Merriam-Webster's Collegiate® Thesaurus

SECOND EDITION

Merriam-Webster's Collegiate® Thesaurus

SECOND EDITION

Merriam-Webster, Incorporated
Springfield, Massachusetts, U.S.A.

A GENUINE MERRIAM-WEBSTER

The name *Webster* alone is no guarantee of excellence. It is used by a number of publishers and may serve mainly to mislead an unwary buyer.

Merriam-Webster™ is the name you should look for when you consider the purchase of dictionaries or other fine reference books. It carries the reputation of a company that has been publishing since 1831 and is your assurance of quality and authority.

Library of Congress Cataloging-in-Publication Data

Merriam-Webster's collegiate thesaurus.—2nd ed.
p. cm.
Spine title: Thesaurus
Includes bibliographical references.
ISBN 978-0-87779-269-7 (alk. paper)
1. English language—Synonyms and antonyms. I. Merriam-Webster, Inc. II. Title: Collegiate thesaurus. III. Title: Thesaurus.
PE1591.W38 2010
423′.12—dc22 2009042161

Made in the United States of America

234567CDS:QGV13121110

Preface

Merriam-Webster's Collegiate Thesaurus, Second Edition, is the first major revision of a work that was originally published in 1976 with the title *Webster's Collegiate Thesaurus.* In the more than three decades since the publication of the first edition, we have developed an improved understanding of what people look for in a thesaurus and of how a thesaurus ought to be constructed to meet those needs. As a result, we have made some significant changes in the book's format and emphasis, all the while preserving the general conception and underlying philosophy of the first edition. The principles regarding synonymy that guided *Webster's Collegiate Thesaurus* remain fundamentally sound, and our goal has been, first and foremost, to incorporate revisions that better serve those core principles of synonymy.

Like the editors of the first edition, we asked ourselves the one most important and basic question: what is a typical user of a thesaurus most likely looking for? We envision the thesaurus user to be someone who is engaged in the always challenging task of putting words down on paper or on a computer screen, as the case may be, and who feels at least vaguely dissatisfied with his or her original choice of word. Being conscientious, our hypothetical writer embarks on a search for a more appropriate substitute: a word which closely approximates in meaning the word that has tentatively been chosen but which differs from it in tone, connotation, level of formality, or range of application. To accomplish this end, our hypothetical writer is in many cases best served by a thesaurus that offers not only a large and comprehensive selection of words to choose from, but also some guidance as to which words, out of a plethora of possibilities with similar meanings, are words that really do have the same meaning as the word originally chosen. This thesaurus provides such guidance by grouping the true synonyms together and by stating explicitly the meaning that is shared by all of the synonyms in each group.

We are of course aware that not every user of the thesaurus will be looking for a word that means exactly the same as the word he or she already has. With this in mind, we have supplemented our lists of synonyms with lists of "related words"—words which don't exactly match the meaning shared by the words listed as synonyms but which are not so far afield from it that they are likely to be of little interest to the user. Similarly, we have been ever mindful that users are not always looking for true antonyms, and so we have endeavored, under the rubric of "near antonyms," to supplement the antonyms with words that are only approximately opposite in meaning to the synonyms. Above all, we have endeavored to be selective in our offerings of related words and near antonyms so that the user's time is not wasted by long lists of words that have only some vague connection to the meaning shared by the synonyms. One of our guiding tenets has been the belief that quality trumps quantity.

To aid the user in making a selection from this large stock of offerings, we have provided a sentence or phrase that illustrates a typical context for every synonym listed in this book. Including a sample sentence or phrase for every synonym is a new feature to this edition and is intended to provide guidance about how individual synonyms are used, in the hope that this will help the user choose the most appropriate one while avoiding those that are less appropriate.

The vocabulary that is offered in *Merriam-Webster's Collegiate Thesaurus, Second Edition,* is taken from *Merriam-Webster's Collegiate Dictionary, Eleventh Edition.* Containing more than 165,000 entries and 225,000 discrete definitions, this edition of the dictionary has virtually all of the words that the contemporary user of English needs to know. The vocabulary of the thesaurus has not been diluted by the inclusion of obscure or obsolete words. This thesaurus is published with the sincere belief that it offers for the user's consideration a treasury of genuinely useful words.

The editor of the second edition of *Merriam-Webster's Collegiate Thesaurus* has been ably and generously assisted in its composition by the editors Anne P. Bello, Rose Martino Bigelow, Deanna Stathis, and Paul S. Wood. Daniel B. Brandon was responsible for the handling of the electronic data files and contributed essential technical assistance in a number of other ways. The project was supervised in its entirety by Madeline L. Novak, and Thomas F. Pitoniak served as editor in charge of production. The always challenging task of cross referencing the text was expertly accomplished by Christopher Chapin Connor. The necessary but often thankless task of proofreading the galleys and page proofs was done by editors Bigelow and Wood and by James G. Lowe, Joan I. Narmontas, Adrienne M. Scholz, Neil S. Serven, and Emily A. Vezina. Final and most important credit must be given to John M. Morse, President and Publisher of Merriam-Webster, Inc., for his steadfast faith in and support of the *Collegiate Thesaurus.*

Michael G. Belanger
Editor

Introduction

Synonyms

English is an extraordinarily complex language, having been woven from the strands of many languages, both ancient and modern. Because of this diverse heritage, English enjoys a wealth of words, and perhaps no other language is as rich in synonyms. A carefully chosen synonym can lend color and precision to the work of any writer, whether that writer is an experienced professional or a conscientious amateur.

So, just what are synonyms? To the writers of early dictionaries, the meaning was clear enough: synonyms are words that mean the same thing. Words that are somewhat similar in meaning—but definitely do not mean the same thing—are not true synonyms. They are merely related words, and they belong in a different category. In some famous thesauri of the mid-19th century, the distinction between these two types of words started to become blurred. As a result, thesauri became ever-expanding compilations of vaguely related words. We believe that this concept of a thesaurus presents problems. Lumping loosely related words all together is unhelpful to the writer who cares about using words with precision. Often the careful writer will want a word that means the same as the one he or she already has but that carries a distinctly different suggestion or tone. To meet that need, we have adhered to the original notion of what constitutes a synonym. In this thesaurus, a word is classified as a synonym if—and only if—it shares with another word at least one basic meaning.

For an example of how we arrived at the basic meaning shared by a group of words, let's look at the following words as they are defined in *Merriam-Webster's Collegiate Dictionary, Eleventh Edition:*

amenity . . . **2** *usu pl* **:** something (as a conventional social gesture) that conduces to smoothness or pleasantness of social relationships . . .

attention . . . **3 a :** an act of civility or courtesy esp. in courtship . . .

civility . . . **2 b :** a polite act or expression . . .

[1]courtesy . . . **1 b :** a courteous act or expression . . .

formality . . . **3 :** an established form or procedure that is required or conventional . . .

[1]gesture . . . **4 :** something said or done by way of formality or courtesy, as a symbol or token, or for its effect on the attitudes of others . . .

pleasantry . . . **3 :** a polite social remark . . .

None of these words share identically worded definitions, but they do have in common a basic meaning that allows them to be regarded as synonyms. That basic meaning can be concisely expressed as "an act or utterance that is a customary show of good manners," and that is what is shown at *civility,* which is the main-entry word for this word group in this thesaurus. All of the members of the word group essentially mean this, the differences in the wording of their individual dictionary definitions notwithstanding.

If a word is more limited in scope than the basic meaning given at a main entry, then it cannot be regarded as a synonym for that word group. Hence, the words *greetings, regards,* and *respects* are entered only as related words at *civility,* as they refer to specific kinds of conventionally polite remarks.

Related Words

Oftentimes thesaurus users are not looking for something that means exactly the same as the word they already have in mind. To meet this need, the *Collegiate Thesaurus* includes lists of words that are so closely related to the synonymy group that they have been deemed of likely interest to the user. These related words do not qualify as synonyms because they have meanings that differ significantly from the basic meaning shared by the members of the synonymy group. For example, the word *funny* has the meaning of "causing or intended to cause laughter." A person who is making "funny faces" is causing, or at least trying to cause, others to laugh. *Witty,* although closely related to *funny,* has a slightly different meaning: "given to or marked by mature intelligent humor." A witty person is someone who has a habit of making clever remarks that display a grown-up sense of humor. Because of the close relationship between *funny* and *witty,* many, if not all, of the words listed as synonyms at *witty* are given as related words at *funny.* The lists of related words at a main entry in the *Collegiate Thesaurus* may be likened to the hyperlinks that connect one Web site to another on the Internet. Following the links between Web sites often takes one to new and unexpected places. Thesaurus users are encouraged to go from one related entry to another when searching for just the right word for their purpose.

Some words are not true synonyms of anything, but because they are so fundamentally useful, they have been included in this thesaurus among the lists of related words and in places where they are likely to be most helpful. For example, the word *ballast,* which refers to any type of "heavy material used to make a ship steady," is too narrow in meaning to have any synonyms of its own. It is related to the more general term *load,* however, and so, fittingly, it is included as a related word at the entry for the noun *load.*

Antonyms

An antonym is a word whose meaning is directly opposite to another word's meaning. Fundamental to this thesaurus's concept of an antonym is the notion of negation. An antonym has a meaning that completely cancels out another word's meaning. *Short* and *tall* are complete opposites. Something cannot be both short and tall at the same time, and both words suggest about the same degree of deviation from the norm or average for height. *Good* and *evil* are another pair of exact opposites. Logically, something cannot be both *good* and *evil* in the same way and at the same time.

Words that are only opposite in some aspect of their meaning cannot be said to be true antonyms. For example, *sad,* which means "causing unhappiness," is not a true antonym of *funny,* which means "causing or intended to cause laughter." The opposite of unhappiness is happiness, and there are things that make people happy without generating gales of laughter. Similarly, *hurt,* which means "to cause physical pain," is not an antonym of *heal,* which means "to restore to healthy condition." The exact opposite of "to cause physical pain" would be "to cause or give physical pleasure." Hurt and *heal* are certainly contrary words, but they differ in their focus and in what they suggest. Pairs of words like *hurt* and *heal* are better regarded as near antonyms.

In this thesaurus, pairs of true antonyms generally fall into three basic classes: (1) words that are mutually exclusive and have no middle ground between them, as *dead* and *alive,* or *perfect* and *imperfect;* (2) words that are on opposite ends of some spectrum, as *maximum* and *minimum,* or *huge* and *tiny;* (3) words that in effect reverse or undo one another, as *assemble* and *disassemble,* or *prove* and *disprove.*

Near Antonyms

Near antonyms are words that do not qualify as antonyms under the strict definition used for this thesaurus but which are clearly in marked contrast with the members of a synonym group. Just as a user may not be seeking a word that is exactly synonymous with another, he or she may not be seeking a word that is exactly opposite. The user may simply want a word that lies somewhere on the opposite side of the spectrum of meaning. *Afraid* is not so exactly opposite to *courageous* as *cowardly* is, but *afraid* and *courageous* certainly have markedly contrasting meanings and consequently can be considered near antonyms of each other.

Phrases

This thesaurus also includes phrases that, taken as a whole, are synonymous with individual words. Some of these are fixed phrases that contain a word that is entered in the dictionary at its own alphabetical place but is never, or almost never, used except in a fixed phrase. For example, *in jeopardy* appears as a synonymous phrase at *liable* because a person liable (that is, "exposed") to something dangerous or undesirable is a person "in jeopardy." The word *jeopardy* is normally used with this meaning only in the phrase *in jeopardy.*

Idioms constitute the other major class of word combinations that are entered under the heading of phrases. Idioms are phrases that have a figurative meaning that is different from the literal meaning one would get if one were to piece together the meanings of the individual components of the phrase. For example, the phrase *make good* is virtually meaningless if one attempts to piece together the literal meanings of *make* and *good.* As a fixed phrase, however, *make good* means "to reach a desired level of accomplishment" and is a synonym of *succeed.*

Whether fixed combinations of words or actual idioms, the expressions entered under the heading of phrases share the same basic meaning as the members of the synonymy group. Such synonymous phrases qualified for entry in the *Thesaurus* if they are in some manner covered in the pages of *Merriam-Webster's Collegiate Dictionary, Eleventh Edition.*

Verbal Illustrations

It is the firm belief of the editors of this thesaurus that verbal illustrations play a key role in helping users decide which word best suits their purposes. Members of a synonym group of course have the same core meaning, but typically they differ in their nuances, connotations, level of formality, and range of application. For a description of something that is "very pleasing to look at," one's choices include the following adjectives: *aesthetic, attractive, beauteous, beautiful, bonny, comely, cute, drop-dead, fair, fetching, good, good-looking, goodly, gorgeous, handsome, knockout, likely, lovely, lovesome, pretty, ravishing, seemly, sightly, stunning, taking,* and *well-favored.* The thesaurus user is faced with the challenge of deciding which of these words is best for describing, say, a sunset or a city square. Likewise, would *knockout* be an appropriate choice for describing a cathedral—or *ravishing* to describe a hotel lobby? To help guide users, the editors of this thesaurus have provided each member of a synonym group with a distinctive verbal illustration that shows how the word is appropriately and typically used:

⟨sunsets in Hawaii are just *gorgeous*⟩

⟨a *handsome* man with finely chiseled features⟩

⟨a *knockout* sports car that's the talk of the neighborhood⟩

⟨with her red curls falling around her shoulders, she looked *ravishing* in her green dress⟩

⟨had never seen such a *taking* city as Venice⟩

In some cases the thesaurus user may decide, after reviewing all of the verbal illustrations for a synonym group, that he or she still has not found the word that precisely meets the present need. The user should then consider the entry's list of related words:

related words alluring, appealing, charming, cunning, delightful, engaging, fascinating, glamorous (*also* glamourous), prepossessing; elegant, exquisite, glorious, Junoesque, magnificent, resplendent, splendid, statuesque, sublime, superb; flawless, perfect, radiant; dainty, delicate; personable, pleasant, presentable; chocolate-box, prettyish; desirable, dishy, dollish, foxy, hot, luscious, nubile, pulchritudinous, seductive, sexy, tasty, toothsome, yummy; hunky, studly [*slang*]; arresting, eye-catching, flamboyant, flashy, glossy, showstopping, showy, slick, snazzy, splashy, striking, zingy; photogenic, telegenic

These supplementary words, which are quite close in meaning to the members of the synonym list, are intended to expand the user's options. Some related words are too specific in meaning to be members of any synonym group; some other related words are members of synonym lists at other entries. Thesaurus users should regard the lists of related words as departure points for further exploration.

Lastly, users of this thesaurus are urged to consult it in conjunction with a good dictionary. The preferred companion dictionary would of course be *Merriam-Webster's Collegiate Dictionary, Eleventh Edition.* All of the vocabulary of the *Collegiate Thesaurus* also appears in the *Collegiate Dictionary.* As such, the *Collegiate Dictionary* will provide the thesaurus user with the precise definition of any word encountered in the text, and in many cases the *Collegiate Dictionary* will provide the user with another verbal illustration for a word. Regardless of which dictionary is used, thesaurus users should consult a dictionary before attempting to use a word with which they were previously unfamiliar.

Explanatory Notes

Every user of *Merriam-Webster's Collegiate Thesaurus, Second Edition,* is encouraged to read the following Explanatory Notes because a thorough understanding of the *Thesaurus*'s scope, philosophy, and structure is essential to its effective use.

Scope of Merriam-Webster's Collegiate Thesaurus, Second Edition

This thesaurus is intended to be a tool for the conscientious writer who is seeking the precisely right word; hence, it is centered on the general vocabulary of the English language. It is this part of the language that is rich with words that have special nuances, distinctive connotations, and varying degrees of formality. As a consequence, the user generally will not find words that belong to science, technology, or other specialized fields. Obsolete and extremely rare terms have also been omitted, as these would do little to help the writer seeking genuinely useful words. Lastly, words that have been labeled as *vulgar, obscene, disparaging, offensive,* or *nonstandard* in *Merriam-Webster's Collegiate Dictionary, Eleventh Edition,* have been disregarded.

Entry Order

The boldface word or phrase at the beginning of a thesaurus entry is called a **headword.** Headwords appear in alphabetical order for ease of use. Alphabetization is by first letter, then second letter, and so on, regardless of any spaces or hyphens that may separate those letters:

make *vb*

make–believe *adj*

make out *vb*

make over *vb*

Maker *n*

makeshift *adj*

When a headword contains a numeral, the numeral is alphabetized as though it were a spelled-out word:

anywise

A–OK *adj*

A1 *adj*

apace *adv*

Homographs are words that are spelled exactly the same but are different parts of speech or have entirely different etymologies (word origins). Homographs that are different parts of speech are simply entered as separate headwords:

bat *n* **1** a hard strike with a part of the body or an instrument

bat *vb* **1** to deliver a blow to (someone or something) . . .

bear *n* **1** a dull, unpleasant, or difficult piece of work

bear *vb* **1** to bring forth from the womb

If two or more homographs are the same part of speech, they are entered as separate headwords and are grouped together and numbered:

[1]list *n* a record of a series of items (as names or titles) usually arranged according to some system

[2]list *n* the act of positioning or an instance of being positioned at an angle

[3]list *n* a long narrow piece of material

[1]list *vb* **1** to make a list of

[2]list *vb* to set or cause to be at an angle

As discussed below under the heading "Some Notes about Verbs," verbs that are customarily used in combination with a preposition or an adverb appear as headwords in this thesaurus in either of two ways: with the verb itself in boldface type and followed by the preposition or adverb in parentheses and in lightface type, or with both the verb and its companion preposition or adverb in boldface type. Simple verbs are listed first, followed by verbs with parenthetical prepositions or adverbs, which are in turn followed by the boldface verb-adverb or verb-preposition combinations:

run *vb*

run (over) *vb*

run along *vb*

talk *vb*

talk (into) *vb*

talk (to) *vb*

talkative *adj*

talk down *vb*

talk down (to) *vb*

When headwords are compound words, a closed compound (one without a space or hyphen) is entered before a hyphenated compound, and a hyphenated compound is entered before an open compound (one with an intervening space):

> **nosedive** *n*
> **nose–dive** *vb*
> **open–air** *adj*
> **open air** *n*

Plural Nouns

Some nouns are always pluralized or are pluralized when they are used with certain meanings. When a thesaurus entry for a noun includes no senses that are used in the singular, the plural form is given as the headword:

> **leavings** *n pl* a remaining group or portion ⟨the *leavings* of the banquet were packed up and delivered to a shelter for the homeless⟩ — see REMAINDER 1

When a noun is often or usually, but not always, used in the plural form, the singular form is used for the headword, and the plural follows, introduced by the label *often* or *usually*:

> **habiliment** *n, usually* **habiliments** *pl* covering for the human body ⟨the lady's rich *habiliments* and haughty manner made the host's servants think she was someone important⟩ — see CLOTHING

When such a noun appears in a list of synonyms, related words, etc., it is shown as a plural form with parentheses around the final *s* or *es*:

> **clothing** *n* covering for the human body ⟨a store that sells both men's and women's *clothing*⟩
> ***synonyms*** apparel, attire, clobber [*British slang*], clothes, costumery, dress, duds, garments, habiliment(s), habit [*archaic*], rags, raiment, rig, rigging, threads, toggery, togs, vestiary, vestments, vesture, wear, wearables, weeds

When a noun is used in the singular form in one sense and in the plural form in another, the singular form is given as the headword. The plural form is indicated at the appropriate sense or senses:

> **provision** *n* **1** something upon which the carrying out of an agreement or offer depends ⟨loaned them the car with the *provision* that they refill the gas tank before returning it⟩ — see CONDITION 2
> **2 provisions** *pl* substances intended to be eaten ⟨gave them ample *provisions* so they would not get hungry on the trip⟩ — FOOD 1

Variants

An alternate spelling or form of a headword is called a **variant**. Variants are shown in boldface type immediately after the headword and are introduced by *or* or *also*. The label *or* means that the variant is as common, or nearly as common, as the headword. As long as the variants are equally common, the headword is the spelling that comes first alphabetically.

> **egotistic** *or* **egotistical** *adj*
> **theater** *or* **theatre** *n*
> **OK** *or* **okay** *vb*

However, if one of the spellings is used slightly more frequently than the other, the more common one is shown first even if it does not fall first alphabetically:

> **goody** *or* **goodie** *n*

A variant that is introduced by the label *also* is considerably less common than the headword:

> **among** *also* **amongst** *prep*
> **facade** *also* **façade** *n*
> **naught** *also* **nought** *n*

When two variants are separated from the headword by *also* but from each other by *or*, it means that both variants are considerably less common than the headword:

> **bogey** *also* **bogie** *or* **bogy** *n*

Variants are also shown in the word lists within the entries:

> **zero** *n* **1** the numerical symbol 0 or the absence of number or quantity represented by it ⟨anything multiplied by *zero* comes out to *zero*⟩
> ***synonyms*** aught, cipher, goose egg, naught (*also* nought), nil, nothing, o, oh, zilch, zip

Parts of Speech

Every headword is followed by one of the following abbreviated part-of-speech labels: *adj* (adjective), *adv* (adverb), *conj* (conjunction), *interj* (interjection), *n* (noun), *prep* (preposition), *pron* (pronoun), or *vb* (verb). Plural nouns are followed by the *n pl* label.

Kinds of Entries

This thesaurus consists of two types of entries: **main entries** and **cross entries.** Each main entry provides a full treatment of a group of synonyms and is located at the alphabetical place of one of the most important words in the group. The cross entries, which are shorter than the main entries, can be found at the alphabetical place of each of the synonyms listed at the main entries. Every headword with its part-of-speech label is followed by either one or more main entries, one or more cross entries, or a combination of the two. If there is more than one meaning treated at a given headword, all the main entries will come first, followed by all the cross entries, and each will begin with a boldface sense number.

A main entry always includes a statement of the core meaning shared by the members of a synonym group. It is by this means that the user knows in what sense the members of the group are being treated as synonyms. This statement of shared meaning is followed by a verbal illustration for the headword. The illustration is followed by a list of synonyms as well as such related words, phrases, near antonyms, and antonyms as may exist for that meaning.

> **famous** *adj* **1** widely known ⟨a book about some of the most *famous* people of the last century⟩
> ***synonyms*** big-name, celebrated, famed, noted, no-

torious, prominent, renowned, star, visible, well-known
related words fabled, fabulous, legendary; infamous; distinguished, eminent, exceptional, great, illustrious, leading, notable, noteworthy, outstanding, preeminent, prestigious, remarkable, supereminent, superior; important, significant; acknowledged, recognized, respected; favorite, popular, preferred; estimable, honorable, reputable, respectable; formidable, redoubtable
near antonyms insignificant, unimportant; inconspicuous; undistinguished, unexceptional; unpopular
antonyms anonymous, nameless, obscure, uncelebrated, unfamous, unknown, unsung

Every word in the list of synonyms at each main entry is entered at its own alphabetical place as a cross entry. The statement of shared meaning that appears at the main entry will be shown at the cross entry as well. This is done so that the user who is looking at the cross entry will know whether the main entry treats the sense that he or she is interested in. The statement of shared meaning is followed by a verbal illustration for that particular synonym. The cross entry does not repeat the synonyms, related words, phrases, near antonyms, or antonyms given at the main entry. Instead, at the end of the cross entry, there is a reference that points the user to the appropriate main entry:

big–name *adj* widely known ⟨several *big-name* writers gave readings at the book festival⟩ — see FAMOUS 1

fade *vb* **1** to cease to be visible ⟨the departing ship gradually *faded* over the horizon⟩ — see DISAPPEAR
2 to make white or whiter by removing color ⟨years of harsh sunlight had *faded* the car, which was once fire-engine red⟩ — see WHITEN
3 to lose bodily strength or vigor ⟨began to *fade* after battling the disease for years⟩ — see WEAKEN 2

Cross-References

A **cross-reference** is a direction at the end of a cross entry that tells the user where the main entry for that particular shared meaning is located. If there is more than one sense at the headword referred to in the cross-reference, the cross-reference will include the relevant sense number. If there is more than one numbered homograph for a headword, the cross-reference will include the correct homograph number as well:

pain *vb* to feel or cause physical pain ⟨my poor head was *paining* so from all that racket⟩ — see HURT 1

ranking *n* **1** a scheme of rank or order ⟨in one *ranking* of the best places to live, San Francisco surpassed all other cities in the U.S.⟩ — see [3]SCALE 1

Cross-references are always between words having the same part of speech. In the above example, for instance, the cross-reference is to the first sense of the third homograph for the noun *scale,* which is of course the same part of speech as *ranking:*

[3]scale *n* **1** a scheme of rank or order ⟨a student who scored very highly on a standard intelligence *scale*⟩
synonyms graduation, hierarchy, ladder, ordering, ranking

Special Usage Labels

Occasionally words in this thesaurus will bear italicized usage labels. The following labels indicate that a word is limited to regional use: *Australian, British, Irish, Midland, New Zealand, Northwest, Scottish, South African, Southern, Southwest,* and *West.* All of these designations may be used in combination with one another (as *Southern & Midland*) or qualified by the word *chiefly.* Three other labels that have been used for this thesaurus are *dialect, slang,* and *archaic.* The label *dialect* indicates that a word occurs in several regional varieties of American or British English and that the pattern of its usage is too complicated to be concisely labeled. The stylistic label *slang* indicates that the word is used most appropriately in very informal contexts. The temporal label *archaic* indicates that the word is nowadays used only in special contexts, such as poetry or historical fiction:

afore *prep, chiefly dialect* **1**

bobby *n, British*

conk *n, chiefly British slang*

kirk *n, chiefly Scottish*

kloof *n, South African*

sundowner *n, Australian*

[2]waddy *or* **waddie** *n, West*

When a headword has multiple senses and a usage label applies to one or more of them but not to all of them, the label will come after the appropriate sense numbers:

jack *n* **1** *slang* something (as pieces of stamped metal or printed paper) customarily and legally used as a medium of exchange, a measure of value, or a means of payment ⟨I'd buy that watch, but I don't have the *jack* right now⟩ — see MONEY 1
2 a piece of cloth with a special design that is used as an emblem or for signaling ⟨a Portuguese ship flying the national *jack*⟩ — see FLAG 1

In the word lists at main entries, special usage labels appear in square brackets immediately after the words to which they apply:

before *prep* **1** earlier than ⟨since I'm a faster runner, I got there *before* him⟩
synonyms afore [*chiefly dialect*], ahead of, ere, fore (*also* (fore) [*chiefly dialect*], of, previous to, prior to, to

Shared Meanings

Every entry contains a statement of the meaning shared by members of a synonym group. This shared meaning is the "thing" that is referred to when we say that two or more words "mean the same thing"and thus qualify as synonyms. The statement of shared meaning follows the part-of-speech label in single-sense entries and the sense number in multisense entries.

Sometimes there are parenthetical elements within these statements of shared meaning, as in the following entry:

> **payment** *n* . . .
> **2** something (as money) that is given or received in return for goods or services ⟨our *payment* for all the work we did barely covered our expenses⟩ ⟨we finally mailed our last car *payment* last week⟩
> ***synonyms*** compensation, consideration, pay, recompense, remittance, remuneration, requital

The parenthetical element is intended to suggest the usual range of application of a group of words, but it should not be interpreted as a strict limitation of a word's application.

Some Notes about Verbs

Verbs that have a given meaning only when they are followed by a particular word appear as headwords in this thesaurus in one of several ways. Sometimes both the verb and the following adverb or preposition are shown in boldface:

> **belly up** *vb* to come near or nearer ⟨*belly up* to the buffet table and help yourselves⟩

Sometimes the verb is shown in boldface followed by a lightface adverb, preposition, or other word in parentheses:

> **comply** (with) *vb* **1** to act according to the commands of ⟨the guards rushed to *comply with* the warden's orders⟩

> **knock** (about) *vb* to move about from place to place aimlessly ⟨we *knocked about* from town to town, looking for work⟩

> **leg** (it) *vb* to go on foot ⟨the car was in the shop so we had to *leg it* to work for a couple of days⟩

And sometimes both styles are combined:

> **hold off** (on) *vb* to assign to a later time ⟨we *held off on* accepting the invitation in the hopes that something better would come along⟩

These different stylings are intended to help the user who wants to look these verbs up in *Merriam-Webster's Collegiate Dictionary, Eleventh Edition,* the companion dictionary for this thesaurus. In all cases, the boldface part of the thesaurus headword will match the headword of the corresponding *Collegiate Dictionary* entry.

If there are two words inside the parentheses and they are separated by *or,* then either word can be used with the verb:

> **fit** (in *or* into) *vb* to put among or between others ⟨do you think that you can *fit* this picture *into* the album?⟩ ⟨I can *fit* you *in* between my two o'clock and three o'clock appointments⟩

A verb that has a parenthesized element when shown as a headword has that same parenthesized element when the verb appears in a word list. Users who encounter such a verb in a list should remember that the complete verb combination must be used for it to match the shared meaning of its synonym group:

> **obey** *vb* to act according to the commands of . . .
> ***synonyms*** adhere (to), comply (with), conform (to), follow, goose-step (to), mind, observe

When the statement of shared meaning calls for a direct object, all of the members of a synonym group will take a direct object. If the statement of shared meaning does not call for a direct object, then none of the synonyms will take an object. One frequent clue that the members of a word group take an object is the fact that the statement of shared meaning ends with a preposition:

> **constitute** *vb* **1** to be all the substance of ⟨nine players *constitute* a baseball team⟩

Not all verbs requiring an object are worded this way, however, so the user may need to study the verbal illustration to determine the need for a direct object. A check of the verbal illustration at a verb's cross entry may be needed for further confirmation.

Verbal Illustrations

Every synonym in this thesaurus is illustrated with an example of its typical use. This **verbal illustration** appears after the statement of shared meaning and is set off by angle brackets. The word being illustrated is italicized in each verbal illustration.

> **fight** *vb* **1** to oppose (someone) in physical conflict ⟨a proud people who have fiercely *fought* all invaders of their homeland⟩

> **hold back** *vb* **1** to create difficulty for the work or activity of ⟨the only thing *holding* Joe *back* from joining the swim team is lack of transportation⟩

> **loony** *also* **looney** *adj* **1** showing or marked by a lack of good sense or judgment ⟨that's got to be the *looniest* idea I've ever heard⟩

When the headword includes a parenthesized lightface element, that element will also be italicized in the verbal illustration:

> **conk** (out) *vb* **1** to lose consciousness ⟨after three days without eating, he simply *conked out*⟩

All verbal illustrations in this thesaurus begin with a lowercase letter unless the initial word is normally capitalized. Question marks and exclamation points are used when appropriate at the end of a verbal illustration, but otherwise no ending punctuation is used.

Synonyms Used in Defining

The central word in a dictionary definition is known as the defining term, and every definition has to have one. Likewise, each statement of shared meaning in this thesaurus includes a defining term:

> **gadget** *n* an interesting and often novel device with a practical use ⟨she tried out a new *gadget* for weeding the garden⟩
> ***synonyms*** appliance, contraption, contrivance, gimmick, gizmo (*also* gismo), jigger, widget

In the above example, the verb *device* is the defining term. If *device* had not been used as the defining term, it could have been included with good justification in the list of synonyms. However, since it was in fact used as the defining term, *device* was omitted from the list in accordance with our practice of not using a word both as a defining term and as a synonym at the same main entry.

Related Words

The cornerstone of every entry in this thesaurus is the list of synonyms. For the vast majority of main entries, an often generous supply of related words is provided to supplement the synonyms. The lists of related words are meant to suggest to the user an array of paths that might be taken in search of the precisely right word. The number of related words often exceeds that of the synonyms because related words do not have to match the synonyms' shared meaning: they need only relate to some aspect of that statement of shared meaning. Where appropriate, related words are divided into subgroups which are separated by semicolons. Words within each subgroup are usually closer in meaning to each other than to members of neighboring subgroups. The subgroups are generally presented in order of most relevant to least relevant.

> **conceited** *adj* having too high an opinion of oneself ⟨a *conceited* basketball player who was always too busy even to sign autographs⟩
> ***synonyms*** assured, biggety (*or* biggity) [*Southern & Midland*], bigheaded, complacent, consequential, egoistic (*also* egoistical), egotistic (*or* egotistical), important, overweening, pompous, prideful, proud, self-conceited, self-important, self-opinionated, self-satisfied, smug, stuck-up, swell-headed, vain, vainglorious
> ***related words*** blusterous, blustery, boastful, bombastic, braggart, bragging, braggy, cocky, swaggering; arrogant, assumptive, bumptious, cavalier, chesty, disdainful, fastuous, haughty, high-and-mighty, high-hat, huffy, lofty, lordly, masterful, peremptory, pontifical, self-asserting, self-assertive, snobbish, snobby, snooty, supercilious, superior, toplofty (*also* toploftical), uppish, uppity; domineering, high-handed, imperious; highfalutin (*also* hifalutin), holier-than-thou, pretentious; overconfident, presuming, presumptuous; confident, self-assured, self-confident; self-adulatory, self-congratulatory, self-contented, self-gratulatory; self-applauding, self-dramatizing, self-glorifying, self-promoting; self-affected, self-centered, self-engrossed, selfish; condescending, patronizing

Phrases

The heading **phrases** is reserved for expressions that, taken as a whole, are synonymous with their entry's synonym group. These expressions are shown in a list of their own but do not have their own cross entries and thus do not have verbal illustrations in this thesaurus. These expressions are often colorful figures of speech that add interest and variety to one's writing, but the writer is advised to look up unfamiliar expressions in a dictionary before attempting to use them.

Near Antonyms

Just as related words are not exact synonyms, near antonyms are not exact antonyms. Not every synonym group will have near antonyms, but in general they are more plentiful than exact antonyms. As is the case with related words, near antonyms are typically divided into subgroups separated by semicolons. And as with related words, near antonyms are generally listed in order of relevancy.

> **maintenance** *n* the act or activity of keeping something in an existing and usually satisfactory condition ⟨I was hired to perform basic *maintenance* until the property could be sold⟩
> ***synonyms*** care and feeding, conservation, conserving, keep, preservation, preserving, sustentation, upkeep
> ***related words*** conservancy; support, sustaining; care, custody, guardianship; defense, guarding, protection, safeguarding, safekeeping
> ***near antonyms*** dereliction, disregard, ignoring, inattention, neglect, negligence; damage, demolition, destruction, harm, hurt, injury, ruin, ruination

Antonyms

The words in a main entry's antonym list are exactly opposite in meaning to the headword and its list of synonyms. A true antonym is a word whose meaning completely cancels out another word's meaning. True antonyms do not exist for many words in this thesaurus. There are no words that completely cancel out the shared meaning at *car*: "a self-propelled passenger vehicle on four wheels." There is no word in English that essentially means "not a car." A word like *truck* may be used in contradistinction to car, but *truck* and *car* are not antonyms. In this thesaurus words listed as antonyms are given their own cross entries only if they appear as synonyms at some other entry. The word *torrid* has its own cross entry; the cross-reference is to *hot* 1, where the word is a synonym, and not to *cold* 1, where it is an antonym.

At most main entries all of the members of an antonym list are synonyms of each other. At some entries, however, while all the listed antonyms are opposite in meaning to the synonym group, they are not opposite in exactly the same way. The following is an example of such an entry:

> **colorful** *adj* marked by a variety of usually vivid colors ⟨the *colorful* robes and blankets of the Native Americans of the Southwest⟩
> ***synonyms*** chromatic, colored, kaleidoscopic, motley, multicolored, multihued, polychromatic, polychrome, prismatic, rainbow, varicolored, varied, variegated, various . . .
> ***antonyms*** colorless; monochromatic, monochromic, monotone, self-colored, solid

The opposite meaning of "marked by a variety of usually vivid colors is "not marked by a variety of usually vivid colors." All of the words in the antonym list fit that meaning. The word *colorless* means "lacking an addition of color." The other antonyms, *monochromatic, monochromic, monotone, self-colored,* and *solid,* mean "having or consisting of a single color" and so, of course, are not synonyms of *colorless.* Antonyms that are not synonymous with each other are separated by semicolons.

A Note Regarding the Number of Times a Word Will Appear in an Entry

In this thesaurus no word will appear in more than one list at any single main entry. The general vocabulary of the English language has a plethora of words with more than one sense. One sense of a multisense word in *Merriam-Webster's Collegiate Dictionary, Eleventh Edition,* might be exactly synonymous with a thesaurus entry's statement of shared meaning. Another sense of that same multisense word might be properly regarded as being no more than closely related to it. To avoid confusion, this thesaurus enters such words only in the entry's synonym list and not in the list of related words as well. For example, the much-used word *nice* is in the synonym list at *pleasant,* where the shared meaning is "giving pleasure or contentment to the mind or senses." *Nice* can also be found in the synonym list at *amiable,* where the shared meaning is "having an easygoing and pleasing manner especially in social situations." Since *amiable* is in the list of related words at *pleasant,* one might expect to find *nice* there as well. But finding the same word at two places in the same entry would be confusing for many users, so *nice* is included only in the list of synonyms.

Sometimes multisense words have meanings that are opposite to one another—or nearly so. For example, *Merriam-Webster's Collegiate Dictionary, Eleventh Edition,* defines one sense of *nervy* as "showing or expressive of calm courage," or the equivalent of "bold," and another sense of the word as "excitable, nervous." Thus, at the thesaurus entry for *nervous,* where the shared meaning for the first given sense is "feeling or showing uncomfortable feelings of uncertainty," *nervy* appears alongside of *jittery, jumpy, tense, uneasy, uptight,* and several other synonyms. The list of near antonyms for this same sense of *nervous* includes *confident, self-assured, self-confident,* and *sure. Nervy* might well have been added to the list, in light of the fact that it has a sense meaning "showing or expressive of calm courage." *Nervy* was omitted from the list of near antonyms to avoid unnecessary confusion.

Guide Words

Guide words are boldface words that are separated by a dot and placed at the top of each page. They are there to indicate the alphabetical range of entries on that page, thereby facilitating the user's search for entries. The first guide word is the headword of the first entry beginning on that page, and the second guide word is the headword of the page's final entry.

aback *adv* without warning ⟨completely taken *aback* by the neighbors' announcement that they were moving⟩ — see UNAWARES

abaft *adv* near, toward, or in the stern of a ship or the tail of an aircraft ⟨the lookout in the crow's nest warned that there was an enemy frigate *abaft* and bearing down hard on their ship⟩ see AFT

abaft *prep* at, to, or toward the rear of ⟨a school of porpoises swam *abaft* the fishing boat⟩ — see BEHIND 1

abandon *n* carefree freedom from constraint ⟨added spices to the stew with complete *abandon*⟩
synonyms abandonment, ease, lightheartedness, naturalness, spontaneity, spontaneousness, unconstraint, uninhibitedness, unrestraint
related words ardor, enthusiasm, exuberance, fervor, spirit, warmth, zeal, zealotry, zealousness; carelessness, heedlessness, impulsiveness, impulsivity, indiscretion, insouciance, recklessness, thoughtlessness; unselfconsciousness; casualness, offhandedness; excess, excessiveness, immoderacy, incontinence, indulgence, intemperance, licentiousness, permissiveness, wantonness, wildness; blank check, carte blanche, free hand
near antonyms embarrassment, reserve, reticence, self-consciousness, uneasiness; inhibition, repression, self-restraint, suppression; carefulness, discreetness, discretion, heedfulness; discipline, self-command, self-control, self-denial, self-discipline, self-mastery, willpower
antonyms constraint, restraint

abandon *vb* **1** to give (oneself) over to something especially unrestrainedly ⟨more than ready to *abandon* himself to a life of complete idleness for the duration of his vacation⟩
synonyms deliver, give up, indulge, surrender, yield
related words overdo, overindulge; bask, luxuriate, revel, roll, wallow
near antonyms abstain (from), eschew, forbear, forgo (*also* forego), refrain (from); check, inhibit, restrain
antonyms deny
2 to cause to remain behind ⟨*abandoned* the group that he had been hiking with and struck out on his own⟩ — see LEAVE 1
3 to put an end to (something planned or previously agreed to) ⟨the bad weather forced NASA to *abandon* the launch⟩ — see CANCEL 1
4 to stop doing (something) permanently ⟨marriage customs that were *abandoned* decades ago⟩ — see QUIT 2

abandoned *adj* **1** left unoccupied or unused ⟨she consciously avoided walking past the *abandoned* house, with its broken windows and sagging porch⟩
synonyms derelict, deserted, desolate, disused, forgotten, forsaken, rejected, vacant, vacated, void
related words ignored, neglected, unattended, untended; castaway, cast-off, discarded, jettisoned, junked, refuse, waste; godforsaken, miserable, shabby, wretched; empty, idle
near antonyms reclaimed, recovered, redeemed, rescued, retrieved, salvaged, saved; reconditioned, rehabbed, rehabilitated, restored; repeopled
2 showing no signs of being under control ⟨wild, *abandoned* dancing that shocked the staid chaperones at the debutante ball⟩ — see RAMPANT 1

abandonment *n* **1** carefree freedom from constraint ⟨sang at the top of her lungs with complete *abandonment* in the shower⟩ — see ABANDON
2 the act of abandoning ⟨the law says *abandonment* by the owner of any building for more than a year entitles the city to sell it⟩ — see DERELICTION 1
3 the act of putting an end to something planned or previously agreed to ⟨the park commissioner cited cost considerations as the main reason for the project's *abandonment*⟩ — see CANCELLATION 1

abase *vb* **1** to lower in character, dignity, or quality ⟨was unwilling to *abase* himself by pleading guilty to a crime that he did not commit⟩ — see DEBASE 1
2 to reduce to a lower standing in one's own eyes or in others' eyes ⟨I certainly don't *abase* myself when I do good, honest manual labor⟩ — see HUMBLE

abash *vb* to throw into a state of self-conscious distress ⟨felt terribly *abashed* when she walked into the wrong hotel room⟩ — see EMBARRASS 1

abashment *n* the emotional state of being made self-consciously uncomfortable ⟨his friends shared his *abashment* when his wife scolded him right in front of them⟩ — see EMBARRASSMENT 1

abate *vb* **1** to grow less in scope or intensity especially gradually ⟨interest in the author's home *abated* as her novels waned in popularity⟩ — see DECREASE 2
2 to make smaller in amount, volume, or extent ⟨a couple of aspirin should *abate* the pain⟩ — see DECREASE 1
3 to put an end to by formal action ⟨asked the appellate court to *abate* the lower court's ruling allowing the patient to be removed from life support⟩ — see ABOLISH 1
4 to take away (an amount or number) from a total ⟨I managed to get the used car dealer to *abate* $200 from the sticker price⟩ — see SUBTRACT
5 to take something away from ⟨recurring problems could not *abate* her of her enthusiasm for the project⟩ — see DEPRIVE 1

abatement *n* **1** something that is or may be subtracted ⟨entitled to a tax *abatement* for child care expenses⟩ — see DEDUCTION 1
2 the amount by which something is lessened ⟨there's been a significant *abatement* in noise from the floor above since the upstairs neighbors installed carpets⟩ — see DECREASE
3 the doing away with something by formal action ⟨sought an *abatement* of the court proceeding on the grounds that the plaintiff had no legal standing in the case⟩ — see ABOLITION

abbey *n* a residence for men under religious vows ⟨the monks in the *abbey* grow all their own vegetables⟩ — see MONASTERY

abbreviate *vb* to make less in extent or duration ⟨had to *abbreviate* his vacation in France in order to travel to Oslo to receive the Nobel Prize⟩ — see SHORTEN

abbreviation *n* a shortened version of a written work ⟨a recording of musical *abbreviations* that introduces the listener to the great composers⟩ — see ABRIDGMENT

ABC *n, usually* **ABC's** *or* **ABCs** *pl* general or basic truths on which other truths or theories can be based ⟨a book on the *ABCs* of computer usage⟩ — see PRINCIPLES 1

abdicate *vb* to give up (as a position of authority) formally ⟨the revolutionary government forced Nicholas II to *abdicate* the Russian throne⟩
synonyms abnegate, cede, relinquish, renounce, resign, step aside (from), step down (from), surrender
related words abjure, demit, deny, disavow, disclaim, disown, waive; forsake, give up, hand over, yield; abandon, desert, quit, vacate
near antonyms appropriate, arrogate, assume, claim, confiscate; seize, take over, usurp, wrest; defend, guard, protect, safeguard, secure

abdomen *n* the part of the body between the chest and the pelvis ⟨showed us a tiny tattoo on her *abdomen*, right next to her belly button⟩ — see STOMACH 1

abduct *vb* to carry away (as a person) forcibly or unlawfully ⟨the gangsters planned to *abduct* the industrialist's young daughter and demand a huge ransom from her family⟩ — see KIDNAP

abduction *n* the unlawful or forcible carrying away of a person or animal ⟨discredited reports of *abductions* by aliens⟩
synonyms hijacking (*also* highjacking), kidnapping (*also* kidnaping), rape, snatch [*slang*]
related words impressment, seizure, shanghaiing

abecedarian *adj* of or relating to the simplest facts or theories of a subject ⟨an *abecedarian* approach to historical study⟩ — see ELEMENTARY

abecedarian *n* a person who is just starting out in a field of activity ⟨*abecedarians* soon learn that martial arts have a spiritual as well as physical side⟩ — see BEGINNER

aberrant *adj* **1** being out of the ordinary ⟨a year of *aberrant* weather—record rainfall in the summer, record heat in the autumn⟩ — see EXCEPTIONAL 1
2 departing from some accepted standard of what is normal ⟨*aberrant* behavior can be a sign of rabies in a wild animal⟩ — see DEVIANT

aberrated *adj* being out of the ordinary ⟨you may have taken an *aberrated* path to the correct answer, but you got there⟩ — see EXCEPTIONAL 1

aberration *n* **1** a serious mental disorder that prevents one from living a safe and normal life ⟨Joan of Arc was certain the voices she had been hearing were not a manifestation of some sort of *aberration*⟩ — see INSANITY 1
2 something that is different from what is ordinary or expected ⟨there are some slight *aberrations* in the type due to the nature of old printing presses⟩ — see ANOMALY 1

aberrational *adj* departing from some accepted standard of what is normal ⟨in wartime what was once regarded as clearly *aberrational* becomes the new norm⟩ — see DEVIANT

abet *vb* **1** to bring (something volatile or intense) into being ⟨the belief that violent entertainment *abets* violent behavior in the people who partake of it⟩ — see INCITE 1
2 to provide (someone) with what is useful or necessary to achieve an end ⟨car thieves are often unwittingly *abetted* by owners foolishly leaving the keys in the ignition⟩ — see HELP 1

abetment *n* an act or instance of helping ⟨the proposed government bailout of the company is being decried as an ill-advised *abetment* of managerial ineptitude⟩ — see HELP 1

abettor *also* **abetter** *n* **1** one associated with another in wrongdoing ⟨the man who drove the getaway car in the bank robbery was arrested as an aider and *abettor*⟩ — see ACCOMPLICE
2 someone associated with another to give assistance or moral support ⟨without all the neighborhood kids as *abettors*, I would never have gotten all my chickens back in their coop⟩ — see ALLY

abeyance *n* a state of temporary inactivity ⟨our weekend plans were held in *abeyance* until we could get a weather forecast⟩
synonyms cold storage, deep freeze, doldrums, dormancy, holding pattern, latency, moratorium, quiescence, suspended animation, suspense, suspension
related words inaction, inertia, inertness, motionlessness; impasse, standstill; coma, hibernation, hypnosis, repose, rest, sleep, slumber, torpor; recess, recession, remission; downtime, idleness, layoff
near antonyms recommencement, renewal, resumption, resuscitation
antonyms continuance, continuation

abhor *vb* to dislike strongly ⟨*abhors* the way people leave their trash at the picnic sites in the park⟩ — see HATE

abhorrence *n* **1** something or someone that is hated ⟨one of the changes in American society that remains a particular *abhorrence* of social conservatives⟩ — see HATE 2
2 a very strong dislike ⟨my firm *abhorrence* of all forms of hypocrisy⟩ — see HATE 1

abhorrent *adj* **1** causing intense displeasure, disgust, or resentment ⟨he considers it *abhorrent* the way she keeps her dogs penned up all the time⟩ — see OFFENSIVE 1
2 feeling or showing open dislike for someone or something regarded as undeserving of respect or concern ⟨she's *abhorrent* of the nonsense that the tabloid media pass off as news⟩ — see CONTEMPTUOUS 1

abidance *n* **1** the following of a custom, rule, or law ⟨the FDA requires strict *abidance* by food manufacturers of its definitions for certain terms used on product labels⟩ — see OBSERVANCE 1
2 uninterrupted or lasting existence ⟨the reassuring *abidance* of their friendship through times both good and bad⟩ — see CONTINUATION

abide *vb* **1** to continue to be in a place for a significant amount of time ⟨refused to *abide* where it was clear that he wasn't wanted⟩ — see [1]STAY 1
2 to have a home ⟨the charming fantasy that fairies *abide* in the cup-shaped flowers dotting the woodland floor⟩ — see LIVE 1
3 to put up with (something painful or difficult) ⟨cannot *abide* being in huge crowds⟩ — see BEAR 2
4 to remain indefinitely in existence or in the same state ⟨the village's once-honored ways no longer *abide* and now exist only in the memories of a few elders⟩ — see CONTINUE 1

abiding *adj* having an existence or validity that does not change or diminish ⟨I have an *abiding* interest in animal welfare—it's not just a phase I'm going through⟩
synonyms ageless, continuing, dateless, enduring, eternal, everlasting, immortal, imperishable, lasting, ongoing, perennial, perpetual, timeless, undying
related words ceaseless, endless, permanent; changeless, constant, stable, stationary, steady, unchanging, unvarying
near antonyms antiquated, archaic, dated, obsolete, outdated, outmoded, out-of-date, outworn, passé

ability *n* the physical or mental power to do something

⟨as a result of the accident the once-vigorous athlete lost the *ability* to walk⟩
synonyms capability, capableness, capacity, competence, competency, faculty
related words aptitude, aptness, endowment, equipment, facility, gift, knack, talent; address, adroitness, deftness, dexterity, hand, prowess, skill; gray matter, instinct, intelligence, ken, reason, understanding; might, potency, puissance, staying power, stuff; adequacy, effectiveness, effectualness, fitness, form, influence, resourcefulness, usefulness; means, resources, wherewithal
near antonyms helplessness, impotence, paralysis, powerlessness, weakness; defectiveness, deficiency, inadequacy, inadequateness, ineffectiveness, ineffectuality, ineffectualness, inefficaciousness, inefficacy, uselessness; debilitation, disablement, impairment, incapacitation
antonyms disability, inability, incapability, incapableness, incapacity, incompetence, incompetency, ineptitude, ineptness

abject *adj* showing, expressing, or offered in a spirit of humility or unseemly submissiveness ⟨demanded nothing less than an *abject* apology from them⟩
synonyms base, humble, menial, servile, slavish
related words hangdog, lamblike, sheepish; demure, lowly, meek, modest, retiring, unassuming, unpretentious; fawning, sycophant, sycophantic, toadyish
near antonyms arrogant, haughty, high-handed, imperious, lordly, supercilious, superior, uppity

abjection *n* a sinking to a state of low moral standards and behavior ⟨sees the corporate scandal as yet another sign of the general *abjection* of our society⟩ — see CORRUPTION 2

abjectly *adv* in a manner showing no signs of pride or self-assertion ⟨she was so sincerely and *abjectly* apologetic that he was won over⟩ — see LOWLY

abjure *vb* **1** to solemnly or formally reject or go back on (as something formerly adhered to) ⟨*abjured* some long-held beliefs when she converted to another religion⟩
synonyms abnegate, forswear (*also* foreswear), recant, renege, renounce, repeal, repudiate, retract, take back, unsay, withdraw
related words contradict, deny, disavow, disclaim, disown, gainsay, negate, negative; abandon, bolt, forsake, give up, relinquish, spurn, surrender; controvert, disagree (with), disprove, dispute, rebut, refute; back down, back off, backtrack; disallow, recall, revoke
near antonyms acknowledge, admit, affirm, assert, avow, claim, contend, declare, maintain, proclaim, profess, state, vouch, vow; back, confirm, defend, endorse (*also* indorse), espouse, maintain, support, uphold; accept, adopt, embrace
antonyms adhere (to)
2 to resist the temptation of ⟨a strict religious sect that *abjures* the luxuries, comforts, and conveniences of the modern world⟩ — see FORBEAR

ablaze *adj* **1** being on fire ⟨the entire block was *ablaze* by the time firefighters arrived⟩
synonyms afire, aflame, alight [*chiefly British*], blazing, burning, combusting, conflagrant, fiery, flaming, ignited, inflamed (*also* enflamed), kindled, lit (*or* lighted)
related words aglow, flaring, flickering, glowing, live, smoldering (*or* smouldering); broiling, hot, piping hot, red-hot, roasting, scalding, scorching, searing, sizzling; burned (*or* burnt), charred, incinerated, scorched, seared, singed
near antonyms choked, damped, dead, doused (*also* dowsed), extinguished, quenched, smothered, snuffed (out), stamped (out), suffocated
2 filled with much light ⟨that night the ballroom, *ablaze* with light, looked very different from the curtained room it usually was by day⟩ — see BRIGHT 2

able *adj* having the required skills for an acceptable level of performance ⟨looking for an *able* and reliable assistant⟩ — see COMPETENT 1

able-bodied *adj* enjoying health and vigor ⟨every *able-bodied* young man in the village had been sent off to fight in the war⟩ — see HEALTHY 1

ably *adv* in a skillful or expert manner ⟨*ably* maneuvered the boat up to the dock⟩ — see WELL 3

abnegate *vb* **1** to give up (as a position of authority) formally ⟨*abnegated* all claims to the deceased lord's domain⟩ — see ABDICATE
2 to solemnly or formally reject or go back on (as something formerly adhered to) ⟨felt that if the Congress adopted these security measures, it would be *abnegating* the nation's fundamental commitment to individual rights⟩ — see ABJURE 1

abnegation *n* the act or practice of giving up or rejecting something once enjoyed or desired ⟨the couple's sudden *abnegation* of life in the fast lane for work as missionaries stunned everyone⟩ — see RENUNCIATION

abnormal *adj* **1** being out of the ordinary ⟨a completely *abnormal* school day, because half of the kids were out sick⟩ — see EXCEPTIONAL 1
2 departing from some accepted standard of what is normal ⟨noticed his *abnormal* breathing and took him to the emergency room⟩ — see DEVIANT

abnormality *n* **1** a person, thing, or event that is far from normal ⟨the *abnormalities* in the tree's leaves are caused by disease⟩ — see FREAK 1
2 something that is different from what is ordinary or expected ⟨let the vet know if you notice any *abnormalities* in your pet's behavior⟩ — see ANOMALY 1

abode *n* the place where one lives ⟨welcome to my humble *abode*⟩ — see HOME 1

aboil *adj* marked by much life, movement, or activity ⟨even in the wee hours of the morning, his mind is *aboil* with new ideas⟩ — see ALIVE 2

abolish *vb* **1** to put an end to by formal action ⟨the U.S. *abolished* slavery by constitutional amendment on December 6, 1865⟩
synonyms abate, abrogate, annul, avoid, cancel, disannul, dissolve, invalidate, negate, null, nullify, quash, repeal, rescind, roll back, strike down, vacate, void
related words countermand, override, overrule, overturn, veto; abort, call, call off, drop, recall, retract, reverse, revoke, suspend, withdraw; ban, enjoin, forbid, outlaw, prohibit; disallow, dismiss, reject; annihilate, break down, eliminate, eradicate, erase, liquidate, remove, throw out, write off
phrases do away with, set aside
near antonyms enact, lay down, legislate; establish, found, institute; formalize, legalize, legitimate, legitimize, validate; pass, ratify; allow, approve, authorize, clear, endorse (*also* indorse), permit, sanction, warrant; command, decree, mandate, order, prescribe
2 to destroy all traces of ⟨if only there were a way that we could *abolish* hatred and intolerance⟩ — see ANNIHILATE 1

abolishment *n* the doing away with something by formal action ⟨recurrent calls for the *abolishment* of the electoral college⟩ — see ABOLITION

abolition *n* the doing away with something by formal action ⟨calls for the *abolition* of the death penalty⟩
synonyms abatement, abolishment, abrogation, annulment, avoidance, cancellation (*also* cancelation), defeasance, dissolution, invalidation, negation, nullification, quashing, repeal, rescindment, voiding
related words abortion, calling off, recall; countermand, override, overruling, overturn, veto; retraction, reversal, revocation, suspension, withdrawal; banning,

enjoining, forbiddance, outlawing, prohibition; disallowance, dismissal, rejection; elimination, eradication, erasure, liquidation, removal
near antonyms enactment, legislation; establishment, founding, institution; formalization, legalization, legitimation, legitimization, validation; passing, ratification; approval, authorization, clearance, endorsement (*also* indorsement), permission, sanctioning; commandment, decreeing, mandating, ordering, prescription

abominable *adj* causing intense displeasure, disgust, or resentment ⟨your table manners are *abominable*!⟩ — see OFFENSIVE 1

abominate *vb* to dislike strongly ⟨we *abominate* jokes that make fun of people who have mental or physical disabilities⟩ — see HATE

abomination *n* **1** something or someone that is hated ⟨although once common, torture is now an *abomination* to the civilized peoples of the earth⟩ — see HATE 2
2 a very strong dislike ⟨the townspeople have such an *abomination* of taxes that they have even voted down increases that would have given their schools badly needed funds⟩ — see HATE 1

aboriginal *adj* belonging to a particular place by birth or origin ⟨the *aboriginal* peoples of northern Alaska are known as Inupiats, which in their language literally means "real people"⟩ — see NATIVE 1

aboriginal *n* a member of the first race to inhabit a region ⟨for a long time the *aboriginals* were not even included in the censuses, as they were viewed as part of the region's fauna⟩ — see ABORIGINE

aborigine *n* a member of the first race to inhabit a region ⟨the *aborigines* had no immunity against the raft of diseases brought by the invaders⟩
synonyms aboriginal, autochthon, indigene (*also* indigen), native
related words primitive
near antonyms alien, foreigner
antonyms nonnative

aborning *adj* beginning to come into existence ⟨the new governor will have to deal with the state's *aborning* fiscal crisis⟩ — see NASCENT

abort *vb* to put an end to (something planned or previously agreed to) ⟨had to *abort* the mission to Mars when they lost contact with the satellite⟩ — see CANCEL 1

abortion *n* the act of putting an end to something planned or previously agreed to ⟨the *abortion* of the space mission caused the whole space program to be reexamined⟩ — see CANCELLATION 1

abortive *adj* producing no results ⟨an *abortive* attempt to recover the sunken pirate ship⟩ — see FUTILE 1

abound *vb* to be copiously supplied ⟨a city that *abounds* with art museums and private galleries⟩
synonyms brim, bristle, bulge, burst, bustle, buzz, crawl, hum, overflow, pullulate, swarm, teem
near antonyms lack, need, want

abounding *adj* possessing or covered with great numbers or amounts of something specified ⟨a city *abounding* with inviting parks⟩ — see RIFE

about *adv* **1** on all sides or in every direction ⟨people standing *about* waiting for a salesclerk to assist them⟩ — see AROUND 1
2 toward the opposite direction ⟨turned *about* and saw the dog following him⟩ — see AROUND 2
3 very close to but not completely ⟨*about* as many women as men signed up for the course in auto repair⟩ — see ALMOST
4 close to but not exactly ⟨it's *about* a mile to the nearest gas station⟩ — see APPROXIMATELY
5 in one place and another ⟨his garage was a dirty, cluttered place with various tools and engine parts just lying *about*⟩ — see HERE AND THERE 1

about *prep* **1** having to do with ⟨a poignant story *about* a young man who goes off to war⟩
synonyms apropos, apropos of, as far as, as for, as regards (*also* as respects), as to, concerning, of, on, regarding, respecting, touching, toward (*or* towards)
related words over
phrases in regard to, in respect to, in view of, with regard to, with respect to
2 close to ⟨*about* the hedge there was a picket fence⟩ — see AROUND 1
3 in random positions within the boundaries of ⟨sparrows hopping *about* the lawn near the bird feeder⟩ — see AROUND 2

about-face *n* a changing from one policy or point of view to virtually its exact opposite ⟨the candidate's frequent *about-faces* on issues disturbs many voters⟩
synonyms about-turn [*British*], flip-flop, reversal, turnabout, turnaround, U-turn, volte-face
related words bait and switch, switcheroo; denial, disaffirmance, disavowal, disownment, recantation, renunciation, repudiation, retraction; reconsideration, retreat, second thought; hesitation, indecision, irresolution, shilly-shallying, vacillation, wavering, wobbling (*also* wabbling)
phrases change of heart

about-turn *n, British* a changing from one policy or point of view to virtually its exact opposite ⟨more than one London newspaper accused the prime minister of doing an *about-turn* on the issue⟩ — see ABOUT-FACE

above *adv* to or in a higher place ⟨we eventually got used to the planes constantly flying *above*⟩
synonyms aloft, over, overhead
related words skyward, upward (*or* upwards)
near antonyms underneath
antonyms below, beneath, under

above *n* a dwelling place of perfect happiness for the soul after death ⟨in her dying days she was supposedly visited by an angel from *above*⟩ — see HEAVEN 1

above *prep* higher than ⟨one minute our kite was *above* the telephone wires; the next minute it was tangled in them⟩
synonyms over
related words atop
near antonyms underneath
antonyms below, beneath, under

abracadabra *n* **1** a spoken word or set of words believed to have magic power ⟨originally, an *abracadabra* was a cryptogram of the word "abracadabra" that was repeated in diminishing form until it disappeared entirely—supposedly just like the targeted evil or misfortune⟩ — see SPELL 1
2 unintelligible or meaningless talk ⟨after some *abracadabra* the spiritualist announced that we had made contact with "the other side"⟩ — see GIBBERISH 1

abrade *vb* **1** to damage or diminish by continued friction ⟨ropes *abraded* by the rocks were a huge danger to the climbers⟩
synonyms chafe, corrade, erode, fray, frazzle, fret, gall, rasp, rub, wear
related words file, gnaw, grate, graze, grind, nibble, sandblast, sandpaper, scour, scrape, scuff, shave; erase, reduce, rub out, wear out, wipe (away); bite, break down, break up, chew, corrode, decompose, disintegrate, dissolve, eat; hone, sharpen, whet
2 to make sore by continued rubbing ⟨the prisoner's manacles *abraded* his wrists and ankles until they bled⟩ — see CHAFE 1
3 to damage by rubbing against a sharp or rough surface ⟨the yacht's once-flawless wooden hull had been badly *abraded* by years of rough dockings⟩ — see SCRAPE 2

abrasion *n* an area of skin roughened or worn away by harsh rubbing against another surface ⟨walked away

from the auto accident with only minor *abrasions*⟩
synonyms bruise, graze, scrape
related words bedsore, gall

abrasive *adj* causing annoyance ⟨an *abrasive* display of rude behavior⟩ — see ANNOYING

abreast *adj* having information especially as a result of study or experience ⟨keeping *abreast* of the latest fashion trends⟩ — see FAMILIAR 2

abridge *vb* to make less in extent or duration ⟨the library's hours have been drastically *abridged* to cut costs⟩ — see SHORTEN

abridgment *or* **abridgement** *n* a shortened version of a written work ⟨this Italian-English pocket dictionary is an *abridgment* of the hardback edition⟩
synonyms abbreviation, bowdlerization, condensation, digest
related words abstract, aperçu, brief, capsule, outline, overview, précis, recap, recapitulation, résumé (*or* resume *also* resumé), review, sketch, sum, summarization, summary, summation, survey, syllabus, synopsis, tabloid, wrap-up
near antonyms amplification, elaboration, enlargement, expansion

abrogate *vb* to put an end to by formal action ⟨the U.S. Congress can *abrogate* old treaties that are unfair to Native Americans⟩ — see ABOLISH 1

abrogation *n* the doing away with something by formal action ⟨staunch opposition to any legislation that would result in the *abrogation* of the rights of religious minorities⟩ — see ABOLITION

abrupt *adj* **1** being or characterized by direct, brief, and potentially rude speech or manner ⟨the policeman's *abrupt* manner discouraged me from trying to claim that I hadn't seen the red light⟩ — see BLUNT 1
2 having an incline approaching the perpendicular ⟨the gentle, rolling hills gradually give way to high mountains with *abrupt* sides⟩ — see STEEP 1
3 not expected ⟨his *abrupt* reappearance seems to have caught everyone off guard⟩ — see UNEXPECTED

abruptly *adv* with great suddenness ⟨the car in front stopped *abruptly*, and we almost hit it⟩ — see SHORT

abscond *vb* to get free from a dangerous or confining situation ⟨the burglar was trying to *abscond* with the jewels when he tumbled down the stairs⟩ — see ESCAPE 1

absence *n* **1** a state of being without something necessary, desirable, or useful ⟨the *absence* of volunteers to be troop leaders is putting the scouting program in real jeopardy⟩ — see NEED 1
2 the fact or state of being absent ⟨in the *absence* of ferry service to the island, the ecotourists had to charter a plane⟩ — see LACK 1

absent *adj* **1** not at a certain place ⟨three students were *absent* because of the flu⟩
synonyms away, missing, out
related words AWOL, truant; departed, gone, retired; abroad, vacationing
near antonyms accompanying, attending, participating
antonyms here, in, present
2 not present or in evidence ⟨the city's usual stir of activity was conspicuously *absent* due to the report of an escaped lion from the zoo⟩
synonyms lacking, missing, nonexistent, wanting
related words dead, departed, extinct, lost, perished, vanished; defunct, done, expired, finished, lapsed, obsolete, over, passé; inadequate, insufficient, rare, scarce, sparse, uncommon
near antonyms active, alive, animate, living, thriving; current, going, prevailing, uncanceled; common, prevalent; apparent, conspicuous, evident, obvious, plain
antonyms existent, present
3 lost in thought and unaware of one's surroundings or actions ⟨seemed *absent* when I told him you were coming because he nodded but didn't say anything⟩ — see ABSENTMINDED 1

absent *prep* not having ⟨*absent* a significant source of investment funds, the fledgling company continues to struggle⟩ — see WITHOUT 1

absentminded *adj* **1** lost in thought and unaware of one's surroundings or actions ⟨the grieving woman was so *absentminded* that she left her key in the lock after opening the door⟩
synonyms absent, abstracted, distracted, preoccupied
related words absorbed, daydreaming, dreaming, dreamy, engrossed, faraway, intent, pensive, rapt; heedless, inattentive, insensible, oblivious, unaware, unconscious, unheeding, unknowing, unmindful, unperceptive, unthinking, unwary, unwitting, vacant; befogged, befuddled, bemused, bewildered, birdbrained, clueless, confused, dazed, flighty, foggy, forgetful, forgetting, hazy, muddled, scatterbrained, unfocused (*also* unfocussed)
near antonyms alive, attentive, aware, conscious, engaged, heads-up, heedful, mindful, observant, observing, open-eyed, sharp, vigilant, wary, watchful, wide-awake; clearheaded, unconfused
antonyms alert
2 inclined to forget what one has learned or to do what one should ⟨an *absentminded* aunt who some years sends me two birthday checks⟩ — see FORGETFUL

absolute *adj* **1** exercising power or authority without interference by others ⟨Russia's *absolute* monarchy effectively ceased to be when Czar Nicholas II promised to share power with a legislative body⟩
synonyms arbitrary, autocratic (*also* autocratical), czarist (*also* tsarist *or* tzarist), despotic, dictatorial, monocratic, tyrannical (*also* tyrannic), tyrannous
related words authoritarian, jackbooted, oppressive, totalitarian; antidemocratic, antirepublican; high-handed, magisterial; domineering, imperious, masterful; all-powerful, almighty, omnipotent; autonomous, self-governing, self-ruling, sovereign (*also* sovran); unconditional, unlimited
near antonyms circumscribed, restrained, restricted; constitutional, lawful; democratic, republican
antonyms limited
2 having no exceptions or restrictions ⟨ironing is an *absolute* bore⟩ ⟨I want the *absolute* truth⟩
synonyms all-out, arrant, blank, blooming [*chiefly British*], bodacious [*Southern & Midland*], categorical (*also* categoric), clean, complete, consummate, cotton-picking, crashing, damn, damned, dead, deadly, definite, downright, dreadful, fair, flat, flat-out, out-and-out, outright, perfect, plumb, profound, pure, rank, regular, sheer, simple, stark, stone, straight-out, thorough, thoroughgoing, total, unadulterated, unalloyed, unconditional, unmitigated, unqualified, utter, very
related words authentic, classic, genuine, real, veritable; constant, endless, eternal, perpetual, undying, unremitting; extreme, unrestricted; confirmed, habitual, hopeless, inveterate; extraordinary, frightful, horrible, huge, main, superlative, supreme, surpassing, terrible, terrific
near antonyms doubtful, dubious, equivocal, qualified, questionable, restricted, uncertain
3 being entirely without fault or flaw ⟨a formal living room decorated with *absolute* taste⟩ — see PERFECT 1
4 free from added matter ⟨*absolute* alcohol⟩ — see PURE 1
5 serving to put an end to all debate or questioning ⟨*absolute* proof of her innocence⟩ — see CONCLUSIVE 1

absoluteness *n* the quality or state of being without restriction, exception, or qualification ⟨the *absoluteness* of my belief in God should be apparent⟩ — see ENTIRENESS

absolution *n* release from the guilt or penalty of an offense ⟨the jury's verdict of "not guilty" was *absolution* in the eyes of the law, but the verdict would always be "guilty" in the court of public opinion⟩ — see PARDON

absolutism *n* a system of government in which the ruler has unlimited power ⟨concerning *absolutism* Lord Acton famously observed that "absolute power corrupts absolutely"⟩ — see DESPOTISM

absolve *vb* to free from a charge of wrongdoing ⟨no amount of remorse will *absolve* shoplifters who are caught, and all cases will be prosecuted to the full extent of the law⟩ — see EXCULPATE

absorb *vb* **1** to take in (something liquid) through small openings ⟨most of the spilled water was *absorbed* by the tablecloth⟩
synonyms drink, imbibe, soak (up), sponge, suck (up), take up
related words gulp, guzzle, quaff, sip, slurp, swallow, swig, swill
2 to hold the attention of ⟨chatting on the phone doesn't *absorb* me so much that I can't do something else at the same time⟩ — see ENGAGE 1
3 to make a part of a body or system ⟨local schools will seek to *absorb* the new immigrants into the regular curriculum as quickly as possible⟩ — see EMBODY 1
4 to make complete use of ⟨cleaning the house *absorbed* the rest of his energy⟩ — see DEPLETE 1
5 to put up with (something painful or difficult) ⟨somehow she managed to *absorb* whatever hardships life offered⟩ — see BEAR 2

absorbed *adj* having the mind fixed on something ⟨Lori was so *absorbed* in her book that she didn't hear the bell ring⟩ — see ATTENTIVE 1

absorbent *also* **absorbant** *adj* able to soak up liquids especially readily ⟨highly *absorbent* material that is really good for wiping off automobiles⟩
synonyms bibulous, spongy, thirsty
related words osmotic
antonyms nonabsorbent

absorbing *adj* holding the attention or provoking interest ⟨shell collecting can be so *absorbing* that you don't notice the tide coming in⟩ — see INTERESTING

absorption *n* a focusing of the mind on something ⟨forgot to return the phone call due to his *absorption* in setting up the new computer system⟩ — see ATTENTION 1

abstain (from) *vb* to resist the temptation of ⟨had to *abstain from* solid food before her surgery⟩ — see FORBEAR

abstainer *n* a person who abstains from alcoholic beverages ⟨for religious reasons she's been a total *abstainer* her entire life⟩ — see NONDRINKER

abstemious *adj* given to or marked by restraint in the satisfaction of one's appetites ⟨being *abstemious* diners, they avoid restaurants with all-you-can-eat buffets⟩
synonyms abstentious, abstinent, continent, self-abnegating, self-denying, sober, temperate
related words ascetic (*also* ascetical), austere; disciplined, self-controlled, self-disciplined, self-governed
near antonyms gluttonous, greedy, rapacious, voracious; Cyrenaic, hedonistic, self-pleasing, sensual, sybaritic, voluptuous, voluptuary; masturbatory, onanistic
antonyms self-indulgent

abstentious *adj* given to or marked by restraint in the satisfaction of one's appetites ⟨*abstentious* by nature, she eats only to satisfy actual hunger—never just for the sake of eating⟩ — see ABSTEMIOUS

abstinence *n* **1** voluntary restraint in the satisfaction of one's appetites ⟨a cleric vainly preaching *abstinence* in a world where self-indulgence is regarded as almost a virtue⟩
synonyms continence, self-abnegation, self-denial, sobriety, temperance
related words control, forbearance, restraint; discipline, self-command, self-control, self-discipline, self-mastery; asceticism, austerity
near antonyms gluttony, greed, rapaciousness, rapacity, voraciousness, voracity; hedonism, sensuality, sybaritism
antonyms self-indulgence
2 abstention from sexual intercourse ⟨an AIDS-prevention program that relies primarily on *abstinence*⟩ — see CELIBACY

abstinent *adj* given to or marked by restraint in the satisfaction of one's appetites ⟨grew up in a family where *abstinent* behavior was expected and self-indulgence of any kind was scorned and castigated⟩ — see ABSTEMIOUS

abstract *adj* **1** dealing with or expressing a quality or idea ⟨the book deals with *abstract* matters such as honesty and integrity on the job as well as practical subjects such as asking for a raise⟩
synonyms conceptual, ideal, ideational, metaphysical, notional, theoretical (*also* theoretic)
related words conjectural, hypothetical, speculative; cosmic (*also* cosmical), intellectual, mental, spiritual; ethereal, immaterial, incorporeal, insubstantial, nonmaterial, nonphysical, unsubstantial; impalpable, imperceptible, insensible, intangible, invisible; impractical, romantic, transcendent, transcendental, unreal, utopian, visionary
near antonyms material, physical; appreciable, detectable, discernible (*also* discernable), noticeable, observable, palpable, perceptible, sensible, substantial, tangible, visible; defined, definite, distinct; actual, factual, real
antonyms concrete, nonabstract
2 using elements of form (as color, line, or texture) with little or no attempt at creating a realistic picture ⟨Cubism is a style of *abstract* art in which natural forms are broken up into geometric shapes⟩
synonyms nonfigurative, nonobjective, nonrealistic, nonrepresentational
related words expressionist, expressionistic, impressionist, impressionistic; symbolist, symbolistic
near antonyms lifelike, natural
antonyms figurative, naturalistic (*also* naturalist), nonabstract, objective, realistic, representational

abstract *n* **1** a short statement of the main points ⟨the scientist wrote a bare-bones *abstract* of his research and conclusions⟩ — see SUMMARY
2 a visible representation of something abstract (as a quality) ⟨a recent college valedictorian who's been hailed as the very *abstract* of what's right with today's young people⟩ — see EMBODIMENT

abstract *vb* **1** to draw the attention or mind to something else ⟨personal problems *abstracted* him so persistently that he struggled to keep his mind on his work⟩ — see DISTRACT 1
2 to make into a short statement of the main points (as of a report) ⟨took the 135-page report and *abstracted* it in three short paragraphs⟩ — see SUMMARIZE

abstracted *adj* lost in thought and unaware of one's surroundings or actions ⟨the man on the train seemed somewhat *abstracted*, and he did indeed forget to get off at his stop⟩ — see ABSENTMINDED 1

abstraction *n* something imagined or pictured in the mind ⟨to a people who have lived under one dictatorship after another, democracy and freedom are mere *abstractions*⟩ — see IDEA 1

abstruse *adj* difficult for one of ordinary knowledge or intelligence to understand ⟨you're not the only one who finds Einstein's theory of relativity *abstruse*⟩ — see PROFOUND 1

absurd *adj* **1** conceived or made without regard for reason or reality ⟨*absurd* claims of having been abducted by UFO's⟩ — see FANTASTIC 1
2 showing or marked by a lack of good sense or judgment ⟨an *absurd* rule that bicycles are not allowed in the park⟩ — see FOOLISH 1
3 so foolish or pointless as to be worthy of scornful laughter ⟨it's *absurd* to expect to make a killing in the stock market overnight⟩ — see RIDICULOUS 1

absurdity *n* **1** a foolish act or idea ⟨to say men can't cook as well as women is of course an *absurdity*⟩ — see FOLLY 1
2 lack of good sense or judgment ⟨the *absurdity* of expecting a 98-year-old woman to adequately supervise four six-year-olds⟩ — see FOOLISHNESS 1

abubble *adj* marked by much life, movement, or activity ⟨when the grandkids come to stay, the house is *abubble* with their chatter and horseplay⟩ — see ALIVE 2

abundance *n* **1** a considerable amount ⟨an *abundance* of flowers for the wedding⟩ ⟨grew up with an *abundance* of cousins⟩ — see LOT 2
2 an amount or supply more than sufficient to meet one's needs ⟨we have an *abundance* of food, so eat as much as you want⟩ — see PLENTY 1

abundant *adj* **1** being more than enough without being excessive ⟨claimed that the needy were already receiving *abundant* help from both the government and charitable organizations⟩ — see PLENTIFUL
2 possessing or covered with great numbers or amounts of something specified ⟨a savory soup that is *abundant* with kale, potatoes, and linguica⟩ — see RIFE

abuse *n* **1** harsh insulting language ⟨hometown fans hurled *abuse* at the visiting team⟩
synonyms billingsgate, fulmination, invective, obloquy, scurrility, vitriol, vituperation
related words blackguardism; blasphemy, curse, execration, imprecation, malediction, profanity; epithet, insult, put-down, slur; expletive, swearword; aspersion, bad-mouthing, belittlement, disparagement, revilement, vilification; castigation, chastisement, criticism, excoriation, opprobrium, rebuke, reprimand, reproof; broadside, diatribe, harangue, polemic, tirade
near antonyms acclaim, applause, commendation, praise; compliments, congratulations, endearments, felicitations; adulation, blarney, flattery, overpraise, soft soap
2 incorrect or improper use ⟨naturally the furniture had received a lot of *abuse* from the 10 kids in the family⟩ — see MISUSE

abuse *vb* **1** to inflict physical or emotional harm upon ⟨if you *abuse* your pet, he will always have an ugly disposition⟩
synonyms brutalize, bully, ill-treat, ill-use, kick around, maltreat, manhandle, mess over [*slang*], mishandle, mistreat, misuse
related words molest, outrage, violate; harass, harm, hurt, injure, oppress, persecute, torment, torture; burn, sandbag, victimize, wrong; beat (up), mess (up), rough (up), work (over)
phrases take apart
near antonyms care (for), cherish, foster, nurture; baby, cater (to), coddle, favor, gratify, humor, indulge, mollycoddle, pamper, spoil
2 to criticize harshly and usually publicly ⟨a demanding, difficult patient who constantly *abuses* the nurses and aides⟩ — see ATTACK 2
3 to put to a bad or improper use ⟨if you *abuse* your baseball bat by using it to hammer nails, don't expect it to last long⟩ — see MISAPPLY
4 to take unfair advantage of ⟨*abused* his parents' trust, pilfering small amounts from them that he hoped they wouldn't notice⟩ — see EXPLOIT 1

abusive *adj* marked by harsh insulting language ⟨never one to believe that honorable people can disagree honorably, he invariably launches *abusive* attacks against anyone who dares to challenge him⟩
synonyms contumelious, invective, opprobrious, scurrile (*or* scurril), scurrilous, truculent, vitriolic, vituperative, vituperatory
related words affronting, insulting, offending, offensive, outrageous, outraging; coarse, crude, dirty, filthy, foul, foulmouthed, gross, indecent, nasty, obscene, potty-mouthed, vulgar; contemptuous, disdainful, scornful; defamatory, libelous (*or* libellous), scandalous, slanderous; maligning, traducing, vilifying; hateful, malevolent, malicious, spiteful; immoderate, intemperate, unbridled, unrestrained
near antonyms moderate, temperate; deferential, respectful; civil, courteous, gracious, mannerly, polite; discreet, judicious, tempered; encomiastic, laudative, laudatory, praiseful

abut *vb* to be adjacent to ⟨our land *abuts* a nature preserve, so we see a lot of wildlife⟩ — see ADJOIN 1

abutting *adj* having a border in common ⟨the new neighbors promptly erected fences between their property and the *abutting* properties⟩ — see ADJACENT

abuzz *adj* marked by much life, movement, or activity ⟨the classroom was *abuzz* with preparations for that evening's open house for the parents⟩ — see ALIVE 2

abysm *n* an immeasurable depth or space ⟨a recurrent dream in which he would fall helplessly into a dark and silent *abysm*⟩ — see ABYSS

abysmal *adj* extending far downward ⟨a desperate cry echoing from the *abysmal* reaches of the cave⟩ — see DEEP 1

abyss *n* an immeasurable depth or space ⟨looking down at the dark ocean from the ship's rail, the cruise passenger felt as though he was staring into an *abyss*⟩
synonyms abysm, chasm, deep, gulf, ocean
related words cleft, crevasse, crevice, fissure; cavern, hole, hollow, pit; breadth, expanse, extent, reach, spread, stretch; black hole, emptiness, nothingness, vacancy, vacuity, vacuum, void

academe *n* a place or establishment for teaching and learning ⟨the cloistered and privileged world inhabited by the students in that suburban *academe*⟩ — see SCHOOL

academic *also* **academical** *adj* **1** of or relating to schooling or learning especially at an advanced level ⟨"If you spent more time in *academic* pursuits and less time in social ones, you could easily make good grades," the dean told Valerie⟩
synonyms educational, intellectual, scholarly, scholastic
related words bookish, donnish, geeky, nerdish, nerdy, pedagogical (*also* pedagogic), pedantic, professorial, tweedy; curricular; educative, instructive; collegiate, graduate, postgraduate
near antonyms cocurricular, extracurricular; noncollegiate
antonyms nonacademic, noneducational, unacademic, unscholarly
2 very learned or educated but inexperienced in practical matters ⟨*academic* thinkers who have no understanding of realpolitik⟩
synonyms ivory-tower, ivory-towered, ivory-towerish
related words cerebral, eggheaded, highbrow, intellectual
near antonyms astute, canny, clear-sighted, hard-

headed, hard-nosed, knowing, sharp, sharp-witted, shrewd, tough-minded
3 existing only as an assumption or speculation ⟨your arguments are merely *academic*—such a worst-case scenario is unlikely to ever occur⟩ — see THEORETICAL 1

academy *n* a place or establishment for teaching and learning ⟨a military *academy*⟩ ⟨an *academy* of the fine arts⟩ — see SCHOOL

accede *vb* to give or express one's approval (as to a proposal) ⟨finally *acceded* to their pleas for more time to complete the project⟩
synonyms acquiesce, agree, assent, come round, consent, subscribe
related words adopt, embrace, espouse; abide, bear (with), endure, stand, suffer, tolerate; stomach, swallow, take; bow, knuckle under, relent, submit, succumb, yield
near antonyms rebuff, refuse, reject, scorn, spurn; deny, gainsay
antonyms dissent

accelerate *vb* **1** to become greater in size, extent, volume, amount, or number ⟨toy purchases *accelerate* dramatically during the Christmas season⟩ — see INCREASE 2
2 to cause to move or proceed fast or faster ⟨we *accelerated* preparations for the hurricane upon hearing weather reports that it had gained speed⟩ — see HURRY 1
3 to make greater in size, amount, or number ⟨the company *accelerated* its advertising purchases even as the economy appeared to be in recession⟩ — see INCREASE 1

accent *n* a special notice or importance given to something ⟨although we dutifully carried binoculars on our bird walk, the *accent* was on recognizing avifauna by their song⟩ — see EMPHASIS 1

accent *vb* to indicate the importance of by centering attention on ⟨the town's promotional literature *accents* its vital role in American history⟩ — see EMPHASIZE 1

accentuate *vb* **1** to indicate the importance of by centering attention on ⟨let's *accentuate* the saxophones during this piece by having the sax players stand up⟩ — see EMPHASIZE 1
2 to make markedly greater in measure or degree ⟨the foul weather merely *accentuated* my feelings of depression⟩ — see INTENSIFY
3 to make more apparent ⟨unfortunately, the new bedspread just *accentuates* the dinginess of the curtains behind the bed⟩ — see EMPHASIZE 2

accentuation *n* a special notice or importance given to something ⟨the school's *accentuation* on math skills has resulted in its students being among the highest math scorers in the state⟩ — see EMPHASIS 1

accept *vb* **1** to agree to receive whether willingly or reluctantly ⟨some merchants in town will *accept* Canadian coins⟩ — see TAKE 2
2 to have a favorable opinion of ⟨her husband feels that he has never been truly *accepted* by his wife's family⟩ — see APPROVE (OF)
3 to regard as right or true ⟨refused to *accept* that her friend had said those mean things⟩ — see BELIEVE 1
4 to take to or upon oneself ⟨*accepted* the responsibility of sending out the invitations⟩ — see ASSUME 1
5 to put up with (something painful or difficult) ⟨he *accepted* all of life's vicissitudes without complaint⟩ — see BEAR 2

acceptability *n* the quality or state of meeting one's needs adequately ⟨the *acceptability* of a broken key or two on a secondhand piano might depend on which keys are broken⟩ — see SUFFICIENCY

acceptable *adj* of a level of quality that meets one's needs or standards ⟨told the bike rental man that a ten-speed with four broken gears was not *acceptable*⟩ — see ADEQUATE

acceptably *adv* in a satisfactory way ⟨the previous renters had left the cottage's kitchen *acceptably* clean⟩ — see WELL 1

access *n* **1** a sudden experiencing of a physical or mental disorder ⟨a sudden *access* of hay fever was making him feel miserable⟩ — see ATTACK 2
2 the means or right of entering or participating in ⟨in the evening the only *access* to the building is through the side door⟩ — see ENTRANCE 1

access *vb* to go or come in or into ⟨could not *access* the bank vault because the lock was controlled by a timer⟩ — see ENTER 1

accessible *adj* **1** being within the financial means of most people ⟨a store offering stylish clothes at *accessible* prices⟩
synonyms affordable, popular
related words bargain-basement, budget, cheap, discount, inexpensive, low, low-end, rock-bottom; moderate, modest, reasonable
near antonyms costly, dear, expensive, high, high-end, upscale
2 possible to get ⟨the phone line is not *accessible* without your personal identification number⟩ — see AVAILABLE 1
3 situated within easy reach ⟨with the elevator broken, the second floor is not *accessible* to people in wheelchairs⟩ — see CONVENIENT
4 capable of being understood ⟨one of the more *accessible* works of a poet who can often be difficult and obscure⟩ — see INTELLIGIBLE

accession *n* **1** something added to an existing supply ⟨an exhibit of the museum's latest *accessions*⟩
synonyms acquisition, obtainment
related words accomplishment, acquirement, attainment
2 the means or right of entering or participating in ⟨joining the army was his emancipation from his family as well as his *accession* to adulthood⟩ — see ENTRANCE 1

accessorial *adj* available to supply something extra when needed ⟨an *accessorial* service, such as packing, will add substantially to the moving company's basic fee⟩ — see AUXILIARY

accessory *adj* available to supply something extra when needed ⟨most phone services offer *accessory* features such as call-waiting⟩ — see AUXILIARY

accessory *also* **accessary** *n* **1** something that is not necessary in itself but adds to the convenience or performance of the main piece of equipment ⟨bought a new car with lots of high-tech *accessories*⟩
synonyms accoutrement (*or* accouterment), adapter (*also* adaptor), add-on, adjunct, appendage, appliance, attachment, option
related words accompaniment, additive, complement, supplement; auxiliary, subsidiary; amenity, doodad, embroidery, extra, filler, frill, incidental, luxury, nonessential, nonnecessity; appurtenances, bells and whistles, equipment, furnishings, habiliment(s), paraphernalia, trappings; adornment, decoration, embellishment, enhancement, garnish, ornament, trim, trimming
near antonyms essential, necessity, requirement, requisite
2 one associated with another in wrongdoing ⟨two *accessories*, the driver of the getaway car and the dishonest bank teller, were charged in the robbery case⟩ — see ACCOMPLICE

accident *n* **1** a chance and usually sudden event bringing loss or injury ⟨was involved in a minor *accident* on her way home from work⟩

synonyms casualty, mischance, mishap
related words calamity, cataclysm, catastrophe, cropper, deathblow, disaster, tragedy; bummer, knock, misadventure, misfortune; collision, crack-up, crash, smashup, wreck
near antonyms boon, break, fluke, godsend, miracle, strike, windfall; fortune, luck, serendipity
2 the uncertain course of events ⟨you shouldn't leave it to *accident* to decide where you'll be lodging in the course of your trip across the country⟩ — see CHANCE 1

accidental *adj* **1** happening by chance ⟨finding the gold was all the more remarkable because its discovery was entirely *accidental*⟩
synonyms casual, chance, fluky (*also* flukey), fortuitous, inadvertent, incidental, unintended, unintentional, unplanned, unpremeditated, unwitting
related words coincidental; freak, odd; aimless, arbitrary, desultory, haphazard, random; uncertain, unexpected, unforeseeable, unforeseen; coerced, forced, involuntary; unconscious, unprompted
near antonyms certain, destined, expected, fixed, foreordained, foreseeable, foreseen, inevitable, predestined, predetermined, predictable, preordained, prescribed, sure; conscious, freewill, knowing, unforced, voluntary, volunteer, willful (*or* wilful)
antonyms calculated, deliberate, intended, intentional, planned, premeditated, premeditative, prepense, set
2 not being a vital part of or belonging to something ⟨we're considering the painting's merit as a work of art, its commercial value being entirely *accidental* as far as we're concerned⟩ — see EXTRINSIC

acclaim *n* public acknowledgment or admiration for an achievement ⟨many people were involved in the search, but the person who actually found the missing girl got all the *acclaim*⟩ — see GLORY 1

acclaim *vb* to declare enthusiastic approval of ⟨she has long been *acclaimed* by the critics for her realistic acting⟩
synonyms accredit, applaud, cheer, crack up, hail, laud, praise, salute, tout
related words bravo, clap, rise (to); ballyhoo; approve, commend, endorse (*also* indorse), favor, recommend, root (for), support; celebrate, emblazon, eulogize, extol (*also* extoll), glorify, magnify, sing; adulate, belaud, flatter, overpraise; deify, idolize
phrases doff one's hat to (*or* doff one's cap to)
near antonyms belittle, discommend, disparage, put down; blame, censure, reprehend, reprobate; admonish, chide, criticize, rebuke, reprimand, reproach, reprove; castigate, excoriate, keelhaul, lambaste (*or* lambast), skewer, slag [*chiefly British*], vilify
antonyms knock, pan, slam

acclamation *n* enthusiastic and usually public expression of approval ⟨the young piano prodigy has received *acclamation* from audiences worldwide⟩ — see APPLAUSE 1

acclimate *vb* to change (something) so as to make it suitable for a new use or situation ⟨never could *acclimate* himself to a nine-to-five office job⟩ — see ADAPT

acclimation *n* the act or process of changing something to fit a new use or situation ⟨a period of *acclimation* to the region's rising temperatures⟩ — see ADAPTATION

acclimatization *n* the act or process of changing something to fit a new use or situation ⟨the *acclimatization* of the immigrants to the culture of their adopted homeland has proven to be unexpectedly difficult⟩ — see ADAPTATION

acclimatize *vb* to change (something) so as to make it suitable for a new use or situation ⟨had lived through several northern winters before she fully *acclimatized* her wardrobe⟩ — see ADAPT

acclivity *n* an upward slope ⟨the steep *acclivity* was especially daunting for the novice hikers⟩ — see ASCENT 2

accolade *n* **1** a formal expression of praise ⟨for their exceptional bravery the firefighters received *accolades* from both local and national officials⟩ — see ENCOMIUM
2 public acknowledgment or admiration for an achievement ⟨winning the Nobel Prize for Physics is generally regarded as the highest *accolade* for a physicist⟩ — see GLORY 1
3 something given in recognition of achievement ⟨a screen performance that won virtually every *accolade* that the film world has to offer⟩ — see AWARD 1

accommodate *vb* **1** to make or have room for ⟨the back seat *accommodates* three people comfortably⟩
synonyms fit, hold, take
related words carry, contain, seat; enclose (*also* inclose), encompass, enfold; harbor, house
2 to bring to a state free of conflicts, inconsistencies, or differences ⟨let's *accommodate* the difference in their voices by moving the mike closer to Sarah, whose voice is softer⟩ — see HARMONIZE 2
3 to change (something) so as to make it suitable for a new use or situation ⟨*accommodated* the lectern to the height of the guest speaker, who turned out to be quite short⟩ — see ADAPT
4 to do a service or favor for ⟨couldn't *accommodate* everyone who wanted a free T-shirt⟩ — see OBLIGE 1
5 to provide with living quarters or shelter ⟨regards the tent as entirely inadequate for *accommodating* them through the winter⟩ — see HOUSE 1

accommodating *adj* willing to do a favor ⟨an *accommodating* waiter who readily honored our request to make substitutions in our order⟩
synonyms accommodative, friendly, indulgent, obliging
related words helpful, solicitous; considerate, thoughtful; agreeable, amenable, complaisant, gracious; lenient, overindulgent, permissive

accommodation *n* **1** *usually* **accommodations** *pl* a place to sleep and related amenities for the temporary use of a tourist or traveler ⟨a resort offering a wide range of *accommodations*⟩
synonyms lodging, lodgment (*or* lodgement)
related words berth, shelter; crash pad
2 the act or practice of each side giving up something in order to reach an agreement ⟨the twins each made an *accommodation*: Jane agreed to Joan's pink curtains and Joan agreed to Jane's purple rug⟩ — see CONCESSION 1
3 something that adds to one's ease of living ⟨a village that wants to attract tourists but doesn't even provide public *accommodations* for their sanitary needs⟩ — see COMFORT 2
4 the act or process of changing something to fit a new use or situation ⟨an *accommodation* to changing economic conditions will be necessary if the church is to remain open⟩ — see ADAPTATION

accommodative *adj* willing to do a favor ⟨owing to the efforts of an *accommodative* desk clerk, we were moved to a quieter section of the hotel⟩ — see ACCOMMODATING

accompaniment *n* something that is found along with something else ⟨the sound of crickets was the perfect *accompaniment* to our summer evenings on the porch⟩
synonyms attendant, companion, concomitant, corollary, incident, obbligato
related words accessory (*also* accessary), adjunct, appendage; complement, supplement; counterpart, fellow, mate; consequence, follow-up; fixings, trimmings

accompany *vb* **1** to go along with in order to provide

assistance, protection, or companionship ⟨children using the pool must be *accompanied* by a parent at all times⟩
synonyms attend, chaperone (*or* chaperon), companion, company, convoy, escort, see, squire
related words walk; associate, consort, pal (around), team (up); defend, guard, protect; bring, conduct, guide, lead, pilot, steer, usher; follow, shadow, tag, tag along, tail; hang (around), hover (over)
near antonyms abandon, desert, ditch, dump, forsake
2 to occur or exist at the same time ⟨a general feeling of weariness often *accompanies* a cold⟩ — see COINCIDE 1

accompanying *adj* present at the same time and place ⟨you can enjoy your video games in here, but preferably without the *accompanying* sound effects⟩ — see COINCIDENT 1

accomplice *n* one associated with another in wrongdoing ⟨the thief and his *accomplices* were eventually caught and brought to justice⟩
synonyms abettor (*also* abetter), accessory (*also* accessary), cohort, confederate
related words collaborationist, collaborator, informant, informer; evidence, state's evidence; companion, comrade, crony, henchman, partner; conspirator, plotter, traitor; gangster, mobster, racketeer

accomplish *vb* to carry through (as a process) to completion ⟨you've *accomplished* your assigned task with your usual efficiency⟩ — see PERFORM 1

accomplished *adj* **1** having or showing a taste for the fine arts and gracious living ⟨a year as an exchange student in Europe had transformed the tomboy into an *accomplished* young woman⟩ — see CULTIVATED
2 having or showing exceptional knowledge, experience, or skill in a field of endeavor ⟨an *accomplished* performance of a difficult violin concerto⟩ ⟨a delicate eye operation that only the most *accomplished* surgeon would attempt⟩ — see PROFICIENT
3 not capable of being challenged or proved wrong ⟨it is an *accomplished* fact that 10th century Norsemen established settlements in Newfoundland⟩ — see IRREFUTABLE

accomplishment *n* **1** a successful result brought about by hard work ⟨our biggest *accomplishment* this week was finishing the living room makeover⟩
synonyms achievement, acquirement, attainment, baby, coup, success, triumph
related words blockbuster, hit, jackpot, megahit, miracle, smash, winner; conquest, gain, victory, win; skill; deed, feat, performance; arrival, completion, consummation, culmination, execution, fruition, fulfillment (*or* fulfilment), implementation, realization
phrases a feather in one's cap
near antonyms botch, cock-up [*British*], mess, muddle, shambles; bummer, bust, catastrophe, debacle (*also* débâcle), disaster, dud, failure, fiasco, fizzle, flop, washout; disappointment, letdown, loss, setback
antonyms nonachievement
2 the doing of an action ⟨your prompt *accomplishment* of this urgent project is much appreciated⟩ — see COMMISSION 2
3 the state of being actual or complete ⟨a long, difficult project whose *accomplishment* we wondered if we would ever see⟩ — see FRUITION
4 a high level of taste and enlightenment as a result of extensive intellectual training and exposure to the arts ⟨what his wife lacked in traditional *accomplishment* she made up for with a great generosity of spirit⟩ — see CULTURE 1

accord *n* **1** a formal agreement between two or more nations or peoples ⟨hoped to bring about a peace *accord* between the warring nations⟩ — see TREATY
2 a state of consistency ⟨this undated map doesn't seem to be in *accord* with the current layout of the streets⟩ — see CONFORMITY 1
3 an arrangement about action to be taken ⟨the judges have reached an *accord*: the match will have to be replayed⟩ — see AGREEMENT 2
4 the state of being of one opinion about something ⟨is everyone in *accord* about where to go for lunch?⟩ — see AGREEMENT 1
5 the act or power of making one's own choices or decisions ⟨did not move to a different workstation of her own *accord*⟩ — see FREE WILL

accord *vb* **1** to be in agreement on every point ⟨claims that the newspaper's quote does not *accord* with what he actually said⟩ — see CHECK 1
2 to give the ownership or benefit of (something) formally or publicly ⟨women were finally *accorded* the right to vote in 1920⟩ — see CONFER 1

accordance *n* a state of consistency ⟨make sure the fund-raiser is in *accordance* with the school rules⟩ — see CONFORMITY 1

accordant *adj* not having or showing any apparent conflict ⟨a decision *accordant* with previous policy regarding unpaid leave⟩ — see CONSISTENT

accordingly *adv* for this or that reason ⟨the application deadline was yesterday; *accordingly*, only applications mailed before midnight can be considered⟩ — see THEREFORE

accouchement *n* the act or process of giving birth to children ⟨for her second *accouchement*, she was attended by a more sympathetic doctor⟩ — see CHILDBIRTH

account *n* **1** a relating of events usually in the order in which they happened ⟨newspaper reporters must strive to provide an accurate *account* of what happened⟩
synonyms chronicle, chronology, commentary (*usually* commentaries), history, narration, narrative, record, report, story
related words version; deposition, documentation, testament, testimonial, testimony, witness; annals, blog, diary, journal, log, logbook, memoir; minutes, procès-verbal; anecdote, tale, yarn; epic, saga; gest (*or* geste), romance; recital, recitation; case history, case study
2 a presentation of an artistic work (as a piece of music) from a particular point of view ⟨the pianist gave an *account* of the sonata that revealed a very mature understanding of the work⟩
synonyms interpretation, performance, reading, rendition, version
related words adaptation, reworking, variation
3 a record of goods sold or services performed together with the costs due ⟨please add this meal to my restaurant *account*⟩ — see [1]BILL 1
4 a sum of money set aside for a particular purpose ⟨after paying the tuition, there was still money left for books in her special *account* for college expenses⟩ — see FUND 1
5 the capacity for being useful for some purpose ⟨all the planning came to no *account* when the event was abruptly cancelled⟩ — see USE 2
6 the relative usefulness or importance of something as judged by specific qualities ⟨the position of publicity agent for a star is of considerable *account* in Hollywood⟩ — see WORTH 1
7 a careful weighing of the reasons for or against something ⟨take into *account* the potential problems that come with keeping a horse⟩ — see CONSIDERATION 1
8 a feeling of great approval and liking ⟨held her grandmother, a pioneer in aviation, in high *account*⟩ — see ADMIRATION 1
9 a person who buys a product or uses a service from a business ⟨the company sends out holiday cards to all its *accounts*⟩ — see CUSTOMER 1

10 a statement given to explain a belief or act ⟨he could offer no credible *account* for why he had been absent from work for two hours⟩ — see REASON 1
11 something (as a belief) that serves as the basis for another thing ⟨for that *account* alone you should agree that the system needs overhauling⟩ — see REASON 2
12 the quality or state of being important ⟨where we go for dinner is of no *account* to me⟩ — see IMPORTANCE

account *vb* to think of in a particular way ⟨*account* themselves lucky to be alive⟩ — see CONSIDER 1

account (for) *vb* to give the reason for or cause of ⟨could not *account for* the huge difference in price between the two practically identical handbags⟩ — see EXPLAIN 2

accountable *adj* being the one who must meet an obligation or suffer the consequences for failing to do so ⟨the owner was held *accountable* for his dog's biting of the child⟩ — see RESPONSIBLE 1

accounting *n* a statement given to explain a belief or act ⟨what *accounting* can you give for your bizarre actions on the night in question?⟩ — see REASON 1

accoutre *or* **accouter** *vb* to provide (someone) with what is needed for a task or activity ⟨hikers *accoutred* with walking sticks, water bottles, trail maps, and compasses⟩ — see FURNISH 1

accoutrement *or* **accouterment** *n* **1** something that is not necessary in itself but adds to the convenience or performance of the main piece of equipment ⟨this vacuum cleaner has all of the *accoutrements* for cleaning furniture as well as floors⟩ — see ACCESSORY 1
2 accoutrements *or* **accouterments** *pl* items needed for the performance of a task or activity ⟨has all the *accoutrements* that the home pastry chef could ever want⟩ — see EQUIPMENT

accredit *vb* **1** to explain (something) as being the result of something else ⟨*accredits* his good choice of movies to reading a reviewer who seldom steers him wrong⟩ — see CREDIT 1
2 to give official or legal power to ⟨took a course that *accredited* her to teach first aid⟩ — see AUTHORIZE 1
3 to declare enthusiastic approval of ⟨generally *accredited* as the finest American dramatist of the postwar generation⟩ — see ACCLAIM
4 to give official acceptance of as satisfactory ⟨thus far the board has refused to *accredit* the school⟩ — see APPROVE

accreditation *n* the granting of power to perform various acts or duties ⟨the only body empowered with the *accreditation* of medical schools in the state⟩ — see COMMISSION 1

accrete *vb* to gradually form into a layer, pile, or mass ⟨silt *accreting* at the mouth of the river over time⟩ — see COLLECT 2

accretion *n* **1** a mass or quantity that has piled up or that has been gathered over a period of time ⟨a thick *accretion* of ice in a freezer that obviously had not been cleaned for some time⟩ — see ACCUMULATION 1
2 something added (as by growth) ⟨*accretions* of lime have thickened the cave's stalactites and stalagmites over the centuries⟩ — see INCREASE 1

accretive *adj* produced by a series of additions of identical or similar things ⟨the story of his encounter with the bear was awash with *accretive* exaggeration, the bear becoming larger with each retelling of the tale⟩ — see CUMULATIVE

accrual *n* something added (as by growth) ⟨had an *accrual* of $100 through interest on my savings account last year⟩ — see INCREASE 1

accumulate *vb* **1** to become greater in extent, volume, amount, or number ⟨the number of complaints about that mail order firm is really *accumulating*⟩ — see INCREASE 2
2 to bring together in one body or place ⟨finally *accumulated* enough donated books to hold a book sale⟩ — see GATHER 1
3 to gradually form into a layer, pile, or mass ⟨clouds *accumulating* on the western horizon⟩ — see COLLECT 2

accumulating *n* the act or process of becoming greater in number ⟨the *accumulating* of newspapers in the basement over the years is really getting out of hand⟩ — see MULTIPLICATION

accumulation *n* **1** a mass or quantity that has piled up or that has been gathered over a period of time ⟨a vast *accumulation* of evidence about the dangers of smoking⟩
synonyms accretion, assemblage, collection, cumulation, cumulus, gathering, lodgment (*or* lodgement), pileup
related words agglomerate, assortment, congeries, conglomerate, conglomeration, hodgepodge, hotchpotch, jumble, medley, mélange, mishmash, mix, mixture, motley, potpourri; agglomeration, clutter, hash, heap, litter, mass, pile; aggregate, aggregation, sum, totality; backlog, cache, fund, hoard, inventory, kitty, nest egg, reserve, stock, stockpile, store, supply
2 the act or process of becoming greater in number ⟨the *accumulation* of leaves on the ground is proceeding at a much faster rate than my raking⟩ — see MULTIPLICATION

accumulative *adj* produced by a series of additions of identical or similar things ⟨the *accumulative* effect of all her worries was to seriously undermine her health⟩ — see CUMULATIVE

accuracy *n* the quality or state of being very accurate ⟨obviously, with brain surgery the *accuracy* of the incision is incredibly important⟩ — see PRECISION

accurate *adj* **1** being in agreement with the truth or a fact or a standard ⟨an *accurate* count of the number of people coming to the wedding reception⟩ — see CORRECT 1
2 following an original exactly ⟨an *accurate* translation of the original story⟩ — see FAITHFUL 2
3 meeting the highest standard of accuracy ⟨an *accurate* thermometer⟩ ⟨*accurate* measurements⟩ — see PRECISE 1

accurateness *n* the quality or state of being very accurate ⟨a local weatherman whose popularity seems to rest more on the attractiveness of his personality than on the *accurateness* of his predictions⟩ — see PRECISION

accursed *or* **accurst** *adj* deserving of one's condemnation or displeasure ⟨the video store is charging another *accursed* late fee⟩ — see DAMNABLE

accuse *vb* to make a claim of wrongdoing against ⟨she was *accused* of lying on the employment application⟩
synonyms charge, criminate, defame [*archaic*], impeach, incriminate, indict
related words blame, call (on), castigate, censure, condemn, criticize, damn, denounce, fault, impugn, reproach, reprobate; chide, rebuke, reprove, tax; appeal, arraign, book, cite, summon; prosecute, sue, try; frame, implicate, inculpate, inform (against), name, report; recriminate, retaliate
near antonyms advocate, champion, defend; excuse, forgive, justify, pardon, remit, shrive
antonyms absolve, acquit, clear, exculpate, exonerate, vindicate

accustom *vb* to impart knowledge of a new thing or situation to ⟨the task of *accustoming* new recruits to shipboard life⟩ — see ACQUAINT 1

accustomed *adj* being in the habit or custom ⟨Josh felt uncomfortably full, as he was not *accustomed* to eating so much⟩

synonyms given, habituated, used, wont
related words apt, inclined, liable, likely, prone; hardened, inured; experienced, practiced (*or* practised), seasoned, veteran; addicted, hooked
near antonyms unapt, unlikely; averse, disinclined, opposed; inexperienced, new, unseasoned; disaccustomed, weaned
antonyms unaccustomed, unused, unwonted

ace *adj* having or showing exceptional knowledge, experience, or skill in a field of endeavor ⟨an *ace* computer programmer⟩ — see PROFICIENT

ace *n* **1** a person with a high level of knowledge or skill in a field ⟨took a few lessons with a tennis *ace* to improve his backhand⟩ — see EXPERT
2 a very small amount ⟨not an *ace* of truth in what she said⟩ — see PARTICLE 1
3 a very small distance or degree ⟨came within an *ace* of being chosen for the part⟩ — see HAIR 1

acerb *adj* marked by the use of wit that is intended to cause hurt feelings ⟨a professor with a rather *acerb* sense of humor⟩ — see SARCASTIC

acerbic *adj* marked by the use of wit that is intended to cause hurt feelings ⟨whispered a steady stream of *acerbic* comments as the lecturer droned on⟩ — see SARCASTIC

acerbity *n* a harsh or sharp quality ⟨the customer made his displeasure known with more *acerbity* than was necessary⟩ — see EDGE 1

ache *n* a sharp unpleasant sensation usually felt in some specific part of the body ⟨a dull pounding *ache* in his head⟩ — see PAIN 1

ache *vb* to feel or cause physical pain ⟨my feet *ache* from all that walking⟩ — see HURT 1

ache (for) *vb* **1** to have sympathy for ⟨I *ache for* those people who have to spend the holidays alone⟩ — see PITY
2 to have an earnest wish to own or enjoy ⟨*aching for* some quiet time to himself⟩ — see DESIRE 1

achievable *adj* capable of being done or carried out ⟨I think that retirement at 55 is an *achievable* goal⟩ — see POSSIBLE 1

achieve *vb* **1** to obtain (as a goal) through effort ⟨finally *achieved* stardom⟩
synonyms attain, bag, chalk up, clock (up) [*chiefly British*], gain, hit, log, make, notch (up), rack up, ring up, score, win
related words acquire, capture, carry, draw, garner, get, land, make, obtain, procure, realize, secure; amount (to), approach, equal, match, measure up (to), meet, rival, tie, touch; beat, excel, outdo, surpass, top
near antonyms fall short (of), miss; fail (at); lose
2 to carry through (as a process) to completion ⟨finally *achieved* his purpose, which was to form a first-class boys' choir made up of inner-city kids⟩ — see PERFORM 1

achievement *n* **1** a successful result brought about by hard work ⟨this improvement in your time for a 10K road race is quite an *achievement*!⟩ — see ACCOMPLISHMENT 1
2 the doing of an action ⟨what you're asking is the *achievement* of a miracle⟩ — see COMMISSION 2
3 the state of being actual or complete ⟨you should be proud of the *achievement* of your goals⟩ — see FRUITION

Achilles' heel *n* a vulnerable point ⟨the food supply proved to be the nation's *Achilles' heel* in its defense against terrorist attacks⟩
synonyms back, chink, jugular, soft spot, underbelly
related words downfall, ruin, undoing; hamartia, tragic flaw

aching *adj* **1** causing or feeling bodily pain ⟨my poor, *aching* back⟩ — see PAINFUL 1
2 expressing or suggesting mourning ⟨another one of those *aching* country songs about a woman who done him wrong⟩ — see MOURNFUL 1

achingly *adv* to a great degree ⟨an *achingly* funny movie⟩ — see VERY 1

achy *adj* causing or feeling bodily pain ⟨unable to play in tomorrow's football game because of an *achy* right knee⟩ — see PAINFUL 1

acid *adj* **1** causing or characterized by the one of the four basic taste sensations that is produced chiefly by acids ⟨an *acid*-tasting medicine⟩ — see SOUR 1
2 having or showing a habitually bad temper ⟨with her *acid* personality, my aunt could be relied upon to bring some much-needed balance to the holiday gush⟩ — see ILL-TEMPERED
3 marked by the use of wit that is intended to cause hurt feelings ⟨a cultural gadfly known for an *acid* tongue that spares no one⟩ — see SARCASTIC

acidic *adj* **1** causing or characterized by the one of the four basic taste sensations that is produced chiefly by acids ⟨the *acidic* flavor of lemon goes nicely with broiled fish⟩ — see SOUR 1
2 marked by the use of wit that is intended to cause hurt feelings ⟨her often *acidic* reviews have ruffled more than a few toques in the restaurant kitchens of New York⟩ — see SARCASTIC

acidity *n* **1** a harsh or sharp quality ⟨detected a certain *acidity* in the way he responded⟩ — see EDGE 1
2 biting sharpness of feeling or expression ⟨the *acidity* of their relationship was well known to their mutual acquaintances⟩ — see ACRIMONY 1

acidness *n* **1** a harsh or sharp quality ⟨there's an irritating *acidness* to the writer's comments on just about everything⟩ — see EDGE 1
2 biting sharpness of feeling or expression ⟨the *acidness* in his remarks hurt her to the core⟩ — see ACRIMONY 1

acidulous *adj* **1** causing or characterized by the one of the four basic taste sensations that is produced chiefly by acids ⟨a slightly *acidulous* drink that is far more refreshing than the overly sweet iced tea that is also available⟩ — see SOUR 1
2 marked by the use of wit that is intended to cause hurt feelings ⟨a gently *acidulous* writing style that never becomes annoying⟩ — see SARCASTIC

acknowledge *vb* to accept the truth or existence of (something) usually reluctantly ⟨finally had to *acknowledge* that she'd outgrown her favorite jacket⟩ — see ADMIT 1

acknowledgment *or* **acknowledgement** *n* **1** a formal recognition of an achievement or praiseworthy deed ⟨an *acknowledgment* to the food committee for the delicious refreshments⟩ — see COMMENDATION 1
2 an open declaration of something (as a fault or the commission of an offense) about oneself ⟨a surprising *acknowledgment* that he had been faking his injury in order to scam the insurance company⟩ — see CONFESSION

acme *n* **1** the highest part or point ⟨the *acme* of their basketball season was their hard-won victory over last year's state champs⟩ — see HEIGHT 1
2 the most perfect type or example ⟨a movie that has come to be regarded as the *acme* of the Hollywood musical⟩ — see QUINTESSENCE 1

acolyte *n* one who follows the opinions or teachings of another ⟨a highly influential economist whose *acolytes* can be found at many major universities⟩ — see FOLLOWER 1

acoustic *or* **acoustical** *adj* of, relating to, or experienced through the sense of hearing ⟨is a bird's *acoustic* organ similar to a human's?⟩ — see AUDITORY

acquaint *vb* **1** to impart knowledge of a new thing or situation to ⟨Mr. King spent the first week of the summer

internship *acquainting* everyone with the new computers⟩
synonyms accustom, familiarize, initiate, introduce, orient, orientate
related words habituate, wont; apprise, brief, clue (in), fill in, inform; educate, enlighten, ground, instruct, school, train, verse; expose, present, subject; advise, tell, tip (off), warn, wise (up); reacquaint
2 to give information to ⟨his sailor friend *acquainted* him with the latest navigational aids for weekend yachtsmen⟩ — see ENLIGHTEN 1
3 to make (one person) known (to another) socially ⟨hoping that someone would *acquaint* them with the new neighbors⟩ — see INTRODUCE 1

acquaintance *n* knowledge gained by personal experience ⟨Tiffany's *acquaintance* with cows is limited to a long-ago visit to a petting zoo when she was three⟩
synonyms cognizance, familiarity
related words association, experience, exposure, intimacy, involvement; initiation, introduction; awareness, comprehension, conception, inkling, notion, understanding; education, enlightenment, grounding, information, instruction, learning, schooling, training
near antonyms callowness, greenness, ignorance, inexperience
antonyms unfamiliarity

acquainted *adj* having information especially as a result of study or experience ⟨would like to see students become *acquainted* with all the services that the university has to offer⟩ — see FAMILIAR 2

acquiesce *vb* to give or express one's approval (as to a proposal) ⟨apparently the contractor expected me to *acquiesce* to my own fleecing⟩ — see ACCEDE

acquiescence *n* a readiness or willingness to yield to the wishes of others ⟨good manners demanded our cheerful *acquiescence* to our host's plans for dinner⟩ — see COMPLIANCE 1

acquiescent *adj* receiving or enduring without offering resistance ⟨was not as *acquiescent* about sharing her room as her parents seemed to think she should be⟩ — see PASSIVE

acquirable *adj* possible to get ⟨is a decent bagel *acquirable* in this town?⟩ — see AVAILABLE 1

acquire *vb* **1** to come to have gradually ⟨from years of working two jobs, he has *acquired* the ability to get by on only a few hours of sleep a day⟩ — see DEVELOP 2
2 to receive as return for effort ⟨*acquired* a reputation for always arriving at his friends' house just as they were sitting down to dinner⟩ — see EARN 1

acquirement *n* a successful result brought about by hard work ⟨the contention that the candidate's *acquirements* in the business world would stand him in good stead in the political arena⟩ — see ACCOMPLISHMENT 1

acquisition *n* something added to an existing supply ⟨every vacation trip inevitably resulted in new *acquisitions* to our array of bric-a-brac⟩ — see ACCESSION 1

acquisitive *adj* having or marked by an eager and often selfish desire especially for material possessions ⟨*acquisitive* developers are trying to tear down the historic home and build a shopping mall⟩ — see GREEDY 1

acquisitiveness *n* an intense selfish desire for wealth or possessions ⟨the queen's *acquisitiveness* would not be satisfied until she owned the largest diamond in the world⟩ — see GREED

acquit *vb* **1** to free from a charge of wrongdoing ⟨*acquitted* of the robbery charge after proving he was nowhere near the scene of the crime⟩ — see EXCULPATE
2 to manage the actions of (oneself) in a particular way ⟨the king promised handsome rewards to all who *acquitted* themselves well in the battle⟩ — see BEHAVE

acquittal *n* a setting free from a charge of wrongdoing ⟨confidently predicted that his client's trial would result in a full *acquittal*⟩
synonyms clearing, exculpation, exoneration, vindication
related words absolution, condonation, forgiveness, pardon, remission; atonement, expiation; compurgation; whitewash
near antonyms accusation, arraignment, impeachment, incrimination, indictment; prosecution; castigation, censure, condemnation, denunciation
antonyms conviction

acrid *adj* **1** having or showing deep-seated resentment ⟨there have been *acrid* relations between the two families ever since they fought over that strip of land⟩ — see BITTER 1
2 marked by the use of wit that is intended to cause hurt feelings ⟨Phillipa's *acrid* comments about the new employee's clothes were met by laughter from everyone at the lunch table⟩ — see SARCASTIC

acridity *n* **1** a harsh or sharp quality ⟨the *acridity* of the stand-up's comic rant was a little unexpected⟩ — see EDGE 1
2 biting sharpness of feeling or expression ⟨the *acridity* of the supervisor's reprimands was detrimental to morale in the department⟩ — see ACRIMONY 1

acridness *n* **1** a harsh or sharp quality ⟨an *acridness* in her voice when she said she hoped that we would get what we deserve⟩ — see EDGE 1
2 biting sharpness of feeling or expression ⟨over the years the *acridness* he felt toward his stepfather softened somewhat⟩ — see ACRIMONY 1

acrimonious *adj* having or showing deep-seated resentment ⟨an *acrimonious* parting between the two former friends⟩ — see BITTER 1

acrimoniousness *n* a harsh or sharp quality ⟨*acrimoniousness* lay beneath his words, which on their face seemed harmless enough⟩ — see EDGE 1

acrimony *n* **1** biting sharpness of feeling or expression ⟨she responded with such *acrimony* that he never brought the subject up again⟩
synonyms acidity, acidness, acridity, acridness, asperity, bile, bitterness, cattiness, corrosiveness, mordancy, tartness, virulence, virulency, vitriol
related words gruffness, harshness, hostility, relentlessness, severity, sternness, vehemence; coldness, crossness, discourteousness, iciness, impoliteness, incivility, nastiness, rudeness, sourness, surliness, ungraciousness; anger, animosity, gall, jaundice, malevolence, malice, rancor, scorn, spite, spleen, venom, vindictiveness; jealousy, pique, resentment, sour grapes
near antonyms civility, cordiality, courtesy, diplomacy, geniality, graciousness, kindness, politeness, tactfulness; compassion, softness, sweetness, sympathy, tenderness, warmth; oiliness, smoothness, suaveness, suavity, unctuousness, urbanity
2 a harsh or sharp quality ⟨the *acrimony* of his parting words shocked everyone in the office⟩ — see EDGE 1

acrobat *n* **1** one who performs feats of physical strength, balance, and agility on special apparatus ⟨a child who is a natural *acrobat* with a superb sense of balance⟩
synonyms gymnast, turner
related words exerciser, tumbler; contortionist, equilibrist; aerialist, ropedancer, ropewalker, trampoliner, trampolinist, trapeze artist, trapezist
2 a person who dexterously and expediently changes or adopts opinions ⟨a political *acrobat* whose opinion on any issue is whatever will get the most votes⟩
synonyms chameleon, chancer [*British*], opportunist, temporizer, timeserver, trimmer, weathercock
related words egoist, egotist, self-seeker; conniver, machinator, plotter, schemer

acrobatics *n pl* a spectacular display or performance of artistic or technical skill ⟨an operatic role that gives the coloratura the opportunity to indulge in a goodly amount of vocal *acrobatics*⟩
synonyms fireworks, pyrotechnics
related words extravaganza, pageant, spectacle

across *adv* from one side to the other of an intervening space ⟨will you go *across* to the Bentley's and see if their phone is working?⟩ — see OVER 1

across *prep* **1** to the opposite side of ⟨we rowed *across* the lake and visited the other couple for the evening⟩
synonyms athwart, over, through
related words around, round; beyond, past
2 in random positions within the boundaries of ⟨sheep scattered *across* the field⟩ — see AROUND 2

across–the–board *adj* belonging or relating to the whole ⟨an *across-the-board* reduction in the state's budget because of declining revenues⟩ — see GENERAL 1

act *n* **1** a performance regularly presented by an individual or group ⟨in his nightclub *act* he impersonates a veritable galaxy of movie stars⟩
synonyms bit, number, routine, shtick (*also* schtick *or* shtik), turn
related words signature
2 a display of emotion or behavior that is insincere or intended to deceive ⟨was putting on an *act* when she said she didn't mind being left out of the outing⟩ — see MASQUERADE
3 a rule of conduct or action laid down by a governing authority and especially a legislature ⟨the Americans with Disabilities *Act* requires public buildings to have wheelchair access⟩ — see LAW 1
4 something done by someone ⟨it's *acts* such as this—lying about having to work late—that make me feel like I can't trust you⟩ — see ACTION 1

act *vb* **1** to present a portrayal or performance of ⟨a local student *acted* the part of Tiny Tim in our theater company's production of *A Christmas Carol*⟩
synonyms do, impersonate, interpret, perform, play, portray
related words depict, dramatize, render, represent; act out, enact, pantomime, playact, role-play, take on; overact, overplay, underplay; ape, clown, ham, imitate, masquerade, mime, mimic, pose (as); star (in); coact, costar
2 to produce a desired effect ⟨the painkiller *acted* surprisingly quickly⟩
synonyms operate, perform, take, work
related words behave, react, respond; affect, influence, sway; pan out, redound, result
phrases take effect, take hold
near antonyms backfire; fizzle
3 to give the impression of being ⟨always *acting* helpless, just to get attention⟩ — see SEEM
4 to have a certain purpose ⟨the tail feathers of woodpeckers *act* as props while the birds excavate tree trunks for insects⟩ — see FUNCTION
5 to present a false appearance of ⟨if you *act* confident long enough, you'll begin to actually feel it⟩ — see FEIGN
6 to pretend to be (what one is not) in appearance or behavior ⟨someone who is willing to *act* the helpless little thing when she wants attention⟩ — see IMPERSONATE 1

act (toward) *vb* to behave toward in a stated way ⟨I would never *act toward* my boss that way⟩ — see TREAT 1

acting *adj* serving in a position for the time being ⟨will serve as *acting* president of the university until a permanent replacement can be found⟩
synonyms ad interim, interim, provisional, provisionary, provisory, temporary
related words alternate, backup, jackleg, make-do, makeshift, proxy, stopgap, substitute
antonyms long-term, permanent

action *n* **1** something done by someone ⟨judge people by their *actions*, not by their words⟩
synonyms act, deed, doing, exploit, feat, thing
related words accomplishment, achievement, attainment; adventure, experience; emprise, enterprise, initiative, undertaking; handiwork, performance, work; stunt, trick; activity, dealing; maneuver, measure, move, operation, procedure, proceeding, step, tactic; coaction
2 the unfolding of events in a dramatic or literary work ⟨the mystery writer displays a sure hand in managing the novel's complicated but never incoherent *action*⟩
synonyms plot, story, story line
related words subplot; arc, development; design, outline, plan, scheme; argument, mythos, subject, theme
3 a court case for enforcing a right or claim ⟨filed an *action* in county court to recover his lawn mower from his neighbor, who claims he "gave" it to her⟩ — see LAWSUIT
4 active fighting during the course of a war ⟨the battalion saw *action* soon after it arrived in France⟩ — see COMBAT 1
5 actions *pl* the way or manner in which one conducts oneself ⟨observing the *actions* of mice in various controlled settings helps scientists understand the effects of certain drugs⟩ — see BEHAVIOR
6 readiness to engage in daring or difficult activity ⟨the wilderness was tamed by men and women of *action*⟩ — see ENTERPRISE 2

actionable *adj* capable of being put to use or account ⟨the authorities had no *actionable* intelligence with which to foil the terrorist plot⟩ — see PRACTICAL 1

action figure *n* a small figure often of a human being used especially as a child's plaything ⟨a collection of *action figures* of his favorite superheroes⟩ — see DOLL 1

activate *vb* to cause to function ⟨the thermostat is set to *activate* the heating system only when the temperature drops below 65 degrees⟩
synonyms actuate, crank (up), drive, move, run, set off, spark, start, touch off, trigger, turn on
related words kick over, turn over; charge, electrify, energize, fire, fuel, generate, power, push; discharge, launch, release, switch, trip; reactivate, recharge; arouse, excite, jump-start, kick-start, stimulate, vitalize; ignite, incite, instigate, provoke, quicken, stir up; accelerate, catalyze, speed (up), step up
near antonyms arrest, brake, check, cut off, draw up, halt, jam, stall, stick, stop; decelerate, repress, slow, stunt, suppress
antonyms cut, cut out, deactivate, kill, shut off, turn off

active *adj* **1** being in effective operation ⟨the abandoned factory had not been *active* for years⟩
synonyms alive, functional, functioning, going, live, living, on, operating, operational, operative, running, working
related words effective, effectual; employable, operable, usable (*also* useable), viable, workable; performing, producing, productive, serving, useful, yielding; astir, bustling, busy, dynamic, flourishing, humming, roaring, thriving
phrases in commission (*or* into commision), in force, in gear, on line
near antonyms deactivated, decommissioned; ineffective, ineffectual, useless; inoperable, unusable, unworkable; arrested, asleep, dormant, fallow, idle, inert, latent, lifeless, nonproductive, quiescent, sleepy, stagnating, unproductive, vegetating
antonyms broken, dead, inactive, inoperative, kaput (*also* kaputt), nonactivated, nonfunctional, nonfunc-

tioning, nonoperating, nonoperational, nonoperative
2 having much high-spirited energy and movement ⟨the fish are *active* today, but we still haven't caught anything⟩ — see LIVELY 1
3 involved in often constant activity ⟨all morning the crowd at the coffeehouse kept Marion and her helper pretty *active*⟩ — see BUSY 1

actively *adv* in a manner involving great or constant activity ⟨he's been working *actively* toward the goal of opening his own restaurant⟩ — see BUSILY

activity *n* energetic movement of the body for the sake of physical fitness ⟨had to restrict his *activity* after the surgery, which meant letting the weeds take over the garden⟩ — see EXERCISE 1

actor *n* 1 one who acts professionally (as in a play, movie, or television show) ⟨my sister went to drama school to become an *actor*⟩
synonyms impersonator, mummer, player, thesp, thespian, trouper
related words barnstormer, enactor, entertainer, performer; actress, starlet; lead, leading lady, leading man, star; coactor, costar; extra, spear-carrier, supernumerary, walk-on; monologuist (*or* monologist); prima donna, scene-stealer; double, understudy; comedian, farceur; tragedian, tragedienne; ape, aper, ham, imitator, impressionist, masker, masquerader, mime, mimic, pantomime, pantomimist, personator, poser; buffoon, clown, harlequin, stooge, zany
antonyms nonactor
2 one who takes part in something ⟨Benjamin Franklin was a major *actor* in many of the events leading up to the founding of our nation⟩ — see PARTICIPANT

act out *vb* to behave badly ⟨because his parents spent so much time with his chronically ill sister, the boy resorted to *acting out* in order to get attention⟩ — see MISBEHAVE

actual *adj* existing in fact and not merely as a possibility ⟨the *actual* outcome of the election was quite different from what everybody had expected⟩
synonyms concrete, de facto, effective, existent, factual, genuine, real, sure-enough, true, very
related words attested, authenticated, confirmed, demonstrated, established, proven, substantiated, valid, validated, verified; incontestable, incontrovertible, indisputable, indubitable, inescapable, irrefutable, undeniable, unquestionable; believable, convincing, literal, realistic, unmistakable, verifiable; authentic, bona fide, real-life, real-world; absolute, certain, final, hard, objective, palpable, positive, substantial, tangible; authoritative, certifiable, certified
near antonyms alleged, assumed, reputed, supposed; conceived, envisaged, envisioned, imagined, pictured, visualized; chimerical (*also* chimeric), fabled, fanciful, fictional, fictitious, illusory, legendary; fabricated, fake, imaginary, invented, made-up, make-believe, pretend, romantic; abstract, symbolic, unreal; virtual
antonyms conjectural, hypothetical, ideal, inexistent, nonexistent, platonic, possible, potential, suppositional, theoretical (*also* theoretic)

actuality *n* 1 the fact of being or of being real ⟨the *actuality* of the Abominable Snowman is not taken seriously by scientists⟩ — see EXISTENCE
2 the quality of being actual ⟨the *actuality* of equal opportunity depends on more than just having laws that supposedly ensure it⟩ — see FACT 1
3 the state of being actual or complete ⟨the *actuality* of a manned flight to the moon would never have been believed a hundred years ago⟩ — see FRUITION
4 something that actually exists ⟨these estimated tax revenues, from casinos that have yet to be built, are being treated as *actualities*⟩ — see FACT 2

actualization *n* the state of being actual or complete ⟨an operatic performance that was the long-promised *actualization* of her musical potential⟩ — see FRUITION

actualize *vb* to come into existence ⟨several years passed before any profits from the enterprise *actualized*⟩ — see BEGIN 2

actually *adv* 1 to tell the truth ⟨*actually*, I'd rather spend the evening at home⟩
synonyms admittedly, forsooth, frankly, honestly, indeed, really, truly, truthfully, verily
related words absolutely, certainly, indisputably, indubitably, positively, realistically, undoubtedly, unquestionably, veritably
phrases as a matter of fact, in actuality, in fact, in point of fact, in reality, in truth, to be sure
2 in actual fact ⟨I call her Aunt Emily, but she is *actually* my cousin, not my aunt⟩ — see VERY 2

actuate *vb* 1 to cause to function ⟨a light *actuated* by a motion detector⟩ ⟨the alarm system *actuates* the door locks⟩ — see ACTIVATE
2 to set or keep in motion ⟨hearing depends on sound vibrations that *actuate* the complex mechanism of that sensory organ, the ear⟩ — see MOVE 2

act up *vb* 1 to behave badly ⟨the two-year-old was *acting up* in church so much that her dad had to take her outside⟩ — see MISBEHAVE
2 to engage in attention-getting playful or boisterous behavior ⟨you should have seen the boys *acting up* when they put on their aprons⟩ — see CUT UP

acuity *n* the state or quality of being able to sense slight impressions or differences ⟨a worrisome deterioration in the *acuity* of his hearing over the years⟩
synonyms acuteness, delicacy, keenness, perceptiveness, perceptivity, sensitiveness, sensitivity, sharpness
related words hyperacuity, hypersensitiveness, hypersensitivity, oversensitiveness, oversensitivity, supersensitivity; accuracy, exactitude, exactness, fineness

acumen *n* exceptional discernment and judgment especially in practical matters ⟨had the business *acumen* to know that the market for sportswear was becoming oversaturated⟩
synonyms astuteness, caginess (*also* cageyness), canniness, clear-sightedness, foxiness, hardheadedness, intelligence, keenness, knowingness, sharpness, shrewdness, wit
related words discernment, insight, perception, perceptiveness, perceptivity, percipience, sagaciousness, sagacity, sageness, sapience, wisdom; artfulness, artifice, craft, craftiness, cunning, deviousness, guile, slickness, slyness, sneakiness, subtleness, subtlety, wiliness; brain(s), gray matter, intellect, reason, sense
near antonyms artlessness, greenness, guilelessness, ingenuousness, innocence, naiveness, naïveté (*also* naivete *or* naiveté), simplemindedness, simpleness, simplicity, unsophistication, unworldliness; brainlessness, density, doltishness, dopiness, dumbness, fatuity, foolishness, half-wittedness, mindlessness, oafishness, obtuseness, senselessness, slowness, stupidity, stupidness, vacuity, witlessness

acute *adj* 1 able to sense slight impressions or differences ⟨dogs, with their *acute* sense of smell, are used for finding toxic substances undetectable by humans⟩
synonyms delicate, fine, keen, perceptive, quick, sensitive, sharp
related words accurate, clear, discerning, good, piercing, precise, receptive, sensible, subtle; hair-trigger, hyperacute, hypersensitive, oversensitive, supersensitive
near antonyms bad, deadened, dimmed, dull, dulled, fading; dead, imperceptive, insensible, insensitive, numb; imprecise, inaccurate
2 needing immediate attention ⟨famine caused by an *acute* shortage of grain⟩
synonyms burning, clamant, compelling, critical, cry-

ing, dire, emergent, exigent, imperative, imperious, importunate, instant, necessitous, pressing, urgent
related words demanding, extreme, immediate, insistent, intense, overriding; crucial, desperate, grave, life-and-death (*also* life-or-death), serious, severe, vital; dangerous, explosive, hazardous, perilous, precarious, unstable
near antonyms incidental, low-pressure, minor, negligible, trivial, unimportant; nonthreatening, safe, stable
antonyms noncritical, nonurgent
3 extreme in degree, power, or effect ⟨experiencing *acute* distress over the misunderstanding with her best friend⟩ — see INTENSE 1

acuteness *n* **1** a harsh or sharp quality ⟨judging by the *acuteness* in his tone when he congratulated me, I think he was actually quite resentful that I won⟩ — see EDGE 1
2 the state or quality of being able to sense slight impressions or differences ⟨the *acuteness* of the bird's eyesight is amazing⟩ — see ACUITY

ad *n* a published statement informing the public of a matter of general interest ⟨did you see the *ads* in the paper for cheap round-trip flights to Florida?⟩ — see ANNOUNCEMENT

adage *n* an often stated observation regarding something from common experience ⟨that old *adage*, "the early bird gets the worm"⟩ — see SAYING

adamant *adj* sticking to an opinion, purpose, or course of action in spite of reason, arguments, or persuasion ⟨remained *adamant* about getting the actor's autograph even after he had disappeared backstage⟩ — see OBSTINATE

adamantine *adj* sticking to an opinion, purpose, or course of action in spite of reason, arguments, or persuasion ⟨the *adamantine* opposition of his parents to his marriage to a girl from a poor family⟩ — see OBSTINATE

adapt *vb* to change (something) so as to make it suitable for a new use or situation ⟨it always takes freshmen a little while to *adapt* themselves to high school⟩
synonyms acclimate, acclimatize, accommodate, adjust, condition, conform, doctor, edit, fashion, fit, put, shape, suit, tailor
related words readapt, readjust; customize, gear, match, model, pattern; attune, correct, harmonize, square, tune; establish, root, settle; acquaint, familiarize, orient, orientate; equip, prepare, prime, rehearse; harden, inure, season, toughen; alter, convert, make over, modify, recast, reclaim, recycle, redesign, redevelop, redo, reengineer, refashion, refigure, refit, refocus, reinvent, rejigger, remake, remodel, revamp, revise, rework, transform; accustom, condition, habilitate, habituate, naturalize; ready, season; bend; fiddle (with), fine-tune, phase, register, regulate, rig
near antonyms misadjust

adaptable *adj* **1** able to do many different kinds of things ⟨an activities director who's *adaptable* to any kind of situation⟩ — see VERSATILE
2 capable of being readily changed ⟨the caterer's menu is *adaptable* to specific dietary needs, such as vegan, kosher, or low-fat⟩ — see FLEXIBLE 1

adaptation *n* the act or process of changing something to fit a new use or situation ⟨a careful *adaptation* of the book for the silver screen could take several years⟩
synonyms acclimation, acclimatization, accommodation, adaption, adjustment, conformation
related words readaptation, readjustment; attunement, correction, harmonization; alteration, conversion, makeover, modification, refit, revision, transformation
near antonyms maladaptation

adapter *also* **adaptor** *n* something that is not necessary in itself but adds to the convenience or performance of the main piece of equipment ⟨*adapters* for the food mixer include a meat grinder and an ice cream maker⟩ — see ACCESSORY 1

adaption *n* the act or process of changing something to fit a new use or situation ⟨the store's slow *adaption* to shoppers' changing tastes spelled its doom⟩ — see ADAPTATION

add *vb* **1** to join (something) to a mass, quantity, or number so as to bring about an overall increase ⟨the band recently *added* a saxophonist and a keyboard player to its ranks⟩ ⟨*add* another cup of flour to the mixture⟩
synonyms adjoin, annex, append, subjoin, tack (on)
related words affix, attach, fasten, fix, graft, hitch, tag, tie; infuse, inject, insert, interfuse, introduce; aggrandize, amplify, augment, beef (up), boost, compound, enlarge, escalate, expand, extend, increase, multiply, raise, swell up; elongate, lengthen, prolong, protract; enhance, heighten, intensify, magnify; complement, supplement, supply; enforce, reinforce (*also* reenforce), strengthen; maximize
near antonyms detach, disconnect, disjoin, separate, unfasten; amputate, cut, excise, lop (off), sever; contract, decrease, diminish, lessen, lower, reduce; abbreviate, abridge, curtail, shorten; compress, condense, constrict, cut back, retrench
antonyms abate, bate, deduct, knock off, remove, subtract, take off
2 to combine (numbers) into a single sum ⟨when she *added* all the phone charges herself, she discovered an error in her bill⟩
synonyms cast (up), foot (up), sum, summate, tot (up), total, totalize, tote (up)
related words calculate, cipher, compute, figure, reckon, table, tabulate, tally, work out; divide, multiply, subtract; count, enumerate, number, tell; recompute, refigure
phrases put together

add (to) *vb* to make greater in size, amount, or number ⟨the need to be back home before 5:00 p.m. *adds to* the difficulty of arranging the trip⟩ — see INCREASE 1

added *adj* resulting in an increase in amount or number ⟨ever since his mother got sick, he's had the *added* responsibility of getting his little sister ready for school⟩ — see ADDITIONAL

addendum *n* **1** a part added at the end of a book or periodical ⟨there's an *addendum* from the author to explain certain stylistic choices that she made⟩
synonyms afterword, appendix, codicil, excursus, supplement
related words coda, epilogue (*also* epilog), postlude; conclusion, ending, finale; accompaniment, addition, complement, postscript; follow-up, sequel; documentation; allonge, rider
antonyms foreword, introduction, preface, prologue (*also* prolog)
2 something added (as by growth) ⟨with each new *addendum* the list of demands simply got more absurd⟩ — see INCREASE 1

addict *n* **1** a person who regularly uses drugs especially illegally ⟨an inspiring story about *addicts* who seek help and manage to kick their habit⟩ — see DOPER
2 a person with a strong and habitual liking for something ⟨science-fiction *addicts* who eagerly await each new installment in the series⟩ — see FAN

addicting *adj* causing or relating to a physiological need for certain drugs ⟨cocaine is highly *addicting*⟩ — see ADDICTIVE

addiction *n* a physiological need for certain drugs ⟨an *addiction* to heroin⟩
synonyms dependence (*also* dependance), habit, jones [*slang*], monkey

related words alcoholism, heroinism, morphinism; habituation, tolerance

addictive *adj* causing or relating to a physiological need for certain drugs ⟨an *addictive* painkiller⟩
synonyms addicting, habit-forming
related words hard; narcotic
near antonyms soft
antonyms nonaddictive

addition *n* **1** a smaller structure added to a main building ⟨a new *addition* to the library providing space for an expanded video collection⟩ — see ANNEX
2 something added (as by growth) ⟨the cache of old stamps I found in the discarded desk was a huge *addition* to my stamp collection⟩ — see INCREASE 1
3 the act or process of becoming greater in number ⟨how do you account for the *addition* of more paint stains on your shirt after you put on a smock?⟩ — see MULTIPLICATION

additional *adj* resulting in an increase in amount or number ⟨there turned out to be *additional* reasons for her unauthorized absence⟩
synonyms added, another, else, farther, fresh, further, more, other
related words accessory, adjunct, collateral, extraneous, peripheral, side, supplemental, supplementary; new; excess, extra, plus, spare, supernumerary, supervenient, surplus; complementary, contributory
near antonyms fewer, less

additionally *adv* in addition to what has been said ⟨the diet recommends fruit juice for breakfast and, *additionally*, fresh fruit once a day⟩ — see MORE 1

additive *adj* produced by a series of additions of identical or similar things ⟨certain drugs have *additive* effects when taken in conjunction with each other that one doesn't see when any one is used alone⟩ — see CUMULATIVE

addle *adj* suffering from mental confusion ⟨my brain grew more and more *addle* as I made my way through the tax instructions⟩ — see DIZZY 2

addle *vb* to throw into a state of mental uncertainty ⟨after slipping on the ice, Bethany was so *addled* that she left her groceries where they'd fallen⟩ — see CONFUSE 1

addled *adj* **1** having undergone organic breakdown ⟨*addled* eggs found on a long abandoned hen's nest⟩ — see ROTTEN 1
2 suffering from mental confusion ⟨one of the more *addled* audience members confused Ghana with Guyana⟩ — see DIZZY 2

addlepated *adj* suffering from mental confusion ⟨some *addlepated* clerk had confused our hotel reservation with that of another, similarly named, party⟩ — see DIZZY 2

add–on *n* something that is not necessary in itself but adds to the convenience or performance of the main piece of equipment ⟨a blow-dryer that comes with a couple of *add-ons* for people who are serious about styling their hair⟩ — see ACCESSORY 1

address *n* **1** a usually formal discourse delivered to an audience ⟨George Washington's Farewell *Address*⟩ ⟨a papal *address*⟩ — see SPEECH 1
2 the way or manner in which one conducts oneself ⟨a gentleman with all of poise and social *address* that one would expect of someone coming from old money⟩ — see BEHAVIOR

address *vb* **1** to deal with (something) usually skillfully or efficiently ⟨the problem will only get worse if you don't *address* it now⟩ — see HANDLE 1
2 to occupy (oneself) diligently or with close attention ⟨please *address* yourself to what I'm saying and not to the television⟩ — see APPLY 2
3 to transmit information or requests to ⟨you may *address* the manager about your problems tomorrow⟩ — see CONTACT

adduce *vb* to give as an example ⟨in support of a 12-month school year, the committee *adduced* data from other school districts⟩ — see QUOTE 1

add up (to) *vb* **1** to be the same in meaning or effect ⟨whether we take the 4:00 train or the 4:15 bus, it *adds up to* the same thing: they both get us back too late⟩ — see AMOUNT (TO) 2
2 to have a total of ⟨even if we pool all our money, it won't *add up to* enough to rent a beach house for a week⟩ — see AMOUNT (TO) 1

adept *adj* having or showing exceptional knowledge, experience, or skill in a field of endeavor ⟨he's an *adept* pitcher, and the team is lucky to have him⟩ — see PROFICIENT

adept *n* a person with a high level of knowledge or skill in a field ⟨even by the standards of Washington, he's an *adept* at political intrigue and power politics⟩ — see EXPERT

adeptly *adv* in a skillful or expert manner ⟨*adeptly* sank the ball in the basket with a hook shot⟩ — see WELL 3

adeptness *n* subtle or imaginative ability in inventing, devising, or executing something ⟨his *adeptness* at thinking on his feet makes him a formidable debater⟩ — see SKILL 1

adequacy *n* the quality or state of meeting one's needs adequately ⟨the fire department sent someone to determine the *adequacy* of the building's evacuation plan⟩ — see SUFFICIENCY

adequate *adj* of a level of quality that meets one's needs or standards ⟨this old computer is probably *adequate* if you just want to type a term paper⟩
synonyms acceptable, all right, decent, fairish, fine, good, OK (*or* okay), passable, respectable, satisfactory, serviceable, tolerable
related words agreeable, bearable, endurable, sufferable; average, fair, indifferent, mediocre, middling, minimal; common, ordinary, run-of-the-mill, run-of-the-mine (*or* run-of-mine), second-rate, so-so; standard, unexceptional; appropriate, correct, due, fitting, meet, proper, right, seemly, suitable, useful, worthy; gratifying, satisfying
phrases up to snuff
near antonyms disagreeable, disreputable, improper, indecent, objectionable, unfit, unsuitable, unworthy, useless, wrong; bad, cheap, defective, faulty, imperfect, incomplete, lamentable, pitiful, shoddy; dissatisfying; insufficient, meager (*or* meagre), mean, miserly, niggardly, poor, scanty, shabby, short, skimpy, spare, stingy; insufferable, intolerable, unbearable, unendurable; atrocious, execrable, miserable, vile, wretched; exceptional, exquisite, extreme, fancy, first-class, high-grade, matchless, maximized, maximum, optimal, optimum, peerless, preeminent, premium, special, supreme, unmatched, unparalleled; A1, bang-up, banner, boss [*slang*], capital, classic, crackerjack, dandy, divine, fabulous, fine, first-rate, grand, great, groovy, heavenly, jim-dandy, keen, marvelous (*or* marvellous), mean, neat, nifty, noble, par excellence, prime, sensational, splendid, stellar, sterling, superb, superior, superlative, supernal, swell, terrific, tip-top, top, top-notch, unsurpassed, wonderful
antonyms deficient, inadequate, insufficient, lacking, unacceptable, unsatisfactory, wanting

adequately *adv* **1** in a satisfactory way ⟨we weren't completely bowled over by the performance, but the band certainly played more than *adequately*⟩ — see WELL 1
2 in or to a degree or quantity that meets one's requirements or satisfaction ⟨*adequately* provided with candles

and freshwater in case of a power outage⟩ — see ENOUGH 1

adhere *vb* to hold to something firmly as if by adhesion ⟨everyone started calling her "Cookie" when she was little and the name *adhered*⟩ — see STICK 1

adhere (to) *vb* **1** to give steadfast support to ⟨our coach *adheres to* the belief that we can win this game if we just have a positive attitude⟩

synonyms cling (to), hew (to), keep (to), stand by, stick (to *or* with)

related words cleave (to); advocate, back, champion, confirm, defend, endorse (*also* indorse), espouse, support, uphold; accept, adopt, cherish, cultivate, embrace, follow, foster, heed; backstop, bolster, boost, buttress, enforce, reinforce (*also* reenforce)

phrases abide by, hold to, live up to

near antonyms abandon, abnegate, desert, forsake, give up, relinquish, spurn, surrender; abjure, recall, recant, reconsider, renege, renounce, retract, revoke, take back, unsay, withdraw; controvert, disagree (with), disprove, dispute, rebut, refute; contradict, deny, disavow, disclaim, disown, gainsay, negate, negative, repudiate; back down, back off, backtrack

antonyms defect (from)

2 to act according to the commands of ⟨*adhere to* the terms of the deceased's will⟩ — see OBEY

adherence *n* **1** a physical sticking to as if by glue ⟨you'd think these refrigerator magnets would have better *adherence*—they fall off every time I open the door⟩ — see ADHESION 1

2 the following of a custom, rule, or law ⟨*adherence* to convention requires that the couple send out formal wedding invitations⟩ — see OBSERVANCE 1

adherent *adj* tending to adhere to objects upon contact ⟨the bandage is made from a mildly *adherent* fiber⟩ — see STICKY 1

adherent *n* one who follows the opinions or teachings of another ⟨the Flat Earth Society surely doesn't have many *adherents*⟩ — see FOLLOWER 1

adhesion *n* **1** a physical sticking to as if by glue ⟨discourages the use of photo albums that keep the pictures in place by *adhesion* to the pages⟩

synonyms adherence, bonding, cling

related words agglutination, clumping, cohesion; adhesiveness, attachment, cohesiveness, tenacity; cementing, gluing (*also* glueing)

antonyms unsticking

2 adherence to something to which one is bound by a pledge or duty ⟨she has always shown steadfast *adhesion* to psychiatry's code of ethics⟩ — see FIDELITY

adhesive *adj* tending to adhere to objects upon contact ⟨walked barefoot through *adhesive*, clayey mud⟩ — see STICKY 1

adhesive *n* a substance used to stick things together ⟨prefers postage stamps coated with *adhesive* so that she doesn't have to do any licking⟩ — see GLUE

ad hoc *adj* made or done without previous thought or preparation ⟨upon learning that it was her birthday, we had an *ad hoc* celebration right there in the restaurant⟩ — see EXTEMPORANEOUS

adieu *n* an expression of good wishes at parting ⟨we bid our *adieus* and were off⟩ — see GOOD-BYE

ad interim *adj* **1** intended to last, continue, or serve for a limited time ⟨will serve as the *ad interim* CEO until the merger of the two corporations is complete⟩ — see TEMPORARY 1

2 serving in a position for the time being ⟨an *ad interim* government until the new constitution goes into effect⟩ — see ACTING

adipose *adj* containing animal fat especially in unusual amounts ⟨seals have a thick layer of *adipose* tissue, which acts as insulation against the cold and contributes to buoyancy as well⟩ — see FATTY

adiposity *n* the condition of having an excess of body fat ⟨beneath that *adiposity* of flesh lay a nobility of spirit that only the wisest could discern⟩ — see CORPULENCE

adjacency *n* the state or condition of being near ⟨environmentalists are concerned about the proposed shopping plaza's *adjacency* to the river⟩ — see PROXIMITY

adjacent *adj* having a border in common ⟨their house is *adjacent* to a wooded park⟩

synonyms abutting, adjoining, bordering, conterminous, contiguous, flanking, flush, fringing, joining, juxtaposed, neighboring, skirting, touching, verging

related words approximate, close, closest, immediate, near, nearby, nearest, next-door, nigh; attached, communicating, connected, connecting, interconnecting, joined, linked, united; bounding, circumjacent, embracing, encircling, enclosing (*also* inclosing), fencing, rimming, surrounding; marginal, peripheral, tangent, tangential; ambient, encompassing

near antonyms apart, detached, disconnected, discrete, free-standing, isolate, isolated, removed, separate, single, unattached, unconnected, unlinked; away, distant, far, faraway, far-off, farthest, remote; discontinuous, noncontinuous; broken up, disjoined, dissevered, dissociated, disunited, divided, divorced, parted, ramified, resolved, severed, split, sundered, uncoupled, unyoked

antonyms nonadjacent, noncontiguous

adjoin *vb* **1** to be adjacent to ⟨the bedroom of their apartment *adjoins* their neighbor's living room⟩

synonyms abut, border (on), butt (on *or* against), flank, fringe, join, march (with), neighbor, skirt, touch, verge (on)

related words attach (to), communicate (with), connect (with), link (with); bound, embrace, encircle, enclose (*also* inclose), fence, line, margin, rim, surround; contact, converge, meet

2 to join (something) to a mass, quantity, or number so as to bring about an overall increase ⟨after the dictionary writer's talk, the principal *adjoined* a few remarks about her own love of words⟩ — see ADD 1

adjoining *adj* having a border in common ⟨the cows had broken through the fence and were grazing in the *adjoining* field⟩ — see ADJACENT

adjourn *vb* to bring to a formal close for a period of time ⟨the meeting was *adjourned* by the chairperson until further notice⟩

synonyms prorogate, prorogue, recess, suspend

related words break off, disband, discontinue, disperse, intermit, interrupt; defer, hold off, postpone, put off, reserve, shelve, table; dissolve, end, halt, stop, terminate; break up, close, conclude, wind up, wrap up; abort, call, call off, drop, recall, repeal, rescind, revoke; abrogate, annul, invalidate, negate, nullify, quash, void

near antonyms inaugurate, launch, open; carry on, continue, draw out, extend, proceed, prolong; renew, reopen, resume; assemble, call, convene, convoke, muster, rally, summon

adjudge *vb* to give an opinion about (something at issue or in dispute) ⟨his version of what had happened was generally *adjudged* to be completely fictitious⟩ — see JUDGE 1

adjudicate *vb* to give an opinion about (something at issue or in dispute) ⟨when we asked the salesclerk to *adjudicate* our disagreement, she agreed with me that the white shoes looked better⟩ — see JUDGE 1

adjudicator *n* **1** a person who impartially decides or resolves a dispute or controversy ⟨since they seemed to be in a hopeless stalemate, both labor and management agreed to use an independent *adjudicator* to decide the terms of the contract⟩ — see JUDGE 1

2 a public official having authority to decide questions of law ⟨the appellate court refused to hear the case, thus allowing the judgment of previous *adjudicators* to stand⟩ — see JUDGE 2

adjunct *n* **1** a person who helps a more skilled person ⟨serving as an *adjunct* to the congressional delegation on its fact-finding mission⟩ — see HELPER

2 something that is not necessary in itself but adds to the convenience or performance of the main piece of equipment ⟨you can spend a lot on camera accessories, but this nifty little battery recharger is the one *adjunct* that will pay for itself⟩ — see ACCESSORY 1

adjuration *n* **1** an earnest request ⟨though he was loath to take over the family business, he couldn't refuse his ailing father's *adjuration*⟩ — see PLEA 1

2 an opinion suggesting a wise or proper course of action ⟨an *adjuration* to check the facts carefully before publishing the exposé on corruption in the statehouse⟩ — see ADVICE 1

adjure *vb* **1** to give advice to ⟨*adjured* them not to break the drug laws of any of the countries they would be visiting⟩ — see ADVISE 1

2 to issue orders to (someone) by right of authority ⟨by all that is holy, I *adjure* you to tell us the whereabouts of the missing child⟩ — see COMMAND 1

adjust *vb* to change (something) so as to make it suitable for a new use or situation ⟨after going on the night shift, he found it difficult to *adjust* his sleep schedule⟩ ⟨*adjust* the amount of sugar in the recipe to your taste⟩ — see ADAPT

adjustable *adj* capable of being readily changed ⟨quantities that are easily *adjustable* if you're cooking for a larger crowd⟩ — see FLEXIBLE 1

adjustment *n* the act or process of changing something to fit a new use or situation ⟨the publishing industry's necessary *adjustment* to the age of electronic media⟩ — see ADAPTATION

adjutant *n* a person who helps a more skilled person ⟨the senator's *adjutants* and aides always arrive ahead of him on the campaign trail⟩ — see HELPER

ad–lib *adj* made or done without previous thought or preparation ⟨not bad for an *ad-lib* comedy routine⟩ — see EXTEMPORANEOUS

ad–lib *n* something that is performed, made, or done without preparation ⟨you would never suspect that that stirring speech was an *ad-lib*⟩ — see IMPROVISATION

ad–lib *vb* to perform, make, or do without preparation ⟨had to *ad-lib* constructing a piñata because she'd never actually seen it being done⟩ — see IMPROVISE

admeasurement *n* the act or process of giving out something to each member of a group ⟨the *admeasurement* of the company's profits among its employees is based strictly upon seniority⟩ — see DISTRIBUTION 1

administer *vb* **1** to give out (something) to appropriate individuals ⟨the principal *administers* discipline fairly when students break the rules⟩
synonyms allocate, apportion, deal (out), dispense, distribute, dole out, hand out, mete (out), parcel (out), portion, prorate
related words admeasure, allot, allow, appropriate, assign, dish out, divide, divvy (up), dollop (out), lot, measure (out), part, proportion, ration, redistribute, set, share (out), split; bestow, disburse, furnish, issue, provide, share, supply; circulate, disperse, disseminate, scatter, spread; chip in, contribute, donate, pledge; reallocate, reapportion
near antonyms begrudge, decline, deny, deprive (of), disallow, refuse, reject, withhold; niggle (out), pinch, skimp, stint
antonyms misallocate

2 to carry out effectively ⟨local officials should see that the fair housing laws are rigorously *administered*⟩ — see ENFORCE

3 to look after and make decisions about ⟨the lieutenant governor *administers* the affairs of the state in the absence of the governor⟩ — see CONDUCT 1

administer (to) *vb* to attend to the needs and comforts of ⟨volunteers *administering to* the terminally ill at a hospice⟩ — see NURSE 1

administrant *n* a person who manages or directs something ⟨an *administrant* of the nation's largest private charitable foundation⟩ — see EXECUTIVE

administrate *vb* to look after and make decisions about ⟨they're looking for someone to *administrate* the new division⟩ — see CONDUCT 1

administration *n* **1** lawful control over the affairs of a political unit (as a nation) ⟨the fair and just *administration* of the U.S. territories⟩ — see RULE 2

2 the act or activity of looking after and making decisions about something ⟨*administration* of the funds was left in the hands of a committee⟩ — see CONDUCT 1

administrative *adj* suited for or relating to the directing of things ⟨among his other *administrative* duties is the appointment of transit authority officials⟩ — see EXECUTIVE

administrator *n* a person who manages or directs something ⟨a hospital *administrator*⟩ — see EXECUTIVE

admirable *adj* deserving of high regard or great approval ⟨it's *admirable* the way she helps her elderly neighbor with chores and errands every Saturday⟩
synonyms applaudable, commendable, creditable, estimable, laudable, meritorious, praiseworthy
related words deserving, worthy; awesome, distinctive, distinguished, excellent, heady, honorable, impressive, noteworthy, noticeable, outstanding, redoubtable, reputable, respectable; invaluable, precious, priceless, valuable; delightful, enjoyable, pleasing, satisfying; ethical, good, high-minded, moral, noble, principled
near antonyms base, contemptible, deplorable, despicable, detestable, dirty, infamous, lousy, nasty, notorious, pitiable, pitiful, scabby, scummy, scurvy, sorry, unlikable, unworthy, vile, worthless, wretched; disgraceful, dishonorable, disreputable, ignominious, low, mean, scandalous, seamy, shady, shameful, shocking, sordid, unethical, unsavory
antonyms censurable, discreditable, illaudable, reprehensible

admiration *n* **1** a feeling of great approval and liking ⟨my *admiration* for her increased when I discovered she had learned English only since coming to the U.S.⟩
synonyms account, appreciation, esteem, estimation, favor, regard, respect
related words appetite, fancy, fondness, like, love, partiality, preference, relish, shine, taste, use; acclamation, adoration, adulation, approbation, deference, hero worship, homage, honor, idolatry, infatuation, lionization, praise, props [*slang*], reverence, veneration, worship; delight, enjoyment; amazement, awe, wonder, wonderment; enthusiasm, interest, passion; bias, prejudice; affection, attachment, devotion, passion
near antonyms condemnation, disapproval, disdain, opprobrium, scorn; disappointment, discontent, disenchantment, disgruntlement, disillusionment, displeasure, indignation, unhappiness; aversion, contempt, disfavor, disgust, disinclination, dislike, disliking, disregard, distaste; hate, hatred, loathing, nausea, repugnance, repulsion, revulsion; abomination, antipathy, detestation; deprecation, displeasure, dissatisfaction
antonyms disfavor

2 the rapt attention and deep emotion caused by the sight of something extraordinary ⟨gaped in *admiration* as one flower-bedecked float after another paraded past them⟩ — see WONDER 2

admire *vb* to think very highly or favorably of ⟨I *admire* the way you handled such a touchy situation⟩
synonyms appreciate, consider, esteem, regard, respect
related words acclaim, accredit, applaud, approve, commend, compliment, credit, praise; delight (in), drink (in), enjoy, relish, revel (in), savor (*also* savour); dig, fancy, favor, groove (on), like, love; adore, adulate, canonize, deify, dote (on), hallow, idolize, revere, reverence, venerate, worship; cherish, love, prize, treasure, value
phrases set store by (*or* on)
near antonyms abhor, abominate, despise, detest, execrate, hate, loathe; condemn, decry, deplore, disapprove, discount, discountenance, disdain, disfavor, dislike, dismiss, disregard, frown (on *or* upon), kiss off, scorn, vilify

admiring *adj* expressing approval ⟨the smartly dressed couple drew *admiring* glances⟩ — see FAVORABLE 1

admiringly *adv* in an approving manner ⟨we gazed *admiringly* at the portrait⟩
synonyms appreciatively, approvingly, complimentarily, favorably, positively
related words lovingly, regardfully, respectfully; reverently, worshipfully
near antonyms captiously, hypercritically; deploringly, disdainfully, scornfully, unflatteringly
antonyms adversely, disapprovingly, negatively, unfavorably

admissible *adj* that may be permitted ⟨using direct quotations without naming your source is not *admissible*⟩ — see PERMISSIBLE

admission *n* **1** an open declaration of something (as a fault or the commission of an offense) about oneself ⟨by her own *admission*, her cooking is not the greatest⟩ — see CONFESSION
2 the means or right of entering or participating in ⟨no *admission* unless accompanied by an adult⟩ — see ENTRANCE 1

admit *vb* **1** to accept the truth or existence of (something) usually reluctantly ⟨the host of the talk show eventually *admitted* that she hadn't actually read the book⟩ ⟨you can't bring yourself to *admit* your mistakes⟩
synonyms acknowledge, agree, allow, concede, confess, fess (up), grant, own (up to)
related words disburden, unburden, unload; affirm, avow, confirm, profess; accept, recognize, yield; announce, break, broadcast, communicate, declare, disclose, divulge, impart, proclaim, publish, reveal, spill, tell, unveil; betray, blab, expose, give away, inform, leak, rat, squeal, talk, tattle, tip (off), warn, wise (up); breathe, say, whisper
phrases come clean (about)
near antonyms disallow, disavow, disclaim, disown; contradict, dispute, gainsay, negate, negative; rebut, refute, reject, repudiate; conceal, cover (up), hide, obscure, veil; kid (oneself)
antonyms deny
2 to offer entrance (as to a place, school, or privilege) to ⟨she was *admitted* to Harvard⟩
synonyms enter, receive, take
related words entertain, welcome; fellowship; confirm, ratify
near antonyms decline, disallow, disapprove, dismiss, refuse, reject; blackball, blacklist, ostracize; banish, deport, exile, expel, oust, throw out
antonyms ban, bar
3 to make an acknowledgment of something unpleasant as true or valid ⟨I *admit* to some suspicions about the new neighbors⟩ — see CONFESS 1

admit (of) *vb* to make possible especially to the exclusion of other possibilities ⟨your question does not *admit of* a simple "yes" or "no" answer⟩ — see ALLOW (OF)

admittance *n* the means or right of entering or participating in ⟨*admittance* to the country club requires sponsorship from a current member⟩ — see ENTRANCE 1

admittedly *adv* to tell the truth ⟨*admittedly*, I should not have lost my temper like that⟩ — see ACTUALLY 1

admixture *n* a distinct entity formed by the combining of two or more different things ⟨an *admixture* of rose petals and lavender for a fragrant potpourri⟩ — see BLEND

admonish *vb* **1** to criticize (someone) usually gently so as to correct a fault ⟨*admonished* her for littering⟩ — see REBUKE 1
2 to give advice to ⟨my physician is always *admonishing* me to eat more healthy foods⟩ — see ADVISE 1

admonishing *adj* serving as or offering a warning ⟨shot an *admonishing* glance at me just as I was about to spill the beans⟩ — see CAUTIONARY

admonishment *n* **1** an opinion suggesting a wise or proper course of action ⟨wintertime *admonishments* about remembering to wear a coat and hat⟩ — see ADVICE 1
2 the act or an instance of telling beforehand of danger or risk ⟨that near miss with the guardrail was all the *admonishment* I needed to slow down⟩ — see WARNING 1

admonition *n* **1** an opinion suggesting a wise or proper course of action ⟨a heartfelt *admonition* to the graduates to make the most of their lives⟩ — see ADVICE 1
2 the act or an instance of telling beforehand of danger or risk ⟨ignored the ranger's *admonitions* and took the road over the mountain, only to be stranded by the blizzard⟩ — see WARNING 1

admonitory *adj* serving as or offering a warning ⟨*admonitory* articles abound around Halloween, warning parents of the hazards of trick-or-treating⟩ — see CAUTIONARY

ado *n* a state of noisy, confused activity ⟨a bride-to-be caught up in the usual prenuptial *ado*⟩ — see COMMOTION

adolescence *n* the transitional period between childhood and adulthood ⟨*adolescence* can be a turbulent time for teenagers and parents alike⟩
synonyms minority, nonage
related words boyhood, girlhood, preadolescence, youth; bloom, flush, heyday, prime; majority, maturity; manhood, womanhood; babyhood, infancy

adolescent *adj* **1** being in the early stage of life, growth, or development ⟨an *adolescent* sheepdog, who hasn't quite gotten the hang of keeping the sheep huddled together⟩ — see YOUNG
2 having or showing the annoying qualities (as silliness) associated with children ⟨would hope that the college students had outgrown such *adolescent* behavior⟩ — see CHILDISH
3 lacking in adult experience or maturity ⟨took a group of *adolescent* recruits and turned them into professional warriors⟩ — see CALLOW

adopt *vb* to take for one's own use (something originated by another) ⟨shortly after moving to the U.S., the family dutifully *adopted* the American tradition of having turkey for Thanksgiving⟩
synonyms borrow, embrace, espouse, take on, take up
related words domesticate, naturalize; appropriate, arrogate, take over, usurp; absorb, assimilate, incorporate, quote; cherish, prize, treasure; cultivate, follow, heed, honor; use, utilize; bring up, foster, nurture, raise, rear; affect, assume, copy, imitate, pretend, put on, simulate
phrases pick up on
near antonyms abandon, forsake, give up, relinquish,

surrender; abjure, abnegate, disown; reject, renounce, repudiate, spurn; discard, jettison, junk, throw away, throw out

adorable *adj* having qualities that tend to make one loved ⟨what an *adorable* old lady, so kind and sweet⟩ ⟨an *adorable* little cottage⟩ — see LOVABLE

adore *vb* **1** to feel passion, devotion, or tenderness for ⟨an attentive, solicitous husband who clearly *adores* his wife⟩ — see LOVE 2

2 to love or admire too much ⟨*adores* her older sister so much that she cannot see her considerable faults⟩ — see IDOLIZE

3 to offer honor or respect to (someone) as a divine power ⟨the Roman soldier was beheaded for *adoring* the Christian god⟩ — see WORSHIP 1

4 to take pleasure in ⟨I *adore* those earrings—wherever did you get them?⟩ — see ENJOY 1

adoring *adj* **1** feeling or showing love ⟨*adoring* grandparents who love to spoil their grandchildren⟩ — see LOVING 1

2 reflecting great admiration or devotion ⟨the *adoring* attention of the girls' gymnastics team when our local Olympic hero spoke to them⟩ — see WORSHIPFUL

adorn *vb* to make more attractive by adding something that is beautiful or becoming ⟨the Sultan's tent was richly *adorned* with thick tapestries and gleaming gold candlesticks⟩ — see DECORATE

adorning *adj* serving to add beauty ⟨*adorning* garlands of greenery can be seen all over the mansion at Christmastime⟩ — see DECORATIVE

adornment *n* something that decorates or beautifies ⟨the only *adornment* in the sparely furnished bedroom was a small portrait of the poet Walt Whitman⟩ — see DECORATION 1

adroit *adj* accomplished with trained ability ⟨with an *adroit* flick of the wrist, flipped the omelet into the air and landed it squarely back in the pan⟩ — see SKILLFUL 1

adroitly *adv* in a skillful or expert manner ⟨the captain *adroitly* navigated his vessel through the treacherous waters⟩ — see WELL 3

adroitness *n* **1** mental skill or quickness ⟨shows a remarkable *adroitness* in identifying birds the moment they land at the feeder⟩ — see DEXTERITY 1

2 subtle or imaginative ability in inventing, devising, or executing something ⟨with the *adroitness* of a magician, she twisted the balloons into the shape of a monkey⟩ — see SKILL 1

adulate *vb* **1** to love or admire too much ⟨it's ridiculous how she *adulates* that airheaded rock star⟩ — see IDOLIZE

2 to praise too much ⟨a business executive who unwisely surrounds herself with incompetent assistants who spend all their time *adulating* her⟩ — see FLATTER 1

adulation *n* **1** excessive admiration of or devotion to a person ⟨the pathetic *adulation* of the leader of the cult by her misguided followers⟩ — see WORSHIP

2 excessive praise ⟨more objective critics have observed that the artist never deserved the *adulation* heaped upon her mediocre paintings⟩ — see FLATTERY

adulatory *adj* **1** overly or insincerely flattering ⟨an office flunky who can be counted on to make an *adulatory* response to the boss's every suggestion⟩ — see FULSOME 1

2 reflecting great admiration or devotion ⟨an *adulatory* eulogy delivered at a beloved teacher's retirement party⟩ — see WORSHIPFUL

adult *adj* **1** relating to or typical of adults; displaying proper maturity ⟨an *adult* reaction to the issue⟩

synonyms grown-up, mature

near antonyms childish, infantile, kiddish

antonyms adolescent, immature

2 dealing in or with explicitly sexual material ⟨an *adult* magazine⟩

synonyms mature, pornographic, porny, X-rated

related words hard-core, soft-core; bedroom, erotic (*also* erotical), sexy, suggestive; bawdy, coarse, crude, dirty, filthy, foul, gross, indecent, lascivious, lewd, lustful, nasty, obscene, ribald, salacious, smutty, unprintable, vulgar, wanton; immodest, kinky, prurient; earthy, racy, salty; indecorous, unbecoming; debasing, perverted, profane; naughty, wicked

near antonyms priggish, prim, prudish, puritanical, straitlaced (*or* straightlaced), Victorian; correct, decent, decorous, genteel, polite, proper, seemly

antonyms clean, G-rated

3 fully grown or developed ⟨insects that are butterflies in their *adult* stage⟩ — see MATURE 1

adult *n* a fully grown person ⟨at the beach, the *adults* sat under broad umbrellas while the children splashed in the water⟩

synonyms grown-up

related words middle-ager; ancient, elder, gaffer, graybeard, oldster, old-timer, senior, senior citizen

near antonyms bairn [*chiefly Scottish*], child, cub, kid, moppet, tad, toddler, tot, tyke (*also* tike); baby, infant; adolescent, juvenile, minor, youngling, youngster, youth; preteen, preteen-ager, teen, teenager, teener, teenybopper, tween

adulterant *n* something that is or that makes impure ⟨concerned about *adulterants* in the town's water supply coming from the discharge from the factory⟩ — see IMPURITY 1

adulterate *adj* **1** containing foreign or lower-grade substances ⟨the pharmacist was convicted of selling *adulterate* drugs in order to maximize profits⟩ — see IMPURE 1

2 relating to or being a sexual encounter or relationship between a married person and someone other than their spouse ⟨caught red-handed in what he claimed was his first *adulterate* encounter⟩ — see ADULTEROUS

adulterate *vb* to alter (something) for the worse with the addition of foreign or lower-grade substances ⟨the company was fined for *adulterating* its "all beef" frankfurters with cereal⟩

synonyms cut, dilute, extend, lace, sophisticate, thin, water down, weaken

related words load; befoul, contaminate, corrupt, defile, dirty, envenom, foul, infect, poison, pollute, soil, spoil, sully, taint; cheapen, debase, degrade; manipulate, misrepresent, tamper (with); counterfeit, fake, falsify, fudge; doctor, spike; attenuate, moderate, qualify, temper

near antonyms fertilize, lard; augment, reinforce (*also* reenforce), supplement; decontaminate, purify; clarify, clean, cleanse, distill (*also* distil), filter, flush, leach, pasteurize, purge, refine; better, enhance, improve; compact, concentrate, condense

antonyms enrich, fortify, richen, strengthen

adulterated *adj* containing foreign or lower-grade substances ⟨the outbreak of food poisoning was traced to *adulterated* ground beef⟩ — see IMPURE 1

adulterine *adj* relating to or being a sexual encounter or relationship between a married person and someone other than their spouse ⟨*adulterine* fiction often portrays the illicit lovers sympathetically⟩ — see ADULTEROUS

adulterous *adj* relating to or being a sexual encounter or relationship between a married person and someone other than their spouse ⟨had an *adulterous* affair that nearly destroyed his marriage⟩

synonyms adulterate, adulterine, extracurricular, extramarital, two-timing

related words premarital; promiscuous

adultery *n* a sexual encounter or relationship between a married person and someone other than their spouse ⟨*adultery* is the cause of many divorces⟩
synonyms cheating, infidelity, misconduct, two-timing, unfaithfulness
related words criminal conversation; free love, promiscuity; disloyalty, faithlessness, falseness, inconstancy, perfidiousness, perfidy, treachery; affair (*also* affaire), amour, fling, love, love affair, romance; intrigue; attachment, infatuation; entanglement, flirtation; liaison, passion
near antonyms allegiance, constancy, dedication, devotedness, devotion, fealty, loyalty, steadfastness
antonyms faithfulness, fidelity

adulthood *n* the state of being fully grown or developed ⟨the period between childhood and *adulthood* is called adolescence⟩ — see MATURITY 1

adultness *n* the state of being fully grown or developed ⟨decorating her own house gave her a sense of *adultness* and independence⟩ — see MATURITY 1

adumbrate *vb* to give a slight indication of beforehand ⟨the strife in Bloody Kansas in the 1850s *adumbrated* the civil war that would follow⟩ — see FORESHADOW

advance *n* **1** forward movement in time or place ⟨during her long convalescence, the housebound woman was barely aware of the *advance* of the seasons⟩
synonyms advancement, furtherance, going, headway, march, onrush, passage, process, procession, progress, progression
related words current, drift, flow, flux, stream, way; advent, approach, arrival, coming, nearing; bound, jump, leap, step, stride; impetus, momentum
near antonyms backwash, ebb, reflux; retraction, return, reversal, reverse; about-face, turnabout, turnaround
antonyms recess, recession, regress, regression, retreat, retrogression
2 an instance of notable progress in the development of knowledge, technology, or skill ⟨under her new teacher, the aspiring violinist has made noticeable *advances* in her technique in just a few weeks⟩
synonyms advancement, breakthrough, enhancement, improvement, refinement
related words quantum leap; amelioration, boost, heightening, increase, melioration, strengthening, upgrade, uplift, upswing, uptrend, upturn; betterment, development, elaboration, evolution, expansion, gestation, growth, maturation, perfection, ripening; civilization, edification, education, enlightenment; renaissance, renascence, revival; discovery, find, windfall; innovation, invention
near antonyms breakdown, collapse, crash; hindrance, impediment, stumbling block; decadence, decay, declension, decline, decrease, degeneration, descent, deterioration, diminishment, downgrade, ebbing, failing, flagging, languishment, lapse, lessening, reduction, sinking, slowing, weakening, worsening; detriment, disablement, drawback, glitch, impairment, shortcoming
antonyms setback

advance *vb* **1** to give to another for temporary use with the understanding that it or a like thing will be returned ⟨*advanced* her some cash with the understanding that the amount would be deducted from her first paycheck⟩ — see LEND
2 to help the growth or development of ⟨great thinkers who did much to *advance* modern science⟩ — see FOSTER 1
3 to move forward along a course ⟨as the technology *advances*, electronic devices keep getting smaller and smarter⟩ — see GO 1
4 to move higher in rank or position ⟨within six months was *advanced* to the position of head waiter, to the dismay of the waiters who had been there much longer⟩ — see PROMOTE 1
5 to set before the mind for consideration ⟨let me explain my reasons for *advancing* this proposal⟩ — see PROPOSE 1
6 to move closer to ⟨*advanced* cautiously toward the snarling dog⟩ — see COME 1

advanced *adj* **1** being far along in development ⟨an *advanced* civilization, among the first anywhere to use the plow, developed on the banks of the Nile River thousands of years ago⟩
synonyms developed, evolved, forward, high, higher, improved, late, progressive, refined
related words precocious; full-blown, full-fledged, full-scale; aged, grown, mature, matured, perfected, ripe, ripened; civilized, educated, enhanced, enlightened; contemporary, current, cutting-edge, latest, leading-edge, mod, modern, new, newest, newfangled, new-fashioned, novel, now, present-day, recent, space-age, supermodern, ultramodern, up-to-date
near antonyms green, immature, underdeveloped, undersized (*also* undersize), underweight, unripe, unripened; savage, uncivilized, uneducated; early, embryonic, germinal, primeval, primordial; antediluvian, antiquated, antique, dated, fusty, hoary, musty, Neanderthal (*or* Neandertal), obsolete, old, oldfangled, old-fashioned, old-time, out-of-date, outworn, passé, past
antonyms backward, low, lower, nonprogressive, primitive, retarded, rude, rudimentary, undeveloped
2 being or employing the latest concepts, styles, or techniques ⟨went to a very *advanced* school for gifted children⟩ — see AVANT

advancement *n* **1** a raising or a state of being raised to a higher rank or position ⟨the young man's rapid *advancement* in the company came as no surprise to those who knew he was the president's nephew⟩
synonyms ascent, creation, elevation, preference, preferment, promotion, rise, upgrade, upgrading
related words aggrandizement, ennoblement, exaltation, glorification, magnification
near antonyms deposition, dethronement, discharge, dismissal, expulsion, impeachment, ouster, overthrow, removal, suspension, unmaking, unseating; downfall, fall
antonyms abasement, comedown, degradation, demotion, disrating, downgrade, reduction
2 an instance of notable progress in the development of knowledge, technology, or skill ⟨science has made huge *advancements* in the field of genetics in recent years⟩ — see ADVANCE 2
3 forward movement in time or place ⟨wondered why we hadn't made any *advancement* in the long checkout line for at least 10 minutes⟩ — see ADVANCE 1

advantage *n* **1** the more favorable condition or position in a competition ⟨your experience volunteering at the hospital will put you at an *advantage* when you're applying for a job there⟩
synonyms better, bulge, catbird seat, drop, edge, high ground, inside track, jump, pull, stead, upper hand, vantage, whip hand
related words allowance, head start, lead, leg up, margin, odds, start; ascendancy (*also* ascendency), command, dominance, mastery, predominance, superiority, supremacy, transcendence, transcendency; precedence, preference, prerogative, privilege, seniority; break, foothold, opportunity; benefit, blessing, boon, felicity, godsend, manna, windfall
phrases coign of vantage
near antonyms detriment, stranglehold; disparity, imbalance, inequality, unevenness; disability, failing, impairment, shortcoming; bar, catch, check, clog, crimp,

embarrassment, hindrance, hitch, hurdle, impediment, interference, let, manacle, obstacle, obstruction, rub, shackle, stop, trammel; lurch, setback
antonyms disadvantage, drawback, handicap, liability, minus, penalty, strike
2 a thing that helps ⟨had all the *advantages* of being born into a wealthy and powerful family⟩ — see HELP 2

advantage *vb* to provide with something useful or desirable ⟨there's no question that that bicycle racer was significantly *advantaged* by a great set of genes⟩ — see BENEFIT

advantageous *adj* promoting or contributing to personal or social well-being ⟨a trade agreement that is *advantageous* to both countries⟩ — see BENEFICIAL

advent *n* the act of coming upon a scene ⟨with the *advent* of the mass-produced automobile, the need for a better system of roads and highways soon became apparent⟩ — see ARRIVAL

adventitious *adj* not being a vital part of or belonging to something ⟨the point of view that art should be for art's sake and that moral considerations are *adventitious* to the study of art⟩ — see EXTRINSIC

adventure *n* **1** an exciting or noteworthy event that one experiences firsthand ⟨our quiet hike turned into quite an *adventure* when we encountered a bear and her cub⟩
synonyms emprise, experience, exploit, gest (*or* geste), happening, time
related words escapade, lark, ploy; act, action, deed, doing, feat; episode, occasion; baptism, ordeal, test, trial, tribulation; enterprise, risk, venture; expedition, exploration, mission, performance, quest, stunt
near antonyms bore, bummer, bust, downer, drag
2 a risky undertaking ⟨a bold *adventure* in deep-sea exploration that could imperil the submarine and its crew⟩ — see GAMBLE

adventure *vb* **1** to place in danger ⟨*adventured* all his savings in a very risky investment scheme⟩ — see ENDANGER
2 to take a chance on ⟨if I had to *adventure* a guess, I'd say she's about 35⟩ — see RISK 1

adventuresome *adj* inclined or willing to take risks ⟨not inclined to be *adventuresome* when it comes to foreign travel, preferring guided bus tours that stick to the beaten path⟩ — see BOLD 1

adventurous *adj* inclined or willing to take risks ⟨let's be *adventurous* and take a bus into the city for New Year's Eve this year⟩ — see BOLD 1

ad verbum *adv* in the same words ⟨an *ad verbum* translation⟩ ⟨if the giver of the oath mangles the wording, should one repeat after him *ad verbum*?⟩ — see VERBATIM

adversarial *adj* marked by opposition or ill will ⟨the relationship between the president and the congress should not be *adversarial* if anything is to get done⟩ — see HOSTILE 1

adversary *adj* marked by opposition or ill will ⟨there was a long history of *adversary* dealings between the two nations⟩ — see HOSTILE 1

adversary *n* **1** one that is hostile toward another ⟨our old cat seemed to consider the new kitten an *adversary*⟩ — see ENEMY
2 one that takes a position opposite another in a competition or conflict ⟨our *adversaries* in tomorrow's meet are from one of the top schools in the league⟩ — see OPPONENT 1

adverse *adj* **1** opposed to one's interests ⟨all the *adverse* publicity really caused the movie star's popularity to suffer⟩
synonyms counter, disadvantageous, hostile, inimical, negative, prejudicial, unfavorable, unfriendly, unsympathetic, untoward
related words bad, baleful, baneful, evil; damaging, deleterious, destructive, detrimental, fatal, harmful, hurtful, ill, injurious, lethal, malignant, murderous, noxious, pernicious, poisonous, ruinous, threatening, troublesome, unhealthy, wounding; dangerous, hazardous, imperiling (*or* imperilling), jeopardizing, parlous, perilous, risky, unsafe; calumnious, defamatory, detractive, offensive, scathing, slanderous; antagonistic, antipathetic, inhospitable, intolerant, uncongenial, uncooperative; competing, conflicting, counteracting, countering, opposing, resistant, resisting
near antonyms beneficial, good, helpful, propitious, useful; harmless, innocent, innocuous, inoffensive, nondestructive, nonfatal, nonlethal, nonthreatening; unresistant; tolerant, understanding; affable, agreeable, amiable, amicable, benign, benignant, complying, congenial, cordial, friendly, hospitable
antonyms advantageous, favorable, friendly, positive, supportive, sympathetic, well-disposed
2 causing or capable of causing harm ⟨the *adverse* effects of the drug are too severe to allow it to be marketed⟩ — see HARMFUL

adversity *n* **1** bad luck or an example of this ⟨many people came face-to-face with life-altering *adversity* when the stock market crashed⟩ — see MISFORTUNE
2 something that is a cause for suffering or special effort especially in the attainment of a goal ⟨some overcame all the *adversities* of the Great Depression and rebuilt their fortunes⟩ — see DIFFICULTY 1

advert *n, chiefly British* a published statement informing the public of a matter of general interest ⟨busily perusing the job *adverts* in the Sunday Times⟩ — see ANNOUNCEMENT

advert (to) *vb* to make reference to or speak about briefly but specifically ⟨when our hosts *adverted to* the lateness of the hour we took the hint, and prepared to leave⟩ — see MENTION 1

advertence *n* a state of being aware ⟨a greater *advertence* to the feelings of others is what that insensitive clod needs⟩ — see ATTENTION 2

advertency *n* a state of being aware ⟨a history textbook that has been widely criticized for its lack of *advertency* to the contributions of minorities⟩ — see ATTENTION 2

advertise *vb* to make known openly or publicly ⟨I wouldn't *advertise* my bad credit rating to the whole world if I were you⟩ — see ANNOUNCE

advertisement *n* a published statement informing the public of a matter of general interest ⟨an *advertisement* for special low fares to Florida and Cancún during spring break⟩ — see ANNOUNCEMENT

advice *n* **1** an opinion suggesting a wise or proper course of action ⟨we got some good *advice* from the vet about dealing with our dog's habit of chasing cars⟩
synonyms adjuration, admonishment, admonition, counsel, guidance, input
related words recommendation, suggestion; hint, pointer, tip; data, feedback, information; answer, solution; advisement, consideration, thought; alarm (*also* alarum), alert, caution, cautioning, expostulation, forewarning, remonstrance, remonstration, urging, warning; judgment (*or* judgement), observation, verdict; assistance, briefing, coaching, direction, instruction, mentoring, priming, prompting, teaching, tutoring; interference, kibitzing (*also* kibbitzing), meddling; moralizing, pontificating, preaching; exhortation, lecture, lesson, sermon, speech
2 *usually* **advices** *pl* a report of recent events or facts not previously known ⟨had *advices* that the city could hold out against an invasion force for at most a week⟩ — see NEWS

advisability *n* suitability for bringing about a desired result under the circumstances ⟨questioned the *advis-*

ability of betting everything on the outcome of a single race⟩ — see EXPEDIENCY

advisable *adj* suitable for bringing about a desired result under the circumstances ⟨it's never *advisable* to ride double on a bicycle⟩ — see EXPEDIENT

advisableness *n* suitability for bringing about a desired result under the circumstances ⟨doubts about the *advisableness* of using the Internet to meet a significant other⟩ — see EXPEDIENCY

advise *vb* **1** to give advice to ⟨a popular guidance counselor who has been *advising* students about their college plans for two decades⟩
synonyms adjure, admonish, counsel
related words alert, caution, forewarn, warn; brief, clue (in), fill in, inform, tell, wise (up); coach, direct, guide, instruct, lead, mentor, shepherd, show, teach, tutor; direct, pilot, steer; acquaint, apprise, familiarize; convince, encourage, induce, persuade, talk (into); beg, exhort, implore, prevail (upon), urge; propose, recommend, suggest

2 to put (something) forward as one's choice for a wise or proper course of action ⟨she *advised* calling ahead for a reservation at the new restaurant⟩
synonyms counsel, recommend, suggest
related words advocate, back, champion, espouse, favor, support; exhort, urge; advance, offer, propose, submit

3 to exchange viewpoints or seek advice for the purpose of finding a solution to a problem ⟨the doctor *advised* with his partner before recommending the patient's treatment⟩ — see CONFER 2

4 to give information to ⟨*advised* her as to the best way to get to the art museum by public transportation⟩ — see ENLIGHTEN 1

5 to give notice to beforehand especially of danger or risk ⟨*advised* us not to invest our money in what looked like a pyramid scheme⟩ — see WARN

advised *adj* decided on as a result of careful thought ⟨his *advised* use of the inflammatory term set off a firestorm, just as he had intended⟩ — see DELIBERATE 1

advisedly *adv* with full awareness of what one is doing ⟨I'm calling him a traitor, and I use that term *advisedly*⟩ — see INTENTIONALLY

advisement *n* a careful weighing of the reasons for or against something ⟨we'll take that matter under *advisement* and get back to you later⟩ — see CONSIDERATION 1

adviser *also* **advisor** *n* a person who gives advice especially professionally ⟨our financial *adviser* had some words of caution about buying a second home⟩ — see CONSULTANT

advocate *n* **1** a person who actively supports or favors a cause ⟨Mark Twain, Noah Webster, and President Theodore Roosevelt are among past *advocates* of a reformed spelling system⟩ — see EXPONENT 1

2 a person whose profession is to conduct lawsuits for clients or to advise about legal rights and obligations ⟨with such a strong case against him, he's going to need the best *advocate* that money can buy⟩ — see LAWYER

advocate *vb* to promote the interests or cause of ⟨environmentalists *advocating* agricultural methods designed to slow the destruction of rain forests⟩ — see SUPPORT 1

advocator *n* a person who actively supports or favors a cause ⟨a strong *advocator* of musical education in the schools⟩ — see EXPONENT 1

aegis *also* **egis** *n* **1** means or method of defending ⟨having no claim to the land under the *aegis* of the law, the cattle baron decided to claim it by force⟩ — see DEFENSE 1

2 the financial support and general guidance for an undertaking ⟨a medical study that was questioned by many because it was done under the *aegis* of a major pharmaceutical company⟩ — see AUSPICE 1

aeon *or* **eon** *n* a long or seemingly long period of time ⟨it's been *aeons* since I saw a movie at the multiplex⟩ ⟨glaciers that formed *aeons* ago⟩ — see AGE 2

aerodrome *n, chiefly British* a place from which aircraft operate that usually has paved runways and a terminal ⟨landed at the *aerodrome* in Surrey, south of London⟩ — see AIRPORT

aeroplane *n, chiefly British* a vehicle for traveling through the air that has fixed wings for lift ⟨an exhibit of a few of the *aeroplanes* that won the Battle of Britain⟩ — see AIRPLANE

aesthetic *also* **esthetic** *or* **aesthetical** *or* **esthetical** *adj* very pleasing to look at ⟨an *aesthetic* arrangement of the floral decorations⟩ — see BEAUTIFUL 1

aesthetics *also* **esthetics** *n pl* the qualities in a person or thing that as a whole give pleasure to the senses ⟨what the building lacks in *aesthetics* it makes up for in practicality⟩ — see BEAUTY 1

afar *n* a long distance ⟨the experienced birder was able to identify birds from *afar*⟩ — see MILE

affability *n* the state or quality of having a pleasant or agreeable manner in socializing with others ⟨First Lady Dolley Madison was beloved by the nation for her *affability* toward people from all walks of life⟩ — see AMIABILITY 1

affable *adj* **1** having a relaxed, casual manner ⟨as the show's *affable* host, she keeps the freewheeling gabfest from getting out of hand⟩ — see EASYGOING 1

2 having an easygoing and pleasing manner especially in social situations ⟨as an experienced event planner, he knows that having an *affable* emcee is critical⟩ — see AMIABLE

3 showing a natural kindness and courtesy especially in social situations ⟨although First Lady Lucretia Hayes didn't particularly enjoy her role as White House hostess, she was always *affable*⟩ — see GRACIOUS 1

affair *n* **1** *also* **affaire** a brief romantic relationship ⟨an *affair* between two singles spending the summer at the same beach resort⟩
synonyms amour, fling, love, love affair, romance
related words intrigue, liaison; dalliance, hanky-panky; attachment, infatuation; entanglement, flirtation; idyll (*also* idyl), passion; calf-love, puppy love

2 a social gathering ⟨the annual country club dance is a really fancy *affair*⟩ — see PARTY 1

3 something produced by physical or intellectual effort ⟨the lead float in the parade was a pretty impressive *affair*, a giant eagle's head with equally huge wings⟩ — see PRODUCT 1

4 something that happens ⟨the whole *affair* from start to finish took a total of 15 minutes⟩ — see EVENT 1

5 something to be dealt with ⟨it's none of your *affair* whom I'm going out with tonight⟩ — see MATTER 2

[1]affect *vb* **1** to act upon (a person or a person's feelings) so as to cause a response ⟨their son claims that scary movies don't *affect* him in the least⟩
synonyms impact, impress, influence, move, reach, strike, sway, tell (on), touch
related words carry away, dazzle, enrapture, entrance, enthrall (*or* enthral), ravish, transport; bias, color; inspire, stir; engage, interest, involve, penetrate, pierce; afflict, agitate, bother, concern, discomfort, discompose, disquiet, distress, disturb, fluster, harass, harry, perturb, pester, plague, smite, strain, stress, trouble, try, upset, worry, wring; allure, attract, bewitch, captivate, charm, enchant, fascinate
phrases get to
near antonyms bore, jade, pall, tire, weary; underwhelm

2 to be the business or affair of ⟨fortunately, hurricane season doesn't *affect* the West Coast⟩ — see CONCERN 2

[2]**affect** *vb* **1** to present a false appearance of ⟨she *affected* complete unawareness that we were talking about her, though she must have overheard⟩ — see FEIGN
2 to go to or spend time in often ⟨a power couple known to *affect* all the fancy parties in town⟩ — see FREQUENT

affectation *n* the quality or state of appearing or trying to appear more important or more valuable than is the case ⟨a woman of great *affectation* at social gatherings⟩ — see PRETENSE 1

affected *adj* **1** lacking in natural or spontaneous quality ⟨*affected* laughter at the boss's jokes⟩ ⟨an *affected* southern accent⟩ — see ARTIFICIAL 1
2 self-consciously trying to present an appearance of grandeur or importance ⟨with her pinkie extended, the four-year-old held her tiny teacup in that *affected* manner that some women have⟩ — see PRETENTIOUS 1
3 having a liking or affection ⟨after years of being well *affected* toward their grandchildren, they did not want to lose access to them because of a bitter divorce⟩ — see FOND 1

affectedness *n* the quality or state of appearing or trying to appear more important or more valuable than is the case ⟨bowed and sat down at the piano with a degree of *affectedness* that was laughable⟩ — see PRETENSE 1

affecting *adj* having the power to affect the feelings or sympathies ⟨the *affecting* final scene in the play, when the children are reunited with their father⟩ — see MOVING

affection *n* **1** a feeling of strong or constant regard for and dedication to someone ⟨an elderly couple showing their *affection* for each other by little acts of kindness⟩ — see LOVE 1
2 an abnormal state that disrupts a plant's or animal's normal bodily functioning ⟨born with a heart *affection* that later caused him problems⟩ — see DISEASE
3 a habitual attraction to some activity or thing ⟨I'm rooting for the Cubs—just my natural *affection* for the underdog, I guess⟩ — see INCLINATION 1
4 something that sets apart an individual from others of the same kind ⟨religion, of one kind or another, is an *affection* common to every society known to have existed⟩ — see CHARACTERISTIC

affectionate *adj* feeling or showing love ⟨an *affectionate* child who gives hugs and kisses freely⟩ — see LOVING 1

affectless *adj* **1** having or showing a lack of sympathy or tender feelings ⟨an *affectless* analysis of the cost of the war purely in pecuniary terms⟩ — see HARD 1
2 not feeling or showing emotion ⟨the accused remained *affectless* throughout the long trial⟩ — see IMPASSIVE 1

affectlessness *n* a lack of emotion or emotional expressiveness ⟨though she always acts so blasé about everything, I think her air of *affectlessness* is largely put on⟩ — see APATHY 1

affianced *adj* pledged in marriage ⟨the *affianced* couple are much-sought-after guests for this year's holiday parties⟩ — see ENGAGED 1

affiliate *n* a local unit of an organization ⟨our local Humane Society is an *affiliate* of a national organization⟩ — see CHAPTER 1

affiliated *adj* having a close connection like that between family members ⟨costuming and set design are *affiliated* arts, both requiring research into the period of the play or film⟩ — see RELATED

affiliation *n* the state of having shared interests or efforts (as in social or business matters) ⟨the Little League team, despite its name, the Northern Dynamites, has no *affiliation* with the Northern Dynamite Company⟩ — see ASSOCIATION 1

affinity *n* **1** a habitual attraction to some activity or thing ⟨always had an *affinity* for nurturing living things⟩ — see INCLINATION 1
2 the fact or state of having something in common ⟨a study showing an *affinity* between obesity and socioeconomic status⟩ — see CONNECTION 1

affirm *vb* **1** to state as a fact usually forcefully ⟨unwilling to *affirm* without further study that the painting is an original Rembrandt⟩ — see CLAIM 1
2 to state clearly and strongly ⟨our business partner *affirmed* his trust in us, and we in turn promised not to let him down⟩ — see ASSERT 1

affirmation *n* a solemn and often public declaration of the truth or existence of something ⟨a sworn *affirmation* that he had never acted as a spy for the enemy⟩ — see PROTESTATION

affirmative *n* a vote or decision for something ⟨we have five *affirmatives* and two negatives for forming the committee⟩ — see YES

affix *vb* to cause (something) to hold to another ⟨*affix* a first-class stamp to the envelope⟩ — see FASTEN 1

afflict *vb* to cause persistent suffering to ⟨the South was *afflicted* by a severe drought⟩ ⟨he's been *afflicted* by nightmares ever since the accident⟩
synonyms agonize, anguish, bedevil, beset, besiege, curse, excruciate, harrow, persecute, plague, rack, torment, torture
related words assail, attack; badger, dog, hound, pursue, ride; aggravate, agitate, annoy, bother, bug, chafe, distress, disturb, exasperate, gall, get, grate, gripe, hagride, harass, harry, irk, irritate, molest, nettle, peeve, pester, pique, put out, rasp, rile, vex; discomfort, discompose, disquiet, fluster, grieve, perturb, strain, stress, trouble, try, upset, worry; crush, oppress, overpower, overwhelm, smite, strike, tyrannize, victimize; hurt, pain, pang, prick, smart, stab, sting, wring; martyr
near antonyms abet, aid, assist, help; deliver, release, relieve, reprieve; comfort, console, content, quiet, solace, soothe, succor

afflicting *adj* hard to accept or bear especially emotionally ⟨the *afflicting* sight of so many earthquake victims was too much even for some hardened rescue workers⟩ — see BITTER 2

affliction *n* **1** a state of great suffering of body or mind ⟨she listened with deep *affliction* as her daughter told her about the latest trouble she was in⟩ — see DISTRESS 1
2 deep sadness especially for the loss of someone or something loved ⟨felt such great *affliction* over the destruction of the beautiful old home⟩ — see SORROW
3 a source of harm or misfortune ⟨alcohol has been his *affliction* ever since he took his first drink at the age of 12⟩ — see BANE 1
4 a source of persistent emotional distress ⟨suffered from *afflictions* that only a professional therapist could deal with⟩ — see DEMON 2
5 something that causes loss or pain ⟨cronyism and corruption are *afflictions* on the body politic⟩ — see INJURY 1

afflictive *adj* causing or feeling bodily pain ⟨the *afflictive* disease known as shingles is a reactivation of the virus that causes chicken pox⟩ — see PAINFUL 1

affluence *n* a flowing or coming in ⟨this *affluence* of new students is straining an already crowded school system⟩ — see INFLUX

affluent *adj* having goods, property, or money in abundance ⟨he is *affluent* and can afford to send his children to the best schools⟩ — see RICH 1

affluent *n* a stream that flows into a larger body of water ⟨the Nipigon and the St. Louis rivers are *affluents* of Lake Superior⟩ — see TRIBUTARY

afford *vb* to have enough money for ⟨we can't *afford* new clothes this month⟩
synonyms go, swing
related words cover; expend, finance, outlay, pay (for), pony up, spring (for); pick up, purchase, take; acquire, get, obtain, procure, secure; bid, offer; bankroll, endow, subsidize, underwrite

affordable *adj* **1** being within the financial means of most people ⟨once those electronic devices became *affordable*, sales skyrocketed⟩ — see ACCESSIBLE 1
2 costing little ⟨they've added some *affordable* options⟩ — see CHEAP 1

affray *n, chiefly British* a rough and often noisy fight usually involving several people ⟨an *affray* broke out in the parking lot when someone shouted a racial slur⟩ — see BRAWL 1

affright *vb* to strike with fear ⟨a ghastly sight that would *affright* any person⟩ — see FRIGHTEN

affrighted *adj* filled with fear or dread ⟨the *affrighted* villagers ran in all directions at the first sight of the monster⟩ — see AFRAID

affront *n* an act or expression showing scorn and usually intended to hurt another's feelings ⟨took it as an *affront* that she wasn't asked to help cook Thanksgiving dinner⟩ — see INSULT

affront *vb* to cause hurt feelings or deep resentment in ⟨did not mean to *affront* you when I told you I didn't need your help⟩ — see INSULT

aficionado *also* **afficionado** *n* a person with a strong and habitual liking for something ⟨an *aficionado* of the sci-fi series who has seen all the movies several times⟩ — see FAN

afield *adv* off the desired or intended path or course ⟨how did we get so far *afield* from the subject we intended to discuss?⟩ — see WRONG 1

afire *adj* being on fire ⟨looked down upon the city, which was all *afire* from the bombing⟩ — see ABLAZE 1

aflame *adj* being on fire ⟨the kindling in the wood stove was *aflame* as soon as I held a match to it⟩ — see ABLAZE 1

afloat *adj* riding upon the surface of a body of liquid ⟨the boat can't stay *afloat* much longer⟩
synonyms floating
related words buoyant, floaty, unsinkable; free-floating; awash, drifting, gliding, hanging, hovering, poised, sailing, wafting
near antonyms aground, high and dry
antonyms sinking, sunk

aflutter *adj* feeling or showing uncomfortable feelings of uncertainty ⟨Jonathan was all *aflutter* about proposing to Shelley that evening⟩ — see NERVOUS 1

afoot *adj* being in progress or development ⟨plans are *afoot* for a new sports stadium in the city⟩ — see ONGOING 1

afoot *adv* in progress ⟨although the drug just got released, research for a more effective medication is already *afoot*⟩ — see UNDER WAY

afore *adv, chiefly dialect* so as to precede something in order of time ⟨some young boys raced *afore* to tell onlookers that there were elephants in the circus parade⟩ — see AHEAD 1

afore *prep, chiefly dialect* **1** earlier than ⟨my father, his father, and even his father *afore* him farmed this land⟩ — see BEFORE 1
2 preceding in space ⟨a majestic sailing ship going full speed *afore* the wind⟩ — see BEFORE 2

aforementioned *adj* mentioned previously ⟨with the *aforementioned* reservation, I would recommend the play for serious-minded theatergoers⟩ — see AFORESAID

aforesaid *adj* mentioned previously ⟨with the *aforesaid* objections in mind, I think we should reconsider the proposal⟩
synonyms aforementioned, foregoing, forenamed, said
related words above; such; antecedent, anterior, precedent, preceding, prior; introductory, preliminary; erstwhile, former, whilom
near antonyms below; ensuing, following, subsequent, succeeding

afraid *adj* filled with fear or dread ⟨Melissa is *afraid* of flying, so she takes a train from Boston to visit her brother in Chicago⟩
synonyms affrighted, aghast, alarmed, fearful, frightened, horrified, horror-struck, hysterical (*also* hysteric), scared, scary, shocked, spooked, terrified, terrorized
related words chicken, fainthearted, fearsome, shrinking, shy, timid, timorous, tremulant, tremulous; agitated, anxious, apprehensive, disconcerted, disquieted, disturbed, funky, jittery, jumpy, nervous, panicked, panicky, panic-stricken, perturbed, skittish, uneasy, upset, worried; phobic; appalled, dismayed, startled; cowed, daunted, intimidated, unnerved; coward, cowardly, craven, gutless, lily-livered, pusillanimous; careful, cautious, heedful, prudent, unadventurous, wary
near antonyms adventuresome, adventurous, audacious, bold, daredevil, daring, dashing, gutsy, plucky, spirited, spunky, venturesome, venturous; brave, courageous, gallant, hardy, heroic (*also* heroical), intrepid, lionhearted, manful, stalwart, stout, stouthearted, valiant, valorous; assured, collected, composed, confident, cool, sanguine, sure, unperturbed; dauntless, resolute, undaunted
antonyms fearless, unafraid

afresh *adv* yet another time ⟨the shooting broke out *afresh* when the bandits reappeared at the crest of the hill⟩ — see AGAIN 1

aft *adj* being at or in the part of something opposite the front part ⟨the *aft* part of the cruise ship turned out to be the noisier section⟩ — see BACK

aft *adv* near, toward, or in the stern of a ship or the tail of an aircraft ⟨after transferring the controls to the copilot, the captain went *aft* to see what the disturbance was⟩
synonyms abaft, astern, sternward (*or* sternwards)
related words after, back, backward (*or* backwards), behind, posteriorly, rearward (*also* rearwards)
near antonyms anteriorly; ahead, before
antonyms fore, forward

after *adj* **1** being at or in the part of something opposite the front part ⟨had heard that the *after* section of an aircraft is safer in the event of a crash⟩ — see BACK
2 being, occurring, or carried out at a time after something else ⟨in *after* years the government set up a special fund for disabled veterans of the war⟩ — see SUBSEQUENT

after *adv* following in time or place ⟨upon seeing *The Nutcracker* for the first time, and for a long time *after*, Irma wanted to play the part of the Mouse King⟩
synonyms afterward (*or* afterwards), later, latterly, subsequently, thereafter
related words next; by and by, hereafter, presently, since, soon, then, thereupon; hereinbelow, infra
near antonyms formerly; heretofore, theretofore
antonyms afore [*chiefly dialect*], ahead, antecedently, anteriorly, before, beforehand, earlier, previously

after *prep* subsequent to in time or order ⟨the brass band came right *after* the mayor in the parade⟩
synonyms après, behind, below, following, next to, past
related words since
near antonyms toward (*or* towards)

antonyms afore [*chiefly dialect*], ahead of, before, ere, of, previous to, prior to, to

aftereffect *n* a condition or occurrence traceable to a cause ⟨in the U.S. slavery was abolished in 1865, but its *aftereffects* remained keenly felt long afterwards⟩ — see EFFECT 1

afterlife *n* **1** a later period of one's life ⟨written in *afterlife*, his memoirs reveal a kinder, more forgiving man⟩ — see AGE 3
2 unending existence after death ⟨hoping to join her deceased parents in the *afterlife*⟩ — see ETERNITY 2

aftermath *n* a condition or occurrence traceable to a cause ⟨the surgery was successful, but she now had to deal with its *aftermath*: a huge bill⟩ — see EFFECT 1

afternoon *n* a later period of one's life ⟨literary fame did not arrive until the *afternoon* of her life⟩ — see AGE 3

afterward *or* **afterwards** *adv* following in time or place ⟨we'll go to the play, then have supper *afterward*⟩ — see AFTER

afterword *n* a part added at the end of a book or periodical ⟨the author included an *afterword* about developments in cancer treatment since the book was written⟩ — see ADDENDUM 1

again *adv* **1** yet another time ⟨now I have to mop the floor *again* because you didn't wipe your feet⟩
synonyms afresh, anew, de novo, over
related words always, consistently, constantly, continuously, endlessly, ever, evermore, forever, incessantly, invariably, perpetually, unfailingly; continually, frequently, oft, often, oftentimes (*or* ofttimes); recurrently, repeatedly; freshly, newly
near antonyms ne'er, never; infrequently, little, rarely, seldom, unusually; intermittently, occasionally, periodically, sometimes, sporadically
antonyms nevermore
2 in addition to what has been said ⟨a green pillow will go fine with my living room; *again*, the best colors are blues and greens⟩ — see MORE 1
3 just the opposite being true ⟨I might take swimming lessons this summer; then *again*, I might not⟩ — see CONTRARIWISE

again and again *adv* many times ⟨as she's gotten older, Grandma has tended to ask the same things *again and again*⟩ — see OFTEN

against *prep* **1** in or into contact with ⟨he leaned *against* the fence and it collapsed⟩ ⟨unwittingly rubbed his leg *against* some poison ivy⟩
synonyms on, upon
related words alongside, next, next to; upside
2 opposed to; not for ⟨I'm *against* going to see the parade if it's raining⟩ — see ANTI

agape *adj* having or showing signs of eagerly awaiting something ⟨at the sound of the sleigh bells the children were all *agape*, waiting for Santa to appear⟩ — see EXPECTANT 1

age *n* **1** an extent of time associated with a particular person or thing ⟨the Bronze *Age* marks the beginning of the use of metal by ancient peoples⟩
synonyms day, epoch, era, period, time
related words cycle, generation, year; bit, space, span, spell, stretch, while; date, vintage
2 a long or seemingly long period of time ⟨it took *ages* for the clerk to ring up three items⟩
synonyms aeon (*or* eon), blue moon, coon's age, cycle, donkey's years [*chiefly British*], eternity, forever, long, months, moon
related words infinity; lifetime
near antonyms flash, instant, jiffy, minute, moment, second, shake, split second, trice, twinkle, twinkling, wink; microsecond, nanosecond
3 a later period of one's life ⟨stoically endures all of the aches and pains that come with *age*⟩
synonyms afterlife, afternoon, autumn, evening
related words sunset, twilight, winter; anecdotage, dotage, senility; elderliness, golden years, oldness, seniority; adulthood, majority, maturity, middle, middle age, midlife, ripeness
near antonyms adolescence, youth
antonyms springtime
4 the state of being an old person ⟨at 88, she gets frustrated by the feebleness that is inevitable with *age*⟩ — see ANCIENTNESS 1
5 the state of being something old ⟨the copper monument has acquired the patina of *age*⟩ — see ANCIENTNESS 2

age *vb* to become mature ⟨as your cat *ages* and becomes less active, you should change her diet⟩ — see MATURE

aged *adj* **1** being of advanced years and especially past middle age ⟨all the young men went to fight in the war; and only the *aged* and infirm remained behind⟩ — see ELDERLY
2 dating or surviving from the distant past ⟨a forest of *aged* and gnarled oaks⟩ — see ANCIENT 1

agedness *n* **1** the state of being an old person ⟨the advanced *agedness* of the patient was immediately obvious to the emergency room staff⟩ — see ANCIENTNESS 1
2 the state of being something old ⟨the sheer *ancientness* of the Middle East impresses many first-time visitors⟩ — see ANCIENTNESS 2

ageless *adj* having an existence or validity that does not change or diminish ⟨a screen icon whose *ageless* beauty still entrances audiences today⟩ — see ABIDING

agency *n* **1** a large unit of a governmental, business, or educational organization ⟨the federal *agency* charged with enforcing laws and regulations regarding the use of firearms⟩ — see DIVISION 2
2 something used to achieve an end ⟨by what *agency* do you plan to acquire this fortune?⟩ — see AGENT 1

agenda *n* a listing of things to be presented or considered (as at a concert or play) ⟨unless your proposal is on the meeting's *agenda*, it won't be addressed⟩ — see PROGRAM 1

agent *n* **1** something used to achieve an end ⟨the whitening *agent* in the detergent is chlorine bleach⟩ ⟨the Church has been the traditional *agent* for social justice in impoverished countries⟩
synonyms agency, instrument, instrumentality, machinery, means, medium, ministry, organ, vehicle
related words determinant, expedient, factor, influence, ingredient, mechanism, tool; weapon; activator, animator, catalyst, driver, energizer, executor, generator, impetus, incentive, inspiration, instigation, instigator, launcher, mover, power, stimulus, trigger; antecedent, cause, occasion, reason; subagency, subagent
2 a person who acts or does business for another ⟨the sports *agent* negotiated a record-breaking contract for the baseball player⟩
synonyms assignee, attorney, commissary, delegate, deputy, envoy, factor, minister, procurator, proxy, rep, representative
related words ambassador, diplomat, diplomatist, emissary, foreign minister, legate, plenipotentiary; alternate, backup, pinch hitter, relief, replacement, stand-in, sub, substitute, surrogate, understudy; informer, operative, spy; broker, distributor, manager; arbiter, arbitrator, comprador (*or* compradore), conciliator, go-between, intercessor, intermediary, interposer, liaison, mediator, middleman, peacemaker; mouthpiece, point man, point person, prophet, speaker, spokesman, spokesperson
3 a person sent on a mission to represent another ⟨an undercover *agent* of the Crown⟩ — see AMBASSADOR

4 a person who tries secretly to obtain information for one country in the territory of another usually unfriendly country ⟨an *agent* feeding information about enemy troop movements⟩ — see SPY

age–old *adj* dating or surviving from the distant past ⟨*age-old* customs and beliefs⟩ — see ANCIENT 1

agglomerate *n* an unorganized collection or mixture of various things ⟨the Holy Roman Empire was an ever-varying *agglomerate* of central European states that managed to survive for 1,000 years⟩ — see MISCELLANY 1

agglomerate *vb* to form into a round compact mass ⟨breakfast cereal consisting of *agglomerated* clusters of wheat, rice, and nuts stays crunchy in milk⟩ — see WAD

agglomeration *n* an unorganized collection or mixture of various things ⟨a mere *agglomeration* of warring tribes, it was far from being a unified nation⟩ — see MISCELLANY 1

aggrandize *vb* **1** to assign a high status or value to ⟨a movie that *aggrandizes* the bad guys and makes the cops look like dopes⟩ — see EXALT 1

2 to make greater in size, amount, or number ⟨a generous grant, enabling the library to significantly *aggrandize* its collection of books on tape⟩ — see INCREASE 1

aggravate *vb* **1** to disturb the peace of mind of (someone) especially by repeated disagreeable acts ⟨it really *aggravates* me when I arrive 10 minutes before the stated closing time, and the store's closed already⟩ — see IRRITATE 1

2 to make more severe ⟨overheated rhetoric that only *aggravated* racial tension in the city⟩ — see EXACERBATE

aggravated *adj* subjected to and reacting with irritation ⟨*aggravated* customers looking in vain for a salesclerk for assistance⟩ — see ANNOYED

aggravating *adj* causing annoyance ⟨there's nothing so *aggravating* as a blaring car alarm that no one is paying any attention to⟩ — see ANNOYING

aggravation *n* **1** something that is a source of irritation ⟨drivers distracted by cell phones was one *aggravation* we didn't need⟩ — see ANNOYANCE 3

2 the act of making unwelcome intrusions upon another ⟨the neighbors' constant *aggravations* prompted us to move out of town⟩ — see ANNOYANCE 1

3 the feeling of impatience or anger caused by another's repeated disagreeable acts ⟨informed her children that she didn't need the extra *aggravation* of hearing them fight in the back seat while they were stuck in traffic⟩ — see ANNOYANCE 2

aggregate *n* a complete amount of something ⟨numerous episodes of pilferage, taken in the *aggregate*, can really add up to a significant sum⟩ — see WHOLE

aggregate *vb* to have a total of ⟨over time, her petty thefts *aggregated* a significant shortfall in the company's books⟩ — see AMOUNT (TO) 1

aggression *n* **1** an inclination to fight or quarrel ⟨Japanese *aggression* in the years preceding the attack on Pearl Harbor had strained relations with the U.S.⟩ — see BELLIGERENCE

2 the act or action of setting upon with force or violence ⟨Japan's act of *aggression*—the attack on Pearl Harbor—brought the U.S. into World War II⟩ — see ATTACK 1

aggressive *adj* **1** having or showing a bold forcefulness in the pursuit of a goal ⟨if you don't take a more *aggressive* approach to this yard pretty soon, the weeds are going to take over completely⟩

synonyms ambitious, assertive, enterprising, fierce, go-getting, high-pressure, in-your-face, militant, pushy, self-asserting, self-assertive

related words argumentative, bellicose, belligerent, combative, contentious, discordant, disputatious, gladiatorial, militant, pugnacious, quarrelsome, trigger-happy, truculent, warlike; hyperaggressive, overambitious; dynamic, energetic, enterprising, gung ho, hustling, strenuous, vigorous; emphatic, obtrusive; adventuresome, adventurous, daring, dashing, emboldened, gutsy, venturesome, venturous; audacious, bold, brash, brassy, bumptious, cheeky, cocksure, cocky, confident, determined, forward, impudent, insolent, overconfident, presumptuous, unapologetic, unsubdued, unyielding; bare-knuckle (*also* bare-knuckled *or* bare-knuckles), feisty, scrappy; dominating, domineering, imperious, lordly, magisterial, overbearing

near antonyms easygoing, laid-back, relaxed; acquiescent, amenable, compliant, deferential, docile, resigned, submissive, tractable, yielding; cowering, cringing, groveling (*or* grovelling), shrinking; bashful, demure, diffident, humble, lowly, meek, mild, modest, mousy (*or* mousey), overmodest, passive, quiet, reserved, retiring, shy, subdued, timid, unobtrusive; obsequious, servile, slavish, subservient

antonyms ambitionless, low-pressure, nonassertive, unaggressive, unambitious, unassertive, unenterprising

2 feeling or displaying eagerness to fight ⟨a kindergarten teacher who discourages *aggressive* behavior, like pushing, by rewarding those children who wait their turn⟩ — see BELLIGERENT

3 marked by or uttered with forcefulness ⟨an *aggressive* campaign to win the African-American vote⟩ — see EMPHATIC 1

aggressiveness *n* **1** readiness to engage in daring or difficult activity ⟨because of the mayor's *aggressiveness* in tackling problems, there have been significant changes for the better⟩ — see ENTERPRISE 2

2 the quality or state of being forceful (as in expression) ⟨has the *aggressiveness* one needs to pursue a career in show business⟩ — see VEHEMENCE 1

3 an inclination to fight or quarrel ⟨male bettas, known for their *aggressiveness*, are best raised alone⟩ — see BELLIGERENCE

aggressor *n* one that starts armed conflict against another especially without reasonable cause ⟨these pocket-size states had formed an alliance to deter potential *aggressors*⟩

synonyms invader, raider

related words initiator, instigator; ambuscader, ambusher, assailant, attacker, forayer, pillager, plunderer; hawk, jingo, jingoist, militant, militarist, war hawk, warmonger; belligerent, cobelligerent, combatant

near antonyms defender; dove, pacifist, peacemaker; nonbelligerent

aggrieved *adj* having a feeling that one has been wronged or thwarted in one's ambitions ⟨a line of *aggrieved* ticket-holders, demanding a refund for the cancelled concert⟩ — see DISCONTENTED

aggro *n, British* **1** the feeling of impatience or anger caused by another's repeated disagreeable acts ⟨we simply decided that trying to get our son to tidy up his room was not worth the *aggro*⟩ — see ANNOYANCE 2

2 something that is a source of irritation ⟨just another *aggro* that commuters on the tube have to put up with⟩ — see ANNOYANCE 3

aghast *adj* filled with fear or dread ⟨I stood there, *aghast*, as the vile monster made its way toward me⟩ — see AFRAID

agile *adj* moving easily ⟨the expressive movements of *agile* dancers⟩ ⟨*agile* herons wading in the marsh⟩ — see GRACEFUL 1

agility *n* ease and grace in physical activity ⟨a gymnast whose *agility* on the parallel bars has won him several medals⟩ — see DEXTERITY 2

agin *prep, dialect* opposed to; not for ⟨Grandpa was

generally *agin* any music created after the Second World War⟩ — see ANTI

aging *or* **ageing** *adj* being of advanced years and especially past middle age ⟨more and more middle-aged adults must care for *aging* parents⟩ — see ELDERLY

agita *n* an uneasy state of mind usually over the possibility of an anticipated misfortune or trouble ⟨took a deep breath to dispel her *agita* as she stepped onstage⟩ — see ANXIETY 1

agitate *vb* **1** to cause (as a liquid) to move about in a circle especially repeatedly ⟨this room could use a ceiling fan to *agitate* the stuffy air a bit⟩ — see STIR 1

2 to trouble the mind of; to make uneasy ⟨there's no need to *agitate* the patient about little things⟩ — see DISTURB 1

3 to make a series of small irregular or violent movements ⟨set the washing machine so it will *agitate* for four minutes before going into the rinse cycle⟩ — see SHAKE 1

4 to talk about (an issue) usually from various points of view and for the purpose of arriving at a decision or opinion ⟨a question which has been *agitated* by the legislature time and time again⟩ — see DISCUSS

agitated *adj* **1** being in a state of increased activity or agitation ⟨all ferry crossings were cancelled because of the *agitated* waters around the islands⟩ — see FEVERISH 1

2 feeling overwhelming fear or worry ⟨by the time they finally showed up, long after midnight, we'd become so *agitated* that we never did get to sleep that night⟩ — see FRANTIC 1

agitating *adj* marked by or causing agitation or uncomfortable feelings ⟨no more *agitating* waits to find out sports scores—get them instantly online!⟩ — see NERVOUS 2

agitation *n* **1** a state of wildly excited activity or emotion ⟨knew immediately, from the horses' *agitation*, that something terrible was happening⟩ — see FRENZY

2 an uneasy state of mind usually over the possibility of an anticipated misfortune or trouble ⟨experienced a great deal of *agitation* over whether she had an appropriate dress for her husband's inauguration⟩ — see ANXIETY 1

agitator *n* a person who stirs up public feelings especially of discontent ⟨a political *agitator* who led an unsuccessful revolt against the government⟩

synonyms demagogue (*also* demagog), exciter, firebrand, fomenter, incendiary, inciter, instigator, kindler, provocateur, rabble-rouser

related words demonstrator, marcher, objector, picketer, protester (*or* protestor); advocate, apostle, backer, booster, champion, exponent, persuader, promoter, proponent, reformer, reformist, supporter; alarmist, extremist, insurgent, insurrectionist, radical, rebel, revolter, revolutionary, revolutionist, subversive, troublemaker; goader, prodder, prompter, provoker; agent provocateur

near antonyms peacemaker, reconciler, uniter

aglow *adj* having or being an outward sign of good feelings (as of love, confidence, or happiness) ⟨all *aglow* as she was awarded first place in the spelling bee⟩ — see RADIANT 1

ago *adv* earlier than the present time ⟨he left here long *ago*⟩

synonyms agone [*archaic*], back, since, syne [*chiefly Scottish*]

antonyms hence

agog *adj* **1** having or showing signs of eagerly awaiting something ⟨parents *agog* for the latest news from the children away at college⟩ — see EXPECTANT 1

2 showing urgent desire or interest ⟨all *agog* to get started on their journey⟩ — see EAGER

agone *adv, archaic* earlier than the present time ⟨'tis long *agone* since last I saw my lady⟩ — see AGO

agonistic *adj* feeling or displaying eagerness to fight ⟨clearly a writer with a chip on his shoulder, he's very *agonistic* even when stating indisputable facts⟩ — see BELLIGERENT

agonize *vb* **1** to cause persistent suffering to ⟨got into more trouble, further *agonizing* her poor mother⟩ — see AFFLICT

2 to feel deep sadness or mental pain ⟨*agonized* for days over whether she'd done the right thing⟩ — see GRIEVE

agonized *adj* expressing or suggesting mourning ⟨one look at his *agonized*, tearful eyes and it was clear that something was terribly wrong⟩ — see MOURNFUL 1

agonizing *adj* **1** hard to accept or bear especially emotionally ⟨*agonizing* cries rose up from the dungeon⟩ — see BITTER 2

2 intensely or unbearably painful ⟨died an *agonizing* death⟩ — see EXCRUCIATING 1

agonizingly *adv* with feelings of bitterness or grief ⟨*agonizingly* made the decision to have her beloved cat put to sleep⟩ — see HARD 2

agony *n* **1** a situation or state that causes great suffering and unhappiness ⟨waiting all those hours to hear if he'd survived the plane crash was pure *agony*⟩ — see HELL 2

2 a state of great suffering of body or mind ⟨the *agony* of never knowing what happened to her son⟩ — see DISTRESS 1

3 a sudden intense expression of strong feeling ⟨the announcement that the war was over unleashed a mass *agony* of joy⟩ — see OUTBURST 1

agrarian *adj* engaged in or concerned with agriculture ⟨an *agrarian* community⟩ ⟨the nation's *agrarian* history⟩ — see AGRICULTURAL

agree *vb* **1** to have or come to the same opinion or point of view ⟨My husband and I *agree* on just about every aspect of child-rearing⟩

synonyms coincide, concur

related words accede (to), accept, acquiesce, assent (to), comply (with), consent (to), go (by), subscribe; affiliate, ally, associate, unite; collaborate, cooperate, get along, get on

phrases see eye to eye

near antonyms clash, collide, conflict; bicker, counter, dispute, dissent, diverge, fall out, object, oppose, protest, quarrel, resist, rival; dissociate, separate, split

antonyms differ, disagree

2 to come to an arrangement as to a course of action ⟨since we couldn't *agree*, we tossed a coin to decide the matter⟩

synonyms bargain, contract, covenant

related words come around, come round; subscribe, underwrite; arrange, settle

phrases come to terms, strike a bargain

near antonyms differ, dissent; cancel, renege, revoke; argue, contest, dispute, object

antonyms disagree

3 to accept the truth or existence of (something) usually reluctantly ⟨finally *agreed* that the paint job was sloppy and would have to be redone⟩ — see ADMIT 1

4 to be in agreement on every point ⟨the robber's story didn't *agree* with the cop's report on the incident⟩ — see CHECK 1

5 to form a pleasing relationship ⟨this warm climate seems to *agree* with you⟩ — see HARMONIZE 1

6 to give or express one's approval (as to a proposal) ⟨we'll have to get the author to *agree* to the revisions before the article can be published⟩ — see ACCEDE

agree (on) *vb* to come to an agreement or decision concerning the details of ⟨I'm sure we can all *agree on* what to do next⟩ — see ARRANGE 1

agree (with) *vb* to give satisfaction to ⟨her new job,

which is much less stressful than her old one, *agrees with* her⟩ — see PLEASE 1

agreeability *n* the state or quality of having a pleasant or agreeable manner in socializing with others ⟨the general *agreeability* of everyone in the tour group made for a pleasant trip⟩ — see AMIABILITY 1

agreeable *adj* **1** being to one's liking ⟨is the zoo an *agreeable* alternative for everyone, since the aquarium is closed?⟩ — see SATISFACTORY 1
2 giving pleasure or contentment to the mind or senses ⟨put on some *agreeable* music for dinner⟩ — see PLEASANT 1
3 having an easygoing and pleasing manner especially in social situations ⟨an *agreeable* art teacher who lets me do pretty much whatever I want⟩ — see AMIABLE
4 having or marked by agreement in feeling or action ⟨the belief that these new security measures are not *agreeable* with our core concepts of personal freedom⟩ — see HARMONIOUS 3

agreeableness *n* the state or quality of having a pleasant or agreeable manner in socializing with others ⟨the impression that the couple give to first-time visitors is one of well-bred *agreeableness*⟩ — see AMIABILITY 1

agreeably *adv* in a pleasing way ⟨an *agreeably* warm day, just right for a picnic⟩ — see WELL 5

agreement *n* **1** the state of being of one opinion about something ⟨we were in *agreement* about one thing at least: that we'd never worked so hard in all our lives⟩
synonyms accord, concurrence, concurrency, consensus, unanimity, unison
related words accession, adhesion, assent, assentation, consent; acceptance, acquiescence, concession, embrace, embracement; approbation, approval, favor; alliance, collaboration, collusion, complicity, conspiracy; compliance, concert, concertedness, concord, concordance, conformity, consonance, harmony, oneness, solidarity, understanding, union; empathy, rapport, sympathy
phrases meeting of minds
near antonyms discord, dissension (*also* dissention); dissent, opposition, resistance; disapprobation, disapproval, disfavor
antonyms conflict, disagreement, dissensus
2 an arrangement about action to be taken ⟨we finally reached an *agreement* regarding a fair division of the housework⟩
synonyms accord, bargain, compact, contract, convention, covenant, deal, disposition, pact, settlement, understanding
related words charter, treaty; binder, pledge, promise; alliance, association, entente, entente cordiale, league, partnership; acceptance, approval, assent, concurrence, consent, OK (*or* okay)
3 a state of consistency ⟨the amount in column A needs to be in *agreement* with the total receipts minus expenses⟩ — see CONFORMITY 1

agricultural *adj* engaged in or concerned with agriculture ⟨he grew up in an *agricultural* community and farming was still in his blood⟩
synonyms agrarian, farming
related words agronomic, arable [*British*], monocultural; bucolic, georgic, pastoral, pastoralist; garden; aquacultural, arboricultural; country, rural, rustic (*also* rustical), villatic
near antonyms metro, metropolitan, urban; industrial, industrialized
antonyms nonagricultural

agriculture *n* the science or occupation of cultivating the soil, producing crops, and raising livestock ⟨the forest was cut down, and the land given over to *agriculture*⟩
synonyms farming, husbandry
related words cultivation, culture, farmwork, gardening, horticulture, tillage; agribusiness, agroecology, agronomy; agroforestry, arboriculture, pomology; aquaculture (*also* aquiculture), hydroponics; animal husbandry, mixed farming, monoculture, pastoralism; sharecropping

agriculturist *or* **agriculturalist** *n* a person who cultivates the land and grows crops on it ⟨*agriculturists* who adhere to the organization's standards of organic farming⟩ — see FARMER

agronomist *n* a person who cultivates the land and grows crops on it ⟨went from being a simple soybean farmer to an *agronomist* specializing in soil management⟩ — see FARMER

aground *adj* resting on the shore or bottom of a body of water ⟨the villagers came to stare at the foreign ship that was *aground* on their beach and at the strangely dressed sailors on board⟩
synonyms beached, grounded, stranded
related words landed; alongshore; high and dry
near antonyms offshore
antonyms afloat

ah *interj* how surprising, doubtful, or unbelievable ⟨*ah*—so that's the way it is!⟩ — see NO

aha *interj* how surprising, doubtful, or unbelievable ⟨*aha*! so the money was never missing in the first place!⟩ — see NO

ahead *adv* **1** so as to precede something in order of time ⟨call *ahead* for reservations⟩
synonyms afore [*chiefly dialect*], already, antecedently, anteriorly, before, beforehand, earlier, formerly, preliminarily, previously
related words a priori, early, prematurely; first, first off, now; before long, erelong [*archaic*], presently, shortly, soon
phrases in advance
near antonyms behind, by and by, next, subsequently
antonyms after, afterward (*or* afterwards), later
2 toward a point ahead in space or time ⟨sent me *ahead* to get a place in the check-out line while she went to get the eggs and milk⟩ — see ONWARD 1
3 toward or at a point lying in advance in space or time ⟨the line moved *ahead* at a snail's pace⟩ — see ALONG

ahead of *prep* **1** earlier than ⟨always arrives at school *ahead of* the bus⟩ ⟨we were cautioned not to fill out any of the test answers *ahead of* time⟩ — see BEFORE 1
2 preceding in space ⟨the three lost children emerged from the forest, with the family dog walking proudly *ahead of* them⟩ — see BEFORE 2

aid *n* **1** a person who helps a more skilled person ⟨Jack is his mother's preferred *aid* in the kitchen, as his sister Janice is clumsy when it comes to chopping and peeling⟩ — see HELPER
2 a thing that helps ⟨a dictionary is a handy *aid* for working crossword puzzles⟩ — see HELP 2
3 an act or instance of helping ⟨the clerk asked if she needed any *aid* carrying out her purchases⟩ — see HELP 1

aid *vb* to provide (someone) with what is useful or necessary to achieve an end ⟨sought to *aid* her in her search for a dachshund puppy by looking online⟩ — see HELP 1

aide *n* a person who helps a more skilled person ⟨the nurse's *aide* will bring you an extra pillow⟩ ⟨served as an *aide* in his father's senatorial campaign⟩ — see HELPER

ail *n* an abnormal state that disrupts a plant's or animal's normal bodily functioning ⟨half of the staff is out sick with the usual wintertime *ails*⟩ — see DISEASE

ail *vb* to trouble the mind of; to make uneasy ⟨parents who were at a loss to explain what was *ailing* their normally vivacious daughter⟩ — see DISTURB 1

ailing *adj* **1** chronically or repeatedly suffering from poor health ⟨when his *ailing* wife had to go to a nursing home, he visited her every day⟩ — see SICKLY 1
2 temporarily suffering from a disorder of the body ⟨he was *ailing* from some sort of infection in his eye that made it look all red and puffy⟩ — see SICK 1

ailment *n* an abnormal state that disrupts a plant's or animal's normal bodily functioning ⟨people who have AIDS are more susceptible to other *ailments* as well⟩ — see DISEASE

aim *n* something that one hopes or intends to accomplish ⟨the main *aim* of a trip to the city is to shop for school clothes, but we always go to the artisans' market, too⟩ — see GOAL

aim *vb* **1** to point or turn (something) toward a target or goal ⟨the anti-drug campaign was *aimed* primarily at preteens⟩
synonyms bend, cast, direct, head, hold, level, pinpoint, set, train
related words sight; bear, face; concentrate, focus; incline, orient, steer
near antonyms avert, curve, deflect, detour, divert, rechannel, shunt, sidetrack
2 to have in mind as a purpose or goal ⟨*aimed* to have his paper all done in time to go to the movies⟩ — see INTEND 1

aimless *adj* lacking a definite plan, purpose, or pattern ⟨this *aimless* walking through stores isn't going to get your Christmas shopping done⟩ — see RANDOM

aimlessly *adv* without definite aim, direction, rule, or method ⟨wandered *aimlessly* through the forest until we were hopelessly lost⟩ — see HIT OR MISS

air *n* **1** a rhythmic series of musical tones arranged to give a pleasing effect ⟨played a lively *air* on his fiddle⟩ — see MELODY
2 a slight or gentle movement of air ⟨we sailed into the bay on a light *air* and just in time to enjoy a spectacular sunset⟩ — see BREEZE 1
3 a special quality or impression associated with something ⟨Naomi's the only person I know who can wear old jeans and a T-shirt with an *air* of elegance⟩ — see AURA 1
4 airs *pl* a display of emotion or behavior that is insincere or intended to deceive ⟨ever since she joined the country club she's been putting on *airs* of being too "high society" for us ordinary folks⟩ — see MASQUERADE

air *vb* to make known (as an idea, emotion, or opinion) ⟨suggested we *air* any complaints about the seating arrangements to the person who actually planned the event⟩ — see EXPRESS 1

airdrome *n* a place from which aircraft operate that usually has paved runways and a terminal ⟨helicopters taking off from a military *airdrome* near Moscow⟩ — see AIRPORT

airfield *n* a place from which aircraft operate that usually has paved runways and a terminal ⟨the passenger jet made an emergency landing at an abandoned *airfield*⟩ — see AIRPORT

airhead *n* a stupid person ⟨among his intimates the consensus is that his new girlfriend is an *airhead*⟩ — see IDIOT

airheaded *adj* not having or showing an ability to absorb ideas readily ⟨he insisted that beauty pageants were nothing but a collection of overdressed, *airheaded* women prancing around⟩ — see STUPID 1

airily *adv* in a quick and spirited manner ⟨sang the ditty *airily*, tapping his foot in time⟩ — see GAILY 2

airman *n* one who flies or is qualified to fly an aircraft or spacecraft ⟨her father was an *airman* who was shot down in Vietnam⟩ — see PILOT

airplane *n* a vehicle for traveling through the air that has fixed wings for lift ⟨my uncle learned how to fly an *airplane* during World War II⟩
synonyms aeroplane [*chiefly British*], plane
related words airbus, airliner, air taxi, liner; aerodyne, aircraft, air-cushion vehicle, airframe, airship, ship, tractor; freighter, tanker; jet, jetliner, superjet, supersonic, supersonic transport, trijet, turbojet, turboprop; aerospace plane, rocket plane; bomber, fighter, jump jet, torpedo bomber, torpedo plane, warplane; amphibian, seaplane; biplane, lightplane, tilt-rotor, towplane, trimotor, triplane; glider, sailplane

airport *n* a place from which aircraft operate that usually has paved runways and a terminal ⟨the *airport* nearest us has plane service on only one major airline⟩
synonyms aerodrome [*chiefly British*], airdrome, airfield, field
related words air base, air park, helipad, heliport, jetport; airstrip, landing field, landing strip, runway; launchpad, pad

airy *adj* **1** resembling air in lightness ⟨Aunt Helen's lemon pies are famous for their *airy* meringues⟩
synonyms ethereal, fluffy, gossamer, gossamery, light
related words cobwebby, dainty, delicate, diaphanous, downy, feathery, flimsy, gauzelike, gauzy, insubstantial, tender, wispy; buoyant, lighter-than-air, lightweight, rarefied, unsubstantial, vaporous, weightless; cumulous, pillowy
near antonyms firm, solid, substantial; bulky, burdensome, cumbersome, hefty, hulking, lumpish, ponderous, unwieldy, weighty
antonyms heavy, leaden
2 open to the free circulation of air ⟨a pleasant, *airy* room⟩
synonyms breezy, ventilated
related words atmosphered, vented
near antonyms close, stifling, suffocating
antonyms breathless, stuffy, unventilated
3 located at a greater height than average or usual ⟨*airy* mountain villages⟩ — see HIGH 3
4 having much high-spirited energy and movement ⟨the *airy* revelry of their latest album is a departure from the slower and more somber music of the band's previous work⟩ — see LIVELY 1
5 satisfying or pleasing because of fineness or mildness ⟨an *airy* cologne that would be appropriate to wear to the office⟩ — see DELICATE 1

akin *adj* **1** having a close connection like that between family members ⟨foxes are closely *akin* to dogs⟩ — see RELATED
2 having qualities in common ⟨mathematics and computer programming are *akin* in that they both require logical thinking⟩ — see ALIKE

alack *interj* used to express sorrow or distress ⟨*alack*, it's true—the only good restaurant in town is closing!⟩ — see ALAS

alacritous *adj* having or showing the ability to respond without delay or hesitation ⟨his *alacritous* response to every request is "Right away, mate!"⟩ — see QUICK 1

alacrity *n* cheerful readiness to do something ⟨having just acquired his driver's license that morning, the teen agreed with *alacrity* to drive his cousin to the airport⟩
synonyms amenability, gameness, goodwill, obligingness, willingness
related words celerity, quickness, rapidity, speed, speediness, swiftness; dispatch, promptitude, promptness; ardor, avidity, eagerness, enthusiasm, exuberance, fervor, gusto, keenness, relish, zeal, zest; agreeableness, geniality, good-naturedness, heartiness, warmth; open-mindedness, receptiveness, receptivity, responsiveness
near antonyms leisureliness, pokiness, slowness, sluggishness; apathy, disinterestedness, halfheartedness, indifference, lukewarmness, perfunctoriness; delay, dila-

toriness, doubt, equivocation, hesitance, hesitancy, hesitation, reluctance, reservation, reticence, uncertainty, vacillation; disinclination, indisposition, recalcitrance, resistance, unwillingness; antipathy, averseness, aversion

à la mode *also* **a la mode** *adj* being in the latest or current fashion ⟨we discovered that what is *à la mode* for teens to wear in the U.S. isn't all that different from what they wear in Europe⟩ — see STYLISH

alarm *also* **alarum** *n* **1** suspicion or fear of future harm or misfortune ⟨observed with *alarm* the man staggering toward the edge of the cliff⟩ — see APPREHENSION 1
2 the act or an instance of telling beforehand of danger or risk ⟨in a daring midnight ride Paul Revere gave the *alarm* that British troops were approaching⟩ — see WARNING 1
3 the emotion experienced in the presence or threat of danger ⟨filled with *alarm* when the flood waters reached their front steps⟩ — see FEAR 1

alarm *also* **alarum** *vb* **1** to strike with fear ⟨I don't want to *alarm* you, but I think you should know there's a bear on your back porch⟩ — see FRIGHTEN
2 to trouble the mind of; to make uneasy ⟨*alarmed* at the skyrocketing cost of home heating fuel⟩ — see DISTURB 1

alarmed *adj* filled with fear or dread ⟨the Mohawks were the trapper's friends, so he was not the least bit *alarmed* at the sight of the band of Mohawk hunters⟩ — see AFRAID

alarming *adj* causing fear ⟨an *alarming* rise in her fever, causing the doctor to fear the worst⟩ — see FEARFUL 1

alarums and excursions *n pl* a state of noisy, confused activity ⟨the city is preparing for the *alarums and excursions* that inevitably accompany a presidential visit⟩ — see COMMOTION

alas *interj* used to express sorrow or distress ⟨Juliet's pitiful lament, "*alas*, poor Romeo, he is already dead!"⟩
synonyms alack, ay, wirra [*Irish*], woe
related words ouch, ow; aw, phooey, rats, sheesh, shucks; bah, boo, faugh, fie, ho hum, humph, pish, pooh, pshaw, tsk, tush, tut, yuck (*also* yuk)
near antonyms alleluia, glory, hallelujah; ha, hey, hooray (*also* hurrah *or* hurray), hot dog, wahoo [*chiefly West*], whee, whoopee, wow, yahoo, yippee

albeit *conj* in spite of the fact that ⟨she felt that her script was still too long, *albeit* it was much shorter than any of her previous scripts⟩ — see ALTHOUGH

album *n* a collection of writings ⟨a special anniversary *album* of his poetry published 100 years after his death⟩ — see ANTHOLOGY

alchemize *vb* to change in form, appearance, or use ⟨time and fiction writers have *alchemized* these Wild West thugs into romantic heroes⟩ — see CONVERT 2

alcohol *n* a distilled beverage that can make a person drunk ⟨after his daughter was born, the man never again touched *alcohol*⟩
synonyms aqua vitae, ardent spirits, booze, bottle, drink, firewater, grog, hooch [*slang*], inebriant, intoxicant, John Barleycorn, juice [*slang*], liquor, lush [*slang*], moonshine, potable, rum, sauce [*slang*], spirits, stimulant, strong drink, tipple
related words aperitif, bracer, chaser, digestif, nightcap; belt, load, nip, peg [*British*], pop, shooter, shot, slug, snifter, snort, tot, whet; cocktail, mixed drink; ale, beer, brew, brewage, brewski [*slang*], home brew, malt liquor, microbrew, mum, nappy [*chiefly Scottish*]; mead, sake (*or* saki), wine; barley-bree (*also* barley-broo) [*chiefly Scottish*], brandy, gin, liqueur, mao-tai, mescal, schnapps, tequila, vodka, whiskey (*or* whisky); Dutch courage
antonyms nonintoxicant

alcoholic *n* a person who makes a habit of getting drunk ⟨one can be a social drinker without turning into an *alcoholic*⟩ — see DRUNK 1

alcoholism *n* habitual or excessive drinking of intoxicants ⟨a treatment center for those suffering from *alcoholism*⟩ — see INTEMPERANCE 1

alcove *n* **1** a freestanding airy structure in a scenic setting (as a park) typically offering commanding views ⟨a small *alcove* in one corner of the backyard garden⟩ — see BELVEDERE
2 a hollowed-out space in a wall ⟨an ancient vase in an *alcove* and a sculpture of Achilles on a stand in the museum's Greek Hall⟩ — see NICHE 1

alert *adj* **1** paying close attention usually for the purpose of anticipating approaching danger or opportunity ⟨she needed to stay *alert* throughout the train ride so as not to miss her stop⟩
synonyms Argus-eyed, attentive, awake, observant, open-eyed, tenty (*also* tentie) [*Scottish*], vigilant, watchful, wide-awake
related words alive, aware, conscious, sensitive; cognizant, heedful, keen, mindful, observing, regardful, sharp, sharp-eyed; hyperalert, hypervigilant, sleepless, wakeful; careful, cautious, chary, wary; prepared, ready
phrases on guard, on one's toes, on the alert, on the ball, on the qui vive, on tiptoe
near antonyms absent, absentminded, absorbed, abstracted, daydreaming, dazed, distracted, dreaming, dreamy, engrossed, faraway, insensible, oblivious, preoccupied; sleeping, unaware, unconscious, unknowing, unwitting; careless, heedless, inattentive, unheeding, unmindful, unthinking, unwary; unprepared, unready
antonyms asleep
2 having or showing a close attentiveness to avoiding danger or trouble ⟨warned us to be *alert* to the presence of pickpockets on the crowded bus⟩ — see CAREFUL 1
3 having or showing quickness of mind ⟨an *alert* and well-trained sheep dog who can handle difficult situations⟩ — see INTELLIGENT 1
4 having or showing the ability to respond without delay or hesitation ⟨an *alert* force of commandos, ready to go on a mission at a moment's notice⟩ — see QUICK 1

alert *n* **1** the act or an instance of telling beforehand of danger or risk ⟨the white flash of the doe's raised tail, giving the "danger" *alert* to her fawns⟩ — see WARNING 1
2 the state of being constantly attentive and responsive to signs of opportunity, activity, or danger ⟨the doctor told the patient to be on the *alert* for any signs of infection⟩ — see VIGILANCE

alert *vb* to give notice to beforehand especially of danger or risk ⟨*alerted* us to the possibility that the roads would be flooded and we might have to take a detour⟩ — see WARN

alertness *n* **1** a close attentiveness to avoiding danger ⟨drove through the fog with extra *alertness*, as the road signs repeatedly warned of deer and moose crossings⟩ — see CAUTION 1
2 the state of being constantly attentive and responsive to signs of opportunity, activity, or danger ⟨we observed the U.S. border patrol's intensified *alertness* for drug smugglers at the border stations⟩ — see VIGILANCE

alfresco *adj* of, relating to, or held in the open air ⟨during the summer months, the theater company puts on a series of *alfresco* performances⟩ — see OUTDOOR

alfresco *adv* in or into the open air ⟨the restaurant's shaded terrace is highly recommended for those seeking to dine *alfresco*⟩ — see OUTDOORS

algid *adj* having a low or subnormal temperature ⟨the

rescuers searching the *algid* waters of the Bering Sea⟩ — see COLD 1

alias *n* **1** a descriptive or familiar name given instead of or in addition to the one belonging to an individual ⟨a dressmaker whom everyone knows as "Bet," her adopted *alias* in the dressmaking business that she named after Betsy Ross⟩ — see NICKNAME

2 a fictitious or assumed name ⟨the English author Eric Blair, better known under the *alias* of George Orwell⟩ — see PSEUDONYM

alibi *n* an explanation that frees one from fault or blame ⟨a student who always has a very creative *alibi* for undone homework or late papers⟩ — see EXCUSE

alien *adj* **1** being, relating to, or characteristic of a country other than one's own ⟨new immigrants with customs *alien* to the community where they have settled⟩ — see FOREIGN 1

2 not being a vital part of or belonging to something ⟨it's completely *alien* to her nature to wish evil of anyone⟩ — see EXTRINSIC

alien *vb* **1** to cause to change from friendly or loving to unfriendly or uncaring ⟨such emotional cruelty will rapidly *alien* any friends you might possibly have left⟩ — see ESTRANGE

2 to give over the legal possession or ownership of ⟨the couple plans to *alien* the adjoining house lot to their eldest son⟩ — see TRANSFER 1

alienate *vb* **1** to cause to change from friendly or loving to unfriendly or uncaring ⟨his heartless treatment of their mother during the divorce proceeding has completely *alienated* the two children⟩ — see ESTRANGE

2 to give over the legal possession or ownership of ⟨a landowner has a right to *alienate* his right of ownership—in other words, he can sell the land if he wants to⟩ — see TRANSFER 1

alienation *n* the loss of friendship or affection ⟨after years of *alienation* from her family, she became reconciled with them when her father fell ill⟩ — see ESTRANGEMENT

alight *adj* **1** filled with much light ⟨we approached the clearing, *alight* with torches, and observed a reenactment of ancient rites by Druids⟩ — see BRIGHT 2

2 *chiefly British* being on fire ⟨the pub, one of London's oldest, was completely *alight* by the time firefighters arrived⟩ — see ABLAZE 1

alight *vb* **1** to come to rest after descending from the air ⟨a flock of eight swans circled above, then *alighted* on the pond⟩

synonyms land, light, perch, roost, settle, touch down

related words belly-land, crash-land

near antonyms arise, ascend, climb, rise; float, fly, glide, plane, soar, wing; hang, hover

antonyms blast off, take off

2 to come down from something (as a vehicle) ⟨as she *alighted* from the coach, she momentarily lost her footing⟩

synonyms descend, disembark, dismount, get down, light

related words deplane, detrain

near antonyms board, climb (aboard), get in, mount; enplane (*also* emplane), entrain

antonyms embark

alike *adj* having qualities in common ⟨all the houses in the neighborhood are *alike* in that they all have a one-car garage and a fenced-in backyard⟩

synonyms akin, analogous, cognate, comparable, connate, correspondent, corresponding, ditto, like, matching, parallel, resemblant, resembling, similar, such, suchlike

related words commensurate, proportionate; tantamount, virtual; allied, congeneric, congenerous, congenial, connatural, kin, kindred, relatable, related; approaching, approximating, close, coextensive, coincident, conformable, conforming, consistent, consonant, duplicate, equal, equivalent, fungible, identical, indistinguishable, interchangeable, me-too, redundant, same, selfsame, substitutable, synonymous, twin; entire, homogeneous, homogenous, unchanging, uniform, unvaried, unvarying

phrases on the order of

near antonyms disparate, distinct, distinguishable, nonequivalent, noninterchangeable; variable, varied, various, varying; imprecise, inaccurate, inexact; unconnected, unrelated

antonyms different, dissimilar, diverse, unakin, unlike

alike *adv* in like manner ⟨regulations that are disapproved of by teachers and students *alike*⟩ — see ALSO 1

alikeness *n* the quality or state of having many qualities in common ⟨since they're identical twins, you shouldn't be so surprised at the *alikeness* of their personal tastes⟩ — see SIMILARITY 1

aliment *n* something that maintains or stimulates the intellect ⟨complained that he had to drive for hours to find any sort of cultural *aliment* when visiting his parents' rural home⟩ — see SUSTENANCE

A–list *n* individuals carefully selected as being the best of a class ⟨the ceremony featured an *A-list* of Hollywood stars⟩ — see ELITE 1

alive *adj* **1** having or showing life ⟨after crashing into the plate glass window the little bird was not only still *alive*, it seemed merely dazed⟩

synonyms animate, breathing, live, living, quick

related words active, animated, dynamic, lively, thriving, vibrant, vigorous, vital, vivacious; current, existent, existing, extant, going, prevailing, surviving; resurrected

near antonyms dying, fading, moribund; stillborn; reposing, resting; ghostlike, ghostly, ghosty, zombielike; absent, extinct, fallen, finished, gone, lapsed, lost, nonexistent, perished, terminated, vanished, wiped out; barren, desert

antonyms asleep, breathless, cold, dead, deceased, defunct, departed, expired, inanimate, lifeless, nonliving

2 marked by much life, movement, or activity ⟨the mall was *alive* with holiday shoppers⟩

synonyms aboil, abubble, abuzz, animated, astir, brisk, bustling, busy, buzzing, flourishing, happening, hopping, humming, kinetic, lively, rousing, stirring, thriving, vibrant

related words abounding, crowded, overflowing, populous, swarming, teeming, thronging

antonyms asleep, dead, inactive, lifeless, sleepy

3 being in effective operation ⟨kept the cause of peace *alive* despite severe setbacks in relations between the two nations⟩ — see ACTIVE 1

4 having being at the present time ⟨insists that her new boyfriend is the handsomest guy *alive*⟩ — see EXTANT 1

5 having specified facts or feelings actively impressed on the mind ⟨*alive* to the need for major improvements in the school system⟩ — see CONSCIOUS 1

alkie *or* **alky** *n, slang* a person who makes a habit of getting drunk ⟨most of the guys at that fraternity seem destined to spend their lives as *alkies*⟩ — see DRUNK 1

all *adj* not divided or scattered among several areas of interest or concern ⟨you need to focus *all* your attention on this matter⟩ — see WHOLE 1

all *adv* **1** to a full extent or degree ⟨we are *all* out of milk⟩ ⟨I was *all* ready to leave at least ten minutes ago⟩ — see FULLY 1

2 for each one ⟨the score is three *all*⟩ — see APIECE

all *pron* every person ⟨a joyous holiday to one and *all*!⟩ — see EVERYBODY

Allah *n* the being worshipped as the creator and ruler of the universe ⟨Muslims worship *Allah*⟩ — see DEITY 2

all–around *also* **all–round** *adj* **1** not limited or specialized in application or purpose ⟨an *all-around* garden rake that adjusts for any raking task, from raking lawns to delicate flower beds⟩ — see GENERAL 4
2 relating to the main elements and not to specific details ⟨this saw has the top rating for *all-around* performance, but for small detail work it might not be your best choice⟩ — see GENERAL 2
3 able to do many different kinds of things ⟨an *all-around* player, as skilled on the pitcher's mound as he is at the batting plate⟩ — see VERSATILE

all around *adv* with everyone or everything taken into account at the same time ⟨*all around*, she's our best athlete⟩
synonyms all told, altogether, collectedly, collectively, inclusively, overall, together
related words broadly, generally, liberally, loosely, macroscopically; all over, completely, comprehensively, encyclopedically, entirely, exhaustively, fully, sweepingly, thoroughly, totally, wholly
phrases across the board, all in all, in the aggregate, on the whole
near antonyms detailedly, microscopically, minutely; literally, narrowly, restrictedly, strictly; alone, categorically, distinctly, exclusively, fractionally, individually, separately, singly, singularly, soley, solitarily, specifically

allay *vb* to make more bearable or less severe ⟨a gentle breeze would *allay* the heat⟩ — see HELP 2

all but *adv* very close to but not completely ⟨dinner is *all but* on the table, so don't go anywhere⟩ — see ALMOST

allege *vb* to state as a fact usually forcefully ⟨*alleged* that the restaurant chain was engaging in discriminatory hiring practices⟩ — see CLAIM 1

allegiance *n* adherence to something to which one is bound by a pledge or duty ⟨torn between his *allegiance* to his native country and the opportunities a sports career in the U.S. could offer⟩ — see FIDELITY

allegory *n* a story intended to teach a basic truth or moral about life ⟨Dr. Seuss's story "The Sneetches" is a telling *allegory* about tolerance for people's differences⟩
synonyms apologue, fable, parable
related words beast fable, bestiary; morality play; legend, myth, mythology, narrative, tale

all–embracing *adj* covering everything or all important points ⟨an *all-embracing* explanation for the great diversity of life on the planet⟩ — see ENCYCLOPEDIC

allergic *adj* having a natural dislike for something ⟨a lover of the outdoors who claims to be *allergic* to desk jobs⟩ — see ANTIPATHETIC 1

allergy *n* a strong feeling of not liking or approving ⟨independent-minded people who seem to have an *allergy* to any control from the government⟩ — see DISLIKE 1

alleviate *vb* to make more bearable or less severe ⟨a car pool *alleviates* some of the stress of driving the kids to and from school every day⟩ — see HELP 2

alleviation *n* reduction of or freedom from pain ⟨hoping a couple of aspirin would provide some *alleviation* of the pain in his shoulder⟩ — see EASE 1

alliance *n* **1** a formal agreement between two or more nations or peoples ⟨the smaller countries signed an *alliance* pledging to protect one another against the belligerent behemoth in their midst⟩ — see TREATY
2 an association of persons, parties, or states for mutual assistance and protection ⟨an *alliance* between the French and the Algonquians to check Iroquois advances into their territory⟩ — see CONFEDERACY
3 the state of having shared interests or efforts (as in social or business matters) ⟨in *alliance* with booksellers, the nation's schools are promoting National Reading Month⟩ — see ASSOCIATION 1

allied *adj* having a close connection like that between family members ⟨people with foreign language fluency and an *allied* skill such as the ability to relate to people from different cultures⟩ — see RELATED

all–important *adj* impossible to do without ⟨that *all-important* item for a successful birthday party: a fancily decorated cake with candles⟩ — see ESSENTIAL 1

all–in *adj, chiefly British* covering everything or all important points ⟨*all-in* seven-day tour of Scotland⟩ — see ENCYCLOPEDIC

all in *adj* depleted in strength, energy, or freshness ⟨was *all in* after an evening of dancing and partying⟩ — see WEARY 1

all–inclusive *adj* covering everything or all important points ⟨an *all-inclusive* look at the threat posed by a global pandemic⟩ — see ENCYCLOPEDIC

allocate *vb* **1** to give as a share or portion ⟨not enough computers to *allocate* one to every student⟩ — see ALLOT
2 to give out (something) to appropriate individuals ⟨*allocated* the housework in such a way that the older kids got more than the younger ones⟩ — see ADMINISTER 1
3 to keep or intend for a special purpose ⟨sliced the strawberries after first *allocating* all the nicest ones for the top of the cake⟩ — see DEVOTE 1

allocation *n* **1** a sum of money allotted for a specific use by official or formal action ⟨recognizing the importance of the arts in the health of a city, the council increased the *allocation* for the city's annual jazz festival⟩ — see APPROPRIATION 1
2 the act or process of giving out something to each member of a group ⟨the *allocation* of Halloween candy became my job when I was too old to go trick-or-treating myself⟩ — see DISTRIBUTION 1

all of *adv* to a full extent or degree ⟨the boat is *all of* 15 feet long⟩ — see FULLY 1

allot *vb* to give as a share or portion ⟨each speaker was *allotted* five minutes to present his or her opinion in the debate⟩
synonyms allocate, allow, apportion, assign, distribute, lot, ration
related words admeasure, administer, deal, dispense, divide, dole out, hand out, measure, mete (out), meter, parcel (out), part, portion, prorate, share (out), split; accord, award, give, grant; earmark, reserve; chip in, contribute, donate; reallocate, reapportion, reassign, redistribute
near antonyms begrudge, deny, deprive (of); keep, retain, stint, withhold; appropriate, arrogate, confiscate

allotment *n* **1** a sum of money allotted for a specific use by official or formal action ⟨the library budget was reduced, while *allotments* for city officials' travel expenses were increased⟩ — see APPROPRIATION 1
2 something belonging to, due to, or contributed by an individual member of a group ⟨every kindergartner received colored paper, scissors, and an *allotment* of paste to make paper chains⟩ — see SHARE 1
3 the act or process of giving out something to each member of a group ⟨the *allotment* of exhibition space at the annual trade show is always fraught with politics and infighting⟩ — see DISTRIBUTION 1

all–out *adj* **1** having no exceptions or restrictions ⟨Grandpa got the *all-out* support of the family when he decided to remarry at age 72⟩ — see ABSOLUTE 2
2 trying all possibilities ⟨an *all-out* effort to break open the door⟩ — see EXHAUSTIVE 1

all out *adv* with all power or resources being used ⟨went *all out* for her New Year's Eve party—she even had fireworks!⟩ — see FULL BLAST

all over *adv* **1** in every place or in all places ⟨I've looked

all over—even outside—and I can't find my other shoe⟩ — see EVERYWHERE
2 to a full extent or degree ⟨his writing style is his mentor's *all over*⟩ — see FULLY 1
allow *vb* **1** to give permission for or to approve of ⟨flash photography is not *allowed* inside the church⟩
synonyms green-light, have, permit, suffer
related words authorize, commission, license (*also* licence); accede (to), acquiesce, agree (to), assent (to), consent (to), OK (*or* okay), warrant; accord, concede, grant, sanction, vouchsafe; admit, brook, condone, countenance, endure, support, tolerate
phrases stand for
near antonyms hinder, impede, obstruct; censure, disallow, disapprove, deny, interdict, refuse, reject, revoke, suppress, withhold; deplore, discountenance, disfavor, dislike, frown (at *or* on), grudge; check, curb, keep, repress, restrain
antonyms ban, enjoin, forbid, prohibit, proscribe, veto
2 to give permission to ⟨a boarding school that does not *allow* students to go on weekend trips without written permission⟩
synonyms leave, let, permit
related words authorize, commission, empower, license (*also* licence); approve, endorse (*also* indorse), sanction; free, liberate, release; cater (to), give in (to), humor, indulge
near antonyms deter, discourage; bar, block, constrain, curb, frustrate, hold back, impede, inhibit, obstruct, prevent
antonyms enjoin, forbid, prohibit
3 to fail to prevent (some behavior on someone's part) especially from neglect or indifference ⟨only a lazy gardener would *allow* the weeds to grow that high⟩
synonyms let, permit, suffer, tolerate
related words brush (aside *or* off), condone, disregard, ignore, overlook, shrug off, wink (at); excuse, forgive, pardon; brook, cater (to), give in (to), humor, indulge
phrases put up with
near antonyms forbid, prohibit; curb, deter, discourage, frustrate, hold back, impede, inhibit, interfere (with)
antonyms bar, block, constrain, prevent
4 to accept the truth or existence of (something) usually reluctantly ⟨I'll *allow* I probably said more than I should have⟩ — see ADMIT 1
5 to give as a share or portion ⟨*allowed* each camper one match to light his fire⟩ — see ALLOT
6 to make able or possible ⟨a patient's canceled appointment *allowed* the doctor to squeeze in a few extra phone calls⟩ — see ENABLE 1
7 to make a statement of one's opinion ⟨he *allowed* that their new house looked very nice⟩ — see REMARK 1
8 *chiefly Southern & Midland* to have as an opinion ⟨people in these parts *allow* that everyone is entitled to one mistake in life, even if it's a doozy⟩ — see BELIEVE 2
9 *chiefly Southern & Midland* to have in mind as a purpose or goal ⟨I *allow* to go hunting before the season is over⟩ — see INTEND 1
allow (for) *vb* to give consideration to (as unexpected circumstances or contingencies) ⟨budget your time to *allow for* the possibility of unexpected problems⟩
synonyms consider, factor (in *or* into), provide (for), regard
related words accommodate, adapt, adjust, condition; anticipate, contemplate, envisage, expect, foresee; assume, presume, presuppose; plan; calculate, face
phrases figure on, reckon with, take account of, take into account
near antonyms factor (out)
antonyms discount, disregard
allow (of) *vb* to make possible especially to the exclusion of other possibilities ⟨I'm afraid the problem doesn't *allow of* any other solution⟩
synonyms admit (of), permit (of)
related words open up; favor, justify, support, sustain, validate; need, take, want, warrant
near antonyms close out, disallow, enjoin, exclude, forbid, negative, preclude, rule out
allowable *adj* that may be permitted ⟨international travel without a passport isn't *allowable*⟩ — see PERMISSIBLE
allowance *n* **1** something belonging to, due to, or contributed by an individual member of a group ⟨as the war progressed, each family's *allowance* of sugar and flour was reduced⟩ — see SHARE 1
2 the approval by someone in authority for the doing of something ⟨without the official *allowance* of the school board, no organization can hold its meetings on school property⟩ — see PERMISSION
alloy *n* a distinct entity formed by the combining of two or more different things ⟨brass is an *alloy*, consisting of copper and zinc⟩ — see BLEND
alloyed *adj* containing foreign or lower-grade substances ⟨*alloyed* aluminum, containing either copper or silicon, is much stronger than pure aluminum for cookware⟩ — see IMPURE 1
all–powerful *adj* having unlimited power or authority ⟨that country's monarch was never an *all-powerful* ruler, but one who shared power with a parliament⟩ — see OMNIPOTENT
all–purpose *adj* not limited or specialized in application or purpose ⟨there's nothing wrong with *all-purpose* flour for baking bread, but flour with more gluten is better⟩ — see GENERAL 4
all right *adj* **1** being to one's liking ⟨it's *all right* with me if you wear jeans to the party⟩ — see SATISFACTORY 1
2 not exposed to the threat of loss or injury ⟨as soon as we heard the rescue helicopter, we knew we were *all right*⟩ — see SAFE 1
3 of a level of quality that meets one's needs or standards ⟨it wasn't a great meal, but it was *all right*⟩ — see ADEQUATE
4 conforming to a high standard of morality or virtue ⟨he's an *all right* guy, so if he says that's the way it happened, I believe him⟩ — see GOOD 2
all right *adv* **1** in a satisfactory way ⟨if everything goes *all right*, I should be back in a day or two⟩ — see WELL 1
2 used to express agreement ⟨*all right*, I'll try one tiny bite of octopus⟩ — see YES
3 without any question ⟨he was there *all right*—I saw him sitting in the back row⟩ — see INDEED 1
all told *adv* with everyone or everything taken into account at the same time ⟨*all told*, we made $14.64⟩ — see ALL AROUND
allude *vb* to convey an idea indirectly ⟨Mrs. Simons *alluded* to some health problems, without being specific⟩ — see HINT
allure *n* the power of irresistible attraction ⟨the nostalgic *allure* of America's Wild West still attracts vacationers to ghost towns⟩ — see CHARM 2
allure *vb* **1** to attract or delight as if by magic ⟨was so *allured* by his sister's college roommate that before long he was asking her for a date⟩ — see CHARM 1
2 to lead away from a usual or proper course by offering some pleasure or advantage ⟨*allured* by the promise of big bucks, he decided to have a go at a job on the trading floor of the stock market⟩ — see LURE
allurement *n* **1** something that persuades one to perform an action for pleasure or gain ⟨for him the *allurement* of gambling is not the prospect of getting rich but rather the excitement of the game⟩ — see LURE 1
2 the act or pressure of giving in to a desire especially

when ill-advised ⟨difficult to ignore the *allurements* of the sideshow posters at the carnival⟩ — see TEMPTATION 1

alluring *adj* having an often mysterious or magical power to attract ⟨the *alluring* beauty of the swans on the lake held us spellbound⟩ — see FASCINATING 1

alluvion *n* a great flow of water or of something that overwhelms ⟨the nonstop torrential rains were threatening to produce an *alluvion* of biblical proportions⟩ — see FLOOD

ally *n* someone associated with another to give assistance or moral support ⟨in trying to convince his parents to send him to soccer camp, the youngster had a strong *ally* in his coach⟩
synonyms abettor (*also* abetter), backer, bedfellow, confederate, fellow traveler, supporter, sympathizer
related words empathizer, well-wisher; accessory (*also* accessary), accomplice, coalitionist, collaborationist, collaborator; adjunct, assistant, coadjutor, helper; associate, cohort, colleague, fellow, partner; buddy, chum, companion, comrade, confidant, crony, familiar, friend, intimate, mate, pal
near antonyms belittler, detractor; adversary, enemy, foe, opponent

ally *vb* to form or enter into an association that furthers the interests of its members ⟨the area's small grape growers have *allied* and formed a cooperative that will help them get the best prices⟩
synonyms associate, band (together), club, coalesce, cohere, confederate, conjoin, cooperate, federate, league, unite
related words cabal, collaborate, gang up, hang together, team (up); incorporate, organize, unionize; affiliate; amalgamate, combine, conglomerate, consolidate, converge, group, join, merge; knot, link, tie, wed
phrases close ranks, pull together
near antonyms detach, disengage, dissolve, disunite, divorce, part, segregate, separate, sever, split, sunder; alienate, estrange, fall out
antonyms break up, disband

almighty *adj* **1** extreme in degree, power, or effect ⟨the *almighty* shock that we got when we received the bill⟩ — see INTENSE 1
2 having unlimited power or authority ⟨when we are young, we want our parents to be *almighty* and to be able to make everything right when something goes wrong⟩ — see OMNIPOTENT

almighty *adv* to a great degree ⟨that's an *almighty* large pumpkin you've grown there⟩ — see VERY 1

Almighty *n* the being worshipped as the creator and ruler of the universe ⟨the missionaries gave thanks to the *Almighty* for their miraculous deliverance from death⟩ — see DEITY 2

almost *adj* being such only when compared to something else ⟨burdened with impossibly high expectations, the movie came to be regarded as an *almost* failure⟩ — see COMPARATIVE

almost *adv* very close to but not completely ⟨we were *almost* finished with dinner when an unexpected visitor showed up⟩ ⟨there were *almost* enough seats for everybody on the bus⟩
synonyms about, all but, borderline, fair [*chiefly British*], fairly, feckly [*chiefly Scottish*], more or less, most, much, near, nearly, next to, nigh, practically, somewhere, virtually, well-nigh
related words appreciably, by and large, chiefly, largely, mainly, mostly; kind of, partially, partly, somewhat
phrases as good as, just about, pretty much, within an inch of
near antonyms absolutely, altogether, completely, entirely, fully, plain, plumb [*chiefly dialect*], quite, thoroughly; totally, utterly, well, wholly; barely, hardly, scarcely

alms *n pl* a gift of money or its equivalent to a charity, humanitarian cause, or public institution ⟨believes that giving *alms* to the poor is a moral duty⟩ — see CONTRIBUTION

almsgiving *n* the giving of necessities and especially money to the needy ⟨good works such as *almsgiving*, tending the sick and visiting the imprisoned⟩ — see CHARITY 1

aloft *adv* to or in a higher place ⟨the ease with which he can hold a ballerina *aloft* with one hand is awesome⟩ — see ABOVE

alone *adj* **1** not being in the company of others ⟨no one realized the boy was *alone* in his room so they all left for the movies without him⟩
synonyms lone, lonely, lonesome, single, solitary, solo, unaccompanied
related words unattended, unchaperoned; forlorn, friendless; cloistered, disassociated, hermetic (*also* hermetical), insulated, isolate, isolated, remote, retired, secluded, withdrawn; quarantined, segregated, separated, sequestered; separate, unattached, unconnected, unlinked; detached, disconnected, disjointed, dissociated, disunited, divided, fractionated; abandoned, adrift, deserted, desolate, forgotten, forsaken, lorn, neglected
phrases on one's own
near antonyms attended, chaperoned, escorted; adjacent, adjoining, communicating, contiguous, neighboring, next-door; attached, connected, coupled, linked
antonyms accompanied
2 being the one or ones of a class with no other members ⟨he is *alone* among the actors of his generation in his exceptional ability to play both comedic and serious parts⟩ — see ONLY 2

alone *adv* **1** without aid or support ⟨completely new to the big city, she nevertheless managed to find her way home *alone*⟩
synonyms independently, single-handed, single-handedly, singly, solely, unaided, unassisted
related words individually, separately; solo
phrases by one's own bootstraps, on one's own, on one's own hook, on one's own initiative
near antonyms collectively, conjointly, cooperatively, hand in glove (*or* hand and glove), hand in hand, jointly, mutually, together; en masse
2 for nothing other than ⟨would willingly play professional baseball for the sheer enjoyment *alone*⟩ — see SOLELY 1

aloneness *n* the state of being alone or kept apart from others ⟨it was an overwhelming sense of *aloneness* that eventually drove the island castaway mad⟩ — see ISOLATION

along *adv* toward or at a point lying in advance in space or time ⟨traffic was inching *along* at a snail's pace⟩ ⟨work on the project is moving right *along*⟩
synonyms ahead, forth, forward, forwards, on, onward (*also* onwards)
related words before, fore, frontward (*or* frontwards)
near antonyms back, backward (*or* backwards), behind, rearward (*also* rearwards)

alongshore *adj* of, relating to, or situated in the waters near the shore ⟨temperatures are moderated by an *alongshore* current⟩ — see INSHORE

aloof *adj* having or showing a lack of friendliness or interest in others ⟨the new kid was really not so *aloof* as we thought him at first, just painfully shy⟩ — see COOL 1

aloud *adv* with one's normal voice speaking the words ⟨the mischievous teacher likes to call on the sleepiest-looking students to read *aloud* from the textbook⟩
synonyms audibly, out, out loud

related words verbally, vocally; clearly, discernibly, distinctly, distinguishably, perceptibly, plainly; blatantly, bloody murder, boisterously, clamorously, loudly, lustily, mightily, noisily, resonantly, resoundingly, stridently, thunderously, uproariously, vociferously
near antonyms faintly, feebly, low, noiselessly, quietly, softly
antonyms inaudibly, silently, soundlessly, voicelessly

alp *n* an elevation of land higher than a hill ⟨an adventurer who has scaled *alps*, explored ocean depths, and flown into the stratosphere⟩ — see MOUNTAIN 1

alpha *n* the point at which something begins ⟨money is not the *alpha* and omega—the beginning and end—of life's purpose⟩ — see BEGINNING

alphabet *n* general or basic truths on which other truths or theories can be based ⟨you need to learn the *alphabet* of genealogy before you can move on to more advanced study⟩ — see PRINCIPLES 1

alphabet soup *n* an unorganized collection or mixture of various things ⟨the *alphabet soup* of designer drugs that were available to patrons of the once-notorious disco⟩ — see MISCELLANY 1

already *adv* so as to precede something in order of time ⟨when we got back to the house, the movers had *already* left⟩ — see AHEAD 1

alright *adj* **1** being to one's liking ⟨an *alright* movie, but I wouldn't pay to see it again⟩ — see SATISFACTORY 1
2 not exposed to the threat of loss or injury ⟨we got the plane's nose back up, and after that we were *alright*⟩ — see SAFE 1

alright *adv* **1** in a satisfactory way ⟨the audition for the orchestra position seemed to go *alright*, but one never knows⟩ — see WELL 1
2 used to express agreement ⟨*alright*, you can buy me lunch, but next time it's my treat⟩ — see YES
3 without any question ⟨she passed the test *alright*—she had the highest score in the class⟩ — see INDEED 1

also *adv* **1** in like manner ⟨we stayed at a historic London hotel, the same establishment that had *also* welcomed our grandparents many years ago⟩
synonyms alike, correspondingly, ditto, likewise, similarly, so
related words equally, equivalently, identically
phrases as well
near antonyms contrarily, conversely, inversely, oppositely, vice versa; diversely, unequally, variously
antonyms differently, dissimilarly, otherwise
2 in addition to what has been said ⟨I'd like a motorcycle for my birthday; *also*, I'd like a new CD player⟩ — see MORE 1

alter *vb* **1** to make different in some way ⟨can't you *alter* your plans just slightly so we can leave 10 minutes earlier?⟩ — see CHANGE 1
2 to remove the sex organs of ⟨contends that cats and dogs that have been *altered* make better pets⟩ — see NEUTER

alterable *adj* capable of being readily changed ⟨if my vacation plans were *alterable*, I'd change them⟩ — see FLEXIBLE 1

alteration *n* the act, process, or result of making different ⟨there's been an *alteration* in the intended route of our bird walk⟩ — see CHANGE 1

altercate *vb* to express different opinions about something often angrily ⟨this discussion is so silly we might as well *altercate* on how many angels can dance on the point of a needle⟩ — see ARGUE 2

altercation *n* an often noisy or angry expression of differing opinions ⟨judging from all the slamming and banging, I'd say there was some sort of *altercation* going on next door⟩ — see ARGUMENT 1

alter ego *n* **1** a person who has a strong liking for and trust in another ⟨over the years the state's other senator became his *alter ego* as well as his political ally⟩ — see FRIEND 1
2 something or someone that strongly resembles another ⟨the hero of the novel is clearly the author's *alter ego*, right down to his receding hairline and middle-aged paunch⟩ — see IMAGE 1

alternative *n* the power, right, or opportunity to choose ⟨there's no *alternative*: we must cross the stream to reach our destination⟩ — see CHOICE 1

although *also* **altho** *conj* in spite of the fact that ⟨*although* I've been to his house several times, I still can't remember how to get there⟩
synonyms albeit, as, howbeit, much as, notwithstanding, though, when, whereas, while, whilst [*chiefly British*]
related words but, if

altiplano *n* a broad flat area of elevated land ⟨a cold wind from the Andes swept across the *altiplano*⟩ — see PLATEAU

altitude *n* **1** the distance of something or someone from bottom to top ⟨the *altitude* of the highest mountain in the U.S. is only about two thirds that of the highest mountain in the world⟩ — see HEIGHT 3
2 the most extreme or advanced point ⟨a man whose arrogance continues to reach new *altitudes*⟩ — see HEIGHT 2
3 *usually* **altitudes** *pl* an area of high ground ⟨the air is thinner at higher *altitudes*⟩ — see HEIGHT 4

altitudinous *adj* extending to a great distance upward ⟨the brochure described the seaside hotel as "an imposing edifice graced by old world charm, situated atop an *altitudinous* promontory with panoramic views"⟩ — see HIGH 1

altogether *adv* **1** for the most part ⟨*altogether*, I'd say we had a pretty good time⟩ — see CHIEFLY
2 to a full extent or degree ⟨I was not *altogether* prepared for such bad news⟩ — see FULLY 1
3 with everyone or everything taken into account at the same time ⟨we spent six months in Europe *altogether*⟩ — see ALL AROUND

altogether *n* the state of having no clothes on one's body ⟨had never posed in the *altogether* for a photographer before⟩ see NUDITY

altruistic *adj* having or showing a concern for the welfare of others ⟨I'm not being *altruistic* in giving you these books, since I was going to have to lug them with me if you hadn't come along⟩ — see CHARITABLE 1

always *adv* **1** on every relevant occasion ⟨although we never intend more than an afternoon visit, she *always* insists we stay for dinner⟩
synonyms aye (*also* ay), consistently, constantly, continually, ever, forever, incessantly, invariably, night and day, perpetually, unfailingly
related words commonly, frequently, oft, often, oftentimes (*or* ofttimes), recurrently, repeatedly; continuously, steadily, uninterruptedly, unremittingly; dependably, generally, habitually, normally, ordinarily, regularly, routinely, typically, usually; inevitably; eternally, everlastingly
phrases at every turn
near antonyms intermittently, occasionally, periodically, sometimes, sporadically; infrequently, rarely, seldom, unusually; variously
antonyms ne'er, never
2 whatever else is done or is the case ⟨you can *always* take a cab if the buses aren't running⟩
synonyms anyhow, anyway, leastways [*dialect*], leastwise
phrases at all events, at any rate, at least, in any case, in any event
3 for all time ⟨I will love you *always*⟩ — see EVER 1

amain *adv* with great effort or determination ⟨conflicting ideals that social philosophers have struggled *amain* to reconcile⟩ — see HARD 1

amalgam *n* a distinct entity formed by the combining of two or more different things ⟨a church that is an *amalgam* of traditional and modern architectural styles⟩ — see BLEND

amalgamate *vb* to turn into a single mass or entity that is more or less the same throughout ⟨silver *amalgamated* with mercury is used for tooth fillings⟩ — see BLEND 1

amalgamated *adj* made from the joining of two or more parts or elements ⟨the *Amalgamated* Clothing and Textile Workers Union was formed from the merger of the clothing workers' and textile workers' unions⟩ — see COMPOSITE

amalgamation *n* a distinct entity formed by the combining of two or more different things ⟨an *amalgamation* of peat moss and vermiculite is a good medium for starting vegetable seedlings⟩ — see BLEND

amanuensis *n* one who writes from dictation or copies manuscripts ⟨thanks to the efforts of his dutiful *amanuensis*, copies of most of the author's letters and unpublished manuscripts have been preserved⟩ — see SCRIBE 1

amass *vb* **1** to bring together in one body or place ⟨*amassed* a truckload of donations in the course of their canned food drive⟩ — see GATHER 1

2 to gradually form into a layer, pile, or mass ⟨over the last month a huge mound of paperwork has *amassed* on my desk⟩ — see COLLECT 2

amateur *adj* **1** being such only for recreation ⟨an *amateur* cabinetmaker, he derives immense satisfaction from finely crafting his own furniture⟩ — see AVOCATIONAL

2 lacking or showing a lack of expert skill ⟨in every room there were *amateur* watercolors, apparently the work of the innkeeper's wife⟩ — see AMATEURISH

amateur *n* **1** a person who regularly or occasionally engages in an activity as a pastime rather than as a profession ⟨an *amateur* photographer who has won a number of photo contests⟩

synonyms dabbler, dilettante, hobbyist, layman, nonexpert, nonprofessional, potterer, putterer, tinkerer

related words all-rounder [*British*], generalist, general practitioner, jack-of-all-trades; aficionado (*also* afficionado), buff, devotee, enthusiast, fan

antonyms authority, expert, pro, professional, specialist

2 a person who lacks experience and competence in an art or science ⟨a homemade doghouse that looked like it was built by an *amateur* who hadn't mastered basic carpentry⟩

synonyms hack, hacker, inexpert, jackleg, trifler

related words beginner, freshman, greenhorn, kid, learner, neophyte, newcomer, novice, rookie, tenderfoot, tyro

near antonyms maestro, virtuoso, whiz, wizard; old hand, old-timer, vet, veteran

antonyms ace, adept, crackerjack (*also* crackajack), craftsman, expert, hand, master, past master, shark, sharp

amateurish *adj* lacking or showing a lack of expert skill ⟨that's an *amateurish* wallpapering job—the pattern doesn't match at the seams⟩

synonyms amateur, dilettante, dilettantish, inexperienced, inexpert, jackleg, nonprofessional, unprofessional, unskilled, unskillful

related words curbstone, self-taught, uninitiated, unprepared, unqualified, unschooled, untaught, untrained, untutored; awkward, clumsy, ham-fisted, ham-handed, heavy-handed; crude, defective, faulty, flawed, primitive, unfinished, unpolished; beginning, entry-level, fresh, green, new, raw, unseasoned, untested, untried, would-be; incapable, incompetent, talentless, unable, unfit, ungifted, untalented

near antonyms able, accomplished, capable, competent, dexterous (*also* dextrous), gifted, habile, handsome, proficient, skilled, skillful, talented; experienced, practiced (*also* practised), seasoned, veteran; educated, fitted, initiated, knowledgeable, prepared, qualified, schooled, taught, trained, tutored, versed; all-around (*also* all-round), ambidextrous, versatile, well-rounded; finished, polished, slick

antonyms ace, adept, consummate, crackerjack, expert, master, masterful, masterly, professional, virtuosic, virtuoso

amateurishness *n* a lack of the level of skill associated with an expert or professional ⟨I was surprised at the *amateurishness* of the dance presentation, considering it was put on by supposed professionals⟩

synonyms amateurism, dilettantism, inexpertness

related words inexperience, unpreparedness; clumsiness, crudeness, ham-handedness, heavy-handedness; inability, inaptitude, incompetence, incompetency, unskillfulness

near antonyms finish, polish; ability, adeptness, competence, proficiency, skill, skillfulness, talent, virtuosity

antonyms expertness, masterfulness, masterliness, professionalism

amateurism *n* a lack of the level of skill associated with an expert or professional ⟨the new defense secretary proceeded to criticize the *amateurism* of the nation's war effort up to that point⟩ — see AMATEURISHNESS

amatory *adj* of, relating to, exciting, or expressing sexual attraction or desire ⟨*amatory* letters that kept their love alive during the years they were separated by war⟩ — see EROTIC

amaze *vb* to make a strong impression on (someone) with something unexpected ⟨your ability to remember names and faces *amazes* me⟩ — see SURPRISE 1

amazed *adj* **1** affected with sudden and great wonder or surprise ⟨you'd be *amazed* at the destruction one small squirrel can cause inside a house⟩ — see THUNDERSTRUCK

2 filled with amazement or wonder ⟨a visitor cannot help but be *amazed* by the size of the Great Pyramid⟩ — see OPENMOUTHED

amazement *n* **1** the rapt attention and deep emotion caused by the sight of something extraordinary ⟨Israelites watched in *amazement* as the Red Sea parted so that they could cross on dry land⟩ — see WONDER 2

2 the state of being strongly impressed by something unexpected or unusual ⟨imagine Dorothy's *amazement* when she discovered that the Wizard of Oz was just an ordinary man⟩ — see SURPRISE 2

amazing *adj* **1** causing a strong emotional reaction because of unexpectedness ⟨it was rather *amazing* that the store let me return the sweater after I'd worn and even washed it⟩ — see SURPRISING 1

2 causing wonder or astonishment ⟨the *amazing* feats of the circus acrobats simply enthralled the audience⟩ — see MARVELOUS 1

ambassador *n* a person sent on a mission to represent another ⟨a beloved entertainer who has often been sent abroad by the president as his country's goodwill *ambassador*⟩

synonyms agent, delegate, emissary, envoy, legate, minister, representative

related words ambassadress; attaché, chargé d'affaires, consul, deputy, diplomat, foreign minister, nuncio, procurator, proxy; apostle, evangelist, missionary; deputation, detachment, legation; courier, messenger; mouthpiece, spokesperson

ambience *or* **ambiance** *n* a special quality or impression associated with something ⟨the exurb has the unmistakable *ambience* of old money⟩ — see AURA 1

ambient *n* the circumstances, conditions, or objects by which one is surrounded ⟨observing how the survival techniques of primates vary with the *ambient*⟩ — see ENVIRONMENT

ambiguity *n* the quality or state of having a veiled or uncertain meaning ⟨the *ambiguity* of the clairvoyant's messages from the deceased allowed the grieving relatives to interpret them however they wished⟩ — see OBSCURITY 1

ambiguous *adj* having an often intentionally veiled or uncertain meaning ⟨the exact reason for the change in plans is *ambiguous*, but I suspect it has something to do with money⟩ — see OBSCURE 1

ambiguousness *n* the quality or state of having a veiled or uncertain meaning ⟨the *ambiguousness* of her "I'll come if I can" left us wondering if we should find someone to take her place⟩ — see OBSCURITY 1

ambit *n* an area over which activity, capacity, or influence extends ⟨many feel that church leaders stray outside of their proper *ambit* when they make specific political endorsements⟩ — see RANGE 2

ambition *n* **1** eager desire for personal advancement ⟨"Talent without *ambition* will not make you a star," the singer's voice coach liked to remind her⟩
synonyms ambitiousness, aspiration, go-getting
related words determination, diligence, drive, energy, enterprise, go, hustle, industry, initiative, motivation, push; aggression, competitiveness, killer instinct; opportunism, overambitiousness, pretentiousness, pushiness; assertiveness, daring, spirit; ardor, avidity, eagerness, keenness, passion; avarice, greed, hunger
near antonyms apathy, halfheartedness, indifference, unconcern; idleness, indolence, inertia, laziness, lethargy, shiftlessness, sloth
2 readiness to engage in daring or difficult activity ⟨the *ambition* shown by the undersea explorers of the Mariana Trench, the deepest in the world⟩ — see ENTERPRISE 2
3 something that one hopes or intends to accomplish ⟨his *ambition* is to study international business, then get a job overseas⟩ — see GOAL

ambitious *adj* **1** having a strong desire for personal advancement ⟨an *ambitious* child actor and his even more ambitious mother, who will do anything to get him in commercials⟩
synonyms aspiring, go-getting, hard-driving, pushing, self-seeking
related words determined, diligent, driving, dynamic, enterprising, gung ho, hungry, hustling, industrious, motivated, scrappy, venturesome, venturous; animated, lively, spirited; ardent, avid, eager, energetic, impassioned, keen, raring, vigorous; aggressive, assertive, high-flying, opportunistic, overambitious, pretentious, pushy, self-assertive; competing, competitive, rival, rivalrous
near antonyms apathetic, disinterested, indifferent, uneager, unenthusiastic, unexcited, uninterested; casual, easygoing, lackadaisical, lazyish; halfhearted, lukewarm, tepid; lazy, lethargic, listless, shiftless, sluggish, spiritless; unaggressive, unassertive
antonyms ambitionless, unambitious
2 having or showing a bold forcefulness in the pursuit of a goal ⟨cleaning up the vacant lot in one weekend was an *ambitious* undertaking⟩ — see AGGRESSIVE 1

ambitiousness *n* eager desire for personal advancement ⟨for sheer *ambitiousness*, few professions can rival the modeling world⟩ — see AMBITION 1

ambivalent *adj* having a mixture of opposing feelings ⟨she's somewhat *ambivalent* about the relationship⟩ — see CONFLICTED

amble *n* a relaxed journey on foot for exercise or pleasure ⟨we had a lovely *amble* about the quaint village before continuing our drive⟩ — see WALK 1

amble *vb* to travel by foot for exercise or pleasure ⟨the couple enjoys *ambling* along the many footpaths that meander through the park⟩ — see HIKE 1

ambler *n* a person who travels by foot for exercise or pleasure ⟨the state park has a number of easy trails which even the most casual of *amblers* can enjoy⟩ — see HIKER

ambrosial *adj* **1** having a pleasant smell ⟨the *ambrosial* air of a greenhouse filled with orchids⟩ — see FRAGRANT
2 very pleasing to the sense of taste ⟨a platter heaped with exotic and *ambrosial* tropical fruits⟩ — see DELICIOUS 1

ambulant *adj* traveling from place to place ⟨a scattering of *ambulant* vendors can be found on the downtown plaza⟩ — see ITINERANT

ambulate *vb* to go on foot ⟨a progressive disease that compromises a patient's ability to *ambulate*⟩ — see WALK 1

ambulatory *adj* traveling from place to place ⟨*ambulatory* theatrical companies that brought live theater to small towns across America⟩ — see ITINERANT

ambuscade *n* a setup in which hidden attackers lie in wait ⟨warned by one of their scouts of an Apache *ambuscade*, the Comanches took a different path through the mountains⟩ — see AMBUSH 1

ambuscade *vb* to lie in wait for and attack by surprise ⟨marching to the rescue of the beseiged Fort Stanwix, 800 colonial militiamen were *ambuscaded* by a force of Loyalist troops and their Native American allies⟩ — see AMBUSH

ambush *n* **1** a setup in which hidden attackers lie in wait ⟨revolutionaries laid an *ambush* for the king along the route his carriage would travel⟩
synonyms ambuscade, ambushment, surprise (*also* surpize), trap
related words assault, attack, charge, sally; capture, entrapment, mousetrap, snare; hunting, stalking
2 a device or scheme for capturing another by surprise ⟨thinking that he was getting into his assigned limousine, the diplomat did not realize that he was the victim of an *ambush* as he was being lured into his captor's car⟩ — see TRAP 1

ambush *vb* to lie in wait for and attack by surprise ⟨the king's enemies planned to *ambush* the royal coach on the way to Paris and capture the king⟩
synonyms ambuscade, surprise (*also* surprize), waylay
related words assail, assault, attack, storm, strike; jump, mug, pounce (on), tackle; charge, sally; capture, ensnare, entrap, mousetrap, net, snare, trap; hunt, prey (on *or* upon), stalk

ambushment *n* a setup in which hidden attackers lie in wait ⟨*ambushments* were a constant threat to travelers along the road to London⟩ — see AMBUSH 1

ameliorate *vb* to make better ⟨social legislation that must be given credit for *ameliorating* the lot of millions of deprived people⟩ — see IMPROVE

amenability *n* **1** a desire or disposition to please ⟨our circle of friends tends to take advantage of Will's *amenability*, usually not even bothering to ask him what he wants to do⟩ — see COMPLAISANCE
2 cheerful readiness to do something ⟨our cat Figaro hasn't shown much *amenability* to going outside now that the weather's cold⟩ — see ALACRITY

amenable *adj* **1** having a desire or inclination (as for a specified course of action) ⟨whatever you decide to do, I'm *amenable*—just let me know⟩ — see WILLING 1

2 readily giving in to the command or authority of another ⟨our normally balky cat becomes the most *amenable* of creatures when confronted with the strange environment of the veterinary clinic⟩ — see OBEDIENT
3 being the one who must meet an obligation or suffer the consequences for failing to do so ⟨even our nation's highest leaders must remain *amenable* to the law⟩ — see RESPONSIBLE 1

amend *vb* **1** to make better ⟨trying to *amend* the situation of the striking workers by supplying them with minimal food supplies⟩ — see IMPROVE
2 to remove errors, defects, deficiencies, or deviations from ⟨the Bill of Rights was adopted in an effort to *amend* a constitution that seemed to many to be deficient in guaranteeing individual rights⟩ — see CORRECT 1
3 to change one's behavior or character for the better ⟨the judge had heard the defendant promise before that he would *amend*⟩ — see REFORM 2

amendatory *adj* serving to raise or adjust something to some standard or proper condition ⟨a bill of rights was seen as a much-needed *amendatory* supplement to the national constitution⟩ — see CORRECTIVE 1

amendment *n* a change designed to correct or improve a written work ⟨the article as written requires only one factual *amendment*⟩ — see CORRECTION 1

amenity *n* **1** an act or utterance that is a customary show of good manners ⟨an unhappy, bickering couple who, at least in public, observe all the *amenities* of polite behavior⟩ — see CIVILITY 1
2 something adding to pleasure or comfort but not absolutely necessary ⟨we don't need an expensive hotel with all the *amenities*—just a place to sleep⟩ — see LUXURY 1
3 something that adds to one's ease of living ⟨that campground has so many of the *amenities* of home that it is best left to those who only like to pretend they are camping⟩ — see COMFORT 2
4 the state or quality of having a pleasant or agreeable manner in socializing with others ⟨at the nursing home Mr. Crawford's natural *amenity* charms the ladies and puts the men at ease⟩ — see AMIABILITY 1

American dream *n* a life marked by material wealth and comfort ⟨with the acquisition of a big house in the suburbs, they felt as though the *American dream* had indeed become a reality for them⟩ — see GOOD LIFE

amiability *n* **1** the state or quality of having a pleasant or agreeable manner in socializing with others ⟨the waitress's *amiability* is what makes eating at the diner so much fun⟩
synonyms affability, agreeability, agreeableness, amenity, amiableness, geniality, good-naturedness, good-temperedness, graciousness, niceness, personableness, pleasantness, sweetness
related words amenability, complaisance, mellowness, sweetness and light; amicability, amicableness, amity, cordiality, empressement, friendliness, gemütlichkeit; benignity, gentleness, kindliness, kindness; cheerfulness, cheeriness, sunniness; civility, comity, considerateness, consideration, courteousness, courtesy, politeness, thoughtfulness; attractiveness, delightfulness, enjoyableness, likability, likableness, pleasingness
near antonyms boorishness, discourtesy, impoliteness, incivility, rudeness, ungraciousness; biliousness, cantankerousness, churlishness, crankiness, fussiness, grouchiness, grumpiness, irascibility, irascibleness, irritability, peevishness, petulance, testiness; contentiousness, contrariness, orneriness, quarrelsomeness, querulousness; hostility, unfriendliness; sourness, vinegar
antonyms disagreeableness, unpleasantness
2 a desire or disposition to please ⟨we had expected our rich cousin to be pushy and snobby, so we were pleasantly surprised by her *amiability*⟩ — see COMPLAISANCE

amiable *adj* having an easygoing and pleasing manner especially in social situations ⟨the owner of the inn is an *amiable*, talkative widow who treats guests like family⟩
synonyms affable, agreeable, genial, good-natured, good-tempered, gracious, mellow, nice, pleasant, sweet, well-disposed
related words amicable, clever [*dialect*], cordial, friendly, neighborly; benign, gentle, kind; cheerful, cheery, glad [*archaic*], sunny; companionable, conversable, sociable; civil, considerate, courteous, polite, thoughtful; accommodating, amenable, obliging; attractive, delightful, enjoyable, likable (*or* likeable)
near antonyms boorish, discourteous, ill-mannered, impolite, inconsiderate, rude, surly, uncivil, unkind, unmannerly, unsociable; bearish, bilious, cantankerous, choleric, churlish, crabby, cranky, dyspeptic, fussy, grouchy, grumpy, ill-humored, irascible, irritable, peevish, petulant, quick-tempered, snappish, testy, touchy; argumentative, contentious, contrary, ornery, querulous; unappealing, unattractive; sour, vinegary
antonyms disagreeable, ill-natured, ill-tempered, unamiable, ungenial, ungracious, unpleasant

amiableness *n* the state or quality of having a pleasant or agreeable manner in socializing with others ⟨the dance instructor's natural *amiableness* puts new students immediately at ease⟩ — see AMIABILITY 1

amicable *adj* **1** having or marked by agreement in feeling or action ⟨the contract negotiations between the hotel workers and management were reasonably *amicable*⟩ — see HARMONIOUS 3
2 having or showing kindly feeling and sincere interest ⟨finds his coworkers at his new job just as *amicable* as he ever could have hoped⟩ — see FRIENDLY 1

amid *or* **amidst** *prep* **1** in or into the middle of ⟨having grown up *amid* farmers and ranchers, Keith still thinks of himself as a country boy at heart⟩ — see AMONG
2 in the course of ⟨*amidst* the messy divorce proceedings they never forgot that their children mattered most⟩ — see DURING

amigo *n* a person who has a strong liking for and trust in another ⟨is it all right if I bring my *amigo* Ben to the party?⟩ — see FRIEND 1

amiss *adj* **1** having a fault ⟨that engine noise indicates that something is clearly *amiss*⟩ — see FAULTY
2 not appropriate for a particular occasion or situation ⟨official recognition would not be *amiss* after that spectacular effort⟩ — see INAPPROPRIATE

amiss *adv* **1** in a mistaken or inappropriate way ⟨I hope that my suggestion that you might be more comfortable in a larger chair was not taken *amiss*⟩ — see WRONGLY
2 off the desired or intended path or course ⟨the reenactment of the Wright Brothers' first flight went *amiss* when the wind died on the makeshift runway and the plane stopped short in a mud puddle⟩ — see WRONG 1

amity *n* kindly concern, interest, or support ⟨a youth club fostering *amity* among the city's many and diverse ethnic groups⟩ — see GOODWILL 1

ammunition *n* means or method of defending ⟨be certain that all of your accusations are true, lest you just give them *ammunition* to claim that all of them are false⟩ — see DEFENSE 1

amnesty *n* release from the guilt or penalty of an offense ⟨the president of France traditionally grants *amnesty* to specially selected prisoners on Bastille Day⟩ — see PARDON

amok *or* **amuck** *adv* in a confused and reckless manner ⟨returned to the classroom to find an escaped snake and her students running *amok*⟩ — see HELTER-SKELTER 1

among *also* **amongst** *prep* in or into the middle of ⟨a

gull landed *among* the burgers-and-fries eaters at the outdoor snack bar, clearly looking for handouts⟩
synonyms amid (*or* amidst), mid, midst, through
related words between, betwixt
phrases in the thick of
near antonyms from, out of

amorous *adj* of, relating to, exciting, or expressing sexual attraction or desire ⟨male birds engage in *amorous* behavior—nest-building, singing, showing off their finery—in order to attract females⟩ — see EROTIC

amorphous *adj* having no definite or recognizable form ⟨*amorphous* lumps of clay magically transformed by a skilled potter's hands into works of art⟩ — see FORMLESS 1

amount *n* a given or particular mass or aggregate of matter ⟨is this small *amount* of food supposed to feed the whole hockey team?⟩
synonyms measure, quantity, quantum, volume
related words coefficient, degree; body, portion; many, number

amount (to) *vb* **1** to have a total of ⟨the expenses of the trip *amounted to* nearly double what we'd budgeted for⟩
synonyms add up (to), aggregate, come (to), count (up to), number, sum (to *or* into), total
related words average, equal, measure, reach; compose, comprise, constitute, make up
phrases clock in at
2 to be the same in meaning or effect ⟨it makes no difference whether you're going to the game or the movies, for it *amounts to* the same thing—that you can't babysit⟩
synonyms add up (to), come (to), correspond (to), emulate, equal
related words approach, match, measure (up), meet, rival, touch; connote, denote, express, import, mean, signify, smack (of), spell, suggest

amour *n* a brief romantic relationship ⟨in her memoirs the diva candidly recalls her *amours* with some of opera's best-known tenors and baritones⟩ — see AFFAIR 1

amour propre *n* an often unjustified feeling of being pleased with oneself or with one's situation or achievements ⟨if *amour propre* is a virtue, then this actress's memoirs are among the greatest declarations of love ever written⟩ — see COMPLACENCE 1

amp (up) *vb* **1** to give life, vigor, or spirit to ⟨an important news story that doesn't need to be *amped up* with sensationalism⟩ — see ANIMATE
2 to make markedly greater in measure or degree ⟨inflammatory rhetoric that served only to *amp up* the civil unrest that was overspreading the city⟩ — see INTENSIFY

amphitheater *n* a large room or building for enclosed public gatherings ⟨the conference attendees crowded into the *amphitheater* for the keynote address⟩ — see HALL 3

ample *adj* **1** being more than enough without being excessive ⟨there's *ample* time to order a pizza before the show⟩ — see PLENTIFUL
2 more than adequate or average in capacity ⟨a husky fellow, he always heads for the most *ample* chair in the room⟩ — see SPACIOUS

amplify *vb* **1** to express more fully and in greater detail ⟨after filing a report of missing luggage, he was asked to *amplify* a bit as to the circumstances⟩ — see EXPAND 1
2 to make greater in size, amount, or number ⟨the number of blood volunteers was significantly *amplified* by the promise of thank-you gifts to donors⟩ — see INCREASE 1
3 to make markedly greater in measure or degree ⟨a fox's large ears serve to *amplify* such sounds as little critters skittering among stones⟩ — see INTENSIFY

amplitude *n* an area over which activity, capacity, or influence extends ⟨the *amplitude* of Thomas Jefferson's interests—government, architecture, agriculture, science, philosophy—is truly awesome⟩ — see RANGE 2

amply *adv* in a generous manner ⟨*amply* rewarded the boy who had found her necklace⟩ — see WELL 2

amulet *n* something worn or kept to bring good luck or keep away evil ⟨a small cross made of goat bone was worn in the Middle Ages as an *amulet* to ward off evil⟩ — see CHARM 1

amuse *vb* to cause (someone) to pass the time agreeably occupied ⟨the older girl *amused* her four-year-old sister at the family reunion by showing her off to all the relatives⟩
synonyms disport, divert, entertain, regale, solace
related words absorb, busy, distract, engage, engross, immerse, interest, involve, occupy; beguile, bewitch, captivate, charm, delight, enchant, enthrall (*or* enthral), fascinate; grip, hypnotize, intrigue, mesmerize; coddle, gratify, humor, indulge, mollycoddle, pamper, please, pleasure, spoil; appease, comfort, conciliate, console, content, mollify, oblige, pacify, placate, propitiate, soothe
near antonyms bore, jade; drain, enervate, exhaust, fatigue, tire, wear, wear out, weary; aggravate, annoy, bother, bug, chafe, disturb, exasperate, fret, gall, grate, harass, harry, irk, nettle, peeve, perturb, pester, pique, upset, vex

amusement *n* the act or activity of providing pleasure or amusement especially for the public ⟨with the opening of Disneyland in 1955, the film producer Walt Disney greatly expanded his *amusement* empire⟩ — see ENTERTAINMENT 1

amusing *adj* providing amusement or enjoyment ⟨Grandma told an *amusing* story about Dad when he was little⟩ — see FUN

analgesic *n* something (as a drug) that relieves pain ⟨the doctor prescribed an *analgesic* and rest for my injured knee⟩ — see PAINKILLER

analogize *vb* to describe as similar ⟨*analogized* the White House scandal to a cancer that was spreading to every internal organ of the body⟩ — see COMPARE 1

analogous *adj* having qualities in common ⟨badmouthing your sister is *analogous* to slapping her in the face—it's just as bad⟩ — see ALIKE

analphabetic *adj* lacking in education or the knowledge gained from books ⟨this *analphabetic* society left no written records so archaeologists must piece together their culture from a variety of nonverbal artifacts⟩ — see IGNORANT 1

analysis *n* **1** the separation and identification of the parts of a whole ⟨investigators took the mysterious powder to the lab for *analysis*⟩
synonyms anatomizing, anatomy, assay, breakdown, deconstruction, dissection
related words assessment, diagnosis, evaluation, examination, inspection, investigation, muster, scrutiny; arrangement, assortment, cataloging (*or* cataloguing), categorization, classification, codification, indexing; enumeration, inventory, itemization, tabulation; division, reduction, segmentation, separation, subdivision
near antonyms agglomeration, aggregation, amalgamation, assimilation, coalescence, conglomeration, consolidation, integration, synthesis, unification
2 a series of explanations or observations on something (as an event) ⟨gave a thorough *analysis* of the main character's motives⟩ — see COMMENTARY 1

analytic *or* **analytical** *adj* according to the rules of logic ⟨presented a very *analytical* argument for the defendant's guilt⟩ — see LOGICAL 1

analyze *vb* to identify and examine the basic elements or parts of (something) especially for discovering inter-

relationships ⟨*analyze* the park's ecosystem before deciding whether hunting should be allowed⟩
synonyms anatomize, assay, break down, cut, deconstruct, dissect
related words assess, diagnose, evaluate, examine, inspect, investigate, scrutinize; arrange, assort, catalog (*or* catalogue), categorize, classify, codify, diagram, enumerate, index, order, schematize, sort, tabulate; divide, reduce, segment, separate, subdivide
near antonyms agglomerate, aggregate, amalgamate, assimilate, coalesce, conglomerate, consolidate, integrate, synthesize, unify

anamnesis *n* a particular act or instance of recalling or the thing remembered ⟨an extended, highly fruitful *anamnesis* that was triggered by the simple act of biting into a madeleine⟩ — see MEMORY 2

anarchic *also* **anarchical** *adj* not restrained by or under the control of legal authority ⟨the citywide blackouts caused *anarchic* looting and rioting⟩ — see LAWLESS 1

anarchy *n* a state in which there is widespread wrongdoing and disregard for rules and authority ⟨the *anarchy* that the country experienced after the dictator drained the treasury and fled the country⟩
synonyms lawlessness, misrule
related words anarchism; commotion, tumult, uproar; chaos, confusion, disarray, disorder, disorderliness, disorganization, misorder; disruption, disturbance, havoc, riot, strife, turbulence, turmoil, unrest, upheaval; mutiny, rebellion, revolution, uprising; criminality, outlawry
near antonyms law, law-abidingness, lawfulness, legality, legitimacy, rule; calmness, harmony, order, orderliness, peace, peaceableness, peacefulness, quiet, tranquillity (*or* tranquility)

anathema *n* **1** a prayer that harm will come to someone ⟨uttered an *anathema* before driving the would-be robber from the his shop⟩ — see CURSE 1
2 something or someone that is hated ⟨the use of animals in the testing of cosmetics is *anathema* to animal-rights activists⟩ — see HATE 2

anathematize *vb* **1** to ask a divine power to send harm or evil upon ⟨heretics *anathematized* by the church leaders⟩ — see CURSE 1
2 to declare to be morally wrong or evil ⟨fundamentalist preachers who *anathematize* any departure from a literal interpretation of the Bible⟩ — see CONDEMN 1

anatomize *vb* to identify and examine the basic elements or parts of (something) especially for discovering interrelationships ⟨if you *anatomize* the problem, you'll see it stems from a combination of her bad behavior and your unwillingness to speak to her about it⟩ — see ANALYZE

anatomizing *n* the separation and identification of the parts of a whole ⟨your *anatomizing* of the situation is quite insightful⟩ — see ANALYSIS 1

anatomy *n* the separation and identification of the parts of a whole ⟨a minutely detailed *anatomy* of the "perfect crime"⟩ — see ANALYSIS 1

ancestor *n* **1** a person who is several generations earlier in an individual's line of descent ⟨Bridie's Irish *ancestors* immigrated to the United States in the 19th century during the Great Potato Famine⟩
synonyms father, forebear (*also* forbear), forebearer, forefather, grandfather, primogenitor, progenitor
related words antecessor, predecessor [*archaic*]; ancestress, foremother, grandmother, matriarch; grandsire [*archaic*], patriarch, sire [*archaic*]; ancestry, antecedents, roots
near antonyms children, family, issue, lineage, offspring, posterity, progeny, seed, stock; daughter, heir, inheritor, scion, son, successor
antonyms descendant (*also* descendent)
2 something belonging to an earlier time from which something else was later developed ⟨pinball machines—the *ancestors* of today's video games—go back to the 19th century⟩
synonyms antecedent, archetype, daddy, foregoer, forerunner, granddaddy (*also* grandaddy), precursor, predecessor, prototype
related words model, original; originator, sire; father, mother
near antonyms by-product, derivative, offshoot, outgrowth, spin-off; daughter, son
antonyms descendant (*also* descendent)

ancestry *n* the line of ancestors from whom a person is descended ⟨a Cambodian immigrant who can trace her Khmer *ancestry* as far back as the 16th century⟩
synonyms birth, blood, bloodline, breeding, descent, extraction, family tree, genealogy, line, lineage, origin, parentage, pedigree, stock, strain
related words heredity, succession; family, house; kin, kindred, relations, relatives; race
near antonyms offspring; child, heir, inheritor, son, successor
antonyms issue, posterity, progeny, seed

anchor *n* **1** one who reads and introduces news reports on a news program ⟨the news *anchor* coordinated the reports of the correspondents from around the state⟩ — see ANCHORPERSON
2 something or someone to which one looks for support ⟨my best friend has been my *anchor* throughout this crisis⟩ — see DEPENDENCE 2

anchor *vb* **1** to put securely in place or in a desired position ⟨used ropes and sandbags to *anchor* the hot-air balloon to the ground⟩ — see FASTEN 2
2 to stop at or near a place along the shore ⟨we'll *anchor* at Praia, Cape Verde⟩ — see LAND 1

anchorage *n* a part of a body of water protected and deep enough to be a place of safety for ships ⟨sailed into a quiet *anchorage* to wait out the storm⟩ — see HARBOR 1

anchorite *n* a person who lives away from others ⟨many Christian saints were *anchorites* who removed themselves from the world to focus on their spirituality⟩ — see RECLUSE

anchorperson *n* one who reads and introduces news reports on a news program ⟨the new *anchorperson* did an admirable job of dealing with the late-breaking news story⟩
synonyms anchor, newscaster, newsreader [*chiefly British*]
related words anchorman, anchorwoman, coanchor; announcer, broadcaster, commentator, linkman [*British*], telecaster; correspondent, foreign correspondent, interviewer, journalist, newshound, newsie, newsman, newsperson, newswoman, reporter, stringer

ancient *adj* **1** dating or surviving from the distant past ⟨Rome's *ancient* ruins remain carefully preserved even in the midst of the bustle of the modern city⟩
synonyms aged, age-old, antediluvian, antique, dateless, hoar, hoary, immemorial, old, venerable
related words aging (*or* ageing), mature; antiquated, archaic, archaistic, dated, fusty, geriatric, medieval (*also* mediaeval), moldy, Noachian, obsolete, outmoded, out-of-date, passé; old-fashioned, old-time, old-world, retro, vintage; durable, enduring, lasting, long-lived, permanent; ageless, hallowed, time-honored, timeless, time-tested, timeworn, traditional, tried, tried-and-true; classic, classical; prehistoric (*also* prehistorical), primeval, primordial
near antonyms fresh, vernal, young, youthful; contemporary, current, latest, mod, novel, present-day, ultramodern; untested, untried; brand-new, unused, unworn
antonyms modern, new, recent

2 being of advanced years and especially past middle age ⟨used to think that age 40 was *ancient* until I turned 40 myself⟩ — see ELDERLY
3 relating to or occurring near the beginning of a process, series, or time period ⟨the *ancient* Inca built a vast network of roads⟩ — see EARLY 1

ancient *n* a person of advanced years ⟨*ancients* in the tribe are accorded great respect and valued for their wisdom⟩ — see SENIOR CITIZEN

ancientness *n* **1** the state of being an old person ⟨if nothing else, the patriarch had achieved a degree of *ancientness* worthy of veneration⟩
synonyms age, agedness, elderliness, maturity
related words senectitude; venerableness; anecdotage, anility, caducity, dotage, second childhood, senescence, senility; feebleness, infirmity
near antonyms freshness, prime, youthfulness; adolescence, immaturity, juvenility, minority, nonage
antonyms youngness, youth
2 the state of being something old ⟨the *ancientness* of the papyrus was authenticated by carbon dating⟩
synonyms age, agedness, antiquity, hoariness
related words antiquation, datedness, obsolescence, obsoleteness, old-fashionedness; fustiness; agelessness
near antonyms currency, currentness, freshness, modernity, modernness, novelty, recentness
antonyms newness

androgynous *adj* suitable to or for either sex ⟨the *androgynous* hairdos favored by the hip⟩ ⟨an actor whose *androgynous* looks are at the heart of his appeal⟩ — see GENDERLESS

anecdote *n* a brief account of something interesting that happened especially to one personally ⟨told us once again that *anecdote* about the dog and the bike⟩ — see STORY 2

anesthetic *n* **1** something (as a drug) that relieves pain ⟨the dentist waited until the *anesthetic* took effect⟩ — see PAINKILLER
2 something that soothes, calms, or induces passivity or a sense of security ⟨he used total immersion in his job as an *anesthetic* for the empty shell that his marriage had become⟩ — see OPIATE

anew *adv* yet another time ⟨junked what he had written and began the essay *anew*⟩ — see AGAIN 1

angel *n* **1** an innocent or gentle person ⟨would like to think that her child is a perfect *angel*⟩ — see LAMB
2 one that announces or indicates the later arrival of another ⟨looking forward to seeing those red-breasted *angels* of the spring—robins⟩ — see FORERUNNER 1
3 one that helps another with gifts or money ⟨over the years the industrialist frequently served as the symphony orchestra's anonymous *angel*⟩ — see BENEFACTOR

anger *n* an intense emotional state of displeasure with someone or something ⟨managed to stifle his *anger* when the receptionist put him on hold for the third time⟩
synonyms angriness, birse [*chiefly Scottish*], choler, furor, fury, indignation, irateness, ire, lividity, lividness, mad, madness, mood [*archaic*], outrage, rage, spleen, wrath, wrathfulness
related words aggravation, annoyance, exasperation, irritation, vexation; acrimoniousness, acrimony, animosity, antagonism, antipathy, bile, biliousness, bitterness, contempt, embitterment, empoisonment, enmity, grudge, hostility, rancor; envy, jaundice, jealousy, pique, resentment; malevolence, malice, spite, vengefulness, venom, vindictiveness, virulence, vitriol; belligerence, contentiousness, contrariness, crankiness, disputatiousness, hot-headedness, irascibility, irascibleness, irritability, orneriness, pugnaciousness, pugnacity, quarrelsomeness, querulousness; blowup, flare, flare-up, outburst; chafe, dander, dudgeon, huff, pet, rise, ruffle, temper; air rage, road rage; delirium, heat, passion, warmth
phrases slow burn
near antonyms calmness, forbearance, patience
antonyms delight, pleasure

anger *vb* to make angry ⟨it's virtually impossible to *anger* Mrs. Peterson—she's the most easygoing person I've ever known⟩
synonyms enrage, incense, inflame (*also* enflame), infuriate, ire, madden, outrage, rankle, rile, roil, steam up, tick off
related words affront, aggravate, annoy, burn (up), cross, exasperate, get, huff, irritate, miff, nettle, offend, peeve, pique, provoke, put out, ruffle, vex; antagonize, embitter, envenom
phrases get one's goat, rub the wrong way
near antonyms allay, assuage, relieve; comfort, console, soothe; appease, conciliate, mollify, pacify, placate; calm, lull, quiet, settle; beguile, bewitch, captivate, charm, disarm, enchant
antonyms delight, gratify, please

angered *adj* feeling or showing anger ⟨*angered* residents demanded to know why their street hadn't been plowed three days after the snowstorm⟩ — see ANGRY

angle *n* **1** a certain way in which something appears or may be regarded ⟨from this *angle*, that car looks gray, not brown⟩ — see ASPECT 1
2 a way of looking at or thinking about something ⟨what's your *angle* on the problem?⟩ — see PERSPECTIVE 1
3 something that curves or is curved ⟨the road around the peninsula is all *angles* and hairpin turns⟩ — see BEND 1

angle *vb* to set or cause to be at an angle ⟨*angle* the camera this way and the Leaning Tower of Pisa will look straight⟩ — see LEAN 1

angling *n* the act of positioning or an instance of being positioned at an angle ⟨his *angling* of the picture made everything else on the wall look crooked⟩ — see TILT

angriness *n* an intense emotional state of displeasure with someone or something ⟨his constant *angriness* makes him unpleasant to work with⟩ — see ANGER

angry *adj* feeling or showing anger ⟨my sister gets really *angry* and practically throws a tantrum if her soccer team loses⟩
synonyms angered, apoplectic, ballistic, cheesed off [*chiefly British*], choleric, enraged, foaming, fuming, furious, hopping, horn-mad, hot, incensed, indignant, inflamed (*also* enflamed), infuriate, infuriated, irate, ireful, livid, mad, outraged, rabid, rankled, riled, riley, roiled, shirty [*chiefly British*], sore, steamed up, steaming, teed off, ticked, wrathful, wroth
related words ranting, raving, stormy; boiling, bristling, bristly, burning, cross, huffy, passionate, seething, sizzling, smoldering (*or* smouldering), worked up, wrought (up); acrid, acrimonious, antagonistic, antipathetic, bitter, embittered, inimical, malevolent, piqued, rancorous, resentful, spiteful, vengeful, vindictive, virulent, vitriolic; antisocial, cold, cool, disagreeable, disapproving, distant, frigid, icy, ill-tempered, sorehead (*or* soreheaded), sulky, unfriendly, unpleasant; aggravated, annoyed, bearish, bilious, cantankerous, churlish, crabby, cranky, dyspeptic, exasperated, fretful, fussy, grouchy, grumpy, ill-humored, inflammable, irascible, irritable, peevish, perturbed, petulant, put out, quick-tempered, snappish, testy, touchy; argumentative, belligerent, contentious, contrary, disputatious, ornery, pugnacious, quarrelsome, querulous
phrases bent out of shape, blue in the face, fit to be tied, going crook [*Australian & New Zealand*], hopping mad, hot under the collar, in a fume, in a huff, in a pet

near antonyms accepting, accommodating, obliging; agreeable, amenable, complaisant; amicable, cordial, friendly; content, happy, satisfied; empathetic, sympathetic, tolerant, understanding; calm, pacific, peaceable, placid, serene, tranquil, unembittered; affable, amiable, easygoing, genial, good-natured, good-tempered, kind, pleasant, sweet

antonyms angerless, delighted, pleased

anguish *n* **1** a state of great suffering of body or mind ⟨as a new teacher, she was in real *anguish* over the decision to report the cheating⟩ — see DISTRESS 1

2 deep sadness especially for the loss of someone or something loved ⟨words can't express my *anguish* at losing my cat⟩ — see SORROW

anguish *vb* **1** to cause persistent suffering to ⟨she was *anguished* by the fear that her sons would die in the war⟩ — see AFFLICT

2 to feel deep sadness or mental pain ⟨I *anguished* over the loss of my father for years afterwards⟩ — see GRIEVE

anguished *adj* expressing or suggesting mourning ⟨an *anguished* cry⟩ ⟨the military's explanation of the accident did nothing to console the *anguished* widow⟩ — see MOURNFUL 1

animal *adj* of or relating to the human body ⟨had intellectual as well as *animal* needs⟩ — see PHYSICAL 1

animal *n* one of the lower animals as distinguished from human beings ⟨we saw a lot of *animals* at the wildlife refuge—cranes, alligators, deer, a fox, even an armadillo⟩

synonyms beast, beastie, brute, creature, critter

related words blastie [*Scottish*], varmint, vermin; biped, quadruped; carnivore, herbivore, insectivore; invertebrate, vertebrate; domestic animal, pet; feral; livestock, stock

animalism *n* the manifestation of the traits or the gratification of the appetites of a lower animal ⟨without law and order, society would quickly devolve into a state of *animalism*⟩ — see BESTIALITY

animalistic *adj* having or showing the nature and appetites of a lower animal ⟨with *animalistic* fury the boxer tore into his opponent⟩ — see BESTIAL

animality *n* the manifestation of the traits or the gratification of the appetites of a lower animal ⟨in his portrayal the actor emphasizes the working-class hunk's fundamental *animality*⟩ — see BESTIALITY

animalize *vb* to make (someone) feel or behave more like an animal than a human being ⟨six months of solitary living in the jungle would *animalize* anyone⟩ — see BRUTALIZE 1

animal magnetism *n* the power of irresistible attraction ⟨a photograph that captures the athlete's *animal magnetism*⟩ — see CHARM 2

animate *adj* **1** having much high-spirited energy and movement ⟨an *animate* dance routine that will really get the blood pumping⟩ — see LIVELY 1

2 having or showing life ⟨had a dream about a sandwich that becomes *animate*⟩ — see ALIVE 1

animate *vb* to give life, vigor, or spirit to ⟨Mr. Clark *animates* history for his sixth graders by frequently showing up for class dressed like some famous historical figure⟩

synonyms amp (up), brace, energize, enliven, fillip, fire, ginger (up), invigorate, jazz (up), juice up, jump-start, liven (up), pep (up), quicken, spike, stimulate, vitalize, vivify, zip (up)

related words arouse, awake, awaken, raise, rouse, stir, wake (up); activate, actuate, drive, impel, motivate, motive, move, propel; charge, electrify, galvanize; enkindle, excite, ferment, foment, incite, inflame (*also* enflame), instigate, kindle, provoke, set off, spark, trigger, turn on, whip (up); abet, boost, buoy, cheer, embolden, fortify, hearten, infuse, inspire, lift, rally, steel, strengthen; reactivate, reanimate, reawake, reawaken, recharge, recreate, reenergize, refresh, refreshen, regenerate, reinvigorate, rejuvenate, rekindle, renew, restimulate, resurrect, resuscitate, revitalize, revive

near antonyms burn out, debilitate, do in, drain, enervate, enfeeble, exhaust, fag, fatigue, harass, kayo, knock out, sap, tucker (out), undermine, wash out, weaken, wear, wear out, weary; check, curb, inhibit, jade, quell, quench, repress, restrain, slow, still, stunt, suppress; daunt, demoralize, discourage, dishearten, dispirit

antonyms damp, dampen, deaden, dull, kill

animated *adj* **1** having much high-spirited energy and movement ⟨an *animated* group of girls loudly running down the hall⟩ — see LIVELY 1

2 marked by much life, movement, or activity ⟨an *animated* marketplace full of vendors and holiday shoppers⟩ — see ALIVE 2

animatedly *adv* in a quick and spirited manner ⟨*animatedly* raced into the living room to open Christmas presents⟩ — see GAILY 2

animately *adv* in a quick and spirited manner ⟨began talking *animately* about her favorite subject: horses⟩ — see GAILY 2

animation *n* the quality or state of having abundant or intense activity ⟨the *animation* of any city depends upon an abundance of street-level restaurants, shops, and places of entertainment⟩ — see VITALITY 1

animosity *n* a deep-seated ill will ⟨his open *animosity* towards us made our meeting very uncomfortable⟩ — see ENMITY

animus *n* a deep-seated ill will ⟨feeling no *animus* toward those who had wronged her⟩ — see ENMITY

annalist *n* a student or writer of history ⟨a new book by America's best-known *annalist* of the Civil War⟩ — see HISTORIAN

annals *n pl* an account of important events in the order in which they happened ⟨his *annals* of the reigns of English kings was used as a source by Shakespeare⟩ — see HISTORY 1

annex *n* a smaller structure added to a main building ⟨a new *annex* that will serve as the permanent home for the school library⟩

synonyms addition, extension, penthouse

related words arm, ell, wing

annex *vb* to join (something) to a mass, quantity, or number so as to bring about an overall increase ⟨plans to *annex* the supply room so as to make the classroom bigger⟩ — see ADD 1

annihilate *vb* **1** to destroy all traces of ⟨the family's attempts to *annihilate* the roach population in their apartment had met with little success⟩

synonyms abolish, black out, blot out, cancel, clean (up), efface, eradicate, erase, expunge, exterminate, extirpate, liquidate, obliterate, root (out), rub out, snuff (out), stamp (out), sweep (away), wipe out

related words decimate, demolish, destroy, devastate, ravage; dismantle, flatten, mow (down), raze, tear down; ruin, total, waste, wreck; blast, blow up, dash, dynamite, smash; atomize, consume, devour, dissolve, fragment, powder, pulverize, shatter, splinter; doom, finish, kill, kill off, terminate, zap; cancel, cut, discard, ditch, eject, excise, expel, jettison, oust, throw out

near antonyms conserve, preserve, protect, save; build, construct, create, fabricate, fashion, forge, form, frame, make, manufacture, shape; fix, mend, patch, rebuild, recondition, reconstruct, renew, renovate, repair, restore, revamp

2 to bring to a complete end the physical soundness, existence, or usefulness of ⟨the tornado simply *annihilated* the family's home⟩ — see DESTROY 1

3 to defeat by a large margin ⟨we didn't just win; we absolutely *annihilated* them!⟩ — see WHIP 2

annihilation *n* the state or fact of being rendered nonexistent, physically unsound, or useless ⟨idealists who seek the *annihilation* of all forms of prejudice⟩ — see DESTRUCTION 1

annihilatory *adj* causing or tending to cause destruction ⟨the *annihilatory* power of atomic bombs⟩ — see DESTRUCTIVE 1

announce *vb* to make known openly or publicly ⟨the excited coworker *announced* to everyone within hearing distance that she and her husband were expecting⟩
synonyms advertise, annunciate, blare, blaze, blazon, broadcast, declare, enunciate, flash, give out, herald, placard, post, proclaim, promulgate, publicize, publish, release, sound, trumpet
related words bark, call (off *or* out), cry; bill, billboard, bulletin, gazette [*chiefly British*]; knell, ring, toll; blurb, feature, pitch, plug, promote, puff; disseminate, spread; disclose, divulge, introduce, kithe [*chiefly Scottish*], manifest, report, reveal, show; advise, apprise, hand down, inform, notify; communicate, impart, intimate
phrases beat the drum (for *or* about), run with
near antonyms conceal, hush (up), silence, suppress, withhold; recall, recant, retract, revoke

announcement *n* a published statement informing the public of a matter of general interest ⟨an *announcement* was in today's paper regarding the merger of the two banks⟩
synonyms ad, advert [*chiefly British*], advertisement, bulletin, communiqué, notice, notification, posting, release
related words broadside, brochure, circular, flyer (*also* flier), fly sheet, gazette [*British*], handbill, handout; bill, billboard, placard, playbill, poster, show bill, sign; broadcast, cablecast, newscast, telecast; advertising, billing, blurb, come-on, commercial, message, pitch, plugola, spot, word; communication, dispatch, report; annunciation, declaration, edict, proclamation, promulgation, pronouncement, pronunciamento, rescript, signification; ballyhoo, boost, buildup, campaign, plug, promo, promotion, propaganda, publicity

announcer *n* a person who conducts a program of entertainment by making introductions and providing continuity ⟨*announcer* for the Indy 500⟩
synonyms emcee, host, MC
related words mistress of ceremonies; DJ, disc jockey (*or* disk jockey), shock jock, veejay, VJ; huckster, pitchman; anchor, anchorman, anchorperson, anchorwoman, newscaster; CBer, ham, radioman
phrases master of ceremonies

annoy *vb* to disturb the peace of mind of (someone) especially by repeated disagreeable acts ⟨deliberately *annoyed* the elderly neighbor by walking across his lawn⟩ — see IRRITATE 1

annoyance *n* **1** the act of making unwelcome intrusions upon another ⟨they have an unlisted number in the hopes that it will reduce the constant *annoyance* by telemarketers⟩
synonyms aggravation, bedevilment, botheration, bothering, bugging, disturbance, harassment, harrying, importunity, pestering, teasing, vexation
related words aggro [*British*], molestation, offense (*or* offence), persecution, provocation, torment, torture; devilment, devilry, mischief
2 the feeling of impatience or anger caused by another's repeated disagreeable acts ⟨Carlene made known her *annoyance* at having to pick up her sister's dirty clothes⟩
synonyms aggravation, aggro [*British*], bother, botheration, exasperation, frustration, grief, irritation, pip [*chiefly British*], vexation
related words agitation, discomfort, displeasure, distress, disturbance, upset; irritability, irritableness, peeve, perturbation, pet, pique, resentment, snappishness, trouble; anger, angriness, chafe, dander, dudgeon, gall, huff, indignation, irateness, ire, outrage, umbrage
near antonyms delight, pleasure
3 something that is a source of irritation ⟨flashing ads, visual clutter, and other *annoyances* that are the price for free information on the Internet⟩
synonyms aggravation, aggro [*British*], bother, botheration, bugbear, exasperation, frustration, hair shirt, hassle, headache, inconvenience, irk, irritant, nuisance, peeve, pest, rub, ruffle, thorn, trial, vexation
related words discomfort, fleabite, pinprick; affront, insult, offense (*or* offence); upset, worry; affliction, albatross, burden, cross, curse, menace, millstone, plague, sore; anxiety, plight, predicament, tribulation, trouble; hang-up, pet peeve, problem; annoyer, disturber, harasser, mischief, offender; pandora's box
near antonyms delight, joy, pleasure
4 one who is obnoxiously annoying ⟨younger brothers can be an *annoyance* sometimes⟩ — see NUISANCE 1

annoyed *adj* subjected to and reacting with irritation ⟨I was extremely *annoyed* when she changed her mind for the third time⟩
synonyms aggravated, bothered, exasperated, galled, irked, irritated, narked [*British*], peeved, put out, scunnered [*chiefly Scottish*], teed off, vexed
related words displeased, distressed, disturbed, perturbed, troubled, upset; angered, angry, indignant, inflamed (*also* enflamed), infuriated, irate, ireful, mad, outraged, rankled, riled, roiled, shirty [*chiefly British*], sore, steaming; bristly, cross, disapproving, huffy, piqued, resentful; bearish, bilious, cantankerous, choleric, churlish, crabby, cranky, dyspeptic, fretful, fussy, grouchy, grumpy, ill-humored, irascible, irritable, peevish, petulant, snappish, snuffy, testy, touchy; badgered, bedeviled, frustrated, haggled, harassed, harried, hassled, inconvenienced, persecuted, pestered, pinpricked, plagued, provoked, tested, tormented, tortured, tried
near antonyms delighted, pleased; content, happy, satisfied; calm, pacific, peaceable, placid, serene, tranquil

annoyer *n* one who is obnoxiously annoying ⟨a bratty *annoyer* who wouldn't leave me alone⟩ — see NUISANCE 1

annoying *adj* causing annoyance ⟨my partner has the *annoying* habit of eating all the pickles and leaving a jar full of pickle juice in the refrigerator⟩
synonyms abrasive, aggravating, bothersome, carking, chafing, disturbing, exasperating, frustrating, galling, irksome, irritating, maddening, nettlesome, nettling, peeving, pesky, pestiferous, pestilent, pestilential, pesty, plaguey (*also* plaguy), rankling, rebarbative, riling, vexatious, vexing
related words burdensome, discomforting, displeasing, disquieting, distressing, importunate, importune, inconveniencing; angering, enraging, infuriating; brattish, bratty, mischievous, offensive, troublesome, upsetting; distractive, painful, stressful, tiresome, troubling, trying, worrisome; biting, grating, jangling, jarring, spiny, thorny
near antonyms delightful, pleasing

annuity *n* a sum of money allotted for a specific use by official or formal action ⟨his grandfather's will provided him with an *annuity* of $5,000 a year to be used for school expenses⟩ — see APPROPRIATION 1

annul *vb* **1** to balance with an equal force so as to make ineffective ⟨unfortunately, his arrogant attitude *annuls* the many generous favors he does for people⟩ — see OFFSET
2 to put an end to by formal action ⟨plans to *annul* their

short-lived, ill-advised marriage⟩ — see ABOLISH 1

annulment *n* the doing away with something by formal action ⟨an *annulment* of that hastily conceived marriage can't come too soon⟩ — see ABOLITION

annunciate *vb* to make known openly or publicly ⟨a politician is wise to *annunciate* past minor transgressions before the media make something major of them⟩ — see ANNOUNCE

anodyne *adj* not causing or being capable of causing injury or hurt ⟨the otherwise *anodyne* comments sounded quite inflammatory when taken out of context⟩ — see HARMLESS

anodyne *n* **1** something (as a drug) that relieves pain ⟨the dentist prescribed an *anodyne* after the root canal⟩ — see PAINKILLER

2 something that soothes, calms, or induces passivity or a sense of security ⟨as an *anodyne* for the stress and superficiality of the modern world, there's nothing better than reading a literary classic of substance and insight⟩ — see OPIATE

anoint *vb* to rub an oily or sticky substance over ⟨*anoint* the wound with antiseptic to prevent infection⟩ — see SMEAR 1

anomalous *adj* **1** being out of the ordinary ⟨that was an *anomalous* year for the housing industry, so the number of starts is anything but typical⟩ — see EXCEPTIONAL 1

2 departing from some accepted standard of what is normal ⟨an *anomalous* burst of anger from this usually easygoing person⟩ — see DEVIANT

anomaly *n* **1** something that is different from what is ordinary or expected ⟨her C grade is an *anomaly*, as she's never made anything except A's and B's before⟩

synonyms aberration, abnormality, exception, oddity, oddment, rarity

related words curiosity, peculiarity, singularity; accident, bizarrerie, phenomenon, quirk, vagary; distortion, kink, mutation, variation; difference, disparity, inconsistence, inconsistency; error, mistake; contradiction, paradox

near antonyms norm, ordinary, usual

2 a person, thing, or event that is far from normal ⟨snow in July is an *anomaly* in most of the northern hemisphere⟩ — see FREAK 1

anon *adv* at or within a short time ⟨be ready—we will begin our Yuletide Boar's Head Feast *anon*⟩ — see SHORTLY 2

anonymity *n* the quality or state of being mostly or completely unknown ⟨oddly enough we like the *anonymity* of being a part of an enormous crowd⟩ — see OBSCURITY 2

anonymous *adj* **1** known but not named ⟨I heard the news from a person who will remain *anonymous*⟩ — see CERTAIN 1

2 not named or identified by a name ⟨a beautiful manuscript illuminated by an *anonymous* medieval monk⟩ — see NAMELESS 1

another *adj* resulting in an increase in amount or number ⟨add *another* thing to the shopping list⟩ — see ADDITIONAL

answer *n* **1** something spoken or written in reaction especially to a question ⟨the standard *answer* of "Fine, thank you" when asked, "How are you?"⟩

synonyms comeback, rejoinder, replication, reply, response, retort, return

related words back talk, banter, persiflage, repartee; acknowledgment (*or* acknowledgement), comment, communication, correspondence, feedback, non sequitur, observation, reaction, remark; defense, explanation, justification, plea, rebuttal, refutation

near antonyms challenge, charge, cross-examination, grilling, interrogation, interrogatory, quiz; poll, questionnaire, survey

antonyms inquiry, query, question

2 something attained by mental effort and especially by computation ⟨the *answers* to the odd-numbered problems are at the back of the book⟩

synonyms result, solution

related words conclusion, determination, explanation, finding; clue, key

3 action or behavior that is done in return to other action or behavior ⟨a cold stare was her withering *answer* to that gratuitous insult⟩ — see REACTION

answer *vb* **1** to speak or write in reaction to a question or to another reaction ⟨didn't *answer* right away when the detective asked him where he'd been for the last three hours⟩

synonyms come back, rejoin, reply, respond, retort, return, riposte

related words acknowledge, comment, communicate, correspond, react, remark; counter, defend, deny, explain, field, rebut, refute

near antonyms challenge, cross-examine, examine, grill, interrogate, pump, quiz; poll, query, survey

antonyms ask, inquire, question

2 to be in agreement on every point ⟨sorry, I haven't seen anyone *answering* to that description⟩ — see CHECK 1

3 to do what is required by the terms of ⟨I don't have a box cutter as such, but will this knife *answer* the purpose?⟩ — see FULFILL 1

4 to find an answer for through reasoning ⟨try to *answer* this riddle⟩ — see SOLVE

answerable *adj* **1** being the one who must meet an obligation or suffer the consequences for failing to do so ⟨you are *answerable* for your own conduct at all times⟩ — see RESPONSIBLE 1

2 capable of having the reason for or cause of determined ⟨they say this equation is not *answerable*⟩ — see SOLVABLE

antagonism *n* a deep-seated ill will ⟨the *antagonism* between them was so bad they couldn't even sit near each other⟩ — see ENMITY

antagonist *n* **1** one that is hostile toward another ⟨please name the novel's hero and his *antagonist*⟩ — see ENEMY

2 one that takes a position opposite another in a competition or conflict ⟨his *antagonist* in the boxing match⟩ — see OPPONENT 1

antagonistic *adj* marked by opposition or ill will ⟨countries that have been *antagonistic* towards each other for centuries⟩ — see HOSTILE 1

antagonize *vb* to implant bitter feelings in ⟨everything he said just *antagonized* the other side even more⟩ — see EMBITTER

ante *n* the amount of money that is demanded as payment for something ⟨the base price is $500, but any additional repairs will up the *ante*⟩ — see PRICE 1

ante (up) *vb* to give what is owed for ⟨if we can't *ante up* at least half of the overdue rent, we are going to be evicted⟩ — see PAY 2

antecede *vb* to go or come before in time ⟨the 19th-century Pre-Raphaelites claimed to base their principles and practices on the Italian art that *anteceded* Raphael and other masters of the High Renaissance⟩ — see PRECEDE

antecedent *adj* going before another in time or order ⟨I'd like to follow up on an *antecedent* question from another reporter⟩ — see PREVIOUS

antecedent *n* **1** someone or something responsible for a result ⟨what are the *antecedents* of the American Revolutionary War?⟩ — see CAUSE 1

2 something belonging to an earlier time from which

something else was later developed ⟨the typewriter is the *antecedent* of the computer keyboard⟩ — see ANCESTOR 2

antecedently *adv* so as to precede something in order of time ⟨make credit card payments *antecedently* to their due date just in case there's a delay in mail delivery⟩ — see AHEAD 1

antedate *vb* to go or come before in time ⟨dinosaurs *antedate* cavemen by millions of years⟩ — see PRECEDE

antediluvian *adj* dating or surviving from the distant past ⟨found evidence in the Middle East of an *antediluvian* people previously unknown to history⟩ — see ANCIENT 1

antediluvian *n* a person with old-fashioned ideas ⟨an *antediluvian* who thought women shouldn't work outside the home⟩ — see FOGY

anterior *adj* **1** being at or in the forward part or surface of something ⟨the *anterior* chamber of the eye is bounded in front by the cornea⟩ — see FRONT
2 going before another in time or order ⟨fossils from an *anterior* geologic age⟩ — see PREVIOUS

anteriorly *adv* so as to precede something in order of time ⟨archaeological artifacts are all that we have of those ancient people who flourished *anteriorly* of the invention of writing⟩ — see AHEAD 1

anthem *n* a religious song ⟨fervently sang an *anthem* of praise to the Lord⟩ — see HYMN 1

anthologize *vb* to bring together from several sources into a single volume or list ⟨*anthologized* an impressive array of essays championing freedom of the press⟩ — see COMPILE

anthology *n* a collection of writings ⟨an *anthology* of American short stories⟩
synonyms album, collectanea, compendium, compilation, florilegium, miscellany, reader
related words almanac, ana, analects, chapbook, digest, garland, symposium; casebook, sourcebook; archives, corpus, library, miscellanea

anti *prep* opposed to; not for ⟨if you ask me, she's *anti* anything that sounds like the least bit of fun⟩
synonyms against, agin [*dialect*], contra
related words athwart, contrary to; versus, with
antonyms for, pro

antic *adj* **1** causing or intended to cause laughter ⟨*antic* shenanigans that made me nearly fall over with laughter⟩ — see FUNNY 1
2 given to good-natured joking or teasing ⟨an *antic* group of kids at summer camp⟩ — see PLAYFUL

antic *n* a playful or mischievous act intended as a joke ⟨we'll have no more of your *antics*, so just settle down⟩ — see PRANK

anticipant *adj* having or showing signs of eagerly awaiting something ⟨*anticipant* of receiving a holiday bonus, she had mentally spent the money by Thanksgiving⟩ — see EXPECTANT 1

anticipate *vb* **1** to believe in the future occurrence of (something) ⟨I *anticipate* that we'll be seeing you for New Year's⟩ — see EXPECT
2 to realize or know about beforehand ⟨I *anticipated* this unhelpful response⟩ — see FORESEE

anticipated *adj* being in accordance with the prescribed, normal, or logical course of events ⟨the *anticipated* date of delivery is July 14th⟩ — see DUE 2

anticipation *n* the act or state of looking forward to some occurrence ⟨in *anticipation* of a marriage proposal, she had already begun looking at wedding dresses⟩ — see EXPECTATION

anticipatory *adj* having or showing signs of eagerly awaiting something ⟨couldn't control his *anticipatory* excitement on Christmas morning⟩ — see EXPECTANT 1

antidote *n* something that corrects or counteracts something undesirable ⟨hoped that taking dance lessons would prove to be an *antidote* for her loneliness⟩ — see CURE 1

antipathetic *adj* **1** having a natural dislike for something ⟨a series of adventure books that turned boys who had been *antipathetic* to reading into avid readers⟩
synonyms allergic, averse
related words afraid, disinclined, loath (*also* loth *or* loathe), reluctant, unwilling; antagonistic, hostile, intolerant, negative, opposed, opposing, resistant, resisting, uncongenial, unfriendly, unsympathetic; disgusted, nauseated, repelled, repulsed, revolted, shocked, squeamish, turned off
phrases down on
near antonyms friendly, sympathetic, tolerant, understanding; admiring, appreciative, charmed, delighted, fond, pleased, tickled
2 marked by opposition or ill will ⟨the mayor has always had an openly *antipathetic* relationship with the local press⟩ — see HOSTILE 1

antipathy *n* **1** a deep-seated ill will ⟨I feel no *antipathy* towards any of my opponents in the tournament⟩ — see ENMITY
2 something or someone that is hated ⟨cruelty to animals is one of my most deeply felt *antipathies*⟩ — see HATE 2

antipodal *adj* being as different as possible ⟨love is *antipodal* to hate⟩ — see OPPOSITE

antipode *n* something that is as different as possible from something else ⟨my jock brother is an *antipode* to my bookworm sister⟩ — see OPPOSITE

antipodean *adj* being as different as possible ⟨since freedom and equality are often *antipodean* goals, a democratic society must find ways of striking a balance between the two⟩ — see OPPOSITE

antiquated *adj* having passed its time of use or usefulness ⟨saw an *antiquated* hand-cranked rope-making machine at the textiles museum⟩ — see OBSOLETE

antique *adj* **1** dating or surviving from the distant past ⟨studied shards from *antique* pots made by the Pueblos of the Southwest⟩ — see ANCIENT 1
2 pleasantly reminiscent of an earlier time ⟨loved to collect *antique* sugar tongs⟩ — see OLD-FASHIONED 1

antique *n* something belonging to or surviving from an earlier period ⟨their house is filled with rare *antiques*, including a collection of 19th-century African masks⟩
synonyms museum piece, relic
related words artifact, fossil; dinosaur; antiquities, ruins; hangover, remains, remnant, trace, vestige

antiquity *n* the state of being something old ⟨despite their indisputable *antiquity*, many of the carvings look like they could have been made yesterday⟩ — see ANCIENTNESS 2

antiseptic *adj* **1** being clean and in good order ⟨known for keeping a strenuously *antiseptic* kitchen, the floor of which does indeed seem fit for eating off of⟩ — see NEAT 1
2 free from dirt or stain ⟨for such an expensive, elegant Sunday brunch, one would expect the attendants at the buffet tables to be professionally attired in starched, *antiseptic* white jackets⟩ — see CLEAN 1
3 lacking in friendliness or warmth of feeling ⟨an *antiseptic* assessment of the chances of survival for their cancer-stricken mother⟩ — see COLD 2

antisocial *adj* having or showing a lack of friendliness or interest in others ⟨she's not *antisocial*, just extremely shy⟩ — see COOL 1

antithesis *n* something that is as different as possible from something else ⟨true love for another is the *antithesis* of the desire to control that person's life⟩ — see OPPOSITE

antithetical *adj* being as different as possible ⟨spiritual concerns and ideals that are *antithetical* to the materialism embraced by modern society⟩ — see OPPOSITE

antre *n* a naturally formed underground chamber with an opening to the surface ⟨a fantasy in which an intrepid band of adventurers enter a vast *antre* and discover a hidden world filled with monsters and wonders⟩ — see CAVE

antsy *adj* **1** feeling or showing uncomfortable feelings of uncertainty ⟨he was feeling understandably *antsy* about the tax audit⟩ — see NERVOUS 1
2 making jerky or restless movements ⟨after a few minutes in the formal restaurant, the kids got *antsy*⟩ — see FIDGETY
3 showing urgent desire or interest ⟨she's been *antsy* to start what promises to be an exciting new job⟩ — see EAGER

anxiety *n* **1** an uneasy state of mind usually over the possibility of an anticipated misfortune or trouble ⟨Dorothy's *anxiety* about her brother's operation kept her awake all night⟩
synonyms agita, agitation, anxiousness, apprehension, apprehensiveness, care, concern, concernment, disquiet, disquietude, fear, nervosity, nervousness, perturbation, solicitude, sweat, unease, uneasiness, worry
related words strain, stress, tension; alarm (*also* alarum), anguish, consternation, desperateness, desperation, discomfort, discomposure, dismay, distraction, distress, disturbance, edginess, franticness, hand-wringing, jitters, jumpiness, panic, tremor; angst, fearfulness, torment, upset, vexation; cold feet, doubt, dread, foreboding, incertitude, misgiving, presentiment, suspense, uncertainty; compunction, qualm, scruple
near antonyms calm, calmness, content, contentment, ease, easiness, peace, peacefulness, placidity, placidness, quiet, quietude, sereneness, serenity, tranquillity (*or* tranquility), tranquilness; comfort, consolation, relief, solace
antonyms unconcern
2 the emotion experienced in the presence or threat of danger ⟨the newly discovered virus is creating considerable *anxiety* in the public at large⟩ — see FEAR 1

anxious *adj* **1** feeling or showing uncomfortable feelings of uncertainty ⟨was *anxious* about the play tryouts scheduled for the following day⟩ — see NERVOUS 1
2 marked by or causing agitation or uncomfortable feelings ⟨the whole crowd seemed to make an *anxious* gasp as the home team almost fumbled the ball⟩ — see NERVOUS 2
3 showing urgent desire or interest ⟨I'm *anxious* for my birthday party⟩ — see EAGER

anxiousness *n* an uneasy state of mind usually over the possibility of an anticipated misfortune or trouble ⟨don't be overcome with *anxiousness* about things that may never happen⟩ — see ANXIETY 1

any *adj* being one of a group ⟨*any* person who comes in the store today is eligible for the discount⟩ — see EACH

anyhow *adv* **1** in spite of everything ⟨even though it's raining, I'm going to the golf course *anyhow*⟩ — see REGARDLESS
2 without definite aim, direction, rule, or method ⟨clothes that were hurriedly stuffed *anyhow* into the suitcase⟩ — see HIT OR MISS
3 whatever else is done or is the case ⟨your mother called and said you don't need to stop by, but I think you should *anyhow*⟩ — see ALWAYS 2

anymore *adv* at the present time ⟨they don't sell that kind of sandwich *anymore*⟩ — see NOW 1

anyway *adv* **1** in spite of everything ⟨I know I really can't afford it, but I'm buying that new car *anyway*⟩ — see REGARDLESS
2 without definite aim, direction, rule, or method ⟨do it *anyway* you feel like⟩ — see HIT OR MISS
3 whatever else is done or is the case ⟨pack an extra sweater *anyway*, as you never know when you might end up needing it⟩ — see ALWAYS 2

anyways *adv, chiefly dialect* in spite of everything ⟨I don't care what you say—I'm going *anyways*!⟩ — see REGARDLESS

anywise *adv* **1** in any way or respect ⟨nor is it *anywise* important what you wear to the party⟩ — see AT ALL
2 without definite aim, direction, rule, or method ⟨just stuffed his newly cleaned clothes *anywise* back into the drawers⟩ — see HIT OR MISS

A-OK *adj* of the very best kind ⟨rated by his colleagues as an *A-OK* investigative reporter⟩ — see EXCELLENT

A1 *adj* of the very best kind ⟨an *A1* mom deserves only the very best Mother's Day card⟩ — see EXCELLENT

apace *adv* with great speed ⟨the end of another year is hastening *apace*⟩ — see FAST 1

apart *adv* into parts or pieces ⟨the fancy new adjustable rake came *apart* the first time I tried to use it⟩
synonyms asunder, piecemeal
phrases to pieces
antonyms together

apart from *prep* not including ⟨*apart from* the saggy roof, the cottage is in pretty good shape⟩ — see EXCEPT

apartment *n* **1** a room or set of rooms in a private house or a block used as a separate dwelling place ⟨a spacious six-room *apartment* that occupies the entire upper floor of a two-family house⟩
synonyms diggings [*chiefly British*], digs, flat [*chiefly British*], lodgings, suite, tenement
related words bed-sitter (*also* bedsit *or* bed-sitting-room) [*British*], cohousing, condo, condominium, duplex, duplex apartment, efficiency, efficiency apartment, flatlet [*British*], floor-through, garden apartment, granny flat [*chiefly British*], maisonette, penthouse, railroad flat, salon, saloon [*chiefly British*], studio, studio apartment, triplex, walk-up; gallery, wing; apartment building, apartment house, tenement house
2 an area within a building that has been set apart from surrounding space by a wall ⟨the museum sets aside this large central *apartment* to display special exhibitions⟩ — see ROOM 2

apathetic *adj* **1** having or showing a lack of interest or concern ⟨people of conscience cannot be *apathetic* about the great suffering in this world⟩ — see INDIFFERENT 1
2 not feeling or showing emotion ⟨gave nothing more than an *apathetic* gaze to his interrogators⟩ — see IMPASSIVE 1

apathy *n* **1** a lack of emotion or emotional expressiveness ⟨the *apathy* of the people of that war-torn country comes from their having seen too many horrors⟩
synonyms affectlessness, emotionlessness, impassiveness, impassivity, insensibility, numbness, phlegm
related words bloodlessness, callosity, callousness, coldness, coolness, halfheartedness, hard-heartedness, hardness, heartlessness, imperturbability, insensitivity, obduracy; blankness, deadness, emptiness, vacancy; aloofness, detachment, indifference, unconcern; stiffness, woodenness
near antonyms compassion, empathy, pity, sympathy; receptiveness, receptivity, responsiveness, sensitivity; solicitude, tenderness, understanding, warmth; hand-wringing, histrionics, hysteria, hysterics, melodrama; vehemence
antonyms emotion, feeling, sensibility
2 lack of interest or concern ⟨her poor grades are proof enough of her *apathy* concerning all matters academic⟩ — see INDIFFERENCE

ape *vb* to use (someone or something) as the model for one's speech, mannerisms, or behavior ⟨was caught *ap-*

ing the substitute teacher's thick accent⟩ — see IMITATE 1

aper *n* a person who adopts the appearance or behavior of another especially in an obvious way ⟨they're just no-talent *apers* of whatever rock band has the current number one record⟩ — see COPYCAT

aperiodic *adj* lacking in steadiness or regularity of occurrence ⟨released *aperiodic* reports on the results of their cancer research⟩ — see FITFUL

aperture *n* a place in a surface allowing passage into or through a thing ⟨you can adjust the *aperture* on this camera's lens by pushing this button⟩ — see HOLE 1

apex *n* **1** the highest part or point ⟨she reached the *apex* of fame, only to find it wasn't what she expected⟩ — see HEIGHT 1

2 the last and usually sharp or tapering part of something long and narrow ⟨the *apex* of the spear⟩ — see POINT 2

aphorism *n* an often stated observation regarding something from common experience ⟨what does the *aphorism* "Hindsight is 20/20" mean?⟩ — see SAYING

aphoristic *adj* marked by the use of few words to convey much information or meaning ⟨retorted with the *aphoristic* comment, "No one said life is fair"⟩ — see CONCISE

aphrodisiac *also* **aphrodisiacal** *adj* of, relating to, exciting, or expressing sexual attraction or desire ⟨the tomato's supposed *aphrodisiac* qualities have caused it to be also known as "the love apple"⟩ — see EROTIC

apiece *adv* for each one ⟨when you figure that they usually sell for six dollars *apiece*, you're getting quite a bargain⟩

synonyms all, each, per, per capita

related words apart, discretely, independently, individually, respectively, separately, singly

phrases a pop, a shot, a throw

near antonyms aggregately, altogether, collectively, together

apish *adj* using or marked by the use of something else as a basis or model ⟨whenever I smiled, the baby would respond with an *apish* grin⟩ — see IMITATIVE 1

aplenty *adj* being more than enough without being excessive ⟨there will be food and drink *aplenty*, so please come⟩ — see PLENTIFUL

aplomb *n* **1** evenness of emotions or temper ⟨you've handled a difficult situation with perfect *aplomb*⟩ — see EQUANIMITY

2 great faith in oneself or one's abilities ⟨carried herself with the dignity and *aplomb* of a born leader⟩ — see CONFIDENCE 1

apocalypse *n* a sudden violent event that brings about great loss or destruction ⟨the fear that the next global pandemic could be an *apocalypse* of biblical proportions⟩ — see DISASTER 1

apocalyptic *also* **apocalyptical** *adj* of, relating to, or being a major turning point ⟨the *apocalyptic* Battle of Stalingrad, which led to the ultimate defeat of Nazi Germany⟩ — see CLIMACTIC

apogee *n* the highest part or point ⟨shag carpeting reached the *apogee* of its popularity in the 1970s but is now considered outdated⟩ — see HEIGHT 1

apologetic *adj* feeling sorrow for a wrong that one has done ⟨was profusely *apologetic* after accidentally breaking a treasured plate⟩ — see CONTRITE

apologue *n* a story intended to teach a basic truth or moral about life ⟨the film is an *apologue* of sorts, but the message is couched in a zany and action-filled plot⟩ — see ALLEGORY

apology *n* an explanation that frees one from fault or blame ⟨her standard *apology* for her chronic tardiness is the ever-present congestion on the highways⟩ — see EXCUSE

apoplectic *adj* feeling or showing anger ⟨the coach was so *apoplectic* when the player missed the free throw that he threw his clipboard onto the court⟩ — see ANGRY

apostate *n* **1** a person who abandons a cause or organization usually without right ⟨an *apostate* from communism, he later became one of its harshest critics⟩ — see RENEGADE

2 one who betrays a trust or an allegiance ⟨became an *apostate* to liberalism after he had gotten wealthy⟩ — see TRAITOR

apostle *n* a person who actively supports or favors a cause ⟨a fervent *apostle* of universal health care⟩ — see EXPONENT 1

apothecary *n* **1** a person who prepares drugs according to a doctor's prescription ⟨in olden days the *apothecary* had few drugs that actually cured anything, most substances being little more than pain relievers⟩ — see DRUGGIST

2 a retail store where medicines and miscellaneous articles are sold ⟨the historic village boasts an old-fashioned *apothecary* that's been there for almost a century and a half⟩ — see DRUGSTORE

apothegm *n* an often stated observation regarding something from common experience ⟨her mother endlessly repeated the *apothegm* "cleanliness is next to godliness"⟩ — see SAYING

apothegmatic *adj* marked by the use of few words to convey much information or meaning ⟨his clear-sighted assessments of today's political leaders are delivered with an *apothegmatic* forcefulness⟩ — see CONCISE

apotheosis *n* the most perfect type or example ⟨the *apotheosis* of the picaresque novel⟩ — see QUINTESSENCE 1

appall *also* **appal** *vb* to cause an unpleasant surprise for ⟨conditions inside the house overrun with cats simply *appalled* animal control officers⟩ — see SHOCK 1

appalling *adj* **1** causing intense displeasure, disgust, or resentment ⟨opening your mouth to show me your half-chewed food is absolutely *appalling*⟩ — see OFFENSIVE 1

2 extremely disturbing or repellent ⟨*appalling* crimes against humanity⟩ — see HORRIBLE 1

appanage *also* **apanage** *n* **1** something granted as a special favor ⟨use of the grounds was just one *appanage* he bestowed upon the caretakers of his estate⟩ — see PRIVILEGE

2 something to which one has a just claim ⟨wealthy people who believe that political power is their natural *appanage*⟩ — see RIGHT 1

apparatus *n* items needed for the performance of a task or activity ⟨the hospital's operating rooms boast the very latest medical *apparatus*⟩ — see EQUIPMENT

apparel *n* covering for the human body ⟨a sale on summer *apparel* for women⟩ — see CLOTHING

apparel *vb* to outfit with clothes and especially fine or special clothes ⟨a designer who regularly *apparels* several of the presenters at the Oscar ceremonies⟩ — see CLOTHE 1

apparent *adj* **1** appearing to be true on the basis of evidence that may or may not be confirmed ⟨at the start of the investigation, the *apparent* cause of the plane crash was mechanical failure⟩

synonyms assumed, evident, ostensible, ostensive, presumed, prima facie, putative, reputed, seeming, supposed

related words demonstrable, external, outward, superficial, visible; conceivable, plausible, possible, supposable; likely, probable; clear, distinct, manifest, obvious, plain; deceptive, delusive, delusory, illusive, illusory, imaginary; misleading, specious; fake, faked, feigned, phony (*also* phoney), pretended, pseudo, put-on; al-

leged, claimed, professed, purported, so-called
near antonyms hidden, inapparent; implausible, impossible, improbable, inconceivable, unlikely; actual, authenticated, confirmed, corroborated, established, genuine, real, substantiated, sure, valid, validated, verified
2 capable of being seen ⟨as the fog lifts, the town in the valley below us will become more *apparent*⟩ — see VISIBLE 1
3 not subject to misinterpretation or more than one interpretation ⟨it's *apparent* from the smile on her face that she got a part in the play⟩ — see CLEAR 2

apparently *adv* to all outward appearances ⟨*apparently*, her husband didn't know the cake was for the raffle, since he helped himself to a piece⟩
synonyms evidently, ostensibly, ostensively, presumably, putatively, seemingly, supposedly
related words externally, outwardly, visibly; believably, credibly; assumably, likely, presumedly, probably; conceivably, maybe, mayhap, perchance, perhaps, possibly, professedly, supposably; allegedly, purportedly, reportedly, reputedly; clearly, distinctly, manifestly, obviously, plainly, self-evidently; assuredly, positively, surely
phrases on the surface
near antonyms implausibly, impossibly, improbably, incredibly

apparition *n* the soul of a dead person thought of especially as appearing to living people ⟨an eccentric who claimed to have photographed an *apparition* in her very own house⟩ — see GHOST 1

appeal *n* **1** an earnest request ⟨made an *appeal* to the public to donate desperately needed blood⟩ — see PLEA 1
2 the power of irresistible attraction ⟨that hot new actress has a certain indescribable *appeal*⟩ — see CHARM 2

appeal (to) *vb* to make a request to (someone) in an earnest or urgent manner ⟨when supplies at the food bank ran desperately low, officials *appealed to* the public for some much-needed replacements⟩ — see BEG

appealing *adj* having an often mysterious or magical power to attract ⟨the idea of living on Mars is *appealing* to space enthusiasts⟩ — see FASCINATING 1

appear *vb* **1** to come into view ⟨a police car *appeared* just as I ran a red light⟩
synonyms come out, materialize, show, show up, turn up, unfold
related words reappear, resurface; bulk, loom; arrive, come; dawn, debut; arise, blossom, bob (up), break, break out, crop (up), emerge, erupt, issue, outcrop, rise, shoot (up), spring (up), surface; happen, occur; reappear, rematerialize
near antonyms depart, leave, retire, withdraw
antonyms clear, disappear, dissolve, evanesce, evaporate, fade, go (away), melt (away), vanish
2 to give the impression of being ⟨it *appears* that he doesn't hear you⟩ — see SEEM
3 to come into existence ⟨the benefits of the exercise program should *appear* almost immediately⟩ — see BEGIN 2
4 to get to a destination ⟨a friend who daily manages to *appear* at our door just as dinner is being served⟩ — see COME 2

appearance *n* **1** the outward form of someone or something especially as indicative of a quality ⟨the dignified *appearance* of this church leader⟩ ⟨the country club's manicured lawns and well-groomed *appearance* in general⟩
synonyms aspect, dress, figure, garb, look, mien, outside, presence, regard [*archaic*]
related words air, attitude, bearing, behavior, comportment, demeanor, deportment, manner, poise, pose; carriage, posture, stance; cast, mold, shape, turn; color, coloring, complexion; countenance, face, features, habit, habitus, person [*archaic*], physiognomy, superficies, visage
phrases cut of one's jib
2 outward and often deceptive indication ⟨can't you at least give the *appearance* of listening to what I say?⟩
synonyms face, guise, name, outward, seeming, semblance, show
related words air, effect, impression; hint, implication, insinuation, resemblance, suggestion; affectation, demonstration, display, fiction, image, imitation, imposture, likeness, make-believe (*also* make-belief), pose, pretense (*or* pretence), representation, simulation; cloak, disguise, exterior, facade (*also* façade), front, gloss, mask, masquerade, patina, Potemkin village, shape, shell, surface, veneer
phrases first blush
3 the act of coming upon a scene ⟨his *appearance* at the party caused considerable speculation⟩ — see ARRIVAL

appease *vb* to lessen the anger or agitation of ⟨candy often *appeases* an upset toddler⟩ — see PACIFY 1

appeasing *adj* tending to lessen or avoid conflict or hostility ⟨we had been feuding with the people next door, so inviting them to the party was intended as an *appeasing* gesture⟩ — see PACIFIC 1

appellation *n* a word or combination of words by which a person or thing is regularly known ⟨a twisting road that deserved the *appellation* "Sidewinder Lane"⟩ — see NAME 1

appellative *n* a word or combination of words by which a person or thing is regularly known ⟨the brochure had advertised a sandy beach, but we didn't see anything that remotely merited that *appellative*⟩ — see NAME 1

append *vb* to join (something) to a mass, quantity, or number so as to bring about an overall increase ⟨*append* the prefix "un-" to each of these words⟩ — see ADD 1

appendage *n* something that is not necessary in itself but adds to the convenience or performance of the main piece of equipment ⟨pasta makers became the must-have *appendage* for tabletop mixers⟩ — see ACCESSORY 1

appendix *n* a part added at the end of a book or periodical ⟨an *appendix* listing all of the artist's known works and their current locations⟩ — see ADDENDUM 1

appertain *vb* **1** to be the property of a person or group of persons ⟨the doctrine that the swath of land between the Atlantic and the Pacific naturally *appertained* to the United States⟩ — see BELONG 2
2 to have a relation or connection ⟨list some of the things *appertaining* to public health⟩ — see APPLY 1

appetency *n* a strong wish for something ⟨television commercials create *appetency* for products that the consumer may not have known even existed⟩ — see DESIRE 1

appetite *n* **1** a need or desire for food ⟨don't eat before dinner, as it will spoil your *appetite*⟩ — see HUNGER 1
2 a strong wish for something ⟨an *appetite* for adventure⟩ — see DESIRE 1
3 positive regard for something ⟨his girlfriend has expensive *appetites*⟩ — see LIKING
4 urgent desire or interest ⟨an athlete with an *appetite* for in-your-face competition⟩ — see EAGERNESS

appetizing *adj* very pleasing to the sense of taste ⟨that dish looks very *appetizing*⟩ — see DELICIOUS 1

applaud *vb* to declare enthusiastic approval of ⟨I *applaud* your decision to take that advanced course⟩ — see ACCLAIM

applaudable *adj* deserving of high regard or great approval ⟨the *applaudable* goal of working one's way through college⟩ — see ADMIRABLE

applauding *adj* expressing approval ⟨a student encouraged by his teacher's *applauding* comments⟩ — see FAVORABLE 1

applause *n* **1** enthusiastic and usually public expression of approval ⟨a design for a memorial for the victims of the attack that has received nothing but *applause* from officials, commentators, and the general public⟩
synonyms acclamation, cheer, cheering, ovation, plaudit(s), rave(s), réclame
related words clapping; bravo, hail, hallelujah, hurrah (*also* hooray *or* hoorah), hosanna, huzzah (*or* huzza); acclaim, accolade, citation, commendation, compliment, encomium, eulogy, homage, kudo, paean, panegyric, salutation, tribute; kudos, praise
near antonyms boo, hiss, hoot, jeer, raspberry, smirk, sneer, snicker, snigger, snort, whistle; gibe (*or* jibe), put-down, taunt
antonyms booing, hissing
2 public acknowledgment or admiration for an achievement ⟨a heroic effort by the fire department that deserves the *applause* of everyone in the city⟩ — see GLORY 1

apple–polish *vb* to use flattery or the doing of favors in order to win approval especially from a superior ⟨a departmental supervisor who *apple-polishes* shamelessly whenever higher-ups are about⟩ — see FAWN

apple–polisher *n* a person who flatters another in order to get ahead ⟨a transparent *apple-polisher* whose fulsome praise fooled no one⟩ — see SYCOPHANT

applesauce *n, slang* language, behavior, or ideas that are absurd and contrary to good sense ⟨all that talk about taking up the farming life was just a lot of spoiled *applesauce*⟩ — see NONSENSE 1

appliance *n* **1** an interesting and often novel device with a practical use ⟨since the invention of the cork, all manner of *appliances* have been invented for the extraction of these sometimes troublesome stoppers⟩ — see GADGET
2 something that is not necessary in itself but adds to the convenience or performance of the main piece of equipment ⟨an *appliance* that allows the machine to be used as a sander⟩ — see ACCESSORY 1

applicability *n* the fact or state of being pertinent ⟨we have to question the *applicability* of much of the information he has included in his report⟩ — see PERTINENCE

applicable *adj* **1** capable of being put to use or account ⟨is that information *applicable* in this case?⟩ — see PRACTICAL 1
2 having to do with the matter at hand ⟨that comment isn't *applicable* to our discussion⟩ — see PERTINENT
3 meeting the requirements of a purpose or situation ⟨a knack for selecting the most *applicable* word⟩ — see FIT 1

applicant *n* one who seeks an office, honor, position, or award ⟨have numerous *applicants* for the job⟩ — see CANDIDATE

application *n* the act or practice of employing something for a particular purpose ⟨fixing a snag in panty hose is not the intended *application* of nail polish, but it's a handy one⟩ — see USE 1

applicative *adj* capable of being put to use or account ⟨certain basic work skills that are *applicative* to almost any job and work environment⟩ — see PRACTICAL 1

applied *adj* capable of being put to use or account ⟨used some *applied* psychology to get the teenager to become more responsible⟩ — see PRACTICAL 1

applier *n* one who seeks an office, honor, position, or award ⟨first-time *appliers* for federal grant money⟩ — see CANDIDATE

apply *vb* **1** to have a relation or connection ⟨does your rule about calling home *apply* to me as well?⟩
synonyms appertain, bear, pertain, refer, relate
related words affect, concern, interest, involve, touch; associate, connect, couple, interrelate, link, tie in; deal (with), treat
phrases have to do with
2 to occupy (oneself) diligently or with close attention ⟨Sam *applied* himself to writing thank-you letters to everyone who'd helped sponsor him for the charity walk⟩
synonyms address, bend, buckle, devote, give
related words readdress, reapply; knuckle down, set (to), settle (down); busy, commit, concern, engage, involve; exert, exhaust, put out, spend, strain, stress, tax, trouble, wear out; carry on, pitch in, plunge (in); grind, hump, hustle, peg (away), plod, plow, plug (away), work
phrases get cracking, get one's act together, get with it, turn one's hand (*or* turn a hand)
near antonyms dally, dawdle, dillydally, fiddle (around), fool around, idle, mess around, monkey (around), play, potter (around), putter (around), trifle
3 to put a layer of on a surface ⟨*apply* the ointment liberally⟩ — see SPREAD 2
4 to put into action or service ⟨*apply* the laws of motion to this physics problem⟩ — see USE 1
5 to bring to bear especially forcefully or effectively ⟨*apply* pressure to the area to stop the bleeding⟩ — see EXERT
6 to carry out effectively ⟨a police officer *applying* the law⟩ — see ENFORCE

appoint *vb* **1** to decide upon (the time or date for an event) usually from a position of authority ⟨at the *appointed* hour we were in our places⟩
synonyms designate, fix, name, set
related words adopt, assign, choose, determine, establish, opt (for), pick, pin (down), prefer, select, settle, single (out), specify; arrange, coordinate, orchestrate; advertise, announce, declare, publish
2 to pick (someone) by one's authority for a specific position or duty ⟨was *appointed* to the council on national security⟩
synonyms assign, attach, commission, constitute, designate, detail, name, nominate, place
related words authorize, delegate, depute, deputize; anoint, consecrate, create, inaugurate, induct, install, instate, institute, invest, make, ordain; crown, enthrone, throne; choose, destine, draft, elect, handpick, select, single (out), vote (in)
near antonyms blackball, depose, dethrone, displace, eject, evict, oust, overthrow, remove, throw out, uncrown, unmake, unseat
antonyms discharge, dismiss, expel, fire

appointee *n* one who has been chosen by some authority for a specific position or duty ⟨the announcement of the presidential *appointees* to the cabinet⟩
synonyms designee, nominee, selectee
related words candidate; assignee, licensee, licentiate, permittee; inductee; agent, delegate, delegatee, deputy; choice, draftee, endorsee, pick, selection

appointment *n* **1** the state or fact of being chosen for a position or duty ⟨the *appointment* of the mayor's husband to the Board of Health came as a surprise⟩
synonyms assignment, commission, designation
related words billet, gig, job, office, place, position, situation, spot, station; authorization, delegation, deputation, emplacement, placement, ranking; anointing, anointment, induction, installation, installment (*also* instalment), instating, investiture, investment, ordination; choice, choosing, destination, election, nomination, picking, selection, singling (out)
near antonyms blackball, rejection; deposition, de-

thronement, ejection, eviction, ouster, overthrow, removal
antonyms discharge, dismissal, dismission, expulsion, firing
2 an agreement to be present at a specified time and place ⟨I have a dental *appointment* for two o'clock tomorrow afternoon⟩ — see ENGAGEMENT 2
3 an assignment at which one regularly works for pay ⟨loved her latest *appointment* as an aide at the governor's office⟩ — see JOB 1
4 appointments *pl* the movable articles (such as tables and chairs) in a room ⟨the yacht's staterooms have the most luxurious *appointments* imaginable⟩ — see FURNITURE

apportion *vb* **1** to give as a share or portion ⟨*apportioned* the profits according to years of service with the company⟩ — see ALLOT
2 to give out (something) to appropriate individuals ⟨*apportioned* the grant money to the winners of the competition⟩ — see ADMINISTER 1

apportionment *n* the act or process of giving out something to each member of a group ⟨the *apportionment* of the estate will happen this Friday⟩ — see DISTRIBUTION 1

apposite *adj* having to do with the matter at hand ⟨enriched his essay on patriotism with some very *apposite* quotations from famous people on the subject⟩ — see PERTINENT

appositely *adv* in a manner suitable for the occasion or purpose ⟨the young painter has been *appositely* compared with the most prominent artists of the previous century⟩ ⟨such inexcusably boorish behavior is fully deserving of an *appositely* harsh reprimand⟩ — see PROPERLY

appositeness *n* the quality or state of being especially suitable or fitting ⟨questioned the *appositeness* of such racy illustrations to a serious text on human sexuality⟩ — see APPROPRIATENESS

appraisal *n* **1** an opinion on the nature, character, or quality of something ⟨gave us a positive *appraisal* of his artistic talents⟩ — see ESTIMATION 1
2 the act of placing a value on the nature, character, or quality of something ⟨the *appraisal* of the house's value took place yesterday⟩ — see ESTIMATE 1

appraise *vb* to make an approximate or tentative judgment regarding ⟨take a moment to *appraise* the current situation⟩ — see ESTIMATE 1

appraisement *n* **1** an opinion on the nature, character, or quality of something ⟨offered us her *appraisement* of the band's latest album⟩ — see ESTIMATION 1
2 the act of placing a value on the nature, character, or quality of something ⟨was too harsh in his *appraisement* of us⟩ — see ESTIMATE 1

appreciable *adj* able to be perceived by a sense or by the mind ⟨there doesn't seem to be any *appreciable* difference between this piece and that one⟩ — see PERCEPTIBLE

appreciate *vb* **1** to become greater in extent, volume, amount, or number ⟨the value of that antique should *appreciate* over time⟩ — see INCREASE 2
2 to hold dear ⟨I *appreciate* my parents more than I can express⟩ — see LOVE 1
3 to have a clear idea of ⟨I hope you *appreciate* just how much that collector's CD costs⟩ — see COMPREHEND 1
4 to think very highly or favorably of ⟨many great artists and musicians have not been *appreciated* in their own lifetimes⟩ — see ADMIRE

appreciation *n* **1** a feeling of great approval and liking ⟨my *appreciation* of her great contributions to women's sports⟩ — see ADMIRATION 1
2 acknowledgment of having received something good from another ⟨if you can do that, you'll have our heartfelt *appreciation*⟩ — see THANKS
3 the knowledge gained from the process of coming to know or understand something ⟨a course intended to give students an *appreciation* of abstract art⟩ — see COMPREHENSION

appreciative *adj* **1** expressing approval ⟨his latest novel has received a number of *appreciative* reviews⟩ — see FAVORABLE 1
2 feeling or expressing gratitude ⟨very *appreciative* after we helped him change his flat tire⟩ — see GRATEFUL 1

appreciatively *adv* in an approving manner ⟨he tasted the wine *appreciatively* as his host looked on⟩ — see ADMIRINGLY

appreciativeness *n* acknowledgment of having received something good from another ⟨a note expressing their *appreciativeness* of all that we had done for them⟩ — see THANKS

appreciatory *adj* feeling or expressing gratitude ⟨as the name of each contributor was announced, the audience responded with *appreciatory* applause⟩ — see GRATEFUL 1

apprehend *vb* **1** to have a clear idea of ⟨do you *apprehend* the importance of this discovery?⟩ — see COMPREHEND 1
2 to take or keep under one's control by authority of law ⟨the agency charged with *apprehending* criminals who have violated federal law⟩ — see ARREST 1

apprehended *adj* taken and held prisoner ⟨an *apprehended* crime lord who can easily post the million-dollar bail⟩ — see CAPTIVE

apprehensible *adj* **1** able to be perceived by a sense or by the mind ⟨some of the moon's more interesting features are *apprehensible* even to someone with a more modestly powered telescope⟩ — see PERCEPTIBLE
2 capable of being understood ⟨a teacher who favored preachy stories that had an easily *apprehensible* moral⟩ — see INTELLIGIBLE

apprehension *n* **1** suspicion or fear of future harm or misfortune ⟨the hikers entered the dark cave with a great deal of *apprehension*⟩
synonyms alarm (*also* alarum), apprehensiveness, dread, foreboding, misgiving
related words agitation, anxiety, anxiousness, concern, disquiet, disquietude, distress, disturbance, fearfulness, funk, perturbation, solicitude, suspense, unease, uneasiness; scruple, worry; doubt, incertitude, mistrust, suspiciousness, uncertainty, wariness; defeatism, pessimism; foreknowledge, premonition, presage, presentiment
near antonyms anticipation, excitement, hope, hopefulness; confidence, optimism, sanguinity
2 the act of taking into one's control by authority of law ⟨*apprehension* of the burglar set the neighborhood at ease⟩ — see ARREST 1
3 an uneasy state of mind usually over the possibility of an anticipated misfortune or trouble ⟨felt a great deal of *apprehension* about the trip and about arriving safely⟩ — see ANXIETY 1
4 the knowledge gained from the process of coming to know or understand something ⟨a good *apprehension* of how computer systems work⟩ — see COMPREHENSION

apprehensive *adj* having specified facts or feelings actively impressed on the mind ⟨I'm fully *apprehensive* of the options, I assure you⟩ — see CONSCIOUS 1

apprehensiveness *n* **1** an uneasy state of mind usually over the possibility of an anticipated misfortune or trouble ⟨her *apprehensiveness* about starting college is keeping her awake at night⟩ — see ANXIETY 1
2 suspicion or fear of future harm or misfortune ⟨my *apprehensiveness* about raw fish disagreeing with me is keeping me from even trying sushi⟩ — see APPREHENSION 1

apprentice *n* **1** a person who helps a more skilled person ⟨decided to be an *apprentice* to an electrician after he graduated⟩ — see HELPER
2 a person who is just starting out in a field of activity ⟨aware that she's only an *apprentice* in the medical field, she readily defers to her more experienced colleagues⟩ — see BEGINNER

apprenticeship *n* a period of undergoing practical instruction in one's job or career ⟨only after long *apprenticeship* as a camera operator was he appointed director of photography on a major motion picture⟩
synonyms externship, internship, practicum, training
related words basic training, boot camp, cadetship; education, grounding, instruction, schooling, tutelage; candidacy, probation, trial
near antonyms tenure

apprise *vb* to give information to ⟨let me *apprise* you of the current situation⟩ — see ENLIGHTEN 1

approach *n* **1** an established course for traveling from one place to another ⟨will take the standard landing *approach* from the south⟩ — see PASSAGE 1
2 the means or procedure for doing something ⟨that's a different *approach* to knitting, but it seems to work⟩ — see METHOD

approach *vb* **1** to come near or nearer ⟨the parade's *approaching*! I can hear the band playing!⟩
synonyms belly up, close, close in, come up, draw on, near, nigh
related words arrive, attain, come, gain, hit, land, make, reach, show up, turn up, waltz up; creep up, sneak up; adjoin, border, touch, verge
near antonyms clear out, depart, exit, go, leave, light out, pull out, quit, remove, run away, shove (off), take off, walk out
antonyms back (up *or* away), recede, retire, retreat, withdraw
2 to move closer to ⟨*approach* the bull with caution⟩ — see COME 1
3 to come near or nearer to in character or quality ⟨his store-bought dessert doesn't even *approach* your homemade version of it⟩ — see APPROXIMATE

approaching *adj* being soon to appear or take place ⟨the *approaching* holiday has everyone in a state of excitement⟩ — see FORTHCOMING 1

approbate *vb* to give official acceptance of as satisfactory ⟨Congress must *approbate* the President's nominees to the U.S. Supreme Court⟩ — see APPROVE

approbation *n* an acceptance of something as satisfactory ⟨that plan has the *approbation* of the school board⟩ — see APPROVAL 1

approbatory *adj* expressing approval ⟨the candidate's views on taxes received overwhelmingly *approbatory* nods from the conservative audience⟩ — see FAVORABLE 1

appropriate *adj* meeting the requirements of a purpose or situation ⟨I don't think jeans and a T-shirt are *appropriate* attire for a wedding⟩ — see FIT 1

appropriate *vb* **1** to take or make use of under a guise of authority but without actual right ⟨archaeologists once freely *appropriated* artifacts excavated at ancient African sites for their museums in Europe⟩
synonyms arrogate, commandeer, convert, expropriate, pirate, preempt, press, seize, take over, usurp
related words annex, attach, claim, confiscate, impound, repossess, sequester; assume, collar, grab, grasp, snatch, steal, wrench, wrest; despoil, loot, pillage; encroach, infringe, invade, occupy, preoccupy, trespass; embezzle, misapply, misappropriate, misuse, peculate
2 to take (something) without right and with an intent to keep ⟨you can't just *appropriate* somebody's term paper and put your name on it!⟩ — see STEAL 1

appropriately *adv* in a manner suitable for the occasion or purpose ⟨make sure you greet your elders *appropriately*⟩ — see PROPERLY

appropriateness *n* the quality or state of being especially suitable or fitting ⟨visitors remarked on the *appropriateness* of window boxes on the cottage, noting they gave it a quaint, cheerful look⟩
synonyms appositeness, aptness, felicitousness, felicity, fitness, fittingness, happiness, properness, propriety, rightness, seemliness, suitability, suitableness
related words agreeableness, compatibility, congruity, harmoniousness; applicability, bearing, connection, justifiability, materiality, pertinence, relevance, relevancy, validity; acceptability, adequacy, adequateness, convenience, expedience, expediency, satisfactoriness, serviceableness, usefulness
near antonyms disagreeableness, incompatibility, incongruence, incongruity, incongruousness, inexpedience, inexpediency, inharmoniousness, unbecomingness; immateriality, inapplicability, irrelevance, irrelevancy; meaninglessness, pointlessness
antonyms improperness, impropriety, inappositeness, inappropriateness, inaptness, infelicity, unfitness, unseemliness, unsuitability, wrongness

appropriation *n* **1** a sum of money allotted for a specific use by official or formal action ⟨the National Park Service received an increased *appropriation* for wildlife management⟩
synonyms allocation, allotment, annuity, entitlement, grant, subsidy, subvention
related words aid, assistance, block grant, grant-in-aid, set-aside; foreign aid, relief, state aid; advance, allowance, benefit, bequest, endowment, fund, legacy, stipend, trust, trust fund
2 the unlawful taking or withholding of something from the rightful owner under a guise of authority ⟨the insurgents' *appropriation* of the house for their headquarters⟩
synonyms arrogation, commandeering, detainer, expropriation, preemption, seizure, takeover, usurpation
related words annexation, assumption, attachment, confiscation, grab, impoundment, repossession, sequestration; defalcation, embezzlement, misapplication, misappropriation, misuse, peculation, theft; despoilment, looting, pillaging; encroachment, infringement, piracy; invasion, occupancy, occupation, preoccupancy, trespass; deforcement, disfurnishment, dispossession, ejection, stripping

approval *n* an acceptance of something as satisfactory ⟨does this dress I bought for the wedding meet with your *approval*?⟩
synonyms approbation, blessing, favor, imprimatur, OK (*or* okay)
related words backing, cachet, endorsement (*also* indorsement), finalization, formalization, homologation, nod, ratification, rubber stamp, sanction, support, thumbs-up, vote; benediction, goodwill; acceptation, accession, agreement, assent, concurrence, consent; countenance, liking, satisfaction
phrases clean bill of health, pat on the back
near antonyms refusal, rejection, repudiation; dislike, dissatisfaction; censure, condemnation, criticism, denunciation, deprecation, depreciation, disparagement, opprobrium, reprehension, reproach, reprobation
antonyms disapprobation, disapproval, disfavor

approve *vb* to give official acceptance of as satisfactory ⟨as soon as the pond project was *approved*, the bulldozers were at the site⟩
synonyms accredit, approbate, authorize, clear, confirm, finalize, formalize, homologate, OK (*or* okay), ratify, sanction, warrant
related words accept, acknowledge, affirm; certify, endorse (*also* indorse), validate; bless, canonize, sanctify;

initial, rubber-stamp, sign, sign off (on); allow, enable, legalize, license (*also* licence), pass, permit; reapprove
near antonyms ban, enjoin, forbid, illegalize, interdict, prohibit, proscribe; disregard, ignore, neglect, overlook; rebuff, rebut, refuse, spurn
antonyms decline, deny, disallow, disapprove, negative, reject, turn down, veto

approve (of) *vb* to have a favorable opinion of ⟨we don't *approve of* people who stand in the "12 items or less" lane with 13 items⟩
synonyms accept, care (for), countenance, favor, OK (*or* okay), subscribe (to)
related words acclaim, applaud, laud, praise, salute; back (up), concur (in), stand by, support, sustain, uphold; bear, endure, tolerate; assent (to), consent (to); commend, recommend; enjoy, like
phrases go for, hold with, take kindly to
near antonyms blacklist, censure, condemn, criticize, damn, denounce, deprecate, depreciate, disparage, reprehend, reprobate; dislike, mind; detest, hate, loathe; dissent (from), object (to), oppose
antonyms disapprove (of), discountenance, disfavor, frown (on *or* upon)

approving *adj* expressing approval ⟨the play did not receive a single *approving* notice⟩ — see FAVORABLE 1

approvingly *adv* in an approving manner ⟨she smiled *approvingly* at the child who was performing onstage⟩ — see ADMIRINGLY

approximate *adj* **1** being such only when compared to something else ⟨the movie's an *approximate* success, if you can overlook the overblown publicity that preceded it⟩ — see COMPARATIVE
2 not precisely correct ⟨police could only give us an *approximate* count of the number of people who attended the air show⟩ — see INEXACT 1

approximate *vb* to come near or nearer to in character or quality ⟨Rob's violin performance last night didn't even *approximate* what he's really capable of when he's not feeling sick⟩
synonyms approach, compare (with), measure up (to), stack up (against *or* with)
related words add up (to), amount (to), come (to); duplicate, equal, match; mirror, parallel, reflect; border (on), touch (on), verge (on)
phrases hold a candle to

approximately *adv* close to but not exactly ⟨it takes *approximately* three hours to drive to Dallas⟩
synonyms about, around, like, more or less, much, near, plus or minus, roughly, say, some
related words generally, kind of, loosely; nearly, nominally, practically, virtually, well-nigh
phrases after a fashion, somewhere about, somewhere around
near antonyms due, even, just, sharp, smack-dab, squarely
antonyms exactly, precisely

approximative *adj* not precisely correct ⟨until we receive more information, the sales figures are only *approximative*⟩ — see INEXACT 1

appurtenant *adj* available to supply something extra when needed ⟨a store selling tents, sleeping bags, and all manner of *appurtenant* equipment for a week of roughing it⟩ — see AUXILIARY

après *prep* subsequent to in time or order ⟨*après* dinner, we retired to the living room for cigars and conversation⟩ — see AFTER

a priori *adj* being or provable by reasoning in which the conclusion follows necessarily from given information ⟨an *a priori* argument for the defendant's innocence⟩ — see DEDUCTIVE

apropos *adj* having to do with the matter at hand ⟨the actor announced to reporters that he would regard as *apropos* only questions about the movie and would ignore inquiries about his love life⟩ — see PERTINENT

apropos *adv* by way of interjection or digression ⟨I went up to New York last weekend; *apropos*, have you seen your New York cousins lately?⟩
synonyms en passant, incidentally
related words digressively, excursively, interjectionally, parenthetically, secondarily, tangentially
phrases by the by (*or* by the bye), by the way, in passing

apropos *prep* having to do with ⟨makes a number of telling observations *apropos* the current political situation⟩ — see ABOUT 1

apropos of *prep* having to do with ⟨*apropos of* our earlier conversation, here's that file I mentioned⟩ — see ABOUT 1

apt *adj* **1** having a tendency to be or act in a certain way ⟨that dog is *apt* to run off if you don't put him on a leash⟩ — see PRONE 1
2 meeting the requirements of a purpose or situation ⟨"gingerbread" is certainly an *apt* description for that house with all the ornate trim⟩ — see FIT 1

aptitude *n* **1** a habitual attraction to some activity or thing ⟨bored teenagers with an *aptitude* for getting into trouble⟩ — see INCLINATION 1
2 a special and usually inborn ability ⟨has an *aptitude* for math⟩ — see TALENT

aptness *n* **1** an established pattern of behavior ⟨an unfortunate *aptness* to interrupt people in mid sentence⟩ — see TENDENCY 1
2 the quality or state of being especially suitable or fitting ⟨I'd question the *aptness* of that goofy sympathy card⟩ — see APPROPRIATENESS

aquatic *adj* living, lying, or occurring below the surface of the water ⟨a lifelong fascination with sharks and other fearsome *aquatic* creatures⟩ — see UNDERWATER

aqua vitae *n* a distilled beverage that can make a person drunk ⟨*aqua vitae* has been part of human culture since ancient times⟩ — see ALCOHOL

aqueduct *n* an open man-made passageway for water ⟨marveled at the ancient Roman *aqueducts* that still carry water to distant villages⟩ — see CHANNEL 1

aquiver *adj* marked by or given to small uncontrollable bodily movements ⟨a puppy *aquiver* with anticipation as his owner held out a treat⟩ — see SHAKY 1

arbiter *n* a person who impartially decides or resolves a dispute or controversy ⟨the dean of student affairs is the proper *arbiter* when a student disputes a grade⟩ — see JUDGE 1

arbitrary *adj* **1** having or showing a tendency to force one's will on others without any regard to fairness or necessity ⟨an *arbitrary* piano teacher who makes all her students do the same exercises over and over again⟩
synonyms dictatorial, high-handed, imperious, peremptory, willful (*or* wilful)
related words arrogant, commanding, demanding, dominant, domineering, haughty, imperative, lordly, masterful, overbearing, presumptuous; authoritarian, autocratic (*also* autocratical), despotic, totalitarian, tyrannical (*also* tyrannic), tyrannous; capricious, changeable, erratic, inconsistent, mercurial, whimsical; biased, inequitable, partisan, prejudiced, unequal, unfair, unjust, unrealistic, unreasonable; unconscionable, unethical, unprincipled, unscrupulous
near antonyms balanced, disinterested, dispassionate, equal, equitable, evenhanded, fair, impartial, just, nonpartisan, objective; rational, reasonable, understanding; unbiased, unprejudiced; ethical, honorable, irreproachable, law-abiding, moral, principled, unimpeachable
2 lacking a definite plan, purpose, or pattern ⟨the order of the names of the 10 semifinalists is entirely *arbitrary*⟩ — see RANDOM

3 exercising power or authority without interference by others ⟨a nation with no tradition of democracy, only a long history of *arbitrary* rulers⟩ — see ABSOLUTE 1

arbitrate *vb* to give an opinion about (something at issue or in dispute) ⟨will *arbitrate* the dispute between the company and the labor union⟩ — see JUDGE 1

arbitrator *n* a person who impartially decides or resolves a dispute or controversy ⟨the couple finally agreed to let the salesclerk be the final *arbitrator* and tell them which shirt looked best⟩ — see JUDGE 1

arc *n* something that curves or is curved ⟨the stars seemed to align themselves into one vast glittering *arc*⟩ — see BEND 1

arc *vb* to turn away from a straight line or course ⟨the ball *arced* toward the batter and nearly hit him⟩ — see CURVE 1

arcadian *adj* free from disturbing noise or uproar ⟨the painter is fond of depicting mute, slightly mysterious figures in *arcadian* settings⟩ — see QUIET 1

arcane *adj* **1** difficult for one of ordinary knowledge or intelligence to understand ⟨grammatical rules that seem *arcane* to generations of students who were never taught grammar in the first place⟩ — see PROFOUND 1
2 having an often intentionally veiled or uncertain meaning ⟨the rebate form uses *arcane* language, the only purpose of which seems to be to disqualify buyers from actually getting a rebate⟩ — see OBSCURE 1
3 being beyond one's powers to know, understand, or explain ⟨my predecessor in this job obviously had his own *arcane* system for filing things, and so I haven't a clue as to where anything is⟩ — see MYSTERIOUS 1

arch *adj* **1** coming before all others in importance ⟨since the start of her acting career her parents have steadfastly remained her *arch* supporters⟩ — see FOREMOST 1
2 displaying or marked by rude boldness ⟨was so *arch* as to ask him outright if he was wearing a toupee⟩ — see NERVY 1
3 tending to or exhibiting reckless playfulness ⟨the *arch* look on the girl's face betrayed her as the one who had tricked the babysitter into believing that the house was haunted⟩ — see MISCHIEVOUS 1

arch *n* something that curves or is curved ⟨the limestone *arch* is a natural formation that is the product of many years of erosion⟩ — see BEND 1

arch *vb* **1** to cause to turn away from a straight line ⟨the cat *arched* her back whenever she was stroked⟩ — see BEND 1
2 to turn away from a straight line or course ⟨the path gradually *arches* off into the woods⟩ — see CURVE 1

archaic *adj* having passed its time of use or usefulness ⟨a man with some *archaic* notions about the proper sphere for women⟩ — see OBSOLETE

archconservative *adj* tending to favor established ideas, conditions, or institutions ⟨his moderate views on social issues means that he has no chance with *archconservative* voters⟩ — see CONSERVATIVE 1

archconservative *n* a person whose political beliefs are centered on tradition and keeping things the way they are ⟨*archconservatives* refused to accept any change in the definition of marriage⟩ — see CONSERVATIVE

archetypal *also* **archetypical** *adj* **1** constituting, serving as, or worthy of being a pattern to be imitated ⟨St. Peter's basilica in Rome is considered by some art historians to be the *archetypal* structure in the baroque style⟩ — see MODEL
2 having or showing the qualities associated with the members of a particular group or kind ⟨the movie's hero is pretty *archetypal*, lacking in any distinctive qualities that would distinguish him from countless other masked avengers⟩ — see TYPICAL 1

archetype *n* **1** something belonging to an earlier time from which something else was later developed ⟨the abacus is sometimes cited as the *archetype* of the modern digital calculator⟩ — see ANCESTOR 2
2 something from which copies are made ⟨*Beowulf* is considered by some scholars to be the *archetype* for medieval British heroic tales⟩ — see ORIGINAL 1

archfiend *n* the supreme personification of evil often represented as the ruler of hell ⟨he sold his soul to the *archfiend*⟩ — see DEVIL 1

architect *n* a person who designs and guides a plan or undertaking ⟨the *architect* of the economic plan that rebuilt Europe after World War II⟩ — see ENGINEER

architecture *n* the arrangement of parts that gives something its basic form ⟨the nonlinear *architecture* of the novel reflects a postmodern sensibility⟩ — see FRAME 1

archive *n* a place where books, periodicals, and records are kept for use but not for sale ⟨asked that the rare book be brought from the *archive*⟩ ⟨sent the novelist's letters to the *archive* for preservation⟩ — see LIBRARY 1

archly *adv* to a great degree ⟨an *archly* competitive young executive⟩ — see VERY 1

archon *n* a person who manages or directs something ⟨as *archon* of the nation's most prestigious university, he became something of a national figure⟩ — see EXECUTIVE

arctic *adj* **1** having a low or subnormal temperature ⟨the *arctic* air of deep winter⟩ — see COLD 1
2 lacking in friendliness or warmth of feeling ⟨received the usual *arctic* reception from her in-laws at Thanksgiving⟩ — see COLD 2

ardency *n* depth of feeling ⟨the *ardency* in the social worker's voice surprised me⟩ — see ARDOR 1

ardent *adj* **1** having or expressing great depth of feeling ⟨made *ardent* declarations of love to the woman he someday hoped to marry⟩ — see FERVENT 1
2 showing urgent desire or interest ⟨an *ardent* science-fiction fan who has read virtually all of his favorite author's many works⟩ — see EAGER
3 having a notably high temperature ⟨under an *ardent* sun the band of bedouins made their way across the sandy wastes⟩ — see HOT 1

ardent spirits *n pl* a distilled beverage that can make a person drunk ⟨in the 1800s, laws against selling *ardent spirits* in "Indian country" were mostly ignored⟩ — see ALCOHOL

ardor *n* **1** depth of feeling ⟨candidates for citizenship reciting the oath of allegiance to the United States with all the *ardor* that they could muster⟩
synonyms ardency, emotion, enthusiasm, fervency, fervidness, fervor, fire, heat, intenseness, intensity, passion, passionateness, vehemence, violence, warmth, white heat
related words cathexis; emotionalism, emotionality, histrionics, mawkishness, melodrama, sappiness, sentimentality; eagerness, earnestness, excitement, gusto, keenness, zest; fanaticism, fever, hot-bloodedness, infatuation, mania, obsession, zeal; compassion, responsiveness, sentiment, sympathy, tenderness; torridity, torridness
near antonyms aloofness, calmness, collectedness, composure, detachedness, dryness, phlegm, reserve, reservedness, reticence, taciturnity; apathy, indifference, stoicism, stoniness, unconcern; stiffness, woodenness; chilliness, coldness, coolness, frigidity, frigidness
antonyms impassiveness, impassivity, insensibility, insensibleness, insensitiveness, insensitivity
2 urgent desire or interest ⟨his *ardor* for combat cooled once he began experiencing the horrors of war⟩ — see EAGERNESS

3 intense sexual desire ⟨her revealing outfit only inflamed his *ardor* all the more⟩ — see LUST 1

arduous *adj* **1** requiring considerable physical or mental effort ⟨climbing Mount Everest is an *arduous*, exhausting challenge⟩ — see HARD 2

2 requiring much time, effort, or careful attention ⟨the *arduous* task of doing the research for my term paper⟩ — see DEMANDING 1

arduously *adv* with great effort or determination ⟨*arduously* made their way through the dense jungle⟩ — see HARD 1

area *n* **1** a part or portion having no fixed boundaries ⟨I last saw your dog over in that general *area*⟩ — see REGION 1

2 a region of activity, knowledge, or influence ⟨a top researcher in the *area* of human genetics⟩ — see FIELD 2

arena *n* **1** a large room or building for enclosed public gatherings ⟨watched the hockey game in the new sports *arena*⟩ — see HALL 3

2 a region of activity, knowledge, or influence ⟨has a lot of influence in the local business *arena*⟩ — see FIELD 2

argentine *adj* of the color gray ⟨an *argentine* sky hinted at a coming storm⟩ — see GRAY 1

argle–bargle *n, chiefly British* an often noisy or angry expression of differing opinions ⟨after a lot of *argle-bargle* even with members of his own party, the prime minister managed to get the measure through parliament⟩ — see ARGUMENT 1

argosy *n* an abundant source ⟨a book that is an *argosy* of stories and legends about the golden age of Hollywood⟩ — see MINE 1

argot *n* the special terms or expressions of a particular group or field ⟨used the *argot* of figure skaters⟩ — see TERMINOLOGY

arguable *adj* open to question or dispute ⟨frankly, it's *arguable* whether you deserve the promotion⟩ — see DEBATABLE 1

argue *vb* **1** to state (something) as a reason in support of or against something under consideration ⟨*argued* that a bake sale would make a lot less money than a car wash⟩

synonyms assert, contend, maintain, plead, reason

related words adduce, cite, mention; claim, insist; affirm, aver, avouch, avow; advance, give, offer, propose, submit; advise, counsel, recommend, suggest, urge; convince, persuade; advocate, champion, defend, enforce, espouse, support; explain, justify, rationalize; consider, debate, discuss; confute, counter, disprove, rebut, refute

2 to express different opinions about something often angrily ⟨that couple *argues* so incessantly it's a miracle they're still together⟩

synonyms altercate, argufy, bicker, brabble, brawl, controvert, dispute, fall out, fight, hassle, jar, quarrel, quibble, row, scrap, spat, squabble, tiff, wrangle

related words challenge, dare, defy; clash, contend, contest, tangle; cavil, fuss, nitpick; consider, debate, discuss; kick, object, protest

phrases bandy words, butt heads, lock horns, mix it up

near antonyms coexist, get along; accept, agree, assent, concur, consent

3 to cause (someone) to agree with a belief or course of action by using arguments or earnest requests ⟨*argued* my boss into letting me telecommute for four days a week⟩ — see PERSUADE

4 to talk about (an issue) usually from various points of view and for the purpose of arriving at a decision or opinion ⟨candidates *arguing* gun control in a nationally televised debate⟩ — see DISCUSS

5 to give evidence or testimony to the truth or factualness of ⟨the security video *argues* that it was a taller man who entered the building⟩ — see CONFIRM 1

arguer *n* a person who takes part in a dispute ⟨he's is demand on the Sunday morning political shows because he's an eager and indefatigable *arguer*⟩ — see DISPUTANT

argufier *n* a person who takes part in a dispute ⟨she's a relentless, petty *argufier* who never concedes even the most trivial point⟩ — see DISPUTANT

argufy *vb* to express different opinions about something often angrily ⟨tedious departmental meetings at which staffers would *argufy* endlessly⟩ — see ARGUE 2

argument *n* **1** an often noisy or angry expression of differing opinions ⟨the couple's *arguments* were often loud enough to be heard all over the neighborhood⟩

synonyms altercation, argle-bargle [*chiefly British*], argy-bargy [*chiefly British*], battle royal, bicker, brawl, contretemps, controversy, cross fire, disagreement, dispute, donnybrook, falling-out, fight, hassle, imbroglio, kickup, misunderstanding, quarrel, rhubarb, row, scrap, set-to, spat, squabble, tiff, wrangle

related words clash, run-in, skirmish, tangle, tussle; logomachy; feud, vendetta; attack, contention, dissension (*also* dissention); debate, difference, disputation; fuss, objection, protest, protestation; affray [*chiefly British*], fisticuffs, fracas, fray, free-for-all, melee (*also* mêlée); catfight

2 a statement given to explain a belief or act ⟨gave a solid *argument* for the redeeming value of the shockingly violent movie⟩ — see REASON 1

3 an exchange of views for the purpose of exploring a subject or deciding an issue ⟨the president of the Senate has allotted a week for the *argument* of the treaty⟩ — see DISCUSSION 1

4 an idea or opinion that is put forth in a discussion or debate ⟨it's my *argument* that we have too many problems here on earth to concern ourselves with manned trips to Mars⟩ — see CONTENTION 1

argumentation *n* an exchange of views for the purpose of exploring a subject or deciding an issue ⟨the matter is not subject to *argumentation*; my decision is final⟩ — see DISCUSSION 1

argumentative *adj* **1** given to arguing ⟨he's too *argumentative* to be part of a project in which teamwork is critical⟩

synonyms contentious, controversial, disputatious, polemical (*also* polemic), quarrelsome, scrappy

related words aggressive, bellicose, belligerent, combative, gladiatorial, militant, pugnacious, truculent, warlike; feisty, fractious, surly; balky, contrary, ornery, perverse, restive, wayward; disobedient, froward, insubordinate, intractable, recalcitrant, refractory; hardheaded, headstrong, mulish, obdurate, obstinate, pigheaded, resistant, self-opinionated, self-willed, stubborn, unbending, uncompromising, uncooperative, unreasonable, unyielding, willful (*or* wilful); acidic, bearish, bilious, cantankerous, captious, choleric, crabby, cranky, cross, disagreeable, dyspeptic, fretful, grouchy, grumpy, huffy, ill-humored, ill-natured, ill-tempered, irascible, irritable, peevish, pettish, petulant, querulous, rude, snappish, snappy, splenetic, testy, touchy, waspish; battling, fighting, warring

near antonyms affable, amiable, amicable, benevolent, cordial, easygoing, friendly, genial, good-natured, good-tempered, gracious, ingratiating, pleasant, sociable; acquiescent, agreeable, amenable, complaisant, compliant, complying, conciliatory, cooperative, obliging; docile, obedient, submissive, tractable; pacific, peaceable, peaceful

2 feeling or displaying eagerness to fight ⟨an *argumentative* gang of bullies always looking for a fight⟩ — see BELLIGERENT

3 relating to or causing the expression of opposing opinions ⟨a topic that sparked more than a few *argu-*

mentative conversations around the watercooler⟩ — see CONTROVERSIAL 1

Argus–eyed *adj* paying close attention usually for the purpose of anticipating approaching danger or opportunity ⟨an *Argus-eyed* photographer known for capturing on film many celebrity meltdowns⟩ — see ALERT 1

argy–bargy *n, chiefly British* **1** an exchange of views for the purpose of exploring a subject or deciding an issue ⟨wouldn't be a cricket match without a little *argy-bargy* over the umpire's every call⟩ — see DISCUSSION 1

2 an often noisy or angry expression of differing opinions ⟨the perennial *argy-bargy* over whether the monarchy should be abolished⟩ — see ARGUMENT 1

arid *adj* **1** causing weariness, restlessness, or lack of interest ⟨an *arid* speech about duty and responsibility⟩ — see BORING

2 marked by little or no precipitation or humidity ⟨*arid* wastelands unfit for human habitation⟩ — see DRY 1

arise *vb* **1** to leave one's bed ⟨the travelers *arose* before dawn and were on their way as the sun came up⟩

synonyms get up, rise, roll out, turn out, uprise

related words arouse, awake, awaken, bestir, stir, wake

near antonyms catnap, doze, drop off, lie up, nap, nod, rest, sleep, slumber, snooze; bunk, perch, roost, settle; couch, doss (down) [*chiefly British*], flop (down), lie (down), recline

antonyms bed (down), retire, turn in

2 to come to one's attention especially gradually or unexpectedly ⟨note in your report any problems that *arise* while you are conducting the experiment⟩

synonyms come up, crop (up), emerge, materialize, spring (up), surface

related words appear, come out, show up, turn up; chance, come, come about, fall out, go (on), go off, hap, happen, occur, pass, transpire; interfere, interpose, intervene, intrude

3 to come into existence ⟨it is not known exactly how mammals *arose*, but scientists date the earliest mammals to the Triassic period⟩ — see BEGIN 2

4 to move or extend upward ⟨slowly the hot-air balloon *arose*, and the round-the-world flight was begun⟩ — see ASCEND

aristocracy *n* **1** the highest class in a society ⟨at one time in China only the *aristocracy* could own land⟩

synonyms elite, gentility, gentlefolk (*also* gentlefolks), gentry, nobility, patriciate, quality, upper class, upper crust

related words A-list, beau monde, beautiful people, café society, Four Hundred (*or* 400), glitterati, haut monde (*also* haute monde), jet set, society; carriage trade, plutocracy

near antonyms commoners, (the) crowd, (the) masses, peasantry, peonage, (the) people, plebeians, plebs, (the) populace, (the) public, rank and file; bourgeoisie, middle class, working class; dregs, (the) herd, (the) mob, rabble, rabblement, riffraff, scum, trash

antonyms proletarians, proletariat

2 individuals carefully selected as being the best of a class ⟨membership in the society is reserved for the literary world's *aristocracy*⟩ — see ELITE 1

aristocrat *n* a person of high birth or social position ⟨could trace his lineage to an English *aristocrat* of the 17th century⟩ — see GENTLEPERSON

aristocratic *adj* **1** being or characteristic of a person who has an offensive air of superiority and tends to ignore or disdain anyone regarded as inferior ⟨the restaurant's cuisine is truly superb, but the maître d's *aristocratic* demeanor is a bit much⟩ — see SNOBBISH

2 of high birth, rank, or station ⟨an impoverished dowager who never lets people forget about her *aristocratic* origins⟩ — see NOBLE 1

arithmetic *n* the act or process of performing mathematical operations to find a value ⟨I haven't actually done the *arithmetic* yet, but I suspect we're losing money on the deal⟩ — see CALCULATION

[1]arm *n* a portable weapon from which a shot is discharged by gunpowder ⟨soldiers grabbing their *arms* and helmets and heading into battle⟩ — see GUN 1

[2]arm *n* **1** a large unit of a governmental, business, or educational organization ⟨a company that needs to beef up its marketing *arm* if it wants to compete in today's business world⟩ — see DIVISION 2

2 a part of a body of water that extends beyond the general shoreline ⟨this *arm* of the Atlantic is surprisingly peaceful, as the stronger ocean currents do not reach this far⟩ — see GULF 1

3 an area of land that juts out into a body of water ⟨Maine has so many long, narrow *arms* that jut out into the ocean that early coastal settlers found it much easier to travel by sea⟩ — see [2]CAPE

4 the right or means to command or control others ⟨few criminals manage to permanently escape the long *arm* of the law⟩ — see POWER 1

armada *n* a group of vehicles traveling together or under one management ⟨an *armada* of ships sailing up the coast⟩ — see FLEET

armature *n* the arrangement of parts that gives something its basic form ⟨the rigid *armature* of a highly stratified society⟩ — see FRAME 1

armed forces *n pl* the combined army, air force, and navy of a nation ⟨our nation's *armed forces* are stationed throughout the world⟩

synonyms colors, military, service, troops

related words GIs (*or* GI's), men-at-arms, rank and file, servicemen, servicewomen, soldiers, soldiery; force; militia, reserves; armor, defense; gendarmerie (*or* gendarmery)

near antonyms civilians, noncombatants

armistice *n* a temporary stopping of fighting ⟨both sides in the conflict agreed to an *armistice* during the solemn holy days⟩ — see TRUCE

armor *n* **1** means or method of defending ⟨the skunk's primary *armor* is the foul-smelling fluid that it can eject⟩ — see DEFENSE 1

2 something that encloses another thing especially to protect it ⟨the crab's *armor* makes it difficult prey for some smaller predators⟩ — see [1]CASE

armory *n* a place where military arms are stored ⟨the soldier was sent to the *armory* to get a replacement weapon for the one that had been stolen⟩

synonyms arsenal, depot, dump, magazine

related words fort, fortress, stronghold; repository, storehouse, warehouse

arm–twisting *n* the use of power to impose one's will on another ⟨it took some *arm-twisting*, but they eventually agreed to make a donation⟩ — see FORCE 2

army *n* **1** a large body of men and women organized for land warfare ⟨In 218 B.C., Hannibal crossed the Alps with an *army* of 26,000 men and, most famously, a number of elephants⟩

synonyms array, battalion, host, legion

related words militia, national guard, standing army; infantry, ranks, regulars, soldiers, troopers, troops

2 a great number of persons or creatures massed together ⟨a vast *army* of loyal fans in line for the band's farewell concert⟩ — see CROWD 1

3 a group of people working together on a task ⟨an *army* of rescue workers descended on the tornado-stricken town⟩ — see GANG 1

aroma *n* **1** a sweet or pleasant smell ⟨I love the *aroma* of bread baking in the oven⟩ — see FRAGRANCE

2 the quality of a thing that makes it perceptible to the sense organs in the nose ⟨the ripe *aroma* of a sweatshirt that's in dire need of laundering⟩ — see SMELL 1

3 a special quality or impression associated with something ⟨the *aroma* of wealth and privilege that pervades the manicured confines of the country club⟩ — see AURA 1

aromatic *adj* having a pleasant smell ⟨*aromatic* flowers can add greatly to the ambience of a room⟩ — see FRAGRANT

around *adj* having being at the present time ⟨she's generally regarded as one of the most talented singers *around*⟩ — see EXTANT 1

around *adv* **1** on all sides or in every direction ⟨he looked *around*⟩ ⟨butterflies were flying all *around*⟩
synonyms about, round
related words all over, everyplace, everywhere; abroad, afloat, hereabouts (*or* hereabout)
2 toward the opposite direction ⟨she turned *around* and saw him⟩
synonyms about, back, backward (*or* backwards), round
related words behind, down, downward (*or* downwards), rearward (*also* rearwards); obversely, reversely; across, athwart, counter, counterclockwise, widdershins (*also* withershins)
near antonyms clockwise, deasil
3 at, within, or to a short distance or time ⟨our dog usually stays *around* our yard⟩ ⟨he'll be getting in *around* 6:00⟩ — see NEAR 1
4 from beginning to end ⟨a team that plays all year *around*⟩ — see THROUGH 1
5 close to but not exactly ⟨there's *around* a hundred books still left to be packed in boxes⟩ — see APPROXIMATELY
6 in one place and another ⟨while typewriters can still be seen *around*, they are no longer the common office fixtures they once were⟩ — see HERE AND THERE 1

around *prep* **1** close to ⟨I wouldn't stand *around* those rocks—there could be snakes under them⟩
synonyms about, by, near, next to, nigh
related words alongside, beside; across, along, at; circa; toward (*or* towards)
phrases next door to
2 in random positions within the boundaries of ⟨huge, strangely shaped rocks were scattered *around* the canyon floor⟩
synonyms about, across, over, round, through, throughout
related words on

arouse *vb* **1** to cause to stop sleeping ⟨the rooster's crow *aroused* me from my deep sleep⟩ — see WAKE 1
2 to cease to be asleep ⟨set the alarm so we would *arouse* at 5:00 a.m.⟩ — see WAKE 2
3 to rouse to strong feeling or action ⟨the court's controversial decision *aroused* many to protest and to lobby the legislature for a constitutional amendment⟩ — see PROVOKE 1

arrange *vb* **1** to come to an agreement or decision concerning the details of ⟨*arrange* a time for the meeting⟩ ⟨*arrange* money matters for your trip⟩
synonyms agree (on), decide, fix, set, settle
related words contract, pledge, promise; blueprint, calculate, chart, concert, design, draft, frame, hammer out, intrigue, lay out, maneuver, map (out), plan, program (*also* programme), schematize, scheme, shape, square away, work out; choose, conclude, determine, figure, opt, resolve; affirm, approve, authorize, clear, confirm, OK (*or* okay), sanction, warrant; close, complete, end, finalize, finish, round (off *or* out), wind up, wrap up; bargain, chaffer, deal, dicker, haggle, horse-trade, negotiate
phrases dispose of
near antonyms abort, call, call off, drop, recall, repeal, rescind, revoke; differ (over), disagree (with); counter, debate, object, oppose, protest, resist; contest, dispute
2 to put into a particular arrangement ⟨*arrange* the flowers so that the taller ones are at the center of the bouquet⟩ — see ORDER 1
3 to bring about through discussion and compromise ⟨I'll *arrange* your free movie pass with the cinema's manager⟩ — see NEGOTIATE 1
4 to work out the details of (something) in advance ⟨we need to *arrange* our European vacation so that we can get the best deals⟩ — see PLAN 1

arrangement *n* **1** a method worked out in advance for achieving some objective ⟨will work out a visitation *arrangement* in court⟩ — see PLAN 1
2 the way in which something is sized, arranged, or organized ⟨an artistic *arrangement* of the vases on the shelf⟩ — see FORMAT 1
3 the way in which the elements of something (as a work of art) are arranged ⟨the close *arrangement* of the figures in the family portrait is meant to be symbolic of their close emotional attachment⟩ — see COMPOSITION 3
4 the way objects in space or events in time are arranged or follow one another ⟨the ill-advised *arrangement* of works in the piano recital resulted in pieces of similar mood being played back-to-back⟩ — see ORDER 1

arrant *adj* having no exceptions or restrictions ⟨that statement is complete and *arrant* nonsense⟩ — see ABSOLUTE 2

array *n* **1** a number of things considered as a unit ⟨an *array* of baseball gloves in the corner of his room⟩ — see GROUP 1
2 a usually small number of persons considered as a unit ⟨a motley *array* of travelers waiting for the bus⟩ — see GROUP 2
3 dressy clothing ⟨dressed in festive *array* for the city's annual New Year's Eve celebration⟩ — see FINERY
4 the way objects in space or events in time are arranged or follow one another ⟨a marching band's carefully choreographed *array*⟩ — see ORDER 1
5 a large body of men and women organized for land warfare ⟨feudal lords depended upon their *array* for defense⟩ — see ARMY 1

array *vb* **1** to make more attractive by adding something that is beautiful or becoming ⟨a door *arrayed* for the holidays with a beautiful evergreen wreath⟩ — see DECORATE
2 to outfit with clothes and especially fine or special clothes ⟨*arrayed* in a wedding dress that has been handed down in the family for generations⟩ — see CLOTHE 1
3 to put into a particular arrangement ⟨*arrayed* his baseball cards in order of their rarity and consequent monetary value⟩ — see ORDER 1

arrearage *n* something (as money) which is owed ⟨the new buyer must pay the *arrearage* on the home before moving in⟩ — see DEBT 1

arrears *n pl* something (as money) which is owed ⟨since it lost the discrimination lawsuit, the employer will have to pay the worker all *arrears* in salary⟩ — see DEBT 1

arrest *n* **1** the act of taking into one's control by authority of law ⟨there have been only two *arrests* for driving while intoxicated in the county in the last six months⟩
synonyms apprehension, arrestment, bust [*slang*], collar, pinch
related words raid; house arrest; capture, entrapment, seizure; captivity, confinement, detention, enchainment, hold, immurement, imprisonment, incarceration, restraint; rearrest; remand
near antonyms emancipation, liberation, release
antonyms discharge

2 the stopping of a process or activity ⟨"hemostasis" is the technical term for *arrest* of bleeding⟩ — see END 1

arrest *vb* **1** to take or keep under one's control by authority of law ⟨the inept robber was promptly *arrested* by the off-duty policeman he had tried to hold up⟩
synonyms apprehend, bust [*slang*], collar, nab, nail, nick [*British slang*], pick up, pinch, pull in, restrain, run in, seize
related words bag, capture, catch, get, grab, grapple, hook, land, snap (up), snare, snatch, trap; commit, confine, detain, hold, immure, imprison, incarcerate, intern, jail, jug, lock (up); bind, enchain, fetter, handcuff, manacle, shackle, trammel; rearrest; remand
near antonyms emancipate, free, liberate, loose, loosen, release, spring; unbind, unchain
antonyms discharge
2 to bring (something) to a standstill ⟨cryogenics is based on the idea that extreme cold can almost *arrest* molecular motion⟩ — see [1]HALT 1
3 to hold the attention of as if by a spell ⟨the sight of the daredevil walking a tightrope between high-rises *arrested* area pedestrians and motorists alike⟩ — see ENTHRALL 1

arrested *adj* taken and held prisoner ⟨a line of *arrested* suspects waiting to be booked on a variety of charges⟩ — see CAPTIVE

arresting *adj* **1** holding the attention or provoking interest ⟨an *arresting* film about tribal traditions in Africa⟩ — see INTERESTING
2 likely to attract attention ⟨at seven feet tall, he's an *arresting* figure in any crowd⟩ — see NOTICEABLE

arrestment *n* **1** the act of taking or holding under one's control by authority of law ⟨the *arrestment* of the bank president for embezzlement was accomplished as quietly as possible⟩ — see ARREST 1
2 the stopping of a process or activity ⟨the *arrestment* of all brain activity in the patient⟩ — see END 1

arrival *n* the act of coming upon a scene ⟨spring's late *arrival* meant we were still skiing in mid-April⟩ ⟨the groom blamed his belated *arrival* for the wedding on a huge traffic snarl⟩
synonyms advent, appearance, coming, incoming
related words approach, entrance, ingress; beginning, birth, commencement, dawn, dawning, debut (*also* début), genesis, inception, morning, onset, start
near antonyms dissipation, dissolution, evaporation, fadeaway, fading, melting, passing, vanishing; clearing out, egress, leaving, retirement, retreat, withdrawal; emigration, evacuation, exodus
antonyms decamping, decampment, departing, departure, disappearance, exit, exiting, farewell, going, leave-taking, parting, quitting

arrive *vb* **1** to get to a destination ⟨when will the guests *arrive*?⟩ — see COME 2
2 to reach a desired level of accomplishment ⟨the actress knew she'd *arrived* when she received an Oscar nomination⟩ — see SUCCEED 2

arriviste *n* one who has recently acquired wealth and social position ⟨the town's old money immediately shunned these vulgar *arrivistes*, who may have had the cash but certainly not the class⟩ — see NOUVEAU RICHE

arrogance *n* an exaggerated sense of one's importance that shows itself in the making of excessive or unjustified claims ⟨in his *arrogance* the president of the club made all the arrangements for the annual banquet without consulting the members⟩
synonyms assumption, bumptiousness, consequence, haughtiness, hauteur, high horse, huffiness, imperiousness, loftiness, lordliness, masterfulness, peremptoriness, pomposity, pompousness, presumptuousness, pretense (*or* pretence), pretension, pretentiousness, self-consequence, self-importance, superciliousness, superiority, toploftiness
related words authoritativeness, bossiness, bowwow, brag, dominance, high-handedness; condescension, disdain, scorn; chest-thumping, inflation, self-assertion, side [*chiefly British*], snobbery, snobbishness, snobbism, snootiness; attitude, cheek, cheekiness, impertinence, impudence, sauciness; boastfulness, bombast, braggadocio, bravado, strut, swagger, triumphalism, vaingloriousness, vainglory; cockiness, complacence, conceit, egoism, egotism, pride, pridefulness, self-assumption, self-centeredness, self-complacency, self-conceit, self-content, self-contentment, self-opinion, self-partiality, self-satisfaction, smugness, swelled head, vanity; superiority complex
near antonyms bashfulness, demureness, retiringness, shyness; diffidence, self-distrust, self-doubt, timidity, timidness; lowliness, meekness, mousiness, passiveness, passivity, submissiveness; quietness, reserve, reservedness
antonyms humility, modesty, unassumingness, unpretentiousness

arrogant *adj* having a feeling of superiority that shows itself in an overbearing attitude ⟨the *arrogant* young lawyer elbowed his way to the head of the line of customers, declaring that he was too busy to wait like everybody else⟩
synonyms assumptive, bumptious, cavalier, chesty, haughty, highfalutin (*also* hifalutin), high-and-mighty, high-handed, high-hat, huffish, huffy, imperious, important, lofty, lordly, masterful, overweening, peremptory, pompous, presuming, presumptuous, pretentious, self-asserting, self-assertive, sniffy, stiff-necked, supercilious, superior, toplofty (*also* toploftical), uppish, uppity
related words authoritarian, bossy, dominant, dominating, domineering, magisterial, pontifical, pontificating; condescending, disdainful, patronizing; impertinent, impudent, saucy; snobbish, snobby, snooty; blusterous, blustery, boastful, bombastic, braggart, bragging, braggy, cocky, swaggering, vain, vainglorious; complacent, conceited, egocentric, egoistic (*also* egoistical), egotistic (*or* egotistical), hubristic, narcissistic, orgulous, prideful, proud, self-affected, self-applauding, self-centered, self-complacent, self-conceited, self-pleased, self-satisfied, smug, stuck-up; self-flattering, self-loving, self-promoting; brash, forward, uninhibited, unreserved; extroverted (*also* extraverted), immodest
near antonyms bashful, cowering, cringing, demure, diffident, introverted, mousy (*or* mousey), overmodest, self-critical, self-doubting, sheepish, shrinking, shy, subdued, timid; acquiescent, compliant, deferential, meek, passive, submissive, unaggressive, unassertive, unassuming, unobtrusive, yielding; quiet, reserved, retiring
antonyms humble, lowly, modest, unarrogant, unpretentious

arrogate *vb* to take or make use of under a guise of authority but without actual right ⟨*arrogated* the corner office without obtaining prior approval⟩ — see APPROPRIATE 1

arrogation *n* the unlawful taking or withholding of something from the rightful owner under a guise of authority ⟨the legislature's *arrogation* of certain powers that are explicitly reserved by the constitution for the judiciary⟩ — see APPROPRIATION 2

arsenal *n* a place where military arms are stored ⟨sent the ordnance officer to the *arsenal* for weapons⟩ — see ARMORY

arsonist *n* a person who deliberately and unlawfully sets fire to a building or other property ⟨they finally

caught the *arsonist*, but only after he'd set fire to four barns⟩
synonyms firebug, incendiary, torch
related words pyromaniac; flamer, igniter (*also* ignitor), immolator, inflamer, kindler

art *n* **1** an occupation requiring skillful use of the hands ⟨one of the country's finest practitioners of the *art* of cabinetmaking⟩ — see CRAFT 1
2 subtle or imaginative ability in inventing, devising, or executing something ⟨while some people see it simply as mindless fun or exercise, there is an *art* to skateboarding⟩ — see SKILL 1

arterial *n* a passage cleared for public vehicular travel ⟨one of the main *arterials* connecting the airport with the city⟩ — see WAY 1

artery *n* a passage cleared for public vehicular travel ⟨there's an accident on the main *artery* into town, so I'll be late⟩ — see WAY 1

artful *adj* **1** clever at attaining one's ends by indirect and often deceptive means ⟨the *artful* lawyer got the witness to admit he had been lying⟩
synonyms beguiling, cagey (*also* cagy), crafty, cunning, cute, designing, devious, dodgy [*chiefly British*], foxy, guileful, scheming, shrewd, slick, sly, subtle, tricky, wily
related words astute, facile, glib, sharp; crooked, deceitful, deceptive, dishonest, fraudulent, insinuating, knavish, Machiavellian, oblique, serpentine, shady, shifty, slippery, sneaky, treacherous, underhand, underhanded, unscrupulous; backhanded, double-dealing, hypocritical, insincere, left-handed, mealy, mealy-mouthed, smooth-tongued, two-faced; circuitous, circular, roundabout; clandestine, concealed, covert, furtive, hugger-mugger, secret, stealthy, surreptitious, undercover; calculating, plotting
near antonyms obvious, open, patent, plain, public, unconcealed; aboveboard, candid, direct, forthright, frank, honest, natural, outspoken, plainspoken, real, simple, sincere, straightforward, unaffected, unpretending, unpretentious, unvarnished; childlike, impressionable, simpleminded, unsophisticated, unworldly; unforced, unstudied; trustful, trusting
antonyms artless, guileless, ingenuous, innocent, undesigning
2 showing a noteworthy use of the imagination and creativity especially in inventing ⟨that kitchen gadget is an *artful* tool for extracting cherry pits⟩ — see CLEVER 1
3 accomplished with trained ability ⟨that was an *artful* way to handle a very delicate situation⟩ — see SKILLFUL

artfully *adv* in a skillful or expert manner ⟨the sushi chef *artfully* filleted the salmon⟩ — see WELL 3

artfulness *n* **1** skill in achieving one's ends through indirect, subtle, or underhanded means ⟨with well-practiced *artfulness*, he convinced his mother he was sick enough to stay home from school but not sick enough for a visit to the doctor's office⟩ — see CUNNING 1
2 subtle or imaginative ability in inventing, devising, or executing something ⟨building a ship model requires a painstaking *artfulness* I don't have⟩ — see SKILL 1

article *n* a short piece of writing typically expressing a point of view ⟨read an *article* extolling the benefits of vegetarianism⟩ — see ESSAY 1

articulacy *n, chiefly British* the art or power of speaking or writing in a forceful and convincing way ⟨the impressive *articulacy* of the members of the debating society known as the Oxford Union⟩ — see ELOQUENCE

articulate *adj* able to express oneself clearly and well ⟨the television crew covering the science fair were looking for photogenic and *articulate* students to explain their projects on the air⟩
synonyms eloquent, fluent, silver-tongued, well-spoken
related words facile, glib, smooth-tongued, voluble; expressive, outspoken, verbal, vocal; blabby, chatty, garrulous, loquacious, talkative, verbose; unfaltering, unhesitating
near antonyms faltering, halting, hesitant, maundering, mumbling, muttering, sputtering, stammering, stumbling, stuttering; mute, speechless, tongueless, tongue-tied, voiceless
antonyms inarticulate, ineloquent, unvocal

articulate *vb* **1** to utter clearly and distinctly ⟨uses a very measured tone and *articulates* every syllable when issuing scoldings⟩
synonyms enunciate
related words express, pronounce, say, speak, talk, tell, utter, verbalize, vocalize, voice; speak out, speak up
near antonyms falter, grunt, halt, hesitate, maunder, splutter, sputter, stammer, stumble, stutter; mouth, mumble, murmur, mutter, whisper; breathe, drawl, gasp
2 to convey in appropriate or telling terms ⟨an essay that masterfully *articulates* the case for a greater commitment to space exploration⟩ — see PHRASE
3 to express (a thought or emotion) in words ⟨I'm not *articulating* my thoughts very well⟩ — see SAY 1

articulateness *n* the art or power of speaking or writing in a forceful and convincing way ⟨obviously, *articulateness* was not what got that politician elected⟩ — see ELOQUENCE

articulation *n* **1** an act, process, or means of putting something into words ⟨her boyfriend's *articulation* of his feelings for her was long overdue⟩ — see EXPRESSION 1
2 the clear and accurate pronunciation of words especially in public speaking ⟨you will have to work on your *articulation* if you want to be an announcer on TV⟩ — see DICTION 1

artifice *n* **1** a clever often underhanded means to achieve an end ⟨used the *artifice* of saying his grandmother had died so that he could get the last seat on the plane⟩ — see TRICK 1
2 skill in achieving one's ends through indirect, subtle, or underhanded means ⟨using their *artifice*, the Greeks crafted a hollow wooden horse to hide inside and thereby gained entry into the city of Troy⟩ — see CUNNING 1
3 subtle or imaginative ability in inventing, devising, or executing something ⟨a painting that could only have been created with the *artifice* of a master⟩ — see SKILL 1
4 the inclination or practice of misleading others through lies or trickery ⟨a crook who is a master of *artifice* and manipulation⟩ — see DECEIT 1
5 the use of clever underhanded actions to achieve an end ⟨if she has to resort to *artifice* to get a man, well, she's prepared to do that⟩ — see TRICKERY

artificer *n* a person whose occupation requires skill with the hands ⟨the oil tycoon insisted that the best stone masons, cabinetmakers, and *artificers* in every other craft be employed to create a mansion of unequalled splendor⟩ — see ARTISAN

artificial *adj* **1** lacking in natural or spontaneous quality ⟨the beauty-pageant contestants' *artificial* smiles looked like they were glued on their faces⟩
synonyms affected, assumed, bogus, contrived, factitious, fake, false, feigned, forced, mechanical, mock, phony (*also* phoney), plastic, pretended, pseudo, put-on, sham, simulated, spurious, strained, unnatural
related words automatic, canned, concocted, fabricated, hokey, labored, manufactured, pat, unauthentic, unreal, unrealistic; double-dealing, empty, facile, hol-

low, hypocritical, insincere, left-handed, mealy, mealy-mouthed, two-faced, unctuous; exaggerated, histrionic, melodramatic, overacted, overdone, theatrical (*also* theatric); cute, cutesy, genteel, goody-goody, mincing, overrefined, simpering; conventional, formal, impersonal, inflexible, rigid, stiff, stylized, wooden; artful, calculated, conscious, cultivated, deliberate, premeditated, studied
near antonyms authentic, bona fide, real, realistic, right, true; honest, ingenuous, sincere, unpretending; easy, effortless, smooth; extemporaneous, impromptu, impulsive, instinctive, unconscious, unprompted, unrehearsed, unstudied
antonyms artless, genuine, natural, spontaneous, unaffected, uncontrived, unfeigned, unforced
2 not being or expressing what one appears to be or express ⟨the familiar sight of the award winner accepting the *artificial* congratulations of the other nominees⟩ — see INSINCERE
3 being such in appearance only and made with or manufactured from usually cheaper materials ⟨*artificial* fruit made from wax⟩ — see IMITATION
4 produced by humans rather than natural processes ⟨I find that *artificial* sweeteners often have an odd aftertaste⟩ — see SYNTHETIC 1

artillery *n* large firearms (as cannon or rockets) ⟨during the brutal *artillery* attack families hid in their cellars⟩
synonyms guns, ordnance
related words ammunition, armament, arms, munitions, weaponry, weapons

artisan *n* a person whose occupation requires skill with the hands ⟨we visited a re-created 19th-century New England village that features an array of *artisans*—a cooper, a carpenter, a blacksmith, a potter, a glassblower⟩
synonyms artificer, crafter, craftsman, craftsperson, handcraftsman, handicrafter, handicraftsman, handworker, tradesman
related words craftswoman; artist, maker; journeyman, master; mechanic, operative, shaper, smith, technician, wright; handyman, handyperson, workman

artist *n* a person with a high level of knowledge or skill in a field ⟨a pitcher who is a strikeout *artist*⟩ — see EXPERT

artistic *adj* of or relating to the fine arts ⟨funding for *artistic* endeavors is crucial if the city is to survive and prosper⟩ — see CULTURAL

artistry *n* subtle or imaginative ability in inventing, devising, or executing something ⟨the high level of *artistry* involved in painting miniatures⟩ — see SKILL 1

artless *adj* **1** free from any intent to deceive or impress others ⟨a genuine and *artless* girl⟩ — see GUILELESS
2 hastily or roughly constructed ⟨*artless* though it may be, our homemade doghouse has a certain charm to it⟩ — see RUDE 1

artlessly *adv* without any attempt to impress by deception or exaggeration ⟨*artlessly* commented that the dress looked good⟩ ⟨informed his host rather *artlessly* that the food was okay but not fantastic⟩ — see NATURALLY 3

artlessness *n* the quality or state of being simple and sincere ⟨the *artlessness* of young children should be cherished while it lasts⟩ — see NAÏVETÉ 1

as *conj* **1** at or during the time that ⟨he slipped *as* he was walking to his car⟩ — see WHEN 1
2 for the reason that ⟨had his meals delivered to him *as* he couldn't navigate the icy sidewalk with his walker⟩ — see SINCE
3 in spite of the fact that ⟨silly *as* it sounds, that's exactly the way that it happened⟩ — see ALTHOUGH
4 the way it would be or one would do if ⟨his face looked *as* he'd gotten a terrible shock⟩ — see AS IF

ascend *vb* to move or extend upward ⟨the path *ascended* so steeply at one point that we had to scramble up on our hands and knees⟩
synonyms arise, aspire, climb, lift, mount, rise, soar, thrust, up, uprise, upthrust, upturn
related words surge, tower; boost, elevate, raise, upheave, uplift, upraise; balloon, blast off, take off, zoom; crest, scale, surmount, top; cant, incline, lean, list, recline, slant, slope, tilt, tip
near antonyms dive, nose-dive, plummet, sink, slide
antonyms decline, descend, dip, drop, fall (off), plunge

ascendance *also* **ascendence** *n* controlling power or influence over others ⟨studied the *ascendance* of modernism in 20th-century art and design⟩ — see SUPREMACY 1

ascendancy *also* **ascendency** *n* controlling power or influence over others ⟨a book chronicling the *ascendancy* of fascism in Europe after World War I⟩ — see SUPREMACY 1

ascension *n* the act or an instance of rising or climbing up ⟨her *ascension* from the freshman to the varsity team was evidence of how much she had improved in one season⟩ — see ASCENT 1

ascent *n* **1** the act or an instance of rising or climbing up ⟨our plane broke through some heavy low clouds during its *ascent* and leveled off once we were above them⟩
synonyms ascension, climb, rise, rising, soar
related words boost, hike, increase, raise; blastoff, elevation, hoist, levitation, liftoff, raising, takeoff; heave, thrust, upheaval, uplifting, upraising, upsurge, upsweep, upswing, upthrust, uptrend, upturn, upwelling
near antonyms plop, plummeting, sinking; decline, decrease, down; comedown, downfall, downgrade
antonyms descent, dip, dive, drop, fall, nosedive, plunge
2 an upward slope ⟨we'd reached the final *ascent* of the trail to the summit⟩
synonyms acclivity, hill, rise, upgrade, uphill, uprise
related words cant, diagonal, glacis, grade, gradient, inclination, incline, lean, pitch, rake, tilt; climb, hump, mound, ridge, swell
near antonyms basin, depression, hollow
antonyms declension, decline, declivity, descent, dip, downgrade, downhill, drop-off, fall, hang, hanging
3 a raising or a state of being raised to a higher rank or position ⟨his long, gradual *ascent* into the ranks of management⟩ — see ADVANCEMENT 1

ascertain *vb* **1** to come to an awareness of ⟨was immediately able to *ascertain* that the girl was uncomfortable talking about her life at home⟩ — see DISCOVER 1
2 to come upon after searching, study, or effort ⟨*ascertained* that their old colonial-era house had once functioned as a tavern⟩ — see FIND 1

ascribe *vb* to explain (something) as being the result of something else ⟨*ascribed* their stunning military victory to good intelligence beforehand⟩ — see CREDIT 1

aseptic *adj* free from filth, infection, or dangers to health ⟨patients with compromised immune systems must be treated in *aseptic* environments⟩ — see SANITARY

as far as *prep* having to do with ⟨*as far as* a menu for the event, I haven't given it any thought⟩ — see ABOUT 1

as for *prep* having to do with ⟨*as for* the others, let them get their own dinner⟩ — see ABOUT 1

ashamed *adj* suffering from or expressive of a feeling of responsibility for wrongdoing ⟨was *ashamed* that she had lied to the interviewer⟩ ⟨wearing a very *ashamed* look⟩ — see GUILTY

ashen *adj* lacking a healthy skin color ⟨still looking *ashen* from his bout with the flu⟩ — see PALE 2

ashes *n pl* the portion or bits of something left over or behind after it has been destroyed ⟨a new and more splendid city was built on the *ashes* of the old⟩ — see REMAINS 1

ashy *adj* lacking a healthy skin color ⟨paramedics knew she was in shock because she was *ashy* and shaking⟩ — see PALE 2

aside *n* a departure from the subject under consideration ⟨as an *aside*, something similar happened to me years ago⟩ — see TANGENT

aside from *prep* not including ⟨*aside from* the C in geometry, he made all A's this term⟩ — see EXCEPT

as if *conj* the way it would be or one would do if ⟨she looked *as if* she wanted to ask one more question before we left⟩
synonyms as, as though, like

asinine *adj* showing or marked by a lack of good sense or judgment ⟨it was *asinine* to run into the street like that⟩ — see FOOLISH 1

asininity *n* **1** a foolish act or idea ⟨a serious journalist who refuses to take part in the *asininity* of reporting celebrity gossip as real news⟩ — see FOLLY 1
2 lack of good sense or judgment ⟨the *asininity* of your public ridicule of the boss is beyond belief⟩ — see FOOLISHNESS 1

ask *vb* **1** to put a question or questions to ⟨my coworkers *asked* me all about my trip to Machu Picchu⟩
synonyms catechize, grill, inquire (of), interrogate, query, question, quiz
related words besiege, bombard, cross-examine, cross-question, examine, pump; poll, survey
near antonyms rejoin, retort; comment, observe, remark; avoid, duck
antonyms answer, reply, respond
2 to make a request of ⟨*ask* the salesclerk for assistance⟩
synonyms hit (up), request, solicit
related words appeal (to), beg, beseech, conjure, entreat, implore, importune, invite, invoke, petition, plead (to), pray, supplicate; demand, enjoin, exact, press, require
phrases call on (*or* upon)
near antonyms coerce, compel, constrain, force, oblige, require
3 to set or receive as a price ⟨they are only *asking* $300 for that antique grandfather clock⟩ — see CHARGE 1
4 to request the presence or participation of ⟨a fixture on the party circuit, that couple is always *asking* people over for dinner⟩ — see INVITE 1

ask (for) *vb* **1** to make a request for ⟨don't be afraid to *ask for* help if you need it⟩
synonyms bespeak, call (for), desire, plead (for), quest, request, seek, solicit, speak (for), sue (for)
related words apply (for), beg (for), claim, clamor (for), importune, urge, wish (for); demand, enjoin, exact, insist (on), petition (for), press (for), require, requisition; invite, invoke
2 to act so as to make (something) more likely ⟨you are *asking for* trouble if you invite her ex to the wedding⟩ — see COURT 1
3 to give a request or demand for ⟨the surgeon *asked for* the scalpel⟩ — see ORDER 2

askance *also* **askant** *adv* with distrust ⟨we looked *askance* at the dealer's assertion that the car had never been in an accident⟩
synonyms distrustfully, doubtfully, doubtingly, dubiously, mistrustfully, sideways, skeptically, suspiciously
related words hesitantly, hesitatingly, incredulously, questioningly, quizzically, unbelievingly; charily, guardedly, warily; captiously, critically, cynically, deprecatingly, disapprovingly, disparagingly, negatively, reproachfully, reproachingly, reprovingly, unfavorably; anxiously, apprehensively, uncomfortably, uneasily
phrases with a grain of salt
near antonyms approvingly, favorably, positively; confidently, sanguinely; credulously, uncritically, unquestioningly
antonyms trustfully, trustingly

askew *adj* inclined or twisted to one side ⟨his hat was *askew* because of the wind⟩ — see AWRY

aslant *adj* inclined or twisted to one side ⟨that picture is *aslant*—would you mind straightening it?⟩ — see AWRY

asleep *adj* **1** being in a state of suspended consciousness ⟨was sound *asleep* when the earthquake struck⟩
synonyms dormant, dozing, napping, resting, sleeping, slumbering
related words drowsy, nodding, sleepy, slumberous (*or* slumbrous), somnolent; dreaming, reposing; hypnotized, mesmerized; comatose, semiconscious; sleepwalking, somnambulant
phrases at rest
near antonyms aware, conscious; sleepless; aroused, astir, awakened, roused, up, wakened; reawakened, revived
antonyms awake, sleepless, wakeful, wide-awake
2 lacking in sensation or feeling ⟨after sitting cross-legged all afternoon, I arose only to discover that my right foot was *asleep*⟩ — see NUMB 1
3 no longer living ⟨let us pray for those who are now *asleep*⟩ — see DEAD 1

as long as *conj* for the reason that ⟨*as long as* I've got my boots on, I might as well go out and get the firewood⟩ — see SINCE

asocial *adj* having or showing a lack of friendliness or interest in others ⟨an *asocial* and grumpy artist lives alone on the top floor⟩ — see COOL 1

aspect *n* **1** a certain way in which something appears or may be regarded ⟨depending on what *aspect* of college life you consider most important, there are several colleges which might be good for you⟩
synonyms angle, facet, hand, phase, side
related words air, appearance, character, color, complexion, condition, face, look, semblance, shape, state, visage; period, stage, step; outlook, perspective, position, posture, shoes, slant, stance, standpoint, view, viewpoint; interpretation, reading, rendering, translation, version; article, case, component, count, detail, dimension, element, factor, instance, item, matter, part, particular, point, regard, respect
2 the outward form of someone or something especially as indicative of a quality ⟨he has the *aspect* of a man used to giving orders and seeing them obeyed⟩ — see APPEARANCE 1
3 the state or fact of facing a particular direction ⟨the harbor's northern *aspect* means that vessels are often exposed to strong winds⟩ — see EXPOSURE 2
4 *archaic* a fixed intent look ⟨his *aspect* was focused on the distant shore⟩ — see GAZE

asperity *n* **1** a harsh or sharp quality ⟨doesn't like the *asperity* of most experimental music⟩ — see EDGE 1
2 biting sharpness of feeling or expression ⟨she responded with such *asperity* that we knew she was deeply offended by the question⟩ — see ACRIMONY 1
3 something that is a cause for suffering or special effort especially in the attainment of a goal ⟨as a physically challenged person, he has encountered more than his share of *asperities* on the road to success⟩ — see DIFFICULTY 1

asperse *vb* to make untrue and harmful statements about ⟨how dare you *asperse* the character of our dedicated pastor!⟩ — see SLANDER

aspersing *n* the making of false statements that damage another's reputation ⟨she has refused to take part in the mean-spirited *aspersing* in which so many political candidates indulge⟩ — see SLANDER

asphalt jungle *n* a thickly settled, highly populated area ⟨a realistic novel about life in the *asphalt jungle*⟩ — see CITY

aspirant *n* one who seeks an office, honor, position, or award ⟨a bevy of ever-smiling *aspirants* for the Miss America title⟩ — see CANDIDATE

aspiration *n* **1** eager desire for personal advancement ⟨a combination of *aspiration* and hard work made her the top female tennis player in the state⟩ — see AMBITION 1
2 something that one hopes or intends to accomplish ⟨college is his immediate *aspiration* after he graduates from high school⟩ — see GOAL

aspire *vb* **1** to have in mind as a purpose or goal ⟨*aspire* to great deeds, and you have a better chance of doing good deeds⟩ — see INTEND 1
2 to move or extend upward ⟨a tower *aspiring* towards the heavens⟩ — see ASCEND

aspiring *adj* having a strong desire for personal advancement ⟨an *aspiring* young pianist eager to win the prestigious competition⟩ — see AMBITIOUS 1

as regards *also* **as respects** *prep* having to do with ⟨*as regards* her suggestions, I think the less said the better⟩ — see ABOUT 1

ass *n* a sturdy and patient domestic mammal that is used especially to carry things ⟨the farm kept a few *asses* for hauling hay in and out of the field⟩ — see DONKEY 1

assail *vb* **1** to criticize harshly and usually publicly ⟨the union organizers *assailed* the chemical company for failing to provide a safe working environment⟩ — see ATTACK 2
2 to take sudden, violent action against ⟨a band of hooligans *assailed* the homeless man, punching and kicking him senseless⟩ — see ATTACK 1

assailant *n* one who violently sets upon another ⟨the darkness prevented me from getting a good look at my *assailant*⟩ — see ATTACKER

assassin *n* a person who kills another person ⟨shot down by an unknown *assassin*⟩
synonyms cutthroat, homicide, killer, manslayer, murderer
related words bravo, hit man, torpedo, triggerman; butcher, executioner, massacrer, slaughterer, slayer; murderess

assassinate *vb* to put to death deliberately ⟨Marat was *assassinated* by Charlotte Corday⟩ — see MURDER 1

assault *n* **1** the act of forcing a person to engage in sexual activity and especially intercourse ⟨the body of the murdered woman also showed signs of *assault*⟩ — see RAPE 1
2 the act or action of setting upon with force or violence ⟨was arrested for his *assault* of the bystander⟩ — see ATTACK 1

assault *vb* **1** to engage in sexual activity and especially intercourse with a person unwilling or unable to give consent ⟨she could not give a full description of the person who had *assaulted* her⟩ — see RAPE
2 to take sudden, violent action against ⟨roving bands of hoodlums randomly *assaulted* people on the street⟩ — see ATTACK 1

assaulter *n* one who violently sets upon another ⟨a cowardly *assaulter* of defenseless senior citizens out for a stroll⟩ — see ATTACKER

assaultive *adj* feeling or displaying eagerness to fight ⟨with viciously *assaultive* prose the writer takes on her critics⟩ — see BELLIGERENT

assaultiveness *n* an inclination to fight or quarrel ⟨an accustomed *assaultiveness* that really gets out of control when he's drunk⟩ — see BELLIGERENCE

assay *n* **1** the separation and identification of the parts of a whole ⟨a metallurgist did an *assay* on the metal and determined it contained nickel⟩ — see ANALYSIS 1
2 *archaic* an effort to do or accomplish something ⟨the poem about a frustrated man's last *assay* at greatness⟩ — see ATTEMPT 1

assay *vb* **1** to identify and examine the basic elements or parts of (something) especially for discovering interrelationships ⟨the company *assayed* a sample of the rock to see if it contained gold in quantities worth mining⟩ — see ANALYZE
2 to make an effort to do ⟨*assaying* the task of writing his autobiography⟩ — see ATTEMPT

assemblage *n* **1** a body of people come together in one place ⟨an *assemblage* of onlookers at the construction site⟩ — see GATHERING 1
2 a mass or quantity that has piled up or that has been gathered over a period of time ⟨tried to sort through the *assemblage* of ripped wrapping paper and boxes for the missing toy⟩ — see ACCUMULATION 1
3 a number of things considered as a unit ⟨an *assemblage* of brass candlesticks on the table⟩ — see GROUP 1
4 an organized group of objects acquired and maintained for study, exhibition, or personal pleasure ⟨donated his *assemblage* of 18th-century miniature paintings to the museum⟩ — see COLLECTION 1

assemble *vb* **1** to come together into one body or place ⟨the graduates were told to *assemble* in the cafeteria an hour before the ceremony⟩
synonyms cluster, collect, concenter, concentrate, conglomerate, congregate, convene, converge, forgather (*or* foregather), gather, meet, rendezvous
related words affiliate, ally, associate, band (together), caucus, club, collaborate, confederate, conjoin, consolidate, consort, cooperate, couple, federate, gang up, join, merge, unite; reassemble, reconvene, regather, remeet
phrases get together
near antonyms depart, leave, take off; disjoin, dissociate, disunite
antonyms break up, disband, disperse, split (up)
2 to form by putting together parts or materials ⟨it took a lot more time to *assemble* the model train set than the box said it would⟩ — see BUILD
3 to bring together in assembly by or as if by command ⟨we *assembled* the club members to decide who would be traveling with whom on the trip⟩ — see CONVOKE
4 to bring together in one body or place ⟨*assembled* an assortment of fancy desserts for the reception⟩ — see GATHER 1

assembly *n* **1** a body of people come together in one place ⟨the usual *assembly* of early morning commuters waiting at the train station⟩ — see GATHERING 1
2 a body of persons gathered for religious worship ⟨the preacher addressed the *assembly* in somber tones⟩ — see CONGREGATION 1
3 a coming together of a number of persons for a specified purpose ⟨attendance at the awards *assembly* is mandatory⟩ — see MEETING 1

assent *vb* to give or express one's approval (as to a proposal) ⟨are we to conclude from your silence that you *assent*?⟩ — see ACCEDE

assert *vb* **1** to state clearly and strongly ⟨a superpatriot who is never afraid to *assert* her allegiance to flag and country⟩
synonyms affirm, aver, avouch, avow, declare, guarantee, lay down, profess
related words advance, advertise, boost, plug, promote, publicize; announce, blaze, call, proclaim, pronounce, say; accent, accentuate, emphasize, stress, underline, underscore; advocate, champion, defend, espouse, support, uphold; assure, convince, persuade; explain, justify, rationalize; reaffirm, reassert

near antonyms minimize, understate; disregard, ignore, neglect, overlook
2 to state (something) as a reason in support of or against something under consideration ⟨*asserted* that a new roof would be necessary if the church was to remain open⟩ — see ARGUE 1
3 to state as a fact usually forcefully ⟨vigorously *asserted* that what passes for art these days is absolute rubbish⟩ — see CLAIM 1
assertion *n* **1** a solemn and often public declaration of the truth or existence of something ⟨the *assertion* that all men have certain unalienable rights is set forth in the Declaration of Independence⟩ — see PROTESTATION
2 an idea or opinion that is put forth in a discussion or debate ⟨made the unlikely *assertion* that gravity affects light⟩ — see CONTENTION 1
assertive *adj* **1** having or showing a bold forcefulness in the pursuit of a goal ⟨some reef fish are *assertive* in defending their territory⟩ — see AGGRESSIVE 1
2 marked by or uttered with forcefulness ⟨after months of *assertive* declarations that he would not run for president, he announced he was running⟩ — see EMPHATIC 1
assertiveness *n* the quality or state of being forceful (as in expression) ⟨the *assertiveness* with which he voices his opinions intimidates some people⟩ — see VEHEMENCE 1
assess *vb* **1** to establish or apply as a charge or penalty ⟨the utility company will *assess* a fee if your payment is late⟩ — see IMPOSE
2 to make an approximate or tentative judgment regarding ⟨let's step back and *assess* the situation⟩ — see ESTIMATE 1
assessment *n* **1** a charge usually of money collected by the government from people or businesses for public use ⟨hated paying the annual *assessment* on his car⟩ — see TAX
2 an opinion on the nature, character, or quality of something ⟨I'm far too quiet, in the *assessment* of my new boss⟩ — see ESTIMATION 1
3 the act of placing a value on the nature, character, or quality of something ⟨we may have been too hasty in our *assessment* of the value of the property⟩ — see ESTIMATE 1
asset *n* **1** a person who tries secretly to obtain information for one country in the territory of another usually unfriendly country ⟨rumors persisted that CIA *assets* were behind the coup d'état⟩ — see SPY
2 a thing that helps ⟨the team's strong pitching staff has become a real *asset* in its pursuit of a pennant⟩ — see HELP 2
3 assets *pl* the total of one's money and property ⟨as a result of the booming economy, the college's *assets* grew dramatically over the course of the decade⟩ — see WEALTH 1
asseveration *n* a solemn and often public declaration of the truth or existence of something ⟨despite the reporter's *asseverations* about journalistic integrity, there is little doubt that he is guilty of fabricating a number of details in his stories⟩ — see PROTESTATION
assiduity *n* attentive and persistent effort ⟨this project has been successful only through the *assiduity* of a lot of people⟩ — see DILIGENCE
assiduous *adj* involved in often constant activity ⟨the fascinating sight of *assiduous* ants carrying food into the anthill⟩ — see BUSY 1
assiduously *adv* **1** in a manner involving great or constant activity ⟨trying *assiduously* to organize everything for the walkathon⟩ — see BUSILY
2 with great effort or determination ⟨*assiduously* pursued a law degree when continuing to work full-time during the day⟩ — see HARD 1
assiduousness *n* attentive and persistent effort ⟨with painstaking *assiduousness* investigators finally cracked the case of the stolen works of art⟩ — see DILIGENCE
assign *vb* **1** to give a task, duty, or responsibility to ⟨*assigned* the class with the task of finding something in the state constitution they felt needed changing⟩ — see ENTRUST 1
2 to give as a share or portion ⟨each new employee is *assigned* a cubicle and a computer⟩ — see ALLOT
3 to give over the legal possession or ownership of ⟨*assigned* all rights to and royalties from the song to the Boy Scouts⟩ — see TRANSFER 1
4 to pick (someone) by one's authority for a specific position or duty ⟨the mayor *assigned* the panel with the task of luring a major sports franchise to the city⟩ — see APPOINT 2
assignation *n* an agreement to be present at a specified time and place ⟨a midnight *assignation* between adulterers at a downtown hotel⟩ — see ENGAGEMENT 2
assignee *n* a person who acts or does business for another ⟨you are hereby authorized as my *assignee* for the duration of the case⟩ — see AGENT 2
assignment *n* **1** a piece of work that needs to be done regularly ⟨his first newspaper *assignment* was writing obituaries⟩ — see CHORE 1
2 a specific task with which a person or group is charged ⟨the spy team's *assignment* was to steal the plans for the nuclear reactor⟩ — see MISSION
3 something assigned to be read or studied ⟨have you read the *assignment* for tomorrow?⟩ — see LESSON
4 the state or fact of being chosen for a position or duty ⟨her *assignment* to the board of directors was a point of considerable pride for her⟩ — see APPOINTMENT 1
assimilate *vb* **1** to describe as similar ⟨*assimilated* the 19th-century American captains of industry and commerce to the medieval barons who exorbitantly taxed shipping along the Rhine⟩ — see COMPARE 1
2 to have a clear idea of ⟨still trying to *assimilate* the doctor's diagnosis of my heart condition⟩ — see COMPREHEND 1
3 to make a part of a body or system ⟨social workers will need time to *assimilate* the new arrivals into the community⟩ — see EMBODY 1
assist *n* an act or instance of helping ⟨with an *assist* from his dad, the youngster built a doghouse any canine would be proud to call home⟩ — see HELP 1
assist *vb* to provide (someone) with what is useful or necessary to achieve an end ⟨you can *assist* families in need by donating old clothes in good condition⟩ — see HELP 1
assistance *n* an act or instance of helping ⟨thank you for your *assistance* in helping me change my flat tire⟩ — see HELP 1
assistant *n* a person who helps a more skilled person ⟨the chief *assistant* to the director⟩ — see HELPER
associate *n* **1** a person frequently seen in the company of another ⟨a number of his *associates* were members of organized crime, so he was a person of interest to the FBI⟩
synonyms cohort, companion, compatriot, compeer, comrade, crony, fellow, hobnobber, mate, running mate
related words colleague, coworker, equal, peer, workmate; accomplice, affiliate, ally, collaborator, confederate, half, partner; buddy, chum, confidant, familiar, friend, hearty, intimate, pal; countryman; classmate, housemate, messmate, playfellow, playmate, roommate (*also* roomie), schoolmate, shipmate, teammate; attendant, escort; hanger-on, leech, parasite
2 a fellow worker ⟨my *associates* at the office⟩ — see COLLEAGUE
associate *vb* **1** to come or be together as friends ⟨a so-

cially ambitious couple who joined the country club in order to *associate* with the right sort of people⟩

synonyms chum, company, consociate, consort, fraternize, hang (around *or* out), hobnob, hook up, mess around, pal (around), run, sort, travel

related words affiliate, ally, attach, band, bond, club, collaborate, collude, confederate, conjoin, connect, cooperate, couple, gang, get along, get on, group, interrelate, join, knot, league, link, mingle, mix, rally, relate, side, socialize, team, tie, wed; befriend, friend

phrases be friends with, fall in with, keep company (with), rub elbows (with) *or* rub shoulders (with), take up with

near antonyms avoid, cold-shoulder, shun, snub; alienate, estrange; break up, disband, disperse, split (up); disjoin, dissociate, disunite, divorce, sever, split, sunder

2 to think of (something) in combination ⟨she still *associates* Memorial Day with her long-ago fiancé, who died in Vietnam⟩

synonyms connect, correlate, identify, link, relate

related words compare, equate, liken; group, join, lump (together), tie (together)

near antonyms contrast, differentiate, discriminate, distinguish, separate, set off

3 to come together to form a single unit ⟨the elements hydrogen and oxygen *associate* to form molecules of water⟩ — see UNITE 1

4 to form or enter into an association that furthers the interests of its members ⟨nations deciding to *associate* in order to remove trade barriers⟩ — see ALLY

5 to take part in social activities ⟨you should try to *associate* with people your own age⟩ — see SOCIALIZE

association *n* **1** the state of having shared interests or efforts (as in social or business matters) ⟨the public television station is producing the series in *association* with a foundation for the arts⟩

synonyms affiliation, alliance, collaboration, confederation, connection, cooperation, hookup, liaison, linkup, partnership, relation, relationship, tie-up, union

related words business, dealings, interaction; exchange, interconnection, interrelation, mutualism, reciprocity, symbiosis; incorporation, integration, merger, unification; affinity, attachment, closeness, intimacy, rapport, sympathy; kinship, oneness, solidarity, togetherness, unity; colleagueship, companionship, company, fellowship; bed, cahoots, league

near antonyms breakup, dissolution, disunion; division, parting, separation, severance, split; alienation, divorce, estrangement

antonyms disaffiliation, dissociation

2 a group of persons formally joined together for some common interest ⟨all *associations* meeting on town property must be registered with and approved by the registrar's office⟩

synonyms board, brotherhood, chamber, club, college, congress, consortium, council, fellowship, fraternity, guild (*also* gild), institute, institution, league, order, organization, society, sodality

related words collective, commune, community, cooperative; alliance, bloc, camp, coalition, partnership; body, cadre, group; circle, clan, clique, coterie, junta, junto, klatch (*also* klatsch), lot, set; crew, outfit, party, squad, team; branch, chapter, local; faithful, fold, membership; sisterhood, sorority; cabal, camarilla, camorra, confederacy, conspiracy; band, gang, ring; cartel, combine, syndicate

3 the fact or state of having something in common ⟨what's the *association* between cat hair and my allergic reaction to certain proteins?⟩ — see CONNECTION 1

as soon as *conj* just at the moment that ⟨let us know *as soon as* you get the news from the hospital⟩ — see WHEN 2

assort *vb* **1** to arrange or assign according to type ⟨*assort* these butterfly specimens according to geographic origin⟩ — see CLASSIFY 1

2 to form a pleasing relationship ⟨somewhat surprisingly, the collection of ancient Egyptian art *assorts* rather well with the museum's modern design⟩ — see HARMONIZE 1

assorted *adj* consisting of many things of different sorts ⟨a box of *assorted* chocolates⟩ — see MISCELLANEOUS

assortment *n* **1** an unorganized collection or mixture of various things ⟨an *assortment* of nails at the bottom of my tool box⟩ — see MISCELLANY 1

2 the quality or state of being composed of many different elements or types ⟨we were disappointed in the small clothing store's lack of *assortment*⟩ — see VARIETY 1

assuage *vb* **1** to make more bearable or less severe ⟨a mother cooing to her toddler and *assuaging* his fear of the dark⟩ — see HELP 2

2 to put a complete end to (a physical need or desire) ⟨that huge meal certainly *assuaged* my hunger⟩ — see SATISFY 1

3 to lessen the anger or agitation of ⟨nothing would *assuage* the angry parent except the prompt dismissal of the teacher who had used corporal punishment without authorization⟩ — see PACIFY 1

assumably *adv* by reasonable assumption ⟨*assumably*, the package deal for the cruise includes air fare⟩ — see PROBABLY

assume *vb* **1** to take to or upon oneself ⟨we promised to *assume* responsibility for any damage to the flower beds caused by the volleyball game in the backyard⟩

synonyms accept, bear, shoulder, take over, undertake

related words adopt, embrace, take up; advocate, back, champion, endorse (*also* indorse), espouse, stand by, support, uphold; accede, acquiesce, agree, assent, consent; reaccept, reassume

near antonyms abjure, recant, renounce, retract, take back, unsay, withdraw; decline, refuse, reject, spurn, turn down; abstain (from), forbear, refrain (from); avoid, bypass, detour; abandon, abnegate, forsake, give up, relinquish, spurn, surrender; back down, back off, backtrack

antonyms disavow, disclaim, disown, repudiate

2 to take as true or as a fact without actual proof ⟨everyone *assumed*, wrongly, that someone else was bringing dessert⟩

synonyms hypothecate, hypothesize, postulate, premise, presume, presuppose, say, suppose

related words accept, believe, credit, swallow; conclude, deduce, gather, infer, judge, take; conjecture, figure, guess, reckon [*chiefly dialect*], surmise, suspect, suspicion [*chiefly dialect*], think; conceive, dream, fancy, imagine, perceive, preconceive; speculate, theorize; affirm, allege, assert, aver, avouch, avow, claim, contend, declare, insist, maintain, profess

phrases take for granted

near antonyms challenge, controvert, disagree (with), disbelieve, discount, discredit, dispute, distrust, doubt, mistrust, question, wonder (about); deny, disavow, disclaim, disown, reject, repudiate; belie, confute, disprove, rebut, refute

3 to form an opinion from little or no evidence ⟨as I just *assumed* it was too late to go out, I didn't think to ask⟩ — see GUESS 1

4 to present a false appearance of ⟨she *assumed* an air of nonchalance even though she was wildly ecstatic she was going on the date⟩ — see FEIGN

5 to provide with a paying job ⟨*assumed* as partner by the prestigious law firm⟩ — see EMPLOY 1

assumed *adj* **1** appearing to be true on the basis of evi-

dence that may or may not be confirmed ⟨an *assumed* connection between the two species that has yet to be confirmed by fossil findings⟩ — see APPARENT 1
2 lacking in natural or spontaneous quality ⟨the salesclerk's *assumed* friendliness vanished as soon as I assured her I was just looking⟩ — see ARTIFICIAL 1
assumption *n* **1** something taken as being true or factual and used as a starting point for a course of action or reasoning ⟨the widespread *assumption* that violent entertainment leads to violent behavior in children⟩ ⟨your argument is faulty because it's based on erroneous *assumptions*⟩
synonyms given, hypothetical, if, postulate, premise (*also* premiss), presumption, presupposition, supposition
related words hypothesis, proposition, theory, thesis; axiom, truism, verity; belief, canon, doctrine, dogma, gospel, law; precept, principle, rule, standard, tenet; basis, foundation, ground; conclusion, deduction, inference; affirmation, assertion, avouchment, declaration; dictum, ipse dixit
2 an exaggerated sense of one's importance that shows itself in the making of excessive or unjustified claims ⟨his air of *assumption* tended to put people off rather quickly⟩ — see ARROGANCE
assumptive *adj* having a feeling of superiority that shows itself in an overbearing attitude ⟨an *assumptive* and tiresome woman⟩ — see ARROGANT
assurance *n* **1** a state of mind in which one is free from doubt ⟨I can state with complete *assurance* that no harm will ever come to you⟩ — see CONFIDENCE 2
2 great faith in oneself or one's abilities ⟨her *assurance* was evident in the way she carried herself onto the playing field⟩ — see CONFIDENCE 1
assure *vb* **1** to ease the grief or distress of ⟨a minister choosing just the right words to *assure* the grieving parents of the fallen soldier⟩ — see COMFORT
2 to make sure, certain, or safe ⟨security measures that *assured* our safety⟩ — see ENSURE
assured *adj* **1** having or showing a mind free from doubt ⟨a man who seemed very *assured* of the outcome of the election⟩ — see CERTAIN 2
2 having or showing great faith in oneself or one's abilities ⟨an *assured* attorney, he dominates any coutroom proceeding⟩ — see CONFIDENT 1
3 having too high an opinion of oneself ⟨he's rather *assured* for a moviemaker with one hit movie to his name⟩ — see CONCEITED
assuredly *adv* without any question ⟨I am most *assuredly* the person you are looking for⟩ — see INDEED 1
assuredness *n* a state of mind in which one is free from doubt ⟨the complete *assuredness* with which the cocky jock would ask for dates⟩ — see CONFIDENCE 2
astern *adv* near, toward, or in the stern of a ship or the tail of an aircraft ⟨if you turn around and look *astern*, you'll see dolphins following the boat⟩ — see AFT
asthenia *n* the quality or state of lacking physical strength or vigor ⟨headache, nausea, fever, and *asthenia* are side effects of the drug⟩ — see WEAKNESS 1
asthenic *adj* lacking bodily strength ⟨resistance training can benefit the *asthenic* individual⟩ — see WEAK 1
as though *conj* the way it would be or one would do if ⟨the applause was so great it was *as though* the toddler's dance class had been the Bolshoi Ballet⟩ — see AS IF
astir *adj* marked by much life, movement, or activity ⟨the mall was *astir* with throngs of holiday shoppers⟩ — see ALIVE 2
as to *prep* having to do with ⟨I'm in a quandary *as to* how to deal with the problem⟩ — see ABOUT 1
astonish *vb* to make a strong impression on (someone) with something unexpected ⟨the news that you and she broke up absolutely *astonishes* me⟩ — see SURPRISE 1
astonished *adj* **1** affected with sudden and great wonder or surprise ⟨was *astonished* at seeing a cow wandering down Main Street⟩ — see THUNDERSTRUCK
2 filled with amazement or wonder ⟨grandparents *astonished* at how much their grandchildren had grown in the past year⟩ — see OPENMOUTHED
astonishing *adj* **1** causing a strong emotional reaction because of unexpectedness ⟨gave us the *astonishing* news she was getting married⟩ — see SURPRISING 1
2 causing wonder or astonishment ⟨an *astonishing* view of the Grand Canyon that few tourists get to see⟩ — see MARVELOUS 1
astonishment *n* **1** the rapt attention and deep emotion caused by the sight of something extraordinary ⟨the Midwesterner's *astonishment* at seeing the ocean for the first time⟩ — see WONDER 2
2 the state of being strongly impressed by something unexpected or unusual ⟨the suddenness of the thunderstorm left the picnickers in a state of *astonishment*⟩ — see SURPRISE 2
astound *vb* to make a strong impression on (someone) with something unexpected ⟨it *astounds* me that you flew all the way out here just for my birthday⟩ — see SURPRISE 1
astounded *adj* **1** affected with sudden and great wonder or surprise ⟨were *astounded* to realize that we were holding the winning lottery ticket⟩ — see THUNDERSTRUCK
2 filled with amazement or wonder ⟨the *astounded* look on the tourists' faces when the police ordered them to leave the country immediately⟩ — see OPENMOUTHED
astounding *adj* **1** causing a strong emotional reaction because of unexpectedness ⟨the *astounding* sight of their cat returning home after having been missing for two years⟩ — see SURPRISING 1
2 causing wonder or astonishment ⟨experiencing the *astounding* sight of the aurora borealis for the first time⟩ — see MARVELOUS 1
astral *adj* **1** of or relating to the stars ⟨gave the astronomy students the assignment of charting *astral* movement for the next month⟩ — see STELLAR 1
2 standing above others in rank, importance, or achievement ⟨after his film became an unexpected blockbuster, the director was suddenly welcome in the most *astral* circles of Hollywood society⟩ — see EMINENT
astray *adv* off the desired or intended path or course ⟨I think we were led *astray* by the unfortunate similarity of the two names⟩ — see WRONG 1
astronomical *also* **astronomic** *adj* unusually large ⟨a googol is an *astronomical* number, and the whimsical coinage of the name was intended to suggest that fact⟩ — see HUGE
astronomically *adv* to a large extent or degree ⟨their battalion was *astronomically* outnumbered by enemy forces⟩ — see GREATLY 2
astute *adj* having or showing a practical cleverness or judgment ⟨a police detective known to be an *astute* judge of character⟩ — see SHREWD 1
astuteness *n* exceptional discernment and judgment especially in practical matters ⟨a political observer renowned for her *astuteness*⟩ — see ACUMEN
asunder *adv* into parts or pieces ⟨the environmental organization was torn *asunder* by bitter rivalries⟩ — see APART
as well as *prep* in addition to ⟨we offer electronic toys *as well as* rent out video games⟩ — see BESIDES 1
aswoon *adj* having a feeling of being whirled about and in danger of falling down ⟨I don't know what was in that cocktail, but I was all *aswoon* after drinking it⟩ — see DIZZY 1
asylum *n* **1** a place where insane people are cared for

⟨volunteered to play piano for the residents of the state *asylum* on weekends⟩ — see MADHOUSE 1
2 something (as a building) that offers cover from the weather or protection from danger ⟨the embassy serves as an *asylum* for that country's nationals in need of help⟩ — see SHELTER
at all *adv* in any way or respect ⟨wasn't *at all* pleased with the way the family portrait came out⟩
synonyms anywise, ever, half
related words somehow, someway (*also* someways); remotely
athirst *adj* showing urgent desire or interest ⟨was *athirst* for any news at all about family members serving in the war zone⟩ — see EAGER
athwart *adv* **1** from one side to the other of an intervening space ⟨after it enters the Gulf of Mexico, the hurricane is predicted to advance *athwart* to the Texas coastline⟩ — see OVER 1
2 in a line or direction running from corner to corner ⟨we hung the twisted strips of crepe paper *athwart* to the floor and ceiling so that they formed giant crosses on all four walls⟩ — see CROSSWISE
athwart *prep* to the opposite side of ⟨*athwart* the road was farmland as far as the eye could see⟩ — see ACROSS 1
atilt *adj* inclined or twisted to one side ⟨cuts quite a dashing figure with a jauntily *atilt* beret⟩ — see AWRY
atmosphere *n* **1** a special quality or impression associated with something ⟨the fireplace and cozy armchairs give the bookstore the *atmosphere* of a comfortable home⟩ — see AURA 1
2 the circumstances, conditions, or objects by which one is surrounded ⟨liked the quiet and scholarly *atmosphere* of his prep school⟩ — see ENVIRONMENT
atom *n* a very small piece ⟨give me just one *atom* of information about the novel's surprise ending⟩ — see BIT 1
atomic *adj* very small in size ⟨made *atomic* adjustments to the clock's mechanism to keep it from whirring as it ran⟩ — see TINY
atomize *vb* to reduce to fine particles ⟨this medication for athlete's foot is *atomized* so that it can be sprayed on from an aerosol can⟩ — see POWDER
atone (for) *vb* to make up for (an offense) ⟨tried to *atone for* forgetting their anniversary by giving his wife a truly extravagant gift⟩ — see EXPIATE
atremble *adj* marked by or given to small uncontrollable bodily movements ⟨*atremble* with fright at the sound of the booming howitzers⟩ — see SHAKY 1
atrocious *adj* **1** extremely disturbing or repellent ⟨an *atrocious* crime that shocked even hardened members of the police force⟩ — see HORRIBLE 1
2 extremely unsatisfactory ⟨the picture quality on the pirated DVD was *atrocious*⟩ — see WRETCHED 1
3 having or showing the desire to inflict severe pain and suffering on others ⟨the *atrocious* treatment of prisoners at the camps⟩ — see CRUEL 1
atrociousness *n* **1** the quality of inspiring intense dread or dismay ⟨George Orwell's novel *1984* captures the *atrociousness* of tyranny⟩ — see HORROR 1
2 the state or quality of being utterly evil ⟨the unspeakable *atrociousness* of the mass genocide that was perpetrated in that African nation⟩ — see ENORMITY 1
3 disposition to willfully inflict pain and suffering on others ⟨for sheer *atrociousness* the murders committed by Jack the Ripper occupy a special place in the annals of crime⟩ — see CRUELTY
atrocity *n* **1** the quality of inspiring intense dread or dismay ⟨the undeniable *atrocity* of the forced march of Cherokees known as the Trail of Tears⟩ — see HORROR 1
2 the state or quality of being utterly evil ⟨was appalled by the *atrocity* of Stalin's mass executions⟩ — see ENORMITY 1
3 disposition to willfully inflict pain and suffering on others ⟨wars often unleash a level of *atrocity* that would be unimaginable in peacetime⟩ — see CRUELTY
atrophy *vb* to become worse or of less value ⟨in the years following the closing of the last textile mill, the town *atrophied*⟩ — see DETERIORATE 1
attach *vb* **1** to cause (something) to hold to another ⟨you can *attach* the buttons to the puppet with fabric glue⟩ — see FASTEN 1
2 to pick (someone) by one's authority for a specific position or duty ⟨*attached* the colonel to the new regiment⟩ — see APPOINT 2
3 to take ownership or control of (something) by right of one's authority ⟨*attached* the house for nonpayment of property taxes⟩ — see CONFISCATE
attached *adj* having a liking or affection ⟨was rather *attached* to her old stuffed animals⟩ — see FOND 1
attachment *n* **1** a feeling of strong or constant regard for and dedication to someone ⟨I doubt that there's any permanent *attachment* between the two teenagers⟩ — see LOVE 1
2 something that is not necessary in itself but adds to the convenience or performance of the main piece of equipment ⟨bought a grinder *attachment* for the kitchen mixer⟩ — see ACCESSORY 1
3 adherence to something to which one is bound by a pledge or duty ⟨an unflinching *attachment* to the marriage, through times both good and bad⟩ — see FIDELITY
attack *n* **1** the act or action of setting upon with force or violence ⟨The USS Constitution was nicknamed "Old Ironsides" after its oaken hull successfully withstood a British *attack*⟩
synonyms aggression, assault, attempt, blitz, blitzkrieg, charge, coup de main, descent, offense (*or* offence), offensive, onset, onslaught, raid, rush, strike
related words ambuscade, ambush; counteraggression, counterassault, counterattack, counteroffensive, counterstrike; sally, sortie; envelopment, flanking; breakthrough, foray, incursion, invasion; pillage, ravage, sack; air raid, bombardment, bombing; siege, storm; barrage, cannonade, fusillade, hail, salvo, volley; whammy
near antonyms defense, defensive, guard, shield; opposition, resistance; protection, security, shelter
2 a sudden experiencing of a physical or mental disorder ⟨malaria is characterized by periodic *attacks* of chills and fever⟩
synonyms access, bout, case, fit, seizure, siege, spell, turn
related words recurrence, relapse; brainstorm, convulsion, eclampsia, pang, paroxysm, spasm, throe; agitation, frenzy; breakdown, collapse, prostration
near antonyms arrest, relief, remission
attack *vb* **1** to take sudden, violent action against ⟨our dog unexpectedly *attacked* the mailman, sinking his teeth into the startled man's leg⟩
synonyms assail, assault, beset, bushwhack, charge, descend (on *or* upon), go in (on), jump (on), pounce (on *or* upon), raid, rush, set on, sic (*also* sick), storm, strike, trash, turn (on)
related words bum-rush, gang up (on), mob, swarm; mug, rob; ambuscade, ambush, surprise (*also* surprize), waylay; blitz, bomb, bombard, nuke; barrage, cannon, cannonade; bang away (at), batter, buffet, plaster; beleaguer, besiege, press; harry, loot, pillage, plunder, ravage, sack; foray, invade, overrun; envelop, flank
phrases beat up on, fly at, go at, light into, pitch into, round on, set at, set upon, tear into

near antonyms cover, defend, guard, protect, secure, shield

2 to criticize harshly and usually publicly ⟨the mayor and all his aides were *attacked* mercilessly in the press when the scandal erupted⟩

synonyms abuse, assail, bash, belabor, blast, castigate, excoriate, jump (on), lambaste (*or* lambast), potshot, savage, scathe, slam, trash, vituperate

related words berate, harangue, harass, harry, revile, scold, whip; blaspheme, curse, execrate, imprecate, profane; affront, insult, slur; asperse, bad-mouth, belittle, blackguard, disparage, put down; libel, slander, traduce, vilify; chastise, chide, criticize, lace (into), rebuke, reprimand, reproof; fulminate, lash (out)

phrases beat up on, light into, sail into, tie into

near antonyms acclaim, commend, compliment, hail, laud, praise

3 to start work on energetically ⟨Courtney *attacked* the huge mess in her room with determination and enthusiasm⟩

synonyms dive (into), tackle, wade (in *or* into)

related words address, approach, face; buckle (down to), concentrate (on), focus (on), knuckle down (to), zero (in on); fall (to), pitch in, plunge (in), settle (down); pursue, take up, undertake

phrases go at, have at, light into, pitch into, sail into, tear into

near antonyms avoid, evade, shun; dally, dawdle, dilly-dally, fiddle (around), fool, idle, lag, mess, monkey (around), play, poke, potter (around), putter (around), trifle

attack dog *n* one who makes harsh, personal attacks against opponents ⟨his reputation as a political *attack dog* earned him the vice presidential spot on the ticket⟩

synonyms mudslinger

related words polemicist, polemist; hatchet man, hired gun, hit man; barracuda, shark

attacker *n* one who violently sets upon another ⟨was able to pick her *attacker* out of the police lineup⟩

synonyms assailant, assaulter, bushwhacker

related words mugger, robber; molester, predator, raper, rapist, ravager; aggressor, besieger, invader, raider; counterattacker

attain *vb* **1** to obtain (as a goal) through effort ⟨Napoléon had *attained* mastery of much of Europe at that point⟩ — see ACHIEVE 1

2 to receive as return for effort ⟨with hard work she will inevitably *attain* success in her chosen profession⟩ — see EARN 1

attainable *adj* **1** capable of being done or carried out ⟨set *attainable* goals, not impracticable ones⟩ — see POSSIBLE 1

2 possible to get ⟨I don't know if those blue jeans are *attainable* overseas⟩ — see AVAILABLE 1

attainment *n* **1** a successful result brought about by hard work ⟨first place in the state journalism competition is quite an *attainment*⟩ — see ACCOMPLISHMENT 1

2 the state of being actual or complete ⟨the *attainment* of man's age-old dream of flying was at last realized in 1903 by Orville and Wilbur Wright⟩ — see FRUITION

attar *also* **otto** *n* a sweet or pleasant smell ⟨exuding the *attar* of jasmine, the beautifully bejeweled woman set off for the ball⟩ — see FRAGRANCE

attempt *n* **1** an effort to do or accomplish something ⟨it took several *attempts* before we made good ice cream with an old-fashioned hand-cranked ice cream freezer⟩

synonyms assay [*archaic*], bash [*chiefly British*], bid, crack, endeavor, essay, fling, go, offer, pass, shot, stab, trial, try, whack, whirl

related words striving, struggle, throes, undertaking; trial and error

2 the act or action of setting upon with force or violence ⟨several *attempts* on the life of the country's chief drug enforcement official⟩ — see ATTACK 1

attempt *vb* to make an effort to do ⟨after *attempting*—and failing—to start the lawn mower on my own, I finally succeeded with a neighbor's help⟩ ⟨don't even *attempt* walking on your broken foot⟩

synonyms assay, endeavor, essay, seek, strive, try

related words fight, strain, struggle, toil, trouble, work; aim, aspire, hope; assume, take up, undertake

phrases have a go at, shoot at (*or* shoot for), try one's hand (at)

near antonyms drop, give up, quit

attend *vb* **1** to go along with in order to provide assistance, protection, or companionship ⟨a passel of assistants *attend* the movie star wherever she goes⟩ — see ACCOMPANY 1

2 to pay attention especially through the act of hearing ⟨I'm sorry, but all the noise means I'm having a hard time *attending* to the conversation⟩ — see LISTEN

3 to take charge of especially on behalf of another ⟨tired of *attending* other people's children, the nanny was eager to have a child of her own⟩ — see [2]TEND 1

4 to occur or exist at the same time ⟨all the pomp and circumstance that *attend* the opening of the Olympic Games⟩ — see COINCIDE 1

attendant *adj* **1** coming as a result ⟨dreaded the coming flu season and the *attendant* flood of school absences⟩ — see RESULTANT

2 present at the same time and place ⟨the movie stars' divorce and the *attendant* press coverage about it⟩ — see COINCIDENT 1

attendant *n* **1** one that accompanies another for protection, guidance, or as a courtesy ⟨let the hotel *attendant* help them with their bags⟩ — see ESCORT

2 something that is found along with something else ⟨disease is the inevitable *attendant* of poor sanitation⟩ — see ACCOMPANIMENT

attending *adj* **1** being within the confines of a specified place ⟨a surprise arrest of the operator of an illegal gambling joint and all *attending* employees⟩ — see PRESENT 2

2 present at the same time and place ⟨dislikes flying and all of its *attending* inconveniences⟩ — see COINCIDENT 1

attention *n* **1** a focusing of the mind on something ⟨I need your full *attention* right now⟩

synonyms absorption, concentration, engrossment, enthrallment, immersion

related words fixation, obsession, preoccupation; alertness, application, awareness, consciousness, consideration, heedfulness, intentness, raptness, regard; contemplation, meditation, musing, pondering, rumination

near antonyms absence, absentmindedness, abstractedness, abstraction, detachment, distraction, obliviousness, remoteness, unawareness, unconsciousness, withdrawal; disinterest, indifference, mindlessness, unconcern; befuddlement, bemusement, bewilderment, confusion

antonyms inattention

2 a state of being aware ⟨several mothers brought to the committee's *attention* the deplorable condition of the playground⟩

synonyms advertence, advertency, awareness, cognizance, consciousness, ear, eye, heed, knowledge, mindfulness, note, notice, observance, observation

related words hyperawareness, hyperconsciousness; advisement, care, concern, consideration, regard, watch; apprehension, discernment, grasp, mind, perception, recognition, thought, understanding

near antonyms disregard, neglect, obliviousness, unawareness

3 an act or utterance that is a customary show of good manners ⟨she enjoyed her suitor's old-school *attentions*⟩ — see CIVILITY 1

attentive *adj* **1** having the mind fixed on something ⟨Susan became particularly *attentive* when the sportscaster turned to women's tennis, her favorite sport⟩
synonyms absorbed, deep, engrossed, enthralled, focused (*also* focussed), immersed, intent, observant, rapt
related words engaged, interested, intrigued, involved; hypnotized, mesmerized; alert, alive, conscious, open-eyed, watchful, wide-awake
phrases all ears
near antonyms daydreaming, dreamy, faraway, foggy, hazy, lost, oblivious, preoccupied, remote; apathetic, disinterested, uninterested
antonyms absent, absentminded, abstracted, distracted, inattentive, inobservant, unabsorbed, unfocused (*also* unfocussed)
2 given to or made with heedful anticipation of the needs and happiness of others ⟨an *attentive* neighbor who helps out whenever and wherever she spots a need⟩ — see THOUGHTFUL 1
3 paying close attention usually for the purpose of anticipating approaching danger or opportunity ⟨if only for your own safety, you need to stay *attentive* when you are hunting⟩ — see ALERT 1

attentiveness *n* the state of being constantly attentive and responsive to signs of opportunity, activity, or danger ⟨your *attentiveness* prevented a potentially bad accident⟩ — see VIGILANCE

attenuate *vb* to diminish the price or value of ⟨an investment *attenuated* by significant inflation over the years⟩ — see DEPRECIATE 1

attest *vb* **1** to declare (something) to be true or genuine ⟨the appraiser *attests* that the lamp is indeed an original Tiffany⟩ — see CERTIFY 1
2 to make a solemn declaration under oath for the purpose of establishing a fact ⟨an eyewitness who will *attest* to my innocence⟩ — see TESTIFY
3 to give evidence or testimony to the truth or factualness of ⟨I'll *attest* that she was at the party⟩ — see CONFIRM 1

attestation *n* something presented in support of the truth or accuracy of a claim ⟨the fact that he spent hours standing in line for the sequel should be *attestation* enough that he's a die-hard fan of the movie series⟩ — see PROOF

attic *n* a room or unfinished space directly beneath the roof of a building ⟨rented the *attic* out to a college student⟩
synonyms cockloft, garret, loft
related words hayloft

attire *n* covering for the human body ⟨needed some snazzy *attire* for the job interview⟩ — see CLOTHING

attire *vb* to outfit with clothes and especially fine or special clothes ⟨men *attired* in tuxedos for the awards banquet⟩ — see CLOTHE 1

attitude *n* a general way of holding the body ⟨had the ramrod straight *attitude* of a man who had spent all of his life in the military⟩ — see POSTURE 1

attorney *n* **1** a person who acts or does business for another ⟨talked to the count's *attorney* about buying land from his estate⟩ — see AGENT 2
2 a person whose profession is to conduct lawsuits for clients or to advise about legal rights and obligations ⟨finished law school and became an *attorney*⟩ — see LAWYER

attorney–at–law *n* a person whose profession is to conduct lawsuits for clients or to advise about legal rights and obligations ⟨the sign on the door read "Blalock Smith, *Attorney-at-Law*"⟩ — see LAWYER

attraction *n* something that attracts interest ⟨a park with the world's fastest roller coaster and other *attractions*⟩ — see MAGNET

attractive *adj* **1** having an often mysterious or magical power to attract ⟨world travel has always been very *attractive* to me⟩ — see FASCINATING 1
2 very pleasing to look at ⟨generally the star of a TV commercial is an *attractive* person⟩ — see BEAUTIFUL 1

attractiveness *n* **1** the power of irresistible attraction ⟨she had a certain *attractiveness* that came from her witty conversation⟩ — see CHARM 2
2 the qualities in a person or thing that as a whole give pleasure to the senses ⟨the *attractiveness* of the Greek countryside has inspired poets since ancient times⟩ — see BEAUTY 1

attribute *n* something that sets apart an individual from others of the same kind ⟨list the *attributes* of a mammal⟩ — see CHARACTERISTIC

attribute *vb* **1** to explain (something) as being the result of something else ⟨*attributed* the quick rescue to the well-trained police force⟩ — see CREDIT 1
2 to give the reason for or cause of ⟨a psychotherapist who's a little too quick to *attribute* every emotional problem or character defect to an unhappy childhood⟩ — see EXPLAIN 2

attribution *n* something that sets apart an individual from others of the same kind ⟨a genuine respect for one another is one of the most commonly cited *attributions* of a happily married couple⟩ — see CHARACTERISTIC

attrition *n* a gradual weakening, loss, or destruction ⟨took the machinery out of operation since *attrition* had led to the main mechanism's breaking⟩ — see CORROSION

attune *vb* to bring to a state free of conflicts, inconsistencies, or differences ⟨after years spent in academia, he's finding it difficult to *attune* himself to the corporate culture⟩ — see HARMONIZE 2

atwitter *adj* feeling or showing uncomfortable feelings of uncertainty ⟨the whole office was *atwitter* with speculation that there might be another round of layoffs⟩ — see NERVOUS 1

atypical *adj* **1** being out of the ordinary ⟨the postal service delivered the package with *atypical* speed⟩ — see EXCEPTIONAL 1
2 departing from some accepted standard of what is normal ⟨since that's an *atypical* response for an infant, you might want to have her hearing tested⟩ — see DEVIANT

auberge *n* a place that provides rooms and usually a public dining room for overnight guests ⟨they spent their honeymoon at a little French *auberge* that overflowed with charm⟩ — see HOTEL

au courant *adj* **1** keenly aware of and responsive to the latest developments especially in fashion and entertainment ⟨*au courant* filmgoers have dismissed Hollywood's latest effects-laden actioner as so last year⟩
synonyms cool [*slang*], def [*slang*], downtown, groovy, hep, hip, in, mod, now, trendy, turned-on, with-it
related words à la mode (*also* a la mode), chic, fashionable, modish, sharp, smart, snappy, stylish, voguish
near antonyms geeky, nerdish, nerdy; dowdy, styleless, unfashionable, unstylish
antonyms out, uncool, unhip, untrendy
2 being in the latest or current fashion ⟨glossy magazines full of reed-thin models in *au courant* outfits⟩ — see STYLISH
3 having information especially as a result of study or experience ⟨doctors try to stay *au courant* with the latest advances in medicine⟩ — see FAMILIAR 2

audacious *adj* **1** displaying or marked by rude boldness ⟨with an *audacious* disregard for innocent bystanders, rival gang members opened fire⟩ — see NERVY 1
2 foolishly adventurous or bold ⟨an *audacious* effort to

start her own business with no real plan or funding⟩ — see FOOLHARDY 1

3 inclined or willing to take risks ⟨*audacious* adventurers risking everything they had for a shot at glory⟩ — see BOLD 1

audaciousness *n* shameless boldness ⟨she had the *audaciousness* to complain when I refused to do her job as well as my own⟩ — see EFFRONTERY

audacity *n* shameless boldness ⟨I can't believe she had the *audacity* to tell me to shut up!⟩ — see EFFRONTERY

audial *adj* of, relating to, or experienced through the sense of hearing ⟨a specialist in *audial* disorders in children⟩ — see AUDITORY

audibly *adv* with one's normal voice speaking the words ⟨don't mumble your lines—speak *audibly* so the audience can hear you⟩ — see ALOUD

audience *n* a group of people showing intense devotion to a cause, person, or work (as a film) ⟨that mystery novelist, although long deceased, continues to have an enthusiastic *audience*⟩ — see CULT 1

audile *adj* of, relating to, or experienced through the sense of hearing ⟨the claim that a blind person has an enhanced *audile* capability⟩ — see AUDITORY

audit *n* a close look at or over someone or something in order to judge condition ⟨an energy *audit* of our house showed that we were losing lots of heat and needed to upgrade the insulation⟩ — see INSPECTION

audit *vb* to look over closely (as for judging quality or condition) ⟨*audited* the equipment to make sure that everything was in working order⟩ — see INSPECT

auditorium *n* a large room or building for enclosed public gatherings ⟨will hold the town meeting in the high school *auditorium*⟩ — see HALL 3

auditory *adj* of, relating to, or experienced through the sense of hearing ⟨I have a bad *auditory* memory—unless I see a word in writing, and not just hear it, I forget it easily⟩

synonyms acoustic (*or* acoustical), audial, audile, aural, auricular

related words audiovisual; audible, clear, discernible (*also* discernable), distinct, distinguishable, heard, perceptible

near antonyms faint, feeble, imperceptible, inaudible, indistinct, indistinguishable; low, noiseless, quiet, silent, soft, soundless

antonyms nonauditory

Augean *adj* requiring considerable physical or mental effort ⟨dreaded the *Augean* task of cleaning the bathroom after an overflow of the toilet⟩ — see HARD 2

Augean stable *n* a place of great vice and corruption ⟨as a gubernatorial candidate he claimed that the state capitol was an *Augean stable* that desperately needed to be cleaned out⟩

synonyms cesspool, Gomorrah, sink

related words tenderloin; den, dump, pigpen, pigsty; hellhole, hole

aught *n* the numerical symbol 0 or the absence of number or quantity represented by it ⟨for dates, the year is automatically listed as a pair of *aughts*, so the user has to scroll down to the correct figure⟩ — see ZERO 1

augment *vb* to make greater in size, amount, or number ⟨our volleyball team was *augmented* by some of the exchange team's players⟩ — see INCREASE 1

augmentation *n* something added (as by growth) ⟨*augmentations* to the benefits package over the years have resulted in a total of 12 paid holidays for employees⟩ — see INCREASE 1

augur *n* one who predicts future events or developments ⟨ancient Roman *augurs* who predicted the future by reading the flight of birds⟩ — see PROPHET 1

augur *vb* **1** to show signs of a favorable or successful outcome ⟨the extended interview *augurs* well for your acceptance into that law school⟩ — see BODE

2 to tell of or describe beforehand ⟨the fortune-teller *augured* nothing but a series of calamities for me⟩ — see FORETELL

auguring *n* a declaration that something will happen in the future ⟨it's a good thing that people don't remember the tabloid's *augurings* a year later, since very few come to pass⟩ — see PREDICTION

augury *n* **1** a declaration that something will happen in the future ⟨a yearbook *augury* that of all the graduates, he would be the most likely to succeed⟩ — see PREDICTION

2 something believed to be a sign or warning of a future event ⟨some people believe that a broken mirror is an *augury* of seven years' bad luck⟩ — see OMEN

3 the art or practice of foretelling future events by interpreting omens ⟨the gift of *augury* that Nostradamus purportedly possessed⟩ — see DIVINATION

august *adj* **1** having or showing a formal and serious or reserved manner ⟨unsurprisingly, the head of the bank is an *august* white-haired gentleman⟩ — see DIGNIFIED

2 large and impressive in size, grandeur, extent, or conception ⟨an *august* golden anniversary celebration for the company⟩ — see GRAND 1

augustness *n* **1** a dignified bearing or appearance befitting someone of royal status ⟨the opera star carries herself with the *augustness* of a queen⟩ — see MAJESTY 1

2 impressiveness of beauty on a large scale ⟨the *augustness* of the Lincoln Memorial in our nation's capital⟩ — see MAGNIFICENCE

auld lang syne *n* the events or experience of former times ⟨let us bid farewell to *auld lang syne* and welcome in the new year⟩ — see PAST

au naturel *adj* lacking or shed of clothing ⟨for vacationers who prefer to be *au naturel*, the tropical resort features a secluded, private beach⟩ — see NAKED 1

aura *n* **1** a special quality or impression associated with something ⟨the monastery perched high on a mountaintop had an *aura* of unreality and mystery about it⟩

synonyms air, ambience (*or* ambiance), aroma, atmosphere, climate, flavor, halo, karma, mood, nimbus, note, odor, patina, smell, temper, vibration(s)

related words aureole (*or* aureola), mystique, romance; genius loci; feel, feeling, sensation, sense, spirit; attribute, character, characteristic, image, mark, notion, peculiarity, picture, property, trait; color, illusion, overtone, semblance, suggestion, tone

2 a spiritual force that is held to emanate from or give animation to living beings ⟨alternative medical treatments that rely on the practitioner's ability to detect a patient's *aura*⟩ — see ENERGY 1

aural *adj* of, relating to, or experienced through the sense of hearing ⟨a quiet room for people seeking relief from the overload of *aural* stimulus just outside⟩ — see AUDITORY

aureate *adj* full of fine words and fancy expressions ⟨the *aureate* speeches that are traditionally given at graduation ceremonies⟩ — see FLOWERY 1

aureole *or* **aureola** *n* an artistic rendering of radiant light around the head or body of a sacred personage ⟨the white marble sculpture of the saint in the throes of divine ecstasy is strikingly offset by a gilt *aureole*⟩

synonyms glory, halo, nimbus

related words starburst, sunburst; aura, corona

au revoir *n* an expression of good wishes at parting ⟨the noise of the street was so loud that the quieter *au revoirs* of her friends went unheard⟩ — see GOOD-BYE

auricular *adj* of, relating to, or experienced through the sense of hearing ⟨had *auricular* proof that the sun was up, as the birds began chirping⟩ — see AUDITORY

aurora *n* the first appearance of light in the morning or the time of its appearance ⟨a gorgeous pink *aurora* aroused us out of our slumber⟩ — see DAWN 1

auspice *n* **1 auspices** *pl* the financial support and general guidance for an undertaking ⟨a program for inner-city youths that is under the *auspices* of a national corporation⟩
synonyms aegis (*also* egis), backing, patronage, sponsorship
related words bankrolling, endowment, financing, funding, subsidy; encouragement, fosterage; aid, assistance, help
2 something believed to be a sign or warning of a future event ⟨interpreted the teacher's smile as an *auspice* that he would get an A on his presentation⟩ — see OMEN

auspicious *adj* **1** having qualities which inspire hope ⟨told him she couldn't dance with him just then, but her *auspicious* smile encouraged him to ask again later⟩ — see HOPEFUL 1
2 pointing toward a happy outcome ⟨began the season with an *auspicious* win against their strongest football rival⟩ — see FAVORABLE 2

austere *adj* **1** given to exacting standards of discipline and self-restraint ⟨an *austere* conductor who is as tough on himself as he is on the orchestra⟩ — see SEVERE 1
2 harsh and threatening in manner or appearance ⟨an *austere* fortress at the top of some formidable cliffs⟩ — see GRIM 1
3 providing only the essentials and nothing fancy or luxurious ⟨for the private office of the CEO of the large corporation, the room is unexpectedly *austere*⟩ — see NO-FRILLS

autarchy *n* a system of government in which the ruler has unlimited power ⟨having just thrown off the yoke of Great Britain, the American Founding Fathers were adamantly opposed to establishing some form of homegrown *autarchy*⟩ — see DESPOTISM

authentic *adj* **1** being exactly as appears or as claimed ⟨found an *authentic* Native American arrowhead⟩
synonyms bona fide, certifiable, certified, dinkum [*Australian & New Zealand*], echt, genuine, honest, pukka (*also* pucka), real, right, sure-enough, true
related words actual, historical, original; lawful, legal, legitimate; identifiable, recognizable, verifiable; proven, substantiated, validated, verified; incontestable, incontrovertible, indisputable, indubitable, irrefutable, undeniable, undoubted, unmistakable, unquestionable; veritable, very; accurate, correct, proper; pure, unadulterated, unalloyed
phrases for real
near antonyms artificial, factitious, imitation, manmade, simulated, synthetic, unnatural; concocted, fabricated, manufactured; deceptive, delusive, delusory, misleading
antonyms bogus, counterfeit, fake, false, mock, phony (*also* phoney), pseudo, sham, spurious, suppositious, supposititious, unauthentic, unreal
2 following an original exactly ⟨an *authentic* reconstruction of the Parthenon as it is believed to have looked when first built⟩ — see FAITHFUL 2

authentically *adv* in actual fact ⟨people are surprised to learn that he is an *authentically* certified graduate of clown college⟩ — see VERY 2

authenticate *vb* **1** to declare (something) to be true or genuine ⟨a jeweler *authenticated* the diamond as real⟩ — see CERTIFY 1
2 to give evidence or testimony to the truth or factualness of ⟨we require more than simply your word to *authenticate* this story⟩ — see CONFIRM 1

author *n* **1** a person who creates a written work ⟨a brilliant novel by a first-time *author*⟩
synonyms litterateur (*or* littérateur), pen, penman, scribe, scrivener, writer
related words auteur, belletrist (*also* belle-lettrist), stylist, wordsmith; coauthor, coscenarist, cowriter; ghostwriter, hack, hatchet man, scribbler, wordmonger; biographer, hagiographer; autobiographer, memoirist, memorialist; fabulist, fictioneer, fictionist, novelist, romancer, storyteller; essayist, pamphleteer, satirist; dramatist, playwright, scenarist, screenwriter, scriptwriter; prosaist, prosateur, proser; bard, poet, rhymer, versifier; blogger, columnist, journalist, newspaperman, paragrapher, reporter, sportswriter
phrases man of letters, woman of letters
antonyms nonauthor
2 a person who establishes a whole new field of endeavor ⟨the *author* of modern genetics⟩ — see FATHER 2
3 *cap* the being worshipped as the creator and ruler of the universe ⟨let us thank the *Author* of our being for all the blessings He has bestowed⟩ — see DEITY 2

author *vb* to compose and set down on paper the words of ⟨*authored* a new biography of Thomas Jefferson⟩ — see WRITE 1

authoritarian *adj* **1** fond of ordering people around ⟨grew up with an *authoritarian* older sister who thought she was queen of the world⟩ — see BOSSY
2 given to exacting standards of discipline and self-restraint ⟨an *authoritarian* coach who runs football practice like it's boot camp⟩ — see SEVERE 1

authoritarianism *n* a system of government in which the ruler has unlimited power ⟨a critical period that saw a number of third-world countries abandon *authoritarianism* for democracy⟩ — see DESPOTISM

authoritative *adj* **1** being the most accurate and apparently thorough ⟨this book is considered the most *authoritative* source on that subject⟩ — see DEFINITIVE 1
2 having power over the minds or behavior of others ⟨after a couple of *authoritative* critics panned the movie, the other reviewers rushed to say how awful it was⟩ — see INFLUENTIAL 1
3 fond of ordering people around ⟨she's very *authoritative* for someone who doesn't actually outrank us⟩ — see BOSSY

authority *n* **1** a person with a high level of knowledge or skill in a field ⟨the leading *authority* on neural anatomy⟩ — see EXPERT
2 lawful control over the affairs of a political unit (as a nation) ⟨the sheriff had *authority* over the whole county⟩ — see RULE 2
3 the power to direct the thinking or behavior of others usually indirectly ⟨speaks with a persuasive *authority* on matters of public health⟩ — see INFLUENCE 1
4 the right or means to command or control others ⟨by the *authority* vested in me, I now pronounce you married⟩ — see POWER 1
5 something (as a belief) that serves as the basis for another thing ⟨I had good *authority* to believe that the information was correct⟩ — see REASON 2
6 something mentioned in a text as providing related and especially supporting information ⟨the Bible is the sole *authority* for his impassioned defense of creationism⟩ — see REFERENCE 1
7 the capacity to persuade ⟨a strict grammarian whose pronouncements carried plenty of *authority* with my third-grade English teacher⟩ — see COGENCY 1

authorization *n* **1** the approval by someone in authority for the doing of something ⟨you will need the *authorization* of the council before you can act⟩ — see PERMISSION
2 the granting of power to perform various acts or duties ⟨his *authorization* to go ahead with the project was finally given⟩ — see COMMISSION 1
3 the right to act or move freely ⟨granted *authorization* to enter the military facility⟩ — see FREEDOM 2

authorize *vb* **1** to give official or legal power to ⟨only the school nurse is *authorized* to give any necessary shots⟩
synonyms accredit, certify, charter [*British*], commission, empower, enable, invest, license (*also* licence), qualify, vest, warrant
related words approve, clear, credential, endorse (*also* indorse), OK (*or* okay), sanction; affirm, confirm, validate; inaugurate, induct, initiate, install, instate, swear in; allow, let, permit; enfranchise, entitle, privilege
near antonyms ban, bar, block, constrain, deny, disallow, disbar, discourage, disenfranchise, disfranchise, exclude, hinder, hold back, impede, inhibit, obstruct, prevent, shut out, stop; enjoin, forbid, interdict, outlaw, prohibit, proscribe, veto
antonyms disqualify
2 to give a right to ⟨this pass will *authorize* you to go backstage⟩ — see ENTITLE 1
3 to give official acceptance of as satisfactory ⟨a system for sound reproduction that has been *authorized* as meeting the electronic industry's highest standards⟩ — see APPROVE

authorized *adj* ordered or allowed by those in authority ⟨an *authorized* biography of the former president⟩ — see OFFICIAL

auto *n* a self-propelled passenger vehicle on four wheels ⟨the *auto* gave people a level of mobility that they had never known before⟩ — see CAR

autochthon *n* a member of the first race to inhabit a region ⟨descendants of the island's earliest settlers regard themselves as a sort of aristocracy of *autochthons*, with all others being brash interlopers⟩ — see ABORIGINE

autochthonous *adj* belonging to a particular place by birth or origin ⟨an illegally introduced Asian fish that has virtually wiped out the lake's *autochthonous* species⟩ — see NATIVE 1

autocracy *n* a system of government in which the ruler has unlimited power ⟨the Magna Carta is historically important because it signified the British rejection of *autocracy* and constituted the first formal restraining of the power of the monarch⟩ — see DESPOTISM

autocrat *n* one who rules over a people with a sole, supreme, and usually hereditary authority ⟨European *autocrats* once commonly believed that they had received the right to rule directly from God⟩ — see MONARCH 1

autocratic *also* **autocratical** *adj* **1** exercising power or authority without interference by others ⟨democracy is supposed to protect the people against the rise of *autocratic* rulers⟩ — see ABSOLUTE 1
2 fond of ordering people around ⟨an *autocratic* Boy Scout leader who is under the delusion that he's still an army colonel⟩ — see BOSSY

autodidactic *adj* having skills or knowledge acquired through one's own efforts without formal training ⟨an *autodidactic* painter, John Singleton Copley learned his craft from books purchased from England⟩ — see SELF-TAUGHT

autograph *n* a person's name written in their own handwriting often given to indicate awareness or consent ⟨she added her *autograph* to the joint tax return⟩ — see SIGNATURE

autograph *vb* to write one's name on (as a document) ⟨asked the baseball player to *autograph* the bill of his cap⟩ — see SIGN

automated *adj* designed to replace or decrease human labor and especially physical labor ⟨an *automated* facility in which you can get your car washed without having encountered a single human being⟩ — see LABORSAVING

automatic *adj* **1** done instantly and without conscious thought or decision ⟨Carl's *automatic* use of the brakes narrowly averted a collision⟩
synonyms instinctive, instinctual, involuntary, knee-jerk, mechanic, mechanical, robotic, spontaneous
related words conditioned, natural, Pavlovian, reactive, reflex, simple, subliminal, unconscious, unforced, visceral; blind, inadvertent, unintended, unintentional, unwilling, unwitting; abrupt, quick, ready, sudden; ad-lib, extemporaneous, extempore, impromptu, improvised, offhand, offhanded, off-the-cuff, snap, spur-of-the-moment, unconsidered, unplanned, unpremeditated, unprepared, unprompted, unreasoned, unrehearsed, unstudied; casual, chance, chancy, haphazard, hasty, hit-or-miss, impetuous, impulsive, mindless, random, rash
near antonyms calculated, conscious, cultivated, deliberate, designed, intended, intentional, predetermined, prepared, projected, refined, rehearsed, volitional, voluntary, willed, willful (*or* wilful); advised, aforethought, careful, considered, foresighted, forethoughtful, measured, meticulous, reasoned, studied, thoughtful
antonyms nonmechanical
2 designed to replace or decrease human labor and especially physical labor ⟨liked the ease of an *automatic* CD changer⟩ — see LABORSAVING

automation *n* the process of putting an apparatus, operation, or system under the control or regulation of mechanical or electronic devices ⟨feared that *automation* would add millions to the ranks of the unemployed⟩
synonyms mechanization, robotization
related words computerization, cybernation; electrification, motorization

automobile *n* a self-propelled passenger vehicle on four wheels ⟨browsed the classified ads for used *automobiles* for sale⟩ — see CAR

automobile *vb* to travel by a motorized vehicle ⟨would rather *automobile* across the country than fly over it at 35,000 feet⟩ — see DRIVE 2

automobilist *n* a person who travels by automobile ⟨with the introduction of affordable, mass-produced cars, more and more people left their horses at home and became *automobilists*⟩ — see MOTORIST

autonomous *adj* not being under the rule or control of another ⟨Native American nations are regarded as *autonomous* in many respects and thus not subject to a number of state and local laws⟩ — see FREE 1

autonomy *n* **1** the act or power of making one's own choices or decisions ⟨the director agreed to make the film only on the condition that she be given complete *autonomy* for the casting⟩ — see FREE WILL
2 the state of being free from the control or power of another ⟨finding the mother country's treatment of them oppressive and intolerable, the 13 British colonies made the momentous decision to seek *autonomy*⟩ — see FREEDOM 1

autopsy *n* examination of a dead body especially to find out the cause of death ⟨the *autopsy* revealed an advanced stage of cancer⟩
synonyms necropsy, postmortem, postmortem examination
related words dissection
near antonyms biopsy, vivisection

autumn *n* a later period of one's life ⟨with *autumn* came a mellowness of spirit that she had never shown before⟩ — see AGE 3

auxiliary *adj* available to supply something extra when needed ⟨the auditorium has an *auxiliary* cooling system used only on particularly sweltering days⟩
synonyms accessorial, accessory, appurtenant, peripheral, supplemental, supplementary
related words backup, makeshift, substitute; added, additional, another, further; complementary, contribu-

tory; adjuvant, assistant, assisting, helping, supportive, tributary; secondary, subordinate, subservient, subsidiary; dispensable, excess, nonessential, superfluous, surplus, unessential
near antonyms basic, fundamental, primary, prime; all-important, essential, imperative, indispensable, integral, necessary, needed, needful, required, requisite, vital
antonyms chief, main, principal

avail *n* the capacity for being useful for some purpose ⟨although I appreciate the concern, your help would be of little *avail* in this situation⟩ — see USE 2

avail *vb* to provide with something useful or desirable ⟨all your begging will not *avail* you in the least⟩ — see BENEFIT

available *adj* **1** possible to get ⟨the nursery's orchids are *available* by mail order only⟩ ⟨fare information is readily *available* by using the toll-free number⟩
synonyms accessible, acquirable, attainable, obtainable, procurable
related words getatable, reachable; appropriable, purchasable, rentable; furnished, provided, supplied; common, omnipresent, prevalent, ubiquitous, universal, widespread; free, free-for-all, open, public, unrestricted
phrases at the ready, on hand, on file, on tap
near antonyms limited, off-limits, restricted; deficient, lacking, missing, rare, scarce, uncommon
antonyms inaccessible, unattainable, unavailable, unobtainable
2 capable of or suitable for being used for a particular purpose ⟨my car is *available* should you need a way to get to the mall⟩ — see USABLE 1

avant *adj* being or employing the latest concepts, styles, or techniques ⟨readers of this very *avant* novel should not expect to find much in the way of traditional narrative structure⟩
synonyms advanced, avant-garde, cutting-edge, progressive, state-of-the-art
related words pioneering, revolutionary, trailblazing; alternative, antiestablishment, nontraditional, unconventional, underground; bizarre, far-out, outré, way-out; fresh, new, novel, original; strange, unaccustomed, unfamiliar, unheard-of, unknown, unprecedented; contemporary, current, hot, mod, modern, modernistic, newfangled, new-fashioned, present-day, red-hot, space-age, ultramodern, up-to-date
near antonyms conventional, customary, established, orthodox, traditional

avant-garde *adj* being or employing the latest concepts, styles, or techniques ⟨a very *avant-garde* artist whose works wouldn't even be considered art by many traditionalists⟩ — see AVANT

avant-garde *n* the innovators of new concepts, styles, and techniques especially in the arts ⟨to the theater world's *avant-garde*, the melodrama seemed like a very old-fashioned play whose time had come and gone⟩
synonyms cutting edge, van, vanguard
related words underground; avant-gardist, forerunner, pioneer, precursor, trailblazer
near antonyms establishment, old guard

avarice *n* an intense selfish desire for wealth or possessions ⟨the bank official's embezzlement was motivated by pure *avarice*⟩ — see GREED

avaricious *adj* having or marked by an eager and often selfish desire especially for material possessions ⟨an *avaricious* scheme to con the elderly couple out of thousands of dollars⟩ — see GREEDY 1

avariciousness *n* an intense selfish desire for wealth or possessions ⟨their all-consuming *avariciousness* blinds them to the suffering of people just beyond their doorstep⟩ — see GREED

avatar *n* a visible representation of something abstract (as a quality) ⟨our genial hosts, *avatars* of Southern hospitality⟩ — see EMBODIMENT

ave *n* an expression of good wishes at parting ⟨after a final *ave*, we turned our backs on the Tuscan village that had been our home for a year⟩ — see GOOD-BYE

avenge *vb* to punish in kind the wrongdoer responsible for ⟨a play about a prince who struggles to *avenge* his father's death⟩
synonyms redress, requite, retaliate, revenge, venge [*archaic*]
related words castigate, fix, get, penalize, punish, scourge; chasten, chastise, correct, discipline; right; compensate, pay (back), recompense, repay
phrases get even (for)
near antonyms absolve, condone, excuse, forgive, pardon, remit

avenger *n* one who inflicts punishment in return for an injury or offense ⟨a novel about a man who becomes the obsessed *avenger* of his sister's death⟩ — see NEMESIS 1

avenue *n* **1** a passage cleared for public vehicular travel ⟨a city famous for its broad, tree-lined *avenues*⟩ — see WAY 1
2 an established course for traveling from one place to another ⟨the two main *avenues* available to those joining in the California gold rush were the trail across the Southwest desert or the hazard-filled loop around Central and South America⟩ — see PASSAGE 1

aver *vb* **1** to state as a fact usually forcefully ⟨was tearfully *averring* his innocence⟩ — see CLAIM 1
2 to state clearly and strongly ⟨*averred* that she didn't need any help choosing her own clothes⟩ — see ASSERT 1

average *adj* **1** being about midway between extremes of amount or size ⟨since a Chihuahua seems as impractical as a Saint Bernard, let's get a dog of more *average* dimensions⟩ — see MIDDLE 2
2 being of the type that is encountered in the normal course of events ⟨just an *average* day at the office⟩ — see ORDINARY 1
3 having or showing the qualities associated with the members of a particular group or kind ⟨the company's marketing people want to interview *average* teenagers to see what kinds of clothes appeal to them⟩ — see TYPICAL 1

average *n* what is typical of a group, class, or series ⟨my cat's a cut above the *average* when it comes to being a finicky eater⟩
synonyms norm, normal, par, standard
related words golden mean, mean, median, middle; commonplace, ordinary, rule, run, status quo, usual; exemplar, representative
near antonyms abnormality, anomaly, deviation, exception, rarity

averse *adj* having a natural dislike for something ⟨I'm not *averse* to broccoli if it's cooked right⟩ — see ANTIPATHETIC 1

averseness *n* a strong feeling of not liking or approving ⟨our dog's strong *averseness* to getting a bath⟩ — see DISLIKE 1

aversion *n* **1** a dislike so strong as to cause stomach upset or queasiness ⟨I simply have this ingrained *aversion* to the sight of bloodshed⟩ — see DISGUST
2 a strong feeling of not liking or approving ⟨couldn't overcome her *aversion* to her brother-in-law and pointedly avoided his company⟩ — see DISLIKE 1
3 something or someone that is hated ⟨clichés should be the pet *aversion* of every good writer⟩ — see HATE 2

avert *vb* to keep from happening by taking action in advance ⟨her careful planning *averted* disaster⟩ — see PREVENT

averting *n* the act or practice of keeping something

from happening ⟨the *averting* of forest fires can be helped by the clearing of dry underbrush⟩ — see PREVENTION

aviate *vb* to move through the air with or as if with outstretched wings ⟨once humankind learned how to *aviate*, the world became a much smaller place⟩ — see FLY 1

aviator *n* one who flies or is qualified to fly an aircraft or spacecraft ⟨the solo flight from New York to Paris by the *aviator* Charles Lindbergh captured the imagination of people around the world⟩ — see PILOT

avid *adj* **1** having or marked by an eager and often selfish desire especially for material possessions ⟨stared at the array of jewels with an *avid* glint in his eye⟩ — see GREEDY 1

2 showing urgent desire or interest ⟨an *avid* baseball card collector⟩ — see EAGER

avidity *n* **1** an intense selfish desire for wealth or possessions ⟨an advanced case of *avidity* that led to shoplifting at the tender age of 13⟩ — see GREED

2 urgent desire or interest ⟨in her *avidity* to express her opinions, she frequently and unthinkingly interrupts people⟩ — see EAGERNESS

avidness *n* **1** an intense selfish desire for wealth or possessions ⟨with the *avidness* of a child in a candy store, scores of holiday shoppers raced to grab the early-bird specials⟩ — see GREED

2 urgent desire or interest ⟨he approaches every new challenge in life with the *avidness* of a man half his age⟩ — see EAGERNESS

avocation *n* an activity outside of one's regular occupation that is engaged in primarily for pleasure ⟨photography is merely an *avocation* for me—I've never tried to make money off of it⟩

synonyms hobby, hobbyhorse, pursuit, recreation

related words amusement, distraction, diversion, entertainment, pastime, relaxation, sport

avocational *adj* being such only for recreation ⟨just a bunch of *avocational* rockers who get together in a garage on weekends⟩

synonyms amateur, backyard, jackleg, nonprofessional, Sunday

related words naive (*or* naïve), primitive, self-taught; amateurish, dilettante, inexperienced, inexpert, unprofessional, unskilled; uninitiated, unprepared, unqualified, unschooled, untaught, untrained, untutored; part-time, weekend

avoid *vb* **1** to get or keep away from (as a responsibility) through cleverness or trickery ⟨trying to *avoid* writing thank-you notes for the gifts he didn't like⟩ — see ESCAPE 2

2 to put an end to by formal action ⟨asked the court to *avoid* the contract because it was signed under duress⟩ — see ABOLISH 1

avoidance *n* **1** the act or a means of getting or keeping away from something undesirable ⟨her congenital *avoidance* of conflict makes talking about problems with her difficult⟩ — see ESCAPE 2

2 the doing away with something by formal action ⟨plans to petition the court for an *avoidance* of the prenuptial agreement⟩ — see ABOLITION

avoirdupois *n* **1** the amount that something weighs ⟨the coach limited his recruiting to linebackers of a certain *avoirdupois*⟩ — see WEIGHT 1

2 the state or quality of being heavy ⟨told his patient that he had to do something about his unhealthy *avoirdupois* and that exercising would be a good start⟩ — see WEIGHTINESS 1

avouch *vb* **1** to declare (something) to be true or genuine ⟨a note from my doctor *avouching* that my medical condition did indeed disqualify me from gym class⟩ — see CERTIFY 1

2 to state as a fact usually forcefully ⟨*avouched* that he had never cheated on his taxes in his life⟩ — see CLAIM 1

3 to state clearly and strongly ⟨she tends to *avouch* her opinions in such a way as to imply that anyone who thinks otherwise is an idiot⟩ — see ASSERT 1

avouchment *n* a solemn and often public declaration of the truth or existence of something ⟨your *avouchment* of his good intentions means he won't be disciplined⟩ — see PROTESTATION

avow *vb* **1** to state as a fact usually forcefully ⟨*avowed* that the colonization of Mars in our lifetime is not only possible but probable⟩ — see CLAIM 1

2 to state clearly and strongly ⟨*avowed* their undying love for each other⟩ — see ASSERT 1

avowal *n* **1** a solemn and often public declaration of the truth or existence of something ⟨with jingoism rampant, the peace candidate felt compelled to make an *avowal* of his patriotism⟩ — see PROTESTATION

2 an open declaration of something (as a fault or the commission of an offense) about oneself ⟨her own *avowal* that she was to blame for the accident⟩ — see CONFESSION

await *vb* **1** to believe in the future occurrence of (something) ⟨members of the sect are confidently *awaiting* the imminent end of the world⟩ — see EXPECT

2 to remain in place in readiness or expectation of something ⟨crowds had been *awaiting* in the streets for hours⟩ — see WAIT

awaited *adj* being in accordance with the prescribed, normal, or logical course of events ⟨at the *awaited* moment the President walked up to the lectern and began his address to the nation⟩ — see DUE 2

awake *adj* **1** not sleeping or able to sleep ⟨was *awake* until 3:00 a.m.⟩ — see WAKEFUL

2 paying close attention usually for the purpose of anticipating approaching danger or opportunity ⟨*awake* to the possibility of trouble at the demonstration⟩ — see ALERT 1

awake *vb* **1** to cause to stop sleeping ⟨*awoke* the boys for breakfast⟩ — see WAKE 1

2 to cease to be asleep ⟨at the sound of breaking glass she *awoke* with a start⟩ — see WAKE 2

awaken *vb* **1** to cause to stop sleeping ⟨be quiet or you'll *awaken* the kids⟩ — see WAKE 1

2 to cease to be asleep ⟨guests at the B and B usually *awaken* to the smell of fresh pancakes⟩ — see WAKE 2

award *n* **1** something given in recognition of achievement ⟨Faye received the highest *award* in the 16 and under category for her poem⟩

synonyms accolade, blue ribbon, decoration, distinction, honor, kudo, plume, premium, prize

related words badge, crown, cup, laurel, medal, order, plaque, plate, ribbon, trophy; applause, bravo, encomium, eulogy, hallelujah, homage, paean, panegyric, plaudit, tribute; citation, commendation, compliment, honorable mention

2 a position arrived at after consideration ⟨in their *award* the board of arbitrators declared that both writers deserved screen credit for their contributions to the final screenplay⟩ — see DECISION 1

award *vb* **1** to give something as a token of gratitude or admiration for a service or achievement ⟨we will *award* the top three contestants in the essay competition⟩ — see REWARD

2 to give the ownership or benefit of (something) formally or publicly ⟨custody of the boy was *awarded* to the grandparents⟩ — see CONFER 1

aware *adj* having specified facts or feelings actively impressed on the mind ⟨as she was being wheeled out of surgery, she became dimly *aware* that her parents were in the room⟩ — see CONSCIOUS 1

awareness *n* a state of being aware ⟨while strolling in the big city, maintain an *awareness* of what's going on around you⟩ — see ATTENTION 2

awash *adj* **1** containing, covered with, or thoroughly penetrated by water ⟨the streets were *awash* from the heavy rains⟩ — see WET 1

2 possessing or covered with great numbers or amounts of something specified ⟨the literary review is currently *awash* in submissions and will not be accepting any more until next year⟩ — see RIFE

away *adj* **1** not close in time or space ⟨the store is far *away* from here⟩ ⟨Passover is still three months *away*⟩ — see DISTANT 1

2 not at a certain place ⟨he's *away* right now, but he should be back at the office next week⟩ — see ABSENT 1

away *adv* from this or that place ⟨don't walk *away* while I'm still talking to you⟩

synonyms down, fro, hence, off, out

related words apart, aside, elsewhere; abroad, afar, afield, astray

awe *n* the rapt attention and deep emotion caused by the sight of something extraordinary ⟨was in *awe* of the sinewy Olympic runners⟩ — see WONDER 2

aweary *adj, archaic* depleted in strength, energy, or freshness ⟨the famous lament of Tennyson's Mariana: "I am *aweary* . . . I would that I were dead!"⟩ — see WEARY 1

awed *adj* filled with amazement or wonder ⟨gave the nationally known golfer an *awed* look⟩ — see OPEN-MOUTHED

awesome *adj* **1** causing wonder or astonishment ⟨the *awesome* power of the sea⟩ — see MARVELOUS 1

2 of the very best kind ⟨the food at the Sunday brunch was just *awesome*⟩ — see EXCELLENT

awestruck *also* **awestricken** *adj* **1** affected with sudden and great wonder or surprise ⟨the crowds were *awestruck* by the aerial feats of the stunt pilots⟩ — see THUNDERSTRUCK

2 filled with amazement or wonder ⟨*awestruck* by the majesty of the Sierra Nevada Mountains⟩ — see OPEN-MOUTHED

awful *adj* **1** causing intense displeasure, disgust, or resentment ⟨that's an *awful* thing to say about someone⟩ — see OFFENSIVE 1

2 causing wonder or astonishment ⟨the *awful* power of Niagara Falls⟩ — see MARVELOUS 1

3 extremely disturbing or repellent ⟨spare me the *awful* details of the murder⟩ — see HORRIBLE 1

4 extremely unsatisfactory ⟨I can't believe I spent good money to see that movie—it was *awful*⟩ — see WRETCHED 1

awful *adv* to a great degree ⟨that's *awful* sweet of you⟩ — see VERY 1

awfully *adv* to a great degree ⟨I'm *awfully* sorry⟩ — see VERY 1

awfulness *n* the quality of inspiring intense dread or dismay ⟨the *awfulness* of the car accident can scarcely be described⟩ — see HORROR 1

awkward *adj* **1** lacking social grace and assurance ⟨preteens feeling *awkward* at their first formal dance⟩

synonyms clumsy, gauche, graceless, inelegant, roughhewn, rustic (*also* rustical), stiff, stilted, uncomfortable, uneasy, ungraceful, wooden

related words angular, gawky, lubberly, ungainly; boorish, clownish, uncouth; abashed, discomfited, discomforted, discomposed, disconcerted, discountenanced, embarrassed; self-conscious; agitated, bothered, chagrined, dismayed, disquieted, distressed, disturbed, fazed, flustered, jittery, jumpy, mortified, nervous, nonplussed (*also* nonplused), perturbed, rattled, unhinged, unsettled, upset; diffident, insecure, meek, modest, self-doubting, timid, unassertive, unassuming, unpretentious

near antonyms assured, calm, collected, composed, confident, cool, placid, poised, secure, self-assured, self-confident, self-possessed, serene, tranquil, undisturbed, unperturbed

antonyms graceful, suave, urbane

2 showing or marked by a lack of skill and tact (as in dealing with a situation) ⟨her *awkward* handling of the seating arrangements at the wedding reception resulted in many hurt feelings⟩

synonyms botched, bungling, clumsy, fumbled, inept, inexpert, maladroit

related words amateur, amateurish, crude, green, incompetent, ineffectual, inefficient, inexperienced, unpolished, unprofessional, unskilled, unskillful; careless, sloppy, tacky, tactless, undiplomatic; ill-advised, ineffective, ineffectual, misdirected, misguided

near antonyms able, accomplished, adept, capable, clever, competent, consummate, crackerjack, expert, masterful, masterly, polished, professional, proficient, skilled, skillful, talented; diplomatic, easy, effortless, gracious, smooth, tactful

antonyms adroit, deft, dexterous (*also* dextrous), facile

3 causing embarrassment ⟨the *awkward* situation of having to listen as your host and hostess quarrel loudly in the next room⟩

synonyms discomfiting, disconcerting, disturbing, embarrassing, flustering, uncomfortable

related words confusing, difficult, disagreeable, impossible, inconvenient, intolerable, troublesome, unpleasant, unwieldy; unsettling; debasing, degrading, demeaning, humbling, humiliating, mortifying

near antonyms agreeable, comfortable, convenient, pleasing

4 causing difficulty, discomfort, or annoyance ⟨our surprise guests came at a very *awkward* time⟩ — see INCONVENIENT 1

5 difficult to use or operate especially because of size, weight, or design ⟨that manual can opener is *awkward* to hold⟩ — see CUMBERSOME

6 having or showing an inability to move in a graceful manner ⟨an *awkward* person who is always tripping over herself⟩ — see CLUMSY 2

7 lacking or showing a lack of nimbleness in using one's hands ⟨an *awkward* catch of a fly ball⟩ — see CLUMSY 1

awning *n* a raised covering over something for decoration or protection ⟨stayed under the *awning* outside the shop during the rainstorm⟩ — see CANOPY

awry *adj* inclined or twisted to one side ⟨the shutters that still remained on the run-down old house were all *awry*⟩

synonyms askew, aslant, atilt, cock-a-hoop, cockeyed, crazy, crooked, listing, lopsided, oblique, off-kilter, pitched, skewed, slanted, slanting, slantwise, tilted, tipping, uneven

related words asymmetrical (*or* asymmetric), unbalanced, unsymmetrical; contorted, disordered, distorted, irregular

phrases out of plumb (*or* off plumb)

near antonyms ordered, orderly, regular, uniform; balanced, symmetrical (*or* symmetric)

antonyms even, level, straight

awry *adv* off the desired or intended path or course ⟨their plans for an outdoor wedding went *awry* when they got a freak hailstorm the night before⟩ — see WRONG 1

aw–shucks *adj* lacking in worldly wisdom or informed judgment ⟨his persona may be that of an *aw-shucks* country singer, but offstage he is anything but⟩ — see NAIVE 1

ax *or* **axe** *n* the termination of the employment of an employee or a work force often temporarily ⟨the company was hemorrhaging money, so 700 employees would soon be given the *ax*⟩ — see LAYOFF 1

ax *or* **axe** *vb* to let go from office, service, or employment ⟨the boss will *ax* anyone who leaks company secrets⟩ — see DISMISS 1

axiomatic *adj* not needing proof in order to be accepted ⟨it's *axiomatic* that the instinct for self-preservation is universal throughout the animal kingdom⟩
synonyms prima facie, self-evident
related words self-explanatory; apparent, clear, evident, hands-down, manifest, obvious, open-and-shut, patent, plain, transparent, unmistakable; incontestable, incontrovertible, indisputable, indubitable, undeniable, unquestionable; accepted, given, granted
near antonyms arguable, contestable, debatable, disputable, doubtable, dubious, moot, problematic (*also* problematical), questionable

axis *n* **1** a thing or place that is of greatest importance to an activity or interest ⟨in addition to being the suburb's social *axis*, the country club is the place where deals are made and partnerships are forged⟩ — see CENTER 1
2 an association of persons, parties, or states for mutual assistance and protection ⟨an *axis* of previously nonaligned nations⟩ — see CONFEDERACY

ay *interj* used to express sorrow or distress ⟨*ay* me, we are doomed to listen to that noise all night!⟩ — see ALAS

[1]**aye** *also* **ay** *adv* **1** on every relevant occasion ⟨I *aye* thought that she was the loveliest woman I ever laid eyes on⟩ — see ALWAYS 1
2 for all time ⟨a friendship that will *aye* endure⟩ — see EVER 1

[2]**aye** *also* **ay** *adv* used to express agreement ⟨*aye*, you're right about that⟩ — see YES

B

babble *n* unintelligible or meaningless talk ⟨the baby's good-natured *babble* and random gurglings were cute, but not very helpful in determining what he wanted⟩ — see GIBBERISH 1

babble *vb* **1** to speak rapidly, inarticulately, and usually unintelligibly ⟨in such a rush to tell us the news that she just *babbled*⟩
synonyms bumble, chat, chatter, drivel, drool, gabble, gibber, jabber, prattle, sputter
related words blabber, blather, bleat, blither, gab, jangle, jaw, patter, prate, rattle, run on, smatter, tittle-tattle, troll, yak (*also* yack); chunter [*British*], maunder, mouth, mumble, murmur, mutter; stammer, stutter; screech, shout, shriek
near antonyms articulate, enunciate, pronounce
2 to engage in casual or rambling conversation ⟨the little girls *babbled* contentedly for the whole ride home⟩ — see CHAT 1

babbler *n* a person who talks constantly ⟨spending too much time with that *babbler* gives me a headache⟩ — see CHATTERBOX

babe *n* **1** a person who is just starting out in a field of activity ⟨although I worked with film for years, I'm just a *babe* as far as digital photography is concerned⟩ — see BEGINNER
2 a recently born person ⟨a *babe* in arms, too young even to crawl⟩ — see BABY 1
3 *slang* a lovely woman ⟨that woman's a total *babe*⟩ — see BEAUTY 2
4 *slang* a physically attractive person ⟨a beach resort that attracts well-tanned *babes* of both sexes⟩ — see DOLL 2

babel *n* **1** a place of uproar or confusion ⟨on opening day the area's newest big-box store was an incredible *babel*⟩ — see MADHOUSE 2
2 loud, confused, and usually inharmonious sound ⟨the *babel* of languages and accents that can be heard at the city's farmers' market every weekend⟩ — see NOISE 1

babushka *n* a scarf worn on the head ⟨an elderly Russian woman with a *babushka*⟩ — see BANDANNA

baby *n* **1** a recently born person ⟨the *baby* is just learning to sit up, so be careful⟩
synonyms babe, bambino, child, infant, neonate, newborn
related words cherub; foundling, nursling, suckling; preemie (*also* premie); papoose; bantling, kid, kiddie (*also* kiddy), kiddo, moppet, toddler, tot, tyke (*also* tike); boy, nipper, tad; juvenile, minor, youngling, youngster, youth; brat, imp, squirt, urchin, whippersnapper; girl, hoyden, tomboy
near antonyms adult, grown-up; elder, graybeard, oldster, old-timer, senior, senior citizen
2 a member of the human race ⟨I don't care what you want, there'll be no housecleaning for this *baby*⟩ — see HUMAN
3 a successful result brought about by hard work ⟨a small film that was a labor of love and the *baby* that the director was proudest of⟩ — see ACCOMPLISHMENT 1
4 a person who makes frequent complaints usually about little things ⟨he becomes a big *baby* when his wife is out of town and he's expected to fend for himself at suppertime⟩ — see CRYBABY

baby *vb* to treat with great or excessive care ⟨he *babied* his car, faithfully washing it every week⟩
synonyms cocker, coddle, cosset, dandle, indulge, mollycoddle, nurse, pamper, spoil, wet-nurse
related words cater (to), humor; content, delight, gladden, gratify, mother, oblige, please, satisfy; appease, mollify, pacify, placate, soothe
near antonyms control, discipline, restrain; oppress; neglect, overlook, slight; molest, outrage, violate; harass, harm, hurt, injure, oppress, persecute, torment, torture, victimize
antonyms abuse, ill-treat, ill-use, maltreat, manhandle, mishandle, mistreat, misuse

baby buggy *n* a small four-wheeled vehicle designed for pushing a baby around in ⟨a reluctant father who isn't looking forward to pushing a *baby buggy* around the park⟩ — see BABY CARRIAGE

baby carriage *n* a small four-wheeled vehicle designed

for pushing a baby around in ⟨twins in a double *baby carriage*⟩
synonyms baby buggy, buggy, perambulator [*chiefly British*], pram [*chiefly British*], pushchair [*chiefly British*], stroller
related words bassinet, cradle, crib; carry-cot [*British*]

babyish *adj* having or showing the annoying qualities (as silliness) associated with children ⟨the boy now thinks that playing with blocks is a rather *babyish* activity⟩ — see CHILDISH

Babylonian *adj* showing obvious signs of wealth and comfort ⟨the *Babylonian* glitter of the city's gold coast⟩ — see LUXURIOUS 1

babysitter *n* a girl or woman employed to care for a young child or children ⟨a *babysitter* who is a great favorite with the kids because she's always thinking of fun things to do⟩ — see NURSE

bach *n, New Zealand* an often small house for recreational or seasonal use ⟨maintains a *bach* in South Island's Fiordland⟩ — see COTTAGE

back *adj* being at or in the part of something opposite the front part ⟨she carried all the presents in the *back* door, as the children were playing in the front yard⟩
synonyms aft, after, hind, hinder, hindmost, posterior, rear, rearward
related words dorsal
near antonyms ventral
antonyms anterior, fore, forward, front, frontal

back *adv* **1** earlier than the present time ⟨that's longer *back* than I can remember⟩ — see AGO
2 toward the opposite direction ⟨turned *back* for one last comment⟩ — see AROUND 2
3 toward the rear ⟨staring *back*, the newly convicted felon vowed revenge⟩ — see BACKWARD 1

back *n* **1** a behind part or surface ⟨the *back* of the page was blank⟩ — see REAR 1
2 a vulnerable point ⟨a candidate needing a loyal aide who can be relied upon to always watch his *back*⟩ — see ACHILLES' HEEL

back *vb* **1** to promote the interests or cause of ⟨she enthusiastically *backed* the plan to renovate and upgrade the school's facilities⟩ — see SUPPORT 1
2 to provide (someone) with what is useful or necessary to achieve an end ⟨a number of influential people have already agreed to *back* the candidate⟩ — see HELP 1
3 to provide evidence or information for (as a claim or idea) ⟨the author needs to *back* her thesis with more facts⟩ — see SUPPORT 4

back-and-forth *n* **1** a giving or taking of one thing of value in return for another ⟨after the usual *back-and-forth* of official gifts, the two leaders entered into a serious discussion⟩ — see EXCHANGE 1
2 an exchange of views for the purpose of exploring a subject or deciding an issue ⟨the others listened with relish to the *back-and-forth* between the two noted professors⟩ — see DISCUSSION 1

back away *vb* to move back or away (as from something difficult, dangerous, or disagreeable) ⟨*backed away* from the snake very slowly and carefully⟩ — see RETREAT 1

backbone *n* **1** a column of bones supporting the trunk of a vertebrate animal ⟨found the *backbone* of a fish lying on the beach⟩ — see SPINE
2 the strength of mind that enables a person to endure pain or hardship ⟨it takes *backbone* to stand up to the kind of suffering that some cancer patients must endure⟩ — see FORTITUDE

backbreaking *adj* requiring considerable physical or mental effort ⟨modern machinery has significantly eased the *backbreaking* work of farming⟩ — see HARD 2

backchat *n* **1** disrespectful or argumentative talk given in response to a command or request ⟨there'll be no *backchat* from you, young lady⟩ — see BACK TALK
2 friendly, informal conversation or an instance of this ⟨bored with the usual *backchat* with which people whiled away the lunch hour⟩ — see CHAT 1
3 good-natured teasing or exchanging of clever remarks ⟨outsiders sometimes mistook their constant *backchat* for spiteful bickering⟩ — see BANTER

backcountry *n* a rural region that forms the edge of the settled or developed part of a country ⟨he took a month's supplies and headed out to the *backcountry*⟩ — see FRONTIER 2

back down *vb* to break a promise or agreement ⟨if you *back down* about dinner again, I'm not going to agree to another date⟩ — see RENEGE 1

backdrop *n* the physical conditions or features that form the setting against which something is viewed ⟨visitors dine at the restaurant with a dramatic stretch of the Pacific Ocean as a jaw-dropping *backdrop*⟩ — see BACKGROUND 1

backer *n* **1** a person who actively supports or favors a cause ⟨*backers* of prison reform held a rally in front of the statehouse⟩ — see EXPONENT 1
2 a person who takes the responsibility for some other person or thing ⟨all financial *backers* will be expected to offer some input into the company's decisions⟩ — see SPONSOR
3 someone associated with another to give assistance or moral support ⟨the student's *backers* spoke at the school board meeting on her behalf⟩ — see ALLY

backfire *vb* to have the reverse of the desired or expected effect ⟨my plan to throw her a surprise party *backfired* when she ended up sobbing that everyone had forgotten her birthday⟩
synonyms boomerang
related words collapse, flop, flunk, fold, wash out; flounder, struggle; decline, slip, slump, wane
near antonyms succeed; flourish, prosper, thrive

background *n* **1** the physical conditions or features that form the setting against which something is viewed ⟨they got married on a mountain top with the sunset as *background*⟩
synonyms backdrop, ground
related words mise-en-scène, scene, scenery, set, stage; entourage, environment, milieu, setting, surroundings
near antonyms foreground; center, focal point, focus, heart
2 the place and time in which the action for a portion of a dramatic work (as a movie) is set ⟨the *background* of that movie is the World War II era⟩ — see SCENE 1

backhanded *adj* not being or expressing what one appears to be or express ⟨"You throw okay, for a girl" is a bit of a *backhanded* compliment⟩ — see INSINCERE

backhander *n, British* something given or promised in order to improperly influence a person's conduct or decision ⟨the customs official let us know that he might be prepared to look the other way if an appropriate *backhander* was slipped into his palm⟩ — see BRIBE

backing *n* **1** an act or instance of helping ⟨the teacher's *backing* on the science project was invaluable⟩ — see HELP 1
2 the financial support and general guidance for an undertaking ⟨the museum exhibition would not have been possible without corporate *backing*⟩ — see AUSPICE 1

backland *n, usually* **backlands** *pl* a rural region that forms the edge of the settled or developed part of a country ⟨they purposely vacationed in the *backlands* to get away from people⟩ — see FRONTIER 2

back of *prep* at, to, or toward the rear of ⟨the equipment shed is a concrete structure *back of* the school⟩ — see BEHIND 1

back off *vb* to break a promise or agreement ⟨you'd better not *back off* on your promise to do all the planning for the big dance⟩ — see RENEGE 1

back out *vb* to break a promise or agreement ⟨she *backed out* on her offer to help with the wedding planning⟩ — see RENEGE 1

backpack *n* a soft-sided case designed for carrying belongings especially on the back ⟨stuffed her *backpack* with so many books that she could barely walk⟩ — see PACK 1

backside *n* the part of the body upon which someone sits ⟨our *backsides* were sore after sitting on those hard benches for so long⟩ — see BUTTOCKS

backslapper *n* a gregarious and unreserved person ⟨a career in politics appeals to him, but he's not a *backslapper* by nature⟩ — see EXTROVERT

backslider *n* a person who has sunk below the normal moral standard ⟨the evangelist was determined to win back the *backsliders* who had fallen away⟩ — see DEGENERATE

backstab *vb* to be unfaithful or disloyal to ⟨knew what it felt like to be *backstabbed* by a so-called friend⟩ — see BETRAY 1

backstabber *n* one who betrays a trust or an allegiance ⟨a *backstabber* taking credit for work she didn't do while bad-mouthing the rest of the team to the boss⟩ — see TRAITOR

backstabbing *n* the act or fact of violating the trust or confidence of another ⟨a reality TV show that seems to have raised *backstabbing* to an art form⟩ — see BETRAYAL

backstage *adv* in a manner intended to prevent knowledge or awareness by others ⟨some of the most important decisions were made *backstage*, and only presented to the full committee afterward⟩ — see PRIVATELY

backstairs *adj* undertaken or done so as to escape being observed or known by others ⟨an influential Washington lobbyist who has been involved in a number of *backstairs* deals to limit regulation of financial institutions⟩ — see SECRET 1

backstop *vb* to provide (someone) with what is useful or necessary to achieve an end ⟨the Nobel-winning geneticist was of course *backstopped* in his research by a team of highly talented assistants⟩ — see HELP 1

back talk *n* disrespectful or argumentative talk given in response to a command or request ⟨his mother sent him to his room because of his constant *back talk*⟩
synonyms backchat, cheek, impertinence, impudence, insolence, mouth, sass, sauce
related words comeback, rejoinder, retort, riposte, wisecrack; cuteness, discourtesy, disrespect, guff, impoliteness, nonsense, rudeness, tactlessness; audaciousness, audacity, boldness, brazenness; coarseness, crassness, crudity, vulgarity; abruptness, bluffness, bluntness, brusqueness, crossness, curtness, gruffness, surliness
near antonyms civility, cordiality, courtesy, diplomacy, politeness, tactfulness; consideration, gallantry, gentility, graciousness, smoothness, suaveness, suavity; deference, respect; affability

back-to-back *adj* following one after another without others coming in between ⟨the new governor was soon facing several *back-to-back* crises⟩ — see CONSECUTIVE

back-to-back *adv* in succession without others coming in between ⟨the three movies in the series were filmed *back-to-back* so that the cast members wouldn't age visibly on screen⟩ — see CONSECUTIVELY

backup *n* **1** a crowded mass (as of cars) that impedes or blocks movement ⟨there was the inevitable *backup* of travelers trying to pass through airport security⟩ — see JAM 1
2 a person or thing that takes the place of another ⟨you didn't get the lead position, but you can be the *backup* to the chosen singer⟩ — see SUBSTITUTE

backward *adj* **1** directed, turned, or done toward the back ⟨a *backward* turn on ice skates is hard to learn because you can't see where you're going⟩
synonyms rearward, retrograde
related words reverse, reversed; aft, after, hind, posterior, rear; astern, sternforemost
near antonyms forward
2 not comfortable around people ⟨curiously, the quiet, *backward* man opened up when around other introverts⟩ — see SHY 2

backward *or* **backwards** *adv* **1** toward the rear ⟨looking *backward*, we could see the town receding in the distance⟩
synonyms back, rearward (*also* rearwards)
related words astern, sternforemost; anticlockwise [*chiefly British*], counterclockwise, left-handed, left-handedly, retrograde, reversely, widdershins (*also* withershins)
near antonyms before
antonyms ahead, along, forth, forward, forwards, on, onward (*also* onwards)
2 toward the opposite direction ⟨the loud noise prompted him to glance *backward* to see what was happening⟩ — see AROUND 2

backwash *n* a condition or occurrence traceable to a cause ⟨a general recession was the *backwash* of the crisis in the housing market⟩ — see EFFECT 1

backwater *n* a rural region that forms the edge of the settled or developed part of a country ⟨a distant *backwater* that didn't even have electricity at that time⟩ — see FRONTIER 2

backwoods *n pl* a rural region that forms the edge of the settled or developed part of a country ⟨lived far out in the *backwoods* and raised hogs for a living⟩ — see FRONTIER 2

backyard *adj* being such only for recreation ⟨an orchid that is a favorite with *backyard* horticulturists⟩ — see AVOCATIONAL

backyard *n* an adjoining region or space ⟨shocked to learn that the wind farm would be right in our own *backyard*⟩ — see ENVIRONS 2

bad *adj* **1** falling short of a standard ⟨a *bad* first attempt at making meat loaf resulted in a soggy, inedible mess⟩
synonyms bastard, bush, bush-league, crummy (*also* crumby), deficient, dissatisfactory, ill, inferior, lame, lousy, off, paltry, poor, punk, sour, suboptimal, subpar, substandard, unacceptable, unsatisfactory, wack [*slang*], wanting, wretched, wrong
related words abysmal, atrocious, awful, bitchin' [*slang*], brutal, damnable, deplorable, detestable, disastrous, dreadful, execrable, gnarly [*slang*], horrendous, horrible, pathetic, stinky, sucky [*slang*], terrible, unspeakable; defective, faulty, flawed; egregious, flagrant, gross; bum, cheesy, coarse, common, crappy [*slang*], cut-rate, junky, lesser, low-grade, low-rent, mediocre, miserable, reprehensible, rotten, rubbishy, second-rate, shoddy, sleazy, trashy; abominable, odious, vile; useless, valueless, worthless; inadequate, insufficient, lacking, meager (*or* meagre), mean, miserly, niggardly, scanty, shabby, short, skimp, skimpy, spare, stingy; miscreant, scurrilous, villainous; counterfeit, fake, phony (*also* phoney), sham
phrases below (*or* under) par, from hunger
near antonyms classic, classical; A1, bang-up, banner, boss [*slang*], capital, choice, crackerjack, dandy, divine, excellent, exceptional, fabulous, fine, first-class, first-rate, grand, great, groovy, heavenly, high-test, jim-dandy, keen, marvelous (*or* marvellous), mean, neat, nifty, noble, par excellence, perfect, premium, prime, sensational, slick, splendid, stellar, sterling, superb, superior, superlative, supernal, swell, terrific, tip-top, top, top-notch, unsurpassed, wonderful; better, exceptional,

fancy, high-grade, special, sufficient; average, borderline, fair, mediocre, middling, minimal, so-so, unexceptional; suitable, useful, worthy; gratifying, satisfying
antonyms acceptable, adequate, all right, decent, fine, OK (*or* okay), passable, respectable, satisfactory, standard, tolerable
2 not conforming to a high moral standard; morally unacceptable ⟨stealing is just plain *bad*⟩
synonyms black, dark, evil, immoral, iniquitous, nefarious, rotten, sinful, unethical, unlawful, unrighteous, unsavory, vicious, vile, villainous, wicked, wrong
related words base, contemptible, despicable, dirty, disreputable, evil-minded, ignoble, ill, infernal, low, mean, snide, sordid; atrocious, cruel, infamous, nasty; blamable, blameworthy, censurable, objectionable, obscene, offensive, reprehensible; corrupt, debased, debauched, degenerate, depraved, dissolute, libertine, loose, low-minded, perverted, reprobate, scrofulous, sick, unhealthy; cursed (*also* curst), cussed, defiling, noxious, pernicious, pestilential, ugly, ungodly, unwholesome; banned, barred, condemned, discouraged, forbidden, illegal, interdicted, outlawed, prohibited, proscribed, unauthorized, unclean; disallowed; execrable, lousy, miserable, wretched; errant, erring, fallen, unprincipled, unscrupulous; improper, incorrect, indecent, indecorous, naughty, unbecoming, unseemly, vulgar; dishonest, dishonorable
near antonyms elevated, high, high-minded, law-abiding, legitimate, lofty, noble, principled, reputable, scrupulous; allowed, authorized, legal, licensed, permissible, permitted; approved, endorsed (*also* indorsed), sanctioned; abetted, encouraged, promoted, supported; clean, correct, decent, decorous, exemplary, proper, seemly; blameless, commendable, creditable, guiltless, legitimate; chaste, immaculate, incorruptible, innocent, inoffensive, irreproachable, lily-white, perfect, pure, spotless, squeaky-clean, uncorrupted, unerring, unfallen, unobjectionable, venerable, white, wholesome; esteemed, respected, upstanding, worthy
antonyms decent, ethical, good, honest, honorable, just, moral, right, righteous, sublime, upright, virtuous
3 causing or capable of causing harm ⟨sitting too close to the television is said to be *bad* for the eyes⟩ — see HARMFUL
4 engaging in or marked by childish misbehavior ⟨the children were *bad*, so they didn't get dessert⟩ — see NAUGHTY
5 feeling unhappiness ⟨hearing about the world's miseries always makes him feel *bad*⟩ — see SAD 1
6 having a fault ⟨a *bad* video connection that is causing some picture loss⟩ — see FAULTY
7 having undergone organic breakdown ⟨I think the milk has turned *bad*⟩ — see ROTTEN 1
8 not giving pleasure to the mind or senses ⟨the air in the damp basement had a very *bad* smell⟩ — see UNPLEASANT
9 of low quality ⟨*bad* shoes that fell apart within a week⟩ — see CHEAP 2
10 temporarily suffering from a disorder of the body ⟨I've been feeling *bad* all week with this cold⟩ — see SICK 1
11 having no legal or binding force ⟨all known claims on the property were dismissed by the court as *bad*⟩ — see NULL 1
12 *slang* having or showing a desire to cause someone pain or suffering for the sheer enjoyment of it ⟨with all of his tattoos and piercings, that skinhead looks like one really *bad* dude⟩ — see HATEFUL

bad *adv* in an unsatisfactory way ⟨you didn't do too *bad* on the treadmill test⟩ — see BADLY 1

bad *n* that which is morally unacceptable ⟨there's *bad* and good in people of every race and nationality⟩ — see EVIL

bad blood *n* a deep-seated ill will ⟨there's been *bad blood* between the two families for years⟩ — see ENMITY

baddie *or* **baddy** *n* a mean, evil, or unprincipled person ⟨the actor has never been cast as a hero, but he's played every kind of *baddie* imaginable⟩ — see VILLAIN

badinage *n* good-natured teasing or exchanging of clever remarks ⟨the sophisticated *badinage* of the characters in plays by Oscar Wilde⟩ — see BANTER

badly *adv* **1** in an unsatisfactory way ⟨I'm afraid you performed quite *badly* in our last rehearsal⟩
synonyms bad, deficiently, inadequately, lousily, poorly, unacceptably, unsatisfactorily, wretchedly
related words abysmally, atrociously, awfully, damnably, deplorably, detestably, disastrously, dreadfully, execrably, horrendously, horribly, horrifically, rottenly, terribly; intolerably, unbearably; inappropriately, incorrectly, indecently, reprehensibly, unsuitably, vulgarly; naughtily; egregiously, flagrantly, grossly; miserably, shoddily, sleazily, trashily, unspeakably; abominably, odiously, vilely; inferiorly, insufficiently, meagerly, meanly, niggardly, scantily, scantly, shabbily, skimpily, sparely, stingily
near antonyms appropriately, congruously, correctly, decently, decorously, felicitously, fittingly, meetly, rightly, seemly, suitably; exactly, faithfully, ideally, precisely, respectably; gratifyingly, satisfyingly
antonyms acceptably, adequately, all right, fine, good, nicely, OK (*or* okay), palatably, passably, satisfactorily, so-so, tolerably, well
2 to a great degree ⟨blood donors are *badly* needed this time of year⟩ — see VERY 1

bad–mouth *vb* to express scornfully one's low opinion of ⟨she promptly *bad-mouthed* that awful movie to everyone she knew⟩ — see DECRY 1

badness *n* the state or quality of being utterly evil ⟨the villain's complete *badness* made him a good foil for the unfailingly virtuous hero⟩ — see ENORMITY 1

baffle *vb* **1** to prevent from achieving a goal ⟨the language barrier *baffled* everyone and discouraged us from attempting another teleconference⟩ — see FRUSTRATE 1
2 to throw into a state of mental uncertainty ⟨she was *baffled* by the wording of the clause in the insurance policy⟩ — see CONFUSE 1

baffled *adj* faced with difficulty or uncertainty about what to say, think, or do ⟨*baffled* viewers didn't know what to make of the strange antics of the talk show host⟩ — see HARD PUT

bafflegab *n* language marked by abstractions, jargon, euphemisms, and circumlocutions ⟨I kept asking the telemarketer what the final cost of the "special offer" was, and all I got was more *bafflegab* about deferred payments, option to cancel at any point, etc.⟩ — see GIBBERISH 2

bafflement *n* a state of mental uncertainty ⟨his complete *bafflement* as to the point of the joke was in itself funny⟩ — see CONFUSION 1

bag *n* **1** a container made of a flexible material (as paper or plastic) ⟨she carries her towel and other supplies to the beach in a bright, colorful *bag* slung over her arm⟩
synonyms poke [*chiefly Southern & Midland*], pouch, sack
related words carryall, portmanteau, traveling bag, wallet; bundle, pack, package, packet, parcel; backpack, barracks bag, duffel bag, haversack, knapsack, rucksack, satchel, tote; handbag, pocketbook, purse, tote bag; ditty bag, flight bag, garment bag, kit bag, shopping bag, work bag
2 a container for carrying money and small personal

items ⟨a very carefully dressed woman who makes sure that her *bag* always matches the color of her shoes⟩ — see PURSE

bag *vb* **1** to extend outward beyond a usual point ⟨the shirt *bagged* at the waist⟩ — see BULGE 1
2 to take physical control or possession of (something) suddenly or forcibly ⟨*bagged* a deer while hunting last weekend⟩ — see CATCH 1
3 to give up (a job or office) ⟨if the supervisor says one more nasty thing to me, I'm going to *bag* this stupid job⟩ — see QUIT 1
4 to obtain (as a goal) through effort ⟨*bagged* a full fellowship at one of the nation's leading universities⟩ — see ACHIEVE 1
5 to receive as return for effort ⟨*bagged* an acting nomination for a truly inspired performance⟩ — see EARN 1

bagatelle *n* something of little importance ⟨the question of who will pick up the coffee is a mere *bagatelle* in the overall planning of the conference⟩ — see TRIFLE

bagnio *n* a building in which prostitutes are available ⟨the police staged a raid on the London *bagnio*, causing great inconvenience to its well-heeled clientele⟩ — see BORDELLO

bail *vb* to leave a place often for another ⟨after two hours of that boring party, we were ready to *bail*⟩ — see GO 2

bailiwick *n* a region of activity, knowledge, or influence ⟨questions about organization of the fund drive are my *bailiwick*⟩ — see FIELD 2

bail out *vb* **1** to leave a place often for another ⟨if the meeting seems like it will never end, find an excuse to *bail out*⟩ — see GO 2
2 to remove from danger or harm ⟨the government *bailed out* the savings and loan industry⟩ — see SAVE 2

bairn *n, chiefly Scottish* a young person who is between infancy and adulthood ⟨at the Scottish festival there were traditional contests of strength and endurance, Celtic fiddlers, and groups of *bairns* performing Highland flings⟩ — see CHILD 1

bait *n* **1** something used to attract animals to a hook or into a trap ⟨cheese is the traditional *bait* for trapping mice⟩
synonyms decoy, lure
related words ambush, net, trap; hook, snare, troll; plug, scent, spinner, stool pigeon; appeal, attraction, call, draw, incentive, pull; enticement, seducement, seduction, temptation; entanglement, entrapment
near antonyms repellent (*also* repellant)
2 something that persuades one to perform an action for pleasure or gain ⟨the promise of free vacation is surefire *bait* to get people to agree to be chaperones for school trips⟩ — see LURE 1

bait *vb* **1** to attack repeatedly with mean put-downs or insults ⟨as the first woman to work in the mines, she was mercilessly *baited* by the men on her shift⟩ — see TEASE 2
2 to lead away from a usual or proper course by offering some pleasure or advantage ⟨the investment scheme cunningly *baits* the greedy and the unscrupulous⟩ — see LURE

baiter *n* **1** a person who causes repeated emotional pain, distress, or annoyance to another ⟨vowed revenge someday on the *baiters* who were making his life miserable⟩ — see TORMENTOR
2 one that tries to get a person to give in to a desire ⟨my sister is quite the mischievous *baiter*, always offering candy even though she knows I'm on a diet⟩ — see TEMPTER

balance *n* **1** a condition in which opposing forces are equal to one another ⟨in order to determine the weight of that beaker, you need to get the two pans of the scale in perfect *balance*⟩
synonyms counterpoise, equilibration, equilibrium, equipoise, poise, stasis
related words counterbalance, offset; firmness, fixedness, security, stability, steadiness
near antonyms changeability, fluctuation, inconstancy, insecurity, instability, mutability, precariousness, shakiness, unsteadiness, volatility
antonyms disequilibration, disequilibrium, imbalance, nonequilibrium, unbalance
2 a balanced, pleasing, or suitable arrangement of parts ⟨the *balance* of the landscaping is in keeping with the symmetry of so many 18th-century mansions⟩ — see HARMONY 1
3 a device for measuring weight ⟨use a *balance* to make sure you get the amounts precisely correct⟩ — see [1]SCALE
4 a force or influence that makes an opposing force ineffective or less effective ⟨the *balance* to the mountain of complaints are the many letters of praise that we also receive⟩ — see COUNTERBALANCE
5 a remaining group or portion ⟨and the *balance* of the contestants should stand in that last corner⟩ — see REMAINDER 1

balance *vb* **1** to make equal in amount, degree, or status ⟨tried to *balance* the total amount of money spent on gifts for each child⟩ — see EQUALIZE
2 to show uncertainty about the right course of action ⟨his tendency to *balance* and waffle on certain hot-button issues may hurt him in the general election⟩ — see HESITATE
3 to give what is owed for ⟨she had to *balance* her account with the video store before being allowed to rent more movies⟩ — see PAY 2

balanced *adj* **1** having full use of one's mind and control over one's actions ⟨no *balanced* person would believe that their dog's bark was actually the voice of God⟩ — see SANE
2 having the parts agreeably related ⟨a *balanced* arrangement of the furniture made the room look more spacious⟩ — see HARMONIOUS 2

balcony *n* a flat roofless structure attached to a building ⟨on summer mornings I often have breakfast out on the *balcony*⟩ — see SUNDECK

bald *adj* **1** lacking a usual or natural covering ⟨trees that are *bald* in the winter aren't the best for giving a home year-round privacy⟩ — see NAKED 2
2 free from all additions or embellishment ⟨try to avoid the *bald* statement "You're wrong!" when trying to reason with someone⟩ — see PLAIN 1
3 not subject to misinterpretation or more than one interpretation ⟨her angry neighbor's *bald* threats made her want to call the police⟩ — see CLEAR 2

balderdash *n* language, behavior, or ideas that are absurd and contrary to good sense ⟨a combat veteran himself, he could not believe the *balderdash* he was hearing from whippersnappers with no war experience at all⟩ — see NONSENSE 1

bald–faced *adj* not subject to misinterpretation or more than one interpretation ⟨I took the remark as a *bald-faced* accusation that I had cheated⟩ — see CLEAR 2

baleful *adj* **1** being or showing a sign of evil or calamity to come ⟨a dark, *baleful* sky portending a tornado⟩ — see OMINOUS
2 causing or capable of causing harm ⟨contends that the violent content of so much of popular entertainment is a *baleful* influence on our society⟩ — see HARMFUL
3 likely to cause or capable of causing death ⟨a medicine that is beneficial in small doses but *baleful* in large⟩ — see DEADLY 1

balk *n* something that makes movement or progress difficult ⟨the extravagant centerpiece proved to be a *balk* to the flow of conversation⟩ — see ENCUMBRANCE

balk *vb* to prevent from achieving a goal ⟨a young man with big dreams who refused to be *balked* by the daily obstacles of his inner-city existence⟩ — see FRUSTRATE 1

balk (at) *vb* to show unwillingness to accept, do, engage in, or agree to ⟨she *balked at* lending him any more money⟩ — see DECLINE 1

balkiness *n* refusal to obey ⟨the teen's unrelenting *balkiness* was truly frustrating⟩ — see DISOBEDIENCE

balky *adj* given to resisting authority or another's control ⟨a *balky* toddler who only seemed to know the word "no" when told to do something⟩ — see DISOBEDIENT

[1]ball *n* **1** a more or less round body or mass ⟨the little rubber *ball* used in racquetball⟩ ⟨a *ball* of string⟩
synonyms globe, orb, sphere
related words bead, globule; egg, ellipse, loop, oval, spheroid; circle, ring, rondure, round; chunk, clump, gob, hunk, lump, nugget, wad
near antonyms block, cube, rectangle, square
2 a usually round or cone-shaped little piece of lead made to be fired from a firearm ⟨found a cache of musket *balls* while excavating the old fort⟩ — see BULLET

[2]ball *n* a social gathering for dancing ⟨a *ball* to celebrate the inauguration⟩ — see DANCE

ball *vb* to form into a round compact mass ⟨*balled* up the paper and threw it at the garbage can⟩ — see WAD

ballad *n* a short musical composition for the human voice often with instrumental accompaniment ⟨a haunting *ballad* about lost love and loneliness⟩ — see SONG 1

ball game *n* **1** an earnest effort for superiority or victory over another ⟨don't count me out yet, for I'm still in this *ball game*⟩ — see CONTEST 1
2 position with regard to conditions and circumstances ⟨with the new regulations in place, investors are facing a whole new *ball game*⟩ — see SITUATION 1

ballistic *adj* feeling or showing anger ⟨she went *ballistic* when she discovered her sister using her nail polish⟩ — see ANGRY

balloon *vb* **1** to become greater in extent, volume, amount, or number ⟨the number of students who stay home sick *balloons* every winter⟩ — see INCREASE 2
2 to extend outward beyond a usual point ⟨the paper bag *ballooned* and blew away as the wind lifted it skyward⟩ — see BULGE 1

ballot *n* **1** a piece of paper indicating a person's preferences in an election ⟨we collected all of the *ballots* from the students voting for class president⟩
synonyms vote
related words aye (*also* ay), yea; nay, no, non placet; blackball; referendum; ticket; absentee ballot, Australian ballot, secret ballot, short ballot, write-in
2 the right to formally express one's position or will in an election ⟨believes that even convicted felons should have the *ballot*⟩ — see VOTE 1

ballpark *adj* not precisely correct ⟨I suspect that the *ballpark* costs we were quoted for the kitchen renovation will turn out to be too low⟩ — see INEXACT 1

ballyhoo *n* **1** a state of noisy, confused activity ⟨it turned out that the *ballyhoo* was the result of a movie being filmed on the street⟩ — see COMMOTION
2 information released to the media that is designed to gain public attention or support for a person, business, or cause ⟨the usual *ballyhoo* intended to fill the seats at megaplexes around the country⟩ — see PUBLICITY

ballyhoo *vb* **1** to praise or publicize lavishly and often excessively ⟨that reviewer always *ballyhoos* any book by one of his pet authors⟩ — see TOUT 1
2 to provide publicity for ⟨the TV networks usually spend the summer months *ballyhooing* their new fall shows⟩ — see PUBLICIZE 1

balm *n* a sweet or pleasant smell ⟨the *balm* of the restaurant's backyard garden enhances the aura of romance⟩ — see FRAGRANCE

balminess *n* lack of good sense or judgment ⟨only sheer *balminess* would possess someone to invest in that loser of a stock⟩ — see FOOLISHNESS 1

balmy *adj* **1** having or showing a very abnormal or sick state of mind ⟨a completely *balmy* but harmless old man who talked intently to plants and believed they answered back⟩ — see INSANE 1
2 marked by temperatures that are neither too high nor too low ⟨a *balmy* spring day⟩ — see CLEMENT 1
3 not harsh or stern especially in nature or effect ⟨a pleasant, *balmy* breeze was all that stirred the wildflowers growing near the shore⟩ — see GENTLE 1
4 showing or marked by a lack of good sense or judgment ⟨the *balmy* notion that the IRS wouldn't collect taxes on his lottery winnings⟩ — see FOOLISH 1

baloney *also* **boloney** *n* language, behavior, or ideas that are absurd and contrary to good sense ⟨just follow my orders, and stop the *baloney*⟩ — see NONSENSE 1

balustrade *n* a protective barrier consisting of a horizontal bar and its supports ⟨an ornately carved *balustrade* for the staircase⟩ — see RAILING

bambino *n* **1** a recently born person ⟨a new mother cuddling a *bambino* in her lap⟩ — see BABY 1
2 a young person who is between infancy and adulthood ⟨bouncing a *bambino* on her knee⟩ — see CHILD 1

bamboozle *vb* **1** to cause to believe what is untrue ⟨*bamboozled* by con men into buying worthless land in the desert⟩ — see DECEIVE
2 to throw into a state of mental uncertainty ⟨she's completely *bamboozled* by the latest changes in the tax code⟩ — see CONFUSE 1

bamboozlement *n* a state of mental uncertainty ⟨their *bamboozlement* is understandable, considering the lame instructions they got⟩ — see CONFUSION 1

ban *n* **1** a prayer that harm will come to someone ⟨a father's *ban* upon his ungrateful son⟩ — see CURSE 1
2 an order that something not be done or used ⟨a quiet seaside resort with a *ban* on the drinking of alcohol in public places⟩ — see PROHIBITION 2

ban *vb* **1** to order not to do or use or to be done or used ⟨the company absolutely *bans* smoking within its buildings⟩ — see FORBID
2 to prevent the participation, consideration, or inclusion of ⟨the university *banned* those caught in the cheating scandal from graduation ceremonies⟩ — see EXCLUDE

banal *adj* **1** lacking in qualities that make for spirit and character ⟨the sort of *banal* woman who appeals to men not looking for intellectual stimulation⟩ — see WISHY-WASHY 1
2 used or heard so often as to be dull ⟨please find new ways of phrasing your thoughts instead of relying on *banal* expressions⟩ — see STALE 1

banality *n* an idea or expression that has been used by many people ⟨another sitcom based on the *banality* that men avoid committed relationships⟩ — see COMMONPLACE

[1]band *n* **1** a circular strip ⟨a *band* of cloth tied around his wrist⟩ — see [1]RING 2
2 something that physically prevents free movement ⟨the dog was forced to wear a *band* around its muzzle until it learned not to nip people⟩ — see BOND 1
3 a line or long narrow section differing in color from the background ⟨skunks have a *band* of white down their backs⟩ — see [1]STRIPE 1

[2]band *n* **1** a usually large group of musicians playing to-

gether ⟨that traveling *band* needs to find a new singer⟩
synonyms orchestra, philharmonic, symphony, symphony orchestra
related words brass band, chamber orchestra, sinfonietta; brasses, strings, woodwinds; combo, ensemble, group; company, troupe; duo, octet, quartet (*also* quartette), quintet, septet, sextet, trio
2 a group of people working together on a task ⟨a *band* of volunteer searchers found the lost child⟩ — see GANG 1
3 a usually small number of persons considered as a unit ⟨a *band* of explorers⟩ — see GROUP 2
4 a number of things considered as a unit ⟨a *band* of songbirds⟩ — see GROUP 1

band *vb* **1** to encircle or bind with or as if with a belt ⟨*banded* the waist of the dress with a speckled belt⟩ — see GIRD 1
2 to gather into a tight mass by means of a line or cord ⟨*banded* the newspapers together for delivery⟩ — see TIE 1
3 to make stripes on ⟨*banded* the sleeves of the robe with strips of contrasting material⟩ — see STRIPE

band (together) *vb* **1** to participate or assist in a joint effort to accomplish an end ⟨we're *banding together* to oppose the construction of one of those big-box stores in our town⟩ — see COOPERATE 1
2 to form or enter into an association that furthers the interests of its members ⟨small farmers *banded together* to oppose the interests of the agricultural giants⟩ — see ALLY

bandage *vb* to cover with a bandage ⟨her mother always *bandages* her scraped knees very carefully⟩
synonyms bind, dress, swathe
related words attend, care (for), doctor, medicate, minister (to), nurse, treat; cure, heal, mend, rehabilitate, remedy
near antonyms unbandage

bandanna *or* **bandana** *n* a scarf worn on the head ⟨she uses her colorful print *bandanna* to keep the hair out of her eyes⟩
synonyms babushka, do-rag, handkerchief, kerchief, madras, mantilla
related words shawl; hankie (*or* hanky)

bandbox *adj* being clean and in good order ⟨a small *bandbox* bed-and-breakfast decorated with taste and charm⟩ — see NEAT 1

banded *adj* having stripes ⟨the red, black, and yellow *banded* king snake is sometimes mistaken for the venomous coral snake⟩ — see STRIPED

banderole *or* **banderol** *n* a piece of cloth with a special design that is used as an emblem or for signaling ⟨during the festival this ancient Italian city is bestrewn with *banderoles* celebrating its illustrious medieval heritage⟩ — see FLAG 1

bandwagon *n* a series of activities undertaken to achieve a goal ⟨tried to get everyone on the *bandwagon* about forming a neighborhood crime watch⟩ — see CAMPAIGN

bandy *vb* to talk about (an issue) usually from various points of view and for the purpose of arriving at a decision or opinion ⟨*bandied* around the idea of going out to dinner for their anniversary⟩ — see DISCUSS

bane *n* **1** a source of harm or misfortune ⟨regarding the new laborsaving machinery as a *bane*, the 19th-century Luddites went about destroying it in protest⟩
synonyms affliction, curse, nemesis, scourge
related words hex, hoodoo, jinx; danger, hazard, menace, peril, risk, threat, trouble; booby trap, catch, pitfall, snag
near antonyms advantage, aid, assistance, gift, help, relief, support; comfort, consolation, solace; delight, joy, pleasure; armor, defense, guard, protection, safeguard, safety, security, shield
antonyms benefit, blessing, boon, felicity, godsend, good, manna, windfall
2 a substance that by chemical action can kill or injure a living thing ⟨a plant that is believed to be the *bane* of the wolf⟩ — see POISON

baneful *adj* causing or capable of causing harm ⟨the incredibly *baneful* effect that drug dealing has on so many inner-city neighborhoods⟩ — see HARMFUL

bang *adv* without delay ⟨the reform movement was just beginning when it *bang* ran into opposition⟩ — see IMMEDIATELY

bang *n* **1** a hard strike with a part of the body or an instrument ⟨delivered a sharp *bang* that rattled the door⟩ — see [1]BLOW
2 a loud explosive sound ⟨a sudden *bang* made the cat jump⟩ — see CLAP 1
3 a pleasurably intense stimulation of the feelings ⟨tried to get the most *bang* for her money at the attractions at the county fair⟩ — see THRILL

bang *vb* **1** to come into usually forceful contact with something ⟨the toy car *banged* into the wall and stopped⟩ — see HIT 2
2 to deliver a blow to (someone or something) usually in a strong vigorous manner ⟨idly *banged* trees with a stick⟩ — see HIT 1
3 to shove into a closed position with force and noise ⟨stomped off to his room and *banged* the door⟩ — see SLAM 1

bang away *vb* to devote serious and sustained effort ⟨the design team has been *banging away* at that project for months⟩ — see LABOR

bang–bang *adj* marked by bursts of destructive force or intense activity ⟨the film lacks compelling characters, but it has plenty of *bang-bang* action⟩ — see VIOLENT 1

banger *n, British* a rod-shaped portion of seasoned ground meat in a casing ⟨*bangers* and mash is classic British pub cuisine⟩ — see SAUSAGE

bangle *n* an ornament worn on a chain around the neck or wrist ⟨wore a bracelet with small silver *bangles* on it⟩ — see PENDANT 1

bang on *adj, chiefly British* being in agreement with the truth or a fact or a standard ⟨a London theatre critic who can generally be relied upon for his *bang on* assessments of new plays in the West End⟩ — see CORRECT 1

bang–up *adj* of the very best kind ⟨you did a *bang-up* job on this sales report⟩ — see EXCELLENT

banish *vb* **1** to force to leave a country ⟨in the old days, criminals were sometimes *banished* to distant lands⟩
synonyms deport, displace, exile, expatriate, relegate, transport
related words cast out, dismiss, eject, eliminate, evict, exclude, expel, expulse, kick out, oust, run out, throw out; excommunicate, ostracize, reject, repudiate, spurn; dispossess
near antonyms naturalize, repatriate; accept, admit, receive, take in; entertain, harbor, house, shelter
2 to drive or force out ⟨permanently *banished* the troublemakers from the youth recreational center⟩ — see EJECT 1

banishment *n* the forced removal from a homeland ⟨some members of the tribe of Native Americans believe they are still owed compensation for their *banishment* from their homeland⟩ — see EXILE 1

banister *also* **bannister** *n* a protective barrier consisting of a horizontal bar and its supports ⟨a much-needed new *banister* for the rickety staircase⟩ — see RAILING

[1]**bank** *n* **1** a number of things considered as a unit ⟨a *bank* of telephones set up for the telethon⟩ — see GROUP 1

2 a series of people or things arranged side by side ⟨a *bank* of elevators⟩ — see [1]ROW 1

[2]bank *n* a pile or ridge of granular matter (as sand or snow) ⟨a *bank* of dirt that the construction workers left behind⟩
synonyms bar, drift, mound
related words snowbank, snowdrift; embankment, sandbar; heap, hill, mass, mountain, stack, tuft

bank *vb* **1** to form into a pile or ridge of earth ⟨*banked* sand into little mounds on the beach⟩ — see MOUND 1
2 to put in an account ⟨she always *banks* half of her paycheck⟩ — see DEPOSIT 1

banknote *n* a piece of printed paper used as money in the United States ⟨the new nation immediately printed up its own *banknotes*⟩ — see [1]BILL 2

bankroll *n* available money ⟨my total *bankroll* right now is $2,000⟩ — see FUND 2

bankroll *vb* to provide money for ⟨several corporations *bankrolled* the Broadway musical⟩ — see FINANCE 1

bankrupt *adj* utterly lacking in something needed, wanted, or expected ⟨she's a kind soul, but *bankrupt* of all common sense, I'm afraid⟩ — see DEVOID 1

bankrupt *vb* to cause to lose one's fortune and become unable to pay one's debts ⟨several bad investments *bankrupted* him⟩ — see RUIN 1

bankruptcy *n* the inability to pay one's debts ⟨learned the hard way the costs of declaring *bankruptcy*⟩ — see INSOLVENCY

banned *adj* that may not be permitted ⟨at one time books, movies, and plays could use "*banned* in Boston" as a selling point⟩ — see IMPERMISSIBLE

banner *adj* of the very best kind ⟨it's been a *banner* year for the petroleum business⟩ — see EXCELLENT

banner *n* **1** a piece of cloth with a special design that is used as an emblem or for signaling ⟨the boat flew a bright red *banner* for the seaport's harbor festival⟩ — see FLAG 1
2 an attention-getting word or phrase used to publicize something (as a campaign or product) ⟨after the near accident, the nuclear power station is now operating under the *banner* of "safety first"⟩ — see SLOGAN

banning *n* the act of ordering that something not be done or used ⟨the *banning* of the use of foul language at town council meetings was long overdue⟩ — see PROHIBITION 1

banquet *n* a large fancy meal often accompanied by ceremony or entertainment ⟨prepared a celebratory *banquet* for the graduating class⟩ — see FEAST 1

banquet *vb* to entertain with a fancy meal ⟨*banqueted* the returning troops at the military base⟩ — see FEAST 1

bantam *adj* of a size that is less than average ⟨a *bantam* comedian who is known to fellow performers for his oversize ego⟩ — see SMALL 1

banter *n* good-natured teasing or exchanging of clever remarks ⟨members of the Algonquin Round Table were known for their brilliant and witty *banter*⟩
synonyms backchat, badinage, chaff, give-and-take, jesting, joshing, persiflage, raillery, repartee
related words barb, crack, dig, gag, gambit, jest, joke, laugh, pleasantry, quip, sally, waggery, wisecrack, witticism; drollness, facetiousness, funniness, hilariousness, humorousness, richness; fooling, kidding, mocking, razzing, ribbing, ridiculing; humor, wit, wordplay; nothings; chatter, chitchat, gossip, small talk

banter *vb* to make jokes ⟨the teacher *bantered* pleasantly, albeit a bit awkwardly, with the students at the school dance⟩ — see JOKE 1

bantering *adj* marked by or expressive of mild or good-natured teasing ⟨the gently *bantering* tone of the couple's conversation⟩ — see QUIZZICAL

baptism *n* the process or an instance of being formally placed in an office or organization ⟨the *baptism* of the new members of the college fraternity⟩ — see INSTALLATION 1

baptize *vb* **1** to give a name to ⟨*baptized* the child "Anne"⟩ — see NAME 1
2 to put into an office or welcome into an organization with special ceremonies ⟨the new sisters will be *baptized* with special initiation rites at the sorority house⟩ — see INSTALL 1

bar *n* **1** a straight piece (as of wood or metal) that is longer than it is wide ⟨all of the prison's windows are partially covered with steel *bars*⟩
synonyms billet, rod
related words arbor, beam, board, crossbar, crossbeam, girder; band, strip; bloom, ingot, slab, stick
2 a line or long narrow section differing in color from the background ⟨the cat had a *bar* of white down her throat⟩ — see [1]STRIPE 1
3 a pile or ridge of granular matter (as sand or snow) ⟨more than one boater has run aground on that treacherous *bar* of sand in the river⟩ — see [2]BANK
4 a place of business where alcoholic beverages are sold to be consumed on the premises ⟨a *bar* that serves meals as well as drinks⟩ — see BARROOM
5 an assembly of persons for the administration of justice ⟨rather than try and convict the alleged murderer in the mass media, let justice be done at the *bar*⟩ — see COURT 3
6 something that makes movement or progress difficult ⟨the complication of the molecule is the biggest *bar* to reproducing it⟩ — see ENCUMBRANCE
7 something set up as an example against which others of the same type are compared ⟨we need to raise the *bar* for what is acceptable behavior in this situation⟩ — see STANDARD 1

bar *prep* not including ⟨everyone in the company is invited, *bar* none⟩ — see EXCEPT

bar *vb* **1** to make stripes on ⟨*barred* the fence with white strips⟩ — see STRIPE
2 to order not to do or use or to be done or used ⟨corporal punishment has long been *barred* in most public schools⟩ — see FORBID
3 to prevent the participation, consideration, or inclusion of ⟨gangs of rowdy teenagers have been *barred* from the mall⟩ — see EXCLUDE
4 to disallow entry into (a place) by means of a physical barrier at the entry point ⟨the bikeway was *barred* by a huge fallen tree⟩ — see CLOSE (OFF)

barb *n* an act or expression showing scorn and usually intended to hurt another's feelings ⟨delivered one last *barb* to his ex-girlfriend as he stalked away⟩ — see INSULT

barbarian *adj* not civilized ⟨people who were regarded as *barbarian* by the ancient Romans⟩ — see SAVAGE 1

barbarian *n* an uncivilized person ⟨in those times European explorers tended to regard any people having a different language, culture, or religion as a race of *barbarians*⟩ — see HEATHEN 2

barbaric *adj* **1** having or showing the desire to inflict severe pain and suffering on others ⟨a *barbaric* dictator who tortured his own people with no qualms⟩ — see CRUEL 1
2 not civilized ⟨the *barbaric* forebears of modern mankind⟩ — see SAVAGE 1

barbarity *n* disposition to willfully inflict pain and suffering on others ⟨more than one reluctant dental patient has been tempted to level the charge of *barbarity* against their dentist⟩ — see CRUELTY

barbarous *adj* **1** having or showing the desire to inflict severe pain and suffering on others ⟨the *barbarous* treatment of the native peoples of the New World by those bent on conquest at any cost⟩ — see CRUEL 1

2 not civilized ⟨an aunt who abhors *barbarous* behavior such as eating with your fingers⟩ — see SAVAGE 1

barbarousness *n* disposition to willfully inflict pain and suffering on others ⟨the utter *barbarousness* of slavery outraged the abolitionists⟩ — see CRUELTY

barbed *adj* marked by the use of wit that is intended to cause hurt feelings ⟨*barbed* satire on American academia⟩ — see SARCASTIC

barber *n* a person who cuts and arranges hair ⟨went to the *barber* to get his hair cut and his beard trimmed⟩ — see HAIRDRESSER

bard *n* a person who writes poetry ⟨a *bard* best known for a series of love poems to his raven-haired beloved⟩ — see POET

bardic *adj* having qualities suggestive of poetry ⟨"Now the trumpet summons us again" is one of the many *bardic* phrases in President Kennedy's inaugural address⟩ — see POETIC

bare *adj* **1** being this and no more ⟨impoverished people who can no longer afford the *bare* necessities⟩ — see MERE

2 free from all additions or embellishment ⟨do you want to know the *bare* truth?⟩ — see PLAIN 1

3 lacking a usual or natural covering ⟨the ground was *bare*, without a trace of grass⟩ — see NAKED 2

4 lacking or shed of clothing ⟨the toddler liked to run around *bare*⟩ — see NAKED 1

5 lacking contents that could or should be present ⟨the cupboard was *bare*—not a thing to eat⟩ — see EMPTY 1

6 utterly lacking in something needed, wanted, or expected ⟨the cupboard was *bare* of baking supplies⟩ — see DEVOID 1

bare *vb* to make known (as information previously kept secret) ⟨finally *bared* the secret that she had kept to herself for so long⟩ — see REVEAL 1

barefaced *adj* not subject to misinterpretation or more than one interpretation ⟨a *barefaced* challenge for a fight⟩ — see CLEAR 2

barely *adv* by a very small margin ⟨we *barely* made it to the church on time⟩ — see JUST 2

bareness *n* **1** the quality or state of being empty ⟨the stark *bareness* of the refrigerator suggested it was time to go shopping⟩ — see VACANCY 2

2 the state of having no clothes on one's body ⟨as she encountered more and more nude people at the resort, she became less conscious of her own *bareness*⟩ — see NUDITY

barf *vb* to discharge the contents of the stomach through the mouth ⟨the movie's in-your-face violence made us want to *barf*⟩ — see VOMIT

bargain *n* **1** something bought or offered for sale at a desirable price ⟨those shoes were a *bargain* because the store was going out of business⟩

synonyms buy, deal, pennyworth, snip [*British*], steal

related words clearance, closeout, markdown; cheapie; bonus, freebie (*or* freebee), gift, giveaway, premium, present; boon, windfall

near antonyms gouging, overcharge, rip-off, soaking; markup, surcharge; extravagance, luxury

2 an arrangement about action to be taken ⟨made a *bargain* that one would help the other next week⟩ — see AGREEMENT 2

bargain *vb* **1** to talk over or dispute the terms of a purchase ⟨they *bargained* with the car salesman for half an hour before settling on a price⟩

synonyms chaffer, deal, dicker, haggle, horse-trade, negotiate, palter

related words argue, bicker, clash, fight, hassle, quarrel, quibble, squabble, wrangle; comparison shop, shop (around); barter, exchange, trade; hawk, peddle; buy, purchase

phrases cut a deal, wheel and deal

2 to come to an arrangement as to a course of action ⟨I really hadn't *bargained* on buying a whole case of Girl Scout cookies, just a couple of boxes⟩ — see AGREE 2

3 to bring about through discussion and compromise ⟨*bargained* the price of the painting down to a figure that the artist could still live with⟩ — see NEGOTIATE 1

bargain–basement *adj* **1** costing little ⟨throughout the trip we ate at *bargain-basement* restaurants in order to save money⟩ — see CHEAP 1

2 of low quality ⟨*bargain-basement* shoes that fell apart after a week⟩ — see CHEAP 2

barge *vb* to move heavily or clumsily ⟨the big man *barged* into the room⟩ — see LUMBER 1

[1]**bark** *vb* to remove the natural covering of ⟨*barking* a tree will probably kill it⟩ — see PEEL

[2]**bark** *vb* to speak sharply or irritably ⟨the new supervisor found that speaking to people with a civil tongue got better results than *barking* at them⟩ — see SNAP 1

bark *n* a boat equipped with one or more sails ⟨took a small *bark* out on the lake⟩ — see SAILBOAT

barmy *adj, chiefly British* having or showing a very abnormal or sick state of mind ⟨a farm in Yorkshire that seemed to be run by a *barmy* old man⟩ — see INSANE 1

barometer *n* something set up as an example against which others of the same type are compared ⟨a legendary Broadway flop that has subsequently become the *barometer* by which failure in the theater is judged⟩ — see STANDARD 1

baron *n* a person of rank, power, or influence in a particular field ⟨a media *baron* who owns newspapers, television and radio stations, and even several cable networks⟩ — see MAGNATE

baronial *adj* large and impressive in size, grandeur, extent, or conception ⟨a *baronial* mansion with dozens of spacious, luxurious rooms⟩ — see GRAND 1

barony *n* a region of activity, knowledge, or influence ⟨no longer is the city's social and cultural life the *barony* of a few old-line families⟩ — see FIELD 2

baroque *adj* **1** going beyond a normal or acceptable limit in degree or amount ⟨eventually even the movie seems bored by its *baroque* violence⟩ — see EXCESSIVE

2 having many parts or aspects that are usually interrelated ⟨a thriller with a *baroque* plot that is sure to baffle many readers⟩ — see COMPLEX 1

barracuda *n* an aggressive and fiercely determined person ⟨the governor-elect is too nice and easygoing, so he'll need a *barracuda* as his chief of staff⟩ — see PIT BULL

barrage *n* a rapid or overwhelming outpouring of many things at once ⟨the teacher's rapid-fire *barrage* of homework assignments went by too fast for me to write them all down⟩

synonyms blitz, blitzkrieg, bombardment, cannonade, drumbeat, drumfire, flurry, fusillade, hail, salvo, shower, storm, volley

related words broadside, earful; avalanche, burst, cataclysm, cataract, deluge, discharge, engulfment, flood, flood tide, flush, gush, inundation, outburst, outflow, outpouring, overflow, rash, spate, surge, torrent; current, river, stream, tide; excess, glut, overabundance, overage, overkill, overmuch, oversupply, superabundance, superfluity, surfeit, surplus

near antonyms dribble, drip, trickle

barrage *vb* to attack with a rapid or overwhelming outpouring of many things at once ⟨the star athlete was *barraged* with requests for an autograph⟩ — see BOMBARD 2

barranca *also* **barranco** *n* a steep wall of rock, earth, or ice ⟨the intimidating *barrancas* that can be found in the Sierra Nevada⟩ — see CLIFF

barred *adj* **1** having stripes ⟨a tabby is a *barred* cat, often with black stripes⟩ — see STRIPED

2 that may not be permitted ⟨smoking is *barred* inside the restaurant⟩ — see IMPERMISSIBLE

barrel *n* **1** a considerable amount ⟨a visit to an amusement park should be a *barrel* of laughs⟩ — see LOT 2
2 a metal container in the shape of a cylinder ⟨a trash *barrel*⟩ — see CAN 1
3 an enclosed wooden vessel for holding beverages ⟨*barrels* of fine wine aging in the winery's cellar⟩ — see CASK

barrel *vb* to proceed or move quickly ⟨faced with a firm deadline, we *barreled* through the project at a furious pace⟩ — see HURRY 2

barren *adj* **1** producing inferior or only a small amount of vegetation ⟨if tobacco fields aren't allowed to lie idle once every few years, they will become *barren*⟩
synonyms bony (*also* boney), dead, desolate, hardscrabble, impoverished, infertile, poor, stark, unfertile, unproductive, waste
related words bleak, inhospitable, lifeless; uncultivable, untillable; bankrupted, consumed, debilitated, depleted, diminished, drained, dried-up, enfeebled, exhausted, expended, lessened, reduced, spent, used up; arid, desert, droughty, dry, rainless, sere (*also* sear), thirsty, waterless; baked, dehydrated, parched, sunbaked
near antonyms arable, tillable; green, sylvan, verdant
antonyms fertile, fruitful, lush, luxuriant, productive, rich
2 not able to produce fruit or offspring ⟨the pear tree appears to be *barren*⟩ — see STERILE 1
3 producing no results ⟨that line of investigation proved *barren*, so the police tried other avenues⟩ — see FUTILE 1
4 utterly lacking in something needed, wanted, or expected ⟨their proposal for revitalizing the downtown business district is utterly *barren* of useful ideas⟩ — see DEVOID 1

barren *n* land that is uninhabited or not fit for crops ⟨lived out in the *barrens* where it was impossible to grow anything⟩ — see WASTELAND

barricade *n* a physical object that blocks the way ⟨the police put up *barricades* to block off the parade route⟩ — see BARRIER

barricade *vb* to disallow entry into (a place) by means of a physical barrier at the entry point ⟨the city *barricaded* the flooded streets⟩ — see CLOSE (OFF)

barrier *n* a physical object that blocks the way ⟨there was a big *barrier* plastered with signs saying "Keep Out" around the trash compactor⟩
synonyms barricade, fence, hedge, wall
related words bar, pale, paling; block, chain, clog, crimp, deterrent, drag, embarrassment, encumbrance, handicap, hindrance, hurdle, impediment, inhibition, interference, let, obstacle, obstruction, roadblock, stop, stumbling block, trammel; fetter, hobble, manacle, shackle(s); constraint, curb, restraint, snag; buffer, bulwark, bumper, cushion, dam, fender, pad, rampart
near antonyms door, doorway, entrance, entranceway, entry, entryway, gate, portal; break, gap, pass

barring *n* the act of ordering that something not be done or used ⟨most of the restaurant's customers applauded the *barring* of the use of cell phones in the dining room⟩ — see PROHIBITION 1

barring *prep* not including ⟨we'll be there, *barring* rain or some other unexpected problem⟩ — see EXCEPT

barroom *n* a place of business where alcoholic beverages are sold to be consumed on the premises ⟨her mother didn't like her even to walk past the *barroom* because she was worried that there might be drunk people inside⟩
synonyms bar, café (*also* cafe), cantina [*Southwest*], dramshop, gin mill, grogshop [*chiefly British*], pub, public house [*chiefly British*], saloon, taproom, tavern, watering hole, watering place
related words alehouse, barrelhouse, bistro, bottle club, brewpub, cabaret, dive, joint, nightclub, roadhouse, speakeasy, sports bar, wineshop; package store

bar sinister *n* the state or fact of being born out of wedlock ⟨back in the days when the *bar sinister* was a real obstacle to social acceptance⟩ — see ILLEGITIMACY

barter *n* a giving or taking of one thing of value in return for another ⟨according to our *barter* agreement, I do all of the mechanical work on my neighbor's car, and he does all of my snow removal⟩ — see EXCHANGE 1

basal *adj* of or relating to the simplest facts or theories of a subject ⟨she clearly lacked even a *basal* familiarity with the topic⟩ — see ELEMENTARY

base *adj* **1** not following or in accordance with standards of honor and decency ⟨a *base* and sneaky act that is a clear violation of international law⟩ — see IGNOBLE 2
2 showing, expressing, or offered in a spirit of humility or unseemly submissiveness ⟨her *base* obedience to every unprincipled action ordered by her boss⟩ — see ABJECT

base *n* **1** an immaterial thing upon which something else rests ⟨the firm belief that complete trust between husband and wife is the *base* of any successful marriage⟩
synonyms basis, bedrock, bottom, cornerstone, footing, foundation, ground, groundwork, keystone, root, underpinning, warp, warp and woof
related words anchorage, bed, brace, bulwark, buttress, framework, infrastructure, mount, prop, shore, stay, substratum, substructure, support; assumption, justification, premise (*also* premiss), presumption, presupposition, rationale, supposition, theory, thesis, warrant; backbone, center, core, cornerstone, eye, focus, heart, hub, kernel, keystone, nucleus, seat; essence, quintessence, soul, touchstone
2 a place from which an advance (as for military operations) is made ⟨the army's *base* of attack was kept top secret until the battle began⟩
synonyms bridgehead, foothold
related words staging area, staging ground; beachhead, camp, center, emplacement, footing, front, headquarters, installation, station; airbase; bastion, fastness, fortress, stronghold; battlefront, field; toehold
3 a thing or place that is of greatest importance to an activity or interest ⟨the *base* of the industry is California's Silicon Valley⟩ — see CENTER 1
4 the lowest part, place, or point ⟨the *base* of the mountain extends over a huge area⟩ — see BOTTOM 3
5 the place from which a commander runs operations ⟨the army *base* is three miles down the road⟩ — see COMMAND 3

base *vb* to find a basis ⟨she *based* her argument against the death penalty on careful research⟩
synonyms ground, hang, predicate, rest
related words establish, found; assume, postulate, premise, presume, presuppose, suppose

baseborn *adj* **1** belonging to the class of people of low social or economic rank ⟨in the Middle Ages, a *baseborn* person simply had to accept his or her station in life⟩ — see IGNOBLE 1
2 born to a father and mother who are not married ⟨a *baseborn* child who didn't even know his father's name⟩ — see ILLEGITIMATE 1

baseless *adj* having no basis in reason or fact ⟨*baseless* rumors that the baseball player was using steroids⟩ — see GROUNDLESS

baseline *n* the point at which something begins ⟨any

year or event we use as the *baseline* for the Renaissance is going to be at least somewhat arbitrary⟩ — see BEGINNING

basement *n* **1** a room or set of rooms below the surface of the ground ⟨we store our bicycles in the *basement* during the winter⟩ — see CELLAR
2 the lowest part, place, or point ⟨the *basement* of the outdoor fountain needs a lot of restoration work⟩ — see BOTTOM 3

bash *n* **1** a hard strike with a part of the body or an instrument ⟨he hasn't been the same ever since he received that *bash* on his head⟩ — see [1]BLOW
2 *chiefly British* an effort to do or accomplish something ⟨while golf isn't my game, I had to give it a *bash* while at Saint Andrews in Scotland⟩ — see ATTEMPT 1
3 a social gathering ⟨I'm throwing a New Year's *bash* this year⟩ — see PARTY 1

bash *vb* **1** to come into usually forceful contact with something ⟨the car *bashed* into the tree with glass-shattering force⟩ — see HIT 2
2 to deliver a blow to (someone or something) usually in a strong vigorous manner ⟨you have to *bash* that door hard in order to get it open⟩ — see HIT 1
3 to strike repeatedly ⟨the angry child kept *bashing* her toy with a hammer until it broke⟩ — see BEAT 1
4 to criticize harshly and usually publicly ⟨in all of talk radio no other host seems to enjoy *bashing* liberals as much as he does⟩ — see ATTACK 2

bashful *adj* not comfortable around people ⟨a *bashful* child who hid in his room whenever there were visitors in the house⟩ — see SHY 2

basic *adj* of or relating to the simplest facts or theories of a subject ⟨you'll need a *basic* knowledge of computers to get any sort of office work⟩ — see ELEMENTARY

basically *adv* for the most part ⟨your answer is *basically* correct⟩ — see CHIEFLY

basics *n pl* general or basic truths on which other truths or theories can be based ⟨if you don't learn the *basics* of algebra now, you'll never master calculus⟩ — see PRINCIPLES 1

basis *n* an immaterial thing upon which something else rests ⟨the sole *basis* for the rumor is someone's overactive imagination⟩ — see BASE 1

bask *vb* to refrain from labor or exertion ⟨we blissfully *basked* at the seashore over the long holiday⟩ — see REST 1

basketful *n* a considerable amount ⟨the movie showed off a *basketful* of eye-popping special effects⟩ — see LOT 2

bass *adj* having a low musical pitch or range ⟨a man with an impressive *bass* voice⟩ — see DEEP 2

bastard *adj* **1** born to a father and mother who are not married ⟨Alexander Hamilton appears to have been bothered by the fact that he was a *bastard* child⟩ — see ILLEGITIMATE 1
2 falling short of a standard ⟨a *bastard* knockoff of a far superior thriller⟩ — see BAD 1

bastard *n* **1** an illegitimate child ⟨one of history's most illustrious *bastards* was England's first Norman king, William the Conqueror⟩
synonyms by-blow, love child, whoreson
related words nephew, niece
2 an adult male human being ⟨that lucky *bastard* has won the raffle three times in a row⟩ — see MAN 1
3 a person whose behavior is offensive to others ⟨that *bastard's* behavior was completely out of line⟩ — see JERK 1

bastardize *vb* to lower in character, dignity, or quality ⟨*bastardize* the art form by adapting it to popular taste⟩ — see DEBASE 1

bastardy *n* the state or fact of being born out of wedlock ⟨acutely conscious of his *bastardy*, he always felt the need to prove himself⟩ — see ILLEGITIMACY

baste *vb* **1** to criticize (someone) severely or angrily especially for personal failings ⟨a tyrannical father who used the dinner hour to *baste* his children for their many perceived shortcomings⟩ — see SCOLD
2 to strike repeatedly ⟨*basted* the thief with a stick while he cried out for help⟩ — see BEAT 1

bastille *n* a place of confinement for persons held in lawful custody ⟨were amazed by the squalid, cramped quarters in the town's historic *bastille*⟩ — see JAIL

bastinado *or* **bastinade** *n* a heavy rigid stick used as a weapon or for punishment ⟨the guards savagely beat the prisoner's feet with a *bastinado*⟩ — see CLUB 1

bastion *n* a structure or place from which one can resist attack ⟨the rebel army retreated to its *bastion* in the mountains to regroup⟩ — see FORT

bat *n* **1** a hard strike with a part of the body or an instrument ⟨a sharp *bat* with a rolled-up newspaper and that fly was a goner⟩ — see [1]BLOW
2 a heavy rigid stick used as a weapon or for punishment ⟨riot policemen armed with *bats* and tear gas⟩ — see CLUB 1

bat *vb* **1** to deliver a blow to (someone or something) usually in a strong vigorous manner ⟨*batted* the lamp off the table with one strike⟩ — see HIT 1
2 to strike repeatedly ⟨*batted* the piñata until it finally broke open⟩ — see BEAT 1
3 to move about from place to place aimlessly ⟨on Sunday afternoons we'd pile into Father's car and *bat* around the countryside⟩ — see WANDER 1

bat (around *or* **back and forth)** *vb* to talk about (an issue) usually from various points of view and for the purpose of arriving at a decision or opinion ⟨the issue's been *batted around*, but nothing's ever been done⟩ — see DISCUSS

batch *n* **1** a number of things considered as a unit ⟨a *batch* of essays to correct⟩ — see GROUP 1
2 a usually small number of persons considered as a unit ⟨send in the next *batch* of applicants⟩ — see GROUP 2

bath *n* **1** a great flow of water or of something that overwhelms ⟨after a night in that tropical heat I was practically drowning in a *bath* of sweat⟩ — see FLOOD
2 a room furnished with a fixture for flushing body waste ⟨retired to the upstairs *bath* to freshen up⟩ — see TOILET

bathe *vb* **1** to flow along or against ⟨the cool waters of the North Atlantic *bathe* the island's shores⟩ — see WASH 1
2 to make wet ⟨*bathe* your contact lens with the solution before inserting them⟩ — see WET
3 to supply with light ⟨the walls of the canyon were *bathed* with the warm rays of the setting sun⟩ — see ILLUMINATE 1

bathed *adj* containing, covered with, or thoroughly penetrated by water ⟨covered the victim's burns with *bathed* bandages⟩ — see WET 1

bathos *n* the state or quality of having an excess of tender feelings (as of love, nostalgia, or compassion) ⟨a novel that wallows in *bathos*⟩ — see SENTIMENTALITY

bathroom *n* a room furnished with a fixture for flushing body waste ⟨everyone should use the *bathroom* before we leave on the long trip⟩ — see TOILET

baton *n* a heavy rigid stick used as a weapon or for punishment ⟨the detainee claimed that the police had beat him with their *batons* even after he had been shackled⟩ — see CLUB 1

bats *adj* having or showing a very abnormal or sick state of mind ⟨by film's end it's obvious that faded movie star Norma Desmond is completely *bats*⟩ — see INSANE 1

battalion *n* a large body of men and women organized

for land warfare ⟨the nation's *battalions* were forced to fight on two fronts simultaneously⟩ — see ARMY 1

batter *vb* **1** to strike repeatedly ⟨intruders *battered* the door until it fell down⟩ — see BEAT 1
2 to use bombs or artillery against ⟨planes *battered* the city for weeks⟩ — see BOMBARD 1

battery *n* **1** a number of things considered as a unit ⟨a *battery* of tests to determine the cause of the medical disorder⟩ see GROUP 1
2 a usually small number of persons considered as a unit ⟨a *battery* of specialists worked on the problem until it was fixed⟩ — see GROUP 2

battle *n* **1** a forceful effort to reach a goal or objective ⟨passing the driving test was an uphill *battle*, but she finally succeeded⟩ — see STRUGGLE 1
2 a physical dispute between opposing individuals or groups ⟨a *battle* between rival gangs left two people lying dead on the street⟩ — see FIGHT 1
3 active fighting during the course of a war ⟨soldiers who desperately wanted to forget the horrors that they had witnessed in *battle*⟩ — see COMBAT 1
4 an earnest effort for superiority or victory over another ⟨the chess game was a real *battle* between two of the world's best players⟩ — see CONTEST 1

battle *vb* **1** to engage in a contest ⟨the two teams, which have long been archrivals, will *battle* on the court for the state championship⟩ — see COMPETE
2 to enter into contest or conflict with ⟨the two top-seeded tennis players *battled* each other for almost three hours⟩ — see ENGAGE 2
3 to oppose (someone) in physical conflict ⟨Andrew Jackson first gained fame as a military commander *battling* the Creek Indians during the War of 1812⟩ — see FIGHT 1
4 to strive to reduce or eliminate ⟨we must *battle* hunger and poverty wherever they exist⟩ — see FIGHT 2

battle–ax *or* **battle–axe** *n* a bad-tempered scolding woman ⟨at the office he's very much the take-charge executive; at home he meekly cowers before his *battle-ax* wife⟩ — see SHREW

battlefield *n* a place where a battle takes place ⟨wounded soldiers being carried off the *battlefield*⟩
synonyms battleground, field
related words battle line, front, front line, ground; beachhead, bridgehead, foothold; killing field
phrases field of honor

battleground *n* a place where a battle takes place ⟨the verdant hill suddenly turned into a bloody *battleground*⟩ — see BATTLEFIELD

battle royal *n* an often noisy or angry expression of differing opinions ⟨the dysfunctional couple next door had another one of their *battles royal* last night⟩ — see ARGUMENT 1

batty *adj* having or showing a very abnormal or sick state of mind ⟨a *batty* old lady who lives with 100 cats⟩ — see INSANE 1

bauble *n* a small object displayed for its attractiveness or interest ⟨picked up some cheap *baubles* at the fair⟩ — see KNICKKNACK

bawd *n* a woman who engages in sexual activities for money ⟨in the 17th century the port was a notorious hangout for Caribbean pirates and their *bawds*⟩ — see PROSTITUTE

bawdiness *n* the quality or state of being obscene ⟨the *bawdiness* of the song makes it inappropriate for children⟩ — see OBSCENITY 1

bawdy *adj* **1** depicting or referring to sexual matters in a way that is unacceptable in polite society ⟨a *bawdy* comment about someone you work with could get you fired⟩ — see OBSCENE 1
2 hinting at or intended to call to mind matters regarded as indecent ⟨a *bawdy* limerick that mischievous storytellers love to recite⟩ — see SUGGESTIVE 1

bawdy house *n* a building in which prostitutes are available ⟨a frontier mining town that had few diversions other than the local *bawdy house*⟩ — see BORDELLO

bawl *vb* **1** to shed tears often while making meaningless sounds as a sign of pain or distress ⟨he *bawled* for days after his dog died⟩ — see CRY 1
2 to speak so as to be heard at a distance ⟨the mover was *bawling* for help as the refrigerator was about to slip out of his hands⟩ — see CALL 1

bawl out *vb* to criticize (someone) severely or angrily especially for personal failings ⟨got loudly *bawled out* by the coach for making mistake after stupid mistake⟩ — see SCOLD

1bay *n* one of the parts into which an enclosed space is divided ⟨the garage has three separate *bays* for cars⟩ — see COMPARTMENT

2bay *n* a part of a body of water that extends beyond the general shoreline ⟨the *bay* is a favorite cruising ground for weekend yachtsmen⟩ — see GULF 1

3bay *n, usually* **bays** *pl* public acknowledgment or admiration for an achievement ⟨he wrote for his own personal satisfaction, not for any *bays* that the literary establishment might deign to bestow⟩ — see GLORY 1

bay *vb* **1** to speak so as to be heard at a distance ⟨the mob was *baying* for revenge⟩ — see CALL 1
2 to make a long loud mournful sound ⟨the lonesome beagle *bayed* whenever someone walked by⟩ — see HOWL 1

bayou *n* a stream that flows into a larger body of water ⟨a small creek that is the *bayou* of a larger stream⟩ — see TRIBUTARY

bay window *n* an enlarged or bulging abdomen ⟨if his *bay window* gets any bigger, it's going to need its own draw curtains⟩ — see POTBELLY

bazaar *n* an establishment where goods are sold to consumers ⟨we wandered around the *bazaar* looking to buy gifts⟩ — see SHOP 1

be *vb* **1** to have life ⟨stories that begin with the familiar line "once upon a time there *was* a beautiful maiden"⟩
synonyms breathe, exist, live, subsist
related words abide, continue, endure, hold on, hold up, keep (on), kick, last, lead, persist, rule, run on, survive; move; flourish, prosper, thrive
near antonyms disappear, evaporate, vanish; cease, desist, discontinue, end, quit, stop; abate, die (down), ebb, let up, moderate, subside, wane
antonyms depart, die, expire, pass away, perish, succumb
2 to occupy a place or location ⟨we'll *be* there waiting for you⟩ — see STAND 1
3 to take or have a certain position within a group arranged in vertical classes ⟨our school's football team *is* first in its division⟩ — see RANK 1
4 to take place ⟨the party *is* next Saturday⟩ — see HAPPEN

be (to) *vb* to behave toward in a stated way ⟨you need to *be* nice *to* your brother⟩ — see TREAT 1

beach *n* the usually sandy or gravelly land bordering a body of water ⟨she loves walking along the *beach*, looking for shells that the waves cast up⟩
synonyms beachfront, sand(s), strand
related words seaboard, seacoast, seashore, seaside; coast, coastland, coastline, shore, shoreline; oceanfront, shorefront, waterfront; bank, riverbank, riverfront, riverside; esplanade; littoral; lido, plage

beached *adj* resting on the shore or bottom of a body of water ⟨the *beached* whale had to be helped back out to sea⟩ — see AGROUND

beachfront *n* the usually sandy or gravelly land bordering a body of water ⟨the town's *beachfront* extends for more than a mile⟩ — see BEACH

beacon *n* something that provides illumination ⟨the floodlit skyscraper is one of the city's most beloved nighttime *beacons*⟩ — see LIGHT 2

beacon *vb* to supply with light ⟨a lone lighthouse *beacons* the entrance to the island's only harbor⟩ — see ILLUMINATE 1

bead *n* the quantity of fluid that falls naturally in one rounded mass ⟨squeeze a *bead* or two of glue onto the seam⟩ — see DROP 1

beak *n* **1** the jaws of a bird together with their hornlike covering ⟨the bird cracked the walnut shell with its *beak* and ate its nut⟩
synonyms bill, neb, nib
related words mouth; muzzle; mandible, maw, maxilla
2 the part of the face bearing the nostrils and nasal cavity ⟨the man's prominent *beak* gives him a somewhat aquiline appearance⟩ — see NOSE 1
3 *chiefly British* a public official having authority to decide questions of law ⟨received a stiff sentence from one of the harshest *beaks* in all of London⟩ — see JUDGE 2

beam *n* a narrow sharply defined line of light radiating from an object ⟨we'll need a flashlight that casts a broader *beam* in order to really see anything⟩ — see SHAFT 1

beam *vb* **1** to emit rays of light ⟨a lighthouse has *beamed* from this site since the 1790s⟩ — see SHINE 1
2 to express an emotion (as amusement) by curving the lips upward ⟨my father *beamed* when I showed him my new car⟩ — see SMILE 1

beaming *adj* **1** giving off or reflecting much light ⟨the orchestra began its season of outdoor concerts under a *beaming* moon⟩ — see BRIGHT 1
2 having or being an outward sign of good feelings (as of love, confidence, or happiness) ⟨Mom's *beaming* face shone with love as we all gathered for a family photo⟩ — see RADIANT 1

bean *n* **1** the upper or front part of the body that contains the brain, the major sense organs, and the mouth ⟨he tried to duck, but the pitch still hit him squarely on the *bean*⟩ — see HEAD 1
2 beans *pl* active strength of body or mind ⟨nine-year-old twins who are full of *beans*⟩ — see VIGOR 1
3 beans *pl* language, behavior, or ideas that are absurd and contrary to good sense ⟨I know something about gardening, and you're full of *beans*⟩ — see NONSENSE 1
4 beans *pl* the smallest amount or part imaginable ⟨had trouble finding a job because he didn't know *beans* about computers⟩ — see JOT

beanery *n* a public establishment where meals are served to paying customers for consumption on the premises ⟨that jerkwater town doesn't boast a single decent *beanery*⟩ — see RESTAURANT

bear *n* **1** a dull, unpleasant, or difficult piece of work ⟨the upcoming kitchen renovation sounds like a real *bear*⟩ — see CHORE 2
2 an irritable and complaining person ⟨you've been a real *bear* lately—are you having a bad week?⟩ — see GROUCH 1

bear *vb* **1** to bring forth from the womb ⟨luckily, she turned out to be able to *bear* children after all⟩
synonyms birth [*chiefly dialect*], deliver, drop, have, mother, produce
related words labor; breed, multiply, propagate, reproduce, spawn; beget, father, generate, get, sire; calve, kid, kindle, kitten, litter, pup, whelp
phrases give birth to
near antonyms abort, lose, miscarry
2 to put up with (something painful or difficult) ⟨I can't *bear* the thought of losing another loved one⟩
synonyms abide, absorb, accept, bide [*chiefly dialect*], brook, countenance, endure, go, hack, handle, meet, pocket, stand, stick out, stomach, support, sustain, sweat out, take, tolerate, wear [*British*]
related words allow, permit, suffer, swallow; reconcile (to); acquiesce, agree (with *or* to), assent (to), capitulate, consent (to), respect, submit (to), yield (to)
phrases live with, lump (it), stand for, tough (it) out
near antonyms decline, dismiss, refuse, reject, repudiate, spurn, turn down; combat, contest, fight, oppose, resist; avoid, bypass, circumvent, dodge, elude, escape, evade, miss; abstain (from), forbear, refrain (from)
3 to have a relation or connection ⟨I just found another fact that *bears* on this issue⟩ — see APPLY 1
4 to go on a specified course or in a certain direction ⟨the road *bears* left after the second traffic light⟩ — see HEAD 1
5 to hold up or serve as a foundation for ⟨the wooden bridge will only *bear* one truck at a time⟩ — see SUPPORT 3
6 to keep in one's mind or heart ⟨I'm not one to *bear* grudges⟩ — see HARBOR 1
7 to manage the actions of (oneself) in a particular way ⟨she *bore* herself well in her first public speaking event⟩ — see BEHAVE
8 to support and take from one place to another ⟨the rescue team came *bearing* much-needed food and supplies⟩ — see CARRY 1
9 to take to or upon oneself ⟨I *bear* some responsibility for the mishap⟩ — see ASSUME 1
10 to wear or have on one's person ⟨the right to *bear* arms⟩ — see CARRY 2
11 to be positioned along a certain course or in a certain direction ⟨the path will *bear* north after that marked tree⟩ — see RUN 3
12 to have as a requirement ⟨the violence in that country *bears* watching if the world wants to avoid a serious international conflict⟩ — see NEED 1
13 to have within ⟨gold-*bearing* ore⟩ — see CONTAIN 1
14 to occupy a place or location ⟨a hot, humid air mass is now *bearing* just south of the Gulf Coast⟩ — see STAND 1
15 to produce as revenue ⟨an interest-*bearing* savings account⟩ — see YIELD 2

bear (down on) *vb* to push steadily against with some force ⟨you need to *bear down on* that cap a bit to get it to latch tightly⟩ — see [2]PRESS 1

bearable *adj* capable of being endured ⟨the pain from a sprained ankle is annoying but *bearable*⟩
synonyms endurable, sufferable, supportable, sustainable, tolerable
related words livable (*also* liveable), survivable; acceptable, adequate, admissible, allowable, permissible, reasonable, satisfactory
near antonyms agonizing, appalling, awful, bad, cruel, dire, dreadful, excruciating, frightful, ghastly, grisly, gruesome (*also* grewsome), harrowing, harsh, hideous, horrendous, horrible, horrid, horrifying, lurid, macabre, monstrous, nasty, nightmarish, painful, rotten, shocking, terrible, tormenting, torturous, unfortunate, vicious, vile, wretched; unacceptable; acute, extreme, intense, piercing; abhorrent, deplorable, disgusting, distasteful, loathsome, nauseating, obnoxious, offensive, repugnant, repulsive, revolting, sickening; abominable, evil, foul, heinous, noxious, odious, unspeakable
antonyms insufferable, insupportable, intolerable, unbearable, unendurable, unsupportable

beard *vb* to oppose (something hostile or dangerous) with firmness or courage ⟨a man of integrity who was never afraid to *beard* the lion in his den⟩ — see FACE 2

bear-hug *vb* to put one's arms around and press tightly ⟨elated team members *bear-hugging* everyone in sight⟩ — see EMBRACE 1

bearing *n* **1** the fact or state of being pertinent ⟨these new facts have some *bearing* on the case⟩ — see PERTINENCE

2 the fact or state of having something in common ⟨I don't see any *bearing* between the quality of this bottle of wine and its rather exorbitant price⟩ — see CONNECTION 1

3 the way or manner in which one conducts oneself ⟨always retained his military *bearing*, even after he entered politics⟩ — see BEHAVIOR

bearish *adj* **1** emphasizing or expecting the worst ⟨some studio execs are *bearish* about this summer's box office⟩ — see PESSIMISTIC 1

2 having or showing a habitually bad temper ⟨a *bearish* recluse who ordered everyone to stay off his property⟩ — see ILL-TEMPERED

bear out *vb* to give evidence or testimony to the truth or factualness of ⟨the newly discovered papers *bore out* the rumors about the president's personal life⟩ — see CONFIRM 1

bear up *vb* to fill with courage or strength of purpose ⟨repeatedly *borne up* in times of adversity by his faith⟩ — see ENCOURAGE 1

beast *n* **1** a mean, evil, or unprincipled person ⟨she's a real *beast* to anyone who makes the mistake of crossing her⟩ — see VILLAIN

2 a person whose behavior is offensive to others ⟨he always has to act like a *beast* whenever things don't go his way⟩ — see JERK 1

3 one of the lower animals as distinguished from human beings ⟨a frigid night that was fit for neither man nor *beast*⟩ — see ANIMAL

4 a dull, unpleasant, or difficult piece of work ⟨controlling the state's vast bureaucracy has always been a *beast*⟩ — see CHORE 2

beastie *n* one of the lower animals as distinguished from human beings ⟨I've become used to sharing our cabin in the woods with all sorts of little *beasties*⟩ — see ANIMAL

beastliness *n* the manifestation of the traits or the gratification of the appetites of a lower animal ⟨a film depicting the sheer *beastliness* of life in a street gang⟩ — see BESTIALITY

beastly *adj* having or showing the nature and appetites of a lower animal ⟨left to shift for himself on an isolated farm, he gradually sank into a *beastly*, purposeless existence⟩ — see BESTIAL

beastly *adv* to a great degree ⟨it's *beastly* hot today⟩ — see VERY 1

beat *adj* depleted in strength, energy, or freshness ⟨can we pick this up tomorrow, because I'm *beat*?⟩ — see WEARY 1

beat *n* **1** a hard strike with a part of the body or an instrument ⟨delivered one hard *beat* on the drums⟩ — see [1]BLOW

2 a rhythmic expanding and contracting ⟨a single *beat* of the heart is said to be all that separates the vice president from the presidency⟩ — see PULSATION

3 the recurrent pattern formed by a series of sounds having a regular rise and fall in intensity ⟨moved to the *beat* of the music⟩ — see RHYTHM

4 a very small space of time ⟨within a *beat* he was on the phone complaining about an error in his bill⟩ — see INSTANT

beat *vb* **1** to strike repeatedly ⟨they attacked and *beat* him, but fortunately he'll be fine⟩
synonyms bash, baste, bat, batter, belabor, belt, birch, bludgeon, buffet, bung up, club, curry, do, drub, fib [*British*], flog, hammer, hide, lace, lambaste (*or* lambast), lash, lather, lick, maul, mess (up), paddle, pelt, pommel, pound, pummel, punch out, rough (up), slate, slog, switch, tan, thrash, thresh, thump, tromp, wallop, whale, whip, whop (*or* whap), whup, work over
related words assail, assault, attack, beset, box, bust, chop, clobber, clout, crack, cudgel, cuff, descend (on *or* upon), hit, jump (on), knock, lam, lay on, paste, pounce (on *or* upon), punch, raid, rush, slam, slap, smack, smash, sock, spank, storm, swat, swipe, thwack, whack, wham, whomp; blackjack, cane, cowhide, flagellate, fustigate, horsewhip, leather, pistol-whip, rawhide, scourge, strap; gore, lacerate, wound; maim, mangle, mutilate
phrases beat up on

2 to achieve a victory over ⟨she always *beats* everyone at checkers, but she's not as good at chess⟩
synonyms best, conquer, defeat, dispatch, do down [*British*], get, get around, lick, master, overbear, overcome, overmatch, prevail (over), skunk, stop, subdue, surmount, take, trim, triumph (over), upend, win (against), worst
related words sweep; edge (out), nose out, pip [*British*]; annihilate, blow away, blow out, bomb, break, bury, clobber, cream, crush, drub, finish, flatten, overwhelm, rout, shellac, skin, slaughter, smoke [*slang*], snow under, thrash, trounce, upset, wallop, wax [*slang*], whip; cap, excel, flourish, score, succeed; knock off, knock over, overpower, overthrow, subjugate, unseat, vanquish; ace (out), better, eclipse, exceed, excel, outdistance, outdo, outfight, outshine, outstrip, overtop, surpass, top, transcend
phrases get the better of, knock for a loop
near antonyms fall, give up, go down, go under; collapse, fail, flop, flunk, fold, wash out
antonyms lose (to)

3 to be greater, better, or stronger than ⟨this new animated feature sure *beats* everything else that's ever been done in animation⟩ — see SURPASS 1

4 to expand and contract in a rhythmic manner ⟨the patient's heart *beats* roughly 60 times per minute⟩ — see PULSATE

5 to move or cause to move with a striking motion ⟨the bird's wings *beat* strongly as it soared in the air⟩ — see FLAP

6 to prevent from achieving a goal ⟨you *beat* me to it⟩ — see FRUSTRATE 1

7 to shape with a hammer ⟨the medieval artisans who *beat* iron into exquisite swords⟩ — see HAMMER 1

8 to shine with a bright harsh light ⟨the tropical sun *beat* down on our heads without mercy⟩ — see GLARE 1

9 to strike or cause to strike lightly and usually rhythmically ⟨*beat* the drum in a marching rhythm⟩ — see [1]TAP

10 to throw into a state of mental uncertainty ⟨it *beats* me how that slipup happened⟩ — see CONFUSE 1

11 to avoid having to comply with (something) especially through cleverness ⟨he spends all of his time trying to *beat* the system⟩ — see CIRCUMVENT 1

12 to reduce to fine particles ⟨years of pounding had *beaten* the pebbles to a fine dust⟩ — see POWDER

13 to rob by the use of trickery or threats ⟨the screenwriter has filed a lawsuit, accusing the production company of *beating* him out of his share of the film's net profits⟩ — see FLEECE

beaten *adj* depleted in strength, energy, or freshness ⟨felt *beaten* after three months of 90-hour workweeks⟩ — see WEARY 1

beater *n* **1** a dilapidated old automobile ⟨he drives a *beater* that just barely runs⟩
synonyms clunker, crate, jalopy, junker
related words flivver, hulk, wreck; lemon

2 one that defeats an enemy or opponent ⟨no one likes to see the *beater* of our team in the play-offs⟩ — see VICTOR 1

beating *n* **1** a rhythmic expanding and contracting ⟨he wears a pacemaker to help maintain a regular *beating* of his heart⟩ — see PULSATION

2 failure to win a contest ⟨took a *beating* and ended up in second place⟩ — see DEFEAT 1

beatitude *n* a feeling or state of well-being and contentment ⟨not from earthly riches but from the milk of human kindness comes true *beatitude*⟩ — see HAPPINESS 1

beat off *vb* to drive back ⟨the defense managed to *beat off* those offensive players who were taking shots at the goalie⟩ — see REPEL 1

beat–up *adj* showing signs of advanced wear and tear and neglect ⟨drives the same *beat-up* truck he had in high school⟩ — see SHABBY 1

beau *n* **1** a male romantic companion ⟨her new *beau* brought flowers when he picked her up for their first date⟩ — see BOYFRIEND

2 a man extremely interested in his clothing and personal appearance ⟨in his youth he had been a flashy *beau* and a hit with all the ladies⟩ — see DANDY 1

Beau Brummell *n* a man extremely interested in his clothing and personal appearance ⟨the *Beau Brummells* at the health club spend more time in front of the mirror than some supermodels⟩ — see DANDY 1

beaucoup *adj, slang* being of a large but indefinite number ⟨we were able to make *beaucoup* bucks working overtime at the power plant⟩ — see MANY

beau ideal *n* **1** someone of such unequaled perfection as to deserve imitation ⟨she is the *beau ideal* of the beautiful but unassuming film actress⟩ — see IDEAL 1

2 the most perfect type or example ⟨Frank Lloyd Wright's most famous architectural creation, Falling Water, is widely regarded as the *beau ideal* of a building in harmony with its setting⟩ — see QUINTESSENCE 1

beaut *n* something very good of its kind ⟨that new bike of yours is a real *beaut*⟩ — see JIM-DANDY

beauteous *adj* very pleasing to look at ⟨a *beauteous* woman in a ball gown⟩ — see BEAUTIFUL 1

beauteousness *n* the qualities in a person or thing that as a whole give pleasure to the senses ⟨the *beauteousness* of the starlit evening put the couple in a very romantic mood⟩ — see BEAUTY 1

beautifier *n* something that decorates or beautifies ⟨a flawless complexion like that doesn't need any *beautifiers*⟩ — see DECORATION 1

beautiful *adj* **1** very pleasing to look at ⟨a strikingly *beautiful* child who is being eagerly pursued by all the modeling agencies⟩

synonyms aesthetic (*also* esthetic *or* aesthetical *or* esthetical), attractive, beauteous, bonny (*also* bonnie) [*chiefly British*], comely, cute, drop-dead, fair, fetching, good, good-looking, goodly, gorgeous, handsome, knockout, likely, lovely, lovesome, pretty, ravishing, seemly, sightly, stunning, taking, well-favored

related words alluring, appealing, charming, cunning, delightful, engaging, fascinating, glamorous (*also* glamourous), prepossessing; elegant, exquisite, glorious, Junoesque, magnificent, resplendent, splendid, statuesque, sublime, superb; flawless, perfect, radiant; dainty, delicate; personable, pleasant, presentable; chocolate-box, prettyish; desirable, dishy, dollish, foxy, hot, luscious, nubile, pulchritudinous, seductive, sexy, tasty, toothsome, yummy; hunky, studly [*slang*]; arresting, eye-catching, flamboyant, flashy, glossy, showstopping, showy, slick, snazzy, splashy, striking, zingy; photogenic, telegenic

near antonyms abhorrent, abominable, bad, disagreeable, disgusting, dreadful, foul, frightful, ghastly, horrible, loathsome, nasty, nauseating, objectionable, offensive, repellent (*also* repellant), repugnant, repulsive, revolting, shocking, sickening, terrible, vile; unappealing, unappetizing, unimposing, unpleasant, unprepossessing; frumpish, frumpy, unbecoming, unshapely; Gorgonian, haggish, witchy

antonyms grotesque, hideous, homely, ill-favored, plain, ugly, unaesthetic, unattractive, unbeautiful, uncomely, uncute, unhandsome, unlovely, unpleasing, unpretty, unsightly

2 of the very best kind ⟨you've done a *beautiful* job of illustrating that children's story⟩ — see EXCELLENT

beautifulness *n* the qualities in a person or thing that as a whole give pleasure to the senses ⟨she had a *beautifulness* of soul that made any consideration of her physical plainness irrelevant⟩ — see BEAUTY 1

beautify *vb* to make more attractive by adding something that is beautiful or becoming ⟨*beautified* the roadside landscape by planting flowers⟩ — see DECORATE

beautifying *adj* serving to add beauty ⟨added one last *beautifying* ornament to the wreath and hung it on the door⟩ — see DECORATIVE

beauty *n* **1** the qualities in a person or thing that as a whole give pleasure to the senses ⟨her *beauty* was enough to take your breath away⟩

synonyms aesthetics (*also* esthetics), attractiveness, beauteousness, beautifulness, comeliness, cuteness, fairness, gorgeousness, handsomeness, looks, loveliness, prettiness, sightliness

related words allure, appeal, attraction, fascination, glamour (*also* glamor); charm, delightfulness, elegance, exquisiteness, gloriousness, radiance, radiancy, resplendence, resplendency, splendidness, splendiferousness, sublimeness, sublimity, superbness; desirability, desirableness, foxiness, lusciousness, nubility, pulchritude, seductiveness, sex appeal, sexiness, shapeliness, tastiness, toothsomeness, yumminess; flawlessness, perfection; daintiness, delicacy; flamboyance, flashiness, glossiness, showiness, slickness, splashiness

near antonyms disagreeableness, dreadfulness, foulness, ghastliness, horribleness, loathsomeness, nastiness, offensiveness, repellency, repulsiveness, terribleness, vileness; blemish, flaw, imperfection

antonyms grotesqueness, hideousness, homeliness, plainness, ugliness, unattractiveness, unbecomingness, unloveliness, unsightliness

2 a lovely woman ⟨she was quite a *beauty* in her younger days⟩

synonyms babe [*slang*], beauty queen, cookie (*or* cooky), cutie (*or* cutey), dolly bird [*British*], enchantress, eyeful, fox, goddess, honey, knockout, queen, stunner

related words belle, charmer, peach; bathing beauty, cover girl, pinup girl; bimbette [*slang*], bunny, houri, sex kitten, sexpot, sex symbol; cutie-pie, dish, doll, dreamboat [*slang*], hottie, looker, pretty; coquette, femme fatale, siren, temptress, vamp

near antonyms bag, dog, frump; crone, hag, horror, witch; gorgon, monster

3 something very good of its kind ⟨that fish is a *beauty*⟩ — see JIM-DANDY

beauty queen *n* a lovely woman ⟨every loving husband considers his wife a *beauty queen*⟩ — see BEAUTY 2

beaver (away) *vb* to devote serious and sustained effort ⟨he's been *beavering away* at his acceptance speech all afternoon⟩ — see LABOR

becalm *vb* to free from distress or disturbance ⟨*becalmed* at last, she slept soundly for the first time in weeks⟩ — see CALM 1

because *conj* for the reason that ⟨I simply can't go to work today *because* I don't feel well⟩ — see SINCE

because of *prep* as the result of ⟨I was late for work *because of* the snowstorm, which made driving a nightmare⟩

synonyms due to, owing to, through, with

phrases on account of

beck *n, British* a natural body of running water smaller than a river ⟨when we were lads, we raced our toy boats in the narrow *beck* that bordered the lane⟩ — see CREEK 1

beckon *vb* to direct or notify by a movement or gesture ⟨*beckoned* the bashful child to come closer⟩ — see MOTION

becloud *vb* **1** to make (something) unclear to the understanding ⟨don't *becloud* the discussion by raising unrelated issues⟩ — see CONFUSE 2
2 to make dark, dim, or indistinct ⟨the smog from the city's steel mills was once so oppressive that it *beclouded* the local landscape even at noon⟩ — see CLOUD 1

beclouded *adj* **1** covered over by clouds ⟨a gloomy, *beclouded* sky that aptly matched our mood⟩ — see OVERCAST
2 filled with or dimmed by fine particles (as of dust or water) in suspension ⟨the water was so *beclouded* by mud that I couldn't see the bottom⟩ — see HAZY 1

become *vb* to eventually have as a state or quality ⟨many people *became* sick with the flu⟩ ⟨with the arrival of autumn the days *become* crisper and breezier⟩
synonyms come, get, go, grow, run, turn, wax
related words alter, change, metamorphose, modify, mutate, transfigure, transform, transmute
near antonyms abide, be, continue, linger, remain, stay

becoming *adj* meeting the requirements of a purpose or situation ⟨that's a particularly *becoming* dress for the dance⟩ — see FIT 1

bed *n* **1** a place set aside for sleeping ⟨the sofa in the living room will be your *bed* for the night⟩
synonyms bunk, doss [*chiefly British*], hay [*slang*], kip, lair [*British dialect*], pad, rack, sack
related words bedstead, futon, mattress, pallet; bunk bed, cot, couch, daybed, feather bed, four-poster, hammock, Murphy bed, shakedown, sleigh bed, sofa, sofa bed, studio couch, trundle bed, water bed; bassinet, carry-cot [*British*], cradle, crib
2 the surface upon which a body of water lies ⟨some prospectors supposedly found gold in the *bed* of that mountain stream⟩ — see BOTTOM 2
3 a natural periodic loss of consciousness during which the body restores itself ⟨I always brush my teeth and floss before going to *bed*⟩ — see SLEEP 1

bed *vb* **1** to go to one's bed in order to sleep ⟨the campers all *bedded* down for the night around 9:00 p.m.⟩
synonyms crash [*slang*], doss (down) [*chiefly British*], retire, turn in
related words bunk, perch, roost, settle; doze, drop off, nap, nod, sleep, slumber, snooze; couch, lie (down), recline
phrases hit the hay (*or* sack)
near antonyms arouse, awake, awaken, rouse, wake, waken; bestir, stir; reawake, reawaken; shift, stir
antonyms arise, get up, rise, uprise
2 to set solidly in or as if in surrounding matter ⟨a walkway of flagstones firmly *bedded* in the earth⟩ — see ENTRENCH

bedaub *vb* to rub an oily or sticky substance over ⟨the toddler delightedly *bedaubed* herself with her mother's makeup⟩ — see SMEAR 1

bedazzle *vb* **1** to hold the attention of as if by a spell ⟨don't let their promises of immense riches *bedazzle* you⟩ — see ENTHRALL 1
2 to overpower with light ⟨the theater's enormous chandelier *bedazzled* me as a child⟩ — see DAZZLE

bedazzling *adj* giving off or reflecting much light ⟨*bedazzling* Christmas decorations that added to the holiday cheer⟩ — see BRIGHT 1

bedcover *also* **bedcovering** *n* a decorative cloth used as a top covering for a bed ⟨antique *bedcovers* that should be handled with extreme care⟩ — see COUNTERPANE

bedeck *vb* **1** to make more attractive by adding something that is beautiful or becoming ⟨*bedecked* the house with hundreds of miniature lights for the party⟩ — see DECORATE
2 to outfit with clothes and especially fine or special clothes ⟨the ladies arrived *bedecked* in furs⟩ — see CLOTHE 1

bedevil *vb* to cause persistent suffering to ⟨a lingering cold *bedeviled* me for over a month⟩ — see AFFLICT

bedeviled *adj* suffering from mental confusion ⟨some *bedeviled* motorists have complained that the road maps are more a hindrance than a help⟩ — see DIZZY 2

bedevilment *n* the act of making unwelcome intrusions upon another ⟨constant *bedevilments* from a pesty neighbor kept me from finishing my work⟩ — see ANNOYANCE 1

bedew *vb* to make or become slightly or moderately wet ⟨her forehead gently *bedewed* with perspiration⟩ — see MOISTEN

bedfellow *n* someone associated with another to give assistance or moral support ⟨a child-welfare cause that has made *bedfellows* of activists who are normally on opposite ends of the political spectrum⟩ — see ALLY

bedim *vb* to make dark, dim, or indistinct ⟨the view from the mountain's summit is often *bedimmed* by haze⟩ — see CLOUD 1

bedizen *vb* to make more attractive by adding something that is beautiful or becoming ⟨an elderly actress *bedizening* herself with makeup and jewelry⟩ — see DECORATE

bedizened *adj* elaborately and often excessively decorated ⟨a *bedizened* dress that looked more like a Christmas tree than an article of clothing⟩ — see ORNATE 1

bedlam *adj* having or showing a very abnormal or sick state of mind ⟨*bedlam* ravings that suggest that the man is in need of some serious therapy⟩ — see INSANE 1

bedlam *n* **1** a place where insane people are cared for ⟨French physician Philippe Pinel was instrumental in the transformation of *bedlams* from filthy hellholes to well-ordered, humane institutions⟩ — see MADHOUSE 1
2 a place of uproar or confusion ⟨there's no way I can get any reading done in this *bedlam*, so I'm going to the library⟩ — see MADHOUSE 2

bedraggle *vb* to make wet ⟨I was so *bedraggled* by the relentless rain that I couldn't wait to get into some dry clothes⟩ — see WET

bedraggled *adj* **1** containing, covered with, or thoroughly penetrated by water ⟨the cat looked rather funny, all *bedraggled* and fit to be tied after her bath⟩ — see WET 1
2 not clean ⟨found flood victims in *bedraggled* clothes⟩ — see DIRTY 1

bedrock *n* **1** an immaterial thing upon which something else rests ⟨my religious faith is the *bedrock* of my life⟩ — see BASE 1
2 the lowest point or level ⟨knew that his acting career was at *bedrock* when all he could get were bit parts in campy horror movies⟩ — see NADIR 1

bedspread *n* a decorative cloth used as a top covering for a bed ⟨a beautiful *bedspread* that is a reproduction of an 18th-century design⟩ — see COUNTERPANE

bee *n* a sudden impulsive and apparently unmotivated idea or action ⟨she got a sudden *bee* to quit her job and move to South Carolina⟩ — see WHIM

beef *n* **1** an expression of dissatisfaction, pain, or resentment ⟨had to deal with an angry customer with a *beef* about our service⟩ — see COMPLAINT 1
2 muscular strength ⟨a heavyweight wrestler with a good deal of *beef*⟩ — see MUSCLE 1

beef *vb* to express dissatisfaction, pain, or resentment usually tiresomely ⟨he tends to stand around and *beef* for hours about any slight, real or imagined⟩ — see COMPLAIN

beef (up) *vb* **1** to increase the ability of (as a muscle) to exert physical force ⟨*beefed up* the walls with iron bars⟩ — see STRENGTHEN 1
2 to make markedly greater in measure or degree ⟨will *beef up* security for the next few days while the president is in town⟩ — see INTENSIFY

beefcake *n* a physically attractive man ⟨an iconic *beefcake* of Hollywood in the 1940s, he always appeared shirtless in at least one scene⟩ — see HUNK 1

beefy *adj* strongly and heavily built ⟨a *beefy* man who worked in a warehouse all his life⟩ — see [1]HUSKY 1

Beelzebub *n* the supreme personification of evil often represented as the ruler of hell ⟨*Beelzebub* himself could not change her mind⟩ — see DEVIL 1

beer and skittles *n pl* a situation or state of carefree comfort ⟨a job at a beach resort isn't all *beer and skittles*—it's still work⟩
synonyms easy street, fun and games, hog heaven, picnic
related words primrose path; heaven, paradise, utopia; American dream, good life; ease, relaxation, rest
phrases bed of roses, the lap of luxury, life of Riley (*also* life of Reilly)
near antonyms agony, hell, horror, misery, murder, nightmare, torment, torture

beer–bellied *adj* having a large protruding abdomen ⟨at the reunion, former players of the championship baseball squad gathered for a group photo in all their gray-haired and *beer-bellied* glory⟩ — see PAUNCHY

beer belly *n* an enlarged or bulging abdomen ⟨a former jock whose most impressive physical asset these days is his bloated *beer belly*⟩ — see POTBELLY

bee's knees *n pl* something very good of its kind ⟨can't get enough of your apple pie—it's the *bee's knees* as my grandmother would say⟩ — see JIM-DANDY

beetle *vb* to extend outward beyond a usual point ⟨houses in the town commonly have second stories that *beetle* over the ground floors, and the overhang is known as a "bump"⟩ — see BULGE 1

befall *vb* to take place ⟨whatever *befalls*, we'll make the best of it and carry on⟩ — see HAPPEN

befit *vb* to be fitting or proper ⟨spoke politely of the deceased, as *befitted* the occasion⟩ — see DO 1

befitting *adj* **1** following the established traditions of refined society and good taste ⟨many voters feel that the womanizing governor has not acted in a *befitting* manner for someone who serves as the state's chief executive⟩ — see PROPER 1
2 meeting the requirements of a purpose or situation ⟨a *befitting* reply to a civil question⟩ — see FIT 1

befog *vb* **1** to make (something) unclear to the understanding ⟨the professor's convoluted explanation only *befogged* the textbook's presentation of this scientific principle⟩ — see CONFUSE 2
2 to make dark, dim, or indistinct ⟨the morning murk *befogged* our view of the harbor⟩ — see CLOUD 1
3 to throw into a state of mental uncertainty ⟨completely *befogged* by the sudden change of subject⟩ — see CONFUSE 1

befogged *adj* **1** filled with or dimmed by fine particles (as of dust or water) in suspension ⟨the *befogged* air of the construction site was so clogged with dust that I starting coughing⟩ — see HAZY 1
2 suffering from mental confusion ⟨became hopelessly *befogged* after trying to understand the instructions for the latest handheld device⟩ — see DIZZY 2

before *adv* so as to precede something in order of time ⟨their arrival was completely expected because a messenger had gone *before*⟩ — see AHEAD 1

before *prep* **1** earlier than ⟨since I'm a faster runner, I got there *before* him⟩
synonyms afore [*chiefly dialect*], ahead of, ere, fore (*also* 'fore) [*chiefly dialect*], of, previous to, prior to, to
related words till, until, up to
phrases in advance of
near antonyms next, next to, since
antonyms after, following
2 preceding in space ⟨the children always insisted on running *before* their parents⟩
synonyms afore [*chiefly dialect*], ahead of, fore (*also* 'fore) [*chiefly dialect*]
related words against
phrases in advance of, in front of
antonyms after, following

beforehand *adv* **1** before the usual or expected time ⟨if you arrive *beforehand*, we won't be entirely prepared yet⟩ — see EARLY
2 so as to precede something in order of time ⟨if you get ready *beforehand*, you won't have to rush at the last minute⟩ — see AHEAD 1

before long *adv* at or within a short time ⟨the painters ought to be done *before long*⟩ — see SHORTLY 2

befoul *vb* **1** to make dirty ⟨unsightly mud and slush *befouls* the family car every winter⟩ — see DIRTY
2 to make unfit for use by the addition of something harmful or undesirable ⟨the enemy had *befouled* the water in all of the area's wells with animal carcasses⟩ — see CONTAMINATE

befouled *adj* not clean ⟨given the task of cleaning the animals' *befouled* pens⟩ — see DIRTY 1

befuddle *vb* to throw into a state of mental uncertainty ⟨most of the applicants were *befuddled* by the wording of one of the questions on the driving test⟩ — see CONFUSE 1

befuddled *adj* suffering from mental confusion ⟨the perennially *befuddled* professor was always forgetting where she'd left her glasses⟩ — see DIZZY 2

befuddlement *n* a state of mental uncertainty ⟨the library patron was in obvious *befuddlement* over where to find the appropriate references⟩ — see CONFUSION 1

beg *vb* to make a request to (someone) in an earnest or urgent manner ⟨she *begged* her husband to give up extreme skiing⟩
synonyms appeal (to), beseech, besiege, conjure, entreat, impetrate, implore, importune, petition, plead (to), pray, solicit, supplicate
related words bludge [*chiefly Australian & New Zealand*], cadge, mooch, sponge; ask, desire, invoke, request, sue; claim, coerce, command, compel, demand, force, insist, require
phrases call on (*or* upon)
near antonyms hint, imply, intimate, suggest; appease, conciliate, gratify, mollify, oblige, pacify, placate, please, satisfy; comfort, console, content, quiet

beget *vb* **1** to be the cause of (a situation, action, or state of mind) ⟨one change in the natural environment will *beget* others⟩ — see EFFECT
2 to become the father of ⟨the racehorse *begot* several Kentucky Derby winners⟩ — see FATHER

begetter *n* a person who establishes a whole new field of endeavor ⟨Michael Faraday is widely hailed as one of the *begetters* of electromagnetism, the field of study that sparked a technological revolution⟩ — see FATHER 2

beggar *n* a person who lives by public begging ⟨the pitiful *beggars* that are such a common sight in underdeveloped countries⟩
synonyms mendicant, panhandler
related words bohemian, bum, clochard, drifter, hobo, tramp, vagabond, vagrant; guttersnipe, urchin, waif; miserable, pauper; bludger [*chiefly Australian & New Zealand*], cadger, hanger-on, leech, moocher, parasite,

schnorrer, sponge, sponger; dependent; deadbeat, derelict, idler, ne'er-do-well

beggared *adj* lacking money or material possessions ⟨the family was completely *beggared* after the stock market crash⟩ — see POOR 1

beggarly *adj* lacking money or material possessions ⟨the dictator and his inner circle lived in unconscionable luxury while the *beggarly* masses eked out a pitiful existence⟩ — see POOR 1

beggary *n* the state of lacking sufficient money or material possessions ⟨too many people are homeless and living in shameful *beggary* in this country⟩ — see POVERTY 1

begin *vb* **1** to take the first step in (a process or course of action) ⟨she *began* walking to work for exercise⟩
synonyms commence, embark (on *or* upon), enter (into *or* upon), fall (to), get off, kick off, launch, lead off, open, start, strike (into)
related words create, generate, inaugurate, initiate, innovate, invent, originate; adopt, embrace, take on, take up; establish, father, found, institute, organize, pioneer, set up, spawn; get around (to), get down (to), get round (to)
phrases get going, get to, set about
near antonyms cease, desist, discontinue, halt, knock off, lay off, quit, stop; close, complete; abandon, forsake, leave; abolish, demolish, destroy, exterminate, extinguish, phase out
antonyms conclude, end, finish, terminate
2 to come into existence ⟨the storm *began* late in the day and lasted all night⟩
synonyms actualize, appear, arise, break, commence, dawn, engender, form, materialize, originate, set in, spring, start
related words be, breathe, exist, live, subsist; arrive, come on, emerge; coalesce, cohere, shape (up); continue, endure, last, persist, survive
near antonyms conclude, desist, discontinue, finish, halt, quit, terminate; disappear, dissolve, evaporate, vanish; depart, die, expire, pass away, perish
antonyms cease, end, stop
3 to be responsible for the creation and early operation or use of ⟨the religious sect was *begun* by a small breakaway faction⟩ — see FOUND

beginner *n* a person who is just starting out in a field of activity ⟨although our son is only a *beginner* at swimming, he is making excellent progress⟩
synonyms abecedarian, apprentice, babe, colt, cub, fledgling, freshman, greenhorn, neophyte, newbie, newcomer, novice, novitiate, punk, recruit, rook, rookie, tenderfoot, tyro, virgin
related words boot; amateur, dabbler, dilettante; learner, student, trainee; candidate, entrant, probationer
near antonyms expert, master, pro, professional
antonyms old hand, old-timer, vet, veteran

beginning *adj* **1** coming before the main part or item usually to introduce or prepare for what follows ⟨the *beginning* part of the book is a portrait of Europe on the eve of the World War I⟩ — see PRELIMINARY
2 of or relating to the simplest facts or theories of a subject ⟨a course in *beginning* geology for nonscience majors⟩ — see ELEMENTARY

beginning *n* the point at which something begins ⟨the actual *beginning* of the universe is still under debate, with some scientists continuing to uphold the big bang theory⟩
synonyms alpha, baseline, birth, commencement, dawn, day one, genesis, get-go (*also* git-go), inception, incipience, incipiency, kickoff, launch, morning, nascence, nascency, onset, outset, start, threshold
related words drawing board, first base, ground zero, square one; creation, founding, inauguration, initiation, institution, origination; cradle, fountain, fountainhead, germ, origin, root, seedbed, source, spring, well, wellspring; dawning, opening; advent, appearance, arrival, debut (*also* début), emergence; childhood, infancy, youth
near antonyms cessation, closing, closure, completion, finale, finish, period, stop, termination, windup
antonyms close, conclusion, end, ending, omega

begird *vb* to encircle or bind with or as if with a belt ⟨a white granite boulder *begirt* with a band of dark gray⟩ — see GIRD 1

begone *vb* to leave a place often for another ⟨in his frustration the beleaguered actor cried out to the autograph seekers, "*Begone* and let me finish my meal in peace!"⟩ — see GO 2

begrime *vb* to make dirty ⟨years of spattered mud had thoroughly *begrimed* the mailbox by the side of the road⟩ — see DIRTY

begrimed *adj* not clean ⟨*begrimed* miners emerging from the coal mines⟩ — see DIRTY 1

begrudge *vb* to have a resentful awareness of and desire for (another's possessions or advantages) or to feel resentment toward (someone) over possessions or advantages ⟨I don't *begrudge* you your success—you earned it⟩ — see ENVY

beguile *vb* **1** to attract or delight as if by magic ⟨the magician effortlessly *beguiled* and amazed the children⟩ — see CHARM 1
2 to cause to believe what is untrue ⟨*beguiled* her into believing that yet another worthless item would enhance her life⟩ — see DECEIVE
3 to lead away from a usual or proper course by offering some pleasure or advantage ⟨was *beguiled* by the promise of easy money as a drug dealer⟩ — see LURE

beguiling *adj* **1** clever at attaining one's ends by indirect and often deceptive means ⟨a smart and *beguiling* child who can manipulate her parents with alarming ease⟩ — see ARTFUL 1
2 tending or having power to deceive ⟨the *beguiling* allure of a life of crime⟩ — see DECEPTIVE 1

behave *vb* to manage the actions of (oneself) in a particular way ⟨if the children *behave* themselves properly and sit quietly during church, they'll get their ice cream afterward⟩
synonyms acquit, bear, carry, comport, conduct, demean, deport, quit
related words check, collect, compose, constrain, contain, control, curb, handle, inhibit, quiet, repress, restrain; moderate, modulate, temper; act, impersonate, play
near antonyms act up, carry on, cut up, misbehave, misconduct

behavior *n* the way or manner in which one conducts oneself ⟨usually the enfant terrible, he's promising to be on his best *behavior* for the party⟩
synonyms actions, address, bearing, comportment, conduct, demeanor, deportment, geste (*also* gest) [*archaic*]
related words etiquette, form, manners, mores, proprieties; p's and q's; amenity, civility, courtesy, decorum, politeness; air, attitude, carriage, poise, pose, posture, presence; aspect, look, mien; formality, protocol, rules; custom, habit, habitude, pattern, practice (*also* practise), trick, wont; convention, fashion, form, mode, style; affectation, attribute, characteristic, mark, trait; distinctiveness, oddity, peculiarity, singularity, strangeness, uniqueness, weirdness

behead *vb* to cut off the head of ⟨Mary, Queen of Scots, was *beheaded* for plotting against Queen Elizabeth⟩ — see DECAPITATE

behemoth *n* something that is unusually large and

powerful ⟨the newest SUV is a gas-guzzling *behemoth* that doesn't even fit in a standard parking space⟩ — see GIANT

behest *n* a statement of what to do that must be obeyed by those concerned ⟨I only made the change at the author's *behest*⟩ — see COMMAND 1

behind *adj* not arriving, occurring, or settled at the due, usual, or proper time ⟨the required work was *behind*, so now we're running late⟩ — see LATE 1

behind *n* the part of the body upon which someone sits ⟨cleaned the baby's *behind*⟩ — see BUTTOCKS

behind *prep* **1** at, to, or toward the rear of ⟨she preferred to be *behind* the lead hikers, who were always too much in a rush to enjoy the scenery⟩
synonyms abaft, back of
phrases in back of
near antonyms ahead of
antonyms before
2 subsequent to in time or order ⟨we arrived *behind* them⟩ — see AFTER

behindhand *adj* not arriving, occurring, or settled at the due, usual, or proper time ⟨the response was *behindhand*, just like everything else the company did⟩ — see LATE 1

behind–the–scenes *adj* **1** not known or meant to be known by the general populace ⟨a tell-all book about the *behind-the-scenes* negotiations that got him the vice presidential nomination⟩ — see PRIVATE 1
2 undertaken or done so as to escape being observed or known by others ⟨*behind-the-scenes* negotiations that resulted in the hostages being released unharmed⟩ — see SECRET 1

behold *vb* **1** to have a clear idea of ⟨to anyone who *beholds* the immense complexity of life on earth⟩ — see COMPREHEND 1
2 to make note of (something) through the use of one's eyes ⟨I opened the window blinds and *beheld* snow everywhere⟩ — see SEE 1

beholden *adj* being under obligation for a favor or gift ⟨not wanting to be *beholden* to anyone, he insisted on paying his own way⟩
synonyms bounden [*archaic*], indebted, obligated, obliged
related words appreciative, grateful, thankful

beige *adj* lacking in distinctive features or qualities ⟨some food critics have dismissed that chef's version of French cuisine as *beige* and boring⟩ — see NONDESCRIPT

being *n* **1** a member of the human race ⟨no one has the right to enslave another *being*⟩ — see HUMAN
2 one that has a real and independent existence ⟨new parents are typically in awe at having created this separate *being*⟩ — see ENTITY
3 the quality or qualities that make a thing what it is ⟨music is such a large part of her *being* that she could never give up performing⟩ — see ESSENCE 1

being (as *or* as how *or* that) *conj, chiefly dialect* for the reason that ⟨*being as how* I paid for lunch, I'd appreciate it if you picked up the tab for dinner⟩ — see SINCE

belabor *vb* **1** to speak or write about insistently and usually tiresomely ⟨stop *belaboring* the fact that they're already in debt⟩
synonyms dwell (on *or* upon), harp (on)
related words accent, accentuate, emphasize, pay (up), point (up), stress, underline, underscore
antonyms disregard, forget, ignore, overlook, overpass, pass over, slight, slur (over)
2 to criticize harshly and usually publicly ⟨there's no need to *belabor* other people's flaws when you're hardly perfect yourself⟩ — see ATTACK 2
3 to strike repeatedly ⟨with a whip he *belabored* a horse almost to the point of death⟩ — see BEAT 1

belated *adj* not arriving, occurring, or settled at the due, usual, or proper time ⟨a *belated* birthday card⟩ — see LATE 1

belatedly *adv* after the due, usual, or proper time ⟨she *belatedly* realized that it had been her friend's birthday the day before⟩ — see LATE 1

belatedness *n* the quality or state of being late ⟨the *belatedness* of the payment resulted in us being charged overdue fees⟩ — see LATENESS

belaud *vb* to praise too much ⟨critically *belauded* in his heyday, that early 20th-century novelist is now largely forgotten⟩ — see FLATTER 1

belch *n* an expulsion of stomach gas through the mouth ⟨with a loud *belch* he concluded his pig-out and rose at last from the table⟩
synonyms burp, eructation
related words hiccup (*also* hiccough)

belch *vb* to violently throw out or off (something from within) ⟨the volcano *belched* lava and ash for days⟩ — see ERUPT 1

beldam *or* **beldame** *n* a mean or ugly old woman ⟨knocking on the *beldam's* door on Halloween was once an annual ritual for the kids in the neighborhood⟩ — see CRONE

beleaguer *vb* to surround (as a fortified place) with armed forces for the purpose of capturing or preventing commerce and communication ⟨*beleaguered* the castle for months⟩ — see BESIEGE 1

beleaguerment *n* the cutting off of an area by military means to stop the flow of people or supplies ⟨the devastating *beleaguerment* of Leningrad that lasted from September 1941 to January 1944⟩ — see BLOCKADE

belie *vb* **1** to give a misleading impression of ⟨his bright smile *belied* his actual mood, which was really one of great sadness⟩
synonyms misrepresent
related words contradict; camouflage, cloak, conceal, counterfeit, disguise, hide, mask, obscure; color, deceive, distort, falsify, garble, mislead, misrender, misreport, twist; dissemble, feign, pretend
near antonyms bare, demonstrate, disclose, discover, evince, exhibit, expose, reveal; flaunt, parade, show off
antonyms betray, represent
2 to prove to be false ⟨the latest information *belies* the old theory⟩ — see DISPROVE
3 to keep secret or shut off from view ⟨the security council issued false assurances that *belied* the true gravity of the situation⟩ — see [1]HIDE 2

belief *n* **1** mental conviction of the truth of some statement or the reality of some being or phenomenon ⟨a *belief* in UFO's led him to relentlessly scan the nighttime skies⟩
synonyms credence, credit, faith
related words axiom, law, precept, principle, tenet; assurance, certainty, certitude, conviction, positiveness, sureness; confidence, dependence (*also* dependance), reliance, trust; hope; doctrine, dogma, philosophy; dogmatism, fanaticism, insistence
phrases article of faith
near antonyms distrust, mistrust, skepticism, suspicion, uncertainty
antonyms disbelief, discredit, doubt, nonbelief, unbelief
2 an idea that is believed to be true or valid without positive knowledge ⟨it's my *belief* that the sky is blue because our eyes perceive the color blue easily⟩ — see OPINION 1

believable *adj* worthy of being accepted as true or reasonable ⟨she had a *believable* excuse for missing the deadline⟩
synonyms credible, creditable, likely, plausible, presumptive, probable

related words cogent, compelling, conclusive, convincing, decisive, effective, forceful, persuasive, satisfying, strong, telling; acceptable, cogitable, conceivable, imaginable, possible, practical, reasonable; dependable, reliable, trustworthy; sophistic (*or* sophistical), specious

near antonyms absurd, doubtful, dubious, fantastic (*also* fantastical), flimsy, outlandish, preposterous, questionable, ridiculous; impossible, inconceivable, unimaginable, unthinkable; skeptical, suspect, suspicious, uncertain, unsure; hopeless, unworkable, useless

antonyms far-fetched, implausible, improbable, incredible, unbelievable, unlikely, unplausible

believe *vb* **1** to regard as right or true ⟨only the most naive car buyer would have *believed* the salesman's claim that the dealership was actually losing money on the deal⟩

synonyms accept, buy, credit, swallow, take, trust

related words account, accredit, understand; assume, presume, suppose; conclude, deduce, infer

phrases set store by (*or* on)

near antonyms distrust, doubt, misdoubt, mistrust, question, suspect; challenge, dispute

antonyms disbelieve, discredit, reject

2 to have as an opinion ⟨despite the horrors she witnessed and endured, Anne Frank steadfastly *believed* that "people are really good at heart"⟩

synonyms allow [*chiefly Southern & Midland*], conceive, consider, deem, esteem, feel, figure, guess, hold, imagine, judge, reckon [*chiefly dialect*], suppose, think

related words regard, view; accept, perceive; depend, rely, trust; assume, presume, presuppose, surmise; conclude, deduce, infer

near antonyms distrust, doubt, mistrust, question, suspect; disbelieve, discredit, reject

believer *n* one who professes a religious faith ⟨for *believers*, it was sufficient proof that a miracle had occurred⟩

synonyms religionist

related words fundamentalist; cultist, pietist, zealot; deist, monotheist, polytheist, theist; churchgoer, communicant, congregant

belittle *vb* to express scornfully one's low opinion of ⟨*belittled* the movie hunk's acting ability⟩ — see DECRY 1

belittlement *n* the act of making a person or a thing seem little or unimportant ⟨an unconscionable *belittlement* of his spouse in public⟩ — see DEPRECIATION

belittling *adj* intended to make a person or thing seem of little importance or value ⟨there's no need for *belittling* comments about your brother's trumpet playing⟩ — see DEROGATORY

belle epoque *or* **belle époque** *n* a period of high artistic or cultural development ⟨that 19th-century *belle epoque* when Paris seemed to be the artistic center of the universe⟩

synonyms golden age, renaissance

related words silver age; millennium; bloom, blossom, flower, flush, glory, heyday, prime, salad days; acme, apex, climax, meridian, peak, pinnacle, summit, zenith

antonyms dark age

bellicose *adj* feeling or displaying eagerness to fight ⟨*bellicose* hockey players who always seem to spend more time fighting than playing⟩ — see BELLIGERENT

bellicosity *n* an inclination to fight or quarrel ⟨the notorious *bellicosity* of the countries on the Balkan Peninsula over the centuries⟩ — see BELLIGERENCE

belligerence *n* an inclination to fight or quarrel ⟨among the Native American tribes of the colonial period, the Iroquois were known for their *belligerence*⟩

synonyms aggression, aggressiveness, assaultiveness, bellicosity, belligerency, combativeness, contentiousness, defiance, disputatiousness, feistiness, fight, militance, militancy, militantness, pugnacity, quarrelsomeness, scrappiness, truculence

related words antagonism, fierceness, hostility, hyperaggressiveness, unfriendliness; imperialism, jingoism, militarism; acidity, biliousness, captiousness, crabbiness, crankiness, crossness, disagreeableness, fractiousness, fretfulness, grouchiness, grumpiness, huffiness, irascibility, irascibleness, irritability, irritableness, orneriness, peevishness, pettishness, petulance, querulousness, rudeness, surliness, testiness, waspishness

phrases chip on one's shoulder

near antonyms antiaggression, anti-imperialism, antimilitarism; affability, amiability, amicability, benevolence, cordiality, friendliness, geniality, graciousness, pleasantness, sociability; gentleness, kindliness, mildness; amenability, complaisance, placability

antonyms nonaggression, pacifism

belligerency *n* an inclination to fight or quarrel ⟨an inveterate *belligerency* that needs to be addressed by classes in anger management⟩ — see BELLIGERENCE

belligerent *adj* feeling or displaying eagerness to fight ⟨the coach became quite *belligerent* and spit at an umpire after being thrown out of the game⟩

synonyms aggressive, agonistic, argumentative, assaultive, bellicose, brawly, chippy, combative, confrontational, contentious, discordant, disputatious, feisty, gladiatorial, militant, pugnacious, quarrelsome, scrappy, truculent, warlike

related words antagonistic, fierce, hostile, hot-tempered; acidic, bearish, bilious, bristly, choleric, crabby, cranky, cross, disagreeable, dyspeptic, fractious, fretful, grouchy, grumpy, huffy, ill-humored, ill-natured, ill-tempered, irascible, irritable, ornery, peevish, pettish, petulant, prickly, querulous, rude, snappish, snappy, stroppy [*British*], surly, testy, touchy, ugly, waspish; savage, vicious; battling, fighting, warring

phrases on the warpath

near antonyms anti-imperialist, antimilitarist, unwarlike; affable, amiable, amicable, benevolent, complaisant, conciliatory, cordial, easygoing, friendly, genial, good-natured, good-tempered, gracious, ingratiating, kindhearted, obliging, pleasant, sociable; calm, quiet, relaxed, serene, tranquil; benign, gentle, kindly, mild

antonyms nonaggressive, nonbelligerent, pacific, peaceable, peaceful, unbelligerent, uncombative, uncontentious

bellow *vb* **1** to make a long loud deep noise or cry ⟨the cow *bellowed* for her calf⟩ — see ROAR 1

2 to speak so as to be heard at a distance ⟨down in the servants' quarters the housekeeper was *bellowing* at one of the parlor maids⟩ — see CALL 1

bellwether *n* one that takes the lead or sets an example ⟨the state has a long history of being an early and reliable *bellwether* in presidential elections⟩

synonyms leader, pacemaker, pacer, pacesetter, trendsetter

related words foregoer, forerunner, harbinger, herald, precursor; groundbreaker, innovator, pioneer

near antonyms Johnny-come-lately, me-tooer

antonyms follower, imitator

belly *n* **1** a need or desire for food ⟨his one concern in life seemed to be for his *belly*⟩ — see HUNGER 1

2 an enlarged or bulging abdomen ⟨vowed to get rid of his *belly* in time to attend his class reunion⟩ — see POTBELLY

3 the part of the body between the chest and the pelvis ⟨a baby with a round little *belly*⟩ — see STOMACH 1

4 the seat of one's deepest thoughts and emotions ⟨in my *belly* I knew that he wasn't telling the truth, as the details of his story just didn't add up⟩ — see CORE 1

belly *vb* **1** to extend outward beyond a usual point ⟨the sails slowly *bellied* as the wind picked up⟩ — see BULGE 1

2 to move slowly with the body close to the ground ⟨recruits were forced to *belly* over the obstacle course under simulated enemy fire⟩ — see CRAWL 1

bellyache *n* abdominal pain especially when focused in the digestive organs ⟨eating too many apples will give you a *bellyache*⟩ — see STOMACHACHE

bellyache *vb* to express dissatisfaction, pain, or resentment usually tiresomely ⟨tired of the kids *bellyaching* every time they're asked to mow the lawn or take out the trash⟩ — see COMPLAIN

bellyacher *n* **1** a person who makes frequent complaints usually about little things ⟨one of the biggest *bellyachers* about the lousy coffee at work⟩ — see CRYBABY

2 an irritable and complaining person ⟨there's always at least one *bellyacher* who doesn't like the food on the cruise ship⟩ — see GROUCH 1

bellyful *n* the state or an instance of going beyond what is usual, proper, or needed ⟨a *bellyful* of complaints about the new security procedures⟩ — see EXCESS 1

belly laugh *n* an explosive sound that is a sign of amusement ⟨humorous anecdotes that are likely to evoke lots of smiles but few *belly laughs*⟩ — see LAUGH 1

belly up *vb* to come near or nearer ⟨*belly up* to the buffet table and help yourselves⟩ — see APPROACH 1

belong *vb* **1** to have or be in a usual or proper place ⟨your shoes *belong* in the closet, not in the middle of the living room where people will trip on them⟩

synonyms go

related words place, stay; fit (in)

2 to be the property of a person or group of persons ⟨those textbooks *belong* to the school system and not to the students⟩

synonyms appertain, pertain

related words have, hold, own, possess

belonging *n* **1** the state of being in a very personal or private relationship ⟨her adoptive family gave the young girl a sense of *belonging* that she had never felt before⟩ — see FAMILIARITY 1

2 belongings *pl* transportable items that one owns ⟨packed up all their *belongings* and moved across the country⟩ — see POSSESSION 2

beloved *adj* granted special treatment or attention ⟨her *beloved* cat sleeps in its own little bed⟩ — see DARLING 1

beloved *n* a person with whom one is in love ⟨searching for some incredibly romantic spot in which to ask his *beloved* to marry him⟩ — see SWEETHEART 1

below *adv* **1** in or to a lower place ⟨the skipper climbed *below* to fix the engine⟩

synonyms beneath, under, underneath

related words beside, near, nearby

near antonyms aloft, overhead

antonyms up

2 toward or in a lower position ⟨when rock climbing I just know that if I look *below*, I'll become paralyzed with fear⟩ — see DOWN 1

below *prep* **1** in a lower position than ⟨for the photo she sat *below* everyone else, on the floor actually⟩

synonyms beneath, neath [*dialect*], under

related words underneath

antonyms above, over

2 subsequent to in time or order ⟨that ranks a little *below* a root canal on my list of things I'd want to experience⟩ — see AFTER

belowground *adj* being, situated, or operating beneath the surface of the earth ⟨a vast *belowground* network of tunnels⟩

synonyms subsurface, subterranean, underground

antonyms aboveground, surface

[1]**belt** *n* **1** a hard strike with a part of the body or an instrument ⟨delivered a shattering *belt* to the rock with a hammer⟩ — see [1]BLOW

2 the portion of a serving of a beverage that is swallowed at one time ⟨he knocked back a *belt* of whiskey before leaving⟩ — see DRINK 2

[2]**belt** *n* **1** a strip of flexible material (as leather) worn around the waist ⟨a drugstore cowboy who loves his fancily decorated *belt*⟩

synonyms ceinture, cincture, cummerbund (*also* cumberbund), girdle, sash, self-belt

related words band, waistband; circle, loop, ribbon, ring; baldric, bandolier (*or* bandoleer), Sam Browne belt; cestus, obi

2 a broad geographical area ⟨that part of the country is sometimes called "the farm *belt*" because of the number of farms there⟩ — see REGION 2

belt *vb* **1** to deliver a blow to (someone or something) usually in a strong vigorous manner ⟨*belted* the baseball out of the park⟩ — see HIT 1

2 to encircle or bind with or as if with a belt ⟨*belted* the little boy's pants tightly so they would stay up⟩ — see GIRD 1

3 to strike repeatedly ⟨*belted* the punching bag relentlessly⟩ — see BEAT 1

4 to proceed or move quickly ⟨the boy went *belting* along on his skateboard⟩ — see HURRY 2

belt (down) *vb* to swallow in liquid form ⟨I *belted down* a can of soda and rushed back out to the game⟩ — see DRINK 1

belt up *vb, British* to stop talking ⟨the schoolboy ordered his mates to *belt up* about the prank⟩ — see SHUT UP 1

belvedere *n* a freestanding airy structure in a scenic setting (as a park) typically offering commanding views ⟨a Greek revival *belvedere* stands majestically on a grassy knoll overlooking the river⟩

synonyms alcove, casino, gazebo, kiosk, pavilion, summerhouse

related words trellis

bemire *vb* to make dirty ⟨I was not thrilled to have my brand-new car *bemired* by the spattering mud⟩ — see DIRTY

bemired *adj* not clean ⟨tired and *bemired* after a day spent working outdoors⟩ — see DIRTY 1

bemoan *vb* **1** to feel or express sorrow for ⟨*bemoaned* the death of his wife by writing a series of poignant letters addressed to her⟩ — see LAMENT 1

2 to feel sorry or dissatisfied about ⟨a think piece *bemoaning* the coarsening of our society over the last several decades⟩ — see REGRET

bemoaning *adj* expressing or suggesting mourning ⟨one parishioner who always seems to have a *bemoaning* expression on her face⟩ — see MOURNFUL 1

bemuse *vb* **1** to hold the attention of ⟨a public that seemed more *bemused* by the shenanigans of celebrities than by a war being waged half a world away⟩ — see ENGAGE 1

2 to throw into a state of mental uncertainty ⟨the stage mishap momentarily *bemused* the actress⟩ — see CONFUSE 1

bemused *adj* suffering from mental confusion ⟨new federal regulations that the easily *bemused* should make no attempt to read and understand⟩ — see DIZZY 2

bemusement *n* a state of mental uncertainty ⟨an expression of utter *bemusement*⟩ — see CONFUSION 1

bench *n* **1** a public official having authority to decide questions of law ⟨appealed to the *bench* for leniency⟩ — see JUDGE 2

2 an assembly of persons for the administration of justice ⟨a ruling from the *bench* is expected any day now⟩ — see COURT 3

benchmark *n* something set up as an example against which others of the same type are compared ⟨this prize-winning biography will be the *benchmark* against which all others will be judged in future years⟩ — see STANDARD 1

bend *n* **1** something that curves or is curved ⟨it's hard to see around that *bend* in the road, so be careful⟩
synonyms angle, arc, arch, bow, crook, curvature, curve, inflection, turn, wind
related words kink, warp; circle, ring, ringlet, round; coil, curl, curlicue (*also* curlycue); buckle, convolution, flexure, fold, loop, spiral, swirl, twist, winding; incurvature, reflection; decline, inclination, incline, slope; corner, turnoff; dogleg, hairpin
2 the act of positioning or an instance of being positioned at an angle ⟨did knee *bends* for exercise⟩ — see TILT

bend *vb* **1** to cause to turn away from a straight line ⟨she *bent* the blade of the knife when she got it jammed in the drawer⟩
synonyms arch, bow, crook, curve, hook, swerve
related words arc, round; incurvate, incurve, inflect, reflect; deflect, divert; entwine, kink, swirl, turn, twine, twist, veer, warp; coil, curl, enroll (*also* enrol), loop, spiral; dent, dimple; meander, wave, weave, wind; decline, incline, slope
antonyms straighten, unbend, uncurl
2 to occupy (oneself) diligently or with close attention ⟨*bent* herself to the task for the rest of the day⟩ — see APPLY 2
3 to point or turn (something) toward a target or goal ⟨*bent* all of his efforts toward making his first documentary film⟩ — see AIM 1
4 to turn away from a straight line or course ⟨the stream *bends* slightly to the east⟩ — see CURVE 1
5 to change so much as to create a wrong impression or alter the meaning of ⟨attorneys *bending* the facts to put their client in the most favorable light⟩ — see GARBLE 1
6 to cause (something) to hold to another ⟨*bend* a leash to the dog's collar⟩ — see FASTEN 1

bender *n* a bout of prolonged or excessive drinking ⟨didn't remember a thing after the all-night *bender*⟩ — see CAROUSE

bending *adj* marked by a long series of irregular curves ⟨the river takes a long *bending* path to the sea⟩ — see CROOKED 1

bendy *adj, chiefly British* able to bend easily without breaking ⟨the kids love to use *bendy* straws⟩ — see WILLOWY

beneath *adv* in or to a lower place ⟨a ranch house with all of the rooms on one floor and a combined basement and garage *beneath*⟩ — see BELOW 1

beneath *prep* in a lower position than ⟨sat *beneath* him, on the floor, for the group photo⟩ — see BELOW 1

benediction *n* **1** a prayer calling for divine care, protection, or favor ⟨the priest offered a *benediction* for the missing children⟩ — see BLESSING 1
2 something that provides happiness or does good for a person or thing ⟨the library's silence was a welcome *benediction* to someone, like me, who needed to concentrate⟩ — see BLESSING 2

benefaction *n* a gift of money or its equivalent to a charity, humanitarian cause, or public institution ⟨the generous *benefaction* from an anonymous donor meant the animal shelter could stay open⟩ — see CONTRIBUTION

benefactor *n* one that helps another with gifts or money ⟨an anonymous *benefactor* gave the school a dozen new computers⟩
synonyms angel, donator, donor, fairy godmother, Maecenas, patron, sugar daddy
related words benefactress, patroness; almoner, almsgiver, philanthropist; altruist, bestower, contributor, giver; helper, subscriber, supporter; guardian angel, protector, savior (*or* saviour)
near antonyms beneficiary, donee, giftee, recipient

benefic *adj* promoting or contributing to personal or social well-being ⟨the belief that participation in sports has a *benefic* influence on a young person⟩ — see BENEFICIAL

beneficence *n* **1** a gift of money or its equivalent to a charity, humanitarian cause, or public institution ⟨the town library stays open primarily through *beneficences* from concerned residents⟩ — see CONTRIBUTION
2 sympathetic concern for the well-being of others ⟨a religious leader whose *beneficence* is felt by all who meet him⟩ — see BENIGNANCY

beneficent *adj* **1** having or marked by sympathy and consideration for others ⟨a *beneficent* couple who are regular volunteers at a homeless shelter⟩ — see HUMANE 1
2 having or showing a concern for the welfare of others ⟨a *beneficent* effort to help out the needy during the holidays⟩ — see CHARITABLE 1
3 promoting or contributing to personal or social well-being ⟨cultural activities have a *beneficent* effect on a community that can't be measured in dollars and cents⟩ — see BENEFICIAL

beneficial *adj* promoting or contributing to personal or social well-being ⟨tutoring can often be as *beneficial* and rewarding for the tutor as for the student receiving the help⟩
synonyms advantageous, benefic, beneficent, benignant, favorable, friendly, good, helpful, kindly, profitable, salutary
related words gratifying, rewarding, satisfying; auspicious, promising, propitious; advisable, desirable, healthful, healthy, salubrious, salutiferous, wholesome; gainful, lucrative, remunerative; ameliorative, amelioratory, bettering, constructive, supportive
near antonyms damaging, deleterious, harmful, injurious, insalubrious
antonyms bad, disadvantageous, unfavorable, unfriendly, unhelpful, unprofitable

benefit *n* **1** a thing that helps ⟨it would be a real *benefit* if you could keep track of what you have already bought⟩ — see HELP 2
2 something that provides happiness or does good for a person or thing ⟨the meal service is a great *benefit* to invalids and the elderly⟩ — see BLESSING 2

benefit *vb* to provide with something useful or desirable ⟨his summer internship *benefited* him in two ways: by giving him some tuition funds and by offering vital work experience⟩
synonyms advantage, avail, help, profit, serve
related words succeed, work (for); aid, assist; better, improve; content, delight, gladden, gratify, please, satisfy; bless
near antonyms hinder, impede; damage, harm, hurt, impair, injure; afflict, distress, upset

benevolence *n* **1** an act of kind assistance ⟨self-effacing as well as selfless, he refused all public acknowledgement of his many *benevolences* to the community⟩ — see FAVOR 1
2 kindly concern, interest, or support ⟨her *benevolence* towards her employees was such that she actually let one live in her home temporarily⟩ — see GOODWILL 1
3 sympathetic concern for the well-being of others ⟨an actress who was admired for her *benevolence* as for her beauty⟩ — see BENIGNANCY

benevolent *adj* **1** having or marked by sympathy and consideration for others ⟨a *benevolent* willingness to

provide veterinary services to low-income families at greatly reduced prices⟩ — see HUMANE 1
2 having or showing a concern for the welfare of others ⟨a *benevolent* businessman who has donated money and time to helping inner-city youths⟩ — see CHARITABLE 1

benighted *adj* lacking in education or the knowledge gained from books ⟨the poor *benighted* souls who do not know the joys of reading⟩ — see IGNORANT 1

benightedness *n* the state of being unaware or uninformed ⟨takes perverse pride in his *benightedness* regarding popular culture⟩ — see IGNORANCE 1

benign *adj* **1** not causing or being capable of causing injury or hurt ⟨around campus he's known as a real character, but one whose eccentricities are entirely *benign*⟩ — see HARMLESS
2 not harsh or stern especially in nature or effect ⟨basking under a *benign* sun on a day in early spring⟩ — see GENTLE 1

benignancy *n* sympathetic concern for the well-being of others ⟨through posture and facial expression the artist has been able to convey the serene *benignancy* that is traditionally associated with the saint⟩
synonyms beneficence, benevolence, benignity, compassionateness, good-heartedness, humaneness, kindheartedness, kindliness, kindness, softheartedness, tenderheartedness, tenderness, warmheartedness
related words attentiveness, considerateness, thoughtfulness; affability, friendliness, good-naturedness, good-temperedness, warmth; graciousness, niceness, pleasantness; clemency, leniency, mercifulness; patience, tolerance, understanding; altruism, charitableness, charity; generosity, greatheartedness, magnanimity, philanthropy, unselfishness
near antonyms mercilessness, pitilessness, ruthlessness; inconsiderateness, insensitivity, thoughtlessness; grimness, harshness, severity, sternness, toughness; hatefulness, malevolence, maliciousness, meanness, spitefulness, virulence, vitriol
antonyms barbarity, barbarousness, bestiality, brutality, brutishness, callousness, cold-bloodedness, cruelty, hard-heartedness, heartlessness, inhumanity, insensateness, savageness, savagery, unfeelingness, unkindliness, unkindness

benignant *adj* **1** having or marked by sympathy and consideration for others ⟨a *benignant* understanding of the daily struggles of the economically disadvantaged⟩ — see HUMANE 1
2 promoting or contributing to personal or social well-being ⟨firmly believes that religion is a *benignant* force in society⟩ — see BENEFICIAL

benignity *n* sympathetic concern for the well-being of others ⟨a doctor who extends to all of her patients, both rich and poor, the same measure of gentle *benignity*⟩ — see BENIGNANCY

benison *n* a prayer calling for divine care, protection, or favor ⟨during the harbor festival the parish priest offered a *benison* for the local fishermen⟩ — see BLESSING 1

bent *adj, chiefly British* given to or marked by cheating and deception ⟨the drug dealer knew which of the cops were *bent*⟩ — see DISHONEST 2

bent *n* **1** a habitual attraction to some activity or thing ⟨the perfect gift for a person of a literary *bent*⟩ — see INCLINATION 1
2 a special and usually inborn ability ⟨having a decided *bent* for languages, he picked up Italian in no time⟩ — see TALENT

bent (on *or* **upon)** *adj* fully committed to achieving a goal ⟨a bride-to-be *bent on* having the perfect wedding⟩ — see DETERMINED

benumb *vb* to reduce or weaken in strength or feeling ⟨a succession of personal tragedies had *benumbed* him to all grief⟩ — see DULL 1

benumbed *adj* lacking in sensation or feeling ⟨my *benumbed* ears took a few minutes to warm up after the frigid air outside⟩ — see NUMB 1

bepaint *vb, archaic* to give color or a different color to ⟨when one gazes upon the *bepainted* sky of dawn⟩ — see COLOR 1

bequeath *vb* to give by means of a will ⟨having no heir, he *bequeathed* his house to his local church⟩ — see LEAVE 2

bequest *n* something that is or may be inherited ⟨left small *bequests* to all of her nieces and nephews⟩ — see INHERITANCE

berate *vb* to criticize (someone) severely or angrily especially for personal failings ⟨there's no need to *berate* someone for making a mistake during the first day on the job⟩ — see SCOLD

bereave *vb* to take something away from ⟨news of a death in the family *bereaved* them of the unmitigated joy that normally prevails at a wedding⟩ — see DEPRIVE 1

bereaved *adj* suffering the death of a loved one ⟨the grief of the *bereaved* parents seemed to be without limit⟩
synonyms bereft
related words orphaned, widowed; distressed, grieving, melancholy, miserable, mournful, mourning, sad, sorrowing, suffering, unhappy, upset; bemoaning, crying, lamenting, wailing, weeping

bereft *adj* **1** suffering the death of a loved one ⟨to one investigator, the *bereft* woman seemed to be taking the sudden death of her rich husband amazingly well⟩ — see BEREAVED
2 utterly lacking in something needed, wanted, or expected ⟨a cheap motel completely *bereft* of all amenities⟩ — see DEVOID 1

berk *n, British* a person who lacks good sense or judgment ⟨I wouldn't like some silly *berk* from Fleet Street following me about⟩ — see FOOL 1

berserk *adv* in a confused and reckless manner ⟨the familiar scene in horror movies where everyone runs *berserk* as the monster destroys everything in sight⟩ — see HELTER-SKELTER 1

berserkly *adv* in a confused and reckless manner ⟨reports of a crazed man running *berserkly* through traffic at a major intersection⟩ — see HELTER-SKELTER 1

berth *n* an assignment at which one regularly works for pay ⟨found a *berth* at a travel agency⟩ — see JOB 1

beseech *vb* to make a request to (someone) in an earnest or urgent manner ⟨parishioners ardently *beseeched* the local bishop not to close their beloved church⟩ — see BEG

beseeching *adj* asking humbly ⟨a *beseeching* letter from his parents asking him to bring the grandchildren for a long overdue visit⟩ — see SUPPLIANT

beseem *vb, archaic* to be fitting or proper ⟨ordered his servants to deck the hall with such adornments as might *beseem* for the holidays⟩ — see DO 1

beset *vb* **1** to cause persistent suffering to ⟨he's been *beset* by a lack of self-confidence virtually his entire life⟩ — see AFFLICT
2 to take sudden, violent action against ⟨the unsuspecting tourists were suddenly *beset* by robbers⟩ — see ATTACK 1

besetting *adj* caused by or suggestive of an irresistible urge ⟨that woman's *besetting* need to meddle in the affairs of others⟩ — see COMPULSIVE

beshrew *vb, archaic* to ask a divine power to send harm or evil upon ⟨I would *beshrew* anyone who is untrue to his word⟩ — see CURSE 1

beside *prep* **1** in addition to ⟨I'll need one more helper *beside* all of you⟩ — see BESIDES 1

2 not including ⟨I need four books *beside* this one⟩ — see EXCEPT

besides *adv* in addition to what has been said ⟨"*Besides*," Dan exclaimed, "Who are you to tell me what to do?"⟩ — see MORE 1

besides *prep* **1** in addition to ⟨*besides* me, there are five people working on this project⟩

synonyms as well as, beside, beyond, over and above

related words plus; including

phrases along with, at that, together with

near antonyms except (*also* excepting); less, minus, wanting

2 not including ⟨the book is 800 pages long *besides* the bibliography⟩ — see EXCEPT

besiege *vb* **1** to surround (as a fortified place) with armed forces for the purpose of capturing or preventing commerce and communication ⟨armies *besieged* the city for six months before it finally surrendered⟩

synonyms beleaguer, blockade, invest, leaguer [*archaic*]

related words barricade, block, cut off, dam, encircle; assail, assault, attack, beset; confine, insulate, isolate, quarantine

phrases lay siege to

near antonyms emancipate, free, liberate, release, rescue

2 to cause persistent suffering to ⟨a family *besieged* by worries about the faltering economy⟩ — see AFFLICT

3 to make a request to (someone) in an earnest or urgent manner ⟨bereaved parents continued to *besiege* the president with pleas to end the war⟩ — see BEG

besmear *vb* to rub an oily or sticky substance over ⟨*besmeared* the mirror with jelly⟩ — see SMEAR 1

besmirch *vb* to make dirty ⟨inconsiderately *besmirched* the white bedsheets with their dirty feet⟩ — see DIRTY

besmirched *adj* not clean ⟨wiped the toddler's *besmirched* face with a damp cloth⟩ — see DIRTY 1

besotted *adj* being under the influence of alcohol ⟨when he staggered in and tripped over the cat, she knew he was *besotted* again⟩ — see DRUNK

besotted (by) *adj* filled with an intense or excessive love for ⟨was so *besotted by* the movies that as a kid he'd sometimes spend all day staring up at the silver screen⟩ — see ENAMORED (OF)

bespatter *vb* to wet or soil by striking with something liquid or mushy ⟨vehicle after passing vehicle *bespattered* the sides of my once-clean car with that wintry slush⟩ — see SPLASH 2

bespeak *vb* **1** to arrange to have something (as a hotel room) held for one's future use ⟨*bespoke* the rental car weeks in advance of their trip⟩ — see RESERVE 1

2 to make known (something abstract) through outward signs ⟨her expression throughout the meeting *bespoke* great boredom⟩ — see SHOW 2

3 to make a request for ⟨milady *bespoke* our indulgence, inviting us to wait in the foyer while she attended to other matters⟩ — see ASK (FOR) 1

4 to serve as a sign or symptom of ⟨her impressive virtuosity as a pianist *bespeaks* years of diligent practice⟩ — see INDICATE 1

bespoke *also* **bespoken** *adj* **1** made or fitted to the needs or preferences of a specific customer ⟨a wealthy man who can easily afford *bespoke* suits⟩ — see CUSTOM-MADE

2 *dialect* pledged in marriage ⟨once the last decent-looking woman in town was *bespoke*, it was time for the luckless bachelor to move on⟩ — see ENGAGED 1

best *n* **1** dressy clothing ⟨a family that still believes that you should wear your *best* to church⟩ — see FINERY

2 individuals carefully selected as being the best of a class ⟨only the *best* will go on to the finals⟩ — see ELITE 1

best *vb* to achieve a victory over ⟨at last she's *bested* her card-playing mother at the game of hearts⟩ — see BEAT 2

bestial *adj* having or showing the nature and appetites of a lower animal ⟨investigators were appalled by the degree of *bestial* debauchery depicted in the pornographic materials⟩

synonyms animalistic, beastly, brutal, brute, brutish, feral, ferine, subhuman, swinish

related words animal, bodily, carnal, corporal, corporeal, fleshly, physical, sensual; barbaric, barbarous, cruel, heartless, inhumane, sadistic, savage, vicious, wanton; coarse, crass, crude, gross, ill-bred, lowbred, rude, uncouth, uncultivated, uncultured, unrefined, vulgar

near antonyms chivalrous, elevated, gallant, great, greathearted, high, high-minded, lofty, lordly, magnanimous, noble, sublime; angelic (*or* angelical), spiritual; beneficent, benevolent, benignant, compassionate, good-hearted, kind, kindhearted, kindly, softhearted, tenderhearted; cultivated, cultured, genteel, polished, refined, well-bred

bestiality *n* the manifestation of the traits or the gratification of the appetites of a lower animal ⟨by the end of hostilities the populace had been reduced to a level of *bestiality* that would have been unthinkable before the war⟩

synonyms animalism, animality, beastliness, brutality, brutishness, swinishness

related words carnality, physicality, sensuality; boorishness, coarseness, crudeness, grossness, loutishness, rudeness; barbarity, cruelty, sadism, savagery, viciousness, wantonness

near antonyms intellectuality, spirituality; greatheartedness, high-mindedness, magnanimity, nobility; beneficence, benevolence, benignity, compassion, goodheartedness, kindheartedness, kindliness, kindness, tenderheartedness

bestialize *vb* to make (someone) feel or behave more like an animal than a human being ⟨men who had been *bestialized* by war⟩ — see BRUTALIZE 1

bestow *vb* **1** to make a present of ⟨*bestowed* a new car on their son for graduation⟩ — see GIVE 1

2 to provide with living quarters or shelter ⟨eventually the refugee family was *bestowed* in its own apartment⟩ — see HOUSE 1

bestowal *n* something given to someone without expectation of a return ⟨the company's annual Yuletide *bestowals* include a holiday party and substantial bonuses⟩ — see GIFT 1

bestrew *vb* to cover by or as if by scattering something over or on ⟨the flower girl delightedly *bestrewed* the aisle with rose petals⟩ — see SCATTER 2

bet *n* **1** the money or thing risked on the outcome of an uncertain event ⟨she offered the *bet* of a free lunch if her team won the World Series⟩

synonyms stake, wager

related words collateral; handle, jackpot, kitty, pool, pot

2 a person or thing that is chosen ⟨your best *bet* would be the scenic route along the coast⟩ — see CHOICE 2

bet *vb* to risk (something) on the outcome of an uncertain event ⟨foolishly *bet* a month's allowance on the World Series⟩

synonyms gamble, go, lay, play, put, stake, wager

related words bid, offer; adventure, chance, hazard, speculate, venture; endanger, imperil, jeopardize

bête noire *n* **1** something or someone that causes fear or dread especially without reason ⟨doing my own tax return is the *bête noire* that haunts me every April⟩ — see BOGEY 1

2 something or someone that is hated ⟨in that organization's view, society's number one *bête noire* should be the drunk driver of a motor vehicle⟩ — see HATE 2

betide *vb* to take place ⟨we will be happy in our new home, whatever may *betide*⟩ — see HAPPEN

bêtise *n* a foolish act or idea ⟨writing a sequel to a Jane Austen novel must be regarded as a literary *bêtise* of the highest order⟩ — see FOLLY 1

betoken *vb* to serve as a sign or symptom of ⟨the humor in his writing is never cruel, and *betokens* a warm and compassionate heart⟩ — see INDICATE 1

betray *vb* **1** to be unfaithful or disloyal to ⟨childhood friends of movie stars often *betray* them by telling their secrets to the supermarket tabloids⟩
synonyms backstab, cross, double-cross, sell (out), two-time
related words give away; inform (on), peach, rat (on), shop [*British*], snitch (on), split (on) [*British*], tell (on), turn in
phrases go back on, sell down the river, stab in the back
near antonyms defend, guard, protect, safeguard, save, shield
antonyms stand by

2 to make known (something abstract) through outward signs ⟨his face *betrayed* his exasperation with his nosy neighbor⟩ — see SHOW 2

3 to lead away from a usual or proper course by offering some pleasure or advantage ⟨she was *betrayed* by a false show of friendship into covering up the crime⟩ — see LURE

betrayal *n* the act or fact of violating the trust or confidence of another ⟨the terrible *betrayal* of having her best friend reveal her confidences to others⟩
synonyms backstabbing, business, disloyalty, double cross, faithlessness, falseness, falsity, infidelity, perfidy, sellout, treachery, treason, two-timing, unfaithfulness
related words abandonment, desertion; deceit, deception, double-dealing, duplicity, guile, two-facedness; fraud, informing, lying, snitching, talebearing, trickery
near antonyms dependability, reliability, trustworthiness; defense, protection, safeguard, shield
antonyms allegiance, devotion, faithfulness, fealty, fidelity, loyalty, staunchness, steadfastness

betrayer *n* **1** a person who provides information about another's wrongdoing ⟨the arrested drug dealer vowed that he would get his revenge on his *betrayer*⟩ — see INFORMER

2 one who betrays a trust or an allegiance ⟨the *betrayer* of Anne Frank's family in Amsterdam has never been identified for certain⟩ — see TRAITOR

betrothal *n* the act or state of being engaged to be married ⟨the couple's *betrothal* lasted four years⟩ — see ENGAGEMENT 1

betrothed *adj* pledged in marriage ⟨a splendid party in honor of the *betrothed* couple⟩ — see ENGAGED 1

betrothed *n* the person to whom one is engaged to be married ⟨he gazed lovingly at his *betrothed* throughout the dinner⟩
synonyms fiancé, fiancée, intended
related words admirer, beau, beloved, boyfriend, darling, dear, favorite, fellow, flame, girlfriend, honey, love, lover, steady, swain, sweet, sweetheart, sweetie, sweetie pie, valentine; bride, groom

better *adv* to a greater or higher extent ⟨he knows property law *better* than anyone else⟩ — see MORE 2

better *n* **1** one who is above another in rank, station, or office ⟨be polite to your *betters* and to your inferiors in equal measure⟩ — see SUPERIOR

2 the more favorable condition or position in a competition ⟨she got the *better* of her opponents very early in the race⟩ — see ADVANTAGE 1

better *vb* **1** to be greater, better, or stronger than ⟨this year's profits should *better* last year's by a wide margin⟩ — see SURPASS 1

2 to make better ⟨social workers and reformers trying to *better* the lives of inner-city residents⟩ — see IMPROVE

better half *n* the person to whom another is married ⟨"Allow me to introduce you to my *better half*, Joan"⟩ — see SPOUSE

bettor *or* **better** *n* one that bets (as on the outcome of a contest or sports event) ⟨*bettors* on the horse race have to place their bets at least 20 minutes before the start of the race⟩
synonyms gambler, gamester, punter [*chiefly British*], wagerer
related words high roller, piker; dicer; bluffer, punger, sharper, speculator; bookmaker, handicapper, oddsmaker, tipster

beverage *n* a liquid suitable for drinking ⟨would anyone like a *beverage* with their snack?⟩ — see DRINK 1

bewail *vb* to feel or express sorrow for ⟨he invariably spends more time *bewailing* his predicament than trying to fix it⟩ — see LAMENT 1

bewailing *adj* expressing or suggesting mourning ⟨the doctor assured us that my father was not in any danger of dying, hence those *bewailing* looks on our faces were uncalled-for⟩ — see MOURNFUL 1

beware (of) *vb* to be cautious of or on guard against ⟨*beware of* that parrot because it bites⟩
synonyms guard (against), look out (for), mind, ware, watch out (for)
related words attend, heed, mark, note, notice; behold, discern, observe, perceive, see, watch
phrases be on the lookout for, keep one's eyes open for (*or* keep one's eyes peeled for)
near antonyms discount, disregard, ignore, miss, overlook

bewilder *vb* to throw into a state of mental uncertainty ⟨the change in policy seems to have *bewildered* many of our customers⟩ — see CONFUSE 1

bewildered *adj* suffering from mental confusion ⟨the *bewildered* child wandered aimlessly around the playground⟩ — see DIZZY 2

bewilderedness *n* a state of mental uncertainty ⟨he gave her a look of inexpressible *bewilderedness*⟩ — see CONFUSION 1

bewilderment *n* a state of mental uncertainty ⟨the slightest change in her daily routine leaves her in complete *bewilderment*⟩ — see CONFUSION 1

bewitch *vb* **1** to cast a spell on ⟨a Wiccan who believes that it is indeed possible to *bewitch* someone⟩
synonyms charm, enchant, ensorcell (*or* ensorcel), hex, overlook, spell, strike
related words curse, jinx, possess, voodoo; attract, beguile, captivate, fascinate, mesmerize, spellbind; entice, lure, seduce, tempt
near antonyms bless

2 to attract or delight as if by magic ⟨an animated film that *bewitches* children and adults alike⟩ — see CHARM 1

bewitched *adj* being or appearing to be under a magic spell ⟨the *bewitched* princess who could be awakened only by a kiss from the prince destined to be her husband⟩ — see ENCHANTED

bewitchery *n* the power to control natural forces through supernatural means ⟨would have thought that only an act of *bewitchery* could make snow fall in Florida, but the state has a history of modest snow accumulations⟩ — see MAGIC 1

bewitching *adj* having an often mysterious or magical

power to attract ⟨a *bewitching* woman who has never lacked for suitors⟩ — see FASCINATING 1

bewitchment *n* **1** a spoken word or set of words believed to have magic power ⟨the hope that there was some *bewitchment* that would turn their jerky son-in-law into a prince⟩ — see SPELL 1
2 the power to control natural forces through supernatural means ⟨while stuck in traffic, I could have used a bit of *bewitchment* to clear the road of other drivers⟩ — see MAGIC 1

beyond *adv* at or to a greater distance or more advanced point ⟨the dream that someday we will journey to the outer reaches of our solar system and *beyond*⟩ — see FARTHER

beyond *n* unending existence after death ⟨who knows how we'll fare in the *beyond*?⟩ — see ETERNITY 2

beyond *prep* **1** on or to the farther side of ⟨the arrow flew *beyond* the fence and into the woods⟩
synonyms over, past
related words outside
phrases on the far side of
near antonyms inside
2 out of the reach or sphere of ⟨although the town has ordinances against public drunkenness, any degree of intoxication under your own roof is *beyond* their authority⟩
synonyms outside, outside of, without
related words except (*also* excepting)
near antonyms inside
antonyms within
3 in addition to ⟨*beyond* the asking price of the house, there's also the cost of fixing up this "handyman's dream"⟩ — see BESIDES 1

bias *adv* in a line or direction running from corner to corner ⟨made of fabric cut *bias*⟩ — see CROSSWISE

bias *n* **1** an attitude that always favors one way of feeling or acting especially without considering any other possibilities ⟨he has a powerful *bias* towards sentimentality, which comes through even in his grittier stories⟩
synonyms favor, nonobjectivity, one-sidedness, partiality, parti pris, partisanship, ply, prejudice, tendentiousness
related words chauvinism, cronyism, favoritism, nepotism; self-opinionatedness, self-partiality; bent, inclination, leaning, penchant, predilection, predisposition, proclivity, propensity, tendency; preconception, prejudgment, prepossession
near antonyms calm, detachment, dispassion, indifference; aversion, dislike, distaste, hate, scunner
antonyms impartiality, neutrality, objectivity, open-mindedness, unbiasedness
2 a habitual attraction to some activity or thing ⟨from her youth she revealed a strong *bias* toward a life of the mind⟩ — see INCLINATION 1

bias *vb* to cause to have often negative opinions formed without sufficient knowledge ⟨bad reviews *biased* her against the movie, even though it starred one of her favorite actors⟩ — see PREJUDICE

biased *adj* inclined to favor one side over another ⟨in my admittedly *biased* opinion, my wife is always the prettiest woman in whatever room she graces⟩ — see PARTIAL 1

bib *vb* to partake excessively of alcoholic beverages ⟨the old professor has been known to *bib* on occasion⟩ — see DRINK 2

bibelot *n* a small object displayed for its attractiveness or interest ⟨practically every horizontal surface in the Victorian parlor was blanketed with fussy little *bibelots*⟩ — see KNICKKNACK

Bible *n* a book made up of the writings accepted by Christians as coming from God ⟨she received a lovely *Bible* as a First Communion gift⟩
synonyms Book, Good Book, Holy Writ, Scripture
related words Polyglot

bibliolator *n* one who is keenly devoted to books ⟨a *bibliolator* who regards vandalism to a library as being equal to desecration of a church⟩ — see BIBLIOPHILE

bibliomaniac *n* one who is keenly devoted to books ⟨an incorrigible *bibliomaniac*, he's already bought more books than anyone could read in a lifetime⟩ — see BIBLIOPHILE

bibliophile *n* one who is keenly devoted to books ⟨for *bibliophiles*, no electronic device could possibly give the tactile pleasure of a beautifully bound book⟩
synonyms bibliolator, bibliomaniac, bookman
related words bookworm; antiquarian, bibliopole, bookseller; bibliopegist, bookbinder, bookmaker

bibulous *adj* **1** able to soak up liquids especially readily ⟨special drying cloths that are so *bibulous* that they can absorb 10 times their weight in water⟩ — see ABSORBENT
2 given to excessive use of alcoholic beverages ⟨a campaign to make the *bibulous* fraternity brother a collegiate archetype of the past⟩ — see CRAPULOUS

bicker *n* an often noisy or angry expression of differing opinions ⟨after a prolonged *bicker*, they finally managed to find a movie that both of them were interested in seeing⟩ — see ARGUMENT 1

bicker *vb* to express different opinions about something often angrily ⟨if you two don't stop *bickering* about where to go to eat, we're not going out at all!⟩ — see ARGUE 2

bickerer *n* a person who takes part in a dispute ⟨perpetual *bickerers*, the Taylors think nothing of having their private quarrels in public places⟩ — see DISPUTANT

bicycle *n* a two-wheeled vehicle that is propelled by the use of pedals and steered through the use of handlebars ⟨the range of the boy's explorations vastly expanded when he acquired his first *bicycle*⟩
synonyms bike, cycle, push-bike (*also* push bicycle) [*British*], two-wheeler, velocipede [*archaic*]
related words mountain bike, tandem bicycle, ten-speed

bid *n* an effort to do or accomplish something ⟨a dramatic film that is widely regarded as the comedian's last-ditch *bid* to be taken seriously as an actor⟩ — see ATTEMPT 1

bid *vb* **1** to issue orders to (someone) by right of authority ⟨the servants were expected to do exactly as they were *bidden*⟩ — see COMMAND 1
2 to request the presence or participation of ⟨as company president, I *bid* you all to come to our annual holiday party!⟩ — see INVITE 1

biddability *n* a readiness or willingness to yield to the wishes of others ⟨a pastor who longs for the days when the *biddability* of parishioners could be taken for granted⟩ — see COMPLIANCE 1

biddable *adj* readily giving in to the command or authority of another ⟨the elderly widower was one of the more *biddable* and cooperative residents at the nursing home⟩ — see OBEDIENT

biddy *n* a female domestic servant ⟨those poor old *biddies* were mostly Irishwomen who worked for old-line Yankee families⟩ — see MAID 1

bide *vb* **1** to remain indefinitely in existence or in the same state ⟨how long are you going to *bide* in this unhappy marriage?⟩ — see CONTINUE 1
2 *chiefly dialect* to put up with (something painful or difficult) ⟨at my advanced age I simply cannot *bide* young children⟩ — see BEAR 2
3 to remain in place in readiness or expectation of something ⟨I promise you that if you *bide* yet a little longer, all will come to pass just as you desire⟩ — see WAIT

bier *n* a boxlike container for holding a dead body ⟨lifted the *bier* from its stand and placed it in the hearse for its final journey⟩ — see COFFIN

biff *n* a hard strike with a part of the body or an instrument ⟨he got a *biff* in the noggin as his reward for trying to intervene in the fight⟩ — see [1]BLOW

biff *vb* to deliver a blow to (someone or something) usually in a strong vigorous manner ⟨the elderly woman swung her purse and *biffed* the mugger upside the head⟩ — see HIT 1

bifurcation *n* **1** a movement in different directions away from a common point ⟨a thoughtful book about the nation's *bifurcation* into two distinct and antagonistic cultures⟩ — see DIVERGENCE 1
2 the act or process of a whole separating into two or more parts or pieces ⟨a divisive issue that caused the *bifurcation* of the political party⟩ — see SEPARATION 1

big *adj* **1** having great meaning or lasting effect ⟨there will be a *big* meeting to resolve the issue⟩ — see IMPORTANT 1
2 of a size greater than average of its kind ⟨bought a *big* apple to quench his raging appetite⟩ — see LARGE 1
3 having, characterized by, or arising from a dignified and generous nature ⟨how *big* of you to give your subordinates most of the credit⟩ — see NOBLE 2
4 having an abundance of some characteristic quality (as flavor) ⟨inexperienced wine drinkers should not start with such a *big* wine⟩ — see FULL-BODIED
5 coming before all others in importance ⟨the *big* story that year was the assassination of the president⟩ — see FOREMOST 1
6 enjoying widespread favor or approval ⟨jackets with very wide lapels were *big* that year⟩ — see POPULAR 1
7 containing unborn young within the body ⟨a mare *big* with a foal⟩ — see PREGNANT 1

big *n* **1** one of high position or importance within a group ⟨with that new promotion he's now one of the *bigs* in the company⟩ — see BIG SHOT
2 *usually* **bigs** *pl* the highest level of a field of endeavor ⟨when a candidate is running for president, he's playing in the *bigs* and cannot afford to make major mistakes⟩ — see BIG TIME

big boy *n* one of high position or importance within a group ⟨when she became the network's White House correspondent, she knew that she was now playing with the *big boys*⟩ — see BIG SHOT

big bucks *n pl* a very large amount of money ⟨I hear she's been offered *big bucks* to take that job⟩ — see FORTUNE 2

big cheese *n* one of high position or importance within a group ⟨thinks he's a *big cheese* just because he's got a business card⟩ — see BIG SHOT

bigfoot *n* one of high position or importance within a group ⟨a *bigfoot* in the field of genetics⟩ — see BIG SHOT

biggety *or* **biggity** *adj, Southern & Midland* having too high an opinion of oneself ⟨he's gotten *biggety* since he got promoted to director of sales⟩ — see CONCEITED

biggie *n* one of high position or importance within a group ⟨among food and beverage magazines, it's one of the *biggies*⟩ — see BIG SHOT

biggish *adj* **1** of a size greater than average of its kind ⟨a rather *biggish* table for a dining room of modest dimensions⟩ — see LARGE 1
2 sufficiently large in size, amount, or number to merit attention ⟨a *biggish* wart that should be removed⟩ — see CONSIDERABLE 1

big gun *n* one of high position or importance within a group ⟨for a high-profile case like this, the law firm uses only its *big guns*⟩ — see BIG SHOT

bighead *n* an often unjustified feeling of being pleased with oneself or with one's situation or achievements ⟨the kind of early success that can give a young performer a *bighead*⟩ — see COMPLACENCE 1

bigheaded *adj* having too high an opinion of oneself ⟨she's become *bigheaded* since winning that literary award⟩ — see CONCEITED

bighearted *adj* giving or sharing in abundance and without hesitation ⟨a *bighearted* guy who can't seem to ever say "no"⟩ — see GENEROUS 1

bigheartedness *n* **1** the capacity for feeling for another's unhappiness or misfortune ⟨because of the *bigheartedness* of her coworkers, she was able to present the charity with a fat check⟩ — see HEART 1
2 the quality or state of being generous ⟨the commendable *bigheartedness* of that upscale restaurateur, who uses a portion of her profits to fund a soup kitchen⟩ — see LIBERALITY

big house *n, slang* a place of confinement for persons held in lawful custody ⟨told harrowing stories of his years spent in the *big house*⟩ — see JAIL

bight *n* a part of a body of water that extends beyond the general shoreline ⟨the *bight* known as the Bay of Fundy is known for its fast-running tides⟩ — see GULF 1

big league *n, often* **big leagues** *pl* the highest level of a field of endeavor ⟨Broadway is the *big leagues*, and for big bucks theatergoers expect professionalism⟩ — see BIG TIME

big leaguer *n* one of high position or importance within a group ⟨the once-tiny ad agency is now a *big leaguer* that attracts clients on the A-list⟩ — see BIG SHOT

big–name *adj* widely known ⟨several *big-name* writers gave readings at the book festival⟩ — see FAMOUS 1

bigness *n* the quality or state of being large in size ⟨the sheer *bigness* of the 50-pound pumpkin made us want to buy it⟩ — see LARGENESS

bigot *n* one who stubbornly or intolerantly adheres to his or her own opinions and prejudices ⟨an incorrigible *bigot* who hasn't entertained a new thought in years⟩
synonyms dogmatist, dogmatizer, partisan (*also* partizan), sectarian
related words doctrinaire, fanatic, purist; jingoist, nationalist; racialist, racist, supremacist; chauvinist, sexist
near antonyms freethinker, latitudinarian, liberal

bigoted *adj* unwilling to grant other people social rights or to accept other viewpoints ⟨*bigoted* people once believed that black people were naturally inferior and unqualified to vote⟩ — see INTOLERANT 2

bigotry *n* stubborn or intolerant adherence to one's opinions or prejudices ⟨a deeply ingrained *bigotry* prevented her from even considering the counterarguments⟩
synonyms dogmatism, illiberalism, illiberality, illiberalness, intolerance, intolerantness, narrow-mindedness, opinionatedness, partisanship, sectarianism, small-mindedness
related words conservatism, reactionaryism; insularism, insularity, parochialism, provincialism
near antonyms progressiveness, progressivism
antonyms broad-mindedness, liberalism, liberality, open-mindedness, tolerance

big screen *n* the art or business of making a movie ⟨many a television star has failed to make it on the *big screen*⟩ — see MOVIE 2

big shot *n* one of high position or importance within a group ⟨a meeting at which all of the *big shots* in the company were present⟩
synonyms big, big boy, big cheese, bigfoot, biggie, big gun, big leaguer, big-timer, big wheel, bigwig, fat cat, heavy, heavy hitter, heavyweight, high-muck-a-muck (*or* high-muckety-muck), honcho, kahuna, kingfish, kingpin, major leaguer, muckety-muck (*also* muck-a-

muck *or* mucky-muck), nabob, nawab, nibs, nob [*chiefly British*], pooh-bah (*also* poo-bah), wheel
related words baron, czar (*also* tsar *or* tzar), king, lion, magnate, mogul, prince, tycoon; VIP
near antonyms inferior, subordinate, underling; mediocrity, obscurity
antonyms lightweight, nobody, nonentity, nothing, shrimp, twerp, whippersnapper, zero, zilch

big–ticket *adj* commanding a large price ⟨with the tough economy, fewer people are likely to be making *big-ticket* purchases⟩ — see COSTLY

big–time *adv* to a large extent or degree ⟨wow, those renovations improved the library *big-time*⟩ — see GREATLY 2

big time *n* the highest level of a field of endeavor ⟨the young ad execs knew that their agency had hit the *big time* when major corporations came calling⟩
synonyms big(s), big league(s), major league
related words establishment, old guard

big–timer *n* one of high position or importance within a group ⟨a field in which one can go from being a *big-timer* to a small-timer in practically no time at all⟩ — see BIG SHOT

big wheel *n* one of high position or importance within a group ⟨brags that her son is a *big wheel* on Wall Street⟩ — see BIG SHOT

bigwig *n* one of high position or importance within a group ⟨interviewed by several *bigwigs* on the hospital's staff⟩ — see BIG SHOT

[1]**bike** *n* a two-wheeled vehicle that is propelled by the use of pedals and steered through the use of handlebars ⟨likes to ride her mountain *bike* on weekends⟩ — see BICYCLE

[2]**bike** *n, chiefly Scottish* a great number of persons or creatures massed together ⟨the boisterous *bike* that annually descends upon Edinburgh for the Fringe⟩ — see CROWD 1

bile *n* biting sharpness of feeling or expression ⟨with considerable *bile*, the author recounts a childhood filled with misery and loneliness⟩ — see ACRIMONY 1

bilge *n* language, behavior, or ideas that are absurd and contrary to good sense ⟨tried to justify his bigoted tirade with a lot of stale and insincere *bilge*⟩ — see NONSENSE 1

bilious *adj* having or showing a habitually bad temper ⟨a *bilious* old dog who snaps at everyone⟩ — see ILL-TEMPERED

biliousness *n* readiness to show annoyance or impatience ⟨her *biliousness* was such that most people simply avoided her⟩ — see PETULANCE

bilk *n* a dishonest person who uses clever means to cheat others out of something of value ⟨people who lost money in the scheme discovered that the investment company was a fake and the "owner" just a *bilk*⟩ — see TRICKSTER 1

bilk *vb* to rob by the use of trickery or threats ⟨an investigation revealed that the garage had been *bilking* motorists for repairs that had never been made⟩ — see FLEECE

bilker *n* a dishonest person who uses clever means to cheat others out of something of value ⟨the "victim" of the staged car crash turned out to be a serial *bilker* of insurance companies⟩ — see TRICKSTER 1

[1]**bill** *n* **1** a record of goods sold or services performed together with the costs due ⟨why is the electric *bill* so high this month?⟩
synonyms account, check, invoice, statement, tab
related words receipt, reckoning; document, ledger, record; charge, cost, expense, fee, price, rate, toll; score, tally
2 a piece of printed paper used as money in the United States ⟨the $20 *bill* has a picture of Andrew Jackson on the front⟩
synonyms banknote, greenback, note
related words dead presidents [*slang*], paper money, scrip; buck, dollar, simoleon [*slang*], smacker [*slang*]; C-note, fifty, fin [*slang*], five, fiver [*slang*], hundred, one, sawbuck [*slang*], ten, tenner, twenty, two; cash, chips, currency, dough, legal tender, lucre, money, pelf; check, draft, money order
3 a sheet bearing an announcement for posting in a public place ⟨posted a *bill* advertising the new play⟩ — see POSTER
4 the amount owed at a bar or restaurant or the slip of paper stating the amount ⟨although they were all working adults, their father still insisted on paying the *bill* whenever they went out to eat⟩ — see CHECK 1
5 a rule of conduct or action laid down by a governing authority and especially a legislature ⟨the fair housing *bill* of the 1960s⟩ — see LAW 1

[2]**bill** *n* **1** the jaws of a bird together with their hornlike covering ⟨parrots have very strong *bills* so they can break open nuts⟩ — see BEAK 1
2 the projecting front part of a hat or cap ⟨the hat was blue, but the *bill* was red⟩ — see VISOR

billabong *n, Australian* a small often deep body of water ⟨taking a break from our trek through the outback, we bathed our tired feet in the still waters of a *billabong*⟩ — see [1]POOL

[1]**billet** *n* a straight piece (as of wood or metal) that is longer than it is wide ⟨a stack of gold *billets* in the vault⟩ — see BAR 1

[2]**billet** *n* an assignment at which one regularly works for pay ⟨found a *billet* at one of the leading brokerage houses in New York⟩ — see JOB 1

billet *vb* to provide with living quarters or shelter ⟨every colonial household was expected to *billet* a British soldier⟩ — see HOUSE 1

billingsgate *n* harsh insulting language ⟨the intemperate *billingsgate* to which the staff in customer service were sometimes subjected⟩ — see ABUSE 1

billow *n* a moving ridge on the surface of water ⟨the great *billows* created by the ocean storm threatened to swamp the fishing boat⟩ — see WAVE

billow *vb* to extend outward beyond a usual point ⟨the curtains in the open windows *billowed* in the summer wind⟩ — see BULGE 1

billy *n* a heavy rigid stick used as a weapon or for punishment ⟨police officers carry a *billy* for protection⟩ — see CLUB 1

billy club *n* a heavy rigid stick used as a weapon or for punishment ⟨rapping the shoes of the sleeping vagrant with his *billy club*, the policeman told him to move on⟩ — see CLUB 1

bimbo *n, slang* a boldly flirtatious or sexually promiscuous woman ⟨a scandal involving a *bimbo* that effectively ended the congressman's career⟩ — see FLOOZY

bin *n* a covered rectangular container for storing or transporting things ⟨a storage *bin* for hats and gloves⟩ — see CHEST

binary *adj* consisting of two members or parts that are usually joined ⟨a *binary* star is a system of two stars that revolve around each other under their mutual gravitation⟩ — see DOUBLE 1

bind *n* **1** a difficult, puzzling, or embarrassing situation from which there is no easy escape ⟨with our vacation week fast approaching, and no arrangements for the care of our pets, we were in a serious *bind*⟩ — see PREDICAMENT
2 something that physically prevents free movement ⟨the burglar was held in a makeshift *bind* until the law officers could arrive⟩ — see BOND 1

bind *vb* **1** to confine or restrain with or as if with chains

⟨prisons tend to *bind* convicted criminals for transport⟩
synonyms chain, enchain, enfetter, fetter, gyve, handcuff, manacle, pinion, shackle, trammel
related words bit, hobble, hog-tie, iron, lash, secure, tie, truss; attach, fasten, join, link; confine, constrain, curb, hamper, hinder, impede; limit, restrict; entangle, tangle
near antonyms emancipate, free, liberate, loose, release, rescue; undo, unfasten, untangle, untie; detach, disengage
antonyms unbind, unfetter, unshackle
2 to cover with a bandage ⟨*bind* the wound to stop the bleeding⟩ — see BANDAGE
3 to gather into a tight mass by means of a line or cord ⟨*bind* the asparagus spears carefully before packing the bunches⟩ — see TIE 1

bindle stiff *n* a homeless wanderer who may beg or steal for a living ⟨upon graduation from college he wandered around the country as a *bindle stiff*, naively believing that he was at one with the downtrodden⟩ — see TRAMP 1

binge *n* **1** a bout of prolonged or excessive drinking ⟨weekend *binges* are a serious problem at many colleges and universities⟩ — see CAROUSE
2 a time or instance of carefree fun ⟨a shopping *binge* at the mall⟩ — see FLING 1
3 a social gathering ⟨what should we wear to this *binge* at the country club?⟩ — see PARTY 1

binge *vb* to take part in drunken revelry ⟨a program designed to educate college students about the dangers of *bingeing*⟩ — see CAROUSE

bio *n* a history of a person's life ⟨you can read a *bio* of the author on her home page⟩ — see BIOGRAPHY

biography *n* a history of a person's life ⟨an unauthorized *biography* of the actor gave him some serious headaches⟩
synonyms bio, life, memoir
related words autobiography; hagiography; psychobiography; pathography, tell-all; chronicle, history, past, story; obituary; character sketch, profile

biological *also* **biologic** *adj* being such by blood and not by adoption or marriage ⟨the rights of the *biological* father in this case⟩ — see NATURAL 3

bipartite *adj* consisting of two members or parts that are usually joined ⟨separated the *bipartite* rock⟩ — see DOUBLE 1

birch *vb* **1** to strike repeatedly with something long and thin or flexible ⟨students at the private school were once routinely *birched* for violating the rules⟩ — see WHIP 1
2 to strike repeatedly ⟨always a stern disciplinarian, our father *birched* anyone who talked back⟩ — see BEAT 1

bird *n* **1** a member of the human race ⟨they're a couple of tough old *birds* who can manage without any interference from their grandchildren⟩ — see HUMAN
2 *chiefly British* a vocal sound made to express scorn or disapproval ⟨the Liverpool fans were quick to give the visiting footballers the *bird*⟩ — see CATCALL

birdbrain *n* **1** a silly flighty person ⟨those *birdbrains* who eagerly adopt every fad diet that comes along⟩ — see FLIBBERTIGIBBET
2 a stupid person ⟨some *birdbrain* left the water running⟩ — see IDIOT

birdbrained *adj* **1** lacking in seriousness or maturity ⟨a *birdbrained* neighbor who is forever giving me tacky tchotchkes⟩ — see GIDDY 1
2 not having or showing an ability to absorb ideas readily ⟨a group of apparently *birdbrained* teenagers were clearly bored by the memorial⟩ — see STUPID 1

bird–dog *vb* to go after or on the track of ⟨suspecting infidelity, he hired a private detective to *bird-dog* his wife⟩ — see FOLLOW 2

birdman *n* one who flies or is qualified to fly an aircraft or spacecraft ⟨in the early days of aviation, *birdmen* would travel around the country in their biplanes, putting on flying shows⟩ — see PILOT

bird's–eye *adj* relating to the main elements and not to specific details ⟨a *bird's-eye* look at the current situation in that part of the world⟩ — see GENERAL 2

birl *vb, chiefly Scottish* to take part in drunken revelry ⟨spent a good part of his time in Edinburgh *birling* into the wee small hours of the night⟩ — see CAROUSE

birse *n, chiefly Scottish* an intense emotional state of displeasure with someone or something ⟨as the lad's *birse* is fair up, it'd be best to leave him alone⟩ — see ANGER

birth *adj* being such by blood and not by adoption or marriage ⟨argued that the *birth* mother had not been informed of all of her options at the time of the adoption⟩ — see NATURAL 3

birth *n* **1** the act or instance of being born ⟨almost from *birth*, he showed all the marks of future greatness⟩
synonyms geniture, nativity
related words creation, genesis, nascency, origination, rise; accouchement, bearing, childbearing, labor, parturition; begetting, breeding, fathering, generation, mothering, parenting, reproduction, siring, spawning; fatherhood, maternity, motherhood, parenthood, paternity
near antonyms abortion, miscarriage; stillbirth
2 the line of ancestors from whom a person is descended ⟨a man of noble *birth*⟩ — see ANCESTRY
3 the point at which something begins ⟨that 12-second flight by Orville Wright marked the *birth* of aviation⟩ — see BEGINNING

birth *vb, chiefly dialect* to bring forth from the womb ⟨back in those days a woman her age would have *birthed* several children⟩ — see BEAR 1

birthday suit *n* the state of having no clothes on one's body ⟨with all of the resort guests in their *birthday suits*, socioeconomic differences became invisible and irrelevant⟩ — see NUDITY

birthplace *n* a place of origin ⟨Montgomery, Alabama, is considered the *birthplace* of the civil rights movement⟩
synonyms cradle, home, mother country, motherland
related words hometown; Blighty [*chiefly British*], country, nativity, old country, roots

birthright *n* **1** something that is or may be inherited ⟨believed that the house was her *birthright*⟩ — see INHERITANCE
2 something to which one has a just claim ⟨the promotion is his *birthright*, after the work he put in⟩ — see RIGHT 1

bisect *vb* to divide by passing through or across ⟨the infamous concrete wall that once *bisected* the city of Berlin, Germany⟩ — see INTERSECT

bistro *n* a bar or restaurant offering special nighttime entertainment (as music, dancing, or comedy acts) ⟨a section of the city populated with casual *bistros* offering entertainment to suit nearly every taste⟩ — see NIGHTCLUB

bit *n* **1** a very small piece ⟨she left only a *bit* of the broccoli on her plate⟩
synonyms atom, crumb, dribble, fleck, flyspeck, grain, granule, molecule, morsel, mote, nubbin, nugget, particle, patch, scrap, scruple, snip, snippet, speck, tittle
related words ace, dab, dash, driblet, drop, fraction, haet [*chiefly Scottish*], halfpenny, ha'penny, iota, jot, kenning [*chiefly Scottish*], lick, minim, mite, modicum, nutshell, ounce, pinch, shred, smatter, smidgen (*also* smidgeon *or* smidgin *or* smidge), spot, strain, streak, suspicion, taste, touch, trace, whisper, whit; bite, mouthful, nibble, tidbit (*also* titbit); fragment, part, portion, section; chip, flake, shard, shiver, sliver, splinter; clipping, paring, shaving; smithereens

near antonyms chunk, gob, hunk, lump, slab; abundance, barrel, bucket, bushel, deal, heaps, loads, mass, mountain, peck, pile, pot, profusion, quantity, raft, scads, stack, volume, wad, wealth

2 a broken or irregular part of something that often remains incomplete ⟨*bits* of cookie scattered on the table⟩ — see FRAGMENT

3 a very small amount ⟨I'll have only a *bit* of food right now⟩ — see PARTICLE 1

4 an indefinite but usually short period of time ⟨this will only take a *bit*⟩ — see WHILE 1

5 a performance regularly presented by an individual or group ⟨known for a comedic *bit* in which she portrayed a very nervous student driver⟩ — see ACT 1

6 something that is pleasing to eat because it is rare or a luxury ⟨wielding silver trays, the servers offered partygoers a variety of exotic-looking *bits*⟩ — see DELICACY 1

bitch *n* an expression of dissatisfaction, pain, or resentment ⟨tiresome members of the tour group who had one *bitch* after another⟩ — see COMPLAINT 1

bitch *vb* to express dissatisfaction, pain, or resentment usually tiresomely ⟨those lowly wage earners are always *bitching* about something⟩ — see COMPLAIN

bitchily *adv* in a mean or spiteful manner ⟨the *bitchily* funny put-downs of the satirist Dorothy Parker⟩ — see NASTILY

bitchy *adj* having or showing a desire to cause someone pain or suffering for the sheer enjoyment of it ⟨a *bitchy* and vindictive boss who has punished workers who have had the gall to call attention to her mistakes⟩ — see HATEFUL

bite *n* **1** a harsh or sharp quality ⟨the fall winds had a real *bite*⟩ — see EDGE 1

2 a small piece or quantity of food ⟨had only a *bite* to eat before rushing off⟩ — see MORSEL 1

3 an uncomfortable degree of coolness ⟨weather with a *bite* that suggested winter was right around the corner⟩ — see CHILL

bite *vb, slang* to be objectionable or unsatisfactory ⟨man, that really *bites* that you have to work on Christmas⟩ — see STINK 2

bite (at) *vb* to consume or wear away gradually ⟨the waves were *biting at* the sand castle I had worked so hard on⟩ — see EAT 2

bite (on) *vb* to crush or grind with the teeth ⟨she tends to *bite on* her pencils when she thinks hard⟩

synonyms champ, chaw, chew, chomp (on), crunch (on), gnaw (on), masticate, nibble

related words ruminate; munch, nosh, snack; consume, eat, ingest, swallow; bolt, devour, gobble (up *or* down), gorge, gulp, scarf, scoff, snack, wolf; nip, peck (at), pick (at); gum, mumble

phrases sink one's teeth into

biting *adj* **1** causing intense discomfort to one's skin ⟨a *biting* wind that only the toughest football fans were willing to endure⟩ — see CUTTING 1

2 marked by the use of wit that is intended to cause hurt feelings ⟨the *biting* comments by the popular girls about the new kid in class⟩ — see SARCASTIC

bitsy *adj* very small in size ⟨it's just a *bitsy* blister, but it's right on my heel so that I feel it every time I take a step⟩ — see TINY

bitter *adj* **1** having or showing deep-seated resentment ⟨a *bitter* attitude about always having to work on Saturday⟩ ⟨she's still *bitter* about the way her boyfriend broke up with her⟩

synonyms acrid, acrimonious, embittered, hard, rancorous, resentful, sore

related words disaffected, discontented, disgruntled, malcontent; contemptuous, cynical, disdainful, misanthropic, scornful; angry, cruel, harsh, irritated, mad, rough, savage, vehement, vicious, virulent, vitriolic; acid, caustic, cutting, mordant, sarcastic, trenchant; knock-down, drag-out (*or* knock-down-and-drag-out)

near antonyms caring, forgiving, gentle, kind, kindhearted, loving, sweet, sympathetic, tender, warm, warmhearted

antonyms unbitter

2 hard to accept or bear especially emotionally ⟨discovering that he had been cut from the crew team was a *bitter* disappointment⟩

synonyms afflicting, agonizing, cruel, excruciating, galling, grievous, harrowing, harsh, heartrending, hurtful, painful, tormenting, torturous

related words insufferable, insupportable, intolerable, unacceptable, unbearable, unendurable, unsupportable; appalling, awful, bad, dire, dreadful, ghastly, horrible, miserable, nasty, rotten, severe, terrible, vile, wretched; acute, extreme, intense, piercing

near antonyms bearable, endurable, supportable, sustainable, tolerable; livable (*also* liveable), sufferable, survivable; acceptable, allowable, reasonable

antonyms gratifying, pleasing, sweet

3 causing intense discomfort to one's skin ⟨a *bitter* wind was stinging the faces of the skiers⟩ — see CUTTING 1

4 difficult to endure ⟨a *bitter* lesson about money and friendship⟩ — see HARSH 1

5 having a low or subnormal temperature ⟨a *bitter* February day for this part of the country⟩ — see COLD 1

6 uncomfortably cool ⟨a *bitter*, rainy day⟩ — see CHILLY 1

7 expressing or suggesting mourning ⟨a *bitter* cry of grief⟩ — see MOURNFUL 1

8 not giving pleasure to the mind or senses ⟨had to face the *bitter* truth about their marriage⟩ — see UNPLEASANT

bitterly *adv* with feelings of bitterness or grief ⟨cried *bitterly* after her grandmother died⟩ — see HARD 2

bitterness *n* **1** a deep-seated ill will ⟨he still harbored an implacable *bitterness* against the company that had fired him⟩ — see ENMITY

2 a harsh or sharp quality ⟨the *bitterness* of the coffee suggested that it had been reheated⟩ — see EDGE 1

3 an uncomfortable degree of coolness ⟨there's a *bitterness* in the air, so let's build a fire in the fireplace⟩ — see CHILL

4 biting sharpness of feeling or expression ⟨complained with great *bitterness* about the ill treatment he had always received from his in-laws⟩ — see ACRIMONY 1

bitty *adj* very small in size ⟨a little *bitty* kitten that I could hold in my hand⟩ — see TINY

bivouac *n* a place where a group of people live for a short time in tents or cabins ⟨soldiers setting up a *bivouac* by the stream⟩ — see CAMP 1

bivouac *vb* **1** to live in a camp or the outdoors ⟨the army *bivouacked* for the night by the lake⟩ — see CAMP (OUT)

2 to provide with living quarters or shelter ⟨survivors of the tornado were *bivouacked* in the church basement⟩ — see HOUSE 1

bizarre *adj* **1** conceived or made without regard for reason or reality ⟨a *bizarre* invention that no one could figure out how to use⟩ — see FANTASTIC 1

2 different from the ordinary in a way that causes curiosity or suspicion ⟨a *bizarre* tattoo that suggested he might be a member of a gang⟩ — see ODD 2

bizarro *adj* **1** different from the ordinary in a way that causes curiosity or suspicion ⟨the cat was acting pretty *bizarro* this morning, and I'm worried about him⟩ — see ODD 2

2 excitingly or mysteriously unusual ⟨entered the *bizarro* world of all-night raves⟩ — see EXOTIC

blab *vb* **1** to engage in casual or rambling conversation

⟨frequently calls her best friend and *blabs* for an hour⟩ — see CHAT 1

2 to relate sometimes questionable or secret information of a personal nature ⟨he *blabs* a lot, so never share a secret with him⟩ — see GOSSIP

blabber *n* **1** a person who talks constantly ⟨a *blabber* who always wastes my time with drivel⟩ — see CHATTERBOX

2 unintelligible or meaningless talk ⟨doting, overindulgent parents who take their toddler's *blabber* a little too seriously⟩ — see GIBBERISH 1

blabbermouth *n* a person who talks constantly ⟨told the *blabbermouth* to put a lid on it⟩ — see CHATTERBOX

blabby *adj* fond of talking or conversation ⟨she is a sweet woman, but so *blabby* that you need to escape her after a while⟩ — see TALKATIVE

black *adj* **1** having the color of soot or coal ⟨a little *black* dress blends into the night very well⟩

synonyms ebony, pitch-black, pitch-dark, pitchy, raven, sable

related words dark, dusky, inky; blackish, brunet (*or* brunette)

near antonyms bright, brilliant, light, pale, palish

antonyms white

2 causing or marked by an atmosphere lacking in cheer ⟨the Friday of the stock market crash was indeed a *black* day for the country⟩ — see GLOOMY 1

3 not conforming to a high moral standard; morally unacceptable ⟨the *black* deeds of the brigands along the Scottish border⟩ — see BAD 2

4 not having a light complexion ⟨a *black* Irishman, Tyrone Power had the classic looks of a Hollywood leading man⟩ — see DARK 2

5 being without light or without much light ⟨on a *black* night such as this, the imagination runs wild⟩ — see DARK 1

6 not clean ⟨don't you dare touch my curtains with those *black* hands!⟩ — see DIRTY 1

black *n* a time or place of little or no light ⟨a serial killer who always did his evil deeds in the *black* of night⟩ — see DARK 1

blackball *vb* to reject by or as if by a vote ⟨the club secretly *blackballs* applicants who belong to that religion⟩ — see NEGATIVE 1

black beast *n* something or someone that causes fear or dread especially without reason ⟨Form 1040 has always been his personal *black beast*, and he puts off dealing with it for as long as he can⟩ — see BOGEY 1

blacken *vb* **1** to make dirty ⟨*blackened* the towels with their dirty hands⟩ — see DIRTY

2 to make untrue and harmful statements about ⟨the politician maliciously *blackened* his opponent's reputation⟩ — see SLANDER

3 to make dark, dim, or indistinct ⟨thick smoke from the forest fires *blackened* the sky for many miles⟩ — see CLOUD 1

4 to grow dark ⟨the auditorium *blackened* suddenly, and a spotlighted performer appeared alone on stage⟩ — see DARKEN 2

blackened *adj* not clean ⟨the church's *blackened* ceiling is the result of centuries of candle smoke⟩ — see DIRTY 1

blackening *n* the making of false statements that damage another's reputation ⟨*blackening* of the senator's good name disgusted voters⟩ — see SLANDER

black hole *n* empty space ⟨a psychopath who seemingly has a *black hole* where his heart should be⟩ — see VACANCY 1

blackjack *vb* **1** to cause (a person) to give in to pressure ⟨you cannot *blackjack* me into going along with this⟩ — see FORCE 1

2 to make timid or fearful by or as if by threats ⟨a couple of thugs trying to *blackjack* a shopkeeper into paying protection money⟩ — see INTIMIDATE

blackmailer *n* a person who gets money from another by using force or threats ⟨the *blackmailer* threatened to tell the media about the mayor's arrest as a teenager⟩ — see RACKETEER

blackness *n* **1** a time or place of little or no light ⟨strange nocturnal noises emanated from the forbidding *blackness* of the forest⟩ — see DARK 1

2 the state or quality of being dirty ⟨judging from the *blackness* of the carpet, I'd say that it had never been cleaned⟩ — see DIRTINESS 1

blackout *n* a temporary state of unconsciousness ⟨even though you experienced only a brief *blackout*, you still ought to be checked by a doctor⟩ — see FAINT

black out *vb* **1** to destroy all traces of ⟨had spent most of her adulthood trying to *black out* memories of a wretched childhood⟩ — see ANNIHILATE 1

2 to grow dark ⟨with the delivery of the knockout punch, the screen *blacks out*, and in the next scene the boxer wakes up in the hospital⟩ — see DARKEN 2

3 to lose consciousness ⟨*blacked out* after hitting her head on the beam⟩ — see FAINT

blade *n* **1** a hand weapon with a length of metal sharpened on one or both sides and usually tapered to a sharp point ⟨dueled with *blades* rather than guns⟩ — see SWORD

2 an instrument with a metal length that has a sharp edge for cutting ⟨used a small *blade* to cut the rope⟩ — see KNIFE

blah *also* **blah–blah** *n* **1** language, behavior, or ideas that are absurd and contrary to good sense ⟨gave me the usual *blah* that my manuscript did not meet their current publishing needs but thanks for considering them⟩ — see NONSENSE 1

2 blahs *pl* the state of being bored ⟨I've just been stuck in the *blahs* lately⟩ — see BOREDOM

blamable *adj* deserving reproach or blame ⟨an honest mistake is hardly a *blamable* offense⟩ — see BLAMEWORTHY

blame *n* **1** responsibility for wrongdoing or failure ⟨willingly accepted the *blame* for not seeing that the kitchen was properly cleaned⟩

synonyms culpability, fault, guilt, onus, rap

related words blameworthiness, complicity, guiltiness, sinfulness; accusation, censure, condemnation, denunciation, finger-pointing, reproach; regret, remorse, self-reproach, shame

antonyms blamelessness, faultlessness, guiltlessness, innocence

2 the state of being held as the cause of something that needs to be set right ⟨*blame* for the school's poor performance in standardized tests was attributed to several factors⟩ — see RESPONSIBILITY 1

blame *vb* to express one's unfavorable opinion of the worth or quality of ⟨more concerned with pleasing audiences, the playwright has always claimed to be indifferent to whether critics praise his comedies or *blame* them without mercy⟩ — see CRITICIZE

blameless *adj* free from guilt or blame ⟨a *blameless* baby shouldn't have to suffer for his parents' mistakes⟩ — see INNOCENT 2

blamelessness *n* the quality or state of being free from guilt or blame ⟨your *blamelessness* in this incident is obvious, so you won't be punished⟩ — see INNOCENCE 1

blameworthy *adj* deserving reproach or blame ⟨we were all equally *blameworthy*, whether we had openly approved the free-speech restrictions or simply kept quiet about them⟩

synonyms blamable, censurable, culpable, reprehensible, reproachable

related words bad, guilty, sinful, wicked; foolish, irresponsible, reckless; amerciable, chargeable, disciplinable, impeachable, indictable, punishable; criminal, illegal, illicit, unlawful; illegitimate, improper, wrongful
phrases at fault
near antonyms flawless, perfect, pure; guiltless, innocent
antonyms blameless, faultless, impeccable, irreproachable

blanch *vb* to make white or whiter by removing color ⟨a good washing with bleach should *blanch* these yellowed sheets⟩ — see WHITEN

blanched *adj* lacking a healthy skin color ⟨looking *blanched* and feeble after a long illness⟩ — see PALE 2

bland *adj* not harsh or stern especially in nature or effect ⟨*bland* food that was good for babies and invalids⟩ — see GENTLE 1

blandish *vb* to get (someone) to do something by gentle urging, special attention, or flattery ⟨*blandished* her into doing their work for them by complimenting her shamelessly⟩ — see COAX

blank *adj* **1** not expressing any emotion ⟨the teacher knew no one was paying attention when she looked out and saw all those *blank* faces⟩
synonyms catatonic, deadpan, empty, expressionless, impassive, inexpressive, numb, stolid, vacant
related words dull, vacuous, vague, vapid; enigmatic (*also* enigmatical), impenetrable, inscrutable, mysterious; motionless, static, still, wooden; reserved, restrained, reticent, taciturn; aloof, apathetic, cold, cool, detached, indifferent, phlegmatic, unresponsive
near antonyms engaged, interested, responsive; active, alive, animated, bright, busy, dynamic, effervescent, energetic, expansive, exuberant, lively, vivacious; eloquent, revealing, revelatory; gestic, gesticulant, gesticulative, gesticulatory, gestural; emotional, melodramatic, theatrical (*also* theatric), unreserved, unrestrained
antonyms demonstrative, expressive
2 lacking contents that could or should be present ⟨the page of instructions actually turned out to be *blank*⟩ — see EMPTY 1
3 having no exceptions or restrictions ⟨his *blank* refusal to even consider my request for an unpaid leave of absence⟩ — see ABSOLUTE 2

blank *n* **1** a piece of paper with information written or to be written on it ⟨handed him an employment *blank* to fill out⟩ — see FORM 2
2 empty space ⟨a *blank* on the form for the patient's insurance policy number⟩ — see VACANCY 1

blanket *adj* belonging or relating to the whole ⟨a *blanket* promise of amnesty for everyone with overdue library books⟩ — see GENERAL 1

blanket *n* something that covers or conceals like a piece of cloth ⟨a *blanket* of fog concealed the view of the harbor⟩ — see CLOAK 1

blanket *vb* **1** to form a layer over ⟨leaves *blanketed* all of the land around the house⟩ — see COVER 2
2 to keep secret or shut off from view ⟨*blanketed* the secret memo from the news media⟩ — see [1]HIDE 2
3 to cause to cease burning ⟨firefighters managed to *blanket* the fire with foam⟩ — see EXTINGUISH 1

blankness *n* empty space ⟨a conspicuous *blankness* surrounds the figure of the woman, for the artist is trying to suggest her deep isolation and loneliness⟩ — see VACANCY 1

blare *n* loud, confused, and usually inharmonious sound ⟨the *blare* of horns arising from the long line of cars behind him did nothing to help the motorist get his car started again⟩ — see NOISE 1

blare *vb* to make known openly or publicly ⟨was it really necessary to *blare* that private quarrel to the whole world?⟩ — see ANNOUNCE

blaring *adj* marked by a high volume of sound ⟨some teens drove by and woke us up with *blaring* music⟩ — see LOUD 1

blarney *n* **1** excessive praise ⟨laid the *blarney* on thick in order to get special treatment from the waitress⟩ — see FLATTERY
2 language, behavior, or ideas that are absurd and contrary to good sense ⟨his excuse was his usual *blarney* about how he'd love to help out but he was just so darned busy⟩ — see NONSENSE 1

blarney *vb* **1** to get (someone) to do something by gentle urging, special attention, or flattery ⟨attendants at the nursing home sometimes have to *blarney* the patients to take their medicine⟩ — see COAX
2 to praise too much ⟨an eager, young assistant who *blarneys* the boss shamelessly⟩ — see FLATTER 1

blaspheme *vb* to use offensive or indecent language ⟨shocked that someone would *blaspheme* in church, of all places⟩ — see SWEAR 1

blasphemous *adj* not showing proper reverence for the holy or sacred ⟨Catholics used to believe that anyone but a priest touching a consecrated wafer was *blasphemous*⟩ — see IRREVERENT

blasphemy *n* an act of great disrespect shown to God or to sacred ideas, people, or things ⟨in the 17th century the Quakers were persecuted for beliefs and practices that older churches regarded as *blasphemies*⟩
synonyms defilement, desecration, impiety, irreverence, profanation, sacrilege
related words cursing, profanity, swearing; affront, insult; violation; contamination, corruption, debasement, pollution; sin, trespass
near antonyms consecration, purification, sanctification; reverence, veneration
antonyms adoration, glorification, worship

blast *n* **1** a loud explosive sound ⟨a sharp *blast* of the horn startled the other driver⟩ — see CLAP 1
2 a sudden brief rush of wind ⟨a surprise *blast* stole the umbrella right out of his hands⟩ — see GUST 1
3 the act or an instance of exploding ⟨the *blast* destroyed the building completely⟩ — see EXPLOSION 1
4 a social gathering ⟨a wild fraternity *blast* that lasted a whole weekend⟩ — see PARTY 1

blast *vb* **1** to cause to break open or into pieces by or as if by an explosive ⟨the highway engineers will have to *blast* that hill in order to put a road through here⟩
synonyms blow, blow up, burst, demolish, explode, pop, shatter, smash
related words dynamite; annihilate, decimate, destroy; ruin, wreck; detonate, discharge; fragment, splinter
near antonyms collapse, implode
2 to cause (a projectile) to be driven forward with force ⟨artillery that could *blast* cannonballs from hundreds of yards⟩ — see SHOOT 1
3 to cause a weapon to release a missile with great force ⟨the recruits were all *blasting* away at the target range⟩ — see SHOOT 2
4 to criticize harshly and usually publicly ⟨*blasted* the new governor for every little misstep⟩ — see ATTACK 2
5 to proceed or move quickly ⟨rowdy teenagers *blasting* down the road in a sports car⟩ — see HURRY 2

blasted *adj* **1** deserving of one's condemnation or displeasure ⟨that *blasted* car salesman cheated us⟩ — see DAMNABLE
2 *slang* being under the influence of a recreational drug ⟨the members of the rock band were all so *blasted* they could barely perform⟩ — see STONED 1
3 *slang* being under the influence of alcohol ⟨the number of empty wineglasses before her does not suggest

"connoisseur" so much as "completely *blasted*"⟩ — see DRUNK

blasting *adj* marked by a high volume of sound ⟨carried a *blasting* radio wherever he went⟩ — see LOUD 1

blasting *n* a directed propelling of a missile by a firearm or artillery piece ⟨the next *blasting* by the artillery scored a direct hit⟩ — see SHOT

blastoff *n* a rising from a surface at the start of a flight (as of a rocket) ⟨the mission was scrubbed just minutes before *blastoff*⟩ — see LIFTOFF

blat *vb* to utter with a sudden burst of strong feeling ⟨*blatted* an obscene expletive before biting the dust⟩ — see EXCLAIM

blatant *adj* **1** engaging in or marked by loud and insistent cries especially of protest ⟨a *blatant* clamor for the impeachment of the scandal-plagued governor⟩ — see VOCIFEROUS

2 very noticeable especially for being incorrect or bad ⟨I take off points for *blatant* spelling errors⟩ — see EGREGIOUS

blather *n* **1** a state of noisy, confused activity ⟨wanted to retire quietly and without all the *blather* of an office send-off⟩ — see COMMOTION

2 language, behavior, or ideas that are absurd and contrary to good sense ⟨dismissed the whole election as just so much *blather*⟩ — see NONSENSE 1

blather (on) *vb* to talk at length without sticking to a topic or getting to a point ⟨my attention wandered as she *blathered on* about her endlessly active social life⟩ — see RAMBLE 1

blatherskite *n* language, behavior, or ideas that are absurd and contrary to good sense ⟨a Scottish uncle who regards any pronouncement from the government as ignorable *blatherskite*⟩ — see NONSENSE 1

blaze *n* **1** a sudden intense expression of strong feeling ⟨she felt a *blaze* of resentment upon hearing that she had been passed over for promotion⟩ — see OUTBURST 1

2 the steady giving off of the form of radiation that makes vision possible ⟨temporarily blinded by the *blaze* of dozens of camera lights⟩ — see LIGHT 1

[1]blaze *vb* to make known openly or publicly ⟨the White House didn't waste a minute in *blazing* the lower unemployment figures⟩ — see ANNOUNCE

[2]blaze *vb* **1** to be on fire especially brightly ⟨the house *blazed* for over three hours in the late-night fire⟩ — see BURN 1

2 to shine with a bright harsh light ⟨the spotlight *blazed* through my window⟩ — see GLARE 1

3 to proceed or move quickly ⟨an extreme skier went *blazing* down the ski slope at a reckless pace⟩ — see HURRY 2

blaze (up) *vb* to develop suddenly and violently ⟨after years of decline, street crime *blazed up* again⟩ — see ERUPT 2

blazing *adj* **1** being on fire ⟨the *blazing* logs in the fireplace cast a warm glow on our holiday party⟩ — see ABLAZE 1

2 having or expressing great depth of feeling ⟨a *blazing* speech affirming the value of every individual in this world⟩ — see FERVENT 1

blazon *vb* **1** to make known openly or publicly ⟨their very public canoodling has pretty much *blazoned* the fact that they are having an affair⟩ — see ANNOUNCE

2 to make more attractive by adding something that is beautiful or becoming ⟨the city's waterfront has been *blazoned* with banners celebrating the festival of tall ships⟩ — see DECORATE

bleach *vb* to make white or whiter by removing color ⟨*bleached* the stained shirt back to its original white⟩ — see WHITEN

bleak *adj* **1** causing or marked by an atmosphere lacking in cheer ⟨a *bleak* outlook for the team for the rest of the season⟩ — see GLOOMY 1

2 marked by wet and windy conditions ⟨it was a dark and *bleak* wintry day⟩ — see FOUL 1

3 uncomfortably cool ⟨a *bleak* December morning⟩ — see CHILLY 1

bleakness *n* an uncomfortable degree of coolness ⟨the morning *bleakness* prompted me to get a fire going⟩ — see CHILL

blear *adj* not seen or understood clearly ⟨I can't describe him; all I saw was a *blear* figure for an instant⟩ — see FAINT 1

blear *vb* to make dark, dim, or indistinct ⟨her image was *bleared*, as if I were staring at it through a watery lens⟩ — see CLOUD 1

bleary *adj* **1** depleted in strength, energy, or freshness ⟨disoriented, *bleary* passengers departing from the red-eye⟩ — see WEARY 1

2 not seen or understood clearly ⟨the *bleary* outline of a fishing boat could just be seen through the fog⟩ — see FAINT 1

bleat *n* an expression of dissatisfaction, pain, or resentment ⟨a very patient, understanding person who accepts life's inconveniences without a *bleat*⟩ — see COMPLAINT 1

bleat *vb* **1** to express dissatisfaction, pain, or resentment usually tiresomely ⟨as far as the slumlord was concerned, the unhappy tenants were just *bleating* about nothing⟩ — see COMPLAIN

2 to utter feeble plaintive cries ⟨the baby *bleated* softly as he woke up, then smiled⟩ — see WHIMPER 1

bleed *vb* **1** to feel deep sadness or mental pain ⟨her heart *bleeds* for the homeless people she sees on her way to work⟩ — see GRIEVE

2 to flow forth slowly through small openings ⟨pitch was *bleeding* from cuts in the tree bark⟩ — see EXUDE

3 to remove (liquid) gradually or completely ⟨*bleed* water from the radiators⟩ — see DRAIN 1

4 to rob by the use of trickery or threats ⟨the confidence men coldheartedly *bled* the elderly couple of their life savings⟩ — see FLEECE

bleed (for) *vb* to have sympathy for ⟨the young man *bleeds for* his friend, who just lost his father⟩ — see PITY

bleeder *n, British* a person whose behavior is offensive to others ⟨don't let the insults of those lousy *bleeders* get you down, old chap⟩ — see JERK 1

blemish *n* something that spoils the appearance or completeness of a thing ⟨the first mirror had a *blemish* on its surface, so we took it back to the store⟩

synonyms blight, blotch, defect, deformity, disfigurement, excrescence, excrescency, fault, flaw, imperfection, mar, mark, pockmark, scar

related words abnormality, distortion, irregularity, malformation, misshape; bug, glitch, kink; blot, blur, spot, stain, taint; damage, defacement, impairment, injury; failing, weakness

near antonyms adornment, decoration, embellishment, enhancement, ornament

blemish *vb* **1** to affect slightly with something morally bad or undesirable ⟨a single indiscretion *blemished* the rabbi's reputation for years⟩ — see TAINT 1

2 to reduce the soundness, effectiveness, or perfection of ⟨a scratch *blemished* the finish on the car⟩ — see DAMAGE 1

[1]blench *vb* to draw back in fear, pain, or disgust ⟨she *blenched* from the horrible sight⟩ — see FLINCH

[2]blench *vb* to make white or whiter by removing color ⟨we'll have to *blench* the sheets with bleach to restore that snow-white look⟩ — see WHITEN

blend *n* a distinct entity formed by the combining of two or more different things ⟨that fabric is a cotton and

polyester *blend*, so it shouldn't shrink as much as pure cotton⟩
synonyms admixture, alloy, amalgam, amalgamation, cocktail, combination, composite, compound, conflation, emulsion, fusion, intermixture, meld, mix, mixture, synthesis
related words half-and-half; absorption, blending, coalescence, coalition, commingling, commixture, compost, concretion, homogenization, immingling, immixture, incorporation, integration, interfusion, intermingling, mergence, merger, merging, mingling; assortment, hash, hodgepodge, hotchpotch, jumble, medley, mélange, mishmash, motley, patchwork, potpourri, variety; accumulation, aggregation, conglomeration
near antonyms component, constituent, element, ingredient

blend *vb* **1** to turn into a single mass or entity that is more or less the same throughout ⟨she *blended* the ingredients for the brownies very thoroughly to eliminate lumps in the batter⟩
synonyms amalgamate, combine, comingle, commingle, commix, composite, concrete, conflate, fuse, homogenize, immingle, immix, incorporate, integrate, interfuse, intermingle, intermix, meld, merge, mingle, mix
related words add, admix, beat (in), cut in, fold, stir, toss; coalesce, compound, emulsify; conjoin, join, knit, link, unite; intertwine, interweave, weave
near antonyms cleave, disjoin, disunite, divide, divorce, part, rupture, sever, sunder; disperse, dissolve, scatter; detach, disengage, split
antonyms break down, break up, separate, unmix
2 to form a pleasing relationship ⟨the colors *blend* nicely in that rug⟩ — see HARMONIZE 1

bless *vb* **1** to make holy through prayers or ritual ⟨the priest *blessed* the water, thus allowing it to be used as holy water for various rites⟩
synonyms consecrate, hallow, sacralize, sanctify
related words baptize, canonize, spiritualize; chasten, cleanse, lustrate, purify; exorcise (*also* exorcize), expurgate; commit, dedicate, devote; reconsecrate
near antonyms defile, desecrate, profane; dirty, foul, pollute, soil, taint, violate; blaspheme, curse, cuss, damn, execrate; cast out, condemn, damn, punish
antonyms deconsecrate, desacralize, desanctify
2 to proclaim the glory of ⟨*bless* the name of God⟩ — see PRAISE 1
3 to furnish freely or naturally with some power, quality, or attribute ⟨*blessed* with a knack for glib conversation⟩ — see ENDOW 1

blessed *also* **blest** *adj* **1** of, relating to, or being God ⟨a prayer to the *blessed* Savior⟩ — see HOLY 3
2 set apart or worthy of veneration by association with God ⟨statues honoring an array of *blessed* saints are scattered throughout the cathedral⟩ — see HOLY 2
3 giving pleasure or contentment to the mind or senses ⟨the *blessed* sight of home after a long journey⟩ — see PLEASANT 1

blessedness *n* **1** a feeling or state of well-being and contentment ⟨the proud parents can scarcely describe the *blessedness* of having four healthy children⟩ — see HAPPINESS 1
2 the quality or state of being spiritually pure or virtuous ⟨Mother Teresa's renowned *blessedness* made her an obvious candidate for sainthood⟩ — see HOLINESS

blessing *n* **1** a prayer calling for divine care, protection, or favor ⟨that rabbi always ends the service with a short *blessing*⟩
synonyms benediction, benison
related words Godspeed; appeal, entreaty, grace, intercession, invocation, orison, petition, plea, prayer, supplication; sanctification
phrases laying on of hands
antonyms anathema, curse, execration, imprecation, malediction
2 something that provides happiness or does good for a person or thing ⟨winning the lottery shortly after being laid off was an unexpected *blessing*⟩
synonyms benediction, benefit, boon, felicity, godsend, good, manna, windfall
related words grace, mercy; favor, kindness, mitzvah; advantage, aid, assistance, gift, help, relief, support; anodyne, comfort, consolation, solace; bonus, extra, lagniappe; delight, joy, pleasure
near antonyms hex, hoodoo, jinx; bother, irritant, nuisance, pest; disadvantage; cross, misery, trial, tribulation
antonyms affliction, bane, curse, evil, plague, scourge
3 an acceptance of something as satisfactory ⟨Mr. Roberts promptly gave his *blessing* to his daughter's choice of husband⟩ — see APPROVAL 1
4 the act of making something holy through religious ritual ⟨traditionally, worshippers kneel during the *blessing* of the communion wafers⟩ — see CONSECRATION

blight *n* something that spoils the appearance or completeness of a thing ⟨the expanding urban sprawl is a *blight* on the countryside⟩ — see BLEMISH

blighter *n, chiefly British* a person whose behavior is offensive to others ⟨if the old chap gets unruly, just tell the *blighter* to leave you alone⟩ — see JERK 1

blind *adj* **1** lacking the power of sight ⟨our old *blind* cat kept walking into walls and furniture⟩
synonyms eyeless, sightless, stone-blind, visionless
related words blinded, blindfold, blindfolded, unsighted; gravel-blind, purblind
near antonyms observant, observing, seeing; clear-eyed, clear-sighted; gimlet-eyed, lynx-eyed, sharp-eyed, sharp-sighted
antonyms sighted
2 being under the influence of alcohol ⟨you'd have to be really *blind* to think that was a good idea⟩ — see DRUNK

blind *vb* to overpower with light ⟨the bright lights in the TV studio momentarily *blinded* the quiz show contestants⟩ — see DAZZLE

blindsiding *adj* causing a strong emotional reaction because of unexpectedness ⟨the last-minute *blindsiding* allegations that almost derailed the candidate's campaign⟩ — see SURPRISING 1

blink *vb* **1** to shine with light at regular intervals ⟨she loves to sit in the dark and watch the lights on the Christmas tree *blink* in ever-changing patterns⟩
synonyms flash, twinkle, wink
related words coruscate, flare, flicker, glance, glimmer, glint, glisten, glister, glitter, scintillate, shimmer, spangle, spark, sparkle
2 to rapidly open and close one's eyes ⟨I *blinked* for a few seconds after the camera flashed⟩ — see WINK 1
3 to cease resistance (as to another's arguments, demands, or control) ⟨for two days the nations stood on the brink of war, until one finally *blinked*⟩ — see YIELD 3
4 to look long and hard in wonder or surprise ⟨stood *blinking* at the ridiculous scene before him in utter disbelief⟩ — see GAPE

blink (at) *vb* to dismiss as of little importance ⟨the firm conviction that we should never *blink at* any instances of plagiarism, whether in academia or in commercial publishing⟩ — see EXCUSE 1

bliss *n* **1** a dwelling place of perfect happiness for the soul after death ⟨the godly life she has lived will surely lead to infinite *bliss* after death⟩ — see HEAVEN 1
2 a feeling or state of well-being and contentment ⟨the

enviable *bliss* of a happily married couple⟩ — see HAPPINESS 1

blissful *adj* experiencing pleasure, satisfaction, or delight ⟨a *blissful* cat who obviously loves being stroked⟩ — see GLAD 1

blissfulness *n* a feeling or state of well-being and contentment ⟨the *blissfulness* that only a full stomach and a warm bed can bring⟩ — see HAPPINESS 1

blistering *adj* **1** extreme in degree, power, or effect ⟨even after a *blistering* attack from the enemy, the fortress held⟩ — see INTENSE 1
2 moving, proceeding, or acting with great speed ⟨a major-league pitcher known for his *blistering* fastballs⟩ — see FAST 1

blisteringly *adv* to a great degree ⟨a *blisteringly* harsh review of the new musical⟩ — see VERY 1

blithe *adj* **1** having or showing a good mood or disposition ⟨a *blithe*, obedient child⟩ — see CHEERFUL 1
2 indicative of or marked by high spirits or good humor ⟨a *blithe* remark that good food enjoyed with good company makes good wine seem even better⟩ — see MERRY
3 having or showing freedom from worries or troubles ⟨he has a *blithe* attitude about ever having to earn a living because he knows there's a trust fund in his future⟩ — see CAREFREE

blither *n* language, behavior, or ideas that are absurd and contrary to good sense ⟨a boss who isn't inclined to accept any *blither* on why something isn't finished on time⟩ — see NONSENSE 1

blithesome *adj* **1** having or showing a good mood or disposition ⟨a *blithesome* girl who never seems to be sad or angry⟩ — see CHEERFUL 1
2 indicative of or marked by high spirits or good humor ⟨a *blithesome* and silly joke among old friends⟩ — see MERRY

blitz *n* **1** a rapid or overwhelming outpouring of many things at once ⟨a multimedia *blitz* of advertisements for the summer blockbuster⟩ — see BARRAGE
2 the act or action of setting upon with force or violence ⟨a massive aerial *blitz* that was supposed to shock and awe the enemy into immediate surrender⟩ — see ATTACK 1
3 a series of activities undertaken to achieve a goal ⟨an all-out advertising *blitz* to promote the new soft drink⟩ — see CAMPAIGN

blitz *vb* to use bombs or artillery against ⟨in 1940 and 1941 the German air force *blitzed* London night after horrible night⟩ — see BOMBARD 1

blitzed *adj, slang* **1** being under the influence of a recreational drug ⟨she says she was too *blitzed* to remember most of the party⟩ — see STONED 1
2 being under the influence of alcohol ⟨most weekends those frat boys are utterly *blitzed*⟩ — see DRUNK

blitzkrieg *n* **1** a rapid or overwhelming outpouring of many things at once ⟨the stunned survivors of the crash were then confronted with a *blitzkrieg* of insensitive questions from the media⟩ — see BARRAGE
2 the act or action of setting upon with force or violence ⟨the war began with a *blitzkrieg* that was designed to shock the enemy into submission⟩ — see ATTACK 1

blitzkrieg *vb* to use bombs or artillery against ⟨the Germans were determined to *blitzkrieg* London until the British surrendered⟩ — see BOMBARD 1

bloated *adj* **1** extended beyond normal or realistic bounds ⟨a *bloated* sense of his own importance⟩
synonyms exaggerated, hyperbolized, inflated, outsize (*also* outsized), overblown, overdrawn, overweening
related words elaborated, embellished, embroidered, enlarged, hyped-up, magnified, overdone, overemphasized, overplayed, overstated, padded, stretched; grandiose, preposterous, unreal, unrealistic, unreasonable
near antonyms realistic, reasonable
2 enlarged beyond normal from internal pressure ⟨a *bloated* stomach⟩
synonyms blown, distended, overinflated, puffed, swollen, tumescent, tumid, turgid, varicose (*also* varicosed)
related words ballooned, blown up, expanded; bulging, dilated, protuberant; ventricose; ballooning, dilating, turgescent
near antonyms collapsed, deflated, detumescent

blob *n* **1** a small uneven mass ⟨flicked a *blob* of jelly on the toast and began to spread it around⟩ — see LUMP 1
2 the quantity of fluid that falls naturally in one rounded mass ⟨got a *blob* of honey on his sweater⟩ — see DROP 1

bloc *n* **1** a group of people acting together within a larger group ⟨a whole *bloc* of students got together to complain⟩ — see FACTION
2 an association of persons, parties, or states for mutual assistance and protection ⟨the *bloc* that the United States and most of western Europe formed during the Cold War⟩ — see CONFEDERACY

block *n* **1** a number of things considered as a unit ⟨bought a *block* of stocks⟩ — see GROUP 1
2 something that makes movement or progress difficult ⟨constant bickering that is only a *block* to the completion of the project⟩ — see ENCUMBRANCE
3 *slang* the upper or front part of the body that contains the brain, the major sense organs, and the mouth ⟨threatened to knock the *block* off the jerk next door if he didn't can the noise⟩ — see HEAD 1
4 a group of people acting together within a larger group ⟨a more conservative *block* within the political party⟩ — see FACTION
5 an association of persons, parties, or states for mutual assistance and protection ⟨a *block* of oil-producing nations⟩ — see CONFEDERACY

block *vb* **1** to close up so that no empty spaces remain ⟨*block* up the opening in the wall where a window once was⟩ — see FILL 2
2 to prevent passage through by filling with something ⟨one of the patient's arteries was so *blocked* with fatty deposits that blood flow had been reduced to a trickle⟩ — see CLOG 1
3 to stop, seize, or interrupt while in progress or on course ⟨a thug suddenly stepped out of a doorway and *blocked* his escape down the alley⟩ — see INTERCEPT

block (off) *vb* to disallow entry into (a place) by means of a physical barrier at the entry point ⟨the square is temporarily *blocked off* for the street fair⟩ — see CLOSE (OFF)

blockade *n* the cutting off of an area by military means to stop the flow of people or supplies ⟨it was the *blockade* of all the enemy's major ports that finally won the war⟩
synonyms beleaguerment, investment, leaguer, siege
related words counterblockade; containment, encirclement, encompassment; confinement, insulation, isolation, quarantine, seclusion, segregation, sequestration; incarceration, internment

blockade *vb* **1** to disallow entry into (a place) by means of a physical barrier at the entry point ⟨the militant protestors *blockaded* the whole area around city hall⟩ — see CLOSE (OFF)
2 to surround (as a fortified place) with armed forces for the purpose of capturing or preventing commerce and communication ⟨*blockaded* the city until it surrendered⟩ — see BESIEGE 1

blockbuster *n* **1** a person or thing that is successful ⟨the movie is expected to be the biggest *blockbuster* of the summer⟩ — see HIT 1
2 something that is unusually large and powerful ⟨a

blockbuster of a fighter plane⟩ — see GIANT

blockhead *n* a stupid person ⟨only a real *blockhead* would think that she had literally said it a million times⟩ — see IDIOT

bloke *n, chiefly British* an adult male human being ⟨a couple of friendly *blokes* offered to show us the sights of London⟩ — see MAN 1

blond *or* **blonde** *adj* of a pale yellow or yellowish brown color ⟨the little boy's *blond* hair darkened to brown as he grew older⟩
synonyms fair, flaxen, golden, sandy, straw, tawny
related words ocherous (*or* ochreous); ash-blond (*or* ash-blonde), blondish, strawberry blonde (*or* strawberry blond), towheaded; gold, light, white
near antonyms black-a-vised, brown, brunet (*or* brunette), dark, olive, swart, swarthy; black, ebony, raven

blood *n* **1** a group of persons who come from the same ancestor ⟨in his mind, *blood* came before anything else, and he would not betray his criminal brother to the police⟩ — see FAMILY 1
2 the line of ancestors from whom a person is descended ⟨the language expert was certain that a young woman with such an upper-class accent had to be of royal *blood*⟩ — see ANCESTRY
3 the seat of one's deepest thoughts and emotions ⟨in your *blood* you know this business deal just isn't right⟩ — see CORE 1
4 the intentional and unlawful taking of another person's life ⟨*blood* will always have *blood*, and so the killing never ends⟩ — see HOMICIDE 1

blood–and–guts *adj* marked by bursts of destructive force or intense activity ⟨a hockey team known for its *blood-and-guts* play⟩ — see VIOLENT 1

bloodbath *n* the killing of a large number of people ⟨one side was so much better armed that the battle quickly turned into a *bloodbath*⟩ — see MASSACRE

blooded *adj* of unmixed ancestry ⟨the expansive farm on which *blooded* Arabian horses are raised⟩ — see PUREBRED

bloodline *n* the line of ancestors from whom a person is descended ⟨came from a *bloodline* that could be traced back to the 12th century⟩ — see ANCESTRY

bloodstained *adj* smeared or stained with blood ⟨had to throw away the *bloodstained* washcloth after a particularly bad nosebleed⟩ — see BLOODY 1

bloodsucker *n* **1** a person who is supported by or seeks support from another without making an adequate return ⟨the union accused the company executives of being *bloodsuckers*, since they had given themselves raises at a time when the rank and file were forced to take cuts in their benefits⟩ — see LEECH
2 a person who habitually preys upon others ⟨a sleazy lawyer who had a reputation for being a shyster, an ambulance chaser, and an all-around *bloodsucker*⟩ — see PREDATOR

bloodthirsty *adj* eager for or marked by the shedding of blood, extreme violence, or killing ⟨the Goths were a wild and *bloodthirsty* people⟩
synonyms bloody, bloody-minded, homicidal, murdering, murderous, sanguinary, sanguine, sanguineous
related words barbaric, barbarous, brutal, cold-blooded, cruel, heartless, inhumane, sadistic, savage, vicious, wanton; antagonistic, ferocious, fierce, gladiatorial, hostile; aggressive, assertive, bellicose, belligerent, combative, contentious, discordant, pugnacious, quarrelsome, scrappy, truculent, violent; merciless, pitiless, ruthless; bloodstained, fell, gory, grim; despiteful, hateful, malevolent, malicious, malign, malignant, mean, nasty, spiteful
near antonyms appeasing, conciliatory, disarming, dovish, mollifying, pacific, pacifying, peaceable, peaceful, peacemaking, placating, placative, placatory, propitiatory; unaggressive, unassertive; benign, benignant, compassionate, good-hearted, humane, kind, kindhearted, sympathetic, tenderhearted; tender, warm, warmhearted; clement, lenient, merciful; affable, amiable, amicable, benevolent, gentle, kindly; submissive, surrendering, yielding

bloody *adj* **1** smeared or stained with blood ⟨after the fight, her shirt was all *bloody*⟩
synonyms bloodstained, gory
related words bloodred, carmine, crimson, incarnadine, red, reddish, ruby, sanguine, sanguineous; sanguinary
2 eager for or marked by the shedding of blood, extreme violence, or killing ⟨a *bloody* battle⟩ ⟨a *bloody* movie that is unsuitable for children⟩ — see BLOODTHIRSTY

bloody *vb* to reduce the soundness, effectiveness, or perfection of ⟨the politician's reputation was permanently *bloodied* by the rumors of corruption⟩ — see DAMAGE 1

bloody–minded *adj* **1** eager for or marked by the shedding of blood, extreme violence, or killing ⟨some *bloody-minded* individuals wanted to castrate the alleged rapists even without so much as a word of sworn testimony⟩ — see BLOODTHIRSTY
2 *chiefly British* having or showing a habitually bad temper ⟨according to palace gossip, behind closed doors the prince was a *bloody-minded* bore⟩ — see ILL-TEMPERED

bloom *n* **1** a state or time of great activity, thriving, or achievement ⟨a handsome young man in the full *bloom* of youth⟩
synonyms blossom, florescence, floruit, flower, flush, heyday, high noon, prime, salad days, springtime
related words autumn, Indian summer; blooming, blossoming, efflorescence, flowering; acme, apex, climax, meridian, peak, pinnacle, summit, zenith; glory, grandeur, splendor; belle epoque (*or* belle époque), golden age, silver age; comeback, recovery, revivial
near antonyms decay, decline, downfall; bottom, nadir; shriveling (*or* shrivelling), wilting, withering
2 a rosy appearance (of the cheeks) ⟨after a snowball fight, she came inside with a *bloom* on her cheeks⟩
synonyms blush, color, flush
related words brightness, brilliance, glow; pinkness, reddishness, redness, rosiness, ruddiness, sanguineness
near antonyms paleness, pallidness, pallor, pastiness, wanness, whiteness; greenishness, greenness, sallowness
3 the usually showy plant part that produces seeds ⟨the rosebush produces *blooms* only in midsummer⟩ — see FLOWER 1

bloom *vb* **1** to produce flowers ⟨forsythias only *bloom* at the beginning of spring⟩
synonyms blossom, blow, burgeon (*also* bourgeon), effloresce, flower, unfold
related words leaf, leave; bud; open
near antonyms dry up, fade, shrivel, wilt, wither; die, drop, expire, perish
2 to develop a rosy facial color (as from excitement or embarrassment) ⟨she arrived at the house, *blooming* from her vigorous walk⟩ — see BLUSH

blooming *adj* **1** having a healthy reddish skin tone ⟨the *blooming* faces of children at play in the great outdoors⟩ — see RUDDY
2 *chiefly British* having no exceptions or restrictions ⟨thought that the royals were *blooming* idiots for making such indiscreet statements⟩ — see ABSOLUTE 2

blossom *n* **1** a state or time of great activity, thriving, or achievement ⟨in the full *blossom* of her career as a writer⟩ — see BLOOM 1
2 the usually showy plant part that produces seeds ⟨the

marigolds are finally showing *blossoms*⟩ — see FLOWER 1

blossom *vb* to produce flowers ⟨the fruit tree seemed to *blossom* overnight once the warm spring weather arrived⟩ — see BLOOM

blot *n* a mark of guilt or disgrace ⟨the bribery scandal was a *blot* on his reputation⟩ — see STAIN 1

blotch *n* **1** a small area that is different (as in color) from the main part ⟨a dog with a single small *blotch* of black⟩ — see SPOT 1

2 something that spoils the appearance or completeness of a thing ⟨that cell tower is another *blotch* on the landscape⟩ — see BLEMISH

blotch *vb* **1** to mark with blotches especially of different colors or shades ⟨*blotched* the bedroom walls with various shades of blue to give them a textured effect⟩ — see MOTTLE 1

2 to mark with small spots especially unevenly ⟨my pen leaked and *blotched* my shirt pocket⟩ — see SPOT 1

blotched *adj* having blotches of two or more colors ⟨a *blotched* black-and-white rabbit⟩ — see PIED

blotchy *adj* having blotches of two or more colors ⟨using that bronzer just made my face look *blotchy*⟩ — see PIED

blot out *vb* **1** to destroy all traces of ⟨*blotted out* all evidence of tampering with the explosive device⟩ — see ANNIHILATE 1

2 to keep secret or shut off from view ⟨bushes *blotted out* the shed from our view⟩ — see [1]HIDE 2

blotto *adj, slang* being under the influence of alcohol ⟨someone call for a taxi; the guy's *blotto* and in no condition to drive⟩ — see DRUNK

[1]**blow** *n* a hard strike with a part of the body or an instrument ⟨he was dizzy for the rest of the day after the *blow* to his head⟩

synonyms bang, bash, bat, beat, belt, biff, bop, box, buffet, bust, chop, clap, clip, clout, crack, cuff, dab, douse [*British*], fillip, hack, haymaker, hit, hook, knock, larrup [*dialect*], lash, lick, pelt, pick, plump, poke, pound, punch, rap, slam, slap, slug, smack, smash, sock, spank, stinger, stripe, stroke, swat, swipe, switch, thud, thump, thwack, wallop, welt, whack, wham, whop (*also* whap)

related words counter, counterblow, counterpunch, counterstroke; body blow, hand, kick, knee, left, one-two, rabbit punch, right, right-hander, roundhouse, shiver, sidewinder, sucker punch, swing, uppercut; cruncher, kayo, knockdown, knockout, KO; bastinado (*or* bastinade), battering, beating, bludgeoning, clobbering, cudgeling (*or* cudgelling), drubbing, hammering, lambasting, licking, pasting, pounding, pummeling (*also* pummelling), thrashing; flogging, walloping, whip, whipping

[2]**blow** *n* a sudden brief rush of wind ⟨the ocean *blows* that sweep over the island are so strong that only the hardiest shrubs can grow there⟩ — see GUST 1

[1]**blow** *vb* **1** to breathe hard, quickly, or with difficulty ⟨that horse was really *blowing* after the race⟩ — see GASP

2 to use up carelessly ⟨each year he *blows* his holiday bonus on a trip to Las Vegas⟩ — see WASTE 1

3 to break open or into pieces usually because of internal pressure ⟨a huge crater was formed when the volcano last *blew*⟩ — see EXPLODE 1

4 to cause to break open or into pieces by or as if by an explosive ⟨one false move and we would be *blown* to bits⟩ — see BLAST 1

5 to proceed or move quickly ⟨that car *blew* past us as if we were standing still⟩ — see HURRY 2

6 to make or do (something) in a clumsy or unskillful way ⟨he keeps *blowing* every job interview that comes his way⟩ — see BOTCH

7 to praise or express pride in one's own possessions, qualities, or accomplishments often to excess ⟨another self-made millionaire *blowing* about how much he'd achieved⟩ — see BOAST 1

[2]**blow** *vb* to produce flowers ⟨longing for a grassy field in some far-off land where the wildflowers *blow*⟩ — see BLOOM

blow (out) *vb* to let or force out of the lungs ⟨*blew out* a smoke ring and began to tell us a good yarn⟩ — see EXHALE 1

blow away *vb* to defeat by a large margin ⟨the chess prodigy completely *blew away* the reigning world champion⟩ — see WHIP 2

blow–by–blow *adj* including many small descriptive features ⟨a *blow-by-blow* account of what had changed in her life since they last met⟩ — see DETAILED 1

blower *n* someone who boasts ⟨although he's not the first person to blow his own horn, he's about the most obnoxious *blower* I've ever met⟩ — see BRAGGART

blowhard *n* **1** a person who talks constantly ⟨a politician who is the stereotypical backslapping *blowhard*⟩ — see CHATTERBOX

2 someone who boasts ⟨a *blowhard* who always had to act like she was better than anyone else⟩ — see BRAGGART

blown *adj* enlarged beyond normal from internal pressure ⟨if the tin can is *blown*, throw it away—the food inside is spoiled⟩ — see BLOATED 2

blow off *vb* **1** to end a usually intimate relationship with ⟨before she embarks on another relationship, she should try to figure out why all those other men have *blown* her *off*⟩ — see DITCH 1

2 to fail to attend ⟨*blew off* the committee meeting, thinking that it would just be a colossal waste of time⟩ — see CUT 2

blowout *n* a social gathering ⟨staged a huge *blowout* for Halloween⟩ — see PARTY 1

blowsy *also* **blowzy** *adj* lacking neatness in dress or person ⟨a large, *blowsy* woman in frumpy clothes runs the diner⟩ — see SLOPPY 1

blowup *n* **1** an outburst or display of excited anger ⟨the boss had another *blowup* when someone fouled up the copy machine⟩ — see TANTRUM

2 the act or an instance of exploding ⟨the last *blowup* of the volcano flattened trees for miles around⟩ — see EXPLOSION 1

blow up *vb* **1** to become very angry ⟨she *blew up* at everybody after a very long and very bad day⟩

synonyms flare (up), flip (out) [*slang*]

related words anger, fulminate, rage, rant, rave, snap, snarl, sputter, storm, tee off, vent, vituperate; bristle, burn, foam, fume, glare, glower, seethe, sizzle, smolder (*or* smoulder), steam, warm; burst, explode, flare (out), flash, inflame (*also* enflame), madden

phrases blow a gasket, blow one's cool, blow one's stack, blow one's top, fly into a rage, fly off the handle, forget oneself, go ballistic, have a fit, hit the ceiling, hit the roof, lose one's cool, lose one's temper

near antonyms chill out [*slang*], cool (off *or* down), relax; hush, quiet (down)

antonyms calm (down), simmer down

2 to break open or into pieces usually because of internal pressure ⟨the building *blew up* because of a gas leak⟩ — see EXPLODE 1

3 to cause to break open or into pieces by or as if by an explosive ⟨*blew up* the biggest rocks and then cleared them away⟩ — see BLAST 1

4 to praise or publicize lavishly and often excessively ⟨the advertisement *blows* the new soda *up* to the point where I half expected to be transported to a higher level of consciousness⟩ — see TOUT 1

blowy *adj* marked by strong wind or more wind than

usual ⟨a *blowy* day that resulted in most of the fall foliage being knocked off the trees⟩ — see [1]WINDY 1

blub *vb, chiefly British* to shed tears often while making meaningless sounds as a sign of pain or distress ⟨the girl was *blubbing* so uncontrollably that we couldn't understand what she was trying to tell us⟩ — see CRY 1

blubber *vb* to shed tears often while making meaningless sounds as a sign of pain or distress ⟨the poor child was *blubbering* because she had fallen and skinned her knee⟩ — see CRY 1

blubbery *adj* having an excess of body fat ⟨the sort of *blubbery* person you hope you never see naked⟩ — see FAT 1

bludgeon *n* a heavy rigid stick used as a weapon or for punishment ⟨guards armed with *bludgeons* roamed the compound⟩ — see CLUB 1

bludgeon *vb* **1** to deliver a blow to (someone or something) usually in a strong vigorous manner ⟨*bludgeoned* the door with an iron bar in a senseless act of vandalism⟩ — see HIT 1
2 to strike repeatedly ⟨*bludgeoned* the victim to death⟩ — see BEAT 1

blue *adj* **1** depicting or referring to sexual matters in a way that is unacceptable in polite society ⟨shocked at the *blue* banter she heard on that satellite-radio talk show⟩ — see OBSCENE 1
2 feeling unhappiness ⟨a cold, dreary day always leaves me *blue*⟩ — see SAD 1
3 hinting at or intended to call to mind matters regarded as indecent ⟨she was one of the first female comics to use *blue* humor in her act⟩ — see SUGGESTIVE 1
4 much given to learning and thinking ⟨a book club that had been founded many years earlier by the *blue*, progressive women of the city⟩ — see INTELLECTUAL 1

blue *n* **1** the expanse of air surrounding the earth ⟨the plane flew off into the *blue* and was never seen again⟩ — see SKY 1
2 the whole body of salt water that covers nearly three-fourths of the earth ⟨pirate ships that sailed the vasty *blue* in search of treasure⟩ — see OCEAN 1

blue blood *n* a man or woman of high birth or social position ⟨one need not be a *blue blood* to enjoy the amenities at the Royal Crown Hotel⟩ — see GENTLEPERSON

blue-blooded *adj* of high birth, rank, or station ⟨given his working-class roots, he's wondering how he'll fit in with his *blue-blooded* in-laws⟩ — see NOBLE 1

blue-chip *adj* of the very best kind ⟨because of his *blue-chip* crew, he's won yachting's biggest prize several times⟩ — see EXCELLENT

blue devils *n pl* a state or spell of low spirits ⟨eating alone always gives me a fit of the *blue devils*⟩ — see SADNESS

blue moon *n* a long or seemingly long period of time ⟨once in a *blue moon* we'll get dressed up and eat in a fancy restaurant⟩ — see AGE 2

blueness *n* the quality or state of being obscene ⟨a comedy act without any hint of *blueness*⟩ — see OBSCENITY 1

bluenose *n* a person who is greatly concerned with seemly behavior and morality especially regarding sexual matters ⟨the editorial lambasts those *bluenoses* who feel they have the moral authority to dictate how other people should conduct themselves in private⟩ — see PRUDE

bluenosed *adj* given to or marked by very conservative standards regarding personal behavior or morals ⟨intimations of homosexuality in the author's diary and correspondence were later excised by *bluenosed* editors⟩ — see STRAITLACED

blue-pencil *vb* to show (something written) to be no longer valid by drawing a cross over or a line through it ⟨military censors *blue-penciled* any remarks that could possibly be deemed critical⟩ — see X (OUT)

blueprint *n* a method worked out in advance for achieving some objective ⟨an ambitious young man with a remarkably detailed *blueprint* for becoming a millionaire by the age of 25⟩ — see PLAN 1

blueprint *vb* to work out the details of (something) in advance ⟨*blueprinted* the schedule of events for the festival right down to the last detail⟩ — see PLAN 1

blue-ribbon *adj* of the very best kind ⟨your work on this project has been of *blue-ribbon* quality⟩ — see EXCELLENT

blue ribbon *n* something given in recognition of achievement ⟨the Pritzker Prize is widely regarded as the ultimate *blue ribbon* for architectural achievement⟩ — see AWARD 1

blues *n pl* a state or spell of low spirits ⟨failing the driving test gave me the *blues* for the rest of the day⟩ — see SADNESS

blue-water *adj* of, relating to, or occurring in the open sea ⟨an experienced hand at *blue-water* sailing in the South Pacific⟩ — see DEEP-SEA

bluff *adj* being or characterized by direct, brief, and potentially rude speech or manner ⟨he's a *bluff* but goodhearted teacher⟩ — see BLUNT 1

bluff *n* a steep wall of rock, earth, or ice ⟨fossils embedded in a stone *bluff* that date from the Jurassic period⟩ — see CLIFF

bluff *vb* **1** to cause to believe what is untrue ⟨I *bluffed* the interviewer into believing that I could really speak French and thus would be the perfect person to serve in the newspaper's Paris bureau⟩ — see DECEIVE
2 to present a false appearance of ⟨the basketball player *bluffed* a shot, then passed instead⟩ — see FEIGN

blunder *n* an unintentional departure from truth or accuracy ⟨fixed a minor *blunder* in the advertising flyer⟩ — see ERROR 1

blunder *vb* **1** to make a mistake ⟨even though the prosecution had *blundered* several times in presenting its case, it ultimately prevailed⟩ — see ERR 1
2 to proceed or act clumsily or ineffectually ⟨*blundered* his way through an acceptance speech⟩ — see FLOUNDER 1

blunderbuss *n* someone who bungles an effort ⟨leave it to that *blunderbuss* to bungle a job that a child could do⟩ — see BUTCHER

blunderer *n* someone who bungles an effort ⟨those *blunderers* at city hall sent me the wrong tax bill⟩ — see BUTCHER

blunt *adj* **1** being or characterized by direct, brief, and potentially rude speech or manner ⟨he values honesty and is quite *blunt* about telling people what he doesn't like about them⟩
synonyms abrupt, bluff, brusque (*also* brusk), crusty, curt, downright, short, short-spoken, snippy, unceremonious
related words gruff, rough, snappish; candid, direct, forthright, foursquare, frank, free-spoken, open, outspoken, plain, plainspoken, point-blank, straightforward, straight-out; artless, discourteous, disrespectful, impertinent, impolite, inconsiderate, insensitive, rude, tactless, undiplomatic; brief, closemouthed, laconic, reserved, reticent, terse, tight-lipped; earnest, honest, sincere; coarse, crass, crude, low, uncouth, vulgar
near antonyms civil, considerate, courteous, diplomatic, gracious, polite, politic, smooth, suave, tactful; loquacious, talkative, voluble; long-winded, prolix, verbose; courtly, cultivated, gallant, genteel, polished, refined
antonyms circuitous, mealymouthed
2 lacking sharpness of edge or point ⟨a *blunt* knife won't open that package⟩ — see DULL 1

blunt *vb* to reduce or weaken in strength or feeling ⟨the mushy music *blunted* the effect of the movie's final tragic scene⟩ — see DULL 1

blunted *adj* lacking sharpness of edge or point ⟨the *blunted* saw was worthless for fine woodworking⟩ — see DULL 1

bluntness *n* the free expression of one's true feelings and opinions ⟨the refreshing *bluntness* of the former president in assessing those who followed him in the Oval Office⟩ — see CANDOR 1

blur *vb* **1** to make (something) unclear to the understanding ⟨an article for the layman that *blurs* the distinction between the two kinds of cholesterol⟩ — see CONFUSE 2
2 to make dark, dim, or indistinct ⟨evening shadows *blurred* the view of the valley from the overlook⟩ — see CLOUD 1

blurry *adj* not seen or understood clearly ⟨a *blurry* image in the foreground of the photograph⟩ — see FAINT 1

blurt (out) *vb* to utter with a sudden burst of strong feeling ⟨"I'm very sad!" the toddler *blurted out*⟩ — see EXCLAIM

blush *n* a rosy appearance (of the cheeks) ⟨a baby with a healthy *blush*⟩ — see BLOOM 2

blush *vb* to develop a rosy facial color (as from excitement or embarrassment) ⟨she *blushed* when she realized she had walked into the boys' bathroom by mistake⟩
synonyms bloom, color, crimson, flush, glow, redden
related words incarnadine, rouge, ruddle; abash, chagrin, discomfit, disconcert, embarrass, faze, humiliate, mortify
phrases turn color

bluster *n* **1** boastful speech or writing ⟨all the *bluster* in the campaign speech was intended to hide a lack of specifics⟩ — see BOMBAST 1
2 loud, confused, and usually inharmonious sound ⟨I can't work with all the *bluster* in here⟩ — see NOISE 1
3 a state of noisy, confused activity ⟨a mayor who got things done without a lot of *bluster* and self-serving publicity⟩ — see COMMOTION

bluster *vb* to talk loudly and wildly ⟨the rude customer *blustered* and yelled threats about lawsuits, but eventually left⟩ — see RANT

blustery *adj* marked by strong wind or more wind than usual ⟨it can be a bit risky to drive across the bridge on a *blustery* day⟩ — see [1]WINDY 1

board *n* **1** a group of persons formally joined together for some common interest ⟨a proposal that is likely to meet with strong opposition from the local *board* of undertakers⟩ — see ASSOCIATION 2
2 a leg-mounted piece of furniture with a broad flat top designed for the serving of food ⟨in preparation for the governor's visit, the taverner arranged an array of fancy dishes and silverware on the inn's finest *board*⟩ — see TABLE 1

board *vb* **1** to provide food or meals for ⟨housed and *boarded* many foster children over the years⟩ — see FEED 1
2 to provide with living quarters or shelter ⟨*boarded* the stray cat until a permanent home could be found⟩ — see HOUSE 1

boarder *n* one who rents a room or apartment in another's house ⟨a *boarder* who paid $100 per week for a room and meals⟩ — see TENANT 1

boardwalk *n* a public place for strolling ⟨the town's old-fashioned beachfront *boardwalk* has been a tourist attraction since the 1920s⟩ — see PROMENADE

boast *n* an asset that brings praise or renown ⟨the school's *boast* was a winning football team⟩ — see GLORY 2

boast *vb* **1** to praise or express pride in one's own possessions, qualities, or accomplishments often to excess ⟨he *boasted* about his latest killing in real estate so I thought he should be the one to pay for dinner⟩
synonyms blow, brag, bull [*slang*], crow, gasconade, swagger, vapor, vaunt
related words bluster, harangue, puff; pride; gush; exult, glory, rejoice; brandish, display, exhibit, expose, flaunt, glorify, parade, show off; magnify, maximize
phrases blow smoke
near antonyms belittle, deprecate, diminish, discount, laugh off, minimize, play down, pooh-pooh (*also* pooh), shrug off, underrate, undervalue; bemoan, lament, mourn, regret
2 to have within ⟨the hotel *boasts* nearly 50 rooms⟩ — see CONTAIN 1

boaster *n* someone who boasts ⟨I'm tired of hearing about that *boaster's* new car⟩ — see BRAGGART

boat *n* **1** a small buoyant structure for travel on water ⟨paddling the little *boat* across the lake is great exercise, but tiring⟩
synonyms bottom, craft, vessel, watercraft
related words catboat, ketch, sailboat, schooner, yacht; bateau, caïque, canoe, catamaran, coracle, curragh (*or* currach), dhow, dinghy, dink, dory, dugout, flatboat, garvey, gig, johnboat, kayak, outrigger, paddleboat, pinnace, piragua, pirogue, pontoon, pram, punt, raft, rowboat, rowing boat [*chiefly British*], sampan, scow, scull, shallop, shell, skiff, surfboat, umiak, wherry; cruiser, inboard, motorboat, outboard, powerboat; houseboat, riverboat; auxiliary, bumboat, cutter, jolly boat, launch, lifeboat, longboat, tender, yawl; barge, hoy, keel, keelboat, lighter, narrow boat [*British*]; towboat, tug, tugboat; ferry, ferryboat, gondola, taxi, water taxi; banker, coble, dragger, gillnetter, hooker, lugger, scalloper, seiner, shrimper, trawler, whaleboat, whaler, workboat; cockleshell, tub; airboat, air-cushion vehicle, hovercraft; hydrofoil, hydroplane; assault boat, PT boat, torpedo boat
2 a large craft for travel by water ⟨you'll have to take a passenger *boat* to get to the island⟩ — see SHIP

boat *vb* to travel on water in a vessel ⟨*boated* to the picnic site on an island in the bay⟩ — see SAIL 1

boatload *n* a considerable amount ⟨a *boatload* of publicity for the new handheld devices⟩ — see LOT 2

[1]**bob** *vb* to make (something) shorter or smaller with the use of a cutting instrument ⟨*bobbed* her waist-length hair herself on her 18th birthday⟩ — see CLIP 1

[2]**bob** *vb* **1** to make short up-and-down movements ⟨a family of ducks *bobbing* on the water⟩ — see NOD
2 to deliver a blow to (someone or something) usually in a strong vigorous manner ⟨he playfully *bobbed* his brother on the nose to get his attention⟩ — see HIT 1

bob *n, Scottish* a bunch of flowers ⟨the lassie carried only a little *bob* on her wedding day⟩ — see BOUQUET 1

bobbery *n* a state of noisy, confused activity ⟨proponents of a silent birth believe that the *bobbery* that accompanies most births is harmful to the newborn⟩ — see COMMOTION

bobble *n* an unintentional departure from truth or accuracy ⟨she's terrified that she'll make some silly *bobble* during the important presentation⟩ — see ERROR 1

bobble *vb* **1** to make or do (something) in a clumsy or unskillful way ⟨the first baseman *bobbled* the catch, so the runner was safe⟩ — see BOTCH
2 to make short up-and-down movements ⟨the little doll's head *bobbled* when you poked it⟩ — see NOD

bobby *n, British* a member of a force charged with law enforcement at the local level ⟨asked a passing London *bobby* for directions⟩ — see OFFICER 1

bod *n, British* a member of the human race ⟨I know several *bods* who work on Fleet Street⟩ — see HUMAN

bodacious *adj* **1** likely to attract attention ⟨the *bodacious* decor of the boutique hotel is intended to appeal to the young and the hip⟩ — see NOTICEABLE
2 *Southern & Midland* having no exceptions or restrictions ⟨had the *bodacious* gall to tell me that he'd return my lawn mower when he felt like it⟩ — see ABSOLUTE 2
3 sexually attractive ⟨she's got a *bodacious* bod that's definitely swimsuit-friendly⟩ — see SEXY 1

bode *vb* to show signs of a favorable or successful outcome ⟨her natural gift for reading *boded* well for her future in school⟩
synonyms augur, forebode (*also* forbode), promise
related words forecast, foretell, predict, presage, prognosticate, prophesy; forewarn, warn; anticipate, divine, foreknow, foresee; betoken, foreshadow, harbinger, portend, prefigure, presignify; indicate, signify; allude, connote, hint, imply, insinuate, intimate, suggest
phrases bid fair

bodement *n* a declaration that something will happen in the future ⟨the continuing fascination with the obscure *bodements* of the 16th-century astrologer Nostradamus⟩ — see PREDICTION

bodiless *adj* not composed of matter ⟨ghosts are supposed to be *bodiless*⟩ — see IMMATERIAL 1

bodily *adj* of or relating to the human body ⟨the old man suffered from a number of *bodily* ailments⟩ — see PHYSICAL 1

boding *n* something believed to be a sign or warning of a future event ⟨among some ancient peoples, solar eclipses were often seen as celestial *bodings* of earthly calamities⟩ — see OMEN

body *vb* to represent in visible form ⟨abstract sculpture that *bodies* forth the artist's aesthetic of minimalism⟩ — see EMBODY 2

body *n* **1** the main or greater part of something as distinguished from its subordinate parts ⟨the *body* of the novel was quite good, even if the beginning was a bit slow⟩
synonyms brunt, bulk, chief, core, generality, heft [*archaic*], main, mass, staple, weight
related words majority; aggregate, amount, entirety, quantum, sum, sum total, total, totality, whole; bottom, essence, essentiality, marrow, meat, nature, pith, quintessence, root, soul, stuff, substance; center, heart, hub, kernel, middle, nucleus, nut, seat; affair, argument, burden, crux, focus, gist, nub, pitch, point, purport; matter, motif, subject, text, theme, topic
near antonyms accessory (*also* accessary), adjunct, appendage, extension, offshoot; component, constituent, element, ingredient; division, part, piece, section, segment; angle, aspect, facet, feature, quality, side
2 a distinct and separate portion of matter ⟨to the early explorers the Atlantic was a gigantic and forbidding *body* of water⟩
synonyms mass
related words aggregate, amount, bulk, quantity, quantum, volume; item, object, thing; material, stuff, substance; entirety, totality, whole
3 a group of people acting together within a larger group ⟨feared that there was a *body* of extremists within the labor union⟩ — see FACTION
4 a group of people sharing a common interest and relating together socially ⟨a hangout where, it seems, much of the student *body* can be found on a Saturday night⟩ — see GANG 2
5 a member of the human race ⟨the most intelligent *body* in this entire place⟩ — see HUMAN
6 a usually small number of persons considered as a unit ⟨a *body* of security men accompany the president at all times⟩ — see GROUP 2

boff *or* **boffo** *n* **1** an explosive sound that is a sign of amusement ⟨an old joke dating from the days of vaudeville that's still good for a *boff*⟩ — see LAUGH 1
2 something said or done to cause laughter ⟨the emcee told some good *boffs* that kept the ceremony from becoming too serious⟩ — see JOKE 1

boffo *adj* of the very best kind ⟨a *boffo* performance that wowed even Broadway's toughest critics⟩ — see EXCELLENT

boffola *n* **1** an explosive sound that is a sign of amusement ⟨the audience could be heard chuckling throughout the play, but there were few theater-filling *boffolas*⟩ — see LAUGH 1
2 something said or done to cause laughter ⟨if that was the wannabe comic's best *boffola*, he'd be well-advised not to quit his day job⟩ — see JOKE 1

[1]**bog** *n* spongy land saturated or partially covered with water ⟨got a shoe stuck in the *bog*⟩ — see SWAMP 1

[2]**bog** *n, British* a room furnished with a fixture for flushing body waste ⟨they're out of paper in the *bog* again⟩ — see TOILET

bog (down) *vb* to place in conflict or difficulties ⟨we were *bogged down* by the endless changes, and of course finished late⟩ — see EMBROIL

bogart *vb* to make timid or fearful by or as if by threats ⟨his friends tried to *bogart* him into doing the right thing and marrying the girl⟩ — see INTIMIDATE

bogey *also* **bogie** *or* **bogy** *n* **1** something or someone that causes fear or dread especially without reason ⟨math and math tests have long been *bogeys* for many students⟩
synonyms bête noire, black beast, bugaboo, bugbear, dread, hobgoblin, ogre
related words apparition, ghost, phantasm (*also* fantasm), phantom, poltergeist, shade, specter (*or* spectre), spirit, spook, wraith; banshee, bogeyman (*also* bogyman), demon (*or* daemon), devil, fiend, ghoul, imp, incubus; fright, horrible, horror, monster, monstrosity, terror; bane, curse, enemy, plague, scourge, torment; abomination, anathema
2 the soul of a dead person thought of especially as appearing to living people ⟨the child believed *bogeys* lived in the closet⟩ — see GHOST 1

boggle *vb* to make or do (something) in a clumsy or unskillful way ⟨she *boggled* her first effort to make Christmas cookies⟩ — see BOTCH

bogus *adj* **1** being such in appearance only and made with or manufactured from usually cheaper materials ⟨for that price, you're only going to get furniture covered in *bogus* leather and not the real stuff⟩ — see IMITATION
2 being such in appearance only and made or manufactured with the intention of committing fraud ⟨the "designer" watches sold on the street are usually *bogus*⟩ — see COUNTERFEIT 1
3 lacking in natural or spontaneous quality ⟨there was often a lot of *bogus* conviviality at the company's parties⟩ — see ARTIFICIAL 1

bohemian *n* a person who does not conform to generally accepted standards or customs ⟨he spent a few years living as a *bohemian* in the artists' quarter of the city⟩ — see NONCONFORMIST 1

boho *n* a person who does not conform to generally accepted standards or customs ⟨after living among the *bohos* for a while, she realized that there was a disenchanting conformity to their nonconformity⟩ — see NONCONFORMIST 1

boil *n* a small, inflamed swelling of the skin ⟨the dermatologist lanced the infected *boil* that had formed on the patient's neck⟩ — see POCK

boil *vb* **1** to be excited or emotionally stirred up with anger ⟨she was *boiling* at the thought of her so-called best friend trying to steal her boyfriend⟩

synonyms burn, foam, fume, rage, rankle, seethe, sizzle, steam, storm
related words fulminate, rant, rave; smolder (*or* smoulder); bristle, flare (up), inflame (*also* enflame); chafe, fret, stew; agitate, convulse, roil, shake
phrases see red
2 to cook in a liquid heated to the point that it gives off steam ⟨*boil* the potatoes until they are tender before you try to mash them⟩
synonyms coddle, parboil, poach, simmer, stew
related words scald; braise, fricassee, pressure-cook, smother, steam; reboil
3 to be in a state of violent rolling motion ⟨the sea *boiled* and frothed during the storm⟩ — see SEETHE 1

boil down *vb* to make into a short statement of the main points (as of a report) ⟨the discussion of the problem can be *boiled down* to a couple of critical points⟩ — see SUMMARIZE

boiling *adj* having a notably high temperature ⟨it was *boiling* in that car, and the owners had foolishly left their pet in it⟩ — see HOT 1

boiling point *n* a time or state of affairs requiring prompt or decisive action ⟨when the situation reached the *boiling point*, the President had no choice but to order out the National Guard⟩ — see EMERGENCY

boisterous *adj* being rough or noisy in a high-spirited way ⟨the fans at the baseball game became particularly *boisterous* after the home run⟩
synonyms hell-raising, knockabout, rambunctious, raucous, robustious, roisterous, rollicking, rowdy, rumbustious [*chiefly British*]
related words callithumpian, carnival, carnivalesque, larrikin [*chiefly Australian*], raffish, rampageous, raucous, riotous, rowdyish, ruffianly; stormy, tempestuous, turbulent, violent; headstrong, intractable, obstreperous, recalcitrant, uncontrollable, uncontrolled, undisciplined, ungovernable, uninhibited, unmanageable, unreserved, unrestrained, unruly, wild, willful (*or* wilful); bubbly, buoyant, effervescent, exuberant, high-spirited, impassioned, lively, sprightly, vivacious; clamorous, loudmouthed, noisy, openmouthed, rackety, strident, vociferous; howling, screaming, yelling
phrases wild and woolly
near antonyms sedate, sober, solemn, somber (*or* sombre), staid; decorous, dignified, proper, seemly; calm, hushed, noiseless, peaceful, placid, quiet, restrained, serene, silent, soundless, tranquil; collected, composed, constrained, controlled, imperturbable, inhibited, repressed, self-controlled, unflappable, unruffled; moderate, reasonable, subdued, temperate; impassive, phlegmatic, stoic (*or* stoical), stolid; depressed; aloof, detached, indifferent
antonyms orderly

boîte *n* a bar or restaurant offering special nighttime entertainment (as music, dancing, or comedy acts) ⟨a funky *boîte* on Paris's Left Bank that offers hot jazz to a self-consciously cool crowd⟩ — see NIGHTCLUB

bold *adj* **1** inclined or willing to take risks ⟨our youngest brother was the *boldest* one in the family, instantly taking to everything from skiing to skateboarding⟩
synonyms adventuresome, adventurous, audacious, daring, dashing, emboldened, enterprising, free-swinging, gutsy, hardy, nerved, nervy, venturesome, venturous
related words brash, daredevil, foolhardy, heedless, hotheaded, impetuous, imprudent, impulsive, incautious, madcap, overbold, overconfident, rash, reckless, thoughtless, wild; brave, courageous, dauntless, fearless, gallant, greathearted, heroic (*also* heroical), intrepid, lionhearted, stalwart, stout, stouthearted, swashbuckling, unafraid, undaunted, valiant, valorous; gritty, plucky, spirited, spunky; gadarene, hasty, headlong, precipitate; absurd, asinine, balmy, brainless, crazy, foolish, half-witted, harebrained, insane, lunatic, mad, nutty, scatterbrained, silly, wacky (*also* whacky), witless; unnecessary; dumb, idiotic (*also* idiotical), moronic, stupid; irrational, unreasonable
near antonyms chickenhearted, coward, cowardly, craven, lily-livered, milk-livered, milky, poltroon, pusillanimous, shy, timid, timorous; careful, cautious, heedful, prudent, wary; overcareful, overcautious; affrighted, afraid, alarmed, fainthearted, fearful, frightened, horrified, scared, shocked, spooked, startled, terrified, terrorized; unnerved; calm, cool, levelheaded, rational, reasonable, sage, sane, sensible, sound, wise; appalled, concerned, dismayed, upset, worried
antonyms unadventurous, unenterprising
2 displaying or marked by rude boldness ⟨you're a *bold* little brat for trying to steal my stuff while I'm right here⟩ — see NERVY 1
3 likely to attract attention ⟨an interior decorator who likes to use *bold* colors⟩ — see NOTICEABLE
4 showing a lack of proper social reserve or modesty ⟨a *bold* child who interrupts the adults at his parents' parties⟩ — see PRESUMPTUOUS 1
5 having an incline approaching the perpendicular ⟨the advanced climbers chose a *bold* cliff to test themselves⟩ — see STEEP 1
6 feeling or displaying no fear by temperament ⟨the *bold* explorers who will someday journey to other planets⟩ — see BRAVE 1

bold–faced *adj* displaying or marked by rude boldness ⟨the child proceeded to tell a *bold-faced* lie despite the evidence right in front of us⟩ — see NERVY 1

boldly *adv* in a fearless manner ⟨she strode *boldly* into the political fray⟩ — see BRAVELY 1

bollix (up) *vb* to make or do (something) in a clumsy or unskillful way ⟨you've *bollixed up* the whole thing⟩ — see BOTCH

bolster *vb* **1** to hold up or serve as a foundation for ⟨used additional beams to *bolster* the ceiling⟩ — see SUPPORT 3
2 to provide evidence or information for (as a claim or idea) ⟨a couple of tournament wins would *bolster* the extravagant claims that have been made on behalf of the young golfer⟩ — see SUPPORT 4

bolt *vb* **1** to move suddenly and sharply (as in surprise) ⟨I *bolted* as I read the winning lottery numbers⟩ — see START 1
2 to proceed or move quickly ⟨the cat *bolted* for the food dish the minute he spied it⟩ — see HURRY 2
3 to hasten away from something dangerous or frightening ⟨the rabbit *bolted* when it saw the fox approaching⟩ — see RUN 2
4 to utter with a sudden burst of strong feeling ⟨*bolted* out the cuss word without thinking⟩ — see EXCLAIM
5 to swallow or eat greedily ⟨the way you *bolted* those hot dogs, it's no wonder you're feeling a little queasy⟩ — see GOBBLE

bolt–hole *n, chiefly British* something (as a building) that offers cover from the weather or protection from danger ⟨her cottage in the Lake District served as her *bolt-hole* whenever the stresses of London became too great⟩ — see SHELTER

bomb *n* **1** something that has failed ⟨her tell-all book was a *bomb* that landed on the remainder tables with a thud⟩ — see FAILURE 3
2 *British* a very large amount of money ⟨that stay at Claridge's cost a *bomb*, but it was worth it⟩ — see FORTUNE 2

bomb *vb* **1** to attack with a rapid or overwhelming outpouring of many things at once ⟨following the reporter's obscene outburst, viewers *bombed* the television station with an unprecedented number of complaints⟩ — see BOMBARD 2

2 *slang* to proceed or move quickly ⟨a snowboarder *bombing* down the slope almost crashed into me⟩ — see HURRY 2

3 to be unsuccessful ⟨the chichi restaurant *bombed* big-time, lasting only six months⟩ — see FAIL 2

4 to defeat by a large margin ⟨it's no surprise that the inexperienced baseball team got totally *bombed* in its first game⟩ — see WHIP 2

5 to use bombs or artillery against ⟨the enemy has *bombed* the city again⟩ — see BOMBARD 1

bombard *vb* **1** to use bombs or artillery against ⟨the Allies *bombarded* Germany for a great many months during World War II⟩

synonyms batter, blitz, blitzkrieg, bomb, cannonade, shell

related words enfilade; rake, strafe; assail, assault, attack, devastate, hit, pound, ravage, strike

2 to attack with a rapid or overwhelming outpouring of many things at once ⟨reporters *bombarded* the company spokesman with sharp questions⟩

synonyms barrage, bomb

related words examine, grill, interrogate, pump, query, question, quiz; debrief; cross-examine; catechize; annoy, harass, hound, pester; flood, inundate

bombardment *n* a rapid or overwhelming outpouring of many things at once ⟨the *bombardment* of so many instructions meant that I missed some of the information⟩ — see BARRAGE

bombast *n* **1** boastful speech or writing ⟨the other world leaders at the international conference had little interest in being subjected to the president's *bombast*⟩

synonyms bluster, brag, braggadocio, bull [*slang*], cockalorum, fanfaronade, gas, gasconade, grandiloquence, hot air, magniloquence, rant, rodomontade (*also* rhodomontade)

related words oratory, rhapsody, rhetoric; pomposity, turgidity, wind; bloviation, verbosity, windiness; babble, blab, chatter, drivel, gabble, gibber, gibberish, jabber, prattle; jawing, patter, prating, yammering; egotism, self-conceit, self-importance, swagger, vaunt

2 language that is impressive-sounding but not meaningful or sincere ⟨you need less *bombast* and more substance in this speech on human rights⟩ — see RHETORIC 1

bombastic *adj* marked by the use of impressive-sounding but mostly meaningless words and phrases ⟨a *bombastic* speech intended to impress the voters in her congressional district⟩ — see RHETORICAL 1

bombed *adj* **1** being under the influence of alcohol ⟨my handwriting gets much worse when I'm *bombed*⟩ — see DRUNK

2 being under the influence of a recreational drug ⟨the pop star was clearly *bombed* out of her skull during the interview⟩ — see STONED 1

bombed–out *adj* showing signs of advanced wear and tear and neglect ⟨a *bombed-out* section of the city seemingly frequented only by hookers and heroin addicts⟩ — see SHABBY 1

bombproof *adj* marked by the ability to withstand stress without structural damage or distortion ⟨the manufacturer's *bombproof* powerboats can take a lot of punishment⟩ — see STABLE 1

bombshell *n* something that makes a strong impression because it is so unexpected ⟨discovering that I had a long-lost sister was an absolute *bombshell*⟩ — see SURPRISE 1

bona fide *adj* being exactly as appears or as claimed ⟨a *bona fide* war hero⟩ — see AUTHENTIC 1

bond *n* **1** something that physically prevents free movement ⟨before they could release the captive, they had to undo a number of *bonds*⟩

synonyms band, bind, bracelet, chain, cuff(s), fetter, handcuff(s), irons, ligature, manacle(s), shackle

related words captivity, confinement, constraint, curb, enchainment, enslavement, hindrance, immurement, imprisonment, incarceration, restraint, restriction; entanglement, net, trammel, trap; collar, straitjacket (*also* straightjacket); fastener, hobble, hold, hold-down, holding, tie

2 a uniting or binding force or influence ⟨the *bond* of love between them was so strong that even death could not break it⟩

synonyms cement, cord, knot, ligature, link, tie

related words attachment, connection, fastening, hookup, joint, linkage, linkup, nexus, tie-up, union, yoke; affection, fondness, sympathy; fetter, handcuff, manacle, shackle, trammel; constraint, curb, hampering, limit, limitation, restraint, restriction

near antonyms detaching, disengaging, parting, separation; unbinding, unfastening, unfettering, untying (*or* untieing); emancipation, freedom, liberation, release

3 a formal agreement to fulfill an obligation ⟨signed a *bond* to repay the money⟩ — see GUARANTEE 1

4 a substance used to stick things together ⟨what type of *bond* works best on ceramics?⟩ — see GLUE

bond *vb* to form a close personal relationship ⟨a man attempting to *bond* with his new and mistrustful stepson⟩ — see COMMUNE

bondage *n* the state of being a slave ⟨the Civil War ended over 200 years of *bondage* for black Africans in America⟩ — see SLAVERY 1

bonding *n* a physical sticking to as if by glue ⟨this epoxy has good *bonding* for glass and ceramics⟩ — see ADHESION 1

bondman *also* **bondsman** *n* a person who is considered the property of another person ⟨would rather die as an insurgent than live as a *bondman*⟩ — see SLAVE 1

bone *adv* to a great degree ⟨grew up in a backwoods area that was *bone* poor⟩ — see VERY 1

bone *n* **1** a habitual attraction to some activity or thing ⟨he hasn't a competitive *bone* in his body⟩ — see INCLINATION 1

2 bones *pl* a small cube marked on each side with one to six spots and usually played in pairs in various games ⟨the pirates decided their captives' fate with a toss of the *bones*⟩ — see DIE

3 *usually* **bones** *pl* the seat of one's deepest thoughts and emotions ⟨I could feel in my *bones* that I had just met my future wife⟩ — see CORE 1

4 *slang* a U.S. currency bill representing 100 cents ⟨I hadn't a *bone* to my name⟩ — see DOLLAR

5 bones *pl* a dead body ⟨requested that his *bones* be buried in the country of his birth⟩ — see CORPSE

bone (up) *vb* to use the mind to acquire knowledge ⟨I suggest you *bone up* a bit on torts before the next attempt at the bar exam⟩ — see STUDY 1

bone–chilling *adj* having a low or subnormal temperature ⟨we stood in line for hours in the *bone-chilling* weather⟩ — see COLD 1

bonehead *adj* not having or showing an ability to absorb ideas readily ⟨dreaded spending the holidays with his *bonehead* relatives⟩ — see STUPID 1

bonehead *n* a stupid person ⟨the package's directions seem to suggest that anyone who would buy such a product is a *bonehead*⟩ — see IDIOT

boneheaded *adj* not having or showing an ability to absorb ideas readily ⟨a product with a warning label that even the most *boneheaded* consumer should be able to understand⟩ — see STUPID 1

boneheadedness *n* the quality or state of lacking intelligence or quickness of mind ⟨the sheer *boneheaded-*

ness shown by the state's politicians, who have ignored the problem for decades⟩ — see STUPIDITY 1

boneyard *n* a piece of land used for burying the dead ⟨a once-notorious gunslinger who now lies in the forlorn *boneyard* of an Old West ghost town⟩ — see CEMETERY

bong *vb* to make the clear sound heard when metal vibrates ⟨church bells across the city *bonged* to mark the solemn occasion⟩ — see ²RING

bonhomous *adj* having or showing kindly feeling and sincere interest ⟨*bonhomous* talk about their lives⟩ ⟨the talk show's *bonhomous* host has an easy rapport with television viewers⟩ — see FRIENDLY 1

boniface *n* the owner or manager of an inn ⟨the operator of the inn is the very epitome of the genial and gracious *boniface*⟩ — see INNKEEPER

bonk *vb* to deliver a blow to (someone or something) usually in a strong vigorous manner ⟨an overhead branch suddenly fell and *bonked* him on the head⟩ — see HIT 1

bonkers *adj* having or showing a very abnormal or sick state of mind ⟨spent her last years as a totally *bonkers* recluse in a decaying mansion⟩ — see INSANE 1

bonny *also* **bonnie** *adj, chiefly British* **1** of the very best kind ⟨one of several inns in the Lake District offering *bonny* accommodations and bountiful breakfasts⟩ — see EXCELLENT

2 very pleasing to look at ⟨a *bonny* child dressed in traditional Scottish clothing⟩ — see BEAUTIFUL 1

bonus *n* something given in addition to what is ordinarily expected or owed ⟨this job offers a nice Christmas *bonus* in addition to the salary⟩

synonyms cumshaw, dividend, donative, extra, gratuity, gravy, gravy train, lagniappe, perk, perquisite, throw-in, tip

related words pension; bestowal, presentation; benefaction, beneficence, benevolence, bounty, charity, generosity, largesse (*also* largess), philanthropy; contribution, donation, gift, offering, present; grant, subsidy; boon, manna, windfall; favor, freebie (*or* freebee), giveaway, premium; award, prize, reward; fringe benefit, icing

bon vivant *n* a person with refined tastes in food and wine ⟨a *bon vivant* who loves to hold dinner parties and serve exquisite, elaborate meals⟩ — see EPICURE

bon voyage *n* an expression of good wishes at parting ⟨everyone said their *bon voyages* as the happy couple left on a cruise for their honeymoon⟩ — see GOOD-BYE

bony *also* **boney** *adj* **1** having a noticeably small amount of body fat ⟨that *bony* old horse may have been deliberately starved⟩ — see THIN 1

2 producing inferior or only a small amount of vegetation ⟨*bony* hills from which sheepherders eked out a meager existence⟩ — see BARREN 1

boo *n* a vocal sound made to express scorn or disapproval ⟨the referee's questionable call was greeted with a chorus of *boos*⟩ — see CATCALL

boob *n, British* an unintentional departure from truth or accuracy ⟨made an embarrassing *boob* on a chat show that had all of London laughing⟩ — see ERROR 1

boob *vb, British* to make a mistake ⟨it was an important speech, and the prime minister knew that he could not afford to *boob* on it⟩ — see ERR 1

boo-boo *n* an unintentional departure from truth or accuracy ⟨the president should not be making *boo-boos* in something as important as the State of the Union Address⟩ — see ERROR 1

boob tube *n* an electronic device with a screen and speakers that reproduces images and sound ⟨tonight I just want to unwind in front of the *boob tube*⟩ — see TELEVISION

booby *n* a person who lacks good sense or judgment ⟨what kind of *booby* goes out into the snow barefoot?⟩ — see FOOL 1

booby-trap *vb* to place hidden explosive devices in or under ⟨*booby-trapped* the field bordering the army's camp⟩ — see MINE

booby trap *n* **1** a usually concealed explosive device designed to go off when disturbed ⟨luckily, the bomb squad didn't find any *booby traps*⟩

synonyms mine

related words claymore mine, land mine; torpedo; bomb, explosive; hazard, pitfall, snare, trap; ambush, net, web

2 a danger or difficulty that is hidden or not easily recognized ⟨he noticed the *booby trap* in the interviewer's question just a little too late⟩ — see PITFALL 1

boodle *n* **1** a usually small number of persons considered as a unit ⟨a *boodle* of teenagers boarded the bus together⟩ — see GROUP 2

2 a very large amount of money ⟨we saved a *boodle* by buying a house that's off the beaten path⟩ — see FORTUNE 2

3 something given or promised in order to improperly influence a person's conduct or decision ⟨an IRS agent was caught accepting some *boodle* from people she was auditing⟩ — see BRIBE

book *n* **1** a set of printed sheets of paper bound together between covers and forming a work of fiction or nonfiction ⟨I bought another new *book* yesterday, and I can't wait to read it⟩

synonyms tome, volume

related words hardback, hardcover, paper, paperback, paperbound, pocket book, pocket edition, softback, softcover, trade book, trade edition; folio, quarto; guidebook, handbook, how-to, manual; catalog (*or* catalogue), cyclopedia (*also* cyclopaedia), dictionary, encyclopedia; monograph, primer, text, textbook, tract, treatise; novel, novelette, pulp; album, almanac, anthology, casebook, chapbook, nonbook, omnibus, picture book

2 *cap* a book made up of the writings accepted by Christians as coming from God ⟨offered to swear on the *Book* that everything had happened just as he said⟩ — see BIBLE

3 a publication that appears at regular intervals ⟨older people in these parts still tend to call a magazine a *book*⟩ — see JOURNAL 1

4 information not generally available to the public ⟨what's the *book* on the new company president?⟩ — see DOPE 1

book *vb* **1** to arrange to have something (as a hotel room) held for one's future use ⟨we *booked* a conference room for the meeting next week⟩ — see RESERVE 1

2 *slang* to leave a place often for another ⟨I'm running late, so I've got to *book*⟩ — see GO 2

bookish *adj* suggestive of the vocabulary used in books ⟨"fealty" is a *bookish* synonym for "loyalty"⟩

synonyms erudite, learned, literary

related words academic (*also* academical), donnish, inkhorn, pedantic, scholastic; belletristic (*also* belle-lettristic); highbrow, highbrowed, intellectual; educated, schooled; elevated, eloquent, formal, high-flown, lofty, majestic, stately, towering; bombastic, declamatory, florid, flowery, grandiloquent, highfalutin (*also* hifalutin), pompous, stilted

near antonyms chatty, conversational; familiar, informal; slangy; illiterate

antonyms colloquial, nonliterary, unbookish

booklet *n* a short printed publication with no cover or with a paper cover ⟨there's an instruction *booklet* next to the computer⟩ — see PAMPHLET

bookman *n* one who is keenly devoted to books ⟨a

bookman since toddlerhood, he's never shown much interest in television or video games⟩ — see BIBLIOPHILE

bookworm *n* a person slavishly devoted to intellectual or academic pursuits ⟨a *bookworm* who prefers reading to just about any other activity⟩ — see NERD 1

boom *n* a loud explosive sound ⟨the nerve-jangling *boom* of a car backfiring⟩ — see CLAP 1

boom *vb* **1** to become greater in size, extent, volume, amount, or number ⟨requests for hybrid cars are *booming*⟩ — see INCREASE 2
2 to make a long loud deep noise or cry ⟨the cannons *boomed* throughout the night⟩ — see ROAR 1

boomerang *vb* to have the reverse of the desired or expected effect ⟨the well-meaning gesture *boomeranged*, since he ended up being offended by it⟩ — see BACKFIRE

booming *adj* **1** marked by a high volume of sound ⟨a *booming* bass drum⟩ — see LOUD 1
2 marked by vigorous growth and well-being especially economically ⟨a *booming* business that has grown every year since it was founded⟩ — see PROSPEROUS 1

boomy *adj* marked by vigorous growth and well-being especially economically ⟨a Web designer who made a fortune during the *boomy* days of the dot-com bubble⟩ — see PROSPEROUS 1

boon *adj* likely to seek or enjoy the company of others ⟨I and my *boon* companions celebrated that afternoon's victory on the gridiron with a night at a local dance club⟩ — see CONVIVIAL

boon *n* **1** a thing that helps ⟨the couple's generous donation was a great *boon* to the charity's fund-raising campaign⟩ — see HELP 2
2 an act of kind assistance ⟨a softhearted man who finds it hard to deny any *boon*, whether it be for friend or stranger⟩ — see FAVOR 1
3 something granted as a special favor ⟨at the prep school, seniors are given certain *boons* that make them the envy of underclassmen⟩ — see PRIVILEGE
4 something that provides happiness or does good for a person or thing ⟨the unexpected rain was a *boon* for the farmers who had been struggling with drought⟩ — see BLESSING 2

boondocks *n pl* the open rural area outside of big towns and cities ⟨a former city girl who was still adjusting to life in the *boondocks*⟩ — see COUNTRY 2

boonies *n pl, slang* the open rural area outside of big towns and cities ⟨this is the *boonies*, so don't expect to find a lot of places selling cappuccino⟩ — see COUNTRY 2

boor *n* a person whose behavior is offensive to others ⟨a loudmouthed *boor* who embarrassed his family at every social event they attended⟩ — see JERK 1

boorish *adj* having or showing crudely insensitive or impolite manners ⟨*boorish* behavior, such as yelling for service in restaurants⟩ — see CLOWNISH

boost *n* **1** an act or instance of helping ⟨she always liked to give struggling families in the neighborhood a *boost*⟩ — see HELP 1
2 something added (as by growth) ⟨a sudden *boost* in sales⟩ — see INCREASE 1
3 something that arouses action or activity ⟨according to the President, a tax cut is just the *boost* that the economy needs⟩ — see IMPULSE 1

boost *vb* **1** to lift with effort ⟨*boosted* the child into her car seat⟩ — see HEAVE 1
2 to make greater in size, amount, or number ⟨a promotion that *boosted* the number of interested customers milling about the showroom⟩ — see INCREASE 1
3 to make markedly greater in measure or degree ⟨let's *boost* the volume on the radio so everyone can hear⟩ — see INTENSIFY
4 to move from a lower to a higher place or position ⟨*boosted* the box onto the top shelf⟩ — see RAISE 1
5 to provide publicity for ⟨*boosted* the singer's latest release with a round of appearances on all the talk and entertainment shows⟩ — see PUBLICIZE 1
6 *slang* to take (something) without right and with an intent to keep ⟨the woman was nabbed trying to *boost* a couple of bottles of perfume⟩ — see STEAL 1

booster *n* a person who actively supports or favors a cause ⟨rah-rah *boosters* for the sports team will be attending the game and carrying large signs⟩ — see EXPONENT 1

boot *n* a pleasurably intense stimulation of the feelings ⟨the fans got a real *boot* out the team's lopsided victory over its longtime rivals⟩ — see THRILL

boot *vb* to make or do (something) in a clumsy or unskillful way ⟨he *booted* the answer of what should have been an easy question⟩ — see BOTCH

boot (out) *vb* to drive or force out ⟨the theater manager *booted out* the teens who were making a disturbance⟩ — see EJECT 1

bootleg *n* illegally produced liquor ⟨getting caught with *bootleg* during Prohibition could have resulted in a jail sentence⟩ — see MOONSHINE 1

bootlegger *n* a person who imports or exports goods secretly and illegally ⟨a *bootlegger* of counterfeit electronics⟩ — see SMUGGLER

bootless *adj* producing no results ⟨a *bootless* effort to get tickets to the sold-out game⟩ — see FUTILE 1

bootlick *vb* to use flattery or the doing of favors in order to win approval especially from a superior ⟨the kind of office in which people feel they have to *bootlick* in order to get ahead⟩ — see FAWN

bootlicker *n* a person who flatters another in order to get ahead ⟨she's such a *bootlicker* that I don't take any of her compliments seriously⟩ — see SYCOPHANT

bootstrapper *n* an ambitious person who eagerly goes after what is desired ⟨he was the proverbial *bootstrapper*, having worked his way up from the mail room to the corner office⟩ — see GO-GETTER

[1]**booty** *n* valuables stolen or taken by force ⟨no one knows where Captain Kidd hid his *booty*, but that hasn't deterred hopeful adventurers from looking for it for the last 300 years⟩ — see LOOT 1

[2]**booty** *also* **bootie** *n, slang* the part of the body upon which someone sits ⟨she's got a nice *booty*⟩ — see BUTTOCKS

booze *n* a distilled beverage that can make a person drunk ⟨this will be a birthday party without *booze*⟩ — see ALCOHOL

booze *vb* to partake excessively of alcoholic beverages ⟨he went out *boozing* with his friends on his 21st birthday⟩ — see DRINK 2

boozehound *n* a person who makes a habit of getting drunk ⟨he's a famous writer and an infamous *boozehound*⟩ — see DRUNK 1

boozer *n* a person who makes a habit of getting drunk ⟨the *boozer* finally checked herself into rehab⟩ — see DRUNK 1

boozy *adj* being under the influence of alcohol ⟨I know I said that I liked the party, but you have to remember: I was *boozy* at the time⟩ — see DRUNK

bop *n* a hard strike with a part of the body or an instrument ⟨a *bop* to the television set sometimes fixes it⟩ — see [1]BLOW

bop *vb* to deliver a blow to (someone or something) usually in a strong vigorous manner ⟨*bopped* the dog on the nose to discourage bad behavior⟩ — see HIT 1

bordello *n* a building in which prostitutes are available ⟨the cabdriver offered to show me what he claimed was the fanciest *bordello* in town⟩
synonyms bagnio, bawdy house, brothel, cathouse, disorderly house, sporting house, stew, whorehouse

related words call house, crib; massage parlor; harem, seraglio

border *n* **1** the line or relatively narrow space that marks the outer limit of something ⟨a rug with a fancily embroidered *border*⟩
synonyms borderline, bound, boundary, brim, circumference, compass, confines, edge, edging, end, frame, fringe, hem, margin, perimeter, periphery, rim, skirt, skirting, verge
related words ambit; brink, crest, curb, cusp, lip; ceiling, maximum; demarcation, extent, limitation, measure, mere, restriction, termination; borderland, frontier, march, outskirts, pale, selvage; lap; shore
near antonyms center, core, heart; inner, inside, interior, middle, within
2 a region along the dividing line between two countries ⟨people who live on an international *border* get used to carrying a passport⟩ — see FRONTIER 1

border *vb* to serve as a border for ⟨that velvet *bordered* the sleeves on this shirt, until it fell off⟩
synonyms bound, edge, frame, fringe, margin, rim, skirt
related words hem, trim; circumscribe, define, delineate, demarcate, outline, silhouette, sketch, trace; circle, compass, encircle, enclose (*also* inclose), environ, girdle, girth, loop, ring, round, surround, wall; check, confine, control, curb, limit, restrain, restrict

border (on) *vb* **1** to come very close to being ⟨that comment *borders on* insubordination, and you should be more careful in the future⟩
synonyms touch (on), trench (on), verge (on)
related words approach, near; appear, look, resemble, seem, suggest; approximate, compare (with), measure up (to), stack up (against *or* with)
2 to be adjacent to ⟨that state *borders on* three others⟩ — see ADJOIN 1

bordering *adj* having a border in common ⟨a country given to constant disagreements with *bordering* nations⟩ — see ADJACENT

borderland *n* a region along the dividing line between two countries ⟨I grew up on the *borderland*, so I speak both languages⟩ — see FRONTIER 1

borderline *adj* located at or near a border ⟨a *borderline* region that is claimed by both countries⟩
synonyms frontier, marginal
related words outermost, outmost; exterior, external, outer, outside, outward
near antonyms inner, inside, internal, inward; inmost, innermost; central, mid, middle
antonyms interior

borderline *adv* very close to but not completely ⟨your answer was *borderline* rude, so I would advise you to be more diplomatic in the future⟩ — see ALMOST

borderline *n* the line or relatively narrow space that marks the outer limit of something ⟨the actual *borderline* separating the two properties is now being disputed⟩ — see BORDER 1

[1]**bore** *vb* **1** to make a hole or series of holes in ⟨some woodpecker *bored* holes in our tree in the backyard⟩ — see PERFORATE
2 to force one's way ⟨with some effort, she *bored* through the throng of yelling protestors⟩ — see [2]PRESS 4

[2]**bore** *vb* to make weary and restless by being dull or monotonous ⟨the professor's lifeless and unimaginative teaching style *bored* the students to death⟩
synonyms jade, tire, weary
related words pall; burn out, do in, drain, enervate, exhaust, fag, fatigue, tucker (out), wash out, wear, wear out; debilitate, disable, enfeeble; deject, demoralize, discourage, dishearten, dispirit
phrases put to sleep
near antonyms activate, animate, energize, enliven, excite, galvanize, invigorate, stimulate, strengthen, vitalize; amuse, entertain; allure, attract, beguile, bewitch, captivate, charm, enchant, hypnotize, mesmerize; monopolize, preoccupy; busy, immerse, involve, occupy; pump up, rally, rouse, stir
antonyms absorb, busy, engage, engross, enthrall (*or* enthral), fascinate, grip, interest, intrigue

bore *n* someone or something boring ⟨for once, the graduation speaker wasn't a real *bore*⟩ — see DRAG 1

bored *adj* having one's patience, interest, or pleasure exhausted ⟨I was completely *bored* during that speech⟩ — see WEARY 2

boredom *n* the state of being bored ⟨she spent that whole meeting in a state of complete *boredom*, waiting for lunch⟩
synonyms blahs, doldrums, ennui, listlessness, restlessness, tedium, weariness
related words cheerlessness, dispiritedness, joylessness, melancholy; languidness, languor, lassitude, lethargy, lifelessness, torpidity, torpor; dullness (*also* dulness), monotonousness, monotony, sameness; apathy, indifference, unconcern
near antonyms beguilement, bewitchment, captivation, enchantment, fascination; absorption, engagement, engrossment, immersion, involvement; animation, enlivenment, excitement, invigoration, stimulation; amusement, entertainment; diversion, relief

boring *adj* causing weariness, restlessness, or lack of interest ⟨I wish this book weren't so *boring*; I keep falling asleep whenever I try to read it⟩
synonyms arid, colorless, drab, dreary, drudging, dry, dull, dusty, flat, heavy, ho-hum, humdrum, jading, jejune, leaden, mind-numbing, monochromatic, monotonous, numbing, old, pedestrian, ponderous, slow, stale, stodgy, stuffy, stupid, tame, tedious, tiresome, tiring, uninteresting, wearisome, weary, wearying
related words aseptic, barren, blah, dullish, pleasureless, prosaic, prosy, soggy, spiritless; blank, earthbound, gray (*also* grey), inanimate, pallid, pedantic, sterile, suspenseless, undramatic, uneventful, unexciting, unimaginative, uninspiring, unnewsworthy, unrewarding, unsensational, unspectacular; annoying, bothersome, irksome, irritating; longsome; palling; draining, enervating, exhausting, fatiguing, wearing; debilitating, enfeebling; demoralizing, discouraging, disheartening, dispiriting; common, commonplace, ordinary, tepid, unexceptional, unsurprising, vapid; cumbersome, lumbering, plodding, poky (*or* pokey)
near antonyms amazing, astonishing, astounding, awesome, eye-opening, fabulous, marvelous (*or* marvellous), sensational, spectacular, surprising, wonderful, wondrous; animating, breathtaking, electrifying, energizing, enlivening, exciting, exhilarating, galvanizing, hair-raising, inspiring, invigorating, rip-roaring, rousing, stimulating, stirring, thrilling; amusing, diverting, entertaining; moving, poignant, touching; alluring, attracting, attractive, beguiling, bewitching, captivating, charming, enchanting, enthralling, entrancing, fascinating; mesmerizing, spellbinding; suspenseful; arresting, provocative, tantalizing
antonyms absorbing, engaging, engrossing, gripping, interesting, intriguing, involving, riveting

born *adj* **1** being such from birth or by nature ⟨a *born* artist and largely self-taught, John Singleton Copley was producing accomplished portraits by the time he was in his late teens⟩ — see NATURAL 1
2 belonging to a particular place by birth or origin ⟨a *born* Texan and very proud of it⟩ — see NATIVE 1

borrow *vb* to take for one's own use (something originated by another) ⟨*borrowed* the basic plot from a book of tales, but put her personal stamp on the story⟩ — see ADOPT

boscage *also* **boskage** *n* a thick patch of shrubbery, small trees, or underbrush ⟨hidden from prying eyes by a leafy *boscage*, the cottage was the perfect trysting place⟩ — see THICKET

bosh *n* language, behavior, or ideas that are absurd and contrary to good sense ⟨a pseudoscientific examination of UFO claims that was utter *bosh*⟩ — see NONSENSE 1

bosk *also* **bosque** *n* a thick patch of shrubbery, small trees, or underbrush ⟨the thorny branches of the mesquite *bosk* provide quail and other desert birds with a safe haven from predators⟩ — see THICKET

bosom *adj* closely acquainted ⟨promised to remain *bosom* friends for the rest of their lives⟩ — see FAMILIAR 1

bosom *n* the seat of one's deepest thoughts and emotions ⟨his friend's sudden death pained him to his very *bosom*⟩ — see CORE 1

bosom *vb* to surround or cover closely ⟨*bosomed* by overgrown shrubbery, the abandoned cottage seemed like the ideal place for an afternoon tryst⟩ — see ENFOLD 1

bosquet *n* a thick patch of shrubbery, small trees, or underbrush ⟨a dense *bosquet* shields the trailhead from the bridle path⟩ — see THICKET

boss *adj, slang* of the very best kind ⟨that's a really *boss* stereo you've got⟩ — see EXCELLENT

boss *n* the person (as an employer or supervisor) who tells people and especially workers what to do ⟨every morning the *boss* hands out a list of top-priority tasks⟩

synonyms boss man, captain, chief, foreman, head, headman, helmsman, honcho, jefe, kingpin, leader, master, taskmaster

related words directress, mistress; administrator, commander, director, executive, general, governor, hierarch, higher-up; leadman, manager, overseer, principal, skipper, standard-bearer, steward, straw boss, superintendent, superior, supervisor; dominator, lord, overlord, potentate, ruler, sovereign (*also* sovran); figurehead; slave driver; baron, czar (*also* tsar *or* tzar), king, magnate, mogul, president, prince; big cheese, big gun, bigwig, top dog, top gun; cohead, coleader; employer, gaffer [*British*], ganger [*British*]; micromanager; subchief, subdirector

near antonyms dependent, inferior, junior, secondary, subject, subordinate, underling

boss *vb* **1** to be in charge of ⟨she *bossed* that project for years, until she was promoted again⟩

synonyms captain, handle, head, overlook, oversee, quarterback, superintend, supervise

related words administer, command, control, direct, guide, manage, order, run, shepherd, show, steer; monitor, preside (over); govern, reign, rule

phrases call the shots (of), call the tune (for), ride herd on, watch over

2 to exercise authority or power over ⟨*bossed* the entire job site for a year⟩ — see GOVERN 1

3 to serve as leader of ⟨*bossed* the entire gang of electricians on the construction project⟩ — see LEAD 2

boss (around) *vb* to issue orders to (someone) by right of authority ⟨that regional manager certainly likes to *boss* people *around*⟩ — see COMMAND 1

boss man *n* the person (as an employer or supervisor) who tells people and especially workers what to do ⟨maybe we should ask the *boss man* how to handle this⟩ — see BOSS

bossy *adj* fond of ordering people around ⟨I don't want to work with him because he's so *bossy* and always runs roughshod over me⟩

synonyms authoritarian, authoritative, autocratic (*also* autocratical), despotic, dictatorial, domineering, imperious, masterful, overbearing, peremptory, tyrannical (*also* tyrannic), tyrannous

related words arrogant, assumptive, disdainful, fastuous, haughty, highfalutin (*also* hifalutin), high-and-mighty, high-hat, huffy, important, lofty, lordly, overweening, presuming, presumptuous, pretentious, proud, self-asserting, supercilious, superior, toplofty (*also* toploftical), uppish, uppity; commanding, controlling, dictating, regimental; arbitrary, high-handed, imperial; directorial, magisterial; aggressive, assertive, self-assertive; imperative; conceited, narcissistic, pompous, vain; all-powerful, almighty, omnipotent; firm, stern

near antonyms humble, meek, modest, unassuming; amenable, docile, obedient, tractable; indecisive, irresolute; acquiescent, compliant, passive, resigned, submissive, yielding

botch *n* an unorganized collection or mixture of various things ⟨this police procedural is basically a *botch* of plot elements stolen from other (and better) novels⟩ — see MISCELLANY 1

botch *vb* to make or do (something) in a clumsy or unskillful way ⟨the first time we tried to make a cake, we *botched* the job completely⟩

synonyms blow, bobble, boggle, bollix (up), boot, bugger (up), bumble, bungle, butcher, dub, flub, fluff, foozle, foul up, fumble, goof (up), louse up, mangle, mess (up), muck up, muff, murder, screw up

related words blunder, gum (up), muddle, piffle; blemish, blight, damage, flaw, harm, hurt, impair, injure, mar, mutilate, ruin, spoil, vitiate; destroy, wreck; mishandle, mismanage

near antonyms ameliorate, better, enhance, help, improve, meliorate, rectify, refine, reform, remedy; doctor, fix, patch, recondition, renovate, repair, revamp

botched *adj* showing or marked by a lack of skill and tact (as in dealing with a situation) ⟨a *botched* attempt to mend relations with our disaffected European allies⟩ — see AWKWARD 2

botcher *n* someone who bungles an effort ⟨she has few rivals as a *botcher* of operatic arias⟩ — see BUTCHER

bother *n* **1** a state of noisy, confused activity ⟨the whole household was in a *bother*, as our overnight guests were expected to arrive any minute⟩ — see COMMOTION

2 one who is obnoxiously annoying ⟨the woman nextdoor is such a *bother*—always dropping in at the most inopportune moments!⟩ — see NUISANCE 1

3 something that is a source of irritation ⟨returning damaged goods is a real *bother*⟩ — see ANNOYANCE 3

4 the feeling of impatience or anger caused by another's repeated disagreeable acts ⟨never let his personal *bothers* interfere with his responsibilities at work⟩ — see ANNOYANCE 2

bother *vb* **1** to thrust oneself upon (another) without invitation ⟨I am never going to get this work done if people don't stop wandering into the room and *bothering* me⟩

synonyms bug, chivy (*or* chivvy), disturb, intrude (upon), pester

related words inconvenience, trouble; aggravate, annoy, bedevil, chafe, devil, dog, dun, exasperate, fret, gall, get, gnaw, grate, hassle, irk, irritate, nettle, peeve, persecute, pique, put out, rankle, rasp, rile, roil, torment, vex, worry; beleaguer, beset, besiege; distress, plague; afflict, harass, provoke; anger, antagonize, enrage, incense, inflame (*also* enflame), infuriate, madden, outrage; agitate, perturb; butt in, cut in (on), obtrude; encroach, infringe, invade, trespass

near antonyms disregard, forget, ignore, leave, slight; appease, conciliate, disarm, mollify, oblige, placate; delight, gladden, gratify, please, satisfy; comfort, console, content

2 to disturb the peace of mind of (someone) especially

by repeated disagreeable acts ⟨it *bothers* me when obviously sick people go to concerts and spend the whole time coughing and sneezing⟩ — see IRRITATE 1
3 to experience concern or anxiety ⟨just get the basic concept right and don't *bother* about the details⟩ — see WORRY 1
4 to trouble the mind of; to make uneasy ⟨the stranger lurking outside her office building *bothered* her⟩ — see DISTURB 1

botheration *n* **1** the act of making unwelcome intrusions upon another ⟨if I'm to get any work done, this incessant *botheration* has to stop⟩ — see ANNOYANCE 1
2 the feeling of impatience or anger caused by another's repeated disagreeable acts ⟨my life at that point seemed destined to be one endless *botheration*⟩ — see ANNOYANCE 2
3 something that is a source of irritation ⟨I hope that during my visit my special dietary needs won't be a *botheration*⟩ — see ANNOYANCE 3

bothered *adj* subjected to and reacting with irritation ⟨she finally learned not to get all hot and *bothered* over his insensitive remarks⟩ — see ANNOYED

bothering *n* the act of making unwelcome intrusions upon another ⟨one more *bothering*, and I'm going to kick you out of here⟩ — see ANNOYANCE 1

bothersome *adj* causing annoyance ⟨a *bothersome* habit of dropping trash on the floor right next to the garbage can⟩ — see ANNOYING

bottle *n* **1** a distilled beverage that can make a person drunk ⟨a talented writer whose fondness for the *bottle* was the stuff of legend⟩ — see ALCOHOL
2 *British slang* strength of mind to carry on in spite of danger ⟨I wanted to confront the neighbors about the excessive noise coming from their flat, but I lost my *bottle*⟩ — see COURAGE

bottleneck *n* a crowded mass (as of cars) that impedes or blocks movement ⟨a *bottleneck* inevitably forms at the start of a construction zone when the highway narrows from three to two lanes⟩ — see JAM 1

bottom *adj* of, relating to, or located at the bottom ⟨was sitting on the *bottom* step of the stairway⟩
synonyms bottommost, low, lowermost, nethermost, rock-bottom, undermost
related words below, lower, low-grade, lowly, nether, under; lowered, low-lying, sunken
near antonyms higher, loftier, upper; elevated, escalated, heightened, jacked (up), lifted, raised, uplifted, upraised
antonyms highest, loftiest, top, topmost, upmost, uppermost

bottom *n* **1** the side or part facing downward from something ⟨that side of the shelf is supposed to be the *bottom*, so turn it over before you assemble the bookcase⟩
synonyms underbelly, underbody, underpart, underside, undersurface
related words belly, sole, toe; base, floor, foot, ground, seat, underpinning; undercarriage
near antonyms acme, apex, climax, crest, crown, culmination, height, high-water mark, meridian, peak, pinnacle, roof, summit; cusp, head, point, tip, tip-top, zenith
antonyms face, top
2 the surface upon which a body of water lies ⟨my missing fishing pole is probably lying on the *bottom* of the lake⟩
synonyms bed, floor
related words riverbed; base, basement, foundation, ground
near antonyms surface
3 the lowest part, place, or point ⟨sliding all the way to the *bottom* of the snow-covered slope⟩
synonyms base, basement, foot, nadir, rock bottom
related words basis, bed, bedrock, foundation, ground, groundwork, keystone, seat, underpinning
near antonyms acme, apex, climax, crest, culmination, height, meridian, peak, pinnacle, summit, tip, tip-top, zenith
antonyms head, top, vertex
4 the part of the body upon which someone sits ⟨the baby fell backwards onto her *bottom*⟩ — see BUTTOCKS
5 a small buoyant structure for travel on water ⟨the cargo will be carried by a local *bottom*⟩ — see BOAT 1
6 the lowest point or level ⟨their marriage had really hit *bottom* when they began sleeping in separate rooms⟩ — see NADIR 1
7 an immaterial thing upon which something else rests ⟨the *bottom* of his thesis is the assumption that people are fundamentally good⟩ — see BASE 1

bottom–feeder *n* one who does things only for his own benefit and with little regard for right and wrong ⟨that *bottom-feeder* would run over his own mother if it would help him get ahead⟩ — see SELF-SEEKER

bottomless *adj* **1** being or seeming to be without limits ⟨the wealthy couple are generous hosts, providing a *bottomless* supply of food and drink⟩ — see INFINITE
2 extending far downward ⟨the killer threw the gun into what he thought was a *bottomless* pit⟩ — see DEEP 1
3 lacking or shed of clothing ⟨after one bar began featuring topless dancers, its chief competitor upped the ante with *bottomless* performers of the terpsichorean art⟩ — see NAKED 1

bottomlessness *n* the state of having no clothes on one's body ⟨as far as the city council was concerned, toplessness in bars was not a problem, but *bottomlessness* was⟩ — see NUDITY

bottom line *n* the central part or aspect of something under consideration ⟨why don't we stop talking around it and get to the *bottom line*⟩ — see CRUX

bottommost *adj* **1** following all others of the same kind in order or time ⟨the *bottommost* part of the wine list is where you'll find the bargains⟩ — see LAST 1
2 of, relating to, or located at the bottom ⟨the *bottommost* rung of the ladder is broken⟩ — see BOTTOM

bough *n* a major outgrowth from the main stem of a woody plant ⟨a tree *bough* fell on my car during the windstorm⟩ — see BRANCH 1

bought *adj* made beforehand in large numbers ⟨a *bought* dress that looked like a high-end designer item⟩ — see READY-MADE

boulevard *n* a passage cleared for public vehicular travel ⟨the city is celebrated for its broad, tree-lined *boulevards*⟩ — see WAY 1

bouleversement *n* a violent disturbance (as of the political or social order) ⟨the *bouleversement* in the print media since the rise of the Internet⟩ — see CONVULSION

bounce *n* active strength of body or mind ⟨the new pop singer has real *bounce* that serves her well in her videos⟩ — see VIGOR 1

bounce *vb* **1** to drive or force out ⟨the bar doesn't hesitate to *bounce* customers for getting rowdy⟩ — see EJECT 1
2 to strike and fly off at an angle ⟨most of my shots *bounce* off the rim of the basket⟩ — see GLANCE 1
3 to let go from office, service, or employment ⟨I'll *bounce* you if I catch you talking that way again⟩ — see DISMISS 1
4 to set before the mind for consideration ⟨we *bounced* several script suggestions off the producers, but they weren't interested in any of them⟩ — see PROPOSE 1
5 to move with a light springing step ⟨the girl *bounced* excitedly alongside her parents as they hurried toward

the entrance to the amusement park⟩ — see SKIP 1

bounce (back) *vb* to regain a former or normal state ⟨once the cleanup from the hurricane is completed, business owners are hoping that tourism quickly *bounces back*⟩ — see RECOVER 2

bouncily *adv* in a quick and spirited manner ⟨came *bouncily* into the room⟩ — see GAILY 2

bouncing *adj* **1** enjoying health and vigor ⟨a *bouncing* new baby in the family⟩ — see HEALTHY 1
2 having much high-spirited energy and movement ⟨a *bouncing* dance routine that should be good for an aerobics class⟩ — see LIVELY 1

bouncy *adj* **1** able to revert to original size and shape after being stretched, squeezed, or twisted ⟨*bouncy* seat cushions⟩ — see ELASTIC 1
2 joyously unrestrained ⟨unsurprisingly, the *bouncy* talk show hostess was a cheerleader in high school⟩ — see EXUBERANT

[1]bound *n* **1** a real or imaginary point beyond which a person or thing cannot go ⟨the language in the novel really is beyond the *bounds* of decency⟩ — see LIMIT 1
2 the line or relatively narrow space that marks the outer limit of something ⟨colored outside the *bounds* of the drawing⟩ — see BORDER 1

[2]bound *n* an act of leaping into the air ⟨the kangaroo took one giant *bound* and was gone⟩ — see JUMP 1

[1]bound *vb* **1** to mark the limits of ⟨the country is *bounded* by water on two sides⟩ — see LIMIT 2
2 to serve as a border for ⟨being *bounded* on all sides by the Alps has helped Switzerland maintain its neutrality⟩ — see BORDER

[2]bound *vb* **1** to move with a light springing step ⟨the child giggled and *bounded* off to play with her friends⟩ — see SKIP 1
2 to propel oneself upward or forward into the air ⟨a rabbit *bounded* down the garden path⟩ — see JUMP 1

bound *adj* fully committed to achieving a goal ⟨I am *bound* and determined to write a novel before I turn 30⟩ — see DETERMINED 1

boundary *n* **1** a real or imaginary point beyond which a person or thing cannot go ⟨parents have to set *boundaries* for their children, and the children want them to⟩ — see LIMIT 1
2 the line or relatively narrow space that marks the outer limit of something ⟨that chalk line marks the *boundary* of our playing field⟩ — see BORDER 1

bounded *adj* having distinct or certain limits ⟨in their paintings the Impressionists played down *bounded* figures and concentrated on the subtle, fleeting effects of light⟩ — see LIMITED 1

bounden *adj, archaic* being under obligation for a favor or gift ⟨a rugged individualist who refused to be *bounden* to any man⟩ — see BEHOLDEN

bounder *n* a person whose behavior is offensive to others ⟨a good-for-nothing *bounder* who always leaves it to someone else to pick up the tab⟩ — see JERK 1

boundless *adj* being or seeming to be without limits ⟨her *boundless* energy and enthusiasm make her a natural for the cheerleading squad⟩ — see INFINITE

bounteous *adj* **1** being more than enough without being excessive ⟨offered a *bounteous* reward for finding the lost ring⟩ — see PLENTIFUL
2 giving or sharing in abundance and without hesitation ⟨a *bounteous* king who made sure all his subjects were well-fed⟩ — see GENEROUS 1

bounteously *adv* in a generous manner ⟨our host handed us *bounteously*-filled plates and invited us to sit out by the pool⟩ — see WELL 2

bountiful *adj* **1** being more than enough without being excessive ⟨a *bountiful* supply of apples for the harvest festival⟩ — see PLENTIFUL
2 giving or sharing in abundance and without hesitation ⟨a *bountiful* host who makes sure that everyone has plenty to eat at his dinners⟩ — see GENEROUS 1

bountifully *adv* in a generous manner ⟨Grandma makes sure that everyone in the family is *bountifully* supplied with her hand-knit sweaters and scarves⟩ — see WELL 2

bountifulness *n* the quality or state of being generous ⟨because of the restaurant owner's *bountifulness*, a number of homeless people were fed that day⟩ — see LIBERALITY

bounty *n* **1** something offered or given in return for a service performed ⟨a *bounty* was offered for information leading to the capture of the criminal⟩ — see REWARD
2 the quality or state of being generous ⟨her *bounty* at Halloween was known throughout the neighborhood⟩ — see LIBERALITY
3 the total amount collected or obtained especially at one time ⟨the record-breaking *bounty* from this year's corn harvest⟩ — see HAUL 1

bouquet *n* **1** a bunch of flowers ⟨I bought my wife a nice *bouquet* for her birthday⟩
synonyms bob [*Scottish*], nosegay, posy
related words boutonniere, corsage; arrangement; garland, lei
2 a sweet or pleasant smell ⟨this wine has a good *bouquet*⟩ — see FRAGRANCE
3 an admiring personal remark ⟨an evening dress of daring design that attracted *bouquets* as well as brickbats⟩ — see COMPLIMENT 1

bourg *n* a small residential settlement ⟨the invaders captured the castle and sacked the *bourg*⟩ — see VILLAGE

bourn *or* **bourne** *n* a natural body of running water smaller than a river ⟨idyllic days that were spent rambling the length of the *bourn* that flowed through that peaceful vale⟩ — see CREEK 1

bourne *also* **bourn** *n* something that one hopes or intends to accomplish ⟨still searching for the *bourne* that would give his life meaning⟩ — see GOAL

bout *n* **1** a competitive encounter between individuals or groups carried on for amusement, exercise, or in pursuit of a prize ⟨undoubtedly the team's best wrestler, he hasn't lost a *bout* yet⟩ — see GAME 1
2 a sudden experiencing of a physical or mental disorder ⟨she's currently suffering from a *bout* of the flu⟩ — see ATTACK 2

[1]bow *vb* **1** to cease resistance (as to another's arguments, demands, or control) ⟨finally *bowed* to the judge's insistence that she change her outfit⟩ — see YIELD 3
2 to give up and cease resistance (as to a liking, temptation, or habit) ⟨*bowed* to the craving for fresh coffee⟩ — see YIELD 1

[2]bow *vb* **1** to turn away from a straight line or course ⟨the river *bows* gently to the north before it reaches the sea⟩ — see CURVE 1
2 to cause to turn away from a straight line ⟨you'll have to gently *bow* the strip of wood in order to fit it in⟩ — see BEND 1

bow *n* something that curves or is curved ⟨her full lips form a pair of perfect *bows*⟩ — see BEND 1

bowdlerization *n* a shortened version of a written work ⟨this *bowdlerization* of "Moby Dick" simply eliminates all the chapters on whaling and cetology⟩ — see ABRIDGMENT

bowdlerize *vb* to remove objectionable parts from ⟨a *bowdlerized* version of "Gulliver's Travels" that purportedly makes it unobjectionable for children⟩ — see CENSOR

bowed *adj* **1** bending downward or forward ⟨the *bowed* branches of the weeping willow offered some protection from the rain⟩ — see NODDING

2 directed down ⟨with *bowed* heads the mourners recited a prayer for the repose of her soul⟩ — see DOWNCAST 1

bower *vb* to surround or cover closely ⟨*bowered* by a canopy of grapevines, we enjoyed a serene and very private picnic⟩ — see ENFOLD 1

bowing *adj* bending downward or forward ⟨the *bowing* blossoms indicated that the petunia plant desperately needed water⟩ — see NODDING

bowl *n* a large usually roofless building for sporting events with tiers of seats for spectators ⟨a new *bowl* for the football team⟩ — see STADIUM

bowl *vb* **1** to move or proceed smoothly and readily ⟨*bowling* along in my spiffy new car⟩ — see FLOW 2
2 to proceed or move quickly ⟨*bowled* through the test and was the first one to hand in the booklet⟩ — see HURRY 2

bowl (down *or* **over)** *vb* to strike (someone) so forcefully as to cause a fall ⟨the exuberant dog *bowled over* several children⟩ — see FELL 1

bowled over *adj* affected with sudden and great wonder or surprise ⟨I was *bowled over* when the appraiser told me what the painting was worth⟩ — see THUNDERSTRUCK

bowl over *vb* to make a strong impression on (someone) with something unexpected ⟨she was *bowled over* to learn that she had a long-lost sister⟩ — see SURPRISE 1

bow out *vb* to undergo defeat ⟨quite embarrassingly, the top-seeded player *bowed out* in the first round of competition⟩ — see LOSE 3

bowwow *n* loud, confused, and usually inharmonious sound ⟨the *bowwow* coming from the store's returns desk on the day after Christmas⟩ — see NOISE 1

[1]box *n* **1** a covered rectangular container for storing or transporting things ⟨filled a whole *box* with books⟩ — see CHEST
2 a boxlike container for holding a dead body ⟨the only way I'm ever leaving this hospital room is in a *box*⟩ — see COFFIN
3 an electronic device with a screen and speakers that reproduces images and sound ⟨would you switch on the *box* so that we can watch the news?⟩ — see TELEVISION
4 a difficult, puzzling, or embarrassing situation from which there is no easy escape ⟨with our new home still unfinished, and the buyers of our condo eager to move in, we were in a real *box*⟩ — see PREDICAMENT

[2]box *n* a hard strike with a part of the body or an instrument ⟨the vicious bully delivered a *box* to the child's ear⟩ — see [1]BLOW

box *vb* to deliver a blow to (someone or something) usually in a strong vigorous manner ⟨his mother threatened to *box* his ears if he didn't show a bit more respect⟩ — see HIT 1

box (in) *vb* to close or shut in by or as if by barriers ⟨upon attempting to leave, we discovered we were completely *boxed in* by other cars⟩ — see ENCLOSE 1

boxcar *adj* of a size greater than average of its kind ⟨a *boxcar* pile of paper⟩ ⟨*boxcar* amounts of money⟩ — see LARGE 1

boxer *n* one that engages in the sport of fighting with the fists ⟨that *boxer* is quite famous for being the youngest heavyweight champion ever⟩
synonyms fighter, gladiator, prizefighter, pug, pugilist
related words palooka, slugger, stumblebum; bantamweight, cruiserweight, featherweight, flyweight, heavyweight, light heavyweight, lightweight, middleweight, superheavyweight, welterweight

boy *n* **1** a male person who has not yet reached adulthood ⟨a giggling little *boy* ran by⟩
synonyms boychick (*or* boychik), boyo [*Irish*], callant [*chiefly Scottish*], lad, laddie, nipper, shaveling, shaver, sonny, stripling, tad, youth
related words adolescent, juvenile, kid, kiddie (*also* kiddy), kiddo, minor, moppet, teenager, tween, youngling, youngster; brat, gamin, guttersnipe, hobbledehoy, imp, squirt, urchin, whippersnapper; schoolboy; toddler, tot, tyke (*also* tike); mama's boy, mollycoddle
2 a male romantic companion ⟨their teenaged daughter has a new *boy*, and she's just crazy about him⟩ — see BOYFRIEND

boychick *or* **boychik** *n* a male person who has not yet reached adulthood ⟨my favorite *boychick* is getting tall, isn't he?⟩ — see BOY 1

boyfriend *n* a male romantic companion ⟨her *boyfriend* always brings her flowers for Valentine's Day⟩
synonyms beau, boy, fellow, man, old man, swain
related words admirer, crush, steady; gallant, suitor, wooer; beloved, darling, dear, favorite, flame, honey, love, lover, significant other, soul mate, spark, sparker, squeeze [*slang*], sweet, sweetheart, sweetie, sweetie pie, valentine; fancy man, gigolo; date, escort; groom, husband; fiancé, intended

boyo *n, Irish* a male person who has not yet reached adulthood ⟨a novel about a self-assertive, self-reliant *boyo* growing up in working-class Dublin⟩ — see BOY 1

brabble *vb* to express different opinions about something often angrily ⟨bored children *brabbling* in the back seat⟩ — see ARGUE 2

brace *n* **1** a structure that holds up or serves as a foundation for something else ⟨wore a *brace* for the injured knee⟩ — see SUPPORT 1
2 two things of the same or similar kind that match or are considered together ⟨bagged a *brace* of pheasants⟩ — see PAIR

brace *vb* **1** to give life, vigor, or spirit to ⟨the pep talk *braced* the team up for the second half⟩ — see ANIMATE
2 to hold up or serve as a foundation for ⟨several boards *braced* the wall⟩ — see SUPPORT 3
3 to prepare (oneself) mentally or emotionally ⟨she *braced* herself for the job interview⟩ — see FORTIFY 1

bracelet *n* something that physically prevents free movement ⟨putting the handcuffs on the jewel thief, the detective asked him how he liked those *bracelets*⟩ — see BOND 1

bracing *adj* having a renewing effect on the state of the body or mind ⟨a chilly but *bracing* day⟩ — see TONIC 1

bracket *n* one of the units into which a whole is divided on the basis of a common characteristic ⟨they're in the same income *bracket*⟩ — see CLASS 2

bracket *vb* to describe as similar ⟨I wouldn't exactly *bracket* your paintings with those of Michelangelo and Leonardo da Vinci⟩ — see COMPARE 1

brackish *adj* **1** disagreeable or disgusting to the sense of taste ⟨the office coffee is often some *brackish* brew that's been sitting around for a couple of hours⟩ — see DISTASTEFUL 1
2 of, relating to, or containing salt ⟨the river becomes *brackish* as we approach the tidemark⟩ — see SALTY 1

brag *adj* of the very best kind ⟨he did a really *brag* job on restoring that classic car⟩ — see EXCELLENT

brag *n* **1** boastful speech or writing ⟨for all his *brag* about diving, he actually does very little⟩ — see BOMBAST 1
2 someone who boasts ⟨he's an irritating *brag* whose sense of selfhood is defined by what he owns⟩ — see BRAGGART

brag *vb* to praise or express pride in one's own possessions, qualities, or accomplishments often to excess ⟨she *bragged* that she was richer than anyone else in the state⟩ — see BOAST 1

braggadocio *n* **1** boastful speech or writing ⟨his *brag-*

gadocio hid the fact that he felt personally inadequate⟩ — see BOMBAST 1
2 someone who boasts ⟨the swaggering *braggadocio* is a stock figure of American folklore, with Davy Crockett and Mike Fink being prime examples⟩ — see BRAGGART
braggart *n* someone who boasts ⟨a *braggart* who was always talking about how much money he made⟩
synonyms blower, blowhard, boaster, brag, braggadocio, bragger, cockalorum, cracker [*chiefly dialect*], gascon, gasconader, swaggerer, vaunter
related words blusterer, cock; self-advertiser, self-dramatizer, self-promoter
bragger *n* someone who boasts ⟨she's a tiresome *bragger* who should be put in her place⟩ — see BRAGGART
braid *n* a length of something formed of three or more strands woven together ⟨until she was 15, she had a *braid* that reached to her knees⟩
synonyms lace, lacing, plait, plat
related words rickrack (*or* ricrac), stripe; cornrow, dreadlock, pigtail, queue; braiding
braid *vb* to form into a braid ⟨they taught each other how to *braid* yarn into bracelets⟩
synonyms plait, plat, pleat
related words interlace, interweave, weave
brain *n* **1** a very smart person ⟨the *brains* all sit together at lunch⟩ — see GENIUS 1
2 *often* **brains** *pl* the ability to learn and understand or to deal with problems ⟨you have the *brains* to figure out that problem on your own⟩ — see INTELLIGENCE 1
3 the part of a person that feels, thinks, perceives, wills, and especially reasons ⟨I'd love to get inside his *brain* and experience the world as he experiences it⟩ — see MIND 1
brainchild *n* something (as a device) created for the first time through the use of the imagination ⟨the artificial language Esperanto was the *brainchild* of L. L. Zamenhof, a Polish oculist⟩ — see INVENTION 1
brain-dead *adj* not having or showing an ability to absorb ideas readily ⟨it seems like she's always doing some *brain-dead* thing or another⟩ — see STUPID 1
brainiac *n* a very smart person ⟨a techie who always has to have the latest gadget that the *brainiacs* in Silicon Valley have cooked up⟩ — see GENIUS 1
brainless *adj* **1** not having or showing an ability to absorb ideas readily ⟨a teacher who affirms that there are no *brainless* students, only lazy ones⟩ — see STUPID 1
2 showing or marked by a lack of good sense or judgment ⟨a *brainless* decision to talk on her cell phone while weaving in and out of traffic⟩ — see FOOLISH 1
brainlessness *n* **1** lack of good sense or judgment ⟨had the inexplicable *brainlessness* to sell his car for half of what it was worth⟩ — see FOOLISHNESS 1
2 the quality or state of lacking intelligence or quickness of mind ⟨the turkey is one bird that has often been cited for its *brainlessness*⟩ — see STUPIDITY 1
brainpower *n* the ability to learn and understand or to deal with problems ⟨the president's inner circle of advisers just didn't seem to have the *brainpower* to deal with the crisis⟩ — see INTELLIGENCE 1
brainsick *adj* having or showing a very abnormal or sick state of mind ⟨today he is regarded as a *brainsick* genius who produced some of the greatest paintings in the history of art⟩ — see INSANE 1
brainstorm *vb* to engage in an exchange of information or ideas ⟨they *brainstormed* about ways to raise money for their organization⟩ — see COMMUNICATE 2
brainy *adj* having or showing quickness of mind ⟨a *brainy* student who didn't fit in socially⟩ — see INTELLIGENT 1
brake *n* a thick patch of shrubbery, small trees, or underbrush ⟨built a small shelter in the *brake* to watch for deer⟩ — see THICKET
brake *vb* to cause to move or proceed at a less rapid pace ⟨*braked* the car sharply when someone pulled out in front of us⟩ — see SLOW 1
braking *n* a usually gradual decrease in the pace or level of activity of something ⟨there's always a *braking* in sales after lunch⟩ — see SLOWDOWN
brambly *adj* having leaves or branches which are likely to cause a scratch ⟨be careful of the *brambly* blackberry bushes⟩ — see SCRATCHY 1
branch *n* **1** a major outgrowth from the main stem of a woody plant ⟨I loved climbing among the *branches* of that old tree⟩
synonyms bough, limb
related words branchlet, offshoot, outgrowth, shoot, spur; spray, sprig, twig
2 a local unit of an organization ⟨a bank with many neighborhood *branches*⟩ — see CHAPTER 1
3 a stream that flows into a larger body of water ⟨the Blue Nile, the Atbara, and the White Nile are the three primary *branches* of the Nile River⟩ — see TRIBUTARY
4 a large unit of a governmental, business, or educational organization ⟨the two *branches* of the U.S. Congress⟩ — see DIVISION 2
branch *vb* to extend outwards from or as if from a central point ⟨threads *branched* from the center of the spider web⟩ — see RADIATE 1
branch (out) *vb* to go or move in different directions from a central point ⟨the vine *branched out* as it climbed the trellis⟩ — see SEPARATE 2
brand *n* **1** a device (as a word) identifying the maker of a piece of merchandise and legally reserved for the exclusive use of that person or company ⟨a company that was sued for using a name that was very similar to a rival's *brand*⟩ — see TRADEMARK 1
2 a mark of guilt or disgrace ⟨always felt that her shabby clothes showed the *brand* of poverty⟩ — see STAIN 1
3 a hand weapon with a length of metal sharpened on one or both sides and usually tapered to a sharp point ⟨on the battlefield lies our hero, slain by some fell *brand*⟩ — see SWORD
brand *vb* to produce a vivid impression of ⟨the exact words my father spoke as he left us are *branded* in my memory⟩ — see ENGRAVE 2
brand-new *adj* **1** being in an original and unused or unspoiled state ⟨his car is so well cared for that three years later it still looks *brand-new*⟩ — see FRESH 1
2 recently made and never used before ⟨a *brand-new* disk still in its original packaging⟩ — see NEW 3
brash *adj* **1** displaying or marked by rude boldness ⟨a *brash* request to get something for free⟩ — see NERVY 1
2 foolishly adventurous or bold ⟨that *brash* motorcyclist likes to show off by riding on only one wheel⟩ — see FOOLHARDY 1
3 showing poor judgment especially in personal relationships or social situations ⟨he was reprimanded for his *brash* comments to the media about the team's coaching staff⟩ — see INDISCREET
brashness *n* shameless boldness ⟨for sheer *brashness* it would be hard to beat the customer who wanted a refund on merchandise bought elsewhere⟩ — see EFFRONTERY
brass *n* shameless boldness ⟨had the *brass* to demand a refund for something they had broken themselves!⟩ — see EFFRONTERY
brassbound *adj* **1** not allowing for any exceptions or loosening of standards ⟨a person of *brassbound* honesty⟩ — see RIGID 1
2 tending to favor established ideas, conditions, or institutions ⟨the *brassbound* military leadership had failed

to realize that this time the nation was fighting a different kind of war⟩ — see CONSERVATIVE 1

3 displaying or marked by rude boldness ⟨some *brass-bound* upstart who thought that he could waltz in here and start issuing orders⟩ — see NERVY 1

brassiness *n* shameless boldness ⟨the *brassiness* with which he would blame his mistakes on others left me speechless⟩ — see EFFRONTERY

brass tacks *n pl* the specific practical details of something ⟨after the usual introductions and requisite pleasantries, we got down to the *brass tacks* of our business proposal⟩ — see NITTY-GRITTY

brassy *adj* displaying or marked by rude boldness ⟨a *brassy* customer insisted on arriving late and still being taken first⟩ — see NERVY 1

brave *adj* **1** feeling or displaying no fear by temperament ⟨despite considerable risk to their own safety, the *brave* team of rescuers rushed into the collapsed building⟩

synonyms bold, courageous, dauntless, doughty, fearless, gallant, greathearted, gutsy, gutty, heroic (*also* heroical), intrepid, lionhearted, manful, stalwart, stout, stouthearted, undauntable, undaunted, valiant, valorous

related words determined, firm, game, gamy (*or* gamey), gritty, plucky, resolute, Spartan, undeterred, undismayed, unflinching, unswerving; mettlesome, spirited, spunky; adventuresome, adventurous, audacious, daring, dashing, hardy, venturesome, venturous; crazy, foolish, half-witted, insane, lunatic, mad, nutty; brash, brazen, daredevil, foolhardy, heedless, hotheaded, impetuous, imprudent, impulsive, incautious, madcap, overbold, overconfident, rash, reckless, thoughtless, wild; hasty, headlong, precipitate; comforted, emboldened, encouraged, heartened, reassured, unafraid

near antonyms diffident, mousy (*or* mousey), scary, shy, skittish, timid; anxious, apprehensive, nervous; careful, cautious, heedful, prudent, unadventurous; afraid, agitated, disconcerted, disquieted, disturbed, frightened, horrified, panicked, panic-stricken, perturbed, scared, shocked, spooked, startled, terrified, terrorized, unnerved, upset; appalled, concerned, dismayed, worried; unmanly, weak, wimpy

antonyms chicken, chickenhearted, chicken-livered, coward, cowardly, craven, dastardly, fainthearted, fearful, gutless, lily-livered, milk-livered [*archaic*], nerveless, poltroon, poor-spirited, pusillanimous, spineless, spiritless, timorous, uncourageous, ungallant, unheroic, weakhearted, yellow

2 of the very best kind ⟨the gourmet food shop is off to a *brave* start⟩ — see EXCELLENT

brave *vb* to oppose (something hostile or dangerous) with firmness or courage ⟨a soldier who *braved* enemy fire to rescue her wounded comrade⟩ — see FACE 2

bravely *adv* **1** in a fearless manner ⟨confronted the fact that he had inoperable cancer calmly and *bravely*⟩

synonyms boldly, courageously, dauntlessly, doughtily, fearlessly, gallantly, gutsily, heroically, intrepidly, manfully, stalwartly, stoutheartedly, valiantly, valorously

related words determinedly, firmly, gamely, grittily, pluckily, resolutely; spiritedly, spunkily, stoutly; adventurously, audaciously, daringly, hardily, venturesomely, venturously; self-confidently; crazily, foolishly, insanely; brashly, brazenly, foolhardily, heedlessly, hotheadedly, impetuously, imprudently, impulsively, incautiously, overconfidently, rashly, recklessly, thoughtlessly, wildly; hastily, precipitately

near antonyms diffidently, mousily, shyly, skittishly, timidly; anxiously, apprehensively, nervously; carefully, cautiously, heedfully, prudently

antonyms cowardly, cravenly, fearfully, pusillanimously, spinelessly, spiritlessly, timorously

2 in a manner that is colorful and tends to arouse gaiety ⟨*bravely* decked houses in celebration of Independence Day⟩ — see GAILY 3

bravery *n* **1** dressy clothing ⟨children in their Sunday *bravery*⟩ — see FINERY

2 strength of mind to carry on in spite of danger ⟨it took great *bravery* to rescue the baby trapped in the burning building⟩ — see COURAGE

bravura *adj* accomplished with trained ability ⟨a truly *bravura* performance of the ballet that brought the crowd to its feet⟩ — see SKILLFUL 1

brawl *n* **1** a rough and often noisy fight usually involving several people ⟨they were thrown out of the party after starting a *brawl*⟩

synonyms affray [*chiefly British*], broil, donnybrook, fracas, fray, free-for-all, melee (*also* mêlée), rough-and-tumble, row, ruckus, ruction

related words battle, clash, combat, conflict, contest, fisticuffs, handgrips, hassle, scrap, scrimmage, scuffle, skirmish, struggle, tussle; horseplay, roughhousing; altercation, argument, dispute, kickup, quarrel, spat, squabble, tiff, wrangle

2 an often noisy or angry expression of differing opinions ⟨the student drama society's decision to put on the controversial play prompted a *brawl* at the school board meeting⟩ — see ARGUMENT 1

3 loud, confused, and usually inharmonious sound ⟨we could hear the *brawl* of the river rapids ahead of us before we could actually see them⟩ — see NOISE 1

brawl *vb* to express different opinions about something often angrily ⟨the Wilsons were always loudly *brawling*, and the neighbors were always shutting their windows⟩ — see ARGUE 2

brawler *n* a person who takes part in a dispute ⟨every couple has marital problems, but those two are heavyweight *brawlers* in a seriously dysfunctional relationship⟩ — see DISPUTANT

brawly *adj* feeling or displaying eagerness to fight ⟨a bar that was once a favorite haunt of *brawly* servicemen from the nearby military base⟩ — see BELLIGERENT

brawn *n* muscular strength ⟨an actor who is more famous for his *brawn* than for his talent⟩ — see MUSCLE 1

brawny *adj* **1** having muscles capable of exerting great physical force ⟨the store manager always asked the *brawniest* person there to do the heavy lifting⟩ — see STRONG 1

2 marked by a well-developed musculature ⟨*brawny* arms that weren't developed in the gym but by years of work in the construction business⟩ — see MUSCULAR 1

3 strongly and heavily built ⟨a tough little boy who's going to be a *brawny* man someday⟩ — see [1]HUSKY 1

bray *vb* to reduce to fine particles ⟨*bray* the seeds using a mortar and pestle⟩ — see POWDER

brazen *adj* displaying or marked by rude boldness ⟨a *brazen* demand for special treatment just because she's rich⟩ — see NERVY 1

brazen *vb* to oppose (something hostile or dangerous) with firmness or courage ⟨a filmmaker willing to *brazen* the criticism that such a violent film was sure to provoke⟩ — see FACE 2

brazen–faced *adj* displaying or marked by rude boldness ⟨shocked by his *brazen-faced* insistence that he had never uttered the insult, even though it was heard by a score of onlookers⟩ — see NERVY 1

brazenness *n* shameless boldness ⟨she had the *brazenness* to expect us to let her tap into our cable connection⟩ — see EFFRONTERY

breach *n* **1** a failure to uphold the requirements of law, duty, or obligation ⟨the president's deliberate misstatements were widely seen as a *breach* of the public trust⟩

synonyms contravention, infraction, infringement, transgression, trespass, violation
related words misconduct, misdemeanor, misfeasance, misprision, offense (*or* offence), sin, wrong; disregard, forgetting, ignoring, nonobservance, overlooking; delinquency, dereliction, neglect; encroachment, intrusion, invasion
near antonyms respecting, upholding
antonyms noninfringement, nonviolation, observance
2 a breaking of a moral or legal code ⟨cheating on the exam was a serious *breach* of the military academy's honor code⟩ — see OFFENSE 1
3 an open space in a barrier (as a wall or hedge) ⟨the cat got out of the yard through a *breach* in the hedge⟩ — see GAP 1

breach *vb* to fail to keep ⟨a builder being sued by a homeowner for *breaching* a contract⟩ — see VIOLATE 1

bread *n* **1** *slang* something (as pieces of stamped metal or printed paper) customarily and legally used as a medium of exchange, a measure of value, or a means of payment ⟨I'll buy that tomorrow, when I get some *bread*⟩ — see MONEY 1
2 substances intended to be eaten ⟨supplied his charges with *bread* and a place to stay⟩ — see FOOD 1

breadbasket *n, slang* the part of the body between the chest and the pelvis ⟨got hit right in the *breadbasket*⟩ — see STOMACH 1

breadth *n* **1** a wide space or area ⟨a great *breadth* of land awaited those who were brave and hardy enough to settle it⟩ — see EXPANSE
2 an area over which activity, capacity, or influence extends ⟨the *breadth* of his knowledge on the subject is awesome⟩ — see RANGE 2

break *n* **1** a momentary halt in an activity ⟨there was a brief *break* after the first movement as the doors to the concert hall were opened and the latecomers were allowed in⟩ — see PAUSE 1
2 a period during which the usual routine of school or work is suspended ⟨most of the students at the boarding school are going home for Christmas *break*⟩ — see VACATION
3 an open space in a barrier (as a wall or hedge) ⟨the rancher repaired the *break* in the fence where the horse had gotten through⟩ — see GAP 1
4 a favorable combination of circumstances, time, and place ⟨in classic fashion, her big *break* came when, as an understudy, she took over for an ailing star⟩ — see OPPORTUNITY
5 an unexpected benefit or advantage resulting from the uncertain course of events ⟨a guy who just seems to get all the *breaks* in life⟩ — see FLUKE
6 the act or an instance of getting free from danger or confinement ⟨a desperate *break* from that hellhole⟩ — see ESCAPE 1

break *vb* **1** to cause to separate into pieces usually suddenly or forcibly ⟨hated telling her that I had *broken* her favorite glass vase⟩
synonyms break up, bust, distintegrate, dismember, disrupt, fracture, fragment, rive
related words atomize, crush, grind, powder, pulverize, reduce; blast, blow up, burst, detonate, explode; crack, pop, shatter, shiver, smash; chip, sliver, splinter, split; implode; destroy, ruin, wreck
near antonyms doctor, fix, heal, mend, patch, rebuild, recondition, reconstruct, renovate, repair
2 to bring (as an action or operation) to an immediate end ⟨the final vote *broke* the deadlock⟩ — see STOP 1
3 to bring to a lower grade or rank ⟨the captain was *broken* to lieutenant commander for disobeying a direct order from his group commander⟩ — see DEMOTE
4 to change (as a secret message) from code into ordinary language ⟨Alan Turing and the Bletchley Park mathematicians *broke* the Enigma code being used by the Nazis⟩ — see DECODE 1
5 to come to a temporary halt in one's activity ⟨she *broke* from her ruminations to find that it was already dinnertime⟩ — see PAUSE
6 to cut into and turn over the sod of (a piece of land) using a bladed implement ⟨farmers once *broke* fields with horse-drawn plows⟩ — see PLOW 1
7 to fail to keep ⟨had *broken* his promise not to share their conversation with anyone⟩ — see VIOLATE 1
8 to find an answer for through reasoning ⟨Professor Bates *broke* the problem when she realized that it was possible to synthesize the necessary compounds⟩ — see SOLVE
9 to reduce the soundness, effectiveness, or perfection of ⟨I *broke* a tooth on the hard candy⟩ — see DAMAGE 1
10 to stop functioning ⟨after working for 30 years, the pump simply *broke* one day⟩ — see FAIL 1
11 to hasten away from something dangerous or frightening ⟨the herd of gazelles *broke* when they saw the lions racing toward them from the ridge above⟩ — see RUN 2
12 to use up all the physical energy of ⟨the trek up the mountain just about *broke* me⟩ — see EXHAUST 1
13 to become known ⟨as soon as the scandal *broke*, the CEO fled the country⟩ — see GET OUT 1
14 to cause to lose one's fortune and become unable to pay one's debts ⟨another bad investment could *break* him⟩ — see RUIN 1
15 to come into existence ⟨the crisis had passed, and a new day was *breaking*⟩ — see BEGIN 2
16 to depart abruptly from a straight line or course ⟨the running back *broke* to his left before running out of bounds⟩ — see SWERVE 1
17 to diminish the price or value of ⟨distressing economic news that will *break* many energy stocks⟩ — see DEPRECIATE 1
18 to go beyond the limit of ⟨a menu with prices that is likely to *break* the budgets of all but the wealthiest of diners⟩ — see EXCEED 1
19 to penetrate the surface (as of water) from below ⟨dolphins were *breaking* all around the boat⟩ — see BROACH 1

breakable *adj* easily broken ⟨elderly people's bones can be highly *breakable* if they haven't gotten enough calcium during their lifetimes⟩ — see FRAGILE 1

breakdown *n* **1** a mental or nervous collapse ⟨if you don't ease your workload, you're going to have a *breakdown*⟩
synonyms crack-up, nervous breakdown, tailspin
related words frazzle, freak-out, meltdown; alarm (*also* alarum), anxiety, apprehension, disquiet; excitability, nervousness; disturbance; agitation, discomposure, perturbation; basket case
near antonyms aplomb, calmness, composure, coolness, imperturbability, placidity, self-possession, sereneness, serenity, tranquillity (*or* tranquility), tranquilness
2 the process by which dead organic matter separates into simpler substances ⟨the *breakdown* of the body was arrested by the embalming process⟩ — see CORRUPTION 1
3 the separation and identification of the parts of a whole ⟨a demographic *breakdown* revealed that the ethnic composition of the area had changed significantly since the last census⟩ — see ANALYSIS 1

break down *vb* **1** to arrange or assign according to type ⟨when presented with the pile of files, the first thing he did was to *break* them *down* by month, order within the month, and region⟩ — see CLASSIFY 1
2 to go through decomposition ⟨the enamel of a human

tooth will begin to *break down* when exposed to sugar for too long⟩ — see DECAY 1
3 to identify and examine the basic elements or parts of (something) especially for discovering interrelationships ⟨if we *break* the problem *down* into what appear to be three aspects of it, we'll have a better chance of solving it⟩ — see ANALYZE
4 to stop functioning ⟨the computer finally *broke down* and had to be replaced⟩ — see FAIL 1
5 to yield to mental or emotional stress ⟨began to *break down* when he realized that he was on the verge of bankruptcy⟩ — see CRACK 2
6 to take apart ⟨the crew was *breaking down* the party tent when we arrived⟩ — see DISASSEMBLE 1
7 to cause to break with violence and much noise ⟨firefighters had to *break down* the wall to rescue the kitten⟩ — see SMASH 1

break in *vb* **1** to enter a house or building by force usually with illegal intent ⟨the burglars *broke in* by smashing a window⟩
synonyms burglarize, burgle
related words invade, trespass; hold up, loot, plunder, rip off, rob, stick up; ransack, rifle; despoil, devastate, maraud, pillage, ravage, sack
2 to cause a disruption in a conversation or discussion ⟨he rudely *broke in* to drop the names of several celebrities that he had met⟩ — see INTERRUPT

breaking point *n* a time or state of affairs requiring prompt or decisive action ⟨tensions between the two nations had risen to the *breaking point*⟩ — see EMERGENCY

breakneck *adj* moving, proceeding, or acting with great speed ⟨the *breakneck* production of naval vessels during World War II⟩ — see FAST 1

break off *vb* **1** to bring (as an action or operation) to an immediate end ⟨the judge *broke off* court proceedings until after lunch⟩ — see STOP 1
2 to come to an end ⟨talks between the two sides *broke off* when one began making unreasonable demands⟩ — see CEASE 1

break off (with) *vb* to end a usually intimate relationship with ⟨sincerely wants to *break off with* him without hurting his feelings⟩ — see DITCH 1

breakout *n* the act or an instance of getting free from danger or confinement ⟨the captives had been planning to stage a *breakout* at the next change in shift for the guards⟩ — see ESCAPE 1

break out *vb* to develop suddenly and violently ⟨in the wake of news reports of deaths from the flu, panic *broke out*, and there was a mad rush for flu shots⟩ — see ERUPT 2

break out (of) *vb* to get free from a dangerous or confining situation ⟨at last she decided to *break out of* her suffocating marriage⟩ — see ESCAPE 1

breakthrough *n* an instance of notable progress in the development of knowledge, technology, or skill ⟨Alexander Fleming's discovery of penicillin was one of medicine's great *breakthroughs*, for penicillin became the first antibiotic to successfully combat bacterial infections in humans⟩ — see ADVANCE 2

breakup *n* the act or process of a whole separating into two or more parts or pieces ⟨the *breakup* of the Soviet Union and the collapse of communism pretty much signaled the end of the Cold War⟩ — see SEPARATION 1

break up *vb* **1** to cease to exist or cause to cease to exist as a group or organization ⟨the band *broke up* when their arguments over money grew too stressful⟩ — see DISBAND 1
2 to come to an end ⟨the meeting *broke up* when all the business for the day had been completed⟩ — see CEASE 1
3 to set or force apart ⟨he *broke up* the rocks in the old stone wall with a crowbar, sending them tumbling to the ground⟩ — see SEPARATE 1
4 to yield to mental or emotional stress ⟨the sort of person who would be among the first to *break up* in a prisoner of war camp⟩ — see CRACK 2
5 to bring (as an action or operation) to an immediate end ⟨police arrived at the scene and immediately *broke up* the fracas⟩ — see STOP 1
6 to cause to separate into pieces usually suddenly or forcibly ⟨*break up* the feta cheese and spread it over the salad⟩ — see BREAK 1
7 to show mirth with an explosive vocal sound ⟨if you *break up* during the skit, the audience will know that you're in on the joke⟩ — see LAUGH 1

breast *n* the seat of one's deepest thoughts and emotions ⟨deep in his *breast*, he knew that his father had a great love for him that did not need to be expressed in words⟩ — see CORE 1

breast *vb* to oppose (something hostile or dangerous) with firmness or courage ⟨*breasted* the diagnosis of cancer with fortitude and optimism⟩ — see FACE 2

breast-feed *vb* to give milk to from the breast ⟨believes that all women should *breast-feed* their babies⟩ — see NURSE 2

breath *n* **1** a momentary halt in an activity ⟨let's all take a *breath* before continuing this discussion⟩ — see PAUSE 1
2 a slight or gentle movement of air ⟨a sweet *breath* caressed her cheek as she sat in the garden⟩ — see BREEZE 1
3 an almost imperceptible sign of something ⟨the mornings are already getting warmer, and there is a *breath* of spring in the air⟩ — see HINT 2

breathe *vb* **1** to inhale and exhale air ⟨sometimes it gets so hot in here that it's hard to even *breathe*⟩
synonyms respire
related words blow (out), draw, expire, inbreathe, inspire; gasp, huff, pant, puff, suspire, wheeze; sniff, snore, snort, snuff, snuffle, whiff; yawn
near antonyms asphyxiate, choke, gag, smother, suffocate; garrote (*or* garotte), stifle, strangle, throttle
2 to have life ⟨as long as I *breathe*, you will have a place to stay⟩ — see BE 1

breathe (out) *vb* to let or force out of the lungs ⟨leaned back in his chair and *breathed out* the smoke from his pipe⟩ — see EXHALE 1

breather *n* a momentary halt in an activity ⟨took a *breather* from the seemingly endless task of sorting through years of stuff stored in the attic⟩ — see PAUSE 1

breathing *adj* having or showing life ⟨realized that he didn't need a comic-book superhero, since he had a real, *breathing* hero in his father⟩ — see ALIVE 1

breathless *adj* **1** lacking fresh air ⟨the room was hot and *breathless*⟩ — see STUFFY 1
2 moving, proceeding, or acting with great speed ⟨ran at a *breathless* pace to get help⟩ — see FAST 1
3 no longer living ⟨carried the *breathless* body of his beloved dog back home⟩ — see DEAD 1

breathtaking *adj* causing great emotional or mental stimulation ⟨a truly *breathtaking* view of the majestic waterfall⟩ — see EXCITING 1

bred-in-the-bone *adj* **1** being such by habit and not likely to change ⟨a *bred-in-the-bone* Democrat who always votes a straight ticket⟩ — see HABITUAL 1
2 firmly established over time ⟨*bred-in-the-bone* honesty earned him the nickname of "Honest Abe"⟩ — see INVETERATE 1

breech *n* **1** the part of the body upon which someone sits ⟨plant yourselves on your *breeches* on that bench and listen to what I have to say⟩ — see BUTTOCKS
2 breeches *pl* an outer garment covering each leg sepa-

rately from waist to ankle ⟨the mounted riders look striking in their red coats and white *breeches*⟩ — see PANTS

breed *n* a number of persons or things that are grouped together because they have something in common ⟨some people say that honest politicians are a rare *breed*⟩ — see SORT 1

breed *vb* **1** to bring forth offspring ⟨rabbits will *breed* very frequently unless they're kept separated⟩ — see PROCREATE

2 to bring to maturity through care and education ⟨he was *bred* to a life in the military by his father, himself an army captain⟩ — see BRING UP 1

3 to be the cause of (a situation, action, or state of mind) ⟨this habit of favoring one employee over the others will *breed* resentment⟩ — see EFFECT

4 to engage in sexual intercourse ⟨cats *breeding* outside our window made a horrible racket last night⟩ — see COPULATE

5 to set permanently in the consciousness or mind-set ⟨parents who *breed* in their children a deep respect for people of all classes⟩ — see IMPLANT 1

breeding *n* the line of ancestors from whom a person is descended ⟨a family of good *breeding* that is well respected in the community⟩ — see ANCESTRY

breeding ground *n* a place or environment that favors the development of something ⟨unwashed skin is a *breeding ground* for bacteria⟩

synonyms hotbed, hothouse, nest, nidus, nursery, seedbed, seminary

related words crucible; base, capital, center, core, cynosure, eye, focus, heart, hub, mecca, nucleus, seat; focus, headquarters

breeze *n* **1** a slight or gentle movement of air ⟨a warm spring *breeze* ruffled our hair⟩

synonyms air, breath, puff, waft, zephyr

related words current, draft, whiff; sea breeze; blast, blow, flurry, gale, headwind, northeaster, norther, northwester, southeaster, southwester, tailwind, westerly, wind; squall, tempest, tornado, windstorm; airflow

near antonyms calm

2 something that is easy to do ⟨that assignment will be a *breeze*⟩ — see CINCH 1

breeze *vb* **1** to move or proceed smoothly and readily ⟨we *breezed* through the line for customs at the airport⟩ — see FLOW 2

2 to proceed or move quickly ⟨the doctor *breezed* past the people in the waiting room, apparently on his way to an emergency⟩ — see HURRY 2

breezy *adj* **1** having a relaxed, casual manner ⟨a *breezy* tour guide who remains completely unfazed no matter what the mishap⟩ — see EASYGOING 1

2 marked by strong wind or more wind than usual ⟨a *breezy* day usually finds the waters of the bay studded with sail⟩ — see [1]WINDY 1

3 open to the free circulation of air ⟨let's sit on the front porch; it's *breezier* there⟩ — see AIRY 2

breviary *n* a short statement of the main points ⟨a speech that could serve as a *breviary* for impeachment⟩ — see SUMMARY

brevity *n* **1** the condition of being short ⟨the best quality a graduation speech can have is *brevity*⟩

synonyms briefness, conciseness, shortness

related words abbreviation, abridgment (*or* abridgement), compression, condensation, contraction, curtailment; decreasing, diminishing, lessening, reducing, shortening, shrinking; abruptness, brusqueness, curtness; compendiousness, crispness, laconism, pithiness, succinctness, tautness, terseness; littleness, minuteness, smallness, tininess

near antonyms extensiveness; elongating, elongation, extending, extension, prolongation, prolonging, protraction, stretching; expansion, growth, spread; diffuseness, garrulousness, long-windedness, prolixity, talkativeness, talkiness, verboseness, volubility, wordiness; bigness, bulkiness, greatness, heftiness, largeness

antonyms lengthiness

2 the quality or state of being marked by or using only few words to convey much meaning ⟨if *brevity* is the soul of wit, then that speech wasn't at all witty⟩ — see SUCCINCTNESS

brew *vb* **1** to bring (something volatile or intense) into being ⟨they accused her of deliberately trying to *brew* dissension within the rank and file⟩ — see INCITE 1

2 to be about to happen ⟨there's trouble *brewing* in the department⟩ — see LOOM

bribable *adj* open to improper influence and especially bribery ⟨corruption in that country is so widespread that there are few public officials who are not *bribable*⟩ — see VENAL

bribe *n* something given or promised in order to improperly influence a person's conduct or decision ⟨that judge refused a huge *bribe* to dismiss the charges against the wealthy defendant⟩

synonyms backhander [*British*], boodle, cumshaw, fix, sop

related words baksheesh, kickback, payoff; slush fund; incentive, incitement, instigation, motivation, provocation, spur, stimulation, stimulus; boost, encouragement, goad, inducement; allurement, bait, enticement, lure, seduction, temptation, turn-on; flattery, persuasion; decoy, snare, trap

bribe *vb* to influence someone with a bribe ⟨meat inspectors were *bribed*, and the contaminated beef was sold to the public⟩

synonyms buy, corrupt, have, pay off, square

related words fix, tamper (with); abase, debase, debauch, defile, degrade, demean, deprave, dishonor, pervert, poison, profane, prostitute, subvert, taint, warp; allure, bait, beguile, entice, lead on, lure, seduce, tempt; motivate, provoke, spur, stimulate; goad, induce; flatter, persuade; snare, trap

phrases get at, grease the hand of (*or* grease the palm of), oil the hand of (*or* oil the palm of)

brick *n* an unintentional departure from truth or accuracy ⟨he dropped a *brick* that had his friends helpless with laughter⟩ — see ERROR 1

brickbat *n* an act or expression showing scorn and usually intended to hurt another's feelings ⟨the *brickbats* were flying the night that those two bitchy divas were seated at the same table⟩ — see INSULT

brickle *adj, dialect* having a texture that readily breaks into little pieces under pressure ⟨that stuff's so *brickle* that it breaks into pieces as soon as you touch it⟩ — see CRISP 1

bridal *n* a ceremony in which two people are united in matrimony ⟨an old-fashioned country *bridal*⟩ — see WEDDING

bridewell *n* a place of confinement for persons held in lawful custody ⟨the citadel was later converted into a *bridewell* to house the city's growing criminal population⟩ — see JAIL

bridgehead *n* a place from which an advance (as for military operations) is made ⟨established a *bridgehead* on the beach before beginning the land invasion⟩ — see BASE 2

bridle *vb* to keep from exceeding a desirable degree or level (as of expression) ⟨try to *bridle* your criticism next time so that it is helpful and not hurtful⟩ — see CONTROL 1

brief *adj* **1** marked by the use of few words to convey much information or meaning ⟨a *brief* but crucial admonition to keep quiet⟩ — see CONCISE

2 not lasting for a considerable time ⟨fortunately, the

meeting was *brief*⟩ — see SHORT 2
3 lasting only for a short time ⟨a *brief* flash of light⟩ — see MOMENTARY

brief *n* **1** a short statement of the main points ⟨a one-page *brief* of the intelligence report⟩ — see SUMMARY
2 a specific task with which a person or group is charged ⟨the soldiers' *brief* was to secure the village from enemy attacks⟩ — see MISSION

brief *vb* **1** to give information to ⟨the lieutenant *briefed* his superior officers on the state of the enemy's fortifications⟩ — see ENLIGHTEN 1
2 to make into a short statement of the main points (as of a report) ⟨his duties include *briefing* intelligence reports for the president⟩ — see SUMMARIZE

briefly *adv* in a few words ⟨tell us *briefly* why you chose this position⟩ — see SHORTLY 1

briefness *n* **1** the condition of being short ⟨the *briefness* of the instructions rendered them less than helpful⟩ — see BREVITY 1
2 the quality or state of being marked by or using only few words to convey much meaning ⟨in this case the *briefness* of the essay is not a drawback because it says all that needs to be said and does so with eloquence⟩ — see SUCCINCTNESS

brig *n* a place of confinement for persons held in lawful custody ⟨the captain ordered that the prisoner be thrown into the *brig* immediately⟩ — see JAIL

brigade *n* a group of people working together on a task ⟨a clean-up *brigade* put the parish hall back in good order⟩ — see GANG 1

bright *adj* **1** giving off or reflecting much light ⟨in the desert the sun was so *bright* that it hurt my eyes⟩ ⟨the moon is *bright* tonight⟩
synonyms beaming, bedazzling, brilliant, candescent, clear, dazzling, effulgent, fulgent, glowing, incandescent, lambent, lucent, lucid, luminous, lustrous, radiant, refulgent, sheeny, shining, shiny, splendid
related words ablaze, ardent, blazing, burning, combusting, fiery, flaming, red-hot; agleam, aglitter, blinding, coruscant, flaring, flashing, flickering, gemmy, glancing, glaring, gleaming, glimmering, glinting, glistening, glistering, glittering, scintillant, scintillating, shimmering, shimmery, sparkling, sunny, twinkling, winking; burnished, polished, shined; superbright, ultrabright
near antonyms blackened, dark, darkened, darkish, darkling, darksome, dimmed, dusky, gloomy, lightless, murky, obscure, obscured, pitch-black, pitch-dark, somber (*or* sombre), sunless, tenebrous, unlit; cloudy, shadowlike, shadowy, shady; gray (*also* grey), leaden, pale, palish
antonyms dim, dull, lackluster, unbright, unbrilliant
2 filled with much light ⟨the display windows of department stores are especially *bright* at Christmastime⟩
synonyms ablaze, alight, brightened, illuminated, illumined, light, lightsome, lit (*or* lighted)
related words floodlit (*also* floodlighted), highlighted, spotlighted (*or* spotlit); ignited, kindled; moonlit, shiny, sunlit, sunny, sunshiny
near antonyms gloomy, somber (*or* sombre), sunless; cloudy, murky, obscured, shadowlike, shadowy; gray (*also* grey), leaden, pale; lightproof
antonyms blackened, dark, darkened, darkish, darkling, dimmed, dusk, dusky, lightless, pitch-black, pitch-dark, tenebrous, unlit
3 having or showing a good mood or disposition ⟨always walks into work with a *bright* smile on his face⟩ — see CHEERFUL 1
4 having or showing quickness of mind ⟨a company that is always looking for *bright*, ambitious college graduates⟩ — see INTELLIGENT 1
5 having qualities which inspire hope ⟨predicted a *bright* future for the young math whiz⟩ — see HOPEFUL 1
6 pointing toward a happy outcome ⟨all the signs are *bright* right now for an economic boom⟩ — see FAVORABLE 2
7 serving to lift one's spirits ⟨a *bright* and beautiful morning to begin planting our garden⟩ — see CHEERFUL 2
8 standing above others in rank, importance, or achievement ⟨a *bright* new star on the operatic scene⟩ — see EMINENT
9 having or being an outward sign of good feelings (as of love, confidence, or happiness) ⟨a room full of summer interns with *bright*, eager faces⟩ — see RADIANT 1
10 not stormy or cloudy ⟨we'll have a picnic on the next *bright* day⟩ — see FAIR 1

bright *adv* in a manner marked by the shining or reflecting of much light ⟨the storm passed, and once again the sun shone *bright*⟩ — see BRIGHTLY 1

brighten *vb* to become glad or hopeful ⟨the glum soccer player started to *brighten* upon being told that his injury would not jeopardize his career⟩ — see CHEER (UP) 1

brightened *adj* filled with much light ⟨the *brightened* room is now a much more cheerful place for the recuperating patients⟩ — see BRIGHT 2

bright–line *adj* not subject to misinterpretation or more than one interpretation ⟨there is no *bright-line* rule governing the issue⟩ — see CLEAR 2

brightly *adv* **1** in a manner marked by the shining or reflecting of much light ⟨the light glowed *brightly*⟩
synonyms bright, brilliantly, dazzlingly, fulgently, glowingly, incandescently, lambently, luminously, lustrously, radiantly, splendidly
related words blazingly, burningly, flamingly; blindingly, flaringly, flickeringly, glaringly, glitteringly, opalescently; pellucidly
near antonyms darkly, duskily, gloomily, murkily, obscurely, somberly; cloudily, shadily, shadowily
antonyms dimly, dully
2 in a cheerful or happy manner ⟨"And how are we today?" the nurse asked *brightly*⟩ — see GAILY 1
3 in a manner that is colorful and tends to arouse gaiety ⟨parade marchers carrying *brightly* painted banners⟩ — see GAILY 3

brightness *n* the quality or state of having or giving off light ⟨the *brightness* of the sunshine made me squint after an afternoon spent in a darkened movie theater⟩ — see BRILLIANCE 1

brilliance *n* **1** the quality or state of having or giving off light ⟨the *brilliance* of the flash from the camera was so intense that I was blinded for a moment afterwards⟩
synonyms brightness, brilliancy, candor, dazzle, effulgence, illumination, lambency, lightness, luminance, luminosity, luminousness, luster (*or* lustre), lustrousness, radiance, refulgence, splendor
related words blaze, flare, flash, flicker, light; fluorescence, incandescence, luminescence; burnish, gloss, polish, sheen, shine, shininess; fire, flame, glare, glow; flash, gleam, glimmer, glint, glisten, glitter, scintillation, shimmer, sparkle, twinkle
near antonyms dimness, gloominess, somberness; cloudiness, haziness, murkiness, obscureness, obscurity; colorlessness, grayness, lackluster, paleness, shadiness, shadowiness
antonyms blackness, dark, darkness, dullness (*also* dulness), duskiness
2 impressiveness of beauty on a large scale ⟨the *brilliance* of the palace is really quite staggering⟩ — see MAGNIFICENCE

brilliancy *n* the quality or state of having or giving off light ⟨the *brilliancy* of the diamond is shown to good effect by the museum's lighting⟩ — see BRILLIANCE 1

brilliant *adj* **1** giving off or reflecting much light ⟨a *brilliant* chandelier graces the hotel lobby⟩ — see BRIGHT 1
2 having or showing quickness of mind ⟨a *brilliant* boy who left for college at the age of 16⟩ — see INTELLIGENT 1
3 likely to attract attention ⟨a *brilliant* example of government waste⟩ — see NOTICEABLE

brilliant *n* a usually valuable stone cut and polished for ornament ⟨the diamond cutter set out an array of *brilliants* to show the various ways the diamond could be cut⟩ — see GEM 1

brilliantly *adv* **1** in a manner marked by the shining or reflecting of much light ⟨the diamond necklace sparkled *brilliantly*⟩ — see BRIGHTLY 1
2 in a manner that is colorful and tends to arouse gaiety ⟨a chorus of *brilliantly* costumed Las Vegas showgirls⟩ — see GAILY 3

brim *n* **1** the line or relatively narrow space that marks the outer limit of something ⟨the *brim* of the teacup was banded with gold⟩ — see BORDER 1
2 the projecting front part of a hat or cap ⟨touched the *brim* of his cap by way of salute⟩ — see VISOR

brim *vb* **1** to be copiously supplied ⟨a secondhand bookstore that was *brimming* with bargains⟩ — see ABOUND
2 to put into (something) as much as can be held or contained ⟨he *brimmed* the glass with milk, and now I'm sure to spill it⟩ — see FILL 1

brimful *adj* containing or seeming to contain the greatest quantity or number possible ⟨a book *brimful* of stories about people who overcome childhood adversities to achieve great things⟩ — see FULL 1

brimming *adj* containing or seeming to contain the greatest quantity or number possible ⟨bins *brimming* with coffee beans from a wide array of tropical localities⟩ — see FULL 1

brine *n* the whole body of salt water that covers nearly three-fourths of the earth ⟨for hundreds of years people from Atlantic Canada have made their living from the *brine*⟩ — see OCEAN 1

bring *vb* **1** to be the cause of (a situation, action, or state of mind) ⟨in the end, the lawsuit *brought* distress to everyone, including the plaintiff⟩ — see EFFECT
2 to cause (someone) to agree with a belief or course of action by using arguments or earnest request ⟨nothing will ever *bring* her to admit she's wrong⟩ — see PERSUADE
3 to have a price of ⟨the antique will probably *bring* at least $1000 at auction⟩ — see COST

bring about *vb* to be the cause of (a situation, action, or state of mind) ⟨I promise: making one mistake will not *bring about* the apocalypse⟩ — see EFFECT

bring around *vb* to cause (someone) to agree with a belief or course of action by using arguments or earnest request ⟨an airtight argument is the only thing that will ever *bring* him *around*⟩ — see PERSUADE

bringdown *n* something that disappoints ⟨meeting one's literary hero is usually a bad idea—almost inevitably it's a *bringdown*⟩ — see DISAPPOINTMENT 2

bring in *vb* to receive as return for effort ⟨she's *bringing in* good money selling houses⟩ — see EARN 1

bring off *vb* **1** to carry through (as a process) to completion ⟨the cast and crew were able to *bring off* an eccentric but engaging reinterpretation of *King Lear*⟩ — see PERFORM 1
2 to remove from danger or harm ⟨had it been alerted in time, a nearby ship might have been able to *bring off* all of the passengers from the Titanic⟩ — see SAVE 2

bring on *vb* to be the cause of (a situation, action, or state of mind) ⟨this legislation will surely *bring on* some unintended consequences⟩ — see EFFECT

bring out *vb* **1** to express (a thought or emotion) in words ⟨he ever so casually *brings out* the names of celebrities with whom he's supposedly buddy-buddy⟩ — see SAY 1
2 to make more apparent ⟨a blue scarf would *bring out* the color of your eyes⟩ — see EMPHASIZE 2

bring up *vb* **1** to bring to maturity through care and education ⟨it takes an immense commitment and a lot of love to *bring up* a child properly⟩
synonyms breed, foster, nourish, nurse, raise, rear
related words father, mother; attend, care (for), cradle, cultivate, mind, minister (to), nurture, watch; discipline, educate, instruct, mentor, school, teach, train, tutor; edify, enlighten, indoctrinate; feed, provide (for), supply; advance, forward, further, promote; prepare; direct, guide, lead, shepherd, show
near antonyms abuse, ill-treat, ill-use, maltreat, mishandle, mistreat; ignore, neglect; harm, hurt, injure
2 to present or bring forward for discussion ⟨I hate to *bring* this *up*, but we're running short of money⟩ — see INTRODUCE 2
3 to bring (something) to a standstill ⟨wasn't expecting the operator to *bring up* the carnival ride so suddenly⟩ — see [1]HALT 1

brininess *n* the quality or state of being salty ⟨the *brininess* of the soup rendered it inedible⟩ — see SALTINESS

brink *n* an interval of time just before the onset of something ⟨was at the *brink* of death when the rescuers arrived⟩ — see POINT 3

briny *adj* of, relating to, or containing salt ⟨a *briny* liquid that is often used to make pickles⟩ — see SALTY 1

brio *n* active strength of body or mind ⟨impressed the interviewers with his poise and *brio*⟩ — see VIGOR 1

brisk *adj* **1** having much high-spirited energy and movement ⟨a *brisk* exercise that many athletes use to warm up⟩ — see LIVELY 1
2 moving, proceeding, or acting with great speed ⟨moved at a *brisk* walk through the exhibit⟩ — see FAST 1
3 marked by much life, movement, or activity ⟨*brisk* trading on the stock market⟩ — see ALIVE 2

briskly *adv* with great speed ⟨strode off *briskly* to deal with the problem⟩ — see FAST 1

briskness *n* the quality or state of having abundant or intense activity ⟨the *briskness* of the shopping scene at the mall makes it a good candidate for our next store⟩ — see VITALITY 1

bristle *n* a thin, flexible structure that resembles a hair ⟨a hairbrush with plastic *bristles*⟩ — see HAIR 2

bristle *vb* **1** to be copiously supplied ⟨a recent college grad thrilled to be starting a new life in a city *bristling* with possibilities⟩ — see ABOUND
2 to express one's anger usually violently ⟨the man *bristled* at the accusation, and threatened to file a lawsuit⟩ — see RAGE 1

bristly *adj* covered with or as if with hair ⟨although pigs look hairless, they're actually *bristly* creatures⟩ — see HAIRY 1

britches *n pl* an outer garment covering each leg separately from waist to ankle ⟨a traditional riding outfit consisting of red jacket, tan *britches*, and black boots⟩ — see PANTS

brittle *adj* **1** having a texture that readily breaks into little pieces under pressure ⟨a *brittle* cracker that turned into crumbs in my pocket⟩ — see CRISP 1
2 lacking in friendliness or warmth of feeling ⟨a *brittle* apology that was anything but heartfelt⟩ — see COLD 2

broach *vb* **1** to penetrate the surface (as of water) from below ⟨the immense whales *broaching* was a magnificent sight⟩
synonyms break, surface
related words emerge, rise
near antonyms dive, drop, drown, founder, plunge, sink, submerge, submerse

2 to present or bring forward for discussion ⟨*broached* the topic of plans for next year's parade⟩ — see INTRODUCE 2

broad *adj* **1** having a greater than usual measure across ⟨an unusually *broad* expanse of water in the island-dotted lake⟩ — see WIDE 1
2 having considerable extent ⟨her *broad* knowledge of American politics makes her a much-sought-after guest on talk shows⟩ — see EXTENSIVE
3 not subject to misinterpretation or more than one interpretation ⟨gave them a *broad* hint that it was time to leave⟩ — see CLEAR 2
4 relating to the main elements and not to specific details ⟨a *broad* overview of the topic⟩ — see GENERAL 2

broad-brush *adj* belonging or relating to the whole ⟨an unfair, *broad-brush* accusation of corruption in the statehouse⟩ — see GENERAL 1

broadcast *vb* **1** to cause to be known over a considerable area or by many people ⟨*broadcast* the information only to people who needed to know⟩ — see SPREAD 1
2 to make known openly or publicly ⟨please don't *broadcast* this news, as it's not being publicly announced yet⟩ — see ANNOUNCE

broad-gauge *or* **broad-gauged** *adj* covering everything or all important points ⟨a *broad-gauge* book about roses that covers just about everything you could want to know about roses⟩ — see ENCYCLOPEDIC

broadly *adv* to a large extent or degree ⟨the new policy is *broadly* applicable⟩ — see GREATLY 2

broad-minded *adj* **1** not bound by traditional ways or beliefs ⟨a *broad-minded* philosophy of parenting⟩ — see LIBERAL 1
2 willing to consider new or different ideas ⟨we have to be *broad-minded* on this issue, since traditional solutions no longer work⟩ — see OPEN-MINDED 1

broadside *adv* with one side faced forward ⟨one car hit the other *broadside* and crushed the passenger door⟩ — see SIDEWAYS 1

Brobdingnagian *adj* unusually large ⟨a *Brobdingnagian* billboard stood at the entrance to the theme park⟩ — see HUGE

brochure *n* a short printed publication with no cover or with a paper cover ⟨handed out *brochures* giving practical hints about environment-friendly practices that every family can adopt⟩ — see PAMPHLET

broil *n* a rough and often noisy fight usually involving several people ⟨a noisy *broil* broke out at the bar⟩ — see BRAWL 1

broil *vb* to place in conflict or difficulties ⟨instead of *broiling* themselves in internal strife, they should band together against the common enemy⟩ — see EMBROIL

broiling *adj* having a notably high temperature ⟨the office was *broiling* because the air conditioning was on the blink⟩ — see HOT 1

broke *adj* lacking money or material possessions ⟨too *broke* to afford even a used car⟩ — see POOR 1

broken *adj* **1** forcibly separated into many pieces ⟨a *broken* vase that could not be repaired⟩
synonyms busted, fractured, fragmented, shattered, smashed
related words blasted, detonated, exploded; cracked, slivered, splintered, split; collapsed, imploded; demolished, destroyed, devastated, pulverized, ruinate, ruined, wrecked; damaged, defaced, disintegrated, dynamited, mangled, mutilated; eradicated, exterminated, extirpated, obliterated, wiped out; breakable, brittle, delicate, fragile, frail, frangible
near antonyms fixed, healed, mended, patched, rebuilt, reconstructed, repaired; infrangible, unbreakable
antonyms unbroken
2 having an uneven edge or outline ⟨the *broken* rim of the antique vase greatly reduces its value⟩ — see RAGGED 1
3 not having a level or smooth surface ⟨that portion of the hiking trail consists of a long, *broken* mountain ridge⟩ — see UNEVEN 1

brokenhearted *adj* feeling unhappiness ⟨she was *brokenhearted* when the relationship ended⟩ — see SAD 1

broker *n* **1** one who works with opposing sides in order to bring about an agreement ⟨the *broker* in the hostage situation was a prominent reporter that the gunman felt he could trust⟩ — see MEDIATOR
2 the person in a business deal who hands over an item in exchange for money ⟨all of the local yacht *brokers* were at the boat show⟩ — see VENDOR

bromide *n* an idea or expression that has been used by many people ⟨a newspaper editorial offering the time-worn *bromide* that people should settle their differences peacefully⟩ — see COMMONPLACE

Bronx cheer *n* a vocal sound made to express scorn or disapproval ⟨a baseball legend who seems never to have forgotten the *Bronx cheer* he once received from the hometown ingrates⟩ — see CATCALL

brood *vb* to cover and warm eggs as the young inside develop ⟨don't disturb the hen while she's *brooding*⟩ — see SET 1

broody *adj* given to or marked by long, quiet thinking ⟨he spent a long, *broody* weekend trying to figure out where his relationship with his girlfriend was headed⟩ — see CONTEMPLATIVE

brook *n* a natural body of running water smaller than a river ⟨there are tiny fish and frogs in that *brook*⟩ — see CREEK 1

brook *vb* to put up with (something painful or difficult) ⟨I will not *brook* insults from my own employees⟩ — see BEAR 2

brooklet *n* a natural body of running water smaller than a river ⟨a little *brooklet* trickled past the house⟩ — see CREEK 1

brothel *n* a building in which prostitutes are available ⟨the district is infamous for its *brothels* and drug dealers⟩ — see BORDELLO

brotherhood *n* **1** a group of persons formally joined together for some common interest ⟨they're a *brotherhood* of retired war veterans⟩ — see ASSOCIATION 2
2 the body of people in a profession or field of activity ⟨a family that has been part of the *brotherhood* of police officers for four generations⟩ — see CORPS
3 the feeling of closeness and friendship that exists between companions ⟨the *brotherhood* that existed between the medical missionaries and the villagers they served⟩ — see COMPANIONSHIP
4 kindly concern, interest, or support ⟨in a display of *brotherhood*, other writers rushed to the defense of the jailed journalist⟩ — see GOODWILL 1

brotherly *adj* of, relating to, or befitting brothers ⟨the *brotherly* love that exists between the members of the scout troop⟩ — see FRATERNAL

browbeat *vb* to make timid or fearful by or as if by threats ⟨they would often *browbeat* the younger child until he cried⟩ — see INTIMIDATE

brownie *n* an imaginary being usually having a small human form and magical powers ⟨some people believe that *brownies* will clean your house if you leave them milk⟩ — see FAIRY

brownnoser *n* a person who flatters another in order to get ahead ⟨surrounded himself with brainless *brownnosers*, so no wonder the company went down the tubes⟩ — see SYCOPHANT

browse *vb* **1** to feed on grass or herbs ⟨cows *browsing* in fields are a common sight along that stretch of the road⟩ — see [1]GRAZE
2 to take a quick or hasty look ⟨*browsed* through the

stacks looking for interesting books⟩ — see GLANCE 2

bruise *n* **1** a bodily injury in which small blood vessels are broken but the overlying skin is not ⟨she got quite a big *bruise* from walking into the corner of the table⟩ — see CONTUSION
2 an area of skin roughened or worn away by harsh rubbing against another surface ⟨*bruises* caused by ill-fitting hiking boots⟩ — see ABRASION

bruit *n, archaic* loud, confused, and usually inharmonious sound ⟨a film that captures the thunderous fury of medieval warfare and the *bruit* of a thousand clashing swords⟩ — see NOISE 1

bruit (about) *vb* to make (as a piece of information) the subject of common talk without any authority or confirmation of accuracy ⟨please don't *bruit* accusations *about* without confirming them first⟩ — see RUMOR

brume *n* an atmospheric condition in which suspended particles in the air rob it of its transparency ⟨cloaked in the early-morning *brume*, the village did indeed look like some long-lost Brigadoon⟩ — see HAZE 1

brumous *adj* filled with or dimmed by fine particles (as of dust or water) in suspension ⟨the village was slumbering peacefully beneath the *brumous* morning sky⟩ — see HAZY 1

brunet *or* **brunette** *adj* not having a light complexion ⟨a *brunette* woman who favored dark red lipstick⟩ — see DARK 2

brunt *n* the main or greater part of something as distinguished from its subordinate parts ⟨the *brunt* of the responsibility fell on her shoulders⟩ — see BODY 1

brush *n* a brief clash between enemies or rivals ⟨the two advance parties had a *brush*, but no one was wounded⟩ — see ENCOUNTER

[1]**brush** *vb* to move or proceed smoothly and readily ⟨a pop star *brushing* past a crowd of autograph seekers⟩ — see FLOW 2

[2]**brush** *vb* to pass lightly across or touch gently especially in passing ⟨spiderwebs *brushed* her cheek as she walked through the basement⟩
synonyms graze, kiss, nudge, shave, skim
related words bump, contact, scrape, sideswipe, strike, sweep, swipe, touch; bounce, carom, glance, rebound, ricochet, skip; caress, cuddle, fondle, love, pat, pet, stroke; miss, skirt
near antonyms bang, bash, bump, clash, collide, crash, hit, impact, impinge, knock, punch, ram, slam, slap, smack, smash, swipe, thud, thwack, whack

brush (aside *or* **off)** *vb* to dismiss as of little importance ⟨*brushed off* their complaints as the whining of people who were never satisfied⟩ — see EXCUSE 1

brush–off *n* treatment that is deliberately unfriendly ⟨the mayor tends to give anyone under voting age the *brush-off*⟩ — see COLD SHOULDER

brushwood *n* a thick patch of shrubbery, small trees, or underbrush ⟨cleared away the *brushwood* in order to build a shed⟩ — see THICKET

brushy *adj* covered with or as if with hair ⟨the vogue for *brushy* cheeks on men reached a whimsical apex in the 19th century when muttonchop whiskers came in fashion⟩ — see HAIRY 1

brusque *also* **brusk** *adj* being or characterized by direct, brief, and potentially rude speech or manner ⟨a *brusque* and unhelpful reply from the clerk in the hardware store⟩ — see BLUNT 1

brutal *adj* **1** difficult to endure ⟨*brutal* hard labor in the hot sun⟩ — see HARSH 1
2 having or showing the desire to inflict severe pain and suffering on others ⟨a *brutal* child who liked to torture animals⟩ — see CRUEL 1
3 having or showing the nature and appetites of a lower animal ⟨a coarse, *brutal* man who has no sense of what it means to be refined or sensitive or cultured⟩ — see BESTIAL

brutality *n* **1** disposition to willfully inflict pain and suffering on others ⟨the police were accused of *brutality* for using excessive force in making arrests⟩ — see CRUELTY
2 the manifestation of the traits or the gratification of the appetites of a lower animal ⟨the disconcerting ease with which the people adopted the *brutality* of the enemy invaders⟩ — see BESTIALITY

brutalize *vb* **1** to make (someone) feel or behave more like an animal than a human being ⟨three years in a prison camp so *brutalized* him that he couldn't remember how to eat with a fork⟩
synonyms animalize, bestialize, dehumanize
related words abase, corrupt, debauch, degrade, demean, deprave, pervert, poison, profane, prostitute, subvert, warp; contaminate, pollute, taint; disgrace, humble, humiliate
near antonyms dignify, exalt, honor; amend, improve; cleanse, purify, restore; respect; elevate, ennoble, uplift
2 to inflict physical or emotional harm upon ⟨Red Cross workers reported that prisoners had been *brutalized* in truly shocking ways⟩ — see ABUSE 1

brutally *adv* in a manner so as to cause loss or suffering ⟨the prisoners were treated *brutally* at the hands of the sadistic guards⟩ — see HARDLY 1

brute *adj* **1** having or showing the desire to inflict severe pain and suffering on others ⟨the *brute* attacks on innocent civilians had taken the war to a whole new level⟩ — see CRUEL 1
2 having or showing the nature and appetites of a lower animal ⟨a man of *brute* instinct, he deals with conflict the only way he knows how—by physical force⟩ — see BESTIAL

brute *n* **1** one of the lower animals as distinguished from human beings ⟨it is a fundamental sense of right and wrong that separates us from the *brutes*⟩ — see ANIMAL
2 a mean, evil, or unprincipled person ⟨only a *brute* would deliberately break someone's arm⟩ — see VILLAIN

brutish *adj* having or showing the nature and appetites of a lower animal ⟨as the months of recurrent combat dragged on, the daily existence of the soldiers became increasingly *brutish*⟩ — see BESTIAL

brutishness *n* the manifestation of the traits or the gratification of the appetites of a lower animal ⟨approached sex with the same *brutishness* that he manifested in every other aspect of his life⟩ — see BESTIALITY

bubble *vb* to flow in a broken irregular stream ⟨the soapy water *bubbled* down the drain⟩ — see GURGLE

bubblehead *n* a stupid person ⟨a murder mystery so obvious that even *bubbleheads* need not tax their brains⟩ — see IDIOT

bubbleheaded *adj* **1** not having or showing an ability to absorb ideas readily ⟨she's regarded as the brains behind her popular but *bubbleheaded* husband⟩ — see STUPID 1
2 showing or marked by a lack of good sense or judgment ⟨a coworker who should keep her *bubbleheaded* opinions on current events to herself⟩ — see FOOLISH 1

bubbly *adj* joyously unrestrained ⟨offered their *bubbly* congratulations to the expectant parents⟩ — see EXUBERANT

bubkes *also* **bupkes** *or* **bupkus** *n pl* the smallest amount or part imaginable ⟨she always eats out and proudly admits that she doesn't know *bubkes* about cooking⟩ — see JOT

buccaneer *n* someone who engages in robbery of ships at sea ⟨*buccaneers* who preyed upon treasure-laden ships in the Caribbean⟩ — see PIRATE

buck *n* **1** a man extremely interested in his clothing and personal appearance ⟨a vain *buck* who spends an hour before the bathroom mirror every morning⟩ — see DANDY 1
2 an adult male human being ⟨found some strong young *bucks* to help move her furniture⟩ — see MAN 1
3 a U.S. currency bill representing 100 cents ⟨dropped a *buck* in the collection basket⟩ — see DOLLAR
4 bucks *pl* something (as pieces of stamped metal or printed paper) customarily and legally used as a medium of exchange, a measure of value, or a means of payment ⟨hoping to win some major *bucks* at the slot machines⟩ — see MONEY 1

buck *vb* **1** to move or cause to move with a sharp quick motion ⟨the car *bucked* and stalled⟩ — see JERK 1
2 to refuse to give in to ⟨*bucked* the trend to outdo everyone else and just wore the same clothes they had in previous years⟩ — see RESIST
3 to shift possession of (something) from one person to another ⟨*buck* each box to the next person in line, and the last person will stack them in the storeroom⟩ — see PASS 1

buckaroo *also* **buckeroo** *n* a hired hand who tends cattle or horses at a ranch or on the range ⟨a rip-roaring *buckaroo* of the Old West⟩ — see COWBOY

bucket *n* **1** a considerable amount ⟨made *buckets* of money in the stock market⟩ — see LOT 2
2 a round container that is open at the top and outfitted with a handle ⟨carried water from the well in a *bucket*⟩ — see PAIL

bucket *vb* **1** to lift out with something that holds liquid ⟨*bucketing* water from the well, we raced to put out the fire⟩ — see DIP 2
2 to make a series of small irregular or violent movements ⟨getting the troops into the *bucketing* landing craft proved to be challenging⟩ — see SHAKE 1

buckle *vb* **1** to fall down or in as a result of physical pressure ⟨the flimsy bridge *buckled* under the weight of the caravan of trucks⟩ — see COLLAPSE 1
2 to occupy (oneself) diligently or with close attention ⟨*buckled* himself down and finished the assignment in record time⟩ — see APPLY 2

buckler *n* means or method of defending ⟨a strong and free press is our best *buckler* against tyranny⟩ — see DEFENSE 1

buck up *vb* **1** to become glad or hopeful ⟨*buck up*, kids, it's not so bad as you're making it out to be⟩ — see CHEER (UP) 1
2 to fill with courage or strength of purpose ⟨a surprise presidential visit to *buck up* the troops⟩ — see ENCOURAGE 1

bucolic *adj* of, relating to, associated with, or typical of open areas with few buildings or people ⟨a *bucolic* region where farms are still common⟩ — see RURAL

bud *n* a young person who is between infancy and adulthood ⟨that sitcom star is still a *bud*, so all he needs right now are looks and personality⟩ — see CHILD 1

budding *adj* beginning to come into existence ⟨the *budding* romance between the coworkers was the talk of the office⟩ — see NASCENT

buddy *n* a person who has a strong liking for and trust in another ⟨my old college *buddy* is the one person I can always turn to⟩ — see FRIEND 1

buddy–buddy *adj* **1** closely acquainted ⟨those two army officers have been *buddy-buddy* for years⟩ — see FAMILIAR 1
2 having or showing kindly feeling and sincere interest ⟨he's even *buddy-buddy* to people he's only just met⟩ — see FRIENDLY 1

budge *vb* **1** to cease resistance (as to another's arguments, demands, or control) ⟨despite hours of intense pressure, she refused to *budge* from her position⟩ — see YIELD 3
2 to change one's position ⟨he finally *budged* from his beach blanket when the tide started swirling up around him⟩ — see MOVE 3
3 to change the place or position of ⟨the bureau was so heavy that two people couldn't *budge* it⟩ — see MOVE 1

budget *adj* costing little ⟨a *budget* phone plan for people on fixed incomes⟩ — see CHEAP 1

budget *n* **1** a sum of money set aside for a particular purpose ⟨we've spent a little more than our *budget* this year⟩ — see FUND 1
2 the number of individuals or amount of something available at any given time ⟨the tour group had a whole *budget* of complaints⟩ — see SUPPLY

budget *vb* to work out the details of (something) in advance ⟨the vacationers carefully *budgeted* how they would spend their limited time in Italy⟩ — see PLAN 1

buff *n* **1** a person with a strong and habitual liking for something ⟨he's such a film *buff* that he owns over 3,000 movies⟩ — see FAN
2 the state of having no clothes on one's body ⟨protected by a fully enclosed backyard, the couple would frequently sunbathe in the *buff*⟩ — see NUDITY

buff *vb* **1** to make smooth by friction ⟨she learned to *buff* semiprecious stones in order to make her own jewelry⟩ — see GRIND 1
2 to make smooth or glossy usually by repeatedly applying surface pressure ⟨the janitor *buffed* the lobby floor until it shone⟩ — see POLISH 1

buffalo *vb* **1** to cause to believe what is untrue ⟨I'm not some newcomer that you can *buffalo* with that nonsense⟩ — see DECEIVE
2 to throw into a state of mental uncertainty ⟨in this debate I refuse to be *buffaloed* by a flurry of irrelevant issues⟩ — see CONFUSE 1

buffed *adj* having a shiny surface or finish ⟨a beautiful, *buffed* antique table⟩ — see GLOSSY

buffer *n* **1** one who works with opposing sides in order to bring about an agreement ⟨it took a friend serving as a *buffer* between the feuding siblings to get them to speak to one another again⟩ — see MEDIATOR
2 something that serves as a protective barrier ⟨the excelsior acts as an additional *buffer* for the marble bust during shipping⟩ — see CUSHION

buffer *vb* to lessen the shock of ⟨during my walk an umbrella and thick coat *buffered* the freezing rain⟩ — see CUSHION

[1]**buffet** *n* a hard strike with a part of the body or an instrument ⟨delivered a powerful *buffet* to the side of the prisoner's head⟩ — see [1]BLOW

[2]**buffet** *n* a storage case typically having doors and shelves ⟨a *buffet* completed the kitchen set⟩ — see CABINET

buffet *vb* to strike repeatedly ⟨fierce winds *buffeted* the small sailboat⟩ — see BEAT 1

buffo *n* a comically dressed performer (as at a circus) who entertains with playful tricks and ridiculous behavior ⟨in the comic opera, the *buffo* shared his entrance aria with a grimacing mime⟩ — see CLOWN 1

buffoon *n* a comically dressed performer (as at a circus) who entertains with playful tricks and ridiculous behavior ⟨the children at the birthday party giggled at the *buffoon's* silly tricks⟩ — see CLOWN 1

buffoonery *n* wildly playful or mischievous behavior ⟨their madcap *buffoonery* turned the duo into the nation's hottest comedy act⟩ — see HORSEPLAY

bug *n* **1** a person with a strong and habitual liking for something ⟨a camera *bug* who loves taking candid shots at fairs and festivals⟩ — see FAN
2 an abnormal state that disrupts a plant's or animal's normal bodily functioning ⟨I can't go to work today be-

cause I've caught some *bug* that's going around⟩ — see DISEASE
3 a person judged to be legally or medically insane ⟨a *bug* with a fascination for tormenting small animals and setting fires⟩ — see LUNATIC 1
bug *vb* **1** to disturb the peace of mind of (someone) especially by repeated disagreeable acts ⟨these incessant phone calls are really starting to *bug* me⟩ — see IRRITATE 1
2 to thrust oneself upon (another) without invitation ⟨I hate to *bug* you, but could you help me move this table?⟩ — see BOTHER 1
bugaboo *n* something or someone that causes fear or dread especially without reason ⟨doing one's tax returns are a real *bugaboo* for some people⟩ — see BOGEY 1
bugbear *n* **1** something or someone that causes fear or dread especially without reason ⟨communism was once the nation's biggest *bugbear*⟩ — see BOGEY 1
2 something that is a source of irritation ⟨hated all the *bugbears* of modern life, especially those long commutes to work⟩ — see ANNOYANCE 3
bugger *n* a person whose behavior is offensive to others ⟨a cranky *bugger* who's always at odds with his neighbors⟩ — see JERK 1
bugger (up) *vb* to make or do (something) in a clumsy or unskillful way ⟨I've somehow *buggered up* the program again⟩ — see BOTCH
bugger off *vb, British slang* to leave a place often for another ⟨*bugger off*, or I'll call the police!⟩ — see GO 2
bugging *n* the act of making unwelcome intrusions upon another ⟨this perpetual *bugging* while I'm trying to concentrate is driving me nuts!⟩ — see ANNOYANCE
buggy *n* a small four-wheeled vehicle designed for pushing a baby around in ⟨we'll need a new *buggy* if we have another baby⟩ — see BABY CARRIAGE
bughouse *adj, slang* having or showing a very abnormal or sick state of mind ⟨anyone would go *bughouse* after spending a week with her relatives⟩ — see INSANE 1
bug off *vb* to leave a place often for another ⟨*bug off*, or I'll sic my dogs on you!⟩ — see GO 2
bug out *vb* **1** to hasten away from something dangerous or frightening ⟨the ground soldiers *bugged out* just before the start of the aerial bombing⟩ — see RUN 2
2 to leave a place often for another ⟨the strange visitor *bugged out* without so much as saying a word⟩ — see GO 2
build *n* the type of body that a person has ⟨she has a slender *build*⟩ — see PHYSIQUE
build *vb* to form by putting together parts or materials ⟨he spent hours *building* a model airplane from a kit⟩
synonyms assemble, confect, construct, erect, fabricate, make, make up, piece, put up, raise, rear, set up
related words carpenter, fashion, forge, frame, hammer, handcraft, manufacture, mold, produce, shape; prefabricate; begin, coin, create, generate, inaugurate, initiate, innovate, invent, originate; constitute, establish, father, found, institute, organize; conceive, concoct, contrive, cook (up), design, devise, imagine, think (up); reassemble, rebuild, reconstruct, redevelop, reedify [*British*], retrofit; jerry-build, rig (up), throw up; combine, unite
phrases put together
near antonyms demolish, destroy, devastate, flatten, level, pull down, pulverize, raze, ruin, ruinate, shatter, smash, wreck; blow up, explode; detach, disengage; disconnect, disjoin, disunite, divide, separate
antonyms demount, disassemble, dismantle, dismember, knock down, strike, take down, tear down
building *n* something built as a dwelling, shelter, or place for human activity ⟨English class will be in that big stone *building* over there⟩
synonyms edifice, structure
related words construction, erection; bungalow, cabin, chalet, cottage, house, lodge, summerhouse; hovel, hut, hutment, shack, shanty, shed; castle, château, estate, hall, manor, mansion, palace, pile, villa; skyscraper, tower
building block *n* one of the parts that make up a whole ⟨historically the infantry division has been a basic *building block* of armies⟩ — see ELEMENT 1
build up *vb* **1** to become greater in extent, volume, amount, or number ⟨static electricity *built up* on the cat's fur⟩ — see INCREASE 2
2 to gradually increase in ⟨the roller coaster *built up* momentum⟩ — see GAIN 1
3 to gradually form into a layer, pile, or mass ⟨evidence that the toxic chemical *builds up* in the bloodstream to unhealthy levels⟩ — see COLLECT 2
4 to make greater in size, amount, or number ⟨he patiently *built up* his coin collection over several decades⟩ ⟨the young stockbroker worked hard to *build up* a clientele⟩ — see INCREASE 1
built–in *adj* being a part of the innermost nature of a person or thing ⟨a poker player with a seemingly *built-in* ability to read his opponents' faces⟩ — see INHERENT
bulge *n* **1** a part that sticks out from the general mass of something ⟨several *bulges* in the old vinyl flooring in the dingy bathroom⟩
synonyms bunch, convexity, jut, overhang, projection, protrusion, protuberance, swell
related words dome; blob, bump, dilatation, gibbosity, hump, knob, knot, knurl, lump, nub, obtrusion, puff, snag, swelling; block, piece, portion, section; enlargement, escalation, expansion, increase; hill, mound
near antonyms crater, hole, well; basin, bowl, dip, valley; furrow, groove, trench, trough; dimple, gouge, impression, notch, pocket
antonyms cavity, concave, concavity, dent, depression, dint, hollow, indent, indentation, indenture, pit, recess
2 the more favorable condition or position in a competition ⟨somehow she got the *bulge* on him in the race for the statehouse⟩ — see ADVANTAGE 1
bulge *vb* **1** to extend outward beyond a usual point ⟨the sides of the returning camper's suitcase *bulged* with a month's worth of dirty laundry⟩
synonyms bag, balloon, beetle, belly, billow, bunch, jut, overhang, poke, pooch [*chiefly dialect*], pouch, pout, project, protrude, stand out, start, stick out, swell
related words dome; blow up, inflate; dilate, distend, expand; mushroom, snowball; elongate, extend, lengthen, stretch
near antonyms compress, condense, constrict, contract, shrink
2 to be copiously supplied ⟨this guidebook to San Francisco positively *bulges* with useful information⟩ — see ABOUND
bulk *n* **1** the largest part or quantity of something ⟨agriculture makes up the *bulk* of the country's economy⟩ — see MAJORITY 1
2 the main or greater part of something as distinguished from its subordinate parts ⟨the cookie lost a few crumbs, but the *bulk* of it remained⟩ — see BODY 1
3 the total amount of measurable space or surface occupied by something ⟨due to its *bulk*, we were unable to get the television set into the backseat of the car⟩ — see [1]SIZE
bulk (up) *vb* to bring together in one body or place ⟨she *bulked up* her hair with one hand as she reached for the shears with the other⟩ — see GATHER 1
bulkiness *n* the quality or state of being large in size

⟨the box wasn't heavy, but its *bulkiness* made it awkward to carry⟩ — see LARGENESS

bulky *adj* of a size greater than average of its kind ⟨*bulky* packages might cost more to mail⟩ — see LARGE 1

[1]bull *n* an order publicly issued by an authority ⟨the head office issued a *bull* banning the use of alcohol at all on-site social functions⟩ — see EDICT 1

[2]bull *n, slang* a member of a force charged with law enforcement at the local level ⟨the town's drug pushers and *bulls* were well acquainted with one another⟩ — see OFFICER 1

[3]bull *n, slang* **1** boastful speech or writing ⟨an interview filled with the usual *bull* about how seriously she takes the art of acting⟩ — see BOMBAST 1
2 language, behavior, or ideas that are absurd and contrary to good sense ⟨a guy who's always trying to sell some sucker a line of *bull*⟩ — see NONSENSE 1

[1]bull *vb* to force one's way ⟨the beleaguered governor *bulled* through the crowd of reporters without answering a single question⟩ — see [2]PRESS 4

[2]bull *vb, slang* to praise or express pride in one's own possessions, qualities, or accomplishments often to excess ⟨no one bought all his *bulling* about how he had bedded every woman in the bar⟩ — see BOAST 1

bulldoze *vb* **1** to force one's way ⟨*bulldozed* through the crowd at the arena, urgently trying to find the bathroom⟩ — see [2]PRESS 4
2 to make timid or fearful by or as if by threats ⟨one of those gatherings at which high-pressure sales reps try to *bulldoze* naive people into buying time-shares⟩ — see INTIMIDATE

bullet *n* a usually round or cone-shaped little piece of lead made to be fired from a firearm ⟨it is possible to make your own *bullets*, but it takes a lot of patience and some extra money⟩
synonyms ball, pellet
related words ammunition, cannonball, cap, cartridge, charge, dumdum, gunshot, lead, load, missile, pop, projectile, round, shell, shot, slug
near antonyms blank

bulletin *n* **1** a publication that appears at regular intervals ⟨picks up a church *bulletin* every Sunday after Mass⟩ — see JOURNAL 1
2 a published statement informing the public of a matter of general interest ⟨a Web site that allows visitors to read the latest news *bulletins* free of charge⟩ — see ANNOUNCEMENT

bulletproof *adj* incapable of being defeated, overcome, or subdued ⟨this year the city's football team seems *bulletproof*⟩ — see INVINCIBLE

bullheaded *adj* sticking to an opinion, purpose, or course of action in spite of reason, arguments, or persuasion ⟨a *bullheaded* government official who refused to bend the rules even just a little bit⟩ — see OBSTINATE

bullheadedness *n* a steadfast adherence to an opinion, purpose, or course of action in spite of reason, arguments, or persuasion ⟨*bullheadedness* runs in that family⟩ — see OBSTINACY

bullishness *n* an inclination to believe in the most favorable outcome ⟨the customary *bullishness* of the company's executives is more credible in light of the most recent earnings report⟩ — see OPTIMISM

bull's–eye *n* the central part or aspect of something under consideration ⟨you hit the *bull's-eye* when you noted that the real issue here is money⟩ — see CRUX

bully *adj* of the very best kind ⟨that's a *bully* idea for reviving the town's retail center⟩ — see EXCELLENT

bully *n* **1** a person who teases, threatens, or hurts smaller or weaker persons ⟨officials were warned that if they wished to avoid a school shooting, they had to deal with the local *bullies*⟩
synonyms bullyboy, hector, intimidator
related words antagonist, enemy; abuser, baiter, giber (*or* jiber), harasser, harrier, heckler, mocker, needler, oppressor, persecutor, ridiculer, taunter, tease, teaser, torturer; goon, homeboy, homey (*or* homie), hood, hoodlum, hooligan, mug, punk, rough, roughneck, rowdy, ruffian, thug, tough, toughie (*also* toughy); cutthroat, felon, gangster, gunman, mobster, racketeer
2 a violent, brutal person who is often a member of an organized gang ⟨the local loan shark and his *bullies* have ways of making people pay up⟩ — see HOODLUM

bully *vb* **1** to inflict physical or emotional harm upon ⟨children who had been *bullied* by their father since infancy⟩ — see ABUSE 1
2 to make timid or fearful by or as if by threats ⟨the older boys constantly *bullied* him to the point where he was afraid to walk home alone⟩ — see INTIMIDATE

bullyboy *n* a person who teases, threatens, or hurts smaller or weaker persons ⟨unfortunately, some local *bullyboys* had made the park their turf, and families avoided it⟩ — see BULLY 1

bullyrag *vb* to make timid or fearful by or as if by threats ⟨the kind of neighborhood in which it was standard practice for young teens to be *bullyragged* into joining a street gang⟩ — see INTIMIDATE

bulwark *vb* to drive danger or attack away from ⟨vowed to use any means necessary to *bulwark* the country against a terrorist attack⟩ — see DEFEND 1

bum *adj* of low quality ⟨that was *bum* advice that you got from that chat room⟩ — see CHEAP 2

[1]bum *n* the part of the body upon which someone sits ⟨a woman with a big *bum*⟩ — see BUTTOCKS

[2]bum *n* **1** an idle worthless person ⟨asked his future son-in-law if he was planning on being a *bum* all his life⟩ — see NE'ER-DO-WELL
2 a homeless wanderer who may beg or steal for a living ⟨I feel sorry for *bums* and occasionally give them money⟩ — see TRAMP 1

bum *vb* to spend time doing nothing ⟨spent most of the summer just *bumming* around the house⟩ — see IDLE

bum (out) *vb* to make sad ⟨that sort of news really *bums* me *out*⟩ — see DEPRESS 1

[1]bumble *vb* to fly, turn, or move rapidly with a fluttering or vibratory sound ⟨a fly *bumbling* around the room while we were trying to sleep⟩ — see WHIR

[2]bumble *vb* **1** to make or do (something) in a clumsy or unskillful way ⟨accused the White House staff of *bumbling* the confirmation of the nominee for the cabinet post⟩ — see BOTCH
2 to proceed or act clumsily or ineffectually ⟨I sort of *bumbled* through the dance number, hoping that it would soon end⟩ — see FLOUNDER 1
3 to speak rapidly, inarticulately, and usually unintelligibly ⟨overcome with stage fright, I could only *bumble* through the speech⟩ — see BABBLE 1

bumbler *n* someone who bungles an effort ⟨we can't trust that *bumbler* to do anything right⟩ — see BUTCHER

[1]bummer *n* **1** something (as a situation or event) that is depressing ⟨boy, breaking your leg right before vacation is a *bummer*⟩ — see DOWNER
2 something that disappoints ⟨the cancellation of the holiday office party was a total *bummer*⟩ — see DISAPPOINTMENT 2
3 something that has failed ⟨that dot-com proved to be a real *bummer*⟩ — see FAILURE 3

[2]bummer *n* a homeless wanderer who may beg or steal for a living ⟨a lifelong *bummer*, he never knew the satisfaction of having to work for a living⟩ — see TRAMP 1

bump *n* **1** a small rounded mass of swollen tissue ⟨that's a nasty *bump* on your arm where you hit the table⟩
synonyms knot, lump, node, nodule, swelling

related words growth, tumor, wart; hump, hunch; bruise, contusion, welt; blister, boil; blob, chunk, clod, clump, gob, gobbet, hunk, knob, nub, nubble, nugget, wad
2 the act or an instance of bringing to a lower grade or rank ⟨the *bump* was punishment for insubordination⟩
synonyms demotion, reduction
related words disrating, downgrade; dismissal, firing, layoff, sacking; abasement, debasement, humiliation
3 a forceful coming together of two things ⟨I felt the *bump* of the other car, but there was no damage to either vehicle⟩ — see IMPACT 1

bump *vb* to come into usually forceful contact with something ⟨that police officer *bumped* into me and should have apologized⟩ — see HIT 2

bumper *adj* **1** of the very best kind ⟨it's been a *bumper* year for movies aimed at intelligent adults⟩ — see EXCELLENT
2 unusually large ⟨a *bumper* crop of pumpkins that year⟩ — see HUGE

bumper *n* something that serves as a protective barrier ⟨cars have *bumpers* to protect them from damage in minor collisions⟩ — see CUSHION

bumpkin *n* an awkward or simple person especially from a small town or the country ⟨the *bumpkin* was overwhelmed by the city's confusing subway system⟩ — see HICK

bump off *vb* to put to death deliberately ⟨these drug dealers mean business, and they'll *bump off* anyone who gets in their way⟩ — see MURDER 1

bumptious *adj* having a feeling of superiority that shows itself in an overbearing attitude ⟨a *bumptious* young man whose family wealth gave him a sense of entitlement⟩ — see ARROGANT

bumptiousness *n* an exaggerated sense of one's importance that shows itself in the making of excessive or unjustified claims ⟨for unbridled *bumptiousness*, it would be hard to beat that upstart⟩ — see ARROGANCE

bumpy *adj* **1** marked by a series of sharp quick motions ⟨a *bumpy* ride over a badly rutted road⟩ — see JERKY 1
2 not having a level or smooth surface ⟨the *bumpy* road made the jeep bounce all over⟩ — see UNEVEN 1

bunch *n* **1** a group of people sharing a common interest and relating together socially ⟨that *bunch* goes out to lunch together every Friday⟩ — see GANG 2
2 a number of things considered as a unit ⟨bought a *bunch* of grapes⟩ — see GROUP 1
3 a usually small number of persons considered as a unit ⟨a small *bunch* of people were sent to clean up the place⟩ — see GROUP 2
4 a part that sticks out from the general mass of something ⟨a *bunch* in the blanket⟩ — see BULGE 1
5 a considerable amount ⟨I have a *bunch* of thoughts on the matter, so grab a notepad⟩ — see LOT 2

bunch *vb* **1** to extend outward beyond a usual point ⟨the dress *bunches* a bit at the waist⟩ — see BULGE 1
2 to gather into a closely packed group ⟨the slow service caused the customers at the pick-up counter to *bunch* up⟩ — see [2]PRESS 3

bunco *or* **bunko** *n* an instance of the use of dishonest methods to acquire something of value ⟨they were experts at that *bunco*, having fleeced wide-eyed tourists for years⟩ — see FRAUD 1

bundle *n* **1** a considerable amount ⟨a bundle of *plans* for the winter carnival⟩ — see LOT 2
2 a wrapped or sealed case containing an item or set of items ⟨a *bundle* of newspapers⟩ — see PACKAGE 1
3 a very large amount of money ⟨he dropped a *bundle* on that new sports car⟩ — see FORTUNE 2

bundle *vb* **1** to cause to move or proceed fast or faster ⟨the tour guide *bundled* us off before we had a chance to ask any questions⟩ — see HURRY 1
2 to proceed or move quickly ⟨a group of servants came *bundling* out of the palace to attend to the returning royals⟩ — see HURRY 2

bung *vb* to close up so that no empty spaces remain ⟨we had *bunged* up the moving van so much that we couldn't have possibly squeezed in one more thing⟩ — see FILL 2

bungle *vb* to make or do (something) in a clumsy or unskillful way ⟨*bungled* the job the first time she tried to do it⟩ — see BOTCH

bungler *n* someone who bungles an effort ⟨a hopeless *bungler* at fixing things around the house⟩ — see BUTCHER

bunglesome *adj* difficult to use or operate especially because of size, weight, or design ⟨get rid of that *bunglesome* old suitcase and buy something with wheels⟩ — see CUMBERSOME

bungling *adj* showing or marked by a lack of skill and tact (as in dealing with a situation) ⟨I refuse to let that *bungling* incompetent insult me again⟩ — see AWKWARD 2

bung up *vb* to strike repeatedly ⟨he's a bit of a mess, but he says he *bunged up* the other guy in the fight even worse⟩ — see BEAT 1

[1]**bunk** *n* a place set aside for sleeping ⟨crawled into their *bunks* and went to sleep immediately⟩ — see BED 1

[2]**bunk** *n* language, behavior, or ideas that are absurd and contrary to good sense ⟨the idea that the Great Wall of China is visible from the moon is pure *bunk*⟩ — see NONSENSE 1

[3]**bunk** *n, British* the act or an instance of getting free from danger or confinement ⟨he waited until everyone was looking the other way, then did a *bunk* from the room⟩ — see ESCAPE 1

bunk *vb* to provide with living quarters or shelter ⟨*bunked* the guest in the spare room⟩ — see HOUSE 1

bunkum *or* **buncombe** *n* language, behavior, or ideas that are absurd and contrary to good sense ⟨a cinematic depiction of the Middle Ages that was derided as pure *bunkum* by historians⟩ — see NONSENSE 1

buns *n pl* the part of the body upon which someone sits ⟨he's got cute little *buns*⟩ — see BUTTOCKS

buoy (up) *vb* to fill with courage or strength of purpose ⟨the sudden improvement in his health *buoyed* him *up*⟩ — see ENCOURAGE 1

buoyant *adj* **1** having or showing a good mood or disposition ⟨all the fans were *buoyant* the day after the big win in the play-offs⟩ — see CHEERFUL 1
2 joyously unrestrained ⟨gave him a *buoyant* hug and kiss upon meeting him at the airport⟩ — see EXUBERANT

buoyantly *adv* in a quick and spirited manner ⟨went about her chores cheerfully and *buoyantly*⟩ — see GAILY 2

burble *n* unintelligible or meaningless talk ⟨the *burble* of babies can be so endearing⟩ — see GIBBERISH 1

[1]**burden** *n* **1** a mass or quantity of something taken up and carried, conveyed, or transported ⟨the early settlers often used horses to carry their *burdens*⟩ — see LOAD 1
2 something one must do because of prior agreement ⟨the *burden* of homework prevented the youngster from joining his friends at the game⟩ — see OBLIGATION 1

[2]**burden** *n* a part of a song or hymn that is repeated every so often ⟨had some trouble coming up with a *burden* for the song⟩ — see CHORUS 2

burden *vb* **1** to place a weight or burden on ⟨*burdened* the dog with a little backpack⟩ — see LOAD 1
2 to make sad ⟨refuses to let everyday problems *burden* her⟩ — see DEPRESS 1

burdensome *adj* **1** difficult to endure ⟨the *burdensome* living conditions that the early settlers had to endure⟩ — see HARSH 1

2 requiring much time, effort, or careful attention ⟨the *burdensome* task of finishing the tax return⟩ — see DEMANDING 1

bureau *n* a large unit of a governmental, business, or educational organization ⟨the federal revenue *bureau*⟩ — see DIVISION 2

bureaucrat *n* a worker in a government agency ⟨the *bureaucrats* at the town hall seem to think that we need a building permit to build a tree house⟩

synonyms civil servant, functionary, mandarin, public servant

related words clerk, officeholder, official, officiary; employee (*also* employe), hand, hireling, jobholder, underling, worker

burg *n* a thickly settled, highly populated area ⟨moved from a small town into a much bigger *burg*⟩ — see CITY

burgeon *also* **bourgeon** *vb* **1** to become greater in extent, volume, amount, or number ⟨the trout population in the stream is *burgeoning* now that the water is clean⟩ — see INCREASE 2

2 to grow vigorously ⟨the spring flowers *burgeoned* once the warm weather set in for good⟩ — see THRIVE 1

3 to produce flowers ⟨chrysanthemums usually *burgeon* in early fall⟩ — see BLOOM

burgher *n* a person who lives in a town on a permanent basis ⟨many of the college students are regarded by the local *burghers* as obnoxious louts⟩

synonyms citizen, townie (*or* towny), townsman, villager

related words townswoman; cliff dweller, denizen, dweller, habitant, inhabitant, national, native, occupant, resident, resider, subject; town, townsfolk, townspeople; suburbanite, urbanite

near antonyms alien, foreigner, guest, nonnative, tourist, transient, visitor; gownsman

antonyms noncitizen

burglarize *vb* **1** to enter a house or building by force usually with illegal intent ⟨the Watergate scandal began when Republican operatives *burglarized* the Democratic Party's headquarters in Washington, D.C.⟩ — see BREAK IN 1

2 to remove valuables from (a place) unlawfully ⟨before they were caught, the thieves had *burglarized* dozens of houses around the city⟩ — see ROB

burgle *vb* **1** to enter a house or building by force usually with illegal intent ⟨someone *burgled* the lab when no one was there and let the animals out of their cages⟩ — see BREAK IN 1

2 to remove valuables from (a place) unlawfully ⟨the neighbors returned from vacation to find that their house had been *burgled*⟩ — see ROB

burial *n* **1** the act or ceremony of putting a dead body in its final resting place ⟨the children wanted to give the dead bird a proper *burial* in the backyard⟩

synonyms burying, entombing, entombment, inhumation, interment, interring, obsequy (*usually* obsequies), sepulture

related words embalmment, funeral; immurement, inurnment; reburial, reinterment

near antonyms cremation

antonyms disinterment, exhumation, unearthing

2 a final resting place for a dead person ⟨archaeologically significant artifacts, such as stone tools, have been discovered in Neanderthal *burials*⟩ — see GRAVE 1

burke *vb* to keep from being publicly known ⟨the executives knew that the drug had dangerous side effects, but they *burked* the findings⟩ — see SUPPRESS 1

burlesque *n* a work that imitates and exaggerates another work for comic effect ⟨it is interesting to note that the first novel ever written in English was followed by a *burlesque* of it⟩ — see PARODY 1

burlesque *vb* to copy or exaggerate (someone or something) in order to make fun of ⟨*burlesquing* the teacher's nervous tic isn't very nice⟩ — see MIMIC 1

burly *adj* strongly and heavily built ⟨a *burly* delivery man brought the furniture⟩ — see [1]HUSKY 1

burn *n, British* a natural body of running water smaller than a river ⟨the walkers forded the shallow *burn* and then came upon a field of gorse⟩ — see CREEK 1

burn *vb* **1** to be on fire especially brightly ⟨all evening long we just sat there, contentedly watching the Yule log *burn*⟩

synonyms blaze, combust, flame, glow

related words catch, enkindle; deflagrate, fire, ignite, kindle; flare (up), light (up); flicker, gutter, waver; bake, broil, char, cook, melt, roast, scorch, swelter; smolder (*or* smoulder), spark, sputter; beam, brighten, radiate; beat (down), flash, glare, gleam, glimmer, glint, glisten, glitter, scintillate, shimmer, shine, sparkle, twinkle

phrases go up in flames

2 to set (something) on fire ⟨it is not a good idea to try to *burn* old papers in the sink⟩

synonyms enkindle, fire, ignite, inflame (*also* enflame), kindle, light, torch

related words immolate; deflagrate; char, frizzle, scorch; bake, broil, cook; ash, cremate, incinerate, kiln; set off; brighten, illuminate, illumine, irradiate, lighten, radiate; scald, scathe, sear; reignite, rekindle, relight; bank, stoke

near antonyms choke, smother, suffocate; stamp (out); blacken, darken, dim, dull, obscure

antonyms douse (*also* dowse), extinguish, put out, quench, snuff (out)

3 to be excited or emotionally stirred up with anger ⟨he came home *burning* with anger because of a reprimand at work⟩ — see BOIL 1

4 to shine with a bright harsh light ⟨the bright streetlight outside our motel room *burned* all night long⟩ — see GLARE 1

5 to cause to believe what is untrue ⟨he's been *burned* before, so he's careful to double-check such claims now⟩ — see DECEIVE

6 to make complete use of ⟨heedlessly *burning* the country's resources without any concern for future generations⟩ — see DEPLETE 1

burn (up) *vb* to disturb the peace of mind of (someone) especially by repeated disagreeable acts ⟨seeing people violate smoking bans really *burns* me *up*⟩ — see IRRITATE 1

burnable *adj* capable of catching or being set on fire ⟨don't put something so *burnable* as a towel next to the stove⟩ — see COMBUSTIBLE

burned–out *or* **burnt–out** *adj* depleted in strength, energy, or freshness ⟨I'm feeling so *burned-out* that I can't wait for vacation⟩ — see WEARY 1

burning *adj* **1** being on fire ⟨a firefighter must be that rare soul who rushes into a *burning* house, not away from it⟩ — see ABLAZE 1

2 having a notably high temperature ⟨a *burning* sauna seems like a welcome retreat after a day of shoveling snow⟩ — see HOT 1

3 having or expressing great depth of feeling ⟨the *burning* enthusiasm of that candidate's campaign workers⟩ — see FERVENT 1

4 needing immediate attention ⟨once again the media ignored the *burning* issues and focused on fluff⟩ — see ACUTE 2

burnish *n* brightness created by light reflected from a surface ⟨after some much-needed polishing, the silver tea set had a brilliant *burnish*⟩ — see SHINE 1

burnish *vb* to make smooth or glossy usually by repeatedly applying surface pressure ⟨*burnished* the floor of the ballroom to a soft luster⟩ — see POLISH 1

burnished *adj* having a shiny surface or finish ⟨bright *burnished* metal is used extensively in that boutique's decor⟩ — see GLOSSY

burnout *n* a complete depletion of energy or strength ⟨people in that job often suffer *burnout* and have to retire at a relatively early age⟩ — see FATIGUE 1

burn out *vb* to use up all the physical energy of ⟨working 12-hour days at that job just *burned* me *out*⟩ — see EXHAUST 1

burp *n* an expulsion of stomach gas through the mouth ⟨felt embarrassed when a *burp* escaped from his lips as the table was being cleared⟩ — see BELCH

burr *n* a monotonous sound like that of an insect in motion ⟨heard the *burr* of a distant engine⟩ — see HUM

burr *vb* to fly, turn, or move rapidly with a fluttering or vibratory sound ⟨the pitch *burred* past the batter's ear⟩ — see WHIR

burro *n* a sturdy and patient domestic mammal that is used especially to carry things ⟨used a *burro* to carry the supplies⟩ — see DONKEY 1

burrow *n* the shelter or resting place of a wild animal ⟨the chipmunk retreated to its *burrow* to have its babies⟩ — see DEN 1

burst *n* **1** a sudden and usually temporary growth of activity ⟨a sudden *burst* of industriousness whenever the boss appeared⟩ — see OUTBREAK 1

2 a sudden intense expression of strong feeling ⟨a *burst* of anger that startled the other members on the panel⟩ — see OUTBURST 1

3 the act or an instance of exploding ⟨one *burst* after another could be heard in the distance⟩ — see EXPLOSION 1

burst *vb* **1** to break open or into pieces usually because of internal pressure ⟨the turnover's crust *burst* when the filling expanded⟩ — see EXPLODE 1

2 to cause to break open or into pieces by or as if by an explosive ⟨finally *burst* the piñata open with one mighty swing of the bat⟩ — see BLAST 1

3 to be copiously supplied ⟨a young singer/dancer who seems to be *bursting* with energy and talent⟩ — see ABOUND

burst (forth) *vb* to develop suddenly and violently ⟨hives *burst forth* on the child's arms and face whenever she goes near that plant⟩ — see ERUPT 2

bursting *adj* containing or seeming to contain the greatest quantity or number possible ⟨the store was *bursting* with bargain hunters on the day of the big sale⟩ — see FULL 1

bursting *n* the act or an instance of exploding ⟨narrowly escaped the *bursting* of the car's gas tank⟩ — see EXPLOSION 1

bury *vb* **1** to place (a dead body) in the earth, a tomb, or the sea ⟨he died on Tuesday and was *buried* on Friday⟩
synonyms entomb, hearse, inhume, inter, lay, put away, tomb
related words immure, inurn; enshrine; conceal, cover, ensconce, hide; obscure, shade, shield; cloak, curtain, enshroud, shroud; rebury, reinter; coffin
near antonyms burn, cremate; bare, disclose, discover, display, exhibit, expose, reveal, show; uncoffin
antonyms disinter, exhume, unearth

2 to put into a hiding place ⟨*buried* his face in his hands as his wife recounted the embarrassing incident⟩ — see [1]HIDE 1

3 to defeat by a large margin ⟨if we don't work harder, the other softball team will *bury* us⟩ — see WHIP 2

burying *n* the act or ceremony of putting a dead body in its final resting place ⟨all the grandchildren attended the *burying* of their grandfather in his homeland⟩ — see BURIAL 1

bus *n* a self-propelled passenger vehicle on four wheels ⟨this old *bus* is still running—but barely⟩ — see CAR

bush *adj* falling short of a standard ⟨a hopelessly *bush* effort at creating a romantic comedy⟩ — see BAD 1

bush *n* a rural region that forms the edge of the settled or developed part of a country ⟨a guide who specializes in taking adventurous tourists through the *bush*⟩ — see FRONTIER 2

bushed *adj* **1** depleted in strength, energy, or freshness ⟨I'm *bushed* after a day of moving boxes from the cellar to the attic⟩ — see WEARY 1

2 *chiefly Australian* suffering from mental confusion ⟨we were thoroughly *bushed* after listening to the convoluted directions from a well-meaning Sydneysider⟩ — see DIZZY 2

bushel *n* a considerable amount ⟨picked up a *bushel* of decorations at the after-Christmas sale⟩ — see LOT 2

bush–league *adj* falling short of a standard ⟨that's just a *bush-league* ploy to get cast on a TV reality show⟩ — see BAD 1

bushwhack *vb* to take sudden, violent action against ⟨a remote area of the park in which gangs of hoodlums have been known to *bushwhack* lone joggers⟩ — see ATTACK 1

bushwhacker *n* one who violently sets upon another ⟨*bushwhackers* have made that lonely stretch of road very dangerous⟩ — see ATTACKER

busily *adv* in a manner involving great or constant activity ⟨the deadline is in two days, so everyone in the department has been working *busily*⟩
synonyms actively, assiduously, diligently, industriously, laboriously
related words energetically, vigorously; indefatigably, tirelessly
near antonyms lifelessly, sleepily
antonyms idly, inactively

business *n* **1** transactions or economic support provided by customers ⟨only places that are equal opportunity employers will get my *business*⟩
synonyms custom, patronage
related words marketplace, trade, traffic; free trade; affairs, dealings, horse-trading; merchandising, retailing, wholesaling

2 a commercial or industrial activity or organization ⟨most of the local *businesses* belong to the association⟩ — see ENTERPRISE 1

3 something to be dealt with ⟨we have one piece of *business* remaining for today's meeting⟩ — see MATTER 2

4 the buying and selling of goods especially on a large scale and between different places ⟨this bookstore is a place of *business*, not a free library, so please do your reading elsewhere⟩ — see COMMERCE 1

5 the action for which a person or thing is specially fitted or used or for which a thing exists ⟨plants going about the *business* of photosynthesis provide the Earth with a renewable source of oxygen⟩ — see ROLE

6 a region of activity, knowledge, or influence ⟨if you want a medical malpractice lawyer, he's the best in the *business*⟩ — see FIELD 2

7 a specific task with which a person or group is charged ⟨the interrogators demanded to know what *business* the suspect had in the restricted area at that time of night⟩ — see MISSION

8 the act or fact of violating the trust or confidence of another ⟨the price for giving the drug lord the *business* was certain death⟩ — see BETRAYAL

bust *n* **1** a hard strike with a part of the body or an instrument ⟨delivered a *bust* to the boxer's chops⟩ — see [1]BLOW

2 something that has failed ⟨the first movie was a hit, but the sequel was an unexpected *bust*⟩ — see FAILURE 3

3 *slang* the act of taking or holding under one's control by authority of law ⟨those lowlifes were nabbed for drug dealing in a massive *bust* last month⟩ — see ARREST 1
4 a bout of prolonged or excessive drinking ⟨a bunch of underage kids having a beer *bust* while the parents were away for the weekend⟩ — see CAROUSE

bust *vb* **1** to bring to a lower grade or rank ⟨the commander threatened to *bust* her for failing to salute⟩ — see DEMOTE
2 to cause to lose one's fortune and become unable to pay one's debts ⟨gambling is a dangerous habit that has *busted* many unfortunate souls⟩ — see RUIN 1
3 to cause to separate into pieces usually suddenly or forcibly ⟨the butterfingered husband had *busted* more plates than he cared to remember⟩ — see BREAK 1
4 to deliver a blow to (someone or something) usually in a strong vigorous manner ⟨*busted* the storekeeper on the nose and was promptly arrested for it⟩ — see HIT 1
5 *slang* to take or keep under one's control by authority of law ⟨the cops *busted* the revelers for drinking in public⟩ — see ARREST 1
6 to use up all the physical energy of ⟨I had to *bust* my butt in order to get the project done on time⟩ — see EXHAUST 1

busted *adj* forcibly separated into many pieces ⟨a *busted* headlight⟩ — see BROKEN 1

bustle *n* a state of noisy, confused activity ⟨I couldn't concentrate in all the *bustle* of the student lounge⟩ — see COMMOTION

bustle *vb* **1** to be copiously supplied ⟨on Saturdays the city's downtown *bustles* with activity as a farmers' market sets up shop⟩ — see ABOUND
2 to proceed or move quickly ⟨the hostess *bustled* about, taking care of last-minute preparations for the party⟩ — see HURRY 2

bustling *adj* **1** involved in often constant activity ⟨a *bustling* greeter was there to welcome guests to the grand opening⟩ — see BUSY 1
2 marked by much life, movement, or activity ⟨a *bustling* shopping center during the Christmas season⟩ — see ALIVE 2

busy *adj* **1** involved in often constant activity ⟨the deadline is in two days, so everyone at work has been extremely *busy*⟩
synonyms active, assiduous, bustling, diligent, employed, engaged, hopping, industrious, laborious, occupied, sedulous, tied-up, working
related words knee-deep, swamped; animated, astir, buzzing, flourishing, happening, humming, lively, thriving, vibrant; absorbed, concentrating, engrossed, focused (*also* focussed), immersed, intent, preoccupied; alive, functional, functioning, going, living, operating, operational, operative, running; energetic, vigorous; hardworking; indefatigable, tireless, untiring
near antonyms free; asleep, dormant, latent, lifeless, quiescent, sleepy; inert, passive; dead, dull, slow; inoperative, nonoperating
antonyms idle, inactive, unbusy, unemployed, unoccupied
2 marked by much life, movement, or activity ⟨the *busy*, often hectic floor of the New York Stock Exchange⟩ — see ALIVE 2
3 thrusting oneself where one is not welcome or invited ⟨she's one of those *busy* production facilitators—always concerned about other people's work and never her own⟩ — see INTRUSIVE

busy *vb* to hold the attention of ⟨the video game *busied* the child for hours⟩ — see ENGAGE 1

busybody *n* a person who meddles in the affairs of others ⟨that *busybody* across the street is always telling me how to tend to my own garden⟩
synonyms buttinsky (*also* buttinski), interferer, interloper, intermeddler, intruder, kibitzer (*also* kibbitzer), meddler, nosey parker [*chiefly British*]
related words gaper, gawker, gawper [*chiefly British*], gazer, peeper, peeping Tom, prier (*also* pryer), rubberneck, rubbernecker, snoop, snooper, spy; blabber, discloser, gossip, gossiper, prattler, quidnunc, revealer, teller; betrayer, talebearer, tattler, tattletale, telltale; snake, sneak; informant, informer, snitcher, squealer, stool pigeon

but *adv* nothing more than ⟨she is *but* a child and too young to understand such things⟩ — see JUST 3

but *conj* if it were not for the fact that ⟨I would have said something *but* I was too chicken⟩ — see EXCEPT

but *prep* not including ⟨brought everything *but* the kitchen table to the campground⟩ — see EXCEPT

butcher *n* someone who bungles an effort ⟨the newest intern on the campaign is a *butcher* when it comes to writing press releases⟩
synonyms blunderbuss, blunderer, botcher, bumbler, bungler, fumbler, screwup
related words incompetent, muddler
near antonyms ace, adept, crackerjack (*also* crackajack), expert, maestro, master, virtuoso, wizard

butcher *vb* **1** to kill on a large scale ⟨the barbarians *butchered* the monks in the monasteries without mercy⟩ — see MASSACRE
2 to make or do (something) in a clumsy or unskillful way ⟨the new piano student *butchered* the sonatina⟩ — see BOTCH

butcherly *adj* having or showing the desire to inflict severe pain and suffering on others ⟨Genghis Khan and his *butcherly* horde even massacred the livestock of the villages they overran⟩ — see CRUEL 1

butchery *n* the killing of a large number of people ⟨*butchery* on a scale that horrified the civilized world⟩ — see MASSACRE

[1]**butt** *n* the part of the body upon which someone sits ⟨park your *butts* in the seats and keep quiet, or I'm turning this car around⟩ — see BUTTOCKS

[2]**butt** *n* **1** a person or thing that is made fun of ⟨the social outcast got tired of being the *butt* of everyone's jokes⟩ — see LAUGHINGSTOCK
2 a person or thing that is the object of abuse, criticism, or ridicule ⟨usually the U.S. Congress is the *butt* of the radio commentator's scathing wit⟩ — see TARGET 1

[3]**butt** *n* an enclosed wooden vessel for holding beverages ⟨a *butt* of hard cider that we had pressed ourselves⟩ — see CASK

butt (on *or* against) *vb* to be adjacent to ⟨our property *butts on* a swamp⟩ — see ADJOIN 1

butter *n* excessive praise ⟨a junior exec who was laying on the *butter* so thickly that her colleagues were ready to gag⟩ — see FLATTERY

butterfingered *adj* lacking or showing a lack of nimbleness in using one's hands ⟨I'm so *butterfingered* this morning—I keep dropping things⟩ — see CLUMSY 1

butterfingers *n pl* a clumsy, awkward person ⟨I declined her offer to help us move; I'm not letting that *butterfingers* near my antiques⟩ — see KLUTZ

butterflies *n pl* a sense of panic or extreme nervousness ⟨even experienced actors sometimes get *butterflies* before a performance⟩ — see JITTERS

butter up *vb* to praise too much ⟨a flunky who shamelessly *butters up* the boss⟩ — see FLATTER 1

butt in *vb* to interest oneself in what is not one's concern ⟨stop *butting in* on my personal life⟩ — see INTERFERE

buttinsky *also* **buttinski** *n* a person who meddles in the affairs of others ⟨there's always some *buttinsky* who has to tell you there's a better way to do whatever you're doing⟩ — see BUSYBODY

buttocks *n pl* the part of the body upon which someone

sits ⟨she slipped in the mud puddle and hit the ground square on her *buttocks*⟩
synonyms backside, behind, booty (*also* bootie) [*slang*], bottom, breech, bum, buns, butt, caboose, can, cheeks, derriere (*or* derrière), duff, fanny, fundament, hams, haunches, heinie [*slang*], hunkers, keister (*also* keester) [*slang*], nates, posterior, rear, rear end, rump, seat, tail, tail end, tush [*slang*]
related words beam, stern; moon [*slang*]

button–down *or* **buttoned–down** *adj* tending to favor established ideas, conditions, or institutions ⟨a *button-down* architectural firm would never have the imagination to produce such a cutting-edge design⟩ — see CONSERVATIVE 1

buttoned–up *adj* having or showing a lack of friendliness or interest in others ⟨a *buttoned-up* colleague who had no interest in talking about anything but work, even at parties⟩ — see COOL 1

buttress *n* **1** something or someone to which one looks for support ⟨the mother had always been the *buttress* of our family in trying times⟩ — see DEPENDENCE 2
2 a structure that holds up or serves as a foundation for something else ⟨after the wall collapsed, the construction company agreed to rebuild it with a *buttress*⟩ — see SUPPORT 1

buttress *vb* **1** to hold up or serve as a foundation for ⟨a brace *buttressed* the wall⟩ — see SUPPORT 3
2 to provide evidence or information for (as a claim or idea) ⟨a mass of circumstantial evidence *buttresses* the prosecutor's case⟩ — see SUPPORT 4

buy *n* something bought or offered for sale at a desirable price ⟨four cartons of ice cream for four dollars is a real *buy*⟩ — see BARGAIN 1

buy *vb* **1** to get possession of (something) by giving money in exchange for ⟨I really want to *buy* that new book, but I don't have enough money right now⟩
synonyms cop [*slang*], pick up, purchase, take
related words acquire, gain, garner, get, obtain, procure, secure, win; finance, pay (for), spring (for); barter (for), deal (for), dicker (over), exchange (for), haggle (for), negotiate (about), trade (for); bargain (with), chaffer (with), horse-trade (with), palter (with); bid, offer; rebuy, repurchase
near antonyms deal (in), market, merchandise (*also* merchandize), retail, sell, vend
2 to influence someone with a bribe ⟨there were rumors that the mobster had *bought* the judge⟩ — see BRIBE
3 to regard as right or true ⟨if you *buy* that story, then I have a bridge in Brooklyn you might be interested in⟩ — see BELIEVE 1

buzz *n* **1** a communication by telephone ⟨give me a *buzz* when you decide⟩ — see CALL 3
2 a monotonous sound like that of an insect in motion ⟨the motor made a soft *buzz*⟩ — see HUM
3 information or opinion that is widely disseminated without any authority or confirmation of accuracy ⟨the *buzz* is that this would-be blockbuster will be the bomb of the summer⟩ — see RUMOR
4 a practice or interest that is very popular for a short time ⟨longer hairstyles are the *buzz* this season⟩ — see FAD

buzz *vb* **1** to be copiously supplied ⟨for months the area has been *buzzing* with rumors that a megacorporation plans to locate its headquarters here⟩ — see ABOUND
2 to proceed or move quickly ⟨we've been *buzzing* around all morning getting ready for the meeting with the VIPs from the head office⟩ — see HURRY 2
3 to fly, turn, or move rapidly with a fluttering or vibratory sound ⟨the little plane *buzzed* past the crowd⟩ — see WHIR

buzz (off) *vb* to leave a place often for another ⟨you've outstayed your welcome, so *buzz off*⟩ — see GO 2

buzzard *n* **1** a person who habitually preys upon others ⟨the real estate *buzzards* were really putting pressure on the one homeowner who was still refusing to sell⟩ — see PREDATOR
2 a person whose behavior is offensive to others ⟨that crotchety old man can be a real *buzzard* when he's in a bad mood—which is usually the case⟩ — see JERK 1

buzzing *adj* marked by much life, movement, or activity ⟨the arena is really *buzzing* tonight⟩ — see ALIVE 2

by *adv* at, within, or to a short distance or time ⟨the library is close *by*⟩ — see NEAR 1

by *prep* **1** along the way of ⟨went *by* the woods to get to the summer cottage⟩
synonyms through, via
related words across, along, alongside, beyond, near, nearby, over; below, beneath, under, underneath; outside, past; throughout
phrases by way of
2 using the means or agency of ⟨try to convince them *by* reason alone, if possible⟩
synonyms in, per, through, via, with
phrases by dint of, by means of, by (*or* in) virtue of
3 close to ⟨that house is right *by* the ocean⟩ — see AROUND 1
4 in the course of ⟨she attends college *by* day and works at the club *by* night⟩ — see DURING

by–and–by *n* time that is to come ⟨we shall meet again in the *by-and-by*⟩ — see FUTURE 1

by and by *adv* at or within a short time ⟨we'll get under way *by and by*⟩ — see SHORTLY 2

by and large *adv* for the most part ⟨*by and large*, that information is accurate⟩ — see CHIEFLY

by–blow *n* an illegitimate child ⟨prior to his election as pope, Alexander VI fathered four *by-blows*, including the notorious siblings Cesare and Lucrezia Borgia⟩ — see BASTARD 1

bygone *adj* no longer existing ⟨elderly people reminiscing about *bygone* fashions⟩ — see EXTINCT

bylaw *n* a statement spelling out the proper procedure or conduct for an activity ⟨the club's *bylaws* bar any member whose annual dues remain unpaid from voting in the election⟩ — see RULE 1

byname *n* a descriptive or familiar name given instead of or in addition to the one belonging to an individual ⟨Thomas Edward Lawrence is better known to most people by his *byname*, Lawrence of Arabia⟩ — see NICKNAME

bypass *vb* **1** to avoid by going around ⟨we can *bypass* the traffic jam if we take this other road⟩ — see DETOUR 1
2 to fail to give proper attention to ⟨a serious news event that was *bypassed* by the mainstream media so that they could concentrate on celebrity gossip⟩ — see NEGLECT 1
3 to avoid having to comply with (something) especially through cleverness ⟨you can *bypass* the graduation requirements if you do enough extra credit⟩ — see CIRCUMVENT 1

bypast *adj* no longer existing ⟨those *bypast* days when gasoline was cheap⟩ — see EXTINCT

by–product *n* something that naturally develops or is developed from something else ⟨hydrogen is one *by-product* of that chemical reaction⟩ — see DERIVATIVE

bystander *n* someone who sees or watches something ⟨*bystanders* rushed to help the victim of the mugging⟩ — see SPECTATOR

byword *n* **1** an often stated observation regarding something from common experience ⟨Mom's favorite *byword* is "You can get more flies with honey than with vinegar"⟩ — see SAYING
2 the most perfect type or example ⟨nationally, Beverly

Hills' Rodeo Drive has become a *byword* for luxury retailing〉 — see QUINTESSENCE 1

byzantine *adj* having many parts or aspects that are usually interrelated 〈spent his first year at the Pentagon just trying to fathom its *byzantine* workings〉 — see COMPLEX 1

C

cab *n* an automobile that carries passengers for a fare usually determined by the distance traveled 〈called a *cab* to get back to the hotel〉 — see TAXICAB

cabal *n* a group involved in secret or criminal activities 〈a conspiracy theory about the existence of an international *cabal* devoted to world domination〉 — see [1]RING 1

cabaret *n* a bar or restaurant offering special nighttime entertainment (as music, dancing, or comedy acts) 〈a singing superstar who got her start singing in the *cabarets* of New York City〉 — see NIGHTCLUB

cabbage *n, slang* something (as pieces of stamped metal or printed paper) customarily and legally used as a medium of exchange, a measure of value, or a means of payment 〈he suddenly has a lot of *cabbage* for someone who's never done an honest day's work in his life〉 — see MONEY 1

cabin *n* **1** a small, simply constructed, and often temporary dwelling 〈a small *cabin* that hikers along the Appalachian Trail use for overnight stays〉 — see SHACK

2 an often small house for recreational or seasonal use 〈kept a *cabin* in the mountains for vacations during skiing season〉 — see COTTAGE

3 one of the parts into which an enclosed space is divided 〈an airplane *cabin*〉 — see COMPARTMENT

cabinet *n* a storage case typically having doors and shelves 〈the most precious knickknacks were kept in a *cabinet* with glass doors〉

synonyms buffet, closet, console, cupboard, hutch, locker, press, sideboard

related words bookcase, breakfront, chest, china closet, credence, credenza, étagère (*or* etagere), secretary, showcase, taboret (*or* tabouret), vitrine; cuddy, dresser, pie safe; armoire, clothespress, garderobe, wardrobe; cabinetry, shelving

cabinetwork *n* the movable articles (such as tables and chairs) in a room 〈18th-century *cabinetwork* from Newport, Rhode Island, is among the most prized of all American furniture〉 — see FURNITURE

cable *n* a length of braided, flexible material that is used for tying or connecting things 〈a mass of *cables* connecting the audio and video components〉 — see CORD 1

caboose *n* the part of the body upon which someone sits 〈a 1950s sex symbol who was famous for swinging her *caboose* as she walked〉 — see BUTTOCKS

cache *n* **1** a collection of things kept available for future use or need 〈a *cache* of medical supplies in case of emergency〉 — see STORE 1

2 a supply stored up and often hidden away 〈the squirrel kept a *cache* of nuts in the hollow of the tree〉 — see HOARD 1

cache *vb* **1** to put (something of future use or value) in a safe or secret place 〈an eccentric who *cached* money in odd places, such as under the boards of the floor〉 — see HOARD

2 to put into a hiding place 〈*cached* the fugitive slaves in their cellar until they could make their way to Canada〉 — see [1]HIDE 1

caching *n* the placing of something out of sight 〈the *caching* of holiday gifts in the weeks before Christmas〉 — see CONCEALMENT 1

cachinnation *n* an explosive sound that is a sign of amusement 〈as is common in some forms of schizophrenia, the patient would often erupt in *cachinnation*, often at the most inappropriate times〉 — see LAUGH 1

cack–handed *adj, British* lacking or showing a lack of nimbleness in using one's hands 〈some duffer with a *cack-handed* grip on his golf club〉 — see CLUMSY 1

cackle *n* **1** an explosive sound that is a sign of amusement 〈erupted in a high-pitched *cackle* at the absurdity of the suggestion〉 — see LAUGH 1

2 friendly, informal conversation or an instance of this 〈the constant *cackle* of his seat companion made the long flight seem even longer〉 — see CHAT 1

cackle *vb* **1** to engage in casual or rambling conversation 〈*cackled* on the phone with her friends about the latest soap opera plots〉 — see CHAT 1

2 to show mirth with an explosive vocal sound 〈she *cackled* with glee when her tax-evading neighbor finally got caught〉 — see LAUGH 1

cackler *n* a person who talks constantly 〈steadfastly avoids that *cackler* in the lunchroom, who doesn't mind wasting other people's time〉 — see CHATTERBOX

cacodemon *n* an evil spirit 〈he'd often wrestle with his conscience, but inevitably the *cacodemons* would win〉 — see DEMON 1

cacodemonic *adj* of, relating to, or worthy of an evil spirit 〈narcotics seemed to have a *cacodemonic* hold on him, and they inevitably ruined his life〉 — see FIENDISH 1

cacophonous *adj* marked by or producing a harsh combination of sounds 〈the *cacophonous* chaos on the floor of the New York Stock Exchange〉 — see DISSONANT

cacophony *n* loud, confused, and usually inharmonious sound 〈the *cacophony* of a pet store full of animals〉 — see NOISE 1

cad *n* a person whose behavior is offensive to others 〈he's the type of *cad* who readily bad-mouths every girl who's ever dumped him〉 — see JERK 1

cadaver *n* a dead body 〈medical students who train by using *cadavers*〉 — see CORPSE

cadaverous *adj* **1** lacking a healthy skin color 〈everyone always looks *cadaverous* in the winter〉 — see PALE 2

2 suffering extreme weight loss as a result of hunger or disease 〈a *cadaverous* cancer patient living out his final days with dignity and courage〉 — see EMACIATED

caddy *n* a covered rectangular container for storing or transporting things ⟨an antique tea *caddy* from the colonial period⟩ — see CHEST

cadence *n* the recurrent pattern formed by a series of sounds having a regular rise and fall in intensity ⟨the soothing *cadence* of the lecturer's voice nearly put me to sleep⟩ — see RHYTHM

cadenced *adj* marked by or occurring with a noticeable regularity in the rise and fall of sound ⟨a very *cadenced* voice, as one would expect of an instructor in a meditation class⟩ — see RHYTHMIC

cadent *adj* marked by or occurring with a noticeable regularity in the rise and fall of sound ⟨the song's *cadent* repetitions quickly became mesmerizing⟩ — see RHYTHMIC

cadet *n, slang* a man who solicits clients for a woman who is willing to engage in sexual activities for money ⟨the hooker claims she turned all her dough in to her *cadet* last night⟩ — see PIMP

cadre *n* the arrangement of parts that gives something its basic form ⟨claims that the problem will never be solved within the existing *cadre* of the state bureaucracy⟩ — see FRAME 1

caducity *n* the state or period of mental decline that typically accompanies old age ⟨forgetting the name of an old friend was another painful reminder of her progressive *caducity*⟩ — see DOTAGE

caesar *n* a person who uses power or authority in a cruel, unjust, or harmful way ⟨like many another third-world *caesar*, he cared little for the destitute class into which he himself had been born⟩ — see DESPOT

Caesarism *n* a system of government in which the ruler has unlimited power ⟨a military-led coup would almost certainly result in ironfisted *Caesarism* for that unstable nation⟩ — see DESPOTISM

café *also* **cafe** *n* **1** a bar or restaurant offering special nighttime entertainment (as music, dancing, or comedy acts) ⟨the *café* presents nationally known jazz performers in an intimate setting⟩ — see NIGHTCLUB
2 a place of business where alcoholic beverages are sold to be consumed on the premises ⟨a speakeasy that became a fashionable *café* with the repeal of prohibition⟩ — see BARROOM
3 a public establishment where meals are served to paying customers for consumption on the premises ⟨they met at a little *café* in Paris⟩ — see RESTAURANT

caff *n, British* a public establishment where meals are served to paying customers for consumption on the premises ⟨a simple East End *caff* that serves fish-and-chips and the like to a largely working-class clientele⟩ — see RESTAURANT

cage *n* an enclosure with an open framework for keeping animals ⟨the dogs and cats at the animal shelter looked so sad in their *cages*⟩
synonyms coop, corral, hutch, pen, pound
related words kennel, run; kraal, stockade; cote, dovecote (*also* dovecot), henhouse; fold, sheepfold; pigpen; aquarium, terrarium; live-box; fence

cage *vb* to close or shut in by or as if by barriers ⟨*caged* the rabbit at night so she wouldn't wake everyone up⟩ — see ENCLOSE 1

cagey *also* **cagy** *adj* **1** clever at attaining one's ends by indirect and often deceptive means ⟨a *cagey* old politician who is exceptionally skilled at getting federal money for his district⟩ — see ARTFUL 1
2 slow to begin or proceed with a course of action because of doubts or uncertainty ⟨when it came time to sign the contract, he suddenly got *cagey* about taking on the job⟩ — see HESITANT

caginess *also* **cageyness** *n* **1** exceptional discernment and judgment especially in practical matters ⟨most consumers should possess sufficient *caginess* to see through that scam⟩ — see ACUMEN
2 skill in achieving one's ends through indirect, subtle, or underhanded means ⟨the lawyer's celebrated *caginess* makes her the first choice of the hopelessly guilty⟩ — see CUNNING 1

caitiff *n* a mean, evil, or unprincipled person ⟨upon entering the store, I was beset by a *caitiff* in the guise of a salesman set on separating me from my money⟩ — see VILLAIN

cajole *vb* to get (someone) to do something by gentle urging, special attention, or flattery ⟨*cajoled* her into doing his laundry for him⟩ — see COAX

cake *n* **1** a small usually rounded mass of minced food that has been fried ⟨the rich, tender *cakes* of crabmeat had been lightly fried⟩
synonyms croquette, cutlet, fritter, galette, patty (*also* pattie)
related words finger, stick; gâteau (*or* gateau)
2 something easily done or dealt with ⟨today's assignment is *cake* compared to yesterday's⟩ — see CINCH 1

cake *vb* to cover with a hardened layer ⟨shoes *caked* with dried mud⟩ — see ENCRUST

cakewalk *n* something easily done or dealt with ⟨no one was pretending that winning the election would be a *cakewalk*⟩ — see CINCH 1

calaboose *n* a place of confinement for persons held in lawful custody ⟨fittingly, the *calaboose* in that one-horse town consisted of a single cell⟩ — see JAIL

calamitous *adj* **1** bringing about ruin or misfortune ⟨a *calamitous* decision to sell their products online exclusively ruined the business⟩ — see FATAL 1
2 causing or tending to cause destruction ⟨a *calamitous* flood that destroyed the town's central business district⟩ — see DESTRUCTIVE 1

calamity *n* a sudden violent event that brings about great loss or destruction ⟨this latest breakdown of the car is inconvenient, but not a *calamity*⟩ — see DISASTER 1

calculable *adj* worthy of one's trust ⟨his performance as a pitcher is as *calculable* as the daily tides⟩ — see DEPENDABLE

calculate *vb* **1** to determine (a value) by doing the necessary mathematical operations ⟨the family has been *calculating* what a week at the beach resort would end up costing⟩
synonyms cipher, compute, figure, reckon, work out
related words add up, average, sum, tally, total, totalize; add, divide, multiply, subtract; allow (for), deduct, factor (in *or* into *or* out), figure in; figure out, solve (for); count, itemize, number; calibrate, gauge (*also* gage), measure, scale; assess, appraise, estimate, evaluate, rate, value; recalculate, recompute, refigure
2 to decide the size, amount, number, or distance of (something) without actual measurement ⟨I *calculate* that this job will take another two days to finish⟩ — see ESTIMATE 2
3 to work out the details of (something) in advance ⟨*calculated* the best route to take to the coast⟩ — see PLAN 1
4 to have in mind as a purpose or goal ⟨I *calculate* to run a marathon from start to finish—even if it kills me⟩ — see INTEND 1
5 to place reliance or trust ⟨we know we can *calculate* on you following through, whatever the assignment⟩ — see DEPEND 2

calculated *adj* decided on as a result of careful thought ⟨took a *calculated* risk and got in on the ground floor of the new enterprise⟩ — see DELIBERATE 1

calculation *n* the act or process of performing mathematical operations to find a value ⟨by my *calculation*, it

should take me a month to save up for the weekend getaway⟩
synonyms arithmetic, calculus, ciphering, computation, figures, figuring, math, mathematics, number crunching, numbers, reckoning
related words addition, division, multiplication, subtraction; calibration, measurement, mensuration; appraisal, assessment, estimation, evaluation, valuation

calculus *n* the act or process of performing mathematical operations to find a value ⟨by my *calculus* the more efficient air conditioner will have paid for itself within a span of five years⟩ — see CALCULATION

calendar *n* a listing of things to be presented or considered (as at a concert or play) ⟨the *calendar* of upcoming events at the state fair will be available tomorrow⟩ — see PROGRAM 1

caliber *or* **calibre** *n* degree of excellence ⟨musicians of the highest *caliber* perform at that concert hall⟩ — see QUALITY 1

caliginous *adj* being without light or without much light ⟨what horrors were committed within the *caliginous* confinements of that torture chamber⟩ — see DARK 1

call *n* **1** a natural vocal sound made by an animal ⟨a ranger who could immediately identify the *call* of every creature in the forest⟩
synonyms cry, note
related words bark, bay, bellow, blat, bleat, bray, cackle, calling, caterwaul, caw, cheep, chirp, cluck, coo, crake, croak, crow, grunt, honk, hoot, howl, low, meow (*also* miaow), mew, moo, neigh, oink, peep, quack, roar, screech, squall, squawk, squeak, squeal, trumpet, tu-whit tu-whoo, twitter, whinny, yap, yelp, yip, yowl
2 a coming to see another briefly for social or business reasons ⟨we paid a *call* on the new neighbors the day after they moved in⟩
synonyms visit, visitation
related words drop-in, stopover; get-together, meeting, rendezvous, tryst
3 a communication by telephone ⟨give me a *call* as soon as you arrive, so I'll know you got there safely⟩
synonyms buzz, ring
related words callback, cold call, conference call, message, toll call, voice mail
4 an act or instance of asking for information ⟨put out a *call* for background information about the suspect⟩ — see QUESTION 2
5 an entitlement to something ⟨you have no *call* to insult people⟩ — see CLAIM 1
6 a position arrived at after consideration ⟨I told you my preference for a cruise destination, but it's your *call*⟩ — see DECISION 1
7 the state of being sought after especially for purchase ⟨there's not much *call* for classical music in this neck of the woods⟩ — see DEMAND 2

call *vb* **1** to speak so as to be heard at a distance ⟨we could hear someone *calling* for help from the other side of the wall⟩
synonyms bawl, bay, bellow, cry, holler, hollo (*or* halloo *also* hallo), roar, shout, sound off, thunder, vociferate, yell
related words crow, whoop; scream, screech, shriek, shrill, squeak, squeal; caterwaul, howl, ululate, wail, yawp (*or* yaup), yowl; hail; speak out, speak up
near antonyms breathe, mumble, murmur, mutter, whisper
2 to make a telephone call to ⟨use this cell phone to *call* me if there's an emergency⟩
synonyms dial, phone, ring (up) [*chiefly British*], telephone
related words beep, buzz; call in; cold-call
3 to make a brief visit ⟨the hospital posts the hours during which friends and relatives may *call*⟩
synonyms come by, come over, drop by, drop in, pop (in), run (over), run in, step in, stop (by *or* in), visit
related words barge (in); look up, see; bop (into), happen (by); frequent, hang (at), haunt, resort (to)
4 to put an end to (something planned or previously agreed to) ⟨the game was *called* on account of rain⟩ — see CANCEL 1
5 to think of in a particular way ⟨I wouldn't quite *call* that cheating, but it's not entirely ethical either⟩ — see CONSIDER 1
6 to utter one's distinctive animal sound ⟨the dog *called* whenever it flushed a quail⟩ — see CRY 2
7 to bring together in assembly by or as if by command ⟨*called* all the night workers in for a meeting⟩ — see CONVOKE
8 to decide the size, amount, number, or distance of (something) without actual measurement ⟨let's *call* that five feet for now, and we'll measure it out later⟩ — see ESTIMATE 2
9 to demand or request the presence or service of ⟨rushed to *call* a repairman when the furnace broke⟩ — see SUMMON 1
10 to give a name to ⟨we've decided to *call* the kitten "Molly"⟩ — see NAME 1
11 to request the doing of by virtue of one's authority ⟨the union president is refusing to *call* a strike⟩ — see COMMAND 2
12 to tell of or describe beforehand ⟨somehow the political pundit *called* the race results within a mere percentage point⟩ — see FORETELL

call (for) *vb* **1** to ask for (something) earnestly or with authority ⟨with an eye to the expected rush, the manager *called for* additional waiters⟩ — see DEMAND 1
2 to make a request for ⟨*called for* someone to help with planning the club's party⟩ — see ASK (FOR) 1

call (on *or* **upon)** *vb* to make a social call upon ⟨lots of well-wishers *called on* the new mother in the weeks following the birth of her first child⟩ — see VISIT 1

callant *n, chiefly Scottish* a male person who has not yet reached adulthood ⟨ever since he was a *callant*, he's been fishing off the eastern coast of Scotland⟩ — see BOY 1

call down *vb* to criticize (someone) severely or angrily especially for personal failings ⟨I was *called down* by my supervisor for not catching the accounting error sooner⟩ — see SCOLD

caller *n* a person who visits another ⟨a number of *callers* have been by since they heard you weren't feeling well⟩ — see GUEST 1

call girl *n* a woman who engages in sexual activities for money ⟨before the actress made it big, she worked for a time as a *call girl*⟩ — see PROSTITUTE

calligrapher *n* one who writes from dictation or copies manuscripts ⟨a gorgeous copy of the text that was produced by one of the finest *calligraphers* of the age⟩ — see SCRIBE 1

calligraphy *n* writing done by hand ⟨she specializes in scrollwork with beautiful *calligraphy*⟩ — see HANDWRITING 2

calling *n* **1** the act of putting an end to something planned or previously agreed to ⟨the *calling* of the match was a disappointment to both players⟩ — see CANCELLATION 1
2 the activity by which one regularly makes a living ⟨I think my true *calling* will be as a commercial artist⟩ — see OCCUPATION 1

calling off *n* the act of putting an end to something planned or previously agreed to ⟨the *calling off* of the senior prom is not going to go over well⟩ — see CANCELLATION 1

call off *vb* **1** to draw the attention or mind to something else ⟨she was about to tell me the big news when her attention was *called off* by the arrival of another guest⟩ — see DISTRACT 1
2 to put an end to (something planned or previously agreed to) ⟨*called off* the party after half of those invited couldn't make it⟩ — see CANCEL 1

callous *adj* having or showing a lack of sympathy or tender feelings ⟨the *callous* comment "It's just a fish," when the boy's pet died, made him cry⟩ — see HARD 1

callow *adj* lacking in adult experience or maturity ⟨a story about a *callow* youth who learns the value of hard work and self-reliance⟩
synonyms adolescent, green, immature, inexperienced, juvenile, puerile, raw, unfledged, unformed, unripe, unripened
related words babyish, childish, infantile, infantilized, infantine; boyish, girlish, juvenescent, kiddish, young, youngish, youthful; maidenly, virginal; ingenuous, innocent, naive (*or* naïve), tender; unknowing, unseasoned, unsophisticated, untrained, untried
phrases wet behind the ears
near antonyms advanced, precocious; knowing, savvy, sophisticated, worldly, worldly-wise
antonyms adult, experienced, grown-up, mature, ripe

calm *adj* **1** free from storms or physical disturbance ⟨after a stormy night of high winds and driving rains, the day dawned on a *calm* sea⟩
synonyms halcyon, hushed, lown [*dialect*], peaceful, placid, quiet, serene, still, stilly, tranquil, untroubled
related words balmy, clement, equable, gentle, mild, moderate, temperate; clear, cloudless, fair, rainless, sunny, sunshiny, windless
near antonyms blizzardy (*also* blizzardly), blustery, squally, windy; extreme, foul, intemperate, nasty, severe
antonyms agitated, angry, inclement, restless, rough, stormy, tempestuous, turbulent, unquiet, unsettled
2 free from emotional or mental agitation ⟨bystanders tried to help the injured person remain *calm* while they waited for the ambulance to arrive⟩
synonyms collected, composed, cool, coolheaded, equal, level, limpid, peaceful, placid, possessed, recollected, sedate, self-composed, self-possessed, serene, smooth, together, tranquil, undisturbed, unperturbed, unruffled, unshaken, untroubled, unworried
related words even, even-keeled, steady, well-adjusted, well-balanced; imperturbable, nerveless, unflappable, unshakable; centered, disciplined, equable, self-contained, self-controlled; affable, breezy, devil-may-care, easygoing, happy-go-lucky, laid-back, loosey-goosey, mellow; carefree, nonchalant, unconcerned; assured, confident, self-assured; aloof, detached, dispassionate, indifferent; bovine, impassive, phlegmatic, sober, stolid; relaxed, relieved, tranquilized (*also* tranquillized)
phrases at peace
near antonyms anxious, bothered, distressed, uneasy, unquiet, unsettled, worried; jittery, jumpy, nervous, restless, skittish, tense; high-strung, unstable, uptight
antonyms agitated, discomposed, disturbed, flustered, perturbed, unglued, unhinged, unstrung, upset
3 free from disturbing noise or uproar ⟨the room became much *calmer* once the rowdy tour group had left⟩ — see QUIET 1

calm *n* **1** a state of freedom from storm or disturbance ⟨vacationing city dwellers who are tired of the hustle and bustle enjoy the *calm* of the secluded mountain village⟩
synonyms calmness, hush, peace, peacefulness, placidity, quiet, quietness, quietude, repose, restfulness, sereneness, serenity, still, stillness, tranquillity (*or* tranquility)
related words lull, pause, respite; silence; mildness, soothingness; comity, concord, harmony; casualness, easygoingness, informality, laid-backness, relaxedness
near antonyms clamor, din, noise, racket
antonyms bustle, commotion, hubbub, hurly-burly, pandemonium, tumult, turmoil, unquietness, unrest, uproar
2 freedom from disquieting or oppressive thoughts or emotions ⟨the batter always exudes an aura of *calm*, even in clutch situations⟩ — see PEACE 2

calm *vb* **1** to free from distress or disturbance ⟨the president's reassuring words did much to *calm* the public during the national emergency⟩
synonyms becalm, compose, lull, lullaby, quiet, quieten [*chiefly British*], salve, settle, soothe, still, tranquilize (*also* tranquillize)
related words appease, conciliate, hush, mollify, pacify, placate; allay, alleviate, assuage, ease, lay, mitigate, quell, relax, relieve, solace; narcotize, sedate, stupefy
near antonyms aggravate, heighten, intensify; arouse, excite, foment, incite, rouse, stir (up), work up
antonyms agitate, discompose, disquiet, disturb, key (up), perturb, upset, vex
2 to gain emotional or mental control of ⟨he *calmed* himself before continuing the eulogy⟩ — see COLLECT 1

calm (down) *vb* to become still and orderly ⟨the sea finally *calmed down*, making it safe for small craft to venture forth once again⟩ — see QUIET 1

calming *adj* tending to calm the emotions and relieve stress ⟨a *calming* glass of warm milk⟩ — see SOOTHING 1

calmness *n* **1** a state of freedom from storm or disturbance ⟨the unusual *calmness* of the lake gave its surface a strikingly glassy appearance⟩ — see CALM 1
2 evenness of emotions or temper ⟨her resolute *calmness* in a crisis serves her well as a nurse in the emergency room⟩ — see EQUANIMITY
3 freedom from disquieting or oppressive thoughts or emotions ⟨a teacher who handles even the most vexing situations with a clearheaded *calmness*⟩ — see PEACE 2

calumniate *vb* to make untrue and harmful statements about ⟨the short-lived Sedition Act of 1798 made it illegal to *calumniate* the President of the United States⟩ — see SLANDER

calumniation *n* the making of false statements that damage another's reputation ⟨his campaign's reliance on *calumniation* seems out of keeping with his claim that he's a new kind of politician⟩ — see SLANDER

calumnious *adj* causing or intended to cause unjust injury to a person's good name ⟨a *calumnious* campaign ad that went well beyond the negativity to which voters had become so richly accustomed⟩ — see LIBELOUS

calumny *n* the making of false statements that damage another's reputation ⟨a blogger whose site is little more than a foulmouthed forum for *calumny* and rumormongering⟩ — see SLANDER

camaraderie *n* the feeling of closeness and friendship that exists between companions ⟨weekend retreats that are intended to foster *camaraderie* within the upper echelons of the corporation⟩ — see COMPANIONSHIP

Camelot *n* an often imaginary place or state of utter perfection and happiness ⟨that year spent in Spain studying art was their personal *Camelot*⟩ — see PARADISE 1

camouflage *n* clothing put on to hide one's true identity or imitate someone or something else ⟨the soldiers must wear protective jungle *camouflage* while on patrol⟩ — see DISGUISE 1

camouflage *vb* to change the dress or looks of so as to conceal true identity ⟨*camouflaged* the military camp as a native village⟩ — see DISGUISE 1

camp *n* **1** a place where a group of people live for a short time in tents or cabins ⟨the war forced people to flee their homes and to live in crowded *camps* along the border⟩
synonyms bivouac, campground, campsite, encampment, hutment
related words canvas (*also* canvass), tentage; colony, plantation, settlement; Hooverville, jungle, shantytown; concentration camp, prison camp; barracks, cantonment, installation, laager [*South African*], leaguer, post
2 a small, simply constructed, and often temporary dwelling ⟨a hunter's *camp* deep in the woods⟩ — see SHACK
3 an often small house for recreational or seasonal use ⟨years ago the wealthy industrialists built some rather grand *camps* along the lake⟩ — see COTTAGE

camp *vb* to provide with living quarters or shelter ⟨some out-of-town delegates to the convention were *camped* in university dorms⟩ — see HOUSE 1

camp (out) *vb* to live in a camp or the outdoors ⟨rather than stay in motels, my family usually *camps out* when we're on vacation⟩
synonyms bivouac, encamp
related words sleep out, tent; bed (down); backpack, caravan
phrases rough it

campaign *n* a series of activities undertaken to achieve a goal ⟨an all-out *campaign* to bring a minor league baseball team to the city⟩
synonyms bandwagon, blitz, cause, crusade, drive, juggernaut, movement, push
related words assault, attack, maneuver, march, offensive; action, bid, enterprise, initiative, mission, project, undertaking

campaigner *n* one who seeks an office, honor, position, or award ⟨an experienced *campaigner* who knows that one televised mistake can put an end to one's candidacy⟩ — see CANDIDATE

camper *n* a motor vehicle that is specially equipped for living while traveling ⟨the family loaded up the *camper* and headed off for the tour of several national parks⟩
synonyms caravan, motor home, recreational vehicle, RV, trailer
related words house trailer, mobile home; coach, van

campground *n* a place where a group of people live for a short time in tents or cabins ⟨at last the weary vacationers pulled into a *campground* for the night⟩ — see CAMP 1

campo *n* a broad area of level or rolling treeless country ⟨vaqueros driving their herd of cattle across the *campo*⟩ — see PLAIN 1

campsite *n* a place where a group of people live for a short time in tents or cabins ⟨the *campsite* at least offers shower and bathroom facilities⟩ — see CAMP 1

can *n* **1** a metal container in the shape of a cylinder ⟨the shelter stores huge *cans* of water for an emergency⟩
synonyms barrel, canister (*also* cannister), drum, tin
related words bucket, pail; cannikin; tin can
2 a place of confinement for persons held in lawful custody ⟨the protesters were rounded up and thrown in the *can*⟩ — see JAIL
3 a room furnished with a fixture for flushing body waste ⟨excuse me, I need to use the *can*⟩ — see TOILET
4 the part of the body upon which someone sits ⟨she claims a guy on the subway gave her a pinch on the *can*⟩ — see BUTTOCKS

can *vb* **1** *slang* to bring (as an action or operation) to an immediate end ⟨*can* the chatter, or I'm kicking you out of this library⟩ — see STOP 1
2 to let go from office, service, or employment ⟨the cashier was summarily *canned* for stealing from the registers⟩ — see DISMISS 1

canal *n* an open man-made passageway for water ⟨the Panama *Canal* opened a much easier and shorter passageway from the Atlantic to the Pacific⟩ — see CHANNEL 1

canalize *vb* to cause to move to a central point or along a restricted pathway ⟨the director of the charity should be *canalizing* the flow of donations so that the money ends up where it is most needed⟩ — see CHANNEL

canard *n* a rumor or report of a personal or sensational nature ⟨it's a popular *canard* that the actress died under scandalous circumstances⟩ — see TALE 1

canary *n, slang* a person who provides information about another's wrongdoing ⟨a *canary* who was singing and giving up the names of some of the city's most notorious drug lords⟩ — see INFORMER

cancel *vb* **1** to put an end to (something planned or previously agreed to) ⟨please call to *cancel* your appointment with the dentist if you can't make it⟩
synonyms abandon, abort, call, call off, cry off, drop, recall, repeal, rescind, revoke, scrap, scrub
related words abrogate, annul, invalidate, nullify, void, write off; recant, retract, take back, withdraw; countermand, reverse, roll back; break off, discontinue, end, halt, stop, terminate; hold back, interrupt, suspend; give up, relinquish, surrender
near antonyms engage, pledge, promise; begin, commence, initiate, start; take on, take up, undertake
antonyms continue, keep
2 to put an end to by formal action ⟨the agreement can be *canceled* by either side with a formal written notice⟩ — see ABOLISH 1
3 to show (something written) to be no longer valid by drawing a cross over or a line through it ⟨*canceled* the check and wrote a new one⟩ — see X (OUT)
4 to destroy all traces of ⟨it seemed as though all honor and decency had been *canceled* by the war's new moral order⟩ — see ANNIHILATE 1

cancel (out) *vb* to balance with an equal force so as to make ineffective ⟨unfortunately, this one indiscretion will *cancel out* a long record of accomplishment⟩ — see OFFSET

canceler *or* **canceller** *n* a force or influence that makes an opposing force ineffective or less effective ⟨his dispassionate manner can be a welcome *canceler* of his wife's emotional response to every little thing⟩ — see COUNTERBALANCE

cancellation *also* **cancelation** *n* **1** the act of putting an end to something planned or previously agreed to ⟨the misbehavior of a few bad apples at the end of the football game resulted in the *cancellation* of the victory party⟩
synonyms abandonment, abortion, calling, calling off, dropping, recall, recision, repeal, rescission, revocation
related words annulment, invalidation, neutralization, nullification, voidance; abolishment, abolition, ending, halting, stopping, termination; giving up, relinquishment, surrender; reversal, rollback
near antonyms beginning, commencement, initiation; engagement, undertaking
antonyms continuation
2 the doing away with something by formal action ⟨a blanket *cancellation* of all military leave for the duration of the crisis⟩ — see ABOLITION

candescent *adj* giving off or reflecting much light ⟨the campers were transfixed by the *candescent* coals of their seashore fire⟩ — see BRIGHT 1

candid *adj* **1** free in expressing one's true feelings and opinions ⟨a *candid* woman who never hesitates to say exactly what's on her mind⟩ — see FRANK
2 marked by justice, honesty, and freedom from bias ⟨a *candid* listing of the advantages and disadvantages of each medical insurance plan⟩ — see FAIR 2

candidate *n* one who seeks an office, honor, position, or award ⟨each *candidate* for town council was allowed to speak at the candidates' forum⟩
synonyms applicant, applier, aspirant, campaigner, contender, expectant, hopeful, prospect, seeker
related words competitor, contestant, entrant, entry, favorite, qualifier; dark horse, spoiler, stalking horse; crown prince, favorite son; claimant, pretender; nominee, running mate
near antonyms incumbent, officeholder; awardee, honoree, inductee; dropout
antonyms noncandidate

candidness *n* the free expression of one's true feelings and opinions ⟨*candidness* is something that we claim to admire—except when we are on the receiving end of a brutally honest assessment⟩ — see CANDOR 1

candlelight *n* a time or place of little or no light ⟨at *candlelight* carolers would gather in the village green before beginning their stroll⟩ — see DARK 1

candor *n* **1** the free expression of one's true feelings and opinions ⟨an interview in which the members of the rock band speak with *candor* about their recent squabbling⟩
synonyms bluntness, candidness, directness, forthrightness, frankness, honesty, openheartedness, openness, outspokenness, plainness, plainspokenness, plumpness, straightforwardness, unguardedness, unreserve, unreservedness
related words earnestness, sincerity, sobriety; artlessness, genuineness, naïveté (*also* naivete *or* naiveté), simplicity, unsophistication; communicativeness, freedom, license (*or* licence), uninhibitedeness, unrestrainedness, unrestraint
near antonyms circuitousness, evasiveness, secretiveness; inhibition, reserve, restraint, reticence, shyness; diplomacy, tact
antonyms dissembling, dissimulation, indirection
2 the quality or state of having or giving off light ⟨the desert sun shone down on the intrepid travelers with fiery *candor*⟩ — see BRILLIANCE 1

candy *vb* to make more desirable ⟨the publisher hopes the flashy cover will *candy* up the novel for impulse buyers⟩ — see SWEETEN

candyfloss *n, British* something attractive but lacking in substance ⟨the composer's works have generally been dismissed as *candyfloss* by music critics⟩ — see COTTON CANDY

cane *n* a heavy rigid stick used as a weapon or for punishment ⟨in those days corporal punishment was common, and the *cane* was regarded as another one of the schoolmaster's educational tools⟩ — see CLUB 1

canine *n* a domestic mammal that is related to the wolves and foxes ⟨in the minds of some, the winner of this prestigious dog show has a fair claim to the title of King of the *Canines*⟩ — see DOG 1

canister *also* **cannister** *n* a metal container in the shape of a cylinder ⟨she put the store-bought cookies in a fancy *canister* to make them look homemade⟩ — see CAN 1

canker *vb* to lower in character, dignity, or quality ⟨such shameless ambulance chasing *cankers* the legal profession⟩ — see DEBASE 1

canned *adj* **1** using or marked by the use of something else as a basis or model ⟨there's a *canned* quality to the screenplay that reminds you of countless other action movies⟩ — see IMITATIVE 1
2 *slang* being under the influence of alcohol ⟨if you think she's boring now, you should talk to her when she's *canned*⟩ — see DRUNK

canniness *n* **1** exceptional discernment and judgment especially in practical matters ⟨negotiates business deals with all of the proverbial *canniness* of an old-time horse trader⟩ — see ACUMEN
2 skill in achieving one's ends through indirect, subtle, or underhanded means ⟨the *canniness* with which she negotiated her contract as spokesperson for the shoe manufacturer⟩ — see CUNNING 1

cannonade *n* a rapid or overwhelming outpouring of many things at once ⟨the director of the sporting event was greeted at the scene with a *cannonade* of complaints⟩ — see BARRAGE

cannonade *vb* to use bombs or artillery against ⟨the artillery *cannonaded* the enemy encampment all night⟩ — see BOMBARD 1

cannonball *vb* to proceed or move quickly ⟨a dune buggy came recklessly *cannonballing* down the crowded beach⟩ — see HURRY 2

canny *adj* **1** having or showing a practical cleverness or judgment ⟨a *canny* card player, good at psyching out his opponents⟩ — see SHREWD 1
2 *chiefly Scottish* enjoying physical comfort ⟨warm and *canny* under the woolen bedcovers, we didn't mind the chilly Scottish nights⟩ — see COMFORTABLE 2

canon *n* **1** a statement or body of statements concerning faith or morals proclaimed by a church ⟨members of the church must abide by its *canons*⟩ — see DOCTRINE 1
2 a record of a series of items (as names or titles) usually arranged according to some system ⟨the *canon* of plays that are attributed to William Shakespeare⟩ — see [1]LIST
3 a collection or system of rules of conduct ⟨the ABA Model Code of Professional Responsibility is a lawyer's *canon*⟩ — see CODE

canonize *vb* **1** to love or admire too much ⟨a singing star so *canonized* by his fans that they refuse to believe anything bad about him⟩ — see IDOLIZE
2 to assign a high status or value to ⟨those movie buffs who have *canonized* Alfred Hitchcock as filmdom's preeminent director⟩ — see EXALT 1

canopy *n* a raised covering over something for decoration or protection ⟨trees line both sides of the garden path, with their foliage forming a leafy *canopy* for walkers⟩
synonyms awning, ceiling, cover, roof, tent
related words dome, marquee, pavilion; arbor, bower, pergola; screen, shade, shelter, shield, sunshade, umbrella; canvas (*also* canvass), fly

canorous *adj* having a pleasing mixture of notes ⟨a *canorous* chorus of birdsong filled the morning air⟩ — see HARMONIOUS 1

[1]**cant** *n* the degree to which something rises up from a position level with the horizon ⟨a steep *cant* of the riverbank at that turn in the river⟩ — see SLANT

[2]**cant** *n* **1** the pretending of having virtues, principles, or beliefs that one in fact does not have ⟨many accused the evangelist of *cant*, since his lavish lifestyle seemed to bear little resemblance to what he was preaching⟩ — see HYPOCRISY
2 the special terms or expressions of a particular group or field ⟨the colorful *cant* used by movie producers and publicity agents in Hollywood⟩ — see TERMINOLOGY

cant *adj* running in a slanting direction ⟨the *cant* buttresses on the interior walls are made of solid oak⟩ — see DIAGONAL

cant *vb* to set or cause to be at an angle ⟨carefully *canted* the ladder against the wall⟩ — see LEAN 1

cantankerous *adj* having or showing a habitually bad temper ⟨a *cantankerous* old woman who insisted that nothing should ever be allowed to change⟩ — see ILL-TEMPERED

canted *adj* running in a slanting direction ⟨an odd little house, built with deliberately *canted* windows and not one right angle⟩ — see DIAGONAL

canticle *n* a religious song ⟨the monks offered up a *canticle* at dawn on Easter morning⟩ — see HYMN 1

cantina *n, Southwest* a place of business where alcoholic beverages are sold to be consumed on the premises ⟨we spent an interesting evening in that desert town's lone *cantina*⟩ — see BARROOM

can't–miss *adj* not likely to fail ⟨my uncle's willingness to see every get-rich-quick scheme as a *can't-miss* opportunity⟩ — see INFALLIBLE 2

canty *adj, British dialect* having or showing a good mood or disposition ⟨a bloke with a perpetually *canty* attitude⟩ — see CHEERFUL 1

canvas *also* **canvass** *n* a picture created with oil paint ⟨one *canvas* by Picasso is worth more money than most of us can imagine⟩ — see PAINTING

canvass *also* **canvas** *vb* **1** to go around and approach (people) with a request for opinions or information ⟨we *canvassed* people all over town, asking if they would be interested in participating in a recycling program⟩
synonyms interview, poll, solicit, survey
related words circularize; interrogate, question; feel (out), sound (out)
near antonyms report
2 to talk about (an issue) usually from various points of view and for the purpose of arriving at a decision or opinion ⟨*canvassed* all the items on the agenda⟩ — see DISCUSS

canvasser *also* **canvaser** *n* a person who goes around and approaches people with a request for opinions or information ⟨worked as a *canvasser* for a public interest research group⟩
synonyms interviewer, poller, pollster
related words asker, inquirer, querier, querist, questioner
near antonyms answerer, replier, responder; attester, informant, reporter, testifier, witness
antonyms interviewee, pollee, respondent

canyon *also* **cañon** *n* a narrow opening between hillsides or mountains that can be used for passage ⟨as the scouts made their way through the *canyon*, they marveled at the sheer walls of rock on both sides⟩
synonyms col, couloir, defile, flume, gap, gill [*British*], gorge, gulch, gulf, kloof [*South African*], linn [*chiefly Scottish*], notch, pass, ravine, saddle
related words abyss, chasm, cirque, cleft, crevasse, crevice, cwm [*chiefly British*], fissure; combe (*also* coombe *or* coomb) [*British*], dale, dell, glen, hollow, shut-in, vale, valley; basin, floodplain, kettle; arroyo, barranca (*also* barranco), coulee, draw, gully (*also* gulley), gutter, nullah, trench, trough, wadi, wash [*West*]

[1]**cap** *n* a small mass containing medicine to be taken orally ⟨I prefer to take my medicine as *caps* rather than in liquid form⟩ — see PILL 1

[2]**cap** *n* **1** a covering for the head usually having a shaped crown ⟨grabbed a *cap* and plopped it on his head before running out⟩ — see HAT
2 a piece placed over an open container to hold in, protect, or conceal its contents ⟨I can't find the *cap* to the milk bottle⟩ — see COVER 1
3 a real or imaginary point beyond which a person or thing cannot go ⟨a *cap* on player salary expenditures was suggested as a way to keep small market teams competitive⟩ — see LIMIT 1

cap *vb* to set bounds or an upper limit for ⟨the senator will propose a bill to *cap* prices for home heating oil⟩ — see LIMIT 1

cap (off) *vb* to bring to a triumphant conclusion ⟨*capped off* the baseball season with 10–0 shutout⟩ — see CROWN

capability *n* **1** a skill, an ability, or knowledge that makes a person able to do a particular job ⟨the nature of the tasks to which you are assigned will depend on your *capabilities*⟩ — see QUALIFICATION 1
2 the physical or mental power to do something ⟨the natural *capability* some people seem to have for teaching⟩ — see ABILITY
3 something that can develop or become actual ⟨there are great *capabilities* in the property, either as a bed-and-breakfast or as a private home⟩ — see POTENTIAL

capable *adj* having the required skills for an acceptable level of performance ⟨a *capable* and efficient editor⟩ — see COMPETENT 1

capableness *n* the physical or mental power to do something ⟨the very *capableness* of such a young child to commit a criminal act of any kind is questionable⟩ — see ABILITY

capably *adv* in a skillful or expert manner ⟨the summer intern performed all assigned tasks at the television station *capably* and quickly⟩ — see WELL 3

capacious *adj* more than adequate or average in capacity ⟨that car has a *capacious* trunk that makes it a good choice for families⟩ — see SPACIOUS

capacity *n* **1** the largest number or amount that something can hold ⟨the seating *capacity* of the school auditorium is 800 people⟩
synonyms complement, cubage, real estate, volume
related words burden, fill, fullness, load, measure; area, room, space, stowage
2 an assignment at which one regularly works for pay ⟨served in the *capacity* of the network's White House correspondent for a year⟩ — see JOB 1
3 the action for which a person or thing is specially fitted or used or for which a thing exists ⟨offered advice in his *capacity* as a lawyer⟩ — see ROLE
4 the physical or mental power to do something ⟨not everyone has the *capacity* for learning higher math⟩ — see ABILITY

caparison *n* **1** dressy clothing ⟨attended the masquerade ball in the *caparison* of an Indian maharaja⟩ — see FINERY
2 something that decorates or beautifies ⟨horses dressed in Old-West *caparison* for the parade⟩ — see DECORATION 1

caparison *vb* **1** to outfit with clothes and especially fine or special clothes ⟨used to seeing him in a T-shirt and jeans, we were startled by the sight of strapping youth *caparisoned* for the prom in a tuxedo⟩ — see CLOTHE 1
2 to make more attractive by adding something that is beautiful or becoming ⟨the state's rolling hills are even more becoming when they are *caparisoned* in the glorious colors of autumn⟩ — see DECORATE

[1]**cape** *n* a sleeveless garment worn so as to hang over the shoulders, arms, and back ⟨the mysterious figure wrapped his *cape* tightly around his shoulders⟩
synonyms capote, cloak, frock, manteau, mantle
related words burnoose (*or* burnous), capelet, capuchin, cowl, domino, joseph, manta, mantelet, mantilla, palatine, pelerine, pelisse, poncho, roquelaure, tippet; serape (*or* sarape), shawl, stole, wrap

[2]**cape** *n* an area of land that juts out into a body of water ⟨residents fled the *cape* as the hurricane roared up the coast⟩
synonyms arm, foreland, headland, ness, peninsula, point, promontory, spit
related words breakwater, jetty

caper *n* a playful or mischievous act intended as a joke ⟨long-ago college *capers* that have become more rollicking and daring with each recounting⟩ — see PRANK

caper *vb* to play and run about happily ⟨as summer drew to a close, the children spent their days wistfully *capering* on the beach⟩ — see FROLIC 1

capital *adj* **1** coming before all others in importance ⟨the *capital* goal of the effort is to assimilate the new

immigrants⟩ — see FOREMOST 1
2 of the very best kind ⟨a truly *capital* idea, which I highly endorse⟩ — see EXCELLENT

capital *n* **1** a thing or place that is of greatest importance to an activity or interest ⟨during the 1980s Silicon Valley became the *capital* of the computer industry⟩ — see CENTER 1
2 the total of one's money and property ⟨invested nearly all of their *capital* in the new business⟩ — see WEALTH 1

capitalist *n* a wealthy person ⟨*capitalists* who lost everything in the '29 Crash⟩
synonyms Croesus, deep pocket, fat cat, have, money, moneybags, plutocrat, silk stocking
related words moneymaker, money-spinner [*chiefly British*]; magnate, nabob, tycoon; billionaire, gazillionaire, millionaire, multibillionaire, multimillionaire, multimillionairess, zillionaire; heir, heiress, jet-setter, jeunesse dorée
near antonyms bankrupt, beggar
antonyms have-not, pauper

capitalize *vb* to provide money for ⟨several investors agreed to *capitalize* the new venture⟩ — see FINANCE 1

capitalize (on) *vb* to take unfair advantage of ⟨*capitalized on* her coworker's absence to take full credit for the joint project⟩ — see EXPLOIT 1

capitol *n* the building in which a state legislature meets ⟨the legislators were called to the *capitol* for an emergency session⟩
synonyms statehouse
related words meetinghouse; chamber, hall; house, senate

capitulate *vb* **1** to cease resistance (as to another's arguments, demands, or control) ⟨one side finally *capitulated* when it became clear that they couldn't win the argument⟩ — see YIELD 3
2 to yield to the control or power of enemy forces ⟨the city reluctantly *capitulated* to the invaders after a three-day siege⟩ — see FALL 2

capitulating *n* the usually forced yielding of one's person or possessions to the control of another ⟨the tug-of-war will continue until the *capitulating* of one side or the other⟩ — see SURRENDER

capitulation *n* the usually forced yielding of one's person or possessions to the control of another ⟨her sudden *capitulation* surprised everyone; she usually debated for hours⟩ — see SURRENDER

capote *n* a sleeveless garment worn so as to hang over the shoulders, arms, and back ⟨the traveler wore a long hooded *capote* as he walked over the moors⟩ — see [1]CAPE

capper *n* **1** the last part of a process or action ⟨the *capper* to the campaign rally was an appearance by the candidate himself⟩ — see FINALE
2 something (as a fact or argument) that is decisive or overwhelming ⟨she was smart, she was pretty, but here's the *capper*—she was kind, unlike the other girls⟩ — see CLINCHER

capriccio *n* a playful or mischievous act intended as a joke ⟨the sort of innocuous *capriccio* intended to liven up a stuffy dinner party⟩ — see PRANK

caprice *n* **1** a sudden impulsive and apparently unmotivated idea or action ⟨an out-of-character *caprice* led him to take the day off from work and go to the beach⟩ — see WHIM
2 an inclination to sudden illogical changes of mind, ideas, or actions ⟨his knack for picking racetrack winners appears to owe as much to *caprice* as it does to a canny assessment of horseflesh⟩ — see WHIMSICALITY

capricious *adj* **1** likely to change frequently, suddenly, or unexpectedly ⟨*capricious* weather that was balmy one day and freezing cold the next⟩ — see FICKLE 1
2 prone to sudden illogical changes of mind, ideas, or actions ⟨a *capricious* woman who changed her mind dozens of times about what color to paint the bathroom⟩ — see WHIMSICAL

capriciousness *n* an inclination to sudden illogical changes of mind, ideas, or actions ⟨the client's *capriciousness* frustrated the building contractor to no end⟩ — see WHIMSICALITY

capsize *vb* to turn on one's side or upside down ⟨a huge wave out of nowhere caused our little sailboat to *capsize*⟩
synonyms overturn, turn over, upset
related words invert, overset, overthrow, pitchpole, topple, tump (over) [*chiefly Southern*], upend; careen, heel, keel, lean, list, tilt, tip; collapse, fall, founder, give
phrases turn turtle
near antonyms stand up, straighten (up); erect, raise
antonyms right

capstone *n* the highest part or point ⟨her election as the state's first woman governor was a *capstone* of a long political career⟩ — see HEIGHT 1

capsule *adj* marked by the use of few words to convey much information or meaning ⟨*capsule* reviews of the latest offerings at the multiplex⟩ — see CONCISE

capsule *n* **1** a small mass containing medicine to be taken orally ⟨took an antibiotic *capsule* three times a day for a week⟩ — see PILL 1
2 something that encloses another thing especially to protect it ⟨a *capsule* containing all sorts of items from our era that is to be opened 100 years from now⟩ — see [1]CASE 1
3 a short statement of the main points ⟨*capsules* of the day's major news stories appear on the paper's second page⟩ — see SUMMARY

capsule *vb* to reduce in size or volume by or as if by pressing parts or members together ⟨newscasts that *capsule* complex, important stories into one-minute bits for easy digestion by viewers⟩ — see COMPRESS 1

capsulize *vb* to reduce in size or volume by or as if by pressing parts or members together ⟨*capsulized* accounts of the breach in national security failed to convey its gravity⟩ — see COMPRESS 1

captain *n* **1** a person in overall command of a ship ⟨the *captain* is responsible for everything that happens to his ship in the course of a voyage⟩
synonyms commander, skip, skipper
related words sea captain; master, pilot; commanding officer; admiral, commodore, vice admiral; mate, officer
near antonyms crew, crewman, crewmate
2 one in official command especially of a military force or base ⟨the *captain* of the largest army ever marshaled for battle in this country⟩ — see COMMANDER 1
3 the person (as an employer or supervisor) who tells people and especially workers what to do ⟨we only do what the *captain* tells us to, so it's not our fault when things don't work out⟩ — see BOSS
4 a person of rank, power, or influence in a particular field ⟨a fascinating magazine article profiling the *captains* of the American auto industry⟩ — see MAGNATE

captain *vb* **1** to be in charge of ⟨if you do well on this, you'll be asked to *captain* the next mission⟩ — see BOSS 1
2 to exercise authority or power over ⟨*captained* the project for a few days while the boss was out of town⟩ — see GOVERN 1
3 to serve as leader of ⟨you did a good job of *captaining* the team⟩ — see LEAD 2

caption *n* **1** an explanation or description accompanying a pictorial illustration ⟨for the school yearbook, funny *captions* were written for snapshots showing a typical day at school⟩

synonyms cutline, legend
related words key; closed-captioning, subtitle, translation; motto, posy, slogan, tagline
2 a word or series of words often in larger letters placed at the beginning of a passage or at the top of a page in order to introduce or categorize ⟨the textbook features cleverly worded *captions* to capture the reader's attention⟩ — see HEADING

captious *adj* given to making or expressing unfavorable judgments about things ⟨a *captious* and cranky eater who's never met a vegetable he didn't hate⟩ — see CRITICAL 1

captivate *vb* to attract or delight as if by magic ⟨the clown *captivated* the toddlers with his balloon tricks⟩ — see CHARM 1

captivating *adj* having an often mysterious or magical power to attract ⟨a *captivating* performance by the young singing sensation⟩ — see FASCINATING 1

captivation *n* the power of irresistible attraction ⟨by some mysterious method of *captivation*, the therapist is able to evoke a response from even the shiest of children⟩ — see CHARM 2

captive *adj* taken and held prisoner ⟨the *captive* soldiers were treated humanely by the guards⟩
synonyms apprehended, arrested, captured, caught, confined, imprisoned, incarcerated, interned, jailed
related words bound, enslaved, indentured; ensnared, trapped; abducted, kidnapped (*also* kidnaped); subdued, subjugated; occupied
phrases behind bars
near antonyms unconfined, unrestrained; delivered, emancipated, enfranchised, freed, liberated, paroled, released
antonyms free

captive *n* one that has been taken and held in confinement ⟨the *captives* in the concentration camp had devised a daring plan of escape⟩
synonyms capture, internee, prisoner
related words coprisoner; convict, jailbird; arrestee; abductee, kidnappee (*or* kidnapee)
near antonyms custodian, guard, guardian, jailer (*also* jailor), keeper, marshal (*also* marshall), warden; abductor, kidnapper (*also* kidnaper)
antonyms captor

captivity *n* the act of confining or the state of being confined ⟨the wildlife refuge raises endangered species in *captivity* and then releases them into the wild⟩ — see INTERNMENT

capture *n* one that has been taken and held in confinement ⟨a Spanish treasure ship was the most valuable *capture* ever taken by that privateer⟩ — see CAPTIVE

capture *vb* **1** to receive as return for effort ⟨the movie's producers *captured* several awards for their work⟩ — see EARN 1
2 to take physical control or possession of (something) suddenly or forcibly ⟨*captured* the cat just as it was about to escape out the front door⟩ — see CATCH 1

captured *adj* taken and held prisoner ⟨a *captured* American business executive held for ransom by insurgents⟩ — see CAPTIVE

car *n* a self-propelled passenger vehicle on four wheels ⟨every teenager's dream of getting a driver's license and a first *car*⟩
synonyms auto, automobile, bus, horseless carriage, machine, motor, motorcar, motor vehicle, wheels [*slang*]
related words coach, jitney, microbus, minibus, minivan, omnibus, van; convertible, fastback, hardtop, hatchback, notchback, ragtop, sports car, sport-utility vehicle, station wagon, SUV, town car, wagon, woody (*or* woodie); compact, coupe (*or* coupé), intermediate, limousine, mini, minicar, sedan, subcompact, V-8; gas-guzzler, land yacht; muscle car, stock car, turbocar; beater, clunker, crate, flivver, jalopy, junker; cream puff; phaeton, roadster, tin lizzie, touring car; hybrid

caravan *n* **1** a group of vehicles traveling together or under one management ⟨a funeral *caravan* slowly making its way down the street⟩ — see FLEET
2 a motor vehicle that is specially equipped for living while traveling ⟨bought a *caravan* and drove cross-country to California⟩ — see CAMPER

caravansary *or* **caravanserai** *n* a place that provides rooms and usually a public dining room for overnight guests ⟨a *caravansary* designed specifically for self-styled cheapskates⟩ — see HOTEL

carbon *n* **1** something or someone that strongly resembles another ⟨this new digital camera is a *carbon* of a well-known model costing almost twice as much⟩ — see IMAGE 1
2 something that is made to look exactly like something else ⟨the bell tower is a *carbon* of an earlier one that toppled in an earthquake⟩ — see COPY

carbon copy *n* **1** something or someone that strongly resembles another ⟨the child is a *carbon copy* of his father⟩ — see IMAGE 1
2 something that is made to look exactly like something else ⟨a clothing company that makes *carbon copies* of designer duds⟩ — see COPY

carcass *n* a dead body ⟨the *carcass* of a squirrel that had been run over⟩ — see CORPSE

card *n* **1** a list of foods served at or available for a meal ⟨the diners asked if there were any specials on the *card* for the evening⟩ — see MENU 1
2 a person (as a writer) noted for or specializing in humor ⟨you're really a *card*, but save the jokes for after class⟩ — see HUMORIST

cardinal *adj* coming before all others in importance ⟨the *cardinal* rule of medicine: do no harm⟩ — see FOREMOST 1

cardinal virtue *n* a quality that gives something special worth ⟨the *cardinal virtue* of wool is that it retains its insulating properties even when wet⟩ — see EXCELLENCE 2

care *n* **1** strict attentiveness to what one is doing ⟨reading the report with more *care* the second time, she detected several errors⟩
synonyms carefulness, closeness, conscientiousness, heed, heedfulness, meticulosity, meticulousness, pains, scrupulousness
related words advertence, advertency, attention, concentration, focus, observance, observation; alertness, mindfulness, vigilance, watchfulness; dutifulness, irreproachability, irreproachableness, punctiliousness, responsibility; bother, effort, painstaking, trouble; exactness, particularity, precision
near antonyms inadvertence, inadvertency, inattention, inobservance
antonyms heedlessness, inattentiveness, negligence
2 attention accompanied by protectiveness and responsibility ⟨that's an extremely valuable violin, so handle it with *care*⟩
synonyms carefulness, lovingness, solicitousness, solicitude
related words concern, considerateness, consideration, kindness, thoughtfulness; babying, coddling, pampering
near antonyms inconsiderateness, inconsideration, thoughtlessness, unconcern, unkindness
antonyms carelessness
3 a close attentiveness to avoiding danger ⟨take *care* while crossing the street⟩ — see CAUTION 1
4 an uneasy state of mind usually over the possibility of an anticipated misfortune or trouble ⟨on vacation, without a *care* in the world⟩ — see ANXIETY 1

5 responsibility for the safety and well-being of someone or something ⟨while you're under my *care*, you'll do as you're told⟩ — see CUSTODY

6 the duty or function of watching or guarding for the sake of proper direction or control ⟨you'll have *care* of the project from its beginning to its completion⟩ — see SUPERVISION 1

7 the act or activity of looking after and making decisions about something ⟨she stepped up and took over the *care* of the bank after her father retired⟩ — see CONDUCT 1

care *vb* to have an interest or concern for ⟨a teacher who *cares* what happens to her students long after they leave her classroom⟩
synonyms look out (for), mind, watch
related words attend, heed, regard; note, notice, observe; empathize (with), feel (for), sympathize (with)
near antonyms disregard, ignore, overlook

care (for) *vb* **1** to take charge of especially on behalf of another ⟨will you *care for* the lawn while we're gone?⟩ — see [2]TEND 1
2 to attend to the needs and comforts of ⟨he is *caring for* his mother while she's sick⟩ — see NURSE 1
3 to have a favorable opinion of ⟨I don't really *care for* what you're doing with that dog⟩ — see APPROVE (OF)
4 to wish to have ⟨I don't particularly *care for* rice cereal, but I'll eat it⟩ — see LIKE 1
5 to show partiality toward ⟨she generally doesn't *care for* war movies⟩ — see PREFER 1

care and feeding *n* the act or activity of keeping something in an existing and usually satisfactory condition ⟨devotes too much time to the *care and feeding* of her buggy computer⟩ — see MAINTENANCE

careen *vb* **1** to make a series of unsteady side-to-side motions ⟨the sled *careened* as it barreled down the hill⟩ — see ROCK 1
2 to move forward while swaying from side to side ⟨he *careened* unsteadily to the couch after hitting his head⟩ — see STAGGER 1
3 to proceed or move quickly ⟨sounding its siren, an ambulance *careened* through the intersection⟩ — see HURRY 2

career *vb* to proceed or move quickly ⟨she *careered* off to the class she'd almost forgotten⟩ — see HURRY 2

carefree *adj* having or showing freedom from worries or troubles ⟨passengers on a luxury cruise ship enjoying a *carefree* vacation⟩ ⟨*carefree* college students on spring break⟩
synonyms blithe, debonair, devil-may-care, gay, happy-go-lucky, insouciant, lighthearted, lightsome, slaphappy, unconcerned
related words blasé (*also* blase), breezy, cavalier, nonchalant; casual, easygoing, informal, laid-back, low-pressure, relaxed, unfussy
near antonyms earnest, grave, serious, serious-minded, somber (*or* sombre); careful, cautious, heedful, wary; anxious, concerned, upset, worried; long-suffering, overburdened, sorrowful
antonyms careworn

careful *adj* **1** having or showing a close attentiveness to avoiding danger or trouble ⟨*careful* drivers slow down on slick or icy roadways⟩
synonyms alert, cautious, chary, circumspect, conservative, considerate, gingerly, guarded, heedful, safe, wary
related words advertent, attentive, awake, observant, regardful, vigilant, watchful; hypercautious; foresighted, foresightful, forethoughtful, provident, thoughtful; cagey (*also* cagy), calculating, canny, shrewd; deliberate, slow; ultracareful, ultracautious
near antonyms bold, brash, impetuous, rash, reckless, venturesome; asleep, inattentive, regardless; inconsiderate, thoughtless; lax, neglectful, negligent, remiss; imprudent, indiscreet, injudicious; absentminded, forgetful; inadvertent, unintentional, unplanned
antonyms careless, heedless, incautious, unguarded, unmindful, unsafe, unwary
2 taking, showing, or involving great care and effort ⟨that furniture maker was known to be a most *careful* worker, so his output was small⟩ — see PAINSTAKING

carefulness *n* **1** a close attentiveness to avoiding danger ⟨her natural *carefulness* keeps her from having car accidents and the high insurance premiums that go with them⟩ — see CAUTION 1
2 strict attentiveness to what one is doing ⟨a degree of *carefulness* is required to get the details just right⟩ — see CARE 1
3 *archaic* attention accompanied by protectiveness and responsibility ⟨with what *carefulness* they tended the frail princess day and night!⟩ — see CARE 2

caregiver *n* a person who has responsibility for the care of another ⟨he could no longer keep up his role as *caregiver* for his sick wife⟩
synonyms carer, caretaker, guardian
related words foster parent; babysitter, minder, nanny (*also* nannie), nurse, sitter; custodian, guard, keep, keeper, protector; attendant, chaperone (*or* chaperon), companion
near antonyms charge, client, dependent, ward

careless *adj* **1** not paying or showing close attention especially for the purpose of avoiding trouble ⟨a *careless* reporter who often doesn't get his facts straight⟩ ⟨a *careless* mistake that caused the plane to crash⟩
synonyms heedless, incautious, mindless, unguarded, unsafe, unwary
related words bold, impetuous, rash, reckless; inattentive, regardless; blithe, inconsiderate, thoughtless; absentminded, forgetful, unmindful; lax, neglectful, negligent, remiss, slipshod; imprudent, indiscreet, injudicious; inadvertent, unintentional, unplanned
near antonyms attentive, chary, observant, vigilant, watchful; foresighted, forethoughtful, provident; calculating, scheming, shrewd; considerate, thoughtful; ultracareful, ultracautious
antonyms alert, cautious, circumspect, gingerly, guarded, heedful, safe, wary
2 failing to give proper care and attention ⟨a *careless* effort that made an unnecessary mess⟩ — see NEGLIGENT

carelessness *n* failure to take the care that a cautious person usually takes ⟨the only errors you made were from *carelessness*, not lack of knowledge⟩ — see NEGLIGENCE 1

carer *n* a person who has responsibility for the care of another ⟨a workshop for parents and other *carers* of autistic children⟩ — see CAREGIVER

caress *vb* to touch or handle in a tender or loving manner ⟨gently *caressed* her hair⟩ — see FONDLE

caretaker *n* **1** a person who takes care of a property sometimes for an absent owner ⟨hired a *caretaker* for the mansion during the winter months⟩ — see CUSTODIAN 1
2 a person who has responsibility for the care of another ⟨most primary *caretakers* of elderly parents are women⟩ — see CAREGIVER

cargo *n* a mass or quantity of something taken up and carried, conveyed, or transported ⟨we put all of our *cargo* on the pack animals and began our journey through the canyon⟩ — see LOAD 1

caricature *n* **1** a poor, insincere, or insulting imitation of something ⟨that TV network's reporting is a mere *caricature* of real journalism⟩ — see MOCKERY 1
2 a work that imitates and exaggerates another work for comic effect ⟨the artist creates *caricatures* of fa-

mous paintings by replacing humans with cats⟩ — see PARODY 1
3 the representation of something in terms that go beyond the facts ⟨the mayor has presented only a *caricature* of his opponent's views⟩ — see EXAGGERATION
caricature *vb* to copy or exaggerate (someone or something) in order to make fun of ⟨*caricatured* the supervisor's distinctive walk⟩ — see MIMIC 1
carking *adj* causing annoyance ⟨sometimes she's overwhelmed by the *carking* anxieties of being a single parent⟩ — see ANNOYING
carline *or* **carlin** *n, chiefly Scottish* a mean or ugly old woman ⟨there's no appeasing the auld *carline* who lives at the far end of the loch⟩ — see CRONE
carload *n* a considerable amount ⟨he always has a *carload* of ideas for a new product launch⟩ — see LOT 2
carnage *n* the killing of a large number of people ⟨the appalling *carnage* in that war-torn country requires that the outside world intervene⟩ — see MASSACRE
carnal *adj* **1** having to do with life on earth especially as opposed to that in heaven ⟨the preacher warned that those who were interested only in *carnal* pursuits would not see the kingdom of heaven⟩ — see EARTHLY
2 of or relating to the human body ⟨a missionary who tends to the *carnal* needs of the people as well as to their spiritual concerns⟩ — see PHYSICAL 1
3 pleasing to the physical senses ⟨*carnal* attractions of that gambling mecca in the desert⟩ — see SENSUAL
carnality *n* excessive pursuit of fleshly pleasures ⟨a rich playboy who was undone by his own *carnality*⟩ — see SENSUALITY
carnival *n* a time or program of special events and entertainment in honor of something ⟨the town's annual Fourth of July *carnival*⟩ — see FESTIVAL
carol *n* a religious song ⟨sang *carols* at the Christmas Eve service⟩ — see HYMN 1
carol *vb* **1** to produce musical sounds with the voice ⟨she *caroled* with glee when she heard the good news⟩ — see SING 1
2 to proclaim the glory of ⟨landscape photographs that *carol* the majesty and monumentality of Yosemite Valley⟩ — see PRAISE 1
caroler *or* **caroller** *n* one who sings ⟨those feathered *carolers* outside my window every morning⟩ — see SINGER
carom *vb* to strike and fly off at an angle ⟨a ball *caromed* off the wall⟩ — see GLANCE 1
carousal *n* a bout of prolonged or excessive drinking ⟨came home tired and hungover after an all-night *carousal* with his friends⟩ — see CAROUSE
carouse *n* a bout of prolonged or excessive drinking ⟨the Old West custom of heading to the saloon at night for an all-out *carouse* and some poker playing⟩
synonyms bender, binge, bust, carousal, drunk, jamboree, spree, toot, wassail
related words blowout, kegger (*also* keg party); bacchanalia, orgy, revel, revelry; bibbery, bibulousness, drunkenness, inebriation, inebriety, intoxication, jag, tipsiness
carouse *vb* to take part in drunken revelry ⟨spent all of shore leave *carousing* with his mates⟩
synonyms binge, birl [*chiefly Scottish*], revel, roister, wassail
related words booze, drink, guzzle, liquor (up), soak, tipple
carp *n* an expression of dissatisfaction, pain, or resentment ⟨the usual *carp* about that restaurant is that the service is slow⟩ — see COMPLAINT 1
carp *vb* **1** to express dissatisfaction, pain, or resentment usually tiresomely ⟨someone who *carps* and whines about everything is a pain⟩ — see COMPLAIN
2 to make often peevish criticisms or objections about matters that are minor, unimportant, or irrelevant ⟨*carped* about the order of names on the wedding invitations⟩ — see QUIBBLE 1
carper *n* a person given to harsh judgments and to finding faults ⟨eventually, almost everyone learned to avoid the ski school's resident *carper*⟩ — see CRITIC 1
carpet *vb* to form a layer over ⟨leaves *carpeted* the lawn⟩ — see COVER 2
carping *adj* given to making or expressing unfavorable judgments about things ⟨a peevish and *carping* old woman who is not a favorite at the nursing home⟩ — see CRITICAL 1
carrefour *n* a place where roads meet ⟨our hotel in Montreal was adjacent to a noisy *carrefour*⟩ — see CROSSROAD 1
carriage *n* **1** a horse-drawn wheeled vehicle for carrying passengers ⟨a museum with a large collection of beautiful, old *carriages*⟩
synonyms equipage, rig
related words barouche, brougham, buckboard, buggy, cab, cabriolet, calash, calèche (*or* caleche), caroche, carryall, chaise, chariot, coach, coupé (*or* coupe), curricle, diligence, dogcart, droshky (*also* drosky), four-in-hand, gig, go-cart, hackney (*or* hackney coach), hansom (*or* hansom cab), jaunting car, landau, phaeton, post chaise, roadster, rockaway, stage, stagecoach, stanhope, surrey, tandem, tilbury, tonga, trap, troika, victoria; turnout
2 a general way of holding the body ⟨her Ladyship's *carriage* is upright and regal⟩ — see POSTURE 1
carriageway *n, British* a passage cleared for public vehicular travel ⟨an American who apparently was not used to driving in England, as he was traveling down the wrong side of the *carriageway*⟩ — see WAY 1
carry *vb* **1** to support and take from one place to another ⟨each camper must be able to *carry* his or her own backpack⟩
synonyms bear, cart, convey, ferry, haul, lug, pack, tote, transport
related words deliver, hand over, transfer; forward, send, ship, transmit; bring, fetch, take; move, remove, shift
2 to wear or have on one's person ⟨I always *carry* a camera with me so as to never miss a great shot⟩
synonyms bear, pack
related words flaunt, show off, sport; display, exhibit, parade, show
3 to bring before the public in performance or exhibition ⟨all of the television networks will *carry* the president's speech⟩ — see PRESENT 1
4 to have as part of a whole ⟨the idea of equality *carries* with it a number of other concepts⟩ — see INCLUDE 1
5 to hold up or serve as a foundation for ⟨erected a trellis to *carry* the vine⟩ — see SUPPORT 3
6 to receive as return for effort ⟨*carried* off the award for best picture of the year⟩ — see EARN 1
7 to manage the actions of (oneself) in a particular way ⟨during that difficult time the grieving parents *carried* themselves with unfailing grace and dignity⟩ — see BEHAVE
carryall *n* a bag carried by hand and designed to hold a traveler's clothing and personal articles ⟨took only a small *carryall* on the plane⟩ — see TRAVELING BAG
carry away *vb* to fill with overwhelming emotion (as wonder or delight) ⟨the beauty of the music *carried* him *away*⟩ — see ENTRANCE
carry off *vb* **1** to carry through (as a process) to completion ⟨the con artist would never have been able to *carry off* his schemes if it were not for the greed of his eager victims⟩ — see PERFORM 1
2 to deprive of life ⟨pray that the pestilence does not

carry off any more souls than it already has⟩ — see KILL 1

carry–on *n* a bag carried by hand and designed to hold a traveler's clothing and personal articles ⟨the airline allows two *carry-ons* per person⟩ — see TRAVELING BAG

carry on *vb* **1** to behave badly ⟨a toddler crying and *carrying on* in the store⟩ — see MISBEHAVE

2 to continue despite difficulties, opposition, or discouragement ⟨she bravely *carried on* despite the loss of her husband⟩ — see PERSEVERE

3 to look after and make decisions about ⟨*carries on* a business and still manages to run the household⟩ — see CONDUCT 1

carry out *vb* to carry through (as a process) to completion ⟨*carried out* the task efficiently and cheerfully⟩ — see PERFORM 1

cart *n* a wheeled usually horse-drawn vehicle used for hauling ⟨a *cart* piled up with hay⟩

synonyms wagon, wain

related words dray, jolt-wagon [*Midland*], oxcart, spring wagon, wagonette; barrow, hand truck, pushcart, tram, truck, wheelbarrow

cart *vb* to support and take from one place to another ⟨*carted* a knapsack filled with books from class to class⟩ — see CARRY 1

cartel *n* a number of businesses or enterprises united for commercial advantage ⟨a *cartel* of oil-producing nations that controls production and influences prices⟩

synonyms combination, combine, syndicate, trust

related words chain, conglomerate, megacorporation, multinational; association, guild (*also* gild), organization, partnership, pool, union; big business

cartoon *n* **1** a picture using lines to represent the chief features of an object or scene ⟨a political *cartoon* mocking the state legislature⟩ — see DRAWING

2 a series of drawings that tell a story or part of a story ⟨reading the *cartoons* in the Sunday newspaper⟩ — see COMIC STRIP

3 a poor, insincere, or insulting imitation of something ⟨in this biopic the life of a complex man is reduced to a *cartoon*⟩ — see MOCKERY 1

carve *vb* to create a three-dimensional representation of (something) using solid material ⟨*carved* a statue out of rare marble⟩ — see SCULPT

carve (out) *vb* to produce or bring about especially by long or repeated effort ⟨finally *carved out* a niche for the sport in the school's athletic program⟩ — see HAMMER OUT

Casanova *n* a man given to seducing women ⟨to hear him tell it, he was his college's number one *Casanova*⟩ — see DON JUAN

cascade *n* a fall of water usually from a great height ⟨the river forms a series of *cascades* as it drops a total of 200 feet in elevation⟩ — see WATERFALL

¹case *n* **1** something that encloses another thing especially to protect it ⟨those binoculars come with their own *case*⟩

synonyms armor, capsule, casing, cocoon, cover, covering, encasement, housing, hull, husk, jacket, pod, sheath, shell

related words cartridge, cassette (*also* casette); bark, crust; carapace, house, mail, panoply, plate, plating, shield; cuticle, hide, skin; envelope, package, wrapper; backing, coating, coverture, facing

2 a covered rectangular container for storing or transporting things ⟨a handy little cosmetics *case* that matches the rest of her luggage⟩ — see CHEST

²case *n* **1** an individual awaiting or under medical care and treatment ⟨her doctor wishes that all of his *cases* were as cooperative as she is⟩ — see PATIENT

2 one of a group or collection that shows what the whole is like ⟨this is a perfect *case* of people jumping to the wrong conclusion before all the facts are known⟩ — see EXAMPLE

3 something that actually exists ⟨this has never been the *case* before⟩ — see FACT 2

4 a statement given to explain a belief or act ⟨you'll get a chance to make your *case*, but unless you're very convincing, your request will be denied⟩ — see REASON 1

5 a sudden experiencing of a physical or mental disorder ⟨a young boy suffering from a *case* of chicken pox⟩ — see ATTACK 2

6 something that might happen ⟨it may be the *case* that the cause of the fire will forever remain a mystery⟩ — see EVENT 2

7 something that requires thought and skill for resolution ⟨that's a tough *case* to solve⟩ — see PROBLEM 1

case–hardened *adj* having or showing a lack of sympathy or tender feelings ⟨a *case-hardened* homicide detective who has seen it all⟩ — see HARD 1

cash *n* something (as pieces of stamped metal or printed paper) customarily and legally used as a medium of exchange, a measure of value, or a means of payment ⟨went to the ATM to get more *cash*⟩ — see MONEY 1

cashier *vb* **1** to let go from office, service, or employment ⟨was abruptly *cashiered* after money was found missing from the safe⟩ — see DISMISS 1

2 to get rid of as useless or unwanted ⟨the company is giving away a clutter of computers that have recently been *cashiered* for obsolescence⟩ — see DISCARD

cash in (on) *vb* to take unfair advantage of ⟨some observers thought the lawyers were *cashing in on* the tragedy⟩ — see EXPLOIT 1

casing *n* something that encloses another thing especially to protect it ⟨the egg of this bird has an unusually hard *casing*⟩ — see ¹CASE 1

casino *n* a freestanding airy structure in a scenic setting (as a park) typically offering commanding views ⟨on summer evenings dance bands would perform in the seaside *casino*⟩ — see BELVEDERE

cask *n* an enclosed wooden vessel for holding beverages ⟨*casks* of wine that had been in the castle for many years⟩

synonyms barrel, butt, firkin, hogshead, keg, kilderkin, pipe, puncheon, rundlet (*or* runlet), tun

related words scuttlebutt; cistern, tub, vat; can, drum

casket *n* **1** a boxlike container for holding a dead body ⟨bought a beautiful *casket* when her grandmother died⟩ — see COFFIN

2 a covered rectangular container for storing or transporting things ⟨a small *casket* of jewels⟩ — see CHEST

Cassandra *n* one given to forebodings and predictions of impending calamity ⟨more than one *Cassandra* on Wall Street had warned that the market was overdue for a major correction⟩ — see DOOMSAYER

cast *n* **1** a declaration that something will happen in the future ⟨stock market analysts offered an optimistic *cast* for the coming year⟩ — see PREDICTION

2 a property that becomes apparent when light falls on an object and by which things that are identical in form can be distinguished ⟨the walls had a slight yellowish *cast*⟩ — see COLOR 1

3 an instance of looking especially briefly ⟨a mischievous *cast* in his eye when we asked what our destination would be⟩ — see LOOK 2

4 facial appearance regarded as an indication of mood or feeling ⟨his face took on a somewhat sad *cast* when we asked how his ill wife was faring⟩ — see LOOK 1

5 the outward appearance of something as distinguished from its substance ⟨the lovely *cast* of the baby's features⟩ — see FORM 1

cast *vb* **1** to throw or give off ⟨spermaceti candles, made

from whale oil, are known to *cast* an exceptionally bright light⟩ — see EMIT 1
2 to point or turn (something) toward a target or goal ⟨*cast* her eyes skyward for signs of the rescue plane⟩ — see AIM 1
3 to put (something) into proper and usually carefully worked out written form ⟨carefully *cast* the letter of complaint as politely as possible⟩ — see COMPOSE 1
4 to send through the air especially with a quick forward motion of the arm ⟨*cast* a rock into the stream⟩ — see THROW 1

cast (off) *vb* to get rid of as useless or unwanted ⟨once she became rich and didn't need them anymore, she *cast off* all her old friends like so much junk⟩ — see DISCARD

cast (up) *vb* to combine (numbers) into a single sum ⟨had worked as a clerk in a countinghouse, mainly *casting up* long columns of figures every day⟩ — see ADD 2

cast about (for) *vb* to go in search of ⟨*cast about for* an answer to the question of why so many people had ignored the victim's cries for help⟩ — see SEEK 1

cast around (for) *vb* to go in search of ⟨*cast around for* a last minute replacement for the lead actor in the movie⟩ — see SEEK 1

castaway *n* one who is cast out or rejected by society ⟨one theory is that Easter Island was first settled by *castaways* from Polynesia⟩ — see OUTCAST

cast down *adj* feeling unhappiness ⟨newly widowed, he was *cast down* at the thought of being alone once again⟩ — see SAD 1

caste *n* one of the segments of society into which people are grouped ⟨a member of the upper *caste*⟩ — see CLASS 1

castigate *vb* **1** to criticize (someone) severely or angrily especially for personal failings ⟨*castigated* him for his constant tardiness⟩ — see SCOLD
2 to criticize harshly and usually publicly ⟨a newspaper editorial *castigating* the city council for approving the project in the first place⟩ — see ATTACK 2
3 to inflict a penalty on for a fault or crime ⟨a judge who believes in *castigating* criminals to the full extent of the law⟩ — see PUNISH

castigating *adj* inflicting, involving, or serving as punishment ⟨a *castigating* task that succeeds in doing nothing more than making the lives of the inmates miserable⟩ — see PUNITIVE

castigation *n* suffering, loss, or hardship imposed in response to a crime or offense ⟨the loss of his father's trust was the harshest *castigation* that the boy could have possibly received for having told the lie⟩ — see PUNISHMENT

castigator *n* **1** a person given to harsh judgments and to finding faults ⟨even Broadway's most famously caustic *castigator* liked the play⟩ — see CRITIC 1
2 one who inflicts punishment in return for an injury or offense ⟨the principal seems to enjoy his role as the tireless *castigator* of classroom pranksters⟩ — see NEMESIS 1

cast–iron *adj* **1** not allowing for any exceptions or loosening of standards ⟨lost weight only after a *cast-iron* adherence to his diet⟩ — see RIGID 1
2 able to withstand hardship, strain, or exposure ⟨he has a *cast-iron* faith in his innate ability to overcome any adversity that life might throw against him⟩ — see HARDY 1

castle *n* **1** a structure or place from which one can resist attack ⟨the implacable attackers placed the *castle* under a prolonged siege⟩ — see FORT
2 a large impressive residence ⟨the mining tycoon built a magnificent *castle* on the hill overlooking the town⟩ — see MANSION

castoff *n* one who is cast out or rejected by society ⟨a *castoff* who later became a famous poet⟩ — see OUTCAST

cast out *vb* to drive or force out ⟨*cast* them *out* of the tribe for violating sacred traditions⟩ — see EJECT 1

castrate *vb* to deprive of emotional or intellectual vitality ⟨a movie version that *castrates* the hard-hitting novel⟩ — see DEHYDRATE 1

casual *adj* **1** not designed to be worn only on special occasions ⟨a restaurant where people in *casual* clothes are always welcome⟩
synonyms everyday, informal, workaday
related words dégagé, relaxed, sporty; dressed down; shabby, sloppy, slovenly, unkempt
near antonyms best, Sunday; dressed up; chic, elegant, fashionable, smart, stylish; neat, tidy, trim; semiformal
antonyms dressy, formal, noncasual
2 happening by chance ⟨a *casual* meeting with the next-door neighbors on a beach in Hawaii⟩ — see ACCIDENTAL 1
3 having or showing a lack of interest or concern ⟨only a *casual* examination of the bicycle before buying it⟩ — see INDIFFERENT 1
4 lacking in steadiness or regularity of occurrence ⟨a *casual* attendance at their son's hockey games⟩ — see FITFUL

casualness *n* lack of interest or concern ⟨her *casualness* distressed everyone who took the issue seriously⟩ — see INDIFFERENCE

casualty *n* **1** a person or thing harmed, lost, or destroyed ⟨the real *casualties* in the war against drugs are millions of innocent children⟩
synonyms fatality, loss, prey, victim
related words loser, underdog; martyr, sacrifice; collateral damage; murderee
near antonyms gainer, victor, winner; harmer, injurer; assassin, killer, murderer
2 a chance and usually sudden event bringing loss or injury ⟨*casualties* at sea that sometimes resulted in great losses of men or even of entire ships⟩ — see ACCIDENT 1
3 *archaic* the uncertain course of events ⟨believes finding one's true love is too important a matter to be left to mere *casualty*⟩ — see CHANCE 1

cat *n* **1** a small domestic animal known for catching mice ⟨the family's *cat* did an exemplary job of keeping the house and yard free of all rodents⟩
synonyms feline, house cat, kitty, moggy (*also* moggie) [*British*], puss, pussy, pussycat
related words mouser; kit, kitten; alley cat, tabby; gib, tomcat
2 an adult male human being ⟨he was one cool *cat* driving around in his new sports car⟩ — see MAN 1

cataclysm *n* **1** a great flow of water or of something that overwhelms ⟨an ancient *cataclysm* that may have been the basis for the Flood described in the Bible⟩ — see FLOOD
2 a sudden violent event that brings about great loss or destruction ⟨the earthquake that struck Lisbon in 1755, killing 30,000 people, was one of the greatest *cataclysms* ever recorded⟩ — see DISASTER 1
3 a violent disturbance (as of the political or social order) ⟨a social *cataclysm* that gave rise to a new world order⟩ — see CONVULSION

cataclysmal *or* **cataclysmic** *adj* **1** bringing about ruin or misfortune ⟨a *cataclysmal* decision to plunge the nation into war⟩ — see FATAL 1
2 causing or tending to cause destruction ⟨a *cataclysmal* landslide that virtually wiped out the village⟩ — see DESTRUCTIVE 1
3 marked by sudden or violent disturbance ⟨the French Revolution was one of the great *cataclysmal* events in modern history⟩ — see CONVULSIVE 1

catacomb *n, usually* **catacombs** *pl* an underground burial chamber ⟨explored the *catacombs* looking for evidence about burial customs of that ancient society⟩ — see CRYPT

catalog *or* **catalogue** *n* a record of a series of items (as names or titles) usually arranged according to some system ⟨a *catalog* of music album titles⟩ — see [1]LIST

catalog *or* **catalogue** *vb* to put (someone or something) on a list ⟨*cataloged* the latest additions to the collection⟩ — see [1]LIST 2

catalyze *vb* to be the cause of (a situation, action, or state of mind) ⟨a reinstitution of the draft would *catalyze* protests around the country⟩ — see EFFECT

catamount *n* a large tawny cat of the wild ⟨found the footprints of a *catamount* on the mountain trail⟩ — see COUGAR

cat–a–mountain *n* a large tawny cat of the wild ⟨tracks that looked to be those of a *cat-a-mountain*⟩ — see COUGAR

cataplasm *n* a medicated covering used to heal an injury ⟨the doctor ordered the placement of a *cataplasm* on the wound until it closed up⟩ — see DRESSING 1

catapult *vb* to send through the air especially with a quick forward motion of the arm ⟨*catapulted* a pumpkin into the next yard⟩ — see THROW 1

cataract *n* **1** a fall of water usually from a great height ⟨the roaring *cataract* is one of the park's most majestic sights⟩ — see WATERFALL

2 a great flow of water or of something that overwhelms ⟨in spring the melting snows usually produce a *cataract* that inundates the valley⟩ — see FLOOD

catastrophe *n* **1** a sudden violent event that brings about great loss or destruction ⟨more than one natural *catastrophe* has threatened to destroy their farm over the years⟩ — see DISASTER 1

2 something that has failed ⟨the movie was a *catastrophe*, nearly bankrupting the studio that produced it⟩ — see FAILURE 3

catastrophic *adj* bringing about ruin or misfortune ⟨a *catastrophic* tornado destroyed the hamlet's only house of worship⟩ — see FATAL 1

catatonic *adj* not expressing any emotion ⟨a *catatonic* stare was all that the neglected resident of the nursing home seemed capable of⟩ — see BLANK 1

catbird seat *n* **1** the more favorable condition or position in a competition ⟨your fluency in French should put you in the *catbird seat* for getting the Paris posting⟩ — see ADVANTAGE 1

2 the center of public attention ⟨in the wake of the natural disaster, this obscure bureaucrat was suddenly and unexpectedly thrust into the *catbird seat*⟩ — see CENTER STAGE

catcall *n* a vocal sound made to express scorn or disapproval ⟨the band's sloppy playing produced only *catcalls* from the crowd⟩

synonyms bird [*chiefly British*], boo, Bronx cheer, hiss, hoot, jeer, raspberry, razz, snort

related words smirk, sneer, snicker, snigger; gibe (*or* jibe), put-down, taunt; whistle

near antonyms applause, clapping

antonyms cheer

catch *n* **1** a danger or difficulty that is hidden or not easily recognized ⟨the *catch* is that you have to come up with the money by tomorrow⟩ — see PITFALL 1

2 someone or something unusually desirable ⟨everyone thought the captain of the football team was a real *catch*⟩ — see PRIZE 1

3 the total amount collected or obtained especially at one time ⟨the total *catch* for our day at the creek was six fish and a crab⟩ — see HAUL 1

catch *vb* **1** to take physical control or possession of (something) suddenly or forcibly ⟨we tried to *catch* the kitten before she could sneak out the door⟩

synonyms bag, capture, collar, cop [*slang*], corral, get, glom, grab, grapple, hook, land, nab, nail, net, nobble [*British slang*], rap, seize, snag, snap (up), snare, snatch, trap

related words glove, halter, lasso, rope; apprehend, arrest, detain; bay, corner; clasp, clutch, fasten (on), fist, grasp, grip, hold, latch (on *or* onto), secure; rend, wrest; enmesh (*also* immesh), ensnare, entangle, entrap, mesh; abduct, kidnap, spirit (away *or* off)

phrases take hold (of)

near antonyms discharge, free, liberate, release; drop, loosen, unhand

antonyms miss

2 to become affected with (a disease or disorder) ⟨you'll *catch* the flu for sure if you don't get a shot⟩ — see CONTRACT 1

3 to bring (something) to a standstill ⟨I *caught* myself just as I was about to step into the freshly poured concrete⟩ — see [1]HALT 1

4 to put securely in place or in a desired position ⟨*caught* back her hair with a barrette⟩ — see FASTEN 2

5 to have a clear idea of ⟨I didn't *catch* the point you were making about our nation's foreign policy⟩ — see COMPREHEND 1

6 to cause to believe what is untrue ⟨a number of media outlets were *caught* by the woman's hard-luck story⟩ — see DECEIVE

7 to come upon face-to-face or as if face-to-face ⟨I'll *catch* you at the library tomorrow⟩ — see MEET 1

8 to make note of (something) through the use of one's eyes ⟨I looked out the window just in time to *catch* the neighbor's dog digging up my flower bed⟩ — see SEE 1

9 to move fast enough to get even with ⟨despite the suspect's considerable lead, the fleet-footed police officer was able to *catch* him and make an arrest⟩ — see OVERTAKE

catch–as–catch–can *adj* lacking a definite plan, purpose, or pattern ⟨we're always having drop-in guests at our beachfront cottage, and sleeping arrangements tend to be *catch-as-catch-can*⟩ — see RANDOM

catching *adj* **1** capable of being passed by physical contact from one person to another ⟨a cold is often *catching* before the symptoms even begin⟩ — see CONTAGIOUS 1

2 exciting a similar feeling or reaction in others ⟨a *catching* smile that instantly puts patients at ease⟩ — see CONTAGIOUS 2

catch on (to) *vb* **1** to come to an awareness of ⟨she *caught on to* the fact that they were planning a surprise party⟩ — see DISCOVER 1

2 to have a clear idea of ⟨he finally *caught on to* the concept of phototaxis⟩ — see COMPREHEND 1

catchpenny *adj* arousing a strong and usually superficial interest or emotional reaction ⟨the novel's *catchpenny* title belies its serious literary ambitions⟩ — see SENSATIONAL 1

catchphrase *n* an attention-getting word or phrase used to publicize something (as a campaign or product) ⟨one of those advertising *catchphrases* that, if you think about them, don't mean much of anything⟩ — see SLOGAN

catch–22 *n* **1** a danger or difficulty that is hidden or not easily recognized ⟨the drug lowers cholesterol, but the *catch-22* is that it mainly lowers good cholesterol⟩ — see PITFALL 1

2 a difficult, puzzling, or embarrassing situation from which there is no easy escape ⟨the *catch-22* faced by every first-time loan applicant: how to get a loan without a credit history⟩ — see PREDICAMENT

3 a situation in which one has to choose between two or more equally unsatisfactory choices ⟨an environmental *catch-22*: building wind farms results in scenic eyesores; not building wind farms results in greater pollution from fossil fuels⟩ — see DILEMMA 1

catch up *vb* **1** to catch or hold as if in a net ⟨a young idealist who got *caught up* in the political fanaticism of the times⟩ — see ENTANGLE 2

2 to hold the attention of as if by a spell ⟨completely *caught up* in opera ever since he saw *La Traviata*⟩ — see ENTHRALL 1

3 to hold the attention of ⟨so *caught up* in the game that she didn't note the passage of time⟩ — see ENGAGE 1

4 to give information to ⟨*catch* me *up* on what's been happening at the office⟩ — see ENLIGHTEN 1

catch up (with) *vb* to move fast enough to get even with ⟨I walked faster to *catch up with* my friends⟩ — see OVERTAKE

catchy *adj* **1** likely to attract attention ⟨will need a *catchy* slogan to sell the new product, which is actually pretty boring⟩ — see NOTICEABLE

2 requiring exceptional skill or caution in performance or handling ⟨Professor Hartman's exams always include at least one *catchy* question⟩ — see TRICKY 1

3 lacking in steadiness or regularity of occurrence ⟨she was so winded that her breathing came in *catchy* gasps⟩ — see FITFUL

cate *n, archaic* something that is pleasing to eat because it is rare or a luxury ⟨with *cates* as luscious as her lips did he woo her⟩ — see DELICACY 1

catechize *vb* **1** to put a question or questions to ⟨her roommates *catechized* her about every detail of her date with her new boyfriend⟩ — see ASK 1

2 to put a series of questions to ⟨applicants are rigorously *cathechized* by the seminary's rector regarding their motives for joining the priesthood⟩ — see EXAMINE 1

categorical *also* **categoric** *adj* having no exceptions or restrictions ⟨a *categorical* denial of the rumors that the celebrities were planning to get married⟩ — see ABSOLUTE 2

categorize *vb* to arrange or assign according to type ⟨*categorized* the questions by topic⟩ — see CLASSIFY 1

category *n* one of the units into which a whole is divided on the basis of a common characteristic ⟨divide the essays into *categories* based on difficulty of comprehension⟩ — see CLASS 2

catena *n* a series of things linked together ⟨a *catena* of lies that ultimately proved to be her undoing⟩ — see CHAIN 1

catenate *vb* to put or bring together so as to form a new and longer whole ⟨a Broadway musical that *catenates* a series of pop hits by means of a flimsy libretto⟩ — see CONNECT 1

catenation *n* a series of things linked together ⟨a *catenation* of missteps and miscalculations that ultimately grew into a colossal blunder⟩ — see CHAIN 1

cater *vb* to provide food or meals for ⟨a local firm will *cater* the awards banquet for high school athlete of the year⟩ — see FEED 1

cater (to) *vb* to give in to (a desire) ⟨the gooey dessert *catered to* the children's sweet tooth⟩ — see INDULGE 1

caterwaul *vb* to express dissatisfaction, pain, or resentment usually tiresomely ⟨like other small-town teens, they were *caterwauling* about the lack of things to do⟩ — see COMPLAIN

caterwauling *adj* engaging in or marked by loud and insistent cries especially of protest ⟨"The *caterwauling* liberals have done nothing but block legislation this year," the conservative pundit complained⟩ — see VOCIFEROUS

cathedral *n* a large, magnificent, or massive building ⟨the company didn't want just a new office building—it demanded a *cathedral* that proclaimed its place among the giants of finance⟩ — see EDIFICE 1

catholic *adj* not limited or specialized in application or purpose ⟨a museum director with *catholic* tastes in art⟩ — see GENERAL 4

catholicon *n* something that cures all ills or problems ⟨the vain notion that there could ever be an easy, painless *catholicon* for obesity⟩ — see CURE-ALL

cathouse *n* a building in which prostitutes are available ⟨soldiers on leave looking for a *cathouse* in the tenderloin⟩ — see BORDELLO

catnap *n* a short sleep ⟨a *catnap* left me refreshed enough to face the rest of the day⟩ — see [1]NAP

catnap *vb* **1** to be in a state of sleep ⟨the children are *catnapping*, so please be quiet⟩ — see SLEEP 1

2 to sleep lightly or briefly ⟨*catnapped* for 10 minutes and then went back to work⟩ — see NAP 1

catnapping *n* a natural periodic loss of consciousness during which the body restores itself ⟨indulged in some quick *catnapping* between appointments with patients⟩ — see SLEEP 1

cat's meow *n* something very good of its kind ⟨this flapper-style dress was the *cat's meow* back in the roaring 1920s⟩ — see JIM-DANDY

cat's–paw *n* one that is or can be used to further the purposes of another ⟨these changes to the zoning laws have only confirmed for many that the town council has become the *cat's-paw* of local real estate developers⟩ — see [1]PAWN

cattily *adv* in a mean or spiteful manner ⟨commented *cattily* that the woman onstage was wearing an ugly dress⟩ — see NASTILY

cattiness *n* **1** biting sharpness of feeling or expression ⟨the *cattiness* of the commentary for the televised awards was neither nice nor necessary⟩ — see ACRIMONY 1

2 the desire to cause pain for the satisfaction of doing harm ⟨there's no reason for saying such hurtful things except sheer *cattiness*⟩ — see MALICE

catty *adj* having or showing a desire to cause someone pain or suffering for the sheer enjoyment of it ⟨a *catty* remark that served its only purpose: to make someone cry⟩ — see HATEFUL

caught *adj* **1** containing unborn young within the body ⟨worried that the heedless girl would get *caught* before the summer was over⟩ — see PREGNANT 1

2 taken and held prisoner ⟨after seeing how the *caught* soldiers had been treated, we resolved never to be taken alive⟩ — see CAPTIVE

causality *n* someone or something responsible for a result ⟨a supreme being is a being that, by definition, has no *causality* of its own⟩ — see CAUSE 1

causation *n* someone or something responsible for a result ⟨presented data that supports the thesis that poverty is the primary *causation* of crime⟩ — see CAUSE 1

cause *n* **1** someone or something responsible for a result ⟨the much-debated *causes* of the American Civil War⟩

synonyms antecedent, causality, causation, occasion, reason

related words consideration, determinant, factor; alpha and omega, be-all and end-all; impetus, incentive, inspiration, instigation, stimulus; mother, origin, root, source, spring

near antonyms ramification; denouement (*also* dénouement), repercussion; conclusion, end; by-product, side effect (*also* side reaction)

antonyms aftereffect, aftermath, consequence, corollary, development, effect, fate, fruit, issue, outcome, outgrowth, product, result, resultant, sequel, sequence, upshot

2 a series of activities undertaken to achieve a goal

⟨joined the freedom fighters' *cause* as a young man⟩ — see CAMPAIGN

cause *vb* to be the cause of (a situation, action, or state of mind) ⟨the ice storm *caused* a massive power outage⟩ — see EFFECT

'cause *conj* for the reason that ⟨he left *'cause* I told him to bug off⟩ — see SINCE

cause célèbre *also* **cause celebre** *n* a person who is widely known and usually much talked about ⟨a *cause célèbre* from some reality TV show whose fame hadn't even lasted the proverbial 15 minutes⟩ — see CELEBRITY 1

causerie *n* friendly, informal conversation or an instance of this ⟨the monthly departmental *causeries* did much to foster a sense of community⟩ — see CHAT 1

caustic *adj* marked by the use of wit that is intended to cause hurt feelings ⟨*caustic* movie reviews that serve mainly to show how clever the reviewer is⟩ — see SARCASTIC

cauterize *vb* to reduce or weaken in strength or feeling ⟨time had *cauterized* his bitterness, and he was willing to let bygones be bygones⟩ — see DULL 1

caution *n* **1** a close attentiveness to avoiding danger ⟨the extreme *caution* with which the zookeeper handled the snake⟩
synonyms alertness, care, carefulness, cautiousness, chariness, circumspection, gingerliness, guardedness, heedfulness, prudence, wariness
related words attentiveness, observance, vigilance, watchfulness; foresight, foresightedness, providence; calculation, canniness, deliberateness, deliberation, shrewdness
near antonyms abruptness, hastiness, impetuousness, precipitousness, rashness, suddenness; inconsiderateness, inconsideration, thoughtlessness
antonyms brashness, carelessness, heedlessness, incaution, incautiousness, recklessness, unwariness
2 something extraordinary or surprising ⟨how she manages to drive her car without destroying the neighborhood is a *caution*⟩ — see WONDER 1
3 something that tells of approaching danger or risk ⟨this is just a *caution* that the following paragraph practically gives away the entire plot of the movie⟩ — see WARNING 2
4 the act or an instance of telling beforehand of danger or risk ⟨we heeded the police officer's *caution* about the road ahead⟩ — see WARNING 1
5 a measure taken to preclude loss or injury ⟨the standard *caution* of donning surgical gloves before performing any kind of dental work⟩ — see PRECAUTION

caution *vb* to give notice to beforehand especially of danger or risk ⟨the doctor *cautioned* that I should still be careful using my sprained wrist for the next several days⟩ — see WARN

cautionary *adj* serving as or offering a warning ⟨the story of King Midas is a *cautionary* tale about the perils of wishing for something—you just might get it⟩
synonyms admonishing, admonitory, cautioning, exemplary, monitory, premonitory, warning
related words didactic, moralistic, moralizing; advisory, counseling (*or* counselling); punishing, punitive

cautioning *adj* serving as or offering a warning ⟨a *cautioning* story about how envy can destroy a friendship⟩ — see CAUTIONARY

cautious *adj* having or showing a close attentiveness to avoiding danger or trouble ⟨a *cautious* approach to everyday living⟩ — see CAREFUL 1

cautiousness *n* a close attentiveness to avoiding danger ⟨the *cautiousness* of drivers on the icy roadways was largely responsible for the accident-free day⟩ — see CAUTION 1

cavalcade *n* **1** a group of vehicles traveling together or under one management ⟨the longest *cavalcade* of floats in the history of the parade⟩ — see FLEET
2 a staged presentation often with music that consists of a procession of narrated or enacted scenes ⟨a *cavalcade* presenting major events in the town's history⟩ — see PAGEANT 1

cavalier *adj* having a feeling of superiority that shows itself in an overbearing attitude ⟨a *cavalier* and pompous boss, indifferent to the feelings of her subordinates⟩ — see ARROGANT

cavalier *n* an honorable and courteous man ⟨a novel about the dashing *cavaliers* and gracious ladies of the South before the Civil War⟩
synonyms gentleman
related words Galahad, knight, prince; beau, Beau Brummell, blade, blood, buck, dandy, dude, fop, gallant, jay, petit-maître; captivator, charmer, ladies' man (*also* lady's man), smoothy (*or* smoothie); aristocrat, patrician, swell, toff [*chiefly British*]

cave *n* a naturally formed underground chamber with an opening to the surface ⟨Kentucky's Mammoth *Cave* is actually a series of large chambers on five levels⟩
synonyms antre, cavern, delve [*archaic*], grot, grotto
related words abyss, chasm, gulf, hollow; crawlway, gallery, subway, tunnel; excavation, mine, pit, shaft, well; bunker, dugout, foxhole; burrow, covert, den, hole, lair, lodge, shelter

cave (in) *vb* **1** to fall down or in as a result of physical pressure ⟨the wall *caved in* when a tree fell on it⟩ — see COLLAPSE 1
2 to give up and cease resistance (as to a liking, temptation, or habit) ⟨I *caved in* to my bibliomania and bought two more books last week⟩ — see YIELD 1

caveman *n* a man with crude manners and habits and outmoded attitudes ⟨married a *caveman* who spends all his free time swigging beer and watching sports on TV⟩
synonyms Neanderthal, troglodyte
related words barbarian, heathen, primitive, savage; animal, beast, brute; boor, cad, churl, creep, cretin, cur, heel, jerk, louse, lout, swine

cavern *n* a naturally formed underground chamber with an opening to the surface ⟨a *cavern* with beautiful stalactites⟩ — see CAVE

cavil *vb* to make often peevish criticisms or objections about matters that are minor, unimportant, or irrelevant ⟨*caviled* for hours about a single sentence⟩ — see QUIBBLE 1

caviler *or* **caviller** *n* a person given to harsh judgments and to finding faults ⟨the chronic *cavilers* who are going to complain no matter what the mayor does⟩ — see CRITIC 1

caviling *or* **cavilling** *adj* given to making or expressing unfavorable judgments about things ⟨a *caviling* theater critic who has yet to see a play she likes⟩ — see CRITICAL 1

cavity *n* a sunken area forming a separate space ⟨a *cavity* in the lawn where a tree stump had been removed⟩ — see HOLE 2

cavort *vb* to play and run about happily ⟨children *cavorting* on the first sunny day of spring⟩ — see FROLIC 1

cease *n* the stopping of a process or activity ⟨worked without *cease* for the betterment of humanity⟩ — see END 1

cease *vb* **1** to come to an end ⟨the rain finally *ceased*, and we were able to continue the baseball game⟩
synonyms break off, break up, close, conclude, dead-end, determine, die, discontinue, elapse, end, expire, finish, go, halt, lapse, leave off, let up, pass, quit, stop, terminate, wind up, wink (out)
related words desist (from), lay off (of), refrain (from); give over [*British*], knock off, pack (up *or* in); break

down, conk (out), cut out, stall; pause, stay, suspend; abate, peter (out), wind down
phrases bite the dust
near antonyms draw out, extend, prolong, protract
antonyms continue, hang on, persist
2 to bring (as an action or operation) to an immediate end ⟨*cease* chattering and get down to work, please⟩ — see STOP 1

cease–fire *n* a temporary stopping of fighting ⟨the two armies declared a *cease-fire* for the holiday⟩ — see TRUCE

ceaseless *adj* **1** going on and on without any interruptions ⟨there has been *ceaseless* rain for three days⟩ — see CONTINUOUS
2 lasting forever ⟨promised her *ceaseless* happiness if she would only marry him⟩ — see EVERLASTING 1

ceaselessness *n* uninterrupted or lasting existence ⟨the *ceaselessness* of the noise was as irritating as its loudness⟩ — see CONTINUATION

cede *vb* **1** to give (something) over to the control or possession of another usually under duress ⟨she reluctantly *ceded* her position as leader⟩ — see SURRENDER 1
2 to give over the legal possession or ownership of ⟨Spain *ceded* Puerto Rico to the United States as part of the settlement of the Spanish-American War⟩ — see TRANSFER 1
3 to give up (as a position of authority) formally ⟨the President officially *cedes* his position on the January 20th immediately following the presidential election⟩ — see ABDICATE

ceiling *n* **1** a real or imaginary point beyond which a person or thing cannot go ⟨there's a *ceiling* on prices⟩ — see LIMIT 1
2 a raised covering over something for decoration or protection ⟨we sat around the campfire under a *ceiling* of stars⟩ — see CANOPY

ceinture *n* a strip of flexible material (as leather) worn around the waist ⟨the designer's dresses typically are accessorized with eye-catching *ceintures*⟩ — see [2]BELT 1

celeb *n* a person who is widely known and usually much talked about ⟨a trendy restaurant much favored by Tinseltown *celebs*⟩ — see CELEBRITY 1

celebrant *n* one who engages in merrymaking especially in honor of a special occasion ⟨all of the *celebrants* at the birthday party received a favor to take home⟩
synonyms celebrator, merrymaker, partyer (*also* partier), partygoer, reveler (*or* reveller), roisterer
related words bacchanal, binger, carouser, party animal, wassailer; cutup, skylarker; noisemaker
antonyms killjoy, party pooper

celebrate *vb* **1** to proclaim the glory of ⟨a personal essay that *celebrates* the single life⟩ — see PRAISE 1
2 to mark with an appropriate practice, rite, or ceremony ⟨a mixed family that *celebrates* both the Christian and Jewish religious holidays⟩ — see KEEP 1

celebrated *adj* widely known ⟨a *celebrated* author making an appearance on a talk show⟩ — see FAMOUS 1

celebration *n* a time or program of special events and entertainment in honor of something ⟨a *celebration* of the company's 100th anniversary⟩ — see FESTIVAL

celebrator *n* one who engages in merrymaking especially in honor of a special occasion ⟨some rowdy Super Bowl *celebrators* had to be given friendly warnings by the police⟩ — see CELEBRANT

celebrity *n* **1** a person who is widely known and usually much talked about ⟨*celebrities* from sports and entertainment attended the opening ceremonies of the Olympic Games⟩
synonyms big name, cause célèbre (*also* cause celebre), celeb, figure, icon (*also* ikon), light, luminary, megastar, name, notability, notable, notoriety, personage, personality, somebody, standout, star, superstar, VIP
related words favorite, heartthrob, hero, idol; demigod, dignitary, eminence, immortal, monument, pillar, worthy; baron, big shot, bigwig, kahuna, magnate, mogul, nabob, panjandrum
near antonyms lightweight, mediocrity; has-been
antonyms nobody, noncelebrity
2 the fact or state of being known to the public ⟨an actor who reportedly feels very uncomfortable with his *celebrity*⟩ — see FAME 1

celerity *n* a high rate of movement or performance ⟨a journalist who writes his well-crafted stories with remarkable *celerity*⟩ — see SPEED 1

celestial *adj* of, relating to, or suggesting heaven ⟨movie scenes depicting life after death are usually accompanied by *celestial* music⟩
synonyms elysian, empyreal, empyrean, ethereal, heavenly, supernal
related words supernatural, transcendent, transcendental, unearthly, unworldly; angelic (*or* angelical), beatific, blissful; Olympian, paradisiacal (*or* paradisiac), utopian; cosmic (*also* cosmical), galactic, stellar
near antonyms earthly, mundane, terrestrial, worldly; anti-utopian, dystopian
antonyms chthonic (*also* chthonian), hellish, infernal, plutonian, sulfurous, Tartarean

celibacy *n* abstention from sexual intercourse ⟨a widower who has maintained absolute *celibacy* since the death of his wife⟩
synonyms abstinence, chasteness, chastity, continence
related words modesty, purity; honor, innocence, virginity, virtue
near antonyms debauchery, lechery, licentiousness, venery, wenching, whoring

cell *n* **1** an area within a building that has been set apart from surrounding space by a wall ⟨a jail *cell*⟩ — see ROOM 2
2 one of the parts into which an enclosed space is divided ⟨*cells* in a honeycomb⟩ — see COMPARTMENT
3 a local unit of an organization ⟨his mission was to locate and infiltrate the terrorist *cell* that was believed to be hiding in the city⟩ — see CHAPTER 1

cellar *n* a room or set of rooms below the surface of the ground ⟨an amazing array of interesting things were found in the *cellar* of the old house⟩
synonyms basement
related words cellarage; bunker, crawlway, foundation, hold, vault; cyclone cellar, storm cellar

cement *n* **1** a substance used to stick things together ⟨what kind of *cement* works best on glass and pottery?⟩ — see GLUE
2 a uniting or binding force or influence ⟨she is the *cement* that holds that often quarrelsome group together⟩ — see BOND 2

cemetery *n* a piece of land used for burying the dead ⟨many of the soldiers who died in the battle are buried in a *cemetery* nearby⟩
synonyms boneyard, God's acre, graveyard, memorial park, necropolis, potter's field
related words catacombs, churchyard; crypt, grave, mausoleum, sepulchre (*or* sepulcher), sepulture, tomb, vault

censor *vb* to remove objectionable parts from ⟨the producers were told that they would have to *censor* their movie if they wanted a PG rating⟩
synonyms bowdlerize, clean (up), expurgate, launder, red-pencil
related words cleanse, purge, purify; abbreviate, blue-pencil, edit, shorten; bleep, blip, cut (out), delete, excise, expunge, gut, x (out); black out, repress, silence,

suppress; censure, condemn, denounce; examine, review, screen, scrutinize
near antonyms approve, authorize, sanction

censurable *adj* **1** deserving reproach or blame ⟨*censurable* conduct that should get that student expelled⟩ — see BLAMEWORTHY
2 provoking or likely to provoke protest ⟨the *censurable* language on the poster resulted in it being taken down⟩ — see OBJECTIONABLE

censure *n* an often public or formal expression of disapproval ⟨a rare *censure* of a senator by the full United States Senate for misconduct⟩
synonyms commination, condemnation, denunciation, excoriation, objurgation, rebuke, reprimand, reproach, reproof, riot act, stricture
related words admonishment, admonition, castigation, chastisement, damnation, punishment, remonstrance; business, devil, dressing-down, lash, lecture, lesson, rap, scolding, talking-to, tongue-lashing; belittlement, criticism, deprecation, depreciation, disparagement, pan
near antonyms acclamation, honor, tribute; encomium, eulogy, panegyric, plaudit(s), praise; approval, blessing, sanction
antonyms citation, commendation, endorsement (*also* indorsement)

censure *vb* **1** to express public or formal disapproval of ⟨a vote to *censure* the President for conduct that was unbecoming to his office⟩
synonyms condemn, denounce, objurgate, rebuke, reprimand, reproach, reprove
related words admonish, chastise; castigate, punish; bawl out, berate, chew out, cut up, dress down, flay, gibbet, jaw, keelhaul, lambaste (*or* lambast), lecture, rag, rail (at *or* against), rate, scold, score, tell off, upbraid; belittle, criticize, deprecate, depreciate, disparage
phrases bring to account, call to account
near antonyms acclaim, applause, hail, honor; eulogize, laud, praise; approve, bless, sanction
antonyms cite, commend, endorse (*also* indorse)
2 to declare to be morally wrong or evil ⟨our society generally *censures* the taking of another person's life⟩ — see CONDEMN 1
3 to express one's unfavorable opinion of the worth or quality of ⟨critics have striven to outdo each other in *censuring* that pop novelist's latest work⟩ — see CRITICIZE

censurer *n* a person given to harsh judgments and to finding faults ⟨there's more malicious fun in being a *censurer* than in being a celebrator, so many theater critics are the latter⟩ — see CRITIC 1

census *n* a total number obtained or recorded by noting each thing as it was being added ⟨a thorough *census* of all the grizzly bears living within the national park⟩ — see COUNT 1

center *n* **1** a thing or place that is of greatest importance to an activity or interest ⟨a stretch of coastline that has long been the area's *center* of tourism⟩
synonyms axis, base, capital, central, core, cynosure, epicenter, eye, focus, ground zero, heart, hub, locus, mecca, navel, nerve center, nexus, nucleus, omphalos, seat
related words headquarters; happy hunting ground, hive, hotbed, hot spot, playground, playland; kernel, nub, pith; deep, thick; essence, quintessence, soul; attraction, lodestone (*also* loadstone), magnet, polestar
phrases where it's at
2 an area or point that is an equal distance from all points along an edge or outer surface ⟨the *center* of the earth⟩
synonyms core, middle, midpoint, midst
related words inside, interior
antonyms perimeter, periphery

center *vb* **1** to bring (something) to a central point or under a single control ⟨*centered* administrative duties under the command of a single person⟩ — see CENTRALIZE
2 to fix (as one's attention) steadily toward a central objective ⟨the students *centered* their attention on final exams⟩ — see CONCENTRATE 2

centerpiece *n* the central part or aspect of something under consideration ⟨resolution of the original dispute became the *centerpiece* of the negotiations⟩ — see CRUX

center stage *n* the center of public attention ⟨a public health problem that has moved to *center stage* in recent years⟩
synonyms catbird seat, limelight, spotlight, top billing
related words front burner; attention, heed, notice
near antonyms back burner

central *adj* **1** coming before all others in importance ⟨the *central* theme of the book⟩ — see FOREMOST 1
2 occupying a position equally distant from the ends or extremes ⟨will hold the conference in the *central* part of the country in order to encourage delegates from both coasts⟩ — see MIDDLE 1
3 avoiding major social change or extreme political ideas ⟨with all of the attention being paid to the party's right and left wings, the vast *central* core has been largely ignored⟩ — see MODERATE 2

central *n* a thing or place that is of greatest importance to an activity or interest ⟨a health club that has become dating *central* for singles in the area⟩ — see CENTER 1

centralize *vb* to bring (something) to a central point or under a single control ⟨the company decided to *centralize* all of its operations at its Ohio plant⟩
synonyms center, compact, concenter, concentrate, consolidate, polarize, unify, unite
related words coordinate, harmonize, integrate, orchestrate; blend, coalesce, combine, fuse, incorporate, merge, reduce; conjoin, join, link; assemble, collect, colligate, gather; reunify, reunite
near antonyms segregate, separate
antonyms decentralize, deconcentrate, spread (out)

centrist *adj* avoiding major social change or extreme political ideas ⟨several *centrist* candidates were elected, apparently in a reaction against the extremists⟩ — see MODERATE 2

centrist *n* a person who holds moderate views ⟨the *centrists* will most likely rally behind the candidate who favors reforming the government program—not abolishing it entirely⟩
synonyms middle-of-the-roader, moderate
related words progressive, reformer; accommodationist, compromiser
near antonyms conservative, reactionary, rightist, right-winger; leftist, left-winger, liberal
antonyms extremist, radical, revolutionary, revolutionist, ultraist

cerebral *adj* **1** much given to learning and thinking ⟨a very *cerebral* jurist who has given much thought to what makes our nation's constitution work⟩ — see INTELLECTUAL 1
2 of or relating to the mind ⟨a young man given more to *cerebral* pursuits than to sporting activities⟩ — see MENTAL 1

cerebrum *n* the part of a person that feels, thinks, perceives, wills, and especially reasons ⟨you'll need the patience of a saint and the *cerebrum* of a rocket scientist to figure out the solution to this brainteaser⟩ — see MIND 1

ceremonial *adj* following or agreeing with established form, custom, or rules ⟨a *ceremonial* presentation of the ambassador's credentials⟩ — see FORMAL 1

ceremonial *n* an oft-repeated action or series of actions performed in accordance with tradition or a set of rules ⟨the funeral of a pope is usually marked by rich pageantry and elaborate *ceremonials*⟩ — see RITE

ceremonious *adj* **1** marked by or showing careful attention to set forms and details ⟨a century ago everyday life was much more *ceremonious* than in our anything-goes era⟩
synonyms correct, decorous, formal, nice, proper, punctilious, starchy, stiff, stiff-necked, stilted
related words sober, solemn, stately; chivalrous, courtly, gallant; genteel, polished, refined; civil, courteous, polite, red-carpet
near antonyms improper, indecorous, unmannerly; discourteous, impolite, rude
antonyms casual, easygoing, informal, laid-back, unceremonious
2 following or agreeing with established form, custom, or rules ⟨the *ceremonious* regalia of the Swiss Guards, the pope's traditional body guards⟩ — see FORMAL 1

ceremony *n* an oft-repeated action or series of actions performed in accordance with tradition or a set of rules ⟨a beautiful, old-fashioned wedding *ceremony*⟩ — see RITE

certain *adj* **1** known but not named ⟨a *certain* person told me that today is your birthday⟩
synonyms anonymous, given, one, some, unidentified, unnamed, unspecified
related words particular, specific
near antonyms known, named, specified
2 having or showing a mind free from doubt ⟨I'm *certain* that they'll arrive on time⟩
synonyms assured, clear, cocksure, confident, doubtless, implicit, positive, sanguine, sure
related words self-assured, self-conceited, self-confident; decisive, resolute, unfaltering, unhesitating, unquestioning, unwavering
near antonyms hesitant, indecisive, vacillating, wavering; diffident, unassuming
antonyms doubtful, dubious, uncertain, unsure
3 having been established and usually not subject to change ⟨a *certain* percentage of the profits will go to charity⟩ — see FIXED 1
4 impossible to avoid or evade ⟨as he got older, the athlete began to feel the *certain* effects of the aging process on his body⟩ — see INEVITABLE
5 not likely to fail ⟨chicken soup is grandma's *certain* cure for pretty much whatever ails you⟩ — see INFALLIBLE 2
6 not capable of being challenged or proved wrong ⟨up to this point there's been no *certain* evidence that a crime has been committed⟩ — see IRREFUTABLE

certainly *adv* without any question ⟨*certainly*, you can come to the party⟩ — see INDEED 1

certainty *n* **1** a state of mind in which one is free from doubt ⟨I have full *certainty* that I'll pass the test⟩ — see CONFIDENCE 2
2 the quality or state of being impossible to avoid or evade ⟨the proverbial *certainty* of death and taxes⟩ — see INEVITABILITY

certifiable *adj* **1** being exactly as appears or as claimed ⟨a professor who is regarded by his colleagues as a *certifiable* genius⟩ — see AUTHENTIC 1
2 having or showing a very abnormal or sick state of mind ⟨raised by a feckless father and a mother who was clearly *certifiable*⟩ — see INSANE 1

certifiably *adv* in actual fact ⟨this is *certifiably* the worst pizza I've ever had⟩ — see VERY 2

certificate *n* a written or printed paper giving information about or proof of something ⟨a *certificate* will be awarded to each person who completes the course in lifesaving⟩
synonyms certification, document, instrument
related words credentials; diploma, parchment; record; warrant, writ; warranty; coupon, voucher

certification *n* a written or printed paper giving information about or proof of something ⟨submitted the required *certifications*⟩ — see CERTIFICATE

certified *adj* being exactly as appears or as claimed ⟨presumably his chauffeured limousine qualifies him as *certified* big shot⟩ — see AUTHENTIC 1

certify *vb* **1** to declare (something) to be true or genuine ⟨experts *certified* the letter as indeed having been written by Abraham Lincoln⟩
synonyms attest, authenticate, avouch, testify (to), vouch (for), witness
related words guarantee, warrant; affirm, assert, aver, avow, profess, vow
2 to give official or legal power to ⟨*certified* her as a teacher⟩ — see AUTHORIZE 1
3 to give evidence or testimony to the truth or factualness of ⟨please bring in a doctor's note to *certify* that you were really sick⟩ — see CONFIRM 1

certitude *n* a state of mind in which one is free from doubt ⟨believes with *certitude* that he is the best candidate for the job⟩ — see CONFIDENCE 2

cessation *n* the stopping of a process or activity ⟨the *cessation* of the snowstorm was a relief⟩ — see END 1

cession *n* the usually forced yielding of one's person or possessions to the control of another ⟨the *cession* of the southern territories was part of the peace treaty⟩ — see SURRENDER

cesspool *n* a place of great vice and corruption ⟨over the decades the once-respectable neighborhood had become an urban *cesspool*⟩ — see AUGEAN STABLE

chafe *vb* **1** to make sore by continued rubbing ⟨ill-fitting boots that had badly *chafed* my heels⟩
synonyms abrade, excoriate, fret, gall, irritate
related words graze, scrape, scratch; burn, inflame (*also* enflame); flay, peel, skin
2 to damage or diminish by continued friction ⟨constant stepping on a rope will gradually *chafe* it, rendering it unsafe for rock climbing⟩ — see ABRADE 1
3 to disturb the peace of mind of (someone) especially by repeated disagreeable acts ⟨nothing *chafes* us so much as those telemarketers who call during the dinner hour⟩ — see IRRITATE 1

[1]**chaff** *n* discarded or useless material ⟨there's a lot of *chaff* in this book, and the reader should be on the alert for it⟩ — see GARBAGE 1

[2]**chaff** *n* good-natured teasing or exchanging of clever remarks ⟨I got no end of *chaff* about my accent when I was in the military⟩ — see BANTER

chaff *vb* **1** to make fun of in a good-natured way ⟨*chaffed* her about the brightly colored shirt she had received as a gift⟩ — see TEASE 1
2 to make jokes ⟨a coworker who likes to *chaff* at others' expense, and this often results in hurt feelings⟩ — see JOKE 1

chaffer *vb* **1** to talk over or dispute the terms of a purchase ⟨in that country you're expected to *chaffer* with the vendors at the bazaar⟩ — see BARGAIN 1
2 *British* to engage in casual or rambling conversation ⟨just a couple of blokes *chaffering* at the neighborhood pub⟩ — see CHAT 1

chaffing *adj* marked by or expressive of mild or good-natured teasing ⟨a *chaffing* tone to Dad's discussion of my sister's new boyfriend⟩ — see QUIZZICAL

chaffy *adj* having no usefulness ⟨a decidedly *chaffy* book that is basically a collection of old interviews with celebrities⟩ — see WORTHLESS

chafing *adj* causing annoyance ⟨learned to ignore those *chafing* comments that his mother-in-law was constantly making⟩ — see ANNOYING

chain *n* **1** a series of things linked together ⟨the *chain* of events that led the American colonies to seek independence from Great Britain⟩
synonyms catena, catenation, concatenation, consecution, nexus, progression, sequence, string, train
related words chain reaction; belt, circle, cycle, vicious circle (*also* vicious cycle); continuum, gamut, gauntlet (*also* gantlet), scale, spectrum; flow, river, stream; file, line, queue, range, row, succession
2 something that makes movement or progress difficult ⟨this community will grow and prosper only after it has thrown off the *chains* of ignorance and prejudice⟩ — see ENCUMBRANCE
3 something that physically prevents free movement ⟨*chains* on the prisoner's ankles⟩ — see BOND 1

chain *vb* **1** to confine or restrain with or as if with chains ⟨*chaining* up the dog in the backyard⟩ — see BIND 1
2 to put or bring together so as to form a new and longer whole ⟨the prosecutor meticulously and brilliantly *chained* all the evidence together in his closing argument⟩ — see CONNECT 1

chair *n* **1** a person in charge of a meeting ⟨all questions and comments should be directed to the *chair*⟩
synonyms chairman, chairperson, moderator, president, presider, prolocutor, speaker
related words chairwoman; cochair, cochairman, cochairperson, cochairwoman, copresident
2 the place of leadership or command ⟨the *chair* of the English department at the university⟩ — see HEAD 2

chairman *n* a person in charge of a meeting ⟨the *chairman* called the meeting to order⟩ — see CHAIR 1

chairperson *n* a person in charge of a meeting ⟨the *chairperson* will determine the order in which people will speak⟩ — see CHAIR 1

chalet *n* an often small house for recreational or seasonal use ⟨a mountain *chalet* for weekend getaways⟩ — see COTTAGE

chalk up *vb* **1** to explain (something) as being the result of something else ⟨let's *chalk up* her weird behavior to simple nervousness⟩ — see CREDIT 1
2 to obtain (as a goal) through effort ⟨*chalked up* a record in singles tennis that is likely to stand for a long time⟩ — see ACHIEVE 1

challenge *n* **1** a feeling or declaration of disapproval or dissent ⟨there were no serious *challenges* to the legislative bill, so it passed easily⟩ — see OBJECTION
2 something that requires thought and skill for resolution ⟨the many *challenges* facing developing countries in the 21st century⟩ — see PROBLEM 1

challenge *vb* **1** to demand proof of the truth or rightness of ⟨don't hesitate to *challenge* any statement that generalizes about people⟩
synonyms contest, dispute, impeach, oppugn, query, question
related words doubt, mistrust; kick (about), object (to), protest; combat, fight, oppose, resist
phrases call in (*or* into) question
near antonyms back, defend, support; advocate, champion, promote; abide, endure, stomach, tolerate
antonyms accept, believe, embrace, swallow
2 to invite (someone) to take part in a contest or to perform a feat ⟨I *challenge* you to swim to the other side of the pond⟩
synonyms dare, defy, stump
related words beard, brave, brazen, breast, confront, face, outbrave, outface
3 to have as a requirement ⟨having to put up with an overbearing boss *challenges* forbearance⟩ — see NEED 1

challenged *adj* deprived of the power to perform one or more natural bodily activities ⟨all parts of the sports complex are fully accessible to the physically *challenged*⟩ — see DISABLED

challenger *n* one who strives for the same thing as another ⟨the third-party *challenger* in the presidential election⟩ — see COMPETITOR

challenging *adj* **1** requiring considerable physical or mental effort ⟨an exceptionally *challenging* brainteaser⟩ — see HARD 2
2 requiring much time, effort, or careful attention ⟨a *challenging* test designed to whittle down the number of contestants⟩ — see DEMANDING 1

chamber *n* **1** an area within a building that has been set apart from surrounding space by a wall ⟨the inner *chamber* is the president's private office⟩ — see ROOM 2
2 one of the parts into which an enclosed space is divided ⟨if the camera doesn't work, check to see that the battery has been properly installed in its *chamber*⟩ — see COMPARTMENT
3 a group of persons formally joined together for some common interest ⟨joined the local *chamber* of commerce⟩ — see ASSOCIATION 2

chamber *vb* to provide with living quarters or shelter ⟨*chambered* the lost hikers in the barn until the next morning⟩ — see HOUSE 1

chameleon *n* a person who dexterously and expediently changes or adopts opinions ⟨at the summer resort he acquired a reputation as a social *chameleon*—someone who could be whatever his hosts wanted him to be⟩ — see ACROBAT 2

champ *n* the person who comes in first in a competition ⟨the wrestling *champ*⟩ — see CHAMPION 1

champ *vb* **1** to crush or grind with the teeth ⟨kept *champing* a cigar as he barked out orders⟩ — see BITE (ON)
2 to tread on heavily so as to crush or injure ⟨watch the horses so they don't *champ* the flower beds⟩ — see TRAMPLE

champaign *n* a broad area of level or rolling treeless country ⟨after days of trudging through dense forest, the explorers came upon a vast *champaign*⟩ — see PLAIN 1

champion *n* **1** the person who comes in first in a competition ⟨the *champion* of the national spelling bee⟩
synonyms champ, titleholder, titlist, victor, winner
related words cochampion, cowinner; placer; finalist, quarterfinalist, semifinalist; medalist (*or* medallist), prizewinner; megastar, star, superstar; world-beater
near antonyms loser
2 a person who actively supports or favors a cause ⟨she's the biggest *champion* of budget reform in the Congress⟩ — see EXPONENT 1

champion *vb* to promote the interests or cause of ⟨he has always *championed* the protection of abused animals⟩ — see SUPPORT 1

championship *n* the position occupied by the one who comes in first in a competition ⟨the Yankees have won the *championship* many times⟩ — see CROWN 2

chance *adj* happening by chance ⟨a *chance* advantage that I immediately recognized and made full use of⟩ — see ACCIDENTAL 1

chance *n* **1** the uncertain course of events ⟨rather than leave everything to *chance*, let's plan how we're going to spend our time in New York City⟩
synonyms accident, casualty [*archaic*], circumstance, hap, hazard, luck
related words fortuitousness, fortuity, haphazardry, randomness, uncertainty; fluke, happenchance, happenstance; destiny, doom, fate, fortune, lot; danger, peril, risk
near antonyms intent, intention, purpose; design, outline, plan, scheme
2 a favorable combination of circumstances, time, and

place ⟨this is my one *chance* to succeed⟩ — see OPPORTUNITY
3 a measure of how often an event will occur instead of another ⟨the *chance* of being struck by lightning is very low⟩ — see PROBABILITY 2
4 a risky undertaking ⟨it's a *chance*, but I think the business will be profitable⟩ — see GAMBLE
chance *vb* **1** to take a chance on ⟨I don't think we should *chance* driving in this snowstorm⟩ — see RISK 1
2 to take place ⟨there *chanced* to be a beautiful day when we were touring that part of Scotland⟩ — see HAPPEN
chance (upon) *vb* **1** to come upon face-to-face or as if face-to-face ⟨*chanced upon* my archenemy as I rounded a corner⟩ — see MEET 1
2 to come upon unexpectedly or by chance ⟨I *chanced upon* your mother in the grocery store yesterday⟩ — see HAPPEN (ON *OR* UPON)
chance–medley *n* a state in which everything is out of order ⟨priceless artworks that disappeared in the *chance-medley* of World War II's closing days⟩ — see CHAOS
chancer *n, British* **1** a person who dexterously and expediently changes or adopts opinions ⟨a two-faced *chancer*, he doesn't hesitate to dump people when they are no longer of any use⟩ — see ACROBAT 2
2 one who does things only for his own benefit and with little regard for right and wrong ⟨betrayed by a *chancer* who, she mistakenly thought, was her friend⟩ — see SELF-SEEKER
change *n* **1** the act, process, or result of making different ⟨the positive *change* in our students' attitude toward people who are somehow different was a long and gradual process⟩
synonyms alteration, difference, modification, redoing, refashioning, remaking, remodeling, revamping, review, revise, revision, reworking, variation
related words amendment, correction, rectification, reform; conversion, deformation, distortion, metamorphosis, mutation, transfiguration, transformation; fluctuation, oscillation, shift; displacement, replacement, substitution; adjustment, modulation, regulation, tweak; redesign, redo
antonyms fixation, stabilization
2 the frequent and usually sudden passing from one condition to another ⟨there is nothing so constant as *change* itself⟩ — see FLUX 1
3 something (as pieces of stamped metal or printed paper) customarily and legally used as a medium of exchange, a measure of value, or a means of payment ⟨she spent quite a chunk of *change* on that car⟩ — see MONEY 1
change *vb* **1** to make different in some way ⟨my wife has *changed* the look of our living room more times than we care to remember⟩
synonyms alter, make over, modify, recast, redo, refashion, remake, remodel, revamp, revise, rework, vary
related words deform, metamorphose, mutate; regenerate, revolutionize, transfigure, transform, transmute; commute, convert, exchange; rejigger, retool
antonyms fix, freeze, set, stabilize
2 to pass from one form, state, or level to another ⟨the weather in New England is constantly *changing*⟩
synonyms fluctuate, mutate, shift, snap, vary
related words metamorphose, morph, transmute; better, improve; deteriorate, worsen; turn around; seesaw, teeter, vacillate, waver
antonyms plateau, stabilize
3 to give up (something) and take something else in return ⟨would you mind *changing* your seat so my friends can sit together?⟩
synonyms commute, exchange, shift, substitute, swap, switch, trade
related words interchange; displace, replace, supersede; cede, hand over, surrender, yield; reciprocate
changeable *adj* **1** capable of being readily changed ⟨an easily *changeable* color scheme for the nursery⟩ — see FLEXIBLE 1
2 likely to change frequently, suddenly, or unexpectedly ⟨the *changeable* nature of the business is such that you either have too much or too little to do⟩ — see FICKLE 1
changeful *adj* likely to change frequently, suddenly, or unexpectedly ⟨a confusingly *changeful* attitude toward his so-called best friend⟩ — see FICKLE 1
changeless *adj* not undergoing a change in condition ⟨apparently *changeless* mountains⟩ — see CONSTANT 1
changelessness *n* the state of continuing without change ⟨the *changelessness* of the scenery is actually an illusion⟩ — see CONSTANCY 1
changeover *n* a change in form, appearance, or use ⟨the region's *changeover* from an agricultural economy to one based on manufacturing⟩ — see CONVERSION 1
changing *adj* not staying constant ⟨a *changing* wind made sailing a challenge⟩ — see UNEVEN 2
channel *n* **1** an open man-made passageway for water ⟨water was drained from the swamp through a specially constructed *channel*⟩
synonyms aqueduct, canal, conduit, course, flume, racecourse, raceway, watercourse, waterway
related words millrace, millstream; floodway, sluice, sluiceway, spillway; swash, tideway, torrent; gutter, trough; river, rivulet, stream
2 a narrow body of water between two land masses ⟨the world record for swimming the *channel* between France and Great Britain⟩
synonyms narrows, neck, sound, strait
related words arm, bay, gulf, inlet; roads, roadstead; reach, stretch
3 a direct way of passing along information or supplies ⟨you need to make arrangements through the proper *channels*⟩ — see PIPELINE
4 a long hollow cylinder for carrying a substance (as a liquid or gas) ⟨had to replace the main water *channel*⟩ — see PIPE 1
5 a person who claims to speak with or for the spirits of the dead ⟨the *channel* went into a trance and began speaking in what was purported to be the voice of the deceased woman⟩ — see CHANNELER
channel *vb* to cause to move to a central point or along a restricted pathway ⟨an athletic youth who *channeled* all of his energy into sports⟩
synonyms canalize, channelize, conduct, direct, funnel, pipe, siphon (*also* syphon)
related words carry, convey, transmit; concentrate, consolidate, focus
channeler *n* a person who claims to speak with or for the spirits of the dead ⟨a *channeler* who claims to receive messages from a medieval warrior⟩
synonyms channel, medium, psychic, spiritist, spiritualist
related words clairvoyant; mentalist, mind reader, telepath; sensitive
channelize *vb* to cause to move to a central point or along a restricted pathway ⟨*channelized* all of his resources into winning that state's crucial primary⟩ — see CHANNEL
chant *vb* **1** to utter in musical or drawn out tones ⟨the frustrated crowd at the rock concert started to *chant*, "We want the show to start!"⟩
synonyms intonate, intone, sing
related words bellow, belt, roar; chime, chorus
2 to produce musical sounds with the voice ⟨monks

chanting fervently at matins⟩ — see SING 1

chaos *n* a state in which everything is out of order ⟨the boy's room is in such *chaos* that it looks as though a tornado had struck⟩
synonyms chance-medley, confusion, disarrangement, disarray, dishevelment, disorder, disorderedness, disorderliness, disorganization, free-for-all, havoc, heck, hell, jumble, mare's nest, mess, messiness, misorder, muddle, muss, shambles, snake pit, tumble, welter
related words anarchy, lawlessness, misrule, riot; knot, snarl, tangle; labyrinth, maze, web; maelstrom, storm; bollix, clutter, litter, mishmash, shuffle; hodgepodge, medley, miscellany, morass, motley
near antonyms method, pattern, plan, system
antonyms order, orderliness

chaotic *adj* lacking in order, neatness, and often cleanliness ⟨a *chaotic* cellar sorely in need of some straightening up⟩ — see MESSY

chap *n* **1** *chiefly British* an adult male human being ⟨a couple of *chaps* kindly gave us directions to Buckingham Palace⟩ — see MAN 1
2 *Southern & Midland* a young person who is between infancy and adulthood ⟨a cute little *chap*⟩ — see CHILD 1

chaparral *n* a thick patch of shrubbery, small trees, or underbrush ⟨the rabbit darted into the *chaparral*⟩ — see THICKET

chapeau *n* a covering for the head usually having a shaped crown ⟨with her *chapeau* cocked jauntily to one side, the French actress was the very picture of Gallic insouciance⟩ — see HAT

chaperone *or* **chaperon** *vb* to go along with in order to provide assistance, protection, or companionship ⟨three parents will *chaperone* the students on the school trip⟩ — see ACCOMPANY 1

chaplet *n* a decorative band or wreath worn about the head as a symbol of victory or honor ⟨maidens wove a *chaplet* of flowers round the champion's head⟩ — see CROWN 1

chappie *n, British* an adult male human being ⟨a good-humored *chappie* from the London office⟩ — see MAN 1

chapter *n* **1** a local unit of an organization ⟨our *chapter* was well represented at the Jaycees' national convention⟩
synonyms affiliate, branch, cell, council, local
related words arm, division, wing; offshoot, subchapter; lodge, post
2 an individual part of a process, series, or ranking ⟨a horror movie that marks a new *chapter* in vicarious sadism⟩ — see DEGREE 1

char *n, British* a female domestic servant ⟨a busy executive who leaves most of the cooking and cleaning to the *char*⟩ — see MAID 1

char *vb* to burn on the surface ⟨I'd like my hamburger *charred*, but not cooked through⟩ — see SCORCH 1

character *n* **1** a written or printed mark that is meant to convey information to the reader ⟨the pictorial *characters* of the ancient Egyptians had long been a mystery⟩
synonyms glyph, icon (*also* ikon), sign, symbol
related words cipher, letter, numeral; hieroglyph, ideogram, pictogram, pictograph; rune
2 a person of odd or whimsical habits ⟨the junk dealer is certainly a *character*, but he's as honest as they come⟩ — see ECCENTRIC
3 conduct that conforms to an accepted standard of right and wrong ⟨we need more people of sound *character* in public office⟩ — see MORALITY 1
4 overall quality as seen or judged by people in general ⟨the general *character* of the business appears to be good⟩ — see REPUTATION
5 something that sets apart an individual from others of the same kind ⟨one of the distinguishing *characters* of mammals⟩ — see CHARACTERISTIC
6 the set of qualities that make a person different from other people ⟨she regards each of her children as having a distinctive *character* that should be valued for what it is⟩ — see INDIVIDUALITY 1
7 the set of qualities that makes a person, a group of people, or a thing different from others ⟨the basic *character* of the work requires that an employee be able to work quietly and independently⟩ — see NATURE 1
8 a member of the human race ⟨you wouldn't believe what kind of *characters* hang around the bus station⟩ — see HUMAN

character *vb* to point out the chief quality or qualities of an individual or group ⟨formerly *charactered* as "the dark ages," that period of history may not have been quite so benighted as once thought⟩ — see CHARACTERIZE 1

character assassination *n* **1** the making of false statements that damage another's reputation ⟨the actor's lawyers charge that the tabloid engaged in a deliberate campaign of *character assassination*⟩ — see SLANDER
2 the use of personal attacks or insults in order to undermine an opponent ⟨refused to resort to *character assassination* even if it meant losing his bid for governor⟩ — see NAME-CALLING

characteristic *adj* **1** serving to identify as belonging to an individual or group ⟨the *characteristic* taste of licorice⟩
synonyms classic, diagnostic (*also* diagnostical), discriminating, distinct, distinctive, distinguishing, identifying, individual, peculiar, proper, symptomatic, typical
related words idiosyncratic; identifiable, pronounced, unmistakable; general, generic; common, normal, regular, usual; especial, particular, special, specific; archetypal (*also* archetypical), model, paradigmatic
antonyms atypical, nontypical, uncharacteristic, untypical
2 having or showing the qualities associated with the members of a particular group or kind ⟨the *characteristic* wit and good-naturedness of the Irish⟩ — see TYPICAL 1

characteristic *n* something that sets apart an individual from others of the same kind ⟨the ability to fashion tools and other *characteristics* that distinguish human beings from other animals⟩
synonyms affection, attribute, attribution, character, criterion, diagnostic, differentia, feature, fingerprint, hallmark, mark, marker, note, particularity, peculiarity, point, property, quality, specific, stamp, touch, trait
related words badge, indication, sign; emblem, symbol, token; charm, grace; excellence, merit, virtue; eccentricity, idiosyncrasy, oddity, quirk; individuality, singularity, uniqueness

characterize *vb* **1** to point out the chief quality or qualities of an individual or group ⟨how would you *characterize* the mission of this environmental organization?⟩
synonyms character, define, depict, describe, portray, represent
related words categorize, classify, pigeonhole, type; color, identify, indicate, name, specify; distinguish, individualize, mark, particularize, stamp
2 to be an important feature of ⟨an unsightly rash *characterizes* chicken pox⟩
synonyms distinguish, mark
related words differentiate; customize, individualize, particularize

characterless *adj* **1** lacking in distinctive features or qualities ⟨*characterless* suburban houses that have nothing going for them but their newness⟩ — see NONDESCRIPT
2 lacking strength of will or character ⟨a *characterless*

person who never has an opinion of his own⟩ — see WEAK 2

charade *n* a display of emotion or behavior that is insincere or intended to deceive ⟨put on a convincing *charade* to keep her from knowing about the surprise party⟩ — see MASQUERADE

charge *n* **1** a formal claim of criminal wrongdoing against a person ⟨*charges* of burglary and armed robbery that have yet to be proved⟩
synonyms complaint, count, indictment, rap
related words accusation, allegation, plea; crimination; counteraccusation, countercharge; arraignment, impeachment; implication, imputation, innuendo, insinuation; censure, condemnation, denunciation; incrimination, recrimination
2 a specific task with which a person or group is charged ⟨your *charge* is to keep everyone else organized and busy⟩ — see MISSION
3 a statement of what to do that must be obeyed by those concerned ⟨we've received an official *charge* about how to handle the situation⟩ — see COMMAND 1
4 something one must do because of prior agreement ⟨the first *charge* of our armed forces is to defend this country against enemy attack⟩ — see OBLIGATION 1
5 the act or action of setting upon with force or violence ⟨the famously disastrous *charge* led by General George Pickett at Gettysburg⟩ — see ATTACK 1
6 the amount of money that is demanded as payment for something ⟨the *charge* for the book will be five dollars⟩ — see PRICE 1
7 the duty or function of watching or guarding for the sake of proper direction or control ⟨was given *charge* of the business during the owner's absence⟩ — see SUPERVISION 1
8 a payment made in the course of achieving a result ⟨the *charges* mounted at a dizzying pace as the building project went way over budget⟩ — see EXPENSE
9 a pleasurably intense stimulation of the feelings ⟨the slopes at this resort aren't particularly challenging and aren't likely to give expert skiers much of a *charge*⟩ — see THRILL
10 the act or activity of looking after and making decisions about something ⟨he inherited *charge* of the Paris bureau after his supervisor quit⟩ — see CONDUCT 1

charge *vb* **1** to set or receive as a price ⟨any shop would *charge* $100 to repair that thing⟩
synonyms ask, command, demand
related words overcharge, undercharge; bring, fetch, sell (for); discount, mark down, mark up; assess, bill, invoice; price, value
2 to establish or apply as a charge or penalty ⟨*charges* a restocking fee for returned merchandise⟩ — see IMPOSE
3 to give a task, duty, or responsibility to ⟨we're *charging* you with the care of your little sister while we're gone for the evening⟩ — see ENTRUST 1
4 to issue orders to (someone) by right of authority ⟨*charged* the soldier to keep watch over the prisoner⟩ — see COMMAND 1
5 to make a claim of wrongdoing against ⟨he has not yet been *charged* with any crime⟩ — see ACCUSE
6 to put into (something) as much as can be held or contained ⟨*charge* a blast furnace with iron ore⟩ — see FILL 1
7 to take sudden, violent action against ⟨plans to *charge* the enemy's fortification at daybreak⟩ — see ATTACK 1
8 to cause a pleasurable stimulation of the feelings of ⟨the players are going into this game still *charged* from their upset victory the week before⟩ — see THRILL

charged *adj* **1** causing great emotional or mental stimulation ⟨an abstract expressionist who uses a palette of *charged* colors to great effect⟩ — see EXCITING 1
2 having or expressing great depth of feeling ⟨a very *charged* speech that got everyone worked up⟩ — see FERVENT 1
3 serving or likely to arouse a strong reaction ⟨a muralist who creates politically *charged* and often controversial works⟩ — see PROVOCATIVE

chariness *n* a close attentiveness to avoiding danger ⟨approached the can't-miss investment opportunity with the *chariness* of someone who's been burned before⟩ — see CAUTION 1

charisma *n* the power of irresistible attraction ⟨a movie star with great *charisma*⟩ — see CHARM 2

charismatic *adj* having an often mysterious or magical power to attract ⟨the cult's *charismatic* leader had managed to persuade seemingly rational people to obey him blindly⟩ — see FASCINATING 1

charitable *adj* **1** having or showing a concern for the welfare of others ⟨a *charitable* couple who have donated a sizable chunk of their fortune to the local university⟩
synonyms altruistic, beneficent, benevolent, do-good, eleemosynary, good, humanitarian, philanthropic (*also* philanthropical)
related words selfless, self-sacrificing; bighearted, bounteous, bountiful, free, freehanded, generous, greathearted, handsome, liberal, magnanimous, munificent, openhanded, openhearted, unselfish, unsparing; compassionate, humane, kind, kindhearted; social-minded
near antonyms self-indulgent, self-seeking; cheap, closefisted, miserly, niggardly, parsimonious, stingy, tight, tightfisted; hard-hearted, pitiless, unfeeling; self-obsessed
antonyms self-centered, self-concerned, selfish
2 giving or sharing in abundance and without hesitation ⟨a *charitable* woman who helped everyone who needed it⟩ — see GENEROUS 1
3 tolerant and kind in the judgment of and expectations for others ⟨her best friend, who was inclined towards a more *charitable* interpretation of her actions, let it pass⟩ — see INDULGENT 1

charity *n* **1** the giving of necessities and especially money to the needy ⟨after amassing a fortune in the computer industry, the brothers devoted themselves to *charity*⟩
synonyms almsgiving, dole, philanthropy
related words altruism, do-gooding, do-goodism, humanism, humanitarianism; beneficence, benevolence, goodwill; alms, benefaction, contribution, donation; relief, welfare; endowment, fund, grant, subsidy
2 a gift of money or its equivalent to a charity, humanitarian cause, or public institution ⟨donated his mansion and all of its land as a *charity* to the people of his beloved home state⟩ — see CONTRIBUTION
3 kind, gentle, or compassionate treatment especially towards someone who is undeserving of it ⟨can't you show a little *charity* to a guy who's the first to admit he's not perfect?⟩ — see MERCY 1
4 the capacity for feeling for another's unhappiness or misfortune ⟨his *charity* is such that he's a sucker for every panhandler's tale of woe⟩ — see HEART 1
5 kindly concern, interest, or support ⟨Lincoln's famous promise that the period of Reconstruction would be marked by "*charity* for all"⟩ — see GOODWILL 1

charlatan *n* one who makes false claims of identity or expertise ⟨the famed faith healer turned out to be a *charlatan*⟩ — see IMPOSTOR

charley horse *n* a painful sudden tightening of a muscle ⟨had to stop and rest because of a *charley horse* in his leg⟩ — see [1]CRAMP

charlie *also* **charley** *n, British* a person who lacks good sense or judgment ⟨he's a nice enough bloke, but a real *charlie* when choosing his girlfriends⟩ — see FOOL 1

charm *n* **1** something worn or kept to bring good luck or keep away evil ⟨an old cap that I use as a *charm* for whenever I play softball⟩
synonyms amulet, fetish (*also* fetich), mascot, mojo, periapt, phylactery, talisman
related words gris-gris (*also* grigri), juju, philter, toadstone; emblem, symbol, token, totem
near antonyms curse, hex, spell
antonyms hoodoo, jinx
2 the power of irresistible attraction ⟨a young singer with the kind of *charm* that turns a performer into a star⟩
synonyms allure, animal magnetism, appeal, attractiveness, captivation, charisma, duende, enchantment, fascination, force field, glamour (*also* glamor), magic, magnetism, oomph, pizzazz (*or* pizazz), seductiveness, witchery
related words allurement, attraction, call, lure, seduction; agreeableness, darlingness, delightfulness, desirability, desirableness, niceness, pleasantness, pleasingness, sweetness; sex appeal
near antonyms disagreeableness, distastefulness, obnoxiousness, offensiveness, unpleasantness
antonyms repulsion, repulsiveness
3 a spoken word or set of words believed to have magic power ⟨recited a *charm* to make the prince fall in love with her⟩ — see SPELL 1
4 an ornament worn on a chain around the neck or wrist ⟨a dangling *charm* in the figure of a horse on her bracelet⟩ — see PENDANT 1

charm *vb* **1** to attract or delight as if by magic ⟨a quaint seaside village that *charms* all who visit it⟩
synonyms allure, beguile, bewitch, captivate, enchant, fascinate, kill, magnetize, wile, witch [*archaic*]
related words disarm, draw, entice, lure, pull, seduce, tempt; delight, gratify, please; arrest, enrapture, enthrall (*or* enthral), entrance; appeal (to), interest, intrigue; beckon, court, invite, solicit, woo
near antonyms disgust, offend, repel, revolt; annoy, displease, irk; bore, tire, weary
2 to cast a spell on ⟨in one version of the tale, it is a vengeful fairy who *charms* Sleeping Beauty so that she falls into a sleep for a hundred years⟩ — see BEWITCH 1

charmed *adj* being or appearing to be under a magic spell ⟨you must be living a *charmed* life if you haven't caught the flu that's going around⟩ — see ENCHANTED

charmer *n* a person skilled in using supernatural forces ⟨the legendary *charmer* known as the Pied Piper of Hamelin⟩ — see MAGICIAN 1

charming *adj* having an often mysterious or magical power to attract ⟨a *charming* man who had no problem winning women's hearts⟩ — see FASCINATING 1

charmingly *adv* in a pleasing way ⟨a *charmingly* old-fashioned country inn⟩ — see WELL 5

chart *n* an illustration of certain features of a geographical area ⟨a *chart* of that section of the coastline will show any possible hazards⟩ — see MAP

chart *vb* **1** to give an oral or written account of in some detail ⟨the book *charts* the years between the two World Wars⟩ — see TELL 1
2 to work out the details of (something) in advance ⟨*charted* the entire campaign for governor before she even agreed to run⟩ — see PLAN 1

charter *vb* **1** to take or get the temporary use of (something) for a set sum ⟨*charter* a boat⟩ — see HIRE 1
2 *British* to give official or legal power to ⟨a London firm seeking the services of a *chartered* accountant⟩ — see AUTHORIZE 1

charwoman *n* a female domestic servant ⟨the couple finally hired a *charwoman* as they were just too busy to clean⟩ — see MAID 1

chary *adj* having or showing a close attentiveness to avoiding danger or trouble ⟨*chary* investors who weren't burned by the dot-com bust⟩ — see CAREFUL 1

chase *n* **1** an animal that is hunted or killed ⟨the gazelle is a favorite *chase* of lions⟩ — see PREY 1
2 the act of going after or in the tracks of another ⟨a high-speed car *chase*⟩ — see PURSUIT 1

chase *vb* **1** to drive or force out ⟨*chased* the cat out of the garden⟩ — see EJECT 1
2 to go after or on the track of ⟨a dog that likes to *chase* cars⟩ — see FOLLOW 2
3 to seek out (game) for food or sport ⟨owls often *chase* mice in the dark⟩ — see HUNT 1
4 to proceed or move quickly ⟨they *chased* all over the place to find the missing child⟩ — see HURRY 2

chase (down) *vb* to go in search of ⟨a historian who has spent two decades *chasing down* firsthand accounts of the drafting of the U.S. Constitution⟩ — see SEEK 1

chasing *n* the act of going after or in the tracks of another ⟨despite our determined *chasing*, the rabbit got away⟩ — see PURSUIT 1

chasm *n* an immeasurable depth or space ⟨a *chasm* in the ocean floor⟩ — see ABYSS

chaste *adj* **1** free from any trace of the coarse or indecent ⟨as one would expect, the minister's small talk is always *chaste*, even though he likes a joke as much as the next person⟩
synonyms clean, decent, G-rated, immaculate, modest, pure, vestal, virgin, virginal
related words lily-white, spotless, stainless, unblemished, undefiled, unsoiled, unspotted, unstained, unsullied, untainted, untarnished; decorous, proper, seemly; cultivated, refined, tasteful; harmless, innocent, innocuous, inoffensive
near antonyms blemished, defiled, soiled, spotted, stained, sullied, tainted, tarnished; improper, indecorous, indelicate, ribald, unseemly; crude, tacky, tasteless, unrefined
antonyms coarse, dirty, filthy, immodest, impure, indecent, obscene, smutty, unchaste, unclean, vulgar
2 free from dirt or stain ⟨the *chaste* white carpet is a key element in the living room's stark, minimalist design⟩ — see CLEAN 1

chastely *adv* with purity of thought and deed ⟨for living so *chastely* Kateri Tekakwitha became known as the "Lily of the Mohawks"⟩ — see PURELY 1

chasten *vb* **1** to inflict a penalty on for a fault or crime ⟨*chastened* the child with five minutes of sitting in the corner⟩ — see PUNISH
2 to reduce to a lower standing in one's own eyes or in others' eyes ⟨the unexpected loss to a second-rate player really *chastened* the tournament's top-seeded tennis star⟩ — see HUMBLE

chasteness *n* **1** the quality or state of being morally pure ⟨her unchallenged *chasteness* put her on the fast track for sainthood⟩ — see CHASTITY 1
2 abstention from sexual intercourse ⟨their marriage of consensual *chasteness* seems to have worked for both the composer and his wife⟩ — see CELIBACY

chastening *adj* inflicting, involving, or serving as punishment ⟨a *chastening* hour spent cleaning floors should discourage them from further pranks⟩ — see PUNITIVE

chastise *vb* **1** to criticize (someone) severely or angrily especially for personal failings ⟨a cold, distant father who rarely paid attention to his children except to *chastise* them⟩ — see SCOLD
2 to inflict a penalty on for a fault or crime ⟨the division of opinion regarding the appropriate way to *chastise* juvenile perpetrators of adult crimes⟩ — see PUNISH

chastisement *n* suffering, loss, or hardship imposed in response to a crime or offense ⟨missing the field trip should be sufficient *chastisement* for the schoolyard fight⟩ — see PUNISHMENT

chastiser *n* one who inflicts punishment in return for an injury or offense ⟨the highway patrolman who is the committed *chastiser* of those motorists who regard speed limits as no more than suggestions⟩ — see NEMESIS 1

chastising *adj* inflicting, involving, or serving as punishment ⟨a *chastising* lecture on the proper care and feeding of the dog⟩ — see PUNITIVE

chastity *n* **1** the quality or state of being morally pure ⟨a saint who is often held up as a model of *chastity*⟩
synonyms chasteness, immaculacy, innocence, modesty, purity
related words goodness, righteousness, virtue, virtuousness; morality, probity, rectitude; decency, decorum, propriety, seemliness
near antonyms badness, evil, sinfulness, unrighteousness, wickedness; impropriety, indecency, vulgarity
antonyms immodesty, impurity, unchasteness, unchastity
2 abstention from sexual intercourse ⟨vows of poverty, *chastity*, and obedience⟩ — see CELIBACY

chat *n* **1** friendly, informal conversation or an instance of this ⟨short *chats* between parents and teachers during the school's open house⟩
synonyms backchat, cackle, causerie, chatter, chin music, chin-wag [*slang*], chitchat, confab, confabulation, gab, gabfest, gossip, jangle, jaw, natter [*chiefly British*], palaver, patter, rap, schmooze, small talk, table talk, talk, tête-à-tête
related words colloquy, conference, discourse, parley, powwow, symposium; debate, dialogue (*also* dialog), exchange, give-and-take; crosstalk, happy talk; yak (*also* yack), yammer, yap
2 talking or a talk between two or more people ⟨a fireside *chat* between two of America's foremost men of letters⟩ — see CONVERSATION

chat *vb* **1** to engage in casual or rambling conversation ⟨the coffeehouse became the favored place to meet friends and *chat* for hours⟩
synonyms babble, blab, cackle, chaffer [*British*], chatter, chin [*slang*], converse, gab, gabble, gas, jabber, jaw, kibitz (*also* kibbitz), natter, palaver, patter, prate, prattle, rap, rattle, run on, schmooze (*or* shmooze), talk, twitter, visit
related words gossip, tattle; descant, discuss, expatiate; yak (*also* yack), yammer, yap
phrases blow smoke, chew the fat (*also* chew the rag), shoot the breeze, talk a blue streak
2 to speak rapidly, inarticulately, and usually unintelligibly ⟨lost in his own world, the toddler *chatted* happily for hours⟩ — see BABBLE 1

chat (with) *vb* to communicate with by means of spoken words ⟨*chatting with* the other expectant couples before the start of Lamaze class⟩ — see TALK 1

château *n* a large impressive residence ⟨a gorgeous *château* on a hill⟩ — see MANSION

chattel *n* **1** a person who is considered the property of another person ⟨at one time, the children of black slaves were also considered *chattel*⟩ — see SLAVE 1
2 chattels *pl* transportable items that one owns ⟨packed up all her *chattels* and moved to a new state⟩ — see POSSESSION 2

chatter *n* **1** friendly, informal conversation or an instance of this ⟨pleasant *chatter* over morning coffee⟩ — see CHAT 1
2 loud, confused, and usually inharmonious sound ⟨the *chatter* of the ship's engine kept us awake all night⟩ — see NOISE 1

chatter *vb* **1** to engage in casual or rambling conversation ⟨*chattered* idly while waiting in line⟩ — see CHAT 1
2 to speak rapidly, inarticulately, and usually unintelligibly ⟨the parrot *chatters* all day⟩ — see BABBLE 1

chatterbox *n* a person who talks constantly ⟨my seat companion was a *chatterbox* who never once shut up during the whole trip⟩
synonyms babbler, blabber, blabbermouth, blowhard, cackler, chatterer, conversationalist, gabbler, gasbag, jabberer, jay, magpie, motormouth, prattler, talker, windbag
related words gossip, gossiper, talebearer, tattler, tattletale; blatherer, blatherskite; converser, discourser

chatterer *n* a person who talks constantly ⟨that precocious little boy is a real *chatterer*⟩ — see CHATTERBOX

chattery *adj* having the style and content of everyday conversation ⟨writes a *chattery* advice column for the local paper⟩ — see CHATTY 1

chatty *adj* **1** having the style and content of everyday conversation ⟨a time when campers were expected to write a *chatty* letter to their folks every week⟩
synonyms chattery, colloquial, conversational, dishy, gossipy, newsy
related words casual, familiar, informal, intimate, tell-all; digressive, discursive, rambling; communicative, expansive, garrulous, talkative
near antonyms ceremonious, dignified, elevated, formal, solemn, stately
antonyms bookish, literary
2 fond of talking or conversation ⟨a *chatty* older woman who talked to everyone that walked by⟩ — see TALKATIVE

chauvinism *n* excessive favoritism towards one's own country ⟨their ingrained *chauvinism* has blinded them to their country's faults⟩
synonyms jingoism, nationalism, superpatriotism
related words loyalty, patriotism; nativism, xenophobia
near antonyms internationalism

chauvinist *adj* having or showing excessive favoritism towards one's own country ⟨wrote a history of World War II that was widely criticized for its *chauvinist* slant⟩ — see NATIONALIST 1

chauvinist *n* one who shows excessive favoritism towards his or her country ⟨*chauvinists* who express their patriotism by plastering flag decals all over their cars⟩ — see NATIONALIST

chauvinistic *adj* having or showing excessive favoritism towards one's own country ⟨other nations were decidedly irked by the American media's *chauvinistic* coverage of the Olympic Games⟩ — see NATIONALIST 1

chaw *vb* to crush or grind with the teeth ⟨the farmer was intently *chawing* a carrot⟩ — see BITE (ON)

chawbacon *n* an awkward or simple person especially from a small town or the country ⟨the townspeople were offended by the documentary's portrayal of them as an unwashed mass of *chawbacons*⟩ — see HICK

cheap *adj* **1** costing little ⟨e-mail is so popular because it's a *cheap* way to send messages⟩
synonyms affordable, bargain-basement, budget, cheapie, cheapo, chintzy, cut-price [*chiefly British*], cut-rate, dime-store, dirt cheap, el cheapo, inexpensive, low, low-end, popular, reasonable
related words cheapish, moderate; discount, discounted, fire-sale, lowered, reduced; wholesale; valueless, worthless; supercheap, ultracheap
near antonyms increased, inflated; exorbitant, extravagant, overpriced, prohibitive, prohibitory, steep, stiff, superexpensive, ultraexpensive, unreasonable; invaluable, priceless; luxurious
antonyms costly, dear, deluxe, expensive, high, high-ticket, precious, premium, pricey (*also* pricy), spendy [*chiefly Northwest*], valuable

2 of low quality ⟨a *cheap* sweater that started to unravel almost as soon as I bought it⟩
synonyms bad, bargain-basement, bum, cheapjack, cheesy, coarse, common, crappy [*slang*], cut-rate, el cheapo, execrable, gimcrack, inferior, junky, lousy, low-grade, low-rent, mediocre, miserable, poor, rotten, rubbishy, schlock (*or* schlocky *also* shlock *or* shlocky), second-rate, shoddy, sleazy, terrible, trashy, trumpery, wretched
related words useless, valueless, worthless; indifferent, lackluster, second-class; brummagem, flashy, garish, gaudy, glitzy, kitsch, kitschy, meretricious, ostentatious, showy, splashy, swank (*or* swanky), tawdry; seedy, shabby, tacky; counterfeit, fake, phony (*also* phoney), sham; supercheap, ultracheap
near antonyms elegant, handsome, tasteful; handcrafted, polished, refined
antonyms excellent, fine, first-class, first-rate, good, high-grade, superior, top-notch
3 giving or sharing as little as possible ⟨a *cheap* co-worker who never contributes to the collections taken up in the office⟩ — see STINGY 1
4 arousing or deserving of one's loathing and disgust ⟨that was a *cheap* thing to say to someone who never did you any harm⟩ — see CONTEMPTIBLE 1
5 involving minimal difficulty or effort ⟨the boxer's early bouts were *cheap* wins, but now he's moving up to the top ranks of boxing⟩ — see EASY 1

cheapen *vb* **1** to diminish the price or value of ⟨a glutted market *cheapened* cranberries to the point where they were selling for less than what it cost to grow them⟩ — see DEPRECIATE 1
2 to lower in character, dignity, or quality ⟨a politician who would *cheapen* herself by caving in to lobbyists⟩ — see DEBASE 1
3 to reduce to a lower standing in one's own eyes or in others' eyes ⟨she really *cheapens* herself by shamelessly pursuing men like that⟩ — see HUMBLE

cheapie *adj* costing little ⟨we'll crash in some *cheapie* motel room⟩ — see CHEAP 1

cheapjack *adj* of low quality ⟨a *cheapjack* little watch that I wear on camping trips⟩ — see CHEAP 2

cheapness *n* the quality or practice of being overly sparing with money ⟨his chronic *cheapness* is such that he never takes vacations or replaces old, worn-out household goods⟩ — see PARSIMONY 1

cheapo *adj* costing little ⟨I picked up a *cheapo* souvenir watch as gag gift⟩ — see CHEAP 1

cheapskate *n* a mean grasping person who is usually stingy with money ⟨a *cheapskate* who lived like a pauper, she was reputedly the wealthiest woman in the U.S. at the time of her death⟩ — see MISER

cheat *n* a dishonest person who uses clever means to cheat others out of something of value ⟨a *cheat* at cards⟩ — see TRICKSTER 1

cheat *vb* **1** to use dishonest methods to achieve a goal ⟨students who *cheat* on tests end up never knowing anything⟩
synonyms chicane, finagle, fudge
related words crib; color, distort, falsify, misinterpret, misrepresent, misstate, pervert, twist, warp; doctor, fake, tamper (with); elaborate, embellish, embroider, exaggerate, magnify, pad, stretch; dodge, evade, hedge
2 to be sexually unfaithful ⟨he suspects that his girlfriend is *cheating* on him⟩
synonyms philander, screw around, step out
related words cat (around), fool around, fornicate, play (around), tomcat (around), womanize; copulate, couple, lie, make out, mate, sleep; lust
3 to fall short in satisfying the expectation or hope of ⟨the daredevil survived his plunge over the falls with barely a scratch, having *cheated* death once again⟩ — see DISAPPOINT
4 to rob by the use of trickery or threats ⟨a despicable confidence man who heartlessly *cheated* elderly people out of their savings⟩ — see FLEECE

cheater *n* a dishonest person who uses clever means to cheat others out of something of value ⟨gambling casinos have very elaborate means of detecting *cheaters*⟩ — see TRICKSTER 1

cheating *n* **1** the inclination or practice of misleading others through lies or trickery ⟨a conscienceless adventuress who never earned anything except through *cheating*⟩ — see DECEIT 1
2 a sexual encounter or relationship between a married person and someone other than their spouse ⟨she swore that if there was ever any *cheating*, she'd leave in a heartbeat⟩ — see ADULTERY

check *n* **1** the amount owed at a bar or restaurant or the slip of paper stating the amount ⟨diners at that temple of gastronomy often look shocked when they receive the *check*⟩
synonyms bill, tab
related words invoice, receipt; account, reckoning, record, statement; charge, cost, damage, expense, fee, figure; score, tally
2 a close look at or over someone or something in order to judge condition ⟨made a careful *check* of the antique table before buying it⟩ — see INSPECTION
3 a record of goods sold or services performed together with the costs due ⟨request a detailed *check* from the company before sending any money⟩ — see [1]BILL 1
4 a small sheet of plastic, paper, or paperboard showing that the bearer has a claim to something (as admittance) ⟨handed over a *check* for his coat⟩ — see TICKET 1
5 something that limits one's freedom of action or choice ⟨the judiciary is intended to be a *check* on the executive and legislative branches of government⟩ — see RESTRICTION 1
6 an irregular usually narrow break in a surface created by pressure ⟨the network of fine *checks* on the surface would indicate that the painting is quite old⟩ — see CRACK 1
7 the stopping of a process or activity ⟨the announcement of bad news gave a sudden *check* to the celebration⟩ — see END 1

check *vb* **1** to be in agreement on every point ⟨their story of what happened *checks* with the report of the eyewitness⟩
synonyms accord, agree, answer, chord, cohere, coincide, comport, conform, consist, correspond, dovetail, fit, go, harmonize, jibe, rhyme (*also* rime), sort, square, tally
related words equal, match, parallel; align (*also* aline), line up, register
phrases fall in with
near antonyms contradict, dispute, gainsay; negate, nullify; clash, conflict, jar
antonyms differ (from), disagree (with)
2 to bring (something) to a standstill ⟨a tree finally *checked* the skidding car⟩ — see [1]HALT 1
3 to keep from exceeding a desirable degree or level (as of expression) ⟨*check* your enthusiasm a bit, and think before you marry someone you just met⟩ — see CONTROL 1

check (out) *vb* to look over closely (as for judging quality or condition) ⟨*check out* the house and let me know if you think it's worth buying⟩ — see INSPECT

checkable *adj* capable of being proven as true or real ⟨all of the statistics cited by the news reporter are readily *checkable*, but it would appear that the article was never fact-checked before publication⟩ — see VERIFIABLE

checklist *n* a record of a series of items (as names or titles) usually arranged according to some system ⟨a *checklist* of things to do before the flight⟩ — see [1]LIST

checkmate *vb* to prevent from achieving a goal ⟨finally *checkmated* the billionaire in his attempt to take over the movie studio⟩ — see FRUSTRATE 1

check out *vb* to stop living ⟨there are a lot of sights around the world that I want to see before I *check out*⟩ — see DIE 1

checkup *n* a close look at or over someone or something in order to judge condition ⟨the vet gave the kitten a *checkup*, then reassuringly declared her in fine health⟩ — see INSPECTION

cheek *n* **1** disrespectful or argumentative talk given in response to a command or request ⟨any more *cheek* in this classroom and you'll get a detention⟩ — see BACK TALK

2 shameless boldness ⟨she had the *cheek* to blame me for the fact that she had forgotten about the staff meeting⟩ — see EFFRONTERY

3 cheeks *pl* the part of the body upon which someone sits ⟨he dropped his pants and flashed his *cheeks* at the opposing team⟩ — see BUTTOCKS

cheekiness *n* shameless boldness ⟨the *cheekiness* of the restaurant's demand that we pay for unordered food was breathtaking⟩ — see EFFRONTERY

cheeky *adj* displaying or marked by rude boldness ⟨a *cheeky* comment about something that was none of her business⟩ — see NERVY 1

cheep *vb* to make a short sharp sound like a small bird ⟨the toaster *cheeps* to indicate that the toast is done⟩ — see CHIRP

cheer *n* **1** a mood characterized by high spirits and amusement and often accompanied by laughter ⟨a birthday celebration filled with affection and *cheer*⟩ — see MIRTH

2 a feeling of ease from grief or trouble ⟨the visiting general had some words of *cheer* for each of the hospital's recuperating soldiers⟩ — see COMFORT 1

3 a state of mind dominated by a particular emotion ⟨be of good *cheer* in this Christmas season⟩ — see MOOD 1

4 enthusiastic and usually public expression of approval ⟨all three movies in the series received *cheers* from fans of the novels⟩ — see APPLAUSE 1

cheer *vb* **1** to declare enthusiastic approval of ⟨critics and fans alike have *cheered* the latest addition to the author's series of fantasy novels⟩ — see ACCLAIM

2 to ease the grief or distress of ⟨let's hope that these flowers will *cheer* my ailing aunt at least a little⟩ — see COMFORT

cheer (up) *vb* **1** to become glad or hopeful ⟨*cheer up*—things are bound to get better⟩

synonyms brighten, buck up, lighten, look up, perk (up)

related words rejoice; liven (up), revive; beam, glow, radiate, sparkle; encourage, gladden, hearten

near antonyms despair, despond; brood, fret, mope

antonyms darken, sadden

2 to fill with courage or strength of purpose ⟨the general's speech *cheered up* the troops tremendously⟩ — see ENCOURAGE 1

cheerful *adj* **1** having or showing a good mood or disposition ⟨a *cheerful* person who is always fun to work with and a pleasure to be around⟩

synonyms blithe, blithesome, bright, buoyant, canty [*British dialect*], cheery, chipper, eupeptic, gay, gladsome, lightsome, sunny, upbeat, winsome

related words hopeful, optimistic, rosy, sanguine; animated, chirpy, jaunty, lilting, lively, perky, sprightful, sprightly, vivacious; carefree, careless, cavalier, devil-may-care, easygoing, happy-go-lucky, insouciant, lighthearted, unconcerned; boon, gleeful, jocund, jolly, jovial, merry, mirthful; blissful, delighted, glad, gratified, happy, joyful, joyous, pleased, satisfied, tickled; beaming, grinning, laughing, smiling

near antonyms joyless, sad, unhappy, unsatisfied; dull, lethargic, listless, sluggish, torpid; blue, brokenhearted, crestfallen, dejected, depressed, despondent, disconsolate, disheartened, down, downcast, downhearted, droopy, forlorn, hangdog, heavyhearted, inconsolable, low, low-spirited, melancholy, mirthless, sorrowful

antonyms dour, gloomy, glum, morose, saturnine, sulky, sullen

2 serving to lift one's spirits ⟨a hospital with sunny, *cheerful* rooms that are designed to make a patient's stay as pleasant as possible⟩

synonyms bright, cheering, cheery, gay, glad

related words gladdening, heartening, heartwarming; gleaming, radiant, sparkling

near antonyms discouraging, disheartening; colorless, drab, dull, lackluster, lusterless; black, desolate, dispiriting

antonyms bleak, cheerless, dark, depressing, dismal, dreary, gloomy, gray (*also* grey)

cheerfully *adv* in a cheerful or happy manner ⟨*cheerfully* announced, "It's a beautiful morning!"⟩ — see GAILY 1

cheerfulness *n* a mood characterized by high spirits and amusement and often accompanied by laughter ⟨his constant *cheerfulness* makes him a pleasure to be around⟩ — see MIRTH

cheerily *adv* in a cheerful or happy manner ⟨waving *cheerily* as they drove off⟩ — see GAILY 1

cheeriness *n* a mood characterized by high spirits and amusement and often accompanied by laughter ⟨a moment of *cheeriness* interrupted the solemn discussion⟩ — see MIRTH

cheering *adj* **1** making one feel good inside ⟨the *cheering* sight of a child being reunited with a pet that had been lost⟩ — see HEARTWARMING

2 serving to lift one's spirits ⟨*cheering* words from the doctor that the worst of the treatment was over⟩ — see CHEERFUL 2

cheering *n* enthusiastic and usually public expression of approval ⟨a raucous *cheering* welcomed the newlyweds⟩ — see APPLAUSE 1

cheerless *adj* causing or marked by an atmosphere lacking in cheer ⟨a dank and *cheerless* castle that was once the site of unspeakable horrors⟩ — see GLOOMY 1

cheery *adj* **1** having or showing a good mood or disposition ⟨a *cheery* grin on the host of the holiday party⟩ — see CHEERFUL 1

2 serving to lift one's spirits ⟨a *cheery*, unexpected compliment can really make another person's day⟩ — see CHEERFUL 2

cheese *n* that which is of low quality or worth ⟨you wouldn't believe the *cheese* that the movie studio puts out⟩ — see JUNK 1

cheesed off *adj, chiefly British* feeling or showing anger ⟨I was really *cheesed off* that they made me go to the back of the queue⟩ — see ANGRY

cheeseparing *n* the quality or practice of being overly sparing with money ⟨Ebenezer Scrooge is portrayed as a taskmaster so dedicated to *cheeseparing* that he would prefer that his employees freeze to death rather than splurge on heat⟩ — see PARSIMONY 1

cheesy *adj* **1** marked by an obvious lack of style or good taste ⟨*cheesy* plastic knickknacks lined the fireplace mantel⟩ — see [1]TACKY 1

2 of low quality ⟨a *cheesy* watch that he bought from a sidewalk vendor preying on tourists⟩ — see CHEAP 2

chef *n* a person who prepares food by some manner of heating ⟨the restaurant hired a famous *chef* to raise the quality of its cuisine⟩ — see COOK

chef d'oeuvre *n* something (as a work of art) that is a great achievement and often its creator's greatest achievement ⟨the sculptor labored for 15 years on his *chef d'oeuvre*⟩ — see MASTERPIECE

chemist *n, British* a person who prepares drugs according to a doctor's prescription ⟨let's ask the *chemist* whether it's safe to take these two drugs together⟩ — see DRUGGIST

cherish *vb* **1** to feel passion, devotion, or tenderness for ⟨promised to love and *cherish* her husband forever⟩ — see LOVE 2
2 to hold dear ⟨we shall always *cherish* the keepsakes that our grandmother left us⟩ — see LOVE 1
3 to keep in one's mind or heart ⟨after all these years, she still *cherishes* the memory of her first summer romance⟩ — see HARBOR 1

cherished *adj* granted special treatment or attention ⟨a *cherished* heirloom that has been in the family for generations⟩ — see DARLING 1

cherry–pick *vb* to decide to accept (someone or something) from a group of possibilities ⟨*cherry-picked* the spacious corner office for his corporate fief⟩ — see CHOOSE 1

cherry–picked *adj* singled out from a number or group as more to one's liking ⟨claims that the committee used only *cherry-picked* facts in their report on the state of the nation's economy⟩ — see SELECT 1

chest *n* a covered rectangular container for storing or transporting things ⟨a *chest* containing almost every tool that the home do-it-yourselfer is likely to need⟩
synonyms bin, box, caddy, case, casket, locker, trunk
related words carton, crate; footlocker, locker, sea chest; coffer, lockbox, safe, safe-deposit box, strongbox; coffin; compartment, vault; canteen; caisson, hope chest; minaudière; bandbox, hatbox, jewel box, snuffbox, tinderbox

chesterfield *n* a long upholstered piece of furniture designed for several sitters ⟨bought a huge new *chesterfield* for the living room⟩ — see COUCH

chestnut *n* an idea or expression that has been used by many people ⟨an op-ed piece that's offers nothing but warmed-over *chestnuts* for solving the city's financial woes⟩ — see COMMONPLACE

chesty *adj* having a feeling of superiority that shows itself in an overbearing attitude ⟨obnoxiously *chesty* self-made millionaires⟩ — see ARROGANT

chew *vb* to crush or grind with the teeth ⟨please *chew* your food thoroughly so you don't choke⟩ — see BITE (ON)

chew out *vb* to criticize (someone) severely or angrily especially for personal failings ⟨the coach *chews out* even the stars of the team if they fail to show up for practice⟩ — see SCOLD

chew over *vb* to give serious and careful thought to ⟨yet another senator *chewing over* the idea of running for president⟩ — see PONDER

chewy *adj* not easily chewed ⟨a flavorful but *chewy* piece of meat⟩ — see TOUGH 1

chi *or* **ch'i** *also* **qi** *n* a spiritual force that is held to emanate from or give animation to living beings ⟨the concept of *chi* is of central importance in acupuncture⟩ — see ENERGY 1

chic *adj* being in the latest or current fashion ⟨a *chic* new hairstyle that makes her look very sophisticated⟩ — see STYLISH

chic *n* a practice or interest that is very popular for a short time ⟨mockumentaries are the latest filmmaking *chic*⟩ — see FAD

chicane *n* the use of clever underhanded actions to achieve an end ⟨most get-rich-quick schemes involve more than a smidgen of *chicane*⟩ — see TRICKERY

chicane *vb* to use dishonest methods to achieve a goal ⟨a lawyer who is so notorious for *chicaning* that the guilty invariably seek his services⟩ — see CHEAT 1

chicanery *n* the use of clever underhanded actions to achieve an end ⟨that candidate only won the election through *chicanery*⟩ — see TRICKERY

chick *n* a young person who is between infancy and adulthood ⟨those innocent little *chicks* can scarcely imagine what life has in store for them⟩ — see CHILD 1

chicken *adj* **1** having or showing a shameful lack of courage ⟨too *chicken* to go through with the stunt⟩ — see COWARDLY
2 so small or unimportant as to warrant little or no attention ⟨just concentrate on the important duties of the job and forget about the *chicken* stuff⟩ — see NEGLIGIBLE 1

chicken *n* a person who shows a shameful lack of courage in the face of danger ⟨a staunch hawk during the drumbeat for war, he proved to be a *chicken* when it came to actually fighting it⟩ — see COWARD

chicken feed *n, slang* a very small sum of money ⟨I'm sick of working for *chicken feed*—I want a job where I can bring home some real dough⟩ — see MITE 1

chickenhearted *adj* having or showing a shameful lack of courage ⟨too *chickenhearted* to speak up, even though she knew a terrible injustice was being committed⟩ — see COWARDLY

Chicken Little *n* one given to forebodings and predictions of impending calamity ⟨some called him *Chicken Little*, but the climatologist had the data to back up his warning on global warming⟩ — see DOOMSAYER

chicken–livered *adj* having or showing a shameful lack of courage ⟨a *chicken-livered* newspaper editor who has been afraid to take on the town's powerful business elite⟩ — see COWARDLY

chide *vb* to criticize (someone) usually gently so as to correct a fault ⟨my wife *chided* me for forgetting to offer our guests some refreshments⟩ — see REBUKE 1

chief *adj* **1** coming before all others in importance ⟨our *chief* priority this year will be cutting the budget⟩ — see FOREMOST 1
2 highest in rank or authority ⟨the *chief* administrator will be retiring soon⟩ — see HEAD

chief *n* **1** the main or greater part of something as distinguished from its subordinate parts ⟨the *chief* of the estate was left to the eldest son⟩ — see BODY 1
2 the person (as an employer or supervisor) who tells people and especially workers what to do ⟨our *chief* is out on a business trip right now⟩ — see BOSS

chiefly *adv* for the most part ⟨our video collection consists *chiefly* of comedies, but we have a few horror movies⟩
synonyms altogether, basically, by and large, generally, largely, mainly, mostly, overall, predominantly, primarily, principally, substantially
related words about, more or less, most, much, near, nearly, next to, nigh, practically, some, virtually, well-nigh; approximately, broadly, plus or minus, roughly; commonly, frequently, generally, normally, ordinarily, typically, usually; incompletely, partially, partly, rather, somewhat
phrases in general, on the whole
near antonyms completely, entirely, fully, perfectly, thoroughly, totally, wholly; barely, hardly, just, marginally, minimally, scarcely; absolutely, categorically, unqualifiedly

child *n* **1** a young person who is between infancy and adulthood ⟨an imaginative animated film that appeals to adults as well as to *children*⟩
synonyms bairn [*chiefly Scottish*], bambino, bud, chap [*Southern & Midland*], chick, cub, juvenile, kid, kiddie (*also* kiddy), kiddo, moppet, sprat, sprout, squirt,

whelp, youngling, youngster, youth
related words adolescent, minor; kindergartner (*also* kindergartener), preschooler, rug rat [*slang*], schoolboy, schoolchild, schoolgirl, schoolkid; babe, baby, bantling, infant, neonate, nestling, newborn, toddler, tot, tyke (*also* tike), weanling; brat, devil, hellion, imp, jackanapes, mischief, monkey, rapscallion, rascal, rogue, urchin, whippersnapper; cherub; preteen, preteen-ager, subteen, teen, teenager, teener, teenybopper, tween; lad, nipper, shaver, stripling, tad; bobby-soxer, hoyden, tomboy
near antonyms middle-ager; ancient, elder, golden-ager, oldster, old-timer, senior, senior citizen
antonyms adult, grown-up
2 a recently born person ⟨wrapped the *child* in a blanket before taking him outside in the cold⟩ — see BABY 1
3 a condition or occurrence traceable to a cause ⟨widespread stress is the *child* of the frenetic pace of the modern world⟩ — see EFFECT 1

childbearing *n* the act or process of giving birth to children ⟨in olden days many women died in *childbearing*⟩ — see CHILDBIRTH

childbirth *n* the act or process of giving birth to children ⟨women who choose to undergo *childbirth* without the use of anesthetics and other drugs⟩
synonyms accouchement, childbearing, delivery, labor, parturition, travail
related words birth pang, contraction, pains; pregnancy; abortion, miscarriage; cesarean section (*or* caesarean section), natural childbirth; childbed, confinement, lying-in

childhood *n* the state or time of being a child ⟨enjoy your *childhood*—it won't last forever⟩
synonyms nonage, springtime, youth
related words boyhood, girlhood, toddlerhood; adolescence, juvenescence, minority; immaturity, juvenility; babyhood, infancy
near antonyms majority; middle age, midlife; senectitude, sunset, winter
antonyms adulthood

childish *adj* having or showing the annoying qualities (as silliness) associated with children ⟨you almost spoiled the ceremony for everyone with your *childish* giggling⟩
synonyms adolescent, babyish, immature, infantile, jejune, juvenile, kiddish, puerile
related words boyish, brattish, bratty, girlie (*or* girly), girlish; childlike, innocent, naive (*or* naïve), simple, simplistic, unsophisticated
near antonyms unchildlike; cosmopolitan, experienced, knowing, smart, sophisticated, worldly, worldly-wise
antonyms adult, grown-up, mature

child's play *n* **1** something of little importance ⟨the injury is *child's play*, just a scratch⟩ — see TRIFLE
2 something that is easy to do ⟨winning the game against those guys will be *child's play*⟩ — see CINCH 1

chill *adj* **1** lacking in friendliness or warmth of feeling ⟨were met with a *chill* gaze when they arrived home late from the party⟩ — see COLD 2
2 uncomfortably cool ⟨this *chill* weather is making my teeth chatter⟩ — see CHILLY 1
3 having a low or subnormal temperature ⟨no one should be coatless on a *chill* night as this⟩ — see COLD 1
4 causing or marked by an atmosphere lacking in cheer ⟨the house's design may be cutting-edge, but it has a *chill* sterility about it that is anything but homey⟩ — see GLOOMY 1

chill *n* an uncomfortable degree of coolness ⟨there's a *chill* in the air, so you'd better wear a sweater⟩
synonyms bite, bitterness, bleakness, chilliness, nip, nippiness, rawness, sharpness
related words briskness, crispness; coldness, frigidity, frigidness, frostiness, gelidity, iciness, wintriness; cold, freeze, snap
near antonyms balminess, warmness, warmth; heat, hotness, sultriness

chill *vb* **1** to cause to lose heat ⟨*chill* the gelatin for two hours, until it sets⟩ — see COOL 1
2 to get rid of nervous tension or anxiety ⟨you want to hang out with us and just *chill* this weekend?⟩ — see RELAX 1
3 to lessen the courage or confidence of ⟨investors *chilled* by the floundering economy⟩ — see DISCOURAGE 1
4 to spend time doing nothing ⟨instead of going out tonight, let's stay in and *chill*⟩ — see IDLE

chilliness *n* an uncomfortable degree of coolness ⟨the lingering *chilliness* in the church prompted everyone to put on jackets⟩ — see CHILL

chilling *adj* uncomfortably cool ⟨a Southern visitor who was unused to the *chilling* air of a Northeast winter⟩ see CHILLY 1

chill out *vb, slang* **1** to become still and orderly ⟨stop making that racket, and just *chill out*!⟩ — see QUIET 1
2 to get rid of nervous tension or anxiety ⟨if you don't *chill out*, you're going to get an ulcer⟩ — see RELAX 1

chilly *adj* **1** uncomfortably cool ⟨those *chilly* nights when a warm fire can be especially comforting⟩
synonyms bitter, bleak, chill, chilling, nipping, nippy, raw, sharp
related words bracing, brisk, crisp, invigorating, rigorous, snappy; arctic, bitter, cold, coolish, freezing, frigid, frosty, glacial, ice-cold, icy, numbing, polar, shivery, wintry (*also* wintery); subfreezing, subzero; frore, frosted, frozen, iced, refrigerated, unheated
near antonyms balmy, warm; lukewarm, tepid; heated, warmed
2 lacking in friendliness or warmth of feeling ⟨a *chilly* glare directed at the person who tried to go to the head of the line⟩ — see COLD 2
3 having a low or subnormal temperature ⟨a *chilly* spring morning⟩ — see COLD 1

chime *n* **1** *usually* **chimes** *pl* a series of short high ringing sounds ⟨the welcoming *chimes* on our doorbell⟩ — see TINKLE
2 peaceful coexistence ⟨firmly believes that science and religion can keep *chime* with one another⟩ — see HARMONY 2

chime *vb* **1** to form a pleasing relationship ⟨the restaurant's manor-house decor *chimes* perfectly with the chef's traditionalist take on haute cuisine⟩ — see HARMONIZE 1
2 to make the clear sound heard when metal vibrates ⟨the doorbell *chimed* just as we were sitting down to eat⟩ — see [2]RING
3 to say or state again ⟨TV commercial that *chimes* the same message over and over⟩ — see REPEAT 1

chime in *vb* **1** to cause a disruption in a conversation or discussion ⟨"I don't like that show at all," my friend *chimed in*⟩ — see INTERRUPT
2 to form a pleasing relationship ⟨unfortunately, his views on child rearing don't *chime in* with those of his new wife, who has two children from a previous marriage⟩ — see HARMONIZE 1

chimera *n* a conception or image created by the imagination and having no objective reality ⟨a monster in the closet would not have been the first *chimera* that the boy had seen in his mind's eye⟩ — see FANTASY 1

chimerical *also* **chimeric** *adj* not real and existing only in the imagination ⟨for the time being, interplanetary travel remains a *chimerical* feature of life in the 21st century⟩ — see IMAGINARY

chin *vb, slang* to engage in casual or rambling conversation ⟨the kind of work environment in which staffers can knock off early on Friday and *chin* with the boss⟩ — see CHAT 1

chine *n* a column of bones supporting the trunk of a vertebrate animal ⟨uncovered the *chine* of some animal while digging in the backyard⟩ — see SPINE

chink *n* **1** a vulnerable point ⟨before the tournament she studied tapes of her chief rival, looking for the *chink* in her game⟩ — see ACHILLES' HEEL
2 an irregular usually narrow break in a surface created by pressure ⟨plugged the *chinks* in the walls with mortar⟩ — see CRACK 1

chink *vb* to make a repeated sharp light ringing sound ⟨in the breeze the flag's chain *chinked* against the flagpole⟩ — see JINGLE

chin music *n* friendly, informal conversation or an instance of this ⟨after listening to *chin music* all afternoon, I was ready for the sounds of silence⟩ — see CHAT 1

chintzy *adj* **1** costing little ⟨for the party I want *chintzy* plates that we can throw away afterward⟩ — see CHEAP 1
2 giving or sharing as little as possible ⟨her husband can be pretty *chintzy* when it comes to buying gifts for others⟩ — see STINGY 1

chin–wag *n, slang* friendly, informal conversation or an instance of this ⟨a tireless practitioner of *chin-wag*, she makes every other talker seem a little taciturn⟩ — see CHAT 1

chip *n* **1** a small flat piece separated from a whole ⟨wood *chips* were spread over the ground between the plants⟩
synonyms flake, sliver, spall, splint, splinter
related words bit, disk (*or* disc), fragment, part, particle, portion, scrap, section, shard; flinders, shiver, smithereens; shred, tatter; clipping, paring, shave, shaving, snippet; leaf, sheet, slice
near antonyms chunk, hunk, lump, slab
2 a V-shaped cut usually on an edge or a surface ⟨watch out for the *chip* on the rim of that drinking glass⟩ — see NOTCH 1
3 chips *pl* something (as pieces of stamped metal or printed paper) customarily and legally used as a medium of exchange, a measure of value, or a means of payment ⟨was in the *chips* after hitting it big in the lottery⟩ — see MONEY 1

chip in *vb* **1** to make a donation as part of a group effort ⟨we all *chipped in* and bought flowers for the secretaries⟩ — see CONTRIBUTE 1
2 *chiefly British* to cause a disruption in a conversation or discussion ⟨forgive me in *chipping in* like this, but I think I know a better way to get to Trafalgar Square⟩ — see INTERRUPT

chipper *adj* having or showing a good mood or disposition ⟨you're awfully *chipper* this morning⟩ — see CHEERFUL 1

chippie *also* **chippy** *n* a boldly flirtatious or sexually promiscuous woman ⟨detectives wanted to talk to the *chippies* who were regulars at the bar—to learn if they had seen anything⟩ — see FLOOZY

chippy *adj* feeling or displaying eagerness to fight ⟨a *chippy*, defensive fellow whose alma mater was the school of hard knocks⟩ — see BELLIGERENT

chirk (up) *vb* to fill with courage or strength of purpose ⟨presented her with an inspirational book to *chirk* her *up* during her prolonged hospitalization⟩ — see ENCOURAGE 1

chirp *vb* to make a short sharp sound like a small bird ⟨the sparrows were *chirping* up a storm in the backyard⟩
synonyms cheep, chirrup, chitter, jargon, peep, pip, pipe, tweet, twitter
related words cackle, chatter, jabber; sing, trill, warble

chirr *n* a monotonous sound like that of an insect in motion ⟨the *chirr* of dragonflies⟩ — see HUM

chirrup *vb* to make a short sharp sound like a small bird ⟨the kitten *chirruped* insistently for her dinner⟩ — see CHIRP

chisel *vb* to rob by the use of trickery or threats ⟨ruthlessly *chiseled* other students out of their lunch money⟩ — see FLEECE

chiseler *or* **chiseller** *n* a dishonest person who uses clever means to cheat others out of something of value ⟨the *chiseler* made off with nearly a million dollars before anyone realized what was going on⟩ — see TRICKSTER 1

chitchat *n* friendly, informal conversation or an instance of this ⟨a bit of *chitchat* over lunch with people we hadn't seen in a while⟩ — see CHAT 1

chitter *vb* to make a short sharp sound like a small bird ⟨the *chittering* birds outside were driving the cat crazy⟩ ⟨the cell phone *chittered* in his pocket⟩ — see CHIRP

chivalrous *adj* having, characterized by, or arising from a dignified and generous nature ⟨still engages in *chivalrous* behavior, such as holding doors for people⟩ — see NOBLE 2

chivy *or* **chivvy** *vb* to thrust oneself upon (another) without invitation ⟨a boss with a reputation for *chivying* his workers about every little thing⟩ — see BOTHER 1

chockablock *adj* containing or seeming to contain the greatest quantity or number possible ⟨the mantel was *chockablock* with knickknacks⟩ — see FULL 1

chock–full *or* **chockful** *adj* containing or seeming to contain the greatest quantity or number possible ⟨returned from the buffet with a plate *chock-full* of food⟩ — see FULL 1

chocolate–box *adj* appealing to the emotions in an obvious and tiresome way ⟨a dog calendar that features the animals in cutesy, *chocolate-box* poses and robs them of their dignity⟩ — see CORNY 1

choice *adj* **1** having qualities that appeal to a refined taste ⟨*choice* chocolates for which chocolate lovers are willing to pay extra⟩
synonyms dainty, delicate, elegant, exquisite, fine, rare, recherché, select
related words bijou, jewellike; better, exceptional, fancy, high-grade, special; elite, exclusive; classic, excellent, fabulous, first-class, first-rate, grand, great, marvelous (*or* marvellous), noble, outstanding, par excellence, premium, prime, sensational, splendid, stellar, sterling, superb, superior, superlative, supernal, terrific, tip-top, top, top-notch, transcendant, unsurpassed, wonderful; ultrarare
near antonyms coarse, gross, kitsch, kitschy, lowbrow, raffish, rough, rough-hewn, tasteless, uncultivated, uncultured, unpolished, unrefined, vulgar; commercial, mass-produced, popular; common, ordinary; average, lesser, mediocre, run-of-the-mill, run-of-the-mine (*or* run-of-mine), second-class, second-rate; deficient, inferior, low-grade, substandard, unacceptable, unsatisfactory, wanting
2 of the very best kind ⟨thus far, the pool of applicants for the job has been less than *choice*⟩ — see EXCELLENT
3 singled out from a number or group as more to one's liking ⟨the restaurant offers a small but *choice* list of wines from some of Europe's finest viticultural regions⟩ — see SELECT 1

choice *n* **1** the power, right, or opportunity to choose ⟨you have no *choice*: you have to go to the conference⟩
synonyms alternative, discretion, druthers [*dialect*], election, liberty, option, pick, preference, selection, volition, way
related words determination, free will, will; say, voice, vote; inclination, liking, partiality, penchant, predilec-

tion, proclivity, propensity, tendency; discernment, judgment (*or* judgement), perspicacity

near antonyms coercion, duress, force; duty, obligation; Hobson's choice

2 a person or thing that is chosen ⟨my *choice* for best song of all time⟩

synonyms bet, chosen, pick, selection

related words favorite, like, liking, preference; elective, option; appointment, designation, nomination; appointee, candidate, nominee, selectee; preselection

antonyms rejectee

3 individuals carefully selected as being the best of a class ⟨that school accepts only the *choice* of the city's crop of high school students⟩ — see ELITE 1

4 the act or power of making one's own choices or decisions ⟨the prisoner had no *choice* but to do what he was told⟩ — see FREE WILL

5 the act or process of selecting ⟨you'll have to make a *choice* eventually⟩ — see SELECTION 1

choiceness *n* exceptionally high quality ⟨a chocolatier renowned for the *choiceness* of the cacao beans it uses⟩ — see EXCELLENCE 1

choir *n* an organized group of singers ⟨joined the *choir* for next year⟩ — see CHORUS 1

choke *vb* **1** to keep (someone) from breathing by exerting pressure on the windpipe ⟨let go of my throat—you're *choking* me!⟩

synonyms garrote (*or* garotte), strangle, suffocate, throttle

related words asphyxiate, smother, stifle; scrag

near antonyms restore, resuscitate, revive

2 to experience complete or partial blockage of the windpipe ⟨the recommended procedure for helping someone who is *choking*⟩

synonyms gag, suffocate

related words heave, retch, throw up, vomit; asphyxiate, smother, stifle

near antonyms breathe, respire; expire, inspire

3 to be or cause to be killed by lack of breathable air ⟨thick, black smoke *choked* the trapped firefighters⟩ — see SMOTHER 1

4 to prevent passage through by filling with something ⟨overgrown bushes *choked* the narrow alleyway between the buildings⟩ — see CLOG 1

choke (back) *vb* to refrain from openly showing or uttering ⟨*choked back* a sarcastic reply to an insulting question⟩ — see SUPPRESS 2

choker *n* an ornamental chain or string (as of beads) worn around the neck ⟨a pearl *choker* closely wrapped around her throat⟩ — see NECKLACE

choler *n* **1** an intense emotional state of displeasure with someone or something ⟨he felt his *choler* rising and choked back an angry reply⟩ — see ANGER

2 readiness to show annoyance or impatience ⟨the boss's reputation for *choler* made many employees reluctant to ask questions⟩ — see PETULANCE

choleric *adj* **1** easily irritated or annoyed ⟨watch out for the *choleric* librarian at the reference desk⟩ — see IRRITABLE

2 feeling or showing anger ⟨I absolutely get *choleric* when a telemarketer calls during the dinner hour⟩ — see ANGRY

chomp (on) *vb* to crush or grind with the teeth ⟨loudly *chomped on* popcorn during the movie⟩ — see BITE (ON)

choose *vb* **1** to decide to accept (someone or something) from a group of possibilities ⟨*choose* a computer that best suits your needs⟩

synonyms cherry-pick, cull, elect, handpick, name, opt (for), pick, prefer, select, single (out), tag, take

related words preselect; appoint, designate, fix, mark, nominate, set, tab, tap; accept, adopt, embrace, espouse; settle (on *or* upon)

near antonyms disapprove, negative, repudiate, spurn; discard, jettison, throw away, throw out

antonyms decline, refuse, reject, turn down

2 to see fit ⟨you can wear whatever you *choose* to the party⟩

synonyms like, please, want, will, wish

related words ache (for), covet, crave, desire, die (for), fancy, hanker (for), hunger (for), itch (for), long (for), lust (for *or* after), pant (after), pine (for), repine (for), sigh (for), thirst (for), yearn (for); decide, determine, resolve

3 to come to a judgment about after discussion or consideration ⟨*chose* to write on a controversial topic for the local newspaper⟩ — see DECIDE 1

chooser *n* someone with the right or responsibility for making a selection ⟨among other things, the president must be a good *chooser* of competent individuals, both for his cabinet and for the U.S. Supreme Court⟩ — see SELECTOR

choosing *n* the act or process of selecting ⟨the *choosing* of a new mayor is often left to a few voters, unfortunately⟩ — see SELECTION 1

choosy *or* **choosey** *adj* **1** hard to please ⟨a *choosy* dog who refuses all but the fanciest food⟩ — see FINICKY

2 tending to select carefully ⟨a *choosy* man when it came to clothes for the office⟩ — see SELECTIVE

chop *n* a hard strike with a part of the body or an instrument ⟨delivered a sharp *chop* to his opponent's neck⟩ — see [1]BLOW

chop *vb* to cut into small pieces ⟨*chop* the onions before adding them to the pot⟩

synonyms dice, hash, mince

related words chip, grate, grind, kibble, mash, puree (*or* purée), slice; butcher, carve, dissect

chop (down) *vb* to bring down by cutting ⟨we have to *chop down* that tree out front before it falls on the house⟩ — see FELL 2

chop–chop *adv* with great speed ⟨I need this project done *chop-chop*⟩ — see FAST 1

chopper *n* a vehicle for traveling through the air that obtains its lift from rotors which spin horizontally ⟨army *choppers* evacuated refugees from the war zone⟩ — see HELICOPTER

choppy *adj* **1** lacking in steadiness or regularity of occurrence ⟨a sharp, *choppy* wind coming off the lake⟩ — see FITFUL

2 marked by a series of sharp quick motions ⟨the old cable car provides a picturesque but *choppy* ride to the mountain's peak⟩ — see JERKY 1

3 not clearly or logically connected ⟨the plot was intriguing, but the author's style was so *choppy* that I finally gave up in frustration⟩ — see INCOHERENT 1

chops *n pl* **1** knowledge gained by actually doing or living through something ⟨that pianist really doesn't yet have the musical *chops* to do that piece justice⟩ — see EXPERIENCE 1

2 the opening through which food passes into the body of an animal ⟨the toddler popped a candy into his *chops* and grinned stickily⟩ — see MOUTH 1

chorale *n* **1** a religious song ⟨practiced a *chorale* to perform in church⟩ — see HYMN 1

2 an organized group of singers ⟨a *chorale* that is regarded as being among the best in the state⟩ — see CHORUS 1

chord *n* a subjective response to a person, thing, or situation ⟨the story of the family's woes struck a sympathetic *chord* with newspaper readers⟩ — see FEELING 1

chord *vb* to be in agreement on every point ⟨the revised system *chords* perfectly with the original goals⟩ — see CHECK 1

chore *n* **1** a piece of work that needs to be done regularly ⟨everyone in this household is expected to do weekly *chores*⟩
synonyms assignment, duty, job, task
related words chare (*or* char); endeavor, enterprise, project, stint, undertaking; care, charge, commission, responsibility; function, mission, office, operation, post; errand; circuit, round, route
2 a dull, unpleasant, or difficult piece of work ⟨cleaning everything out of the attic was a real *chore*⟩
synonyms bear, beast, headache, job, killer, labor
related words drudgery, grind, heavy lifting, lucubration; effort, strain, sweat; burden, load, weight; bother, nuisance, trouble
near antonyms breeze, child's play, cinch, duck soup, kid stuff, setup, snap

choreograph *vb* to work out the details of (something) in advance ⟨the advance team completely *choreographed* the candidate's campaign appearances⟩ — see PLAN 1

chorography *n* the physical features of a region as a whole ⟨a detailed map of the region's *chorography*⟩ — see GEOGRAPHY

chortle *n* an explosive sound that is a sign of amusement ⟨the joke provoked a sudden *chortle* from a bystander⟩ — see LAUGH 1

chortle *vb* to show mirth with an explosive vocal sound ⟨audiences might *chortle* gently during the movie's amusing bits, but there are few knee-slappers⟩ — see LAUGH 1

chorus *n* **1** an organized group of singers ⟨the annual Christmas program presented by the church's *chorus*⟩
synonyms choir, chorale, consort, glee club
related words ensemble; minstrelsy
2 a part of a song or hymn that is repeated every so often ⟨the whole congregation will join in for the *chorus*⟩
synonyms burden, refrain
related words repeat, response

chosen *adj* singled out from a number or group as more to one's liking ⟨the *chosen* few who are invited to a gathering at the CEO's house at the end of the year⟩ — see SELECT 1

chosen *n* a person or thing that is chosen ⟨of the five sons in the family, he was his father's *chosen* and thus showered with attention and special gifts⟩ — see CHOICE 2

chouse *vb* to rob by the use of trickery or threats ⟨an open-air bazaar where generations of unwary tourists have been *choused*⟩ — see FLEECE

chow *n* **1** food eaten or prepared for eating at one time ⟨that evening's *chow* was pretty basic because we were in a hurry⟩ — see MEAL
2 substances intended to be eaten ⟨there's always at least some *chow* in the house⟩ — see FOOD 1

chowderhead *n* a stupid person ⟨instantly concluded his new son-in-law was a *chowderhead*⟩ — see IDIOT

christen *vb* to give a name to ⟨*christened* the new baby "Ophelia"⟩ — see NAME 1

Christian name *n* a name that is placed before one's family name ⟨although his *Christian name* is ordinary, his last name is quite distinctive⟩ — see FORENAME

Christmastide *n* the season celebrating Christmas ⟨may everyone be filled with peace and joy, this *Christmastide*!⟩ — see YULETIDE

Christmastime *n* the season celebrating Christmas ⟨there are always lots of lights on the neighborhood's houses around *Christmastime*⟩ — see YULETIDE

chromatic *adj* marked by a variety of usually vivid colors ⟨the strikingly *chromatic* paintings of Matisse and the other Fauvists⟩ — see COLORFUL

chronic *adj* being such by habit and not likely to change ⟨a *chronic* smoker who has quit—many, many times⟩ — see HABITUAL 1

chronicle *n* **1** a relating of events usually in the order in which they happened ⟨a *chronicle* of their adventure on the river⟩ — see ACCOUNT 1
2 an account of important events in the order in which they happened ⟨only sketchy information about King Arthur can be found in the *chronicles* of ancient England⟩ — see HISTORY 1

chronicle *vb* to give an oral or written account of in some detail ⟨the book *chronicles* the efforts of two climbers to scale Mount Everest⟩ — see TELL 1

chronicler *n* a student or writer of history ⟨*chroniclers* who gave often conflicting accounts of battles, depending upon which side they favored⟩ — see HISTORIAN

chronology *n* a relating of events usually in the order in which they happened ⟨in his *chronology* of their relationship, they had communication problems right from the start⟩ — see ACCOUNT 1

chronometer *n* a device to measure time ⟨a fancy new *chronometer* that is light-years more advanced than your average wristwatch⟩ — see TIMEPIECE

chubbiness *n* the condition of having an excess of body fat ⟨a bit of *chubbiness* is normal in very small children⟩ — see CORPULENCE

chubby *adj* having an excess of body fat ⟨the *chubby* baby had slimmed down by the time she was a toddler⟩ — see FAT 1

chuck *n, chiefly West* substances intended to be eaten ⟨after a long day, the cowboys lined up for some *chuck*⟩ — see FOOD 1

chuck *vb* **1** to get rid of as useless or unwanted ⟨after the power outage we reluctantly *chucked* everything that had been sitting in the fridge⟩ — see DISCARD
2 to give up (a job or office) ⟨I swear, I have half a mind to *chuck* this job and become a hermit!⟩ — see QUIT 1
3 to send through the air especially with a quick forward motion of the arm ⟨*chucked* a wad of paper at his friend's back⟩ — see THROW 1

chuckle *n* an explosive sound that is a sign of amusement ⟨a quick *chuckle* at the funny comment⟩ — see LAUGH 1

chuckle *vb* to show mirth with an explosive vocal sound ⟨everyone dutifully *chuckled* at the professor's intended jokes⟩ — see LAUGH 1

chucklehead *n* a stupid person ⟨most of the summer interns strike me as *chuckleheads*⟩ — see IDIOT

chuckleheaded *adj* not having or showing an ability to absorb ideas readily ⟨a comedy about a pair of *chuckleheaded* guys who always blunder into trouble⟩ — see STUPID 1

chucklesome *adj* causing or intended to cause laughter ⟨an inadvertently *chucklesome* comment sent titters through the audience⟩ — see FUNNY 1

chuff *n* a person whose behavior is offensive to others ⟨the sort of ostentatious London townhouse that some greedy *chuff* of a billionaire might own⟩ — see JERK 1

chuffed *adj, British* experiencing pleasure, satisfaction, or delight ⟨I was feeling rather *chuffed* with myself, having competed in a cricket tournament with some of England's best⟩ — see GLAD 1

chum *n* a person who has a strong liking for and trust in another ⟨college *chums* who go way back⟩ — see FRIEND 1

chum *vb* to come or be together as friends ⟨they always *chum* around together⟩ — see ASSOCIATE 1

chumminess *n* the state of being in a very personal or private relationship ⟨her *chumminess* with the boss did not sit well with some of her coworkers⟩ — see FAMILIARITY 1

chummy *adj* **1** closely acquainted ⟨the neighboring

families know each other but are hardly *chummy*⟩ — see FAMILIAR 1
2 having or showing kindly feeling and sincere interest ⟨she was so *chummy* to me that I sensed that she had put our quarrel behind her⟩ — see FRIENDLY 1

chump *n* one who is easily deceived or cheated ⟨the guy trying to unload that used car must have thought that I was a *chump*⟩ — see [1]DUPE

chump change *n* a very small sum of money ⟨what seems like a huge amount of money to most people is only *chump change* to a billionaire⟩ — see MITE 1

chunk *n* **1** a considerable amount ⟨that new sports car must have cost a real *chunk* of change⟩ — see LOT 2
2 a small uneven mass ⟨a little *chunk* of dirt⟩ — see LUMP 1

chunky *adj* **1** having small pieces or lumps spread throughout ⟨*chunky* peanut butter adds an interesting layer of texture when paired with jelly⟩
synonyms clumpy, curdy, lumpy, nubbly, nubby
related words ropy (*also* ropey), thick, viscous; knobbed, knobbly, knobby, lumpish; clabbered, clotted, coagulated, congealed, curdled, gelled, thickened; broken, bumpy, coarse, irregular, jagged, knotted, knotty, pebbly
antonyms smooth
2 being compact and broad in build and often short in stature ⟨a *chunky* little toddler⟩ — see STOCKY
3 having or being of relatively great depth or extent from one surface to its opposite ⟨a *chunky* piece of bread⟩ — see THICK 1

chunter *vb, British* to speak softly and unclearly ⟨in Hyde Park a clearly disturbed man was *chuntering* about something⟩ — see MUMBLE

church *n* **1** a building for public worship and especially Christian worship ⟨a city that is noted for its many historic *churches*⟩
synonyms kirk [*chiefly Scottish*], tabernacle, temple
related words abbey, bethel, cathedral, chapel, minster, mission, oratory, sanctuary, shrine; meetinghouse; mosque, pagoda, shul, synagogue (*also* synagog)
2 a body of persons gathered for religious worship ⟨spoke to the whole *church* at once⟩ — see CONGREGATION 1
3 the group ordained to perform clerical functions in the Christian church ⟨a time when few young men seem to want to join the *church*⟩ — see CLERGY

churchly *adj* of or relating to a church ⟨refused to discuss *churchly* matters except on Sundays⟩ — see ECCLESIASTICAL

churl *n* **1** an awkward or simple person especially from a small town or the country ⟨as far as he was concerned, anyone from outside the city was a backwater *churl*⟩ — see HICK
2 a mean grasping person who is usually stingy with money ⟨don't bother asking for donations at that house—the *churl* who lives there believes that charity begins and ends at home⟩ — see MISER
3 a person whose behavior is offensive to others ⟨a *churl* who gets thrown out of parties with remarkable regularity⟩ — see JERK 1

churlish *adj* having or showing crudely insensitive or impolite manners ⟨it would be *churlish* for any dinner guest to express anything but gratitude for his host's generous hospitality⟩ — see CLOWNISH

churn *vb* **1** to be in a state of violent rolling motion ⟨a *churning* sea made getting to the island a risky undertaking⟩ — see SEETHE 1
2 to cause (as a liquid) to move about in a circle especially repeatedly ⟨*churn* the cream until it turns into butter⟩ — see STIR 1

churr *n* a monotonous sound like that of an insect in motion ⟨the *churr* of grasshoppers in the field⟩ — see HUM

chutzpah *also* **chutzpa** *or* **hutzpah** *or* **hutzpa** *n* shameless boldness ⟨had the *chutzpah* to demand that he be treated as a special case and be given priority in settling his insurance claim⟩ — see EFFRONTERY

Cimmerian *adj* causing or marked by an atmosphere lacking in cheer ⟨a wealthy recluse who lived in *Cimmerian* isolation in a decaying Victorian mansion⟩ — see GLOOMY 1

cinch *n* **1** something that is easy to do ⟨the clear instructions made setting up the audiovisual system a *cinch*⟩
synonyms breeze, cake, cakewalk, child's play, cream puff, duck soup, kid stuff, picnic, pushover, roses, snap
related words no-brainer, nothing; sitting duck; gimme, laugher, walkaway
phrases piece of cake, walk in the park
near antonyms brainteaser, poser, stumper, toughie (*also* toughy); bother, nuisance, trouble
antonyms bear, beast, chore, headache, horror show, killer, labor, murder, pain, sticky wicket, stinker [*slang*]
2 one that is certain to succeed ⟨after that hole in one, she's a *cinch* to make the cut for the next round of the tournament⟩ — see SURE THING

cinch *vb* to make sure, certain, or safe ⟨the team's latest victory *cinches* a trip to the play-offs⟩ — see ENSURE

cincture *n* a strip of flexible material (as leather) worn around the waist ⟨wrapped a *cincture* around the dress as a stylish accessory⟩ — see [2]BELT 1

cinema *n* **1** the art or business of making a movie ⟨felt that the *cinema* was one of the most challenging and fulfilling forms of artistic expression⟩ — see MOVIE 2
2 a building or part of a building where movies are shown ⟨got a job cleaning the *cinemas* at the multiplex⟩ — see THEATER 1

cipher *n* **1** the numerical symbol 0 or the absence of number or quantity represented by it ⟨remember to put the *cipher* after the decimal point⟩ — see ZERO 1
2 a person of no importance or influence ⟨it was either write the Great American Novel or be consigned to the status of a *cipher* in the annals of literature⟩ — see NOBODY

cipher *vb* to determine (a value) by doing the necessary mathematical operations ⟨were surprised by how much we had spent on the cruise after we had *ciphered* out the grand total⟩ — see CALCULATE 1

ciphering *n* the act or process of performing mathematical operations to find a value ⟨he wasn't very good at *ciphering*, but he had excellent language skills⟩ — see CALCULATION

circle *n* **1** something with a perfectly round circumference ⟨a *circle* of columns surrounds the memorial to the fallen heroes⟩
synonyms cirque, ring, round, roundel
related words circlet, ringlet; ellipse, loop, oval; ball, globe, orb, sphere
2 a circular strip ⟨a decorative *circle* of silver on the rim of the commemorative plate for their 25th wedding anniversary⟩ — see [1]RING 2
3 a group of people sharing a common interest and relating together socially ⟨got together with her social *circle* once a week⟩ — see GANG 2
4 a series of events or actions that repeat themselves regularly and in the same order ⟨with the birth of a child coming so soon after the death of a grandparent, we were once again reminded of the *circle* of life⟩ — see CYCLE 1
5 a region of activity, knowledge, or influence ⟨that lies outside the *circle* of our investigation⟩ — see FIELD 2

circle *vb* **1** to form a circle around ⟨everyone *circled* the lectern and waited their turn to read from the Bible⟩ — see SURROUND

2 to travel completely around ⟨with a look of extreme frustration, the commander *circled* the new recruit⟩ — see ENCIRCLE 1

circuit *vb* to travel completely around ⟨after *circuiting* the exterior of the church, the procession headed inside⟩ — see ENCIRCLE 1

circuitous *adj* **1** not straightforward or direct ⟨we took a *circuitous* route to the airport so as to avoid the massive traffic jam on the highway⟩ — see INDIRECT

2 using or containing more words than necessary to express an idea ⟨a *circuitous* explanation for what seems like a fairly basic concept⟩ — see WORDY 1

circular *adj* not straightforward or direct ⟨a rather *circular* discussion of the problem that never addresses it directly⟩ — see INDIRECT

circular *n* a short printed publication with no cover or with a paper cover ⟨promptly tosses out those advertising *circulars* that come in the newspaper⟩ — see PAMPHLET

circulate *vb* **1** to cause to be known over a considerable area or by many people ⟨*circulate* the plans for the new stadium around town to get people's reaction⟩ — see SPREAD 1

2 to make (as a piece of information) the subject of common talk without any authority or confirmation of accuracy ⟨*circulated* a rumor that someone was about to be fired⟩ — see RUMOR

3 to become known ⟨the prince denies the story about an extramarital affair that's been *circulating* in the tabloids⟩ — see GET OUT 1

circulator *n* a person who habitually reveals personal or sensational facts about others ⟨an ugly rumor about one of our staffers was circulating, and, as usual, the chief *circulator* was the in-house busybody⟩ — see GOSSIP 1

circumference *n* **1** the distance around a round body ⟨the *circumference* of the earth at the equator⟩
synonyms girth
related words ambit, circuit, compass; waistline; equator; diameter, radius; perimeter, periphery

2 the line or relatively narrow space that marks the outer limit of something ⟨a silly little affair that's of interest to no one beyond the *circumference* of this campus⟩ — see BORDER 1

circumfuse *vb* to surround or cover closely ⟨*circumfused* in darkness, the isolated house seemed the perfect spot for a clandestine meeting⟩ — see ENFOLD 1

circumlocution *n* **1** deliberate evasion in speech ⟨rather than answering the question directly, he resorted to *circumlocution*, which made her suspect that he was hiding something⟩
synonyms equivocation, shuffle, tergiversation
related words quibbling; ambiguity, ambiguousness, equivocalness, murkiness, nebulousness, obscureness, obscurity, opacity
near antonyms candor, directness, forthrightness, frankness, openheartedness, openness, plainness, plumpness, straightforwardness

2 the use of too many words to express an idea ⟨your papers have to be five pages long, but that's five pages of substance, not *circumlocution*⟩ — see VERBIAGE 1

circumlocutory *adj* using or containing more words than necessary to express an idea ⟨the studio's statement that "the film's earnings did not live up to expectations" was a *circumlocutory* admission that the movie was a flop⟩ — see WORDY 1

circumnavigate *vb* **1** to travel completely around ⟨the first ship to *circumnavigate* the globe⟩ — see ENCIRCLE 1

2 to avoid by going around ⟨we can *circumnavigate* the traffic jam if we take the next exit⟩ — see DETOUR 1

circumscribe *vb* **1** to set bounds or an upper limit for ⟨*circumscribed* his enthusiasm so as not to make the losing side feel worse⟩ — see LIMIT 1

2 to mark the limits of ⟨Lake Michigan *circumscribes* the city of Chicago on the east⟩ — see LIMIT 2

circumscribed *adj* having distinct or certain limits ⟨the powers of that state's governor are so sharply *circumscribed* that often his hands are tied by the state legislature⟩ — see LIMITED 1

circumscription *n* **1** something that limits one's freedom of action or choice ⟨such *circumscriptions* on the freedom of speech are antithetical to a free and open society⟩ — see RESTRICTION 1

2 the act or practice of keeping something (as an activity) within certain boundaries ⟨electronic monitoring bracelets are sometimes used to impose a *circumscription* of movement on people awaiting trial⟩ — see RESTRICTION 2

circumspect *adj* having or showing a close attentiveness to avoiding danger or trouble ⟨she has a reputation for being quiet and *circumspect* in investigating charges of child abuse⟩ — see CAREFUL 1

circumspection *n* a close attentiveness to avoiding danger ⟨*circumspection* is always good when considering charging someone with cheating⟩ — see CAUTION 1

circumstance *n* **1** a state or end that seemingly has been decided beforehand ⟨the condemned murderer seemed indifferent to his *circumstance*⟩ — see FATE 1

2 something that happens ⟨due to unexpected *circumstances*, the test will be postponed⟩ — see EVENT 1

3 the uncertain course of events ⟨I was a victim of *circumstance*, for nothing that I could have done would have made a difference⟩ — see CHANCE 1

circumstantial *adj* including many small descriptive features ⟨the *circumstantial* account of his surgery told us more than we really wanted to know about the stomach⟩ — see DETAILED 1

circumvent *vb* **1** to avoid having to comply with (something) especially through cleverness ⟨employees who try to *circumvent* the company's dress code⟩
synonyms beat, bypass, dodge, get around, shortcut, sidestep, skirt
related words avoid, duck, elude, end-run, escape, eschew, evade, outflank, shake, shirk, shun; disobey, disregard, flout, ignore; avert, deflect, divert, obviate, parry, prevent, ward (off)
near antonyms accede (to), acquiesce (to), assent (to); accept, court, embrace, pursue, seek, welcome; catch, contract, incur
antonyms comply (with), follow, keep, obey, observe

2 to avoid by going around ⟨*circumvented* the traffic jam by taking an alternate route⟩ — see DETOUR 1

3 to travel completely around ⟨most casual joggers will be able to *circumvent* the reservoir without too much of a strain⟩ — see ENCIRCLE 1

circus *n* **1** a large usually roofless building for sporting events with tiers of seats for spectators ⟨the Roman *circus* is believed to have held 50,000 spectators in ancient times⟩ — see STADIUM

2 a place of uproar or confusion ⟨with seven kids in the house, it's a *circus* most of the time⟩ — see MADHOUSE 2

3 an elaborate, visually exciting show or event ⟨the media *circus* that took place outside the courthouse every day of the murder trial⟩ — see EXTRAVAGANZA

cirque *n* something with a perfectly round circumference ⟨the harvest moon was a glowing *cirque* in autumn sky⟩ — see CIRCLE 1

citable *adj* worth remembering or mentioning ⟨she has a lot of annoying little habits but none are really *citable*⟩ — see NOTEWORTHY 1

citadel *n* a structure or place from which one can resist attack ⟨a massive stone *citadel* continues to command the city of Halifax, Nova Scotia⟩ — see FORT

citation *n* **1** a formal expression of praise ⟨the *citation* for the Nobel Prize winner noted his major contributions to quantum theory⟩ — see ENCOMIUM

2 a formal recognition of an achievement or praiseworthy deed ⟨a police officer who has received several *citations* for his work with troubled youths in the city⟩ — see COMMENDATION 1

3 a passage referred to, repeated, or offered as an example ⟨in your paper be sure to include *citations* to back up any points you make about the play⟩ — see QUOTATION

cite *vb* **1** to give as an example ⟨*cited* several experts' opinions to back up her argument⟩ — see QUOTE 1

2 to make reference to or speak about briefly but specifically ⟨*cited* a number of similar instances of people surviving plane crashes⟩ — see MENTION 1

citify *vb* to accustom to the ways of the city ⟨we've become so *citified* that many people have no idea where their food comes from⟩

synonyms urbanize

related words civilize, cultivate

citizen *n* **1** a person who owes allegiance to a government and is protected by it ⟨conscientious *citizens* who regard voting as a duty as well as a right⟩

synonyms freeman, national, subject

related words compatriot, countryman; inhabitant, native, nonimmigrant, resident

near antonyms foreigner, stranger; immigrant, nonnative

antonyms alien, noncitizen

2 a person who lives in a town on a permanent basis ⟨claimed that the good *citizens* of the town were sick of high property taxes⟩ — see BURGHER

city *n* a thickly settled, highly populated area ⟨commuters who drive every day between their homes in the suburbs and their jobs in the *city*⟩

synonyms asphalt jungle, burg, cosmopolis, megacity, megalopolis, metropolis, municipality, town

related words borough; conurbation; urban sprawl; exurb, suburb, suburbia; central city, edge city, garden city; core city, downtown, inner city, midtown

city slicker *n* a person with the outlook, experience, and manners thought to be typical of big city dwellers ⟨with their snotty attitude, the *city slickers* quickly wore out their welcome⟩ — see COSMOPOLITAN

civil *adj* **1** of or relating to a nation ⟨the country was not destroyed by outside enemies but by a series of *civil* wars⟩ — see NATIONAL

2 showing consideration, courtesy, and good manners ⟨please try to be *civil* to your ex-husband at the upcoming family wedding⟩ — see POLITE 1

civility *n* **1** an act or utterance that is a customary show of good manners ⟨after the usual *civilities*, the parents and the principal had a serious talk about the boy⟩

synonyms amenity, attention, courtesy, formality, gesture, pleasantry, politeness

related words honors; ceremony, observance, rite, ritual; decorum, etiquette, form, manners, mores, proprieties; addresses, devoirs, greetings, regards, respects; favor, grace, kindliness, kindness; protocol, rules

2 speech or behavior that is a sign of good breeding ⟨treated people from all walks of life with the same unfailing *civility*⟩ — see POLITENESS 1

civilization *n* **1** the way people live at a particular time and place ⟨a documentary on the advanced *civilization* created by the Mayas over a thousand years ago⟩

synonyms culture, life, lifestyle, society

related words customs, manners, mores, values; folklore, heritage, legacy, tradition; subculture, subsociety

2 a high level of taste and enlightenment as a result of extensive intellectual training and exposure to the arts ⟨by the 18th century Boston had reached a level of *civilization* sufficiently advanced to support a circle of portrait painters⟩ — see CULTURE 1

civilized *adj* having or showing a taste for the fine arts and gracious living ⟨a *civilized* older couple who are celebrated for holding dinner parties that are attended by the city's best and brightest⟩ — see CULTIVATED

civil servant *n* a worker in a government agency ⟨took the examination to become a *civil servant* in the defense department⟩ — see BUREAUCRAT

clack *vb* to make a series of short sharp noises ⟨her teeth *clacked* because she was freezing while waiting for the bus⟩ — see RATTLE 1

clad *vb* to cover with something that protects ⟨if the vehicles are not *clad* in armor, they will remain vulnerable to roadside bombs⟩ — see SHEATHE

claim *n* **1** an entitlement to something ⟨I'm announcing my *claim* to that last slice of pizza⟩

synonyms call, dibs, pretense (*or* pretence), pretension, right

related words birthright, prerogative, title; favor, privilege; refusal

near antonyms disclaimer, quitclaim, release, waiver

2 a legal right to participation in the advantages, profits, and responsibility of something ⟨a shareholder has a *claim* in the business⟩ — see INTEREST 1

3 a solemn and often public declaration of the truth or existence of something ⟨Galileo's *claim* that the moon has a very irregular surface and thus is not the perfect sphere that the ancients had imagined⟩ — see PROTESTATION

4 something that someone insists upon having ⟨young children make great *claims* on their parents' time⟩ — see DEMAND 1

claim *vb* **1** to state as a fact usually forcefully ⟨people who *claim* that they have been kidnapped by aliens from other worlds⟩

synonyms affirm, allege, assert, aver, avouch, avow, contend, declare, insist, maintain, profess, protest, purport, warrant

related words announce, broadcast, proclaim; argue, rationalize, reason; confirm, justify, vindicate; defend, persevere, support, uphold; reaffirm, reassert

phrases put forth

near antonyms abandon; disavow, disclaim, disown, negate, negative, reject, repudiate; challenge, dispute, question; confute, disprove, rebut, refute; contradict, counter

antonyms deny, gainsay

2 to ask for (something) earnestly or with authority ⟨after many years had passed, he suddenly appeared to *claim* his inheritance⟩ — see DEMAND 1

3 to deprive of life ⟨cancer *claims* hundreds of thousands of Americans each year⟩ — see KILL 1

4 to have as a requirement ⟨caring for her three small children *claims* virtually all of her time⟩ — see NEED 1

clairvoyance *n* the power of seeing or knowing about things that are not present to the senses ⟨people who claim to have *clairvoyance* are sometimes asked to help locate missing persons⟩

synonyms extrasensory perception, second sight, sixth sense

related words foreknowledge, foresight, prescience; precognition; telepathy; parapsychology

clam *n* a U.S. currency bill representing 100 cents ⟨it must take a whole lot of *clams* to buy a car like that⟩ — see DOLLAR

clamant *adj* **1** engaging in or marked by loud and insistent cries especially of protest ⟨*clamant* students gathered outside the college president's office, protesting the denial of tenure for the popular professor⟩ — see VOCIFEROUS

2 needing immediate attention ⟨faced with utter bankruptcy, she didn't think that moist skin was one of her *clamant* needs at that moment⟩ — see ACUTE 2

clamber *vb* to move (as up or over something) often with the help of the hands in holding or pulling ⟨*clambered* over a wall and was never seen again⟩ — see CLIMB 1

clammy *adj* lacking in friendliness or warmth of feeling ⟨after a *clammy* handshake, the two bitter rivals squared off for a no-holds-barred debate⟩ — see COLD 2

clamor *n* **1** a violent shouting ⟨a *clamor* arose from the crowd as the prisoner was brought forward⟩
synonyms howl, hubbub, hue and cry, hullabaloo, noise, outcry, roar, tumult, uproar, vociferation
related words clangor, din, jangle, racket; cri de coeur, outburst, protest
near antonyms mumble, mumbling, murmur, murmuring, rumble, rumbling
2 loud, confused, and usually inharmonious sound ⟨the *clamor* of a dozen people practicing the trumpet at once⟩ — see NOISE 1

clamor (for) *vb* to ask for (something) earnestly or with authority ⟨a dozen customers *clamoring for* service all at once⟩ — see DEMAND 1

clamorous *adj* **1** engaging in or marked by loud and insistent cries especially of protest ⟨a *clamorous* objection to the play that the students have chosen to put on this year⟩ — see VOCIFEROUS
2 full of or characterized by the presence of noise ⟨a *clamorous* kindergarten classroom that would try the patience of any sane adult⟩ — see NOISY 2
3 marked by a high volume of sound ⟨a rock band whose *clamorous* concerts will rattle your bones⟩ — see LOUD 1

clamp *vb* to put securely in place or in a desired position ⟨*clamped* the headphones to her ears and began to listen⟩ — see FASTEN 2

clamp down (on) *vb* to put a stop to (something) by the use of force ⟨the need to *clamp down on* petty crime in the city⟩ — see QUELL 1

clam up *vb* to stop talking ⟨the little girl *clammed up* when the doctor came into the room⟩ — see SHUT UP 1

clan *n* **1** a group of people sharing a common interest and relating together socially ⟨that *clan* of football fans has parties every weekend on which the New England Patriots play⟩ — see GANG 2
2 a group of persons who come from the same ancestor ⟨the whole *clan* gets together only for holidays⟩ — see FAMILY 1

clandestine *adj* undertaken or done so as to escape being observed or known by others ⟨I took a *clandestine* peek at the price tag on the diamond necklace⟩ — see SECRET 1

clang *n* the loud sound made when metal strikes metal ⟨the horseshoe hit the stake with a satisfying *clang*⟩
synonyms clangor, clank, clash, whang
related words chime, ding-dong, knell, peal, ping, plink, ring, tintinnabulation; chink, clink, clinkety-clank, jangle, jingle, rattle, tang, tinkle, twang; clap, clip-clop, clop, crack, crash, crunch; clump, clunk, thump

clanger *n, British* an unintentional departure from truth or accuracy ⟨a newsreader who memorably dropped a *clanger* when she referred to Robert Burns as an English poet⟩ — see ERROR 1

clangor *n* **1** loud, confused, and usually inharmonious sound ⟨the *clangor* of pots and pans coming from the kitchen as the cooks threw together an impromptu meal⟩ — see NOISE 1
2 the loud sound made when metal strikes metal ⟨the *clangor* of a battle in the Middle Ages, as steel hit against steel a thousand times⟩ — see CLANG

clangorous *adj* **1** full of or characterized by the presence of noise ⟨grew up in a *clangorous* but warmhearted household⟩ — see NOISY 2
2 making loud, confused, and usually unharmonious sounds ⟨the teen's *clangorous* efforts to learn to play the drums⟩ — see NOISY 1
3 marked by a high volume of sound ⟨a *clangorous* sheet metal factory⟩ — see LOUD 1

clank *n* the loud sound made when metal strikes metal ⟨the car is making a funny *clank*, and this can't be good⟩ — see CLANG

clannish *adj* bound together by feelings of very close association ⟨a *clannish* family that can be rather cool to outsiders⟩ — see CLOSE-KNIT

clap *n* **1** a loud explosive sound ⟨a *clap* of thunder that woke the whole house up⟩
synonyms bang, blast, boom, crack, crash, pop, report, slam, smash, snap, thunderclap, thwack, whack, whomp, whump
related words thunk, wham; clang, clangor, clank, clash; knock, rap, tap; blare, clamor, howl, hubbub, hue and cry, hullabaloo, outcry, roar, tumult, uproar
2 a hard strike with a part of the body or an instrument ⟨a sharp *clap* to the head of the disrespectful youth⟩ — see [1]BLOW

clap *vb* to deliver a blow to (someone or something) usually in a strong vigorous manner ⟨*clapped* him on the back as a friendly gesture⟩ — see HIT 1

clap (together *or* up) *vb* to perform, make, or do without preparation ⟨we can *clap together* a repair on the tire that should last until we get home⟩ — see IMPROVISE

claptrap *n* language, behavior, or ideas that are absurd and contrary to good sense ⟨the idea that you can get a cold from not dressing warmly is *claptrap*⟩ — see NONSENSE 1

clarification *n* a statement that makes something clear ⟨after that *clarification*, I find I actually agree with you⟩ — see EXPLANATION 1

clarify *vb* **1** to remove usually visible impurities from ⟨*clarify* the melted butter by skimming off the milky bits⟩
synonyms clear, distill (*also* distil), filter, fine, garble, purify
related words process, rectify, refine; clean, cleanse, decontaminate, elutriate, purge, wash; extract, leach; bolt, screen, sieve, sift; disinfect, sanitize
near antonyms cloud, dull, muddy; contaminate, dirty, soil; defile, pollute, taint; begrime, besmirch, foul, sully
2 to make plain or understandable ⟨it would help if you could *clarify* your position for us⟩ — see EXPLAIN 1

clarity *n* **1** the state or quality of being easily seen through ⟨mountain streams with water of incredible *clarity*⟩
synonyms clearness, limpidity, limpidness, lucency, translucence, translucency, transparency
related words brightness, brilliance, effulgence, luminosity, luminousness; definition, resolution, sharpness; apparentness, observability, visibility
near antonyms fogginess, haziness, milkiness, mistiness, murkiness
antonyms cloudiness, opacity, opaqueness, turbidity, turbidness
2 clearness of expression ⟨this explanation of the greenhouse effect is a marvel of *clarity*⟩ — see SIMPLICITY 2

clash *n* **1** a physical dispute between opposing individuals or groups ⟨a *clash* between rival gangs that resulted in some serious injuries⟩ — see FIGHT 1
2 the loud sound made when metal strikes metal ⟨the *clash* of cymbals⟩ — see CLANG

clash *vb* to be out of harmony or agreement usually no-

ticeably ⟨the colors of your shirt and pants *clash*⟩ ⟨a parent's idea of proper dress often *clashes* with a teenager's⟩
synonyms collide, conflict, disaccord, discord, jar
related words battle, combat, engage, fight, war (against); chafe, gall, grate, jangle; differ, disagree, dissent
near antonyms agree, assent, coincide, concur, correspond
antonyms accord, blend, conform (to *or* with), fit, harmonize, match

clash (with) *vb* to oppose (someone) in physical conflict ⟨the Iroquois often *clashed with* the other Native American nations in the region⟩ — see FIGHT 1

clashing *adj* not being in agreement or harmony ⟨freedom and equality are often a *clashing* set of ideals⟩ — see INCONSISTENT 1

clasp *n* the act or manner of holding ⟨be careful that your *clasp* on the cat isn't too tight, or she could get hurt⟩ — see HOLD 1

clasp *vb* **1** to put one's arms around and press tightly ⟨*clasped* his long-lost sister and cried without restraint⟩ — see EMBRACE 1
2 to reach for and take hold of by embracing with the fingers or arms ⟨*clasped* a crayon and began drawing⟩ — see TAKE 1

class *n* **1** one of the segments of society into which people are grouped ⟨a politician who appeals to people of every *class*⟩
synonyms caste, estate, folk, gentry, order, stratum
related words bracket, echelon, grade, layer, level, tier; place, position, rank, standing, status; food chain, grouping, hierarchy, stratification; clan, family, fraternity, people, race, tribe; subcaste
2 one of the units into which a whole is divided on the basis of a common characteristic ⟨a new *class* of wireless devices that could be used for Internet access as well as personal communication⟩
synonyms bracket, category, classification, division, family, genus, grade, group, kind, league, order, rank(s), rubric, set, species, tier, type
related words description, feather, ilk, kidney, like, manner, nature, sort; branch, section, speciality, specialty, subclass, subdivision, subgroup, subspecies, variety; breed, race; generation; heading, label, title
3 a number of persons or things that are grouped together because they have something in common ⟨only a particular *class* of burglar would do that⟩ — see SORT 1
4 a series of lectures on a subject ⟨took a *class* on modern art⟩ — see COURSE 2
5 degree of excellence ⟨only horses of great *class* are allowed to enter the Kentucky Derby⟩ — see QUALITY 1
6 dignified or restrained beauty of form, appearance, or style ⟨an old mansion with tremendous *class* that puts today's gaudy behemoths to shame⟩ — see ELEGANCE
7 high position within society ⟨the woman exudes an aura of *class* and breeding⟩ — see RANK 2

class *vb* to arrange or assign according to type ⟨I would *class* that suggestion as helpful, so let's make a note of it⟩ — see CLASSIFY 1

classic *adj* **1** constituting, serving as, or worthy of being a pattern to be imitated ⟨*classic* designs in furniture that never go out of style⟩ — see MODEL
2 of the very best kind ⟨one of the really *classic* comedies in the history of movies⟩ — see EXCELLENT
3 serving to identify as belonging to an individual or group ⟨the anthropologist noted the *classic* facial features of the inhabitants of those islands⟩ — see CHARACTERISTIC 1
4 being the most accurate and apparently thorough ⟨the *classic* study of the alienation of the individual in modern urban society⟩ — see DEFINITIVE 1

classic *n* **1** someone of such unequaled perfection as to deserve imitation ⟨among women who have devoted themselves to a life of scientific inquiry, Marie Curie is one of the acknowledged *classics*⟩ — see IDEAL 1
2 something (as a work of art) that is a great achievement and often its creator's greatest achievement ⟨the works of Michelangelo are regarded as *classics* of the sculptor's art⟩ — see MASTERPIECE
3 the most perfect type or example ⟨his journey of discovery was a *classic* of arduous effort and fierce determination⟩ — see QUINTESSENCE 1

classical *adj* **1** based on customs usually handed down from a previous generation ⟨the *classical* preparation of a ham for Easter⟩ — see TRADITIONAL 1
2 being the most accurate and apparently thorough ⟨a writer celebrated for his *classical* profiles of eminent Victorians⟩ — see DEFINITIVE 1

classification *n* one of the units into which a whole is divided on the basis of a common characteristic ⟨dinosaur remains that do not fit any existing *classification*⟩ — see CLASS 2

classify *vb* **1** to arrange or assign according to type ⟨*classify* the baseball cards in your collection on the basis of rarity⟩
synonyms assort, break down, categorize, class, codify, compartment, compartmentalize, digest, distinguish, distribute, grade, group, peg, place, range, rank, relegate, separate, sort, type
related words array, dispose, draw up, marshal (*also* marshall), order, organize, systematize; alphabetize, catalog (*or* catalogue), file, index, list, refer; pigeonhole, shelve; identify, recognize; cull, screen, set, sieve, sift, winnow; clump, cluster, colligate; recategorize, reclassify, regroup; subcategorize
near antonyms confuse, disarrange, jumble, lump, mix (up), scramble; misclassify, missort, mistype
2 to put into a particular arrangement ⟨*classify* the information you got from the Internet by source⟩ — see ORDER 1

classiness *n* dignified or restrained beauty of form, appearance, or style ⟨the *classiness* of the hotel's facade is in stark contrast to the kitsch of the casinos that surround it⟩ — see ELEGANCE

classless *adj* having or showing crudely insensitive or impolite manners ⟨I object not so much to what he did as the *classless* way he did it⟩ — see CLOWNISH

classy *adj* having or showing elegance ⟨a *classy* seaside resort that reeks of old money⟩ — see ELEGANT 1

clatter *n* a state of noisy, confused activity ⟨the *clatter* of a crowded cafeteria⟩ — see COMMOTION

clatter *vb* to make a series of short sharp noises ⟨horses' hooves *clattering* on the pavement⟩ — see RATTLE 1

clattering *adj* full of or characterized by the presence of noise ⟨a huge, *clattering* warehouse⟩ — see NOISY 2

clattery *adj* full of or characterized by the presence of noise ⟨a *clattery* diner serving hordes of hungry workers⟩ — see NOISY 2

clay *n* the set of qualities that makes a person, a group of people, or a thing different from others ⟨had the feeling that the natives were of a different *clay* than us and that neither side would ever understand the other⟩ — see NATURE 1

clean *adj* **1** free from dirt or stain ⟨although the soccer team always starts out with *clean* uniforms, they don't stay that way for long⟩
synonyms antiseptic, chaste, fair, immaculate, pristine, spick-and-span (*or* spic-and-span), spotless, squeaky-clean, stainless, unsoiled, unstained, unsullied
related words pure, taintless, undefiled, unpolluted, untainted, wholesome; cleanly, germfree, hygienic, sanitary, sterile; abluted, bleached, cleansed, purified, scrubbed, washed, whitened; milky, snowy, white; flaw-

less, unblemished; bright, shiny, sparkling
near antonyms dingy, greasy, grimy, mucky, muddy, unwashed; defiled, germy, polluted, tainted, unsterile, unsterilized; blackened, discolored
antonyms besmirched, dirty, filthy, foul, grubby, smirched, soiled, spotted, stained, sullied, unclean, uncleaned
2 following or according to the rules ⟨a *clean* check from the other hockey player⟩ — see FAIR 3
3 free from any trace of the coarse or indecent ⟨only *clean* songs will be permitted for the performances on the last night of summer camp⟩ — see CHASTE 1
4 trying all possibilities ⟨police made a *clean* sweep of the area before the governor's arrival⟩ — see EXHAUSTIVE 1
5 having no exceptions or restrictions ⟨the *clean* joy of running that young children experience⟩ — see ABSOLUTE 2
6 lacking contents that could or should be present ⟨the ship returned with a *clean* hold⟩ — see EMPTY 1

clean *adv* **1** according to the rules or the law ⟨a boxer who doesn't fight *clean*⟩ — see FAIRLY 2
2 to a full extent or degree ⟨the thief got *clean* away⟩ — see FULLY 1

clean *vb* **1** to remove the dirt from ⟨we *cleaned* the clothes before donating them to charity⟩
synonyms cleanse, deterge, GI, turn out
related words decontaminate, purge, purify; disinfect, sanitize; brush, comb, dry-clean, dust, launder, mop, muck (out), rinse, scour, scrub, shampoo, sponge, swab, sweep, vacuum, wash, wipe; brighten, deodorize, freshen, spruce (up), sweeten; pick up, straighten (up), tidy, unclutter
near antonyms begrime, muddy; defile, pollute, taint; blacken, discolor
antonyms besmirch, dirty, foul, soil, spot, stain, sully
2 to take the internal organs out of ⟨*cleaned* the rabbit before cooking it⟩ — see GUT

clean (up) *vb* **1** to make a place neat and orderly by removing extraneous stuff ⟨you're expected to *clean up* after you use the workroom⟩
synonyms pick up, tidy (up)
related words houseclean, housekeep; clean (off), clean (up), neaten, police (up), straighten (up), turn out, unclutter; arrange, order
phrases clean house, set straight
near antonyms clutter, disarrange, mess (up)
2 to remove objectionable parts from ⟨*cleaned up* the rock star's interview before publishing it in the newspaper⟩ — see CENSOR
3 to destroy all traces of ⟨hurriedly *cleaned up* the mess that they had created in the kitchen⟩ — see ANNIHILATE 1

cleaner *n* a substance used for cleaning ⟨a kitchen shelf loaded with household *cleaners*⟩
synonyms cleanser, detergent, soap
related words disinfectant, purifier, solvent; scrub, shampoo

cleanhanded *adj* free from guilt or blame ⟨none of us is exactly *cleanhanded* in this affair⟩ — see INNOCENT 2

cleanly *adv* according to the rules or the law ⟨it was a *cleanly* fought match, so you have no grounds for complaint⟩ — see FAIRLY 2

cleanse *vb* **1** to free from moral guilt or blemish especially ceremonially ⟨in an elaborate ritual the priestess *cleansed* the gathering of supplicants⟩ — see PURIFY 1
2 to remove the dirt from ⟨*cleanse* the wound with soap and water before applying the bandage⟩ — see CLEAN 1

cleanser *n* a substance used for cleaning ⟨a bathroom *cleanser*⟩ — see CLEANER

cleansing *n* the act or fact of freeing from sin or moral guilt ⟨underwent a *cleansing* before he could enter the temple's most sacred chamber⟩ — see PURIFICATION

clear *adj* **1** easily seen through ⟨the *clear* glass walls of the aquarium's giant ocean tank⟩
synonyms crystal, crystal clear, crystalline, limpid, liquid, lucent, pellucid, see-through, transparent
related words colorless, uncolored; diaphanous, lucid, semitranslucent, semitransparent, sheer, translucent, transparentized; glassy, vitreous
near antonyms colored, dark, glazed, tinted; filmy, foggy, hazy, misty, nebulous, smoky (*also* smokey); dense, muddy, murky, turbid
antonyms cloudy, opaque
2 not subject to misinterpretation or more than one interpretation ⟨the meaning of her broad smile was *clear* to the whole class⟩
synonyms apparent, bald, bald-faced, barefaced, bright-line, broad, clear-cut, crystal clear, decided, distinct, evident, lucid, luculent, luminous, manifest, nonambiguous, obvious, open-and-shut, palpable, patent, pellucid, perspicuous, plain, ringing, straightforward, transparent, unambiguous, unambivalent, unequivocal, unmistakable
related words cognizable, cognoscible, comprehendible, comprehensible, digestible, fathomable, graspable, intelligible, knowable, understandable; self-evident, self-explanatory; clean-cut, simple, tidy, uncomplicated; overt, undisguised; appreciable, perceptible, recognizable, sensible, tangible; discernible (*also* discernable), noticeable, observable, visible; black-and-white, explicit, trenchant, well-defined; clean, decipherable, fair, legible, readable
near antonyms incomprehensible, indecipherable, unfathomable, unintelligible, unknowable; impalpable, imperceptible, inappreciable, indiscernible, insensible; cloudy, gauzy, gray (*also* grey), hazy, imprecise, indefinite, indeterminate, misty, murky, nebulous, noncommital, sketchy, slippery, subtle, vague; illegible, undecipherable, unreadable
antonyms ambiguous, clouded, cryptic, dark, enigmatic (*also* enigmatical), equivocal, indistinct, mysterious, nonobvious, obfuscated, obscure, unapparent, unclarified, unclear, unclouded
3 having or showing a mind free from doubt ⟨I need to be absolutely *clear* about what you're saying⟩ — see CERTAIN 2
4 not stormy or cloudy ⟨novice pilots can only fly on *clear* days⟩ — see FAIR 1
5 serving to put an end to all debate or questioning ⟨the evidence is *clear*: he's innocent⟩ — see CONCLUSIVE 1
6 allowing passage without obstruction ⟨flooding was widespread, and only some roads are *clear* so far⟩ — see OPEN 1
7 free from guilt or blame ⟨slept with a *clear* conscience⟩ — see INNOCENT 2
8 giving off or reflecting much light ⟨spermaceti candles were once highly prized for the *clear* flame that they produced⟩ — see BRIGHT 1

clear *vb* **1** to rid the surface of (as an area) from things in the way ⟨the early settlers worked hard to *clear* the land for crops⟩
synonyms free, open, unblock
related words ease, facilitate, loosen (up), smooth, unchoke, unclog, unplug, unstop; unclutter; strip
near antonyms clog, close, dam, obstruct, plug, stop; clutter (up)
antonyms block
2 to set (a person or thing) free of something that encumbers ⟨*cleared* the woods of brush⟩ — see RID
3 to give what is owed for ⟨finally *cleared* the last debt⟩ — see PAY 2
4 to remove the contents of ⟨*cleared* a drawer so there would be a place to store his clothes⟩ — see EMPTY

5 to remove usually visible impurities from ⟨*cleared* the car windows⟩ — see CLARIFY 1
6 to set free from entanglement or difficulty ⟨*cleared* himself of any involvement in the matter⟩ — see EXTRICATE
7 to make passage through (something) possible by removing obstructions ⟨plows promptly *cleared* the roads of snow⟩ — see OPEN 2
8 to free from a charge of wrongdoing ⟨she had once been accused of embezzlement, but an investigation by the bank *cleared* her⟩ — see EXCULPATE
9 to give official acceptance of as satisfactory ⟨the administration *cleared* the plan, and building should begin shortly⟩ — see APPROVE
10 to take away from a place or position ⟨*cleared* the dishes from the table⟩ — see REMOVE 2
11 to give information to ⟨please *clear* my mind about the new arrangement regarding reimbursement for traveling expenses⟩ — see ENLIGHTEN 1
12 to receive after charges and deductions have been made ⟨*cleared* enough from that stock transaction to be able to afford a new luxury automobile⟩ — see [2]NET

clear (up) *vb* to make plain or understandable ⟨a simple explanation *cleared* the matter *up*⟩ — see EXPLAIN 1

clearance *n* the approval by someone in authority for the doing of something ⟨we'll need official *clearance* before publishing this editorial⟩ — see PERMISSION

clear–cut *adj* **1** not subject to misinterpretation or more than one interpretation ⟨a *clear-cut* case of plagiarism that resulted in her immediate dismissal⟩ — see CLEAR 2
2 so clearly expressed as to leave no doubt about the meaning ⟨*clear-cut* instructions that even an idiot should be able to follow⟩ — see EXPLICIT

cleared *adj* allowing passage without obstruction ⟨for safety reasons, there must be a *cleared* staircase at all times⟩ — see OPEN 1

clear–eyed *adj* having or showing a practical cleverness or judgment ⟨shows a *clear-eyed* understanding of what it takes to be successful in business⟩ — see SHREWD 1

clearheaded *adj* **1** having full use of one's mind and control over one's actions ⟨waited until she was *clearheaded* to make the decision⟩ — see SANE
2 not having one's mind affected by alcohol ⟨woke up *clearheaded* and alert the next morning⟩ — see SOBER 1

clearing *n* **1** a setting free from a charge of wrongdoing ⟨the *clearing* of his good name became his obsession⟩ — see ACQUITTAL
2 a small area of usually open land ⟨deer browsing in a *clearing* in the woods⟩ — see FIELD 1

clearly *adv* without any question ⟨your grandmother *clearly* needs to get her finances organized before she gets into further trouble⟩ — see INDEED 1

clearness *n* the state or quality of being easily seen through ⟨the *clearness* of a diamond is one of the factors used to judge its quality⟩ — see CLARITY 1

clear off *vb, chiefly British* to leave a place often for another ⟨told the onlookers to *clear off* so that the police could do their work⟩ — see GO 2

clear out *vb* **1** to cause (members of a group) to move widely apart ⟨police used tear gas to *clear out* the demonstrators⟩ — see SCATTER 1
2 to get free from a dangerous or confining situation ⟨everyone *cleared out* as soon as the fire alarm began sounding⟩ — see ESCAPE 1
3 to leave a place often for another ⟨the lunch crowd usually *clears out* by 2:00 p.m. at the latest⟩ — see GO 2

clear–sighted *adj* **1** having or showing a practical cleverness or judgment ⟨a *clear-sighted* businessman who doesn't let sentimentality or compassion affect his decisions⟩ — see SHREWD 1
2 having unusually keen vision ⟨a *clear-sighted* person could see for almost 20 miles from the observatory⟩ — see SHARP-EYED

clear–sightedness *n* exceptional discernment and judgment especially in practical matters ⟨a loan officer who has the *clear-sightedness* to know when a business venture is a sure loser⟩ — see ACUMEN

cleavage *n* the act or process of a whole separating into two or more parts or pieces ⟨the *cleavages* of an egg as an embryo develops⟩ — see SEPARATION 1

cleave *vb* to hold to something firmly as if by adhesion ⟨you should resolutely *cleave* to the facts in your report⟩ — see STICK 1

cleft *n* an irregular usually narrow break in a surface created by pressure ⟨my fishing line managed to get wedged in a *cleft* in the rocks⟩ — see CRACK 1

clemency *n* kind, gentle, or compassionate treatment especially towards someone who is undeserving of it ⟨the judge chose to show *clemency* to the truly repentant embezzler⟩ — see MERCY 1

clement *adj* **1** marked by temperatures that are neither too high nor too low ⟨Hawaii is known for its delightfully *clement* climate⟩
synonyms balmy, equable, genial, gentle, mild, moderate, soft, temperate
related words clear, cloudless, fair, rainless, sunny, sunshiny; calm, halcyon, peaceful, placid, tranquil; delightful, fine, pleasant
near antonyms blustering, blustery, breezy, gusty, rough, squally, stormy, windy; misty, rainy, showery; bleak, cloudy, dismal, foggy, gloomy, gray (*also* grey), hazy, overcast, sunless; bitter, dirty, foul, nasty, raw
antonyms harsh, inclement, intemperate, severe
2 tolerant and kind in the judgment of and expectations for others ⟨his *clement* application of authority was a welcome change after years of managerial heavy-handedness⟩ — see INDULGENT 1

clench *n* the act or manner of holding ⟨fearful that his suitcase might be stolen, he never once relaxed his *clench* on the handle⟩ — see HOLD 1

clench *vb* to have or keep in one's hands ⟨*clenched* a tissue in his hands as he told his story of misfortune⟩ — see HOLD 1

clepe *vb, archaic* to give a name to ⟨the brewpub, *yclept* Ye Olde Taverne, has been decorated in Merrie Olde England to within an inch of its life⟩ — see NAME 1

clergy *n* the group ordained to perform clerical functions in the Christian church ⟨when people find out she's a member of the *clergy*, they suddenly change their manner⟩
synonyms church, cloth, first estate, ministry, spirituality, spiritualty
related words diaconate, episcopate, hierarchy, presbytery; clerkship, monkhood, priesthood
antonyms laity

clergyperson *n* a person specially trained and authorized to conduct religious services in a Christian church ⟨a *clergyperson* of your choice would be the best one to advise on this spiritual matter⟩
synonyms cleric, clerical, clerk, deacon, divine, dominie, ecclesiastic, minister, preacher, priest, reverend
related words churchman, clergyman, father, Holy Joe [*slang*], padre; clergywoman, deaconess, priestess; abbot, archbishop, archpriest, bishop, dean, diocesan, monsignor, pope, prelate, presbyter; abbé, curate, curé, parson, pastor, rector, shepherd, vicar; chaplain, confessor, sky pilot; evangelist, missionary, missioner, missionizer, revivalist; friar, mendicant, monastic, monk, oblate, religious; high priest, high priestess
near antonyms lay reader, lector
antonyms layman, layperson, secular

cleric *n* a person specially trained and authorized to

conduct religious services in a Christian church ⟨*clerics* were sharply divided on the issue of whether the war was morally justified⟩ — see CLERGYPERSON

clerical *adj* of, relating to, or characteristic of the clergy ⟨*clerical* duties such as providing spiritual counseling and leading Bible study classes⟩
synonyms clerkly, ministerial, pastoral, priestly, sacerdotal
related words evangelical (*also* evangelic), missionary; apostolic, canonical, diaconal, diocesan, episcopal, papal, patriarchal, pontifical; churchly, ecclesiastic, ecclesiastical; divine, holy, religious, sacramental; conventual, mendicant, monachal, monastic; caliphal, rabbinic (*or* rabbinical)
antonyms lay, nonclerical, secular, temporal

clerical *n* a person specially trained and authorized to conduct religious services in a Christian church ⟨some of the state's most prominent *clericals* have spoken out against the measure⟩ — see CLERGYPERSON

clerisy *n* intellectuals considered as a social class ⟨a society lacking a well-established *clerisy* with a strong commitment to democratic ideals⟩ — see INTELLIGENTSIA

clerk *n* **1** an official whose job is to keep records ⟨you'll need to get a copy of your birth certificate from the office of the town *clerk*⟩
synonyms register, registrar, scribe, secretary
related words archivist, bookkeeper, recorder, reporter, transcriptionist; annalist, chronicler, documenter, historian
2 a person employed to sell goods or services especially in a store ⟨the *clerk* suggested a different brand⟩ — see SALESPERSON
3 a person specially trained and authorized to conduct religious services in a Christian church ⟨the *clerks* in the rural parishes were for the most part sons of merchants⟩ — see CLERGYPERSON

clerkly *adj* of, relating to, or characteristic of the clergy ⟨a time when the *clerkly* duties of a country parson might include long rides on horseback to visit the more isolated members of the flock⟩ — see CLERICAL

clever *adj* **1** showing a noteworthy use of the imagination and creativity especially in inventing ⟨an inventor who was constantly coming up with *clever* devices for doing everyday chores⟩
synonyms artful, creative, imaginative, ingenious, innovative, inventive
related words adventurous, fresh, groundbreaking, novel, original, visionary; cleverish, gadgety, gimmicky; convenient, handy, neat, nifty, practical, useful; complex, sophisticated; adroit, deft, dexterous (*also* dextrous), expert, handsome, tricky; brainy, intelligent, sharp, smart
near antonyms dull, pedantic, pedestrian, stodgy; assembly-line, canned, cookie-cutter, derivative, hackneyed, unoriginal; impractical, useless
antonyms uncreative, unimaginative
2 having or showing quickness of mind ⟨a *clever* student figured out a trick to do the assignment faster⟩ — see INTELLIGENT 1
3 skillful with the hands ⟨the Shakers were *clever* artisans who created many ingenious and highly useful devices⟩ — see DEXTEROUS 1
4 given to or marked by mature intelligent humor ⟨a *clever* joke that requires a little bit of thought on the part of the listener⟩ — see WITTY
5 having the skill and imagination to create new things ⟨I wonder what *clever* person thought of the digital camera⟩ — see CREATIVE 1

cleverness *n* **1** mental skill or quickness ⟨it takes real *cleverness* to find a way around the rules⟩ — see DEXTERITY 1
2 subtle or imaginative ability in inventing, devising, or executing something ⟨the undeniable *cleverness* of the negotiator, who managed to get each side to believe that they had won⟩ — see SKILL 1
3 the skill and imagination to create new things ⟨Cole Porter's overall *cleverness* with words, including his effortless ability to rhyme and pun⟩ — see CREATIVITY 1

cliché *also* **cliche** *adj* used or heard so often as to be dull ⟨a *cliché* tale of lust and betrayal among the fabulously rich⟩ — see STALE 1

cliché *also* **cliche** *n* an idea or expression that has been used by many people ⟨try to write a love story without resorting to well-worn *clichés*⟩ — see COMMONPLACE

clichéd *adj* used or heard so often as to be dull ⟨a *clichéd* joke about sex and the elderly⟩ — see STALE 1

click *vb* **1** to form a close personal relationship ⟨we just *clicked* from the moment we met⟩ — see COMMUNE
2 to turn out as planned or desired ⟨sometimes an idea simply *clicks*⟩ — see SUCCEED 1

client *n* a person who buys a product or uses a service from a business ⟨a law firm soliciting new *clients* through television advertising⟩ — see CUSTOMER 1

cliff *n* a steep wall of rock, earth, or ice ⟨the *cliff* rises 200 feet from the island's south shore⟩
synonyms barranca (*also* barranco), bluff, crag, escarpment, palisade, precipice, scar, scarp
related words butte, cuesta, hogback, tor; bulwark, embankment; declivity, drop-off, pitch

cliff-hanger *n* something (as a close contest) that induces much suspense as to its outcome ⟨finally, a Super Bowl game that turned out to be a real *cliff-hanger*⟩ — see NAIL-BITER

climacteric *adj* of, relating to, or being a major turning point ⟨as the war reached its *climacteric* phase, the atrocities dramatically increased, both in number and brutality⟩ — see CLIMACTIC

climacteric *n* a point in a chain of events at which an important change (as in one's fortunes) occurs ⟨historians attempting to pinpoint the Roman Empire's *climacteric*, that precise moment when it began its long downhill slide⟩ — see TURNING POINT

climactic *adj* of, relating to, or being a major turning point ⟨the French Revolution is usually regarded as one of the *climactic* events in modern European history⟩
synonyms apocalyptic (*also* apocalyptical), climacteric
related words apical, apogean, crestal, crowning, culminating, high, highest, meridian; critical, crossover, crucial, fateful, life-and-death (*also* life-or-death), vital; cataclysmal (*or* cataclysmic), earthshaking, epochal, momentous; deciding, decisive, payoff, pivotal, watershed; go-no-go, make-or-break
near antonyms anticlimactic (*also* anticlimactical); inconsequential, indecisive, insignificant, noncritical, trivial, unimportant

climate *n* **1** a special quality or impression associated with something ⟨a new inner-city school designed to encourage a *climate* of learning⟩ — see AURA 1
2 the circumstances, conditions, or objects by which one is surrounded ⟨it's hard to concentrate in this hectic *climate*⟩ — see ENVIRONMENT

climax *n* **1** a point in a chain of events at which an important change (as in one's fortunes) occurs ⟨the *climax* of the story occurs when the hero discovers the identity of his father⟩ — see TURNING POINT
2 the highest part or point ⟨the *climax* of her career as a performer⟩ — see HEIGHT 1

climax *vb* to bring to a triumphant conclusion ⟨organizers *climaxed* the county fair with a down and dirty pie-eating contest⟩ — see CROWN

climb *n* the act or an instance of rising or climbing up ⟨a long hard *climb* up the mountain⟩ — see ASCENT 1

climb *vb* **1** to move (as up or over something) often with the help of the hands in holding or pulling ⟨visitors should use caution when *climbing* over the wet rocks along the shore⟩

synonyms clamber, scrabble, scramble, swarm

related words shimmy, shin, shinny, skin; ascend, breast [*chiefly British*], free-climb, get up, mount, scale, summit, surmount; claw, sprawl, struggle

2 to move or extend upward ⟨smoke from the cabin *climbing* in the still mountain air⟩ — see ASCEND

3 to become greater in size, extent, volume, amount, or number ⟨complaints to the cable company *climbed* after the changeover⟩ — see INCREASE 2

clime *n* the circumstances, conditions, or objects by which one is surrounded ⟨a nonconformist who left his jerkwater hometown for the more welcoming *clime* of the big city⟩ — see ENVIRONMENT

clinch *vb* to make final, definite, or beyond dispute ⟨the rain *clinched* the matter: we would have the party indoors⟩

synonyms decide, determine, nail, settle

related words demonstrate, establish, nail (down), prove, show; affirm, assure, ensure, insure, secure; define, specify, state, stipulate; clarify, clear (up), illuminate; conclude, end, finish

near antonyms confuse, muddle, muddy, unsettle

clincher *n* something (as a fact or argument) that is decisive or overwhelming ⟨the fact that the resort had tennis courts was the *clincher* in our deciding to stay there⟩

synonyms capper, coup de grâce (*or* coup de grace), crusher, topper

related words confutation, deathblow, knockout; determinant, factor

phrases ace in the hole

cling *n* a physical sticking to as if by glue ⟨for certain types of materials that plastic wrap has very little *cling*⟩ — see ADHESION 1

cling *vb* to hold to something firmly as if by adhesion ⟨a dozen magnets *clinging* to the refrigerator⟩ — see STICK 1

cling (to) *vb* **1** to give steadfast support to ⟨continued to *cling to* the old ideas of child rearing long after they had gone out of fashion⟩ — see ADHERE (TO) 1

2 to have or keep in one's hands ⟨*clung to* a pole in the subway car to keep from falling as it lurched along⟩ — see HOLD 1

clingy *adj* tending to adhere to objects upon contact ⟨it took forever to clean up the *clingy* Styrofoam pellets that had been used as packing material for the lamp⟩ — see STICKY 1

clink *n, slang* a place of confinement for persons held in lawful custody ⟨I once spent a night in the *clink*, and it's an experience I don't want to repeat⟩ — see JAIL

clink *vb* to make a repeated sharp light ringing sound ⟨coins *clinking* in his pocket as he traipsed down the street⟩ — see JINGLE

clinker *n* **1** an unintentional departure from truth or accuracy ⟨a documentary that had such *clinkers* as a reference to Iran as an Arab nation⟩ — see ERROR 1

2 something that has failed ⟨all of the toy company's new offerings for the Christmas season proved to be *clinkers*⟩ — see FAILURE 3

clip *n* a hard strike with a part of the body or an instrument ⟨an unexpectedly low branch dealt him a *clip* to the head⟩ — see [1]BLOW

clip *vb* **1** to make (something) shorter or smaller with the use of a cutting instrument ⟨a mother who's sad to see her little boy's curls *clipped* for the first time⟩

synonyms bob, crop, cut, cut back, dock, lop (off), nip, pare, poll, prune, shave, shear, snip, trim

related words skive, whittle; manicure, mow; pinch, stump; curtail, shorten

near antonyms elongate, extend, lengthen

2 to deliver a blow to (someone or something) usually in a strong vigorous manner ⟨the pitch *clipped* the batter's helmet with enough force to knock it clean off his head⟩ — see HIT 1

clique *n* a group of people sharing a common interest and relating together socially ⟨that *clique* refuses to even talk to outsiders at their lunch table⟩ — see GANG 2

cliquey *adj* bound together by feelings of very close association ⟨found the people at the brokerage house to be just as *cliquey* as a gaggle of high school cheerleaders⟩ — see CLOSE-KNIT

cliquish *adj* bound together by feelings of very close association ⟨the *cliquish* White House press corps soon let him know that he was not on the A-list⟩ — see CLOSE-KNIT

cloak *n* **1** something that covers or conceals like a piece of cloth ⟨the *cloak* of mystery that surrounds the royal family⟩

synonyms blanket, cope, cover, covering, coverture, cover-up, curtain, hood, mantle, mask, pall, penumbra, robe, shroud, veil, wraps

related words blind, concealer, screen, shield; fig leaf, Potemkin village, Trojan horse; camouflage, disguise, facade (*also* façade), face, mask, veneer; gloss, varnish

2 a sleeveless garment worn so as to hang over the shoulders, arms, and back ⟨threw a *cloak* around his shoulders⟩ — see [1]CAPE

cloak *vb* **1** to change the dress or looks of so as to conceal true identity ⟨the outlaw nation had *cloaked* its chemical weapons plant as a fertilizer factory⟩ — see DISGUISE 1

2 to keep secret or shut off from view ⟨*cloaked* their military maneuvers from the outside world⟩ — see [1]HIDE 2

cloakroom *n, British* a room furnished with a fixture for flushing body waste ⟨the lady discreetly whispered that she would be ready after a moment in the *cloakroom*⟩ — see TOILET

clobber *n, British slang* covering for the human body ⟨still wearing the same *clobber* he wore as an undergrad at Cambridge⟩ — see CLOTHING

clobber *vb* **1** to deliver a blow to (someone or something) usually in a strong vigorous manner ⟨he *clobbered* the ball, sending it in a high arc toward the back wall⟩ — see HIT 1

2 to defeat by a large margin ⟨they *clobbered* the opposing team⟩ — see WHIP 2

clock *n* a device to measure time ⟨the *clock* reads 5:00 p.m.⟩ — see TIMEPIECE

clock *vb* to deliver a blow to (someone or something) usually in a strong vigorous manner ⟨sick of being insulted, he swung around and *clocked* his tormentor hard enough to knock him off his bar stool⟩ — see HIT 1

clock (up) *vb, chiefly British* to obtain (as a goal) through effort ⟨among British actors he holds the distinction of having *clocked up* the most performances of *Hamlet* on the London stage⟩ — see ACHIEVE 1

clod *n* **1** a big clumsy often slow-witted person ⟨despite his imposing size, he's no simple *clod*⟩ — see OAF 1

2 a small uneven mass ⟨a *clod* of dirt stuck to the bottom of the bucket⟩ — see LUMP 1

3 the loose surface material in which plants naturally grow ⟨faced with the task of burying his beloved wife in the cold, hard *clod* of the frontier⟩ — see DIRT 1

cloddish *adj* having or showing crudely insensitive or impolite manners ⟨the *cloddish* behavior of the frat boys at the party⟩ — see CLOWNISH

clodhopper *n* **1** an awkward or simple person especially from a small town or the country ⟨a stereotypical

depiction of *clodhoppers* visiting the city for the first time⟩ — see HICK
2 a big clumsy often slow-witted person ⟨I do not want that *clodhopper* handling my rare antiques!⟩ — see OAF 1
clodpoll *or* **clodpole** *n* a stupid person ⟨mistook the local farmers for a bunch of *clodpolls* who could be easily fleeced⟩ — see IDIOT
clog *n* something that makes movement or progress difficult ⟨she's not one to let moral principle be a *clog* upon her conscience⟩ — see ENCUMBRANCE
clog *vb* **1** to prevent passage through by filling with something ⟨the discovery that a ton of hair was *clogging* the drain in the tub⟩
synonyms block, choke, clot, congest, dam, gum (up), jam, obstruct, occlude, plug (up), stop (up), stuff
related words bung, cork, spile, stopper, stopple; fill, gridlock, pack; fur, silt; flood, glut, inundate, overwhelm, swamp
near antonyms excavate, hollow (out), scoop (out); empty, lighten
antonyms clear, free, open (up), unblock, unclog, unplug, unstop
2 to create difficulty for the work or activity of ⟨a court system *clogged* by frivolous suits⟩ — see HAMPER
cloister *n* a residence for men under religious vows ⟨monks living in a *cloister* in the country⟩ — see MONASTERY
cloistered *adj* screened or sequestered from view ⟨behind the stately townhouses lie *cloistered* gardens that the public never sees⟩ — see SECLUDED
clone *n* **1** something that is made to look exactly like something else ⟨the car is a *clone* under a different brand name—it's even manufactured in the same plant as its cousin⟩ — see COPY
2 something or someone that strongly resembles another ⟨the new television series is a *clone* of half a dozen police procedurals already on the air⟩ — see IMAGE 1
clone *vb* to make an exact likeness of ⟨will *clone* the designer outfit for the ready-to-wear market⟩ — see COPY 1
[1]**close** *n* an open space wholly or partly enclosed (as by buildings or walls) ⟨a garden in a *close* at the center of the complex⟩ — see COURT 2
[2]**close** *n* **1** the stopping of a process or activity ⟨at the *close* of the evening⟩ — see END 1
2 the last part of a process or action ⟨managed to conduct the negotiations to a satisfactory *close*⟩ — see FINALE
close *adj* **1** having little space between items or parts ⟨the soldiers marched in *close* formation against the enemy⟩
synonyms compact, crowded, dense, jam-packed, packed, serried, thick, tight
related words crammed, jammed, overcrowded; crushed, massed, pressed, squeezed, wall-to-wall; airtight, snug; compacted, compressed, condensed, congested; firm, hard, solid; impenetrable, impermeable, impervious
near antonyms commodious, roomy, spacious
antonyms airy, loose, open, uncrowded
2 not being distant in time, space, or significance ⟨my birthday is *close* to Christmas⟩ ⟨a shopping mall that is very *close* to the highway⟩ ⟨these words are *close* synonyms⟩
synonyms close-up, immediate, near, nearby, neighboring, next-door, nigh, proximate
related words abutting, adjacent, adjoining, bordering, contiguous; approaching, coming, forthcoming, oncoming, upcoming; accessible, convenient, handy; close-in, hand-to-hand
phrases at hand, to hand
near antonyms divorced, removed, separated
antonyms away, deep, distant, far, faraway, far-off, remote
3 showing little difference in the standing of the competitors ⟨the election results were so *close* that the votes had to be recounted⟩
synonyms down-to-the-wire, hairbreadth, narrow, neck and neck, nip and tuck, tight
related words crowded
4 closely acquainted ⟨a small wedding ceremony that was limited to *close* friends⟩ — see FAMILIAR 1
5 given to keeping one's activities hidden from public observation or knowledge ⟨she was as *close* as a stone when it came to talking about her love life⟩ — see SECRETIVE
6 giving or sharing as little as possible ⟨the kind of folks who are very *close* when charity calls⟩ — see STINGY 1
7 lacking fresh air ⟨a small room with an uncomfortably *close* atmosphere⟩ — see STUFFY 1
8 meeting the highest standard of accuracy ⟨a *close* analysis of the box-office performance of action movies⟩ — see PRECISE 1
close *adv* at, within, or to a short distance or time ⟨the stranded passengers drew *close* for reassurance⟩ — see NEAR 1
close *vb* **1** to position (something) so as to prevent passage through an opening ⟨be sure to *close* the gate when you leave⟩
synonyms make [*chiefly dialect*], shut, steek [*chiefly Scottish*]
related words bar, batten (down), bolt, chain, fasten, latch, lock; plug, seal, stopper; secure; bang, clap, slam
near antonyms unbar, unbolt, unchain, unfasten, unlatch, unlock, unseal
antonyms open
2 to stop the operations of ⟨the merchant will *close* the store if business doesn't improve⟩
synonyms close (down), close out, shut
related words phase out, turn off; extinguish, quell, suppress; gag, muzzle, silence; fail, fold
near antonyms build, expand
antonyms open, start
3 to bring (an event) to a natural or appropriate stopping point ⟨we'll *close* the assembly with the singing of our national anthem⟩
synonyms close out, complete, conclude, end, finish, round (off *or* out), terminate, wind up, wrap up
related words climax, crown; consummate, perfect; halt, stop, suspend
phrases put paid to [*chiefly British*], ring down the curtain (on)
antonyms begin, commence, inaugurate, open, start
4 to come to an end ⟨the services *closed* with a short prayer⟩ — see CEASE 1
5 to come near or nearer ⟨the two groups *closed* with each other from opposite sides of the field⟩ — see APPROACH 1
close (down) *vb* to stop the operations of ⟨the coal mine was *closed down* in the 1930s⟩ — see CLOSE 2
close (off) *vb* to disallow entry into (a place) by means of a physical barrier at the entry point ⟨museum officials *closed off* the west wing after the fire⟩
synonyms bar, barricade, blockade, block (off), guard, wall (off)
related words curtain (off), screen (off); dike, fence, gate, hedge; bolt, lock; obstruct
near antonyms reopen, unblock, unbolt
antonyms open, unbar
close call *n* a barely successful escape from something undesirable ⟨the doctor said I'd had a *close call*, and was lucky to be alive⟩
synonyms close shave, near miss

related words squeaker
phrases hairbreadth escape, narrow escape, near escape
near antonyms misfire

closed book *n* something hard to understand or explain ⟨the couple's unorthodox marriage is definitely a *closed book* to those outside of the relationship⟩ — see MYSTERY

closedown *n* the stopping of a process or activity ⟨ordered a *closedown* of operations until the cause of the mine explosion could be determined⟩ — see END 1

closefisted *adj* giving or sharing as little as possible ⟨*closefisted* administrators objecting to legitimate office expenses⟩ — see STINGY 1

close in *vb* **1** to come near or nearer ⟨the eagle *closed in* on its prey⟩ — see APPROACH 1
2 to grow dark ⟨with evening *closing in* we knew we had to find shelter fairly soon⟩ — see DARKEN 2

close–knit *adj* bound together by feelings of very close association ⟨a *close-knit* family that constantly keeps in touch⟩
synonyms clannish, cliquey, cliquish
related words bosom, chummy, close, familiar, friendly, inseparable, intimate, pack [*chiefly Scottish*], pally, palsy, palsy-walsy [*slang*], thick, tight; exclusive, snobbish, snobby; incestuous; forbidding, inhospitable, unfriendly
near antonyms receptive, welcoming

closely *adv* to a close degree ⟨*closely* resembling a normal outfit⟩ — see NEAR 2

closemouthed *adj* **1** given to keeping one's activities hidden from public observation or knowledge ⟨he remained *closemouthed* about their activities⟩ — see SECRETIVE
2 tending not to speak frequently (as by habit or inclination) ⟨encourage the *closemouthed* children to speak up and not be shy⟩ — see SILENT 2

closeness *n* **1** the practice or habit of keeping secrets or keeping one's affairs secret ⟨we tried to penetrate her strange *closeness* about her domestic life⟩ — see SECRECY
2 the quality or practice of being overly sparing with money ⟨rebelled against his parents' *closeness* with his allowance⟩ — see PARSIMONY 1
3 the quality or state of being very accurate ⟨the body was too decomposed to estimate the time of death with any great *closeness*⟩ — see PRECISION
4 the state of being in a very personal or private relationship ⟨the *closeness* of their relationship was a matter of intense speculation among their coworkers⟩ — see FAMILIARITY 1
5 the state or condition of being near ⟨we were surprised by the *closeness* of everything to our downtown loft⟩ — see PROXIMITY
6 strict attentiveness to what one is doing ⟨how much you get out of the sermon will depend on the *closeness* with which you listen to it⟩ — see CARE 1

close out *vb* **1** to bring (an event) to a natural or appropriate stopping point ⟨the team *closed out* the season with major losses⟩ — see CLOSE 3
2 to prevent the participation, consideration, or inclusion of ⟨don't assume an attitude that *closes out* any possibility of a compromise⟩ — see EXCLUDE
3 to stop the operations of ⟨failing health forced the cardiologist to *close out* his practice⟩ — see CLOSE 2

closer *adj* being the less far of two ⟨the *closer* gas station was also more expensive⟩ — see NEAR 1

close shave *n* a barely successful escape from something undesirable ⟨the passengers in the jeep had a *close shave* when a mine exploded just a few yards away⟩ — see CLOSE CALL

closet *n* **1** a built-in space for storage behind a door ⟨a broom *closet* for the vacuum, carpet sweeper, ironing board, etc.⟩
synonyms cuddy, cupboard, pantry, press
related words ambry [*chiefly British dialect*], buttery [*chiefly dialect*], larder, spence [*chiefly British dialect*]; cloakroom, coatroom, garderobe, vestiary, wardrobe
2 an area within a building that has been set apart from surrounding space by a wall ⟨a huge walk-in *closet*⟩ — see ROOM 2
3 a storage case typically having doors and shelves ⟨a china *closet* in the Hepplewhite style⟩ — see CABINET

closet *vb* to close or shut in by or as if by barriers ⟨he *closeted* himself in his study, vowing not to emerge until he had finished the term paper⟩ — see ENCLOSE 1

close–up *adj* not being distant in time, space, or significance ⟨come over here and get a *close-up* view of the painting⟩ — see CLOSE 2

closing *adj* following all others of the same kind in order or time ⟨the orchestra's *closing* piece is traditionally the national anthem⟩ — see LAST 1

closing *n* the last part of a process or action ⟨a stand-up comedian has to have a strong *closing* if he wants a spirited round of applause⟩ — see FINALE

closure *n* the stopping of a process or activity ⟨after the *closure* of the region's last copper mine, the population simply withered away⟩ — see END 1

clot *n* **1** a number of things considered as a unit ⟨a *clot* of daisies occupied one corner of the flower bed⟩ — see GROUP 1
2 a small uneven mass ⟨*clots* of dirt that were flung up by the horses' hooves⟩ — see LUMP 1
3 *British* a stupid person ⟨was of the opinion that most of the people running for parliament were *clots*⟩ — see IDIOT

clot *vb* **1** to prevent passage through by filling with something ⟨phone lines *clotted* by Internet traffic⟩ — see CLOG 1
2 to turn from a liquid into a substance resembling jelly ⟨scabs form over cuts when your blood starts to *clot*⟩ — see COAGULATE

cloth *n* **1** a woven or knitted material (as of cotton or nylon) ⟨cotton canvas was the *cloth* traditionally used for a ship's sails⟩
synonyms fabric, textile
related words fiber, thread, yarn; rag
2 the group ordained to perform clerical functions in the Christian church ⟨he's a member of the *cloth*, but that doesn't keep him from enjoying a stiff drink every now and then⟩ — see CLERGY

clothe *vb* **1** to outfit with clothes and especially fine or special clothes ⟨they liked to *clothe* the twins in identical outfits just to confuse people⟩
synonyms apparel, array, attire, bedeck, caparison, costume, deck (out), do up, dress, dress up, enrobe, garb, garment, get up, gown, habit, invest, rig (out), robe, suit, tog (up *or* out), toilet, vesture
related words cloak, frock, jacket, mantle, vest; drape, enswathe, hap [*dialect*], huddle, swaddle, swathe, wrap; accoutre (*or* accouter), bedight [*archaic*], equip, furnish, habilitate, outfit, tailor, uniform; dress down, underdress
near antonyms denude, divest, uncover, undrape, unveil
antonyms disarray, disrobe, strip, unclothe, undress, untruss [*archaic*]
2 to convey in appropriate or telling terms ⟨regulations *clothed* in obscure terminology⟩ — see PHRASE

clothes *n pl* covering for the human body ⟨put on your warmest *clothes*—it's freezing outside⟩ — see CLOTHING

clothing *n* covering for the human body ⟨a store that sells both men's and women's *clothing*⟩

synonyms apparel, attire, clobber [*British slang*], clothes, costumery, dress, duds, garments, gear, habiliment(s), habit [*archaic*], rags, raiment, rig, rigging, threads, toggery, togs, vestiary, vestments, vesture, wear, wearables, weeds
related words garderobe, wardrobe; array, bravery, caparison, finery, gaiety (*also* gayety), glad rags, pretties, regalia, trim; foofaraw, frippery, gaudery, tawdry, trumpery [*archaic*]; tatters; costume, ensemble, frock, garb, getup, guise, livery, outfit; civvies (*also* civies), mufti; couture, prêt-à-porter (*or* pret-a-porter), ready-to-wear, tailoring; activewear, loungewear, outerwear, playwear, sportswear; nightclothes, sleepwear, smallclothes, underclothes, underwear; haberdashery, menswear

cloud *n* an overspreading element that produces an atmosphere of gloom ⟨all day we were under a *cloud* until we heard the good news⟩
synonyms darkness, pall, shadow
related words fog, haze, mist, murk, penumbra, umbra; midnight, night; mantle, shroud, veil

cloud *vb* **1** to make dark, dim, or indistinct ⟨the diner's dark interior, *clouded* with smoke and grease⟩
synonyms becloud, bedim, befog, blacken, blear, blur, darken, dim, dislimn, fog, fuzz (up), haze, mist, obscure, overcast, overcloud, overshadow, shadow, shroud
related words adumbrate, blot out, conceal, eclipse, hide, obliterate, screen, shade; camouflage, cloak, cover, curtain, disguise, mask, veil
near antonyms expose, reveal, uncover, unveil
antonyms brighten, illuminate, illumine, light (up), lighten
2 to make (something) unclear to the understanding ⟨*cloud* the issue with obscure statistics⟩ — see CONFUSE 2

cloudburst *n* a steady falling of water from the sky in significant quantity ⟨the weatherman warned of possible *cloudbursts* in the afternoon⟩ — see RAIN 1

clouded *adj* **1** covered over by clouds ⟨*clouded* skies did not diminish our fun⟩ — see OVERCAST
2 filled with or dimmed by fine particles (as of dust or water) in suspension ⟨with only a *clouded* view of the valley before, we canceled the hang gliding⟩ — see HAZY 1

cloudless *adj* not stormy or cloudy ⟨playing in the park on a *cloudless* summer day⟩ — see FAIR 1

cloud nine *n* a state of overwhelming usually pleasurable emotion ⟨I've been on *cloud nine* ever since I landed my dream job⟩ — see ECSTASY

cloudy *adj* **1** having visible particles in liquid suspension ⟨the water coming out of the faucet was unusually *cloudy*⟩
synonyms muddy, riley, roiled, turbid
related words dingy, filmy, hazy, scummy, unfiltered; inky, muddied, muddled, murky, puddled, sludgy; opaque
near antonyms clarified, filtered, purified; colorless, transparent, uncolored
antonyms clear, crystal clear, crystalline
2 covered over by clouds ⟨the skies grew *cloudy* and we headed home⟩ — see OVERCAST
3 filled with or dimmed by fine particles (as of dust or water) in suspension ⟨the room grew *cloudy* with smoke from the fire⟩ — see HAZY 1
4 causing or marked by an atmosphere lacking in cheer ⟨after his third failed marriage, he seemed destined to live the rest of his life in a permanently *cloudy* mood⟩ — see GLOOMY 1

clout *n* **1** a hard strike with a part of the body or an instrument ⟨gave the stubborn handle a solid *clout* to make it turn⟩ — see [1]BLOW
2 the power to direct the thinking or behavior of others usually indirectly ⟨has a great deal of *clout* in the film industry⟩ — see INFLUENCE 1

clout *vb* to deliver a blow to (someone or something) usually in a strong vigorous manner ⟨*clouted* the nail with the hammer and drove it all the way into the wood⟩ — see HIT 1

clown *n* **1** a comically dressed performer (as at a circus) who entertains with playful tricks and ridiculous behavior ⟨a *clown* wearing big floppy shoes and a red wig⟩
synonyms buffo, buffoon, harlequin, zany
related words cutup, madcap; antic [*archaic*], fool, gracioso, jester, motley, scaramouch (*or* scaramouche); mime, mimic, mummer, pantaloon; comedian, comedienne, comic, droll, farceur, funnyman, gagger, gagman, gagster, humorist, joker, jokester, merry-andrew, second banana, stand-up, top banana, wag, wit
2 a person whose behavior is offensive to others ⟨you should stay away from that *clown*⟩ — see JERK 1

clown (around) *vb* to engage in attention-getting playful or boisterous behavior ⟨as a youngster he was always *clowning around* in the classroom⟩ — see CUT UP

clownery *n* wildly playful or mischievous behavior ⟨it was *clownery* like that that resulted in an expensive vase being broken⟩ — see HORSEPLAY

clowning *n* wildly playful or mischievous behavior ⟨our coworker's *clowning* was distracting, but fun to watch⟩ — see HORSEPLAY

clownish *adj* having or showing crudely insensitive or impolite manners ⟨the *clownish* antics of some of the teenagers at the wedding reception⟩
synonyms boorish, churlish, classless, cloddish, loutish, uncouth
related words coarse, ill-bred, uncultivated, unpolished, unrefined, unsophisticated; tasteless, vulgar; beastly, bestial; doltish, oafish, stupid; discourteous, impolite, mannerless, misleared [*chiefly Scottish*], rude, uncivil, ungracious, unmannerly; awkward, ungainly
near antonyms couth, cultivated, polished, refined, sophisticated, well-bred; classy, courtly, genteel, gentlemanly, ladylike; civil, courteous, polite

cloying *adj* appealing to the emotions in an obvious and tiresome way ⟨the *cloying* sentiments of so many Mother's Day cards⟩ — see CORNY 1

club *n* **1** a heavy rigid stick used as a weapon or for punishment ⟨hit the prisoner with a *club* if he tries anything funny⟩
synonyms bastinado (*or* bastinade), bat, baton, billy, billy club, bludgeon, cane, cudgel, nightstick, rod, rung [*Scottish*], sap, shillelagh (*also* shillalah), staff, truncheon, waddy [*Australian*]
related words blackjack, knobkerrie, mace; birch, crabstick, hickory, rattan, stave, switch; beetle, gavel, hammer, mallet, maul, sledgehammer; crook, crosier (*or* crozier), walking stick, whangee
2 the meeting place of an organization ⟨the Elks gather at their *club* every Monday evening⟩
synonyms clubhouse, lodge
related words den, hangout, haunt, hideaway, hideout, lair; camp, headquarters; conventicle, hall, house, meetinghouse
3 a group of persons formally joined together for some common interest ⟨an alumni *club*⟩ — see ASSOCIATION 2
4 a bar or restaurant offering special nighttime entertainment (as music, dancing, or comedy acts) ⟨a weekly newspaper column devoted to current happenings on the local *club* scene⟩ — see NIGHTCLUB

club *vb* **1** to form or enter into an association that furthers the interests of its members ⟨*clubbed* together to share their love of model rockets⟩ — see ALLY
2 to strike repeatedly ⟨frustrated, the gardener *clubbed*

the inoffensive weed into submission⟩ — see BEAT 1

clubbable *also* **clubable** *adj* likely to seek or enjoy the company of others ⟨a frequenter of coffeehouses, Samuel Johnson has been called the most *clubbable* man in English literature⟩ — see CONVIVIAL

clubby *adj* likely to seek or enjoy the company of others ⟨new in town, she was hoping some of her *clubbier* coworkers might show her the city's hot spots⟩ — see CONVIVIAL

clubhouse *n* the meeting place of an organization ⟨we plan to meet at the *clubhouse* each week⟩ — see CLUB 2

cluck *n* a stupid person ⟨stuck with a bunch of *clucks* on an extended bus tour⟩ — see IDIOT

clue *n* a slight or indirect pointing to something (as a solution or explanation) ⟨vainly searched for a *clue* to the answer⟩ — see HINT 1

clue (in) *vb* to give information to ⟨would you *clue* him *in* on the plan?⟩ — see ENLIGHTEN 1

clueless *adj* not informed about or aware of something ⟨television producers who seem utterly *clueless* about the concerns and interests of today's teenagers⟩ — see IGNORANT 2

cluelessness *n* the state of being unaware or uninformed ⟨the utter *cluelessness* of the parents astounded the police who raided the underage drinking party⟩ — see IGNORANCE 1

clump *n* **1** a number of things considered as a unit ⟨scattered *clumps* of houses were visible from the air⟩ — see GROUP 1
2 a small uneven mass ⟨a *clump* of dirt⟩ — see LUMP 1

clump *vb* to move heavily or clumsily ⟨a child *clumping* around the house in her father's oversized boots⟩ — see LUMBER 1

clumpy *adj* having small pieces or lumps spread throughout ⟨the soil was a little too *clumpy* to make for a good garden⟩ — see CHUNKY 1

clumsy *adj* **1** lacking or showing a lack of nimbleness in using one's hands ⟨diamond cutting is no job for a *clumsy* person⟩
synonyms awkward, butterfingered, cack-handed [*British*], graceless, ham-fisted, ham-handed, handless, heavy-handed, left-handed, maladroit, unhandy
related words uncoordinated; bunglesome, bungling, gauche, inept, inexpert, unskilled, unskillful
phrases all thumbs
near antonyms expert, masterly, skilled, skillful; coordinated
antonyms deft, dexterous (*also* dextrous), handy, surehanded
2 having or showing an inability to move in a graceful manner ⟨a *clumsy* bow⟩ ⟨*clumsy* on the dance floor⟩
synonyms awkward, gawkish, gawky, graceless, klutzy, uncoordinated, ungainly
related words galumphing, larruping [*dialect*], lubberly, lumbering, lumpish, shambling, shuffling, unsteady, wobbly (*also* wabbly)
near antonyms light, light-footed (*also* light-foot), lissome (*also* lissom), lithe, nimble, sure-footed
antonyms coordinated, graceful
3 lacking social grace and assurance ⟨felt *clumsy* in the unfamiliar uniform⟩ — see AWKWARD 1
4 showing or marked by a lack of skill and tact (as in dealing with a situation) ⟨a *clumsy* joke⟩ — see AWKWARD 2
5 difficult to use or operate especially because of size, weight, or design ⟨a *clumsy* contraption, but it got the job done⟩ — see CUMBERSOME
6 hastily or roughly constructed ⟨a *clumsy* mock-up of the real thing⟩ — see RUDE 1

clunk *n* a stupid person ⟨don't be such a *clunk* and just get on with it⟩ — see IDIOT

clunker *n* **1** a dilapidated old automobile ⟨she drove a *clunker* because she couldn't afford anything better⟩ — see BEATER 1
2 something that has failed ⟨a real *clunker*, the movie was soon littering the shelves of video stores everywhere⟩ — see FAILURE 3

clunky *adj* difficult to use or operate especially because of size, weight, or design ⟨even my five-year-old laptop seems *clunky* next to some of the really slim new models⟩ — see CUMBERSOME

cluster *n* **1** a number of things considered as a unit ⟨a *cluster* of stars in the southern sky⟩ — see GROUP 1
2 a usually small number of persons considered as a unit ⟨a small *cluster* of reporters waited by the courthouse door⟩ — see GROUP 2

cluster *vb* **1** to come together into one body or place ⟨the mice *clustered* together into a small burrow⟩ — see ASSEMBLE 1
2 to gather into a closely packed group ⟨all the cottages are *clustered* on one end of the lake⟩ — see [2]PRESS 3

[1]**clutch** *n* **1** a number of things considered as a unit ⟨a *clutch* of medals adorned the general's chest⟩ — see GROUP 1
2 a usually small number of persons considered as a unit ⟨a *clutch* of people traveling together⟩ — see GROUP 2

[2]**clutch** *n* **1** a time or state of affairs requiring prompt or decisive action ⟨a football quarterback who always comes through in the *clutch*⟩ — see EMERGENCY
2 the right or means to command or control others ⟨a nation no longer living in the *clutch* of a cruel tyrant⟩ — see POWER 1

clutch *vb* to have or keep in one's hands ⟨he *clutched* the eggs carefully so he wouldn't drop them⟩ — see HOLD 1

clutter *n* **1** an unorganized collection or mixture of various things ⟨a scrapbook that was a *clutter* of snapshots, diary entries, letters, and newspaper clippings⟩ — see MISCELLANY 1
2 *chiefly dialect* a state of noisy, confused activity ⟨the *clutter* created by the exhibitors setting up for the annual state fair⟩ — see COMMOTION

cluttered *adj* lacking in order, neatness, and often cleanliness ⟨keeping a *cluttered* workshop makes it hard to find the right tool⟩ — see MESSY

coach *n* a person who trains performers or athletes ⟨a *coach* who is highly respected by all of the baseball players⟩
synonyms trainer
related words handler, manager; instructor, teacher, tutor; driller, drillmaster; adviser (*also* advisor), cicerone, counselor (*or* counsellor), guide, mentor

coach *vb* to give advice and instruction to (someone) regarding the course or process to be followed ⟨carefully *coached* her through the home-buying process⟩ — see GUIDE 1

coadjutor *n* a person who helps a more skilled person ⟨he was appointed *coadjutor* to the president⟩ — see HELPER

coagulate *vb* to turn from a liquid into a substance resembling jelly ⟨the blood *coagulated*, and a scab formed on the wound⟩
synonyms clot, congeal, gel, gelate, gelatinize, jell, jelly, set
related words cake, concrete, firm (up), fix, freeze, harden, indurate, solidify, stiffen; condense, thicken; clump, curd, curdle, gum, lump (up)
near antonyms deliquesce, flux, fuse, liquefy (*also* liquify), melt, thaw

coalesce *vb* **1** to come together to form a single unit ⟨several small townships have *coalesced* into a single metropolis⟩ — see UNITE 1
2 to form or enter into an association that furthers the

interests of its members ⟨the historic preservation movement gained momentum when the two groups *coalesced*⟩ — see ALLY

coalition *n* **1** a group of people acting together within a larger group ⟨rival *coalitions* struggling for control of the party⟩ — see FACTION
2 an association of persons, parties, or states for mutual assistance and protection ⟨preservationists formed a *coalition* with the theater owners to preserve these historic structures⟩ — see CONFEDERACY

coarse *adj* **1** made up of large particles ⟨*coarse* rock salt was sprinkled on the icy walkway⟩
synonyms grained, grainy, granular, granulated
related words unfiltered, unrefined; earthy, gravelly, gritty, sandy; pebbly, rocky, stony (*also* stoney); coarse-grained, cracked, kibbled, lumpy, mealy
near antonyms buttery, smooth, velvety; filtered, levigated, refined; close-grained, comminuted, ground, micronized, milled, mulled, pestled, pulverized, reduced, triturated
antonyms dusty, fine, floury, powdery, superfine, ultrafine
2 lacking in refinement or good taste ⟨the hockey player's *coarse* manners turned his date off completely⟩
synonyms common, crass, crude, gross, ill-bred, illiberal [*archaic*], incult, insensible, low, lowbred, lowbrow, raffish, rough, rough-hewn, roughneck, rude, rugged, tasteless, uncouth, uncultivated, uncultured, unpolished, unrefined, vulgar
related words boorish, churlish, cloddish, clownish, loutish, ungentlemanly; clumsy, lubberly, lumpish, oafish; inconsiderate, indelicate, insensitive, thoughtless; countrified (*also* countryfied), provincial, rustic (*also* rustical), unsophisticated; graceless, inelegant, tacky; animallike, barbaric, barbarous, uncivilized; mannerless, unmannered, unmannerly
near antonyms aristocratic, courtly, patrician; elegant, graceful, restrained; considerate, gracious, sensitive, thoughtful; citified, sophisticated, urbane
antonyms civilized, cultivated, cultured, genteel, polished, refined, smooth, tasteful, ultrarefined, well-bred
3 depicting or referring to sexual matters in a way that is unacceptable in polite society ⟨offended by the *coarse* humor at the celebrity roast⟩ — see OBSCENE 1
4 harsh and dry in sound ⟨a *coarse* laugh⟩ — see HOARSE
5 not having a level or smooth surface ⟨the *coarse* surface of the sandpaper⟩ — see UNEVEN 1
6 of low quality ⟨*coarse* imitations of quality merchandise⟩ — see CHEAP 2

coarseness *n* **1** the quality or state of being obscene ⟨the *coarseness* of the movie's humor makes it unsuitable for children⟩ — see OBSCENITY 1
2 the quality or state of lacking refinement or good taste ⟨there was a *coarseness* about her that really bothered her boyfriend's well-bred friends⟩ — see VULGARITY 1

coast *vb* to move or proceed smoothly and readily ⟨*coasting* along easily in the light traffic⟩ — see FLOW 2

coastal *adj* of, relating to, or situated in the waters near the shore ⟨in the summer, *coastal* traffic is significantly increased by pods of weekend yachtsmen⟩ — see INSHORE

coat *n* the hairy covering of a mammal especially when fine, soft, and thick ⟨a poodle's *coat* is often extremely curly⟩ — see FUR 1

coat *vb* to form a layer over ⟨thicken the sauce until it will *coat* the back of a spoon⟩ — see COVER 2

coax *vb* to get (someone) to do something by gentle urging, special attention, or flattery ⟨trying to *coax* their father into taking them on a ski trip, the teens mentioned what a great skier he is⟩
synonyms blandish, blarney, cajole, palaver, soft-soap, sweet-talk, wheedle
related words adulate, flatter, overpraise; butter up, charm, massage, woo; beg, beseech, importune, urge; beguile, cozen, finagle, juggle, wangle, wile; entice, lure, seduce, tempt
near antonyms bug, harass, nag, pester, tease; browbeat, bulldoze, bully, cow, intimidate; coerce, compel, constrain, demand, force, make, oblige, require

cobble (together *or* **up)** *vb* to make or assemble roughly or hastily ⟨the stranded hikers *cobbled together* a rickety shelter for the night⟩
synonyms jury-rig, patch (together), throw up
related words dash (off); jerry-build
phrases knock together, throw together
near antonyms craft, handcraft; fashion, forge, hammer out, pound (out)

cobwebby *adj* **1** being of a material lacking in sturdiness or substance ⟨wore a gown of *cobwebby* georgette⟩ — see FLIMSY 1
2 used or heard so often as to be dull ⟨*cobwebby* bits of cracker-barrel philosophy that were stale even 200 years ago⟩ — see STALE 1
3 very thin and easy to see through ⟨a *cobwebby* crocheted doily⟩ — see SHEER 1

[1]**cock** *n* a fixture for controlling the flow of a liquid ⟨an automobile radiator *cock*⟩ — see FAUCET

[2]**cock** *n* a quantity of things thrown or stacked on one another ⟨a *cock* of hay⟩ — see [1]PILE 1

[3]**cock** *n* the act of positioning or an instance of being positioned at an angle ⟨a slight *cock* of his head suggested that he was listening in on our conversation⟩ — see TILT

cock *vb* to set or cause to be at an angle ⟨*cocked* his head to the side as he listened to her quizzically⟩ — see LEAN 1

cock–a–hoop *adj* **1** having or expressing feelings of joy or triumph ⟨the district attorney's office was positively *cock-a-hoop* upon obtaining a conviction in the case against the mobster⟩ — see EXULTANT
2 inclined or twisted to one side ⟨topped with 50 burning candles all *cock-a-hoop* and dripping wax, the birthday cake made its dramatic appearance⟩ — see AWRY

Cockaigne *n* an often imaginary place or state of utter perfection and happiness ⟨many gourmets still regard Paris as a culinary *Cockaigne*⟩ — see PARADISE 1

cockalorum *n* **1** boastful speech or writing ⟨a boxer who was as famous for his prefight *cockalorum* as for his knockouts in the ring⟩ — see BOMBAST 1
2 someone who boasts ⟨Muhammad Ali's reputation as boxing's most colorful *cockalorum*⟩ — see BRAGGART

cockamamy *or* **cockamamie** *adj* so foolish or pointless as to be worthy of scornful laughter ⟨a *cockamamy* plan that could only have been dreamt up by a cartoonish mad scientist⟩ — see RIDICULOUS 1

cockcrow *n* the first appearance of light in the morning or the time of its appearance ⟨by *cockcrow* the mysterious stranger had vanished⟩ — see DAWN 1

cocker *vb* to treat with great or excessive care ⟨overjoyed to be parents at last, they will likely *cocker* that child shamelessly⟩ — see BABY

cockeyed *adj* **1** inclined or twisted to one side ⟨rakishly wears his hat a little *cockeyed*⟩ — see AWRY
2 showing or marked by a lack of good sense or judgment ⟨a *cockeyed* scheme to build a shopping mall in the middle of nowhere⟩ — see FOOLISH 1
3 being under the influence of alcohol ⟨don't trust a thing that Wilson tells you when he's *cockeyed*⟩ — see DRUNK

cockloft *n* a room or unfinished space directly beneath the roof of a building ⟨the ski chalet features additional sleeping quarters in its *cockloft*, which is accessible through a pull-down ladder⟩ — see ATTIC

cocksure *adj* **1** displaying or marked by rude boldness ⟨his *cocksure* assertion that he could bed any woman of his choice⟩ — see NERVY 1

2 having or showing a mind free from doubt ⟨you're always so *cocksure* about everything⟩ — see CERTAIN 2

cocksureness *n* a state of mind in which one is free from doubt ⟨the *cocksureness* with which he presented his investment scheme convinced others to jump in⟩ — see CONFIDENCE 2

cocktail *n* a distinct entity formed by the combining of two or more different things ⟨an autopsy found a lethal *cocktail* of banned substances in the actor's body⟩ — see BLEND

cocky *adj* displaying or marked by rude boldness ⟨a *cocky* young actor who thought that he was God's gift to the theater⟩ — see NERVY 1

cocoon *n* **1** something that encloses another thing especially to protect it ⟨he retired to the *cocoon* of his study whenever he'd had enough of the company⟩ — see [1]CASE 1

2 something that serves as a protective barrier ⟨as the TV had been packed in a *cocoon* of Styrofoam, it arrived in one piece⟩ — see CUSHION

cocoon *vb* to surround or cover closely ⟨*cocooned* in puffy down parkas, we braved the bitter cold as best we could⟩ — see ENFOLD 1

cocotte *n* a woman who engages in sexual activities for money ⟨in the new play, she takes on the somewhat racy role of a *cocotte* in fin de siècle Paris⟩ — see PROSTITUTE

coddle *vb* **1** to cook in a liquid heated to the point that it gives off steam ⟨a hearty, traditional breakfast that included *coddled* eggs⟩ — see BOIL 2

2 to treat with great or excessive care ⟨accused the judiciary of *coddling* criminals⟩ — see BABY

code *n* a collection or system of rules of conduct ⟨Hammurabi was an ancient king of Babylon with a famous *code* of laws⟩ ⟨the tax *code*⟩

synonyms canon, constitution, decalogue, law

related words discipline, establishment; common law, legislation

codger *n* a person of odd or whimsical habits ⟨just an old *codger* who never harmed anyone⟩ — see ECCENTRIC

codicil *n* a part added at the end of a book or periodical ⟨a *codicil* to the treaty was necessary to clarify certain provisos that had proved to be ambiguous⟩ — see ADDENDUM 1

codify *vb* **1** to arrange or assign according to type ⟨*codify* these ancient cultures according to their political structures⟩ — see CLASSIFY 1

2 to put into a particular arrangement ⟨the rules for the game were *codified* over a hundred years ago⟩ — see ORDER 1

codswallop *n, British* language, behavior, or ideas that are absurd and contrary to good sense ⟨a trendy London restaurant serving bizarre concoctions that anyone with a brain and a stomach would dismiss as *codswallop*⟩ — see NONSENSE 1

coequal *adj* resembling another in every respect ⟨in my mind illegally downloading a music file is *coequal* to stealing a CD from a store⟩ — see SAME 1

coequal *n* one that is equal to another in status, achievement, or value ⟨viewing himself as the *coequal* of the Caesars of ancient Rome, Napoléon surrounded himself with the emblems of classical antiquity⟩ — see EQUAL

coequality *n* the state or fact of being exactly the same in number, amount, status, or quality ⟨felt that the success of their marriage was due to the *coequality* of their positions, with neither one being master of the other⟩ — see EQUIVALENCE

coerce *vb* to cause (a person) to give in to pressure ⟨was *coerced* into signing the document⟩ — see FORCE 1

coerced *adj* not made or done willingly or by choice ⟨*coerced* participation that couldn't last⟩ — see INVOLUNTARY 1

coercion *n* the use of power to impose one's will on another ⟨a promise obtained by *coercion* is never binding⟩ — see FORCE 2

coetaneous *adj* existing or occurring at the same period of time ⟨the Spanish founding of San Francisco and the British colonies' declaration of independence from the mother country were *coetaneous* events that occurred on opposite ends of the continent⟩ — see CONTEMPORARY 1

coeval *adj* existing or occurring at the same period of time ⟨two stars thought to be *coeval* because they have nearly the same mass and brightness⟩ — see CONTEMPORARY 1

coeval *n* a person who lives at the same time or is about the same age as another ⟨somewhat surprisingly, Saint Patrick and Attila the Hun were *coevals*⟩ — see CONTEMPORARY

coexist *vb* to occur or exist at the same time ⟨two nations that should be able to *coexist* without conflict⟩ — see COINCIDE 1

coexistence *n* the occurrence or existence of several things at once ⟨the home video market could not long tolerate the *coexistence* of competing formats⟩ — see CONCURRENCE 1

coexistent *adj* **1** existing or occurring at the same period of time ⟨the theory that there were two *coexistent* hominids inhabiting that region⟩ — see CONTEMPORARY 1

2 present at the same time and place ⟨a disorder that is often *coexistent* with a deficiency of certain vitamins⟩ — see COINCIDENT 1

coexisting *adj* **1** existing or occurring at the same period of time ⟨*coexisting* but widely separated cultures that had no knowledge of one another⟩ — see CONTEMPORARY 1

2 present at the same time and place ⟨*coexisting* beliefs⟩ — see COINCIDENT 1

coextensive *adj* **1** occupying the same space ⟨South Dakota's Todd County is *coextensive* with the Rosebud Sioux Reservation⟩

synonyms coincident, coinciding, conterminous, coterminous

related words allover, overlaying, superimposed, superposed, underlying; conjoining, crisscrossing, intersecting, overlapping; coaxial, concurrent, convergent; congruent, conjunctional

near antonyms nonconcurrent, noncongruent

2 existing or occurring at the same period of time ⟨the golden age of Dutch culture was roughly *coextensive* with the Netherlands' reign as a world power⟩ — see CONTEMPORARY 1

coffer *n* **1** a specially reinforced container to keep valuables safe ⟨kept the jewels in a locked *coffer*⟩ — see SAFE

2 coffers *pl* available money ⟨let me see what's in the household *coffers* and I'll get back to you about making a donation⟩ — see FUND 2

coffin *n* a boxlike container for holding a dead body ⟨*coffins* are said to be the preferred sleeping places of vampires⟩

synonyms bier, box, casket, pall, sarcophagus

related words charnel (*also* charnel house), crypt, sepulchre (*or* sepulcher), sepulture, tomb, vault; urn; body bag

cogency *n* **1** the capacity to persuade ⟨the *cogency* of

Thomas Paine's celebrated case for American independence⟩

synonyms authority, conclusiveness, convincingness, effectiveness, force, forcefulness, persuasion, persuasiveness, suasiveness

related words impact, might, power, punch, strength, weight; believability, credibility, soundness, validity; authoritativeness, definitiveness; influence, sway; appeal, seductiveness

near antonyms invalidity, shakiness, unsoundness; feebleness, powerlessness, weakness

antonyms inconclusiveness, ineffectiveness, ineffectuality, ineffectualness

2 the quality of an utterance that provokes interest and produces an effect ⟨satirical comments of great *cogency*⟩ — see [1]PUNCH 1

cogent *adj* having the power to persuade ⟨the results of the DNA fingerprinting were the most *cogent* evidence for acquittal⟩

synonyms compelling, conclusive, convincing, decisive, effective, forceful, persuasive, satisfying, strong, telling

related words authoritative, definitive; sound, valid, well-founded; important, significant, weighty; material, pertinent, relevant

near antonyms groundless, invalid, shaky, unfounded, unsound; inconsequential, insignificant, unimportant; immaterial, irrelevant; feeble, weak

antonyms inconclusive, indecisive, ineffective, uncompelling, unconvincing, unpersuasive

cogitate *vb* to give serious and careful thought to ⟨by the time he finishes *cogitating* what to do with his life, it'll be almost over⟩ — see PONDER

cogitation *n* something imagined or pictured in the mind ⟨as long as there's a national deficit, interplanetary exploration will most likely remain an agreeable *cogitation* and nothing more⟩ — see IDEA 1

cogitative *adj* given to or marked by long, quiet thinking ⟨a *cogitative* woman who was given to long silences, even in the company of her own family⟩ — see CONTEMPLATIVE

cognate *adj* having qualities in common ⟨alcoholism and drug addiction are *cognate* disorders⟩ — see ALIKE

cognizance *n* **1** a state of being aware ⟨take *cognizance* of what is happening⟩ — see ATTENTION 2

2 knowledge gained by personal experience ⟨seemed to have no *cognizance* of last night's events⟩ — see ACQUAINTANCE

cognizant *adj* having specified facts or feelings actively impressed on the mind ⟨not fully *cognizant* of the details of the trade agreement⟩ — see CONSCIOUS 1

cognize *vb* to have a clear idea of ⟨the philosopher's claim that we can never *cognize*—in a fundamental sense—anything⟩ — see COMPREHEND 1

cognomen *n* **1** a descriptive or familiar name given instead of or in addition to the one belonging to an individual ⟨richly deserved the *cognomen* of "Butterfingers"⟩ — see NICKNAME

2 a word or combination of words by which a person or thing is regularly known ⟨"Christopher Columbus" is the Latinized *cognomen* of the navigator who was known to his Spanish crewmates as Cristóbal Colón⟩ — see NAME 1

cognoscente *n* **1** a person having a knowledgeable and fine appreciation of the arts ⟨a *cognoscente* of medieval painting⟩ — see CONNOISSEUR 1

2 a person with a high level of knowledge or skill in a field ⟨*cognoscenti* in the art world knew that most of the works being auctioned off were second-rate stuff⟩ — see EXPERT

cohere *vb* **1** to be in agreement on every point ⟨the account in his journal *coheres* with the official report of the battle⟩ — see CHECK 1

2 to form or enter into an association that furthers the interests of its members ⟨beset by personal animosities, the people of the neighborhood could not *cohere* into an effective civic association⟩ — see ALLY

coherence *n* a balanced, pleasing, or suitable arrangement of parts ⟨the house has been expanded and remodeled so many times that now it's a jumbled mess that lacks *coherence*⟩ — see HARMONY 1

coherent *adj* **1** according to the rules of logic ⟨a *coherent* blueprint to hooking up a home theater system with a minimum of fuss⟩ — see LOGICAL 1

2 capable of being understood ⟨the victim of the attack was too distraught to make a *coherent* statement⟩ — see INTELLIGIBLE

3 not having or showing any apparent conflict ⟨a business venture that is *coherent* with the company's long-range goals⟩ — see CONSISTENT

cohort *n* **1** a person frequently seen in the company of another ⟨if you're trying to give up drinking, your *cohorts* shouldn't be confirmed party animals⟩ — see ASSOCIATE 1

2 one associated with another in wrongdoing ⟨she and her *cohorts* were arrested for shoplifting⟩ — see ACCOMPLICE

coiffure *n* a style or arrangement of hair ⟨with his flashy suit and carefully sculpted *coiffure*, he looks like a slick car dealer⟩ — see HAIRDO

coil *n* a state of noisy, confused activity ⟨amidst the *coil* of the office renovations, we even managed to get some work done⟩ — see COMMOTION

coil *vb* to follow a circular or spiral course ⟨a vine *coiling* around a pillar⟩ — see WIND 1

coiling *adj* turning around an axis like the thread of a screw ⟨the *coiling* strands of rope⟩ — see SPIRAL

coin *n* something (as pieces of stamped metal or printed paper) customarily and legally used as a medium of exchange, a measure of value, or a means of payment ⟨seeking a job that pays plenty of *coin*⟩ — see MONEY 1

coinage *n* something (as a device) created for the first time through the use of the imagination ⟨this latest *coinage* from the minds who gave us the MP3 player⟩ — see INVENTION 1

coincide *vb* **1** to occur or exist at the same time ⟨the heaviest snowfall of the season *coincided* with the start of our weeklong ski vacation⟩

synonyms accompany, attend, coexist, concur, co-occur, synchronize

related words chance, hap, happen, transpire

near antonyms antedate, precede, predate; follow, succeed

2 to be in agreement on every point ⟨the two lists *coincide*⟩ — see CHECK 1

3 to have or come to the same opinion or point of view ⟨their wishes *coincide* exactly with my desire⟩ — see AGREE 1

coincidence *n* the occurrence or existence of several things at once ⟨the *coincidence* of the last note of the violin with the sound of the bell⟩ — see CONCURRENCE 1

coincident *adj* **1** present at the same time and place ⟨the hard economic times and the *coincident* increase in crime were a double strain on the city's social services⟩

synonyms accompanying, attendant, attending, coexistent, coexisting, coincidental, concomitant, concurrent

related words contemporaneous, contemporary, simultaneous, synchronous; associated, collateral, connected, linked, related; consequent, resultant, resulting; ensuing, following, subsequent; accidental, casual, chance, fluky (*also* flukey), fortuitous, freak, incident, incidental

near antonyms unassociated, unconnected, unrelated
2 occupying the same space ⟨a study to determine whether the areas with the highest family incomes were *coincident* with the locations boasting the highest percentage of college graduates⟩ — see COEXTENSIVE 1
3 existing or occurring at the same period of time ⟨*coincident* changes in the region's demographic makeup that were little noted at the time⟩ — see CONTEMPORARY 1

coincidental *adj* **1** existing or occurring at the same period of time ⟨the nearly *coincidental* deaths of Princess Diana and Mother Teresa⟩ — see CONTEMPORARY 1
2 present at the same time and place ⟨claims a connection between the proliferation of fast-food restaurants and the *coincidental* surge in the rate of obesity⟩ — see COINCIDENT 1

coincidentally *adv* at one and the same time ⟨the final stages of the Napoleonic Wars were fought *coincidentally* with the U.S.-British conflict known as the War of 1812⟩ — see TOGETHER 1

coincidently *adv* at one and the same time ⟨the outdoor concert is timed so that its rousing finale occurs *coincidently* with the setting of the summer sun⟩ — see TOGETHER 1

coinciding *adj* occupying the same space ⟨the *coinciding* bases of the two triangles⟩ — see COEXTENSIVE 1

coition *n* sexual union involving penetration of the vagina by the penis ⟨studied the frequency of *coition* in animals that mate for life⟩ — see SEXUAL INTERCOURSE

coitus *n* sexual union involving penetration of the vagina by the penis ⟨the act of *coitus* is the natural method by which conception occurs⟩ — see SEXUAL INTERCOURSE

col *n* a narrow opening between hillsides or mountains that can be used for passage ⟨a remote *col* in the Alps⟩ — see CANYON

cold *adj* **1** having a low or subnormal temperature ⟨the *cold* climate of the Yukon⟩ ⟨an unusually *cold* spring that was followed by a sweltering summer⟩
synonyms algid, arctic, bitter, bone-chilling, chill, chilly, coldish, cool, coolish, freezing, frigid, frosty, gelid, glacial, ice-cold, icy, nipping, nippy, numbing, polar, shivery, snappy, wintry (*also* wintery)
related words cryogenic, subfreezing, subzero, ultracold; cutting, keen, penetrating, piercing, sharp; bracing, brisk, crisp, invigorating, rigorous; chilled, cooled, frosted, frozen, iced, refrigerated, unheated
near antonyms lukewarm, tepid; heated, overheated, reheated, warmed; snug, toasty, warm; feverish, flushed, inflamed (*also* enflamed); canicular, equatorial, muggy, steamy, summery, tropical
antonyms ardent, blazing, boiling, broiling, burning, fervent, fervid, fiery, glowing, hot, igneous, molten, piping hot, red-hot, roasting, scalding, scorching, searing, seething, sizzling, sultry, sweltering, torrid, ultrahot, warming, white-hot
2 lacking in friendliness or warmth of feeling ⟨the prisoners got only a *cold* stare when they tried to befriend the guard⟩
synonyms antiseptic, arctic, brittle, chill, chilly, clammy, cold-blooded, cold-eyed, coldish, cool, frigid, frosty, frozen, gelid, glacial, hard-eyed, icy, unfriendly, unsympathetic, wintry (*also* wintery)
related words bloodless, coldhearted, hard-hearted, heartless, kindless, pitiless, uncaring, unfeeling; reserved, soulless, undemonstrative, unemotional, unresponsive; apathetic, indifferent, unenthusiastic, uninterested; aloof, detached, dispassionate, impersonal, offish, standoffish; antisocial, unsociable, unsocial
near antonyms compassionate, kind, kindhearted; demonstrative, emotional, expressive; eager, enthusiastic, passionate
antonyms cordial, friendly, genial, happy, hearty, sympathetic, warm, warm-blooded, warmhearted
3 having or showing a lack of friendliness or interest in others ⟨received a *cold* reception from the hostess⟩ — see COOL 1
4 having lost consciousness ⟨the boxer was out *cold* for a few minutes⟩ — see UNCONSCIOUS 1
5 causing or marked by an atmosphere lacking in cheer ⟨the couple practiced a *cold* civility with each other, but they hadn't had a heart-to-heart talk in years⟩ — see GLOOMY 1
6 no longer living ⟨paramedics tried to revive him, but he was already *cold*⟩ — see DEAD 1

cold *n* a weather condition marked by low temperatures ⟨the *cold* will stay with us for another day, then temperatures should rise⟩
synonyms cold wave, deep freeze, freeze, snap
related words cold front; frost; bite, chill, chilliness, chillness, coldness, frigidness, nip, wintriness
near antonyms dog days; torridity, torridness
antonyms heat, heat wave

cold-blooded *adj* **1** having or showing a lack of sympathy or tender feelings ⟨a *cold-blooded* criminal who never once showed an ounce of mercy to his victims⟩ — see HARD 1
2 lacking in friendliness or warmth of feeling ⟨the *cold-blooded* selfishness shown by the miser when confronted by people in need⟩ — see COLD 2
3 not feeling or showing emotion ⟨a *cold-blooded* assessment of the situation showed that the company needed either to lay off workers or go bankrupt⟩ — see IMPASSIVE 1
4 *or* **coldblood** being offspring produced by parents of different races, breeds, species, or genera ⟨he may not be as fancy as the other horses they own, but that *cold-blooded* gelding is safe and gentle⟩ — see MIXED 1

cold-eyed *adj* **1** having or showing a lack of friendliness or interest in others ⟨the attendant's *cold-eyed* stare discouraged any thoughts about having a conversation⟩ — see COOL 1
2 lacking in friendliness or warmth of feeling ⟨under the *cold-eyed* gaze of the director, I auditioned for the part⟩ — see COLD 2

cold fish *n* a cold aloof person ⟨her husband is such a *cold fish* that I'm reluctant to have them over for dinner⟩
synonyms cold turkey, iceberg, icicle
related words clam, stick, wallflower; prig, snob, snoot, snot, stuffed shirt
near antonyms dear, sweetheart, sweetie

coldish *adj* **1** having a low or subnormal temperature ⟨believe it or not, the weather was *coldish* the whole time we were in Florida⟩ — see COLD 1
2 lacking in friendliness or warmth of feeling ⟨a *coldish* reply that told me that she wasn't prepared to bury the hatchet just yet⟩ — see COLD 2

coldness *n* the absence of emotional involvement ⟨her clinical *coldness* allows her to function in a job where she sees human misery every day⟩ — see COOL 1

cold-shoulder *vb* to deliberately ignore or treat rudely ⟨*cold-shouldered* by his old friends after his family had lost all of its money⟩ — see SNUB 1

cold shoulder *n* treatment that is deliberately unfriendly ⟨at the party the two former friends consciously gave each other the *cold shoulder*⟩
synonyms brush-off, rebuff, repulse, silent treatment, snub
related words dismissal, kiss-off, rejection; banishment, blackball, ostracism

near antonyms acceptance, embrace, welcome; glad hand, welcome mat
antonyms open arms

cold storage *n* a state of temporary inactivity ⟨the president's domestic programs had been in *cold storage* while he attended to a string of international crises⟩ — see ABEYANCE

cold turkey *n* a cold aloof person ⟨my new boss is a *cold turkey* and definitely not one for chitchat⟩ — see COLD FISH

cold wave *n* a weather condition marked by low temperatures ⟨the unseasonable *cold wave* in the Northeast has already put a strain on oil supplies⟩ — see COLD

coliseum *n* a large usually roofless building for sporting events with tiers of seats for spectators ⟨the local *coliseum* is a standard stop for rock bands on tour⟩ — see STADIUM

collaborate *vb* to participate or assist in a joint effort to accomplish an end ⟨a trio of museums *collaborated* to mount this once-in-a-lifetime exhibit of van Gogh's major portraits⟩ — see COOPERATE 1

collaboration *n* **1** the state of having shared interests or efforts (as in social or business matters) ⟨a documentary film on the battle that was produced in *collaboration* with a society of historical reenactors⟩ — see ASSOCIATION 1
2 the work and activity of a number of persons who individually contribute toward the efficiency of the whole ⟨our *collaboration* produced a better result than any of us could have achieved alone⟩ — see TEAMWORK

collaborative *adj* used or done by a number of people as a group ⟨a culture in which the raising of children is regarded as a *collaborative* endeavor for a whole village⟩ — see COLLECTIVE

collage *n* an unorganized collection or mixture of various things ⟨my scrapbook is just a *collage* of articles, pictures, cartoons, and observations that I have deemed worth saving⟩ — see MISCELLANY 1

collapse *n* **1** a complete depletion of energy or strength ⟨suffered a mental *collapse* under the strain of studying for his bar exam⟩ — see FATIGUE 1
2 a falling short of one's goals ⟨the complete *collapse* of the invasion set off a round of finger-pointing and recrimination⟩ — see FAILURE 2

collapse *vb* **1** to fall down or in as a result of physical pressure ⟨the motel balcony *collapsed* under the weight of so many people⟩
synonyms buckle, cave (in), crumple, founder, give, go, go out, implode, tumble, yield
related words deflate, flatten, melt, melt down; break, break down, conk (out), crash, die, fail, give out, stall; burst, shatter, smash, splinter, split; crack, crumble, pop, snap
phrases give way
near antonyms inflate, rise, swell
2 to be unsuccessful ⟨the legal case *collapsed* in the face of the opposition's evidence⟩ — see FAIL 2
3 to reduce in size or volume by or as if by pressing parts or members together ⟨the novel *collapses* events from four separate trips into one long odyssey⟩ — see COMPRESS 1

collar *n* **1** an ornamental chain or string (as of beads) worn around the neck ⟨a simple gold *collar* is all that little black cocktail dress needs⟩ — see NECKLACE
2 the act of taking or holding under one's control by authority of law ⟨when the murderer was finally apprehended, the detective who doggedly checked every single lead got credit for the *collar*⟩ — see ARREST 1

collar *vb* **1** to take or keep under one's control by authority of law ⟨the juvenile delinquent was *collared* for robbing houses⟩ — see ARREST 1
2 to take physical control or possession of (something) suddenly or forcibly ⟨she *collared* the boy before he could get into the cookie jar⟩ — see CATCH 1

colleague *n* a fellow worker ⟨on her first day at work her *colleagues* went out of their way to make her feel welcome⟩
synonyms associate, confrere (*also* confrère), coworker
related words equal, fellow, peer; accomplice, ally, cohort, collaborator, confederate, copartner, half, partner; buddy, chum, companion, comrade, crony, pal; compatriot, countryman

collect *vb* **1** to gain emotional or mental control of ⟨applicants should *collect* their thoughts while waiting to be interviewed⟩
synonyms calm, compose, contain, control, re-collect, settle
related words hold back, restrain; rally, recover; lull, quiet, soothe, still, tranquilize (*also* tranquillize)
2 to gradually form into a layer, pile, or mass ⟨dust has been *collecting* under my bed for years⟩
synonyms accrete, accumulate, amass, build up, concentrate, conglomerate, gather, mass, pile (up), stack (up)
related words agglutinate, clump, lump; bank, drift, ridge
near antonyms disperse, dissipate, scatter
3 to bring together from several sources into a single volume or list ⟨*collected* the author's early short stories, which were originally published in several obscure sci-fi magazines⟩ — see COMPILE
4 to bring together in one body or place ⟨she *collects* antique silverware⟩ — see GATHER 1
5 to come together into one body or place ⟨a crowd *collected* at the beach as the sun slowly set over the horizon⟩ — see ASSEMBLE 1

collectanea *n* a collection of writings ⟨in the library I discovered a three-volume *collectanea* containing all of the author's known writings⟩ — see ANTHOLOGY

collected *adj* free from emotional or mental agitation ⟨stayed calm and *collected* while she was in the MRI unit⟩ — see CALM 2

collectedly *adv* with everyone or everything taken into account at the same time ⟨*collectedly*, the fund-raisers for the museum raised $300,000⟩ — see ALL AROUND

collectedness *n* evenness of emotions or temper ⟨with the *collectedness* of an old pro, the new governor responded to the other hostile questions of the press corps⟩ — see EQUANIMITY

collection *n* **1** an organized group of objects acquired and maintained for study, exhibition, or personal pleasure ⟨his stamp *collection* has become quite valuable⟩
synonyms assemblage, library
related words assortment, kaleidoscope, miscellanea, mixed bag, omnium-gatherum, phantasmagoria, treasure, treasure trove, trove; arsenal, cache, hoard, repertoire, repertory, reserve, stock, stockpile, store, supply; accumulation, assembly, gathering
near antonyms bric-a-brac, clutter, heap, jumble, litter, pile, ragbag
2 a mass or quantity that has piled up or that has been gathered over a period of time ⟨a *collection* of lint underneath the dryer⟩ — see ACCUMULATION 1
3 a number of things considered as a unit ⟨the historic village boasts an interesting *collection* of gift shops and antique stores⟩ — see GROUP 1

collective *adj* used or done by a number of people as a group ⟨the cleanup of the neighborhood park was a *collective* effort for which many people should be thanked⟩
synonyms collaborative, combined, common, communal, concerted, conjoint, conjunct, cooperative, joint, multiple, mutual, pooled, public, shared, united

related words bilateral, consensual, reciprocal, symbiotic, synergic, synergistic, two-way; mass, popular; general, generic, universal
near antonyms personal, private; independent, separate, several; esoteric, particular, special, specialized
antonyms exclusive, individual, one-man, one-sided, one-way, single, sole, solitary, unilateral

collectively *adv* with everyone or everything taken into account at the same time ⟨*collectively*, the firm's partners have 107 years of experience⟩ — see ALL AROUND

college *n* a group of persons formally joined together for some common interest ⟨a *college* of craftsmen dedicated to preserving the traditional crafts of Appalachia⟩ — see ASSOCIATION 2

collegial *adj* having or showing kindly feeling and sincere interest ⟨company luncheons that are designed to instill a *collegial* spirit among coworkers⟩ — see FRIENDLY 1

collide *vb* **1** to be out of harmony or agreement usually noticeably ⟨a story of what happens when modern American mores and traditional Asian values *collide*⟩ — see CLASH
2 to come into usually forceful contact with something ⟨fortunately, I wasn't hurt when my bike *collided* with that fence⟩ — see HIT 2

collision *n* **1** a forceful coming together of two things ⟨the *collision* of two opposing philosophies regarding the rearing of children⟩ — see IMPACT 1
2 the violent coming together of two bodies into destructive contact ⟨a horrendous car *collision* on the highway⟩ — see CRASH 1

colloquial *adj* **1** used in or suitable for speech and not formal writing ⟨the new coworker's rudeness soon began—to use a *colloquial* expression—to rub me the wrong way⟩
synonyms conversational, informal, nonformal, nonliterary, unbookish, unliterary, vernacular, vulgar
related words dialectal, dialectical (*also* dialectic), nonstandard, regional; incorrect, nongrammatical, substandard, uneducated, ungrammatical, unlearned; slang, slangy
near antonyms standard, undialectical; correct, educated, genteel, grammatical, proper
antonyms bookish, formal, learned, literary
2 having the style and content of everyday conversation ⟨a *colloquial* essay on what makes a marriage successful⟩ — see CHATTY 1

colloquy *n* **1** a meeting featuring a group discussion ⟨attended a *colloquy* on economic globalization⟩ — see FORUM 1
2 an exchange of views for the purpose of exploring a subject or deciding an issue ⟨the subject of the spirited *colloquy* was the disputed authorship of the plays attributed to Shakespeare⟩ — see DISCUSSION 1
3 talking or a talk between two or more people ⟨a casual *colloquy* between two old colleagues in the faculty lounge⟩ — see CONVERSATION

collude *vb* to engage in a secret plan to accomplish evil or unlawful ends ⟨accused of *colluding* to block the sale of the vacant land⟩ — see PLOT

collusion *n* a secret agreement or cooperation between two parties for an illegal or dishonest purpose ⟨there was *collusion* between the two companies to fix prices⟩
synonyms complicity, connivance, conspiracy
related words chicanery, foul play, skulduggery (*or* skullduggery); double-dealing, duplicity; cover-up, frame-up, setup; conspiration, intrigue, plot, scheme

collywobbles *n pl* abdominal pain especially when focused in the digestive organs ⟨her heavy meals always give me the *collywobbles*⟩ — see STOMACHACHE

Colonel Blimp *n* a person with old-fashioned ideas ⟨felt like a *Colonel Blimp* who had outlived his time⟩ — see FOGY

colonial *adj* tending to group with others of the same kind ⟨*colonial* organisms⟩
synonyms gregarious, sociable, social
related words associational, consociational, subsocial; dependent, parasitic (*also* parasitical), precocial, symbiotic
near antonyms autonomous, independent, self-contained, semiautonomous, semi-independent; altricial, self-subsistent, self-sufficient, self-supporting, self-sustaining; lone, recluse, reclusive, unsociable
antonyms nonsocial, solitary

colonial *n* a person who settles in a new region ⟨European *colonials* who built coffee plantations in East Africa⟩ — see FRONTIERSMAN

colonist *n* a person who settles in a new region ⟨over time the *colonists* began to sense that they were becoming a people unto themselves⟩ — see FRONTIERSMAN

colonize *vb* to supply with inhabitants ⟨citizens who were sent abroad to *colonize* the conquered lands⟩ — see SETTLE 2

colonizer *n* a person who settles in a new region ⟨the first *colonizers* of Easter Island must have faced untold challenges⟩ — see FRONTIERSMAN

colony *n* **1** a settlement in a new country or region ⟨the early history of New York City when it was a Dutch *colony*⟩
synonyms plantation
related words camp, diaspora, exclave, habitation, outpost, post; dependency, mandate, possession, protectorate, territory
2 a group of people with a common interest living in one place ⟨New Hampshire's MacDowell *colony* was founded as a summer residence for writers and composers⟩ — see COMMUNITY 2

color *n* **1** a property that becomes apparent when light falls on an object and by which things that are identical in form can be distinguished ⟨a shirt that is available in every *color* of the rainbow⟩
synonyms cast, hue, shade, tincture, tinge, tint, tone
related words overtone, undertone; primary color, secondary color, tertiary color; brightness, chroma, chromaticity, contrast, lightness, saturation, value; coloration, coloring, colorway, pigmentation
near antonyms achromatism
2 a substance used to color other materials ⟨added some red *color* to the base paint⟩ — see PIGMENT
3 the hue or appearance of the skin and especially of the face ⟨her *color* hasn't been good since she got sick⟩ — see COMPLEXION 1
4 colors *pl* a piece of cloth with a special design that is used as an emblem or for signaling ⟨flew their country's *colors* atop the highest mast on the ship⟩ — see FLAG 1
5 a rosy appearance (of the cheeks) ⟨the stay in the country brought *color* to her cheeks⟩ — see BLOOM 2
6 colors *pl* the combined army, air force, and navy of a nation ⟨she hopes to carry on the family tradition and serve with the *colors*⟩ — see ARMED FORCES
7 colors *pl* the set of qualities that makes a person, a group of people, or a thing different from others ⟨we saw his true *colors* during the emergency⟩ — see NATURE 1

color *vb* **1** to give color or a different color to ⟨she's *colored* her hair for so long and so often that no one knows what her natural color is⟩
synonyms bepaint [*archaic*], dye, paint, pigment, stain, tincture, tinge, tint
related words brighten, lighten; darken, embrown, tone (down); checker, dapple, daub, fleck, marble, mottle, pattern, polychrome, speck, speckle, streak, striate, stripe, variegate

near antonyms blanch, bleach, whiten
antonyms decolorize
2 to add to the interest of by including made-up details ⟨he gave a highly *colored* version of a rather mundane experience⟩ — see EMBROIDER
3 to change so much as to create a wrong impression or alter the meaning of ⟨his news reporting is *colored* by his prejudices⟩ — see GARBLE 1
4 to develop a rosy facial color (as from excitement or embarrassment) ⟨she *colored* after hearing the nasty remarks about her weight⟩ — see BLUSH

colorant *n* a substance used to color other materials ⟨in ancient times, a mollusk was used to produce a rich purple *colorant* for clothing and linens⟩ — see PIGMENT

colored *adj* marked by a variety of usually vivid colors ⟨the highly *colored* glassware that is the studio's hallmark⟩ — see COLORFUL

colorful *adj* marked by a variety of usually vivid colors ⟨the *colorful* robes and blankets of the Native Americans of the Southwest⟩
synonyms chromatic, colored, kaleidoscopic, motley, multicolored, multihued, polychromatic, polychrome, prismatic, rainbow, varicolored, varied, variegated, various
related words iridescent, opalescent; brave, bright, brilliant, gay, vibrant; flashy, garish, gaudy, loud, showy, splashy; checkered, dotted, patterned, plaid, plaided, striped; dappled (*also* dapple), marbled, mottled, parti-color (*or* parti-colored), piebald, pied, pinto; flecked, specked, speckled, spotted; banded, barred, brindled (*or* brindle), streaked, striated; bichrome, bicolored (*or* bicolor), dichromatic, trichromatic, tricolor (*or* tricolored), two-tone, two-toned
near antonyms achromatic; bleached, decolorized, faded, washed-out; dull, faint, gray (*also* grey), neutral, pale, pallid, unbrilliant
antonyms colorless; monochromatic, monochromic, monotone, self-colored, solid

colorfully *adv* in a manner that is colorful and tends to arouse gaiety ⟨a *colorfully* illustrated children's alphabet book⟩ — see GAILY 3

coloring *n* **1** a substance used to color other materials ⟨added more *coloring* to the buttercream frosting to get the perfect shade of blue⟩ — see PIGMENT
2 the hue or appearance of the skin and especially of the face ⟨the pale *coloring* of people of Irish descent⟩ — see COMPLEXION 1
3 the representation of something in terms that go beyond the facts ⟨the unexciting facts were given a sensational *coloring* in the local news⟩ — see EXAGGERATION

colorless *adj* **1** lacking an addition of color ⟨since we can't decide what color to paint the doghouse, our latest home project remains *colorless* for the time being⟩
synonyms tintless [*archaic*], uncolored, undyed, unpainted, unstained, white
related words clear, limpid, liquid, lucent, pellucid, transparent; bleached, faded, palish, washed-out, washy; dull, faint, gray (*also* grey), neutral, pale, pallid; snow-white, snowy, whited
near antonyms colorful, multicolored, polychromatic, polychrome, varicolored, variegated
antonyms colored, colorized, dyed, hued, painted, pigmented, stained, tinct, tinctured, tinged, tinted
2 causing weariness, restlessness, or lack of interest ⟨page after page of *colorless* prose without even one neat turn of phrase⟩ — see BORING

colossal *adj* unusually large ⟨a *colossal* statue of the town's founder⟩ — see HUGE

colossally *adv* **1** to a great degree ⟨after reading all the praise from critics, I found the play to be *colossally* disappointing⟩ — see VERY 1
2 to a large extent or degree ⟨the most *colossally* rude person she had ever met⟩ — see GREATLY 2

colosseum *n* a large usually roofless building for sporting events with tiers of seats for spectators ⟨run 10 laps around the *colosseum*⟩ — see STADIUM

colossus *n* something that is unusually large and powerful ⟨Leonardo da Vinci remains a *colossus* in the history of art⟩ — see GIANT

colt *n* a person who is just starting out in a field of activity ⟨a *colt* who looked to the team's more experienced players for advice⟩ — see BEGINNER

coltish *adj* given to good-natured joking or teasing ⟨off camera the actor is high-spiritedly *coltish*, but turns serious once the camera starts rolling⟩ — see PLAYFUL

coltishness *n* a natural disposition for playful behavior ⟨although she's now in her 30s, she still displays the *coltishness* of a high-spirited teenager⟩ — see PLAYFULNESS

column *n* **1** a series of persons or things arranged one behind another ⟨a *column* of ants stretched between the fallen hot dog and the ant hill⟩ — see LINE 1
2 an upright shaft that supports an overhead structure ⟨engraved *columns* supported the arch on either side⟩ — see PILLAR 1

coma *n* a temporary or permanent state of unconsciousness ⟨the girl lay in a *coma* for three days after the accident⟩ — see FAINT

comatose *adj* lacking in gaiety, movement, or animation ⟨the city's downtown has been *comatose* for years⟩ — see DEAD 2

comb *vb* to look through (as a place) carefully or thoroughly in an effort to find or discover something ⟨*combed* the library for the missing book⟩ — see SEARCH 1

combat *n* **1** active fighting during the course of a war ⟨a soldier who served throughout the war without actually seeing *combat*⟩
synonyms action, battle, field
related words attack, fire, firefight, pitched battle, single combat; hostilities, operations, warfare; duty, service
2 a physical dispute between opposing individuals or groups ⟨the two stags entered a furious *combat* for dominance of the herd⟩ — see FIGHT 1
3 an earnest effort for superiority or victory over another ⟨the fierce ideological *combat* between the religionists and the secularists⟩ — see CONTEST 1

combat *vb* **1** to oppose (someone) in physical conflict ⟨a general eager to *combat* the enemy on his own ground⟩ — see FIGHT 1
2 to strive to reduce or eliminate ⟨must marshal all of our resources to *combat* this disease⟩ — see FIGHT 2

combative *adj* feeling or displaying eagerness to fight ⟨channeling his naturally *combative* impulses into sports⟩ — see BELLIGERENT

combativeness *n* an inclination to fight or quarrel ⟨the boxer was known more for his unbridled *combativeness* than for his technical skill⟩ — see BELLIGERENCE

combination *n* **1** a distinct entity formed by the combining of two or more different things ⟨a victory that was due to a *combination* of luck and planning⟩ — see BLEND
2 the act or an instance of joining two or more things into one ⟨the *combination* of mint and chocolate in a delicious dessert⟩ — see UNION 1
3 a number of businesses or enterprises united for commercial advantage ⟨the companies formed a *combination* in an attempt to establish a monopoly in the rubber market⟩ — see CARTEL
4 an association of persons, parties, or states for mutual assistance and protection ⟨a *combination* of citizens

dedicated to fighting higher property taxes⟩ — see CONFEDERACY

combine *n* **1** a number of businesses or enterprises united for commercial advantage ⟨charged that the cable companies had formed an illegal *combine* for the purpose of keeping rates artificially high⟩ — see CARTEL

2 an association of persons, parties, or states for mutual assistance and protection ⟨one of the most notorious *combines* in the history of organized crime⟩ — see CONFEDERACY

combine *vb* **1** to come together to form a single unit ⟨the room's highly varied design elements *combine* to form a harmonious whole⟩ — see UNITE 1

2 to turn into a single mass or entity that is more or less the same throughout ⟨*combine* the sugar and flour in a bowl⟩ — see BLEND 1

combined *adj* used or done by a number of people as a group ⟨a *combined* effort on the part of all of the members⟩ — see COLLECTIVE

combining *n* the act or an instance of joining two or more things into one ⟨abhors the *combining* of business and pleasure at sales conferences⟩ — see UNION 1

combust *vb* to be on fire especially brightly ⟨anthracite, which is naturally hard, *combusts* more cleanly than bituminous coal⟩ — see BURN 1

combustible *adj* capable of catching or being set on fire ⟨don't store oily rags and other *combustible* materials in a hot attic⟩

synonyms burnable, combustive, fiery, flammable, ignitable (*also* ignitible), inflammable, touchy

related words explosive, incendiary

near antonyms nonexplosive

antonyms fireproof, incombustible, nonburnable, noncombustible, nonflammable, noninflammable, unburnable

combusting *adj* being on fire ⟨*combusting* oxygen tanks turned the fire on the evacuees' bus into a raging inferno⟩ — see ABLAZE 1

combustive *adj* capable of catching or being set on fire ⟨with such a highly *combustive* inventory, the ropewalk was engulfed in flames in a matter of minutes⟩ — see COMBUSTIBLE

come *vb* **1** to move closer to ⟨*come* here and sit by the fire⟩

synonyms advance, approach, near, nigh

related words drop in, enter, pop (in)

near antonyms depart, exit, leave

antonyms go, recede (from), retreat, withdraw

2 to get to a destination ⟨when do you think they'll *come*?⟩

synonyms appear, arrive, get in, get through, land, show up, turn up

related words fetch, hit, make, reach; pull in, touch down; debark, disembark; barge (in), blow in, breeze (in), burst (in *or* into), waltz (in); check in, clock (in)

near antonyms check out, clock (out); flee, vamoose

antonyms go, leave

3 to eventually have as a state or quality ⟨your dreams can *come* true⟩ — see BECOME

4 to take place ⟨whatever may *come* we'll always be together⟩ — see HAPPEN

5 to move forward along a course ⟨how is the remodeling job *coming*?⟩ — see GO 1

come (to) *vb* **1** to have a total of ⟨your bill *comes to* $53.74⟩ — see AMOUNT (TO) 1

2 to be the same in meaning or effect ⟨it all *comes to* nothing in the end⟩ — see AMOUNT (TO) 2

3 to enter the mind of ⟨the actual name of the item didn't *come to* me until I was walking out of the store⟩ — see OCCUR (TO)

come about *vb* to take place ⟨how did all this *come about*?⟩ — see HAPPEN

come across (as) *vb* to give the impression of being ⟨the law professor *comes across as* a bit of an ogre at first, but he's actually quite personable⟩ — see SEEM

come along *vb* to move forward along a course ⟨our backyard makeover is *coming along* nicely⟩ — see GO 1

come around *vb* to gain consciousness again ⟨she *came around* surprisingly quickly after falling off the horse⟩ — see COME TO

comeback *n* **1** a quick witty response ⟨always ready with a *comeback* for every insult⟩ — see RETORT 1

2 something spoken or written in reaction especially to a question ⟨regardless of the question posed by the prosecutor, the witness had a plausible *comeback*⟩ — see ANSWER 1

3 the process or period of gradually regaining one's health and strength ⟨trying to make a *comeback* after a career-threatening injury⟩ — see CONVALESCENCE

come back *vb* **1** to become healthy and strong again after illness or weakness ⟨she's slowly *coming back* after being in a coma⟩ — see CONVALESCE

2 to regain a former or normal state ⟨the American bald eagle was once nearly extinct but has *come back* strong⟩ — see RECOVER 2

3 to speak or write in reaction to a question or to another reaction ⟨he *came back* with another one of his smart remarks⟩ — see ANSWER 1

come by *vb* **1** to make a brief visit ⟨*come by* after work and I'll give you some clothes for the rummage sale⟩ — see CALL 3

2 to receive as return for effort ⟨a literary award like that isn't easy to *come by*⟩ — see EARN 1

comedian *n* a person (as a writer) noted for or specializing in humor ⟨struggled to eke out a living as a *comedian* in nightclubs⟩ — see HUMORIST

comedic *adj* causing or intended to cause laughter ⟨my friends insist that this new television show is the most *comedic* thing ever created by the mind of man⟩ — see FUNNY 1

comedown *n* a loss of status ⟨after a rapid rise to stardom, the rock band's *comedown* was just as quick⟩

synonyms decline, dégringolade, demise, descent, down, downfall, fall, flameout, Götterdämmerung

related words breakdown, burnout, collapse, crash, meltdown, ruin, undoing; defeat, disappointment, reversal, setback; bottom, nadir; abasement, disgrace, humiliation

near antonyms advance, headway, progress; flower, heyday, prime

antonyms aggrandizement, ascent, exaltation, rise, up

come down *vb* to take place ⟨let's wait and see what *comes down* at the meeting⟩ — see HAPPEN

come down (with) *vb* to become affected with (a disease or disorder) ⟨I hope that you're not *coming down with* a cold⟩ — see CONTRACT 1

comedy *n* **1** humorous entertainment ⟨presented a night of *comedy* as part of the weeklong celebrations⟩

synonyms farce, humor, slapstick

related words high comedy, low comedy; burlesque, parody, satire; improv, stand-up; banter, drollery, persiflage, wit; foolery, fun, horseplay, knockabout, monkeyshine(s), shenanigan(s)

2 the amusing quality or element in something ⟨I just don't see the *comedy* in someone flunking a driving test that they really needed to pass⟩ — see HUMOR 1

comeliness *n* the qualities in a person or thing that as a whole give pleasure to the senses ⟨a verdant countryside of uncommon *comeliness*⟩ — see BEAUTY 1

comely *adj* very pleasing to look at ⟨a brood of *comely* children that any parent would be proud to claim⟩ — see BEAUTIFUL 1

come off *vb* **1** to take place ⟨couldn't believe that the wedding would actually *come off*—they've been "just dating" for years⟩ — see HAPPEN
2 to turn out as planned or desired ⟨the attempted revival of the city's downtown never really *came off*, and even more stores eventually closed⟩ — see SUCCEED 1

come off (as) *vb* to give the impression of being ⟨she is an intelligent debater, but she can sometimes *come off as* arrogant⟩ — see SEEM

come–on *n* something that persuades one to perform an action for pleasure or gain ⟨the spectacular sale was enough of a *come-on* to get many shoppers to try the store for the first time⟩ — see LURE 1

come on *interj* how surprising, doubtful, or unbelievable ⟨*come on*, you can't be serious in making such an offer!⟩ — see NO

come out *vb* **1** to come to be ⟨in the end everything *came out* OK⟩
synonyms fall out, pan out, prove, shake out, turn out
related words develop, emerge, evolve, germinate, play out, unfold, work out
2 to come into view ⟨*come out, come out* wherever you are!⟩ — see APPEAR 1
3 to become known ⟨if the truth of his sexuality ever *came out*, the actor's career would be ruined⟩ — see GET OUT 1

come over *vb* to make a brief visit ⟨*come over* sometime and I'll show you my roses⟩ — see CALL 3

come round *vb* **1** to gain consciousness again ⟨the medic waved smelling salts under his nose until he *came round*⟩ — see COME TO
2 to give or express one's approval (as to a proposal) ⟨she's cool to the idea right now, but sooner or later she'll *come round*⟩ — see ACCEDE

comestible *adj* suitable for use as food ⟨some mushrooms are comfortably *comestible*, but others are decidedly poisonous⟩ — see EDIBLE

comestibles *n pl* substances intended to be eaten ⟨the gourmet food shop stocks a wide variety of *comestibles* from around the world⟩ — see FOOD 1

come to *vb* to gain consciousness again ⟨after being in a coma for months, the patient quite unexpectedly *came to*⟩
synonyms come around, come round, revive
related words pull through, rally, recover; awake, awaken, wake up
near antonyms black out, faint, pass out

come up *vb* **1** to come near or nearer ⟨the girl *came up* to the counter and asked if she could have her order prepared to go⟩ — see APPROACH 1
2 to come to one's attention especially gradually or unexpectedly ⟨let me know if anything else *comes up* during the project⟩ — see ARISE 2

comeuppance *n* suffering, loss, or hardship imposed in response to a crime or offense ⟨as with many action movies, this one ends with a wild chase and an over-the-top fight sequence in which the bad guys finally get their *comeuppance*⟩ — see PUNISHMENT

comfort *n* **1** a feeling of ease from grief or trouble ⟨the mourners found *comfort* in their pastor's words⟩
synonyms cheer, consolation, relief, solace
related words encouragement, inspiration, uplift; assurance, reassurance; alleviation, assuagement, mitigation; contentment, gladness, happiness; commiseration, empathy, sympathy; aid, assistance, help, succor
near antonyms cold comfort; anguish, distress, heartache, heartbreak, torment, torture
2 something that adds to one's ease of living ⟨a family campground with all the *comforts* of home⟩
synonyms accommodation, amenity, convenience, creature comfort, luxury, mod con [*chiefly British*], nicety
related words bonus, extra; benefit, help, service; anodyne, solace; delight, indulgence, joy, pleasure
antonyms burden, millstone, weight
3 reduction of or freedom from pain ⟨a life of *comfort*⟩ — see EASE 1
4 something adding to pleasure or comfort but not absolutely necessary ⟨a hotel room featuring an array of domestic *comforts*⟩ — see LUXURY 1

comfort *vb* to ease the grief or distress of ⟨the minister did his best to *comfort* the victims of the terrible tornado⟩
synonyms assure, cheer, console, reassure, solace, soothe
related words commiserate, condole, empathize, sympathize; boost, buoy (up), elevate, lift, uplift; allay, alleviate, assuage, relieve; calm, quiet, relax, tranquilize (*also* tranquillize)
near antonyms demoralize, discourage, dishearten; fret, upset, worry; aggravate, intensify, worsen; annoy, irk, irritate; harass, pester
antonyms distress, torment, torture, trouble

comfortable *adj* **1** providing physical comfort ⟨a large, overstuffed chair that is very *comfortable*⟩
synonyms comfy, cozy, cushy, easy, snug, soft
related words easeful, relaxing, reposeful, restful; gemütlich, genial, hospitable, inviting, pleasant; commodious, roomy, spacious; homelike, homely, homey (*also* homy), intimate
near antonyms hard, harsh, severe; inhospitable, uninviting, unpleasant
antonyms uncomfortable
2 enjoying physical comfort ⟨make yourself *comfortable* in the living room while I fix us some snacks⟩
synonyms canny [*chiefly Scottish*], comfy, cozy, relaxed, snug
related words toasty, warm; content, contented, pleased, satisfied; easeful, peaceful, resting; easygoing, laid-back; undisturbed, unperturbed, untroubled
phrases at ease, at home
near antonyms discontented, displeased, dissatisfied; agitated, disturbed, perturbed, troubled
antonyms uncomfortable
3 being more than enough without being excessive ⟨enjoying retirement with a *comfortable* income⟩ — see PLENTIFUL

comforting *adj* **1** making one feel good inside ⟨the *comforting* smell of fresh bread⟩ — see HEARTWARMING
2 tending to calm the emotions and relieve stress ⟨a long *comforting* soak in a hot bath⟩ — see SOOTHING 1

comforting *n* the giving of hope and strength in times of grief, distress, or suffering ⟨the *comforting* of the sick has always been regarded as one of the major acts of charity⟩ — see CONSOLATION 1

comfortless *adj* **1** causing discomfort ⟨one of those modern *comfortless* sofas that are more pleasurable to look at than to sit on⟩ — see UNCOMFORTABLE 1
2 causing or marked by an atmosphere lacking in cheer ⟨spent a night in a sleazy *comfortless* hotel⟩ — see GLOOMY 1

comfort station *n* a room furnished with a fixture for flushing body waste ⟨a theme park abundantly supplied with *comfort stations*⟩ — see TOILET

comfy *adj* **1** providing physical comfort ⟨couldn't wait to return home and sleep in his own *comfy* bed⟩ — see COMFORTABLE 1
2 enjoying physical comfort ⟨customers are not likely to get too *comfy* in the restaurant's unforgiving chairs⟩ — see COMFORTABLE 2

comic *adj* causing or intended to cause laughter ⟨a *comic* monologue about his misadventures as a first-time camper⟩ — see FUNNY 1

comic *n* **1** a person (as a writer) noted for or specializing in humor ⟨a well-known TV *comic*⟩ — see HUMORIST
2 a series of drawings that tell a story or part of a story ⟨posted an especially funny *comic* by the watercooler⟩ — see COMIC STRIP
3 the amusing quality or element in something ⟨a celebrated humorist who, without fail, could find the *comic* in even the most mundane of situations⟩ — see HUMOR 1

comical *adj* **1** causing or intended to cause laughter ⟨the *comical* antics of the circus clowns⟩ — see FUNNY 1
2 so foolish or pointless as to be worthy of scornful laughter ⟨the *comical* expression on his face when he realized that he had been swindled⟩ — see RIDICULOUS 1

comicality *n* the amusing quality or element in something ⟨there's a certain *comicality* to the outcome of the election: the candidate who ran against Washington, D.C., is now going there⟩ — see HUMOR 1

comic strip *n* a series of drawings that tell a story or part of a story ⟨a *comic strip* that is beloved by both children and adults⟩
synonyms cartoon, comic, funny, strip
related words comic book, funny paper(s), graphic novel; animated cartoon, animation; caricature

coming *adj* **1** being soon to appear or take place ⟨a listing of the *coming* attractions⟩ — see FORTHCOMING 1
2 being the one that comes immediately after another ⟨in the *coming* year⟩ — see NEXT
3 of a time after the present ⟨over the *coming* weeks we'll be adding to the staff⟩ — see FUTURE

coming *n* the act of coming upon a scene ⟨the *coming* of the children meant we could finally get the party started⟩ — see ARRIVAL

comingle *vb* to turn into a single mass or entity that is more or less the same throughout ⟨the chemicals, when *comingled*, will spontaneously ignite⟩ — see BLEND 1

comity *n* peaceful coexistence ⟨the *comity* that has always existed among the town's houses of worship⟩ — see HARMONY 2

command *n* **1** a statement of what to do that must be obeyed by those concerned ⟨the captain's *commands* were followed without question⟩
synonyms behest, charge, commandment, decree, dictate, direction, directive, do, edict, imperative, injunction, instruction, order, word
related words demand, requirement; mandate; countermand, counterorder; law, precept, prescript, prescription, rule; ordinance, regulation, statute
near antonyms appeal, entreaty, petition, plea, urging; proposal, recommendation, suggestion
2 a highly developed skill in or knowledge of something ⟨a *command* of French that is the result of a year spent in France as an exchange student⟩
synonyms IQ, mastership, mastery, proficiency
related words virtuosity; facility, hang; fluency, literacy; experience, expertise, know-how, practice (*also* practise), skill(s); acquaintance, familiarity, intimacy
near antonyms incompetence, incompetency; ignorance, illiteracy, unfamiliarity
3 the place from which a commander runs operations ⟨the general set up his *command* in the old port city⟩
synonyms base, command post, headquarters
related words home, seat
4 a place from which authority is exercised ⟨central *command*⟩ — see SEAT 1
5 the right or means to command or control others ⟨the army officer in *command* during the attack⟩ — see POWER 1
6 all that can be seen from a certain point ⟨from his mountain perch, the scout had a *command* of the entire valley⟩ — see VIEW 1

command *vb* **1** to issue orders to (someone) by right of authority ⟨the general *commanded* his troops with Caesar-like imperiousness⟩
synonyms adjure, bid, boss (around), charge, direct, enjoin, instruct, order, tell
related words ask, petition, request; beg, beseech, entreat; advise, counsel, warn; appoint, assign, authorize, commission; oversee, superintend, supervise; conduct, control, lead, manage; coerce, compel, constrain, force, oblige, require
near antonyms comply (with), follow, keep, observe
antonyms mind, obey
2 to request the doing of by virtue of one's authority ⟨the governor has *commanded* that all state flags be flown at half-mast⟩
synonyms call, decree, dictate, direct, mandate, ordain, order
related words ask, petition, request; demand, require
phrases call for
near antonyms cancel, countermand, rescind
3 to ask for (something) earnestly or with authority ⟨an act of courage that *commands* the admiration of all who witnessed it⟩ — see DEMAND 1
4 to exercise authority or power over ⟨a cabinet secretary who *commands* the largest department in the federal government⟩ — see GOVERN 1
5 to keep, control, or experience as one's own ⟨local government does not *command* the resources that are needed to respond to such a huge disaster⟩ — see HAVE 1
6 to look down on ⟨for centuries an imposing castle has *commanded* that stretch of the river⟩ — see OVERLOOK 1
7 to serve as leader of ⟨the head of the agency *commands* an army of workers trained to respond to the immediate needs of disaster victims⟩ — see LEAD 2
8 to set or receive as a price ⟨*commands* a high fee for his decorating services⟩ — see CHARGE 1

commandant *n* one in official command especially of a military force or base ⟨the *commandant* of a naval district⟩ — see COMMANDER 1

commandeer *vb* **1** to take control of (a vehicle) by force ⟨an airliner *commandeered* by terrorists⟩
synonyms hijack (*also* highjack)
related words carjack, skyjack; appropriate, confiscate, expropriate, seize
2 to take or make use of under a guise of authority but without actual right ⟨*commandeered* all of the equipment, as if the chem lab belonged solely to him⟩ — see APPROPRIATE 1

commandeering *n* the unlawful taking or withholding of something from the rightful owner under a guise of authority ⟨the Spanish navy's *commandeering* of fishing boats and impressment of fishermen⟩ — see APPROPRIATION 2

commander *n* **1** one in official command especially of a military force or base ⟨a surrender of the fort by the *commander* without a single shot having been fired⟩
synonyms captain, commandant, commanding officer
related words commissioned officer, field officer
phrases commander in chief
2 a person in overall command of a ship ⟨the intrepid *commander* of the HMS Surprise⟩ — see CAPTAIN 1

commanding *adj* **1** highest in rank or authority ⟨with the death of the general, he instantly became the *commanding* officer on the field of battle⟩ — see HEAD
2 likely to attract attention ⟨even in a room filled with world leaders, he was a *commanding* presence⟩ — see NOTICEABLE

commanding officer *n* one in official command especially of a military force or base ⟨reported directly to the fort's *commanding officer*⟩ — see COMMANDER 1

commandment *n* a statement of what to do that must be obeyed by those concerned ⟨the boss left behind a list of *commandments* for running the office while he was away⟩ — see COMMAND 1

command post *n* the place from which a commander runs operations ⟨a historic home that for a time served as Washington's *command post* during the American Revolution⟩ — see COMMAND 3

commemorate *vb* **1** to be a memorial of ⟨a stone obelisk *commemorates* the Battle of Bunker Hill⟩
synonyms memorialize, monumentalize
related words celebrate, keep, observe, remember; enshrine, exalt, glorify, honor; bless, consecrate, sanctify, solemnize
near antonyms disgrace, dishonor
2 to mark with an appropriate practice, rite, or ceremony ⟨let's *commemorate* Martin Luther King Day with readings of some of Dr. King's speeches⟩ — see KEEP 1

commemorating *adj* serving to preserve the memory of a person, thing, or an event ⟨a *commemorating* reenactment of the Civil War battle on the occasion of its 150th anniversary⟩ — see COMMEMORATIVE

commemorative *adj* serving to preserve the memory of a person, thing, or an event ⟨*commemorative* stamps for the stars of American popular music⟩
synonyms commemorating, honorary, memorial, memorializing
related words epitaphial, epitaphic; dedicatory, testimonial; canonizing, enshrining, exalting, glorifying

commemorative *n* something that serves to keep alive the memory of a person or event ⟨a stamp was issued as a *commemorative* of the event⟩ — see MEMORIAL

commence *vb* **1** to take the first step in (a process or course of action) ⟨*commence* the festivities⟩ — see BEGIN 1
2 to come into existence ⟨the games *commenced* early in the morning⟩ — see BEGIN 2

commencement *n* the point at which something begins ⟨there was a large turnout at the *commencement* of the conference, but the numbers dwindled as it progressed⟩ — see BEGINNING

commend *vb* to put (something) into the possession or safekeeping of another ⟨I *commend* my fate into your hands⟩ — see GIVE 2

commendable *adj* deserving of high regard or great approval ⟨a *commendable* interest in classical music⟩ — see ADMIRABLE

commendation *n* **1** a formal recognition of an achievement or praiseworthy deed ⟨a firefighter who has been awarded several *commendations* for bravery⟩
synonyms acknowledgment (*or* acknowledgement), citation, mention
related words decoration, medal, ribbon; accolade, award, honor, kudo, prize, tribute; dedication
2 a formal expression of praise ⟨a new novel that has received enthusiastic *commendations* from most of the critics⟩ — see ENCOMIUM
3 commendations *pl, archaic* best wishes ⟨his Lordship extends his hearty *commendations*⟩ — see COMPLIMENT 2

commendatory *adj* expressing approval ⟨on the basis of several *commendatory* letters from his teachers, the student was admitted to the advanced studies program⟩ — see FAVORABLE 1

commensurable *adj* corresponding in size, amount, extent, or degree ⟨though his new job pays less, the pay is at least *commensurable* with the amount of work and the level of stress he must contend with⟩ — see PROPORTIONAL

commensurate *adj* corresponding in size, amount, extent, or degree ⟨was given a job *commensurate* with her abilities and experience⟩ — see PROPORTIONAL

comment *n* **1** a briefly expressed opinion ⟨just ate the food without offering even a single *comment*⟩ — see REMARK
2 comments *pl* a series of explanations or observations on something (as an event) ⟨the pundit's *comments* on the political events of the previous week were astute as usual⟩ — see COMMENTARY 1

comment *vb* to make a statement of one's opinion ⟨*commenting* on recent developments in the Middle East⟩ — see REMARK 1

commentary *n* **1** a series of explanations or observations on something (as an event) ⟨the TV anchors provided a running *commentary* on the parade⟩
synonyms analysis, comment, exposition, play-by-play
related words annotation, explication; descant (*also* discant), note, observation, remark; report, review, write-up
2 *usually* **commentaries** *pl* a relating of events usually in the order in which they happened ⟨the general's *commentaries* on his military campaigns rank among the best firsthand accounts of the war⟩ — see ACCOUNT 1

commerce *n* **1** the buying and selling of goods especially on a large scale and between different places ⟨a government agency in charge of regulating interstate *commerce*⟩
synonyms business, marketplace, trade, traffic
related words free trade; black market, gray market; dealings, horse-trading; e-tail, merchandising, retailing, wholesaling; bartering
2 doings between individuals or groups ⟨when I was doing outside consulting for the company, I never had much *commerce* with the in-house staff⟩ — see RELATION 1
3 sexual union involving penetration of the vagina by the penis ⟨rumors of *commerce* between the lady and the knight spread throughout the court⟩ — see SEXUAL INTERCOURSE

commercial *adj* fit or likely to be sold especially on a large scale ⟨the *commercial* fare produced by the Hollywood movie studios⟩
synonyms corporate, marketable, mass-market, salable (*or* saleable)
related words mass-produced, wholesale
antonyms noncommercial, nonsalable, uncommercial, unmarketable, unsalable

commie *n* an adherent or advocate of an economic system in which the means of production are owned and controlled by the state ⟨alleged that *commies* had infiltrated every level of the federal government⟩ — see COMMUNIST

commination *n* an often public or formal expression of disapproval ⟨the tendency by some to regard every unfortunate natural disaster as a sign of the Almighty's *commination* of mankind's sinfulness⟩ — see CENSURE

commingle *vb* to turn into a single mass or entity that is more or less the same throughout ⟨*commingled* the remaining dry ingredients before adding them to the batter⟩ — see BLEND 1

comminute *vb* to reduce to fine particles ⟨eons of incessant pounding by the waves have *comminuted* the once-rocky shoreline into a bed of fine-grained sand⟩ — see POWDER

commiserate (with) *vb* to have sympathy for ⟨we *commiserated with* him but there was little we could do to make the situation better⟩ — see PITY

commiseration *n* **1** sorrow or the capacity to feel sorrow for another's suffering or misfortune ⟨letters of *commiseration* sent to the hospitalized student⟩ — see SYMPATHY 1

2 the capacity for feeling for another's unhappiness or misfortune ⟨a heartless businessman with no *commiseration* for the less fortunate⟩ — see HEART 1

commiserative *adj* having or showing the capacity for sharing the feelings of another ⟨the two passengers exchanged *commiserative* looks as another delay was announced over the loudspeaker⟩ — see SYMPATHETIC 1

commissary *n* a person who acts or does business for another ⟨will serve as *commissary* of religious education for the whole diocese⟩ — see AGENT 2

commission *n* **1** the granting of power to perform various acts or duties ⟨President Jefferson's *commission* to Lewis and Clark to explore the Louisiana Territory⟩
synonyms accreditation, authorization, delegation, empowerment, license (*or* licence), mandate
related words commendation, consignment, entrustment; facilitation, fostering, promotion; commanding, directing, ordering
2 the doing of an action ⟨a single burglar was responsible for the *commission* of all the break-ins⟩
synonyms accomplishment, achievement, discharge, enactment, execution, fulfillment (*or* fulfilment), implementation, performance, perpetration, prosecution, pursuance
related words dispatch, expedition; administration, direction, handling, management; application, operation, practice (*also* practise)
antonyms nonfulfillment, nonperformance
3 a select group of persons assigned to consider or take action on some matter ⟨reported to a UN *commission* on the AIDS crisis⟩ — see COMMITTEE
4 the state or fact of being chosen for a position or duty ⟨her *commission* as head of the investigation⟩ — see APPOINTMENT 1

commission *vb* **1** to appoint as one's representative ⟨plans to *commission* a deputy to investigate the matter⟩ — see DELEGATE 1
2 to give official or legal power to ⟨was *commissioned* lieutenant⟩ — see AUTHORIZE 1
3 to give a task, duty, or responsibility to ⟨was *commissioned* to do the biography⟩ — see ENTRUST 1
4 to pick (someone) by one's authority for a specific position or duty ⟨*commissioned* him to head the office of veterans affairs⟩ — see APPOINT 2

commit *vb* **1** to carry through (as a process) to completion ⟨accused of *committing* a felony⟩ — see PERFORM 1
2 to obligate by prior agreement ⟨we were *committed* to finishing the project⟩ — see PLEDGE 1
3 to put (something) into the possession or safekeeping of another ⟨*commit* only some power to each official⟩ — see GIVE 2
4 to put in or as if in prison ⟨*committed* the rapist to prison⟩ — see IMPRISON

commitment *n* **1** adherence to something to which one is bound by a pledge or duty ⟨his frequent absences made others question his *commitment* to the political campaign⟩ — see FIDELITY
2 something one must do because of prior agreement ⟨they made a *commitment* to pay the bill upon receipt of their order⟩ — see OBLIGATION 1

committee *n* a select group of persons assigned to consider or take action on some matter ⟨a *committee* in charge of planning the organization's annual Christmas party⟩
synonyms commission, panel
related words standing committee, steering committee; subcommittee; delegation, mission; assembly, body, congress, convocation, council, synod

commix *vb* to turn into a single mass or entity that is more or less the same throughout ⟨I learned which spices are *commixed* to make curry powder⟩ — see BLEND 1

commodious *adj* more than adequate or average in capacity ⟨a house with exceptionally *commodious* closets⟩ — see SPACIOUS

commodity *n* **1** one that has a real and independent existence ⟨the docudrama really wasn't a *commodity* until the television networks started creating their own feature-length movies⟩ — see ENTITY
2 commodities *pl* products that are bought and sold in business ⟨*commodities* such as sugar and oil⟩ — see MERCHANDISE

common *adj* **1** often observed or encountered ⟨horse ranches are a *common* sight in that part of the state⟩
synonyms common or garden [*chiefly British*], commonplace, everyday, familiar, frequent, garden-variety, household, ordinary, quotidian, routine, ubiquitous, usual
related words normal, regular, standard; de rigueur, mandatory, obligatory; general, universal; ceaseless, constant, continual, continuous, incessant, unceasing; endemic, popular, prevailing, prevalent, rampant; perennial, recurrent, repeated
phrases a dime a dozen
near antonyms aberrant, abnormal, irregular, unnatural; intermittent, occasional, sporadic
antonyms extraordinary, infrequent, rare, seldom, uncommon, unfamiliar, unusual
2 being of the type that is encountered in the normal course of events ⟨just a *common* house cat but an extraordinary friend⟩ — see ORDINARY 1
3 belonging or relating to the whole ⟨facts of *common* knowledge⟩ — see GENERAL 1
4 belonging to the class of people of low social or economic rank ⟨a man of wealth and privilege who mingled without pretense with the *common* folk⟩ — see IGNOBLE 1
5 held by or applicable to a majority of the people ⟨a politician who works not for the special interests but for the *common* good⟩ — see GENERAL 3
6 used or done by a number of people as a group ⟨used a *common* bathroom while at the campground⟩ — see COLLECTIVE
7 of average to below average quality ⟨has a *common* singing voice that's good enough for performing at those venues⟩ — see MEDIOCRE 1
8 of low quality ⟨furniture of *common* workmanship that did not justify the high prices⟩ — see CHEAP 2
9 lacking in refinement or good taste ⟨embarrassed by the *common* manners of his new in-laws⟩ — see COARSE 2

commonality *n* a point which two or more things share in common ⟨one *commonality* between the two very different women is their passion for charity work⟩ — see SIMILARITY 2

common denominator *n* a point which two or more things share in common ⟨the only *common denominator* between the novel and the movie allegedly based on it appears to be the name of the main character⟩ — see SIMILARITY 2

commoners *n pl* the body of the community as contrasted with the elite ⟨the British nobles used to believe that they were fundamentally better than the *commoners*⟩ — see MASS 1

commonly *adv* according to the usual course of things ⟨the clusters of idle teens that can *commonly* be found hanging around any mall⟩ — see NATURALLY 2

commonness *n* **1** the fact or state of happening often ⟨tardiness of as much *commonness* as the rising of the sun⟩ — see FREQUENCY
2 the quality or state of lacking refinement or good taste ⟨the socialites were appalled by the newcomer's

commonness⟩ — see VULGARITY 1

common or garden *adj, chiefly British* often observed or encountered ⟨lives in a *common or garden* row house in a nondescript suburb of London⟩ — see COMMON 1

commonplace *adj* **1** being of the type that is encountered in the normal course of events ⟨a *commonplace* occurrence⟩ — see ORDINARY 1
2 often observed or encountered ⟨the large corporate mergers that have become *commonplace*⟩ — see COMMON 1
3 used or heard so often as to be dull ⟨a thriller that uses the *commonplace* plot twist of the evil twin⟩ — see STALE 1

commonplace *n* an idea or expression that has been used by many people ⟨the familiar summertime *commonplace* that "It's not the heat, it's the humidity"⟩
synonyms banality, bromide, chestnut, cliché (*also* cliche), groaner, homily, platitude, shibboleth, trope, truism
related words conventional wisdom, party line, routine; inanity; generality, generalization, simplification; adage, proverb, saw, saying; old wives' tale, stereotype
near antonyms profundity

commons *n pl* the body of the community as contrasted with the elite ⟨the aristocracy feared what would happen if the *commons* were enfranchised⟩ — see MASS 1

commonsense *adj* based on sound reasoning or information ⟨the *commonsense* interpretation of this so-called mysterious sighting⟩ — see GOOD 1

common sense *n* the ability to make intelligent decisions especially in everyday matters ⟨*common sense* should tell you not to meet face-to-face with someone who is just an online acquaintance⟩
synonyms discreetness, discretion, gumption [*chiefly dialect*], horse sense, levelheadedness, nous [*chiefly British*], policy, prudence, sense, sensibleness, wisdom, wit
related words street smarts; farsightedness, forehandedness, foresight, foresightedness, forethoughtfulness, judgment (*or* judgement); brains, gray matter, intelligence; logicality, logicalness, practicality, rationality, rationalness; discernment, discrimination, insight, sagacity, sapience; acumen, astuteness, clearheadedness, keenness, penetration, perspicacity, shrewdness; care, caution, circumspection, precaution, premeditation
near antonyms shortsightedness; brainlessness, foolishness, half-wittedness, idiocy, senselessness, stupidity; carelessness, heedlessness; unreasonableness
antonyms imprudence, indiscretion

commonsensible *adj* based on sound reasoning or information ⟨she takes a *commonsensible* approach to child rearing, blithely ignoring what the so-called experts suggest⟩ — see GOOD 1

commonsensical *adj* based on sound reasoning or information ⟨the only *commonsensical* solution would be to divide the children into groups according to age⟩ — see GOOD 1

commonwealth *n* a body of people composed of one or more nationalities usually with its own territory and government ⟨laws that will benefit all the citizens of the *commonwealth*⟩ — see NATION 1

commotion *n* a state of noisy, confused activity ⟨the *commotion* created when the nation's top rock band arrived in town⟩
synonyms ado, alarums and excursions, ballyhoo, blather, bluster, bobbery, bother, bustle, clatter, clutter [*chiefly dialect*], coil, corroboree [*Australian*], disturbance, do [*chiefly dialect*], foofaraw, fun, furor, furore, fuss, helter-skelter, hoo-ha (*also* hoo-hah), hoopla, hubble-bubble, hubbub, hullabaloo, hurly, hurly-burly, hurricane, hurry, hurry-scurry (*or* hurry-skurry), kerfuffle [*chiefly British*], moil, pandemonium, pother, row, ruckus, ruction, rumpus, shindy, splore [*Scottish*], squall, stew, stir, storm, to-do, tumult, turmoil, uproar, welter, whirl, williwaw, zoo
related words cacophony, clamor, din, howl, hue and cry, noise, outcry, racket, roar; disorder, unrest, upheaval; eruption, flare-up, flurry, flutter, outbreak, outburst; brawl, fracas, fray, hassle, melee (*also* mêlée), scuffle; dither, fever, fret, lather, tizzy
near antonyms calm, hush, peace, quiet, quietude, rest, stillness, tranquillity (*or* tranquility); order, orderliness

communal *adj* used or done by a number of people as a group ⟨the swimming pool is part of the *communal* property of the condo complex⟩ — see COLLECTIVE

commune *vb* to form a close personal relationship ⟨after a week in the wilderness, the scouts were really starting to *commune* with nature⟩
synonyms bond, click, relate
related words befriend; empathize, identify, sympathize
phrases hit it off

communicable *adj* capable of being passed by physical contact from one person to another ⟨*communicable* diseases that are usually transmitted sexually⟩ — see CONTAGIOUS 1

communicate *vb* **1** to cause (something) to pass from one to another ⟨the infected cook unknowingly *communicated* the disease to hundreds of people⟩
synonyms conduct, convey, give, impart, spread, transfer, transfuse, transmit
related words deliver, hand over, surrender, turn over; broadcast, diffuse, disseminate, propagate; hand down, hand on; contaminate, infect, poison
near antonyms catch, come down (with), contract
2 to engage in an exchange of information or ideas ⟨for decades the two medical centers have been *communicating* about cancer research⟩
synonyms brainstorm, intercommunicate
related words correspond; converse, talk; message; bond, commune, relate; accost, approach, board, contact
3 to make known (something abstract) through outward signs ⟨his voice *communicated* a certain distrust and wariness⟩ — see SHOW 2

communicate (with) *vb* to transmit information or requests to ⟨*communicating with* other ham radio enthusiasts⟩ — see CONTACT

communication *n* **1** a piece of conveyed information ⟨the latest *communication* from the crew of the space station⟩
synonyms dispatch, message
related words bulletin, communiqué, express [*British*], report; memo, memorandum, notice; epistle, letter, missive, note; electronic mail, e-mail, voice mail; intelligence, news, tidings, word; command, directive, instruction, order
2 the state or fact of being able to exchange information regarding one's current situation ⟨we haven't been in *communication* with him since he left for the Alaskan wilderness⟩ — see TOUCH 1

communion *n* a friendly relationship marked by ready communication and mutual understanding ⟨gradually established a feeling of *communion* with her fellow physicians⟩ — see RAPPORT

communiqué *n* a published statement informing the public of a matter of general interest ⟨a White House *communiqué*⟩ — see ANNOUNCEMENT

communist *n* an adherent or advocate of an economic system in which the means of production are owned and controlled by the state ⟨*communists* were plotting an overthrow of the government⟩
synonyms commie, comrade, Red, socialist

related words leftist, lefty, pink, pinko, social democrat; Bolshevik, Leninist, Leninite, Maoist, Marxist, Stalinist, Trotskyist, Trotskyite; extremist, radical, revolutionary, revolutionist
antonyms capitalist

community *n* **1** the people living in a particular area ⟨the whole *community* rallied to the aid of the family who had lost its home⟩
synonyms neighborhood
related words city, commune, hamlet, town, village; denizens, dwellers, inhabitants, residents; citizenry, culture, people, populace, public, society
2 a group of people with a common interest living in one place ⟨a picturesque seacoast village that is known for its sizable *community* of artists⟩
synonyms colony
related words circle, clique, coterie, set, society; band, company, troop; clan, family
3 a group of people sharing a common interest and relating together socially ⟨a large *community* of retired people in the coastal town⟩ — see GANG 2
4 the body of people in a profession or field of activity ⟨members of the medical *community*⟩ — see CORPS
5 the quality or state of having many qualities in common ⟨there's a *community* of aesthetics that makes a very modern-looking gallery an especially appropriate setting for primitive art⟩ — see SIMILARITY 1
6 the feeling of closeness and friendship that exists between companions ⟨interactive features that are designed to foster a sense of *community* among the visitors to the Web site⟩ — see COMPANIONSHIP

commutable *adj* capable of being substituted in place of one another ⟨for most of the book's recipes, fresh and dried herbs are not *commutable*⟩ — see INTERCHANGEABLE

commutation *n* a giving or taking of one thing of value in return for another ⟨an international *commutation* of food for oil⟩ — see EXCHANGE 1

commute *vb* to give up (something) and take something else in return ⟨*commuting* foreign currency to domestic⟩ — see CHANGE 3

comp *n* something given to someone without expectation of a return ⟨this hotel offers its guests more *comps*, including a free bottle of champagne, than most in its class⟩ — see GIFT 1

compact *adj* **1** having a consistency that does not easily yield to pressure ⟨a mattress with a *compact* foam core⟩ — see FIRM 2
2 having little space between items or parts ⟨*compact* soil that should provide good support for the plant⟩ — see CLOSE 1
3 marked by the use of few words to convey much information or meaning ⟨*compact* prose without a single wasted word⟩ — see CONCISE

compact *n* **1** a formal agreement between two or more nations or peoples ⟨a five-nation *compact* to control drug traffic⟩ — see TREATY
2 an arrangement about action to be taken ⟨the two made a *compact* never to artificially prolong the other's life in the event of incapacitating illness or injury⟩ — see AGREEMENT 2

compact *vb* **1** to bring (something) to a central point or under a single control ⟨the media giant decided to *compact* all of its far-flung operations onto a single site⟩ — see CENTRALIZE
2 to reduce in size or volume by or as if by pressing parts or members together ⟨*compact* the snow into a tight ball for throwing⟩ — see COMPRESS 1

compacting *n* the act or process of reducing the size or volume of something by or as if by pressing ⟨the *compacting* of wool fibers into felt⟩ — see COMPRESSION

compaction *n* the act or process of reducing the size or volume of something by or as if by pressing ⟨the *compaction* of a complex topic into a short article means that a lot of niceties are going to get crushed⟩ — see COMPRESSION

compactly *adv* in a few words ⟨write the instructions as *compactly* as possible⟩ — see SHORTLY 1

compactness *n* the quality or state of being marked by or using only few words to convey much meaning ⟨the *compactness* of his prose requires a close, careful reading⟩ — see SUCCINCTNESS

compadre *n* a person who has a strong liking for and trust in another ⟨they're longtime *compadres* who have been through a lot together⟩ — see FRIEND 1

companion *n* **1** a person frequently seen in the company of another ⟨the reckless *companions* of one's youth⟩ — see ASSOCIATE 1
2 one that accompanies another for protection, guidance, or as a courtesy ⟨a dapper gentleman who's a frequent *companion* of widowed dowagers at society galas⟩ — see ESCORT
3 either of a pair matched in one or more qualities ⟨a sketch that is a *companion* to the original drawing⟩ — see MATE 1
4 something that is found along with something else ⟨the report and its *companion* recommendations for action⟩ — see ACCOMPANIMENT

companion *vb* to go along with in order to provide assistance, protection, or companionship ⟨movie heroes are often *companioned* by wisecracking sidekicks⟩ — see ACCOMPANY 1

companionable *adj* **1** having or showing kindly feeling and sincere interest ⟨a *companionable* pat on the back let me know that my shipmates were now my friends⟩ — see FRIENDLY 1
2 likely to seek or enjoy the company of others ⟨a good club for *companionable* enthusiasts of the great outdoors⟩ — see CONVIVIAL

companionship *n* the feeling of closeness and friendship that exists between companions ⟨the widow's pet cats provided her with her only *companionship*⟩
synonyms brotherhood, camaraderie, community, company, comradery, comradeship, fellowship, society
related words amity, benevolence, cordiality, friendliness, friendship, goodwill, kindliness; civility, comity, concord, harmony, rapport; charity, generosity; affinity, compassion, empathy, sympathy; chumminess, familiarity, inseparability, intimacy, nearness; affection, devotion, fondness, love
near antonyms forlornness, loneliness, lonesomeness

company *n* **1** an organized group of stage performers ⟨a city that is fortunate enough to have two thriving opera *companies*⟩
synonyms troop, troupe
related words stock company; cast, dramatis personae, ensemble
2 a group of people working together on a task ⟨a *company* of carpenters constructed the frame of the house in no time⟩ — see GANG 1
3 a commercial or industrial activity or organization ⟨she works for a construction *company*⟩ — see ENTERPRISE 1
4 the feeling of closeness and friendship that exists between companions ⟨enjoying each other's *company*⟩ — see COMPANIONSHIP
5 a position within view ⟨I would prefer that you not mock your so-called friends while in my *company*⟩ — see PRESENCE 1

company *vb* **1** to come or be together as friends ⟨in her sermon the minister noted that Jesus had *companied* with the least privileged and most disadvantaged members of society⟩ — see ASSOCIATE 1
2 to go along with in order to provide assistance, pro-

tection, or companionship ⟨may the Good Lord *company* you on your journey home⟩ — see ACCOMPANY 1

comparability *n* the quality or state of having many qualities in common ⟨there's little *comparability* between the two vehicles: one's basic transportation and the other's a luxurious salon on wheels⟩ — see SIMILARITY 1

comparable *adj* having qualities in common ⟨two *comparable* selections that are hard to choose between⟩ — see ALIKE

comparative *adj* being such only when compared to something else ⟨if you consider the multimillionaire's yearly income, we're living in *comparative* poverty⟩
synonyms almost, approximate, near, relative
related words alike, comparable, similar; equal, equivalent
near antonyms genuine, real, true
antonyms absolute, complete, downright, out-and-out, outright, perfect, pure, unqualified

compare *vb* **1** to describe as similar ⟨reviews that *compared* the adventure movie to a thrilling ride on a roller coaster⟩
synonyms analogize, assimilate, bracket, equate, liken
related words associate, connect, couple, link; allude, refer, relate; equal, match, parallel
antonyms contrast
2 to regard or represent as equal or comparable ⟨*compared* the restaurant's food to the nectar of the gods⟩ — see EQUATE 1

compare (with) *vb* to come near or nearer to in character or quality ⟨nothing *compares with* the literary achievement of Shakespeare⟩ — see APPROXIMATE

compartment *n* one of the parts into which an enclosed space is divided ⟨a backpack with many handy *compartments* for storing your camping gear⟩
synonyms bay, cabin, cell, chamber, cube, cubicle
related words cubbyhole, pigeonhole, snuggery [*chiefly British*]; alcove, niche, nook, recess; cabinet, drawer, locker; cavity, hole, hollow; booth, box, crib, loge, stall; bunker, crypt, vault

compartment *vb* to arrange or assign according to type ⟨*compartment* the responses according to country of origin⟩ — see CLASSIFY 1

compartmentalize *vb* to arrange or assign according to type ⟨we shouldn't *compartmentalize* the students into such restrictive categories as scholar and athlete, which are not mutually exclusive⟩ — see CLASSIFY 1

compass *n* **1** a guiding or motivating purpose or principle ⟨a young go-getter who lost his moral *compass* in the course of his quest for fame and fortune⟩
synonyms cynosure, direction, focus, lodestar (*also* loadstar), polestar
related words benchmark, criterion, grade, mark, measure, par, standard, touchstone, yardstick; aim, ambition, aspiration, dream, goal, intention, object, objective, purpose, target
2 an area over which activity, capacity, or influence extends ⟨within the *compass* of my voice⟩ — see RANGE 2
3 the line or relatively narrow space that marks the outer limit of something ⟨within the *compass* of the city walls⟩ — see BORDER 1

compass *vb* **1** to carry through (as a process) to completion ⟨attempting more than his modest abilities could *compass*⟩ — see PERFORM 1
2 to travel completely around ⟨the great age of exploration, when ships of sail *compassed* the earth⟩ — see ENCIRCLE 1
3 to engage in a secret plan to accomplish evil or unlawful ends ⟨the rebels are *compassing* the assassination of the king⟩ — see PLOT
4 to form a circle around ⟨a mysterious isle, *compassed* by treacherous seas⟩ — see SURROUND
5 to have a clear idea of ⟨the concept that the earth is billions of years old is one that the average mind struggles to *compass*⟩ — see COMPREHEND 1

compassion *n* **1** sorrow or the capacity to feel sorrow for another's suffering or misfortune ⟨treats the homeless with great *compassion*⟩ — see SYMPATHY 1
2 the capacity for feeling for another's unhappiness or misfortune ⟨has no *compassion* for people who squander their money⟩ — see HEART 1

compassionate *adj* **1** having or marked by sympathy and consideration for others ⟨a *compassionate* person by nature⟩ — see HUMANE 1
2 having or showing the capacity for sharing the feelings of another ⟨a *compassionate* smile made the refugees feel a little better⟩ — see SYMPATHETIC 1

compassionate *vb* to have sympathy for ⟨a gentle soul who could *compassionate* even the most reprobate of scoundrels and villains⟩ — see PITY

compassionateness *n* sympathetic concern for the well-being of others ⟨the unfailing *compassionateness* of the staff at the hospice⟩ — see BENIGNANCY

compassionless *adj* having or showing a lack of sympathy or tender feelings ⟨shocked by the mother's *compassionless* treatment of her autistic child⟩ — see HARD 1

compatibility *n* peaceful coexistence ⟨the remarkable *compatibility* of roommates from such widely divergent backgrounds⟩ — see HARMONY 2

compatible *adj* **1** having or marked by agreement in feeling or action ⟨didn't think that they'd be *compatible* as roommates⟩ — see HARMONIOUS 3
2 not having or showing any apparent conflict ⟨a theory that is *compatible* with what we already know about early man⟩ — see CONSISTENT

compatriot *n* **1** a person living in or originally from the same country as another ⟨an appeal to all of his *compatriots* to come to their country's aid in its hour of need⟩
synonyms countryman, landsman
related words countrywoman; nationalist, patriot; citizen, national, subject; aborigine, native; homeboy, resident
near antonyms alien, foreigner, immigrant, outsider
2 a person frequently seen in the company of another ⟨doesn't indulge in the lavish lifestyle of his *compatriots* in the movie business⟩ — see ASSOCIATE 1

[1]**compeer** *n* a person frequently seen in the company of another ⟨like so many of his twentysomething *compeers*, he just had to get a tattoo⟩ — see ASSOCIATE 1

[2]**compeer** *n* one that is equal to another in status, achievement, or value ⟨contends that no military commander of modern times ranks as the *compeer* of Alexander the Great⟩ — see EQUAL

compel *vb* to cause (a person) to give in to pressure ⟨public opinion *compelled* her to fire her scandal-plagued aide⟩ — see FORCE 1

compellation *n* a word or combination of words by which a person or thing is regularly known ⟨apparently no one dares to enter the world of professional wrestling without a catchy *compellation*⟩ — see NAME 1

compelling *adj* **1** having the power to persuade ⟨made a *compelling* argument against military intervention⟩ — see COGENT
2 needing immediate attention ⟨no *compelling* need to raise taxes at this time⟩ — see ACUTE 2

compendious *adj* **1** covering everything or all important points ⟨her *compendious* knowledge of the monarch butterfly⟩ — see ENCYCLOPEDIC
2 marked by the use of few words to convey much information or meaning ⟨a *compendious* summary of the referendum before the voters⟩ — see CONCISE

compendium *n* a collection of writings ⟨a book entirely devoted to poodles—a *compendium* of writings by breeders, trainers, and others in love with the breed⟩ — see ANTHOLOGY

compensate *vb* **1** to provide (someone) with a just payment for loss or injury ⟨you'll have to *compensate* the neighbors for cutting down their tree⟩
synonyms indemnify, recompense, recoup, remunerate, requite, satisfy
related words refund, reimburse, repay; redress, remedy, repair; discharge, pay, quit
2 to give (someone) the sum of money owed for goods or services received ⟨*compensate* them well for their efforts⟩ — see PAY 1

compensate (for) *vb* to balance with an equal force so as to make ineffective ⟨a mafioso thinking that he can *compensate for* the evil he's done by giving to charity⟩ — see OFFSET

compensation *n* **1** payment to another for a loss or injury ⟨a warehouse worker who received a large *compensation* for his crippling injury while on the job⟩
synonyms damages, indemnification, indemnity, quittance, recompense, recoupment, redress, remuneration, reparation, reprisal(s), requital, restitution, satisfaction
related words punitive damage, solatium; amends, atonement, expiation; refund, reimbursement, repayment; adjustment, settlement; punishment, retaliation
2 something (as money) that is given or received in return for goods or services ⟨fair *compensation* for his work on the project⟩ — see PAYMENT 2
3 the act of offering money in exchange for goods or services ⟨his generous *compensation* was greatly appreciated⟩ — see PAYMENT 1

compete *vb* to engage in a contest ⟨prizefighters *competing* for the world heavyweight championship⟩
synonyms battle, contend, face off, fight, race, rival, vie
related words challenge, engage, play; jockey, jostle, maneuver; go out, try out; train, work

competence *n* the physical or mental power to do something ⟨questioned his *competence* to finish the task without help⟩ — see ABILITY

competency *n* the physical or mental power to do something ⟨she's proved that she has the *competency* to run a major company⟩ — see ABILITY

competent *adj* **1** having the required skills for an acceptable level of performance ⟨any *competent* mechanic should be able to fix that⟩
synonyms able, capable, equal, fit, good, qualified, suitable
related words accomplished, ace, adept, experienced, expert, master, masterful, masterly, practiced (*also* practised), proficient, seasoned, skilled, skillful, veteran; overqualified; prepared, schooled, trained; apt, ready, willing; all-around (*also* all-round), protean, versatile
phrases on the ball
near antonyms inexperienced, inexpert, unseasoned, unskilled, unskillful; unprepared, unschooled, untrained; beginning, green, new, raw, untested, untried
antonyms incompetent, inept, poor, unfit, unfitted, unqualified
2 being what is called for by accepted standards of right and wrong ⟨the arbiter has all the necessary information to make a *competent* decision on the matter⟩ — see JUST 1

competently *adv* in a skillful or expert manner ⟨performed the piece at least *competently*, if not superbly⟩ — see WELL 3

competition *n* **1** a competitive encounter between individuals or groups carried on for amusement, exercise, or in pursuit of a prize ⟨a *competition* between two fierce football rivals⟩ — see GAME 1
2 one who strives for the same thing as another ⟨tried to analyze his major *competition* in the tennis tournament⟩ — see COMPETITOR
3 an earnest effort for superiority or victory over another ⟨the intense *competition* for bragging rights to being the city's best French restaurant⟩ — see CONTEST 1

competitor *n* one who strives for the same thing as another ⟨the *competitors* for this prestigious science award come from the best high schools in the country⟩
synonyms challenger, competition, contender, contestant, corrival, rival
related words archrival; finalist, semifinalist; also-ran, entrant, entry, player; adversary, antagonist, opponent
antonyms noncompetitor

compilation *n* a collection of writings ⟨the poet bound a *compilation* of her best work into a single volume⟩ — see ANTHOLOGY

compile *vb* to bring together from several sources into a single volume or list ⟨*compiled* the best short stories ever written into one fat book⟩
synonyms anthologize, collect
related words edit, recompile, redact, redraft, reedit, revamp, revise, rework; accumulate, amass, assemble, collate, gather, group

complacence *n* **1** an often unjustified feeling of being pleased with oneself or with one's situation or achievements ⟨the *complacence* of some of the rich kids at the exclusive private school⟩
synonyms amour propre, bighead, complacency, conceit, conceitedness, ego, egotism, pomposity, pompousness, pride, pridefulness, self-admiration, self-assumption, self-conceit, self-congratulation, self-esteem, self-glory, self-importance, self-love, self-opinion, self-satisfaction, smugness, swelled head, swellheadedness, vaingloriousness, vainglory, vainness, vanity
related words assurance, confidence, self-assurance, self-confidence; self-righteousness; arrogance, disdainfulness, haughtiness, imperiousness, lordliness, self-assertion, snobbishness, superciliousness, superiority; hubris, overconfidence, presumption; pretense (*or* pretence), pretension, pretentiousness; egoism, self-centeredness, selfishness; self-pride, self-respect
near antonyms diffidence, self-doubt; self-disgust, self-hate, self-loathing; altruism, unselfishness; bashfulness, demureness, shyness, timidity, timidness; passiveness, passivity
antonyms humbleness, humility, modesty
2 lack of interest or concern ⟨someone who displayed a startling *complacence* toward his own financial plight⟩ — see INDIFFERENCE

complacency *n* an often unjustified feeling of being pleased with oneself or with one's situation or achievements ⟨a momentary *complacency* that was quickly dispelled by the shock of cold reality⟩ — see COMPLACENCE 1

complacent *adj* **1** having or showing a lack of interest or concern ⟨the auditors were taken aback by his *complacent* response to their findings of fraud⟩ — see INDIFFERENT 1
2 having too high an opinion of oneself ⟨a *complacent* junior exec who was certain of his indispensability to the company⟩ — see CONCEITED

complain *vb* to express dissatisfaction, pain, or resentment usually tiresomely ⟨the time-honored tradition of new recruits *complaining* about the food in the mess hall⟩
synonyms beef, bellyache, bitch, bleat, carp, caterwaul, crab, croak, fuss, gripe, grizzle, grouch, grouse, growl, grumble, grump, holler, inveigh, keen, kick, kvetch, maunder [*chiefly British*], moan, murmur, mutter, nag, repine, scream, squawk, squeal, wail, whimper, whine, whinge [*British*], yammer, yawp (*or* yaup), yowl

related words object (to), protest, quarrel (with); cavil, quibble; fret, stew, worry; blubber, cry, sob; bemoan, bewail, deplore, lament
phrases kick up a fuss
near antonyms accept, bear, countenance, endure, take, tolerate; applaud, cheer, commend
antonyms crow, delight, rejoice

complainant *n* the person in a legal proceeding who makes a charge of wrongdoing against another ⟨the *complainant* charged that the defendant had broken the ironclad contract that both had signed⟩
synonyms plaintiff, suer
related words accuser; litigant, party, suitor; appellant, petitioner, pleader
near antonyms accused
antonyms defendant

complainer *n* **1** a person who makes frequent complaints usually about little things ⟨she early on got a reputation as a *complainer* after finding fault with her work space⟩ — see CRYBABY
2 an irritable and complaining person ⟨a chronic *complainer*⟩ — see GROUCH 1

complaint *n* **1** an expression of dissatisfaction, pain, or resentment ⟨a warning that if there were any more *complaints*, we were turning around and not going to the beach after all⟩
synonyms beef, bitch, bleat, carp, fuss, grievance, gripe, grouch, grouse, grumble, holler, kvetch, lament, miserere, moan, murmur, plaint, squawk, wail, whimper, whine, whinge [*British*], yammer
related words challenge, demur, expostulation, kick, niggle [*chiefly British*], objection, protest, quibble, remonstrance, stink
near antonyms commendation, compliment, plaudit; acclaim, applause, praise; approval, endorsement (*also* indorsement), sanction
2 a feeling or declaration of disapproval or dissent ⟨the condo development proceeded despite the *complaints* of the neighborhood residents⟩ — see OBJECTION
3 a formal claim of criminal wrongdoing against a person ⟨filed a *complaint* in court⟩ — see CHARGE 1
4 an abnormal state that disrupts a plant's or animal's normal bodily functioning ⟨takes a slew of medicines for his many *complaints*⟩ — see DISEASE

complaisance *n* a desire or disposition to please ⟨the *complaisance* of his girlfriend is such that she meekly goes along with everything he says⟩
synonyms amenability, amiability, good-naturedness
related words affability, amicability, amicableness, congeniality, cordiality, friendliness, geniality, sociability; agreeableness, graciousness, pleasantness; kindheartedness, kindliness, warmheartedness; acquiescence, compliance, docility, passivity, submissiveness
near antonyms disagreeableness, sullenness, surliness, ungraciousness; disobedience, intractability, recalcitrance

compleat *adj* **1** having or showing exceptional knowledge, experience, or skill in a field of endeavor ⟨a training course that transformed the former technophobe into the *compleat* computer geek almost overnight⟩ — see PROFICIENT
2 not lacking any part or member that properly belongs to it ⟨an exhaustive how-to guide for anyone planning the *compleat* wedding⟩ — see COMPLETE 1

complement *n* **1** something that serves to complete or make up for a deficiency in something else ⟨with his practicality and her refreshing enthusiasm, they are perfect *complements* to each other⟩
synonyms correlate, supplement
related words addendum, addition, appendix; adjunct, annex, appendage, extension; accessory (*also* accessary), accompaniment, appliance, attachment; additive, filler
2 the largest number or amount that something can hold ⟨a full *complement* of sailors on the ship⟩ — see CAPACITY 1

complement *vb* to serve as a completing element to ⟨this silk handkerchief will *complement* your suit very nicely and give it a bit of dash⟩
synonyms complete, round (off *or* out)
related words finish (off), flesh (out); adorn, beautify, decorate, embellish; better, enhance, improve; constitute, form, make up; enrich, perfect

complementary *adj* related to each other in such a way that one completes the other ⟨the *complementary* contributions of the cooking and cleanup committees were essential to the success of the church barbecue⟩
synonyms correlative, reciprocal, supplemental, supplementary
related words cooperative, mutual, symbiotic; collective, combined, common, communal, conjoint, joint, shared, united
antonyms noncomplementary, nonreciprocal

complete *adj* **1** not lacking any part or member that properly belongs to it ⟨a *complete* deck of cards⟩
synonyms compleat, comprehensive, entire, full, grand, intact, integral, perfect, plenary, total, whole
related words unabridged, uncut, undiminished; all-out, exhaustive, extensive, maximal; full-blooded, full-blown, full-bore, full-fledged, full-on, full-out, full-scale
near antonyms abbreviated, abridged, cut, diminished, reduced
antonyms imperfect, incomplete, partial
2 brought or having come to an end ⟨your education is never *complete*—there's always something more to learn⟩
synonyms completed, concluded, done, down, ended, finished, over, over with, terminated, through, up
related words accomplished, achieved, attained, compassed, realized; dead, defunct, extinct, kaput (*also* kaputt), obsolete; expired
phrases out of hand, out of the way
antonyms continuing, incomplete, ongoing, uncompleted, undone, unfinished
3 covering everything or all important points ⟨will present *complete* coverage of the tennis tournament⟩ — see ENCYCLOPEDIC
4 having no exceptions or restrictions ⟨he's a *complete* lunatic⟩ — see ABSOLUTE 2
5 trying all possibilities ⟨a *complete* search of the computer file⟩ — see EXHAUSTIVE 1
6 having or showing exceptional knowledge, experience, or skill in a field of endeavor ⟨a riding school that will teach you all skills required of the *complete* equestrian⟩ — see PROFICIENT

complete *vb* **1** to bring (something) to a state where nothing remains to be done ⟨managed to *complete* the assignment with time to spare⟩ — see FINISH 1
2 to serve as a completing element to ⟨the bird's beautiful song simply *completes* its appeal for pet owners⟩ — see COMPLEMENT
3 to bring (an event) to a natural or appropriate stopping point ⟨the well-attended concert *completed* a great weekend of arts and entertainment events⟩ — see CLOSE 3
4 to do what is required by the terms of ⟨no payments will be made until the contract is *completed*⟩ — see FULFILL 1

completed *adj* brought or having come to an end ⟨unlike most *completed* construction projects, this one came in under budget⟩ — see COMPLETE 2

completely *adv* **1** to a full extent or degree ⟨she waited

until we were *completely* finished before starting the next part⟩ — see FULLY 1
2 with attention to all aspects or details ⟨an allegation that was *completely* investigated and found to be groundless⟩ — see THOROUGHLY 1

completeness *n* the quality or state of being without restriction, exception, or qualification ⟨the *completeness* of my respect for the theory of relativity is in no way diminished by the incompleteness of my understanding of the details⟩ — see ENTIRENESS

complex *adj* **1** having many parts or aspects that are usually interrelated ⟨this camera is a *complex* instrument that requires careful handling⟩ ⟨*complex* issues regarding free speech and school discipline⟩
synonyms baroque, byzantine, complicate, complicated, convoluted, daedal, elaborate, intricate, involute, involved, knotty, labyrinthian, labyrinthine, sophisticated, tangled
related words overcomplex, overcomplicated; composite, compound, heterogeneous, mixed, multibranched, multifaceted, multifarious, multipart, varied; challenging, difficult, tough; impenetrable, incomprehensible, inexplicable, Kafkaesque, unfathomable, unintelligible
near antonyms oversimplified, simplified, simplistic; homogeneous, uniform, unvaried
antonyms noncomplex, noncomplicated, plain, simple, uncomplicated
2 made or done with great care or with much detail ⟨a *complex* plan for evacuating the city in the event of a natural disaster⟩ — see ELABORATE 1

complex *n* **1** a structure that is designed and built for a particular purpose ⟨an apartment *complex*⟩ — see FACILITY
2 something made up of many interdependent or related parts ⟨a *complex* of goverment programs designed to assist the needy⟩ — see SYSTEM 1

complex *vb* to make complex or difficult ⟨there's no need to *complex* what should be a simple process for obtaining a building permit⟩ — see COMPLICATE 1

complexify *vb* to make complex or difficult ⟨my proposal would simplify the process, whereas yours would needlessly *complexify* it⟩ — see COMPLICATE 1

complexion *n* **1** the hue or appearance of the skin and especially of the face ⟨a sunscreen for people with very light *complexions*⟩
synonyms color, coloring
related words shade, tint, tone; features, lineaments, looks; countenance, face, visage
2 the set of qualities that makes a person, a group of people, or a thing different from others ⟨changing the *complexion* of the department to reflect changing needs⟩ — see NATURE 1

complexity *n* **1** the state or quality of having many interrelated parts or aspects ⟨the *complexity* of the company's computer system is such that a full-time repairman is needed⟩
synonyms complexness, complicacy, complicatedness, complication, elaborateness, intricacy, intricateness, involution, knottiness, sophistication
related words diversity, heterogeneity, heterogeneousness, multifariousness; impenetrability, incomprehensibility, inexplicability
near antonyms simplification; homogeneity, uniformity
antonyms plainness, simpleness, simplicity
2 something that makes a situation more complicated or difficult ⟨the political *complexities* that the secretary-general must deal with⟩ — see COMPLICATION 1

complexness *n* the state or quality of having many interrelated parts or aspects ⟨a coffee-making machine of such staggering *complexness* as to be worthy of Rube Goldberg himself⟩ — see COMPLEXITY 1

compliance *n* **1** a readiness or willingness to yield to the wishes of others ⟨a strong-willed pop star who is not known for her *compliance*⟩
synonyms acquiescence, biddability, compliancy, deference, docility, obedience, submissiveness
related words amenability, amiability, complaisance, good-naturedness; obsequiousness, servility, slavishness, subservience, subserviency; conformity; cooperativeness, receptiveness, receptivity; humoring, indulgence; acceptance, assent, consent; capitulation, submission, surrender; affability, amicability, congeniality, cordiality, friendliness, geniality, sociability
near antonyms animosity, antipathy, enmity, hostility, ill will
antonyms defiance, disobedience, intractability, recalcitrance
2 a bending to the authority or control of another ⟨an administrator who demands prompt and unquestioning *compliance* from his subordinates⟩ — see OBEDIENCE 1
3 the following of a custom, rule, or law ⟨*compliance* with the statute was far from universal⟩ — see OBSERVANCE 1

compliancy *n* a readiness or willingness to yield to the wishes of others ⟨a husband who apparently doesn't know that the days of wifely *compliancy* are over⟩ — see COMPLIANCE 1

compliant *adj* readily giving in to the command or authority of another ⟨a corrupt regime aided by a *compliant* press⟩ — see OBEDIENT

complicacy *n* **1** something that makes a situation more complicated or difficult ⟨the difference in time zones was yet another *complicacy* that had to be dealt with⟩ — see COMPLICATION 1
2 the state or quality of having many interrelated parts or aspects ⟨the *complicacy* of the theory of relativity is such that it cannot be reduced to a few words that are readily comprehensible to the layman⟩ — see COMPLEXITY 1

complicate *adj* having many parts or aspects that are usually interrelated ⟨the kind of *complicate* machinery that is used in the field of robotics⟩ — see COMPLEX 1

complicate *vb* **1** to make complex or difficult ⟨the need to go to both a PTA conference and condo board meeting really *complicates* tonight's schedule⟩
synonyms complex, complexify, embarrass, entangle, perplex, sophisticate
related words develop, elaborate, expand; intensify, magnify; confound, confuse, mess (up), mix (up), muddle; snarl, tangle
near antonyms abbreviate, cut, shorten; ease, facilitate; disentangle, straighten (out), unravel, untangle; oversimplify
antonyms simplify, streamline
2 to make more severe ⟨asthma that has recently been *complicated* by a bout of bronchitis⟩ — see EXACERBATE

complicated *adj* **1** having many parts or aspects that are usually interrelated ⟨a *complicated* apparatus⟩ — see COMPLEX 1
2 made or done with great care or with much detail ⟨*complicated* plans for redeveloping the urban slum that involve both the private and public sectors⟩ — see ELABORATE 1

complicatedness *n* the state or quality of having many interrelated parts or aspects ⟨the *complicatedness* of the home theater system may require that it be installed by a professional⟩ — see COMPLEXITY 1

complication *n* **1** something that makes a situation more complicated or difficult ⟨the food allergies of the guests were just another *complication* for the couple trying to plan their wedding reception⟩

synonyms complexity, complicacy, convolution, difficulty, intricacy
related words aftereffect, ramification, side effect (*also* side reaction); subtlety, technicality; annoyance, bitch, bother, headache, inconvenience, matter, trouble
phrases fly in the ointment
2 an abnormal state that disrupts a plant's or animal's normal bodily functioning ⟨*complications* set in after the surgery⟩ — see DISEASE
3 the state or quality of having many interrelated parts or aspects ⟨a problem of such irreducible *complication* as to defy any easy solution⟩ — see COMPLEXITY 1

complicity *n* a secret agreement or cooperation between two parties for an illegal or dishonest purpose ⟨the two major auction houses acting in *complicity* to drive up the prices of art works⟩ — see COLLUSION

compliment *n* **1** an admiring personal remark ⟨a woman who does not know how to accept a *compliment* graciously⟩
synonyms bouquet, kudo
related words accolade, citation, commendation, encomium, eulogy, homage, paean, panegyric, salutation, tribute, valentine
near antonyms affront, barb, dart, dig, epithet, insult, put-down, slight, slur
2 compliments *pl* best wishes ⟨please extend our *compliments* to the chef for a great meal⟩
synonyms commendations [*archaic*], congratulations, felicitations, greetings, regards, respects
related words approval, benediction, blessing, endorsement (*also* indorsement); acknowledgment (*or* acknowledgement), citation, commendation; adulation, flattery, praise; well-wishing
near antonyms dig, gibe (*or* jibe), insult, put-down, taunt

compliment *vb* to express to (someone) admiration for his or her success or good fortune ⟨*complimented* her on her election victory⟩ — see CONGRATULATE

complimentarily *adv* in an approving manner ⟨a gigantic mall that was *complimentarily* hailed by its developer as "a total shopping experience"⟩ — see ADMIRINGLY

complimentary *adj* **1** expressing approval ⟨the novel received overwhelmingly *complimentary* reviews⟩ — see FAVORABLE 1
2 not costing or charging anything ⟨the airline will continue to give out *complimentary* soft drinks on all domestic flights⟩ — see FREE 4

comply (with) *vb* **1** to act according to the commands of ⟨the guards rushed to *comply with* the warden's orders⟩ — see OBEY
2 to do what is required by the terms of ⟨were summarily threatened with a lawsuit if they did not *comply with* the contract⟩ — see FULFILL 1

component *n* one of the parts that make up a whole ⟨each set is composed of several distinct *components*⟩ — see ELEMENT 1

comport *vb* **1** to be in agreement on every point ⟨an outfit that most definitely does not *comport* with the company's guidelines for dress-down days⟩ — see CHECK 1
2 to manage the actions of (oneself) in a particular way ⟨the grieving relatives *comported* themselves with grace and dignity during that difficult time⟩ — see BEHAVE

comportment *n* the way or manner in which one conducts oneself ⟨the *comportment* of visitors who know that they are in effect their country's goodwill ambassadors⟩ — see BEHAVIOR

compose *vb* **1** to put (something) into proper and usually carefully worked out written form ⟨*composed* a statement on this hot-button issue that managed to satisfy absolutely no one⟩
synonyms cast, craft, draft, draw up, formulate, frame, prepare
related words fabricate, fashion, form, mold, sculpture, shape; couch, express, phrase, state, verbalize, word; author, indite, pen, write; conceive, concoct, devise; build, construct, make; assemble, compound, piece (together); redraft, reformulate, reframe
phrases put together
2 to be all the substance of ⟨the earth's crust is *composed* of mostly silicon with several other elements in smaller amounts⟩ — see CONSTITUTE 1
3 to free from distress or disturbance ⟨the first order of business was to *compose* the injured pedestrian⟩ — see CALM 1
4 to gain emotional or mental control of ⟨she took a deep breath and *composed* herself⟩ — see COLLECT 1

composed *adj* free from emotional or mental agitation ⟨stayed *composed* and focused despite all of the distractions⟩ — see CALM 2

composedness *n* evenness of emotions or temper ⟨he coped with the medical emergency with his usual *composedness*⟩ — see EQUANIMITY

composer *n* a person who writes musical compositions ⟨a versatile *composer* whose works include operas, symphonies, concertos, and sonatas⟩
synonyms melodist, musician
related words cocomposer; songsmith, songwriter, tunesmith; symphonist; arranger, orchestrator (*also* orchestrater), scorer; librettist, lyricist, lyrist

composite *adj* made from the joining of two or more parts or elements ⟨the movie's special effects included the use of many *composite* photographs⟩
synonyms amalgamated, compound
related words blended, combined, commingled, mingled, mixed; coalescent, fused, integrated; interlaced, intermixed, intertwined, interwoven; cut-and-paste
near antonyms uncombined, unmixed
antonyms noncompound, simple

composite *n* a distinct entity formed by the combining of two or more different things ⟨a striking *composite* of two separate images⟩ — see BLEND

composite *vb* to turn into a single mass or entity that is more or less the same throughout ⟨wood chips can be *composited* or sold as mulch⟩ — see BLEND 1

composition *n* **1** a literary, musical, or artistic production ⟨the *compositions* of Michelangelo include the dome of St. Peter's, the ceiling of the Sistine Chapel, and his monumental statue of David⟩
synonyms number, opus, piece, work
related words classic, magnum opus, masterpiece, pièce de résistance, showpiece; model, outline, sketch; étude; canon, corpus, oeuvre
2 a short piece of writing done as a school exercise ⟨a teacher who is fond of having her class write *compositions*⟩
synonyms paper, theme
related words article, essay, story
3 the way in which the elements of something (as a work of art) are arranged ⟨student photographers learn the importance of *composition* in creating striking images⟩
synonyms arrangement, configuration, constellation, design, form, format, getup, layout, makeup, ordonnance, pattern
related words motif, theme
4 a short piece of writing typically expressing a point of view ⟨submitted a *composition* to the local newspaper for its special section marking Martin Luther King Day⟩ — see ESSAY 1

compos mentis *adj* having full use of one's mind and control over one's actions ⟨went to court to prove that her grandmother was no longer *compos mentis* and needed a legal guardian⟩ — see SANE

composure *n* evenness of emotions or temper ⟨kept his *composure* in spite of the repeated provocations⟩ — see EQUANIMITY

compound *adj* made from the joining of two or more parts or elements ⟨a *compound* word⟩ — see COMPOSITE

compound *n* a distinct entity formed by the combining of two or more different things ⟨mixed the chemicals together to form a new *compound*⟩ — see BLEND

compound *vb* **1** to make greater in size, amount, or number ⟨we *compounded* our error by waiting too long to call for help⟩ — see INCREASE 1

2 to put or bring together so as to form a new and longer whole ⟨the German language's propensity for *compounding* words⟩ — see CONNECT 1

comprehend *vb* **1** to have a clear idea of ⟨the age at which children can *comprehend* the difference between right and wrong⟩

synonyms appreciate, apprehend, assimilate, behold, catch, catch on (to), cognize, compass, conceive, cotton (to *or* on to), decipher, decode, dig, discern, get, grasp, grok, intuit, know, make, make out, perceive, recognize, register, savvy, see, seize, sense, tumble (to), twig, understand

related words absorb, digest, take in; realize; fathom, penetrate, pierce

phrases pick up on

near antonyms misapprehend, misconceive, misconstrue, misinterpret, misperceive, misread, mistake, misunderstand

antonyms miss

2 to have a practical understanding of ⟨it took me a while to *comprehend* algebra⟩ — see KNOW 1

3 to have as part of a whole ⟨our notion of morality should *comprehend* much more than proper sexual behavior⟩ — see INCLUDE 1

comprehendible *adj* capable of being understood ⟨much of what the theoretical physicist wrote is hardly *comprehendible* by the average person⟩ — see INTELLIGIBLE

comprehensible *adj* capable of being understood ⟨a book that makes the subject of longitude *comprehensible* to most laymen⟩ — see INTELLIGIBLE

comprehension *n* the knowledge gained from the process of coming to know or understand something ⟨the president's *comprehension* of the current situation in the Middle East⟩

synonyms appreciation, apprehension, grasp, grip, hold, perception, percipience, understanding

related words absorption, assimilation, digestion, uptake; conception, visualization; awareness, consciousness, enlightenment, realization

near antonyms misapprehension, miscomprehension, misinterpretation, misperception, misunderstanding

antonyms incomprehension, noncomprehension

comprehensive *adj* **1** covering everything or all important points ⟨a *comprehensive* overview of European history since the French Revolution⟩ — see ENCYCLOPEDIC

2 not lacking any part or member that properly belongs to it ⟨a *comprehensive* listing of all the paintings generally attributed to the Dutch artist Rembrandt⟩ — see COMPLETE 1

3 trying all possibilities ⟨*comprehensive* plans for covering just about any conceivable terrorist attack⟩ — see EXHAUSTIVE 1

comprehensively *adv* with attention to all aspects or details ⟨no period in American history has been as *comprehensively* studied as the Civil War⟩ — see THOROUGHLY 1

compress *vb* **1** to reduce in size or volume by or as if by pressing parts or members together ⟨a science textbook that *compresses* a lot of information about human reproduction into a few short chapters⟩

synonyms capsule, capsulize, collapse, compact, condense, constrict, constringe, contract, narrow (down), squeeze, telescope

related words cram, crowd, jam, jam-pack, pack; abbreviate, abridge, curtail, shorten; boil down, downsize, shrink; concentrate, consolidate; simplify, streamline; decrease, diminish, lessen

near antonyms dilate, disperse, dissipate, scatter; distend, inflate, swell

antonyms decompress, expand, open, outspread, outstretch

2 to become smaller in size or volume through the drawing together of particles of matter ⟨the substance can *compress* under pressure⟩ — see CONTRACT 2

compression *n* the act or process of reducing the size or volume of something by or as if by pressing ⟨the *compression* of a long, complicated story into a two-hour movie is never easy⟩

synonyms compacting, compaction, condensation, condensing, constricting, constriction, contracting, contraction, squeeze, squeezing, telescoping

related words abbreviation, abridgment (*or* abridgement), curtailment, shortening; concentration, consolidation; simplification, streamlining; decreasing, diminishment, lessening

near antonyms dilation, dispersion, dissipation, scattering; distension (*or* distention), inflation, swelling

antonyms decompression, expansion

comprise *vb* **1** to be made up of ⟨the mall *comprises* three department stores and 80 smaller shops selling specialized goods⟩

synonyms consist (of), contain, muster

related words comprehend, embrace, encompass, entail, include, involve, take in; assimilate, embody, incorporate

2 to be all the substance of ⟨at the time, about 100,000 fighting men and women *comprised* our military force in that country⟩ — see CONSTITUTE 1

compromise *n* the act or practice of each side giving up something in order to reach an agreement ⟨eventually we reached a *compromise* on the number of hours per week that would be devoted to piano practice⟩ — see CONCESSION 1

compromise *vb* **1** to place in danger ⟨officials at the state department were concerned that his statements would *compromise* national security⟩ — see ENDANGER

2 to reduce the soundness, effectiveness, or perfection of ⟨the deletion of several critical points for space considerations really *compromised* the essay⟩ — see DAMAGE 1

compulsion *n* the use of power to impose one's will on another ⟨in that class I read books under *compulsion* that I ordinarily wouldn't have considered⟩ — see FORCE 2

compulsive *adj* caused by or suggestive of an irresistible urge ⟨his *compulsive* clowning around can sometimes be annoying⟩

synonyms besetting, driven, impulsive, obsessional, obsessive

related words irrepressible, uncontrollable; automatic, instinctive, involuntary, knee-jerk, reflex, spontaneous; conditioned, mechanical; unconscious, unthinking, unwitting; capricious, unpredictable, whimsical

near antonyms unforced, voluntary, willful (*or* wilful); controllable, manageable, resistible

compulsory *adj* forcing one's compliance or participation by or as if by law ⟨*compulsory* retirement at age 70⟩ — see MANDATORY

compunction *n* an uneasy feeling about the rightness of what one is doing or going to do ⟨throughout her school years she cheated without *compunction*⟩ — see QUALM

compunctious *adj* feeling sorrow for a wrong that one has done ⟨he appeared not the least bit *compunctious* about ditching his date at the bar and walking off with the woman he had just met⟩ — see CONTRITE

computation *n* the act or process of performing mathematical operations to find a value ⟨we were able to divide the dinner bill fairly with a little *computation*⟩ — see CALCULATION

compute *vb* to determine (a value) by doing the necessary mathematical operations ⟨for the test we were required to *compute* the answers without using a calculator⟩ — see CALCULATE 1

comrade *n* **1** a person frequently seen in the company of another ⟨the boy, and two others who are known to be his *comrades*, are wanted for questioning by the police⟩ — see ASSOCIATE 1
2 a person who has a strong liking for and trust in another ⟨we expect to be *comrades* for the rest of our lives⟩ — see FRIEND 1
3 an adherent or advocate of an economic system in which the means of production are owned and controlled by the state ⟨a novel about an aging *comrade's* eventual disenchantment with communism and its excesses⟩ — see COMMUNIST

comradely *adj* having or showing kindly feeling and sincere interest ⟨a *comradely* handshake from an old friend whom he hadn't seen in years⟩ — see FRIENDLY 1

comradery *n* the feeling of closeness and friendship that exists between companions ⟨the special *comradery* that exists between soldiers that have experienced the crucible of combat together⟩ — see COMPANIONSHIP

comradeship *n* the feeling of closeness and friendship that exists between companions ⟨nursing home residents are able to offer each other support and *comradeship*⟩ — see COMPANIONSHIP

[1]**con** *n* a person convicted as a criminal and serving a prison sentence ⟨was uneasy with the fact that an ex-*con* was living next door⟩ — see CONVICT

[2]**con** *n* an instance of the use of dishonest methods to acquire something of value ⟨the explanation was so plausible that I never suspected it was all a *con* to make off with my car⟩ — see FRAUD 1

[1]**con** *vb* **1** to commit to memory ⟨usually candidates *con* their entire campaign speech, right down to the jokes they supposedly ad-lib⟩ — see MEMORIZE
2 to look over closely (as for judging quality or condition) ⟨seemed to be *conning* his face for any sign of romantic interest⟩ — see INSPECT

[2]**con** *vb* **1** to rob by the use of trickery or threats ⟨a fly-by-night operator who had *conned* hundreds of would-be homeowners out of their hard-earned money⟩ — see FLEECE
2 to cause to believe what is untrue ⟨tried to *con* me into thinking that he had actually won the lottery⟩ — see DECEIVE

concatenate *vb* **1** to put or bring together so as to form a new and longer whole ⟨*concatenate* several lists of instructions into a single master file⟩ — see CONNECT 1
2 to put together into a series by means of or as if by means of a thread ⟨the movie actually *concatenates* into one extended narrative several episodes from various books in the series⟩ — see THREAD 2

concatenation *n* a series of things linked together ⟨a complicated *concatenation* of events leading to the freak accident⟩ — see CHAIN 1

concave *adj* curved inward ⟨a *concave* lens⟩ — see HOLLOW

concavity *n* a sunken area forming a separate space ⟨water collected in a shallow *concavity* on the floor of the cave⟩ — see HOLE 2

conceal *vb* **1** to put into a hiding place ⟨wisely *concealed* the documents in a drawer beneath a false bottom⟩ — see [1]HIDE 1
2 to keep secret or shut off from view ⟨tried to *conceal* her true intentions from immigration officials⟩ — see [1]HIDE 2

concealment *n* **1** the placing of something out of sight ⟨your choice of the oven for the *concealment* of the money was unwise⟩
synonyms caching, hiding, secretion, stashing
related words burial, burying, entombment, interment, interring
near antonyms disinterment, unearthing
antonyms display, exhibition, exposure, parading, showing
2 a place where a person goes to hide or to avoid others ⟨cave-riddled mountains that offer a multitude of *concealments* where a fugitive could hide indefinitely⟩ — see HIDEOUT

concede *vb* **1** to accept the truth or existence of (something) usually reluctantly ⟨she grudgingly *conceded* his point⟩ — see ADMIT 1
2 to cease resistance (as to another's arguments, demands, or control) ⟨he *conceded* as soon as it became clear that he could not win⟩ — see YIELD 3

conceit *n* **1** an elaborate or fanciful way of expressing something ⟨the *conceit* that the crowd at the outdoor rock concert was a vast sea of people waving to the beat of the music⟩
synonyms metaphor
related words device; analogy, circumlocution, code word, crank, dead metaphor, euphemism, simile; catachresis, mixed metaphor
phrases figure of speech
2 a conception or image created by the imagination and having no objective reality ⟨his dream of swimming in the Olympics is nothing more than a *conceit*⟩ — see FANTASY 1
3 an often unjustified feeling of being pleased with oneself or with one's situation or achievements ⟨even though her novels are enormously popular, the writer is more prone to insecurity than to *conceit*⟩ — see COMPLACENCE 1

conceit *vb, chiefly dialect* to form a mental picture of ⟨after a huge meal like that, I cannot *conceit* eating another thing for the rest of the day⟩ — see IMAGINE 1

conceited *adj* having too high an opinion of oneself ⟨a *conceited* basketball player who was always too busy even to sign autographs⟩
synonyms assured, biggety (*or* biggity) [*Southern & Midland*], bigheaded, complacent, consequential, egoistic (*also* egoistical), egotistic (*or* egotistical), important, overweening, pompous, prideful, proud, self-conceited, self-important, self-opinionated, self-satisfied, smug, stuck-up, swellheaded, vain, vainglorious
related words blusterous, blustery, boastful, bombastic, braggart, bragging, braggy, cocky, swaggering; arrogant, assumptive, bumptious, cavalier, chesty, disdainful, fastuous, haughty, high-and-mighty, high-hat, huffy, lofty, lordly, masterful, peremptory, pontifical, self-asserting, self-assertive, snobbish, snobby, snooty, supercilious, superior, toplofty (*also* toploftical), uppish, uppity; domineering, high-handed, imperious; highfalutin (*also* hifalutin), holier-than-thou, pretentious; overconfident, presuming, presumptuous; confident, self-assured, self-confident; self-adulatory, self-congratulatory, self-contented, self-gratulatory; self-applauding, self-dramatizing, self-glorifying, self-promot-

ing; self-affected, self-centered, self-engrossed, selfish; condescending, patronizing
near antonyms diffident, self-critical, self-distrustful, self-doubting, self-reproachful, self-reproving; meek, timid, unassertive; down-to-earth, unarrogant, unassuming, unpretentious; bashful, demure, introverted, mousy (*or* mousey), overmodest, retiring, sheepish, shrinking, shy
antonyms egoless, humble, modest, uncomplacent

conceitedness *n* an often unjustified feeling of being pleased with oneself or with one's situation or achievements ⟨she was annoyed by his persistent air of *conceitedness*⟩ — see COMPLACENCE 1

conceivably *adv* it is possible ⟨we could *conceivably* finish the project next week⟩ — see PERHAPS

conceive *vb* **1** to form a mental picture of ⟨it takes an idealist to *conceive* a world without war, and an activist to make it happen⟩ — see IMAGINE 1
2 to have a clear idea of ⟨I cannot *conceive* the reason for such pointless vandalism⟩ — see COMPREHEND 1
3 to have as an opinion ⟨I just can't *conceive* that he would have lied⟩ — see BELIEVE 2

concenter *vb* **1** to bring (something) to a central point or under a single control ⟨you'll have to *concenter* your nebulous thoughts on the subject before even attempting to write⟩ — see CENTRALIZE
2 to come together into one body or place ⟨most of the local motels have *concentered* around the theme park, which is the region's biggest attraction by far⟩ — see ASSEMBLE 1

concentrate *vb* **1** to increase the amount of (a substance in a mixture) by removing other substances ⟨prolonged boiling is required to *concentrate* the sap when making maple syrup⟩
synonyms condense
related words clarify, clean, cleanse, distill (*also* distil), flush, leach, purge, purify, refine; boil down, decoct, reduce; compact, harden, solidify; deepen, enhance, heighten, intensify; evaporate, extract, remove; enrich, fortify, richen, strengthen; reconcentrate, recondense
near antonyms adulterate, cut, thin, weaken
antonyms dilute, water (down)
2 to fix (as one's attention) steadily toward a central objective ⟨a president who will try to *concentrate* public attention on the problems of inner cities⟩
synonyms center, fasten, focus, rivet, train
related words aim, direct, home (in on), hone in (on), level, nail, point, set, zero (in on); attend, heed, mind; fixate (on), obsess (over); refocus
3 to bring (something) to a central point or under a single control ⟨time to *concentrate* our efforts on the really important problems that confront us⟩ — see CENTRALIZE
4 to bring together in one body or place ⟨*concentrate* your forces on the right side of the battlefield⟩ — see GATHER 1
5 to come together into one body or place ⟨recent immigrants tend to *concentrate* in port cities⟩ — see ASSEMBLE 1
6 to gradually form into a layer, pile, or mass ⟨the ozone layer is *concentrated* 20 to 30 miles above the Earth's surface⟩ — see COLLECT 2

concentrated *adj* **1** having an abundance of some characteristic quality (as flavor) ⟨a *concentrated* mixture of lemonade and iced tea⟩ — see FULL-BODIED
2 not divided or scattered among several areas of interest or concern ⟨when you get a private conference with that financial adviser, you get nothing but his *concentrated* attention⟩ — see WHOLE 1

concentration *n* a focusing of the mind on something ⟨the noise from the party next door threatened to disturb the law student's *concentration*⟩ — see ATTENTION 1

concept *n* **1** an idea or statement about all of the members of a group or all the instances of a situation ⟨trying to change the public's *concept* of a nightly newscast⟩ — see GENERALIZATION
2 something imagined or pictured in the mind ⟨a *concept* for a new kind of automobile that could revolutionize the industry⟩ — see IDEA 1

conception *n* **1** an idea or statement about all of the members of a group or all the instances of a situation ⟨the false *conception* that wheelchair users are homebound and helpless⟩ — see GENERALIZATION
2 something imagined or pictured in the mind ⟨our changing *conceptions* of what constitutes art⟩ — see IDEA 1

conceptual *adj* dealing with or expressing a quality or idea ⟨*conceptual* thinking is often the most demanding kind of mental activity⟩ — see ABSTRACT 1

concern *n* **1** a commercial or industrial activity or organization ⟨several banking *concerns* in the area⟩ — see ENTERPRISE 1
2 an uneasy state of mind usually over the possibility of an anticipated misfortune or trouble ⟨the recent crime wave has caused a great deal of *concern* in the neighborhood⟩ — see ANXIETY 1

concern *vb* **1** to have (something) as a subject matter ⟨the book *concerns* the challenges faced by children growing up in single-parent households⟩
synonyms cover, deal (with), pertain (to), treat (of)
related words appertain (to), bear (on *or* upon), refer (to), relate (to); advert (to), allude (to), cite, glance (upon), instance, mention, name, note, notice, quote, specify, touch (upon); offer, present; contain, embrace, encompass, entail, include, incorporate
phrases have to do with
near antonyms exclude, omit; disregard, forget, ignore, neglect, overlook, overpass, pass over, slight, slur (over); brush (aside *or* off), reject, shrug off
2 to be the business or affair of ⟨the problems of air and water pollution that *concern* all of us⟩
synonyms affect, involve, touch
related words appertain (to), apply (to), bear (on), pertain (to), refer (to), relate (to); embroil, ensnare, entangle, implicate
3 to trouble the mind of; to make uneasy ⟨we were greatly *concerned* by reports that yet another previously unknown virus is now posing a threat⟩ — see DISTURB 1

concerning *prep* having to do with ⟨we had a meeting with the principal today *concerning* the new policy on student-run organizations⟩ — see ABOUT 1

concernment *n* an uneasy state of mind usually over the possibility of an anticipated misfortune or trouble ⟨as my layoff from work grew longer and longer, how I was going to pay my bills became a matter of *concernment*⟩ — see ANXIETY 1

concert *n* an entertainment featuring singing or the playing of musical instruments ⟨during the summer various groups give *concerts* on the town green⟩
synonyms musicale
related words performance, presentation; recital, symphony; ceilidh (*also* ceili) [*Scottish & Irish*], hootenanny, jam, jam session, sing, songfest; festival, fete (*or* fête), shindig

concert *vb* **1** to bring about through discussion and compromise ⟨warned that the rain forests are in danger of extinction unless the world's industrial powers *concert* a plan to prevent such an occurrence⟩ — see NEGOTIATE 1
2 to participate or assist in a joint effort to accomplish an end ⟨the governor is eager to *concert* with the federal

authorities on this matter⟩ — see COOPERATE 1

concerted *adj* used or done by a number of people as a group ⟨a victory like that results only from the *concerted* effort of the entire team⟩ — see COLLECTIVE

concertedly *adv* in or by combined action or effort ⟨the two ball players seemed to be *concertedly* trying to shatter every batting record in the American League⟩ — see TOGETHER 2

concession *n* **1** the act or practice of each side giving up something in order to reach an agreement ⟨when trying to get a raise in your salary, it's good to know the art of *concession*⟩
synonyms accommodation, compromise, give-and-take, negotiation
related words haggle, horse trade; accord, arrangement, bargain, concurrence, consensus, deal, understanding; agreement, settlement; mediation, treaty
2 an open declaration of something (as a fault or the commission of an offense) about oneself ⟨an abject *concession* of guilt from the governor is the only thing that will save her political career⟩ — see CONFESSION
3 something granted as a special favor ⟨a *concession* to sell their T-shirts at the village fair⟩ — see PRIVILEGE

conciliate *vb* **1** to bring to a state free of conflicts, inconsistencies, or differences ⟨it will be hard to *conciliate* the views of labor and management regarding health benefits⟩ — see HARMONIZE 2
2 to lessen the anger or agitation of ⟨a principal trying to *conciliate* the parents who did not receive their tickets to the graduation ceremonies⟩ — see PACIFY 1

conciliating *adj* tending to lessen or avoid conflict or hostility ⟨small *conciliating* acts designed to win the trust of the new neighbors⟩ — see PACIFIC 1

conciliator *n* one who works with opposing sides in order to bring about an agreement ⟨his genius as a *conciliator* is that he is able to convince both sides that they got everything they wanted⟩ — see MEDIATOR

conciliatory *adj* tending to lessen or avoid conflict or hostility ⟨eased the tension with *conciliatory* remarks⟩ — see PACIFIC 1

concinnity *n* a balanced, pleasing, or suitable arrangement of parts ⟨a choral work admired for its seamless *concinnity* of music and dance⟩ — see HARMONY 1

concise *adj* marked by the use of few words to convey much information or meaning ⟨a *concise* article on violence in the media that manages to say more than most books on the subject⟩
synonyms aphoristic, apothegmatic, brief, capsule, compact, compendious, crisp, curt, elliptical (*or* elliptic), epigrammatic, laconic, monosyllabic, pithy, sententious, succinct, summary, telegraphic, terse, thumbnail
related words abrupt, blunt, brusque (*also* brusk), short, snippety, snippy; abbreviated, abridged, condensed, curtailed, shortened; meaty, substantial; meaningful, significant; well-turned
near antonyms pleonastic, redundant, repetitious, tautological, tautologous; enlarged, expanded, supplemented; embellished, embroidered, exaggerated, inflated
antonyms circuitous, circumlocutory, diffuse, long-winded, prolix, rambling, verbose, windy, wordy

concisely *adv* in a few words ⟨since there's little room on the form, you'll have to state *concisely* the reason why you're returning the merchandise⟩ — see SHORTLY 1

conciseness *n* **1** the condition of being short ⟨we were disappointed by the unexpected *conciseness* of the presentation, since we wanted more details⟩ — see BREVITY 1
2 the quality or state of being marked by or using only few words to convey much meaning ⟨many have admired the restrained *conciseness* of Emily Dickinson's poetry⟩ — see SUCCINCTNESS

concision *n* the quality or state of being marked by or using only few words to convey much meaning ⟨the essay is a marvel of *concision* and clarity⟩ — see SUCCINCTNESS

conclude *vb* **1** to bring (an event) to a natural or appropriate stopping point ⟨a brief reminder of tonight's game *concluded* the announcements⟩ — see CLOSE 3
2 to come to an end ⟨the concert *concluded* late in the evening⟩ — see CEASE 1
3 to bring about through discussion and compromise ⟨*concluded* an economic agreement among the world's leading industrial nations⟩ — see NEGOTIATE 1
4 to come to a judgment about after discussion or consideration ⟨he *concluded* that the reprimand could wait until later⟩ — see DECIDE 1
5 to form an opinion or reach a conclusion through reasoning and information ⟨*concluded* that only the murderer could possibly have known that information⟩ — see INFER 1

concluded *adj* brought or having come to an end ⟨with another recently *concluded* fiscal year behind us, we are now ready to face new challenges⟩ — see COMPLETE 2

concluding *adj* following all others of the same kind in order or time ⟨the *concluding* statement will be read by the secretary⟩ — see LAST 1

conclusion *n* **1** an opinion arrived at through a process of reasoning ⟨the detective's *conclusion* that the murderer had to be left-handed⟩
synonyms consequence, deduction, determination, eduction, induction, inference, sequitur
related words decision, deliverance, diagnosis, judgment (*or* judgement), resolution, ruling, verdict; conjecture, guess, surmise; assumption, presumption, supposition
2 a position arrived at after consideration ⟨came to the *conclusion* that we couldn't go on vacation while the dog was sick⟩ — see DECISION 1
3 a condition or occurrence traceable to a cause ⟨all their efforts came to no practical *conclusion*⟩ — see EFFECT 1
4 the last part of a process or action ⟨the *conclusion* of the speech was a national call to arms⟩ — see FINALE
5 the stopping of a process or activity ⟨a bell signaled the *conclusion* of the event⟩ — see END 1

conclusive *adj* **1** serving to put an end to all debate or questioning ⟨the archeological discovery was *conclusive* proof that the Vikings had indeed settled in North America around 1000 A.D.⟩
synonyms absolute, clear, deciding, decisive, definitive, last
related words determinate, determinative, dispositive, hands-down, inarguable, incontestable, incontrovertible, indisputable, indubitable, irrefutable, unanswerable, undebatable, undeniable, undisputable, unquestionable; unchallenged, uncontested, undisputed; unambiguous, unequivocal; certain, definite, positive, sure; cogent, compelling, convincing, persuasive, telling
near antonyms debatable, disputable, doubtable, doubtful, moot, problematic (*also* problematical), questionable, refutable; ambiguous, equivocal; controversial, debated, disputed
antonyms inconclusive, indecisive, unclear
2 having the power to persuade ⟨a *conclusive* argument for allowing the students to put on a play of their own choosing⟩ — see COGENT

conclusiveness *n* the capacity to persuade ⟨the *conclusiveness* of DNA testing in paternity suits⟩ — see COGENCY 1

concoct *vb* to create or think of by clever use of the imagination ⟨trying to *concoct* an explanation for how the lamp got broken by itself⟩ — see INVENT

concoction *n* something (as a device) created for the first time through the use of the imagination ⟨the first submarine must have seemed like the looniest *concoction* ever to spring from the human mind⟩ — see INVENTION 1

concomitant *adj* present at the same time and place ⟨an improvement in the facilities led to a *concomitant* improvement in morale⟩ — see COINCIDENT 1

concomitant *n* something that is found along with something else ⟨disease is all too often one of the *concomitants* of poverty⟩ — see ACCOMPANIMENT

concord *n* peaceful coexistence ⟨living in *concord* with people of different races and religions⟩ — see HARMONY 2

concordant *adj* not having or showing any apparent conflict ⟨the movie's opening-weekend gross was fairly *concordant* with box-office returns for that genre⟩ — see CONSISTENT

concourse *n* a typically long narrow way connecting parts of a building ⟨airline passengers had to pass through the security checkpoints before being allowed in the *concourse*⟩ — see HALL 2

concrete *adj* **1** existing in fact and not merely as a possibility ⟨*concrete* evidence, and not just a theory, must be presented at a trial⟩ — see ACTUAL

2 relating to or composed of matter ⟨*concrete* objects like rocks and trees⟩ — see MATERIAL 1

3 of a particular or exact sort ⟨while there was a lot of hand-wringing, no one offered a practical, *concrete* plan for the energy shortage⟩ — see EXPRESS 1

concrete *vb* **1** to become physically firm or solid ⟨the mortar slowly *concreted* in the mold⟩ — see HARDEN 1

2 to turn into a single mass or entity that is more or less the same throughout ⟨a choral work that *concretes* music and dance into a stunning theatrical experience⟩ — see BLEND 1

concubine *n* ⟨spent an exorbitant sum on furnishing living quarters for his *concubine*⟩ — see MISTRESS

concupiscence *n* **1** sexual appetite ⟨the Puritans did not condemn *concupiscence* but rather the satisfaction of it in ways they deemed illicit⟩ — see DESIRE 2

2 intense sexual desire ⟨according the church theologian St. Augustine, *concupiscence* is a consequence of original sin⟩ — see LUST 1

concupiscent *adj* having a strong sexual desire ⟨such was Giacomo Casanova's notoriety as a promiscuous lover that his name became an epithet for a *concupiscent* man of the world⟩ — see LUSTFUL

concur *vb* **1** to have or come to the same opinion or point of view ⟨I *concur* with your assessment of the political situation⟩ — see AGREE 1

2 to occur or exist at the same time ⟨the lively 1960s, a decade in which the Cold War, the race to the moon, the Vietnam War, and the civil rights movement all *concurred*⟩ — see COINCIDE 1

3 to participate or assist in a joint effort to accomplish an end ⟨all sides *concurred* to pass the reform legislation on campaign financing⟩ — see COOPERATE 1

concurrence *n* **1** the occurrence or existence of several things at once ⟨the *concurrence* of my birthday and the concert by my favorite rock band made my preference for a birthday present pretty obvious⟩

synonyms coexistence, coincidence, concurrency

related words development, happening, occurrence; coevality, contemporaneousness, simultaneousness, synchronism, synchrony

near antonyms asynchrony (*or* asynchronism)

2 the state of being of one opinion about something ⟨looked for some sign of *concurrence* among the delegates to the conference⟩ — see AGREEMENT 1

3 the approval by someone in authority for the doing of something ⟨we needed the *concurrence* of the boss before proceeding with the project⟩ — see PERMISSION

concurrency *n* **1** the occurrence or existence of several things at once ⟨the *concurrency* of several life-threatening emergencies made for a busy night at the trauma center⟩ — see CONCURRENCE 1

2 the state of being of one opinion about something ⟨there is general *concurrency* that the rule concerning the writing of thank-you notes still pertains⟩ — see AGREEMENT 1

concurrent *adj* **1** existing or occurring at the same period of time ⟨*concurrent* expeditions to the Antarctic that were in a race to reach the South Pole⟩ — see CONTEMPORARY 1

2 present at the same time and place ⟨the postwar period of prosperity and the *concurrent* baby boom are the major topics in this history of the 1950s⟩ — see COINCIDENT 1

concurrently *adv* at one and the same time ⟨two major trade shows running *concurrently* at the convention center⟩ — see TOGETHER 1

concussion *n* **1** a forceful coming together of two things ⟨the *concussion* of the airliner slamming into the skyscraper was felt for several blocks in all directions⟩ — see IMPACT 1

2 the violent coming together of two bodies into destructive contact ⟨the theory that such a *concussion*, by a giant asteroid or comet millions of years ago, led to the extinction of the dinosaurs⟩ — see CRASH 1

condemn *vb* **1** to declare to be morally wrong or evil ⟨it is a sign of human progress that slavery, which was once common, is now universally *condemned*⟩

synonyms anathematize, censure, damn, decry, denounce, execrate, reprehend, reprobate

related words attack, blame, blast, criticize, dis (*also* diss) [*slang*], dispraise, fault, knock, pan, slam; belittle, deprecate, disparage; doom, sentence; convict; blacklist, excommunicate, ostracize; castigate, chastise, rebuke, reprimand, reproach; admonish, chide, reprove; berate, lambaste (*or* lambast), rake, scold, upbraid, vituperate; curse, imprecate; abhor, abominate, detest, hate, loathe, revile

near antonyms approve, endorse (*also* indorse), sanction; eulogize, exalt, extol (*also* extoll), glorify, laud, praise; acclaim, applaud, commend, hail, salute, tout; consecrate, hallow, sanctify; honor, revere, venerate

antonyms bless

2 to express one's unfavorable opinion of the worth or quality of ⟨a report that *condemns* the working conditions in the factories of many developing countries⟩ — see CRITICIZE

3 to express public or formal disapproval of ⟨the philosopher's works were once *condemned* by the church and placed on its list of forbidden books⟩ — see CENSURE 1

4 to find or pronounce guilty ⟨the accused was *condemned* by the news media even before the trial began⟩ — see CONVICT

5 to impose a judicial punishment on ⟨a stern judge who does not hesitate to *condemn* a felon to life behind bars⟩ — see SENTENCE

condemnation *n* an often public or formal expression of disapproval ⟨a *condemnation* of the war by the conference of bishops⟩ — see CENSURE

condensation *n* **1** a shortened version of a written work ⟨a *condensation* of the opinion issued by the state's supreme court⟩ — see ABRIDGMENT

2 the act or process of reducing the size or volume of something by or as if by pressing ⟨a staff employed in the *condensation* of magazine articles⟩ — see COMPRESSION

condense *vb* **1** to become smaller in size or volume through the drawing together of particles of matter

⟨over time the once-fluffy material in the pillow had *condensed* into a lumpy wad⟩ — see CONTRACT 2
2 to reduce in size or volume by or as if by pressing parts or members together ⟨*condense* the information into as brief a report as possible⟩ — see COMPRESS 1
3 to increase the amount of (a substance in a mixture) by removing other substances ⟨added *condensed* milk to the mix⟩ — see CONCENTRATE 1

condensing *n* the act or process of reducing the size or volume of something by or as if by pressing ⟨after the *condensing* of our stored junk, we actually had room in the garage for the car⟩ — see COMPRESSION

condescend *vb* 1 to descend to a level that is beneath one's dignity ⟨I will not *condescend* to answer the sore loser's charge that I cheated in order to win the race⟩
synonyms deign, stoop
related words abase, debase, degrade, demean, discredit, disgrace, dishonor, humble, humiliate, lower, shame
near antonyms rise
2 to assume or treat with an air of superiority ⟨wealthy people who tend to be *condescending* toward their poor relations⟩
synonyms lord (it over), patronize, talk down (to)
related words cold-shoulder, cut, high-hat, slight, snub; queen (it over)

condign *adj* being what is called for by accepted standards of right and wrong ⟨a suspension without pay is *condign* punishment for breaking the company's code of business ethics⟩ — see JUST 1

condiment *n* something used to enhance the flavor of cooked or prepared food ⟨the cafeteria's self-serve table has a full array of *condiments*⟩
synonyms seasoning
related words herb, savory, spice; relish, sauce; flavoring

condition *n* 1 a state of being or fitness ⟨a car that was 10 years old but in still good *condition*⟩
synonyms estate, fettle, form, health, keeping, kilter, nick [*British*], order, repair, shape, trim
related words practice (*also* practise); pass, phase, stage; footing, picture, posture, scene, status, situation; rank, standing
near antonyms disorder, disrepair
2 something upon which the carrying out of an agreement or offer depends ⟨you'll get a bonus with the *condition* that we meet our sales forecast⟩
synonyms contingency, if, provision, proviso, qualification, reservation, stipulation
related words strings, terms; precondition, prerequisite, requirement, requisite; limitation, modification, restriction; exception, exemption; demand, essential, must, necessity, need
3 an abnormal state that disrupts a plant's or animal's normal bodily functioning ⟨a skin *condition* that prevents me from staying out in the sun for very long⟩ — see DISEASE
4 something necessary, indispensable, or unavoidable ⟨water is a *condition* for life on Earth⟩ — see ESSENTIAL 1
5 something that limits one's freedom of action or choice ⟨their parents placed several *conditions* on their weekend plans⟩ — see RESTRICTION 1

condition *vb* 1 to bring to a proper or desired state of fitness ⟨the length of time that it takes for runners to *condition* their bodies for a marathon⟩
synonyms season, train
related words fit, habilitate, prepare, ready; acclimate, acclimatize, accommodate, adapt, adjust, break in, orient, orientate, shape; accustom, familiarize, habituate, naturalize; fortify, harden, inure, season, shape up, steel, strengthen, toughen
antonyms decondition
2 to change (something) so as to make it suitable for a new use or situation ⟨an immigrant family that must *condition* its traditional attitudes regarding child rearing to the realities of modern American life⟩ — see ADAPT

conditional *adj* determined by something else ⟨the sale of the house is *conditional* upon the approval of a mortgage for the prospective buyer⟩ — see DEPENDENT 2

conditioning *n* energetic movement of the body for the sake of physical fitness ⟨the actor went through months of *conditioning* in order to play the role of the buffed hero in the action film⟩ — see EXERCISE 1

condole (with) *vb* to have sympathy for ⟨*condole with* them in their hour of grief⟩ — see PITY

condonable *adj* worthy of forgiveness ⟨she doesn't think infidelity is ever *condonable*⟩ — see VENIAL

condone *vb* to dismiss as of little importance ⟨he is too quick to *condone* his friend's faults⟩ — see EXCUSE 1

conducive *adj* 1 tending to promote or assist the development of something ⟨the claim that the state's long-standing antitax attitude is *conducive* to entrepreneurship⟩
synonyms facilitative
related words advantageous, beneficial, favorable, helpful, profitable, propitious, salutary
near antonyms bad, damaging, deleterious, disadvantageous, harmful, injurious, unfavorable, unhelpful
2 providing service or assistance ⟨the noisy environment of the dorms was not very *conducive* to studying⟩ — see HELPFUL 1

conduct *n* 1 the act or activity of looking after and making decisions about something ⟨the President was happy to leave the *conduct* of foreign affairs to his secretary of state⟩
synonyms administration, care, charge, control, direction, governance, government, guidance, handling, intendance, management, operation, oversight, presidency, regulation, running, stewardship, superintendence, superintendency, supervision
related words generalship, leadership, rulership; agency; aegis (*also* egis), custody, guardianship, keeping, lap, protection, safekeeping, trust, tutelage, ward; engineering, logistics, machination, manipulation; coadministration, codirection, comanagement
2 the way or manner in which one conducts oneself ⟨a child who has often been scolded for poor *conduct* in public⟩ — see BEHAVIOR

conduct *vb* 1 to look after and make decisions about ⟨the company's president continues to *conduct* the everyday affairs of the software firm he founded many years ago⟩
synonyms administer, administrate, carry on, control, direct, govern, guide, handle, keep, manage, operate, overlook, oversee, preside (over), regulate, run, steward, superintend, supervise, tend
related words care (for), mind, watch; lead, pilot, steer; guard, protect, safeguard; micromanage, stage-manage; codirect, comanage
phrases watch over
2 to cause to move to a central point or along a restricted pathway ⟨the gutter *conducts* water to the curb, thus protecting the house's basement⟩ — see CHANNEL
3 to manage the actions of (oneself) in a particular way ⟨*conducted* themselves at the party like perfect ladies and gentlemen⟩ — see BEHAVE
4 to point out the way for (someone) especially from a position in front ⟨a job *conducting* tourists through the historical museum⟩ — see LEAD 1
5 to cause (something) to pass from one to another ⟨a material that *conducts* heat quite efficiently⟩ — see COMMUNICATE 1

conduit *n* **1** a long hollow cylinder for carrying a substance (as a liquid or gas) ⟨the major *conduit* for carrying water to the military base⟩ — see PIPE 1
2 an open man-made passageway for water ⟨water flowed along the *conduit* to the fountain⟩ — see CHANNEL 1

confab *n* **1** an exchange of views for the purpose of exploring a subject or deciding an issue ⟨we had a little *confab* about the merits of the plan⟩ — see DISCUSSION 1
2 friendly, informal conversation or an instance of this ⟨after the requisite *confab*, we got down to business⟩ — see CHAT 1

confab *vb* to exchange viewpoints or seek advice for the purpose of finding a solution to a problem ⟨the members of the condo board have been *confabbing* about the security problem⟩ — see CONFER 2

confabulate *vb* to exchange viewpoints or seek advice for the purpose of finding a solution to a problem ⟨an Alzheimer's support group in which caregivers can *confabulate* as well as commiserate⟩ — see CONFER 2

confabulation *n* **1** an exchange of views for the purpose of exploring a subject or deciding an issue ⟨there seemed to be some sort of lengthy *confabulation* going on in the next room⟩ — see DISCUSSION 1
2 friendly, informal conversation or an instance of this ⟨began our *confabulation* with that traditional icebreaker: an innocuous discussion of the weather⟩ — see CHAT 1

confect *vb* to form by putting together parts or materials ⟨a cook who can *confect* a magnificent dinner from whatever ingredients are in the cupboards⟩ — see BUILD

confection *n* a food having a high sugar content ⟨following the main course there were assorted *confections* so delicious-looking as to tempt even determined dieters⟩ — see SWEET 1

confederacy *n* an association of persons, parties, or states for mutual assistance and protection ⟨a *confederacy* of several small nations who had promised to come to one another's aid if any were attacked⟩
synonyms alliance, axis, bloc, block, coalition, combination, combine, confederation, federation, league, union
related words cabal, conspiracy, junto; cartel, syndicate, trust; faction, front, fusion, side, wing; association, group, organization; affiliation, cooperative, partnership; circuit, conference

confederate *n* **1** one associated with another in wrongdoing ⟨the police were able to track down his *confederates* once the thief started talking⟩ — see ACCOMPLICE
2 someone associated with another to give assistance or moral support ⟨relied on her *confederates* in the medical community for support⟩ — see ALLY

confederate *vb* to form or enter into an association that furthers the interests of its members ⟨the nations *confederated* in order to lower international trade barriers⟩ — see ALLY

confederation *n* **1** an association of persons, parties, or states for mutual assistance and protection ⟨the smaller nations were forced to form a *confederation* out of self-defense⟩ — see CONFEDERACY
2 the state of having shared interests or efforts (as in social or business matters) ⟨the big-budget movie was produced by the studio in *confederation* with another in order to lower the risk⟩ — see ASSOCIATION 1

confer *vb* **1** to give the ownership or benefit of (something) formally or publicly ⟨the British monarch continues to *confer* knighthood on those who are outstanding in their fields of endeavor⟩
synonyms accord, award, grant, vest
related words bestow, contribute, donate, give, present, show; furnish, provide, supply; extend, offer, proffer; allocate, appropriate, assign; appoint, designate, dub, fix, name, set
near antonyms abort, call, call off, drop, recall, repeal, rescind, revoke; abrogate, annul, invalidate, nullify, void, write off; recant, retract, take back, withdraw
2 to exchange viewpoints or seek advice for the purpose of finding a solution to a problem ⟨my parents are going to *confer* with a financial adviser about saving for their retirement⟩
synonyms advise, confab, confabulate, consult, counsel, parley, powwow, treat
related words argue, bandy, bat (around), chew over, debate, deliberate, discuss, dispute, hash (over), kick around, moot, palaver, talk, talk over, ventilate; rehash; coach, guide, tutor; recommend, suggest; direct, refer (to)

conference *n* **1** a body of people come together in one place ⟨the *conference* voted to conclude that day's meeting and to resume discussions the next morning⟩ — see GATHERING 1
2 a meeting featuring a group discussion ⟨a *conference* on the need for international cooperation in combating emerging viruses⟩ — see FORUM 1
3 an exchange of views for the purpose of exploring a subject or deciding an issue ⟨a parent-teacher *conference* to discuss a student having trouble in school⟩ — see DISCUSSION 1

confess *vb* **1** to make an acknowledgment of something unpleasant as true or valid ⟨the thief *confessed* to dozens of robberies⟩
synonyms admit, cop (to) [*slang*], fess (up), own (up)
related words blab, talk, tattle; babble, spill
near antonyms clam up, hush, quiet (down), shut up
2 to accept the truth or existence of (something) usually reluctantly ⟨political prisoners, under threat of torture, forced to *confess* their guilt⟩ — see ADMIT 1

confession *n* an open declaration of something (as a fault or the commission of an offense) about oneself ⟨a *confession* that he had been lying all along⟩
synonyms acknowledgment (*or* acknowledgement), admission, avowal, concession, self-confession
related words self-accusation, self-betrayal, self-revelation; self-incrimination, self-recrimination, self-reproach; affirmation, assertion, avouchment, claim, confirmation, declaration, insistence, profession; allowance; apology, hand-wringing; betrayal, disclosure, divulgence, giveaway, revelation; announcement, declaration, proclamation, pronouncement; blame, fault, responsibility; contriteness, contrition, penitence, regret, remorse, remorsefulness, repentance, rue
near antonyms denial, disallowance, disclaimer, recantation, rejection, renouncement, repudiation
antonyms disavowal, nonadmission

confidant *n* a person who has a strong liking for and trust in another ⟨she's my *confidant*; I tell her everything without reservation⟩ — see FRIEND 1

confidante *n* a person who has a strong liking for and trust in another ⟨only her closest *confidantes* know what she's going through⟩ — see FRIEND 1

confide *vb* to put (something) into the possession or safekeeping of another ⟨the local SPCA was looking for homes for a number of exotic animals *confided* to its care⟩ — see GIVE 2

confidence *n* **1** great faith in oneself or one's abilities ⟨a lifelong *confidence* that enabled her to achieve great things despite powerful obstacles⟩
synonyms aplomb, assurance, self-assurance, self-assuredness, self-confidence, self-esteem, self-trust
related words cockiness, complacence, complacency, conceit, conceitedness, ego, egoism, egotism, hubris, overconfidence, pomposity, pompousness, pride, pride-

fulness, self-admiration, self-applause, self-assumption, self-complacency, self-conceit, self-consequence, self-content, self-contentment, self-glorification, self-importance, self-opinion, self-partiality, self-satisfaction, smugness, vaingloriousness, vainglory, vanity; calmness, composure, coolness, equanimity; self-poise, self-possession; assumption, bumptiousness, haughtiness, hauteur, huffiness, imperiousness, loftiness, lordliness, peremptoriness, presumptuousness, pretentiousness, superciliousness, superiority, toploftiness

near antonyms apprehension, doubt, misgiving

antonyms diffidence, insecurity, self-distrust, self-doubt

2 a state of mind in which one is free from doubt ⟨the *confidence* with which the game show contestant answered every question⟩

synonyms assurance, assuredness, certainty, certitude, cocksureness, conviction, doubtlessness, face, positiveness, satisfaction, sureness, surety

related words authoritarianism, dogmatism; decisiveness, determination, firmness, purposefulness, resoluteness, resolution, resolve

near antonyms hesitancy, hesitation, indecisiveness, irresolution; disbelief, incredulity, unbelief; anxiety, concern, misgiving; distrust, mistrust, suspicion

antonyms doubt, incertitude, nonconfidence, uncertainty

3 firm belief in the integrity, ability, effectiveness, or genuineness of someone or something ⟨as players, we have complete *confidence* in our coach⟩ — see TRUST 1

4 information shared only with another or with a select few ⟨accused him of betraying an important *confidence*⟩ — see SECRET 1

confidence man *n* a dishonest person who uses clever means to cheat others out of something of value ⟨taken in by a persuasive *confidence man* using the Internet⟩ — see TRICKSTER 1

confident *adj* **1** having or showing great faith in oneself or one's abilities ⟨you'll need to be *confident*—even in the face of rejection—if you want to pursue a career in show business⟩

synonyms assured, secure, self-asserting, self-assured, self-confident

related words collected, composed, cool, coolheaded, poised, recollected, self-possessed, serene, tranquil, unperturbed, unshaken; hopeful, optimistic, rosy, sanguine, upbeat; complacent, conceited, egoistic (*also* egoistical), egotistic (*or* egotistical), important, overweening, pompous, prideful, proud, self-affected, self-applauding, self-centered, self-complacent, self-conceited, self-contented, self-important, self-pleased, self-satisfied; self-promoting, smug, stuck-up, vain, vainglorious; imperturbable, nerveless, unflappable, unselfconscious, unshakable; disciplined, self-collected, self-composed, self-contained, self-controlled, self-poised; self-reliant, self-sufficient

near antonyms meek, timid, unassertive; humble, modest, unassuming, unpretentious; jittery, jumpy, nervous; bashful, demure, mousy (*or* mousey), overmodest, quiet, reserved, shy; self-critical, self-reproachful, self-reproving

antonyms diffident, insecure, self-distrustful, self-doubting

2 having or showing a mind free from doubt ⟨we were *confident* that the directions we had been given were accurate⟩ — see CERTAIN 2

confidential *adj* not known or meant to be known by the general populace ⟨someone leaked *confidential* government information to the press⟩ — see PRIVATE 1

confidentially *adv* in a manner intended to prevent knowledge or awareness by others ⟨he was furious when his friend revealed to others information that he had shared *confidentially*⟩ — see PRIVATELY

confiding *adj* having or showing trust in another ⟨a very *confiding* child who is a little too eager to trust total strangers⟩ — see TRUSTING 1

configuration *n* **1** the arrangement of parts that gives something its basic form ⟨the basic *configuration* of the building is that of a geodesic dome⟩ — see FRAME 1

2 the way in which something is sized, arranged, or organized ⟨a small business computer system in its simplest *configuration*⟩ — see FORMAT 1

3 the way in which the elements of something (as a work of art) are arranged ⟨his photographs have an intentionally loose *configuration*, with no single object intended as the primary center of interest⟩ — see COMPOSITION 3

4 the outward appearance of something as distinguished from its substance ⟨a birthday cake in the *configuration* of a top hat⟩ — see FORM 1

confine *vb* **1** to set bounds or an upper limit for ⟨will *confine* my remarks to the subject we came here to discuss⟩ — see LIMIT 1

2 to put in or as if in prison ⟨the accused was *confined* until the trial could take place⟩ — see IMPRISON

confined *adj* taken and held prisoner ⟨*confined* citizens have basic rights under that nation's constitution⟩ — see CAPTIVE

confinement *n* **1** the act of confining or the state of being confined ⟨some wild animals take to *confinement* very poorly⟩ — see INTERNMENT

2 the act or practice of keeping something (as an activity) within certain boundaries ⟨the *confinement* of commercial development to one stretch of roadway is intended to help preserve the town's rural character⟩ — see RESTRICTION 2

confines *n pl* **1** a real or imaginary point beyond which a person or thing cannot go ⟨within the *confines* of the city⟩ — see LIMIT 1

2 the line or relatively narrow space that marks the outer limit of something ⟨outside the *confines* of the school walls⟩ — see BORDER 1

3 an area over which activity, capacity, or influence extends ⟨that's beyond the *confines* of my power as dean of the college⟩ — see RANGE 2

confirm *vb* **1** to give evidence or testimony to the truth or factualness of ⟨several eyewitnesses who can *confirm* the defendant's account of what happened⟩

synonyms argue, attest, authenticate, bear out, certify, corroborate, substantiate, support, validate, verify, vindicate

related words avouch, back (up), testify (to), vouch (for), witness; guarantee, warrant; affirm, assert, aver, avow, declare, profess; demonstrate, document, establish, prove, reinforce (*also* reenforce)

near antonyms contradict, gainsay; deny, disavow, disclaim; challenge, contest, dispute, question

antonyms disprove, rebut, refute

2 to give official acceptance of as satisfactory ⟨the senate must *confirm* an appointment to an ambassadorship⟩ — see APPROVE

confirmable *adj* capable of being proven as true or real ⟨the theory was not *confirmable*, and eventually it had to be discarded in favor of one that was⟩ — see VERIFIABLE

confirmation *n* something presented in support of the truth or accuracy of a claim ⟨regards the finding as a *confirmation* of the theory that extraterrestrial impacts were responsible for the demise of the dinosaurs⟩ — see PROOF

confirmational *adj* serving to give support to the truth or factualness of something ⟨that's an interesting hypothesis but one that still awaits *confirmational* data⟩ — see CORROBORATIVE

confirmatory *adj* serving to give support to the truth or factualness of something ⟨a *confirmatory* test for pregnancy⟩ — see CORROBORATIVE

confirmed *adj* **1** being such by habit and not likely to change ⟨a *confirmed* grouch who never seems to smile⟩ — see HABITUAL 1
2 firmly established over time ⟨a *confirmed* tendency to exaggerate about everything⟩ — see INVETERATE 1

confirming *adj* serving to give support to the truth or factualness of something ⟨in the absence of *confirming* evidence, we should give him the benefit of the doubt⟩ — see CORROBORATIVE

confiscate *vb* to take ownership or control of (something) by right of one's authority ⟨anything that might be used as a weapon will be *confiscated* by the security guards⟩
synonyms attach, expropriate, sequester
related words garnishee; appropriate, arrogate, preempt, usurp; commandeer, seize, take over
near antonyms cede, deliver, forfeit, give up, hand over, release, relinquish, render, surrender, turn over, yield

conflagrant *adj* being on fire ⟨smoke from the *conflagrant* forest spread over hundreds of square miles⟩ — see ABLAZE 1

conflagration *n* **1** a destructive burning ⟨the historic tavern burned to the ground in a horrible *conflagration*⟩ — see FIRE 1
2 a state of armed violent struggle between states, nations, or groups ⟨what began as a skirmish over disputed territory erupted into a *conflagration* that swept the continent⟩ — see WAR 1

conflate *vb* **1** to fail to differentiate (a thing) from something similar or related ⟨be careful not to *conflate* gossip with real news⟩ — see CONFUSE 3
2 to turn into a single mass or entity that is more or less the same throughout ⟨the movie *conflates* documentary footage and dramatized reenactments so seamlessly and ingeniously that viewers may not know what is real and what is not⟩ — see BLEND 1

conflation *n* a distinct entity formed by the combining of two or more different things ⟨the word "robustious" is probably a *conflation* of "robust" and "boisterous"⟩ — see BLEND

conflict *n* **1** a lack of agreement or harmony ⟨the *conflict* between absolute freedom and personal responsibility⟩ — see DISCORD
2 a physical dispute between opposing individuals or groups ⟨an armed *conflict* between strikers and strikebreakers⟩ — see FIGHT 1
3 a state of armed violent struggle between states, nations, or groups ⟨the United Nations strives to prevent international *conflicts*⟩ — see WAR 1
4 an earnest effort for superiority or victory over another ⟨the eternal *conflict* between the forces of good and evil⟩ — see CONTEST 1

conflict *vb* to be out of harmony or agreement usually noticeably ⟨his statement *conflicts* with the facts, as given in the police report⟩ — see CLASH

conflicted *adj* having a mixture of opposing feelings ⟨I'm *conflicted* about the prospect of our only child going away to college⟩
synonyms ambivalent, equivocal
related words doubtful, faltering, irresolute, questioning, uncertain, undecided, unsure, vacillating, wobbly (*also* wabbly); afraid, disinclined, dubious, hesitant, indisposed, loath (*also* loth *or* loathe), reluctant
near antonyms certain, decided, resolute, sure, unquestioning
antonyms unambivalent

conflicting *adj* not being in agreement or harmony ⟨*conflicting* reports from the witnesses at the scene⟩ — see INCONSISTENT 1

confluence *n* the coming together of two or more things to the same point ⟨a happy *confluence* of beautiful weather and spectacular scenery during our vacation⟩ — see CONVERGENCE

confluent *n* a stream that flows into a larger body of water ⟨several *confluents* slowly winding their way to the main river⟩ — see TRIBUTARY

conform *vb* **1** to be in agreement on every point ⟨the list *conforms* with the contents of the trunk⟩ — see CHECK 1
2 to form a pleasing relationship ⟨last-minute changes in the schedule that *conform* with our plans nicely⟩ — see HARMONIZE 1
3 to bring to a state free of conflicts, inconsistencies, or differences ⟨we'll have to *conform* this new rule with existing policy regarding student-run organizations on campus⟩ — see HARMONIZE 2
4 to change (something) so as to make it suitable for a new use or situation ⟨I can be funny or serious, for I always *conform* my behavior to the situation⟩ — see ADAPT

conform (to) *vb* to act according to the commands of ⟨an independent-minded person who refuses to *conform to* the dictates of society⟩ — see OBEY

conformable *adj* readily giving in to the command or authority of another ⟨one of the more *conformable* inmates in a prison that's filled with unruly ones⟩ — see OBEDIENT

conformable (to) *adj* not having or showing any apparent conflict ⟨student conduct must be at all times *conformable to* the principles and values of the school⟩ — see CONSISTENT

conformance *n* **1** a state of consistency ⟨behavior found to be not in *conformance* with all company policies regarding sexual harassment⟩ — see CONFORMITY 1
2 the following of a custom, rule, or law ⟨a woman with no interest in *conformance* to the dictates of fashion⟩ — see OBSERVANCE 1

conformation *n* **1** the outward appearance of something as distinguished from its substance ⟨an ice sculpture in the *conformation* of a swan⟩ — see FORM 1
2 the way in which something is sized, arranged, or organized ⟨the regular *conformation* of particles in a crystal⟩ — see FORMAT 1
3 the act or process of changing something to fit a new use or situation ⟨the *conformation* of their lives to the changing social order⟩ — see ADAPTATION

conformity *n* **1** a state of consistency ⟨the simple lifestyle of the Amish is in *conformity* with their ascetic religious beliefs⟩
synonyms accord, accordance, agreement, conformance, congruence, congruency, congruity, consonance, harmony, tune
related words compatibility; assimilation, integration; oneness, solidarity, togetherness; affinity, empathy, sympathy
near antonyms contrast, discrepancy, disparateness, disparity, dissimilarity, distinction, distinctiveness, distinctness, diverseness, diversity, unlikeness; deviance, divergence; discord, discordance, dissension (*also* dissention), dissent, dissidence, disunity, friction, strife; variability, variance; incompatibility
antonyms conflict, disagreement, incongruence, incongruity, incongruousness
2 the action of following a custom, rule, or law ⟨a rebellious artist who has never shown any interest in *conformity* to social custom⟩ — see OBSERVANCE 1
3 the following of a custom, rule, or law ⟨a small community that still expected *conformity* to traditional gen-

der roles⟩ — see OBSERVANCE 1

confound *vb* **1** to throw into a state of mental uncertainty ⟨we were *confounded* by the player's remote control, which wasn't at all user-friendly⟩ — see CONFUSE 1

2 to throw into a state of self-conscious distress ⟨his renewed popularity has *confounded* the critics who said his singing career was dead⟩ — see EMBARRASS 1

3 to fail to differentiate (a thing) from something similar or related ⟨I think you've *confounded* astrology with astronomy⟩ — see CONFUSE 3

4 to prove to be false ⟨new discoveries that *confound* much of what archaeologists thought they knew about the Mayan civilization⟩ — see DISPROVE

confounded *adj* **1** deserving of one's condemnation or displeasure ⟨that *confounded* dog chewed up my shoe⟩ — see DAMNABLE

2 faced with difficulty or uncertainty about what to say, think, or do ⟨the sudden burden of familial responsibility has left him anxious and *confounded*⟩ — see HARD PUT

3 suffering from mental confusion ⟨since their house is old and impressive-looking, they are frequently imposed upon by *confounded* tourists⟩ — see DIZZY 2

confrere *also* **confrère** *n* a fellow worker ⟨many of the judge's *confreres* on the Fifth Circuit bench don't feel as she does on the issue⟩ — see COLLEAGUE

confront *vb* to oppose (something hostile or dangerous) with firmness or courage ⟨you must *confront* your fear in order to conquer it⟩ — see FACE 2

confrontation *n* an earnest effort for superiority or victory over another ⟨the softball rivals met in an epic *confrontation* on the last weekend of the summer⟩ — see CONTEST 1

confrontational *adj* feeling or displaying eagerness to fight ⟨her *confrontational*, in-your-face manner doesn't help get legislation passed⟩ — see BELLIGERENT

confuse *vb* **1** to throw into a state of mental uncertainty ⟨the similar-sounding words "censure" and "censor" often *confuse* people⟩
synonyms addle, baffle, bamboozle, beat, befog, befuddle, bemuse, bewilder, buffalo, confound, discombobulate, disorient, flummox, fox, fuddle, get, gravel, maze, muddle, muddy, mystify, perplex, pose, puzzle, vex
related words stick, stump, weird out; abash, discomfit, disconcert, discountenance, embarrass, faze, fluster, mortify, nonplus, rattle; agitate, bother, chagrin, discomfort, discompose, dismay, disquiet, distress, disturb, perturb, stun, unhinge, unsettle, upset; beguile, cozen, deceive, delude, dupe, fool, gull, hoax, hoodwink, humbug, misguide, mislead, snow, string along, take in, trick
phrases blow one's mind, go to one's head
near antonyms assure, reassure, satisfy; enlighten, inform

2 to make (something) unclear to the understanding ⟨stop *confusing* the issue with irrelevant facts⟩
synonyms becloud, befog, blur, cloud, fog, muddy, obfuscate
related words complicate, perplex, sophisticate; entangle, snarl, tangle; disarrange, disarray, discompose, dishevel, disorder, disrupt, disturb, jumble, mess (up), mix (up), muddle, scramble, shuffle, tousle, upset
near antonyms simplify, streamline; disentangle, straighten (out), undo, unravel, unscramble, untangle; decipher, decode; analyze, break down
antonyms clarify, clear (up), illuminate

3 to fail to differentiate (a thing) from something similar or related ⟨a lot of people *confuse* popular fame with enduring achievement⟩
synonyms conflate, confound, mistake, mix (up)
related words lump (together); misapply, miscall, misidentify, misname
antonyms difference, differentiate, discriminate, distinguish, separate

4 to throw into a state of self-conscious distress ⟨she was *confused* by the shocking bluntness of his marriage proposal⟩ — see EMBARRASS 1

5 to undo the proper order or arrangement of ⟨vandals had hopelessly *confused* the papers in the office files⟩ — see DISORDER

confused *adj* **1** lacking in order, neatness, and often cleanliness ⟨the cans were lying in a *confused* jumble in the basement⟩ — see MESSY

2 suffering from mental confusion ⟨she was briefly *confused* after her fall from the horse⟩ — see DIZZY 2

confusedness *n* a state of mental uncertainty ⟨such *confusedness* was laughable as well as pitiable⟩ — see CONFUSION 1

confusion *n* **1** a state of mental uncertainty ⟨the farmer's driving directions to the fairground just left us in total *confusion*⟩
synonyms bafflement, bamboozlement, befuddlement, bemusement, bewilderedness, bewilderment, confusedness, discombobulation, distraction, fog, head-scratching, maze [*chiefly dialect*], muddle, mystification, perplexity, puzzlement, tangle, whirl
related words abashment, discomfiture, disconcertment, embarrassment, mortification; agitation, chagrin, discomfort, dismay, disquiet, distress, disturbance, perturbation, upset; bother, commotion, dither, flurry, fluster, fuss, stew, turmoil
near antonyms assurance, certainty, certitude, confidence, conviction, positiveness, sureness

2 a state in which everything is out of order ⟨it was hard to find anything in that *confusion* in the attic⟩ — see CHAOS

3 the emotional state of being made self-consciously uncomfortable ⟨thrown into speechless *confusion* by the wild accusations⟩ — see EMBARRASSMENT 1

confutation *n* something (as an argument) that serves to disprove ⟨he crafted an elegant *confutation* to the argument that animals do not feel pain⟩
synonyms disconfirmation, disproof, rebuttal, refutation
related words counterargument, counterevidence
near antonyms attestation, confirmation, corroboration, documentation, evidence, substantiation, testament, testimony, validation, witness; authentication, identification, manifestation, verification
antonyms proof

confute *vb* to prove to be false ⟨theories which will eventually be confirmed or *confuted* by experience⟩ — see DISPROVE

congé *also* **congee** *n* an expression of good wishes at parting ⟨with an elaborately ceremonious *congé*, the ambassador took his leave⟩ — see GOOD-BYE

congeal *vb* **1** to become physically firm or solid ⟨the surface of the pond *congealed* after several days of frigid temperatures⟩ — see HARDEN 1

2 to turn from a liquid into a substance resembling jelly ⟨the gravy had already started to *congeal* by the time the waiter served our dinners⟩ — see COAGULATE

congenial *adj* **1** giving pleasure or contentment to the mind or senses ⟨a couple relaxing in the *congenial* atmosphere of a luxury health spa⟩ — see PLEASANT 1

2 having or marked by agreement in feeling or action ⟨*congenial* traveling companions who made our tour of Italy even more enjoyable than we had anticipated⟩ — see HARMONIOUS 3

congenital *adj* being such from birth or by nature ⟨a *congenital* liar who couldn't speak the truth if his life depended on it⟩ — see NATURAL 1

congenitally *adv* by natural character or ability ⟨she appeared to be *congenitally* incapable of telling the truth⟩ — see NATURALLY 1

congest *vb* to prevent passage through by filling with something ⟨the usual weekend traffic *congested* the region's highways⟩ — see CLOG 1

conglomerate *n* a group of businesses or enterprises under one control ⟨the huge media *conglomerate* owns TV and radio stations, a cable company, and a movie studio⟩
synonyms empire
related words multinational; cartel, combination, combine, syndicate, trust; chain; association, corporation, organization, pool

conglomerate *vb* **1** to come together into one body or place ⟨people *conglomerated* in the downtown streets for an impromptu victory celebration⟩ — see ASSEMBLE 1
2 to gradually form into a layer, pile, or mass ⟨over the years the town's discarded junk *conglomerated* at the bottom of the river⟩ — see COLLECT 2

conglomerative *adj* produced by a series of additions of identical or similar things ⟨the overabundance of historical detail has the *conglomerative* effect of overwhelming and boring the reader⟩ — see CUMULATIVE

congratulate *vb* to express to (someone) admiration for his or her success or good fortune ⟨let me be the first to *congratulate* you on winning the award⟩
synonyms compliment, felicitate, hug
related words applaud, cheer, commend, hail, salute; extol (*also* extoll), glorify, laud, praise
near antonyms bad-mouth, belittle, cry down, decry, deprecate, depreciate, diminish, discount, disparage, minimize, put down, write off; jeer, mock, ridicule, taunt, tease

congratulations *n pl* best wishes ⟨a gift for you with our *congratulations*⟩ — see COMPLIMENT 2

congregate *vb* **1** to bring together in one body or place ⟨both captains *congregated* their team members for some pregame strategizing⟩ — see GATHER 1
2 to come together into one body or place ⟨pilgrims have been *congregating* in the town's historic square for centuries⟩ — see ASSEMBLE 1

congregation *n* **1** a body of persons gathered for religious worship ⟨the whole *congregation* began to sing with great fervor⟩
synonyms assembly, church
related words flock, laity, parish; communion, confession, denomination, fold, sect
2 a body of people come together in one place ⟨a *congregation* of journalists were at the hotel bar, discussing the latest developments⟩ — see GATHERING 1

congress *n* **1** the highest lawmaking body of a political unit ⟨the national emergency required a special session of *congress*⟩
synonyms parliament
related words assembly, chamber, council, diet, house, legislative, legislature; general assembly, legislative assembly
2 a coming together of a number of persons for a specified purpose ⟨following World War I a great *congress* of world leaders took place in Paris to plan the postwar world⟩ — see MEETING 1
3 a group of persons formally joined together for some common interest ⟨the Canada Trades and Labor *Congress*⟩ — see ASSOCIATION 2
4 sexual union involving penetration of the vagina by the penis ⟨laws that once prohibited *congress* between people of different races⟩ — see SEXUAL INTERCOURSE

congruence *n* a state of consistency ⟨little apparent *congruence* between her professed concern for the poor and her own extravagant lifestyle⟩ — see CONFORMITY 1

congruency *n* a state of consistency ⟨at least he acts in *congruency* with his avowed beliefs and values⟩ — see CONFORMITY 1

congruent *adj* not having or showing any apparent conflict ⟨a theory *congruent* with the known facts of the case⟩ — see CONSISTENT

congruity *n* **1** a point which two or more things share in common ⟨the book alleges certain *congruities* between several political assassinations that were thought to be unrelated⟩ — see SIMILARITY 2
2 a state of consistency ⟨there's little *congruity* between your professed religious beliefs and your actual behavior⟩ — see CONFORMITY 1

congruous *adj* **1** having the parts agreeably related ⟨the *congruous* layout of the mansion's formal gardens conveys a sense of both grandeur and intimacy⟩ — see HARMONIOUS 2
2 not having or showing any apparent conflict ⟨when performing his official duties, the president must be dressed in clothes that are *congruous* with his high position⟩ — see CONSISTENT

congruously *adv* in a manner suitable for the occasion or purpose ⟨in a *congruously* solemn voice, he recited the oath of office⟩ — see PROPERLY

conjectural *adj* existing only as an assumption or speculation ⟨a necessarily *conjectural* account of Shakespeare's life, since there is so little hard information⟩ — see THEORETICAL 1

conjecture *n* an opinion or judgment based on little or no evidence ⟨the many *conjectures* about the true identity of Jack the Ripper⟩
synonyms guess, shot, supposition, surmise
related words hypothesis, hypothetical, theory, thesis; dead reckoning, guessing, guesswork, speculation; hunch, intuition; belief, faith
phrases shot in the dark

conjecture *vb* **1** to decide the size, amount, number, or distance of (something) without actual measurement ⟨he *conjectured* that the theater could seat 1000 people more or less⟩ — see ESTIMATE 2
2 to form an opinion from little or no evidence ⟨you're only *conjecturing* that he was the culprit⟩ — see GUESS 1

conjoin *vb* **1** to come together to form a single unit ⟨several streets *conjoin* to form the crossroads known as New York's Times Square⟩ — see UNITE 1
2 to form or enter into an association that furthers the interests of its members ⟨small farmers had to *conjoin* in order to compete with the agricultural conglomerates⟩ — see ALLY
3 to participate or assist in a joint effort to accomplish an end ⟨government agencies and private charities have *conjoined* to bring relief to the famine-stricken nation⟩ — see COOPERATE 1

conjoint *adj* used or done by a number of people as a group ⟨only through the *conjoint* effort of the entire department could we have finished this project on time⟩ — see COLLECTIVE

conjointly *adv* in or by combined action or effort ⟨the two departments worked *conjointly* to finish the project in less than half the usual time⟩ — see TOGETHER 2

conjugal *adj* of or relating to marriage ⟨newlyweds still in a rapturous state of *conjugal* happiness⟩ — see MARITAL

conjugality *n* a union representing a special kind of social and legal partnership between two people ⟨the level of mutual affection and respect that comes only with decades of contented *conjugality*⟩ — see MARRIAGE 1

conjugate *vb* **1** to come together to form a single unit

⟨biological cells *conjugating* under a microscope⟩ — see UNITE 1

2 to put or bring together so as to form a new and longer whole ⟨*conjugate* polymers in a chemistry lab⟩ — see CONNECT 1

conjunct *adj* used or done by a number of people as a group ⟨the supreme commander of the *conjunct* operations of the allied armies⟩ — see COLLECTIVE

conjunction *n* the coming together of two or more things to the same point ⟨the *conjunction* of the two major highways creates a massive influx of cars into the city⟩ — see CONVERGENCE

conjuncture *n* a time or state of affairs requiring prompt or decisive action ⟨an unfortunate *conjuncture* of events—peak demand at a time of reduced output from hurricane-ravished refineries—resulted in skyrocketing gas prices⟩ — see EMERGENCY

conjuration *n* **1** a spoken word or set of words believed to have magic power ⟨the preposterous claim that he could raise the spirits of the dead with a mystical *conjuration*⟩ — see SPELL 1

2 an earnest request ⟨a *conjuration* for divine guidance during a time of national crisis⟩ — see PLEA 1

conjure *vb* to make a request to (someone) in an earnest or urgent manner ⟨I *conjure* you to hear my plea for mercy⟩ — see BEG

conjure (up) *vb* **1** to form a mental picture of ⟨with certain flowers I instantly *conjure up* memories of our Caribbean honeymoon⟩ — see IMAGINE 1

2 to call into being through the use of one's inner resources or powers ⟨managed to *conjure up* the courage to ask the boss for a raise⟩ — see SUMMON 2

conjurer *or* **conjuror** *n* **1** a person skilled in using supernatural forces ⟨in the book the *conjurer* battles a barbarian swordsman⟩ — see MAGICIAN 1

2 one who practices tricks and illusions for entertainment ⟨a *conjurer* in Las Vegas who must make audiences believe in the impossible eight shows a week⟩ — see MAGICIAN 2

conjuring *n* **1** the power to control natural forces through supernatural means ⟨his attempts at *conjuring* demonstrated the vanity of human wishes⟩ — see MAGIC 1

2 the art or skill of performing tricks or illusions for entertainment ⟨she's so good at *conjuring* that she's a much-sought-after entertainer at children's parties⟩ — see MAGIC 2

conk *n, chiefly British slang* the part of the face bearing the nostrils and nasal cavity ⟨a feisty cockney who had got his *conk* broken more than once in street brawls⟩ — see NOSE 1

conk (out) *vb* **1** to lose consciousness ⟨after three days without eating, he simply *conked out*⟩ — see FAINT

2 to stop functioning ⟨the engine *conked out* just as we were approaching the exact middle of nowhere⟩ — see FAIL 1

3 to stop living ⟨a list of people whose chief claim to fame is the unusual manner in which they *conked out*⟩ — see DIE 1

conn *also* **con** *vb* to operate or control the course of ⟨there was white-knuckle tension as the captain *conned* the gunboat through the mine-infested harbor⟩ — see NAVIGATE 1

connate *adj* having qualities in common ⟨the central premise of the comedy is that organized crime and moviemaking are pretty much *connate* activities⟩ — see ALIKE

connect *vb* **1** to put or bring together so as to form a new and longer whole ⟨*connect* all the sets of lights and attach them to the branches of the Christmas tree⟩

synonyms catenate, chain, compound, concatenate, conjugate, couple, hitch, hook, interconnect, interlink, join, link, yoke

related words articulate, dovetail, integrate, interlock, intermesh; cord, string, wire; cement, coalesce, combine, fuse, unite, weld

near antonyms detach, disengage, divide, part, split; cleave, rupture, sever, sunder

antonyms disconnect, disjoin, disjoint, dissever, disunite, separate, unchain, uncouple, unhitch, unlink, unyoke

2 to come together to form a single unit ⟨the two interstate highways *connect*, so a driver can go from one corner of the state to the other without much trouble⟩ — see UNITE 1

3 to think of (something) in combination ⟨opera is popularly *connected* with high society⟩ — see ASSOCIATE 2

connecting *n* the act or an instance of joining two or more things into one ⟨the *connecting* of the truck to the trailer was easily accomplished⟩ — see UNION 1

connection *n* **1** the fact or state of having something in common ⟨the endless debate about the *connection* between crime and poverty⟩

synonyms affinity, association, bearing, kinship, liaison, linkage, relation, relationship

related words correlation, interrelation; materiality, pertinence, relevance; bond, link, tie; affiliation, alliance, union; identicalness, sameness; alikeness, community, likeness, resemblance, similarity; accordance, agreement, conformity, congruity, correspondence

near antonyms variability, variance; incompatibility, incongruence, incongruity, incongruousness

2 a place where two or more things are united ⟨there's a problem at the *connection* where the outside wire is hooked up to the inside wiring⟩ — see JOINT 1

3 an acquaintance who has influence especially in the business or political world ⟨I have a *connection* in Hollywood who might be able to get you a part in a movie⟩ — see CONTACT

4 the act or an instance of joining two or more things into one ⟨that bridge is the only *connection* between the island and the mainland⟩ — see UNION 1

5 the fact or state of being pertinent ⟨that last comment of yours has no *connection* with what we've been talking about for the last hour⟩ — see PERTINENCE

6 the state of having shared interests or efforts (as in social or business matters) ⟨in a truly secular society there is no *connection* between church and state⟩ — see ASSOCIATION 1

7 an assignment at which one regularly works for pay ⟨enjoyed self-employment and never wanted a *connection* with a big company⟩ — see JOB 1

connivance *n* a secret agreement or cooperation between two parties for an illegal or dishonest purpose ⟨was able to sneak out at night with the *connivance* of a camp counselor⟩ — see COLLUSION

connive *vb* **1** to secretly sympathize with or pretend ignorance of something improper or unlawful ⟨the principal *connived* at all the school absences that were recorded on the day of the city's celebration of its Super Bowl victory⟩

synonyms wink

related words brush (aside *or* off), condone, disregard, excuse, forgive, gloss (over), gloze (over), ignore, overlook, pardon, pass over, shrug off, tolerate

near antonyms disapprove (of), frown (on *or* upon); deny, disallow, refuse

2 to engage in a secret plan to accomplish evil or unlawful ends ⟨suspects that his coworkers are *conniving* to get him fired⟩ — see PLOT

connoisseur *n* **1** a person having a knowledgeable and fine appreciation of the arts ⟨a forthcoming exhibit at

the art museum that is eagerly awaited by *connoisseurs* of ancient Greek pottery⟩
synonyms cognoscente, dilettante
related words adept, authority, expert, maestro, master, past master, scholar, virtuoso; critic, reviewer; amateur, dabbler; collector; specialist; aficionado (*also* afficionado), buff, devotee, enthusiast, fan
near antonyms groundling, lowbrow, materialist, philistine
2 a person with a high level of knowledge or skill in a field ⟨works that are highly prized by *connoisseurs* of art glass⟩ — see EXPERT

connubial *adj* of or relating to marriage ⟨a happy couple celebrating half a century of *connubial* bliss⟩ — see MARITAL

connubiality *n* a union representing a special kind of social and legal partnership between two people ⟨the sudden craze for *connubiality* had claimed its latest victim: a bachelor who swore that he'd never marry⟩ — see MARRIAGE 1

conquer *vb* **1** to bring under one's control by force of arms ⟨before his final defeat, Napoléon had managed to *conquer* much of Europe⟩
synonyms dominate, overpower, pacify, subdue, subject, subjugate, subordinate, vanquish
related words annihilate, beat, clobber, crush, defeat, drub, lick, mow (down), overcome, prevail (over), reduce, rout, skunk, smash, thrash, triumph (over), trounce, wallop, whip; enslave; break, clamp down (on), crack down (on), put down, quash, quell, repress, silence, smother, snuff (out), squash, squelch, suppress
near antonyms discharge, emancipate, enfranchise, free, liberate, manumit, release, spring, unbind, uncage, unchain, unfetter
2 to achieve a victory over ⟨love *conquers* all, or so romance novels would have us believe⟩ — see BEAT 2
3 to achieve victory (as in a contest) ⟨a coach who demands that his team *conquer*, whatever the cost⟩ — see WIN 1

conqueror *n* one that defeats an enemy or opponent ⟨hailed as *conqueror* of the barbarian forces⟩ — see VICTOR 1

conquest *n* the act or process of bringing someone or something under one's control ⟨the *conquest* of much of North and South America by the Spanish during the 16th century⟩
synonyms dominating, domination, overpowering, subduing, subjecting, subjection, subjugating, subjugation, vanquishing
related words triumph, victory, win, winning; beating, defeat, drubbing, licking, shellacking, trimming, trouncing, whipping; enslavement; takeover
near antonyms emancipation, enfranchisement, freeing, liberation, manumission, release

consanguineous *adj* being such by blood and not by adoption or marriage ⟨felt just as close to his adopted brother as he did to his two *consanguineous* siblings⟩ — see NATURAL 3

conscientious *adj* **1** guided by or in accordance with one's sense of right and wrong ⟨operated on the belief that most people are *conscientious*, the unattended farm stand has a price list and a money drawer for customers to leave payment for their purchases⟩
synonyms conscionable, ethical, honest, honorable, just, moral, principled, scrupulous
related words decent, good, righteous, right-minded, straight, upright, virtuous; dutiful, observant, respectful; overconscientious; reliable, responsible, solid, tried-and-true, true, trustworthy, trusty; esteemed, law-abiding, reputable, respected, upstanding, worthy
near antonyms bad, black, evil, evil-minded, immoral, indecent, sinful, unrighteous, wicked; unreliable, untrustworthy; corrupt, debased, debauched, degenerate, depraved, dissolute, perverted, reprobate; atrocious, infamous, villainous; base, low, mean, vicious, vile; iniquitous, nefarious
antonyms cutthroat, dishonest, dishonorable, immoral, unconscionable, unethical, unjust, unprincipled, unscrupulous
2 taking, showing, or involving great care and effort ⟨a counselor who serves patients by first being a *conscientious* listener⟩ — see PAINSTAKING

conscientiousness *n* strict attentiveness to what one is doing ⟨finished the last details with as much *conscientiousness* as the first⟩ — see CARE 1

conscionable *adj* guided by or in accordance with one's sense of right and wrong ⟨rejecting the title of hero, he insisted that any *conscionable* person would have done the same thing⟩ — see CONSCIENTIOUS 1

conscious *adj* **1** having specified facts or feelings actively impressed on the mind ⟨*conscious* of the fact that my hands were sweating the whole time that I was making my presentation⟩
synonyms alive, apprehensive, aware, cognizant, mindful, sensible, sentient, ware, witting
related words alert, attentive, careful, cautious, heedful, observant, open-eyed, regardful, safe, vigilant, wary, watchful, wide-awake; hyperaware, hyperconscious
near antonyms careless, heedless, inattentive, incautious, mindless, unguarded, unheeding, unwary
antonyms insensible, oblivious, unaware, unconscious, unmindful, unwitting
2 made, given, or done with full awareness of what one is doing ⟨a *conscious* effort to instill discord in the family⟩ — see INTENTIONAL

consciously *adv* with full awareness of what one is doing ⟨she *consciously* chose to take the more dangerous route down the mountain⟩ — see INTENTIONALLY

consciousness *n* a state of being aware ⟨a glaring problem that somehow has yet to penetrate the *consciousness* of the people that run this company⟩ — see ATTENTION 2

conscribe *vb* to pick especially for required military service ⟨young men worried about whether they would be *conscribed* to fight in this latest conflict⟩ — see DRAFT 1

conscript *n* a person forced or required to enroll in military service ⟨as the war continued, the body of enlisted soldiers was supplemented by an increasing number of *conscripts*⟩
synonyms draftee, inductee, selectee
related words levy; recruit, rookie
near antonyms enlistee, volunteer

conscript *vb* to pick especially for required military service ⟨was *conscripted* into the army shortly after turning 18⟩ — see DRAFT 1

consecrate *adj* set apart or worthy of veneration by association with God ⟨the *consecrate* gold tablets which Joseph Smith claimed to have found⟩ — see HOLY 2

consecrate *vb* **1** to keep or intend for a special purpose ⟨a philanthropist who *consecrated* his considerable fortune to an array of charitable causes⟩ — see DEVOTE 1
2 to make holy through prayers or ritual ⟨plans to *consecrate* the altar in the new church with great ceremony⟩ — see BLESS 1

consecrated *adj* set apart or worthy of veneration by association with God ⟨built the cemetery on *consecrated* ground⟩ — see HOLY 2

consecration *n* the act of making something holy through religious ritual ⟨the *consecration* of the Host during Communion⟩
synonyms blessing, hallowing, sanctification
related words purification; dedication; adoration, glo-

rification, reverence, veneration, worship
near antonyms debasement, defilement, desecration, impiety, irreverence, profanation, sacrilege

consecution *n* a series of things linked together ⟨a *consecution* of schoolboy misdeeds, juvenile offenses, and misdemeanors that eventually led to a life as a career criminal⟩ — see CHAIN 1

consecutive *adj* following one after another without others coming in between ⟨the team's winning streak has lasted for seven *consecutive* games⟩
synonyms back-to-back, sequent, sequential, straight, succeeding, successional, successive
related words serial; constant, continuous, uninterrupted; ensuing, following, later, next, posterior, subsequent
near antonyms in series
antonyms inconsecutive, inconsequent, nonconsecutive, nonsequential

consecutively *adv* following one after another without others coming in between ⟨talked of retirement after winning the title four times *consecutively*⟩
synonyms back-to-back, hand running [*dialect*], running, sequentially, seriatim, successionally, successively, together
related words serially; constantly, continually, continuingly, continuously, night and day, repeatedly, unceasingly, uninterruptedly; subsequently
phrases on end
near antonyms discontinuously, intermittently, interruptedly

consensus *n* the state of being of one opinion about something ⟨finally reached a *consensus* on how to spend the money that the club had raised⟩ — see AGREEMENT 1

consent *n* the approval by someone in authority for the doing of something ⟨we had to get our neighbor's *consent* in order to trim the tree from his side⟩ — see PERMISSION

consent *vb* to give or express one's approval (as to a proposal) ⟨refused to *consent* to the marriage⟩ — see ACCEDE

consequence *n* **1** a condition or occurrence traceable to a cause ⟨the flood was an inevitable *consequence* of the prolonged, heavy rains⟩ — see EFFECT 1
2 the quality or state of being important ⟨a mistake that was of no great *consequence*⟩ — see IMPORTANCE
3 an exaggerated sense of one's importance that shows itself in the making of excessive or unjustified claims ⟨a junior executive who strutted around the office with all of the *consequence* of a peacock in pinstripes⟩ — see ARROGANCE
4 an opinion arrived at through a process of reasoning ⟨I am able to deduce several *consequences* from those premises⟩ — see CONCLUSION 1

consequent *adj* **1** according to the rules of logic ⟨the conclusion that you have reached is neither *consequent* nor plausible⟩ — see LOGICAL 1
2 coming as a result ⟨her new job and *consequent* relocation added to the stress⟩ — see RESULTANT

consequential *adj* **1** coming as a result ⟨his high-fat diet and the *consequential* weight gain⟩ — see RESULTANT
2 having great meaning or lasting effect ⟨the American Civil War is often regarded as the nation's most *consequential* event since its founding⟩ — see IMPORTANT 1
3 having too high an opinion of oneself ⟨for such a *consequential* businessman, he's head of a rather small company⟩ — see CONCEITED

consequently *adv* for this or that reason ⟨taxes were lowered, and *consequently* complaints were fewer⟩ — see THEREFORE

conservancy *n* the careful maintaining and protection of something valuable especially in its natural or original state ⟨she's devoted her life to *conservancy* of the rain forest⟩ — see CONSERVATION 1

conservation *n* **1** the careful maintaining and protection of something valuable especially in its natural or original state ⟨everyone has a duty to aid in the *conservation* of our nation's wilderness areas⟩
synonyms conservancy, preservation, sustentation
related words care, maintenance, upkeep; salvation, saving; defense, guardianship, guarding, keeping, protection, safeguarding, safekeeping; economy, husbandry, management
near antonyms dereliction, ignoring, neglect, squandering, waste; destruction, ruin; damage, harm, hurt, injury
2 the act or activity of keeping something in an existing and usually satisfactory condition ⟨the *conservation* of the nation's monuments and memorials⟩ — see MAINTENANCE

conservatism *n* attitudes or opinions tending to favor established ideas, conditions, or institutions ⟨the state's well-known *conservatism* means that progressive legislation always has an uphill battle⟩
synonyms conservativeness, die-hardism, reactionaryism, traditionalism, ultraconservatism
related words neoconservatism, Toryism; bigotry, illiberalism; conventionalism, conventionality, fogyism (*or* fogeyism)
near antonyms neoliberalism; extremism, radicalism; nonconformism, nonconformity, unconventionalism, unorthodoxy
antonyms broad-mindedness, liberalism, liberalness, open-mindedness, progressivism

conservative *adj* **1** tending to favor established ideas, conditions, or institutions ⟨*conservative* baseball fans consider the new ballpark too modern-looking and plain ugly⟩
synonyms archconservative, brassbound, button-down (*or* buttoned-down), die-hard, hidebound, mossbacked, old-fashioned, old-line, old-school, orthodox, paleoconservative, reactionary, standpat, traditional, traditionalistic, ultraconservative, unprogressive
related words conventional, square; devoted, faithful, loyal, staunch (*also* stanch), steadfast, steady, true, true-blue; blimpish, neoconservative, Tory, ultraright, ultrarightist; dowdy, fogyish (*or* fogeyish), fuddy-duddy, ossified, set, stodgy; right, right-wing; antiliberal, antimodern, antiprogressive, antireform, antirevolutionary
near antonyms anticonventional, antiestablishment, antitraditional, extremist, radical, revolutionary; nonconformist; advanced, contemporary, modern; lefty, radical, ultraleft, ultraleftist, ultraprogressive, ultraradical
antonyms broad-minded, large-minded, liberal, nonconservative, nonconventional, nonorthodox, nontraditional, open-minded, progressive, unconventional, unorthodox
2 not excessively showy ⟨dressing in *conservative* outfits so as to make a good impression at job interviews⟩ — see QUIET 2
3 having or showing a close attentiveness to avoiding danger or trouble ⟨made *conservative* investments, and so he wasn't ruined when the market went into a free fall⟩ — see CAREFUL 1

conservative *n* a person whose political beliefs are centered on tradition and keeping things the way they are ⟨proposed legislation that was opposed by *conservatives* throughout the state⟩
synonyms archconservative, paleoconservative, reactionary, rightist, right-winger, Tory, traditionalist
related words right, right-wing; conformist; neocon,

neoconservative; diehard, standpatter; bourbon, Colonel Blimp, fuddy-duddy, square, stuffed shirt
near antonyms extremist, radical, red, revolutionary, revolutionist; reformer, reformist
antonyms leftist, left-winger, lefty, liberal, progressive

conservativeness *n* attitudes or opinions tending to favor established ideas, conditions, or institutions ⟨the judge is noted for his gentlemanly politeness and his judicial *conservativeness*⟩ — see CONSERVATISM

conservatory *n* a glass-enclosed building for growing plants ⟨the college's *conservatory* is entirely devoted to cultivating and displaying orchids⟩
synonyms glasshouse [*chiefly British*], greenhouse, hothouse
related words cold frame, hot bed; nursery; botanical garden (*also* botanic garden)

conserve *vb* **1** to avoid the wasteful or destructive use of ⟨the need to *conserve* oil and other finite fossil fuels⟩
synonyms husband
related words economize, save, scrimp, skimp; preserve, protect, save; hoard, lay by, lay up
near antonyms clean (out), consume, deplete, drain, exhaust, expend, impoverish, spend, use up
antonyms blow, dissipate, fritter (away), lavish, misspend, run through, squander, throw away, waste
2 to keep in good condition ⟨*conserve* our national parks so that they may be enjoyed by future generations⟩ — see MAINTAIN 1

conserving *n* the act or activity of keeping something in an existing and usually satisfactory condition ⟨the *conserving* of such national treasures as the flag that flew over Fort McHenry during its famous bombardment⟩ — see MAINTENANCE

consider *vb* **1** to think of in a particular way ⟨I *consider* him a very good friend⟩
synonyms account, call, count, esteem, hold, look (on *or* upon), rate, reckon, regard, set down, view
related words believe, deem, feel, sense, think; conceive, fancy, imagine
phrases take for
2 to give serious and careful thought to ⟨carefully *considering* our options⟩ — see PONDER
3 to have as an opinion ⟨*consider* the price too high⟩ — see BELIEVE 2
4 to give consideration to (as unexpected circumstances or contingencies) ⟨I had to *consider* the commute in deciding whether to take the job⟩ — see ALLOW (FOR)
5 to think very highly or favorably of ⟨her well-*considered* novels have seldom been best sellers⟩ — see ADMIRE

considerable *adj* **1** sufficiently large in size, amount, or number to merit attention ⟨the *considerable* number of auto accidents that resulted from the surprise snowstorm⟩
synonyms biggish, good, goodly, handsome, healthy, largish, major, respectable, significant, sizable (*or* sizeable), substantial, substantive, tidy
related words big, bulky, hefty, hulking, outsize (*also* outsized), oversize (*or* oversized), voluminous; astronomical (*also* astronomic), bumper, colossal, elephantine, enormous, gigantic, great, herculean, huge, immense, jumbo, king-size (*or* king-sized), mammoth, massive, monstrous, monumental, prodigious, titanic, tremendous, whopping
near antonyms measly, minute, paltry, petty, picayune, picayunish, piddling, puny, trifling, trivial, unimportant; marginal, meager (*or* meagre), slight; little, small, tiny, undersized (*also* undersize); bitty, diminutive, miniature, pint-size (*or* pint-sized), pocket, pocket-size (*also* pocket-sized), pygmy, smallish
antonyms inconsequential, inconsiderable, insignificant, insubstantial, negligible, nominal
2 of a size greater than average of its kind ⟨a house with a *considerable* barn in back⟩ — see LARGE 1

considerably *adv* to a large extent or degree ⟨home electronic devices that have fallen *considerably* in price⟩ — see GREATLY 2

considerate *adj* **1** given to or made with heedful anticipation of the needs and happiness of others ⟨a kindly woman who is very *considerate* of other people's feelings⟩ — see THOUGHTFUL 1
2 having or showing a close attentiveness to avoiding danger or trouble ⟨you need to develop a more *considerate* temperament and learn to think before you speak⟩ — see CAREFUL 1

considerately *adv* with good reason or courtesy ⟨he *considerately* made breakfast for all of the exhausted rescue workers⟩ — see WELL 4

consideration *n* **1** a careful weighing of the reasons for or against something ⟨after much *consideration* we decided to make an offer on the house⟩
synonyms account, advisement, debate, deliberation, reflection, study, thought
related words cogitation, contemplation, meditation, pondering, rumination; introspection; agonizing, hesitation, indecision; premeditation
antonyms short shrift
2 something (as money) that is given or received in return for goods or services ⟨since it was pro bono work, no *consideration* was made⟩ — see PAYMENT 2

considered *adj* decided on as a result of careful thought ⟨my *considered* opinion is that this is the best movie I've ever seen⟩ — see DELIBERATE 1

considering *conj* for the reason that ⟨*considering* the police have almost nothing to go on, I wouldn't expect the case to be solved anytime soon⟩ — see SINCE

consigliere *n* a person who gives advice especially professionally ⟨the President's trusted *consigliere* and chief political strategist⟩ — see CONSULTANT

consign *vb* **1** to cause to go or be taken from one place to another ⟨*consigned* the prisoner to the dungeon⟩ — see SEND
2 to put (something) into the possession or safekeeping of another ⟨the deliveryman had *consigned* our package to a next-door neighbor⟩ — see GIVE 2

consist *vb* to be in agreement on every point ⟨that account *consists* with the information in the other reports⟩ — see CHECK 1

consist (of) *vb* to be made up of ⟨those cookies *consist of* flour, butter, sugar, chocolate, and vanilla⟩ — see COMPRISE 1

consistence *n* the degree to which a fluid can resist flowing ⟨the mixture should have the *consistence* of pancake batter⟩ — see CONSISTENCY

consistency *n* the degree to which a fluid can resist flowing ⟨beat the egg whites until they take on the *consistency* of whipped cream⟩
synonyms consistence, density, thickness, viscidity, viscosity
related words compactness, firmness, solidity; ropiness, stickiness

consistent *adj* not having or showing any apparent conflict ⟨the clothes you wear to work must be *consistent* with the company's dress code⟩
synonyms accordant, coherent, compatible, concordant, conformable (to), congruent, congruous, consonant, correspondent (with *or* to), harmonious, nonconflicting
related words self-consistent; appropriate, befitting, felicitous, fit, fitting, meet, proper, right, suitable
phrases of a piece
near antonyms improper, inapposite, inappropriate, inapt, infelicitous, unsuitable
antonyms conflicting, conflictive, incompatible, incon-

gruous, inconsistent, inharmonious, noncompatible

consistently *adv* on every relevant occasion ⟨he *consistently* brings a sandwich for lunch⟩ — see ALWAYS 1

consociate *vb* to come or be together as friends ⟨you'll be judged by those with whom you *consociate*⟩ — see ASSOCIATE 1

consolation *n* **1** the giving of hope and strength in times of grief, distress, or suffering ⟨the *consolation* of the grieving family by their pastor⟩
synonyms comforting, consoling, reassurance, solace, solacing
related words commiseration, compassion, condolence, feeling, sympathy; counseling (*or* counselling); humanity, kindheartedness, kindliness, kindness, mercy, pity
2 a feeling of ease from grief or trouble ⟨the *consolation* that our favorite foods give us when we're having a bad day⟩ — see COMFORT 1

console *n* a storage case typically having doors and shelves ⟨a custom-built walnut *console* holds all of their home-theater components⟩ — see CABINET

console *vb* to ease the grief or distress of ⟨the military officer who must *console* the bereaved at a soldier's funeral⟩ — see COMFORT

consolidate *vb* **1** to bring (something) to a central point or under a single control ⟨plans to *consolidate* several branches into one regional office⟩ — see CENTRALIZE
2 to make markedly greater in measure or degree ⟨another win would *consolidate* their hold on first place in their division⟩ — see INTENSIFY

consolidation *n* the act or an instance of joining two or more things into one ⟨the *consolidation* of several intelligence agencies into one super agency⟩ — see UNION 1

consoling *n* the giving of hope and strength in times of grief, distress, or suffering ⟨the responsibility for the *consoling* of the families of the firefighters fell to the mayor⟩ — see CONSOLATION 1

consonance *n* **1** a balanced, pleasing, or suitable arrangement of parts ⟨at present, the living room lacks *consonance* because all of the furniture is on one side⟩ — see HARMONY 1
2 a state of consistency ⟨in good writing there is always *consonance* of thought and expression, as the use of simple words for simple thoughts⟩ — see CONFORMITY 1

consonancy *n* a balanced, pleasing, or suitable arrangement of parts ⟨what makes *Citizen Kane* so great is the *consonancy* between its larger-than-life subject and its bravura style⟩ — see HARMONY 1

consonant *adj* **1** having the parts agreeably related ⟨the temples and palaces of ancient Greece are among the most *consonant* buildings in architectural history⟩ — see HARMONIOUS 2
2 not having or showing any apparent conflict ⟨his gentle behavior is *consonant* with his expressed belief in pacifism⟩ — see CONSISTENT

[1]**consort** *n* **1** a usually small number of persons considered as a unit ⟨a *consort* of doctors attended the case⟩ — see GROUP 2
2 an organized group of singers ⟨hired a *consort* of madrigal singers to perform at the wedding reception⟩ — see CHORUS 1

[2]**consort** *n* the person to whom another is married ⟨it is the queen's eldest son and not her *consort* who is next in line for the throne⟩ — see SPOUSE

consort *vb* **1** to come or be together as friends ⟨at college she began *consorting* with drug users, eventually becoming an addict herself⟩ — see ASSOCIATE 1
2 to form a pleasing relationship ⟨the restaurant's sophisticated menu *consorts* seamlessly with its sleek, modern ambience⟩ — see HARMONIZE 1

consortium *n* a group of persons formally joined together for some common interest ⟨a *consortium* for the prevention of animal cruelty⟩ — see ASSOCIATION 2

conspectus *n* a short statement of the main points ⟨a book that could serve as a *conspectus* of the work thus far on the development of artificial intelligence⟩ — see SUMMARY

conspicuous *adj* **1** likely to attract attention ⟨the seven-foot-tall basketball player is *conspicuous* in any crowd⟩ — see NOTICEABLE
2 very noticeable especially for being incorrect or bad ⟨*conspicuous* bureaucratic waste that drives taxpayers crazy⟩ — see EGREGIOUS

conspiracy *n* **1** a group involved in secret or criminal activities ⟨members of the *conspiracy* recognized each other by a secret handshake⟩ — see [1]RING 1
2 a secret agreement or cooperation between two parties for an illegal or dishonest purpose ⟨a *conspiracy* among the leading manufacturers to fix prices⟩ — see COLLUSION
3 a secret plan for accomplishing evil or unlawful ends ⟨several generals were engaged in a *conspiracy* to overthrow the government⟩ — see PLOT 1

conspire *vb* **1** to engage in a secret plan to accomplish evil or unlawful ends ⟨*conspired* to replace the leader with someone more easily influenced⟩ — see PLOT
2 to participate or assist in a joint effort to accomplish an end ⟨foul weather and airline foul-ups seemed to be *conspiring* to ruin our vacation⟩ — see COOPERATE 1

constable *n, chiefly British* a member of a force charged with law enforcement at the local level ⟨reported the crime to the local *constable*⟩ — see OFFICER 1

constabulary *n* a body of officers of the law ⟨all members of the local *constabulary* were on the alert for the escaped convict⟩ — see POLICE 2

constancy *n* **1** the state of continuing without change ⟨the mistaken notion that there is *constancy* in language—words do indeed change their meanings over time⟩
synonyms changelessness, fixedness, immutability, immutableness, invariability, stability, steadiness, unchangeableness
related words consistency, regularity, sameness, uniformity; durability, enduringness, lastingness, permanence
near antonyms aperiodicity, inconsistence, inconsistency, irregularity, unevenness; caducity, evanescence, impermanence
antonyms capriciousness, changeability, changeableness, fickleness, instability, mutability, unpredictability, unsteadiness, variability, variableness, volatileness, volatility
2 adherence to something to which one is bound by a pledge or duty ⟨soldiers serving with *constancy* and devotion to country⟩ — see FIDELITY
3 the strength of mind that enables a person to endure pain or hardship ⟨it takes determination and *constancy* to get through law school⟩ — see FORTITUDE

constant *adj* **1** not undergoing a change in condition ⟨change is the only *constant* thing in the world of fashion⟩
synonyms changeless, stable, stationary, steady, unchanging, unvarying
related words fast, fixed, hard-and-fast, immutable, inflexible, invariable, unalterable, unchangeable; established, set, settled; ceaseless, continuing, durable, enduring, lasting, permanent
phrases on an even keel (*also* on even keel)
near antonyms adaptable, alterable, changeable, flexible, mutable, variable; ephemeral, evanescent, fleeting, momentary, transient, transitory; kaleidoscopic, phantasmagoric (*or* phantasmagorical)

antonyms capricious, changeful, changing, fickle, fluctuating, fluid, inconstant, mercurial, skittish, uncertain, unpredictable, unsettled, unstable, unsteady, varying, volatile

2 appearing or occurring repeatedly from time to time ⟨I get *constant* headaches during humid weather⟩ — see REGULAR 1

3 firm in one's allegiance to someone or something ⟨*constant* friends during times both good and bad⟩ — see FAITHFUL 1

constantly *adv* **1** many times ⟨a crackpot who *constantly* wrote angry letters to the local newspaper⟩ — see OFTEN

2 on every relevant occasion ⟨stay *constantly* on guard until the danger of forest fire is past⟩ — see ALWAYS 1

constellate *vb* to bring together in one body or place ⟨the museum has *constellated* many of the artist's most glorious paintings into one stunning exhibition⟩ — see GATHER 1

constellation *n* **1** a number of things considered as a unit ⟨the *constellation* of beliefs, attitudes, and values that serve to define liberalism today⟩ — see GROUP 1

2 a usually small number of persons considered as a unit ⟨the organization invited an impressive *constellation* of guest speakers⟩ — see GROUP 2

3 the way in which the elements of something (as a work of art) are arranged ⟨there's a constantly shifting *constellation* of relationships among the characters of the novel⟩ — see COMPOSITION 3

constituent *n* one of the parts that make up a whole ⟨the soil contained all of the necessary *constituents* for growing crops⟩ — see ELEMENT 1

constitute *vb* **1** to be all the substance of ⟨nine players *constitute* a baseball team⟩
synonyms compose, comprise, form, make up
related words embody, epitomize, incarnate, incorporate, integrate, materialize, personify, substantiate; complement, complete, supplement; fill (out), flesh (out)

2 to be responsible for the creation and early operation or use of ⟨a fund was *constituted* to help needy students attend the prep school⟩ — see FOUND

3 to pick (someone) by one's authority for a specific position or duty ⟨the legally *constituted* authorities with jurisdiction in this matter⟩ — see APPOINT 2

4 to put into effect through legislative or authoritative action ⟨charged with enforcing such regulations as are *constituted* by the government⟩ — see ENACT

constitution *n* **1** the set of qualities that makes a person, a group of people, or a thing different from others ⟨the question of whether violent conflict is part of the *constitution* of human society⟩ — see NATURE 1

2 the type of body that a person has ⟨that marathon runner is known more for her strong *constitution* than for her speed⟩ — see PHYSIQUE

3 a collection or system of rules of conduct ⟨our society's *constitution* requires that every member in good standing pay yearly dues⟩ — see CODE

4 a rule of conduct or action laid down by a governing authority and especially a legislature ⟨the *constitution* against murder is universal among civilized societies⟩ — see LAW 1

constitutional *adj* being a part of the innermost nature of a person or thing ⟨a man notable for his poor hygiene and apparently *constitutional* aversion to soap⟩ — see INHERENT

constitutional *n* a relaxed journey on foot for exercise or pleasure ⟨went for my evening *constitutional* in the park⟩ — see WALK 1

constitutionally *adv* by natural character or ability ⟨I'm afraid that I'm *constitutionally* incapable of carrying a tune⟩ — see NATURALLY 1

constitutive *adj* being a part of the innermost nature of a person or thing ⟨the proposition that liberty and justice are *constitutive* elements of an enlightened society⟩ — see INHERENT

constrain *vb* **1** to cause (a person) to give in to pressure ⟨*constrained* by conscience to tell only the truth⟩ — see FORCE 1

2 to keep from exceeding a desirable degree or level (as of expression) ⟨*constrained* his anger at the needless interruption⟩ — see CONTROL 1

constraint *n* **1** the checking of one's true feelings and impulses when dealing with others ⟨in civilized society people do not just say or do whatever they feel like—they exercise some *constraint*⟩
synonyms continence, discipline, discretion, inhibition, refrainment, repression, reserve, restraint, self-command, self-control, self-restraint, suppression
related words command, control, mastery, possession; self-censorship, self-containment, self-denial, self-discipline, self-government, self-mastery, will, willpower; composure, self-poise, self-possession; aloofness, detachedness, distance; bashfulness, modesty, shyness; reticence, silence, taciturnity
near antonyms self-abandonment, uninhibitedness; unrestrainedness; gratification, indulgence, overindulgence, self-indulgence; bluntness, candor, frankness; immoderacy, intemperance
antonyms disinhibition, incontinence, unconstraint

2 something that limits one's freedom of action or choice ⟨put legal *constraints* on the board's activities⟩ — see RESTRICTION 1

3 the use of power to impose one's will on another ⟨parental *constraint* can take several different forms, including a denial of the approval that children usually seek from their parents⟩ — see FORCE 2

constrict *vb* **1** to become smaller in size or volume through the drawing together of particles of matter ⟨the vessel *constricted*, thereby reducing the flow of blood⟩ — see CONTRACT 2

2 to reduce in size or volume by or as if by pressing parts or members together ⟨*constricted* the opening with a clamp⟩ — see COMPRESS 1

constricting *n* the act or process of reducing the size or volume of something by or as if by pressing ⟨the constant *constricting* of the animal's throat had caused permanent damage⟩ — see COMPRESSION

constriction *n* the act or process of reducing the size or volume of something by or as if by pressing ⟨tried to ease the tie's *constriction* of his neck⟩ — see COMPRESSION

constringe *vb* to reduce in size or volume by or as if by pressing parts or members together ⟨a styptic pencil stops the bleeding by *constringing* the small blood vessels at the site of cut⟩ — see COMPRESS 1

construct *vb* **1** to create or think of by clever use of the imagination ⟨he managed to *construct* a theory that fits all the facts⟩ — see INVENT

2 to form by putting together parts or materials ⟨*constructed* a hydroelectric dam across the river⟩ — see BUILD

construction *n* **1** something put together by arranging or connecting an array of parts ⟨the swing set turned out to be a more complicated *construction* than the "some assembly required" warning suggested⟩
synonyms erection, structure
related words arrangement, assembly; configuration, frame, framework, shell, skeleton; geography, geometry

2 a statement that makes something clear ⟨could you give us your *construction* of this passage in the Bible?⟩ — see EXPLANATION 1

constructive *adj* having a role in deciding something's final form ⟨his experiences as an exchange student played a *constructive* part in the course that his life would take⟩ — see FORMATIVE

construe *vb* to make plain or understandable ⟨the role of the justices of the Supreme Court in *construing* the constitution⟩ — see EXPLAIN 1

consult *n* an exchange of views for the purpose of exploring a subject or deciding an issue ⟨it was time for a change of do, which called for a *consult* with her hairdresser⟩ — see DISCUSSION 1

consult *vb* **1** to exchange viewpoints or seek advice for the purpose of finding a solution to a problem ⟨will *consult* with several experts on the disease before deciding which course of treatment to pursue⟩ — see CONFER 2
2 to use or seek out as a source of aid, relief, or advantage ⟨I often *consult* the dictionary when I am uncertain of a word's exact meaning⟩ — see RESORT (TO) 1

consultant *n* a person who gives advice especially professionally ⟨a *consultant* in public relations to a number of large corporations⟩
synonyms adviser (*also* advisor), consigliere, counsel, counselor (*or* counsellor)
related words authority, expert, pro, professional, specialist; confidant; cabinet, kitchen cabinet; sounding board
near antonyms counselee

consultation *n* an exchange of views for the purpose of exploring a subject or deciding an issue ⟨holding frequent *consultations* with his lawyer to discuss the case⟩ — see DISCUSSION 1

consume *vb* **1** to destroy all trace of ⟨massive fires had *consumed* hundreds of square miles of forest⟩
synonyms devour, eat (up)
related words gut; deplete, drain, exhaust, expend, spend, use up; annihilate, decimate, demolish, desolate, devastate, do in, pulverize, raze, ruin, shatter, smash, tear down, waste, wreck; annihilate, blot out, eradicate, exterminate, extinguish, extirpate, obliterate, remove, rub out, stamp (out), wipe out
near antonyms conserve, preserve, protect, save; build, construct, erect, put up, raise
2 to make complete use of ⟨the mining company *consumed* all of the local mineral resources and then moved on⟩ — see DEPLETE 1
3 to take in as food ⟨hungry enough to *consume* most of the pie⟩ — see EAT 1

consuming *adj* holding the attention or provoking interest ⟨didn't find the plot of the novel particularly *consuming*⟩ — see INTERESTING

consummate *adj* **1** having or showing exceptional knowledge, experience, or skill in a field of endeavor ⟨*consummate* cabinetmakers, they produced desks and chests of drawers that are now regarded as masterpieces of American furniture⟩ — see PROFICIENT
2 having no exceptions or restrictions ⟨a *consummate* liar who has practically made mendacity an art form⟩ — see ABSOLUTE 2
3 of the greatest or highest degree or quantity ⟨a ballerina renowned for her *consummate* grace⟩ — see ULTIMATE 1

consummate *vb* to bring (something) to a state where nothing remains to be done ⟨willing to do whatever it takes to *consummate* a business deal⟩ — see FINISH 1

consummately *adv* in a skillful or expert manner ⟨the archaeologist unearthed a *consummately* carved bust from the fourth century BC⟩ — see WELL 3

consummation *n* **1** the last part of a process or action ⟨the signing of the contract marked the *consummation* of six months of negotiations⟩ — see FINALE
2 the state of being actual or complete ⟨the opening of the performing arts center brought to *consummation* years of planning⟩ — see FRUITION

contact *n* **1** an acquaintance who has influence especially in the business or political world ⟨an intern who got her summer job in the governor's office through *contacts*⟩
synonyms connection
related words in, insider; big shot, bigwig, somebody, VIP; arbiter, arbitrator, conciliator, go-between, intercessor, intermediary, interposer, mediator, middleman, peacemaker
2 the state or fact of being able to exchange information regarding one's current situation ⟨she had moved to the other side of the country, but continued to stay in *contact* with her closest friends⟩ — see TOUCH 1

contact *vb* to transmit information or requests to ⟨you can *contact* me at this number⟩
synonyms address, communicate (with), get, reach
related words get through (to); acquaint, advise, apprise, brief, clue, enlighten, familiarize, fill in, inform, instruct, notify, tell, wise (up); buzz, call, phone, ring (up) [*chiefly British*], telephone; keep up (with)
phrases get hold of, get (*or* keep) in touch with, touch base (with)

contagious *adj* **1** capable of being passed by physical contact from one person to another ⟨chicken pox, measles, German measles, and other *contagious* diseases⟩
synonyms catching, communicable, pestilent, transmissible, transmittable
related words infectious, infective
near antonyms noninfectious
antonyms noncommunicable
2 exciting a similar feeling or reaction in others ⟨the enthusiasm of the new club members was *contagious*⟩
synonyms catching, epidemic, infectious, spreading
related words palpable, perceptible, tangible; irresistible (*also* irresistable), overpowering, overwhelming; disarming, endearing, fetching, inviting, winning, winsome

contain *vb* **1** to have within ⟨the top drawer of the cabinet *contains* my stamp collection⟩
synonyms bear, boast, hold
related words accommodate, fit, take; case, encase, enclose (*also* inclose), encompass; harbor, house, lodge, shelter
2 to have as part of a whole ⟨the contract *contains* several new clauses⟩ — see INCLUDE 1
3 to be made up of ⟨the recipe *contains* several parts⟩ — see COMPRISE 1
4 to gain emotional or mental control of ⟨could hardly *contain* herself when she heard that she had won the scholarship⟩ — see COLLECT 1
5 to keep from exceeding a desirable degree or level (as of expression) ⟨frantic efforts to *contain* the spread of the disease⟩ — see CONTROL 1

container *n* something into which a liquid or smaller objects can be put for storage or transportation ⟨save the plastic *containers* from the deli for other uses⟩
synonyms holder, receptacle, vessel
related words carrier; cartridge; basket, bin, box, caddy, carton, case, casket, crate, handbasket, locker, trunk; bag, hamper, pocket, sack; cooler, warmer; basin, bottle, bowl, bucket, can, jar, jug, keg, kettle, kit, pack, pail, pitcher, pot, tub, vat

contaminant *n* something that is or that makes impure ⟨a filter to remove *contaminants* from the drinking water⟩ — see IMPURITY 1

contaminate *vb* to make unfit for use by the addition of something harmful or undesirable ⟨a supply of drinking water that was *contaminated* by a toxic waste dump⟩
synonyms befoul, defile, foul, poison, pollute, taint
related words infect; begrime, besmirch, blacken, dirty, foul up, grime, mire, muddy, smirch, smudge,

soil, stain, sully; corrupt, rot, spoil; adulterate, doctor; dilute, water down
near antonyms clarify, clean, cleanse, clear, distill (*also* distil), purge; filter; disinfect, sanitize, sterilize
antonyms decontaminate, purify

contaminated *adj* containing foreign or lower-grade substances ⟨the hospitals had no choice but to throw out the *contaminated* blood supply⟩ — see IMPURE 1

contamination *n* something that is or that makes impure ⟨swimming in the lake is banned until the *contamination* is identified and neutralized⟩ — see IMPURITY 1

contemn *vb* to show contempt for ⟨arrogant critics who *contemn* the general public's taste in art⟩ — see SCORN 1

contemplate *vb* **1** to give serious and careful thought to ⟨she *contemplated* the problem for several hours before reaching a decision⟩ — see PONDER
2 to have in mind as a purpose or goal ⟨he waited patiently, *contemplating* revenge all the while⟩ — see INTEND 1

contemplation *n* **1** long or deep thinking about spiritual matters ⟨the decision to enter a monastery and to spend one's life in prayer and *contemplation*⟩
synonyms meditation
related words brown study, daydreaming, introspection, muse, navel-gazing, reflection, retrospection, reverie, study, trance, woolgathering; cogitation, deliberation, musing, pondering, rumination
2 the act or state of looking forward to some occurrence ⟨in *contemplation* of their children's college expenses, they started saving early⟩ — see EXPECTATION

contemplative *adj* given to or marked by long, quiet thinking ⟨a *contemplative* person who likes to go on solitary walks⟩ ⟨the *contemplative* life of the monks at the abbey⟩
synonyms broody, cogitative, meditative, melancholy, musing, pensive, reflective, ruminant, ruminative, thoughtful
related words introspective, retrospective, self-reflective; earnest, grave, sedate, serious, serious-minded, severe, sober, solemn, somber (*or* sombre), weighty; philosophical (*also* philosophic); analytic (*or* analytical), logical, rational; deliberate, purposeful; absent-minded, abstracted, preoccupied
near antonyms featherbrained, flighty, flippant, frivolous, goofy, harebrained, light-headed, scatterbrained; brainless, mindless, silly, thoughtless, unthinking
antonyms unreflective

contemporaneous *adj* existing or occurring at the same period of time ⟨*contemporaneous* accounts of the battle from officers on both sides⟩ — see CONTEMPORARY 1

contemporaneously *adv* at one and the same time ⟨Mozart was writing music *contemporaneously* with Haydn⟩ — see TOGETHER 1

contemporary *adj* **1** existing or occurring at the same period of time ⟨the absurd notion that early cave dwellers were *contemporary* with the dinosaurs⟩
synonyms coetaneous, coeval, coexistent, coexisting, coextensive, coincident, coincidental, concurrent, contemporaneous, coterminous, simultaneous, synchronic, synchronous
related words accompanying, attendant, attending, concomitant, incident
antonyms asynchronous, noncontemporary, nonsimultaneous, nonsynchronous
2 being or involving the latest methods, concepts, information, or styles ⟨a magazine devoted to *contemporary* fashions⟩ — see MODERN

contemporary *n* a person who lives at the same time or is about the same age as another ⟨Abraham Lincoln and Charles Darwin were exact *contemporaries*, actually being born on the same day in 1809⟩
synonyms coeval
related words accompaniment, companion, concomitant; coordinate, counterpart, equal, equivalent, match, peer, rival

contemporize *vb* to adapt to modern needs, taste, or usage ⟨the new owners of the old-line French restaurant plan to *contemporize* the menu and make the place seem less intimidating⟩ — see MODERNIZE

contempt *n* open dislike for someone or something considered unworthy of one's concern or respect ⟨my undying *contempt* for people who abuse animals⟩
synonyms contemptuousness, despisement, despite, despitefulness, disdain, misprision, scorn
related words abhorrence, abomination, detestation, execration, hate, hatred, loathing, lovelessness; cattiness, hatefulness, invidiousness, malevolence, malice, maliciousness, malignancy, malignity, meanness, spite, spitefulness; aversion, disgust, distaste, horror, odium, repugnance, repulsion, revulsion; animosity, antagonism, antipathy, bitterness, enmity, gall, grudge, hostility, jealousy, pique, resentment; bile, jaundice, rancor, spleen, venom, vindictiveness, virulence, vitriol; aspersion, belittlement, deprecation, depreciation, detraction, diminishment, disparagement; derision, mockery, ridicule; abuse, invective, vituperation; censure, condemnation, denunciation
near antonyms acceptance, tolerance; adoration, adulation, deference, deification, glorification, idolatry, idolization, lionization, reverence, veneration, worship; affection, fancy, fondness, liking, love
antonyms admiration, esteem, estimation, favor, regard, respect

contemptible *adj* **1** arousing or deserving of one's loathing and disgust ⟨the *contemptible* thieves who stole the Christmas gifts intended for needy children⟩
synonyms cheap, cruddy, deplorable, despicable, dirty, grubby, lame, lousy, mean, nasty, paltry, pitiable, pitiful, ratty, scabby, scummy, scurvy, sneaking, sorry, wretched
related words abhorrent, abominable, condemnable, detestable, execrable, hateful, loathsome, odious; disgusting, reptilian, repugnant, repulsive, revolting, revulsive; discreditable, disgraceful, dishonorable, disreputable, ignominious, shameful; base, ignoble, low, shabby, sordid, squalid, vile; blamable, censurable, reprehensible, reproachable; cowardly, craven, dastardly; unethical, unprincipled, unscrupulous
near antonyms high-minded, honest, honorable, noble, principled, redoubtable, reputable, right-minded, scrupulous, upright; ethical, good, moral, right, righteous, virtuous
antonyms admirable, commendable, creditable, laudable, meritorious, praiseworthy
2 deserving pitying scorn (as for inadequacy) ⟨a *contemptible* attempt at science fiction by someone with no understanding of the genre⟩ — see PITIFUL 1
3 not following or in accordance with standards of honor and decency ⟨the *contemptible* behavior of the students who took part in the hazing⟩ — see IGNOBLE 2

contemptuous *adj* **1** feeling or showing open dislike for someone or something regarded as undeserving of respect or concern ⟨loutish tourists who are *contemptuous* of the ways and traditions of their host countries⟩
synonyms abhorrent, disdainful, scornful
related words bold-faced, brash, brassy, brazen, cheeky, cocky, discourteous, disrespectful, fresh, impertinent, impudent, insolent, sassy, saucy; arrogant, cavalier, highfalutin (*also* hifalutin), high-handed, high-hat, pretentious, uppish, uppity; haughty, lofty, lordly, prideful, sniffish, snobbish, supercilious; pompous, self-important, superior; catty, cruel, despiteful, hateful,

malevolent, malicious, malign, malignant, mean, nasty, spiteful
near antonyms deferential, regardful, respectful; accepting, tolerant; courteous, polite
antonyms admiring, applauding, appreciative, approving
2 intended to make a person or thing seem of little importance or value ⟨*contemptuous* comments about the baseball team's pathetic showings⟩ — see DEROGATORY

contemptuousness *n* open dislike for someone or something considered unworthy of one's concern or respect ⟨a glance filled with unrestrained *contemptuousness* for the rest of us⟩ — see CONTEMPT

contend *vb* **1** to engage in a contest ⟨two traditional rivals *contending* for the championship⟩ — see COMPETE
2 to state (something) as a reason in support of or against something under consideration ⟨*contended* that the senator's considerable experience made him the best candidate⟩ — see ARGUE 1
3 to state as a fact usually forcefully ⟨*contended* that his opponent was wrong about practically everything⟩ — see CLAIM 1

contend (with) *vb* **1** to deal with (something) usually skillfully or efficiently ⟨a multitude of problems to *contend with* as soon as he returned to the office⟩ — see HANDLE 1
2 to strive to reduce or eliminate ⟨medical missionaries who daily *contend with* disease and poverty⟩ — see FIGHT 2

contender *n* **1** one who seeks an office, honor, position, or award ⟨a strong *contender* for the mayoral position⟩ — see CANDIDATE
2 one who strives for the same thing as another ⟨several *contenders* competing for the title of the city's best Italian restaurant⟩ — see COMPETITOR

content *adj* feeling that one's needs or desires have been met ⟨are you *content* with your present salary?⟩
synonyms contented, gratified, happy, pleased, satisfied
related words blissful, delighted, glad, joyful, joyous, jubilant, rejoicing, tickled; ecstatic, elated, enraptured, euphoric, overjoyed, rapturous, thrilled; appeased, mollified, pacified, placated
near antonyms disaffected, disgruntled, displeased, unsatisfied; abject, aggrieved, anguished, brokenhearted, dejected, depressed, despondent, disconsolate, discouraged, disheartened, dispirited, downcast, downhearted
antonyms discontent, discontented, displeased, dissatisfied, malcontent, malcontented, unhappy

[1]**content** *n* **1** a major object of interest or concern (as in a discussion or artistic composition) ⟨although I appreciate the poem's lyrical qualities, I don't understand its *content*⟩ — see MATTER 1
2 the amount of something (as subject matter) included ⟨judging from the table of *contents*, I'd have to say that this book covers most of the major topics in American history⟩ — see COVERAGE
3 the idea that is conveyed or intended to be conveyed to the mind by language, symbol, or action ⟨the speech was filled with fine words but devoid of any real *content*⟩ — see MEANING 1

[2]**content** *n* the feeling experienced when one's wishes are met ⟨slept to her heart's *content* on weekends⟩ — see PLEASURE 1

content *vb* to give satisfaction to ⟨a person easily *contented* by life's simple pleasures⟩ — see PLEASE 1

contented *adj* feeling that one's needs or desires have been met ⟨having had her fill of candy, the *contented* girl sank back into the easy chair and dozed off⟩ — see CONTENT

contentedness *n* the feeling experienced when one's wishes are met ⟨the look of *contentedness* on the sleeping child's face⟩ — see PLEASURE 1

contention *n* **1** an idea or opinion that is put forth in a discussion or debate ⟨my *contention* is that today's lower batting averages are the result of better pitching⟩
synonyms argument, assertion, thesis
related words conjecture, guess, hunch, hypothesis, speculation, surmise, theory; proposal, proposition; assumption, presupposition, supposition; position, stand; case, explanation, rationale, reason
2 an earnest effort for superiority or victory over another ⟨several actresses seem to be in heated *contention* for the title of "worst dressed"⟩ — see CONTEST 1

contentious *adj* **1** feeling or displaying eagerness to fight ⟨the Tartars were a *contentious* people who terrorized much of Asia and eastern Europe during the Middle Ages⟩ — see BELLIGERENT
2 given to arguing ⟨a tiresomely *contentious* person who likes to argue for the sake of arguing⟩ — see ARGUMENTATIVE 1
3 relating to or causing the expression of opposing opinions ⟨gun control is likely to be a *contentious* subject in any group discussion⟩ — see CONTROVERSIAL 1

contentiousness *n* an inclination to fight or quarrel ⟨his natural tendency towards *contentiousness* made him a poor choice for a diplomatic post⟩ — see BELLIGERENCE

contentment *n* the feeling experienced when one's wishes are met ⟨a couple of golden-agers looking over their life together with a feeling of *contentment* and accomplishment⟩ — see PLEASURE 1

conterminous *adj* **1** having a border in common ⟨for two nations that are *conterminous* from the Atlantic to the Pacific, the U.S. and Canada have had remarkably little strife⟩ — see ADJACENT
2 occupying the same space ⟨the county and the school district are *conterminous*⟩ — see COEXTENSIVE 1

contest *n* **1** an earnest effort for superiority or victory over another ⟨the eternal *contest* between the forces of good and the forces of evil⟩
synonyms ball game, battle, combat, competition, conflict, confrontation, contention, dogfight, duel, face-off, grapple, match, rivalry, strife, struggle, sweepstakes (*also* sweep-stake), tug-of-war, war, warfare
related words horse race, nail-biter; showdown; clash, collision, discord, friction; argument, controversy, debate, disagreement, disputation, dispute, dissension (*also* dissention), quarrel, row, wrangle
near antonyms concord, harmony, peace
2 a competitive encounter between individuals or groups carried on for amusement, exercise, or in pursuit of a prize ⟨a *contest* for the gold medal in diving⟩ — see GAME 1
3 a physical dispute between opposing individuals or groups ⟨what mighty *contests* have been waged on trivial matters⟩ — see FIGHT 1

contest *vb* to demand proof of the truth or rightness of ⟨vowed to *contest* the claim in court⟩ — see CHALLENGE 1

contestant *n* one who strives for the same thing as another ⟨three *contestants* will compete on live TV for the cash prize⟩ — see COMPETITOR

contestation *n* variance of opinion on a matter ⟨the statement is certainly open to *contestation* among reasonable people⟩ — see DISAGREEMENT 1

context *n* the circumstances, conditions, or objects by which one is surrounded ⟨in the *context* of the Great Depression, communism had a certain allure for some disillusioned Americans⟩ — see ENVIRONMENT

contexture *n* the circumstances, conditions, or objects by which one is surrounded ⟨the whole *contexture* of

Las Vegas is focused on escapism⟩ — see ENVIRONMENT

contiguity *n* the state or condition of being near ⟨because of the *contiguity* of the mall to the border, it attracts many shoppers from out of state⟩ — see PROXIMITY

contiguous *adj* having a border in common ⟨Connecticut and Massachusetts are *contiguous* states⟩ — see ADJACENT

continence *n* **1** abstention from sexual intercourse ⟨argued for a pregnancy-prevention program that did not put so much faith in the *continence* of teenagers⟩ — see CELIBACY

2 the checking of one's true feelings and impulses when dealing with others ⟨experiencing a moment of unusual *continence*, I refrained from returning her gratuitous insult⟩ — see CONSTRAINT 1

3 the power to control one's actions, impulses, or emotions ⟨a religious sect that demanded nearly superhuman *continence* from its adherents⟩ — see WILL 1

4 voluntary restraint in the satisfaction of one's appetites ⟨a gambling mecca that has a reputation for being the sort of place where caution and *continence* are thrown to the wind⟩ — see ABSTINENCE 1

continent *adj* given to or marked by restraint in the satisfaction of one's appetites ⟨a religous sect that expects its unmarried members to be completely celibate and its married adherents to maintain *continent* relationships⟩ — see ABSTEMIOUS

continent *n* one of the great divisions of land on the globe or the main part of such a division ⟨Europe and Asia are sometimes considered together to be one *continent*⟩ — see MAINLAND

continental *n* the smallest amount or part imaginable ⟨complained that today's youth doesn't care a *continental* about their elders⟩ — see JOT

contingence *n* something that might happen ⟨the collapse of that nation's economy was one *contingence* that the architects of the war hadn't planned on⟩ — see EVENT 2

contingency *n* **1** something that might happen ⟨agencies trying to provide for every *contingency* in a national emergency⟩ — see EVENT 2

2 something upon which the carrying out of an agreement or offer depends ⟨an offer to buy the house, with the *contingency* that it pass inspection⟩ — see CONDITION 2

contingent *n* **1** a body of persons chosen as representatives of a larger group ⟨the local Scout troop traditionally sends a large *contingent* to the jamboree⟩
synonyms delegacy, delegation
related words embassy, legation, mission; band, company, crew, detachment, gang, outfit, party, squad, team

2 something that might happen ⟨officials in charge of managing the national emergency tried to prepare for every *contingent*, no matter how improbable⟩ — see EVENT 2

contingent (on *or* upon) *adj* determined by something else ⟨the train's scheduled departure is *contingent on* the prompt fixing of the mechanical fault⟩ — see DEPENDENT 2

continual *adj* **1** going on and on without any interruptions ⟨the castaways hoped that the *continual* broadcast of the distress signal would eventually attract attention⟩ — see CONTINUOUS

2 occurring or appearing at intervals ⟨a history of *continual* invasions from countries to the west⟩ — see INTERMITTENT 1

continually *adv* **1** many times ⟨grew up in a time when children were *continually* being told to mind their manners⟩ — see OFTEN

2 on every relevant occasion ⟨the computer program *continually* updates the file with new information⟩ — see ALWAYS 1

continuance *n* **1** the period during which something exists, lasts, or is in progress ⟨the feud between the two families was bitter and of long *continuance*⟩ — see DURATION 1

2 uninterrupted or lasting existence ⟨the *continuance* of hunger in the world despite some valiant efforts to solve the problem⟩ — see CONTINUATION

continuation *n* uninterrupted or lasting existence ⟨the *continuation* of high unemployment has cost the government much support⟩
synonyms abidance, ceaselessness, continuance, continuity, continuousness, durability, duration, endurance, persistence, subsistence
related words drawing out, elongation, extension, lengthening, prolongation, prolonging, stretching; enduringness, permanence; survival
near antonyms abridgment (*or* abridgement), curtailment, cutback, shortening
antonyms cessation, close, discontinuance, discontinuity, end, ending, expiration, finish, stoppage, surcease, termination

continue *vb* **1** to remain indefinitely in existence or in the same state ⟨the heavy snow *continued* throughout the night⟩
synonyms abide, bide, endure, hold on, hold up, keep up, last, perdure, persist, remain, run on
related words linger, stay, stick around, tarry; carry through, prevail, survive
near antonyms abate, die (down), ebb, let up, moderate, subside, wane
antonyms cease, close, conclude, desist, die, discontinue, end, expire, finish, lapse, leave off, pass, quit, stop, terminate, wind up

2 to begin again or return to after an interruption ⟨we'll *continue* this discussion after we've eaten⟩ — see RESUME

continued *adj* going on and on without any interruptions ⟨the *continued* drought is starting to take its toll on the region's farms⟩ — see CONTINUOUS

continuing *adj* **1** going on and on without any interruptions ⟨the *continuing* success of the chain as it opens stores around the country⟩ — see CONTINUOUS

2 having an existence or validity that does not change or diminish ⟨the public's *continuing* interest in every aspect of the lives of celebrities⟩ — see ABIDING

continuity *n* uninterrupted or lasting existence ⟨after being shuttled from one foster home to another, the child needs some *continuity* of care⟩ — see CONTINUATION

continuous *adj* going on and on without any interruptions ⟨a city that has been under *continuous* bombardment for three days⟩
synonyms ceaseless, continual, continued, continuing, incessant, nonstop, perpetual, running, unbroken, unceasing, uninterrupted, unremitting
related words dateless, deathless, endless, eternal, everlasting, immortal, interminable, permanent, undying, unending; changeless, constant, stable, steady, unchanging, unvarying; durable, enduring, lasting, persistent; imperishable, indestructible
near antonyms intermittent, periodic, periodical, recurrent, recurring; alternate, alternating, cyclic (*or* cyclical), rhythmic (*or* rhythmical), seasonal, serial; erratic, fitful, irregular, occasional, spasmodic, sporadic, spotty, unsteady
antonyms discontinuous, noncontinuous

continuousness *n* uninterrupted or lasting existence ⟨although their bickering wasn't particularly vicious, its merciless *continuousness* was wearying⟩ — see CONTINUATION

contort *vb* to twist (something) out of a natural or normal shape or condition ⟨the acrobat is able to *contort* his body so that it almost looks like a pretzel⟩
synonyms deform, distort, misshape, screw, squinch, torture, warp
related words deface, disfigure; wrench, wrest, wring; coil, curl, loop, spiral, twine, wind, wreathe
near antonyms straighten, unbend, uncurl

contortion *n* the twisting of something out of its natural or normal shape or condition ⟨the comedian is renowned for his seemingly endless variety of facial *contortions*⟩
synonyms deformation, distortion, misshaping, screwing, squinching, torturing, warping
related words defacement, deformity, disfigurement, malformation

contour *n* a line that traces the outer limits of an object or surface ⟨a car with flowing *contours*⟩ — see OUTLINE 1

contra *prep* opposed to; not for ⟨a roundup of editorials pro and *contra* the proposed constitutional amendment⟩ — see ANTI

contrabandist *n* a person who imports or exports goods secretly and illegally ⟨*contrabandists* supplying the rebels with guns⟩ — see SMUGGLER

contract *n* **1** a formal agreement to fulfill an obligation ⟨accused her of breaking their *contract* by not completing the decorating job on budget⟩ — see GUARANTEE 1
2 an arrangement about action to be taken ⟨a *contract* outlining what needed to be done by each person⟩ — see AGREEMENT 2

contract *vb* **1** to become affected with (a disease or disorder) ⟨before vaccines were invented, people lived in fear of *contracting* polio⟩
synonyms catch, come down (with), get, go down (with) [*chiefly British*], sicken (with), take
related words break out (with); die (from), succumb (to); fail, languish, sink, waste (away), weaken, wilt, wither, worsen
near antonyms come back, gain, heal, mend, recoup, recover, recuperate, snap back; rally, rebound, recover (from), shake (off)
2 to become smaller in size or volume through the drawing together of particles of matter ⟨metal *contracts* at low temperatures⟩
synonyms compress, condense, constrict, shrink
related words collapse, deflate, flatten; dry up, shrivel, wilt, wither; abate, decrease, diminish, dwindle, lessen; recede, retreat, withdraw
near antonyms accumulate, grow, increase; balloon, inflate, puff (up)
antonyms balloon, expand, snowball, swell
3 to reduce in size or volume by or as if by pressing parts or members together ⟨*contract* the calf muscles in your legs⟩ — see COMPRESS 1
4 to come to an arrangement as to a course of action ⟨the farmer *contracted* for delivery of the hay by the first of July⟩ — see AGREE 2

contracting *n* the act or process of reducing the size or volume of something by or as if by pressing ⟨the *contracting* of the time frame for the primaries tends to favor candidates who are already well-known⟩ — see COMPRESSION

contraction *n* the act or process of reducing the size or volume of something by or as if by pressing ⟨most substances undergo *contraction* when cooled⟩ — see COMPRESSION

contradict *vb* **1** to make an assertion that is contrary to one made by (another) ⟨no matter what I say, you always have to *contradict* me⟩
synonyms disagree (with), gainsay
related words challenge, contest, dispute, question; confute, rebut, refute; cross, fight, oppose, resist
near antonyms confirm, corroborate, substantiate, verify; attest, authenticate, avouch, certify, testify (to), vouch (for), witness
antonyms agree (with), concur (with)
2 to declare not to be true ⟨his account *contradicted* the story that they had gotten earlier⟩ — see DENY 1

contradiction *n* **1** someone or something with qualities or features that seem to conflict with one another ⟨a loving father as well as a ruthless killer, the gangster is a living *contradiction*⟩
synonyms dichotomy, incongruity, paradox
related words antinomy; conundrum, enigma, mystery, mystification, puzzle, puzzlement, riddle
2 a refusal to confirm the truth of a statement ⟨the actress's *contradiction* of the marriage rumor caused quite a stir⟩ — see DENIAL 2

contradictory *adj* being as different as possible ⟨*contradictory* predictions regarding stock prices that were of no help to investors at all⟩ — see OPPOSITE

contraption *n* an interesting and often novel device with a practical use ⟨built a *contraption* for automatically buttering toast⟩ — see GADGET

contrariety *n* the quality or state of being as different as possible ⟨the inescapable *contrariety* of her chief interests: food and a desire for supermodel svelteness⟩
synonyms contrariness, oppositeness, opposition, polarity
related words contradictoriness; antipode, antithesis; disparateness, disparity, dissimilarity, divergence, unlikeness; inequality; conflict, disagreement, discrepancy, variance; incompatibility, incongruence, incongruity, incongruousness
near antonyms agreement, alikeness, conformity, congruity, correspondence, likeness, parallelism, resemblance, similarity, similitude; analogousness; correlation, relationship
antonyms identicalness, sameness

contrarily *adv* just the opposite being true ⟨*contrarily*, the most authentic novel about the American Civil War was written by someone born six years after it had ended⟩ — see CONTRARIWISE

contrariness *n* **1** refusal to obey ⟨cursed the *contrariness* of her beloved mutt when it refused to come back inside the house⟩ — see DISOBEDIENCE
2 the quality or state of being as different as possible ⟨a *contrariness* between his professed altruism and his blatant selfishness⟩ — see CONTRARIETY

contrariwise *adv* just the opposite being true ⟨the rock singer is hardly a carouser; *contrariwise*, he totally abstains from alcohol⟩
synonyms again, contrarily, conversely
phrases if anything, on the contrary, to the contrary
near antonyms even, indeed, nay, true, truly, verily, yea

contrary *adj* **1** being as different as possible ⟨the other jurors seemed sure the defendant was guilty, but I came to the *contrary* conclusion⟩ — see OPPOSITE
2 engaging in or marked by childish misbehavior ⟨a *contrary* child who wouldn't behave⟩ — see NAUGHTY
3 given to resisting authority or another's control ⟨the *contrary* soldier is facing a court-martial for insubordination⟩ — see DISOBEDIENT

contrary *n* something that is as different as possible from something else ⟨the admonition that we should not return hate with hate, but rather with its *contrary*—love⟩ — see OPPOSITE

contrast *n* the quality or state of being different ⟨the *contrast* between the two approaches to the problem of overeating could not be greater⟩ — see DIFFERENCE 1

contrast *vb* to be unlike; to not be the same ⟨her depressed mood today *contrasts* sharply with her good spirits yesterday⟩ — see DIFFER 1

contravene *vb* to fail to keep ⟨the unauthorized reproduction of the image *contravenes* copyright laws⟩ — see VIOLATE 1

contravention *n* a failure to uphold the requirements of law, duty, or obligation ⟨a clandestine weapons program that was a *contravention* of the international arms agreement⟩ — see BREACH 1

contretemps *n* an often noisy or angry expression of differing opinions ⟨there was a bit of a *contretemps* over the seating arrangements for the upcoming wedding⟩ — see ARGUMENT 1

contribute *vb* **1** to make a donation as part of a group effort ⟨would you like to *contribute* to the Thanksgiving fund for needy families?⟩
synonyms chip in, kick in, pitch in
related words bestow, donate, give, present; award, confer, dole (out), endow; afford, furnish, provide
2 to make a present of ⟨*contributes* money to a variety of worthy causes⟩ — see GIVE 1

contribution *n* a gift of money or its equivalent to a charity, humanitarian cause, or public institution ⟨*contributions* for the victims of the earthquake began pouring in⟩
synonyms alms, benefaction, beneficence, charity, donation, philanthropy
related words offering, tithe; bequest, endowment, legacy; aid, assistance, dole, handout, relief, welfare; grant, subsidy; benevolence, bestowal, largesse (*also* largess), present, presentation

contrite *adj* feeling sorrow for a wrong that one has done ⟨being *contrite* is not enough to spare you an arrest if you're caught shoplifting⟩
synonyms apologetic, compunctious, penitent, regretful, remorseful, repentant, rueful, sorry
related words ashamed, shamefaced, sheepish; dolorous, grieving, lugubrious, mournful, plaintive, sorrowful, wailing, weeping, woeful
near antonyms compassionless, cruel, merciless, pitiless, ruthless, unmerciful; shameless, unashamed
antonyms impenitent, remorseless, unapologetic, unrepentant

contriteness *n* a feeling of responsibility for wrongdoing ⟨his determination to make things right again was seen as a sign of his sincere *contriteness*⟩ — see GUILT 1

contrition *n* a feeling of responsibility for wrongdoing ⟨once again she heard her abusive husband's tearful expressions of *contrition*⟩ — see GUILT 1

contrivance *n* **1** an interesting and often novel device with a practical use ⟨a new *contrivance* for cleaning computer keyboards⟩ — see GADGET
2 something (as a device) created for the first time through the use of the imagination ⟨despite the many modern *contrivances* for saving time and labor, we seem to have less leisure and energy than ever before⟩ — see INVENTION 1
3 the ability to form mental images of things that either are not physically present or have never been conceived or created by others ⟨in that writer's hands, narrative *contrivance* can often deteriorate into pointless gimmickry⟩ — see IMAGINATION 1

contrive *vb* **1** to create or think of by clever use of the imagination ⟨*contrived* abstract metal sculptures using old household utensils⟩ — see INVENT
2 to engage in a secret plan to accomplish evil or unlawful ends ⟨the mischievous boys were always *contriving* and trying to pull the prank that would be the talk of the school⟩ — see PLOT
3 to plan out usually with subtle skill or care ⟨*contrived* a way of helping the needy family without their knowing it⟩ — see ENGINEER

contrived *adj* lacking in natural or spontaneous quality ⟨the *contrived* applause of a TV studio audience that has been told when to clap⟩ — see ARTIFICIAL 1

contriver *n* one who creates or introduces something new ⟨a *contriver* of yet another piece of exercise equipment guaranteed to take off the pounds⟩ — see INVENTOR

control *n* **1** a mechanism for adjusting the operation of a device, machine, or system ⟨the *controls* for the player are well marked⟩
synonyms controller, regulator
related words actuator; button, dial, key, knob, lever, push button, selector, switch
2 the ability to direct the course of something ⟨after the tail fell off, the plane went out of the pilot's *control*⟩ ⟨firefighters keeping *control* of the blaze⟩
synonyms grasp, hand(s)
related words clutch, grip, hold, mastery; arm, command, dominion, helm, sway; authority, domination, jurisdiction, might, power; administration, direction, governance, government, guidance, management, operation, oversight, regulation, running, superintendence, supervision
near antonyms helplessness, weakness; impotence, impotency, powerlessness
3 the act or activity of looking after and making decisions about something ⟨*control* of manufacturing operations was given to a new manager with fresh ideas⟩ — see CONDUCT 1
4 the fact or state of having (something) at one's disposal ⟨took *control* of the process of selecting candidates for the scholarship⟩ — see POSSESSION 1
5 the right or means to command or control others ⟨teachers are responsible for the students under their *control*⟩ — see POWER 1

control *vb* **1** to keep from exceeding a desirable degree or level (as of expression) ⟨you must learn to *control* your temper⟩
synonyms bridle, check, constrain, contain, curb, govern, hold, inhibit, keep, measure, pull in, regulate, rein (in), restrain, rule, tame
related words bottle (up), choke (back), hold back, mince, muffle, pocket, repress, sink, smother, squelch, stifle, strangle, suppress, swallow; arrest, interrupt, stop; block, hamper, handcuff, hinder, impede, obstruct; gag, muzzle, silence
near antonyms liberate, loose, loosen, unleash; air, express, take out, vent
antonyms lose
2 to gain emotional or mental control of ⟨he *controlled* himself only with the greatest difficulty in the face of his opponent's insulting remarks⟩ — see COLLECT 1
3 to exercise authority or power over ⟨circumstances often *control* the choices we make in life⟩ — see GOVERN 1
4 to look after and make decisions about ⟨during the period that she *controlled* the company it was highly profitable⟩ — see CONDUCT 1

controller *n* a mechanism for adjusting the operation of a device, machine, or system ⟨the *controllers* for the video game system seem fairly well designed⟩ — see CONTROL 1

controversial *adj* **1** relating to or causing the expression of opposing opinions ⟨racial segregation was a *controversial* topic in the 1960s⟩
synonyms argumentative, contentious, disputatious, hot-button, polemical (*also* polemic)
related words delicate, difficult, knotty, problematic (*also* problematical), spiny, thorny, ticklish, touchy, tough

near antonyms incontestable, incontrovertible, indisputable, indubitable, undeniable, unquestionable; irrefutable; uncontested, undisputed
antonyms noncontroversial, safe, uncontroversial
2 given to arguing ⟨*controversial* by temperament, she's the sort of political attack dog who kills all hope of bipartisanship⟩ — see ARGUMENTATIVE 1

controversy *n* **1** an often noisy or angry expression of differing opinions ⟨the seemingly imperishable *controversy* over the teaching of evolution⟩ — see ARGUMENT 1
2 variance of opinion on a matter ⟨there is considerable *controversy* regarding the assassination of President Kennedy⟩ — see DISAGREEMENT 1

controvert *vb* to express different opinions about something often angrily ⟨ever since the poem was first published, critics and scholars have *controverted* over the meaning of its concluding lines⟩ — see ARGUE 2

controvertible *adj* open to question or dispute ⟨a *controvertible* decision to permit smoking in certain public spaces around town⟩ — see DEBATABLE 1

contumacious *adj* given to resisting authority or another's control ⟨the judge threatened to charge the *contumacious* witness with contempt of court⟩ — see DISOBEDIENT

contumacy *n* refusal to obey ⟨a rogue archbishop who was excommunicated on grounds of *contumacy*⟩ — see DISOBEDIENCE

contumelious *adj* marked by harsh insulting language ⟨a well-reasoned thesis that merited more than just a scornful, *contumelious* response⟩ — see ABUSIVE

contusion *n* a bodily injury in which small blood vessels are broken but the overlying skin is not ⟨suffered multiple *contusions* as a result of a car accident⟩
synonyms bruise
related words abrasion, boo-boo, bump, lump, scrape, scratch; black eye, hickey; discoloration

conundrum *n* something hard to understand or explain ⟨the *conundrum* of how an ancient people were able to build such massive structures without the benefit of today's knowledge and technology⟩ — see MYSTERY

convalesce *vb* to become healthy and strong again after illness or weakness ⟨the long months that the soldier spent in the hospital slowly *convalescing*⟩
synonyms come back, gain, heal, mend, pull round [*chiefly British*], rally, recoup, recover, recuperate, snap back
related words come around, come round, come to, improve, pick up, revive; cheer (up), perk (up); pull through, survive; recruit
near antonyms ail, collapse, come down, sicken; decline, degenerate, deteriorate, fade, fail, languish, sink, waste (away), weaken, wilt, wither, worsen; regress, relapse

convalescence *n* the process or period of gradually regaining one's health and strength ⟨her release from the hospital was followed by a long *convalescence* at home⟩
synonyms comeback, healing, mending, rally, recovery, recuperation, rehab, rehabilitation, snapback
related words resuscitation, revival; survival
near antonyms decline, degeneration, deterioration, fading, failing, languishing, sinking, wasting (away), weakening, wilting, withering, worsening; regression, relapse

convene *vb* **1** to bring together in assembly by or as if by command ⟨*convened* the members of the council for an emergency session⟩ — see CONVOKE
2 to come together into one body or place ⟨the conventioneers *convened* in the auditorium to hear the guest speaker⟩ — see ASSEMBLE 1

convenience *n* **1** something that adds to one's ease of living ⟨a house with all the modern *conveniences* that buyers have come to expect⟩ — see COMFORT 2
2 *chiefly British* a room furnished with a fixture for flushing body waste ⟨it can be hard to find a public *convenience* in an unfamiliar train station⟩ — see TOILET

convenient *adj* situated within easy reach ⟨the shopping mall is *convenient* to all of the area's major highways⟩
synonyms accessible, handy, reachable
related words close, near, nearby, nigh; abutting, adjacent, adjoining; approachable, attainable, getatable, obtainable; ultraconvenient
phrases at hand, to hand
near antonyms away, distant, far, faraway, far-off, remote, removed; unapproachable, unattainable, unavailable, unobtainable
antonyms inaccessible, inconvenient, unhandy, unreachable, untouchable

convention *n* **1** a coming together of a number of persons for a specified purpose ⟨attended a *convention* of mathematicians in California⟩ — see MEETING 1
2 a formal agreement between two or more nations or peoples ⟨an international *convention* banning the spread of nuclear weapons⟩ — see TREATY
3 an arrangement about action to be taken ⟨the Geneva *Convention* details proper treatment of prisoners of war⟩ — see AGREEMENT 2
4 an inherited or established way of thinking, feeling, or doing ⟨the bride decided to follow *convention* and to have her father give her away⟩ — see TRADITION 1

conventional *adj* **1** accepted, used, or practiced by most people ⟨*conventional* wisdom holds that an incumbent president has an overwhelming advantage over his opponent⟩ — see CURRENT 1
2 based on customs usually handed down from a previous generation ⟨tried to break from the *conventional* attitudes regarding the proper roles for men and women⟩ — see TRADITIONAL 1
3 following or agreeing with established form, custom, or rules ⟨*conventional* courtesy demands that the bridal couple send written thank-you notes for their gifts⟩ — see FORMAL 1

converge *vb* to come together into one body or place ⟨hungry students *converged* on the cafeteria almost as soon as the class bell rang⟩ — see ASSEMBLE 1

convergence *n* the coming together of two or more things to the same point ⟨the *convergence* of the city's major arteries on a single rotary⟩
synonyms confluence, conjunction, convergency, meeting
related words combination, combining, connecting, connection, consolidation, coupling, joining, junction, juncture, linking, merging, unification, union
antonyms divergence

convergency *n* the coming together of two or more things to the same point ⟨the *convergency* of several trade routes brought the city immense wealth during the Middle Ages⟩ — see CONVERGENCE

conversant *adj* having information especially as a result of study or experience ⟨a world traveler who is highly *conversant* with the customs of foreign cultures⟩ — see FAMILIAR 2

conversation *n* talking or a talk between two or more people ⟨Thomas Jefferson was celebrated for his brilliant, wide-ranging *conversations* with a host of friends and acquaintances⟩
synonyms chat, colloquy, converse, dialogue (*also* dialog), discourse, discussion, exchange
related words banter, chaff, cross fire, give-and-take, persiflage, raillery, repartee; conference, parley, powwow; babble, chatter, chin-wag [*slang*], chitchat, confabulation, gabfest, gossip, natter [*chiefly British*], palaver, prate, prattle, rap, small talk, table talk; round-

robin, roundtable, symposium; debate, deliberation
conversational *adj* **1** fond of talking or conversation ⟨the antiques dealer is not the *conversational* sort, so customers should not expect any impromptu chats⟩ — see TALKATIVE
2 having the style and content of everyday conversation ⟨struck a very *conversational* tone in his reports of his travels through foreign countries⟩ — see CHATTY 1
3 used in or suitable for speech and not formal writing ⟨uses *conversational* language instead of more stilted expressions in her campaign speeches⟩ — see COLLOQUIAL 1
conversationalist *n* a person who talks constantly ⟨she was known as a compulsive *conversationalist*, so much so that it was often impossible to stop her once she got going⟩ — see CHATTERBOX
converse *n* talking or a talk between two or more people ⟨ideally, the college classroom should be a place of intellectual *converse* between student and teacher⟩ — see CONVERSATION
converse *vb* to engage in casual or rambling conversation ⟨jurors are not allowed to *converse* while the attorneys go off to one side to confer with the judge⟩ — see CHAT 1
converse (with) *vb* to communicate with by means of spoken words ⟨in a press conference, the president is not just addressing reporters—he's *conversing with* the public⟩ — see TALK (TO)
conversely *adv* just the opposite being true ⟨she cannot stand sugary food; *conversely*, her husband is fond of sweets⟩ — see CONTRARIWISE
conversion *n* **1** a change in form, appearance, or use ⟨the *conversion* of the spare bedroom into a home office was easily accomplished⟩
synonyms changeover, metamorphosis, transfiguration, transformation
related words shift, transition; adjustment, alteration, modification; reconstruction, reconversion, redo, redoing, refashioning, reformation, remaking, remodeling, revamping, revision, reworking, variation; deformation, disfigurement, distortion, mutation, transmutation; displacement, replacement, substitution, supplantation
2 the act of reasoning or pleading with someone to accept a belief or course of action ⟨the *conversion* of the natives to Christianity proved to be much more difficult than anticipated⟩ — see PERSUASION 1
convert *n* **1** a person who has recently been persuaded to join a religious sect ⟨the *converts* were the most vocal and fervent worshippers in the church⟩
synonyms neophyte, proselyte
related words regenerate; newcomer, novice, novitiate, recruit; catechumen
2 one who follows the opinions or teachings of another ⟨the British biologist T. H. Huxley was one of the earliest *converts* to Darwin's theory of evolution⟩ — see FOLLOWER 1
convert *vb* **1** to persuade to change to one's religious faith ⟨young missionaries who go door-to-door trying to *convert* people⟩
synonyms proselyte, proselytize
related words missionize; brainwash, influence, sway; propagate
near antonyms secularize; dissuade
2 to change in form, appearance, or use ⟨the old factory was *converted* into an apartment building⟩
synonyms alchemize, make over, metamorphose, transfigure, transform, transmute, transpose, transubstantiate
related words adjust, alter, modify, recast; redefine, redesign, redo, reengineer, refashion, regenerate, remake, remodel, revamp, revise, rework, vary; deform, disfigure, distort, mutate, transmogrify; displace, replace, substitute, supplant
3 to cause (someone) to agree with a belief or course of action by using arguments or earnest request ⟨many who used to insist that global warming was a myth have since been *converted*⟩ — see PERSUADE
4 to take or make use of under a guise of authority but without actual right ⟨the bailee *converted* the goods to his own use⟩ — see APPROPRIATE 1
convexity *n* a part that sticks out from the general mass of something ⟨he had been gaining weight, as the *convexity* over his belt buckle clearly showed⟩ — see BULGE 1
convey *vb* **1** to cause (something) to pass from one to another ⟨intends to personally *convey* the message to the governor⟩ — see COMMUNICATE 1
2 to support and take from one place to another ⟨*conveying* a package to his relatives⟩ — see CARRY 1
3 to give over the legal possession or ownership of ⟨upon her death, the house will be *conveyed* to a predesignated charity⟩ — see TRANSFER 1
conveyance *n* something used to carry goods or passengers ⟨the covered wagon was the major *conveyance* that transported settlers and their belongings across the frontier⟩
synonyms transport, transportation, vehicle
related words carrier, hauler, mover; transit
convict *n* a person convicted as a criminal and serving a prison sentence ⟨a warning that the three escaped *convicts* were armed and dangerous⟩
synonyms con, jailbird
related words lifer, trusty; parolee, probationer; captive, capture, inmate, internee, prisoner
convict *vb* to find or pronounce guilty ⟨an accused person is presumed innocent until *convicted* in a court of law⟩
synonyms condemn
related words accuse, arraign, charge, impeach, indict; censure, damn, denounce, rebuke, reprimand, reproach, reprove; admonish, castigate, chastise; penalize, punish, sentence
near antonyms cite, commend, endorse (*also* indorse); approve, bless, sanction
antonyms absolve, acquit, clear, exculpate, exonerate, vindicate
conviction *n* **1** a state of mind in which one is free from doubt ⟨spoke with *conviction* about her political beliefs⟩ — see CONFIDENCE 2
2 an idea that is believed to be true or valid without positive knowledge ⟨held deep *convictions* about life after death⟩ — see OPINION 1
convince *vb* to cause (someone) to agree with a belief or course of action by using arguments or earnest requests ⟨we *convinced* him to keep silent about our activities until we could spring the surprise⟩ — see PERSUADE
convincing *adj* having the power to persuade ⟨*convincing* evidence for the guilt of the accused⟩ — see COGENT
convincing *n* the act of reasoning or pleading with someone to accept a belief or course of action ⟨it will take a great deal of *convincing* to make them see our point of view⟩ — see PERSUASION 1
convincingness *n* the capacity to persuade ⟨he spoke with such *convincingness* that we never dreamed he was lying⟩ — see COGENCY 1
convivial *adj* likely to seek or enjoy the company of others ⟨the hiking club attracts a wide range of *convivial* people who share a love of the outdoors⟩
synonyms boon, clubbable (*also* clubable), clubby, companionable, extroverted (*also* extraverted), gregarious, outgoing, sociable, social

related words cordial, folksy, forthcoming, friendly, hospitable; affable, genial, gracious; agreeable, amiable, congenial, kindly, neighborly; animated, gay, jaunty, jolly, jovial, lively, peppy, perky, pert, spirited, sprightful, sprightly, vivacious; communicative, expansive, garrulous, talkative; bright, buoyant, cheerful, chipper, effervescent, upbeat; bubbly, exuberant, high-spirited
near antonyms misanthropic; aloof, cold, cool, detached, distant, frosty, remote, reserved, standoffish; mum, mute, reticent, silent, taciturn
antonyms antisocial, insociable, introverted, nongregarious, reclusive, unsociable, unsocial

conviviality *n* **1** joyful or festive activity ⟨fondly remembers the many evenings spent in *conviviality* with her basketball teammates⟩ — see MERRYMAKING
2 the quality or state of being social ⟨his *conviviality*, warmth, and good nature are irresistible⟩ — see SOCIABILITY

convocation *n* **1** a body of people come together in one place ⟨the first speaker to address the *convocation*⟩ — see GATHERING 1
2 a coming together of a number of persons for a specified purpose ⟨called for a national *convocation* of both the clergy and the laity to discuss the crisis in the church⟩ — see MEETING 1

convoke *vb* to bring together in assembly by or as if by command ⟨*convoked* the leading experts on juvenile delinquency to study the situation⟩
synonyms assemble, call, convene, muster, summon
related words rally; call in, call out, call up, knell; amass, collect, gather, group, round up; reassemble, reconvene
near antonyms break up, dissolve

convoluted *adj* having many parts or aspects that are usually interrelated ⟨a *convoluted* explanation that left the listeners even more confused than they were before⟩ — see COMPLEX 1

convolution *n* something that makes a situation more complicated or difficult ⟨the inevitable *convolutions* involved in setting up an international teleconference⟩ — see COMPLICATION 1

convoy *vb* to go along with in order to provide assistance, protection, or companionship ⟨will *convoy* the shipment to its destination in the war zone⟩ — see ACCOMPANY 1

convulse *vb* to make a series of small irregular or violent movements ⟨*convulsing* with silent laughter as the inept pianist blithely played on⟩ — see SHAKE 1

convulsion *n* a violent disturbance (as of the political or social order) ⟨the Russian Revolution was one of the major *convulsions* of the 20th century⟩
synonyms bouleversement, cataclysm, earthquake, paroxysm, storm, tempest, tumult, upheaval, uproar
related words insurgency, insurrection, mutiny, overthrow, overturn, rebellion, revolt, revolution, subversion, unrest, uprising, upset; fit, seizure, spasm; eruption, flare-up, outbreak, outburst; bluster, bobbery, bustle, coil, commotion, furor, furore, fuss, hubbub, hullabaloo, hurly-burly, pandemonium, rout, row, ruckus, ruction, rumpus, shindy, squall, stew, stir, to-do, turmoil, welter, williwaw; quaking, rocking, shaking, trembling

convulsive *adj* **1** marked by sudden or violent disturbance ⟨the assassination of Martin Luther King was one of the most *convulsive* events of the 1960s⟩
synonyms cataclysmal (*or* cataclysmic), stormy, tempestuous, tumultuous, turbulent
related words fitful, spasmodic, sporadic; boisterous, clamorous, furious, noisy, riotous
near antonyms calm, peaceful, placid, serene, tranquil, undisturbed, unperturbed, unshaken, untroubled
2 marked by bursts of destructive force or intense activity ⟨after a day of *convulsive* trading, the stock market was down 300 points⟩ — see VIOLENT 1

co–occur *vb* to occur or exist at the same time ⟨the chronic depression that so often *co-occurs* with drug abuse⟩ — see COINCIDE 1

cook *n* a person who prepares food by some manner of heating ⟨the hearty meals prepared by the *cook* at summer camp⟩
synonyms chef, cooker, culinarian
related words baker, pâtissier (*or* patissier); barbecuer, griller

cook *vb* **1** to change so much as to create a wrong impression or alter the meaning of ⟨it turns out the pharmaceutical researcher had *cooked* her data⟩ — see GARBLE 1
2 to take place ⟨wondered what was *cooking* when several police cars pulled up to their neighbor's house⟩ — see HAPPEN

cook (up) *vb* to create or think of by clever use of the imagination ⟨*cooked up* a scheme to get out of doing the dishes⟩ — see INVENT

cooker *n* **1** an appliance that prepares food for consumption by heating it ⟨a portable gas-fired *cooker* that's perfect for camping trips⟩
synonyms cookstove, range
related words broiler, fryer (*also* frier), microwave, microwave oven, oven, roaster, rotisserie, stove, toaster, toaster oven
2 a person who prepares food by some manner of heating ⟨Dad was the traditional *cooker* of the big Sunday breakfast⟩ — see COOK

cookery *n* the art or style of preparing food (as in a specified region) ⟨tacos represented my introduction to Mexican *cookery*⟩
synonyms cooking, cuisine
related words haute cuisine; gastronomy

cookie *or* **cooky** *n* **1** a lovely woman ⟨every time I see him, he's got some new *cookie* on his arm⟩ — see BEAUTY 2
2 a member of the human race ⟨the new CEO is said to be one sharp *cookie*⟩ — see HUMAN

cooking *n* the art or style of preparing food (as in a specified region) ⟨a TV show that teaches viewers the basics of French *cooking*⟩ — see COOKERY

cookstove *n* an appliance that prepares food for consumption by heating it ⟨a small *cookstove* that would be appropriate for an apartment⟩ — see COOKER 1

cool *adj* **1** having or showing a lack of friendliness or interest in others ⟨the locals were *cool* towards outsiders⟩ ⟨the schoolmaster's *cool* manner did not encourage chitchat⟩
synonyms aloof, antisocial, asocial, buttoned-up, cold, cold-eyed, detached, distant, dry, frosty, offish, remote, standoff, standoffish, unbending, unclubbable, unsociable
related words indrawn, introverted, nongregarious, recessive, reclusive, reserved, unsocial, withdrawn; misanthropic; apathetic, hard, indifferent, unconcerned; clinical, dispassionate, impersonal, professional; disinterested, incurious, uninterested; reticent, silent, taciturn, uncommunicative; diffident, shy, timid; cliquey, cliquish, clubbish
near antonyms boon, clubbable (*also* clubable), clubby, companionable, convivial, extroverted (*also* extraverted), gregarious, outgoing; communicative, expansive, garrulous, talkative; affable, folksy, genial, gracious, hospitable; agreeable, amiable, congenial, kindly, neighborly
antonyms cordial, friendly, sociable, social, warm
2 free from emotional or mental agitation ⟨in a crisis keep a *cool* head, even if no one else is⟩ — see CALM 2
3 having a low or subnormal temperature ⟨a *cool* base-

ment that would be perfect for storing wine⟩ — see COLD 1

4 lacking in friendliness or warmth of feeling ⟨directed a *cool* glance at the student who was sneaking into class late⟩ — see COLD 2

5 *slang* being in the latest or current fashion ⟨the outfit you're wearing is so not *cool* on this campus⟩ — see STYLISH

6 *slang* keenly aware of and responsive to the latest developments especially in fashion and entertainment ⟨a Greek island that's the current favorite of the *cool* crowd⟩ — see AU COURANT 1

7 *slang* of the very best kind ⟨a really *cool* garage band that's starting to get some attention from the music industry⟩ — see EXCELLENT

cool *n* **1** the absence of emotional involvement ⟨the judge's customary *cool* stood him in good stead during the sensational trial⟩

synonyms coldness, detachment, dispassion, dispassionateness

related words equitability, equitableness, fairness; disinterest, disinterestedness, impartiality, nonpartisanship, objectivity, unbiasedness; balance, rationality, rationalness, reasonability, reasonableness; calm, calmness, peace, peacefulness, placidity, quiet, quietness, quietude, repose, restfulness, sereneness, serenity, tranquillity (*or* tranquility), tranquilness; reserve, undemonstrativeness, unresponsiveness; apathy, indifference

near antonyms emotionalism; bias, favor, one-sidedness, partiality, partisanship, prejudice

2 the quality or state of being fashionable ⟨I envy you your *cool*⟩

synonyms coolness, fashionableness, hip, hipness, hipsterism, modishness, stylishness, trendiness, voguishness

related words chic, chicness, dapperness, elegance, poshness, smartness, style, swank, swankiness; class, grace, gracefulness, majesty, stateliness; artfulness, polish, sophistication, taste, tastefulness

near antonyms flashiness, garishness, gaudiness, gracelessness, grotesqueness, tackiness, tastelessness, tawdriness

antonyms unfashionableness

3 evenness of emotions or temper ⟨despite the flood of insults, the fledgling stand-up comic never lost his *cool*⟩ — see EQUANIMITY

cool *vb* **1** to cause to lose heat ⟨*cool* your drinks in the icy mountain stream⟩

synonyms chill, refrigerate

related words air-condition; freeze, frost, ice, quick-freeze, supercool; ventilate

near antonyms bake, boil, broil, steam; heat-treat, temper; microwave

antonyms heat, toast, warm

2 to become still and orderly ⟨after the recess, tempers had *cooled*, and we could have a civil, rational discussion⟩ — see QUIET 1

cooler *n* a place of confinement for persons held in lawful custody ⟨plea-bargained to avoid spending time in the *cooler*⟩ — see JAIL

coolheaded *adj* free from emotional or mental agitation ⟨a *coolheaded* response to the crisis⟩ — see CALM 2

coolish *adj* having a low or subnormal temperature ⟨made the mistake of wearing shorts on a *coolish* day⟩ — see COLD 1

coolness *n* **1** evenness of emotions or temper ⟨his *coolness* under pressure makes him everyone's first choice to head a project with an ironclad deadline⟩ — see EQUANIMITY

2 the quality or state of being fashionable ⟨the *coolness* of their clothes is something that high schoolers tend to obsess over⟩ — see COOL 2

coon's age *n* a long or seemingly long period of time ⟨I haven't seen you in a *coon's age*!⟩ — see AGE 2

coop *n* **1** a place of confinement for persons held in lawful custody ⟨like many of the city's hookers, she was back in the *coop* within a week of her release⟩ — see JAIL

2 an enclosure with an open framework for keeping animals ⟨a chicken *coop*⟩ — see CAGE

coop (up) *vb* to close or shut in by or as if by barriers ⟨restless kids *cooped up* in the house on a rainy day⟩ — see ENCLOSE 1

cooperate *vb* **1** to participate or assist in a joint effort to accomplish an end ⟨conservation groups *cooperated* with state authorities to find a humane way to manage the area's overpopulation of deer⟩

synonyms band (together), collaborate, concert, concur, conjoin, conspire, join, league, team (up), unite

related words connive; affiliate, ally, associate, combine, confederate, hang together, interface

phrases make common cause, play ball, pull together

2 to form or enter into an association that furthers the interests of its members ⟨several industrialized nations *cooperated* in a trade agreement to reduce or eliminate tariffs⟩ — see ALLY

cooperation *n* **1** the state of having shared interests or efforts (as in social or business matters) ⟨a series of televised announcements made in *cooperation* with the tobacco companies warning teenagers about the hazards of smoking⟩ — see ASSOCIATION 1

2 the work and activity of a number of persons who individually contribute toward the efficiency of the whole ⟨everyone's *cooperation* will make the project go much faster⟩ — see TEAMWORK

cooperative *adj* used or done by a number of people as a group ⟨a *cooperative* space project undertaken by Russia and the U.S.⟩ — see COLLECTIVE

co–opt *vb* to make a part of a body or system ⟨younger immigrants are inevitably *co-opted* by the culture of their adopted country, even as their elders struggle against the cultural assimilation⟩ — see EMBODY 1

coordinate *n* one that is equal to another in status, achievement, or value ⟨the Nobel Memorial Award for Economic Science is universally regarded as the *coordinate* of the original Nobel Prizes for peace, literature, medicine, physics, and chemistry⟩ — see EQUAL

coordinate *vb* **1** to bring to a state free of conflicts, inconsistencies, or differences ⟨*coordinating* the plans for the surprise party⟩ — see HARMONIZE 2

2 to form a pleasing relationship ⟨a very meticulous hostess, who makes sure that every aspect of her dinner parties—table settings, food, flowers—*coordinate* right down to the last detail⟩ — see HARMONIZE 1

coordinateness *n* the state or fact of being exactly the same in number, amount, status, or quality ⟨legislation that would enhance the power of the presidency and threaten the supposed *coordinateness* of the three branches of the federal government⟩ — see EQUIVALENCE

coordination *n* the work and activity of a number of persons who individually contribute toward the efficiency of the whole ⟨an operation requiring precise *coordination* among all branches of the armed forces⟩ — see TEAMWORK

cop *n* a member of a force charged with law enforcement at the local level ⟨a *cop* stopped her for speeding⟩ — see OFFICER 1

cop *vb, slang* **1** to get possession of (something) by giving money in exchange for ⟨I *copped* a great outfit for only $50⟩ — see BUY 1

2 to take physical control or possession of (something)

suddenly or forcibly ⟨some concertgoers rush pell-mell through the doors so that they could *cop* the seats down front⟩ — see CATCH 1

cop (to) *vb, slang* to make an acknowledgment of something unpleasant as true or valid ⟨that thug will make a deal with the prosecutor and end up *copping to* a charge of simple assault⟩ — see CONFESS 1

copacetic *also* **copasetic** *or* **copesetic** *adj* being to one's liking ⟨don't worry, because I assure you that everything's *copacetic*⟩ — see SATISFACTORY 1

cope *n* something that covers or conceals like a piece of cloth ⟨committed their nefarious deeds under the dark *cope* of night⟩ — see CLOAK 1

cope *vb* to meet one's day-to-day needs ⟨a young man learning to *cope* on his own at college⟩ — see GET ALONG 1

cope (with) *vb* to deal with (something) usually skillfully or efficiently ⟨*coped with* the latest foul-up gracefully⟩ — see HANDLE 1

copious *adj* pouring forth in great amounts ⟨a *copious* rush of words just poured out of the two friends who hadn't seen each other in years⟩ — see PROFUSE

cop–out *n* the act or a means of getting or keeping away from something undesirable ⟨I think that saying you're sick is just a *cop-out* to get out of going to work⟩ — see ESCAPE 2

cop out *vb* to break a promise or agreement ⟨don't *cop out* on your promise to pay for the damage⟩ — see RENEGE 1

copper *n* a member of a force charged with law enforcement at the local level ⟨a crime novel set in the days when policemen were *coppers* and safecrackers were "yeggs"⟩ — see OFFICER 1

coppice *n* a thick patch of shrubbery, small trees, or underbrush ⟨the deer bounded off into the *coppice*⟩ — see THICKET

copse *n* a thick patch of shrubbery, small trees, or underbrush ⟨a small *copse* of trees shaded the back of the house⟩ — see THICKET

copter *n* a vehicle for traveling through the air that obtains its lift from rotors which spin horizontally ⟨*copters* from the local TV stations made the obligatory reports on the bumper-to-bumper traffic at the start of the holiday weekend⟩ — see HELICOPTER

copulate *vb* to engage in sexual intercourse ⟨the time of year when deer in the wild are likely to *copulate*⟩
synonyms breed, mate, sleep
related words fool around, fornicate
phrases do it, have sex

copulating *n* sexual union involving penetration of the vagina by the penis ⟨our Puritan forebears imposed severe penalties for *copulating* outside of marriage⟩ — see SEXUAL INTERCOURSE

copulation *n* sexual union involving penetration of the vagina by the penis ⟨laws against *copulation* between an adult and one who has not reached the legal age of consent⟩ — see SEXUAL INTERCOURSE

copy *n* something that is made to look exactly like something else ⟨a *copy* of the famous painting "Washington Crossing the Delaware"⟩
synonyms carbon, carbon copy, clone, dummy, dupe, duplicate, duplication, facsimile, imitation, mock, reduplication, replica, replication, reproduction
related words counterfeit, fake, forgery, knockoff, phony (*also* phoney), rip-off, rubber stamp, sham; miniature, mock-up, simulation; reconstruction, re-creation; image, likeness, semblance, shadow; impression, imprint, print; approximation, reincarnation, version; extra, reserve, spare
antonyms archetype, original, prototype

copy *vb* **1** to make an exact likeness of ⟨for the movie, set designers *copied* the Oval Office in the White House down to the smallest detail⟩
synonyms clone, copycat, duplicate, imitate, reduplicate, render, replicate, reproduce
related words counterfeit, fake, forge, knock off, rip off; mimic, simulate; reconstruct, re-create
near antonyms create, imagine, initiate, invent
antonyms originate
2 to use (someone or something) as the model for one's speech, mannerisms, or behavior ⟨she shamelessly *copies* her idol's hairstyle and fashion choices⟩ — see IMITATE 1

copycat *n* a person who adopts the appearance or behavior of another especially in an obvious way ⟨every rock singer who makes it big soon has a whole cluster of *copycats*⟩
synonyms aper, copyist, echo, follower, imitator, rubber stamp, wannabe (*also* wannabee)
related words parrot; ape, emulator, impersonator, impressionist, mimic

copycat *vb* **1** to make an exact likeness of ⟨asked her stylist to *copycat* a hairstyle from the magazine⟩ — see COPY 1
2 to use (someone or something) as the model for one's speech, mannerisms, or behavior ⟨a performer who slavishly *copycats* another never rises to the level of true stardom⟩ — see IMITATE 1

copyist *n* **1** a person who adopts the appearance or behavior of another especially in an obvious way ⟨she prides herself on being an innovator in fashion, and not a mere *copyist*⟩ — see COPYCAT
2 one who writes from dictation or copies manuscripts ⟨some scholars argue that the vexing passage reflects a misreading of the text by an early *copyist*⟩ — see SCRIBE 1

coquet *or* **coquette** *vb* to show a sexual attraction for someone just for fun ⟨at the country club she would often brazenly *coquet* with the husbands of the women to whom she was giving golf lessons⟩ — see FLIRT 1

coquetry *n* the attitude or behavior of one who insincerely courts the amorous attentions of others ⟨her compulsive *coquetry* at parties was embarrassing for her husband⟩
synonyms coquettishness, coyness, flirtation, flirtatiousness, kittenishness
related words dalliance, play

coquettish *adj* affecting shyness or modesty in order to attract masculine interest ⟨an 18th-century painting of a *coquettish* maiden dallying with a young moonstruck gallant⟩ — see COY 1

coquettishness *n* the attitude or behavior of one who insincerely courts the amorous attentions of others ⟨such displays of girlish *coquettishness* are really out of place in a business office⟩ — see COQUETRY

cord *n* **1** a length of braided, flexible material that is used for tying or connecting things ⟨a vacuum cleaner with an extra long *cord*⟩
synonyms cable, lace, lacing, line, rope, string, wire
related words guy, halyard, lanyard, stay; bungee cord, whipcord
2 a uniting or binding force or influence ⟨the *cords* of trust and affection that exist between the longtime friends⟩ — see BOND 2

cordial *adj* **1** having or showing kindly feeling and sincere interest ⟨a *cordial* inquiry about her mother's health⟩ — see FRIENDLY 1
2 showing a natural kindness and courtesy especially in social situations ⟨a *cordial* hostess who makes sure everyone is comfortable⟩ — see GRACIOUS 1
3 having a renewing effect on the state of the body or mind ⟨he insisted that a *cordial* nip of brandy would be

just the thing for someone suffering from shock⟩ — see TONIC 1

cordiality *n* kindly concern, interest, or support ⟨everyone appreciated the *cordiality* and thoughtfulness of the welcoming committee⟩ — see GOODWILL 1

cordialness *n* kindly concern, interest, or support ⟨an affluent suburb that has never been known for its *cordialness* toward the downtrodden⟩ — see GOODWILL 1

core *n* **1** the seat of one's deepest thoughts and emotions ⟨in my very *core* I knew that an injustice was being committed⟩
synonyms belly, blood, bone(s), bosom, breast, gut, heart, heartstrings, inner space, inside, quick, soul
related words conscience, mind
2 a thing or place that is of greatest importance to an activity or interest ⟨the capitol building is the *core* of the political life of the state⟩ — see CENTER 1
3 the central part or aspect of something under consideration ⟨at last, we come to the *core* of the issue that has been dividing us⟩ — see CRUX
4 the main or greater part of something as distinguished from its subordinate parts ⟨a starfish can even survive the division of its *core* into two parts; both halves then regenerate⟩ — see BODY 1
5 an area or point that is an equal distance from all points along an edge or outer surface ⟨the mountain rises from ground that is almost precisely at the island's *core*⟩ — see CENTER 2

corker *n* something very good of its kind ⟨that last race was a real *corker*!⟩ — see JIM-DANDY

corking *adj* of the very best kind ⟨they've done a really *corking* job on restoring that old house⟩ — see EXCELLENT

corking *adv* to a great degree ⟨the novel is a *corking* good read⟩ — see VERY 1

corkscrew *adj* turning around an axis like the thread of a screw ⟨an angelic child with beautiful *corkscrew* curls⟩ — see SPIRAL

corkscrew *vb* **1** to draw out by force or with effort ⟨practically every word had to be *corkscrewed* out of the tight-lipped witness⟩ — see EXTRACT
2 to follow a circular or spiral course ⟨the trail *corkscrews* through dense woods to the top of the steep hill⟩ — see WIND 1

cormorant *n* one who eats greedily or too much ⟨Diamond Jim Brady was perhaps the most celebrated *cormorant* of the Gilded Age⟩ — see GLUTTON

corn *n* something (as a work of literature or music) that is too sentimental ⟨a story about a lost puppy that was pure *corn*⟩
synonyms goo, mush, schmaltz (*also* schmalz), sludge, slush, soap opera, sorghum
related words claptrap, drivel, rubbish, tripe

cornball *adj* tiresomely obvious and unsophisticated ⟨the show's shamelessly *cornball* jokes appealed to small-town America⟩ — see CORNY 2

cornball *n* an awkward or simple person especially from a small town or the country ⟨a movie about a *cornball* making his way through a world of cynical sophisticates⟩ — see HICK

corner *n* **1** a difficult, puzzling, or embarrassing situation from which there is no easy escape ⟨the writers have gotten themselves into a *corner* on that TV show⟩ — see PREDICAMENT
2 a place where roads meet ⟨we'll meet at the *corner* tomorrow⟩ — see CROSSROAD 1
3 a point in a chain of events at which an important change (as in one's fortunes) occurs ⟨the president believes that we have turned a *corner* in the war on drugs⟩ — see TURNING POINT

cornerstone *n* an immaterial thing upon which something else rests ⟨a concern for basic human rights was the *cornerstone* of the president's foreign policy⟩ — see BASE 1

cornerways *adv* in a line or direction running from corner to corner ⟨buttered toast cut *cornerways*⟩ — see CROSSWISE

cornerwise *adv* in a line or direction running from corner to corner ⟨fold the napkin *cornerwise* and then fold it again⟩ — see CROSSWISE

cornet *n* something shaped like a hollow cone and used as a container ⟨*cornets* of pastry dough that were baked and later filled with cream⟩
synonyms cornucopia, horn
related words funnel, tube

corn–fed *adj* tiresomely obvious and unsophisticated ⟨the musical's *corn-fed* humor harkens back to a more innocent, unjaded era⟩ — see CORNY 2

cornpone *adj* tiresomely obvious and unsophisticated ⟨the comedian's *cornpone* wisecracks were old even in the days of vaudeville⟩ — see CORNY 2

cornucopia *n* **1** an abundant source ⟨even to the computer-addicted children, the old-fashioned toy chest was a *cornucopia* of delights⟩ — see MINE 1
2 an amount or supply more than sufficient to meet one's needs ⟨the rabbits found a *cornucopia* of food in the vegetable garden⟩ — see PLENTY 1
3 something shaped like a hollow cone and used as a container ⟨a *cornucopia* filled with fruits and vegetables in celebration of the harvest⟩ — see CORNET

cornucopian *adj* **1** being more than enough without being excessive ⟨there were *cornucopian* profits for the last three quarters⟩ — see PLENTIFUL
2 producing abundantly ⟨one of the most *cornucopian* sources of all of literature, the legend of King Arthur has inspired everything from epic poems to musical dramas⟩ — see FERTILE

corny *adj* **1** appealing to the emotions in an obvious and tiresome way ⟨*corny* violin music during the movie's love scenes⟩
synonyms chocolate-box, cloying, drippy, fruity, gooey, lovey-dovey, maudlin, mawkish, mushy, novelettish, saccharine, sappy, schmaltzy, sentimental, sloppy, slushy, soppy, soupy, spoony (*or* spooney), sticky, sugarcoated, sugary, wet
related words dreamy, misty-eyed, moonstruck, moony, nostalgic, starry-eyed; feel-good, fuzzy; melodramatic, soap-operatic, soapy, sudsy; flat, insipid, soft-boiled, tasteless, vapid, watery; cutesy, twee [*chiefly British*]
near antonyms unadulterated, unvarnished; antisentimental, cynical, hard-boiled, hard-edged, hardheaded
antonyms unsentimental
2 tiresomely obvious and unsophisticated ⟨the audience groaned as the emcee told one *corny* joke after another⟩
synonyms cornball, corn-fed, cornpone, hokey
related words countrified (*also* countryfied), down-home, folksy, rustic (*also* rustical); hick, hickish
near antonyms cosmopolitan, smart, sophisticated, worldly, worldly-wise; hip, trendy, with-it

corollary *n* **1** a condition or occurrence traceable to a cause ⟨one *corollary* of the rise of television was a massive makeover of radio's programming⟩ — see EFFECT 1
2 something that is found along with something else ⟨increased taxes—or expanding deficits—are the inevitable *corollary* to any new government spending program⟩ — see ACCOMPANIMENT

coronal *also* **coronel** *n* a decorative band or wreath worn about the head as a symbol of victory or honor ⟨a Renaissance portrait of a nobel woman of Florence wearing a bejeweled *coronal*⟩ — see CROWN 1

coronet *n* a decorative band or wreath worn about the

head as a symbol of victory or honor ⟨the prince wore a small gold *coronet* to denote his rank⟩ — see CROWN 1

corporal *adj* of or relating to the human body ⟨started to suffer the *corporal* ailments that come with advancing age⟩ — see PHYSICAL 1

corporality *n* the fact of being or of being real ⟨the age-old debate about the *corporality* of the human soul⟩ — see EXISTENCE

corporate *adj* fit or likely to be sold especially on a large scale ⟨chain hotels, even high-end ones, tend to all have the same *corporate* decor that doesn't evoke a sense of place⟩ — see COMMERCIAL

corporation *n* an enlarged or bulging abdomen ⟨a substantial *corporation* that showed that he was a sucker for all-you-can-eat buffets⟩ — see POTBELLY

corporeal *adj* of or relating to the human body ⟨*corporeal* cravings such as hunger and thirst⟩ — see PHYSICAL 1

corporeality *n* the fact of being or of being real ⟨a philosophical discussion about the *corporeality* of the intellect, as distinct from the brain⟩ — see EXISTENCE

corps *n* the body of people in a profession or field of activity ⟨a reporter who is widely respected throughout the press *corps*⟩
synonyms brotherhood, community, fellowship, fraternity, sodality, vocation
related words calling, profession; association, club, federation, guild (*also* gild), organization, society

corps d'elite *n* individuals carefully selected as being the best of a class ⟨the atomic bomb developers for the Manhattan Project constituted the *corps d'elite* of American science⟩ — see ELITE 1

corpse *n* a dead body ⟨the startling discovery of a *corpse* required a call to the police⟩
synonyms bones, cadaver, carcass, corpus, corse [*archaic*], relics, remains, stiff
related words mummy; carnage, carrion; ashes; deceased, decedent

corpulence *n* the condition of having an excess of body fat ⟨the doctor warned that the patient's *corpulence* was unhealthy and not merely unattractive⟩
synonyms adiposity, chubbiness, corpulency, embonpoint, fat, fatness, fattiness, fleshiness, grossness, obesity, plumpness, portliness, pudginess, pursiness, rotundity, weight
related words bulkiness, heaviness; huskiness, stoutness; brawniness, burliness; endomorphy
near antonyms fitness, trimness; gauntness, scrawniness, skinniness, weediness
antonyms leanness, reediness, slenderness, slimness, svelteness, thinness

corpulency *n* the condition of having an excess of body fat ⟨her *corpulency* is such that she requires two seats on public conveyances⟩ — see CORPULENCE

corpulent *adj* having an excess of body fat ⟨a *corpulent*, elegantly dressed opera singer came out and sang, and we knew it was over⟩ — see FAT 1

corpus *n* **1** the complete works of an author ⟨Jane Austen's *corpus* is modest in number but magnificent in achievement⟩
synonyms oeuvre
related words output; canon
2 a dead body ⟨international conventions requiring that the *corpus* of the enemy combatant be treated with respect and dignity⟩ — see CORPSE

corrade *vb* to damage or diminish by continued friction ⟨the desert's windblown sands had *corraded* much of the ancient stone's inscription⟩ — see ABRADE 1

corral *n* an enclosure with an open framework for keeping animals ⟨the horses live in our *corral*, along with a cow⟩ — see CAGE

corral *vb* **1** to close or shut in by or as if by barriers ⟨*corralled* everyone in the conference room for a speech by the CEO⟩ — see ENCLOSE 1
2 to take physical control or possession of (something) suddenly or forcibly ⟨*corralled* a scattering of stray pens and quickly stuffed them in the drawer to tidy the desk⟩ — see CATCH
3 to bring together in one body or place ⟨*corral* all the members of the tour group in the lounge⟩ — see GATHER 1

correct *adj* **1** being in agreement with the truth or a fact or a standard ⟨a real brainteaser with only one *correct* solution to it⟩
synonyms accurate, bang on [*chiefly British*], dead-on, exact, good, on-target, precise, proper, right, so, spot-on, true, veracious
related words legitimate, logical, sound, valid; errorless, faultless, flawless, impeccable, inerrant, infallible, letter-perfect, perfect; rigorous, strict, stringent
phrases on target, on the money
near antonyms defective, faulty, flawed, imperfect
antonyms false, improper, inaccurate, incorrect, inexact, off, untrue, wrong
2 following the established traditions of refined society and good taste ⟨painfully *correct* dress for the state dinner at the White House⟩ — see PROPER 1
3 marked by or showing careful attention to set forms and details ⟨the *correct* method for folding the American flag⟩ — see CEREMONIOUS 1

correct *vb* **1** to remove errors, defects, deficiencies, or deviations from ⟨more time will be needed to *correct* the computer program⟩
synonyms amend, debug, emend, rectify, red-pencil, reform, remedy
related words redraft, redraw, restyle, revise, rework, rewrite; blue-pencil, cut, shorten; redress, right; ameliorate, better, improve; perfect, polish, touch up; fix, mend, repair; adjust, modulate, regulate; alter, change, modify
near antonyms damage, harm, hurt, impair, injure, mar, spoil; aggravate, worsen
2 to balance with an equal force so as to make ineffective ⟨hopefully the young entrepreneur's professionalism will serve to *correct* his partner's extreme enthusiasm in the eyes of investors⟩ — see OFFSET
3 to inflict a penalty on for a fault or crime ⟨an insensitive boss who liked to *correct* subordinates in front of their colleagues⟩ — see PUNISH

correctable *adj* capable of being corrected ⟨a racehorse with some minor, *correctable* faults⟩ — see REMEDIABLE

correcting *adj* inflicting, involving, or serving as punishment ⟨questions the value of such *correcting* measures as prison sentences for drug addicts⟩ — see PUNITIVE

correction *n* **1** a change designed to correct or improve a written work ⟨the copy editor's *corrections* were marked in red⟩
synonyms amendment, emendation
related words cut, deletion; addition, amplification, supplement; adjustment, alteration, modification, revision; improvement, renovation; clarification, explanation, explication
2 suffering, loss, or hardship imposed in response to a crime or offense ⟨received a severe *correction* after the third offense⟩ — see PUNISHMENT

correctional *adj* inflicting, involving, or serving as punishment ⟨threatened to take *correctional* measures if the household chores were not done⟩ ⟨the state's largest *correctional* institution⟩ — see PUNITIVE

corrective *adj* **1** serving to raise or adjust something to some standard or proper condition ⟨eyeglasses are

called *corrective* lenses by the department of motor vehicles⟩
synonyms amendatory, rectifying, remedial, remedying, reformative, reformatory
related words curative, medicinal, therapeutic; reparative, restorative; beneficial, helpful, salutary, wholesome; antidotal, counteractive, counterbalancing
2 inflicting, involving, or serving as punishment ⟨a *corrective* sentence of five years' hard labor⟩ — see PUNITIVE

corrective *n* **1** a force or influence that makes an opposing force ineffective or less effective ⟨a substantial outflow of people proved to be the necessary *corrective* for the spiraling cost of housing⟩ — see COUNTERBALANCE
2 something that corrects or counteracts something undesirable ⟨the only *corrective* to bad behavior is good, firm discipline⟩ — see CURE 1

correctly *adv* in a manner suitable for the occasion or purpose ⟨dressed *correctly* for an appearance in court⟩ — see PROPERLY

correlate *n* something that serves to complete or make up for a deficiency in something else ⟨the often uneasy relationship between the employer and his *correlate*, the employee⟩ — see COMPLEMENT 1

correlate *vb* to think of (something) in combination ⟨a demanding father who always *correlated* success with hard work⟩ — see ASSOCIATE 2

correlative *adj* related to each other in such a way that one completes the other ⟨the *correlative* contributions that both teacher and student make to the learning process⟩ — see COMPLEMENTARY

correspond *vb* **1** to engage in an exchange of written messages ⟨old friends who have been *corresponding* for years⟩
synonyms write
related words communicate, intercommunicate; airmail, e-mail, telegraph; mail, post; answer, reply
2 to be in agreement on every point ⟨the menu for the wedding banquet *corresponds* exactly with everyone's special requests⟩ — see CHECK 1

correspond (to) *vb* **1** to be the exact counterpart of ⟨the British chancellor of the exchequer *corresponds to* the U.S. secretary of the treasury⟩ — see MATCH 1
2 to be the same in meaning or effect ⟨"shut up" and "please be quiet" may *correspond to* each other in meaning, but please use the more polite phrase⟩ — see AMOUNT (TO) 2

correspondence *n* **1** a point which two or more things share in common ⟨the *correspondence* in hair color is about all that the siblings have in common⟩ — see SIMILARITY 2
2 the quality or state of having many qualities in common ⟨the best friends' *correspondence* in looks is so striking that they could pass for twins⟩ — see SIMILARITY 1
3 communications or parcels sent or carried through the postal system ⟨piles of unanswered *correspondence* littered the office of the reclusive author⟩ — see MAIL

correspondent *adj* having qualities in common ⟨reading and writing are actually *correspondent* activities⟩ — see ALIKE

correspondent *n* a person employed by a newspaper, magazine, or radio or television station to gather, write, or report news ⟨a *correspondent* in the Middle East bureau just filed a new report on the coup⟩ — see REPORTER

correspondent (with *or* **to)** *adj* not having or showing any apparent conflict ⟨the new regulation regarding cell phones is *correspondent with* existing policy on the use of electronic devices⟩ — see CONSISTENT

corresponding *adj* having qualities in common ⟨solving a crime and diagnosing a disease are *corresponding* tasks: they both require a meticulous search for clues⟩ — see ALIKE

correspondingly *adv* in like manner ⟨if you're nice to someone, they'll probably be *correspondingly* polite⟩ — see ALSO 1

corridor *n* **1** a broad geographical area ⟨the urban *corridor* along the state's eastern coast is considerably more liberal than the rural areas to the west⟩ — see REGION 2
2 a typically long narrow way connecting parts of a building ⟨the long, sterile *corridors* give the government building a forbidding air⟩ — see HALL 2

corrigible *adj* capable of being corrected ⟨there are *corrigible* lapses in the author's grammar, but nothing that a good editor cannot readily fix⟩ — see REMEDIABLE

corrival *n* one who strives for the same thing as another ⟨two universities that are long-standing *corrivals* for the title of best in the nation⟩ — see COMPETITOR

corroborate *vb* **1** to give evidence or testimony to the truth or factualness of ⟨the witnesses *corroborated* the policeman's testimony⟩ — see CONFIRM 1
2 to provide evidence or information for (as a claim or idea) ⟨my personal experience does not *corroborate* your faith in the essential goodness of people⟩ — see SUPPORT 4

corroborating *adj* serving to give support to the truth or factualness of something ⟨*corroborating* information on the activities of the terrorists⟩ — see CORROBORATIVE

corroboration *n* something presented in support of the truth or accuracy of a claim ⟨that's a serious charge, so you certainly should have *corroboration* for it⟩ — see PROOF

corroborative *adj* serving to give support to the truth or factualness of something ⟨the results of the DNA fingerprinting was all the *corroborative* evidence the jury needed to convict⟩
synonyms confirmational, confirmatory, confirming, corroborating, corroboratory, probative, probatory, substantiating, supporting, supportive, verifying, vindicating
related words auxiliary, supplementary; beneficial, helpful
near antonyms contradictory, contrary, counter, opposing
antonyms confuting, disproving, refuting

corroboratory *adj* serving to give support to the truth or factualness of something ⟨offered *corroboratory* testimony for the defendant's alibi⟩ — see CORROBORATIVE

corroboree *n, Australian* a state of noisy, confused activity ⟨quite a *corroboree* when Britain's royal couple paid a visit to Sydney⟩ — see COMMOTION

corrode *vb* to consume or wear away gradually ⟨water slowly *corrodes* iron⟩ — see EAT 2

corrosion *n* a gradual weakening, loss, or destruction ⟨the *corrosion* of family values that is often brought on by great wealth⟩
synonyms attrition, erosion, undermining, waste
related words breakdown, decay, decomposition, disintegration, dissolution
near antonyms gain, increase
antonyms buildup

corrosive *adj* marked by the use of wit that is intended to cause hurt feelings ⟨a *corrosive* satire on the fashion industry and its movers and shakers⟩ — see SARCASTIC

corrosiveness *n* biting sharpness of feeling or expression ⟨the unconscionable *corrosiveness* with which he voiced his criticisms diminished their value and effectiveness⟩ — see ACRIMONY 1

corrupt *adj* having or showing lowered moral character

or standards ⟨*corrupt* businessmen who are out to fleece the public⟩ ⟨*corrupt* business practices that should be investigated⟩
synonyms debased, debauched, decadent, degenerate, degraded, demoralized, depraved, dissipated, dissolute, jackleg, libertine, loose, perverse, perverted, rakehell (*or* rakehelly), rakish, reprobate, sick, unclean, unwholesome, warped
related words bent [*chiefly British*], crooked, cutthroat, dishonest, unethical, unprincipled, unscrupulous; contaminated, spoiled, tainted; bad, evil, immoral, iniquitous, miscreant, nefarious, sinful, vicious, wicked
near antonyms incorruptible; ethical, honest, principled; good, moral, righteous, virtuous
antonyms pure, uncorrupt, uncorrupted

corrupt *vb* **1** to go through decomposition ⟨a dead mouse *corrupting* in the walls produced a terrible smell⟩ — see DECAY 1
2 to lower in character, dignity, or quality ⟨some observers believe that grossly violent movies *corrupt* the people who watch them as well as the people who make them⟩ — see DEBASE 1
3 to influence someone with a bribe ⟨he bragged about having *corrupted* half of the officials on the city council⟩ — see BRIBE

corrupted *adj* having undergone organic breakdown ⟨*corrupted* corpses that sickened the animal control officers sent to investigate⟩ — see ROTTEN 1

corruptible *adj* open to improper influence and especially bribery ⟨there's a rumor that that judge is eminently *corruptible*⟩ — see VENAL

corruption *n* **1** the process by which dead organic matter separates into simpler substances ⟨the ancient Egyptians used special preservatives to spare their dead from complete *corruption*⟩
synonyms breakdown, decay, decomposition, festering, putrefaction, putrescence, rot, spoilage
related words crumbling, disintegration, dissolution; curdling, fermentation, moldering, souring
near antonyms growth, maturation, ripening
2 a sinking to a state of low moral standards and behavior ⟨the *corruption* of the upper classes eventually led to the fall of the Roman empire⟩
synonyms abjection, corruptness, debasement, debauchery, decadence, decadency, degeneracy, degenerateness, degeneration, degradation, demoralization, depravity, dissipatedness, dissipation, dissoluteness, libertinage, libertinism, perversion, pervertedness, rakishness, turpitude
related words evil, immorality, sinfulness, villainy, wickedness; filth, gangrene, rot, squalor
near antonyms goodness, morality, righteousness, virtue
3 immoral conduct or practices harmful or offensive to society ⟨Socrates was put to death because the ancient Athenians believed he was spreading *corruption* to their youth⟩ — see VICE 1

corruptness *n* a sinking to a state of low moral standards and behavior ⟨such *corruptness* in government threatens our democratic institutions⟩ — see CORRUPTION 2

corsair *n* someone who engages in robbery of ships at sea ⟨no one knows the fate of the *corsair's* treasure-filled ship⟩ — see PIRATE

corse *n, archaic* a dead body ⟨would have to inter the *corse* of many a fallen comrade before the war's end⟩ — see CORPSE

cortege *also* **cortège** *n* **1** a body of employees or servants who accompany and wait on a person ⟨the movie star's *cortege* included her hair stylist, makeup artist, personal assistant, and press agent⟩
synonyms entourage, following, posse, retinue, suite, tail, train
related words crew, personnel, staff; court; assistant, attendant, helper, retainer
2 a body of individuals moving along in an orderly and often ceremonial way ⟨the funeral *cortege* of mourners stretched for three city blocks⟩
synonyms parade, procession
related words progress; callithump; column, line, string, train

coruscate *vb* to shoot forth bursts of light ⟨a classic car from the 1950s, replete with yards of *coruscating* chrome⟩ — see FLASH 1

cosmetic *adj* serving to add beauty ⟨changes in the original design of the building were purely *cosmetic*⟩ — see DECORATIVE

cosmetics *n pl* preparations intended to beautify the face ⟨I need to buy some fresh *cosmetics* to use for the wedding⟩ — see MAKEUP 1

cosmic *also* **cosmical** *adj* unusually large ⟨predicted that the war would forever be regarded as a *cosmic* error⟩ — see HUGE

cosmopolis *n* a thickly settled, highly populated area ⟨a sprawling *cosmopolis* where ambitious people from all over come to make their fortune⟩ — see CITY

cosmopolitan *adj* having a wide and refined knowledge of the world especially from personal experience ⟨a college student who now seems conspicuously *cosmopolitan* after spending his junior year abroad⟩ — see WORLDLY-WISE

cosmopolitan *n* a person with the outlook, experience, and manners thought to be typical of big city dwellers ⟨as someone who had lived in Paris for a year as an exchange student, she seemed very much the *cosmopolitan* to her old classmates⟩
synonyms city slicker, cosmopolite, metropolitan, slicker, sophisticate
related words urbanite; worldling
antonyms bumpkin, hick, provincial, rustic, yokel

cosmopolite *n* a person with the outlook, experience, and manners thought to be typical of big city dwellers ⟨having sung in opera houses all over the world, she has the confident demeanor of a seasoned *cosmopolite*⟩ — see COSMOPOLITAN

cosmos *n* the whole body of things observed or assumed ⟨an essay that ponders the place of humankind in the vast *cosmos*⟩ — see UNIVERSE

cosset *vb* to treat with great or excessive care ⟨a luxury spa where guests are *cosseted* with no expense spared⟩ — see BABY

cost *n* **1** a payment made in the course of achieving a result ⟨the newlyweds spared no *cost* in building the kitchen of their dreams⟩ — see EXPENSE
2 the amount of money that is demanded as payment for something ⟨we can't afford the *cost* of a house just yet, so we're renting an apartment⟩ — see PRICE 1
3 the loss or penalty involved in achieving a goal ⟨they won the war, but at a terrible *cost* in lives⟩ — see PRICE 2

cost *vb* to have a price of ⟨the raffle tickets *cost* a dollar each⟩
synonyms bring, fetch, go (for), run, sell (for)
related words list (for); amount (to), come (to), total; command, exact; ask, demand

costless *adj* not costing or charging anything ⟨maintaining a checking account with the bank is not the *costless* service that its advertising would have you believe⟩ — see FREE 4

costly *adj* commanding a large price ⟨running is one sport that does not require a lot of *costly* equipment⟩
synonyms big-ticket, dear, expensive, extravagant, high, high-end, high-ticket, precious, premium, price-

less, pricey (*also* pricy), spendy [*chiefly Northwest*], ultraexpensive, valuable
related words exorbitant, overpriced, prohibitive, sky-high, steep, stiff, unaffordable, uneconomic (*or* uneconomical), unreasonable; inestimable, invaluable; deluxe, luxurious, sumptuous
near antonyms moderate, reasonable; valueless, worthless; discounted
antonyms cheap, inexpensive

costume *n* **1** clothing chosen as appropriate for a specific situation ⟨a tuxedo is the only acceptable *costume* for men attending a formal event⟩ — see OUTFIT 1
2 clothing put on to hide one's true identity or imitate someone or something else ⟨Halloween *costumes* that caricature some of the "celebrities" created by the media over the past year⟩ — see DISGUISE 1

costume *vb* to outfit with clothes and especially fine or special clothes ⟨the days when people, *costumed* in their Sunday best, would parade along the grand avenue on Easter⟩ — see CLOTHE 1

costumery *n* covering for the human body ⟨a museum exhibit devoted to the *costumery* of women since the classical period⟩ — see CLOTHING

coterie *n* a group of people sharing a common interest and relating together socially ⟨a *coterie* of old friends who attend all of the home games of the high school basketball team⟩ — see GANG 2

coterminous *adj* **1** existing or occurring at the same period of time ⟨the Alfred Lunt–Lynn Fontanne partnership was more or less *coterminous* with Broadway's golden age⟩ — see CONTEMPORARY 1
2 occupying the same space ⟨Massachusetts' Nantucket County isn't quite *coterminous* with the island of the same name, as the county includes two small nearby islets⟩ — see COEXTENSIVE 1

cotillion *also* **cotillon** *n* a social gathering for dancing ⟨young men hoping to meet the women of their dreams at the *cotillion*⟩ — see DANCE

cottage *n* an often small house for recreational or seasonal use ⟨for a month every summer we rent a *cottage* on the ocean⟩
synonyms bach [*New Zealand*], cabin, camp, chalet, lodge
related words dacha, summerhouse; bungalow, cot; hut, shack, shanty

cotton (to *or* **on to)** *vb* to have a clear idea of ⟨failed to *cotton on to* the fact that her senatorial campaign was going nowhere⟩ — see COMPREHEND 1

cotton candy *n* something attractive but lacking in substance ⟨the beauty pageant is a variety of *cotton candy* that the public has clearly started to grow tired of⟩
synonyms candyfloss [*British*], eye candy, tinsel
related words window dressing; fluff, froth, gossamer; glitter, gloss

cotton–picking *adj* **1** deserving of one's condemnation or displeasure ⟨that *cotton-picking* scoundrel ought to be ashamed of himself⟩ — see DAMNABLE
2 having no exceptions or restrictions ⟨a perennial malcontent who is always sputtering about the *cotton-picking* idiocy of state officials and bureaucrats⟩ — see ABSOLUTE 2

cottony *adj* **1** covered with or as if with hair ⟨that gray, *cottony* spot on the bread is mold⟩ — see HAIRY 1
2 smooth or delicate in appearance or feel ⟨fluffy, *cottony* hair⟩ — see SOFT 2

couch *n* a long upholstered piece of furniture designed for several sitters ⟨find yourself a place on the *couch* and make yourself at home⟩
synonyms chesterfield, davenport, divan, lounge, settee, sofa, squab
related words lounger, love seat, recamier, tête-à-tête; daybed, sofa bed, studio couch; banquette, bench, ottoman

couch *vb* **1** to convey in appropriate or telling terms ⟨I'm trying to *couch* this delicately: I don't think we should date anymore⟩ — see PHRASE
2 to lie low with the limbs close to the body ⟨I *couched* behind the partition so as to avoid an awkward situation with my ex⟩ — see CROUCH

couch potato *n* a lazy person ⟨a *couch potato* who refused to budge no matter what needed to be done⟩ — see LAZYBONES

cougar *n* a large tawny cat of the wild ⟨in many regions, suburban developments have encroached upon the habitat of the *cougar*⟩
synonyms catamount, cat-a-mountain, mountain lion, panther, puma

cough up *vb* to give (something) over to the control or possession of another usually under duress ⟨finally got my brother to *cough up* the dough he owed me⟩ — see SURRENDER 1

couloir *n* a narrow opening between hillsides or mountains that can be used for passage ⟨at one point the steep, ice-encrusted walls of the *couloir* are no more than 50 feet apart⟩ — see CANYON

council *n* **1** a coming together of a number of persons for a specified purpose ⟨a war *council* attended by the top commanders of each of the armed services⟩ — see MEETING 1
2 a group of persons formally joined together for some common interest ⟨the neighborhood *council* decided to campaign for a new park⟩ — see ASSOCIATION 2
3 a meeting featuring a group discussion ⟨summoned to a *council* to discuss ways that the state could improve medical care for the elderly⟩ — see FORUM 1
4 a local unit of an organization ⟨the scout's own *council* chose to ignore the national organization's discriminatory policies⟩ — see CHAPTER 1
5 an exchange of views for the purpose of exploring a subject or deciding an issue ⟨an unscheduled *council* in the judge's chambers⟩ — see DISCUSSION 1

counsel *n* **1** a person whose profession is to conduct lawsuits for clients or to advise about legal rights and obligations ⟨if you cannot afford *counsel*, one will be provided for you⟩ — see LAWYER
2 an opinion suggesting a wise or proper course of action ⟨I suggest you take the teacher's *counsel*⟩ — see ADVICE 1
3 a person who gives advice especially professionally ⟨the toy manufacturer hired a public relations *counsel* to do some damage control⟩ — see CONSULTANT
4 an exchange of views for the purpose of exploring a subject or deciding an issue ⟨she approved the move after a *counsel* with her advisers⟩ — see DISCUSSION 1

counsel *vb* **1** to exchange viewpoints or seek advice for the purpose of finding a solution to a problem ⟨concerned parents *counseling* about the problem of substance abuse in their community⟩ — see CONFER 2
2 to give advice and instruction to (someone) regarding the course or process to be followed ⟨every year the admissions officer *counsels* thousands of students about the process of applying to college⟩ — see GUIDE 1
3 to give advice to ⟨perhaps a psychologist would be better qualified to *counsel* you⟩ — see ADVISE 1
4 to put (something) forward as one's choice for a wise or proper course of action ⟨I would *counsel* caution and deliberation in this sensitive matter⟩ — see ADVISE 2

counselor *or* **counsellor** *n* **1** a person who gives advice especially professionally ⟨a young couple going to a marriage *counselor*⟩ — see CONSULTANT
2 a person whose profession is to conduct lawsuits for clients or to advise about legal rights and obligations

⟨get the best *counselor* that money can buy, especially if you're guilty⟩ — see LAWYER

counselor–at–law *n* a person whose profession is to conduct lawsuits for clients or to advise about legal rights and obligations ⟨enjoyed a distinguished career as a *counselor-at-law* for more than 40 years⟩ — see LAWYER

count *n* **1** a total number obtained or recorded by noting each thing as it was being added ⟨my *count* for the number of bird species and subspecies that visited the sanctuary that weekend was 43⟩
synonyms census, tale, tally
related words score; amount, gross, sum, total, whole; recount
2 a formal claim of criminal wrongdoing against a person ⟨she's been charged with two *counts* of larceny⟩ — see CHARGE 1

count *vb* **1** to find the sum of (a collection of things) by noting each one as it is being added ⟨*count* the baseball gloves in the storage locker to see if there are enough to go around⟩
synonyms enumerate, number, tell
related words add (up), tally, total; calculate, compute, reckon, table, tabulate; check, mark, tick (off); recount
2 to be of importance ⟨punctuality and a neat appearance *count* during a job interview⟩ — see MATTER
3 to place reliance or trust ⟨I'm *counting* on you to show up tomorrow to help me move⟩ — see DEPEND 2
4 to think of in a particular way ⟨I'm not sure I'd *count* that as a serious effort⟩ — see CONSIDER 1

count (out) *vb* to prevent the participation, consideration, or inclusion of ⟨I don't feel well, so *count* me *out* for the party tonight⟩ — see EXCLUDE

count (up to) *vb* to have a total of ⟨that *counts up to* a pretty sum over the course of several years⟩ — see AMOUNT (TO) 1

countenance *n* **1** facial appearance regarded as an indication of mood or feeling ⟨a pleasant *countenance* that puts visitors at ease⟩ — see LOOK 1
2 the front part of the head ⟨a fairly pretty *countenance*⟩ — see FACE 1
3 evenness of emotions or temper ⟨the EMT's purposeful *countenance* was in stark contrast to everyone else's hysteria⟩ — see EQUANIMITY

countenance *vb* **1** to have a favorable opinion of ⟨I don't *countenance* such behavior in children of any age⟩ — see APPROVE (OF)
2 to put up with (something painful or difficult) ⟨*countenanced* the delays and inconveniences of traveling by air with good grace⟩ — see BEAR 2

counter *adj* opposed to one's interests ⟨was unprepared for such a strong *counter* campaign by opponents of the legislative bill⟩ — see ADVERSE 1

counter *n* **1** a force or influence that makes an opposing force ineffective or less effective ⟨strong moral guidance at home is the best *counter* to the pernicious allure of popular culture⟩ — see COUNTERBALANCE
2 something that is as different as possible from something else ⟨her version of the domestic dispute was almost the exact *counter* of what actually happened⟩ — see OPPOSITE

counter *vb* to strive to reduce or eliminate ⟨efforts to *counter* poverty in every sector of our country⟩ — see FIGHT 2

counteract *vb* to balance with an equal force so as to make ineffective ⟨this medication will *counteract* the symptoms but it won't kill the infection⟩ — see OFFSET

counteraction *n* a force or influence that makes an opposing force ineffective or less effective ⟨the wind serves as a *counteraction* to gravity, making it possible for a kite to remain airborne⟩ — see COUNTERBALANCE

counterassault *n* an attack made to counter an enemy's attack ⟨a feeble *counterassault* that proved to be entirely futile⟩ — see COUNTERATTACK

counterattack *n* an attack made to counter an enemy's attack ⟨suddenly the tide of battle turned, and the rebels, who had been falling back, made a furious *counterattack*⟩
synonyms counterassault, counteroffensive, counterpunch, counterstrike
related words sally, sortie; blitzkrieg, charge; assault, attack, offensive, onslaught

counterbalance *n* a force or influence that makes an opposing force ineffective or less effective ⟨charitable giving is usually a good *counterbalance* to the self-indulgent commercialism of the Christmas season⟩
synonyms balance, canceler (*or* canceller), corrective, counter, counteraction, counterforce, counterpoise, counterweight, equipoise, neutralizer, offset
related words trade-off; ballast, weight

counterbalance *vb* to balance with an equal force so as to make ineffective ⟨a hearty dinner might *counterbalance* missing lunch⟩ — see OFFSET

counterculturist *n* a person who does not conform to generally accepted standards or customs ⟨the daughter of *counterculturists*, she had a very interesting, albeit undisciplined, childhood⟩ — see NONCONFORMIST 1

counterfeit *adj* **1** being such in appearance only and made or manufactured with the intention of committing fraud ⟨*counterfeit* currency that had been passed all over town⟩
synonyms bogus, fake, false, forged, inauthentic, phony (*also* phoney), queer, sham, snide, spurious, unauthentic
related words artificial, factitious, imitation, manmade, mimic, mock, simulated, substitute, synthetic; dummy, nonfunctioning, ornamental; cultured, fabricated, manufactured; deceptive, delusive, misleading
near antonyms natural; actual, true, valid
antonyms authentic, bona fide, genuine, real, unfaked
2 not being or expressing what one appears to be or express ⟨when it comes to the poor, his compassion is so *counterfeit*—he gives a damn, and that's all that he gives⟩ — see INSINCERE

counterfeit *n* an imitation that is passed off as genuine ⟨the will as well as the other documents turned out to be *counterfeits*⟩ — see FAKE 1

counterfeit *vb* **1** to imitate or copy especially in order to deceive ⟨an expert at *counterfeiting* money⟩ — see FAKE 1
2 to present a false appearance of ⟨managing to *counterfeit* a happy expression while visiting a sick friend⟩ — see FEIGN

counterforce *n* a force or influence that makes an opposing force ineffective or less effective ⟨the belief that higher interest rates are an effective *counterforce* to inflationary pressures⟩ — see COUNTERBALANCE

counteroffensive *n* an attack made to counter an enemy's attack ⟨the army launched a *counteroffensive* at dawn⟩ — see COUNTERATTACK

counterpane *n* a decorative cloth used as a top covering for a bed ⟨a beautiful *counterpane* that was a family heirloom⟩
synonyms bedcover (*also* bedcovering), bedspread, coverlet, hap [*dialect*], spread
related words comforter, puff, quilt; bedclothes, bedding, clothes

counterpart *n* **1** one that is equal to another in status, achievement, or value ⟨she worked with her *counterpart* in the other office to get the job done⟩ — see EQUAL
2 something or someone that strongly resembles another ⟨the daughter is her mother's *counterpart* in

somewhat reduced form⟩ — see IMAGE 1

counterpoise *n* **1** a condition in which opposing forces are equal to one another ⟨a musical piece with a *counterpoise* of loud and soft passages⟩ — see BALANCE 1
2 a force or influence that makes an opposing force ineffective or less effective ⟨the happiness brought by a new baby was a timely *counterpoise* to the grief occasioned by a death in the family⟩ — see COUNTERBALANCE

counterpoise *vb* to balance with an equal force so as to make ineffective ⟨her overall healthiness largely *counterpoised* the virulence of the infection⟩ — see OFFSET

counterproductive *adj* not producing the desired result ⟨harsh disciplinary measures that prove to be *counterproductive*⟩ — see INEFFECTIVE 1

counterpunch *n* an attack made to counter an enemy's attack ⟨the last, desperate *counterpunch* of the German armies, known as the Battle of the Bulge⟩ — see COUNTERATTACK

countersign *n* a word or phrase that must be spoken by a person in order to pass a guard ⟨the guard demanded the *countersign*⟩ — see PASSWORD

counterstrike *n* an attack made to counter an enemy's attack ⟨after countless strikes and *counterstrikes*, the positions of both armies remained essentially unchanged⟩ — see COUNTERATTACK

counterweight *n* a force or influence that makes an opposing force ineffective or less effective ⟨hard work can often be a *counterweight* to modest intelligence⟩ — see COUNTERBALANCE

countless *adj* too many to be counted ⟨I've told you *countless* times not to do that⟩
synonyms innumerable, innumerous, myriad, numberless, uncountable, uncounted, unnumbered, untold
related words endless, infinite, unlimited, vast; many, multitudinous, numerous
phrases beyond number
near antonyms finite, limited
antonyms countable, enumerable, numberable

country *adj* of, relating to, associated with, or typical of open areas with few buildings or people ⟨plain *country* living among unpretentious people⟩ — see RURAL

country *n* **1** the land of one's birth, residence, or citizenship ⟨a great love for my *country*⟩
synonyms fatherland, home, homeland, mother country, motherland, sod
related words old country; community, neighborhood
2 the open rural area outside of big towns and cities ⟨out in the *country*, where the air is fresh and the rivers are clean⟩
synonyms boondocks, boonies [*slang*], countryside, nowhere, sticks
related words exurbia; backcountry, backwater, backwoods, bush, frontier, hinterland, outback, up-country; wild, wilderness
phrases middle of nowhere
near antonyms conurbation, megalopolis, urban sprawl
3 a body of people composed of one or more nationalities usually with its own territory and government ⟨usually in time of war, the whole *country* unites behind the president⟩ — see NATION 1

countryman *n* **1** a person living in or originally from the same country as another ⟨met a fellow Canadian *countryman* while traveling in France⟩ — see COMPATRIOT 1
2 an awkward or simple person especially from a small town or the country ⟨though neither well-educated nor well-dressed, the *countryman* presented the farmers' case before the state legislature⟩ — see HICK

country mile *n* a long distance ⟨the distance from the car to the concert hall felt like a *country mile* in her new high heels⟩ — see MILE

countryside *n* the open rural area outside of big towns and cities ⟨everyone hates to see the *countryside* ruined by new developments⟩ — see COUNTRY 2

coup *n* a successful result brought about by hard work ⟨winning that big contract was a real *coup*⟩ — see ACCOMPLISHMENT 1

coup de grâce *or* **coup de grace** *n* something (as a fact or argument) that is decisive or overwhelming ⟨the prosecutor presented his *coupe de grâce*—a videotape of the beating⟩ — see CLINCHER

coup de main *n* the act or action of setting upon with force or violence ⟨the Continental Army's attack on the British-Hessian encampment at Trenton, New Jersey, ranks as one of the most brilliant *coups de main* of the war⟩ — see ATTACK 1

couple *n* **1** a small number ⟨there are only a *couple* of errors in the computer program⟩ — see FEW
2 two things of the same or similar kind that match or are considered together ⟨a *couple* of socks⟩ — see PAIR

couple *vb* **1** to come together to form a single unit ⟨at Pittsburgh, the Allegheny and Monongahela Rivers *couple* to form the Ohio⟩ — see UNITE 1
2 to put or bring together so as to form a new and longer whole ⟨if you *couple* the two extension cords, the connection should be long enough to reach the next room⟩ — see CONNECT 1

couplet *n* two things of the same or similar kind that match or are considered together ⟨a *couplet* of statues flank the entrance to the church⟩ — see PAIR

coupling *n* **1** a place where two or more things are united ⟨the *coupling* between two train cars⟩ — see JOINT 1
2 the act or an instance of joining two or more things into one ⟨credited with the *coupling* of several existing ideas into a single thesis⟩ — see UNION 1
3 sexual union involving penetration of the vagina by the penis ⟨the zoo announced that the giant pandas' most recent *coupling* was successful and that a cub was expected in March⟩ — see SEXUAL INTERCOURSE

coupon *n* a small sheet of plastic, paper, or paperboard showing that the bearer has a claim to something (as admittance) ⟨a book of discount *coupons*⟩ — see TICKET 1

courage *n* strength of mind to carry on in spite of danger ⟨the moral *courage* to speak out against injustice when no one else will⟩
synonyms bottle [*British slang*], bravery, courageousness, daring, daringness, dauntlessness, doughtiness, fearlessness, gallantry, greatheartedness, guts, gutsiness, hardihood, heart, heroism, intestinal fortitude, intrepidity, intrepidness, moxie, nerve, pecker [*chiefly British*], prowess, stoutness, valor, virtue
related words backbone, fiber, fortitude, grit, gumption, mettle, pluck, pluckiness, spunk, temper; determination, perseverance, resolution; endurance, stamina, stomach, tenacity; audacity, boldness, brazenness, cheek, cojones [*slang*], effrontery, gall, temerity
near antonyms cold feet, faintheartedness, fearfulness, mousiness, timidity, timorousness; feebleness, softness, weakness; impotence, ineffectualness; hesitation, indecision, indecisiveness, irresolution
antonyms cowardice, cowardliness, cravenness, dastardliness, poltroonery, spinelessness

courageous *adj* feeling or displaying no fear by temperament ⟨the *courageous* decision to quit rather than obey an illegal order⟩ — see BRAVE 1

courageously *adv* in a fearless manner ⟨he *courageously* demanded fair treatment for those who could not speak for themselves⟩ — see BRAVELY 1

courageousness *n* strength of mind to carry on in spite of danger ⟨the soldiers' exceptional *courageous-*

ness was credited with saving the mission from near disaster⟩ — see COURAGE

courier *n* **1** a person who imports or exports goods secretly and illegally ⟨under wartime rationing, the only way to obtain some foods was from a *courier*⟩ — see SMUGGLER

2 one that carries a message or does an errand ⟨a *courier* just delivered a package for you⟩ — see MESSENGER

course *n* **1** a way of acting or proceeding ⟨the president's usual *course* has been to obtain advice from several people and then make up his own mind⟩
synonyms line, methodology, policy, procedure, program
related words blueprint, design, plan, scheme, strategy; intent, intention, purpose; approach, direction, method, path, pathway, tack

2 a series of lectures on a subject ⟨a *course* on American history from the colonial period to the present⟩
synonyms class
related words elective, refresher; clinic, institute, seminar, survey course; minicourse; core, curriculum
phrases course of study

3 a usually fixed or ordered series of actions or events leading to a result ⟨set out on the *course* that would lead to a college degree⟩ — see PROCESS 1

4 the direction along which something or someone moves ⟨the river follows a southeasterly *course* to the ocean⟩ — see PATH 1

5 an open man-made passageway for water ⟨the Erie Canal was replaced by a much larger *course*, the New York State Barge Canal⟩ — see CHANNEL 1

course *vb* **1** to go after or on the track of ⟨after *coursing* the conspirators for months, the federal agents closed in and made the arrests⟩ — see FOLLOW 2

2 to make one's way through, across, or over ⟨once the threat of terrorism became apparent, fighter jets began *coursing* that corridor on a daily basis⟩ — see TRAVERSE

3 to proceed or move quickly ⟨racehorses *coursing* down the track⟩ — see HURRY 2

court *n* **1** the residence of a ruler ⟨Hampton *Court* was the imposing residence of King Henry VIII⟩
synonyms palace
related words castle, château, estate, mansion, villa; alcazar, seraglio

2 an open space wholly or partly enclosed (as by buildings or walls) ⟨the art museum boasts a glass-sided *court* that is filled with an array of greenery and sculpture⟩
synonyms close, courtyard, enclosure (*also* inclosure), patio, quad, quadrangle, yard
related words atrium, galleria, parvis (*also* parvise), peristyle; forecourt, place, plaza, square; deck, terrace; curtilage

3 an assembly of persons for the administration of justice ⟨this *court* is now called to order⟩
synonyms bar, bench, forum, tribunal
related words criminal court, judicatory, judicature, judiciary; high court, supreme court; court-martial, drumhead court-martial; inquisition, kangaroo court
phrases court of law

4 a public official having authority to decide questions of law ⟨if it please the *court*, I'd like to approach the bench⟩ — see JUDGE 2

court *vb* **1** to act so as to make (something) more likely ⟨you're *courting* disaster if you keep playing with matches⟩
synonyms ask (for), flirt (with), invite, woo
related words angle (for), fish (for); hunt, search, seek; provoke, tempt
phrases look for

2 to go on dates that may eventually lead to marriage ⟨they *courted* for a year before getting married⟩
synonyms date
related words attend, gallant, romance, spark, woo; escort, see, take out; go out, step out
phrases go steady, keep company, make love

courteous *adj* showing consideration, courtesy, and good manners ⟨their customer service department always gives *courteous* responses, even to rude people⟩ — see POLITE 1

courteously *adv* with good reason or courtesy ⟨*courteously* suggested that we try other bookstores⟩ — see WELL 4

courteousness *n* speech or behavior that is a sign of good breeding ⟨a gentleman of unfailing *courteousness*⟩ — see POLITENESS 1

courtesan *n* a woman who engages in sexual activities for money ⟨the protagonist of the novel is a composite of several real-life *courtesans* who plied their trade among the decadent aristocracy⟩ — see PROSTITUTE

courtesy *n* **1** an act of kind assistance ⟨did me the *courtesy* of loaning me his jacket⟩ — see FAVOR 1

2 an act or utterance that is a customary show of good manners ⟨the greeting "How are you?" is often intended as no more than a *courtesy*⟩ — see CIVILITY 1

3 speech or behavior that is a sign of good breeding ⟨a woman who responds to every situation with *courtesy* and kindness⟩ — see POLITENESS 1

courting *n* the series of social engagements shared by a couple looking to get married ⟨after two years of *courting*, they finally married⟩ — see COURTSHIP

courtliness *n* dignified or restrained beauty of form, appearance, or style ⟨there's a *courtliness* to rococo furniture that makes you feel like you should be wearing fine clothes and sipping champagne⟩ — see ELEGANCE

courtly *adj* having or showing elegance ⟨his *courtly* manners made him a favorite escort of widowed socialites⟩ — see ELEGANT 1

courtship *n* the series of social engagements shared by a couple looking to get married ⟨a long-married couple who look back on their whirlwind *courtship* with fondness and laughter⟩
synonyms courting, dating, lovemaking, suit
related words suit, wooing; affair (*also* affaire), love affair, romance; betrothal, engagement

courtyard *n* an open space wholly or partly enclosed (as by buildings or walls) ⟨a series of lunchtime concerts in the museum's open-air *courtyard*⟩ — see COURT 2

cousin *n* a person connected with another by blood or marriage ⟨we both were surprised to learn that we are distant *cousins*⟩ — see RELATIVE

couth *adj* having or showing a taste for the fine arts and gracious living ⟨he's remarkably *couth* for someone who grew up in a small town with limited cultural opportunities⟩ — see CULTIVATED

couth *n* a high level of taste and enlightenment as a result of extensive intellectual training and exposure to the arts ⟨their future son-in-law's lack of *couth* was of some concern to this patrician couple⟩ — see CULTURE 1

cove *n* a part of a body of water that extends beyond the general shoreline ⟨a secluded *cove* that smugglers once used⟩ — see GULF 1

coven *n* a group of people sharing a common interest and relating together socially ⟨a *coven* of epicures who gather for monthly wine tastings⟩ — see GANG 2

covenant *n* **1** a formal agreement between two or more nations or peoples ⟨the two countries signed a peace *covenant* that, it was hoped, would put an end to decades of bitter conflict⟩ — see TREATY

2 a formal agreement to fulfill an obligation ⟨I had to

sign a *covenant* that I would return the rental car on time⟩ — see GUARANTEE 1

3 an arrangement about action to be taken ⟨the *covenant* that existed among neighbors in olden times whereby they would quickly respond to the call to help put out one another's house fires⟩ — see AGREEMENT 2

covenant *vb* **1** to come to an arrangement as to a course of action ⟨a traditional rule held that a husband could not enter into a covenant with his wife, because that was the equivalent of *covenanting* with himself⟩ — see AGREE 2

2 to make a solemn declaration of intent ⟨the home buyers had to *covenant* that they would restore and keep the house for at least 10 years in exchange for a low mortgage rate⟩ — see PROMISE 1

cover *n* **1** a piece placed over an open container to hold in, protect, or conceal its contents ⟨where's the *cover* for the cookie jar?⟩

synonyms cap, lid, top

related words dome, hood, roof; capsule, case, casing, covering, housing, jacket, sheath, shell

2 means or method of defending ⟨provided *cover* while their comrades ran for safety⟩ — see DEFENSE 1

3 something that encloses another thing especially to protect it ⟨put the restaurant menus in clear plastic *covers* so that they would last longer⟩ — see [1]CASE 1

4 a person or thing that takes the place of another ⟨people may only skip their shifts if they find a *cover* for themselves first⟩ — see SUBSTITUTE

5 a raised covering over something for decoration or protection ⟨all of the exhibits at the fair are under *cover*, so the weather won't be a factor⟩ — see CANOPY

6 something that covers or conceals like a piece of cloth ⟨under *cover* of friendship the con man insinuated himself in the lives of the unsuspecting couple⟩ — see CLOAK 1

cover *vb* **1** to serve as a replacement usually for a time only ⟨a friend *covered* for me as a hospital volunteer while my family went on vacation⟩

synonyms fill in, pinch-hit, stand in, step in, sub, substitute, take over

related words understudy; relieve, spell; double (as)

2 to form a layer over ⟨by morning a foot of snow *covered* the ground⟩

synonyms blanket, carpet, coat, overlay, overlie, overspread, sheet

related words enclose (*also* inclose), enrobe, enshroud, enswathe, envelop, enwrap, mantle, shawl, shroud, swathe, wrap; cloak, clothe, curtain, veil; circle, encircle, encompass

3 to place a protective layer over ⟨better *cover* your skin with sunblock if you don't want a sunburn, not to mention skin cancer⟩

synonyms screen, shield

related words cloak, clothe, veil; drape, pall; canopy, cap, crown; disguise, mask, obscure

near antonyms bare, expose, uncover

4 to have (something) as a subject matter ⟨this section of the book *covers* kitchen makeovers for the enterprising do-it-yourselfer⟩ — see CONCERN 1

5 to keep secret or shut off from view ⟨*covered* the foxhole with grass and leaves⟩ — see [1]HIDE 2

6 to make one's way through, across, or over ⟨we usually manage to *cover* a lot of ground in a single day⟩ — see TRAVERSE

7 to pay continued close attention to (something) for a particular purpose ⟨I'll *cover* the reception desk while you take a break⟩ — see MONITOR

8 to drive danger or attack away from ⟨*covered* the wounded soldier until he could be rescued from the downed chopper⟩ — see DEFEND 1

cover (up) *vb* to keep from being publicly known ⟨the governor vainly tried to *cover up* the growing scandal⟩ — see SUPPRESS 1

coverage *n* the amount of something (as subject matter) included ⟨the biographical dictionary's *coverage* is limited to people no longer living⟩

synonyms content

related words compass, gamut, range, scope, sweep; membership, participation

cover–all *adj* covering everything or all important points ⟨a detailed plan for *cover-all* health insurance⟩ — see ENCYCLOPEDIC

covering *n* **1** something that covers or conceals like a piece of cloth ⟨with the commotion on the dance floor as a *covering*, we were able to slip out undetected⟩ — see CLOAK 1

2 something that encloses another thing especially to protect it ⟨the plastic *coverings* on lamp shades should be removed⟩ — see [1]CASE 1

coverlet *n* a decorative cloth used as a top covering for a bed ⟨bought a beautiful new *coverlet* to match the sheets⟩ — see COUNTERPANE

covert *adj* **1** screened or sequestered from view ⟨a *covert* little hideaway that provides a lot of privacy⟩ — see SECLUDED

2 undertaken or done so as to escape being observed or known by others ⟨a *covert* operation to provide aid to the rebels⟩ — see SECRET 1

covert *n* **1** a place where a person goes to hide or to avoid others ⟨set up a *covert* from which to watch wildlife without being detected⟩ — see HIDEOUT

2 a thick patch of shrubbery, small trees, or underbrush ⟨the rabbit rushed to the safety of the nearest *covert*⟩ — see THICKET

coverture *n* something that covers or conceals like a piece of cloth ⟨under the *coverture* of a raging snowstorm, the rebels undertook their surprise attack on the fortress⟩ — see CLOAK 1

cover–up *n* something that covers or conceals like a piece of cloth ⟨that contrived burglary was just a *cover-up* for murder⟩ — see CLOAK 1

covet *vb* to have an earnest wish to own or enjoy ⟨I've been *coveting* that sleek sports car in the showroom for some time now⟩ — see DESIRE 1

coveting *adj* having or marked by an eager and often selfish desire especially for material possessions ⟨cast a *coveting* glance at her friend's diamond necklace⟩ — see GREEDY 1

covetous *adj* **1** having or marked by an eager and often selfish desire especially for material possessions ⟨one aggressive bargain hunter rushed to make a *covetous* grab for the last marked-down TV⟩ — see GREEDY 1

2 having or showing mean resentment of another's possessions or advantages ⟨a *covetous* child who must destroy what he cannot have⟩ — see ENVIOUS

covetousness *n* **1** a painful awareness of another's possessions or advantages and a desire to have them too ⟨his *covetousness* for his neighbors' things spoils any enjoyment he might have of his own possessions⟩ — see ENVY

2 an intense selfish desire for wealth or possessions ⟨an insatiable *covetousness* made her work long hours so that she could afford expensive things⟩ — see GREED

cow *vb* to make timid or fearful by or as if by threats ⟨a sharp glare *cowed* the child into being quiet⟩ — see INTIMIDATE

coward *n* a person who shows a shameful lack of courage in the face of danger ⟨the soldiers who ran as soon as the first shots were fired were branded as *cowards*⟩

synonyms chicken, craven, cur, dastard, funk, poltroon, recreant, sissy

related words defeatist, quitter; cream puff, milquetoast, pushover, pussy [*slang*], weakling, wimp; caitiff,

snake, sneak; ostrich, scaramouch (*or* scaramouche)
near antonyms daredevil
antonyms hero, stalwart, valiant

cowardice *n* a shameful lack of courage in the face of danger ⟨the *cowardice* shown by political leaders who were willing to give the Nazis whatever they wanted⟩
synonyms cowardliness, cravenness, dastardliness, gutlessness, poltroonery, pusillanimity, spinelessness
related words diffidence, faintheartedness, fearfulness, timidity, timorousness; carefulness, cautiousness, wariness; bashfulness, shyness; feebleness, softness, weakness
near antonyms audacity, boldness, brazenness; backbone, fiber, fortitude, grit, gumption, mettle, pluck, spunk; determination, perseverance, resolution; endurance, stamina, tenacity
antonyms bravery, courage, courageousness, daring, dauntlessness, doughtiness, fearlessness, gallantry, greatheartedness, guts, hardihood, heart, heroism, intrepidity, intrepidness, nerve, stoutness, valiance, valor, virtue

cowardliness *n* a shameful lack of courage in the face of danger ⟨the soldier was court-martialed for *cowardliness* under fire⟩ — see COWARDICE

cowardly *adj* having or showing a shameful lack of courage ⟨a *cowardly* bully who picks on the weak and defenseless⟩ ⟨vile charges that were made in a *cowardly*, unsigned letter⟩
synonyms chicken, chickenhearted, chicken-livered, craven, dastardly, gutless, lily-livered, milk-livered [*archaic*], poltroon, pusillanimous, recreant, spineless, unheroic, yellow
related words diffident, fainthearted, fearful, timid, timorous; afraid, frightened, scared; careful, cautious, wary; bashful, coy, shy; feeble, soft, unmanly, weak
near antonyms audacious, bold, brazen, cheeky, nervy; plucky, spirited, spunky; determined, resolute
antonyms brave, courageous, daring, dauntless, doughty, fearless, gallant, greathearted, gutsy, hardy, heroic (*also* heroical), intrepid, lionhearted, stalwart, stout, stouthearted, valiant, valorous

cowboy *n* a hired hand who tends cattle or horses at a ranch or on the range ⟨*cowboys* were rounding up the cattle for branding⟩
synonyms buckaroo (*also* buckeroo), cowhand, cowman, cowpoke, cowpuncher, waddy (*or* waddie) [*West*], wrangler
related words cowgirl; caballero [*chiefly Southwest*], gaucho, vaquero; horseman, horsewoman; cattleman, rancher, stockman; cowherd, drover, herder, herdsman

cower *vb* to draw back or crouch down in fearful submission ⟨the abused dog always *cowered* in the presence of its master⟩
synonyms cringe, grovel, quail
related words flinch, recoil, shrink, squinch; blanch, blench, whiten; fawn, kowtow, toady

cowhand *n* a hired hand who tends cattle or horses at a ranch or on the range ⟨we need to hire a new *cowhand* to help out⟩ — see COWBOY

cowhide *vb* to strike repeatedly with something long and thin or flexible ⟨was *cowhiding* the horse until a police officer intervened⟩ — see WHIP 1

cowman *n* a hired hand who tends cattle or horses at a ranch or on the range ⟨an expert *cowman* who can round up the livestock in no time⟩ — see COWBOY

coworker *n* a fellow worker ⟨my *coworkers* and I often send facetious e-mails to one another⟩ — see COLLEAGUE

cowpoke *n* a hired hand who tends cattle or horses at a ranch or on the range ⟨it takes a long time to train a good *cowpoke*⟩ — see COWBOY

cowpuncher *n* a hired hand who tends cattle or horses at a ranch or on the range ⟨*cowpunchers* hanging out and telling stories during branding time⟩ — see COWBOY

coy *adj* **1** affecting shyness or modesty in order to attract masculine interest ⟨not wanting him to know that she was interested in him, she acted very *coy* at the dance⟩
synonyms coquettish, demure, kittenish
related words flirtatious, flirty, girlish; goody-goody, governessy, overmodest, priggish, prim, prudish
antonyms uncoy
2 not comfortable around people ⟨a *coy* toddler who hides whenever anyone comes to the house⟩ — see SHY 2

coyness *n* the attitude or behavior of one who insincerely courts the amorous attentions of others ⟨an actress better known for her come-hither *coyness* than for her acting chops⟩ — see COQUETRY

cozen *vb* **1** to cause to believe what is untrue ⟨*cozened* several elderly ladies into believing that he was intending marriage⟩ — see DECEIVE
2 to rob by the use of trickery or threats ⟨*cozened* scores of people by persuading them to hand over funds that he would "invest"⟩ — see FLEECE

cozenage *n* the inclination or practice of misleading others through lies or trickery ⟨through *cozenage* and flattery, the art dealer coaxed the unwary into selling their family treasures for a song⟩ — see DECEIT 1

cozener *n* a dishonest person who uses clever means to cheat others out of something of value ⟨he was a "career" *cozener* who had worked one racket or another his whole life⟩ — see TRICKSTER 1

cozy *adj* **1** enjoying physical comfort ⟨the cat looked very *cozy*, all cuddled up in the blankets⟩ — see COMFORTABLE 2
2 providing physical comfort ⟨a coffeehouse with soft, *cozy* chairs⟩ — see COMFORTABLE 1

crab *n* an irritable and complaining person ⟨you're always such a *crab* in the morning!⟩ — see GROUCH 1

crab *vb* **1** to express dissatisfaction, pain, or resentment usually tiresomely ⟨their two-year-old whined and *crabbed* for the whole car trip⟩ — see COMPLAIN
2 to reduce the soundness, effectiveness, or perfection of ⟨*crabbed* the blossoming romance by becoming moody and demanding⟩ — see DAMAGE 1

crabby *adj* **1** easily irritated or annoyed ⟨a *crabby* old dog who snapped at passersby⟩ — see IRRITABLE
2 given to complaining a lot ⟨a bunch of *crabby* kids who don't want to do any work⟩ — see FUSSY 1

crabwise *adv* with one side faced forward ⟨she inched *crabwise* out of the room, hoping no one would notice⟩ — see SIDEWAYS 1

crack *adj* having or showing exceptional knowledge, experience, or skill in a field of endeavor ⟨known as one of the college's *crack* tennis players⟩ — see PROFICIENT

crack *n* **1** an irregular usually narrow break in a surface created by pressure ⟨a pebble struck the car's windshield and left a spidery *crack* in it⟩
synonyms check, chink, cleft, cranny, crevice, fissure, rift, split
related words crevasse; craze, hairline; fracture, rupture; breach, gap, opening; cut, gash, incision, slit
2 a hard strike with a part of the body or an instrument ⟨a disciplinary *crack* on the hand with a ruler was once common in schoolrooms⟩ — see [1]BLOW
3 a loud explosive sound ⟨the tree fell with a sharp *crack*⟩ — see CLAP 1
4 an effort to do or accomplish something ⟨this is my first *crack* at painting⟩ — see ATTEMPT 1
5 something said or done to cause laughter ⟨a whispered *crack* made the whole back row start laughing⟩ — see JOKE 1

6 a person of odd or whimsical habits ⟨that conspiracy theorist has been labeled a *crack* by the ballistics experts⟩ — see ECCENTRIC

crack *vb* **1** to break suddenly with an explosive sound ⟨the tree branch unexpectedly *cracked* under our weight⟩
synonyms pop, snap
related words rend, rive, split; crackle, hiss, sizzle, sputter; burst, explode, shatter; clack, clatter, click
2 to yield to mental or emotional stress ⟨after hours of tough questioning the suspect finally *cracked* and blurted out a confession⟩
synonyms break down, break up, flip (out) [*slang*], freak (out), melt down, wig (out) [*slang*]
related words choke
phrases blow one's cool, fall apart, go off the deep end, go to pieces, lose it
3 to change (as a secret message) from code into ordinary language ⟨the United States military used the Navajo language as a code during World War II, and the enemy never *cracked* it⟩ — see DECODE 1
4 to deliver a blow to (someone or something) usually in a strong vigorous manner ⟨*cracked* him on the bottom with a paddle⟩ — see HIT 1
5 to find an answer for through reasoning ⟨I've been mulling this riddle, but I just can't *crack* it⟩ — see SOLVE
6 to cause to go insane or as if insane ⟨*cracked* by years in solitary confinement, the prisoner could only maunder incoherently⟩ — see CRAZE

crack (on) *vb* to proceed or move quickly ⟨the postman *cracked on* in an effort to get the mail delivered on time⟩ — see HURRY 2

crackbrain *n* **1** a person judged to be legally or medically insane ⟨once a brilliant dancer, he died a *crackbrain* in a mental institution⟩ — see LUNATIC 1
2 a person of odd or whimsical habits ⟨a *crackbrain* who wore bedroom slippers to the grocery shop⟩ — see ECCENTRIC

crackbrained *adj* having or showing a very abnormal or sick state of mind ⟨had the *crackbrained* idea that he was receiving radio signals from outer space⟩ — see INSANE 1

crack down (on) *vb* to put a stop to (something) by the use of force ⟨the government *cracked down on* political demonstrations with unprecedented brutality⟩ — see QUELL 1

cracked *adj* having or showing a very abnormal or sick state of mind ⟨are you completely *cracked*?⟩ — see INSANE 1

cracker *n* **1** a person who illegally gains access to a computer system and sometimes tampers with its information ⟨a *cracker* who had broken into the intelligence agency's database attempted to leak the classified information⟩ — see HACKER 1
2 *chiefly dialect* someone who boasts ⟨you're a fool if you believe half of what that *cracker* says⟩ — see BRAGGART

cracker-barrel *adj* having or showing an unpretentious informality ⟨his *cracker-barrel* campaign speeches strike a chord with voters⟩
synonyms down-home, folksy, homespun
related words modest, unassuming, unpretentious; colloquial, conversational, informal; casual, familiar, fireside, intimate
near antonyms affected, grandiose, highfalutin (*also* hifalutin), ostentatious, pompous, pretentious

crackerjack *adj* **1** having or showing exceptional knowledge, experience, or skill in a field of endeavor ⟨a *crackerjack* photographer who gets the news photo that is reprinted around the world⟩ — see PROFICIENT
2 of the very best kind ⟨a *crackerjack* book on the history of rock music⟩ — see EXCELLENT

crackerjack *also* **crackajack** *n* **1** a person with a high level of knowledge or skill in a field ⟨a young prospect who's supposed to be a *crackerjack* on the baseball diamond⟩ — see EXPERT
2 something very good of its kind ⟨the cheese maker's aged cheddar is a real *crackerjack*⟩ — see JIM-DANDY

crackers *adj* having or showing a very abnormal or sick state of mind ⟨prisoners in that hellhole either died of disease or went *crackers*⟩ — see INSANE 1

cracking *adj* of the very best kind ⟨a writer renowned for her *cracking* tales of mystery and suspense⟩ — see EXCELLENT

cracking *adv* to a great degree ⟨tells a *cracking* good tale of a search for a lost city⟩ — see VERY 1

crackpot *adj* **1** having or showing a very abnormal or sick state of mind ⟨all it took to bring down a president was one *crackpot* malcontent⟩ — see INSANE 1
2 showing or marked by a lack of good sense or judgment ⟨a *crackpot* scheme to get rich quick⟩ — see FOOLISH 1

crackpot *n* a person of odd or whimsical habits ⟨everyone is tolerant of the town *crackpot*, a man who never hurt anyone⟩ — see ECCENTRIC

crack-up *n* **1** a mental or nervous collapse ⟨a *crack-up* required him to take a year off from work⟩ — see BREAKDOWN 1
2 the violent coming together of two bodies into destructive contact ⟨two people were injured in a serious *crack-up* on the interstate⟩ — see CRASH 1

crack up *vb* **1** to declare enthusiastic approval of ⟨that sports car isn't all it's *cracked up* to be⟩ — see ACCLAIM
2 to praise or publicize lavishly and often excessively ⟨the movie is being *cracked up* as the blockbuster of the summer⟩ — see TOUT 1
3 to show mirth with an explosive vocal sound ⟨try not to *crack up* at your own punch lines—it's funnier if you keep a straight face⟩ — see LAUGH 1

cradle *n* **1** a place of origin ⟨Philadelphia is known as "the *cradle* of liberty" because it was there that the Declaration of Independence was signed⟩ — see BIRTHPLACE
2 a point or place at which something is invented or provided ⟨the 1848 meeting at Seneca Falls, New York, is often regarded as the *cradle* of the women's suffrage movement⟩ — see SOURCE 1

craft *n* **1** an occupation requiring skillful use of the hands ⟨the *craft* of cabinetmaking was much admired in colonial times⟩
synonyms art, handcraft, handicraft, trade
related words skill; calling, métier (*also* metier), occupation, profession, vocation
2 a small buoyant structure for travel on water ⟨borrowed a *craft* to get across the river⟩ — see BOAT 1
3 the inclination or practice of misleading others through lies or trickery ⟨never hesitated to resort to *craft* to get what she wanted in life⟩ — see DECEIT 1
4 skill in achieving one's ends through indirect, subtle, or underhanded means ⟨celebrated in political circles for his *craft*, he's the legislator who knows how to get bills passed⟩ — see CUNNING 1
5 subtle or imaginative ability in inventing, devising, or executing something ⟨a really ingenious household appliance that shows a lot of *craft* on the part of its inventors⟩ — see SKILL 1

craft *vb* to put (something) into proper and usually carefully worked out written form ⟨spent hours *crafting* the perfect letter of recommendation for her prize student⟩ — see COMPOSE 1

crafter *n* a person whose occupation requires skill with the hands ⟨as a *crafter* of handmade bedsteads, he's about the best there is⟩ — see ARTISAN

craftiness *n* **1** skill in achieving one's ends through indirect, subtle, or underhanded means ⟨other antique dealers envied her for her *craftiness* in getting people to sell their treasures for a song⟩ — see CUNNING 1
2 the inclination or practice of misleading others through lies or trickery ⟨according to the confidence man's credo of *craftiness*, "There's a sucker born every minute"⟩ — see DECEIT 1

craftsman *n* a person whose occupation requires skill with the hands ⟨if you want good work, hire a *craftsman*⟩ — see ARTISAN

craftsperson *n* a person whose occupation requires skill with the hands ⟨at the fair you should be able to find a *craftsperson* who can design and make a 19th-century style sunbonnet⟩ — see ARTISAN

crafty *adj* clever at attaining one's ends by indirect and often deceptive means ⟨a *crafty* real estate broker who got people to sell their property at bargain prices⟩ — see ARTFUL 1

crag *n* a steep wall of rock, earth, or ice ⟨a menacing *crag* overhangs the hiking trail⟩ — see CLIFF

craggy *adj* having an uneven edge or outline ⟨goats scrambled nimbly up the *craggy* side of the mountain⟩ — see RAGGED 1

cram *n* a great number of persons or things massed together ⟨battling the rush-hour *cram* in the subway⟩ — see CROWD 1

cram *vb* **1** to fit (people or things) into a tight space ⟨tried to *cram* one more book into the backpack⟩ — see CROWD 1
2 to put into (something) as much as can be held or contained ⟨*crammed* his mouth with candy⟩ — see FILL 1
3 to fill with food to capacity ⟨one of those eating contests in which competitors attempt to *cram* themselves with as many hot dogs as they can in three minutes⟩ — see GORGE 1
4 to swallow or eat greedily ⟨the thoughtless guest *crammed* a dinner that had taken hours to prepare⟩ — see GOBBLE

crammed *adj* containing or seeming to contain the greatest quantity or number possible ⟨the auditorium is usually *crammed* when that candidate makes an appearance⟩ — see FULL 1

[1]**cramp** *n* a painful sudden tightening of a muscle ⟨I was suddenly awakened by a *cramp* in my leg⟩
synonyms charley horse, crick, kink, spasm
related words contraction, jerk, pang, stitch, twinge, twitch

[2]**cramp** *n* something that makes movement or progress difficult ⟨an antismoking ordinance that was seen as just another *cramp* on business by bar owners⟩ — see ENCUMBRANCE

cramp *vb* to create difficulty for the work or activity of ⟨having to constantly entertain guests at the summer cottage was really *cramping* my writing efforts⟩ — see HAMPER

crane *vb* to move from a lower to a higher place or position ⟨*craned* her head to see the roof⟩ — see RAISE 1

cranium *n* the case of bone that encloses the brain and supports the jaws of vertebrates ⟨the *cranium* of a Neanderthal is striking for its brow ridges⟩ — see SKULL

crank *adj, chiefly dialect* **1** having or expressing feelings of joy or triumph ⟨you shouldn't feel so *crank*, considering that you beat the worst softball team in the league⟩— see EXULTANT
2 joyously unrestrained ⟨folks around here are downright *crank* that a local boy won a gold medal in the Olympics⟩ — see EXUBERANT

crank *n* **1** a person of odd or whimsical habits ⟨she's a bit of a *crank*, but still a good-hearted person⟩ — see ECCENTRIC
2 an irritable and complaining person ⟨he's always a *crank* until he has his morning coffee⟩ — see GROUCH 1
3 a sudden impulsive and apparently unmotivated idea or action ⟨his endless and unpredictable *cranks* made spending time with him exhausting⟩ — see WHIM

crank (up) *vb* to cause to function ⟨*crank up* the CD player so we can dance⟩ — see ACTIVATE

crankiness *n* readiness to show annoyance or impatience ⟨overtired children are often prone to *crankiness*⟩ — see PETULANCE

cranky *adj* **1** difficult to use or operate especially because of size, weight, or design ⟨that old typewriter is handy sometimes, but rather *cranky* these days⟩ — see CUMBERSOME
2 easily irritated or annoyed ⟨the baby was *cranky* after not being fed for hours⟩— see IRRITABLE
3 given to complaining a lot ⟨if *cranky* children don't appreciate what they already have, then they shouldn't get a thing more⟩ — see FUSSY 1
4 different from the ordinary in a way that causes curiosity or suspicion ⟨that's just another of his *cranky* theories about the CIA⟩ — see ODD 2
5 *dialect* having or showing a very abnormal or sick state of mind ⟨the man would inflict on innocent bystanders his *cranky* ruminations on world events⟩ — see INSANE 1

cranny *n* an irregular usually narrow break in a surface created by pressure ⟨one climbing shoe got wedged into a *cranny* on the face of the cliff⟩ — see CRACK 1

crapola *n, slang* **1** language, behavior, or ideas that are absurd and contrary to good sense ⟨her book, in which she details the things that are purportedly wrong with the country, is *crapola* of the first magnitude⟩ — see NONSENSE 1
2 that which is of low quality or worth ⟨it's a sin that such *crapola* gets shown on TV⟩ — see JUNK 1

crappy *adj, slang* of low quality ⟨a *crappy* radio that immediately broke⟩ — see CHEAP 2

crapshoot *n* a risky undertaking ⟨there are almost no sure bets in the movie business—almost everything is a *crapshoot*⟩ — see GAMBLE

crapulous *adj* given to excessive use of alcoholic beverages ⟨a *crapulous* wastrel who went through the family's once-fabulous fortune in less than a decade⟩
synonyms bibulous, drunken, intemperate, sottish
related words debauched, dissipated, dissolute; drunk, high, inebriated, intoxicated, loaded [*slang*], soused, tipsy
near antonyms clearheaded, sober, straight; abstemious, abstinent, teetotal
antonyms temperate

crash *n* **1** the violent coming together of two bodies into destructive contact ⟨the fiery *crash* of two jumbo jet airplanes in midair⟩
synonyms collision, concussion, crack-up, smash, smashup, wreck
related words accident, pileup; demolishment, destruction, ruin
2 a falling short of one's goals ⟨refused to be discouraged by the *crash* of her hairdressing business⟩ — see FAILURE 2
3 a loud explosive sound ⟨the *crash* of cymbals⟩ — see CLAP 1
4 a forceful coming together of two things ⟨a story about the *crash* of two alien cultures and the unfortunate consequences⟩ — see IMPACT 1

crash *vb* **1** to cause to break with violence and much noise ⟨*crashed* the vase against the wall⟩ — see SMASH 1
2 to come into usually forceful contact with something ⟨the speeding car *crashed* into the tree with horrifying results⟩ — see HIT 2
3 to stop functioning ⟨my computer *crashed* yet again⟩ — see FAIL 1

4 to force one's way ⟨the drunken partygoer *crashed* into my room and promptly passed out⟩ — see [2]PRESS 4
5 to go to a lower level especially abruptly ⟨sales of that digital camera have *crashed* since the competing version came out⟩ — see DROP 2
6 *slang* to go to one's bed in order to sleep ⟨I'm so exhausted that I'm just going to *crash* as soon as we get home⟩ — see BED 1
7 *slang* to reside as a temporary guest ⟨I'm going to *crash* at my sister's apartment when I'm in New York⟩ — see VISIT 2

crashing *adj* having no exceptions or restrictions ⟨a *crashing* bore, he can turn any party into a funeral⟩ — see ABSOLUTE 2

crass *adj* lacking in refinement or good taste ⟨a loud-mouthed jerk given to rude jokes and *crass* comments⟩ — see COARSE 2

crassness *n* the quality or state of lacking refinement or good taste ⟨the *crassness* of the observation shocked everyone into silence⟩ — see VULGARITY 1

crate *n* a dilapidated old automobile ⟨he keeps sinking money into that old *crate*⟩ — see BEATER 1

crater *vb* 1 to be unsuccessful ⟨a time when dot-coms were *cratering* left and right⟩ — see FAIL 2
2 to go to a lower level especially abruptly ⟨the stock price *cratered* when the company filed for Chapter 11⟩ — see DROP 2

crave *vb* to have an earnest wish to own or enjoy ⟨*craves* ice cream at all hours of the day⟩ — see DESIRE 1

craven *adj* having or showing a shameful lack of courage ⟨a *craven* refusal to deliver the unwelcome news personally⟩ — see COWARDLY

craven *n* a person who shows a shameful lack of courage in the face of danger ⟨a *craven* who ran away and left everyone else behind to deal with the crisis⟩ — see COWARD

cravenness *n* a shameful lack of courage in the face of danger ⟨it was sheer *cravenness* to avoid the consequences of your actions⟩ — see COWARDICE

craving *n* a strong wish for something ⟨a pregnant woman with a *craving* for pickles⟩ — see DESIRE 1

crawl *vb* 1 to move slowly with the body close to the ground ⟨the time we had to *crawl* through a narrow passageway from one cave to another⟩
synonyms belly, creep, grovel, slide, slither, snake, worm, wriggle
related words crouch, squat; edge, inch, nose; skulk, sneak, steal, tiptoe
2 to move slowly ⟨the weekend traffic on the road to the beach just *crawled*⟩
synonyms creak (along), creep, drag, inch, limp, nose, ooze, plod, poke, slouch, snail
related words lumber, shamble, shuffle, tramp, trudge
near antonyms float, glide, sail; hurry, tear
antonyms fly, race, speed, whiz (*or* whizz), zip
3 to move or act slowly ⟨the deadline is fast approaching, so this is no time to *crawl*⟩ — see DELAY 1
4 to be copiously supplied ⟨something must be up, as city hall is *crawling* with reporters⟩ — see ABOUND

crawler *n* someone who moves slowly or more slowly than others ⟨he's always the *crawler* who makes everyone else late⟩ — see SLOWPOKE

crawling *adj* moving or proceeding at less than the normal, desirable, or required speed ⟨the *crawling* pace of the narrative is really frustrating⟩ — see SLOW 1

craze *n* a practice or interest that is very popular for a short time ⟨if history is any guide, this latest diet for losing weight is just another *craze*⟩ — see FAD

craze *vb* to cause to go insane or as if insane ⟨soldiers who had been *crazed* by months of combat and chaos in the countryside⟩
synonyms crack, derange, frenzy, loco, madden, unbalance, unhinge, unstring
related words agitate, bother, confuse, discompose, disquiet, distract, disturb, perturb, unsettle, upset; annoy, irritate, vex
near antonyms calm, quiet, relax, settle, soothe, tranquilize (*also* tranquillize)

crazed *adj* having or showing a very abnormal or sick state of mind ⟨the inmate's *crazed* and disturbing stare⟩ — see INSANE 1

craziness *n* lack of good sense or judgment ⟨this latest example of juvenile *craziness* does not incline us to trust you⟩ — see FOOLISHNESS 1

crazy *adj* 1 conceived or made without regard for reason or reality ⟨the mansion is a *crazy* construction of several different styles⟩ — see FANTASTIC 1
2 having or showing a very abnormal or sick state of mind ⟨a *crazy* woman who tried to throw her baby out of a window⟩ — see INSANE 1
3 showing or marked by a lack of good sense or judgment ⟨a *crazy* plan to climb Mount Everest without proper equipment⟩ — see FOOLISH 1
4 showing urgent desire or interest ⟨*crazy* for the latest entertainment news⟩ — see EAGER
5 different from the ordinary in a way that causes curiosity or suspicion ⟨a downtown musician with *crazy* notions of what's stylish and what's not⟩ — see ODD 2
6 inclined or twisted to one side ⟨surrounded by *crazy* stacks of books, she began writing her paper⟩ — see AWRY
7 marked by a long series of irregular curves ⟨walked down a *crazy* path deep in the woods to a secluded swimming hole⟩ — see CROOKED 1

crazy *n* 1 a person judged to be legally or medically insane ⟨one unsympathetic homeowner insisted that all homeless people are *crazies*⟩ — see LUNATIC 1
2 a person who favors rapid and sweeping changes especially in laws and methods of government ⟨beleaguered government officials tried to dismiss the protesters as a bunch of leftist *crazies*⟩ — see RADICAL

crazy (about *or* over) *adj* filled with an intense or excessive love for ⟨he's just *crazy about* that new drummer⟩ — see ENAMORED (OF)

crazy quilt *n* an unorganized collection or mixture of various things ⟨an environmental issue that brought together a *crazy quilt* of people from all points on the political spectrum⟩ — see MISCELLANY 1

creak *n* a harsh grating sound ⟨the *creak* of a floorboard⟩ — see RASP

creak (along) *vb* to move slowly ⟨the line at the registry of motor vehicles was just *creaking along*⟩ — see CRAWL 2

cream *n* individuals carefully selected as being the best of a class ⟨the school accepts only the *cream* of the world's young violinists⟩ — see ELITE 1

cream *vb* 1 to bring to a complete end the physical soundness, existence, or usefulness of ⟨the head-on collision *creamed* the brand-new car in an instant⟩ — see DESTROY 1
2 to defeat by a large margin ⟨the novice player was *creamed* in her first tennis tournament⟩ — see WHIP 2

cream puff *n* something easily done or dealt with ⟨everyone thinks tonight's game will be a *cream puff*, and so it hasn't generated a lot of interest⟩ — see CINCH 1

crease *n* a small fold in a soft and otherwise smooth surface ⟨rolling, rather than folding, your clothes when you pack will usually prevent a lot of *creases*⟩ — see WRINKLE 1

crease *vb* to develop creases or folds ⟨her face *creased* with worry⟩ — see WRINKLE 1

create *vb* to be the cause of (a situation, action, or state of mind) ⟨it was your negligence that *created* this mess⟩ — see EFFECT

creation *n* **1** something (as a device) created for the first time through the use of the imagination ⟨Dr. Frankenstein was divinely proud of his *creation*, at least at first⟩ — see INVENTION 1
2 the whole body of things observed or assumed ⟨an unshakable belief in a primal source, a fount of all *creation*⟩ — see UNIVERSE
3 a raising or a state of being raised to a higher rank or position ⟨the *creation* of an unprecedented number of new cardinals by the pope⟩ — see ADVANCEMENT 1

creative *adj* **1** having the skill and imagination to create new things ⟨Thomas Edison's status as perhaps America's greatest *creative* genius⟩
synonyms clever, imaginative, ingenious, innovational, innovative, innovatory, inventive, original, originative, Promethean
related words gifted, inspired, talented; resourceful; fecund, fertile, fruitful, generative, germinal, productive, prolific
near antonyms imitative, uninspired; infertile, unproductive; talentless
antonyms uncreative, unimaginative, uninventive, unoriginal
2 showing a noteworthy use of the imagination and creativity especially in inventing ⟨always coming up with *creative* ways to use hamburger⟩ — see CLEVER 1

creativeness *n* the skill and imagination to create new things ⟨a child with the *creativeness* to build his own figure of a superhero out of the parts of several toys⟩ — see CREATIVITY 1

creativity *n* **1** the skill and imagination to create new things ⟨the arts and crafts fair showed the remarkable *creativity* of local artists and artisans⟩
synonyms cleverness, creativeness, imagination, imaginativeness, ingeniousness, ingenuity, innovativeness, invention, inventiveness, originality
related words fecundity, fertility, fruitfulness, productiveness, productivity, prolificacy, prolificity, prolificness; capableness, resourcefulness; genius, giftedness, talent; fire, inspiration, muse
near antonyms dryness, dullness (*also* dulness)
2 the ability to form mental images of things that either are not physically present or have never been conceived or created by others ⟨while his imaginary friend is a little annoying, you have to admire his *creativity* in thinking her up⟩ — see IMAGINATION 1

creator *n* **1** a person who establishes a whole new field of endeavor ⟨although some people see Freud as the *creator* of psychology, that isn't really true⟩ — see FATHER 2
2 *cap* the being worshipped as the creator and ruler of the universe ⟨she humbly gave thanks to her *Creator* for each new day⟩ — see DEITY 2

creature *n* **1** a member of the human race ⟨we must try to be kind to our fellow *creatures*⟩ — see HUMAN
2 one of the lower animals as distinguished from human beings ⟨a saint who is celebrated for his love of birds and other small *creatures*⟩ — see ANIMAL

creature comfort *n* something that adds to one's ease of living ⟨she's too addicted to *creature comforts* to enjoy roughing it, even for a few days⟩ — see COMFORT 2

crèche *n* a school for children who are generally less than five years old ⟨one of the first cities to establish *crèches* so that poor women with children could work outside of the home⟩ — see NURSERY SCHOOL

credence *n* **1** firm belief in the integrity, ability, effectiveness, or genuineness of someone or something ⟨I'm afraid I don't put much *credence* in common gossip⟩ — see TRUST 1
2 mental conviction of the truth of some statement or the reality of some being or phenomenon ⟨a foolish theory that, incredibly, once had wide *credence* among educated people⟩ — see BELIEF 1

credentials *n pl* a skill, an ability, or knowledge that makes a person able to do a particular job ⟨she certainly has the *credentials* for the position⟩ — see QUALIFICATION 1

credible *adj* worthy of being accepted as true or reasonable ⟨it's at least a *credible* explanation⟩ — see BELIEVABLE

credit *n* **1** the right to take possession of goods before paying for them ⟨because of their reputation for not paying their bills, no store will extend the family *credit*⟩
synonyms trust
related words installment plan, layaway; charge account, credit line
2 an asset that brings praise or renown ⟨your intelligence and dedication are a *credit* to you, our choice for teacher of the year⟩ — see GLORY 2
3 mental conviction of the truth of some statement or the reality of some being or phenomenon ⟨I give full *credit* to this report on the prevalence of cheating among college students today⟩ — see BELIEF 1
4 public acknowledgment or admiration for an achievement ⟨she deserves all the *credit*, since she did all the work⟩ — see GLORY 1
5 the power to direct the thinking or behavior of others usually indirectly ⟨despite his legal woes, he has not yet lost all his *credit* with the administration in the White House⟩ — see INFLUENCE 1

credit *vb* **1** to explain (something) as being the result of something else ⟨has to *credit* his success in picking winning lottery numbers to pure luck⟩
synonyms accredit, ascribe, attribute, chalk up, impute, lay, put down
related words blame, charge, father (on), impute (to), pin (on); assign, refer; associate, attach, connect, link
2 to regard as right or true ⟨I simply cannot *credit* that story about the boy who was supposedly raised by wolves⟩ — see BELIEVE 1

creditable *adj* **1** deserving of high regard or great approval ⟨a *creditable* effort, even if it didn't succeed completely⟩ — see ADMIRABLE
2 worthy of being accepted as true or reasonable ⟨let's look for a scientifically *creditable* explanation before going off into the realm of the supernatural⟩ — see BELIEVABLE

creditably *adv* in a satisfactory way ⟨he performed the part *creditably* even though he had no experience acting on stage⟩ — see WELL 1

credo *n* **1** a body of beliefs and practices regarding the supernatural and the worship of one or more deities ⟨the *credo* of the ancient Egyptians involved a variety of polytheism⟩ — see RELIGION 1
2 the basic beliefs or guiding principles of a person or group ⟨we must abide by the simple *credo* that "The customer is always right"⟩ — see CREED 1

credulity *n* readiness to believe the claims of others without sufficient evidence ⟨the quack pushing the phony medicine was taking advantage of the *credulity* of people hoping for miracle cures⟩
synonyms credulousness, gullibility, naiveness, naïveté (*also* naivete *or* naiveté), simpleness
related words artlessness, simplicity, unsophistication, unwariness, unworldliness; belief, credibility, faith, trust
near antonyms sophistication, worldliness; distrust, misdoubt, mistrust, suspicion, suspiciousness, wariness; doubt, uncertainty
antonyms incredulity, skepticism

credulousness *n* readiness to believe the claims of others without sufficient evidence ⟨her inveterate *credulousness* makes her an easy target for practical jokes⟩ — see CREDULITY

creed *n* **1** the basic beliefs or guiding principles of a person or group ⟨central to the *creed* of this organization of medical volunteers is the belief that health care is a basic human right⟩
synonyms credo, doctrine, dogma, gospel, ideology (*also* idealogy), philosophy, testament
related words manifesto; metaphysic, theory; axiom, tenet, watchword
2 a body of beliefs and practices regarding the supernatural and the worship of one or more deities ⟨the Amish live by a strict *creed* that rejects many of the values and practices of modern society⟩ — see RELIGION 1

creek *n* **1** a natural body of running water smaller than a river ⟨the shallow *creek* that runs in back of our house⟩
synonyms beck [*British*], bourn (*or* bourne), brook, brooklet, burn [*British*], gill [*British*], rill, rivulet, run [*chiefly Midland*], runlet, runnel, streamlet
related words arroyo, billabong [*Australian*], fresh, freshet, runoff; bayou, coulee, slough (*also* slew *or* slue), stream, wash; canal, channel, cut, cutoff, gut, kill, millrace, millstream, race, watercourse, waterway; affluent, branch, confluent, distributary, influent, tributary
2 *chiefly British* a part of a body of water that extends beyond the general shoreline ⟨explored many of the *creeks* along the Cornwall coast of England⟩ — see GULF 1

creep *n* a person whose behavior is offensive to others ⟨after he had sent her several obnoxious e-mails, she reported the *creep* to the director of human resources⟩ — see JERK 1

creep *vb* **1** to advance gradually beyond the usual or desirable limits ⟨water *crept* slowly over the top of the tub and onto the floor⟩ — see ENCROACH
2 to move or act slowly ⟨that Friday afternoon we were just *creeping*, waiting for the buzzer to sound so that we could start the long weekend⟩ — see DELAY 1
3 to move slowly with the body close to the ground ⟨the kitten *crept* silently across the floor before suddenly pouncing on the mouse⟩ — see CRAWL 1
4 to move slowly ⟨the class hour seems to *creep* by⟩ — see CRAWL 2

creeping *adj* moving or proceeding at less than the normal, desirable, or required speed ⟨at this *creeping* pace of progress we'll never have the float ready for the parade⟩ — see SLOW 1

creepy *adj* **1** fearfully and mysteriously strange or fantastic ⟨a fascinating but *creepy* stage show by an offbeat magician⟩ — see EERIE
2 marked by or causing agitation or uncomfortable feelings ⟨a *creepy* aura about the abandoned farmhouse—as though something horrific had happened there⟩ — see NERVOUS 2

crème de la crème *n* individuals carefully selected as being the best of a class ⟨a list of titles that represents the *crème de la crème* of the multitude of books published over the past year⟩ — see ELITE 1

crepuscule *or* **crepuscle** *n* the time from when the sun begins to set to the onset of total darkness ⟨from the deck of our sloop we watched as the island slowly faded from sight in the golden *crepuscule* of a beautiful Caribbean day⟩ — see DUSK 1

crescendo *n* the highest part or point ⟨their divorce was merely the formal *crescendo* of a long period of marital stress and estrangement⟩ — see HEIGHT 1

crest *n* **1** the highest part or point ⟨at that point the filmmaker was at the *crest* of his critical acclaim, which included winning an Oscar⟩ — see HEIGHT 1
2 the line formed when two sloping surfaces come together along their topmost edge ⟨the hiking party reached the *crest* of the mountain just as it began to thunder⟩ — see RIDGE

crestfallen *adj* feeling unhappiness ⟨she was *crestfallen* when she found out she hadn't got the job⟩ — see SAD 1

cretin *n* **1** a person whose behavior is offensive to others ⟨a *cretin* who's constantly forwarding e-mails filled with racist and sexist jokes⟩ — see JERK 1
2 a stupid person ⟨in discussions anyone who disagrees with her is inevitably called a *cretin*⟩ — see IDIOT

crevice *n* an irregular usually narrow break in a surface created by pressure ⟨steam escaped from a long *crevice* in the volcano⟩ — see CRACK 1

crew *n* **1** a group involved in secret or criminal activities ⟨when one boy turned informant, the police were able to nab the drug kingpin and the rest of his *crew*⟩ — see [1]RING 1
2 a group of people working together on a task ⟨we'll need the whole *crew* to stay late tomorrow⟩ — see GANG 1

crick *n* a painful sudden tightening of a muscle ⟨got a *crick* in my neck from sleeping while sitting up⟩ — see [1]CRAMP

crime *n* **1** activities that are in violation of the laws of the state ⟨a promise by the president to step up the war against *crime*⟩
synonyms criminality, lawbreaking, lawlessness
related words outlawry; gangsterism, hooliganism, racketeering; malfeasance, misconduct; wrongdoing; evil, immorality, sin, wickedness; corruption, depravity; malefaction, misdeed, misdoing, offense (*or* offence), transgression, trespass
2 a regrettable or blameworthy act ⟨it's a *crime* to waste food, so give the rest of the pizza to me⟩
synonyms disgrace, pity, shame, sin
related words outrage, scandal
3 a breaking of a moral or legal code ⟨anyone who commits a *crime* should expect to be punished for it⟩ — see OFFENSE 1

criminal *adj* contrary to or forbidden by law ⟨people should know with certainty that *criminal* behavior will be punished⟩ — see ILLEGAL 1

criminal *n* a person who has committed a crime ⟨car thieves, pickpockets, burglars, and other *criminals*⟩
synonyms crook, culprit, felon, lawbreaker, malefactor, miscreant, offender
related words misdemeanant; accomplice, principal; desperado, outlaw; convict, jailbird; perp, perpetrator; evildoer, gallows bird, misdoer, misfeasor, sinner, transgressor, trespasser, villain, wrongdoer; blackhander, button man, gangster, hoodlum, hooligan, mobster, racketeer, thug; enforcer, gun, gunman, gunsel [*slang*], hit man, triggerman; backslider, recidivist, relapser, repeater; accused, arrestee, defendant, detainee, fish, suspect
near antonyms gangbuster, lawman

criminality *n* activities that are in violation of the laws of the state ⟨*criminality* and physical violence often go hand in hand⟩ — see CRIME 1

criminalize *vb* to make or declare contrary to the law ⟨wanted to *criminalize* an activity that the mountaineers had been engaging in for generations⟩ — see ILLEGALIZE

criminate *vb* to make a claim of wrongdoing against ⟨scornfully declaring that he was not the school's lone drug dealer, he immediately began *criminating* a host of confederates⟩ — see ACCUSE

crimp *n* **1** a small fold in a soft and otherwise smooth surface ⟨a small *crimp* in the dollar bill prevented it from being accepted by the bill changer⟩ ⟨made a tiny little *crimp* in the corner of the Queen of Spades⟩ — see WRINKLE 1
2 something that makes movement or progress difficult

⟨the strike could put a real *crimp* in the production schedule⟩ — see ENCUMBRANCE

crimson *vb* to develop a rosy facial color (as from excitement or embarrassment) ⟨he *crimsoned* the minute he realized the foolishness of what he'd said⟩ — see BLUSH

cringe *vb* **1** to draw back in fear, pain, or disgust ⟨gruesome crime scene photos that made several jurors *cringe*⟩ — see FLINCH
2 to draw back or crouch down in fearful submission ⟨the puppy *cringed* when his master raised the rolled-up newspaper⟩ — see COWER

crinkle *n* a small fold in a soft and otherwise smooth surface ⟨little *crinkles* at the corners of his mouth showed whenever he smiled⟩ — see WRINKLE 1

crinkle *vb* **1** to make small sounds usually by rubbing or moving ⟨a paper seat cover that *crinkles* with every move⟩
synonyms rustle
related words crackle, crepitate; creak, squeak; swoosh, whoosh; babble, gurgle, murmur, sigh, whisper
2 to create (as by crushing) an irregular mass of creases in ⟨*crinkled* the candy wrapper up and threw it away⟩ — see CRUMPLE 1
3 to develop creases or folds ⟨her forehead *crinkled* in consternation when her guests failed to arrive on time⟩ — see WRINKLE 1

cripple *vb* **1** to cause severe or permanent injury to ⟨the car crash may have *crippled* two people for life⟩ — see MAIM
2 to reduce the soundness, effectiveness, or perfection of ⟨the collision so severely *crippled* the ship that it had to be towed into port⟩ — see DAMAGE 1
3 to render powerless, ineffective, or unable to move ⟨a wave of strikes *crippled* that nation's steel industry⟩ — see PARALYZE 1

crisis *n* a time or state of affairs requiring prompt or decisive action ⟨the governor responded swiftly and surely to the *crisis*⟩ — see EMERGENCY

crisp *adj* **1** having a texture that readily breaks into little pieces under pressure ⟨the bag of *crisp* cookies had a lot of crumbs on the bottom⟩
synonyms brickle [*dialect*], brittle, crispy, crumbly, embrittled, flaky (*also* flakey), friable, short
related words crackly, crisped, crispened, crunchy, crusty; breakable, delicate, fragile
near antonyms elastic, flexible, pliable, pliant, resilient; strong, sturdy, tough
2 being clean and in good order ⟨a pretty, *crisp* bedspread for the guest room⟩ — see NEAT 1
3 marked by the use of few words to convey much information or meaning ⟨a *crisp* suggestion about what they could do with their boom box⟩ — see CONCISE

crisply *adv* in a few words ⟨the teacher *crisply* commanded the rubbernecking students to direct their attention forward⟩ — see SHORTLY 1

crispness *n* the quality or state of being marked by or using only few words to convey much meaning ⟨the *crispness* of the writing is such that this writer says more in nine paragraphs than some others say in nine pages⟩ — see SUCCINCTNESS

crispy *adj* having a texture that readily breaks into little pieces under pressure ⟨the *crispy* potato chips snapped satisfyingly in my mouth⟩ — see CRISP 1

criterion *n* **1** something set up as an example against which others of the same type are compared ⟨one *criterion* for grading these essays will be their conformity to the rules of traditional grammar⟩ — see STANDARD 1
2 something that sets apart an individual from others of the same kind ⟨an exceptionally high degree of physical risk is the preeminent *criterion* of an extreme sport⟩ — see CHARACTERISTIC

critic *n* **1** a person given to harsh judgments and to finding faults ⟨the president's hard-core *critics* are going to attack him no matter what he does⟩
synonyms carper, castigator, caviler (*or* caviller), censurer, criticizer, disparager, faultfinder, hypercritic, knocker, niggler, nitpicker
related words condemner (*or* condemnor), denouncer; belittler, decrier, denigrator, derider, detractor; assailant, attacker, crucifier; criticaster, hairsplitter, pettifogger, quibbler; admonisher, haranguer, railer, ranter, rebuker, reproacher, reprover, scold, upbraider; bellyacher, complainer, crybaby, fusser, griper, grouch, grouser, grumbler, whiner
near antonyms commender, praiser
2 a person who makes or expresses a judgment on the quality of offerings in some field of endeavor ⟨the restaurant *critic* said that the fries at that fast-food outlet were the worst she'd ever eaten⟩
synonyms pundit, reviewer
related words analyst, annotator, columnist, commentator, observer; appraiser, evaluator, judge, referee

critical *adj* **1** given to making or expressing unfavorable judgments about things ⟨adults tend to be *critical* of teenagers' taste in music and movies⟩
synonyms captious, carping, caviling (*or* cavilling), faultfinding, hypercritical, judgmental, overcritical, rejective
related words discerning, discriminating, judicious; demanding, exacting, fastidious, finical, finicky, fussy, nitpicky, particular, picky; pettifogging, quibbling; harsh, merciless, uncharitable, unforgiving
near antonyms undiscriminating; undemanding, unfussy; charitable, forgiving
antonyms uncritical
2 needing immediate attention ⟨this problem isn't *critical*, so we can go home now and tend to it in the morning⟩ — see ACUTE 2
3 of the greatest possible importance ⟨this is the *critical* exam that will largely determine your college career⟩ — see CRUCIAL
4 impossible to do without ⟨*critical* information for an informed medical diagnosis⟩ — see ESSENTIAL 1

criticism *n* an essay evaluating or analyzing something ⟨every *criticism* of the movie has noted that there are major holes in its plot⟩
synonyms critique, examen, notice, review
related words column, commentary, editorial, punditry; appraisal, assessment, evaluation; analysis, examination, opinion, outline, study, survey

criticize *vb* to express one's unfavorable opinion of the worth or quality of ⟨people who *criticize* every single idea that the principal has for improving the school⟩
synonyms blame, censure, condemn, denounce, dis (*also* diss) [*slang*], dispraise, fault, knock, pan, reprehend, slag [*chiefly British*]
related words skewer, tweak; assail, attack, blast, clobber, slam, slash; nick (at), snipe (at); beef, bellyache, bitch, carp, cavil, complain, crab, croak, fuss, gripe, grouse, growl, grumble, kick, kvetch, moan, murmur, mutter, niggle, quibble, whine; admonish, chide, drub, rebuke, reprimand, reproach, reprove; berate, castigate, crucify, excoriate, flay, gibbet, hammer, keelhaul, lambaste (*or* lambast), lash, pillory, scold, upbraid; badmouth, belittle, decry, deride, discommend, disparage, put down
phrases come down hard (on), find fault (with), take to task
near antonyms approve, commend, endorse (*also* indorse), recommend, sanction
antonyms extol (*also* extoll), laud, praise

criticizer *n* a person given to harsh judgments and to

finding faults ⟨those perennial *criticizers* of the local school board⟩ — see CRITIC 1

critique *n* an essay evaluating or analyzing something ⟨in a *critique* of the retrospective, the reviewer faulted it for not including more of the painter's mature works⟩ — see CRITICISM

critter *n* one of the lower animals as distinguished from human beings ⟨she's so fond of every kind of *critter* that she ought to be a veterinarian⟩ — see ANIMAL

croak *vb* **1** to express dissatisfaction, pain, or resentment usually tiresomely ⟨the cranky patient was always *croaking* to the nurses about something⟩ — see COMPLAIN

2 *slang* to stop living ⟨I wouldn't go around saying your great-grandmother "*croaked*"⟩ — see DIE 1

3 *slang* to deprive of life ⟨"I *croaked* the old bugger," he bragged⟩ — see KILL 1

4 *slang* to put to death deliberately ⟨hooligans had *croaked* the street corner wino just for the hell of it⟩ — see MURDER 1

croaker *n* **1** an irritable and complaining person ⟨she becomes a real *croaker* when she's overtired⟩ — see GROUCH 1

2 *slang* a person specially trained in healing human medical disorders ⟨ever more ornery as he grew older, he swore that he didn't need some *croaker* telling him that smoking was bad for his health⟩ — see DOCTOR

croaking *adj* harsh and dry in sound ⟨a *croaking* voice from smoking too many cigarettes⟩ — see HOARSE

croaky *adj* harsh and dry in sound ⟨a week of constant coughing left her with a *croaky* voice⟩ — see HOARSE

crock *n* language, behavior, or ideas that are absurd and contrary to good sense ⟨that whole thing about how surprised she was to win the award was a *crock*⟩ — see NONSENSE 1

crocked *adj* being under the influence of alcohol ⟨she found that after only three drinks she would be completely *crocked*⟩ — see DRUNK

crockery *n* articles made of baked clay ⟨a display of beautifully hand-painted *crockery* on the kitchen countertop⟩

synonyms earthenware, pottery, stoneware

related words ceramics; china, ironstone china, porcelain, redware

Croesus *n* a wealthy person ⟨if you have to ask the price, you're not the *Croesus* for whom this palatial yacht is intended⟩ — see CAPITALIST

crone *n* a mean or ugly old woman ⟨a run-down house that was inhabited by a cantankerous *crone* who kept to herself⟩

synonyms beldam (*or* beldame), carline (*or* carlin) [*chiefly Scottish*], hag, hellcat, trot, witch

related words harpy, shrew, virago

crony *n* **1** a person frequently seen in the company of another ⟨the criminal's *cronies* were also closely questioned about the illegal gambling operation⟩ — see ASSOCIATE 1

2 a person who has a strong liking for and trust in another ⟨only my *cronies* can call me by my nickname⟩ — see FRIEND 1

crook *n* **1** a person who has committed a crime ⟨a guy at the bar was raving about how all politicians are basically *crooks*⟩ — see CRIMINAL

2 something that curves or is curved ⟨carried the baby in the *crook* of her arm⟩ — see BEND 1

crook *vb* **1** to cause to turn away from a straight line ⟨*crooked* a finger⟩ — see BEND 1

2 to turn away from a straight line or course ⟨the road suddenly *crooked* to the left⟩ — see CURVE 1

crooked *adj* **1** marked by a long series of irregular curves ⟨a long, *crooked* line of people had formed in front of the ticket booth⟩

synonyms bending, crazy, curled, curling, curved, curving, curvy, devious, serpentine, sinuous, tortuous, twisted, twisting, winding, windy

related words zigzag, zigzagging; circling, coiled, coiling, corkscrew, looping, spiral, spiraling (*or* spiralling), swirling; circuitous, indirect, roundabout; meandering, rambling, wandering; irregular, jagged, uneven

near antonyms direct, linear

antonyms straight, straightaway

2 given to or marked by cheating and deception ⟨the common belief that gambling casinos are often *crooked* businesses⟩ — see DISHONEST 2

3 inclined or twisted to one side ⟨the photo on that wall is *crooked*⟩ — see AWRY

4 marked by, based on, or done by the use of dishonest methods to acquire something of value ⟨a *crooked* scheme to bill the government for medical services never performed⟩ — see FRAUDULENT 1

crookedness *n* the inclination or practice of misleading others through lies or trickery ⟨for sheer *crookedness* it would be hard to beat the used-car dealer who sold me that lemon⟩ — see DECEIT 1

crookery *n* the inclination or practice of misleading others through lies or trickery ⟨the dealer encouraged his sales reps to engage in *crookery* of all sorts, so long as it sold cars⟩ — see DECEIT 1

crop *n* **1** the quantity of an animal or vegetable product gathered at the end of a season ⟨the wheat *crop* is going to be exceptionally large this year⟩

synonyms harvest

related words return, yield; cut, cutting

2 a usually small number of persons considered as a unit ⟨the school's latest *crop* of graduates is its most academically gifted so far⟩ — see GROUP 2

crop *vb* **1** to look after or assist the growth of by labor and care ⟨a family that's been *cropping* potatoes on that piece of land for generations⟩ — see GROW 1

2 to make (something) shorter or smaller with the use of a cutting instrument ⟨grass *cropped* short by repeated grazing⟩ ⟨*cropped* the painting to fit the frame⟩ — see CLIP 1

crop (up) *vb* to come to one's attention especially gradually or unexpectedly ⟨a new issue has just *cropped up* in the campaign⟩ — see ARISE 2

cropper *n* a falling short of one's goals ⟨more than a few people were glad to see the obnoxiously smug skater come a *cropper* at the national championships⟩ — see FAILURE 2

croquette *n* a small usually rounded mass of minced food that has been fried ⟨a fish *croquette* that tasted more of filler than of fish⟩ — see CAKE 1

cross *adj* **1** being offspring produced by parents of different races, breeds, species, or genera ⟨raises both purebred and *cross* lambs⟩ — see MIXED 1

2 easily irritated or annoyed ⟨she was *cross* all day because of a nagging headache⟩ — see IRRITABLE

cross *n* **1** a test of faith, patience, or strength ⟨dyslexia is just my *cross* to bear, and I accepted it long ago⟩ — see TRIAL 1

2 an offspring of parents with different genes especially when of different races, breeds, species, or genera ⟨the mare is an Arabian-Thoroughbred *cross*⟩ — see HYBRID

cross *vb* **1** to be unfaithful or disloyal to ⟨people who *cross* the local mob boss usually are found floating in the river⟩ — see BETRAY 1

2 to divide by passing through or across ⟨there's a light where that street *crosses* Main Street⟩ — see INTERSECT

3 to make one's way through, across, or over ⟨you may have to *cross* some woods on the way⟩ — see TRAVERSE

4 to enter the mind of ⟨the idea did *cross* me that he might be pulling my leg⟩ — see OCCUR (TO)

cross (out) *vb* to show (something written) to be no longer valid by drawing a cross over or a line through it ⟨*cross out* the old phone number and write in the new one⟩ — see X (OUT)

cross (up) *vb* to reduce the soundness, effectiveness, or perfection of ⟨your refusal to cooperate will *cross up* the whole investigation⟩ — see DAMAGE 1

crossbred *adj* being offspring produced by parents of different races, breeds, species, or genera ⟨a beautiful *crossbred* dog who had the pleading eyes of a beagle and the body of a greyhound⟩ — see MIXED 1

crossbred *n* an offspring of parents with different genes especially when of different races, breeds, species, or genera ⟨a puppy that was clearly a *crossbred* of a beagle and a dachshund⟩ — see HYBRID

crossbreed *n* an offspring of parents with different genes especially when of different races, breeds, species, or genera ⟨a Siamese *crossbreed* who was atypically black, but had the build and voice of a Siamese⟩ — see HYBRID

cross fire *n* an often noisy or angry expression of differing opinions ⟨viewers tune in to witness the weekly *cross fire* between the liberal and conservative commentators⟩ — see ARGUMENT 1

crossing *n* **1** a journey over water in a vessel ⟨an uneventful *crossing* from the United States to Britain⟩ — see SAIL

2 a place where roads meet ⟨turn left at the next *crossing* and then stay on that road for two miles⟩ — see CROSSROAD 1

crossness *n* readiness to show annoyance or impatience ⟨a librarian who had a reputation for chronic *crossness*⟩ — see PETULANCE

crosspatch *n* an irritable and complaining person ⟨that sweet little girl turns into a real *crosspatch* when she's hungry⟩ — see GROUCH 1

crossroad *n* **1** *usually* **crossroads** *pl* a place where roads meet ⟨the fast-food chain has a restaurant at practically every *crossroads*⟩
synonyms carrefour, corner, crossing, crossway(s), intersection, junction
related words cloverleaf, interchange, overpass, underpass; circle, rotary, roundabout [*British*], traffic circle

2 *usually* **crossroads** *pl* a time or state of affairs requiring prompt or decisive action ⟨we've come to a *crossroads*, and we have to make a decision⟩ — see EMERGENCY

cross section *n* a number of things selected from a group to stand for the whole ⟨a television ratings service that monitors the viewing of a representative *cross section* of the general population⟩ — see SAMPLE 1

crossway *n, often* **crossways** *pl* a place where roads meet ⟨carolers assembling at the village *crossways* on Christmas Eve⟩ — see CROSSROAD 1

crossways *adv* in a line or direction running from corner to corner ⟨the van had been deliberately parked *crossways* so as to take up both parking spaces⟩ — see CROSSWISE

crosswise *adv* in a line or direction running from corner to corner ⟨first cut the sandwiches *crosswise* and then trim the crusts⟩
synonyms athwart, bias, cornerways, cornerwise, crossways, diagonally, kitty-corner (*also* catty-corner *or* catercorner *or* kitty-cornered *or* catty-cornered *or* catercornered), obliquely, transversely
related words across
phrases on the bias, on the diagonal
near antonyms lengthwise, longitudinally

crotchet *n* an odd or peculiar habit ⟨her one *crotchet* is a fondness for eating cookies while soaking in the tub⟩ — see IDIOSYNCRASY

crotchetiness *n* readiness to show annoyance or impatience ⟨the understandable *crotchetiness* of an overworked teacher⟩ — see PETULANCE

crotchety *adj* easily irritated or annoyed ⟨I get *crotchety* after a long day at work⟩ — see IRRITABLE

crouch *vb* to lie low with the limbs close to the body ⟨the cat *crouched* in the bushes, waiting for the right moment to pounce on the chipmunk⟩
synonyms couch, huddle, hunch, hunker (down), scrunch, squat, squinch
related words curl up

crow *vb* **1** to feel or express joy or triumph ⟨being the home of the new Super Bowl champs was the first thing that city residents had to *crow* about in a very long time⟩ — see EXULT

2 to praise or express pride in one's own possessions, qualities, or accomplishments often to excess ⟨the in-your-face *crowing* by some of the winning athletes at the Olympics was embarrassing⟩ — see BOAST 1

crowd *n* **1** a great number of persons or creatures massed together ⟨a huge *crowd* of fans was on hand to greet the returning World Series champions⟩
synonyms army, bike [*chiefly Scottish*], cram, crush, drove, flock, herd, horde, host, legion, mass, mob, multitude, press, rout, scrum, swarm, throng
related words masses, millions, rabble, rabblement, riffraff; gaggle; heap, mountain, pile; jam, logjam

2 a group of people sharing a common interest and relating together socially ⟨the fashionable *crowd* at the polo tournament⟩ — see GANG 2

3 the body of the community as contrasted with the elite ⟨no national leader was ever more hated by the *crowd*⟩ — see MASS 1

crowd *vb* **1** to fit (people or things) into a tight space ⟨*crowded* all the boats into the harbor before the storm struck⟩
synonyms cram, crush, jam, ram, sandwich, shoehorn, squeeze, stuff, wedge
related words fill, heap, jam-pack, load, pack

2 to move upon or fill (something) in great numbers ⟨cars *crowded* the roads over the long holiday weekend⟩
synonyms flock, mob, swarm, throng
related words beset, infest, invade, overrun; clog, dam, jam, obstruct, plug (up)

3 to gather into a closely packed group ⟨everyone *crowded* around to see the baby being shown off by his proud parents⟩ — see [2]PRESS 3

crowded *adj* **1** containing or seeming to contain the greatest quantity or number possible ⟨we kept circling around the *crowded* parking lot at the mall⟩ — see FULL 1

2 having little space between items or parts ⟨a *crowded* design that made the bedroom wallpaper a little overwhelming⟩ — see CLOSE 1

crowd–pleasing *adj* enjoying widespread favor or approval ⟨an actor who rarely ventures far afield from *crowd-pleasing* comedies and actioners⟩ — see POPULAR 1

crowing *adj* having or expressing feelings of joy or triumph ⟨in a *crowing* speech, the mayor thanked all who had helped get her reelected⟩ — see EXULTANT

crown *n* **1** a decorative band or wreath worn about the head as a symbol of victory or honor ⟨the *crown* of laurel leaves that is traditionally placed on the winner of the marathon⟩
synonyms chaplet, coronal (*also* coronel), coronet, diadem
related words anadem [*archaic*], tiara; garland, laurel

2 the position occupied by the one who comes in first in a competition ⟨his lifelong dream of someday winning the heavyweight boxing *crown*⟩
synonyms championship, title

3 the highest part or point ⟨covered in mud from the soles of his feet to the *crown* of his head⟩ — see HEIGHT 1

crown *vb* to bring to a triumphant conclusion ⟨the Olympic Games were *crowned* by spectacular closing ceremonies⟩
synonyms cap (off), climax, culminate
related words complete, conclude, finish, round (off *or* out), terminate, wrap up

crown jewel *n* an asset that brings praise or renown ⟨the city's *crown jewel* is an emerald necklace of lushly landscaped parks⟩ — see GLORY 2

crucial *adj* of the greatest possible importance ⟨water is *crucial* to our survival⟩
synonyms critical, key, pivotal, vital
related words decisive, life-and-death (*also* life-or-death), weighty; basic, elementary, fundamental; essential, indispensable, necessary, requisite; pressing, urgent
near antonyms inconsequential, insignificant, minor, trivial, unimportant

crucible *n* a test of faith, patience, or strength ⟨soldiers who had withstood the *crucible* of war⟩ — see TRIAL 1

crud *n* **1** foul matter that mars the purity or cleanliness of something ⟨you must have stepped in something, because there's *crud* all over your shoe⟩ — see FILTH 1
2 *slang* a person whose behavior is offensive to others ⟨I don't care how hip that clothing store is, their employees behave like absolute *cruds*⟩ — see JERK 1

cruddy *adj* **1** arousing or deserving of one's loathing and disgust ⟨her *cruddy* treatment of her now-destitute parents, who had put her through medical school⟩ — see CONTEMPTIBLE 1
2 not clean ⟨the refrigerator's *cruddy* shelves were a sign that the interior had never been cleaned⟩ — see DIRTY 1

crude *adj* **1** being such as found in nature and not altered by processing or refining ⟨a sizable spill of *crude* oil along a coastline is the worst kind of environmental disaster⟩
synonyms native, natural, raw, rude, undressed, unprocessed, unrefined, untreated
related words undeveloped; rough-hewn, semifinished, unfinished, unpolished; uncooked; impure, unfiltered
phrases in the raw, in the rough
near antonyms filtered, pure, purified
antonyms dressed, processed, refined, treated
2 belonging to or characteristic of an early level of skill or development ⟨the *crude* stone tools that those prehistoric peoples used⟩ — see PRIMITIVE 1
3 depicting or referring to sexual matters in a way that is unacceptable in polite society ⟨*crude* jokes can be considered sexual harassment⟩ — see OBSCENE 1
4 lacking in refinement or good taste ⟨any discussion of one's money is considered *crude* by the club's blue-blooded members⟩ — see COARSE 2
5 hastily or roughly constructed ⟨a *crude* hut that was constructed by some shipwrecked sailors⟩ — see RUDE 1

crudeness *n* **1** the quality or state of being obscene ⟨the blatant *crudeness* of the remark first made him blush and then made him angry⟩ — see OBSCENITY 1
2 the quality or state of lacking refinement or good taste ⟨the lowbrow *crudeness* of the commentary at the fashion show horrified her⟩ — see VULGARITY 1

crudity *n* **1** the quality or state of being obscene ⟨shocked by the *crudity* of the youngster's language⟩ — see OBSCENITY 1
2 the quality or state of lacking refinement or good taste ⟨appalled by the *crudity* of the way her nephews referred to women⟩ — see VULGARITY 1

cruel *adj* **1** having or showing the desire to inflict severe pain and suffering on others ⟨a *cruel* dictator who tortured anyone who dared to speak out against him⟩ ⟨*cruel* and unusual punishments are forbidden by the U.S. Constitution⟩
synonyms atrocious, barbaric, barbarous, brutal, brute, butcherly, fiendish, heartless, inhuman, inhumane, sadistic, savage, truculent, vicious, wanton
related words hard-hearted, ironhearted, merciless, pitiless, ruthless, stonyhearted, unfeeling; fell, ferocious, grim; bloodthirsty, cutthroat, murderous, sanguinary, sanguine; catty, despiteful, hateful, malevolent, malicious, malign, malignant, mean, nasty, spiteful, vindictive; draconian, draconic, hardhanded, harsh, heavy-handed, oppressive
phrases red in tooth and claw
near antonyms tender, warm, warmhearted; charitable, clement, lenient, merciful, pitying; pacific, peaceable, peaceful
antonyms benign, benignant, compassionate, goodhearted, humane, kind, kindhearted, sympathetic, tenderhearted
2 difficult to endure ⟨the *cruel* climate of the Arctic⟩ — see HARSH 1
3 hard to accept or bear especially emotionally ⟨the *cruel* situation of being orphaned at an early age⟩ — see BITTER 2
4 having or showing a desire to cause someone pain or suffering for the sheer enjoyment of it ⟨the bully was fond of making *cruel* little jabs at his victim's sore points⟩ — see HATEFUL

cruelness *n* disposition to willfully inflict pain and suffering on others ⟨far from being healers, the doctors in the Nazi death camps were notable for their senseless *cruelness*⟩ — see CRUELTY

cruelty *n* disposition to willfully inflict pain and suffering on others ⟨centuries after he ravaged Europe, Attila the Hun remains notorious for his *cruelty*⟩
synonyms atrociousness, atrocity, barbarity, barbarousness, brutality, cruelness, fiendishness, heartlessness, inhumanity, inhumanness, sadism, savageness, savagery, truculence, viciousness, wantonness
related words hard-heartedness, mercilessness, pitilessness, ruthlessness, unfeelingness; fellness, ferociousness, ferocity, fierceness, grimness; bloodlust, bloodthirstiness, murderousness, sanguineness, sanguinity; cattiness, despitefulness, hatefulness, malevolence, maliciousness, malignity, meanness, nastiness, spitefulness; hardhandedness, harshness, heavy-handedness, oppressiveness
near antonyms tenderness, warmheartedness, warmness, warmth; charitableness, clemency, leniency, mercifulness, mercy, pity
antonyms benignity, compassion, good-heartedness, humaneness, humanity, kindheartedness, kindness, sympathy, tenderheartedness

cruise *n* a journey over water in a vessel ⟨took a luxury *cruise* for their first wedding anniversary⟩ — see SAIL

cruise *vb* **1** to move about from place to place aimlessly ⟨the girls happily *cruised* around the mall for hours⟩ — see WANDER 1
2 to move or proceed smoothly and readily ⟨she's been *cruising* through her daily physical therapy with remarkable ease⟩ — see FLOW 2
3 to travel on water in a vessel ⟨*cruised* to the Bahamas in their yacht⟩ — see SAIL 1

crumb *n* **1** a very small amount ⟨a neglected dog who is desperate for any *crumb* of affection he might get from strangers⟩ — see PARTICLE 1
2 a very small piece ⟨eating pretzels in bed got *crumbs* between the sheets⟩ — see BIT 1
3 *slang* a person whose behavior is offensive to others ⟨if I ever start behaving as obnoxiously as those *crumbs*,

be sure to give me a good slap on the kisser⟩ — see JERK 1

crumble *vb* to become worse or of less value ⟨the stock of the energy company *crumbled* after the revelations of fraud and mismanagement⟩ — see DETERIORATE 1

crumbly *adj* having a texture that readily breaks into little pieces under pressure ⟨a *crumbly* shortbread cookie⟩ — see CRISP 1

crummy *also* **crumby** *adj* falling short of a standard ⟨the dry cleaners did a *crummy* job of pressing my suit⟩ — see BAD 1

crump *vb* to break open or into pieces usually because of internal pressure ⟨one aerial bomb failed to *crump* as it landed⟩ — see EXPLODE 1

crumple *vb* **1** to create (as by crushing) an irregular mass of creases in ⟨*crumpled* the piece of paper and angrily threw it in the wastebasket⟩
synonyms crinkle, rumple, scrunch, wrinkle
related words corrugate, crease, crimp, fold, pleat, pucker, ruck; crisp, ripple, ruffle; contract, furrow, knit; mess (up), muss (up)
near antonyms even, iron, press, straighten; unfold; neaten, tidy
antonyms flatten, iron out, smooth, smoothen, uncrumple
2 to fall down or in as a result of physical pressure ⟨the box *crumpled* when I accidentally dropped a brick on it⟩ — see COLLAPSE 1

crunch *n* **1** a falling short of an essential or desirable amount or number ⟨a severe energy *crunch* that resulted in long lines at the gas pumps⟩ — see DEFICIENCY
2 a time or state of affairs requiring prompt or decisive action ⟨a player who's always good in a *crunch*, like when we need a goal to win the soccer match⟩ — see EMERGENCY

crunch *vb* to press or strike against or together so as to make a scraping sound ⟨I could hear the bicycle gears *crunch* as I shifted the derailleur⟩ — see GRIND 2

crunch (on) *vb* to crush or grind with the teeth ⟨people who *crunch on* hard candies during movies really annoy me⟩ — see BITE (ON)

crunch time *n* a time or state of affairs requiring prompt or decisive action ⟨with only three minutes left in the game, it was definitely *crunch time*⟩ — see EMERGENCY

crusade *n* a series of activities undertaken to achieve a goal ⟨a grassroots *crusade* for spending more money on our public schools⟩ — see CAMPAIGN

crusader *n* one who is intensely or excessively devoted to a cause ⟨a *crusader* for improved safety in coal mines⟩ — see ZEALOT

crush *n* **1** a strong but often short-lived liking for another person ⟨fondly remembers the *crush* that she had on a boy one summer long ago⟩
synonyms infatuation, mash, passion
related words fixation, obsession; affection, devotion, fondness, love; craze, fad, rage, vogue
2 a great number of persons or creatures massed together ⟨the huge *crush* in the store must have far exceeded safety limits⟩ — see CROWD 1

crush *vb* **1** to cause to become a pulpy mass ⟨dark-colored grapes that will be *crushed* to make red wine⟩
synonyms mash, pulp, squash
related words press, squeeze; beat, pound, powder, pulverize
2 to put a stop to (something) by the use of force ⟨the government is doing everything to *crush* the latest guerrilla uprising⟩ — see QUELL 1
3 to reduce to fine particles ⟨*crushed* the baby's medicine tablet and mixed it with applesauce⟩ — see POWDER
4 to subject to incapacitating emotional or mental stress ⟨the terrible news of her death simply *crushed* the entire family⟩ — see OVERWHELM 1
5 to apply external pressure on so as to force out the juice or contents of ⟨after *crushing* the grapes, let the skins soak in the juice in order to extract some color⟩ — see [2]PRESS 2
6 to fit (people or things) into a tight space ⟨the desperate refugees were *crushed* into the back of the truck⟩ — see CROWD 1
7 to put one's arms around and press tightly ⟨she tearfully *crushed* the child to her breast⟩ — see EMBRACE 1

crushed *adj* suffering grave abuse or injustice at the hands of one in authority ⟨a tyrant seemingly untroubled by the *crushed* masses that he left in his wake⟩ — see DOWNTRODDEN

crusher *n* something (as a fact or argument) that is decisive or overwhelming ⟨the *crusher* was that we would be out of town that weekend in any event⟩ — see CLINCHER

crust *n* shameless boldness ⟨the grandchildren had the *crust* to ask for more money after wasting the first handout⟩ — see EFFRONTERY

crust *vb* to cover with a hardened layer ⟨pipes *crusted* with mineral deposits⟩ — see ENCRUST

crusty *adj* being or characterized by direct, brief, and potentially rude speech or manner ⟨a *crusty* old fisherman who doesn't care to have his picture taken with silly tourists⟩ — see BLUNT 1

crux *n* the central part or aspect of something under consideration ⟨the *crux* of the problem is that the school's current budget is totally inadequate⟩
synonyms bottom line, bull's-eye, centerpiece, core, essence, gist, heart, kernel, keynote, meat, meat and potatoes, net, nub, nubbin, nucleus, pith, pivot, point, root, sum
related words course, direction, drift, tenor; body, content, substance; hypothesis, proposition, purport, subject, theme, thesis
phrases sum and substance, the long and short (*or* the long and the short)

cry *n* **1** a loud vocal expression of strong emotion ⟨a *cry* of despair arose when the smoke of the bomb blast cleared⟩ — see SHOUT
2 a natural vocal sound made by an animal ⟨the lonesome *cry* of a coyote⟩ — see CALL 1
3 an attention-getting word or phrase used to publicize something (as a campaign or product) ⟨"A chance to change America" was the *cry* on which the candidate was hoping to win the White House⟩ — see SLOGAN
4 an earnest request ⟨the king was deaf to their *cries*⟩ — see PLEA 1
5 a sudden short emotional utterance ⟨*cries* of disbelief greeted the announcement of the surprise winner for best picture⟩ — see EXCLAMATION

cry *vb* **1** to shed tears often while making meaningless sounds as a sign of pain or distress ⟨some kids started to *cry* even before the doctor had given them their shot⟩
synonyms bawl, blub [*chiefly British*], blubber, sob, weep
related words greet [*Scottish*], grieve, keen, lament, mourn; howl, scream, squall, wail, yowl; bleat, mewl, pule, whimper, whine; sniffle, snivel; groan, moan, sigh
2 to utter one's distinctive animal sound ⟨we knew that we were getting very close to the ocean when we could hear sea gulls *crying*⟩
synonyms call, sing
3 to speak so as to be heard at a distance ⟨a mother *crying* for help⟩ — see CALL 1

cry (out) *vb* to utter with a sudden burst of strong feeling ⟨"I can't stand it!" he *cried out*⟩ — see EXCLAIM

crybaby *n* a person who makes frequent complaints

usually about little things ⟨car trips that were often spoiled by a couple of *crybabies* in the back seat⟩
synonyms baby, bellyacher, complainer, fussbudget, fusser, fusspot, griper, grumbler, kvetch, kvetcher, sniveler, whiner
related words bawler, bleater, moaner, screamer, squawker, wailer, weeper; crab, grump, malcontent
near antonyms happy camper

cry down *vb* to express scornfully one's low opinion of ⟨she *cried down* any party to which she wasn't invited⟩ — see DECRY 1

crying *adj* needing immediate attention ⟨a *crying* need for more activities for young people in this town⟩ — see ACUTE 2

cry off *vb* to put an end to (something planned or previously agreed to) ⟨their film deal had been abruptly *cried off*, and now the filmmakers were back to square one⟩ — see CANCEL 1

crypt *n* an underground burial chamber ⟨the old church's *crypt* is the final resting place for the president and his beloved wife⟩
synonyms catacomb(s), vault
related words mausoleum, sepulchre (*or* sepulcher), sepulture, tomb

cryptic *adj* **1** being beyond one's powers to know, understand, or explain ⟨puzzled by the *cryptic* e-mail message left on his computer⟩ — see MYSTERIOUS 1
2 having an often intentionally veiled or uncertain meaning ⟨the oracle offered only *cryptic* predictions that could be interpreted any number of different ways⟩ — see OBSCURE 1

crystal *adj* easily seen through ⟨an unspoiled region with majestic mountains and *crystal* streams⟩ — see CLEAR 1

crystal clear *adj* **1** easily seen through ⟨drank thirstily of the *crystal-clear* water from the spring⟩ — see CLEAR 1
2 not subject to misinterpretation or more than one interpretation ⟨what could be more *crystal-clear* than an emphatic "No!"⟩ — see CLEAR 2

crystalline *adj* easily seen through ⟨we could see fish swimming beneath the *crystalline* ice of the frozen lake⟩ — see CLEAR 1

crystallize *also* **crystalize** *vb* to take on a definite form ⟨after months of planning, the project is finally starting to *crystallize*⟩ — see FORM 1

cry up *vb* to praise or publicize lavishly and often excessively ⟨in exchange for his hefty endorsement fee, the basketball player is expected to *cry up* that brand of sneaker at every opportunity⟩ — see TOUT 1

cub *n* **1** a person who is just starting out in a field of activity ⟨the kind of big story that can propel a *cub* reporter into the stratosphere of the newspaper world⟩ — see BEGINNER
2 a young person who is between infancy and adulthood ⟨assigned to teach a bunch of young *cubs* how to play baseball⟩ — see CHILD 1

cubage *n* the largest number or amount that something can hold ⟨pipes with a *cubage* of over 1,000 cubic meters⟩ — see CAPACITY 1

Cuban sandwich *n* a large sandwich on a long split roll ⟨my favorite place to get a *Cuban sandwich* is in Chicago⟩ — see SUBMARINE

cube *n* one of the parts into which an enclosed space is divided ⟨even though they worked in adjoining *cubes*, the two coworkers rarely acknowledged one another's existence⟩ — see COMPARTMENT

cubicle *n* one of the parts into which an enclosed space is divided ⟨data entry clerks busily typing in *cubicles*⟩ — see COMPARTMENT

cuckoo *adj* **1** having or showing a very abnormal or sick state of mind ⟨a *cuckoo* woman who wandered around town carefully gathering up useless trash⟩ — see INSANE 1
2 showing or marked by a lack of good sense or judgment ⟨offered a completely *cuckoo* suggestion for using the defunct strip mall⟩ — see FOOLISH 1

cuckoo *n* **1** a person who lacks good sense or judgment ⟨one *cuckoo* at the campground tried to boil soup in a plastic cup⟩ — see FOOL 1
2 a silly flighty person ⟨didn't want to be among those *cuckoos* who race around the mall the day before Christmas⟩ — see FLIBBERTIGIBBET

cuddle *vb* to lie close ⟨kittens *cuddling* in a basket⟩ — see NUZZLE

[1]**cuddy** *n* a built-in space for storage behind a door ⟨kept his stash of liquor in a small *cuddy* by the dining room⟩ — see CLOSET 1

[2]**cuddy** *or* **cuddie** *n, British dialect* a stupid person ⟨the pub seemed to be the favorite haunt of every *cuddy* in the village⟩ — see IDIOT

cudgel *n* a heavy rigid stick used as a weapon or for punishment ⟨a farmer armed with a *cudgel* drove us off his land⟩ — see CLUB 1

[1]**cue** *n* a slight or indirect pointing to something (as a solution or explanation) ⟨taking a *cue* from nature, scientists are developing safe and effective insecticides using insect hormones⟩ — see HINT 1

[2]**cue** *n* a series of persons or things arranged one behind another ⟨the *cue* to get tickets to the concert moved with agonizing slowness⟩ — see LINE 1

[1]**cuff** *n* a hard strike with a part of the body or an instrument ⟨the mama cat would give her kittens a *cuff* with a paw whenever they played too rough⟩ — see [1]BLOW

[2]**cuff** *n, usually* **cuffs** *pl* something that physically prevents free movement ⟨the policeman snapped the *cuffs* on and led the prisoner away to the car⟩ — see BOND 1

cuisine *n* the art or style of preparing food (as in a specified region) ⟨spent several years in Tuscany mastering Italian *cuisine*⟩ — see COOKERY

culinarian *n* a person who prepares food by some manner of heating ⟨a celebrated *culinarian* who started his own cooking school⟩ — see COOK

cull *n* something separated from a group or lot for not being as good as the others ⟨the unbruised apples will be packed in bags, and the *culls* will be used for cider⟩
synonyms discard, reject, rejection, second
related words castaway, throwaway; hand-me-down, white elephant; rubbish, scrap, trash, waste

cull *vb* to decide to accept (someone or something) from a group of possibilities ⟨*culled* the best short stories from the author's body of writings⟩ — see CHOOSE 1

culminate *vb* to bring to a triumphant conclusion ⟨*culminated* the school year with a trip to New York⟩ — see CROWN

culmination *n* the highest part or point ⟨an acting performance that was seen as the *culmination* of a brilliant career on the stage⟩ — see HEIGHT 1

culpability *n* responsibility for wrongdoing or failure ⟨cannot find *culpability* where there is neither knowledge that a crime has been committed nor evidence of intent to commit a crime⟩ — see BLAME 1

culpable *adj* deserving reproach or blame ⟨are you any less *culpable* for murder if you acted in the heat of passion?⟩ — see BLAMEWORTHY

culprit *n* a person who has committed a crime ⟨the police caught the *culprit* a mere two blocks from the scene of the crime⟩ — see CRIMINAL

cult *n* **1** a group of people showing intense devotion to a cause, person, or work (as a film) ⟨long after it had gone off the air, the TV series continued to have a huge *cult*⟩
synonyms audience, followership, following
related words discipleship; fandom

2 a body of beliefs and practices regarding the supernatural and the worship of one or more deities ⟨an ancient *cult* that centered on the worship of the earth as the source of all life⟩ — see RELIGION 1

cultivate *vb* **1** to come to have gradually ⟨*cultivated* a taste for opera in order to fit in with his new circle of friends⟩ — see DEVELOP 2
2 to help the growth or development of ⟨*cultivated* a passion for learning among his students over the years⟩ — see FOSTER 1
3 to look after or assist the growth of by labor and care ⟨in an attempt to produce New World counterparts of the wines that he had enjoyed in Europe, Jefferson *cultivated* several varieties of grapes at Monticello⟩ — see GROW 1
4 to work by plowing, sowing, and raising crops on ⟨we ought to *cultivate* the field out back⟩ — see FARM

cultivated *adj* having or showing a taste for the fine arts and gracious living ⟨the museum's annual gala for charity attracts not only a very wealthy, but also a very *cultivated* crowd⟩
synonyms accomplished, civilized, couth, cultured, genteel, polished, refined
related words cerebral, highbrow, highbrowed, high-toned, intellectual, intellectualist, intellectualistic; bourgeois, middlebrow; educated, erudite, knowledgeable, learned, literate, scholarly, well-read; civil, courteous, mannerly, polite, well-bred; cosmopolitan, sophisticated, urbane; hypercivilized, overcivilized, oversophisticated
near antonyms ignorant, illiterate, uneducated, unlettered; lowbrow, unintelligent; coarse, ill-bred, ill-mannered; backwoods, provincial, rustic (*also* rustical); inelegant, polyester, unsophisticated; boorish, churlish, cloddish, clownish, crude, uncouth, vulgar
antonyms barbaric, barbarous, philistine, uncivilized, uncultured, ungenteel, unpolished, unrefined

cultivation *n* a high level of taste and enlightenment as a result of extensive intellectual training and exposure to the arts ⟨people of *cultivation* appreciate the special experience that only live theater can provide⟩ — see CULTURE 1

cultivator *n* a person who cultivates the land and grows crops on it ⟨encountered an indigenous people who were experienced *cultivators* of the soil as well as highly skilled craftsmen⟩ — see FARMER

cultural *adj* of or relating to the fine arts ⟨with its many museums, theaters, and opera and ballet companies, the city is a *cultural* paradise⟩
synonyms artistic
related words aesthetic (*also* esthetic *or* aesthetical *or* esthetical), tasteful
near antonyms nonaesthetic
antonyms nonartistic, noncultural

culture *n* **1** a high level of taste and enlightenment as a result of extensive intellectual training and exposure to the arts ⟨because of its wide reputation as a place of *culture*, Boston became known as "the Athens of America"⟩
synonyms accomplishment, civilization, couth, cultivation, polish, refinement
related words education, erudition, intellectualism, intellectuality, knowledge, learning, literacy, scholarship; cosmopolitanism, sophistication, urbanity; breeding, genteelness, gentility, manners; class, elegance, grace, taste; civility, courteousness, courtesy, politeness
near antonyms ignorance, illiteracy; parochialism, provincialism, rusticity, unsophistication; boorishness, churlishness, clownishness, coarseness, crudeness, vulgarity
antonyms barbarianism, barbarism, philistinism
2 the way people live at a particular time and place ⟨a study of ancient Anasazi *culture* as it existed in the canyons of the American Southwest⟩ — see CIVILIZATION 1

culture *vb* to look after or assist the growth of by labor and care ⟨*culture* bacteria in laboratory dishes⟩ — see GROW 1

cultured *adj* having or showing a taste for the fine arts and gracious living ⟨the most highly *cultured* period of the country's long history⟩ — see CULTIVATED

cumbersome *adj* difficult to use or operate especially because of size, weight, or design ⟨a long-handled wrench that is too *cumbersome* for tight spots, such as under the sink⟩
synonyms awkward, bunglesome, clumsy, clunky, cranky, cumbrous, ponderous, ungainly, unhandy, unwieldy
related words uncontrollable, unmanageable; bulky, dinosaurian, dinosauric, elephantine, heavy, hulking, massive; impracticable, impractical
near antonyms functional, practicable, practical, serviceable, useful
antonyms handy

cumbrous *adj* difficult to use or operate especially because of size, weight, or design ⟨it took two people to haul the *cumbrous* machine into the garage⟩ — see CUMBERSOME

cummerbund *also* **cumberbund** *n* a strip of flexible material (as leather) worn around the waist ⟨a *cummerbund* is the perfect accessory for a man's tuxedo⟩ — see ²BELT 1

cumshaw *n* **1** something given in addition to what is ordinarily expected or owed ⟨the clerk at Calcutta airport was clearly angling for a little *cumshaw* on the side⟩ — see BONUS
2 something given or promised in order to improperly influence a person's conduct or decision ⟨the captain slipped the customs official his customary *cumshaw* at the Port of Shanghai⟩ — see BRIBE

cumulation *n* a mass or quantity that has piled up or that has been gathered over a period of time ⟨the *cumulation* of grime on the stove was really disgusting⟩ — see ACCUMULATION 1

cumulative *adj* produced by a series of additions of identical or similar things ⟨a *cumulative* weight gain of 20 pounds over the course of a year⟩
synonyms accretive, accumulative, additive, conglomerative, incremental
related words gradual, step-by-step, stepwise; increscent, progressive; accruable, accrued, aggregated, amassed, built-up, compiled, conglomerated
near antonyms decremental, decrescent, degressive, regressive

cumulus *n* a mass or quantity that has piled up or that has been gathered over a period of time ⟨the *cumulus* of sundry things that fill up one's attic and somehow sum up a lifetime of experiences⟩ — see ACCUMULATION 1

cunning *adj* **1** clever at attaining one's ends by indirect and often deceptive means ⟨a *cunning*, underhanded plan to win the election by preying on people's fears and prejudices⟩ — see ARTFUL 1
2 skillful with the hands ⟨only the most *cunning* cabinetmaker could have crafted such a beautifully proportioned chest of drawers⟩ — see DEXTEROUS 1

cunning *n* **1** skill in achieving one's ends through indirect, subtle, or underhanded means ⟨the *cunning* with which Tom Sawyer was able to get others to whitewash the fence for him⟩
synonyms artfulness, artifice, caginess (*also* cageyness), canniness, craft, craftiness, cunningness, deviousness, foxiness, guile, guilefulness, slickness, slyness, sneakiness, subtleness, subtlety, wiliness
related words calculation, care, design; savvy, sharp-

ness, shrewdness; cleverness, ingeniousness, ingenuity, inventiveness; ease, facility, finesse; deceitfulness, duplicity, shiftiness, underhandedness

2 subtle or imaginative ability in inventing, devising, or executing something ⟨the unmatched *cunning* of the scout who led them safely through the trackless wilderness⟩ — see SKILL 1

3 the inclination or practice of misleading others through lies or trickery ⟨used *cunning* and subterfuge to work her way up the corporate ladder⟩ — see DECEIT 1

cunningness *n* **1** skill in achieving one's ends through indirect, subtle, or underhanded means ⟨it took a certain amount of *cunningness* on the photographer's part to obtain such revealing portraits of his rich and famous subjects⟩ — see CUNNING 1

2 the inclination or practice of misleading others through lies or trickery ⟨people should remember that it was *cunningness* and not kindness that made him a very wealthy lawyer⟩ — see DECEIT 1

cup *n* a round vessel equipped with a handle and designed for drinking ⟨a large *cup* that can hold almost a pint of hot chocolate⟩

synonyms mug

related words beaker, blackjack, stein, tankard; chalice, goblet; demitasse, noggin; teacup

cupboard *n* **1** a built-in space for storage behind a door ⟨the colonial dining room features a double-door corner *cupboard* for the family's finest china⟩ — see CLOSET 1

2 a storage case typically having doors and shelves ⟨dishes go in the *cupboard* next to the sink⟩ — see CABINET

cupidity *n* an intense selfish desire for wealth or possessions ⟨reports of great treasure in the Indies inflamed the *cupidity* of Columbus's crew⟩ — see GREED

cur *n* **1** a person who shows a shameful lack of courage in the face of danger ⟨denounced as *curs* those police officers who deserted their posts during the hurricane and its aftermath⟩ — see COWARD

2 a person whose behavior is offensive to others ⟨only a clueless *cur* would tell his girlfriend that, yes, a certain outfit did make her look fat⟩ — see JERK 1

curative *adj* tending to cure disease or restore health ⟨some believe that the herb has *curative* properties⟩ — see MEDICINAL 1

curative *n* something that corrects or counteracts something undesirable ⟨the best *curative* for her depression might be volunteer work at a local animal shelter⟩ — see CURE 1

curb *n* something that limits one's freedom of action or choice ⟨these international regulations act as a *curb* on the plundering of a nation's archaeological treasures⟩ — see RESTRICTION 1

curb *vb* to keep from exceeding a desirable degree or level (as of expression) ⟨try to *curb* your curiosity when it comes to your neighbors' business⟩ — see CONTROL 1

curdy *adj* having small pieces or lumps spread throughout ⟨*curdy* cottage cheese⟩ — see CHUNKY 1

cure *n* **1** something that corrects or counteracts something undesirable ⟨a fun hobby is always a good *cure* for boredom⟩

synonyms antidote, corrective, curative, rectifier, remedy, therapeutic, therapy

related words cure-all, elixir, panacea; answer, solution; aid, help, relief, succor; balm, medicinal, medicine, palliative

2 a substance or preparation used to treat disease ⟨researchers tirelessly working to find a *cure* for cancer⟩ — see MEDICINE

cure *vb* **1** to bring about recovery from ⟨do you have anything that will *cure* my headache?⟩

synonyms heal, mend, remedy

related words allay, alleviate, assuage, relieve; palliate, salve, soothe; ease, lighten, moderate, temper; doctor, nurse; medicate, treat; diagnose

near antonyms aggravate, worsen; misdiagnose, overdiagnose, underdiagnose

2 to restore to a healthy condition ⟨the antibiotic *cured* the sick boy of the bacterial infection⟩ — see HEAL 1

cure–all *n* something that cures all ills or problems ⟨raising a young person's self-esteem is not the *cure-all* that some people think⟩

synonyms catholicon, elixir, nostrum, panacea, theriac

related words magic bullet, silver bullet; corrective, cure, remedy; miracle drug, wonder drug

curio *n* **1** a small object displayed for its attractiveness or interest ⟨be careful of the fragile *curios* on the end tables⟩ — see KNICKKNACK

2 something strange or unusual that is an object of interest ⟨a museum's collection of *curios* brought back from the Far East by 19th-century traders⟩ — see CURIOSITY 2

curiosity *n* **1** an eager desire to find out about things that are often none of one's business ⟨our neighbor's *curiosity* about what we were doing last night was really offensive⟩

synonyms curiousness, inquisitiveness, nosiness

related words attentiveness, concern, interest, regard, wonderment; inquiry, interrogation, prying, questioning; interference, intrusiveness, meddlesomeness, obtrusiveness, officiousness; eavesdropping, rubbernecking

near antonyms apathy, disinterestedness, disregard, indifference, unconcern

antonyms incuriosity, incuriousness

2 something strange or unusual that is an object of interest ⟨the museum's *curiosities* include items constructed entirely out of toothpicks⟩

synonyms curio, exotic, objet d'art (*also* objet), oddity, oddment, rarity

related words found object, objet trouvé; curiosa, ephemera, virtu (*or* vertu); marvel, prodigy, rara avis, rare bird, wonder; abnormality, anomaly, freak, monster, monstrosity; malformation, mutant, mutation

3 a small object displayed for its attractiveness or interest ⟨an assortment of *curiosities* from around the world that the family picked up during various vacations⟩ — see KNICKKNACK

4 an odd or peculiar habit ⟨Charles Dickens typically endowed his characters with an array of endearing *curiosities*⟩ — see IDIOSYNCRASY

curious *adj* **1** interested in what is not one's own business ⟨*curious* neighbors peered out of their windows as the new people moved in⟩

synonyms inquisitive, nosy (*or* nosey), prying, snoopy

related words interfering, intrusive, meddlesome, meddling, obtrusive, officious; inquisitional, inquisitorial, interrogative, questioning, quizzical; concerned, interested

near antonyms apathetic, disinterested, indifferent, unconcerned, uninterested

antonyms incurious, uncurious

2 different from the ordinary in a way that causes curiosity or suspicion ⟨that's a *curious* argument to make in favor of legalizing certain drugs⟩ — see ODD 2

3 noticeably different from what is generally found or experienced ⟨a *curious* hairstyle for a young girl⟩ — see UNUSUAL 1

curiousness *n* an eager desire to find out about things that are often none of one's business ⟨children have a natural *curiousness* about where babies come from⟩ — see CURIOSITY 1

curl *n* a length of hair that forms a loop or series of loops ⟨a little girl with beautiful golden *curls*⟩
synonyms frizz, frizzle, ringlet
related words kink; crimp, wave; perm, permanent, set; lock, tress

curl *vb* to follow a circular or spiral course ⟨an inviting path for joggers *curls* around the reservoir⟩ — see WIND 1

curled *adj* **1** forming or styled into loops ⟨the strokes of the capital letters were elaborately *curled*⟩ — see CURLY
2 marked by a long series of irregular curves ⟨a *curled* and complicated route through a series of caves⟩ — see CROOKED 1

curling *adj* marked by a long series of irregular curves ⟨a *curling* labyrinth designed to discourage grave robbers from ever finding the inner burial chamber⟩ — see CROOKED 1

curl up *vb* to sit or recline comfortably or cozily ⟨I love to *curl up* in a big chair with a book⟩ — see SNUGGLE 1

curly *adj* forming or styled into loops ⟨the boy's naturally *curly* locks⟩
synonyms curled
related words crimped, crimpy, crisp, frizzled, frizzy, kinky, waved, wavy
near antonyms lank, limp; straightened
antonyms straight, uncurled

curmudgeon *n* an irritable and complaining person ⟨only a *curmudgeon* would object to the nursing home's holiday decorations⟩ — see GROUCH 1

currency *n* something (as pieces of stamped metal or printed paper) customarily and legally used as a medium of exchange, a measure of value, or a means of payment ⟨I prefer to carry only paper *currency*, as coins are too heavy⟩ — see MONEY 1

current *adj* **1** accepted, used, or practiced by most people ⟨*current* wisdom on parenting favors allowing children lots of self-expression⟩
synonyms conventional, customary, going, popular, prevailing, prevalent, standard, stock, usual
related words average, common, everyday, normal, ordinary; regular, routine; epidemic, ubiquitous, universal, widespread; accustomed, wonted; fashionable, in, modish, stylish
near antonyms abnormal, exceptional, extraordinary, uncommon
antonyms nonstandard, unconventional, unpopular, unusual
2 being or involving the latest methods, concepts, information, or styles ⟨*current* therapies for treating cancer have success rates that were undreamed of only a few decades ago⟩ — see MODERN
3 existing or in progress right now ⟨the *current* fund-raising effort⟩ — see PRESENT 1

current *n* **1** a prevailing or general movement or inclination ⟨the *currents* of fashion are always changing⟩ — see TREND 1
2 noticeable movement of air in a particular direction ⟨curtains that were being lightly lifted by a fresh *current* from the open window⟩ — see [1]WIND 1

currently *adv* at the present time ⟨we're *currently* working on three separate projects⟩ — see NOW 1

currish *adj* not following or in accordance with standards of honor and decency ⟨a coarse brute of a man who was prone to *currish* acts of violence against women⟩ — see IGNOBLE 2

curry *vb* to strike repeatedly ⟨vowed to *curry* the hide of the person who stole his wallet⟩ — see BEAT 1

curse *n* **1** a prayer that harm will come to someone ⟨uttered a *curse* upon his persecutor from the scaffold⟩
synonyms anathema, ban, execration, imprecation, malediction, malison, winze [*Scottish*]
related words censure, condemnation, damnation, denunciation, excommunication; hex, hoodoo, jinx, mojo, spell, voodoo, whammy; pox
near antonyms citation, commendation, endorsement (*also* indorsement)
antonyms benediction, benison, blessing
2 a disrespectful or indecent word or expression ⟨started muttering *curses* after hitting his thumb with the hammer⟩ — see SWEARWORD
3 a source of harm or misfortune ⟨intolerance of personal differences is a *curse* of humanity⟩ — see BANE 1

curse *vb* **1** to ask a divine power to send harm or evil upon ⟨I *curse* the guy who had the idea of having annoying salespeople call up innocent people to sell them things they don't want⟩
synonyms anathematize, beshrew [*archaic*], imprecate, maledict
related words condemn, damn, denounce, execrate, reprobate; hex, jinx, voodoo; dang, darn (*also* durn), dash; cuss (out), fulminate (against), rail (against), revile
near antonyms applaud, commend, congratulate
antonyms bless
2 to cause persistent suffering to ⟨misfortunes and problems seem to have *cursed* everyone ever associated with that house⟩ — see AFFLICT
3 to use offensive or indecent language ⟨you'll have to put a quarter in the jar every time you *curse*⟩ — see SWEAR 1
4 to use profane or obscene language at or about ⟨*cursed* him for showing up late—and drunk at that⟩ — see DAMN

cursed *also* **curst** *adj* deserving of one's condemnation or displeasure ⟨that *cursed* tree fell and blocked the road⟩ — see DAMNABLE

cursorily *adv* with excessive or careless speed ⟨*cursorily* glanced over the report before tossing it to one side⟩ — see HASTILY 1

cursory *adj* acting or done with excessive or careless speed ⟨your essays require more than a *cursory* effort at proofreading⟩ — see HASTY 1

curt *adj* **1** being or characterized by direct, brief, and potentially rude speech or manner ⟨she was offended by the *curt* reply to her well-meaning question⟩ — see BLUNT 1
2 marked by the use of few words to convey much information or meaning ⟨on a daily basis she e-mailed to her commanders *curt* reports on the situation⟩ — see CONCISE

curtail *vb* to make less in extent or duration ⟨*curtailed* the school day because of the stormy weather⟩ — see SHORTEN

curtain *n* **1** something that covers or conceals like a piece of cloth ⟨there has long been a *curtain* of secrecy surrounding that religious sect⟩ — see CLOAK 1
2 curtains *pl* pieces of cloth hung to darken, decorate, or divide a room ⟨the kittens keep climbing the *curtains*⟩ — see DRAPERY
3 curtains *pl* the permanent stopping of all the vital bodily activities ⟨if you're caught in a government facility with a bomb, it's *curtains* for you⟩ — see DEATH 1

curtain *vb* to keep secret or shut off from view ⟨she dropped her head and in shame *curtained* her face with her hair⟩ — see [1]HIDE 2

curtain-raiser *n* a performance, activity, or event that precedes and sets the stage for the main event ⟨the opening of the performing arts center proved to be a *curtain-raiser* for the rebirth of the city's downtown⟩ — see PRELUDE 1

curtly *adv* in a few words ⟨the beleaguered mayor *curtly* answered all questions with a simple "No comment"⟩ — see SHORTLY 1

curvaceous *also* **curvacious** *adj* having a well-proportioned feminine figure ⟨*curvaceous* swimsuit models⟩
synonyms curvy, pneumatic, shapely
related words Junoesque, statuesque; plump, round, Rubenesque, voluptuous, zaftig (*also* zoftig); bosomy, built, busty, buxom, chesty, stacked, well-endowed; callipygian (*also* callipygous); well-turned
near antonyms shapeless

curvature *n* something that curves or is curved ⟨*curvature* of the spine is called scoliosis⟩ — see BEND 1

curve *n* something that curves or is curved ⟨the bold *curve* of the racing yacht's hull⟩ — see BEND 1

curve *vb* **1** to turn away from a straight line or course ⟨after following a straight path most of the way down the mountain, the ski trail abruptly *curves* to the right⟩
synonyms arc, arch, bend, bow, crook, fall off, hook, round, sweep, swerve, trend, wheel
related words circle, coil, curlicue, curl, loop, spiral; turn, twist, wind; deviate, veer
antonyms straighten
2 to cause to turn away from a straight line ⟨*curved* the wood to make a bow⟩ — see BEND 1

curved *adj* marked by a long series of irregular curves ⟨a *curved* strip of metal that had sheared off during the collision⟩ — see CROOKED 1

curving *adj* marked by a long series of irregular curves ⟨the *curving* shoreline on the island's south side is a beachcomber's paradise⟩ — see CROOKED 1

curvy *adj* **1** having a well-proportioned feminine figure ⟨a *curvy* brunette with lots of male admirers⟩ — see CURVACEOUS
2 marked by a long series of irregular curves ⟨a perilously *curvy* stretch of a corniche along the Riviera⟩ — see CROOKED 1

cushion *n* something that serves as a protective barrier ⟨used a blanket as a *cushion* between the two tables in the moving van⟩
synonyms buffer, bumper, cocoon, cushioning, fender, pad
related words baffle, muffler; padding; safeguard, shield; barricade, cordon

cushion *vb* to lessen the shock of ⟨a substantial nest egg helped to *cushion* the sudden loss of her job⟩
synonyms buffer, gentle, soften
related words baffle, dampen, deaden, dull, obtund; moderate, modulate, temper; allay, alleviate, assuage, ease; lighten, mitigate, relieve
near antonyms heighten, intensify, sharpen

cushioning *n* something that serves as a protective barrier ⟨put plenty of *cushioning* around that bottle of wine if you're going to carry it home in your suitcase⟩ — see CUSHION

cushy *adj* providing physical comfort ⟨a big *cushy* chair that's perfect for watching television⟩ — see COMFORTABLE 1

cusp *n* **1** an interval of time just before the onset of something ⟨medical researchers who are on the *cusp* of a major breakthrough⟩ — see POINT 3
2 the last and usually sharp or tapering part of something long and narrow ⟨the *cusp* of a fang⟩ — see POINT 2

cuss *n* a disrespectful or indecent word or expression ⟨a man who has never uttered a single *cuss*⟩ — see SWEARWORD

cuss *vb* to use offensive or indecent language ⟨the little girl clapped her hands over her ears when her brother started *cussing*⟩ — see SWEAR 1

cussed *adj* deserving of one's condemnation or displeasure ⟨that *cussed* cat once again woke us up last night⟩ — see DAMNABLE

cussword *n* a disrespectful or indecent word or expression ⟨was reprimanded for teaching his little brother *cusswords*⟩ — see SWEARWORD

custodian *n* **1** a person who takes care of a property sometimes for an absent owner ⟨the *custodian* made his usual rounds of the building to make sure that everything was OK⟩
synonyms caretaker, guardian, janitor, keeper, warden, watchman
related words cocurator, curator; sexton, steward
2 a person or group that watches over someone or something ⟨served as *custodian* of the prisoner until he could be turned over to federal authorities⟩ — see GUARD 1
3 someone that protects ⟨we must regard ourselves as *custodians* of the Earth so that its natural resources may be enjoyed by many generations to come⟩ — see PROTECTOR

custodianship *n* responsibility for the safety and well-being of someone or something ⟨a museum that regards its mission as nothing less than the *custodianship* of the nation's cultural heritage⟩ — see CUSTODY

custody *n* responsibility for the safety and well-being of someone or something ⟨the government department having *custody* of all official state gifts⟩
synonyms care, custodianship, guardianship, keeping, safekeeping, trust, ward
related words control, governorship, hand(s), management, superintendence, supervision

custom *adj* made or fitted to the needs or preferences of a specific customer ⟨that business tycoon wears only *custom* suits⟩ — see CUSTOM-MADE

custom *n* **1** a usual manner of behaving or doing ⟨it is my *custom* to have half a bagel and coffee for breakfast⟩ — see HABIT 1
2 an inherited or established way of thinking, feeling, or doing ⟨the *custom* around here is that the bride's family pays for the wedding⟩ — see TRADITION 1
3 transactions or economic support provided by customers ⟨that restaurant certainly lost my *custom* after they were cited for health code violations⟩ — see BUSINESS 1

customary *adj* **1** accepted, used, or practiced by most people ⟨the *customary* response to the greeting "How are you?" is "Fine, thanks"⟩ — see CURRENT 1
2 based on customs usually handed down from a previous generation ⟨the *customary* toasting of the bride and groom at their wedding reception⟩ — see TRADITIONAL 1

customer *n* **1** a person who buys a product or uses a service from a business ⟨the store greatly values its regular *customers*⟩
synonyms account, client, guest, patron, punter [*chiefly British*]
related words consumer, end user, user; buyer, correspondent, purchaser, vendee; browser, prospect, shopper, window-shopper; bargainer, haggler; regular
near antonyms broker, merchant, seller, vendor (*also* vender); shopkeeper, tradesman; black marketer (*or* black marketeer), fence
2 a member of the human race ⟨he's one tough *customer*, so you'd better not cross him⟩ — see HUMAN

customized *adj* made or fitted to the needs or preferences of a specific customer ⟨a *customized* car for a physically challenged person⟩ — see CUSTOM-MADE

custom–made *adj* made or fitted to the needs or preferences of a specific customer ⟨an odd-sized window that will require the purchase of *custom-made* curtains⟩
synonyms bespoke (*also* bespoken), custom, customized, custom-tailored, made-to-order, tailored, tailor-made
related words particular, special, specialized; custom-built, handcrafted, handmade; made-to-measure
antonyms mass-produced, ready-made

custom–tailored *adj* made or fitted to the needs or preferences of a specific customer ⟨a filing system that is *custom-tailored* to the needs of your office⟩ — see CUSTOM-MADE

cut *n* **1** a piece that has been separated from the whole by cutting ⟨choose *cuts* of meat that have very little visible fat⟩
synonyms cutting, slice
related words chop, cutlet; length, part, portion, section, segment; chunk, hunk, lump; clipping, paring, shaving, sliver, snippet, splinter
2 an individual part of a process, series, or ranking ⟨one of the new recruits is a *cut* above the rest in intelligence⟩ — see DEGREE 1
3 something belonging to, due to, or contributed by an individual member of a group ⟨received my *cut* of the profits from the garage sale⟩ — see SHARE 1
4 a style or arrangement of hair ⟨she decided she needed a new *cut* after wearing her hair the same way for years⟩ — see HAIRDO
5 an act or expression showing scorn and usually intended to hurt another's feelings ⟨completely ignoring her was the unkindest *cut* of all⟩ — see INSULT

cut *vb* **1** to penetrate with a sharp edge (as a knife) ⟨I *cut* my hand on a piece of broken glass⟩
synonyms gash, incise, rip, shear, slash, slice, slit
related words crosscut, hacksaw, saw, scissor; cleave, rive, split; pierce, stab; bruise, butcher, hack, haggle, lacerate, mangle; rend, tear; carve, chip, chisel, notch; anatomize, dissect, section; chop, dice, mince; amputate, cut off, sever
2 to fail to attend ⟨a warning that she had been *cutting* too many classes without valid excuses⟩
synonyms blow off, miss, skip
related words ignore, neglect, pass over
phrases absent oneself, play hooky
antonyms attend, show up (for)
3 to deliberately ignore or treat rudely ⟨the snobbish lady *cut* anyone who didn't meet her standards of wealth and social standing⟩ — see SNUB 1
4 to make (something) shorter or smaller with the use of a cutting instrument ⟨when you *cut* the pad, make it a little smaller than the carpet⟩ — see CLIP 1
5 to shorten the standing leafy plant cover of ⟨you need to *cut* the lawn very soon—before it becomes a jungle⟩ — see MOW 1
6 to alter (something) for the worse with the addition of foreign or lower-grade substances ⟨the fruit juice was so *cut* with water that it was barely a fruit-flavored drink⟩ — see ADULTERATE
7 to depart abruptly from a straight line or course ⟨*cut* towards the goal, eluding a defender⟩ — see SWERVE 1
8 to divide by passing through or across ⟨a long mountain range virtually *cuts* that country in half⟩ — see INTERSECT
9 to identify and examine the basic elements or parts of (something) especially for discovering interrelationships ⟨whichever way you *cut* it, we won't be seeing any profits from the business for at least three years⟩ — see ANALYZE

cut (across) *vb* to make one's way through, across, or over ⟨*cut across* the field on the way to school⟩ — see TRAVERSE

cut (down) *vb* to bring down by cutting ⟨we need to *cut down* that dying tree⟩ — see FELL 2

cut–and–dried *also* **cut–and–dry** *adj* being of the type that is encountered in the normal course of events ⟨a *cut-and-dried* session of the convention just to get required business out of the way⟩ — see ORDINARY 1

cut back *vb* **1** to make (something) shorter or smaller with the use of a cutting instrument ⟨we need to *cut back* the bushes a bit so that the house number is visible from the street⟩ — see CLIP 1
2 to make less in extent or duration ⟨*cut back* the meeting so everyone could leave early for the long weekend⟩ — see SHORTEN

cute *adj* **1** clever at attaining one's ends by indirect and often deceptive means ⟨she's very nice, but she's not afraid to get *cute* when there's something she wants⟩ — see ARTFUL 1
2 making light of something usually regarded as serious or sacred ⟨we're having a serious discussion here, so cut the *cute* remarks⟩ — see FLIPPANT
3 very pleasing to look at ⟨a *cute* baby that no one could resist cooing over⟩ — see BEAUTIFUL 1

cuteness *n* the qualities in a person or thing that as a whole give pleasure to the senses ⟨that kitten's *cuteness* is simply overwhelming!⟩ — see BEAUTY 1

cutie *or* **cutey** *n* **1** a lovely woman ⟨in her days as a chorus girl she was a real *cutie*⟩ — see BEAUTY 2
2 a physically attractive person ⟨a director hoping to find among that crowd of *cuties* someone who could actually act⟩ — see DOLL 2

cut in *vb* to cause a disruption in a conversation or discussion ⟨a stranger *cut in* with unsolicited advice on how we could fix our relationship⟩ — see INTERRUPT

cutlet *n* a small usually rounded mass of minced food that has been fried ⟨a breaded veal *cutlet*⟩ — see CAKE 1

cutline *n* an explanation or description accompanying a pictorial illustration ⟨the *cutline* wrongly identified the people in the photo⟩ — see CAPTION 1

cutoff *n* the stopping of a process or activity ⟨with a *cutoff* for funding the war, military operations soon ground to a halt⟩ — see END 1

cut off *vb* **1** to bring (as an action or operation) to an immediate end ⟨the majority party *cut off* debate and forced a vote on the bill⟩ — see STOP 1
2 to set or keep apart from others ⟨the dog *cut off* the one sheep that had to be sheared⟩ — see ISOLATE

cut out *vb* **1** to stop functioning ⟨the engine abruptly *cut out*⟩ — see FAIL 1
2 to bring (as an action or operation) to an immediate end ⟨now *cut* that *out*, or I'm turning this car around!⟩ — see STOP 1
3 to leave a place often for another ⟨after a few minutes of their brainless conversation I was ready to *cut out*⟩ — see GO 2
4 to take the place of ⟨this ambitious new friend of hers seems to be *cutting out* people that she's known for years⟩ — see REPLACE 1

cut–price *adj, chiefly British* costing little ⟨a *cut-price* purse that looked like a much more expensive brand⟩ — see CHEAP 1

cut–rate *adj* **1** costing little ⟨opted for a *cut-rate* insurance policy because we didn't need anything more⟩ — see CHEAP 1
2 of low quality ⟨a *cut-rate* motel that looked like the kind at which people in horror movies always end up⟩ — see CHEAP 2

cutter *n* an instrument with a metal length that has a sharp edge for cutting ⟨a fabric *cutter*⟩ — see KNIFE

cutthroat *adj* not guided by or showing a concern for what is right ⟨*cutthroat* business practices intended to drive competitors out of business⟩ — see UNPRINCIPLED

cutthroat *n* a person who kills another person ⟨while traveling the ancient Silk Road, traders were constant prey to *cutthroats* and thieves⟩ — see ASSASSIN

cutting *adj* **1** causing intense discomfort to one's skin ⟨a frigid day with a *cutting* wind that made it seem even colder⟩
synonyms biting, bitter, keen, penetrating, piercing, raw, sharp, shrewd, smarting, stinging

related words brisk, invigorating, nippy, snappy; needlelike, prickly, tingling; caustic, corrosive
near antonyms balmy, gentle, mild, soothing
2 having an edge thin enough to cut or pierce something ⟨the *cutting* side of the sword blade⟩ — see SHARP 1
3 marked by the use of wit that is intended to cause hurt feelings ⟨her *cutting* comments serve only one purpose: to make someone cry⟩ — see SARCASTIC

cutting *n* a piece that has been separated from the whole by cutting ⟨a bag full of grass *cuttings*⟩ — see CUT 1

cutting–edge *adj* being or employing the latest concepts, styles, or techniques ⟨his insistent tracking shots and rapid-fire pacing earned him a reputation as a *cutting-edge* filmmaker⟩ — see AVANT

cutting edge *n* **1** the innovators of new concepts, styles, and techniques especially in the arts ⟨an urban enclave that has an established reputation for being hospitable to artists who are part of the *cutting edge*⟩ — see AVANT-GARDE
2 the leading or most important part of a movement ⟨a company that has always been on the *cutting edge* of the new electronic media⟩ — see FOREFRONT

cut up *vb* to engage in attention-getting playful or boisterous behavior ⟨high-spirited cousins who *cut up* at every family gathering⟩
synonyms act up, clown (around), fool around, horse around, hotdog, monkey (around), showboat, show off, skylark
related words carry on, misbehave; roughhouse; caper, cavort, disport, frisk, frolic, gambol, lark, rollick, romp; carouse, maffick, revel, roar, wassail

cybercitizen *n* an active participant in the online community of the Internet ⟨*cybercitizens* have an obligation to treat one another with respect⟩ — see NETIZEN

cybernaut *n* an active participant in the online community of the Internet ⟨a *cybernaut* who bookmarks all of the weird sites that he stumbles across⟩ — see NETIZEN

cyberpunk *n* a person who illegally gains access to a computer system and sometimes tampers with its information ⟨the bank had to overhaul its online banking system after a *cyberpunk* broke into the accounts of thousands of customers⟩ — see HACKER 1

cybersurfer *n* an active participant in the online community of the Internet ⟨a *cybersurfer* who is constantly amazed by the length of her daily history⟩ — see NETIZEN

cycle *n* **1** a series of events or actions that repeat themselves regularly and in the same order ⟨the *cycle* of birth, growth, decline, and death that is experienced by all life forms⟩
synonyms circle, merry-go-round, round, wheel, zodiac
related words pattern, syndrome; course, development, progression, run; beat, circuit, loop, ring; rotation, revolution, turn, turnover; chain, sequence, series, string, succession, train
2 a long or seemingly long period of time ⟨years, centuries, and *cycles* will pass before I budge on that issue⟩ — see AGE 2
3 a two-wheeled vehicle that is propelled by the use of pedals and steered through the use of handlebars ⟨a top-of-the-line *cycle* incorporating the latest technology⟩ — see BICYCLE

cyclonic *adj* marked by bursts of destructive force or intense activity ⟨a man who was given to *cyclonic* rages⟩ — see VIOLENT 1

cyclopean *adj* unusually large ⟨a *cyclopean* granite statue that the dictator himself had commissioned⟩ — see HUGE

cyclopedic *adj* covering everything or all important points ⟨she has a *cyclopedic* memory—she just doesn't have a clue as to what's important and what isn't⟩ — see ENCYCLOPEDIC

cynic *n* a person who distrusts other people and believes that everything is done for selfish reasons ⟨a *cynic* who believes that nobody does a good deed without expecting something in return⟩
synonyms misanthrope, naysayer, pessimist
related words misandrist, misogynist; doubter, negativist, skeptic; belittler, critic, derider, detractor, scoffer; malcontent; defeatist, quitter
near antonyms optimist, Pollyanna, positivist; idealist, sentimentalist

cynical *adj* having or showing a deep distrust of human beings and their motives ⟨so *cynical* that he can't understand why anyone would volunteer to help out at a homeless shelter⟩
synonyms misanthropic, pessimistic
related words distrustful, mistrustful, negativist, negativistic, skeptical, suspicious; derisive, mocking, sardonic, scornful; defeatist, fatalistic, negative; ironic (*also* ironical), sarcastic; jaded, sophisticated, worldly-wise; hard-bitten, hard-boiled, hardcase, hard-edged, unsentimental
near antonyms trustful, trusting, unsuspicious; cheerful, optimistic, positive, positivist, positivistic, rose-colored; ingenuous, innocent, naive (*or* naïve), unsophisticated; idealistic, impractical, romantic; maudlin, mushy, saccharine, sappy, sentimental
antonyms uncynical

cynosure *n* **1** a guiding or motivating purpose or principle ⟨with an unwavering commitment to equal rights for all as his only *cynosure*⟩ — see COMPASS 1
2 a thing or place that is of greatest importance to an activity or interest ⟨that company is the *cynosure* for anyone wishing to make it in the music business⟩ — see CENTER

czar *also* **tsar** *or* **tzar** *n* a person of rank, power, or influence in a particular field ⟨a showbiz *czar* who is said to be able to make or break a career⟩ — see MAGNATE

czarism *also* **tsarism** *or* **tzarism** *n* a system of government in which the ruler has unlimited power ⟨historically, during times of national crisis, people have looked to *czarism* as an answer to their fears⟩ — see DESPOTISM

czarist *also* **tsarist** *or* **tzarist** *adj* exercising power or authority without interference by others ⟨the trustees felt that the university needed a strong, *czarist* leader who could propel it to world-class status⟩ — see ABSOLUTE 1

D

[1]dab *n* **1** a quick thrust ⟨one more quick *dab* of the brush and he would be finished with his painting⟩ — see [1]POKE 1
2 a very small amount ⟨she added a *dab* of sesame oil to the dressing before pouring it on the salad⟩ — see PARTICLE 1
3 a hard strike with a part of the body or an instrument ⟨a bear can knock a man down with a simple *dab* of his paw⟩ — see [1]BLOW

[2]dab *n, chiefly British* a person with a high level of knowledge or skill in a field ⟨a *dab* at finding unappreciated collectibles and reselling them at a considerable profit⟩ — see EXPERT

dabbler *n* a person who regularly or occasionally engages in an activity as a pastime rather than as a profession ⟨he was a *dabbler*, learning the basics of many arts but mastering none⟩ — see AMATEUR 1

dab hand *n, chiefly British* a person with a high level of knowledge or skill in a field ⟨a British mystery writer who's an undisputed *dab hand* at building suspense⟩ — see EXPERT

dad *n* a male human parent ⟨my *dad* did most of the cooking for dinner because he usually got home earlier than my mom⟩ — see FATHER 1

daddy *n* **1** a male human parent ⟨I stopped calling my father "*Daddy*" because I thought it sounded childish⟩ — see FATHER 1
2 something belonging to an earlier time from which something else was later developed ⟨Cook's Tours can be considered the *daddy* of all organized travel tours⟩ — see ANCESTOR 2

daedal *adj* having many parts or aspects that are usually interrelated ⟨the *daedal* workings of the chime clock are a marvel to behold⟩ — see COMPLEX 1

daffy *adj* **1** having or showing a very abnormal or sick state of mind ⟨lurid newspaper reports that portrayed the serial killer as clearly *daffy*⟩ — see INSANE 1
2 showing or marked by a lack of good sense or judgment ⟨their *daffy* antics made generations of movie audiences laugh⟩ — see FOOLISH 1

daft *adj* **1** having or showing a very abnormal or sick state of mind ⟨the king was clearly *daft*, talking to trees and rocks as if they were people⟩ — see INSANE 1
2 showing or marked by a lack of good sense or judgment ⟨a *daft* plan, doomed to wretched failure and merciless ridicule⟩ — see FOOLISH 1

daftness *n* lack of good sense or judgment ⟨his dithery *daftness* makes him unfit for any position but that of class clown⟩ — see FOOLISHNESS 1

daily *adj* occurring, done, produced, or appearing every day ⟨they made their *daily* stop at the coffee shop after work to relax before dinner⟩
synonyms day-to-day, diurnal, quotidian
related words alternate, cyclic (*or* cyclical), intermittent, periodic, recurrent, recurring, regular; ceaseless, continual, continued, continuing, continuous, everlasting, frequent, incessant, nonstop, perpetual, unbroken, unceasing, uninterrupted, unremitting
near antonyms monthly, weekly, yearly; erratic, infrequent, irregular; occasional, spasmodic, spastic, sporadic; interrupted

daily *n, British* a person hired to perform household or personal services ⟨hired a *daily* to come in each morning to cook and clean⟩ — see SERVANT

daintiness *n* the state or quality of having a delicate structure ⟨we were less impressed by the *daintiness* of the etching on the crystal vase than by the heftiness of its price⟩ — see DELICACY 2

dainty *adj* **1** hard to please ⟨you can't afford to be *dainty* about food when you're starving⟩ — see FINICKY
2 having qualities that appeal to a refined taste ⟨the *dainty* hors d'oeuvres were delicious, but not terribly filling⟩ — see CHOICE 1
3 satisfying or pleasing because of fineness or mildness ⟨a set of *dainty* teacups that would be perfect for an elderly lady⟩ — see DELICATE 1
4 very pleasing to the sense of taste ⟨the sort of *dainty* finger foods that might be served at afternoon tea⟩ — see DELICIOUS 1

dainty *n* something that is pleasing to eat because it is rare or a luxury ⟨the widow plied her suitor with *dainties* and endless glasses of sherry⟩ — see DELICACY 1

dais *n* a level usually raised surface ⟨the speaker took his place at the front of the *dais*⟩ — see PLATFORM 1

daisy *n* something very good of its kind ⟨while the old crooner is now well past his prime, Grandma still harkens back to the "*daisy* of a performance" he could give in his heyday⟩ — see JIM-DANDY

dale *n* an area of lowland between hills or mountains ⟨a hunting lodge in a secluded *dale* in the country⟩ — see VALLEY

dalliance *n* activity engaged in to amuse oneself ⟨an extremely serious scientist who is not much given to *dalliance* or idle chitchat⟩ — see PLAY 1

dallier *n* someone who moves slowly or more slowly than others ⟨the *dalliers* began to hurry when they realized a violent storm was brewing⟩ — see SLOWPOKE

dally *vb* **1** to engage in activity for amusement ⟨he spent his college years *dallying*, seemingly determined to acquire as little knowledge as possible⟩ — see PLAY 1
2 to move or act slowly ⟨don't *dally* on the way to the interview⟩ — see DELAY 1
3 to show a sexual attraction for someone just for fun ⟨she spent the summer *dallying* with a guy renting the neighboring beach house⟩ — see FLIRT 1
4 to spend time doing nothing ⟨I kept *dallying* at my desk until I couldn't put off doing my work any longer⟩ — see IDLE

dallying *adj* moving or proceeding at less than the normal, desirable, or required speed ⟨the *dallying* diners seemed oblivious to the fact that other customers were impatiently waiting for tables⟩ — see SLOW 1

dam *n* a bank of earth constructed to control water ⟨the river backed up behind the *dam* until it formed a new lake⟩
synonyms dike, embankment, head, levee
related words breakwater, jetty, seawall; breastwork, bulwark, earthwork, rampart; canal, channel, ditch, gutter, trough; lock; barricade, barrier, block; floodgate, sluice; barrage, milldam, stank [*British*], weir

dam *vb* **1** to prevent passage through by filling with something ⟨ice floes were *damming* the river⟩ — see CLOG 1
2 to close up so that no empty spaces remain ⟨*dam* up the pipes⟩ — see FILL 2

damage *n* **1** something that causes loss or pain ⟨the collision did a great deal of *damage* to her car⟩ — see INJURY 1
2 damages *pl* a sum of money to be paid as a punish-

ment ⟨ordered by the court to pay $1000 in *damages*⟩ — see FINE

3 damages *pl* payment to another for a loss or injury ⟨the company was forced to pay millions in *damages* to the permanently disabled worker⟩ — see COMPENSATION 1

4 the amount of money that is demanded as payment for something ⟨he winced when he saw the *damage* after the family's shopping spree⟩ — see PRICE 1

damage *vb* **1** to reduce the soundness, effectiveness, or perfection of ⟨the explosion in the sewers *damaged* the entire city's water supply⟩
synonyms blemish, bloody, break, compromise, crab, cripple, cross (up), deface, disfigure, endamage, flaw, harm, hurt, impair, injure, mar, spoil, vitiate
related words deteriorate, enervate, enfeeble, undermine, weaken; erode, scour, wash out, wear (away); blight, tarnish; dent, ding, dint; botch, gum (up), queer; lacerate, wound; disable, hamstring, lame, maim, mangle, mutilate, torment, torture; annihilate, bang up, bash, batter, clobber, crush, dash, decimate, demolish, desolate, destroy, devastate, do in, pulverize, raze, ruin, scourge, shatter, smash, tear down, total, waste, wipe out, wreck
near antonyms cure, heal, help, rectify, rehabilitate, remedy; edit, remodel, revise; ameliorate, better, enhance, enrich, improve, meliorate, perfect, refine
antonyms doctor, fix, mend, patch, rebuild, recondition, reconstruct, renovate, repair, revamp
2 to cause bodily damage to ⟨his knee was badly *damaged* in the accident, and he walked with a limp for months⟩ — see INJURE 1

damaging *adj* causing or capable of causing harm ⟨the *damaging* effects of the sun on unprotected skin⟩ — see HARMFUL

dame *n* **1** a dignified usually elderly woman of some rank or authority ⟨as the grand *dames* of local society, they determined which charities received support⟩ — see MATRIARCH
2 a woman of high birth or social position ⟨the lords and *dames* of the shire eagerly awaited the royal visit⟩ — see GENTLEWOMAN

damn *adj* having no exceptions or restrictions ⟨that dilapidated house is a *damn* eyesore and should be torn down⟩ — see ABSOLUTE 2

damn *adv* to a great degree ⟨told her she'd never get married because she was too *damn* picky⟩ — see VERY 1

damn *n* the smallest amount or part imaginable ⟨I don't want to hear about your problems—I just don't give a *damn*⟩ — see JOT

damn *vb* **1** to use profane or obscene language at or about ⟨*damned* the car for once again breaking down⟩
synonyms curse
related words imprecate, maledict; criticize, reprove; admonish, chide, rebuke, reprimand, reproach; blame, censure, reprehend, reprobate
near antonyms bless, extol (*also* extoll), glorify, laud, magnify, praise; acclaim, applaud, commend, compliment, hail, salute
2 to declare to be morally wrong or evil ⟨a heresy that was quickly *damned* by a hastily called church council⟩ — see CONDEMN 1
3 to impose a judicial punishment on ⟨*damned* him to life in prison without the possibility of parole⟩ — see SENTENCE

damnable *adj* deserving of one's condemnation or displeasure ⟨this *damnable* couch is falling apart⟩
synonyms accursed (*or* accurst), blasted, confounded, cotton-picking, cursed (*also* curst), cussed, dang, danged, darn (*also* durn), darned (*also* durned), deuced, doggone (*or* doggoned), freaking, goddamned (*or* goddamn *or* goddam), infernal
related words atrocious, awful, bum, detestable, execrable, lousy, punk, rotten, terrible, wretched; abominable, odious, vile; contemptible, despicable, miserable, nasty, pitiable, pitiful, scabby, scummy, scurvy, shameful, sorry
near antonyms commendable, creditable, laudable, praiseworthy; great, marvelous (*or* marvellous), wonderful

damned *adj* having no exceptions or restrictions ⟨only a *damned* fool would say such a thing⟩ — see ABSOLUTE 2

damned *adv* to a great degree ⟨it's a *damned* fine day⟩ — see VERY 1

damning *adj* bringing about ruin or misfortune ⟨a *damning* flaw in the program cost the company millions of dollars⟩ — see FATAL 1

damp *adj* **1** containing or characterized by an uncomfortable amount of moisture ⟨the *damp* air made 85 degrees feel like 105⟩ — see HUMID
2 slightly or moderately wet ⟨marks can usually be removed with a *damp* cloth⟩ — see MOIST

damp *n* the amount of water suspended in the air in tiny droplets ⟨we bought a dehumidifier for the basement when the *damp* down there began causing mold to grow⟩ — see MOISTURE

damp *vb* **1** to deprive of emotional or intellectual vitality ⟨refused to let the setbacks *damp* his drive for success⟩ — see DEHYDRATE 1
2 to make or become slightly or moderately wet ⟨*damp* the shirt slightly before ironing it⟩ — see MOISTEN
3 to reduce or weaken in strength or feeling ⟨nothing seemed to *damp* the unwelcome attentions of her suitor⟩ — see DULL 1

dampen *vb* **1** to make or become slightly or moderately wet ⟨*dampen* a paper towel with water and use it to clean up the mess⟩ — see MOISTEN
2 to reduce or weaken in strength or feeling ⟨the oppressive heat *dampened* our spirits⟩ — see DULL 1
3 to deprive of emotional or intellectual vitality ⟨nothing could *dampen* their enthusiasm⟩ — see DEHYDRATE 1

damper *n* a device on a musical instrument that deadens or softens its tone ⟨the pianist used the *damper* pedal on the piano for the quiet passages⟩ — see MUTE

dampish *adj* slightly or moderately wet ⟨the basement is still *dampish* even a week after that last rain caused some flooding⟩ — see MOIST

dampness *n* the amount of water suspended in the air in tiny droplets ⟨the *dampness* in the air made a mess of my new hairstyle⟩ — see MOISTURE

damsel *n* a young unmarried woman ⟨knights are celebrated in fairy tales for rescuing *damsels* in distress⟩ — see GIRL 1

dance *n* a social gathering for dancing ⟨who are you taking to the *dance* on Saturday night?⟩
synonyms ball, cotillion (*also* cotillon), formal, hop, prom
related words blowout, celebration, event, festival, festivity, fete (*or* fête), gala, masque (*also* mask), masquerade, mixer, party, reception, shindig, soiree (*or* soirée); hoedown, square dance

dance *vb* **1** to perform a series of usually rhythmic bodily movements to music ⟨she can't resist *dancing* to her favorite rock bands⟩
synonyms foot (it), hoof (it), step
related words prance, strut, trip; boogie (*also* boogy *or* boogey), bop, fox-trot, gavotte, jig, jitterbug, jive, mambo, polka, shag, shimmy, shuffle, tango, tap-dance, twist, waltz; tread
phrases shake a leg, trip the light fantastic

2 to make an irregular series of quick, sudden movements ⟨the lithe boxer *danced* around the ring, staying just out of the reach of his opponent⟩ — see FLIT

dandle *vb* to treat with great or excessive care ⟨the college president is a past master at *dandling* wealthy alumni⟩ — see BABY

dandy *adj* of the very best kind ⟨that's a *dandy* new racing bike⟩ — see EXCELLENT

dandy *n* **1** a man extremely interested in his clothing and personal appearance ⟨that *dandy* was willing to spend all day and hundreds of dollars just to get the perfect pair of shoes⟩
synonyms beau, Beau Brummell, buck, dude, fop, gallant, jay, lounge lizard, macaroni, pretty boy, toff [*chiefly British*]
related words coxcomb, fancy Dan, popinjay; blade, cavalier, dasher; clotheshorse, exquisite, swell
near antonyms slob, sloven
2 something very good of its kind ⟨that new PDA is a *dandy*⟩ — see JIM-DANDY

dang *adj* deserving of one's condemnation or displeasure ⟨we need to go shovel the *dang* snow again⟩ — see DAMNABLE

dang *adv* to a great degree ⟨we've driven too *dang* far to turn around now⟩ — see VERY 1

danged *adj* deserving of one's condemnation or displeasure ⟨that *danged* company lost our payment again⟩ — see DAMNABLE

danger *n* **1** the state of not being protected from injury, harm, or evil ⟨he knew he was in *danger* when he received the threatening phone calls at home⟩
synonyms distress, endangerment, harm's way, imperilment, jeopardy, peril, risk, trouble
related words exposure, liability, openness, vulnerability; precariousness, threat; susceptibility, susceptibleness; defenselessness, helplessness, weakness
near antonyms preservation, salvation; defense, protection; exemption, immunity, impunity, inviolability, invulnerability
antonyms safeness, safety, secureness, security
2 something that may cause injury or harm ⟨willing to face the *dangers* of the Arctic in quest of the Northwest Passage⟩
synonyms hazard, imminence, menace, peril, pitfall, risk, threat, trouble
related words snare, trap; booby trap
near antonyms guard, protection, safeguard, shield, ward; asylum, harbor, haven, refuge, retreat, shelter

dangerous *adj* **1** involving potential loss or injury ⟨the soldiers were specially selected to go on a *dangerous* mission behind enemy lines⟩
synonyms grave, grievous, hazardous, jeopardizing, menacing, parlous, perilous, risky, serious, threatening, unhealthy, unsafe, venturesome
related words dicey, insecure, precarious, treacherous, uncertain; ultrahazardous; chance, haphazard, random; distressing, sickening, unpleasant; ugly, wicked; adverse, bad, baleful, baneful, deleterious, detrimental, evil, harmful, hurtful, ill, inimical, injurious, malignant, nasty, noxious, pernicious, pestilent; deadly, deathly, destructive, dire, fatal, fateful, fell, killer, lethal, mortal, murderous
near antonyms advantageous, beneficial, good; ultrasafe
antonyms harmless, innocent, innocuous, nonhazardous, nonthreatening, safe, unthreatening
2 causing or capable of causing harm ⟨the common knowledge that smoking is *dangerous* to one's health hasn't stopped some people⟩ — see HARMFUL

dangle *vb* to place on an elevated point without support from below ⟨he *dangled* the string in front of the cat, hoping that it was in the mood for play⟩ — see HANG 1

dangling *adj* extending freely from a support from above ⟨there was a *dangling* banner in one corner of the room⟩ — see DEPENDENT 1

dank *adj* slightly or moderately wet ⟨vegetables tended to go bad quickly in the *dank* cellar⟩ — see MOIST

dapper *adj* being strikingly neat and trim in style or appearance ⟨the *dapper* gentleman drew admiring glances from all over the ballroom⟩ — see SMART 1

dapple *n* a small area that is different (as in color) from the main part ⟨the clouds threw *dapples* of shadow over the eerily quiet street⟩ — see SPOT 1

dapple *vb* to mark with small spots especially unevenly ⟨sunlight *dappled* the canopy of vines over our heads⟩ — see SPOT 1

dappled *also* **dapple** *adj* **1** marked with spots ⟨a *dappled* fawn⟩ — see SPOTTED 1
2 having blotches of two or more colors ⟨a forest that was vibrant with the *dappled* foliage of autumn⟩ — see PIED

dare *vb* **1** to invite (someone) to take part in a contest or to perform a feat ⟨I *dare* you to repeat that to my face!⟩ ⟨he *dared* his friend to race to the end of the block⟩ — see CHALLENGE 2
2 to oppose (something hostile or dangerous) with firmness or courage ⟨every day the old fisherman *dared* the elements to make his meager living⟩ — see FACE 2

daredevil *adj* **1** foolishly adventurous or bold ⟨his *daredevil* stunts are sure to end in disaster someday⟩ — see FOOLHARDY 1
2 having or showing a lack of concern for the consequences of one's actions ⟨a *daredevil* driver who thinks that drag racing on city streets is a harmless game⟩ — see RECKLESS 1

daredevil *n* a person who seeks out very dangerous or foolhardy adventures with no apparent fear ⟨that little *daredevil* has broken an arm and an ankle this year alone⟩
synonyms devil, madcap, madman
related words berserk (*or* berserker), cowboy, hotdog, showboat

daresay *vb* to form an opinion from little or no evidence ⟨I *daresay* we might manage to finish on time after all⟩ — see GUESS 1

daring *adj* inclined or willing to take risks ⟨*daring* acrobats who risk life and limb every day for the entertainment of the crowds at the circus⟩ — see BOLD 1

daring *n* strength of mind to carry on in spite of danger ⟨the *daring* that the early explorers of Oceania must have had⟩ — see COURAGE

daringness *n* strength of mind to carry on in spite of danger ⟨the sheer *daringness* of Hannibal's trek over the Alps with the aid of elephants⟩ — see COURAGE

dark *adj* **1** being without light or without much light ⟨a *dark* alley that most people wisely avoided⟩
synonyms black, caliginous, darkened, darkish, darkling, darksome, dim, dimmed, dusk, dusky, gloomy, lightless, murky, obscure, obscured, pitch-black, pitch-dark, pitchy, rayless, somber (*or* sombre), stygian, tenebrific, tenebrous, unlit
related words crepuscular, twilit; moonless, starless, sunless; cloudy, dull, dulled, lackluster; shadowlike, shadowy, shady; gray (*also* grey), leaden, pale; beclouded, befogged, clouded, foggy, fuliginous, misty, smoggy, soupy
near antonyms ablaze, agleam, aglitter, alight, beaming, beamy, effulgent, glaring, glowing, incandescent, lambent, radiant, relucent, resplendent, shining, sparkling; ultrabright; glossy, lustrous, shiny; floodlit (*also* floodlighted), highlighted, spotlighted (*or* spotlit); moonlit, moony, starlit, sunlit
antonyms bright, brightened, brilliant, illuminated, il-

lumined, light, lit (*or* lighted), lightsome, lucent, lucid, luminous

2 not having a light complexion ⟨because of her *dark* good looks, the actress was usually cast as sultry temptresses⟩

synonyms black, brunet (*or* brunette), swart, swarthy

near antonyms ashen, ashy, pale, palish, pallid, pasty, peaked, peaky, sallow, wan

antonyms light

3 causing or marked by an atmosphere lacking in cheer ⟨her mind was filled with *dark* thoughts as she waited for the results of the medical test⟩ — see GLOOMY 1

4 given to keeping one's activities hidden from public observation or knowledge ⟨the actor was always quite *dark* about his life before his arrival in Hollywood⟩ — see SECRETIVE

5 having an often intentionally veiled or uncertain meaning ⟨a troubled kid who was always muttering *dark* threats that someday they'd all be sorry⟩ — see OBSCURE 1

6 lacking in education or the knowledge gained from books ⟨a *dark* period in European history when people lived in ignorance, fear, and want⟩ — see IGNORANT 1

7 not conforming to a high moral standard; morally unacceptable ⟨*dark* deeds that resulted in the Russian czar being known to history as Ivan the Terrible⟩ — see BAD 2

dark *n* **1** a time or place of little or no light ⟨I have a bad habit of running into tables in the *dark*⟩

synonyms black, blackness, candlelight, darkness, dusk, gloaming, gloom, murk, night, semidarkness, shade, shadows, twilight, umbra

related words midnight; blackout, brownout, dimout; shadiness, umbrage; dullness (*also* dulness), somberness; cloudiness, fogginess, haziness, mistiness, murkiness; dimness, faintness, gloominess, grayness, paleness; half-light

near antonyms moonlight, starlight, sunlight; effulgence, radiance, radiancy, shine, sunshine; incandescence, luminance, luminescence, luminosity, luminousness

antonyms blaze, brightness, brilliance, day, daylight, glare, glow, light, lightness

2 the time from sunset to sunrise when there is no visible sunlight ⟨we were going to wait until *dark* to go trick-or-treating⟩ — see NIGHT 1

darken *vb* **1** to take on a gloomy or forbidding look ⟨his face slowly *darkened* as we told him the sad news⟩

synonyms gloom, glower, lower (*also* lour)

related words frown, scowl; glare, stare; brood, mope, pet, pout, sulk; anger, bristle, fume, rage, steam, storm; intimidate, menace, threaten

antonyms brighten, cheer (up), lighten, perk (up)

2 to grow dark ⟨the sky *darkened* as a storm moved in⟩

synonyms blacken, black out, close in, dusk

related words dim, fade, wane; gloom, lower (*also* lour)

near antonyms dawn; beam, glow, radiate, shine

antonyms brighten, light, lighten

3 to make dark, dim, or indistinct ⟨years of accumulated grime have *darkened* the painting until it can barely be seen⟩ — see CLOUD 1

4 to affect slightly with something morally bad or undesirable ⟨posthumous revelations of marital infidelity have *darkened* the President's reputation somewhat⟩ — see TAINT 1

darkened *adj* being without light or without much light ⟨wanting to surprise her, we waited in the *darkened* room for her to get home⟩ — see DARK 1

darkening *adj* causing or marked by an atmosphere lacking in cheer ⟨a *darkening* sky that seemed to match our downcast spirits⟩ — see GLOOMY 1

darkish *adj* being without light or without much light ⟨the *darkish* galleries do not show off the museum's paintings to their best advantage⟩ — see DARK 1

darkling *adj* being without light or without much light ⟨the *darkling* valleys of Transylvania, where tales of vampires have long existed⟩ — see DARK 1

darkness *n* **1** a time or place of little or no light ⟨the raiding party snuck up under cover of *darkness*⟩ — see DARK 1

2 the quality or state of having a veiled or uncertain meaning ⟨the *darkness* of certain passages in the Book of Revelation⟩ — see OBSCURITY 1

3 the time from sunset to sunrise when there is no visible sunlight ⟨let's wait for *darkness* before telling ghost stories⟩ — see NIGHT 1

4 an overspreading element that produces an atmosphere of gloom ⟨the *darkness* of that period of my life is best forgotten⟩ — see CLOUD

darksome *adj* being without light or without much light ⟨a pile of *darksome* ruins in the heart of the forest⟩ — see DARK 1

darling *adj* **1** granted special treatment or attention ⟨they poured gifts and affection on their *darling* child⟩

synonyms beloved, cherished, dear, fair-haired, favored, favorite, fond, loved, pet, precious, special, sweet, white-headed

related words admired, adored, appreciated, esteemed, relished, revered; prized, treasured; preferred

near antonyms abhorred, abominated, despised, detested, disdained, disfavored, disliked, execrated, hated, loathed, unfavorite; abandoned, forgotten, ignored; alienated, estranged

antonyms unbeloved

2 having qualities that tend to make one loved ⟨a *darling* child that any couple would want to adopt⟩ — see LOVABLE

3 giving pleasure or contentment to the mind or senses ⟨what a *darling* set of dishes!⟩ — see PLEASANT 1

darling *n* **1** a person or thing that is preferred over others ⟨for a while that candidate was the *darling* of the news media and could do no wrong⟩ — see FAVORITE

2 a person with whom one is in love ⟨anything you say, *darling*⟩ — see SWEETHEART 1

darn *n* the smallest amount or part imaginable ⟨nobody gave a *darn* about us when we were poor, but now that we are rich, we have friends we never knew about!⟩ — see JOT

darn *vb* to close up with a series of interlacing stitches ⟨in the old days, holes in socks had to be *darned* by hand⟩ — see SEW

darn *also* **durn** *adj* deserving of one's condemnation or displeasure ⟨I can't seem to tie this *darn* shoe⟩ — see DAMNABLE

darned *also* **durned** *adj* deserving of one's condemnation or displeasure ⟨the *darned* computer is broken⟩ — see DAMNABLE

dart *n* an act or expression showing scorn and usually intended to hurt another's feelings ⟨the *darts* flew fast and furiously when the two former friends bumped into each other at the party⟩ — see INSULT

dart *vb* to make an irregular series of quick, sudden movements ⟨the housefly *darted* about the room until it found an open window and flew out⟩ — see FLIT

dash *n* active strength of body or mind ⟨the cavalry officer's *dash* and enthusiasm inspired his men to follow him into battle⟩ — see VIGOR 1

dash *vb* **1** to go at a pace faster than a walk ⟨one sprinter *dashed* to the finish line in record-breaking time⟩ — see RUN 1

2 to proceed or move quickly ⟨we *dashed* about in a panic, trying to get everything organized before the guests were scheduled to arrive⟩ — see HURRY 2

3 to send through the air especially with a quick forward motion of the arm ⟨she *dashed* water in his face in an attempt to wake him up⟩ — see THROW 1
4 to wet or soil by striking with something liquid or mushy ⟨our clothes were *dashed* with the mud of passing cars⟩ — see SPLASH 2
5 to cause (something liquid or mushy) to move along in sheets ⟨a sudden jolt *dashed* the hot coffee onto the driver's lap⟩ — see SPLASH 1
6 to make sad ⟨she's always *dashed* by the failure of her matchmaking efforts⟩ — see DEPRESS 1

dashing *adj* inclined or willing to take risks ⟨the *dashing* heroes in stories about the American West⟩ — see BOLD 1

dashingly *adv* in a strikingly neat and trim manner ⟨a handsome young man *dashingly* dressed in a tuxedo for the prom⟩ — see SMARTLY

dastard *n* a person who shows a shameful lack of courage in the face of danger ⟨the villain of the story is a *dastard* indeed⟩ — see COWARD

dastardliness *n* a shameful lack of courage in the face of danger ⟨the *dastardliness* of the enemy's surprise attack⟩ — see COWARDICE

dastardly *adj* having or showing a shameful lack of courage ⟨his *dastardly* conduct in a critical moment haunted him for the rest of his life⟩ — see COWARDLY

data *n pl* a collection of factual knowledge about something ⟨we are putting together all the *data* we have obtained on the local housing market⟩ — see INFORMATION 1

date *n* **1** an agreement to be present at a specified time and place ⟨I have a *date* to meet my financial consultant at seven o'clock⟩ — see ENGAGEMENT 2
2 the period during which something exists, lasts, or is in progress ⟨the embarrassingly short *date* of most of his romances⟩ — see DURATION 1

date *vb* **1** to go on a social engagement with ⟨I don't want to *date* him—I'd rather just be friends⟩
synonyms go out (with), take out
related words accompany, escort, see; court, woo
2 to go on dates that may eventually lead to marriage ⟨we *dated* for two years before we got engaged⟩ — see COURT 2

dated *adj* having passed its time of use or usefulness ⟨his jokes are awfully *dated*, referring to things that happened years ago⟩ — see OBSOLETE

dateless *adj* **1** dating or surviving from the distant past ⟨*dateless* artifacts left by an obscure people of the distant past⟩ — see ANCIENT 1
2 lasting forever ⟨the *dateless* cycle of the seasons⟩ — see EVERLASTING 1
3 having an existence or validity that does not change or diminish ⟨it is because of their *dateless* themes that the plays of Shakespeare are still performed today⟩ — see ABIDING

dating *n* the series of social engagements shared by a couple looking to get married ⟨their *dating* had been going on for so long that she was starting to wonder if she'd ever take that trip down the aisle⟩ — see COURTSHIP

datum *n* a single piece of information ⟨let's begin our discussion of this matter with a *datum* from actual experience⟩ — see FACT 3

daub *vb* **1** to make dirty ⟨a tablecloth *daubed* with too many spills to ignore any longer⟩ — see DIRTY
2 to rub an oily or sticky substance over ⟨he begins his nightly transformation into a circus clown by *daubing* greasepaint on his face⟩ — see SMEAR 1

daunt *vb* to lessen the courage or confidence of ⟨the raging inferno didn't *daunt* the firefighters for a moment⟩ — see DISCOURAGE 1

dauntless *adj* feeling or displaying no fear by temperament ⟨*dauntless* heroes who are inclined to rush to danger, not away from it⟩ — see BRAVE 1

dauntlessly *adv* in a fearless manner ⟨the early suffragettes *dauntlessly* pursued their cause, even in the face of public ridicule⟩ — see BRAVELY 1

dauntlessness *n* strength of mind to carry on in spite of danger ⟨the inspiring *dauntlessness* of the soldiers who led the charge up the hill⟩ — see COURAGE

davenport *n* a long upholstered piece of furniture designed for several sitters ⟨we seated ourselves on the *davenport* while we waited for him to get ready⟩ — see COUCH

dawdle *vb* **1** to move or act slowly ⟨if you continue to *dawdle*, we'll be late for sure⟩ — see DELAY 1
2 to spend time doing nothing ⟨accused the city council of *dawdling* even as the crime rate was spiraling out of control⟩ — see IDLE

dawdler *n* someone who moves slowly or more slowly than others ⟨we encouraged the *dawdlers* to pick up the pace⟩ — see SLOWPOKE

dawdling *adj* moving or proceeding at less than the normal, desirable, or required speed ⟨the *dawdling* pace of the movie was really making us restless⟩ — see SLOW 1

dawn *n* **1** the first appearance of light in the morning or the time of its appearance ⟨we stayed up talking until *dawn*⟩
synonyms aurora, cockcrow, dawning, day, daybreak, daylight, light, morn, morning, sun, sunrise, sunup
related words daytime; forenoon
near antonyms dark, darkness, midnight, night, nighttime; afternoon, midday; dusk, evening, eventide, gloaming, twilight
antonyms nightfall, sundown, sunset
2 the point at which something begins ⟨the *dawn* of civilization⟩ — see BEGINNING

dawn *vb* to come into existence ⟨a smile *dawned* on his face as he got the joke⟩ — see BEGIN 2

dawn (on) *vb* to enter the mind of ⟨it finally *dawned on* me that I had been going the wrong way⟩ — see OCCUR (TO)

dawning *n* the first appearance of light in the morning or the time of its appearance ⟨the cold, gray *dawning* of a wintry day⟩ — see DAWN 1

day *n* **1** the hours of light between one night and the next ⟨during the *day*, we like to go play ball in the park⟩
synonyms daylight, daytime
related words light, sunlight, sunshine; dawn, dawning, daybreak, forenoon, morn, morning, sunrise; afternoon, noon; dusk, eve, evening, gloaming, nightfall, sundown, sunset, twilight
near antonyms black, blackness, dark, darkness
antonyms night, nighttime
2 an extent of time associated with a particular person or thing ⟨the brief but glorious *day* of the clipper ship⟩ — see AGE 1
3 the first appearance of light in the morning or the time of its appearance ⟨at the break of *day* I was relieved to realize that I had survived another night in the wilderness⟩ — see DAWN 1

daybook *n* a record of personal experiences, reflections, or ideas kept regularly for private use ⟨each night, before bed, she jots down her thoughts in a *daybook*⟩ — see JOURNAL 2

daybreak *n* the first appearance of light in the morning or the time of its appearance ⟨I always seem to wake up at *daybreak*, regardless of what the clock says⟩ — see DAWN 1

daydream *n* a conception or image created by the imagination and having no objective reality ⟨hoped that one day world peace would be a reality and not just a *daydream*⟩ — see FANTASY 1

daydreaming *n* the state of being lost in thought ⟨if you're bored while traveling, *daydreaming* is a perfectly normal state to be in, regardless of what the road signs say⟩ — see REVERIE

daylight *n* **1** the first appearance of light in the morning or the time of its appearance ⟨*daylight* was just breaking when we stumbled out of bed⟩ — see DAWN 1

2 the hours of light between one night and the next ⟨there isn't a lot of *daylight* left, so we'd better get home soon⟩ — see DAY 1

3 daylights *pl* the normal or healthy condition of the mental abilities ⟨nearly terrified the *daylights* out of him with that scream⟩ — see MIND 2

day nursery *n* a school for children who are generally less than five years old ⟨committed to the needs of its employees with young children, the insurance company has its own on-site *day nursery*⟩ — see NURSERY SCHOOL

day one *n* the point at which something begins ⟨since *day one* of this project, we've always insisted that we would create the best product possible without any consideration of cost⟩ — see BEGINNING

daytime *n* the hours of light between one night and the next ⟨it's a lot easier to find your way through a strange neighborhood in the *daytime*⟩ — see DAY 1

day–to–day *adj* occurring, done, produced, or appearing every day ⟨the *day-to-day* routine of commuting to work⟩ — see DAILY

daze *n* a state of mental confusion ⟨she was in a *daze* for a minute after being hit on the head by a volleyball⟩ — see HAZE 2

daze *vb* **1** to make senseless or dizzy by a blow ⟨the fall *dazed* him for a moment, causing him to become disoriented⟩ — see STUN 1

2 to overpower with light ⟨a skier *dazed* by the glare from the snow⟩ — see DAZZLE

dazed *adj* suffering from mental confusion ⟨the *dazed* goalie could only watch as the winning point went flying past him⟩ — see DIZZY 2

dazedness *n* a state of mental confusion ⟨a degree of *dazedness* that only the truly dissolute ever get to experience⟩ — see HAZE 2

dazzle *n* the quality or state of having or giving off light ⟨the *dazzle* of the stars on a cold but clear winter's night⟩ — see BRILLIANCE 1

dazzle *vb* to overpower with light ⟨skiers were *dazzled* by the glare off of the slopes of freshly packed snow⟩
synonyms bedazzle, blind, daze
related words confuse, overpower, overwhelm, stun

dazzling *adj* giving off or reflecting much light ⟨the attraction that the *dazzling* lights of Broadway have for many young performers⟩ — see BRIGHT 1

dazzlingly *adv* in a manner marked by the shining or reflecting of much light ⟨the *dazzlingly* colorful costumes worn by Las Vegas showgirls⟩ — see BRIGHTLY 1

deacon *n* a person specially trained and authorized to conduct religious services in a Christian church ⟨my cousin was married by his uncle, who is also a *deacon* in his church⟩ — see CLERGYPERSON

deactivate *vb* to cause to stop functioning ⟨*deactivate* the machine carefully, or you'll risk an electric shock⟩
synonyms kill, shut off, turn off
related words flick (off); dismantle, mothball, phase out; arrest, brake, chock, cut off, draw up, halt, jam, stall, stick
near antonyms charge, electrify, energize, fire, fuel, generate, power, push; discharge, launch, release, switch, trip; reactivate, recharge
antonyms activate, actuate, crank (up), drive, move, propel, run, set off, spark, start, touch off, trigger, turn on

dead *adj* **1** no longer living ⟨I inherited this heirloom from my *dead* great-grandfather⟩
synonyms asleep, breathless, cold, deceased, defunct, demised, departed, fallen, gone, late, lifeless, low
related words extinct; dying, fading, moribund; stillborn; finished, lapsed, terminated; inanimate, insensate, nonliving
phrases bitten the dust
near antonyms animated; dynamic, lively, thriving, vibrant, vital, vivacious; active, functioning, operative, running
antonyms alive, animate, breathing, going, live, living, quick

2 lacking in gaiety, movement, or animation ⟨the store is often *dead* after 4:00 p.m.⟩
synonyms comatose, sleepy, slow
related words lethargic, sluggish, torpid; dormant, fallow, free, idle, inactive, inert, inoperative, latent, off, vacant
near antonyms abounding, overflowing, swarming, teeming, thronging
antonyms alive, animated, astir, bustling, busy, buzzing, flourishing, humming, lively, thriving, vibrant

3 depleted in strength, energy, or freshness ⟨a long day of traveling left them just *dead*⟩ — see WEARY 1

4 having no exceptions or restrictions ⟨there was a *dead* silence following that incredibly moving performance⟩ — see ABSOLUTE 2

5 lacking in sensation or feeling ⟨my foot was *dead* after I absentmindedly sat on it for an hour⟩ — see NUMB 1

6 no longer existing ⟨the *dead* Babylonian culture⟩ — see EXTINCT

7 not being in a state of use, activity, or employment ⟨local coal mines that have been *dead* for years⟩ — see INACTIVE 2

8 of, relating to, or suggestive of death ⟨fell into a *dead* faint upon hearing the news⟩ — see DEATHLY 1

9 facing certain defeat, disaster, or death ⟨if we don't finish this project on time, we're *dead*⟩ — see DONE FOR

10 lacking in taste or flavor ⟨from the first sip I could tell that the wine hadn't aged well and was pretty much *dead*⟩ — see INSIPID 1

11 producing inferior or only a small amount of vegetation ⟨the *dead* wastes of the far country to the west⟩ — see BARREN 1

dead *adv* **1** in a direct line or course ⟨the finish line is *dead* ahead⟩ — see DIRECTLY 1

2 to a full extent or degree ⟨I'm *dead* certain that's the one I want⟩ — see FULLY 1

dead *n* the state of being dead ⟨it's impossible to raise someone from the *dead*⟩ — see DEATH 2

deadbeat *n* a lazy person ⟨he snapped instructions to the *deadbeats* who were standing around watching the work pile up⟩ — see LAZYBONES

deaden *vb* **1** to deprive of emotional or intellectual vitality ⟨an excess of detail *deadens* much of the mystery novel's suspense⟩ — see DEHYDRATE 1

2 to reduce or weaken in strength or feeling ⟨a couple of aspirins *deadened* the headache⟩ — see DULL 1

dead–end *vb* to come to an end ⟨after several fruitless years, the research seems to have simply *dead-ended*⟩ — see CEASE 1

deadhead *n* a stupid person ⟨people knew that he was a *deadhead* and voted for him anyway⟩ — see IDIOT

dead heat *n* a situation in which neither participant in a contest, competition, or struggle comes out ahead of the other ⟨the horses crossed the finish line in a *dead heat*⟩ — see TIE 1

deadlock *n* a point in a struggle where neither side is capable of winning or willing to give in ⟨the jury sent a note to the judge that it was hopelessly stuck in a *deadlock*⟩ — see IMPASSE 1

deadly *adj* **1** likely to cause or capable of causing death ⟨the doctors were alarmed about the outbreak of the *deadly* new virus⟩
synonyms baleful, deathly, fatal, fell, killer, lethal, mortal, murderous, pestilent, terminal, vital
related words baneful, deleterious, destructive, harmful, injurious, noxious, pernicious, truculent; infectious, infective, pestilential, poisonous, sublethal, toxic, virulent; dangerous, grave, grievous, hazardous, jeopardizing, menacing, parlous, perilous, risky, serious, threatening, ugly, unhealthy, unsound; bloody, internecine, sanguinary, sanguine
near antonyms beneficial, restorative, salubrious, salutary; alleviative, corrective, curative, remedial, tonic; advantageous, beneficial, useful; nonpoisonous, nontoxic, safe
antonyms healthful, healthy, nonfatal, nonlethal, wholesome
2 having no exceptions or restrictions ⟨the *deadly* tedium of waiting for the fog to lift⟩ — see ABSOLUTE 2
3 of, relating to, or suggestive of death ⟨a *deadly* pallor spread across her face as the tragic news gradually sank in⟩ — see DEATHLY 1

deadly *adv* to a great degree ⟨I'm *deadly* serious about making an offer on the house⟩ — see VERY 1

deadness *n* the state of being dead ⟨the sheer *deadness* of the corpse was the creepiest thing about it⟩ — see DEATH 2

dead–on *adj* being in agreement with the truth or a fact or a standard ⟨a stand-up comedian known for her *dead-on* impressions of various divas of stage and screen⟩ — see CORRECT 1

deadpan *adj* not expressing any emotion ⟨he delivered the joke in such a *deadpan* voice that we thought at first that he was serious⟩ — see BLANK 1

deadwood *n* discarded or useless material ⟨much of the material in the file cabinets is just *deadwood*⟩ — see GARBAGE 1

deafening *adj* marked by a high volume of sound ⟨a boom box blasting *deafening* music⟩ — see LOUD 1

[1]**deal** *n* a considerable amount ⟨there is a great *deal* of waste in government⟩ — see LOT 2

[2]**deal** *n* **1** an arrangement about action to be taken ⟨we made a *deal* to cooperate on the next assignment⟩ — see AGREEMENT 2
2 the transfer of ownership of something from one person to another for a price ⟨we closed the *deal* for the house last week⟩ — see SALE
3 a formal agreement to fulfill an obligation ⟨if the other party backs out of the *deal* after it's signed, you can sue⟩ — see GUARANTEE 1
4 position with regard to conditions and circumstances ⟨we don't yet know what the *deal* is with the new manager⟩ — see SITUATION 1
5 something bought or offered for sale at a desirable price ⟨that mail-order sweater isn't such a great *deal* after you factor in the cost of shipping and handling⟩ — see BARGAIN 1

deal *vb* **1** to carry on the business of buying and selling goods or other property ⟨that store *deals* in used furniture⟩ — see TRADE 1
2 to talk over or dispute the terms of a purchase ⟨you're going to have to learn how to *deal* if you want to buy a car at a fair price⟩ — see BARGAIN 1

deal (in) *vb* to offer for sale to the public ⟨the company *deals in* virtually all types of insurance⟩ — see MARKET

deal (out) *vb* to give out (something) to appropriate individuals ⟨aid workers *dealt out* a packet of emergency supplies to each earthquake victim⟩ — see ADMINISTER 1

deal (with) *vb* **1** to behave toward in a stated way ⟨it's important to *deal with* others fairly⟩ — see TREAT 1
2 to have (something) as a subject matter ⟨this textbook *deals with* the history of France⟩ — see CONCERN 1

dealer *n* **1** a buyer and seller of goods for profit ⟨a *dealer* in fine fabrics⟩ — see MERCHANT
2 the person in a business deal who hands over an item in exchange for money ⟨if both the *dealer* and the buyer are happy, then the item sold at a fair price⟩ — see VENDOR

dealings *n pl* doings between individuals or groups ⟨I've had *dealings* with those guys before⟩ — see RELATION 1

dean *n* the senior member of a group ⟨the *dean* of the Aspen ski instructors oversaw the training of the rescue team⟩
synonyms doyen, elder, elder statesman, éminence grise, nestor, senior
related words better, superior; old hand, old-timer, vet, veteran
near antonyms doyenne; inferior, subordinate, underling; beginner, colt, fledgling, freshman, greenhorn, neophyte, newbie, newcomer, novice, recruit, rookie, tenderfoot, tyro
antonyms baby, junior

dear *adj* **1** commanding a large price ⟨caviar has always been among the *dearest* of foods⟩ — see COSTLY
2 granted special treatment or attention ⟨spared no expense when caring for and feeding her *dear* little dog⟩ — see DARLING 1
3 having qualities that tend to make one loved ⟨a *dear* friend that I would do anything for⟩ — see LOVABLE

dear *n* a person with whom one is in love ⟨I love you, *dear*⟩ — see SWEETHEART 1

dearth *n* **1** a falling short of an essential or desirable amount or number ⟨there was a *dearth* of usable firewood at the campsite⟩ — see DEFICIENCY
2 the fact or state of being absent ⟨the *dearth* of salesclerks at the shoe store annoyed us⟩ — see LACK 1

death *n* **1** the permanent stopping of all the vital bodily activities ⟨we were all saddened by the *death* of our friend⟩
synonyms curtains, decease, demise, dissolution, doom, end, exit, expiration, expiry, fate, grave, great divide, passage, passing, quietus, sleep
related words casualty, fatality; martyrdom, self-destruction, self-murder, self-slaughter, suicide; annihilation, destruction, ending, extermination, ruin; assassination, execution, killing, massacre, slaughter
near antonyms existence, life; creation, genesis, origination, rise
antonyms birth, nativity
2 the state of being dead ⟨*death* is one of the few constants in the universe⟩
synonyms dead, deadness, grave, lifelessness, nothingness, sleep
related words mortality
near antonyms immortality; life span, lifetime
antonyms existence, life
3 the act of ceasing to exist ⟨the *death* of the Soviet economic system in the wake of the breakup of the USSR⟩
synonyms demise, expiration, expiry, termination
related words dispersion, dissolution; cessation, close, conclusion, decease, discontinuance, doom, end, ending, finish, halt, lapse, passing, quietus, shutdown, shutoff, stop, stoppage, surcease; suicide; annihilation, destruction, ruin
near antonyms existence, persistence, prolongation; inauguration, initiation, institution, origination
antonyms alpha, beginning, birth, commencement, creation, dawn, genesis, inception, incipience, incipiency, launch, morning, onset, outset, start

4 something that is the cause of one's ultimate failure or loss of life ⟨that muscle car will be the *death* of him yet⟩ — see DOWNFALL 1

5 the killing of a large number of people ⟨thousands of soldiers were lost on the field of *death*⟩ — see MASSACRE

death grip *n* the right or means to command or control others ⟨the cult leader had such a *death grip* on his followers that all orders were carried out without the slightest objection⟩ — see POWER 1

deathless *adj* lasting forever ⟨an author who craved *deathless* fame⟩ — see EVERLASTING 1

deathly *adj* **1** of, relating to, or suggestive of death ⟨his *deathly* pallor suggested that any attempt to find a pulse would be futile⟩

synonyms dead, deadly, mortal, mortuary

related words cadaverous; ghostlike, ghostly, phantom, spectral; inactive, inert, inoperative, lifeless, quiescent, still; macabre; baleful, fatal, fateful, fell, killer, lethal, murderous, pestilent

near antonyms active, alive, animate, breathing, live, living; animated, bouncing, brisk, energetic, frisky, gay, jaunty, jazzy, lively, peppy, perky, pert, racy, snappy, spanking, sparky, spirited, sprightful, sprightly, springy, vigorous, vital, vivacious, zippy; able-bodied, chipper, fit, hale, healthy, hearty, robust, sound, well, whole, wholesome

2 likely to cause or capable of causing death ⟨smallpox is one *deathly* disease that medical science has been able to conquer⟩ — see DEADLY 1

debacle *also* **débâcle** *n* **1** a sudden violent event that brings about great loss or destruction ⟨the financial *debacle* that was the stock market crash of 1929⟩ — see DISASTER 1

2 something that has failed ⟨the movie, which some had predicted would be a blockbuster, turned out to be the summer's biggest *debacle* at the multiplexes⟩ — see FAILURE 3

debar *vb* to prevent the participation, consideration, or inclusion of ⟨the judge *debarred* all of the reporters from the courtroom⟩ — see EXCLUDE

debark *vb* to go ashore from a ship ⟨the seasick passengers *debarked* as soon as the ship dropped anchor⟩ — see DISEMBARK 1

debase *vb* **1** to lower in character, dignity, or quality ⟨we *debase* ourselves when we adopt the moral code and behavior of our despised enemies⟩

synonyms abase, bastardize, canker, cheapen, corrupt, debauch, degrade, demean, demoralize, deprave, deteriorate, lessen, pervert, poison, profane, prostitute, subvert, vitiate, warp

related words befoul, begrime, contaminate, defile, dilute, dirty, pollute, taint, thin, water down, weaken; descend; disgrace, dishonor, humble, humiliate, shame, take down; blemish, damage, deface, destroy, flaw, harm, hurt, impair, mar, ruin, spoil, stain, tarnish, wreck; depreciate, downgrade

near antonyms dignify, exalt, honor; ameliorate, amend, better, enhance, enrich, improve, meliorate, perfect; clarify, clean, cleanse, purify, refine, restore; respect

antonyms elevate, ennoble, uplift

2 to reduce to a lower standing in one's own eyes or in others' eyes ⟨our failure to win a single game completely *debased* us⟩ — see HUMBLE

debased *adj* having or showing lowered moral character or standards ⟨a book that examines the *debased* character of the criminal mind⟩ — see CORRUPT

debasement *n* a sinking to a state of low moral standards and behavior ⟨the *debasement* of professional sports to a shamelessly commercial enterprise⟩ — see CORRUPTION 2

debatable *adj* **1** open to question or dispute ⟨it's always *debatable* which college football team is really number one, since there's more than one ranking system⟩

synonyms arguable, controvertible, disputable, doubtable, doubtful, issuable, moot, negotiable, questionable

related words contradictable, refutable; controversial, debated, disputed; dubious, iffy, inconclusive, indecisive, problematic (*also* problematical), shaky, uncertain; academic (*also* academical), hypothetical, speculative, theoretical (*also* theoretic); ambiguous, equivocal

near antonyms irrefutable; definite; unambiguous, unequivocal; absolute, clear, conclusive, decisive; uncontested, undisputed

antonyms accomplished, certain, hands-down, inarguable, incontestable, incontrovertible, indisputable, indubitable, irrefragable, positive, questionless, settled, sure, unanswerable, unarguable, unchallengeable, undebatable, undeniable, unquestionable

2 giving good reason for being doubted, questioned, or challenged ⟨the *debatable* wisdom of going back for another helping from the buffet⟩ — see DOUBTFUL 2

debate *n* **1** a careful weighing of the reasons for or against something ⟨after much *debate*, I decided to get the chocolate ice cream⟩ — see CONSIDERATION 1

2 variance of opinion on a matter ⟨there was a great deal of *debate* over the need for cutting costs by eliminating some programs⟩ — see DISAGREEMENT 1

3 an exchange of views for the purpose of exploring a subject or deciding an issue ⟨there was no *debate* over the expenditures before the vote⟩ — see DISCUSSION 1

debate *vb* **1** to give serious and careful thought to ⟨still *debating* what to do⟩ — see PONDER

2 to talk about (an issue) usually from various points of view and for the purpose of arriving at a decision or opinion ⟨we *debated* the advantages versus the disadvantages of the proposed waterfront development⟩ — see DISCUSS

debater *n* a person who takes part in a dispute ⟨the *debater* was unable to come up with a convincing rebuttal for his opponent's argument⟩ — see DISPUTANT

debauch *vb* to lower in character, dignity, or quality ⟨the long stay on a tropical isle had *debauched* the ship's crew to the point where they no longer acted liked naval professionals⟩ — see DEBASE 1

debauched *adj* having or showing lowered moral character or standards ⟨the *debauched* philanderer was the talk of the town⟩ — see CORRUPT

debauchee *n* **1** a person who has sunk below the normal moral standard ⟨the *debauchees* that are legendarily found at any fraternity party⟩ — see DEGENERATE

2 a person whose life is devoted to luxury and sensual pleasures ⟨the biography of a *debauchee* who underwent a late-life religious conversion and became a monk⟩ — see VOLUPTUARY

debaucher *n* a person who has sunk below the normal moral standard ⟨in his youth the man had been a *debaucher* of the worst sort⟩ — see DEGENERATE

debauchery *n* **1** immoral conduct or practices harmful or offensive to society ⟨the fraternity brothers indulged in shameless *debauchery* all weekend⟩ — see VICE 1

2 a sinking to a state of low moral standards and behavior ⟨the minister decried what he called the *debauchery* of today's society⟩ — see CORRUPTION 2

3 excessive pursuit of fleshly pleasures ⟨a night of drinking and *debauchery* at the gentleman's club⟩ — see SENSUALITY

debilitate *vb* to diminish the physical strength of ⟨the heart surgery *debilitated* the college athlete beyond his worst fears⟩ — see WEAKEN 1

debilitated *adj* lacking bodily strength ⟨the *debilitated* prisoners could barely stand⟩ — see WEAK 1

debilitation *n* **1** a gradual sinking and wasting away of mind or body ⟨the *debilitation* that all the prisoners of war had experienced during their captivity⟩ — see DECLINE 1

2 the quality or state of lacking physical strength or vigor ⟨attributed the patient's general *debilitation* to an iron deficiency⟩ — see WEAKNESS 1

debility *n* the quality or state of lacking physical strength or vigor ⟨our grandmother's *debility* is due in large part to her advanced age⟩ — see WEAKNESS 1

debit *n* a feature of someone or something that creates difficulty for achieving success ⟨one of the *debits* of living in the country was the lack of easy accessibility to health care⟩ — see DISADVANTAGE 1

debonair *adj* **1** having or showing freedom from worries or troubles ⟨his *debonair* dismissal of my inquiry concerning his financial situation led me to believe that nothing was wrong⟩ — see CAREFREE

2 having or showing very polished and worldly manners ⟨the *debonair* gentleman charmed all of the ladies in the room⟩ — see SUAVE

debris *n* **1** discarded or useless material ⟨the unsightly *debris* left after mining operations had ceased⟩ — see GARBAGE 1

2 the portion or bits of something left over or behind after it has been destroyed ⟨the demolition workers cleared away all of the *debris* from the demolished building⟩ — see REMAINS 1

debt *n* **1** something (as money) which is owed ⟨he filed for bankruptcy when his *debts* exceeded his assets⟩

synonyms arrearage, arrears, indebtedness, liability (*usually* liabilities), obligation, score

related words bond, debit, delinquency; bankruptcy, default, embarrassment, insolvency

near antonyms quietus, quittance, repayment; asset

2 a breaking of a moral or legal code ⟨forgive us our *debts*⟩ — see OFFENSE 1

debug *vb* to remove errors, defects, deficiencies, or deviations from ⟨the computer program ran much faster after it was *debugged*⟩ — see CORRECT 1

debunk *vb* **1** to prove to be false ⟨a Web site that assiduously *debunks* urban legends⟩ — see DISPROVE

2 to reveal the true nature of ⟨the investigative reporter easily *debunked* the charlatan's claims of clairvoyance⟩ — see EXPOSE 1

decadence *n* **1** a change to a lower state or level ⟨a symbol of the *decadence* of their once-mighty civilization⟩ — see DECLINE 2

2 a sinking to a state of low moral standards and behavior ⟨clergymen striving to combat *decadence* and sin in their communities⟩ — see CORRUPTION 2

decadency *n* a sinking to a state of low moral standards and behavior ⟨a novel that examines the *decadency* of a group of overprivileged teens in an affluent suburb⟩ — see CORRUPTION 2

decadent *adj* **1** having lost forcefulness, courage, or spirit ⟨social critics claimed that their culture had become *decadent* and weak⟩ — see EFFETE 1

2 having or showing lowered moral character or standards ⟨opponents of gambling casinos claim that gambling is a *decadent* form of entertainment⟩ — see CORRUPT

3 given to or marked by excessive gratification of one's desires ⟨the impressionable heiress couldn't resist the *decadent* temptations of the jet-set life⟩ — see HEDONISTIC

decadent *n* **1** a person who has sunk below the normal moral standard ⟨avant-garde artists who were scorned by the bourgeoisie as talentless *decadents*⟩ — see DEGENERATE

2 a person whose life is devoted to luxury and sensual pleasures ⟨a *decadent* who squandered her once considerable family fortune⟩ — see VOLUPTUARY

decalogue *n* a collection or system of rules of conduct ⟨the *decalogue* for scouting known as the Scout Oath⟩ — see CODE

decamping *n* the act of leaving a place ⟨the mass *decamping* for the mountains or the shore by city dwellers that occurs every summer weekend⟩ — see DEPARTURE 1

decampment *n* the act of leaving a place ⟨the simultaneous *decampment* of tens of thousands of sports fans from the stadium created the inevitable traffic jam⟩ — see DEPARTURE 1

decapitate *vb* to cut off the head of ⟨a particularly gruesome series of murders in which the victims were *decapitated*⟩

synonyms behead, guillotine, head

related words decollate; prune, shorten, trim; scalp

decay *n* **1** a gradual sinking and wasting away of mind or body ⟨middle-aged people who fervently hope that daily exercise will arrest the physical *decay* that usually accompanies advancing age⟩ — see DECLINE 1

2 the process by which dead organic matter separates into simpler substances ⟨the cycle by which the *decay* of dead plants on the forest floor provides soil and nutrients for the next generation of plants⟩ — see CORRUPTION 1

decay *vb* **1** to go through decomposition ⟨the logs *decayed* on the rain forest floor⟩ ⟨the atom of plutonium *decayed* in the test chamber⟩

synonyms break down, corrupt, decompose, disintegrate, fester, foul, mold, molder, perish [*chiefly British*], putrefy, rot, spoil

related words sour, turn, turn off [*British*]; contaminate, defile, pollute, taint; addle, curdle, ferment; mortify; rust; crumble, decline, degenerate, descend, deteriorate, dilapidate, sink, wither

phrases fall apart, go to seed (*or* run to seed)

near antonyms age, develop, grow, mature, ripen; refresh, renew, restore; cleanse, purify; assemble, compose, integrate; ameliorate, better, improve, meliorate

2 to become worse or of less value ⟨the restaurant's standards for food and service had *decayed* over the years⟩ — see DETERIORATE 1

3 to lose bodily strength or vigor ⟨having reached her 80s, the woman could sense that her body was *decaying*⟩ — see WEAKEN 2

decayed *adj* **1** having lost forcefulness, courage, or spirit ⟨a candidate who vehemently rejects the idea that liberalism is a *decayed* political philosophy⟩ — see EFFETE 1

2 having undergone organic breakdown ⟨we routinely throw all *decayed* or unwanted organic matter into our compost heap⟩ — see ROTTEN 1

decaying *n* a gradual sinking and wasting away of mind or body ⟨the *decaying* of the bone mass that is so regrettably common in elderly women⟩ — see DECLINE 1

decease *n* the permanent stopping of all the vital bodily activities ⟨in the event of the *decease* of the president, the vice president will immediately assume his duties⟩ — see DEATH 1

decease *vb* to stop living ⟨no one knows what happened to the family fortune after the spinster *deceased*⟩ — see DIE 1

deceased *adj* no longer living ⟨the recently *deceased* tenant was found by a concerned neighbor⟩ — see DEAD 1

deceit *n* **1** the inclination or practice of misleading others through lies or trickery ⟨a rise to power that was marked by treachery and *deceit*⟩

synonyms artifice, cheating, cozenage, craft, craftiness, crookedness, crookery, cunning, cunningness, deceitfulness, deception, deceptiveness, dishonesty, dissembling, dissimulation, double-dealing, dupery, du-

plicity, fakery, foxiness, fraud, guile, guilefulness, wiliness
related words equivocation, lying, mendacity, prevarication; chicane, chicanery, fraudulence, hanky-panky, jugglery, legerdemain, mountebankery, obliquity, skulduggery (*or* skullduggery), subterfuge, swindling, trickery, wile; falsehood, falsity, fib, untruth; hypocrisy, insincerity, sanctimoniousness, two-facedness; artfulness, caginess (*also* cageyness), deviousness, shrewdness; treacherousness, underhandedness, unscrupulousness; covertness, furtiveness, secrecy, shadiness, sneakiness, stealthiness; oiliness, shiftiness, slickness, slipperiness, slyness, smoothness
near antonyms candidness, candor, directness, frankness, openness, plainness, plainspokenness; honesty, probity; dependability, reliability, reliableness, solidity, trustability, trustiness, trustworthiness; decency, goodness, incorruptibility, integrity, righteousness, truthfulness, uprightness, virtuousness
antonyms artlessness, forthrightness, good faith, guilelessness, ingenuousness, sincerity
2 the tendency to tell lies ⟨she's completely free of *deceit*⟩ — see DISHONESTY 1

deceitful *adj* **1** marked by, based on, or done by the use of dishonest methods to acquire something of value ⟨charged the store owner with such *deceitful* practices as inflating the list prices for items only so he could put them on sale at drastically reduced prices⟩ — see FRAUDULENT 1
2 tending or having power to deceive ⟨the *deceitful* salesman neglected to mention some important information about the used car⟩ — see DECEPTIVE 1

deceitfulness *n* **1** the inclination or practice of misleading others through lies or trickery ⟨her *deceitfulness* about the long-term effects of her weight-loss program was finally exposed⟩ — see DECEIT 1
2 the tendency to tell lies ⟨his lifelong *deceitfulness* began when he was just a toddler⟩ — see DISHONESTY 1

deceive *vb* to cause to believe what is untrue ⟨he went to great lengths to *deceive* his family about the nature of his new job at the mall⟩
synonyms bamboozle, beguile, bluff, buffalo, burn, catch, con, cozen, delude, dupe, fake out, fool, gaff, gammon, gull, have, have on [*chiefly British*], hoax, hoodwink, hornswoggle, humbug, juggle, misguide, misinform, mislead, snooker, snow, spoof, string along, sucker, suck in, take in, trick
related words kid, put on, tease; bleed, cheat, chisel, defraud, diddle, euchre, flam, fleece, gyp, hustle, mulct, rook, shortchange, skin, squeeze, stick, sting, swindle
phrases do a number on, lead one down the garden path (*also* lead one up the garden path), pull one's leg, pull the wool over one's eyes
near antonyms debunk, expose, reveal, show up, uncloak, uncover, unmask; disclose, divulge, tell, unveil; disabuse, disenchant, disillusion
antonyms undeceive

deceiving *adj* tending or having power to deceive ⟨the *deceiving* nature of most flat maps of the globe causes some people to believe erroneously that Greenland is actually bigger than South America⟩ — see DECEPTIVE 1

decelerate *vb* to cause to move or proceed at a less rapid pace ⟨she *decelerated* the car as we entered the school zone⟩ — see SLOW 1

deceleration *n* a usually gradual decrease in the pace or level of activity of something ⟨demand for our product is dropping, so I have ordered a *deceleration* of production⟩ — see SLOWDOWN

decency *n* **1** socially acceptable behavior ⟨the standards of basic *decency* demanded that they help the old lady with her groceries⟩
synonyms decorum, form, propriety
related words etiquette; civility, courteousness, courtesy, gentilesse, gentility, graciousness, mannerliness, politeness, politesse; dignity, grace, refinement; discretion, prudence; appropriateness, correctitude, correctness, decorousness, fitness, rightness, seemliness; attention, attentiveness, care, carefulness; character, goodness, high-mindedness, honesty, honor, integrity, morality, probity, rectitude, righteousness, straightness, uprightness, virtue, virtuousness
near antonyms coarseness, crudeness, gracelessness; discourtesy, impoliteness, incivility, vulgarity; imprudence, indiscretion; badness, evil, immorality, wickedness; debauchery, degeneracy, degradation, depravity, perversion; crookedness, dishonesty, underhandedness, unscrupulousness
antonyms impropriety, indecency, indecorum
2 conduct that conforms to an accepted standard of right and wrong ⟨expected all of the scouts in his troop to be models of *decency*⟩ — see MORALITY 1

decent *adj* **1** conforming to a high standard of morality or virtue ⟨as *decent* and kind a couple as you could ever hope to meet⟩ — see GOOD 2
2 following the accepted rules of moral conduct ⟨demanded nothing less than *decent* behavior by the troops serving overseas⟩ — see HONORABLE 1
3 following the established traditions of refined society and good taste ⟨*decent* clothing for someone attending a funeral, if only as a friend of a friend⟩ — see PROPER 1
4 free from any trace of the coarse or indecent ⟨students were warned that their skits could be funny but still had to remain *decent*⟩ — see CHASTE 1
5 of a level of quality that meets one's needs or standards ⟨he did a *decent* job on the project, but there's still room for improvement⟩ — see ADEQUATE

decently *adv* in a satisfactory way ⟨her latest novel is selling *decently*, if not spectacularly⟩ — see WELL 1

deception *n* the inclination or practice of misleading others through lies or trickery ⟨a telemarketing company with a reputation for *deception*⟩ — see DECEIT 1

deceptive *adj* **1** tending or having power to deceive ⟨in his *deceptive* answer about the vehicle's history, the salesman said that the used car had never been hit by another car⟩
synonyms beguiling, deceitful, deceiving, deluding, delusive, delusory, fallacious, false, misleading, specious
related words artful, crafty, cunning, devious, foxy, guileful, shady, shifty, slick, sly, sneaking, sneaky, subtile, subtle, trick, trickish, tricky, underhand, underhanded, wily; inaccurate, incorrect, wrong; bewildering, confounding, distracting, perplexing, puzzling; ambidextrous, crooked, defrauding, dishonest, dissembling, double-dealing, duplicitous, faithless, fast, fraudulent, knavish, lying, mendacious, untrustworthy, untruthful; bogus, counterfeit, fake, feigned, forged, jive [*slang*], phony (*also* phoney), sham, spurious; insidious, perfidious, treacherous; ambiguous, circuitous, equivocal, evasive; artificial, backhanded, hypocritical, insincere, left-handed, two-faced
near antonyms candid, direct, foursquare, frank, freespoken, open, openhearted, outspoken, plain, plainspoken, straight; clarifying, elucidative, explanatory, illuminating; revealing, revelatory; honest, trustworthy, truthful
antonyms aboveboard, forthright, nondeceptive, straightforward
2 given to or marked by cheating and deception ⟨a mail-order firm indicted for *deceptive* business practices⟩ — see DISHONEST 2

deceptiveness *n* the inclination or practice of misleading others through lies or trickery ⟨numerous complaints about the *deceptiveness* of the ad campaign⟩ — see DECEIT 1

decibel *n, usually* **decibels** *pl* loud, confused, and usually inharmonious sound ⟨the crowd *decibels* increased dramatically as the horses neared the finish line⟩ — see NOISE 1

decide *vb* **1** to come to a judgment about after discussion or consideration ⟨they *decided* to go out for pizza after the movie was over⟩
synonyms choose, conclude, determine, figure, name, opt, resolve, settle (on *or* upon)
related words decree, rule; cull, elect, handpick, pick, prefer, select, single (out); adjudge, adjudicate, arbitrate, find, judge, referee, rule (on), umpire; chew over, cogitate, consider, contemplate, debate, deliberate, entertain, meditate, mull (over), ponder, question, ruminate, study, think (about *or* over), weigh
near antonyms abstain, decline, refuse, reject, turn down; delay, halt, hesitate, stall, temporize; shilly-shally, vacillate, waffle, waver
2 to give an opinion about (something at issue or in dispute) ⟨the judge *decided* that the defendant was not liable for damages⟩ — see JUDGE 1
3 to come to an agreement or decision concerning the details of ⟨we waited for our captors to *decide* our fate⟩ — see ARRANGE 1
4 to make final, definite, or beyond dispute ⟨the huge sum that they were offering *decided* the matter: we would sell the house⟩ — see CLINCH
5 to form an opinion or reach a conclusion through reasoning and information ⟨the commanding officer *decided* that the soldier was indeed telling the truth⟩ — see INFER 1

decided *adj* not subject to misinterpretation or more than one interpretation ⟨a *decided* hint of perfume on her skin⟩ — see CLEAR 2

decidedness *n* firm or unwavering adherence to one's purpose ⟨for two years he pursued the presidential nomination with an undeviating *decidedness*⟩ — see DETERMINATION 1

deciding *adj* serving to put an end to all debate or questioning ⟨the project's prohibitive cost was the *deciding* factor in its cancellation⟩ — see CONCLUSIVE 1

deciduous *adj* lasting only for a short time ⟨he chose not to fret about the *deciduous* discomforts of his existence⟩ — see MOMENTARY

decimate *vb* to bring to a complete end the physical soundness, existence, or usefulness of ⟨the army's attack *decimated* the enemy's defenses beyond repair⟩ — see DESTROY 1

decimation *n* the state or fact of being rendered nonexistent, physically unsound, or useless ⟨the virtual *decimation* of the coastal town by the hurricane⟩ — see DESTRUCTION 1

decipher *vb* **1** to change (as a secret message) from code into ordinary language ⟨we *deciphered* the hidden message to find out when we were supposed to meet⟩ — see DECODE 1
2 to have a clear idea of ⟨a convoluted thriller, the plot of which I was never able to actually *decipher*⟩ — see COMPREHEND 1

decision *n* **1** a position arrived at after consideration ⟨after much deliberation, we made a *decision* about what to have on our pizza⟩
synonyms award, call, conclusion, deliverance, determination, diagnosis, judgment (*or* judgement), opinion, resolution, verdict
related words behest, charge, commandment, decree, dictate, directive, edict, instruction, mandate, order, word; last word, say-so; adjudication, disposition, doom, finding, ruling, sentence; choice, option, selection; consensus; belief, conviction, eye, feeling, mind, notion, persuasion, sentiment, view
near antonyms deadlock, draw, halt, stalemate, standoff, tie
2 firm or unwavering adherence to one's purpose ⟨acted with swift *decision*⟩ — see DETERMINATION 1

decisive *adj* **1** fully committed to achieving a goal ⟨only a team with a *decisive* attitude is going to win a state championship⟩ — see DETERMINED 1
2 having the power to persuade ⟨a lawyer who knows how to construct the kind of *decisive* argument that sways a jury⟩ — see COGENT
3 serving to put an end to all debate or questioning ⟨the *decisive* finding of the coroner regarding the cause of death⟩ — see CONCLUSIVE 1

decisiveness *n* firm or unwavering adherence to one's purpose ⟨moved with speed and *decisiveness* in investigating the charges of the use of excessive force by the police⟩ — see DETERMINATION 1

deck *n* a flat roofless structure attached to a building ⟨the family usually ate on the *deck* on summer evenings⟩ — see SUNDECK

deck *vb* to make more attractive by adding something that is beautiful or becoming ⟨*deck* the halls with boughs of holly⟩ — see DECORATE

deck (out) *vb* to outfit with clothes and especially fine or special clothes ⟨all *decked out* in our finest outfits for the wedding⟩ — see CLOTHE 1

declaim *vb* **1** to give a formal often extended talk on a subject ⟨over the last two centuries some of the most illustrious personages of their times have *declaimed* in the town's historic lyceum⟩ — see TALK 1
2 to talk as if giving an important and formal speech ⟨he *declaimed* at some length about the nation's obligation to spread democratic values around the world⟩ — see ORATE 1

declamation *n* a usually formal discourse delivered to an audience ⟨inspired *declamations* about the global triumph of democracy within our lifetimes⟩ — see SPEECH 1

declaration *n* a solemn and often public declaration of the truth or existence of something ⟨once the delegates had made the *declaration* that the colonies were henceforth independent of Great Britain, their fate was sealed⟩ — see PROTESTATION

declare *vb* **1** to make known openly or publicly ⟨she chose to *declare* her presidential aspirations at her college alma mater⟩ — see ANNOUNCE
2 to state as a fact usually forcefully ⟨she would *declare* her innocence to the whole world if she could⟩ — see CLAIM 1
3 to state clearly and strongly ⟨our guest enthusiastically *declared* that the pie was the best he had ever eaten⟩ — see ASSERT 1
4 to make known (something abstract) through outward signs ⟨though she was silent, her expression *declared* her unwillingness to go along with the others⟩ — see SHOW 2

declension *n* **1** a gradual sinking and wasting away of mind or body ⟨a noticeable *declension* of the fitness of the baseball players over the winter⟩ — see DECLINE 1
2 a change to a lower state or level ⟨a *declension* in her acting career from leading roles to cameos eventually⟩ — see DECLINE 2
3 a downward slope ⟨from this region to the seacoast there's a gentle *declension* of the landscape⟩ — see DECLINE 3

declination *n* **1** a change to a lower state or level ⟨there's been a *declination* in basic civility in our society⟩ — see DECLINE 2
2 an unwillingness to grant something asked for ⟨congressional *declinations* of cabinet appointments have been relatively infrequent, most senators believing that

the president is entitled to pick his own advisors⟩ — see DENIAL 1

decline *n* **1** a gradual sinking and wasting away of mind or body ⟨her sad *decline* from a robust athlete to an old woman with arthritis⟩
synonyms debilitation, decay, decaying, declension, degeneration, descent, deterioration, ebbing, enfeeblement, weakening
related words atrophy; exhaustion; drooping, flagging, limping; regression, relapse, setback
near antonyms invigoration, strengthening; progress; rejuvenation, rejuvenescence
antonyms comeback, improvement, rally, recovery, recuperation, rehabilitation, revitalization, snapback
2 a change to a lower state or level ⟨the *decline* of the Roman Empire⟩
synonyms decadence, declension, declination, degeneracy, degeneration, degradation, dégringolade, descent, deterioration, devolution, downfall, downgrade, ebb, eclipse, fall
related words dark age, nadir, sunset; decay, rotting, spoiling; breakup, crumbling, decomposition, disintegration, dissolution; abasement, debasement; depreciation, lessening; decimation, demolishment, demolition, desolation, destruction, havoc, ruin, ruination; abatement, decrease, decrement, de-escalation, deflation, diminishment, diminution, dip, downslide, downtrend, downturn, drop, drop-off, falloff, loss, lowering, reduction, sag, shrinkage, slip, slump
near antonyms advancement, development, evolution, growth; blossoming, flourishing, flowering; renewal, restoration, revitalization; heightening; accretion, accrual, addendum, addition, augmentation, boost, enhancement, gain, increase, increment, raise, supplement
antonyms ascent, rise, upswing
3 a downward slope ⟨the bicyclist lost control on the unexpectedly steep *decline*⟩
synonyms declension, declivity, descent, dip, downgrade, downhill, fall, hang, hanging
related words basin, depression, hollow
near antonyms glacis, grade, gradient, hill, inclination, incline, lean, pitch, rake, tilt
antonyms acclivity, ascent, rise, upgrade, uphill, uprise
4 a loss of status ⟨the engagement at the small club was an unmistakable sign of the rock band's *decline*⟩ — see COMEDOWN
5 the amount by which something is lessened ⟨a huge *decline* in the value of the artwork after its authenticity was questioned⟩ — see DECREASE

decline *vb* **1** to show unwillingness to accept, do, engage in, or agree to ⟨he *declined* the invitation to the party⟩ ⟨she *declined* to participate in the soccer game⟩
synonyms balk (at), deselect, disapprove, negative, nix, pass, pass up, refuse, reject, reprobate, repudiate, spurn, throw out, throw over, turn down
related words blow off, disdain, rebuff, scorn, scout, shoot down; overrule, veto; forbid, prohibit, proscribe; dismiss, ignore; abstain (from), forbear, refrain (from); deny, disavow, disclaim, dispute, gainsay; stick; abjure, forswear (*also* foreswear), recant, renounce, retract, take back, unsay, withdraw; avoid, bypass, detour; contradict, deny, disown, negate; controvert, disagree (with), disprove, dispute, rebut, refute; back down, back off, backtrack; disallow, recall, renege, revoke
phrases turn one's back on
near antonyms condone, countenance, swallow, tolerate; adopt, embrace, receive, take, welcome; accede, acquiesce, agree, assent, consent; choose, handpick, select; espouse, support
antonyms accept, agree (to), approve
2 to be unwilling to grant ⟨*declined* our request to hold a party⟩ — see DENY 2
3 to go to a lower level especially abruptly ⟨new-car sales *declined* to their lowest level in years⟩ — see DROP 2
4 to become worse or of less value ⟨his reputation as a writer began to *decline* not long after his death⟩ — see DETERIORATE 1
5 to grow less in scope or intensity especially gradually ⟨the winds should *decline* as soon as the cold front passes⟩ — see DECREASE 2
6 to lead or extend downward ⟨the bike path *declines* toward the riverbank and then follows the river for several miles⟩ — see DESCEND 1

declined *adj* bending downward or forward ⟨we awaited our punishment with *declined* heads⟩ — see NODDING

declining *adj* bending downward or forward ⟨the *declining* flowers perked up with the gentle rainfall⟩ — see NODDING

declivity *n* a downward slope ⟨the cabin is precariously perched on a *declivity* of the mountain's northern face⟩ — see DECLINE 3

decode *vb* **1** to change (as a secret message) from code into ordinary language ⟨the agents worked into the night to *decode* the intercepted message from the enemy spy⟩
synonyms break, crack, decipher, decrypt
related words descramble, unscramble; render, translate; dope (out), figure out, puzzle (out), solve, unravel, unriddle, work, work out
near antonyms garble, jumble (up), mix (up)
antonyms cipher, code, encipher, encode, encrypt
2 to have a clear idea of ⟨I was never able to *decode* the strange relationship that existed between those two people⟩ — see COMPREHEND 1

decolorize *vb* to make white or whiter by removing color ⟨the sample was *decolorized* before being examined under a microscope⟩ — see WHITEN

decompose *vb* to go through decomposition ⟨detectives needed to know how long it would take a corpse to *decompose* to that advanced state⟩ — see DECAY 1

decomposed *adj* having undergone organic breakdown ⟨the *decomposed* remains of an old tree trunk⟩ — see ROTTEN 1

decomposition *n* the process by which dead organic matter separates into simpler substances ⟨the unmistakable smell of *decomposition* led us to some fruit that had fallen behind the refrigerator⟩ — see CORRUPTION 1

decompress *vb* to get rid of nervous tension or anxiety ⟨after she gets home from work, she needs some time to *decompress* before preparing dinner⟩ — see RELAX 1

decompression *n* freedom from activity or labor ⟨the waitstaff gets a welcome period of *decompression* between the lunch and dinner rushes⟩ — see [1]REST 1

deconsecrate *vb* to remove the sacred qualities or status of ⟨hoping to raise much-needed funds, the church elders *deconsecrated* the 18th-century silver chalice and consigned it to a high-end auction house⟩ — see DESANCTIFY

deconstruct *vb* to identify and examine the basic elements or parts of (something) especially for discovering interrelationships ⟨*deconstructing* the economic theories of John Maynard Keynes⟩ — see ANALYZE

deconstruction *n* the separation and identification of the parts of a whole ⟨a lengthy *deconstruction* of the president's speech by a panel of pundits⟩ — see ANALYSIS 1

decor *or* **décor** *n* the array of painted backgrounds and furnishings used to establish the setting in a stage production ⟨a minimalist approach has been taken with the stage *decor* for this production of the play⟩ — see SCENERY

decorate *vb* to make more attractive by adding something that is beautiful or becoming ⟨*decorated* the mansion's hallways with priceless paintings and luxurious tapestries⟩
synonyms adorn, array, beautify, bedeck, bedizen, blazon, caparison, deck, do, doll up, do up, drape, dress, embellish, emblaze, emboss, enrich, fancify, fancy up, festoon, garnish, glitz (up), grace, gussy up, ornament, pretty (up), trim
related words accessorize, dress up, trap, trick (out); brighten, freshen, smarten, spruce (up); boss, chase; braid, embroider, feather, figure, filigree, fillet, flounce, frill, fringe, furbelow, garland, hang, lace, ribbon, swag, wreathe; appliqué, gild, paint; diamond, gem, impearl, jewel, pearl; redecorate, redo
near antonyms simplify, streamline; bare, denude, dismantle, display, divest, expose, reveal, strip, uncover; uglify
antonyms blemish, deface, disfigure, mar, scar, spoil

decoration *n* **1** something that decorates or beautifies ⟨traditionally the family puts lots of *decorations* on and around the Christmas tree⟩
synonyms adornment, beautifier, caparison, doodad, embellisher, embellishment, frill, garnish, garnishment, garniture, ornament, ornamentation, setoff, trim
related words apparel, bells and whistles, blazonry, bric-a-brac, chichi, emblazonry, filigree, finery, foofaraw, frippery, frosting, froufrou; fal-lal, flounce, flourish, furbelow, ruffle; enhancement, enrichment, improvement; appliqué, embossment, embroidery, fancywork; bedizenment, gilt, glitter; design, figure, pattern; furnishings, regalia, trappings
near antonyms blemish, defacement, disfigurement, scar; blot, spot, stain
2 something given in recognition of achievement ⟨an army veteran proudly wearing his old military *decorations*⟩ — see AWARD 1

decorative *adj* serving to add beauty ⟨a necklace of *decorative* flowers was planted along the path to the cottage⟩
synonyms adorning, beautifying, cosmetic, embellishing, ornamental
related words alluring, appealing, attractive, charming, delightful, glamorous (*also* glamourous), pleasing, prepossessing; beauteous, beautiful, bonny (*also* bonnie) [*chiefly British*], comely, fair, gorgeous, handsome, lovely, pretty, stunning; detailed, elaborate, fancy, ornate
antonyms functional, utilitarian

decorous *adj* **1** following the established traditions of refined society and good taste ⟨we were asked to be on our most *decorous* behavior at the formal event⟩ — see PROPER 1
2 marked by or showing careful attention to set forms and details ⟨the oppressively *decorous* standards of a royal court⟩ — see CEREMONIOUS 1

decorum *n* socially acceptable behavior ⟨high standards of *decorum* are usually required when attending the opera⟩ — see DECENCY 1

decouple *vb* to set or force apart ⟨to have a fruitful discussion, we need to *decouple* fact from opinion⟩ — see SEPARATE 1

decoy *n* something used to attract animals to a hook or into a trap ⟨we set the *decoy* afloat in the marsh and from the blind waited for the ducks to arrive⟩ — see BAIT 1

decoy *vb* to lead away from a usual or proper course by offering some pleasure or advantage ⟨tacky souvenir shops to which first-time tourists had been *decoyed* into spending their hard-earned money⟩ — see LURE

decrease *n* the amount by which something is lessened ⟨the average *decrease* in the price of milk was five cents per gallon⟩
synonyms abatement, decline, decrement, dent, depletion, depression, diminishment, diminution, drop, drop-off, fall, falloff, loss, reduction, shrinkage, step-down
related words deduction, subtraction; downturn, slip, slump; curtailment, cut, cutback, retrenchment, shortening
near antonyms accretion, accrual, accumulation, addition, supplement; continuation, extension; upswing, uptrend, upturn
antonyms boost, enlargement, gain, increase, increment, raise, rise, step-up, uptick

decrease *vb* **1** to make smaller in amount, volume, or extent ⟨workers *decreased* the volume of water flowing through the pipes in order to prevent an overflow⟩
synonyms abate, de-escalate, dent, deplete, diminish, downscale, downsize, drop, dwindle, ease, knock down, lessen, lower, reduce
related words compress, condense, constrict, contract; abbreviate, abridge, clip, crop, curtail, cut, cut back, cut down, dock, nick, pare, prune, retrench, shorten, slash, trim, truncate, whittle; deflate, shrink; minimize; moderate, modify, modulate, qualify
near antonyms blow up, dilate, distend, inflate, swell; elongate, extend, lengthen, prolong, protract; add (to), complement, supplement; enhance, heighten, intensify; redouble
antonyms aggrandize, amplify, augment, boost, enlarge, escalate, expand, increase, raise
2 to grow less in scope or intensity especially gradually ⟨the force of the wind slowly *decreased* until the flowers were standing upright again⟩
synonyms abate, decline, de-escalate, die (away *or* down *or* out), diminish, drain (away), drop (off), dwindle, ease, ebb, fall, fall away, lessen, let up, lower, moderate, pall, phase down, ratchet (down) *also* rachet (down), recede, relent, remit, shrink, subside, taper, taper off, wane
related words compress, condense, constrict, contract; evaporate, fade (away), fritter (away), give out, melt (away), peter (out), tail (off), vanish; slacken, slow (down); alleviate, relax; flag, sink, weaken; cave (in), collapse, deflate
near antonyms appear, emerge, show up; blow up, distend, elongate, lengthen
antonyms accumulate, balloon, build, burgeon (*also* bourgeon), enlarge, escalate, expand, grow, increase, intensify, mount, mushroom, pick up, rise, snowball, soar, swell, wax

decree *n* **1** a statement of what to do that must be obeyed by those concerned ⟨the boss doesn't give out many *decrees*, but he does expect those that are issued to be fully obeyed⟩ — see COMMAND 1
2 an order publicly issued by an authority ⟨a *decree* issued by the state's supreme court to the legislature⟩ — see EDICT 1

decree *vb* to request the doing of by virtue of one's authority ⟨the new supervisor *decreed* that thenceforth coffee breaks would have a 15-minute limit⟩ — see COMMAND 2

decrement *n* the amount by which something is lessened ⟨each *decrement* in amount is limited to one third of the previous total⟩ — see DECREASE

decry *vb* **1** to express scornfully one's low opinion of ⟨scientists were quick to *decry* the claims of the psychic⟩
synonyms bad-mouth, belittle, cry down, denigrate, deprecate, depreciate, derogate, diminish, dis (*also* diss) [*slang*], discount, dismiss, disparage, kiss off, minimize, play down, poor-mouth, put down, run down, talk

down, trash, trash-talk, vilipend, write off
related words discommend; abuse, scold; disapprove (of), dislike; censure, condemn, criticize, denounce, reprehend, reprobate; asperse, defame, malign, rip, slander, slur, traduce, vilify; discredit, disgrace
phrases dump on
near antonyms approve, countenance, endorse (*also* indorse), favor, recommend, sanction; commend, compliment, eulogize
antonyms acclaim, applaud, exalt, extol (*also* extoll), glorify, laud, magnify, praise
2 to declare to be morally wrong or evil ⟨a statement by the church *decrying* modern society's liberal attitude regarding marriage and divorce⟩ — see CONDEMN 1

decrying *adj* intended to make a person or thing seem of little importance or value ⟨the usual *decrying* remarks about the clothes that the stars wore to the awards ceremony⟩ — see DEROGATORY

decrypt *vb* to change (as a secret message) from code into ordinary language ⟨*decrypting* the Germans' code was one of the Allies' greatest triumphs⟩ — see DECODE 1

dedicate *vb* to keep or intend for a special purpose ⟨a young attorney who has decided to *dedicate* her career to helping the poor receive justice⟩ — see DEVOTE 1

dedicated *adj* firm in one's allegiance to someone or something ⟨a *dedicated* follower of the television show who wouldn't dream of missing an episode⟩ — see FAITHFUL 1

dedication *n* adherence to something to which one is bound by a pledge or duty ⟨her *dedication* to the ideals of the organization is indeed admirable⟩ — see FIDELITY

deduce *vb* to form an opinion or reach a conclusion through reasoning and information ⟨I can *deduce* from the simple observation of your behavior that you're trying to hide something from me⟩ — see INFER 1

deducible *adj* being or provable by reasoning in which the conclusion follows necessarily from given information ⟨the killer's identity is clearly *deducible* from the clues scattered throughout the novel⟩ — see DEDUCTIVE

deduct *vb* to take away (an amount or number) from a total ⟨after *deducting* taxes, what's left is your net pay for the week⟩ — see SUBTRACT

deduction *n* **1** something that is or may be subtracted ⟨contestants get a *deduction* from their scores for every incorrect guess⟩
synonyms abatement, discount, reduction
related words giveback, kickback, rebate; dent, depreciation; decline, decrement, diminishment, diminution, drop, fall, loss; forfeit, forfeiture, penalty
near antonyms accretion, accrual, augmentation, boost, gain, increase, increment, raise, rise; appreciation
antonyms accession, addition
2 the act or an instance of taking away from a total ⟨the *deduction* of the amount awarded to the plaintiff in order to pay the legal fees⟩ — see SUBTRACTION
3 an opinion arrived at through a process of reasoning ⟨his impressive *deduction* of the correct answer from only a few hints⟩ — see CONCLUSION 1

deductive *adj* being or provable by reasoning in which the conclusion follows necessarily from given information ⟨using *deductive* reasoning we must conclude that since everyone eventually dies, sooner or later it's going to be our turn⟩
synonyms a priori, deducible, derivable, inferable (*also* inferrible), inferential, reasoned
related words conjectural, hypothetical, purported, supposed, suppositional; academic (*also* academical), speculative, theoretical (*also* theoretic); logical, rational
near antonyms inducible, inductive; absolute, categorical (*also* categoric), definite, explicit, express; instinctive, intuitive; illogical, irrational
antonyms nondeductive

deed *n* **1** an act of notable skill, strength, or cleverness ⟨traditionally heroes have been celebrated for their great *deeds* in song and story⟩ — see FEAT 1
2 something done by someone ⟨*deeds* always carry greater weight than words⟩ — see ACTION 1

deed *vb* to give over the legal possession or ownership of ⟨the philanthropist unexpectedly *deeded* his entire fortune to the animal shelter⟩ — see TRANSFER 1

deem *vb* to have as an opinion ⟨I *deem* it fitting that we mark this solemn occasion with a day of prayer and thanksgiving⟩ — see BELIEVE 2

de–emphasize *vb* to reduce in apparent importance ⟨you're at a point in your career where you can *de-emphasize* your academic record and emphasize your work experience⟩ — see SOFT-PEDAL

deep *adj* **1** extending far downward ⟨lowered their bucket down a *deep* well⟩ ⟨the ax made a *deep* cut into the wood⟩
synonyms abysmal, bottomless, profound
related words abyssal, unfathomable; boundless, endless, immeasurable, inestimable, infinite, limitless, measureless, unlimited, vast
near antonyms depthless, two-dimensional; even, flat, flush, horizontal, level, plane, smooth; confined, finite, limited, measured, restricted
antonyms shallow, shoal, skin-deep, superficial, surface
2 having a low musical pitch or range ⟨the tour guide had an impressively *deep* voice⟩
synonyms bass, grave, low, throaty
related words boomy, tubby; gruff, hoarse, husky, rough, smoky (*also* smokey)
near antonyms squeaking, squeaky, squealing, thin; earsplitting, penetrating, piercing, strident; peeping, tinny
antonyms acute, high, high-pitched, piping, sharp, shrill, treble
3 being beyond one's powers to know, understand, or explain ⟨a *deep*, dark secret that he took to his grave⟩ — see MYSTERIOUS 1
4 difficult for one of ordinary knowledge or intelligence to understand ⟨her poetry is now regarded as sentimental and not very *deep*⟩ — see PROFOUND 1
5 having an often intentionally veiled or uncertain meaning ⟨one of those *deep* passages in the Bible that can be interpreted in any number of different ways⟩ — see OBSCURE 1
6 extreme in degree, power, or effect ⟨fell into a *deep* sleep after taking the potion⟩ — see INTENSE 1
7 firmly established over time ⟨a *deep* devotion to obtaining justice for all, even society's most disadvantaged⟩ — see INVETERATE 1
8 having considerable extent ⟨an economist with a *deep* understanding of the forces that propel the global economy⟩ — see EXTENSIVE
9 having the mind fixed on something ⟨I was so *deep* in the mystery novel that I didn't hear the doorbell⟩ — see ATTENTIVE 1
10 not close in time or space ⟨an episode in her *deep* past that she had never spoken about, even to her husband⟩ — see DISTANT 1

deep *n* **1** the most intense or characteristic phase of something ⟨the kind of cold weather that we usually have only in the *deep* of winter⟩ — see THICK
2 the whole body of salt water that covers nearly three-fourths of the earth ⟨sailors exploring the farther reaches of the briny *deep*⟩ — see OCEAN 1
3 an immeasurable depth or space ⟨the belief that

somewhere in the *deep* of outer space humankind will meet its ultimate destiny⟩ — see ABYSS

deepen *vb* to make markedly greater in measure or degree ⟨this book really *deepens* our knowledge of how the brain works⟩ — see INTENSIFY

deep freeze *n* **1** a state of temporary inactivity ⟨his hunt for a new house was put in the *deep freeze* while he recovered from the auto accident⟩ — see ABEYANCE
2 a weather condition marked by low temperatures ⟨the *deep freeze* had everyone thinking that global warming might not be so bad⟩ — see COLD

deepness *n* **1** distance measured from the top to the bottom of something ⟨the *deepness* of the well could not be determined by visual means⟩ — see DEPTH 1
2 the quality of being great in extent (as of insight) ⟨the *deepness* of his knowledge on the subject is truly impressive⟩ — see DEPTH 2

deep pocket *n* a wealthy person ⟨argued that the *deep pockets* will benefit most from the tax cuts⟩ — see CAPITALIST

deep-pocketed *adj* having goods, property, or money in abundance ⟨thanks to a *deep-pocketed* benefactor, she can pursue her dream of becoming an artist without worrying about how to pay the rent⟩ — see RICH 1

deep-rooted *adj* firmly established over time ⟨he had had a *deep-rooted* fear of the dark from the time he was a small child⟩ — see INVETERATE 1

deep-sea *adj* of, relating to, or occurring in the open sea ⟨chartered a boat to do some *deep-sea* fishing⟩
synonyms blue-water, oceanic, pelagic
related words deepwater; marine, maritime, nautical
near antonyms littoral

deep-seated *adj* firmly established over time ⟨has *deep-seated* convictions about religion that no one is ever going to change⟩ — see INVETERATE 1

deep-six *vb* to get rid of as useless or unwanted ⟨*deep-sixed* the documents with the incriminating evidence⟩ — see DISCARD

deep throat *n* a person who provides information about another's wrongdoing ⟨an accountant who had turned *deep throat*, he was the first to leak the information that the company had been cooking its books for years⟩ — see INFORMER

de-escalate *vb* **1** to make smaller in amount, volume, or extent ⟨first, the mediator tried to *de-escalate* the tension in the room⟩ — see DECREASE 1
2 to grow less in scope or intensity especially gradually ⟨the fighting *de-escalated* as the peace talks progressed⟩ — see DECREASE 2

def *adj, slang* keenly aware of and responsive to the latest developments especially in fashion and entertainment ⟨of the rappers on the scene, he was definitely the most *def*⟩ — see AU COURANT 1

deface *vb* **1** to deliberately cause the damage or destruction of another's property ⟨the principal vowed to get the punks who *defaced* the statue in front of the school⟩ — see VANDALIZE 1
2 to reduce the soundness, effectiveness, or perfection of ⟨years of wear had *defaced* the fine engraving on the coins⟩ — see DAMAGE 1

defacement *n* deliberate damaging or destroying of another's property ⟨the *defacement* of the school's property ended up costing hundreds of dollars⟩ — see VANDALISM

defacer *n* a person who damages or destroys property on purpose ⟨so far the police have no leads on the identity of the *defacer* of the street signs⟩ — see VANDAL

defacing *n* deliberate damaging or destroying of another's property ⟨the neo-Nazis' *defacing* of the synagogue was condemned by the entire community⟩ — see VANDALISM

de facto *adj* existing in fact and not merely as a possibility ⟨with the death of his father, he became the *de facto* head of the family⟩ — see ACTUAL

defamation *n* the making of false statements that damage another's reputation ⟨accused the newspaper columnist of *defamation* of character⟩ — see SLANDER

defamatory *adj* causing or intended to cause unjust injury to a person's good name ⟨*defamatory* remarks that were published in the newspaper⟩ — see LIBELOUS

defame *vb* **1** to make untrue and harmful statements about ⟨of course I want to win the election, but I refuse to *defame* my opponent in order to do so⟩ — see SLANDER
2 *archaic* to make a claim of wrongdoing against ⟨so the harmless old woman was *defamed* of witchcraft⟩ — see ACCUSE

defaming *n* the making of false statements that damage another's reputation ⟨the callous *defaming* of the popular actress by the unscrupulous tabloid reporter⟩ — see SLANDER

default *n* the nonperformance of an assigned or expected action ⟨a *default* in the repayment of a bank loan⟩ — see FAILURE 1

defeasance *n* the doing away with something by formal action ⟨the kind of gross misconduct that could result in the *defeasance* of the athlete's contract to endorse their products⟩ — see ABOLITION

defeat *n* **1** failure to win a contest ⟨sore losers still griping about their *defeat* in the basketball game earlier that week⟩
synonyms beating, drubbing, licking, loss, lump, overthrow, plastering, rout, shellacking, trimming, trouncing, whipping
related words collapse, debacle (*also* débâcle), failure, fiasco, fizzle, flop, nonsuccess, setback, upset; lurch, shutout, washout, whitewash
near antonyms accomplishment, achievement; blowout, cakewalk, landslide, romp, runaway, sweep, walkaway, walkover
antonyms success, triumph, victory, win
2 a falling short of one's goals ⟨truly disheartened by the *defeat* of his plans to revitalize downtown⟩ — see FAILURE 2

defeat *vb* to achieve a victory over ⟨they *defeated* their archrivals easily and moved into the next round of the play-offs⟩ — see BEAT 2

defeatist *adj* emphasizing or expecting the worst ⟨your *defeatist* attitude is depressing everyone else on the team!⟩ — see PESSIMISTIC 1

defeatist *n* one who emphasizes bad aspects or conditions and expects the worst ⟨we told her that if she was going to be such a *defeatist*, she should keep her thoughts to herself⟩ — see PESSIMIST 1

defect *n* something that spoils the appearance or completeness of a thing ⟨the statue has a slight *defect* on the base, so it's being sold at a discount⟩ — see BLEMISH

defect (from) *vb* to leave (a cause or party) often in order to take up another ⟨soldiers *defected from* the rebel army en masse as the failure of their cause became apparent⟩
synonyms desert, rat (on)
related words abandon, abdicate, abjure, apostatize, cut off, disown, forsake, quit, reject, renounce, repudiate, spurn; renege; depart, go, leave, withdraw
phrases go back on, jump ship, run out on, walk out on
near antonyms adhere (to), cling (to), stick (to *or* with); cherish, cultivate, foster

defective *adj* having a fault ⟨promptly took the *defective* microwave oven back to the store for a replacement⟩ — see FAULTY

defector *n* a person who abandons a cause or organization usually without right ⟨the *defector* demanded political asylum in exchange for information about his nation's spying operations⟩ — see RENEGADE

defend *vb* **1** to drive danger or attack away from ⟨a solemn oath to *defend* the mother country at any cost⟩
synonyms bulwark, cover, fence, fend, forfend, guard, keep, protect, safeguard, screen, secure, shield, ward
related words avert, prevent; oppose, resist, withstand; battle, contend, fight, war; conserve, preserve, save; buffer, palisade, picket, wall
phrases stand up for
near antonyms bombard, storm; beset, besiege, overrun; capitulate, cave, submit, yield
antonyms assail, assault, attack
2 to continue to declare to be true or proper despite opposition or objections ⟨she will pigheadedly *defend* any claim regardless of all evidence to the contrary⟩ — see MAINTAIN 2

defendable *adj* **1** capable of being defended against physical attack ⟨that nation has long insisted on having borders that it regards as *defendable*⟩ — see TENABLE 1
2 capable of being defended with good reasoning against verbal attack ⟨your thesis had better be *defendable* for the attacks are going to be withering⟩ — see TENABLE 2

defender *n* someone that protects ⟨one of the traditional roles of an older brother is that of schoolyard *defender*⟩ — see PROTECTOR

defense *n* **1** means or method of defending ⟨thorns are a rose's *defense* against grazing animals⟩
synonyms aegis (*also* egis), ammunition, armor, buckler, cover, guard, protection, safeguard, screen, security, shield, wall, ward
related words arm, armament, munitions, weapon, weaponry; fastness, fort, fortress, palisade, stronghold
near antonyms aggression, assault, attack, offense (*or* offence), offensive
2 an explanation that frees one from fault or blame ⟨there's absolutely no *defense* for your actions⟩ — see EXCUSE

defenseless *adj* lacking protection from danger or resistance against attack ⟨the lack of warm clothing left the hikers *defenseless* against the unexpected cold snap⟩ — see HELPLESS 1

defenselessness *n* the quality or state of having little resistance to some outside agent ⟨our utter *defenselessness* against the rising floodwaters quickly became apparent⟩ — see SUSCEPTIBILITY

defensible *adj* **1** capable of being defended against physical attack ⟨the pioneers retreated to a *defensible* hillside to take a stand against the raiders⟩ — see TENABLE 1
2 capable of being defended with good reasoning against verbal attack ⟨there's simply no *defensible* reason for dropping out of school⟩ — see TENABLE 2

defensive *adj* intended to resist or prevent attack or aggression ⟨a *defensive* alliance among the small nations against the aggressors⟩
synonyms protective, self-protective
related words deterrent, preventive; safe, secure
near antonyms aggressive, bellicose, belligerent, combative, contentious, in-your-face, militant, pugnacious, quarrelsome, scrappy, truculent, warlike
antonyms offensive

defensive *n* a position of readiness to oppose actual or expected attack ⟨their unexpectedly harsh words put him on the *defensive*⟩
synonyms guard
related words alert, lookout, qui vive, watch
antonyms offensive

defer *vb* to assign to a later time ⟨we agreed to *defer* a discussion of the issue until we had more information⟩ — see POSTPONE

deference *n* a readiness or willingness to yield to the wishes of others ⟨the sycophantic *deference* with which the hotel treats celebrity guests⟩ — see COMPLIANCE 1

deferent *adj* marked by or showing proper regard for another's higher status ⟨though he's already attained star status, the rookie remains *deferent* to the team's veteran players⟩ — see RESPECTFUL

deferential *adj* marked by or showing proper regard for another's higher status ⟨the man had the *deferential* attitude of someone who had been a servant his entire life⟩ — see RESPECTFUL

deferentially *adv* in a manner showing no signs of pride or self-assertion ⟨behaved *deferentially* when approaching someone in authority⟩ — see LOWLY

defiance *n* **1** refusal to obey ⟨any *defiance* of the authoritarian regime would have dire consequences⟩ — see DISOBEDIENCE
2 the inclination to resist ⟨the troubled youth seems to have an ingrained *defiance* to authority of any sort⟩ — see RESISTANCE 1
3 an inclination to fight or quarrel ⟨a deeply troubled person who seemed the very soul of *defiance*⟩ — see BELLIGERENCE

defiant *adj* given to resisting authority or another's control ⟨the *defiant* puppy refused to let go of the football⟩ — see DISOBEDIENT

deficiency *n* a falling short of an essential or desirable amount or number ⟨there is a *deficiency* of fresh food in the diet of many of the working poor⟩
synonyms crunch, dearth, deficit, drought (*also* drouth), failure, famine, inadequacy, inadequateness, insufficiency, lack, lacuna, paucity, pinch, poverty, scantiness, scarceness, scarcity, shortage, undersupply, want
related words absence, omission; meagerness, poorness, skimpiness; necessity, need, privation
near antonyms bountifulness, copiousness; excess, overabundance, oversupply, surfeit, surplus
antonyms abundance, adequacy, amplitude, opulence, plenitude, plenty, sufficiency, wealth

deficient *adj* **1** lacking some necessary part ⟨a diet *deficient* in calcium can lead to weak bones⟩ — see INCOMPLETE
2 falling short of a standard ⟨woefully *deficient* eyesight kept him out of military service⟩ — see BAD 1
3 not coming up to an expected measure or meeting a particular need ⟨too *deficient* in common sense to be trusted to stay by himself⟩ — see SHORT 3

deficiently *adv* in an unsatisfactory way ⟨the road to the mountain lodge is so *deficiently* marked that we had a terrible time finding it⟩ — see BADLY 1

deficit *n* a falling short of an essential or desirable amount or number ⟨a growing *deficit* in the number of hours devoted to sleep⟩ — see DEFICIENCY

defile *n* a narrow opening between hillsides or mountains that can be used for passage ⟨the cattle, once they were cornered in the *defile*, were quickly rounded up⟩ — see CANYON

defile *vb* **1** to make unfit for use by the addition of something harmful or undesirable ⟨supplies of meat that had been *defiled* by maggots⟩ — see CONTAMINATE
2 to treat (a sacred place or object) shamefully or with great disrespect ⟨art conservators were careful not to do anything that might *defile* the holy relic⟩ — see DESECRATE

defilement *n* **1** an act of great disrespect shown to God or to sacred ideas, people, or things ⟨for two centuries the Christian monasteries in England suffered *defilements* at the hands of Viking invaders⟩ — see BLASPHEMY
2 something that is or that makes impure ⟨souvenir shops, observation towers, and other tacky *defilements* on Civil War battlefields that should be considered hal-

lowed ground⟩ — see IMPURITY 1

define *vb* **1** to draw or make apparent the outline of ⟨the glass skyscraper's sleek silhouette was strikingly *defined* by the setting sun to its west⟩ — see OUTLINE 1
2 to mark the limits of ⟨the river *defines* the town on the south⟩ — see LIMIT 2
3 to point out the chief quality or qualities of an individual or group ⟨a woman who is *defined* by her unswerving loyalty to her friends⟩ — see CHARACTERIZE 1
4 to give the rules about (something) clearly and exactly ⟨let me *define* the task so that there is no doubt in your minds about what needs to be done⟩ — see PRESCRIBE

defined *adj* having distinct or certain limits ⟨well *defined* guidelines on the range of activities in which the intelligence agency can engage⟩ — see LIMITED 1

definite *adj* **1** having distinct or certain limits ⟨there should be a *definite* scope to your paper on the campaign for women's rights because you obviously cannot cover the whole history in five pages⟩ — see LIMITED 1
2 so clearly expressed as to leave no doubt about the meaning ⟨a *definite* instruction not to let anyone in the house while the parents were out for the evening⟩ — see EXPLICIT
3 having no exceptions or restrictions ⟨the house is a *definite* bargain by today's standards⟩ — see ABSOLUTE 2

definitely *adv* without any question ⟨that is *definitely* the kind of dog we're looking to adopt⟩ — see INDEED 1

definition *n* a vivid representation in words of someone or something ⟨he gave us his *definition* of the perfect romantic evening on the town⟩ — see DESCRIPTION 1

definitive *adj* **1** being the most accurate and apparently thorough ⟨the *definitive* work on the attack on Pearl Harbor⟩
synonyms authoritative, classic, classical, magisterial
related words conclusive, decisive; approved, official, sanctioned; accurate, correct; complete, comprehensive, exhaustive, thorough
2 serving to put an end to all debate or questioning ⟨a *definitive* answer that put an immediate end to the discussion⟩ — see CONCLUSIVE 1
3 so clearly expressed as to leave no doubt about the meaning ⟨the insurance company's *definitive* statement on the types of surgical operations that are covered⟩ — see EXPLICIT
4 constituting, serving as, or worthy of being a pattern to be imitated ⟨Dashiell Hammett's Sam Spade is often cited as the *definitive* hard-boiled private detective⟩ — see MODEL

deflect *vb* to change the course or direction of (something) ⟨the wind *deflected* the Frisbee just as I was about to lunge for it⟩ — see TURN 2

deflection *n* a turning away from a course or standard ⟨a stern father who would not tolerate the slightest *deflection* from the strict moral code that he imposed on his children⟩ — see DIVERGENCE 2

deform *vb* to twist (something) out of a natural or normal shape or condition ⟨a cynic whose face seems to be permanently *deformed* by a sneer⟩ — see CONTORT

deformation *n* the twisting of something out of its natural or normal shape or condition ⟨the catastrophic *deformation* of the steel girders under the enormous weight of the bridge⟩ — see CONTORTION

deformed *adj* badly or imperfectly formed ⟨his first sculpture looked more like a *deformed* rabbit than a galloping horse⟩ — see MALFORMED

deformity *n* something that spoils the appearance or completeness of a thing ⟨a primitive culture that cast aside infants born with *deformities*, allowing them to die of exposure to the elements⟩ — see BLEMISH

defraud *vb* to rob by the use of trickery or threats ⟨senior citizens generally were too smart to fall for the fast-talking salesman's attempts to *defraud* them⟩ — see FLEECE

defrauder *n* a dishonest person who uses clever means to cheat others out of something of value ⟨the state's department of consumer protection has to contend with *defrauders* of every ilk⟩ — see TRICKSTER 1

defrauding *adj* marked by, based on, or done by the use of dishonest methods to acquire something of value ⟨every new technology has brought with it a raft of *defrauding* schemes that make full use of it⟩ — see FRAUDULENT 1

defrock *vb* to remove from a position of prominence or power (as a throne) ⟨the movie's director was *defrocked* for going way over budget⟩ — see DEPOSE 1

defrosted *adj* freed from a frozen state by exposure to warmth ⟨I tossed a *defrosted* steak under the broiler for dinner⟩ — see THAWED

deft *adj* **1** accomplished with trained ability ⟨a luthier whose *deft* craftsmanship is prized by violinists the world over⟩ — see SKILLFUL 1
2 skillful with the hands ⟨the *deft* jeweler quickly attached the diamond to its mount on the gold band⟩ — see DEXTEROUS 1

deftly *adv* in a skillful or expert manner ⟨the company spokesperson *deftly* sidestepped the investigative reporter's questions⟩ — see WELL 3

deftness *n* **1** ease and grace in physical activity ⟨the effortless *deftness* with which he plays the piano⟩ — see DEXTERITY 2
2 subtle or imaginative ability in inventing, devising, or executing something ⟨with *deftness* and aplomb she managed to keep the bickering relatives apart for the duration of the reception⟩ — see SKILL 1

defunct *adj* **1** no longer existing ⟨a stack of brochures and a few faded placards are all that remain of the *defunct* organization⟩ — see EXTINCT
2 no longer living ⟨a *defunct* species that we know only through fossil remains⟩ — see DEAD 1

defy *vb* **1** to go against the commands, prohibitions, or rules of ⟨in those days a woman was brave if she *defied* fashion and wore white after Labor Day⟩ — see DISOBEY
2 to invite (someone) to take part in a contest or to perform a feat ⟨after missing the target, she *defied* her boyfriend to do better⟩ — see CHALLENGE 2
3 to oppose (something hostile or dangerous) with firmness or courage ⟨a rescue team willing to *defy* the raging storm⟩ — see FACE 2
4 to refuse to give in to ⟨a bicyclist who regularly *defies* illness and infirmity in order to compete in races⟩ — see RESIST

degeneracy *n* **1** a change to a lower state or level ⟨the sad *degeneracy* of the old neighborhood into a slum⟩ — see DECLINE 2
2 a sinking to a state of low moral standards and behavior ⟨the *degeneracy* of the family into a gang of petty thieves⟩ — see CORRUPTION 2

degenerate *adj* **1** having lost forcefulness, courage, or spirit ⟨a *degenerate* society in which people had no sense of being citizens, only consumers⟩ — see EFFETE 1
2 having or showing lowered moral character or standards ⟨a movie about a gang of *degenerate* drug dealers⟩ — see CORRUPT

degenerate *n* a person who has sunk below the normal moral standard ⟨a *degenerate* who is uninterested in anything but his own gratification⟩
synonyms backslider, debauchee, debaucher, decadent, deviate, libertine, perv, pervert, profligate, rake, rakehell, rip
related words bankrupt, delinquent, derelict, incorrigi-

ble; blackguard, cad, heel, knave, miscreant, rascal, reprobate, rogue, scoundrel, villain; lecher, playboy, playgirl, satyr
near antonyms saint

degenerate *vb* to become worse or of less value ⟨over the years the community-minded organization *degenerated* into a club for loafers⟩ — see DETERIORATE 1

degenerateness *n* a sinking to a state of low moral standards and behavior ⟨the sad *degenerateness* of the writer's last booze-filled days⟩ — see CORRUPTION 2

degeneration *n* **1** a change to a lower state or level ⟨the organization's *degeneration* from a movement for political reform to just another political party⟩ — see DECLINE 2
2 a gradual sinking and wasting away of mind or body ⟨the troubling *degeneration* of his memory since he reached middle age⟩ — see DECLINE 1
3 a sinking to a state of low moral standards and behavior ⟨the general *degeneration* that characterized so many old mining towns, which had only drinking and gambling for entertainment⟩ — see CORRUPTION 2

degradation *n* **1** a change to a lower state or level ⟨English teachers bemoaning the *degradation* of the language that e-mail and instant messaging have allegedly brought about⟩ — see DECLINE 2
2 a sinking to a state of low moral standards and behavior ⟨the belief that moral *degradation* is an unmistakable sign of a nation in decline⟩ — see CORRUPTION 2

degrade *vb* **1** to bring to a lower grade or rank ⟨the view that such a system *degrades* doctors to the status of medical employees who ultimately are not in charge of their patients' health care⟩ — see DEMOTE
2 to lower in character, dignity, or quality ⟨*degrading* the school's animal mascot with a silly costume⟩ — see DEBASE 1
3 to reduce to a lower standing in one's own eyes or in others' eyes ⟨the players *degraded* themselves with their crude antics off the field⟩ — see HUMBLE

degraded *adj* having or showing lowered moral character or standards ⟨many observers deplored the fact that the city's festivities for Mardi Gras had become a *degraded*, drunken celebration⟩ — see CORRUPT

degrading *adj* intended to make a person or thing seem of little importance or value ⟨made *degrading* comments about his so-called friend behind his back⟩ — see DEROGATORY

degree *n* **1** an individual part of a process, series, or ranking ⟨they worked on the project by *degrees* and eventually it got done⟩
synonyms chapter, cut, grade, inch, notch, peg, phase, place, point, stage, step
related words angle, aspect, facet, side; amount, measure, plane; decrement, increment
2 the placement of someone or something in relation to others in a vertical arrangement ⟨a Freemason of the 32nd *degree*⟩ — see RANK 1

dégringolade *n* **1** a change to a lower state or level ⟨the sad *dégringolade* of the holiday from a solemn day of remembrance to just another excuse to go shopping⟩ — see DECLINE 2
2 a loss of status ⟨a sad *dégringolade* for a theater company that once premiered important American plays⟩ — see COMEDOWN

dehumanize *vb* to make (someone) feel or behave more like an animal than a human being ⟨being deprived of clothes *dehumanized* the prisoners⟩ — see BRUTALIZE 1

dehydrate *vb* **1** to deprive of emotional or intellectual vitality ⟨years of being trapped in a loveless marriage had *dehydrated* his spirit⟩
synonyms castrate, damp, dampen, deaden, desiccate, devitalize, enervate, geld, lobotomize, petrify
related words burn out, debilitate, do in, drain, enfeeble, exhaust, fatigue, sap, tucker (out), undermine, weaken, wear, wear out; daunt, demoralize, discourage, dishearten, dispirit
near antonyms arouse, rouse, stir; charge, electrify, galvanize; excite, ferment, fire, foment, incite, inflame (*also* enflame), instigate, kindle, provoke, spark, trigger, whip (up); abet, boost, buoy, cheer, embolden, fortify, hearten, inspire, lift; reactivate, reanimate, reawake, reawaken, recharge, reenergize, refresh, regenerate, rejuvenate, rekindle, renew, resurrect, resuscitate, revitalize, revive
antonyms brace, energize, enliven, invigorate, quicken, stimulate, vitalize, vivify
2 to make dry ⟨bought a dehumidifier in order to *dehydrate* the damp basement⟩ — see DRY 1

deification *n* excessive admiration of or devotion to a person ⟨the instant *deification* by the press of the country's newest war hero⟩ — see WORSHIP

deify *vb* **1** to love or admire too much ⟨materialistic people who *deify* money⟩ — see IDOLIZE
2 to offer honor or respect to (someone) as a divine power ⟨some ancient pagans *deified* such objects of nature as trees and rivers⟩ — see WORSHIP 1
3 to assign a high status or value to ⟨the sense of entitlement felt by athletes who have been *deified* all their lives⟩ — see EXALT 1

deifying *adj* reflecting great admiration or devotion ⟨the *deifying* descriptions of military heroes that are often published in wartime⟩ — see WORSHIPFUL

deign *vb* to descend to a level that is beneath one's dignity ⟨I wouldn't *deign* to answer that absurd accusation⟩ — see CONDESCEND 1

deity *n* **1** a being having superhuman powers and control over a particular part of life or the world ⟨to the ancient Greeks, Zeus was the *deity* who ruled over the sky and weather, and Poseidon was god of the sea⟩
synonyms divinity, god
related words angel, demigod, demon (*or* daemon), devil, spirit, supernatural
2 *cap* the being worshipped as the creator and ruler of the universe ⟨we prayed to the *Deity* for guidance⟩
synonyms Allah, Almighty, Author, Creator, Divinity, Eternal, Everlasting, Father, God, Godhead, Jehovah, Lord, Maker, Providence, Supreme Being, Yahweh (*also* Jahveh *or* Yahveh)
3 the quality or state of being divine ⟨the repudiation of the claim of *deity* by the Japanese emperor after the end of World War II⟩ — see DIVINITY

deject *vb* to make sad ⟨nothing *dejects* a TV pundit more than the reality check that nobody cares what he thinks⟩ — see DEPRESS 1

dejected *adj* feeling unhappiness ⟨the *dejected* players slowly made their way back to the locker room, where they could mourn their defeat in private⟩ — see SAD 1

dejection *n* a state or spell of low spirits ⟨I find that ice cream often works wonders when trying to overcome *dejection*⟩ — see SADNESS

deke *vb* to elude (an opponent in a sports contest) by making a deceptive or agile movement ⟨*deked* the lone defenseman with a deft move of his stick and went in for the breakaway⟩ — see JUKE

delay *n* an instance or period of being prevented from going about one's business ⟨there was a *delay* for our boarding while the airplane unloaded incoming passengers⟩
synonyms detainment, detention, holdback, holding pattern, holdup, wait
related words deferment, deferral, postponement; reprieve, respite; foot-dragging, hesitation, lag, pause, setback, slowdown

near antonyms haste, rush; dispatch, promptitude, promptness

delay *vb* **1** to move or act slowly ⟨she ordered the kids to stop *delaying* and to get to bed⟩
synonyms crawl, creep, dally, dawdle, diddle, dilly-dally, drag, lag, linger, loiter, lollygag (*also* lallygag), mope, poke, shilly-shally, tarry
related words fiddle (around), fool around, mess around, monkey (around), play, potter (around), putter (around), trifle; hang (around *or* out), idle, loaf, loll, lounge; amble, ease, inch, lumber, plod, saunter, shuffle, stagger, stroll; decelerate, slow (down *or* up); filibuster, procrastinate, stall, temporize
phrases drag one's feet (*also* drag one's heels), drop behind, fall behind, hang fire, mark time, take one's time
near antonyms bowl, breeze, dart, hump, hurtle, hustle, scramble, stampede; gallop, jog, run, sprint, trot; accelerate, quicken, speed (up); catch up, fast-forward, outpace, outrun, outstrip, overtake
antonyms barrel, bolt, career, course, dash, fly, hasten, hotfoot (it), hurry, race, rip, rocket, run, rush, scoot, scud, scurry, speed, tear, whirl, whisk, whiz (*or* whizz), zip
2 to assign to a later time ⟨our guests *delayed* their departure until after dinner⟩ — see POSTPONE

dele *vb* to show (something written) to be no longer valid by drawing a cross over or a line through it ⟨the proofreader was instructed to *dele* stray characters and other typos⟩ — see X (OUT)

delectability *n* the quality of being delicious ⟨frozen entrées of surprising *delectability*⟩ — see DELICIOUSNESS

delectable *adj* **1** giving pleasure or contentment to the mind or senses ⟨a *delectable* melody to listen to after a hard day⟩ — see PLEASANT 1
2 very pleasing to the sense of taste ⟨a *delectable* roast turkey lay on the table⟩ — see DELICIOUS 1

delectable *n* something that is pleasing to eat because it is rare or a luxury ⟨a gourmet shop filled with *delectables* for every palate, albeit not for every pocketbook⟩ — see DELICACY 1

delectably *adv* in a pleasing way ⟨a *delectably* witty comedy⟩ — see WELL 5

delectation *n* **1** a source of great satisfaction ⟨tourists enjoying the *delectations* of this tropical paradise for the first time⟩ — see DELIGHT 1
2 the feeling experienced when one's wishes are met ⟨a musical concert was presented for the *delectation* of the guests⟩ — see PLEASURE 1

delegacy *n* a body of persons chosen as representatives of a larger group ⟨the committee chose a five-person *delegacy* to attend the national conference⟩ — see CONTINGENT 1

delegate *n* **1** a person sent on a mission to represent another ⟨the *delegate* had a list of concerns to discuss with the country's new prime minister⟩ — see AMBASSADOR
2 a person who acts or does business for another ⟨the real estate developer sent a *delegate* to the town meeting to represent his interests⟩ — see AGENT 2

delegate *vb* **1** to appoint as one's representative ⟨he *delegated* his son to go pick up the tickets for him⟩
synonyms commission, depute, deputize
related words assign, charge; appoint, designate, name, nominate
near antonyms abrogate; abdicate
2 to put (something) into the possession or safekeeping of another ⟨a manager who is reluctant to *delegate* authority to subordinates⟩ — see GIVE 2

delegation *n* **1** a body of persons chosen as representatives of a larger group ⟨a *delegation* from the local scout troop is being sent to the national jamboree⟩ — see CONTINGENT 1
2 the granting of power to perform various acts or duties ⟨the *delegation* by the president to the secretary of state of complete control of the nation's foreign policy⟩ — see COMMISSION 1

delete *vb* to show (something written) to be no longer valid by drawing a cross over or a line through it ⟨the teacher *deleted* the last line of the student's essay, wisely sensing that it lessened the impact⟩ — see X (OUT)

deleterious *adj* causing or capable of causing harm ⟨nicotine has long been recognized as a *deleterious* substance⟩ — see HARMFUL

deletion *n* something left out ⟨one of the *deletions* from the final cut of the movie turned out to be my one line of dialogue⟩ — see OMISSION

Delhi belly *n* abnormally frequent intestinal evacuations with more or less fluid stools ⟨her long-planned vacation was spoiled by a bad case of *Delhi belly*⟩ — see DIARRHEA

deliberate *adj* **1** decided on as a result of careful thought ⟨the judge made a *deliberate* decision to impose the maximum sentence⟩
synonyms advised, calculated, considered, knowing, measured, reasoned, studied, thoughtful, thought-out, weighed
related words aforethought, premeditated, prepense; educated, informed; intentional, purposeful; designed, intended, planned, projected; careful, meticulous; foresighted, forethoughtful, provident, prudent
near antonyms half-cocked, ill-advised; chance, haphazard, hit-or-miss, random; aimless, desultory, purposeless; hasty, hurried, rushed; abrupt, impetuous, sudden; automatic, extemporaneous, impromptu, instinctive, spontaneous
antonyms casual, unadvised, uncalculated, unconsidered, unstudied
2 made, given, or done with full awareness of what one is doing ⟨a *deliberate* act of vandalism that should not go unpunished⟩ — see INTENTIONAL

deliberate *vb* to give serious and careful thought to ⟨the jury *deliberated* the case for three days before returning a verdict⟩ — see PONDER

deliberately *adv* with full awareness of what one is doing ⟨*deliberately* chose to break the rules⟩ — see INTENTIONALLY

deliberation *n* **1** a careful weighing of the reasons for or against something ⟨gave the matter full *deliberation* before reaching a decision⟩ — see CONSIDERATION 1
2 an exchange of views for the purpose of exploring a subject or deciding an issue ⟨there was a great deal of *deliberation* among the representatives about the wording of the public statement⟩ — see DISCUSSION 1

delicacy *n* **1** something that is pleasing to eat because it is rare or a luxury ⟨presented with a plate of national *delicacies* while they waited for the queen⟩
synonyms bit, cate [*archaic*], dainty, delectable, goody (*or* goodie), kickshaw, tidbit (*also* titbit), treat, viand
related words morsel; candy, dessert, junket, sweet, sweetmeat
2 the state or quality of having a delicate structure ⟨we never cease to marvel at the *delicacy* of a snowflake⟩
synonyms daintiness, exquisiteness, fineness, fragility, frangibility
related words diaphanousness, flimsiness, insubstantiality, wispiness; brittleness, crumbliness, friability
near antonyms firmness, solidity; strength
antonyms coarseness, crudeness, crudity, roughness, rudeness
3 the tendency to be or state of being squeamish ⟨the urgent need for blood prompted many people to overcome their habitual *delicacy* and become first-time donors⟩
synonyms qualmishness, queasiness, squeamishness

related words daintiness, fastidiousness, finicalness, finickiness, fussiness
near antonyms boldness, gutsiness
antonyms indelicacy
4 the quality or state of being very accurate ⟨the *delicacy* of the watch movement is incredible⟩ — see PRECISION
5 the quality or state of lacking physical strength or vigor ⟨all of her life the shy poet gave the appearance of extreme *delicacy*⟩ — see WEAKNESS 1
6 the state or quality of being able to sense slight impressions or differences ⟨the *delicacy* of the sensor is such that it will be affected by the slightest vibration⟩ — see ACUITY

delicate *adj* **1** satisfying or pleasing because of fineness or mildness ⟨a heavy sauce would spoil the *delicate* flavor of this fish⟩
synonyms airy, dainty, exquisite, nuanced, refined, subtle
related words choice, elegant, extraordinary, incomparable, peerless, preeminent, prime, rare, select, superior, superlative, supreme, transcendent, unsurpassed; picked, selected; fine, fragile, frail
near antonyms coarse, crude, rough; common, ordinary; average, fair, indifferent, mediocre, medium, middling, run-of-the-mill, second-rate
antonyms robust, strong, sturdy
2 able to sense slight impressions or differences ⟨only a person with *delicate* taste buds could tell the difference between these two wines⟩ — see ACUTE 1
3 accomplished with trained ability ⟨the *delicate* handling of a difficult diplomatic situation⟩ — see SKILLFUL
4 easily broken ⟨*delicate* glassware that must be carefully wrapped for shipping⟩ — see FRAGILE 1
5 easily injured without careful handling ⟨the *delicate* ecosystem of the wetlands⟩ — see TENDER 1
6 hard to please ⟨a person of *delicate* tastes⟩ — see FINICKY
7 having qualities that appeal to a refined taste ⟨*delicate* perfumes that only a connoisseur of scents would appreciate⟩ — see CHOICE 1
8 lacking bodily strength ⟨a *delicate* child who was never allowed to play sports⟩ — see WEAK 1
9 made or done with extreme care and accuracy ⟨*delicate* measurements of brain tumors that are only possible using the latest medical technology⟩ — see FINE 2
10 meeting the highest standard of accuracy ⟨extremely *delicate* instruments such as an atomic clock⟩ — see PRECISE 1
11 not harsh or stern especially in nature or effect ⟨a *delicate* breeze was floating in from the open window⟩ — see GENTLE 1
12 requiring exceptional skill or caution in performance or handling ⟨the *delicate* challenge of inviting two people who don't like each other to the same party⟩ — see TRICKY 1

delicious *adj* **1** very pleasing to the sense of taste ⟨the family sat down to a *delicious* Thanksgiving dinner⟩
synonyms ambrosial, appetizing, dainty, delectable, delish, flavorful, flavorsome, luscious, lush, mouthwatering, palatable, savory (*also* savoury), scrumptious, succulent, tasteful, tasty, toothsome, toothy, yummy
related words digestible, eatable, edible; delightful, heavenly, pleasing; agreeable, gratifying, pleasant; satisfying; choice, delicate, exquisite, rare
near antonyms banal, boring, commonplace, tedious; noisome, smelly, stinky; noxious, unwholesome; miserable, wretched; abhorrent, abominable, awful, detestable, disagreeable, disgusting, foul, horrid, nauseating, offensive, repellent (*also* repellant), repugnant, repulsive, sickening, unpleasant
antonyms distasteful, flat, flavorless, insipid, stale, tasteless, unappetizing, unpalatable, unsavory, yucky (*also* yukky)
2 giving pleasure or contentment to the mind or senses ⟨a *delicious* breeze gave us welcome relief from the tropical heat⟩ — see PLEASANT 1

deliciously *adv* in a pleasing way ⟨a *deliciously* told anecdote on the DVD's commentary track⟩ — see WELL 5

deliciousness *n* the quality of being delicious ⟨the fancy feast was *deliciousness* itself⟩
synonyms delectability, lusciousness, palatability, palatableness, savor (*also* savour), savoriness, tastiness, toothsomeness
related words digestability, edibility, edibleness; choiceness, daintiness, delicacy
antonyms distastefulness, flatness, insipidity, staleness, tastelessness, unpalatability

delight *n* **1** a source of great satisfaction ⟨the opportunity for travel was one of the major *delights* of the couple's golden years⟩
synonyms delectation, feast, gas [*slang*], joy, kick, manna, pleasure, treat
related words amusement, diversion, entertainment, fun, recreation; comfort, relief, solace; gratification, indulgence; ambrosia
2 someone or something that provides amusement or enjoyment ⟨with his great sense of humor and bubbly personality, he is a *delight* to be around⟩ — see FUN 1
3 the feeling experienced when one's wishes are met ⟨we were filled with *delight* at the sight of everyone in the family together at last for the holidays⟩ — see PLEASURE 1

delight *vb* **1** to feel or express joy or triumph ⟨I *delighted* at the sight of my old schoolyard tormentor standing behind the fast-food counter, asking customers if they wanted fries⟩ — see EXULT
2 to give satisfaction to ⟨the news that you had won the Pulitzer *delighted* us beyond words⟩ — see PLEASE 1

delight (in) *vb* to take pleasure in ⟨I've been *delighting in* your company, so I was wondering if we might have another date⟩ — see ENJOY 1

delighted *adj* experiencing pleasure, satisfaction, or delight ⟨we're *delighted* to meet you finally!⟩ — see GLAD 1

delightful *adj* **1** giving pleasure or contentment to the mind or senses ⟨a *delightful* rendition of our favorite song⟩ — see PLEASANT 1
2 providing amusement or enjoyment ⟨we had a *delightful* time at the party⟩ — see FUN

delightfully *adv* in a pleasing way ⟨a *delightfully* silly song about dancing bears⟩ — see WELL 5

delightsome *adj* giving pleasure or contentment to the mind or senses ⟨any man would find it most *delightsome* to gaze upon her lovely face⟩ — see PLEASANT 1

delimit *vb* to mark the limits of ⟨the highway *delimits* the eastern edge of the downtown area⟩ — see LIMIT 2

delineate *vb* **1** to draw or make apparent the outline of ⟨the man's roly-poly shape was softly *delineated* by the glow of the fire⟩ — see OUTLINE 1
2 to give a representation or account of in words ⟨the story does a remarkable job of *delineating* the emotions that immigrants feel upon their arrival in a strange country⟩ — see DESCRIBE 1

delineated *adj* producing a mental picture through clear and impressive description ⟨the finely *delineated* characters of the novel will seem real to the reader⟩ — see GRAPHIC 1

delineation *n* **1** a picture using lines to represent the chief features of an object or scene ⟨his simple but striking *delineations* of Dutch landscapes⟩ — see DRAWING
2 a vivid representation in words of someone or some-

thing ⟨a finely wrought *delineation* of a young woman's first experience with romantic love⟩ — see DESCRIPTION 1

delinquency *n* **1** the nonperformance of an assigned or expected action ⟨we received a notice in the mail informing us of our *delinquency* in paying our utility bill⟩ — see FAILURE 1
2 the quality or state of being late ⟨*delinquency* of our mortgage payment meant that we would have to pay a surcharge⟩ — see LATENESS

delinquent *adj* not arriving, occurring, or settled at the due, usual, or proper time ⟨the bank was annoyed because our check was *delinquent*⟩ — see LATE 1

delinquently *adv* after the due, usual, or proper time ⟨he always paid his bills, but usually *delinquently*⟩ — see LATE 1

deliquesce *vb* to go from a solid to a liquid state ⟨a rotting tomato slowly *deliquescing* in the hot summer sun⟩ — see LIQUEFY

delirious *adj* **1** feeling overwhelming fear or worry ⟨we were *delirious* with anxiety when the boy failed to return home⟩ — see FRANTIC 1
2 marked by great and often stressful excitement or activity ⟨rushing about in a *delirious* state during the holidays⟩ — see FURIOUS 1

deliriousness *n* a state of wildly excited activity or emotion ⟨in the *deliriousness* of the emergency evacuation, a lot of things were overlooked⟩ — see FRENZY

delirium *n* a state of wildly excited activity or emotion ⟨shoppers running around in a *delirium* the day before Christmas⟩ — see FRENZY

delish *adj* very pleasing to the sense of taste ⟨the homemade chocolate sauce was absolutely *delish*⟩ — see DELICIOUS 1

deliver *vb* **1** to free from the penalties or consequences of sin ⟨*deliver* us from evil⟩ — see SAVE 1
2 to remove from danger or harm ⟨the doomed passengers kept hoping that a ship would miraculously appear and *deliver* them⟩ — see SAVE 2
3 to give (something) over to the control or possession of another usually under duress ⟨*delivered* up the ransom money⟩ — see SURRENDER 1
4 to put (something) into the possession of someone for use or consumption ⟨the inn endeavors to *deliver* the luxuries that its well-heeled guests have come to expect⟩ — see FURNISH 2
5 to put (something) into the possession or safekeeping of another ⟨*delivered* the prisoners to the sheriff⟩ — see GIVE 2
6 to turn out as planned or desired ⟨finally, a summer blockbuster that *delivers*⟩ — see SUCCEED 1
7 to bring forth from the womb ⟨she *delivered* four healthy babies⟩ — see BEAR 1
8 to give (oneself) over to something especially unrestrainedly ⟨deeply dissatisfied with his dissolute lifestyle, he resolved to *deliver* himself over to the ways of the Lord⟩ — see ABANDON 1

deliverance *n* **1** the saving from danger or evil ⟨looked to the European powers for *deliverance* from their country's cruel tyrant⟩ — see SALVATION
2 a position arrived at after consideration ⟨the jury's *deliverance* shocked the courtroom⟩ — see DECISION 1

deliverer *n* **1** a person who delivers goods to customers usually over a regular local route ⟨we eagerly took the food and tipped the *deliverer*⟩ — see DELIVERYMAN
2 one that saves from danger or destruction ⟨the surviving passengers thanked their *deliverers* profusely⟩ — see SAVIOR

delivery *n* **1** a freeing from an obligation or responsibility ⟨the school bell signaled our *delivery* from the tortures of math class⟩ — see RELEASE 1
2 the act or process of giving birth to children ⟨her second *delivery* took only three hours⟩ — see CHILDBIRTH

deliveryman *n* a person who delivers goods to customers usually over a regular local route ⟨the *deliveryman* dropped off a package for us while we were at the store⟩
synonyms deliverer
related words delivery boy; bearer, carrier, courier, go-between, liaison, messenger

Delphic *adj* having an often intentionally veiled or uncertain meaning ⟨the *Delphic* pronouncements that are so typical of many stock market prognosticators⟩ — see OBSCURE 1

delude *vb* to cause to believe what is untrue ⟨we *deluded* ourselves into thinking that the ice cream wouldn't affect our diet⟩ — see DECEIVE

deluding *adj* tending or having power to deceive ⟨the *deluding* appearance of the surface of the river, which is actually quite polluted⟩ — see DECEPTIVE 1

deluge *n* **1** a great flow of water or of something that overwhelms ⟨a *deluge* of thanks and appreciation for the returning troops⟩ — see FLOOD
2 a steady falling of water from the sky in significant quantity ⟨the exiting moviegoers were caught in the *deluge* without umbrellas⟩ — see RAIN 1

deluge *vb* to cover with a flood ⟨*deluged* with requests for help⟩ — see FLOOD

delusion *n* **1** a conception or image created by the imagination and having no objective reality ⟨her idea that her new man is a long lost prince is surely just a *delusion*⟩ — see FANTASY 1
2 a false idea or belief ⟨he appears to suffer from the *delusion* that he's the best reporter in the business⟩ — see FALLACY 1

delusive *adj* tending or having power to deceive ⟨*delusive* promises of high-paying jobs for the illegal immigrants⟩ see DECEPTIVE 1

delusory *adj* tending or having power to deceive ⟨the *delusory* notion that wealth invariably brings happiness⟩ — see DECEPTIVE 1

deluxe *adj* showing obvious signs of wealth and comfort ⟨a classy hotel with truly *deluxe* accommodations⟩ — see LUXURIOUS 1

delve *n, archaic* a naturally formed underground chamber with an opening to the surface ⟨a poem in which a medieval knight encounters a mysterious beauty in a darkened *delve*⟩ — see CAVE

delve (into) *vb* to search through or into ⟨we uncovered many interesting stories as we *delved into* the history of the house we were restoring⟩ — see EXPLORE 1

delving *n* a systematic search for the truth or facts about something ⟨we didn't want to pry and did as little personal *delving* as possible⟩ — see INQUIRY 1

demagogue *also* **demagog** *n* a person who stirs up public feelings especially of discontent ⟨that politician is just a *demagogue* who preys upon people's fears and prejudices⟩ — see AGITATOR

demand *n* **1** something that someone insists upon having ⟨the terrorists presented their list of *demands*⟩
synonyms claim, dun, importunity, requisition, ultimatum
related words desire, request, want, wish; drive, need, requirement, stipulation; basic, essential, must; imposition; condition, provision
2 the state of being sought after especially for purchase ⟨a steadily declining *demand* for film cameras⟩
synonyms call, market, request
related words bear market, bull market; buyer's market, seller's market
3 something necessary, indispensable, or unavoidable ⟨we are very confident that our new employee is fully equal to the *demands* of the job⟩ — see ESSENTIAL 1

demand *vb* **1** to ask for (something) earnestly or with

authority ⟨the losing party *demanded* a recount of the votes cast in the election⟩
synonyms call (for), claim, clamor (for), command, enjoin, exact, insist (on), press (for), quest, stipulate (for)
related words ask, plead (for), request, want; cry (for), necessitate, need, require, take, warrant; requisition; impose; badger, dun, harass, hound
near antonyms give up, relinquish, surrender, yield
2 to have as a requirement ⟨a task that *demands* one's unremitting attention⟩ — see NEED 1
3 to set or receive as a price ⟨superstars who *demand* millions for appearing in a movie⟩ — see CHARGE 1

demanding *adj* **1** requiring much time, effort, or careful attention ⟨the *demanding* assignment kept them working all night long⟩
synonyms arduous, burdensome, challenging, exacting, grueling (*or* gruelling), killing, laborious, onerous, persnickety, taxing, toilsome
related words difficult, formidable, hard, herculean, rough, rugged, stiff, strenuous, testing, tough; oppressive, trying; rigid, rigorous, severe, stern, strict, stringent
near antonyms easy, effortless, facile, simple, smooth
antonyms light, nondemanding, unchallenging, undemanding
2 hard to please ⟨will play before a *demanding* audience of music critics, who are not easily impressed⟩ — see FINICKY
3 requiring considerable physical or mental effort ⟨the *demanding* task of reading and grading student compositions⟩ — see HARD 2

demarcate *vb* to mark the limits of ⟨a yellow line *demarcated* the county on the road map⟩ — see LIMIT 2

demarcation *n* the state of being kept distinct ⟨the lines of *demarcation* between art and entertainment are often blurry⟩ — see SEPARATION 2

demark *vb* to mark the limits of ⟨the Connecticut River *demarks* the eastern edge of the state of Vermont⟩ — see LIMIT 2

dematerialize *vb* to cease to be visible ⟨the image suddenly *dematerialized*, and once again we were staring at a blank screen⟩ — see DISAPPEAR

[1]demean *vb* **1** to lower in character, dignity, or quality ⟨it *demeans* the political process to demand that candidates make promises that everyone knows are unrealistic⟩ — see DEBASE 1
2 to reduce to a lower standing in one's own eyes or in others' eyes ⟨we were *demeaned* by our shabby appearance at the funeral⟩ — see HUMBLE

[2]demean *vb* to manage the actions of (oneself) in a particular way ⟨I shall endeavor to *demean* myself with utmost respect when our pastor comes to visit⟩ — see BEHAVE

demeaning *adj* intended to make a person or thing seem of little importance or value ⟨demanded an apology from the men's football coach for his *demeaning* comments on women athletes⟩ — see DEROGATORY

demeanor *n* the way or manner in which one conducts oneself ⟨the director of the opera company has a haughty *demeanor* that can be irritating⟩ — see BEHAVIOR

demented *adj* having or showing a very abnormal or sick state of mind ⟨a poor, *demented* animal that had obviously suffered years of abuse⟩ — see INSANE 1

dementia *n* a serious mental disorder that prevents one from living a safe and normal life ⟨doctors were able to treat the patient's *dementia* with drugs and thus allow him to function on his own⟩ — see INSANITY 1

demerit *n* a defect in character ⟨as a typist she has the advantage of speed but the *demerit* of inaccuracy⟩ — see FAULT 1

demesne *n* **1** a part or portion having no fixed boundaries ⟨the vast and frozen *demesne* of the northern tundra⟩ — see REGION 1
2 a region of activity, knowledge, or influence ⟨the view that the issue is not in the *demesne* of the courts and is something that should be decided by the state legislature⟩ — see FIELD 2
3 the area around and belonging to a building ⟨the mansion's huge *demesne* covers more than 100 acres⟩ — see GROUND 1

demilitarization *n* the reduction or elimination of a country's armed forces or weapons ⟨the *demilitarization* of some formerly warlike nations that occurred in the aftermath of World War II⟩ — see DISARMAMENT

demilitarize *vb* to reduce the size and strength of the armed forces of ⟨the two nations agreed to *demilitarize* themselves reciprocally⟩ — see DISARM 1

demimonde *n* a social sphere that exists outside of the mainstream ⟨a documentary examining the *demimonde* to which homosexuals were relegated before the start of the gay rights movement⟩ — see NETHERWORLD

de minimis *adj* so small or unimportant as to warrant little or no attention ⟨stock dividends that were decidedly *de minimis*⟩ — see NEGLIGIBLE 1

demise *n* **1** the permanent stopping of all the vital bodily activities ⟨inherited all of the estate upon the sudden *demise* of his grandfather⟩ — see DEATH 1
2 the act of ceasing to exist ⟨the gradual *demise* of the Roman Empire over the course of several centuries⟩ — see DEATH 3
3 a loss of status ⟨after her *demise* as the doyenne of New York society, the mere mention of her name was regarded as a faux pas⟩ — see COMEDOWN

demise *vb* to stop living ⟨our much beloved, recently *demised* leader⟩ — see DIE 1

demised *adj* no longer living ⟨a cemetery reserved for *demised* family pets⟩ — see DEAD 1

demiworld *n* a social sphere that exists outside of the mainstream ⟨a runaway teenager who ended up in the *demiworld* of street prostitution⟩ — see NETHERWORLD

demo *n, British* a mass meeting for the purpose of displaying or arousing support for a cause or person ⟨a *demo* to support the Prime Minister⟩ — see RALLY 2

democracy *n* government in which the supreme power is held by the people and used by them directly or indirectly through representation ⟨under our *democracy* the people have some control over their lives by being able to select their own political leaders⟩
synonyms republic, self-government, self-rule
related words pure democracy; home rule, self-determination; autonomy, sovereignty (*also* sovranty)
near antonyms despotism, dictatorship, monarchy, monocracy, totalitarianism, tyranny

democrat *n* one who advocates or practices social equality ⟨a true *democrat*, he has always abhorred that nation's class system⟩
synonyms egalitarian, leveler (*or* leveller)
related words populist; communist, Marxist, social democrat, socialist
near antonyms snob, snoot

democratic *adj* of, relating to, or favoring political democracy ⟨the *democratic* system ensures that every citizen's voice is heard⟩
synonyms popular, republican, self-governing, self-ruling
related words representative; libertarian, nontotalitarian
near antonyms autocratic (*also* autocratical), despotic, dictatorial, monarchal (*or* monarchial), monarchical (*also* monarchic), tyrannical (*also* tyrannic)
antonyms nondemocratic, undemocratic

démodé *adj* having passed its time of use or usefulness

⟨an old-line French restaurant with stodgy food and a *démodé* decor straight out of the 1950s⟩ — see OBSOLETE

demoded *adj* having passed its time of use or usefulness ⟨with its *demoded* '70s look—shag carpeting, no less—that split-level is in need of some serious updating⟩ — see OBSOLETE

demoiselle *n* a young unmarried woman ⟨fell in love with a pretty *demoiselle* from a neighboring village⟩ — see GIRL 1

demolish *vb* **1** to destroy (as a building) completely by knocking down or breaking to pieces ⟨developers *demolished* the old warehouse to make room for the new shopping mall⟩
synonyms level, pull down, raze, tear down, unbuild
related words blow up, dynamite; abolish, annihilate, crack up, crush, dash, decimate, destroy, devastate, devour, dissolve, do in, eradicate, extirpate, finish, flatten, obliterate, overturn, pulverize, ravage, ruin, scourge, smash, total, unmake, waste, wipe out, wreck
near antonyms build, construct, erect, put up, raise; rebuild, renew, renovate, restore; create, fabricate, fashion, forge, form, make, manufacture, shape
2 to bring to a complete end the physical soundness, existence, or usefulness of ⟨most of the buildings in the town had been *demolished* in the bombing raid⟩ — see DESTROY 1
3 to cause to break open or into pieces by or as if by an explosive ⟨terrorists used a powerful pipe bomb to *demolish* the concrete wall around the compound⟩ — see BLAST 1

demolishment *n* the state or fact of being rendered nonexistent, physically unsound, or useless ⟨in the aftermath of its *demolishment* by the tornado, the house looked like nothing more than a discarded plaything⟩ — see DESTRUCTION 1

demolition *n* the state or fact of being rendered nonexistent, physically unsound, or useless ⟨several condemned buildings around the city are undergoing *demolition* as part of the revitalization program⟩ — see DESTRUCTION 1

demon *or* **daemon** *n* **1** an evil spirit ⟨only in rare cases is the ancient rite of exorcism performed to cast out a troublesome *demon*⟩
synonyms cacodemon, devil, fiend, ghost, ghoul, ghoulie, imp, shaitan
related words hag [*archaic*], lamia, vampire; incubus, nightmare, succubus; afreet (*or* afrit), genie, jinni (*or* jinn *also* djinni *or* djinn); apparition, banshee, bogey (*also* bogie *or* bogy), bugbear, familiar, familiar spirit, genius, phantasm (*also* fantasm), phantom, poltergeist, shade, shadow, specter (*or* spectre), spirit, spook, vision, wraith; brownie, dwarf, elf, faerie (*also* faery), fairy, fay, gnome, goblin, gremlin, hobgoblin, kobold, leprechaun, pixie (*also* pixy), puck, sprite, troll; monster, ogre
near antonyms angel
2 a source of persistent emotional distress ⟨a man who was finally able to conquer his *demons* and kick his drug habit⟩
synonyms affliction, hang-up, terror, torment
related words bête noire, bogey (*also* bogie *or* bogy), bugaboo, bugbear, hobgoblin, ogre

demoniac *also* **demoniacal** *adj* of, relating to, or worthy of an evil spirit ⟨the murderer seemed possessed by a *demoniac* wish to destroy life⟩ — see FIENDISH 1

demonian *adj* of, relating to, or worthy of an evil spirit ⟨a *demonian* laugh echoed through the haunted house⟩ — see FIENDISH 1

demonic *also* **demonical** *adj* of, relating to, or worthy of an evil spirit ⟨the villain in the movie cackled with *demonic* laughter⟩ — see FIENDISH 1

demonstrable *adj* capable of being proven as true or real ⟨as a serious scientist, she is only interested in *demonstrable* phenomena⟩ — see VERIFIABLE

demonstrate *vb* **1** to gain full recognition or acceptance of ⟨you must *demonstrate* your scientific thesis before a jury of your professional peers⟩ — see ESTABLISH 1
2 to show the existence or truth of by evidence ⟨the paleontologist hopes to *demonstrate* that dinosaurs once existed in central Peru by unearthing the fossil evidence⟩ — see PROVE 1
3 to make known (something abstract) through outward signs ⟨the babysitter's actions during the emergency *demonstrate* beyond doubt her general dependability⟩ — see SHOW 2
4 to make plain or understandable ⟨a few striking facts should *demonstrate* the complex nature of our topic⟩ — see EXPLAIN 1
5 to show or make clear by using examples ⟨the visiting physicist *demonstrated* very graphically several basic scientific principles⟩ — see ILLUSTRATE 1

demonstration *n* **1** a mass meeting for the purpose of displaying or arousing support for a cause or person ⟨disgruntled students organized a *demonstration* to protest the change in university policy⟩ — see RALLY 2
2 an outward and often exaggerated indication of something abstract (as a feeling) for effect ⟨staged a grand *demonstration* of her love for her husband with a candlelight-and-champagne Valentine's Day dinner⟩ — see SHOW 1

demonstrative *adj* **1** showing feeling freely ⟨my grandmother was always very *demonstrative* when we visited, showering us with hugs and kisses⟩
synonyms effusive, emotional, touchy-feely, uninhibited, unreserved, unrestrained
related words dramatic, histrionic, hyperemotional, melodramatic, theatrical (*also* theatric); gushing, gushy, maudlin, mawkish, mushy, schmaltzy, sentimental; communicative, expansive; extroverted (*also* extraverted), outgoing; affectionate, feeling, intense, loving, passionate, sensitive, soulful, warm; blunt, candid, frank, outspoken, plain
near antonyms constrained; quiet, reticent, silent, taciturn; bashful, modest, retiring, shy; introverted, self-directed; aloof, detached, dispassionate, emotionless, impassive, indifferent, phlegmatic, stolid, unconcerned, unfeeling; chilly, cold, frigid, glacial, hard-boiled, hard-edged, hard-hearted, icy, unfriendly
antonyms inhibited, reserved, restrained, undemonstrative, unemotional
2 having or expressing great depth of feeling ⟨a *demonstrative* welcome for the returning troops by their families and friends⟩ — see FERVENT 1

demoralization *n* **1** a sinking to a state of low moral standards and behavior ⟨a general state of *demoralization* prevailed at every level of the government⟩ — see CORRUPTION 2
2 the state of being discouraged ⟨the officers struggled to combat the *demoralization* of the troops as their tour of duty grew longer⟩ — see DISCOURAGEMENT

demoralize *vb* **1** to deprive of courage or confidence ⟨the mere sight of the forbidding cliffs *demoralized* the climbers⟩ — see UNNERVE 1
2 to lessen the courage or confidence of ⟨we refused to be *demoralized* by our humiliating defeat and vowed to come roaring back the following week⟩ — see DISCOURAGE 1
3 to lower in character, dignity, or quality ⟨felt society as a whole has been *demoralized* by the widespread availability of pornography⟩ — see DEBASE 1

demoralized *adj* having or showing lowered moral character or standards ⟨a *demoralized* nation that had forgotten the values that once made it great⟩ — see CORRUPT

demote *vb* to bring to a lower grade or rank ⟨the court-martial's decision was to *demote* the officer responsible for the failed mission⟩
synonyms break, bust, degrade, disrate, downgrade, reduce
related words can, cashier, dismiss, downsize, fire, lay off, sack; abase, debase, demean, humble, humiliate, lower
near antonyms hire
antonyms advance, elevate, promote, raise

demotion *n* the act or an instance of bringing to a lower grade or rank ⟨anyone who objects will get a *demotion*⟩ — see BUMP 2

demount *vb* to take apart ⟨soldiers were expected to be able to *demount* and reassemble their weapons⟩ — see DISASSEMBLE 1

demur *n* a feeling or declaration of disapproval or dissent ⟨we accepted his offer to pay for our dinners without *demur*⟩ — see OBJECTION

demur *vb* to present an opposing opinion or argument ⟨don't hesitate to *demur* to the idea if you have any qualms⟩ — see OBJECT

demure *adj* **1** affecting shyness or modesty in order to attract masculine interest ⟨the previously *demure* maiden began making some surprisingly shocking remarks⟩ — see COY 1
2 not comfortable around people ⟨hesitant and *demure*, she hardly spoke a word at the banquet table⟩ — see SHY 2
3 not having or showing any feelings of superiority, self-assertiveness, or showiness ⟨wore a very *demure* outfit to the interview for the job at the church's headquarters⟩ — see HUMBLE 1

demureness *n* the absence of any feelings of being better than others ⟨her excessive *demureness* will be to her disadvantage if she wants a career in show business⟩ — see HUMILITY

demurral *n* a feeling or declaration of disapproval or dissent ⟨surprisingly, she wrote the check for the parking fine without *demurral*⟩ — see OBJECTION

demurrer *n* a feeling or declaration of disapproval or dissent ⟨the only *demurrer* voiced by most music critics was that the piece was too short⟩ — see OBJECTION

demystify *vb* to make plain or understandable ⟨a wine book that does a lot to *demystify* the subject for the casual drinker who just wants a good bottle for dinner⟩ — see EXPLAIN 1

den *n* **1** the shelter or resting place of a wild animal ⟨the foxes hid in their *den* until the bear finally left the area⟩
synonyms burrow, hole, house, lair, lodge
related words nest; territory
2 a place where a person goes to hide or to avoid others ⟨an abandoned building that is often used as a *den* by the city's petty criminals⟩ — see HIDEOUT

dene *n, British* an area of lowland between hills or mountains ⟨there are some deeply wooded *denes* in that part of Northumberland⟩ — see VALLEY

denegation *n* a refusal to confirm the truth of a statement ⟨this recent flip-flop is merely the latest in a series of *denegations* by the governor of previously held positions⟩ — see DENIAL 2

denial *n* **1** an unwillingness to grant something asked for ⟨our supervisor's *denial* of unpaid personal leave got mixed reactions from the staff⟩
synonyms declination, disallowance, nay, no, nonacceptance, refusal, rejection, turndown
related words rebuff, repudiation, repulse, spurn; negative; ban, injunction, veto; deterrence, discouragement, repression, suppression
near antonyms acceptance, accession, acquiescence, agreement, assent, authorization, clearance, concurrence, consent, leave, license (*or* licence), permission, sanction, sufferance; imprimatur, seal, signature, stamp
antonyms allowance, approval, grant, OK (*or* okay)
2 a refusal to confirm the truth of a statement ⟨the senator issued a flat *denial* of the accusation against her⟩
synonyms contradiction, denegation, disallowance, disavowal, disclaimer, disconfirmation, negation, rejection, repudiation
related words disproof, rebuttal, refutation; negative
near antonyms concession, confession; affirmation, assertion, declaration; attestation, corroboration, documentation, substantiation, testament, testimony, validation
antonyms acknowledgment (*or* acknowledgement), admission, avowal, confirmation

denigrate *vb* to express scornfully one's low opinion of ⟨theater critics have been *denigrating* her acting ability for years⟩ — see DECRY 1

denigration *n* the act of making a person or a thing seem little or unimportant ⟨the unfair *denigration* of the social sciences by some people in the natural sciences⟩ — see DEPRECIATION

denigrative *adj* intended to make a person or thing seem of little importance or value ⟨thanked her for the gift and then added the *denigrative* aside, "Not that it's anything special!"⟩ — see DEROGATORY

denigratory *adj* intended to make a person or thing seem of little importance or value ⟨a *denigratory* observation that the novel wasn't half bad—considering it was written by an actor⟩ — see DEROGATORY

denizen *n* **1** someone who regularly spends time in a particular place ⟨one of those muscle-bound *denizens* of the gym⟩
synonyms familiar, frequenter, habitué (*also* habitue), haunter, rat, regular
related words client, customer, guest, patron; addict, aficionado (*also* afficionado), buff, bug, devotee, enthusiast, fan, fanatic, fancier, fiend, freak, lover, maniac, nut
2 one who lives permanently in a place ⟨the polar bear is an iconic *denizen* of the snowy Arctic⟩ — see INHABITANT

denominate *vb* to give a name to ⟨stargazing is nothing more than that, and *denominating* it as astrology does not make it a science⟩ — see NAME 1

denomination *n* a word or combination of words by which a person or thing is regularly known ⟨a variety of creative works that today come under the *denomination* of "art"⟩ — see NAME 1

denotation *n* **1** a word or combination of words by which a person or thing is regularly known ⟨"soul" is the common *denotation* for that mysterious force within the human body that gives it life and yet is separate from it⟩ — see NAME 1
2 the idea that is conveyed or intended to be conveyed to the mind by language, symbol, or action ⟨although most people exercise for fitness, the *denotation* of the term "fitness" varies from exerciser to exerciser⟩ — see MEANING 1

denotative *adj* indicating something ⟨a string of absences from this course will be seen as *denotative* of the student's lack of interest in it⟩ — see INDICATIVE

denote *vb* **1** to communicate or convey (as an idea) to the mind ⟨a flashing red light that *denotes* danger⟩ — see MEAN 1
2 to serve as a sign or symptom of ⟨the unkempt yard *denotes* a homeowner with little concern for the well-being of his neighborhood⟩ — see INDICATE 1

denoting *adj* indicating something ⟨an arrow is a common *denoting* symbol for direction⟩ — see INDICATIVE

denounce *vb* **1** to declare to be morally wrong or evil

⟨the church council *denounced* the bishop's teachings, officially declaring them to be heresy⟩ — see CONDEMN 1
2 to express one's unfavorable opinion of the worth or quality of ⟨*denounced* the shoddy merchandise that the local shops were foisting on tourists⟩ — see CRITICIZE
3 to express public or formal disapproval of ⟨the governor has *denounced* the court's decision and vows to press for a constitutional amendment⟩ — see CENSURE 1

de novo *adv* yet another time ⟨since a mistrial was declared, the case will have to be tried *de novo*⟩ — see AGAIN 1

dense *adj* **1** having little space between items or parts ⟨the *dense* soil in the garden⟩ — see CLOSE 1
2 not having or showing an ability to absorb ideas readily ⟨she accused him of being *dense* when he didn't seem to understand her at first⟩ — see STUPID 1

denseness *n* the quality or state of lacking intelligence or quickness of mind ⟨complained about the indefensible *denseness* of the shipping clerks who had misplaced his order⟩ — see STUPIDITY 1

density *n* **1** the degree to which a fluid can resist flowing ⟨the simple fact that molasses has greater *density* than room-temperature water⟩ — see CONSISTENCY
2 the quality or state of lacking intelligence or quickness of mind ⟨only a person with the proverbial *density* of concrete could have missed that clue⟩ — see STUPIDITY 1

dent *n* **1** a sunken area forming a separate space ⟨there was a big *dent* in the car's hood where something had hit it⟩ — see HOLE 2
2 the amount by which something is lessened ⟨a little belt-tightening would at least make a small *dent* in our credit-card debt⟩ — see DECREASE

dent *vb* to make smaller in amount, volume, or extent ⟨hopefully this vacation won't *dent* our bank account too much⟩ — see DECREASE 1

dented *adj* curved inward ⟨the *dented* car fender bore silent testament to an accident that no one in the family was owning up to⟩ — see HOLLOW

denuded *adj* lacking a usual or natural covering ⟨the *denuded* trees left behind after the forest fire had passed⟩ — see NAKED 2

denunciation *n* an often public or formal expression of disapproval ⟨the official *denunciation* of the congresswoman's actions before the full house⟩ — see CENSURE

deny *vb* **1** to declare not to be true ⟨the congressman *denied* all charges of wrongdoing⟩
synonyms contradict, disaffirm, disallow, disavow, disclaim, disconfirm, disown, gainsay, negate, negative, refute, reject, repudiate
related words traverse; challenge, confute, disprove, rebut; disagree (with), dispute
near antonyms accept, adopt, embrace, espouse; affirm, announce, assert, aver, claim, declare, maintain, profess, submit; authenticate, corroborate, substantiate, validate, verify
antonyms acknowledge, admit, allow, avow, concede, confirm, own
2 to be unwilling to grant ⟨the director *denied* access to the top secret files to all but those with a need to know⟩
synonyms decline, disallow, disapprove, negative, nix, refuse, reject, reprobate, withhold
related words ban, enjoin, forbid, prohibit, proscribe, veto; rebuff, repel, spurn; check, constrain, curb, hold, keep, repress, restrain, restrict; balk (at), hinder, impede, obstruct
near antonyms afford, furnish, give, provide, supply; authorize, commission, license (*also* licence); accede (to), acquiesce, agree (to), assent (to), consent (to), warrant; accord, sanction, vouchsafe
antonyms allow, concede, grant, let, OK (*or* okay), permit
3 to refuse to acknowledge as one's own or as one's responsibility ⟨in a futile attempt to get out of the contract, he even *denied* his own signature⟩ — see DISCLAIM 1

deodorize *vb* to make (something) seem less bad by offering excuses ⟨the propaganda film attempts to *deodorize* the dictator's history of human rights abuses⟩ — see PALLIATE 1

depart *vb* **1** to leave a place often for another ⟨I'll sing one more song before I *depart*⟩ — see GO 2
2 to stop living ⟨a special tribute for those members of the motion picture academy who have *departed* over the past year⟩ — see DIE 1

departed *adj* **1** no longer existing ⟨a few crumbling ruins are all that remain of that *departed* civilization⟩ — see EXTINCT
2 no longer living ⟨our dear *departed* friend⟩ — see DEAD 1

departing *n* the act of leaving a place ⟨his *departing* was accompanied by tears and heartfelt good wishes⟩ — see DEPARTURE 1

department *n* **1** a large unit of a governmental, business, or educational organization ⟨the *Department* of the Interior⟩ — see DIVISION 2
2 a region of activity, knowledge, or influence ⟨that's not my *department*, but maybe I can help you anyway⟩ — see FIELD 2

departure *n* **1** the act of leaving a place ⟨his sudden *departure* left them wondering if they'd upset him⟩
synonyms decamping, decampment, departing, exit, exiting, farewell, going, leave, leave-taking, lighting out, outgo, parting, quitting, walking out
related words flight, retirement, retreat, running away, withdrawal; diaspora, emigration, evacuation, exodus; embarkation, embarkment; disembarkation, egress; abandonment, forsaking, relinquishment
near antonyms coming; approach, entrance, ingress
antonyms advent, appearance, arrival
2 a turning away from a course or standard ⟨any *departure* from the modernist orthodoxy was scorned by the city's cultural elite⟩ — see DIVERGENCE 2

depend *vb* **1** to be determined by, based on, or subject (to) ⟨whether or not we play baseball will *depend* on how much rain we get⟩
synonyms hang, hinge, ride, turn
related words base, establish, found, rest, stay; ground
2 to place reliance or trust ⟨I know I can always *depend* on you for help when I really need it⟩
synonyms calculate, count, lean, reckon, rely
related words commit, confide, entrust (*also* intrust), trust
phrases bank on, call on (*or* upon), figure on, look to, stand on
near antonyms distrust, mistrust, question, suspect

dependability *n* worthiness as the recipient of another's trust or confidence ⟨her *dependability* as a friend, in good times and bad, is legendary⟩ — see RELIABILITY

dependable *adj* worthy of one's trust ⟨seeking a *dependable* person to look after their summer home in the off-season⟩
synonyms calculable, good, reliable, responsible, safe, secure, solid, steady, sure, tried, tried-and-true, true, trustable, trustworthy, trusty
related words constant, devoted, faithful, fast, loyal, staunch (*also* stanch), steadfast, true-blue; honest, sincere, single-minded; infallible, unerring; bedrock, firm, sound, strong; effective, telling; attested, authenticated, confirmed, proven, valid, validated, verified; blameless, faultless, guiltless, impeccable, inerrant, irreproachable, unimpeachable, unquestionable

near antonyms disloyal, faithless, false, fickle, inconstant, perfidious, recreant, traitorous, treacherous, unfaithful, untrue; deceitful, dishonest, lying, mendacious, untruthful; debatable, disputable, doubtable, doubtful, dubious, fishy, problematic (*also* problematical), questionable, shady, shaky, suspect, uncertain, unsound; hazardous, risky; unconfirmed, untried
antonyms dodgy [*chiefly British*], uncertain, undependable, unreliable, unsafe, untrustworthy

dependableness *n* worthiness as the recipient of another's trust or confidence ⟨the questionable *dependableness* of the no-name televisions being sold at a discount store⟩ — see RELIABILITY

dependence *also* **dependance** *n* **1** the quality or state of needing something or someone ⟨a baby's total *dependence* upon his or her parents for every one of life's needs⟩
synonyms dependency, reliance
related words reciprocity, relativity; confidence, credence, faith, stock, trust
near antonyms autonomy, self-determination, sovereignty (*also* sovranty)
antonyms independence, independency, self-dependence, self-reliance, self-sufficiency, self-support
2 something or someone to which one looks for support ⟨ultimately rice became the chief *dependence* in that state⟩
synonyms anchor, buttress, mainstay, pillar, reliance, standby
related words backbone, sinew(s), spine; right hand; bolsterer, crutch, handmaiden (*also* handmaid), prop, stay; anchorage, harbor, refuge
3 a physiological need for certain drugs ⟨acquired a *dependence* on prescription painkillers following back surgery⟩ — see ADDICTION

dependency *n* the quality or state of needing something or someone ⟨she was concerned about his heavy *dependency* on coffee to get him moving in the morning⟩ — see DEPENDENCE 1

dependent *adj* **1** extending freely from a support from above ⟨the *dependent* willow branches swayed in the gentle breeze⟩
synonyms dangling, hanging, pendent (*or* pendant), pendulous, suspended
related words drooping, flagging, lolling, sagging, wilting
2 determined by something else ⟨our going to the movies tonight is *dependent* on whether or not we have any money left after we eat out⟩
synonyms conditional, contingent (on *or* upon), subject (to), tentative
related words liable, open, susceptible; limited, modified, qualified, restricted; debatable, disputable, doubtable, doubtful, iffy, problematic (*also* problematical), questionable, shady, shaky, suspect, uncertain
near antonyms absolute, all-out, arrant, categorical (*also* categoric), complete, consummate, out-and-out, outright, perfect, simple, total, ultimate, unadulterated, unalloyed, unconditional, unequivocal, unmitigated, unqualified, utter; basal, basic, fundamental, primary
antonyms independent, unconditional

depict *vb* **1** to give a representation or account of in words ⟨this letter from an eyewitness *depicts* the battle in greater detail than any other account⟩ — see DESCRIBE 1
2 to point out the chief quality or qualities of an individual or group ⟨the report *depicted* him as a reliable assistant and an employee who could be entrusted with any task⟩ — see CHARACTERIZE 1
3 to present a picture of ⟨the painting *depicts* a pastoral landscape on a summer day⟩ — see PICTURE 1

depiction *n* a vivid representation in words of someone or something ⟨the set piece of the novel is a *depiction* of the battle that makes readers feel like they were there⟩ — see DESCRIPTION 1

deplete *vb* **1** to make complete use of ⟨miners *depleted* the vein of copper ore after only a few months⟩
synonyms absorb, burn, consume, devour, drain, draw down, exhaust, expend, play out, spend, use up
related words abate, decrease, de-escalate, diminish, downsize, dwindle, lessen, lower, reduce; eat, use; bankrupt, clean (out), impoverish; cripple, debilitate, disable, enfeeble, sap, undermine, weaken; dry up, empty; blow, dissipate, fritter (away), guzzle, lavish, misspend, run through, squander, throw away, waste
phrases run out of
near antonyms augment, enlarge, increase; bolster, enforce, fortify, reinforce (*also* reenforce), strengthen; rebuild, repair, restore, revive; conserve, preserve, save
antonyms renew, replace
2 to make smaller in amount, volume, or extent ⟨disease and battlefield casualties had *depleted* troop strength to dangerously low levels⟩ — see DECREASE 1

depletion *n* the amount by which something is lessened ⟨the kind of catastrophic illness that can make a sizable *depletion* in a family's savings⟩ — see DECREASE

deplorable *adj* **1** arousing or deserving of one's loathing and disgust ⟨we will not tolerate such *deplorable* behavior in a house of worship⟩ — see CONTEMPTIBLE 1
2 of a kind to cause great distress ⟨condemned the *deplorable* conditions in which the family was living⟩ — see REGRETTABLE

deplore *vb* **1** to feel or express sorrow for ⟨a statement from the bishops *deploring* the loss of life in the war overseas⟩ — see LAMENT 1
2 to feel sorry or dissatisfied about ⟨*deplored* the fact that his guests were seeing his apartment at its messiest⟩ — see REGRET

deploring *adj* expressing or suggesting mourning ⟨a *deploring* look on his face long after the funeral had ended⟩ — see MOURNFUL 1

deport *vb* **1** to force to leave a country ⟨*deported* them back to their country of birth⟩ — see BANISH 1
2 to manage the actions of (oneself) in a particular way ⟨*deported* herself with grace and propriety at the country club cotillion⟩ — see BEHAVE

deportation *n* the forced removal from a homeland ⟨the *deportation* of the Jews from Spain in 1492⟩ — see EXILE 1

deportee *n* a person forced to emigrate for political reasons ⟨the *deportee* vowed that he would someday return to a liberated nation⟩ — see ÉMIGRÉ 1

deportment *n* the way or manner in which one conducts oneself ⟨her *deportment* during the bitter divorce was a model of self-restraint and class⟩ — see BEHAVIOR

depose *vb* **1** to remove from a position of prominence or power (as a throne) ⟨a military junta *deposed* the dictator after he had bankrupted the country⟩
synonyms defrock, deprive, dethrone, displace, oust, uncrown, unmake, unseat, unthrone
related words can, cashier, discharge, dismiss, fire, muster out, remove, retire, sack; overthrow, subvert, supplant, topple, usurp; banish, boot (out), bounce, cast out, chase, drum (out), eject, expel, extrude, rout, run off, throw out
near antonyms baptize, inaugurate, induct, initiate, install, instate, invest; appoint, designate, elect
antonyms crown, enthrone, throne
2 to make a solemn declaration under oath for the purpose of establishing a fact ⟨she was nervous when the time to *depose* before the jury finally arrived⟩ — see TESTIFY
3 to arrange something in a certain spot or position ⟨*de-*

posed her fan and gloves on the dressing table⟩ — see PLACE 1

deposit *n* **1** matter that settles to the bottom of a body of liquid ⟨a *deposit* of silt on the river bed⟩
synonyms deposition, dregs, grounds, precipitate, sediment, settlings
related words lees; ooze, silt, sludge; dross, slag, waste
2 a collection of things kept available for future use or need ⟨a *deposit* of ammunition under lock and key⟩ — see STORE 1
3 a sum of money set aside for a particular purpose ⟨made a *deposit* at the bank every week⟩ — see FUND 1

deposit *vb* **1** to put in an account ⟨we quickly *deposited* the check in a bank account⟩
synonyms bank
related words cache, hoard, lay away, reserve, salt away, save, squirrel (away), stash, store, stow; invest
near antonyms remove, take out; disburse, expend, give, lay out, pay, spend
antonyms withdraw
2 to arrange something in a certain spot or position ⟨*deposited* their luggage at the foot of the hotel bed⟩ — see PLACE 1

deposition *n* matter that settles to the bottom of a body of liquid ⟨several types of *deposition* on the bottom of the lake⟩ — see DEPOSIT 1

depository *n* a building for storing goods ⟨a book *depository*⟩ — see STOREHOUSE

depot *n* **1** a building for storing goods ⟨a distribution *depot* for auto parts⟩ — see STOREHOUSE
2 a place where military arms are stored ⟨the guns and ammunition were stored in a *depot* in Concord⟩ — see ARMORY

deprave *vb* to lower in character, dignity, or quality ⟨the belief that pornography *depraves* society as a whole⟩ — see DEBASE 1

depraved *adj* having or showing lowered moral character or standards ⟨the *depraved* actions of a gang of madmen who had gained control of an entire nation⟩ — see CORRUPT

depravedness *n* the state or quality of being utterly evil ⟨the prosecutor argued that the murders in their utter *depravedness* called for a sentence of nothing less than the death penalty⟩ — see ENORMITY 1

depravity *n* **1** a sinking to a state of low moral standards and behavior ⟨regards the widespread acceptance of gambling as another sign of the *depravity* of today's society⟩ — see CORRUPTION 2
2 immoral conduct or practices harmful or offensive to society ⟨a section of the city long known as den of *depravity*⟩ — see VICE 1
3 the state or quality of being utterly evil ⟨the *depravity* of the demons and devils in many tales of horror⟩ — see ENORMITY 1

deprecate *vb* **1** to express scornfully one's low opinion of ⟨movie critics tried to outdo one another in *deprecating* the comedy as the stupidest movie of the year⟩ — see DECRY 1
2 to hold an unfavorable opinion of ⟨*deprecates* TV sitcoms as childish and simpleminded⟩ — see DISAPPROVE (OF)

deprecation *n* **1** refusal to accept as right or desirable ⟨considering that he's a member of the old school, his *deprecation* of contemporary manners isn't surprising⟩ — see DISAPPROVAL
2 the act of making a person or a thing seem little or unimportant ⟨she had low self-esteem, so she made up for it with a near-constant *deprecation* of other people⟩ — see DEPRECIATION

deprecatory *adj* intended to make a person or thing seem of little importance or value ⟨he typically followed up any mention of his accomplishments with some *deprecatory* comments about his perceived failures⟩ — see DEROGATORY

depreciate *vb* **1** to diminish the price or value of ⟨a faded finish will really *depreciate* your car when you decide to trade it in⟩
synonyms attenuate, break, cheapen, depress, devaluate, devalue, downgrade, lower, mark down, reduce, sink, write down, write off
related words debase, demonetize; underestimate, underprice, underrate, undervalue; abridge, compress, contract, de-escalate, deflate, downsize, dwindle, lessen, moderate, shrink
near antonyms bloat, blow up, inflate; overestimate, overprice, overrate, overvalue; add, aggrandize, amplify, augment, balloon, boost, compound, dilate, enlarge, escalate, expand, extend, heighten, increase, maximize, multiply, raise, swell, up
antonyms appreciate, enhance, mark up, upgrade
2 to express scornfully one's low opinion of ⟨dared to *depreciate* Shakespeare, saying his works have no relevance for modern audiences⟩ — see DECRY 1

depreciation *n* the act of making a person or a thing seem little or unimportant ⟨a *depreciation* of the role of minorities in the building of the nation was once a common feature of history books⟩
synonyms belittlement, denigration, deprecation, derogation, detraction, diminishment, disparagement, putdown
related words aspersion, backbiting, calumny, defamation, libel, slander, vilification; derision, mockery, ridicule; abuse, invective, vituperation; censure, condemnation, criticism, denouncement, denunciation; de-emphasis, minimization, soft-pedaling
near antonyms acclaim, praise; approbation, approval, blessing, commendation; hype, puffery
antonyms aggrandizement, ennoblement, exaltation, glorification, magnification

depreciative *adj* intended to make a person or thing seem of little importance or value ⟨the usual *depreciative* comments by the troops about the food in the mess hall⟩ — see DEROGATORY

depreciatory *adj* intended to make a person or thing seem of little importance or value ⟨a customer making *depreciatory* remarks about the quality of the service at the restaurant⟩ — see DEROGATORY

depress *vb* **1** to make sad ⟨the thought of once again failing the bar exam *depressed* me⟩
synonyms bum (out), burden, dash, deject, get down, oppress, sadden, weigh down
related words ail, distress, trouble; afflict, torment, torture; daunt, demoralize, discourage, dishearten, dismay, dispirit, get down, unnerve; agitate, bother, concern, discomfort, discompose, disquiet, disturb, exercise, freak (out), perturb, undo, unhinge, unsettle, upset, worry
near antonyms animate, enliven, invigorate; assure, comfort, console, reassure, solace, soothe; excite, inspire, stimulate; elate, exhilarate; encourage, hearten; delight, gratify, please; boost, elevate, lift, uplift
antonyms brighten, buoy, cheer (up), gladden, lighten, rejoice
2 to cause to fall intentionally or unintentionally ⟨construction workers *depressed* the roadbed in order to make way for an overpass⟩ — see DROP 1
3 to diminish the price or value of ⟨the glut of wheat on the market has *depressed* that commodity for most of the past year⟩ — see DEPRECIATE 1
4 to push steadily against with some force ⟨*depressed* the lever to start the machine⟩ — see [2]PRESS 1

depressed *adj* **1** curved inward ⟨the *depressed* sections of the highway under the overpasses constantly get flooded during heavy rainstorms⟩ — see HOLLOW

2 feeling unhappiness ⟨I was *depressed* and didn't feel much like going to the party⟩ — see SAD 1
3 kept from having the necessities of life or a healthful environment ⟨a *depressed* class of people whose living conditions are abominable even by third world standards⟩ — see DEPRIVED

depressing *adj* **1** causing or marked by an atmosphere lacking in cheer ⟨the *depressing* atmosphere of the funeral⟩ — see GLOOMY 1
2 causing unhappiness ⟨more *depressing* news about the famine overseas⟩ — see SAD 2

depression *n* **1** a period of decreased economic activity ⟨during the 1930s the U.S. suffered a great *depression*⟩
synonyms recession, slump
related words bust, crash, panic; stagnation; downbeat, downdraft, downswing, downtrend, downturn, slowdown
near antonyms development, growth; advancement, progress; rally, recovery
antonyms boom
2 a state or spell of low spirits ⟨we threw our friend a party just to jar him out of his *depression*⟩ — see SADNESS
3 a sunken area forming a separate space ⟨the water generally collects in the patchwork of *depressions* in the city plaza⟩ — see HOLE 2
4 the amount by which something is lessened ⟨a *depression* in the number of new homes being built⟩ — see DECREASE

depressive *adj* causing or marked by an atmosphere lacking in cheer ⟨the *depressive* air of a dingy barroom where locals went to drown their sorrows⟩ — see GLOOMY 1

deprivation *n* the state of being robbed of something normally enjoyed ⟨the concern of some that there has been a *deprivation* of rights since the passing of laws to combat the threat of terrorism⟩ — see PRIVATION

deprive *vb* **1** to take something away from ⟨working those long hours was *depriving* him of his sleep⟩
synonyms abate, bereave, divest, strip
related words denude; cheat, clean (out), defraud, shortchange; bankrupt, disfurnish, impoverish
2 to remove from a position of prominence or power (as a throne) ⟨one of scores of bishops who had been *deprived* after the anticlericals came to power⟩ — see DEPOSE 1

deprived *adj* kept from having the necessities of life or a healthful environment ⟨*deprived* children growing up in the slums⟩
synonyms depressed, disadvantaged, underprivileged
related words beggared, broke, destitute, impecunious, impoverished, indigent, needy, penniless, penurious, poor, poverty-stricken, unprivileged; bankrupt, bankrupted, insolvent; pinched, reduced, straitened; displaced, dispossessed
near antonyms blessed (*also* blest), fortunate, lucky; affluent, flush, loaded, moneyed (*also* monied), opulent, rich, wealthy, well-heeled, well-off, well-to-do; coddled, indulged, pampered, spoiled; comfortable, propertied, prosperous, successful; flourishing, prospering, thriving
antonyms advantaged, privileged

depth *n* **1** distance measured from the top to the bottom of something ⟨be sure to check the *depth* of the water before diving off the dock⟩
synonyms deepness, drop
related words lowness; draft, sounding
near antonyms shallowness; altitude, elevation, height, stature
2 the quality of being great in extent (as of insight) ⟨the *depth* of the poet's understanding of human nature has given his works a timeless appeal⟩
synonyms deepness, profoundness, profundity
related words discernment, perception, perceptiveness, perceptivity, percipience, sagacity, sapience, sense, sensibility, wisdom; braininess, brightness, brilliance, intellect, intelligence, judgment (*or* judgement), reason, sense, smartness, wit; acuity, acuteness, keenness, penetration, perspicacity, sensitivity, sharpness
near antonyms shallowness, superficiality; brainlessness, idiocy, imbecility, mindlessness, simpleness, stupidity, witlessness; illogic, irrationality, unreasonableness, unsoundness
3 the most intense or characteristic phase of something ⟨I was in the *depths* of profound thought when I was rudely interrupted⟩ — see THICK
4 the lowest point or level ⟨at the *depth* of her depression she had even contemplated suicide⟩ — see NADIR 1
5 the most extreme or advanced point ⟨even in the *depth* of the Great Depression people never lost hope⟩ — see HEIGHT 2

depthless *adj* lacking significant physical depth ⟨three inches of water may seem rather *depthless*, but unattended babies have drowned in bathtubs with that amount⟩ — see SHALLOW 1

depute *vb* to appoint as one's representative ⟨the governor has the authority to *depute* anyone he wants⟩ — see DELEGATE 1

deputize *vb* to appoint as one's representative ⟨he *deputized* a local citizen to take charge of the situation while he went for reinforcements⟩ — see DELEGATE 1

deputy *n* **1** a person who acts or does business for another ⟨the club president sent a *deputy* to the conference to vote on our behalf⟩ — see AGENT 2
2 a person who helps a more skilled person ⟨a *deputy* supervisor to help out with routine tasks⟩ — see HELPER

derail *vb* to trouble the mind of; to make uneasy ⟨according to police, the suspect had been *derailed* in recent months by mounting financial problems⟩ — see DISTURB 1

derange *vb* **1** to cause to go insane or as if insane ⟨being stranded at night on a lonely road would derange anyone⟩ — see CRAZE
2 to undo the proper order or arrangement of ⟨the storage room had all been *deranged* by the earthquake, and it took hours to sort out things⟩ — see DISORDER

deranged *adj* having or showing a very abnormal or sick state of mind ⟨a *deranged* prisoner who had been in that rat-infested hole for 20 years⟩ — see INSANE 1

derangement *n* **1** a serious mental disorder that prevents one from living a safe and normal life ⟨given powerful drugs to treat his *derangement*⟩ — see INSANITY 1
2 an act or instance of the order of things being disturbed ⟨the *derangement* of the carefully organized event by a single freak accident⟩ — see UPSET

derelict *adj* **1** failing to give proper care and attention ⟨the guards were judged *derelict* in their duty⟩ — see NEGLIGENT
2 left unoccupied or unused ⟨an old *derelict* mansion that was rumored to be haunted⟩ — see ABANDONED 1

derelict *n* an idle worthless person ⟨a section of the city that seemed to be frequented mostly by *derelicts*⟩ — see NE'ER-DO-WELL

dereliction *n* **1** the act of abandoning ⟨the family's shameful *dereliction* of their pets at the end of the summer season⟩
synonyms abandonment, desertion, forsaking
related words defection; tergiversation; discard, dumping, jettisoning
near antonyms retention; recoupment, repossession, retrieval
antonyms reclamation
2 failure to take the care that a cautious person usually

takes ⟨the ski area was not held responsible for the injury on account of the skier's own manifest *dereliction*⟩ — see NEGLIGENCE 1

3 the nonperformance of an assigned or expected action ⟨both sentries were to be court-martialed for *dereliction* of duty⟩ — see FAILURE 1

4 a defect in character ⟨believes that society is guilty of a moral *dereliction* if it does not care for those unable to care for themselves⟩ — see FAULT 1

deride *vb* to make (someone or something) the object of unkind laughter ⟨my brothers *derided* our efforts, but were forced to eat their words when we won first place⟩ — see RIDICULE

de rigueur *adj* following the established traditions of refined society and good taste ⟨though he was wearing a dinner jacket and a black bow tie, his jeans and tennis shoes were hardly *de rigueur*⟩ — see PROPER 1

derision *n* **1** a person or thing that is made fun of ⟨in the 19th century any supporter of women's rights could expect to become a *derision* to her neighbors⟩ — see LAUGHINGSTOCK

2 the making of unkind jokes as a way of showing one's scorn for someone or something ⟨her absurd behavior on the awards show became a source of *derision* for comedians⟩ — see RIDICULE

derisive *adj* so foolish or pointless as to be worthy of scornful laughter ⟨the *derisive* performances of some of the singers on the talent show⟩ — see RIDICULOUS 1

derisory *adj* **1** intended to make a person or thing seem of little importance or value ⟨a literary snob, she invariably used the *derisory* term "the boob tube" when referring to television⟩ — see DEROGATORY

2 so foolish or pointless as to be worthy of scornful laughter ⟨the pawnbroker offered what I regarded as a *derisory* amount for the diamond ring⟩ — see RIDICULOUS 1

derivable *adj* being or provable by reasoning in which the conclusion follows necessarily from given information ⟨the solution was easily *derivable* from the clues we were given⟩ — see DEDUCTIVE

derivate *n* something that naturally develops or is developed from something else ⟨a cuisine that is regarded by some as a *derivate* of creole cookery⟩ — see DERIVATIVE

derivation *n* something that naturally develops or is developed from something else ⟨the noun is a *derivation* of a much earlier verb⟩ — see DERIVATIVE

derivative *adj* taken or created from something original or basic ⟨a *derivative* style that she took from earlier and better painters⟩ — see SECONDARY 1

derivative *n* something that naturally develops or is developed from something else ⟨the whole field of industrial robots is a *derivative* of technology developed for the space program⟩

synonyms by-product, derivate, derivation, offshoot, outgrowth, spin-off

related words descendant (*also* descendent); aftermath, consequence, corollary, development, fruit, growth, issue, outcome, product, result, sequel, sequence, upshot; denouement (*also* dénouement), repercussion; aftereffect, side effect (*also* side reaction); copy, duplicate, facsimile, replica, reproduction

near antonyms archetype, original, prototype; antecedent, cause, determinant, occasion, reason

antonyms origin, root, source

derive *vb* to form an opinion or reach a conclusion through reasoning and information ⟨from the summit, he was able to *derive* his location from the position of several prominent landmarks⟩ — see INFER 1

dernier cri *n* a practice or interest that is very popular for a short time ⟨when deconstructionism became the *dernier cri* in literary criticism⟩ — see FAD

derogate *vb* to express scornfully one's low opinion of ⟨there's no need to *derogate* him as a human being just because you disagree with him politically⟩ — see DECRY 1

derogation *n* the act of making a person or a thing seem little or unimportant ⟨those remarks were not intended as a *derogation* of popular music⟩ — see DEPRECIATION

derogative *adj* intended to make a person or thing seem of little importance or value ⟨since "housewife" is now regarded by some as a *derogative* word, designations such as "stay-at-home mom" have emerged⟩ — see DEROGATORY

derogatory *adj* intended to make a person or thing seem of little importance or value ⟨fans made a steady stream of *derogatory* remarks about the players on the visiting team⟩

synonyms belittling, contemptuous, decrying, degrading, demeaning, denigrative, denigratory, deprecatory, depreciative, depreciatory, derisory, derogative, detractive, disdainful, disparaging, pejorative, scornful, slighting, uncomplimentary

related words aspersing, calumnious, defamatory, insulting, libelous (*or* libellous), maligning, slandering, slanderous, vilifying; abusive, opprobrious, scurrilous; catty, cruel, despiteful, hateful, malevolent, malicious, malign, malignant, mean, nasty, spiteful, unkind, virulent; critical, denunciative, denunciatory; acrimonious, bitter, envious, jaundiced, jealous, rancorous, resentful; acrid, caustic, scathing, venomous

near antonyms admiring, adulatory, applauding, approving, friendly, positive; appreciative, respectful; kind, kindhearted, kindly, sympathetic, unmalicious, warm, warmhearted

antonyms commendatory, complimentary, laudative, laudatory

derriere *or* **derrière** *n* the part of the body upon which someone sits ⟨swimsuits that should be worn only by those with tight little *derrieres*⟩ — see BUTTOCKS

desacralize *vb* to remove the sacred qualities or status of ⟨deplores how contemporary society has *desacralized* and trivialized the celebration of Christmas⟩ — see DESANCTIFY

desanctify *vb* to remove the sacred qualities or status of ⟨*desanctified* the church building and converted it into condos⟩

synonyms deconsecrate, desacralize

related words defile, desecrate, profane, violate

near antonyms canonize, deify, venerate; spiritualize; chasten, cleanse, purify; exorcise (*also* exorcize), expurgate

antonyms bless, consecrate, hallow, sacralize, sanctify

descant *vb* **1** to give a formal often extended talk on a subject ⟨an English professor who loves to *descant* on his beloved Shakespeare⟩ — see TALK 1

2 to produce musical sounds with the voice ⟨the soprano *descanted* above the melody line⟩ — see SING 1

descend *vb* **1** to lead or extend downward ⟨the pathway *descends* to the river bank⟩

synonyms decline, dip, drop, fall, plunge, sink

related words angle, cant, cock, heel, incline, lean, list, recline, slant, slope, tilt, tip

near antonyms even, flatten, level, plane, smooth, straighten

antonyms arise, ascend, climb, mount, rise, uprise, upsweep, upturn

2 to become worse or of less value ⟨the family's economic fortunes *descended* to the point where they were finally homeless⟩ — see DETERIORATE 1

3 to go to a lower level especially abruptly ⟨leaves slowly *descended* from the branches in the gentle autumn wind⟩ — see DROP 2

4 to come down from something (as a vehicle) ⟨the driver *descended* from the truck's cab, dreading to see what he had hit⟩ — see ALIGHT 2

descend (on *or* upon) *vb* to take sudden, violent action against ⟨the shock troops *descended on* the village without warning⟩ — see ATTACK 1

descendant *also* **descendent** *adj* bending downward or forward ⟨the *descendant* branches of a weeping willow⟩ — see NODDING

descending *adj* bending downward or forward ⟨with *descending* heads the mourners made their way to the burial site⟩ — see NODDING

descent *n* **1** the act or process of going to a lower level or altitude ⟨the airplane began its gradual *descent* to the landing field⟩

synonyms dip, dive, down, drop, fall, nosedive, plunge

related words comedown, decline, downfall, downgrade; plummeting, sinking

near antonyms advance, headway, progress, progression; betterment, improvement

antonyms ascent, climb, rise, rising, soaring, upswing, upturn

2 a gradual sinking and wasting away of mind or body ⟨the family patriarch's heartbreaking *descent* into infirmity and senility⟩ — see DECLINE 1

3 a change to a lower state or level ⟨the nation's rapid *descent* into anarchy after the revolution⟩ — see DECLINE 2

4 a loss of status ⟨for throwing the game, the ballplayer underwent a huge *descent* in the eyes of the fans⟩ — see COMEDOWN

5 a sudden attack on and entrance into hostile territory ⟨the lightning *descent* of the invading army on that unsuspecting border town⟩ — see RAID 1

6 the act or action of setting upon with force or violence ⟨the *descent* of the voracious locusts on the wheat fields⟩ — see ATTACK 1

7 the line of ancestors from whom a person is descended ⟨a person of Finnish *descent*⟩ — see ANCESTRY

8 a downward slope ⟨on bicycle tours the ascents always seem to outnumber the *descents*⟩ — see DECLINE 3

describe *vb* **1** to give a representation or account of in words ⟨he tried to *describe* the dream he had last night as accurately as he could⟩

synonyms delineate, depict, draw, image, limn, paint, picture, portray, render, set out, sketch

related words characterize, define, label, qualify, represent; demonstrate, illustrate; narrate, recite, recount, rehearse, relate, report, tell; display, exhibit, show; hint, suggest; draft, outline, silhouette, trace, vignette; summarize, sum up, touch off; redescribe, reimage

near antonyms color, distort, falsify, garble, misdescribe, misrepresent, misstate, pervert, twist, warp

2 to give an oral or written account of in some detail ⟨a biography of Washington that *describes* the decisive Battle of Yorktown at great length⟩ — see TELL 1

3 to point out the chief quality or qualities of an individual or group ⟨how would you *describe* the Inupiat people you encountered in Alaska?⟩ — see CHARACTERIZE 1

description *n* **1** a vivid representation in words of someone or something ⟨we immediately recognized the man from our cousin's *description* of him⟩

synonyms definition, delineation, depiction, picture, portrait, portraiture, portrayal, rendering, sketch, vignette

related words account, anecdote, chronicle, narrative, report, story, tale, yarn; demonstration, exemplification, illustration; clarification, elucidation, explanation, explication, exposition

2 a number of persons or things that are grouped together because they have something in common ⟨fixes small appliances and other things of that *description*⟩ — see SORT 1

descry *vb* **1** to come upon after searching, study, or effort ⟨we couldn't *descry* the reasons for his sudden departure⟩ — see FIND 1

2 to make note of (something) through the use of one's eyes ⟨could just *descry* the ship coming over the horizon⟩ — see SEE 1

desecrate *vb* to treat (a sacred place or object) shamefully or with great disrespect ⟨vandals *desecrated* the cemetery last night by covering the tombstones with graffiti⟩

synonyms defile, profane, violate

related words deconsecrate, desacralize, desanctify; blaspheme, curse, swear; befoul, contaminate, foul, poison, pollute, soil, sully, taint; affront, defame, insult, offend, outrage; annihilate, crush, decimate, demolish, desolate, destroy, devastate, ravage, raze, ruin, waste, wreck; despoil, loot, pillage, plunder, raid, ransack, rob, sack, spoil, strip

near antonyms bless, consecrate, dedicate, hallow, sanctify; honor, respect; cleanse, purge, purify

desecration *n* an act of great disrespect shown to God or to sacred ideas, people, or things ⟨the communicants were aghast at the *desecration* of the altar⟩ — see BLASPHEMY

deselect *vb* to show unwillingness to accept, do, engage in, or agree to ⟨he'll *deselect* any plan that doesn't put him in total control⟩ — see DECLINE 1

desensitized *adj* having or showing a lack of sympathy or tender feelings ⟨having lived through the horrors of war, the soldiers had seemingly become *desensitized* to virtually all human suffering⟩ — see HARD 1

[1]**desert** *n* land that is uninhabited or not fit for crops ⟨we were lost in the *desert* for days without food⟩ — see WASTELAND

[2]**desert** *n, usually* **deserts** *pl* suffering, loss, or hardship imposed in response to a crime or offense ⟨the robbers got their just *deserts*⟩ — see PUNISHMENT

desert *vb* **1** to leave (a cause or party) often in order to take up another ⟨the volunteer became disillusioned with his candidate and *deserted* to a political rival⟩ — see DEFECT (FROM)

2 to cause to remain behind ⟨*deserted* the kids at the food court for some independent shopping⟩ — see LEAVE 1

deserted *adj* left unoccupied or unused ⟨we had the *deserted* beach all to ourselves⟩ — see ABANDONED 1

deserter *n* a person who abandons a cause or organization usually without right ⟨we had orders to find and capture the *deserters* before they could reveal our location⟩ — see RENEGADE

desertion *n* the act of abandoning ⟨the soldiers were imprisoned for *desertion* of their posts⟩ — see DERELICTION 1

deserve *vb* to be or make worthy of (as a reward or punishment) ⟨the team really *deserved* that victory after the way they played⟩ — see EARN 2

deserved *adj* being what is called for by accepted standards of right and wrong ⟨a well *deserved* promotion for a hard worker⟩ — see JUST 1

deserving *adj* having sufficient worth or merit to receive one's honor, esteem, or reward ⟨gifts donated to *deserving* children every Christmas⟩ — see WORTHY

desex *vb* to remove the sex organs of ⟨*desex* the baby chickens destined for market⟩ — see NEUTER

desiccate *vb* **1** to deprive of emotional or intellectual vitality ⟨that historian's dryasdust prose *desiccates* what is actually an exciting period in European history⟩ — see DEHYDRATE 1

2 to make dry ⟨add a cup of *desiccated* coconut to the mix⟩ — see DRY 1

desiderate *vb* to have an earnest wish to own or enjoy ⟨a wide gulf between what they *desiderate* and what they deserve⟩ — see DESIRE 1

design *n* **1** a method worked out in advance for achieving some objective ⟨she always achieves her objective by *design* rather than by luck⟩ — see PLAN 1

2 a secret plan for accomplishing evil or unlawful ends ⟨the adventurer had devised an elaborate *design* to get the widow's fortune⟩ — see PLOT 1

3 something that one hopes or intends to accomplish ⟨the immigrant laborer had ambitious *designs* in mind for his daughter⟩ — see GOAL

4 a unit of decoration that is repeated all over something (as a fabric) ⟨the curtains have a lovely floral *design*⟩ — see PATTERN 1

5 the way in which the elements of something (as a work of art) are arranged ⟨the *design* of the building's lobby encourages the free flow of traffic⟩ — see COMPOSITION 3

design *vb* **1** to have in mind as a purpose or goal ⟨early on she had *designed* to a top position in a major insurance company⟩ — see INTEND 1

2 to work out the details of (something) in advance ⟨the foreman *designed* a better layout for the factory floor to improve efficiency⟩ — see PLAN 1

designate *vb* **1** to decide upon (the time or date for an event) usually from a position of authority ⟨the *designated* time for the meeting⟩ — see APPOINT 1

2 to pick (someone) by one's authority for a specific position or duty ⟨he has yet to *designate* his successor as head of the firm⟩ — see APPOINT 2

3 to give a name to ⟨he was *designated* "Air Jordan" by his fans⟩ — see NAME 1

designated hitter *n* a person or thing that takes the place of another ⟨you'll have to be my *designated hitter* in the office while I'm on business trips⟩ — see SUBSTITUTE

designation *n* **1** a word or combination of words by which a person or thing is regularly known ⟨we've never given the homemade gadget a proper *designation*⟩ — see NAME 1

2 the state or fact of being chosen for a position or duty ⟨his surprising *designation* as the running mate raised a few eyebrows⟩ — see APPOINTMENT 1

designedly *adv* with full awareness of what one is doing ⟨the puzzle was *designedly* difficult to decipher⟩ — see INTENTIONALLY

designee *n* one who has been chosen by some authority for a specific position or duty ⟨the director or his *designee* shall sign the report⟩ — see APPOINTEE

designer *adj* being or involving the latest methods, concepts, information, or styles ⟨that car manufacturer is claiming that their new models are the last word in *designer* technology⟩ — see MODERN

designer *n* one who creates or introduces something new ⟨credited as the *designer* of the first sneaker specifically intended for distance running⟩ — see INVENTOR

designing *adj* clever at attaining one's ends by indirect and often deceptive means ⟨he suspected his new admirer of being a *designing* woman who only wanted his money⟩ — see ARTFUL 1

desirability *n* suitability for bringing about a desired result under the circumstances ⟨the *desirability* of immortality becomes a little less certain after some consideration of the consequences⟩ — see EXPEDIENCY

desirable *adj* **1** sexually attractive ⟨the *desirable* young stars of a television reality show⟩ — see SEXY 1

2 suitable for bringing about a desired result under the circumstances ⟨a *desirable* location for the new house⟩ — see EXPEDIENT

desirableness *n* suitability for bringing about a desired result under the circumstances ⟨began to question the *desirableness* of a life of indolence on a tropical isle⟩ — see EXPEDIENCY

desire *n* **1** a strong wish for something ⟨a *desire* for adventure and excitement prompted him to travel to Africa⟩

synonyms appetency, appetite, craving, drive, hankering, hunger, itch, jones [*slang*], letch, longing, lust, passion, pining, thirst, thirstiness, urge, yearning, yen

related words compulsion, impulse, impulsion, will, zeal; liking, love, taste, weakness; eagerness, impatience; want, wish; necessity, need, requirement; obsession; acquisitiveness, avarice, avariciousness, avidity, covetousness, cupidity, greed, greediness, rapaciousness, rapacity; cacoëthes, mania

near antonyms abhorrence, abomination, allergy, averseness, aversion, disfavor, disgust, disinclination, dislike, disliking, distaste, hatred, loathing, nausea, repugnance, repulsion, revulsion; apathy, indifference, insouciance, nonchalance, unconcern

2 sexual appetite ⟨the nude pictures were clearly intended to provoke *desire*⟩

synonyms concupiscence, eroticism, horniness, hots, itch, lech, letch, libidinousness, lust, lustfulness, lustihood, passion, salaciousness

related words libido; ardor, heat, rut; erotomania, hypersexuality, lecherousness, lechery, nymphomania, satyriasis; venery

near antonyms abstinence, celibacy, chastity; frigidity, frigidness

3 an earnest request ⟨at the delegate's *desire*, the voice vote on the controversial measure was followed by an actual roll call⟩ — see PLEA 1

desire *vb* **1** to have an earnest wish to own or enjoy ⟨he greatly *desired* a new mountain bike for his next birthday⟩

synonyms ache (for), covet, crave, desiderate, die (for), hanker (for *or* after), hunger (for), itch (for), jones (for) [*slang*], long (for), lust (for *or* after), pant (after), pine (for), repine (for), salivate (for), sigh (for), thirst (for), want, wish (for), yearn (for), yen (for)

related words spoil (for); adore, delight (in), dig, enjoy, fancy, groove (on), like, love, relish, revel (in); favor, prefer; admire, appreciate, cherish, prize, treasure, value

phrases set one's heart on

near antonyms abhor, abominate, despise, detest, execrate, hate, loathe; decline, refuse, reject, spurn

2 to make a request for ⟨the host *desires* a response to the dinner invitation by tomorrow⟩ — see ASK (FOR) 1

desirous *adj* showing urgent desire or interest ⟨management is very *desirous* of finishing the project on time and within budget⟩ — see EAGER

desirousness *n* urgent desire or interest ⟨her *desirousness* for advancement in the corporation is such that she'll stamp on anyone in her way⟩ — see EAGERNESS

desist (from) *vb* to bring (as an action or operation) to an immediate end ⟨ordered to *desist from* all attempts to contact his estranged wife⟩ — see STOP 1

desk *n* a large unit of a governmental, business, or educational organization ⟨the city *desk* of a prominent newspaper⟩ — see DIVISION 2

desolate *adj* **1** causing or marked by an atmosphere lacking in cheer ⟨a *desolate* house abandoned many years ago⟩ — see GLOOMY 1

2 sad from lack of companionship or separation from others ⟨destitute and *desolate* since her husband walked out on her⟩ — see LONESOME 1

3 left unoccupied or unused ⟨a *desolate* mining town that had its brief heyday more than a century ago⟩ — see ABANDONED 1

4 producing inferior or only a small amount of vegetation ⟨wild, *desolate* plains on which only the hardiest could survive⟩ — see BARREN 1

desolate *vb* to bring to a complete end the physical soundness, existence, or usefulness of ⟨totally *desolated* the city with aerial bombs⟩ — see DESTROY 1

desolation *n* **1** a state or spell of low spirits ⟨his *desolation* after his twin brother died was incurable⟩ — see SADNESS

2 land that is uninhabited or not fit for crops ⟨looked out over the vast untamed *desolation* to the north⟩ — see WASTELAND

3 the state of being unattended to or not cared for ⟨the *desolation* of the abandoned garden⟩ — see NEGLECT 1

4 the state or fact of being rendered nonexistent, physically unsound, or useless ⟨the nuclear attack resulted in a scene of utter *desolation*⟩ — see DESTRUCTION 1

despair *n* **1** utter loss of hope ⟨the endless drought drove the farmers to *despair*⟩

synonyms desperation, despond, despondence, despondency, forlornness, hopelessness

related words blue devils, blues, dejection, depression, desolation, disconsolateness, dispiritedness, doldrums, dolor, downheartedness, dreariness, dumps, gloom, gloominess, joylessness, melancholy, mopes, oppression, sadness, sorrow, unhappiness; self-despair, self-pity; dolefulness, mournfulness, sorrowfulness, woefulness; agony, distress, pain; misery, woe, wretchedness; cynicism, pessimism; acceptance, resignation

phrases slough of despond

near antonyms cheer, cheerfulness, sunniness; optimism; gaiety (*also* gayety), glee, gleefulness, jollity, joviality, lightheartedness, merriment, mirth, mirthfulness; bliss, blissfulness, ecstasy, elatedness, elation, euphoria, exhilaration, exuberance, exultation, gladness, happiness, joy, joyfulness, joyousness, jubilation, rapture, rapturousness

antonyms hope, hopefulness

2 the state of being discouraged ⟨the other team's temporary lead caused some momentary *despair*⟩ — see DISCOURAGEMENT

despair *vb* to lose all hope or confidence ⟨we *despaired* when we saw how little time we had left to complete our project⟩

synonyms despond

related words give up, surrender, yield; darken, sadden; agonize, bleed, grieve, hurt, mourn, sorrow, suffer; discourage, dishearten, dispirit

phrases lose heart

near antonyms exult, rejoice; assure, encourage, hearten, reassure; hope

antonyms brighten, cheer (up), perk (up)

despairing *adj* **1** emphasizing or expecting the worst ⟨*despairing* predictions regarding the effects of global overpopulation⟩ — see PESSIMISTIC 1

2 feeling or showing no hope ⟨*despairing* applicants need to be reminded that most students are eventually accepted somewhere⟩ — see DESPONDENT 1

desperate *adj* feeling or showing no hope ⟨*desperate* cancer patients who are vulnerable to the claims of unscrupulous quacks⟩ — see DESPONDENT 1

desperately *adv* to a great degree ⟨all of a sudden everything went *desperately* wrong⟩ — see VERY 1

desperation *n* utter loss of hope ⟨during the famine her *desperation* drove her to do things she wouldn't have normally considered⟩ — see DESPAIR 1

despicable *adj* **1** arousing or deserving of one's loathing and disgust ⟨even within the prison population, pedophiles are regarded as particularly *despicable*⟩ — see CONTEMPTIBLE 1

2 not following or in accordance with standards of honor and decency ⟨the cad's *despicable* behavior toward women⟩ — see IGNOBLE 2

3 deserving pitying scorn (as for inadequacy) ⟨a *despicable* attempt at making a movie comedy⟩ — see PITIFUL 1

despise *vb* **1** to dislike strongly ⟨I *despise* anchovies on pizza, and I refuse to eat them!⟩ — see HATE

2 to ignore in a disrespectful manner ⟨a traitor hated and *despised* by the whole community⟩ — see SCORN 2

despisement *n* open dislike for someone or something considered unworthy of one's concern or respect ⟨an expression of total *despisement* for the "unwashed masses"⟩ — see CONTEMPT

despite *n* **1** open dislike for someone or something considered unworthy of one's concern or respect ⟨pointedly ignored his false friend out of *despite*⟩ — see CONTEMPT

2 the desire to cause pain for the satisfaction of doing harm ⟨sheer *despite* was the sole reason for her hurtful comments⟩ — see MALICE

3 the negative result caused by something that creates difficulty for achieving success ⟨baffled as to why working-class voters would vote in *despite* of their own economic interests⟩ — see DISADVANTAGE 2

despite *prep* without being prevented by ⟨we went to the party *despite* the bad weather outside⟩

synonyms notwithstanding, regardless of, with

phrases in defiance of, in despite of, in spite of

despiteful *adj* having or showing a desire to cause someone pain or suffering for the sheer enjoyment of it ⟨*despiteful* treatment of his poor relations during their visit⟩ — see HATEFUL

despitefully *adv* in a mean or spiteful manner ⟨a theater critic known for his *despitefully* negative reviews⟩ — see NASTILY

despitefulness *n* open dislike for someone or something considered unworthy of one's concern or respect ⟨the undisguised *despitefulness* with which the fashion designer announces his "10 worst" list⟩ — see CONTEMPT

despoil *vb* to search through with the intent of committing robbery ⟨the burglars *despoiled* the art museum in search of treasures they thought they could sell to a fence⟩ — see RANSACK 1

despond *n* **1** a state or spell of low spirits ⟨he sank into a crushing *despond* after his wife left him⟩ — see SADNESS

2 utter loss of hope ⟨loss of his job threw him into a deep *despond*⟩ — see DESPAIR 1

despond *vb* to lose all hope or confidence ⟨we must not *despond* even though we live in trying times⟩ — see DESPAIR

despondence *n* **1** a state or spell of low spirits ⟨her slumping posture betrayed a growing *despondence*⟩ — see SADNESS

2 utter loss of hope ⟨the ability to endure defeat without *despondence* has allowed him to weather the ups and downs of an acting career⟩ — see DESPAIR 1

despondency *n* **1** a state or spell of low spirits ⟨in *despondency* because he couldn't seem to settle into a lasting relationship⟩ — see SADNESS

2 the state of being discouraged ⟨in their *despondency* they seemingly forgot that losing teams can become winning teams in a single season⟩ — see DISCOURAGEMENT

3 utter loss of hope ⟨never once gave into *despondency* and self-pity during her long recovery from her injuries in the car crash⟩ — see DESPAIR 1

despondent *adj* **1** feeling or showing no hope ⟨after four days and still no word that the missing plane had been located, the relatives were *despondent*⟩

synonyms despairing, desperate, forlorn, hopeless

related words blue, brokenhearted, crestfallen, de-

jected, depressed, disconsolate, doleful, down, downcast, downhearted, gloomy, glum, hangdog, heartbroken, heartsick, heartsore, inconsolable, joyless, low, low-spirited, melancholy, miserable, mournful, sad, saddened, sorrowful, sorry, unhappy, woebegone, woeful, wretched; abject, disappointed, discouraged, disheartened, dispirited; grieving, wailing, weeping; bleak, cheerless, comfortless, dark, depressing, desolate, dismal, drear, dreary, funereal; cynical, pessimistic; accepting, resigned
near antonyms ecstatic, elated, enraptured, entranced, euphoric, exhilarated, exuberant, exultant; blithe, blithesome, gay, jocund, jolly, jovial, lightsome, merry, mirthful; encouraged, heartened; animated, jaunty, lively, perky, sprightful, sprightly, vivacious; blissful, buoyant, cheerful, cheery, chipper, delighted, glad, gladdened, gladsome, gleeful, happy, joyful, joyous, jubilant, sunny, upbeat
antonyms hopeful, optimistic
2 feeling unhappiness ⟨feeling *despondent* over the death of another close friend⟩ — see SAD 1

despot *n* a person who uses power or authority in a cruel, unjust, or harmful way ⟨the *despot* exiled political dissidents to remote labor camps, where they were left to rot⟩
synonyms caesar, dictator, führer (*or* fuehrer), oppressor, pharaoh, strongman, tyrannizer, tyrant
related words autarch, autocrat, monocrat; authoritarian, Big Brother, paramount, potentate, totalitarian; caudillo, overlord, warlord; boss, captain, chief, dominator, kingpin, leader, master, overlord, ruler; king, lord, monarch, prince, queen, sovereign (*also* sovran); baron, czar (*also* tsar *or* tzar), magnate, mogul, tycoon; disciplinarian, discipliner, enforcer, martinet, taskmaster
phrases man on horseback

despotic *adj* **1** exercising power or authority without interference by others ⟨a nation ruled by a series of *despotic* rulers, each seemingly worse than the last⟩ — see ABSOLUTE 1
2 fond of ordering people around ⟨the *despotic* coach demands that his players obey him without question⟩ — see BOSSY

despotism *n* a system of government in which the ruler has unlimited power ⟨by the end of the 20th century many countries around the world had rejected *despotism* in favor of democracy⟩
synonyms absolutism, autarchy, authoritarianism, autocracy, Caesarism, czarism (*also* tsarism *or* tzarism), dictatorship, totalism, totalitarianism, tyranny
related words monarchism, monarchy, monocracy; Big Brother, Big Brotherism, Communism, fascism, Nazism; domination, oppression
near antonyms democracy, self-governance, self-government, self-rule; freedom, self-determination; autonomy, sovereignty (*also* sovranty)

destine *vb* to determine the fate of in advance ⟨his extreme height seemed to *destine* him for a career in basketball⟩
synonyms doom, fate, foredoom, foreordain, ordain, predestine, predetermine, preordain
related words predestinate; augur, forecast, foretell, predict, presage, prognosticate, prophesy; preconceive, prejudge; condemn, sentence; bode, forebode (*also* forbode), portend; anticipate, divine, foreknow, foresee

destiny *n* a state or end that seemingly has been decided beforehand ⟨I just knew that it wasn't my *destiny* to end up in a dead-end job⟩ — see FATE 1

destitute *adj* **1** lacking money or material possessions ⟨many families were left *destitute* by the horrible fire⟩ — see POOR 1
2 utterly lacking in something needed, wanted, or expected ⟨a lingering drought and a sky *destitute* of rain clouds⟩ — see DEVOID 1

destituteness *n* the state of lacking sufficient money or material possessions ⟨the appalling *destituteness* of the people in that underdeveloped country⟩ — see POVERTY 1

destitution *n* the state of lacking sufficient money or material possessions ⟨widespread *destitution* in Third World countries⟩ — see POVERTY 1

de–stress *vb* to get rid of nervous tension or anxiety ⟨he watches classic movie comedies as a way to *de-stress*⟩ — see RELAX 1

destroy *vb* **1** to bring to a complete end the physical soundness, existence, or usefulness of ⟨they practically *destroyed* the safe in order to get at the money inside⟩ ⟨their poor scores on the final exam *destroyed* any chance they might have had to pass the course⟩
synonyms annihilate, cream, decimate, demolish, desolate, devastate, do in, extinguish, nuke, pull down, pulverize, raze, rub out, ruin, shatter, smash, tear down, total, vaporize, waste, wrack, wreck
related words beat, best, clobber, conquer, crush, defeat, drub, lick, master, overbear, overcome, overmatch, prevail (over), rout, scotch, skunk, subdue, surmount, thrash, trim, triumph (over), trounce, wallop, whip, win (against); blast, blow up, break, cripple, damage, deface, deteriorate, disfigure, disintegrate, dissolve, dynamite, harm, impair, injure, mangle, mar, mutilate, spoil, vitiate; erode, scour, sweep (away), wash out, wear (away); dilapidate, disassemble, dismantle, gut, take down, unbuild, undo, unmake; blot out, efface, eradicate, expunge, exterminate, extirpate, liquidate, obliterate, remove, root (out), snuff (out), stamp (out), wipe out; despoil, havoc, loot, pillage, plunder, ravage, sack, trample, trash, vandalize; assassinate, butcher, cut down, dispatch, execute, fell, kill, kill off, massacre, mow (down), murder, slaughter, slay, take out, zap
near antonyms doctor, fix, mend, patch, recondition, repair, revamp; create, invent; assemble, fabricate, fashion, forge, form, frame, make, manufacture, mold, produce, shape; bring about, constitute, establish, father, found, institute, organize; conserve, preserve, protect, save; rebuild, reconstruct, remodel, renovate, restore
antonyms build, construct, erect, put up, raise, rear, set up
2 to bring destruction to (something) through violent action ⟨wildfires *destroyed* thousands of acres in forests across the state⟩ — see RAVAGE
3 to deprive of life ⟨regrettably, the veterinarian was forced to *destroy* the injured horse⟩ — see KILL 1

destruction *n* **1** the state or fact of being rendered nonexistent, physically unsound, or useless ⟨the violent storm resulted in the *destruction* of their tree house⟩
synonyms annihilation, decimation, demolishment, demolition, desolation, devastation, extermination, extinction, havoc, loss, mincemeat, obliteration, ruin, ruination, wastage, wreckage
related words depredation, despoilment, despoliation; breakup, collapse, disintegration, dissolution; assassination, execution, killing, massacre, slaughter; dismantlement, effacement, eradication
near antonyms rescue, salvage, salvation, saving; conservation, preservation, protection; reclamation, reconstruction, re-creation, refurbishment, regeneracy, remodeling, renovation, restoration
antonyms building, construction, erection, raising
2 something that is the cause of one's ultimate failure or loss of life ⟨alcohol will be her *destruction* if we don't intervene to help her⟩ — see DOWNFALL 1

destructive *adj* **1** causing or tending to cause destruction ⟨the *destructive* storm blew down trees all over

town, and blew the roof off our neighbor's house⟩
synonyms annihilatory, calamitous, cataclysmal (*or* cataclysmic), devastating, devastative, disastrous, ruinous
related words antibiotic, biocidal; baleful, deadly, deathly, fatal, fell, killer, lethal, mortal, murderous, pestilent, poisonous, virulent, vital; deleterious, detrimental, harmful, pernicious
near antonyms preservative, protective; constructive, creative, formative, productive; harmless, innocent, innocuous, inoffensive; ameliorative, helpful, useful; healthful, healthy, nonfatal, nonlethal, salubrious, wholesome
antonyms nondestructive
2 bringing about ruin or misfortune ⟨technology used for *destructive* ends⟩ — see FATAL 1

desuetude *n* lack of use ⟨despite the long years of *desuetude*, the old manual typewriter seemed to work just fine⟩ — see DISUSE

desultorily *adv* without definite aim, direction, rule, or method ⟨sat watching the movie, *desultorily* eating popcorn⟩ — see HIT OR MISS

desultory *adj* **1** lacking a definite plan, purpose, or pattern ⟨a *desultory* search for something of interest on TV⟩ — see RANDOM
2 passing from one topic to another ⟨a *desultory* discussion about the news of the day⟩ — see DISCURSIVE

detached *adj* **1** having or showing a lack of friendliness or interest in others ⟨a *detached* observer at company parties, taking it all in and saying very little⟩ — see COOL 1
2 not physically attached to another unit ⟨a *detached* garage on the side of the house⟩ — see SEPARATE 2

detachment *n* **1** lack of favoritism toward one side or another ⟨the judge showed commendable *detachment* when deciding the controversial case⟩
synonyms disinterest, disinterestedness, equity, evenhandedness, fair-mindedness, fairness, impartiality, justice, neutralism, neutrality, nonpartisanship, objectiveness, objectivity
related words apathy, indifference, unconcern; broad-mindedness, open-mindedness, tolerance; fence-sitting, straddling
near antonyms chauvinism, nepotism; subjectiveness, subjectivity; bent, inclination, leaning, penchant, predilection, predisposition, proclivity, propensity, tendency; preconception, prejudgment
antonyms bias, favor, favoritism, nonobjectivity, one-sidedness, partiality, partisanship, prejudice
2 a small military unit with a special task or function ⟨the general sent a *detachment* ahead to scout the enemy's position⟩
synonyms detail
related words commando, firing squad, outpost, paratroops, patrol, picket, rear guard, sentry, watch; battalion, command, company, corps, division, platoon, regiment, squad, squadron, troop, wing
3 the absence of emotional involvement ⟨his *detachment* allowed him a clearer perspective on the child custody case⟩ — see COOL 1

detail *n* **1** a separate part in a list, account, or series ⟨every *detail* was accounted for⟩ — see ITEM 1
2 a single piece of information ⟨didn't leave out a single *detail* in his police report on the burglary⟩ — see FACT 3
3 a small military unit with a special task or function ⟨the officer sent out a *detail* to patrol the perimeter of the compound⟩ — see DETACHMENT 2
4 a specific task with which a person or group is charged ⟨the soldier was placed on guard *detail* at the border crossing⟩ — see MISSION

detail *vb* **1** to assign to a place or position ⟨once again he was *detailed* to guard duty⟩ — see ²POST
2 to pick (someone) by one's authority for a specific position or duty ⟨the new assistant was *detailed* to accompany the boss on the business trip⟩ — see APPOINT 2
3 to specify one after another ⟨*detailed* all of the reasons that the plan was a bad idea⟩ — see ENUMERATE 1

detailed *adj* **1** including many small descriptive features ⟨a *detailed* report on all the activities that their Scout troop had been involved in over the past year⟩
synonyms blow-by-blow, circumstantial, elaborate, full, minute, particular, particularized, thorough
related words enumerated, inventoried, itemized, listed, numerated; delineated, specific, specified; abundant, copious; comprehensive, encyclopedic, exhausting, exhaustive, inclusionary, inclusive, in-depth, omnibus, panoramic, thoroughgoing; accurate, correct, exact, precise; complete, entire, replete; distinct, explicit, sharp; mapped (out); descriptive, graphic (*also* graphical), picturesque, vivid
near antonyms brief, compact, concise, crisp, pithy, short, succinct, terse; abbreviated, abridged, curtailed, cut, pruned, shortened, trimmed; ambiguous, indeterminate, nebulous, nondescript, sketchy, vague; bird's-eye, broad, general, nonspecific, overall, unspecified
antonyms compendious, summary
2 made or done with great care or with much detail ⟨a *detailed* miniature of the royal palace⟩ — see ELABORATE 1

detailedly *adv* with attention to all aspects or details ⟨went over the proposal somewhat more *detailedly* than he had the first time⟩ — see THOROUGHLY 1

detainer *n* **1** the state of being held in lawful custody ⟨keep him in *detainer* for at least 72 hours⟩ — see DETENTION 1
2 the unlawful taking or withholding of something from the rightful owner under a guise of authority ⟨she filed an action for unlawful *detainer* of land after nonpayment of rent⟩ — see APPROPRIATION 2

detainment *n* **1** an instance or period of being prevented from going about one's business ⟨the returning vacationers' *detainment* at the border only lasted a few minutes⟩ — see DELAY
2 the state of being held in lawful custody ⟨she'll be kept in *detainment* until the trial if she can't post bail⟩ — see DETENTION 1

detect *vb* to come upon after searching, study, or effort ⟨I can *detect* just a hint of lemon in the soup⟩ — see FIND 1

detectable *adj* able to be perceived by a sense or by the mind ⟨there was a barely *detectable* hum coming from the refrigerator⟩ — see PERCEPTIBLE

detection *n* the act or process of sighting or learning the existence of something for the first time ⟨my *detection* of the scent of baked apple pie led me to the kitchen⟩ — see DISCOVERY 1

detective *n* a person not on the police force who investigates criminal or illicit activity or searches for missing persons ⟨the code used by the serial killer in his letters to the police was actually cracked by an amateur *detective*⟩
synonyms dick, gumshoe, hawkshaw, investigator, operative, private detective, private eye, private investigator, shamus [*slang*], sherlock, sleuth, sleuthhound
related words shadow, tail, tracer, tracker; fed, Federal, G-man, narc (*or* nark) [*slang*], plainclothesman

detector *n* a device that detects some physical quantity and responds usually with a transmitted signal ⟨a motion *detector* to thwart burglaries⟩ — see SENSOR

detention *n* **1** the state of being held in lawful custody ⟨he's been in *detention* since the arrest⟩
synonyms detainer, detainment, hold, immurement, imprisonment, incarceration
related words captivity, confinement, internment; ap-

prehension, arrest, arrestment, bust [*slang*], collar, pinch; capture, entrapment, seizure; enchainment, restraint
near antonyms emancipation, freedom, liberation
antonyms discharge, release
2 an instance or period of being prevented from going about one's business ⟨an inane joke about a bomb netted the airline passenger no laughs, only a two-hour *detention* that caused him to miss his flight⟩ — see DELAY

deter *vb* to steer (a person) from an activity or course of action ⟨we tried to *deter* him from his crazy scheme, but to no avail⟩ — see DISCOURAGE 2

deterge *vb* to remove the dirt from ⟨*deterge* the surface using an industrial-strength commercial soap⟩ — see CLEAN 1

detergent *n* a substance used for cleaning ⟨add the *detergent* to the washing machine before putting in the clothes⟩ — see CLEANER

deteriorate *vb* **1** to become worse or of less value ⟨the garden slowly *deteriorated* after months of neglect⟩
synonyms atrophy, crumble, decay, decline, degenerate, descend, devolve, ebb, regress, retrograde, rot, sink, worsen
related words abate, de-escalate, diminish, downsize, dwindle, recede, wane; break down, corrupt, decompose, degrade, dilapidate, disintegrate, molder, putrefy; sour, spoil; lessen, lower, reduce; debilitate, undermine; droop, fail, fall, flag, lag, languish, run down, sag, slip, waste (away), weaken, wilt
phrases go to pot, go to seed (*or* run to seed)
near antonyms better, upgrade; enhance, enrich, fortify, heighten, intensify, strengthen; advance, develop, march, proceed, progress
antonyms ameliorate, improve, meliorate
2 to lower in character, dignity, or quality ⟨childish name-calling that merely *deteriorates* what should be a serious discussion on an important issue⟩ — see DEBASE 1

deterioration *n* **1** a gradual sinking and wasting away of mind or body ⟨muscle *deterioration* resulting from prolonged disuse⟩ — see DECLINE 1
2 a change to a lower state or level ⟨a *deterioration* in the quality of food at that once-thriving restaurant⟩ — see DECLINE 2

determinate *adj* **1** having been established and usually not subject to change ⟨a *determinate* order of succession to the throne⟩ — see FIXED 1
2 having distinct or certain limits ⟨contestants have a *determinate* length of time to answer the questions⟩ — see LIMITED 1

determination *n* **1** firm or unwavering adherence to one's purpose ⟨the *determination* with which the pioneers settled the land despite many hardships and setbacks⟩
synonyms decidedness, decision, decisiveness, determinedness, firmness, granite, purposefulness, resoluteness, resolution, resolve, stick-to-itiveness
related words doggedness, obduracy, obdurateness, obstinacy, obstinateness, perseverance, persistence, persistency, stubbornness, tenaciousness, tenacity; certainty, certitude, confidence, sureness; alacrity, eagerness, gameness, readiness; backbone, fortitude, grit, iron, pluck, sand
near antonyms doubt, incertitude, indetermination, uncertainty; aversion, disinclination, indisposition, reluctance, unwillingness
antonyms hesitation, indecision, indecisiveness, irresoluteness, irresolution, vacillation
2 a position arrived at after consideration ⟨a *determination* by the judge regarding an appropriate sentence⟩ — see DECISION 1
3 an opinion arrived at through a process of reasoning ⟨his *determination* of the truth of the matter⟩ — see CONCLUSION 1

determine *vb* **1** to give an opinion about (something at issue or in dispute) ⟨a three-member panel will *determine* the case⟩ — see JUDGE 1
2 to come to a judgment about after discussion or consideration ⟨trying to *determine* which direction we were facing⟩ — see DECIDE 1
3 to come upon after searching, study, or effort ⟨we failed to *determine* the answer to the riddle⟩ — see FIND 1
4 to come to an end ⟨your participation in the savings plan *determines* with the termination of your employment here⟩ — see CEASE 1
5 to make final, definite, or beyond dispute ⟨your choice of college could *determine* the rest of your life⟩ — see CLINCH

determined *adj* **1** fully committed to achieving a goal ⟨his *determined* opponent would not be bluffed or shaken⟩
synonyms bent (on *or* upon), bound, decisive, do-or-die, firm, hell-bent (on *or* upon), intent, out, purposeful, resolute, resolved, set, single-minded
related words bitter, vehement; certain, cocksure, confident, positive, sure; earnest, serious; steady, unfaltering, unhesitating, unswerving, unwavering; adamant, adamantine, dogged, hard, hardened, hardheaded, headstrong, immovable, implacable, inflexible, mulish, obdurate, persistent, pertinacious, perverse, pigheaded, rigid, self-willed, stubborn, tenacious, unbending, uncompromising, unrelenting, unyielding, willful (*or* wilful)
phrases on one's mettle
near antonyms distrustful, doubtful, dubious, mistrustful, skeptical, suspicious, uncertain, unconvinced, undecided, unsettled, unsure; disinclined, indisposed, loath (*also* loth *or* loathe), reluctant
antonyms faltering, hesitant, indecisive, irresolute, undetermined, unresolved, vacillating, wavering, weak-kneed
2 showing no signs of slackening or yielding in one's purpose ⟨a *determined* effort to finish first in the race⟩ — see UNYIELDING 1

determinedly *adv* with great effort or determination ⟨*determinedly* unhip, the restaurant serves old-fashioned comfort food⟩ — see HARD 1

determinedness *n* firm or unwavering adherence to one's purpose ⟨she set about her goal of landing a rich husband with such *determinedness* that one could not observe the proceedings with anything but the greatest admiration⟩ — see DETERMINATION 1

deterrent *n* something that makes movement or progress difficult ⟨the homeowner put up a fence around his garden as a *deterrent* for animals⟩ — see ENCUMBRANCE

detest *vb* to dislike strongly ⟨I *detest* pepperoni, and wouldn't eat it if you paid me!⟩ — see HATE

detestable *adj* not following or in accordance with standards of honor and decency ⟨the *detestable* actions of a nasty little man⟩ — see IGNOBLE 2

detestation *n* **1** a very strong dislike ⟨a congenital *detestation* of injustice, which drove her to become an activist for civil rights⟩ — see HATE 1
2 something or someone that is hated ⟨the family's pickiest eater is quite vehement in expressing his feelings about boiled cabbage, a particular *detestation* of his⟩ — see HATE 2

dethrone *vb* to remove from a position of prominence or power (as a throne) ⟨the nation's last monarch was *dethroned* in a popular uprising many years ago⟩ — see DEPOSE 1

detonate *vb* to break open or into pieces usually because of internal pressure ⟨the bomb *detonated* with a thunder that could be heard for blocks in all directions⟩ — see EXPLODE 1

detonation *n* the act or an instance of exploding ⟨there was a series of *detonations* around the base of the condemned building, causing it to come crashing down in a matter of minutes⟩ — see EXPLOSION 1

detour *n* a turning away from a course or standard ⟨we'll regard this relapse as just a brief *detour* on your road to recovery from substance abuse⟩ — see DIVERGENCE 2

detour *vb* **1** to avoid by going around ⟨we had to *detour* the construction zone in order to get to the stadium⟩
synonyms bypass, circumnavigate, circumvent, skirt
related words leapfrog; avoid, dodge, duck, elude, escape, eschew, evade, flee, shake, shun
near antonyms confront, face, meet; accept, court, embrace, pursue, seek, welcome
2 to change one's course or direction ⟨we had to *detour* for a few miles around the section of highway under construction⟩ — see TURN 3

detract *vb* to draw the attention or mind to something else ⟨numerous typos in the text *detract* the reader's attention from the novel's intricate plot⟩ — see DISTRACT 1

detraction *n* the act of making a person or a thing seem little or unimportant ⟨her inevitable *detraction* of every new idea is annoying to the other club members⟩ — see DEPRECIATION

detractive *adj* intended to make a person or thing seem of little importance or value ⟨used the *detractive* epithet "McJob" to describe what his feckless son-in-law did for work⟩ — see DEROGATORY

detriment *n* **1** something that causes loss or pain ⟨opponents of casino gambling claim that it is a *detriment* to society at large⟩ — see INJURY 1
2 the negative result caused by something that creates difficulty for achieving success ⟨the requirement that runners wear shoes for the race worked to his *detriment* since he was used to running barefoot⟩ — see DISADVANTAGE 2

detrimental *adj* causing or capable of causing harm ⟨there were serious concerns that the factory's waste was *detrimental* to the local environment⟩ — see HARMFUL

detritus *n* the portion or bits of something left over or behind after it has been destroyed ⟨the expanse of tree stumps represented the *detritus* of a vast forest that had been mercilessly clear-cut⟩ — see REMAINS 1

deuced *adj* deserving of one's condemnation or displeasure ⟨this *deuced* washing machine always gives me trouble⟩ — see DAMNABLE

devaluate *vb* to diminish the price or value of ⟨plans to *devaluate* the peso⟩ — see DEPRECIATE 1

devalue *vb* to diminish the price or value of ⟨normally, significant damage would *devalue* an antique⟩ — see DEPRECIATE 1

devastate *vb* **1** to bring destruction to (something) through violent action ⟨the city was *devastated*, first by the earthquake and then by fires⟩ — see RAVAGE
2 to bring to a complete end the physical soundness, existence, or usefulness of ⟨the explosion *devastated* an entire city block⟩ — see DESTROY 1
3 to subject to incapacitating emotional or mental stress ⟨we were *devastated* by the awful news of his death⟩ — see OVERWHELM 1

devastating *adj* causing or tending to cause destruction ⟨a *devastating* blow to our morale⟩ — see DESTRUCTIVE 1

devastation *n* the state or fact of being rendered nonexistent, physically unsound, or useless ⟨the sheer *devastation* of the housing development by the forest fire⟩ — see DESTRUCTION 1

devastative *adj* causing or tending to cause destruction ⟨that kind of *devastative* tornado can tear the roof off of a house in a matter of seconds⟩ — see DESTRUCTIVE 1

develop *vb* **1** to gradually become clearer or more detailed ⟨as the story of the bombing *developed*, the scope of the tragedy became more apparent⟩
synonyms elaborate, evolve, unfold
related words advance, fare, forge, get along, get on, march, proceed, progress; blossom, grow, mature, ripen; materialize; emerge, play out
2 to come to have gradually ⟨the youngster *developed* a taste for green olives⟩
synonyms acquire, cultivate, form
related words absorb, adopt, embrace, take in, take on; gain, get, obtain; achieve, attain, reach; foster, nourish, nurture, promote
near antonyms abandon, desert, forsake; cast, discard, ditch, dump, fling (off *or* away), jettison, junk, reject, scrap, shed, shuck (off), slough (*also* sluff), throw away, throw out, unload
antonyms lose
3 to become mature ⟨the wine is *developing* nicely in the new oak barrels⟩ — see MATURE
4 to express more fully and in greater detail ⟨marketing people *developed* the initial idea into a complete promotional campaign⟩ — see EXPAND 1
5 to produce or bring about especially by long or repeated effort ⟨outside consultants helped the company *develop* an effective marketing strategy⟩ — see HAMMER OUT

developed *adj* being far along in development ⟨a highly *developed* society with a rigid class system⟩ — see ADVANCED 1

developer *n* one who creates or introduces something new ⟨the *developer* of software that is used the world over⟩ — see INVENTOR

development *n* **1** the act or process of going from the simple or basic to the complex or advanced ⟨the *development* of an idea into a marketable product⟩
synonyms elaboration, evolution, expansion, growth, progress, progression
related words advancement, betterment, improvement, perfection, refinement; incubation, maturation, maturing, ripening; blossoming, flourishing, flowering; addition, augmentation, enhancement, supplementation; emergence, evolvement, metamorphosis
near antonyms backslide, lapse, relapse; decadence, decay, decaying, declension, declination, decline, degeneracy, degeneration, degradation, descent, deterioration, devaluation, downfall, downgrade, ebbing, falling, weakening
antonyms regress, regression, retrogression, reversion
2 a condition or occurrence traceable to a cause ⟨a *development* that the writers of the law never anticipated or intended⟩ — see EFFECT 1
3 the process of becoming mature ⟨a tulip's *development* from a bulb into a flower⟩ — see MATURATION

developmental *adj* made or done as an experiment ⟨*developmental* weaponry that is classified as top secret by the Pentagon⟩ — see EXPERIMENTAL 1

deviant *adj* departing from some accepted standard of what is normal ⟨some studies show that many violent criminals begin exhibiting *deviant* behavior in early childhood⟩
synonyms aberrant, aberrational, abnormal, anomalous, atypical, deviate, devious, irregular, unnatural, untypical
related words unrepresentative; extraordinary, preternatural; rare, uncommon, uncustomary, unusual, unwonted; bizarre, curious, far-out, funny, kinky, odd,

outlandish, out-of-the-way, outré, peculiar, quaint, queer, queerish, quirky, remarkable, screwy, strange, wacky (*also* whacky), way-out, weird, wild; eccentric, freakish, idiosyncratic, nonconformist, unconventional, unorthodox; extraordinary, preternatural; rare, uncommon, uncustomary, unusual, unwonted; odd, peculiar, strange

near antonyms common, commonplace, everyday, familiar, ordinary, routine, run-of-the-mill, run-of-the-mine (*or* run-of-mine), unexceptional, unremarkable, workaday; customary, usual, wonted; archetypal (*also* archetypical), average, characteristic, representative

antonyms natural, normal, regular, standard, typical

deviant *n* a person who does not conform to generally accepted standards or customs ⟨branded as social *deviants* by a society that did not value self-expression⟩ — see NONCONFORMIST 1

deviate *adj* departing from some accepted standard of what is normal ⟨the mother's *deviate* response to her child's death aroused suspicions⟩ — see DEVIANT

deviate *n* a person who has sunk below the normal moral standard ⟨a sleazy bar that seemed to be an informal clubhouse for *deviates*⟩ — see DEGENERATE

deviate *vb* to change one's course or direction ⟨sailors forced to *deviate* from their course in order to avoid the storm⟩ — see TURN 3

deviation *n* a turning away from a course or standard ⟨a memoir that was discovered to contain numerous *deviations* from fact⟩ — see DIVERGENCE 2

device *n* **1** a clever often underhanded means to achieve an end ⟨used every *device* and stratagem he knew to prevent his son's marriage⟩ — see TRICK 1

2 an article intended for use in work ⟨the salesclerk tried to sell me a new *device* for grooming cats⟩ — see IMPLEMENT

3 devices *pl* a habitual attraction to some activity or thing ⟨left to her own *devices* she'd eat at a fast-food restaurant every night of the week⟩ — see INCLINATION 1

devil *n* **1** *cap* the supreme personification of evil often represented as the ruler of hell ⟨the *Devil* is traditionally seen as a being who relentlessly tempts people to commit evil⟩

synonyms archfiend, Beelzebub, fiend, Lucifer, Old Nick, Satan, serpent

related words deuce, dickens; Mephistopheles

2 an evil spirit ⟨acted as if possessed by some *devil*⟩ — see DEMON 1

3 a member of the human race ⟨that poor *devil* never did achieve his dream⟩ — see HUMAN

4 an appealingly mischievous person ⟨why, you little *devil*!⟩ — see SCAMP 1

5 a mean, evil, or unprincipled person ⟨he's a *devil* to everyone he does business with⟩ — see VILLAIN

6 a person who seeks out very dangerous or foolhardy adventures with no apparent fear ⟨originally snowboarders were regarded as *devils* on the slopes and a menace to skiers⟩ — see DAREDEVIL

devilfish *n* any of several extremely large rays ⟨they saw a *devilfish* when they went scuba diving in the Caribbean, but it swam away quickly⟩

synonyms manta, manta ray, sea devil

related words ray, skate

devilish *adj* **1** going beyond a normal or acceptable limit in degree or amount ⟨that's a *devilish* amount of bad luck for any person to have to endure⟩ — see EXCESSIVE

2 of, relating to, or worthy of an evil spirit ⟨a *devilish* plan to sabotage the other party's political convention⟩ — see FIENDISH 1

3 tending to or exhibiting reckless playfulness ⟨a *devilish* grin that told us he was up to something⟩ — see MISCHIEVOUS 1

devilishly *adv* beyond a normal or acceptable limit ⟨a *devilishly* clever scheme to make money⟩ — see TOO 1

devilishness *n* playful, reckless behavior that is not intended to cause serious harm ⟨the children always concoct some sort of *devilishness* on Halloween⟩ — see MISCHIEF 1

devil–may–care *adj* **1** having a relaxed, casual manner ⟨a *devil-may-care* golfer who knows that it's only a game⟩ — see EASYGOING 1

2 having or showing a lack of concern for the consequences of one's actions ⟨the *devil-may-care* speed with which he drives his sports car is going to cause a lot of grief someday⟩ — see RECKLESS 1

3 having or showing freedom from worries or troubles ⟨the *devil-may-care* attitude that some people have about needlessly contributing to global warming⟩ — see CAREFREE

devilment *n* playful, reckless behavior that is not intended to cause serious harm ⟨his *devilment* at school remains the stuff of local legend⟩ — see MISCHIEF 1

devilry *or* **deviltry** *n* **1** playful, reckless behavior that is not intended to cause serious harm ⟨children always getting into some *devilry*⟩ — see MISCHIEF 1

2 the power to control natural forces through supernatural means ⟨superstitious villagers who were quick to attribute an unexpected occurrence to *devilry*⟩ — see MAGIC 1

devious *adj* **1** clever at attaining one's ends by indirect and often deceptive means ⟨we always left it to our most *devious* friends to find out the latest information⟩ — see ARTFUL 1

2 marked by a long series of irregular curves ⟨a *devious* trail through the swampland⟩ — see CROOKED 1

3 departing from some accepted standard of what is normal ⟨her behavior is *devious* because of a developmental disorder⟩ — see DEVIANT

deviousness *n* skill in achieving one's ends through indirect, subtle, or underhanded means ⟨his *deviousness* was almost as awesome as his lack of scruples⟩ — see CUNNING 1

devise *vb* to create or think of by clever use of the imagination ⟨she quickly *devised* a new scheme when the first one failed⟩ — see INVENT

deviser *n* one who creates or introduces something new ⟨Melvil Dewey was the *deviser* of a new system for organizing books⟩ — see INVENTOR

devitalize *vb* **1** to deprive of emotional or intellectual vitality ⟨overuse has *devitalized* many a once-striking figure of speech⟩ — see DEHYDRATE 1

2 to diminish the physical strength of ⟨she was *devitalized* by the infection⟩ — see WEAKEN 1

devoid *adj* **1** utterly lacking in something needed, wanted, or expected ⟨the so-called comedy is totally *devoid* of intelligence, originality, and even laughs⟩

synonyms bankrupt, bare, barren, bereft, destitute, void

related words blank, empty, innocent, stark, vacant, wanting; deficient, fragmental, fragmentary, incomplete, insufficient, partial, short; absent, missing

near antonyms furnished, provided, supplied; brimming, bulging, bursting, chock-full (*or* chockful), crammed, crowded, fat, jammed, jam-packed, loaded, packed, saturated, stuffed; abounding, swarming, teeming, thick, thronging

antonyms filled, flush, fraught, full, replete, rife

2 lacking contents that could or should be present ⟨the picnic jug was completely *devoid* of juice after only a few minutes⟩ — see EMPTY 1

devoir *n* something one must do because of prior agreement ⟨patient confidentiality has long been an integral part of a physician's professional *devoir*⟩ — see OBLIGATION 1

devolution *n* a change to a lower state or level ⟨the gradual *devolution* of the neighborhood from a thriving community of close-knit families to a drug-ridden slum⟩ — see DECLINE 2

devolve *vb* to become worse or of less value ⟨the once-lovely neighborhood has *devolved* into a squalid slum⟩ — see DETERIORATE 1

devote *vb* **1** to keep or intend for a special purpose ⟨I conscientiously *devote* several hours every weekend to playing with my dog⟩
synonyms allocate, consecrate, dedicate, earmark, give up (to), reserve, save, set by
related words bless, hallow, sanctify; commit, confide, consign, entrust (*also* intrust); apply, bestow, employ, use
phrases set apart, set aside
near antonyms ignore, neglect; misapply, misuse
2 to occupy (oneself) diligently or with close attention ⟨planning a diplomatic career, she's been intensely *devoting* herself to the study of foreign languages in college⟩ — see APPLY

devoted *adj* **1** feeling or showing love ⟨a *devoted* couple who enjoy sharing their lives with one another⟩ — see LOVING 1
2 firm in one's allegiance to someone or something ⟨remembered her most *devoted* servants in her will⟩ — see FAITHFUL 1

devotedness *n* **1** a feeling of strong or constant regard for and dedication to someone ⟨the heartwarming *devotedness* that the newlywed couple felt for each other⟩ — see LOVE 1
2 adherence to something to which one is bound by a pledge or duty ⟨the kind of *devotedness* that only a dog can show for its master⟩ — see FIDELITY

devotee *n* a person with a strong and habitual liking for something ⟨a *devotee* of stamp collecting⟩ — see FAN

devotion *n* **1** a feeling of strong or constant regard for and dedication to someone ⟨Albert Schweitzer was world-renowned for his *devotion* to his fellow man⟩ — see LOVE 1
2 adherence to something to which one is bound by a pledge or duty ⟨the knight's fierce *devotion* to his lord⟩ — see FIDELITY
3 belief and trust in and loyalty to God ⟨a people of deep spirituality and indomitable *devotion*⟩ — see FAITH 1

devotional *adj* of, relating to, or used in the practice or worship services of a religion ⟨a religious bookstore with an extensive stock of *devotional* literature⟩ — see RELIGIOUS 1

devour *vb* **1** to destroy all trace of ⟨a series of devastating storms *devoured* the beach on the south side of the island⟩ — see CONSUME 1
2 to make complete use of ⟨a catastrophic medical event that *devoured* their savings⟩ — see DEPLETE 1
3 to swallow or eat greedily ⟨the starving villagers simply *devoured* the relief food⟩ — see GOBBLE

devout *adj* **1** firm in one's allegiance to someone or something ⟨*devout* Red Sox fans never lost faith during the long World Series drought⟩ — see FAITHFUL 1
2 showing a devotion to God and to a life of virtue ⟨*devout* monks living a life of prayer and solitude⟩ — see HOLY 1

devoutness *n* the quality or state of being spiritually pure or virtuous ⟨a figure of such *devoutness* that a campaign for her canonization was begun shortly after her death⟩ — see HOLINESS

dewy *adj* lacking in worldly wisdom or informed judgment ⟨another version of the story of the *dewy* small-town girl hoping to make it big on Broadway⟩ — see NAIVE 1

dewy–eyed *adj* **1** lacking in worldly wisdom or informed judgment ⟨*dewy-eyed* newlyweds who had yet to experience the trials and tribulations of married life⟩ — see NAIVE 1
2 readily taken advantage of ⟨*dewy-eyed* young women who thought that they were going to a legitimate modeling agency⟩ — see EASY 2

dexterity *n* **1** mental skill or quickness ⟨the ambassador showed great *dexterity* in his handling of the touchy situation⟩
synonyms adroitness, cleverness, finesse, sleight
related words ability, aptitude, capability, capacity, faculty, knack, prowess, talent; competence, competency, efficiency, expertise, know-how, proficiency; ingeniousness, ingenuity, resourcefulness; savvy, sharpness, shrewdness; artfulness, artifice, caginess (*also* cageyness), canniness, craft, craftiness, cunning, cunningness, deviousness, foxiness, guile, slickness, slyness, sneakiness, subtleness, wiliness
near antonyms inadequacy, incompetence, incompetency, ineptitude, ineptness; brainlessness, denseness, density, doltishness, dopiness, dullness (*also* dulness), dumbness, fatuity, foolishness, mindlessness, obtuseness, senselessness, simpleness, slowness, stupidity, stupidness, witlessness
2 ease and grace in physical activity ⟨the juggler needed lots of *dexterity* in order to keep all five balls in the air at the same time⟩
synonyms agility, deftness, nimbleness, sleight, spryness
related words coordination; flexibility, gracefulness, limberness, litheness, loose-jointedness, suppleness; handiness, sure-handedness; sure-footedness; adeptness, adroitness, finesse, prowess
near antonyms disability, inability, incapability, incapacity; debilitation, disablement, impairment, incapacitation; unhandiness
antonyms awkwardness, clumsiness, gaucheness, gawkiness, gawkishness, gracelessness, ham-handedness, heavy-handedness, klutziness, ungainliness

dexterous *also* **dextrous** *adj* **1** skillful with the hands ⟨the *dexterous* watchmaker was able to repair the antique watch's delicate gears and parts⟩
synonyms clever, cunning, deft, handy
related words agile, flexible, graceful, limber, lissome (*also* lissom), lithe, lithesome, nimble, spry; coordinated; able, adept, capable, competent, expert, habile, masterful, masterly, proficient, qualified, skilled, skillful, sure-handed; double-jointed, loose-jointed
near antonyms awkward, bungling, clumsy, fumbling, gauche, gawky, graceless, klutzy, rough-hewn, stiff, stilted, uncomfortable, uneasy, ungainly, ungraceful, wooden; uncoordinated; incapable, incompetent, inept, inexpert, maladroit
antonyms butterfingered, ham-fisted, ham-handed, handless, heavy-handed, unhandy
2 accomplished with trained ability ⟨*dexterous* handling of a potentially embarrassing situation⟩ — see SKILLFUL

diablerie *n* **1** playful, reckless behavior that is not intended to cause serious harm ⟨the boy, who was once filled with *diablerie*, grew up to be a staid and rather dull man⟩ — see MISCHIEF 1
2 the power to control natural forces through supernatural means ⟨since the common folk had an unshakable belief in a personal devil, a charge of *diablerie* was taken seriously⟩ — see MAGIC 1

diabolical *or* **diabolic** *adj* of, relating to, or worthy of an evil spirit ⟨the police quickly mobilized to track down the *diabolical* serial killer⟩ — see FIENDISH 1

diabolicalness *n* the state or quality of being utterly evil ⟨the *diabolicalness* of the serial killer's acts, which included cannibalism, defy belief⟩ — see ENORMITY 1

diadem *n* a decorative band or wreath worn about the head as a symbol of victory or honor ⟨Miss America's *diadem* was auctioned off for charity⟩ — see CROWN 1

diagnosis *n* a position arrived at after consideration ⟨my *diagnosis* of the situation is that immediate action needs to be taken⟩ — see DECISION 1

diagnostic *also* **diagnostical** *adj* serving to identify as belonging to an individual or group ⟨studies that show that cultural diversity is a *diagnostic* feature of a thriving city⟩ — see CHARACTERISTIC 1

diagnostic *n* something that sets apart an individual from others of the same kind ⟨the thesis that moral decline is the infallible *diagnostic* of a decadent society⟩ — see CHARACTERISTIC

diagonal *adj* running in a slanting direction ⟨the *diagonal* design ran up the wall all the way from the lower left to the upper right-hand corner⟩
synonyms cant, canted, graded, inclined, leaning, listing, oblique, pitched, raked, slant, slanted, slantwise, sloped, sloping, tilted, tilting
near antonyms horizontal, level; plumb, up-and-down, vertical; parallel, perpendicular

diagonal *n* the degree to which something rises up from a position level with the horizon ⟨the ramp was set at a low *diagonal* to make it easier for physically challenged patrons⟩ — see SLANT

diagonally *adv* in a line or direction running from corner to corner ⟨placed two strips of pimiento *diagonally* on each deviled egg⟩ — see CROSSWISE

diagram *n* something that visually explains or decorates a text ⟨the explanation of the process of photosynthesis is accompanied by a very useful *diagram*⟩ — see ILLUSTRATION 1

dial *vb* to make a telephone call to ⟨*dialed* 911 and asked for the police⟩ — see CALL 2

dialect *n* the special terms or expressions of a particular group or field ⟨the promotional team for the new computer used a *dialect* full of acronyms that the press found difficult to follow⟩ — see TERMINOLOGY

dialogue *also* **dialog** *n* **1** an exchange of views for the purpose of exploring a subject or deciding an issue ⟨calling for an international *dialogue* on human rights⟩ — see DISCUSSION 1
2 talking or a talk between two or more people ⟨coworkers having a short *dialogue* about politics at the watercooler before heading back to work⟩ — see CONVERSATION

diametric *or* **diametrical** *adj* being as different as possible ⟨that husband and wife have seemingly *diametric* personalities, but somehow their marriage works⟩ — see OPPOSITE

diapason *n* the distance or extent between possible extremes ⟨the survey ultimately recorded the full *diapason* of seemingly possible replies regarding sexual practices⟩ — see RANGE 3

diaphanous *adj* very thin and easy to see through ⟨the bride wore a *diaphanous* veil⟩ — see SHEER 1

diarrhea *n* abnormally frequent intestinal evacuations with more or less fluid stools ⟨I was taken with severe *diarrhea* while attending the conference⟩
synonyms Delhi belly, flux, Montezuma's revenge, runs, trots, turista
related words dysentery, shigellosis; scour(s)

diary *n* a record of personal experiences, reflections, or ideas kept regularly for private use ⟨has diligently kept a *diary* since she was 15⟩ — see JOURNAL 2

diatribe *n* a long angry speech or scolding ⟨he was forced to sit through a long *diatribe* after he came home late once too often⟩ — see TIRADE

dibs *n pl* an entitlement to something ⟨I get *dibs* on the front seat!⟩ — see CLAIM 1

dice *n* a small cube marked on each side with one to six spots and usually played in pairs in various games ⟨she anxiously rolled the *dice*, hoping to win the jackpot⟩ — see DIE

dice *vb* to cut into small pieces ⟨quickly *diced* some peppers and onions and threw them into the stew⟩ — see CHOP

dichotomy *n* someone or something with qualities or features that seem to conflict with one another ⟨her outfit is a sartorial *dichotomy*: an elegant gown and ratty old tennis shoes⟩ — see CONTRADICTION 1

dick *n* a person not on the police force who investigates criminal or illicit activity or searches for missing persons ⟨a novel about a hard-boiled *dick* and the softhearted madam who loves him⟩ — see DETECTIVE

dicker *n* a giving or taking of one thing of value in return for another ⟨was hoping to make a *dicker* with another collector of records from the 1950s⟩ — see EXCHANGE 1

dicker *vb* to talk over or dispute the terms of a purchase ⟨they *dickered* over the price of the car for a few minutes⟩ — see BARGAIN 1

dictate *n* a statement of what to do that must be obeyed by those concerned ⟨a starchily worded *dictate* from on high concerning the company's dress code⟩ — see COMMAND 1

dictate *vb* to request the doing of by virtue of one's authority ⟨*dictated* that the terms of surrender be negotiated by his senior staff⟩ — see COMMAND 2

dictator *n* a person who uses power or authority in a cruel, unjust, or harmful way ⟨the *dictator* had a fierce stranglehold on the country, keeping its people in poverty and ignorance⟩ — see DESPOT

dictatorial *adj* **1** exercising power or authority without interference by others ⟨a *dictatorial* leader with total control over people's lives⟩ — see ABSOLUTE 1
2 fond of ordering people around ⟨no surprise that the *dictatorial* manager is highly unpopular among employees⟩ — see BOSSY
3 having or showing a tendency to force one's will on others without any regard to fairness or necessity ⟨even the teachers chafed under the *dictatorial* rule of the principal⟩ — see ARBITRARY 1

dictatorship *n* a system of government in which the ruler has unlimited power ⟨a revolution that only ended up replacing one *dictatorship* with another⟩ — see DESPOTISM

diction *n* **1** the clear and accurate pronunciation of words especially in public speaking ⟨Shakespearean actors with very good *diction*⟩
synonyms articulation, enunciation
related words elocution, expression, utterance; speech, wording
2 the way in which something is put into words ⟨the spare *diction* that is the hallmark of the poetry of Robert Frost⟩ — see WORDING 1

dictionary *n* a reference book giving information about the meanings, pronunciations, uses, and origins of words listed in alphabetical order ⟨try to develop the habit of going to the *dictionary* whenever you encounter an unfamiliar word⟩
synonyms lexicon, wordbook
related words gloss, glossary, nomenclator, thesaurus, vocabulary

didactic *adj* marked by or given to preaching moral values ⟨the poet's works became increasingly *didactic* after his religious conversion⟩ — see SERMONIC

diddle *vb* **1** to move or act slowly ⟨even though the hurricane was fast approaching, federal and local polticians wasted precious time *diddling*⟩ — see DELAY 1

2 to rob by the use of trickery or threats ⟨an unscrupulous Broadway producer *diddles* little old ladies by persuading them to invest in a surefire flop⟩ — see FLEECE

diddle (with) *vb* to handle thoughtlessly, ignorantly, or mischievously ⟨if you use my home theater system, don't *diddle with* the settings—everything has been professionally calibrated⟩ — see TAMPER (WITH)

diddly *n, slang* the smallest amount or part imaginable ⟨that jerk doesn't know *diddly* about half the things he spouts off about⟩ — see JOT

diddly–squat *n, slang* the smallest amount or part imaginable ⟨your apology is long overdue and doesn't mean *diddly-squat* to me⟩ — see JOT

dido *n* a playful or mischievous act intended as a joke ⟨known for cutting *didoes* at the holiday party held each year at the office⟩ — see PRANK

die *n* a small cube marked on each side with one to six spots and usually played in pairs in various games ⟨he rolled the *die*, hoping for a six⟩
synonyms bones, dice

die *vb* **1** to stop living ⟨the king *died* of old age after a long and fruitful reign⟩
synonyms check out, conk (out), croak [*slang*], decease, demise, depart, drop, end, exit, expire, fall, flatline, go, kick in [*slang*], kick off [*slang*], pass (on), pass away, part, peg out [*chiefly British*], perish, pop off, step out, succumb
related words predecease; consume, disappear, dry up, fade, fail
phrases bite the dust, buy it (*or* buy the farm), give up the ghost, kick the bucket, snuff it [*British*]
near antonyms come to, revive; linger; be, exist, subsist; flourish, prosper, thrive
antonyms breathe, live
2 to come to an end ⟨the storm *died* just as dawn was breaking over the horizon⟩ — see CEASE 1
3 to stop functioning ⟨fortunately, when the engine *died* we were only two blocks from home⟩ — see FAIL 1

die (away *or* down *or* out) *vb* to grow less in scope or intensity especially gradually ⟨the fuss gradually *died down* as people found other things with which to concern themselves⟩ — see DECREASE 2

die (for) *vb* to have an earnest wish to own or enjoy ⟨I'd *die for* some ice cream right now⟩ — see DESIRE 1

die–hard *adj* tending to favor established ideas, conditions, or institutions ⟨the *die-hard* purists are never going to accept certain words, no matter who uses them⟩ — see CONSERVATIVE 1

die–hardism *n* attitudes or opinions tending to favor established ideas, conditions, or institutions ⟨a professor of economics who regards himself as the lone bastion of political *die-hardism* on an overwhelmingly liberal campus⟩ — see CONSERVATISM

differ *vb* **1** to be unlike; to not be the same ⟨my brother and I *differ* markedly in the way we handle money⟩
synonyms contrast, vary
related words deviate, diverge, divide, fluctuate, separate
near antonyms accord, agree, conform, correspond
antonyms compare, match
2 to have a different opinion ⟨after much arguing, we simply have agreed to *differ* about the issue⟩ — see DISAGREE

difference *n* **1** the quality or state of being different ⟨there's a great *difference* between claiming to care about the environment and living like you really do⟩
synonyms contrast, disagreement, discrepancy, disparateness, disparity, dissimilarity, dissimilitude, distance, distinction, distinctiveness, distinctness, diverseness, diversity, otherness, unlikeness
related words deviance, divergence; differentiability, discriminability, distinguishability; change, modification, variation; conflict, discord, discordance, dissension (*also* dissention), dissent, dissidence, disunity, friction, strife; variability, variance; anomalousness, dichotomy, incompatibility, incongruence, incongruity, incongruousness, nonconformity; disproportion, imbalance, inequality, nonequivalence
near antonyms identicalness, identity; accordance, agreement, conformity, congruity, correspondence, parallelism, similitude; equality, equivalence, equivalency; homogeneity, homogeneousness, uniformity
antonyms alikeness, analogousness, analogy, community, likeness, resemblance, sameness, similarity
2 variance of opinion on a matter ⟨we must try to settle our *differences* without fighting⟩ — see DISAGREEMENT 1
3 the act, process, or result of making different ⟨it won't make any *difference* which one you choose⟩ — see CHANGE 1

difference *vb* to understand or point out the difference in ⟨people who cannot *difference* God's will from their own selfish desires and prejudices⟩ — see DISTINGUISH

different *adj* **1** being not of the same kind ⟨how are plantains *different* from bananas?⟩
synonyms disparate, dissimilar, distant, distinct, distinctive, distinguishable, diverse, nonidentical, other, unalike, unlike
related words divers, miscellaneous, mixed, several, sundry, variant, varied, various; differentiable, discriminable; alternate, alternative, individual, particular, peculiar, single; disproportionate, divergent, unequal
near antonyms equal, selfsame; equivalent, tantamount; akin, analogous, comparable, homological, homologous, related; homogeneous, homogenous, uniform
antonyms alike, identical, indistinguishable, kin, kindred, like, parallel, same, similar
2 not the same or shared ⟨my brother and I sleep in *different* rooms when we travel⟩ — see SEPARATE 1

differentia *n* something that sets apart an individual from others of the same kind ⟨a list of the chief *differentiae* between a controlling cult and a legitimate religious sect⟩ — see CHARACTERISTIC

differential *adj* favoring, applying, or being unequal treatment of different classes of people ⟨did away with *differential* pay scales for men and women doing the same work⟩ — see DISCRIMINATORY

differentiate *vb* to understand or point out the difference in ⟨it was hard at first to *differentiate* between the two styles of music⟩ — see DISTINGUISH 1

differently *adv* in a different way ⟨we do things *differently* around here⟩ — see OTHERWISE

differently abled *adj* deprived of the power to perform one or more natural bodily activities ⟨won a gold metal in the Paralympics, an international Olympic competition for the *differently abled*⟩ — see DISABLED

difficult *adj* **1** requiring considerable physical or mental effort ⟨*difficult* questions on the exam that required analytical thinking⟩ — see HARD 2
2 requiring exceptional skill or caution in performance or handling ⟨it's a *difficult* situation when two of your friends are quarreling and you're trying to stay out of it⟩ — see TRICKY 1

difficulty *n* **1** something that is a cause for suffering or special effort especially in the attainment of a goal ⟨the many *difficulties* that he encountered on the road from poor orphan to head of a major corporation⟩
synonyms adversity, asperity, hardness, hardship, rigor
related words discomfort, inconvenience, nuisance; affliction, trial, tribulation; knock, misfortune, mishap, tragedy; bar, catch, check, clog, crimp, embarrassment,

handicap, hindrance, hitch, hurdle, impediment, interference, let, manacle, obstacle, obstruction, pons asinorum, rub, shackle, snag, stop, trammel; block, chain, deterrent, encumbrance, fetter, inhibition; hump
near antonyms advantage, break, opportunity
2 something that makes a situation more complicated or difficult ⟨there was a minor *difficulty* when we realized that the store had already closed⟩ — see COMPLICATION 1
3 a feeling or declaration of disapproval or dissent ⟨the only *difficulty* I have with the dress is its color—does it come in anything besides purple?⟩ — see OBJECTION
4 variance of opinion on a matter ⟨the theologian's ongoing *difficulties* with the Vatican⟩ — see DISAGREEMENT 1

diffident *adj* not comfortable around people ⟨for someone who makes a living performing for other people, the actress is remarkably *diffident* in real life⟩ — see SHY 2

diffuse *adj* using or containing more words than necessary to express an idea ⟨a *diffuse* speech that took a great deal of time to make a very small point⟩ — see WORDY 1

diffuseness *n* the use of too many words to express an idea ⟨I was bored by the *diffuseness* of the Victorian novel I was trying to read⟩ — see VERBIAGE 1

diffusion *n* the use of too many words to express an idea ⟨the author's tendency toward *diffusion* makes the novel a tedious read⟩ — see VERBIAGE 1

dig *n* **1** a quick thrust ⟨gave him a *dig* in the ribs with my elbow⟩ — see [1]POKE 1
2 an act or expression showing scorn and usually intended to hurt another's feelings ⟨got in a couple of *digs* about lawyers at my friend's expense⟩ — see INSULT
3 digs *pl* a room or set of rooms in a private house or a block used as a separate dwelling place ⟨check out my new *digs* on the north side of town⟩ — see APARTMENT 1

dig *vb* **1** to hollow out or form (something) by removing earth ⟨a backhoe *dug* a hole in the backyard to make a swimming pool⟩
synonyms excavate, shovel
related words dredge; burrow, claw, grub; dig in; scoop, spade; delve; mine, quarry
near antonyms fill (in); smooth (out *or* over)
2 to take pleasure in ⟨I really *dig* bluegrass music⟩ — see ENJOY 1
3 to have a clear idea of ⟨can you *dig* what I'm saying?⟩ — see COMPREHEND 1
4 to urge or push forward with or as if with a pointed object ⟨every time I slowed down, he'd *dig* me in the ribs⟩ — see PROD 1

dig (away) *vb* to devote serious and sustained effort ⟨it took days of *digging away* at the subject, but he understands it thoroughly now⟩ — see LABOR

dig (into) *vb* to search through or into ⟨we anxiously *dug into* the old records that we found in the 19th-century house that we were restoring⟩ — see EXPLORE 1

dig (through) *vb* to look through (as a place) carefully or thoroughly in an effort to find or discover something ⟨I roughly *dug through* the closet looking for my shoes⟩ — see SEARCH 1

digest *n* **1** a short statement of the main points ⟨a *digest* of yesterday's departmental meeting⟩ — see SUMMARY
2 a shortened version of a written work ⟨on the ballot there will be a *digest* of the proposed law that is to be submitted for voter approval⟩ — see ABRIDGMENT

digest *vb* **1** to arrange or assign according to type ⟨this volume *digests* the state's laws regarding drugs and alcohol for easy reference by local authorities⟩ — see CLASSIFY 1
2 to make into a short statement of the main points (as of a report) ⟨I *digested* the results of my experiments into a few pages⟩ — see SUMMARIZE

diggings *n pl* **1** the place where one lives ⟨he hasn't been seen around these *diggings* lately⟩ — see HOME 1
2 *chiefly British* a room or set of rooms in a private house or a block used as a separate dwelling place ⟨while at Oxford, his *diggings* were the envy of all the other undergraduates⟩ — see APARTMENT 1

digit *n* a character used to represent a mathematical value ⟨you only need to fill in the last two *digits* of the year in which you were born⟩ — see NUMBER 1

dignified *adj* having or showing a formal and serious or reserved manner ⟨assumed a *dignified* stance and ignored the taunting⟩ ⟨*dignified* funeral services for the fallen firemen⟩
synonyms august, distingué, distinguished, imposing, portly, solemn, staid, stately
related words decorous, proper, seemly; grave, grim, po-faced [*British*], sober, somber (*or* sombre); aristocratic, elegant, elevated, handsome, lordly, magisterial, majestic, noble
near antonyms coarse, crass, crude, improper, indecent, uncouth, unseemly, vulgar
antonyms flighty, frivolous, giddy, goofy, silly, undignified

dignify *vb* to assign a high status or value to ⟨our graduation ceremony was *dignified* by a visit from the mayor⟩ — see EXALT 1

dignity *n* high position within society ⟨the archbishop is very conscious of his *dignity*⟩ — see RANK 2

dig out *vb* **1** to come upon after searching, study, or effort ⟨she *dug* her old art supplies *out* of the basement⟩ — see FIND 1
2 to leave a place often for another ⟨without saying where she was going, the young woman *dug out* early the next morning⟩ — see GO 2

digression *n* a departure from the subject under consideration ⟨the professor's frequent and extended *digressions* are the stuff of campus legend⟩ — see TANGENT

digressional *adj* passing from one topic to another ⟨the freely *digressional* routines that many stand-up comedians employ⟩ — see DISCURSIVE

digressionary *adj* passing from one topic to another ⟨the professor's *digressionary* style is appealing to some students and completely off-putting to others⟩ — see DISCURSIVE

digressive *adj* passing from one topic to another ⟨a *digressive* lecture on current events around the world⟩ — see DISCURSIVE

dig up *vb* to come upon after searching, study, or effort ⟨she tried to *dig up* any information she could for the report on sharks⟩ — see FIND 1

dike *n* **1** a bank of earth constructed to control water ⟨an elaborate system of *dikes* built to protect the lowlands from the relentless onslaught of the sea⟩ — see DAM
2 a long narrow channel dug in the earth ⟨water flowed along the *dike* to the small pond⟩ — see DITCH

diktat *n* an order publicly issued by an authority ⟨a democratic government has to be something wanted by that nation's citizens and not something created by a foreign power's *diktat*⟩ — see EDICT 1

dilapidated *adj* showing signs of advanced wear and tear and neglect ⟨a *dilapidated* car that had seen better days⟩ — see SHABBY 1

dilapidation *n* the state of being unattended to or not cared for ⟨the sad *dilapidation* of the old downtown movie theater has finally prompted local preservationists to mount a restoration campaign⟩ — see NEGLECT 1

dilate (on *or* upon) *vb* to express more fully and in greater detail ⟨refused to *dilate upon* his alleged plan for improving the economy in the event that he won the election⟩ — see EXPAND 1

dilatory *adj* moving or proceeding at less than the normal, desirable, or required speed ⟨the homeowner is claiming that local firefighters were *dilatory* in responding to the call⟩ — see SLOW 1

dilemma *n* **1** a situation in which one has to choose between two or more equally unsatisfactory choices ⟨faced with a *dilemma* whether to spend the night out in the cold or go inside and face his father⟩
synonyms catch-22, double bind, quandary
related words deadlock, impasse, quagmire, stalemate, standoff; knot, problem; bind, difficulty, fix, hole, jam, pickle, pinch, plight, predicament, spot
near antonyms breeze, cinch, duck soup, snap
2 a difficult, puzzling, or embarrassing situation from which there is no easy escape ⟨with home prices in a free fall, sellers were in a terrible *dilemma*⟩ — see PREDICAMENT

dilettante *adj* lacking or showing a lack of expert skill ⟨many *dilettante* efforts could be seen at the sidewalk art show⟩ — see AMATEURISH

dilettante *n* **1** a person having a knowledgeable and fine appreciation of the arts ⟨she writes about art not from the point of view of an artist but from that of a committed *dilettante*⟩ — see CONNOISSEUR 1
2 a person who regularly or occasionally engages in an activity as a pastime rather than as a profession ⟨a *dilettante* at heart, she was never willing to commit the time and effort that ballet demands⟩ — see AMATEUR 1

dilettantish *adj* lacking or showing a lack of expert skill ⟨independently wealthy, she can afford to pursue a resolutely *dilettantish* interest in sculpture⟩ — see AMATEURISH

dilettantism *n* a lack of the level of skill associated with an expert or professional ⟨no charge of *dilettantism* could ever be leveled at English physicist Henry Cavendish, whose immense wealth allowed him to devote his life to scientific pursuits⟩ — see AMATEURISHNESS

diligence *n* attentive and persistent effort ⟨through the *diligence* and ingenuity of a single detective, the gang's ringleader was finally caught⟩
synonyms assiduity, assiduousness, industriousness, industry, sedulity, sedulousness
related words application, attentiveness, attention, care, concentration; doggedness, perseverance, persistence, tenacity, tirelessness; bother, effort, effortfulness, pains, painstaking, trouble
near antonyms carelessness, negligence, slackness; idleness, indolence, laziness

diligent *adj* involved in often constant activity ⟨a student who has been unceasingly *diligent* in pursuit of a degree in mathematics⟩ — see BUSY 1

diligently *adv* **1** in a manner involving great or constant activity ⟨struggling *diligently* to contact everyone who might need a ride to the polls⟩ — see BUSILY
2 with great effort or determination ⟨working *diligently* to finish his documentary in time for the film festival⟩ — see HARD 1

dilly *n* something very good of its kind ⟨came up with a *dilly* of an idea to get the fledgling company off the ground⟩ — see JIM-DANDY

dillydally *vb* **1** to move or act slowly ⟨don't *dillydally* on the way to the store⟩ — see DELAY 1
2 to spend time doing nothing ⟨restaurant employees who, during the slow periods, would rather be doing something instead of just *dillydallying*⟩ — see IDLE

dillydallying *adj* moving or proceeding at less than the normal, desirable, or required speed ⟨the *dillydallying* congress hadn't passed any legislation, and the term was almost over⟩ — see SLOW 1

dilute *adj* **1** not containing very much of some important element ⟨a *dilute* acid that's safe to handle in the classroom⟩ — see WEAK 3
2 containing foreign or lower-grade substances ⟨a *dilute* solution of ammonia⟩ — see IMPURE 1

dilute *vb* to alter (something) for the worse with the addition of foreign or lower-grade substances ⟨the pharmacist was convicted of *diluting* prescription drugs in order to increase profits⟩ — see ADULTERATE

diluted *adj* **1** not containing very much of some important element ⟨a glass of *diluted* wine for the children on special occasions only⟩ — see WEAK 3
2 containing foreign or lower-grade substances ⟨a *diluted* solution of sulfuric acid⟩ — see IMPURE 1

dim *adj* **1** being without light or without much light ⟨a *dim* room in the basement that is very depressing⟩ — see DARK 1
2 lacking a surface luster or gloss ⟨over time, exposure to ultraviolet light will make bright pigments turn *dim*⟩ — see MATTE
3 not seen or understood clearly ⟨have only a *dim* knowledge of the subject⟩ — see FAINT 1
4 not having or showing an ability to absorb ideas readily ⟨she's kind of *dim*, but really sweet⟩ — see STUPID 1

dim *vb* to make dark, dim, or indistinct ⟨the storm clouds *dimmed* our view of the city from the airplane⟩ — see CLOUD 1

dim bulb *n, slang* a stupid person ⟨she's a *dim bulb* for sure, but he certainly didn't marry her for her brains⟩ — see IDIOT

dime *n* a very small sum of money ⟨the beauty of this deal is that all the extras won't cost you a *dime*⟩ — see MITE 1

dimension *n* **1** the total amount of measurable space or surface occupied by something ⟨the mansion is great in *dimension* but not in splendor⟩ — see [1]SIZE
2 dimensions *pl* an area over which activity, capacity, or influence extends ⟨the vast *dimensions* of the subject will require years of study⟩ — see RANGE 2

dime–store *adj* costing little ⟨a *dime-store* tablecloth that is certainly good enough for a picnic⟩ — see CHEAP 1

diminish *vb* **1** to express scornfully one's low opinion of ⟨tends to *diminish* any rival's accomplishments with snide remarks⟩ — see DECRY 1
2 to make smaller in amount, volume, or extent ⟨the state's blood supplies were severely *diminished* by the two consecutive disasters⟩ — see DECREASE 1
3 to grow less in scope or intensity especially gradually ⟨the sound of the train *diminished* as our distance from it increased⟩ — see DECREASE 2

diminishment *n* **1** the act of making a person or a thing seem little or unimportant ⟨she grew increasingly resentful of her husband's constant *diminishment* of her flourishing catering business⟩ — see DEPRECIATION
2 the amount by which something is lessened ⟨there was a sharp *diminishment* in our checking account after Christmas shopping season⟩ — see DECREASE

diminution *n* the amount by which something is lessened ⟨a *diminution* of 60 percent over the course of the month⟩ — see DECREASE

diminutive *adj* of a size that is less than average ⟨a single *diminutive* shrub on the edge of the lawn⟩ — see SMALL 1

diminutive *n* a living thing much smaller than others of its kind ⟨dik-diks, the *diminutives* of the antelope family⟩ — see DWARF 1

diminutiveness *n* the quality or state of being little in size ⟨the *diminutiveness* of jockeys prompts some people to make them the butt of jokes⟩ — see SMALLNESS 1

dimmed *adj* being without light or without much light ⟨a *dimmed* lounge where students like to rest and sleep⟩ — see DARK 1

dimwit *n* a stupid person ⟨you're a *dimwit* if you think I'll sell my house for that price⟩ — see IDIOT

dim–witted *adj* not having or showing an ability to absorb ideas readily ⟨the show's amateur sleuth always has to explain to the *dim-witted* police chief who really committed the murder⟩ — see STUPID 1

dim–wittedness *n* the quality or state of lacking intelligence or quickness of mind ⟨frustrated by the apparent *dim-wittedness* of the clerks in customer service⟩ — see STUPIDITY 1

din *n* loud, confused, and usually inharmonious sound ⟨there's always a great *din* from the cafeteria during lunch⟩ — see NOISE 1

din *vb* to say or state again ⟨safety lessons *dinned* into us over and over⟩ — see REPEAT 1

dine *vb* **1** to take a meal ⟨they *dined* elegantly at the city's finest restaurant before taking in an opera downtown⟩
synonyms eat, fare, feed, partake, refresh, victual
related words banquet, feast, repast; chow (down), dig in; glut, gorge, gormandize, overeat, overfeed, pig out; graze, nibble, nosh, pick, snack; board, mess, dine out; breakfast, lunch, sup; picnic
phrases break bread
near antonyms diet, fast
2 to entertain with a fancy meal ⟨the advertising agency lavishly wines and *dines* prospective clients⟩ — see FEAST 1

diner *n* a public establishment where meals are served to paying customers for consumption on the premises ⟨we'll just grab a quick hamburger at the local *diner*⟩ — see RESTAURANT

ding–a–ling *n* a person who lacks good sense or judgment ⟨some *ding-a-ling* set off the fire alarm by burning paper in a wastebasket⟩ — see FOOL 1

dingbat *n* a person who lacks good sense or judgment ⟨a *dingbat* who was constantly firing off nonsensical letters to the editor⟩ — see FOOL 1

ding–dong *n* a person who lacks good sense or judgment ⟨there's always one *ding-dong* in the tour group who wanders off and gets lost⟩ — see FOOL 1

dinge *n* the state or quality of being dirty ⟨a photograph that captures the *dinge*, the dreariness, and the despair of an addict's apartment⟩ — see DIRTINESS 1

dinghy *n* a boat equipped with one or more sails ⟨we went sailing on the secluded lake in a little two-person *dinghy*⟩ — see SAILBOAT

dinginess *n* the state or quality of being dirty ⟨she was appalled by the *dinginess* of the curtains that came with the apartment and took them all down to be cleaned⟩ — see DIRTINESS 1

dingus *n* a small article the actual name of which one either does not know or cannot remember ⟨it seems to be missing some little *dingus* that holds everything in place⟩ — see DOODAD 1

dingy *adj* not clean ⟨the bed sheets were pretty *dingy* so we threw them in the laundry pile⟩ — see DIRTY 1

dink *n, slang* a person slavishly devoted to intellectual or academic pursuits ⟨in those days a *dink* had a better chance of winning the lottery than of dating a cheerleader⟩ — see NERD 1

dinkum *adj, Australian & New Zealand* being exactly as appears or as claimed ⟨somewhat surprised to learn that our guide through the outback was a fair *dinkum* crocodile hunter⟩ — see AUTHENTIC 1

dinky *adj* of a size that is less than average ⟨recent college graduates crowding into a *dinky* New York City apartment⟩ — see SMALL 1

dinner *n* a large fancy meal often accompanied by ceremony or entertainment ⟨there will be a celebratory *dinner* at a local restaurant for the entire team⟩ — see FEAST 1

dinnerware *n* dishes used for eating or serving food or drink ⟨received three sets of *dinnerware* as wedding gifts⟩ — see TABLEWARE 2

dinning *adj* making loud, confused, and usually unharmonious sounds ⟨*dinning* honks and beeps arose from cars stuck in the massive traffic jam⟩ — see NOISY 1

dinosaur *n* **1** one that has passed the peak of effectiveness or popularity ⟨as an old-time big-city boss, he's become something of a *dinosaur* in today's political world⟩ — see HAS-BEEN
2 something or someone that is unusually large and powerful ⟨not that his small lawn needed such a *dinosaur*, but he bought a riding mower anyway⟩ — see GIANT

dint *n* a sunken area forming a separate space ⟨left a small *dint* in the car's fender⟩ — see HOLE 2

[1]**dip** *n* **1** a downward slope ⟨marathoners have one last *dip* before the race course levels off and the finish line comes into view⟩ — see DECLINE 3
2 the act or process of going to a lower level or altitude ⟨the city's population has taken a slight *dip* since the last census⟩ — see DESCENT 1

[2]**dip** *n* a stupid person ⟨how did that *dip* get through medical school?⟩ — see IDIOT

dip *vb* **1** to sink or push (something) briefly into or as if into a liquid ⟨first *dip* a paper towel in water⟩ ⟨she *dipped* a hand into her pocket and pulled out a piece of candy⟩
synonyms douse (*also* dowse), duck, dunk, immerse, souse, sop, submerge, submerse
related words bathe, moisten, soak, steep, wet; drench, drown, flood; dive, plunge, thrust
2 to lift out with something that holds liquid ⟨carefully *dipped* water from the bucket to the kettle⟩
synonyms bucket, lade, ladle, scoop, spoon
related words bail; deplete, drain, eliminate, empty, exhaust; bleed, draw (off); dish; slop; decant, draw, pump, siphon (*also* syphon), suction
near antonyms pour; fill
3 to go to a lower level especially abruptly ⟨the temperature *dipped* a bit in the evening⟩ — see DROP 2
4 to lead or extend downward ⟨slow down, the road *dips* here⟩ — see DESCEND 1
5 to take a quick or hasty look ⟨I *dipped* into the book, but I didn't have a chance to study it thoroughly⟩ — see GLANCE 2

diplomacy *n* the ability to deal with others in touchy situations without offending them ⟨that candidate is thought to lack the *diplomacy* necessary in dealing with people of power and influence⟩ — see TACT

diplomatic *adj* having or showing tact ⟨a *diplomatic* attempt at preventing any hurt feelings⟩ — see TACTFUL

dipper *n* a utensil with a bowl and a handle that is used especially in cooking and serving food ⟨the metal *dipper* left in the stew pot was too hot to touch⟩ — see SPOON

dippiness *n* lack of good sense or judgment ⟨I'll have none of this latest-thing fashion *dippiness*—I buy clothes with the classic look⟩ — see FOOLISHNESS 1

dippy *adj* showing or marked by a lack of good sense or judgment ⟨a mindless movie about a bunch of *dippy* teenagers⟩ — see FOOLISH 1

dipsomaniac *n* a person who makes a habit of getting drunk ⟨few suspected that this pillar of the community, ensconced in her suburban colonial, was a closet *dipsomaniac*⟩ — see DRUNK 1

dipstick *n* a person who lacks good sense or judgment ⟨which *dipstick* used the good china as a dog dish?⟩ — see FOOL 1

dire *adj* **1** being or showing a sign of evil or calamity to come ⟨a *dire* forecast of a plunge in stock prices⟩ — see OMINOUS
2 causing fear ⟨a series of *dire* tremors that hinted at a huge volcanic eruption⟩ — see FEARFUL
3 needing immediate attention ⟨a *dire* need for food and medicine in the famine-stricken country⟩ — see ACUTE 2
4 causing or marked by an atmosphere lacking in cheer ⟨with stock prices steadily falling, these are *dire* days on the trading floor⟩ — see GLOOMY 1

direct *adj* **1** done or working without something else coming in between ⟨a zoologist whose works are based entirely on her *direct* observation of animals in the wild⟩ ⟨the virus was the *direct* cause of the disease⟩
synonyms firsthand, immediate, primary, unmediated
related words clinical, empirical (*also* empiric); efficient, proximate; hands-on
antonyms indirect, secondhand
2 free in expressing one's true feelings and opinions ⟨our coach is very *direct*, never hesitating for a moment to tell a player whenever he isn't performing up to snuff⟩ — see FRANK
3 going straight to the point clearly and firmly ⟨clear and *direct* instructions that left no room for misinterpretation⟩ — see STRAIGHTFORWARD 1
4 free from irregularities or digressions in course ⟨this road provides the most *direct* route to your destination⟩ — see STRAIGHT 1

direct *adv* in a direct line or course ⟨flew *direct* to the coast⟩ — see DIRECTLY 1

direct *vb* **1** to cause to move to a central point or along a restricted pathway ⟨the aqueduct *directs* the water into an artificial lake⟩ — see CHANNEL
2 to issue orders to (someone) by right of authority ⟨our tour guide *directed* us to wait in front of the building until she could rejoin us⟩ — see COMMAND 1
3 to request the doing of by virtue of one's authority ⟨the caretaker *directed* that all of the windows be closed before we left⟩ — see COMMAND 2
4 to look after and make decisions about ⟨the music teacher *directs* both the student orchestra and the marching band⟩ — see CONDUCT 1
5 to point or turn (something) toward a target or goal ⟨we quickly *directed* our attention toward the noise coming from the rear⟩ — see AIM 1
6 to point out the way for (someone) especially from a position in front ⟨the guide *directed* the tour through the museum with commendable efficiency and expertise⟩ — see LEAD 1

direction *n* **1** a statement of what to do that must be obeyed by those concerned ⟨we were given very specific *directions* for the first part of the exam⟩ — see COMMAND 1
2 the act or activity of looking after and making decisions about something ⟨working under the close *direction* of the engineering supervisor⟩ — see CONDUCT 1
3 a guiding or motivating purpose or principle ⟨a life that seemed to lack any *direction* other than the mindless pursuit of empty pleasures⟩ — see COMPASS 1
4 a prevailing or general movement or inclination ⟨some older people worry about the overall *direction* that political discourse has taken lately⟩ — see TREND 1

directive *n* **1** a statement of what to do that must be obeyed by those concerned ⟨the company president regularly issues *directives* intended for all staff members⟩ — see COMMAND 1
2 an order publicly issued by an authority ⟨a *directive* issued by the archbishop that is to be read during Sunday services at every parish⟩ — see EDICT 1
3 a written communication giving information or directions ⟨a growing stack of unread *directives* from the company's senior vice president⟩ — see MEMORANDUM 1

directly *adv* **1** in a direct line or course ⟨we went *directly* to the site without stopping to pick up extra supplies⟩
synonyms dead, direct, due, plumb, plump, right, straight, straightway
phrases as the crow flies
near antonyms circuitously, deviously, veeringly
antonyms indirectly
2 in an honest and direct manner ⟨the instructor deals with her art students very *directly*, always telling them the plain truth⟩ — see STRAIGHTFORWARD
3 in the same words ⟨quoted *directly* from the encyclopedia⟩ — see VERBATIM
4 without delay ⟨in case of a medical emergency, do not try to contact your doctor but instead go *directly* to the hospital⟩ — see IMMEDIATELY
5 at or within a short time ⟨dinner should be ready *directly*⟩ — see SHORTLY 2

directness *n* the free expression of one's true feelings and opinions ⟨his *directness* is much appreciated by his patients⟩ — see CANDOR 1

director *n* **1** a person who manages or directs something ⟨the new *director* of the company plans to make a number of changes in daily operations⟩ — see EXECUTIVE
2 a person who supervises the production of a stage show ⟨the *director* of the drama club's next production will be a student⟩ — see REGISSEUR

directorial *adj* suited for or relating to the directing of things ⟨an applicant with a number of *directorial* positions on his résumé⟩ — see EXECUTIVE

direful *adj* **1** being or showing a sign of evil or calamity to come ⟨the stock market crash was the first *direful* indication of the dark days to come⟩ — see OMINOUS
2 causing fear ⟨heard the *direful* howling of the wolves during the night⟩ — see FEARFUL 1

dirge *n* a composition expressing one's grief over a loss ⟨bagpipes played a haunting *dirge* at the funeral for the fallen leader⟩ — see LAMENT 2

dirt *n* **1** the loose surface material in which plants naturally grow ⟨dig into the *dirt* to a depth of about three inches⟩
synonyms clod, earth, ground, mold, soil
related words blackland, clay, gault [*chiefly British*], gley, guck (*or* gook), gumbo, kaolin, muck, mud; dust, gravel, sand; humus, loam, topsoil; alluvium, colluvium, detritus, loess, marl, sediment, shingle, silt; duff, mull; subsoil, substratum
2 the solid part of our planet's surface as distinguished from the sea and air ⟨at the first sound of gunfire we hit the *dirt*⟩ — see EARTH 2
3 foul matter that mars the purity or cleanliness of something ⟨there's some *dirt* on your shoes⟩ — see FILTH 1
4 the quality or state of being obscene ⟨appalled by the *dirt* in the author's novels⟩ — see OBSCENITY 1
5 solid matter discharged from an animal's alimentary canal ⟨tread carefully, as there's cow *dirt* all over the pasture⟩ — see DROPPING 1

dirtbag *n, slang* a person whose behavior is offensive to others ⟨forgetting my birthday was the final straw—I had to dump the *dirtbag*⟩ — see JERK 1

dirt cheap *adj* costing little ⟨a *dirt cheap* little house that was the proverbial fixer-upper⟩ — see CHEAP 1

dirtiness *n* **1** the state or quality of being dirty ⟨the health inspector took the manager to task over the general *dirtiness* of the restaurant⟩
synonyms blackness, dinge, dinginess, dustiness, filthiness, foulness, griminess, grubbiness, nastiness, smuttiness, soilage, sordidness, squalidness, uncleanliness, uncleanness

related words discoloration, staining; impureness, impurity; messiness, mussiness, sloppiness, untidiness; insanitation, squalor; muckiness, muddiness, sootiness
near antonyms purity
antonyms cleanliness, immaculateness, spotlessness
2 the quality or state of being obscene ⟨the incontestable *dirtiness* of the film demands an adult rating⟩ — see OBSCENITY 1

dirt–poor *adj* lacking money or material possessions ⟨growing up *dirt-poor* in the rural South⟩ — see POOR 1

dirty *adj* **1** not clean ⟨after working in the factory all day, his clothes are very *dirty*⟩
synonyms bedraggled, befouled, begrimed, bemired, besmirched, black, blackened, cruddy, dingy, draggled, dusty, filthy, foul, grimy, grotty [*chiefly British*], grubby, grungy, mucky, muddy, nasty, smudged, smutty, soiled, sordid, stained, sullied, unclean, uncleanly
related words contaminated, defiled, germy, impure, polluted, tainted; insanitary, uncleaned, unsanitary, unsterile, unsterilized, unwashed; greasy, gunky; chaotic, cluttered, confused, disarranged, disarrayed, disheveled (*or* dishevelled), disordered, jumbled, littered, messed, messy, muddled, mussed, mussy, rumpled, scruffy, sloppy, slovenly, unkempt, untidy; raunchy, scuzzy [*slang*], shabby, skanky [*slang*], sleazy, squalid; collied [*chiefly British dialect*], crocked [*dialect*], fuliginous, sooty
near antonyms clear, limpid, pure; cleaned, cleansed, combed, groomed, neat, ordered, orderly, tidy; bleached, purified, whitened; bright, flawless, perfect, shiny, sparkling, unspotted, untouched; taintless, unblemished, undefiled, unpolluted, untainted, virgin, wholesome
antonyms clean, cleanly, immaculate, spick-and-span (*or* spic-and-span), spotless, stainless, ultraclean, unsoiled, unstained, unsullied
2 depicting or referring to sexual matters in a way that is unacceptable in polite society ⟨some radio stations refused to play the song because of the *dirty* lyrics⟩ — see OBSCENE 1
3 marked by wet and windy conditions ⟨they were unknowingly sailing into *dirty* weather⟩ — see FOUL 1
4 not being in accordance with the rules or standards of what is fair in sport ⟨the school is known for the *dirty* football it plays⟩ — see FOUL 2
5 not following or in accordance with standards of honor and decency ⟨accused the other campaign of playing *dirty* tricks⟩ — see IGNOBLE 2
6 arousing or deserving of one's loathing and disgust ⟨laying off longtime employees was a *dirty* way for the company for reduce labor costs⟩ — see CONTEMPTIBLE 1
7 open to improper influence and especially bribery ⟨a movie about a *dirty* cop paid to protect a mafioso⟩ — see VENAL

dirty *vb* to make dirty ⟨she *dirtied* her new sneakers when she splashed in the puddle⟩
synonyms befoul, begrime, bemire, besmirch, blacken, daub, distain [*archaic*], foul, gaum [*dialect*], grime, mire, muck, muddy, smirch, smudge, soil, stain, sully
related words contaminate, defile, pollute, taint; discolor; confuse, disarrange, disarray, dishevel, disorder, draggle, jumble, mess, muddle; colly [*chiefly British dialect*], crock [*dialect*]
near antonyms decontaminate, purge, purify; disinfect, sanitize; brush, dry-clean, dust, launder, mop, rinse, scour, scrub, sweep, wash, wipe; brighten, deodorize, freshen, renew, spruce (up); straighten (up), tidy (up)
antonyms clean, cleanse

dirty word *n* a disrespectful or indecent word or expression ⟨I'm afraid I won't be much help on the trip—the only Spanish I know is a handful of *dirty words*⟩ — see SWEARWORD

dis *also* **diss** *n, slang* **1** an act or expression showing scorn and usually intended to hurt another's feelings ⟨that's a *dis* that a person of any color should find offensive⟩ — see INSULT
2 rude behavior ⟨in the hood any *dis* is dealt with harshly⟩ — see DISCOURTESY

dis *also* **diss** *vb, slang* **1** to show contempt for ⟨don't you go *dissing* somebody just because you've got a few more dead presidents than they do⟩ — see SCORN 1
2 to express scornfully one's low opinion of ⟨a DJ who has *dissed* every album that rapper has put out⟩ — see DECRY 1
3 to cause hurt feelings or deep resentment in ⟨are you *dissing* me?⟩ — see INSULT
4 to express one's unfavorable opinion of the worth or quality of ⟨never *dis* a person's style of dressing in front of her friends⟩ — see CRITICIZE

disable *vb* **1** to cause severe or permanent injury to ⟨a promising athlete who was severely *disabled* in a plane crash⟩ — see MAIM
2 to render powerless, ineffective, or unable to move ⟨*disabled* the controls for unauthorized users⟩ — see PARALYZE 1

disabled *adj* deprived of the power to perform one or more natural bodily activities ⟨the *disabled* man was unable to climb the stairs without help⟩
synonyms challenged, differently abled, exceptional, impaired, incapacitated
related words special-needs; halt, lame, paralyzed, quadriplegic; immobile, immobilized; ailing, diseased, ill, sick, unfit, unhealthy, unsound, unwell; blind, deaf, hard of hearing, mute
near antonyms bouncing, chipper, fit, hale, healthy, hearty, robust, sound, well, whole, wholesome
antonyms able-bodied, abled, nondisabled, unimpaired

disabuse *vb* to free from mistaken beliefs or foolish hopes ⟨let me *disabuse* you of your foolish notions about married life⟩ — see DISILLUSION

disaccord *n* a lack of agreement or harmony ⟨the perennial question of whether there's an irreconcilable *disaccord* between science and religion⟩ — see DISCORD

disaccord *vb* to be out of harmony or agreement usually noticeably ⟨national security measures that *disaccord* with our cherished right to free expression⟩ — see CLASH

disadvantage *n* **1** a feature of someone or something that creates difficulty for achieving success ⟨their lack of height was a *disadvantage* on the basketball court⟩
synonyms debit, disbenefit, downside, drawback, handicap, incommodity, liability, minus, negative, strike
related words albatross, millstone, stranglehold; disability, impairment; failing, shortcoming; bar, catch, check, clog, crimp, embarrassment, hindrance, hitch, hurdle, impediment, interference, let, manacle, obstacle, obstruction, rub, shackle, stop, trammel
near antonyms vantage; head start, jump, lead, margin, start; ascendancy (*also* ascendency), better, command, control, drop, mastery, predominance, superiority, supremacy, transcendence, upper hand; prerogative, privilege; break, opportunity; aid, assistance, help
antonyms advantage, asset, edge, plus
2 the negative result caused by something that creates difficulty for achieving success ⟨intense pretrial publicity worked to our *disadvantage*⟩
synonyms despite, detriment, disfavor, penalty
related words deficit, deprivation, expense, loss; damage, harm, hurt, injury; prejudice
near antonyms gain

antonyms advantage, favor

disadvantaged *adj* kept from having the necessities of life or a healthful environment ⟨*disadvantaged* families struggling to get by in the inner city⟩ — see DEPRIVED

disadvantageous *adj* opposed to one's interests ⟨such an arrangement with the wholesalers would be *disadvantageous* for small farmers⟩ — see ADVERSE 1

disaffect *vb* **1** to cause to change from friendly or loving to unfriendly or uncaring ⟨a *disaffected* boyfriend was responsible for the vandalism to her home⟩ — see ESTRANGE

2 to make discontented ⟨the troops were *disaffected* by the extension of their tours of duty⟩ — see DISCONTENT

disaffection *n* the loss of friendship or affection ⟨widespread *disaffection* with the governor's administration in its final year⟩ — see ESTRANGEMENT

disaffirm *vb* to declare not to be true ⟨her sullen mood *disaffirmed* her repeated protestations that everything was just fine⟩ — see DENY 1

disagree *vb* to have a different opinion ⟨the leader thought we were still headed north on the trail, but I *disagreed*⟩
synonyms differ, dissent, nonconcur
related words clash, collide, conflict, contrast; counter, debate, object, oppose, protest, resist; contest, dispute; argue, bicker, fall out, quarrel
phrases take issue
near antonyms accede, accept, acquiesce, comply, consent, defer, subscribe; affiliate, ally, associate, collaborate, collude, come round, compromise, cooperate, get along, side
antonyms agree, assent, concur

disagree (with) *vb* to make an assertion that is contrary to one made by (another) ⟨she *disagreed with* me when I said that the jacket was dark blue⟩ — see CONTRADICT 1

disagreeable *adj* **1** having or showing a habitually bad temper ⟨a *disagreeable* old grouch with no friends⟩ — see ILL-TEMPERED

2 not giving pleasure to the mind or senses ⟨a *disagreeable* smell coming from the closet⟩ — see UNPLEASANT

disagreeing *adj* not being in agreement or harmony ⟨the teenagers' *disagreeing* accounts of what happened that night make me wonder if either is telling the truth⟩ — see INCONSISTENT 1

disagreement *n* **1** variance of opinion on a matter ⟨there was some *disagreement* about what color the missing sweater actually was⟩
synonyms contestation, controversy, debate, difference, difficulty, disputation, dispute, dissension (*also* dissention), dissensus, firestorm, nonconcurrence
related words clash, collision, conflict, confliction, disaccord, discord, dissonance; apartness, divarication, division; combat, contention, strife, struggle; altercation, argument, bicker, falling-out, fight, kickup, misunderstanding, quarrel, set-to
near antonyms acceptance, compliance; concord, peace
antonyms accord, agreement, consensus, harmony, unanimity

2 an often noisy or angry expression of differing opinions ⟨a loud *disagreement* started as soon as we tried to order pizza for everyone⟩ — see ARGUMENT 1

3 the quality or state of being different ⟨there is some *disagreement* between the accounts on the sequence of events⟩ — see DIFFERENCE 1

disallow *vb* **1** to declare not to be true ⟨*disallowing* the philosophical concept of free will⟩ — see DENY 1

2 to be unwilling to grant ⟨*disallowed* the defendant's request for a new trial⟩ — see DENY 2

disallowance *n* **1** an unwillingness to grant something asked for ⟨the taxpayer was notified of the *disallowance* of his claim for medical expenses⟩ — see DENIAL 1

2 a refusal to confirm the truth of a statement ⟨a categorical *disallowance* of all charges⟩ — see DENIAL 2

disannul *vb* to put an end to by formal action ⟨the new administration seems intent on *disannulling* every social program instituted by its predecessor⟩ — see ABOLISH 1

disappear *vb* to cease to be visible ⟨the stranger *disappeared* into the mists, never to be seen again⟩
synonyms dematerialize, dissolve, evanesce, evaporate, fade, flee, fly, go (away), melt, sink, vanish
related words blank (out), clear, die (away *or* down *or* out), disperse, dissipate, dissolve, dry up; blur, dim
phrases drop out of sight
near antonyms arrive, break out, come out, emerge, issue, loom, show up
antonyms appear, materialize

disappoint *vb* to fall short in satisfying the expectation or hope of ⟨they were *disappointed* by the outcome of the big game⟩
synonyms cheat, dissatisfy, fail, let down
related words bum (out), chagrin, discontent, disgruntle, displease, distress, upset; disenchant, disillusion; deceive, delude, mock
near antonyms fulfill (*or* fulfil); gladden
antonyms content, gratify, satisfy

disappointment *n* **1** the emotion felt when one's expectations are not met ⟨we felt keen *disappointment* when our offer on the house was rejected⟩
synonyms dismay, dissatisfaction, frustration, letdown
related words crestfallenness, discontent, discontentedness, discontentment, disgruntlement, displeasure; disenchantment, disillusionment; blues, dejectedness, dejection, depression, desolateness, desolation, despondency, disconsolateness, distress, doldrums, dolefulness, dolor, downheartedness, dreariness, dumps, gloom, gloominess, joylessness, melancholy, mopes, oppression, sadness, sorrow, unhappiness; chagrin, discomfiture
near antonyms fulfillment (*or* fulfilment); bliss, felicity, gladness, happiness, joy
antonyms content, contentedness, contentment, gratification, satisfaction

2 something that disappoints ⟨after all the publicity and high expectations, the sequel to the movie blockbuster was a huge *disappointment*⟩
synonyms bringdown, bummer, letdown
related words anticlimax, failure, fiasco, fizzle; lemon, loser
near antonyms success, winner; relief

disapprobation *n* refusal to accept as right or desirable ⟨there was widespread *disapprobation* of their mixed marriage in that narrow-minded community⟩ — see DISAPPROVAL

disapproval *n* refusal to accept as right or desirable ⟨thus far, every one of her boyfriends has met with her parents' *disapproval*⟩
synonyms deprecation, disapprobation, discountenance, disesteem, disfavor, dislike, displeasure
related words disrelish, distaste; rejection, thumbs-down; blame, censure, condemnation, criticism, denunciation, dispraise, opprobrium, reprehension, reproach, reprobation; antagonism, antipathy, hostility; belittlement, disparagement, objection, opposition
near antonyms acclaim, commendation, praise; endorsement (*also* indorsement), sanction, thumbs-up; empathy, sympathy
antonyms approbation, approval, favor

disapprove *vb* **1** to be unwilling to grant ⟨the committee *disapproved* the proposal to allow casino gambling in the state⟩ — see DENY 2

2 to show unwillingness to accept, do, engage in, or

agree to ⟨*disapproved* the first set of blueprints submitted by the firm⟩ — see DECLINE 1

disapprove (of) *vb* to hold an unfavorable opinion of ⟨my sister *disapproves of* my smoking⟩
synonyms deprecate, discountenance, disesteem, disfavor, dislike, frown (on *or* upon), mislike, reprove, tsk-tsk, tut (over *or* about), tut-tut (over *or* about)
related words disrelish, object (to), pooh-pooh (*also* pooh), reject, reprehend, reprobate, scorn; censure, condemn, criticize, denounce, discommend; chide, rebuke, reproach, scold
phrases look down one's nose (on)
near antonyms endorse (*also* indorse), sanction, support; adore, delight (in), dig, enjoy, fancy, groove (on), love, relish, revel (in)
antonyms approve, favor, like

disarm *vb* **1** to reduce the size and strength of the armed forces of ⟨the defeated nation was *disarmed* so that it would never again be a threat to international order⟩
synonyms demilitarize
related words demobilize; denuclearize
near antonyms equip, reequip, weapon; embattle, mechanize, mobilize
antonyms arm, militarize
2 to lessen the anger or agitation of ⟨her future father-in-law was totally *disarmed* by her easy charm⟩ — see PACIFY 1

disarmament *n* the reduction or elimination of a country's armed forces or weapons ⟨the ambassador spoke at length about the possible unilateral *disarmament* of his country⟩
synonyms demilitarization
related words demobilization; denuclearization
near antonyms equipment, reequipment; mechanization, mobilization
antonyms armament, militarization

disarming *adj* **1** having qualities that tend to make one loved ⟨a thoroughly *disarming* little rascal who can talk his way out of any trouble⟩ — see LOVABLE
2 likely or intended to win one's affection ⟨there's a *disarming* lack of pretension about the girl⟩ — see INGRATIATING
3 tending to lessen or avoid conflict or hostility ⟨the secretary's *disarming* smile made me forget why I was angry⟩ — see PACIFIC 1

disarrange *vb* to undo the proper order or arrangement of ⟨the wind had hopelessly *disarranged* my hair⟩ — see DISORDER

disarranged *adj* lacking in order, neatness, and often cleanliness ⟨a *disarranged* collection of sports memorabilia scattered about the room⟩ — see MESSY

disarrangement *n* a state in which everything is out of order ⟨the *disarrangement* of the files makes it almost impossible to find anything⟩ — see CHAOS

disarray *n* a state in which everything is out of order ⟨the boys' bedroom was in its usual *disarray*⟩ — see CHAOS

disarray *vb* to undo the proper order or arrangement of ⟨he had accidentally *disarrayed* his brother's CDs, leaving a telltale sign of borrowing without permission⟩ — see DISORDER

disarrayed *adj* lacking in order, neatness, and often cleanliness ⟨a *disarrayed* pile of rugs in the attic⟩ — see MESSY

disassemble *vb* **1** to take apart ⟨they had to *disassemble* the television set in order to replace the wiring⟩
synonyms break down, demount, dismantle, dismember, dismount, knock down, strike, take down
related words detach, disengage; break up, disaggregate, disarticulate, disconnect, disjoin, disjoint, dissever, disunite, divide, separate
near antonyms build, erect, pitch; combine, unite
antonyms assemble, construct
2 to go off in different directions and cease to exist as a body or unified whole ⟨the class was slow to *disassemble*, many waiting around to ask the instructor some questions⟩ — see DISPERSE 1

disassociate *vb* to set or force apart ⟨the company tried to *disassociate* itself from the rest of the industry, which is widely viewed as corrupt⟩ — see SEPARATE 1

disaster *n* **1** a sudden violent event that brings about great loss or destruction ⟨hurricanes are natural *disasters*⟩
synonyms apocalypse, calamity, cataclysm, catastrophe, debacle (*also* débâcle), tragedy
related words bloodbath, collapse, crash, meltdown; Armageddon, doomsday, end-time; convulsion, paroxysm, upheaval; accident, casualty, fatality; misadventure, mischance, misfortune, mishap; blast, blow, double whammy, one-two (*or* one-two punch)
near antonyms godsend, manna, windfall
2 something that has failed ⟨an utter *disaster*, the play opened and closed on the same miserable night⟩ — see FAILURE 3

disastrous *adj* **1** bringing about ruin or misfortune ⟨a split-second, *disastrous* decision that I would forever regret⟩ — see FATAL 1
2 causing or tending to cause destruction ⟨a *disastrous* fire from which the town never fully recovered⟩ — see DESTRUCTIVE 1

disavow *vb* **1** to declare not to be true ⟨*disavowed* the testimony that she had given earlier in the trial⟩ — see DENY 1
2 to refuse to acknowledge as one's own or as one's responsibility ⟨the government will *disavow* any knowledge of your mission⟩ — see DISCLAIM 1

disavowal *n* a refusal to confirm the truth of a statement ⟨the mayor's *disavowal* of the rumor that a terrorist threat had been received put our minds at rest⟩ — see DENIAL 2

disband *vb* **1** to cease to exist or cause to cease to exist as a group or organization ⟨the university *disbanded* the committee after the report had been submitted⟩ ⟨the rock group *disbanded* upon finishing their farewell tour⟩
synonyms break up, disperse, dissolve
related words demobilize
near antonyms incorporate; consolidate; hang together
antonyms band, join, unite
2 to cause (members of a group) to move widely apart ⟨police *disbanded* the rioters with tear gas⟩ — see SCATTER 1

disbandment *n* an act or process in which something scatters or is scattered ⟨the *disbandment* of the crowd at the end of the outdoor rock concert⟩ — see SCATTERING 1

disbelief *n* refusal to accept something as true ⟨their story explaining their absence was met with frank *disbelief*⟩
synonyms incredulity, nonbelief, unbelief
related words discredit, distrust, doubt, mistrust, skepticism, suspicion, uncertainty; denial, rejection, repudiation, unfaith
near antonyms acceptance, conviction, faith; trust
antonyms belief, credence, credit

disbelieve *vb* to think not to be true or real ⟨many *disbelieved* the medium's claims that she could communicate with the spirits of the dead⟩
synonyms discredit, negate
related words deny, reject, repudiate; distrust, doubt, mistrust, suspect; debunk, disprove, refute; deride, pooh-pooh (*also* pooh), scoff (at)
near antonyms trust

antonyms accept, believe, credit, swallow

disbeliever *n* a person who is always ready to doubt or question the truth or existence of something ⟨the usual *disbelievers* refused to accept the president's claim that he was acting only in the public interest⟩ — see SKEPTIC

disbelieving *adj* inclined to doubt or question claims ⟨the senator stated her case before a *disbelieving* press corps⟩ — see SKEPTICAL 1

disbenefit *n* a feature of someone or something that creates difficulty for achieving success ⟨the question whether allowing the big-box stores in would be a *disbenefit* to the community⟩ — see DISADVANTAGE 1

disburden *vb* **1** to empty or rid of cargo ⟨*disburdened* the oil tanker before it could leak any more oil⟩ — see UNLOAD 1

2 to set (a person or thing) free of something that encumbers ⟨the cinema was a place where we could *disburden* ourselves of our cares, if only for a couple of hours⟩ — see RID

disburse *vb* to hand over or use up in payment ⟨the foundation *disburses* money to many worthy causes⟩ — see SPEND 1

disbursement *n* **1** a payment made in the course of achieving a result ⟨substantial *disbursements* for research and development⟩ — see EXPENSE

2 the act of offering money in exchange for goods or services ⟨the *disbursement* of the foundation's funds to several cancer research centers⟩ — see PAYMENT 1

3 the act or process of giving out something to each member of a group ⟨the agency whose responsibilities included the *disbursement* of strains of the virus to medical research labs around the country⟩ — see DISTRIBUTION 1

discard *n* something separated from a group or lot for not being as good as the others ⟨toss all of your *discards* in the garbage⟩ — see CULL

discard *vb* to get rid of as useless or unwanted ⟨*discard* an old, torn sweater⟩

synonyms cashier, cast (off), chuck, deep-six, ditch, dump, eighty-six (*or* 86), exorcise (*also* exorcize), fling (off *or* away), jettison, junk, lay by, lose, pitch, reject, scrap, shed, shuck (off), slough (off) *also* sluff (off), throw away, throw out, toss, unload

related words abandon, abdicate, desert, forsake; dismiss, kick out; abolish, annihilate, eliminate, eradicate, expunge, exterminate, extinguish, extirpate, liquidate, remove, root (out), stamp (out), wipe out

phrases dispose of, set aside

near antonyms adopt, embrace, take on; employ, use, utilize; hold, hold back, keep, retain

discarding *n* the getting rid of whatever is unwanted or useless ⟨the daily *discarding* of all unwanted e-mail⟩ — see DISPOSAL 1

discern *vb* **1** to make note of (something) through the use of one's eyes ⟨barely able to *discern* the garden gate through the mist⟩ — see SEE 1

2 to understand or point out the difference in ⟨too young to *discern* between right and wrong⟩ — see DISTINGUISH 1

3 to have a clear idea of ⟨we're still trying to *discern* the meaning of that cryptic remark⟩ — see COMPREHEND 1

discernible *also* **discernable** *adj* able to be perceived by a sense or by the mind ⟨*discernible* differences in the two authors' writing styles⟩ — see PERCEPTIBLE

discerning *adj* having or showing deep understanding and intelligent application of knowledge ⟨a *discerning* critic of modern art⟩ — see WISE 1

discernment *n* the ability to understand inner qualities or relationships ⟨the *discernment* to know when someone is a true friend⟩ — see WISDOM 1

discharge *n* **1** a directed propelling of a missile by a firearm or artillery piece ⟨the thunderous *discharge* of the cannons⟩ — see SHOT

2 a freeing from an obligation or responsibility ⟨a full *discharge* from responsibility for the accident⟩ — see RELEASE 1

3 the termination of the employment of an employee or a work force often temporarily ⟨she was resentful over what she felt was a wrongful *discharge*⟩ — see LAYOFF 1

4 the doing of an action ⟨aided in the *discharge* of his duties by a capable assistant⟩ — see COMMISSION 2

discharge *vb* **1** to cause (a projectile) to be driven forward with force ⟨Robert Goddard was the first to *discharge* a rocket containing an instrument package⟩ — see SHOOT 1

2 to empty or rid of cargo ⟨docks for *discharging* containerships⟩ — see UNLOAD 1

3 to give what is owed for ⟨*discharge* a debt in full⟩ — see PAY 2

4 to set free (as from slavery or confinement) ⟨*discharged* the prisoners upon the signing of the peace treaty⟩ — see FREE 1

5 to throw or give off ⟨the mighty river *discharges* its waters into the ocean⟩ — see EMIT 1

6 to cause a weapon to release a missile with great force ⟨felt a strong recoil as the rifle *discharged*⟩ — see SHOOT 2

7 to let go from office, service, or employment ⟨15 people were *discharged* when the embezzling ring was discovered⟩ — see DISMISS 1

disciple *n* one who follows the opinions or teachings of another ⟨a circle of dedicated *disciples* who conscientiously wrote down everything the prophet said⟩ — see FOLLOWER 1

disciplinary *adj* inflicting, involving, or serving as punishment ⟨called for *disciplinary* actions in response to the outrageous behavior⟩ — see PUNITIVE

discipline *n* **1** a region of activity, knowledge, or influence ⟨you must choose a *discipline* to focus on in college⟩ — see FIELD 2

2 suffering, loss, or hardship imposed in response to a crime or offense ⟨harsh *discipline* was imposed to keep order within the ranks⟩ — see PUNISHMENT

3 the checking of one's true feelings and impulses when dealing with others ⟨she lacks the *discipline* that's essential for a job in customer relations⟩ — see CONSTRAINT 1

discipline *vb* to inflict a penalty on for a fault or crime ⟨the pranksters were severely *disciplined* for their irresponsible stunt⟩ — see PUNISH

disciplining *adj* inflicting, involving, or serving as punishment ⟨*disciplining* actions taken in response to the rowdiness⟩ — see PUNITIVE

disclaim *vb* **1** to refuse to acknowledge as one's own or as one's responsibility ⟨the prisoner *disclaimed* any part in the prank⟩

synonyms deny, disavow, disown, repudiate

related words contradict, disallow, gainsay, negate, negative, refuse, reject; challenge, confute, criticize, disprove, rebut, refute; dispute, question; abdicate, abjure, recant, renounce, retract

phrases wash one's hands of

near antonyms accept, adopt, embrace, espouse; admit, concede, confess, grant; affirm, announce, assert, aver, declare, maintain, profess, submit; authenticate, confirm, corroborate, substantiate, validate, verify

antonyms acknowledge, avow, claim, own, recognize

2 to declare not to be true ⟨her spokesperson flatly *disclaimed* the marriage rumor circulating in the press⟩ — see DENY 1

disclaimer *n* **1** a document containing a declaration of an intentional giving up of a right, claim, or privilege

⟨one brother filed a *disclaimer*, allowing all of the estate to go to his poorer siblings⟩ — see WAIVER
2 a refusal to confirm the truth of a statement ⟨the intelligence agency's pro forma *disclaimer* of any involvement in the assassination plot⟩ — see DENIAL 2

disclose *vb* to make known (as information previously kept secret) ⟨the informer *disclosed* all sorts of details about the secret organization⟩ — see REVEAL 1

disclosure *n* the act or an instance of making known something previously unknown or concealed ⟨he offered full *disclosure* of the government files on the assassination⟩ — see REVELATION

discombobulate *vb* to throw into a state of mental uncertainty ⟨our grandmother seems a bit *discombobulated* by all of this birthday fuss⟩ — see CONFUSE 1

discombobulation *n* a state of mental uncertainty ⟨in my *discombobulation* I mistook a bathroom door for an exit⟩ — see CONFUSION 1

discomfit *vb* **1** to prevent from achieving a goal ⟨constant interruptions *discomfited* her in her attempt to finish the speech, and she finally gave up⟩ — see FRUSTRATE 1
2 to throw into a state of self-conscious distress ⟨he was *discomfited* by the awkward situation of having his ex-girlfriend meet his current one⟩ — see EMBARRASS 1

discomfiting *adj* causing embarrassment ⟨the *discomfiting* scrutiny of an audience of music critics⟩ — see AWKWARD 3

discomfiture *n* the emotional state of being made self-consciously uncomfortable ⟨blushed and lowered her eyes in evident *discomfiture*⟩ — see EMBARRASSMENT 1

discomfort *vb* to trouble the mind of; to make uneasy ⟨the harsh criticism of his musical talent did not *discomfort* him in the least⟩ — see DISTURB 1

discomforting *adj* **1** causing discomfort ⟨a *discomforting* perch on the thin balcony rail⟩ — see UNCOMFORTABLE 1
2 causing worry or anxiety ⟨the layoff rumors created a *discomforting* situation for the workers who depend on the factory for a living⟩ — see TROUBLESOME

discommode *vb* to cause discomfort to or trouble for ⟨the breakdown of her car didn't *discommode* her seriously⟩ — see INCONVENIENCE

discommoding *adj* causing difficulty, discomfort, or annoyance ⟨the thoroughly unpleasant and *discommoding* experience of changing a flat tire in the rain⟩ — see INCONVENIENT 1

discompose *vb* **1** to trouble the mind of; to make uneasy ⟨*discomposed* by the tone of the message left on his answering machine⟩ — see DISTURB 1
2 to undo the proper order or arrangement of ⟨the wind ruffled her hair and *discomposed* her carefully arranged papers⟩ — see DISORDER

discomposing *adj* causing worry or anxiety ⟨a *discomposing* response to our routine query about her health⟩ — see TROUBLESOME

disconcert *vb* to throw into a state of self-conscious distress ⟨we were *disconcerted* by the unexpected changes to the program⟩ — see EMBARRASS 1

disconcerting *adj* causing embarrassment ⟨a *disconcerting* habit of chewing with his mouth open⟩ — see AWKWARD 3

disconcertment *n* the emotional state of being made self-consciously uncomfortable ⟨his *disconcertment* over having to tell the landlord he'd lost his key for the third time⟩ — see EMBARRASSMENT 1

disconfirm *vb* **1** to declare not to be true ⟨later updates on the news story *disconfirmed* many details of the initial report⟩ — see DENY 1
2 to prove to be false ⟨contends that we will never be able to confirm or *disconfirm* the existence of God⟩ — see DISPROVE

disconfirmation *n* **1** a refusal to confirm the truth of a statement ⟨an official *disconfirmation* of the rumors that the military was planning an invasion⟩ — see DENIAL 2
2 something (as an argument) that serves to disprove ⟨members of the sect refused to accept the scientific evidence as being in any way a *disconfirmation* of their deeply held religious beliefs⟩ — see CONFUTATION

disconnect *vb* to set or force apart ⟨*disconnected* the two parts of the light fixture⟩ — see SEPARATE 1

disconnected *adj* **1** not clearly or logically connected ⟨a *disconnected* narrative of her time in a mental hospital⟩ — see INCOHERENT 1
2 not physically attached to another unit ⟨a *disconnected* computer terminal⟩ — see SEPARATE 2

disconsolate *adj* **1** causing or marked by an atmosphere lacking in cheer ⟨spent her last years in the *disconsolate* environs of a cheap boarding house⟩ — see GLOOMY 1
2 feeling unhappiness ⟨she was utterly *disconsolate* when her best friend moved away⟩ — see SAD 1

disconsolateness *n* a state or spell of low spirits ⟨his *disconsolateness* over the loss of his dog threatened to last forever⟩ — see SADNESS

discontent *adj* having a feeling that one has been wronged or thwarted in one's ambitions ⟨a novel about a woman who is desperately *discontent* with the stifling limitations of her small-town life⟩ — see DISCONTENTED

discontent *n* the condition of being dissatisfied with one's life or situation ⟨the rebels worked to stir up *discontent* among the citizens⟩
synonyms discontentedness, discontentment, disgruntlement, displeasure, dissatisfaction
related words bitterness, resentment; aggrievement, disquiet, perturbation, uneasiness; blues, dejection, depression, desolateness, desolation, despondency, disconsolateness, doldrums, dolefulness, dolor, downheartedness, dreariness, dumps; misery, sadness, sorrow, unhappiness, wretchedness
near antonyms bliss, felicity, gladness, happiness, joy, lightheartedness; elatedness, exultation, jubilation, triumph
antonyms contentedness, contentment, pleasure, satisfaction

discontent *vb* to make discontented ⟨the ongoing lack of decent food *discontented* and demoralized the soldiers in the rebel army⟩
synonyms disaffect, disgruntle, displease, dissatisfy
related words alienate, estrange; aggrieve, agitate, discompose, disquiet, disturb, perturb, upset; annoy, irk, irritate, nettle, peeve; depress, sadden
near antonyms delight, gladden, tickle; calm, soothe, tranquilize (*also* tranquillize)
antonyms content, gratify, please, satisfy

discontented *adj* having a feeling that one has been wronged or thwarted in one's ambitions ⟨he was becoming increasingly *discontented* with his dead-end job and his dead-end life⟩
synonyms aggrieved, discontent, disgruntled, displeased, dissatisfied, malcontent
related words disappointed, disenchanted, disillusioned, frustrated, unfulfilled; disquieted, disturbed, perturbed, upset; dejected, depressed, despairing, despondent, disconsolate, doleful, down, downcast, downhearted, forlorn, hangdog, inconsolable, joyless, low-spirited, miserable, mournful, sad, sorrowful, unhappy
phrases out of joint
near antonyms blissful, delighted, glad, happy, joyful, joyous; elated, exultant, jubilant, triumphant
antonyms content, contented, gratified, pleased, satisfied

discontentedness *n* the condition of being dissatisfied with one's life or situation ⟨he was left with a vague feeling of *discontentedness* even after he got the car he had always wanted⟩ — see DISCONTENT

discontentment *n* the condition of being dissatisfied with one's life or situation ⟨widespread *discontentment* with the way the club was being run⟩ — see DISCONTENT

discontinuance *n* the stopping of a process or activity ⟨the possible *discontinuance* of one of the town's big holiday traditions⟩ — see END 1

discontinuation *n* the stopping of a process or activity ⟨*discontinuation* of treatment would almost certainly result in a reappearance of the cancer⟩ — see END 1

discontinue *vb* **1** to bring (as an action or operation) to an immediate end ⟨the editors were told to *discontinue* the printing of rumors in the student paper immediately⟩ — see STOP 1
2 to stop doing (something) permanently ⟨we have *discontinued* the manufacture of that item⟩ — see QUIT 2
3 to come to an end ⟨publication of the magazine will *discontinue* at the end of the year⟩ — see CEASE 1

discontinuity *n* **1** an open space in a barrier (as a wall or hedge) ⟨microscopic *discontinuities* in the connecting wires⟩ — see GAP 1
2 a break in continuity ⟨a noticeable *discontinuity* in the flow of the story⟩ — see GAP 2

discontinuous *adj* lacking in steadiness or regularity of occurrence ⟨the novel captures the *discontinuous* nature of a soldier's life: long stretches of boredom interrupted by flashes of chaos and panic⟩ — see FITFUL

discord *n* a lack of agreement or harmony ⟨the *discord* between two of the members threatened to tear our team of researchers apart⟩
synonyms conflict, disaccord, discordance, discordancy, disharmony, dissension (*also* dissention), dissent, dissidence, dissonance, disunion, disunity, division, friction, infighting, inharmony, schism, strife, variance, war, warfare
related words clash, collision, competition, contention; altercation, argument, bicker, brawl, debate, disagreement, dispute, divide, fissure; falling-out, fight, hassle, jar, miff, mix-up, quarrel, row, run-in, scrap, spat, squabble, tiff, wrangle; incompatibility, incongruence, incongruity, incongruousness, inconsistence, inconsistency, inconsonance, inharmoniousness; animosity, antagonism, antipathy, cold war, enmity, hostility, ill will, rancor
near antonyms concurrence, cooperation
antonyms accord, agreement, concord, concordance, harmony, peace

discord *vb* to be out of harmony or agreement usually noticeably ⟨the evangelist's lavish lifestyle *discords* with his professed religious beliefs⟩ — see CLASH

discordance *n* **1** a lack of agreement or harmony ⟨there was a real *discordance* between the tough guys that the actor played in the movies and the wimp that he was in real life⟩ — see DISCORD
2 loud, confused, and usually inharmonious sound ⟨the jarring *discordance* coming from the garage where the band was rehearsing⟩ — see NOISE 1

discordancy *n* a lack of agreement or harmony ⟨the *discordancy* between the film's flamboyant cinematography and its otherwise somber mood⟩ — see DISCORD

discordant *adj* **1** marked by or producing a harsh combination of sounds ⟨*discordant* tones coming from the poorly tuned instrument⟩ — see DISSONANT
2 making loud, confused, and usually unharmonious sounds ⟨the *discordant* cries of gulls fighting over the fishing boat's castoffs⟩ — see NOISY 1
3 feeling or displaying eagerness to fight ⟨a troubled, *discordant* family that would benefit from professional counseling⟩ — see BELLIGERENT
4 not being in agreement or harmony ⟨his views on the proper role of women are certainly *discordant* with most contemporary opinions on the subject⟩ — see INCONSISTENT 1

discount *n* something that is or may be subtracted ⟨a *discount* of 20% from the original price⟩ — see DEDUCTION 1

discount *vb* **1** to dismiss as of little importance ⟨even while acknowledging the primacy of the director, we should not *discount* the contributions of all the others who worked on the film⟩ — see EXCUSE 1
2 to express scornfully one's low opinion of ⟨shouldn't *discount* their contributions to our fund-raising efforts⟩ — see DECRY 1

discountenance *n* refusal to accept as right or desirable ⟨made known his long-standing *discountenance* of any form of religious belief⟩ — see DISAPPROVAL

discountenance *vb* **1** to hold an unfavorable opinion of ⟨a social philosopher who *discountenanced* all programs for helping the needy, claiming that society should encourage survival of the fittest⟩ — see DISAPPROVE (OF)
2 to throw into a state of self-conscious distress ⟨the political party was *discountenanced* by the actions of a few of its overly zealous members⟩ — see EMBARRASS 1

discourage *vb* **1** to lessen the courage or confidence of ⟨I didn't let losing *discourage* me from trying again⟩
synonyms chill, daunt, demoralize, dishearten, dismay, dispirit, frustrate, unman, unnerve
related words browbeat, bully, cow, intimidate; depress, sadden, weigh; afflict, try; damp, dampen, deaden; distress, trouble; bother, irk, vex, worry; debilitate, enfeeble, undermine, weaken; frighten, horrify, scare
phrases throw cold water on
near antonyms buoy (up), cheer, gladden; animate, enliven, invigorate; enforce, fortify, reinforce (*also* reenforce), strengthen; assure, reassure; boost, energize, excite, galvanize, inspire, lift, provoke, quicken, rally, stimulate, stir
antonyms embolden, encourage, hearten, nerve, steel
2 to steer (a person) from an activity or course of action ⟨the higher fines may help *discourage* drivers from speeding on the highway⟩
synonyms deter, dissuade, inhibit
related words divert; unsell; repel
near antonyms egg (on), exhort, goad, prod, urge; impel, induce, prompt
antonyms encourage, persuade

discouragement *n* the state of being discouraged ⟨I tried desperately to avoid *discouragement* after failing the bar exam twice⟩
synonyms demoralization, despair, despondency, disheartenment, dismay, dispiritedness
related words blues, dejection, depression, dumps, gloom, melancholy, mopes; defeatism, pessimism, resignation
near antonyms optimism, sanguinity
antonyms encouragement

discourse *n* talking or a talk between two or more people ⟨Thomas Jefferson is said to have been able to participate in knowledgeable *discourse* on a breathtaking array of subjects⟩ — see CONVERSATION

discourse *vb* **1** to give a formal often extended talk on a subject ⟨the guest lecturer *discoursed* at some length on the long-term results of the war⟩ — see TALK 1
2 to talk as if giving an important and formal speech ⟨grandly *discoursed* as though he were an expert on every subject⟩ — see ORATE 1

discourteous *adj* showing a lack of manners or consideration for others ⟨wouldn't tolerate anything so *dis-*

courteous as the interruption of another speaker during a discussion⟩ — see IMPOLITE

discourteousness *n* rude behavior ⟨a campaign to try to remedy the increasing *discourteousness* of the state's drivers⟩ — see DISCOURTESY

discourtesy *n* rude behavior ⟨the courtiers shuddered at the *discourtesy* shown to the king⟩
synonyms dis (*also* diss) [*slang*], discourteousness, disrespect, disrespectfulness, impertinence, impertinency, impoliteness, impudence, incivility, inconsiderateness, inconsideration, insolence, rudeness, ungraciousness
related words audacity, boldness, brashness, brassiness, forwardness, sauciness, shamelessness; boorishness, caddishness, churlishness, clownishness, crudeness, loutishness, vulgarity; abruptness, bluntness, brusqueness, crustiness, curtness, gruffness, sharpness; crabbedness, crossness, disagreeableness, grumpiness, sullenness, surliness; improperness, impropriety, inappropriateness, incorrectness, indecency, unfitness, unsuitability; arrogance, conceit, conceitedness, presumption, pretense (*or* pretence), pretension, pretentiousness
near antonyms humility, meekness, modesty; deference, dutifulness, respectfulness, submissiveness; acceptability, appropriateness, correctness, decency, decorousness, fitness, goodness, propriety, respectability, respectableness, rightness, seemliness, suitability, suitableness; affability, cordiality, friendliness, geniality, hospitality, kindness; felicitousness, grace, gracefulness
antonyms civility, considerateness, consideration, courtesy, genteelness, gentility, graciousness, politeness, politesse, thoughtfulness

discover *vb* **1** to come to an awareness of ⟨I was startled to *discover* that my keys were missing⟩
synonyms ascertain, catch on (to), find out, get on (to), hear, learn, realize, see, wise (up)
related words hit (on *or* upon), tumble (to); descry, detect, encounter, espy, see, spot; calculate, dope (out), figure out, find, puzzle (out); discern, mind, note, observe, perceive; divine
phrases get wind of
near antonyms miss, overlook; disregard, ignore; forget, unlearn; blanket, blot out, cloak, conceal, cover, curtain, enshroud, hide, mask, occult, screen, shroud, veil
2 to come upon after searching, study, or effort ⟨we hope to *discover* the real reason for his odd behavior⟩ — see FIND 1
3 to make known (as information previously kept secret) ⟨*discovered* to his friend how people whom he had trusted had betrayed him⟩ — see REVEAL 1

discovery *n* **1** the act or process of sighting or learning the existence of something for the first time ⟨the *discovery* of a new species of starfish⟩
synonyms detection, finding, spotting, unearthing
related words awareness, espial, notice; disclosure, exposure, revelation, uncovering, unveiling; creation, invention; exploration; rediscovery
near antonyms disappearance, loss; concealment, hiding
2 something discovered ⟨his many zoological *discoveries* include several species of birds⟩
synonyms find
related words pay dirt, strike, treasure trove; breakthrough

discredit *n* the state of having lost the esteem of others ⟨to his everlasting *discredit*, the coach was found to have placed bets against his own team⟩ — see DISGRACE 1

discredit *vb* **1** to reduce to a lower standing in one's own eyes or in others' eyes ⟨attempted to *discredit* her political opponents by deliberately spreading false rumors⟩ — see HUMBLE
2 to think not to be true or real ⟨I *discredit* the story that the old inn is haunted⟩ — see DISBELIEVE
3 to prove to be false ⟨the pseudoscience of phrenology has been thoroughly *discredited*⟩ — see DISPROVE

discreditable *adj* not respectable ⟨the *discreditable* conduct of drunken college students celebrating a win by their team⟩ — see DISREPUTABLE

discreet *adj* **1** having or showing good judgment and restraint especially in conduct or speech ⟨he was very *discreet*, only saying what was necessary⟩
synonyms intelligent, judgmatic (*or* judgmatical), judicious, prudent
related words cautious, chary, circumspect, cozy; forehanded, foresighted, foresightful, forethoughtful; discerning, discriminating, sage, sane, sapient, senseful, sensible, wise; canny, provident; astute, perspicacious, sagacious, shrewd
near antonyms careless, heedless, incautious, rash; improvident, shortsighted; foolish, unwise
antonyms imprudent, indiscreet, injudicious
2 not readily seen or noticed ⟨with a *discreet* gesture, she signalled to her husband that she was ready to leave the party⟩ — see UNOBTRUSIVE

discreetness *n* the ability to make intelligent decisions especially in everyday matters ⟨I appreciated her *discreetness* in keeping quiet about my inability to pay for our date⟩ — see COMMON SENSE

discrepancy *n* the quality or state of being different ⟨the *discrepancy* of the calculations of my bill by the hotel and myself was a matter of concern⟩ — see DIFFERENCE 1

discrepant *adj* not being in agreement or harmony ⟨widely *discrepant* conclusions on the impact the real estate development would have on the local environment⟩ — see INCONSISTENT 1

discrete *adj* not physically attached to another unit ⟨several *discrete* sections to this vast medical complex, including a college of pharmacology and a research center⟩ — see SEPARATE 2

discreteness *n* the state of being kept distinct ⟨the *discreteness* of the sonnets is given visual emphasis by having each one on a separate page⟩ — see SEPARATION 2

discretion *n* **1** the ability to make intelligent decisions especially in everyday matters ⟨we'll rely on your *discretion* in handling this accusation of cheating⟩ — see COMMON SENSE
2 the power, right, or opportunity to choose ⟨ambassadorships are generally regarded as subject to the president's *discretion*⟩ — see CHOICE 1
3 the checking of one's true feelings and impulses when dealing with others ⟨in that job you'll be expected to show *discretion* and act like a professional at all times⟩ — see CONSTRAINT 1

discretionary *adj* subject to one's freedom of choice ⟨*discretionary* spending on luxuries dropped dramatically last year⟩ — see OPTIONAL

discriminate *vb* to understand or point out the difference in ⟨the human eye can *discriminate* between very slight gradations of color⟩ — see DISTINGUISH 1

discriminating *adj* **1** favoring, applying, or being unequal treatment of different classes of people ⟨accused of *discriminating* practices in the hiring of employees⟩ — see DISCRIMINATORY
2 serving to identify as belonging to an individual or group ⟨a *discriminating* feature of poison ivy is a compound leaf with three mitten-shaped leaflets⟩ — see CHARACTERISTIC 1

discrimination *n* the state of being kept distinct ⟨in her mind there did not exist a *discrimination* between the imaginary and the real⟩ — see SEPARATION 2

discriminational *adj* favoring, applying, or being unequal treatment of different classes of people ⟨are you guilty of *discriminational* behavior toward people unlike yourself?⟩ — see DISCRIMINATORY

discriminative *adj* favoring, applying, or being unequal treatment of different classes of people ⟨fighting laws which were grossly *discriminative*⟩ — see DISCRIMINATORY

discriminatory *adj* favoring, applying, or being unequal treatment of different classes of people ⟨a company that was fined for its *discriminatory* practices in the hiring of women⟩
synonyms differential, discriminating, discriminational, discriminative
related words biased, inequitable, partial, partisan, prejudiced, prejudicial, unequal, unfair, unjust; clubby, elitist, selective; segregative
near antonyms equal, equitable, fair, just; impartial, neutral, objective, unbiased, uncolored, unprejudiced
antonyms nondiscriminatory

discursive *adj* passing from one topic to another ⟨the speaker's *discursive* style made it difficult to understand his point⟩
synonyms desultory, digressional, digressionary, digressive, excursive, leaping, maundering, meandering, rambling, wandering
related words circuitous, deviating, devious, indirect, roundabout
near antonyms coherent, consistent, logical; direct, focused (*also* focussed), straightforward, undeviating

discuss *vb* to talk about (an issue) usually from various points of view and for the purpose of arriving at a decision or opinion ⟨we *discussed* the new proposal for the school stadium⟩
synonyms agitate, argue, bandy, bat (around *or* back and forth), canvass (*also* canvas), debate, dispute, hash (over *or* out), moot, talk over
related words review, speak (about), talk (about); broach, introduce, propound, raise, stir up; forge, hammer out, talk out, thrash (out), wrestle (with); chew over, consider, deliberate, weigh

discussion *n* **1** an exchange of views for the purpose of exploring a subject or deciding an issue ⟨the *discussion* about the club budget went on for hours⟩
synonyms argument, argumentation, argy-bargy [*chiefly British*], back-and-forth, colloquy, confab, confabulation, conference, consult, consultation, council, counsel, debate, deliberation, dialogue (*also* dialog), give-and-take, palaver, parley, talk
related words bull session, chat room, forum, meeting, powwow, roundtable, seminar, skull session (*also* skull practice), symposium, talkathon; chat, conversation, rap, words; discourse, disquisition; bargaining, consultancy, negotiation, pourparler
2 talking or a talk between two or more people ⟨*discussions* around the watercooler at work⟩ — see CONVERSATION

disdain *n* open dislike for someone or something considered unworthy of one's concern or respect ⟨showing undisguised *disdain* for the other employees⟩ — see CONTEMPT

disdain *vb* to show contempt for ⟨*disdained* the deserter as a coward⟩ — see SCORN 1

disdainful *adj* **1** feeling or showing open dislike for someone or something regarded as undeserving of respect or concern ⟨a *disdainful* attitude toward people who work as waiters and waitresses⟩ — see CONTEMPTUOUS 1
2 having or displaying feelings of scorn for what is regarded as beneath oneself ⟨*disdainful* of manual labor of any kind⟩ — see PROUD 1
3 intended to make a person or thing seem of little importance or value ⟨*disdainful* remarks regarding the cheap clothes that the local people were wearing⟩ — see DEROGATORY

disease *n* an abnormal state that disrupts a plant's or animal's normal bodily functioning ⟨they caught a rare *disease* while they were traveling in Africa and were sick for weeks⟩
synonyms affection, ail, ailment, bug, complaint, complication, condition, disorder, distemper, distemperature, fever, ill, illness, infirmity, malady, sickness, trouble
related words contagion, contagious disease; contagium, infection; attack, bout, fit, spell; debility, decrepitude, feebleness, frailness, lameness, sickliness, unhealthiness, unsoundness, unwellness, weakness; malaise, matter, pip; epidemic, pest, pestilence, plague
near antonyms fitness, healthiness, heartiness, robustness, soundness, wholeness, wholesomeness; fettle, shape
antonyms health, wellness

disembark *vb* **1** to go ashore from a ship ⟨the cruise passengers *disembarked* as soon as they got to the terminal in Miami⟩
synonyms debark, land
related words beach; anchor, dock, put in
near antonyms board, get (on); weigh (anchor)
antonyms embark
2 to come down from something (as a vehicle) ⟨before you *disembark*, make sure you haven't left anything on your seat⟩ — see ALIGHT 2

disembarrass *vb* to set free from entanglement or difficulty ⟨still struggling to *disembarrass* herself of the emotional baggage of a failed relationship⟩ — see EXTRICATE

disembowel *vb* to take the internal organs out of ⟨ancient Roman prophets would *disembowel* animals in order to read the future from their entrails⟩ — see GUT

disenchant *vb* to free from mistaken beliefs or foolish hopes ⟨if you thought that you could pass this course without doing any work, let me be the first to *disenchant* you⟩ — see DISILLUSION

disencumber *vb* **1** to empty or rid of cargo ⟨we *disencumbered* our pack animals as soon as we made camp that night⟩ — see UNLOAD 1
2 to set (a person or thing) free of something that encumbers ⟨a simple statement of the terms of the contract *disencumbered* of legal jargon⟩ — see RID

disencumbered *adj* no longer burdened with something unpleasant or painful ⟨the paying off of my loan left me feeling delightfully *disencumbered*⟩ — see FREE 2

disengage *vb* to set free from entanglement or difficulty ⟨sought to *disengage* myself from the embarrassing situation⟩ — see EXTRICATE

disentangle *vb* **1** to separate the various strands of ⟨it took forever to *disentangle* the knot⟩ — see UNRAVEL 1
2 to set free from entanglement or difficulty ⟨the years that it took to *disentangle* ourselves from our troubles after someone started using our social security numbers⟩ — see EXTRICATE

disenthrall *also* **disenthral** *vb* to set free (as from slavery or confinement) ⟨we must *disenthrall* ourselves from time-honored ways of doing things, or we will never progress as a society⟩ — see FREE 1

disesteem *n* **1** refusal to accept as right or desirable ⟨made clear his *disesteem* of her decision to pursue an acting career⟩ — see DISAPPROVAL
2 the state of having lost the esteem of others ⟨the medical researcher had fallen into great *disesteem* after having been caught faking her lab results⟩ — see DISGRACE 1

disesteem *vb* to hold an unfavorable opinion of ⟨a survey showing that both candidates are *disesteemed* by the majority of eligible voters⟩ — see DISAPPROVE (OF)

disfavor *n* **1** a strong feeling of not liking or approving ⟨made no attempt to hide his *disfavor* of his wife's relatives⟩ — see DISLIKE 1

2 refusal to accept as right or desirable ⟨their suggestion was met with *disfavor* by virtually all of the other club members⟩ — see DISAPPROVAL

3 the negative result caused by something that creates difficulty for achieving success ⟨the defendant certainly acted to his own *disfavor* with his frequent outbursts⟩ — see DISADAVANTAGE 2

disfavor *vb* **1** to feel dislike for ⟨a style of stage acting that is *disfavored* by most theatergoers today⟩ — see DISLIKE 1

2 to hold an unfavorable opinion of ⟨polls showing that this political candidate is highly *disfavored* by most voters⟩ — see DISAPPROVE (OF)

disfigure *vb* to reduce the soundness, effectiveness, or perfection of ⟨the statue was seriously *disfigured* by falling rubble during the earthquake⟩ — see DAMAGE 1

disfigurement *n* something that spoils the appearance or completeness of a thing ⟨a plastic surgeon who occasionally donates his services to treat the *disfigurements* of needy children⟩ — see BLEMISH

disgorge *vb* to violently throw out or off (something from within) ⟨the volcano *disgorged* lava in a spectacular nighttime show⟩ — see ERUPT 1

disgrace *n* **1** the state of having lost the esteem of others ⟨the players who threw the game were in *disgrace* with their schoolmates⟩
synonyms discredit, disesteem, dishonor, disrepute, ignominy, infamy, obloquy, odium, opprobrium, reproach, shame
related words scandal; contempt, despite, disdain, scorn; deprecation, disapprobation, disapproval, disfavor; abasement, debasement, debasing, degradation, dust, humbling, humiliation; blot, brand, shadow, slur, smirch, spot, stain, stigma, taint
near antonyms admiration, appreciation, estimation, regard; awe, fear, reverence; fame, glory, renown, repute
antonyms esteem, honor, respect

2 a cause of shame ⟨the exposure of his criminal record was a huge *disgrace* for the councilman⟩
synonyms dishonor, opprobrium, reflection, reproach, scandal
related words blot, brand, slur, smirch, spot, stain, stigma, taint
near antonyms boast, glory, jewel, pride, treasure
antonyms credit, honor

3 a regrettable or blameworthy act ⟨it's a *disgrace* to let all the leftover food from the banquet go to waste, so let's deliver it to the homeless shelter⟩ — see CRIME 2

disgrace *vb* to reduce to a lower standing in one's own eyes or in others' eyes ⟨*disgraced* by the shameful actions of their leader⟩ — see HUMBLE

disgraceful *adj* not respectable ⟨*disgraceful* disruptions at the graduation ceremonies⟩ — see DISREPUTABLE

disgruntle *vb* **1** to cause to change from friendly or loving to unfriendly or uncaring ⟨an employee, *disgruntled* by the restaurant owner's shabby treatment, turned him in to the IRS⟩ — see ESTRANGE

2 to make discontented ⟨a crew *disgruntled* by a long voyage that provided no opportunity for recreation onshore⟩ — see DISCONTENT

disgruntled *adj* having a feeling that one has been wronged or thwarted in one's ambitions ⟨a *disgruntled* postal worker was responsible for the vandalism⟩ — see DISCONTENTED

disgruntlement *n* **1** the condition of being dissatisfied with one's life or situation ⟨a survey showing the extent of people's satisfaction—or *disgruntlement*—with their marriages⟩ — see DISCONTENT

2 the loss of friendship or affection ⟨feelings of neglect that inevitably lead to *disgruntlement* among employees⟩ — see ESTRANGEMENT

disguise *n* **1** clothing put on to hide one's true identity or imitate someone or something else ⟨Mardi Gras revelers dressed in a colorful array of outlandish *disguises*⟩
synonyms camouflage, costume, guise
related words domino, mask, veil, visor (*also* vizor), vizard; costumery, dress, getup, outfit, rig; coloring, cosmetic, makeup, paint

2 a display of emotion or behavior that is insincere or intended to deceive ⟨somehow, he managed to put on a *disguise* of happiness as he watched his secret crush marry someone else⟩ — see MASQUERADE

disguise *vb* **1** to change the dress or looks of so as to conceal true identity ⟨the spies *disguised* themselves as harmless tourists⟩
synonyms camouflage, cloak, dress up, mask
related words blanket, blot out, conceal, cover, curtain, enshroud, hide, obscure, occult, screen, shroud, veil; affect, assume, counterfeit, dissemble, dissimulate, feign, pose, pretend, sham, simulate; act, fake, impersonate, masquerade, play; cosmeticize, gild, gloss (over), varnish, whitewash
near antonyms display, exhibit, expose, flaunt, parade, show, uncloak, unclothe, uncover, undrape, unveil; bare, betray, disclose, discover, divulge, expose, reveal
antonyms unmask

2 to keep secret or shut off from view ⟨that investigative reporter usually does a good job of *disguising* her true motives for interviewing a person⟩ — see [1]HIDE 2

disgust *n* a dislike so strong as to cause stomach upset or queasiness ⟨we turned from the grisly scene with *disgust*⟩
synonyms aversion, distaste, horror, loathing, nausea, repugnance, repulsion, revulsion
related words abhorrence, abomination, antipathy, execration, hate, hatred; allergy, averseness, disapproval, disfavor, disinclination, dislike, disliking, displeasure
near antonyms appetite, bent, fancy, favor, fondness, like, liking, love, partiality, penchant, predilection, preference, propensity, relish, shine, taste, use

disgust *vb* to cause to feel disgust ⟨the movie's graphic, nonstop violence *disgusted* us⟩
synonyms gross out, nauseate, put off, repel, repulse, revolt, sicken, turn off
related words displease, distress; appall (*also* appal), disquiet, horrify; affront, insult, offend, outrage, shock
phrases turn one's stomach
near antonyms allure, attract, beguile, bewitch, captivate, charm, disarm, draw, enchant, entice, fascinate, lure, pull, seduce, tempt; delight, gratify, please, rejoice, tickle; enrapture, enthrall (*or* enthral), entrance; appeal (to), interest, intrigue

disgusted *adj* filled with disgust ⟨the *disgusted* diners left, vowing to report the restaurant to the board of health⟩ — see SICK 2

disgusting *adj* causing intense displeasure, disgust, or resentment ⟨when we cleaned the room, we found a *disgusting* plate of moldy food under the bed⟩ — see OFFENSIVE 1

dish *n* **1** a usually circular utensil for holding something (as food) ⟨we threw all of the ingredients for the salsa into a *dish* and mixed them together⟩
synonyms vessel
related words bowl, casserole, charger, cup, plate, platter, salver, saucer, server, tray, waiter

2 a physically attractive person ⟨what a *dish* my blind date turned out to be!⟩ — see DOLL 2

3 information or opinion that is widely disseminated

without any authority or confirmation of accuracy ⟨she's the one to go to if you want the latest office *dish*⟩ — see RUMOR

dish *vb* to relate sometimes questionable or secret information of a personal nature ⟨for someone who claims to mind her own business, she sure knows how to *dish*⟩ — see GOSSIP

disharmony *n* a lack of agreement or harmony ⟨having witnessed so much domestic *disharmony* while growing up, he was in no rush to join the ranks of the married⟩ — see DISCORD

dishearten *vb* to lessen the courage or confidence of ⟨we were *disheartened* by the news that our grandmother was seriously ill⟩ — see DISCOURAGE 1

disheartenment *n* the state of being discouraged ⟨our excusable *disheartenment* in the face of overwhelming odds against winning the game⟩ — see DISCOURAGEMENT

dished *adj* curved inward ⟨Arabian horses are noted for their *dished* muzzles and large eyes⟩ — see HOLLOW

dishevel *vb* to undo the proper order or arrangement of ⟨decorations for the garden wedding that had been *disheveled* by the wind⟩ — see DISORDER

disheveled *or* **dishevelled** *adj* lacking in order, neatness, and often cleanliness ⟨a slovenly woman with *disheveled* hair and a cigarette hanging out of her mouth⟩ — see MESSY

dishevelment *n* a state in which everything is out of order ⟨given the degree of *dishevelment* in your workstation, it's a miracle that you can ever find anything⟩ — see CHAOS

dishonest *adj* **1** telling or containing lies ⟨*dishonest* kids who lie about their ages in order to get into R-rated movies⟩ ⟨*dishonest* statements on the claims form⟩
synonyms lying, mendacious, untruthful
related words erroneous, fallacious, false, misleading, untrue; double-dealing, hypocrite, hypocritical, insincere, mealymouthed, smooth-tongued, two-faced; perjurious
near antonyms candid, open, plainspoken, straightforward; earnest, sincere, true; conscientious, moral, principled, scrupulous; dependable, reliable, trustable, trustworthy, trusty; decent, ethical, honorable, just, respectable, righteous, right-minded, straight, upright, upstanding, virtuous
antonyms honest, truthful, veracious
2 given to or marked by cheating and deception ⟨*dishonest* car dealers who roll back mileage gauges⟩ ⟨*dishonest* business deals that landed him in jail⟩
synonyms bent [*chiefly British*], crooked, deceptive, double-dealing, duplicitous, fast, fraudulent, guileful, rogue, shady, sharp, shifty, underhand, underhanded
related words unconscionable, unethical, unprincipled, unscrupulous; deceitful, deceiving, deluding, delusive, delusory, false; artful, beguiling, cagey (*also* cagy), crafty, cunning, foxy, slick, sly, subtle, wily; defrauding, devious, furtive, slippery, sneaking, sneaky, trickish, tricky; insidious, perfidious, treacherous
near antonyms conscientious, decent, ethical, honorable, just, scrupulous, upright; forthright, straightforward
antonyms aboveboard, honest, straight
3 marked by, based on, or done by the use of dishonest methods to acquire something of value ⟨*dishonest* appraisals of art works that were part of an elaborate scheme to defraud insurance companies⟩ — see FRAUDULENT 1

dishonesty *n* **1** the tendency to tell lies ⟨if you gain a reputation for *dishonesty*, no one will believe you even when you're telling the truth⟩
synonyms deceit, deceitfulness, falsehood, mendaciousness, mendacity, untruthfulness
related words artifice, craft, craftiness, crookedness, cunning, dissembling, dissimulation, double-dealing, duplicity, fakery, foxiness, guile, guilefulness, insincerity, trickishness, wiliness; falseness; hypocrisy
near antonyms honor, incorruptibility; candidness, candor, frankness, good faith, plainspokenness, sincerity, straightforwardness; dependability, reliability, reliableness, trustworthiness; accuracy, objectivity; authenticity, correctness, genuineness; credibility
antonyms honesty, integrity, probity, truthfulness, veraciousness, veracity, verity
2 the inclination or practice of misleading others through lies or trickery ⟨a religious cult that recruits members through *dishonesty* and subterfuge⟩ — see DECEIT 1

dishonor *n* **1** the state of having lost the esteem of others ⟨a person of integrity who would prefer death to *dishonor*⟩ — see DISGRACE 1
2 a cause of shame ⟨your expulsion from the military academy for cheating is a *dishonor* to this family⟩ — see DISGRACE 2

dishonor *vb* to reduce to a lower standing in one's own eyes or in others' eyes ⟨*dishonored* herself by fixing the results of her medical research⟩ — see HUMBLE

dishonorable *adj* **1** not following or in accordance with standards of honor and decency ⟨resorted to *dishonorable* tactics in order to win first place in the science fair⟩ — see IGNOBLE 2
2 not respectable ⟨*dishonorable* conduct shown by some people while visiting foreign countries⟩ — see DISREPUTABLE

dishy *adj* **1** having the style and content of everyday conversation ⟨twice a week he churns out a *dishy* column on the latest tidings from Tinseltown⟩ — see CHATTY 1
2 sexually attractive ⟨cast a *dishy* redhead in the main role, even though her acting skills seem minimal⟩ — see SEXY 1

disillusion *vb* to free from mistaken beliefs or foolish hopes ⟨we were *disillusioned* when we saw how the movie star acted in real life⟩
synonyms disabuse, disenchant, undeceive
related words sophisticate; advise, apprise, clue (in), fill in, wise (up); debunk, expose, refute, show up, uncloak, uncover, unmask; disclose, divulge, spill, tell, unveil
near antonyms beguile, bluff, cozen, delude, dupe, fool, gull, hoax, hoodwink, kid, misguide, misinform, mislead, misrepresent, snow, take in, trick

disinclination *n* **1** a lack of willingness or desire to do or accept something ⟨it's an understatement to say that our dog shows a *disinclination* to get into the car to go to the vet⟩ — see RELUCTANCE
2 a strong feeling of not liking or approving ⟨a strong *disinclination* for Brussels sprouts since birth⟩ — see DISLIKE 1

disinclined *adj* slow to begin or proceed with a course of action because of doubts or uncertainty ⟨*disinclined* to pay his friends a visit without calling first⟩ — see HESITANT

disintegrate *vb* **1** to go through decomposition ⟨fallen leaves slowly *disintegrate* over the course of the winter⟩ — see DECAY 1
2 to reduce to fine particles ⟨modern air pollution is gradually *disintegrating* the ancient temple's irreplaceable friezes⟩ — see POWDER

disinter *vb* to remove from place of burial ⟨the Egyptian mummy was carefully *disinterred* in hopes that it would yield secrets about the Old Kingdom⟩ — see EXHUME

disinterest *n* lack of favoritism toward one side or another ⟨since the coach has a son on the team, his *disin-*

terest in the selection of a team captain cannot be assumed⟩ — see DETACHMENT 1

disinterested *adj* **1** having or showing a lack of interest or concern ⟨the city's philistines, naturally *disinterested* in art, voted to cut the museum's budget⟩ — see INDIFFERENT 1

2 marked by justice, honesty, and freedom from bias ⟨a judge who is widely respected for his *disinterested* decisions⟩ — see FAIR 2

disinterestedness *n* **1** lack of favoritism toward one side or another ⟨the *disinterestedness* with which the newspaper reports stories earns it the respect and trust of the community⟩ — see DETACHMENT 1

2 lack of interest or concern ⟨a fair measure of the level of *disinterestedness* in the proceedings was the near-constant yawning by both participants and observers⟩ — see INDIFFERENCE

disjoin *vb* to set or force apart ⟨*disjoined* the two drinking glasses, which were stuck together, only with the greatest difficulty⟩ — see SEPARATE 1

disjoint *vb* **1** to set or force apart ⟨*disjoint* the parts of a chicken for frying⟩ — see SEPARATE 1

2 to undo the proper order or arrangement of ⟨the author deliberately *disjoints* his narrative in favor of a more impressionistic account of the war⟩ — see DISORDER

disjointed *adj* not clearly or logically connected ⟨a *disjointed* harangue about a hodgepodge of things that are supposedly wrong with our society⟩ — see INCOHERENT 1

dislike *n* **1** a strong feeling of not liking or approving ⟨we have a strong *dislike* for olives and wouldn't eat them even if we were paid⟩

synonyms allergy, averseness, aversion, disfavor, disinclination, disliking, disrelish, down [*chiefly British*], mislike

related words disgust, distaste, loathing, nausea, repugnance, repulsion, revulsion; abhorrence, abomination, antipathy, detestation, execration, hate, hatred; deprecation, disapproval, displeasure, dissatisfaction; jaundice

near antonyms affection, attachment, devotedness, devotion, love, passion; bent, leaning, penchant, predilection, propensity, tendency

antonyms appetite, favor, fondness, like, liking, partiality, preference, relish, shine, taste, use

2 refusal to accept as right or desirable ⟨the public's general *dislike* of negative campaign ads⟩ — see DISAPPROVAL

dislike *vb* **1** to feel dislike for ⟨the two dogs *disliked* each other the first time they met, and never did become friends⟩

synonyms disfavor, disrelish, mislike

related words abhor, abominate, detest, execrate, hate, loathe, resent; condemn, despise, scorn; cringe (at), disapprove (of), frown (on *or* upon), mind, object (to), shy (from *or* away from)

near antonyms admire, appreciate, cherish, esteem, regard, respect; adore, deify, idolize, revere, reverence, venerate, worship; prize, treasure, value; drink (in), savor (*also* savour); dote (on), idolize; favor, prefer

antonyms adore, cotton (to), delight (in), dig, enjoy, fancy, groove (on), like, love, relish, revel (in)

2 to hold an unfavorable opinion of ⟨*dislike* the governor's heavy-handed way of pushing his agenda⟩ — see DISAPPROVE (OF)

disliking *n* a strong feeling of not liking or approving ⟨I had taken an instant *disliking* to the new neighbors⟩ — see DISLIKE 1

dislimn *vb* to make dark, dim, or indistinct ⟨the apparition hovered, became *dislimned* by the fog, then disappeared altogether⟩ — see CLOUD 1

dislocate *vb* **1** to change the place or position of ⟨*dislocated* his shoulder in the accident⟩ — see MOVE 1

2 to undo the proper order or arrangement of ⟨the country's entire social structure was *dislocated* by the war⟩ — see DISORDER

dislocation *n* an act or instance of the order of things being disturbed ⟨the slightest *dislocation* in her daily routine bothered the elderly woman⟩ — see UPSET

disloyal *adj* not true in one's allegiance to someone or something ⟨we sensed that he was *disloyal* and would eventually turn on us⟩ — see FAITHLESS

disloyalty *n* **1** lack of faithfulness especially to one's husband or wife ⟨she was greatly pained by her husband's *disloyalty*⟩ — see INFIDELITY 1

2 the act or fact of violating the trust or confidence of another ⟨sexual abuse of a young person by a clergyman is usually regarded as the ultimate *disloyalty*⟩ — see BETRAYAL

dismal *adj* **1** causing or marked by an atmosphere lacking in cheer ⟨a suitably *dismal* setting for a haunted house⟩ — see GLOOMY 1

2 causing unhappiness ⟨the *dismal* failure of our hopes for the championship⟩ — see SAD 2

3 extremely unsatisfactory ⟨the quarterback's *dismal* performance suggested that he had not fully recovered from his recent injury⟩ — see WRETCHED 1

dismantle *vb* to take apart ⟨*dismantle* the table for easier transport⟩ — see DISASSEMBLE 1

dismay *n* **1** the emotion felt when one's expectations are not met ⟨filled with *dismay* at not making the finals⟩ — see DISAPPOINTMENT 1

2 the state of being discouraged ⟨in my *dismay* I failed to realize that there would be other chances⟩ — see DISCOURAGEMENT

dismay *vb* **1** to lessen the courage or confidence of ⟨the imposing climb up the mountain *dismayed* us even before we got started⟩ — see DISCOURAGE 1

2 to trouble the mind of; to make uneasy ⟨parents who became increasingly *dismayed* by their son's foundering marriage⟩ — see DISTURB 1

dismember *vb* **1** to cause to separate into pieces usually suddenly or forcibly ⟨quickly *dismembered* the old toolshed and hauled it off to the dump⟩ — see BREAK 1

2 to take apart ⟨*dismembered* the stage settings after the last performance⟩ — see DISASSEMBLE 1

dismiss *vb* **1** to let go from office, service, or employment ⟨the secretary was *dismissed* after it was discovered that she was stealing office supplies⟩

synonyms ax (*or* axe), bounce, can, cashier, discharge, fire, muster out, pink-slip, release, remove, retire, sack, terminate, turn off

related words downsize, excess, furlough, lay off, trim; boot (out), chuck (out), drum (out), kick out, throw out, unseat; separate

phrases send packing, show (one) the door

near antonyms keep; reemploy, rehire; contract, subcontract; recruit

antonyms employ, engage, hire, retain, sign (up *or* on), take on

2 to drive or force out ⟨the sick boy's nurse *dismissed* the visitors so he could get some rest⟩ — see EJECT 1

3 to express scornfully one's low opinion of ⟨critics *dismissed* his music as mere noise⟩ — see DECRY 1

dismissal *n* the termination of the employment of an employee or a work force often temporarily ⟨numerous *dismissals* from the company during the economic slump⟩ — see LAYOFF 1

dismount *vb* **1** to come down from something (as a vehicle) ⟨the coachman *dismounted* from his seat in order to assist the weary travelers⟩ — see ALIGHT 2

2 to take apart ⟨*dismount* a revolver for cleaning⟩ — see DISASSEMBLE 1

disobedience *n* refusal to obey ⟨they gave up on training the dog to fetch because of his constant *disobedience*⟩
synonyms balkiness, contrariness, contumacy, defiance, frowardness, insubordination, intractability, obstreperousness, rebellion, rebelliousness, recalcitrance, refractoriness, unruliness, waywardness, willfulness
related words civil disobedience, noncooperation; discourteousness, disrespect, impertinence, impoliteness, impudence, inconsiderateness, inconsideration, insolence, rudeness, ungraciousness; doggedness, hardheadedness, mulishness, obduracy, obdurateness, obstinacy, obstinateness, peevishness, pertinaciousness, pertinacity, perversity, pigheadedness, self-will, stubbornness, tenaciousness, tenacity; knavery, mischievousness, naughtiness
near antonyms agreeability, amenability, amiability; slavishness, submissiveness, subservience, subserviency; trainability; deference, docility, dutifulness
antonyms compliance, obedience, submission, subordinateness, subordination, tractability, tractableness

disobedient *adj* given to resisting authority or another's control ⟨the *disobedient* child refused to eat his vegetables⟩
synonyms balky, contrary, contumacious, defiant, froward, incompliant, insubordinate, intractable, obstreperous, rebel, rebellious, recalcitrant, recusant, refractory, restive, ungovernable, unruly, untoward, wayward, willful (*or* wilful)
related words noncooperative, uncooperative; insurgent, mutinous; adamant, adamantine, dogged, hardheaded, headstrong, immovable, implacable, inflexible, mulish, negativistic, obdurate, obstinate, opinionated, peevish, pertinacious, pigheaded, rigid, self-willed, stubborn, unbending, uncompromising, unrelenting, unyielding; fractious, restive, uncontrollable, unmanageable, wild; perverse, resistant, wrongheaded; bad, disorderly, errant, misbehaving, mischievous, monkeying, monkeyish, naughty; undisciplined; dissident, nonconformist; discourteous, disrespectful, ill-bred, ill-mannered, ill-natured, impertinent, impolite, impudent, inconsiderate, insolent, ornery, rude, uncivil, uncouth, ungracious, unmannerly
near antonyms acquiescent, agreeable, amiable, cooperative, deferential, obliging; yielding; behaved, disciplined, well-bred; courteous, polite, respectful; kowtowing, obsequious, servile, slavish, subservient; decorous, mannerly, orderly, proper; controllable, governable, manageable, trainable
antonyms amenable, biddable, compliant, conformable, docile, obedient, ruly, submissive, tractable

disobey *vb* to go against the commands, prohibitions, or rules of ⟨students who *disobey* their teachers and use cell phones in class⟩ ⟨drivers who consistently *disobey* traffic laws⟩
synonyms defy, mock, rebel (against)
related words disoblige; mutiny (against), revolt (against); disregard, ignore, overlook, overpass, pass over, tune out; brush off, dismiss, flout, pooh-pooh (*also* pooh), reject, scoff (at), scorn, shrug off, wink (at); breach, break, infringe, transgress, violate; buck, combat, contest, dispute, fight, oppose, resist, withstand
near antonyms capitulate (to), concede (to), defer (to), goose-step (to), serve, stoop (to), submit (to), surrender (to), yield (to); cooperate (with); keep, observe; accede (to), acquiesce (to), agree (to), assent (to), oblige; attend, hear, heed, listen (to), mark, note, notice, regard, watch
antonyms comply (with), conform (to), follow, mind, obey

disoblige *vb* to cause discomfort to or trouble for ⟨didn't want to *disoblige* her relatives by spending the night at their place⟩ — see INCONVENIENCE

disobliging *adj* causing difficulty, discomfort, or annoyance ⟨a friend with the *disobliging* habit of never having the cash to pay his fair share of the restaurant check⟩ — see INCONVENIENT 1

disorder *n* **1** a state in which everything is out of order ⟨the general *disorder* of the room after the guests finally left the party⟩ — see CHAOS
2 an abnormal state that disrupts a plant's or animal's normal bodily functioning ⟨afflicted all her life with a nervous *disorder*⟩ — see DISEASE

disorder *vb* to undo the proper order or arrangement of ⟨be careful not to *disorder* the carefully arranged contents of the dresser⟩
synonyms confuse, derange, disarrange, disarray, discompose, dishevel, disjoint, dislocate, disorganize, disrupt, disturb, hash, jumble, mess (up), mix (up), muddle, muss, rumple, scramble, shuffle, tousle, tumble, upset
related words embroil, entangle, snarl, tangle; agitate, perturb, stir (up), unsettle; clutter
near antonyms align (*also* aline), line, line up, queue; classify, codify, methodize, systematize, systemize; adjust, fix; groom, make up, spruce (up); unscramble
antonyms arrange, array, dispose, draw up, marshal (*also* marshall), order, organize, range, regulate, straighten (up), tidy

disordered *adj* lacking in order, neatness, and often cleanliness ⟨the doctor's *disordered* clothing was obviously thrown on in a hurry⟩ — see MESSY

disorderedness *n* a state in which everything is out of order ⟨the disarray in his car seemed to be a reflection of the general *disorderedness* of his life⟩ — see CHAOS

disorderliness *n* a state in which everything is out of order ⟨the studio had that studied *disorderliness* that appears to be de rigueur for bohemian artists⟩ — see CHAOS

disorderly *adj* **1** not restrained by or under the control of legal authority ⟨*disorderly* mobs roamed the streets after the fall of the city⟩ — see LAWLESS 1
2 lacking in order, neatness, and often cleanliness ⟨*disorderly* piles of clothes on various tables about the room⟩ — see MESSY

disorderly house *n* a building in which prostitutes are available ⟨the penalty for anyone convicted of running a *disorderly house* in the city⟩ — see BORDELLO

disorganization *n* a state in which everything is out of order ⟨all of her notes were in a state of *disorganization*⟩ — see CHAOS

disorganize *vb* to undo the proper order or arrangement of ⟨those unexpected problems that can *disorganize* an entire plan⟩ — see DISORDER

disorient *vb* to throw into a state of mental uncertainty ⟨troops *disoriented* by the sudden change in battle plans⟩ — see CONFUSE 1

disown *vb* **1** to declare not to be true ⟨he steadfastly *disowned* that he was having an affair⟩ — see DENY 1
2 to refuse to acknowledge as one's own or as one's responsibility ⟨the dictatorial father angrily *disowned* his rebellious son⟩ — see DISCLAIM 1

disparage *vb* to express scornfully one's low opinion of ⟨*disparaged* polo as a sport for the idle rich⟩ — see DECRY 1

disparagement *n* the act of making a person or a thing seem little or unimportant ⟨his predictable *disparagement* of the latest fashions among young people⟩ — see DEPRECIATION

disparager *n* a person given to harsh judgments and to finding faults ⟨those professional *disparagers* of the minister care nothing about all the good work that he has done⟩ — see CRITIC 1

disparaging *adj* intended to make a person or thing

seem of little importance or value ⟨*disparaging* comments about the lack of talent among the musical performers⟩ — see DEROGATORY

disparate *adj* being not of the same kind ⟨*disparate* notions among adults and adolescents about when middle age begins⟩ — see DIFFERENT 1

disparateness *n* the quality or state of being different ⟨the *disparateness* of their notions of an ideal weekend may indicate that they would not make a compatible couple⟩ — see DIFFERENCE 1

disparity *n* the quality or state of being different ⟨an enormous *disparity* in the lives of the rich and the poor in that country⟩ — see DIFFERENCE 1

dispassion *n* the absence of emotional involvement ⟨viewed the problem with the weary *dispassion* of a police officer who seen everything⟩ — see COOL 1

dispassionate *adj* marked by justice, honesty, and freedom from bias ⟨*dispassionate* refereeing is all that we ask⟩ — see FAIR 2

dispassionateness *n* the absence of emotional involvement ⟨your heated tone makes me question your professed *dispassionateness*⟩ — see COOL 1

dispatch *n* **1** a message on paper from one person or group to another ⟨a soldier sending daily *dispatches* to friends and family back home⟩ — see [1]LETTER
2 a piece of conveyed information ⟨a *dispatch* from headquarters regarding a change in battle plans⟩ — see COMMUNICATION 1

dispatch *vb* **1** to cause to go or be taken from one place to another ⟨*dispatched* a messenger with urgent news⟩ — see SEND
2 to deprive of life ⟨the exterminator *dispatched* the termites with professional efficiency⟩ — see KILL 1
3 to put to death deliberately ⟨during his reign of terror the dictator *dispatched* thousands without the slightest qualm⟩ — see MURDER 1
4 to achieve a victory over ⟨they *dispatched* the other team without breaking a sweat⟩ — see BEAT 2
5 to cause to go or be taken from one place to another ⟨*dispatched* a messenger to warn the colonel about the attack⟩ — see SEND

dispel *vb* to cause (members of a group) to move widely apart ⟨the sudden downpour *dispelled* the throng of street revelers⟩ — see SCATTER 1

dispensable *adj* not needed by the circumstances or to accomplish an end ⟨a new invention that renders the old methods eminently *dispensable*⟩ — see UNNECESSARY

dispensation *n* the act or process of giving out something to each member of a group ⟨the emergency *dispensation* of medicine to the sick⟩ — see DISTRIBUTION 1

dispense *vb* to give out (something) to appropriate individuals ⟨a conscientious pharmacist never *dispenses* pills to people without assurances that they understand the instructions⟩ — see ADMINISTER 1

dispersal *n* an act or process in which something scatters or is scattered ⟨the *dispersal* of plant seeds in the forests through natural means⟩ — see SCATTERING 1

disperse *vb* **1** to go off in different directions and cease to exist as a body or unified whole ⟨the crowd *dispersed* once the show ended⟩
synonyms disassemble, dissipate, dissolve, scatter
related words branch (out), break up, disband, diverge, divide, fork, separate, spill; clear, disappear, evanesce, evaporate, fade, flee, go (away), melt
near antonyms congregate, gather, meet
2 to cause (members of a group) to move widely apart ⟨the family of the missing woman *dispersed* searchers to all corners of the national park⟩ — see SCATTER 1
3 to cease to exist or cause to cease to exist as a group or organization ⟨the campaign staff *dispersed* almost immediately after the election⟩ — see DISBAND 1

dispersion *n* an act or process in which something scatters or is scattered ⟨the *dispersion* of energy from a source⟩ — see SCATTERING 1

dispirit *vb* to lessen the courage or confidence of ⟨*dispirited* by the overwhelming amount of information needed to write the report⟩ — see DISCOURAGE 1

dispiritedness *n* **1** a state or spell of low spirits ⟨experienced a period of general *dispiritedness* following the birth of her first child⟩ — see SADNESS
2 the state of being discouraged ⟨the *dispiritedness* experienced by the losing team in the Super Bowl must be staggering⟩ — see DISCOURAGEMENT

displace *vb* **1** to change the place or position of ⟨the slight tremor *displaced* the dishes on the shelves, but didn't do any real damage⟩ — see MOVE 1
2 to force to leave a country ⟨World War II *displaced* people all over Europe⟩ — see BANISH 1
3 to take the place of ⟨inefficient methods *displaced* by newer ones⟩ — see REPLACE 1
4 to remove from a position of prominence or power (as a throne) ⟨the CEO was summarily *displaced* after the hostile takeover⟩ — see DEPOSE 1

displacement *n* the forced removal from a homeland ⟨the *displacement* of Jews from the land of their ancestors⟩ — see EXILE 1

displant *vb* to take the place of ⟨long ago *displanted* by the automobile, the horse and buggy have become icons of a slower, gentler time⟩ — see REPLACE 1

display *n* **1** a public showing of objects of interest ⟨a *display* of paintings by masters of French Impressionism⟩ — see EXHIBITION 1
2 an outward and often exaggerated indication of something abstract (as a feeling) for effect ⟨a *display* of sympathy that was totally phony⟩ — see SHOW 1

display *vb* **1** to present so as to invite notice or attention ⟨*display* the best items at the front of the showcase⟩ — see SHOW 1
2 to make known (something abstract) through outward signs ⟨an actress who can *display* a great range of emotion⟩ — see SHOW 2

displease *vb* to make discontented ⟨her coworkers' tendency to pry *displeased* her⟩ — see DISCONTENT

displeased *adj* having a feeling that one has been wronged or thwarted in one's ambitions ⟨feeling vaguely *displeased* by the way his relationship with his girlfriend seemed to be going⟩ — see DISCONTENTED

displeasing *adj* not giving pleasure to the mind or senses ⟨the new hotel is a *displeasing* mix of architectural styles⟩ — see UNPLEASANT

displeasure *n* **1** refusal to accept as right or desirable ⟨fans showed their *displeasure* by loudly booing the umpire⟩ — see DISAPPROVAL
2 the condition of being dissatisfied with one's life or situation ⟨his *displeasure* with his job intensified as the years wore on⟩ — see DISCONTENT

disport *vb* **1** to cause (someone) to pass the time agreeably occupied ⟨*disported* themselves with silly games while they waited in the airport⟩ — see AMUSE
2 to engage in activity for amusement ⟨a full-service resort where vacationers may *disport* at a variety of indoor and outdoor activities⟩ — see PLAY 1
3 to play and run about happily ⟨the puppies *disported* in the backyard while we ate on the patio⟩ — see FROLIC 1
4 to present so as to invite notice or attention ⟨football fans triumphantly *disported* the sports memorabilia for which they had just paid extravagant prices⟩ — see SHOW 1

disposal *n* **1** the getting rid of whatever is unwanted or useless ⟨trash *disposal* is on Wednesday in our neighborhood⟩

synonyms discarding, disposition, dumping, jettison, junking, removal, riddance, scrapping, throwing away
related words clearance, clearing; decimation, demolishment, demolition, destruction
near antonyms accumulation, acquirement, acquisition, collection, deposit, gathering
2 the way objects in space or events in time are arranged or follow one another ⟨the *disposal* of troops along the ridge⟩ — see ORDER 1

dispose *vb* **1** to arrange something in a certain spot or position ⟨looking for the perfect spot to *dispose* the new knickknack⟩ — see PLACE 1
2 to put into a particular arrangement ⟨*disposed* the surgical instruments in the exact order in which they would be needed⟩ — see ORDER 1

disposed *adj* having a desire or inclination (as for a specified course of action) ⟨a dog that is *disposed* to bite⟩ — see WILLING 1

disposition *n* **1** one's characteristic attitude or mood ⟨he has a cheerful *disposition* and is very rarely depressed⟩
synonyms grain, nature, temper, temperament
related words cheer, frame, habit, humor, inclination, mode, spirit; angle, attitude, mind-set, outlook, perspective, slant, standpoint, viewpoint; emotion, feeling, heart, passion, sentiment, spirit; strain; belief, conviction, judgment (*or* judgement), mind, notion, opinion, persuasion, view; expression, tone, vein; character, identity, individuality, makeup, mettle, personality, selfhood, self-identity, setup; responsiveness, sensibility, sensitiveness, sensitivity
2 a habitual attraction to some activity or thing ⟨a woman with a *disposition* to fuss about trivial matters⟩ — see INCLINATION 1
3 the getting rid of whatever is unwanted or useless ⟨we'll have to find some means for the *disposition* of all of this junk⟩ — see DISPOSAL 1
4 the way objects in space or events in time are arranged or follow one another ⟨planned the *disposition* of events at her wedding with a precision that military commanders would envy⟩ — see ORDER 1
5 an arrangement about action to be taken ⟨all that remains is a *disposition* regarding the custody of the two children⟩ — see AGREEMENT 2

dispossess *vb* to end the occupancy or possession of ⟨opponents of gentrification claim that the process unfairly *dispossesses* poorer residents of their long-established homes⟩
synonyms divest, expropriate, oust
related words deforce, evict; disfurnish, strip; bereave, deprive, disinherit; annex, appropriate, commandeer, impound, seize, take over, usurp

dispraise *vb* to express one's unfavorable opinion of the worth or quality of ⟨the movie is an old-fashioned romance, and in calling it that, I don't mean to *dispraise* it at all⟩ — see CRITICIZE

disproof *n* something (as an argument) that serves to disprove ⟨the DNA evidence was all the *disproof* needed to overturn the wrongful conviction⟩ — see CONFUTATION

disprove *vb* to prove to be false ⟨Magellan's circumnavigation of the globe *disproved* any lingering notions that the earth is flat⟩
synonyms belie, confound, confute, debunk, disconfirm, discredit, falsify, rebut, refute, shoot down
related words overthrow, overturn; challenge, contest, query, question; doubt, mistrust; debate, discuss, hash (over), moot, talk over
phrases give the lie to
near antonyms document, evidence, evince, record, show, support, witness; back (up), buttress, corroborate, substantiate; adduce, attest, authenticate, certify, identify; demonstrate, display, illustrate, manifest
antonyms confirm, establish, prove, validate, verify

disputable *adj* **1** giving good reason for being doubted, questioned, or challenged ⟨a speech full of *disputable* generalizations about people⟩ — see DOUBTFUL
2 open to question or dispute ⟨all *disputable* claims must be referred to the committee⟩ — see DEBATABLE 2

disputant *n* a person who takes part in a dispute ⟨there were only three *disputants* in the argument, but they made enough noise for a dozen⟩
synonyms arguer, argufier, bickerer, brawler, debater, disputer, fighter, quarreler (*or* quarreller), scrapper, squabbler, wrangler
related words advocate, codefendant, defendant, plaintiff, pleader; challenger, contender, contestant, skirmisher; fusser, nitpicker, pettifogger, quibbler

disputation *n* variance of opinion on a matter ⟨a heated *disputation* over the true authorship of the poem popularly known as "The Night Before Christmas"⟩ — see DISAGREEMENT 1

disputatious *adj* **1** feeling or displaying eagerness to fight ⟨a long history of little wars waged by the *disputatious* countries occupying that European peninsula⟩ — see BELLIGERENT
2 given to arguing ⟨a *disputatious* professor who could give you an argument on just about anything⟩ — see ARGUMENTATIVE 1
3 relating to or causing the expression of opposing opinions ⟨dismayed at the prospect of enduring another *disputatious* meeting of the school board⟩ — see CONTROVERSIAL 1

disputatiousness *n* an inclination to fight or quarrel ⟨the stubborn *disputatiousness* of the committee members kept them from getting much accomplished⟩ — see BELLIGERENCE

dispute *n* **1** variance of opinion on a matter ⟨a *dispute* over the proper pronunciation of "nuclear"⟩ — see DISAGREEMENT 1
2 an often noisy or angry expression of differing opinions ⟨after much *dispute*, the school committee decided that all backpacks would have to be stored in lockers during class hours⟩ — see ARGUMENT 1

dispute *vb* **1** to demand proof of the truth or rightness of ⟨a whole slew of relatives eager to *dispute* his claim to being the sole heir⟩ — see CHALLENGE 1
2 to express different opinions about something often angrily ⟨hometown fans *disputing* with visiting fans over which had the better team⟩ —see ARGUE 2
3 to talk about (an issue) usually from various points of view and for the purpose of arriving at a decision or opinion ⟨in an extended session the city council *disputed* the need for a new high school⟩ — see DISCUSS

disputer *n* a person who takes part in a dispute ⟨in debate she's a dogged *disputer* who never gives an inch⟩ — see DISPUTANT

disquiet *n* **1** a disturbed or uneasy state ⟨a period of *disquiet* before the results of the close election were confirmed⟩ — see UNREST
2 an uneasy state of mind usually over the possibility of an anticipated misfortune or trouble ⟨was filled with *disquiet* as the hours passed without any sign of the missing children⟩ — see ANXIETY 1

disquiet *vb* to trouble the mind of; to make uneasy ⟨we were *disquieted* by the strange noises we heard outside our tent at night⟩ — see DISTURB 1

disquieting *adj* **1** causing worry or anxiety ⟨*disquieting* news of troubles downtown⟩ — see TROUBLESOME
2 marked by or causing agitation or uncomfortable feelings ⟨with a *disquieting* voice she asked me to investigate the strange noise coming from the basement⟩ — see NERVOUS 2

disquietude *n* an uneasy state of mind usually over the possibility of an anticipated misfortune or trouble ⟨as updates of the devastation caused by the earthquake poured in, our *disquietude* only increased⟩ — see ANXIETY 1

disquisition *n* a systematic search for the truth or facts about something ⟨Adam Smith's celebrated *disquisition* on the factors contributing to the wealth of nations⟩ — see INQUIRY 1

disrate *vb* to bring to a lower grade or rank ⟨several noncommissioned officers had been *disrated*⟩ — see DEMOTE

disregard *n* lack of interest or concern ⟨revelers firing guns in the air with complete *disregard* for the possible consequences⟩ — see INDIFFERENCE

disregard *vb* **1** to ignore in a disrespectful manner ⟨*disregarded* the wishes of his tradition-conscious family in his choice of a bride⟩ — see SCORN 2
2 to fail to give proper attention to ⟨*disregarded* the posted warnings of avalanche danger and went skiing anyway⟩ — see NEGLECT 1
3 to dismiss as of little importance ⟨this essay is so good that I can safely *disregard* a couple of spelling errors⟩ — see EXCUSE 1

disregardful *adj* failing to give proper care and attention ⟨rebuked by the judge for being *disregardful* of her responsibilities as a mother of two young children⟩ — see NEGLIGENT

disrelish *n* a strong feeling of not liking or approving ⟨she showed a clear *disrelish* for the task of cleaning the fish that her husband had caught⟩ — see DISLIKE 1

disrelish *vb* to feel dislike for ⟨I *disrelish* the thought of sitting through endless meetings on the matter⟩ — see DISLIKE 1

disremember *vb* to be unable to recall or think of ⟨with advancing age I seem to *disremember* quite a lot of things⟩ — see FORGET 1

disrepair *n* the state of being unattended to or not cared for ⟨the old house was in such *disrepair* that the roof had caved in⟩ — see NEGLECT 1

disreputable *adj* not respectable ⟨a *disreputable* Internet retailer that had a record of hundreds of complaints for shoddy merchandise and slow refunds⟩
synonyms discreditable, disgraceful, dishonorable, ignominious, infamous, louche, notorious, opprobrious, shady, shameful, shoddy, shy, unrespectable
related words bad, criminal, immoral, seamy, sordid, unethical, unsavory, wicked; base, contemptible, despicable, detestable, dirty, low, mean, miserable, vile, wretched; black, evil, iniquitous, nefarious, rotten, sinful, unrighteous, vicious, villainous, wrong; blamable, blameworthy, censurable, inglorious, reprehensible; corrupt, debased, debauched, degenerate, depraved, dissolute, gamy (*or* gamey), libertine, loose, perverted, reprobate
near antonyms decent, ethical, good, honest, just, moral, noble, principled, righteous, upright, upstanding; esteemed, prestigious, reputed, respected; authorized, legal, licensed, permissible, permitted; approved, endorsed (*also* indorsed), sanctioned; clean, correct, decorous, exemplary, proper, seemly; blameless, commendable, creditable, guiltless
antonyms honorable, reputable, respectable

disrepute *n* the state of having lost the esteem of others ⟨a once proud name fallen into *disrepute*⟩ — see DISGRACE 1

disrespect *n* rude behavior ⟨treated the resort's service workers with haughty *disrespect*⟩ — see DISCOURTESY

disrespect *vb* **1** to cause hurt feelings or deep resentment in ⟨a comedian who shuns jokes that *disrespect* people because of their race or ethnicity⟩ — see INSULT
2 to show contempt for ⟨the player once again *disrespected* fans by refusing to sign autographs⟩ — see SCORN 1

disrespectful *adj* showing a lack of manners or consideration for others ⟨being four hours late is *disrespectful* of the people you promised to meet⟩ — see IMPOLITE

disrespectfulness *n* rude behavior ⟨she was now at an age when the *disrespectfulness* of young people really bothered her⟩ — see DISCOURTESY

disrobe *vb* to remove clothing from ⟨the doctor instructed the patient to *disrobe* himself before the examination⟩ — see UNDRESS 1

disrobed *adj* lacking or shed of clothing ⟨a statue of a partially *disrobed* woman⟩ — see NAKED 1

disrupt *vb* **1** to cause to separate into pieces usually suddenly or forcibly ⟨an earthquake that had *disrupted* the elevated highway in several places⟩ — see BREAK 1
2 to undo the proper order or arrangement of ⟨the arrival of a baby in the household would totally *disrupt* their established routine⟩ — see DISORDER

disruption *n* an act or instance of the order of things being disturbed ⟨the flat tire resulted in an unfortunate *disruption* of the schedule for our road trip⟩ — see UPSET

dissatisfaction *n* **1** the condition of being dissatisfied with one's life or situation ⟨a vague *dissatisfaction* with the state of their marriage, which seemed a little stale⟩ — see DISCONTENT
2 the emotion felt when one's expectations are not met ⟨she felt keen *dissatisfaction* at the hurried job the house painters had done⟩ — see DISAPPOINTMENT 1

dissatisfactory *adj* falling short of a standard ⟨this report is completely *dissatisfactory* on several counts⟩ — see BAD 1

dissatisfied *adj* having a feeling that one has been wronged or thwarted in one's ambitions ⟨the store prides itself on never allowing a customer to walk away *dissatisfied*⟩ — see DISCONTENTED

dissatisfy *vb* **1** to fall short in satisfying the expectation or hope of ⟨a restaurant serving portions that will not *dissatisfy* even the heartiest eater⟩ — see DISAPPOINT
2 to make discontented ⟨an administrative assistant *dissatisfied* by her meager paycheck⟩ — see DISCONTENT

dissect *vb* to identify and examine the basic elements or parts of (something) especially for discovering interrelationships ⟨let's *dissect* the plot of this thriller to see what makes it thrilling⟩ — see ANALYZE

dissection *n* the separation and identification of the parts of a whole ⟨the book's *dissection* of the problem of obesity in this country⟩ — see ANALYSIS 1

dissemble *vb* **1** to present a false appearance of ⟨he *dissembled* happiness at the news that his old girlfriend was getting married—to someone else⟩ — see FEIGN
2 to take on a false or deceptive appearance ⟨children learn to *dissemble* at a surprisingly early age⟩ — see PRETEND 1

dissembling *n* **1** the inclination or practice of misleading others through lies or trickery ⟨a crafty child given to frequent *dissembling* to get what she wants⟩ — see DECEIT 1
2 the pretending of having virtues, principles, or beliefs that one in fact does not have ⟨in the end the preacher's smarmy *dissembling* is discovered, and he is exposed as a fraud⟩ — see HYPOCRISY

disseminate *vb* to cause to be known over a considerable area or by many people ⟨missionaries sent by their church to *disseminate* their faith⟩ — see SPREAD 1

dissension *also* **dissention** *n* **1** a lack of agreement or harmony ⟨religious *dissension* threatened to split the colony⟩ — see DISCORD
2 variance of opinion on a matter ⟨continued *dissension* among historians on the exact spot of Columbus's first landing⟩ — see DISAGREEMENT 1

dissensus *n* variance of opinion on a matter ⟨a democracy relies on *dissensus* as much as on consensus⟩ — see DISAGREEMENT 1

dissent *n* **1** a lack of agreement or harmony ⟨considerable *dissent* within the party's rank and file⟩ — see DISCORD
2 departure from a generally accepted theory, opinion, or practice ⟨the church reacted to any form of *dissent* by promptly excommunicating its proponents⟩ — see HERESY

dissent *vb* to have a different opinion ⟨anyone who *dissented* was encouraged to speak out while they had the chance⟩ — see DISAGREE

dissenter *n* a person who believes, teaches, or advocates something opposed to accepted beliefs ⟨a society that prized conformity very highly and treated *dissenters* of any kind very harshly⟩ — see HERETIC 1

dissentient *adj* deviating from commonly accepted beliefs or practices ⟨the communist party did not look favorably on *dissentient* opinions⟩ — see HERETICAL

dissentient *n* a person who believes, teaches, or advocates something opposed to accepted beliefs ⟨traditionalists who feared that their church was falling into the hands of *dissentients* and malcontents⟩ — see HERETIC 1

dissenting *adj* deviating from commonly accepted beliefs or practices ⟨*dissenting* views were ruthlessly suppressed under the dictatorship⟩ — see HERETICAL

disservice *n* unfair or inadequate treatment of someone or something or an instance of this ⟨you do a great *disservice* to the professionals at the day-care center when you refer to them as "babysitters"⟩
synonyms inequity, injury, injustice, raw deal, shaft, unfairness, unjustness, wrong
related words affront, indignity, insult, offense (*or* offence), outrage, put-down, slight, slur; beef, complaint, grievance
near antonyms cricket
antonyms equitableness, equity, fairness, justice

dissever *vb* to set or force apart ⟨placed the *dissevered* pieces of chicken in the roasting pan⟩ — see SEPARATE 1

dissidence *n* **1** a lack of agreement or harmony ⟨political *dissidence* had plagued the country for years⟩ — see DISCORD
2 departure from a generally accepted theory, opinion, or practice ⟨after abstract art became established, its proponents became just as intolerant of *dissidence* as earlier schools of art had been⟩ — see HERESY

dissident *adj* deviating from commonly accepted beliefs or practices ⟨*dissident* elements within the Catholic Church⟩ — see HERETICAL

dissident *n* a person who believes, teaches, or advocates something opposed to accepted beliefs ⟨the conference drew political *dissidents* of every ilk⟩ — see HERETIC 1

dissimilar *adj* being not of the same kind ⟨a place where people with *dissimilar* backgrounds can interact⟩ — see DIFFERENT 1

dissimilarity *n* the quality or state of being different ⟨the effectiveness of a metaphor largely depends upon the superficial *dissimilarity* of the two things being compared⟩ — see DIFFERENCE 1

dissimilitude *n* the quality or state of being different ⟨there's a real *dissimilitude* between literature and film, and a critic shouldn't evaluate one in terms of the other⟩ — see DIFFERENCE 1

dissimulate *vb* to take on a false or deceptive appearance ⟨as an actress she had been trained to *dissimulate*, so she had no trouble hiding her true feelings offstage as well⟩ — see PRETEND 1

dissimulation *n* **1** the inclination or practice of misleading others through lies or trickery ⟨got whatever she wanted through shameless *dissimulation*⟩ — see DECEIT 1
2 the pretending of having virtues, principles, or beliefs that one in fact does not have ⟨teenagers indulging in *dissimulation* simply in order to be one of the in crowd⟩ — see HYPOCRISY

dissipate *vb* **1** to cause (members of a group) to move widely apart ⟨*dissipated* the enemy forces with unremitting artillery fire⟩ — see SCATTER 1
2 to use up carelessly ⟨*dissipated* the family fortune in reckless business ventures⟩ — see WASTE 1
3 to go off in different directions and cease to exist as a body or unified whole ⟨the fog should *dissipate* once the sun comes out in full force⟩ — see DISPERSE 1

dissipated *adj* having or showing lowered moral character or standards ⟨the *dissipated* and drunken son of the wealthiest man in the county⟩ — see CORRUPT

dissipatedness *n* a sinking to a state of low moral standards and behavior ⟨a novel chronicling the *dissipatedness* of a generation born to great wealth⟩ — see CORRUPTION 2

dissipation *n* **1** a sinking to a state of low moral standards and behavior ⟨the wasting of a once promising life in *dissipation* and drunkenness⟩ — see CORRUPTION 2
2 an act or process in which something scatters or is scattered ⟨the *dissipation* of the clouds by the early morning winds⟩ — see SCATTERING 1

dissociate *vb* to set or force apart ⟨attempts to *dissociate* herself from her troubled past⟩ — see SEPARATE 1

dissolute *adj* having or showing lowered moral character or standards ⟨literature dealing with the *dissolute* and degrading aspects of human experience⟩ — see CORRUPT

dissoluteness *n* a sinking to a state of low moral standards and behavior ⟨the growing *dissoluteness* of the Roman nobles as the empire declined⟩ — see CORRUPTION 2

dissolution *n* **1** the act or process of a whole separating into two or more parts or pieces ⟨the *dissolution* of the empire into a patchwork of petty kingdoms⟩ — see SEPARATION 1
2 the doing away with something by formal action ⟨one of the junta's first acts was the *dissolution* of the national assembly⟩ — see ABOLITION
3 the permanent stopping of all the vital bodily activities ⟨she believed that her leukemia, although in remission, would eventually be the cause of her *dissolution*⟩ — see DEATH 1

dissolve *vb* **1** to cease to be visible ⟨as the mist *dissolved* in the morning sun⟩ — see DISAPPEAR
2 to cease to exist or cause to cease to exist as a group or organization ⟨the company formally *dissolved* three months after declaring bankruptcy⟩ — see DISBAND 1
3 to put an end to by formal action ⟨the king simply *dissolved* parliament⟩ — see ABOLISH 1
4 to go off in different directions and cease to exist as a body or unified whole ⟨the clouds gradually *dissolved*, and the sun came out⟩ — see DISPERSE 1

dissonance *n* a lack of agreement or harmony ⟨the *dissonance* between what we are told and what we see with our own eyes⟩ — see DISCORD

dissonant *adj* marked by or producing a harsh combination of sounds ⟨a *dissonant* chorus of noises arose from the busy construction site⟩
synonyms cacophonous, discordant, inharmonious, unmelodious, unmusical, unvocal
related words blaring, clanging, clangorous, clashing, clattering, dinning, grating, harsh, jangling, jangly, jarring, metallic, noisy, raspy, raucous, scratching, screeching, shrill, squeaky, strident; disagreeable, unpleasant, unpleasing; atonal, off-key, tuneless; resound-

ing, sonorous; clamorous, uproarious
near antonyms dulcet, euphonious, mellifluent, mellifluous, mellow, melodic, sweet, tuneful; resonant, sonorous; quavering, trilling, warbling; agreeable, appealing, pleasant; cadenced, lilting, lyric, lyrical, rhythmic (*or* rhythmical); chordal, harmonic, homophonic, orchestral, polyphonic (*or* polyphonous), symphonic, symphonious, tonal; calm, hushed; noiseless, quiet, silent, soundless, still
antonyms harmonious, harmonizing, melodious, musical

dissuade *vb* to steer (a person) from an activity or course of action ⟨tried to *dissuade* her from her intention to drop out of college⟩ — see DISCOURAGE 2

distain *vb, archaic* to make dirty ⟨weary soldiers with hands *distained* with blood⟩ — see DIRTY

distance *n* **1** the space or amount of space between two points, lines, surfaces, or objects ⟨the *distance* between the earth and the sun is about 93 million miles⟩
synonyms lead, length, remove, spacing, spread, stretch, way
related words altitude, area, breadth, depth, height, rise, space, volume, width; extension, extent; cast, range, reach, scope, shot, sweep, throw; drop, fall, flight, haul; berth, clearance
2 a wide space or area ⟨a region marked by great, featureless *distances*⟩ — see EXPANSE
3 the quality or state of being different ⟨the brothers' personalities are like the *distance* between night and day⟩ — see DIFFERENCE 1

distant *adj* **1** not close in time or space ⟨the *distant* towers were barely visible in the fog⟩
synonyms away, deep, far, faraway, far-flung, far-off, remote, removed
related words apart, devious, isolated, lonesome, nowhere, obscure, odd, outlying, out-of-the-way, retired, secluded, secret, sequestered
near antonyms adjacent, adjoining, contiguous
antonyms close, near, nearby, nigh
2 having or showing a lack of friendliness or interest in others ⟨was *distant* and distracted all throughout the interview⟩ — see COOL 1
3 being not of the same kind ⟨a marriage between two people from very *distant* cultures⟩ — see DIFFERENT 1

distaste *n* a dislike so strong as to cause stomach upset or queasiness ⟨usually views abstract paintings with *distaste*⟩ — see DISGUST

distasteful *adj* **1** disagreeable or disgusting to the sense of taste ⟨cod-liver oil is so *distasteful* that it's worse than anything it cures⟩
synonyms brackish, unappetizing, unpalatable, unsavory, yucky (*also* yukky)
related words abominable, awful, bad, filthy, foul, horrible, loathsome, nasty, nauseating, noisome, obnoxious, offensive, repellent (*also* repellant), repugnant, repulsive, revolting, shocking, sickening; bland, flat, flavorless, insipid, savorless, tasteless
near antonyms appealing, attractive, flavorful, piquant, rich
antonyms appetizing, delectable, delicious, delish, palatable, savory (*also* savoury), tasty, toothsome, yummy
2 not giving pleasure to the mind or senses ⟨concerned mothers who find some recent musical trends *distasteful*⟩ — see UNPLEASANT
3 causing intense displeasure, disgust, or resentment ⟨the *distasteful* nature of his job as a bill collector⟩ — see OFFENSIVE 1

distemper *n* an abnormal state that disrupts a plant's or animal's normal bodily functioning ⟨contracted some tropical *distemper* while he was doing research in the jungles of Borneo⟩ — see DISEASE

distemper *vb* to trouble the mind of; to make uneasy ⟨despite his career success, he has been *distempered* by nagging feelings of inadequacy his whole life⟩ — see DISTURB 1

distemperature *n* an abnormal state that disrupts a plant's or animal's normal bodily functioning ⟨a guinea pig with some sort of *distemperature*⟩ — see DISEASE

distended *adj* enlarged beyond normal from internal pressure ⟨bees with abdomens *distended* with honey are less apt to sting⟩ — see BLOATED 2

distill *also* **distil** *vb* **1** to fall or let fall in or as if in drops ⟨the basement walls *distill* water every time it rains heavily⟩ — see DRIP
2 to remove usually visible impurities from ⟨*distill* the water before pouring it in the steam iron⟩ — see CLARIFY 1

distinct *adj* **1** being not of the same kind ⟨two *distinct* approaches to the same problem⟩ — see DIFFERENT 1
2 not subject to misinterpretation or more than one interpretation ⟨a person with a *distinct* Scottish accent⟩ — see CLEAR 2
3 of a particular or exact sort ⟨I left *distinct* instructions that my books were not to be touched⟩ — see EXPRESS 1
4 serving to identify as belonging to an individual or group ⟨one of the *distinct* traits of a preliterate society⟩ — see CHARACTERISTIC 1

distinction *n* **1** exceptionally high quality ⟨a shop selling native handicrafts of *distinction*⟩ — see EXCELLENCE 1
2 a quality that gives something special worth ⟨has the *distinction* of being the oldest house in the city⟩ — see EXCELLENCE 2
3 public acknowledgment or admiration for an achievement ⟨I did all of the work, and the other guy got all the *distinction*⟩ — see GLORY 1
4 the fact or state of being above others in rank or importance ⟨a number of physicians of national *distinction* serve on the staff of the teaching hospital⟩ — see EMINENCE 1
5 something given in recognition of achievement ⟨won a number of *distinctions* in her long career as an actress⟩ — see AWARD 1
6 the quality or state of being different ⟨the *distinction* between the two photographic prints escapes me⟩ — see DIFFERENCE 1
7 the state of being kept distinct ⟨the *distinction* between liberty and license is often violated in today's freewheeling society⟩ — see SEPARATION 2

distinctive *adj* **1** being not of the same kind ⟨she seems to alternate between two *distinctive* hairstyles⟩ — see DIFFERENT 1
2 serving to identify as belonging to an individual or group ⟨the *distinctive* odor of a barnyard⟩ — see CHARACTERISTIC 1

distinctiveness *n* the quality or state of being different ⟨the pronounced *distinctiveness* of his style of playing the violin⟩ — see DIFFERENCE 1

distinctness *n* the quality or state of being different ⟨the *distinctness* of Jane Austen's writing makes it easy to recognize on a test⟩ — see DIFFERENCE 1

distingué *adj* having or showing a formal and serious or reserved manner ⟨had the *distingué* air of a senior diplomat⟩ — see DIGNIFIED

distinguish *vb* **1** to understand or point out the difference in ⟨even at such a young age, he could *distinguish* the calls of various birds⟩
synonyms difference, differentiate, discern, discriminate, secern, separate
related words contradistinguish; comprehend, grasp, know, understand; divide, part, sever; demarcate, mark (off), set off
near antonyms confound, lump (together), mingle

antonyms confuse, mistake, mix (up)
2 to be an important feature of ⟨muffin recipes *distinguished* by their ease and simplicity⟩ — see CHARACTERIZE 2
3 to find out or establish the identity of ⟨learned at an early age to *distinguish* the sound of a piano in an orchestra⟩ — see IDENTIFY 1
4 to make note of (something) through the use of one's eyes ⟨could barely *distinguish* the garden gate through the mist⟩ — see SEE 1
5 to arrange or assign according to type ⟨please *distinguish* the specimens by acidity⟩ — see CLASSIFY 1

distinguishable *adj* **1** able to be perceived by a sense or by the mind ⟨an evening star easily *distinguishable* by the naked eye⟩ — see PERCEPTIBLE
2 being not of the same kind ⟨snowflakes are *distinguishable* from each other under a microscope⟩ — see DIFFERENT 1

distinguished *adj* **1** having or showing a formal and serious or reserved manner ⟨heads turned as the well-dressed, *distinguished* couple strode through the hotel lobby⟩ — see DIGNIFIED
2 standing above others in rank, importance, or achievement ⟨a *distinguished* astronomer who is widely respected in the field⟩ — see EMINENT

distinguishing *adj* serving to identify as belonging to an individual or group ⟨a novice birder still learning the *distinguishing* features of various finches⟩ — see CHARACTERISTIC 1

distintegrate *vb* to cause to separate into pieces usually suddenly or forcibly ⟨a tornado *disintegrated* the house in a matter of seconds⟩ — see BREAK 1

distort *vb* **1** to change so much as to create a wrong impression or alter the meaning of ⟨the coach's message was so *distorted* after passing through so many people that it was unintelligible⟩ — see GARBLE 1
2 to twist (something) out of a natural or normal shape or condition ⟨if you keep *distorting* your face like that, someday it's going to freeze in that position⟩ — see CONTORT

distorted *adj* badly or imperfectly formed ⟨surgery to correct a *distorted* foot⟩ — see MALFORMED

distortion *n* the twisting of something out of its natural or normal shape or condition ⟨a *distortion* of the car chassis resulting from collision⟩ — see CONTORTION

distract *vb* **1** to draw the attention or mind to something else ⟨we were *distracted* from our discussion by the noise outside⟩
synonyms abstract, call off, detract, divert, throw off
related words amuse, beguile, entertain; stray, wander
near antonyms concentrate, focus
2 to trouble the mind of; to make uneasy ⟨*distracted* by the looming tax deadline⟩ — see DISTURB 1

distracted *adj* **1** feeling overwhelming fear or worry ⟨she's been *distracted* about her son ever since he left on that polar expedition⟩ — see FRANTIC 1
2 lost in thought and unaware of one's surroundings or actions ⟨the *distracted* driver rear-ended the pickup truck that had stopped for the red light⟩ — see ABSENT-MINDED 1
3 suffering from mental confusion ⟨she's been chronically depressed and *distracted* since her husband's death⟩ — see DIZZY 2

distraction *n* **1** a state of mental uncertainty ⟨in my *distraction* I forgot where I was⟩ — see CONFUSION 1
2 a state of wildly excited activity or emotion ⟨driven to *distraction* by the constant screaming and bickering in the house⟩ — see FRENZY
3 the act or activity of providing pleasure or amusement especially for the public ⟨a minister who certainly doesn't view gambling as a harmless *distraction* for people of modest means⟩ — see ENTERTAINMENT 1
4 someone or something that provides amusement or enjoyment ⟨a harmless *distraction* for children at the playground⟩ — see FUN 1

distrait *adj* feeling overwhelming fear or worry ⟨he grew more and more *distrait* as hours passed without confirmation that there were survivors of the plane crash⟩ — see FRANTIC 1

distraught *adj* feeling overwhelming fear or worry ⟨*distraught* relatives waiting to learn whether there were any survivors of the plane crash⟩ — see FRANTIC 1

distress *n* **1** a state of great suffering of body or mind ⟨the upcoming bar exam is causing us considerable *distress*⟩ ⟨the survivors were in extreme *distress* after having been stranded on the island for a week with no food⟩
synonyms affliction, agony, anguish, excruciation, hurt, misery, pain, rack, strait(s), torment, torture, travail, tribulation, woe
related words discomfort; cross, crucible, trial; heartache, heartbreak, joylessness, sadness, sorrow, unhappiness; emergency, pinch; asperity, difficulty, hardship, rigor; ache, pang, smarting, soreness, stitch, throe, twinge; danger, jeopardy, trouble
near antonyms comfort, consolation, solace; alleviation, assuagement, ease, relief; peace, security; well-being
2 the state of not being protected from injury, harm, or evil ⟨a ship in *distress*⟩ — see DANGER 1

distress *vb* to trouble the mind of; to make uneasy ⟨don't let all the bad news *distress* you⟩ — see DISTURB 1

distressful *adj* **1** marked by or causing agitation or uncomfortable feelings ⟨the *distressful* period during which we waited to learn who had made the cut⟩ — see NERVOUS 2
2 of a kind to cause great distress ⟨the *distressful* living conditions in the refugee camp⟩ — see REGRETTABLE

distressing *adj* **1** causing worry or anxiety ⟨*distressing* signs that another war might be imminent⟩ — see TROUBLESOME
2 of a kind to cause great distress ⟨the *distressing* death of our favorite actor⟩ — see REGRETTABLE
3 marked by or causing agitation or uncomfortable feelings ⟨the *distressing* habit of constantly fiddling with her hair⟩ — see NERVOUS 2

distribute *vb* **1** to arrange or assign according to type ⟨*distribute* the assignments according to seniority⟩ — see CLASSIFY 1
2 to give as a share or portion ⟨committed to *distributing* the school's limited scholarship money so that it benefits more students⟩ — see ALLOT
3 to give out (something) to appropriate individuals ⟨*distributed* pamphlets on recycling to everyone in the neighborhood⟩ — see ADMINISTER 1

distribution *n* **1** the act or process of giving out something to each member of a group ⟨aid workers oversaw the *distribution* of medicine to the natives⟩
synonyms admeasurement, allocation, allotment, apportionment, disbursement, dispensation, division, issuance
related words reallocation, reapportionment, redistribution, redivision, repartition; division, partition, separation
2 the way objects in space or events in time are arranged or follow one another ⟨the *distribution* of those stars has long suggested the form of a dipper⟩ — see ORDER 1

district *n* an area (as of a city) set apart for some purpose or having some special feature ⟨Independence Hall in Philadelphia's historic *district*⟩
synonyms nabe, neighborhood, quarter, section
related words belt, zone; department, division, part;

precinct, ward; area, backyard, locality, place, region; barrio, enclave, ghetto, hood (*or* 'hood)

distrust *n* a feeling or attitude that one does not know the truth, truthfulness, or trustworthiness of someone or something ⟨the psychic's bold claims were greeted with *distrust* and outright scorn⟩ — see DOUBT

distrust *vb* to have no trust or confidence in ⟨we instinctively *distrust* those phone calls that tell us we have won a free vacation or car⟩
synonyms doubt, misdoubt, mistrust, question, suspect
related words disbelieve, discount, discredit, negate
near antonyms bank (on *or* upon), count (on *or* upon), depend (on *or* upon), rely (on *or* upon)
antonyms trust

distrustful *adj* **1** inclined to doubt or question claims ⟨she was *distrustful* of her boyfriend's claim of having saved the kitten from a raging fire⟩ — see SKEPTICAL 1
2 not feeling sure about the truth, wisdom, or trustworthiness of someone or something ⟨naturally *distrustful* of politicians who claim to have all the answers⟩ — see DOUBTFUL 1

distrustfully *adv* with distrust ⟨to say that I read the stories in the tabloids *distrustfully* is putting it mildly⟩ — see ASKANCE

distrustfulness *n* a feeling or attitude that one does not know the truth, truthfulness, or trustworthiness of someone or something ⟨one voter who usually listens to campaign promises with an air of *distrustfulness*⟩ — see DOUBT

disturb *vb* **1** to trouble the mind of; to make uneasy ⟨all that talk of war *disturbed* us⟩
synonyms agitate, ail, alarm (*also* alarum), bother, concern, derail, discomfort, discompose, dismay, disquiet, distemper, distract, distress, exercise, flurry, frazzle, freak (out), fuss, hagride, perturb, undo, unhinge, unsettle, upset, weird out, worry
related words aggravate, anger, annoy, bug, chafe, chivy (*or* chivvy), exasperate, fret, gall, get, grate, harass, harry, irk, irritate, nettle, peeve, pester, pique, put off, put out, rile, vex; bedevil, haunt, plague; abash, confound, confuse, discomfit, disconcert, discountenance, embarrass, faze, fluster, jar, mortify, nonplus, rattle, shake up; daunt, demoralize, discourage, dishearten, dispirit, unnerve
near antonyms allay, alleviate, assuage; appease, conciliate, mollify, pacify, placate, propitiate
antonyms calm, compose, quiet, settle, soothe, tranquilize (*also* tranquillize)
2 to change the place or position of ⟨the items on her desk had been *disturbed* by someone⟩ — see MOVE 1
3 to undo the proper order or arrangement of ⟨her careful filing system is sure to be *disturbed* during the move⟩ — see DISORDER
4 to thrust oneself upon (another) without invitation ⟨sorry to *disturb* you while you're working⟩ — see BOTHER 1
5 to cause discomfort to or trouble for ⟨please do not *disturb* yourself—I'll get my own drink⟩ — see INCONVENIENCE

disturbance *n* **1** a state of noisy, confused activity ⟨went to investigate the *disturbance* outside⟩ — see COMMOTION
2 an act or instance of the order of things being disturbed ⟨caused a *disturbance* in the carefully ordered proceedings⟩ — see UPSET
3 the act of making unwelcome intrusions upon another ⟨the assistant apologized for the *disturbance* and got straight to the point⟩ — see ANNOYANCE 1

disturbing *adj* **1** causing annoyance ⟨a *disturbing* visit by the next-door neighbor while I was trying to study⟩ — see ANNOYING
2 causing embarrassment ⟨there was a *disturbing* silence as I struggled to remember her name⟩ — see AWKWARD 3
3 causing worry or anxiety ⟨a *disturbing* trend in the nation's energy consumption⟩ — see TROUBLESOME
4 marked by or causing agitation or uncomfortable feelings ⟨a *disturbing* pause in the normally smooth operation of the machinery⟩ — see NERVOUS 2

disunion *n* **1** a lack of agreement or harmony ⟨political union may longer no possible for a country continuously racked by religious *disunion*⟩ — see DISCORD
2 the act or process of a whole separating into two or more parts or pieces ⟨in the 19th century the volatile issue of slavery resulted in the *disunion* of several Protestant denominations⟩ — see SEPARATION 1

disunite *vb* to set or force apart ⟨attempted to *disunite* the members of the club by vicious gossip⟩ — see SEPARATE 1

disunited *adj* disagreeing with each other ⟨the *disunited* members of the committee couldn't accomplish anything⟩ — see DIVIDED

disunity *n* a lack of agreement or harmony ⟨troubling signs of *disunity* within the normally peaceful organization⟩ — see DISCORD

disuse *n* lack of use ⟨since the car has experienced years of *disuse*, starting it up won't be easy⟩
synonyms desuetude, idleness, inactivity
related words abandonment, desertion, neglect; abeyance, dormancy, latency, quiescence
antonyms use

disused *adj* left unoccupied or unused ⟨a *disused* warehouse that had become a den for drug dealers⟩ — see ABANDONED 1

ditch *n* a long narrow channel dug in the earth ⟨after skidding on the ice, our car went right into the *ditch*⟩
synonyms dike, fosse (*or* foss), gutter, sheugh [*chiefly Scottish*], trench, trough
related words acequia [*Southwest*], culvert, drain, draw, gully (*also* gulley), ravine; drill, furrow; ha-ha, moat, stank [*British dialect*], sunk fence; kennel

ditch *vb* **1** to end a usually intimate relationship with ⟨*ditched* his wife for a woman 30 years his junior⟩
synonyms blow off, break off (with), dump, jilt, kiss off, leave
related words brush (aside *or* off), cold-shoulder, cut, high-hat, slight, snub; abandon, desert, forsake, maroon, quit
phrases kiss good-bye
near antonyms hook up (with), take; befriend, latch (on *or* onto)
2 to get rid of as useless or unwanted ⟨we *ditched* the old table at the town dump⟩ — see DISCARD

dither *n* **1** a state of nervous or irritated concern ⟨Grandma usually gets in a *dither* if I don't make my weekly call⟩ — see FRET
2 a sense of panic or extreme nervousness ⟨we were all in a *dither* while we waited for the test results⟩ — see JITTERS

dither *vb* to show uncertainty about the right course of action ⟨we *dithered* all afternoon over whether to go to the park or to the movies and ended up doing neither⟩ — see HESITATE

dithery *adj* feeling or showing uncomfortable feelings of uncertainty ⟨an expectant father in a high state of *dithery* alarm⟩ — see NERVOUS 1

dithyramb *n* a formal expression of praise ⟨a tongue-in-cheek *dithyramb* in honor of the chocolate chip cookie⟩ — see ENCOMIUM

ditto *adj* having qualities in common ⟨another mega mall filled with chain stores selling *ditto* merchandise⟩ — see ALIKE

ditto *adv* in like manner ⟨Tuesday was spent working all day, and Wednesday was spent *ditto*⟩ — see ALSO 1

ditto *vb* to say after another ⟨since you've said what I wanted to say—only better—I will just *ditto* your comments in my final report⟩ — see REPEAT 3

ditty *n* a short musical composition for the human voice often with instrumental accompaniment ⟨sung a little *ditty* in a minor key⟩ — see SONG 1

ditz *n* a silly flighty person ⟨it's surprising that such a serious guy would have a total *ditz* for a girlfriend⟩ — see FLIBBERTIGIBBET

ditzy *or* **ditsy** *adj* lacking in seriousness or maturity ⟨tried to have a serious conversation with her, but she kept saying *ditzy* things like "Ooh, you're so cute!"⟩ — see GIDDY 1

diurnal *adj* occurring, done, produced, or appearing every day ⟨a love as constant and certain as the *diurnal* tides⟩ — see DAILY

diurnal *n* a publication that appears at regular intervals ⟨a microfilm containing a collection of *diurnals* published by 19th-century American abolitionists⟩ — see JOURNAL 1

diva *n* a usually glamorous woman who is preeminent in her field of activity ⟨the reigning *diva* of daytime television⟩
synonyms goddess, princess, queen
related words high priestess, priestess; prima donna

divagation *n* **1** a departure from the subject under consideration ⟨this may well appear to be a *divagation* at first, but I hope to establish the relevance⟩ — see TANGENT
2 a turning away from a course or standard ⟨a self-consciously "literary" novel that represents a major *divagation* from traditional narrative⟩ — see DIVERGENCE 2

divan *n* a long upholstered piece of furniture designed for several sitters ⟨whenever I stayed over at their house I usually slept on the *divan* in the living room⟩ — see COUCH

divarication *n* a movement in different directions away from a common point ⟨the *divarication* of the various dialects of Latin that occurred with the decline of the Roman Empire⟩ — see DIVERGENCE 1

dive *n* **1** an act or instance of diving ⟨the penguin took a *dive* off of the ice sheet⟩
synonyms pitch, plunge
related words dip, immersion, submersion; fall, plump, slip, spill, stumble, tumble; descent, drop; belly flop, header, jackknife, swan dive
near antonyms jump, leap
2 the act or process of going to a lower level or altitude ⟨stock prices took a long, steady *dive*⟩ — see DESCENT 1

dive *vb* **1** to cast oneself head first into deep water ⟨we watched her *dive* in after the drowning man⟩
synonyms pitch, plunge, sound
related words dip, immerse, submerge; belly flop, plump, plunk (*or* plonk)
near antonyms surface
2 to go to a lower level especially abruptly ⟨sales figures for existing homes *dived* dramatically when mortgage rates skyrocketed⟩ — see DROP 2

dive (into) *vb* to start work on energetically ⟨the first morning back at work was spent *diving into* the huge pile of e-mails that had accumulated over the previous two weeks⟩ — see ATTACK 3

diverge *vb* **1** to change one's course or direction ⟨the deer abruptly *diverged* from its intended path the moment it spied the waiting lynx⟩ — see TURN 3
2 to go or move in different directions from a central point ⟨at that point the road and the railroad tracks *diverge*⟩ — see SEPARATE 2

divergence *n* **1** a movement in different directions away from a common point ⟨a growing *divergence* of opinion about that U.S. president's place in history⟩
synonyms bifurcation, divarication, divergency, separation
related words difference, disagreement, discrepancy, disparateness, disparity, dissidence, dissimilarity, distinction, distinctiveness, distinctness, diversity, unlikeness
phrases parting of the ways
near antonyms accord, agreement; likeness, similarity
antonyms convergence
2 a turning away from a course or standard ⟨any *divergence* from the community's strict moral code was met with social ostracism⟩
synonyms deflection, departure, detour, deviation, divagation, divergency, diversion
related words regression, retrogression, reversion
near antonyms adherence

divergency *n* **1** a movement in different directions away from a common point ⟨a growing *divergency* of opinion on that hot-button issue⟩ — see DIVERGENCE 1
2 a turning away from a course or standard ⟨a warning that no *divergency* from the church's traditional teachings on the subject would be permitted⟩ — see DIVERGENCE 2

divers *adj* being of many and various kinds ⟨the state fair offers *divers* amusements for the whole family⟩ — see MANIFOLD

diverse *adj* being not of the same kind ⟨a movement supported by people with *diverse* interests but one common goal⟩ — see DIFFERENT 1

diverseness *n* **1** the quality or state of being composed of many different elements or types ⟨the *diverseness* of the offerings at the art fair made judging a challenge⟩ — see VARIETY 1
2 the quality or state of being different ⟨the *diverseness* of the two top movies in the running for Best Picture could not be more striking⟩ — see DIFFERENCE 1

diversion *n* **1** someone or something that provides amusement or enjoyment ⟨a scavenger hunt was organized as a *diversion* for the guests at the party⟩ — see FUN 1
2 the act or activity of providing pleasure or amusement especially for the public ⟨movies and television became two of the most popular and influential *diversions* of the 20th century⟩ — see ENTERTAINMENT 1
3 a turning away from a course or standard ⟨carefully weighed testimony that did not contain the slightest *diversion* from the truth⟩ — see DIVERGENCE 2

diversity *n* **1** the quality or state of being composed of many different elements or types ⟨the *diversity* of plant life on that tropical island is staggering⟩ — see VARIETY 1
2 the quality or state of being different ⟨there's considerable *diversity* in the platforms for the two major parties⟩ — see DIFFERENCE 1

divert *vb* **1** to cause (someone) to pass the time agreeably occupied ⟨a light comedy to *divert* the tired business executive⟩ — see AMUSE
2 to change the course or direction of (something) ⟨the bike race was *diverted* around the construction zone⟩ — see TURN 2
3 to draw the attention or mind to something else ⟨trying to *divert* the child with a toy while the doctor was giving her a shot⟩ — see DISTRACT 1

diverting *adj* providing amusement or enjoyment ⟨some tall and *diverting* tales were told by the festival's roving storyteller⟩ — see FUN

divertissement *n* someone or something that provides amusement or enjoyment ⟨for visitors seeking more cerebral *divertissement*, the city boasts a fine performing arts center⟩ — see FUN 1

divest *vb* **1** to end the occupancy or possession of ⟨un-

able to make their mortgage payments, they were summarily *divested* of their house⟩ — see DISPOSSESS
2 to set (a person or thing) free of something that encumbers ⟨the former CEO has *divested* himself of most of his responsibilities but will continue to work with the company as a consultant⟩ — see RID
3 to take something away from ⟨he was *divested* of the boxing title when the fraud was uncovered⟩ — see DEPRIVE 1

divide *vb* **1** to set or force apart ⟨volunteers *divided* the donated groceries into several dozen piles⟩ — see SEPARATE 1
2 to go or move in different directions from a central point ⟨the group *divided* based on those who wanted to go swimming and those who didn't⟩ — see SEPARATE 2

divided *adj* disagreeing with each other ⟨the club members are sharply *divided* on the need for more fund-raising⟩
synonyms disunited, split
related words balkanized, fractionalized, fractionated; cohesionless, factious
phrases at loggerheads, at odds
antonyms unanimous, undivided, united

dividend *n* something given in addition to what is ordinarily expected or owed ⟨the reward money was an unexpected *dividend* for our good deed⟩ — see BONUS

divider *n* something that divides, separates, or marks off ⟨placed a *divider* across the gym so we could have two activities going on at once⟩ — see DIVISION 1

divination *n* the art or practice of foretelling future events by interpreting omens ⟨if her powers of *divination* are so great, why doesn't she know what the stock market will do?⟩
synonyms augury
related words astrology, crystal gazing, geomancy, hydromancy, oneiromancy, pyromancy, rhabdomancy

divine *adj* **1** of the very best kind ⟨how about a piece of the most *divine* apple pie I've ever tasted!⟩ — see EXCELLENT
2 of, relating to, or being God ⟨for these *divine* gifts let us be truly thankful⟩ — see HOLY 3

divine *n* a person specially trained and authorized to conduct religious services in a Christian church ⟨the great influence exerted by the Puritan *divines* in the Massachusetts Bay Colony⟩ — see CLERGYPERSON

divine *vb* to realize or know about beforehand ⟨it was easy to *divine* his intention of asking his girlfriend to marry him⟩ — see FORESEE

diviner *n* one who predicts future events or developments ⟨somehow the *diviner* failed to foresee her own misfortunes with the law⟩ — see PROPHET 1

divinity *n* **1** the quality or state of being divine ⟨Henry David Thoreau felt the presence of *divinity* in every part of nature⟩
synonyms deity, godhead, godhood
related words blessedness, godliness, holiness, piousness, saintliness
2 a being having superhuman powers and control over a particular part of life or the world ⟨a modest temple built for one of the minor *divinities* in ancient Greek mythology⟩ — see DEITY 1
3 *cap* the being worshipped as the creator and ruler of the universe ⟨communal worship of the *Divinity* was expected of every member of the colony⟩ — see DEITY 2

divisible *adj* capable of being split into two or more parts or pieces ⟨easily *divisible* into enough pieces for everyone⟩ — see SEPARABLE

division *n* **1** something that divides, separates, or marks off ⟨we poked our heads over the *division* between the yards to see what the fuss was about⟩
synonyms divider, partition, separation, separator
related words barrier, fence, wall; border, boundary, limit
2 a large unit of a governmental, business, or educational organization ⟨the complaints *division* handled all of the calls from the angry townsfolk⟩
synonyms agency, arm, branch, bureau, department, desk, office, service
related words subdepartment, subdivision
3 one of the units into which a whole is divided on the basis of a common characteristic ⟨one of the major *divisions* of birds⟩ — see CLASS 2
4 the act or process of a whole separating into two or more parts or pieces ⟨the assembly line was a major development in the *division* of labor among workers⟩ — see SEPARATION 1
5 the act or process of giving out something to each member of a group ⟨the person in charge of the *division* of the profits among the business partners⟩ — see DISTRIBUTION 1
6 a lack of agreement or harmony ⟨that church has been racked by *division* for some time now, and a split into two denominations seems unavoidable⟩ — see DISCORD

divorce *vb* to set or force apart ⟨in your head you need to *divorce* your wishes and fantasies from the realities of the world as it is⟩ — see SEPARATE 1

divulge *vb* to make known (as information previously kept secret) ⟨we tried to make him *divulge* the name of the winner, but he wouldn't budge⟩ — see REVEAL 1

divulgence *n* the act or an instance of making known something previously unknown or concealed ⟨the government strictly prohibits the *divulgence* of classified information⟩ — see REVELATION

dizzy *adj* **1** having a feeling of being whirled about and in danger of falling down ⟨I felt very *dizzy* after I got off of the roller coaster⟩
synonyms aswoon, giddy, light-headed, reeling, swimmy, vertiginous, whirling, woozy
related words faint, weak; addled, befuddled, confused, dazed, groggy
near antonyms clearheaded; stable, steady
2 suffering from mental confusion ⟨he felt *dizzy* from trying to remember all of the dates and names that were sure to be asked on the test⟩
synonyms addle, addled, addlepated, bedeviled, befogged, befuddled, bemused, bewildered, bushed [*chiefly Australian*], confounded, confused, dazed, distracted, dopey (*also* dopy), fogged, mixed-up, muddleheaded, muzzy, pixilated (*also* pixillated), punch-drunk, punchy, raddled, shell-shocked, silly, slaphappy, spaced-out (*or* spaced), spacey (*also* spacy), stunned, stupefied, zonked, zonked-out
related words senseless, unconscious
phrases at sea, out of it
near antonyms alert, conscious
antonyms clearheaded, unconfused
3 moving, proceeding, or acting with great speed ⟨prices climbing at a *dizzy* rate⟩ — see FAST 1
4 lacking in seriousness or maturity ⟨Marilyn Monroe never entirely succeeded in shaking off her *dizzy* blonde image⟩ — see GIDDY 1

do *n* **1** a social gathering ⟨it's supposed to be some sort of fancy *do*⟩ — see PARTY 1
2 a statement of what to do that must be obeyed by those concerned ⟨issued a long list of *dos* and don'ts before we even started the project⟩ — see COMMAND 1
3 a style or arrangement of hair ⟨you can tell that the picture was taken in the 1980s from my permed *do*⟩ — see HAIRDO
4 *archaic* something one must do because of prior agreement ⟨in this hour of national crisis everyone must do their *do*⟩ — see OBLIGATION 1

5 *chiefly dialect* a state of noisy, confused activity ⟨in that small town a great deal of *do* could come from very little indeed⟩ — see COMMOTION

do *vb* **1** to be fitting or proper ⟨that outfit just won't *do* for the opera⟩
synonyms befit, beseem [*archaic*], fit [*archaic*], go, serve, suit
related words satisfy, suffice; function, work
phrases fill the bill (*or* fit the bill)
2 to be enough ⟨even half of that amount of sugar will *do*⟩ — see SERVE 2
3 to carry through (as a process) to completion ⟨*do* as much as you can and leave the rest⟩ — see PERFORM 1
4 to make more attractive by adding something that is beautiful or becoming ⟨*did* the living room in French provincial style⟩ — see DECORATE
5 to meet one's day-to-day needs ⟨I'm *doing* just fine⟩ — see GET ALONG 1
6 to be the cause of (a situation, action, or state of mind) ⟨this neighborhood cleanup effort might just *do* some good⟩ — see EFFECT
7 to copy or exaggerate (someone or something) in order to make fun of ⟨the laughing partygoers begged their host to *do* Marlon Brando again⟩ — see MIMIC 1
8 to move forward along a course ⟨how are you *doing* with the house restoration?⟩ — see GO 1
9 to present a portrayal or performance of ⟨she's *done* Eliza Doolittle on the stage so many times that she can probably play the flower girl in her sleep⟩ — see ACT 1
10 to rob by the use of trickery or threats ⟨*did* them out of their savings with surprising ease⟩ — see FLEECE
11 to strike repeatedly ⟨no one is sure who *did* them in that alley⟩ — see BEAT 1
12 to take place ⟨nothing's ever *doing* in this boring little town⟩ — see HAPPEN

doable *adj* capable of being done or carried out ⟨the assignment will be just barely *doable* in the time allowed⟩ — see POSSIBLE 1

doc *n* a person specially trained in healing human medical disorders ⟨currently completing a residency as an emergency room *doc*⟩ — see DOCTOR

docile *adj* readily giving in to the command or authority of another ⟨a *docile* young pony that went wherever it was led⟩ — see OBEDIENT

docility *n* a readiness or willingness to yield to the wishes of others ⟨dogs bred for *docility* instead of aggressiveness⟩ — see COMPLIANCE 1

dock *n* a structure used by boats and ships for taking on or landing cargo and passengers ⟨the boat remained tied up at the *dock* for a week, waiting for the weather to clear⟩
synonyms float, jetty, landing, levee, pier, quai, quay, wharf
related words berth, mooring, slip; embarcadero [*West*]; dockyard, marina, quayage, shipyard, wharfage

[1]dock *vb* **1** to make less in extent or duration ⟨the editorial was *docked* by about a hundred words to make it fit on the page⟩ — see SHORTEN
2 to make (something) shorter or smaller with the use of a cutting instrument ⟨the boxer's tail was *docked* soon after birth⟩ — see CLIP 1

[2]dock *vb* to stop at or near a place along the shore ⟨the cruise ship *docked* at the first port of call early the next morning⟩ — see LAND 1

docker *n, chiefly British* one who loads and unloads ships at a port ⟨*dockers* threatened to go on strike and shut down all shipping on the Thames⟩ — see DOCKWORKER

docket *n* a listing of things to be presented or considered (as at a concert or play) ⟨on the Broadway *docket* for the early part of this season⟩ — see PROGRAM 1

dockhand *n* one who loads and unloads ships at a port ⟨a trade embargo that was especially hard on the nation's *dockhands*⟩ — see DOCKWORKER

dockworker *n* one who loads and unloads ships at a port ⟨the *dockworkers* spent all afternoon taking crates off of the ship⟩
synonyms docker [*chiefly British*], dockhand, longshoreman, roustabout, rouster, stevedore

doctor *n* a person specially trained in healing human medical disorders ⟨we called a *doctor* as soon as we realized the baby was sick⟩
synonyms croaker [*slang*], doc, medic, medico, physician, sawbones [*slang*]
related words family doctor, family physician, family practitioner, general practitioner; anesthesiologist, dermatologist, gynecologist, internist, neurologist, ob-gyn, obstetrician, ophthalmologist, orthopedist, pathologist, pediatrician (*also* pediatrist), physiatrist, podiatrist, radiologist, urologist; attending, clinician, hospitalist; specialist; plastic surgeon, surgeon; intern (*also* interne), resident; aidman, nurse, nurse-practitioner; EMT, paramedic (*also* paramedical); physical therapist, physiotherapist
antonyms nondoctor, nonphysician

doctor *vb* **1** to give medical treatment to ⟨a pledge to *doctor* the burn victims until they were whole again⟩
synonyms treat
related words cure, heal, mend, rehabilitate, remedy; attend, care (for), dose, drug, hospitalize, minister (to), nurse
2 to put into good shape or working order again ⟨spends his spare time *doctoring* old clocks⟩ — see MEND 1
3 to change (something) so as to make it suitable for a new use or situation ⟨slightly *doctored* his standard campaign speech for a collegiate audience⟩ — see ADAPT

doctrinaire *adj* given to or marked by the forceful expression of strongly held opinions ⟨a *doctrinaire* conservative, the columnist takes special delight in baiting liberals⟩ — see DOGMATIC

doctrine *n* **1** a statement or body of statements concerning faith or morals proclaimed by a church ⟨the Catholic Church's *doctrine* on the Eucharist⟩
synonyms canon, dogma
related words canon law; belief, conviction, tenet; credo, creed, ideology (*also* idealogy), philosophy, theology; axiom, precept, principle; symbol
2 the basic beliefs or guiding principles of a person or group ⟨the *doctrine* of quantum physicists⟩ — see CREED 1

document *n* **1** a piece of paper with information written or to be written on it ⟨filled out the *documents* for a bank loan⟩ — see FORM 2
2 a written or printed paper giving information about or proof of something ⟨have your *documents* ready as you approach the border⟩ — see CERTIFICATE

document *vb* to show the existence or truth of by evidence ⟨he tried in vain to *document* a link between ancient civilizations and extraterrestrials⟩ — see PROVE 1

documentary *adj* restricted to or based on fact ⟨a *documentary* film about the surprise attack on Pearl Harbor⟩ — see FACTUAL 1

documentation *n* something presented in support of the truth or accuracy of a claim ⟨the archaeologist presented convincing *documentation* of her theory at the conference⟩ — see PROOF

dodder *vb* to move forward while swaying from side to side ⟨was *doddering* down the walk outside the nursing home⟩ — see STAGGER 1

dodge *n* a clever often underhanded means to achieve an end ⟨just another *dodge* to get out of working in the yard⟩ — see TRICK 1

dodge *vb* **1** to move suddenly aside or to and fro ⟨*dodging* through the crowd on his way to the exit⟩
synonyms duck, jink, sidestep, slalom, weave, zigzag
related words avoid, elude, escape, evade, parry, shirk, skirt; deflect, turn; slide, slip
2 to avoid having to comply with (something) especially through cleverness ⟨always trying to *dodge* the landlord's rule prohibiting pets⟩ — see CIRCUMVENT 1
3 to get or keep away from (as a responsibility) through cleverness or trickery ⟨*dodged* the horde of paparazzi by leaving through the service entrance⟩ — see ESCAPE 2

dodger *n* a dishonest person who uses clever means to cheat others out of something of value ⟨one of the most artful *dodgers* in the annals of American crime⟩ — see TRICKSTER 1

dodging *n* the act or a means of getting or keeping away from something undesirable ⟨the governor's repeated *dodging* of tough questions at the press conference⟩ — see ESCAPE 2

dodgy *adj, chiefly British* **1** requiring exceptional skill or caution in performance or handling ⟨getting the trade unions to go along with the agreement will be a rather *dodgy* piece of work⟩ — see TRICKY 1
2 clever at attaining one's ends by indirect and often deceptive means ⟨needed a *dodgy* barrister to get him acquited of the charge⟩ — see ARTFUL 1
3 giving good reason for being doubted, questioned, or challenged ⟨the authenticity of the "lost" Shakespearean sonnet was more than a little *dodgy*⟩ — see DOUBTFUL 2

dodo *n* **1** a person with old-fashioned ideas ⟨youngsters helping old *dodos* learn to use computers⟩ — see FOGY
2 a stupid person ⟨she called him a *dodo* after he lost the concert tickets⟩ — see IDIOT

do down *vb, British* to achieve a victory over ⟨you'll *do* her *down* at cards, but she'll probably win at croquet⟩ — see BEAT 2

doff *vb* to rid oneself of (a garment) ⟨the blazing sun soon had the men *doffing* their jackets⟩ — see REMOVE 1

dog *n* **1** a domestic mammal that is related to the wolves and foxes ⟨a *dog* who needs a loving home⟩
synonyms canine, doggy (*or* doggie), hound, pooch, tyke (*also* tike)
related words cur, mongrel, mutt; bitch; lapdog, pup, puppy, puppy dog, whelp; bandog, bird dog, coonhound, courser, gundog, hunter, sheepdog, sled dog, watchdog, wolf dog, wolfhound; guide dog, police dog, working dog
2 a person whose behavior is offensive to others ⟨she must think that you're a real *dog* after hearing those tasteless jokes you told last night⟩ — see JERK 1

dog *vb* **1** to go after or on the track of ⟨star athletes being *dogged* by fans when they're out in public⟩ — see FOLLOW 2
2 to subject (someone) to constant scoldings and sharp reminders ⟨tired of constantly having to *dog* their son about cleaning his room⟩ — see NAG 1

dog collar *n* an ornamental chain or string (as of beads) worn around the neck ⟨a gala at which one can expect to see a number of trophy wives wearing diamond-encrusted *dog collars*⟩ — see NECKLACE

dog–eared *adj* showing signs of advanced wear and tear and neglect ⟨an old *dog-eared* copy of a beloved book⟩ — see SHABBY 1

dogface *n* a person engaged in military service ⟨during World War II journalist Ernie Pyle gained fame for his sympathetic reports on the wartime experiences of the common *dogface*⟩ — see SOLDIER

dogfight *n* an earnest effort for superiority or victory over another ⟨the playful competition over who would get the new office turned into a real *dogfight*⟩ — see CONTEST 1

dogged *adj* **1** continuing despite difficulties, opposition, or discouragement ⟨a madman who spent his life in *dogged* pursuit of power⟩ — see PERSISTENT
2 sticking to an opinion, purpose, or course of action in spite of reason, arguments, or persuasion ⟨your *dogged* adherence to a really lame argument is embarrassing⟩ — see OBSTINATE
3 showing no signs of slackening or yielding in one's purpose ⟨a *dogged* search for the missing piece of the puzzle⟩ — see UNYIELDING 1

doggedly *adv* with great effort or determination ⟨the detective *doggedly* pursued the suspect through the city's teeming streets⟩ — see HARD 1

doggedness *n* a steadfast adherence to an opinion, purpose, or course of action in spite of reason, arguments, or persuasion ⟨being an effective detective requires *doggedness* as well as cleverness⟩ — see OBSTINACY

dogging *n* the act of going after or in the tracks of another ⟨the merciless *dogging* of the Hollywood couple by the press⟩ — see PURSUIT 1

doggone *or* **doggoned** *adj* deserving of one's condemnation or displeasure ⟨yet another *doggone* problem in the phone lines⟩ — see DAMNABLE

doggy *or* **doggie** *n* a domestic mammal that is related to the wolves and foxes ⟨what a good little *doggy*!⟩ — see DOG 1

dogma *n* **1** a statement or body of statements concerning faith or morals proclaimed by a church ⟨the Catholic *dogma* of the bodily assumption of the Virgin Mary⟩ — see DOCTRINE 1
2 the basic beliefs or guiding principles of a person or group ⟨the Golden Rule encompasses a *dogma* that can serve all mankind⟩ — see CREED 1

dogmatic *also* **dogmatical** *adj* given to or marked by the forceful expression of strongly held opinions ⟨a critic's *dogmatic* insistence that abstract expressionism is the only school of 20th century art worthy of serious study⟩
synonyms doctrinaire, opinionated, opinionative, opinioned, pontifical, self-opinionated
related words adamant, adamantine, hardheaded, headstrong, implacable, inflexible, mulish, obdurate, obstinate, pertinacious, perverse, pigheaded, rigid, self-willed, stubborn, unbending, unyielding
near antonyms broadminded, open, open-minded, receptive
antonyms latitudinarian, undoctrinaire, undogmatic

dogmatism *n* stubborn or intolerant adherence to one's opinions or prejudices ⟨a man much given to inflexible *dogmatism* when it came to the role of government in regulating the economy⟩ — see BIGOTRY

dogmatist *n* one who stubbornly or intolerantly adheres to his or her own opinions and prejudices ⟨a *dogmatist* as far as economics are concerned, he's an unquestioning supporter of the supply-side theory⟩ — see BIGOT

dogmatizer *n* one who stubbornly or intolerantly adheres to his or her own opinions and prejudices ⟨in his foreign policy speech the secretary of state showed that he is anything but a *dogmatizer*⟩ — see BIGOT

do–good *adj* having or showing a concern for the welfare of others ⟨a *do-good* social program that never worked out in the way that was intended⟩ — see CHARITABLE 1

dogsbody *n, chiefly British* a person who does very hard or dull work ⟨I worked for several years as a gofer and general *dogsbody* for a London publishing house⟩ — see SLAVE 2

do in *vb* **1** to bring to a complete end the physical sound-

ness, existence, or usefulness of ⟨a business venture that was *done in* by poor planning⟩ — see DESTROY 1
2 to deprive of life ⟨the early frost *did in* all of our tender plants⟩ — see KILL 1
3 to put to death deliberately ⟨somebody *did* the old man *in* late last night⟩ — see MURDER 1
4 to use up all the physical energy of ⟨the long day of hard work really *did* me *in*⟩ — see EXHAUST 1
5 to rob by the use of trickery or threats ⟨too savvy an investor to be *done in* by preposterous claims of astronomical returns⟩ — see FLEECE

doing *n* something done by someone ⟨is that mess in the kitchen your *doing*?⟩ — see ACTION 1

doldrums *n pl* 1 a state of temporary inactivity ⟨the theater scene is usually in the *doldrums* during the summer⟩ — see ABEYANCE
2 a state or spell of low spirits ⟨the team had been in the *doldrums* ever since losing the championship⟩ — see SADNESS
3 the state of being bored ⟨in the *doldrums* while we waited for something to happen⟩ — see BOREDOM

dole *n* the giving of necessities and especially money to the needy ⟨an eccentric millionaire who was known for his annual Christmas *dole* to needy-looking strangers he met on the street⟩ — see CHARITY 1

doleful *adj* 1 expressing or suggesting mourning ⟨a *doleful* expression on their faces as they said good-bye to the friends they had made over the summer⟩ — see MOURNFUL 1
2 feeling unhappiness ⟨the visibly *doleful* players, heartbroken about their loss⟩ — see SAD 1

dolefully *adv* with feelings of bitterness or grief ⟨the novelist *dolefully* remarked that the proceeds from his last book would scarcely buy a dollhouse, let alone a real house⟩ — see HARD 2

dolefulness *n* 1 a state or spell of low spirits ⟨with the resigned *dolefulness* of an athlete who knows his playing days are over, he cleared out his locker for the last time⟩ — see SADNESS
2 deep sadness especially for the loss of someone or something loved ⟨a period of *dolefulness* that seemed to last forever for the widower⟩ — see SORROW

dole out *vb* to give out (something) to appropriate individuals ⟨she *doles out* office supplies as if she were paying for them out of her own pocket⟩ — see ADMINISTER 1

dolesome *adj* expressing or suggesting mourning ⟨the *dolesome* sound of a lone harmonica arising from the darkened encampment⟩ — see MOURNFUL 1

doll *n* 1 a small figure often of a human being used especially as a child's plaything ⟨there was a row of *dolls* along the shelf in the bedroom⟩
synonyms action figure, dolly, poppet [*Midland*], puppet
related words rag doll; figure, figurine; handpuppet, marionette
2 a physically attractive person ⟨her new boyfriend is a real *doll*⟩
synonyms babe [*slang*], cutie (*or* cutey), dish, dreamboat [*slang*], fox, glamour-puss, hottie, knockout, looker, showstopper, ten
related words beauty, eyeful, goddess, lovely, stunner; beefcake, hunk, stud, superstud; bimbette [*slang*], bimbo [*slang*], himbo
antonyms dog

dollar *n* a U.S. currency bill representing 100 cents ⟨a wad of *dollars* in his pocket⟩
synonyms bone [*slang*], buck, clam, one, smacker [*slang*]
related words greenback; dead presidents [*slang*]

dollars-and-cents *adj* of or relating to money, banking, or investments ⟨a *dollars-and-cents* analysis of the situation⟩ — see FINANCIAL

dollop *n* a small uneven mass ⟨served crackers topped with *dollops* of caviar as an appetizer⟩ — see LUMP 1

doll up *vb* 1 to make more attractive by adding something that is beautiful or becoming ⟨if you were to *doll up* those Shaker-style rooms, you'd ruin their simple elegance⟩ — see DECORATE
2 to put on one's best or formal clothes ⟨got all *dolled up* for the party⟩ — see DRESS UP

dolly *n* a small figure often of a human being used especially as a child's plaything ⟨my kid sister was always playing with her *dollies*⟩ — see DOLL 1

dolly bird *n, British* a lovely woman ⟨back in the swinging '60s she was one of London's most celebrated *dolly birds*⟩ — see BEAUTY 2

dolor *n* deep sadness especially for the loss of someone or something loved ⟨her sad poems grew out of a deep *dolor* that lasted for months⟩ — see SORROW

dolorous *adj* expressing or suggesting mourning ⟨*dolorous* ballads of death and regret⟩ — see MOURNFUL 1

dolorously *adv* with feelings of bitterness or grief ⟨another country singer wailing *dolorously* about the faithless woman who done him wrong⟩ — see HARD 2

dolt *n* a stupid person ⟨he's always jokingly calling his best friend a *dolt*⟩ — see IDIOT

doltish *adj* not having or showing an ability to absorb ideas readily ⟨foolish and *doltish* behavior that was really beneath you⟩ — see STUPID 1

doltishness *n* the quality or state of lacking intelligence or quickness of mind ⟨she's usually quite bright, with only occasional moments of inexplicable *doltishness*⟩ — see STUPIDITY 1

domain *n* a region of activity, knowledge, or influence ⟨a museum director who is one of the most powerful figures in the art *domain*⟩ — see FIELD 2

dome *n* the upper or front part of the body that contains the brain, the major sense organs, and the mouth ⟨the fitted cap is too small for my large *dome*⟩ — see HEAD 1

domestic *adj* 1 of or relating to a household or family ⟨the surest way to maintain *domestic* peace and harmony is to have everyone pitch in on chores⟩
synonyms familial, household
related words homelike, homely, homey (*also* homy); residential
antonyms nondomestic, nonfamilial
2 changed from the wild state so as to become useful and obedient to humans ⟨*domestic* animals in a barnyard⟩ — see TAME 1
3 belonging to a particular place by birth or origin ⟨the *domestic* bird population has been virtually wiped out by the brown tree snake⟩ — see NATIVE 1

domestic *n* a person hired to perform household or personal services ⟨working as a team, the man and his wife hired themselves out as *domestics* for wealthy homeowners⟩ — see SERVANT

domesticated *adj* changed from the wild state so as to become useful and obedient to humans ⟨the *domesticated* horses are kept in a corral⟩ — see TAME 1

domicile *n* the place where one lives ⟨welcome to my *domicile*, humble though it may be⟩ — see HOME 1

domicile *vb* to provide with living quarters or shelter ⟨the university *domiciles* students in a variety of buildings in and around its urban campus⟩ — see HOUSE 1

dominance *n* 1 controlling power or influence over others ⟨although Napoléon had achieved *dominance* over the European continent, Great Britain still ruled the waves⟩ — see SUPREMACY 1
2 the fact or state of being above others in rank or importance ⟨the professor's *dominance* in the field of ancient Greek history⟩ — see EMINENCE 1

dominant *adj* coming before all others in importance ⟨the *dominant* authority on the English language⟩ — see FOREMOST 1

dominate *vb* **1** to bring under one's control by force of arms ⟨by 1941 Hitler had *dominated* much of Europe⟩ — see CONQUER 1
2 to look down on ⟨the ruined fortress *dominates* the town⟩ — see OVERLOOK 1

dominating *n* the act or process of bringing someone or something under one's control ⟨the gradual *dominating* of Europe by a few ruling families⟩ — see CONQUEST

domination *n* **1** controlling power or influence over others ⟨auction houses battling for *domination* in the high-end art market⟩ — see SUPREMACY 1
2 the act or process of bringing someone or something under one's control ⟨the Spanish *domination* of the Americas in the 16th century⟩ — see CONQUEST

domineering *adj* fond of ordering people around ⟨the younger children in the family were controlled by a *domineering* older sister⟩ — see BOSSY

dominie *n* a person specially trained and authorized to conduct religious services in a Christian church ⟨a small village where the doctor and the *dominie* were the two pillars of society⟩ — see CLERGYPERSON

dominion *n* **1** controlling power or influence over others ⟨in the Bible, man is given *dominion* over all the animals⟩ — see SUPREMACY 1
2 the right or means to command or control others ⟨was granted *dominion* over the household servants⟩ — see POWER 1

don *vb* to place on one's person ⟨she *donned* her best gown for the ball⟩ — see PUT ON 1

donate *vb* to make a present of ⟨we plan to *donate* all the profits from the rummage sale to charity⟩ — see GIVE 1

donation *n* **1** a gift of money or its equivalent to a charity, humanitarian cause, or public institution ⟨a generous *donation* to the orphanage from an anonymous benefactor⟩ — see CONTRIBUTION
2 something given to someone without expectation of a return ⟨a chocolate cake was my *donation* to the office party⟩ — see GIFT 1

donative *n* **1** something given in addition to what is ordinarily expected or owed ⟨the support of the military was bought with a large *donative* to a couple of well-placed generals⟩ — see BONUS
2 something given to someone without expectation of a return ⟨regarded her annual bonus as a just recompense for her job performance and not as some corporate *donative*⟩ — see GIFT 1

donator *n* one that helps another with gifts or money ⟨a frequent *donator* of funds to research foundations⟩ — see BENEFACTOR

done *adj* **1** brought or having come to an end ⟨the demanding job was finally *done*⟩ — see COMPLETE 2
2 depleted in strength, energy, or freshness ⟨after bicycling 30 miles we were completely *done*⟩ — see WEARY 1
3 facing certain defeat, disaster, or death ⟨at this point retailing in the city's downtown is *done*⟩ — see DONE FOR
4 no longer existing ⟨the day of the small independent grocer is *done*⟩ — see EXTINCT

done for *adj* facing certain defeat, disaster, or death ⟨with no means of escape, the stranded climbers knew that they were *done for*⟩
synonyms dead, done, doomed, finished, kaput (*also* kaputt), ruined, sunk
related words endangered, imperiled (*or* imperilled)

Don Juan *n* a man given to seducing women ⟨at the hotel bar she was immediately hit on by the local *Don Juan*⟩
synonyms Casanova, lecher, lothario, lounge lizard, masher, philanderer, satyr, wolf, womanizer
related words amorist, gallant, ladies' man (*also* lady's man), lady-killer, lover, paramour, Romeo; debaucher, romancer, seducer; whoremaster, whoremonger

donkey *n* **1** a sturdy and patient domestic mammal that is used especially to carry things ⟨we put our bags on the *donkey* and headed down the canyon⟩
synonyms ass, burro, jackass, moke [*British slang*]
related words jack, jennet, jenny; hinny, mule; pack animal
2 a stupid person ⟨called him a *donkey* when he refused to go along with their plans⟩ — see IDIOT

donkey's years *n, chiefly British* a long or seemingly long period of time ⟨the greengrocer and the fishmonger haven't spoken in *donkey's years*⟩ — see AGE 2

donkeywork *n* very hard or unpleasant work ⟨the *donkeywork* involved in setting up one's own start-up software firm⟩ — see [1]TOIL

donnybrook *n* **1** a rough and often noisy fight usually involving several people ⟨a dozen people were arrested after the *donnybrook* at the stadium⟩ — see BRAWL 1
2 an often noisy or angry expression of differing opinions ⟨the kind of hot-button issue that inevitably creates a *donnybrook* in the halls of the statehouse⟩ — see ARGUMENT 1

donor *n* one that helps another with gifts or money ⟨a list of *donors* in the charitable foundation's annual report⟩ — see BENEFACTOR

do–nothing *n* **1** a lazy person ⟨the new boss quickly figured out who the *do-nothings* were and fired them⟩ — see LAZYBONES
2 an idle worthless person ⟨he indiscriminately dismisses the state legislators as a bunch of *do-nothings* who live at the taxpayers' expense⟩ — see NE'ER-DO-WELL

Don Quixote *n* one whose conduct is guided more by the image of perfection than by the real world ⟨a latter-day *Don Quixote*, she's spent her life fighting the state's big logging companies⟩ — see IDEALIST

doodad *n* **1** a small article the actual name of which one either does not know or cannot remember ⟨where does this little *doodad* go?⟩
synonyms dingus, doohickey, hickey, thingamabob, thingamajig (*or* thingumajig), thingummy, whatchamacallit, whatnot, whatsit (*also* whatsis *or* what-is-it)
2 a small object displayed for its attractiveness or interest ⟨has a habit of buying gadgets and *doodads* sold on television shopping channels⟩ — see KNICKKNACK
3 something that decorates or beautifies ⟨the array of *doodads* that some drivers hang from their rearview mirror⟩ — see DECORATION 1

doodle *vb* to spend time in aimless activity ⟨I plan to spend the entire vacation just *doodling*⟩ — see FIDDLE (AROUND)

doodley–squat *or* **doodly–squat** *n* the smallest amount or part imaginable ⟨tried to act intelligent but it was painfully obvious that he didn't know *doodley-squat* about cosmology⟩ — see JOT

doo–doo *n* solid matter discharged from an animal's alimentary canal ⟨a three-year-old who thought talking about *doo-doo* was the funniest thing ever⟩ — see DROPPING 1

doofus *n, slang* **1** a person who lacks good sense or judgment ⟨I don't want to be partnered on the project with that *doofus*⟩ — see FOOL 1
2 a stupid person ⟨that actor invariably plays a *doofus* on screen but he's anything but one in real life⟩ — see IDIOT

doohickey *n* a small article the actual name of which one either does not know or cannot remember ⟨screw in the *doohickey* at the top of the lamp shade⟩ — see DOODAD 1

doom *n* **1** a decision made by a court or tribunal regarding a case it has heard ⟨the judge solemnly pronounced his *doom* before a hushed courtroom⟩ — see SENTENCE
2 a state or end that seemingly has been decided beforehand ⟨it was her *doom* to be haunted by the memory of that terrible day⟩ — see FATE 1
3 the permanent stopping of all the vital bodily activities ⟨met his *doom* at the hands of a rampaging rhinoceros⟩ — see DEATH 1

doom *vb* **1** to determine the fate of in advance ⟨had always felt that he was *doomed* to remain single forever⟩ — see DESTINE
2 to impose a judicial punishment on ⟨*doomed* the murderer to life in prison without the possibility of parole⟩ — see SENTENCE

doomed *adj* facing certain defeat, disaster, or death ⟨at that point it was obvious to all that the astronauts were *doomed*⟩ — see DONE FOR

doomsayer *n* one given to forebodings and predictions of impending calamity ⟨*doomsayers* had been saying for some time that the housing bubble was going to burst⟩
synonyms Cassandra, Chicken Little, doomsdayer, doomster
related words defeatist, fatalist; naysayer, negativist, pessimist; handwringer, worrier, worrywart
antonyms optimist, Pollyanna

doomsdayer *n* one given to forebodings and predictions of impending calamity ⟨once again *doomsdayers* were issuing warnings about the dangers of nuclear proliferation⟩ — see DOOMSAYER

doomster *n* one given to forebodings and predictions of impending calamity ⟨from time immemorial *doomsters* have been saying that the world is going to hell in a handbasket⟩ — see DOOMSAYER

doomy *adj* being or showing a sign of evil or calamity to come ⟨the surging *doomy* music in the background was an unmistakable sign that things would not end well for the movie's hero⟩ — see OMINOUS

door *n* **1** a barrier by which an entry is closed and opened ⟨we locked the *door* to the room so that no one could get in⟩
synonyms gate, hatch, portal
related words double door, Dutch door, French door, lattice, portcullis, postern, revolving door, storm door, trapdoor, wicket
2 the opening through which one can enter or leave a structure ⟨a steady stream of visitors through the front *door*⟩
synonyms doorway, entrance, gate, gateway, way
related words hatch, hatchway
3 the means or right of entering or participating in ⟨education unlocks the *door* to advancement⟩ — see ENTRANCE 1

do–or–die *adj* fully committed to achieving a goal ⟨a *do-or-die* abolitionist, William Lloyd Garrison refused to give an inch on the issue of slavery⟩ — see DETERMINED 1

doorkeeper *n* a person who tends a door ⟨the *doorkeeper* held the door open for us so we didn't have to put down our packages⟩
synonyms doorman, gatekeeper, janitor, porter [*chiefly British*]

doorman *n* a person who tends a door ⟨we tipped the hotel *doorman* for getting us a cab⟩ — see DOORKEEPER

doormat *n* a person without strength of character ⟨a *doormat* who always gave in to his father's demands⟩ — see WEAKLING 2

doorway *n* **1** the means or right of entering or participating in ⟨the *doorway* to a life of luxury and leisure⟩ — see ENTRANCE 1
2 the opening through which one can enter or leave a structure ⟨he stood in the *doorway* until we finally invited him in⟩ — see DOOR 2

doozy *or* **doozie** *also* **doozer** *n* something very good of its kind ⟨you don't make mistakes very often, but when you do, it's a real *doozy*⟩ — see JIM-DANDY

dope *adj, slang* of the very best kind ⟨dude, there are some really *dope* rhymes on that rapper's latest album⟩ — see EXCELLENT

dope *n* **1** information not generally available to the public ⟨the stool pigeon gave us the *dope* on the deal taking place that night at the warehouse⟩
synonyms book, 411 [*slang*], inside, lowdown, poop [*slang*], scoop, skinny [*slang*], tip
related words dirt, dish, gossip, rumor, story; hint, pointer; information, intelligence, news, tidings, word
near antonyms ancient history, open secret
2 a stupid person ⟨that *dope* thought he could swim across the Colorado River at night⟩ — see IDIOT

dope (out) *vb* to find an answer for through reasoning ⟨tried to *dope out* the answer from the little information we had been given⟩ — see SOLVE

dopehead *n* a person who regularly uses drugs especially illegally ⟨threw his roommate out when he discovered that the guy was a *dopehead*⟩ — see DOPER

doper *n* a person who regularly uses drugs especially illegally ⟨the *doper* had to go straight—there would be some serious jail time if he didn't⟩
synonyms addict, dopehead, druggie (*also* druggy), fiend, freak [*slang*], head, hophead [*slang*], hype [*slang*], junkie (*also* junky), stoner, user
related words acidhead, cokehead, crackhead, pothead, speed freak; burnout
antonyms nonaddict, nonuser

dopey *also* **dopy** *adj* **1** not having or showing an ability to absorb ideas readily ⟨a sweet but *dopey* little dog who never learned any tricks⟩ — see STUPID 1
2 suffering from mental confusion ⟨we were still *dopey* from having all those facts and figures thrown at us⟩ — see DIZZY 2

dopiness *n* the quality or state of lacking intelligence or quickness of mind ⟨amused by the sheer *dopiness* of the movie's plot⟩ — see STUPIDITY 1

doppelgänger *or* **doppelganger** *n* something or someone that strongly resembles another ⟨at the mall today I saw someone who could be your *doppelgänger*⟩ — see IMAGE 1

do–rag *n* a scarf worn on the head ⟨a rapper wearing a nylon *do-rag* over his cornrows⟩ — see BANDANNA

dork *n, slang* **1** a person slavishly devoted to intellectual or academic pursuits ⟨a jock willing to pay to have one of the *dorks* write his term paper for him⟩ — see NERD 1
2 a stupid person ⟨he tried to be suave, but she still thought he was a *dork*⟩ — see IDIOT

dorkiness *n* the quality or state of lacking intelligence or quickness of mind ⟨the delicious *dorkiness* of the vice president made him a ripe target for satirists⟩ — see STUPIDITY 1

dorky *adj, slang* not having or showing an ability to absorb ideas readily ⟨she's always being embarrassed by her *dorky* cousins⟩ — see STUPID 1

dormancy *n* **1** a state of temporary inactivity ⟨some volcanoes have eruptive cycles marked by long stretches of *dormancy*⟩ — see ABEYANCE
2 lack of action or activity ⟨a fighting force that could be roused instantly from *dormancy* to action⟩ — see INACTION

dormant *adj* **1** being in a state of suspended conscious-

ness ⟨the bears lay *dormant* in their den during the winter⟩ — see ASLEEP 1
2 not being in a state of use, activity, or employment ⟨the engine lay *dormant* in the garage until we found a use for it⟩ — see INACTIVE 2

doss *n, chiefly British* a place set aside for sleeping ⟨the living room couch was my *doss* for the weekend I spent at my friend's Lake District cottage⟩ — see BED 1

doss (down) *vb, chiefly British* to go to one's bed in order to sleep ⟨he frequently plays host at his London flat, and overnight guests pretty much *doss down* where they please⟩ — see BED 1

dot *n* a small area that is different (as in color) from the main part ⟨there was just a *dot* on the tablecloth where the food had spattered⟩ — see SPOT 1

dot *vb* **1** to cover by or as if by scattering something over or on ⟨a hillside *dotted* with wildflowers⟩ — see SCATTER 2
2 to mark with small spots especially unevenly ⟨the practice of some chefs of positioning a small portion of food in the center and *dotting* the rest of the plate with sauce⟩ — see SPOT 1

dotage *n* the state or period of mental decline that typically accompanies old age ⟨he's now in that stage of his *dotage* where he has trouble remembering the simplest things⟩
synonyms caducity, second childhood, senility
related words anility; decrepitude, feebleness, infirmity; geezerhood, senectitude, senescence

dote (on) *vb* to love or admire too much ⟨*doted on* her only grandchild⟩ — see IDOLIZE

dotted *adj* marked with spots ⟨a *dotted* tie that didn't go with his striped shirt at all⟩ — see SPOTTED 1

dottiness *n* lack of good sense or judgment ⟨the irrepressible *dottiness* of her aunt was actually rather endearing⟩ — see FOOLISHNESS 1

dotty *adj* showing or marked by a lack of good sense or judgment ⟨*dotty* relatives that we have to endure only on Thanksgiving⟩ — see FOOLISH 1

dotty (over) *adj* filled with an intense or excessive love for ⟨she's *dotty over* begonias—as you can see the minute you enter her house⟩ — see ENAMORED (OF)

double *adj* **1** consisting of two members or parts that are usually joined ⟨an egg with a *double* yolk⟩
synonyms binary, bipartite, double-barreled, double-edged, dual, duplex, twin, twofold
related words mated, paired
near antonyms unpaired
antonyms single
2 being twice as great or as many ⟨after it was ranked the best in the country, the college had *double* the usual number of applicants⟩
synonyms twofold
3 not being or expressing what one appears to be or express ⟨she's known for speaking with a *double* tongue, so I doubt that her concern is very heartfelt⟩ — see INSINCERE

double *adv* to two times the amount or degree ⟨raced to his side *double* quick⟩ — see DOUBLY

double *n* something or someone that strongly resembles another ⟨he looks so much like you that he could be your *double*⟩ — see IMAGE 1

double *vb* **1** to make twice as great or as many ⟨we *doubled* our investment in six months⟩
synonyms duplicate, redouble
related words compound, multiply; accumulate, balloon, build (up), burgeon (*also* bourgeon), enlarge, escalate, expand, increase, mount, mushroom, proliferate, rise, snowball, swell, wax
2 to lay one part over or against another part of ⟨*double* the wet cloth and place it on the victim's forehead⟩ — see FOLD 1

double–barreled *adj* consisting of two members or parts that are usually joined ⟨the *double-barreled* goal of the company is to do well in the marketplace and to do good in the community⟩ — see DOUBLE 1

double bind *n* a situation in which one has to choose between two or more equally unsatisfactory choices ⟨the *double bind* faced by every politician: responding to scurrilous charges only gives them unwarranted publicity; not responding to such charges is often interpreted as an admission of guilt⟩ — see DILEMMA 1

double–cross *vb* to be unfaithful or disloyal to ⟨she promised to share the profits but then *double-crossed* us⟩ — see BETRAY 1

double cross *n* the act or fact of violating the trust or confidence of another ⟨politics is full of *double crosses* and backbiting⟩ — see BETRAYAL

double–crosser *n* one who betrays a trust or an allegiance ⟨we knew he was a *double-crosser* so we didn't tell him our real plans⟩ — see TRAITOR

double–dealer *n* one who betrays a trust or an allegiance ⟨the company seems to have one or two *double-dealers* who are selling information to competitors⟩ — see TRAITOR

double–dealing *adj* **1** marked by, based on, or done by the use of dishonest methods to acquire something of value ⟨*double-dealing* business practices that are being investigated by the state's attorney general⟩ — see FRAUDULENT 1
2 not being or expressing what one appears to be or express ⟨the *double-dealing* salesman never told me that the car had been in an accident and repaired⟩ — see INSINCERE
3 given to or marked by cheating and deception ⟨the *double-dealing* team owners were pitting the two cities against one another, both of whom badly wanted the franchise⟩ — see DISHONEST 2

double–dealing *n* the inclination or practice of misleading others through lies or trickery ⟨a go-between suspected of *double-dealing*⟩ — see DECEIT 1

double–dome *n* a person with strong intellectual interests ⟨*double-domes* in the scientific community probably understand it—but the rest of us don't⟩ — see INTELLECTUAL

double Dutch *n* unintelligible or meaningless talk ⟨the fast-talking con man spouts some *double Dutch*, and it is only afterwards that the victim realizes that he's given two twenties for a ten⟩ — see GIBBERISH 1

double–edged *adj* **1** consisting of two members or parts that are usually joined ⟨the *double-edged* purpose of the sales promotion is to clear out existing stock and to attract new customers⟩ — see DOUBLE 1
2 having an often intentionally veiled or uncertain meaning ⟨her *double-edged* remark that she hoped that I ultimately got what I deserved⟩ — see OBSCURE 1

double–faced *adj* not being or expressing what one appears to be or express ⟨you'll find out how *double-faced* she is when you're no further help to her career⟩ — see INSINCERE

double–quick *adv* with great speed ⟨she changed her mind *double-quick* when she learned that the sales conference would be held in Paris⟩ — see FAST 1

double–talk *n* **1** language marked by abstractions, jargon, euphemisms, and circumlocutions ⟨the reporter listened to the senator's *double-talk* for about 30 seconds, and then repeated the question⟩ — see GIBBERISH 2
2 unintelligible or meaningless talk ⟨the man on the sidewalk rattled off some *double-talk*, shoved the petition in my face, and before I realized it, I had added my signature to the list⟩ — see GIBBERISH 1

doubly *adv* to two times the amount or degree ⟨we were

doubly certain of her guilt after we read the article in the newspaper⟩
synonyms double, twice, twofold

doubt *n* a feeling or attitude that one does not know the truth, truthfulness, or trustworthiness of someone or something ⟨from the beginning I had my *doubts* about the investment scheme⟩
synonyms distrust, distrustfulness, dubiety, dubitation [*archaic*], incertitude, misdoubt, misgiving, mistrust, mistrustfulness, query, reservation, skepticism, suspicion, uncertainty
related words disbelief, incredulity, unbelief; anxiety, concern, paranoia, wariness; compunction, niggle [*chiefly British*], qualm, scruple, tremor
near antonyms credence, faith
antonyms assurance, belief, certainty, certitude, confidence, conviction, sureness, surety, trust

doubt *vb* to have no trust or confidence in ⟨I *doubt* that you can do all that you say⟩ — see DISTRUST

doubtable *adj* **1** giving good reason for being doubted, questioned, or challenged ⟨her argument rested entirely upon some highly *doubtable* logic⟩ — see DOUBTFUL 2
2 open to question or dispute ⟨that his wartime exploit happened at all is very *doubtable*⟩ — see DEBATABLE 1

doubter *n* a person who is always ready to doubt or question the truth or existence of something ⟨there will always be some hard-core *doubters* of the government's denial of the UFO incident⟩ — see SKEPTIC

doubtful *adj* **1** not feeling sure about the truth, wisdom, or trustworthiness of someone or something ⟨he was *doubtful* about the decision to complete the project despite its mounting problems⟩
synonyms distrustful, dubious, hinky [*slang*], mistrustful, skeptical, suspicious, trustless, uncertain, unconvinced, undecided, unsettled, unsure
related words ambivalent, conflicted, equivocal; diffident, insecure; halting, hesitant, indecisive, irresolute, vacillating, wavering
phrases on the fence
near antonyms assured, confident, sanguine, self-assured; decisive, determined, resolute
antonyms certain, convinced, positive, sure
2 giving good reason for being doubted, questioned, or challenged ⟨the election results were highly *doubtful*, so an investigation was begun⟩
synonyms debatable, disputable, dodgy [*chiefly British*], doubtable, dubious, dubitable, equivocal, fishy, problematic (*also* problematical), queer, questionable, shady, shaky, suspect, suspicious
related words alleged, so-called, supposed; moot; ambiguous, open, unclear; uncertain, undecided, undetermined; far-fetched, flimsy, improbable, unlikely, weak
near antonyms decisive, definitive; clear, obvious, open-and-shut, positive
antonyms certain, hands-down, incontestable, indisputable, indubitable, questionless, sure, undeniable, undoubted, unproblematic, unquestionable
3 not likely to be true or to occur ⟨our winning the championship increasingly looks like a *doubtful* outcome⟩ — see IMPROBABLE
4 open to question or dispute ⟨a *doubtful* claim to the property⟩ — see DEBATABLE 1

doubtfully *adv* with distrust ⟨we followed our guide *doubtfully*, keeping our eyes open at all times⟩ — see ASKANCE

doubting *adj* inclined to doubt or question claims ⟨congenitally *doubting* viewers will wonder if there's anything real about that so-called reality show⟩ — see SKEPTICAL 1

doubtingly *adv* with distrust ⟨we looked at her *doubtingly* as she told the story of her life⟩ — see ASKANCE

doubting Thomas *n* a person who is always ready to doubt or question the truth or existence of something ⟨an astronomer who enjoys taking the role of the *doubting Thomas* in debates with UFOlogists⟩ — see SKEPTIC

doubtless *adj* having or showing a mind free from doubt ⟨another one of his *doubtless* predictions that will never come true⟩ — see CERTAIN 2

doubtless *adv* **1** without any question ⟨she is *doubtless* the one and only girl for me⟩ — see INDEED 1
2 by reasonable assumption ⟨*doubtless* you have heard this story before, but I'll tell it anyway⟩ — see PROBABLY

doubtlessness *n* a state of mind in which one is free from doubt ⟨with the *doubtlessness* of a man who never spent a moment in self-reflection, the president barreled down the road to disaster⟩ — see CONFIDENCE 2

dough *n* something (as pieces of stamped metal or printed paper) customarily and legally used as a medium of exchange, a measure of value, or a means of payment ⟨didn't have to spend a lot of *dough* for a new stereo⟩ — see MONEY 1

doughtily *adv* in a fearless manner ⟨*doughtily* persistent in his opposition to casino gambling in his state⟩ — see BRAVELY 1

doughtiness *n* strength of mind to carry on in spite of danger ⟨a new recruit with all of the *doughtiness* of the finest soldiers who ever saw battle⟩ — see COURAGE

doughty *adj* feeling or displaying no fear by temperament ⟨the *doughty* heroes of old⟩ — see BRAVE 1

doughy *adj* lacking a healthy skin color ⟨she worried that her husband was very ill when she saw his *doughy* complexion⟩ — see PALE 2

do up *vb* **1** to make more attractive by adding something that is beautiful or becoming ⟨the whole house had been *done up* for Halloween⟩ — see DECORATE
2 to outfit with clothes and especially fine or special clothes ⟨on Wild West Day some of the women came to the office *done up* as showgirls, while the men were mostly outlaws⟩ — see CLOTHE 1
3 to use up all the physical energy of ⟨all of this fussing about the wedding has *done* me *up*⟩ — see EXHAUST 1

dour *adj* harsh and threatening in manner or appearance ⟨a *dour* prison guard who didn't look like he'd be very understanding⟩ — see GRIM 1

douse *n, British* a hard strike with a part of the body or an instrument ⟨those soccer hooligans need a sound *douse* or two from a police officer's club⟩ — see [1]BLOW

[1]douse *vb* to rid oneself of (a garment) ⟨in those days a gentleman would *douse* his hat when going indoors⟩ — see REMOVE 1

[2]douse *also* **dowse** *vb* **1** to cause to cease burning ⟨*douse* the campfire before leaving in the morning⟩ — see EXTINGUISH 1
2 to make wet ⟨the heavy rains thoroughly *doused* the tourists strolling the town streets⟩ — see WET
3 to sink or push (something) briefly into or as if into a liquid ⟨*douse* the grapes in water to remove any grit⟩ — see DIP 1

doused *also* **dowsed** *adj* containing, covered with, or thoroughly penetrated by water ⟨shook the water out of her thoroughly *doused* hair⟩ — see WET 1

dove *n* **1** a person who opposes war or warlike policies ⟨the *doves* were in favor of using the surplus to improve the nation's schools and not its weapons systems⟩
synonyms pacifist, peacenik
related words peacemaker
near antonyms militarist; chauvinist, nationalist
antonyms hawk, jingo, war hawk, warmonger
2 an innocent or gentle person ⟨he's a *dove* who wouldn't hurt a fly⟩ — see LAMB

dovetail *vb* to be in agreement on every point ⟨the Union and the Confederate accounts of the battle don't *dovetail* at all⟩ — see CHECK 1

dovish *adj* inclined to live in peace and to avoid war ⟨the party's *dovish* faction has regarded the war as a bad idea from the get-go⟩ — see PEACEFUL 1

dowager *n* a dignified usually elderly woman of some rank or authority ⟨the town's *dowagers* frequently shake their heads over the younger generation⟩ — see MATRIARCH

dowdily *adv* in a careless or unfashionable manner ⟨dressed hurriedly and *dowdily* to go do her workout⟩ — see SLOPPILY

dowdy *adj* **1** lacking neatness in dress or person ⟨a *dowdy* old matron⟩ — see SLOPPY 1
2 marked by an obvious lack of style or good taste ⟨the *dowdy*, beat-up furniture at the cheap motel⟩ — see [1]TACKY 1

down *adj* **1** brought or having come to an end ⟨eight *down* and two to go⟩ — see COMPLETE 2
2 directed down ⟨a *down* escalator⟩ — see DOWNCAST 1
3 feeling unhappiness ⟨feeling a bit *down*⟩ — see SAD 1
4 temporarily suffering from a disorder of the body ⟨*down* with the flu⟩ — see SICK 1
5 not being in working order ⟨while my computer was *down*, I attended to some unfinished odds and ends lying about my cubicle⟩ — see INOPERABLE 1
6 *slang* of the very best kind ⟨a small jazz club that showcases some really *down* musicians⟩ — see EXCELLENT

down *adv* **1** toward or in a lower position ⟨the stairs went *down* to the basement⟩
synonyms below, downward (*or* downwards), over
related words facedown; low; downgrade, downhill, downstairs
near antonyms aloft
antonyms up, upward (*or* upwards), upwardly
2 from this or that place ⟨came *down* from New York for the weekend⟩ — see AWAY

[1]**down** *n* a soft airy substance or covering ⟨a comforter filled with goose *down*⟩ — see [1]FUZZ

[2]**down** *n* **1** something (as a situation or event) that is depressing ⟨lately it's been one *down* after another in my life⟩ — see DOWNER
2 *chiefly British* a lingering ill will towards a person for a real or imagined wrong ⟨I don't understand why she'd have such a *down* against me; we've never even spoken to each other!⟩ — see GRUDGE 1
3 *chiefly British* a strong feeling of not liking or approving ⟨for years after the war her grandfather had an unshakable *down* on the Germans⟩ — see DISLIKE 1
4 the act or process of going to a lower level or altitude ⟨suffered with a psychological disorder in which she alternated between emotional ups and *downs*⟩ — see DESCENT 1
5 a loss of status ⟨experienced the ups and *downs* of a career in showbiz⟩ — see COMEDOWN

[3]**down** *n, usually* **downs** a broad area of level or rolling treeless country ⟨hold a festival on the *downs*⟩ — see PLAIN 1

down *vb* **1** to strike (someone) so forcefully as to cause a fall ⟨*downed* his opponent with one stunning blow⟩ — see FELL 1
2 to take into the stomach through the mouth and throat ⟨*downing* slices of pizza and guzzling bottles of soda⟩ — see SWALLOW 1
3 to reject by or as if by a vote ⟨all attempts to ban indoor smoking had been *downed* by the town council⟩ — see NEGATIVE 1

down and dirty *adj* made or done without previous thought or preparation ⟨hoisting aloft the *down and dirty* sign that we had just made, we joined the protest⟩ — see EXTEMPORANEOUS

down–and–out *adj* **1** lacking bodily strength ⟨I'm over the flu, but I still feel *down-and-out*⟩ — see WEAK 1
2 lacking money or material possessions ⟨a soup kitchen where the *down-and-out* daily line up for a hot meal⟩ — see POOR 1

down–at–the–heels *or* **down–at–heel** *also* **down–at–the–heel** *or* **down–at–heels** *adj* showing signs of advanced wear and tear and neglect ⟨the stately mansion where he lives now is a far cry from the *down-at-the-heels* triple-decker in which he grew up⟩ — see SHABBY 1

downbeat *adj* emphasizing or expecting the worst ⟨a *downbeat* prediction for the company's sales performance in the upcoming year⟩ — see PESSIMISTIC 1

downcast *adj* **1** directed down ⟨her *downcast* gaze made us realize that she was shy⟩
synonyms bowed, down, downward, lowered
near antonyms elevated, lifted, raised, uplifted, upward
2 feeling unhappiness ⟨I'm always a little *downcast* on rainy days⟩ — see SAD 1

downer *n* something (as a situation or event) that is depressing ⟨that story of drug addiction was a real *downer*⟩
synonyms bummer, down
related words bore, drag; accident, fatality, mishap, woe; calamity, catastrophe, debacle (*also* débâcle), misfortune, tragedy
near antonyms pick-me-up, trip
antonyms upper

downfall *n* **1** something that is the cause of one's ultimate failure or loss of life ⟨an insatiable love of money would be their *downfall*⟩
synonyms death, destruction, ruin, ruination, undoing
related words bane, curse, torment; Achilles' heel, tragic flaw
phrases kiss of death
2 a change to a lower state or level ⟨the gradual *downfall* of the Roman Empire⟩ — see DECLINE 2
3 a loss of status ⟨an ill-advised speech that proved to be the cause of the candidate's *downfall*⟩ — see COMEDOWN
4 a steady falling of water from the sky in significant quantity ⟨we ducked under an overhang to shelter ourselves from the sudden *downfall*⟩ — see RAIN 1

downgrade *n* **1** a change to a lower state or level ⟨a singing career on the *downgrade*⟩ — see DECLINE 2
2 a downward slope ⟨the gentle *downgrade* of the parking area is designed for drainage⟩ — see DECLINE 3

downgrade *vb* **1** to bring to a lower grade or rank ⟨increased automation resulted in many jobs in the factory being *downgraded*⟩ — see DEMOTE
2 to diminish the price or value of ⟨the company's filing for Chapter 11 *downgraded* the stock to the point where it was selling for pennies a share⟩ — see DEPRECIATE 1

downhearted *adj* feeling unhappiness ⟨*downhearted* because his best friend was taking a job out of state⟩ — see SAD 1

downheartedness *n* a state or spell of low spirits ⟨his *downheartedness* lasted until another girl came along and won his heart⟩ — see SADNESS

downhill *adj* involving minimal difficulty or effort ⟨the project should be all *downhill* after this problem is fixed⟩ — see EASY 1

downhill *n* a downward slope ⟨most runners will have their best splits on the *downhills*⟩ — see DECLINE 3

down–home *adj* having or showing an unpretentious informality ⟨her *down-home* patter as she prepares comfort foods goes over well with television viewers⟩ — see CRACKER-BARREL

down in the mouth *adj* feeling unhappiness ⟨after a disastrous date like that, anyone would be *down in the mouth*⟩ — see SAD 1

downplay *vb* to reduce in apparent importance ⟨he

self-deprecatingly *downplays* his own contributions to the festival's success⟩ — see SOFT-PEDAL

downpour *n* a steady falling of water from the sky in significant quantity ⟨the *downpour* was so heavy that we were soaked by the time we got to the car⟩ — see RAIN 1

downright *adj* **1** being or characterized by direct, brief, and potentially rude speech or manner ⟨rural folks are often known for their *downright* speech, as they are generally not ones to beat around the bush⟩ — see BLUNT 1
2 having no exceptions or restrictions ⟨that's a *downright* lie, and you know it⟩ — see ABSOLUTE 2

downscale *vb* to make smaller in amount, volume, or extent ⟨the poor economy forced the plant to *downscale* production⟩ — see DECREASE 1

downshift *n* a usually gradual decrease in the pace or level of activity of something ⟨there are promising indications of a turnaround in the prolonged economic *downshift*⟩ — see SLOWDOWN

downside *n* a feature of someone or something that creates difficulty for achieving success ⟨the *downside* of living in the country is, of course, the long commute to work⟩ — see DISADVANTAGE 1

downsize *vb* to make smaller in amount, volume, or extent ⟨the company *downsized* its overseas operations in an attempt to cut costs⟩ — see DECREASE 1

down–the–line *adj* firm in one's allegiance to someone or something ⟨a *down-the-line* supporter of the Republican Party⟩ — see FAITHFUL 1

downtime *n* a period of often involuntary inactivity or idleness ⟨a knee operation that could result in months of *downtime* for the ski racer⟩
synonyms layoff, time-out, winter
related words break, breath, breather, interruption, lull, pause, recess; abeyance, doldrums, dormancy, latency, quiescence, suspense, suspension

down–to–earth *adj* **1** not having or showing any feelings of superiority, self-assertiveness, or showiness ⟨we were all impressed by how *down-to-earth* the movie star turned out to be⟩ — see HUMBLE 1
2 willing to see things as they really are and deal with them sensibly ⟨a *down-to-earth* guidance counselor who is frank in telling students which colleges they're likely to get into⟩ — see REALISTIC 1

down–to–earthness *n* the absence of any feelings of being better than others ⟨we were pleasantly surprised by the quiet *down-to-earthness* and self-deprecating humor of the billionaire⟩ — see HUMILITY

down–to–the–wire *adj* showing little difference in the standing of the competitors ⟨a *down-to-the-wire* contest for the pennant⟩ — see CLOSE 3

downtown *adj* keenly aware of and responsive to the latest developments especially in fashion and entertainment ⟨the *downtown* clientele of this bistro come to be seen, and the food is only an afterthought⟩ — see AU COURANT 1

downtrodden *adj* suffering grave abuse or injustice at the hands of one in authority ⟨a war that was supposed to liberate the *downtrodden* citizens of that nation⟩
synonyms crushed, oppressed, persecuted, tyrannized
related words browbeaten, bullied, cowed, hectored, intimidated; abused, maltreated, mistreated; abject, despairing, disheartened, dispirited, downcast, hopeless

downward *adj* directed down ⟨at that age where the *downward* pull of gravity on the body is obvious⟩ — see DOWNCAST 1

downward *or* **downwards** *adv* toward or in a lower position ⟨at this point the river flows gently *downward* to the sea⟩ — see DOWN 1

downwind *adj* being in the direction that the wind is blowing ⟨we were *downwind* of the deer, so it couldn't smell us⟩
synonyms leeward
antonyms upwind, windward

downy *adj* smooth or delicate in appearance or feel ⟨the *downy* surface of a ripe peach⟩ — see SOFT 2

doxy *also* **doxie** *n* **1** a boldly flirtatious or sexually promiscuous woman ⟨before gentrification the city's waterfront was known for sleazy dives that were frequented by hell-raising sailors and drunken *doxies*⟩ — see FLOOZY
2 a female other than his wife with whom a married man has a continuing sexual relationship ⟨he'll never leave his wife and kids for that low-rent *doxy*⟩ — see MISTRESS

doyen *n* **1** a person with long experience in a specified area ⟨considered the *doyen* of American art critics⟩ — see VETERAN
2 the senior member of a group ⟨he's the *doyen* of American museum directors, and his opinion has considerable weight⟩ — see DEAN

doze *n* a short sleep ⟨a brief *doze* in the sun⟩ — see [1]NAP

doze *vb* **1** to be in a state of sleep ⟨likes to *doze* through those lazy summer afternoons⟩ — see SLEEP 1
2 to sleep lightly or briefly ⟨she *dozed* fitfully in the car but never fell completely asleep⟩ — see NAP 1

dozen *n* a considerable amount ⟨*dozens* of new songs were auditioned and rejected⟩ — see LOT 2

dozer *n* one who sleeps ⟨the crash abruptly wakened the *dozers* on the bus⟩ — see SLEEPER

doziness *n* the quality or state of desiring or needing sleep ⟨a heavy lunch usually leaves me fighting off a spell of *doziness* in the afternoon⟩ — see SLEEPINESS

dozing *adj* being in a state of suspended consciousness ⟨the *dozing* dog was running—at least in his dream⟩ — see ASLEEP 1

dozing *n* a natural periodic loss of consciousness during which the body restores itself ⟨*dozing* is a natural response to the stifling heat of summer⟩ — see SLEEP 1

dozy *adj* desiring or needing sleep ⟨the big Thanksgiving dinner left us all feeling satisfied and *dozy*⟩ — see SLEEPY 1

drab *adj* causing weariness, restlessness, or lack of interest ⟨the new city hall promises to be another *drab* pile of masonry for the town⟩ — see BORING

drab *n* a woman who engages in sexual activities for money ⟨in its time, this waterfront dive was decried as a den of iniquity, unfit even for the dissolute men and *drabs* who haunted it⟩ — see PROSTITUTE

draft *n* **1** a mass or quantity of something taken up and carried, conveyed, or transported ⟨the *draft* of an average-sized oil tanker⟩ — see LOAD 1
2 the portion of a serving of a beverage that is swallowed at one time ⟨took a long *draft* of the beer before putting his mug down⟩ — see DRINK 2
3 noticeable movement of air in a particular direction ⟨do you feel a *draft* from beneath the door?⟩ — see [1]WIND 1

draft *vb* **1** to pick especially for required military service ⟨my grandfather was *drafted* to fight in a war that he opposed⟩
synonyms conscribe, conscript, levy
related words impress, press; enlist, enroll (*also* enrol), recruit; call up; sign up, volunteer
near antonyms discharge, muster out
2 to put (something) into proper and usually carefully worked out written form ⟨*draft* a letter to the local newspaper giving your views on the problem⟩ — see COMPOSE 1
3 to remove (liquid) gradually or completely ⟨remember to *draft* the water from the pool so that we can close it up for the winter⟩ — see DRAIN 1

draftee *n* a person forced or required to enroll in mili-

—tary service ⟨the massive mobilization required *draftees* to be rushed through training⟩ — see CONSCRIPT

drag *n* **1** someone or something boring ⟨that lecture was such a *drag* that half of the audience fell asleep⟩
synonyms bore, drip, droner, dullsville, nudnik (*also* nudnick), snooze, snoozer, yawn, yawner
related words bummer, downer; bromide, pill
near antonyms blast, gas [*slang*], kick, rush, upper
2 a passage cleared for public vehicular travel ⟨the main *drag* in town⟩ — see WAY 1
3 something that makes movement or progress difficult ⟨the *drag* of overpopulation on raising the living standards of that developing country⟩ — see ENCUMBRANCE
4 the portion of a serving of a beverage that is swallowed at one time ⟨took a deep *drag* of tequila before speaking his piece⟩ — see DRINK 2
5 a person who spoils the pleasure of others ⟨the teenager was mortified to be seen in public with such *drags*—her parents⟩ — see KILLJOY
6 clothing chosen as appropriate for a specific situation ⟨an undercover cop who sometimes works her beat in streetwalker *drag*⟩ — see OUTFIT 1

drag *vb* **1** to cause to follow by applying steady force on ⟨the deliveryman *dragged* the barrels over against the wall⟩ — see PULL 1
2 to move or act slowly ⟨one of the climbers was beginning to *drag*⟩ — see DELAY 1
3 to move slowly ⟨the play *dragged* and seemed to take forever to get to its predictable conclusion⟩ — see CRAWL 2

drag (out) *vb* to make longer ⟨pointless questions that merely *dragged out* the meeting another hour⟩ — see EXTEND 1

dragger *n* someone who moves slowly or more slowly than others ⟨we quickly left the *draggers* behind and sprinted up the hill⟩ — see SLOWPOKE

dragging *adj* moving or proceeding at less than the normal, desirable, or required speed ⟨a mysterious, cloaked figure with a strange, *dragging* walk⟩ — see SLOW 1

draggled *adj* not clean ⟨the poor *draggled* teddy bear had clearly seen better days⟩ — see DIRTY 1

dragon lady *n* a bad-tempered scolding woman ⟨a conniving *dragon lady*, their mother attempted to dominate their lives well into their adult years⟩ — see SHREW

dragoon *vb* to cause (a person) to give in to pressure ⟨she was *dragooned* into agreeing to the fraudulent scheme⟩ — see FORCE 1

drain *vb* **1** to remove (liquid) gradually or completely ⟨we *drained* the water from the tank before cleaning it⟩
synonyms bleed, draft, draw (off), pump, siphon (*also* syphon), tap
related words milk; suck; clear, empty, evacuate, exhaust, vacate, vacuate, void; decant, effuse; deplete; clean, flush, purge
near antonyms bathe, douse (*also* dowse), drench, soak, souse, wash, water, wet; deluge, drown, flood, inundate, overflow; submerge, swamp
antonyms fill
2 to make complete use of ⟨virtually *drained* the country's natural resources⟩ — see DEPLETE 1
3 to use up all the physical energy of ⟨the long hike *drained* us⟩ — see EXHAUST 1

drain (away) *vb* to grow less in scope or intensity especially gradually ⟨as the city lost population, its political influence *drained away*⟩ — see DECREASE 2

drained *adj* depleted in strength, energy, or freshness ⟨we were completely *drained* after shoveling snow all afternoon⟩ — see WEARY 1

drainpipe *n* a pipe or channel for carrying off water from a roof ⟨our *drainpipe* is always getting clogged with leaves⟩ — see GUTTER 1

dram *n* a very small amount ⟨allow me to offer a *dram* of advice⟩ — see PARTICLE 1

drama *n* **1** the public performance of plays ⟨he has been interested in *drama* from the first time he ever saw a play⟩
synonyms dramatics, stage, theater (*or* theatre), theatricals, theatrics
related words boards; acting, footlights; entertainment, showbiz, show business; amusement, distraction, diversion, recreation; exhibition, pageant, pageantry, presentation, production, show, spectacle
2 a written work in which the story is told through speech and action that is intended to be acted out on stage ⟨wrote a police *drama* that really captured the speech of cops and criminals⟩ — see PLAY 2

dramatic *adj* **1** having the general quality or effect of a stage performance ⟨the basketball player's *dramatic* announcement of his sudden retirement held everybody spellbound⟩
synonyms histrionic, melodramatic, operatic, stagy (*or* stagey), theatrical (*also* theatric)
related words affected, emotional, emotionalistic, sensational; actorish, actorly, actressy, dramaturgic (*or* dramaturgical), ham, hammy; amazing, astonishing, astounding, awesome, exciting, eye-opening, fabulous, marvelous (*or* marvellous), spectacular, surprising, wonderful, wondrous; overdramatic
near antonyms matter-of-fact, monotonous, uneventful, unexciting; uninspiring, unnewsworthy, unrewarding, unsensational, unspectacular; common, commonplace, ordinary, stale, unexceptional
antonyms undramatic
2 given to or marked by attention-getting behavior suggestive of stage acting ⟨oh, don't be so *dramatic*, and just tell us, without the pregnant pauses, what happened⟩ — see THEATRICAL 1
3 likely to attract attention ⟨a *dramatic* drop in the temperature overnight⟩ — see NOTICEABLE

dramatics *n pl* the public performance of plays ⟨took part in *dramatics* while a student at the local university⟩ — see DRAMA

dramatization *n* a written work in which the story is told through speech and action that is intended to be acted out on stage ⟨a *dramatization* of a true story⟩ — see PLAY 2

dramshop *n* a place of business where alcoholic beverages are sold to be consumed on the premises ⟨according to the state's *dramshop* laws, anyone who serves alcohol automatically incurs certain liabilities⟩ — see BARROOM

drape *vb* to make more attractive by adding something that is beautiful or becoming ⟨a trophy wife who invariably appears at events *draped* in furs and diamonds⟩ — see DECORATE

drapery *n* pieces of cloth hung to darken, decorate, or divide a room ⟨the *drapery* for the picture window matched the color of the furniture in the center of the room⟩
synonyms curtains, drapes
related words hanging(s), shade, tapestry, window shade

drapes *n pl* pieces of cloth hung to darken, decorate, or divide a room ⟨we hung new *drapes* in the living room to match the new color scheme⟩ — see DRAPERY

draw *n* **1** a situation in which neither participant in a contest, competition, or struggle comes out ahead of the other ⟨the game ended in a *draw*⟩ — see TIE 1
2 something that attracts interest ⟨city fathers hoped that the new waterfront development would be a big *draw* for tourists⟩ — see MAGNET

3 the act or an instance of applying force on something so that it moves in the direction of the force ⟨took a *draw* on his cigarette and immediately started coughing⟩ — see PULL 1

draw *vb* **1** to make a representation of by producing lines on a surface ⟨see if you can *draw* the bowl of fruit⟩
synonyms picture
related words caricature, cartoon; crayon, ink, pencil; outline, profile; scrawl, scribble, sketch
2 to cause to follow by applying steady force on ⟨*draw* a chair up to the fire and sit with us⟩ — see PULL 1
3 to give a representation or account of in words ⟨a writer who *draws* characters with lifelike clarity⟩ — see DESCRIBE 1
4 to receive as return for effort ⟨*draws* a hefty weekly salary⟩ — see EARN 1
5 to take away from a place or position ⟨*draw* her aside so we can ask a quick question⟩ — see REMOVE 2
6 to take the internal organs out of ⟨hated the thought of having to pluck and *draw* a goose before cooking it⟩ — see GUT
7 to shape with a hammer ⟨*drew* the metal into a thin sheet by pounding it⟩ — see HAMMER 1

draw (off) *vb* to remove (liquid) gradually or completely ⟨*drew off* the fat from the top of the drippings⟩ — see DRAIN 1

drawback *n* a feature of someone or something that creates difficulty for achieving success ⟨this plan has only one *drawback*: it's unworkable⟩ — see DISADVANTAGE 1

draw down *vb* to make complete use of ⟨I *drew down* my bank account just paying for tuition⟩ — see DEPLETE 1

drawing *n* a picture using lines to represent the chief features of an object or scene ⟨with an economy of lines, he created a vivid *drawing* of the tree⟩
synonyms cartoon, delineation, sketch
related words contour, figure, outline, silhouette; caricature, doodle, illustration; depiction, image, likeness, portrait, representation; engraving, etch, etching; aquatint, charcoal, line drawing, pastel, watercolor; blueprint

drawing out *n* the act of making longer ⟨the tedious *drawing out* of wool into thread that was required before weaving⟩ — see EXTENSION 1

draw on *vb* **1** to be the cause of (a situation, action, or state of mind) ⟨the general's imprudent remarks *drew on* a public rebuke by the secretary of defense⟩ — see EFFECT
2 to come near or nearer ⟨night *draws on*, so we should hurry home⟩ — see APPROACH 1

draw out *vb* to make longer ⟨the actor refused to *draw out* the interview any further⟩ — see EXTEND 1

draw up *vb* **1** to bring (something) to a standstill ⟨he *drew up* his horse outside the tavern⟩ — see [1]HALT 1
2 to put into a particular arrangement ⟨*drew up* the troops into a line along the ridge⟩ — see ORDER 1
3 to put (something) into proper and usually carefully worked out written form ⟨*draw up* a proposal and submit it to the committee for approval⟩ — see COMPOSE 1

dread *adj* causing fear ⟨every ship on the Spanish Main was terrified of running into the *dread* pirate⟩ — see FEARFUL 1

dread *n* **1** suspicion or fear of future harm or misfortune ⟨the *dread* felt by people awaiting bad news⟩ — see APPREHENSION 1
2 the emotion experienced in the presence or threat of danger ⟨we were filled with *dread* when we saw the rapids we would be rafting down⟩ — see FEAR 1
3 something or someone that causes fear or dread especially without reason ⟨speaking in public is a perennial *dread* for many people⟩ — see BOGEY 1

dreadful *adj* **1** causing fear ⟨a *dreadful* hurricane⟩ — see FEARFUL 1
2 causing intense displeasure, disgust, or resentment ⟨a *dreadful* performance of a beautiful piece of music⟩ — see OFFENSIVE 1
3 extremely disturbing or repellent ⟨*dreadful* news of a crime wave in the neighborhood⟩ — see HORRIBLE 1
4 extreme in degree, power, or effect ⟨the *dreadful* heat of the desert⟩ — see INTENSE 1
5 having no exceptions or restrictions ⟨made a *dreadful* mess of his first marriage⟩ — see ABSOLUTE 2

dreadfulness *n* the quality of inspiring intense dread or dismay ⟨the *dreadfulness* of an oncoming avalanche can scarcely be described⟩ — see HORROR 1

dreadnought *n* something or someone that is unusually large and powerful ⟨poor gas mileage did little to stem the popularity of that *dreadnought* of the roadways: the SUV⟩ — see GIANT

dream *n* **1** a conception or image created by the imagination and having no objective reality ⟨his invention is only a *dream* right now, but someday it might be a reality⟩ — see FANTASY 1
2 something that one hopes or intends to accomplish ⟨my *dream* is to open my own restaurant⟩ — see GOAL
3 something very good of its kind ⟨the Alaskan cruise exceeded their wildest expectations—it was a *dream* of a vacation⟩ — see JIM-DANDY

dream *vb* to form a mental picture of ⟨I *dreamed* that I was living on that proverbial desert island in the South Pacific⟩ — see IMAGINE 1

dreamboat *n, slang* a physically attractive person ⟨an actor who's still regarded as one of the screen's all-time great *dreamboats*⟩ — see DOLL 2

dreamer *n* one whose conduct is guided more by the image of perfection than by the real world ⟨a *dreamer* who believes that war doesn't have to be part of the human condition⟩ — see IDEALIST

dreamily *adv* in a pleasing way ⟨our date at the restaurant went *dreamily* until the check arrived⟩ — see WELL 5

dreamy *adj* **1** giving pleasure or contentment to the mind or senses ⟨a beach resort that is a perfectly *dreamy* place to relax⟩ — see PLEASANT 1
2 tending to calm the emotions and relieve stress ⟨the kind of *dreamy* music I want after a hard day at work⟩ — see SOOTHING 1

drear *adj* **1** causing or marked by an atmosphere lacking in cheer ⟨it was a *drear* morning in January when I went to take my driving test⟩ — see GLOOMY 1
2 causing unhappiness ⟨a barren and *drear* existence in a remote village⟩ — see SAD 2

dreariness *n* a state or spell of low spirits ⟨my own *dreariness* seemed to match the dismal weather we were having⟩ — see SADNESS

dreary *adj* **1** causing or marked by an atmosphere lacking in cheer ⟨vowed that he would never take a desk job working in a *dreary* office⟩ — see GLOOMY 1
2 causing unhappiness ⟨decided to see a professional counselor in order to save their *dreary* marriage⟩ — see SAD 2
3 causing weariness, restlessness, or lack of interest ⟨another *dreary* social event to suffer through⟩ — see BORING

dreck *also* **drek** *n* **1** discarded or useless material ⟨he poured the *dreck* she called soup down the drain⟩ — see GARBAGE 1
2 that which is of low quality or worth ⟨can you believe that the gallery owner dares to call that *dreck* "art"?⟩ — see JUNK 1

dredge *vb* to look through (as a place) carefully or thoroughly in an effort to find or discover something ⟨I've been *dredging* my memory bank, and I simply can't remember her name⟩ — see SEARCH 1

dredge (up) *vb* to come upon after searching, study, or effort ⟨I might be able to *dredge up* some old baby clothes to donate⟩ — see FIND 1

dregs *n pl* matter that settles to the bottom of a body of liquid ⟨poured the *dregs* into the sink⟩ — see DEPOSIT 1

dreich *adj, chiefly Scottish* causing or marked by an atmosphere lacking in cheer ⟨historically regarded as a *dreich* corner of Britain, Scotland's very name comes from the Greek word for "dark"⟩ — see GLOOMY 1

drench *vb* **1** to make wet ⟨we were *drenched* by the sudden rainstorm⟩ — see WET

2 to wet thoroughly with liquid ⟨when using the carpet shampooer, wet but do not *drench* the carpet⟩ — see SOAK 1

drenched *adj* containing, covered with, or thoroughly penetrated by water ⟨the *drenched* tourists straggled into the visitors' center⟩ — see WET 1

dress *adj* relating to or suitable for wearing to an event requiring elegant dress and manners ⟨the naval commander wore his *dress* uniform to the ball⟩

synonyms dressy, formal

related words costume, costumey; chic, dapper, fashionable, in, modish, natty, sharp, smart, snappy, stylish; custom-made, fitted, tailored; black-tie, evening, white-tie; semiformal

near antonyms street; dowdy, outmoded, styleless, unfashionable, unstylish; frowsy (*or* frowzy), grungy, sloppy, sloven, slovenly, unkempt, untidy; disheveled (*or* dishevelled), messy, mussy, rumpled, wrinkled

antonyms casual, informal, sportif, sporty

dress *n* **1** a garment with a joined blouse and skirt usually worn by a woman or girl ⟨what a lovely *dress* you're wearing today!⟩

synonyms frock, gown

related words chemise, coatdress, granny dress, housedress, jumper, kimono, kirtle, minidress, Mother Hubbard, muumuu, overdress, sack, sheath, shift, shirtdress, shirtwaist, sundress, sweaterdress, tea gown

2 clothing chosen as appropriate for a specific situation ⟨a bagpiper in full Scottish Highlander *dress*⟩ — see OUTFIT 1

3 covering for the human body ⟨a businessman who is very conservative in his *dress*⟩ — see CLOTHING

4 the outward form of someone or something especially as indicative of a quality ⟨another version of the Cinderella story but in modern-romance *dress*⟩ — see APPEARANCE 1

dress *vb* **1** to cover with a bandage ⟨first wash and then *dress* the wound⟩ — see BANDAGE

2 to make more attractive by adding something that is beautiful or becoming ⟨let's *dress* up the room with some greenery for the holiday party⟩ — see DECORATE

3 to make smooth or glossy usually by repeatedly applying surface pressure ⟨*dress* the granite block to be used as the headstone on all four sides⟩ — see POLISH 1

4 to outfit with clothes and especially fine or special clothes ⟨*dressed* the young girl in satin and lace⟩ — see CLOTHE 1

5 to put on one's best or formal clothes ⟨we don't usually *dress* for dinner⟩ — see DRESS UP

6 to look after or assist the growth of by labor and care ⟨*dress* the beans by applying fertilizer once a week⟩ — see GROW 1

dress down *vb* to criticize (someone) severely or angrily especially for personal failings ⟨*dressed down* for boorish behavior at the dance⟩ — see SCOLD

dressing *n* **1** a medicated covering used to heal an injury ⟨nurses put a *dressing* over his cuts so they wouldn't get infected⟩

synonyms cataplasm, plaster, poultice

related words balm, cream, embrocation, liniment, lotion, ointment, salve, unguent

2 a savory fluid food used as a topping or accompaniment to a main dish ⟨tangy salad *dressing* that wasn't overloaded with corn syrup⟩ — see SAUCE 1

dress up *vb* **1** to put on one's best or formal clothes ⟨we always like to *dress up* when going to parties⟩

synonyms doll up, dress

related words preen, primp, prink, smarten (up); accessorize; apparel, array, attire, bedeck, bedizen, caparison, clothe, costume, deck, dude (up), garb, garment, invest, rig (out), robe, suit, tog (out *or* up)

2 to change the dress or looks of so as to conceal true identity ⟨the war was a fiasco that the administration tried to *dress up* as a triumph⟩ — see DISGUISE 1

3 to make more desirable ⟨*dressed up* the house with new windows and a paint job before putting it on the market⟩ — see SWEETEN

4 to outfit with clothes and especially fine or special clothes ⟨the girls were *dressed up* in skirts or dresses, but the boys were wearing jeans⟩ — see CLOTHE 1

dressy *adj* relating to or suitable for wearing to an event requiring elegant dress and manners ⟨shopping for a *dressy* handbag for a New Year's Eve party⟩ — see DRESS

dribble *n* a very small piece ⟨news about the remote earthquake was coming in *dribbles*⟩ — see BIT 1

dribble *vb* **1** to fall or let fall in or as if in drops ⟨water *dribbling* over the lip of the fountain⟩ — see DRIP

2 to flow in a broken irregular stream ⟨rainwater *dribbling* along the partially clogged gutter⟩ — see GURGLE

3 to let saliva or some other substance flow from the mouth ⟨picnickers *dribbling* in eager anticipation of the hamburgers on the grill⟩ — see DROOL 1

driblet *n* **1** a very small amount ⟨money doled out in *driblets* to the workers⟩ — see PARTICLE 1

2 the quantity of fluid that falls naturally in one rounded mass ⟨rain leaked through the roof in solitary *driblets* here and there⟩ — see DROP 1

drift *n* **1** a pile or ridge of granular matter (as sand or snow) ⟨deep *drifts* of snow blocked our driveway⟩ — see ²BANK

2 a prevailing or general movement or inclination ⟨the steady *drift* of the population away from large cities⟩ — see TREND 1

3 the idea that is conveyed or intended to be conveyed to the mind by language, symbol, or action ⟨you should expect a visit from the stork, if you get my *drift*⟩ — see MEANING 1

drift *vb* **1** to move or proceed smoothly and readily ⟨casual conversation *drifting* from one topic to another⟩ — see FLOW 2

2 to rest or move along the surface of a liquid or in the air ⟨the boat *drifted* along on the current⟩ — see FLOAT 1

3 to move about from place to place aimlessly ⟨spent several years *drifting* from town to town, picking up odd jobs whenever he needed cash⟩ — see WANDER 1

drifter *n* a person who roams about without a fixed route or destination ⟨the *drifter* just packed up and moved on to the next dead-end job⟩ — see NOMAD

drill *n* **1** an established and often automatic or monotonous series of actions followed when engaging in some activity ⟨shuttling the kids between extracurricular activities is all part of the suburban *drill*⟩ — see ROUTINE 1

2 something done over and over in order to develop skill ⟨doing vocabulary *drills* all afternoon in preparation for the test⟩ — see EXERCISE 2

¹drill *vb* **1** to make a hole or series of holes in ⟨the nerve-jangling sound when a dentist *drills* a tooth⟩ — see PERFORATE

2 to strike with a missile from a gun ⟨*drilled* the target from 100 yards away⟩ — see SHOOT 3

²**drill** *vb* to put or set into the ground to grow ⟨he *drills* soybeans in the same rows with corn⟩ — see PLANT 1

drink *n* **1** a liquid suitable for drinking ⟨we went inside to have a *drink* after mowing the lawn⟩
synonyms beverage, drinkable, libation, potable, quencher
related words potion; pop, soda, soda pop, soft drink; nectar; alcohol, brew, intoxicant, liquor, spirits; mix, mixer
2 the portion of a serving of a beverage that is swallowed at one time ⟨the thirsty soldier took a long *drink* from his canteen⟩
synonyms belt, draft, drag, gulp, nip, quaff, shot, sip, slug, snort, sup, swallow, swig, swill
related words dram, drop
3 a distilled beverage that can make a person drunk ⟨you can get *drinks* at the bar only if you show them a valid ID⟩ — see ALCOHOL

drink *vb* **1** to swallow in liquid form ⟨the doctor wants her to *drink* lots of water before the examination⟩
synonyms belt (down), gulp, guzzle, hoist, imbibe, knock back, pound (down), quaff, sip, slug (down), slurp, sup, swig, swill, toss (down *or* off)
related words lap, lick, suck; consume, down, ingurgitate, kill, mouth (down), put away; nip, tipple; pledge, toast, wine
2 to partake excessively of alcoholic beverages ⟨we're worried that she's started *drinking* again⟩
synonyms bib, booze, guzzle, liquor (up), lush (up) [*slang*], soak, tipple
related words carouse, revel; imbibe, nip
phrases booze it up, hit the bottle
near antonyms abstain
3 to take in (something liquid) through small openings ⟨the hot surface of the porous rock *drank* water like a sponge⟩ — see ABSORB 1

drink (in) *vb* to receive or accept gladly or readily ⟨the studio audience for the infomercial seemed to *drink in*—a little too readily—every word of the host's spiel⟩ — see WELCOME

drinkable *adj* suitable for drinking ⟨technically, that cheap stuff may be wine, but it's hardly *drinkable*⟩ — see POTABLE

drinkable *n* a liquid suitable for drinking ⟨the thoughtful hostess offered her guests an assortment of alcoholic and nonalcoholic *drinkables*⟩ — see DRINK 1

drinker *n* a person who makes a habit of getting drunk ⟨although he can still hold a job, he's definitely become a problem *drinker*⟩ — see DRUNK 1

drip *n* **1** someone or something boring ⟨he's well-meaning, but kind of a *drip*⟩ — see DRAG 1
2 the quantity of fluid that falls naturally in one rounded mass ⟨the faucet leaked one *drip* after another no matter what I did to try to fix it⟩ — see DROP 1

drip *vb* to fall or let fall in or as if in drops ⟨water from the leaky roof was *dripping* all over the floor⟩ ⟨the cracked bottle *dripped* wine⟩
synonyms distill (*also* distil), dribble, drop, trickle
related words drizzle, sprinkle; flow, pour, roll, run, stream; cascade, gutter, riffle, ripple; bleed, exude, ooze, seep, weep; discharge
near antonyms gush, spout, spurt

dripping *adj* containing, covered with, or thoroughly penetrated by water ⟨*dripping* shoes left on the porch to dry⟩ — see WET 1

drippy *adj* appealing to the emotions in an obvious and tiresome way ⟨*drippy* romance novels that are apparently intended for the terminally lovesick⟩ — see CORNY 1

drive *n* **1** a passage cleared for public vehicular travel ⟨raced our motorcycles along the *drive*⟩ — see WAY 1
2 a series of activities undertaken to achieve a goal ⟨a fund-raising *drive* for the school's marching band⟩ — see CAMPAIGN
3 a strong wish for something ⟨a *drive* to succeed in the television news business⟩ — see DESIRE 1
4 active strength of body or mind ⟨senior citizens who exercise regularly are more likely to have the *drive* to keep up with their grandchildren⟩ — see VIGOR 1
5 readiness to engage in daring or difficult activity ⟨a great opportunity for a sales representative who is full of *drive*⟩ — see ENTERPRISE 2

drive *vb* **1** to urge, push, or force onward ⟨cowboys *drove* the herd of cattle from San Antonio to San Francisco⟩
synonyms herd, punch, run
related words shepherd; wrangle; egg, exhort, flog, goad, hound, press, prick, prod, prompt, scourge, spur, whip
2 to travel by a motorized vehicle ⟨I'm going to *drive* across the country—want to come?⟩
synonyms automobile, motor, tool
related words roll, wheel; joyride; chauffeur, hack, taxi; ride; drag, race
3 to apply force to (someone or something) so that it moves in front of one ⟨*drove* the plunger into the opening⟩ — see PUSH 1
4 to cause (a person) to give in to pressure ⟨the corrupt governor was *driven* out of office⟩ — see FORCE 1
5 to cause to function ⟨machinery *driven* by waterpower⟩ — see ACTIVATE
6 to set or keep in motion ⟨this motor *drives* the gears, which then turn the shaft⟩ — see MOVE 2
7 to proceed or move quickly ⟨the runner *drove* past the finish line and then came to a dead stop⟩ — see HURRY 2

drive–by *adj* acting or done with excessive or careless speed ⟨the administrator's schedule left her with no time to make more than a *drive-by* assessment of the situation⟩ — see HASTY 1

drivel *n* **1** language, behavior, or ideas that are absurd and contrary to good sense ⟨that critic's reviews are nothing but self-important *drivel*⟩ — see NONSENSE 1
2 unintelligible or meaningless talk ⟨my roommate talks in her sleep, but it's just *drivel*⟩ — see GIBBERISH 1

drivel *vb* **1** to let saliva or some other substance flow from the mouth ⟨the panting dog *driveled* on my hand⟩ — see DROOL 1
2 to speak rapidly, inarticulately, and usually unintelligibly ⟨he *driveled* on about his "distinguished" family for what seemed like hours⟩ — see BABBLE 1

driven *adj* caused by or suggestive of an irresistible urge ⟨a man with a *driven* need to be loved or liked by everyone⟩ — see COMPULSIVE

driver *n* a person who travels by automobile ⟨fans arriving by public transportation will find the south entrance most convenient, but *drivers* will have a choice of entrances⟩ — see MOTORIST

driver's seat *n* the place of leadership or command ⟨with her boss's early retirement, she unexpectedly found herself in the *driver's seat*⟩ — see HEAD 2

drizzle *n* a light or fine rain ⟨the intermittent *drizzle* was just heavy enough to spoil all of our outdoor activities⟩
synonyms mist, mizzle, sprinkle
related words precipitation, rainfall, shower
near antonyms cloudburst, deluge, downpour, storm; rainstorm, thunderstorm; monsoon

droll *adj* causing or intended to cause laughter ⟨made a *droll* comment about the commencement speaker's penchant for clichés⟩ — see FUNNY 1

droll *n* a person (as a writer) noted for or specializing in humor ⟨the *drolls* of late-night TV had a field day with that senator's sexual shenanigans⟩ — see HUMORIST

drollery *n* **1** something said or done to cause laughter ⟨the film's sophisticated *drolleries* will elicit smiles and chuckles even upon repeated viewings⟩ — see JOKE 1
2 the amusing quality or element in something ⟨though generally serious, the novel about a seriously dysfunctional family is not without *drollery*⟩ — see HUMOR 1

drollness *n* the amusing quality or element in something ⟨fans of Edward Gorey appreciate the delicious *drollness* of his illustrations of poker-faced individuals caught in macabre situations⟩ — see HUMOR 1

[1]**drone** *n* **1** a lazy person ⟨those *drones* just lie around while we do all the work⟩ — see LAZYBONES
2 a person who does very hard or dull work ⟨after lunch my fellow *drones* and I shuffle back to our cubicles⟩ — see SLAVE 2

[2]**drone** *n* a monotonous sound like that of an insect in motion ⟨heard the *drone* of an airplane overhead⟩ — see HUM

drone *vb* **1** to fly, turn, or move rapidly with a fluttering or vibratory sound ⟨the sound of *droning* bees all around us⟩ — see WHIR
2 to spend time doing nothing ⟨instead of getting a job, he preferred to *drone* and live off his parents⟩ — see IDLE

droner *n* someone or something boring ⟨the movie turned out to be a *droner*⟩ — see DRAG 1

drool *n* **1** language, behavior, or ideas that are absurd and contrary to good sense ⟨the only thing more pathetic than the pop psychologist who gushed such *drool* was the public that lapped it up⟩ — see NONSENSE 1
2 the fluid that is secreted into the mouth by certain glands ⟨the baby left a puddle of *drool* on my shirt⟩ — see SALIVA

drool *vb* **1** to let saliva or some other substance flow from the mouth ⟨the dog *drooled* when we put the steak down on the floor⟩
synonyms dribble, drivel, salivate, slaver, slobber
related words water; expectorate, spit; foam, froth, splutter; sputter
2 to make an exaggerated display of affection or enthusiasm ⟨middle-aged men *drooling* over a starlet half their age⟩ — see GUSH 2
3 to speak rapidly, inarticulately, and usually unintelligibly ⟨stop *drooling*, slow down, and take a deep breath, because I can't understand you⟩ — see BABBLE 1

droop *n* the extent to which something hangs or dips below a straight line ⟨tighten the line at the top of the banner so there won't be so much *droop*⟩ — see SAG

droop *vb* **1** to be limp from lack of water or vigor ⟨the flowers *drooped* on their stalks in the blazing sun⟩
synonyms flag, hang, loll, sag, swag, wilt
related words slouch, slump; cave (in), collapse, crumple, drop, fall, sink, subside, yield
near antonyms distend, stiffen; rise, straighten, unbend, uncurl
2 to lose bodily strength or vigor ⟨as the afternoon wore on, we started to *droop*⟩ — see WEAKEN 2

drooping *adj* bending downward or forward ⟨faded, *drooping* banners lining the walls of the old gym⟩ — see NODDING

droopy *adj* **1** bending downward or forward ⟨the *droopy* heads of tired fans riding home on the bus⟩ — see NODDING
2 not stiff in structure ⟨a *droopy* stalk of celery⟩ — see LIMP 1
3 feeling unhappiness ⟨looking *droopy* and miserable while standing in the pouring rain⟩ — see SAD 1

drop *n* **1** the quantity of fluid that falls naturally in one rounded mass ⟨a *drop* of water fell from the leaky faucet every few seconds⟩
synonyms bead, blob, driblet, drip, droplet, glob, globule
related words gobbet; dewdrop, raindrop, tear, teardrop; spatter; dribble, trickle
2 distance measured from the top to the bottom of something ⟨a *drop* of 10 feet from the roof to the ground⟩ — see DEPTH 1
3 the act or process of going to a lower level or altitude ⟨the sudden *drop* of the plane really shook up the passengers⟩ — see DESCENT 1
4 the amount by which something is lessened ⟨a huge *drop* in pressure⟩ — see DECREASE
5 the more favorable condition or position in a competition ⟨got the *drop* on his opponent very early in the wrestling match⟩ — see ADVANTAGE 1

drop *vb* **1** to cause to fall intentionally or unintentionally ⟨I *dropped* the fly ball⟩ ⟨*drop* the anchor⟩
synonyms depress, lower, throw, throw down
related words flatten, floor, level; knock down, knock over, strike down, topple; plop, plunk down; bobble, bungle, foozle, fumble; immerse, sink, submerge
antonyms lift, pick up, raise
2 to go to a lower level especially abruptly ⟨although they start out high, prices for home electronics eventually *drop*⟩
synonyms crash, crater, decline, descend, dip, dive, fall, lower, nose-dive, plummet, plunge, sink, skid, tumble
related words abate, decrease, de-escalate, die (down), diminish, droop, dwindle, ebb, lessen, let up, moderate, subside, taper off, wane; recede, retreat
near antonyms accumulate, balloon, build, burgeon (*also* bourgeon), enlarge, escalate, expand, grow, increase, intensify, mushroom, pick up, snowball, swell, wax
antonyms arise, ascend, lift, mount, rise, soar, spike, up
3 to bring (as an action or operation) to an immediate end ⟨*drop* what you're doing and come here⟩ — see STOP 1
4 to stop doing (something) permanently ⟨isn't it time you *dropped* that smoking habit and spent your money on better things?⟩ — see QUIT 2
5 to lead or extend downward ⟨the cable car tracks can *drop* suddenly, so be sure to hang onto something⟩ — see DESCEND 1
6 to put an end to (something planned or previously agreed to) ⟨*drop* that plan in favor of another⟩ — see CANCEL 1
7 to bring forth from the womb ⟨the cow *dropped* her calf early this morning⟩ — see BEAR 1
8 to strike (someone) so forcefully as to cause a fall ⟨*dropped* the would-be mugger in his tracks with a single well-aimed blow⟩ — see FELL 1
9 to fail to win, gain, or obtain ⟨the local hockey team has *dropped* two out of the last three contests⟩ — see LOSE 2
10 to fall or let fall in or as if in drops ⟨the cold glass *dropped* condensation⟩ — see DRIP
11 to hand over or use up in payment ⟨I *dropped* $50 on these shoes⟩ — see SPEND 1
12 to make reference to or speak about briefly but specifically ⟨he would ever so "casually" *drop* the names of celebrities he knew personally⟩ — see MENTION 1
13 to make smaller in amount, volume, or extent ⟨with these icy road conditions, drivers should be *dropping* their speed⟩ — see DECREASE 1
14 to stop living ⟨during the Black Death people all over Asia and Europe were *dropping* like flies⟩ — see DIE 1

drop (off) *vb* to grow less in scope or intensity especially gradually ⟨my interest in photography has *dropped off* over the years⟩ — see DECREASE 2

drop back *vb* to move back or away (as from something difficult, dangerous, or disagreeable) ⟨a change in the wind direction forced the firefighters to *drop back*⟩ — see RETREAT 1

drop by *vb* to make a brief visit ⟨I'll either *drop by* on the way there or on the way back⟩ — see CALL 3

drop–dead *adj* very pleasing to look at ⟨a *drop-dead* wedding dress that must have cost a fortune⟩ — see BEAUTIFUL 1

drop–in *n* a person who visits another ⟨we're having open house for New Year's, and *drop-ins* are welcome to come and go as they please⟩ — see GUEST 1

drop in *vb* to make a brief visit ⟨*drop in* any time—we're always home⟩ — see CALL 3

drop in (on) *vb* to make a social call upon ⟨as long as we're in town, we should *drop in on* my aunt⟩ — see VISIT 1

droplet *n* the quantity of fluid that falls naturally in one rounded mass ⟨there were only a few *droplets* left in the canteen⟩ — see DROP 1

drop–off *n* the amount by which something is lessened ⟨the *drop-off* in movie attendance was the greatest in more than a decade⟩ — see DECREASE

dropping *n* **1 droppings** *pl* solid matter discharged from an animal's alimentary canal ⟨the only bad part about owning a rabbit was cleaning the *droppings* out of the litter box every night⟩
synonyms dirt, doo-doo, dung, excrement, excreta, feces, ordure, poop, scat, slops, soil, waste
related words night soil, stool; dunghill, guano, manure, midden, muck; spoor; sewage, sewerage; coprolite
2 the act of putting an end to something planned or previously agreed to ⟨the *dropping* of an act from the talent show should bring it in on time⟩ — see CANCELLATION 1

dross *n* discarded or useless material ⟨get rid of the *dross* before closing up the shop⟩ — see GARBAGE 1

drought *also* **drouth** *n* a falling short of an essential or desirable amount or number ⟨there's been a *drought* of good movies this year⟩ — see DEFICIENCY

droughty *adj* marked by little or no precipitation or humidity ⟨a *droughty* region that could never support settlements⟩ — see DRY 1

drove *n* **1** a great number of persons or creatures massed together ⟨people flocked to the annual festival in *droves*⟩ — see CROWD 1
2 a group of domestic animals assembled or herded together ⟨a *drove* of cattle⟩ — see HERD 1

drown *vb* **1** to cover with a flood ⟨whole villages *drowned* by the rampaging river⟩ — see FLOOD
2 to wet thoroughly with liquid ⟨*drowned* the carpet with shampoo, and so it took forever to dry⟩ — see SOAK 1
3 to make wet ⟨cooked pasta *drowned* in marinara sauce⟩ — see WET

drowse *n* a short sleep ⟨was just falling into a *drowse* when you called⟩ — see [1]NAP

drowse *vb* to sleep lightly or briefly ⟨picnickers *drowsing* in the shade of an oak tree⟩ — see NAP 1

drowsiness *n* the quality or state of desiring or needing sleep ⟨we tried to fight our *drowsiness* but fell asleep anyway⟩ — see SLEEPINESS

drowsy *adj* **1** desiring or needing sleep ⟨the *drowsy* students shuffled into the first-period class⟩ — see SLEEPY 1
2 tending to cause sleep ⟨listened to *drowsy* music while waiting in the dentist's office⟩ — see HYPNOTIC

drub *vb* **1** to strike repeatedly ⟨a crowd was *drubbing* the purse snatcher when the police arrived on the scene⟩ — see BEAT 1
2 to defeat by a large margin ⟨we *drubbed* our traditional football rivals so badly that it was basically no contest⟩ — see WHIP 2

drubbing *n* failure to win a contest ⟨took a terrible *drubbing* in last night's basketball game⟩ — see DEFEAT 1

drudge *n* **1** a person who does very hard or dull work ⟨worked like a *drudge* at a low-paying job that had few benefits⟩ — see SLAVE 2
2 very hard or unpleasant work ⟨it took hours of pure *drudge* to sort through the junk in the basement⟩ — see [1]TOIL

drudge *vb* to devote serious and sustained effort ⟨factory workers who must *drudge* all day at repetitive tasks⟩ — see LABOR

drudger *n* a person who does very hard or dull work ⟨a youth striving to become something more than just a *drudger* working at some dead-end job⟩ — see SLAVE 2

drudgery *n* very hard or unpleasant work ⟨in the "good old days" household servants led lives filled with much *drudgery* and little pleasure⟩ — see [1]TOIL

drudging *adj* causing weariness, restlessness, or lack of interest ⟨the hours of *drudging* effort that went into straightening out the company's books⟩ — see BORING

drug *n* a substance or preparation used to treat disease ⟨prescribed a *drug* to treat the bacterial infection⟩ — see MEDICINE

druggie *also* **druggy** *n* a person who regularly uses drugs especially illegally ⟨an old college classmate who became a *druggie* and ended up on skid row⟩ — see DOPER

druggist *n* a person who prepares drugs according to a doctor's prescription ⟨she got her prescription for antibiotics filled by the *druggist*⟩
synonyms apothecary, chemist [*British*], pharmacist
related words pharmacologist

drugstore *n* a retail store where medicines and miscellaneous articles are sold ⟨we picked up her medicine and some toothpaste at the *drugstore*⟩
synonyms apothecary, pharmacy
related words dispensary; sick bay

drum *n* a metal container in the shape of a cylinder ⟨an oil *drum*⟩ — see CAN 1

drum *vb* to strike or cause to strike lightly and usually rhythmically ⟨absentmindedly *drumming* his fingers on the table⟩ — see [1]TAP

drum (out) *vb* to drive or force out ⟨*drummed out* of the service for conduct unbecoming an officer⟩ — see EJECT 1

drumbeat *n* a rapid or overwhelming outpouring of many things at once ⟨a dizzying *drumbeat* of interviews in the hours following her winning of the Academy Award⟩ — see BARRAGE

drumfire *n* a rapid or overwhelming outpouring of many things at once ⟨a rising *drumfire* of criticism for the president's latest nominee for the U.S. Supreme Court⟩ — see BARRAGE

drum up *vb* to create or think of by clever use of the imagination ⟨anyone who *drums up* a better way of doing this tedious task will make a fortune⟩ — see INVENT

drunk *adj* being under the influence of alcohol ⟨several wedding guests who got a little *drunk*⟩
synonyms besotted, blasted [*slang*], blind, blitzed [*slang*], blotto [*slang*], bombed, boozy, canned [*slang*], cockeyed, crocked, drunken, fried, gassed, hammered [*slang*], high, impaired, inebriate, inebriated, intoxicated, juiced [*slang*], lit, lit up, loaded [*slang*], looped, oiled [*slang*], pickled, pie-eyed, plastered, potted [*slang*], ripped [*slang*], sloshed [*slang*], smashed [*slang*], sottish, soused, sozzled, squiffed (*or* squiffy), stewed, stiff, stinking [*slang*], stoned, tanked [*slang*], tiddly [*chiefly British*], tight, tipsy, wasted [*slang*], wet, wiped out [*slang*]

related words maudlin; beery; befuddled, bleary-eyed, crapulous, dopey (*also* dopy), rocky, strung out, stupefied; debauched, dissipated, dissolute; alcoholic, bibulous, dipsomaniacal
phrases in one's cups, in the bag [*slang*], three sheets in the wind (*or* three sheets to the wind), under the influence, under the weather
near antonyms abstemious, abstinent, dry, temperate, teetotal; clearheaded, cool, level, steady
antonyms sober, straight

drunk *n* **1** a person who makes a habit of getting drunk ⟨you can't trust anything that old *drunk* says⟩
synonyms alcoholic, alkie (*or* alky) [*slang*], boozehound, boozer, dipsomaniac, drinker, drunkard, inebriate, juicehead [*slang*], juicer [*slang*], lush, rummy, soak, soaker, sot, souse, tippler, toper, tosspot
related words swigger, swiller; wino
near antonyms abstainer, nondrinker, teetotaler (*or* teetotaller), teetotalist
2 a bout of prolonged or excessive drinking ⟨after a weeklong *drunk* he was unable to remember anything⟩ — see CAROUSE

drunkard *n* a person who makes a habit of getting drunk ⟨accused him of being a no-good *drunkard* who needed professional help for his problem⟩ — see DRUNK 1

drunken *adj* **1** being under the influence of alcohol ⟨the *drunken* revelers made sure to take taxis home instead of trying to drive⟩ — see DRUNK
2 given to excessive use of alcoholic beverages ⟨*drunken* ne'er-do-wells who had been pressed into service in the British navy⟩ — see CRAPULOUS

drunkenness *n* **1** habitual or excessive drinking of intoxicants ⟨unfortunately most of his time in college had been devoted to *drunkenness* and debauchery⟩ — see INTEMPERANCE 1
2 the condition of being drunk ⟨officials warning that public *drunkenness* would not be tolerated, even during Mardi Gras⟩ — see INTOXICATION 1

druthers *n pl, dialect* the power, right, or opportunity to choose ⟨If I had my *druthers*, I'd stay home tonight⟩ — see CHOICE 1

dry *adj* **1** marked by little or no precipitation or humidity ⟨the *dry* climate of the American Southwest⟩
synonyms arid, droughty, sere (*also* sear), thirsty, waterless
related words air-dry; bone-dry, hyperarid, ultradry; baked, dehydrated, parched, sunbaked; rainless; desert, desertic, desertlike, xerothermic
near antonyms awash, bathed, doused (*also* dowsed), drenched, dripping, saturated, soaked, soaking, sodden, soggy, sopping, soppy, soused, washed, watered, waterlogged, watery; deluged, drowned, flooded, inundated, overflowed; submerged, swamped; hydrated
antonyms damp, dank, humid, moist, wet
2 causing weariness, restlessness, or lack of interest ⟨a very *dry* topic for a lecture at a museum of natural history⟩ — see BORING
3 having or showing a lack of friendliness or interest in others ⟨a *dry* temperament that suited him well in a desk job that required no interaction with the customers⟩ — see COOL 1

dry *vb* **1** to make dry ⟨the wind quickly *dried* their clothes⟩
synonyms dehydrate, desiccate, parch, scorch, sear
related words dehumidify; drain; evaporate; mummify, shrivel, wither, wizen; air-dry, bake
near antonyms bathe, deluge, douse (*also* dowse), drench, drown, flood, inundate, overflow, saturate, soak, sop, souse, waterlog; damp, dampen, humidify, moisten; rehydrate; dip, dunk, submerge, swamp
antonyms hydrate, wash, water, wet
2 to lose liveliness, force, or freshness ⟨his creative talents were just *drying* on the vine in that small, provincial town⟩ — see WITHER 1

dryad *n* a mythical goddess represented as a young girl and said to live outdoors ⟨*dryads* were said to live within trees, their lives ending when the life of the tree ended⟩ — see NYMPH 1

dry nurse *n* a girl or woman employed to care for a young child or children ⟨after years of being a *dry nurse* to other women's children, she longed to have a child of her own⟩ — see NURSE

dry run *n* a private performance or session in preparation for a public appearance ⟨we had time for just one *dry run* of the play before opening night⟩ — see REHEARSAL

dry up *vb* to stop talking ⟨sick of her constant complaining, he angrily told her to *dry up*⟩ — see SHUT UP 1

dual *adj* consisting of two members or parts that are usually joined ⟨*dual* axles⟩ — see DOUBLE 1

dub *n* a clumsy, awkward person ⟨even though I wasn't the most graceful skater on the ice, I thought I did well for a *dub*⟩ — see KLUTZ

dub *vb* **1** to give a name to ⟨I've *dubbed* my car the "Lone Ranger," although "Loan Raider" probably would have been more apt⟩ — see NAME 1
2 to make or do (something) in a clumsy or unskillful way ⟨he *dubbed* his first attempt at homemade wine, but he got it reasonably right on the second⟩ — see BOTCH

dubiety *n* a feeling or attitude that one does not know the truth, truthfulness, or trustworthiness of someone or something ⟨the comfort of having a faith free from all *dubiety* is what attracts people to the religious sect⟩ — see DOUBT

dubious *adj* **1** giving good reason for being doubted, questioned, or challenged ⟨any letter bearing the signature of Geronimo would be of *dubious* authenticity, to say the least⟩ — see DOUBTFUL 2
2 slow to begin or proceed with a course of action because of doubts or uncertainty ⟨I'm *dubious* about our plan to go hang gliding without having had any training⟩ — see HESITANT
3 not likely to be true or to occur ⟨made the *dubious* claim of being of royal blood⟩ — see IMPROBABLE
4 not feeling sure about the truth, wisdom, or trustworthiness of someone or something ⟨*dubious* about a diet that claims I can eat all I want and still lose weight⟩ — see DOUBTFUL 1

dubiously *adv* with distrust ⟨the young girl approached the camel *dubiously*⟩ — see ASKANCE

dubitable *adj* giving good reason for being doubted, questioned, or challenged ⟨some highly *dubitable* "evidence" that the stone tower was built by the Vikings⟩ — see DOUBTFUL 2

dubitation *n, archaic* a feeling or attitude that one does not know the truth, truthfulness, or trustworthiness of someone or something ⟨with considerable *dubitation* we listened to his tall tales of adventure⟩ — see DOUBT

duck *n* a member of the human race ⟨her coworkers regard her as something of an odd *duck*⟩ — see HUMAN

duck *vb* **1** to get or keep away from (as a responsibility) through cleverness or trickery ⟨don't try to *duck* your commitment to spending Thanksgiving with your family by claiming you have to work⟩ — see ESCAPE 2
2 to move suddenly aside or to and fro ⟨*duck* behind a pillar before they see us⟩ — see DODGE 1
3 to sink or push (something) briefly into or as if into a liquid ⟨*ducked* the new camper in the lake as a joke⟩ — see DIP 1

ducking *n* the act or a means of getting or keeping away from something undesirable ⟨the disgraceful *ducking* of your duties to your family⟩ — see ESCAPE 2

duck soup *n* something that is easy to do ⟨hooking up this home theater should be *duck soup*—right?⟩ — see CINCH 1

ducky *adj* being to one's liking ⟨if you don't want to come, that's just *ducky* with me⟩ — see SATISFACTORY 1

duct *n* a long hollow cylinder for carrying a substance (as a liquid or gas) ⟨air *ducts* to provide ventilation⟩ — see PIPE 1

dud *n* **1** something that has failed ⟨our first attempt was a complete *dud*, so we had to start over⟩ — see FAILURE 3
2 duds *pl* covering for the human body ⟨those are some pretty fancy *duds* you're wearing⟩ — see CLOTHING
3 duds *pl* transportable items that one owns ⟨you have one hour to pack up your *duds* and clear out of here⟩ — see POSSESSION 2

dude *n* **1** a man extremely interested in his clothing and personal appearance ⟨a *dude* given to sporting expensive suits and flashy jewelry⟩ — see DANDY 1
2 an adult male human being ⟨OK, *dude*, whatever you say⟩ — see MAN 1

dudgeon *n* the feeling of being offended or resentful after a slight or indignity ⟨stomped off in high *dudgeon* after having his honor questioned⟩ — see PIQUE

due *adj* **1** having reached the date at which payment is required ⟨the loan is *due* next April⟩
synonyms mature
related words delinquent, outstanding, overdue, owed, owing, receivable, unpaid, unsettled; payable
near antonyms cleared, liquidated, paid (off *or* up), repaid, settled; prepaid
antonyms undue
2 being in accordance with the prescribed, normal, or logical course of events ⟨their train is *due* to arrive in half an hour⟩
synonyms anticipated, awaited, expected, scheduled, slated
near antonyms behind, behindhand, belated, delinquent, dilatory, late, latish, overdue, tardy; early, premature, untimely; unanticipated, unforeseen, unlooked-for
3 being what is called for by accepted standards of right and wrong ⟨all the participants in the trial are required to treat the judge with *due* respect⟩ — see JUST 1

due *adv* **1** as stated or indicated without the slightest difference ⟨the island lies *due* south of the headland⟩ — see EXACTLY 1
2 in a direct line or course ⟨a plane flying *due* east⟩ — see DIRECTLY 1

due (to) *adj* coming as a result ⟨success that is *due to* hard work⟩ — see RESULTANT

duel *n* an earnest effort for superiority or victory over another ⟨a *duel* for the title of captain of the team⟩ — see CONTEST 1

duende *n* the power of irresistible attraction ⟨even as a child, she had an unmistakable *duende* that attracted the attention of passersby⟩ — see CHARM 2

due to *prep* as the result of ⟨evening classes were cancelled *due to* heavy snow⟩ — see BECAUSE OF

duff *n* the part of the body upon which someone sits ⟨I've been sitting on my *duff* all day⟩ — see BUTTOCKS

du jour *adj* enjoying widespread favor or approval ⟨that year the yellow tie was the fashion accessory *du jour* for ambitious male executives⟩ — see POPULAR 1

dulcet *adj* giving pleasure or contentment to the mind or senses ⟨although she flashed a *dulcet* smile, she was secretly seething with resentment⟩ — see PLEASANT 1

dull *adj* **1** lacking sharpness of edge or point ⟨the *dull* knife just bounced off the skin of the tomato without cutting it⟩
synonyms blunt, blunted, dulled, obtuse
related words dullish; rounded, smooth; even, flat, flattened, level
near antonyms jagged, needlelike, prickly, spiked, spikelike, spiky (*also* spikey), spiny; jabbing, lacerating, piercing, scratching, stabbing; ultrasharp
antonyms cutting, edged, edgy, ground, honed, keen, pointed, sharp, sharpened, whetted
2 causing weariness, restlessness, or lack of interest ⟨a *dull* dance recital that made us wish that we were someplace else⟩ — see BORING
3 covered over by clouds ⟨*dull* skies plagued most of our vacation days at the beach⟩ — see OVERCAST
4 lacking a surface luster or gloss ⟨a good polish should restore that car's *dull* finish⟩ — see MATTE
5 lacking intensity of color ⟨that canvas shirt should fade to an attractive, *dull* red over time⟩ — see PALE 1
6 not having or showing an ability to absorb ideas readily ⟨the importance of the discovery was lost on the *dull* minds of his colleagues⟩ — see STUPID 1
7 not loud in pitch or volume ⟨a *dull* roar from the distance⟩ — see SOFT 1
8 slow to move or act ⟨a *dull* market for luxury goods this holiday season⟩ — see INACTIVE 1

dull *vb* **1** to reduce or weaken in strength or feeling ⟨the aspirin *dulled* his headache and he was soon feeling better⟩
synonyms benumb, blunt, cauterize, damp, dampen, deaden, numb
related words muffle, mute, tone (down); decrease, diminish, lessen, let up (on), lower, reduce, subdue; debilitate, enfeeble, weaken; dwindle, recede, subside, taper (off), wane; alleviate, ease, lighten; abate, moderate
near antonyms amplify, augment, beef (up), boost, consolidate, deepen, enhance, heighten, intensify, magnify, redouble, step up, strengthen; animate, arouse, stimulate
antonyms sharpen, whet
2 to make white or lighter by removing color ⟨the painting's once-vivid colors have been *dulled* by time⟩ — see WHITEN

dullard *n* a stupid person ⟨often mistaken for a *dullard* because he never said much in discussions⟩ — see IDIOT

dulled *adj* **1** lacking a surface luster or gloss ⟨it might be best to paint the exposed pipes with a *dulled* enamel⟩ — see MATTE
2 lacking intensity of color ⟨the *dulled* colors and brownish tones are characteristic of this painter's works⟩ — see PALE 1
3 lacking sharpness of edge or point ⟨the *dulled* blade of a knife that had been stored in a drawer full of miscellaneous utensils⟩ — see DULL 1

dullness *also* **dulness** *n* the quality or state of lacking intelligence or quickness of mind ⟨the *dullness* of the characters in horror movies cannot be overstated⟩ — see STUPIDITY 1

dullsville *n* someone or something boring ⟨that book is totally *dullsville*—you'll be asleep by page three⟩ — see DRAG 1

duly *adv* in a manner suitable for the occasion or purpose ⟨the perpetrators of this outrageous crime will be *duly* punished⟩ — see PROPERLY

dumb *adj* **1** deliberately refraining from speech ⟨the mayor has chosen to remain *dumb* about her activities that night⟩ — see SILENT 1
2 not having or showing an ability to absorb ideas readily ⟨don't call him *dumb* just because he makes the occasional mistake like the rest of us⟩ — see STUPID 1
3 tending not to speak frequently (as by habit or inclination) ⟨he prefers to remain *dumb*, and replies in monosyllables if really pressed⟩ — see SILENT 2

dumb *vb* to stop the noise or speech of ⟨the terrible

news *dumbed* her for a long moment, and then she burst into tears⟩ — see SILENCE 1

dumbbell *n* a stupid person ⟨if we don't give him a shove, the poor *dumbbell* never will propose to her⟩ — see IDIOT

dumbfound *also* **dumfound** *vb* to make a strong impression on (someone) with something unexpected ⟨the surprise ending will *dumbfound* even the most seasoned mystery reader⟩ — see SURPRISE 1

dumbfounded *also* **dumfounded** *adj* **1** affected with sudden and great wonder or surprise ⟨*dumbfounded* by the realization that he had just won the grand prize in the multistate lottery⟩ — see THUNDERSTRUCK
2 filled with amazement or wonder ⟨*dumbfounded* visitors to the Grand Canyon⟩ — see OPENMOUTHED

dumbfounding *also* **dumfounding** *adj* causing a strong emotional reaction because of unexpectedness ⟨the *dumbfounding* sight of the race car driver walking away from that horrific crash⟩ — see SURPRISING 1

dumbhead *n* a stupid person ⟨the *dumbhead* who designed this contraption should be shot⟩ — see IDIOT

dumbness *n* **1** incapacity for or restraint from speaking ⟨the determined *dumbness* of the accountants who tally the votes for the Academy Awards⟩ — see SILENCE 1
2 the quality or state of lacking intelligence or quickness of mind ⟨couldn't believe the *dumbness* of the people who fell for that scam⟩ — see STUPIDITY 1

dumbstruck *adj* affected with sudden and great wonder or surprise ⟨the *dumbstruck* ecotourists gaped in silence as the enormous whale breached near their vessel⟩ — see THUNDERSTRUCK

dum–dum *n* a stupid person ⟨I'd rather be alone than spend an evening with those *dum-dums*⟩ — see IDIOT

dummkopf *n* a stupid person ⟨a good-looking guy, but a *dummkopf* with the brains of a potato⟩ — see IDIOT

dummy *adj* being such in appearance only and made with or manufactured from usually cheaper materials ⟨the *dummy* shutters on the house are actually made of vinyl and are for decoration only⟩ — see IMITATION

dummy *n* **1** a stupid person ⟨only a *dummy* would think that the mechanical monster was real⟩ — see IDIOT
2 a three-dimensional representation of the human body used especially for displaying clothes ⟨the *dummies* were arranged in the store window as if they were acting out scenes⟩ — see MANNEQUIN 1
3 something that is made to look exactly like something else ⟨for the movie, the props department made a *dummy* of the pistol actually used in the assassination⟩ — see COPY

dummy up *vb* to stop talking ⟨all of a sudden the suspect just *dummied up* and demanded the presence of an attorney⟩ — see SHUT UP 1

dump *n* **1** a place where discarded materials (as trash) are dumped ⟨all of the used packaging eventually ends up in the *dump*⟩
synonyms landfill, sanitary landfill, tip [*chiefly British*]
related words dustbin, dustheap, junkyard, kitchen midden, midden; transfer station; mess, pigpen, pigsty, sty
2 a place where military arms are stored ⟨a daring raid on the ammunition *dump*⟩ — see ARMORY
3 a dirty or messy place ⟨his place is always a *dump*, so he almost never has people over⟩ — see PIGPEN

dump *vb* **1** to end a usually intimate relationship with ⟨all of her friends were telling her to *dump* the jerk already⟩ — see DITCH 1
2 to get rid of as useless or unwanted ⟨*dump* the trash on the curb and go back inside⟩ — see DISCARD

dumping *n* the getting rid of whatever is unwanted or useless ⟨the *dumping* of last year's fashions by the garment manufacturers⟩ — see DISPOSAL 1

dumps *n pl* a state or spell of low spirits ⟨I've been down in the *dumps* all week⟩ — see SADNESS

dumpy *adj* **1** being compact and broad in build and often short in stature ⟨*dumpy* little men trying to look like tough guys⟩ — see STOCKY
2 showing signs of advanced wear and tear and neglect ⟨we could only find rooms at a *dumpy* motel on the outskirts of the city⟩ — see SHABBY 1

dun *n* something that someone insists upon having ⟨it's probably not a good idea to ignore a loan shark's *dun* for repayment⟩ — see DEMAND 1

dunce *n* a stupid person ⟨people with the learning disability dyslexia were once simply dismissed as *dunces*⟩ — see IDIOT

dunderhead *n* a stupid person ⟨wondered how long it would take the *dunderheads* at the head office to screw things up⟩ — see IDIOT

dunderheaded *adj* not having or showing an ability to absorb ideas readily ⟨a novel featuring clever criminals who make fools of the *dunderheaded* cops⟩ — see STUPID 1

dung *n* solid matter discharged from an animal's alimentary canal ⟨researchers tracked the wild gorillas by following the piles of *dung*⟩ — see DROPPING 1

dunk *vb* to sink or push (something) briefly into or as if into a liquid ⟨*dunking* a doughnut in one's morning coffee⟩ — see DIP 1

Dunkirk *n* a time or state of affairs requiring prompt or decisive action ⟨with the company facing a financial *Dunkirk*, it was hoped that the new CEO could turn things around—and fast⟩ — see EMERGENCY

duo *n* two things of the same or similar kind that match or are considered together ⟨the shy boy and his outgoing friend make an unlikely *duo*⟩ — see PAIR

[1]**dupe** *n* one who is easily deceived or cheated ⟨the swindler was able to escape with all of the *dupe's* money⟩
synonyms chump, gull, mug [*chiefly British*], patsy, pigeon, pushover, sap, soft touch, sucker, tool
related words cat's-paw, mark, target, victim; schlemiel (*also* shlemiel); butt, derision, laughingstock, mock, mockery; booby, dodo, fool, goose, half-wit, jackass, lunatic, monkey, nincompoop, ninny, nitwit, simp, simpleton, turkey, yo-yo; loser; blockhead, cretin, dolt, dope, dumbbell, dummy, dunce, idiot, imbecile, moron, schlub (*also* shlub) [*slang*], schlump [*slang*], schnook [*slang*]
near antonyms cheat, cheater, confidence man, cozener, defrauder, dodger, hoaxer, shark, sharper, slicker, swindler, trickster

[2]**dupe** *n* something that is made to look exactly like something else ⟨he built a *dupe* of the original model, which is locked in a vault⟩ — see COPY

dupe *vb* to cause to believe what is untrue ⟨we were *duped* into thinking the dummy was a real alien⟩ — see DECEIVE

dupery *n* the inclination or practice of misleading others through lies or trickery ⟨accusations of widespread *dupery* in the mortgage business⟩ — see DECEIT 1

duplex *adj* consisting of two members or parts that are usually joined ⟨a *duplex* apartment with all of the bedrooms on the second floor⟩ — see DOUBLE 1

duplicate *adj* resembling another in every respect ⟨*duplicate* copies of the portrait that were painted by the artist himself⟩ — see SAME 1

duplicate *n* **1** something or someone that strongly resembles another ⟨doll carriages that are *duplicates* of baby carriages⟩ — see IMAGE 1
2 something that is made to look exactly like something else ⟨a *duplicate* of a house key⟩ — see COPY 1

duplicate *vb* **1** to make an exact likeness of ⟨art students trying to *duplicate* paintings in the museum's collection as part of their training⟩ — see COPY 1

2 to make or do again ⟨we were unable to *duplicate* the experiment in our own lab, so we're suspicious⟩ — see REPEAT 4

3 to make twice as great or as many ⟨the recipe can be easily *duplicated* in order to feed a large family⟩ — see DOUBLE 1

duplication *n* **1** something or someone that strongly resembles another ⟨in adulthood he became sort of a living *duplication* of his late father⟩ — see IMAGE 1

2 something that is made to look exactly like something else ⟨a *duplication* of an ancient Chinese vase for the mass market⟩ — see COPY

3 the act of saying or doing over again ⟨let's avoid *duplication* of effort on this group project if we can⟩ — see REPEAT

duplicative *adj* marked by repetition ⟨*duplicative* efforts in this area that are just a waste of time⟩ — see REPETITIVE

duplicitous *adj* given to or marked by cheating and deception ⟨warned her not to trust the *duplicitous* art dealer⟩ — see DISHONEST 2

duplicity *n* the inclination or practice of misleading others through lies or trickery ⟨we were lucky not to be taken in by his *duplicity*⟩ — see DECEIT 1

durability *n* uninterrupted or lasting existence ⟨the *durability* of the novel's popularity since it was first published in the 1930s⟩ — see CONTINUATION

duration *n* **1** the period during which something exists, lasts, or is in progress ⟨for the whole *duration* of the speech the bored audience fidgeted⟩

synonyms continuance, date, life, life span, lifetime, run, standing, time

related words spell, stretch; span, tenure, term; hitch, tour, turn; half-life; age, longevity

2 uninterrupted or lasting existence ⟨scientists warning that the very *duration* of our civilization depends upon finding a solution to this major environmental problem⟩ — see CONTINUATION

duress *n* the use of power to impose one's will on another ⟨complied with the order only under *duress*⟩ — see FORCE 2

during *prep* in the course of ⟨we wrote notes *during* the boring lecture⟩

synonyms amid (*or* amidst), by, over, pending, through, throughout

dusk *adj* being without light or without much light ⟨under a *dusk* sky, the campers wearily bedded down for the night⟩ — see DARK 1

dusk *n* **1** the time from when the sun begins to set to the onset of total darkness ⟨we stopped playing at *dusk*, since it was getting too dark to see the ball⟩

synonyms crepuscule (*or* crepuscle), eve, evenfall, evening, eventide, gloaming, night, nightfall, sundown, sunset, twilight

related words dark, darkness, nighttime

near antonyms day, daytime, light; forenoon

antonyms aurora, cockcrow, dawn, dawning, daybreak, daylight, morn, morning, sunrise, sunup

2 a time or place of little or no light ⟨legends of fearsome beasts living in the *dusk* of the great forest⟩ — see DARK 1

3 partial darkness due to the obstruction of light rays ⟨the forbidding *dusk* of Germany's famed Black Forest⟩ — see SHADE 1

dusk *vb* to grow dark ⟨the grief-stricken woman continued to sit in the *dusking* room until she was completely enveloped in darkness⟩ — see DARKEN 2

dusky *adj* being without light or without much light ⟨in the *dusky* depths of the dungeon⟩ — see DARK 1

dust *n* **1** discarded or useless material ⟨the piles of *dust* that future archaeologists will sift through for insights into our civilization⟩ — see GARBAGE 1

2 the solid part of our planet's surface as distinguished from the sea and air ⟨laid him out in the *dust* with one blow to the head⟩ — see EARTH 2

dust *vb* to defeat by a large margin ⟨the inexperienced sprinter somehow *dusted* the field of veterans⟩ — see WHIP 2

dustiness *n* the state or quality of being dirty ⟨we were glad for a shower after the *dustiness* of the hike⟩ — see DIRTINESS 1

dustup *n* a physical dispute between opposing individuals or groups ⟨he came home with a black eye from the *dustup* at the bar⟩ — see FIGHT 1

dusty *adj* **1** consisting of very small particles ⟨*dusty* soil⟩ — see FINE 1

2 not clean ⟨old *dusty* clothes⟩ — see DIRTY 1

3 causing weariness, restlessness, or lack of interest ⟨I almost fell asleep reading that *dusty* book of memoirs⟩ — see BORING

dutiful *adj* marked by or showing proper regard for another's higher status ⟨the family showed a *dutiful* deference to their minister when he came to dinner⟩ — see RESPECTFUL

duty *n* **1** a charge usually of money collected by the government from people or businesses for public use ⟨the shop at the airport charges no *duty* on tourist memorabilia⟩ — see TAX

2 a piece of work that needs to be done regularly ⟨the regular *duties* of a lifeguard⟩ — see CHORE 1

3 something one must do because of prior agreement ⟨I must obey the call of *duty* and serve my country⟩ — see OBLIGATION 1

dwarf *n* **1** a living thing much smaller than others of its kind ⟨Shetland ponies are the *dwarfs* of the horse world⟩

synonyms diminutive, midget, mite, peewee, pygmy (*also* pigmy), runt, scrub, shrimp, Tom Thumb

related words nubbin; mini, miniature; bantam; homunculus, hop-o'-my-thumb, manikin (*also* mannikin); half-pint

near antonyms whale, whopper

antonyms behemoth, colossus, giant, jumbo, leviathan, mammoth, monster, titan

2 an imaginary being usually having a small human form and magical powers ⟨Snow White and the seven *dwarfs*⟩ — see FAIRY

3 a person of no importance or influence ⟨it would be ridiculous to compare the two sculptors—one's a giant of the art world and the other's a *dwarf*⟩ — see NOBODY

dwarf *vb* to hold back the normal growth of ⟨shrubs *dwarfed* by the lack of water⟩ — see STUNT

dwarfish *adj* of a size that is less than average ⟨a *dwarfish* people living deep in the rain forest⟩ — see SMALL 1

dwell *vb* **1** to continue to be in a place for a significant amount of time ⟨*dwelling* with a farm family as an exchange student in France⟩ — see [1]STAY 1

2 to have a home ⟨the widow *dwells* in the valley by herself⟩ — see LIVE 1

dwell (on *or* upon) *vb* to speak or write about insistently and usually tiresomely ⟨she was always *dwelling on* past insults and snubs, both real and imagined⟩ — see BELABOR 1

dweller *n* one who lives permanently in a place ⟨the kinds of nuisances that city *dwellers* are all too familiar with⟩ — see INHABITANT

dwelling *n* the place where one lives ⟨the simple *dwellings* in which the Pilgrims spent the first winter at Plymouth⟩ — see HOME 1

dwindle *vb* **1** to make smaller in amount, volume, or extent ⟨the long winter *dwindled* our supply of firewood to practically nothing⟩ — see DECREASE 1

2 to grow less in scope or intensity especially gradually

⟨our hopes *dwindled* as the reports of more casualties came in⟩ — see DECREASE 2

dyad *n* two things of the same or similar kind that match or are considered together ⟨the book examines the doctor-patient *dyad* from several perspectives⟩ — see PAIR

dye *n* a substance used to color other materials ⟨soaked the fabric in blue *dye*⟩ — see PIGMENT

dye *vb* to give color or a different color to ⟨*dyed* her hair a startling red⟩ — see COLOR 1

dyed-in-the-wool *adj* being such by habit and not likely to change ⟨as a *dyed-in-the-wool* skeptic, I give these "confirmed" UFO sightings as much credence as I do the tooth fairy⟩ — see HABITUAL 1

dyestuff *n* a substance used to color other materials ⟨indigo is a *dyestuff* originally from India⟩ — see PIGMENT

dying *adj* nearly dead ⟨we watered the *dying* plants just in time⟩ — see MORIBUND 1

dynamic *adj* **1** having active strength of body or mind ⟨a *dynamic* new challenger for the title of heavyweight champion⟩ — see VIGOROUS 1

2 marked by or uttered with forcefulness ⟨a *dynamic* speech expressing her party's goals and values⟩ — see EMPHATIC 1

dynamically *adv* in a vigorous and forceful manner ⟨presented her ideas so *dynamically* that the other committee members were instantly won over by her proposal⟩ — see HARD 3

dynamism *n* active strength of body or mind ⟨voters were attracted to the young challenger's *dynamism*, charisma, and progressive ideas⟩ — see VIGOR 1

dynamite *adj* of the very best kind ⟨a summer blockbuster that features some really *dynamite* special effects⟩ — see EXCELLENT

dynamo *n* a very energetic person ⟨a *dynamo* who barely needs to sleep, or so it seems⟩ — see PISTOL

dyspeptic *adj* having or showing a habitually bad temper ⟨as might be expected, the newspaper's resident curmudgeon took a *dyspeptic* view of the whole affair⟩ — see ILL-TEMPERED

E

each *adj* being one of a group ⟨*each* park visitor receives a free souvenir⟩
synonyms any, every
related words all; several, various; particular; respective, specific; either
phrases each and every
near antonyms neither

each *adv* for each one ⟨raffle tickets selling for a dollar *each*⟩ — see APIECE

eager *adj* showing urgent desire or interest ⟨Tom was *eager* to try out his new pair of skis⟩
synonyms agog, antsy, anxious, ardent, athirst, avid, crazy, desirous, enthused, enthusiastic, excited, geeked [*slang*], great, greedy, gung ho, hepped up, hopped-up, hot, hungry, impatient, juiced, keen, nuts, pumped, raring, solicitous, stoked [*slang*], thirsty, voracious, wild
related words engaged, interested; happy, hung up, obsessed; ambitious, appetent, covetous, craving, hankering, longing, pining; breathless, restive, restless; amenable, disposed, game, glad, inclined, ready, unreluctant, willing
phrases champing at the bit, chomping at the bit
near antonyms casual, incurious, insouciant, nonchalant, unconcerned, uninterested; aloof, detached, disinterested; impassive, stolid; halfhearted, lackadaisical, languid, languorous, lukewarm, spiritless; averse, disinclined, hesitant, loath (*also* loth *or* loathe), reluctant, unwilling
antonyms apathetic, indifferent, uneager, unenthusiastic

eagerness *n* urgent desire or interest ⟨students with an *eagerness* to learn⟩
synonyms appetite, ardor, avidity, avidness, desirousness, enthusiasm, excitement, hunger, impatience, keenness, lust, thirst
related words alacrity, quickness; ambition, gusto, zest; appetence, appetency, fervency, passion, warmth, zeal; amenability, readiness, willingness
near antonyms casualness, insouciance, nonchalance, unconcern; aloofness, detachment; impassivity, languidness, languor; halfheartedness, lukewarmness
antonyms apathy, indifference

eagle-eyed *adj* having unusually keen vision ⟨my *eagle-eyed* aunt quickly spotted my contact lens on the floor⟩ — see SHARP-EYED

ear *n* a state of being aware ⟨I'm trying to get the boss's *ear* in order to ask for a raise in my pay⟩ — see ATTENTION 2

earlier *adv* so as to precede something in order of time ⟨he had arrived *earlier* to take care of some preliminary matters⟩ — see AHEAD 1

earliest *adj* coming before all others in time or order ⟨the *earliest* computers were massive machines that practically filled up a room⟩ — see FIRST 1

early *adj* **1** relating to or occurring near the beginning of a process, series, or time period ⟨*early* birds of the Jurassic period⟩
synonyms ancient, primal, primeval, primitive, primordial
related words budding, embryonic, germinal, infant; aged, age-old, antediluvian, antiquated, antique, dateless, hoary, old, prehistoric (*also* prehistorical); obsolete, outmoded, out-of-date, passé
near antonyms advanced, complex, developed, evolved, high, higher; full-blown, full-fledged, full-scale
antonyms late

2 occurring before the usual or expected time ⟨we had an *early* dinner so as not to miss the concert⟩
synonyms inopportune, precocious, premature, unseasonable, untimely
related words unanticipated, unexpected, unforeseen, unlooked-for; abrupt, sudden
near antonyms behindhand, belated, delinquent,

latish, overdue, slow, tardy; anticipated, expected; delayed, detained, postponed
antonyms late

early *adv* before the usual or expected time ⟨that year spring arrived *early*⟩
synonyms beforehand, inopportunely, precociously, prematurely, unseasonably
related words immediately, instantly, presently, promptly, pronto, punctually; apropos, betimes, seasonably
antonyms belatedly, late, tardily

earmark *vb* to keep or intend for a special purpose ⟨the earnings from my second job have been *earmarked* for a down payment on a car⟩ — see DEVOTE 1

earn *vb* **1** to receive as return for effort ⟨during my teen years I *earned* pocket money by mowing lawns⟩
synonyms acquire, attain, bag, bring in, capture, carry, come by, draw, gain, garner, get, knock down, land, make, obtain, procure, pull down, realize, reap, secure, win
related words clear, gross, net; accomplish, achieve, notch (up), score; accumulate, amass, draw, rack up; catch, pick up; annex, occupy, take over; reacquire, reattain, recapture, regain, remake
near antonyms accord, give, grant, pay; give up, hand over, part (with), relinquish, surrender, yield
antonyms forfeit, lose
2 to be or make worthy of (as a reward or punishment) ⟨you've *earned* the afternoon off after all that hard work⟩
synonyms deserve, merit, rate
related words entitle, qualify

earnest *adj* not joking or playful in mood or manner ⟨I'll accept only an *earnest* apology from you⟩ — see SERIOUS 1

earnest *n* a mental state free of jesting or trifling ⟨I am in deadly *earnest* about this marriage proposal⟩ — see EARNESTNESS

earnestness *n* a mental state free of jesting or trifling ⟨practiced the art of acting with great *earnestness*⟩
synonyms earnest, graveness, gravity, intentness, serious-mindedness, seriousness, soberness, sobriety, solemnity, solemnness, staidness
related words gravitas, humorlessness; decisiveness, deliberation, determination, firmness, purposefulness, resoluteness, resolve; absorption, attentiveness, concentration, engrossment, enthrallment, immersion, intensity
near antonyms lightness, shallowness, superficiality; dalliance, dilettantism; cheerfulness, gaiety (*also* gayety), glee, high-spiritedness, merriment, mirth
antonyms facetiousness, flightiness, flippancy, frivolity, frivolousness, levity, lightheartedness, lightness, play, unseriousness

earnings *n pl* **1** an increase usually measured in money that comes from labor, business, or property ⟨*earnings* from her babysitting jobs that are being put away for college⟩ — see INCOME 1
2 the amount of money left when expenses are subtracted from the total amount received ⟨after subtracting what we spent on music and refreshments, the *earnings* from our charity gala were still impressive⟩ — see PROFIT 1

earshot *n* range of hearing ⟨babysitters should remain within *earshot* of young children⟩
synonyms hail, hearing, sound
related words volume; distance, sight

earsplitting *adj* marked by a high volume of sound ⟨the *earsplitting* noise coming from the jackhammers at the construction site⟩ — see LOUD 1

earth *n* **1** the celestial body on which we live ⟨environmentalists who are committed to preserving the *earth*⟩
synonyms globe, planet, world
related words cosmos, creation, nature, universe; ball, orb, sphere; macrocosm, microcosm, microcosmos
2 the solid part of our planet's surface as distinguished from the sea and air ⟨after nearly drowning, I was glad to feel the *earth* under my feet⟩
synonyms dirt, dust, ground, land, soil, terra firma
related words continent, landmass, zone; island, isthmus, mainland, peninsula
3 the loose surface material in which plants naturally grow ⟨set the plants deep enough into the *earth* so that they'll be sure to take root⟩ — see DIRT 1
4 a very large amount of money ⟨it'll cost the *earth* to repair that porcelain vase, so make sure that it's worth it⟩ — see FORTUNE 2

earthborn *adj* **1** having to do with life on earth especially as opposed to that in heaven ⟨turned away from *earthborn* concerns during the High Holidays⟩ — see EARTHLY
2 relating to or characteristic of human beings ⟨he claims to be above such *earthborn* concerns as material comfort⟩ — see HUMAN

earthbound *adj* having to do with life on earth especially as opposed to that in heaven ⟨we have too many *earthbound* worries to speculate on the number of angels who can dance on the head of a pin⟩ — see EARTHLY

earthenware *n* articles made of baked clay ⟨a wide array of hand-painted *earthenware* available at the craft fair⟩ — see CROCKERY

earthlike *adj* consisting or suggestive of earth ⟨the basket of garden-fresh mushrooms had that typically *earthlike* smell⟩ — see EARTHY 1

earthly *adj* having to do with life on earth especially as opposed to that in heaven ⟨a sermon against our obsession with *earthly* pursuits⟩
synonyms carnal, earthborn, earthbound, fleshly, material, mundane, sublunary, temporal, terrene, terrestrial, worldly
related words animal, bodily, corporal, corporeal, physical; daily, diurnal; unspiritual; anthropic (*or* anthropical), anthropocentric
near antonyms celestial, Elysian, empyreal, empyrean, supernal; metaphysical; devotional, divine, religious, sacred, spiritual, utopian; extraterrestrial; ethereal, supernatural, transcendent, transcendental
antonyms heavenly, nontemporal, unearthly, unworldly

earthquake *n* **1** a shaking of the earth ⟨the San Andreas Fault is notorious for its *earthquakes*⟩
synonyms quake, shake, temblor, tremor
related words aftershock, foreshock, shock; cataclysm, convulsion, upheaval; microearthquake, microseism, seaquake
2 a violent disturbance (as of the political or social order) ⟨the election of the socialist candidate caused a political *earthquake* that nearly led to a military coup⟩ — see CONVULSION

earthshaking *adj* having great meaning or lasting effect ⟨*earthshaking* news—the President has been assassinated⟩ — see IMPORTANT 1

earth–shattering *adj* having great meaning or lasting effect ⟨scientists have made a few minor discoveries in that area, but nothing *earth-shattering*⟩ — see IMPORTANT 1

earthy *adj* **1** consisting or suggestive of earth ⟨the unmistakably *earthy* aroma of a greenhouse⟩
synonyms earthlike, loamy
related words clayey, dusty, muddy, sandy, silty
2 willing to see things as they really are and deal with them sensibly ⟨the dog trainer was *earthy*, no-nonsense,

and blunt—with us, as well as our dog⟩ — see REALISTIC 1

ease *n* **1** reduction of or freedom from pain ⟨the sunburn medication brought me instant *ease*⟩
synonyms alleviation, comfort, release, relief
related words appeasement, assuagement, decrease, diminishment, mitigation, moderation, mollification; calming, salving, soothing
near antonyms discomfort, unrest; agony, anguish, misery, suffering, torment, torture; ache, pain, pang, prick, smart, sting, stitch, throe, tingle, twinge
2 carefree freedom from constraint ⟨a gymnast who can handle even the most demanding moves on the parallel bars with total *ease*⟩ — see ABANDON
3 freedom from activity or labor ⟨the dream of every lottery player is a life of fabulous luxury and everlasting *ease*⟩ — see [1]REST 1

ease *vb* **1** to free from obstruction or difficulty ⟨measures intended to *ease* the flow of traffic during rush hour⟩
synonyms facilitate, grease, loosen (up), smooth, unclog
related words accelerate, expedite, hasten, hurry, quicken, rush, speed; advance, forward, further, promote; abet, aid, assist, help, improve; disentangle, straighten (out), untangle; simplify, streamline
phrases pave the way (for)
near antonyms hinder, impede; retard; aggravate, worsen; perplex, sophisticate
antonyms complicate
2 to make less taut ⟨the rock climber *eased* the rope a little so that his fellow climber had room to maneuver⟩ — see SLACKEN 1
3 to make more bearable or less severe ⟨grandmother's firm belief that there are few ailments that chicken soup won't *ease*⟩ — see HELP 2
4 to make smaller in amount, volume, or extent ⟨the chairman of the Federal Reserve has promised to *ease* interest rates⟩ — see DECREASE 1
5 to grow less in scope or intensity especially gradually ⟨new investments in the region have *eased* since the rise in interest rates⟩ — see DECREASE 2

easily *adv* **1** without difficulty ⟨a skater who *easily* executes even the most difficult jumps⟩
synonyms easy, effortlessly, facilely, fluently, freely, handily, hands down, lightly, painlessly, readily, smoothly, well
related words ably, adeptly, adroitly, competently, deftly, dexterously, efficiently, expertly, masterfully, proficiently, skillfully; instinctively, intuitively, naturally, spontaneously
phrases in a breeze, no sweat [*slang*], without ado, without a hitch
near antonyms awkwardly, clumsily, gracelessly, hamhandedly, ineptly, maladroitly, unskillfully; meticulously, painfully, painstakingly, thoroughly; assiduously, diligently, indefatigably, industriously, intensely, intently, mightily, sedulously, tirelessly
antonyms arduously, hardly, laboriously, strenuously
2 without any question ⟨we *easily* have enough people to get the project under way⟩ — see INDEED 1

easy *adj* **1** involving minimal difficulty or effort ⟨a minor problem with an *easy* solution⟩
synonyms cheap, downhill, effortless, facile, fluent, fluid, hands-down, light, painless, ready, royal, simple, smooth, snap, soft
related words idiotproof, mindless, quick, straightforward, unchallenging, uncomplicated; apparent, clear, clear-cut, distinct, evident, manifest, obvious, open-and-shut, palpable, patent, perspicuous, plain, transparent, unambiguous, unequivocal, unmistakable
near antonyms burdensome, exhausting, onerous, oppressive, painful, stressful, taxing, troublesome; abstruse, complex, complicated, intricate, involved, knotty, problematic (*also* problematical), recondite
antonyms arduous, demanding, difficult, exacting, formidable, grueling (*or* gruelling), hard, herculean, killer, labored, laborious, murderous, rough, severe, stiff, strenuous, toilful, toilsome, tough
2 readily taken advantage of ⟨senior citizens who are *easy* prey for scam artists⟩
synonyms dewy-eyed, exploitable, gullible (*also* gullable), naive (*or* naïve), susceptible, trusting, unwary, wide-eyed
related words credulous, overcredulous, trustful, uncritical, unsuspecting, unsuspicious; artless, genuine, guileless, innocent, simple, unsophisticated, unworldly; fictile, malleable, pliable, pliant; deceivable; acquiescent, agreeable, amiable, obliging; yielding
near antonyms critical, cynical, mistrustful, skeptical, suspicious, wary; sophisticated; clear-eyed, clear-sighted, hardheaded; shrewd, street-smart, streetwise
3 providing physical comfort ⟨my favorite *easy* chair for watching TV⟩ — see COMFORTABLE 1
4 tolerant and kind in the judgment of and expectations for others ⟨despite her *easy* approach to discipline, she had a remarkably well-behaved class⟩ — see INDULGENT 1

easy *adv* without difficulty ⟨we can make the trip in four hours *easy*⟩ — see EASILY 1

easygoing *adj* **1** having a relaxed, casual manner ⟨counselors at the summer camp are pretty *easygoing*⟩
synonyms affable, breezy, devil-may-care, happy-go-lucky, laid-back, low-pressure, mellow
related words carefree, casual, dégagé, lackadaisical, nonchalant, unaffected, unconcerned, unfussy, unperturbed, untroubled, unworried; familiar, homey (*also* homy), informal; flexible, lax, lenient, permissive, pliable, pliant, soft; accessible, approachable; imperturbable, nerveless, unflappable, unshakable; amicable, companionable, comradely, cordial, genial, hail-fellow-well-met, hearty, neighborly, warm, warmhearted
near antonyms ceremonious, decorous, formal, rigid, strict; anxious, bothered, distressed, worried; jittery, jumpy, nervous, skittish, tense
antonyms high-strung, uptight
2 not bound by rigid standards ⟨some men are pretty *easygoing* about housekeeping⟩
synonyms flexible, lax, loose, relaxed, slack, unrestrained, unrestricted
related words careless, derelict, heedless, irresponsible, lazy, neglectful, negligent, remiss, slipshod, sloppy, sloven, slovenly, unfussy
near antonyms constrained, restrained, restricted, tight; careful, conscientious, exact, fussy, meticulous, painstaking, punctilious, scrupulous; implacable, inflexible
antonyms hard, harsh, rigid, rigorous, severe, stern, strict

easy street *n* a situation or state of carefree comfort ⟨just knew that if I hit the lottery, I'd be on *easy street* for the rest of my life⟩ — see BEER AND SKITTLES

eat *vb* **1** to take in as food ⟨having gone all day without food, we greedily *ate* the hamburgers⟩
synonyms consume, ingest, partake (of), put away, put down, tuck (away *or* in)
related words digest, down, mouth (down), swallow; bolt, chow (down on), devour, glut (on), gobble (up *or* down), gorge, gulp, scoff, slop, snarf (down), swill, wolf; chew, gnaw (at *or* on), gum, lap, lick, nibble (on), nurse, pick (at); relish, savor (*also* savour), taste; banquet, dine, fare, feast, gormandize, pig out, regale; dispatch, polish off; breakfast, lunch, sup; munch, nosh, snack
2 to consume or wear away gradually ⟨the pot's protec-

tive coating was *eaten* away by the acid⟩
synonyms bite (at), corrode, erode, fret, gnaw, nibble
related words break down, break up, decompose, disintegrate, dissolve; decimate, destroy, devastate, ruin, waste, wreck
near antonyms freshen, recreate, refresh, refreshen, regenerate, rejuvenate, renew, restore, revitalize, revive
3 to take a meal ⟨where's the best place to *eat* in this town?⟩ — see DINE 1
4 to disturb the peace of mind of (someone) especially by repeated disagreeable acts ⟨it really *eats* me the way people go to national parks to enjoy nature—and then leave their litter behind⟩ — see IRRITATE 1

eat (up) *vb* **1** to receive or accept gladly or readily ⟨predictably, moviegoers *ate up* the sequel to last summer's blockbuster⟩ — see WELCOME
2 to destroy all trace of ⟨the surf created by a powerful hurricane could really *eat up* what's left of the island's eastern beach⟩ — see CONSUME 1

eatable *adj* suitable for use as food ⟨a survival course in which you learn which wild plants are *eatable*⟩ — see EDIBLE

eatables *n pl* substances intended to be eaten ⟨the buffet table aboard the cruise ship always had a tempting array of *eatables*⟩ — see FOOD 1

eatery *n* a public establishment where meals are served to paying customers for consumption on the premises ⟨we usually go to lunch at an *eatery* that is just around the corner from the office⟩ — see RESTAURANT

eating *adj* suitable for use as food ⟨crab apples are not actually *eating* apples⟩ — see EDIBLE

eats *n pl* substances intended to be eaten ⟨there are some good *eats* at the buffet table⟩ — see FOOD 1

eavesdrop (on) *vb* to listen to (another in private conversation) ⟨a nosy traveler who likes to *eavesdrop on* his fellow airline passengers⟩
synonyms listen in (on), overhear
related words bug, tap, wiretap; monitor, snoop, spy, surveil; attend, hear, hearken, heed, mind

eaves trough *n* a pipe or channel for carrying off water from a roof ⟨rain so heavy that the *eaves trough* couldn't handle it⟩ — see GUTTER 1

ebb *n* a change to a lower state or level ⟨a surprising *ebb* in the quality of workmanship in goods coming from that country⟩ — see DECLINE 2

ebb *vb* **1** to become worse or of less value ⟨the fortunes of the town slowly *ebbed* as factory after textile factory closed⟩ — see DETERIORATE 1
2 to grow less in scope or intensity especially gradually ⟨the howling winds *ebbed* as the hurricane moved into the interior⟩ — see DECREASE 2

ebbing *n* a gradual sinking and wasting away of mind or body ⟨seniors who stay active can keep at bay some of the inevitable *ebbing* of the memory that comes with advanced years⟩ — see DECLINE 1

ebony *adj* having the color of soot or coal ⟨the *ebony* loudspeakers on their chrome stands look very sleek and modern⟩ — see BLACK 1

ebullition *n* a sudden intense expression of strong feeling ⟨the earsplitting *ebullition* of the fans following the from-the-jaws-of-defeat victory⟩ — see OUTBURST 1

eccentric *adj* different from the ordinary in a way that causes curiosity or suspicion ⟨his *eccentric* decorating style isn't going over well with the neighbors⟩ — see ODD 2

eccentric *n* a person of odd or whimsical habits ⟨an *eccentric* who designed his house to look like a Scottish castle⟩
synonyms character, codger, crack, crackbrain, crackpot, crank, flake, fruitcake, head case, kook, nut, nutcase, nutter [*British slang*], oddball, oddity, original, quiz, screwball, weirdo, zany
related words bohemian, maverick, nonconformist, quixote; coot, geezer; curio, rarity; freak; fantast, fantastico
phrases odd duck, piece of work
near antonyms conformer, conformist, follower, sheep

eccentricity *n* an odd or peculiar habit ⟨one of the woman's *eccentricities* was her lifelong habit of reading while soaking in the bathtub for hours⟩ — see IDIOSYNCRASY

ecclesial *adj* of or relating to a church ⟨the waning of *ecclesial* power in Europe as the number of lapsed Christians increases⟩ — see ECCLESIASTICAL

ecclesiastic *adj* of or relating to a church ⟨a council to make final determinations on *ecclesiastic* matters⟩ — see ECCLESIASTICAL

ecclesiastic *n* a person specially trained and authorized to conduct religious services in a Christian church ⟨as the leading *ecclesiastic* for his church in the state, the bishop must be beyond reproach in everything he does⟩ — see CLERGYPERSON

ecclesiastical *adj* of or relating to a church ⟨*ecclesiastical* laws that have been in existence for centuries⟩
synonyms churchly, ecclesial, ecclesiastic
related words blessed (*also* blest), consecrated, divine, hallowed, holy, religious, sacramental, sacred, sacrosanct, sanctified; apostolic, canonical, clerical, episcopal, evangelical (*also* evangelic), ministerial, papal, pastoral, patriarchal, pontifical, priestly, rabbinic (*or* rabbinical), sacerdotal
near antonyms lay, profane, secular, temporal; nonclerical; nondenominational, nonsectarian
antonyms nonchurch, nonecclesiastical

echelon *n* the placement of someone or something in relation to others in a vertical arrangement ⟨jobs in the upper *echelons* of the company pay quite well indeed⟩ — see RANK 1

echo *n* **1** a person who adopts the appearance or behavior of another especially in an obvious way ⟨a younger sister who was her *echo* all the while that they were growing up⟩ — see COPYCAT
2 a tiny often physical indication of something lost or vanished ⟨a few stone carvings are the only *echoes* that remain of a once-mighty civilization⟩ — see VESTIGE 1

echo *vb* **1** to continue or be repeated in a series of reflected sound waves ⟨my calls for help *echoed* off the walls of the abandoned mine shaft⟩ — see REVERBERATE
2 to say after another ⟨the little brats sassed the babysitter by *echoing* in a singsong voice everything she said⟩ — see REPEAT 3

echt *adj* being exactly as appears or as claimed ⟨an *echt* New Englander wouldn't think of putting tomatoes in clam chowder⟩ — see AUTHENTIC 1

eclectic *adj* consisting of many things of different sorts ⟨the museum's *eclectic* collection has everything from a giraffe skeleton to medieval musical instruments⟩ — see MISCELLANEOUS

eclipse *n* a change to a lower state or level ⟨the *eclipse* of the town from a grand seaside resort to a tacky tourist trap⟩ — see DECLINE 2

eclipse *vb* to be greater, better, or stronger than ⟨the brilliant young pianist now *eclipsed* even his own mentor in musical artistry⟩ — see SURPASS 1

economic *adj* yielding a profit ⟨unfortunately, raising employees' salaries would not be *economic*—the business would have to fold⟩ — see PROFITABLE 1

economical *adj* careful in the management of money or resources ⟨we have to be *economical* in our use of the camp's limited supply of electricity⟩ — see FRUGAL

economize *vb* to avoid unnecessary waste or expense ⟨in tough times people learn how to *economize*⟩
synonyms pinch, save, scrimp, skimp, spare

related words conserve, husband, maintain, manage, preserve; scrape; cut back, cut down, retrench; hoard, lay up
phrases pinch pennies
near antonyms blow, dissipate, fritter (away), lavish, misspend, run through, spend, squander, throw away; splurge
antonyms waste

economizing *adj* careful in the management of money or resources ⟨*economizing* drivers aren't so affected by every hike in the price of gasoline⟩ — see FRUGAL

economy *n* careful management of material resources ⟨people on fixed incomes are used to practicing *economy*⟩
synonyms frugality, husbandry, parsimony, penny-pinching, providence, scrimping, skimping, thrift
related words conservation, saving; miserliness, niggardliness, stinginess; belt-tightening, retrenchment; discretion, forehandedness, prudence; austerity, moderation, restraint, temperance
near antonyms extravagance, improvidence, lavishness, prodigality, squandering
antonyms diseconomy, wastefulness

ecstasy *n* a state of overwhelming usually pleasurable emotion ⟨actors are typically in *ecstasy* upon winning an Oscar⟩
synonyms cloud nine, elatedness, elation, euphoria, exhilaration, heaven, high, intoxication, paradise, rapture, rhapsody, seventh heaven, swoon, transport
related words exaltation; blessedness, bliss, blissfulness, delight, enchantment, felicity, gladness, happiness, joy, joyfulness, joyousness, pleasure; reverie, trance; inspiration; fervor, frenzy, madness, passion; cheer, cheerfulness, exuberance, gaiety (*also* gayety), glee, gleefulness, jubilance, jubilation, lightheartedness
near antonyms misery, sadness, unhappiness, woe, wretchedness; blues, dejection, desolation, despair, despondency, disconsolateness, disheartenment, dispiritedness, doldrums, downheartedness, dreariness, dumps, forlornness, gloom, gloominess, heartsickness, melancholy, mopes
antonyms depression

ecstatic *adj* experiencing or marked by overwhelming usually pleasurable emotion ⟨a football player who was *ecstatic* upon receiving a full athletic scholarship to the college of his choice⟩
synonyms elated, elevated, enrapt, enraptured, entranced, euphoric, exhilarated, giddy, heady, intoxicated, rapt, rapturous, rhapsodic (*also* rhapsodical)
related words enchanted, exultant, glorying, jubilant, rejoicing, triumphant; enthusiastic, excited, gung ho, thrilled; blissed-out, blissful, delighted, glad, gratified, happy, joyful, joyous, pleased, satisfied, tickled
phrases on cloud nine, over the moon
near antonyms blue, brokenhearted, crestfallen, dejected, despondent, disconsolate, disheartened, doleful, down, downcast, downhearted, forlorn, gloomy, glum, hangdog, heartbroken, heartsick, heartsore, inconsolable, joyless, low, low-spirited, melancholy, miserable, mournful, sad, saddened, sorrowful, sorry, unhappy, woebegone, woeful, wretched
antonyms depressed

edacious *adj* having a huge appetite ⟨my *edacious* dining companion could always be counted on to order the largest—and often most expensive—item on the menu⟩ — see VORACIOUS 1

Eden *n* an often imaginary place or state of utter perfection and happiness ⟨some of the first Europeans to explore Polynesia thought that they had indeed discovered a tropical *Eden*⟩ — see PARADISE 1

edge *n* **1** a harsh or sharp quality ⟨the teacher's voice had a sarcastic *edge* as she welcomed the tardy student to class⟩
synonyms acerbity, acidity, acidness, acridity, acridness, acrimoniousness, acrimony, acuteness, asperity, bite, bitterness, harshness, keenness, poignance, poignancy, pungency, roughness, sharpness, tartness
related words ginger, punch, spice, tang; raucousness, severeness, severity, shrillness, virulence, vitriol; cattiness, maliciousness; pointedness, thorniness
near antonyms gentleness, kindliness
antonyms mildness, softness
2 the line or relatively narrow space that marks the outer limit of something ⟨the design along the *edge* of the plate is badly worn⟩ — see BORDER 1
3 the more favorable condition or position in a competition ⟨my big feet give me something of an *edge* in swimming⟩ — see ADVANTAGE 1
4 the power to produce a desired result ⟨the utter lack of enforcement provisions totally blunts the *edge* of the law⟩ — see EFFICACY
5 an interval of time just before the onset of something ⟨the nation's economy was on the *edge* of collapse when the Federal Reserve took exceptionally bold action⟩ — see POINT 3

edge *vb* **1** to make sharp or sharper ⟨if you *edge* the tip of that stick, it should be a fine skewer for roasting marshmallows⟩ — see SHARPEN
2 to serve as a border for ⟨pavement *edging* the flower bed⟩ — see BORDER

edged *adj* having an edge thin enough to cut or pierce something ⟨always store your finely *edged* knives in a knife block⟩ — see SHARP 1

edge in *vb* to put among or between others ⟨although she likes to profess journalistic impartiality when covering a story, she seldom refrains from *edging in* her personal observations⟩ — see INSERT

edgeways *adv, chiefly British* with one side faced forward ⟨he shoved the oversized book in *edgeways* so it would fit between the shelves⟩ — see SIDEWAYS 1

edgewise *adv* with one side faced forward ⟨you can squeeze through the narrow passage between the two caves if you go *edgewise*⟩ — see SIDEWAYS 1

edginess *n* a state of nervousness marked by sudden jerky movements ⟨the *edginess* of the basketball players in the moments before the start of the tournament was apparent⟩ — see JUMPINESS

edging *n* the line or relatively narrow space that marks the outer limit of something ⟨the lace *edging* on the sleeves gives a blouse a pleasingly feminine look⟩ — see BORDER 1

edgy *adj* **1** feeling or showing uncomfortable feelings of uncertainty ⟨with an *edgy* voice the spelling-bee contestant started to spell the tongue twister⟩ — see NERVOUS 1
2 having an edge thin enough to cut or pierce something ⟨be careful as you walk along the beach—those broken clam shells are *edgy* enough to cut your feet⟩ — see SHARP 1
3 serving or likely to arouse a strong reaction ⟨a director known for his *edgy*, over-the-top satires on modern life⟩ — see PROVOCATIVE

edible *adj* suitable for use as food ⟨*edible* plant products⟩
synonyms comestible, eatable, eating, esculent
related words absorbable, chewable, digestible, ingestible, swallowable; nourishing, nutritious, nutritive; appetizing, delicious, flavorful, palatable, savory (*also* savoury), succulent, tasty, toothsome, toothy
near antonyms indigestible, nondigestible, nonnutritious, undigestible
antonyms inedible, nonedible, uneatable

edibles *n pl* substances intended to be eaten ⟨even if the storm turns out to be a blizzard, there are enough *edibles* in the refrigerator to last us a week⟩ — see FOOD 1

edict *n* **1** an order publicly issued by an authority ⟨the school board's *edict* put a new student dress code into effect⟩
synonyms bull, decree, diktat, directive, fiat, rescript, ruling, ukase
related words call, conclusion, decision, deliverance, determination, diagnosis, judgment (*or* judgement), opinion, resolution, verdict; announcement, declaration, dictum, manifesto, proclamation, pronouncement; canon, encyclical
2 a statement of what to do that must be obeyed by those concerned ⟨this household's *edict* of long standing: no television until all homework has been completed⟩ — see COMMAND 1

edifice *n* **1** a large, magnificent, or massive building ⟨the U.S. Capitol is one of our nation's most impressive *edifices*⟩
synonyms cathedral, hall, palace, tower
related words construction, erection, structure; castle, château, countryseat, estate, hacienda, manor, manor house, mansion, showplace, villa; mausoleum, memorial, monument
2 something built as a dwelling, shelter, or place for human activity ⟨the first *edifices* built by the colonists were primitive huts with walls of dried mud and roofs covered with thatch⟩ — see BUILDING
3 the arrangement of parts that gives something its basic form ⟨the *edifice* of the argument is quite simple, once you get past the fancy language⟩ — see FRAME 1

edify *vb* to provide (someone) with moral or spiritual understanding ⟨a family-oriented show that tried to *edify* the television audience as well as entertain it⟩ — see ENLIGHTEN 2

edit *vb* **1** to prepare for publication by correcting, rewriting, or updating ⟨the publisher *edited* a new version of its best-selling school dictionary⟩
synonyms redraft, revamp, revise, rework
related words perfect, polish, touch up; copyedit, read, sub [*British*], subedit; reedit; amend, annotate, correct, emend, rectify; fact-check; anthologize, collect, compile; get out, issue, print, publish; abridge, blue-pencil, redact, red-pencil; engross, recopy
2 to change (something) so as to make it suitable for a new use or situation ⟨the restaurant chef has *edited* several of his gourmet dishes for preparation by the home cook⟩ — see ADAPT

edit (out) *vb* to show (something written) to be no longer valid by drawing a cross over or a line through it ⟨anything potentially offensive or disturbing was *edited out* of the newsletter before it was mailed⟩ — see X (OUT)

editorialize *vb* to make a statement of one's opinion ⟨she never misses a chance to *editorialize* on the issues of the day—even the ones she knows nothing about⟩ — see REMARK 1

educate *vb* **1** to cause to acquire knowledge or skill in some field ⟨a revered professor of astronomy who is credited with *educating* many of today's leading astronomers⟩ — see TEACH
2 to provide (someone) with moral or spiritual understanding ⟨the belief that parents better *educate* their children by example than by sending them to Sunday school⟩ — see ENLIGHTEN 2

educated *adj* **1** having or displaying advanced knowledge or education ⟨*educated* people are often more aware and tolerant of cultural and ethnic diversity⟩
synonyms erudite, knowledgeable, learned, lettered, literate, scholarly, well-read
related words civilized, cultivated, cultured; cerebral, highbrow, highbrowed, intellectual; polished, refined, well-bred; academic (*also* academical), bookish, didactic, didactical, inkhorn, pedantic, professorial; informed, instructed, schooled, skilled, trained; homeschooled, self-educated, self-instructed, self-taught; briefed, enlightened, informed, versed; overeducated, polyhistoric, polymath (*or* polymathic)
near antonyms uncivilized, uncultivated, uncultured; lowbrow, semiliterate, unintellectual; ill-bred, unpolished, unrefined; uninformed, unknowledgeable; uninstructed, unschooled, untaught, untutored; semiliterate, undereducated
antonyms benighted, dark, ignorant, illiterate, uneducated, unlearned, unlettered, unscholarly
2 having or showing exceptional knowledge, experience, or skill in a field of endeavor ⟨a violinist caressing the instrument with an *educated* touch⟩ — see PROFICIENT

education *n* **1** the act or process of imparting knowledge or skills to another ⟨a teacher who devoted herself to the *education* of children with special needs⟩
synonyms instruction, schooling, teaching, training, tuition, tutelage, tutoring
related words didactics, pedagogics, pedagogy; higher education, higher learning; coaching, conditioning, cultivation, preparation, readying; development, direction, guidance, nurturance, nurturing; edification, enlightenment, improvement
2 the understanding and information gained from being educated ⟨a person whose extensive *education* was obvious to all who met him⟩
synonyms erudition, knowledge, learnedness, learning, literacy, scholarship
related words culture, edification, enlightenment; reading; bookishness, pedantry
near antonyms functional illiteracy
antonyms ignorance, illiteracy, illiterateness

educational *adj* **1** providing useful information or knowledge ⟨we found the talk on easy ways for families to recycle household products very *educational*⟩ — see INFORMATIVE
2 of or relating to schooling or learning especially at an advanced level ⟨the community college strives to meet the *educational* needs of the residents of its urban location⟩ — see ACADEMIC 1

educationist *n, chiefly British* a person whose occupation is to give formal instruction in a school ⟨*educationists* around the U.K. were largely in support of the reforms⟩ — see TEACHER

educative *adj* providing useful information or knowledge ⟨college students discover that what they experience outside the classroom can be just as *educative* as anything that happens within⟩ — see INFORMATIVE

educator *n* a person whose occupation is to give formal instruction in a school ⟨decided at a fairly young age that there is no more rewarding career than that of an *educator*⟩ — see TEACHER

educe *vb* to draw out (something hidden, latent, or reserved) ⟨the gift of a puppy finally *educed* a response from the shy boy⟩
synonyms elicit, evoke, inspire, raise
related words drag, dredge (up), extort, extract, pull, wangle, wrest, wring; coax (out), gain, get, obtain, procure, secure; bare, disclose, discover, divulge, evince, expose, reveal, uncloak, uncover, unmask, unveil
phrases call forth
near antonyms disregard, forget, ignore, miss, neglect, overlook, overpass, pass over

eduction *n* an opinion arrived at through a process of reasoning ⟨the policeman's *eduction* was that there was more than one murderer involved⟩ — see CONCLUSION 1

e'er *adv* for all time ⟨an act of heroism for which the nation will *e'er* be grateful⟩ — see EVER 1

eerie *also* **eery** *adj* fearfully and mysteriously strange or fantastic ⟨*eerie* noises would occasionally come from locked rooms in the castle⟩
synonyms creepy, haunting, spookish, spooky, uncanny, unearthly, weird
related words ghastly, ghostlike, ghostly, ghoulish, spectral; bizarre, curious, odd, outlandish, outré, peculiar, quaint, queerish, quirky; unaccustomed, uncommon, unusual; metaphysical, preternatural, supernatural; enigmatic (*also* enigmatical), inscrutable, mysterious, puzzling; dreadful, fearsome, horrible, horrifying, terrible, terrifying
near antonyms common, commonplace, everyday, normal, ordinary, prosaic, routine, typical, unexceptional, unremarkable, usual; natural; expected, familiar, predictable

efface *vb* to destroy all traces of ⟨when the supply ship finally arrived, it discovered that virtually all evidence of the colony at Roanoke had been *effaced*⟩ — see ANNIHILATE 1

effect *n* **1** a condition or occurrence traceable to a cause ⟨better health is always one of the *effects* of improved hygiene⟩
synonyms aftereffect, aftermath, backwash, child, conclusion, consequence, corollary, development, fate, fruit, issue, outcome, outgrowth, precipitate, product, result, resultant, sequel, sequence, upshot
related words ramification; denouement (*also* dénouement), echo, implication, repercussion; afterclap, afterglow, aftershock; blowback, by-product, fallout, offshoot, ripple, side effect (*also* side reaction), spin-off
phrases matter of course
near antonyms consideration, determinant, factor; base, basis, foundation, ground, groundwork; impetus, incentive, inspiration, instigation, stimulus; mother, origin, root, source, spring
antonyms antecedent, causation, cause, occasion, reason
2 the power to bring about a result on another ⟨religion has a profound *effect* on our lives⟩
synonyms impact, influence, mark, repercussion, sway
related words authority, clout, prestige, pull, weight; command, domination, dominion, mastery; consequence, importance, significance; sovereignty (*also* sovranty), supremacy
near antonyms helplessness, impotence, impotency, powerlessness, weakness
3 effects *pl* transportable items that one owns ⟨the family packed up its household *effects* and moved to Florida⟩ — see POSSESSION 2

effect *vb* to be the cause of (a situation, action, or state of mind) ⟨classroom discussions designed to *effect* a change in racial attitudes⟩
synonyms beget, breed, bring, bring about, bring on, catalyze, cause, create, do, draw on, effectuate, engender, generate, induce, invoke, make, occasion, produce, prompt, result (in), spawn, translate (into), work, yield
related words conduce (to), contribute (to); decide, determine; begin, establish, father, found, inaugurate, initiate, innovate, institute, introduce, launch, pioneer, set, set up, start; advance, cultivate, develop, encourage, forward, foster, further, nourish, nurture, promote; enact, render, turn out
phrases bring forth, give rise to
near antonyms impede, limit, restrict; clamp down (on), crack down (on), crush, dampen, put down, quash, quell, repress, smother, squash, squelch, stifle, subdue, suppress; arrest, check, control, curb, inhibit, rein (in), restrain, retard; can [*slang*], kill, snuff (out), still; abolish, demolish, destroy, extinguish, liquidate, quench

effective *adj* **1** producing or capable of producing a desired result ⟨an *effective* treatment of the once-dreaded disease⟩
synonyms effectual, efficacious, efficient, fruitful, operative, potent, productive
related words hyperefficient, ultraefficient; adequate, capable, competent; accomplished, adept, consummate, experienced, expert, masterly, practiced (*also* practised), proficient, skilled, skillful, versed, veteran, virtuoso; cogent, convincing, killer, sound, striking, telling, valid; active, dynamic; useful, working; applicable, feasible, functional, practicable, practical, realizable, usable (*also* useable), workable
near antonyms counterproductive; incapable, incompetent, inexperienced, inexpert, unqualified, unseasoned, unskilled, unskillful; abortive, bootless, futile, vain; empty, hollow, idle, pointless, unavailing, unprofitable, unsuccessful; inoperative, worthless
antonyms fruitless, ineffective, ineffectual, inefficient, inoperative, unfruitful, unproductive, useless
2 having the power to persuade ⟨made an *effective* argument in favor of the proposal⟩ — see COGENT
3 existing in fact and not merely as a possibility ⟨made the mistake of confusing the plant's production capacity with its *effective* output⟩ — see ACTUAL

effectiveness *n* **1** the capacity to persuade ⟨the "guilty" verdict was all the proof needed of the *effectiveness* of the prosecutor's closing argument⟩ — see COGENCY 1
2 the power to produce a desired result ⟨the huge upsurge in sales pretty much demonstrated the *effectiveness* of the new ad campaign⟩ — see EFFICACY
3 the quality of an utterance that provokes interest and produces an effect ⟨your writing lacks *effectiveness* because practically every sentence is in the passive voice⟩ — see [1]PUNCH 1

effectual *adj* producing or capable of producing a desired result ⟨acting like a jerk has generally not been a terribly *effectual* dating strategy⟩ — see EFFECTIVE 1

effectualness *n* the power to produce a desired result ⟨the *effectualness* of that new cancer treatment has yet to be proven⟩ — see EFFICACY

effectuate *vb* to be the cause of (a situation, action, or state of mind) ⟨the hope that the greater social interaction between native residents and the immigrants will *effectuate* greater understanding and harmony⟩ — see EFFECT

effeminate *adj* of or relating to a man who has or displays qualities considered more suitable for women ⟨a comedian deliberately affecting *effeminate* mannerisms⟩
synonyms effete, epicene, sissified, sissy, unmanly, womanish
related words feminine, girlish, girlie (*or* girly), womanlike, womanly; old-maidish, overnice, prissy, spinsterish; dandyish, dudish, foppish, sappy; camp, campy; antimacho
antonyms manlike, manly, mannish, masculine, virile

effervescent *adj* joyously unrestrained ⟨candidates for positions on the cheerleading squad should have naturally *effervescent* personalities⟩ — see EXUBERANT

effete *adj* **1** having lost forcefulness, courage, or spirit ⟨the soft, *effete* society that marked the final years of the Roman empire⟩
synonyms decadent, decayed, degenerate, overripe, washed-up
related words effeminate, overrefined, precious; decaying, declining, dying, failing, waning; debilitated, enervate, enervated, enfeebled, feeble, frail, languid, sapped, soft, wasted, weak, weakened, wimpy; dissolute, immoral; debased, debauched, degraded, demoralized, depraved, dissipated, dissolute

antonyms undecadent
2 lacking bodily strength ⟨the Western ranch takes *effete* youths from comfortable suburbs and turns them into rugged wranglers⟩ — see WEAK 1
3 lacking strength of will or character ⟨the governor is too *effete* to take on the powerful special interests that really run this state⟩ — see WEAK 2
4 of or relating to a man who has or displays qualities considered more suitable for women ⟨people were surprised to learn that the *effete* man played football⟩ — see EFFEMINATE

efficacious *adj* producing or capable of producing a desired result ⟨taking a cookie break while studying is one of the most *efficacious* ways of rejuvenating the mind that I have ever discovered⟩ — see EFFECTIVE 1

efficaciousness *n* the power to produce a desired result ⟨the debatable *efficaciousness* of many of the campaigns aimed at reducing smoking among teenagers⟩ — see EFFICACY

efficacity *n* the power to produce a desired result ⟨the limited *efficacity* of the primitive tool as an instrument for cutting raw meat⟩ — see EFFICACY

efficacy *n* the power to produce a desired result ⟨questioned the *efficacy* of the alarms in actually preventing auto theft⟩
synonyms edge, effectiveness, effectualness, efficaciousness, efficacity, efficiency, productiveness
related words ability, capability, capacity; potency, puissance, strength
near antonyms inability, inadequacy, inadequateness, incompetence, incompetency
antonyms ineffectiveness, ineffectuality, ineffectualness, inefficiency

efficiency *n* the power to produce a desired result ⟨the proven *efficiency* of citizen patrols in reducing crime in urban neighborhoods⟩ — see EFFICACY

efficient *adj* producing or capable of producing a desired result ⟨that manual lawn mower is not a very *efficient* tool for doing a huge yard⟩ — see EFFECTIVE 1

effloresce *vb* to produce flowers ⟨created an artificial environment in which plants grew and *effloresced* regardless of season⟩ — see BLOOM 1

effluvium *also* **effluvia** *n* discarded or useless material ⟨the *effluvia* from local sewage treatment plants polluting the river⟩ — see GARBAGE 1

effort *n* the active use of energy in producing a result ⟨the finished parade float was well worth the *effort*⟩
synonyms elbow grease, exertion, expenditure, labor, pains, sweat, trouble, while, work
related words drudgery, grind, slog, strain, toil, travail; dint, energy; force, might, muscle, power, puissance; attempt, endeavor, essay, fling, go, pass, shot, stab, trial, try, whack
near antonyms adroitness, ease, facility, fluency, smoothness; dormancy, idleness, inaction, inactivity, indolence, inertia, languor, laziness, quiescence

effortful *adj* requiring considerable physical or mental effort ⟨the book's abstruse subject matter and dense prose make for *effortful* reading⟩ — see HARD 2

effortless *adj* involving minimal difficulty or effort ⟨using an automatic dishwasher is not quite as *effortless* as I would like—you still have to put the dishes away⟩ — see EASY 1

effortlessly *adv* without difficulty ⟨the pizza worker flung the round of dough into the air and *effortlessly* caught it⟩ — see EASILY 1

effrontery *n* shameless boldness ⟨the little squirt had the *effrontery* to deny eating any cookies, even with the crumbs still on his lips⟩
synonyms audaciousness, audacity, brashness, brass, brassiness, brazenness, cheek, cheekiness, chutzpah (*also* chutzpa *or* hutzpah *or* hutzpa), crust, face, gall, nerve, nerviness, pertness, presumption, presumptuousness, sauce, sauciness, temerity
related words arrogance, assurance, cockiness, confidence, hardihood, overconfidence, sanguinity, self-assurance, self-confidence; discourteousness, disrespect, impertinence, impoliteness, impudence, incivility, inconsiderateness, inconsideration, insolence, rudeness, ungraciousness; back talk, sass; swagger, swash
near antonyms bashfulness, diffidence, faintheartedness, hesitancy, modesty, shyness, timidity, timidness, timorousness; civility, courteousness, courtesy, gentility, graciousness, mannerliness, manners

effulgence *n* the quality or state of having or giving off light ⟨the exceptional *effulgence* of the harvest moon is always a striking sight⟩ — see BRILLIANCE 1

effulgent *adj* giving off or reflecting much light ⟨the stars always seem more *effulgent* when viewed in the country, far away from the distracting lights of the city⟩ — see BRIGHT 1

effuse *vb* to make an exaggerated display of affection or enthusiasm ⟨pundits who should have known better *effused* endlessly about this idealistic but naive senator⟩ — see GUSH 2

effusive *adj* showing feeling freely ⟨often *effusive* no matter what the occasion, my aunt is even more so at weddings and funerals⟩ — see DEMONSTRATIVE 1

egalitarian *n* one who advocates or practices social equality ⟨as *egalitarians*, they have always spurned the thought of hiring domestic help, even though they can well afford it⟩ — see DEMOCRAT

egg *n* a member of the human race ⟨kindhearted and generous, she's a real good *egg* by anyone's standard⟩ — see HUMAN

egg (on) *vb* to try to persuade (someone) through earnest appeals to follow a course of action ⟨though exhausted, I was *egged on* by spectators to finish the marathon⟩ — see URGE

eggbeater *n* a vehicle for traveling through the air that obtains its lift from rotors which spin horizontally ⟨told stories of his days flying *eggbeaters* during the Vietnam War⟩ — see HELICOPTER

egghead *n* a person with strong intellectual interests ⟨the unlikely marriage between a literary *egghead* and a Hollywood sex symbol⟩ — see INTELLECTUAL

eggheaded *adj* much given to learning and thinking ⟨a play that appeals mainly to the small body of *eggheaded* theatergoers⟩ — see INTELLECTUAL 1

ego *n* **1** a reasonable or justifiable sense of one's worth or importance ⟨I have enough *ego* not to want to give up easily in any contest or competition⟩ — see PRIDE 1
2 an often unjustified feeling of being pleased with oneself or with one's situation or achievements ⟨a star athlete with a refreshing lack of *ego*⟩ — see COMPLACENCE 1

egocentric *adj* overly concerned with one's own desires, needs, or interests ⟨the cult attracts *egocentric* people who are preoccupied with reaching their potential as individuals⟩
synonyms egoistic (*also* egoistical), egomaniacal, egotistic (*or* egotistical), narcissistic, self-absorbed, self-centered, self-concerned, self-infatuated, self-interested, self-involved, selfish, self-loving, self-obsessed, self-oriented, self-preoccupied, self-regarding, self-seeking, self-serving, solipsistic
related words inner-directed; complacent, conceited, overweening, pompous, prideful, proud, self-complacent, self-conceited, self-contented, self-directed, self-glorifying, self-important, self-indulgent, self-opinionated, self-pleased, self-satisfied, smug, vain, vainglorious
near antonyms altruistic, beneficent, benevolent, charitable, generous, greathearted, humanitarian, magnani-

mous, philanthropic (*also* philanthropical), self-denying, self-giving, self-sacrificing; other-directed; diffident, self-doubting; self-flagellating; self-questioning, self-reflective

antonyms self-forgetful, self-forgetting, selfless, unselfish

egocentric *n* a person who is overly concerned with his or her own desires, needs, or interests ⟨he's such an *egocentric* that he painstakingly records every detail of his unremarkable life⟩ — see EGOIST

egocentricity *n* excessive interest in oneself ⟨his *egocentricity* is such that he simply cannot fathom that anyone would have an opposing view⟩ — see EGOISM

egocentrism *n* excessive interest in oneself ⟨her exquisite *egocentrism* informs her conception of reality: she thinks the world revolves around her⟩ — see EGOISM

egoism *n* excessive interest in oneself ⟨because of her *egoism*, she never gave a thought to asking how the others felt⟩

synonyms egocentricity, egocentrism, egomania, egotism, narcissism, navel-gazing, self-absorption, self-centeredness, self-concern, self-interest, self-involvement, selfishness, selfness, self-preoccupation, self-regard

related words complacence, complacency, conceit, conceitedness, ego, pomposity, pompousness, pride, pridefulness, self-admiration, self-conceit, self-esteem, self-importance, self-indulgence, self-love, self-partiality, self-respect, self-satisfaction, self-sufficiency, smugness, vaingloriousness, vainglory, vainness, vanity; self-assumption, self-consequence, self-content, self-contentment, self-glorification

near antonyms altruism, generosity, magnanimity, self-sacrifice; detachment, disinterestedness, fairness, impartiality, neutrality, objectivity; self-flagellation; self-annihilation, self-immolation

antonyms self-abandonment, self-forgetfulness, selflessness, unselfishness

egoist *n* a person who is overly concerned with his or her own desires, needs, or interests ⟨their boss is a demanding *egoist* who insists that everything be done her way⟩

synonyms egocentric, egomaniac, egotist, ego-tripper, narcissist

related words megalomaniac; beast, boor, cad, churl, clown, creep, cretin, cur, heel, jerk, joker, louse, lout, skunk, slob, snake, stinker

near antonyms altruist, humanitarian, philanthropist

egoistic *also* **egoistical** *adj* **1** having too high an opinion of oneself ⟨unfortunately, the race car driver is so *egoistic* that he pats himself on the back before anyone else has a chance⟩ — see CONCEITED

2 overly concerned with one's own desires, needs, or interests ⟨they're too *egoistic* to even give a thought to becoming involved in something that benefits the whole community⟩ — see EGOCENTRIC

egomania *n* excessive interest in oneself ⟨even by Hollywood standards, that movie star's *egomania* is of epic proportions⟩ — see EGOISM

egomaniac *n* a person who is overly concerned with his or her own desires, needs, or interests ⟨even in a field rife with *egomaniacs*, that actress sets a new standard for self-absorption⟩ — see EGOIST

egomaniacal *adj* overly concerned with one's own desires, needs, or interests ⟨a brilliant but *egomaniacal* urban planner who ruthlessly sought to impose his vision of the ideal cityscape⟩ — see EGOCENTRIC

egotism *n* **1** an often unjustified feeling of being pleased with oneself or with one's situation or achievements ⟨for someone who has won a Nobel Prize in physics, he is remarkably without *egotism*⟩ — see COMPLACENCE 1

2 excessive interest in oneself ⟨*egotism* is not something that winners of the Nobel Prize for peace usually have time for⟩ — see EGOISM

egotist *n* a person who is overly concerned with his or her own desires, needs, or interests ⟨she's an *egotist* who bores her coworkers with endless ruminations about herself and her problems⟩ — see EGOIST

egotistic *or* **egotistical** *adj* **1** having too high an opinion of oneself ⟨the *egotistic* pro quarterback was always too busy to sign autographs, forgetting that the fans had paid good money to see him play⟩ — see CONCEITED

2 overly concerned with one's own desires, needs, or interests ⟨the true spirit of the Christmas season is the resolve to be less *egotistic* and more altruistic⟩ — see EGOCENTRIC

ego–tripper *n* a person who is overly concerned with his or her own desires, needs, or interests ⟨had been dating a hopeless *ego-tripper* who valued her only as a potential trophy wife⟩ — see EGOIST

egregious *adj* very noticeable especially for being incorrect or bad ⟨the student's theme was marred by a number of *egregious* errors in spelling⟩

synonyms blatant, conspicuous, flagrant, glaring, gross, obvious, patent, pronounced, rank, striking

related words arresting, clear, distinct, dramatic, emphatic, evident, eye-catching, marked, notable, noticeable, outstanding, plain, prominent, remarkable, salient, showy, splashy; absolute, arrant, downright, out-and-out, outright, sheer, stark, utter; detectable, discernible (*also* discernable), observable, perceptible, visible; abominable, atrocious, awful, deplorable, execrable, heinous, lousy, monstrous, outrageous, preposterous, shameful, shocking, terrible, wretched

near antonyms imperceptible, inconspicuous, unnoticeable, unobtrusive; inconsequential, inconsiderable, insignificant, slight, small, trifling, trivial; concealed, hidden, invisible

egress *n* a place or means of going out ⟨the only *egress* from the nightclub was a dark, narrow stairway to the street below⟩ — see EXIT 1

eidolon *n* someone of such unequaled perfection as to deserve imitation ⟨an industrialist who remains an *eidolon* of the visionary and ambitious self-made man⟩ — see IDEAL 1

eighty–six *or* **86** *vb* to get rid of as useless or unwanted ⟨decided to *eighty-six* his birth name the minute he arrived in Hollywood⟩ — see DISCARD

either *adv* in addition to what has been said ⟨you won't convince them, and, in fact, I don't agree *either*!⟩ — see MORE 1

ejaculate *vb* to utter with a sudden burst of strong feeling ⟨"Eureka!" the Greek mathematician Archimedes is said to have *ejaculated* upon discovering a method for determining the purity of gold⟩ — see EXCLAIM

ejaculation *n* a sudden short emotional utterance ⟨uttered a profane *ejaculation* upon stubbing his toe in the dark⟩ — see EXCLAMATION

eject *vb* **1** to drive or force out ⟨we summarily *ejected* the unwanted guest from our party⟩

synonyms banish, boot (out), bounce, cast out, chase, dismiss, drum (out), expel, extrude, kick out, oust, out, rout, run off, throw out, turf (out) [*chiefly British*], turn out

related words deforce, deport, displace, dispossess, evict, exile, expatriate, ostracize, read out, shut out; ax (*or* axe), can, cashier, defenestrate, discharge, fire, muster out, pink-slip, release, remove, retire, sack, terminate

phrases give one the gate [*slang*], send packing

near antonyms accept, admit, receive, take, take in; welcome; entertain, harbor, house, lodge, shelter

2 to violently throw out or off (something from within)

⟨the malfunctioning VCR abruptly stopped rewinding and *ejected* the tape⟩ — see ERUPT 1

eke (out) *vb* to get with great difficulty ⟨*eked out* a living from the family's small farm⟩
synonyms scrape (up *or* together), scrounge, squeeze, wrest, wring
related words acquire, attain, draw, earn, gain, land, obtain, procure, secure

elaborate *adj* **1** made or done with great care or with much detail ⟨*elaborate* festivities for the 200th anniversary of the town's founding⟩
synonyms complex, complicated, detailed, fancy, intricate, involved, sophisticated
related words elegant, exquisite, grand, magnificent, ornate, splendid; chichi, extravagant, exuberant, fancified, flamboyant, frilly, gimmicked (up), grandiose, ostentatious, overwrought, showy, souped-up; Byzantine, convoluted, involute, involuted, labyrinthian, labyrinthine
near antonyms modest, plain, plain-Jane, plain-vanilla, uncomplicated; bald, bare, naked, unadorned, undecorated, unvarnished
antonyms no-frills, simple, unfancy, unsophisticated
2 including many small descriptive features ⟨the *elaborate* world known as Middle Earth that J.R.R. Tolkien created in his richly imagined novels⟩ — see DETAILED 1
3 having many parts or aspects that are usually interrelated ⟨plans for a huge mall that will actually be an *elaborate* center for sports, entertainment, and shopping⟩ — see COMPLEX 1

elaborate *vb* to gradually become clearer or more detailed ⟨as mankind's understanding of the universe has *elaborated*⟩ — see DEVELOP 1

elaborate (on) *vb* **1** to add to the interest of by including made-up details ⟨my friend tends to *elaborate on* his hiking experiences, turning an ordinary walk in the woods into a hair-raising adventure⟩ — see EMBROIDER
2 to express more fully and in greater detail ⟨the candidate for governor refused to *elaborate on* how she would balance the state's budget⟩ — see EXPAND 1

elaborateness *n* the state or quality of having many interrelated parts or aspects ⟨the *elaborateness* of the parade is such that a virtual army of people spend the whole year working on it⟩ — see COMPLEXITY 1

elaboration *n* **1** the act or process of going from the simple or basic to the complex or advanced ⟨the *elaboration* of the Internet from an exclusive computer network into a worldwide communications network of colossal proportions⟩ — see DEVELOPMENT 1
2 the representation of something in terms that go beyond the facts ⟨the eyewitness was deemed unreliable because of his obvious *elaboration* of what he had actually seen⟩ — see EXAGGERATION

elapse *vb* to come to an end ⟨in those coin-operated binoculars at scenic areas your viewing time seems to *elapse* almost before it has begun⟩ — see CEASE 1

elastic *adj* **1** able to revert to original size and shape after being stretched, squeezed, or twisted ⟨*elastic* rubber bands⟩
synonyms bouncy, flexible, resilient, rubberlike, rubbery, springy, stretch, stretchable, stretchy, supple, whippy
related words adaptable, ductile, kneadable, malleable, moldable, plastic, pliable, pliant; limber, lissome (*also* lissom), lithe, lithesome, willowy
near antonyms compact, firm, hard, solid, unyielding; brittle, crisp, crumbly, flaky (*also* flakey), friable, short
antonyms inelastic, inflexible, nonelastic, rigid, stiff
2 capable of being readily changed ⟨when vacationing, we generally have very *elastic* daily sightseeing plans⟩ — see FLEXIBLE 1

elate *vb* to fill with great joy ⟨the winning of the state basketball championship *elated* the whole town⟩
synonyms elevate, enrapture, exhilarate, intoxicate, transport
related words commove, excite, inspire, stimulate, uplift; content, delight, gladden, gratify, please, rejoice, satisfy, warm
near antonyms demoralize, discourage, dishearten, dispirit; distress, oppress, sadden
antonyms depress

elated *adj* experiencing or marked by overwhelming usually pleasurable emotion ⟨she was *elated* upon learning that she had been accepted by her first-choice college⟩ — see ECSTATIC

elatedness *n* a state of overwhelming usually pleasurable emotion ⟨with the *elatedness* of someone who had just won the lottery, he announced that his girlfriend had accepted his marriage proposal⟩ — see ECSTASY

elation *n* a state of overwhelming usually pleasurable emotion ⟨most people can't imagine the kind of *elation* that comes with winning a super lottery's grand prize, but they're dying to find out⟩ — see ECSTASY

elbow *vb* to force one's way ⟨the sort of greedy person who is always the first to *elbow* to the front of the buffet table at every party⟩ — see ²PRESS 4

elbow grease *n* the active use of energy in producing a result ⟨with a little polish and a lot of *elbow grease*, I was able to make the old silver teapot shine again⟩ — see EFFORT

elbow room *n* an extent or area available for or used up by some activity or thing ⟨help me move the furniture so that we'll have enough *elbow room* to do some aerobics⟩ — see ROOM 1

el cheapo *adj* **1** costing little ⟨took an *el cheapo* vacation, staying at a friend's cabin the whole time⟩ — see CHEAP 1
2 of low quality ⟨he bought *el cheapo* sneakers from someone on a street corner⟩ — see CHEAP 2

elder *n* **1** a person of advanced years ⟨in that Asian society *elders* are accorded great respect⟩ — see SENIOR CITIZEN
2 one who is above another in rank, station, or office ⟨as your *elder* in the company, he is within his rights to tell you what to do⟩ — see SUPERIOR
3 one who is older than another ⟨it wouldn't hurt to show a little more respect for your *elders*⟩ — see SENIOR 1
4 the senior member of a group ⟨as the *elder* of the contingent of living former presidents, he was accorded a place of highest honor at the ceremonies⟩ — see DEAN

elderliness *n* the state of being an old person ⟨refuses to let her *elderliness* interfere with her indomitable zest for life⟩ — see ANCIENTNESS 1

elderly *adj* being of advanced years and especially past middle age ⟨*elderly* people who stay active are usually the healthiest and the happiest⟩
synonyms aged, aging (*or* ageing), ancient, geriatric, long-lived, old, older, over-the-hill, senescent, senior, unyoung
related words centenarian, nonagenarian, octogenarian, septuagenarian, sexagenarian; oldish; adult, grown-up, mature, middle-aged; pensioned, retired, superannuated; matriarchal, patriarchal, venerable; anile, decrepit, doddering, senile, spavined, tottery; overage (*also* overaged)
phrases long in the tooth, of a certain age
near antonyms ageless; youngish; adolescent, immature, juvenile, preteen, puerile; minor, underage; callow, green, inexperienced, raw; babyish, childish, childlike, infantile, infantine, kiddish

antonyms young, youthful

elder statesman *n* the senior member of a group ⟨the *elder statesman* of the White House correspondents is finally retiring after nearly a half century of service⟩ — see DEAN

elect *adj* singled out from a number or group as more to one's liking ⟨this *elect* body of students represents the best that the nation's high schools have to offer⟩ — see SELECT 1

elect *n* individuals carefully selected as being the best of a class ⟨the members of this all-American team are the *elect* of collegiate football⟩ — see ELITE 1

elect *vb* to decide to accept (someone or something) from a group of possibilities ⟨I've *elected* to study French as my foreign language⟩ — see CHOOSE 1

election *n* **1** the act or process of selecting ⟨the *election* of a major is something that every college student has to do at some point⟩ — see SELECTION 1
2 the power, right, or opportunity to choose ⟨at the country inn, breakfast in bed is entirely at the *election* of the guest⟩ — see CHOICE 1

elective *adj* subject to one's freedom of choice ⟨a plastic surgeon who mainly does face-lifting and other kinds of *elective* surgery⟩ — see OPTIONAL

electric *adj* causing great emotional or mental stimulation ⟨Dr. King's "I Have a Dream" speech was one of the truly *electric* moments in American oratory⟩ — see EXCITING 1

electrify *vb* to cause a pleasurable stimulation of the feelings ⟨Marian Anderson *electrified* audiences with her soaring operatic voice⟩ — see THRILL

electrifying *adj* causing great emotional or mental stimulation ⟨ranked the U.S. hockey team's victory in 1980 as one of the most *electrifying* moments in Olympic history⟩ — see EXCITING 1

eleemosynary *adj* having or showing a concern for the welfare of others ⟨used his vast fortune for establishing and funding a host of *eleemosynary* institutions⟩ — see CHARITABLE 1

elegance *n* dignified or restrained beauty of form, appearance, or style ⟨the *elegance* of the hotel's French furnishings⟩
synonyms class, classiness, courtliness, elegancy, fineness, grace, gracefulness, handsomeness, majesty, refinement, stateliness
related words augustness, brilliance, gloriousness, glory, grandeur, grandness, lavishness, luxuriance, luxuriousness, luxury, magnificence, nobility, nobleness, opulence, ornateness, plushiness, plushness, resplendence, resplendency, richness, splendor, sumptuousness; artfulness, chic, polish, sophistication, taste, tastefulness; choiceness, classicism, dignity, exquisiteness, restraint, simplicity; affectedness, grandiosity, ostentation, ostentatiousness, pretentiousness, showiness
near antonyms coarseness, crudeness, flamboyance, flashiness, garishness, gaudiness, glitz, grotesqueness, grotesquerie (*also* grotesquery), kitsch, tastelessness, tawdriness, vulgarity
antonyms gracelessness, inelegance

elegancy *n* dignified or restrained beauty of form, appearance, or style ⟨there's a certain *elegancy* about this hotel that other places in Las Vegas don't have⟩ — see ELEGANCE

elegant *adj* **1** having or showing elegance ⟨the most *elegant* First Lady in the nation's history⟩ ⟨the bride's *elegant* gown received nothing but praise⟩
synonyms classy, courtly, fine, graceful, handsome, majestic, refined, stately, tasteful
related words august, baronial, gallant, glorious, grand, heroic (*also* heroical), imposing, lavish, luxurious, magnificent, monumental, noble, ornate, proud, regal, rich, royal, splendid, superb; artful, genteel, polished, sophisticated; classic, conservative, exquisite, quiet, restrained, simple, understated; aristocratic, patrician; à la mode (*also* a la mode), chic, fashionable, in, modish, posh, sharp, sleek, smart, snappy, stylish, swagger, swank (*or* swanky); affected, grandiose, ostentatious, pretentious, recherché
near antonyms cheesy, coarse, crude, flamboyant, flashy, garish, gaudy, glitzy, grotesque, loud, raffish, splashy, tacky, tawdry, ticky-tacky (*also* ticky-tack); rough-edged, rough-hewn, rude, trashy, uncouth, uncultivated, uncultured, unpolished, unrefined, vulgar
antonyms dowdy, graceless, inelegant, styleless, tasteless, unfashionable, unhandsome, unstylish
2 having qualities that appeal to a refined taste ⟨prepared an *elegant* dinner for the honored guests⟩ — see CHOICE 1

elegiac *also* **elegiacal** *adj* causing or marked by an atmosphere lacking in cheer ⟨the sight of an old ruined church or castle can be a pleasantly *elegiac* experience⟩ — see GLOOMY 1

elegy *n* a composition expressing one's grief over a loss ⟨"O Captain! My Captain!" is Walt Whitman's *elegy* on the death of President Lincoln⟩ — see LAMENT 2

element *n* **1** one of the parts that make up a whole ⟨a free press is an essential *element* of a democracy⟩
synonyms building block, component, constituent, factor, ingredient, member
related words basis, part and parcel; detail, item, particular, point; aspect, characteristic, facet, feature, trait; division, fragment, particle, partition, piece, portion, section, sector, segment; subcomponent
near antonyms aggregate, composite, compound, mass; entirety, sum, summation, total, totality; admixture, amalgam, amalgamation, blend, combination, intermixture, mix, mixture
antonyms whole
2 elements *pl* general or basic truths on which other truths or theories can be based ⟨the *elements* of mathematics can be traced back to Euclid⟩ — see PRINCIPLES 1
3 a region of activity, knowledge, or influence ⟨she felt a bit out of her *element* in the mathematics section of the exam⟩ — see FIELD 2

elemental *adj* of or relating to the simplest facts or theories of a subject ⟨even if you're not planning on becoming a scientist, you should have an *elemental* knowledge of chemistry⟩ — see ELEMENTARY

elementary *adj* of or relating to the simplest facts or theories of a subject ⟨students who do not have even an *elementary* knowledge of geography⟩
synonyms abecedarian, basal, basic, beginning, elemental, essential, fundamental, introductory, meat-and-potatoes, rudimental, rudimentary, underlying
related words primal, primary, prime, simple; crude, primeval, primitive, primordial, rude, uncomplicated; preliminary, preparatory; crucial, important, key
near antonyms complex, sophisticated; complicated, convoluted, detailed, elaborate, extensive, intricate; developed, evolved, high, higher, refined
antonyms advanced

elephant *n* something or someone that is unusually large and powerful ⟨by any standard, the new shopping mall will be an *elephant* and one that is certain to alter the retail landscape⟩ — see GIANT

elephantine *adj* unusually large ⟨the wedding reception was held under an *elephantine* tent on the great lawn⟩ — see HUGE

elevate *vb* **1** to fill with great joy ⟨seeing their son ordained as a priest was one of the most *elevating* moments in their lives⟩ — see ELATE
2 to move from a lower to a higher place or position ⟨the old trick of using a fat phone book to *elevate* a

child to a more comfortable position at the table⟩ — see RAISE 1
3 to move higher in rank or position ⟨the announcement that the pope will *elevate* several prelates to the rank of cardinal⟩ — see PROMOTE 1
4 to assign a high status or value to ⟨a decade in which greed and selfishness were *elevated* to the rank of virtues⟩ — see EXALT 1

elevated *adj* **1** being positioned above a surface ⟨an *elevated* monorail that transports visitors all over the theme park⟩
synonyms lifted, raised, uplifted, upraised
related words aerial, suspended; erect, perpendicular, standing, upright, upstanding, vertical
near antonyms low, low-lying, short, squat
antonyms sunken
2 very dignified in form, tone, or style ⟨the *elevated* language of Lincoln's Gettysburg Address⟩
synonyms eloquent, formal, high-flown, lofty, majestic, stately, towering
related words affected, bombastic, declamatory, florid, flowery, grandiloquent, grandiose, highfalutin (*also* hifalutin), oratorical, pompous, pretentious, rhetorical (*also* rhetoric), stilted; Attic, cultured, refined; classy, courtly, fine, graceful, tasteful; aristocratic, genteel, patrician; correct, educated, grammatical, proper; academic (*also* academical), bookish, learned, literary
near antonyms casual, colloquial, conversational, informal, nonformal, slangy, unbookish, unliterary, vernacular; coarse, common, crass, crude, gross, ill-bred, indecent, lowbred, lowbrow, rough, rough-hewn, rude, tasteless, uncouth, uncultivated, uncultured, unpolished, unrefined, vulgar; incorrect, substandard, uneducated, ungrammatical, unlearned
antonyms ineloquent, low, undignified
3 being at a higher level than average ⟨for the next several days temperatures will be a little *elevated* for this time of year⟩ — see HIGH 2
4 having, characterized by, or arising from a dignified and generous nature ⟨the offspring of this very wealthy family have been instilled with the *elevated* notion that they should devote their lives to public service⟩ — see NOBLE 2
5 located at a greater height than average or usual ⟨from their *elevated* position the machine gunners had a commanding view of the whole battlefield⟩ — see HIGH 3
6 experiencing or marked by overwhelming usually pleasurable emotion ⟨she's been in an *elevated* mood all week after hearing that she got the promotion⟩ — see ECSTATIC

elevation *n* **1** a raising or a state of being raised to a higher rank or position ⟨the appointment of Sandra Day O'Connor marked the first *elevation* of a woman to the U.S. Supreme Court⟩ — see ADVANCEMENT 1
2 an area of high ground ⟨Little Round Top is one of the most visited *elevations* in the entire Gettysburg National Military Park⟩ — see HEIGHT 4
3 the distance of something or someone from bottom to top ⟨the *elevation* of Angel Falls is 979 meters, making it the world's highest waterfall⟩ — see HEIGHT 3
4 the most extreme or advanced point ⟨some people contend that Western civilization reached its *elevation* in Greece five centuries before Christ⟩ — see HEIGHT 2

elf *n* an imaginary being usually having a small human form and magical powers ⟨*elves* are often portrayed as rather mischievous⟩ — see FAIRY

elfin *adj* having an often mysterious or magical power to attract ⟨the heroine in the story has an *elfin* beauty that men find irresistible⟩ — see FASCINATING 1

elfish *adj* given to good-natured joking or teasing ⟨an *elfish* comedian who often played lovable drunks and wisecracking sidekicks⟩ — see PLAYFUL

elicit *vb* to draw out (something hidden, latent, or reserved) ⟨the role *elicited* the actress's flair for comedy that previous directors had overlooked⟩ — see EDUCE

elide *vb* **1** to show (something written) to be no longer valid by drawing a cross over or a line through it ⟨some unnecessary verbiage will need to be *elided*, but otherwise the article is publishable⟩ — see X (OUT)
2 to make less in extent or duration ⟨the product presentation was not *elided*—it's always only 15 minutes long⟩ — see SHORTEN

eliminate *vb* to prevent the participation, consideration, or inclusion of ⟨the stiff entry fee is intended to *eliminate* less-than-serious competitors⟩ — see EXCLUDE

elision *n* something left out ⟨unfortunately, when the book was condensed, some of the *elisions* rendered major plot developments incomprehensible⟩ — see OMISSION

elite *n* **1** individuals carefully selected as being the best of a class ⟨the winners of this science award represent the *elite* of our high schools⟩
synonyms A-list, aristocracy, best, choice, corps d'elite, cream, crème de la crème, elect, fat, flower, illuminati, pick, pink, pride, priesthood, prime, royalty, upper crust
related words establishment, gentry, nobility, quality, society, top, top drawer, upper class; caviar (*also* caviare); who's who
phrases cream of the crop, Hall of Fame
near antonyms commoners, herd, hoi polloi, masses, millions, mob, multitude, rank and file, unwashed
2 the highest class in a society ⟨the country's *elite* owned or controlled most of the wealth⟩ — see ARISTOCRACY 1

elitist *adj* being or characteristic of a person who has an offensive air of superiority and tends to ignore or disdain anyone regarded as inferior ⟨the complacent, *elitist* attitude of the members at that suburban country club⟩ — see SNOBBISH

elixir *n* something that cures all ills or problems ⟨warned that casino gambling would not be an *elixir* for all of the region's economic woes⟩ — see CURE-ALL

elliptical *or* **elliptic** *adj* **1** having an often intentionally veiled or uncertain meaning ⟨the poet's *elliptical* style is such that the reader often senses that an allusion is being made—but to what exactly?⟩ — see OBSCURE 1
2 having the shape of an egg ⟨the villa's marble pool is surrounded by an *elliptic* arrangement of ancient Greek statuary⟩ — see OVAL
3 marked by the use of few words to convey much information or meaning ⟨his *elliptical* replies can seem rude to some people, but that's just his way⟩ — see CONCISE

elliptically *adv* in a few words ⟨the characters in Harold Pinter's plays speak *elliptically* leaving much of the meaning to be conveyed by the frequent, lengthy pauses⟩ — see SHORTLY 1

elocution *n* the art of speaking in public eloquently and effectively ⟨the oft-told story that he practiced *elocution* by learning to speak with a mouth full of pebbles⟩ — see ORATORY 1

elongate *vb* to make longer ⟨in his paintings the artist *elongated* the bodies of angels to give them a spiritual quality⟩ — see EXTEND 1

elongate *or* **elongated** *adj* of great extent from end to end ⟨the giraffe's *elongate* neck is thought to be the result of natural selection⟩ — see LONG 1

elongation *n* the act of making longer ⟨the *elongation* of artificial fibers in the manufacturing process⟩ — see EXTENSION 1

eloquence *n* the art or power of speaking or writing in

a forceful and convincing way ⟨the *eloquence* of Martin Luther King's "I Have a Dream" speech⟩
synonyms articulacy [*chiefly British*], articulateness, poetry, rhetoric
related words expression, expressiveness; declamation, elocution, oratory; cogency, force, forcefulness, meaningfulness, persuasion, persuasiveness; ardor, emotion, fervency, fervidness, fervor, heat, intensity, passion, power, vehemence, warmth
phrases gift of gab
antonyms inarticulateness

eloquent *adj* **1** able to express oneself clearly and well ⟨an *eloquent* writer and speaker, Elizabeth Cady Stanton was one of the founders of the women's rights movement⟩ — see ARTICULATE
2 clearly conveying a special meaning (as one's mood) ⟨in an *eloquent* gesture, the defeated general was graciously given back his sword at the surrender ceremonies⟩ — see EXPRESSIVE
3 very dignified in form, tone, or style ⟨President Kennedy's *eloquent* inaugural address is often credited with inspiring a whole generation⟩ — see ELEVATED 2

else *adj* resulting in an increase in amount or number ⟨is there anything *else* you would like to add to your list?⟩ — see ADDITIONAL

else *adv* in a different way ⟨if you could do it over again, how *else* would you have done it?⟩ — see OTHERWISE

elucidate *vb* to make plain or understandable ⟨colored charts that really help to *elucidate* the points made in the text⟩ — see EXPLAIN 1

elucidation *n* a statement that makes something clear ⟨the candidate issued what were supposed to be *elucidations* of his earlier statements, but they did little to quell the controversy⟩ — see EXPLANATION 1

elucidative *adj* serving to explain ⟨most editions of Shakespeare's plays now have *elucidative* footnotes to help the modern reader⟩ — see EXPLANATORY

elude *vb* to get or keep away from (as a responsibility) through cleverness or trickery ⟨the millionaire had been *eluding* his fair share of taxes for years before getting caught⟩ — see ESCAPE 2

eluding *n* the act or a means of getting or keeping away from something undesirable ⟨the bachelor's *eluding* of that dreaded trip to the altar came to an end when his girlfriend issued an ultimatum⟩ — see ESCAPE 2

elusion *n* the act or a means of getting or keeping away from something undesirable ⟨his artful *elusion* of the worst work assignments⟩ — see ESCAPE 2

elusive *adj* hard to find, capture, or isolate ⟨the giant squid is one of the ocean's most *elusive* inhabitants⟩
synonyms evasive, fugitive, slippery
related words cagey (*also* cagy), shifty; ephemeral, evanescent, fleeting, impermanent, momentary, passing, short-lived, temporary, transient, transitory; inaccessible, inconvenient, unapproachable, unattainable, unavailable, unobtainable, unreachable, untouchable
near antonyms accessible, approachable, attainable, available, convenient, obtainable, reachable

elvish *adj* tending to or exhibiting reckless playfulness ⟨with *elvish* glee the fraternity brothers hazed the new members to the point of utter humiliation⟩ — see MISCHIEVOUS 1

elysian *adj* of, relating to, or suggesting heaven ⟨the dream of retiring to a tropical isle and enjoying a life of *elysian* ease⟩ — see CELESTIAL

elysian fields *n pl* a dwelling place of perfect happiness for the soul after death ⟨those that live righteously will find peace in the *elysian fields* of the hereafter⟩ — see HEAVEN 1

Elysium *n* **1** a dwelling place of perfect happiness for the soul after death ⟨the mourners were comforted by their belief that the saintly woman was now experiencing the joys of *Elysium*⟩ — see HEAVEN 1
2 an often imaginary place or state of utter perfection and happiness ⟨the universal pipe dream that there exists somewhere an earthly *Elysium* where people live trouble-free lives⟩ — see PARADISE 1

emaciate *vb* to lose bodily strength or vigor ⟨without adequate medical supplies, doctors could only look on helplessly as cholera victims continued to *emaciate*⟩ — see WEAKEN 2

emaciated *adj* suffering extreme weight loss as a result of hunger or disease ⟨the *emaciated* bodies of the survivors of the concentration camps⟩
synonyms cadaverous, gaunt, haggard, skeletal, wasted
related words bony (*also* boney), lank, lanky, rawboned, scraggy, scrawny, sinewy, skinny, spare, thin; starved, underfed, undernourished; famished, hungry, starving; shriveled (*or* shrivelled), withered, wizened
near antonyms beefy, brawny, burly, fit, hale, healthy, hearty, husky; chubby, corpulent, fat, fleshy, heavyset, obese, overweight, plump, portly, pudgy, roly-poly, rotund, stocky, thickset, tubby; flabby, soft

emanate *vb* to throw or give off ⟨honeysuckle *emanating* such a sweet scent⟩ — see EMIT 1

emancipate *vb* to set free (as from slavery or confinement) ⟨under the cover of darkness animal rights activists *emancipated* the inhabitants of the mink ranch⟩ — see FREE 1

emancipation *n* the act of setting free from slavery ⟨a book discussing the role that the *emancipation* of slaves played in the nation's history⟩ — see LIBERATION

emasculate *vb* to deprive of courage or confidence ⟨being eliminated early in one's very first tennis tournament can be an *emasculating* experience⟩ — see UNNERVE 1

embankment *n* a bank of earth constructed to control water ⟨the *embankment* is steep, so be careful walking along the ridge⟩ — see DAM

embargo *n* an order that something not be done or used ⟨there's a standing *embargo* against the use of foul language in this house⟩ — see PROHIBITION 2

embark (on *or* **upon)** *vb* to take the first step in (a process or course of action) ⟨she's eager to finish college and to *embark upon* a career in teaching⟩ — see BEGIN 1

embarrass *vb* **1** to throw into a state of self-conscious distress ⟨the young soldier was *embarrassed* by the public praise for his heroism⟩
synonyms abash, confound, confuse, discomfit, disconcert, discountenance, faze, fluster, mortify, nonplus, rattle
related words agitate, bother, chagrin, discomfort, discompose, dismay, disquiet, distress, disturb, perturb, put off, put out, unhinge, unsettle, upset; debase, degrade, demean, humble, humiliate, queer, shame
near antonyms calm, comfort, console, relieve, soothe; buoy, cheer, embolden, encourage, hearten; assure, reassure
2 to create difficulty for the work or activity of ⟨a lot of this paperwork is unnecessary and just *embarrasses* the organization⟩ — see HAMPER
3 to make complex or difficult ⟨claims that the new government regulations will needlessly *embarrass* the operations of small businesses in the state⟩ — see COMPLICATE 1

embarrassing *adj* causing embarrassment ⟨an *embarrassing* failure of memory inauspiciously marked my first appearance as an actor⟩ — see AWKWARD 3

embarrassment *n* **1** the emotional state of being made self-consciously uncomfortable ⟨experienced the great *embarrassment* of tripping while on stage⟩

synonyms abashment, confusion, discomfiture, disconcertment, fluster, mortification
related words agitation, bother, chagrin, discomfort, discomposure, dismay, disquiet, distress, disturbance, perturbation, unease, uneasiness, upset; disgrace, ignominy, shame; debasement, degradation, humiliation, mortification; humble pie
phrases egg on one's face
near antonyms aplomb, assurance, composure, confidence, coolness, equanimity, poise, self-assurance, self-confidence, self-possession
2 something that makes movement or progress difficult ⟨a big suitcase filled with clothes proved to be more an *embarrassment* than a convenience on my trip⟩ — see ENCUMBRANCE

embayment *n* a part of a body of water that extends beyond the general shoreline ⟨a fingerlike *embayment* of the Bay of Fundy⟩ ⟨a river *embayment*⟩ — see GULF 1

embed *also* **imbed** *vb* to set solidly in or as if in surrounding matter ⟨the nails were solidly *embedded* in those old plaster walls⟩ — see ENTRENCH

embellish *vb* **1** to add to the interest of by including made-up details ⟨the story of the comic marriage proposal was *embellished* as it passed from one generation to the next in the family⟩ — see EMBROIDER
2 to make more attractive by adding something that is beautiful or becoming ⟨the walls of the French restaurant are *embellished* with scenes of Parisian life⟩ — see DECORATE

embellisher *n* something that decorates or beautifies ⟨that simple dress is beautiful by itself and doesn't need any *embellishers*⟩ — see DECORATION 1

embellishing *adj* serving to add beauty ⟨the chef tends to overuse sprigs of parsley and other *embellishing* garnishes on dishes that don't need them⟩ — see DECORATIVE

embellishment *n* **1** something that decorates or beautifies ⟨a colorful mobile is just the *embellishment* that the soon-to-be nursery needs⟩ — see DECORATION 1
2 the representation of something in terms that go beyond the facts ⟨the actor's penchant for *embellishment* suggests that his memoirs would be more appropriately shelved in the fiction section⟩ — see EXAGGERATION

embitter *vb* to implant bitter feelings in ⟨the family refused to let their devastating collision with a drunk driver permanently *embitter* them⟩
synonyms antagonize, empoison, envenom
related words aggravate, anger, enrage, incense, infuriate, madden; alienate, disaffect, disgruntle, estrange, set (against); curdle, sour
near antonyms endear, ingratiate; appease, assuage, mollify, pacify, placate, propitiate; sweeten

embittered *adj* having or showing deep-seated resentment ⟨gradually the *embittered* woman realized that her lingering feelings of hatred were slowly destroying her⟩ — see BITTER 1

emblaze *vb* **1** to make more attractive by adding something that is beautiful or becoming ⟨the days when movies were shown in palaces that were lavishly *emblazed* to look like ancient Egypt or exotic Arabia⟩ — see DECORATE
2 to supply with light ⟨a time when Broadway was *emblazed* by the lights of dozens of theaters⟩ — see ILLUMINATE 1

emblazon *vb* to proclaim the glory of ⟨colossal statues and other monumental constructions that were intended to *emblazon* his name for eons to come⟩ — see PRAISE 1

emblem *n* a device, design, or figure used as an identifying mark ⟨the oil company uses a scallop shell as its *emblem*⟩
synonyms ensign, hallmark, impresa, logo, symbol, totem, trademark
related words attribute, icon (*also* ikon), pictograph; logogram, logograph; badge, coat of arms, cognizance, crest, insignia, monogram; colophon, stamp, token

emblematic *also* **emblematical** *adj* having the function or meaning of an object or figure that stands for something else ⟨the dove is *emblematic* of the organization's mission to bring some peace to a troubled world⟩ — see SYMBOLIC

emblematize *vb* to serve as a material counterpart of ⟨the burned-out church *emblematizes* how the religious strife has destroyed that nation⟩ — see SYMBOLIZE

embodier *n* a visible representation of something abstract (as a quality) ⟨a devoted caregiver to her elderly parents, she is the flesh-and-blood *embodier* of filial duty⟩ — see EMBODIMENT

embodiment *n* a visible representation of something abstract (as a quality) ⟨Mother Theresa was often regarded as the *embodiment* of selfless devotion to others⟩
synonyms abstract, avatar, embodier, epitome, externalization, genius, icon (*also* ikon), image, incarnation, incorporation, instantiation, manifestation, objectification, personification, personifier
related words actualization, concretization, exemplification, personalization, realization, substantiation; essence, quintessence, soul; archetype, exemplar, model, paradigm, pattern; reincarnation

embody *vb* **1** to make a part of a body or system ⟨they must *embody* their ideas in substantial institutions if they are to survive⟩
synonyms absorb, assimilate, co-opt, incorporate, integrate
related words amalgamate, blend, combine, commingle, fuse, intermingle, merge, mingle; acculturate, accustom, condition, enculturate, habituate, naturalize
2 to represent in visible form ⟨George Washington *embodied* so many of the virtues that Americans hold dear⟩
synonyms body, epitomize, express, externalize, incarnate, incorporate, instantiate, manifest, materialize, personalize, personify, substantiate
related words actualize, concretize, realize; exemplify, illustrate, image, objectify, symbolize, typify
antonyms disembody

embolden *vb* to fill with courage or strength of purpose ⟨his poor showing in his first swim meet just *emboldened* him to train even harder⟩ — see ENCOURAGE 1

emboldened *adj* inclined or willing to take risks ⟨not too surprisingly, rock climbing tends to attract the more *emboldened* seekers of outdoor adventure⟩ — see BOLD 1

embonpoint *n* the condition of having an excess of body fat ⟨clothes for women who may be inclined to *embonpoint* but who still want to look stylish⟩ — see CORPULENCE

embosom *vb* to surround or cover closely ⟨a villa that has been *embosomed* by the verdant hills of northern Italy for three centuries⟩ — see ENFOLD 1

emboss *vb* to make more attractive by adding something that is beautiful or becoming ⟨the simple country church has an aura of serene spirituality that is often missing in more *embossed* houses of worship⟩ — see DECORATE

embower *vb* to surround or cover closely ⟨over the years grapevines have completely *embowered* the summerhouse in the garden⟩ — see ENFOLD 1

embrace *vb* **1** to put one's arms around and press tightly ⟨upon being finally reunited, the overjoyed father *embraced* his son⟩

synonyms bear-hug, clasp, crush, enclasp, enfold, grasp, hug, strain
related words clamp, cling, cradle, grab, grip, hold; bosom, embosom, encircle, entwine, envelop, enwind; fold, lock, twine, wrap; cuddle, fondle, nestle, nuzzle, pat, pet, snuggle, stroke
2 to surround or cover closely ⟨the stone walls that *embrace* the monastery serve to symbolize its function as a retreat from an unquiet world⟩ — see ENFOLD 1
3 to take for one's own use (something originated by another) ⟨rap music came to be *embraced* by people who were far removed from the inner cities where it originated⟩ — see ADOPT
4 to receive or accept gladly or readily ⟨the exchange student was gratified to be so quickly *embraced* by people of the small rural community⟩ — see WELCOME
5 to have as part of a whole ⟨a course in social studies can *embrace* everything from sociology to civics and economics⟩ — see INCLUDE 1
6 to form a circle around ⟨a sleepy village *embraced* by low hills⟩ — see SURROUND

embracive *adj* covering everything or all important points ⟨"pickle" is an *embracive* term for any kind of food preserved in brine or vinegar⟩ — see ENCYCLOPEDIC

embrangle *vb* to place in conflict or difficulties ⟨it seems everyone who was even remotely connected to the man became somehow *embrangled* in the scandal surrounding him⟩ — see EMBROIL

embrittled *adj* having a texture that readily breaks into little pieces under pressure ⟨old, *embrittled* movie film that would never stand up to being run through a projector⟩ — see CRISP 1

embroider *vb* to add to the interest of by including made-up details ⟨Dad likes to *embroider* his fishing stories⟩
synonyms color, elaborate (on), embellish, exaggerate, hyperbolize, magnify, pad, stretch
related words dress up, gussy up; amplify, enhance, enlarge (on *or* upon), expand, flesh (out); fudge, hedge; overdo, overdraw, overemphasize, overplay, overstate; emphasize, play up, stress; caricature; satirize
near antonyms belittle, minimize, play down, understate

embroidering *n* the representation of something in terms that go beyond the facts ⟨with considerable *embroidering* the owners of the bed-and-breakfast have turned a few odd incidents into a full-blown legend of ghostly apparitions⟩ — see EXAGGERATION

embroidery *n* **1** decorative stitching done on cloth with the use of a needle ⟨she's been able to turn her skill at *embroidery* into a second business selling decorative cushions at craft fairs⟩ — see NEEDLEWORK
2 the representation of something in terms that go beyond the facts ⟨it's doubtful that she ever told an anecdote without considerable *embroidery*⟩ — see EXAGGERATION

embroil *vb* to place in conflict or difficulties ⟨the town has been *embroiled* in controversy over the building of the huge shopping mall⟩
synonyms bog (down), broil, embrangle, mire
related words enmesh (*also* immesh), ensnare, ensnarl, entangle, entrap, snare, tangle, trap
near antonyms emancipate, free, liberate, release

emcee *n* a person who conducts a program of entertainment by making introductions and providing continuity ⟨acted as *emcee* for the evening's entertainment at the political convention⟩ — see ANNOUNCER

emend *vb* to remove errors, defects, deficiencies, or deviations from ⟨the first printout quickly revealed that our computer program needed to be *emended*⟩ — see CORRECT 1

emendation *n* a change designed to correct or improve a written work ⟨the governor's numerous *emendations* to the speechwriter's first draft left nary a sentence untouched⟩ — see CORRECTION 1

emerge *vb* to come to one's attention especially gradually or unexpectedly ⟨problems *emerged* almost as soon as the contractor began the excavation for the swimming pool⟩ — see ARISE 2

emergency *n* a time or state of affairs requiring prompt or decisive action ⟨an alert, quick-thinking girl who is good to have around in an *emergency*⟩
synonyms boiling point, breaking point, clutch, conjuncture, crisis, crossroad(s), crunch, crunch time, Dunkirk, exigency, extremity, flash point, head, juncture, tinderbox, zero hour
related words contingency, possibility; climax, turning point; happening, landmark, milestone; condition, pass, situation, strait; deadlock, impasse, stalemate; corner, fix, hole, hot water, jam, last ditch, pinch, predicament, scrape, spot; eleventh hour, last minute
phrases moment of truth, point of no return

emergent *adj* needing immediate attention ⟨since it was not seen as an *emergent* problem, it was continually put off⟩ — see ACUTE 2

emigrant *n* one that leaves one place to settle in another ⟨a city teeming with *emigrants* from many lands⟩
synonyms émigré (*also* emigré), immigrant, incomer [*chiefly British*], in-migrant, migrant, out-migrant, settler
related words defector, deportee, evacuee, exile, expatriate, refugee, relocatee, repatriate; alien, foreigner, illegal, noncitizen, nonnative; colonist, newcomer, squatter; migrator, pilgrim, pioneer, trekker
near antonyms aborigine, native; citizen, habitant, inhabitant, national, resident
antonyms nonimmigrant

émigré *also* **emigré** *n* **1** a person forced to emigrate for political reasons ⟨the revolution resulted in a flood of *émigrés* into neighboring countries⟩
synonyms deportee, evacuee, exile, expat [*chiefly British*], expatriate, refugee
related words alien, fugitive; castoff, outcast, pariah; loyalist, patriot
2 one that leaves one place to settle in another ⟨the *émigrés* had little understanding of what awaited them in America⟩ — see EMIGRANT

eminence *n* **1** the fact or state of being above others in rank or importance ⟨the *eminence* of the Nobel Prize in the field of awards and prizes⟩
synonyms distinction, dominance, noteworthiness, paramountcy, preeminence, preponderance, preponderancy, prepotency, prestigiousness, primacy, superiority, supremacy, transcendence
related words celebrity, fame, famousness, glory, honor, kudos, renown, reputation, repute; megastardom, stardom, superstardom; greatness, illustriousness, nobleness, notableness; ascendance (*also* ascendence), ascendancy (*also* ascendency), authority, domination, dominion; influence, power, prestige, weight; infamy, notoriety
near antonyms insignificance; inferiority, mediocrity; obscureness, obscurity
2 an area of high ground ⟨the old citadel sits on an *eminence* with a commanding view of the city⟩ — see HEIGHT 4

éminence grise *n* the senior member of a group ⟨the revered *éminence grise* of Civil War historians⟩ — see DEAN

eminent *adj* standing above others in rank, importance, or achievement ⟨many *eminent* surgeons are on the hospital's staff⟩
synonyms astral, bright, distinguished, illustrious, lu-

minous, noble, notable, noteworthy, outstanding, preeminent, prestigious, redoubtable, signal, star, superior
related words celebrated, exalted, famed, famous, glorious, honored, renowned, reputable; infamous, notorious; dominant, paramount, predominant
near antonyms insignificant, minor, unimportant; average, inferior, mediocre; obscure, uncelebrated, unsung

eminently *adv* to a great degree ⟨an applicant who is *eminently* qualified for the job⟩ — see VERY 1

emissary *n* **1** a person sent on a mission to represent another ⟨most of the industrialized nations of the world sent *emissaries* to the conference on global warming⟩ — see AMBASSADOR
2 a person who tries secretly to obtain information for one country in the territory of another usually unfriendly country ⟨the embassy's staff likely contains at least one *emissary* who reports to the home country's chief of intelligence⟩ — see SPY

emit *vb* **1** to throw or give off ⟨nuclei that *emit* gamma rays⟩
synonyms cast, discharge, emanate, evolve, exhale, expel, expire [*archaic*], give out, irradiate, issue, radiate, release, send (out), shoot, throw out, vent
related words eliminate, evacuate, excrete, exude, ooze, secrete; eject, erupt, gush, jet, outpour, pour, spew, spout, spray, spurt, squirt
near antonyms absorb, inhale, soak (up), sponge, suck (up), take up
2 to send forth using the vocal chords ⟨I was so scared I couldn't *emit* a peep⟩ — see UTTER 1

emolument *n* the money paid regularly to a person for labor or services ⟨the annual *emolument* for the director of the charity is officially only one dollar⟩ — see WAGE

emotion *n* **1** a subjective response to a person, thing, or situation ⟨my *emotions* after hearing the shocking news went from utter disbelief to overwhelming sorrow⟩ — see FEELING 1
2 depth of feeling ⟨the *emotion* that the singer is able to instill in "Amazing Grace" is truly stirring⟩ — see ARDOR 1

emotional *adj* **1** having or expressing great depth of feeling ⟨worship at revival meetings often takes a markedly *emotional* form⟩ — see FERVENT 1
2 having the power to affect the feelings or sympathies ⟨in one *emotional* scene in the movie the boy must say goodbye to his extraterrestrial friend⟩ — see MOVING
3 showing feeling freely ⟨the fact that he is not a very *emotional* person does not mean that he is not a loving, caring father⟩ — see DEMONSTRATIVE 1

emotionless *adj* not feeling or showing emotion ⟨endured an unsatisfying marriage to a seemingly *emotionless* man⟩ — see IMPASSIVE 1

emotionlessness *n* a lack of emotion or emotional expressiveness ⟨her seeming *emotionlessness* at her husband's funeral masked a grief that was beyond words⟩ — see APATHY 1

empathetic *adj* having or showing the capacity for sharing the feelings of another ⟨an *empathetic* social worker who soon realized that the single mother was at her breaking point⟩ — see SYMPATHETIC 1

empathic *adj* having or showing the capacity for sharing the feelings of another ⟨gave an *empathic* nod as I recounted my repeated efforts to land a decent-paying job in a tough economy⟩ — see SYMPATHETIC 1

emphasis *n* **1** a special notice or importance given to something ⟨a prep school with a long-established *emphasis* on sports⟩
synonyms accent, accentuation, stress, underscoring, weight
related words attention, concentration, focus, spotlight; consequence, import, moment, note, significance, value, worth; precedence, primacy, priority, top billing; consideration, heed, regard
near antonyms minimization, underemphasis; disregard, indifference
antonyms de-emphasis
2 the quality or state of being forceful (as in expression) ⟨the *emphasis* with which my parents issued the warning about smoking left no doubt that they were serious⟩ — see VEHEMENCE 1

emphasize *vb* **1** to indicate the importance of by centering attention on ⟨supermarket tabloids that *emphasize* sensational news stories⟩
synonyms accent, accentuate, feature, foreground, highlight, illuminate, play up, point (up), press, punctuate, stress
related words focus, identify, pinpoint, spotlight; advertise, boost, plug, promote, publicize; overplay
phrases bear down on, make much of
near antonyms tone (down), underemphasize, understate; belittle, discount, disparage, minimize
antonyms de-emphasize, play down
2 to make more apparent ⟨that huge belt buckle only *emphasizes* his big gut⟩
synonyms accentuate, bring out, italicize, stress, underline, underscore
related words amplify, beef (up), boost, reinforce (*also* reenforce), strengthen; augment, deepen, enhance, enlarge, heighten, magnify, maximize, supplement; enliven, jazz (up)
near antonyms decrease, diminish, lessen, minimize, reduce, subdue, tone (down), understate, weaken
antonyms de-emphasize

emphatic *adj* **1** marked by or uttered with forcefulness ⟨the governor issued an *emphatic* denial of all charges⟩
synonyms aggressive, assertive, dynamic, energetic, forceful, full-blooded, muscular, resounding, strenuous, vehement, vigorous, violent
related words decided, insistent, marked, pointed; absolute, categorical (*also* categoric), clear, plain, unambiguous, unequivocal; arresting, compelling, conspicuous, impelling, noticeable, striking
near antonyms guarded, mild, uncompelling, weak, wishy-washy; ambiguous, equivocal, halting, hesitant; understated
antonyms nonassertive, nonemphatic, unemphatic
2 likely to attract attention ⟨with all of the decorative fishing nets, lobster pots, and oars, the seafood restaurant's nautical theme was a little too *emphatic* for my taste⟩ — see NOTICEABLE

empire *n* a group of businesses or enterprises under one control ⟨the media mogul's *empire* consists of newspapers, TV stations, and cable companies⟩ — see CONGLOMERATE

empirical *also* **empiric** *adj* **1** based on observation or experience ⟨guidelines for raising children that are based on *empirical* evidence⟩
synonyms existential, experiential, experimental, objective, observational
related words actual, factual, genuine, hard, material, real; accepted, established, tried, tried-and-true; indisputable, undeniable; demonstrable, provable, verifiable
near antonyms conjectural, hypothetical, speculative; unproven, unsubstantiated; metaphysical, transcendentalist, visionary
antonyms nonempirical, theoretical (*also* theoretic), unempirical
2 capable of being proven as true or real ⟨a philosopher who does not regard "God exists" as an *empirical* statement⟩ — see VERIFIABLE

emplace *vb* to arrange something in a certain spot or position ⟨the plan is to *emplace* more guns on the ridge north of the camp⟩ — see PLACE 1

emplacement *n* the area or space occupied by or intended for something ⟨the *emplacement* of the house, which is between two hulking mansions, makes it seem smaller than it is⟩ — see PLACE 1

employ *n* the state of being provided with a paying job ⟨while you're under our *employ*, you can't do outside work for our competitors⟩ — see HIRE 1

employ *vb* **1** to provide with a paying job ⟨a new factory that will *employ* 500 people⟩
synonyms assume, engage, fee [*chiefly Scottish*], hire, lay on [*chiefly British*], pay, place, recruit, retain, sign (up *or* on), take on
related words reemploy, reengage, rehire; apprentice, contract, job, partner, subcontract; enlist; advance, promote, upgrade; keep (on); headhunt, scout
near antonyms furlough, lay off, lock out
antonyms ax (*or* axe), can, discharge, dismiss, fire, sack
2 to put into action or service ⟨looking for a job in which she can *employ* her considerable writing skills⟩ — see USE 1

employable *adj* capable of or suitable for being used for a particular purpose ⟨this wall map of the bay is for decoration only—it's not *employable* for actual navigation⟩ — see USABLE 1

employed *adj* involved in often constant activity ⟨insisted that the children be *employed* in some useful activity, even during school vacations⟩ — see BUSY 1

employee *also* **employe** *n* one who works for another for wages or a salary ⟨an employer who was loved and admired by generations of *employees*⟩
synonyms hand, hireling, jobholder, retainer, worker
related words assistant, cog, flunky (*also* flunkey *or* flunkie), subordinate, underling, yes-man; drudge, gandy dancer, grub, hack, jobber, laborer, navvy [*chiefly British*], toiler; nine-to-fiver, wage earner, wage slave, wageworker, workingman, workingwoman, workman, workwoman; associate, colleague, coworker; temp, temporary
near antonyms boss, superior, supervisor
antonyms employer, gaffer [*British*]

employment *n* **1** the act or practice of employing something for a particular purpose ⟨the *employment* of the kitchen oven as a storage cupboard had predictably disastrous results⟩ — see USE 1
2 the activity by which one regularly makes a living ⟨his regular *employment* is that of a restaurant waiter, but he always identifies himself as an actor⟩ — see OCCUPATION 1
3 the state of being provided with a paying job ⟨the parents tried to convey to their adult son the joys of steady *employment*⟩ — see HIRE 1

empoison *vb* to implant bitter feelings in ⟨a series of misfortunes had *empoisoned* him against the whole world⟩ — see EMBITTER

emporium *n* an establishment where goods are sold to consumers ⟨an *emporium* for home electronic equipment filled with stuff I didn't know I needed but now desperately want⟩ — see SHOP 1

empower *vb* **1** to give official or legal power to ⟨the federal agency *empowered* to collect taxes⟩ — see AUTHORIZE 1
2 to make able or possible ⟨workshops in financial management to *empower* workers to plan for their retirement⟩ — see ENABLE 1

empowerment *n* the granting of power to perform various acts or duties ⟨the *empowerment* of her husband to make medical decisions on her behalf is clearly stated in her living will⟩ — see COMMISSION 1

emprise *n* an exciting or noteworthy event that one experiences firsthand ⟨he always seems to be having the sort of high *emprise* that most of us experience only in our dreams⟩ — see ADVENTURE 1

emptiness *n* **1** a need or desire for food ⟨the *emptiness* that usually sets in about three o'clock in the afternoon⟩ — see HUNGER 1
2 empty space ⟨there in the vast *emptiness* of the desert was a long-abandoned jeep⟩ — see VACANCY 1
3 the quality or state of being empty ⟨the *emptiness* of the interior of the isolated house just made it seem all the more eerie⟩ — see VACANCY 2

empty *adj* **1** lacking contents that could or should be present ⟨the refrigerator is *empty*, so we'll have to eat out⟩
synonyms bare, blank, clean, devoid, stark, toom [*chiefly Scottish*], vacant, vacuous, void
related words barren, hollow; available, clear, free, open; unfilled, unfurnished; unattended, uninhabited, unoccupied; abandoned, deserted, emptied, forsaken, vacated; depleted, drained, dry, exhausted
near antonyms complete; replete; furnished, provided, supplied; filled, occupied; flush, overflowing, packed, teeming
antonyms full
2 feeling a desire or need for food ⟨as the long car trip wore on, we all started to feel a little *empty*⟩ — see HUNGRY 1
3 having no meaning ⟨spare me your *empty* apologies because if you were truly sorry, you'd change⟩ — see MEANINGLESS
4 having no usefulness ⟨an *empty* task that was assigned just to keep us busy⟩ — see WORTHLESS
5 producing no results ⟨all of the leads in the missing-person case were turning up *empty*⟩ — see FUTILE 1
6 not expressing any emotion ⟨the refugees' faces had the dazed, *empty* look of despair⟩ — see BLANK 1

empty *vb* to remove the contents of ⟨*empty* the room before starting to paint the ceiling⟩
synonyms clear, evacuate, vacate, void
related words deplete, drain, eliminate, exhaust, waste; bleed, draw (off); clean, flush, purge, scour, sweep
antonyms fill, load

empty–headed *adj* not having or showing an ability to absorb ideas readily ⟨she sometimes plays the stereotypical *empty-headed* blonde to trick people into underestimating her⟩ — see STUPID 1

empyreal *adj* of, relating to, or suggesting heaven ⟨a painting depicting the Deity as seated on an *empyreal* throne surrounded by saints and angels⟩ — see CELESTIAL

empyrean *adj* of, relating to, or suggesting heaven ⟨movie scenes set in heaven often suggest that harps are the favored instruments for *empyrean* music⟩ — see CELESTIAL

empyrean *n* **1** a dwelling place of perfect happiness for the soul after death ⟨ascended into the *empyrean* after a life filled with good deeds⟩ — see HEAVEN 1
2 an often imaginary place or state of utter perfection and happiness ⟨most ticket buyers have no trouble envisioning the *empyrean* that winning the lottery would inevitably bring about⟩ — see PARADISE 1

emulate *vb* **1** to be the same in meaning or effect ⟨what they offered at the new resort didn't begin to *emulate* the kind of pampering we were used to getting at the resort that closed down⟩ — see AMOUNT (TO) 2
2 to use (someone or something) as the model for one's speech, mannerisms, or behavior ⟨a pro athlete who has often said that children should *emulate* their parents—not him⟩ — see IMITATE 1

emulative *adj* using or marked by the use of something else as a basis or model ⟨right now she's an *emulative* singer, not having yet created a style of her own⟩ — see IMITATIVE

emulsion *n* a distinct entity formed by the combining

of two or more different things ⟨milk is basically an oil-in-water *emulsion*⟩ — see BLEND

enable *vb* **1** to make able or possible ⟨my new glasses *enable* me to read the fine print⟩
synonyms allow, empower, let, permit
related words fit, habilitate, prepare, qualify, ready; approve, endorse (*also* indorse), sanction; condition, equip
near antonyms inhibit, preclude; disallow, enjoin, forbid, prohibit
antonyms prevent
2 to give official or legal power to ⟨a law that would *enable* the authorities to use wiretaps without obtaining court orders⟩ — see AUTHORIZE 1

enact *vb* to put into effect through legislative or authoritative action ⟨Congress *enacts* all laws relating to foreign trade and immigration⟩
synonyms constitute, lay down, legislate, make, ordain, pass
related words reenact, repass; bring about, effect; allow, authorize, permit, sanction; decree, dictate, proclaim; administer, execute; approve, confirm, ratify
near antonyms abolish, abrogate, annul, cancel, invalidate, kill, nullify; overturn, reverse, void
antonyms repeal, rescind, revoke

enactment *n* **1** a rule of conduct or action laid down by a governing authority and especially a legislature ⟨as a result of an *enactment* by Congress, this breathtaking canyon will be permanently protected from development⟩ — see LAW 1
2 the doing of an action ⟨the *enactment* of the murder is never actually shown on screen⟩ — see COMMISSION 2

enamored (of) *adj* filled with an intense or excessive love for ⟨many teenage girls became *enamored of* the movie idol for his boyish good looks⟩
synonyms besotted (by), crazy (about *or* over), dotty (over), enraptured (by), gaga (over), gone (on), infatuated (with), mad (about), nuts (about)
related words hung up (on), obsessed; foolish, silly, wild; bewitched, captivated, charmed, enchanted, entranced, fascinated
phrases stuck on, sweet on
near antonyms cool, detached, unenchanted, unimpressed; disenchanted, disillusioned; heart-free

encage *vb* to close or shut in by or as if by barriers ⟨a stay-at-home mom who somehow felt *encaged* in her home⟩ — see ENCLOSE 1

encamp *vb* **1** to live in a camp or the outdoors ⟨the hike will take several days, and we plan to *encamp* along the trail⟩ — see CAMP (OUT)
2 to provide with living quarters or shelter ⟨as the hurricane raged outside, the stranded tourists were *encamped* overnight in the high school gym⟩ — see HOUSE 1

encampment *n* a place where a group of people live for a short time in tents or cabins ⟨a recreational area that will serve as this year's *encampment* for the Scouts' jamboree⟩ — see CAMP 1

encapsulate *vb* to make into a short statement of the main points (as of a report) ⟨can you *encapsulate* the president's speech in about a paragraph?⟩ — see SUMMARIZE

encapsulation *n* a short statement of the main points ⟨didn't have time to read the full news article, just the *encapsulation* on the second page⟩ — see SUMMARY

encase *vb* to close or shut in by or as if by barriers ⟨fear of the outside world can *encase* a person just as surely as stone walls⟩ — see ENCLOSE 1

encasement *n* something that encloses another thing especially to protect it ⟨an *encasement* of several inches of silt had helped to preserve the sunken remains of the historic ship⟩ — see [1]CASE 1

enceinte *adj* containing unborn young within the body ⟨back in the days when a bride who was visibly *enceinte* was a cause for family embarrassment⟩ — see PREGNANT 1

enchain *vb* to confine or restrain with or as if with chains ⟨children who were *enchained* by an overprotective mother⟩ — see BIND 1

enchant *vb* **1** to attract or delight as if by magic ⟨the child actress *enchanted* audiences with her bubbly personality⟩ — see CHARM 1
2 to cast a spell on ⟨out of spite, the jealous queen *enchanted* her chief rival for the title of the fairest one of all⟩ — see BEWITCH 1
3 to hold the attention of as if by a spell ⟨the tales about the young wizard have *enchanted* children around the globe⟩ — see ENTHRALL 1

enchanted *adj* being or appearing to be under a magic spell ⟨an *enchanted* isle of the South Pacific⟩
synonyms bewitched, charmed, entranced, magic, magical, spellbound
related words cursed (*also* curst), jinxed, possessed; dreamy, fairy, fairylike; fantastic (*also* fantastical), miraculous, utopian, wondrous; hypnotized, mesmerized; bedazzled, captivated, fascinated

enchanter *n* a person skilled in using supernatural forces ⟨in Shakespeare's play an *enchanter* creates a storm at sea that causes his rivals to be cast upon the shores of his magical isle⟩ — see MAGICIAN 1

enchanting *adj* having an often mysterious or magical power to attract ⟨visitors have long found the Highlands of Scotland to be an *enchanting* place⟩ — see FASCINATING 1

enchantingly *adv* in a pleasing way ⟨we visited an *enchantingly* lovely village in Vermont⟩ — see WELL 5

enchantment *n* **1** a spoken word or set of words believed to have magic power ⟨eventually she realized that there wasn't an *enchantment* in the world that was going to turn her boyfriend into a prince⟩ — see SPELL 1
2 the power of irresistible attraction ⟨there's an *enchantment* about that handsome, young actor that women just adore⟩ — see CHARM 2
3 the power to control natural forces through supernatural means ⟨there are people even today who claim to be skilled in *enchantment*⟩ — see MAGIC 1

enchantress *n* **1** a woman believed to have often harmful supernatural powers ⟨when misfortune occurred, it was not uncommon for some unpopular woman of the village to be branded an *enchantress*⟩ — see WITCH 1
2 a woman whom men find irresistibly attractive ⟨Scarlett O'Hara is one of literature's most celebrated *enchantresses*⟩ — see SIREN
3 a lovely woman ⟨an *enchantress* of the silver screen whose legend has only grown over the years⟩ — see BEAUTY 2

encircle *vb* **1** to travel completely around ⟨communication satellites *encircling* the earth⟩
synonyms circle, circuit, circumnavigate, circumvent, compass, girdle, orbit, ring, round
related words circumambulate, cross, perambulate, traverse
2 to form a circle around ⟨immediately after announcing their engagement, the couple was *encircled* by their applauding friends⟩ — see SURROUND

enclasp *vb* to put one's arms around and press tightly ⟨reached around and *enclasped* all four children at once⟩ — see EMBRACE 1

enclose *also* **inclose** *vb* **1** to close or shut in by or as if by barriers ⟨dogs who spend the day *enclosed* in small cages⟩
synonyms box (in), cage, closet, coop (up), corral, encage, encase, envelop, fence (in), hedge, hem (in),

house, immure, include, mew (up), pen, wall (in)
related words bound, circumscribe, confine, contain, limit, restrict; encircle, encompass, enfold, enframe, enlace, frame, ring, surround; armor, cocoon, encapsulate, encapsule, encyst, ensheathe, ensphere, enwomb
2 to form a circle around ⟨in a show of support, the women rushed to *enclose* their distraught friend⟩ — see SURROUND
3 to surround or cover closely ⟨the house was *enclosed* by a high hedge that shielded it from public view⟩ — see ENFOLD 1

enclosure *also* **inclosure** *n* an open space wholly or partly enclosed (as by buildings or walls) ⟨a fenced-in *enclosure* where the sheep are allowed to graze unattended⟩ — see COURT 2

encomium *n* a formal expression of praise ⟨the *encomiums* bestowed on a teacher at her retirement ceremonies⟩
synonyms accolade, citation, commendation, dithyramb, eulogium, eulogy, homage, hymn, paean, panegyric, salutation, tribute
related words award, decoration, dedication, honor, prize; acclaim, acclamation, laudation; applause, plaudit(s); bravo, hallelujah, kudo; approval, cachet, compliment, recommendation
near antonyms censure, condemnation, denunciation, indictment, rebuke, reprimand, reproof; admonition, correction, harangue, lecture, sermon

encompass *vb* **1** to form a circle around ⟨a necklace of sapphire-blue lakes *encompasses* the town⟩ — see SURROUND
2 to have as part of a whole ⟨textbooks on American history are now likely to *encompass* its social history as well as its political and military history⟩ — see INCLUDE 1
3 to surround or cover closely ⟨a fog of mystery has long *encompassed* this fraternal organization, which is known for its secret rituals⟩ — see ENFOLD 1

encounter *n* a brief clash between enemies or rivals ⟨survived an *encounter* with the school bully at the local park⟩
synonyms brush, hassle, run-in, scrape, skirmish
related words argument, fight, quarrel, row, spat, squabble, tiff; battle, brawl, fray, wrangle

encounter *vb* **1** to come upon face-to-face or as if face-to-face ⟨quite unexpectedly *encountered* our next-door neighbor while vacationing in Europe⟩ — see MEET 1
2 to come upon unexpectedly or by chance ⟨we *encountered* a host of unforeseen problems during the restoration of our 200-year-old house⟩ — see HAPPEN (ON *OR* UPON)
3 to enter into contest or conflict with ⟨the troops *encountered* bands of guerrilla fighters as they made their way across the desert⟩ — see ENGAGE 2

encourage *vb* **1** to fill with courage or strength of purpose ⟨a pep talk that *encouraged* the team to get out there and win⟩
synonyms bear up, buck up, buoy (up), cheer (up), chirk (up), embolden, hearten, inspire, inspirit, steel
related words animate, enliven, invigorate; enforce, fortify, reinforce (*also* reenforce), strengthen; assure, reassure; boost, energize, excite, galvanize, provoke, quicken, rally, stimulate, stir
near antonyms demoralize, depress, sadden; debilitate, enfeeble, hamstring, undermine, weaken; intimidate, psych (out)
antonyms daunt, discourage, dishearten, dispirit
2 to help the growth or development of ⟨asserted that the government should be *encouraging* small businesses, not smothering them with regulations⟩ — see FOSTER 1
3 to rouse to strong feeling or action ⟨the movie's cheap special effects will not *encourage* audiences to sit on the edge of their seats but to roll in the aisles with laughter⟩ — see PROVOKE 1
4 to try to persuade (someone) through earnest appeals to follow a course of action ⟨the pastor continues to *encourage* the couple to work out their problems in hopes of saving their marriage⟩ — see URGE

encouragement *n* something that arouses action or activity ⟨the huge rebates that the auto companies were offering were all the *encouragement* I needed to buy a new car⟩ — see IMPULSE 1

encouraging *adj* **1** having qualities which inspire hope ⟨*encouraging* signs that the economy is improving⟩ — see HOPEFUL 1
2 making one feel good inside ⟨the *encouraging* story of a young girl who overcame great social and physical obstacles to become an outstanding athlete⟩ — see HEARTWARMING
3 pointing toward a happy outcome ⟨we're off to an *encouraging* start on this project⟩ — see FAVORABLE 2

encroach *vb* to advance gradually beyond the usual or desirable limits ⟨each year the sea continues to *encroach* upon the island's beaches⟩
synonyms creep, inch, worm
related words snake, sneak; entrench (*also* intrench), impinge, infringe, intrude, invade; overpass, overreach, overrun, overshoot, overstep

encrust *also* **incrust** *vb* to cover with a hardened layer ⟨refrigerator shelves that were *encrusted* with the residue of many spills⟩
synonyms cake, crust, rime
related words besmear, coat, smear, spread; cover, daub; coagulate, congeal, harden

encumber *vb* **1** to create difficulty for the work or activity of ⟨the claim that all of these regulations *encumber* doctors, taking time away from the actual practice of medicine⟩ — see HAMPER
2 to place a weight or burden on ⟨don't *encumber* your pack animal so much that it can hardly move⟩ — see LOAD 1

encumbrance *n* something that makes movement or progress difficult ⟨without the *encumbrance* of a heavy backpack, I could sprint along the trail⟩
synonyms balk, bar, block, chain, clog, cramp, crimp, deterrent, drag, embarrassment, fetter, handicap, hindrance, holdback, hurdle, impediment, inhibition, interference, let, manacle, obstacle, obstruction, shackles, stop, stumbling block, trammel
related words catch, hitch, rub, snag; barrier, blockade, blockage, brick wall, stone wall; arrest, bit, brake, check, constraint, curb, hobble, rein, restraint; embargo, stoppage; delay, holdup, stall; burden, cumber, load; danger, hazard, peril, reef; adversity, difficulty, disadvantage, drawback, hardship
near antonyms catalyst, goad, impetus, incentive, spur, stimulant, stimulus; advantage, break, edge; aid, assistance, benefit, boost, handmaiden (*also* handmaid), help

encyclopedic *adj* covering everything or all important points ⟨a tour guide with an *encyclopedic* knowledge of New York City and its people⟩
synonyms all-embracing, all-in [*chiefly British*], all-inclusive, broad-gauge (*or* broad-gauged), compendious, complete, comprehensive, cover-all, cyclopedic, embracive, exhaustive, full, global, inclusive, in-depth, omnibus, panoramic, thorough, universal
related words broad, catholic, encyclical, general, inclusionary, overall; cosmic (*also* cosmical), extensive, far, far-reaching, grand, large, panoptic, sweeping, vast, wide, wide-ranging; blanket, indiscriminate, unrestricted
near antonyms circumscribed, limited, narrow, re-

stricted, specialized; exact, precise; individual, singular, specific; incomplete, patchy, sketchy

end *n* **1** the stopping of a process or activity ⟨the *end* of hostilities brought general rejoicing⟩
synonyms arrest, arrestment, cease, cessation, check, close, closedown, closure, conclusion, cutoff, discontinuance, discontinuation, ending, expiration, finish, halt, lapse, offset, shutdown, shutoff, stay, stop, stoppage, surcease, termination
related words mop-up, phaseout; abeyance, break, interruption, layoff, letup, moratorium, pause, standstill, suspension
near antonyms extension, persistence, prolongation
antonyms continuance, continuation
2 a real or imaginary point beyond which a person or thing cannot go ⟨I'm at the *end* of my patience with these little brats⟩ — see LIMIT 1
3 an unused or unwanted piece or item typically of small size or value ⟨a couple of *ends* of wallpaper were all that was left after we finished papering the room⟩ — see [1]SCRAP 1
4 something that one hopes or intends to accomplish ⟨in this case the *ends* definitely do not justify the means⟩ — see GOAL
5 the last and usually sharp or tapering part of something long and narrow ⟨a child's pair of scissors with blunt *ends*⟩ — see POINT 2
6 the last part of a process or action ⟨the war wasn't yet over, but we were definitely at the beginning of the *end*⟩ — see FINALE
7 the line or relatively narrow space that marks the outer limit of something ⟨the *ends* of his shirt cuffs were badly frayed⟩ — see BORDER 1
8 the permanent stopping of all the vital bodily activities ⟨Henry Hudson and eight others were set adrift in the bay in a small boat, and how they met their *end* is unknown⟩ — see DEATH 1
9 something belonging to, due to, or contributed by an individual member of a group ⟨keep up your *end* of the bargain⟩ — see SHARE 1

end *vb* **1** to bring (an event) to a natural or appropriate stopping point ⟨let's *end* the meeting with a short prayer⟩ — see CLOSE 3
2 to bring (as an action or operation) to an immediate end ⟨unfortunately, an argument *ended* their date, and they're still not speaking to each other⟩ — see STOP 1
3 to come to an end ⟨a book so good that you hate to see it *end*⟩ — see CEASE 1
4 to stop living ⟨a great general, who *ended* on the field of battle⟩ — see DIE 1

endamage *vb* to reduce the soundness, effectiveness, or perfection of ⟨a thoughtless indiscretion that *endamaged* a reputation that took a lifetime to build⟩ — see DAMAGE 1

endanger *vb* to place in danger ⟨a reckless use of fireworks that *endangered* the lives of many people⟩
synonyms adventure, compromise, gamble (with), hazard, imperil, jeopard, jeopardize, menace, peril, risk, venture
related words intimidate, threaten; expose; subject; chance, wager
near antonyms guard, protect, shelter, shield; preserve, resume, save

endangered *adj* being in a situation where one is likely to meet with harm ⟨a daring attempt to rescue the *endangered* passengers from the burning boat⟩ — see LIABLE 1

endangerment *n* the state of not being protected from injury, harm, or evil ⟨I didn't think I would be subject to any *endangerment* if I simply dangled my legs over the rock ledge⟩ — see DANGER 1

endearing *adj* **1** having qualities that tend to make one loved ⟨you have to wonder about people who don't find kittens and puppies *endearing*⟩ — see LOVABLE
2 likely or intended to win one's affection ⟨his impish sense of humor is one of his more *endearing* traits⟩ — see INGRATIATING

endeavor *n* an effort to do or accomplish something ⟨the hope that this latest *endeavor* will yield much information about the atmosphere of the planet⟩ — see ATTEMPT 1

endeavor *vb* **1** to devote serious and sustained effort ⟨the trapped climber *endeavored* mightily to get the boulder to budge⟩ — see LABOR
2 to make an effort to do ⟨our club is forever *endeavoring* to find ways to raise more money for activities⟩ — see ATTEMPT

ended *adj* brought or having come to an end ⟨the recently *ended* season was one of the best that the baseball team ever had⟩ — see COMPLETE 2

endemic *adj* belonging to a particular place by birth or origin ⟨the fish is not an *endemic* species of the lake, and it is rapidly devouring the native trout population⟩ — see NATIVE 1

endgame *n* the last part of a process or action ⟨they're now in the *endgame* of the negotiations for a new labor contract⟩ — see FINALE

ending *n* **1** the last part of a process or action ⟨the plagiarism scandal was a disgraceful *ending* to a once-promising academic career⟩ — see FINALE
2 the stopping of a process or activity ⟨the best part about any dental procedure is its *ending*⟩ — see END 1

endless *adj* **1** being or seeming to be without limits ⟨from the promontory visitors can look out over an *endless* sea⟩ — see INFINITE
2 lasting forever ⟨the *endless* roar is what I remember most about Niagara Falls⟩ — see EVERLASTING 1

endorse *also* **indorse** *vb* to promote the interests or cause of ⟨an increase in the number of parents who *endorse* the idea of school uniforms⟩ — see SUPPORT 1

endow *vb* **1** to furnish freely or naturally with some power, quality, or attribute ⟨a young performer *endowed* with a great singing voice⟩
synonyms bless, endue (*or* indue), favor, gift, invest
related words equip, provide, supply; bestow (on *or* upon), clothe, confer (on), cover; accord, award, grant; empower, enable, enhance, enrich, heighten; bequeath, will
near antonyms dispossess, divest, strip; deplete, drain, exhaust; skimp, stint
2 to furnish (as an institution) with a regular source of income ⟨a wealthy businessman who *endowed* several museums⟩
synonyms finance, fund, subsidize
related words establish, found, organize; bequeath, contribute, donate, subscribe, support, underwrite; award, grant; back, promote, sponsor; capitalize, invest (in)
near antonyms draw, receive; subsist
antonyms defund, disendow
3 to provide money for ⟨the program to bring the arts to inner-city youths is *endowed* by a grant from the federal government⟩ — see FINANCE 1

endowment *n* a special and usually inborn ability ⟨it's a sin to waste one's God-given *endowments*⟩ — see TALENT

endue *or* **indue** *vb* **1** to cause (as a person) to become filled or saturated with a certain quality or principle ⟨professional soldiers *endued* with an ironclad sense of duty and honor⟩ — see INFUSE
2 to furnish freely or naturally with some power, quality, or attribute ⟨she's always been *endued* with an unquenchable optimism⟩ — see ENDOW 1

endurable *adj* capable of being endured ⟨a flu shot is

never pleasant, but I find the momentary pain entirely *endurable*⟩ — see BEARABLE

endurance *n* uninterrupted or lasting existence ⟨the *endurance* of his love for his wife was not arrested even by her death⟩ — see CONTINUATION

endure *vb* **1** to come to a knowledge of (something) by living through it ⟨an elderly couple who have *endured* the ups and downs of a half century of married life⟩ — see EXPERIENCE

2 to put up with (something painful or difficult) ⟨at some point we all have to *endure* the loss of a beloved pet⟩ — see BEAR 2

3 to remain indefinitely in existence or in the same state ⟨the fashion business is built on change, since nobody expects a particular clothing style to *endure*⟩ — see CONTINUE 1

enduring *adj* having an existence or validity that does not change or diminish ⟨science fiction's *enduring* fascination with worlds beyond our own⟩ — see ABIDING

enemy *n* one that is hostile toward another ⟨a beloved minister with no known *enemies*⟩

synonyms adversary, antagonist, foe, hostile, opponent

related words archenemy, archfoe, nemesis; ill-wisher; bane, bête noire; assailant, attacker, combatant, invader; competitor, emulator, rival

near antonyms buddy, chum, compadre, crony, fellow, hail-fellow, hail-fellow-well-met, hearty, hobnobber, mate, musketeer, pal; abettor (*also* abetter), accomplice, ally, collaborator, colleague, comrade, confederate, friendly, partner; adherent, disciple, follower; backer, benefactor, exponent, supporter, sympathizer, well-wisher

antonyms amigo, friend

energetic *adj* **1** having active strength of body or mind ⟨a lifelong fitness fanatic, he remained *energetic* well into his 80s⟩ — see VIGOROUS 1

2 having much high-spirited energy and movement ⟨trying to find the right music for an *energetic* aerobics routine⟩ — see LIVELY 1

3 marked by or uttered with forcefulness ⟨the salesperson gave us an *energetic* sales pitch, talking excitedly about the amazing features of this year's cars⟩ — see EMPHATIC 1

energetically *adv* in a vigorous and forceful manner ⟨the crew worked *energetically* to get the parade float done on time⟩ — see HARD 3

energize *vb* to give life, vigor, or spirit to ⟨a teacher who knows how to *energize* history lessons with little-known but interesting facts about long-ago people⟩ — see ANIMATE

energized *adj* made or become fresh in spirits or vigor ⟨after a refreshing lunch, we felt *energized* and ready to hit the bike trail once again⟩ — see NEW 4

energy *n* **1** a spiritual force that is held to emanate from or give animation to living beings ⟨many Eastern cultures believe in the significance of life *energy* in the healing process⟩

synonyms aura, chi (*or* ch'i *also* qi), ki, vibe(s), vibration(s)

related words inner light, light, nature, orgone, soul, spirit; élan vital, life, lifeblood, Shakti (*also* Sakti), world soul; karma, mana

2 active strength of body or mind ⟨for a woman of advanced years, she has remarkable *energy*⟩ — see VIGOR 1

3 something with a usable capacity for doing work ⟨some of the power needs of the house are provided by solar *energy*⟩ — see FUEL

4 the ability to exert effort for the accomplishment of a task ⟨I'm so tired that I don't think I have the *energy* to take another step⟩ — see POWER 2

enervate *vb* **1** to deprive of emotional or intellectual vitality ⟨a lifetime of working in dreary jobs had *enervated* his very soul⟩ — see DEHYDRATE 1

2 to diminish the physical strength of ⟨the surgery really *enervated* me for weeks afterwards⟩ — see WEAKEN 1

enervated *adj* **1** lacking bodily energy or motivation ⟨as the heat wave wore on, everyone really started to feel *enervated*⟩ — see LISTLESS

2 lacking bodily strength ⟨months of recovery in the hospital had rendered the soldiers *enervated* and unfit⟩ — see WEAK 1

enervation *n* the quality or state of lacking physical strength or vigor ⟨took a dip in the pool to alleviate the *enervation* caused by the heat and humidity⟩ — see WEAKNESS 1

enfant terrible *n* a person who does not conform to generally accepted standards or customs ⟨an author who reveled in his role as the *enfant terrible* of American letters⟩ — see NONCONFORMIST 1

enfeeble *vb* to diminish the physical strength of ⟨long periods of being confined to a hospital bed will *enfeeble* anyone⟩ — see WEAKEN 1

enfeebled *adj* lacking bodily strength ⟨the *enfeebled* old woman now needs a companion to help her with everyday tasks⟩ — see WEAK 1

enfeeblement *n* **1** a gradual sinking and wasting away of mind or body ⟨daily exercise can help to halt some of the *enfeeblement* that comes with advanced years⟩ — see DECLINE 1

2 the quality or state of lacking physical strength or vigor ⟨a lot of the *enfeeblement* I've experienced since the accident is being gradually diminished by daily physical therapy⟩ — see WEAKNESS 1

enfetter *vb* to confine or restrain with or as if with chains ⟨*enfettered* by debt, she was in no position to take early retirement⟩ — see BIND 1

enfold *vb* **1** to surround or cover closely ⟨darkness began to *enfold* the lonely house on the hill⟩

synonyms bosom, bower, circumfuse, cocoon, embosom, embower, embrace, enclose (*also* inclose), encompass, enshroud, enswathe, envelop, enwrap, invest, involve, lap, mantle, muffle, shroud, swathe, veil, wrap

related words curtain, drape; embed (*also* imbed), encase; swaddle; blanket, overlay, overspread; camouflage, cloak, disguise, mask; circle, encircle, enlace, enwind

near antonyms bare, denude, expose, strip

2 to put one's arms around and press tightly ⟨the winner *enfolded* the huge bouquet of roses in her arms and thanked the judges⟩ — see EMBRACE 1

enforce *vb* to carry out effectively ⟨the duty of the police is to *enforce* the law⟩

synonyms administer, apply, execute, implement

related words bring about, effect, effectuate; discharge, fulfill (*or* fulfil), render; cite, invoke; enact, legislate; honor, observe, uphold; prosecute; promulgate

near antonyms disregard, ignore, neglect

enfranchise *vb* to set free (as from slavery or confinement) ⟨in a way, modern labor-saving appliances *enfranchised* people, giving them much more leisure time⟩ — see FREE 1

enfranchisement *n* **1** the act of setting free from slavery ⟨the Emancipation Proclamation was merely the first step in the full *enfranchisement* of African-Americans⟩ — see LIBERATION

2 the right to formally express one's position or will in an election ⟨a time when *enfranchisement* was limited to white males who owned property⟩ — see VOTE 1

engage *vb* **1** to hold the attention of ⟨the challenging jigsaw puzzle *engaged* us all evening⟩

synonyms absorb, bemuse, busy, catch up, engross,

enthrall (*or* enthral), enwrap, fascinate, grip, immerse, interest, intrigue, involve, occupy
related words allure, attract, beguile, bewitch, captivate, charm, enchant, obsess; hypnotize, mesmerize; distract, preoccupy; hog, monopolize
phrases catch one's eye
near antonyms bore, jade, pall, tire, weary
2 to enter into contest or conflict with ⟨the daring young captain was eager to *engage* the enemy⟩
synonyms battle, encounter, face, meet, take on
related words emulate, rival; contend, fight, oppose
near antonyms elude, escape, evade; retreat
3 to obligate by prior agreement ⟨we can't go to the dance because we're already *engaged* to attend a piano recital⟩ — see PLEDGE 1
4 to provide with a paying job ⟨the wealthy couple are looking to *engage* a handyman to take care of the estate⟩ — see EMPLOY 1
5 to take or get the temporary use of (something) for a set sum ⟨my sister and her boyfriend have *engaged* a chauffeured limousine for the prom⟩ — see HIRE 1

engaged *adj* **1** pledged in marriage ⟨the *engaged* couple make a charming pair⟩
synonyms affianced, bespoke (*also* bespoken) [*dialect*], betrothed, promised [*chiefly dialect*]
related words committed
antonyms unattached
2 involved in often constant activity ⟨I'm *engaged* right now, so call back some other time⟩ — see BUSY 1

engagement *n* **1** the act or state of being engaged to be married ⟨the fun couple recently announced their *engagement*⟩
synonyms betrothal, espousal, troth
antonyms disengagement
2 an agreement to be present at a specified time and place ⟨a lifelong practice of marking all of my *engagements* on a weekly calendar⟩
synonyms appointment, assignation, date, rendezvous, tryst
related words arrangement; invitation; interview; get-together, meeting; call, visit; schedule
3 the state of being provided with a paying job ⟨his *engagement* as a caddie at the golf club was his first work experience⟩ — see HIRE 1

engaging *adj* **1** having an often mysterious or magical power to attract ⟨movie stars often have an *engaging* aura that is hard to describe⟩ — see FASCINATING 1
2 holding the attention or provoking interest ⟨a movie with an *engaging* story that will hold your interest for a couple of hours⟩ — see INTERESTING

engender *vb* **1** to be the cause of (a situation, action, or state of mind) ⟨a suggestion to go out for pizza that didn't seem to *engender* any interest⟩ — see EFFECT
2 to come into existence ⟨feelings of confidence and independence that were only just beginning to *engender* within her⟩ — see BEGIN 2

engine *n* a device that changes energy into mechanical motion ⟨a car with a 200-horsepower *engine*⟩
synonyms machine, motor
related words converter, transformer; appliance, mechanism; equipment, tool; mill

engineer *n* a person who designs and guides a plan or undertaking ⟨the *engineer* of a movement to eradicate hunger⟩
synonyms architect, mastermind
related words builder, maker, producer; captain, commander, director, handler, leader, manager, quarterback; contriver, designer, formulator, originator, spawner; arranger, hatcher, organizer, planner, plotter, schemer; finagler, machinator, maneuverer; developer, generator, inaugurator, initiator, inspirer, instituter (*or* institutor), pioneer

engineer *vb* to plan out usually with subtle skill or care ⟨the mayor *engineered* an agreement to have a major league team play in our city⟩
synonyms contrive, finagle, finesse, frame, machinate, maneuver, manipulate, mastermind, negotiate, wangle
related words arrange, concert, conclude, hammer out, work out; angle (for), compass, intrigue, plot, scheme; connive; brew, concoct, cook (up), hatch; captain, command, conduct, direct, handle, manage, quarterback, run; gerrymander
near antonyms blow, bobble, botch, bungle, butcher, flub, fumble, gum (up), louse up, mangle, mess (up), mishandle, muff

engird *vb, archaic* to encircle or bind with or as if with a belt ⟨her forehead *engirded* with a band of gold⟩ — see GIRD 1

engirdle *vb* to encircle or bind with or as if with a belt ⟨the cloud-*engirdled* peaks of the Andes⟩ — see GIRD 1

engrave *vb* **1** to cut (as letters or designs) on a hard surface ⟨*engraved* the birth and death dates on the tombstone⟩
synonyms etch, grave, incise, inscribe, insculp [*archaic*]
related words carve, chisel, sculpt, sculpture; chase, groove, indent, notch; score, trace; affix, impress
2 to produce a vivid impression of ⟨a scar that forever *engraved* the killer's face in the witness's mind⟩
synonyms brand, etch, impress, imprint, infix, ingrain (*also* engrain)
related words enroot, imbue, implant, inculcate, infuse, instill; fix, set, stamp
near antonyms blot out, erase, expunge, obliterate

engross *vb* to hold the attention of ⟨a mystery story that will *engross* readers all the way to the surprise ending⟩ — see ENGAGE 1

engrossed *adj* having the mind fixed on something ⟨I was too *engrossed* in the book to notice the time⟩ — see ATTENTIVE 1

engrossing *adj* holding the attention or provoking interest ⟨an *engrossing* lecture on Native American culture before the arrival of Europeans⟩ — see INTERESTING

engrossment *n* a focusing of the mind on something ⟨my *engrossment* in the video game made me lose track of time⟩ — see ATTENTION 1

engulf *vb* to cover with a flood ⟨high waves from the hurricane *engulfed* large areas of the coastal community⟩ — see FLOOD

enhance *vb* **1** to make better ⟨some shrubbery would really *enhance* the curb appeal of that house⟩ — see IMPROVE
2 to make markedly greater in measure or degree ⟨the right makeup would *enhance* the beauty of her eyes⟩ — see INTENSIFY
3 to make more desirable ⟨leather seats and a state-of-the-art stereo system *enhance* the sedan⟩ — see SWEETEN

enhancement *n* an instance of notable progress in the development of knowledge, technology, or skill ⟨the phenomenal *enhancements* that have been made in home electronic equipment⟩ — see ADVANCE 2

enigma *n* something hard to understand or explain ⟨how Thomas Jefferson could be both a slaveholder and a champion of liberty remains an *enigma*⟩ — see MYSTERY

enigmatic *also* **enigmatical** *adj* **1** being beyond one's powers to know, understand, or explain ⟨the discovery of the abandoned ship in mid ocean remains one of the most *enigmatic* episodes in seafaring history⟩ — see MYSTERIOUS 1
2 having an often intentionally veiled or uncertain

meaning ⟨the *Mona Lisa's enigmatic* smile⟩ — see OBSCURE 1

enjoin *vb* **1** to ask for (something) earnestly or with authority ⟨police *enjoined* the community's full cooperation in getting rid of the drug dealers⟩ — see DEMAND 1
2 to issue orders to (someone) by right of authority ⟨undeterred, the captain *enjoined* his crew to sail at full speed into the mine-filled harbor⟩ — see COMMAND 1
3 to order not to do or use or to be done or used ⟨Quakerism *enjoins* the taking of human life⟩ — see FORBID

enjoining *n* the act of ordering that something not be done or used ⟨the *enjoining* of the use of all tobacco products by the director of the baseball camp⟩ — see PROHIBITION 1

enjoy *vb* **1** to take pleasure in ⟨TV and DVDs are OK, but we still *enjoy* seeing movies on the big screen⟩
synonyms adore, delight (in), dig, fancy, get off (on), groove (on), like, love, rejoice (in), relish, revel (in), savor (*also* savour)
related words admire, appreciate, cherish, revere, venerate, worship; prize, treasure, value; devour, drink (in), eat (up), feast (on); dote (on), idolize; cotton (to), favor, prefer; indulge (in), luxuriate (in), wallow (in)
phrases be partial to, get a kick (*or* charge) out of, go for, have a soft spot for, take to
near antonyms abhor, abominate, detest, dislike, hate, loathe; condemn, despise, scorn
2 to keep, control, or experience as one's own ⟨a country where the people *enjoy* the highest living standards in the world⟩ — see HAVE 1

enjoyable *adj* **1** giving pleasure or contentment to the mind or senses ⟨the great food, service, and atmosphere made for a most *enjoyable* dinner⟩ — see PLEASANT 1
2 providing amusement or enjoyment ⟨the theme park's great variety of attractions mean that every member of the family will have an *enjoyable* time⟩ — see FUN

enjoyably *adv* in a pleasing way ⟨an *enjoyably* goofy comedy⟩ — see WELL 5

enjoyment *n* **1** the fact or state of having (something) at one's disposal ⟨a scenic walkway along the ocean shore that is intended for the *enjoyment* of all⟩ — see POSSESSION 1
2 the feeling experienced when one's wishes are met ⟨this new video game should provide countless hours of *enjoyment*⟩ — see PLEASURE 1

enkindle *vb* to set (something) on fire ⟨see if you can *enkindle* some paper in the fireplace while I look for logs⟩ — see BURN 2

enlace *vb* to cause to twine about one another ⟨*enlaced* the strips of leather to create a decorative headband⟩ — see INTERTWINE 1

enlarge *vb* **1** to become greater in extent, volume, amount, or number ⟨as the number of people with cell phones *enlarges*, more transmission towers will have to be built⟩ — see INCREASE 2
2 to make greater in size, amount, or number ⟨with a new member of the family on the way, maybe we should consider *enlarging* the house⟩ — see INCREASE 1
3 to set free (as from slavery or confinement) ⟨like a wild animal *enlarged* from a leghold trap, the freed prisoner raced about⟩ — see FREE 1

enlarge (on *or* upon) *vb* to express more fully and in greater detail ⟨in your complaint, don't just say that your neighbor has been harassing you; *enlarge on* what you mean by that⟩ — see EXPAND 1

enlighten *vb* **1** to give information to ⟨the lecturer at the planetarium *enlightened* us about the latest astronomical discoveries⟩
synonyms acquaint, advise, apprise, brief, catch up, clear, clue (in), familiarize, fill in, hip, inform, instruct, tell, verse, wise (up)
related words advertise, alert, notify; announce (to), disclose (to); assure, certify, convince, reassure, warrant; educate, lecture, school, teach, tutor; disabuse, disenchant, disillusion, undeceive
phrases keep (one) posted, let (one) know
near antonyms misinform, mislead
2 to provide (someone) with moral or spiritual understanding ⟨many people around the world have been *enlightened* by the teachings of Gautama Buddha⟩
synonyms edify, educate, illume, illuminate, illumine, inspire, nurture
related words elevate, ennoble, enrich, ensoul, lift, uplift; better, improve, regenerate, renew, transform; exalt, glorify, transfigure
near antonyms confuse, perplex, puzzle; becloud, cloud, darken, obscure

enlightening *adj* providing useful information or knowledge ⟨an *enlightening* pamphlet about the major changes that consumers can expect from their cable and Internet service providers⟩ — see INFORMATIVE

enlist (in) *vb* to become a member of ⟨young men and women were *enlisting in* the navy in greater numbers⟩ — see ENTER 2

enliven *vb* to give life, vigor, or spirit to ⟨in most instances it's a good idea to *enliven* a speech with a joke or two⟩ — see ANIMATE

enmesh *also* **immesh** *vb* to catch or hold as if in a net ⟨soon after Eli Whitney had invented it, others copied his cotton gin, and he spent the rest of his life *enmeshed* in lawsuits trying to protect his invention⟩ — see ENTANGLE 2

enmity *n* a deep-seated ill will ⟨*enmity* had existed between the two families for generations⟩
synonyms animosity, animus, antagonism, antipathy, bad blood, bitterness, gall, grudge, hostility, jaundice, rancor
related words blood feud, feud, score, vendetta; hate, hatred, loathing; vindictiveness, virulence, vitriol; alienation, disaffection, estrangement; conflict, coolness, discord, friction, strain, tension; inhospitableness, unfriendliness; malice, malignancy, malignity, spite, spitefulness, venom
near antonyms amiability, amicability, civility, cordiality, friendliness, hospitality, neighborliness; comity, empathy, friendship, goodwill, sympathy, understanding
antonyms amity

ennoble *vb* to assign a high status or value to ⟨the heroic actions of firefighters during the terrorist attack did much to *ennoble* the profession of fire fighting in the public mind⟩ — see EXALT 1

ennui *n* the state of being bored ⟨the kind of *ennui* that comes from having too much time on one's hands and too little will to find something productive to do⟩ — see BOREDOM

enormity *n* **1** the state or quality of being utterly evil ⟨the *enormity* of the crimes committed by the Nazis⟩
synonyms atrociousness, atrocity, badness, depravedness, depravity, diabolicalness, evilness, heinousness, hideousness, monstrosity, sinfulness, vileness, wickedness
related words accursedness, baseness, cursedness, devilishness, execrableness, fiendishness, hellishness; corruption, decadence, degeneracy, pervertedness; immorality; infamy, notoriety
near antonyms morality; chasteness, innocence, purity
antonyms goodness, righteousness, virtuousness
2 the quality or state of being very large ⟨the *enormity* of the canyon can only be grasped by taking a trip through its entire length⟩ — see IMMENSITY

enormous *adj* unusually large ⟨that pumpkin is so *enormous* that it has to be a record holder⟩ — see HUGE

enormously *adv* **1** to a great degree ⟨an *enormously* entertaining film⟩ — see VERY 1
2 to a large extent or degree ⟨the neighbors have been *enormously* helpful during this difficult time⟩ — see GREATLY 2

enormousness *n* the quality or state of being very large ⟨the *enormousness* of the mall is such that one could shop at a different store for every day of the year⟩ — see IMMENSITY

enough *adv* **1** in or to a degree or quantity that meets one's requirements or satisfaction ⟨the elevator is big *enough* to hold everyone⟩
synonyms adequately, satisfactorily, sufficiently, suitably
related words acceptably, decently, fairly, moderately, passably, tolerably; meetly, properly, rightly, seemly; agreeably, gratifyingly, satisfyingly; abundantly, amply, aplenty, optimally, plenteously, plentifully; commensurately, proportionately
antonyms inadequately, insufficiently, unsatisfactorily
2 to some degree or extent ⟨I can play the piano well *enough*, but I have no hope for a musical career⟩ — see FAIRLY 1
3 to a full extent or degree ⟨I think we're prepared *enough*—we just lack the will to actually do it⟩ — see FULLY 1

en passant *adv* by way of interjection or digression ⟨she mentioned *en passant* that she'd been to New York⟩ — see APROPOS

enrage *vb* to make angry ⟨the fact that the auto garage bungled the repair and then overcharged him simply *enraged* the customer⟩ — see ANGER

enraged *adj* feeling or showing anger ⟨the repair shop owner tore up the bill when he saw the *enraged* look on the customer's face⟩ — see ANGRY

enrapt *adj* experiencing or marked by overwhelming usually pleasurable emotion ⟨*enrapt* concertgoers just sat there in motionless silence as the pianist flawlessly executed the piece⟩ — see ECSTATIC

enrapture *vb* **1** to fill with great joy ⟨*enraptured* upon learning that he would be attending college on a full sports scholarship⟩ — see ELATE
2 to fill with overwhelming emotion (as wonder or delight) ⟨this classic ballet of the Christmas season never fails to *enrapture* audiences young and old⟩ — see ENTRANCE

enraptured *adj* experiencing or marked by overwhelming usually pleasurable emotion ⟨the *enraptured* look on the fans' faces during the band's concerts⟩ — see ECSTATIC

enraptured (by) *adj* filled with an intense or excessive love for ⟨her friends have noticed that she usually becomes totally *enraptured by* her latest boyfriend—for about a month⟩ — see ENAMORED (OF)

enrich *vb* **1** to make better ⟨a truly great book can *enrich* your life⟩ — see IMPROVE
2 to make more attractive by adding something that is beautiful or becoming ⟨the church's magnificent interior is *enriched* with stunningly beautiful murals⟩ — see DECORATE

enrobe *vb* to outfit with clothes and especially fine or special clothes ⟨dreamed that one day she would be *enrobed* in satins and silks⟩ — see CLOTHE 1

enroll *also* **enrol** *vb* **1** to add (a person) to a list or roll as a participant or member ⟨the community college will *enroll* anyone who has a GED or high school diploma⟩
synonyms inscribe, list, matriculate, register
related words enlist, impanel, induct; conscript, draft, muster; wait-list; book, schedule; check in
near antonyms check off; exclude, expel, expunge, reject; omit, overlook
antonyms delist
2 to put (someone or something) on a list ⟨can I *enroll* you on the list of volunteers for the church supper?⟩ — see [1]LIST 2

enroll (in) *vb* to become a member of ⟨she *enrolled in* the Democratic Party after being a Republican for most of her life⟩ — see ENTER 2

enrollment *also* **enrolment** *n* the number of individuals registered ⟨the school's *enrollment* currently stands at 500⟩ — see REGISTRATION

enroot *vb* **1** to set permanently in the consciousness or mind-set ⟨everyone remembers that special teacher who *enrooted* within them a love of learning⟩ — see IMPLANT 1
2 to set solidly in or as if in surrounding matter ⟨a deeply *enrooted* tradition of respect for the elderly⟩ — see ENTRENCH

ensconce *vb* **1** to establish or place comfortably or snugly ⟨the kids had contentedly *ensconced* themselves on the couch before the TV⟩ ⟨happily *ensconced* in her new home⟩
synonyms install, lodge, nestle, perch, roost, settle
related words deploy, emplace, fix, locate, park, plant, position, set, situate, station; anchor, bivouac, camp, camp (out); burrow, curl up, dig in; harbor, house
2 to put into a hiding place ⟨*ensconced* the spare house key in a place where no intruder would think to look⟩ — see [1]HIDE 1

enshrine *vb* to assign a high status or value to ⟨some teachers tend to *enshrine* their personal preferences as sacred rules of English grammar⟩ — see EXALT 1

enshroud *vb* **1** to keep secret or shut off from view ⟨the criminal organization uses a strictly enforced vow of silence to *enshroud* its villainous doings⟩ — see [1]HIDE 2
2 to surround or cover closely ⟨a dense fog *enshrouded* the bridge spanning the harbor⟩ — see ENFOLD 1

ensign *n* **1** a device, design, or figure used as an identifying mark ⟨that *ensign* of tutorial authority, the hickory stick⟩ — see EMBLEM
2 a piece of cloth with a special design that is used as an emblem or for signaling ⟨fittingly, the organization promoting the welfare of marine life features a dolphin on its *ensign*⟩ — see FLAG 1

ensky *vb* to assign a high status or value to ⟨a society that seems to have *enskied* celebrity as an end in itself⟩ — see EXALT 1

enslavement *n* the state of being a slave ⟨having known the misery of *enslavement* first hand, Frederick Douglass went on devote his life to the cause of making others free⟩ — see SLAVERY 1

ensnare *vb* to catch or hold as if in a net ⟨parked just out of view, the state trooper was lying in wait to *ensnare* unwary speeders⟩ — see ENTANGLE 2

ensnarl *vb* to catch or hold as if in a net ⟨for two years the couple was *ensnarled* in the red tape of an international adoption⟩ — see ENTANGLE 2

ensorcell *or* **ensorcel** *vb* to cast a spell on ⟨a dense, dark forest that is the scene for many a tale in which some unsuspecting traveler is *ensorcelled* by a witch or wizard⟩ — see BEWITCH 1

ensorcellment *n* the power to control natural forces through supernatural means ⟨in the fairy tales collected by the Brothers Grimm, Germany's Black Forest figures prominently as a land of *ensorcellment* and mystery⟩ — see MAGIC 1

ensuing *adj* **1** being the one that comes immediately after another ⟨business was slow in the restaurant's first year, but the *ensuing* year saw a much-needed increase⟩ — see NEXT
2 being, occurring, or carried out at a time after something else ⟨the war and the *ensuing* famine caused unimaginable suffering⟩ — see SUBSEQUENT

ensure *vb* to make sure, certain, or safe ⟨regulations

that *ensure* the wholesomeness of our food⟩
synonyms assure, cinch, guarantee, guaranty, ice, insure, secure
related words attest, certify, vouch, warrant, witness; pledge, promise, swear
near antonyms enfeeble, undermine, weaken

enswathe *vb* to surround or cover closely ⟨swelling buds still *enswathed* in their furry overcoats⟩ — see ENFOLD 1

entail *vb* to have as part of a whole ⟨a lavish wedding *entails* extensive planning and often staggering expense⟩ — see INCLUDE 1

entangle *vb* **1** to twist together into a usually confused mass ⟨in the process of taking down the Christmas tree, we managed to *entangle* the string of lights into a hopeless mess of wires⟩
synonyms interlace, intertwine, intertwist, interweave, knot, snarl, tangle
related words jumble, scrabble, scramble; braid, enlace, entwine, entwist, inweave, plait, twine, weave, wind, wreathe, writhe
near antonyms unknot, unravel, unscramble; unweave
antonyms disentangle, unsnarl, untangle, untwine, untwist
2 to catch or hold as if in a net ⟨the young runaway gradually became *entangled* in a web of lies⟩
synonyms catch up, enmesh (*also* immesh), ensnare, ensnarl, entoil, entrap, mesh, net, snare, tangle, trap
related words bag, birdlime, capture, collar; embroil, implicate, involve, mire
near antonyms detach, disengage, extricate; clear, free, liberate
antonyms disentangle, untangle
3 to make complex or difficult ⟨the history of Alexander the Great is *entangled* by variant accounts of his exploits⟩ — see COMPLICATE 1

entanglement *n* something that catches and holds ⟨his life is greatly complicated by his romantic *entanglements*⟩ — see WEB 1

enter *vb* **1** to go or come in or into ⟨the hikers *entered* the cave with considerable caution⟩
synonyms access, penetrate, pierce
related words barge (in), breeze (in), burst (in *or* into), waltz (in); drop in, pop (in); stray (into), wander (into); crash, encroach, gate-crash, infiltrate, infringe, intrude, invade, trespass
phrases set foot in, step into
antonyms depart, exit, leave
2 to become a member of ⟨patriotic young men and women *entering* the armed services⟩ ⟨debutantes *entering* society⟩
synonyms enlist (in), enroll (in), join, sign on (for), sign up (for)
related words reenlist, reenroll, reenter, rejoin, re-up; get in
near antonyms drop out, quit, withdraw
antonyms demit
3 to put (someone or something) on a list ⟨new voters fill out a form and elections officials *enter* their names into the database⟩ — see [1]LIST 2
4 to offer entrance (as to a place, school, or privilege) to ⟨the club *enters* only five new members a year⟩ — see ADMIT 2

enter (into *or* upon) *vb* to take the first step in (a process or course of action) ⟨a series of counseling sessions intended to help young couples about to *enter into* the trials and tribulations of marriage⟩ — see BEGIN 1

enterprise *n* **1** a commercial or industrial activity or organization ⟨the booming economy witnessed the launch of many small *enterprises*⟩
synonyms business, company, concern, establishment, firm, house, interest, outfit
related words conglomerate, corporation, multinational; association, cartel, chain, combine, syndicate, trust; agency, dealer, outlet; microenterprise
2 readiness to engage in daring or difficult activity ⟨the *enterprise* shown by the early developers and promoters of personal computers⟩
synonyms action, aggressiveness, ambition, drive, go, hustle, initiative
related words grit, gumption, pluck, snap, spirit, spunk, starch; ambitiousness, killer instinct, overambitiousness; assertiveness, self-reliance; energy, hardihood, pep, vigor, vitality
near antonyms inactivity, inertia, passivity; diffidence, faintheartedness, timidity; hesitation, reluctance; indolence, laziness, lethargy
3 a risky undertaking ⟨the general viewed the proposed invasion as a military *enterprise* that offered no easy way out⟩ — see GAMBLE

enterprising *adj* **1** having or showing a bold forcefulness in the pursuit of a goal ⟨the company is claiming that there will be huge financial rewards for *enterprising* sales representatives⟩ — see AGGRESSIVE 1
2 inclined or willing to take risks ⟨*enterprising* people of vision were responsible for the boom in technological industries⟩ — see BOLD 1

entertain *vb* **1** to cause (someone) to pass the time agreeably occupied ⟨*entertain* the kids while I go and prepare dinner⟩ — see AMUSE
2 to give serious and careful thought to ⟨have you ever *entertained* the thought that you could be wrong?⟩ — see PONDER
3 to keep in one's mind or heart ⟨I don't *entertain* the hope of ever getting a girl like that to go out with me⟩ — see HARBOR 1

entertaining *adj* providing amusement or enjoyment ⟨a list of *entertaining* things to do on a snow day⟩ — see FUN

entertainment *n* **1** the act or activity of providing pleasure or amusement especially for the public ⟨we didn't stay for the featured *entertainment* because we don't care for comedy acts⟩ ⟨the film is purely for *entertainment* and not meant to be taken seriously⟩
synonyms amusement, diversion, recreation
related words nightlife, show business; delectation, delight, enjoyment, joy, mirth; gratification, relaxation, relief, satisfaction; exhibition, performance, presentation, presentment, production, show, spectacle; escapism
2 someone or something that provides amusement or enjoyment ⟨what do you do for *entertainment* in this town?⟩ — see FUN 1

enthrall *or* **enthral** *vb* **1** to hold the attention of as if by a spell ⟨*enthralled* by the flickering fire in the hearth, we lost all track of time⟩
synonyms arrest, bedazzle, catch up, enchant, fascinate, grip, hypnotize, mesmerize, spellbind
related words enrapture, entrance, thrill; beguile, bewitch, charm; absorb, engage, engross, involve
2 to fill with overwhelming emotion (as wonder or delight) ⟨for years these master magicians have been *enthralling* audiences with their astounding illusions⟩ — see ENTRANCE
3 to hold the attention of ⟨a play that will *enthrall* you for two hours⟩ — see ENGAGE 1

enthralled *adj* having the mind fixed on something ⟨gave her speech to several hundred *enthralled* listeners⟩ — see ATTENTIVE

enthralling *adj* holding the attention or provoking interest ⟨an *enthralling* account of life in the scientific community in Antarctica⟩ — see INTERESTING

enthrallment *n* a focusing of the mind on something ⟨the child's *enthrallment* with the new toy lasted about

30 minutes⟩ — see ATTENTION 1

enthrone *vb* to assign a high status or value to ⟨the literary world has *enthroned* Shakespeare for so long that his preeminence among writers seems unassailable⟩ — see EXALT 1

enthuse *vb* to make an exaggerated display of affection or enthusiasm ⟨the neighbors invited us over just so we could *enthuse* over their new car⟩ — see GUSH 2

enthused *adj* showing urgent desire or interest ⟨you don't seem that *enthused* about the idea⟩ — see EAGER

enthusiasm *n* **1** a practice or interest that is very popular for a short time ⟨this year's *enthusiasm* is often next year's laughingstock⟩ — see FAD

2 urgent desire or interest ⟨in my *enthusiasm* to get going, I forgot to pack any foul-weather clothing⟩ — see EAGERNESS

3 depth of feeling ⟨spoke about wildlife conservation with evident *enthusiasm*⟩ — see ARDOR 1

enthusiast *n* a person with a strong and habitual liking for something ⟨skiing *enthusiasts* can't wait for the first snowfall of the season⟩ — see FAN

enthusiastic *adj* showing urgent desire or interest ⟨as soon as the gates to the concert area opened, *enthusiastic* fans rushed to get the best seats⟩ — see EAGER

enthusiastically *adv* in an enthusiastic manner ⟨sportswriters have praised this new pitching find so *enthusiastically* you'd think he's going to pitch nothing but no-hitters⟩ — see SKY-HIGH

entice *vb* to lead away from a usual or proper course by offering some pleasure or advantage ⟨every commercial seemed to be for some tempting snack specifically designed to *entice* me from my diet⟩ — see LURE

enticement *n* **1** something that persuades one to perform an action for pleasure or gain ⟨the hospital often offers T-shirts or caps as *enticements* for people to donate blood⟩ — see LURE 1

2 the act or pressure of giving in to a desire especially when ill-advised ⟨the *enticement* of the party buffet was just too great to ignore for very long⟩ — see TEMPTATION 1

entire *adj* **1** not divided or scattered among several areas of interest or concern ⟨this matter is important, so please give me your *entire* attention⟩ — see WHOLE 1

2 not lacking any part or member that properly belongs to it ⟨the *entire* team needs to be present for the photograph⟩ — see COMPLETE 1

entire *adv* to a full extent or degree ⟨a shocking revelation that would destroy *entire* the false little world that she had carefully constructed for herself⟩ — see FULLY 1

entirely *adv* to a full extent or degree ⟨are you *entirely* aware of what you're doing with that thing?⟩ — see FULLY 1

entireness *n* the quality or state of being without restriction, exception, or qualification ⟨impressed by the *entireness* of his commitment to the cause of equal rights for all⟩

synonyms absoluteness, completeness, entirety, fullness, perfectness, wholeness

related words faultlessness, flawlessness, indefectibility, perfection; all-inclusiveness, comprehensiveness, exhaustiveness, extensiveness, inclusiveness, soundness, thoroughness

near antonyms inadequacy, inadequateness; limitedness, narrowness, patchiness, sketchiness

antonyms imperfection, imperfectness, incompleteness, unsoundness

entirety *n* the quality or state of being without restriction, exception, or qualification ⟨I wish that I could find a card for Valentine's Day that expresses the *entirety* of my love⟩ — see ENTIRENESS

entitle *vb* **1** to give a right to ⟨the card *entitles* my grandmother to the discount for senior citizens⟩

synonyms authorize, privilege, qualify

related words empower, enable, enfranchise, license (*also* licence); approve, endorse (*also* indorse); allow, let, permit; accredit, certificate, certify, charter [*British*], ratify; legitimize, sanction, validate, warrant; reaccredit, reapprove, recertify, recharter, revalidate

near antonyms disable, disempower, disenfranchise; decertify; disallow, forbid, proscribe; delegitimize, invalidate, nullify

antonyms disqualify

2 to give a name to ⟨apart from the obvious, she couldn't decide what to *entitle* her painting of a vase with flowers⟩ — see NAME 1

entitlement *n* a sum of money allotted for a specific use by official or formal action ⟨*entitlements* to local school districts⟩ — see APPROPRIATION 1

entity *n* one that has a real and independent existence ⟨the question of whether extrasensory perception will ever be a scientifically recognized *entity*⟩

synonyms being, commodity, existent, individual, individuality, integer, object, reality, something, substance, thing

related words body, subject; material, matter, quantity, stuff

near antonyms nonentity

entoil *vb* to catch or hold as if in a net ⟨*entoiled* by the strings of fate⟩ — see ENTANGLE 2

entomb *vb* to place (a dead body) in the earth, a tomb, or the sea ⟨a number of Boston's historic notables are *entombed* in the Old Granary Burying Ground⟩ — see BURY 1

entombing *n* the act or ceremony of putting a dead body in its final resting place ⟨the *entombing* of the pharaohs in the pyramids must have been a magnificent sight⟩ — see BURIAL 1

entombment *n* the act or ceremony of putting a dead body in its final resting place ⟨the *entombment* of President Kennedy in Arlington National Cemetery⟩ — see BURIAL 1

entourage *n* a body of employees or servants who accompany and wait on a person ⟨the gaggle of hangers-on that passes for the rock star's *entourage*⟩ — see CORTEGE 1

entrails *n pl* the internal organs of the body ⟨in ancient Rome predictions of future events would sometimes be based on an examination of the *entrails* of a sacrificial animal⟩ — see GUT 1

entrance *n* **1** the means or right of entering or participating in ⟨*entrance* to the club is by invitation only⟩

synonyms access, accession, admission, admittance, door, doorway, entrée (*or* entree), entry, gateway, ingress, key, passport, ticket

related words approval, authorization, certification, permission, qualification; open door, welcome mat

near antonyms discharge, dismissal, ejection, expulsion, ouster, rejection, removal

2 the opening through which one can enter or leave a structure ⟨when you come, use the *entrance* on the right side of the building⟩ — see DOOR 2

entrance *vb* to fill with overwhelming emotion (as wonder or delight) ⟨a production of *The Nutcracker* ballet that will *entrance* audiences⟩

synonyms carry away, enrapture, enthrall (*or* enthral), rap, rapture, ravish, transport

related words delight, gladden, gratify, please, satisfy; bewitch, captivate, charm, enchant, fascinate; elate, excite, exhilarate, stir

phrases knock dead, knock one's socks off

entranced *adj* **1** being or appearing to be under a magic spell ⟨a striking beauty who was accustomed to having

entranced and tongue-tied young suitors⟩ — see ENCHANTED
2 experiencing or marked by overwhelming usually pleasurable emotion ⟨the *entranced* look on her face as she danced at the ball⟩ — see ECSTATIC

entranceway *n* the entrance room of a building ⟨the visitor thoughtfully removed her snow-covered hat and gloves in the *entranceway*⟩ — see HALL 1

entrancing *adj* having an often mysterious or magical power to attract ⟨travelers to India say that it has an *entrancing* beauty that is hard to describe⟩ — see FASCINATING 1

entrap *vb* to catch or hold as if in a net ⟨a string of inconsistent statements and outright lies that finally *entrapped* the witness⟩ — see ENTANGLE 2

entreat *vb* to make a request to (someone) in an earnest or urgent manner ⟨she began her letter by *entreating* me to forgive the belatedness of her reply⟩ — see BEG

entreating *adj* asking humbly ⟨it was hard to refuse such an amusingly *entreating* panhandler⟩ — see SUPPLIANT

entreaty *n* an earnest request ⟨our *entreaties* to give us another few minutes to answer the test questions fell on deaf ears⟩ — see PLEA 1

entrée *or* **entree** *n* the means or right of entering or participating in ⟨*entrée* to the country club is through sponsorship by someone who is already a member⟩ — see ENTRANCE 1

entrench *also* **intrench** *vb* to set solidly in or as if in surrounding matter ⟨a father who *entrenched* in our minds the belief that hard work pays off⟩
synonyms bed, embed (*also* imbed), enroot, fix, impact, implant, ingrain (*also* engrain), lodge, root
related words imbue, infuse, instill; beat (into), drive (into); establish, place, put, settle, stick
near antonyms eliminate, eradicate; eject, expel; detach, disconnect, disengage, remove
antonyms dislodge, root (out), uproot

entrenched *also* **intrenched** *adj* firmly established over time ⟨I have an *entrenched* dislike of mimes⟩ — see INVETERATE 1

entrust *also* **intrust** *vb* **1** to give a task, duty, or responsibility to ⟨we *entrusted* our financial adviser with the investment of all of our savings⟩
synonyms assign, charge, commission, task, trust
related words confer, impose; commit, confide, consign, delegate, recommend, relegate, repose; allocate, allot; authorize, empower, invest
2 to put (something) into the possession or safekeeping of another ⟨we *entrusted* our pets to the care of our neighbor while we went on vacation⟩ — see GIVE 2

entry *n* **1** the entrance room of a building ⟨please wait in the *entry* while I get the person you want⟩ — see HALL 1
2 the means or right of entering or participating in ⟨believed that a college education was one's *entry* to a life of luxury⟩ — see ENTRANCE 1

entryway *n* the entrance room of a building ⟨a small *entryway* to receive visitors⟩ — see HALL 1

entwine *vb* **1** to cause to twine about one another ⟨marveled at how the vines had delicately and intricately *entwined* themselves on the trellis⟩ — see INTERTWINE 1
2 to follow a circular or spiral course ⟨the quick-growing vine was soon *entwining* around the fence post⟩ — see WIND 1

enumerate *vb* **1** to specify one after another ⟨I proceeded to *enumerate* the reasons why I would be justified in filing a lawsuit for negligence⟩
synonyms detail, itemize, list, numerate, recite, reel off, rehearse, tick (off)
related words outline; tabulate, tally; catalog (*or* catalogue), inventory; chart, diagram, graph; calculate, compute, estimate, figure, reckon; cite, mention, name
near antonyms generalize
2 to find the sum of (a collection of things) by noting each one as it is being added ⟨there were more birds hovering about the bird feeder than I could possibly *enumerate*⟩ — see COUNT 1
3 to make a list of ⟨let's *enumerate* the top ten reasons why Top Ten lists have gotten out of hand⟩ — see [1]LIST 1

enunciate *vb* **1** to utter clearly and distinctly ⟨*enunciate* your words, and then you won't have to repeat them so often⟩ — see ARTICULATE 1
2 to make known openly or publicly ⟨today the President *enunciated* a new foreign policy⟩ — see ANNOUNCE
3 to express (a thought or emotion) in words ⟨a paper that *enunciates* the goals of the environmental organization⟩ — see SAY 1

enunciation *n* the clear and accurate pronunciation of words especially in public speaking ⟨a radio announcer who is known for his very careful *enunciation*⟩ — see DICTION 1

envelop *vb* **1** to close or shut in by or as if by barriers ⟨a chronic mistrust of outsiders *envelops* that neighborhood, cutting it off from the rest of the city⟩ — see ENCLOSE 1
2 to surround or cover closely ⟨the truth of the presidential assassination is *enveloped* in a dense fog of myths and conspiracy theories⟩ — see ENFOLD 1

envenom *vb* to implant bitter feelings in ⟨thoughtless, self-indulgent antics that only managed to *envenom* his teammates⟩ — see EMBITTER

envenomed *adj* containing or contaminated with a substance capable of injuring or killing a living thing ⟨the *envenomed* spines of these tropical fishes make them a particular hazard of coral reefs⟩ — see POISONOUS

envious *adj* having or showing mean resentment of another's possessions or advantages ⟨a family that is *envious* of their neighbors' big house⟩
synonyms covetous, green-eyed, invidious, jaundiced, jealous, resentful
related words begrudging, grudging; avaricious, grasping, greedy, rapacious; distrustful, suspicious; malicious, petty, spiteful
phrases eating one's heart out, green with envy
near antonyms generous, kind, kindhearted; altruistic, benevolent, charitable; well-meaning
antonyms unenvious

enviousness *n* a painful awareness of another's possessions or advantages and a desire to have them too ⟨Lisa's *enviousness* of Debra's athletic achievements was obvious to all of their friends⟩ — see ENVY

environ *vb* to form a circle around ⟨a decaying, impoverished city *environed* by affluent suburbs⟩ — see SURROUND

environment *n* the circumstances, conditions, or objects by which one is surrounded ⟨the joys of growing up in the *environment* that a small town offers⟩
synonyms ambient, atmosphere, climate, clime, context, contexture, environs, medium, milieu, mise-en-scène, setting, surround, surroundings, terrain
related words location, place, position, space; backdrop, background; element; situation, status; geography, habitat; microenvironment

environs *n pl* **1** the districts adjacent to a city ⟨the city and its *environs* total about a million in population⟩
synonyms outskirts, purlieus, suburbia
related words country, countryside, exurbia
near antonyms core city, downtown, inner city, midtown
2 an adjoining region or space ⟨you can get just about

any kind of ethnic food in the *environs* of the university⟩
synonyms backyard, neighborhood, purlieus, vicinage, vicinity
related words environment, surround, surroundings
3 the circumstances, conditions, or objects by which one is surrounded ⟨growing up in the *environs* of the inner city wasn't easy, but he was determined to make something of himself⟩ — see ENVIRONMENT

envisage *vb* to form a mental picture of ⟨I'm trying to *envisage* you on a surfboard⟩ — see IMAGINE 1

envision *vb* to form a mental picture of ⟨challenged the voters to *envision* a nation in which no child was ever allowed to go hungry⟩ — see IMAGINE 1

envoy *n* **1** a person sent on a mission to represent another ⟨the president sent the secretary of state as his personal *envoy* to gain the support of the country's allies⟩ — see AMBASSADOR
2 a person who acts or does business for another ⟨one of the hostage takers was chosen as the group's *envoy* for all dealings with the authorities⟩ — see AGENT 2

envy *n* a painful awareness of another's possessions or advantages and a desire to have them too ⟨her *envy* of her neighbor's fancy clothes wrecked their friendship⟩
synonyms covetousness, enviousness, green-eyed monster, invidiousness, jealousy, resentment
related words animosity, enmity, hatred, ill will; malice, maliciousness, spitefulness
near antonyms benevolence, goodwill, kindness, sympathy

envy *vb* to have a resentful awareness of and desire for (another's possessions or advantages) or to feel resentment toward (someone) over possessions or advantages ⟨her coworkers *envied* her chummy relationship with the senior vice president⟩ ⟨the other mothers *envied* her because she didn't have to work⟩
synonyms begrudge, resent
related words ache (for), covet, crave, desire, die (for), hanker (for *or* after), hunger (for), itch (for), jones (for) [*slang*], long (for), lust (for *or* after), pant (after), thirst (for), want, wish (for), yearn (for), yen (for); salivate

enwind *vb* to encircle or bind with or as if with a belt ⟨a parcel *enwound* with red ribbons⟩ — see GIRD 1

enwrap *vb* **1** to hold the attention of ⟨*enwrapped* in my own reverie, I failed to notice the coworker standing outside my cubicle⟩ — see ENGAGE 1
2 to surround or cover closely ⟨an air of serene self-satisfaction *enwraps* the leafy, well-to-do suburb⟩ — see ENFOLD 1

ephemeral *adj* lasting only for a short time ⟨the autumnal blaze of colors is always to be treasured, all the more so because it is so *ephemeral*⟩ — see MOMENTARY

ephemerality *n* the state or quality of lasting only for a short time ⟨never has the *ephemerality* of fame been more apparent than in today's pop culture⟩ — see IMPERMANENCE

epic *adj* large and impressive in size, grandeur, extent, or conception ⟨an *epic* plan for the revitalization of the city⟩ — see GRAND 1

epicene *adj* of or relating to a man who has or displays qualities considered more suitable for women ⟨an ancient statue of a young man of graceful, *epicene* beauty⟩ — see EFFEMINATE

epicenter *n* a thing or place that is of greatest importance to an activity or interest ⟨by continually reinventing itself, Las Vegas has managed to remain a national *epicenter* for entertainment⟩ — see CENTER 1

epicure *n* a person with refined tastes in food and wine ⟨Thomas Jefferson was one of America's first great *epicures*⟩
synonyms bon vivant, epicurean, gastronome, gastronomist, gourmand, gourmet
related words connoisseur, dilettante; foodie; savorer; oenophile, turophile
near antonyms glutton, gorger, guzzler, hog, overeater, stuffer, swiller, trencherman

epicurean *n* a person with refined tastes in food and wine ⟨an *epicurean* with a beautifully equipped kitchen⟩ — see EPICURE

epidemic *adj* exciting a similar feeling or reaction in others ⟨the little girl's giggles were *epidemic*, and soon the entire gathering was laughing⟩ — see CONTAGIOUS 2

epigone *n* one who follows the opinions or teachings of another ⟨few of director Alfred Hitchcock's many *epigones* possess much of the master's wit or style⟩ — see FOLLOWER 1

epigonic *or* **epigonous** *adj* using or marked by the use of something else as a basis or model ⟨an epic novel that would eventually spawn a vast body of *epigonic* and decidedly inferior fiction⟩ — see IMITATIVE 1

epigram *n* an often stated observation regarding something from common experience ⟨Benjamin Franklin's famous *epigram*, "Remember that time is money"⟩ — see SAYING

epigrammatic *adj* marked by the use of few words to convey much information or meaning ⟨Oscar Wilde's *epigrammatic* observation, "In America the young are always ready to give to those who are older than themselves the full benefits of their inexperience"⟩ — see CONCISE

episode *n* something that happens ⟨the *episode* in which the Native American Samoset walked into Plymouth Plantation and surprised the Pilgrims with the greeting, "Welcome, Englishman"⟩ — see EVENT 1

episodic *also* **episodical** *adj* **1** appearing in parts or numbers that follow regularly ⟨the long novel was filmed for television as an *episodic* movie that was shown over the course of five evenings⟩ — see SERIAL
2 lacking in steadiness or regularity of occurrence ⟨malaria is characterized by *episodic* attacks of chills and fever that coincide with mass destruction of blood cells⟩ — see FITFUL

epistle *n* a message on paper from one person or group to another ⟨the *epistles* of Saint Paul to various communities of early Christians⟩ — see [1]LETTER

epithet *n* **1** a descriptive or familiar name given instead of or in addition to the one belonging to an individual ⟨King Richard I of England was given the very laudatory *epithet* "the Lion-Hearted"⟩ — see NICKNAME
2 an act or expression showing scorn and usually intended to hurt another's feelings ⟨the school has a strict ban against the use of racial, ethnic, religious, and sexual *epithets*⟩ — see INSULT

epitome *n* **1** a short statement of the main points ⟨the golden rule is often cited as the *epitome* of moral conduct: "Do unto others as you would have them do unto you"⟩ — see SUMMARY
2 a visible representation of something abstract (as a quality) ⟨the prestigious prep school prides itself on being widely regarded as the *epitome* of tradition and old-fashioned values⟩ — see EMBODIMENT
3 the most perfect type or example ⟨Mahatma Gandhi is often cited as the *epitome* of resolute reformer who uses nonviolence to bring about social and political change⟩ — see QUINTESSENCE 1

epitomize *vb* **1** to make into a short statement of the main points (as of a report) ⟨his personal code of behavior on the playing field is *epitomized* by his favorite saying, "Nice guys finish last"⟩ — see SUMMARIZE
2 to represent in visible form ⟨the Parthenon in Athens *epitomizes* the ancient Greek ideal of architectural beauty⟩ — see EMBODY 2

epoch *n* an extent of time associated with a particular person or thing ⟨Sir Isaac Newton is usually credited with establishing the *epoch* of modern science⟩ — see AGE 1

equable *adj* marked by temperatures that are neither too high nor too low ⟨an area with an *equable* climate would be our first choice for a place in which to settle⟩ — see CLEMENT 1

equal *adj* **1** marked by justice, honesty, and freedom from bias ⟨the basic belief that everyone is entitled to *equal* opportunity in employment⟩ — see FAIR 2
2 resembling another in every respect ⟨as far as I can see, except for the high price, the store-brand jacket is *equal* to the jacket with the designer label⟩ — see SAME 1
3 having the required skills for an acceptable level of performance ⟨looking for someone *equal* to the challenge of running a large state university⟩ — see COMPETENT 1
4 free from emotional or mental agitation ⟨he proceeded, in an *equal* tone, to recount the terrible events of the day⟩ — see CALM 2

equal *n* one that is equal to another in status, achievement, or value ⟨a basketball player who truly has no *equal* in his sport⟩
synonyms coequal, compeer, coordinate, counterpart, equivalent, fellow, like, match, parallel, peer, rival
related words analogue (*or* analog); double, half, mate, twin; associate, colleague, companion, copartner, partner; competitor

equal *vb* **1** to produce something equal to (as in quality or value) ⟨no one has *equaled* Shakespeare's plays⟩
synonyms match, meet, tie
related words beat, better, eclipse, excel, outdistance, outdo, outshine, outstrip, overtop, surpass, top, transcend; amount (to), approach, touch; approximate, keep up, measure up (to), parallel, rival, stack up (against *or* with)
2 to be the same in meaning or effect ⟨being confined to home for a whole weekend would *equal* a death sentence in the minds of a lot of teens⟩ — see AMOUNT (TO) 2
3 to be the exact counterpart of ⟨in the British system a public school *equals* an American prep school⟩ — see MATCH 1

equality *n* the state or fact of being exactly the same in number, amount, status, or quality ⟨it's absurd to suggest that there's an *equality* in the evil committed by the Nazis and the crimes of the government of that Asian country⟩ — see EQUIVALENCE

equalize *vb* to make equal in amount, degree, or status ⟨a plan to *equalize* educational opportunities for all the state's children, rich and poor alike⟩
synonyms balance, equate, even, level
related words equilibrate, equipoise; accommodate, adjust, compensate, fit; counterbalance; homogenize, normalize, regularize, standardize; democratize
near antonyms disequilibrate

equanimity *n* evenness of emotions or temper ⟨an Olympic diver who always displays remarkable *equanimity* on the platform⟩
synonyms aplomb, calmness, collectedness, composedness, composure, cool, coolness, countenance, equilibrium, imperturbability, placidity, repose, sangfroid, self-composedness, self-possession, serenity, tranquillity (*or* tranquility), tranquilness
related words assurance, confidence, poise, self-assurance, self-assuredness, self-confidence, self-trust; easygoingness, laid-backness; apathy, detachment, impassivity, indifference, insensibility, numbness, phlegm, unconcern
near antonyms alarm (*also* alarum), anxiety, anxiousness, apprehension, apprehensiveness, care, concern, disquiet, solicitude, uneasiness, worry; excitability, excitableness, nervousness; disturbance
antonyms agitation, discomposure, perturbation

equate *vb* **1** to regard or represent as equal or comparable ⟨a value system that *equates* money with success⟩
synonyms compare, liken
related words associate, connect, correlate, identify, join, link, match, relate; group, lump (together); assort, categorize, class, classify, grade, group, sort
near antonyms differentiate, discern, discriminate, distinguish, separate
2 to describe as similar ⟨you're being silly when you *equate* the talent of that pop star with the musical genius of Mozart⟩ — see COMPARE 1
3 to make equal in amount, degree, or status ⟨you'll stop running up debts when you start *equating* what you spend with what you earn⟩ — see EQUALIZE

equatorial *adj* being near the equator ⟨a lush *equatorial* rain forest that is threatened by rampant development⟩ — see LOW 1

equilibration *n* a condition in which opposing forces are equal to one another ⟨striving to achieve an *equilibration* between the rights of the individual and the needs of society⟩ — see BALANCE 1

equilibrium *n* **1** a condition in which opposing forces are equal to one another ⟨we must find an *equilibrium* between commercial development and conservation of our natural treasures⟩ — see BALANCE 1
2 evenness of emotions or temper ⟨that stunning insult left me speechless, and several minutes passed before I recovered my *equilibrium*⟩ — see EQUANIMITY

equine *n* a large hoofed domestic animal that is used for carrying or drawing loads and for riding ⟨one of the more esteemed *equines* of modern times was the racehorse Seabiscuit⟩ — see HORSE

equip *vb* **1** to make competent (as by training, skill, or ability) for a particular office or function ⟨years of service in the congress and in the cabinet *equipped* him better than most people for the office of the presidency⟩ — see QUALIFY 2
2 to provide (someone) with what is needed for a task or activity ⟨a visit to a ski shop to *equip* ourselves for a week of skiing in the Rockies⟩ — see FURNISH 1

equipage *n* a horse-drawn wheeled vehicle for carrying passengers ⟨for their old-fashioned wedding, the couple arrived at the church in a Victorian-era *equipage*, complete with costumed driver⟩ — see CARRIAGE 1

equipment *n* items needed for the performance of a task or activity ⟨the *equipment* for the polar expedition included ships, instruments, sleds, dogs, and provisions⟩
synonyms accoutrements (*or* accouterments), apparatus, gear, hardware, kit [*chiefly British*], material(s), matériel (*or* materiel), outfit, paraphernalia, stuff, tackle
related words accessories, appurtenances, attachments, fittings; baggage, belongings, impedimenta; appliances, facilities, instruments, machinery, tools; apparel, attire, habiliments, raiment, trappings; armamentarium, armory, arsenal, battery; assets, resources

equipoise *n* **1** a condition in which opposing forces are equal to one another ⟨when participating in any dangerous sport, one should maintain an *equipoise* between fearless boldness and commonsense caution⟩ — see BALANCE 1
2 a force or influence that makes an opposing force ineffective or less effective ⟨her frugality is a much-needed *equipoise* to her husband's spendthrift ways⟩ — see COUNTERBALANCE

equitable *adj* marked by justice, honesty, and freedom from bias ⟨the will calls for an *equitable* distribution of the father's assets among his four children⟩ — see FAIR 2

equity *n* **1** lack of favoritism toward one side or another ⟨the lower wages once paid to women for equal work violated the very notion of *equity*⟩ — see DETACHMENT 1

2 the practice of giving to others what is their due ⟨basic to the notion of *equity* is the principle that all people are of equal standing in the eyes of the law⟩ — see JUSTICE 1

equivalence *n* the state or fact of being exactly the same in number, amount, status, or quality ⟨moviegoers who mistakenly believe that there is an *equivalence* between the personality of an actor and that of his character⟩

synonyms coequality, coordinateness, equality, equivalency, par, parity, sameness

related words comparability, compatibility, correlation, correspondence; alikeness, community, likeness, parallelism, resemblance, similarity, similitude; exchangeability, interchangeability; identicalness, identity

near antonyms difference, disagreement, discrepancy, disparateness, disparity, distinction, distinctiveness, distinctness, divergence, diverseness, diversity; incompatibility; dissimilarity, unlikeness

antonyms imparity, inequality, nonequivalence

equivalency *n* the state or fact of being exactly the same in number, amount, status, or quality ⟨as long as there's a rough *equivalency* in the armaments of the two countries, neither is likely to attack the other⟩ — see EQUIVALENCE

equivalent *n* one that is equal to another in status, achievement, or value ⟨that huge mansion is the *equivalent* of five ordinary houses⟩ — see EQUAL

equivocal *adj* **1** giving good reason for being doubted, questioned, or challenged ⟨the evidence that this latest diet really results in lasting weight loss is certainly *equivocal*⟩ — see DOUBTFUL 2

2 having an often intentionally veiled or uncertain meaning ⟨his demand that I promptly pay what I owe him ended with the *equivocal* threat "or else"⟩ — see OBSCURE 1

3 having a mixture of opposing feelings ⟨a number of people are clearly *equivocal* about allowing casino gambling in the state⟩ — see CONFLICTED

equivocalness *n* the quality or state of having a veiled or uncertain meaning ⟨the intriguing *equivocalness* of her warning that I would get what I had coming to me⟩ — see OBSCURITY 1

equivocate *vb* to avoid giving a definite answer or position ⟨the candidate *equivocated* as long as he could on controversial issues⟩

synonyms fudge, hedge, pussyfoot, tergiversate, waffle, weasel

related words flip-flop, yo-yo; dodge, duck, elude, eschew, evade, shake, shirk, shun, sidestep, skirt; bypass, circumvent; cavil, quibble; straddle

phrases beat around (*or* about) the bush, hem and haw, straddle the fence

equivocation *n* **1** deliberate evasion in speech ⟨your *equivocation* when asked where you were last night is not reassuring⟩ — see CIRCUMLOCUTION 1

2 the quality or state of having a veiled or uncertain meaning ⟨the *equivocation* of the last line of the poem, "That is all ye know on earth, and all ye need to know"⟩ — see OBSCURITY 1

era *n* an extent of time associated with a particular person or thing ⟨the introduction of the mass production of cars on an assembly line ushered in the *era* of the automobile⟩ — see AGE 1

eradicate *vb* to destroy all traces of ⟨the successful effort to *eradicate* smallpox around the globe⟩ — see ANNIHILATE 1

erase *vb* to destroy all traces of ⟨yet another animal species has been *erased* from this earth⟩ — see ANNIHILATE 1

ere *prep* earlier than ⟨an old typewriter that was a relic of that ancient time *ere* the invention of word processors⟩ — see BEFORE 1

erect *adj* rising straight up ⟨a lone tree remained *erect* after the terrible tornado had passed⟩

synonyms perpendicular, plumb, raised, standing, stand-up, upright, upstanding, vertical

related words elevated, lifted, upended, upraised; semierect; freestanding, stand-alone

near antonyms prostrate, supine; diagonal, hanging, sagging, slant, slanted, slanting, slanty

antonyms flat, recumbent

erect *vb* **1** to fix in an upright position ⟨the tribes of the Pacific Northwest *erected* totem poles in front of their dwellings⟩

synonyms pitch, put up, raise, rear, set up, upend, upraise

related words brace, buttress, prop (up), shore (up), support; boost, crane, elevate, heave, heft, heighten, hike, hoist, jack (up), lift, perk (up), pick up, up, uphold, uplift

near antonyms demolish, flatten, knock down, level, raze, tear down

2 to form by putting together parts or materials ⟨we'd better *erect* some sort of shelter before these woods are in total darkness⟩ — see BUILD

erection *n* something put together by arranging or connecting an array of parts ⟨when it was brand-new, the Eiffel Tower was considered as ugly an *erection* as Europe had ever seen⟩ — see CONSTRUCTION 1

eremite *n* a person who lives away from others ⟨an *eremite* wandering the desert alone as a test of his faith⟩ — see RECLUSE

ergo *adv* for this or that reason ⟨according to that line of reasoning, the eyewitness couldn't identify the aircraft, *ergo* it must have been from another planet⟩ — see THEREFORE

erode *vb* **1** to consume or wear away gradually ⟨the fear that inflation will continue to *erode* people's savings⟩ — see EAT 2

2 to damage or diminish by continued friction ⟨the winds and desert sands have *eroded* much of the original surface of these ancient monuments⟩ — see ABRADE 1

erogenous *adj* of, relating to, exciting, or expressing sexual attraction or desire ⟨certain body parts that are known sources of *erogenous* pleasure⟩ — see EROTIC

eros *n* intense sexual desire ⟨dedicated to the poet's lover, the sonnet has *eros* as its theme⟩ — see LUST 1

erosion *n* a gradual weakening, loss, or destruction ⟨the *erosion* of the banks along the river worries flood experts⟩ — see CORROSION

erotic *also* **erotical** *adj* of, relating to, exciting, or expressing sexual attraction or desire ⟨the *erotic* aspects of the story of Beauty and the Beast⟩

synonyms amatory, amorous, aphrodisiac (*also* aphrodisiacal), erogenous, erotogenic, sexy, steamy

related words autoerotic; carnal, fleshly, sensual, sensuous; bawdy, lascivious, lewd, lustful, obscene, prurient, racy, spicy, suggestive, titillating; dirty, filthy, foul, gross, indecent, nasty, pornographic, ribald, smutty, unprintable, vulgar; fetishistic, perversive

near antonyms clean, decent, decorous, polite, proper, seemly; innocuous, inoffensive

antonyms nonerotic, unerotic, unsexy

eroticism *n* **1** intense sexual desire ⟨a novel in which

the heroine is in a way victimized by her own repressed *eroticism*⟩ — see LUST 1
2 sexual appetite ⟨Alfred Kinsey's groundbreaking research in human *eroticism*⟩ — see DESIRE 2
erotogenic *adj* of, relating to, exciting, or expressing sexual attraction or desire ⟨the *erotogenic* component in horror movies⟩ — see EROTIC
err *vb* **1** to make a mistake ⟨we badly *erred* when we calculated the driving distance⟩
synonyms blunder, boob [*British*], flub, fluff, foul up, fumble, goof (up), louse up, mess (up), screw up, slip up, stumble, trip
related words nod; bobble, botch, bungle, butcher, foozle, mangle, mishandle, muff, murder; miscalculate, misconceive, miscount, miscue, misdeem, misgauge, misjudge, mistake; misconstrue, misinterpret, misunderstand
phrases drop the ball, lay an egg
2 to commit an offense ⟨when we *err*, we must be willing to accept the consequences⟩ — see OFFEND 1
errant *adj* **1** engaging in or marked by childish misbehavior ⟨what he considers to be no more than *errant* conduct toward women would be regarded as sexual harassment by most people⟩ — see NAUGHTY
2 traveling from place to place ⟨the *errant* gunslinger as a standard character in western novels⟩ — see ITINERANT
erratic *adj* **1** lacking a definite plan, purpose, or pattern ⟨so far your effort to land a summer job has been very *erratic*⟩ — see RANDOM
2 lacking in steadiness or regularity of occurrence ⟨because of your *erratic* attendance at practice, you're in danger of being cut from the team⟩ — see FITFUL
3 not staying constant ⟨business at the fast-food restaurant has been so *erratic* lately that the manager never knows how much staff to have on hand⟩ — see UNEVEN 2
4 different from the ordinary in a way that causes curiosity or suspicion ⟨the key to the code was the *erratic* punctuation the killer used⟩ — see ODD 2
erratically *adv* without definite aim, direction, rule, or method ⟨the police officer pulled over the driver, who had been driving very *erratically*⟩ — see HIT OR MISS
erraticism *n* an odd or peculiar habit ⟨an overuse of slow motion is one of the filmmaker's more annoying *erraticisms*⟩ — see IDIOSYNCRASY
erroneous *adj* not being in agreement with what is true ⟨a news article about the new virus that was filled with much *erroneous* information⟩ — see FALSE 1
erroneously *adv* in a mistaken or inappropriate way ⟨people *erroneously* believed that the disease was contagious⟩ — see WRONGLY
erroneousness *n* the quality or state of being false ⟨the *erroneousness* of so much that is printed in the tabloids is amazing⟩ — see FALLACY 2
error *n* **1** an unintentional departure from truth or accuracy ⟨a report on the earthquake contained several unfortunate *errors*⟩
synonyms blunder, bobble, boob [*British*], boo-boo, brick, clanger [*British*], clinker, fault, flub, fluff, fumble, gaff, gaffe, goof, inaccuracy, lapse, miscue, misstep, mistake, oversight, screwup, slip, slipup, stumble, trip
related words bloomer, blooper, boner, howler, pratfall; foul-up, snafu; misapprehension, miscalculation, miscomprehension, misconception, misconstruction, miscue, misdescription, misimpression, misinterpretation, misjudgment, misreading, misstatement, misunderstanding
near antonyms accuracy, correctness, exactitude, exactness, preciseness, precision, strictness; inerrancy, infallibility, perfection
2 a breaking of a moral or legal code ⟨we have all committed *errors* in our lives and strayed from the path of righteousness⟩ — see OFFENSE 1
3 a false idea or belief ⟨the church published a list of moral *errors* that it considers to be at odds with its teachings⟩ — see FALLACY 1
ersatz *adj* being such in appearance only and made with or manufactured from usually cheaper materials ⟨like everything else the restaurant served, the whipped cream on the dessert was *ersatz*⟩ — see IMITATION
erstwhile *adj* having been such at some previous time ⟨my *erstwhile* friend ignored me when I ran into her at the mall⟩ — see FORMER 1
erstwhile *adv* at an earlier or previous time ⟨there's now a store where *erstwhile* lay green and pleasant pastures⟩ — see FORMERLY 1
eruct *vb* to violently throw out or off (something from within) ⟨he suddenly snapped and began *eructing* his repressed anger⟩ — see ERUPT 1
eructation *n* an expulsion of stomach gas through the mouth ⟨an enormous *eructation* that startled everyone within earshot⟩ — see BELCH
erudite *adj* **1** having or displaying advanced knowledge or education ⟨the most *erudite* people in medical research attended the conference⟩ ⟨an *erudite* lecture on the latest discoveries in astronomy⟩ — see EDUCATED 1
2 suggestive of the vocabulary used in books ⟨the *erudite* language of a textbook on philosophy⟩ — see BOOKISH
erudition *n* the understanding and information gained from being educated ⟨a theologian of impressive *erudition* but with a down-to-earth manner⟩ — see EDUCATION 2
erupt *vb* **1** to violently throw out or off (something from within) ⟨the volcano *erupted* clouds of poisonous gas and tons of hot ash⟩
synonyms belch, disgorge, eject, eruct, expel, jet, spew, spout, spurt
related words gush, pour, squirt, stream, surge; emanate, exhale, issue, release, shoot, spit, spring, vent; discharge, emit, fire; cast, fling, heave, hurl, launch, pitch, toss
near antonyms bottle (up), contain, restrain, shut (in *or* up)
2 to develop suddenly and violently ⟨a fire *erupted*, and flames soon engulfed the room⟩
synonyms blaze (up), break out, burst (forth), explode, flame, flare (up)
related words rocket, skyrocket; balloon, burgeon (*also* bourgeon), mount, multiply, mushroom, proliferate, snowball, swell, wax; blow up, detonate, touch off
eruption *n* **1** a sudden intense expression of strong feeling ⟨a great *eruption* of glee as it suddenly dawned on her that she had won⟩ — see OUTBURST 1
2 the act or an instance of exploding ⟨the *eruption* of the volcano Krakatoa was one of the most violent in global history⟩ — see EXPLOSION 1
escalate *vb* **1** to become greater in extent, volume, amount, or number ⟨as the war between the two countries *escalated*, it threatened to become a global conflict⟩ — see INCREASE 2
2 to make greater in size, amount, or number ⟨the president promised to *escalate* the government's program to combat the dreaded disease⟩ — see INCREASE 1
escalated *adj* being at a higher level than average ⟨for a time there was an *escalated* interest in the Titanic following the release of the blockbuster movie⟩ — see HIGH 2
escapade *n* a playful or mischievous act intended as a joke ⟨their *escapades* at the prep school became the stuff of boarding-school legend⟩ — see PRANK
escape *n* **1** the act or an instance of getting free from danger or confinement ⟨a daring prison *escape*⟩

synonyms break, breakout, bunk [*British*], flight, getaway, lam, rout, slip
related words jailbreak; deliverance, liberation, redemption, release, rescue, salvation; close call, close shave, near miss
near antonyms captivity, confinement, immurement, imprisonment, incarceration, internment; custody, detention, hold, holding, retention; endangerment, hazard, imperilment, jeopardy, peril, risk, trouble
2 the act or a means of getting or keeping away from something undesirable ⟨the reading of science fiction novels as an *escape* from boring reality⟩
synonyms avoidance, cop-out, dodging, ducking, eluding, elusion, eschewal, eschewing, evasion, out, shaking, shunning
related words bypassing, circumvention, runaround, sidestepping, skirting; averting, deflection, obviation, precluding, prevention
near antonyms abidance, endurance, submission, toleration

escape *vb* **1** to get free from a dangerous or confining situation ⟨everyone managed to *escape* from the burning building in time⟩
synonyms abscond, break out (of), clear out, flee, fly, get out, lam, run away, run off
related words avoid, elude, evade, lose, shun; decamp, depart, elope, exit, go, leave, move, pull out, quit, sally (forth), shove (off), take off, walk out; disentangle, extricate; bring off, emancipate, enfranchise, free, liberate, loose, loosen, manumit, redeem, release, rescue, spring, unbind, uncage, unchain, unfetter
phrases break free
near antonyms abide, dwell, hang around, linger, remain, stay, stick around, tarry; come back, return
2 to get or keep away from (as a responsibility) through cleverness or trickery ⟨a judge who is very determined not to let criminals *escape* punishment⟩
synonyms avoid, dodge, duck, elude, eschew, evade, finesse, get around, scape, shake, shirk, shuffle (out of), shun, weasel (out of)
related words miss; avert, deflect, divert, obviate, parry, prevent, ward (off); ban, bar, debar, eliminate, except, exclude, preclude, rule out; bypass, circumvent, skirt; foil, fox, frustrate, outfox, outsmart, outwit, overreach, thwart
phrases fight shy of, keep clear of, stay clear of, steer clear of
near antonyms accept, court, embrace, pursue, seek, welcome; catch, contract, incur

escarpment *n* a steep wall of rock, earth, or ice ⟨the castle sits atop an *escarpment* that for hundreds of years made it virtually invulnerable to attack⟩ — see CLIFF

eschew *vb* to get or keep away from (as a responsibility) through cleverness or trickery ⟨the minister *eschews* involvement in local politics, since he doesn't want to diminish his moral authority in the community⟩ — see ESCAPE 2

eschewal *n* the act or a means of getting or keeping away from something undesirable ⟨a candidate who is to be admired for her *eschewal* of pat answers and quick fixes⟩ — see ESCAPE 2

eschewing *n* the act or a means of getting or keeping away from something undesirable ⟨the basketball coach's steadfast *eschewing* of favoritism has won her the team's wholehearted respect⟩ — see ESCAPE 2

escort *n* one that accompanies another for protection, guidance, or as a courtesy ⟨the mayor served as the First Lady's *escort* for her tour of the city⟩
synonyms attendant, companion, guard, guide
related words chaperone (*or* chaperon), squire; shadow, sidekick; conductor, leader, pilot; convoy, courier, honor guard, outrider

escort *vb* to go along with in order to provide assistance, protection, or companionship ⟨a student from the college *escorted* my parents and me on our tour of the campus⟩ — see ACCOMPANY 1

esculent *adj* suitable for use as food ⟨harvesting wild mushrooms is no business for amateurs, since some of the *esculent* ones closely resemble poisonous varieties⟩ — see EDIBLE

esoteric *adj* **1** difficult for one of ordinary knowledge or intelligence to understand ⟨metaphysics is such an *esoteric* subject that most people are content to leave it to the philosophers⟩ — see PROFOUND 1
2 not known or meant to be known by the general populace ⟨must have had some *esoteric* motive for leaving his art collection to a museum halfway around the globe⟩ — see PRIVATE 1

especial *adj* **1** being out of the ordinary ⟨a candidate who handled the stunning defeat with *especial* grace⟩ — see EXCEPTIONAL 1
2 closely acquainted ⟨he told his *especial* friends about the job offer but kept everyone else in the dark⟩ — see FAMILIAR 1
3 of a particular or exact sort ⟨with a very ordinary lawn, we don't have any *especial* need for a gardener⟩ — see EXPRESS 1

especially *adv* **1** in the specific case of one person or thing as distinguished from others ⟨all employees, but *especially* the administrative assistants, will need to learn to use the new phone system⟩
synonyms particularly, specifically
related words individually, personally; restrictively, selectively
phrases in especial, in particular
near antonyms broadly, widely
antonyms generally
2 to a great degree ⟨that university is *especially* strong in the sciences⟩ — see VERY 1
3 in regard to something mentioned explicitly or in detail ⟨he *especially* minded the proposed changes to the work schedule⟩ — see SPECIFICALLY 1

espiègle *adj* tending to or exhibiting reckless playfulness ⟨the *espiègle* light in the young princess's eye faded when she contemplated the stifling restrictions of court life⟩ — see MISCHIEVOUS 1

espièglerie *n* **1** a natural disposition for playful behavior ⟨a delightful young woman whose *espièglerie* and sophisticated wit make her a favorite party guest⟩ — see PLAYFULNESS
2 playful, reckless behavior that is not intended to cause serious harm ⟨a femme fatale with a penchant for sophisticated *espièglerie* that men found irresistible⟩ — see MISCHIEF 1

espionage *n* the secret gathering of information on others ⟨the acts of *espionage* on behalf of the Confederacy carried on by Belle Boyd and Rose Greenhow⟩
synonyms spying
related words counterespionage, counterintelligence, intelligence; cloak-and-dagger; tradecraft; observation, reconnaissance, surveillance; bugging, eavesdropping, wiretapping; dope, goods, lowdown

espousal *n* **1** a ceremony in which two people are united in matrimony ⟨the expected *espousal* of the Hollywood actor and the singing superstar should attract the elite of show business⟩ — see WEDDING
2 the act or state of being engaged to be married ⟨considering how long her previous marriage lasted, she'd be wise to have an extended *espousal*⟩ — see ENGAGEMENT 1

espouse *vb* **1** to give in marriage ⟨a couple eager to *espouse* their eldest daughter⟩ — see MARRY 2
2 to take as a spouse ⟨heeded his father's advice to *es-*

pouse someone with whom he had common interests⟩ — see MARRY 3
3 to take for one's own use (something originated by another) ⟨after working among them for two years in the Peace Corps, she felt compelled to *espouse* the peasants' cause for social justice⟩ — see ADOPT

espouser *n* a person who actively supports or favors a cause ⟨became an *espouser* of environmental causes only after she decided to run for office⟩ — see EXPONENT 1

esprit *n* active strength of body or mind ⟨the dance company has an infectious *esprit* that captivates audiences⟩ — see VIGOR 1

espy *vb* to make note of (something) through the use of one's eyes ⟨out of the corner of my eye I *espied* the squirrel making another raid on the bird feeder⟩ — see SEE

essay *n* **1** a short piece of writing typically expressing a point of view ⟨school *essays* on what it means to be a patriot⟩
synonyms article, composition, paper, theme
related words causerie; column, commentary, editorial, feature, report, review, write-up; dissertation, thesis; tract, treatise; discourse, discussion, exposition, prolegomenon, study
2 an effort to do or accomplish something ⟨my first *essay* at baking a cake did not go well⟩ — see ATTEMPT 1
3 a procedure or operation carried out to resolve an uncertainty ⟨a little homemade *essay* to determine the easiest way to strip the paint from the bookcase⟩ — see EXPERIMENT

essay *vb* to make an effort to do ⟨he had been in gymnastics for some time before he even considered *essaying* that move⟩ — see ATTEMPT

essence *n* **1** the quality or qualities that make a thing what it is ⟨the belief that power ultimately rests with the people is the very *essence* of democracy⟩
synonyms being, essentiality, nature, quiddity, quintessence, soul, stuff, substance
related words heart, spirit; alpha and omega, center, core, keynote, marrow, pith, seat; embodiment, epitome, incarnation, manifestation, personification; aspect, attribute, feature, property; gist, kernel, nub
phrases name of the game
2 the central part or aspect of something under consideration ⟨presented the *essence* of weeks of testimony in a 20-minute appeal to the jury⟩ — see CRUX

essential *adj* **1** impossible to do without ⟨a well-stocked public library is *essential* for the well-being of a community⟩
synonyms all-important, critical, imperative, indispensable, integral, must-have, necessary, necessitous, needed, needful, required, requisite, vital
related words prerequisite; compulsory, mandatory, nonelective, obligatory; consequential, crucial, important, major, material, meaningful, momentous, significant, substantial, weighty; basic, central, fundamental, key, organic; insistent, persistent, pressing, urgent
phrases of the essence
near antonyms undesired, unwanted; inconsequential, insignificant, unimportant; excess, external, extra, extraneous, superfluous, surplus
antonyms dispensable, inessential, needless, nonessential, unessential, unnecessary, unneeded
2 of or relating to the simplest facts or theories of a subject ⟨anyone with an *essential* knowledge of human biology can follow the documentary⟩ — see ELEMENTARY
3 being a part of the innermost nature of a person or thing ⟨an unquenchable belief in the *essential* goodness of most people⟩ — see INHERENT

essential *n* **1** something necessary, indispensable, or unavoidable ⟨the *essentials* for success include a willingness to work and the right attitude⟩
synonyms condition, demand, must, must-have, necessary, necessity, need, needful, requirement, requisite, sine qua non
related words precondition, prerequisite; advantage, edge, plus; desideration, desideratum, wish
near antonyms amenity, comfort, extra, extravagance, frill, indulgence, luxury, superfluity, surplus, surplusage
antonyms nonessential, nonnecessity
2 essentials *pl* general or basic truths on which other truths or theories can be based ⟨this will be just an introduction to the *essentials* of computer programming⟩ — see PRINCIPLES

essentiality *n* the quality or qualities that make a thing what it is ⟨physical strength or endurance is the *essentiality* that makes activity a sport and not just a game⟩ — see ESSENCE 1

establish *vb* **1** to gain full recognition or acceptance of ⟨a first novel that *established* him as one of the most promising writers of his generation⟩
synonyms demonstrate, prove, show, substantiate
related words attest, authenticate, bear out, document, evidence, support, sustain, uphold; confirm, corroborate, justify, validate, verify
near antonyms confute, discredit, invalidate, rebut, refute
antonyms disprove
2 to show the existence or truth of by evidence ⟨the developers haven't *established* that there's a need for another shopping center in town⟩ — see PROVE 1
3 to be responsible for the creation and early operation or use of ⟨*established* the first school for the education of Native Americans⟩ — see FOUND

establisher *n* a person who establishes a whole new field of endeavor ⟨Alfred Stieglitz is often credited as the *establisher* of photography as an art form⟩ — see FATHER 2

establishment *n* **1** a building, room, or suite of rooms occupied by a service business ⟨one of the best dining *establishments* in the city⟩ — see PLACE 2
2 a commercial or industrial activity or organization ⟨new business *establishments* sprang up all over in the postwar boom⟩ — see ENTERPRISE 1
3 a public organization with a particular purpose or function ⟨the proposed change in pollution standards was opposed by environmental *establishments* across the board⟩ — see INSTITUTION 1
4 a structure that is designed and built for a particular purpose ⟨the city boasts a host of outstanding medical *establishments*⟩ — see FACILITY

estate *n* **1** a large impressive residence ⟨the *estates* of multimillionaires line the shores of this ocean resort⟩ — see MANSION
2 a state of being or fitness ⟨the mayor pronounced the city's schools to be in their best *estate* ever⟩ — see CONDITION 1
3 one of the segments of society into which people are grouped ⟨the passionate belief that a society is judged by how well it treats and cares for those in the lowest *estate*⟩ — see CLASS 1
4 a piece of land and its buildings used to grow crops or raise livestock ⟨a huge coffee *estate* in Brazil⟩ — see FARM

esteem *n* a feeling of great approval and liking ⟨an athlete who is held in great *esteem* by her peers⟩ — see ADMIRATION 1

esteem *vb* **1** to think of in a particular way ⟨I had *esteemed* the whole affair to be a colossal waste of time⟩ — see CONSIDER 1
2 to think very highly or favorably of ⟨although the

works of the Impressionist painters are *esteemed* today, they met with scorn when they were introduced⟩ — see ADMIRE

3 to have as an opinion ⟨I should have *esteemed* it most unlikely that their marriage had any chance of success⟩ — see BELIEVE 2

esteemed *adj* having a good reputation especially in a field of knowledge ⟨concerned about his heart, my grandfather went to see an *esteemed* cardiac specialist⟩ — see RESPECTABLE 1

estimable *adj* **1** deserving of high regard or great approval ⟨a dramatist with an *estimable* body of work⟩ — see ADMIRABLE

2 having a good reputation especially in a field of knowledge ⟨no *estimable* archaeologist would be fooled by such a crude and obvious hoax⟩ — see RESPECTABLE 1

estimate *n* **1** the act of placing a value on the nature, character, or quality of something ⟨what we owe our war veterans is beyond *estimate*⟩

synonyms appraisal, appraisement, assessment, estimation, evaluation, reckoning, valuation

related words calculation, computation, measurement, mensuration; audit, check, checkup, examination, inspection, review, scan, scrutiny, survey; reassessment, transvaluation; overestimation, overevaluation; underestimation

2 an opinion on the nature, character, or quality of something ⟨the *estimate* of many art specialists that the painting is a fake⟩ — see ESTIMATION 1

estimate *vb* **1** to make an approximate or tentative judgment regarding ⟨experts *estimated* the value of the painting at a million dollars⟩

synonyms appraise, assess, evaluate, guesstimate, rate, set, valuate, value

related words adjudge, deem, judge; ascertain, determine, discover, learn; price, prize; decide, settle; analyze, assay, survey, test; reappraise, reassess, reevaluate, rejudge, revalue; transvaluate, transvalue; misesteem, misjudge, misprize, underestimate, undervalue

2 to decide the size, amount, number, or distance of (something) without actual measurement ⟨we *estimated* the snowfall to be about a foot⟩

synonyms calculate, call, conjecture, figure, gauge (*also* gage), guess, judge, make, place, put, reckon, suppose

related words conclude, deduce, extrapolate, gather, infer, reason, understand

near antonyms calibrate, measure, scale; compute, work out

estimation *n* **1** an opinion on the nature, character, or quality of something ⟨the teacher's *estimation* of her student's scientific aptitude proved to be well-founded when he won a national science award⟩

synonyms appraisal, appraisement, assessment, estimate, evaluation, fix, judgment (*or* judgement), value judgment

related words aperçu, feeling, impression, notion, perception; confidence, faith, stock, trust; belief, conviction, mind, persuasion, sentiment, view; conjecture, guess, hunch, hypothesis, surmise, theory

2 the act of placing a value on the nature, character, or quality of something ⟨I may have been a little too hasty in my *estimation* of his musical abilities⟩ — see ESTIMATE 1

3 a feeling of great approval and liking ⟨a show business superstar who enjoys the *estimation* of fans and fellow performers alike⟩ — see ADMIRATION 1

estrange *vb* to cause to change from friendly or loving to unfriendly or uncaring ⟨she *estranged* several of her coworkers when she let her promotion go to her head⟩

synonyms alien, alienate, disaffect, disgruntle, sour

related words antagonize, embitter, envenom; aggravate, anger, enrage, incense, inflame (*also* enflame), infuriate, madden, outrage, rankle, rile, roil; break up, dissociate, disunite, divide, separate, sever, split, sunder, uncouple, unlink, unyoke; disappoint, disenchant, disillusion; annoy, bother, bug, chafe, exasperate, gall, grate, irk, irritate, nettle, peeve, pique, rile, vex

near antonyms endear, ingratiate; appease, conciliate, disarm, mollify, pacify, placate, propitiate

antonyms reconcile

estrangement *n* the loss of friendship or affection ⟨a silly quarrel that eventually resulted in a complete and lasting *estrangement* between the onetime friends⟩

synonyms alienation, disaffection, disgruntlement, souring

related words antagonism, embitterment, envenoming; breach, breakup, divorce, rift, rupture, schism, separation, split; animosity, antagonism, antipathy, bitterness, hostility, jaundice, rancor; aggravation, furor, fury, incensing, indignation, infuriation, ire, outrage, rage, spleen, wrath; disenchantment, disillusionment

near antonyms endearment, ingratiation; appeasement, conciliation, mollification, pacification, propitiation

antonyms reconcilement, reconciliation

estuary *n* a part of a body of water that extends beyond the general shoreline ⟨the city sits on the shores of a deep *estuary* where the Hudson River meets the Atlantic Ocean⟩ — see GULF 1

esurient *adj* having a huge appetite ⟨the deli is frequented by young, single professionals, *esurient* after those long hours spent staring at the monitor of a computer⟩ — see VORACIOUS 1

etceteras *n pl* small useful items ⟨tossed his razor, shaving cream, and assorted *etceteras* into his toiletry bag⟩ — see NOTION 1

etch *vb* **1** to cut (as letters or designs) on a hard surface ⟨the artist *etched* his landscape on a copper plate⟩ — see ENGRAVE 1

2 to produce a vivid impression of ⟨in just a few pages the writer *etched* an unforgettable portrait of one of the more remarkable First Ladies⟩ — see ENGRAVE 2

eternal *adj* **1** having an existence or validity that does not change or diminish ⟨a charming fable that presents some *eternal* truths in a fresh way⟩ — see ABIDING

2 lasting forever ⟨the quest for some magic potion that promises *eternal* youth⟩ — see EVERLASTING 1

Eternal *n* the being worshipped as the creator and ruler of the universe ⟨spent much time pondering the nature of the *Eternal*⟩ — see DEITY 2

eternalize *vb* to give eternal or lasting existence to ⟨the monument was created to *eternalize* the service and sacrifice of the sons of the village who fought in the American Civil War⟩ — see PERPETUATE

eternally *adv* for all time ⟨we will be *eternally* grateful for your kind generosity⟩ — see EVER 1

eternity *n* **1** endless time ⟨the question whether the universe will end someday or continue to exist in *eternity*⟩

synonyms everlasting, foreverness, infinity, perpetuity

related words boundlessness, endlessness, interminableness, limitlessness, permanence, permanency, timelessness

near antonyms ephemerality, impermanence, temporariness, transience, transitoriness

2 unending existence after death ⟨a firm belief in the *eternity* of the soul⟩

synonyms afterlife, beyond, hereafter, immortality

related words afterworld, otherworld

3 a long or seemingly long period of time ⟨we waited in line for tickets for an *eternity*⟩ — see AGE 2

ethereal *adj* **1** not composed of matter ⟨that *ethereal* attribute that every performer should have—charisma⟩ — see IMMATERIAL 1

2 resembling air in lightness ⟨the bakery's scrumptious pastries have a wonderfully *ethereal* consistency⟩ — see AIRY 1

3 of, relating to, or suggesting heaven ⟨a land of *ethereal* beauty and tranquillity⟩ — see CELESTIAL

ethical *adj* 1 conforming to a high standard of morality or virtue ⟨the *ethical* behavior expected of every member of the police force⟩ — see GOOD 2

2 following the accepted rules of moral conduct ⟨the *ethical* course of action for the senator who lied to Congress would be to resign⟩ — see HONORABLE 1

3 guided by or in accordance with one's sense of right and wrong ⟨*ethical* writers do not use the words of other writers without giving them proper credit⟩ — see CONSCIENTIOUS 1

ethics *n pl* the code of good conduct for an individual or group ⟨the *ethics* of scouting require scouts to be loyal, clean, and reverent⟩

synonyms ethos, morality, morals, norms, principles, standards

related words customs, dictates, etiquette, manners, mores, values; beliefs, dogma, faith, tenets

ethnic *adj* of, relating to, or reflecting the traits exhibited by a group of people with a common ancestry and culture ⟨children who were raised in a home where there was a strong *ethnic* consciousness⟩ — see RACIAL

ethnical *adj* of, relating to, or reflecting the traits exhibited by a group of people with a common ancestry and culture ⟨the marriage flourished, despite the *ethnical* contrast between the partners⟩ — see RACIAL

ethnicity *n* a people having a common language, culture, and body of traditions ⟨a university that aggressively recruits a student body of diverse *ethnicities*⟩ — see NATIONALITY

ethos *n* the code of good conduct for an individual or group ⟨rigorous self-discipline was central to the *ethos* of the ancient Spartans⟩ — see ETHICS

etiolate *vb* to diminish the physical strength of ⟨the long, stressful days and sleepless nights gradually *etiolated* him⟩ — see WEAKEN 1

etiquette *n* personal conduct or behavior as evaluated by an accepted standard of appropriateness for a social or professional setting ⟨the couple exhibited poor *etiquette* when they left the party without saying good-bye to the host and hostess⟩ — see MANNER 1

euchre *vb* to rob by the use of trickery or threats ⟨a fast-talking speculator who thought that *euchring* the tribe out of their land would be easy⟩ — see FLEECE

eulogium *n* a formal expression of praise ⟨on the centennial of its completion, the building received the greatest possible *eulogium*: it remains a unique achievement in architectural design⟩ — see ENCOMIUM

eulogy *n* a formal expression of praise ⟨several *eulogies* were given at the special assembly marking the retirement of the company's longtime president⟩ — see ENCOMIUM

eupeptic *adj* having or showing a good mood or disposition ⟨our *eupeptic* colleague was unfazed by our gloomy expressions and dire predictions⟩ — see CHEERFUL 1

euphonic *adj* having a pleasing mixture of notes ⟨not wanting to burden their newborn with one of those unwieldy hyphenated surnames, the parents are looking for something a little more *euphonic*⟩ — see HARMONIOUS 1

euphonious *adj* 1 having a pleasantly flowing quality suggestive of music ⟨an opera singer with an appropriately *euphonious* name⟩ — see LYRIC 1

2 having a pleasing mixture of notes ⟨the doorbell had a noticeably *euphonious* chime⟩ — see HARMONIOUS 1

euphoria *n* a state of overwhelming usually pleasurable emotion ⟨a general *euphoria* seemed to engulf the city following the World Series win⟩ — see ECSTASY

euphoric *adj* experiencing or marked by overwhelming usually pleasurable emotion ⟨the *euphoric* winner was momentarily speechless⟩ — see ECSTATIC

eurythmic *or* **eurhythmic** *adj* having the parts agreeably related ⟨the ratio of the height of the temple's colonnade to the width of the entablature and pediment make for an eye-pleasing and *eurythmic* facade⟩ — see HARMONIOUS 2

evacuate *vb* to remove the contents of ⟨*evacuate* the cupboards completely before spraying the insecticide⟩ — see EMPTY

evacuee *n* a person forced to emigrate for political reasons ⟨*evacuees* by the thousands poured into the camps for displaced persons⟩ — see ÉMIGRÉ 1

evade *vb* to get or keep away from (as a responsibility) through cleverness or trickery ⟨people who use every loophole in the law to *evade* paying taxes⟩ — see ESCAPE 2

evaluate *vb* to make an approximate or tentative judgment regarding ⟨a trained assistant to *evaluate* the needs of the patients waiting to see the doctor⟩ — see ESTIMATE 1

evaluation *n* 1 an opinion on the nature, character, or quality of something ⟨what's your *evaluation* of her writing ability?⟩ — see ESTIMATION 1

2 the act of placing a value on the nature, character, or quality of something ⟨the *evaluation* of the defendant's mental condition was conducted by a team of psychiatrists⟩ — see ESTIMATE 1

evanesce *vb* to cease to be visible ⟨the kids' rainy-day gloom *evanesced* the minute they heard that we were going out for ice cream⟩ — see DISAPPEAR

evanescence *n* the state or quality of lasting only for a short time ⟨the *evanescence* of a rainbow detracts not a whit from its beauty⟩ — see IMPERMANENCE

evanescent *adj* lasting only for a short time ⟨beauty that is as *evanescent* as a rainbow⟩ — see MOMENTARY

evaporate *vb* to cease to be visible ⟨by mid-morning the fog that had enshrouded the island had just *evaporated*⟩ — see DISAPPEAR

evasion *n* the act or a means of getting or keeping away from something undesirable ⟨pleading chronic back pain is my standard *evasion* for doing any heavy lifting⟩ — see ESCAPE 2

evasive *adj* hard to find, capture, or isolate ⟨believers in Bigfoot have never quite explained how such a large creature can be so *evasive*⟩ — see ELUSIVE

eve *n* the time from when the sun begins to set to the onset of total darkness ⟨from morn to *eve* the settlers toiled to eke a living from the harsh land⟩ — see DUSK 1

even *adj* 1 being neither more nor less than a certain amount, number, or extent ⟨the distance to town is an *even* mile⟩

synonyms exact, flat, precise, round

near antonyms approximate, comparative, near, relative; imprecise

2 having a surface without bends, breaks, or irregularities ⟨let's find an *even* stretch of ground to pitch our tent⟩ — see LEVEL 1

3 resembling another in every respect ⟨the armies of the two countries are fairly *even*⟩ — see SAME 1

4 not varying ⟨energy demands do not stay *even* throughout the day but peak significantly during the afternoon hours⟩ — see UNIFORM

even *adv* 1 not merely this but also ⟨the blue whale is a huge, *even* awesome animal by any measure⟩

synonyms indeed, nay, truly, verily, yea

related words assuredly, certainly, decidedly, definitely, doubtless, incontestably, incontrovertibly, indis-

putably, positively, really, surely, truly, undeniably, undoubtedly, unquestionably
phrases in fact, in reality, in truth
2 to a full extent or degree ⟨I will love you *even* to the end of time⟩ — see FULLY 1
even *vb* **1** to make free from breaks, curves, or bumps ⟨*even* the filling before adding the top layer of the cake⟩
synonyms flatten, level, plane, smooth, smoothen
related words clip, crop, pare, prune, shave, trim; lay, press, spread; card, comb, rake; surface
near antonyms coarsen, rumple, wrinkle; bend, kink; dent, pit
antonyms rough, roughen
2 to make equal in amount, degree, or status ⟨the contention that producing more arms will *even* us with the enemy and therefore make us more secure⟩ — see EQUALIZE
evenfall *n* the time from when the sun begins to set to the onset of total darkness ⟨with the coming of *evenfall* the Greek island takes on an entirely different mood⟩ — see DUSK 1
evenhanded *adj* marked by justice, honesty, and freedom from bias ⟨an *evenhanded* meting out of punishment⟩ — see FAIR 2
evenhandedness *n* lack of favoritism toward one side or another ⟨we trust the *evenhandedness* of our marriage counselor implicitly⟩ — see DETACHMENT 1
evening *n* **1** a later period of one's life ⟨now in the *evening* of their lives, the married couple are ready to hand the family business over to the next generation⟩ — see AGE 3
2 the time from when the sun begins to set to the onset of total darkness ⟨in the *evening* a reddish glow often appears on the mountaintops⟩ — see DUSK 1
even so *adv* in spite of that ⟨I know you claim not to care about the breakup; *even so*, you keep talking about it⟩ — see HOWEVER
event *n* **1** something that happens ⟨dinnertime was devoted to talking over the day's *events*, not to watching television⟩
synonyms affair, circumstance, episode, hap, happening, incident, occasion, occurrence, thing
related words coincidence, co-occurrence, fluke, freak; landmark, milepost, milestone, page, phenomenon, turning point; adventure, experience, time; happenchance, happenstance; accident, crisis, emergency, juncture; achievement, deed, exploit, feat; news, tidings
2 something that might happen ⟨in the *event* of rain, graduation ceremonies will be held indoors⟩
synonyms case, contingence, contingency, contingent, eventuality, possibility
related words probability; accident, chance, hap, hazard, risk
3 a competitive encounter between individuals or groups carried on for amusement, exercise, or in pursuit of a prize ⟨figure skating is usually one of the most popular *events* in the winter Olympics⟩ — see GAME 1
4 a social gathering ⟨the mayor's evenings are often tied up with one *event* after another⟩ — see PARTY 1
eventful *adj* having great meaning or lasting effect ⟨the first moon landing was universally regarded as an *eventful* moment in human history⟩ — see IMPORTANT 1
eventide *n* the time from when the sun begins to set to the onset of total darkness ⟨*eventide* was their favorite time for enjoying a quiet respite in the backyard⟩ — see DUSK 1
eventuality *n* **1** something that can develop or become actual ⟨a cure for that form of cancer seems like a certain *eventuality*—it's just a matter of time⟩ — see POTENTIAL
2 something that might happen ⟨a full-force hurricane on the day of the picnic was one *eventuality* that we hadn't planned on⟩ — see EVENT 2
eventually *adv* at a later time ⟨stop whining about how long it's taking us—we'll get there *eventually*⟩ — see YET 1
ever *adv* **1** for all time ⟨the name of Benedict Arnold will *ever* be linked with treason⟩
synonyms always, aye (*also* ay), e'er, eternally, everlastingly, evermore, forever, forevermore, indelibly, permanently, perpetually
related words enduringly, long, perennially
phrases for good (*also* for good and all), for keeps
near antonyms once
antonyms ne'er, never, nevermore
2 in any way or respect ⟨how can we *ever* repay what you've done for us?⟩ — see AT ALL
3 on every relevant occasion ⟨the boy and his *ever* present dog were a common sight around the village⟩ — see ALWAYS 1
4 to a great degree ⟨boy, was I *ever* embarrassed⟩ ⟨it's been *ever* so long since we've seen you⟩ — see VERY 1
everlasting *adj* **1** lasting forever ⟨valentines typically express the giver's *everlasting* love and devotion⟩
synonyms ceaseless, dateless, deathless, endless, eternal, immortal, permanent, perpetual, undying, unending
related words durable, enduring, lasting, long-lived, persistent, stubborn; imperishable, indefeasible, indefectible, indelible, indestructible, indissoluble, inexpungible; timeless; abiding, stable, standing, steadfast, steady, unfailing, unfaltering; continual, continuing, continuous, incessant, unbroken, unceasing, uninterrupted, unremitting
near antonyms ephemeral, evanescent, fleeting, fugacious, fugitive, momentary, passing, short-lived, transitory; interim, provisional, short-term
antonyms impermanent, mortal, temporary, transient
2 having an existence or validity that does not change or diminish ⟨Shakespeare's plays are still being performed 400 years later because they deal with *everlasting* truths and universal emotions⟩ — see ABIDING
everlasting *n* **1** endless time ⟨that special bond that has existed between mother and child from *everlasting*⟩ — see ETERNITY 1
2 *cap* the being worshipped as the creator and ruler of the universe ⟨people who believe that the magnificence of the natural world is proof of the existence of the *Everlasting*⟩ — see DEITY 2
everlastingly *adv* for all time ⟨the sacrifices made by our brave soldiers on this battlefield will be *everlastingly* remembered⟩ — see EVER 1
evermore *adv* for all time ⟨he promised to love her *evermore*, if only she would consent to be his wife⟩ — see EVER 1
every *adj* being one of a group ⟨*every* man here must decide for himself whether to go or to stay and fight⟩ — see EACH
everybody *pron* every person ⟨*everybody* must do what his or her conscience dictates⟩
synonyms all, everyone
related words anybody, anyone; somebody, someone
phrases each and everyone, one and all
antonyms nobody, none, no one
everyday *adj* **1** being of the type that is encountered in the normal course of events ⟨we're just an *everyday* family, with a dog and a cat and bills to pay⟩ — see ORDINARY 1
2 having to do with the practical details of regular life ⟨even the richest man in town has to do such *everyday* tasks as shaving his face and brushing his teeth⟩ — see MUNDANE 1
3 not designed to be worn only on special occasions ⟨*ev-*

eryday clothes will be fine for this party⟩ — see CASUAL 1

4 often observed or encountered ⟨fortunately, murder is not an *everyday* event around here⟩ — see COMMON 1

everyman *n* an average or ordinary man ⟨despite his superstar status, in his movies the actor is able to play the role of an *everyman* quite convincingly⟩ — see JOE BLOW

everyone *pron* every person ⟨there's plenty of food for *everyone*⟩ — see EVERYBODY

everyplace *adv* in every place or in all places ⟨I can't be *everyplace* at once, so somebody has to help me⟩ — see EVERYWHERE

everywhere *adv* in every place or in all places ⟨freedom and happiness are the goals of people *everywhere*⟩
synonyms all over, everyplace, far and wide, high and low, throughout
related words every which way; right and left
phrases all over the place (*or* map), far and near, in every corner (*or* quarter), on all hands (*or* on every hand)
antonyms nowhere

evidence *n* something presented in support of the truth or accuracy of a claim ⟨do you have any *evidence* that this bike is yours?⟩ — see PROOF

evident *adj* **1** appearing to be true on the basis of evidence that may or may not be confirmed ⟨the *evident* motive for the assault was robbery⟩ — see APPARENT 1
2 not subject to misinterpretation or more than one interpretation ⟨the man was discovered dead in his apartment, but there were no *evident* signs of foul play⟩ — see CLEAR 2

evidently *adv* to all outward appearances ⟨she was *evidently* dissatisfied with her job and abruptly quit⟩ — see APPARENTLY

evil *adj* **1** causing or capable of causing harm ⟨the contention that pornography is an *evil* influence on society⟩ — see HARMFUL
2 not conforming to a high moral standard; morally unacceptable ⟨their *evil* deeds rank among the worst in history⟩ — see BAD 2
3 causing intense displeasure, disgust, or resentment ⟨she refused to eat olives or anything which had their *evil* flavor⟩ — see OFFENSIVE 1

evil *n* that which is morally unacceptable ⟨our free will allows us to choose between good and *evil*⟩
synonyms bad, evildoing, ill, immorality, iniquity, sin, villainy, wrong
related words atrociousness, atrocity, badness, balefulness, darkness, depravedness, devilishness, diabolism, enormity, evilness, heinousness, iniquitousness, satanism, sinfulness, vileness, wickedness; devilry (*or* deviltry), fiendishness; cancer, canker, decay, rot, squalor; corruption, debauchery, degeneracy, depravity, indecency, malefaction, perversion, pervertedness, scurrility, scurrilousness; abomination, anathema, taboo (*also* tabu)
near antonyms decency, goodness, honesty, integrity, probity, rectitude, uprightness; goodness, righteousness, virtuousness
antonyms good, morality, right, virtue

evildoer *n* **1** a person who commits moral wrongs ⟨if good people stand by and do nothing, *evildoers* will triumph⟩
synonyms immoralist, malefactor, sinner, wrongdoer
related words criminal, crook, felon, lawbreaker, miscreant, misdoer, misfeasor, offender, reprobate, transgressor, villain; corrupter (*also* corruptor)
near antonyms angel, innocent, saint
2 a mean, evil, or unprincipled person ⟨the novel's slave owner, Simon Legree, became one of the most notorious *evildoers* in all of literature⟩ — see VILLAIN

evildoing *n* that which is morally unacceptable ⟨a book that ponders the question of the presence of *evildoing* in a universe controlled by a benevolent Supreme Being⟩ — see EVIL

evilness *n* the state or quality of being utterly evil ⟨the *evilness* of the crimes committed by the mass murderer are beyond comprehension⟩ — see ENORMITY 1

evince *vb* to make known (something abstract) through outward signs ⟨the teenager caught shoplifting seemed to *evince* no remorse⟩ — see SHOW 2

eviscerate *vb* to take the internal organs out of ⟨the ancient Egyptians would *eviscerate* the bodies of the dead as part of the process of mummifying them⟩ — see GUT

evocative *adj* provoking a memory or mental association ⟨the Italian-American restaurant is decorated in a manner *evocative* of the charming outdoor cafés in Italy⟩ — see SUGGESTIVE 2

evoke *vb* to draw out (something hidden, latent, or reserved) ⟨the old family photographs we found in the attic *evoked* a wealth of warm memories⟩ — see EDUCE

evolution *n* the act or process of going from the simple or basic to the complex or advanced ⟨the *evolution* of motion pictures from a peep-show novelty into a medium of mass entertainment and an art form⟩ — see DEVELOPMENT 1

evolve *vb* **1** to gradually become clearer or more detailed ⟨as the governor's plans for the reform of state government *evolved*, objections from various groups inevitably arose⟩ — see DEVELOP 1
2 to throw or give off ⟨baking soda and citric acid react with each other and *evolve* carbon dioxide⟩ — see EMIT 1

evolved *adj* being far along in development ⟨whether this is an *evolved* technology or one still in its infancy is a matter of debate⟩ — see ADVANCED 1

ewer *n* a handled container for holding and pouring liquids that usually has a lip or a spout ⟨a silver *ewer* in the elaborately ornamented style favored by the Victorians⟩ — see PITCHER

exacerbate *vb* to make more severe ⟨a misconceived plan that only *exacerbated* the city's traffic problem⟩
synonyms aggravate, complicate, worsen
related words amplify, deepen, intensify, magnify
near antonyms ameliorate, better, improve
antonyms allay, alleviate, assuage, ease, help, mitigate, relieve

exact *adj* **1** being in agreement with the truth or a fact or a standard ⟨maybe I wasn't being very *exact* when I said I had done it a million times—but it sure seemed like it⟩ — see CORRECT 1
2 being neither more nor less than a certain amount, number, or extent ⟨the *exact* number of passengers on that airplane was 147⟩ — see EVEN 1
3 following an original exactly ⟨an *exact* replica of the notorious slave ship *Amistad*⟩ — see FAITHFUL 2
4 made or done with extreme care and accuracy ⟨the company stresses that its optical telescopes are *exact* instruments and should not be handled as toys⟩ — see FINE 2
5 meeting the highest standard of accuracy ⟨in order for the blind to fit properly, we must have the *exact* measurements of the window⟩ — see PRECISE 1

exact *vb* **1** to ask for (something) earnestly or with authority ⟨every war inevitably *exacts* the greatest sacrifice possible from some of the nation's best and brightest⟩ — see DEMAND 1
2 to establish or apply as a charge or penalty ⟨vowed to *exact* a heavy fine from any hockey player engaging in such outrageous behavior on the ice⟩ — see IMPOSE
3 to get (as money) by the use of force or threats ⟨that loan shark can be counted upon to *exact* repayment of his loan by whatever means necessary⟩ — see EXTORT

exacting *adj* **1** hard to please ⟨he was shocked when his normally *exacting* supervisor complimented him on a job well done⟩ — see FINICKY
2 not allowing for any exceptions or loosening of standards ⟨the prep school's *exacting* standards for admission⟩ — see RIGID 1
3 requiring considerable physical or mental effort ⟨the new recruits had to adjust themselves to the *exacting* discipline of military life⟩ — see HARD 2
4 requiring much time, effort, or careful attention ⟨writing will always be an *exacting* task⟩ — see DEMANDING 1

exactingness *n* the quality or state of being demanding or unyielding (as in discipline or criticism) ⟨since I was a guest in their home, I was not about to critique the dinner with the *exactingness* of a professional restaurant reviewer⟩ — see SEVERITY

exactitude *n* the quality or state of being very accurate ⟨after its opening weekend, a movie's final box office gross can be estimated with considerable *exactitude*⟩ — see PRECISION

exactly *adv* **1** as stated or indicated without the slightest difference ⟨we will meet at *exactly* six o'clock⟩
synonyms due, full, just, precisely, right, sharp, smack-dab, squarely
phrases on the button, on the nose
2 in the same manner ⟨he wants to be *exactly* like his father⟩ — see JUST 1
3 in the same words ⟨a plagiarism suit alleging that one historian had copied large segments of another's text *exactly*⟩ — see VERBATIM
4 without any relaxation of standards or precision ⟨follow the rules *exactly* and you won't get into trouble⟩ — see STRICTLY
5 to a full extent or degree ⟨she listened to the advice, then did *exactly* what she wanted to anyway⟩ — see FULLY 1
6 used to express agreement ⟨"Are you calling me a liar?" "*Exactly*."⟩ — see YES

exactness *n* the quality or state of being very accurate ⟨the *exactness* of the bathroom scale isn't such that you could use it in business⟩ — see PRECISION

exaggerate *vb* **1** to add to the interest of by including made-up details ⟨the American colonist John Smith is believed by many historians to have *exaggerated* his adventures⟩ — see EMBROIDER
2 to describe or express in too strong terms ⟨it would be impossible to *exaggerate* the importance of this entrance exam⟩ — see OVERSTATE

exaggerated *adj* extended beyond normal or realistic bounds ⟨loves the *exaggerated* emotions that are part and parcel of grand opera⟩ — see BLOATED 1

exaggeration *n* the representation of something in terms that go beyond the facts ⟨their *exaggeration* was such that a rainstorm became a hurricane⟩
synonyms caricature, coloring, elaboration, embellishment, embroidering, embroidery, hyperbole, magnification, overstatement, padding, stretching
related words amplification, enhancement; fabrication, misrepresentation; fudging, hedging; hype, puffery; superlative
near antonyms belittlement, disparagement, minimizing, poor-mouthing
antonyms meiosis, understatement

exalt *vb* **1** to assign a high status or value to ⟨popular support and media hype have *exalted* Super Bowl Sunday to the level of a national holiday⟩
synonyms aggrandize, canonize, deify, dignify, elevate, ennoble, enshrine, ensky, enthrone, glorify, magnify
related words boost, lift, promote, raise, upgrade, uplift; heighten, intensify; idealize, romanticize, sanitize, sugarcoat; acclaim, extol (*also* extoll), honor, laud, praise
near antonyms belittle, decry, depreciate, detract, disparage, minimize
antonyms abase, degrade, demean, humble, humiliate
2 to proclaim the glory of ⟨monstrous, gaudy gambling palaces that seem to *exalt* the very notion of excess⟩ — see PRAISE 1

exam *n* a set of questions or problems designed to assess knowledge, skills, or intelligence ⟨the *exam* will cover everything we have studied this term⟩ — see EXAMINATION 1

examen *n* **1** a systematic search for the truth or facts about something ⟨an *examen* of the president's assasination that has been plagued by controversy since its original publication⟩ — see INQUIRY 1
2 an essay evaluating or analyzing something ⟨an insightful *examen* of the poet's works⟩ — see CRITICISM

examination *n* **1** a set of questions or problems designed to assess knowledge, skills, or intelligence ⟨applicants to the prep school are required to take a demanding *examination*⟩
synonyms exam, quiz, test
related words aptitude test, intelligence test, placement test; pretest, retest; board(s), midterm, midyear; catechism; audition; final; checkup, inspection, review; inquiry, interrogation, investigation, probe, research
2 a systematic search for the truth or facts about something ⟨an *examination* into the extent and causes of juvenile delinquency in the community⟩ — see INQUIRY 1
3 a close look at or over someone or something in order to judge condition ⟨even a hasty *examination* will tell any jeweler that that is not a real diamond⟩ — see INSPECTION

examine *vb* **1** to put a series of questions to ⟨the defense attorney was eager to *examine* her star witness⟩
synonyms catechize, grill, interrogate, pump, query, question, quiz, sweat [*slang*]
related words debrief; cross-examine, cross-question; annoy, harass, hound, pester; canvass (*also* canvas), poll
phrases give the third degree to, pick the brains of
2 to look over closely (as for judging quality or condition) ⟨the customer painstakingly *examined* the antique piece of furniture from top to bottom before purchasing it⟩ — see INSPECT
3 to search through or into ⟨a groundbreaking study that *examined* the causes of juvenile delinquency⟩ — see EXPLORE 1

example *n* one of a group or collection that shows what the whole is like ⟨a war bonnet that is a fine *example* of Native American handicraft⟩
synonyms case, exemplar, exemplification, illustration, instance, prototype, representative, sample, specimen
related words archetype, classic, locus classicus, paradigm; cross section, microcosm; evidence, indication, manifestation, sign
phrases case in point

exasperate *vb* to disturb the peace of mind of (someone) especially by repeated disagreeable acts ⟨small children can *exasperate* their parents with endless questions about why this or that is so⟩ — see IRRITATE 1

exasperated *adj* subjected to and reacting with irritation ⟨overworked, *exasperated* parents barking at their children over little things⟩ — see ANNOYED

exasperating *adj* causing annoyance ⟨those *exasperating* details that come with almost any job⟩ — see ANNOYING

exasperation *n* **1** something that is a source of irritation ⟨add people who use cell phones inconsiderately to the list of daily *exasperations*⟩ — see ANNOYANCE 3

2 the feeling of impatience or anger caused by another's repeated disagreeable acts ⟨my rising *exasperation* with these constant interruptions⟩ — see ANNOYANCE 2

excavate *vb* to hollow out or form (something) by removing earth ⟨workmen are *excavating* a long tunnel that will eventually replace the aboveground expressway⟩ — see DIG 1

exceed *vb* **1** to go beyond the limit of ⟨by resorting to corporal punishment, the teacher had clearly *exceeded* his authority⟩
synonyms break, outreach, outrun, overpass, overreach, overrun, overshoot, overstep, surpass, transcend
related words encroach, entrench (*also* intrench), infringe, invade, trespass; overdo, overuse, overutilize, overwork
2 to be greater, better, or stronger than ⟨her knowledge of French wines *exceeds* that of anyone else I know⟩ — see SURPASS 1

exceeding *adj* being out of the ordinary ⟨accepted the apology with *exceeding* graciousness⟩ — see EXCEPTIONAL 1

exceedingly *also* **exceeding** *adv* to a great degree ⟨the salesclerk was *exceedingly* patient with one customer who couldn't make up his mind⟩ — see VERY 1

excel *vb* to be greater, better, or stronger than ⟨the special effects in this new sci-fi extravaganza *excel* any that we've seen previously⟩ — see SURPASS 1

excellence *n* **1** exceptionally high quality ⟨the annual awards honor *excellence* in children's literature⟩
synonyms choiceness, distinction, excellency, first-rateness, greatness, perfection, preeminence, primeness, superbness, superiority, supremacy
related words faultlessness, flawlessness, impeccability, perfectness; goodness, value, worth; consequence, importance, notability
near antonyms averageness, badness, crumminess, inferiority, mediocrity, ordinariness, worthlessness
2 a quality that gives something special worth ⟨the particular *excellence* of down in clothing and sleeping bags is its lightness⟩
synonyms cardinal virtue, distinction, excellency, grace, merit, value, virtue
related words advantage, edge, plus, superiority
near antonyms blemish, defect, failing, fault, flaw; drawback, minus, negative
antonyms deficiency, demerit, disvalue

excellency *n* **1** a quality that gives something special worth ⟨claimed that granite has so many *excellencies* as material for countertops that it is well worth the high price⟩ — see EXCELLENCE 2
2 exceptionally high quality ⟨the *excellency* of the violins crafted by Stradivarius is beyond dispute⟩ — see EXCELLENCE 1

excellent *adj* of the very best kind ⟨fast-food fans rate this chain's fries as *excellent*⟩
synonyms A-OK, A1, awesome, bang-up, banner, beautiful, blue-chip, blue-ribbon, boffo, bonny (*also* bonnie) [*chiefly British*], boss [*slang*], brag, brave, bully, bumper, capital, choice, classic, cool [*slang*], corking, crackerjack, cracking, dandy, divine, dope [*slang*], down [*slang*], dynamite, fab, fabulous, famous, fantabulous [*slang*], fantastic, fine, first-class, first-rate, first-string, five-star, four-star, frontline, gangbusters (*also* gangbuster), gilt-edged (*or* gilt-edge), gone [*slang*], grand, great, groovy, heavenly, high-class, hot, hype [*slang*], immense, jim-dandy, keen, lovely, marvelous (*or* marvellous), mean, neat, nifty, noble, number one (*also* No. 1), numero uno, out-of-sight [*slang*], par excellence, peachy, peachy keen, phat [*slang*], prime, primo [*slang*], prize, prizewinning, quality, radical [*slang*], righteous [*slang*], sensational, slick, splendid, stellar, sterling, superb, superior, superlative, supernal, swell, terrific, tip-top, top, top-flight, top-notch, top-of-the-line, topping [*chiefly British*], top-shelf, unsurpassed, wizard [*chiefly British*], wonderful
related words acceptable, adequate, all right, decent, good, OK (*or* okay), passable, satisfactory, tolerable; better, exceptional, fancy, high-grade, high-test, premium, select, special, superfine; classical, standard, traditional
phrases out of this world, too much
near antonyms bad, inferior, low-grade, substandard, unsatisfactory; mediocre, middling, second-class, second-rate
antonyms atrocious, awful, execrable, lousy, pathetic, poor, rotten, terrible, vile, wretched

except *vb* **1** to present an opposing opinion or argument ⟨I must *except* to your remark that there are no great novelists currently living⟩ — see OBJECT
2 to prevent the participation, consideration, or inclusion of ⟨we'll have to *except* members who haven't paid their club dues from voting in the election⟩ — see EXCLUDE

except *also* **excepting** *conj* if it were not for the fact that ⟨I'd go, *except* it's too far⟩
synonyms but, only, saving, yet

except *also* **excepting** *prep* not including ⟨the store is open daily *except* Sundays⟩
synonyms apart from, aside from, bar, barring, beside, besides, but, except for, excluding, exclusive of, other than, outside, outside of, save, saving

except for *prep* not including ⟨*except for* newscasts, I hardly watch any television at all⟩ — see EXCEPT

exception *n* **1** a feeling or declaration of disapproval or dissent ⟨I take strong *exception* to your assessment of his singing ability⟩ — see OBJECTION
2 something that is different from what is ordinary or expected ⟨her tardiness today is an *exception*; usually she's on time⟩ — see ANOMALY 1

exceptionable *adj* provoking or likely to provoke protest ⟨as long as the language is not *exceptionable*, people can discuss any topic they want in the chat room⟩ — see OBJECTIONABLE

exceptional *adj* **1** being out of the ordinary ⟨an *exceptional* amount of snow fell in March⟩
synonyms aberrant, aberrated, abnormal, anomalous, atypical, especial, exceeding, extraordinaire, extraordinary, freak, odd, peculiar, phenomenal, preternatural, rare, singular, uncommon, uncustomary, unique, unusual, unwonted
related words conspicuous, notable, noticeable, outstanding, prominent, remarkable, salient, striking; bizarre, deviant, eccentric, freakish, monstrous, oddball, outlandish, quaint, strange, weird; incomprehensible, inconceivable, incredible, unimaginable, unthinkable
near antonyms everyday, familiar, frequent
antonyms common, customary, normal, ordinary, typical, unexceptional, unextraordinary, usual
2 deprived of the power to perform one or more natural bodily activities ⟨her experience working with *exceptional* children was rewarding and inspiring⟩ — see DISABLED
3 having or showing quickness of mind ⟨a special school for *exceptional* children⟩ — see INTELLIGENT 1

excerpt *n* a part taken from a longer work ⟨he'll read an *excerpt* from the novel at the book signing⟩
synonyms extract, passage
related words clip, snippet, sound bite; citation, quotation; locus classicus, longueur, purple passage; context; sample, selection

excess *adj* being over what is needed ⟨any *excess* food from the party will be donated to a shelter for the homeless⟩ — see SPARE 1

excess *n* **1** the state or an instance of going beyond

what is usual, proper, or needed ⟨a new television season with an *excess* of sitcoms featuring wisecracking teenagers⟩
synonyms bellyful, fat, overabundance, overage, overflow, overkill, overmuch, overplus, oversupply, plethora, plus, redundancy, superabundance, superfluity, surfeit, surplus, surplusage
related words abundance, bounty, plentitude, plenty, profusion, sufficiency; overproduction, overstock
near antonyms dearth, lack, scarcity, want
antonyms deficiency, deficit, insufficiency, undersupply
2 a propensity for extremes in one's actions, beliefs, or habits ⟨the wretched *excess* that is so often found in the world of show business⟩
synonyms excessiveness, exorbitance, immoderacy, immoderation, insobriety, intemperance, intemperateness, nimiety
related words extravagance, prodigality; extremism, irrationality, radicalism, unreasonableness
antonyms moderateness, moderation, temperance, temperateness

excessive *adj* going beyond a normal or acceptable limit in degree or amount ⟨nerdy hackers who spend an *excessive* amount of time sitting in front of their computers⟩
synonyms baroque, devilish, exorbitant, extravagant, extreme, fancy, immoderate, inordinate, insane, intolerable, lavish, overdue, overextravagant, overmuch, overweening, plethoric, steep, stiff, towering, unconscionable, undue, unmerciful
related words boundless, endless, immeasurable, infinite, limitless; unbearable, unjustifiable, unwarranted; improper, inappropriate, thick, unseemly; unrestrained
phrases a bit much, over the top
near antonyms deficient, inadequate, insufficient; minimal, minimum
antonyms middling, moderate, modest, reasonable, temperate

excessively *adv* beyond a normal or acceptable limit ⟨noise from the party was *excessively* loud⟩ — see TOO 1

excessiveness *n* a propensity for extremes in one's actions, beliefs, or habits ⟨the *excessiveness* for which decadent Rome has become famous in history⟩ — see EXCESS 2

exchange *n* **1** a giving or taking of one thing of value in return for another ⟨*exchanges* of commemorative pins are common among Olympic athletes⟩
synonyms back-and-forth, barter, commutation, dicker, quid pro quo, swap, trade, trade-off, truck
related words replacement, substitution; reciprocation, recompense, requital; bargain, deal, horse trade, negotiation, transaction; bargaining, dealing, dickering, haggling, horse trading; logrolling
2 talking or a talk between two or more people ⟨we had a brief *exchange* with the pastor as we passed him on the way out of church⟩ — see CONVERSATION

exchange *vb* to give up (something) and take something else in return ⟨I'd like to *exchange* this sweater for one in a larger size⟩ — see CHANGE 3

exchangeable *adj* capable of being substituted in place of one another ⟨as far as small businesses near the border are concerned, the two currencies are *exchangeable*⟩ — see INTERCHANGEABLE

exchequer *n* available money ⟨their son would make beseeching requests for more money whenever his personal *exchequer* was getting low⟩ — see FUND 2

excitable *adj* easily excited by nature ⟨an *excitable* child who needs a stable home life⟩
synonyms fiddle-footed, flighty, fluttery, high-strung, hyper, hyperactive, hyperexcitable, hyperkinetic, jittery, jumpy, nervous, skittery, skittish, spasmodic, spooky
related words hot-blooded, mercurial, temperamental, unstable, volatile, volcanic; anxious, edgy, flibbertigibbety, nervy, tense, uptight; emotional, emotionalistic, hypersensitive, intense, sensitive, soulful; dramatic, histrionic, melodramatic; irascible, irritable, perturbable, prickly, testy, touchy
near antonyms calm, collected, cool, serene, tranquil; easy, easygoing, laid-back, relaxed
antonyms imperturbable, nerveless, unexcitable, unflappable, unshakable

excite *vb* **1** to cause a pleasurable stimulation of the feelings ⟨for some reason the first snowfall of the season never fails to *excite* us⟩ — see THRILL
2 to rouse to strong feeling or action ⟨televised pictures of the victims of the famine that would *excite* any viewer to pity⟩ — see PROVOKE 1

excited *adj* **1** being in a state of increased activity or agitation ⟨*excited* trading on the stock exchange followed in the wake of the favorable economic report⟩ — see FEVERISH 1
2 showing urgent desire or interest ⟨everyone was *excited* about the upcoming family vacation at the ski resort⟩ — see EAGER

excitement *n* **1** something that arouses a strong response from another ⟨there were few *excitements* of any kind on our very uneventful trip back home⟩ — see PROVOCATION 1
2 urgent desire or interest ⟨in our *excitement* to get going, we forgot to make sure that all of the lights in the house had been turned off⟩ — see EAGERNESS

exciter *n* a person who stirs up public feelings especially of discontent ⟨many of the *exciters* of the so-called "tax revolt" were actually campaign workers for one of the gubernatorial candidates⟩ — see AGITATOR

exciting *adj* **1** causing great emotional or mental stimulation ⟨an *exciting*, come-from-behind victory for the underdogs in the last game of the World Series⟩
synonyms breathtaking, charged, electric, electrifying, exhilarating, exhilarative, galvanic, galvanizing, hair-raising, heart-stopping, inspiring, intoxicating, kicky, mind-bending, mind-blowing, mind-boggling, rip-roaring, rousing, stimulating, stirring, thrilling
related words arresting, interesting, intriguing, provocative, tantalizing, titillating; absorbing, engrossing, gripping, riveting; moving, poignant, touching; enchanting, enthralling, fascinating, spellbinding; dynamic, energetic, high-voltage, kinetic, lively, lusty
near antonyms boring, mind-numbing, tedious, tiresome; dreary, dull, humdrum, monotonous, uninteresting
antonyms unexciting
2 serving or likely to arouse a strong reaction ⟨and what *exciting* news have you for us today?⟩ — see PROVOCATIVE

exclaim *vb* to utter with a sudden burst of strong feeling ⟨the whole team *exclaimed* with one voice, "We won!"⟩
synonyms blat, blurt (out), bolt, cry (out), ejaculate
related words blunder, leak; bellow, bleat, crow, holler, hoot, howl, roar, shout, whoop, yowl; aah (*also* ah), ooh; interject

exclamation *n* a sudden short emotional utterance ⟨the good news was greeted with a chorus of joyous *exclamations*⟩
synonyms cry, ejaculation, interjection
related words aah (*also* ah), ooh; holler, hoot, howl, shout, whoop, yell, yelp, yowl; scream, screech, shriek, squall, squeak, squeal

exclude *vb* to prevent the participation, consideration, or inclusion of ⟨the revelation that the candidate had

once belonged to a country club that *excluded* minorities⟩
synonyms ban, bar, close out, count (out), debar, eliminate, except, freeze out, rule out, shut out
related words blackball, blacklist, excommunicate, ostracize; banish, deport, exile, expel, oust, throw out; obviate, preclude, prevent, prohibit; block, hinder, impede, obstruct; cease, discontinue, halt, suspend; deter, stave off, ward (off); check off, disregard; comb (out), weed (out)
phrases close one's doors to
near antonyms accept, embrace, entertain, receive, take in, welcome; unban
antonyms admit, include

excluding *prep* not including ⟨*excluding* me, plan on five guests for dinner tonight⟩ — see EXCEPT

exclusive *adj* **1** belonging only to the one person, unit, or group named ⟨residents of the apartment complex have *exclusive* use of the pool⟩ — see SOLE 1
2 not divided or scattered among several areas of interest or concern ⟨during interviews she always gives the job applicant her *exclusive* attention⟩ — see WHOLE 1
3 appealing to affluent consumers ⟨a section of the city where the *exclusive* boutiques and fashionable restaurants are concentrated⟩ — see UPSCALE
4 being in the latest or current fashion ⟨an *exclusive* designer gown of the sort that shows up on red carpets⟩ — see STYLISH

exclusively *adv* for nothing other than ⟨his best paintings are the ones that he did *exclusively* for the sheer pleasure they gave him⟩ — see SOLELY 1

exclusive of *prep* not including ⟨all food and beverages are included in the price, *exclusive of* any alcoholic drinks ordered from the bar⟩ — see EXCEPT

excogitate *vb* to create or think of by clever use of the imagination ⟨she's a master at *excogitating* reasons not to do her assigned work⟩ — see INVENT

excoriate *vb* **1** to criticize harshly and usually publicly ⟨the mayor had hardly been in office for a month before she was being *excoriated* for problems of very long standing⟩ — see ATTACK 2
2 to make sore by continued rubbing ⟨the manacles had badly *excoriated* the prisoner's wrists⟩ — see CHAFE 1

excoriation *n* an often public or formal expression of disapproval ⟨the recent *excoriation* of dumbed-down textbooks by a panel of educators⟩ — see CENSURE

excrement *n* solid matter discharged from an animal's alimentary canal ⟨an ordinance that requires dog walkers to remove their animal's *excrement* from city streets⟩ — see DROPPING 1

excrescence *n* **1** an abnormal mass of tissue ⟨concerned about the weird *excrescence* that seemed to be developing on his hand⟩ — see GROWTH 1
2 something that spoils the appearance or completeness of a thing ⟨local residents regard the hulking apartment building as a hideous *excrescence* on their once-lovely street⟩ — see BLEMISH

excrescency *n* **1** an abnormal mass of tissue ⟨fortunately, the *excrescency* could be removed with surgery⟩ — see GROWTH 1
2 something that spoils the appearance or completeness of a thing ⟨some feel that the planned skyscraper would be an *excrescency* on the city's low-rise skyline⟩ — see BLEMISH

excreta *n pl* solid matter discharged from an animal's alimentary canal ⟨the cage badly needed to be cleaned of the rabbit's *excreta*⟩ — see DROPPING 1

excruciate *vb* to cause persistent suffering to ⟨she has long been *excruciated* by a persistent pain in her knee⟩ — see AFFLICT

excruciating *adj* **1** intensely or unbearably painful ⟨those who publicly disagreed with the government were subjected to *excruciating* torture⟩
synonyms agonizing, harrowing, racking, raging, tormenting, torturing, torturous, wrenching
related words acute, exquisite, extreme, fierce, intense, vehement, violent; biting, cutting, penetrating, piercing, sharp, shooting, smarting, stabbing, stinging, tearing, tingling
2 difficult to endure ⟨the *excruciating* heat that the settlers faced as they crossed the deserts of the Southwest⟩ — see HARSH 1
3 hard to accept or bear especially emotionally ⟨most *excruciating* of all was the endless wait for news of any survivors of the plane crash⟩ — see BITTER 2
4 extreme in degree, power, or effect ⟨the *excruciating* grief they felt upon the loss of their child⟩ — see INTENSE 1

excruciation *n* a state of great suffering of body or mind ⟨had never experienced such *excruciation* as when he contracted shingles⟩ — see DISTRESS 1

exculpate *vb* to free from a charge of wrongdoing ⟨I will present evidence that will *exculpate* my client⟩
synonyms absolve, acquit, clear, exonerate, vindicate
related words atone (for), expiate; discharge, liberate, redeem, release, unburden; condone, excuse, whitewash; forgive, pardon, remit; avenge, redress, revenge
near antonyms accuse, arraign, charge, impeach, indict; convict
antonyms criminate, incriminate

exculpation *n* a setting free from a charge of wrongdoing ⟨evidence that might bring about the *exculpation* of the defendant⟩ — see ACQUITTAL

excursion *n* **1** a short trip for pleasure ⟨our weekend *excursions* have encompassed virtually all parts of our home state⟩
synonyms jaunt, junket, outing, ramble, sally, sashay, sortie, spin
related words journey, travel(s), voyage; circuit, tour; expedition, odyssey, safari; detour; hike, peregrination, trek, walk; pilgrimage
2 a departure from the subject under consideration ⟨the professor's frequent and sometimes far-ranging *excursions* in his lectures are the stuff of campus legend⟩ — see TANGENT

excursionist *n* a person who travels for pleasure ⟨a list of things to do for weekend *excursionists* in the city⟩ — see TOURIST

excursive *adj* passing from one topic to another ⟨an *excursive* story line that some readers of Melville's novel find very rewarding⟩ — see DISCURSIVE

excursus *n* a part added at the end of a book or periodical ⟨this biography of Eleanor of Aquitaine contains an interesting *excursus* on the status of women in the Middle Ages⟩ — see ADDENDUM 1

excusable *adj* worthy of forgiveness ⟨an *excusable* lapse of memory in a senior citizen⟩ — see VENIAL

excuse *n* an explanation that frees one from fault or blame ⟨"a really important business call" is no *excuse* for not paying proper attention to one's driving⟩
synonyms alibi, apology, defense, justification, plea, reason
related words color, guise, pretense (*or* pretence), pretext, rationale, rationalization, vindication, whitewash; cop-out, out; acknowledgment (*or* acknowledgement), atonement, confession; extenuation, palliation

excuse *vb* **1** to dismiss as of little importance ⟨more often than not, voters are willing to *excuse* a candidate's youthful indiscretion⟩
synonyms blink (at), brush (aside *or* off), condone, discount, disregard, forgive, gloss (over), gloze (over), ignore, overlook, overpass, paper over, pardon, pass over, remit, shrug off, whitewash, wink (at)
related words explain, justify, rationalize; absolve, ac-

quit, clear, exculpate, exonerate, vindicate; waive, wave (aside *or* off)
phrases close one's eyes to, forgive and forget
near antonyms heed, mark, mind, note, object (to)
2 to be an acceptable reason for ⟨having a female passenger in labor will generally *excuse* a little disregard for the speed limit⟩ — see JUSTIFY 1
3 to make (something) seem less bad by offering excuses ⟨he's always *excusing* his chronic lying by claiming that everybody lies⟩ — see PALLIATE 1

exec *n* a person who manages or directs something ⟨a restaurant where the city's top *execs* like to have power lunches⟩ — see EXECUTIVE

execrable *adj* **1** extremely unsatisfactory ⟨her *execrable* singing finally brought a complaint from the neighbors⟩ — see WRETCHED 1
2 of low quality ⟨another souvenir shop selling *execrable* knickknacks manufactured in some foreign sweatshop⟩ — see CHEAP 2
3 not following or in accordance with standards of honor and decency ⟨a sordid murder case that was covered with *execrable* excess by the newspaper tabloids and cable news outlets⟩ — see IGNOBLE 2

execrate *vb* **1** to declare to be morally wrong or evil ⟨leaders from around the world *execrated* the terrorists responsible for the bomb blast⟩ — see CONDEMN 1
2 to dislike strongly ⟨*execrates* without apology anyone who would physically abuse children or animals⟩ — see HATE

execration *n* **1** a prayer that harm will come to someone ⟨upon discovering that someone had stolen his golf bag, he let loose a volley of *execrations*⟩ — see CURSE 1
2 a very strong dislike ⟨a cowardly betrayal that earned him the *execration* of all who had remained loyal to the cause⟩ — see HATE 1
3 something or someone that is hated ⟨denounced as an abomination before God and man, the heretic would forever be an *execration* even amongst his own people⟩ — see HATE 2

execute *vb* **1** to carry out effectively ⟨the agency charged with *executing* the nation's drug laws⟩ — see ENFORCE
2 to carry through (as a process) to completion ⟨when you *execute* this dance step, try to keep your arms a little higher⟩ — see PERFORM 1
3 to put to death deliberately ⟨during the war those convicted of desertion were summarily *executed*⟩ — see MURDER 1

execution *n* the doing of an action ⟨the *execution* of this magic trick must be accomplished in one fluid motion⟩ — see COMMISSION 2

executive *adj* suited for or relating to the directing of things ⟨the *executive* skills needed to manage a large business office⟩
synonyms administrative, directorial, managerial, supervisory
related words bureaucratic, governmental, ministerial, official, parliamentary; regulatory; authoritarian, despotic, dictatorial
antonyms nonmanagerial, nonsupervisory

executive *n* a person who manages or directs something ⟨a program that teaches company *executives* how to better manage their staffs⟩
synonyms administrant, administrator, archon, director, exec, manager, superintendent, supervisor
related words codirector, comanager, co-organizer; middle manager; boardman, officer, official; commissioner, minister; boss, chief, head, leader, president

exegesis *n* a statement that makes something clear ⟨a psychobiography that purports to be the definitive *exegesis* of the late president's character⟩ — see EXPLANATION 1

exegetical *also* **exegetic** *adj* serving to explain ⟨a new edition of Shakespeare with an abundance of *exegetical* commentary for the modern reader⟩ — see EXPLANATORY

exemplar *n* **1** one of a group or collection that shows what the whole is like ⟨the village's Congregational church could serve as an *exemplar* of the white clapboard church with a steeple that is a fixture in old New England towns⟩ — see EXAMPLE
2 someone of such unequaled perfection as to deserve imitation ⟨few of history's heroes were quite the *exemplars* that generations of schoolteachers made them out to be⟩ — see IDEAL 1
3 the most perfect type or example ⟨the paintings of the French painter Claude Monet are often regarded as *exemplars* of Impressionism⟩ — see QUINTESSENCE 1

exemplary *adj* **1** constituting, serving as, or worthy of being a pattern to be imitated ⟨as a hospital volunteer you have given *exemplary* service to your community⟩ — see MODEL
2 serving as or offering a warning ⟨armies have traditionally used public execution as an *exemplary* punishment for the crime of desertion⟩ — see CAUTIONARY

exemplification *n* one of a group or collection that shows what the whole is like ⟨a futile war that is now regarded as the *exemplification* of national naïveté and arrogance⟩ — see EXAMPLE

exemplify *vb* to show or make clear by using examples ⟨in your review you don't really *exemplify* your points with specific examples from the novel⟩ — see ILLUSTRATE 1

exemption *n* freedom from punishment, harm, or loss ⟨those motorists who think that they can flout the town's parking regulations with *exemption*⟩ — see IMPUNITY

exercise *n* **1** energetic movement of the body for the sake of physical fitness ⟨the doctor ordered plenty of fresh air and *exercise*⟩
synonyms activity, conditioning, exertion
related words training, warm-up, workout; toning, trimming; aerobics, athletics, bodybuilding, body mechanics, calisthenics, gymnastics, isometrics, plyometrics, slimnastics, weight lifting; physical therapy
2 something done over and over in order to develop skill ⟨a young piano student dutifully going through the standard finger *exercises*⟩
synonyms drill, practice (*also* practise), routine, training, workout
related words assignment, homework, lesson; brushup, refresher, review
3 the act or practice of employing something for a particular purpose ⟨the observation that the best exercise for losing weight is the *exercise* of one's ability to say no to food⟩ — see USE 1

exercise *vb* **1** to bring to bear especially forcefully or effectively ⟨a senator who consistently *exercises* his clout in Congress to get pork barrel projects for his state⟩ — see EXERT
2 to do over and over so as to become skilled ⟨the only way to *exercise* your writing skills is to do more writing⟩ — see PRACTICE
3 to put into action or service ⟨commended the firefighters for *exercising* really good judgment in that emergency⟩ — see USE 1
4 to trouble the mind of; to make uneasy ⟨the slightest change in travel plans is enough to get him all *exercised*⟩ — see DISTURB 1

exert *vb* to bring to bear especially forcefully or effectively ⟨parental involvement has consistently been shown to *exert* the most influence over a child's success in school⟩
synonyms apply, exercise, ply, put out, wield

related words employ, use, utilize; abuse, misapply, misuse

exertion *n* **1** energetic movement of the body for the sake of physical fitness ⟨often the television addict's greatest attempt at *exertion* was switching channels on the remote control⟩ — see EXERCISE 1

2 the active use of energy in producing a result ⟨the number of blueberries that we were finding was hardly worth the *exertion*⟩ — see EFFORT

exfoliate *vb* to cast (a natural bodily covering or appendage) aside ⟨a soap that promises to help me *exfoliate* all that dry, flaky skin I've apparently been carrying around⟩ — see SHED 1

exhale *vb* **1** to let or force out of the lungs ⟨before answering, the suspect *exhaled* a cloud of cigarette smoke⟩

synonyms blow (out), breathe (out), expel, expire

related words expectorate

antonyms inbreathe, inhale, inspire

2 to throw or give off ⟨the lilacs were *exhaling* a sweet fragrance that virtually filled the room⟩ — see EMIT 1

exhaust *vb* **1** to use up all the physical energy of ⟨the long day at the county fair had *exhausted* everyone⟩

synonyms break, burn out, bust, do in, do up, drain, fag, fatigue, frazzle, harass, kill, knock out, outwear, tire, tucker (out), wash out, wear, wear out, weary

related words debilitate, enervate, enfeeble, sap, waste, weaken

phrases wear to a frazzle

near antonyms activate, energize, invigorate, rejuvenate, strengthen, vitalize; relax, rest, unwind

2 to make complete use of ⟨we had been at the theme park barely for two hours, and we were on the verge of *exhausting* our spending money⟩ — see DEPLETE 1

exhausted *adj* depleted in strength, energy, or freshness ⟨the *exhausted* runner crossed the finish line and just collapsed⟩ — see WEARY 1

exhaustion *n* a complete depletion of energy or strength ⟨with all of the work and activity that the holiday season brings, the working couple was on the point of *exhaustion*⟩ — see FATIGUE 1

exhaustive *adj* **1** trying all possibilities ⟨after an *exhaustive* search of our house, we still hadn't found the cat⟩

synonyms all-out, clean, complete, comprehensive, full-scale, out-and-out, thorough, thoroughgoing, total

related words broad, extensive, far-reaching, in-depth, sweeping, wide, wide-ranging; general, global, inclusive, methodical (*also* methodic), systematic; no-holds-barred, unhampered, unrestrained

near antonyms aimless, desultory, haphazard, hit-or-miss, random; cursory, shallow, slipshod, superficial; limited, narrow, restricted

2 covering everything or all important points ⟨an *exhaustive* survey of the nation's sexual habits⟩ — see ENCYCLOPEDIC

exhaustively *adv* with attention to all aspects or details ⟨the psychic's claims were *exhaustively* examined by scientific experts and found to be without merit⟩ — see THOROUGHLY 1

exhibit *n* a public showing of objects of interest ⟨a touring *exhibit* of national treasures from the Smithsonian Institution⟩ — see EXHIBITION 1

exhibit *vb* to present so as to invite notice or attention ⟨these naturalists take their birds of prey on tour and *exhibit* them before groups of schoolchildren⟩ — see SHOW 1

exhibition *n* **1** a public showing of objects of interest ⟨an *exhibition* of valuable and fascinating artifacts from a recovered pirate ship⟩

synonyms display, exhibit, expo, exposition, fair, show

related words demonstration, performance, presentation, production; extravaganza, pageant, spectacle; auction, offering, presentment, sale

2 an outward and often exaggerated indication of something abstract (as a feeling) for effect ⟨for the benefit of the crowd, the professional wrestler made a great *exhibition* of ferocity⟩ — see SHOW 1

exhilarate *vb* **1** to cause a pleasurable stimulation of the feelings ⟨the *exhilarating* feeling of flying that hang gliding offers⟩ — see THRILL

2 to fill with great joy ⟨the climactic moment of commencement ceremonies usually *exhilarates* graduates and proud parents alike⟩ — see ELATE

exhilarated *adj* experiencing or marked by overwhelming usually pleasurable emotion ⟨the winner's *exhilarated* glow was seen in newspaper photographs around the globe⟩ — see ECSTATIC

exhilarating *adj* causing great emotional or mental stimulation ⟨no recording can capture the *exhilarating* feeling of being at a live rock concert⟩ — see EXCITING 1

exhilaration *n* **1** a pleasurably intense stimulation of the feelings ⟨the lavish spectacle results in one *exhilaration* after another⟩ — see THRILL

2 a state of overwhelming usually pleasurable emotion ⟨the *exhilaration* of victory that spectators get to witness at the Olympic Games⟩ — see ECSTASY

exhilarative *adj* causing great emotional or mental stimulation ⟨discovered that white-water rafting is an especially *exhilarative* adventure⟩ — see EXCITING 1

exhort *vb* to try to persuade (someone) through earnest appeals to follow a course of action ⟨the speaker *exhorted* the graduating students to go forth and try to make a difference in the world⟩ — see URGE

exhume *vb* to remove from place of burial ⟨the remains of John Paul Jones were *exhumed* in Paris and transported with great ceremony to the U.S. Naval Academy⟩

synonyms disinter, unearth

antonyms bury, entomb, inhume, inter, tomb

exigency *n* a time or state of affairs requiring prompt or decisive action ⟨the *exigencies* requiring snap decisions that traders on the stock exchange face every day⟩ — see EMERGENCY

exigent *adj* needing immediate attention ⟨started his workday with a flood of *exigent* matters that required his quick decision⟩ — see ACUTE 2

exiguous *adj* less plentiful than what is normal, necessary, or desirable ⟨computer equipment that would be prohibitively expensive, given the rural school's *exiguous* resources⟩ — see MEAGER

exile *n* **1** the forced removal from a homeland ⟨the *exile* of French settlers from Nova Scotia resulted in the birth of the Cajun community in the U.S.⟩

synonyms banishment, deportation, displacement, expatriation, expulsion, relegation

related words ostracism; extradition; diaspora, dispersion, scattering; emigration, migration; evacuation; ethnic cleansing, transportation; dispossession, ejection, ouster

near antonyms repatriation, return; immigration

2 a person forced to emigrate for political reasons ⟨after being overthrown in a coup, the dictator spent the remainder of his life as an *exile* in a string of less-than-welcoming countries⟩ — see ÉMIGRÉ 1

exile *vb* to force to leave a country ⟨with their conquest of the Moors complete, Ferdinand and Isabella next *exiled* the Jews from Spain⟩ — see BANISH 1

exist *vb* to have life ⟨strive to have a full, rich life rather than merely *exist*⟩ — see BE 1

existence *n* the fact of being or of being real ⟨the *existence* of UFO's is something that people continue to argue about⟩

synonyms actuality, corporality, corporeality, reality, subsistence, thingness
related words genuineness, realness; activity, animation, life; currency, presence, prevalence
near antonyms absence, dearth, lack, want; potentiality, virtuality
antonyms inexistence, nonbeing, nonexistence, nothingness, unreality

existent *adj* **1** existing in fact and not merely as a possibility ⟨to some people, angels are as *existent* as aardvarks or astronomers⟩ — see ACTUAL
2 having being at the present time ⟨the coelacanth is one *existent* fish that was once thought to be entirely extinct⟩ — see EXTANT 1

existent *n* one that has a real and independent existence ⟨other worlds are *existents* that are generally taken for granted in works of science fiction⟩ — see ENTITY

existential *adj* based on observation or experience ⟨child psychologist Bruno Bettelheim believed that fairy tales help children cope with their *existential* anxieties and dilemmas⟩ — see EMPIRICAL 1

existing *adj* having being at the present time ⟨*existing* breeds of the turkey that graces our Thanksgiving table are said to bear little resemblance to the gamy birds that the Pilgrims enjoyed⟩ — see EXTANT 1

exit *n* **1** a place or means of going out ⟨all of the building's *exits* were being watched by security guards⟩
synonyms egress, issue, outlet
related words escape, escape hatch, release; gate, mouth, opening, passage, vent
near antonyms access, entrée (*or* entree)
antonyms entrance, entranceway, entry, entryway, ingress
2 the act of leaving a place ⟨the movie star's quick *exit* through the back of the hotel went unnoticed by the horde of photographers waiting out front⟩ — see DEPARTURE 1
3 the permanent stopping of all the vital bodily activities ⟨determined that his *exit* be from a place and time of his own choosing, the terminally ill patient opted for suicide⟩ — see DEATH 1

exit *vb* **1** to leave a place often for another ⟨in case of fire, *exit* from the building in a calm and orderly fashion⟩ — see GO 2
2 to stop living ⟨expressed her wish to *exit* surrounded by family and friends⟩ — see DIE 1

exiting *n* the act of leaving a place ⟨their *exiting* of the boring party was swiftly and quietly accomplished⟩ — see DEPARTURE 1

exodus *n* a flowing or going out ⟨the mass *exodus* from the cities for the beaches and the mountains on most summer weekends⟩ — see OUTFLOW

exonerate *vb* to free from a charge of wrongdoing ⟨the results of the DNA fingerprinting finally *exonerated* the man, but only after he had wasted 10 years of his life in prison⟩ — see EXCULPATE

exoneration *n* a setting free from a charge of wrongdoing ⟨the accused refused a plea bargain, asserting that he was innocent and would settle for nothing less than complete *exoneration*⟩ — see ACQUITTAL

exorbitance *n* a propensity for extremes in one's actions, beliefs, or habits ⟨an *exorbitance* that seemed to have been brought about by a midlife crisis⟩ — see EXCESS 2

exorbitant *adj* going beyond a normal or acceptable limit in degree or amount ⟨the cost of our stay was so *exorbitant* you would have thought that we had bought the hotel and not just spent a few nights there⟩ — see EXCESSIVE

exorbitantly *adv* beyond a normal or acceptable limit ⟨the *exorbitantly* priced concert tickets had us wondering if we were personally footing the bill for the band's private jet⟩ — see TOO 1

exorcise *also* **exorcize** *vb* to get rid of as useless or unwanted ⟨please *exorcise* that offensive word from your vocabulary⟩ — see DISCARD

exordium *n* a short section (as of a book) that leads to or explains the main part ⟨in his *exordium* the author warns his readers that they should expect a radically different interpretation of the causes of the war⟩ — see INTRODUCTION

exotic *adj* excitingly or mysteriously unusual ⟨the gradual disappearance of *exotic* lands in a culturally homogenized world⟩
synonyms bizarro, fantastic (*also* fantastical), glamorous (*also* glamourous), marvelous (*or* marvellous), outlandish, romantic, strange
related words colorful, picture-book, picturesque, quaint; alien, foreign; dark, distant, faraway, remote; alluring, captivating, enchanting, fascinating, magical
antonyms familiar, nonexotic, nonglamorous, plain-Jane, unexotic, unglamorous, unromantic

exotic *n* something strange or unusual that is an object of interest ⟨the botanical garden boasts an array of horticultural *exotics* from around the world⟩ — see CURIOSITY 2

expand *vb* **1** to express more fully and in greater detail ⟨an article on the First Ladies that the author later *expanded* into a book⟩
synonyms amplify, develop, dilate (on *or* upon), elaborate (on), enlarge (on *or* upon), flesh (out)
related words add (to), complement, supplement; discourse, expatiate, ramble, run on
near antonyms compress, contract; outline, summarize, sum up
antonyms abbreviate, abridge, condense, shorten
2 to make greater in size, amount, or number ⟨we had to *expand* the list of wedding guests several times in order to accommodate all the relatives Mother wouldn't dream of excluding⟩ — see INCREASE 1
3 to arrange the parts of (something) over a wider area ⟨a spare leaf for those times when we have to *expand* the dining table to accommodate extra guests⟩ — see OPEN 3
4 to become greater in extent, volume, amount, or number ⟨water *expands* when it becomes frozen⟩ — see INCREASE 2

expanse *n* a wide space or area ⟨the great explorers who crossed the vast *expanses* of the seven seas in small ships⟩
synonyms breadth, distance, expansion, extent, field, length, plain, reach, sheet, spread, stretch, waste
related words domain, sphere, territory; compass, range, scope, sweep; gamut, scale, spectrum; depth, emptiness, void; extension, latitude, span; amplitude, immensity, magnitude

expansion *n* **1** something added (as by growth) ⟨the museum's new wing is only the first in a series of *expansions* planned for the next decade⟩ — see INCREASE 1
2 the act or process of going from the simple or basic to the complex or advanced ⟨the *expansion* of remedial reading classes into a district-wide program using school volunteers for a variety of needs⟩ — see DEVELOPMENT 1
3 a wide space or area ⟨we gazed in awe at the star-strewn *expansion* of nighttime sky above us⟩ — see EXPANSE

expansive *adj* having considerable extent ⟨as the river nears the end of its long journey to the sea it becomes quite *expansive* in breadth⟩ — see EXTENSIVE

expat *n, chiefly British* a person forced to emigrate for political reasons ⟨a network of *expats* in London keeps her from missing the family she left behind⟩ — see ÉMIGRÉ

expatiate *vb* to give a formal often extended talk on a subject ⟨the naturalist is known for her willingness to *expatiate* on any number of issues relating to wildlife and the environment⟩ — see TALK 1

expatriate *n* a person forced to emigrate for political reasons ⟨while in exile, the deposed king was accompanied by a small band of loyal *expatriates*⟩ — see ÉMIGRÉ 1

expatriate *vb* to force to leave a country ⟨members of the deposed dictator's once-feared political party were *expatriated* as well⟩ — see BANISH 1

expatriation *n* the forced removal from a homeland ⟨the brutal *expatriation* of thousands of Cherokee to Indian Territory is now commonly referred to as the Trail of Tears⟩ — see EXILE 1

expect *vb* to believe in the future occurrence of (something) ⟨we *expect* their arrival late this afternoon⟩
synonyms anticipate, await, hope (for), watch (for)
related words bank on, count (on *or* upon), depend (on *or* upon), rely (on *or* upon), wait (for); envisage, envision, foresee; foretell, predict, prophesy; assume, presume, presuppose; contemplate, eye, view
phrases look for, look forward to
near antonyms doubt, question

expectance *n* the act or state of looking forward to some occurrence ⟨gave them the painting, with no *expectance* of anything in return⟩ — see EXPECTATION

expectancy *n* the act or state of looking forward to some occurrence ⟨that feeling of optimistic *expectancy* that fills theatergoers as they wait for the curtain to rise⟩ — see EXPECTATION

expectant *adj* **1** having or showing signs of eagerly awaiting something ⟨*expectant* crowds gathered at the spot where the President was scheduled to make an appearance⟩
synonyms agape, agog, anticipant, anticipatory
related words open-eyed, openmouthed; alert, vigilant, watchful; anxious, athirst, breathless, eager, enthusiastic, raring; antsy, impatient, restive, restless
near antonyms apathetic, indifferent, unconcerned, unimpressed, uninterested, unmoved
2 containing unborn young within the body ⟨a medication that should not be taken by *expectant* women without permission from their doctors⟩ — see PREGNANT 1

expectant *n* one who seeks an office, honor, position, or award ⟨divinity students who were all *expectants* for a curacy⟩ — see CANDIDATE

expectation *n* the act or state of looking forward to some occurrence ⟨in *expectation* of a harsh winter, we budgeted more money than usual for the cost of heating our home⟩
synonyms anticipation, contemplation, expectance, expectancy, prospect
related words alarm (*also* alarum), apprehension, dread, foreboding, misgiving

expected *adj* being in accordance with the prescribed, normal, or logical course of events ⟨the children did their chores, but not without the *expected* whining⟩ — see DUE 2

expecting *adj* containing unborn young within the body ⟨the special nutritional needs of *expecting* women⟩ — see PREGNANT 1

expedience *n* suitability for bringing about a desired result under the circumstances ⟨the proven *expedience* of the carrot over the stick in getting the most out of people⟩ — see EXPEDIENCY

expediency *n* suitability for bringing about a desired result under the circumstances ⟨the *expediency* of such a plan is questionable⟩
synonyms advisability, advisableness, desirability, desirableness, expedience, judiciousness, prudence, wisdom
related words advantageousness, beneficialness, profitability; feasibility, practicality, usefulness; opportuneness, seasonableness, timeliness
near antonyms impracticality, infeasibility; inopportuneness, unseasonableness, untimeliness
antonyms imprudence, inadvisability, inexpedience, inexpediency, injudiciousness, unwisdom

expedient *adj* suitable for bringing about a desired result under the circumstances ⟨made the *expedient* decision to sell the land to whomever offered the most money⟩
synonyms advisable, desirable, judicious, politic, prudent, tactical, wise
related words advantageous, beneficial, profitable; useful, utilitarian; feasible, possible, practicable, practical; opportune, seasonable, timely; opportunistic, self-seeking
near antonyms impractical, profitless, unfeasible, unprofitable; inopportune, unseasonable, untimely
antonyms impolitic, imprudent, inadvisable, inexpedient, injudicious, unwise

expedient *n* **1** a temporary replacement ⟨if you're a spectator caught without rainwear at a sporting event, then a plastic garbage bag makes an acceptable, if unfashionable, *expedient*⟩ — see MAKESHIFT
2 an action planned or taken to achieve a desired result ⟨he vowed to use any *expedient* available to get the project done on time⟩ — see MEASURE 1
3 something that one uses to accomplish an end especially when the usual means is not available ⟨since there wasn't a single bandage left in our backpacks, we had to use a bandanna, our only *expedient*⟩ — see RESOURCE 1

expedition *n* a going from one place to another usually of some distance ⟨an avid mountain climber, always on an *expedition* to some far-off corner of the world⟩ — see JOURNEY

expeditious *adj* having or showing the ability to respond without delay or hesitation ⟨a company that is well-regarded for its *expeditious* handling of any request or complaint⟩ — see QUICK 1

expel *vb* **1** to drive or force out ⟨animal lover though I am, I was determined to *expel* the uninvited mouse from my room⟩ — see EJECT 1
2 to throw or give off ⟨something in a wastebasket was *expelling* a foul odor⟩ — see EMIT 1
3 to violently throw out or off (something from within) ⟨ringing and flashing madly, the slot machine *expelled* a bucketful of quarters⟩ — see ERUPT 1
4 to let or force out of the lungs ⟨asked the patient to *expel* a deep breath⟩ — see EXHALE 1

expend *vb* **1** to hand over or use up in payment ⟨redecoration will have to wait, since we've just *expended* our last dollar in buying the house⟩ — see SPEND 1
2 to make complete use of ⟨settlers had to be sure not to *expend* their supply of firewood before the end of the long winter⟩ — see DEPLETE 1

expenditure *n* **1** a payment made in the course of achieving a result ⟨you'll have to drastically cut back on your clothing *expenditures* if you hope to save anything⟩ — see EXPENSE
2 the active use of energy in producing a result ⟨the *expenditure* of the nation's military might on wars that may or may not involve the national interest⟩ — see EFFORT

expense *n* a payment made in the course of achieving a result ⟨they spared no *expense* in building the house of their dreams⟩
synonyms charge, cost, disbursement, expenditure, outgo, outlay

related words overhead; outflow; pocket money, spending money; price, rate, tab, tariff, toll

expensive *adj* commanding a large price ⟨*expensive* clothing that only the truly wealthy can afford⟩ — see COSTLY

expensively *adv* in a luxurious manner ⟨the pop singer's *expensively* decorated mansion was a testament to her commercial success⟩ — see HIGH

experience *n* **1** knowledge gained by actually doing or living through something ⟨the hospital is looking for nurses with operating-room *experience*⟩
synonyms chops, expertise, know-how, moxie, proficiency, savvy, skills
related words background; command, mastery; acquaintance, conversance, familiarity, intimacy
near antonyms ignorance, unawareness, unfamiliarity
antonyms inexperience
2 an exciting or noteworthy event that one experiences firsthand ⟨related in a book his *experiences* as a roving correspondent for network TV news⟩ — see ADVENTURE 1

experience *vb* to come to a knowledge of (something) by living through it ⟨eventually we all have to *experience* the loss of a loved one⟩
synonyms endure, feel, have, know, pass, see, suffer, sustain, taste, undergo, witness
related words encounter, meet; accept, receive; assimilate, digest
phrases go through

experienced *adj* having or showing exceptional knowledge, experience, or skill in a field of endeavor ⟨for this delicate eye operation, seek out an *experienced* eye surgeon⟩ — see PROFICIENT

experiential *adj* based on observation or experience ⟨possesses the kind of *experiential* knowledge that is gained only from a long and eventful life⟩ — see EMPIRICAL 1

experiment *n* a procedure or operation carried out to resolve an uncertainty ⟨Benjamin Franklin's famous *experiment* in which he flew a kite in a thunderstorm to see if lightning and electricity were identical⟩
synonyms essay, experimentation, test, trial
related words trial and error; dry run, shakedown; exercise, practice (*also* practise), rehearsal, tryout, workout; crucible, ordeal; attempt, effort, try

experimental *adj* **1** made or done as an experiment ⟨an *experimental* procedure for patients suffering from leukemia⟩
synonyms developmental, pilot, trial
related words exploratory, investigative, probative; preliminary, preparatory, provisional, temporary, tentative; conjectural, hypothetical, speculative, theoretical (*also* theoretic); untested, untried; unproved, unproven
near antonyms accepted, established, standard; tested, tried; advanced, developed; proved, proven; conclusive, decisive, definitive, final, permanent
2 based on observation or experience ⟨asserted that *experimental* knowledge is vastly superior to idle speculation and theorizing⟩ — see EMPIRICAL 1

experimentation *n* a procedure or operation carried out to resolve an uncertainty ⟨people who oppose *experimentations* involving animals for the testing of cosmetics intended for humans⟩ — see EXPERIMENT

experimenter *n* one who observes or studies by close examination and systematic inquiry ⟨a psychology *experimenter* doing research into the sources of panic attacks⟩ — see INVESTIGATOR 1

expert *adj* **1** accomplished with trained ability ⟨to a serious collector, the *expert* carving on the duck decoy justifies its high price⟩ — see SKILLFUL
2 having or showing exceptional knowledge, experience, or skill in a field of endeavor ⟨people interested in laser eye surgery are advised to seek out an *expert* practitioner⟩ — see PROFICIENT

expert *n* a person with a high level of knowledge or skill in a field ⟨*experts* at the crime lab were able to tell the sex, race, and approximate age of the murderer⟩
synonyms ace, adept, artist, authority, cognoscente, connoisseur, crackerjack (*also* crackajack), dab [*chiefly British*], dab hand [*chiefly British*], fiend, geek, guru, hand, hotshot, maestro, master, maven (*also* mavin), meister, past master, proficient, scholar, shark, sharp, virtuoso, whiz, wizard
related words pro, professional; consultant, hired gun, specialist; addict, aficionado (*also* afficionado), buff, devotee, enthusiast, fan; craftsman, journeyman; all-rounder [*British*], jack-of-all-trades, Renaissance man; mistress
near antonyms apprentice, beginner, neophyte, novice; dabbler, dilettante; layman, nonprofessional
antonyms amateur, inexpert, nonexpert

expertise *n* knowledge gained by actually doing or living through something ⟨new dog owners who were seeking someone with *expertise* in animal obedience⟩ — see EXPERIENCE 1

expertly *adv* in a skillful or expert manner ⟨the apple pie was a traditional but *expertly* made version of an old favorite⟩ — see WELL 3

expiate *vb* to make up for (an offense) ⟨Yom Kippur is the holy day on which Jews are expected to *expiate* sins committed during the past year⟩
synonyms atone (for), mend, redeem
related words compensate, recompense, reimburse, remunerate, repay; amend, correct, rectify, redress; propitiate
phrases make amends for, make good for

expiration *n* **1** the act of ceasing to exist ⟨directed that upon her *expiration* her splendid Italian-style villa be given to the public as a museum⟩ — see DEATH 3
2 the stopping of a process or activity ⟨with the *expiration* of all brain activity there was no point in keeping the patient alive⟩ — see END 1
3 the permanent stopping of all the vital bodily activities ⟨the cancer patient passed away sometime during the night, the exact moment of her *expiration* not being known⟩ — see DEATH 1

expire *vb* **1** to come to an end ⟨speakers will not be allowed to continue after their allotted time has *expired*⟩ — see CEASE 1
2 to let or force out of the lungs ⟨he vows to hold on to that belief until he *expires* his last breath⟩ — see EXHALE 1
3 to stop living ⟨made one last visit to his homeland and *expired* not long afterwards⟩ — see DIE 1
4 *archaic* to throw or give off ⟨linden trees *expiring* their rich perfume⟩ — see EMIT 1

expired *adj* no longer existing ⟨a wildlife organization dedicated to ensuring that the giant panda not be added to the list of *expired* species⟩ — see EXTINCT

expiry *n* **1** the act of ceasing to exist ⟨the *expiry* of a great empire is always a cataclysmic event⟩ — see DEATH 3
2 the permanent stopping of all the vital bodily activities ⟨once upon *expiry*, her soul entered the abode of the blessed dead⟩ — see DEATH 1

explain *vb* **1** to make plain or understandable ⟨a pamphlet that *explains* the medical procedure in language that any layperson can understand⟩
synonyms clarify, clear (up), construe, demonstrate, demystify, elucidate, explicate, expound, get across, illuminate, illustrate, interpret, simplify, spell out, unriddle
related words decipher, decode; analyze, break down;

disentangle, undo, unravel, unscramble, untangle; resolve, solve; define, specify; annotate, commentate, gloss
near antonyms befog, cloud; confound, confuse, obfuscate
antonyms obscure
2 to give the reason for or cause of ⟨can you *explain* your very odd behavior at the wedding reception?⟩
synonyms account (for), attribute, explain away, rationalize
related words condone, excuse, forgive, justify; absolve, acquit, exculpate, exonerate, vindicate

explainable *adj* capable of having the reason for or cause of determined ⟨investigators found that the so-called mysterious happenings at the house were entirely *explainable*⟩ — see SOLVABLE

explain away *vb* **1** to give the reason for or cause of ⟨after the surprise attack, military leaders struggled to *explain away* the nation's unpreparedness⟩ — see EXPLAIN 2
2 to make (something) seem less bad by offering excuses ⟨tried to *explain away* his adulterous affairs by saying that men are promiscuous by nature⟩ — see PALLIATE 1

explanation *n* **1** a statement that makes something clear ⟨an *explanation* of photosynthesis that most museum visitors will be able to understand⟩
synonyms clarification, construction, elucidation, exegesis, explication, exposition, illumination, illustration, interpretation, road map
related words paraphrase, restatement, translation; annotation, comment, commentary, epexegesis, gloss; deciphering, decoding; disentanglement, unscrambling; analysis; edification, enlightenment; definition, meaning; demonstration, enactment; justification, rationale, rationalization, reasoning; caution, caveat, warning
2 a statement given to explain a belief or act ⟨when questioned by authorities, the students were at a loss for an *explanation* for their senseless vandalism⟩ — see REASON 1

explanative *adj* serving to explain ⟨an edition of Melville's novel that could use more *explanative* footnotes about whaling⟩ — see EXPLANATORY

explanatory *adj* serving to explain ⟨the *explanatory* section has as its heading "What the New Tax Changes Mean"⟩
synonyms elucidative, exegetical (*also* exegetic), explanative, explicative, explicatory, expositive, expository, illuminative, illustrative, interpretative, interpretive
related words analytic (*or* analytical), demonstrative, discursive; exculpatory, exonerative

expletive *n* a disrespectful or indecent word or expression ⟨unleashed a slew of *expletives* upon losing the tennis match⟩ — see SWEARWORD

explicable *adj* capable of having the reason for or cause of determined ⟨the mystery of those strange noises became quite *explicable* once we realized that a colony of bats had taken up residence⟩ — see SOLVABLE

explicate *vb* to make plain or understandable ⟨the physicist did his best to *explicate* the wave theory of light for the audience of laymen⟩ — see EXPLAIN 1

explication *n* a statement that makes something clear ⟨any *explication* of Einstein's theory of relativity probably wouldn't help me much⟩ — see EXPLANATION 1

explicative *adj* serving to explain ⟨a dearth of *explicative* material to help the layman understand the difficult subject matter⟩ — see EXPLANATORY

explicatory *adj* serving to explain ⟨most of the medical film's voice-over narration consists of *explicatory* remarks on the images being shown⟩ — see EXPLANATORY

explicit *adj* so clearly expressed as to leave no doubt about the meaning ⟨*explicit* instructions about what to do in an emergency⟩
synonyms clear-cut, definite, definitive, express, specific, unambiguous, unequivocal, univocal
related words avowed, declared, specified, stated; categorical (*also* categoric), complete, comprehensive, exhaustive, full; certain, sure, unmistakable; clear, distinct, lucid, well-defined; exact, precise; direct, literal, plain, simple, straightforward; comprehensible, intelligible, understandable
near antonyms cryptic, dark, enigmatic (*also* enigmatical), obscure, unclear; imprecise, inaccurate, incorrect, inexact; incomprehensible, unintelligible
antonyms implicit, implied, inferred; ambiguous, circuitous; equivocal, indefinite, inexplicit, unspecific, vague

explicitness *n* **1** careful thoroughness of detail ⟨the *explicitness* of the instruction about human reproduction should be appropriate for the age of the students receiving it⟩ — see PARTICULARITY 1
2 clearness of expression ⟨the user's manual is written with such rare *explicitness* that the average consumer actually has a chance of understanding it⟩ — see SIMPLICITY 2

explode *vb* **1** to break open or into pieces usually because of internal pressure ⟨the building was wrecked when a powerful bomb *exploded*⟩
synonyms blow, blow up, burst, crump, detonate, go off, pop
related words fragment, shatter, smash, splinter; discharge, fire, shoot; balloon, burgeon (*also* bourgeon), mushroom
near antonyms collapse, fizzle
antonyms implode
2 to cause to break open or into pieces by or as if by an explosive ⟨the bomb was so powerful that it *exploded* windows in several neighboring buildings⟩ — see BLAST 1
3 to develop suddenly and violently ⟨the mayor's latest unpopular decision caused long-suppressed resentment to *explode* into open anger⟩ — see ERUPT 2

exploit *n* **1** an act of notable skill, strength, or cleverness ⟨the fanciful *exploits* of the giant lumberjack Paul Bunyan⟩ — see FEAT 1
2 something done by someone ⟨once famed as an actor, John Wilkes Booth is now remembered for a single *exploit*, his assassination of Lincoln⟩ — see ACTION 1
3 an exciting or noteworthy event that one experiences firsthand ⟨a memoir recounting three decades of *exploits* as a roving foreign correspondent for TV news⟩ — see ADVENTURE 1

exploit *vb* **1** to take unfair advantage of ⟨the type of person who *exploits* a friend's good nature by constantly sponging off of him⟩
synonyms abuse, capitalize (on), cash in (on), impose (on *or* upon), leverage, milk, pimp, play (on *or* upon), use, work
related words jerk around, manipulate, mistreat; bleed, cheat, fleece, overcharge, skin, soak, stick; commercialize, commodify
phrases trade on, walk on
2 to control or take advantage of by artful, unfair, or insidious means ⟨a politician more than willing to *exploit* any national tragedy for political gain⟩ — see MANIPULATE 1
3 to put into action or service ⟨it will be a shame if you don't *exploit* your artistic talent to the fullest⟩ — see USE 1

exploitable *adj* **1** capable of or suitable for being used

for a particular purpose ⟨claimed that solar power is an *exploitable* form of energy that is being underutilized⟩ — see USABLE 1
2 readily taken advantage of ⟨the group opposes commercials on TV shows for kids, believing that young viewers are too *exploitable* by advertisers⟩ — see EASY 2

exploration *n* a systematic search for the truth or facts about something ⟨an *exploration* into the disappearance of famed aviator Amelia Earhart⟩ — see INQUIRY 1

explore *vb* **1** to search through or into ⟨communities must *explore* new ways of raising money for their cultural institutions⟩
synonyms delve (into), dig (into), examine, inquire (into), investigate, look (into), probe, research
related words inspect, sift, study, view; browse, cruise, peruse, scan, skim (through), surf, thumb (through); coinvestigate, reinvestigate
phrases check into, check up on
2 to go into or range over for purposes of discovery ⟨we must continue to *explore* the depths of the ocean⟩
synonyms hunt, probe, prospect, search, skirr
related words reconnoiter (*or* reconnoitre), scout; disclose, discover, reveal, unearth; fathom, plumb, sound

explosion *n* **1** the act or an instance of exploding ⟨the *explosion* of the first atomic bomb at Hiroshima⟩
synonyms blast, blowup, burst, bursting, detonation, eruption, outburst
related words discharge, firing, shooting; blowout, flare-up; bang, boom, pop; airburst, groundburst
antonyms implosion
2 a sudden intense expression of strong feeling ⟨the *explosion* of patriotic feeling that the country experienced after that momentous event⟩ — see OUTBURST 1
3 an outburst or display of excited anger ⟨the tennis player's expletive-enriched *explosions* on the court tested the patience of officials⟩ — see TANTRUM

explosive *adj* **1** extreme in degree, power, or effect ⟨there's been an *explosive* interest in the sport since the Olympics⟩ — see INTENSE 1
2 marked by bursts of destructive force or intense activity ⟨one of the most *explosive* storms to hit that area of the coast in some time⟩ — see VIOLENT 1

explosively *adv* in a vigorous and forceful manner ⟨the racehorses *explosively* broke from the starting gate⟩ — see HARD 3

expo *n* a public showing of objects of interest ⟨many of the bigger *expos* won't fit into the city's relatively small civic center⟩ — see EXHIBITION 1

exponent *n* **1** a person who actively supports or favors a cause ⟨*exponents* of space exploration earnestly called for more missions to the outer reaches of the solar system⟩
synonyms advocate, advocator, apostle, backer, booster, champion, expounder, espouser, friend, gospeler (*or* gospeller), herald, hierophant, high priest, paladin, promoter, proponent, protagonist, supporter, true believer, tub-thumper, white knight
related words loyalist, partisan (*also* partizan), stalwart; adherent, cohort, disciple, follower; interpreter; applauder, cheerleader, encourager, fellow traveler
near antonyms enemy, foe, rival; belittler, critic, faultfinder
antonyms adversary, antagonist, opponent
2 one who brings an art or science to full realization ⟨has long reigned as the nation's leading *exponent* of modern dance⟩
synonyms expounder, guru, high priest, interpreter, practitioner
related words dean, doyen, grand old man; ideologue (*also* idealogue), philosopher, theorist; advocate, apostle, backer, booster, champion, promoter, proponent, supporter

expose *vb* **1** to reveal the true nature of ⟨a well-researched article that *exposes* the UFO story as a hoax⟩
synonyms debunk, nail, show up, uncloak, uncover, undress, unmask
related words demolish, discredit, disprove; disclose, divulge, tell, unveil
phrases blow the whistle on
near antonyms conceal, hide, secrete, veil
antonyms camouflage, cloak, disguise, mask
2 to make known (as information previously kept secret) ⟨the documentary claims to *expose* how winners of beauty pageants are really picked⟩ — see REVEAL 1
3 to make known (something abstract) through outward signs ⟨the tight race for the championship *exposed* one team's mean streak⟩ — see SHOW 2
4 to present so as to invite notice or attention ⟨I didn't want to *expose* my ignorance in front of the others, so I kept silent⟩ — see SHOW 1

exposed *adj* **1** being in a situation where one is likely to meet with harm ⟨without our immune systems we'd be *exposed* to all sorts of deadly infections⟩ — see LIABLE 1
2 lacking a usual or natural covering ⟨the *exposed* electrical wires were a safety hazard⟩ — see NAKED 2
3 lacking protection from danger or resistance against attack ⟨the soldiers were so *exposed* in the open field that they were the proverbial sitting ducks⟩ — see HELPLESS 1

exposition *n* **1** a public showing of objects of interest ⟨an *exposition* of flying machines from the early days of aviation⟩ — see EXHIBITION 1
2 a series of explanations or observations on something (as an event) ⟨the nonstop *exposition* of the ceremonies by the TV newscasters was both unnecessary and irritating⟩ — see COMMENTARY 1
3 a statement that makes something clear ⟨the astronomer's *exposition* of white dwarfs was a little helpful⟩ — see EXPLANATION 1

expositive *adj* serving to explain ⟨the writer's descriptions are objectively *expositive* and entirely without editorialization⟩ — see EXPLANATORY

expository *adj* serving to explain ⟨an *expository* piece on the workings of the internal-combustion engine⟩ — see EXPLANATORY

expostulate *vb* to present an opposing opinion or argument ⟨the concerned parents tried to *expostulate* with their daughter when she announced her intention to live on her own in New York City⟩ — see OBJECT

expostulation *n* a feeling or declaration of disapproval or dissent ⟨despite the earnest *expostulations* of her friends, Jessica continued to date the foul-tempered guy⟩ — see OBJECTION

exposure *n* **1** the state of being left without shelter or protection against something harmful ⟨some people chronically avoid situations in which there is a high level of *exposure* to germs⟩
synonyms liability, openness, vulnerability
related words predisposition, susceptibility; defenselessness, helplessness, weakness; danger, jeopardy, peril, risk
near antonyms protection, safeguarding, sheltering, shielding
2 the state or fact of facing a particular direction ⟨this plant will need to be in a room with a southern *exposure*⟩
synonyms aspect, frontage, orientation
related words alignment (*also* alinement), arrangement
3 the act or an instance of making known something previously unknown or concealed ⟨the *exposure* by the local newspaper of a kickback scheme in the public

works department⟩ — see REVELATION

expound *vb* **1** to make known (as an idea, emotion, or opinion) ⟨a rambling interview in which the celebrated author *expounds* his views on an array of topics⟩ — see EXPRESS 1

2 to make plain or understandable ⟨at the start of the trial the judge *expounded* the legal difference between libel and slander to the jury⟩ — see EXPLAIN 1

expounder *n* **1** a person who actively supports or favors a cause ⟨an articulate *expounder* of the liberal position on the issue⟩ — see EXPONENT 1

2 one who brings an art or science to full realization ⟨one of the early *expounders* of abstract expressionism⟩ — see EXPONENT 2

express *adj* **1** of a particular or exact sort ⟨a trip to the supermarket with the *express* purpose of buying milk⟩

synonyms concrete, distinct, especial, peculiar, precise, set, special, specific

related words lone, only, separate, single, sole, solitary; distinctive, exclusive, individual, unique; limited, restricted; differentiated, specialized; given, specified

near antonyms general, generalized, generic, nonexclusive, universal

antonyms nonspecific

2 so clearly expressed as to leave no doubt about the meaning ⟨students are not allowed to leave the grounds during school hours unless they have *express* permission from the principal's office⟩ — see EXPLICIT

express *n, British* one that carries a message or does an errand ⟨the solicitors employ an *express* to deliver their summonses⟩ — see MESSENGER

express *vb* **1** to make known (as an idea, emotion, or opinion) ⟨in a true democracy, a person can freely *express* his or her views⟩

synonyms air, expound, give, look, raise, sound, state, vent, ventilate, voice

related words advertise, announce, declare, enounce, enunciate, proclaim, say; broadcast, circulate, disseminate, publish; describe, write, write up; sound off, speak out, speak up; chime in; communicate, convey, put across, put over; offer, submit

phrases give air to, put forth

near antonyms censor, restrain, restrict

antonyms stifle, suppress

2 to apply external pressure on so as to force out the juice or contents of ⟨except as a fun event at festivals, nowadays people do not make wine by *expressing* grapes with their feet⟩ — see [2]PRESS 2

3 to communicate or convey (as an idea) to the mind ⟨an upraised thumb is now universally recognized as a gesture *expressing* approval or encouragement⟩ — see MEAN 1

4 to convey in appropriate or telling terms ⟨could you *express* your opinion of the book in words a little more precise than "lousy"?⟩ — see PHRASE

5 to represent in visible form ⟨towering spires *express* in glass and steel the optimism of the age⟩ — see EMBODY 2

expression *n* **1** an act, process, or means of putting something into words ⟨the poem is his *expression* of his grief upon the loss of his beloved wife⟩

synonyms articulation, formulation, phrasing, statement, utterance, verbalism, voice, wording

related words outlet, vent; observation, reflection, remark, thought; speech, tongue

2 facial appearance regarded as an indication of mood or feeling ⟨we could tell by the fans' *expressions* that the Chicago Cubs had lost again⟩ — see LOOK 1

3 a pronounceable series of letters having a distinct meaning especially in a particular field ⟨the *expression* "John Doe" is used in legal proceedings to refer to a person whose actual name is either unknown or being withheld from the public⟩ — see WORD 1

4 a sequence of words having a specific meaning ⟨the popular *expression* "raining cats and dogs" is meaningless in other languages⟩ — see PHRASE

expressionless *adj* not expressing any emotion ⟨veteran poker players invariably have *expressionless* faces, regardless of the hand they're holding⟩ — see BLANK 1

expressive *adj* clearly conveying a special meaning (as one's mood) ⟨the teacher's *expressive* sigh showed that she had heard that excuse many times before⟩

synonyms eloquent, meaning, meaningful, pregnant, revealing, revelatory, significant, suggestive

related words graphic (*also* graphical), pictorial, vivid; evocative, redolent, reminiscent; sententious, weighty; flavorful, full-bodied, rich

antonyms unexpressive

expressway *n* a passage cleared for public vehicular travel ⟨a baffling maze of high-speed *expressways* encircles the city⟩ — see WAY 1

expropriate *vb* **1** to take or make use of under a guise of authority but without actual right ⟨dissidents were shot, and their lands *expropriated* under his regime⟩ — see APPROPRIATE 1

2 to end the occupancy or possession of ⟨the state will have to *expropriate* scores of homeowners in order to build the new road⟩ — see DISPOSSESS

3 to take ownership or control of (something) by right of one's authority ⟨plans by the city to *expropriate* entire blocks of houses in order to bulldoze them for expansion of the airport⟩ — see CONFISCATE

expropriation *n* the unlawful taking or withholding of something from the rightful owner under a guise of authority ⟨the development of the colony involved *expropriation* of large tracts of fertile farmland from the natives⟩ — see APPROPRIATION 2

expulsion *n* the forced removal from a homeland ⟨the ruthless *expulsion* of the French-speaking Acadians from Nova Scotia by the British⟩ — see EXILE 1

expunge *vb* to destroy all traces of ⟨time and the weather have *expunged* any evidence that a thriving community once existed here⟩ — see ANNIHILATE 1

expurgate *vb* to remove objectionable parts from ⟨the newspaper had to *expurgate* the expletive-laden speech that the criminal made upon being sentenced to life imprisonment⟩ — see CENSOR

exquisite *adj* **1** extreme in degree, power, or effect ⟨felt such *exquisite* anger at being betrayed by a so-called friend that she could hardly think straight⟩ — see INTENSE 1

2 having qualities that appeal to a refined taste ⟨*exquisite* pen-and-ink drawings of city scenes grace the walls of the formal restaurant⟩ — see CHOICE 1

3 satisfying or pleasing because of fineness or mildness ⟨waiters at the wedding reception served *exquisite* hors d'oeuvres from silver trays⟩ — see DELICATE 1

exquisiteness *n* the state or quality of having a delicate structure ⟨marveled at the *exquisiteness* of the lace on the bride's gown⟩ — see DELICACY 2

extant *adj* **1** having being at the present time ⟨a celebrated author who is generally regarded as America's greatest novelist *extant*⟩

synonyms alive, around, existent, existing, living

related words active, busy, flourishing, functioning, operating, working

near antonyms defunct, destroyed, exterminated, kaput (*also* kaputt); departed, gone, lost; nonexistent; idle, inactive, inert

antonyms dead, extinct, nonextant

2 existing or in progress right now ⟨when people envisage the future, they often base their predictions on the assumption that *extant* trends will continue indefinitely⟩ — see PRESENT 1

extemporaneous *adj* made or done without previous thought or preparation ⟨caught by surprise, I had to make an *extemporaneous* speech at the awards banquet⟩
synonyms ad hoc, ad-lib, down and dirty, extemporary, extempore, impromptu, improvisational, improvised, offhand, offhanded, off-the-cuff, snap, spur-of-the-moment, unconsidered, unplanned, unpremeditated, unprepared, unrehearsed, unstudied
related words unscripted; automatic, impulsive, instinctive, involuntary, spontaneous; casual, cursive, informal, unauthorized; half-baked, half-cocked, ill-advised
near antonyms deliberate, intended, intentional
antonyms considered, planned, premeditated, premeditative, prepared, rehearsed
extemporary *adj* made or done without previous thought or preparation ⟨caught red-handed, the would-be embezzler proceeded to give some *extemporary* and not very convincing explanations for her actions⟩ — see EXTEMPORANEOUS
extempore *adj* made or done without previous thought or preparation ⟨after the election both candidates admitted that they had made a number of *extempore* remarks that they later regretted⟩ — see EXTEMPORANEOUS
extemporization *n* something that is performed, made, or done without preparation ⟨a guitar *extemporization*⟩ — see IMPROVISATION
extemporize *vb* to perform, make, or do without preparation ⟨a good talk show host has to be able to *extemporize* the interviews when things don't go as planned⟩ — see IMPROVISE
extend *vb* **1** to make longer ⟨our guests from out of town *extended* their visit by a week⟩
synonyms drag (out), draw out, elongate, lengthen, outstretch, prolong, protract, stretch
related words amplify, enlarge, expand, increase; attenuate, thin
near antonyms decrease, diminish, lessen, reduce; thicken
antonyms abbreviate, abridge, curtail, cut, cut back, shorten
2 to put before another for acceptance or consideration ⟨the couple *extended* an invitation to join them for a get-together at their house after the concert⟩ — see OFFER 1
3 to arrange the parts of (something) over a wider area ⟨you can *extend* that chaise longue so that it lies completely flat⟩ — see OPEN 3
4 to be positioned along a certain course or in a certain direction ⟨our backyard *extends* all the way to that brook⟩ — see RUN 3
5 to make greater in size, amount, or number ⟨embarked on a series of wars intended to *extend* his empire⟩ — see INCREASE 1
6 to alter (something) for the worse with the addition of foreign or lower-grade substances ⟨the company *extends* its ice cream with thickeners and other additives⟩ — see ADULTERATE
extended *adj* **1** expressing one thing in terms normally used for another ⟨the word "snake" in its *extended* sense refers to a contemptible or treacherous person⟩ — see FIGURATIVE
2 having considerable extent ⟨an *extended* portion of the valley is now devoted to the growing of grapes for wine⟩ — see EXTENSIVE
3 lasting for a considerable time ⟨I've met her, but I have never had an *extended* conversation with her⟩ — see LONG 2
4 of great extent from end to end ⟨the two armies clashed along an *extended* line of battle that stretched for miles⟩ — see LONG 1
extended family *n* those who live as a family in one house ⟨their *extended family* includes a grandmother and widowed aunt⟩ — see HOUSEHOLD
extension *n* **1** the act of making longer ⟨the board's *extension* of the school year drew howls of protest⟩
synonyms drawing out, elongation, lengthening, prolongation, prolonging, stretching
antonyms abbreviation, abridgment (*or* abridgement), curtailment, cutback, shortening
2 a smaller structure added to a main building ⟨the new *extension* will connect the house with what is now a freestanding garage⟩ — see ANNEX
extensive *adj* having considerable extent ⟨a rock hound whose *extensive* reading enables him to identify just about any rock or mineral⟩
synonyms broad, deep, expansive, extended, far-flung, far-reaching, rangy, sweeping, wide, wide-ranging, widespread
related words comprehensive, general, global, inclusive; boundless, endless, infinite, limitless, unlimited; capacious, commodious, roomy, spacious
near antonyms circumscribed, limited, restricted
antonyms narrow
extensively *adv* to a large extent or degree ⟨several beaches were *extensively* damaged by the hurricane⟩ — see GREATLY 2
extent *n* **1** a real or imaginary point beyond which a person or thing cannot go ⟨the coach exceeded the *extent* of his authority by exempting some of the players from the requirement⟩ — see LIMIT 1
2 a wide space or area ⟨the seemingly endless *extent* of the windswept prairies⟩ — see EXPANSE
3 an area over which activity, capacity, or influence extends ⟨the *extent* of this criminal investigation has widened considerably since it began⟩ — see RANGE 2
4 the total amount of measurable space or surface occupied by something ⟨looking at the *extent* of the stain on my shirt, you might think that I had spilled a gallon of coffee⟩ — see [1]SIZE
extenuate *vb* to make (something) seem less bad by offering excuses ⟨don't even try to *extenuate* their vandalism of the cemetery with the old refrain of "Boys will be boys"⟩ — see PALLIATE 1
exterior *adj* situated on the outside or farther out ⟨the house's *exterior* walls badly need to be painted⟩ — see OUTER
exterior *n* an outer part or layer ⟨the *exterior* of the tooth consists of very hard enamel⟩
synonyms face, outside, shell, skin, surface, veneer
related words facade (*also* façade), front, top; cover, covering, facing; appearance, disguise, guise, mask, semblance, show
antonyms inside, interior
exterminate *vb* to destroy all traces of ⟨hope that the fumigant *exterminates* the whole colony of cockroaches, for any survivors may be resistant to any poison⟩ — see ANNIHILATE 1
extermination *n* the state or fact of being rendered nonexistent, physically unsound, or useless ⟨the virtual *extermination* of the native tribes by the colonizers⟩ — see DESTRUCTION 1
external *adj* **1** not being a vital part of or belonging to something ⟨the defendant's socioeconomic status must be regarded as entirely *external* to his guilt or innocence⟩ — see EXTRINSIC
2 situated on the outside or farther out ⟨the *external* chambers of the ancient tomb gave little indication of the magnificence of the innermost chamber⟩ — see OUTER
externalization *n* a visible representation of something

abstract (as a quality) ⟨bizarre paintings that are the *externalization* of a very troubled psyche⟩ — see EMBODIMENT

externalize *vb* to represent in visible form ⟨an actress with an expressive face that wonderfully *externalizes* a wide range of emotions⟩ — see EMBODY 2

externship *n* a period of undergoing practical instruction in one's job or career ⟨prior to graduation from the culinary school he had served an *externship* as a sous chef at a high-end restaurant⟩ — see APPRENTICESHIP

extinct *adj* no longer existing ⟨a few overgrown ruins are all that remain of that once mighty but now *extinct* civilization⟩
synonyms bygone, bypast, dead, defunct, departed, done, expired, gone, nonextant, vanished
related words nonexistent; dying, faded, moribund; collapsed, fallen, overthrown; antiquated, dated, obsolete, passé; finished, lapsed, terminated; lost, missing
near antonyms active, dynamic, thriving, vibrant
antonyms alive, existent, existing, extant, living

extinction *n* the state or fact of being rendered nonexistent, physically unsound, or useless ⟨the state's population of moose has been replenished, having once been hunted almost to *extinction*⟩ — see DESTRUCTION 1

extinguish *vb* **1** to cause to cease burning ⟨the fire in the skillet was quickly *extinguished* by slamming the lid on⟩
synonyms blanket, douse (*also* dowse), put out, quench, snuff (out)
related words choke, smother, suffocate; blow out, rub out, snub (out), stamp (out), stub
antonyms fire, ignite, inflame (*also* enflame), kindle, light
2 to bring to a complete end the physical soundness, existence, or usefulness of ⟨a fatal blunder that *extinguished* all hope that the team would actually win the play-offs⟩ — see DESTROY 1
3 to stop the noise or speech of ⟨her final, telling point *extinguished* her opponents on the city council⟩ — see SILENCE 1

extirpate *vb* to destroy all traces of ⟨the triumph of modern medicine in *extirpating* certain diseases⟩ — see ANNIHILATE 1

extol *also* **extoll** *vb* to proclaim the glory of ⟨campaign literature *extolling* the candidate's military record⟩ — see PRAISE 1

extort *vb* to get (as money) by the use of force or threats ⟨a school bully who was used to *extorting* lunch money from weaker kids⟩
synonyms exact, wrest, wring
related words bleed, fleece, gouge, milk, skin, squeeze; cheat, gyp, racketeer, swindle; coerce, compel, force

extortion *n* the exaction of a grossly excessive charge for goods or services ⟨six dollars for a cup of coffee is just plain *extortion*⟩
synonyms fleecing, gouging, highway robbery, overcharging
related words cheating, chiseling (*or* chiselling), defrauding, skinning, swindling

extortioner *n* a person who gets money from another by using force or threats ⟨*extortioners* threatened to beat up the shop owner if he didn't pay the bribe⟩ — see RACKETEER

extortionist *n* a person who gets money from another by using force or threats ⟨tortured by a gang of *extortionists* into revealing the combination for the money vault⟩ — see RACKETEER

extra *adj* being over what is needed ⟨always has *extra* food on hand in the event that unexpected company drops by⟩ — see SPARE 1

extra *adv* to a great degree ⟨the children tried to be *extra* quiet while their mother was recovering⟩ — see VERY 1

extra *n* **1** an interchangeable part or piece of equipment that is kept on hand for replacement of an original ⟨that portable player runs through batteries incredibly fast, so I always keep plenty of *extras* on hand⟩ — see SPARE
2 something adding to pleasure or comfort but not absolutely necessary ⟨the motel is clean and comfortable, but there are no *extras*⟩ — see LUXURY 1
3 something given in addition to what is ordinarily expected or owed ⟨as an *extra*, the dealer filled the tank of my new car⟩ — see BONUS

extract *n* a part taken from a longer work ⟨the anthology includes a long *extract* from the epic poem⟩ — see EXCERPT

extract *vb* to draw out by force or with effort ⟨*extracted* a splinter from my hand⟩
synonyms corkscrew, prize, pry, pull, root (out), tear (out), uproot, wrest, wring, yank
related words mine, pluck, remove, take (out), withdraw
near antonyms implant, insert, install, instill; cram, jam, ram, stuff, wedge

extraction *n* the line of ancestors from whom a person is descended ⟨a family of Italian *extraction*⟩ — see ANCESTRY

extracurricular *adj* relating to or being a sexual encounter or relationship between a married person and someone other than their spouse ⟨hired a private detective to investigate her husband's *extracurricular* activities⟩ — see ADULTEROUS

extramarital *adj* relating to or being a sexual encounter or relationship between a married person and someone other than their spouse ⟨she had several *extramarital* affairs with coworkers⟩ — see ADULTEROUS

extraneous *adj* **1** not being a vital part of or belonging to something ⟨the architect's streamlined modern style shuns any sort of *extraneous* ornamentation⟩ — see EXTRINSIC
2 not having anything to do with the matter at hand ⟨the professor would have covered all of the course material if she had refrained from her *extraneous* remarks on just about everything⟩ — see IRRELEVANT

extraneousness *n* the quality or state of not having anything to do with the matter at hand ⟨the *extraneousness* of the commentators' remarks became more pronounced as the broadcast dragged on⟩ — see IRRELEVANCE

extraordinaire *adj* being out of the ordinary ⟨the sort of chef *extraordinaire* who can whip up a fantastic meal, regardless of the ingredients on hand⟩ — see EXCEPTIONAL 1

extraordinary *adj* **1** being out of the ordinary ⟨the marine is being cited for *extraordinary* courage⟩ — see EXCEPTIONAL 1
2 noticeably different from what is generally found or experienced ⟨no one noticed anything *extraordinary* about the airline passenger⟩ — see UNUSUAL 1

extrapolate *vb* to form an opinion or reach a conclusion through reasoning and information ⟨we can *extrapolate* from past economic recessions the probable course of the current one⟩ — see INFER 1

extrasensory perception *n* the power of seeing or knowing about things that are not present to the senses ⟨discouraged by the lack of progress in the case, the police were willing to listen to a woman claiming *extrasensory perception*⟩ — see CLAIRVOYANCE

extravagance *n* **1** the quality or fact of being free or wasteful in the expenditure of money ⟨Hollywood stars are famous for the *extravagance* of their parties⟩
synonyms extravagancy, lavishness, prodigality, profusion, wastefulness

related words conspicuous consumption, splurge; bountifulness, generosity, liberality; improvidence, squandering; indulgence, overindulgence, self-indulgence; excess, immoderacy, overkill
near antonyms austerity, moderation, restraint, temperance
antonyms economy, frugality, penny-pinching
2 an instance of spending money or resources without care or restraint ⟨the purchase of a fur coat was simply the latest of his wife's *extravagances*⟩ — see WASTE 1

extravagancy *n* the quality or fact of being free or wasteful in the expenditure of money ⟨warned their spendthrift daughter that she would eventually pay the price for her *extravagancy*⟩ — see EXTRAVAGANCE 1

extravagant *adj* **1** given to spending money freely or foolishly ⟨the billionaire's son is the typically *extravagant* playboy who hasn't earned any of what he spends⟩ — see PRODIGAL
2 going beyond a normal or acceptable limit in degree or amount ⟨the book doesn't quite merit the *extravagant* praise that it has received⟩ — see EXCESSIVE
3 commanding a large price ⟨wooed her with an array of *extravagant* gifts⟩ — see COSTLY

extravagantly *adv* in a luxurious manner ⟨the ancient Roman emperors lived as *extravagantly* as any rulers in history⟩ — see HIGH

extravaganza *n* an elaborate, visually exciting show or event ⟨the over-the-top *extravaganzas* that are usually staged at halftime during the Super Bowl⟩
synonyms circus, pageant, raree-show, spectacle, spectacular
related words display, exhibit, exhibition, exposition

extreme *adj* **1** most distant from a center ⟨spacecraft that is specially designed to explore the *extreme* edge of our solar system⟩
synonyms farthermost, farthest, furthermost, furthest, outermost, outmost, remotest, ultimate, utmost
related words aftermost, rearmost, sternmost
near antonyms intermediate, medial, median, mid, middle, midmost
antonyms inmost, innermost, nearest
2 being very far from the center of public opinion ⟨their *extreme* political views attracted only a small band of followers⟩
synonyms extremist, fanatic (*or* fanatical), rabid, radical, revolutionary, revolutionist, ultra
related words subversive, violent, wild; reactionary
near antonyms conservative, moderate, temperate; conventional, orthodox, traditional; liberal, progressive
antonyms middle-of-the-road, nonrevolutionary, unrevolutionary
3 going beyond a normal or acceptable limit in degree or amount ⟨in their *extreme* zeal the members of the cult are willing to do whatever their leader dictates⟩ — see EXCESSIVE

extremely *adv* to a great degree ⟨an *extremely* hot day⟩ — see VERY 1

extremist *adj* being very far from the center of public opinion ⟨their *extremist* views on religious issues set them apart from the rest of the community⟩ — see EXTREME 2

extremist *n* a person who favors rapid and sweeping changes especially in laws and methods of government ⟨*extremists* wanted to do away with everything, even though they had no thought-out plan for what to do afterwards⟩ — see RADICAL

extremity *n* **1** a time or state of affairs requiring prompt or decisive action ⟨made offers of aid to the refugees, and of asylum in *extremity*⟩ — see EMERGENCY
2 the most extreme or advanced point ⟨at its *extremity* the fever was actually life-threatening⟩ — see HEIGHT 2

extricate *vb* to set free from entanglement or difficulty ⟨you've woven such a web of lies that it's hard to see how you can *extricate* yourself now⟩
synonyms clear, disembarrass, disengage, disentangle, free, liberate, release, untangle
related words deliver, redeem, rescue, save; disburden, disencumber, unburden; unravel, unsnarl, untie, untwine
phrases cut loose
near antonyms block, hamper, hinder, impede, obstruct; burden, encumber, load, weigh
antonyms embroil, entangle

extrinsic *adj* not being a vital part of or belonging to something ⟨the fact that the ring belonged to your grandmother is *extrinsic* to its value to a jeweler⟩
synonyms accidental, adventitious, alien, extraneous, external, foreign, supervenient
related words exterior, outside; immaterial, inapplicable, insignificant, irrelevant; nonessential, unessential, unnecessary
near antonyms congenital, deep-seated, inborn, inbred; inside, interior, internal; basic, essential, necessary
antonyms inherent, innate, intrinsic

extrovert *also* **extravert** *n* a gregarious and unreserved person ⟨a natural *extrovert*, he mixes well in any social situation⟩
synonyms backslapper, glad-hander
related words exhibitionist, show-off
antonyms introvert, shrinking violet, wallflower

extroverted *also* **extraverted** *adj* likely to seek or enjoy the company of others ⟨a job in a research lab that is probably not well suited to an *extroverted* person⟩ — see CONVIVIAL

extrude *vb* to drive or force out ⟨the sort of person who is determined to *extrude* every last gob of toothpaste from the tube⟩ — see EJECT 1

exuberance *n* the quality or state of having abundant or intense activity ⟨the *exuberance* of the housing market was an encouraging economic indicator⟩ — see VITALITY 1

exuberant *adj* joyously unrestrained ⟨*exuberant* crowds rushed to greet the returning national champions in collegiate basketball⟩
synonyms bouncy, bubbly, buoyant, crank [*chiefly dialect*], effervescent, frolic, frolicsome, gamesome, gay, high-spirited, vivacious
related words extroverted (*also* extraverted), outgoing, uninhibited; carefree, happy-go-lucky, insouciant, joyful, lighthearted, lively, sprightly; boisterous, raucous, rollicking, rowdy; giddy, light-headed, overexuberant, silly; ecstatic, euphoric, lyric, rapturous; audacious, bold, brash, brazen, impertinent, impudent, insolent, saucy
near antonyms constrained, inhibited, repressed, restrained, subdued; impassive, phlegmatic, stoic (*or* stoical), stolid; depressed, dour, glum, morose, surly
antonyms low-spirited, sullen

exuberantly *adv* in an enthusiastic manner ⟨her last employer sang her praises so *exuberantly* that we just had to hire her⟩ — see SKY-HIGH

exuberate *vb* to feel or express joy or triumph ⟨after their first World Series championship in 86 years, Bostonians felt that they had earned the right to *exuberate* with abandon⟩ — see EXULT

exude *vb* to flow forth slowly through small openings ⟨a sticky resin *exudes* from the bark of the tree⟩
synonyms bleed, ooze, percolate, seep, strain, sweat, transude, weep
related words dribble, drip, trickle; discharge, emit, give off, vent; emanate, flow, spring
near antonyms flood, gush, pour, stream, surge

exult *vb* to feel or express joy or triumph ⟨the winners

of the Super Bowl spent the next week *exulting* in their victory⟩
synonyms crow, delight, exuberate, glory, jubilate, joy, kvell, rejoice, triumph
related words gloat, preen, swell; boast, brag; flaunt, parade, show off, strut, swagger
phrases kick up one's heels
near antonyms bemoan, bewail, grieve, lament, regret, weep

exultant *adj* having or expressing feelings of joy or triumph ⟨the *exultant* winner of the award for best country artist of the year⟩
synonyms cock-a-hoop, crank [*chiefly dialect*], crowing, exulting, glorying, jubilant, prideful, proud, rejoicing, triumphant
related words ecstatic, elated, euphoric; arrogant, boastful, cocky; conquering, victorious, winning
near antonyms crestfallen, defeated, dejected, depressed, disconsolate, dispirited, downcast

exulting *adj* having or expressing feelings of joy or triumph ⟨with an *exulting* smile the winner of the beauty pageant waved to the cheering crowd⟩ — see EXULTANT

eye *n* **1** a circular strip ⟨push the drawstring through the metal *eye* and knot it on one end⟩ — see ¹RING 2
2 a state of being aware ⟨this young actor has the *eye* of every director in Hollywood⟩ — see ATTENTION 2
3 a thing or place that is of greatest importance to an activity or interest ⟨this wilderness area is at the *eye* of the controversy between conservation and development⟩ — see CENTER 1
4 an idea that is believed to be true or valid without positive knowledge ⟨in my *eye*, cats make better pets than dogs⟩ — see OPINION 1
5 an instance of looking especially briefly ⟨all of the guys cast an appreciative *eye* on the new girl as they passed her in the hall⟩ — see LOOK 2
6 the ability to see ⟨her *eyes* are diminishing with age⟩ — see EYESIGHT
7 a fixed intent look ⟨peering through the window with an eager *eye*⟩ — see GAZE

eye *vb* **1** to keep one's eyes on ⟨a lot of his backyard bird watching was spent *eyeing* the squirrels as they depleted the bird feeder of seeds⟩ — see WATCH 1
2 to make note of (something) through the use of one's eyes ⟨I was starting to believe her tale of woe, until I *eyed* the diamond ring on her finger⟩ — see SEE 1
3 to give serious and careful thought to ⟨we're *eyeing* the possibility of buying property there⟩ — see PONDER

eyeball–to–eyeball *adv* in direct confrontation or competition ⟨that inexperienced, upstart candidate will be going *eyeball-to-eyeball* with a senator who's a skilled debater⟩ — see HEAD-TO-HEAD

eyeblink *n* a very small space of time ⟨within an *eyeblink* I accepted their offer on the house⟩ — see INSTANT

eye candy *n* something attractive but lacking in substance ⟨a fashionable portrait painter in his day, he is now regarded as a minor purveyor of *eye candy*⟩ — see COTTON CANDY

eye–catching *adj* likely to attract attention ⟨Brad needs an *eye-catching* slogan for his campaign for president of the student body⟩ — see NOTICEABLE

eyeful *n* a lovely woman ⟨they watched their teenage daughter, once something of an ugly duckling, blossom into quite an *eyeful*⟩ — see BEAUTY 2

eyeglasses *n pl* a pair of lenses set in a frame that is held in place with ear supports and which are usually worn to correct vision ⟨uses her *eyeglasses* only for reading⟩ — see GLASS 1

eyeless *adj* lacking the power of sight ⟨his failing eyesight makes him fear that he may be *eyeless* in old age⟩ — see BLIND 1

eye–opening *adj* **1** causing a strong emotional reaction because of unexpectedness ⟨hunting for a first apartment in a big city is an *eye-opening* experience for young people⟩ — see SURPRISING 1
2 causing wonder or astonishment ⟨that acclaimed animal-cum-magic act had a number of *eye-opening* moments⟩ — see MARVELOUS 1

eyesight *n* the ability to see ⟨the keen *eyesight* of a bird of prey⟩
synonyms eye, sight, vision
related words myopia, nearsightedness; farsightedness, hypermetropia, hyperopia, presbyopia; aniseikonia, astigmatism, diplopia, squint, strabismus; double vision

eyesore *n* something unpleasant to look at ⟨the old abandoned house was a neighborhood *eyesore*⟩
synonyms fright, hideosity, horror, mess, monstrosity, sight
related words eye-catcher; blot, smear, smudge, spot, stain
near antonyms vision

eyespot *n* a small area that is different (as in color) from the main part ⟨a tie having *eyespots* of blue on a light gray background⟩ — see SPOT 1

eye view *n* a way of looking at or thinking about something ⟨from my *eye view*, it looks as if both of you are in the wrong⟩ — see PERSPECTIVE 1

F

fab *adj* of the very best kind ⟨that designer's new line of spring clothing is absolutely *fab*⟩ — see EXCELLENT

fable *n* **1** a story intended to teach a basic truth or moral about life ⟨this classic Christmas film is essentially a *fable* showing how every person's life has meaning and touches the lives of others⟩ — see ALLEGORY
2 a traditional but unfounded story that gives the reason for a current custom, belief, or fact of nature ⟨according to an ancient *fable* the waters of the mountain spring are the tears of a woman weeping for her lost children⟩ — see MYTH 1
3 something that is the product of the imagination ⟨the stories of lost cities of gold may have been *fables* deliberately concocted by Native Americans to dupe the Spanish⟩ — see FICTION
4 a statement known by its maker to be untrue and made in order to deceive ⟨the *fables* that people tell themselves to rationalize their failures and shortcomings⟩ — see LIE

fabled *adj* based on, described in, or being a myth ⟨the *fabled* unicorn continues to be a symbol of elusive and magical beauty⟩ — see MYTHICAL 1

fabric *n* **1** a woven or knitted material (as of cotton or nylon) ⟨a *fabric* that is supposed to repel rain while at the same time allowing the wearer's perspiration to escape⟩ — see CLOTH 1
2 the arrangement of parts that gives something its basic form ⟨you can't expect the *fabric* of society to survive if you do away with all moral imperatives⟩ — see FRAME 1

fabricate *vb* **1** to bring into being by combining, shaping, or transforming materials ⟨with a few inexpensive materials from a craft shop, we were able to *fabricate* our own holiday wreath⟩ — see MAKE 1
2 to create or think of by clever use of the imagination ⟨*fabricated* a daring plan to create an underground explosion that would take the enemy totally by surprise⟩ — see INVENT
3 to form by putting together parts or materials ⟨the house was essentially *fabricated* at the factory and then shipped to the site for assembly⟩ — see BUILD
4 to make a statement one knows to be untrue ⟨since he didn't have a good excuse for not having done his homework, he would have to *fabricate* one⟩ — see [1]LIE

fabrication *n* **1** a statement known by its maker to be untrue and made in order to deceive ⟨her claim that she had been a nurse during the war proved to be a total *fabrication*⟩ — see LIE
2 something that is the product of the imagination ⟨the notion that the Colossus of Rhodes could straddle the harbor was a *fabrication* of medieval writers⟩ — see FICTION

fabricator *n* a person who tells lies ⟨he's been a *fabricator* for so long that it no longer occurs to him to tell the truth⟩ — see LIAR

fabulist *n* a person who tells lies ⟨a once highly admired journalist whose reputation is now that of a disgraced *fabulist*⟩ — see LIAR

fabulous *adj* **1** based on, described in, or being a myth ⟨the city of Phoenix is named after a *fabulous* bird that every 500 years destroys itself with fire, only to rise again from its own ashes⟩ — see MYTHICAL 1
2 causing wonder or astonishment ⟨the *fabulous* sites of dazzlingly lit Las Vegas⟩ — see MARVELOUS 1
3 not real and existing only in the imagination ⟨a story of a *fabulous* land where the people know nothing of war and live together in perfect harmony⟩ — see IMAGINARY
4 of the very best kind ⟨we had a *fabulous* time on our vacation⟩ — see EXCELLENT

fabulously *adv* to a great degree ⟨our *fabulously* wealthy neighbors⟩ — see VERY 1

facade *also* **façade** *n* **1** a forward part or surface ⟨all of the stores in the mall have *facades* that are in keeping with the style of a 19th-century American village⟩ — see FRONT 1
2 a display of emotion or behavior that is insincere or intended to deceive ⟨his interest in acting is just a *facade*—he joined the drama club to meet girls⟩ — see MASQUERADE
3 a deceptively attractive external appearance ⟨the company's *facade* of success collapsed when it was revealed that its financial officers had been cooking the books for years⟩ — see GLOSS 1

face *n* **1** the front part of the head ⟨the criminal hid his *face* from the news cameras as he slumped into the patrol car⟩
synonyms countenance, kisser [*slang*], mug, pan [*slang*], puss [*slang*], visage
related words appearance, aspect, features, lineaments, looks, mien, presence; expression, physiognomy
2 a forward part or surface ⟨the *face* of the store building has been altered many times over the years to meet changing tastes and needs⟩ — see FRONT 1
3 a twisting of the facial features in disgust or disapproval ⟨it's rude to make a *face* when your dinner hostess offers you broccoli⟩ — see GRIMACE
4 an outer part or layer ⟨a much-needed sandblasting revealed that the *face* of the old stone church is actually a pinkish granite⟩ — see EXTERIOR
5 facial appearance regarded as an indication of mood or feeling ⟨a rainy day is no excuse for just moping around with a long *face*, so let's do something⟩ — see LOOK 1
6 outward and often deceptive indication ⟨on the *face* of it, the country went to war for noble reasons⟩ — see APPEARANCE 2
7 a member of the human race ⟨I see they've hired some new *faces*⟩ — see HUMAN
8 shameless boldness ⟨you have to wonder how anyone has the *face* to ask such a personal question⟩ — see EFFRONTERY
9 a state of mind in which one is free from doubt ⟨he managed to maintain *face* despite the endless series of crises⟩ — see CONFIDENCE 2

face *vb* **1** to stand or sit with the face or front toward ⟨the house *faces* the sparkling blue waters of the Pacific Ocean⟩
synonyms front, look (toward), point (toward)
related words abut, adjoin, border, bound, fringe, margin, meet, neighbor, rim, skirt, touch; command, dominate, overlook; look down (on)
2 to oppose (something hostile or dangerous) with firmness or courage ⟨movie superheroes who are ever ready to *face* danger without blinking an eye⟩
synonyms beard, brave, brazen, breast, confront, dare, defy, outbrave, outface
related words face up (to), front; affront; challenge; encounter, meet; accost, approach, corner; repel, resist,

stand, withstand; battle, combat, contend (with), fight, oppose, square (off)
phrases stand up to
near antonyms avoid, eschew, shun; elude, escape, evade, shake
antonyms dodge, duck, funk, shirk, sidestep
3 to cover with something that protects ⟨we decided to *face* our old frame house with aluminum siding⟩ — see SHEATHE
4 to enter into contest or conflict with ⟨the Boston Red Sox were eager to *face* their traditional rivals, the Yankees, in the play-offs⟩ — see ENGAGE 2

faceless *adj* **1** lacking in distinctive features or qualities ⟨it was precisely because he was a *faceless* individual that the serial killer was able to go on for so long without detection⟩ — see NONDESCRIPT
2 not named or identified by a name ⟨*faceless* gossipmongers had been spreading rumors about the actor's sexual identity for years⟩ — see NAMELESS 1

facelessness *n* the quality or state of being mostly or completely unknown ⟨the *facelessness* of those early participants in the American civil rights movement⟩ — see OBSCURITY 2

face–off *n* an earnest effort for superiority or victory over another ⟨the annual fall *face-off* between these traditional rivals is a big event for both football-mad colleges⟩ — see CONTEST 1

face off *vb* to engage in a contest ⟨eager to *face off* with her longtime tennis rival⟩ — see COMPETE

facet *n* a certain way in which something appears or may be regarded ⟨there are so many *facets* to Benjamin Franklin: statesman, scientist, inventor, American original⟩ — see ASPECT 1

facetious *adj* **1** given to or marked by mature intelligent humor ⟨the essay is a *facetious* commentary on the absurdity of war as a solution for international disputes⟩ — see WITTY
2 making light of something usually regarded as serious or sacred ⟨a *facetious* and tasteless remark about people in famine-stricken countries being spared the problem of overeating⟩ — see FLIPPANT

facetiousness *n* a lack of seriousness often at an improper time ⟨underage drinking is a serious problem and not a matter for *facetiousness* and lame jokes⟩ — see FRIVOLITY 1

face–to–face *adv* **1** in person and usually privately ⟨I won't believe that accusation until I meet with him *face-to-face* and ask him myself⟩ — see TÊTE-À-TÊTE
2 in direct confrontation or competition ⟨came *face-to-face* with her lifelong fear of flying even before the plane left the runway⟩ — see HEAD-TO-HEAD

facile *adj* **1** having or showing a lack of depth of understanding or character ⟨the movie takes a *facile* look at what happens when teens enter into serious romantic relationships⟩ — see SUPERFICIAL 2
2 involving minimal difficulty or effort ⟨a few early *facile* victories misled the country into thinking that the war would be short and relatively painless⟩ — see EASY 1

facilely *adv* without difficulty ⟨most TV sitcoms give the impression that family problems can be solved *facilely* and in less than 30 minutes⟩ — see EASILY 1

facilitate *vb* to free from obstruction or difficulty ⟨several religious organizations are involved in the effort to *facilitate* the settlement of the immigrants arriving in the area⟩ — see EASE 1

facilitative *adj* **1** providing service or assistance ⟨managerial attitudes and practices that have proven to be highly *facilitative* of increased worker productivity⟩ — see HELPFUL 1
2 tending to promote or assist the development of something ⟨a well-equipped laboratory *facilitative* to research⟩ — see CONDUCIVE 1

facility *n* a structure that is designed and built for a particular purpose ⟨the city is known for its outstanding medical *facilities*⟩
synonyms complex, establishment, installation
related words building, edifice; institute, institution; business, company, concern, outfit

facsimile *n* **1** something or someone that strongly resembles another ⟨the family resemblance is so strong that the boy is virtually a pint-size *facsimile* of his father⟩ — see IMAGE 1
2 something that is made to look exactly like something else ⟨this is not an antique copy of the Declaration of Independence but a modern *facsimile*⟩ — see COPY

fact *n* **1** the quality of being actual ⟨like other scientists, astronomers deal in the realm of *fact*, not speculation⟩
synonyms actuality, factuality, materiality, reality
related words authenticity, genuineness, truth, verity
near antonyms fancy, fantasy (*also* phantasy), fiction, fictitiousness; dreaminess, surreality
antonyms irreality, unreality
2 something that actually exists ⟨once considered a wild fantasy, the Internet is now a *fact* of everyday life⟩
synonyms actuality, case, materiality, reality
related words certainty, inevitability; circumstance, event, occurrence, phenomenon; element, item, particular, thing
near antonyms eventuality, possibility, potentiality, probability
antonyms fantasy (*also* phantasy), fiction, illusion
3 a single piece of information ⟨a book of little-known *facts* about famous people⟩
synonyms datum, detail, nicety, particular, particularity, point, specific
related words article, item; component, constituent, element, ingredient, member, part; aspect, circumstance, facet, factor; evidence, exhibit; database, information, knowledge
near antonyms error, fallacy, falsehood, inaccuracy, misconception, misstatement, myth
4 facts *pl* a collection of factual knowledge about something ⟨after reading the *facts* on the situation, the president concluded that an outbreak of hostilities was all but certain⟩ — see INFORMATION 1

facticity *n* agreement with fact or reality ⟨the *facticity* of the information is not at issue; it's whether something so private should ever be made public⟩ — see TRUTH

faction *n* a group of people acting together within a larger group ⟨several *factions* within the environmental movement have joined forces to save this wilderness area⟩
synonyms bloc, block, body, coalition, party, sect, set, side, wing
related words splinter, split; crew, gang, pack, team; denomination, persuasion; schism, scission; caucus, movement

factitious *adj* **1** being such in appearance only and made with or manufactured from usually cheaper materials ⟨presumably the statue is of *factitious* marble, because for that price you're not going to get the real stuff⟩ — see IMITATION
2 lacking in natural or spontaneous quality ⟨the *factitious* friendliness shown by the beauty-pageant contestants to one another⟩ — see ARTIFICIAL 1

factor *n* **1** a person who acts or does business for another ⟨at the auction the high bidder for the painting was actually a *factor* for a wealthy art collector⟩ — see AGENT 2
2 one of the parts that make up a whole ⟨price was only

one *factor* in my decision to buy the car⟩ — see ELEMENT 1

factor (in *or* into) *vb* to give consideration to (as unexpected circumstances or contingencies) ⟨you should *factor in* inflation in making investment decisions⟩ — see ALLOW (FOR)

factory *n* a building or set of buildings for the manufacturing of goods ⟨the new *factory* will create hundreds of much-needed jobs⟩
synonyms manufactory, mill, plant, shop, works, workshop
related words sweatshop; atelier, studio, workplace, workroom; yard

factual *adj* **1** restricted to or based on fact ⟨a *factual* biography of George Washington that scoffs at the story about the cherry tree⟩
synonyms documentary, hard, historical, literal, matter-of-fact, nonfictional, objective, true
related words actual, authentic, bona fide, genuine, real, right; documented, established; confirmable, reliable, supportable, sustainable, verifiable; demonstrable, provable; incontestable, incontrovertible, indisputable, irrefutable, undeniable, unquestionable; plain, simple; certain, undoubted
near antonyms hypothetical, speculative, theoretical (*also* theoretic); apocryphal, unauthentic, undocumented; chimerical (*also* chimeric), fabulous, fanciful, fantastic (*also* fantastical), imaginary, imagined, invented, legendary, made-up, make-believe, mythical (*or* mythic), pretend; embroidered, exaggerated; insupportable, unsupportable
antonyms fictional, fictionalized, fictitious, nondocumentary, nonfactual, nonhistorical, unhistorical
2 existing in fact and not merely as a possibility ⟨a serious scientist, she is only interested in *factual* phenomena and lets others speculate about the hypothetical⟩ — see ACTUAL

factuality *n* **1** agreement with fact or reality ⟨some viewers complained that the TV docudrama was short on *factuality* and long on speculation⟩ — see TRUTH
2 the quality of being actual ⟨although this account of the murders seems like it must be fiction, its very *factuality* makes it all the more fascinating⟩ — see FACT 1

faculty *n* **1** a natural ability of the mind or body ⟨although they are well into their 80s, the mental *faculties* of this couple are as sharp as ever⟩ — see POWER 3
2 a special and usually inborn ability ⟨even when he was still at a young age, John Singleton Copley's artistic *faculties* were readily recognizable⟩ — see TALENT
3 the physical or mental power to do something ⟨the belief that if someone loses their sight, all of their other physical *faculties* are heightened⟩ — see ABILITY

fad *n* a practice or interest that is very popular for a short time ⟨once the *fad* for that kind of music had passed, nobody would have been caught dead listening to it⟩
synonyms buzz, chic, craze, dernier cri, enthusiasm, fashion, flavor, go, hot ticket, last word, latest, mode, rage, sensation, style, ton, trend, vogue
related words nine days' wonder (*also* nine day wonder); new wave; crush, infatuation; fervor, passion; furor, fuss, hullabaloo, to-do, uproar; bandwagon, crusade, cult, movement; novelty, wrinkle; caprice, fancy, whim
near antonyms classic, standard

faddish *adj* enjoying widespread favor or approval ⟨a *faddish* novelist who impressed some critics, at least for a time⟩ — see POPULAR 1

faddy *adj* enjoying widespread favor or approval ⟨that chef's *faddy* cuisine was all the rage among foodies back in the 1990s⟩ — see POPULAR 1

fade *vb* **1** to cease to be visible ⟨the departing ship gradually *faded* over the horizon⟩ — see DISAPPEAR
2 to make white or whiter by removing color ⟨years of harsh sunlight had *faded* the car, which was once fire-engine red⟩ — see WHITEN
3 to lose bodily strength or vigor ⟨began to *fade* after battling the disease for years⟩ — see WEAKEN 2

faded *adj* lacking intensity of color ⟨rather than buy *faded* jeans, I get the dark blues and let time and the washing machine do their thing⟩ — see PALE 1

faerie *also* **faery** *n* an imaginary being usually having a small human form and magical powers ⟨in ancient folklore *faeries* were often portrayed as powerful beings who could wreak havoc on the lives of humans⟩ — see FAIRY

fag *n* a person who does very hard or dull work ⟨a rigid class system, with *fags* at the very bottom of it⟩ — see SLAVE 2

fag *vb* **1** to devote serious and sustained effort ⟨the road crew *fagged* mightily to move the boulder out of the way⟩ — see LABOR
2 to use up all the physical energy of ⟨the long hike up the mountain had *fagged* us out⟩ — see EXHAUST 1

fag end *n* an unused or unwanted piece or item typically of small size or value ⟨a patchwork quilt sewn together from the *fag ends* of many bolts of cloth⟩ — see [1]SCRAP 1

fail *vb* **1** to stop functioning ⟨my video camera *failed* just as I was about to shoot the big moment⟩
synonyms break, break down, conk (out), crash, cut out, die, give out, stall
related words fizzle, sputter, wheeze; act up, malfunction; jam
antonyms start (up)
2 to be unsuccessful ⟨despite all the publicity, the movie *failed* miserably at the box office⟩
synonyms bomb, collapse, crater, flame out, flop, flunk, fold, founder, miss, strike out, tank, wash out
related words flounder, struggle; decline, sink, skid, slip, slump, wane; crash, crumble, miscarry, misfire; go under; implode, self-destruct
phrases come a cropper, come to grief, come up empty, die on the vine, fall flat, fall on one's face, fall short, lay an egg
near antonyms cook, flourish, prosper, thrive; prevail, triumph, win
antonyms click, come off, deliver, go, go over, pan out, succeed, work out
3 to fall short in satisfying the expectation or hope of ⟨although the minor-league franchise continues to *fail* local fans, hope springs eternal⟩ — see DISAPPOINT
4 to lose bodily strength or vigor ⟨ever since she reached the age of 90, Grandma has been noticeably *failing*⟩ — see WEAKEN 2
5 to miss the opportunity or obligation ⟨*failed* to mention that he had already been paid for the job by the homeowner's wife⟩ — see NEGLECT 3

failing *n* a defect in character ⟨we could talk about your *failings*, but it would take all night⟩ — see FAULT 1

fail–safe *adj* not likely to fail ⟨men have traditionally regarded flowers as the *fail-safe* gift for Valentine's Day⟩ — see INFALLIBLE 2

fail–safe *n* a measure taken to preclude loss or injury ⟨there are so many *fail-safes* built into the system that a highly unlikely series of mistakes would have to be made before failure could occur⟩ — see PRECAUTION

failure *n* **1** the nonperformance of an assigned or expected action ⟨your *failure* to check the batteries in the smoke detector could have tragic results⟩
synonyms default, delinquency, dereliction, misprision, neglect, negligence, nonfeasance, oversight
related words carelessness, heedlessness, inadvertence, inadvertency, laxity

near antonyms compliance, discharge, fulfillment (*or* fulfilment)
2 a falling short of one's goals ⟨the *failure* of the school's fund-raising drive was a big disappointment to all⟩
synonyms collapse, crash, cropper, defeat, fizzle, nonachievement, nonsuccess
related words futility, uselessness; ineffectiveness, ineffectuality, ineffectualness, inefficaciousness, inefficacy; deficiency, inadequacy, inadequateness, insufficiency; disappointment, letdown, setback
near antonyms victory, win
antonyms accomplishment, achievement, success
3 something that has failed ⟨the students' first attempt to build a homemade rocket was a disappointing *failure*⟩
synonyms bomb, bummer, bust, catastrophe, clinker, clunker, debacle (*also* débâcle), disaster, dud, fiasco, fizzle, flop, frost, lemon, loser, miss, shipwreck, turkey, washout
related words also-ran, disappointment, dog, has-been, near miss; botch, hash, mess, muddle, shambles; nonevent; nonstarter
near antonyms corker, crackerjack (*also* crackajack), dandy, jim-dandy, phenomenon
antonyms blockbuster, hit, smash, success, winner
4 a falling short of an essential or desirable amount or number ⟨the *failure* of the potato crop had a devastating effect on the population of Ireland⟩ — see DEFICIENCY
5 the inability to pay one's debts ⟨years of prolonged economic depression, when business *failures* were common⟩ — see INSOLVENCY

fain *adj* having a desire or inclination (as for a specified course of action) ⟨during the Renaissance most men of science and the arts were *fain* to express their noblest thoughts in Latin, the lingua franca of the learned⟩ — see WILLING 1

fain *adv* by choice or preference ⟨"I would *fain* not marry that suitor, my lord," the princess pleaded⟩ — see RATHER 1

faint *adj* **1** not seen or understood clearly ⟨after wandering in the woods for hours, we had only a *faint* idea of where we were⟩
synonyms blear, bleary, blurry, dim, foggy, fuzzy, gauzy, hazy, indefinite, indistinct, indistinguishable, misty, murky, nebulous, obscure, opaque, pale, shadowy, unclear, undefined, undetermined, vague
related words dark, dusky, gloomy; impalpable, inappreciable, intangible, invisible; hieroglyphic (*also* hieroglyphical), incomprehensible, indecipherable, indiscernible, inexplicable, mysterious, obfuscatory, puzzling
near antonyms bright, distinct, evident, obvious, plain; certain, firm, strong, sure
antonyms clear, definite, pellucid
2 lacking bodily strength ⟨I was starting to feel a little *faint* after going so long without food⟩ — see WEAK 1

faint *n* a temporary state of unconsciousness ⟨shocking news can cause a person to fall into a *faint*⟩
synonyms blackout, insensibility, knockout, swim, swoon, syncope
related words daze, stupor, trance; drowsiness, narcosis, sleep, somnolence

faint *vb* to lose consciousness ⟨the kind of person who *faints* at the sight of blood⟩
synonyms black out, conk (out), keel (over), pass out, swoon
related words break down, collapse; zonk (out)
antonyms come around, come round, come to, revive

fainthearted *adj* easily frightened ⟨the sport of river rafting is not for those who are *fainthearted*⟩ — see SHY 1

faintheartedness *n* lack of willingness to assert oneself and take risks ⟨his *faintheartedness* got the better of him, and he backed off from the ski trail intended for experts⟩ — see TIMIDITY

faintness *n* the quality or state of lacking physical strength or vigor ⟨after a year of increasing *faintness*, the old man quietly died in his sleep⟩ — see WEAKNESS 1

fair *n* a public showing of objects of interest ⟨a dazzling array of sleek cabin cruisers at the annual boat *fair*⟩ — see EXHIBITION 1

fair *adj* **1** not stormy or cloudy ⟨we prayed for *fair* weather during our vacation at the beach⟩
synonyms bright, clear, cloudless, sunny, sunshiny, unclouded
related words balmy, clement, gentle, mild, moderate, temperate; calm, halcyon, peaceful, placid, serene, tranquil; fine, pleasant
near antonyms harsh, inclement, severe; blustering, blustery, breezy, gusty; foggy, hazy, misty, murky, soupy
antonyms bleak, cloudy, dirty, foul, nasty, overcast, rainy, raw, rough, squally, stormy, sunless, tempestuous, turbulent
2 marked by justice, honesty, and freedom from bias ⟨a commanding officer who enjoyed the respect of his soldiers because his decisions were always *fair*⟩
synonyms candid, disinterested, dispassionate, equal, equitable, evenhanded, impartial, indifferent, just, nonpartisan, objective, square, unbiased, unprejudiced
related words frank, forthright, open, straight, straightforward; balanced, rational, reasonable
near antonyms deceitful, deceptive, dishonest; arbitrary, unconscionable, unreasonable; jaundiced, unfriendly, unsympathetic; colored, distorted, warped
antonyms biased, ex parte, inequitable, nonobjective, one-sided, partial, parti pris, partisan, prejudiced, unjust
3 following or according to the rules ⟨a hockey player who is respected for his *fair* play⟩
synonyms clean, legal, sportsmanlike, sportsmanly
related words just, law-abiding; ethical, moral, principled, scrupulous; honorable, irreproachable, unimpeachable
near antonyms immoral, unethical, unprincipled, unrighteous, unscrupulous, vicious, wrong
antonyms dirty, foul, nasty, unfair, unsportsmanlike
4 of light complexion ⟨*fair* people tend to sunburn easily⟩
synonyms light
related words ashen, ashy, pale, paled, palish, pallid, pasty, peaked, peaky, sallow, sallowish, wan, white
antonyms black, brunet (*or* brunette), dark, swart, swarthy
5 having qualities which inspire hope ⟨as long as the team keeps playing as hard as they can, they have a *fair* chance of winning—no matter what the scoreboard says⟩ — see HOPEFUL 1
6 of a pale yellow or yellowish brown color ⟨the abundance of people with *fair* hair in Scandinavia⟩ — see BLOND
7 of average to below average quality ⟨for what they charged us, the painters should have done better than a *fair* job of painting the house⟩ — see MEDIOCRE 1
8 very pleasing to look at ⟨generally considered the *fairest* girl in town, she had no lack of boyfriends⟩ — see BEAUTIFUL 1
9 having no exceptions or restrictions ⟨it would take a *fair* miracle for that project to be finished on time⟩ — see ABSOLUTE 2

10 being what is called for by accepted standards of right and wrong ⟨most thought his dismissal was *fair* since he had been given many chances to clean up his act⟩ — see JUST 1

11 free from dirt or stain ⟨a handwritten thank-you letter requires nothing less than a sheet of *fair* white paper⟩ — see CLEAN 1

fair *adv* **1** according to the rules or the law ⟨we expect everyone on this basketball court to play *fair*⟩ — see FAIRLY 2

2 *chiefly British* very close to but not completely ⟨it *fair* takes your breath away when you find out what properties in London are going for⟩ — see ALMOST

fair–haired *adj* granted special treatment or attention ⟨she had been the teacher's *fair-haired* pupil—the one who could do no wrong⟩ — see DARLING 1

fairing *n*, *British* something given to someone without expectation of a return ⟨business takes him to all corners of the globe, but he never fails to bring back *fairings* for the family back in London⟩ — see GIFT 1

fairish *adj* of a level of quality that meets one's needs or standards ⟨did a *fairish* job of refinishing the old chest, especially since it was her first foray into furniture restoration⟩ — see ADEQUATE

fairly *adv* **1** to some degree or extent ⟨for someone without professional training, she sings *fairly* well⟩

synonyms enough, kindly [*chiefly Southern*], kind of, like, moderately, more or less, pretty, quite, rather, relatively, something, somewhat, sort of

related words acceptably, decently, passably, tolerably; little, negligibly, nominally, slightly, vaguely; half, halfway, incompletely, part, partially, partly, partway

phrases a bit, after a sort, a little, a mite, a tad, a touch, of sorts (*or* of a sort), to a degree

near antonyms awfully, beastly, deadly, especially, exceedingly (*also* exceeding), exceptionally, extremely, frightfully, greatly, heavily, highly, hugely, mightily, mortally, particularly, surpassingly, terribly, very; considerably, extensively, significantly, substantially

2 according to the rules or the law ⟨had acquired the land *fairly*⟩

synonyms clean, cleanly, fair, legally

related words ethically, high-mindedly, morally, nobly; honorably

near antonyms ignobly, immorally, underhandedly, unethically; dishonorably

antonyms dirty, illegally

3 very close to but not completely ⟨he *fairly* knocked me flat on my face as he ran by⟩ — see ALMOST

fair–mindedness *n* lack of favoritism toward one side or another ⟨fortunately, the person chosen to determine custody for the chld is known for her *fair-mindedness*⟩ — see DETACHMENT 1

fairness *n* **1** the qualities in a person or thing that as a whole give pleasure to the senses ⟨a city of incomparable *fairness*, Venice has enchanted travelers for centuries⟩ — see BEAUTY 1

2 lack of favoritism toward one side or another ⟨*fairness* was certainly uppermost in the elderly woman's mind as she made arrangements for dividing the family heirlooms among her many grandchildren⟩ — see DETACHMENT 1

fair shake *n* the practice of giving to others what is their due ⟨it's going to be tough to get a *fair shake* the way this country's legal system is set up⟩ — see JUSTICE 1

fairy *n* an imaginary being usually having a small human form and magical powers ⟨*fairies* are part of the folklore of many countries and cultures⟩

synonyms brownie, dwarf, elf, faerie (*also* faery), fay, gnome, goblin, gremlin, hobgoblin, kobold, leprechaun, pixie (*also* pixy), puck, sprite, troll

related words little people; kelpie, nixie; changeling; imp; banshee, ghoul, hag, ogre

fairy godmother *n* one that helps another with gifts or money ⟨when it came time for the girl to go to college, Aunt Edna once again proved to be a reliable *fairy godmother*⟩ — see BENEFACTOR

fairy tale *n* a statement known by its maker to be untrue and made in order to deceive ⟨did you really see a bear, or are you telling us another one of your *fairy tales*?⟩ — see LIE

faith *n* **1** belief and trust in and loyalty to God ⟨a people who are known for their strong and steadfast *faith*⟩

synonyms devotion, piety, religion

related words devoutness, piousness, religiousness; adoration, reverence, veneration, worship; profession, protestation

near antonyms disbelief, doubt, unbelief, unfaith; agnosticism, know-nothingism; apostasy, lapse, tergiversation

antonyms atheism, godlessness

2 a body of beliefs and practices regarding the supernatural and the worship of one or more deities ⟨the city of Jerusalem is sacred to three *faiths*: Christianity, Islam, and Judaism⟩ — see RELIGION 1

3 adherence to something to which one is bound by a pledge or duty ⟨after they had to declare bankruptcy, the family found out how much *faith* their friends had⟩ — see FIDELITY

4 firm belief in the integrity, ability, effectiveness, or genuineness of someone or something ⟨never having had much *faith* in banks, the old miser kept his money under the mattress⟩ — see TRUST 1

5 mental conviction of the truth of some statement or the reality of some being or phenomenon ⟨she has complete *faith* that the universe is controlled by a benevolent Supreme Being with a master plan⟩ — see BELIEF 1

faithful *adj* **1** firm in one's allegiance to someone or something ⟨fans of the Chicago Cubs are famously *faithful*⟩

synonyms constant, dedicated, devoted, devout, down-the-line, fast, good, loyal, pious, staunch (*also* stanch), steadfast, steady, true, true-blue

related words dependable, dutiful, reliable, responsible, solid, tried, tried-and-true, trustworthy, trusty; unfaltering, unhesitating, unwavering; determined, intent, resolute; confirmed, dyed-in-the-wool, inveterate, sworn; ardent, avid, enthusiastic, fervent, fervid, gung ho, impassioned, passionate, serious

near antonyms irresponsible, undependable, unreliable, untrustworthy; faltering, hesitant, vacillating, wavering; dubious, irresolute, shaky, uncertain; apathetic, dispassionate, uninterested

antonyms disloyal, faithless, false, fickle, inconstant, perfidious, recreant, traitorous, treacherous, unfaithful, untrue

2 following an original exactly ⟨a *faithful* filming of Robert Louis Stevenson's novel *Treasure Island*⟩

synonyms accurate, authentic, exact, precise, right, strict, true, veracious

related words lifelike, realistic; careful, conscientious, meticulous, punctilious, scrupulous; authoritative; bona fide, genuine, real, veridical

near antonyms careless, slack, slipshod, slovenly; erroneous, incorrect, invalid, off, unsound, untrue, untruthful, wrong

antonyms corrupt, corrupted, false, imprecise, inaccurate, inauthentic, inexact, loose, unfaithful

faithfulness *n* adherence to something to which one is bound by a pledge or duty ⟨put the *faithfulness* of his disciples to the test⟩ — see FIDELITY

faithless *adj* not true in one's allegiance to someone or

something ⟨*faithless* friends who deserted him in his time of need⟩
synonyms disloyal, false, fickle, inconstant, perfidious, recreant, traitorous, treacherous, unfaithful, untrue
related words irresponsible, trustless, undependable, unreliable, untrustworthy; faltering, hesitant, vacillating, wavering; dubious, irresolute, uncertain; apathetic, dispassionate, uninterested
near antonyms dependable, dutiful, reliable, responsible, solid, tried, tried-and-true, trustable, trustworthy, trusty; unfaltering, unhesitating, unwavering; determined, intent, resolute; confirmed, dyed-in-the-wool, inveterate, sworn; ardent, avid, enthusiastic, fervent, fervid, impassioned, passionate
antonyms constant, dedicated, devoted, devout, down-the-line, faithful, fast, loyal, staunch (*also* stanch), steadfast, steady, true

faithlessness *n* **1** lack of faithfulness especially to one's husband or wife ⟨a wife who long ago became resigned to the chronic *faithlessness* of her husband⟩— see INFIDELITY 1
2 the act or fact of violating the trust or confidence of another ⟨the former butler's mercenary *faithlessness* shocked and offended the royal family⟩ — see BETRAYAL

fake *adj* **1** being such in appearance only and made with or manufactured from usually cheaper materials ⟨opposed to the unnecessary killing of animals, she'll consider wearing only *fake* furs⟩ — see IMITATION
2 being such in appearance only and made or manufactured with the intention of committing fraud ⟨arrested for peddling "designer" watches that were *fake*⟩ — see COUNTERFEIT 1
3 lacking in natural or spontaneous quality ⟨the boss's pitiful attempts at humor were met with *fake* laughter⟩ — see ARTIFICIAL 1
4 not being or expressing what one appears to be or express ⟨the *fake* friendliness of the sales rep made me want to gag⟩ — see INSINCERE

fake *n* **1** an imitation that is passed off as genuine ⟨experts declared that one of the museum's prized paintings was actually a *fake*⟩
synonyms counterfeit, forgery, hoax, humbug, phony (*also* phoney), sham
related words copycat, knockoff; copy, facsimile, replica, reproduction; dummy, mock-up; fraud, gaff, imposture, spoof, swindle; simulation, synthetic; bastard, brummagem, duffer, shoddy
near antonyms original
2 one who makes false claims of identity or expertise ⟨a hidden-camera investigation revealed that the so-called psychic was a *fake*⟩— see IMPOSTOR

fake *vb* **1** to imitate or copy especially in order to deceive ⟨pranksters *faked* giant footprints and then claimed that they had seen Bigfoot⟩
synonyms counterfeit, forge, phony
related words simulate; duplicate, reduplicate, replicate, reproduce; crib, plagiarize; adulterate, doctor, fudge, juggle, manipulate, tamper (with); concoct, cook (up), fabricate, invent
2 to present a false appearance of ⟨while running for class president, Dan was not above *faking* friendship with people just to get their votes⟩ — see FEIGN
3 to perform, make, or do without preparation ⟨if you give me the gist of the plan, I can probably *fake* enough for the speech⟩ — see IMPROVISE
4 to elude (an opponent in a sports contest) by making a deceptive or agile movement ⟨the running back *faked* the defense by stepping to his left and then quickly cutting to the right⟩ — see JUKE

fake out *vb* **1** to cause to believe what is untrue ⟨my friends *faked* me *out* for a whole day, letting me think that they had forgotten my birthday⟩ — see DECEIVE
2 to elude (an opponent in a sports contest) by making a deceptive or agile movement ⟨used a quick between-the-legs dribble to *fake out* the flat-footed defender⟩ — see JUKE

faker *n* one who makes false claims of identity or expertise ⟨the medium was exposed as a *faker* who was herself making the strange noises that she claimed were from the dead⟩ — see IMPOSTOR

fakery *n* the inclination or practice of misleading others through lies or trickery ⟨if the product were any good, the company wouldn't have to resort to *fakery* to get people to buy it⟩ — see DECEIT 1

fakir *n* **1** a dishonest person who uses clever means to cheat others out of something of value ⟨a traveling carnival that was run by *fakirs* preying on small-town rubes⟩ — see TRICKSTER 1
2 one who makes false claims of identity or expertise ⟨a *fakir* peddling patent medicines that were mostly liquor and sugar⟩ — see IMPOSTOR

fall *n* **1** the act of going down from an upright position suddenly and involuntarily ⟨a bad *fall* that resulted in several broken bones⟩
synonyms slip, spill, stumble, tumble
related words header, pratfall; misstep, trip; descent, dive, plunge, skid, slide; free-fall
2 a change to a lower state or level ⟨last night's record *fall* in temperature was a sure sign that winter's coming, like it or not⟩ — see DECLINE 2
3 a loss of status ⟨being sent back to the minor leagues was quite a *fall* for the once-promising pitcher⟩ — see COMEDOWN
4 the act or process of going to a lower level or altitude ⟨panicked during his first unassisted *fall* when his parachute's rip cord didn't respond to the first tug⟩ — see DESCENT 1
5 the amount by which something is lessened ⟨that year the *fall* in prices was 10 cents for a gallon of regular gas⟩ — see DECREASE
6 *usually* **falls** *pl* a fall of water usually from a great height ⟨tourists were shocked to see a man jump into the water and go over the *falls*⟩ — see WATERFALL
7 a downward slope ⟨the sharp *fall* of the land sends rivers rushing to the seas⟩ — see DECLINE 3

fall *vb* **1** to go down from an upright position suddenly and involuntarily ⟨better sand that walkway before somebody *falls* on the ice⟩
synonyms slip, stumble, topple, trip, tumble
related words collapse, crumple, drop, flump, keel, plop, plunk (*or* plonk), slump (over); crash, free-fall, nose-dive, plummet, plunge, precipitate, wipe out; skid, slide
antonyms get up, rise, stand (up), uprise
2 to yield to the control or power of enemy forces ⟨the city *fell* after weeks of merciless bombardment⟩
synonyms capitulate, give up, knuckle under, submit, succumb, surrender
related words bow, buckle, cave (in), collapse, give (in); hand over, relinquish; lose; concede, fail, fold
near antonyms buck, defy, fight, oppose, repel, resist, withstand; beat, overcome, win; conquer, prevail, triumph
antonyms endure, stand
3 to go to a lower level especially abruptly ⟨word soon got out that the movie was no good, and box-office receipts *fell* like a rock⟩ — see DROP 2
4 to grow less in scope or intensity especially gradually ⟨manufacturing in the area is *falling*, and closing signs are going up all over⟩ — see DECREASE 2
5 to lead or extend downward ⟨the lake bottom *falls* sharply just a few feet from the shoreline, so be careful⟩ — see DESCEND 1

6 to undergo defeat ⟨not surprisingly, the novice player *fell* to a much stronger opponent⟩ — see LOSE 3
7 to commit an offense ⟨even saints can *fall*⟩ — see OFFEND 1
8 to stop living ⟨if their brave leader *falls*, the men will lose their courage⟩ — see DIE 1

fall (to) *vb* to take the first step in (a process or course of action) ⟨after some refreshments, she *fell to* working with renewed vigor⟩ — see BEGIN 1

fallacious *adj* **1** not using or following good reasoning ⟨it's *fallacious* to say that something must exist because science hasn't proven its nonexistence⟩ — see ILLOGICAL
2 tending or having power to deceive ⟨consumers who harbor the *fallacious* belief that credit-card spending will never catch up with them⟩ — see DECEPTIVE 1

fallaciousness *n* the quality or state of being false ⟨the *fallaciousness* of that argument will be apparent as soon as we examine it⟩ — see FALLACY 2

fallacy *n* **1** a false idea or belief ⟨the once-common *fallacy* that girls just weren't any good at math⟩
synonyms delusion, error, falsehood, falsity, hallucination, illusion, misbelief, misconception, myth, old wives' tale, untruth
related words factoid; superstition; fiction, pretense (*or* pretence); distortion, inaccuracy, misapprehension, miscomprehension, misinterpretation, misjudgment, misperception, misunderstanding; misinformation, misknowledge, misreport, misrepresentation, misstatement; sophism, sophistry; fib, half-truth, lie, story, tale
antonyms truth, verity
2 the quality or state of being false ⟨the *fallacy* of the notion of spontaneous generation was demonstrated by the Dutch naturalist Leeuwenhoek⟩
synonyms erroneousness, fallaciousness, falsehood, falseness, falsity, untruth
related words speciousness, spuriousness; deception, deceptiveness, delusion; inaccuracy, incorrectness; dishonesty, mendaciousness, mendacity, untruthfulness
near antonyms accuracy, actuality, correctness, factuality, factualness, genuineness; credibility, honesty, trustworthiness, truthfulness, veracity
antonyms truth, verity

fall away *vb* to grow less in scope or intensity especially gradually ⟨as the years went by, the public's interest in the murder case *fell away*⟩ — see DECREASE 2

fall back *vb* to move back or away (as from something difficult, dangerous, or disagreeable) ⟨resistance from native forces was greater than expected, and the invading army was forced to *fall back*⟩ — see RETREAT 1

fallen *adj* no longer living ⟨let's take a moment to remember our *fallen* comrades⟩ — see DEAD 1

fall guy *n* a person or thing taking the blame for others ⟨the sandlot ball players wanted the littlest kid to be the *fall guy* for the broken window, figuring that he'd have the best chance of escaping punishment⟩ — see SCAPEGOAT

falling–out *n* an often noisy or angry expression of differing opinions ⟨the two friends have been lonely and miserable since they had a *falling-out*⟩ — see ARGUMENT 1

falloff *n* the amount by which something is lessened ⟨the *falloff* in sales was more than the store could weather and so its closing was inevitable⟩ — see DECREASE

fall off *vb* to turn away from a straight line or course ⟨the coastline *falls off* toward the north after you round the bay⟩ — see CURVE 1

fall out *vb* **1** to express different opinions about something often angrily ⟨club members were soon *falling out* about how to spend the money they'd made washing cars⟩ — see ARGUE 2
2 to come to be ⟨I had planned to have a sports career, but things *fell out* otherwise⟩ — see COME OUT 1

fallow *adj* not being in a state of use, activity, or employment ⟨the coal mine has been lying *fallow* since the drop in prices made it unprofitable⟩ — see INACTIVE 2

false *adj* **1** not being in agreement with what is true ⟨early reports about the explosion contained much *false* information⟩
synonyms erroneous, inaccurate, incorrect, inexact, invalid, off, unsound, untrue, untruthful, wrong
related words counterfactual; specious, spurious; deceptive, delusive, delusory, distorted, fallacious, fictitious, illusory, misleading; amiss, askew, awry; deceitful, dishonest, fraudulent, lying, mendacious; unconfirmed, unproven, untested; fabricated, invented, made-up, trumped-up
phrases off base
near antonyms confirmed, demonstrated, established, proven, tested; faultless, flawless, impeccable, letter-perfect, perfect
antonyms accurate, correct, errorless, exact, factual, precise, proper, right, sound, true, valid, veracious
2 being such in appearance only and made with or manufactured from usually cheaper materials ⟨George Washington's *false* teeth were not made of wood but of elephant ivory and cow's teeth⟩ — see IMITATION
3 being such in appearance only and made or manufactured with the intention of committing fraud ⟨arrested for selling *false* ID cards to teenagers⟩ — see COUNTERFEIT 1
4 lacking in natural or spontaneous quality ⟨so much of the sympathy that the widow received was *false* and hypocritical, since it came from people who never liked her husband in the first place⟩ — see ARTIFICIAL 1
5 marked by, based on, or done by the use of dishonest methods to acquire something of value ⟨*false* advertising that claimed that the vegetables were organically grown when they weren't⟩ — see FRAUDULENT 1
6 not true in one's allegiance to someone or something ⟨*false* friends who deserted the prizefighter when all his money was gone⟩ — see FAITHLESS
7 tending or having power to deceive ⟨it turned out that the con man had made *false* promises of marriage to a dozen women⟩ — see DECEPTIVE 1

falsehood *n* **1** a false idea or belief ⟨the possibility of a perpetual motion machine is one *falsehood* that has been disproved by modern physics⟩ — see FALLACY 1
2 a statement known by its maker to be untrue and made in order to deceive ⟨several *falsehoods* in the witness's testimony that may be grounds for perjury⟩ — see LIE
3 the quality or state of being false ⟨scientists eventually demonstrated the *falsehood* of the claim that prehistoric fish did not evolve lungs and legs⟩ — see FALLACY 2
4 the tendency to tell lies ⟨a cynic who believes that politics are a veritable fount of *falsehood*⟩ — see DISHONESTY 1

falseness *n* **1** lack of faithfulness especially to one's husband or wife ⟨so that their love would never know a moment of *falseness*, Thomas Jefferson promised his dying wife that he would never remarry⟩ — see INFIDELITY 1
2 the act or fact of violating the trust or confidence of another ⟨she could not believe that her so-called best friend could ever be guilty of such *falseness*⟩ — see BETRAYAL
3 the quality or state of being false ⟨the *falseness* of your reasoning is so blatant that it's no wonder you reached that absurd conclusion⟩ — see FALLACY 2

falsify *vb* **1** to change so much as to create a wrong impression or alter the meaning of ⟨taking that statement

completely out of context essentially *falsifies* it, whether that's your intention or not⟩ — see GARBLE 1
2 to prove to be false ⟨telephone records *falsified* his claim that he wasn't home that night⟩ — see DISPROVE

falsity *n* **1** a false idea or belief ⟨a papal letter condemning secularism and other movements that the church considered to be *falsities* of the modern age⟩ — see FALLACY 1
2 a statement known by its maker to be untrue and made in order to deceive ⟨when questioned by his parents about his drug use, the teenager told one blatant *falsity* after another⟩ — see LIE
3 lack of faithfulness especially to one's husband or wife ⟨the *falsity* of Guinevere usually figures prominently in medieval and modern tellings of the legend of King Arthur⟩ — see INFIDELITY 1
4 the act or fact of violating the trust or confidence of another ⟨despite being offered a fortune to spill the president's secrets, the trusted aide declared that he'd sooner die than be guilty of such *falsity*⟩ — see BETRAYAL
5 the quality or state of being false ⟨the *falsity* of Columbus's estimate of the earth's circumference was pretty much demonstrated when he made a head-on collision with the western hemisphere⟩ — see FALLACY 2

falter *vb* **1** to show uncertainty about the right course of action ⟨William Lloyd Garrison never once *faltered* in his demand that slavery be unconditionally abolished⟩ — see HESITATE
2 to swing unsteadily back and forth or from side to side ⟨the cut tree seemed to *falter* for a moment before crashing to the ground⟩ — see TEETER 1

faltering *n* a state or an instance of temporary inaction because of uncertainty about the right course of action ⟨when it's so clear that this is the right thing to do, there's no excuse for *faltering*⟩ — see HESITATION

fame *n* **1** the fact or state of being known to the public ⟨many go to Hollywood in search of *fame* and fortune⟩
synonyms celebrity, notoriety, renown
related words infamy; character, mark, name, report, reputability, reputation, repute; cachet, place, position, prestige, rank, standing, stature, status; megastardom, popularity, stardom, superstardom; distinction, eminence, glory, greatness, honor, illustriousness, note, preeminence, prominence, visibility; acclaim, accolade, acknowledgment (*or* acknowledgement), homage, kudos, laurels, praise, recognition; adoration, idolization
near antonyms disgrace, dishonor, disrepute, ignominy, odium, opprobrium, shame; inconspicuousness, invisibility; unpopularity
antonyms anonymity, oblivion, obscureness, obscurity
2 overall quality as seen or judged by people in general ⟨he has some *fame* locally as an honest antiques dealer⟩ — see REPUTATION

famed *adj* widely known ⟨San Francisco's *famed* Golden Gate Bridge⟩ — see FAMOUS 1

familial *adj* of or relating to a household or family ⟨it's a *familial* duty as well as a tradition for everyone in my family to eat dinner together⟩ — see DOMESTIC 1

familiar *adj* **1** closely acquainted ⟨the little inside jokes that people who have long been *familiar* like to share⟩
synonyms bosom, buddy-buddy, chummy, close, especial, friendly, inseparable, intimate, inward, near, thick, tight
related words clannish, close-knit, tight-knit; affable, boon, companionable, convivial, cordial, genial, gracious, hearty; gregarious, sociable, social; comfortable, cozy, easy, snug; amicable, neighborly; confidential, secretive; adoring, affectionate, dear, devoted, fond, loving, tender, tenderhearted, warm
near antonyms aloof, antisocial, cold, cool, detached, distant, frosty, remote, reserved, standoffish, unfriendly, unsociable, withdrawn
antonyms distant
2 having information especially as a result of study or experience ⟨book editors who are *familiar* with what is being taught in the schools⟩
synonyms abreast, acquainted, au courant, conversant, informed, knowledgeable, up, up-to-date, versed, well-informed
related words alive, aware, cognizant, conscious, heedful, mindful, sensible, sentient
phrases at home, in the know
near antonyms insensible, unaware, unconscious, unmindful; blind, oblivious, unknowing, unwitting; inattentive, unheeding
antonyms ignorant, unacquainted, unfamiliar, uninformed, unknowledgeable
3 often observed or encountered ⟨the woman and her pair of Welsh corgis were a *familiar* sight in the quiet neighborhood⟩ — see COMMON 1
4 showing a lack of proper social reserve or modesty ⟨rather too *familiar* for a first-time guest in our home, the woman kept asking how much we paid for this or for that⟩ — see PRESUMPTUOUS 1

familiar *n* **1** someone who regularly spends time in a particular place ⟨a longtime *familiar* of the bar, she would most likely have been there on the night in question⟩ — see DENIZEN 1
2 a person who has a strong liking for and trust in another ⟨with old *familiars* the normally reserved writer can be quite warm and funny⟩ — see FRIEND 1

familiarity *n* **1** the state of being in a very personal or private relationship ⟨the elderly couple enjoys a *familiarity* that is the result of many years of happy marriage⟩
synonyms belonging, chumminess, closeness, inseparability, intimacy, nearness
related words immediacy; affinity, kinship; commitment, devotedness, devotion; affection, attachment, fondness, love, passion; constancy, faithfulness, fidelity; amity, fellowship, friendship, goodwill; affability, conviviality, cordiality, geniality; mutuality; cliquishness, clubbiness
near antonyms aloofness, coldness, coolness, remoteness, reserve
antonyms distance
2 a socially improper or unsuitable act or remark ⟨placing his hand on my shoulder was just one *familiarity* by the car salesman that I did not appreciate⟩ — see IMPROPRIETY 2
3 knowledge gained by personal experience ⟨the restaurant critic's considerable *familiarity* with restaurant kitchens should stand her in good stead⟩ — see ACQUAINTANCE

familiarize *vb* **1** to give information to ⟨the general's day-to-day duties included *familiarizing* the president on international developments⟩ — see ENLIGHTEN 1
2 to impart knowledge of a new thing or situation to ⟨one office worker is assigned with the task of *familiarizing* new staffers with the use of electronic equipment around the office⟩ — see ACQUAINT 1

familiar spirit *n* the soul of a dead person thought of especially as appearing to living people ⟨asked the spiritualist to summon the *familiar spirit* of her late mother for some matrimonial guidance⟩ — see GHOST 1

family *n* **1** a group of persons who come from the same ancestor ⟨the Adams *family* made remarkable contributions to American life for more than two centuries⟩
synonyms blood, clan, folks, house, kin, kindred, kinfolk (*or* kinfolks), kinsfolk, line, lineage, people, race, stock, tribe
related words blended family, nuclear family; ex-

tended family, household, kith; brood; descendant (*also* descendent), issue, offspring, progeny, scion, seed; clansman, kinsman, kinswoman, relative; dynasty
near antonyms ancestry, birth, descent, extraction, origin, pedigree
2 one of the units into which a whole is divided on the basis of a common characteristic ⟨the flute, the clarinet, the oboe, and other members of the woodwind *family*⟩ — see CLASS 2

family name *n* a name shared by members of a family ⟨many women today do not change their *family name* when they marry⟩ — see SURNAME 1

family tree *n* the line of ancestors from whom a person is descended ⟨his *family tree* includes writers, musical composers, and other notables in the arts⟩ — see ANCESTRY

family way *n* the state of containing unborn young within the body ⟨noticing the telltale bump, we guessed that she was in the *family way* again⟩ — see PREGNANCY

famine *n* a falling short of an essential or desirable amount or number ⟨there's a *famine* of good general practitioners in many rural areas⟩ — see DEFICIENCY

famished *adj* **1** feeling a desire or need for food ⟨after a full day of skiing, I was feeling absolutely *famished*⟩ — see HUNGRY 1
2 lacking money or material possessions ⟨do-gooders who were terribly distraught about the poor in other countries but were oblivious to the plight of the *famished* families in their own community⟩ — see POOR 1

famishment *n* a need or desire for food ⟨there's something about outdoor activity that invariably increases one's *famishment*⟩ — see HUNGER 1

famous *adj* **1** widely known ⟨a book about some of the most *famous* people of the last century⟩
synonyms big-name, celebrated, famed, noted, notorious, prominent, renowned, star, visible, well-known
related words fabled, fabulous, legendary; infamous; distinguished, eminent, exceptional, great, illustrious, leading, notable, noteworthy, outstanding, preeminent, prestigious, remarkable, supereminent, superior; important, significant; acknowledged, recognized, respected; favorite, popular, preferred; estimable, honorable, reputable, respectable; formidable, redoubtable
near antonyms insignificant, unimportant; inconspicuous; undistinguished, unexceptional; unpopular
antonyms anonymous, nameless, obscure, uncelebrated, unfamous, unknown, unsung
2 of the very best kind ⟨some truly *famous* Southern-style cooking⟩ — see EXCELLENT

fan *n* a person with a strong and habitual liking for something ⟨lifelong *fans* of country and western music⟩
synonyms addict, aficionado (*also* afficionado), buff, bug, devotee, enthusiast, fanatic, fancier, fiend, fool, freak, habitué (*also* habitue), head, hound, junkie (*also* junky), lover, maniac, maven (*also* mavin), nut, sucker
related words groupie; admirer, amateur, collector, connoisseur, dilettante; authority, expert; adherent, convert, cultist, disciple, follower, hanger-on, votary; advocate, apostle, backer, champion, evangelist, exponent, friend, patron, promoter, proponent, supporter; partisan (*also* partizan), zealot; booster, rooter, well-wisher; faddist
near antonyms nonadmirer; belittler, carper, critic, detractor
antonyms nonfan

fan (out) *vb* **1** to arrange the parts of (something) over a wider area ⟨the accordionist smoothly *fanned out* the bellows of his instrument as he played⟩ — see OPEN 3
2 to extend outwards from or as if from a central point ⟨most of the city's subway lines *fan out* from this central station⟩ — see RADIATE 1

fanatic *n* **1** a person with a strong and habitual liking for something ⟨football *fanatics* are pretty much booked up for weekends from Labor Day to Super Bowl Sunday⟩ — see FAN
2 one who is intensely or excessively devoted to a cause ⟨the vandalism was blamed on *fanatics* within the environmental movement⟩ — see ZEALOT

fanatic *or* **fanatical** *adj* being very far from the center of public opinion ⟨because of her *fanatical* views, her friends know better than to discuss religion with her⟩ — see EXTREME 2

fancier *n* a person with a strong and habitual liking for something ⟨chocolate *fanciers* generally like their favorite confection without the addition of milk or a lot of sugar⟩ — see FAN

fanciful *adj* **1** conceived or made without regard for reason or reality ⟨she harbors the *fanciful* notion that she has a talent for singing⟩ — see FANTASTIC 1
2 not real and existing only in the imagination ⟨the *fanciful* creatures that J.R.R. Tolkien created for his Middle Earth novels⟩ — see IMAGINARY

fancify *vb* to make more attractive by adding something that is beautiful or becoming ⟨you could take a store-bought cake and *fancify* it so that it looks semi-homemade⟩ — see DECORATE

fancy *adj* **1** made or done with great care or with much detail ⟨we're having a little get-together after the concert—nothing *fancy*⟩ — see ELABORATE 1
2 going beyond a normal or acceptable limit in degree or amount ⟨would rather go without than pay the hotel bar's *fancy* prices⟩ — see EXCESSIVE

fancy *n* **1** a conception or image created by the imagination and having no objective reality ⟨a writer with a prodigious talent for creating *fancies* that captivate readers young and old⟩ — see FANTASY 1
2 a sudden impulsive and apparently unmotivated idea or action ⟨is this a serious interest in music, or just your latest *fancy* that will be forgotten after a week?⟩ — see WHIM
3 positive regard for something ⟨now that he's rich he's taken a *fancy* to expensive sports cars⟩ — see LIKING
4 the ability to form mental images of things that either are not physically present or have never been conceived or created by others ⟨to fans of Lewis Carroll, the animal creations of his fertile *fancy* are as real as any creature to be found at the zoo⟩ — see IMAGINATION 1

fancy *vb* **1** to form a mental picture of ⟨try to *fancy*, if you can, our mother on an elephant when she was touring India⟩ — see IMAGINE 1
2 to take pleasure in ⟨the teacher didn't *fancy* the idea of failing the student, even if he was the class clown⟩ — see ENJOY 1

fancy man *n* a man who solicits clients for a woman who is willing to engage in sexual activities for money ⟨an early hard-boiled detective novel featuring a whore who marries her *fancy man* and later murders him⟩ — see PIMP

fancy up *vb* to make more attractive by adding something that is beautiful or becoming ⟨had *fancied up* his van so much that it was virtually a palace on wheels⟩ — see DECORATE

fancy woman *n* a boldly flirtatious or sexually promiscuous woman ⟨in those days acting on stage was considered a profession fit only for a *fancy woman*⟩ — see FLOOZY

fanfaronade *n* boastful speech or writing ⟨all his talk of how he would easily win the boxing match turned out to be so much *fanfaronade*⟩ — see BOMBAST 1

fanny *n* the part of the body upon which someone sits ⟨be careful on that icy walk, unless you want to fall on your *fanny*⟩ — see BUTTOCKS

fantabulous *adj, slang* of the very best kind ⟨shopping at the mall was just *fantabulous*⟩ — see EXCELLENT

fantasied *adj* not real and existing only in the imagination ⟨most of those auditioning had only a *fantasied* talent for singing⟩ — see IMAGINARY

fantasize *vb* to form a mental picture of ⟨all those lottery players *fantasizing* themselves as living in extravagant luxury⟩ — see IMAGINE 1

fantast *n* one whose conduct is guided more by the image of perfection than by the real world ⟨yet another short-lived utopian community that was the brainchild of a naive *fantast*⟩ — see IDEALIST

fantastic *also* **fantastical** *adj* **1** conceived or made without regard for reason or reality ⟨a *fantastic* scheme for getting rich quick⟩

synonyms absurd, bizarre, crazy, fanciful, foolish, insane, nonsensical, preposterous, unreal, wild

related words implausible, inconceivable, incredible, unbelievable, unimaginable, unthinkable; extravagant, grotesque; bizarro, curious, eccentric, far-out, funny, kinky, kooky (*also* kookie), odd, outlandish, out-of-the-way, outré, peculiar, quaint, queer, queerish, quirky, screwy, strange, wacky (*also* whacky), way-out, weird; farcical, laughable, ludicrous, ridiculous; Alice-in-Wonderland, Kafkaesque, nightmarish; dreamlike, surreal

phrases off the wall [*slang*]

antonyms realistic, reasonable

2 excitingly or mysteriously unusual ⟨to European explorers, the Far East was a *fantastic* land filled with unimaginable riches⟩ — see EXOTIC

3 not real and existing only in the imagination ⟨a science fiction writer who can conjure up *fantastic* worlds and make them seem as real as our own⟩ — see IMAGINARY

4 too extraordinary or improbable to believe ⟨concocted some *fantastic* story to try to explain why they had returned home so late⟩ — see INCREDIBLE

5 fantastic of the very best kind ⟨surfing conditions were simply *fantastic*⟩ — see EXCELLENT

fantastically *adv* to a great degree ⟨a community production of the classic musical that featured *fantastically* bad singing⟩ — see VERY 1

fantasy *vb* to form a mental picture of ⟨she regularly *fantasies* sexual encounters that she knows will never happen⟩ — see IMAGINE 1

fantasy *also* **phantasy** *n* **1** a conception or image created by the imagination and having no objective reality ⟨a constant daydreamer who started to believe his own *fantasies*⟩

synonyms chimera, conceit, daydream, delusion, dream, fancy, figment, hallucination, illusion, nonentity, phantasm (*also* fantasm), pipe dream, unreality, vision

related words ignis fatuus, mirage, will-o'-the-wisp; brainchild, idea; concoction, fable, fabrication, fiction, invention; envisaging, imaging, visualization; cloud-cuckoo-land, cloudland, Shangri-la, utopia; daymare, nightmare

phrases castle in Spain, castle in the air

near antonyms actuality, fact, reality

2 the ability to form mental images of things that either are not physically present or have never been conceived or created by others ⟨the painter gave free rein to his *fantasy* to create pictures that capture the kind of reality we experience only in our dreams⟩ — see IMAGINATION 1

3 something that is the product of the imagination ⟨we were coming to the conclusion that the person Karen "saw" in the woods was another one of her *fantasies*⟩ — see FICTION

fantasyland *n* an often imaginary place or state of utter perfection and happiness ⟨a lavish resort casino that transports its patrons to *fantasyland*—at least for a few hours⟩ — see PARADISE 1

far *adj* **1** lasting for a considerable time ⟨the primitive rafts that ancient peoples built for their *far* journeys across the wide expanses of Oceania⟩ — see LONG 2

2 not close in time or space ⟨the dream of someday sending manned spacecraft to explore the *far* reaches of our solar system⟩ — see DISTANT 1

far *adv* to a great degree ⟨the solid advice that if you can't say something good about a person, it is *far* better to say nothing at all⟩ — see VERY 1

far and away *adv* by a considerable margin ⟨that Mexican restaurant is *far and away* the best in the area⟩ — see HEAD AND SHOULDERS

far and wide *adv* in every place or in all places ⟨we searched *far and wide* for a surgeon who could perform that delicate operation⟩ — see EVERYWHERE

faraway *adj* not close in time or space ⟨growing up in a seaport instilled in the youth a restless desire to travel to *faraway* places⟩ — see DISTANT 1

farce *n* **1** a poor, insincere, or insulting imitation of something ⟨the recall of a duly elected official for a frivolous reason is not democracy in action but a *farce*⟩ — see MOCKERY 1

2 humorous entertainment ⟨the rubber-faced, loose-jointed comedian is a master of knockabout *farce*⟩ — see COMEDY 1

farceur *n* a person (as a writer) noted for or specializing in humor ⟨a knockabout comedy that was performed by a trio of accomplished *farceurs*⟩ — see HUMORIST

farcical *adj* **1** causing or intended to cause laughter ⟨the *farcical* behavior of the troupe of circus clowns⟩ — see FUNNY 1

2 so foolish or pointless as to be worthy of scornful laughter ⟨the *farcical* routine that a person has to go through to get a refund from that company⟩ — see RIDICULOUS 1

far cry *n* a long distance ⟨the hotel is a *far cry* from the train station, so you'd better call a cab⟩ — see MILE

fare *n* substances intended to be eaten ⟨that restaurant is well-known for serving only fresh, seasonal *fare* from local suppliers⟩ — see FOOD 1

fare *vb* **1** to meet one's day-to-day needs ⟨residents of the flood-ravaged town are *faring* much better than one might have expected⟩ — see GET ALONG 1

2 to move forward along a course ⟨families can be seen *faring* along the road to the campground while driving or towing all manner of conveyance⟩ — see GO 1

3 to take a meal ⟨diners at this charming country inn will *fare* sumptuously in an authentic colonial atmosphere⟩ — see DINE 1

farewell *adj* given, taken, or performed at parting ⟨the singer's *farewell* tour seemed to last almost as long as her entire career⟩ — see PARTING

farewell *n* **1** an expression of good wishes at parting ⟨the exchange student and her host family said their tearful *farewells*, promising to keep in touch⟩ — see GOOD-BYE

2 the act of leaving a place ⟨before making his final *farewell*, the company president personally spoke to as many employees as he could⟩ — see DEPARTURE 1

3 the act or process of two or more persons going off in different directions ⟨our *farewell* was rushed, and we didn't say all that we wanted to before heading off to colleges at opposite ends of the country⟩ — see PARTING 1

far-fetched *adj* not likely to be true or to occur ⟨an exciting thriller, but one with a *far-fetched* plot that no sensible person could believe⟩ — see IMPROBABLE

far-flung *adj* **1** having considerable extent ⟨it could once be said that the sun never set on the *far-flung* British Empire⟩ — see EXTENSIVE

2 not close in time or space ⟨traveled to *far-flung* towns that had not seen a doctor in years⟩ — see DISTANT 1

farm *n* a piece of land and its buildings used to grow crops or raise livestock ⟨a *farm* that has been in the same family for five generations⟩
synonyms estate, farmstead, grange, ranch
related words cropland, farmland, farmyard; farmhouse, hacienda, homestead, manor, plantation, spread; croft [*chiefly British*], smallholding [*chiefly British*], station, steading; garden, orchard

farm *vb* to work by plowing, sowing, and raising crops on ⟨we're planning on *farming* 50 acres the first year⟩
synonyms cultivate, tend, till
related words crop, plant; harvest, reap; harrow, hoe; sharecrop

farmer *n* a person who cultivates the land and grows crops on it ⟨a young *farmer* whose family has been growing wheat for many generations⟩
synonyms agriculturist (*or* agriculturalist), agronomist, cultivator, grower, planter, tiller
related words farmhand, field hand, gleaner, harvester, plowman, reaper; workfolk (*or* workfolks); crofter [*chiefly British*], cropper, gentleman farmer, sharecropper, subsistence farmer, tenant farmer, yeoman; homesteader, nester [*West*]; granger; rancher, ranchero, ranchman; campesino
antonyms nonfarmer

farming *adj* engaged in or concerned with agriculture ⟨years of drought had a devastating impact on the region's *farming* communities⟩ — see AGRICULTURAL

farming *n* the science or occupation of cultivating the soil, producing crops, and raising livestock ⟨since an ancestor settled there in the 19th century, *farming* has been the only occupation for six generations of the family⟩ — see AGRICULTURE

farmstead *n* a piece of land and its buildings used to grow crops or raise livestock ⟨many of the area's proud, old *farmsteads* have been bulldozed by developers to make way for condominiums⟩ — see FARM

far–off *adj* not close in time or space ⟨many a young person has joined the military with the hope of traveling to *far-off* places⟩ ⟨the impossibility of predicting what life will be like in the *far-off* future⟩ — see DISTANT 1

far–out *adj* different from the ordinary in a way that causes curiosity or suspicion ⟨the religious sect's *far-out* clothes and practices made them the talk of the small town⟩ — see ODD 2

farrago *n* an unorganized collection or mixture of various things ⟨the shop is filled with a whimsical *farrago* of artwork, antiques, and vintage clothing⟩ — see MISCELLANY 1

far–reaching *adj* having considerable extent ⟨to the pioneers the *far-reaching* prairies seemed like an endless sea of grass⟩ — see EXTENSIVE

farseeing *adj* having or showing awareness of and preparation for the future ⟨a *farseeing* corn farmer who realized that the future was in ethanol⟩ — see FORESIGHTED

farsighted *adj* having or showing awareness of and preparation for the future ⟨*farsighted* conservationists long ago realized that wilderness areas of breathtaking beauty needed to be protected from future development⟩ — see FORESIGHTED

farsightedness *n* concern or preparation for the future ⟨thanks to our *farsightedness*, we had sufficient emergency supplies when the storm knocked out our power⟩ — see FORESIGHT 2

farther *adj* resulting in an increase in amount or number ⟨for *farther* information on this condition, you should consult your family physician⟩ — see ADDITIONAL

farther *adv* at or to a greater distance or more advanced point ⟨they had traveled *farther* down the Colorado River than any previous explorers⟩
synonyms beyond, further, yon, yonder

farthermost *adj* most distant from a center ⟨it's a long trip to a major hospital for residents of the *farthermost* corners of the state⟩ — see EXTREME 1

farthest *adj* most distant from a center ⟨for privacy and quiet, we requested a hotel room that was *farthest* from the elevator⟩ — see EXTREME 1

fascinate *vb* **1** to attract or delight as if by magic ⟨for years the zoo's family of giant pandas have *fascinated* visitors⟩ — see CHARM 1
2 to hold the attention of as if by a spell ⟨I can gaze at the sea for hours, *fascinated* by the never-ending waves crashing upon the shore⟩ — see ENTHRALL 1
3 to hold the attention of ⟨the subject of artificial intelligence *fascinates* me⟩ — see ENGAGE 1

fascinating *adj* **1** having an often mysterious or magical power to attract ⟨the *fascinating* cities and peoples of central Asia have been intriguing travelers at least since the time of Marco Polo⟩
synonyms alluring, appealing, attractive, bewitching, captivating, charismatic, charming, elfin, enchanting, engaging, entrancing, fetching, glamorous (*also* glamourous), luring, magnetic, seductive
related words absorbing, arresting, engrossing, enthralling, galvanic, gripping, hypnotic, hypnotizing, mesmerizing, riveting, spellbinding; enticing, tantalizing, tempting; exciting, haunting, interesting, intriguing, titillating; beckoning, inviting, winning; darling, delightful, pleasant, pleasing
near antonyms boring, irksome, tedious, tiresome, wearisome; abhorrent, abominable, appalling, awful, distasteful, hideous, horrendous, horrible, horrid, invidious, loathsome, nauseating, noisome, obnoxious, odious, offensive, shocking, sickening; drab, dreary, dull, flat, humdrum, jading, leaden, monotonous, pedestrian, ponderous
antonyms repellent (*also* repellant), repelling, repugnant, repulsive, revolting, unalluring
2 holding the attention or provoking interest ⟨the *fascinating*—but dubious—legend that Pocahontas rescued John Smith from certain death⟩ — see INTERESTING

fascination *n* the power of irresistible attraction ⟨the *fascination* that the subject of dinosaurs has for most children⟩ — see CHARM 2

fashion *n* **1** a practice or interest that is very popular for a short time ⟨during the 1990s tattoos once again became a hot *fashion* especially for young men⟩ — see FAD
2 a distinctive way of putting ideas into words ⟨when angry, he tends to express himself in a *fashion* that shows that he has a mastery of all of the expletives in which the English language abounds⟩ — see STYLE 1
3 a usual manner of behaving or doing ⟨it has long been my *fashion* to rise early⟩ — see HABIT 1
4 the means or procedure for doing something ⟨you can mix the ingredients in any *fashion* you choose—by hand or by machine⟩ — see METHOD
5 high position within society ⟨a literary salon attended by people of *fashion* from all over the city⟩ — see RANK 2
6 the outward appearance of something as distinguished from its substance ⟨over the millennia, nature had worked the face of the rocky cliff into the *fashion* of a man's head⟩ — see FORM 1

fashion *vb* **1** to change (something) so as to make it suitable for a new use or situation ⟨the ex-governor seems to be *fashioning* his political beliefs to win favor with a more conservative national electorate⟩ — see ADAPT
2 to bring into being by combining, shaping, or trans-

forming materials ⟨for the Christmas pageant the boy's mother was able to *fashion* the length of fabric into something that could pass as a shepherd's outfit⟩ — see MAKE 1

fashionability *n* the state of enjoying widespread approval ⟨doesn't regard the *fashionability* of his fiction as prima facie evidence that it has no literary merit⟩ — see POPULARITY

fashionable *adj* **1** being in the latest or current fashion ⟨a shopping district filled with expensive boutiques selling *fashionable* clothing from the top designers⟩ — see STYLISH
2 enjoying widespread favor or approval ⟨that breed of dog became *fashionable* after it became the preferred dog among Hollywood celebrities⟩ — see POPULAR 1

fashionableness *n* **1** the state of enjoying widespread approval ⟨the *fashionableness* of that look took a nosedive after it began to show up on some very unfashionable people⟩ — see POPULARITY
2 the quality or state of being fashionable ⟨the *fashionableness* of tight jeans⟩ — see COOL 2

fast *adj* **1** moving, proceeding, or acting with great speed ⟨the *fast* pace of construction resulted in our new house being done ahead of schedule⟩
synonyms blistering, breakneck, breathless, brisk, dizzy, fleet, fleet-footed, flying, galloping, hasty, hot, lightning, nippy, quick, rapid, rapid-fire, rattling, snappy, speedy, splitting, swift, whirlwind, zippy
related words expeditious, prompt, ready; accelerated, hastened, hurried, quickened, rushed; breathtaking; energetic, strenuous, strong, vigorous; high-speed; rush; ultrafast, ultrarapid
phrases at speed [*chiefly British*]
near antonyms crawling, dallying, dawdling, dillydallying, dragging, laggard, languid, lingering, plodding, poking, poky (*or* pokey), slowish, sluggish, unhurried; deliberate, leisurely, measured; dilatory, late, tardy; ultraslow
antonyms slow
2 firm in one's allegiance to someone or something ⟨the two girls soon became *fast* and inseparable friends⟩ — see FAITHFUL 1
3 firmly positioned in place and difficult to dislodge ⟨the rusty, old screws are so *fast* in the fitting that there's no hope of getting them out⟩ — see TIGHT 2
4 given to or marked by cheating and deception ⟨rolling back odometers was just one of the *fast* practices that the used-car dealer was guilty of⟩ — see DISHONEST 2
5 marked by the ability to withstand stress without structural damage or distortion ⟨as the storm approached, we checked to see that every thing on the outside of the house was *fast* and locked in position⟩ — see STABLE 1
6 not lasting for a considerable time ⟨after a *fast* explanation of the procedure, we were turned loose to do the work⟩ — see SHORT 2
7 having or showing quickness of mind ⟨I don't know how to operate this machine, but I'm a *fast* learner⟩ — see INTELLIGENT 1

fast *adv* **1** with great speed ⟨run as *fast* as you can to get help⟩
synonyms apace, briskly, chop-chop, double-quick, fleetly, full tilt, hastily, hell-for-leather, hot, lickety-split, posthaste, presto, pronto, quick, quickly, rapidly, snappily, soon, speedily, swift, swiftly
related words immediately, promptly, readily; impetuously, impulsively, rashly, recklessly; abruptly, suddenly; energetically, vigorously
phrases a mile a minute, at full throttle, at full tilt, by leaps and bounds, in a hurry, in short order, like a shot, like gangbusters, like wildfire
near antonyms laggardly, lingeringly, ploddingly, sluggishly; deliberately, leisurely; belatedly, delinquently, tardily
antonyms slow, slowly
2 to a full extent or degree ⟨everyone in camp was *fast* asleep within minutes of hitting the sack⟩ — see FULLY 1

fasten *vb* **1** to cause (something) to hold to another ⟨use this paper clip to *fasten* your picture to the application form⟩
synonyms affix, attach, bend, fix
related words adhere, bolt, cinch, clamp, clasp, clench, clinch, clip, glue, hang, harness, hasp, lace, lash, latch, nail, paste, pin, plaster, rivet, screw, shackle, staple, stick, strap, tack, tackle, tie, toggle, yoke; coapt, connect, join, link, unite; reaffix, reattach, refasten, refix, resecure; batten, belay, button, do up
near antonyms break up, disconnect, disjoin, disjoint, dissever, dissociate, disunite, divide, divorce, part, separate, sever, split, sunder, uncouple, unlink, unyoke; loose, loosen; unbind, unfix, unlash, untie
antonyms detach, undo, unfasten, unhook
2 to put securely in place or in a desired position ⟨don't forget to *fasten* all the lines on your tent⟩
synonyms anchor, catch, clamp, fix, hitch, moor, secure, set
related words embed (*also* imbed), entrench (*also* intrench), implant, ingrain (*also* engrain), lodge, stuff, wedge
near antonyms extract, prize, pry, pull, root (out), tear (out), uproot, wrest, yank
antonyms loose, loosen, unfasten, unfix, unloose, unloosen
3 to fix (as one's attention) steadily toward a central objective ⟨if you could *fasten* your attention on one task for more than a minute, you just might get something done⟩ — see CONCENTRATE 2

fastidious *adj* hard to please ⟨he is very *fastidious* about how he arranges his music collection, and woe to anyone who dares to mess around with it⟩ — see FINICKY

fastness *n* **1** a high rate of movement or performance ⟨the amazing *fastness* with which the boy took his shower had us wondering if he'd used any water⟩ — see SPEED 1
2 a structure or place from which one can resist attack ⟨the guerillas retreated to their network of hidden *fastnesses* deep within the mountains⟩ — see FORT
3 adherence to something to which one is bound by a pledge or duty ⟨his uncompromising *fastness* to the cause of freedom was beyond question⟩ — see FIDELITY

fast–track *vb* to cause to move or proceed fast or faster ⟨we're going to *fast-track* this project so that the product is in the stores for the holiday shopping season⟩ — see HURRY 1

fat *n* **1** individuals carefully selected as being the best of a class ⟨makers of fine wine will pay very high prices for grapes that are the *fat* of the harvest⟩ — see ELITE 1
2 the state or an instance of going beyond what is usual, proper, or needed ⟨claimed that there was absolutely no *fat* in the military's budget⟩ — see EXCESS 1
3 the condition of having an excess of body fat ⟨there's a definite predisposition for *fat* on his wife's side of the family⟩ — see CORPULENCE

fat *adj* **1** having an excess of body fat ⟨the popular image of Santa Claus as a *fat* man in a red suit⟩
synonyms blubbery, chubby, corpulent, fleshy, full, gross, lardy, obese, overweight, plump, podgy [*chiefly British*], portly, pudgy, replete, roly-poly, rotund, round, tubby
related words beefy, bulky, chunky, heavy, heavyset, plumpish, stocky, stout, thick, thickset, weighty;

brawny, burly, hefty, husky; dumpy, squat, stubby; hippy, paunchy, potbellied; flabby, soft; ample, buxom, corn-fed, ripe, zaftig (*also* zoftig); endomorphic
near antonyms angular, bony (*also* boney), gaunt, lank, lanky, rawboned, sinewy; cadaverous, emaciated, haggard, pinched, skeletal, wasted; puny, scraggy, scrawny, slight; rangy, reedy, spindling, spindly, stringy, svelte, sylphlike, twiggy, waspish, weedy, willowy; ectomorphic; anorexic
antonyms lean, skinny, slender, slim, spare, thin
2 containing or seeming to contain the greatest quantity or number possible ⟨the lake is so *fat* with trout that you probably could catch fish with a bare hook⟩ — see FULL 1
3 having a greater than usual measure across ⟨a set of *fat* encyclopedia volumes took up the whole shelf⟩ — see WIDE 1
4 having or being of relatively great depth or extent from one surface to its opposite ⟨the splendid sight of a *fat*, juicy steak cooked to perfection⟩ — see THICK 1
5 producing abundantly ⟨the *fat* soil in the river's delta⟩ — see FERTILE
6 yielding a profit ⟨the highly sought-after baseball player signed a *fat* contract that set a record for the major leagues⟩ — see PROFITABLE 1
7 having goods, property, or money in abundance ⟨while others suffered and sacrificed, the war profiteers grew *fat*⟩ — see RICH 1

fatal *adj* **1** bringing about ruin or misfortune ⟨I made the *fatal* mistake of sharing my secret with the office's biggest blabbermouth⟩
synonyms calamitous, cataclysmal (*or* cataclysmic), catastrophic, damning, destructive, disastrous, fateful, ruinous, unfortunate
related words apocalyptic (*also* apocalyptical); hapless, ill-fated, ill-starred, luckless; adverse, baleful, baneful, damaging, deleterious, detrimental, evil, harmful, hurtful, ill, injurious, noxious, pernicious, prejudicial
near antonyms fluky (*also* flukey), fortuitous, fortunate, happy, lucky, providential; auspicious, bright, encouraging, fair, golden, heartening, hopeful, optimistic, promising, propitious, rose-colored, rosy, upbeat
2 likely to cause or capable of causing death ⟨that snake's venom is *fatal* unless the victim is given the antidote almost immediately⟩ — see DEADLY 1

fatality *n* a person or thing harmed, lost, or destroyed ⟨the grim reminder that every holiday weekend inevitably results in a slew of highway *fatalities*⟩ — see CASUALTY 1

fat–cat *adj* having goods, property, or money in abundance ⟨the economy was in recession, but the *fat-cat* financiers on Wall Street didn't seem to be suffering⟩ — see RICH 1

fat cat *n* **1** a wealthy person ⟨that last recession was particularly hard on the poor, but the *fat cats* barely noticed a dip in their bank accounts⟩ — see CAPITALIST
2 one of high position or importance within a group ⟨a candidate that has the backing of most of the party's *fat cats*⟩ — see BIG SHOT

fate *vb* to determine the fate of in advance ⟨the warning that the lack of an advanced education will *fate* a person to a lifetime of below-average earnings⟩ — see DESTINE

fate *n* **1** a state or end that seemingly has been decided beforehand ⟨the belief that it was this country's *fate* to extend from sea to sea⟩
synonyms circumstance, destiny, doom, fortune, kismet, lot, portion
related words accident, casualty [*archaic*], chance, hap, happenchance, happenstance, hazard, luck; predestination; aftereffect, aftermath, conclusion, consequence, development, effect, fruit, issue, outcome, outgrowth, result, resultant, sequel, sequence, upshot
2 a condition or occurrence traceable to a cause ⟨the *fate* of the presidential election hinged on a few thousand votes in a single state⟩ — see EFFECT 1
3 the permanent stopping of all the vital bodily activities ⟨he met his *fate* in a tragic highway accident⟩ — see DEATH 1

fateful *adj* bringing about ruin or misfortune ⟨a *fateful* encounter with a confidence man that they would long regret⟩ — see FATAL 1

fathead *n* a stupid person ⟨so who's the *fathead* who messed around with my movie collection?⟩ — see IDIOT

father *n* **1** a male human parent ⟨the special relationship that exists between *fathers* and sons⟩
synonyms dad, daddy, old man, pa, papa (*also* poppa), pater [*chiefly British*], pop, sire
related words paterfamilias, patriarch; father figure, father image; stepfather
2 a person who establishes a whole new field of endeavor ⟨Sir Isaac Newton is regarded by many as the *father* of modern science⟩
synonyms author, begetter, creator, establisher, founder, founding father, generator, inaugurator, initiator, instituter (*or* institutor), originator, sire
related words cocreator, cofounder; conceiver, contriver, designer, deviser, formulator, innovator, introducer, inventor, spawner; builder, maker, producer; developer, pioneer, researcher, researchist; organizer, promoter; encourager, galvanizer, inspiration, inspirer
near antonyms disciple, follower, pupil, student, supporter
3 a person who is several generations earlier in an individual's line of descent ⟨our *fathers* founded this nation on the fundamental belief that no person is entitled to rule by divine right⟩ — see ANCESTOR 1
4 *cap* the being worshipped as the creator and ruler of the universe ⟨let us ask humbly for the blessings of our *Father* in heaven⟩ — see DEITY 2

father *vb* to become the father of ⟨Paul Revere somehow found room in his small house for the large family he had *fathered*⟩
synonyms beget, get, sire
related words multiply, procreate, propagate, reproduce, spawn; bear, engender, gender, generate, produce

fatherland *n* the land of one's birth, residence, or citizenship ⟨though they had lived in their adopted country for many years, the immigrant families never broke their ties with the *fatherland* entirely⟩ — see COUNTRY 1

fathom *vb* to measure the depth of (as a body of water) typically with a weighted line ⟨the pilot had to continually *fathom* the river, which drought conditions had lowered to unprecedented levels⟩ — see [2]SOUND 1

fathomable *adj* capable of being understood ⟨acts of vandalism that were committed for no *fathomable* reason⟩ — see INTELLIGIBLE

fathomless *adj* being or seeming to be without limits ⟨impresses everyone with her *fathomless* knowledge of wildcats⟩ — see INFINITE

fatigue *vb* to use up all the physical energy of ⟨the rescue workers pressed on, though their efforts to reach the miners had almost completely *fatigued* them⟩ — see EXHAUST 1

fatigue *n* **1** a complete depletion of energy or strength ⟨the day-long battle against the blaze left firefighters in a state of utter *fatigue*⟩
synonyms burnout, collapse, exhaustion, frazzle, lassitude, prostration, tiredness, weariness
related words debilitation, debility, disablement, enervation, enfeeblement, faintness, feebleness, frailness, frailty, impotence, infirmity, weakness; overfatigue;

languor, lethargy, listlessness; sluggishness, slumber, stupor, torpidity, torpor; apathy, inertia, passiveness, passivity
near antonyms bounce, dash, drive, energy, ginger, go, liveliness, pep, punch, sap, snap, starch, verve, vigor, vim, vitality, zing, zip; might, muscle, potency, power, puissance, strength; briskness, jauntiness, spiritedness, sprightliness, vivaciousness, vivacity
antonyms refreshment, rejuvenation, rejuvenescence, revitalization
2 very hard or unpleasant work ⟨although he had joined the army for action and adventure, much of his day seemed to be devoted to mindless *fatigues*⟩ — see [1]TOIL

fatigued *adj* depleted in strength, energy, or freshness ⟨the *fatigued* hikers paused for some much-needed fun and frolic in the woodland stream⟩ — see WEARY 1

fatless *adj* having a noticeably small amount of body fat ⟨a beer commercial featuring bikini-clad women with shapely, *fatless* bodies⟩ — see THIN 1

fatly *adv* in a luxurious manner ⟨a television evangelist who lives *fatly* on a steady stream of donations from viewers of moderate means and immoderate gullibility⟩ — see HIGH

fatness *n* the condition of having an excess of body fat ⟨advised his patient that her *fatness* wasn't just unsightly—it was unhealthy⟩ — see CORPULENCE

fattiness *n* the condition of having an excess of body fat ⟨the surprising *fattiness* of so many of the children at the school⟩ — see CORPULENCE

fatty *adj* containing animal fat especially in unusual amounts ⟨*fatty* ground beef that was the cheapest available⟩
synonyms adipose
related words blubbery; greasy, oily; lardy, rich
near antonyms fibrous, gristly, stringy, tough; nonfat
antonyms defatted, lean

fatuity *n* **1** a foolish act or idea ⟨building another mall in an area that seems to already have a surplus of them seems like a gross *fatuity*⟩ — see FOLLY 1
2 lack of good sense or judgment ⟨the *fatuity* of the homeowner who used gasoline to burn a pile of brushwood⟩ — see FOOLISHNESS 1
3 the quality or state of lacking intelligence or quickness of mind ⟨the stupidity of the characters on that TV sitcom is probably nothing in comparison to the *fatuity* of its creators⟩ — see STUPIDITY 1

fatuous *adj* **1** not having or showing an ability to absorb ideas readily ⟨the *fatuous* questions that the audience members asked after the lecture suggested to the oceanographer that they had understood little⟩ — see STUPID 1
2 showing or marked by a lack of good sense or judgment ⟨ignoring the avalanche warnings, the *fatuous* skiers continued on their course⟩ — see FOOLISH 1

fatuousness *n* lack of good sense or judgment ⟨the sheer *fatuousness* of the theory precludes any serious discussion⟩ — see FOOLISHNESS 1

faucet *n* a fixture for controlling the flow of a liquid ⟨don't forget to turn off the *faucet*⟩
synonyms cock, gate, spigot, stopcock, tap, valve
related words hydrant, spout; petcock

faugh *interj* used to express disgust ⟨*faugh*! I will not tolerate such ill-mannered behavior in my house!⟩ — see YUCK

fault *vb* to express one's unfavorable opinion of the worth or quality of ⟨you should look at your own work before *faulting* what others have done⟩ — see CRITICIZE

fault *n* **1** a defect in character ⟨the common *fault* of being quick to judge others⟩
synonyms demerit, dereliction, failing, foible, frailty, shortcoming, sin, vice, want, weakness
related words blot, spot, stain; blemish, deficiency, flaw, imperfection, minus, nit; Achilles' heel, soft spot; corruption, depravity, evil, immorality, sinfulness, wickedness
phrases feet of clay
near antonyms excellence, perfection; goodness, integrity, morality, probity, rectitude, righteousness
antonyms merit, virtue
2 an unintentional departure from truth or accuracy ⟨there's a *fault* somewhere in the program⟩ — see ERROR 1
3 responsibility for wrongdoing or failure ⟨getting the time of the performance wrong was entirely my *fault*⟩ — see BLAME 1
4 something that spoils the appearance or completeness of a thing ⟨the minor *faults* in the leather are entirely natural and are what gives it a look different from vinyl⟩ — see BLEMISH
5 the state of being held as the cause of something that needs to be set right ⟨the auto accident was entirely the other driver's *fault*⟩ — see RESPONSIBILITY 1

faultfinder *n* a person given to harsh judgments and to finding faults ⟨no sooner had we finished decorating the church than the parish *faultfinder* decided that she didn't like it⟩ — see CRITIC 1

faultfinding *adj* given to making or expressing unfavorable judgments about things ⟨publishers now have to produce textbooks that pass muster with a slew of *faultfinding* committees⟩ — see CRITICAL 1

faultily *adv* in a mistaken or inappropriate way ⟨discovered that the foreign ambassador's statement had been *faultily* translated⟩ — see WRONGLY

faultless *adj* **1** being entirely without fault or flaw ⟨this 18th-century chest of drawers is considered a *faultless* example of early American craftsmanship⟩ — see PERFECT 1
2 free from guilt or blame ⟨I may have broken my share of things in the past, but in this instance I am entirely *faultless*⟩ — see INNOCENT 2

faultlessly *adv* without any flaws or errors ⟨at the recital the young piano student performed the sonata *faultlessly*⟩ — see PERFECTLY 1

faultlessness *n* the quality or state of being free from guilt or blame ⟨the parents sought to assure the children of their complete *faultlessness* in the breakup of the marriage⟩ — see INNOCENCE 1

faulty *adj* having a fault ⟨the cause of the plane crash was traced to *faulty* wiring⟩
synonyms amiss, bad, defective, flawed, imperfect
related words fallible; blemished, broken, crippled, damaged, defaced, disfigured, harmed, hurt, impaired, injured, marred, spoiled, vitiated; deficient, inadequate, incomplete, insufficient, wanting
phrases on the blink
near antonyms complete, entire, intact, whole; unblemished, undamaged, unimpaired, unspoiled
antonyms faultless, flawless, impeccable, perfect

faux *adj* being such in appearance only and made with or manufactured from usually cheaper materials ⟨even the animal rights activists were fooled by the *faux* furs⟩ — see IMITATION

faux pas *n* a socially improper or unsuitable act or remark ⟨according to an oft-told story, the queen set a guest at ease about a *faux pas* by politely imitating it⟩ — see IMPROPRIETY 2

fave *n* a person or thing that is preferred over others ⟨chocolate ice cream is my absolute *fave*⟩ — see FAVORITE

favor *vb* **1** to do a service or favor for ⟨although she was at the party as a guest, the singer *favored* us with a song⟩ — see OBLIGE 1

2 to have a favorable opinion of ⟨if this measure will reduce our property taxes, then I *favor* it⟩ — see APPROVE (OF)

3 to show partiality toward ⟨older moviegoers tend to *favor* films that have certain extras—like a plot and developed characters⟩ — see PREFER 1

4 to furnish freely or naturally with some power, quality, or attribute ⟨*favored* with good looks⟩ — see ENDOW 1

favor *n* **1** an act of kind assistance ⟨a good and generous friend who is always doing *favors* for others⟩

synonyms benevolence, boon, courtesy, grace, indulgence, kindness, mercy, service, turn

related words dispensation, waiver; advantage, benefit, blessing, godsend, manna; liberty, license (*or* licence), privilege

near antonyms hindrance, hurdle, impediment, interference, obstacle

2 a feeling of great approval and liking ⟨entertainers often learn that the *favor* of the public can be fickle indeed⟩ — see ADMIRATION 1

3 an acceptance of something as satisfactory ⟨over the years that kind of movie fell out of *favor* with the mass audience⟩ — see APPROVAL 1

4 an attitude that always favors one way of feeling or acting especially without considering any other possibilities ⟨although his own son is on the hockey team that he coaches, Mr. Watkins conscientiously avoids any show of *favor*⟩ — see BIAS 1

5 positive regard for something ⟨was willing to do just about anything to keep the boss's *favor*⟩ — see LIKING

6 the state of enjoying widespread approval ⟨after that rock band fell out of *favor*—almost overnight—the stores couldn't give their CDs away⟩ — see POPULARITY

favorable *adj* **1** expressing approval ⟨*favorable* reviews for the movie were few⟩

synonyms admiring, applauding, appreciative, approbatory, approving, commendatory, complimentary, friendly, good, positive

related words accepting, warm; encomiastic, eulogistic, flattering, hagiographic (*also* hagiographical), laudative, laudatory, panegyrical, praiseful; respectful, supportive, sympathetic; adoring, adulatory, idolizing, worshipful, worshipping (*also* worshiping); advisory, recommendatory

near antonyms captious, carping, caviling (*or* cavilling), censuring, critical, faultfinding, hypercritical, overcritical; belittling, contemptuous, disdainful, disparaging, scornful, slighting

antonyms adverse, depreciative, depreciatory, derogatory, disapproving, inappreciative, negative, unappreciative, uncomplimentary, unfavorable, unflattering, unfriendly

2 pointing toward a happy outcome ⟨*favorable* economic conditions for opening a new business⟩

synonyms auspicious, bright, encouraging, golden, heartening, hopeful, promising, propitious

related words fortunate, fortuitous, happy, lucky, providential; advantageous, beneficial, profitable, prosperous, salutary

near antonyms unfortunate, unhappy, unlucky; calamitous, catastrophic, disastrous, fatal, ruinous; baleful, dark, dire, direful, doomy, foreboding, gloomy, ill, ill-boding, menacing, minatory, ominous, portentous, sinister, threatening

antonyms dim, discouraging, disheartening, futureless, hopeless, inauspicious, unfavorable, unpromising, unpropitious

3 promoting or contributing to personal or social well-being ⟨moved to a region with a milder climate in the hope that it would be more *favorable* to his health⟩ — see BENEFICIAL

favorably *adv* **1** in a pleasing way ⟨her violin teacher has been *favorably* impressed with her progress⟩ — see WELL 5

2 in an approving manner ⟨most critics reviewed the movie *favorably*⟩ — see ADMIRINGLY

favored *adj* **1** granted special treatment or attention ⟨the youngest child was also the most *favored*—much to the envy of his siblings⟩ — see DARLING 1

2 singled out from a number or group as more to one's liking ⟨for a *favored* few, the restaurant always has a table available, no matter how busy it is⟩ — see SELECT 1

favorite *adj* **1** granted special treatment or attention ⟨that teacher claims not to have any *favorite* students, although many in the class would disagree⟩ — see DARLING 1

2 singled out from a number or group as more to one's liking ⟨mint chocolate chip is my *favorite* flavor of ice cream⟩ — see SELECT 1

3 enjoying widespread favor or approval ⟨a radio station that mostly plays *favorite* songs from the 1960s and 1970s⟩ — see POPULAR 1

favorite *n* a person or thing that is preferred over others ⟨the youngest child was always Mother's *favorite*⟩

synonyms darling, fave, minion, pet, preference, speed

related words beloved, dear, sweetheart; jewel, prize, treasure

phrases cup of tea

near antonyms abomination, anathema, bête noire, bugbear

fawn *vb* to use flattery or the doing of favors in order to win approval especially from a superior ⟨a student who could not wait to *fawn* over the new teacher⟩

synonyms apple-polish, bootlick, fuss, kowtow, suck (up), toady, truckle

related words drool, gush, slaver, slobber; endear, ingratiate; court, woo; adulate, idolize, worship; blandish, cajole, coax, flatter, overpraise, soft-soap; cower, cringe, grovel; abase, debase, demean; defer, submit, yield

phrases curry favor, kiss up to

near antonyms despise, disdain, scorn; gibe (*or* jibe), jeer, scoff; brave, challenge, defy

fawner *n* a person who flatters another in order to get ahead ⟨having surrounded himself with *fawners* who gave him only good news, the governor had no idea of the true state of affairs⟩ — see SYCOPHANT

fay *adj* given to good-natured joking or teasing ⟨with her slight build and perky manner, the actress was usually cast as the *fay* young woman who charms all the men in town⟩ — see PLAYFUL

fay *n* an imaginary being usually having a small human form and magical powers ⟨in the tale a *fay* appears in the form of a beautiful and serene woman with an angelic air and a billowy gown⟩ — see FAIRY

faze *vb* to throw into a state of self-conscious distress ⟨the collapse of part of the scenery didn't *faze* the actors one bit, and they just carried on⟩ — see EMBARRASS 1

fealty *n* adherence to something to which one is bound by a pledge or duty ⟨as much as I wanted to back my friend up, my *fealty* to the truth was greater, and I could not lie for him⟩ — see FIDELITY

fear *vb* to experience concern or anxiety ⟨her friends *feared* that she was dating a guy who was all wrong for her⟩ — see WORRY 1

fear *n* **1** the emotion experienced in the presence or threat of danger ⟨the sight of the headless horseman filled the schoolmaster with *fear*⟩

synonyms alarm (*also* alarum), anxiety, dread, fearfulness, fright, horror, panic, scare, terror, trepidation

related words phobia; creeps, jitters, nervousness, willies; pang, qualm, twinge; agitation, apprehension, consternation, discomposure, disquiet, funk, perturbation; concern, dismay, worry; cowardice, faintheartedness, timidity, timorousness

near antonyms aplomb, assurance, boldness, confidence, self-assurance, self-confidence; bravery, courage, courageousness, daring, dauntlessness, doughtiness, fearlessness, fortitude, gallantry, hardihood, intrepidity, intrepidness, stoutness, valor; audacity, guts, nerve

2 an uneasy state of mind usually over the possibility of an anticipated misfortune or trouble ⟨*fear* for her family's safety drove her to seek help from neighbors she hardly knew⟩ — see ANXIETY 1

fearful *adj* **1** causing fear ⟨the *fearful* roar of a lion⟩

synonyms alarming, dire, direful, dread, dreadful, fearsome, forbidding, formidable, frightening, frightful, ghastly, hair-raising, horrendous, horrible, horrifying, intimidating, redoubtable, scary, shocking, spine-chilling, terrible, terrifying

related words daunting, demoralizing, disconcerting, discouraging, dismaying, disquieting, distressing, disturbing, perturbing, startling, threatening, troubling, trying, unnerving; bone-chilling, creepy, eerie (*also* eery), weird; appalling, atrocious, awful, grisly, gruesome (*also* grewsome), hideous, horrid, macabre, monstrous, nightmarish

near antonyms calming, comforting, consoling, inviting, lulling, pacifying, quieting, reassuring, relaxing, soothing, tranquilizing (*also* tranquillizing); nonintimidating, nonthreatening

2 easily frightened ⟨the stray cat that we took in is still *fearful*, even around us⟩ — see SHY 1

3 extreme in degree, power, or effect ⟨the *fearful* wind and cold simply made being outside a miserable experience⟩ — see INTENSE 1

4 filled with fear or dread ⟨*fearful* of venturing out onto the dark highway, the stranded motorist decided to wait in the car for help⟩ — see AFRAID

fearfulness *n* the emotion experienced in the presence or threat of danger ⟨the *fearfulness* felt by hostages can scarcely be imagined⟩ — see FEAR 1

fearless *adj* feeling or displaying no fear by temperament ⟨skydiving is one sport that tends to attract *fearless* types⟩ — see BRAVE 1

fearlessly *adv* in a fearless manner ⟨she had *fearlessly* backed the teaching of evolution in her school district⟩ — see BRAVELY 1

fearlessness *n* strength of mind to carry on in spite of danger ⟨the admirable *fearlessness* shown by the pioneers of the civil rights movement⟩ — see COURAGE

fearsome *adj* **1** causing fear ⟨at night the child would always imagine that there were *fearsome* monsters lurking under his bed⟩ — see FEARFUL 1

2 extreme in degree, power, or effect ⟨after working all afternoon in the hot sun, I had developed a *fearsome* thirst⟩ — see INTENSE 1

3 easily frightened ⟨the more *fearsome* of the two children would only peer at the guests from a distance⟩ — see SHY 1

feasible *adj* capable of being done or carried out ⟨would it be *feasible* to build a cabin in so short a time?⟩ — see POSSIBLE 1

feast *n* **1** a large fancy meal often accompanied by ceremony or entertainment ⟨some 90 Native Americans showed up for the *feast* put on by the Pilgrims at Plymouth⟩

synonyms banquet, dinner, feed, regale, spread

related words chow, mess, repast, table; blowout, carnival, festival, fete (*or* fête), gala, party, shindig; festivity; barbecue (*also* barbeque), clambake, cookout, fry, luau, roast; buffet, luncheon, smorgasbord

2 a source of great satisfaction ⟨the colorful Mardi Gras parade is a *feast* for the senses⟩ — see DELIGHT 1

3 an amount or supply more than sufficient to meet one's needs ⟨on the Internet there's a *feast* of information about this medical condition⟩ — see PLENTY 1

feast *vb* **1** to entertain with a fancy meal ⟨the returning war heroes were *feasted* all over the country⟩

synonyms banquet, dine, junket, regale

related words board, cater, feed, provision; fete (*or* fête), honor, recognize

2 to give satisfaction to ⟨*feast* your eyes on all the fresh flowers at the farmers' market⟩ — see PLEASE 1

feat *n* **1** an act of notable skill, strength, or cleverness ⟨Washington's legendary *feat* of tossing a silver dollar across the Rappahannock River⟩

synonyms deed, exploit, number, stunt, tour de force, trick

related words accomplishment, achievement, attainment, coup, success, triumph; adventure; performance

2 something done by someone ⟨famously rich, the oil magnate is today remembered less for his *feats* than for his finances⟩ — see ACTION 1

feather *n* **1** a number of persons or things that are grouped together because they have something in common ⟨the two brothers are sports-obsessed jocks, and most of their friends are of the same *feather*⟩ — see SORT 1

2 dressy clothing ⟨prom couples strutted into the ballroom in full *feather*⟩ — see FINERY

3 a state of mind dominated by a particular emotion ⟨you're in fine *feather* today⟩ — see MOOD 1

featherbrain *n* a silly flighty person ⟨you would not want to have to rely on that *featherbrain* in an emergency⟩ — see FLIBBERTIGIBBET

featherbrained *adj* lacking in seriousness or maturity ⟨some *featherbrained* youngsters giggled through the graduation ceremonies⟩ — see GIDDY 1

featherhead *n* **1** a person who lacks good sense or judgment ⟨she only seems like a *featherhead*; when you least expect it, she'll surprise you⟩ — see FOOL 1

2 a silly flighty person ⟨too important a diplomatic post to assign to some congenial *featherhead*⟩ — see FLIBBERTIGIBBET

featherheaded *adj* showing or marked by a lack of good sense or judgment ⟨a completely *featherheaded* suggestion that would be best ignored⟩ — see FOOLISH 1

featherlight *adj* having little weight ⟨the company has designed a strong but *featherlight* fiber which it hopes to market to manufacturers of body armor⟩ — see [1]LIGHT 1

feathery *adj* having little weight ⟨the apple pie had a wonderfully *feathery* crust⟩ — see [1]LIGHT 1

featly *adj* moving easily ⟨*featly* swans gliding silently across the still waters of the lake⟩ — see GRACEFUL 1

feature *n* something that sets apart an individual from others of the same kind ⟨perhaps the most striking *feature* of that house is the way it was constructed to fit into its hillside site⟩ — see CHARACTERISTIC

feature *vb* **1** to indicate the importance of by centering attention on ⟨a restaurant *featuring* an extensive list of American wines to complement its creative American cuisine⟩ — see EMPHASIZE 1

2 to form a mental picture of ⟨I can't *feature* that guy taking care of a baby, since he can't even take care of himself⟩ — see IMAGINE 1

featureless *adj* lacking in distinctive features or qualities ⟨was surprised to find that the desert was a flat, *featureless*, rock-strewn wasteland⟩ — see NONDESCRIPT

feces *n pl* solid matter discharged from an animal's alimentary canal ⟨examined the animal's *feces* for signs of intestinal parasites⟩ — see DROPPING 1

feckless *adj* not producing the desired result ⟨a well-intentioned but *feckless* response to the rise in school violence⟩ — see INEFFECTIVE 1

feckly *adv, chiefly Scottish* very close to but not completely ⟨an Edinburgh hotel that is *feckly* new⟩ — see ALMOST

fecund *adj* producing abundantly ⟨the Franklin stove, bifocals, and the lightning rod are just a few of the inventions that we owe to the *fecund* creativity of Benjamin Franklin⟩ — see FERTILE

federate *vb* to form or enter into an association that furthers the interests of its members ⟨in the years following World War II, the U.S. and the nations of western Europe made the decision to *federate* as the North Atlantic Treaty Organization⟩ — see ALLY

federation *n* an association of persons, parties, or states for mutual assistance and protection ⟨the new organization is a *federation* of existing organizations that were all dedicated to preserving Civil War battlefields⟩ — see CONFEDERACY

fed up *adj* having one's patience, interest, or pleasure exhausted ⟨*fed up* with the noise and bustle of the big city, the family decided to try country life⟩ — see WEARY 2

fee *n* the amount of money that is demanded as payment for something ⟨my dentist's *fees* seem to increase with every visit⟩ — see PRICE 1

fee *vb, chiefly Scottish* to provide with a paying job ⟨the townspeople *fee* country lasses as housemaids, nurses, and cooks⟩ — see EMPLOY 1

feeble *adj* lacking bodily strength ⟨*feeble* members of the congregation are not expected to stand or kneel during services⟩ — see WEAK 1

feebleness *n* the quality or state of lacking physical strength or vigor ⟨the patient felt a lingering *feebleness* in the weeks following her heart surgery⟩ — see WEAKNESS 1

feed *n* **1** a large fancy meal often accompanied by ceremony or entertainment ⟨the company barbecue was an elaborate *feed* that was enlivened by country music and dancing⟩ — see FEAST 1

2 food eaten or prepared for eating at one time ⟨after soccer practice we were all ready for a hot shower and a satisfying *feed*⟩ — see MEAL

feed *vb* **1** to provide food or meals for ⟨a charity dedicated to *feeding* the hungry⟩

synonyms board, cater, provision, victual

related words serve, wait; nourish, nurture, sustain; banquet, dine, feast, regale; mess; batten, fatten, fill; force-feed, overfeed, surfeit; underfeed; hand-feed, spoon-feed; refeed, reprovision

2 to put (something) into the possession of someone for use or consumption ⟨all week long colleagues have been *feeding* me ideas for a magazine article⟩ — see FURNISH 2

3 to take a meal ⟨an all-you-can-eat buffet where families can *feed* heartily and fairly inexpensively⟩ — see DINE 1

feed (on, upon, *or* off) *vb* to seize and eat (something) as prey ⟨the flycatcher is a bird that—as its name suggests—*feeds on* winged insects in midair⟩ — see PREY (ON *OR* UPON)

feeder *n* a stream that flows into a larger body of water ⟨the lake has several *feeders* that have their headwaters near the Canadian border⟩ — see TRIBUTARY

feel *n* an indefinite physical response to a stimulus ⟨the warm *feel* that fine cashmere gives⟩ — see SENSATION 1

feel *vb* **1** to have a vague awareness of ⟨I *feel* trouble brewing in the town⟩

synonyms perceive, scent, see, sense, smell, taste

related words behold, descry, discern, distinguish, espy, eye, look (at), note, notice, observe, perceive, regard, remark, sight, spy, view, witness; ascertain, catch on (to), discover, find out, hear, learn, realize; anticipate, divine, expect, foreknow, foresee; assume, conjecture, guess, presume, speculate, suppose, surmise, suspect

2 to come into bodily contact with (something) so as to perceive a slight pressure on the skin ⟨*feel* this blanket and perceive how soft it is⟩ — see TOUCH 1

3 to come to a knowledge of (something) by living through it ⟨with the birth of their first child the couple came to *feel* true happiness for the first time⟩ — see EXPERIENCE

4 to have as an opinion ⟨I just *feel* that we haven't explored all of our options for raising funds⟩ — see BELIEVE 2

5 to search for something blindly or uncertainly ⟨the sudden blackout had us *feeling* around in the dark for a flashlight⟩ — see GROPE

6 to give the impression of being ⟨it *felt* like a good idea at the time⟩ — see SEEM

feel (for) *vb* to have sympathy for ⟨a reminder that during the holidays we should all *feel for* those families who have members serving in the military abroad⟩ — see PITY

feeling *n* **1** a subjective response to a person, thing, or situation ⟨an overall *feeling* of happiness about their new home⟩

synonyms chord, emotion, passion, sentiment

related words impression, perception, sensation, sense; angle, attitude, outlook, perspective, standpoint, viewpoint; belief, conviction, judgment (*or* judgement), mind, notion, opinion, persuasion, verdict, view; receptiveness, receptivity, responsiveness, sensibility, sensitiveness, sensitivity

near antonyms insensitiveness, insensitivity, unfeelingness

2 feelings *pl* general emotional condition ⟨a remark that thoughtlessly hurt her *feelings*⟩

synonyms heartstrings, passions, sensibilities

related words cheer, frame, humor, mode, mood, spirit, temper

3 an idea that is believed to be true or valid without positive knowledge ⟨an interesting think piece in which the congresswoman expressed her *feelings* about our nation's most pressing problems⟩ — see OPINION 1

4 an indefinite physical response to a stimulus ⟨that odd *feeling* of forward movement you get when the parked car next to you backs out⟩ — see SENSATION 1

5 sorrow or the capacity to feel sorrow for another's suffering or misfortune ⟨a rich person without much *feeling* for those who are less fortunate⟩ — see SYMPATHY 1

6 the capacity for feeling for another's unhappiness or misfortune ⟨a woman of great *feeling*, the princess wanted to use her status and influence to help the needy⟩ — see HEART 1

feign *vb* to present a false appearance of ⟨I would never *feign* illness just to get out of a test⟩

synonyms act, affect, assume, bluff, counterfeit, dissemble, fake, pass (for), pretend, profess, put on, sham, simulate

related words dissimulate, impersonate, let on, masquerade, play, playact, pose; forge, imitate; camouflage, conceal, disguise, mask; feint; malinger

phrases make believe

feigned *adj* **1** lacking in natural or spontaneous quality ⟨the *feigned* applause that polite people give after a bad concert⟩ — see ARTIFICIAL 1

2 not being or expressing what one appears to be or express ⟨the *feigned* looks of innocence I got when I asked who had broken the lamp⟩ — see INSINCERE

feistiness *n* an inclination to fight or quarrel ⟨a panel of political pundits with a well-earned reputation for unfettered *feistiness*⟩ — see BELLIGERENCE

feisty *adj* feeling or displaying eagerness to fight ⟨a *feisty* hockey player who has spent more than his share of time in the penalty box⟩ — see BELLIGERENT

felicitate *vb* to express to (someone) admiration for his or her success or good fortune ⟨the other pianists rushed to *felicitate* the winner of the piano competition⟩ — see CONGRATULATE

felicitations *n pl* best wishes ⟨our heartfelt *felicitations* on the start of your new business⟩ — see COMPLIMENT 2

felicitous *adj* **1** giving pleasure or contentment to the mind or senses ⟨a *felicitous* accompaniment to dinner is provided by a harpist on weekends at the restaurant⟩ — see PLEASANT 1

2 meeting the requirements of a purpose or situation ⟨the museum's restaurant is featuring a French menu as a *felicitous* complement to the current show on French Impressionism⟩ — see FIT 1

felicitously *adv* in a pleasing way ⟨the evening passed quietly but *felicitously* as we chatted with the other guests at the inn⟩ — see WELL 5

felicitousness *n* the quality or state of being especially suitable or fitting ⟨guests remarked on the perfect *felicitousness* of the rose garden as a site for a June wedding⟩ — see APPROPRIATENESS

felicity *n* **1** a feeling or state of well-being and contentment ⟨told his friends that marriage had brought him a *felicity* that he had never known before⟩ — see HAPPINESS 1

2 something that provides happiness or does good for a person or thing ⟨the elderly couple counted their grandchildren as their most cherished *felicities*⟩ — see BLESSING 2

3 the quality or state of being especially suitable or fitting ⟨the telling *felicity* of the epigraphs that precede each chapter of the novel⟩ — see APPROPRIATENESS

feline *n* a small domestic animal known for catching mice ⟨the commercial claims that the product will please the palate of even the most finicky *feline*⟩ — see CAT 1

feline *adj* moving easily ⟨the thief was eerily *feline* as he moved stealthily through the darkened rooms⟩ — see GRACEFUL 1

fell *adj* **1** likely to cause or capable of causing death ⟨planning in the event that the enemy resorted to biological warfare and released some *fell* virus on the civilian population⟩ — see DEADLY 1

2 violently unfriendly or aggressive in disposition ⟨Captain Cook died in a scuffle with some *fell* natives of the Hawaiian Islands⟩ — see FIERCE 1

fell *vb* **1** to strike (someone) so forcefully as to cause a fall ⟨a boxer who was often *felled* in the first round⟩
synonyms bowl (down *or* over), down, drop, floor, knock down, knock over, level, mow (down), prostrate
related words kayo, knock out, KO; overthrow, throw down, topple; bang, bash, belt, bludgeon, clobber, hammer, hit, jab, paste, poke, pound, punch, slam, slap, slog, slug, smack, smite, sock, swat, swipe, thump, thwack, wallop, whack, whale

2 to bring down by cutting ⟨the settlers began the daunting task of *felling* the mighty trees that blanketed the island⟩
synonyms chop (down), cut (down), hew, mow
related words bulldoze, demolish, flatten, level, raze, tear down

3 to deprive of life ⟨the quest for a cure for malaria, the disease that *felled* so many during the digging of the Panama Canal⟩ — see KILL 1

fella *n* an adult male human being ⟨these *fellas* are the hardest working bunch of players a manager could ever hope to have⟩ — see MAN 1

fellow *n* **1** a male romantic companion ⟨most of the women were bringing their *fellows* to the banquet after the tennis tournament⟩ — see BOYFRIEND

2 a person frequently seen in the company of another ⟨the singer's *fellows* were rumored to have ties to organized crime⟩ — see ASSOCIATE 1

3 an adult male human being ⟨what does a *fellow* have to do to get waited on around here?⟩ — see MAN 1

4 either of a pair matched in one or more qualities ⟨one ice skate isn't much good without its *fellow*⟩ — see MATE 1

5 one that is equal to another in status, achievement, or value ⟨he is well regarded as a chemist by his *fellows* in the field⟩ — see EQUAL

fellowship *n* **1** a friendly relationship marked by ready communication and mutual understanding ⟨the new counselor is eager to develop a trustful *fellowship* with the troubled teens at the center⟩ — see RAPPORT

2 a group of persons formally joined together for some common interest ⟨a *fellowship* of physicians dedicated to administering medical aid without regard to politics⟩ — see ASSOCIATION 2

3 kindly concern, interest, or support ⟨this music festival would not have been a success without the *fellowship* of many people in the community⟩ — see GOODWILL 1

4 the body of people in a profession or field of activity ⟨violated just about every ethical principle that the legal *fellowship* holds dear⟩ — see CORPS

5 the feeling of closeness and friendship that exists between companions ⟨the *fellowship* that exists among members of a college fraternity⟩ — see COMPANIONSHIP

fellow traveler *n* someone associated with another to give assistance or moral support ⟨a cause being promoted by Greenpeace and its *fellow travelers* in the environmental movement⟩ — see ALLY

felonious *adj* contrary to or forbidden by law ⟨the commission found that while the senator's actions were ethically questionable, they were not *felonious*⟩ — see ILLEGAL 1

female *adj* of, relating to, or marked by qualities traditionally associated with women ⟨*female* standards of housekeeping imposed by the women at the vacation cottage weren't especially popular with the men⟩ — see FEMININE

female *n* an adult female human being ⟨the prospect of being in close company with *females* was the main reason why some males joined the amateur theater troupe⟩ — see WOMAN 1

femaleness *n* the set of qualities considered appropriate for or characteristic of women ⟨for some people, maternal instincts are an essential part of *femaleness*⟩ — see FEMININITY

feminine *adj* of, relating to, or marked by qualities traditionally associated with women ⟨the *feminine* furnishings suggested that the bedroom was intended for a girl⟩
synonyms female, womanish, womanlike, womanly
related words girlie (*or* girly), girlish; effeminate, effete, epicene, sissified, sissy, unmanly; ladylike; distaff, petticoat; ultrafeminine
near antonyms boyish, hoydenish, tomboyish; male, manlike, manly, mannish, masculine, virile; androgynous, neuter; Amazonian, butch; hairy-chested, hypermasculine, macho
antonyms unfeminine, unwomanly

femininity *n* the set of qualities considered appropriate for or characteristic of women ⟨she managed to be-

come a CEO without sacrificing her *femininity*⟩
synonyms femaleness, feminity, muliebrity, womanhood, womanishness, womanliness
related words girlishness; effeminacy, effeteness; girlhood, maidenhood
near antonyms androgyny; boyishness, mannishness, tomboyishness
antonyms manhood, manliness, masculinity, virility

feminity *n* the set of qualities considered appropriate for or characteristic of women ⟨she impressed them with her gentle *feminity*⟩ — see FEMININITY

femme fatale *n* a woman whom men find irresistibly attractive ⟨an actress who was often cast as cynical, sexy *femmes fatales*⟩ — see SIREN

fen *n* spongy land saturated or partially covered with water ⟨a day spent trudging through the *fens* in quest of game birds⟩ — see SWAMP 1

fence *n* a physical object that blocks the way ⟨the only way to prevent motorists from trying to use that unsafe bridge is to put a *fence* across the road leading to it⟩ — see BARRIER

fence *vb* to drive danger or attack away from ⟨had worked as a bodyguard, *fencing* a number of pop stars at big events⟩ — see DEFEND 1

fence (in) *vb* to close or shut in by or as if by barriers ⟨*fencing in* the yard would keep our dog in as well as keep unwanted stray dogs out⟩ — see ENCLOSE 1

fence–sitting *n* a state or an instance of temporary inaction because of uncertainty about the right course of action ⟨in Congress there was a lot of *fence-sitting* regarding the war, with many representatives waiting to see which way the political wind was blowing⟩ — see HESITATION

fend *vb* to drive danger or attack away from ⟨uses self-deprecating humor to *fend* herself from serious criticism⟩ — see DEFEND 1

fend (off) *vb* to drive back ⟨several bystanders rushed to help the woman *fend off* the mugger⟩ — see REPEL 1

fender *n* something that serves as a protective barrier ⟨not wanting our brand-new cabin cruiser to get scratched, we put thick rubber *fenders* between it and the dock⟩ — see CUSHION

feral *adj* **1** living outdoors without taming or domestication by humans ⟨animal experts discourage homeowners from trying to adopt *feral* animals as pets⟩ — see WILD 1
2 having or showing the nature and appetites of a lower animal ⟨a novel that reveals just how thin the veneer of civilization is and how *feral* we are at bottom⟩ — see BESTIAL

ferine *adj* having or showing the nature and appetites of a lower animal ⟨the boxer's *ferine* ferocity in the ring is legendary⟩ — see BESTIAL

ferment *n* a disturbed or uneasy state ⟨the city was in *ferment* as its residents nervously awaited the airborne invasion that was sure to come⟩ — see UNREST

ferment *vb* to bring (something volatile or intense) into being ⟨the various social and economic factors that *fermented* the major cultural change in the U.S. during the 1960s⟩ — see INCITE 1

fermentation *n* a disturbed or uneasy state ⟨a wave of immigration followed by a period of social *fermentation*⟩ — see UNREST

ferocious *adj* **1** extreme in degree, power, or effect ⟨the *ferocious* appetite that athletic teenagers have been known to display⟩ — see INTENSE 1
2 marked by bursts of destructive force or intense activity ⟨*ferocious* forest fires threatened to destroy hundreds of homes in the scrubland⟩ — see VIOLENT 1
3 violently unfriendly or aggressive in disposition ⟨Captain Bligh and his castaways bypassed numerous Pacific islands, so afraid were they of the *ferocious* tribesmen⟩ — see FIERCE 1
4 marked by great and often stressful excitement or activity ⟨after a day of *ferocious* trading, the stock market was down 300 points⟩ — see FURIOUS 1

ferret (out) *vb* to come upon after searching, study, or effort ⟨the reporter *ferreted out* massive evidence of corruption at city hall⟩ — see FIND 1

ferry *vb* **1** to support and take from one place to another ⟨there are shuttle buses to *ferry* visitors from the parking lots to the fairground⟩ — see CARRY 1
2 to travel on water in a vessel ⟨we're planning to *ferry* to several islands in the Lesser Antilles⟩ — see SAIL 1

fertile *adj* producing abundantly ⟨the *fertile* mind of Leonardo da Vinci explored art, architecture, engineering, mathematics, and many other fields⟩
synonyms cornucopian, fat, fecund, fructuous, fruitful, lush, luxuriant, productive, prolific, rich
related words bearing, generative, producing, yielding; abounding, abundant, bountiful; copious, generous, liberal, plenteous, plentiful, plentitudinous; blooming, bursting, flourishing, swarming, teeming, thriving; creative, inventive, original
near antonyms meager (*or* meagre), scant, scanty, skimp, skimpy, spare, sparse
antonyms barren, dead, infertile, sterile, unfertile, unfruitful, unproductive

fervency *n* depth of feeling ⟨the guest soloist was able to infuse the familiar hymn with a moving *fervency*⟩ — see ARDOR 1

fervent *adj* **1** having or expressing great depth of feeling ⟨a *fervent* speech that called for tolerance and compassion for those who are different⟩
synonyms ardent, blazing, burning, charged, demonstrative, emotional, fervid, feverish, fiery, flaming, glowing, hot-blooded, impassioned, incandescent, intense, passional, passionate, perfervid, red-hot, religious, superheated, torrid, vehement, warm, warm-blooded
related words gushing, gushy, maudlin, mawkish, mushy, saccharine, sappy, schmaltzy, sentimental, sloppy, sugary; histrionic, melodramatic; enthusiastic, gung ho, keen, zealous; enamored, infatuated, obsessed; uninhibited, unreserved, unrestrained; frenzied, orgiastic, overemotional, overexcited, overheated
phrases on fire
near antonyms detached, dry, impersonal, objective; reserved, undemonstrative
antonyms cold, cool, dispassionate, emotionless, impassive, unemotional
2 having a notably high temperature ⟨in the thick, *fervent* air of a tropical afternoon, a languor set in⟩ — see HOT 1

fervid *adj* **1** having or expressing great depth of feeling ⟨at the school board meeting the librarian delivered a *fervid* speech defending the classic novel against would-be censors⟩ — see FERVENT 1
2 having a notably high temperature ⟨the *fervid* sands of Arabia, where T.E. Lawrence staked his claim to military glory⟩ — see HOT 1

fervidness *n* depth of feeling ⟨the *fervidness* that the actor brought to the part of Romeo made the play fresh all over again⟩ — see ARDOR 1

fervor *n* depth of feeling ⟨surprised by the *fervor* that her parents' old love letters contained when she discovered them in the attic⟩ — see ARDOR 1

fess (up) *vb* **1** to accept the truth or existence of (something) usually reluctantly ⟨he *fessed up* to breaking the vase only after his guilt was obvious⟩ — see ADMIT 1
2 to make an acknowledgment of something unpleasant as true or valid ⟨he immediately *fessed up* once it was clear the cops had the goods on him⟩ — see CONFESS 1

fest *n* a time or program of special events and entertainment in honor of something ⟨a country music *fest*⟩ — see FESTIVAL

fester *n* a small, inflamed swelling of the skin ⟨pus oozed out of the *fester*⟩ — see POCK

fester *vb* to go through decomposition ⟨a week after the battle the corpses of the fallen were still *festering* in the fields⟩ — see DECAY 1

festering *n* the process by which dead organic matter separates into simpler substances ⟨the ghastly *festering* of the corpses abandoned on the battlefield⟩ — see CORRUPTION 1

festival *n* a time or program of special events and entertainment in honor of something ⟨tourists flock to the town for its annual strawberry *festival*⟩
synonyms carnival, celebration, fest, festivity, fete (*or* fête), fiesta, gala, jubilee
related words jamboree, jollification, jollity [*British*], merriment, merrymaking, rejoicing, revel, revelry; exhibit, exhibition, exposition, fair, show; exercises, honors

festive *adj* indicative of or marked by high spirits or good humor ⟨we arrived at the Christmas party to find everyone already in a *festive* mood, perhaps owing in part to the punch⟩ — see MERRY

festivity *n* **1** a mood characterized by high spirits and amusement and often accompanied by laughter ⟨rather than mourn our friend's death we celebrated his life, and his memorial service was more notable for its *festivity* than its funereal gloom⟩ — see MIRTH
2 a time or program of special events and entertainment in honor of something ⟨year-long *festivities* will mark the 300th anniversary of the city's founding⟩ — see FESTIVAL
3 joyful or festive activity ⟨in keeping with their habit of doing everything in a big way, the couple's wedding will entail a whole weekend of *festivity*⟩ — see MERRYMAKING

festoon *vb* to make more attractive by adding something that is beautiful or becoming ⟨for Valentine's Day the dance hall was *festooned* with a riot of red hearts and bow-wielding cupids⟩ — see DECORATE

fetch *vb* to have a price of ⟨those old toys that we tossed away are now *fetching* big bucks as antiques⟩ — see COST

[1]**fetch** *n* a clever often underhanded means to achieve an end ⟨his latest *fetch* to win back his girlfriend smacks of desperation⟩ — see TRICK 1

[2]**fetch** *n* something or someone that strongly resembles another ⟨with its standard assortment of chain stores and central food court, the new mall is pretty much the *fetch* of 1,000 other malls⟩ — see IMAGE 1

fetching *adj* **1** having an often mysterious or magical power to attract ⟨the woman's *fetching* smile has long made the painting a favorite with visitors to the museum⟩ — see FASCINATING 1
2 very pleasing to look at ⟨a most *fetching* outfit in which to go skiing⟩ — see BEAUTIFUL 1

fetchingly *adv* in a pleasing way ⟨the supermodel smiled *fetchingly* for the camera⟩ — see WELL 5

fetch up *vb* to bring (something) to a standstill ⟨the driver *fetched up* the horse-drawn carriage in front of the church⟩ — see [1]HALT 1

fete *or* **fête** *n* **1** a social gathering ⟨the heiress wanted to do something with her life other than shuttle from *fete* to *fete*⟩ — see PARTY 1
2 a time or program of special events and entertainment in honor of something ⟨the island's annual *fete* is a celebration of the daffodil in all of its springtime beauty⟩ — see FESTIVAL

fete *or* **fête** *vb* to show appreciation, respect, or affection for (someone) with a public celebration ⟨the returning servicemen and servicewomen were *feted* with a week's worth of celebrations⟩ — see HONOR

fetid *adj* having an unpleasant smell ⟨that *fetid* cheese from Belgium is definitely an acquired taste⟩ — see MALODOROUS

fetish *also* **fetich** *n* **1** something about which one is constantly thinking or concerned ⟨dieting seems to be a *fetish* with some people⟩ — see FIXATION
2 something worn or kept to bring good luck or keep away evil ⟨an archaeologist discovering an old animal tooth that may have been worn as a *fetish*⟩ — see CHARM 1

fetter *n* **1** something that limits one's freedom of action or choice ⟨a time-honored tradition is fine as long as it doesn't become a *fetter* that prevents us from trying something new⟩ — see RESTRICTION 1
2 something that makes movement or progress difficult ⟨claims that government regulations are unnecessary *fetters* that keep him from achieving his business goals⟩ — see ENCUMBRANCE
3 something that physically prevents free movement ⟨considered a seat belt a pointless *fetter*—until one saved his life in an auto accident⟩ — see BOND 1

fetter *vb* **1** to confine or restrain with or as if with chains ⟨museum artifacts that serve as somber reminders of the days when slaves were *fettered* with irons⟩ — see BIND 1
2 to create difficulty for the work or activity of ⟨the belief that too many rules and restrictions *fetter* children's creativity⟩ — see HAMPER

fettle *n* a state of being or fitness ⟨a visit to the relatives on the other side of the state revealed them all to be in fine *fettle*⟩ — see CONDITION 1

fever *n* **1** an abnormal state that disrupts a plant's or animal's normal bodily functioning ⟨before the days of modern medicine, when death remained a mystery, people said that someone died of a *fever* and left it at that⟩ — see DISEASE
2 a state of wildly excited activity or emotion ⟨in the *fever* of a political campaign a lot of things get said that never should have been said⟩ — see FRENZY

feverish *adj* **1** being in a state of increased activity or agitation ⟨scary stories that were the product of a *feverish* imagination⟩
synonyms agitated, excited, frenzied, heated, hectic, hyperactive, overactive, overwrought
related words hyperexcited, overexcited; afire, aflutter, aquiver, atingle; anxious, dithery, edgy, het up, high-strung, hyped-up, hyper, jittery, jumpy, nervy, nervous, perturbed, tense, troubled, uneasy, unquiet, upset, uptight, wired
phrases in a lather, keyed up
near antonyms calm, collected, composed, cool, coolheaded, placid, serene, tranquil, undisturbed, unperturbed, unshaken, untroubled, unworried
2 having or expressing great depth of feeling ⟨the desperate prisoner made a *feverish* appeal for mercy⟩ — see FERVENT 1
3 marked by great and often stressful excitement or activity ⟨working at a *feverish* pace to get the project done on time⟩ — see FURIOUS 1

feverishness *n* a state of wildly excited activity or emotion ⟨the exhilarating *feverishness* of the final stages of a political campaign⟩ — see FRENZY

few *n* a small number ⟨a *few* of the songs on the album are good, but most are forgettable⟩
synonyms couple, handful, scatter, scattering, smatter, smattering, sprinkle, sprinkling
related words minority; atom, crumb, fragment, grain, iota, jot, modicum, molecule, particle, scrap, shred, tittle, whit
near antonyms majority, most; abundance, excess,

plenty, surplus; deal, gobs, heap, lot, mass, much, peck, pile, plenitude, plenty, pot, profusion, quantity, raft, reams, slather, slew, stack, wad, wealth
antonyms army, crowd, flock, gazillion, horde, host, jillion, kazillion, legion, loads, many, mountain, multitude, oodles, scads, thousands, zillion

fewest *adj* being the least in amount, number, or size possible ⟨the gymnast won the gold medal only because he made the *fewest* mistakes⟩ — see MINIMAL

fiancé *n* the person to whom one is engaged to be married ⟨couldn't wait to show off her *fiancé* to all of her relatives⟩ — see BETROTHED

fiancée *n* the person to whom one is engaged to be married ⟨his *fiancée* is insisting on an elaborate wedding⟩ — see BETROTHED

fiasco *n* something that has failed ⟨undaunted by his early *fiascoes*, he continued his experiments in rocketry⟩ — see FAILURE 3

fiat *n* an order publicly issued by an authority ⟨the school principal issued a *fiat* that caps were not to be worn inside the school, and that was that⟩ — see EDICT 1

fib *n* a statement known by its maker to be untrue and made in order to deceive ⟨the claim that everyday living would be impossible without at least a few innocent *fibs*⟩ — see LIE

[1]fib *vb* to make a statement one knows to be untrue ⟨*fibbed* and said that he had remembered to water her plants while she was away⟩ — see [1]LIE

[2]fib *vb, British* to strike repeatedly ⟨the two drunken pub crawlers proceeded to *fib* each other senseless⟩ — see BEAT 1

fibber *n* a person who tells lies ⟨research that shows that children learn to become *fibbers* at a remarkably early age⟩ — see LIAR

fiber *n* **1** the strength of mind that enables a person to endure pain or hardship ⟨a person of lesser *fiber* would not have spoken out against such an injustice⟩ — see FORTITUDE
2 a thin, flexible structure that resembles a hair ⟨the *fibers* found on the victim's body came from a carpet in the suspect's home⟩ — see HAIR 2

fibrous *adj* resembling or having the texture of a mass of strings ⟨thick, *fibrous* hair that was not easy to comb⟩ — see STRINGY

fickle *adj* **1** likely to change frequently, suddenly, or unexpectedly ⟨a *fickle* friendship that was on and off over the years⟩
synonyms capricious, changeable, changeful, flickery, fluctuating, fluid, inconsistent, inconstant, mercurial, mutable, skittish, temperamental, uncertain, unpredictable, unsettled, unstable, unsteady, variable, volatile
related words aimless, arbitrary, desultory, erratic, haphazard, hit-or-miss, irregular, random, scattered, slapdash, stray; ambivalent, hesitating, shaky, shilly-shally, shilly-shallying, vacillating, wavering; dicey, undependable, unreliable, untrustworthy; adaptable, mobile, protean, versatile
phrases up in the air
near antonyms equable, even, uniform; abiding, durable, lasting, permanent, persistent; dependable, reliable, sure, tried, tried-and-true, true, trustworthy, trusty
antonyms certain, changeless, constant, immutable, invariable, predictable, settled, stable, stationary, steady, unchangeable, unchanging, unvarying
2 not true in one's allegiance to someone or something ⟨when the family's fortune disappeared, so did their *fickle* friends⟩ — see FAITHLESS

fiction *n* something that is the product of the imagination ⟨most stories about famous outlaws of the Old West are *fictions* that have little or nothing to do with fact⟩
synonyms fable, fabrication, fantasy (*also* phantasy), figment, invention
related words anecdote, narrative, novel, story, tale, yarn; fairy tale, falsehood, falsity, fib, lie, mendacity, misrepresentation, prevarication, untruth, whopper; make-believe
near antonyms actuality, realness
antonyms fact, materiality, reality

fictional *adj* not real and existing only in the imagination ⟨the events in the horror movie seemed so real to some fans that they could not believe that the whole thing was *fictional*⟩ — see IMAGINARY

fictitious *adj* not real and existing only in the imagination ⟨his wartime exploits turned out to be entirely *fictitious*, as he had never even been in the military⟩ — see IMAGINARY

fiddle *n* **1** language, behavior, or ideas that are absurd and contrary to good sense ⟨oh, *fiddle*! I've heard that excuse a thousand times before⟩ — see NONSENSE 1
2 *chiefly British* an instance of the use of dishonest methods to acquire something of value ⟨the e-mail was another one of those *fiddles* from some supposed Nigerian millionaire seeking to transfer funds out of his country⟩ — see FRAUD 1

fiddle *vb* **1** to make jerky or restless movements ⟨the executive *fiddled* with a pen as she impatiently waited for the meeting to begin⟩ — see FIDGET
2 to rob by the use of trickery or threats ⟨conscienceless grifters who had spent their lives *fiddling* the naive⟩ — see FLEECE

fiddle (around) *vb* to spend time in aimless activity ⟨we spent the snow day just *fiddling around*⟩
synonyms doodle, fool around, fribble, goof (around), hang about [*British*], kick around, mess around, monkey (around), play, potter (around), putter (around), trifle
related words dally, dawdle, dillydally, hang (around *or* out), idle, loaf, loll, lounge; clown (around), horse around; diddle (with), tinker
near antonyms buckle (down), knuckle down, set (to), settle (down)

fiddle (with) *vb* to handle thoughtlessly, ignorantly, or mischievously ⟨I could tell that someone had been *fiddling with* the carefully set controls on my entertainment system⟩ — see TAMPER (WITH)

fiddle away *vb* to use up carelessly ⟨*fiddled away* the entire evening surfing the Internet⟩ — see WASTE 1

fiddle–faddle *n* language, behavior, or ideas that are absurd and contrary to good sense ⟨a grandmother who routinely pooh-poohed the advice of the so-called experts in child care as so much *fiddle-faddle*⟩ — see NONSENSE 1

fiddle–footed *adj* easily excited by nature ⟨although *fiddle-footed* now, the kitten should settle down once it adjusts to its new home⟩ — see EXCITABLE

fiddlesticks *n pl* language, behavior, or ideas that are absurd and contrary to good sense ⟨some people have one word for the game of golf: *fiddlesticks*!⟩ — see NONSENSE 1

fiddling *adj* lacking importance ⟨you should delegate these *fiddling* matters to your staff so that you can focus on more important issues⟩ — see UNIMPORTANT

fidelity *n* adherence to something to which one is bound by a pledge or duty ⟨they have never wavered in their *fidelity* to the cause of freedom⟩
synonyms adhesion, allegiance, attachment, commitment, constancy, dedication, devotedness, devotion, faith, faithfulness, fastness, fealty, loyalty, piety, steadfastness, troth
related words affection, fondness; determination, firmness, resolution; dependability, reliability, trustability, trustiness, trustworthiness

near antonyms alienation, disaffection, estrangement, separation
antonyms disloyalty, faithlessness, falseness, falsity, inconstancy, infidelity, perfidiousness, perfidy, treachery, unfaithfulness

fidget *vb* to make jerky or restless movements ⟨small children are likely to *fidget* in church⟩
synonyms fiddle, jerk, jig, jiggle, squiggle, squirm, thrash, thresh, toss, twist, twitch, wiggle, wriggle, writhe
related words flit, flutter, twitter; quake, quiver, shake, shiver, shudder, tremble; pace
near antonyms relax, rest, unwind; calm (down), still

fidgetiness *n* a state of nervousness marked by sudden jerky movements ⟨she couldn't stay still before her speech, and by her *fidgetiness* you could tell that she absolutely dreads speaking in public⟩ — see JUMPINESS

fidgets *n pl* a state of nervousness marked by sudden jerky movements ⟨one dental patient in the waiting room had a bad case of the *fidgets*⟩ — see JUMPINESS

fidgety *adj* making jerky or restless movements ⟨I get too *fidgety* to sit after a few minutes in a waiting room⟩
synonyms antsy, squirmy, twitchy, wiggly, wriggly
related words aflutter, fluttery, twittery; quaking, quivering, shaking, shivering, shivery, shuddering, trembling; anxious, dithery, edgy, het up, hung up, jittery, jumpy, nervous, nervy, perturbed, restive, tense, troubled, uneasy, unquiet, upset, uptight, worried
near antonyms calm, collected, cool, easy, relaxed
antonyms motionless, still

fie *interj* **1** how surprising, doubtful, or unbelievable ⟨*fie*! you expect me to believe that sorry excuse?⟩ — see NO
2 used to express disgust ⟨*fie* on anyone who disagrees!⟩ — see YUCK

fief *n* a region of activity, knowledge, or influence ⟨the logistics of the relief effort is the director's *fief*⟩ — see FIELD 2

fiefdom *n* a region of activity, knowledge, or influence ⟨you'll have to ask that guy—the project is his *fiefdom*⟩ — see FIELD 2

field *n* **1** a small area of usually open land ⟨a *field* that is the frequent site of neighborhood softball games⟩
synonyms clearing, ground, lot, parcel, plat, plot, tract
related words common(s), croft [*chiefly British*]; grass, green, greensward, lawn; glade, grassland, heath, heathland, lea (*or* ley), meadow, moor, pasture, pastureland
2 a region of activity, knowledge, or influence ⟨the first woman to enter the *field* of medicine⟩
synonyms area, arena, bailiwick, barony, business, circle, demesne, department, discipline, domain, element, fief, fiefdom, firmament, front, game, kingdom, line, precinct, province, realm, specialty, sphere, terrain, walk
related words frontier; study, subject; territory, turf; occupation, profession, pursuit, racket, vocation; ambit, amplitude, breadth, compass, confine, dimension(s), extent, ken, reach, scope, sweep, width; subfield, subspecialty
3 a part or portion having no fixed boundaries ⟨if you set your camera lens to small aperture, the *field* of sharp focus will be quite large⟩ — see REGION 1
4 a place where a battle takes place ⟨the *field* where two mighty armies met and changed the course of history⟩ — see BATTLEFIELD
5 a place from which aircraft operate that usually has paved runways and a terminal ⟨Worsham *Field* in Corpus Christi used to be home to a sizable crop dusting operation⟩ — see AIRPORT
6 a wide space or area ⟨the cemetery's *field* of crosses for the war's fallen seemed to stretch to infinity⟩ — see EXPANSE
7 active fighting during the course of a war ⟨in the classroom the general had been a brilliant theoretician, but in the *field* he proved to be a wholly incompetent tactician⟩ — see COMBAT 1

field *vb* to deal with (something) usually skillfully or efficiently ⟨gave the waitress a large tip because she kept smiling as she *fielded* their many requests⟩ — see HANDLE 1

fiend *n* **1** a mean, evil, or unprincipled person ⟨even the utter horror of the terrorist attack did not deter some *fiends* from going on a looting spree⟩ — see VILLAIN
2 a person who regularly uses drugs especially illegally ⟨the miserable, wasted lives of narcotic *fiends*⟩ — see DOPER
3 a person with a strong and habitual liking for something ⟨comic-book *fiends* seem to have their own little world⟩ — see FAN
4 an evil spirit ⟨the legend that a *fiend* continues to haunt what was once the castle's torture chamber⟩ — see DEMON 1
5 the supreme personification of evil often represented as the ruler of hell ⟨he swore that not even the *fiend* could tempt him to eat that dessert⟩ — see DEVIL 1
6 a person with a high level of knowledge or skill in a field ⟨our in-house computer *fiend* fixed the problem in no time⟩ — see EXPERT

fiendish *adj* **1** of, relating to, or worthy of an evil spirit ⟨a *fiendish* delight in playing cruel tricks⟩
synonyms cacodemonic, demoniac (*also* demoniacal), demonian, demonic (*also* demonical), devilish, diabolical (*or* diabolic), Luciferian, satanic
related words hellish, infernal; baleful, evil, sinister; malevolent, malicious, malignant; heinous, monstrous; black, immoral, iniquitous, nefarious, vicious, vile, villainous, wicked; barbarous, cruel, ferocious, inhuman, savage
near antonyms celestial, heavenly; beneficent, benevolent, benign, benignant; godly, holy, sainted, saintly; ethical, good, moral, righteous, virtuous
antonyms angelic (*or* angelical)
2 having or showing the desire to inflict severe pain and suffering on others ⟨shook with *fiendish* laughter as he watched his victims writhe in agony⟩ — see CRUEL 1

fiendishness *n* disposition to willfully inflict pain and suffering on others ⟨the unconscionable *fiendishness* of the acts committed by terrorists⟩ — see CRUELTY

fierce *adj* **1** violently unfriendly or aggressive in disposition ⟨the Vikings had a well-earned reputation for being *fierce* warriors⟩
synonyms fell, ferocious, grim, savage, vicious
related words argumentative, assaultive, bellicose, belligerent, brawly, chippy, combative, confrontational, discordant, disputatious, feisty, gladiatorial, militant, pugnacious, scrappy, warlike; bare-knuckle (*also* bare-knuckled *or* bare-knuckles), blood-and-guts, in-your-face, take-no-prisoners; contentious, quarrelsome, truculent; menacing, threatening; bestial, brute, inhuman, inhumane; barbaric, uncivilized, wild; heartless, implacable, merciless, pitiless, relentless, ruthless, unrelenting, wanton; bloodthirsty, bloody, homicidal, murdering, murderous, sanguinary, sanguine; rapacious, ravenous, voracious
near antonyms amicable, companionable, comradely, congenial, cordial, friendly, genial, hearty, warm, warmhearted; compliant, submissive, tame; benign, compassionate, kind, merciful; pacific, peaceable, peaceful; amiable, complaisant, obliging; human, humane; civilized, cultured
antonyms gentle, mild, unaggressive
2 extreme in degree, power, or effect ⟨a *fierce* wind made the frigid temperatures seem even worse⟩ — see INTENSE 1
3 harsh and threatening in manner or appearance ⟨the

fierce faces of the players on the opposing hockey team⟩ — see GRIM 1
4 having or showing a bold forcefulness in the pursuit of a goal ⟨a social reformer of *fierce* and fearless determination⟩ — see AGGRESSIVE 1
5 marked by bursts of destructive force or intense activity ⟨*fierce* fighting raged in the streets of the war-torn city⟩ — see VIOLENT 1
6 marked by great and often stressful excitement or activity ⟨*fierce* early-morning trading sent stocks soaring⟩ — see FURIOUS 1

fiercely *adv* to a great degree ⟨*fiercely* hot weather⟩ — see VERY 1

fierceness *n* the quality or state of being forceful (as in expression) ⟨the *fierceness* of her denial prompted many people to wonder if maybe she was innocent after all⟩ — see VEHEMENCE 1

fiery *adj* **1** being on fire ⟨the *fiery* Yule log made a splendid backdrop for our holiday party⟩ — see ABLAZE 1
2 having a notably high temperature ⟨the long, dangerous trek across the *fiery* desert⟩ — see HOT 1
3 having or expressing great depth of feeling ⟨the *fiery* preacher held the members of the revival meeting spellbound⟩ — see FERVENT 1
4 marked by a lively display of strong feeling ⟨the controversial editorial sparked a page's worth of *fiery* letters to the editor⟩ — see SPIRITED 1
5 capable of catching or being set on fire ⟨with a *fiery* vapor like that, the lighting of a single match could cause an explosion⟩ — see COMBUSTIBLE
6 easily irritated or annoyed ⟨since the governor was known for his *fiery* temper, naturally his aides always shielded him from bad news⟩ — see IRRITABLE

fiesta *n* a time or program of special events and entertainment in honor of something ⟨the city's Latinos have a series of *fiestas* throughout the summer⟩ — see FESTIVAL

fig *n* the smallest amount or part imaginable ⟨they choose to live modestly and don't seem to give a *fig* for the trappings of success⟩ — see JOT

fight *n* **1** a physical dispute between opposing individuals or groups ⟨a troubled youth who got into one *fight* after another⟩
synonyms battle, clash, combat, conflict, contest, dustup, fracas, fray, hassle, scrap, scrimmage, scrum, scuffle, skirmish, struggle, tussle
related words pitched battle, rough-and-tumble; affray [*chiefly British*], battle royal, brawl, broil, donnybrook, free-for-all, melee (*also* mêlée), mix-up, ruckus, ruction; blows, fistfight, fisticuffs, grapple, handgrips, punch-out, punch-up [*chiefly British*], slugfest; confrontation, duel, face-off, joust; altercation, argle-bargle [*chiefly British*], argument, argy-bargy [*chiefly British*], contretemps, controversy, cross fire, disagreement, dispute, falling-out, kickup, misunderstanding, quarrel, row, spat, squabble, tangle, tiff, wrangle; catfight
near antonyms truce
2 a forceful effort to reach a goal or objective ⟨the mayoral candidate pledged to lead a successful *fight* to improve the city's schools⟩ — see STRUGGLE 1
3 an inclination to fight or quarrel ⟨a tough, streetwise kid with a lot of *fight* in him⟩ — see BELLIGERENCE
4 an often noisy or angry expression of differing opinions ⟨the couple have their share of *fights*, but they quickly get over them⟩ — see ARGUMENT 1

fight *vb* **1** to oppose (someone) in physical conflict ⟨a proud people who have fiercely *fought* all invaders of their homeland⟩
synonyms battle, clash (with), combat, scrimmage (with), skirmish (with), war (against)
related words duel, joust; bang, bash, bat, batter, beat, belt, bludgeon, bop, buffet, clobber, hammer, hit, knock, paste, pound, punch, slam, slap, slog, slug, smack, smite, sock, strike, swat, swipe, thump, thwack, wallop, whack, whale; box, spar; brawl; grapple, scuffle, tussle, wrestle; bump, collide
near antonyms give up, submit, surrender
2 to strive to reduce or eliminate ⟨a civil rights leader who dedicated his life to *fighting* prejudice⟩
synonyms battle, combat, contend (with), counter, oppose, oppugn
related words baffle, checkmate, foil, frustrate, resist, thwart, withstand; confront, defy, face, meet
near antonyms abide, bear, endure, suffer; advocate, back, champion, endorse (*also* indorse), support, uphold
antonyms advance, cultivate, encourage, forward, foster, further, nourish, nurture, promote
3 to engage in a contest ⟨everyone on that street seems to be *fighting* to see who can create the gaudiest holiday lighting display⟩ — see COMPETE
4 to express different opinions about something often angrily ⟨if you kids continue to *fight*, I'm turning this car around and we're heading back home!⟩ — see ARGUE 2
5 to refuse to give in to ⟨I tried to *fight* the temptation to eat another cookie—and lost⟩ — see RESIST

fighter *n* **1** a person engaged in military service ⟨the debate whether more *fighters* are needed to bring order to that war-torn country⟩ — see SOLDIER
2 one that engages in the sport of fighting with the fists ⟨a program at the community center for training local youths as *fighters*⟩ — see BOXER
3 a person who takes part in a dispute ⟨kept the two *fighters* apart until they had calmed down and could talk sensibly⟩ — see DISPUTANT

figment *n* **1** a conception or image created by the imagination and having no objective reality ⟨unable to find any tracks in the snow the next morning, I was forced to conclude that the shadowy figure had been a *figment* of my imagination⟩ — see FANTASY 1
2 something that is the product of the imagination ⟨thus far, the invisible human being has been nothing more than a *figment* of fantasy writers⟩ — see FICTION

figural *adj* expressing one thing in terms normally used for another ⟨"a candidate running for office" is just a *figural* expression⟩ — see FIGURATIVE

figurative *adj* expressing one thing in terms normally used for another ⟨the *figurative* use of "allergy" to mean "a feeling of dislike"⟩
synonyms extended, figural, metaphoric (*or* metaphorical), tropical, tropological
related words Aesopian (*also* Aesopic), allegorical, emblematic (*also* emblematical), symbolic (*also* symbolical); catachrestic (*or* catachrestical), sylleptic; euphemistic; nonliteral, veritable
near antonyms literal; nonsymbolic
antonyms nonfigurative, nonmetaphorical

figure *n* **1** a character used to represent a mathematical value ⟨no doubt the *figures* on the price tags at the jewelry store are so small because the zeroes are so many⟩ — see NUMBER 1
2 a line that traces the outer limits of an object or surface ⟨we could gradually see the *figure* of a ship coming our way through the fog⟩ — see OUTLINE 1
3 a person who is widely known and usually much talked about ⟨*figures* from the worlds of sport and entertainment will be guests at the White House dinner⟩ — see CELEBRITY 1
4 a small statue ⟨painted wooden *figures* by untrained artists can be quite valuable on today's antiques market⟩ — see FIGURINE
5 a three-dimensional representation of the human body used especially for displaying clothes ⟨the mu-

seum features a collection of *figures* strikingly attired in suits of medieval armor⟩ — see MANNEQUIN 1

6 a unit of decoration that is repeated all over something (as a fabric) ⟨upholstered the chair with a fabric embossed with *figures* of fleur-de-lis⟩ — see PATTERN 1

7 something that visually explains or decorates a text ⟨the layout editor could have done a better job of getting the *figures* on the same page as the specific portion of text that they are intended to illustrate⟩ — see ILLUSTRATION 1

8 the amount of money that is demanded as payment for something ⟨a number of the paintings at the auction sold at *figures* far higher than had been estimated⟩ — see PRICE 1

9 the outward appearance of something as distinguished from its substance ⟨the ice sculpture at the banquet was in the *figure* of an eagle spreading its wings⟩ — see FORM 1

10 the type of body that a person has ⟨Martha has such a slender *figure* that just about anything looks good on her⟩ — see PHYSIQUE

11 figures *pl* the act or process of performing mathematical operations to find a value ⟨a person with a good head for *figures*⟩ — see CALCULATION

12 the outward form of someone or something especially as indicative of a quality ⟨unshaven and dirty, he presents a sorry *figure*⟩ — see APPEARANCE 1

figure *vb* **1** to come to a judgment about after discussion or consideration ⟨we *figured* that we had better arrive early at the concert in order to get good seats⟩ — see DECIDE 1

2 to decide the size, amount, number, or distance of (something) without actual measurement ⟨let's *figure* the juice in the pan to be about a cup and just add it to the mix⟩ — see ESTIMATE 2

3 to determine (a value) by doing the necessary mathematical operations ⟨the car dealer *figured* that our monthly car payment would be $357⟩ — see CALCULATE 1

4 to have as an opinion ⟨the father *figures* that girls should have the same athletic opportunities as boys and supports his daughter's interest in soccer⟩ — see BELIEVE 2

figure out *vb* to find an answer for through reasoning ⟨a book of brainteasers that even a really clever person won't have an easy time *figuring out*⟩ — see SOLVE

figurine *n* a small statue ⟨his collection of *figurines* includes toy soldiers from every war that America has fought⟩
synonyms figure, statuette
related words doll, dolly, hand puppet, marionette, puppet; bust, figurehead; carving, model, sculpture; dummy, form, manikin (*also* mannikin), mannequin
antonyms colossus

figuring *n* the act or process of performing mathematical operations to find a value ⟨the *figuring* of the cost of the car repair was rushed, and so it bears little resemblance to the actual result⟩ — see CALCULATION

filament *n* a thin, flexible structure that resembles a hair ⟨the cable was made up of fine *filaments* twisted together⟩ — see HAIR 2

filch *vb* to take (something) without right and with an intent to keep ⟨too hungry to wait until the party had started, he *filched* a cookie from the buffet table when no one was looking⟩ — see STEAL 1

file *n* a series of persons or things arranged one behind another ⟨a long *file* of people waiting to get tickets to the game⟩ — see LINE 1

¹file *vb* to make smooth by friction ⟨beautifully *filed* nails that obviously had been done by a manicurist⟩ — see GRIND 1

²file *vb* to move along with a steady regular step especially in a group ⟨to the strains of that familiar music, this year's graduating class *filed* into the auditorium⟩ — see MARCH 1

fill *n* soft material that is used to fill the hollow parts of something ⟨we ripped the tag off years ago, so we have no idea what the *fill* in that pillow is⟩ — see FILLING

fill *vb* **1** to put into (something) as much as can be held or contained ⟨*fill* the basket with apples⟩
synonyms brim, charge, cram, heap, jam, jam-pack, load, pack, stuff
related words drench, flood, glut, swamp; bloat, bulk; crowd, crush, mat, press, ram, shove, squash, squeeze; refill, refresh, reload, repack, replenish; overcharge, overfill, overflow, saturate; honeycomb, penetrate
near antonyms lighten; deplete, drain, eliminate, exhaust; bleed, draw (off); clean, flush, purge, scour, sweep
antonyms clear, empty, evacuate, vacate, void

2 to close up so that no empty spaces remain ⟨before starting to paint, *fill* all the cracks with putty⟩
synonyms block, bung, dam, pack, plug, stop, stuff
related words choke, clog, close (off), clot, congest, jam, obstruct, occlude; caulk, chink, seal; repack, restuff
near antonyms excavate, hollow (out), scoop (out), shovel

3 to do what is required by the terms of ⟨orders received by this date will be *filled* in time for Christmas delivery of the merchandise⟩ — see FULFILL 1

filled *adj* containing or seeming to contain the greatest quantity or number possible ⟨*filled* baskets of every variety of apple were available at the farmers' market⟩ — see FULL 1

filler *n* soft material that is used to fill the hollow parts of something ⟨the vase was packed in Styrofoam *filler* to protect it during shipping⟩ — see FILLING

fill–in *n* a person or thing that takes the place of another ⟨I'm just a *fill-in*, so I have no idea where office supplies are kept⟩ — see SUBSTITUTE

fill in *vb* **1** to give information to ⟨my friend quickly *filled* me *in* on the portion of the movie that I had missed⟩ — see ENLIGHTEN 1

2 to serve as a replacement usually for a time only ⟨she's only *filling in* while the regular secretary is on vacation⟩ — see COVER 1

filling *n* soft material that is used to fill the hollow parts of something ⟨the *filling* for the parka is goose down⟩
synonyms fill, filler, padding, stuffing, wadding
related words packing; interlining, lining, quilting; buffer, bumper, cushion, fender, pad

fillip *n* a hard strike with a part of the body or an instrument ⟨gave him a sharp *fillip* on the noggin with her teakettle⟩ — see ¹BLOW

fillip *vb* to give life, vigor, or spirit to ⟨used a splash of orange-flavored liqueur to *fillip* the otherwise ordinary cranberry sauce⟩ — see ANIMATE

filly *n* a female person who has not yet reached adulthood ⟨she's still a *filly*, so she has plenty of time to decide what she wants to do in life⟩ — see GIRL 2

film *n* **1** a story told by means of a series of continuously projected pictures and a sound track ⟨watched a *film* on the Hopi Indians at the multicultural center⟩ — see MOVIE 1

2 the art or business of making a movie ⟨learned about some of the special-effects techniques used in *film*⟩ — see MOVIE 2

filmdom *n* the art or business of making a movie ⟨that will go down in the annals of *filmdom* as the worst movie ever⟩ — see MOVIE 2

filmland *n* the art or business of making a movie ⟨a master director who is one of the most revered figures of *filmland*⟩ — see MOVIE 2

filmmaking *n* the art or business of making a movie ⟨plans to attend New York University to learn *filmmaking*⟩ — see MOVIE 2

filmy *adj* **1** being of a material lacking in sturdiness or substance ⟨*filmy* cobwebs covering the entryway to the cellar⟩ — see FLIMSY 1
2 very thin and easy to see through ⟨those *filmy* curtains don't block out enough light⟩ — see SHEER 1

filter *vb* **1** to pass through a filter ⟨steep the tea and then *filter* it to get rid of the leaves⟩ — see STRAIN 2
2 to remove usually visible impurities from ⟨after frying the chicken, we *filtered* the oil and kept it in the refrigerator to use again⟩ — see CLARIFY 1

filth *n* **1** foul matter that mars the purity or cleanliness of something ⟨the *filth* in the restaurant's kitchen was unbelievable⟩
synonyms crud, dirt, grime, gunk, muck, smut, soil
related words scum, sewage, sewerage, slime, sludge, swill; dross, dust [*British*], garbage, junk, litter, refuse, rubbish, scrap, trash, waste; crock [*dialect*], soot; dinginess, dirtiness, dustiness, filthiness, foulness, griminess, grubbiness, nastiness, squalidness, uncleanliness, uncleanness
near antonyms cleanliness, cleanness
2 the quality or state of being obscene ⟨films full of *filth* and violence⟩ — see OBSCENITY 1

filthiness *n* **1** the quality or state of being obscene ⟨the book was banned primarily because of the *filthiness* of the language⟩ — see OBSCENITY 1
2 the state or quality of being dirty ⟨the appalling *filthiness* of the oven in the vacated apartment⟩ — see DIRTINESS 1

filthy *adj* **1** depicting or referring to sexual matters in a way that is unacceptable in polite society ⟨you simply cannot use such *filthy* language on the public airwaves⟩ — see OBSCENE 1
2 not clean ⟨you can't go to the concert unless you clean this *filthy* room first⟩ — see DIRTY 1

filthy *adv* to a great degree ⟨grew up *filthy* poor and hated every minute of it⟩ — see VERY 1

finagle *vb* **1** to plan out usually with subtle skill or care ⟨let me look at my schedule and see if I can't *finagle* a visit to the museum⟩ — see ENGINEER
2 to use dishonest methods to achieve a goal ⟨she'll *finagle* until she gets exactly what she wants⟩ — see CHEAT 1

finagler *n* a dishonest person who uses clever means to cheat others out of something of value ⟨financial *finaglers* who were suspected of insider trading⟩ — see TRICKSTER 1

final *adj* **1** following all others of the same kind in order or time ⟨this will be my *final* order⟩ — see LAST 1
2 having been established and usually not subject to change ⟨the wedding date is *final*⟩ — see FIXED 1

finale *n* the last part of a process or action ⟨the *finale* to the festivities was a grand display of fireworks⟩
synonyms capper, close, closing, conclusion, consummation, end, endgame, ending, finis, finish, grand finale, home stretch, mop-up, windup, wrap-up
related words acme, apex, capstone, climax, copestone, coup de grâce (*or* coup de grace), crescendo, crown, culmination, high-water mark, meridian, peak, pinnacle, summit, tip-top, top, zenith; aftermath, anticlimax, coda, epilogue (*also* epilog), postscript; shank, tag end, tail end
near antonyms foreword, introduction, overture, preamble, preface, prelude, prologue (*also* prolog)
antonyms baseline, beginning, dawn, day one, nascence, nascency, opening, start

finalize *vb* **1** to bring (something) to a state where nothing remains to be done ⟨we're still *finalizing* our travel plans but hope to have them done by the end of the week⟩ — see FINISH 1
2 to give official acceptance of as satisfactory ⟨the bank won't *finalize* the loan before Tuesday because of the holiday⟩ — see APPROVE

finally *adv* at a later time ⟨we're making steady progress and may *finally* finish this project⟩ — see YET 1

finance *vb* **1** to provide money for ⟨a local business kindly *financed* the high school band's trip to New York City⟩
synonyms bankroll, capitalize, endow, fund, stake, subsidize, underwrite
related words grubstake; cofinance, refinance; advocate, aid, back, champion, endorse (*also* indorse), patronize, sponsor, support; maintain, nourish, provide (for); clear, defray, discharge, foot, liquidate, pay, pay off, pay up, quit, recompense, settle, spring (for), stand; refund
antonyms defund
2 to furnish (as an institution) with a regular source of income ⟨established a fund to *finance* a visiting lecturer position at the local college⟩ — see ENDOW 2

finances *n pl* available money ⟨will have to take a look at our *finances* to see if we can afford it⟩ — see FUND 2

financial *adj* of or relating to money, banking, or investments ⟨the *financial* world was watching the stock market closely⟩
synonyms dollars-and-cents, fiscal, monetary, pecuniary, pocket
related words capitalist (*or* capitalistic), commercial, economic
antonyms nonfinancial

find *n* something discovered ⟨that antique plate was a great garage sale *find*⟩ — see DISCOVERY 2

find *vb* **1** to come upon after searching, study, or effort ⟨we finally *found* the information after searching dozens of Internet sites⟩
synonyms ascertain, descry, detect, determine, dig out, dig up, discover, dredge (up), ferret (out), find out, get, hit (on *or* upon), hunt (down *or* up), learn, locate, nose out, root (out), rout (out), rummage, run down, scare up, scout (up), track (down), turn up
related words espy, sight, spot; look for, search (for *or* out), seek
near antonyms lose, mislay, misplace, misset
antonyms miss, overlook, pass over
2 to come upon unexpectedly or by chance ⟨hey, I *found* my notebook!⟩ — see HAPPEN (ON *OR* UPON)

finding *n* **1** a decision made by a court or tribunal regarding a case it has heard ⟨the Supreme Court's *finding* was that the state law was unconstitutional⟩ — see SENTENCE
2 the act or process of sighting or learning the existence of something for the first time ⟨the scientists were thrilled with the *finding* of the new fossil⟩ — see DISCOVERY 1

find out *vb* **1** to come to an awareness of ⟨that was around the time that I *found out* I was adopted⟩ — see DISCOVER 1
2 to come upon after searching, study, or effort ⟨*found out* where she lived by checking the phone book⟩ — see FIND 1

fine *adv* in a satisfactory way ⟨you did just *fine* on the stress test⟩ — see WELL 1

fine *adj* **1** consisting of very small particles ⟨the *fine* sand found on the island's beaches⟩
synonyms dusty, floury, powdery
related words smooth; filtered, pulverized, refined; superfine, ultrafine
near antonyms rough; unfiltered, unrefined; gravelly, gritty, sandy; pebbly, rocky, stony (*also* stoney); lumpy, mealy

antonyms coarse, grainy, granular, granulated
2 made or done with extreme care and accuracy ⟨the *fine* distinction between bravery and recklessness⟩
synonyms delicate, exact, finespun, hairline, hairsplitting, minute, nice, nuanced, refined, subtle
related words nitpicking, quibbling; frivolous, inconsequential, inconsiderable, insignificant, negligible, petty, piddling, trifling, trivial; demanding, exacting, fastidious, finical, finicking, finicky, fussy, meticulous, particular, picky
near antonyms apparent, clear, clear-cut, evident, manifest, obvious, open-and-shut, palpable, patent, perspicuous, plain, transparent, unambiguous, unequivocal, unmistakable; broad, indefinite; careless, heedless, incautious, slapdash, slipshod, sloppy
antonyms coarse, inexact, rough
3 being of less than usual width ⟨use a *fine* line for the outline of the facial features you intend to carve into the pumpkin⟩ — see NARROW 1
4 being to one's liking ⟨that arrangement is *fine* with me⟩ — see SATISFACTORY 1
5 free from added matter ⟨that silver is .9600 *fine*⟩ — see PURE 1
6 meeting the highest standard of accuracy ⟨making the final *fine* adjustments on the car's GPS⟩ — see PRECISE 1
7 of a level of quality that meets one's needs or standards ⟨the wine steward declared that the complaint of corkiness was unjustified and that the wine was *fine*⟩ — see ADEQUATE
8 of a size that is less than average ⟨read the *fine* print⟩ — see SMALL 1
9 of the very best kind ⟨a *fine* performance of a classic ballet⟩ — see EXCELLENT
10 having qualities that appeal to a refined taste ⟨savored every morsel of the restaurant's *fine* cuisine⟩ — see CHOICE 1
11 able to sense slight impressions or differences ⟨hearing so *fine* that it can seemingly hear the tiniest twig snap⟩ — see ACUTE 1
12 having or showing elegance ⟨a *fine* old structure in the city's historic district⟩ — see ELEGANT 1

fine *n* a sum of money to be paid as a punishment ⟨a $50 *fine* for speeding⟩
synonyms damages, forfeit, forfeiture, mulct, penalty
related words reparations; assessment, award, compensation; indemnity

[1]fine *vb* to establish or apply as a charge or penalty ⟨the police will *fine* you for driving with one headlight out⟩ — see IMPOSE

[2]fine *vb* to remove usually visible impurities from ⟨the use of egg shells to *fine* wine⟩ — see CLARIFY 1

fineness *n* **1** the quality or state of being little in size ⟨the *fineness* of the grains of sand enhances the appeal of the beach⟩ — see SMALLNESS 1
2 the quality or state of being very accurate ⟨the *fineness* of the telescope's lens and mirror⟩ — see PRECISION
3 the state or quality of having a delicate structure ⟨the *fineness* of the cat's bones⟩ — see DELICACY 2
4 dignified or restrained beauty of form, appearance, or style ⟨there's a *fineness* to the jewelry designs of Fabergé that elevates them to the level of decorative art⟩ — see ELEGANCE

finery *n* dressy clothing ⟨the guests arrived at the wedding in all their *finery*⟩
synonyms array, best, bravery, caparison, feather, frippery, full dress, gaiety (*also* gayety), glad rags, regalia
related words apparel, attire, costume, duds, habiliment(s), rags, raiment, rig, rigging, threads, toggery, togs, vestiary, vesture, wear
phrases best bib and tucker
near antonyms tatters; disarray, dishabille

finespun *adj* made or done with extreme care and accuracy ⟨a *finespun* analysis of what makes an everyday occurrence funny⟩ — see FINE 2

finesse *n* mental skill or quickness ⟨maneuvered his opponent into checkmate with his customary *finesse*⟩ — see DEXTERITY 1

finesse *vb* **1** to plan out usually with subtle skill or care ⟨had to *finesse* the schedule a bit to fit in another patient that afternoon⟩ — see ENGINEER
2 to get or keep away from (as a responsibility) through cleverness or trickery ⟨tried to *finesse* the blame for the foreign policy fiasco, even though he was secretary of state at the time⟩ — see ESCAPE 2

finest *n* a body of officers of the law ⟨proud to be a member of New York's *finest*⟩ — see POLICE 2

finger *vb* to find out or establish the identity of ⟨thus far authorities haven't been able to *finger* the person who's been lighting fires around town⟩ — see IDENTIFY 1

fingerprint *n* something that sets apart an individual from others of the same kind ⟨regards a sense of permanence as one of the *fingerprints* of a civilized society⟩ — see CHARACTERISTIC

finical *adj* hard to please ⟨a newspaper who's old-fashionedly *finical* about proper grammar⟩ — see FINICKY

finicking *adj* hard to please ⟨*finicking* drinkers will find the bar's trendy cocktails far too sweet⟩ — see FINICKY

finicky *adj* hard to please ⟨cats have a reputation for being *finicky* eaters⟩
synonyms choosy (*or* choosey), dainty, delicate, demanding, exacting, fastidious, finical, finicking, fussbudgety, fussy, nice, old-maidish, particular, pernickety [*chiefly British*], persnickety, picky
related words hyperfastidious, overdemanding, ultrafastidious; discerning, discriminating, selective; insightful, knowledgeable; captious, carping, caviling (*or* cavilling), critical, faultfinding, hypercritical, overcritical; careful, meticulous, painstaking, punctilious, scrupulous; queasy (*also* queazy), squeamish; peevish, petulant, prickly, touchy; niminy-piminy, prim, prissy
near antonyms affable, breezy, carefree, devil-may-care, happy-go-lucky, lackadaisical, laid-back, low-pressure, relaxed; flexible, lax, loose; lenient, permissive; uncritical; indiscriminating, undiscriminating
antonyms undemanding, unfastidious, unfussy

finis *n* the last part of a process or action ⟨if the two countries keep up their arms race, the inevitable *finis* to their rivalry will be their mutual destruction⟩ — see FINALE

finish *n* **1** the last part of a process or action ⟨a pie-eating contest is the fair's traditional *finish*⟩ — see FINALE
2 the stopping of a process or activity ⟨an all-out fight right to the *finish*⟩ — see END 1

finish *vb* **1** to bring (something) to a state where nothing remains to be done ⟨we should *finish* the painting of the house by tomorrow⟩
synonyms complete, consummate, finalize, perfect, polish
related words follow through (with), stick out; accomplish, achieve, effect; carry out, carry through, discharge, do, execute, fulfill (*or* fulfil), perform; ameliorate, amend, better, enhance, enrich, improve, meliorate; machine, refine, round (off *or* out), shine, touch up
phrases get through
near antonyms abandon, desert, discontinue, drop, forsake, quit
2 to bring (an event) to a natural or appropriate stopping point ⟨we'll *finish* the concert before dark⟩ — see CLOSE 3

3 to come to an end ⟨the three-day race *finished* yesterday⟩ — see CEASE 1

finished *adj* **1** brought or having come to an end ⟨the frosting isn't *finished* until you've added all of the decorative roses⟩ — see COMPLETE 2

2 facing certain defeat, disaster, or death ⟨since there was no way it could possibly make up the scoring deficit, the team knew that it was *finished*⟩ — see DONE FOR

finite *adj* **1** having a limit ⟨our nation's natural resources are abundant, but they are also *finite*⟩

synonyms limited

related words circumscribed, confined, restricted; definable, defined, definite, determinate, discrete; decided, established, fixed, set; exact, precise, specific; fathomable, measurable, mensurable, numerable

near antonyms unconfined, unrestricted; immeasurable, indefinite, indeterminate, measureless, undefinable, undefined, unfathomable

antonyms boundless, endless, illimitable, infinite, limitless, unbounded, unlimited

2 having distinct or certain limits ⟨we have a *finite* number of options to consider⟩ — see LIMITED 1

fink *n* **1** a person who provides information about another's wrongdoing ⟨his own brother turned out to be the *fink* who ratted them out to the police⟩ — see INFORMER

2 a person whose behavior is offensive to others ⟨that *fink* would sell out every one of us to save her own behind⟩ — see JERK 1

fink *vb* to give information (as to the authorities) about another's improper or unlawful activities ⟨we never would have been caught if he hadn't *finked* on us⟩ — see SQUEAL 1

fink out *vb* to break a promise or agreement ⟨I can't believe you'd *fink out* on me and leave me to go to the party alone!⟩ — see RENEGE 1

fire *n* **1** a destructive burning ⟨a number of suspicious *fires* in the neighborhood recently⟩

synonyms conflagration, holocaust, inferno

related words blaze, flare-up; backfire, bonfire, brush fire, campfire, forest fire, wildfire; arson

2 depth of feeling ⟨had she the *fire* in her heart that a run for the White House requires?⟩ — see ARDOR 1

3 a test of faith, patience, or strength ⟨asked to be sent to the front lines, as he was eager to prove himself in the *fire* of battle⟩ — see TRIAL 1

fire *vb* **1** to cause (a projectile) to be driven forward with force ⟨police officers *firing* rubber bullets⟩ — see SHOOT 1

2 to cause a weapon to release a missile with great force ⟨soldiers *fired* at the enemy in panic-stricken disorder⟩ — see SHOOT 2

3 to give life, vigor, or spirit to ⟨a school outing to the natural history museum *fired* his imagination, and he grew up to become an eminent paleontologist⟩ — see ANIMATE

4 to let go from office, service, or employment ⟨*fired* the secretary for incompetence⟩ — see DISMISS 1

5 to send through the air especially with a quick forward motion of the arm ⟨*fired* a pass to the running back⟩ — see THROW 1

6 to set (something) on fire ⟨lit some kindling before attempting to *fire* the logs⟩ — see BURN 2

fire (up) *vb* to rouse to strong feeling or action ⟨the dynamic speaker *fired up* the audience as no one had previously done⟩ — see PROVOKE 1

firearm *n* a portable weapon from which a shot is discharged by gunpowder ⟨will need a permit to carry a *firearm*⟩ — see GUN 1

fireball *n* a very energetic person ⟨what this club needs is a *fireball* who will bring some sorely needed energy and enthusiasm⟩ — see PISTOL

firebrand *n* a person who stirs up public feelings especially of discontent ⟨a *firebrand* who urged crowds to riot during the blackouts⟩ — see AGITATOR

fire–breather *n* an aggressive and fiercely determined person ⟨the only hope for turning around that failing company would be a CEO who's a real *fire-breather*⟩ — see PIT BULL

firebug *n* a person who deliberately and unlawfully sets fire to a building or other property ⟨after the second suspicious fire, police set a trap for the *firebug*⟩ — see ARSONIST

fire–eater *n* an aggressive and fiercely determined person ⟨if you want to make it in Hollywood, you'll need a *fire-eater* for an agent⟩ — see PIT BULL

firepower *n* the ability to exert effort for the accomplishment of a task ⟨right now the President doesn't have the political *firepower* to push his programs through Congress⟩ — see POWER 2

fireproof *adj* incapable of being burned ⟨remember to store valuable papers in a *fireproof* box⟩ — see INCOMBUSTIBLE

fireside *n* the place where one lives ⟨couldn't wait to get off the plane and back to his comfortable *fireside*⟩ — see HOME 1

firestorm *n* variance of opinion on a matter ⟨a seemingly endless *firestorm* was ignited by that U.S. Supreme Court decision⟩ — see DISAGREEMENT 1

firewater *n* a distilled beverage that can make a person drunk ⟨the bartender recommended a drink made with the local *firewater*, a potent gin⟩ — see ALCOHOL

fireworks *n pl* **1** an outburst or display of excited anger ⟨can we have a calm, rational discussion without the usual *fireworks*?⟩ — see TANTRUM

2 a spectacular display or performance of artistic or technical skill ⟨the theatrical *fireworks* generated by two great stars of the stage⟩ — see ACROBATICS

firing *n* a directed propelling of a missile by a firearm or artillery piece ⟨found a flaw in the gun's *firing*⟩ — see SHOT

firkin *n* an enclosed wooden vessel for holding beverages ⟨the innkeeper opened up a *firkin* of his special ale for the weary travelers⟩ — see CASK

firm *n* a commercial or industrial activity or organization ⟨merged with another *firm* to become a major player in the brokerage business⟩ — see ENTERPRISE 1

firm *adj* **1** not showing weakness or uncertainty ⟨a friendly fellow with a ready smile and a *firm* handshake⟩

synonyms forceful, hearty, iron, lusty, robust, solid, stout, strong, sturdy, vigorous

related words hard, ironclad, mighty, powerful, tough, unyielding; animated, brisk, energetic, frisky, jaunty, jazzy, lively, peppy, perky, spirited, sprightful, sprightly, springy, vital, vivacious, zippy; assured, certain, confident, sanguine, secure, sure

near antonyms feeble, fragile, frail; limp, listless, spiritless; diffident, insecure, self-doubting; characterless, effete, frail, spineless, weakened, weak-kneed, wimpy, wishy-washy

antonyms uncertain, weak

2 having a consistency that does not easily yield to pressure ⟨cold butter that was too *firm* to spread⟩

synonyms compact, hard, rigid, solid, stiff, unyielding

related words case-hardened, compacted, compressed, hardened, indurated, stiffened, tempered; close, dense, heavy, thick, thickset; inelastic, inflexible, ramrod, unbending; compressed, condensed; adamantine, rocklike; sturdy, substantial; impenetrable, impermeable, nonporous

near antonyms loose, scattered, thin; bendable, elastic, flexible, malleable, pliable, pliant, supple; droopy, flac-

cid, floppy, lank, limp, slack; airy, light; permeable, porous; ultrasoft
antonyms flabby, soft, spongy, squashy, squishy
3 firmly positioned in place and difficult to dislodge ⟨was *firm* in the saddle during the canter⟩ — see TIGHT 2
4 fully committed to achieving a goal ⟨asked him to reconsider, but he was *firm* in his commitment to the project⟩ — see DETERMINED 1
5 having been established and usually not subject to change ⟨the selling price of the house is *firm*, so there'll be no dickering⟩ — see FIXED 1
6 marked by the ability to withstand stress without structural damage or distortion ⟨built on a *firm* foundation, so the house hasn't settled⟩ — see STABLE 1
7 based on sound reasoning or information ⟨that assassination theory is far from *firm*, since there's not a shred of actual evidence to back it up⟩ — see GOOD 1

firm (up) *vb* to become physically firm or solid ⟨wait for the modeling clay to *firm up* before handling the finished pot⟩ — see HARDEN 1

firmament *n* **1** the expanse of air surrounding the earth ⟨the stars in the *firmament* twinkled ever so brightly⟩ — see SKY 1
2 a region of activity, knowledge, or influence ⟨a major figure in the classical music *firmament*⟩ — see FIELD 2

firmly *adv* in a vigorous and forceful manner ⟨stomped his feet *firmly* to get the snow off his boots⟩ — see HARD 3

firmness *n* **1** firm or unwavering adherence to one's purpose ⟨a woman of remarkable *firmness* in the achievement of the goals she has set for herself⟩ — see DETERMINATION 1
2 the ability to withstand force or stress without being distorted, dislodged, or damaged ⟨test the *firmness* of the concrete before parking the car on it⟩ — see STABILITY 1

first *adv* **1** as a substitute ⟨eat peas? I'd eat cockroaches *first*⟩ — see INSTEAD
2 by choice or preference ⟨we will not give in, but will fight for our freedom *first*⟩ — see RATHER 1

first *adj* **1** coming before all others in time or order ⟨the much-studied *first*—and last—voyage of the *Titanic*⟩
synonyms earliest, foremost, headmost, inaugural, initial, leadoff, maiden, original, pioneer, premier, virgin
related words ancient, early, primal, primary, prime, primeval, primitive, primordial; antecedent, preceding, previous
near antonyms advanced, late; consequent, ensuing, following, subsequent, succeeding; penultimate
antonyms final, last, latest, latter, terminal, terminating, ultimate
2 coming before all others in importance ⟨there are a number of reasons we can't go, but the *first* is that we don't have the money⟩ — see FOREMOST 1
3 highest in rank or authority ⟨auditioned and got *first* clarinet in the band⟩ — see HEAD

first–class *adj* of the very best kind ⟨a *first-class* production of a classic American musical⟩ — see EXCELLENT

first estate *n* the group ordained to perform clerical functions in the Christian church ⟨a nation in which the *first estate* had long held a privileged position⟩ — see CLERGY

firsthand *adj* done or working without something else coming in between ⟨had *firsthand* knowledge of the events of that evening⟩ — see DIRECT 1

first–line *adj* singled out from a number or group as more to one's liking ⟨surgery is usually not considered a *first-line* treatment for this type of cancer⟩ — see SELECT 1

firstly *adv* in the beginning ⟨*firstly*, gather all the ingredients together⟩ — see ORIGINALLY

first name *n* a name that is placed before one's family name ⟨the parents still haven't picked a *first name* for the baby⟩ — see FORENAME

first–rate *adj* of the very best kind ⟨wanted a *first-rate* bike and not the cheap model she had been using⟩ — see EXCELLENT

first–rateness *n* exceptionally high quality ⟨touristy restaurants generally are not known for the *first-rateness* of their cuisine⟩ — see EXCELLENCE 1

first–string *adj* of the very best kind ⟨a *first-string* rendition of the musical piece⟩ — see EXCELLENT

firth *n* a part of a body of water that extends beyond the general shoreline ⟨the *Firth* of Forth in Scotland⟩ — see GULF 1

fiscal *adj* of or relating to money, banking, or investments ⟨gained some *fiscal* knowledge by taking an economics course⟩ — see FINANCIAL

fish *vb* to search for something blindly or uncertainly ⟨take a minute to *fish* for some change to drop in the donation box⟩ — see GROPE

fish *n* a member of the human race ⟨he's rather an odd *fish*⟩ — see HUMAN

fisher *n* someone who catches fish ⟨few *fishers* of lake trout are more ardent or adept than my father⟩ — see FISHERMAN

fisherman *n* someone who catches fish ⟨*fishermen* sorting out their catch⟩
synonyms fisher
related words fisherfolk, fisherwoman; angler, fly fisherman, giller, surf caster, trawler, trawlerman, troller; waterman

fishy *adj* giving good reason for being doubted, questioned, or challenged ⟨something's *fishy* about the way he's acting⟩ — see DOUBTFUL 2

fissure *n* an irregular usually narrow break in a surface created by pressure ⟨lava flows up through a *fissure* in the earth's crust⟩ — see CRACK 1

fistful *n* a considerable amount ⟨repairing the roof is going to cost a *fistful* of money⟩ — see LOT 2

fit *adj* **1** meeting the requirements of a purpose or situation ⟨clothing that is *fit* for horseback riding⟩
synonyms applicable, appropriate, apt, becoming, befitting, felicitous, fitted, fitting, good, happy, meet, pretty, proper, right, suitable
related words condign, deserved, just, justified; needed, required, requisite; able, capable, competent, cut out, qualified, trained; pitch-perfect; acceptable, adequate, decent, kosher, satisfactory, serviceable, tolerable; correct, decorous, respectable, seemly; balanced, companionate, congruous, consonant, harmonious; rightful
phrases in order
near antonyms incapable, incompetent, inept, inexpert, unqualified, unskilled, unskillful, untrained; inadequate, intolerable, unacceptable, unsatisfactory; graceless, incorrect, indecorous; incompatible, uncongenial
antonyms improper, inapplicable, inapposite, inappropriate, inapt, incongruous, indecent, infelicitous, malapropos, misbecoming, unapt, unbecoming, unbeseeming, unfit, unfitting, unhappy, unmeet, unseemly, unsuitable, wrong
2 being in a state of fitness for some experience or action ⟨*fit* for military service⟩ — see READY 1
3 capable of or suitable for being used for a particular purpose ⟨I don't think those bald tires are *fit* for winter driving⟩ — see USABLE 1
4 enjoying health and vigor ⟨eat well and stay *fit*⟩ — see HEALTHY 1
5 having the required skills for an acceptable level of performance ⟨need to hire someone whose language

skills make them *fit* for the job⟩ — see COMPETENT 1

fit *n* **1** a sudden experiencing of a physical or mental disorder ⟨without her medication, she'd have an epileptic *fit*⟩ — see ATTACK 2

2 a sudden intense expression of strong feeling ⟨helpless *fits* of laughter from the audience⟩ — see OUTBURST 1

3 an outburst or display of excited anger ⟨found out what his wife had spent on clothes and threw a *fit*⟩ — see TANTRUM

fit *vb* **1** *archaic* to be fitting or proper ⟨we hardly know them, so for Christmas a simple card will *fit*⟩ — see DO 1

2 to be in agreement on every point ⟨now that you've explained your absence to me, my records and the office's *fit*⟩ — see CHECK 1

3 to change (something) so as to make it suitable for a new use or situation ⟨I can undo the hem on these old culottes and *fit* them into a skirt⟩ — see ADAPT

4 to make competent (as by training, skill, or ability) for a particular office or function ⟨that final computer course should *fit* him for a career in programming⟩ — see QUALIFY 2

5 to make or have room for ⟨we can *fit* you in the booth if the rest of us squeeze closer together⟩ — see ACCOMMODATE 1

6 to make ready in advance ⟨I won't have time to *fit* the spare room for the guests⟩ — see PREPARE 1

fit (in *or* **into)** *vb* to put among or between others ⟨do you think you can *fit* this picture *into* the album?⟩ ⟨I can *fit* you *in* between my two o'clock and three o'clock appointments⟩ — see INSERT

fit (out) *vb* to provide (someone) with what is needed for a task or activity ⟨*fitted* the hikers *out* with good boots and heavy socks⟩ — see FURNISH 1

fitful *adj* lacking in steadiness or regularity of occurrence ⟨a night of *fitful* sleep did not leave me feeling well rested the next morning⟩

synonyms aperiodic, casual, catchy, choppy, discontinuous, episodic (*also* episodical), erratic, intermittent, irregular, occasional, spasmodic, spastic, sporadic, spotty, unsteady

related words convulsive, sudden, violent; broken, disconnected, fragmentary, interrupted; aimless, arbitrary, desultory, haphazard, hit-and-miss, hit-or-miss, odd, random, scattered, slapdash, stray; capricious, changeful, changing, flickery, fluctuating, fluid, inconstant, mercurial, mutable, temperamental, uncertain, unpredictable, unsettled, unstable, varying, wavering; changeable, fickle, variable, volatile

near antonyms changeless, equable, even, stable, stationary, uniform; unchanging, unvarying, unwavering; methodical (*also* methodic), orderly, systematic; unrelenting, unremitting

antonyms constant, continuous, habitual, periodic, regular, repeated, steady

fitness *n* **1** the condition of being sound in body ⟨a gymnastics program promoting *fitness* and agility in school-aged children⟩ — see HEALTH 1

2 the quality or state of being especially suitable or fitting ⟨I have to question the *fitness* of wearing a bright red dress to a funeral⟩ — see APPROPRIATENESS

fitted *adj* meeting the requirements of a purpose or situation ⟨her personality is well *fitted* to a desk job⟩ — see FIT 1

fitting *adj* meeting the requirements of a purpose or situation ⟨it is only *fitting* that you should be the one to take her back to the airport since she flew out to see you⟩ — see FIT 1

fittingly *adv* in a manner suitable for the occasion or purpose ⟨he was dressed *fittingly* for the prom—all decked out in a spiffy tux⟩ — see PROPERLY

fittingness *n* the quality or state of being especially suitable or fitting ⟨trusted their judgment and didn't have to worry about the *fittingness* of their choice for a school play⟩ — see APPROPRIATENESS

five–star *adj* of the very best kind ⟨at those prices the restaurant's food should be nothing but *five-star*⟩ — see EXCELLENT

fix *n* **1** a difficult, puzzling, or embarrassing situation from which there is no easy escape ⟨what a *fix* we're in!⟩ — see PREDICAMENT

2 something given or promised in order to improperly influence a person's conduct or decision ⟨caught the judge on video accepting the *fix* from the mob boss⟩ — see BRIBE

3 an opinion on the nature, character, or quality of something ⟨what's your *fix* on the military situation over there?⟩ — see ESTIMATION 1

fix *vb* **1** to arrange something in a certain spot or position ⟨*fixed* my hair so that it would stop falling in my eyes⟩ — see PLACE 1

2 to cause (something) to hold to another ⟨first, you need to *fix* those pieces of wood together⟩ — see FASTEN 1

3 to come to an agreement or decision concerning the details of ⟨make sure to *fix* the number of guests with the bride's family before drawing up a list of people from the groom's side⟩ — see ARRANGE 1

4 to decide upon (the time or date for an event) usually from a position of authority ⟨have we *fixed* a day for the party yet?⟩ — see APPOINT 1

5 to make ready in advance ⟨would you mind *fixing* dinner tonight?⟩ — see PREPARE 1

6 to put into good shape or working order again ⟨have to *fix* the car before we can go⟩ — see MEND 1

7 to put securely in place or in a desired position ⟨*fixed* the mittens to the child's snowsuit⟩ — see FASTEN 2

8 to set solidly in or as if in surrounding matter ⟨the image of what Santa Claus looks like is solidly *fixed* in our minds⟩ — see ENTRENCH

9 to remove the sex organs of ⟨the animal shelter requires a pledge from the adoptive owner that they will have their new pet *fixed*⟩ — see NEUTER

10 to restore to a healthy condition ⟨it took surgery and months of physical therapy to completely *fix* her bum knee⟩ — see HEAL 1

fixable *adj* capable of being corrected ⟨don't worry, that mistake in scheduling is *fixable*⟩ — see REMEDIABLE

fixation *n* something about which one is constantly thinking or concerned ⟨their weight is an unfortunate *fixation* for many teenagers⟩

synonyms fetish (*also* fetich), idée fixe, mania, obsession, preoccupation, prepossession

related words monomania; complex, hang-up, problem, trip; appetite, cacoëthes, compulsion, craving, desire, drive, enthusiasm, fascination, hankering, hunger, infatuation, itch, longing, lust, passion, pining, thirst, urge, yearning, yen; idiosyncrasy, quirk; bent, disposition, inclination, leaning, partiality, penchant, predilection, predisposition, proclivity, propensity, tendency

near antonyms apathy, disinterestedness, disregard, indifference, insouciance, nonchalance, unconcern, unconcernedness

fixed *adj* **1** having been established and usually not subject to change ⟨the baseball card dealer's prices were *fixed*, so bargaining was not an option⟩

synonyms certain, determinate, final, firm, flat, frozen, hard, hard-and-fast, inexpugnable, set, settled, stable

related words nonadjustable, noncancelable, nonnegotiable, unchangeable; constant, steady, unchanging, uniform, unwavering; definite, exact, explicit, specific;

given, stated, stipulated; dependable, good, reliable, responsible, safe, solid, sure, tried, tried-and-true, true, trustworthy, trusty
near antonyms adjustable, changeable, negotiable; indefinite, open-ended, unspecified; capricious, changeful, flickery, fluctuating, fluid, inconstant, mercurial, mutable, temperamental, uncertain, unpredictable, unsettled, unstable, unsteady, variable, volatile
2 not capable of changing or being changed ⟨interest accrues at a *fixed* rate⟩ — see INFLEXIBLE 1

fixedness *n* the state of continuing without change ⟨wasn't comfortable with the *fixedness* of her stare⟩ — see CONSTANCY 1

fixture *n* a person who has long been associated with a place or activity ⟨has been a *fixture* in the Republican Party for the last 30 years⟩ — see INSTITUTION 2

fizz *n* a sound similar to the speech sound \s\ stretched out ⟨the light bulb burned out with a quick *fizz*⟩ — see HISS 1

fizz *vb* to make a sound like that of stretching out the speech sound \s\ ⟨soda pop *fizzing* in the glass⟩ — see HISS

fizzle *n* **1** a falling short of one's goals ⟨the home team's unexpected *fizzle* in that last game cost them the championship⟩ — see FAILURE 2
2 something that has failed ⟨the play was a *fizzle*, opening and closing the same night⟩ — see FAILURE 3

fizzle *vb* to make a sound like that of stretching out the speech sound \s\ ⟨oozing gobs of grease, a pair of fatty burgers *fizzled* on the grill⟩ — see HISS

fjord *also* **fiord** *n* a part of a body of water that extends beyond the general shoreline ⟨a cruise through the breathtaking *fjords* along the coast of Norway⟩ — see GULF 1

flabbergast *vb* to make a strong impression on (someone) with something unexpected ⟨your decision to suddenly quit your job *flabbergasts* me⟩ — see SURPRISE 1

flabbergasted *adj* **1** affected with sudden and great wonder or surprise ⟨was *flabbergasted* when we heard she was moving out of the state⟩ — see THUNDERSTRUCK
2 filled with amazement or wonder ⟨responded to the news of his arrival with a *flabbergasted* gasp⟩ — see OPENMOUTHED

flabbergasting *adj* causing a strong emotional reaction because of unexpectedness ⟨the *flabbergasting* sight of the mess that the teens had left in the kitchen⟩ — see SURPRISING 1

flabby *adj* giving easily to the touch ⟨his daughter playfully poked at his *flabby* belly⟩ — see SOFT 3

flaccid *adj* not stiff in structure ⟨the *flaccid* stalks of celery that had been around for far too long⟩ — see LIMP 1

[1]flag *vb* **1** to be limp from lack of water or vigor ⟨flowers *flagging* in the summer heat⟩ — see DROOP
2 to lose bodily strength or vigor ⟨we *flagged* as we neared the end of the long mountain trail⟩ — see WEAKEN 2

[2]flag *vb* to direct or notify by a movement or gesture ⟨*flagged* the cars into the other parking lot⟩ — see MOTION

flag *n* **1** a piece of cloth with a special design that is used as an emblem or for signaling ⟨the *flags* of both countries were prominently displayed at the treaty signing⟩
synonyms banderole (*or* banderol), banner, colors, ensign, guidon, jack, pendant (*also* pendent) [*chiefly British*], pennant, pennon, standard, streamer
related words bunting, gonfalon; black flag, Jolly Roger, tricolor, union jack, white flag; burgee, semaphore, signaler (*or* signaller), waft; badge, coat of arms, crest, insignia
2 an object intended to give public notice or warning ⟨road crews using handheld stop signs as *flags* at both ends of the highway construction zone⟩ — see SIGNAL 1

flagellate *vb* to strike repeatedly with something long and thin or flexible ⟨some medieval monks believed it was necessary to *flagellate* themselves in order to keep their desires in check⟩ — see WHIP 1

flagon *n* a handled container for holding and pouring liquids that usually has a lip or a spout ⟨brought a *flagon* of wine to the table⟩ — see PITCHER

flagrant *adj* very noticeable especially for being incorrect or bad ⟨that was a *flagrant* violation of the rules⟩ — see EGREGIOUS

flag–waver *n* one who shows excessive favoritism towards his or her country ⟨a newspaper columnist who never manages to be anything other than a knee-jerk *flag-waver*⟩ — see NATIONALIST

flail *vb* **1** to move or cause to move with a striking motion ⟨started to *flail* his arms wildly when he spied a bat in the house⟩ — see FLAP
2 to strike repeatedly with something long and thin or flexible ⟨gruesome evidence that the prisoner had been *flailed*⟩ — see WHIP 1

flair *n* a special and usually inborn ability ⟨a person with a *flair* for making friends quickly⟩ — see TALENT

[1]flake *n* a small flat piece separated from a whole ⟨sprinkle the cake with coconut *flakes*⟩ — see CHIP 1

[2]flake *n* a person of odd or whimsical habits ⟨the lady with all those cats is sweet, but kind of a *flake*⟩ — see ECCENTRIC

flaky *also* **flakey** *adj* having a texture that readily breaks into little pieces under pressure ⟨a tender but *flaky* crust on the pastry⟩ — see CRISP 1

flamboyance *n* excessive or unnecessary display ⟨the campy *flamboyance* of her costume almost guaranteed she'd win the masquerade pageant⟩ — see OSTENTATION

flamboyant *adj* **1** likely to attract attention ⟨has a gallery of *flamboyant* gestures that makes him easy to imitate⟩ — see NOTICEABLE
2 excessively showy ⟨Las Vegas showgirls wearing *flamboyant* headdresses⟩ — see GAUDY

flame *n* a person with whom one is in love ⟨decided to look up an old *flame* while she was in town⟩ — see SWEETHEART 1

flame *vb* **1** to be on fire especially brightly ⟨guests gathered around as the Yule log *flamed* brightly in the inn's great stone fireplace⟩ — see BURN 1
2 to develop suddenly and violently ⟨my anger *flamed* when the usher told my friend to shut up⟩ — see ERUPT 2
3 to shine with a bright harsh light ⟨the noonday sun *flamed* down on the desert travelers⟩ — see GLARE 1
4 to shoot forth bursts of light ⟨the actress's ruby necklace *flamed* dazzlingly under the bright lights⟩ — see FLASH 1

flameout *n* a loss of status ⟨before her sudden, self-inflicted *flameout*, she was one of the state's brightest political stars⟩ — see COMEDOWN

flame out *vb* to be unsuccessful ⟨even at the reception, some were predicting that the marriage would *flame out* before the fancy china ever got used⟩ — see FAIL 2

flaming *adj* **1** being on fire ⟨a fancy restaurant serving eye-catching *flaming* desserts⟩ — see ABLAZE 1
2 having or expressing great depth of feeling ⟨a *flaming* speech in support of basic human rights⟩ — see FERVENT 1

flammable *adj* capable of catching or being set on fire ⟨avoid wearing loose *flammable* clothing when using the blowtorch⟩ — see COMBUSTIBLE

flank *n* a place, space, or direction away from or beyond a central point or line ⟨painted the name of the ship along its *flank*⟩ — see SIDE 1

flank *vb* to be adjacent to ⟨the tackles *flank* the center on a football team's offensive line⟩ — see ADJOIN 1
flanking *adj* having a border in common ⟨*flanking* farms that share the same water source⟩ — see ADJACENT
flannel *n, British* **1** excessive praise ⟨the one cabinet minister who never resorts to *flannel*—he always tells it like it is⟩ — see FLATTERY
2 language, behavior, or ideas that are absurd and contrary to good sense ⟨the first serious book about the British royal family that wasn't just *flannel*⟩ — see NONSENSE 1
flap *n* a state of wildly excited activity or emotion ⟨there was a major *flap* when area residents found out that the President would be visiting⟩ — see FRENZY
flap *vb* to move or cause to move with a striking motion ⟨the stirring sight of a huge flock of geese *flapping* their wings⟩
synonyms beat, flail, flop, flutter, whip
related words bang, batter, buffet, knock, pound, smack, spank, thump; flick, flicker, flit; fan, oscillate, sway, swing; undulate, wave; palpitate, pulse, throb
flapdoodle *n* language, behavior, or ideas that are absurd and contrary to good sense ⟨a clear-eyed assessment of the problem minus the usual *flapdoodle*⟩ — see NONSENSE 1
flapjack *n* a flat cake made from thin batter and cooked on both sides (as on a griddle) ⟨for breakfast, there's bacon and *flapjacks* with syrup⟩ — see PANCAKE
flare *n* **1** a sudden and usually temporary growth of activity ⟨a *flare* in antacid sales around the holidays⟩ — see OUTBREAK 1
2 a sudden intense expression of strong feeling ⟨ended the quarrel with a stunning *flare* of swearwords⟩ — see OUTBURST 1
3 the steady giving off of the form of radiation that makes vision possible ⟨in the darkness the *flare* of a single match might be seen by enemy troops⟩ — see LIGHT 1
flare *vb* to shine with a bright harsh light ⟨floodlights *flaring* into the forbidding empty spaces surrounding the prison⟩ — see GLARE 1
flare (out) *vb* to arrange the parts of (something) over a wider area ⟨can we *flare out* the umbrella a little more so that more of the picnic table is sheltered⟩ — see OPEN 3
flare (up) *vb* **1** to become very angry ⟨naturally I *flared up* when he insulted my girlfriend⟩ — see BLOW UP
2 to develop suddenly and violently ⟨her cold sores *flared up* again when she got the flu⟩ — see ERUPT 2
flare–up *n* **1** a sudden and usually temporary growth of activity ⟨took medication to prevent a *flare-up* of her asthma⟩ — see OUTBREAK 1
2 a sudden intense expression of strong feeling ⟨there's no need for an angry *flare-up*, as we'll take care of the problem immediately⟩ — see OUTBURST 1
flaring *adj* excessively showy ⟨*flaring* neon signs advertising all manner of amusement for tourists at the beach town⟩ — see GAUDY
flash *adj* lasting only for a short time ⟨*flash* floods in the local area⟩ — see MOMENTARY
flash *n* **1** a sudden and usually temporary growth of activity ⟨a *flash* of last-minute trips to the video store before the onset of the big snowstorm⟩ — see OUTBREAK 1
2 a sudden intense expression of strong feeling ⟨a much-needed *flash* of humor during the otherwise boring lecture⟩ — see OUTBURST 1
3 a very small space of time ⟨the shower will be over in a *flash*⟩ — see INSTANT
4 something extraordinary or surprising ⟨the new goalie for our hockey team was apparently quite a *flash* in his hometown⟩ — see WONDER 1
5 excessive or unnecessary display ⟨the expensive clothes, the luxury cars, and other apparent signs of success are all *flash* that belie the fact that the family is up to its ears in debt⟩ — see OSTENTATION
flash *vb* **1** to shoot forth bursts of light ⟨the actress's diamond necklace *flashed* as she hurried on stage to accept the award⟩
synonyms coruscate, flame, glance, gleam, glimmer, glint, glisten, glister, glitter, luster (*or* lustre), scintillate, shimmer, spangle, sparkle, twinkle, wink, winkle
related words beam, radiate, shine; bedazzle, blind, daze, dazzle; blaze, burn, flare, glare, glow
2 to present so as to invite notice or attention ⟨*flashed* a wad of cash as he paid for his coffee⟩ — see SHOW 1
3 to shine with light at regular intervals ⟨the disco lights *flashed*, and the revelers danced⟩ — see BLINK 1
4 to make known openly or publicly ⟨*flashed* the news of the royal birth around the world⟩ — see ANNOUNCE
flash back (to) *vb* to bring back to mind ⟨the scent made me *flash back to* the days of my mother's home-cooked Sunday dinners⟩ — see REMEMBER
flashiness *n* excessive or unnecessary display ⟨his penchant for *flashiness*, as evidenced by his expensive, specially tailored suits⟩ — see OSTENTATION
flash point *n* **1** a potentially explosive place or situation ⟨that troubled region remains one of the world's most dangerous *flash points*⟩ — see TINDERBOX 1
2 a time or state of affairs requiring prompt or decisive action ⟨racial tensions in the city were at a *flash point*⟩ — see EMERGENCY
flashy *adj* **1** attractively eye-catching in style ⟨I bought the CD primarily for its *flashy* cover design⟩ — see JAZZY 1
2 excessively showy ⟨wore *flashy* rings on almost all the fingers of his left hand⟩ — see GAUDY
flat *adj* **1** being neither more nor less than a certain amount, number, or extent ⟨industrial growth has been a *flat* two percent for each of the last four quarters⟩ — see EVEN 1
2 causing weariness, restlessness, or lack of interest ⟨a *flat* portrayal of Benjamin Franklin in the new TV series⟩ — see BORING
3 having a surface without bends, breaks, or irregularities ⟨preferred riding her bike on a *flat* road⟩ — see LEVEL 1
4 having been established and usually not subject to change ⟨charged a *flat* rate for overseas calls⟩ — see FIXED 1
5 having no exceptions or restrictions ⟨a *flat* denial of the charges⟩ — see ABSOLUTE 2
6 lacking a surface luster or gloss ⟨used a *flat* paint for the condo's interior walls⟩ — see MATTE
7 lacking in qualities that make for spirit and character ⟨a dull, *flat* person who couldn't come up with an original idea to save her life⟩ — see WISHY-WASHY 1
8 lacking in taste or flavor ⟨this pasta dish tastes a little *flat*⟩ — see INSIPID 1
flat *adv* to a full extent or degree ⟨I am *flat* broke this week⟩ — see FULLY 1
flat *n, chiefly British* a room or set of rooms in a private house or a block used as a separate dwelling place ⟨had to take on a third roommate in order to afford the bigger *flat*⟩ — see APARTMENT 1
flatfoot *n, slang* a member of a force charged with law enforcement at the local level ⟨a comic strip about a square-jawed, trench-coated *flatfoot* who always caught the crooks in suitably dramatic fashion⟩ — see OFFICER 1
flatline *vb* to stop living ⟨the patient was fading fast, and doctors expected him to *flatline* before the night was over⟩ — see DIE 1

flat–out *adj* having no exceptions or restrictions ⟨regarded their son-in-law as a *flat-out* loser and let him know it⟩ — see ABSOLUTE 2

flatten *vb* **1** to make free from breaks, curves, or bumps ⟨*flattened* out the wrinkled paper before attempting to trace the pattern⟩ — see EVEN 1

2 to defeat by a large margin ⟨if you don't understand the rules, you're going to get *flattened* when you try to play⟩ — see WHIP 2

flatter *vb* **1** to praise too much ⟨the billionaire has an army of assistants who are eager to *flatter* him at every opportunity⟩

synonyms adulate, belaud, blarney, butter up, hero-worship, honey, massage, overpraise, puff, soft-soap, stroke

related words blandish, cajole, coax, sweet-talk, wheedle; fawn, kowtow, suck (up to), toady; idolize, worship; eulogize, extol (*also* extoll), laud, praise; applaud, commend, compliment; congratulate, felicitate; drool, gush, slaver, slobber; endear, ingratiate; court, romance, woo

near antonyms bad-mouth, belittle, decry, depreciate, disparage, put down

2 to think highly of (oneself) ⟨don't *flatter* yourself that no one has ever thought of that idea before⟩ — see PRIDE

flattery *n* excessive praise ⟨a talk show host who is known for charming her guests with disingenuous *flattery*⟩

synonyms adulation, blarney, butter, flannel [*British*], incense, overpraise, soft soap, sweet talk, taffy

related words allurements, blandishments, endearments; caresses, compliments, congratulations, felicitations, greetings, regards, respects; adoration, idolatry, worship; fawning, sycophancy, toadying; cajolement, cajolery, ingratiation, smarm; acclaim, applause, commendation, praise

near antonyms bad-mouthing, belittlement, depreciation, detraction, disparagement, put-down

flatulent *adj* marked by the use of impressive-sounding but mostly meaningless words and phrases ⟨on election night TV's self-important pundits let loose a fusillade of *flatulent* pontifications⟩ — see RHETORICAL 1

flatware *n* eating and serving utensils ⟨asked for inexpensive stemware and *flatware* for their wedding⟩ — see TABLEWARE 1

flaunt *vb* to present so as to invite notice or attention ⟨she playfully *flaunted* her engagement ring in all of her coworkers' faces⟩ — see SHOW 1

flaunting *n* an outward and often exaggerated indication of something abstract (as a feeling) for effect ⟨at first, her *flaunting* of her affection for her boyfriend was funny, but after a while it became tiresome⟩ — see SHOW 1

flavor *n* **1** a special quality or impression associated with something ⟨a birthday party whose Caribbean decorations gave it a tropical *flavor*⟩ — see AURA 1

2 something (as a spice or herb) that adds an agreeable or interesting taste to food ⟨a dish that incorporates most of the trademark *flavors* of southeast Asia⟩ — see SEASONING 1

3 the property of a substance that can be identified by the sense of taste ⟨loved the deep *flavor* of the native strawberries⟩ — see TASTE 1

4 a practice or interest that is very popular for a short time ⟨it seems that short skirts are the new *flavor* of the month⟩ — see FAD

flavor *vb* to make more pleasant to the taste by adding something intensely flavored ⟨try *flavoring* the beans with salt and oregano⟩ — see SEASON 1

flavorful *adj* very pleasing to the sense of taste ⟨makes a *flavorful* broth⟩ — see DELICIOUS 1

flavoring *n* something (as a spice or herb) that adds an agreeable or interesting taste to food ⟨soup made with beef *flavoring*⟩ — see SEASONING 1

flavorless *adj* lacking in taste or flavor ⟨a *flavorless* fruitcake that must have been given as a gift many times over⟩ — see INSIPID 1

flavorsome *adj* very pleasing to the sense of taste ⟨a variety of apple that is visually appealing but not very *flavorsome*⟩ — see DELICIOUS 1

flaw *n* something that spoils the appearance or completeness of a thing ⟨noted the *flaw* in the diamond before I bought it⟩ — see BLEMISH

flaw *vb* to reduce the soundness, effectiveness, or perfection of ⟨that crack has *flawed* the vase to the extent that its value in the antiques market is greatly reduced⟩ — see DAMAGE 1

flawed *adj* having a fault ⟨a *flawed* paint job that resulted in some peeling almost as soon as the paint had dried⟩ — see FAULTY

flawless *adj* being entirely without fault or flaw ⟨a *flawless* performance of the piano concerto⟩ — see PERFECT 1

flawlessly *adv* without any flaws or errors ⟨*flawlessly* recited the first 100 digits of pi⟩ — see PERFECTLY 1

flaxen *adj* of a pale yellow or yellowish brown color ⟨fields of *flaxen* wheat waving in the wind⟩ — see BLOND

flay *vb* **1** to criticize (someone) severely or angrily especially for personal failings ⟨her husband *flayed* her constantly for her incessant shopping⟩ — see SCOLD

2 to remove the natural covering of ⟨*flayed* their kill right there in the forest, taking both the meat and the skin home⟩ — see PEEL

fleck *n* **1** a small area that is different (as in color) from the main part ⟨flooring tile that is brown with *flecks* of white⟩ — see SPOT 1

2 a very small piece ⟨wiped a *fleck* of cookie off his jacket⟩ — see BIT 1

fleck *vb* to mark with small spots especially unevenly ⟨to achieve the desired effect, *fleck* the canvas with paint simply by flicking the brush close to the surface⟩ — see SPOT 1

flecked *adj* marked with spots ⟨that *flecked* blue writing paper is so attractive⟩ — see SPOTTED 1

fledgling *n* a person who is just starting out in a field of activity ⟨at hockey he's still a *fledgling* and needs to work on his basic skating skills⟩ — see BEGINNER

flee *vb* **1** to cease to be visible ⟨the fog *fled* with the arrival of the dawn⟩ — see DISAPPEAR

2 to get free from a dangerous or confining situation ⟨a murderer who *fled* on foot⟩ — see ESCAPE 1

3 to hasten away from something dangerous or frightening ⟨a toddler who *fled* when the ladybug he had been quietly watching suddenly began flying around the room⟩ — see RUN 2

fleece *n* the hairy covering of a mammal especially when fine, soft, and thick ⟨learning how to shear the *fleece* off a sheep⟩ — see FUR 1

fleece *vb* to rob by the use of trickery or threats ⟨swindlers who use the telephone to *fleece* senior citizens out of their savings⟩

synonyms beat, bilk, bleed, cheat, chisel, chouse, con, cozen, defraud, diddle, do, do in, euchre, fiddle, flimflam, gaff, gyp, hose [*slang*], hustle, mulct, nobble [*British slang*], pluck, ream, rip off, rook, screw, shake down, short, shortchange, skin, skunk, squeeze, stick, stiff, sting, sucker, swindle, thimblerig, victimize

related words extort, wrench, wrest, wring; clip, gouge, nick, overcharge, soak; exploit, milk; deceive, dupe, fool, gull, trick; rope (in); betray, bitch, double-cross; bamboozle, fast-talk

phrases sell a bill of goods to, take for a ride, take to the cleaners

fleecing *n* the exaction of a grossly excessive charge for goods or services ⟨the *fleecing* of the summer tourists seems to be a time-honored tradition on that resort island⟩ — see EXTORTION

fleecy *adj* covered with or as if with hair ⟨there were signs of the family's *fleecy* poodle all over the upholstery⟩ — see HAIRY 1

fleet *adj* moving, proceeding, or acting with great speed ⟨a jewel thief said to be light of heart and *fleet* of foot⟩ — see FAST 1

fleet *n* a group of vehicles traveling together or under one management ⟨a *fleet* of buses rolling down the highway⟩
synonyms armada, caravan, cavalcade, line, motorcade, train
related words argosy, convoy, flotilla, navy; column, cortege (*also* cortège), parade, procession

fleet–footed *adj* moving, proceeding, or acting with great speed ⟨the Roman god Mercury was the *fleet-footed* messenger of the gods⟩ — see FAST 1

fleeting *adj* lasting only for a short time ⟨had a *fleeting* desire to jump into the cool lake but kept on hiking⟩ — see MOMENTARY

fleetingness *n* the state or quality of lasting only for a short time ⟨nothing makes the *fleetingness* of summer more apparent than the arrival of Labor Day⟩ — see IMPERMANENCE

fleetly *adv* with great speed ⟨horses galloping *fleetly* across the plain⟩ — see FAST 1

fleetness *n* a high rate of movement or performance ⟨clipper ships were renowned for their *fleetness* on the high seas⟩ — see SPEED 1

flesh *n* animal and especially mammal tissue used as food ⟨eats no *flesh* of any kind, only fruits, grains, and vegetables⟩ — see MEAT 1

flesh (out) *vb* to express more fully and in greater detail ⟨a lengthy follow-up that *fleshes out* the original report on the military engagement⟩ — see EXPAND 1

fleshiness *n* **1** the condition of having an excess of body fat ⟨the *fleshiness* of the foreign tourists was in sharp contrast to the gauntness of the native Africans⟩ — see CORPULENCE
2 the quality or state of being full of juice ⟨loves the *fleshiness* of ripe watermelon⟩ — see SUCCULENCE

fleshly *adj* **1** having to do with life on earth especially as opposed to that in heaven ⟨a time of year when people shouldn't focus on *fleshly* concerns, but instead on spiritual matters⟩ — see EARTHLY
2 of or relating to the human body ⟨the *fleshly* eye sees the only finished painting, but the mind's eye sees the genius behind its creation⟩ — see PHYSICAL 1
3 pleasing to the physical senses ⟨returning campers looking forward to all the *fleshly* pleasures of home, including warm baths⟩ — see SENSUAL

fleshy *adj* **1** full of juice ⟨*fleshy* apples, the kind good for making cider⟩ — see JUICY 1
2 having an excess of body fat ⟨the *fleshy* man slowly heaved himself out of his chair⟩ — see FAT 1

flexible *adj* **1** capable of being readily changed ⟨fortunately, that working mother has a very *flexible* schedule for her office job⟩
synonyms adaptable, adjustable, alterable, changeable, elastic, fluid, malleable, modifiable, pliable, variable
related words changing, fluctuating, inconstant, labile, unstable, unsteady, varying, versatile
near antonyms constant, stable, steady, unchanging, uniform, unvarying
antonyms established, fixed, immutable, inelastic, inflexible, invariable, nonmalleable, ramrod, set, unadaptable, unalterable, unbudgeable, unchangeable
2 not bound by rigid standards ⟨parents with a *flexible* attitude when it comes to the children's bedtime⟩ — see EASYGOING 2
3 able to bend easily without breaking ⟨the tent was held up by crisscrossing *flexible* rods threaded through the top⟩ — see WILLOWY
4 able to revert to original size and shape after being stretched, squeezed, or twisted ⟨used a *flexible* plastic for the toy⟩ — see ELASTIC 1

flibbertigibbet *n* a silly flighty person ⟨forced to endure a long flight with a *flibbertigibbet* as a seat companion⟩
synonyms birdbrain, cuckoo, ditz, featherbrain, featherhead, nitwit, rattlebrain, scatterbrain, softhead
related words fool, goose, silly, simpleton
antonyms sobersides

flick *vb* to make an irregular series of quick, sudden movements ⟨the horse's tail *flicked* in restless irritation⟩ — see FLIT

flick *n* a story told by means of a series of continuously projected pictures and a sound track ⟨we could catch a *flick* together next weekend⟩ — see MOVIE 1

flicker *vb* to make an irregular series of quick, sudden movements ⟨a dragonfly *flickering* above the salt marsh⟩ — see FLIT

flicker *n* **1** a story told by means of a series of continuously projected pictures and a sound track ⟨as a child, the future director would spend hours sitting in the theater, totally entranced by the *flickers*⟩ — see MOVIE 1
2 a sudden and usually temporary growth of activity ⟨usually there's a *flicker* in car sales when the new models come out⟩ — see OUTBREAK 1
3 an almost imperceptible sign of something ⟨there was a *flicker* of recognition in her eye when I mentioned his name, but she denied knowing him⟩ — see HINT 2

flickery *adj* likely to change frequently, suddenly, or unexpectedly ⟨wise political leaders don't try to govern according to *flickery* public opinion⟩ — see FICKLE 1

flier *also* **flyer** *n* **1** a risky undertaking ⟨willing to take a *flier* on the bold, new venture⟩ — see GAMBLE
2 one who flies or is qualified to fly an aircraft or spacecraft ⟨a hot-air balloon *flier*⟩ — see PILOT

[1]**flight** *n* travel through the air by the use of wings ⟨for centuries people had been fascinated by the *flight* of birds⟩
synonyms flying
related words aviation; aeronautics; ballooning, gliding, hang gliding, paragliding, skydiving, soaring

[2]**flight** *n* the act or an instance of getting free from danger or confinement ⟨a work of 19th-century Romanticism depicting the ancient Israelites' *flight* from Egypt⟩ — see ESCAPE 1

flightiness *n* **1** a lack of seriousness often at an improper time ⟨a warning that her usual *flightiness* wouldn't be tolerated at the ceremony honoring war veterans⟩ — see FRIVOLITY 1
2 a state of nervousness marked by sudden jerky movements ⟨his *flightiness* before the bar exam was so bad that he nearly made himself sick⟩ — see JUMPINESS

flighty *adj* **1** easily excited by nature ⟨you have to be quiet while the deer are grazing, as they are *flighty* animals and will run if they hear you⟩ — see EXCITABLE
2 lacking in seriousness or maturity ⟨*flighty* and giggly preteens at their first dance⟩ — see GIDDY 1

flimflam *n* **1** a clever often underhanded means to achieve an end ⟨giving the new guy at work her cell phone number—"in case of an emergency"—was just a *flimflam* to pique his romantic interest⟩ — see TRICK 1
2 an instance of the use of dishonest methods to acquire something of value ⟨just the latest Internet *flimflam* to get e-mail recipients to reveal bank account numbers

and other personal information⟩ — see FRAUD 1

flimflam *vb* to rob by the use of trickery or threats ⟨everyone likes to think that they're too smart to be *flimflammed* by anyone⟩ — see FLEECE

flimsy *adj* **1** being of a material lacking in sturdiness or substance ⟨a *flimsy* scarf that was more for decoration than for warmth⟩
synonyms cobwebby, filmy, frothy, gauzy, gossamer, gossamery, insubstantial, sleazy, unsubstantial
related words dainty, delicate, fine; feeble, fragile, frail; diaphanous, sheer, transparent
near antonyms durable, knockabout, lasting, tough; coarse, heavy, rough, rude
antonyms sturdy, substantial
2 not likely to be true or to occur ⟨"The check is in the mail" is a pretty *flimsy* and tired excuse⟩ — see IMPROBABLE

flinch *vb* to draw back in fear, pain, or disgust ⟨there are some patients who *flinch* at the mere sight of a needle⟩
synonyms blench, cringe, quail, recoil, shrink, squinch, wince
related words blanch, pale, whiten; quake, quiver, shake, shudder, tremble; crouch; jerk, start, twitch; recede, retire, retreat, withdraw; falter, hesitate, reel, waver
near antonyms advance, approach, near; beard, challenge, confront, defy, face

fling *n* **1** a time or instance of carefree fun ⟨most families spend Labor Day weekend having one last summer *fling*⟩
synonyms binge, frisk, frolic, gambol, idyll (*also* idyl), lark, ploy, revel, rollick, romp, spree
related words caper, escapade, prank; bender, brannigan, bum, bust, carouse, souse, splore [*Scottish*], toot; antic, monkeyshine(s), shenanigan(s); field day; festivity, merriment, merrymaking; enjoyment, indulgence, pleasure, self-indulgence; amusement, diversion, entertainment, recreation
2 an effort to do or accomplish something ⟨take a *fling* at waterskiing and see how it goes⟩ — see ATTEMPT 1
3 a brief romantic relationship ⟨an ill-advised *fling* with a coworker⟩ — see AFFAIR 1

fling *vb* to send through the air especially with a quick forward motion of the arm ⟨*flinging* rocks into the pond just for the fun of it⟩ — see THROW 1

fling (off *or* away) *vb* to get rid of as useless or unwanted ⟨he *flung away* the used matchstick⟩ ⟨*flinging off* dirty clothes⟩ — see DISCARD

flinty *adj* **1** given to exacting standards of discipline and self-restraint ⟨a *flinty* warrior hardened by years of battle⟩ — see SEVERE 1
2 harsh and threatening in manner or appearance ⟨wrestling opponents intimidating each other with *flinty* stares⟩ — see GRIM 1

flip *adj* making light of something usually regarded as serious or sacred ⟨made some *flip* comment about the marriage between the old man and the considerably younger woman⟩ — see FLIPPANT

flip *vb* **1** to turn over pages in an idle or cursory manner ⟨*flip* through this home decorating book to see if there's anything we could use⟩ — see SKIM 1
2 to change the position of (an object) so that the opposite side or end is showing ⟨*flip* the coin over⟩ — see REVERSE 2

flip (out) *vb, slang* **1** to yield to mental or emotional stress ⟨a movie about a submarine captain who *flips out* when there's an emergency, leaving the crew to deal with it on their own⟩ — see CRACK 2
2 to become very angry ⟨when my wife saw that I had broken her great-grandmother's vase, she absolutely *flipped out*⟩ — see BLOW UP

flip–flop *n* a changing from one policy or point of view to virtually its exact opposite ⟨the governor's frequent *flip-flops* would indicate that she has no core beliefs⟩ — see ABOUT-FACE

flippancy *n* a lack of seriousness often at an improper time ⟨no one appreciates your *flippancy* during our religious services⟩ — see FRIVOLITY 1

flippant *adj* making light of something usually regarded as serious or sacred ⟨his *flippant* comment that the poor save on taxes offended many people⟩
synonyms cute, facetious, flip, pert, smart, smart-aleck, smart-alecky, smart-ass, smart-assed, smarty-pants, wise, wiseass
related words flighty, frivolous; cheeky, cocky, fresh, impertinent, impish, impudent, mischievous, playful, roguish, sassy, saucy, waggish; disrespectful, rude; breezy, casual, glib, inappropriate, thoughtless
near antonyms grave, serious, sober, solemn, somber (*or* sombre)
antonyms earnest, sincere

flirt *n* a person who playfully shows another amorous attention ⟨he's just a harmless *flirt*, so don't take him seriously⟩
synonyms flirter, wanton
related words coquet; coquette, jade, soubrette; vamp

flirt *vb* **1** to show a sexual attraction for someone just for fun ⟨the servers at that restaurant *flirt* with all the customers⟩
synonyms coquet (*or* coquette), dally, frivol, mess around, toy, trifle
related words vamp; court, mash, woo; josh, kid, put on, razz, rib, tease; fool, lead on, string along; manipulate, play (with)
2 to make an irregular series of quick, sudden movements ⟨lazily watched the butterflies *flirting* among the wildflowers⟩ — see FLIT

flirt (with) *vb* to act so as to make (something) more likely ⟨you're *flirting with* death by driving so recklessly⟩ — see COURT 1

flirtation *n* the attitude or behavior of one who insincerely courts the amorous attentions of others ⟨somehow got the bizarre notion that *flirtation* was appropriate during a job interview⟩ — see COQUETRY

flirtatiousness *n* the attitude or behavior of one who insincerely courts the amorous attentions of others ⟨his wink might have been *flirtatiousness*, or just innocent playfulness⟩ — see COQUETRY

flirter *n* a person who playfully shows another amorous attention ⟨she's a compulsive *flirter*, and you're just her prey for the moment⟩ — see FLIRT

flit *vb* to make an irregular series of quick, sudden movements ⟨bargain hunters at the flea market *flitted* from table to table like hummingbirds in a garden⟩
synonyms dance, dart, flick, flicker, flirt, flitter, flutter, zip
related words dash, fly, sail, shoot, speed, sprint, zing, zoom; scamper, scud, scurry, scuttle, skip, skitter; meander, ramble, roam, wander
near antonyms float, hang, hover

flitter *vb* to make an irregular series of quick, sudden movements ⟨the birds *flittered* back and forth between the backyard feeder and the safety of the trees⟩ — see FLIT

float *n* a structure used by boats and ships for taking on or landing cargo and passengers ⟨the crew put the cargo on the *float* before heading back down the river⟩ — see DOCK

float *vb* **1** to rest or move along the surface of a liquid or in the air ⟨a canoe *floating* down the river⟩ ⟨particles of dust *floating* in the air⟩
synonyms drift, glide, hang, hover, poise, ride, sail, swim, waft

related words bob, dangle, suspend; buoy; balloon, raft
near antonyms dive, lunge, plunge; dip, immerse, submerge, submerse
antonyms settle, sink

2 to move about from place to place aimlessly ⟨lost touch with a childhood friend who spent much of his adult life *floating* from place to place⟩ — see WANDER 1

floating *adj* riding upon the surface of a body of liquid ⟨the wreckage remained *floating* for hours⟩ — see AFLOAT

flock *n* **1** a great number of persons or creatures massed together ⟨a *flock* of obstreperous reporters at the press conference⟩ — see CROWD 1

2 a group of domestic animals assembled or herded together ⟨a *flock* of sheep crossing the road⟩ — see HERD 1

flock *vb* to move upon or fill (something) in great numbers ⟨vacationers *flocked* to the towns along the shore in order to escape the August heat⟩ — see CROWD 2

flog *vb* **1** to strike repeatedly with something long and thin or flexible ⟨a graphic depiction of a sailor being *flogged* by the captain for disobeying orders⟩ — see WHIP 1

2 to strike repeatedly ⟨was fined heavily for *flogging* a horse⟩ — see BEAT 1

3 *British* to move heavily or clumsily ⟨for most of the night, searchers *flogged* through the marsh, crying out for the lost child⟩ — see LUMBER 1

4 *British* to proceed or act clumsily or ineffectually ⟨ignoring the groans and catcalls that his speech was provoking, the backbencher *flogged* away⟩ — see FLOUNDER 1

flogger *n* a long thin or flexible tool for striking ⟨a horseman who believes that *floggers* should be used sparingly⟩ — see WHIP

flood *n* a great flow of water or of something that overwhelms ⟨a *flood* nearly wiped out the town⟩ ⟨a *flood* of messages on my computer⟩
synonyms alluvion, bath, cataclysm, cataract, deluge, flood tide, inundation, Niagara, overflow, spate, torrent
related words current, river, stream, tide; cloudburst, discharge, flush, gush, outflow, outpouring; flux, inflow, influx; engulfment, washout; avalanche, blizzard; cascade, waterfall; excess, glut, overabundance, overage, overkill, overmuch, oversupply, superabundance, superfluity, surfeit, surplus
near antonyms dribble, drip, trickle
antonyms drought (*also* drouth)

flood *vb* to cover with a flood ⟨the lowlands were completely *flooded*⟩ ⟨angry calls *flooded* the radio station⟩
synonyms deluge, drown, engulf, gulf, inundate, overflow, overwhelm, submerge, submerse, swamp
related words avalanche, smother; overcome, overrun; flow, flush, gush, pour, sluice, spout, spurt, stream; douse (*also* dowse), drench, soak, wet
near antonyms dehydrate, dry, parch
antonyms drain

flood tide *n* a great flow of water or of something that overwhelms ⟨the *flood tide* of bad manners that seems to be inundating contemporary society⟩ — see FLOOD

floor *n* the surface upon which a body of water lies ⟨discovered a new species of crab living on the ocean *floor*⟩ — see BOTTOM 2

floor *vb* **1** to cause an unpleasant surprise for ⟨that you would say such a rude thing to my mother *floors* me⟩ — see SHOCK 1

2 to make a strong impression on (someone) with something unexpected ⟨as you might expect, winning the lottery simply *floored* us⟩ — see SURPRISE 1

3 to strike (someone) so forcefully as to cause a fall ⟨the boxer *floored* his opponent in the second round, winning the fight by a knockout⟩ — see FELL 1

4 to subject to incapacitating emotional or mental stress ⟨the pushing and shoving at the clearance sale absolutely *floored* me, and I had to leave⟩ — see OVERWHELM 1

floozy *or* **floozie** *n* a boldly flirtatious or sexually promiscuous woman ⟨a *floozy* who was a familiar figure at barrooms around town⟩
synonyms bimbo [*slang*], chippie (*also* chippy), doxy (*also* doxie), fancy woman, hoochie [*slang*], hussy, Jezebel, minx, quean, slut, tramp, trollop, wench, whore
related words siren, temptress, vamp; grisette, harlot, prostitute, trull
phrases woman of easy virtue

flop *n* something that has failed ⟨the movie is such a *flop* that theaters showing it are the loneliest places in town⟩ — see FAILURE 3

flop *vb* **1** to throw or set down clumsily or casually ⟨they lazily *flopped* themselves onto the couch to watch the game⟩ ⟨*flopped* the bag of groceries onto the counter⟩
synonyms flump, plank, plop, plump, plunk (*or* plonk)
related words fling, heave, sling, toss; ensconce, install, plant, settle

2 to be unsuccessful ⟨the attempt to run the ball into the end zone *flopped*, and our team lost by five points⟩ — see FAIL 2

3 to move or cause to move with a striking motion ⟨a fish *flopping* around on the dock⟩ — see FLAP

floppy *adj* not stiff in structure ⟨my basset hound is always tripping over her long, *floppy* ears⟩ — see LIMP 1

flora *n* green leaves or plants ⟨a fascination with the lush *flora* of the South⟩ — see GREENERY

floral *adj* of or relating to flowers ⟨bedroom wallpaper with a somewhat overpowering *floral* pattern⟩
synonyms flowered, flowery
related words florid; abloom, blossomy, floriferous

florescence *n* a state or time of great activity, thriving, or achievement ⟨the *florescence* of Mayan art in the seventh century A.D.⟩ — see BLOOM 1

florid *adj* **1** elaborately and often excessively decorated ⟨a *florid*, gilded mirror that took up most of the wall⟩ — see ORNATE 1

2 full of fine words and fancy expressions ⟨gave a *florid* speech in honor of the queen's visit⟩ — see FLOWERY 1

3 having a healthy reddish skin tone ⟨a jolly fat man with a *florid* complexion⟩ — see RUDDY

florilegium *n* a collection of writings ⟨a *florilegium* of ancient alchemical writings⟩ — see ANTHOLOGY

floruit *n* a state or time of great activity, thriving, or achievement ⟨the *floruit* of Greek art and literature in the fifth century B.C.⟩ — see BLOOM 1

floss *n* a soft airy substance or covering ⟨used cotton *floss* to simulate Santa's beard⟩ — see [1]FUZZ

flotsam *n* the portion or bits of something left over or behind after it has been destroyed ⟨the dispirited family picked through the *flotsam* of their possessions after the hurricane, looking for anything that could be salvaged⟩ — see REMAINS 1

flounce *n* a strip of fabric gathered or pleated on one edge and used as trimming ⟨a prom dress with small *flounces* along the hem⟩ — see RUFFLE 1

flounder *vb* **1** to proceed or act clumsily or ineffectually ⟨unprepared choristers who *floundered* helplessly through the musical number⟩
synonyms blunder, bumble, flog [*British*], limp, lumber, plod, struggle, stumble, trudge
related words jog, shamble, shuffle; wallow, welter; falter, lurch, reel, stagger, sway, teeter, totter; fumble, muddle
near antonyms coast, fly, glide, kilt, sail, zip, zoom

2 to move heavily or clumsily ⟨the car *floundered* through the heavy wet snow, constantly getting stuck⟩ — see LUMBER 1

flourish *vb* **1** to grow vigorously ⟨that plant *flourishes* in cool, wet weather⟩ — see THRIVE 1
2 to reach a desired level of accomplishment ⟨the arts program *flourished* once it received adequate funding⟩ — see SUCCEED 2

flourishing *adj* **1** having attained a desired end or state of good fortune ⟨a *flourishing* actor in the early years of the talkies⟩ — see SUCCESSFUL 1
2 marked by much life, movement, or activity ⟨a *flourishing* market in sports memorabilia⟩ — see ALIVE 2
3 marked by vigorous growth and well-being especially economically ⟨a *flourishing* community that has become a major beneficiary of the high-tech boom⟩ — see PROSPEROUS 1

floury *adj* consisting of very small particles ⟨shelves of old books covered with *floury* dust⟩ — see FINE 1

flout *vb* to ignore in a disrespectful manner ⟨an able-bodied motorist openly *flouting* the law and parking in a space reserved for the disabled⟩ — see SCORN 2

flow *vb* **1** to move in a stream ⟨water was *flowing* over the dam at a tremendous rate⟩
synonyms pour, roll, run, stream
related words arise, disembogue, effuse, emanate, issue, spring; course, race, rush; fountain, gush, spout, spurt; deluge, engulf, flood, inundate, overflow, overrun, swamp; cascade, dribble, drip, gutter, riffle, ripple, sheet, trickle; flush, wash out
near antonyms clot, coagulate, congeal, gel, harden, set
antonyms back up
2 to move or proceed smoothly and readily ⟨as everyone relaxed, the conversation really started to *flow*⟩
synonyms bowl, breeze, brush, coast, cruise, drift, glide, roll, sail, skim, slide, slip, stream, sweep, whisk
related words fly, race, rush, speed
near antonyms limp, lumber, plod, stumble, trudge; shamble, shuffle; stamp, stomp, stump, tramp; labor, toil
antonyms flounder, struggle

flower *vb* to produce flowers ⟨the plant will keep *flowering* if you water it and regularly cut off the dead blossoms⟩ — see BLOOM

flower *n* **1** the usually showy plant part that produces seeds ⟨*flowers* are always a thoughtful gift⟩
synonyms bloom, blossom
related words bud, floret, floweret (*also* flowerette); bouquet, nosegay, posy; arrangement, boutonniere, corsage, garland, lei, spray, wreath
2 a state or time of great activity, thriving, or achievement ⟨the skiing season is usually in full *flower* by Christmas⟩ — see BLOOM 1
3 individuals carefully selected as being the best of a class ⟨without exception, the *flower* of this year's graduating class will be going to prestigious colleges⟩ — see ELITE 1

flowered *adj* of or relating to flowers ⟨a pretty tablecloth with a *flowered* border⟩ — see FLORAL

flowery *adj* **1** full of fine words and fancy expressions ⟨the *flowery* verses that always appear on valentines⟩
synonyms aureate, florid, grandiloquent, highfalutin (*also* hifalutin), high-flown, high-sounding, magnific, ornate, purple, rhetorical (*also* rhetoric)
related words affected, bloated, fancy-pants, grandiose, inflated, pompous, pretentious, stilted; excessive, flattering, fulsome; boastful, bombastic; elevated, eloquent, lofty; bookish, inkhorn, learned
near antonyms prosaic, unpoetic; bald, direct, lean, matter-of-fact, plain, plainspoken, simple, spare, stark, straightforward, unadorned; natural, unaffected, unpretentious
2 of or relating to flowers ⟨Mother's Day cards typically have a *flowery* design on the cover⟩ — see FLORAL

flowing *adj* capable of moving like a liquid ⟨a *flowing* silk scarf⟩ — see FLUID 1

flub *n* an unintentional departure from truth or accuracy ⟨when she was told her information was wrong, she apologized for the *flub* and immediately corrected it⟩ — see ERROR 1

flub *vb* **1** to make or do (something) in a clumsy or unskillful way ⟨added too much flour and *flubbed* the gravy⟩ — see BOTCH
2 to make a mistake ⟨at some point in your training you're going to *flub*, so don't let it rattle you⟩ — see ERR 1

fluctuate *vb* to pass from one form, state, or level to another ⟨temperatures will *fluctuate* between the low and high 50s today⟩ — see CHANGE 2

fluctuating *adj* **1** likely to change frequently, suddenly, or unexpectedly ⟨a *fluctuating* stock market makes it hard for investors to know what to do⟩ — see FICKLE 1
2 not staying constant ⟨our speed was constantly *fluctuating*, so the figure of 50 miles per hour is just an average⟩ — see UNEVEN 2

fluctuation *n* the frequent and usually sudden passing from one condition to another ⟨political instability that resulted in wild *fluctuations* in the overseas stock markets⟩ — see FLUX 1

fluent *adj* **1** able to express oneself clearly and well ⟨a very *fluent* speaker who always communicates his points well⟩ — see ARTICULATE
2 capable of moving like a liquid ⟨heated the wax until it was *fluent*, then poured it into the mold⟩ — see FLUID 1
3 involving minimal difficulty or effort ⟨a *fluent* performance of one of the oldest magic tricks in the book⟩ — see EASY 1

fluently *adv* without difficulty ⟨*fluently* negotiates even the most challenging slalom courses⟩ — see EASILY 1

fluff *n* **1** a soft airy substance or covering ⟨self-consciously picked the *fluff* off his sweater as he answered the officer's questions⟩ — see [1]FUZZ
2 an unintentional departure from truth or accuracy ⟨the flustered newscaster's *fluffs* included a mispronunciation of the town's name⟩ — see ERROR 1

fluff *vb* **1** to make a mistake ⟨unnerved by her earlier missteps, the skater *fluffed* on the final jump as well⟩ — see ERR 1
2 to make or do (something) in a clumsy or unskillful way ⟨I completely *fluffed* the introduction by calling the boss's wife by the wrong name⟩ — see BOTCH

fluffy *adj* resembling air in lightness ⟨big *fluffy* pillows⟩ — see AIRY 1

fluid *adj* **1** capable of moving like a liquid ⟨warm the jam until it is *fluid*, then spread it over the cake⟩
synonyms flowing, fluent, liquid
related words circumfluent, circumfluous; diluted, thin, watery, weak; semiliquid, semisolid
near antonyms clotted, coagulated, gelatinous, gelled, jelled, jellied, thick; gluey, glutinous, gooey, gummy, viscous
antonyms hard, nonliquid, solid
2 capable of being readily changed ⟨the script is still *fluid* at this point, so be prepared for last-minute rewrites⟩ — see FLEXIBLE 1
3 involving minimal difficulty or effort ⟨the dance looked smooth and *fluid*, though backstage we could see the dancer gasping for breath and sweating from the effort⟩ — see EASY 1
4 likely to change frequently, suddenly, or unexpectedly ⟨his arrival plans are *fluid*, so expect him anytime⟩ — see FICKLE 1

fluke *n* an unexpected benefit or advantage resulting from the uncertain course of events ⟨the discovery of oil on their property was just an amazing *fluke*⟩

synonyms break, strike
related words accident, chance, circumstance, hap, happenchance, happenstance, hazard, luck
phrases stroke of luck

fluky *also* **flukey** *adj* **1** coming or happening by good luck especially unexpectedly ⟨a *fluky* coincidence that kept me safely at home when the blizzard hit⟩ — see FORTUNATE 1
2 happening by chance ⟨the *fluky* selection of consecutive numbers on consecutive days of the lottery⟩ — see ACCIDENTAL 1

flume *n* **1** a narrow opening between hillsides or mountains that can be used for passage ⟨hiked through the *flume* and into the meadow beyond it⟩ — see CANYON
2 an open man-made passageway for water ⟨built a *flume* next to the road for runoff⟩ — see CHANNEL 1

flummox *vb* to throw into a state of mental uncertainty ⟨an actor who's easily *flummoxed* by any changes in the script⟩ — see CONFUSE 1

flump *vb* to throw or set down clumsily or casually ⟨for now, just *flump* the rug on the floor—we'll unroll it later⟩ — see FLOP 1

flunk *vb* to be unsuccessful ⟨the movie *flunks*, both as entertainment and as a dramatization of a historical incident⟩ — see FAIL 2

flunky *also* **flunkey** *or* **flunkie** *n* **1** a person hired to perform household or personal services ⟨since I'm just the *flunky* who files his papers, I've no idea where he is⟩ — see SERVANT
2 a person who flatters another in order to get ahead ⟨a rock star who saw through the phonies and the *flunkies*⟩ — see SYCOPHANT

fluorescence *n* the steady giving off of the form of radiation that makes vision possible ⟨studied the *fluorescence* of certain elements⟩ — see LIGHT 1

flurry *n* **1** a sudden and usually temporary growth of activity ⟨a *flurry* of activity on the floor of the stock market as soon as the news spread⟩ — see OUTBREAK 1
2 a sudden brief rush of wind ⟨a *flurry* that scattered the fallen leaves⟩ — see GUST 1
3 a rapid or overwhelming outpouring of many things at once ⟨a patient with a mysterious illness being subjected to a *flurry* of tests⟩ — see BARRAGE

flurry *vb* to trouble the mind of; to make uneasy ⟨*flurried* by visions of falls and broken bones, the parents wouldn't even allow the child to ride a bike⟩ — see DISTURB 1

flush *adj* **1** having a healthy reddish skin tone ⟨was *flushed* after getting out of the hot bath⟩ — see RUDDY
2 having a surface without bends, breaks, or irregularities ⟨the *flush* paneling on the door gives it a very plain and dull look⟩ — see LEVEL 1
3 having active strength of body or mind ⟨a *flush*, healthy man of 65⟩ — see VIGOROUS 1
4 having goods, property, or money in abundance ⟨she's very *flush* now that she has her inheritance⟩ — see RICH 1
5 possessing or covered with great numbers or amounts of something specified ⟨a field *flush* with flowers⟩ — see RIFE
6 having a border in common ⟨the front yard's floral border is *flush* with the sidewalk⟩ — see ADJACENT

flush *n* **1** a rosy appearance (of the cheeks) ⟨looked for a *flush* on her cheeks as evidence of a fever⟩ — see BLOOM 2
2 a state or time of great activity, thriving, or achievement ⟨was in the *flush* of his youth⟩ — see BLOOM 1
3 a sudden intense expression of strong feeling ⟨a *flush* of patriotic pride⟩ — see OUTBURST 1

flush *vb* **1** to pour liquid over or through in order to cleanse ⟨use this cleaner to *flush* the drain in the sink⟩
synonyms irrigate, rinse, sluice, wash, wash out
related words deluge, engulf, flood, inundate, swamp; flow, gush, rush, stream; douche, hose; drench, saturate, soak; douse (*also* dowse), slosh, splash
2 to develop a rosy facial color (as from excitement or embarrassment) ⟨he *flushed* deeply upon hearing the compliment⟩ — see BLUSH

fluster *n* **1** a state of nervous or irritated concern ⟨all the yelling on the bus put the driver in a *fluster*⟩ — see FRET
2 the emotional state of being made self-consciously uncomfortable ⟨there was a palpable *fluster* in the audience when I asked my awkward question⟩ — see EMBARRASSMENT 1

fluster *vb* to throw into a state of self-conscious distress ⟨was *flustered* when her parents dragged out her baby pictures for her new boyfriend⟩ — see EMBARRASS 1

flustering *adj* causing embarrassment ⟨a *flustering* situation that left us all silent⟩ — see AWKWARD 3

flutter *n* **1** a sudden and usually temporary growth of activity ⟨the site saw a *flutter* of construction last month, but nothing's happening now⟩ — see OUTBREAK 1
2 *chiefly British* a risky undertaking ⟨most people regard the lottery as a harmless *flutter*⟩ — see GAMBLE

flutter *vb* **1** to make an irregular series of quick, sudden movements ⟨a lonely butterfly *fluttering* across the lawn⟩ — see FLIT
2 to move or cause to move with a striking motion ⟨*fluttered* my eyelashes as I struck up a conversation with the new guy at work⟩ — see FLAP

fluttery *adj* easily excited by nature ⟨a *fluttery* bus driver who was obviously in the wrong line of work⟩ — see EXCITABLE

flux *n* **1** the frequent and usually sudden passing from one condition to another ⟨the English language is always in a state of *flux*⟩
synonyms change, fluctuation, inconstancy, oscillation
related words metamorphosis, mutation, transformation, transmogrification, transmutation; vacillation, wavering
2 a flowing or coming in ⟨January typically brings a great *flux* of returns to department stores⟩ — see INFLUX
3 abnormally frequent intestinal evacuations with more or less fluid stools ⟨Civil War doctors noted frequent cases of *flux* in the camps⟩ — see DIARRHEA

flux *vb* to go from a solid to a liquid state ⟨a solid will *flux* more quickly under pressure⟩ — see LIQUEFY

fly *vb* **1** to move through the air with or as if with outstretched wings ⟨the Wright brothers realized mankind's age-old wish to *fly*⟩
synonyms aviate, glide, plane, soar, wing
related words drift, float, hang, hover, waft; coast, cruise, sail, sweep; dart, flit, flutter; catapult, helicopter, jet, orbit, rocket; dive, stoop
2 to get free from a dangerous or confining situation ⟨you must *fly* to safety immediately⟩ — see ESCAPE 1
3 to proceed or move quickly ⟨*flew* down the concourse to catch his flight⟩ — see HURRY 2
4 to hasten away from something dangerous or frightening ⟨no one in the movies ever thinks to *fly* from the ax murderer and immediately call the police⟩ — see RUN 2
5 to cease to be visible ⟨the morning mist had *flown*, and a sparkling sea lay before us⟩ — see DISAPPEAR
6 to withstand scrutiny and gain acceptance or approval ⟨the familiar "Because I said so!" is a reason that won't *fly* with most teenagers⟩ — see WASH 2

flyer *also* **flier** *n* a short printed publication with no cover or with a paper cover ⟨came out of the store and saw a *flyer* for a restaurant on my windshield⟩ — see PAMPHLET

flying *adj* **1** acting or done with excessive or careless speed ⟨a *flying* attempt at finishing the work⟩ — see HASTY 1
2 moving, proceeding, or acting with great speed ⟨that car was *flying* as it careened down the streets⟩ — see FAST 1

flying *n* travel through the air by the use of wings ⟨had never had the slightest fear of *flying*⟩ — see [2]FLIGHT

flyspeck *n* a very small piece ⟨surreptitiously removed a *flyspeck* of dirt from the china⟩ — see BIT 1

foam *n* a light mass of fine bubbles formed in or on a liquid ⟨a steaming cup of hot cocoa with a sprinkling of marshmallows drifting through the *foam*⟩
synonyms froth, head, lather, spume, suds, surf
related words mousse; mist, spindrift, spray; scum

foam *vb* to be excited or emotionally stirred up with anger ⟨the old man *foamed* and raged when they told him he would have to give up the farm⟩ — see BOIL 1

foaming *adj* feeling or showing anger ⟨was so upset that he was really *foaming*⟩ — see ANGRY

foamy *adj* covered with, consisting of, or resembling foam ⟨*foamy* milk shakes⟩
synonyms frothy, lathery, sudsy
related words bubbly, effervescent, fizzy, sparkling; soapy

fob off *vb* to offer (something fake, useless, or inferior) as genuine, useful, or valuable ⟨people who try to *fob off* to charities broken-down furniture that is fit only for the junkyard⟩ — see FOIST

focus *n* **1** a thing or place that is of greatest importance to an activity or interest ⟨in the 19th century Paris was the *focus* of the art world⟩ — see CENTER 1
2 a guiding or motivating purpose or principle ⟨a wildlife conservation organization that seems to have lost its *focus*⟩ — see COMPASS 1

focus *vb* to fix (as one's attention) steadily toward a central objective ⟨try to *focus* your attention on the task at hand⟩ — see CONCENTRATE 2

focused *also* **focussed** *adj* **1** having the mind fixed on something ⟨was *focused* on the football game and didn't hear me knock⟩ — see ATTENTIVE 1
2 not divided or scattered among several areas of interest or concern ⟨a *focused* effort to provide shelter for the homeless during the winter⟩ — see WHOLE 1

foe *n* **1** one that is hostile toward another ⟨are you friend or *foe*?⟩ — see ENEMY
2 one that takes a position opposite another in a competition or conflict ⟨this Saturday our team will go up against our longtime *foes* in a game that will determine the champion of the conference⟩ — see OPPONENT 1

fog *n* **1** a state of mental confusion ⟨didn't get enough sleep and now I'm in a *fog*⟩ — see HAZE 2
2 an atmospheric condition in which suspended particles in the air rob it of its transparency ⟨the *fog* lifted once the sun was out⟩ — see HAZE 1
3 a state of mental uncertainty ⟨I wandered around in a *fog* after the shocking news⟩ — see CONFUSION 1

fog *vb* **1** to make (something) unclear to the understanding ⟨extraneous matters that only serve to *fog* the central issue⟩ — see CONFUSE 2
2 to make dark, dim, or indistinct ⟨time will *fog* memories⟩ — see CLOUD 1

fogged *adj* suffering from mental confusion ⟨a discussion that did little more than leave the participants hopelessly *fogged*⟩ — see DIZZY 2

foggy *adj* **1** filled with or dimmed by fine particles (as of dust or water) in suspension ⟨it's pretty *foggy* outside, so be careful driving home⟩ — see HAZY 1
2 not seen or understood clearly ⟨could only see a *foggy* outline of the intruder in the dark⟩ — see FAINT 1

fogy *also* **fogey** *n* a person with old-fashioned ideas ⟨old *fogies* who said that rap music would never last⟩
synonyms antediluvian, Colonel Blimp, dodo, fossil, fud, fuddy-duddy, mossback, reactionary, stick-in-the-mud, stuffed shirt
related words conservative, rightist, Tory; mandarin, old hand, old-timer, veteran; old maid
near antonyms liberal, progressive, radical
antonyms hipster, modern, trendy

foible *n* a defect in character ⟨could tolerate my uncle's *foibles* because we loved him dearly⟩ — see FAULT 1

foil *vb* to prevent from achieving a goal ⟨in popular fiction the hero will always *foil* the villain's plans⟩ — see FRUSTRATE 1

foist *vb* to offer (something fake, useless, or inferior) as genuine, useful, or valuable ⟨shopkeepers who *foist* shoddy souvenirs on unsuspecting tourists⟩
synonyms fob off, palm, palm off, pass off, wish
related words entail, force, impose, inflict; counterfeit, fake, forge; distort, falsify, misrepresent

fold *n* a group of people sharing a common interest and relating together socially ⟨ready to welcome their old Liberal friend back into the *fold*⟩ — see GANG 2

fold *vb* **1** to lay one part over or against another part of ⟨*fold* the blanket so that it will fit inside the trunk⟩
synonyms double
related words overlap, overlay, overlie; collapse, telescope; close, shut; plait, pleat
antonyms extend, open, spread, unfold, unroll
2 to be unsuccessful ⟨the business *folded* after just two months⟩ — see FAIL 2

folder *n* a short printed publication with no cover or with a paper cover ⟨a *folder* offering tips for heating one's home efficiently⟩ — see PAMPHLET

folderol *also* **falderal** *n* language, behavior, or ideas that are absurd and contrary to good sense ⟨wanted a dignified, simple wedding and not the *folderol* that the wedding planner was trying to foist on them⟩ — see NONSENSE 1

foliage *n* green leaves or plants ⟨decided the office needed more *foliage* and bought a few plants⟩ — see GREENERY

folk *n* **1 folks** *pl* a group of persons who come from the same ancestor ⟨her *folks* have farmed that land for five generations⟩ — see FAMILY 1
2 one of the segments of society into which people are grouped ⟨the working-class *folk* with no airs or pretentions⟩ — see CLASS 1
3 folks *pl* human beings in general ⟨c'mon, *folks*, let's get to work⟩ — see PEOPLE 1

folklore *n* the body of customs, beliefs, stories, and sayings associated with a people, thing, or place ⟨the Scottish Highlands are rich in *folklore*⟩
synonyms legend, legendry, lore, myth, mythology, mythos, tradition
related words folklife; information, knowledge, wisdom; anecdote, fable, folktale, old wives' tale, tale, yarn

folksy *adj* having or showing an unpretentious informality ⟨a *folksy* manner that gives television viewers the feeling that they're visiting with a friend for an hour⟩ — see CRACKER-BARREL

follow *vb* **1** to come after in time ⟨a wrap-up always *follows* the Super Bowl broadcast⟩
synonyms postdate, succeed, supervene
related words displace, replace, supersede, supplant; ensue
antonyms antedate, precede, predate
2 to go after or on the track of ⟨let's *follow* the boys to their hiding place⟩
synonyms bird-dog, chase, course, dog, hound, pursue, run, shadow, tag, tail, trace, track, trail
related words accompany, chaperone (*or* chaperon), escort; hunt, search (for), seek; eye, observe, watch
phrases run after

near antonyms head
antonyms guide, lead, pilot
3 to act according to the commands of ⟨*follow* me, and you'll do OK⟩ — see OBEY
4 to make one's way through, across, or over ⟨*followed* the path into the garden⟩ — see TRAVERSE
5 to take notice of and be guided by ⟨don't *follow* his advice⟩ — see HEED 1
6 to keep one's eyes on ⟨stood on the platform and *followed* the departing train until it disappeared from sight⟩ — see WATCH 1

follower *n* **1** one who follows the opinions or teachings of another ⟨the *followers* of Gandhi have spread his philosophy of nonviolence all over the world⟩
synonyms acolyte, adherent, convert, disciple, epigone, liege man, partisan (*also* partizan), pupil, votarist, votary
related words apostle, missionary, proselytizer, soldier; faithful, loyalist; advocate, backer, champion, supporter; protégé, scholar, student; ideologist, ideologue (*also* idealogue), sectarian; admirer, cultist, devotee, enthusiast, fan, idolater (*or* idolator), worshipper (*or* worshiper), zealot; apparatchik, camp follower, flunky (*also* flunkey *or* flunkie), hanger-on, henchman, lackey, lickspittle, minion, myrmidon, satellite, stooge, sycophant, toady, yes-man
near antonyms apostate, defector, renegade, traitor, turncoat
antonyms coryphaeus, leader
2 a person who adopts the appearance or behavior of another especially in an obvious way ⟨Brando's Method acting inspired a whole generation of mumbling *followers*⟩ — see COPYCAT

followership *n* a group of people showing intense devotion to a cause, person, or work (as a film) ⟨the televangelist has a substantial *followership* in the rural South⟩ — see CULT 1

following *adj* being the one that comes immediately after another ⟨the *following* morning, I found the cat was gone⟩ — see NEXT

following *n* **1** a body of employees or servants who accompany and wait on a person ⟨a prince with a large *following* to do practically everything for him⟩ — see CORTEGE 1
2 a group of people showing intense devotion to a cause, person, or work (as a film) ⟨that rock star attracts quite a *following*⟩ — see CULT 1
3 the act of going after or in the tracks of another ⟨took part in the *following* of the coyote⟩ — see PURSUIT 1

following *prep* subsequent to in time or order ⟨*following* the concert, there will be refreshments in the lobby⟩ — see AFTER

follow through (with) *vb* to carry through (as a process) to completion ⟨you said you would put all of the files in order, but you didn't *follow through with* it⟩ — see PERFORM 1

folly *n* **1** a foolish act or idea ⟨the American purchase of Alaska was originally considered a grand *folly*⟩
synonyms absurdity, asininity, bêtise, fatuity, foolery, foppery, idiocy, imbecility, inanity, insanity, lunacy, stupidity
related words absurdness, craziness, foolishness, inaneness, madness, senselessness, witlessness; buffoonery, monkeyshine(s), shenanigan(s), tomfoolery; drivel, humbug, nonsense, twaddle; blunder, bungle, flub, goof, howler
near antonyms discretion, forethought, prudence, sagacity, wisdom; brainstorm, inspiration
2 lack of good sense or judgment ⟨in all my *folly*, I didn't think about how my actions would hurt my father⟩ — see FOOLISHNESS 1
3 language, behavior, or ideas that are absurd and contrary to good sense ⟨enough of this *folly* about moving to the Australian outback⟩ — see NONSENSE 1

foment *vb* to bring (something volatile or intense) into being ⟨John Adams's wife, Abigail, told him that if women were not remembered by the new American government, they would "*foment* a Rebellion and will not hold ourselves bound by any Laws in which we have no voice or Representation"⟩ — see INCITE 1

fomenter *n* a person who stirs up public feelings especially of discontent ⟨sent the *fomenters* of the rebellion to prison⟩ — see AGITATOR

fond *adj* **1** having a liking or affection ⟨even lots of city people are *fond* of country music⟩
synonyms affected, attached, inclined, partial
related words crazy (about *or* over), enamored, enraptured, gone (on), infatuated, mad (about), nuts (about); desirous, eager, enthusiastic, excited, gung ho, keen
phrases big on
near antonyms apathetic, cool, indifferent, uninterested; contemptuous, disdainful, scornful; antagonistic, antipathetic, hostile; alienated, disaffected, disenchanted, estranged
antonyms allergic, averse, disinclined
2 feeling or showing love ⟨gave me a *fond* embrace upon parting⟩ — see LOVING 1
3 granted special treatment or attention ⟨my *fondest* wish is to see my children marry well⟩ — see DARLING 1

fondle *vb* to touch or handle in a tender or loving manner ⟨a cat who enjoys being *fondled* by his loving owners⟩
synonyms caress, gentle, love, pat, pet, stroke
related words bill, canoodle, cuddle, neck, nestle, nose, nuzzle, snuggle, spoon; feel up, paw; cradle, embrace, enfold, hug; bounce, dandle; knead, massage; baby, coddle, indulge, mollycoddle, pamper, spoil

fondness *n* **1** a feeling of strong or constant regard for and dedication to someone ⟨my *fondness* for you will never fail⟩ — see LOVE 1
2 positive regard for something ⟨I have a *fondness* for expensive chocolate⟩ — see LIKING

font *n* a point or place at which something is invented or provided ⟨a domestic diva who is a seemingly endless *font* of new ideas⟩ — see SOURCE 1

food *n* **1** substances intended to be eaten ⟨a simple, little restaurant with excellent *food*⟩
synonyms bread, chow, chuck [*chiefly West*], comestibles, eatables, eats, edibles, fare, foodstuffs, grub, meat, provender, provisions, table, tucker [*chiefly Australian*], viands, victuals, vittles
related words commissary, rations, supplies; aliment, nutriment; diet, nourishment, nurture, sustenance; mess, pap; ensilage, feed, fodder, forage, silage, slop, swill; feast, meal, refreshments, regale, repast, spread; board; dish, plate, platter, serving; finger food, natural food
near antonyms bane, poison, toxin, venom
2 something that maintains or stimulates the intellect ⟨a fascinating, highly readable book that will serve as brain *food* for those long winter evenings⟩ — see SUSTENANCE

foodstuffs *n pl* substances intended to be eaten ⟨stocked up on candles and *foodstuffs* before the hurricane⟩ — see FOOD 1

foofaraw *n* a state of noisy, confused activity ⟨the *foofaraw* that accompanies any big wedding⟩ — see COMMOTION

fool *n* **1** a person who lacks good sense or judgment ⟨only a *fool* would attempt to climb that mountain unprepared⟩
synonyms berk [*British*], booby, charlie (*also* charley) [*British*], cuckoo, ding-a-ling, dingbat, ding-dong, dip-

stick, doofus [*slang*], featherhead, git [*British*], goose, half-wit, jackass, lunatic, mooncalf, nincompoop, ninny, ninnyhammer, nit [*chiefly British*], nitwit, nut, nutcase, simp, simpleton, turkey, yo-yo
related words daredevil; madman, madwoman; airhead, birdbrain, blockhead, cretin, dodo, dolt, donkey, dope, dork [*slang*], dumbbell, dummy, dunce, fathead, gander, goon, half-wit, idiot, ignoramus, imbecile, know-nothing, knucklehead, moron, numskull (*or* numbskull), pinhead, schlub (*also* shlub) [*slang*], schlump [*slang*], schnook [*slang*], stock; featherbrain, scatterbrain; butt, dupe, laughingstock, mockery, monkey; chump, loser, schlemiel (*also* shlemiel); character, codger, crackbrain, crackpot, crank, kook, oddball, screwball, weirdo
near antonyms sage, thinker; brain, genius
2 a person formerly kept in a royal or noble household to amuse with jests and pranks ⟨a king's *fool* could get away with saying things that others in the palace couldn't⟩
synonyms jester, motley
related words buffoon, clown, comedian, comedienne, comic, cutup, droll, harlequin, joker, jokester, madcap, merry-andrew, vice, wag, zany; mime, mummer
3 a person with a strong and habitual liking for something ⟨I'm a *fool* for ice cream—virtually any flavor⟩ — see FAN
4 a person judged to be legally or medically insane ⟨he got out of serving in the army by successfully pretending to be a *fool*⟩ — see LUNATIC 1

fool *adj* showing or marked by a lack of good sense or judgment ⟨he's always got some *fool* plan or other⟩ — see FOOLISH 1

fool *vb* **1** to cause to believe what is untrue ⟨I *fooled* him into thinking that we were driving to the store, not to his surprise birthday party⟩ — see DECEIVE
2 to make jokes ⟨an edgy comedian *fooling* with an appreciative college audience⟩ — see JOKE 1

fool (with) *vb* to handle thoughtlessly, ignorantly, or mischievously ⟨not a good idea to *fool with* power tools before you've read the manual⟩ — see TAMPER (WITH)

fool around *vb* **1** to engage in attention-getting playful or boisterous behavior ⟨quit *fooling around* on the jungle gym, or you'll get hurt⟩ — see CUT UP
2 to spend time in aimless activity ⟨spent the rainy afternoon listening to music and *fooling around*⟩ — see FIDDLE (AROUND)

foolery *n* **1** a foolish act or idea ⟨it's *foolery* to expect me to let you shoplift that DVD⟩ — see FOLLY 1
2 wildly playful or mischievous behavior ⟨let the kids have a little *foolery* once in a while⟩ — see HORSEPLAY

foolhardy *adj* **1** foolishly adventurous or bold ⟨hikers who were *foolhardy* enough to remain on the summit during a thunderstorm⟩
synonyms audacious, brash, daredevil, madcap, overbold, overconfident, reckless, temerarious
related words adventuresome, adventurous, bold, daring, venturesome, venturous; brave, courageous, dauntless, doughty, fearless, gallant, greathearted, gutsy, hardy, heroic (*also* heroical), intrepid, lionhearted, manful, stalwart, stout, stouthearted, undauntable, undaunted, valiant, valorous; hotheaded; impetuous, imprudent, impulsive, incautious, rash; brainless, foolish, harebrained, scatterbrained; careless, heedless, thoughtless; hasty, headlong, precipitate
near antonyms unadventurous, unambitious; fainthearted, fearful, mousy (*or* mousey), scary, shy, skittish, timid, timorous; calm, cool, levelheaded, sensible; alert, intelligent, quick-witted, sharp; chicken, chickenhearted, cowardly, craven, dastardly, lily-livered, pusillanimous, recreant, spineless, unheroic, yellow
antonyms careful, cautious, circumspect, guarded, heedful, prudent, safe, wary
2 having or showing a lack of concern for the consequences of one's actions ⟨it's *foolhardy* to go hiking during late fall without warm clothes⟩ — see RECKLESS 1

fooling *adj* marked by or expressive of mild or good-natured teasing ⟨ribbed him with *fooling* comments about the weight that he had put on⟩ — see QUIZZICAL

foolish *adj* **1** showing or marked by a lack of good sense or judgment ⟨*foolish* people who thought that the world would end in the year 2000⟩ ⟨a *foolish* scheme that was supposed to make us all rich⟩
synonyms absurd, asinine, balmy, brainless, bubbleheaded, cockeyed, crackpot, crazy, cuckoo, daffy, daft, dippy, dotty, fatuous, featherheaded, fool, half-baked, harebrained, half-witted, inept, insane, jerky, kooky (*also* kookie), loony (*also* looney), lunatic, lunkheaded, mad, nonsensical, nutty, preposterous, sappy, screwball, senseless, silly, simpleminded, stupid, tomfool, unwise, wacky (*also* whacky), weak-minded, witless, zany
related words airheaded, birdbrained, boobish, braindead, chowderheaded, chuckleheaded, clueless, dense, dim, dim-witted, doltish, dopey (*also* dopy), dorky [*slang*], dull, dumb, dunderheaded, empty-headed, fatuous, feebleminded, gormless [*chiefly British*], idiotic (*also* idiotical), imbecile (*or* imbecilic), knuckleheaded, lamebrain (*or* lamebrained), mindless, moronic, oafish, obtuse, opaque, pinheaded, simple, slow, slow-witted, soft, softheaded, thoughtless, thick, thickheaded, unintelligent, vacuous, witless; fallacious, illogical, invalid, irrational, nonrational, surd, unreasonable, unreasoning, unsound, weak; farcical, laughable, ludicrous, ridiculous; notional; buffoonish, clownish; ill-advised, unconsidered, unreasoned
phrases out to lunch
near antonyms brainy, bright, clever, intelligent, smart; logical, rational, reasonable, valid; well-advised
antonyms judicious, prudent, sagacious, sage, sane, sapient, sensible, sound, wise
2 conceived or made without regard for reason or reality ⟨*foolish* attempts to construct a perpetual motion machine⟩ — see FANTASTIC 1
3 lacking importance ⟨the current regulations are cluttered with *foolish* details that are unnecessarily burdensome⟩ — see UNIMPORTANT

foolishness *n* **1** lack of good sense or judgment ⟨the *foolishness* of going off to search for the fountain of youth⟩
synonyms absurdity, asininity, balminess, brainlessness, craziness, daftness, dippiness, dottiness, fatuity, fatuousness, folly, imbecility, inanity, insanity, lunacy, madness, nonsensicalness, nuttiness, preposterousness, senselessness, silliness, simplicity, unwisdom, wackiness, witlessness, zaniness
related words denseness, dim-wittedness, doltishness, dopiness, dullness (*also* dulness), dumbness, feeblemindedness, gormlessness [*chiefly British*], idiocy, mindlessness, oafishness, obtuseness, simplemindedness, simpleness, slowness, stupidity, stupidness, vacuity; fallacy, irrationality, unreasonableness; kookiness, weirdness; laughableness, ludicrousness, ridiculousness
near antonyms logicality, logicalness, rationality, rationalness, reasonability, reasonableness, validity; discernment, insight, perception, percipience
antonyms prudence, sagaciousness, sagacity, sageness, sanity, sapience, sensibleness, soundness, wisdom
2 language, behavior, or ideas that are absurd and contrary to good sense ⟨couldn't listen to another second of their *foolishness*, so I told them to be quiet⟩ — see NONSENSE 1
3 the quality or state of lacking intelligence or quick-

ness of mind ⟨you didn't fail the test because of any innate *foolishness* but because of a lack of preparation⟩ — see STUPIDITY 1

foot *n* the lowest part, place, or point ⟨the *foot* of the pedestal⟩ — see BOTTOM 3

foot *vb* to give what is owed for ⟨I'll *foot* the bill for dinner⟩ — see PAY 2

foot (it) *vb* **1** to go on foot ⟨after the car broke down, we had to *foot it* to the movie⟩ — see WALK 1
2 to perform a series of usually rhythmic bodily movements to music ⟨got out onto the dance floor and *footed it* like crazy⟩ — see DANCE 1

foot (up) *vb* to combine (numbers) into a single sum ⟨please *foot up* your traveling expenses from this past month⟩ — see ADD 2

foothold *n* a place from which an advance (as for military operations) is made ⟨don't let the opposing team push us back down the field and gain a *foothold*⟩ — see BASE 2

footing *n* **1** an immaterial thing upon which something else rests ⟨your donations help provide the charity with a firm financial *footing* for its work⟩ — see BASE 1
2 position with regard to conditions and circumstances ⟨the village's two churches are on a friendly *footing*⟩ — see SITUATION 1
3 the placement of someone or something in relation to others in a vertical arrangement ⟨you'll have to work hard to get a better *footing* in the company⟩ — see RANK 1

footle *vb* to spend time doing nothing ⟨spent the morning *footling* about while others were working⟩ — see IDLE

footling *adj* so small or unimportant as to warrant little or no attention ⟨the assistant's job was to shield the president from such *footling* problems⟩ — see NEGLIGIBLE 1

footloose *adj* **1** not bound, confined, or detained by force ⟨after having been chained for so long, the suddenly *footloose* dog ran helter-skelter about the yard⟩ — see FREE 3
2 not held back by rules, duties, or worries ⟨wished I could be as carefree as that *footloose* toddler⟩ — see FREEWHEELING

footmark *n* the mark or impression made by a foot ⟨the police found *footmarks* in the dirt beneath the window⟩ — see FOOTPRINT

footpath *n* a rough course or way formed by or as if by repeated footsteps ⟨found the *footpath* leading down into the valley⟩ — see TRAIL 1

footprint *n* the mark or impression made by a foot ⟨mysterious *footprints* along the beach⟩
synonyms footmark, footstep, step, trace, vestige
related words hoofprint; pug, spoor, track; tread

foot soldier *n* a person who does very hard or dull work ⟨he's been a *foot soldier* for several environmental organizations over the years⟩ — see SLAVE 2

footstep *n* the mark or impression made by a foot ⟨saw muddy *footsteps* on the just-cleaned stairs⟩ — see FOOTPRINT

foozle *vb* to make or do (something) in a clumsy or unskillful way ⟨*foozled* the attempt to move the couch into the apartment and tore the fabric on the arms⟩ — see BOTCH

fop *n* a man extremely interested in his clothing and personal appearance ⟨he's such a *fop* that he drives nearly 50 miles just to get his hair cut by Monsieur Louis⟩ — see DANDY 1

foppery *n* a foolish act or idea ⟨regards the platform shoe as one of the unfortunate *fopperies* of the 1970s that should remain buried in fashion's scrap heap⟩ — see FOLLY 1

for *conj* for the reason that ⟨the bill should be listed as paid, *for* I mailed it in on time⟩ — see SINCE

forage *vb* to feed on grass or herbs ⟨cows *foraging* in the pasture⟩ — see [1]GRAZE

forage (for) *vb* to go in search of ⟨went *foraging for* change for the parking meter⟩ — see SEEK 1

foray *n* a sudden attack on and entrance into hostile territory ⟨made a nighttime *foray* into the enemy camp and took their command post⟩ — see RAID 1

foray (into) *vb* to enter for conquest or plunder ⟨Vikings *foraying into* the village⟩ — see INVADE

forbear *vb* to resist the temptation of ⟨she's old enough to make her own decisions, so we must *forbear* criticizing her taste in clothes⟩
synonyms abjure, abstain (from), forgo (*also* forego), keep (from), refrain (from), withhold (from)
related words avoid, eschew, shun; check, constrain, curb, inhibit; deny, refuse, reject, repudiate; buck, combat, fight
near antonyms acquiesce (to), capitulate, concede (to), knuckle under (to)
antonyms bow (to), give in (to), submit (to), succumb (to), surrender (to), yield (to)

forbearance *n* **1** the capacity to endure what is difficult or disagreeable without complaining ⟨we thank you for your *forbearance* while we attend to the technical difficulties interrupting the TV program⟩ — see PATIENCE
2 kind, gentle, or compassionate treatment especially towards someone who is undeserving of it ⟨the judge showed *forbearance*, and gave the teenaged first offender a suspended sentence⟩ — see MERCY 1

forbearing *adj* accepting pains or hardships calmly or without complaint ⟨she was inspired by the *forbearing* patients of the intensive care unit⟩ — see PATIENT 1

forbid *vb* to order not to do or use or to be done or used ⟨smoking is *forbidden* throughout the building⟩ ⟨we *forbid* you to see him⟩
synonyms ban, bar, enjoin, interdict, outlaw, prohibit, proscribe
related words deter, discourage, dissuade; clamp down (on), crack down (on), crush, put down, quash, quell, repress, silence, snuff (out), squash, squelch, subdue, suppress; halt, preclude, prevent, stop; embargo, exclude, rule out, shut out; debar, deprive, disallow, reject, repudiate, veto; bridle, check, curb, inhibit, rein (in), restrain; block, hinder, impede, obstruct
near antonyms approve, endorse (*also* indorse), sanction; authorize, license (*also* licence), warrant; abet, advance, cultivate, encourage, forward, further, nourish, nurture, promote, support; bid, command, order; abide, bear, brook, countenance, endure, tolerate
antonyms allow, let, permit, suffer

forbidden *adj* that may not be permitted ⟨trespassing is *forbidden*⟩ — see IMPERMISSIBLE

forbidding *adj* **1** causing fear ⟨a dark, *forbidding* house, that is reputed to be haunted⟩ — see FEARFUL 1
2 harsh and threatening in manner or appearance ⟨told us in a *forbidding* voice to stop calling him by that name⟩ — see GRIM 1

forbidding *n* the act of ordering that something not be done or used ⟨the landlord's *forbidding* of loud music after 10:00 p.m.⟩ — see PROHIBITION 1

force *n* **1** a body of persons at work or available for work ⟨the entire *force* of the shipyard will be needed to get this government order done on time⟩
synonyms help, labor force, manpower, personnel, pool, staff, workforce
related words labor, proletariat, rank and file; band, company, crew, gang, outfit, party, squad, team; employee (*also* employe), helper, hireling, worker; blood; support
2 the use of power to impose one's will on another ⟨a

cruel tyrant who disbanded the parliament and ruled by *force*⟩

synonyms arm-twisting, coercion, compulsion, constraint, duress, pressure

related words browbeating, bulldozing, bullying; fear, intimidation, menace, sword, terror, terrorism, threat, violence; squeeze, squeeze play; might, muscle, potency, puissance, strength; hardheadedness, self-will, willfulness; strain, stress

near antonyms agreement, approval, consent, permission; convincing, persuasion, reason, suasion

3 the ability to exert effort for the accomplishment of a task ⟨got through the college board exams by sheer *force* of will⟩ — see POWER 2

4 the capacity to persuade ⟨surely you were influenced by the *force* of his arguments?⟩ — see COGENCY 1

5 the quality of an utterance that provokes interest and produces an effect ⟨felt the full *force* of her denunciation of war as a morally acceptable option⟩ — see [1]PUNCH 1

6 the use of brute strength to cause harm to a person or property ⟨threatened to resort to *force* if he wouldn't listen to reason⟩ — see VIOLENCE 1

7 a body of officers of the law ⟨the new police chief will most likely be someone from the *force*⟩ — see POLICE 2

8 the number of individuals or amount of something available at any given time ⟨the great debate during the Cold War was whether the nation's missile *force* was adequate⟩ — see SUPPLY

force *vb* **1** to cause (a person) to give in to pressure ⟨the government *forced* the natives to sell their land⟩ ⟨hunger *forced* the refugees to steal⟩

synonyms blackjack, coerce, compel, constrain, dragoon, drive, impel, impress, make, muscle, obligate, oblige, press, pressure, sandbag

related words browbeat, bulldoze, bully, cow, hector, intimidate; blackmail, high-pressure, menace, shame, terrorize, threaten; drag; badger, harass, hound

phrases twist one's arm

near antonyms allow, let, permit; argue, convince, induce, move, persuade, prevail (on *or* upon), satisfy, talk (into), win (over)

2 to engage in sexual activity and especially intercourse with a person unwilling or unable to give consent ⟨young men who should realize that there is no excuse for *forcing* a woman⟩ — see RAPE

forced *adj* **1** forcing one's compliance or participation by or as if by law ⟨*forced* attendance at political indoctrination sessions⟩ — see MANDATORY

2 lacking in natural or spontaneous quality ⟨wasn't too excited about their wedding plans and so gave them a *forced* smile⟩ — see ARTIFICIAL 1

3 not made or done willingly or by choice ⟨participation in the program was *forced*⟩ — see INVOLUNTARY 1

force field *n* the power of irresistible attraction ⟨an entrepreneur whose *force field* is intense enough to make you share in his dreams⟩ — see CHARM 2

forceful *adj* **1** having the power to persuade ⟨made a very *forceful* argument against going to war⟩ — see COGENT

2 marked by or uttered with forcefulness ⟨he kept asking me out until I gave him a very *forceful* and blunt "no"⟩ — see EMPHATIC 1

3 not showing weakness or uncertainty ⟨took a *forceful* stand on the highly controversial issue⟩ — see FIRM 1

4 having power over the minds or behavior of others ⟨a *forceful* speaker whose words moved the audience to tears⟩ — see INFLUENTIAL 1

forcefully *adv* in a vigorous and forceful manner ⟨shut the door a little too *forcefully* and broke the glass⟩ — see HARD 3

forcefulness *n* **1** the capacity to persuade ⟨the *forcefulness* of his argument is indisputable⟩ — see COGENCY 1

2 the quality of an utterance that provokes interest and produces an effect ⟨delivered the punch line with appropriate *forcefulness*⟩ — see [1]PUNCH 1

3 the quality or state of being forceful (as in expression) ⟨her clenched teeth only added to the *forcefulness* of her words⟩ — see VEHEMENCE 1

forcibly *adv* in a vigorous and forceful manner ⟨after getting in the ref's face once too often, he was *forcibly* ejected from the game⟩ — see HARD 3

ford *n* a place where a body of water (as a sea or river) is shallow ⟨didn't attempt getting the horses across the stream until we had reached the *ford*⟩ — see SHOAL

fore *adj* being at or in the forward part or surface of something ⟨cats have five *fore* toes but only four hind toes⟩ — see FRONT

fore *also* **'fore** *prep, chiefly dialect* **1** earlier than ⟨*fore* the baby's arrival, the young couple had been able to cope with their problems⟩ — see BEFORE 1

2 preceding in space ⟨*fore* the stranger there swarmed a gaggle of curious street urchins⟩ — see BEFORE 2

forearm *vb* to prepare (oneself) mentally or emotionally ⟨*forearmed* themselves for the championship game with the help of a sports psychologist⟩ — see FORTIFY 1

forebear *also* **forbear** *n* a person who is several generations earlier in an individual's line of descent ⟨his *forebears* came to America on the *Mayflower*⟩ — see ANCESTOR 1

forebearer *n* a person who is several generations earlier in an individual's line of descent ⟨villagers who still practice many of the customs of their *forebearers*⟩ — see ANCESTOR 1

forebode *also* **forbode** *vb* to show signs of a favorable or successful outcome ⟨that police car parked outside the house doesn't *forebode* well⟩ — see BODE

foreboding *adj* being or showing a sign of evil or calamity to come ⟨*foreboding* war clouds began to gather⟩ — see OMINOUS

foreboding *n* **1** a feeling that something bad will happen ⟨I have this strange *foreboding* that your ski vacation will not turn out well, so be extra careful⟩ — see PREMONITION

2 something believed to be a sign or warning of a future event ⟨used to think that if he saw a blackbird fly over his left shoulder it was a *foreboding* of harm⟩ — see OMEN

3 suspicion or fear of future harm or misfortune ⟨a pessimist who is always overcome by a sense of *foreboding* before flying on an airplane⟩ — see APPREHENSION 1

forecast *n* a declaration that something will happen in the future ⟨want to catch the weather *forecast* so I'll know what kind of clothes to pack for the trip tomorrow⟩ — see PREDICTION

forecast *vb* to tell of or describe beforehand ⟨the station's meteorologist *forecasts* sun for the next five days⟩ — see FORETELL

forecaster *n* one who predicts future events or developments ⟨a financial *forecaster* who is widely followed by small investors⟩ — see PROPHET 1

forecasting *n* a declaration that something will happen in the future ⟨the construction company's *forecasting* of a September 1 completion date for the new school was wildly optimistic⟩ — see PREDICTION

foredoom *vb* to determine the fate of in advance ⟨since the dawn of the ages he was *foredoomed* to become king one day⟩ — see DESTINE

forefather *n* a person who is several generations earlier in an individual's line of descent ⟨our *forefathers* bought this farm, and our family has worked it for three generations⟩ — see ANCESTOR 1

forefeel *vb* to realize or know about beforehand ⟨did any of the passengers embarking on the *Titanic*'s maiden voyage *forefeel* their impending doom?⟩ — see FORESEE

forefront *n* the leading or most important part of a movement ⟨a politician who was in the *forefront* of women's rights⟩
synonyms cutting edge, front line, leading edge, van, vanguard
related words spearhead

forego *vb* to go or come before in time ⟨if the sparse crowds are any indication of the public's interest in the presidential candidate, then his reputation obviously *foregoes* him⟩ — see PRECEDE

foregoer *n* **1** one that announces or indicates the later arrival of another ⟨a nearly November snowfall that appears to be a disconcerting *foregoer* of the harsh winter facing us⟩ — see FORERUNNER 1
2 something belonging to an earlier time from which something else was later developed ⟨not many people still have manual typewriters, the *foregoers* to word processors⟩ — see ANCESTOR 2

foregoing *adj* **1** going before another in time or order ⟨your *foregoing* statement contradicts your latest one⟩ — see PREVIOUS
2 mentioned previously ⟨for the *foregoing* reasons, I believe that we have no choice but to deliver a guilty verdict⟩ — see AFORESAID

foreground *vb* to indicate the importance of by centering attention on ⟨repeatedly *foregrounded* his experience in international affairs in the course of his campaign for the presidency⟩ — see EMPHASIZE 1

forehanded *adj* having or showing awareness of and preparation for the future ⟨was *forehanded* enough to stock up on batteries for winter storms⟩ — see FORESIGHTED

forehead *n* a forward part or surface ⟨the *forehead* of the ancient temple features a frieze of dramatically posed figures⟩ — see FRONT 1

foreign *adj* **1** being, relating to, or characteristic of a country other than one's own ⟨more Americans should take an interest in *foreign* languages⟩
synonyms alien, nonnative
related words imported, introduced, naturalized, transplanted; external, international, multiculti, multicultural, multilateral, multinational; foreign-born, nonindigenous; distant, far-off, overseas, remote; bizarre, exotic, outlandish, strange
near antonyms endemic, local; aboriginal, indigenous
antonyms domestic, native
2 not being a vital part of or belonging to something ⟨pediatricians often have to remove peas or other *foreign* bodies from inside the ears of curious toddlers⟩ — see EXTRINSIC
3 relating to or involving two or more nations ⟨*foreign* trade has always been vital to the region's economic health⟩ — see INTERNATIONAL

foreigner *n* a person who is not native to or known to a community ⟨I can tell by your accent you're a *foreigner* in these parts⟩ — see STRANGER

foreknow *vb* to realize or know about beforehand ⟨what couple can possibly *foreknow* the trials and tribulations that marriage will bring?⟩ — see FORESEE

foreknowledge *n* the special ability to see or know about events before they actually occur ⟨a suspenseful story about a man who has a frightening *foreknowledge* of disasters⟩ — see FORESIGHT 1

foreland *n* an area of land that juts out into a body of water ⟨from the plane I could see a *foreland* shaped like a large toe⟩ — see [2]CAPE

foreman *n* the person (as an employer or supervisor) who tells people and especially workers what to do ⟨asked the shift *foreman* if he could take a break⟩ — see BOSS

foremost *adj* **1** coming before all others in importance ⟨Albert Einstein is regarded by many as the *foremost* figure of the 20th century⟩
synonyms arch, big, capital, cardinal, central, chief, dominant, first, grand, great, greatest, highest, key, leading, main, master, number one (*also* No. 1), numero uno, overbearing, overmastering, overriding, paramount, predominant, preeminent, premier, primal, primary, principal, prior, sovereign (*also* sovran), supreme
related words distinguished, eminent, illustrious, noble, notable, noteworthy, outstanding, prestigious, signal, star, stellar, superior; high-level, senior, top; important, influential, major, mighty, momentous, significant; incomparable, matchless, unequaled (*or* unequalled), unparalleled, unsurpassed; celebrated, famed, famous, renowned
near antonyms inconsequential, inconsiderable, insignificant, minor, negligible, slight, trifling, trivial, unimportant; collateral, inferior, secondary, subordinate, subsidiary
antonyms last, least
2 highest in rank or authority ⟨wanted to speak to the *foremost* supervisor in our department⟩ — see HEAD
3 coming before all others in time or order ⟨when the *foremost* person in line tripped, everyone had to stop⟩ — see FIRST 1

forename *n* a name that is placed before one's family name ⟨a long string of *forenames* was given to the latest addition to the royal family⟩
synonyms Christian name, first name, given name, prename
related words appellation, denomination, designation; cognomen, denotation, epithet, handle, nickname, sobriquet (*also* soubriquet), title; alias, nom de plume, pen name, pseudonym; baptismal name

forenamed *adj* mentioned previously ⟨the *forenamed* members of the commission have been asked to serve a second term⟩ — see AFORESAID

forenoon *n* the time from sunrise until noon ⟨enjoy the relatively cool *forenoon*, for the afternoon promises to be a scorcher⟩ — see MORNING 1

foreordain *vb* to determine the fate of in advance ⟨we are such good friends, it's almost like we were *foreordained* to meet⟩ — see DESTINE

forepart *n* a forward part or surface ⟨moved to the *forepart* of the machine to check the mechanism⟩ — see FRONT 1

forerun *vb* to give a slight indication of beforehand ⟨the moral decay that traditionally *foreruns* the decline of a mighty empire⟩ — see FORESHADOW

forerunner *n* **1** one that announces or indicates the later arrival of another ⟨the return of the swallows is traditionally regarded as a *forerunner* of spring⟩
synonyms angel, foregoer, harbinger, herald, outrider, precursor
related words foreboder, foreshadower, foretaste, forewarning; advertiser, announcer, blazoner, crier, proclaimer; courier, messenger, runner; augury, auspice, boding, foreboding, foreshadowing, omen, portent, prefiguring, presage; mark, sign, symptom; bellwether
2 something belonging to an earlier time from which something else was later developed ⟨enjoyed the demonstration of the simple hand loom that was the *forerunner* of today's computer-controlled looms⟩ — see ANCESTOR 2

foresee *vb* to realize or know about beforehand ⟨a freak accident that no one could possibly have *foreseen*⟩
synonyms anticipate, divine, forefeel, foreknow, prevision
related words augur, forecast, foretell, predict,

presage, prognosticate, prophesy; envisage, envision, foreshadow, prefigure, visualize; alert, caution, foretoken, forewarn; preview; descry, discern, perceive; apprehend, dread, fear

foreseeing *adj* having or showing awareness of and preparation for the future ⟨some years ago the senator wrote a *foreseeing* essay on the threat of global terrorism⟩ — see FORESIGHTED

foreseer *n* one who predicts future events or developments ⟨in Greek mythology Cassandra was a *foreseer* who always accurately predicted misfortune but was never believed⟩ — see PROPHET 1

foreshadow *vb* to give a slight indication of beforehand ⟨a series of small tremors that *foreshadowed* the massive earthquake the next day⟩
synonyms adumbrate, forerun, harbinger, herald, prefigure
related words anticipate, foreknow, foresee; forecast, foretell, predict, prognosticate, prophesy; forewarn; augur, bode, forebode (*also* forbode), portend, presage, promise; allude, connote, hint, imply, insinuate, intimate, suggest

foreshadowing *n* something believed to be a sign or warning of a future event ⟨the hero's strange encounter with a grave digger is often seen as a *foreshadowing* of his own death⟩ — see OMEN

foresight *n* **1** the special ability to see or know about events before they actually occur ⟨a mysterious woman who claims to have the gift of *foresight*⟩
synonyms foreknowledge, prescience
related words foreboding, premonition, prenotion, presage, presentiment; clairvoyance, extrasensory perception, sixth sense; omniscience; divination
2 concern or preparation for the future ⟨had the *foresight* to realize the global importance of the Internet⟩
synonyms farsightedness, foresightedness, forethought, prescience, providence, vision
related words precaution, premeditation; discernment, discretion, insight, perception, perceptiveness, prudence, sagaciousness, sagacity, sageness, sapience, wisdom
near antonyms hindsight
antonyms improvidence, myopia, shortsightedness

foresighted *adj* having or showing awareness of and preparation for the future ⟨the *foresighted* conservationists who worked to create the national park system⟩
synonyms farseeing, farsighted, forehanded, foreseeing, forethoughtful, forward, forward-looking, prescient, proactive, provident, visionary
related words careful, cautious, heedful; discerning, insightful, perceptive, percipient, prudent, sagacious, sage, sapient, wise
near antonyms careless, heedless, incautious
antonyms half-baked, half-cocked, improvident, myopic, shortsighted

foresightedness *n* concern or preparation for the future ⟨thanks to your *foresightedness*, we have enough ice and food to last through the blackout⟩ — see FORESIGHT 2

forest *n* a dense growth of trees and shrubs covering a large area ⟨the endless *forest* that the first European settlers encountered⟩
synonyms forestland, timber, timberland, wood(s), woodland
related words brake, brushwood, chaparral, coppice, copse, covert, grove, scrubland, stand, thicket; greenwood, wildwood; woodlot; arboretum, plantation

forestall *vb* to keep from happening by taking action in advance ⟨you can often *forestall* skidding on the ice simply by driving more slowly⟩ — see PREVENT

forestallment *n* the act or practice of keeping something from happening ⟨by raising the necessary funds, the historical society was able to effect a last-minute *forestallment* of the demolition of the town's oldest house⟩ — see PREVENTION

forestland *n* a dense growth of trees and shrubs covering a large area ⟨the region's vanishing *forestland*⟩ — see FOREST

foretell *vb* to tell of or describe beforehand ⟨a 16th-century astrologer who, some claim, accurately *foretold* 20th-century events⟩
synonyms augur, call, forecast, predict, presage, prognosticate, prophesy, read, vaticinate
related words alert, caution, forewarn, warn; bode, forebode (*also* forbode), portend, promise; anticipate, divine, foreknow, foresee; announce, declare, herald, proclaim
near antonyms describe, narrate, recite, recount, relate, report, tell

foreteller *n* one who predicts future events or developments ⟨some regard that 16th-century astrologer as an uncanny *foreteller* of some of the most disastrous events of the 20th century⟩ — see PROPHET 1

foretelling *n* a declaration that something will happen in the future ⟨the ludicrous *foretellings* of self-styled psychics at the end of each year⟩ — see PREDICTION

forethought *n* concern or preparation for the future ⟨in an unusual show of *forethought*, the city had set up a network of well-supplied emergency shelters to accommodate victims of the hurricane⟩ — see FORESIGHT 2

forethoughtful *adj* having or showing awareness of and preparation for the future ⟨doctors encouraging people to be *forethoughtful* and get their flu shots in advance of the flu season⟩ — see FORESIGHTED

forever *adv* **1** for all time ⟨we'll be best friends *forever*⟩ — see EVER 1
2 on every relevant occasion ⟨he is *forever* reminding me to wear my hat and gloves in cold weather⟩ — see ALWAYS 1

forever *n* a long or seemingly long period of time ⟨it took *forever* to fill out all the forms⟩ — see AGE 2

forevermore *adv* for all time ⟨a hero that will be praised *forevermore* for his great deeds⟩ — see EVER 1

foreverness *n* endless time ⟨some men claim that it's the alleged *foreverness* of marriage that makes them fear it⟩ — see ETERNITY 1

forewarn *vb* to give notice to beforehand especially of danger or risk ⟨I should *forewarn* you before you come to visit that we have a dog⟩ — see WARN

forewarning *n* the act or an instance of telling beforehand of danger or risk ⟨heeded the *forewarning* to stay off the ice until the town had checked to see if it was thick enough⟩ — see WARNING 1

foreword *n* a short section (as of a book) that leads to or explains the main part ⟨the editor makes some good points in the *foreword* about the author's life, so be sure to read it⟩ — see INTRODUCTION

forfeit *n* a sum of money to be paid as a punishment ⟨the *forfeit* for each baseball player involved in the brawl was $5,000⟩ — see FINE

forfeiture *n* a sum of money to be paid as a punishment ⟨the *forfeiture* for early withdrawal of the investment savings will be an amount equal to 10 percent of the investment⟩ — see FINE

forfend *vb* to drive danger or attack away from ⟨a place of refuge where the settlers could *forfend* themselves from attack⟩ — see DEFEND 1

forgather *or* **foregather** *vb* to come together into one body or place ⟨asked the townsfolk to *forgather* at the war monument for the Memorial Day ceremony⟩ — see ASSEMBLE 1

¹forge *vb* to move forward along a course ⟨the rescue team *forged* ahead despite the bad weather⟩ — see GO 1

²forge *vb* **1** to imitate or copy especially in order to de-

ceive ⟨arrested for *forging* the doctor's signature on the prescription⟩ — see FAKE 1
2 to produce or bring about especially by long or repeated effort ⟨both sides labored mightily to *forge* a peace treaty⟩ — see HAMMER OUT
3 to shape with a hammer ⟨loved the artisan look of that hand-*forged* copper pot⟩ — see HAMMER 1

forged *adj* being such in appearance only and made or manufactured with the intention of committing fraud ⟨a *forged* ancient document that didn't fool experts in cartography⟩ — see COUNTERFEIT 1

forgery *n* an imitation that is passed off as genuine ⟨that is a cheap *forgery*, not an authentic Ming Dynasty vase⟩ — see FAKE 1

forget *vb* **1** to be unable to recall or think of ⟨I *forget* exactly on which street that the house is⟩
synonyms disremember, unlearn
related words lose, miss; blank; misremember; disregard, ignore, neglect, overlook, overpass, pass over, slight, slur (over)
near antonyms remind
antonyms flash back (to), hark back (to), harken back (to), hearken back (to), mind [*chiefly dialect*], recall, recollect, remember, reminisce (about), think (of)
2 to fail to give proper attention to ⟨she promised not to *forget* her high school friends after she went off to college⟩ — see NEGLECT 1
3 to leave undone or unattended to especially through carelessness ⟨he *forgot* the pot boiling on the stove⟩ — see NEGLECT 2
4 to miss the opportunity or obligation ⟨I *forgot* to call on his birthday⟩ — see NEGLECT 3

forgetful *adj* inclined to forget what one has learned or to do what one should ⟨we become more *forgetful* as we get older⟩
synonyms absentminded
related words absent, abstracted, lost, oblivious, preoccupied, unmindful; amnesiac (*or* amnesic), senile; befogged, befuddled, bemused, bewildered, confused, dazed, muddled, scatterbrained, unfocused (*also* unfocussed); lax, neglectful, negligent, remiss, slack; careless, heedless, inconsiderate, thoughtless; inattentive, insensible, unaware, unconscious, unheeding, unknowing, unperceptive, unthinking
near antonyms alert, attentive, awake, keen, open-eyed, sharp, vigilant, watchful, wide-awake; careful, cautious, circumspect, conscientious, heedful, thoughtful, wary
antonyms retentive

forgetfulness *n* a state of being disregardful or unconscious of one's surroundings, concerns, or obligations ⟨I welcomed the *forgetfulness* of one's worries that only sleep can bring⟩ — see OBLIVION

forgivable *adj* worthy of forgiveness ⟨accidentally spilling your coffee on my newspaper is certainly a *forgivable* mishap⟩ — see VENIAL

forgive *vb* **1** to cease to have feelings of anger or bitterness toward ⟨it is not easy to *forgive* those who have hurt us⟩
synonyms pardon
related words absolve, acquit, clear, exculpate, exonerate, vindicate; remit, shrive; condone, disregard, excuse, ignore, pass over, shrug off; discharge, liberate, redeem, release, unburden
near antonyms abhor, abominate, despise, detest, dislike, execrate, hate, loathe; avenge, redress, requite, retaliate, revenge; discipline, penalize, punish
antonyms resent
2 to dismiss as of little importance ⟨he has so many good qualities that I guess we can *forgive* a slight penchant for exaggeration⟩ — see EXCUSE 1

forgiveness *n* release from the guilt or penalty of an offense ⟨they asked her *forgiveness* for failing to invite her to the party⟩ — see PARDON

forgo *also* **forego** *vb* to resist the temptation of ⟨I'll *forgo* dessert tonight—I'm trying to lose weight⟩ — see FORBEAR

forgotten *adj* left unoccupied or unused ⟨a *forgotten* doll under the bed⟩ ⟨a long-*forgotten* house down a winding dirt road⟩ — see ABANDONED 1

fork *vb* to go or move in different directions from a central point ⟨the road *forks* up ahead and you'll want to take the right fork⟩ — see SEPARATE 2

fork (over, out, *or* **up)** *vb* to hand over or use up in payment ⟨I hated to have to *fork over* that kind of money for a new set of tires⟩ — see SPEND 1

forlorn *adj* **1** feeling unhappiness ⟨she was *forlorn* when she found out the trip had been cancelled⟩ — see SAD 1
2 sad from lack of companionship or separation from others ⟨a *forlorn* wanderer far from home⟩ — see LONESOME 1
3 causing or marked by an atmosphere lacking in cheer ⟨a *forlorn* little town whose brief economic boom ended decades ago⟩ — see GLOOMY 1
4 feeling or showing no hope ⟨the *forlorn* expression of a candidate who knows that he hasn't a prayer of winning the election⟩ — see DESPONDENT 1

forlornness *n* **1** a state or spell of low spirits ⟨seemingly nothing could relieve the losing team's *forlornness*⟩ — see SADNESS
2 utter loss of hope ⟨with the *forlornness* of someone who had been disappointed many times before, he abandoned his quest⟩ — see DESPAIR 1

form *vb* **1** to take on a definite form ⟨my ideas on the subject are just starting to *form*⟩
synonyms crystallize (*also* crystalize), jell, shape (up), solidify
related words associate, coalesce, cohere, fuse; combine, conjoin, conjugate, connect, couple, join, link (up), unify, unite
near antonyms break down, decay, decompose, disintegrate
2 to be all the substance of ⟨this one sentence really *forms* the basis of your argument⟩ — see CONSTITUTE 1
3 to bring into being by combining, shaping, or transforming materials ⟨*formed* the pot out of the clay⟩ — see MAKE 1
4 to come into existence ⟨the new company *formed* from two smaller ones⟩ — see BEGIN 2
5 to come to have gradually ⟨I don't want you beginning skiers to *form* any bad habits⟩ — see DEVELOP 2

form *n* **1** the outward appearance of something as distinguished from its substance ⟨the wood-carver carved the block of wood into the *form* of a duck⟩
synonyms cast, configuration, conformation, fashion, figure, geometry, shape
related words contour, outline, profile, silhouette; frame, framework, shell, skeleton; arrangement, design, format, layout, makeup, organization, pattern, plan, setup
near antonyms composition, material, matter, raw material, stuff, substance
2 a piece of paper with information written or to be written on it ⟨I filled out all the *forms* for applying to the school⟩
synonyms blank, document, paper
related words instrument, writ; filing; sheet
3 personal conduct or behavior as evaluated by an accepted standard of appropriateness for a social or professional setting ⟨it's bad *form* to throw a tantrum on the court just because you lost a tennis match⟩ — see MANNER 1
4 a state of being or fitness ⟨after a long season off, the football team is back in good *form*⟩ — see CONDITION 1

5 a three-dimensional representation of the human body used especially for displaying clothes ⟨put the dress on the *form* to finish pinning it together⟩ — see MANNEQUIN 1
6 an oft-repeated action or series of actions performed in accordance with tradition or a set of rules ⟨we'll use the second *form* in our church missals for today's Lenten service⟩ — see RITE
7 socially acceptable behavior ⟨displayed good *form* throughout the formal dinner⟩ — see DECENCY 1
8 the means or procedure for doing something ⟨there are established *forms* for voting on motions and amendments at meetings⟩ — see METHOD
9 the type of body that a person has ⟨he has the big-boned *form* of a linebacker⟩ — see PHYSIQUE
10 the way in which the elements of something (as a work of art) are arranged ⟨museumgoers liked the asymmetrical *form* of the mobile⟩ — see COMPOSITION 3

formal *n* a social gathering for dancing ⟨he asked her to the *formal* at the end of the year⟩ — see DANCE

formal *adj* **1** following or agreeing with established form, custom, or rules ⟨a *formal* meeting of the board of directors⟩ ⟨a *formal* contract that was legally binding⟩
synonyms ceremonial, ceremonious, conventional, orthodox, regular, routine
related words authorized, certified, official, sanctioned; accepted, correct, decorous, genteel, nice, polite, proper, respectable, seemly; formalistic, ritual, ritualistic; methodical (*also* methodic), orderly, systematic
near antonyms unauthorized, unofficial; graceless, improper, inappropriate, incorrect, indecorous, inept, infelicitous, unapt, unbecoming, unfit, unhappy, unseemly, unsuitable
antonyms casual, freewheeling, informal, irregular, unceremonious, unconventional, unorthodox
2 being something in name or form only ⟨was the *formal* head of the charitable organization though he never attended a single meeting⟩ — see NOMINAL 1
3 marked by or showing careful attention to set forms and details ⟨gave her a *formal* invitation to dinner⟩ — see CEREMONIOUS 1
4 relating to or suitable for wearing to an event requiring elegant dress and manners ⟨the dress code is *formal* for tonight's event⟩ ⟨a shop that rents out *formal* wear⟩ — see DRESS
5 very dignified in form, tone, or style ⟨the *formal* language of the coronation ceremony⟩ — see ELEVATED 2

formality *n* **1** an act or utterance that is a customary show of good manners ⟨bowing to your guest is a *formality* you don't need to perform for me⟩ — see CIVILITY 1
2 an oft-repeated action or series of actions performed in accordance with tradition or a set of rules ⟨churchgoers loved the *formalities* of a traditional Christmas Eve candlelight service⟩ — see RITE

formalize *vb* **1** to make agree with a single established standard or model ⟨we'll need to *formalize* our research results before we submit our study for review⟩ — see STANDARDIZE
2 to give official acceptance of as satisfactory ⟨the plan has yet to be *formalized* by the city council⟩ — see APPROVE

format *n* **1** the way in which something is sized, arranged, or organized ⟨the book's *format* is very user-friendly⟩
synonyms arrangement, configuration, conformation, formation, layout, setout, setup
related words design, plan, scheme; composition, constitution, getup, makeup; build, construction, structure
2 the way in which the elements of something (as a work of art) are arranged ⟨this abstract painter bases the *format* of his works on color and its subtle gradations and not line or form⟩ — see COMPOSITION 3

formation *n* the way in which something is sized, arranged, or organized ⟨geese flying south in a V-*formation*⟩ — see FORMAT 1

formative *adj* having a role in deciding something's final form ⟨a teacher who was a *formative* influence on generations of students⟩
synonyms constructive, productive
related words causal, creative; consequential, influential
antonyms nonconstructive, nonproductive, unproductive

former *adj* **1** having been such at some previous time ⟨the coach is a *former* professional baseball player⟩
synonyms erstwhile, late, old, once, onetime, other, past, quondam, sometime, whilom
related words bygone, dead, defunct, departed, expired, extinct, gone, long-ago, vanished
near antonyms contemporary, current, extant, ongoing, present, present-day; coming, future, prospective, unborn
2 going before another in time or order ⟨the *former* manual had some errors, but the current version has its own problems⟩ — see PREVIOUS

formerly *adv* **1** at an earlier or previous time ⟨the newspaper *formerly* known as "The Newsprint"⟩
synonyms erstwhile, once, onetime
near antonyms lately, recently; currently, now, presently
2 so as to precede something in order of time ⟨if you didn't get a malaria shot *formerly*, you'd better get one now⟩ — see AHEAD 1

formidable *adj* **1** causing fear ⟨a *formidable*, irascible old man who frightened the neighborhood children⟩ — see FEARFUL 1
2 requiring considerable physical or mental effort ⟨running a marathon is a *formidable* undertaking⟩ — see HARD 2

formless *adj* **1** having no definite or recognizable form ⟨a *formless* mass of clay that the potter transformed into an attractive bowl⟩
synonyms amorphous, shapeless, unformed, unshaped, unstructured
related words characterless, featureless, nondescript; chaotic, disorganized, incoherent, systemless, unordered, unorganized; dim, fuzzy, hazy, inchoate, indefinite, indeterminate, indistinct, indistinguishable, murky, nebulous, obscure, unclear, undefined, undetermined, vague
near antonyms coherent, ordered, orderly, organized; clear, decided, definite, distinct
antonyms formed, shaped, shapen, structured
2 not composed of matter ⟨from this *formless* void the universe was supposed to have been created⟩ — see IMMATERIAL 1

formulaic *adj* using or marked by the use of something else as a basis or model ⟨she thought the plots of most action movies were pretty *formulaic*⟩ — see IMITATIVE 1

formulate *vb* **1** to convey in appropriate or telling terms ⟨the doctor was trying to *formulate* a good way to tell her that she would need surgery⟩ — see PHRASE
2 to put (something) into proper and usually carefully worked out written form ⟨a writer planning to *formulate* a response to what he considered a very unfair review of his work⟩ — see COMPOSE 1

formulation *n* an act, process, or means of putting something into words ⟨his letter was a very accurate *formulation* of his thoughts on the matter⟩ — see EXPRESSION 1

formulator *n* one who creates or introduces something new ⟨the *formulator* of the microcomputer⟩ — see INVENTOR

forsake *vb* to cause to remain behind ⟨*forsaking* most of our possessions, we evacuated just before the hurricane struck⟩ — see LEAVE 1

forsaken *adj* left unoccupied or unused ⟨the *forsaken* paper mill was now a rusting wreck⟩ — see ABANDONED

forsaking *n* the act of abandoning ⟨his hard-hearted *forsaking* of his wife and children was truly unforgivable⟩ — see DERELICTION 1

forsooth *adv* **1** to tell the truth ⟨*forsooth*, the rumor is true: this lovely lass and I are getting married!⟩ — see ACTUALLY 1

2 without any question ⟨you're getting married without a penny to your name—a pretty story *forsooth*!⟩ — see INDEED 1

forswear *also* **foreswear** *vb* to solemnly or formally reject or go back on (as something formerly adhered to) ⟨the new government would have to *forswear* the use of torture if it wished to be granted full diplomatic recognition⟩ — see ABJURE 1

fort *n* a structure or place from which one can resist attack ⟨a series of *forts* along the frontier⟩

synonyms bastion, castle, citadel, fastness, fortification, fortress, hold, redoubt, stronghold

related words battlement, breastwork, bulwark, earthwork, embattlement, parapet, rampart; bunker, dugout; blockhouse, garrison house; alcazar, casbah (*also* kasbah)

forte *n* something for which a person shows a special talent ⟨doing funny impressions of people has always been my *forte*⟩

synonyms long suit, métier (*also* metier), speciality, specialty, strong suit, thing

related words area, arena, bailiwick, business, circle, demesne, department, discipline, domain, fief, fiefdom, field, line, precinct, province, realm, sphere, terrain; element; aptitude, aptness, bent, faculty, flair, genius, gift, knack, talent; pursuit, racket, vocation; inclination, leaning, partiality, penchant, predilection, predisposition, proclivity, propensity, tendency

forth *adv* **1** toward a point ahead in space or time ⟨from that day *forth* we were fast friends⟩ — see ONWARD 1

2 toward or at a point lying in advance in space or time ⟨go *forth* into the world with love and hope⟩ — see ALONG

forthcoming *adj* **1** being soon to appear or take place ⟨everyone's excited about the *forthcoming* company gala⟩

synonyms approaching, coming, imminent, impending, nearing, oncoming, pending, proximate, upcoming

related words future; anticipated, awaited, expected, foreseen, predicted

phrases at hand, on hand, on tap, to come

near antonyms bygone, erstwhile, foregone, former, old, onetime, other, past, quondam, sometime, whilom

antonyms late, recent

2 free in expressing one's true feelings and opinions ⟨it's hard to tell what her views on that hot-button issue exactly are, as she's not very *forthcoming*⟩ — see FRANK

forthright *adj* **1** free in expressing one's true feelings and opinions ⟨she sometimes was a little too *forthright* for her own good and ended up saying things that inadvertently offended people⟩ — see FRANK

2 going straight to the point clearly and firmly ⟨I appreciate your *forthright* explanation of the situation⟩ — see STRAIGHTFORWARD 1

forthrightly *adv* in an honest and direct manner ⟨the police commissioner *forthrightly* and unhesitatingly admitted his mistake⟩ — see STRAIGHTFORWARD

forthrightness *n* the free expression of one's true feelings and opinions ⟨I valued her *forthrightness* in telling me she didn't like being called "Susie"⟩ — see CANDOR 1

forthwith *adv* without delay ⟨if the fire alarm rings, leave the building *forthwith*⟩ — see IMMEDIATELY

fortification *n* a structure or place from which one can resist attack ⟨defenders at the border *fortifications* preparing for an attack⟩ — see FORT

fortify *vb* **1** to prepare (oneself) mentally or emotionally ⟨Kelly *fortified* herself for the basketball tournament with a series of confidence-boosting exercises⟩

synonyms brace, forearm, nerve, poise, psych (up), ready, steel, strengthen

related words arm; harden, inure, season, toughen; bolster, boost, buoy (up), buttress, enforce, prop (up), reinforce (*also* reenforce), support, sustain; cheer (up), comfort, embolden, encourage, hearten, inspire; rally, rouse, stir

near antonyms daunt, demoralize, discourage, dishearten, dispirit, psych (out), shake, unnerve; debilitate, enervate, enfeeble, prostrate, sap, soften, tire, undercut, undermine, weaken

2 to increase the ability of (as a muscle) to exert physical force ⟨he downed another granola bar to *fortify* himself for the rest of the bike ride⟩ — see STRENGTHEN 1

3 to make able to withstand physical hardship, strain, or exposure ⟨bought lots of warm clothing to *fortify* ourselves against the cold⟩ — see HARDEN 2

fortitude *n* the strength of mind that enables a person to endure pain or hardship ⟨it was only with the greatest *fortitude* that the Pilgrims were able to survive their first winter in Plymouth⟩

synonyms backbone, constancy, fiber, grit, grittiness, guts, intestinal fortitude, pluck, spunk

related words determination, purposefulness, resoluteness, resolution; bravery, courage, courageousness, daring, dauntlessness, doughtiness, fearlessness, gallantry, greatheartedness, intrepidity, intrepidness, nerve, stoutness, valor; endurance, forbearance, stamina, sufferance, tolerance; heart, mettle, spirit; audacity, boldness, brass, cheek, chutzpah (*also* chutzpa *or* hutzpah *or* hutzpa), effrontery, gall, hardihood, nerve, nerviness, temerity

near antonyms indecisiveness, irresoluteness, irresolution, vacillation; cowardice, cowardliness, cravenness, dastardliness, faintheartedness, pusillanimity, timidity, timorousness

antonyms spinelessness

fortress *n* a structure or place from which one can resist attack ⟨the boys built a snow *fortress* and then challenged the neighborhood kids to an in-your-face snowball fight⟩ — see FORT

fortuitous *adj* **1** coming or happening by good luck especially unexpectedly ⟨your arrival just before the thunderstorm was *fortuitous*⟩ — see FORTUNATE 1

2 happening by chance ⟨firmly believes that the creation of the universe was something other than just the *fortuitous* coming together of particles of matter⟩ — see ACCIDENTAL 1

fortunate *adj* **1** coming or happening by good luck especially unexpectedly ⟨in a *fortunate* turn of events, the motel had one last vacancy⟩

synonyms fluky (*also* flukey), fortuitous, happy, heaven-sent, lucky, providential

related words convenient, opportune, seasonable, timely; unexpected, unforeseen, unlooked-for; accidental, chance, coincidental, serendipitous; auspicious, bright, encouraging, fair, heartening, hopeful, promising, propitious; benign, favorable, golden, good, hal-

cyon; advantageous, beneficial, profitable
near antonyms inconvenient, inopportune, unseasonable, untimely; anticipated, expected, foreseen; deliberate, intentional, planned; inauspicious, unpromising; calamitous, catastrophic, disastrous
antonyms hapless, ill-fated, ill-starred, luckless, star-crossed, unfortunate, unhappy, unlucky
2 having good luck ⟨rabbits' feet are seen as making the carrier of them *fortunate*⟩ — see LUCKY 1

fortunateness *n* success that is partly the result of chance ⟨he attributed his habitual *fortunateness* to the lucky penny that he had long ago stuck in his shoe⟩ — see LUCK 1

fortune *n* **1** what is going to happen to someone in the time ahead ⟨the telephone psychic proceeded to tell me my *fortune*—at great length⟩
synonyms future
related words circumstance, destiny, doom, fate, hap, kismet, lot, portion; futurities, outlook, prospect
near antonyms present
antonyms past
2 a very large amount of money ⟨the billionaire's huge mansion must have cost a *fortune*⟩
synonyms big bucks, bomb [*British*], boodle, bundle, earth, king's ransom, megabucks, mint, packet [*chiefly British*], pile, wad
related words heap, pot; bonanza, mine, treasure trove; assets, capital, means, property, riches, wealth, wherewithal; bread [*slang*], cash, chips, currency, dough, gold, jack [*slang*], legal tender, lucre, pelf, tender, wampum
near antonyms petty cash, pin money, pocket money, spending money
antonyms mite, peanuts, pittance song
3 a state or end that seemingly has been decided beforehand ⟨it was his *fortune* that he should wander in the wilderness before becoming king⟩ — see FATE 1
4 success that is partly the result of chance ⟨in a streak of good *fortune*, she won the lottery twice that year⟩ — see LUCK 1
5 the total of one's money and property ⟨the family *fortune* is mostly in rare paintings and real estate⟩ — see WEALTH 1

fortune–teller *n* one who predicts future events or developments ⟨the carnival's *fortune-teller* should have predicted that I'd pass right by her⟩ — see PROPHET 1

forty winks *n pl* a short sleep ⟨after turning the boat over to the first mate, the captain went below decks for *forty winks*⟩ — see [1]NAP

forum *n* **1** a meeting featuring a group discussion ⟨a public *forum* called to find out how residents felt about a large discount store being built in their neighborhood⟩
synonyms colloquy, conference, council, panel, panel discussion, parley, powwow, round-robin, roundtable, seminar, symposium
related words colloquium; caucus, town meeting; assembly, conclave, congregation, congress, consistory, convention, convocation, synod; debate, deliberation; brainstorming; chat room, newsgroup
2 a place or opportunity for communicating ideas and information ⟨that Web site serves as a *forum* for movie buffs who are passionate about their likes and dislikes⟩ — see VENUE 1
3 an assembly of persons for the administration of justice ⟨a jury may have acquitted Lizzie Borden, but she was guilty of murder in the *forum* of public opinion⟩ — see COURT 3

forward *adj* **1** showing a lack of proper social reserve or modesty ⟨a stranger so *forward* as to ask what medication he was taking and what it was for⟩ — see PRESUMPTUOUS 1
2 being at or in the forward part or surface of something ⟨the ship's *forward* deck⟩ — see FRONT
3 being far along in development ⟨the local citizenry's attitude toward racial equality was very *forward* for its time⟩ — see ADVANCED 1
4 having or showing awareness of and preparation for the future ⟨she was *forward* enough to start investing in her retirement fund at the age of 18⟩ — see FORESIGHTED

forward *adv* **1** toward or at a point lying in advance in space or time ⟨if you keep walking *forward*, you'll hit that wall⟩ — see ALONG
2 toward a point ahead in space or time ⟨from this day *forward*, our two nations will live in peace and harmony⟩ — see ONWARD 1

forward *vb* to help the growth or development of ⟨their foundation will help *forward* better relations between young people from those warring nations⟩ — see FOSTER 1

forward–looking *adj* having or showing awareness of and preparation for the future ⟨a *forward-looking* business plan designed to take full advantage of emerging technologies⟩ — see FORESIGHTED

forwards *adv* toward or at a point lying in advance in space or time ⟨for every step that her campaign takes *forwards*, it seems to take two backwards⟩ — see ALONG

fosse *or* **foss** *n* a long narrow channel dug in the earth ⟨the first line of defense is a water-filled *fosse* that enemy troops would have to cross⟩ — see DITCH

fossil *n* a person with old-fashioned ideas ⟨some old *fossil* who thinks that a boy and a girl shouldn't be together unsupervised until they are engaged⟩ — see FOGY

fossilized *adj* having passed its time of use or usefulness ⟨*fossilized* notions about the proper place of women in society⟩ — see OBSOLETE

foster *vb* **1** to help the growth or development of ⟨the head librarian firmly declared that it is indeed the duty of local government to *foster* learning and a love of reading⟩
synonyms advance, cultivate, encourage, forward, further, incubate, nourish, nurse, nurture, promote
related words advocate, back, champion, endorse (*also* indorse), support, uphold; endow, finance, fund, patronize, stake, subsidize, underwrite; abet, aid, assist; advertise, boost, plug, publicize, tout; agitate (for), campaign (for), work (for)
near antonyms ban, bar, enjoin, forbid, interdict, outlaw, prevent, prohibit, proscribe; battle, combat, contend (with), counter, fight, oppose; repress, snuff (out), squash, squelch, stifle, subdue, suppress; arrest, check, halt, retard; encumber, fetter, hobble, impede, interfere (with), manacle, obstruct, shackle
antonyms discourage, frustrate, hinder, inhibit
2 to bring to maturity through care and education ⟨a greathearted couple *fostering* two adopted children as well as three more of their own⟩ — see BRING UP 1

foul *vb* **1** to make dirty ⟨the mechanic *fouled* the bath towels with axle grease⟩ — see DIRTY
2 to make unfit for use by the addition of something harmful or undesirable ⟨industrial pollution *fouling* the water supply⟩ — see CONTAMINATE
3 to reduce to a lower standing in one's own eyes or in others' eyes ⟨the minister was irreparably *fouled* by baseless rumors and allegations⟩ — see HUMBLE
4 to go through decomposition ⟨unless you want to smell the organic refuse as it *fouls*, locate the compost heap away from the house⟩ — see DECAY 1

foul *adj* **1** marked by wet and windy conditions ⟨the *foul* weather brought out the windbreakers and rain slickers as everyone braced for a day of rough sailing⟩
synonyms bleak, dirty, inclement, nasty, raw, rough,

squally, stormy, tempestuous, turbulent
related words blowy, blustering, blustery, breezy, gusty, windblown, windswept; cloudy, overcast, sunless; rainy, snowy; foggy, hazy, misty, murky, soupy
near antonyms rainless; balmy, calm, halcyon, peaceful, placid, pleasant, serene
antonyms bright, clear, clement, cloudless, fair, sunny, sunshiny, unclouded
2 not being in accordance with the rules or standards of what is fair in sport ⟨an aggressive hockey player who is known for his *foul* play and readiness for a fight⟩
synonyms dirty, illegal, nasty, unfair, unsportsmanlike
related words dishonorable, shabby, shameful; ignoble, low, mean, ungentlemanly; immoral, rotten, unchivalrous, unethical, unjust, unprincipled, unrighteous, unscrupulous
phrases below the belt
near antonyms just, law-abiding; ethical, moral, principled, righteous, scrupulous; honorable, irreproachable, unimpeachable
antonyms clean, fair, legal, sportsmanlike, sportsmanly
3 causing intense displeasure, disgust, or resentment ⟨a *foul* taste that made us gag⟩ — see OFFENSIVE 1
4 depicting or referring to sexual matters in a way that is unacceptable in polite society ⟨that movie features nonstop *foul* language⟩ — see OBSCENE 1
5 having an unpleasant smell ⟨the *foul* fumes from the paper mill⟩ — see MALODOROUS
6 not clean ⟨I wouldn't play in the *foul* rainwater that's collected in the feeding trough⟩ — see DIRTY 1

foulness *n* **1** the quality or state of being obscene ⟨the *foulness* of your language means that your post won't get on the Web site's bulletin board⟩ — see OBSCENITY 1
2 the state or quality of being dirty ⟨she couldn't believe the *foulness* of her daughter's room, and ordered her to clean it⟩ — see DIRTINESS 1

foul play *n* **1** the intentional and unlawful taking of another person's life ⟨the coroner ruled that there was no evidence of *foul play*⟩ — see HOMICIDE 1
2 the use of brute strength to cause harm to a person or property ⟨the suspect has a long history of *foul play*, and was once convicted on assault and battery charges⟩ — see VIOLENCE 1

foul–up *n* an instance of confusion ⟨there was a *foul-up* with our mail order, and not one item arrived as ordered⟩
synonyms mix-up
related words bobble, botch, bungle, fumble; blunder, error, fault, flub, goof, inaccuracy, lapse, miscue, misstep, mistake, oversight, slip, slipup, stumble; chaos, confusion, disarrangement, disarray, disorder, disorganization, hash, jumble, mess, muddle, shambles

foul up *vb* **1** to make or do (something) in a clumsy or unskillful way ⟨tried not to *foul up* the football play⟩— see BOTCH
2 to make a mistake ⟨unfortunately, I *fouled up* and in my e-mail gave everyone the wrong date for the meeting⟩ — see ERR 1

found *vb* to be responsible for the creation and early operation or use of ⟨John Harvard did not actually *found* the university that now bears his name⟩
synonyms begin, constitute, establish, inaugurate, initiate, innovate, institute, introduce, launch, pioneer, plant, set up, start
related words author, father, originate; conceive, concoct, contrive, cook (up), create, devise, fabricate, invent, make up, manufacture, produce, think (up); construct, put up; develop, enlarge, expand; endow, finance, fund, subsidize; arrange, organize, systematize, systemize; refound, reinitiate, reinstitute, relaunch
near antonyms abolish, annihilate, annul, nullify; end, finish, halt, stop, terminate; round (off *or* out), wind up, wrap up
antonyms close (down), phase out, shut (up)

foundation *n* **1** a public organization with a particular purpose or function ⟨donated to a *foundation* that supported cancer research⟩ — see INSTITUTION 1
2 an immaterial thing upon which something else rests ⟨she had a good enough *foundation* in math to pursue an economics degree⟩ — see BASE 1

foundationless *adj* having no basis in reason or fact ⟨a careful investigation proved that the charges were *foundationless*⟩ — see GROUNDLESS

founder *n* a person who establishes a whole new field of endeavor ⟨Maria Montessori was the *founder* of an educational system dedicated to maximizing a child's creative potential⟩ — see FATHER 2

founder *vb* **1** to be unsuccessful ⟨the theater company *foundered* after its corporate funding dried up⟩ — see FAIL 2
2 to fall down or in as a result of physical pressure ⟨the twin towers started to sway and suddenly *foundered*⟩— see COLLAPSE 1

founding father *n* a person who establishes a whole new field of endeavor ⟨Theodor Herzl is often credited as the *founding father* of modern Zionism⟩ — see FATHER 2

fountain *n* a point or place at which something is invented or provided ⟨regards the Bible as the *fountain* of all truth concerning the Divinity⟩ — see SOURCE 1

fountainhead *n* **1** a point or place at which something is invented or provided ⟨historically, California has served as the *fountainhead* of that eclectic group of self-actualization movements known as the New Age⟩ — see SOURCE 1
2 the source from which something grows or develops ⟨a collection of lyrical ballads that became the *fountainhead* of a literary revolution⟩ — see SEED 1

four–letter word *n* a disrespectful or indecent word or expression ⟨clapped her hands over the toddler's ears so he wouldn't hear the *four-letter word*⟩ — see SWEARWORD

411 *n, slang* **1** a report of recent events or facts not previously known ⟨received a call from their daughter, who excitedly gave them the *411* on all that had happened to her since arriving on campus⟩ — see NEWS
2 information not generally available to the public ⟨a guide that will give you the *411* on what's hot and what's not⟩ — see DOPE 1

foursquare *adj* **1** free in expressing one's true feelings and opinions ⟨it's no time to be *foursquare* if you're asked whether a certain outfit makes a person look fat⟩ — see FRANK
2 going straight to the point clearly and firmly ⟨a *foursquare* evaluation of her performance that didn't mince words⟩ — see STRAIGHTFORWARD 1
3 having four equal sides and four right angles ⟨the design of the *foursquare* Georgian mansion is strongly symmetrical, the wide central hallway being flanked by two rooms on either side⟩ — see SQUARE 1

foursquare *adv* in an honest and direct manner ⟨asked him *foursquare* if he was ever going to propose to her⟩ — see STRAIGHTFORWARD

four–star *adj* of the very best kind ⟨a home film library with nothing but *four-star* pictures⟩ — see EXCELLENT

fox *n* **1** a lovely woman ⟨she's a real *fox*—smart, sassy, and sexy⟩ — see BEAUTY 2
2 a physically attractive person ⟨both he and his twin sister are *foxes*⟩ — see DOLL 2

fox *vb* **1** to throw into a state of mental uncertainty ⟨she won't be *foxed* by such telemarketing tricks⟩ — see CONFUSE 1
2 to get the better of through cleverness ⟨no confidence

man will ever *fox* me and get my hard-earned money⟩ — see OUTWIT

foxiness *n* **1** skill in achieving one's ends through indirect, subtle, or underhanded means ⟨it did not take an incredible amount of *foxiness* on his part to get you to spill the beans⟩ — see CUNNING 1
2 the inclination or practice of misleading others through lies or trickery ⟨an imposter of such formidable *foxiness* that a movie was made of his entertaining escapades⟩ — see DECEIT 1
3 exceptional discernment and judgment especially in practical matters ⟨lacks the *foxiness* needed to make it in dog-eat-dog world of show business⟩ — see ACUMEN

foxy *adj* clever at attaining one's ends by indirect and often deceptive means ⟨the oft-told story of the *foxy* flatterer who works her way up the ladder of success by stepping on people as she goes⟩ — see ARTFUL 1

foyer *n* **1** a centrally located room in a building that serves as a gathering or waiting area or as a passageway into the interior ⟨theatergoers crowded the *foyer* during the play's intermission⟩
synonyms hall, lobby
related words entranceway, entry, entryway, hallway, vestibule; concourse, corridor, gallery, passageway; antechamber, anteroom, chamber, waiting room
2 the entrance room of a building ⟨leave your muddy boots in the *foyer* and come into the house⟩ — see HALL 1

fracas *n* **1** a physical dispute between opposing individuals or groups ⟨the police broke up the *fracas* in the bar and threw both combatants in the lockup⟩ — see FIGHT 1
2 a rough and often noisy fight usually involving several people ⟨police preparing for any *fracas* that might follow the soccer game⟩ — see BRAWL 1

fraction *n* a broken or irregular part of something that often remains incomplete ⟨if even a tiny *fraction* of that cookie broke off and fell into the delicate watch works, it could mess things up⟩ — see FRAGMENT

fractionalization *n* the act or process of a whole separating into two or more parts or pieces ⟨new technology has led to the *fractionalization* of the product's traditional market⟩ — see SEPARATION 1

fractionation *n* the act or process of a whole separating into two or more parts or pieces ⟨originally conceived as one novel, *The Lord of the Rings* underwent a *fractionation* into a trilogy when its publisher feared it was too massive to sell as a single volume⟩ — see SEPARATION 1

fracture *vb* **1** to cause to separate into pieces usually suddenly or forcibly ⟨*fractured* his arm in the fall⟩ — see BREAK 1
2 to fail to keep ⟨civil liberties that have been *fractured* by the government's actions⟩ — see VIOLATE 1

fractured *adj* forcibly separated into many pieces ⟨a *fractured* radius that will have to be pieced together with a metal plate and screws⟩ — see BROKEN 1

fragile *adj* **1** easily broken ⟨attaching the beautiful but *fragile* ornaments to the Christmas tree is always a touchy operation⟩
synonyms breakable, delicate, frail, frangible
related words dainty, fine, gossamer; eggshell, flimsy, slight, tenuous; brittle, crisp, crispy, crumbly, crushable, embrittled, flaky (*also* flakey), friable, shaky, shivery, short; feeble, infirm, soft, spindly, tender, weak; inelastic, inflexible, stiff
near antonyms compact, firm, hard, rigid, solid, substantial, unyielding; elastic, flexible, resilient, rubberlike, rubbery, springy, stretch, stretchable, supple
antonyms infrangible, nonbreakable, strong, sturdy, tough, unbreakable
2 easily injured without careful handling ⟨babies are *fragile*, so remember to care for them gently⟩ — see TENDER 1
3 small in degree ⟨a *fragile* possibility that we might emerge from this fiasco unscathed⟩ — see REMOTE 1

fragility *n* **1** the state or quality of having a delicate structure ⟨we marveled at the *fragility* and yet the surprising strength of the bird's wing bones⟩ — see DELICACY 2
2 the quality or state of lacking physical strength or vigor ⟨the *fragility* of the abandoned baby bird⟩ — see WEAKNESS 1

fragment *vb* to cause to separate into pieces usually suddenly or forcibly ⟨you can *fragment* that peanut brittle easily, but how it breaks is basically up to the brittle⟩ — see BREAK 1

fragment *n* a broken or irregular part of something that often remains incomplete ⟨charred *fragments* of the exploded rocket were scattered over a huge area of ground⟩
synonyms bit, fraction, piece, scrap
related words cantle, shred, tatter; end, leftover, oddment, remainder, remnant, stub; portion, section, segment; chip, flake, shard, shatter, shiver, sliver, splinter; clipping, paring, shaving; atom, crumb, dribble, fleck, flyspeck, grain, granule, molecule, morsel, mote, nubbin, nugget, particle, patch, scruple, snip, snippet, speck, tittle

fragmental *adj* lacking some necessary part ⟨we will have to settle for a quick, *fragmental* explanation of what happened⟩ — see INCOMPLETE

fragmentary *adj* lacking some necessary part ⟨the historical record of this pharaoh's life and reign is *fragmentary* at best⟩ — see INCOMPLETE

fragmented *adj* forcibly separated into many pieces ⟨restoring the *fragmented* Roman sculpture was like putting together a jigsaw puzzle⟩ — see BROKEN 1

fragrance *n* a sweet or pleasant smell ⟨the *fragrance* of lilac trees in full bloom⟩
synonyms aroma, attar (*also* otto), balm, bouquet, fragrancy, incense, perfume, redolence, scent, spice
related words essence, odor
antonyms fetor, malodor, reek, stench, stink

fragrancy *n* a sweet or pleasant smell ⟨the *fragrancy* of roses on a warm summer evening⟩ — see FRAGRANCE

fragrant *adj* having a pleasant smell ⟨the balsam fir is a favorite as a Christmas tree because it is so *fragrant*⟩
synonyms ambrosial, aromatic, perfumed, redolent, savory (*also* savoury), scented, sweet
related words flowery, fruity, pungent, spicy; odiferous, odored, odoriferous, odorous; clean, fresh, pure
near antonyms odorless, unscented; fusty, musty, stale; gamy (*or* gamey)
antonyms fetid, foul, malodorous, noisome, putrid, rancid, rank, reeking, reeky, skunky, smelly, stenchful, stenchy, stinking, stinky, strong

frail *adj* **1** easily broken ⟨a *frail* eggshell⟩ — see FRAGILE 1
2 easily injured without careful handling ⟨be careful with your grandmother, as she's very *frail* and a fall would be disastrous⟩ — see TENDER 1
3 lacking bodily strength ⟨he was *frail* after a long battle with bronchitis⟩ — see WEAK 1
4 lacking strength of will or character ⟨a *frail* person, easily swayed by others⟩ — see WEAK 2
5 small in degree ⟨a *frail* hope of success⟩ — see REMOTE 1

frailness *n* **1** the quality or state of lacking physical strength or vigor ⟨his *frailness* prevented him from playing football⟩ — see WEAKNESS 1
2 the quality or state of lacking strength of will or character ⟨don't take advantage of your younger sister's

frailness of character and get her to lie for you⟩ — see WEAKNESS 2

frailty *n* **1** a defect in character ⟨selfishness is a common human *frailty*⟩ — see FAULT 1
2 the quality or state of lacking physical strength or vigor ⟨*frailty* doesn't affect all elderly people, for many are indeed healthy and strong⟩ — see WEAKNESS 1
3 the quality or state of lacking strength of will or character ⟨the *frailty* shown by the apostle Peter when he denied Jesus three times⟩ — see WEAKNESS 2

frame *vb* **1** to bring into being by combining, shaping, or transforming materials ⟨*framed* a unique coffee table from an old, discarded chest of drawers⟩ — see MAKE 1
2 to plan out usually with subtle skill or care ⟨a composer *framing* the structure of a song⟩ — see ENGINEER
3 to put (something) into proper and usually carefully worked out written form ⟨you'll need to *frame* your argument well if you're going to win the debate⟩ — see COMPOSE 1
4 to work out the details of (something) in advance ⟨*framed* a schedule for the project⟩ — see PLAN 1
5 to serve as a border for ⟨trees *framed* the walkway⟩ — see BORDER

frame *n* **1** the arrangement of parts that gives something its basic form ⟨now that the *frame* has been built, we have a better idea of the size of our new house⟩
synonyms architecture, armature, cadre, configuration, edifice, fabric, framework, framing, infrastructure, shell, skeleton, structure
related words cage, lattice, network; contour, figure, outline, profile, shape, silhouette; chassis
2 the type of body that a person has ⟨a tall man with a big *frame*⟩ — see PHYSIQUE
3 the line or relatively narrow space that marks the outer limit of something ⟨a white curtain with a blue *frame*⟩ — see BORDER 1

framework *n* the arrangement of parts that gives something its basic form ⟨you've got the *framework* of the story and just need to fill in the details⟩ — see FRAME 1

framing *n* the arrangement of parts that gives something its basic form ⟨the *framing* of the debate will consist of a predetermined order of turns and follow-up comments⟩ — see FRAME 1

franchise *n* the right to formally express one's position or will in an election ⟨the Territory of Wyoming granted women the *franchise* in 1869, a full 51 years before the 19th Amendment granted women the right to vote in all elections⟩ — see VOTE 1

frangibility *n* the state or quality of having a delicate structure ⟨the *frangibility* of the tree ornaments makes them inappropriate for handling by children⟩ — see DELICACY 2

frangible *adj* easily broken ⟨*frangible* china teacups that were totally inappropriate for a child's birthday party⟩ — see FRAGILE 1

frank *adj* free in expressing one's true feelings and opinions ⟨our ballet teacher is very *frank* about telling her students whether she thinks they have the talent for a career in dance⟩
synonyms candid, direct, forthcoming, forthright, foursquare, freehearted, free-spoken, honest, open, openhearted, out-front, outspoken, plain, plainspoken, straight, straightforward, unguarded, unreserved, upfront
related words artless, earnest, guileless, ingenuous, innocent, naive (*or* naïve), natural, real, sincere, unaffected, undesigning, unpretending, unpretentious; outgoing, uninhibited, unrestrained; vocal, vociferous; abrupt, bluff, blunt, brusque (*also* brusk), crusty, curt, gruff, sharp; impertinent, impolite, inconsiderate, rude, tactless, thoughtless, uncivil, undiplomatic, ungracious, unmannerly, unsubtle
near antonyms inhibited, reserved, restrained; closemouthed, laconic, quiet, reticent, taciturn, tight-lipped, uncommunicative; ambiguous, circuitous, equivocal, evasive; diplomatic, politic, tactful; civil, considerate, courteous, polite
antonyms dissembling, uncandid, unforthcoming

frankly *adv* to tell the truth ⟨*frankly*, I'd rather stay at home than go to the movies tonight⟩ — see ACTUALLY 1

frankness *n* the free expression of one's true feelings and opinions ⟨considering her reputation for *frankness*, I knew she would tell me what she really thought of my dress⟩ — see CANDOR 1

frantic *adj* **1** feeling overwhelming fear or worry ⟨the *frantic* parents were searching all over the fairgrounds for their lost child⟩
synonyms agitated, delirious, distracted, distrait, distraught, frenzied, hysterical (*also* hysteric)
related words alarmed, anxious, disquieted, disturbed, nervous, perturbed, tense, troubled, upset, worried, wrought (up); affrighted, aghast, alarmed, fearful, frightened, horrified, scared, spooked, terrified, terrorized; ballistic, berserk, crazed, demented, deranged, mad, maniacal (*also* maniac), nuclear; raging, ranting, raving
phrases beside oneself
near antonyms calm, peaceful, placid, self-possessed, serene, tranquil; cool, coolheaded, undisturbed, unperturbed, unshaken, untroubled, unworried
antonyms collected, composed, recollected, self-collected, self-composed, self-possessed, unhysterical
2 marked by great and often stressful excitement or activity ⟨the holiday season seems to be moving along at a *frantic* pace⟩ — see FURIOUS 1

frantically *adv* in a confused and reckless manner ⟨the veterinarian ran *frantically* from room to room looking for the escaped hamster⟩ — see HELTER-SKELTER 1

fraternal *adj* of, relating to, or befitting brothers ⟨there was a *fraternal* bond between the two boys all throughout their school years⟩
synonyms brotherly
related words familial, sisterly; chummy, friendly, neighborly

fraternity *n* **1** a group of persons formally joined together for some common interest ⟨a firm believer in community service and a dedicated member of the local *fraternity* of Good Samaritans⟩ — see ASSOCIATION 2
2 the body of people in a profession or field of activity ⟨the *fraternity* of civil engineers⟩ — see CORPS

fraternize *vb* **1** to come or be together as friends ⟨don't *fraternize* just with people of the same race, religion, or social background⟩ — see ASSOCIATE 1
2 to take part in social activities ⟨a group of kids *fraternizing* together after school every day⟩ — see SOCIALIZE

fraud *n* **1** an instance of the use of dishonest methods to acquire something of value ⟨thousands of people lost money when the investment scheme turned out to be a *fraud*⟩
synonyms bunco (*or* bunko), con, fiddle [*chiefly British*], flimflam, gyp, hustle, scam, shell game, sting, swindle
related words cross, fix; Ponzi scheme, pyramid scheme; racket, rip-off; thimblerig, three-card monte; device, dodge, gimmick, jig, ploy, scheme, sleight, stratagem, trick, wile; gouging, overcharging, soaking; counterfeit, fake, forgery, hoax, humbug, phony (*also* phoney), sham
2 one who makes false claims of identity or expertise ⟨the "blind" panhandler was just a *fraud* trying to con holiday shoppers out of their money⟩ — see IMPOSTOR
3 the inclination or practice of misleading others

through lies or trickery ⟨charges that he had gained control of his elderly mother's estate by *fraud*⟩ — see DECEIT 1

fraudster *n, chiefly British* a dishonest person who uses clever means to cheat others out of something of value ⟨an ingenious phishing operation that got him named the year's most inventive online *fraudster*⟩ — see TRICKSTER 1

fraudulent *adj* **1** marked by, based on, or done by the use of dishonest methods to acquire something of value ⟨hoping to get millions from the insurance company, the man made the *fraudulent* claim that he had been seriously injured in the accident⟩
synonyms crooked, deceitful, defrauding, dishonest, double-dealing, false
related words beguiling, deceiving, deceptive, deluding, delusive, delusory, duplicitous, fallacious, misleading, specious; spurious
near antonyms legitimate, true, valid
antonyms aboveboard, honest, truthful
2 given to or marked by cheating and deception ⟨*fraudulent* citizens who cheat on their taxes⟩ — see DISHONEST 2

fraught *adj* **1** possessing or covered with great numbers or amounts of something specified ⟨every room in my childhood home is *fraught* with memories⟩ — see RIFE
2 marked by or causing agitation or uncomfortable feelings ⟨had a *fraught* meeting with his estranged wife to discuss a divorce settlement⟩ — see NERVOUS 2

fray *n* **1** a forceful effort to reach a goal or objective ⟨another generation of scientists entered the *fray* to find a cure for AIDS⟩ — see STRUGGLE 1
2 a physical dispute between opposing individuals or groups ⟨a troubled youth always getting into *frays* at school⟩ — see FIGHT 1
3 a rough and often noisy fight usually involving several people ⟨school officials broke up the *fray* and gave all guilty parties detention⟩ — see BRAWL 1

fray *vb* to damage or diminish by continued friction ⟨constant rubbing against the rock face has badly *frayed* our climbing rope⟩ — see ABRADE 1

frayed *adj* worn or torn into or as if into rags ⟨she wore a beloved but badly *frayed* flannel shirt⟩ — see RAGGED 2

frazzle *n* a complete depletion of energy or strength ⟨months of overtime work have left her worn to a *frazzle*⟩ — see FATIGUE 1

frazzle *vb* **1** to damage or diminish by continued friction ⟨years of use have *frazzled* the cord for the window blinds to the breaking point⟩ — see ABRADE 1
2 to use up all the physical energy of ⟨trying to hold down two full-time jobs had completely *frazzled* him⟩ — see EXHAUST 1
3 to trouble the mind of; to make uneasy ⟨an endless series of dietary warnings that had served only to *frazzle* the general public⟩ — see DISTURB 1

freak *adj* being out of the ordinary ⟨even weather forecasters seemed surprised by the *freak* hailstorm⟩ — see EXCEPTIONAL 1

freak *n* **1** a person, thing, or event that is far from normal ⟨that snowstorm in April was a *freak*, since our weather is usually much balmier by then⟩
synonyms abnormality, anomaly, monster, monstrosity
related words abortion, malformation, miscreation, mutant, mutation; character, crackbrain, crackpot, crank, eccentric, kook, nut, oddball, screwball, weirdo; aberrant, deviant; individualist, maverick, nonconformist; curiosity, peculiarity, singularity; aberration, exception, irregularity, oddity, rarity
near antonyms sample, specimen; commonplace, usual
antonyms average, norm, normal, par, standard
2 a person with a strong and habitual liking for something ⟨I'm a hockey *freak*⟩ — see FAN
3 a sudden impulsive and apparently unmotivated idea or action ⟨suddenly had the bizarre *freak* to take a road trip across the country⟩ — see WHIM
4 *slang* a person who regularly uses drugs especially illegally ⟨he knew that he'd never get his life in order if he continued to hang out with the crystal meth *freaks*⟩ — see DOPER

freak (out) *vb* **1** to trouble the mind of; to make uneasy ⟨don't talk about death, as it totally *freaks* me *out*⟩ — see DISTURB 1
2 to yield to mental or emotional stress ⟨the landlady totally *freaked out* when she saw the dead body in the hall⟩ — see CRACK 2

freaking *adj* deserving of one's condemnation or displeasure ⟨this *freaking* assignment is such a pain in the neck⟩ — see DAMNABLE

freakish *adj* prone to sudden illogical changes of mind, ideas, or actions ⟨had a *freakish* roommate in college who once decided to drive all the way to Canada on the spur of the moment⟩ — see WHIMSICAL

freakishness *n* an inclination to sudden illogical changes of mind, ideas, or actions ⟨though some mistook his *freakishness* for mental illness, it was just a quirk of his personality and nothing more⟩ — see WHIMSICALITY

freckle *vb* to mark with small spots especially unevenly ⟨the baker *freckled* the frosting with flakes of coconut⟩ — see SPOT 1

freckled *adj* marked with spots ⟨a tanned girl with a *freckled* face⟩ — see SPOTTED 1

free *adj* **1** not being under the rule or control of another ⟨the 20th century saw many African countries become *free* after many years of European rule⟩
synonyms autonomous, freestanding, independent, self-governed, self-governing, self-ruling, separate, sovereign (*also* sovran)
related words freeborn; delivered, emancipated, freed, liberated, manumitted, redeemed, released; unconquered, unruled, unsupervised; empowered, enfranchised; democratic, republican
near antonyms bound, captive, conquered, enslaved, fettered, subdued, subjugated; inferior, subordinate, subservient
antonyms dependent, nonautonomous, non-self-governing, subject, unfree
2 no longer burdened with something unpleasant or painful ⟨after our son arrived home safely, we were grateful to be *free* from worry⟩
synonyms disencumbered, quit, shut (of), unburdened
related words delivered, freed, liberated, released; unhampered, unimpeded
near antonyms encumbered, handicapped, hindered, hobbled
3 not bound, confined, or detained by force ⟨all of the animals in the game preserve are *free* to roam all over its vast area⟩
synonyms footloose, loose, unbound, unconfined, unrestrained
related words escaped; uncaged, unchained, unfettered, unleashed; uncaught; unanchored, unbolted, undone, unfastened, untied; clear, disengaged
phrases at large, at liberty
near antonyms caught; caged, chained, enclosed (*also* inclosed), immured, imprisoned, leashed, penned; anchored, bolted, fastened, fettered, manacled, shackled, tied; kidnapped (*also* kidnaped)
antonyms bound, confined, restrained, unfree
4 not costing or charging anything ⟨although the mu-

seum normally charges admission, on Wednesdays it is *free* to all⟩
synonyms complimentary, costless, gratis, gratuitous
related words nominal; bestowed, donated, given; pro bono; discretionary, freewill, optional, voluntary; honorary, uncompensated, unpaid
phrases on the house
near antonyms paid; costly, dear, expensive, high
5 allowing passage without obstruction ⟨make sure the pass is *free* before you attempt the trip through the mountains this winter⟩ — see OPEN 1
6 giving or sharing in abundance and without hesitation ⟨the lottery winner was very *free* with his money⟩ — see GENEROUS 1
7 not being in a state of use, activity, or employment ⟨this computer terminal is *free* if you need to use it⟩ — see INACTIVE 2
8 showing a lack of proper social reserve or modesty ⟨she's a little too *free* with information about her social life⟩ — see PRESUMPTUOUS 1
9 not physically attached to another unit ⟨an arrangement of *free* columns adds interest to the Greco-Roman sculpture garden⟩ — see SEPARATE 2

free *vb* **1** to set free (as from slavery or confinement) ⟨a global crusade to *free* Nelson Mandela from a South African prison had emerged⟩
synonyms discharge, disenthrall (*also* disenthral), emancipate, enfranchise, enlarge, liberate, loose, loosen, manumit, release, spring, unbind, uncage, unchain, unfetter
related words bail (out), deliver, parole, ransom, redeem, rescue, save; adrift, disembarrass, disencumber, disengage, disentangle, extricate; unshackle
phrases turn loose
near antonyms handcuff, manacle, shackle, trammel; commit, immure, imprison, incarcerate, intern, jail, lock (up); conquer, enslave, subdue, subjugate
antonyms bind, confine, enchain, fetter, restrain
2 to make passage through (something) possible by removing obstructions ⟨we'll *free* the river by breaking up the ice jam⟩ — see OPEN 2
3 to rid the surface of (as an area) from things in the way ⟨would you mind *freeing* up the work area so I can work?⟩ — see CLEAR 1
4 to set (a person or thing) free of something that encumbers ⟨a phone call would *free* your parents from worry⟩ — see RID
5 to set free from entanglement or difficulty ⟨this plan should *free* us from debt⟩ — see EXTRICATE

freebie *or* **freebee** *n* something given to someone without expectation of a return ⟨I got this CD as a *freebie* for buying a receiver⟩ — see GIFT 1

freebooter *n* someone who engages in robbery of ships at sea ⟨the ship was captured by *freebooters* who were looking for gold⟩ — see PIRATE

freedom *n* **1** the state of being free from the control or power of another ⟨we owe our *freedom* to the untold numbers of soldiers who have fought in our nation's wars since its founding⟩
synonyms autonomy, independence, independency, liberty, self-determination, self-governance, self-government, sovereignty (*also* sovranty)
related words emancipation, enfranchisement, liberation, manumission, release
near antonyms captivity, enchainment, enslavement, immurement, imprisonment, incarceration, internment, subjugation
antonyms dependence (*also* dependance), heteronomy, subjection, unfreedom
2 the right to act or move freely ⟨as special guests of the owners, the youngsters had full *freedom* of the resort and its private beach⟩
synonyms authorization, free hand, latitude, license (*or* licence), run
related words authority, clutch, command, control, dominion, grip, hold, mandate, mastery, power, sway; range, room, space; blank check, carte blanche

free–for–all *adj* freely available for use or participation by all ⟨the public library has a *free-for-all* lending policy⟩ — see OPEN 2

free–for–all *n* **1** a rough and often noisy fight usually involving several people ⟨during the play-offs, fans of the opposing teams clashed in the streets in several *free-for-alls*⟩ — see BRAWL 1
2 a state in which everything is out of order ⟨it was a *free-for-all* when the doors to the arena opened and the crowd rushed in all at once⟩ — see CHAOS

free hand *n* the right to act or move freely ⟨gave him *free hand* in managing the club⟩ — see FREEDOM 2

freehanded *adj* giving or sharing in abundance and without hesitation ⟨she is very *freehanded* with her friends whenever she gets some extra money⟩ — see GENEROUS 1

freehandedly *adv* in a generous manner ⟨it's not prudent to loan money so *freehandedly*⟩ — see WELL 2

freehearted *adj* **1** free in expressing one's true feelings and opinions ⟨a surprisingly *freehearted* political candidate⟩ — see FRANK
2 giving or sharing in abundance and without hesitation ⟨a nation of *freehearted* people and always among the first to send relief to disaster-stricken areas⟩ — see GENEROUS 1

freeheartedly *adv* in a generous manner ⟨the review for that little restaurant was so *freeheartedly* favorable that I suspect the critic is friends with the owner⟩ — see WELL 2

freeing *n* the act of setting free from slavery ⟨a human rights group that works tirelessly for the *freeing* of political prisoners all over the world⟩ — see LIBERATION

freeload *vb* to live by relying on someone else's generosity or hospitality without sharing in the cost or responsibility ⟨after college, he *freeloaded* off his parents for several years before finally moving out⟩
synonyms mooch, sponge
related words leech; beg; exploit, use

freeloader *n* a person who is supported by or seeks support from another without making an adequate return ⟨a *freeloader* who apparently intends to live off of his long-suffering parents forever⟩ — see LEECH

freely *adv* **1** of one's own free will ⟨I will *freely* give my life for my country⟩ — see VOLUNTARILY
2 without difficulty ⟨the horse broke the halter rope quite *freely*⟩ — see EASILY 1

freeman *n* a person who owes allegiance to a government and is protected by it ⟨after eight years of residency, you will be granted the status of *freeman*⟩ — see CITIZEN 1

free rider *n* a person who is supported by or seeks support from another without making an adequate return ⟨claimed that welfare recipients were a bunch of *free riders* with little or nothing to offer society⟩ — see LEECH

free spirit *n* a person who does not conform to generally accepted standards or customs ⟨an artistically inclined *free spirit* who felt alienated and stifled while growing up in a small town⟩ — see NONCONFORMIST 1

free–spoken *adj* free in expressing one's true feelings and opinions ⟨I pride myself on being *free-spoken* and feel no hesitancy in telling you my honest opinion on just about anything⟩ — see FRANK

freestanding *adj* **1** not physically attached to another unit ⟨a *freestanding* CD player that can easily be hooked up to your existing components⟩ — see SEPARATE 2

2 not being under the rule or control of another ⟨it's a *freestanding* store, not a franchise⟩ — see FREE 1

free–swinging *adj* inclined or willing to take risks ⟨*free-swinging* entrepreneurs who could see that the future lay in biotech and were willing to stake everything on that vision⟩ — see BOLD 1

freeway *n* a passage cleared for public vehicular travel ⟨a new driver who's nervous about driving on the *freeway* for the first time⟩ — see WAY 1

freewheeling *adj* not held back by rules, duties, or worries ⟨James Bond has long been the model of the *freewheeling* hero who encounters danger and excitement in every corner of the globe⟩

synonyms footloose

related words affable, breezy, casual, devil-may-care, easygoing, happy-go-lucky, laid-back, nonchalant, relaxed; unattached, uncommitted; self-abandoned, unbridled, unrestrained; uninhibited; self-assured, self-confident, self-reliant

near antonyms attached, committed, pledged

antonyms tied

freewill *adj* **1** made, given, or done with one's own free will ⟨a *freewill* confession of guilt made by the suspect during police interrogation⟩ — see INTENTIONAL 1

2 done, made, or given with one's own free will ⟨our office staff made a *freewill* offering for UNESCO⟩ — see VOLUNTARY 1

free will *n* the act or power of making one's own choices or decisions ⟨all of the workers at the homeless shelter are unpaid and are there of their own *free will*⟩

synonyms accord, autonomy, choice, self-determination, volition, will

related words election, preference, selection; bent, devices, disposition, inclination, leaning, partiality, penchant, predilection, predisposition, proclivity, propensity, tendency; alternative, discretion, option, pick, way

near antonyms coercion, compulsion, constraint, duress, force, pressure

freeze *n* a weather condition marked by low temperatures ⟨the Midwest will experience an intense *freeze* later in the week⟩ — see COLD

freeze *vb* to become physically firm or solid ⟨add antifreeze to the water in the radiator so it won't *freeze* and damage the engine⟩ — see HARDEN 1

freeze out *vb* to prevent the participation, consideration, or inclusion of ⟨a housing market that effectively *freezes out* people of moderate means⟩ — see EXCLUDE

freezing *adj* having a low or subnormal temperature ⟨why aren't you wearing a coat, as it's *freezing* outside?⟩ — see COLD 1

freight *n* **1** a mass or quantity of something taken up and carried, conveyed, or transported ⟨shipped a large *freight* of steel to the manufacturer⟩ — see LOAD 1

2 the amount of money that is demanded as payment for something ⟨it's all very well to suggest increased government services, but who will pay the *freight* for them?⟩ — see PRICE 1

freight *vb* to place a weight or burden on ⟨it took six hours to *freight* the cargo airplane⟩ — see LOAD 1

frenetic *adj* marked by great and often stressful excitement or activity ⟨the *frenetic* rush to get every member of the cast in place before the curtain went up⟩ — see FURIOUS 1

frenetically *adv* in a confused and reckless manner ⟨we spent all morning *frenetically* searching the house for the lost keys⟩ — see HELTER-SKELTER 1

frenzied *adj* **1** being in a state of increased activity or agitation ⟨the *frenzied* scene at the mall in the final week before Christmas⟩ — see FEVERISH 1

2 feeling overwhelming fear or worry ⟨*frenzied* rescue workers searched through the snow, looking for more victims of the avalanche⟩ — see FRANTIC 1

3 marked by great and often stressful excitement or activity ⟨the *frenzied* pace of the first week of the new school year⟩ — see FURIOUS 1

frenziedly *adv* in a confused and reckless manner ⟨the *frenziedly* scattering protestors were fleeing the tear gas⟩ — see HELTER-SKELTER 1

frenzy *n* a state of wildly excited activity or emotion ⟨in its *frenzy* to flee the danger, the crowd became uncontrollable, and a number of people were trampled to death⟩

synonyms agitation, deliriousness, delirium, distraction, fever, feverishness, flap, furor, furore, fury, hysteria, rage, rampage, uproar

related words chaos, confusion, disorder, havoc, pandemonium, turmoil; bedlam, bother, brouhaha, bustle, clamor, clatter, commotion, disturbance, fuss, hoo-ha (*also* hoo-hah), hubbub, hullabaloo, hurly-burly, ruckus, ruction, rumpus, shindy, squall, stew, stir, storm, to-do, tempest, tumult

near antonyms calm, calmness, peace, peacefulness, placidity, quiet, quietude, repose, restfulness, sereneness, serenity, still, stillness, tranquillity (*or* tranquility), tranquilness

frenzy *vb* to cause to go insane or as if insane ⟨local football fans who were *frenzied* by the fact that their team was going to the Super Bowl⟩ — see CRACK

frequence *n* the fact or state of happening often ⟨the *frequence* of that cough is worrisome; perhaps you should see a doctor⟩ — see FREQUENCY

frequency *n* the fact or state of happening often ⟨the *frequency* of twins in that family is remarkable⟩

synonyms commonness, frequence, frequentness, prevalence

related words chronicity, constancy, continualness, regularity; appearance, incidence, occurrence

antonyms infrequency, rareness, uncommonness, unusualness

frequent *adj* **1** appearing or occurring repeatedly from time to time ⟨our local multiplex usually has *frequent* showings of blockbusters, with starting times about every half hour⟩ — see REGULAR 1

2 often observed or encountered ⟨finches are *frequent* sights in this part of the country⟩ — see COMMON 1

frequent *vb* to go to or spend time in often ⟨like their counterparts elsewhere, the town's teenagers like to *frequent* the local malls⟩

synonyms affect, habituate, hang (at), haunt, resort (to), visit

related words patronize; attend, take in; infest, invade, overrun, swarm; call (on *or* upon), drop by, drop in, pop (in), run (in), stop (in *or* by); camp (out in), sojourn (at), stay (at), stop (over), tarry (in)

near antonyms dodge, duck, elude, escape, eschew, evade, shake

antonyms avoid, shun

frequenter *n* **1** a person who visits another ⟨he's a regular *frequenter* of their home⟩ — see GUEST 1

2 someone who regularly spends time in a particular place ⟨a nightclub *frequenter*, he knows what's hot in music and what's not⟩ — see DENIZEN 1

frequently *adv* many times ⟨our oddball uncle *frequently* lets himself into our house without knocking⟩ — see OFTEN

frequentness *n* the fact or state of happening often ⟨the *frequentness* and the fierceness of the storms that winter were unprecedented⟩ — see FREQUENCY

fresh *adj* **1** being in an original and unused or unspoiled state ⟨the restaurant uses only really *fresh* ingredients in all of its dishes⟩

synonyms brand-new, mint, pristine, span-new, virgin, virginal

related words unaltered, unblemished, unbruised, un-

contaminated, undamaged, undefiled, unharmed, unhurt, unimpaired, uninjured, unmarred, unpolluted, unsoiled, unspoiled, unsullied, untainted, untouched, unworn; new, spick-and-span (*or* spic-and-span)
near antonyms blemished, broken, bruised, damaged, defaced, defiled, disfigured, harmed, hurt, impaired, injured, marred, soiled, sullied, tainted; faded, shopworn, used, well-worn, worn; contaminated, polluted, spoiled; hand-me-down, second hand
antonyms stale
2 displaying or marked by rude boldness ⟨if you are *fresh* with the art teacher, she'll give you a detention immediately⟩ — see NERVY 1
3 not known or experienced before ⟨a *fresh* look at the situation⟩ — see NEW 2
4 resulting in an increase in amount or number ⟨she's making *fresh* changes on top of the existing ones⟩ — see ADDITIONAL
5 *slang* being in the latest or current fashion ⟨those are some *fresh* threads you have on, man!⟩ — see STYLISH

freshen *vb* to bring back to a former condition or vigor ⟨cool glasses of lemonade *freshened* us after a day of hard work outside⟩ — see RENEW 1

freshened *adj* made or become fresh in spirits or vigor ⟨the team came back from the locker room *freshened* and ready for the rest of the game⟩ — see NEW 4

freshly *adv* not long ago ⟨a *freshly*-paved road⟩ — see NEWLY

freshman *n* a person who is just starting out in a field of activity ⟨our senator is just a *freshman* in Congress⟩ — see BEGINNER

freshness *n* the quality or appeal of being new ⟨the *freshness* of that teacher's approach makes his classes fun and interesting⟩ — see NOVELTY 1

fret *vb* **1** to consume or wear away gradually ⟨over the span of thousands of years, the annual spring runoff *fretted* the rock, forming a deep channel⟩ — see EAT 2
2 to damage or diminish by continued friction ⟨don't let the girth *fret* the horse's belly or you won't be able to ride him⟩ — see ABRADE 1
3 to experience concern or anxiety ⟨don't *fret* over whether it will be sunny tomorrow, as there's nothing we can do about it⟩ — see WORRY 1
4 to make sore by continued rubbing ⟨the stiff, starchy collar was *fretting* my neck, and I couldn't wait to change out of that costume⟩ — see CHAFE 1

fret *n* a state of nervous or irritated concern ⟨one of my customers always gets into a *fret* if I'm so much as 15 minutes late delivering his newspaper⟩
synonyms dither, fluster, fuss, huff, lather, pother, stew, sweat, swelter, swivet, tizzy, twitter
related words bother, dudgeon, pique; alarm (*also* alarum), hand-wringing, panic; ado, agitation, delirium, distraction, furor, hysteria, uproar; nervous breakdown

friable *adj* having a texture that readily breaks into little pieces under pressure ⟨sand dollars are *friable*, so handle them carefully⟩ — see CRISP 1

friary *n* a residence for men under religious vows ⟨the Franciscans left the chapel and went to the *friary* for rest⟩ — see MONASTERY

fribble *vb* to spend time in aimless activity ⟨somehow, he managed to spend the whole morning *fribbling* instead of doing his assigned work⟩ — see FIDDLE (AROUND)

friction *n* a lack of agreement or harmony ⟨there was *friction* between the two sides of the family⟩ — see DISCORD

frictionless *adj* having or marked by agreement in feeling or action ⟨enjoys an easygoing and *frictionless* relationship with her mother-in-law⟩ — see HARMONIOUS 3

fried *adj* being under the influence of alcohol ⟨grew up in a family in which Dad got *fried* on every weekend and holiday⟩ — see DRUNK

friend *n* **1** a person who has a strong liking for and trust in another ⟨really close *friends* who like to do everything together and are always sharing secrets⟩
synonyms alter ego, amigo, buddy, chum, compadre, comrade, confidant, confidante, crony, familiar, intimate, mate [*chiefly British*], musketeer, pal
related words acquaintance; associate, cohort, colleague, companion, fellow, hearty, hobnobber, partner, peer, sport; blood brother, brother, main man, sister; abettor (*also* abetter), accomplice, ally, collaborator, confederate; pen pal; benefactor, supporter, sympathizer, well-wisher; friendly
near antonyms adversary, antagonist, competitor, opponent, rival; archenemy, nemesis
antonyms enemy, foe
2 a person who actively supports or favors a cause ⟨hopes that the new governor will be a *friend* to environmental causes⟩ — see EXPONENT 1

friendliness *n* kindly concern, interest, or support ⟨the family was overwhelmed by the *friendliness* of the welcoming committee⟩ — see GOODWILL 1

friendly *adj* **1** having or showing kindly feeling and sincere interest ⟨all of the people in my new department seem *friendly*⟩ ⟨as a *friendly* gesture, we presented our new neighbors with a plate of homemade cookies⟩
synonyms amicable, bonhomous, buddy-buddy, chummy, collegial, companionable, comradely, cordial, genial, hail-fellow, hail-fellow-well-met, hearty, matey [*chiefly British*], neighborly, palsy, palsy-walsy [*slang*], warm, warmhearted
related words affable, agreeable, approachable, good-natured, good-tempered, gracious, nice, sweet; clubby, convivial, folksy, gregarious, hospitable, sociable, social; jolly, jovial, merry; extroverted (*also* extraverted), outgoing; brotherly, fraternal, sisterly; close, familiar, intimate; adoring, affectionate, devoted, fond, lovesome, loving, tender, tenderhearted
near antonyms alienated, estranged; chilly, cold, cold-blooded, cool, frigid, frosty, glacial, icy, wintry (*also* wintery); unsociable, unsocial; aggressive, argumentative, bellicose, belligerent, combative, contentious, disputatious, pugnacious, quarrelsome, scrappy, truculent; inhospitable, inimical
antonyms antagonistic, hostile, unfriendly
2 closely acquainted ⟨we're *friendly* with our neighbors⟩ — see FAMILIAR 1
3 expressing approval ⟨a *friendly* sign that our pet project would be approved⟩ — see FAVORABLE 1
4 willing to do a favor ⟨a kid-*friendly* restaurant with high chairs and a special menu for small-fry appetites⟩ — see ACCOMMODATING
5 promoting or contributing to personal or social well-being ⟨the state's attitude towards commercial development is widely regarded as *friendly* to the business community⟩ — see BENEFICIAL

friendship *n* kindly concern, interest, or support ⟨I appreciate your *friendship* during this difficult time for my family⟩ — see GOODWILL 1

fright *n* **1** something unpleasant to look at ⟨people in our neighborhood think that that orange and green office building is a hideous *fright*⟩ — see EYESORE
2 the emotion experienced in the presence or threat of danger ⟨the earthquake so filled me with *fright* that I still have trouble sleeping⟩ — see FEAR 1

fright *vb* to strike with fear ⟨a ghastly sight that would *fright* even the most stouthearted soul⟩ — see FRIGHTEN

frighten *vb* to strike with fear ⟨around the campfire the campers tried to *frighten* one another with ghostly legends and grisly tales⟩

synonyms affright, alarm (*also* alarum), fright, horrify, panic, scare, scarify, shock, spook, startle, terrify, terrorize
related words appall (*also* appal), bowl over, dismay, floor, jolt, shake, shake up; amaze, astound, awe; chill, daunt, demoralize, dispirit, emasculate, psych (out), undo, unman, unnerve, unstring; discomfort, discompose, disconcert, disquiet, distract, distress, disturb, perturb, unsettle, upset, worry
phrases give one the creeps, make one's flesh creep (*or* crawl)
near antonyms assure, cheer, comfort, console, solace, soothe; embolden, encourage, hearten, inspire, steel
antonyms reassure

frightened *adj* filled with fear or dread ⟨I am *frightened* of the dark⟩ — see AFRAID

frightening *adj* causing fear ⟨a truly *frightening* movie⟩ — see FEARFUL 1

frightful *adj* **1** causing fear ⟨a *frightful* sound emanated from somewhere deep within the forest⟩ — see FEARFUL 1
2 extremely disturbing or repellent ⟨I couldn't listen to the *frightful* details of the murder trial⟩ — see HORRIBLE 1
3 extreme in degree, power, or effect ⟨flew into a *frightful* fit of rage⟩ — see INTENSE 1

frightfully *adv* to a great degree ⟨that coat is *frightfully* expensive, so don't spill anything on it⟩ — see VERY 1

frightfulness *n* the quality of inspiring intense dread or dismay ⟨had heard stories about the *frightfulness* of the entrance exams⟩ — see HORROR 1

frigid *adj* **1** having a low or subnormal temperature ⟨the poor old woman was discovered shivering in a *frigid* apartment⟩ — see COLD 1
2 lacking in friendliness or warmth of feeling ⟨the innkeeper gave us a *frigid* and unnecessarily formal welcome⟩ — see COLD 2

frill *n* **1** a strip of fabric gathered or pleated on one edge and used as trimming ⟨I just had to sew the *frill* onto the bottom of the skirt and the dress was finished⟩ — see RUFFLE 1
2 something adding to pleasure or comfort but not absolutely necessary ⟨didn't get any food or drinks on the no-*frills* flight⟩ — see LUXURY 1
3 something that decorates or beautifies ⟨a birthday cake decorated with *frills* like edible glitter⟩ — see DECORATION 1

fringe *n* the line or relatively narrow space that marks the outer limit of something ⟨was on the *fringes* of the crowd and couldn't see the speaker⟩ — see BORDER 1

fringe *vb* **1** to be adjacent to ⟨the orchestral pit *fringed* the edge of the stage⟩ — see ADJOIN 1
2 to serve as a border for ⟨neat rows of red brick *fringe* the estate's flower beds⟩ — see BORDER

fringing *adj* having a border in common ⟨*fringing* nations fighting over territory on their shared border⟩ — see ADJACENT

frippery *n* **1** dressy clothing ⟨dressed in their most elegant *frippery* for the big gala at the symphony⟩ — see FINERY
2 something of little importance ⟨socialites whose lives were almost entirely consumed by *fripperies*⟩ — see TRIFLE

frisk *vb* to play and run about happily ⟨carefree kids laughing and *frisking* about in their backyard⟩ — see FROLIC 1

frisk *n* a time or instance of carefree fun ⟨fondly remembers the summer before he started college as one long *frisk*⟩ — see FLING 1

friskiness *n* a natural disposition for playful behavior ⟨as your puppy grows older, her *friskiness* will diminish a bit, but this breed is generally very energetic and playful⟩ — see PLAYFULNESS

frisky *adj* **1** given to good-natured joking or teasing ⟨a *frisky* kid who keeps the class in stitches with his jokes⟩ — see PLAYFUL
2 having much high-spirited energy and movement ⟨the *frisky* colt didn't like to be kept in his stall⟩ — see LIVELY 1

frisson *n* a pleasurably intense stimulation of the feelings ⟨those two are still caught up in the giddy *frisson* of a new romance⟩ — see THRILL

fritter *n* a small usually rounded mass of minced food that has been fried ⟨she loves eating corn *fritters* with maple syrup⟩ — see CAKE 1

fritter (away) *vb* to use up carelessly ⟨quit *frittering away* the afternoon playing video games and get some housework done!⟩ — see WASTE 1

fritterer *n* someone who spends money freely or foolishly ⟨a wastrel who had the dubious distinction of being the drunken *fritterer* of one of the largest fortunes ever amassed in America⟩ — see PRODIGAL

frivol *vb* to show a sexual attraction for someone just for fun ⟨my friends warned me not to *frivol* with that guy, as he was likely to take me seriously⟩ — see FLIRT 1

frivolity *n* a lack of seriousness often at an improper time ⟨the boys were scolded for joking during the funeral service, which was hardly the time for *frivolity*⟩
synonyms facetiousness, flightiness, flippancy, frivolousness, frothiness, levity, light-headedness, light-mindedness, lightness, silliness
related words cheer, cheerfulness, festivity, gaiety (*also* gayety), glee, gleefulness, high-spiritedness, hilarity, joviality, lightheartedness, merriment, mirth, mirthfulness; childishness, goofiness, puerility
near antonyms dejection, depression, despondency, dispiritedness, downheartedness, gloom, gloominess, heartsickness, joylessness, melancholy, mopes, moroseness, sadness, sullenness, unhappiness
antonyms earnestness, gravity, seriousness, soberness, solemnity, solemnness

frivolous *adj* **1** lacking importance ⟨judges are getting sick of people bringing *frivolous* lawsuits⟩ — see UNIMPORTANT
2 lacking in seriousness or maturity ⟨when asked by the waiter if we wanted anything else that evening, we made a *frivolous* request for free drinks⟩ — see GIDDY 1

frivolousness *n* a lack of seriousness often at an improper time ⟨his childish *frivolousness* at the awards ceremony wasn't appreciated by anyone⟩ — see FRIVOLITY 1

frizz *n* a length of hair that forms a loop or series of loops ⟨a photograph of a 1920s flapper with that trademark *frizz* on the forehead⟩ — see CURL

frizzle *n* a length of hair that forms a loop or series of loops ⟨the girl has enough *frizzles* to play Little Orphan Annie⟩ — see CURL

fro *adv* from this or that place ⟨ferries carrying passengers to and *fro*⟩ — see AWAY

frock *n* **1** a garment with a joined blouse and skirt usually worn by a woman or girl ⟨please get into your nicest *frock* and join us at the party⟩ — see DRESS 1
2 a sleeveless garment worn so as to hang over the shoulders, arms, and back ⟨the man clutched his heavy *frock* as he made his way through the driving rain⟩ — see [1]CAPE

frolic *n* **1** a playful or mischievous act intended as a joke ⟨we indulgently listened to the senior citizens share memories of long-ago *frolics*⟩ — see PRANK
2 a time or instance of carefree fun ⟨took the long weekend as a three-day *frolic* and spent it at the beach⟩ — see FLING 1
3 activity engaged in to amuse oneself ⟨firmly believes

that childhood should be a time of carefree *frolic*〉 — see PLAY 1

frolic *adj* joyously unrestrained 〈the *frolic* atmosphere that envelops New Orleans during Mardi Gras〉 — see EXUBERANT

frolic *vb* **1** to play and run about happily 〈scores of swimmers were *frolicking* in the ocean surf along the beach〉
synonyms caper, cavort, disport, frisk, gambol, lark, rollick, romp, sport
related words bound, hop, leap, lope, skip, spring, trip, tumble; curvet, dance, prance; carouse, revel, roister; carry on, fool around, horse around; clown, cut up; joyride, roughhouse, skylark; kite
phrases cut capers, kick up one's heels
near antonyms mope, pout, stew, sulk
2 to engage in activity for amusement 〈he would rather *frolic* than do yard work any day of the week〉 — see PLAY 1

frolicking *n* activity engaged in to amuse oneself 〈a night of *frolicking* by three soldiers just before they are sent to the war zone〉 — see PLAY 1

frolicsome *adj* **1** given to good-natured joking or teasing 〈a *frolicsome* uncle who was a favorite among his relatives〉 — see PLAYFUL
2 joyously unrestrained 〈teachers smiling at the *frolicsome* students leaving school for summer vacation〉 — see EXUBERANT

front *vb* to stand or sit with the face or front toward 〈the apartment complex *fronts* the ocean〉 — see FACE 1

front *adj* being at or in the part of something opposite the back part 〈visitors use the *front* door, but family knows to go around to the side entrance〉
synonyms anterior, fore, forward, frontal, frontward (*or* frontwards)
related words ventral
near antonyms dorsal
antonyms aft, after, hind, hinder, hindmost, posterior, rear, rearward

front *n* **1** a forward part or surface 〈the *front* of the church features a magnificent stained-glass window〉
synonyms exterior, facade (*also* façade), face, forehead, forepart
related words outside, skin, surface, veneer
near antonyms innards, inside, interior
antonyms back, rear, rearward, reverse
2 a display of emotion or behavior that is insincere or intended to deceive 〈that smile is just a *front*—I don't think she actually likes me at all〉 — see MASQUERADE
3 a region of activity, knowledge, or influence 〈are we making any progress on the marketing *front*?〉 — see FIELD 2

frontage *n* the state or fact of facing a particular direction 〈the vineyard's southern *frontage* results in earlier-than-usual ripening of the grapes〉 — see EXPOSURE 2

frontal *adj* being at or in the forward part or surface of something 〈most cars have the engine in the *frontal* part〉 — see FRONT

frontier *adj* located at or near a border 〈a *frontier* town with a reputation for vice and lawlessness〉 — see BORDERLINE

frontier *n* **1** a region along the dividing line between two countries 〈the Apaches were once feared on both sides of the U.S.-Mexico *frontier*〉
synonyms border, borderland, march
related words no-man's-land
2 a rural region that forms the edge of the settled or developed part of a country 〈Alaska has been called America's last *frontier*〉
synonyms backcountry, backland(s), backwater, backwoods, bush, hinterland, outback, outlands, upcountry
related words boonies [*slang*], boondocks, country, countryside, sticks
phrases (the) back of beyond

frontiersman *n* a person who settles in a new region 〈the *frontiersmen* were willing to brave harsh living conditions in order to achieve a better life〉
synonyms colonial, colonist, colonizer, homesteader, pioneer, settler
related words explorer, pathfinder, trailblazer; bushranger, mountain man, woodsman

frontline *adj* of the very best kind 〈if I'm having brain surgery, I want it done at a *frontline* hospital〉 — see EXCELLENT

front line *n* the leading or most important part of a movement 〈Susan B. Anthony was on the *front line* of the struggle for woman suffrage〉 — see FOREFRONT

frontward *or* **frontwards** *adj* being at or in the forward part or surface of something 〈ship passengers in the *frontward* cabins were getting the worst of the rough seas〉 — see FRONT

frost *n* **1** a covering of tiny ice crystals on a cold surface 〈the wintertime routine of scraping the *frost* off the car's windshield every morning〉
synonyms hoar, hoarfrost, rime
related words frostwork
2 something that has failed 〈the get-acquainted meeting with his fiancée's parents turned out to be a complete *frost*〉 — see FAILURE 3

frost *vb* to disturb the peace of mind of (someone) especially by repeated disagreeable acts 〈it was the salesclerk's high-handed rudeness that really *frosted* me〉 — see IRRITATE 1

frosty *adj* **1** having a low or subnormal temperature 〈a *frosty* autumn that was a sign of the brutal winter that followed〉 — see COLD 1
2 having or showing a lack of friendliness or interest in others 〈her response was *frosty* enough to tell me she didn't appreciate the question〉 — see COOL 1
3 lacking in friendliness or warmth of feeling 〈she gave the telemarketer on the phone a *frosty* "No, thank you" and hung up〉 — see COLD 2

froth *n* a light mass of fine bubbles formed in or on a liquid 〈*froth* on the ocean waves〉 — see FOAM

frothiness *n* a lack of seriousness often at an improper time 〈try to restrain your natural *frothiness* at least for the duration of the lecture〉 — see FRIVOLITY

frothy *adj* **1** covered with, consisting of, or resembling foam 〈a *frothy* dessert made of whipped egg whites and fruit puree〉 — see FOAMY
2 lacking in seriousness or maturity 〈a *frothy* comedy that wouldn't exert the brain of a gnat〉 — see GIDDY 1
3 being of a material lacking in sturdiness or substance 〈the sort of *frothy* costumes worn by Las Vegas showgirls〉 — see FLIMSY 1

froward *adj* **1** engaging in or marked by childish misbehavior 〈their *froward* pranks are not appropriate in the workplace〉 — see NAUGHTY
2 given to resisting authority or another's control 〈*froward* students sent to the office for chronic disciplinary problems〉 — see DISOBEDIENT
3 given to resisting control or discipline by others 〈acting like a *froward* preschooler is not going to get you what you want〉 — see UNCONTROLLABLE

frowardness *n* refusal to obey 〈the orphan was harshly disciplined for her chronic *frowardness*〉 — see DISOBEDIENCE

frown *n* a twisting of the facial features in disgust or disapproval 〈it was clear from the *frown* on the CEO's face that sales were headed in the wrong direction〉 — see GRIMACE

frown *vb* to look with anger or disapproval 〈the boss

just stood there and *frowned* at his assistant who, once again, was in trouble⟩
synonyms glare, gloom, glower, lower (*also* lour), scowl
related words gape, gaze, ogle, stare; grimace, pout, sulk; growl, snarl, sneer, snigger
phrases look daggers (*or* stare daggers)
antonyms beam, grin, smile

frown (on *or* upon) *vb* to hold an unfavorable opinion of ⟨people of a certain age continue to *frown on* tattoos and body piercings⟩ — see DISAPPROVE (OF)

frowsty *adj, chiefly British* having an unpleasant smell ⟨a *frowsty*, mold-ridden flat in London's East End⟩ — see MALODOROUS

frowsy *or* **frowzy** *adj* **1** lacking neatness in dress or person ⟨a *frowsy* family living in wretched poverty⟩ — see SLOPPY 1
2 having an unpleasant smell ⟨the abandoned house was dank and *frowsy* and barely fit for human habitation⟩ — see MALODOROUS

frozen *adj* **1** firmly positioned in place and difficult to dislodge ⟨the car door was *frozen* ever since an accident had damaged the hinge⟩ — see TIGHT 2
2 having been established and usually not subject to change ⟨pay rates will remain *frozen* until the company does better financially⟩ — see FIXED 1
3 lacking in friendliness or warmth of feeling ⟨responded to my greeting with a *frozen* "hello"and stared straight ahead⟩ — see COLD 2

fructuous *adj* producing abundantly ⟨settlers gradually migrated from the rocky shores to more *fructuous* lands⟩ — see FERTILE

frugal *adj* careful in the management of money or resources ⟨by being *frugal*, the family is able to stretch its monthly budget⟩
synonyms economical, economizing, provident, scrimping, sparing, thrifty
related words conserving, preserving, saving; forehanded, foresighted, foresightful, prudent; penny-wise; cheap, close, closefisted, mean, miserly, niggard, niggardly, parsimonious, penny-pinching, penurious, pinching, spare, stingy, stinting, tight, tightfisted
near antonyms improvident, shortsighted; bountiful, charitable, freehanded, generous, liberal, munificent, openhanded, unselfish, unsparing; extravagant, indulgent, lavish
antonyms prodigal, profligate, spendthrift, squandering, thriftless, unthrifty, wasteful

frugality *n* careful management of material resources ⟨her lifelong *frugality* has enabled her to save enough money to go to college next year⟩ — see ECONOMY

fruit *n* **1** a condition or occurrence traceable to a cause ⟨one *fruit* of your faithfulness in carrying out your duties will be more rewarding responsibilities⟩ — see EFFECT 1
2 something produced by physical or intellectual effort ⟨a "miracle drug" that was the *fruit* of years of research and development⟩ — see PRODUCT 1
3 the descendants of a person, animal, or plant ⟨according to the Bible, God promised Abraham that the *fruit* of his loins would someday become a great nation⟩ — see OFFSPRING

fruitcake *n* **1** a person judged to be legally or medically insane ⟨some *fruitcake* who insisted that he was an alien from another planet⟩ — see LUNATIC 1
2 a person of odd or whimsical habits ⟨the reclusive scientist has been called a loose cannon and a *fruitcake* by his detractors⟩ — see ECCENTRIC

fruitful *adj* **1** producing abundantly ⟨a very *fruitful* tree that gives us plenty of apples every year⟩ — see FERTILE
2 producing or capable of producing a desired result ⟨I hope your efforts to find that missing package are *fruitful*⟩ — see EFFECTIVE 1

fruition *n* the state of being actual or complete ⟨when she landed the lead in a Broadway play, a lifelong dream was brought to *fruition*⟩
synonyms accomplishment, achievement, actuality, actualization, attainment, consummation, fulfillment (*or* fulfilment), pass, realization
related words success, triumph
near antonyms defeat, failure, fizzle, nonsuccess
antonyms naught (*also* nought), nonfulfillment

fruitless *adj* **1** producing no results ⟨this argument is totally *fruitless*, as neither of us will change our position⟩ — see FUTILE 1
2 not able to produce fruit or offspring ⟨a stand of blighted, *fruitless* trees⟩ — see STERILE 1

fruity *adj* **1** appealing to the emotions in an obvious and tiresome way ⟨letters in which his effusive declarations of love are interlaced with snatches of shamelessly *fruity* poetry⟩ — see CORNY 1
2 *slang* having or showing a very abnormal or sick state of mind ⟨dreaded spending the holidays with her husband's *fruity* relatives⟩ — see INSANE 1

frustrate *vb* **1** to prevent from achieving a goal ⟨a multitude of conflicting opinions *frustrated* me in my attempt to find a computer that best suits my needs⟩
synonyms baffle, balk, beat, checkmate, discomfit, foil, thwart
related words bar, block, clog, encumber, fetter, hamper, handicap, hinder, hobble, hold back, impede, inhibit, interfere (with), manacle, obstruct, shackle, tie up, trammel; arrest, check, halt, set back, short-circuit, stall, stop; avert, forestall, obviate, preclude, prevent; negate, neutralize, nullify; counteract, offset; conquer, defeat, overcome
near antonyms abet, aid, assist; ease, facilitate, smooth
antonyms advance, cultivate, encourage, forward, foster, further, nurture, promote
2 to lessen the courage or confidence of ⟨challenge the math student, but don't *frustrate* him or her with overly difficult problems⟩ — see DISCOURAGE 1

frustrating *adj* causing annoyance ⟨these daily traffic jams are *frustrating*⟩ — see ANNOYING

frustration *n* **1** something that is a source of irritation ⟨bad spelling is a constant *frustration* to language-arts teachers⟩ — see ANNOYANCE 3
2 the emotion felt when one's expectations are not met ⟨the kids couldn't hide their *frustration* when they couldn't get the electronic toy to work⟩ — see DISAPPOINTMENT 1
3 the feeling of impatience or anger caused by another's repeated disagreeable acts ⟨the husband's *frustration* over his wife's constant nagging became too much to bear⟩ — see ANNOYANCE 2

fud *n* a person with old-fashioned ideas ⟨a stagnant company that has been run by some old *fuds* for far too long⟩ — see FOGY

fuddle *vb* to throw into a state of mental uncertainty ⟨the hotel staff is completely *fuddled* by the guest's request for a dozen pillows⟩ — see CONFUSE 1

fuddy-duddy *n* a person with old-fashioned ideas ⟨a *fuddy-duddy* who thought that anyone too young to vote shouldn't be out past 8:00 p.m.⟩ — see FOGY

fudge *n* language, behavior, or ideas that are absurd and contrary to good sense ⟨I was starting to realize that Grandpa's tales about when he was a boy were a lot of *fudge*⟩ — see NONSENSE 1

fudge *vb* **1** to avoid giving a definite answer or position ⟨the candidate wouldn't say whether he was for or against gun control but just *fudged* on the issue⟩ — see EQUIVOCATE
2 to use dishonest methods to achieve a goal ⟨she's been

fudging on her taxes for years⟩ — see CHEAT 1
3 to change so much as to create a wrong impression or alter the meaning of ⟨*fudged* the facts about his educational background so he could get the position⟩ — see GARBLE 1

fuel *n* something with a usable capacity for doing work ⟨such nonrenewable *fuels* as coal, petroleum, and natural gas⟩
synonyms energy, power
related words kindling, propellant (*also* propellent); force

fugacious *adj* lasting only for a short time ⟨savor the *fugacious* pleasures of life as intensely as the more enduring ones⟩ — see MOMENTARY

fugitive *adj* **1** hard to find, capture, or isolate ⟨that *fugitive* trait called artistic creativity⟩ — see ELUSIVE
2 lasting only for a short time ⟨had *fugitive* thoughts of leaving town after finishing high school but never acted on them⟩ — see MOMENTARY
3 traveling from place to place ⟨a small *fugitive* circus that traveled the countryside⟩ — see ITINERANT

fugitiveness *n* the state or quality of lasting only for a short time ⟨a sermon on the *fugitiveness* of all earthly existence⟩ — see IMPERMANENCE

führer *or* **fuehrer** *n* a person who uses power or authority in a cruel, unjust, or harmful way ⟨a nation that has suffered under the yoke of one *führer* after another, never knowing the freedoms of a democracy⟩ — see DESPOT

fulfill *or* **fulfil** *vb* **1** to do what is required by the terms of ⟨the football player must remain with the team one more year to *fulfill* his contract⟩
synonyms answer, complete, comply (with), fill, keep, meet, redeem, satisfy
related words conclude, consummate, finalize, finish, perfect; accomplish, achieve, bring about, bring off, carry out, effect; commit, compass, discharge, execute, follow through (with), make, perform
phrases abide by, make good (*or* make good on)
near antonyms default (on); disregard, forget, ignore, neglect, overlook, overpass, pass over, slight
antonyms breach, break, transgress, violate
2 to carry through (as a process) to completion ⟨you have *fulfilled* your duties most admirably⟩ — see PERFORM 1

fulfilling *adj* making one feel good inside ⟨the college student had a *fulfilling* job tutoring inner-city youths⟩ — see HEARTWARMING

fulfillment *or* **fulfilment** *n* **1** the doing of an action ⟨her commendably prompt *fulfillment* of any assignment given her⟩ — see COMMISSION 2
2 the state of being actual or complete ⟨he saw the entire project through, from initial idea to final *fulfillment*⟩ — see FRUITION

fulgent *adj* giving off or reflecting much light ⟨a *fulgent* sun peeked from behind the clouds⟩ — see BRIGHT 1

fulgently *adv* in a manner marked by the shining or reflecting of much light ⟨under a *fulgently* full moon we camped out for the night⟩ — see BRIGHTLY 1

fuliginous *adj* having an often intentionally veiled or uncertain meaning ⟨a *fuliginous* prose style that's not exactly ideal for writing for the mass media⟩ — see OBSCURE 1

full *adv* **1** to a full extent or degree ⟨waited until it was *full* dark to launch the attack⟩ — see FULLY 1
2 to a great degree ⟨he knew *full* well that what he was doing was wrong⟩ — see VERY 1
3 as stated or indicated without the slightest difference ⟨*full* in the center of the square stands an enormous statue of the city's founder⟩ — see EXACTLY 1

full *n* a complete amount of something ⟨the account is now paid in *full*⟩ — see WHOLE

full *adj* **1** containing or seeming to contain the greatest quantity or number possible ⟨at the start of the game everyone was *full* of energy and hope⟩ ⟨the boy's bedroom is *full* of sports trophies and medals⟩
synonyms brimful, brimming, bursting, chockablock, chock-full (*or* chockful), crammed, crowded, fat, filled, jammed, jam-packed, loaded, packed, stuffed
related words overcrowded, overfilled, overflowing, overfull, overladen, overloaded, overstuffed; abounding, flush, fraught, replete, rife, swarming, teeming
near antonyms deficient, inadequate, incomplete, insufficient, short, shortish, shy, wanting; depleted, drained, exhausted
antonyms bare, blank, devoid, empty, stark, vacant, void
2 of the highest degree ⟨even at the age of eighteen he hadn't reached his *full* height⟩ ⟨a boat going at *full* speed⟩
synonyms greatest, maximum, top, topmost, utmost, utter
related words heightened, high
near antonyms lessened, low
antonyms least, littlest, lowest, minimal, minimum, slightest
3 having one's appetite completely satisfied ⟨even the heartiest eaters are sure to be *full* when they leave that restaurant⟩
synonyms replete, sated, satiate, satiated, stuffed, surfeited
related words glutted, gorged, overfed, overfull, overstuffed
near antonyms underfed, undernourished
antonyms empty, famished, hungry, starved, starving
4 covering everything or all important points ⟨a *full* analysis of the problems facing our cities today⟩ — see ENCYCLOPEDIC
5 having an abundance of some characteristic quality (as flavor) ⟨the dessert had a rich, *full* chocolate flavor⟩ — see FULL-BODIED
6 having an excess of body fat ⟨she should have a hairdo that complements her *full* face⟩ — see FAT 1
7 including many small descriptive features ⟨a very *full* description of the city's cultural offerings⟩ — see DETAILED 1
8 not lacking any part or member that properly belongs to it ⟨a *full* deck of cards⟩ — see COMPLETE 1

full blast *adv* with all power or resources being used ⟨the unsuspecting parents arrived home to find the stereo going *full blast* and the kitchen a mess⟩
synonyms all out, full tilt, tooth and nail
related words completely, comprehensively, detailedly, exhaustively, fully, minutely, roundly, thoroughly, totally; extremely, utterly
phrases full steam ahead, in full career, like crazy, to the hilt

full–blood *adj* of unmixed ancestry ⟨her ancestry is *full-blood* Irish⟩ — see PUREBRED

full–blooded *adj* **1** of unmixed ancestry ⟨a *full-blooded* American Indian⟩ — see PUREBRED
2 having a healthy reddish skin tone ⟨had the *full-blooded* complexion of a rugged outdoorsman⟩ — see RUDDY
3 marked by or uttered with forcefulness ⟨mounted a *full-blooded* attack on his opponent's position regarding immigration⟩ — see EMPHATIC 1

full–blown *adj* fully grown or developed ⟨before he became a *full-blown* literary sensation, he wrote articles for little journals that paid even littler money⟩ — see MATURE 1

full–bodied *adj* having an abundance of some characteristic quality (as flavor) ⟨after that huge Sunday brunch, everyone needed a *full-bodied* coffee⟩

synonyms big, concentrated, full, heady, lusty, muscular, plush, potent, rich, robust, strong
related words heavy; straight, undiluted, unmixed; high-octane, high-test; enriched, fortified; concentrated
near antonyms dilute, diluted, watered-down, watery
antonyms delicate, light, mild, thin, thinned, weak, weakened

full dress *n* dressy clothing ⟨suburban teens in *full dress* for the prom at the country club⟩ — see FINERY

full–fledged *adj* fully grown or developed ⟨it was years before he became a *full-fledged* star⟩ — see MATURE 1

fullness *n* the quality or state of being without restriction, exception, or qualification ⟨has regained *fullness* of motor control⟩ — see ENTIRENESS

full–scale *adj* trying all possibilities ⟨a *full-scale* search and rescue for the victims of the rock slide⟩ — see EXHAUSTIVE 1

full tilt *adv* **1** with all power or resources being used ⟨during the war the nation's factories were going *full tilt*⟩ — see FULL BLAST
2 with great speed ⟨the fleeing robber ran *full tilt* down the hill⟩ — see FAST 1

fully *adv* **1** to a full extent or degree ⟨only with daybreak did we *fully* realize the extent of the damage from the storm⟩
synonyms all, all of, all over, altogether, clean, completely, dead, enough, entire, entirely, even, exactly, fast, flat, full, heartily, out, perfectly, plumb [*chiefly dialect*], quite, soundly, thoroughly, through and through, totally, utterly, well, wholly, wide
related words absolutely, categorically, cold, downright, hands down, plain, stone, stone-cold, unqualifiedly; basically, by and large, chiefly, generally, largely, mainly, more or less, mostly, overall, predominantly, predominately, primarily, principally, substantially; abundantly, copiously, generously, greatly
phrases all the way, at length, down the line, down to the ground, for fair, in whole, to bits, to pieces, to the hilt, to the max
near antonyms barely, hardly, just, kind of, marginally, minimally, scarcely, slightly, superficially; approximately, roughly, somewhat
antonyms half, halfway, incompletely, part, partially, partly
2 with attention to all aspects or details ⟨wanted to be *fully* involved in the project⟩ — see THOROUGHLY 1

fulminate *vb* to talk loudly and wildly ⟨she was embarrassed when her friend began *fulminating* at the restaurant about what's wrong with today's kids⟩ — see RANT

fulmination *n* harsh insulting language ⟨players were told they had a right to be spared the foulmouthed *fulmination* of the hockey coach⟩ — see ABUSE 1

fulsome *adj* **1** overly or insincerely flattering ⟨the player's *fulsome* praise for the coach showed just how hard he was trying to be named captain of the team⟩
synonyms adulatory, gushing, gushy, hagiographic (*also* hagiographical), oily, oleaginous, soapy, unctuous
related words drooling, slavering, slobbering; cloying, sickening; demonstrative, effusive, mushy, uninhibited, unreserved, unrestrained; artificial, backhanded, feigned, hypocritical, insincere, left-handed, mealy-mouthed, sanctimonious, two-faced; disarming, endearing, ingratiating, winning, winsome; extravagant, lavish, unrestrained; abundant, copious, profuse
near antonyms artless, earnest, genuine, heartfelt, honest, ingenuous, sincere, true, unaffected, unfeigned, unpretending, unpretentious
2 giving or sharing in abundance and without hesitation ⟨grateful survivors who were *fulsome* in their praise of the rescue team⟩ — see GENEROUS 1
3 causing intense displeasure, disgust, or resentment ⟨the author perpetuates some truly *fulsome* stereotypes in her novel⟩ — see OFFENSIVE 1

fumble *n* an unintentional departure from truth or accuracy ⟨played the entire piano piece without a single *fumble*⟩ — see ERROR 1

fumble *vb* **1** to make or do (something) in a clumsy or unskillful way ⟨her assistant *fumbled* the party plans by getting the time wrong on the invitations⟩ — see BOTCH
2 to search for something blindly or uncertainly ⟨the librarian *fumbled* for the light switch as she entered the dark room⟩ — see GROPE
3 to make a mistake ⟨just when it looked like he was going to get away with the ruse, he *fumbled*⟩ — see ERR 1

fumbled *adj* showing or marked by a lack of skill and tact (as in dealing with a situation) ⟨my future father-in-law shook his head over my *fumbled* attempt to compliment his daughter⟩ — see AWKWARD 2

fumbler *n* someone who bungles an effort ⟨a well-meaning *fumbler* who somehow screwed up our computer network⟩ — see BUTCHER

fume *vb* **1** to be excited or emotionally stirred up with anger ⟨he silently *fumed* as his ex-girlfriend danced with her new beau⟩ — see BOIL 1
2 to express one's anger usually violently ⟨when she found out her driver's license was being suspended, she *fumed*, throwing papers across the room and shouting at the top of her lungs⟩ — see RAGE 1

fuming *adj* feeling or showing anger ⟨I was *fuming* after losing the game by a single point⟩ — see ANGRY

fun *vb* to make jokes ⟨just a couple of old friends *funning* with each other⟩ — see JOKE 1

fun *adj* providing amusement or enjoyment ⟨there were so many *fun* things to do at summer camp that the kids really hated to leave⟩
synonyms amusing, delightful, diverting, enjoyable, entertaining, pleasurable
related words agreeable, beguiling, nice, pleasant, satisfying, welcome; recreational; antic, comic, comical, droll, farcical, funny, hilarious, humorous, laughable, ludicrous, ridiculous, riotous, risible, sidesplitting, uproarious; blithesome, gay, gleeful, happy, jocose, jocund, jolly, jovial, merry, mirthful, sunny; exciting, stimulating, thrilling
near antonyms disagreeable, displeasing, distasteful, uncongenial, unlovely, unpleasant, unpleasing, unwelcome
antonyms boring, drab, dreary, dull, flat, heavy, humdrum, jading, leaden, monotonous, pedestrian, pleasureless, ponderous, stodgy, stuffy, tedious, tiresome, tiring, uninteresting, wearisome, weary, wearying

fun *n* **1** someone or something that provides amusement or enjoyment ⟨theme parks with their rides, shows, and games are great *fun* for the whole family⟩
synonyms delight, distraction, diversion, divertissement, entertainment, pleasure, recreation
related words escape, pastime, time killer; binge, fling, frolic, gambol, lark, revel, rollick, romp, spree; frolicking, rollicking; carousing, conviviality, festivity, gaiety (*also* gayety), hilarity, jollification, jollity, merrymaking, reveling (*or* revelling), revelry, whoopee; picnic; laugh, riot, scream; activity, game
near antonyms killjoy, party pooper
antonyms bore, bummer, downer, drag
2 an attitude or manner not to be taken seriously ⟨when I said that playing the piano like that could get you arrested, I only said it in *fun*⟩
synonyms game, jest, play, sport
related words facetiousness, flightiness, flippancy, frivolity, frivolousness, frothiness, levity, light-mindedness, silliness
near antonyms earnestness, gravity, seriousness, soberness, sobriety, solemnity
antonyms earnest

3 activity engaged in to amuse oneself ⟨came outside to where we were playing touch football and joined the *fun*⟩ — see PLAY 1
4 a state of noisy, confused activity ⟨the *fun* really began when the deer broke out of its pen and started wandering down the street⟩ — see COMMOTION

fun and games *n pl* **1** a situation or state of carefree comfort ⟨soon found out that owning and maintaining a yacht wasn't all *fun and games*⟩ — see BEER AND SKITTLES
2 activity engaged in to amuse oneself ⟨it's not all *fun and games* at the summer music camp, where students are expected to take their studies seriously⟩ — see PLAY 1

function *n* **1** a social gathering ⟨made a brief appearance at the annual holiday *function*⟩ — see PARTY 1
2 an assignment at which one regularly works for pay ⟨what's your *function* in this company?⟩ — see JOB 1
3 the action for which a person or thing is specially fitted or used or for which a thing exists ⟨that machine's *function* is to sort bolts by size⟩ — see ROLE

function *vb* to have a certain purpose ⟨the heart *functions* as a pump for the blood⟩
synonyms act, perform, serve, work
related words operate, run; administer, carry on, control, direct, guide, handle, manage, oversee, regulate, supervise

functional *adj* **1** being in effective operation ⟨I don't think that vending machine is *functional*, so don't put money into it⟩ — see ACTIVE 1
2 capable of being put to use or account ⟨a *functional* knowledge of auto mechanics⟩ — see PRACTICAL 1
3 capable of or suitable for being used for a particular purpose ⟨a very *functional* kitchen utensil for peeling potatoes⟩ — see USABLE 1

functionary *n* **1** a person who holds a public office ⟨spoke to high-ranking *functionaries* at the embassy in the hopes that they could help⟩ — see OFFICIAL
2 a worker in a government agency ⟨the faceless *functionaries* at the Internal Revenue Service⟩ — see BUREAUCRAT

functioning *adj* being in effective operation ⟨looked for a *functioning* washing machine, but the few that weren't broken were in use⟩ — see ACTIVE 1

fund *vb* **1** to furnish (as an institution) with a regular source of income ⟨her will *funded* a new science center for her beloved alma mater⟩ — see ENDOW 2
2 to provide money for ⟨Dad advised me to get a job because he wasn't going to *fund* my social life forever⟩ — see FINANCE 1

fund *n* **1** a sum of money set aside for a particular purpose ⟨our club has a *fund* for parties—which we like to have as often as possible⟩
synonyms account, budget, deposit, kitty, nest egg, pool
related words chest, coffer(s); assets, savings, savings account; bankroll, cache, collection, cushion, hoard, pocketbook, reserve, treasure; petty cash, pin money, pocket money, spending money
2 funds *pl* available money ⟨my *funds* were a little low, so I asked my favorite lending institution—Dad—for a small advance on my first paycheck⟩
synonyms bankroll, coffers, exchequer, finances, pocket, resources, wherewithal
related words shirt; bread [*slang*], cash, chips, currency, dough, gold, jack [*slang*], legal tender, lucre, pelf, scratch [*slang*], tender, wampum; assets, capital, deep pockets, fortune, means, opulence, riches, roll, substance, wealth; purse, treasury; cash flow; financing
near antonyms debts, liabilities; indebtedness
3 the number of individuals or amount of something available at any given time ⟨we have a deep *fund* of volunteers to call on when there is an unexpected need for help⟩ — see SUPPLY

fundament *n* the part of the body upon which someone sits ⟨a naked *fundament* was clearly visible for an instant in the movie⟩ — see BUTTOCKS

fundamental *adj* of or relating to the simplest facts or theories of a subject ⟨the purpose of the course is to furnish students with *fundamental* knowledge of human reproduction⟩ — see ELEMENTARY

fundamentals *n pl* general or basic truths on which other truths or theories can be based ⟨all students at the school of music must take a course in the *fundamentals* of their chosen art⟩ — see PRINCIPLES 1

funeral *adj* expressing or suggesting mourning ⟨a slow and heavy *funeral* song⟩ — see MOURNFUL 1

funeral director *n* a person who manages funerals and prepares the dead for burial or cremation ⟨the *funeral director* instructed the pallbearers on how to proceed⟩
synonyms mortician, undertaker
related words embalmer

funereal *adj* causing or marked by an atmosphere lacking in cheer ⟨shivered with cold in the dark and *funereal* Victorian mansion⟩ — see GLOOMY 1

fungible *adj* capable of being substituted in place of one another ⟨since fruits and vegetables are regarded as *fungible* in this diet, you are allowed a total of five servings of either or both⟩ — see INTERCHANGEABLE

[1]funk *n* a strong unpleasant smell ⟨the overpowering *funk* of rotten meat emanated from the garbage bin⟩ — see STINK 1

[2]funk *n* a person who shows a shameful lack of courage in the face of danger ⟨he may be a strong, athletic guy, but he's a real *funk* when it comes to donating blood⟩ — see COWARD

funky *adj* **1** different from the ordinary in a way that causes curiosity or suspicion ⟨a *funky* antique shop that reflects the owner's decidedly eccentric taste⟩ — see ODD 2
2 having an unpleasant smell ⟨a *funky* pair of old socks lying on the locker room floor⟩ — see MALODOROUS

funnel *vb* to cause to move to a central point or along a restricted pathway ⟨*funneled* endless time and money into his misguided pet project⟩ — see CHANNEL

funniness *n* the amusing quality or element in something ⟨the *funniness* of the situation is often lost on the victim of the prank⟩ — see HUMOR 1

funning *adj* marked by or expressive of mild or good-natured teasing ⟨after he confided to his friends that he had a crush on his science lab partner, they made *funning* comments about the "chemistry" between the two sweethearts⟩ — see QUIZZICAL

funny *n* **1** a series of drawings that tell a story or part of a story ⟨reading the Sunday *funnies* is part of my weekend ritual⟩ — see COMIC STRIP
2 something said or done to cause laughter ⟨let's can the *funnies*—we've got serious work to do here⟩ — see JOKE 1

funny *adj* **1** causing or intended to cause laughter ⟨a very *funny* movie that had audiences rolling in the aisles⟩
synonyms antic, chucklesome, comedic, comic, comical, droll, farcical, hilarious, humoristic, humorous, hysterical (*also* hysteric), killing, laughable, ludicrous, ridiculous, riotous, risible, screaming, sidesplitting, uproarious
related words amusing, diverting, entertaining; clownish, knockabout, slapstick, slapsticky, zany; facetious, flip, flippant, pert, smart, smart-aleck, smart-alecky, snickery; jocular, playful, waggish; campy, jokey (*also* joky); priceless, rich, whimsical, witty, wry; blithesome, gleeful, jocose, jocund, jolly, jovial, laughing, mad, merry, mirthful

near antonyms earnest, grave, no-nonsense, sedate, serious, severe, sober, sobersided, solemn, somber (*or* sombre), staid, unsmiling, weighty; affecting, moving, poignant, touching, tragic (*also* tragical); lachrymose, mournful, sad, sorrowful, tearful, woeful
antonyms humorless, lame, unamusing, uncomic, unfunny, unhumorous, unhysterical
2 different from the ordinary in a way that causes curiosity or suspicion ⟨that's *funny*, for I could have sworn I put my keys right here yesterday⟩ — see ODD 2
3 noticeably different from what is generally found or experienced ⟨that's a *funny*-looking dog—what kind is it?⟩ — see UNUSUAL 1

funnyman *n* a person (as a writer) noted for or specializing in humor ⟨a *funnyman* who honed his shtick in vaudeville, Milton Berle was credited with popularizing the medium of television⟩ — see HUMORIST

fur *n* **1** the hairy covering of a mammal especially when fine, soft, and thick ⟨the chinchilla is known for its exceptionally soft *fur*⟩
synonyms coat, fleece, hair, jacket, pelage, pile, wool
related words undercoat, underfur; hide, leather, pelt, skin
2 a soft airy substance or covering ⟨picked at the *fur* on the chenille pillows⟩ — see [1]FUZZ
3 the outer covering of an animal removed for its commercial value ⟨furriers willing to pay good money for a lynx *fur*⟩ — see HIDE 1

furbelow *n* a strip of fabric gathered or pleated on one edge and used as trimming ⟨she opted for a simple wedding dress that did without all the frills and *furbelows*⟩ — see RUFFLE 1

furbish *vb* to make smooth or glossy usually by repeatedly applying surface pressure ⟨the warrior *furbished* his sword and shield so that they glinted in the sunlight⟩ — see POLISH 1

furious *adj* **1** marked by great and often stressful excitement or activity ⟨everyone worked at a *furious* pace in order to get the float ready for the parade⟩
synonyms delirious, ferocious, feverish, fierce, frantic, frenetic, frenzied, mad, rabid, violent, wild
related words concentrated, high-pressured, intense, intensive, vehement; excessive, exorbitant, extravagant, extreme, immoderate, inordinate, lavish, overmuch, overweening, unconscionable, undue; crazed, crazy, demented, deranged, insane, irrational, lunatic, mad, maniacal (*also* maniac)
near antonyms calm, peaceful, placid, quiet, serene, subdued, tranquil, undisturbed, unperturbed, untroubled; moderate, reasonable, temperate; casual, easygoing, low-pressure; balanced, sane, sound
antonyms relaxed
2 extreme in degree, power, or effect ⟨a *furious* hurricane virtually destroyed the seaside town⟩ — see INTENSE 1
3 feeling or showing anger ⟨a *furious* customer demanding to see the manager⟩ — see ANGRY
4 marked by bursts of destructive force or intense activity ⟨rioters went on a *furious* rampage, doing over $2,000,000 in damage⟩ — see VIOLENT 1

furlough *n* the termination of the employment of an employee or a work force often temporarily ⟨the landscaping company usually has to put most of its personnel on *furlough* during the extremely slow winter months⟩ — see LAYOFF 1

furnish *vb* **1** to provide (someone) with what is needed for a task or activity ⟨the art students were *furnished* with brushes, crayons, pencils, and various other art supplies⟩
synonyms accoutre (*or* accouter), equip, fit (out), gird, kit (up *or* out) [*chiefly British*], outfit, provision, rig, supply
related words stock, store; bestow, contribute, donate, give, present; apportion, deal (out), dispense, distribute, dole out, hand out, mete (out), parcel (out), portion, prorate; allocate, allot, assign; arm, fortify, prepare; reequip, refit, refurnish, reoutfit
near antonyms deprive, dispossess, divest, strip
2 to put (something) into the possession of someone for use or consumption ⟨we'll gladly *furnish* the food for any out-of-town guests⟩
synonyms deliver, feed, give, hand, hand over, provide, supply
related words ply (with); administer, allocate, apportion, deal (out), dispense, distribute, dole out, mete (out), parcel (out), portion, prorate; assign, cede, deed, make over, transfer
near antonyms conserve, keep up, maintain, preserve, save
antonyms hold (back), keep (back), reserve, retain, withhold

furnishings *n pl* the movable articles (such as tables and chairs) in a room ⟨we moved the *furnishings* out of the room so we could sand down and refinish the wood floor⟩ — see FURNITURE

furniture *n* the movable articles (such as tables and chairs) in a room ⟨we bought all new *furniture* for our new house⟩
synonyms appointments, cabinetwork, furnishings, movables (*or* moveables)
related words belongings, chattels, effects, gear, goods, holdings, paraphernalia, possessions, things; case goods
near antonyms built-ins, fixtures

furor *n* **1** a state of noisy, confused activity ⟨the classroom was in a *furor* when the mice escaped from their cage⟩ — see COMMOTION
2 a state of wildly excited activity or emotion ⟨euphoric children in a gift-opening *furor* on Christmas morning⟩ — see FRENZY
3 an intense emotional state of displeasure with someone or something ⟨residents were in a *furor* about the new paper mill being constructed within city limits⟩ — see ANGER

furore *n* **1** a state of noisy, confused activity ⟨the store's going-out-of-business sale caused such a *furore* that security guards had to be called in to restore order⟩ — see COMMOTION
2 a state of wildly excited activity or emotion ⟨baseball fans in a *furore* as the game stretched to 11 innings⟩ — see FRENZY

furred *adj* covered with or as if with hair ⟨a girl who loves all *furred* animals, from hamsters to bears⟩ — see HAIRY 1

furrow *n* a small fold in a soft and otherwise smooth surface ⟨the *furrows* in his usually unwrinkled brow suggested that he was very worried⟩ — see WRINKLE 1

furrow *vb* **1** to cut into and turn over the sod of (a piece of land) using a bladed implement ⟨we had to *furrow* the field before we could plant the wheat⟩ — see PLOW 1
2 to develop creases or folds ⟨his brow *furrowed* in concentration as he tried to figure out the math problem⟩ — see WRINKLE 1

furry *adj* **1** covered with or as if with hair ⟨a *furry* teddy bear that would be so nice to cuddle up with⟩ — see HAIRY 1
2 made of or resembling hair ⟨green *furry* mold on old bread⟩ — see HAIRY 2

further *adj* resulting in an increase in amount or number ⟨I think *further* research is needed before we can say whether that treatment is safe or not⟩ — see ADDITIONAL

further *adv* **1** at or to a greater distance or more advanced point ⟨go *further* along this road and you'll see

the sign for the highway⟩ — see FARTHER
2 in addition to what has been said ⟨I'll say nothing *further* at this time⟩ — see MORE 1
further *vb* to help the growth or development of ⟨she worked hard to *further* her operatic career⟩ — see FOSTER 1
furtherance *n* forward movement in time or place ⟨the 1965 Civil Rights Act was a major step in the *furtherance* of social justice in the U.S.⟩ — see ADVANCE 1
furthermore *adv* in addition to what has been said ⟨I'm not interested in what you are selling, and *furthermore*, I asked your company not to contact me ever again⟩ — see MORE 1
furthermost *adj* most distant from a center ⟨a probe that will travel into the *furthermost* reaches of deep space⟩ — see EXTREME 1
furthest *adj* most distant from a center ⟨this belongs in the aisle *furthest* from the cash registers⟩ — see EXTREME 1
furtive *adj* **1** given to acting in secret and to concealing one's intentions ⟨a *furtive* guy who always seems to be up to something, and usually that something is no-good⟩ — see SNEAKY 1
2 undertaken or done so as to escape being observed or known by others ⟨gave each other *furtive* glances as we watched our friend open the booby-trapped soda⟩ — see SECRET 1
fury *n* **1** a bad-tempered scolding woman ⟨tradition has it that Socrates' wife was such a *fury* that the philosopher's death sentence by the authorities was not an entirely unwelcome fate⟩ — see SHREW
2 a state of wildly excited activity or emotion ⟨the sudden appearance of the rock star whipped the crowd of onlookers into a *fury* of excitement⟩ — see FRENZY
3 an intense emotional state of displeasure with someone or something ⟨in his *fury*, the duped gambler overturned the card table and declared that the game had been fixed⟩ — see ANGER
fuse *vb* **1** to come together to form a single unit ⟨our two local teams *fused* into a larger regional team⟩ — see UNITE 1
2 to go from a solid to a liquid state ⟨the lightning strike was so hot it caused the electrical wires to *fuse* and then drip onto the road⟩ — see LIQUEFY
3 to turn into a single mass or entity that is more or less the same throughout ⟨the many foundries would daily *fuse* copper and zinc to create the brass that made the city famous⟩ — see BLEND 1
fusillade *n* a rapid or overwhelming outpouring of many things at once ⟨responded calmly to the *fusillade* of criticism leveled at his design for the memorial⟩ — see BARRAGE
fusion *n* a distinct entity formed by the combining of two or more different things ⟨a *fusion* of jazz and classical music⟩ — see BLEND
fuss *n* **1** a feeling or declaration of disapproval or dissent ⟨she made a *fuss* over not being picked for the lead role in the play⟩ — see OBJECTION
2 a state of nervous or irritated concern ⟨the new parents are always in a *fuss* over whether the baby is dressed warmly enough⟩ — see FRET
3 a state of noisy, confused activity ⟨the company managed the move into the new building without any undue *fuss*⟩ — see COMMOTION
4 an expression of dissatisfaction, pain, or resentment ⟨none of the employees dared to make a *fuss* over having to come to work in the huge snowstorm⟩ — see COMPLAINT 1
fuss *vb* **1** to express dissatisfaction, pain, or resentment usually tiresomely ⟨the eldest daughter is always *fussing* that she gets stuck with all the chores around the house⟩ — see COMPLAIN
2 to make an exaggerated display of affection or enthusiasm ⟨fans *fussing* over their favorite rock guitarist⟩ — see GUSH 2
3 to make often peevish criticisms or objections about matters that are minor, unimportant, or irrelevant ⟨the picky eater who *fusses* over the arrangement of food on his plate or who won't eat the rice if it touches the salad⟩ — see QUIBBLE 1
4 to use flattery or the doing of favors in order to win approval especially from a superior ⟨given to *fussing* over her father whenever she wants a favor or some ready cash⟩ — see FAWN
5 to experience concern or anxiety ⟨there is no use in *fussing* over things that you can't control⟩ — see WORRY 1
6 to trouble the mind of; to make uneasy ⟨you shouldn't let a little thing like that *fuss* you⟩ — see DISTURB 1
fussbudget *n* a person who makes frequent complaints usually about little things ⟨a customer who's a real *fussbudget* about wanting her food very hot⟩ — see CRYBABY
fussbudgety *adj* hard to please ⟨my *fussbudgety* aunt wouldn't even consider a B and B without private baths⟩ — see FINICKY
fusser *n* **1** a person who makes frequent complaints usually about little things ⟨sat next to an insufferable *fusser*, who whined during the entire bus trip⟩ — see CRYBABY
2 an irritable and complaining person ⟨a natural *fusser* who has never had a glimmer of gratitude for anything done for him⟩ — see GROUCH 1
fusspot *n* a person who makes frequent complaints usually about little things ⟨as a professional gardener with a well-heeled clientele, he's used to dealing with *fusspots*⟩ — see CRYBABY
fussy *adj* **1** given to complaining a lot ⟨predictably, the kids riding in the back were *fussy* passengers, always asking "Are we there yet?"⟩
synonyms crabby, cranky, grouchy, grumpy, querulous
related words antsy, fidgety, restive, restless, squirmy, twitchy, uneasy, wiggly, wriggly; discontented, disgruntled, displeased, dissatisfied; fretful, nervous, worrisome; cantankerous, choleric, cross, crotchety, irascible, irritable, ornery, peevish, perverse, pettish, petulant, quick-tempered, short-tempered, snappish, snappy, snippy, testy, waspish
near antonyms affable, agreeable, amiable, genial, good-humored, good-natured, good-tempered, gracious, well-disposed; accommodating, complaisant, obliging; easygoing, laid-back, relaxed
antonyms forbearing, long-suffering, patient, stoic (*or* stoical), tolerant, uncomplaining
2 hard to please ⟨cats have a well-deserved reputation for being *fussy* eaters⟩ — see FINICKY
3 taking, showing, or involving great care and effort ⟨a *fussy* teacher who reads through papers two and even three times before issuing a grade⟩ — see PAINSTAKING
4 elaborately and often excessively decorated ⟨the room, with its rococo furniture and its overabundance of knickknacks, is just too *fussy* for my taste⟩ — see ORNATE 1
fustian *adj* marked by the use of impressive-sounding but mostly meaningless words and phrases ⟨one of those *fustian* odes to patriotic duty that were so beloved by school teachers⟩ — see RHETORICAL 1
fustian *n* language that is impressive-sounding but not meaningful or sincere ⟨a speech awash in old-fashioned *fustian* and bereft of all substance⟩ — see RHETORIC 1
fusty *adj* having an unpleasant smell ⟨couldn't stay too

long in the *fusty* attic without sneezing⟩ — see MALODOROUS

futile *adj* **1** producing no results ⟨the prison is so well guarded that all attempts to escape have been *futile*⟩
synonyms abortive, barren, bootless, empty, fruitless, ineffective, ineffectual, inefficacious, otiose, profitless, unavailing, unproductive, unprofitable, unsuccessful, useless, vain
related words hollow, idle, meaningless, pointless, valueless, worthless; hopeless, impossible, lost, no-win, unattainable; inadequate, insufficient, lacking, wanting; counterproductive
phrases in vain, no dice, not worth the candle, of no avail
near antonyms meaningful, worthwhile; adequate, sufficient; applicable, feasible, functional, practicable, practical, realizable, usable (*also* useable), workable
antonyms deadly, effective, effectual, efficacious, efficient, fruitful, potent, productive, profitable, successful, virtuous
2 lacking in seriousness or maturity ⟨the *futile* chatter of gossip columnists about the comings and goings of Hollywood celebrities⟩ — see GIDDY 1

future *adj* of a time after the present ⟨we must preserve our national parks in all their glory so that *future* generations can experience the majesty of nature⟩
synonyms coming, unborn
related words approaching, forthcoming, imminent, impending, nearing, oncoming, pending, upcoming; after, ensuing, later, posterior, subsequent; anticipated, awaited, expected, planned, predicted, projected, prospective; eventual, final, last, ulterior, ultimate
near antonyms ancient, olden; antecedent, anterior, precedent, preceding, previous, prior
antonyms bygone, past

future *n* **1** time that is to come ⟨in the *future*, there may be medical discoveries that are beyond our fondest dreams⟩
synonyms by-and-by, futurity, hereafter, offing, tomorrow
related words eventuality, finality; posterity
near antonyms yesterday, yesteryear; antiquity, old, yore; moment, now, present, today
antonyms past
2 what is going to happen to someone in the time ahead ⟨with such a strong academic record, his *future* looks bright⟩ — see FORTUNE 1

futurist *n* one who predicts future events or developments ⟨economic *futurists* predict a new world order in which information is the resource that drives a nation's economy⟩ — see PROPHET 1

futurity *n* time that is to come ⟨we can scarcely imagine what observers in some remote *futurity* will think of civilization as it existed at the dawn of the 21st century⟩ — see FUTURE 1

[1]fuzz *n* a soft airy substance or covering ⟨a comfortable old sweater with clumps of *fuzz* all over it⟩
synonyms down, floss, fluff, fur, lint, nap, pile
related words batting

[2]fuzz *n* **1** a body of officers of the law ⟨we've got to get out of here before the *fuzz* catches on to our scam⟩ — see POLICE 2
2 a member of a force charged with law enforcement at the local level ⟨the weary *fuzz* hauled in yet another drunk⟩ — see OFFICER 1

fuzz (up) *vb* to make dark, dim, or indistinct ⟨picture postcards never show those not-infrequent days when the coastal scenery is *fuzzed up* by fog⟩ — see CLOUD 1

fuzzy *adj* **1** made of or resembling hair ⟨wore a *fuzzy* red wig at the Halloween party⟩ — see HAIRY 2
2 not expressed in precise terms ⟨the specifics of the program proposed by the candidate are rather *fuzzy*, perhaps intentionally so⟩ — see VAGUE 1
3 not seen or understood clearly ⟨saw a *fuzzy* outline through the fog⟩ — see FAINT 1

G

gab *vb* to engage in casual or rambling conversation ⟨spent the time she should have been working *gabbing* with friends instead⟩ — see CHAT 1

gab *n* friendly, informal conversation or an instance of this ⟨a car salesman with the proverbial gift for *gab*⟩ — see CHAT 1

gabble *n* unintelligible or meaningless talk ⟨he claimed he was speaking Arabic, but an Egyptian friend confided that all his murmurings were just *gabble*⟩ — see GIBBERISH 1

gabble *vb* **1** to engage in casual or rambling conversation ⟨heard her parents' guests still *gabbling* in the living room late into the night⟩ — see CHAT 1
2 to speak rapidly, inarticulately, and usually unintelligibly ⟨during the filming of the party scene the extras were told to just *gabble* and act like they were having a great time⟩ — see BABBLE 1

gabbler *n* a person who talks constantly ⟨was a real *gabbler* who never let you get a word in edgewise⟩ — see CHATTERBOX

gabby *adj* fond of talking or conversation ⟨a *gabby* talk-show host whose interviews were almost as much about herself as about her guests⟩ — see TALKATIVE

gabfest *n* friendly, informal conversation or an instance of this ⟨the slumber party was an all-night *gabfest* filled with gossip, giggling, and whispered secrets⟩ — see CHAT 1

gad (about) *vb* to move about from place to place aimlessly ⟨he *gads about* town every Saturday, flirting and gossiping with various shopkeepers and locals⟩ — see WANDER 1

gadabout *n* a person who roams about without a fixed route or destination ⟨she was a thoughtful *gadabout*, always picking up souvenirs for her friends from wherever her travels took her⟩ — see NOMAD

gadarene *adj* acting or done with excessive or careless speed ⟨what began as the defection of a handful of employees soon became a *gadarene* exodus that threatened to leave the advertising agency understaffed⟩ — see HASTY 1

gadfly *n* one who is obnoxiously annoying ⟨a loud sports commentator who was a tactless *gadfly* during post-game interviews with the losing team⟩ — see NUISANCE 1

gadget *n* an interesting and often novel device with a practical use ⟨she tried out a new *gadget* for weeding the garden⟩
synonyms appliance, contraption, contrivance, gimmick, gizmo (*also* gismo), jigger, widget
related words implement, instrument, tool, utensil; ingenuity, innovation, invention; accessory (*also* accessary), adjunct; mechanism, trick; dingus, doodad, doohickey, hickey, hootenanny [*chiefly dialect*], thingamabob, thingamajig (*or* thingumajig), thingummy

gaff *n* **1** a socially improper or unsuitable act or remark ⟨you can expect to make some amusing *gaffs* until you get more familiar with the language⟩ — see IMPROPRIETY 2
2 an unintentional departure from truth or accuracy ⟨double-check her writing, as it's typically riddled with *gaffs*⟩ — see ERROR 1

gaff *vb* **1** to cause to believe what is untrue ⟨a sleazy photographer who *gaffed* small-town girls into thinking he represented a big-city modeling agency⟩ — see DECEIVE
2 to rob by the use of trickery or threats ⟨the operators of the traveling carnival had *gaffed* the gullible with a variety of time-honored ruses⟩ — see FLEECE

gaffe *n* **1** a socially improper or unsuitable act or remark ⟨committed a huge *gaffe* when she started drinking from the finger bowl⟩ — see IMPROPRIETY 2
2 an unintentional departure from truth or accuracy ⟨so-called debates, which were mainly about seeing which candidate made the most *gaffes*⟩ — see ERROR 1

gag *n* **1** something said or done to cause laughter ⟨the movie featured a *gag* involving a chicken driving a car that audiences thought was hysterically funny⟩ — see JOKE 1
2 a playful or mischievous act intended as a joke ⟨the timeworn *gag* of asking a tobacconist if he has "Prince Albert in a can"⟩ — see PRANK

gag *vb* **1** to discharge the contents of the stomach through the mouth ⟨the terrible smell of rotting fish made me *gag*⟩ — see VOMIT
2 to experience complete or partial blockage of the windpipe ⟨took a bite that was too large and began to *gag*⟩ — see CHOKE 2
3 to make jokes ⟨the actor typically mugs and *gags* through his movies, but in his latest vehicle he plays it straight⟩ — see JOKE 1

gaga *adj* having or showing a very abnormal or sick state of mind ⟨after years of being alone in that remote outpost he had become totally *gaga*⟩ — see INSANE 1

gaga (over) *adj* filled with an intense or excessive love for ⟨lately Jack and his friends have been *gaga over* extreme skiing⟩ — see ENAMORED (OF)

gage *n* something given or held to assure that the giver will keep a promise ⟨in the old days a sheriff would take *gage* in the form of personal goods from an accused person who then had to appear in court or forfeit the goods⟩ — see PLEDGE 1

gagger *n* a person (as a writer) noted for or specializing in humor ⟨got her start in comedy as a *gagger* for the host of a talk show⟩ — see HUMORIST

gagman *n* a person (as a writer) noted for or specializing in humor ⟨politicians with no talent for humor often hire *gagmen* to write jokes for them⟩ — see HUMORIST

gagster *n* a person (as a writer) noted for or specializing in humor ⟨*gagsters* tried to outdo one another on jokes about the high-profile box office bomb⟩ — see HUMORIST

gaiety *also* **gayety** *n* **1** dressy clothing ⟨attendees of the masquerade ball arrived dressed in all their *gaiety*⟩ — see FINERY
2 joyful or festive activity ⟨loved the *gaiety* of the annual harvest festival⟩ ⟨the *gaiety* of the wedding reception⟩ — see MERRYMAKING
3 a mood characterized by high spirits and amusement and often accompanied by laughter ⟨the *gaiety* of children enjoying an outing at an amusement park⟩ — see MIRTH

gaily *also* **gayly** *adv* **1** in a cheerful or happy manner ⟨we sat around the table, *gaily* teasing each other and laughing about the good old days⟩
synonyms brightly, cheerfully, cheerily, happily, heartily, jocosely, jovially, merrily, mirthfully, smilingly
related words amusedly, exuberantly, giddily, gigglingly, joyfully, joyously; blithely, blithesomely, breez-

ily, gladly, gladsomely, laughingly, lightheartedly, sunnily; amicably, friendlily, friendly, good-humoredly, good-naturedly, jocularly; hopefully, optimistically, sanguinely; blissfully, elatedly, euphorically, rapturously
near antonyms abjectly, dejectedly, despondently, disconsolately, dispiritedly, wretchedly; dolefully, dolorously, forlornly, mournfully, plaintively, sorrowfully; dourly, glumly, mirthlessly, sourly, sternly, sulkily, sullenly; blackly, dismally, drearily, gloomily, pessimistically
antonyms bleakly, cheerlessly, darkly, heavily, miserably, morosely, unhappily
2 in a quick and spirited manner ⟨children *gaily* running to the buses on the last day of school⟩
synonyms airily, animatedly, animately, bouncily, buoyantly, high-spiritedly, livelily, lively, perkily, pertly, snappily, sparkily, spiritedly, sprightly, trippingly, vivaciously
related words friskily, gamesomely, playfully, skittishly, sportively; briskly, crisply, effervescently, energetically, jazzily, racily, springily; breezily, cockishly, dapperly, dashingly, jauntily; agilely, nimbly, spryly; allegro
near antonyms halfheartedly, idly, indolently, lazily, lethargically, slothfully; heavily, inactively, listlessly, tiredly, wearily
antonyms dully, inanimately, sluggishly, tardily
3 in a manner that is colorful and tends to arouse gaiety ⟨the Mexican dancers were *gaily* dressed in lavish, bright costumes⟩
synonyms bravely, brightly, brilliantly, colorfully
related words flamboyantly, flashily, garishly, gaudily, loud, loudly, ostentatiously; fancily, ornately, swankily; gorgeously, richly, spectacularly, splendidly, strikingly; dapperly, dashingly, gallantly, jazzily, nattily, neatly, pertly, smartly, snappily, spiffily; conspicuously, luridly, shockingly
near antonyms colorlessly, inconspicuously, unobtrusively, unpretentiously; chastely, demurely, modestly; conservatively, plainly, quietly, simply; bleakly, severely, somberly
antonyms boringly, drably, dully

gain *n* **1** something added (as by growth) ⟨attributed her recent weight *gain* to the medication she was taking⟩ — see INCREASE 1
2 the amount of money left when expenses are subtracted from the total amount received ⟨the company posted a substantial fourth-quarter *gain*, signaling an end to their money-losing ventures⟩ — see PROFIT 1
3 *usually* **gains** *pl* an increase usually measured in money that comes from labor, business, or property ⟨net *gains* this year were better than last⟩ — see INCOME 1

gain *vb* **1** to gradually increase in ⟨our hopes were raised as the movement *gained* strength⟩
synonyms build up, gather, grow (in), pick up
related words double (in), triple (in); accrue, accumulate, amass; excite, stimulate; enhance, enlarge, enrich, expand, extend, maximize; boost, elevate, jack (up), mount, ramp (up), step up
near antonyms abate, decline (in), diminish (in), dip, dwindle, fall (in), lessen, taper, taper off
antonyms decrease (in), lose
2 to receive as return for effort ⟨*gained* her affections with his boyishly shy manner⟩ — see EARN 1
3 to become healthy and strong again after illness or weakness ⟨is steadily *gaining* after his bout with the flu and will be back on his feet soon⟩ — see CONVALESCE
4 to become greater in size, extent, volume, amount, or number ⟨the new version of the car *gained* in both width and length compared to the earlier model⟩ — see INCREASE 2
5 to obtain (as a goal) through effort ⟨vowed to *gain* control of the company by any means necessary⟩ — see ACHIEVE 1
6 to cause (someone) to agree with a belief or course of action by using arguments or earnest request ⟨the radical party was able to *gain* some supporters with intense recruitment on college campuses⟩ — see PERSUADE

gainful *adj* yielding a profit ⟨graduated from school and went looking for *gainful* employment⟩ — see PROFITABLE 1

gainsay *vb* **1** to declare not to be true ⟨it can't be *gainsaid* that most people wish they had more time and money⟩ — see DENY 1
2 to make an assertion that is contrary to one made by (another) ⟨repeatedly tried to *gainsay* me, though every point I made was backed up by facts⟩ — see CONTRADICT 1

gal *n* a female romantic companion ⟨after years of dating, Fred finally asked his *gal* to marry him⟩ — see GIRLFRIEND

gala *n* a time or program of special events and entertainment in honor of something ⟨attended the *gala* celebrating the reopening of the museum⟩ — see FESTIVAL

galactic *adj* unusually large ⟨a *galactic* serving of soda that would have been enough for three moviegoers⟩ — see HUGE

galaxy *n* a huge physical or conceptual distance ⟨they're a *galaxy* apart when it comes to politics⟩
synonyms light-year, world
related words country mile, long haul, way; infinity
near antonyms hop, skip, and jump, shouting distance, stone's throw, striking distance; hair, hairbreadth (*or* hairsbreadth), inch

gale *n* a sudden intense expression of strong feeling ⟨the audience responded to the comedian's joke with *gales* of laughter⟩ — see OUTBURST 1

galère *n* a group of people sharing a common interest and relating together socially ⟨charged that the campus newspaper had been completely taken over by a *galère* of right-wing zealots⟩ — see GANG 2

galette *n* a small usually rounded mass of minced food that has been fried ⟨a golden-brown *galette* of lightly buttered and sautéed potato slices⟩ — see CAKE 1

gall *n* **1** a deep-seated ill will ⟨her kindly feelings turned to *gall* when she found out her nephew only wanted her money⟩ — see ENMITY
2 shameless boldness ⟨I can't believe he had the *gall* to ask me how much I weigh⟩ — see EFFRONTERY

gall *vb* **1** to damage or diminish by continued friction ⟨move that rope so the sharp edge of the hull doesn't *gall* it⟩ — see ABRADE 1
2 to disturb the peace of mind of (someone) especially by repeated disagreeable acts ⟨humming through your nose like that absolutely *galls* me⟩ — see IRRITATE 1
3 to make sore by continued rubbing ⟨tie your shoes so they don't *gall* your heels sliding on and off like that⟩ — see CHAFE 1

gallant *adj* **1** feeling or displaying no fear by temperament ⟨a *gallant* firefighter, rushing into the burning house to save the children⟩ ⟨a *gallant* rescue⟩ — see BRAVE 1
2 having, characterized by, or arising from a dignified and generous nature ⟨a *gallant* knight⟩ ⟨the members of that service club are known for their *gallant* service to the community⟩ — see NOBLE 2
3 large and impressive in size, grandeur, extent, or conception ⟨a great and *gallant* sailing ship⟩ — see GRAND 1

gallant *n* **1** a man extremely interested in his clothing and personal appearance ⟨he was quite a *gallant*, primping more than either of his sisters⟩ — see DANDY 1

2 a man who courts a woman usually with the goal of marrying her ⟨she had a whole host of *gallants* vying for her hand in marriage⟩ — see SUITOR 1

gallantly *adv* **1** in a manner befitting a person of the highest character and ideals ⟨*gallantly* offered to personally accompany the lost tourists back to their hotel⟩ — see GREATLY 1

2 in a fearless manner ⟨he ran *gallantly* to the rescue of the woman being mugged⟩ — see BRAVELY 1

gallantry *n* strength of mind to carry on in spite of danger ⟨commended the rescuers for their *gallantry*⟩ — see COURAGE

galled *adj* subjected to and reacting with irritation ⟨I was particularly *galled* when she didn't even offer to pay half the cab fare⟩ — see ANNOYED

gallery *n* **1** a building or part of a building in which objects of interest are displayed ⟨visited an array of art *galleries* while on vacation⟩ — see MUSEUM

2 a typically long narrow way connecting parts of a building ⟨the guest rooms in the east wing rooms open up onto a long windowed *gallery*⟩ — see HALL 2

3 *Southern & Midland* a covered structure adjoining an entrance to a building ⟨a big old house with a wraparound *gallery* just made for a line of rocking chairs⟩ — see PORCH

gallimaufry *n* an unorganized collection or mixture of various things ⟨the collection is a *gallimaufry* of poems, essays, and short stories that have no apparent unifying theme⟩ — see MISCELLANY 1

galling *adj* **1** causing annoyance ⟨her holier-than-thou attitude is *galling*⟩ — see ANNOYING

2 hard to accept or bear especially emotionally ⟨losing in the last round of play-offs was *galling* to our home team⟩ — see BITTER 2

gallivant *also* **galavant** *vb* to move about from place to place aimlessly ⟨*gallivanted* about the country before returning to school in the fall⟩ — see WANDER 1

gallivanting *also* **galavanting** *adj* traveling from place to place ⟨the *gallivanting* entertainers stayed in town for a few days, then moved on⟩ — see ITINERANT

gallop *vb* to go at a pace faster than a walk ⟨dawdles to school but *gallops* coming home⟩ — see RUN 1

galloping *adj* moving, proceeding, or acting with great speed ⟨the *galloping* pace of development in that Sunbelt state⟩ — see FAST 1

galoot *n, slang* an adult male human being ⟨he's a big-hearted *galoot*, even if he's not the sharpest tool in the shed⟩ — see MAN 1

galore *adj* **1** pouring forth in great amounts ⟨there was food *galore* at our Thanksgiving meal⟩ — see PROFUSE

2 being more than enough without being excessive ⟨with restaurants *galore*, the city is an epicure's delight⟩ — see PLENTIFUL

galumph *vb* to move heavily or clumsily ⟨the Great Dane *galumphed* across the floor to greet us⟩ — see LUMBER 1

galvanic *adj* causing great emotional or mental stimulation ⟨her *galvanic* rendition of the song received rapturous applause⟩ — see EXCITING 1

galvanize *vb* to cause a pleasurable stimulation of the feelings ⟨theatergoers were *galvanized* by the actor's powerhouse performance as Hamlet⟩ — see THRILL

galvanizing *adj* causing great emotional or mental stimulation ⟨the presentation on the international aid organization was *galvanizing* and thought-provoking⟩ — see EXCITING 1

gambit *n* a clever often underhanded means to achieve an end ⟨I couldn't tell whether her earlier poor-mouthing had been sincere or just a *gambit* to get me to pick up the dinner check⟩ — see TRICK 1

gamble *n* a risky undertaking ⟨it's a *gamble*, but I'm willing to take the risk⟩
synonyms adventure, chance, crapshoot, enterprise, flier (*also* flyer), flutter [*chiefly British*], speculation, throw, venture
related words bet, hazard, stake, wager; liberty; dark horse, long shot, play
antonyms sure thing

gamble *vb* to risk (something) on the outcome of an uncertain event ⟨a foolish man who *gambled* his life savings on the lottery⟩ — see BET

gamble (on) *vb* to take a chance on ⟨a movie studio willing to *gamble on* a new actress for its summer blockbuster⟩ — see RISK 1

gamble (with) *vb* to place in danger ⟨you don't want to *gamble with* your life, so buckle up⟩ — see ENDANGER

gambler *n* one that bets (as on the outcome of a contest or sports event) ⟨marveled at the huge swarm of *gamblers* in the casino⟩ — see BETTOR

gambol *n* a time or instance of carefree fun ⟨she and her old college roommate headed off for one final European *gambol* before returning to the States to start their separate careers⟩ — see FLING 1

gambol *vb* to play and run about happily ⟨dog owners chat while their pooches *gambol* on the park's great lawn⟩ — see FROLIC 1

game *adj* having a desire or inclination (as for a specified course of action) ⟨are you *game* for going out tonight?⟩ — see WILLING 1

game *n* **1** a competitive encounter between individuals or groups carried on for amusement, exercise, or in pursuit of a prize ⟨decided he would indulge in a friendly basketball *game* with his friends before dinner⟩
synonyms bout, competition, contest, event, match, matchup, meet, sweepstakes (*also* sweep-stake), tournament, tourney
related words athletics, sport; battle, conflict, scrimmage, skirmish, struggle, tug-of-war, tussle; championship, national(s); final, nightcap, play-off, semifinal; derby, field day, gymkhana, open, outing; biathlon, decathlon, heptathlon, pentathlon, triathlon; marathon, race, ultramarathon; heat, round, run, set; rally, volley; round-robin, rubber, runoff, sudden death; dead heat, photo finish, seesaw; classic

2 a method worked out in advance for achieving some objective ⟨the crook told his accomplice, "Here's the *game*: look surprised when the police ask about the money"⟩ — see PLAN 1

3 an attitude or manner not to be taken seriously ⟨there's no need to get upset, all our teasing is only a *game*⟩ — see FUN 2

4 the activity by which one regularly makes a living ⟨stand-up comedy is his *game*, and he's one of a handful of people making a decent living at it⟩ — see OCCUPATION 1

5 a region of activity, knowledge, or influence ⟨the education *game* simply was no longer of interest to her⟩ — see FIELD 2

gameness *n* cheerful readiness to do something ⟨it requires a certain amount of gustatory *gameness* to try something like rattlesnake or alligator⟩ — see ALACRITY

game plan *n* a method worked out in advance for achieving some objective ⟨what's our *game plan* for touring the city?⟩ — see PLAN 1

gamesmanship *n* the use of clever underhanded actions to achieve an end ⟨that author doesn't go in for literary *gamesmanship*, so the reader is never led astray by the novel's narrator⟩ — see TRICKERY

gamesome *adj* joyously unrestrained ⟨a *gamesome* lass

who seemed to revel in the sheer joy of living⟩ — see EXUBERANT

gamester *n* one that bets (as on the outcome of a contest or sports event) ⟨a casino with enough roulette wheels, blackjack tables, and slot machines to satisfy even the most die-hard *gamester*⟩ — see BETTOR

gammon *vb* to cause to believe what is untrue ⟨goodhearted contributors have been *gammoned* into believing that most of the charity's funds go to the needy and not into the pockets of the administrators⟩ — see DECEIVE

gamut *n* the distance or extent between possible extremes ⟨the actress's work runs the *gamut* from goofy comedies to serious historical dramas⟩ — see RANGE 3

gamy *or* **gamey** *adj* hinting at or intended to call to mind matters regarded as indecent ⟨a singles bar where the conversations and come-on lines tend to be *gamy*⟩ — see SUGGESTIVE 1

[1]**gander** *n* an instance of looking especially briefly ⟨suggested that they take a *gander* at the display of classic cars⟩ — see LOOK 2

[2]**gander** *n* a stupid person ⟨the village's chief of police was an ineffectual albeit pleasant *gander*⟩ — see IDIOT

gang *n* **1** a group of people working together on a task ⟨a *gang* of neighborhood residents spent the weekend cleaning up the park⟩
synonyms army, band, brigade, company, crew, outfit, party, platoon, squad, team
related words battalion, corps, troop; force, host, posse, stable, troupe; administration, department, help, personnel, staff
2 a group of people sharing a common interest and relating together socially ⟨the whole *gang* went out for pizza⟩ ⟨the school's computer hackers had their own little *gang*⟩
synonyms body, bunch, circle, clan, clique, community, coterie, coven, crowd, fold, galère, klatch (*also* klatsch), lot, network, pack, ring, set
related words charmed circle, elite, in-group; closed shop; club, college, fellowship, guild (*also* gild), league, organization, society; camp, faction, sect, side, tribe; mess, squad; brotherhood, fraternity, order, sisterhood, sodality, sorority; commune; alliance, bloc, coalition, confederation, congress, council, federation, union
near antonyms loner; individualist
3 a group involved in secret or criminal activities ⟨politicians promising to stop the growth of inner-city *gangs*⟩ — see [1]RING 1

gangbanger *n* a violent, brutal person who is often a member of an organized gang ⟨the argument that the DEA needs to focus more on the kingpins of the drug trade and less on the *gangbangers* in the street⟩ — see HOODLUM

gangbusters *also* **gangbuster** *adj* of the very best kind ⟨most of the pop singers in the competition were anything but *gangbusters*⟩ — see EXCELLENT

gangling *adj* being tall, thin and usually loose-jointed ⟨the riders at the barn just loved the *gangling* newborn colt⟩ — see LANKY

gangly *adj* being tall, thin and usually loose-jointed ⟨a *gangly* teenager who was born to play varsity basketball⟩ — see LANKY

gangsta *n* a violent, brutal person who is often a member of an organized gang ⟨the short, violence-filled life of an inner-city *gangsta*⟩ — see HOODLUM

gangster *n* a violent, brutal person who is often a member of an organized gang ⟨Al Capone remains one of the most notorious *gangsters* in American history⟩ — see HOODLUM

gap *n* **1** an open space in a barrier (as a wall or hedge) ⟨there were several visible *gaps* in the wall where the drywall had pulled away from the wall framing⟩
synonyms breach, break, discontinuity, gulf, hiatus, hole, interstice, interval, opening, rent, rift, separation, void
related words chink, cleft, crack, cranny, crevice, fissure; notch, slit, slot, split; interspace, pore; abyss, aperture, cavity, chasm, gape, orifice; fracture, rupture, severance, sundering
2 a break in continuity ⟨there was a 15-minute *gap* between the two televised sporting events⟩
synonyms discontinuity, hiatus, hiccup (*also* hiccough), interim, interlude, intermission, interregnum, interruption, interstice, interval, parenthesis
related words caesura, comma, interspace, lag, pause, space, time lag, window; entr'acte; bumper; adjournment, discontinuance, lapse, suspension; lull, recess, respite, rest; subinterval
near antonyms continuum, run, stretch; procession, progression
antonyms continuation, continuity
3 an incomplete or deficient area ⟨a *gap* in his understanding⟩
synonyms hiatus, hole, lacuna, space, void
related words defectiveness, detriment, disability, failing, fault, impairment, weakness; deficiency, deficit, imperfection, inadequacy, inadequateness, incompleteness, insufficience, insufficiency, lack, need, shortcoming, shortfall, want
near antonyms completeness, fullness
4 a narrow opening between hillsides or mountains that can be used for passage ⟨thought they were stuck until they found a *gap* in the mountain range that they could hike through⟩ — see CANYON

gape *n* a fixed intent look ⟨I told him to stop staring, that his rather stupid *gape* was annoying⟩ — see GAZE

gape *vb* to look long and hard in wonder or surprise ⟨she suddenly realized she had been *gaping* at the good-looking waiter instead of giving him her order⟩
synonyms blink, gawk, gawp [*chiefly British*], gaze, goggle, peer, rubberneck, stare
related words glare, gloat, glower; consider, eye, fixate, observe, regard, watch; leer, ogle; peruse, pore (over), study; outface, outstare, stare down
near antonyms glance, glimpse, peek, peep; browse, dip (into), scan; wink (at)

garage sale *n* a sale of used household and personal items ⟨prior to the move they held a *garage sale* to clear out all of their unwanted stuff⟩ — see YARD SALE

garb *n* **1** clothing chosen as appropriate for a specific situation ⟨decided to clothe himself in traditional Scottish *garb* for the celebration⟩ — see OUTFIT 1
2 the outward form of someone or something especially as indicative of a quality ⟨a fable about personal redemption presented in the *garb* of a conventional horror story⟩ — see APPEARANCE 1

garb *vb* to outfit with clothes and especially fine or special clothes ⟨firefighters *garbed* in protective gear⟩ — see CLOTHE 1

garbage *n* **1** discarded or useless material ⟨the stray dogs were looking for leftover food in the family's *garbage*⟩
synonyms chaff, deadwood, debris, dreck (*also* drek), dross, dust, effluvium (*also* effluvia), junk, litter, offal, offscouring, raffle, refuse, riffraff, rubbish, scrap, spilth, trash, truck, waste
related words crud, sewage, slop, swill, wash; detritus, remains, rubble, ruins; dump, scrap heap; lumber, odds and ends, trumpery; flotsam, jetsam, wreckage; castoff, cull, discard, hand-me-down, reject, throwaway; nothing, straw, two bits
near antonyms catch, gem, goody (*or* goodie), jewel, pearl, plum, prize, treasure, treasure trove, trove, valuable; booty, find, salvage

2 language, behavior, or ideas that are absurd and contrary to good sense ⟨she was just talking *garbage* when she said that she was taking a loss on the sale of the house⟩ — see NONSENSE 1

garble *vb* **1** to change so much as to create a wrong impression or alter the meaning of ⟨the candidate complained that his views had been deliberately *garbled* by his opponent⟩
synonyms bend, color, cook, distort, falsify, fudge, misinterpret, misrelate, misrepresent, misstate, pervert, slant, twist, warp
related words misdescribe, misspeak, mistranslate; belie, camouflage, disguise, dissemble, gloss (over), mask, veil, whitewash; bowdlerize, censor; complicate, confound, confuse, mistake, mix (up); mystify, obscure; equivocate, fib, lie, palter, prevaricate
near antonyms clarify, clear (up), explain, illuminate, illustrate, interpret, spell out; decipher
2 to remove usually visible impurities from ⟨*garbled* spices are less likely to contaminate a recipe⟩ — see CLARIFY 1

garçon *n* a person who serves food or drink ⟨"*Garçon*, bring another bottle of wine," barked the haughty diner⟩ — see SERVER

garden *n* a large room or building for enclosed public gatherings ⟨we used to go to Boston's historic *garden* to hear concerts and see basketball games⟩ — see HALL 3

garden–variety *adj* **1** being of the type that is encountered in the normal course of events ⟨the once-powerful hurricane eventually abated into just a *garden-variety* tropical storm⟩ — see ORDINARY 1
2 often observed or encountered ⟨the bakery's extravagant creations are not your *garden-variety* wedding cakes⟩ — see COMMON 1

gargantuan *adj* unusually large ⟨people seem to be buying ever more *gargantuan* SUVs these days⟩ — see HUGE

garish *adj* excessively showy ⟨the wedding guest's thick makeup was *garish* and unnecessary⟩ — see GAUDY

garishness *n* excessive or unnecessary display ⟨the *garishness* of the enormous statues in the small yard was almost funny⟩ — see OSTENTATION

garment *vb* to outfit with clothes and especially fine or special clothes ⟨a socialite who was among the most gorgeously *garmented* women of her time⟩ — see CLOTHE 1

garments *n pl* covering for the human body ⟨chimney sweeps wearing the traditional *garments* of their trade⟩ — see CLOTHING

garner *vb* **1** to bring together in one body or place ⟨a prisoner *garnering* food bit by bit and hiding it in his pillow⟩ ⟨an array of rock bands *garnered* from all over the country by the promoters of the festival⟩ — see GATHER 1
2 to receive as return for effort ⟨a novelist that has *garnered* praise for his literate police procedurals⟩ — see EARN 1

garnish *n* something that decorates or beautifies ⟨added a *garnish* of parsley to the plate before serving it⟩ — see DECORATION 1

garnish *vb* to make more attractive by adding something that is beautiful or becoming ⟨a chef who never served any dish without first *garnishing* it⟩ — see DECORATE

garnishment *n* something that decorates or beautifies ⟨a high-end caterer whose dishes feature an array of over-the-top *garnishments*⟩ — see DECORATION 1

garniture *n* something that decorates or beautifies ⟨she prefers a spare style of interior decoration and doesn't go in for a lot of *garnitures*⟩ — see DECORATION 1

garret *n* a room or unfinished space directly beneath the roof of a building ⟨bought a charming Victorian house with a *garret* that she hoped to turn into a writing room⟩ — see ATTIC

garrote *or* **garotte** *vb* to keep (someone) from breathing by exerting pressure on the windpipe ⟨the goons sent by the loan shark threatened to *garrote* the hero with his own necktie⟩ — see CHOKE 1

garrulity *n* the use of too many words to express an idea ⟨in her article the professor resorts to *garrulity* in a vain attempt to disguise the fact that she has very little worth saying⟩ — see VERBIAGE 1

garrulous *adj* **1** fond of talking or conversation ⟨a *garrulous* boy who was in constant trouble for talking out of turn⟩ — see TALKATIVE
2 using or containing more words than necessary to express an idea ⟨now that he's in his anecdotage, Grandpa likes to tell *garrulous*, shaggy-dog accounts of his youthful misadventures⟩ — see WORDY 1

garrulousness *n* the use of too many words to express an idea ⟨the *garrulousness* of the senator's speeches invariably caused every eye in the room to glaze over⟩ — see VERBIAGE 1

gas *n* **1** boastful speech or writing ⟨all that *gas* about being the best fisherman in the world⟩ — see BOMBAST 1
2 language that is impressive-sounding but not meaningful or sincere ⟨the candidate's pledge that he'll fight for the common people is just a lot of *gas*⟩ — see RHETORIC 1
3 *slang* a source of great satisfaction ⟨that movie with the spectacular special effects was a *gas*⟩ — see DELIGHT 1
4 active strength of body or mind ⟨the tennis player ran out of *gas* toward the end of the long match⟩ — see VIGOR 1

gas *vb* **1** to engage in casual or rambling conversation ⟨a group of kids in the mall, *gassing* about their favorite music⟩ — see CHAT 1
2 *slang* to give satisfaction to ⟨a swinging jazz set that really *gassed* the crowd⟩ — see PLEASE 1

gasbag *n* a person who talks constantly ⟨that *gasbag* will talk your ear off about anything⟩ — see CHATTERBOX

gascon *n* someone who boasts ⟨one of history's most celebrated *gascons* was the Baron Münchhausen of Germany⟩ — see BRAGGART

gasconade *n* boastful speech or writing ⟨if you believe the *gasconade* of his memoirs, he pretty much won World War II on his own⟩ — see BOMBAST 1

gasconade *vb* to praise or express pride in one's own possessions, qualities, or accomplishments often to excess ⟨the Baron Münchausen was so notorious for *gasconading* about his purported exploits as soldier and hunter that his name has become synonymous with the telling of tall tales⟩ — see BOAST 1

gasconader *n* someone who boasts ⟨retired military commanders are often portrayed as garrulous *gasconaders* constantly reliving old triumphs⟩ — see BRAGGART

gaseous *adj* marked by the use of impressive-sounding but mostly meaningless words and phrases ⟨a pompous professor known for his *gaseous* lectures that often put students to sleep⟩ — see RHETORICAL 1

gash *vb* to penetrate with a sharp edge (as a knife) ⟨her face had been *gashed* by the rocks as she tumbled down the embankment⟩ — see CUT 1

gash *n* a long deep cut ⟨got a *gash* in his knee that required four stitches⟩
synonyms incision, laceration, rent, rip, slash, slit, tear
related words abrasion, score, scrape, scratch; injury, wound; crack, fracture, rupture, snag

gasp *vb* to breathe hard, quickly, or with difficulty ⟨the runner was audibly *gasping* by the end of the marathon⟩

synonyms blow, heave, hyperventilate, pant, puff, wheeze
related words choke, gag, gulp, huff; asphyxiate, smother, stifle, strangle; snore, snuffle; exhale, expire
phrases be out of breath

gassed *adj* being under the influence of alcohol ⟨he likes to go out and get *gassed* on weekends⟩ — see DRUNK

gassy *adj* marked by the use of impressive-sounding but mostly meaningless words and phrases ⟨another *gassy* speech by a long-winded politician⟩ — see RHETORICAL 1

gastronome *n* a person with refined tastes in food and wine ⟨*gastronomes* from all over make the pilgrimage to this temple of haute cuisine⟩ — see EPICURE

gastronomist *n* a person with refined tastes in food and wine ⟨a *gastronomist* and food historian who is very knowledgeable about Spanish cuisine⟩ — see EPICURE

gate *n* **1** a barrier by which an entry is closed and opened ⟨be sure to latch the *gate* when you leave so the dog doesn't get out⟩ — see DOOR 1
2 the opening through which one can enter or leave a structure ⟨passed through the *gates* of the walled city⟩ — see DOOR 2
3 a fixture for controlling the flow of a liquid ⟨opens the *gate* in the lock so the ships can get through the canal⟩ — see FAUCET

gatekeeper *n* a person who tends a door ⟨those who are hopelessly unhip have little chance of making past the club's *gatekeeper* and his velvet rope⟩ — see DOORKEEPER

gateway *n* **1** something that allows someone to achieve a desired goal ⟨hopefully, my college degree will be a *gateway* to a high-paying job⟩ — see PASSPORT 1
2 the means or right of entering or participating in ⟨Denver is the *gateway* to the West⟩ — see ENTRANCE 1
3 the opening through which one can enter or leave a structure ⟨there are security checkpoints at all of the stadium's *gateways*⟩ — see DOOR 2

gather *vb* **1** to bring together in one body or place ⟨he *gathered* the leftovers from the table and gave them to the dog⟩ ⟨let's *gather* the students and have them line up on the playground before going in from recess⟩
synonyms accumulate, amass, assemble, bulk (up), collect, concentrate, congregate, constellate, corral, garner, group, lump, pick up, round up
related words ball, batch, bunch, cluster, huddle; heap, pile, stack; band, brigade, muster, raise, rally; flock, herd, hive, pack, press, swarm, throng; combine, connect, join, link, merge, pool, unite; archive, arrange, collate, compile, organize, systematize; scrape (up *or* together); re-collect, regather, regroup
phrases get together
near antonyms break up, disband, disintegrate, dissolve, separate, sever, split (up); dismiss, send
antonyms dispel, disperse, dissipate, scatter
2 to catch or collect (a crop or natural resource) for human use ⟨late summer is when we *gather* the tomatoes and begin canning them for the winter⟩ — see HARVEST
3 to come together into one body or place ⟨a crowd *gathered* around the street musician⟩ ⟨ask the faculty to *gather* in the lounge for the meeting⟩ — see ASSEMBLE 1
4 to form an opinion or reach a conclusion through reasoning and information ⟨I *gather* that, since you are back so early, she didn't want to see you?⟩ — see INFER 1
5 to gradually form into a layer, pile, or mass ⟨the newspapers that had been allowed to *gather* on the front doorstep told thieves that the family was away on vacation⟩ — see COLLECT 2
6 to gradually increase in ⟨the movement *gathered* force as election day neared⟩ — see GAIN 1
7 to call into being through the use of one's inner resources or powers ⟨*gathered* the strength to finish the marathon⟩ — see SUMMON 2

gathering *n* **1** a body of people come together in one place ⟨the President spoke before the *gathering* of student leaders⟩
synonyms assemblage, assembly, conference, congregation, convocation, ingathering, meeting, muster
related words company, consort, coterie, gang, pack; caucus, forum, market, panel, rally, symposium, synod; audience, gallery, grandstand, house; crowd, flock, horde, legion, multitude, press, swarm, throng; crush, mob, rabble, rabblement
2 a coming together of a number of persons for a specified purpose ⟨attended a *gathering* for descendants of people who came to America on the Mayflower⟩ — see MEETING 1
3 a mass or quantity that has piled up or that has been gathered over a period of time ⟨a great *gathering* of dust under the bed⟩ — see ACCUMULATION 1

gauche *adj* lacking social grace and assurance ⟨his loud talking at the opera marked him as *gauche* and uncultured⟩ — see AWKWARD 1

gaud *n* a small object displayed for its attractiveness or interest ⟨some tacky little *gaud* that they had picked up at a souvenir stand at an amusement park⟩ — see KNICKKNACK

gaudiness *n* excessive or unnecessary display ⟨the *gaudiness* of the velvety wallpaper and cut-glass lamps made the guests giggle in amusement⟩ — see OSTENTATION

gaudy *adj* excessively showy ⟨*gaudy* decorations on all the doors and windows at festival time⟩
synonyms flamboyant, flaring, flashy, garish, glitzy, loud, noisy, ostentatious, razzle-dazzle, splashy, swank (*or* swanky)
related words excessive, extravagant, fulsome, hammy, overdone, over-the-top, overwrought; pretentious; baroque, bedizened, ornate; fancy, snazzy, zooty; blaring, bright, florid, glaring, glittery, overbright, spectacular; graceless, inelegant, lurid, tacky, tasteless, tawdry, tinselly, vulgar
near antonyms appropriate, fitting, proper; inconspicuous, muted, restrained, subdued, toned (down), unobtrusive; elegant, graceful, tasteful; modest, plain, simple, unpretentious
antonyms conservative, quiet, understated, unflamboyant, unflashy

gauge *also* **gage** *vb* **1** to decide the size, amount, number, or distance of (something) without actual measurement ⟨glance over the pattern and try to *gauge* how much fabric you'll need⟩ — see ESTIMATE 2
2 to find out the size, extent, or amount of ⟨very difficult to *gauge* how upset he really is by his controlled reaction⟩ — see MEASURE 1

gaum *vb, dialect* to make dirty ⟨the kitchen floor was all *gaumed* up from countless spills⟩ — see DIRTY

gaunt *adj* suffering extreme weight loss as a result of hunger or disease ⟨a *gaunt* patient suffering from the side effects of treatment⟩ — see EMACIATED

gauntlet *also* **gantlet** *n* a test of faith, patience, or strength ⟨before being adopted, school textbooks must often run the *gauntlet* of several local and state committees⟩ — see TRIAL

gauze *n* an atmospheric condition in which suspended particles in the air rob it of its transparency ⟨wrapped in the pale *gauze* of a misty afternoon, the city seemed eerily romantic to the strolling lovers⟩ — see HAZE 1

gauzelike *adj* very thin and easy to see through ⟨a beautiful, *gauzelike* fabric⟩ — see SHEER 1

gauzy *adj* **1** being of a material lacking in sturdiness or substance ⟨*gauzy* spiderwebs⟩ — see FLIMSY 1

2 very thin and easy to see through ⟨*gauzy* curtains that let plenty of light through⟩ — see SHEER 1
3 not seen or understood clearly ⟨I have only a *gauzy* recollection of those long-ago events⟩ — see FAINT 1
4 filled with or dimmed by fine particles (as of dust or water) in suspension ⟨the valley was bathed in the soft *gauzy* light of an October morn⟩ — see HAZY 1

gawk *n* a big clumsy often slow-witted person ⟨thought that the linebackers were dumb *gawks* until he got to know them better⟩ — see OAF 1

gawk *vb* to look long and hard in wonder or surprise ⟨couldn't help *gawking* at the exotically dressed guests in the hotel lobby⟩ — see GAPE

gawkish *adj* having or showing an inability to move in a graceful manner ⟨the kind of *gawkish* girl who trips while receiving her high school diploma⟩ — see CLUMSY 2

gawky *adj* having or showing an inability to move in a graceful manner ⟨the stiff, *gawky* gait of a newborn colt⟩ — see CLUMSY 2

gawp *vb, chiefly British* to look long and hard in wonder or surprise ⟨tourists in London *gawping* at royalty⟩ — see GAPE

gay *adj* 1 having much high-spirited energy and movement ⟨couples dancing a *gay*, fast-paced jig⟩ — see LIVELY 1
2 having or showing freedom from worries or trouble ⟨a *gay*, thoughtless girl who didn't care whether her work was done or not⟩ — see CAREFREE
3 indicative of or marked by high spirits or good humor ⟨had a *gay* old time at the party⟩ — see MERRY
4 having or showing a good mood or disposition ⟨with a *gay* toss of his coat over his shoulder, the dapper old gentleman set off for the party⟩ — see CHEERFUL 1
5 serving to lift one's spirits ⟨the skylark's *gay* song lifted me out of my gloom⟩ — see CHEERFUL 2
6 joyously unrestrained ⟨it was the era of the flappers, and young women were *gay*, bold, and defiant of convention⟩ — see EXUBERANT

gayness *n* a mood characterized by high spirits and amusement and often accompanied by laughter ⟨the melancholy-tinged *gayness* of college-bound friends on their last fling together before going their separate ways⟩ — see MIRTH

gaze *vb* to look long and hard in wonder or surprise ⟨just sat there and *gazed* at the panorama before us until it got too dark to see⟩ — see GAPE

gaze *n* a fixed intent look ⟨suddenly aware of her admiring *gaze*, he became self-conscious and uncomfortable⟩
synonyms aspect [*archaic*], eye, gape, regard, scrutiny, stare
related words glare, glower; contemplation, fixation; attention, observance, observation, surveillance, watch; examination, inspection, perusal, study, survey
near antonyms blink [*chiefly Scottish*], flash, glance, glimpse, peek, peep, sight, stime [*chiefly Scottish & Irish*]; oeillade, ogle; browse, scan

gazebo *n* a freestanding airy structure in a scenic setting (as a park) typically offering commanding views ⟨a *gazebo* on the mansion's south lawn⟩ — see BELVEDERE

gazette *n* a publication that appears at regular intervals ⟨picked up the monthly car-buyer's *gazette* when he was in town⟩ — see JOURNAL 1

gear *n* 1 items needed for the performance of a task or activity ⟨grabbed his *gear*, threw on his pads, and headed out to the football field for practice⟩ — see EQUIPMENT
2 transportable items that one owns ⟨you can store your *gear* in the overhead bin during the flight⟩ — see POSSESSION 2
3 covering for the human body ⟨the latest in kid *gear*⟩ — see CLOTHING

geek *n* 1 a person slavishly devoted to intellectual or academic pursuits ⟨was quickly stereotyped as another computer *geek*⟩ — see NERD 1
2 a person with strong intellectual interests ⟨a jock-dominated campus on which *geeks* were either ridiculed or ignored⟩ — see INTELLECTUAL
3 a person with a high level of knowledge or skill in a field ⟨a friend who is an audio-video *geek* set up my home theater for me⟩ — see EXPERT

geeked *adj, slang* showing urgent desire or interest ⟨she's really *geeked* to see the exhibit featuring the latest in home electronics⟩ — see EAGER

geeky *adj* much given to learning and thinking ⟨one university campus on which the *geeky* student will not feel like a social outcast⟩ — see INTELLECTUAL 1

gee–whiz *adj* arousing a strong and usually superficial interest or emotional reaction ⟨most of the movie's budget must have gone for its *gee-whiz* special effects⟩ — see SENSATIONAL 1

Gehenna *n* 1 a situation or state that causes great suffering and unhappiness ⟨the depression that has enshrouded her since the death of her husband is a *Gehenna* from which she may never be released⟩ — see HELL 2
2 the place of punishment for the wicked after death ⟨in a fire-and-brimstone sermon, the evangelist warned those assembled that they faced the fires of *Gehenna* if they failed to repent⟩ — see HELL 1

gel *vb* to turn from a liquid into a substance resembling jelly ⟨the fruit juice should *gel* after you add the pectin⟩ — see COAGULATE

gelate *vb* to turn from a liquid into a substance resembling jelly ⟨biomedical applications for substances that *gelate* in water⟩ — see COAGULATE

gelatinize *vb* to turn from a liquid into a substance resembling jelly ⟨pain relievers with a *gelatinized* coating⟩ — see COAGULATE

geld *vb* to deprive of emotional or intellectual vitality ⟨by the time of the fourth rewrite, the screenplay had pretty much been *gelded* of all originality⟩ — see DEHYDRATE 1

gelid *adj* 1 having a low or subnormal temperature ⟨the Titanic passengers could not long survive the *gelid* waters of the North Atlantic⟩ — see COLD 1
2 lacking in friendliness or warmth of feeling ⟨the judge listened with the *gelid* detachment of someone who had heard it all before⟩ — see COLD 2

gem *n* 1 a usually valuable stone cut and polished for ornament ⟨a ring set with diamonds and other precious *gems*⟩
synonyms brilliant, gemstone, jewel, rock [*slang*]
related words bauble, bijou, trinket; birthstone; baguette, cabochon, cameo, scarab, solitaire, teardrop; paste, rhinestone, zircon; crown jewels, jewelry
near antonyms rough
2 someone or something unusually desirable ⟨that new car is a real *gem*⟩ ⟨she's dating a real *gem* these days⟩ — see PRIZE 1

gemstone *n* a usually valuable stone cut and polished for ornament ⟨traditionally, the *gemstone* for someone born in May is an emerald⟩ — see GEM 1

gemütlichkeit *n* kindly concern, interest, or support ⟨social events that foster a spirit of *gemütlichkeit* among members of the ski club⟩ — see GOODWILL 1

gen *n, chiefly British* a report of recent events or facts not previously known ⟨as he has for decades, he gets most of his *gen* from the BBC over the wireless⟩ — see NEWS

gendarme *n* a member of a force charged with law enforcement at the local level ⟨the senator reiterated his conviction that it is not the role of the United States to be a kind of global *gendarme*⟩ — see OFFICER 1

genderless *adj* suitable to or for either sex ⟨a trendy boutique selling *genderless* accessories—bandannas, caps, bracelets, etc.⟩
synonyms androgynous, unisex, unisexual
related words ambisexual, intersexual; asexual, epicene, neuter, sexless, unsexed; AC/DC, bisexual; homosexual, lesbian; gender-bending, transgender (*or* transgendered), transsexual (*also* transexual), transvestite
near antonyms feminine, masculine
antonyms gendered

genealogy *n* the line of ancestors from whom a person is descended ⟨has a distinguished *genealogy* that traces back to William the Conqueror⟩ — see ANCESTRY

general *adj* **1** belonging or relating to the whole ⟨a *general* increase in postage rates⟩ ⟨there's been a *general* improvement in the economy⟩
synonyms across-the-board, blanket, broad-brush, common, generic, global, overall, universal
related words all-embracing, broad, broad-gauge (*or* broad-gauged), broadscale, comprehensive, extensive, inclusionary, overarching, pervasive, sweeping, ubiquitous, wholesale, wide, widespread; aggregate, collective, complete, full, plenary; planetary, worldwide
near antonyms component, constituent; cross-sectional, divisional, fragmentary, partial; local, localized, regional, sectional
antonyms individual, particular
2 relating to the main elements and not to specific details ⟨gave the *general* impression of being kindhearted⟩ ⟨a *general* course of study in American history⟩
synonyms all-around (*also* all-round), bird's-eye, broad, nonspecific, overall
related words comprehensive, inclusive; absolute, boundless, expansive, extensive, infinite, panoramic, sweeping, vast, wide; indeterminate, nebulous, nondescript, vague; nonspecific, unlimited, unrestricted, unspecified
near antonyms limited, restricted, specified; distinct, explicit, precise, sharp; comprehensive, elaborate, full, mapped (out), thorough; enumerated, inventoried, itemized, listed; individual, singular; particular, peculiar
antonyms close-up, delineated, detailed, molecular, particularized, specific
3 held by or applicable to a majority of the people ⟨it was the *general* opinion that the politician was a liar⟩ ⟨the *general* mood of the nation was one of hope and optimism⟩
synonyms common, majority, overall, popular, prevailing, public, received, ruling, vulgar
related words unanimous, universal; pop; everyday, familiar, household, usual, well-known; contemporary, current, present; dominant, predominant, preponderant; characteristic, typical; pandemic, pervasive, prevalent, rife, widespread; communal, shared
near antonyms rare, strange, unknown, unusual; distinctive, especial, idiosyncratic, peculiar, special, unique; individual, separate, singular; nonpublic, personal, private
antonyms uncommon, unpopular
4 not limited or specialized in application or purpose ⟨a new kitchen tool of *general* usefulness⟩ ⟨a *general* education⟩
synonyms all-around (*also* all-round), all-purpose, catholic, general-purpose, unlimited, unqualified, unrestricted, unspecialized
related words mixed-use, multipurpose; broad, wide; nonspecific, unspecified, vague
near antonyms bounded, circumscribed, confined, definite, demarcated, determinate, finite, qualified; dedicated, selective
antonyms limited, restricted, specialized, technical

generality *n* **1** an idea or statement about all of the members of a group or all the instances of a situation ⟨the idea that all boys are naturally messy is a gross *generality*⟩ — see GENERALIZATION
2 the main or greater part of something as distinguished from its subordinate parts ⟨an important but little-known Scottish inventor whose work was never appreciated by the *generality* of the public⟩ — see BODY 1
3 the largest part or quantity of something ⟨the *generality* of that high school's students will go on to college⟩ — see MAJORITY 1

generalization *n* an idea or statement about all of the members of a group or all the instances of a situation ⟨the *generalization* that children who like violent entertainment grow up to be violent criminals⟩
synonyms concept, conception, generality, notion, stereotype
related words bromide, cliché (*also* cliche), commonplace, platitude, truism; adage, proverb, saw, saying; hypothesis, proposition, theory; oversimplification, simplification, simplism

generally *adv* **1** according to the usual course of things ⟨after lunch we *generally* go for a walk⟩ — see NATURALLY 2
2 for the most part ⟨*generally*, I don't care for raw vegetables⟩ — see CHIEFLY

general–purpose *adj* not limited or specialized in application or purpose ⟨a *general-purpose* glue for routine household repairs⟩ — see GENERAL 4

generate *vb* to be the cause of (a situation, action, or state of mind) ⟨his rabble-rousing speech *generated* a lot of controversy among local taxpayers⟩ — see EFFECT

generator *n* a person who establishes a whole new field of endeavor ⟨the French painter Paul Cézanne is considered to be one of the principal *generators* of modern art⟩ — see FATHER 2

generic *adj* belonging or relating to the whole ⟨a love of big things—big cars, big meals—seems to be a *generic* trait of the American people⟩ — see GENERAL 1

generosity *n* the quality or state of being generous ⟨a sidewalk beggar who benefited from the *generosity* of kindhearted passersby⟩ — see LIBERALITY

generous *adj* **1** giving or sharing in abundance and without hesitation ⟨a civic leader who is very *generous* with his money and time⟩
synonyms bighearted, bounteous, bountiful, charitable, free, freehanded, freehearted, fulsome, liberal, munificent, open, openhanded, unselfish, unsparing, unstinting
related words extravagant, handsome, lavish, overgenerous, profuse; altruistic, beneficent, benevolent, hospitable, humanitarian, philanthropic (*also* philanthropical); big, greathearted, largehearted, magnanimous, openhearted; compassionate, good-hearted, kind, kindly, samaritan, sympathetic
near antonyms mean, petty, small; frugal, spare, sparing, thrifty; chary, stinting; acquisitive, avaricious, avid, coveting, covetous, desirous, grasping, hoggish, itchy, mercenary, rapacious; begrudging, envious, grudging, resentful
antonyms cheap, close, closefisted, costive, illiberal [*archaic*], mingy, miserly, niggardly, parsimonious, penurious, selfish, stingy, stinting, tight, tightfisted, uncharitable, ungenerous
2 being more than enough without being excessive ⟨mashed potatoes with a *generous* serving of butter⟩ — see PLENTIFUL

generously *adv* in a generous manner ⟨gave *generously* to several charities⟩ — see WELL 2

generousness *n* the quality or state of being generous ⟨many of the donations seemed to have been made more out of a nagging sense of guiltiness than in a true spirit of *generousness*⟩ — see LIBERALITY

genesis *n* the point at which something begins ⟨was present at the meeting which was later considered the *genesis* of the new political movement⟩ — see BEGINNING

genetic *also* **genetical** *adj* genetically passed or capable of being passed from parent to offspring ⟨hemophilia and other *genetic* medical disorders⟩ — see HEREDITARY

genial *adj* **1** having an easygoing and pleasing manner especially in social situations ⟨a *genial* host who makes a point of speaking personally to each and every guest⟩ — see AMIABLE

2 having or showing kindly feeling and sincere interest ⟨*genial* new neighbors who helped us unpack boxes and brought us dinner our first night in the new place⟩ — see FRIENDLY 1

3 showing a natural kindness and courtesy especially in social situations ⟨his *genial* offer to give me his seat on the bus⟩ — see GRACIOUS 1

4 marked by temperatures that are neither too high nor too low ⟨wanted to move to a more *genial* clime for health reasons⟩ — see CLEMENT 1

geniality *n* the state or quality of having a pleasant or agreeable manner in socializing with others ⟨her unforced *geniality* never fails to draw fellow passengers into a conversation with her⟩ — see AMIABILITY 1

geniture *n* the act or instance of being born ⟨in astrology, the influence of a planet on a *geniture* depends on the planet's position within the zodiac⟩ — see BIRTH 1

genius *n* **1** a very smart person ⟨the 16-year-old college graduate was considered to be a *genius*⟩

synonyms brain, brainiac, intellect, thinker, whiz, wiz, wizard

related words polyhistor, polymath, Renaissance man; blue, bluestocking, highbrow, intellectual; sage, savant; egghead, geek, longhair, nerd; master, virtuoso; ace, crackerjack (*also* crackajack), natural

near antonyms ignoramus, illiterate, know-nothing, lowbrow; anti-intellectual, philistine; ass, donkey, fool, jackass; beast, boor, cad, churl, clown, creep, cretin, cur, heel, jerk, louse, lout, skunk, snake, stinker

antonyms blockhead, dodo, dolt, dope, dumbbell, dummy, dunce, fathead, goon, half-wit, hammerhead, idiot, imbecile, knucklehead, moron, nitwit, numskull (*or* numbskull), pinhead

2 a special and usually inborn ability ⟨had a *genius* for remembering long strings of numbers⟩ ⟨had a *genius* for saying the wrong thing, no matter what the social situation⟩ — see TALENT

3 a habitual attraction to some activity or thing ⟨a *genius* for gambling over his head⟩ — see INCLINATION 1

4 the set of qualities that makes a person, a group of people, or a thing different from others ⟨putting the needs of the individual before those of society is alien to the *genius* of the Japanese people⟩ — see NATURE 1

5 a visible representation of something abstract (as a quality) ⟨the giant tortoise would seem to be the very *genius* of the unfathomable ancientness that one associates with the Galápagos Islands⟩ — see EMBODIMENT

genre *n* a number of persons or things that are grouped together because they have something in common ⟨the novel's hero is of a different *genre* than the traditional kind⟩ — see SORT 1

gent *n* an adult male human being ⟨ladies and *gents*⟩ — see MAN 1

genteel *adj* **1** following the established traditions of refined society and good taste ⟨those bygone days when young women were taught how to drink tea while wearing long gloves and other *genteel* ways of behaving⟩ — see PROPER 1

2 having or showing a taste for the fine arts and gracious living ⟨she grew up in *genteel* old Savannah⟩ — see CULTIVATED

3 of high birth, rank, or station ⟨the *genteel* ladies never mixed with the servants⟩ ⟨prohibited by reason of her *genteel* birth from marrying the man she loved⟩ — see NOBLE 1

4 showing consideration, courtesy, and good manners ⟨his *genteel* gesture of holding the door for the ladies⟩ — see POLITE 1

genteelness *n* speech or behavior that is a sign of good breeding ⟨the young man displays the kind of old-school *genteelness* that one rarely encounters on today's college campuses⟩ — see POLITENESS 1

gentile *n* a person who does not worship the God of the Bible ⟨a strict sect that believes that fellowship with *gentiles* should exist only for the purposes of conversion⟩ — see HEATHEN 1

gentility *n* **1** speech or behavior that is a sign of good breeding ⟨was full of the same *gentility* and grace that marked the rest of the family⟩ — see POLITENESS 1

2 the highest class in a society ⟨as members of the *gentility*, they felt an obligation to help the less fortunate⟩ — see ARISTOCRACY 1

gentle *adj* **1** not harsh or stern especially in nature or effect ⟨use a *gentle* detergent on that delicate silk blouse⟩ ⟨her *gentle* ways⟩

synonyms balmy, benign, bland, delicate, light, mellow, mild, nonabrasive, soft, soothing, tender

related words calm, pacific, peaceful, placid, quiet, serene, tranquil; clement, compassionate, easy, lenient, merciful; buffering, cushioning, emollient, softening; sleek, slick, smooth

near antonyms exquisite, fierce, intense, powerful, severe; forceful, forcible, savage, violent; roughened, rugged, strong; abrading, irritating, roughening; grim, gruff, rude, stiff; heavy-handed, oppressive, pitiless, tyrannical (*also* tyrannic)

antonyms abrasive, caustic, coarse, hard, harsh, rough, scathing, stern, ungentle

2 marked by temperatures that are neither too high nor too low ⟨whisk the egg yolks in a double boiler set over a *gentle* heat⟩ — see CLEMENT 1

3 of high birth, rank, or station ⟨loved reading about the days when *gentle* lords and ladies danced at fancy balls⟩ — see NOBLE 1

4 not loud in pitch or volume ⟨the mother spoke in a *gentle* voice to her child⟩ — see SOFT 1

gentle *n* a man or woman of high birth or social position ⟨the archbishop treated both the *gentles* and the commoners with respect and kindness⟩ — see GENTLEPERSON

gentle *vb* **1** to lessen the anger or agitation of ⟨employees soon learned that their hot-tempered boss needed to be *gentled* several times a day⟩ — see PACIFY 1

2 to touch or handle in a tender or loving manner ⟨soothingly *gentled* his cat's head as she was being treated by the vet⟩ — see FONDLE

3 to lessen the shock of ⟨adding a bit of sugar to the salsa will *gentle* the hot spiciness of the chili peppers⟩ — see CUSHION

gentlefolk *also* **gentlefolks** *n pl* the highest class in a society ⟨an 18th-century painter whose works are typically of well-dressed *gentlefolk* wooing and frolicking in sylvan settings⟩ — see ARISTOCRACY 1

gentleman *n* **1** a man of high birth or social position ⟨many of the signers of the Declaration of Independence were *gentlemen* who were risking everything⟩

synonyms grandee, lord, milord, nobleman, peer

related words country gentleman, squire; cavalier, chevalier, knight; don, hidalgo, nabob, nawab, seigneur, seignior, sheikh (*or* sheik); baron, baronet, count, duke, earl, esquire, marchese, margrave, marquess (*or* marquis), master, prince, princelet, princeling, raja, viscount; lordship, sire [*archaic*]

near antonyms boor, churl, cottar (*or* cotter), fellah, peasant, peon; commoner, pleb, plebeian; proletarian; toiler

2 an adult male human being ⟨ladies and *gentlemen*, please take your seats⟩ — see MAN 1

3 an honorable and courteous man ⟨was such a *gentleman* that he offered to call a cab for me⟩ — see CAVALIER

gentleperson *n* a man or woman of high birth or social position ⟨*gentlepersons* did not want to be seen keeping company with commoners⟩

synonyms aristocrat, blue blood, gentle, noble, patrician

related words socialite, swell; magnate, magnifico, mogul, nabob; gentlefolk (*also* gentlefolks)

near antonyms canaille, commoner, pleb, plebeian, proletarian, roturier; boor, fellah, peasant, peon

gentlewoman *n* a woman of high birth or social position ⟨in the 19th century a number of American *gentlewomen* used their wealth and influence to further abolitionism, women's rights, and other worthy causes⟩

synonyms dame, lady, milady, noblewoman, peeress

related words baroness, countess, duchess, marchesa, marchioness, marquise, princess, queen, viscountess; dowager, matriarch, matron, mistress; ladyship, madam

gentry *n* **1** the highest class in a society ⟨poor tenant farmers working for landed *gentry*⟩ — see ARISTOCRACY 1

2 one of the segments of society into which people are grouped ⟨the old-line yachting *gentry* frowns on vulgar displays of wealth⟩ — see CLASS 1

genuine *adj* **1** being exactly as appears or as claimed ⟨had a *genuine* van Gogh hanging in their living room⟩ — see AUTHENTIC 1

2 free from any intent to deceive or impress others ⟨*genuine* compliments about her boss's flair for fashion⟩ — see GUILELESS

3 existing in fact and not merely as a possibility ⟨there's *genuine* value in learning how to do household repairs on one's own⟩ — see ACTUAL

genuinely *adv* in actual fact ⟨is *genuinely* fond of her older brother⟩ — see VERY 2

genus *n* one of the units into which a whole is divided on the basis of a common characteristic ⟨the crime novel, written from the criminal's perspective, is sometimes seen as a particular species of the detective story *genus*⟩ — see CLASS 2

geography *n* the physical features of a region as a whole ⟨the *geography* of the region matches ancient descriptions of the location of the lost city⟩

synonyms chorography, geomorphology, landscape, terrain, topography

related words scenery; ground, land, landform, terrane, terrene

geometry *n* the outward appearance of something as distinguished from its substance ⟨the *geometry* of Sydney's famed opera house is suggestive of some modernistic sailing ship⟩ — see FORM 1

geomorphology *n* the physical features of a region as a whole ⟨the unique character of desert *geomorphology*⟩ — see GEOGRAPHY

geriatric *adj* being of advanced years and especially past middle age ⟨went into nursing to work with *geriatric* patients⟩ — see ELDERLY

geriatric *n* a person of advanced years ⟨most of the clinic's outpatients are *geriatrics* living on fixed incomes⟩ — see SENIOR CITIZEN

germ *n* the source from which something grows or develops ⟨this hastily scribbled equation on a cocktail napkin became the *germ* of a new scientific theory⟩ — see SEED 1

germane *adj* having to do with the matter at hand ⟨my personal opinion isn't *germane* to our discussion of the facts of the case⟩ — see PERTINENT

germfree *adj* free from filth, infection, or dangers to health ⟨had to prepare the microscope slides in an isolated and *germfree* environment⟩ — see SANITARY

gest *or* **geste** *n* an exciting or noteworthy event that one experiences firsthand ⟨before packing it all in, he was looking for one grand *gest* that would serve as a fitting finale for his life⟩ — see ADVENTURE 1

gestation *n* the state of containing unborn young within the body ⟨the length of *gestation* for the gray wolf is about 63 days⟩ — see PREGNANCY

geste *also* **gest** *n, archaic* the way or manner in which one conducts oneself ⟨historical fiction in which the hero faces every adversity with honorable *geste*⟩ — see BEHAVIOR

gesticulation *n* a movement of the body or limbs that expresses or emphasizes an idea or feeling ⟨as the argument grew more heated, his *gesticulations* got bigger and wilder⟩ — see GESTURE 1

gesture *vb* to direct or notify by a movement or gesture ⟨the police officer *gestured* me to the side of the road to tell me my headlight was out⟩ — see MOTION

gesture *n* **1** a movement of the body or limbs that expresses or emphasizes an idea or feeling ⟨a teenager who often shrugs her shoulders in a *gesture* of indifference⟩

synonyms gesticulation, mime, pantomime, sign, signal

related words beck, beckon, flourish, shrug, wave; body language, posture; indication, motion; sign language

2 an act or utterance that is a customary show of good manners ⟨sent a handwritten thank-you note as a *gesture* of his gratitude⟩ — see CIVILITY 1

get *vb* **1** to acquire complete knowledge, understanding, or skill in ⟨I'm not sure I ever *got* the new math⟩ — see LEARN 1

2 to become affected with (a disease or disorder) ⟨don't cough on me—I don't want to *get* your cold⟩ — see CONTRACT 1

3 to become the father of ⟨Abraham was quite old when he *got* Isaac, his only son⟩ — see FATHER

4 to cause (someone) to agree with a belief or course of action by using arguments or earnest requests ⟨tried to *get* the mayor to let us stage the concert in the town square, but she refused⟩ — see PERSUADE

5 to come upon after searching, study, or effort ⟨redid the math problem until I *got* the right answer⟩ — see FIND 1

6 to disturb the peace of mind of (someone) especially by repeated disagreeable acts ⟨continuously clearing your throat like that is starting to *get* to me⟩ — see IRRITATE 1

7 to eventually have as a state or quality ⟨it's going to *get* colder as winter approaches⟩ — see BECOME

8 to receive as return for effort ⟨*got* an A on his final paper⟩ — see EARN 1

9 to have a clear idea of ⟨she was speaking so fast—did you *get* what she said?⟩ — see COMPREHEND 1

10 to take physical control or possession of (something) suddenly or forcibly ⟨the defense tackled the running back and *got* the ball⟩ — see CATCH 1

11 to leave a place often for another ⟨will *get* away to the Bahamas for a vacation⟩ — see GO 2

12 to achieve a victory over ⟨you may have won this

game, but I'll *get* you next time⟩ — see BEAT 2
13 to transmit information or requests to ⟨I've been trying all day, but I can't *get* either of them in order to ask the question⟩ — see CONTACT
14 to put to death deliberately ⟨"I'll *get* you if you talk to the cops," the loan shark warned⟩ — see MURDER 1
15 to throw into a state of mental uncertainty ⟨what *gets* me is why she would do such a weird thing⟩ — see CONFUSE 1

get *n* the descendants of a person, animal, or plant ⟨in some animal species, a new mate will refuse to raise another male's *get*⟩ — see OFFSPRING

get about *vb* to become known ⟨it *got about* that the company was having financial difficulties⟩ — see GET OUT 1

get across *vb* to make plain or understandable ⟨what I'm trying to *get across* is that there simply is no money for the project⟩ — see EXPLAIN 1

get along *vb* **1** to meet one's day-to-day needs ⟨most college students can *get along* with just a few hours of sleep at night⟩
synonyms cope, do, fare, get by, get on, make out, manage, shift
related words carry on, contrive, scrape (by *or* through), scrounge; last, survive; eke out, scrape (out), squeeze, wrest, wring; afford, swing
phrases fend for oneself, make do, make ends meet, make shift
near antonyms collapse, fail, fall short, fizzle, flounder; decline, peter (out), slump, wane; give up
2 to move forward along a course ⟨the preparations for the party are *getting along* just fine⟩ — see GO 1

get around *vb* **1** to achieve a victory over ⟨somehow, an inexperienced lawyer managed to *get around* the media giant's stable of high-priced legal eagles⟩ — see BEAT 2
2 to avoid having to comply with (something) especially through cleverness ⟨somehow she managed to *get around* the rules for paying the sales tax on a car bought out of state⟩ — see CIRCUMVENT 1
3 to become known ⟨word of the discovery of gold quickly *got around*⟩ — see GET OUT 1
4 to get or keep away from (as a responsibility) through cleverness or trickery ⟨their lawyer has spent months trying to *get around* certain restrictions in the contract⟩ — see ESCAPE 2

getaway *n* the act or an instance of getting free from danger or confinement ⟨the bank robbers jumped into the waiting car and made their *getaway*⟩ — see ESCAPE 1

get back *vb* to get again in one's possession ⟨the distraught owner cried that she would do anything to *get back* her lost dog⟩ — see RECOVER 1

get by *vb* to meet one's day-to-day needs ⟨working at night paid my college tuition and enabled me to *get by*—but just barely⟩ — see GET ALONG 1

get down *vb* **1** to come down from something (as a vehicle) ⟨I was *getting down* from the seaplane when a gust of wind swept away my hat⟩ — see ALIGHT 2
2 to make sad ⟨it's really *getting* him *down* that there does not seem to be one woman who will date him⟩ — see DEPRESS 1
3 to take into the stomach through the mouth and throat ⟨with her sore throat, liquids are the only thing she can *get down*⟩ — see SWALLOW 1

get–go *also* **git–go** *n* the point at which something begins ⟨from the *get-go*, their relationship was tumultuous and doomed to fail⟩ — see BEGINNING

get in *vb* to get to a destination ⟨it will be late when you *get in*, so you may have trouble finding a taxi⟩ — see COME 2

get off *vb* **1** to leave a place often for another ⟨told him to *get off* for home before it got dark⟩ — see GO 2
2 to take the first step in (a process or course of action) ⟨breakfast helps you *get off* to a good start in the morning⟩ — see BEGIN 1

get off (on) *vb* to take pleasure in ⟨he really *gets off on* being the person in charge of everyone else⟩ — see ENJOY 1

get on *vb* **1** to meet one's day-to-day needs ⟨despite his new job's low pay, he was still *getting on*⟩ — see GET ALONG 1
2 to move forward along a course ⟨find out how the marketing department is *getting on* with the new ad campaign⟩ — see GO 1

get on (to) *vb* to come to an awareness of ⟨by the time the CIA *got on to* the terrorist plot, it was already in progress⟩ — see DISCOVER 1

get out *vb* **1** to become known ⟨news of the rock star's secret wedding *got out* to the news media⟩
synonyms break, circulate, come out, get about, get around, get round, leak (out), out, spread
related words develop, transpire, unfold; disclose, reveal, spill, tell
near antonyms hush (up), suppress; conceal, disguise, hide, mask; secrete
2 to get free from a dangerous or confining situation ⟨tried but couldn't *get out* of the old well without assistance⟩ — see ESCAPE 1
3 to produce and release for distribution in printed form ⟨a romance novelist who *got* a new book *out* every year⟩ — see PUBLISH 1

get round *vb* to become known ⟨word *got round* that a movie star was spending the night at a local motel⟩ — see GET OUT 1

get through *vb* to get to a destination ⟨we had trouble *getting through* because of the heavy snowfall⟩ — see COME 2

get–together *n* **1** a coming together of a number of persons for a specified purpose ⟨promised to meet friends for lunch after that morning's *get-together* for sales reps⟩ — see MEETING 1
2 a social gathering ⟨was invited to a neighborhood *get-together* in the neighbors' backyard⟩ — see PARTY 1

getup *n* **1** clothing chosen as appropriate for a specific situation ⟨went to the prom in some elaborately beaded *getup*⟩ — see OUTFIT 1
2 the way in which the elements of something (as a work of art) are arranged ⟨the wine book's *getup* is pretty standard, with wines being arranged according to country of origin⟩ — see COMPOSITION 3

get up *vb* **1** to leave one's bed ⟨you need to *get* right *up* when the alarm goes off in the morning⟩ — see ARISE 1
2 to outfit with clothes and especially fine or special clothes ⟨all *got up* in her Sunday best⟩ — see CLOTHE 1
3 to call into being through the use of one's inner resources or powers ⟨I'm still trying to *get up* the energy to reply⟩ — see SUMMON 2

get–up–and–go *n* active strength of body or mind ⟨even after her broken hip healed, Grandma never regained her *get-up-and-go*⟩ — see VIGOR 1

gewgaw *also* **geegaw** *n* a small object displayed for its attractiveness or interest ⟨had a shelf devoted just to *gewgaws* featuring his favorite team's mascot⟩ — see KNICKKNACK

ghastliness *n* the quality of inspiring intense dread or dismay ⟨the *ghastliness* of the Holocaust can scarcely be described⟩ — see HORROR 1

ghastly *adj* **1** extremely disturbing or repellent ⟨a *ghastly* murder that shocked even hard-bitten detectives⟩ — see HORRIBLE 1
2 extreme in degree, power, or effect ⟨I'm afraid that there's been a *ghastly* misunderstanding⟩ — see INTENSE 1
3 causing fear ⟨a *ghastly* crime that made local residents

afraid to go out at night⟩ — see FEARFUL 1

ghost *n* **1** the soul of a dead person thought of especially as appearing to living people ⟨looked for *ghosts* in the graveyard on Halloween⟩
synonyms apparition, bogey (*also* bogie *or* bogy), familiar spirit, hant [*dialect*], haunt [*chiefly dialect*], materialization, phantasm (*also* fantasm), phantom, poltergeist, shade, shadow, specter (*or* spectre), spirit, spook, sprite, vision, visitant, wraith
related words angel, daimon, familiar, genie, genius, jinni (*or* jinn *also* djinni *or* djinn), shaitan; double, doppelgänger (*or* doppelganger), fetch; lemures, manes; incubus, lamia, succubus, vampire, zombie (*also* zombi); cacodemon, demon (*or* daemon), devil, fiend, ghoul, imp
2 the smallest amount or part imaginable ⟨she may be a good endurance runner, but she doesn't stand a *ghost* of a chance of winning in a sprint⟩ — see JOT
3 a tiny often physical indication of something lost or vanished ⟨the down-at-the-heels town house is but a *ghost* of the neighborhood's former grandeur⟩ — see VESTIGE 1
4 an evil spirit ⟨the vengeful *ghosts* of seamen who were deliberately shipwrecked upon these shores⟩ — see DEMON 1

ghoul *n* an evil spirit ⟨in Arabic folklore, *ghouls* could change their shapes but had one unchanging feature: donkey's hooves for feet⟩ — see DEMON 1

ghoulie *n* an evil spirit ⟨a tale of a decrepit mansion haunted by a gallery of *ghoulies*⟩ — see DEMON 1

GI *vb* to remove the dirt from ⟨in preparation for one of her mother-in-law's dreaded visits, she had *GI'd* the whole house⟩ — see CLEAN 1

giant *adj* unusually large ⟨the *giant* sycamore tree that dwarfs our house is almost 250 years old⟩ — see HUGE

giant *n* something that is unusually large and powerful ⟨the Great Pyramids of Egypt are *giants* among the world's architectural wonders⟩
synonyms behemoth, blockbuster, colossus, dinosaur, dreadnought, elephant, Goliath, jumbo, leviathan, mammoth, mastodon, monster, titan, whale, whopper
related words amazon, giantess; bulk, hulk; heavyweight; juggernaut, steamroller
near antonyms lightweight, weakling, wimp, wisp; nonentity, twerp, whippersnapper
antonyms diminutive, dwarf, half-pint, midget, mite, peewee, pygmy (*also* pigmy), runt, shrimp

giantism *n* the quality or state of being very large ⟨the American taste for *giantism*: big cars, big houses, big servings of food⟩ — see IMMENSITY

gibber *vb* to speak rapidly, inarticulately, and usually unintelligibly ⟨stop *gibbering*, and pull yourself together!⟩ — see BABBLE 1

gibber *n* unintelligible or meaningless talk ⟨all I could get from her *gibber* was that something had exploded⟩ — see GIBBERISH 1

gibberish *n* **1** unintelligible or meaningless talk ⟨was so excited he could only talk *gibberish*⟩
synonyms abracadabra, babble, blabber, burble, double Dutch, double-talk, drivel, gabble, gibber, jabber, jabberwocky, mumbo jumbo, nonsense, prattle, slobber
related words blah (*also* blah-blah), hocus-pocus, hokeypokey, twaddle; chatter, gab, patter, prate, tattle, twitter; cackle, clack, clatter
2 language marked by abstractions, jargon, euphemisms, and circumlocutions ⟨all I got from the doctor's *gibberish* was that I had a sore throat, which I already knew⟩
synonyms bafflegab, double-talk, gobbledygook (*also* gobbledegook), rigmarole (*also* rigamarole), song and dance
related words bureaucratese, computerese, educationese, governmentese, legalese, Pentagonese, psychobabble, technobabble; bombast, fustian, gas, grandiloquence, hot air, hype, oratory, rhetoric, wind

gibe *or* **jibe** *vb* to make (someone or something) the object of unkind laughter ⟨teammates *gibing* each other when one fouls up an important play⟩ — see RIDICULE

giddy *adj* **1** lacking in seriousness or maturity ⟨the *giddy* youngsters continued to laugh, joke, and make faces during the ceremonies⟩ ⟨the old guy's having an affair with a *giddy* twentysomething⟩
synonyms birdbrained, ditzy (*or* ditsy), dizzy, featherbrained, flighty, frivolous, frothy, futile, goofy, harebrained, light-headed, light-minded, puerile, scatterbrained, silly, yeasty
related words fatuous, foolish, inane, nonsensical, thoughtless, witless; crazy, daffy, daft, fruity; exuberant, flippant, fluttery, giggly, happy, light, lighthearted, playful; sappy, shallow, superficial
near antonyms grave, melancholy, somber (*or* sombre), thoughtful; dignified, heavy, no-nonsense, sedate, severe, solemn, staid
antonyms earnest, serious, serious-minded, sober, unfrivolous
2 having a feeling of being whirled about and in danger of falling down ⟨I love the *giddy* feeling you get riding roller coasters⟩ — see DIZZY 1
3 experiencing or marked by overwhelming usually pleasurable emotion ⟨he's clearly *giddy* at the news that his ailing grandfather will be fine⟩ — see ECSTATIC

gift *n* **1** something given to someone without expectation of a return ⟨gave him an unusual birthday *gift*⟩
synonyms bestowal, comp, donation, donative, fairing [*British*], freebie (*or* freebee), giveaway, handsel, lagniappe, largesse (*also* largess), present, presentation
related words alms, benefaction, beneficence, benevolence, charity, contribution, dole, handout, oblation, offering, philanthropy, tithe; box [*British*], care package, foy [*chiefly Scottish*]; grant, subsidy; remembrance, tribute, valentine; bonus, boon, windfall; courtesy, favor, generosity, sacrifice; gratuity, propine [*Scottish*], tip; award, prize, reward; dowry; bequest, legacy
near antonyms advance, loan; bribe, douceur, peace offering, sop
2 a special and usually inborn ability ⟨has a *gift* for making guests feel right at home⟩ — see TALENT

gift *vb* to furnish freely or naturally with some power, quality, or attribute ⟨*gifted* with an uncanny ability to persuade people to do things they ordinarily wouldn't⟩ — see ENDOW 1

gigantesque *adj* unusually large ⟨a *gigantesque* poster of the rock star covered most of the wall⟩ — see HUGE

gigantic *adj* unusually large ⟨a raccoon got into the trash and now there's a *gigantic* mess in our backyard⟩ — see HUGE

gigantism *n* the quality or state of being very large ⟨the *gigantism* that is this newest ocean liner is impossible to describe⟩ — see IMMENSITY

giggle *n* **1** *chiefly British* something said or done to cause laughter ⟨poking fun at the royal family is nothing new, but this movie comedy has a few *giggles* you haven't heard before⟩ — see JOKE 1
2 an explosive sound that is a sign of amusement ⟨couldn't help but *giggle* at his remark⟩ — see LAUGH 1

giggle *vb* to show mirth with an explosive vocal sound ⟨some audience members thought that they were being clever by *giggling* during the serious scenes⟩ — see LAUGH 1

[1]**gill** *n* a female romantic companion ⟨every Jack must have his *Gill*⟩ — see GIRLFRIEND

[2]**gill** *n, British* **1** a narrow opening between hillsides or mountains that can be used for passage ⟨a narrow *gill* in

the Cumbrian Mountains of the Lake District⟩ — see CANYON

2 a natural body of running water smaller than a river ⟨a narrow but surprisingly deep *gill* runs the length of the rocky gorge⟩ — see CREEK 1

gilt–edged *or* **gilt–edge** *adj* of the very best kind ⟨very little of that network's programming is what you would call *gilt-edged*⟩ — see EXCELLENT

gimcrack *adj* of low quality ⟨a store plastered with "going out of business" signs and notorious for selling *gimcrack* merchandise⟩ — see CHEAP 2

gimcrack *n* a small object displayed for its attractiveness or interest ⟨a remarkable amount of money is spent on *gimcracks* and other unnecessary items each year⟩ ⟨that woman has enough *gimcracks* to fill up a novelty company's mail-order catalog⟩ — see KNICKKNACK

gimmick *n* **1** a clever often underhanded means to achieve an end ⟨that free magazine subscription they offer is just a sales *gimmick* to get you to buy their product⟩ — see TRICK 1

2 an interesting and often novel device with a practical use ⟨a laptop equipped with a carrying handle and other neat *gimmicks*⟩ — see GADGET

3 a danger or difficulty that is hidden or not easily recognized ⟨the deal sounds too good to be true, so make sure there aren't any *gimmicks*⟩ — see PITFALL 1

ginger *n* active strength of body or mind ⟨a 60-year-old with the *ginger* to consider skydiving lessons⟩ — see VIGOR 1

ginger (up) *vb* to give life, vigor, or spirit to ⟨find some human-interest anecdotes that will *ginger up* this news article on the recent downturn in the economy⟩ — see ANIMATE

gingerbread *adj* elaborately and often excessively decorated ⟨marveled at all the woodwork on the historic *gingerbread* cottages that lined the coast⟩ — see ORNATE 1

gingerbreaded *adj* elaborately and often excessively decorated ⟨a *gingerbreaded* gazebo with multicolored shingles and frilly fretwork⟩ — see ORNATE 1

gingerbready *adj* elaborately and often excessively decorated ⟨festooned with Christmas lights and wreaths, the old Victorian house is particularly *gingerbready* in the winter⟩ — see ORNATE 1

gingerliness *n* a close attentiveness to avoiding danger ⟨for someone who usually falls head over heels in love, she's approaching this romance with uncharacteristic *gingerliness*⟩ — see CAUTION 1

gingerly *adj* having or showing a close attentiveness to avoiding danger or trouble ⟨gave the cork on the bottle of champagne a *gingerly* twist⟩ — see CAREFUL 1

gingery *adj* **1** having active strength of body or mind ⟨a *gingery* old lobsterman who goes out every day regardless of the weather⟩ — see VIGOROUS 1

2 marked by a lively display of strong feeling ⟨I got a *gingery* rebuke when I asked the spry old woman if she needed any help crossing the street⟩ — see SPIRITED 1

gin mill *n* a place of business where alcoholic beverages are sold to be consumed on the premises ⟨the streets are full of people staggering home when the area's numerous *gin mills* close⟩ — see BARROOM

gird *n* an act or expression showing scorn and usually intended to hurt another's feelings ⟨in her farewell speech, the departing governor got in some retaliatory *girds* at the media⟩ — see INSULT

gird *vb* **1** to encircle or bind with or as if with a belt ⟨for the celebration of the heroes' return, well-wishers *girded* hundreds of trees with yellow ribbons⟩ ⟨she *girded* her waist with a delicate sash⟩

synonyms band, begird, belt, engird [*archaic*], engirdle, enwind, girdle, girt, girth, wrap

related words tie up, truss; circle, enwreathe, loop, wind, wreathe; bandage, enswathe, swathe; chain, cord, enchain, lash, rope, shackle, tape, wire

near antonyms unbind, unlash, unshackle, untie, unwind

antonyms ungird, unwrap

2 to provide (someone) with what is needed for a task or activity ⟨the Spartan warrior *girded* himself for battle with sword and shield⟩ — see FURNISH 1

3 to form a circle around ⟨a tall hedge *girds* the exclusive estate and shields it from prying eyes⟩ — see SURROUND

girdle *n* a strip of flexible material (as leather) worn around the waist ⟨drew a handkerchief from the *girdle* around her waist and offered it to the knight as a token of affection⟩ — see [2]BELT 1

girdle *vb* **1** to encircle or bind with or as if with a belt ⟨trees *girdled* the campus, essentially hiding it from view⟩ ⟨wire *girdling* the bundle of firewood⟩ — see GIRD

2 to travel completely around ⟨an asteroid belt that *girdles* the inner planets of the solar system⟩ — see ENCIRCLE 1

3 to form a circle around ⟨the rings that famously *girdle* the planet Saturn⟩ — see SURROUND

girl *n* **1** a young unmarried woman ⟨most men would jump at the chance to marry a *girl* like that⟩

synonyms damsel, demoiselle, maid, maiden, miss

related words virgin; deb, debutante, ingenue (*or* ingénue); bird [*chiefly British*], chick [*slang*], chicken, chit, filly, lass, lassie, sheila [*Australian & New Zealand*], sister; colleen, mademoiselle, senhorita, senorita (*or* señorita)

2 a female person who has not yet reached adulthood ⟨when I was a *girl*, I wanted a horse so badly⟩

synonyms filly, lass, lassie, miss, missy, nymph, sheila [*Australian & New Zealand*]

related words bobby-soxer, junior miss, schoolgirl, subdebutante, teenybopper; gamine, hoyden, pixie (*also* pixy), romp, snip, tomboy

3 a female romantic companion ⟨sent her a note asking her to be his *girl*⟩ — see GIRLFRIEND

girlfriend *n* a female romantic companion ⟨he proposed to his *girlfriend* of seven years⟩

synonyms gal, gill, girl, inamorata, lady, ladylove, old lady, woman

related words mistress, moll; beloved, darling, dear, favorite, flame, honey, love, lover, significant other, sweet, sweetheart, valentine

girt *vb* to encircle or bind with or as if with a belt ⟨his wounded leg was *girted* by bandages⟩ — see GIRD 1

girth *n* the distance around a round body ⟨a fallen tree with a *girth* of some 26 feet making it wide enough for a full-grown man to walk through⟩ — see CIRCUMFERENCE 1

girth *vb* **1** to encircle or bind with or as if with a belt ⟨you'll need to make sure you *girth* the saddle tightly or you'll fall off the horse⟩ — see GIRD 1

2 to pass completely around ⟨his arms couldn't quite *girth* the stone column⟩ — see ENCIRCLE 1

gist *n* the central part or aspect of something under consideration ⟨didn't catch every word between them, but heard enough to get the *gist* of the conversation⟩ — see CRUX

git *n, British* a person who lacks good sense or judgment ⟨oh, don't be such a silly *git*, of course your mates want you around⟩ — see FOOL 1

give *vb* **1** to make a present of ⟨math tutors generously *give* their time to help students after school⟩

synonyms bestow, contribute, donate, give away, present, volunteer

related words chip in, kick in, pitch in, throw in;

award, confer, endow, endue (*or* indue), render; afford, comp, furnish, provide; lavish, regale; aid, assist, benefit, help; administer, dish out, dispense, dole out, hand out, impart, issue, mete (out); extend, fork (over, out, *or* up), offer, pay, proffer, pungle (up), put up, tender; sacrifice

phrases give of

near antonyms hold, keep, pocket, retain, withhold; preserve, save; advance, lend, loan; sell

2 to put (something) into the possession or safekeeping of another ⟨*gave* my camera to my father to hold while I went swimming⟩

synonyms commend, commit, confide, consign, delegate, deliver, entrust (*also* intrust), give over, hand, hand over, leave, pass, recommend, repose, transfer, transmit, trust, turn over, vest

related words confer, grant; assign, deal (out), dispense, disperse, distribute, divide; hand in, release, relinquish, submit, surrender, turn in, yield; bequeath, hand down, hand on, will; advance, lend, loan; furnish, supply; recommit, redeliver, regive, retransfer, retransmit

near antonyms detain, hold back, reserve, withhold; own, possess; accept, receive, take in; occupy, take, take over

antonyms hold, keep, retain

3 to bring before the public in performance or exhibition ⟨the author will *give* a reading from her latest work at 7:00 p.m.⟩ — see PRESENT 1

4 to fall down or in as a result of physical pressure ⟨they loaded the shopping cart with so much food it *gave* under all the weight⟩ — see COLLAPSE 1

5 to hand over or use up in payment ⟨I wouldn't *give* a nickel for such a run-down car⟩ — see SPEND 1

6 to make known (as an idea, emotion, or opinion) ⟨she *gave* her opinion on the matter very firmly and unmistakably⟩ — see EXPRESS 1

7 to occupy (oneself) diligently or with close attention ⟨totally *gave* himself to his studies in the hopes of winning a scholarship for next year⟩ — see APPLY 2

8 to produce as revenue ⟨a company that consistently *gives* $30 million in profits to the owner⟩ — see YIELD 2

9 to put (something) into the possession of someone for use or consumption ⟨*gave* him my e-mail address⟩ — see FURNISH 2

10 to put before another for acceptance or consideration ⟨she *gave* the committee her grant proposal⟩ — see OFFER 1

11 to cause (something) to pass from one to another ⟨she *gave* her cold to me, and now I'm so sick that I can barely get out of bed⟩ — see COMMUNICATE 1

give–and–take *n* **1** an exchange of views for the purpose of exploring a subject or deciding an issue ⟨a *give-and-take* about what we should do Saturday night⟩ — see DISCUSSION 1

2 the act or practice of each side giving up something in order to reach an agreement ⟨negotiating the terms of the deal will require some *give-and-take* on both sides⟩ — see CONCESSION 1

3 good-natured teasing or exchanging of clever remarks ⟨enjoyed the flirty *give-and-take* between the two romantic lead characters⟩ — see BANTER

giveaway *n* something given to someone without expectation of a return ⟨offering a Caribbean vacation *giveaway* to the millionth customer⟩ — see GIFT 1

give away *vb* **1** to make known (something abstract) through outward signs ⟨the insincerity of his apology was *given away* by that slight smirk on his face⟩ — see SHOW 2

2 to make a present of ⟨*gave away* all her potted plants when she moved⟩ — see GIVE 1

give in *vb* **1** to give up and cease resistance (as to a liking, temptation, or habit) ⟨*give in* and have some chocolate⟩ — see YIELD 1

2 to cease resistance (as to another's arguments, demands, or control) ⟨after withstanding hours of begging, their father finally *gave in* and let them go to the amusement park⟩ — see YIELD 3

given *adj* **1** being in the habit or custom ⟨a quiet man not *given* to loud expressions of emotion⟩ — see ACCUSTOMED

2 having a tendency to be or act in a certain way ⟨she's *given* to exaggeration⟩ — see PRONE 1

3 known but not named ⟨candidates for the quiz show must complete the qualifying test within a *given* amount of time⟩ — see CERTAIN 1

given *n* something taken as being true or factual and used as a starting point for a course of action or reasoning ⟨it's a *given* that television viewers are influenced by advertising, even consciously or subconsciously⟩ — see ASSUMPTION 1

given name *n* a name that is placed before one's family name ⟨everyone calls me Jack, but my *given name* is John⟩ — see FORENAME

give out *vb* **1** to make known openly or publicly ⟨that's information that I'm not prepared to *give out*⟩ — see ANNOUNCE

2 to throw or give off ⟨this heater *gives out* a funny smell sometimes⟩ — see EMIT 1

3 to stop functioning ⟨waiting for the fuel pump in my old car to *give out*⟩ — see FAIL 1

give over *vb* **1** to bring (as an action or operation) to an immediate end ⟨his wife suggested that he *give over* working such long hours if it was making him so unhappy⟩ — see STOP 1

2 to put (something) into the possession or safekeeping of another ⟨*gave over* his entire savings to an investor⟩ — see GIVE 2

give up *vb* **1** to give (something) over to the control or possession of another usually under duress ⟨was in so much debt he had to *give up* his house and move into a cheaper apartment⟩ — see SURRENDER 1

2 to stop doing (something) permanently ⟨I hope you won't *give up* playing the piano⟩ — see QUIT 2

3 to yield to the control or power of enemy forces ⟨with the prospect of a renewed enemy attack, the regiment decided to simply *give up*⟩ — see FALL 2

4 to give (oneself) over to something especially unrestrainedly ⟨even in the darkest days of her troubled marriage, she refused to *give* herself *up* to feelings of utter hopelessness⟩ — see ABANDON 1

give up (to) *vb* to keep or intend for a special purpose ⟨unfortunately, when he was in college, weekends were largely *given up to* binge drinking⟩ — see DEVOTE 1

giving *n* the act of offering money in exchange for goods or services ⟨a diorama about pioneer life at the museum that depicts the *giving* of beads for clothes⟩ — see PAYMENT 1

gizmo *also* **gismo** *n* an interesting and often novel device with a practical use ⟨found all sorts of interesting woodworking *gizmos* in the garage⟩ — see GADGET

glacial *adj* **1** having a low or subnormal temperature ⟨a *glacial* weather front coming down from Canada will bring freezing temperatures this weekend⟩ — see COLD 1

2 lacking in friendliness or warmth of feeling ⟨her *glacial* manner discouraged him from attempting further conversation⟩ — see COLD 2

glad *adj* **1** experiencing pleasure, satisfaction, or delight ⟨the man was *glad* to see his old college buddies again, after so long an absence⟩

synonyms blissful, chuffed [*British*], delighted, gratified, happy, joyful, joyous, pleased, satisfied, thankful, tickled

related words beaming, blithe, blithesome, buoyant, cheerful, cheery, gay, gladsome, lighthearted, sunny, upbeat; gleeful, jocund, jolly, jovial, laughing, merry, mirthful, smiling; beatific, ecstatic, elated, enraptured, entranced, euphoric, exhilarated, intoxicated, rapturous, rhapsodic (*also* rhapsodical); exuberant, exultant, jubilant, rapt, rejoicing, thrilled; hopeful, optimistic, rosy, sanguine
near antonyms abject, aggrieved, anguished, blue, brokenhearted, dejected, depressed, despondent, disconsolate, disheartened, downcast, downhearted, forlorn, melancholy; doleful, dolorous, lachrymose, mournful, plaintive, sorrowful, sorry, woeful; black, dark, desolate, dispirited, gloomy, glum, gray (*also* grey), grieved, heartbroken, heartsick, miserable, woebegone, wretched
antonyms displeased, dissatisfied, joyless, sad, unhappy, unpleased, unsatisfied
2 having a desire or inclination (as for a specified course of action) ⟨I am *glad* to do the work if it will help the cause⟩ — see WILLING 1
3 serving to lift one's spirits ⟨doctors brought *glad* tidings to the reporters awaiting news of the queen's condition⟩ — see CHEERFUL 2
4 feeling or expressing gratitude ⟨she was *glad* of the offer of a ride home⟩ — see GRATEFUL 1

glad *vb, archaic* to give satisfaction to ⟨it hath *gladded* my heart to see thy face again⟩ — see PLEASE 1

gladden *vb* to give satisfaction to ⟨it would *gladden* me to hear you sing again⟩ — see PLEASE 1

gladdening *adj* making one feel good inside ⟨the overdue change to warm, sunny weather is *gladdening*⟩ — see HEARTWARMING

glad–hander *n* a gregarious and unreserved person ⟨an irrepressible *glad-hander*, she's a natural for the company's public relations department⟩ — see EXTROVERT

gladiator *n* one that engages in the sport of fighting with the fists ⟨the two punch-drunk *gladiators* stumbled to their corners⟩ — see BOXER

gladiatorial *adj* feeling or displaying eagerness to fight ⟨not a reasoned discussion but a shouting match between *gladiatorial* pundits from opposite ends of the political spectrum⟩ — see BELLIGERENT

gladness *n* **1** a feeling or state of well-being and contentment ⟨felt nothing but *gladness* at seeing her best friend beat her out for the award⟩ — see HAPPINESS 1
2 the feeling experienced when one's wishes are met ⟨the children's *gladness* was evident as they opened their Christmas presents⟩ — see PLEASURE 1

glad rags *n pl* dressy clothing ⟨a trendy designer fashioning *glad rags* for the beautiful people⟩ — see FINERY

gladsome *adj* having or showing a good mood or disposition ⟨a *gladsome* group of carolers strolling through the city's historic district⟩ ⟨a *gladsome* smile⟩ — see CHEERFUL 1

glamorize *also* **glamourize** *vb* to represent or think of as better than reality would warrant ⟨most people *glamorize* fame, not thinking of the lack of privacy that accompanies it⟩ — see IDEALIZE

glamorous *also* **glamourous** *adj* **1** excitingly or mysteriously unusual ⟨the *glamorous* sights and scents of a Turkish market⟩ — see EXOTIC
2 having an often mysterious or magical power to attract ⟨*glamorous* Hollywood celebrities whose every move is breathlessly recorded by the media⟩ — see FASCINATING 1

glamour *also* **glamor** *n* **1** a spoken word or set of words believed to have magic power ⟨the children were so preternaturally well-behaved that they must have been under the power of a *glamour* of some sort⟩ — see SPELL 1
2 the power of irresistible attraction ⟨the *glamour* of the fashion industry⟩ — see CHARM 2

glamour (up) *vb* to represent or think of as better than reality would warrant ⟨a movie that does its best to *glamour up* the field of archaeology⟩ — see IDEALIZE

glamour–puss *n* a physically attractive person ⟨not necessarily looking for someone who's a *glamour-puss*—just nice and wholesome⟩ — see DOLL 2

glance *n* an instance of looking especially briefly ⟨she was about to say something rude, but her mother silenced her with a *glance*⟩ — see LOOK 2

glance *vb* **1** to strike and fly off at an angle ⟨the basketball *glanced* off the rim⟩ ⟨her wild pitch *glanced* off my shoulder and landed in the dugout⟩
synonyms bounce, carom, rebound, ricochet, skim, skip
related words brush, graze, nudge, rake, shave, sweep; bump, contact, hit, kiss, touch; sideswipe; reflect
2 to take a quick or hasty look ⟨just *glanced* at the instructions before assembling the bike⟩ ⟨*glanced* over his shoulder to see if she was still there⟩
synonyms browse, dip, glimpse, glint, peek, skim
related words keek [*chiefly Scottish*], peep; blink, squint; look over, peruse, rake, scan
near antonyms examine, overlook, oversee, question, survey; study, view; peer, pry; gawk, goggle, rubberneck; leer, ogle
antonyms gaze, stare
3 to shoot forth bursts of light ⟨diamonds *glancing* in the display case⟩ — see FLASH 1

glare *n* the steady giving off of the form of radiation that makes vision possible ⟨the sudden *glare* of the squad car's headlights in my rearview mirror⟩ — see LIGHT 1

glare *vb* **1** to shine with a bright harsh light ⟨the spotlight *glared* down on the suspect as the police questioned him relentlessly⟩
synonyms beat, blaze, burn, flame, flare
related words beam, glow, radiate; flash, glance, gleam, glimmer, glint, glisten, glister, glitter, scintillate, shimmer, sparkle, twinkle; bedazzle, blind, daze, dazzle
2 to look with anger or disapproval ⟨don't *glare* at me like that when I tell you "no"⟩ — see FROWN

glaring *adj* very noticeable especially for being incorrect or bad ⟨no one missed the *glaring* spelling error in the title⟩ — see EGREGIOUS

glass *n* **1 glasses** *pl* a pair of lenses set in a frame that is held in place with ear supports and which are usually worn to correct vision ⟨I'm a little nearsighted, so I'm going to need *glasses*⟩
synonyms eyeglasses, specs, spectacles
related words bifocals, half-glasses, trifocals; lorgnette, monocle, pince-nez; sunglasses; goggles; contact lens
2 a smooth or polished surface that forms images by reflection ⟨the vain princess spent hours admiring the reflection in her *glass*⟩ — see MIRROR

glasshouse *n, chiefly British* a glass-enclosed building for growing plants ⟨a *glasshouse* for growing tropical plants⟩ — see CONSERVATORY

gleam *n* the steady giving off of the form of radiation that makes vision possible ⟨the door opened a crack and let in a *gleam* of light from the hallway⟩ — see LIGHT 1

gleam *vb* to shoot forth bursts of light ⟨fine china and stemware *gleaming* in the candlelight⟩ — see FLASH 1

glee *n* a mood characterized by high spirits and amusement and often accompanied by laughter ⟨the evident *glee* with which the tabloids report on the misfortunes of celebrities⟩ — see MIRTH

glee club *n* an organized group of singers ⟨sang with the *glee club* in college⟩ — see CHORUS 1

gleeful *adj* indicative of or marked by high spirits or good humor ⟨the *gleeful* atmosphere that envelops the host city of the Super Bowl⟩ — see MERRY

gleefulness *n* a mood characterized by high spirits and amusement and often accompanied by laughter ⟨the infectious *gleefulness* that permeates the town during its annual Christmas stroll⟩ — see MIRTH

glide *vb* **1** to move or proceed smoothly and readily ⟨looking for a college course that he could just *glide* through⟩ — see FLOW 2

2 to move through the air with or as if with outstretched wings ⟨a kite *gliding* on the autumn breeze⟩ — see FLY 1

3 to rest or move along the surface of a liquid or in the air ⟨water striders *gliding* along the surface of the brook⟩ — see FLOAT 1

glimmer *n* **1** a very small amount ⟨a *glimmer* of hope that there will be snow on Christmas⟩ — see PARTICLE 1

2 an almost imperceptible sign of something ⟨most of the students showed not even a *glimmer* of interest in what I had to say⟩ — see HINT 2

glimmer *vb* to shoot forth bursts of light ⟨the waters of the rippling brook *glimmered* in the sun⟩ — see FLASH 1

glimpse *n* an instance of looking especially briefly ⟨I only got a *glimpse* of him as we drove by⟩ — see LOOK 2

glimpse *vb* to take a quick or hasty look ⟨just *glimpsed* at the photo then turned his attention elsewhere⟩ — see GLANCE 2

glint *vb* **1** to shoot forth bursts of light ⟨the cat's eyes *glinted* in the moonlight⟩ — see FLASH 1

2 to take a quick or hasty look ⟨the thief *glinted* around the corner to see if anyone was coming⟩ — see GLANCE 2

glisten *vb* to shoot forth bursts of light ⟨this seemingly dull opal really *glistens* in full light⟩ — see FLASH 1

glistening *adj* having a shiny surface or finish ⟨a *glistening* marble table top⟩ — see GLOSSY

glister *vb* to shoot forth bursts of light ⟨the dew *glistered* in the soft light of the early morning⟩ — see FLASH 1

glitter *vb* to shoot forth bursts of light ⟨the queen's crown *glittered* under the glare of the TV lights⟩ — see FLASH 1

glitz *n* excessive or unnecessary display ⟨a nice dinner, but without all the *glitz* of fancily folded napkins and chichi finger bowls⟩ — see OSTENTATION

glitz (up) *vb* to make more attractive by adding something that is beautiful or becoming ⟨the company's cafeteria had been *glitzed up* for the holiday party⟩ — see DECORATE

glitzy *adj* excessively showy ⟨I think that rhinestone-studded outfit is a little too *glitzy* for church⟩ — see GAUDY

gloaming *n* **1** a time or place of little or no light ⟨lovers would often retreat to the *gloaming* of the park's many secluded recesses to steal a kiss⟩ — see DARK 1

2 the time from when the sun begins to set to the onset of total darkness ⟨with the *gloaming* came the familiar call of the whip-poor-will⟩ — see DUSK 1

glob *n* **1** a small uneven mass ⟨found a *glob* of chewing gum under my theater seat⟩ — see LUMP 1

2 the quantity of fluid that falls naturally in one rounded mass ⟨add a *glob* or two of molasses to the batter⟩ — see DROP 1

global *adj* **1** belonging or relating to the whole ⟨do a *global* search and replace the misspelling throughout the whole document⟩ — see GENERAL 1

2 covering everything or all important points ⟨published a *global* report on the plight of Third World economies⟩ — see ENCYCLOPEDIC

3 having every part of the surface the same distance from the center ⟨one of the fair's more striking pavilions was a *global* structure with a monorail running through its center⟩ — see ROUND 1

globe *n* **1** a more or less round body or mass ⟨the glassblower shaped the molten mass into a *globe* of remarkable thinness and clarity⟩ — see [1]BALL 1

2 the celestial body on which we live ⟨New Year's celebrations around the *globe*⟩ — see EARTH 1

globular *adj* having every part of the surface the same distance from the center ⟨the *globular* streetlights give the pedestrian mall a Gay Nineties look⟩ — see ROUND 1

globule *n* the quantity of fluid that falls naturally in one rounded mass ⟨fat *globules* of hot wax dripping onto the table⟩ — see DROP 1

glom *vb* to take physical control or possession of (something) suddenly or forcibly ⟨the manager *glommed* the shoplifter just as she was about to bolt out of the store⟩ — see CATCH 1

gloom *n* **1** a state or spell of low spirits ⟨has been in a perpetual *gloom* since his dog died⟩ — see SADNESS

2 a time or place of little or no light ⟨the *gloom* of a rainy night is the perfect setting for a mystery story⟩ — see DARK 1

gloom *vb* **1** to look with anger or disapproval ⟨we just sat there, *glooming*, as we waited and waited for our dinners to arrive⟩ — see FROWN

2 to take on a gloomy or forbidding look ⟨he continued to *gloom* over the fact that he had been passed over for promotion to district manager⟩ — see DARKEN 1

gloominess *n* a state or spell of low spirits ⟨even in the depths of her *gloominess* she never lost hope entirely⟩ — see SADNESS

gloomy *adj* **1** causing or marked by an atmosphere lacking in cheer ⟨the cold rain made for a *gloomy* day⟩
synonyms black, bleak, cheerless, chill, Cimmerian, cloudy, cold, comfortless, dark, darkening, depressing, depressive, desolate, dire, disconsolate, dismal, drear, dreary, dreich [*chiefly Scottish*], elegiac (*also* elegiacal), forlorn, funereal, glum, godforsaken, gray (*also* grey), lonely, lonesome, lugubrious, miserable, morbid, morose, murky, plutonian, saturnine, sepulchral, solemn, somber (*or* sombre), sullen, sunless, tenebrific, tenebrous, wretched
related words blue, dejected, depressed, despondent, disconsolate, down, droopy, hangdog, inconsolable, low, melancholic, melancholy, mirthless, sad, unhappy, woebegone, woeful; dim, discomfiting, discouraging, disheartening, dismaying, dispiriting, distressful, distressing, upsetting; desperate, hopeless, pessimistic; lamentable, mournful, plaintive, sorrowful; colorless, drab, dull; dour, grim, lowering (*also* louring), lowery (*also* loury), menacing, negative, oppressive, threatening
near antonyms blithe, blithesome, buoyant, gay, jocund, jolly, joyful, joyous, merry, mirthful; encouraging, hopeful, optimistic; lighthearted, lightsome
antonyms bright, cheerful, cheering, cheery, comforting, cordial, festive, friendly, gay, heartwarming, sunshiny

2 feeling unhappiness ⟨has been *gloomy* ever since the breakup with his girlfriend⟩ — see SAD 1

3 being without light or without much light ⟨that house would be less *gloomy* if some of the overgrown trees and shrubs were cleared away⟩ — see DARK 1

glop *n* a thick semiliquid substance (as food) that is unattractive ⟨the restaurant served *glop* that brought back unpleasant memories of my high school cafeteria⟩
synonyms slop, swill
related words crud, goo, goop, guck (*or* gook), gunk

glorify *vb* **1** to assign a high status or value to ⟨a number of big names were recruited in the hopes that their presence would *glorify* the university's school of medicine in the eyes of the medical world⟩ — see EXALT 1

2 to offer honor or respect to (someone) as a divine power ⟨let us now *glorify* the Lord⟩ — see WORSHIP 1
3 to praise or publicize lavishly and often excessively ⟨fond parents who *glorify* everything that their precious offspring do⟩ — see TOUT 1
4 to proclaim the glory of ⟨the hillsides ablaze in red and gold silently *glorify* New England in the fall⟩ — see PRAISE 1
5 to represent or think of as better than reality would warrant ⟨don't let the job title "team spirit coordinator" fool you—he's nothing more than a *glorified* college cheerleader⟩ — see IDEALIZE

glorious *adj* large and impressive in size, grandeur, extent, or conception ⟨the advent of the printing press in the West ushered in a *glorious* new era of learning⟩ — see GRAND 1

gloriously *adv* in a pleasing way ⟨for Easter services the choir rose to the occasion and sang *gloriously*⟩ — see WELL 5

gloriousness *n* impressiveness of beauty on a large scale ⟨the indisputable *gloriousness* of the Taj Mahal⟩ — see MAGNIFICENCE

glory *vb* to feel or express joy or triumph ⟨the whole city *gloried* in the home team's winning of the World Series⟩ — see EXULT

glory *n* **1** public acknowledgment or admiration for an achievement ⟨the theater director gave the stage crew all the *glory* for the successful production⟩
synonyms acclaim, accolade, applause, bay(s), credit, distinction, homage, honor, kudos, laud, laurels, props [*slang*], réclame, sun
related words celebrity, fame, renown, repute; compliment, encomium, eulogy, panegyric, toast, tribute; acclamation, ovation, plaudit, praise, rave, rhapsody; citation, commendation, kudo, note, recommendation; elevation, enshrinement, enthronement, exaltation, glorification
2 an asset that brings praise or renown ⟨the new art museum has become the *glory* of the college campus⟩
synonyms boast, credit, crown jewel, honor, jewel, pride, treasure, trophy
related words pièce de résistance, showpiece; attraction, feature, highlight; distinction, excellence, merit, value, virtue
phrases a feather in one's cap
near antonyms disgrace, dishonor; blemish, blot, defect, shame, slur, smirch, smudge, stain, stigma; eyesore, fright, horror, mess
3 impressiveness of beauty on a large scale ⟨was overwhelmed by the imperial *glory* of Rome⟩ — see MAGNIFICENCE
4 an artistic rendering of radiant light around the head or body of a sacred personage ⟨an altarpiece depicting God seated on His throne and bathed in celestial *glory*⟩ — see AUREOLE

glory *or* **glory be** *interj* how delightful ⟨*glory*! I thought I'd never see this day come⟩ — see HOORAY

glorying *adj* having or expressing feelings of joy or triumph ⟨the Olympic athletes were told to stifle the *glorying* antics and to accept their medals with some measure of humility⟩ — see EXULTANT

gloss *n* **1** a deceptively attractive external appearance ⟨used a computer to give her astrological predictions the *gloss* of real science⟩
synonyms facade (*also* façade), veneer, window dressing
related words cotton candy, fluff, tinsel; fig leaf; charade, front, guise, masquerade, pose, semblance, show
2 brightness created by light reflected from a surface ⟨the surface has such a high *gloss*, you can see your face reflected in it⟩ — see SHINE 1

gloss *vb* to make smooth or glossy usually by repeatedly applying surface pressure ⟨the action of the water will serve to *gloss* the seal's coat⟩ — see POLISH 1

gloss (over) *vb* **1** to make (something) seem less bad by offering excuses ⟨I don't want to *gloss over* her misbehavior, but keep in mind that she's been under a lot of stress lately⟩ — see PALLIATE 1
2 to dismiss as of little importance ⟨this biographer tends to *gloss over* his subject's many character flaws⟩ — see EXCUSE 1

glossy *adj* having a shiny surface or finish ⟨the *glossy* finish on the gym floor⟩ ⟨a sports car with an interior upholstered with *glossy* leather⟩
synonyms buffed, burnished, glistening, lustrous, polished, rubbed, satin, satiny, sleek
related words brushed, eggshell, semigloss, semilustrous; silken, silky, slick, slippery; glassy, glazed, lacquered, shellacked, varnished; gleaming, glittering, reflective, shining
near antonyms lackluster; unvarnished
antonyms dim, dull, flat, lusterless, matte (*also* mat *or* matt)

glow *n* the steady giving off of the form of radiation that makes vision possible ⟨the *glow* of the restaurant's table lamps is especially flattering to diners⟩ — see LIGHT 1

glow *vb* **1** to be on fire especially brightly ⟨the coals *glowed* red-hot⟩ — see BURN 1
2 to develop a rosy facial color (as from excitement or embarrassment) ⟨when they found out he had won the tournament, his parents *glowed* with pride⟩ — see BLUSH

glower *vb* **1** to look with anger or disapproval ⟨baseball fans *glowering* at their TVs as they watched their favorite team lose⟩ — see FROWN
2 to take on a gloomy or forbidding look ⟨the old man just sat in his rocking chair, his face *glowering* at the prospect of unwanted company⟩ — see DARKEN 1

glowing *adj* **1** giving off or reflecting much light ⟨enjoyed the warmth of the *glowing* fire⟩ — see BRIGHT 1
2 having a healthy reddish skin tone ⟨was *glowing* after spending an afternoon outside splitting firewood⟩ — see RUDDY
3 having or being an outward sign of good feelings (as of love, confidence, or happiness) ⟨her *glowing* face made it evident she'd been offered the job⟩ — see RADIANT 1
4 having or expressing great depth of feeling ⟨*glowing* declarations of everlasting love⟩ — see FERVENT 1

glowingly *adv* in a manner marked by the shining or reflecting of much light ⟨the cat's eyes shone *glowingly* from the dark corner⟩ — see BRIGHTLY 1

gloze (over) *vb* **1** to make (something) seem less bad by offering excuses ⟨he tried to *gloze over* his drinking problem by noting that he had never done drugs⟩ — see PALLIATE 1
2 to dismiss as of little importance ⟨we're certainly willing to *gloze over* a couple of minor historical inaccuracies in an otherwise splendid movie⟩ — see EXCUSE 1

glue *n* a substance used to stick things together ⟨used *glue* to stick the photo in the album⟩
synonyms adhesive, bond, cement, size
related words epoxy, epoxy resin, library paste, mucilage, paste, superglue, water glass; dope, goo, gum

gluey *adj* tending to adhere to objects upon contact ⟨don't overbeat the mashed potatoes, or they will be thick and *gluey* instead of light and fluffy⟩ — see STICKY 1

glum *adj* **1** causing or marked by an atmosphere lacking in cheer ⟨the usual *glum* waiting room at the tax collector's office⟩ ⟨a cold, *glum* day⟩ — see GLOOMY 1
2 feeling unhappiness ⟨how can you be *glum* after such a great day?⟩ — see SAD 1
3 given to or displaying a resentful silence and often ir-

ritability ⟨a chronically *glum* and pouting child⟩ — see SULKY

glumness *n* a state or spell of low spirits ⟨her obvious *glumness* told us that she hadn't gotten the job⟩ — see SADNESS

[1]glut *vb* to fill with food to capacity ⟨prefers not to watch those nature programs where all they show are predators *glutting* themselves on the kill⟩ — see GORGE 1

[2]glut *vb, archaic* to swallow or eat greedily ⟨it seemed that he could *glut* enough food to feed 10 men⟩ — see GOBBLE

glutinous *adj* tending to adhere to objects upon contact ⟨a bad horror movie from the 1950s about a *glutinous* blob that devoured Manhattan⟩ — see STICKY 1

glutton *n* one who eats greedily or too much ⟨he's such a *glutton* that he ate the whole cake⟩
synonyms cormorant, gorger, gormandizer, gourmand, hog, overeater, pig, stuffer, swiller
related words feaster, trencherman; muncher; guzzler
near antonyms dieter, nibbler, picker

gluttonous *adj* having a huge appetite ⟨*gluttonous* customers had practically emptied the all-you-can-eat buffet⟩ — see VORACIOUS 1

gluttonousness *n* the excessive consumption of food ⟨the legendary *gluttonousness* of England's Henry VIII⟩ — see GLUTTONY

gluttony *n* the excessive consumption of food ⟨the view that *gluttony* is a serious failure in self-discipline⟩
synonyms gluttonousness, overeating
related words immoderation, intemperance, overindulgence
near antonyms dieting
antonyms abstemiousness

glyph *n* a written or printed mark that is meant to convey information to the reader ⟨a rock inscribed with mysterious *glyphs* that some have speculated as being of Norse origin⟩ — see CHARACTER 1

gnash *vb* to press or strike against or together so as to make a scraping sound ⟨dogs *gnashing* their teeth⟩ — see GRIND 2

gnaw *vb* to consume or wear away gradually ⟨time has *gnawed* that author's reputation to the point where he rates little more than a footnote⟩ — see EAT 2

gnaw (on) *vb* to crush or grind with the teeth ⟨please don't *gnaw on* that steak bone—it's very unseemly⟩ — see BITE (ON)

gnawer *n* one who is obnoxiously annoying ⟨like a dog who won't let go of a bone, that *gnawer* in the backseat wouldn't quit mentioning that I had made a wrong turn and gotten us lost⟩ — see NUISANCE 1

gnome *n* an imaginary being usually having a small human form and magical powers ⟨in Europe, *gnomes* are thought to guard underground treasure, so that may be why statues of them are commonly placed in gardens⟩ — see FAIRY

go *adj* being in a state of fitness for some experience or action ⟨all systems are *go*⟩ — see READY 1

go *n* **1** a practice or interest that is very popular for a short time ⟨snowboarding is all the *go*⟩ — see FAD
2 active strength of body or mind ⟨a healthy six-year-old full of *go*⟩ — see VIGOR 1
3 an effort to do or accomplish something ⟨it took several *goes* to get the car started⟩ — see ATTEMPT 1
4 readiness to engage in daring or difficult activity ⟨a young executive with the *go* to make this company grow⟩ — see ENTERPRISE 2

go *vb* **1** to move forward along a course ⟨everything is *going* according to our plans⟩
synonyms advance, come, come along, do, fare, forge, get along, get on, go along, go off, march, pace, proceed, progress
related words accelerate, fast-forward, speed; approach, near; journey, pass, repair, run, travel, wend; actuate, drive, impel, propel, push; take out
phrases gain ground
near antonyms arrest, balk, block, check, detain, halt, hinder, hold back, impede, nip, obstruct, slow (down *or* up), stem; repress, retard, stunt, suppress; delay, interrupt, stall; cramp, hamper, inhibit; cease, let up, pause; regress; wait
antonyms remain, stand, stay, stop
2 to leave a place often for another ⟨will *go* on vacation at the end of the year⟩ ⟨decided it would be better to *go* before she got any angrier⟩
synonyms bail, bail out, begone, book [*slang*], bugger off [*British slang*], bug off, bug out, buzz (off), clear off [*chiefly British*], clear out, cut out, depart, dig out, exit, get, get off, go off, move, pack (up *or* off), part, peel off, pike (out *or* off), pull out, push off, push on, quit, run along, sally (forth), scarper [*British*], shove (off), step (along), take off, vamoose, walk out
related words set out, start, strike out; abscond, decamp, escape, evacuate, flee, fly, get out, mizzle [*chiefly British*], run away, scat, scram, skip; go out, light out, step out; abandon, desert, forsake, vacate; emigrate; adjourn, remove, retire, retreat, withdraw
phrases beat it, hit the road, pull stakes (*or* pull up stakes), take a hike (*also* take a walk), take a powder
near antonyms abide, dwell, lodge, remain, settle, stay, tarry; approach, close, near; hit, land, reach
antonyms arrive, come, show up, turn up
3 to be fitting or proper ⟨at Mardi Gras, just about anything *goes*⟩ — see DO 1
4 to be in agreement on every point ⟨your account of how the fire started doesn't *go* with what she said⟩ — see CHECK 1
5 to be positioned along a certain course or in a certain direction ⟨the highway *goes* right along the river⟩ — see RUN 3
6 to eventually have as a state or quality ⟨she *goes* crazy on the dance floor when they start playing 1980s pop⟩ ⟨the room *went* dark⟩ — see BECOME
7 to fall down or in as a result of physical pressure ⟨watched the building *go* after the demolition crew detonated the charges⟩ — see COLLAPSE 1
8 to have or be in a usual or proper place ⟨these plates *go* in this cabinet⟩ — see BELONG 1
9 to lose bodily strength or vigor ⟨when you get old, your eyesight starts to *go*⟩ — see WEAKEN 2
10 to make one's way through, across, or over ⟨I *went* the length of the street before finding an empty parking space⟩ — see TRAVERSE
11 to occur within a continuous range of variation ⟨selling prices for houses in that neighborhood generally *go* between one and two million⟩ — see RUN 4
12 to risk (something) on the outcome of an uncertain event ⟨to play in this game of poker, you have to be willing to *go* at least five dollars per round⟩ — see BET
13 *chiefly Southern & Midland* to have in mind as a purpose or goal ⟨I didn't *go* to fire the gun—it just went off⟩ — see INTEND 1
14 to come to an end ⟨we were having so much fun that the evening just came and *went*⟩ — see CEASE 1
15 to have enough money for ⟨I think I can *go* for the new car after all⟩ — see AFFORD
16 to put up with (something painful or difficult) ⟨I can't *go* the smell of that rotting food for one more minute⟩ — see BEAR 2
17 to stop living ⟨her grandmother *went* peacefully last night⟩ — see DIE 1
18 to turn out as planned or desired ⟨we tried very hard to get the food cooperative to *go*, but it never really worked out⟩ — see SUCCEED 1

go (for) *vb* to have a price of ⟨those cars *go for* $25,000⟩ — see COST

go (to) *vb* to use or seek out as a source of aid, relief, or advantage ⟨when the sales representative refused to help us, we *went to* the store manager⟩ — see RESORT (TO) 1

goad *n* something that arouses action or activity ⟨the threat of skin cancer—not to mention the prospect of wrinkles—should be sufficient *goad* for using sunscreen⟩ — see IMPULSE 1

goad *vb* **1** to try to persuade (someone) through earnest appeals to follow a course of action ⟨tried to *goad* me into auditioning for the play⟩ — see URGE

2 to urge or push forward with or as if with a pointed object ⟨*goading* the horse forward into the stall⟩ — see PROD 1

go–ahead *n* an ambitious person who eagerly goes after what is desired ⟨a born *go-ahead*, he was determined to be the first in his family to graduate from college⟩ — see GO-GETTER

goal *n* something that one hopes or intends to accomplish ⟨leaving the world a better place than I found it is one of my main *goals*⟩

synonyms aim, ambition, aspiration, bourne (*also* bourn), design, dream, end, idea, ideal, intent, intention, mark, meaning, object, objective, plan, point, pretension, purpose, target, thing

related words grail, holy grail; plot, project, scheme; desire, hope, mind, wish; nirvana; destination, terminus

phrases name of the game

near antonyms means, method, way

go along *vb* to move forward along a course ⟨everything was *going along* swimmingly until you interfered⟩ — see GO 1

goat *n* a person or thing taking the blame for others ⟨an unhappy childhood was the *goat* he used to rationalize every failure and shortcoming⟩ — see SCAPEGOAT

goatish *adj* having a strong sexual desire ⟨a seedy grind house that was patronized mainly by *goatish* men wearing raincoats⟩ — see LUSTFUL

[1]**gob** *n* **1** a small uneven mass ⟨grabbed a *gob* of clay from the block and threw it on the pottery wheel⟩ — see LUMP 1

2 gobs *pl* a considerable amount ⟨has *gobs* of money⟩ — see LOT 2

[2]**gob** *n, chiefly British* the opening through which food passes into the body of an animal ⟨he threatened the yob with a punch in the *gob* if he didn't stop insulting everyone⟩ — see MOUTH 1

[3]**gob** *n* one who operates or navigates a seagoing vessel ⟨avast, ye *gobs*, and haul anchor!⟩ — see SAILOR

gobbet *n* a small uneven mass ⟨deftly avoided stepping in a *gobbet* of spit on the sidewalk⟩ — see LUMP 1

gobble *vb* to swallow or eat greedily ⟨*gobbled* the sandwiches like they hadn't eaten for days⟩

synonyms bolt, cram, devour, glut [*archaic*], gorge, gormandize, gulp, ingurgitate, inhale, raven, scarf, scoff, slop, wolf

related words overeat, pig out, swill

near antonyms nibble, peck, pick

gobbledygook *also* **gobbledegook** *n* language marked by abstractions, jargon, euphemisms, and circumlocutions ⟨cut through the *gobbledygook* and just tell me what the final cost of the car would be⟩ — see GIBBERISH 2

go–between *n* **1** one that carries a message or does an errand ⟨I won't act as *go-between* between you and your ex⟩ — see MESSENGER

2 one who works with opposing sides in order to bring about an agreement ⟨acted as *go-between* for the two warring nations during the peace process⟩ — see MEDIATOR

goblin *n* an imaginary being usually having a small human form and magical powers ⟨dressed up the toddlers like *goblins* for Halloween⟩ — see FAIRY

god *n* **1** a being having superhuman powers and control over a particular part of life or the world ⟨in some belief systems, natural forces like the wind and the sea were *gods*⟩ — see DEITY 1

2 *cap* the being worshipped as the creator and ruler of the universe ⟨let us give thanks to *God*⟩ — see DEITY 2

3 a person who is the object of extreme or uncritical devotion ⟨in the eyes of many film critics, Alfred Hitchcock is one of the undisputed *gods* of cinema⟩ — see IDOL

goddamned *or* **goddamn** *or* **goddam** *adj* deserving of one's condemnation or displeasure ⟨the *goddamned* car needs another costly repair⟩ — see DAMNABLE

goddess *n* **1** a lovely woman ⟨like any guy in love, he thought his new girlfriend was a *goddess*⟩ — see BEAUTY 2

2 a usually glamorous woman who is preeminent in her field of activity ⟨one of the *goddesses* of the silver screen during the silent era⟩ — see DIVA

godforsaken *adj* causing or marked by an atmosphere lacking in cheer ⟨grew up in the kind of *godforsaken* town in which everyone drank in order to forget that they were there⟩ — see GLOOMY 1

godhead *n* **1** the quality or state of being divine ⟨in some cultures, the ruler of the people has *godhead* and is worshipped accordingly⟩ — see DIVINITY

2 *cap* the being worshipped as the creator and ruler of the universe ⟨most Christians believe that there are three separate persons—Father, Son, and Holy Spirit—that make up the *Godhead*⟩ — see DEITY 2

godhood *n* the quality or state of being divine ⟨according to Greek myth, Hercules was granted *godhood* after his death⟩ — see DIVINITY

godless *adj* lacking religious emotions, principles, or practices ⟨treated the God-fearing and the *godless* with equal respect and compassion⟩ — see IRRELIGIOUS

godlike *adj* of, relating to, or being God ⟨the *godlike* splendor of creation⟩ — see HOLY 3

godliness *n* the quality or state of being spiritually pure or virtuous ⟨they say that cleanliness is next to *godliness*⟩ — see HOLINESS

godly *adj* **1** showing a devotion to God and to a life of virtue ⟨a *godly* and humble man who will be richly rewarded in the next world⟩ — see HOLY 1

2 of, relating to, or being God ⟨a *godly* voice from the heavens commanded him to build an ark⟩ — see HOLY 3

go down *vb, slang* to take place ⟨when's the drug deal supposed to *go down*?⟩ — see HAPPEN

go down (with) *vb, chiefly British* to become affected with (a disease or disorder) ⟨across the United Kingdom a number of children have *gone down with* chicken pox this week⟩ — see CONTRACT 1

God's acre *n* a piece of land used for burying the dead ⟨was laid in rest in *God's acre*, with a comforting view of the river he loved so much⟩ — see CEMETERY

godsend *n* something that provides happiness or does good for a person or thing ⟨that holiday bonus has proved to be a *godsend* for my bills⟩ — see BLESSING 2

Godspeed *n* an expression of good wishes at parting ⟨a hearty *Godspeed* was extended to all the departing troops⟩ — see GOOD-BYE

go–getter *n* an ambitious person who eagerly goes after what is desired ⟨a *go-getter* with his sights set on the presidency⟩

synonyms bootstrapper, go-ahead, highflier (*or* highflyer), hummer, hustler, live wire, powerhouse, rustler, self-starter

related words eager beaver; achiever, comer, doer, en-

terpriser; he-man, individualist
near antonyms dawdler, idler, loafer, lounger, putterer, trifler; goldbrick, malingerer, procrastinator, shirker, slacker; drone, lazybones, sluggard; dallier, laggard, lingerer, loiterer, slowpoke, stick-in-the-mud; ignorer, ne'er-do-well, neglecter; daydreamer, dreamer; dropout, quitter

go–getting *adj* **1** having a strong desire for personal advancement ⟨this job is a great opportunity for some *go-getting* young person⟩ — see AMBITIOUS 1
2 having or showing a bold forcefulness in the pursuit of a goal ⟨a determined newcomer who made a *go-getting* bid for the governorship⟩ — see AGGRESSIVE 1

go–getting *n* eager desire for personal advancement ⟨with all his *go-getting*, he should move quickly up the corporate ladder⟩ — see AMBITION 1

goggle *vb* to look long and hard in wonder or surprise ⟨*goggled* at the elaborate costumes and floats in the Mardi Gras parade⟩ — see GAPE

go in (on) *vb* to take sudden, violent action against ⟨law enforcement officials decided to wait before *going in on* the barricaded gunman⟩ — see ATTACK 1

going *adj* **1** accepted, used, or practiced by most people ⟨what's the *going* price for a good used washing machine?⟩ — see CURRENT 1
2 being in effective operation ⟨he just can't keep his small bookstore *going*⟩ — see ACTIVE 1
3 having attained a desired end or state of good fortune ⟨our continued partnership with them is a *going* concern⟩ — see SUCCESSFUL 1

going *n* **1** forward movement in time or place ⟨tried to get down the hill quickly, but it was slow *going* with an injured foot⟩ — see ADVANCE 1
2 the act of leaving a place ⟨was so absorbed in her TV show she didn't notice his comings or *goings*⟩ — see DEPARTURE 1

going–over *n* a close look at or over someone or something in order to judge condition ⟨received a thorough *going-over* before being sent on stage⟩ — see INSPECTION

gold *n* something (as pieces of stamped metal or printed paper) customarily and legally used as a medium of exchange, a measure of value, or a means of payment ⟨all the *gold* in the world won't buy happiness⟩ — see MONEY 1

goldbrick *n* one who deliberately avoids work or duty ⟨the *goldbricks* among the colonists were warned: no work, no food⟩ — see SLACKER 1

golden *adj* **1** having qualities which inspire hope ⟨this may be your *golden* moment to impress a baseball scout, so don't blow it⟩ — see HOPEFUL 1
2 marked by conspicuously full and rich sounds or tones ⟨sang in a *golden* alto that filled the concert hall⟩ — see RESONANT
3 marked by vigorous growth and well-being especially economically ⟨the *golden* age of industrialization⟩ — see PROSPEROUS 1
4 of a pale yellow or yellowish brown color ⟨a *golden* Labrador⟩ — see BLOND
5 pointing toward a happy outcome ⟨that new job is a *golden* opportunity⟩ — see FAVORABLE 2

golden age *n* a period of high artistic or cultural development ⟨a memoir of her days as an actress in the *golden age* of Hollywood⟩ — see BELLE EPOQUE

golden–ager *n* a person of advanced years ⟨offered discounts and special tours for *golden-agers*⟩ — see SENIOR CITIZEN

golden mean *n* a middle point between extremes ⟨when it comes to money, the *golden mean* is saving some income, while giving yourself a modest spending allowance⟩ — see MEAN 1

gold mine *n* an abundant source ⟨the estate sale promises to be a *gold mine* for antique dealers⟩ — see MINE 1

gold standard *n* something set up as an example against which others of the same type are compared ⟨the *gold standard* for accurate experimental procedures is the double-blind medication trial⟩ — see STANDARD 1

golem *n* a stupid person ⟨the supervisor was a *golem* who never had an unprogrammed thought in her life⟩ — see IDIOT

Goliath *n* something or someone that is unusually large and powerful ⟨the family-owned company lost the contract to a multibillion-dollar *Goliath*⟩ — see GIANT

Gomorrah *n* a place of great vice and corruption ⟨looks upon Las Vegas as a *Gomorrah* that undermines traditional values⟩ — see AUGEAN STABLE

gone *adj* **1** no longer existing ⟨woolly mammoths have been long *gone*⟩ — see EXTINCT
2 no longer living ⟨doctors came to the waiting room to give the sad news that the operation hadn't been successful and the heart patient was *gone*⟩ — see DEAD 1
3 no longer possessed ⟨I put my watch right here on the table, but now it's *gone*⟩ — see LOST
4 containing unborn young within the body ⟨a woman who's seven months *gone*⟩ — see PREGNANT 1
5 *slang* of the very best kind ⟨in jazz circles he was regarded as a real *gone* trumpeter⟩ — see EXCELLENT

gone (on) *adj* filled with an intense or excessive love for ⟨I've never seen her so *gone on* a man before⟩ — see ENAMORED (OF)

goo *n* something (as a work of literature or music) that is too sentimental ⟨the latest *goo* from a children's author who knows how to lay it on thick⟩ — see CORN

good *adv* in a satisfactory way ⟨things are going *good* for us⟩ — see WELL 1

good *n* **1** something that provides happiness or does good for a person or thing ⟨let us praise God, from Whom all *goods* flow⟩ — see BLESSING 2
2 the state of doing well especially in relation to one's happiness or success ⟨I am doing this for your own *good*⟩ — see WELFARE
3 goods *pl* products that are bought and sold in business ⟨had a hard time selling leftover Easter *goods* that were still on the shelves by Mother's Day⟩ — see MERCHANDISE
4 goods *pl* a skill, an ability, or knowledge that makes a person able to do a particular job ⟨the hiring committee thinks this latest applicant really has the *goods*⟩ — see QUALIFICATION 1
5 goods *pl* transportable items that one owns ⟨before moving to Florida, the couple sold their house and auctioned off their household *goods*⟩ — see POSSESSION 2

good *adj* **1** based on sound reasoning or information ⟨had enough information to make a *good* assessment of the situation⟩
synonyms commonsense, commonsensible, commonsensical, firm, hard, informed, just, justified, levelheaded, logical, rational, reasonable, reasoned, sensible, sober, solid, valid, well-founded
related words actual, real, true; certain, sure; certified, validated, verified; confirmed, corroborated, substantiated; cogent, convincing; colorable, credible, plausible
near antonyms unsubstantiated, unsupported, unwarranted; flimsy, implausible, unconvincing, weak; fallacious, false, misguided, misled
antonyms groundless, illogical, invalid, irrational, nonrational, nonsensical, nonvalid, unfounded, uninformed, unjustified, unreasonable, unreasoned, unsound
2 conforming to a high standard of morality or virtue ⟨a *good* person who seldom did wrong⟩ ⟨*good* behavior will earn you the respect of others⟩
synonyms all right, decent, ethical, honest, honorable,

just, moral, nice, right, righteous, right-minded, straight, true, upright, virtuous
related words correct, decorous, proper, seemly; high-minded, noble, principled; commendable, creditable, exemplary, legitimate; esteemed, law-abiding, menschy, reputable, respected, upstanding, worthy; blameless, clean, guiltless, immaculate, incorrupt (*also* incorrupted), incorruptible, innocent, inoffensive, irreproachable, unobjectionable; angelic (*or* angelical), lily-white, pure, scrupulous, spotless, uncorrupted, unerring; goody-goody, moralistic, pharisaical, rectitudinous, sanctimonious, self-righteous
near antonyms improper, incorrect, indecorous, naughty, unbecoming, unseemly; corrupt, debased, debauched, degenerate, depraved, dissolute, libertine, perverted, reprobate; unprincipled, unscrupulous; atrocious, infamous, villainous; base, low, mean, vicious, vile; blameworthy, objectionable, offensive; iniquitous, nefarious; errant, erring, fallen
antonyms bad, black, dishonest, dishonorable, evil, evil-minded, immoral, indecent, sinful, unethical, unrighteous, wicked, wrong
3 according to the rules of logic ⟨you don't need a *good* reason to stop doing that—it's because I said so⟩ — see LOGICAL 1
4 being to one's liking ⟨that band's music is *good*⟩ — see SATISFACTORY 1
5 expressing approval ⟨gave the restaurant a *good* review⟩ — see FAVORABLE 1
6 firm in one's allegiance to someone or something ⟨a *good* Democrat who wouldn't dream of voting for a Republican candidate⟩ — see FAITHFUL 1
7 giving pleasure or contentment to the mind or senses ⟨we had a *good* time at the movies⟩ — see PLEASANT 1
8 having or showing exceptional knowledge, experience, or skill in a field of endeavor ⟨he's *good* at math⟩ — see PROFICIENT
9 having sufficient worth or merit to receive one's honor, esteem, or reward ⟨she is *good* enough to win a fellowship⟩ — see WORTHY
10 having the required skills for an acceptable level of performance ⟨that electrician is *good* at what he does⟩ — see COMPETENT 1
11 meeting the requirements of a purpose or situation ⟨those rotten apples aren't *good* to eat⟩ — see FIT 1
12 sufficiently large in size, amount, or number to merit attention ⟨had a *good* number of valuable baseball cards in his collection⟩ — see CONSIDERABLE 1
13 worthy of one's trust ⟨a car that should be *good* for another few years⟩ — see DEPENDABLE
14 being in agreement with the truth or a fact or a standard ⟨if these measurements are *good*, the venetian blind should fit the window perfectly⟩ — see CORRECT 1
15 very pleasing to look at ⟨an actress who always looks *good* on-screen⟩ — see BEAUTIFUL 1
16 beneficial to the health of body or mind ⟨eating a *good* breakfast will provide you with more energy during the day⟩ ⟨didn't like broccoli even though he knew it was *good* for him⟩ — see HEALTHFUL
17 having or showing a concern for the welfare of others ⟨if the church is to stay open, it's going to have to receive more than *good* intentions from its members⟩ — see CHARITABLE 1
18 of a level of quality that meets one's needs or standards ⟨the food at that restaurant is *good* but hardly great⟩ — see ADEQUATE
19 promoting or contributing to personal or social well-being ⟨product packaging that is intended to be *good* for the environment⟩ — see BENEFICIAL

Good Book *n* a book made up of the writings accepted by Christians as coming from God ⟨what does the *Good Book* say about temptation?⟩ — see BIBLE

good–bye *or* **good–by** *n* an expression of good wishes at parting ⟨said our *good-byes* and headed for home⟩
synonyms adieu, au revoir, ave, bon voyage, congé (*also* congee), farewell, Godspeed
related words leave-taking, send-off
near antonyms greeting(s), salutation, salute; welcome
antonyms hello

good deal *n* a considerable amount ⟨he knows a *good deal* about the current situation in Africa⟩ — see LOT 2

good–fellowship *n* kindly concern, interest, or support ⟨in the spirit of *good-fellowship*, the opposing softball players asked us to join them for drinks after the game⟩ — see GOODWILL 1

good–for–nothing *adj* having no ambition, success, or value to society ⟨refused to leave anything in his will to his *good-for-nothing* grandchildren⟩ — see NO-ACCOUNT 1

good–for–nothing *n* an idle worthless person ⟨teacher after teacher had predicted that he would never be more than a *good-for-nothing*⟩ — see NE'ER-DO-WELL

good–hearted *adj* having or marked by sympathy and consideration for others ⟨a *good-hearted* doctor who regularly sees poor patients for free⟩ — see HUMANE 1

good–heartedness *n* **1** sympathetic concern for the well-being of others ⟨the woman's inherent *good-heartedness* impelled her to share the little food she had⟩ — see BENIGNANCY
2 the capacity for feeling for another's unhappiness or misfortune ⟨thanks to the *good-heartedness* of its dedicated volunteers, the soup kitchen has never been understaffed⟩ — see HEART 1

good life *n* a life marked by material wealth and comfort ⟨vowed to live the *good life* if he ever won the lottery⟩
synonyms American dream
related words dolce vita (*or* la dolce vita); easy street

good–looking *adj* very pleasing to look at ⟨she's a *good-looking* woman, regardless of her age⟩ — see BEAUTIFUL 1

goodly *adj* **1** of a size greater than average of its kind ⟨$10,000 is a *goodly* reward to offer for a missing wedding ring⟩ — see LARGE 1
2 sufficiently large in size, amount, or number to merit attention ⟨a *goodly* number of people gathered to watch the spectacle⟩ — see CONSIDERABLE 1
3 very pleasing to look at ⟨the smartly dressed soldiers marching snappily along made for a *goodly* sight⟩ — see BEAUTIFUL 1

good–natured *adj* having an easygoing and pleasing manner especially in social situations ⟨the guests at the party were a *good-natured* bunch⟩ — see AMIABLE

good–naturedness *n* **1** a desire or disposition to please ⟨his *good-naturedness* makes him an easy person to work with⟩ — see COMPLAISANCE
2 the state or quality of having a pleasant or agreeable manner in socializing with others ⟨the *good-naturedness* of her response to the teasing made her a hit with the guys⟩ — see AMIABILITY 1

goodness *n* conduct that conforms to an accepted standard of right and wrong ⟨a person of such unaffected *goodness* that his friends were inspired to lead better lives⟩ — see MORALITY 1

good–tempered *adj* having an easygoing and pleasing manner especially in social situations ⟨her children were *good-tempered* and well-behaved in public⟩ — see AMIABLE

good–temperedness *n* the state or quality of having a pleasant or agreeable manner in socializing with others ⟨the volunteer's general *good-temperedness* was infectious and lifted the spirits of those waiting to give blood⟩ — see AMIABILITY 1

goodwill *n* **1** kindly concern, interest, or support ⟨the long tradition of *goodwill* that exists between the United States and Canada⟩
synonyms amity, benevolence, brotherhood, charity, cordiality, cordialness, fellowship, friendliness, friendship, gemütlichkeit, good-fellowship, kindliness, neighborliness
related words bonhomie, camaraderie, collegiality, community, companionship, company, comradeship; civility, comity, concord, harmony, rapport, rapprochement; charity, generosity; affinity, communion, empathy, kindness, sympathy, tolerance; altruism, philanthropy, selflessness, unselfishness
near antonyms disfavor, intolerance; animosity, antagonism, antipathy, enmity, hate, hatred, hostility, incivility, malice, rancor; belligerency, quarrelsomeness, querulousness
antonyms ill will, malevolence, venom
2 cheerful readiness to do something ⟨took on the task of coaching the soccer team with lots of zeal and *goodwill*⟩ — see ALACRITY

goody *or* **goodie** *n* something that is pleasing to eat because it is rare or a luxury ⟨couldn't wait to sample the bonbons, tortes, and other *goodies*⟩ — see DELICACY 1

gooey *adj* appealing to the emotions in an obvious and tiresome way ⟨things get especially *gooey* during the scene in which the lovers are reunited at long last⟩ — see CORNY 1

gooeyness *n* the state or quality of having an excess of tender feelings (as of love, nostalgia, or compassion) ⟨prefers the darkness of the original Grimms' fairy tales to the *gooeyness* of the modern cartoon versions⟩ — see SENTIMENTALITY

goof *n* **1** an unintentional departure from truth or accuracy ⟨that typo is one of the text's rare *goofs*⟩ — see ERROR 1
2 a stupid person ⟨leave it to that *goof* to forget the bait on a fishing trip⟩ — see IDIOT

goof (around) *vb* to spend time in aimless activity ⟨we've been *goofing around* long enough; it's time to get some real work done⟩ — see FIDDLE (AROUND)

goof (off) *vb* to spend time doing nothing ⟨returned home unannounced and found the au pair *goofing off*⟩ — see IDLE

goof (up) *vb* **1** to make a mistake ⟨we must have *goofed up* somewhere, because this cake clearly didn't turn out right⟩ — see ERR 1
2 to make or do (something) in a clumsy or unskillful way ⟨he *goofed up* his first sale at the dealership⟩ — see BOTCH

go off *vb* **1** to break open or into pieces usually because of internal pressure ⟨specialists were able to deactivate the bomb before it *went off*⟩ — see EXPLODE 1
2 to move forward along a course ⟨the wedding *went off* without so much as a single glitch⟩ — see GO 1
3 to leave a place often for another ⟨don't *go off* without telling us where we can find you⟩ — see GO 2

goofy *adj* lacking in seriousness or maturity ⟨it's not appropriate to be *goofy* at a funeral⟩ — see GIDDY 1

goon *n* **1** a stupid person ⟨an unfortunate tendency to call those who disagree with him "brainless *goons*"⟩ — see IDIOT
2 a violent, brutal person who is often a member of an organized gang ⟨the crime boss threatened to send the *goons* after him if he squealed⟩ — see HOODLUM

go on *vb* **1** to take place ⟨what in the world is *going on* in there?⟩ — see HAPPEN
2 to talk at length without sticking to a topic or getting to a point ⟨my, but Aunt Betty does *go on* about all of her aches and pains⟩ — see RAMBLE 1

goose *n* a person who lacks good sense or judgment ⟨don't be such a silly *goose*—you're dressed just fine for the party⟩ — see FOOL 1

goose egg *n* the numerical symbol 0 or the absence of number or quantity represented by it ⟨was such a bad bowler that his final score was a big, fat *goose egg*⟩ — see ZERO 1

goose–step (to) *vb* to act according to the commands of ⟨the new president has everyone *goose-stepping to* her every whim lest they provoke her wrath⟩ — see OBEY

goosey *adj* feeling or showing uncomfortable feelings of uncertainty ⟨have been feeling *goosey* all morning, knowing that I have that driving test hanging over my head⟩ — see NERVOUS 1

go out *vb* **1** to fall down or in as a result of physical pressure ⟨there was concern that the dam would *go out* under the force of the flood waters⟩ — see COLLAPSE 1
2 to take part in social activities ⟨she enjoys *going out* on weekends, but during the week she's a homebody⟩ — see SOCIALIZE

go out (with) *vb* to go on a social engagement with ⟨I'm going to *go out with* that foxy woman from work next Saturday night⟩ — see DATE 1

go over *vb* to turn out as planned or desired ⟨his sales pitch *went over* as expected and he saw a 200% increase in his commissions⟩ — see SUCCEED 1

gore *vb* to penetrate or hold (something) with a pointed object ⟨running with the bulls in Pamplona, Spain, may sound like fun, but the bulls have been known to *gore* runners who get too close⟩ — see IMPALE

gorge *n* a narrow opening between hillsides or mountains that can be used for passage ⟨walked the bridge over the *gorge*, marveling at the spectacular drop⟩ — see CANYON

gorge *vb* **1** to fill with food to capacity ⟨we *gorged* ourselves on the four pies Aunt Martha had brought for Thanksgiving⟩
synonyms cram, glut, sate, stuff, surfeit
related words gobble, gormandize, pig out; gulp, guzzle; cloy, fill; banquet, feast, regale
near antonyms diet, fast
2 to eat greedily or to excess ⟨the kids began *gorging* on Halloween candy the minute they got back from trick-or-treating⟩
synonyms gormandize, overeat, pig out, swill
related words devour, glut, sate, stuff, surfeit, wolf; banquet, feast, regale; bolt, cram, gulp, guzzle
phrases load up on
near antonyms nibble, peck, pick, taste
3 to swallow or eat greedily ⟨the ravenous dogs furiously *gorged* the scraps of meat⟩ — see GOBBLE

gorgeous *adj* very pleasing to look at ⟨sunsets in Hawaii are just *gorgeous*⟩ — see BEAUTIFUL 1

gorgeousness *n* **1** the qualities in a person or thing that as a whole give pleasure to the senses ⟨nothing compares to the *gorgeousness* of the first snow of the winter⟩ — see BEAUTY 1
2 impressiveness of beauty on a large scale ⟨taken aback by the indescribable *gorgeousness* of the Grand Canyon at sunset⟩ — see MAGNIFICENCE

gorger *n* one who eats greedily or too much ⟨a shark that is such a *gorger* it can't move after devouring a meal⟩ — see GLUTTON

gorilla *n* a violent, brutal person who is often a member of an organized gang ⟨the loan shark sent a couple of *gorillas* to "convince" him to pay up⟩ — see HOODLUM

gormandize *vb* **1** to eat greedily or to excess ⟨everybody tends to *gormandize* on Thanksgiving—it's traditional!⟩ — see GORGE 2
2 to swallow or eat greedily ⟨hungry soccer players who will *gormandize* whatever they happen to find in the fridge⟩ — see GOBBLE

gormandizer *n* one who eats greedily or too much ⟨an inconsiderate *gormandizer* who eats his hosts out of house and home⟩ — see GLUTTON

gormless *adj, chiefly British* not having or showing an ability to absorb ideas readily ⟨a comedy show that invariably portrays the British aristocracy as a bunch of *gormless* twits⟩ — see STUPID 1

gormlessness *n, chiefly British* the quality or state of lacking intelligence or quickness of mind ⟨the backbencher professed himself horrified by the *gormlessness* and naïveté of the prime minister⟩ — see STUPIDITY 1

gory *adj* smeared or stained with blood ⟨doesn't watch too many movies that feature *gory* violence⟩ — see BLOODY 1

gospel *n* the basic beliefs or guiding principles of a person or group ⟨her private *gospel* is to do good cheerfully and without any expectation of reward⟩ — see CREED 1

gospeler *or* **gospeller** *n* a person who actively supports or favors a cause ⟨Horatio Alger is remembered as the great *gospeler* of the American success story⟩ — see EXPONENT 1

gossamer *adj* **1** being of a material lacking in sturdiness or substance ⟨fairies are usually depicted as wearing *gossamer* or tattered clothing⟩ — see FLIMSY 1
2 resembling air in lightness ⟨the *gossamer* veil seemed to float about the bride as she walked down the aisle⟩ — see AIRY 1
3 very thin and easy to see through ⟨didn't see the *gossamer* spider webs until the sun hit them just right⟩ — see SHEER 1

gossamery *adj* **1** being of a material lacking in sturdiness or substance ⟨that *gossamery* dress should be washed gently by hand so it doesn't disintegrate⟩ — see FLIMSY 1
2 resembling air in lightness ⟨a *gossamery* feather floating on the breeze⟩ — see AIRY 1
3 very thin and easy to see through ⟨use this *gossamery* cheesecloth to strain the liquid out of the cottage cheese⟩ — see SHEER 1

gossip *n* **1** a person who habitually reveals personal or sensational facts about others ⟨because her friend was such a compulsive *gossip*, she couldn't help but wonder if her private life wasn't also being made the talk of the town⟩
synonyms circulator, gossiper, gossipmonger, newsmonger, quidnunc, talebearer, tale-teller, telltale, yenta
related words betrayer, blabbermouth, informant, informer, snitcher, squealer, stool pigeon, tattler, tattletale; libeler, scandalmonger
2 friendly, informal conversation or an instance of this ⟨lingered at the water fountain for a little *gossip*⟩ — see CHAT 1
3 information or opinion that is widely disseminated without any authority or confirmation of accuracy ⟨idle *gossip* can really damage a person's reputation even if it is later proven to be false⟩ — see RUMOR

gossip *vb* to relate sometimes questionable or secret information of a personal nature ⟨a neighbor who loves to *gossip* with others about that couple's loud arguments⟩
synonyms blab, dish, talk, tattle, wag
related words bandy (about), circulate, noise (about *or* abroad), rumor; blabber, disclose, divulge, reveal, tell; hint, imply, insinuate, intimate, let on, suggest; inform, report, snitch, squeal, tip (off); babble, spill; confide
phrases spill the beans
near antonyms clam up, shut up

gossiper *n* a person who habitually reveals personal or sensational facts about others ⟨the exact nature of the relationship between the two coworkers was a topic that kept the office *gossipers* too busy to do any work⟩ — see GOSSIP 1

gossipmonger *n* a person who habitually reveals personal or sensational facts about others ⟨the upcoming nuptials between the sixtyish businessman and the twentysomething have sent the *gossipmongers* into overdrive⟩ — see GOSSIP 1

gossipy *adj* having the style and content of everyday conversation ⟨this book on the people who have occupied the White House is a little too *gossipy* to qualify as serious history⟩ — see CHATTY 1

gotcha *n* a danger or difficulty that is hidden or not easily recognized ⟨the *gotcha* in the low monthly rate quoted by the cable company is that it is a teaser and good for only six months⟩ — see PITFALL 1

Götterdämmerung *n* a loss of status ⟨a film that chronicles the chaotic *Götterdämmerung* of the Third Reich⟩ — see COMEDOWN

gouge *vb* to charge (someone) too much for goods or services ⟨since I had forgotten the sunscreen, I was forced to buy it from the concession stand at the beach—where they *gouged* me for it⟩ — see OVERCHARGE 1

gouging *n* the exaction of a grossly excessive charge for goods or services ⟨a hotline that consumers may use to report *gouging* at gasoline stations⟩ — see EXTORTION

gourmand *n* **1** a person with refined tastes in food and wine ⟨a finicky *gourmand* who vacationed in Europe every year simply for the wine⟩ — see EPICURE
2 one who eats greedily or too much ⟨the kind of *gourmand* who swallows food without even pausing to taste it⟩ — see GLUTTON

gourmet *n* a person with refined tastes in food and wine ⟨food critics have to be *gourmets* in order to write about food in an informed way⟩ — see EPICURE

govern *vb* **1** to exercise authority or power over ⟨the president is elected in order to *govern* the country, not to follow public opinion polls⟩
synonyms boss, captain, command, control, preside (over), rule, sway [*archaic*]
related words conduct, direct, head, lead; administer, manage, micromanage, oversee, regulate, superintend, supervise; dictate, dominate, domineer, lord (it over), master, oppress, reign (over), tyrannize; conquer, subdue, subjugate
2 to keep from exceeding a desirable degree or level (as of expression) ⟨you need to *govern* your speech and be able to communicate your outrage without resorting to profanity⟩ — see CONTROL 1
3 to look after and make decisions about ⟨the company's finances are *governed* by its chief financial officer⟩ — see CONDUCT 1

governance *n* **1** lawful control over the affairs of a political unit (as a nation) ⟨after World War II, the four Allied nations shared the *governance* of the territory of postwar Germany under the Allied Control Council⟩ — see RULE 2
2 the act or activity of looking after and making decisions about something ⟨while a financial advisor can be helpful, the *governance* of your family finances ultimately rests with you⟩ — see CONDUCT 1

government *n* **1** lawful control over the affairs of a political unit (as a nation) ⟨*government* by the people, for the people⟩ — see RULE 2
2 the act or activity of looking after and making decisions about something ⟨a board involved in the *government* of the distribution of benefits to veterans⟩ — see CONDUCT 1

gown *n* **1** a garment with a joined blouse and skirt usually worn by a woman or girl ⟨a shopping trip for the express purpose of finding the perfect *gown* for the wedding⟩ — see DRESS 1
2 a loose pullover garment worn in bed ⟨answered the front door still dressed in the *gown* that she had been

sleeping in⟩ — see NIGHTGOWN

gown *vb* to outfit with clothes and especially fine or special clothes ⟨a Renaissance portrait of a queen *gowned* in exotic silks and satins⟩ — see CLOTHE 1

grab *n* an instance of theft ⟨a political activist who thinks the government's lease of public lands to logging companies amounts to an illegal land *grab*⟩ — see THEFT 2

grab *vb* to take physical control or possession of (something) suddenly or forcibly ⟨don't *grab* my arm like that⟩ — see CATCH 1

grab bag *n* an unorganized collection or mixture of various things ⟨the festival featured a *grab bag* of independent films from widely disparate genres⟩ — see MISCELLANY 1

grabby *adj* **1** having or marked by an eager and often selfish desire especially for material possessions ⟨very young children tend to be *grabby* and often refuse to share⟩ — see GREEDY 1
2 likely to attract attention ⟨a tabloid that invariably favors *grabby* headlines, even for underwhelming stories⟩ — see NOTICEABLE

grace *n* **1** an act of kind assistance ⟨in Victor Hugo's novel, *Les Misérables*, Jean Valjean's decision to go to jail for the man mistaken for him is a *grace* that goes beyond thanks⟩ — see FAVOR 1
2 dignified or restrained beauty of form, appearance, or style ⟨a beautiful actress who was the epitome of *grace* during her too-brief career⟩ — see ELEGANCE
3 a quality that gives something special worth ⟨as if taste were not enough, red wine has the added *grace* of being healthy for the heart⟩ — see EXCELLENCE 2

grace *vb* to make more attractive by adding something that is beautiful or becoming ⟨I hope that you will *grace* our gathering with your presence⟩ — see DECORATE

graceful *adj* **1** moving easily ⟨the *graceful* ballerina effortlessly leapt across the stage⟩
synonyms agile, featly, feline, gracile, light, light-footed (*also* light-foot), lightsome, lissome (*also* lissom), lithe, lithesome, nimble, spry
related words acrobatic, flexible, limber, loose-jointed, pliable, pliant, supple; adroit, deft, dexterous (*also* dextrous), light-fingered; fleet-footed, sure-footed; athletic, balletic, coordinated
near antonyms uncoordinated; inflexible, rigid, stiff; bungling, inept, maladroit
antonyms awkward, clumsy, gawky, graceless, klutzy, lumbering, ungainly, ungraceful
2 having or showing elegance ⟨sat down in the old plantation home's very *graceful* parlor⟩ — see ELEGANT 1

gracefulness *n* dignified or restrained beauty of form, appearance, or style ⟨a home decorated with all of the *gracefulness* you'd expect of a fashion designer⟩ ⟨impressed by the *gracefulness* of the antebellum mansion⟩ — see ELEGANCE

graceless *adj* **1** lacking or showing a lack of nimbleness in using one's hands ⟨a *graceless* person who was a butterfingered lout when it came to playing basketball⟩ — see CLUMSY 1
2 lacking social grace and assurance ⟨was a *graceless* preteen but evolved into a confident teenager⟩ — see AWKWARD 1
3 not appropriate for a particular occasion or situation ⟨one guest made a *graceless* comment about the bride's bleached hair⟩ — see INAPPROPRIATE
4 having or showing an inability to move in a graceful manner ⟨her *graceless* dancing was painful to watch⟩ — see CLUMSY 2
5 showing poor judgment especially in personal relationships or social situations ⟨indifferent to the nuances of constructive criticism, she sometimes says things which are hurtful or *graceless*⟩ — see INDISCREET

gracile *adj* moving easily ⟨*gracile* as any pair of classically trained dancers, the bride and groom made their way around the dance floor⟩ — see GRACEFUL 1

gracious *adj* **1** showing a natural kindness and courtesy especially in social situations ⟨a *gracious* host who goes out of his way to make every guest feel welcome⟩
synonyms affable, cordial, genial, hospitable, sociable
related words agreeable, amiable, benign, benignant, congenial, convivial, friendly, kind, kindly, neighborly; accommodating, obliging; considerate, courteous, polite, thoughtful; cosmopolitan, sophisticated, urbane; approachable, attentive, outgoing
near antonyms boorish, churlish; abrupt, blunt, brusque (*also* brusk), curt, gruff, sharp, snippy; antisocial, disagreeable, discourteous, ill-mannered, impolite, rude, sullen, surly, uncivil, unfriendly, unkind, unmannerly; crabbed, crabby, cross, crusty, grumpy
antonyms inhospitable, ungenial, ungracious, unsociable
2 having an easygoing and pleasing manner especially in social situations ⟨a *gracious* innkeeper whose jokes and laughter made weary travelers feel right at home⟩ — see AMIABLE
3 showing consideration, courtesy, and good manners ⟨he was a *gracious* man, habitually offering his seat on the bus to elderly women⟩ — see POLITE 1

graciously *adv* with good reason or courtesy ⟨flattered to be asked but unable to attend, she *graciously* turned down the wedding invitation⟩ — see WELL 4

graciousness *n* **1** speech or behavior that is a sign of good breeding ⟨at this type of private school, young women would be taught upper-class *graciousness*⟩ — see POLITENESS 1
2 the state or quality of having a pleasant or agreeable manner in socializing with others ⟨his *graciousness* and wit kept his fellow diners entertained throughout the meal⟩ — see AMIABILITY 1

gradational *adj* proceeding or changing by steps or degrees ⟨*gradational* increases in altitude⟩ — see GRADUAL

gradationally *adv* by small steps or amounts ⟨by adding the white tint drop by drop, she *gradationally* changed the color from dark red to pink⟩ — see GRADUALLY

grade *n* **1** an individual part of a process, series, or ranking ⟨just one *grade* removed from completion⟩ — see DEGREE 1
2 degree of excellence ⟨only motor oil of the highest *grade* for his fancy sports car⟩ — see QUALITY 1
3 one of the units into which a whole is divided on the basis of a common characteristic ⟨there are various *grades* of wool to consider when selecting a fabric⟩ — see CLASS 2
4 something set up as an example against which others of the same type are compared ⟨that painting just doesn't make the *grade*⟩ — see STANDARD 1
5 the degree to which something rises up from a position level with the horizon ⟨the hill rises at a seven percent *grade*⟩ — see SLANT

grade *vb* **1** to arrange or assign according to type ⟨*grade* these apples "extra fancy" and those "fancy"⟩ — see CLASSIFY 1
2 to take or have a certain position within a group arranged in vertical classes ⟨believe it or not, that music *grades* pretty high with young teens⟩ — see RANK 1

graded *adj* running in a slanting direction ⟨a *graded* creek bed, with the creek's center depth being about three feet⟩ — see DIAGONAL

gradient *n* the degree to which something rises up from a position level with the horizon ⟨the path goes up at a pretty steep *gradient* before leveling off⟩ — see SLANT

gradual *adj* proceeding or changing by steps or degrees

⟨a *gradual* drop in gas prices will take place over the next several months⟩

synonyms gradational, incremental, phased, piecemeal, step-by-step

related words progressive, stepped, tapered; imperceptible, inching; decrescent, increscent

near antonyms discontinuous, saltatory; acute, sharp; changeable, dynamic, meteoric, volatile

antonyms abrupt, sudden

gradually *adv* by small steps or amounts ⟨*gradually* worked his way down the class roster⟩ ⟨add the sugar to the beaten egg whites *gradually* to make the meringue⟩

synonyms gradationally, inchmeal, little by little, piece by piece, piecemeal

related words hierarchically; crescively, increasingly, progressively; fractionally, imperceptibly; slowly

phrases bit by bit, by degrees, inch by inch

near antonyms acutely, sharply, steeply; hastily, precipitously

antonyms abruptly, suddenly

graduation *n* a scheme of rank or order ⟨had a *graduation* of testing levels into which to divide the students⟩ — see [3]SCALE 1

grain *n* **1** a very small piece ⟨just give me a *grain* of information about what to expect on the program⟩ — see BIT 1

2 one's characteristic attitude or mood ⟨cheating, even on my income taxes, goes against my *grain*⟩ — see DISPOSITION 1

grained *adj* made up of large particles ⟨the sugar in some countries has a much more *grained* consistency than what we're used to in the U.S.⟩ — see COARSE 1

grainy *adj* made up of large particles ⟨*grainy* sand kept it off the rankings as one of the nation's best beaches⟩ — see COARSE 1

grammar *n* general or basic truths on which other truths or theories can be based ⟨student directors learning the *grammar* of filmmaking⟩ — see PRINCIPLES 1

grand *adj* **1** large and impressive in size, grandeur, extent, or conception ⟨the *grand* ceremonies that typically mark the opening of the Olympic Games⟩

synonyms august, baronial, epic, gallant, glorious, grandiose, heroic (*also* heroical), Homeric, imperial, imposing, magnific, magnificent, majestic, massive, monumental, noble, proud, regal, royal, splendid, stately

related words colossal, monstrous, prodigious, stupendous, tremendous; kingly, lordly, princely, queenly; awesome, awful, cosmic (*also* cosmical), sublime, wondrous; formidable, impressive, prepossessing, redoubtable; apocalyptic (*also* apocalyptical), inflated, operatic, overblown, pompous; marvelous (*or* marvellous), superb, terrific, wonderful; extravagant, lavish, luxurious, opulent, palatial, palatine, sumptuous; gorgeous, resplendent, splendiferous; extraordinary, killer, remarkable, sensational, striking; celestial, divine, heavenly

near antonyms lowly, modest, unprepossessing; average, common, mediocre, ordinary, run-of-the-mill, second-rate; abject, mean, meretricious, shabby, sordid; insignificant, measly, paltry, petty, puny, trifling, trivial

antonyms humble, unheroic, unimposing, unimpressive

2 coming before all others in importance ⟨won the *grand* prize⟩ — see FOREMOST 1

3 not lacking any part or member that properly belongs to it ⟨the *grand* total comes to $350⟩ — see COMPLETE 1

4 of a size greater than average of its kind ⟨in the *grand* ring of the three-ring circus stood the lion tamer himself⟩ — see LARGE 1

5 of high birth, rank, or station ⟨everyone wanted to be seen with Palm Beach society's *grand* dame⟩ — see NOBLE 1

6 of the very best kind ⟨that picnic in the mountains was simply *grand*⟩ — see EXCELLENT

7 unusually large ⟨before them lay a *grand* treeless plain that stretched as far as the eye could see⟩ — see HUGE

granddaddy *also* **grandaddy** *n* something belonging to an earlier time from which something else was later developed ⟨the *granddaddy* of all English mystery novels⟩ — see ANCESTOR 2

grande dame *n* a dignified usually elderly woman of some rank or authority ⟨the city's *grandes dames* still hold considerable sway in its cultural life⟩ — see MATRIARCH

grandee *n* a man of high birth or social position ⟨only a Spanish *grandee*—and no one of lesser rank—can address comments to the king and queen of Spain⟩ — see GENTLEMAN 1

grandeur *n* impressiveness of beauty on a large scale ⟨struck by the *grandeur* of the sun setting over the Golden Gate Bridge⟩ — see MAGNIFICENCE

grandfather *n* a person who is several generations earlier in an individual's line of descent ⟨this tradition has been passed down from our pioneer *grandfathers*⟩ — see ANCESTOR 1

grand finale *n* the last part of a process or action ⟨the award for best picture is traditionally the evening's *grand finale*⟩ — see FINALE

grandiloquence *n* **1** boastful speech or writing ⟨a heavyweight champion who was famous for his entertaining *grandiloquence* prior to every match⟩ — see BOMBAST 1

2 language that is impressive-sounding but not meaningful or sincere ⟨the predictably wearisome *grandiloquence* of the speeches at a political convention⟩ — see RHETORIC 1

grandiloquent *adj* **1** full of fine words and fancy expressions ⟨poets in the 19th century tended to write poetry filled with *grandiloquent* phrases⟩ — see FLOWERY 1

2 marked by the use of impressive-sounding but mostly meaningless words and phrases ⟨at Independence Day celebrations *grandiloquent* speeches by local politicians are as traditional as fireworks⟩ — see RHETORICAL 1

grandiose *adj* **1** large and impressive in size, grandeur, extent, or conception ⟨a *grandiose* plan to upgrade the entire interstate highway system in 10 years⟩ — see GRAND 1

2 self-consciously trying to present an appearance of grandeur or importance ⟨made some *grandiose* claim that she was the descendant of a French princess⟩ — see PRETENTIOUS 1

grandiosity *n* the quality or state of appearing or trying to appear more important or more valuable than is the case ⟨I'd rather be thought of as a person with simple integrity, not a person given to *grandiosity* and exaggeration⟩ — see PRETENSE 1

grandly *adv* **1** in a luxurious manner ⟨we were staying at the Plaza Hotel in New York and living rather *grandly*⟩ — see HIGH

2 in a manner befitting a person of the highest character and ideals ⟨had *grandly* offered to pay the entire cost of the Christmas party at the children's hospital⟩ — see GREATLY 1

grandness *n* **1** impressiveness of beauty on a large scale ⟨wanted to see the Alps in all of their wintertime *grandness*⟩ — see MAGNIFICENCE

2 the quality or state of being large in size ⟨were impressed with the *grandness* of the movie set⟩ — see LARGENESS

grange *n* a piece of land and its buildings used to grow crops or raise livestock ⟨asked the community's farmers to meet at the Howard family *grange* to help raise a new barn⟩ — see FARM

granite *n* firm or unwavering adherence to one's purpose ⟨had the *granite* to see the project out to the end⟩ — see DETERMINATION 1

grant *n* a sum of money allotted for a specific use by official or formal action ⟨applied for a federal *grant* to restore the church, one of the oldest and most architecturally significant in the state⟩ — see APPROPRIATION 1

grant *vb* **1** to accept the truth or existence of (something) usually reluctantly ⟨you will *grant* that she is difficult to work with⟩ — see ADMIT 1

2 to give the ownership or benefit of (something) formally or publicly ⟨by the power vested in me, I *grant* you the keys to the city⟩ — see CONFER 1

granting *n* the approval by someone in authority for the doing of something ⟨your *granting* of an interview for this job opening will be much appreciated⟩ — see PERMISSION

granular *adj* made up of large particles ⟨icy, *granular* snow makes for terrible skiing—if you can, ski on light, powdery snow⟩ — see COARSE 1

granulated *adj* made up of large particles ⟨don't use powdered sugar in that recipe, use *granulated* sugar⟩ — see COARSE 1

granule *n* a very small piece ⟨is there one *granule* of truth in that statement?⟩ — see BIT 1

graphic *n* something that visually explains or decorates a text ⟨the use of *graphics* in the text of the dictionary helps to break up the visual monotony of the page⟩ — see ILLUSTRATION 1

graphic *also* **graphical** *adj* **1** producing a mental picture through clear and impressive description ⟨the report offered many *graphic* details about the devastating earthquake that rocked the area⟩

synonyms delineated, pictorial, picturesque, visual, vivid

related words depicted, descriptive, expressive; concrete, explicit, specific; faithful, lifelike, natural, photographic, realistic; fresh, incisive, sharp

near antonyms indeterminate, nebulous, obscure, sketchy, unclear, vague; bleary, blurry, dark, dim, faint, foggy, fuzzy, hazy, indefinite, indistinct, indistinguishable, muddy, murky, shadowlike, shadowy; ambiguous, cryptic, dark, enigmatic (*also* enigmatical), equivocal, inscrutable, mysterious

2 consisting of or relating to pictures ⟨got a degree in *graphic* design⟩ — see PICTORIAL 1

grapple *n* **1** the act or manner of holding ⟨was simply unable to break my opponent's viselike *grapple* and lost the wrestling match⟩ — see HOLD 1

2 an earnest effort for superiority or victory over another ⟨after a *grapple* with his conscience, he confessed to having an affair⟩ — see CONTEST 1

grapple *vb* **1** to seize and attempt to unbalance one another for the purpose of achieving physical mastery ⟨two sumo wrestlers *grappling* like a pair of mammoth bears⟩ — see WRESTLE

2 to take physical control or possession of (something) suddenly or forcibly ⟨a crane *grappled* the sunken boat and hoisted it above water⟩ — see CATCH 1

grapple (with) *vb* to deal with (something) usually skillfully or efficiently ⟨a medical ethicist who *grapples with* extremely difficult questions all the time⟩ — see HANDLE 1

grasp *n* **1** the ability to direct the course of something ⟨for a time it looked like most of Europe would be within Hitler's *grasp*⟩ — see CONTROL 2

2 the act or manner of holding ⟨during the roller coaster ride, my date clutched my arm with a deathlike *grasp*⟩ — see HOLD 1

3 the knowledge gained from the process of coming to know or understand something ⟨I think I finally have a *grasp* of Spanish grammar⟩ — see COMPREHENSION

grasp *vb* **1** to have a practical understanding of ⟨he just doesn't *grasp* how important it is that he call when he'll be late⟩ — see KNOW 1

2 to put one's arms around and press tightly ⟨the departing soldier *grasped* his children a little closer than usual⟩ — see EMBRACE 1

3 to reach for and take hold of by embracing with the fingers or arms ⟨the attendant *grasped* my arm and steered me towards the door⟩ — see TAKE 1

4 to have a clear idea of ⟨the emergency operator finally *grasped* what he was trying to tell her⟩ — see COMPREHEND 1

graspable *adj* capable of being understood ⟨the immensity of the world is not *graspable* to a child of that age, so the notion of a globe-trotting Santa Claus is plausible⟩ — see INTELLIGIBLE

grasping *adj* having or marked by an eager and often selfish desire especially for material possessions ⟨a *grasping* person who would rather buy a car he didn't need than give a dime to charity⟩ — see GREEDY 1

graspingness *n* an intense selfish desire for wealth or possessions ⟨that period of the 19th century when the *graspingness* of the robber barons knew no bounds is often called the Gilded Age⟩ — see GREED

grass (on) *vb, British slang* to give information (as to the authorities) about another's improper or unlawful activities ⟨that bloke would *grass on* his own mater to save himself⟩ — see SQUEAL 1

grassland *n* a broad area of level or rolling treeless country ⟨stunning pictures of the giraffes and zebras roaming the *grasslands* of Africa⟩ — see PLAIN 1

grate *vb* **1** to disturb the peace of mind of (someone) especially by repeated disagreeable acts ⟨unintentionally or not, you say rude things that *grate* people⟩ — see IRRITATE 1

2 to pass roughly and noisily over or against a surface ⟨the sled *grated* along the bare pavement⟩ — see SCRAPE 1

3 to press or strike against or together so as to make a scraping sound ⟨he *grated* the pieces of metal together⟩ — see GRIND 2

G–rated *adj* free from any trace of the coarse or indecent ⟨the comic's *G-rated* routine is something that the whole family can enjoy⟩ — see CHASTE 1

grateful *adj* **1** feeling or expressing gratitude ⟨she was *grateful* for her neighbor's help after she broke her foot⟩

synonyms appreciative, appreciatory, glad, obliged, thankful

related words beholden, indebted; contented, delighted, gratified, pleased, satisfied, tickled; thanking

near antonyms inhospitable, rude, thoughtless, ungracious

antonyms inappreciative, thankless, unappreciative, ungrateful

2 giving pleasure or contentment to the mind or senses ⟨I'm glad for the *grateful* warmth of the fire on such a cold day⟩ — see PLEASANT 1

gratefulness *n* acknowledgment of having received something good from another ⟨a note expressing her sincere *gratefulness* for our help⟩ — see THANKS

gratification *n* the feeling experienced when one's wishes are met ⟨eating good chocolate gives me a sense of intense *gratification*⟩ — see PLEASURE 1

gratified *adj* **1** experiencing pleasure, satisfaction, or delight ⟨I am deeply *gratified* that you'll be able to come to the wedding⟩ — see GLAD 1

2 feeling that one's needs or desires have been met ⟨a good meal eaten in excellent company is enough to keep me *gratified* for some time⟩ — see CONTENT

gratify *vb* **1** to give in to (a desire) ⟨just *gratify* this one whim of mine⟩ — see INDULGE 1

2 to give satisfaction to ⟨your presence at the holiday table would really *gratify* your grandmother⟩ — see PLEASE 1

gratifying *adj* **1** giving pleasure or contentment to the mind or senses ⟨a spectacular film that is *gratifying* to both the mind and the eyes⟩ — see PLEASANT 1

2 making one feel good inside ⟨your warm welcome sure is *gratifying* to this tired soul⟩ — see HEARTWARMING

gratifyingly *adv* in a pleasing way ⟨the popular television series' *gratifyingly* conclusive finale⟩ — see WELL 5

grating *adj* **1** disagreeable to one's aesthetic or artistic sense ⟨the mix of colors in that painting is terribly *grating*⟩ — see HARSH 2

2 harsh and dry in sound ⟨with a *grating* voice, she croaked a feeble "hello"⟩ — see HOARSE

gratis *adj* not costing or charging anything ⟨if you sign up today, you get a 13-inch TV *gratis*⟩ — see FREE 4

gratitude *n* acknowledgment of having received something good from another ⟨accept these flowers as a token of my *gratitude*⟩ — see THANKS

gratuitous *adj* **1** not costing or charging anything ⟨they will throw in a *gratuitous* box of chocolates when you spend $30 or more in their shop⟩ — see FREE 4

2 not needed by the circumstances or to accomplish an end ⟨that violent scene was completely *gratuitous* and didn't need to be in the movie at all⟩ — see UNNECESSARY

gratuity *n* **1** a small sum of money given for a service over and above what is due ⟨for parties of eight or more, we automatically add a 15% *gratuity* onto the bill⟩ — see [2]TIP 1

2 something given in addition to what is ordinarily expected or owed ⟨got a $100 *gratuity* in addition to his regular pay⟩ — see BONUS

grave *adj* **1** having a matter of importance as its topic ⟨leaving gossip and celebrities to other magazines, this journal focuses on the *grave* issues confronting the nation⟩ — see SERIOUS 2

2 involving potential loss or injury ⟨going over Niagara Falls poses a *grave* danger⟩ — see DANGEROUS 1

3 not joking or playful in mood or manner ⟨when I asked him how his dog was doing, he looked *grave* and said, "Not good"⟩ — see SERIOUS 1

4 having a low musical pitch or range ⟨a *grave* hexachord⟩ — see DEEP 2

grave *vb* to cut (as letters or designs) on a hard surface ⟨the doomed climber *graved* his initials into the rock face⟩ — see ENGRAVE 1

grave *n* **1** a final resting place for a dead person ⟨the forlorn boy put flowers on his mother's *grave*⟩

synonyms burial, sepulchre (*or* sepulcher), sepulture, tomb

related words catacomb, charnel (*also* charnel house), columbarium, crypt, mausoleum, vault; cemetery, churchyard, graveyard, potter's field; barrow, mound, tumulus

2 the permanent stopping of all the vital bodily activities ⟨a rock star who found his early *grave* in a plane crash⟩ — see DEATH 1

3 the state of being dead ⟨a terrible fear of the *grave*⟩ — see DEATH 2

gravel *adj* harsh and dry in sound ⟨after his bout with laryngitis, he had a terribly *gravel* voice⟩ — see HOARSE

gravel *vb* to throw into a state of mental uncertainty ⟨managed to *gravel* his opponent in the debate by focusing on atypical examples⟩ — see CONFUSE 1

gravelly *adj* harsh and dry in sound ⟨his singing voice is a little *gravelly*, but otherwise he's a fine musician⟩ — see HOARSE

graveness *n* a mental state free of jesting or trifling ⟨the doctor's unexpected *graveness* warned us that the news was bad⟩ — see EARNESTNESS

gravestone *n* a shaped stone laid over or erected near a grave and usually bearing an inscription to identify and preserve the memory of the deceased ⟨we love to tour old cemeteries and read the hauntingly poetic inscriptions on the *gravestones*⟩ — see TOMBSTONE

graveyard *n* a piece of land used for burying the dead ⟨reflecting the Quaker avoidance of personal vanity, the *graveyard* is not marked by so much as a single headstone⟩ — see CEMETERY

gravid *adj* containing unborn young within the body ⟨the patient is a *gravid* woman in her seventh month⟩ — see PREGNANT 1

gravidity *n* the state of containing unborn young within the body ⟨a study examining the effects of *gravidity* on women's athletic performance⟩ — see PREGNANCY

gravity *n* a mental state free of jesting or trifling ⟨the hospital waiting room was filled with the kind of *gravity* that inevitably accompanies worry⟩ — see EARNESTNESS

gravy *n* **1** a savory fluid food used as a topping or accompaniment to a main dish ⟨order a large serving of fries with extra *gravy*⟩ — see SAUCE 1

2 something given in addition to what is ordinarily expected or owed ⟨you only pay for three CDs; the fourth one they give you is just *gravy*⟩ — see BONUS

gravy train *n* something given in addition to what is ordinarily expected or owed ⟨the new tax law offers a real *gravy train* to certain categories of investors⟩ — see BONUS

gray *also* **grey** *adj* **1** of the color gray ⟨the *gray* elephant and the gaudily dressed circus performer created a striking contrast⟩

synonyms argentine, grayish, leaden, pewter, silver, silvery, slate, slaty (*also* slatey), steely

related words achromatic, colorless, neutral; dirty, dull, faded, sad, washed-out; ashen, ashy, chalky, livid, mousy (*or* mousey), pale, palish, white, whitish; chocolate, dun, sandy, sepia; brindled (*or* brindle), grizzled, hoar, hoary

near antonyms ablaze, bright, deep, gay, rich; chromatic, colored; colorful, motley, multicolored, polychromatic, polychrome, varicolored, variegated

2 causing or marked by an atmosphere lacking in cheer ⟨a *gray* rainy day⟩ — see GLOOMY 1

grayish *adj* of the color gray ⟨the black stallion and white mare produced a *grayish* filly⟩ — see GRAY 1

gray matter *n* the ability to learn and understand or to deal with problems ⟨she's got the *gray matter* to figure that equation out⟩ — see INTELLIGENCE 1

[1]**graze** *vb* to feed on grass or herbs ⟨cows *grazing* in the meadow⟩

synonyms browse, forage, pasture, rustle

related words eat, feed, nibble; range, stock; overgraze

[2]**graze** *vb* **1** to damage by rubbing against a sharp or rough surface ⟨I *grazed* my elbow diving for the ball⟩ — see SCRAPE 2

2 to pass lightly across or touch gently especially in passing ⟨the volleyball just *grazed* my face, so I'm okay⟩ — see [2]BRUSH

graze *n* an area of skin roughened or worn away by harsh rubbing against another surface ⟨a stumble that resulted in nothing more serious than a *graze* on the knee⟩ — see ABRASION

grease *vb* **1** to coat (something) with a slippery substance in order to reduce friction ⟨make sure you *grease* the pan before you put the batter in⟩ — see LUBRICATE

2 to free from obstruction or difficulty ⟨your help might *grease* the complicated adoption proceedings⟩ — see EASE 1

greased *adj* having or being a surface so smooth as to greatly reduce traction ⟨the floor was *greased* with condensation, and so we slid everywhere we went⟩ — see SLICK 1

greasy *adj* having or being a surface so smooth as to greatly reduce traction ⟨that wet tarmac road is *greasy* enough to send the car into a skid⟩ — see SLICK 1

great *adj* **1** having or showing exceptional knowledge, experience, or skill in a field of endeavor ⟨one of the *great* anthropologists⟩ — see PROFICIENT

2 having, characterized by, or arising from a dignified and generous nature ⟨a *great* humanitarian⟩ ⟨*great* acts of charity⟩ — see NOBLE 2

3 lasting for a considerable time ⟨haven't seen them in a *great* while⟩ — see LONG 2

4 of a size greater than average of its kind ⟨saw a *great* moose calmly walking through our backyard⟩ — see LARGE 1

5 of the very best kind ⟨this cake is *great*!⟩ — see EXCELLENT

6 showing urgent desire or interest ⟨she's *great* on any type of sport that requires endurance⟩ — see EAGER

7 coming before all others in importance ⟨regards global warming as the *great* issue of the day⟩ — see FOREMOST 1

8 of high birth, rank, or station ⟨a descendant of one of the *great* families of Philadelphia⟩ — see NOBLE 1

great *adv* in a pleasing way ⟨the game was going *great* for the home team⟩ — see WELL 5

greatcoat *n* a warm outdoor coat ⟨the men donned their *greatcoats* for the ride in the open carriage⟩ — see OVERCOAT

great divide *n* the permanent stopping of all the vital bodily activities ⟨many religions claim to know what happens after we cross the *great divide*⟩ — see DEATH 1

greatest *adj* **1** coming before all others in importance ⟨the *greatest* achievement in the history of cinema⟩ — see FOREMOST 1

2 of the highest degree ⟨I have the *greatest* respect for the selfless medical missionaries working around the world⟩ — see FULL 2

greathearted *adj* **1** feeling or displaying no fear by temperament ⟨those *greathearted* but otherwise ordinary individuals who answered their country's call for military service⟩ — see BRAVE 1

2 having, characterized by, or arising from a dignified and generous nature ⟨a *greathearted* program to provide basic necessities to millions of children in war-torn countries⟩ — see NOBLE 2

greatheartedly *adv* in a manner befitting a person of the highest character and ideals ⟨*greatheartedly* refusing to profit from his pharmacological discoveries, he never applied for any patents⟩ — see GREATLY 1

greatheartedness *n* strength of mind to carry on in spite of danger ⟨it took a special kind *greatheartedness* for the conscientious objector to remain true to his beliefs⟩ — see COURAGE

greatly *adv* **1** in a manner befitting a person of the highest character and ideals ⟨as commander of the Union army's first black regiment, Robert Gould Shaw died as *greatly* as he had lived⟩

synonyms gallantly, grandly, greatheartedly, heroically, high-mindedly, honorably, magnanimously, nobly

related words loftily, venerably; magnificently, majestically; bravely, chivalrously, courageously, valiantly

near antonyms abominably, contemptibly, despicably, detestably, hatefully, nastily, pitiably, sorrily, wretchedly; degenerately

antonyms basely, currishly, dishonorably, ignobly

2 to a large extent or degree ⟨authorities have *greatly* increased the scope of their investigation of corruption in the mayor's office⟩

synonyms astronomically, big-time, broadly, colossally, considerably, enormously, extensively, highly, hugely, largely, massively, monstrously, monumentally, much, sizably, staggeringly, stupendously, tremendously, utterly, vastly

related words appreciably, noticeably, significantly; abundantly, amply, copiously, healthily, plentifully

phrases a lot, by half, no end

near antonyms modestly; fractionally; imperceptibly, infinitesimally, insignificantly, invisibly, microscopically, minutely; barely, hardly, just, minimally, scarcely

antonyms little, negligibly, nominally, slightly

3 to a great degree ⟨I'm not *greatly* bothered by this setback⟩ — see VERY 1

greatness *n* **1** exceptionally high quality ⟨a poet whose work is of enduring *greatness*⟩ — see EXCELLENCE 1

2 the quality or state of being large in size ⟨the overwhelming *greatness* of the canyon is what visitors first notice⟩ — see LARGENESS

greed *n* an intense selfish desire for wealth or possessions ⟨don't let *greed* for riches control you⟩

synonyms acquisitiveness, avarice, avariciousness, avidity, avidness, covetousness, cupidity, graspingness, greediness, mercenariness, rapaciousness, rapacity

related words commercialism, materialism, possessiveness; gluttonousness, gluttony, piggishness; appetite, craving, desire, drive, hankering, hunger, itch, longing, lust, passion, pining, ravenousness, thirst, voracity, yearning, yen; egoism, egotism, self-centeredness, self-interest, selfishness, self-regard

near antonyms contentment, fulfillment (*or* fulfilment), gratification, satisfaction; bounteousness, bountifulness, bounty, charity, generosity, generousness, largesse (*also* largess), liberality, magnanimity, openhandedness, openheartedness, unselfishness; altruism, selflessness

greediness *n* an intense selfish desire for wealth or possessions ⟨her all-consuming *greediness* blinded her to the pain she caused others in her drive to get rich⟩ — see GREED

greedy *adj* **1** having or marked by an eager and often selfish desire especially for material possessions ⟨a young rocker who was *greedy* for fame and riches⟩ ⟨the *greedy* exploitation of the land by developers⟩

synonyms acquisitive, avaricious, avid, coveting, covetous, grabby, grasping, mercenary, moneygrubbing, rapacious

related words commercialistic, materialistic, philistine; desirous, eager, itchy, lickerish, miserly; hoggish, piggish, piggy, swinish; devouring, gluttonous, gobbling, insatiable, ravenous, unquenchable, voracious; egocentric, egoistic (*also* egoistical), egotistic (*or* egotistical), self-centered, self-seeking; discontent, discontented, malcontent, unsatisfied; begrudging, grudging, resentful

near antonyms nonmaterialistic; altruistic, bounteous, bountiful, charitable, freehanded, generous, greathearted, handsome, liberal, magnanimous, munificent, openhanded, openhearted, selfless, unselfish, unsparing; controlled, moderate, restrained, temperate; content, sated, satisfied

2 having a huge appetite ⟨he's so *greedy* you have to carefully watch your plate during dinner, lest he snatch food off it⟩ — see VORACIOUS 1

3 showing urgent desire or interest ⟨he's *greedy* for new assignments that will really challenge him⟩ — see EAGER

green *adj* **1** covered with a thick, healthy natural

growth ⟨fields *green* with meadow grass⟩ — see LUSH 1
2 lacking in adult experience or maturity ⟨a new pitcher who's pretty *green*, even by rookie standards⟩ — see CALLOW
3 lacking in worldly wisdom or informed judgment ⟨in spite of her age, she's still *green* enough to be hoodwinked by fast-talking scammers⟩ — see NAIVE 1
4 lacking the warm skin color indicative of or associated with good health ⟨after going on the fastest roller coaster in the world, we were all looking a little *green*⟩ — see SICKLY 2

green *n* **1** green leaves or plants ⟨the lonely soldier dreamt of the fields of *green* that he had wandered in as a youth⟩ — see GREENERY
2 something (as pieces of stamped metal or printed paper) customarily and legally used as a medium of exchange, a measure of value, or a means of payment ⟨I need to save up some *green* before I can afford that cruise⟩ — see MONEY 1

greenback *n* a piece of printed paper used as money in the United States ⟨she threw a few *greenbacks* on the counter to pay for the drinks⟩ — see [1]BILL 2

greenery *n* green leaves or plants ⟨Scottish highlands covered with lush *greenery*⟩
synonyms flora, foliage, green, herbage, leafage, vegetation, verdure
related words grassland, prairie; underbrush, undergrowth

green–eyed *adj* having or showing mean resentment of another's possessions or advantages ⟨an anonymous online review of the restaurant that looks like it may have been written by a *green-eyed* competitor⟩ — see ENVIOUS

green–eyed monster *n* a painful awareness of another's possessions or advantages and a desire to have them too ⟨the *green-eyed monster* dogged her whenever she visited her wealthy sister⟩ — see ENVY

greenhorn *n* a person who is just starting out in a field of activity ⟨go easy on him—he's just a *greenhorn* and doesn't have all the experience you do⟩ — see BEGINNER

greenhouse *n* a glass-enclosed building for growing plants ⟨needed to move the plants into the *greenhouse* before the first frost killed them⟩ — see CONSERVATORY

green–light *vb* to give permission for or to approve of ⟨as soon as the project is *green-lighted*, we'll schedule a planning meeting⟩ — see ALLOW 1

green light *n* the approval by someone in authority for the doing of something ⟨we were given the *green light* to use the town commons for our fund-raiser⟩ — see PERMISSION

greenness *n* the quality or state of being simple and sincere ⟨was charmed by her genteel *greenness* and childlike innocence⟩ — see NAÏVETÉ 1

greeting *n* **1** an expression of goodwill upon meeting ⟨the volunteer directed the conference participants towards the coffee after offering them a cheerful *greeting*⟩ — see HELLO
2 greetings *pl* best wishes ⟨when you see him, give him my sincerest *greetings*⟩ — see COMPLIMENT 2

gregarious *adj* **1** likely to seek or enjoy the company of others ⟨a *gregarious* child who ran up to every person on the playground and wanted to be their friend⟩ — see CONVIVIAL
2 tending to group with others of the same kind ⟨walruses are highly *gregarious*⟩ — see COLONIAL

gregariousness *n* the quality or state of being social ⟨his natural *gregariousness* serves him well as a salesman⟩ — see SOCIABILITY

gremlin *n* an imaginary being usually having a small human form and magical powers ⟨during the World Wars, fighter pilots adopted the fanciful notion that *gremlins* were responsible for mechanical failures on their planes⟩ — see FAIRY

griddle cake *n* a flat cake made from thin batter and cooked on both sides (as on a griddle) ⟨buckwheat *griddle cakes* served with strawberry butter⟩ — see PANCAKE

gridlock *n* a point in a struggle where neither side is capable of winning or willing to give in ⟨with the White House controlled by one party and Congress by the other, the nation experienced four years of legislative *gridlock*⟩ — see IMPASSE 1

grief *n* **1** deep sadness especially for the loss of someone or something loved ⟨even the gruff grandfather felt a heartbreaking *grief* when the family dog died⟩ — see SORROW
2 the feeling of impatience or anger caused by another's repeated disagreeable acts ⟨there seemed to be no end to the *grief* that the school bullies were giving to the young boy⟩ — see ANNOYANCE 2

grievance *n* **1** a lingering ill will towards a person for a real or imagined wrong ⟨this is no place to air your *grievances* against him⟩ — see GRUDGE 1
2 an expression of dissatisfaction, pain, or resentment ⟨she decided to file a formal *grievance* against the utility company⟩ — see COMPLAINT 1

grieve *vb* to feel deep sadness or mental pain ⟨we all *grieved* over the lost cat⟩
synonyms agonize, anguish, bleed, hurt, mourn, sorrow, suffer
related words ache, long (for), pine (away), sigh, smart; rack, torment, torture; bemoan, bewail, deplore, lament, rue; bawl, blubber, cry, groan, howl, keen, moan, sob, take on, wail, weep, yammer, yowl; languish; regret
phrases eat one's heart out, tear one's hair
near antonyms beam, cheer, crow, delight, exult, glory, joy, laugh, ravish, rejoice, triumph; assure, cheer, comfort, commiserate, console, reassure, solace, soothe, sympathize

grieve (for) *vb* to feel or express sorrow for ⟨I *grieve for* our loss⟩ — see LAMENT 1

grieving *adj* expressing or suggesting mourning ⟨the *grieving* sobs of the widow could be heard throughout the funeral service⟩ — see MOURNFUL 1

grievous *adj* **1** difficult to endure ⟨the months of chemotherapy seemed almost as *grievous* an affliction as the cancer itself⟩ — see HARSH 1
2 hard to accept or bear especially emotionally ⟨the death of a spouse can be a *grievous* loss from which one never recovers⟩ — see BITTER 2
3 involving potential loss or injury ⟨a *grievous* wound that requires a doctor's immediate attention⟩ — see DANGEROUS 1
4 of a kind to cause great distress ⟨the *grievous* cost of the war in human lives weighed heavily on the president's mind⟩ — see REGRETTABLE

grievously *adv* with feelings of bitterness or grief ⟨I was *grievously* disappointed not to be invited to the wedding⟩ — see HARD 2

grill *n* a public establishment where meals are served to paying customers for consumption on the premises ⟨headed down to the local bar and *grill* for a beer and a burger⟩ — see RESTAURANT

grill *vb* **1** to put a series of questions to ⟨police *grilled* the suspect, but had to release him when it became clear he didn't have the information they were looking for⟩ — see EXAMINE 1
2 to put a question or questions to ⟨*grilled* the children about her ex-husband's new girlfriend⟩ — see ASK 1

grim *adj* **1** harsh and threatening in manner or appearance ⟨a *grim* and desolate landscape⟩ ⟨a *grim* and short-

tempered shopkeeper who didn't exactly invite friendly conversation⟩
synonyms austere, dour, fierce, flinty, forbidding, gruff, intimidating, lowering (*also* louring), rough, rugged, severe, stark, steely, stern, ungentle
related words bleak, cold, hostile, inhospitable, inimical, unfriendly, unsympathetic; adamant, bound, determined, firm, intent, purposeful, resolute, resolved, steadfast, unflinching; fixed, hard, hardened, hardheaded, immovable, implacable, inflexible, ironhanded, mulish, obdurate, obstinate, rigid, self-willed, set, stiff, stubborn, unbending, uncompromising, unrelenting, unyielding, willful (*or* wilful); immutable, unchangeable; black, cheerless, dark, gloomy, glum, joyless, melancholic, moody, morose, sulky, sullen, surly; brooding, grave, humorless, melancholy, serious, sober, sobersided, solemn, somber (*or* sombre), staid, unsmiling, weighty
near antonyms bland, meek, mellow, soft, soothing; easy, quiet, tranquil; agreeable, bright, cheerful, inviting, pleasant, pleasing, sweet; glad, happy, lighthearted, merry, mirthful, sunny; featherbrained, flighty, frivolous, giddy, goofy, harebrained, light-headed, playful, scatterbrained, silly
antonyms benign, benignant, gentle, mild, nonintimidating, tender
2 difficult to endure ⟨this winter is supposed to be particularly *grim*, so stock up on firewood⟩ — see HARSH 1
3 showing no signs of slackening or yielding in one's purpose ⟨with *grim* determination, the woman worked three jobs to put her fatherless children through college⟩ — see UNYIELDING 1
4 violently unfriendly or aggressive in disposition ⟨*grim* warriors heading into battle⟩ — see FIERCE 1

grimace *vb* to distort one's face ⟨playgoers *grimaced* at the actor's terrible attempt at a French accent⟩ — see MUG 1

grimace *n* a twisting of the facial features in disgust or disapproval ⟨he made a *grimace* when he tasted the medicine⟩
synonyms face, frown, lower (*also* lour), moue, mouth, mow, mug, pout, scowl, snoot
related words flinch, squinch, wince; growl, snarl; rictus, simper, smirk; scoff, sneer; glare, glower, look, stare
near antonyms grin, laugh, smile

grime *n* foul matter that mars the purity or cleanliness of something ⟨this new product really cuts through *grime*⟩ — see FILTH 1

grime *vb* to make dirty ⟨countless hours of work were needed to clean the floors of the old warehouse that had been *grimed* from a century of use⟩ — see DIRTY

griminess *n* the state or quality of being dirty ⟨disgusted by the *griminess* in which the previous tenant had left the appliances⟩ — see DIRTINESS 1

grimy *adj* not clean ⟨this mirror is so *grimy* you can barely see your reflection in it⟩ — see DIRTY 1

grin *vb* to express an emotion (as amusement) by curving the lips upward ⟨*grinned* at the kids' fooling around in the pool⟩ — see SMILE 1

grinch *n* a person who spoils the pleasure of others ⟨accused the mayor of being a *grinch* after he cancelled the city's annual holiday parade for budgetary reasons⟩ — see KILLJOY

grind *n* **1** a harsh grating sound ⟨the *grind* of ice in the blender sent the cat running from the room⟩ — see RASP
2 a person slavishly devoted to intellectual or academic pursuits ⟨don't be such a *grind*—go out with your friends and enjoy yourself⟩ — see NERD 1
3 very hard or unpleasant work ⟨yard work is a real *grind*⟩ — see [1]TOIL
4 an established and often automatic or monotonous series of actions followed when engaging in some activity ⟨the daily *grind* of a 50-mile commute was getting old⟩ — see ROUTINE 1

grind *vb* **1** to make smooth by friction ⟨after they are *ground* and polished, these stones can be used for jewelry⟩
synonyms buff, file, hone, rasp, rub, sand
related words plane, scrape; sandblast, scour; burnish, dress, gloss, polish, shine, smooth; edge, hone, sharpen, strop, whet; regrind
near antonyms coarsen, rough (up), roughen, scuff
2 to press or strike against or together so as to make a scraping sound ⟨everyone in the car winced when the driver *ground* the gears trying to shift into second⟩
synonyms crunch, gnash, grate, grit, scrape, scrunch
related words creak, groan, moan, rasp, scratch, whine; clash, collide, jangle, jar
3 to make sharp or sharper ⟨better *grind* down that ax before you even think about trying to cut down that tree⟩ — see SHARPEN
4 to make smooth or glossy usually by repeatedly applying surface pressure ⟨used the finest polishing paper he could to *grind* down the facets of the diamond before dusting it with a soft cloth⟩ — see POLISH 1
5 to pass roughly and noisily over or against a surface ⟨*ground* the rock against the stone wall⟩ — see SCRAPE 1
6 to reduce to fine particles ⟨*grind* whole coffee beans if you want the freshest coffee⟩ — see POWDER

grind (down) *vb* to subject to incapacitating emotional or mental stress ⟨the workers are being *ground down* by the long work hours which leave them little time for anything else⟩ — see OVERWHELM 1

grind (out) *vb* to produce or bring about especially by long or repeated effort ⟨after several years of aborted attempts, the band finally *ground out* a new album⟩ — see HAMMER OUT

grinder *n* a large sandwich on a long split roll ⟨ordered a meatball *grinder* from the beach's concession stand⟩ — see SUBMARINE

grip *n* **1** a bag carried by hand and designed to hold a traveler's clothing and personal articles ⟨she placed her *grip* in the train's overhead rack and seated herself comfortably⟩ — see TRAVELING BAG
2 the act or manner of holding ⟨get a better *grip* on the lid and try to open the jar again⟩ — see HOLD 1
3 the knowledge gained from the process of coming to know or understand something ⟨he has a good *grip* on basic Spanish grammar and spelling⟩ — see COMPREHENSION
4 the right or means to command or control others ⟨a tyrant that keeps the masses tightly in his *grip*⟩ — see POWER 1
5 a part by which an implement is held ⟨bought new pots with heat-resistant *grips*⟩ — see HANDLE 1

grip *vb* **1** to have or keep in one's hands ⟨*gripped* the handlebars tightly and raced down the hill⟩ — see HOLD 1
2 to hold the attention of as if by a spell ⟨that true crime story *gripped* me as much as any whodunit⟩ — see ENTHRALL 1
3 to hold the attention of ⟨that movie will *grip* any true sports car fan⟩ — see ENGAGE 1
4 to reach for and take hold of by embracing with the fingers or arms ⟨the baby *gripped* my fingers and wouldn't let go⟩ — see TAKE 1

gripe *n* an expression of dissatisfaction, pain, or resentment ⟨I would rather not listen to *gripes* about your latest disasters in the dating game⟩ — see COMPLAINT 1

gripe *vb* **1** to disturb the peace of mind of (someone) especially by repeated disagreeable acts ⟨constant com-

plaints from the customers *griped* her to the point where she started snapping back⟩ — see IRRITATE 1
2 to express dissatisfaction, pain, or resentment usually tiresomely ⟨her tendency to *gripe* constantly drove everyone away⟩ — see COMPLAIN

griper *n* **1** a person who makes frequent complaints usually about little things ⟨a petty *griper* who drove us nuts with his merciless nitpicking⟩ — see CRYBABY
2 an irritable and complaining person ⟨driving across the country in four days would make anyone a confirmed *griper*⟩ — see GROUCH 1

gripping *adj* holding the attention or provoking interest ⟨I found the exhibit on the Holocaust intensely *gripping* and quite moving⟩ — see INTERESTING

grisliness *n* the quality of inspiring intense dread or dismay ⟨the *grisliness* of the crime scene was too much for the jury⟩ — see HORROR 1

grisly *adj* extremely disturbing or repellent ⟨recounted the visit to the murder scene in *grisly* detail⟩ — see HORRIBLE 1

grit *n* the strength of mind that enables a person to endure pain or hardship ⟨she was an athlete with true *grit*, continuing her training despite bad weather and an injury⟩ — see FORTITUDE

grit *vb* to press or strike against or together so as to make a scraping sound ⟨the crash victim *gritted* his teeth as a way of coping with the pain⟩ — see GRIND 2

grittiness *n* the strength of mind that enables a person to endure pain or hardship ⟨the movie somewhat exaggerates the frontier *grittiness* of the explorers, but the basic facts are correct⟩ — see FORTITUDE

grizzle *vb* to express dissatisfaction, pain, or resentment usually tiresomely ⟨the kind of person who wouldn't be happy if she didn't have something to *grizzle* about⟩ — see COMPLAIN

groan *n* **1** a crying out in grief ⟨when the underdogs lost the playoffs, the *groans* of millions of disappointed fans were heard throughout the land⟩ — see LAMENT 1
2 a long low sound indicating pain or grief ⟨let out a *groan* when he tried to stand on the sprained ankle⟩ — see MOAN 1

groan *vb* to utter a moan ⟨heard someone *groaning* in pain⟩ — see MOAN 1

groaner *n* an idea or expression that has been used by many people ⟨the play's dialogue featured all of the *groaners* that seem to be de rigueur for any dysfunctional-family drama⟩ — see COMMONPLACE

grog *n* a distilled beverage that can make a person drunk ⟨sailors clamoring for more *grog*⟩ — see ALCOHOL

grogshop *n, chiefly British* a place of business where alcoholic beverages are sold to be consumed on the premises ⟨last saw them heading down to the local *grogshop* for a pint of beer⟩ — see BARROOM

grok *vb* to have a clear idea of ⟨the eternal struggle of the human race to *grok* its place in the grand scheme of the universe⟩ — see COMPREHEND 1

groom *vb* to make ready in advance ⟨the hotel's penthouse suite is being *groomed* for a royal visit⟩ — see PREPARE 1

groomed *adj* being clean and in good order ⟨the front office is always carefully *groomed* in order to give customers a good first impression⟩ — see NEAT 1

groove *n* **1** an established and often automatic or monotonous series of actions followed when engaging in some activity ⟨I can't get into the *groove* on Monday morning without a cup of coffee⟩ — see ROUTINE 1
2 a situation or activity for which a person or thing is best suited ⟨after years of bouncing from job to job, she discovered that her natural *groove* was social work⟩ — see NICHE 2

groove *vb* **1** to mark with or as if with a line or groove ⟨if you *groove* that piece of wood, we should be able to fit this smaller board into it⟩ — see SCORE 1
2 to form a pleasing relationship ⟨surprisingly, his flighty, artistic sensibility and her no-nonsense practicality *groove* together rather well⟩ — see HARMONIZE 1

groove (on) *vb* to take pleasure in ⟨thrill-seekers who *groove on* skiing will love snowboarding⟩ — see ENJOY 1

groovy *adj* **1** of the very best kind ⟨a great movie with *groovy* special effects⟩ — see EXCELLENT
2 keenly aware of and responsive to the latest developments especially in fashion and entertainment ⟨old college buddies fondly recalling the days when bell-bottom jeans were about the *grooviest* thing around⟩ — see AU COURANT 1

grope *vb* to search for something blindly or uncertainly ⟨she nervously *groped* for her car keys⟩ ⟨*groping* for the right answer⟩
synonyms feel, fish, fumble, scrabble
related words grabble; cast about, hunt, look, reach, seek (out); capture, clutch, corral, get, grab, nab, nail, seize, snatch; comb, dig (through), dredge, rake, ransack, rifle, rummage, scour

gross *adj* **1** depicting or referring to sexual matters in a way that is unacceptable in polite society ⟨he was thrown out of class for making a *gross* gesture⟩ — see OBSCENE 1
2 having an excess of body fat ⟨a very *gross* man trying to squeeze into a seat in the plane's coach section⟩ — see FAT 1
3 lacking in refinement or good taste ⟨refused to mix with what she called "the *gross* masses who are unappreciative of fine art"⟩ — see COARSE 2
4 very noticeable especially for being incorrect or bad ⟨a *gross* mistake that some proofreader should have caught⟩ — see EGREGIOUS
5 causing intense displeasure, disgust, or resentment ⟨the little boy insisted that worms are *gross*⟩ — see OFFENSIVE 1

grossness *n* **1** the condition of having an excess of body fat ⟨that level of *grossness* is more than simply unsightly—it's seriously unhealthy⟩ — see CORPULENCE
2 the quality or state of being obscene ⟨a movie of such indisputable *grossness* that people who thought that they had seen everything were proven wrong⟩ — see OBSCENITY 1
3 the quality or state of lacking refinement or good taste ⟨the *grossness* of his table manners disgusted the other wedding guests⟩ — see VULGARITY 1

gross out *vb* to cause to feel disgust ⟨that dead frog in our driveway *grosses* me *out*⟩ — see DISGUST

grot *n* a naturally formed underground chamber with an opening to the surface ⟨the famous Dead Sea Scrolls were discovered in a long-forgotten *grot* by a shepherd boy⟩ — see CAVE

grotesque *adj* **1** disagreeable to one's aesthetic or artistic sense ⟨the gaudy, overdecorated interior of the gambling casino was just too *grotesque* for my taste⟩ — see HARSH 2
2 unpleasant to look at ⟨that bloody Halloween mask is *grotesque*⟩ — see UGLY 1

grotesque *n* a strange or horrible and often frightening creature ⟨a gallery of *grotesques* from some sicko horror movie⟩ — see MONSTER 1

grotesquerie *also* **grotesquery** *n* a strange or horrible and often frightening creature ⟨born Joseph Merrick, the so-called Elephant Man was for a time exhibited as a sideshow *grotesquerie*⟩ — see MONSTER 1

grotto *n* a naturally formed underground chamber with an opening to the surface ⟨at the heart of the shrine is a small rocky *grotto* into which pilgrims can descend⟩ — see CAVE

grotty *adj, chiefly British* not clean ⟨get rid of that *grotty* old rag⟩ — see DIRTY 1

grouch *n* **1** an irritable and complaining person ⟨an uncle who is a real *grouch* when he's sick⟩
synonyms bear, bellyacher, complainer, crab, crank, croaker, crosspatch, curmudgeon, fusser, griper, grouser, growler, grumbler, grump, murmurer, mutterer, sourpuss, whiner
related words hunks; malcontent, sorehead; grinch, killjoy, party pooper, spoilsport; defeatist, pessimist; faultfinder, kicker, nagger, nitpicker, objector, quibbler, repiner; crock [*slang*], hypochondriac
near antonyms optimist, Pollyanna; happy camper
2 a state of resentful silence or irritability ⟨having been proven wrong, he had a *grouch* on for hours afterwards⟩ — see POUT
3 an expression of dissatisfaction, pain, or resentment ⟨it wouldn't be a workday if we didn't hear his daily *grouch* about the coffee⟩ — see COMPLAINT 1

grouch *vb* to express dissatisfaction, pain, or resentment usually tiresomely ⟨a woman who likes to *grouch* about how unappreciated she is⟩ — see COMPLAIN

grouchiness *n* readiness to show annoyance or impatience ⟨while some people thought that toddler's *grouchiness* was cute, it drove me nuts⟩ — see PETULANCE

grouchy *adj* **1** easily irritated or annoyed ⟨a lack of sleep would make anyone *grouchy*⟩ — see IRRITABLE
2 given to complaining a lot ⟨a *grouchy* kid who refuses to eat his vegetables⟩ — see FUSSY 1

ground *adj* having an edge thin enough to cut or pierce something ⟨a finely *ground* axe⟩ — see SHARP 1

ground *n* **1 grounds** *pl* the area around and belonging to a building ⟨an escorted tour of the White House and its surrounding *grounds*⟩
synonyms demesne, park, premises (*also* premisses), yard
related words acres, estate, land, lot, parcel, plot, property, real estate, realty; campus; backyard, churchyard, dooryard, schoolyard; close, enclosure (*also* inclosure), garden, garth, plaza
2 grounds *pl* matter that settles to the bottom of a body of liquid ⟨strain the coffee to remove the *grounds*⟩ — see DEPOSIT 1
3 grounds *pl* something (as a belief) that serves as the basis for another thing ⟨your dislike of her tattoos would be insufficient *grounds* for firing her⟩ — see REASON 2
4 a small area of usually open land ⟨I'll meet you at the parade *ground* in two hours⟩ — see FIELD 1
5 an immaterial thing upon which something else rests ⟨opposed to the notion that religious law should be used as a *ground* for civil law⟩ — see BASE 1
6 the loose surface material in which plants naturally grow ⟨stuck the shovel in the *ground* and went inside for a glass of water⟩ — see DIRT 1
7 the physical conditions or features that form the setting against which something is viewed ⟨take her picture against a blue *ground* in order to bring out her blue eyes⟩ — see BACKGROUND 1
8 the solid part of our planet's surface as distinguished from the sea and air ⟨one of the Nordic creation myths states that the *ground* was formed by the body of the giant Ymir when he was killed by Odin and his brothers⟩ — see EARTH 2

ground *vb* to find a basis ⟨you're *grounding* your entire case on circumstantial evidence⟩ — see BASE

grounded *adj* resting on the shore or bottom of a body of water ⟨once his boat was *grounded*, all he could do was wait for the tide to come back in and raise it off the sand bar⟩ — see AGROUND

groundless *adj* having no basis in reason or fact ⟨please stop making *groundless* accusations against people you happen to dislike⟩ ⟨fears of a strike proved *groundless*⟩
synonyms baseless, foundationless, invalid, nonvalid, unfounded, unreasonable, unsubstantiated, unsupported, unwarranted
related words illogical, irrational, nonlogical, unconscionable, unsound; fallacious, false, misled, wrong; gratuitous, uncalled-for, unnecessary; flimsy, implausible, misleading, specious, unconvincing, untenable, weak; ill-advised, unreasoned; inconsistent; absurd, asinine, brainless, crackpot, crazy, fatuous, foolish, half-witted, harebrained, meaningless, nonsensical, preposterous, senseless, silly, simpleminded, stupid, unwise; insane, lunatic, mad, nutty, wacky (*also* whacky)
near antonyms certified, validated, verified; confirmed, corroborated; informed, logical, rational; commonsense, sane, sensible, sober, wise; actual, genuine, real, true; certain, sure; clear, cogent, compelling, convincing, credible, persuasive, plausible, satisfying, solid, sound
antonyms good, hard, just, justified, reasonable, reasoned, substantiated, valid, well-founded, well-grounded

ground plan *n* a method worked out in advance for achieving some objective ⟨their *ground plan* is first to finish college and then get married⟩ — see PLAN 1

ground rule *n* a statement spelling out the proper procedure or conduct for an activity ⟨before the debate begins, let's lay out some *ground rules*⟩ — see RULE 1

groundwork *n* an immaterial thing upon which something else rests ⟨they had collectively laid the *groundwork* for a new kind of art⟩ — see BASE 1

ground zero *n* a thing or place that is of greatest importance to an activity or interest ⟨a city that was once *ground zero* for the insurance industry⟩ — see CENTER 1

group *vb* **1** to arrange or assign according to type ⟨you should first *group* the invertebrates by genus⟩ — see CLASSIFY 1
2 to bring together in one body or place ⟨*group* the kids together and we'll see who's missing⟩ — see GATHER 1

group *n* **1** a number of things considered as a unit ⟨car buffs stood around admiring a *group* of classic cars in the parking lot⟩
synonyms array, assemblage, band, bank, batch, battery, block, bunch, clot, clump, cluster, clutch, collection, constellation, grouping, huddle, knot, lot, muster, package, parcel, passel, set, suite
related words accumulation, aggregate, aggregation, conglomeration; agglomeration, assortment, hodgepodge, jumble, miscellany, mixture, odds and ends, sundries, variety; cycle, run, series, suit
phrases the whole kit and caboodle
near antonyms entity, item, single, unit
2 a usually small number of persons considered as a unit ⟨the next tour *group* was being seated for dinner⟩
synonyms array, band, batch, battery, body, boodle, bunch, cluster, clutch, consort, constellation, crop, grouping, huddle, knot, lot, parcel, party, passel
related words assembly, collective, congregation, gathering, muster, organization; circle, clan, clique, coterie, fellowship, gang, ring, round, set; faction, guild (*also* gild), order, school, sect; brigade, crew, outfit, phalanx, platoon, posse, task force, team; alliance, bloc, coalition, confederacy, confederation, federation, league, union; battalion, squadron; bevy, brood, covey
phrases the whole kit and caboodle

near antonyms individual, single
3 one of the units into which a whole is divided on the basis of a common characteristic ⟨you'll find both good and bad in every ethnic *group*⟩ — see CLASS 2

grouping *n* **1** a number of things considered as a unit ⟨the standard *grouping* for an average living room: sofa, matching wing chairs, and the inevitable coffee table⟩ — see GROUP 1
2 a usually small number of persons considered as a unit ⟨the next *grouping* of tourists can start the house tour as soon as the last bunch leaves⟩ — see GROUP 2

grouse *vb* to express dissatisfaction, pain, or resentment usually tiresomely ⟨hasn't stopped *grousing* since we started this vacation⟩ — see COMPLAIN

grouse *n* an expression of dissatisfaction, pain, or resentment ⟨a forum in which employees can air their *grouses*⟩ — see COMPLAINT 1

grouser *n* an irritable and complaining person ⟨had the misfortune of waiting on a table full of *grousers*, who sent her back to the kitchen constantly and then refused to tip her⟩ — see GROUCH 1

grovel *vb* **1** to draw back or crouch down in fearful submission ⟨the way in which the abused dog would *grovel* whenever its owner came near⟩ — see COWER
2 to move slowly with the body close to the ground ⟨because of their anatomy, bats can only *grovel* while moving along the ground⟩ — see CRAWL 1

grow *vb* **1** to look after or assist the growth of by labor and care ⟨a dedicated home gardener who *grows* tomatoes in her small garden every summer⟩
synonyms crop, cultivate, culture, dress, promote, raise, rear, tend
related words breed, produce, propagate; plant, sow; gather, glean, harvest, reap; germinate, quicken, ripen, root, sprout
near antonyms kill; dig, extirpate, pick, pluck, pull (up), uproot; cut, hay, mow
2 to become mature ⟨you've *grown* so much since we last saw each other⟩ — see MATURE
3 to eventually have as a state or quality ⟨he will *grow* angry if we don't answer his question⟩ — see BECOME

grow (in) *vb* to gradually increase in ⟨you've *grown in* wisdom over the years⟩ — see GAIN 1

grower *n* a person who cultivates the land and grows crops on it ⟨orange *growers* in Florida were hard hit by the hurricane⟩ — see FARMER

growl *vb* **1** to express dissatisfaction, pain, or resentment usually tiresomely ⟨he was *growling* about how much work he had to do⟩ — see COMPLAIN
2 to make a long loud deep noise or cry ⟨the neighbor's dog *growls* every time we pass the house⟩ — see ROAR 1
3 to make a low heavy rolling sound ⟨I'm sorry my stomach is *growling*, but I'm just really hungry⟩ — see RUMBLE

growler *n* an irritable and complaining person ⟨we can't figure out why our very happy and optimistic friend is dating that chronic *growler*⟩ — see GROUCH 1

grown *adj* covered with a thick healthy natural growth ⟨a field lavishly *grown* with poppies⟩ — see LUSH 1

grown–up *adj* relating to or typical of adults; displaying proper maturity ⟨they have yet to find a *grown-up* way of handling their marital problems⟩ — see ADULT 1

grown–up *n* a fully grown person ⟨once you turn 12, you get to eat with the *grown-ups* at Thanksgiving⟩ — see ADULT

growth *n* **1** an abnormal mass of tissue ⟨found a *growth* on the dog's neck under her collar⟩
synonyms excrescence, excrescency, lump, neoplasm, tumor
related words outgrowth; cancer, carcinoma, lymphoma, malignancy, melanoma, polyp; cyst, tubercle, wart
2 the act or process of going from the simple or basic to the complex or advanced ⟨the *growth* of the gambling industry into an economic mainstay in some locations⟩ — see DEVELOPMENT 1
3 the process of becoming mature ⟨her reflections and mature behavior certainly demonstrate just how much emotional *growth* took place last summer⟩ — see MATURATION

grow up *vb* to become mature ⟨everyone has to *grow up* at some point in their lives⟩ — see MATURE

grub *n* **1** substances intended to be eaten ⟨after the game, we headed to the diner for some hearty *grub*⟩ — see FOOD 1
2 a person who does very hard or dull work ⟨you may have to spend some time working as a *grub* before challenging work comes your way⟩ — see SLAVE 2

grub *vb* to devote serious and sustained effort ⟨*grubbing* away at the yard work before the first snow of the season⟩ — see LABOR

grubber *n* a person who does very hard or dull work ⟨most of the inhabitants of the seedy town are just downtrodden *grubbers* living from paycheck to paycheck⟩ — see SLAVE 2

grubbiness *n* the state or quality of being dirty ⟨the *grubbiness* and general dilapidation of the old house discouraged potential buyers⟩ — see DIRTINESS 1

grubby *adj* **1** not clean ⟨clean off those *grubby* hands before you touch anything⟩ — see DIRTY 1
2 arousing or deserving of one's loathing and disgust ⟨that's a *grubby* reason to stop talking to a friend⟩ — see CONTEMPTIBLE 1

grudge *n* **1** a lingering ill will towards a person for a real or imagined wrong ⟨he's had a *grudge* against her ever since she snubbed him at the dance⟩
synonyms down [*chiefly British*], grievance, resentment, score
related words condemnation; offense (*or* offence), umbrage; complaint; dudgeon, huff, peeve, pique; despite, hatefulness, malevolence, malice, maliciousness, meanness, nastiness, spite, spitefulness, spleen, venom, viciousness; animosity, antagonism, antipathy, bitterness, enmity, hostility, rancor
2 a deep-seated ill will ⟨there's been a *grudge* between the two families for years⟩ — see ENMITY

grueling *or* **gruelling** *adj* **1** requiring considerable physical or mental effort ⟨running a marathon is *grueling*⟩ — see HARD 2
2 requiring much time, effort, or careful attention ⟨cutting diamonds can be *grueling* work⟩ — see DEMANDING 1

gruesome *also* **grewsome** *adj* extremely disturbing or repellent ⟨didn't stick around to hear the *gruesome* details of the car accident⟩ — see HORRIBLE 1

gruesomeness *n* the quality of inspiring intense dread or dismay ⟨permanently scarred by the sheer *gruesomeness* of what she had witnessed during the war⟩ — see HORROR 1

gruff *adj* **1** harsh and dry in sound ⟨she had a *gruff* speaking voice, but a surprisingly sweet singing voice⟩ — see HOARSE
2 harsh and threatening in manner or appearance ⟨I didn't exchange one word with the *gruff* mountaineer who sat next to me in the diner⟩ — see GRIM 1

grumble *n* an expression of dissatisfaction, pain, or resentment ⟨a chorus of moans and *grumbles* when they found out that the overnight camping trip had been cancelled⟩ — see COMPLAINT 1

grumble *vb* **1** to express dissatisfaction, pain, or resentment usually tiresomely ⟨he *grumbled* about how sore his feet were after standing all day⟩ — see COMPLAIN
2 to make a low heavy rolling sound ⟨heavily loaded

trucks *grumbling* as they passed over the steel bridge⟩ — see RUMBLE

grumbler *n* **1** an irritable and complaining person ⟨the motor coach tour would have been okay if I hadn't been paired up with a *grumbler* who whined through the whole thing⟩ — see GROUCH 1
2 a person who makes frequent complaints usually about little things ⟨how can you be such a *grumbler* when so much in your life is going well?⟩ — see CRYBABY

grump *n* an irritable and complaining person ⟨a real *grump* in the morning⟩ — see GROUCH 1

grump *vb* **1** to express dissatisfaction, pain, or resentment usually tiresomely ⟨those incessantly *grumping* patients were generally ignored by the nursing home staff⟩ — see COMPLAIN
2 to silently go about in a bad mood ⟨he's been *grumping* about the house all morning because the golf tournament got rained out⟩ — see SULK

grumpiness *n* readiness to show annoyance or impatience ⟨I don't want your customary *grumpiness* to spoil the evening⟩ — see PETULANCE

grumpy *adj* **1** easily irritated or annoyed ⟨a *grumpy* neighbor whose yard we had long ago learned not to trespass⟩ — see IRRITABLE
2 given to complaining a lot ⟨the baby's sure to be *grumpy* if she doesn't get her afternoon nap⟩ — see FUSSY 1

grungy *adj* **1** not clean ⟨after playing outside, the kids came in *grungy* and in need of a good bath⟩ — see DIRTY 1
2 showing signs of advanced wear and tear and neglect ⟨even though this *grungy* sweatshirt is falling apart, it's still my favorite⟩ — see SHABBY 1

grunt *n* **1** speech that is not clear enough to be understood ⟨preoccupied with what he was doing, the mechanic gave only a *grunt* when I asked when the car would be ready⟩ — see MUMBLE
2 a person who does very hard or dull work ⟨we have an opening in the warehouse if you don't mind doing *grunt* work⟩ — see SLAVE 2

grunt *vb* to speak softly and unclearly ⟨was so absorbed with the video game that when asked what he wanted for dinner, he just *grunted*⟩ — see MUMBLE

grunting *n* speech that is not clear enough to be understood ⟨says he talks in his sleep, but really it's just snorts and *grunting*⟩ — see MUMBLE

guarantee *vb* **1** to assume responsibility for the satisfactory quality or performance of ⟨the shop will *guarantee* all work done on the car for 30 days⟩ — see WARRANT 1
2 to make sure, certain, or safe ⟨I can *guarantee* that you'll feel better after using my product for 30 days⟩ — see ENSURE
3 to state clearly and strongly ⟨I *guarantee* that this movie is better than the last one in the series⟩ — see ASSERT 1

guarantee *n* **1** a formal agreement to fulfill an obligation ⟨the contractors gave us a written *guarantee* that the work on the house would be done by Christmas⟩
synonyms bond, contract, covenant, deal, guaranty, surety, warranty
related words oath, pledge, troth, vow, word; accord, bargain, compact, concordat, convention, pact, treaty; assurance, insurance, seal; bail, deposit, pawn, security
2 something given or held to assure that the giver will keep a promise ⟨you'll have to give your car keys as a *guarantee* that you'll come back⟩ — see PLEDGE 1

guarantor *n* a person who takes the responsibility for some other person or thing ⟨the town police force is the *guarantor* of our safety⟩ — see SPONSOR

guaranty *n* **1** a formal agreement to fulfill an obligation ⟨this fridge comes with a money-back *guaranty* of complete customer satisfaction⟩ — see GUARANTEE 1
2 something given or held to assure that the giver will keep a promise ⟨couples exchange engagement rings as a symbolic *guaranty* that they will marry⟩ — see PLEDGE 1

guaranty *vb* **1** to make sure, certain, or safe ⟨a house *guarantied* against termite damage⟩ — see ENSURE
2 to assume responsibility for the satisfactory quality or performance of ⟨a watch *guarantied* to be water-resistant to a depth of 100 feet⟩ — see WARRANT 1

guard *n* **1** a person or group that watches over someone or something ⟨checked in with the security *guard* at the gate⟩
synonyms custodian, guardian, keeper, lookout, minder, picket, sentinel, sentry, warden, warder, watch, watcher, watchman
related words observer, patrol, spotter, surveillant, watchdog; bodyguard, convoy, defender, escort, honor guard; gatekeeper; hack [*slang*]
2 a position of readiness to oppose actual or expected attack ⟨be on your *guard* against snakes in the swamp⟩ — see DEFENSIVE
3 a protective device (as on a weapon) to prevent accidental operation ⟨slid the *guard* into place over the chainsaw chain⟩ — see SAFETY 2
4 means or method of defending ⟨the boxer's sparring partner managed to get a blow in under his left *guard*⟩ — see DEFENSE 1
5 one that accompanies another for protection, guidance, or as a courtesy ⟨the honor *guards* raised their sabers as the happy couple descended the church steps⟩ — see ESCORT
6 someone that protects ⟨a battalion of burly *guards* surrounding the celebrity⟩ — see PROTECTOR

guard *vb* **1** to drive danger or attack away from ⟨*guard* the quarterback so he doesn't get sacked⟩ — see DEFEND 1
2 to disallow entry into (a place) by means of a physical barrier at the entry point ⟨a fire-breathing dragon *guarded* the entrance to the castle⟩ — see CLOSE (OFF)

guard (against) *vb* to be cautious of or on guard against ⟨unfortunately, you have to *guard against* theft while you're traveling⟩ — see BEWARE (OF)

guarded *adj* having or showing a close attentiveness to avoiding danger or trouble ⟨a *guarded* man who knew better than to reveal such delicate information⟩ ⟨*guarded* actions⟩ — see CAREFUL 1

guardedness *n* a close attentiveness to avoiding danger ⟨you should have shown a little more *guardedness* about sharing personal information with someone you just met online⟩ — see CAUTION 1

guardian *n* **1** a person or group that watches over someone or something ⟨the state became his *guardian* when he was put into protective custody⟩ — see GUARD 1
2 a person who takes care of a property sometimes for an absent owner ⟨the *guardians* of the summer estate awaited the return of the tycoon⟩ — see CUSTODIAN 1
3 someone that protects ⟨the editor defended his newspaper's unrelenting exposure of government corruption, arguing that it is journalism's role to act as a *guardian* of democracy⟩ — see PROTECTOR
4 a person who has responsibility for the care of another ⟨when her parents died, her aunt became her legal *guardian*⟩ — see CAREGIVER

guardian angel *n* someone that protects ⟨his work with the pet rescue center has led many to hail him as a *guardian angel* and friend to all animals⟩ — see PROTECTOR

guardianship *n* responsibility for the safety and well-being of someone or something ⟨gave the *guardianship* of his estate to his children⟩ ⟨has *guardianship* of the dogs while I'm in the hospital⟩ — see CUSTODY

guardrail *n* a protective barrier consisting of a horizontal bar and its supports ⟨the car ran off the road, but fortunately only hit the *guardrail*⟩ — see RAILING

guardroom *n* a place of confinement for persons held in lawful custody ⟨hauled the prisoners of war into the *guardroom* and sent for the doctor on duty⟩ — see JAIL

guck *or* **gook** *n* soft wet earth ⟨don't walk on that clean floor with *guck* on your shoes⟩ — see MUD

guess *n* an opinion or judgment based on little or no evidence ⟨if you don't know the answer for sure, just make a *guess*⟩ — see CONJECTURE

guess *vb* **1** to form an opinion from little or no evidence ⟨though she does not speak with an accent, I would still *guess* that she is a foreigner⟩
synonyms assume, conjecture, daresay, imagine, presume, speculate, suppose, surmise, suspect, suspicion [*chiefly dialect*]
related words conclude, deduce, gather, infer; hypothecate, hypothesize, theorize; believe, conceive, expect, judge, reckon [*chiefly dialect*], take, think
near antonyms demonstrate, document, establish, prove, substantiate, validate; ascertain, determine, find out, learn
2 to decide the size, amount, number, or distance of (something) without actual measurement ⟨I would *guess* the road goes for about two miles before you have to take a left⟩ — see ESTIMATE 2
3 to have as an opinion ⟨I never would have *guessed* that she was capable of such a terrible thing⟩ — see BELIEVE 2

guesstimate *vb* to make an approximate or tentative judgment regarding ⟨I'm going to *guesstimate* that this ring is worth $200 or so⟩ — see ESTIMATE 1

guest *n* **1** a person who visits another ⟨invited the afternoon *guests* to stay for dinner⟩
synonyms caller, drop-in, frequenter, visitant, visitor
related words houseguest; company; invitee; crasher, hanger-on
near antonyms denizen, dweller, habitant, inhabitant, occupant, resident, resider; cohost, cohostess, host, hostess
2 a person who buys a product or uses a service from a business ⟨the headwaiter will seat the *guests* as soon as the waitress clears and sets a table for them⟩ — see CUSTOMER 1

guff *n* language, behavior, or ideas that are absurd and contrary to good sense ⟨and don't give me any of your usual *guff* about having to work late⟩ — see NONSENSE 1

guffaw *n* an explosive sound that is a sign of amusement ⟨managed to keep a straight face for a minute before he let loose with a loud *guffaw*⟩ — see LAUGH 1

guggle *vb* to flow in a broken irregular stream ⟨water *guggled* down the drain⟩ — see GURGLE

guidance *n* **1** an opinion suggesting a wise or proper course of action ⟨sought career *guidance* from the college counselor⟩ — see ADVICE 1
2 the act or activity of looking after and making decisions about something ⟨felt secure under the president's cautious *guidance* of foreign affairs⟩ — see CONDUCT 1
3 the duty or function of watching or guarding for the sake of proper direction or control ⟨an adviser who undertakes the *guidance* of his students' academic careers⟩ — see SUPERVISION 1

guide *n* one that accompanies another for protection, guidance, or as a courtesy ⟨followed our *guide* through the dangerous mountain trails⟩ — see ESCORT

guide *vb* **1** to give advice and instruction to (someone) regarding the course or process to be followed ⟨the pastry chef *guided* her through the creation of the wedding cake, showing her how to ice the layers, fashion the elaborate decorations, and assemble the whole shebang⟩
synonyms coach, counsel, lead, mentor, pilot, shepherd, show, tutor
related words godfather; direct, engineer, steer, sway; accompany, attend, chaperone (*or* chaperon), convoy, escort, see, squire; oversee, superintend, supervise; drill, train; brief, enlighten, inform; instruct, school, teach, tutor; inculcate, indoctrinate; cultivate, foster, nurture
phrases walk through
2 to look after and make decisions about ⟨thought the new superintendent would *guide* the school system well⟩ — see CONDUCT 1
3 to point out the way for (someone) especially from a position in front ⟨would be happy to *guide* you folks to the historic part of town⟩ — see LEAD 1

guidon *n* a piece of cloth with a special design that is used as an emblem or for signaling ⟨each army command unit flew a different color *guidon*, though they were all the same shape⟩ — see FLAG 1

guild *also* **gild** *n* a group of persons formally joined together for some common interest ⟨after his apprenticeship, he was able to join the stonemasons' *guild*⟩ — see ASSOCIATION 2

guile *n* **1** skill in achieving one's ends through indirect, subtle, or underhanded means ⟨a shady salesman who usually relies on a combination of quick thinking and *guile*⟩ — see CUNNING 1
2 the inclination or practice of misleading others through lies or trickery ⟨a person so full of *guile* he can't even be trusted to give you the correct time of day⟩ — see DECEIT 1

guileful *adj* **1** clever at attaining one's ends by indirect and often deceptive means ⟨tried to fix the game with a *guileful* plot to sabotage the other team's bats, but the umpire caught them⟩ — see ARTFUL 1
2 given to or marked by cheating and deception ⟨received a *guileful* answer when I asked the dealer if the used car had ever been in a collision⟩ — see DISHONEST 2

guilefulness *n* **1** skill in achieving one's ends through indirect, subtle, or underhanded means ⟨he had an inherent *guilefulness* that made him a formidable power broker in Washington⟩ — see CUNNING 1
2 the inclination or practice of misleading others through lies or trickery ⟨it was *guilefulness* and not goodness that got the gold digger her millions⟩ — see DECEIT 1

guileless *adj* free from any intent to deceive or impress others ⟨she was an easygoing, *guileless* young woman who was comfortable just being herself⟩
synonyms artless, genuine, honest, ingenuous, innocent, naive (*or* naïve), natural, real, simple, sincere, true, unaffected, unpretending, unpretentious
related words childlike, dewy-eyed, gee-whiz, impressionable, inexperienced, malleable, persuadable, persuasible, simpleminded, unsophisticated, unworldly, wide-eyed; spontaneous, unforced, unstudied; candid, direct, frank, free, free-spoken, open, openhearted, plain, plainspoken, single-minded, straight, straightforward, unguarded; trustful, trusting; exploitable, gullible (*also* gullable), susceptible, unwary
phrases on the level
near antonyms critical, cynical, mistrustful, skeptical, suspicious, wary; cosmopolitan, sophisticated, worldly, worldly-wise; civilized, cultivated, cultured, polished, refined; crooked, deceitful, deceptive, devious, double-dealing, hypocritical, manipulative, two-faced; arch, calculating, canny, crafty, cunning, designing, foxy, knavish, scheming, sharp, shifty, shrewd, slick, slippery, sly, subtle, tricky, underhanded, wily; flattering, mealy-

mouthed, smooth, sycophantic, unctuous; feigned, forced, strained
antonyms affected, artful, artificial, assuming, dishonest, dissembling, dissimulating, fake, false, guileful, insincere, phony (*also* phoney), pretentious

guilelessly *adv* without any attempt to impress by deception or exaggeration ⟨she's a naturally beautiful young woman, *guilelessly* unaware of the effect she has on men⟩ — see NATURALLY 3

guilelessness *n* the quality or state of being simple and sincere ⟨the small-town boy's *guilelessness* is endearing, but it may not serve him well in the ruthless big city⟩ — see NAÏVETÉ 1

guillotine *vb* to cut off the head of ⟨French Revolutionary forces captured and *guillotined* countless aristocrats in the chaotic period following the downfall of the monarchy⟩ — see DECAPITATE

guilt *n* **1** a feeling of responsibility for wrongdoing ⟨he was wracked with *guilt* after he accidentally broke his sister's antique grandfather clock⟩
synonyms contriteness, contrition, penitence, regret, remorse, remorsefulness, repentance, rue, self-reproach, shame
related words compunction, misgiving, prick, qualm, scruple; blame, culpability, fault; liability, rap, responsibility; chagrin, embarrassment; anguish, distress, grief, ruth, sadness, sorrow; bloodguilt, bloodguiltiness; apology, excuses, hand-wringing, mea culpa
antonyms impenitence, remorselessness
2 responsibility for wrongdoing or failure ⟨the chief financial officer was saddled with the *guilt* for the company's failure⟩ — see BLAME 1

guiltless *adj* free from guilt or blame ⟨if the jury acquits him, he is *guiltless* in the eyes of the law⟩ — see INNOCENT 2

guiltlessness *n* the quality or state of being free from guilt or blame ⟨her *guiltlessness* is obvious, since she couldn't possibly have been at the scene of the crime⟩ — see INNOCENCE 1

guilty *adj* suffering from or expressive of a feeling of responsibility for wrongdoing ⟨she was burdened with a *guilty* conscience after stealing the newspaper from the newsstand⟩
synonyms ashamed, shamed, shamefaced
related words apologetic, contrite, penitent, remorseful, repentant, sorry; compunctious, regretful, rueful; penitential; blushing, chagrined, embarrassed, hangdog, sheepish; blamable, blameworthy, culpable
near antonyms impenitent, remorseless, unapologetic, unrepentant; brazen, cheeky, impudent; blameless, guiltless, innocent
antonyms shameless, unashamed

guise *n* **1** a display of emotion or behavior that is insincere or intended to deceive ⟨my new neighbor began seeking my company under the *guise* of friendship, but he turned out to be a member of a religious cult bent on conversion⟩ — see MASQUERADE
2 clothing chosen as appropriate for a specific situation ⟨she felt as though she should be wearing some sort of Germanic *guise*, complete with dirndl, for the fall festival featuring traditional German food and drink⟩ — see OUTFIT 1
3 clothing put on to hide one's true identity or imitate someone or something else ⟨he snuck into the castle to rescue Ivanhoe in the *guise* of a priest coming to give Ivanhoe his last rites⟩ — see DISGUISE 1
4 outward and often deceptive indication ⟨hazing rituals may have the *guise* of harmless fun, but often the reality is serious physical abuse⟩ — see APPEARANCE 2

gulch *n* a narrow opening between hillsides or mountains that can be used for passage ⟨the *gulch* floods in the spring with the runoff from the mountains, so wait until later in the summer to hike it⟩ — see CANYON

gulf *n* **1** a part of a body of water that extends beyond the general shoreline ⟨we dipped our feet in the warm waters of the *gulf*⟩
synonyms arm, bay, bight, cove, creek [*chiefly British*], embayment, estuary, firth, fjord (*also* fiord), inlet, loch [*Scottish*]
related words harbor, port, road(s), roadstead; narrow, sound, strait; bayou; backwater, slough (*also* slew *or* slue)
2 an immeasurable depth or space ⟨the great *gulf* of time and space that separates us from the first inhabitants of North America⟩ — see ABYSS
3 a narrow opening between hillsides or mountains that can be used for passage ⟨the *gulf* was too wide to cross, so we had to hike down into it and go through it⟩ — see CANYON
4 an open space in a barrier (as a wall or hedge) ⟨a wide *gulf* in the defensive wall meant the city was in grave danger⟩ — see GAP 1
5 water moving rapidly in a circle with a hollow in the center ⟨the doomed ship was sucked into the *gulf* and consigned to Davy Jones's locker⟩ — see WHIRLPOOL

gulf *vb* to cover with a flood ⟨with the administration *gulfed* by so many real problems, it's absurd for the president to concern himself with this nonissue⟩ — see FLOOD

gull *n* one who is easily deceived or cheated ⟨that multimillionaire is enough of a *gull* to believe that it's his personality that attracts women⟩ — see [1]DUPE

gull *vb* to cause to believe what is untrue ⟨we were *gulled* into believing that if we answered the e-mail, we'd somehow become millionaires, but instead we just got put on a list for junk mail⟩ — see DECEIVE

gullibility *n* readiness to believe the claims of others without sufficient evidence ⟨teased her about her well-known *gullibility* by repeatedly offering to sell her the Continental Divide⟩ — see CREDULITY

gullible *also* **gullable** *adj* readily taken advantage of ⟨he thought his grandmother was *gullible* simply because she was elderly, but she was sharper than he was in many ways⟩ — see EASY 2

gulp *n* the portion of a serving of a beverage that is swallowed at one time ⟨took a big *gulp* of water⟩ — see DRINK 2

gulp *vb* **1** to swallow in liquid form ⟨hastily *gulping* down the last of her tea before rushing out the door⟩ — see DRINK 1
2 to swallow or eat greedily ⟨you never taste your food—you just *gulp* it⟩ — see GOBBLE

gum (up) *vb* to prevent passage through by filling with something ⟨arteries *gummed up* with atheromas⟩ — see CLOG 1

gumbo *n* an unorganized collection or mixture of various things ⟨drew his artistic inspiration from the city's rich *gumbo* of races and ethnicities⟩ — see MISCELLANY 1

gummy *adj* tending to adhere to objects upon contact ⟨the outside of the bottle was *gummy* with old dribbles of salad oil⟩ — see STICKY 1

gumption *n, chiefly dialect* the ability to make intelligent decisions especially in everyday matters ⟨that girl has no more *gumption* than a grasshopper and is likely to marry the first man who comes along⟩ — see COMMON SENSE

gumshoe *n* a person not on the police force who investigates criminal or illicit activity or searches for missing persons ⟨the suspicious wife paid a *gumshoe* to follow her husband⟩ — see DETECTIVE

gun *vb* to strike with a missile from a gun ⟨traded stories of the Wild West, when outlaws *gunned* men down in broad daylight and in cold blood⟩ — see SHOOT 3

gun *n* **1** a portable weapon from which a shot is discharged by gunpowder ⟨while her father preferred hunting with a crossbow, she preferred a *gun*⟩
synonyms arm, firearm, heat [*slang*], piece, small arm
related words derringer, forty-five (*or* .45), gat [*slang*], handgun, pistol, revolver, rod [*slang*], roscoe [*slang*], sidearm, six-gun, six-shooter, zip gun; self-loader, semiautomatic; blunderbuss, breechloader, culverin, fieldpiece, firelock, flintlock, harquebus (*or* arquebus), matchlock, musket, rifle, shotgun, smoothbore, twenty-two (*or* .22); AK-47, assault rifle, assault weapon, automatic, carbine, machine gun, machine pistol, repeater, submachine gun, tommy gun; speargun
2 guns *pl* large firearms (as cannon or rockets) ⟨the field commander called for the big *guns* to be deployed for the full-scale assault⟩ — see ARTILLERY

gung ho *adj* showing urgent desire or interest ⟨he was *gung ho* about his accounting class⟩ — see EAGER

gunk *n* foul matter that mars the purity or cleanliness of something ⟨I have to wash my hands; I got *gunk* all over them somehow⟩ — see FILTH 1

gurgle *vb* to flow in a broken irregular stream ⟨the tiny stream *gurgled* down the rocky slope and joined the larger river at the bottom of the hill⟩
synonyms bubble, dribble, guggle, lap, plash, ripple, splash, trickle, wash
related words eddy, purl, swirl; swash, swish, swoosh, whish; drip, drop; gush, jet, rush, spew, spout, spurt, squirt
near antonyms run
antonyms pour, roll, stream

guru *n* **1** a person with a high level of knowledge or skill in a field ⟨one of those weather *gurus* that the television networks always drag out whenever there's a big blizzard brewing⟩ — see EXPERT
2 one who brings an art or science to full realization ⟨the leading *guru* of electronic music in the 1960s⟩ — see EXPONENT 2

gush *n* **1** a flowing or going out ⟨the dam burst with a stupendous *gush* of water⟩ — see OUTFLOW
2 a sudden intense expression of strong feeling ⟨with his customary *gush* of tears, he once again begged his long-suffering wife to stay⟩ — see OUTBURST 1

gush *vb* **1** to flow out in great quantities or with force ⟨the dam cracked and water *gushed* from the break⟩
synonyms jet, pour, rush, spew, spout, spurt, squirt, swoosh
related words cascade, issue, roll, run, stream; plash, slosh, splash, wash; surge, swell; flush, sluice; deluge, drown, engulf, flood, inundate, overflow, overwhelm, submerge, submerse, swamp; fountain
near antonyms spatter, sprinkle; bleed, exude, leak, ooze, percolate, seep, strain, weep
antonyms dribble, drip, drop, trickle
2 to make an exaggerated display of affection or enthusiasm ⟨he *gushed* about his favorite basketball player, calling him "the best there ever was"⟩
synonyms drool, effuse, enthuse, fuss, rave, rhapsodize, slobber
related words dote (on), fawn; emote

gushing *adj* **1** overly or insincerely flattering ⟨heaped disgustingly *gushing* praise on her boss's very modest singing skills⟩ — see FULSOME 1
2 pouring forth in great amounts ⟨the *gushing* water from the opened fire hydrant reduced water pressure to a dangerous level⟩ — see PROFUSE

gushy *adj* overly or insincerely flattering ⟨a *gushy* review of a novel by an author who just happened to be a friend of the critic⟩ — see FULSOME 1

gussy up *vb* to make more attractive by adding something that is beautiful or becoming ⟨gone are the days when the high school prom was held in the gym, which had been *gussied up* for the occasion⟩ — see DECORATE

gust *n* **1** a sudden brief rush of wind ⟨a *gust* tore her umbrella from her grip and blew it down the street⟩
synonyms blast, blow, flurry, scud, williwaw, windblast
related words breeze, zephyr; current, draft; air, breath, waft; puff, whiff; bluster, gale, hurricane, squall, tempest, tornado, windstorm; northeaster, norther, northerly, northwester, southeaster, southwester, westerly
2 a sudden intense expression of strong feeling ⟨the stressed-out coworker cried out with a *gust* of emotion that we had never witnessed before⟩ — see OUTBURST 1

gusto *n* active strength of body or mind ⟨I don't have the *gusto* to go on a strenuous hike right now⟩ — see VIGOR 1

gusty *adj* marked by strong wind or more wind than usual ⟨watch out for *gusty* conditions as the storm blows in⟩ — see [1]WINDY 1

gut *n* **1 guts** *pl* the internal organs of the body ⟨the student dissected the frog and looked at its *guts* with a mixture of fascination and disgust⟩
synonyms entrails, innards, inside(s), inwards, viscera, vitals
related words bowel(s), intestine(s); chitterlings (*or* chitlins), giblet(s), variety meat
2 guts *pl* strength of mind to carry on in spite of danger ⟨it took a lot of *guts* to rush into that burning building and save her cat⟩ — see COURAGE
3 guts *pl* the strength of mind that enables a person to endure pain or hardship ⟨had the *guts* to keep running the race even though she felt like quitting⟩ — see FORTITUDE
4 the part of the body between the chest and the pelvis ⟨eating too many french fries will result in a substantial *gut*⟩ — see STOMACH 1
5 an enlarged or bulging abdomen ⟨an ever-expanding *gut* was sorry evidence that she had been neglecting her workouts⟩ — see POTBELLY
6 the seat of one's deepest thoughts and emotions ⟨the film packs an emotional wallop that the viewer will feel in his *gut*⟩ — see CORE 1

gut *vb* to take the internal organs out of ⟨you'll need to *gut* the fish and wash it out before you can cook it⟩
synonyms clean, disembowel, draw, eviscerate
related words bone, dress; cut, excise, extract, remove, withdraw, yank; transplant

gutless *adj* having or showing a shameful lack of courage ⟨a *gutless* attack on a writer who is now deceased and unable to defend herself⟩ — see COWARDLY

gutlessness *n* a shameful lack of courage in the face of danger ⟨the unconscionable *gutlessness* shown by the school board when extremists called for banning certain literary classics from the library⟩ — see COWARDICE

gutsily *adv* in a fearless manner ⟨in her newspaper columns she *gutsily* took on the state's corrupt politicians⟩ — see BRAVELY 1

gutsiness *n* strength of mind to carry on in spite of danger ⟨it takes a certain *gutsiness* to take an unpopular position before a crowd of people⟩ — see COURAGE

gutsy *adj* **1** inclined or willing to take risks ⟨a *gutsy* coach willing to let her team improvise on the court⟩ — see BOLD 1
2 feeling or displaying no fear by temperament ⟨they were *gutsy* enough to attempt a rescue on their own⟩ — see BRAVE 1

gutter *adj* depicting or referring to sexual matters in a way that is unacceptable in polite society ⟨a novel that does a good job of rendering the *gutter* language of that stratum of society⟩ — see OBSCENE 1

gutter *n* **1** a pipe or channel for carrying off water from

a roof ⟨one of his chores is to clean leaves and sticks out of the *gutters* before winter sets in⟩
synonyms drainpipe, eaves trough, rainspout, spout, trough, waterspout
related words drain, flume, sluice; conduit, duct; aqueduct
2 a long narrow channel dug in the earth ⟨rainwater running off the road into the *gutters*⟩ — see DITCH

gutty *adj* feeling or displaying no fear by temperament ⟨standing up for what is right, especially if it's unpopular, is about the *guttiest* thing a person can do⟩ — see BRAVE 1

guy *n* **1** a member of the human race ⟨what would you *guys* like to order?⟩ — see HUMAN
2 an adult male human being ⟨was not the kind of *guy* she ever thought she'd date⟩ — see MAN 1

guzzle *vb* **1** to swallow in liquid form ⟨*guzzled* my soda before I could stop him⟩ — see DRINK 1
2 to partake excessively of alcoholic beverages ⟨teenagers sneaking out to *guzzle* in the woods⟩ — see DRINK 2

gym *n* a building or room used for sports activities and exercising ⟨he decided to get up early and go to the *gym* to lift weights⟩
synonyms gymnasium, health club, health spa, spa
related words arena, bowl, coliseum, colosseum, stadium

gymnasium *n* a building or room used for sports activities and exercising ⟨since it was raining, the kids had recess in the *gymnasium*⟩ — see GYM

gymnast *n* one who performs feats of physical strength, balance, and agility on special apparatus ⟨the years of training required to become a champion *gymnast*⟩ — see ACROBAT 1

gyp *vb* to rob by the use of trickery or threats ⟨*gypped* them into spending a fortune on counterfeit jewels, not real diamonds⟩ — see FLEECE

gyp *n* an instance of the use of dishonest methods to acquire something of value ⟨we were very disappointed when the "free weekend in Las Vegas" offer turned out to be a *gyp*⟩ — see FRAUD 1

gypsy *n* a person who roams about without a fixed route or destination ⟨a guitar-toting *gypsy*, the folk singer tours the country in an endless round of one-night gigs⟩ — see NOMAD

gyrate *vb* to move in circles around an axis or center ⟨the gyroscope got its name for the way the disk inside the instrument *gyrates* around an axis⟩ — see SPIN 1

gyration *n* a rapid turning about on an axis or central point ⟨dizzy from the spirally *gyrations* of the roller coaster⟩ — see SPIN 1

gyve *vb* to confine or restrain with or as if with chains ⟨a woman who was *gyved* by a fear of being alone in the world⟩ — see BIND 1

H

ha *or* **hah** *interj* how delightful ⟨*ha*! I was right all along!⟩ — see HOORAY

habiliment *n, usually* **habiliments** *pl* covering for the human body ⟨the lady's rich *habiliments* and haughty manner made the host's servants think she was someone important⟩ — see CLOTHING

habilitate *vb* to make better in behavior or character ⟨believes that society should be responsible for *habilitating* nonviolent offenders⟩ — see REFORM 1

habit *n* **1** a usual manner of behaving or doing ⟨it was his *habit* to rise early⟩
synonyms custom, fashion, habitude, pattern, practice (*also* practise), ritual, second nature, trick, way, wont
related words addiction; disposition; bent, inclination, proclivity, set, tendency, tenor, turn; bag, convention, form, mode, style; usage, use; deportment, manners, mores; drill, groove, jog trot, regime (*also* régime), regimen, rote, routine, rut; affectation, airs, pose; attribute, characteristic, mark, trait; eccentricity, kink, oddity, peculiarity, quirk, singularity, tic
2 a physiological need for certain drugs ⟨a cocaine *habit* of long standing⟩ — see ADDICTION
3 the type of body that a person has ⟨an imposing man of vigorous *habit*⟩ — see PHYSIQUE
4 *archaic* covering for the human body ⟨dressed in the *habit* of a knight from the golden age of chivalry⟩ — see CLOTHING

habit *vb* to outfit with clothes and especially fine or special clothes ⟨his exclusive clothing store had *habited* the town's upper crust for as long as anyone could remember⟩ — see CLOTHE 1

habitable *adj* suitable for living in ⟨the frigid Arctic is not *habitable* for amphibians and reptiles—or for humans, either, for that matter⟩ — see LIVABLE

habitant *n* one who lives permanently in a place ⟨the *habitants* of Indiana are nicknamed "Hoosiers"⟩ — see INHABITANT

habitat *n* the place where a plant or animal is usually or naturally found ⟨a forest in California is set aside to preserve the unique brushy, rugged *habitat* required by nesting California condors⟩ — see HOME 2

habitation *n* **1** the act or fact of residing in a place ⟨the city declared the area unsafe for *habitation* until it had been decontaminated⟩ — see OCCUPANCY
2 the place where one lives ⟨even though they spend most of their time at their condo in Florida, they still consider their farmhouse in Nebraska their permanent *habitation*⟩ — see HOME 1

habit-forming *adj* causing or relating to a physiological need for certain drugs ⟨warned the patient to be careful, because morphine can be *habit-forming*⟩ — see ADDICTIVE

habitual *adj* **1** being such by habit and not likely to change ⟨she admits she's an *habitual* procrastinator, but she still manages to meet all her deadlines⟩
synonyms bred-in-the-bone, chronic, confirmed, dyed-in-the-wool, inveterate
related words incorrigible, unreconstructed, unregenerate; born, natural; persistent, regular, repeat, serial, steady, unchanging, unfailing; addicted; accustomed, habituated, used, wonted; deep-rooted, deep-seated, entrenched (*also* intrenched), inbred, inherent, innate, intrinsic; apt, inclined, prone; mulish, obstinate, set, stubborn
near antonyms unaccustomed, unused; intermittent, occasional
2 appearing or occurring repeatedly from time to time ⟨her supervisor warned her that she could be fired for *habitual* tardiness⟩ — see REGULAR 1

habituate *vb* to go to or spend time in often ⟨the sort of lounge lizard known to *habituate* bars and nightclubs⟩ — see FREQUENT

habituated *adj* being in the habit or custom ⟨not only did the early-morning anchorman become *habituated* to getting up early, he found he actually liked it⟩ — see ACCUSTOMED

habitude *n* **1** a habitual attraction to some activity or thing ⟨a lifelong *habitude* for talking too much⟩ — see INCLINATION 1
2 a usual manner of behaving or doing ⟨contrary to his long-established *habitude*, he forwent his morning constitutional in favor of a leisurely breakfast⟩ — see HABIT 1

habitué *also* **habitue** *n* **1** a person with a strong and habitual liking for something ⟨confirmed *habitués* of the theater, they support serious dramas as well as comedies and musicals⟩ — see FAN
2 someone who regularly spends time in a particular place ⟨a confirmed *habitué* of the country club, she keeps tabs on who's having an affair⟩ — see DENIZEN 1

hacienda *n* a large impressive residence ⟨the sugar baron spared no expense in building a grand *hacienda* on his plantation near Cuernavaca⟩ — see MANSION

hack *adj* used or heard so often as to be dull ⟨the abrupt revelation of an enemy masquerading as a friend is such a *hack* plot twist⟩ — see STALE 1

[1]**hack** *n* **1** a V-shaped cut usually on an edge or a surface ⟨smallish *hacks* made in the bark of the trees marked the trail through the forest⟩ — see NOTCH 1
2 a hard strike with a part of the body or an instrument ⟨completely stunned by a vicious *hack* across the neck⟩ — see [1]BLOW

[2]**hack** *n* **1** an automobile that carries passengers for a fare usually determined by the distance traveled ⟨after a week of hailing *hacks* and inhabiting hotels, the sales rep was happy to be home⟩ — see TAXICAB
2 a person who lacks experience and competence in an art or science ⟨is he really any good at the piano or just a *hack*?⟩ — see AMATEUR 2

hack *vb* **1** to deal with (something) usually skillfully or efficiently ⟨I doubt that she can *hack* a job with so many responsibilities⟩ — see HANDLE 1
2 to put up with (something painful or difficult) ⟨she's not sure she can *hack* that miserable job much longer⟩ — see BEAR 2

hack (around) *vb* to spend time doing nothing ⟨would prefer to be put to work rather than spend his days at the ranch just *hacking around*⟩ — see IDLE

hack (off) *vb* to disturb the peace of mind of (someone) especially by repeated disagreeable acts ⟨people who ask blatantly stupid questions really *hack* me *off*⟩ — see IRRITATE 1

hacker *n* **1** a person who illegally gains access to a computer system and sometimes tampers with its information ⟨the company's security experts spent days trying to figure out how a *hacker* could have gotten past the firewall⟩
synonyms cracker, cyberpunk
related words computerist; gearhead, geek, propeller-

head, techie, technocrat, technophile; phisher
near antonyms computerphobe, technophobe
2 a person who lacks experience and competence in an art or science ⟨weekend golf *hackers* who are there mainly for the social networking⟩ — see AMATEUR 2

hackney *adj* used or heard so often as to be dull ⟨she quickly learned to ignore her children's *hackney* complaints like "It isn't fair" and "Why me?"⟩ — see STALE 1

hackney *vb* to use so much as to make less appealing ⟨advertisers have *hackneyed* the word "revolutionary" so much that it now just means that a product is new⟩
synonyms overexpose, overuse, stereotype, vulgarize
related words bore, exhaust, overdo; coarsen; deplete, jade, tire, wear out; popularize

hackneyed *adj* used or heard so often as to be dull ⟨it's *hackneyed*, but true—the more you save the more you earn⟩ — see STALE 1

haft *n* a part by which an implement is held ⟨the blade of the adze is still good, but the *haft* is broken and will have to be replaced⟩ — see HANDLE 1

hag *n* **1** a mean or ugly old woman ⟨although she looks like a *hag*, she's really the sweetest old lady you could ever hope to meet⟩ — see CRONE
2 a woman believed to have often harmful supernatural powers ⟨falsely accused of being a *hag* who had caused the plague⟩ — see WITCH 1

haggard *adj* suffering extreme weight loss as a result of hunger or disease ⟨the rescued hiker appeared *haggard* and worn after a week in the woods⟩ — see EMACIATED

haggle *vb* to talk over or dispute the terms of a purchase ⟨had to *haggle* to get his friend to sell his guitar for 20 bucks⟩ — see BARGAIN 1

hagiographic *also* **hagiographical** *adj* overly or insincerely flattering ⟨a *hagiographic* portrait of one of the pioneers of the automotive age⟩ — see FULSOME 1

hagride *vb* to trouble the mind of; to make uneasy ⟨*hagridden* by the specter of a terrorist attack, residents of the city were on edge⟩ — see DISTURB 1

[1]**hail** *n* **1** a heavy fall of objects ⟨a *hail* of small stones warned them of the oncoming avalanche⟩ — see RAIN 2
2 a rapid or overwhelming outpouring of many things at once ⟨even under the *hail* of angry questions, the press secretary stayed cool⟩ — see BARRAGE

[2]**hail** *n* range of hearing ⟨stay within *hail* of the restaurant's front desk so you'll know when your table is ready⟩ — see EARSHOT

hail *vb* **1** to declare enthusiastic approval of ⟨the museum director *hailed* the artist's new installation as a groundbreaking work of genius⟩ — see ACCLAIM
2 to demand or request the presence or service of ⟨let's *hail* a taxi⟩ ⟨*hailed* the waiter for the check⟩ — see SUMMON 1

hail–fellow *adj* having or showing kindly feeling and sincere interest ⟨has the *hail-fellow* manner of an automobile salesman with something up his sleeve⟩ — see FRIENDLY 1

hail–fellow–well–met *adj* having or showing kindly feeling and sincere interest ⟨a *hail-fellow-well-met* politician who genuinely enjoys pressing the flesh⟩ — see FRIENDLY 1

hair *n* **1** a very small distance or degree ⟨a race that was won by a *hair*⟩
synonyms ace, hairbreadth (*or* hairsbreadth), hairline, hop, skip, and jump, inch, neck, shouting distance, step, stone's throw
related words bit, crumb, dab, iota, jot, minim, mite, particle, smidgen (*also* smidgeon *or* smidgin *or* smidge), trace, trifle
near antonyms infinity, light-year
antonyms country mile, long haul, mile
2 a thin, flexible structure that resembles a hair ⟨discovered *hairs* on the plant's stem⟩
synonyms bristle, fiber, filament, thread
related words microfiber; cord, rope, string, wire, yarn; fuzz, tuft
3 the hairy covering of a mammal especially when fine, soft, and thick ⟨has no *hair*, but wears a wig⟩ ⟨a coat made of camel's *hair*⟩ — see FUR 1

hairbreadth *adj* showing little difference in the standing of the competitors ⟨a *hairbreadth* victory, but a victory nevertheless⟩ — see CLOSE 3

hairbreadth *or* **hairsbreadth** *n* a very small distance or degree ⟨just missed the bull's-eye by a *hairbreadth*⟩ — see HAIR 1

haircut *n* a style or arrangement of hair ⟨he hopes the new *haircut* will make him look more mature for the job interview⟩ — see HAIRDO

haircutter *n* a person who cuts and arranges hair ⟨my sister is a perfectly adequate *haircutter*, so I don't see why I should pay to go to some fancy salon⟩ — see HAIRDRESSER

hairdo *n* a style or arrangement of hair ⟨that *hairdo* makes her face look softer and rounder⟩
synonyms coiffure, cut, do, haircut, hairstyle
related words Afro, conk, cornrow, dreadlocks, perm, permanent; beehive, big hair, bun, chignon, French twist, pageboy, pug, updo, upsweep; bob, buzz cut, crew cut, crop, fade, Mohawk, shag, shingle, trim; braid, pigtail, plait, ponytail, queue; comb-over, ducktail, pompadour, roach

hairdresser *n* a person who cuts and arranges hair ⟨she recommended her *hairdresser* to a friend who wanted to get a perm⟩
synonyms barber, haircutter, hairstylist, stylist
related words beautician, coiffeur, coiffeuse, cosmetologist, trichologist

hairline *adj* **1** being of less than usual width ⟨a *hairline* crack in the mug, almost too small to notice, was enough to make the mug break when filled with hot tea⟩ — see NARROW 1
2 made or done with extreme care and accuracy ⟨a *hairline* distinction between her rating of certain things as "necessary" and others as "absolutely necessary"⟩ — see FINE 2
3 meeting the highest standard of accuracy ⟨an ultrasensitive telescope that requires *hairline* placement of the lenses⟩ — see PRECISE 1

hairline *n* a very small distance or degree ⟨the controversial measure passed by a *hairline*, the margin of victory being but a single vote⟩ — see HAIR 1

hairpiece *n* a headpiece made of natural or synthetic hair usually worn to cover a bald area ⟨if no one had told me he wore a *hairpiece*, I would have thought his hair was his own⟩
synonyms rug [*slang*], toupee, wig
related words fright wig; extension, fall, postiche, switch, wiglet

hair–raiser *n* something (as a close contest) that induces much suspense as to its outcome ⟨since they had been dating for five years, her answer to his proposal wasn't exactly a *hair-raiser*⟩ — see NAIL-BITER

hair–raising *adj* **1** causing fear ⟨*hair-raising* stories of headless corpses and disembodied screams⟩ — see FEARFUL 1
2 causing great emotional or mental stimulation ⟨a theme park that is legendary for its lightning-fast roller-coaster and other *hair-raising* rides⟩ — see EXCITING 1

hair shirt *n* something that is a source of irritation ⟨the constant need to cut costs was a *hair shirt*, but one that the theater company had to live with⟩ — see ANNOYANCE 3

hairsplitting *adj* made or done with extreme care and accuracy ⟨usage experts have attempted to make some *hairsplitting* distinctions between the two words, but most writers blithely ignore them⟩ — see FINE 2

hairstyle *n* a style or arrangement of hair ⟨the senator's long parade of *hairstyles* seem to reflect a relentless need to constantly reinvent herself⟩ — see HAIRDO

hairstylist *n* a person who cuts and arranges hair ⟨the *hairstylist* fashioned the model's hair into an elegant updo⟩ — see HAIRDRESSER

hairy *adj* **1** covered with or as if with hair ⟨a *hairy* spider⟩
synonyms bristly, brushy, cottony, fleecy, furred, furry, hirsute, rough, shaggy, silky, unshorn, woolly (*also* wooly)
related words bearded, bewhiskered, mustachioed (*also* moustachioed), whiskered; stubbled, stubbly; downy, fluffy, fuzzy, linty, nappy
near antonyms beardless, shaved, shaven
antonyms bald, furless, glabrous, hairless, shorn, smooth
2 made of or resembling hair ⟨found enough *hairy* clumps around the house to make another cat⟩ ⟨a *hairy* mass of fiberglass insulation⟩
synonyms furry, fuzzy, rough, shaggy, woolly (*also* wooly)
related words downy, fluffy, nappy, puffy; hairlike
3 requiring exceptional skill or caution in performance or handling ⟨landing on that airstrip is always a *hairy* proposition⟩ — see TRICKY 1
4 marked by or causing agitation or uncomfortable feelings ⟨the snowstorm made for a *hairy* commute back home that evening⟩ — see NERVOUS 2

halcyon *adj* **1** free from storms or physical disturbance ⟨a *halcyon* era following the American Civil War⟩ — see CALM 1
2 marked by vigorous growth and well-being especially economically ⟨during those early *halcyon* years the company's potential for growth seemed unlimited⟩ — see PROSPEROUS 1

hale *adj* enjoying health and vigor ⟨still *hale* and strong at 80, often outdoing his younger golfing buddies⟩ — see HEALTHY 1

hale *vb* to cause to follow by applying steady force on ⟨the fishermen *haled* the huge net onto the deck of the ship⟩ — see PULL 1

half *adj* lacking some necessary part ⟨*half* measures that did nothing but prolong the problem⟩ — see INCOMPLETE

half *adv* **1** in any way or respect ⟨this cut on your arm isn't *half* as bad as it looks⟩ — see AT ALL
2 in some measure or degree ⟨what you said is only *half* true⟩ — see PARTLY

half *n* **1** one of two equal or nearly equal parts ⟨to be fair, we should each get *half* the pie⟩
synonyms moiety
related words halvers; hemisphere, meridian, semicircle; component, constituent, division, element, fraction, part, piece, portion, section, segment
near antonyms aggregate, sum, total, whole
2 either of a pair matched in one or more qualities ⟨it's the bottom *half* of the ninth inning, and the Yankees are up at bat⟩ — see MATE 1

half-baked *adj* showing or marked by a lack of good sense or judgment ⟨he's always got some *half-baked* "solution" to a difficult, complex problem⟩ — see FOOLISH 1

halfhearted *adj* showing little or no interest or enthusiasm ⟨a *halfhearted* attempt to clean the house before the arrival of the in-laws⟩ — see TEPID 1

half-pint *adj* of a size that is less than average ⟨one of those *half-pint* refrigerators that are designed for small apartments⟩ — see SMALL 1

half-pint *n* a person of no importance or influence ⟨when I called the company to complain, I was shuttled from one *half-pint* to the next⟩ — see NOBODY

halfway *adj* **1** lacking some necessary part ⟨when *halfway* measures, such as posting signs, failed to keep people off the property, a fence was erected⟩ — see INCOMPLETE
2 occupying a position equally distant from the ends or extremes ⟨by the time she had reached the *halfway* point, she was ready to quit the marathon⟩ — see MIDDLE 1

halfway *adv* in some measure or degree ⟨that was a *halfway* decent performance of a difficult piece⟩ — see PARTLY

half-wit *n* **1** a person who lacks good sense or judgment ⟨some *half-wit* had left the gate open, and all the sheep had gotten loose⟩ — see FOOL 1
2 a stupid person ⟨even a *half-wit* knows that ice cream melts if it's not in the freezer⟩ — see IDIOT

half-witted *adj* **1** not having or showing an ability to absorb ideas readily ⟨the young genius mastered calculus while his peers, who seemed *half-witted* in comparison, labored over basic addition and subtraction⟩ — see STUPID 1
2 showing or marked by a lack of good sense or judgment ⟨had the *half-witted* idea to try to swim across the raging river, and would have drowned if someone hadn't rescued him⟩ — see FOOLISH 1

half-world *n* a social sphere that exists outside of the mainstream ⟨the *half-world* of tattoo addicts who regard the body embellishments not merely as fashion statements but as works of art and fundamental expressions of personal identity⟩ — see NETHERWORLD

hall *n* **1** the entrance room of a building ⟨the dinner guests hung their coats in the *hall*⟩
synonyms entranceway, entry, entryway, foyer, hallway, lobby, vestibule
related words antechamber, anteroom, lounge, waiting room; door, doorway, entrance, portal, threshold
2 a typically long narrow way connecting parts of a building ⟨the bedroom is at the end of the *hall*⟩
synonyms concourse, corridor, gallery, hallway, passage, passageway
related words arcade, breezeway, cloister, loggia, piazza
3 a large room or building for enclosed public gatherings ⟨the concert *hall* was full⟩
synonyms amphitheater, arena, auditorium, garden, theater (*or* theatre)
related words arena theater, music hall, odeum, playhouse, theater-in-the-round; ballroom; lyceum; chamber, house, senate; cafetorium
4 a centrally located room in a building that serves as a gathering or waiting area or as a passageway into the interior ⟨from the main *hall* of the museum, turn left to see the ancient pottery collection and turn right to see the mummies⟩ — see FOYER 1
5 a large impressive residence ⟨Lord Plentiworth has opened his family's hereditary home, Richley *Hall*, to visitors on Tuesdays⟩ — see MANSION
6 a large, magnificent, or massive building ⟨on your right, you will see Parliament *Hall*, a splendid example of Georgian architecture⟩ — see EDIFICE 1

hallelujah *interj* how delightful ⟨*hallelujah*, the bank is approving our loan application⟩ — see HOORAY

hallmark *n* **1** a device, design, or figure used as an identifying mark ⟨the *hallmark* of the Primrose Pottery Works is the small rose emblem etched on each piece⟩ — see EMBLEM
2 something that sets apart an individual from others of the same kind ⟨regards kindness and gentleness as the *hallmarks* of a real man⟩ — see CHARACTERISTIC

hallow *vb* to make holy through prayers or ritual ⟨Lincoln's memorable words at the Gettysburg battlefield, "we cannot dedicate—we cannot consecrate—we cannot *hallow*—this ground"⟩ — see BLESS 1

hallowed *adj* **1** deserving honor and respect especially by reason of age ⟨the college's *hallowed* tradition of ringing the chapel bell one hundred times before commencement ceremonies⟩ — see VENERABLE 1

2 set apart or worthy of veneration by association with God ⟨a church erected on one of Christianity's most *hallowed* sites⟩ — see HOLY 2

3 not to be violated, criticized, or tampered with ⟨*hallowed* traditions that bind the present generation with all those that have gone before⟩ — see SACRED 1

hallowing *n* the act of making something holy through religious ritual ⟨the church's belief that the marriage ceremony is a *hallowing* of the union between a man and a woman⟩ — see CONSECRATION

hallucination *n* **1** a conception or image created by the imagination and having no objective reality ⟨were the voices real, or merely a *hallucination*?⟩ — see FANTASY 1

2 a false idea or belief ⟨the common *hallucination* that gluttony during the holiday season doesn't have consequences⟩ — see FALLACY 1

hallway *n* **1** a typically long narrow way connecting parts of a building ⟨the *hallway* between the bedroom and bathroom was strewn with toys⟩ — see HALL 2

2 the entrance room of a building ⟨visitors to the Georgian mansion are received in a handsomely proportioned *hallway* featuring an open staircase⟩ — see HALL 1

halo *n* **1** a special quality or impression associated with something ⟨the *halo* of unimpeachable honesty in which the politician had long basked⟩ — see AURA 1

2 an artistic rendering of radiant light around the head or body of a sacred personage ⟨a naturalistic depiction of Saint Peter that shows him as a humble fisherman and without the traditional *halo*⟩ — see AUREOLE

halt *n* **1** a point in a struggle where neither side is capable of winning or willing to give in ⟨negotiations are at a *halt*, with neither management nor the union budging on the issue of salary limits⟩ — see IMPASSE 1

2 the stopping of a process or activity ⟨gardening came to a *halt* during the week of solid rain⟩ — see END 1

[1]**halt** *vb* **1** to bring (something) to a standstill ⟨traffic was *halted* by the parade⟩

synonyms arrest, bring up, catch, check, draw up, fetch up, hold up, pull up, stall, stay, still, stop

related words baffle, balk, block, blockade, bottleneck, clog, dam, detain, hinder, hold, hold back, impede, obstruct, snag, stem; conclude, cut off, end, terminate; call, discontinue, suspend; choke off, rein (in), repress, squash, squelch, stanch (*or* staunch), stunt, suppress, turn back

near antonyms carry on, continue, follow through (with), keep (on), keep up, persist, run on; advance, fare, go along, march, move, proceed, progress, wend; actuate, budge, drive, goad, impel, propel, push, spur, stir

2 to bring (as an action or operation) to an immediate end ⟨the private eye abruptly *halted* his surveillance of the building upon being spotted by his subject⟩ — see STOP 1

3 to come to an end ⟨all filming *halted* when the star of the movie quit in a huff⟩ — see CEASE 1

[2]**halt** *vb* **1** to walk while favoring one leg ⟨even with her twisted ankle, she managed to *halt* along and complete her Walk for Peace⟩ — see LIMP 1

2 to show uncertainty about the right course of action ⟨she was often confused, *halting* between the responsibilities of her job and the demands of her home life⟩ — see HESITATE

hamadryad *n* a mythical goddess represented as a young girl and said to live outdoors ⟨the ancients believed that *hamadryads* adopted particular trees as their permanent dwelling places⟩ — see NYMPH 1

ham–fisted *adj* lacking or showing a lack of nimbleness in using one's hands ⟨that's a *ham-fisted* paint job if I ever saw one⟩ — see CLUMSY 1

ham–handed *adj* lacking or showing a lack of nimbleness in using one's hands ⟨much too *ham-handed* to use one of those tiny cell phones⟩ — see CLUMSY 1

hamlet *n* a small residential settlement ⟨she always longed to return to the quiet *hamlet* where she had been born⟩ — see VILLAGE

hammer *vb* **1** to shape with a hammer ⟨medieval artisans *hammered* brass into various bowls and trays, which they then embossed with elaborate designs⟩

synonyms beat, draw, forge, pound

related words chase, planish; fashion, form, knead, model, mold, pat, work; coin, mint, stamp; abate, boast, carve, chisel, cut, grave, hew, knap, sculpt, sculpture

2 to deliver a blow to (someone or something) usually in a strong vigorous manner ⟨*hammer* a nail⟩ ⟨*hammered* the ball for a home run⟩ — see HIT 1

3 to strike repeatedly ⟨tried *hammering* the door to wake them up⟩ ⟨the crops were *hammered* with hail⟩ — see BEAT 1

4 to criticize (someone) severely or angrily especially for personal failings ⟨the critics have long been *hammering* the stage actress for resorting to the same mixed bag of mannerisms over and over⟩ — see SCOLD

hammer–and–tongs *adj* marked by bursts of destructive force or intense activity ⟨the scuffle escalated into a *hammer-and-tongs* fight⟩ — see VIOLENT 1

hammered *adj, slang* being under the influence of alcohol ⟨college students regularly getting *hammered* at keggers⟩ — see DRUNK

hammerhead *n* a stupid person ⟨we despair of ever getting those *hammerheads* to buckle their seat belts without prodding⟩ — see IDIOT

hammer out *vb* to produce or bring about especially by long or repeated effort ⟨the city council *hammered out* new commercial development regulations with input from residents, business owners, and environmental activists⟩

synonyms carve (out), develop, forge, grind (out), thrash (out), work out, work up

related words churn out, crank out, turn out; cobble (together *or* up), throw up; compose, construct, craft, create, engineer, fabricate, fashion, form, frame, generate, manufacture, mint, model, shape, tailor; conceive, concoct, contrive, cook (up), devise, hatch, invent, originate; accomplish, achieve, bring off, carry out, effect

phrases bring forth

near antonyms demolish, destroy, dismantle, raze, tear down; ruin, undo, unmake, wreck

hammy *adj* given to or marked by attention-getting behavior suggestive of stage acting ⟨a *hammy* singer whose overwrought renditions of love songs just beg listeners to cry⟩ — see THEATRICAL 1

hamper *vb* to create difficulty for the work or activity of ⟨fallen branches *hampered* the hikers as they made their way along the narrow path⟩

synonyms clog, cramp, embarrass, encumber, fetter, handcuff, handicap, hinder, hobble, hog-tie, hold back, hold up, impede, inhibit, interfere (with), manacle, obstruct, shackle, short-circuit, stymie, tie up, trammel

related words balk, check, constrain, curb, rein, restrain; bind, chain, halter, leash, tether, tie; arrest, brake, delay, retain, retard; barricade, block, blockade, roadblock; bog (down), mire; choke, smother, stifle, strangle, suffocate; baffle, foil, frustrate, stump, thwart;

derail, disrupt, sabotage; muzzle, repress, suppress; confine, hedge (in), hem (in)
phrases cramp one's style, give a hard time
near antonyms clear, make way, open, unclog, unplug, unstop; free, liberate, release, untie; loosen, smooth; encourage, further, promote
antonyms aid, assist, facilitate, help

hams *n pl* the part of the body upon which someone sits ⟨after sitting on my *hams* all day, I could use a good workout⟩ — see BUTTOCKS

hamstring *vb* to render powerless, ineffective, or unable to move ⟨the downtown development committee claims that it's *hamstrung* by city ordinances protecting historic buildings⟩ — see PARALYZE 1

hamstrung *adj* **1** not producing the desired result ⟨several *hamstrung* attempts to reorganize the local parent-teacher association were made⟩ — see INEFFECTIVE 1
2 unable to act or achieve one's purpose ⟨*hamstrung* by recent congressional limitations on executive power, the president can do little in this situation⟩ — see POWERLESS

hand *n* **1** a certain way in which something appears or may be regarded ⟨on the one *hand*, you would have more storage space in a larger house, but on the other, you would have more rooms to heat⟩ — see ASPECT 1
2 a place, space, or direction away from or beyond a central point or line ⟨tall buildings rose on either *hand*⟩ ⟨nothing but wide open space on either *hand*⟩ — see SIDE 1
3 an arrow-shaped piece on a dial or scale for registering information ⟨both *hands* of the clock pointed to 12⟩ — see POINTER 1
4 one who works for another for wages or a salary ⟨the restaurant always hires several more *hands* for the busy summer season⟩ — see EMPLOYEE
5 the form or style of a particular person's writing ⟨writes with a flowing, old-fashioned *hand*⟩ — see HANDWRITING 1
6 *usually* **hands** *pl* the ability to direct the course of something ⟨the final decision is in your *hands*⟩ — see CONTROL 2
7 hands *pl* the fact or state of having (something) at one's disposal ⟨I'd like to get my *hands* on that vintage Cadillac convertible⟩ — see POSSESSION 1
8 an act or instance of helping ⟨the downstairs tenant gave us a *hand* getting the heavy dresser up the stairs⟩ — see HELP 1
9 a person with a high level of knowledge or skill in a field ⟨once she got her own place, the young woman showed that she was quite a *hand* at interior decoration⟩ — see EXPERT
10 a person's name written in their own handwriting often given to indicate awareness or consent ⟨the subpoena required a lawyer's *hand*⟩ — see SIGNATURE

hand *vb* **1** to put (something) into the possession of someone for use or consumption ⟨was happy to *hand* her grandmother's cookie recipes to the parish ladies to put in their cookbook⟩ — see FURNISH 2
2 to shift possession of (something) from one person to another ⟨the clerk *handed* her the receipt⟩ — see PASS 1
3 to put (something) into the possession or safekeeping of another ⟨*handed* me her bundles while she fished for her house keys⟩ — see GIVE 2

handbag *n* **1** a bag carried by hand and designed to hold a traveler's clothing and personal articles ⟨flies only with a *handbag* so he doesn't have to check his luggage⟩ — see TRAVELING BAG
2 a container for carrying money and small personal items ⟨her *handbag* is just big enough to hold her favorite photos and wallet⟩ — see PURSE

handbook *n* a book used for instruction in a subject ⟨a *handbook* of grammar⟩ — see TEXTBOOK

handcraft *n* an occupation requiring skillful use of the hands ⟨we learned about traditional *handcrafts* like barrel-making and leather-working at the colonial history museum⟩ — see CRAFT 1

handcrafted *adj* created by a hand process rather than by a machine ⟨bought a *handcrafted* wooden bowl at the arts and crafts fair⟩ — see HANDMADE

handcraftsman *n* a person whose occupation requires skill with the hands ⟨using traditional methods, the *handcraftsmen* at the small workshop fashion pieces of wood furniture that are really works of art⟩ — see ARTISAN

handcuff *n, usually* **handcuffs** *pl* something that physically prevents free movement ⟨the man reluctantly held out his wrists so the policeman could snap on *handcuffs*⟩ — see BOND 1

handcuff *vb* **1** to confine or restrain with or as if with chains ⟨wanted to take the trip, but was *handcuffed* by her responsibility to watch her ailing father⟩ — see BIND 1
2 to create difficulty for the work or activity of ⟨the fear that the new mandatory, standardized tests will *handcuff* the state's teachers, who will have to specifically tailor their lesson plans for the test⟩ — see HAMPER

handcuffed *adj* unable to act or achieve one's purpose ⟨*handcuffed* by a dearth of funding, the preservation society can do little but stand by as these historic structures deteriorate⟩ — see POWERLESS

handful *n* a small number ⟨only a *handful* of people signed up for the wintertime hike⟩ — see FEW

handgrip *n* **1** a part by which an implement is held ⟨the vegetable peeler has a no-slip *handgrip*⟩ — see HANDLE 1
2 the act or manner of holding ⟨the tube TV was so bulky that it was difficult for the movers to get a solid *handgrip* on it⟩ — see HOLD 1

handhold *n* the act or manner of holding ⟨she tried to maintain her tight *handhold* on the umbrella as the wind picked up⟩ — see HOLD 1

handicap *n* **1** a feature of someone or something that creates difficulty for achieving success ⟨her natural shyness was not a *handicap* when she played chess⟩ — see DISADVANTAGE 1
2 something that makes movement or progress difficult ⟨her uncomfortable shoes became a *handicap* on the walking tour of the city, as she often had to sit and rest her sore feet⟩ — see ENCUMBRANCE

handicap *vb* to create difficulty for the work or activity of ⟨the baseball player's small size did not *handicap* him in the least⟩ — see HAMPER

handicraft *n* an occupation requiring skillful use of the hands ⟨volunteers demonstrating early American *handicrafts*, such as blacksmithing, glassblowing, and weaving⟩ — see CRAFT 1

handicrafter *n* a person whose occupation requires skill with the hands ⟨an accomplished *handicrafter* who cards, spins, and weaves wool from the sheep she raises⟩ — see ARTISAN

handicraftsman *n* a person whose occupation requires skill with the hands ⟨a *handicraftsman* who makes custom birdhouses⟩ — see ARTISAN

handily *adv* without difficulty ⟨*handily* whipped up a fluffy meringue and spread it on the pie⟩ — see EASILY 1

hand in glove *or* **hand and glove** *adv* in or by combined action or effort ⟨as citizens we must work *hand in glove* with the local police to protect our children from sexual predators⟩ — see TOGETHER 2

handiwork *n* something produced by physical or intellectual effort ⟨proud of his *handiwork*, he was certain that the birdhouse would win first place in its category⟩ — see PRODUCT 1

handkerchief *n* **1** a scarf worn on the head ⟨tied a *handkerchief* around her head and set about cleaning out the dust-covered attic⟩ — see BANDANNA
2 a small, often square piece of material that is used for personal hygiene purposes ⟨usually dries her hands on her *handkerchief* when there are no towels available⟩ — see HANKIE

handle *n* **1** a part by which an implement is held ⟨was given a set a steak knives with wooden *handles*⟩
synonyms grip, haft, handgrip, helve
related words bar, handlebar; bail, bow, loop; hilt, shaft; crop, whipstock; broomstick
2 a word or combination of words by which a person or thing is regularly known ⟨likes to go by the *handle* "Champ"⟩ — see NAME 1
3 a descriptive or familiar name given instead of or in addition to the one belonging to an individual ⟨since it seemed decreed that every new firefighter have a *handle*, his was soon "Hulk"⟩ — see NICKNAME

handle *vb* **1** to deal with (something) usually skillfully or efficiently ⟨as host of a live TV talk show, she must *handle* any situation that comes up⟩
synonyms address, contend (with), cope (with), field, grapple (with), hack, manage, maneuver, manipulate, negotiate, play, swing, take, treat
related words engineer, finesse, jockey; bring off, carry off, carry out, get off, pull; command, direct, guide, steer; control, micromanage, regulate, run; react (to), respond (to)
phrases come to grips with, have a grip on
near antonyms botch, bungle, foozle, fumble, goof (up), louse up, mess (up), mishandle, muff, scamp
2 to behave toward in a stated way ⟨*handles* all requests professionally, even when customers are rude⟩ — see TREAT 1
3 to control the mechanical operation of ⟨learned how to *handle* basic woodworking power tools⟩ — see OPERATE 1
4 to look after and make decisions about ⟨she takes care of the flower beds, and he *handles* all the lawn care⟩ — see CONDUCT 1
5 to put up with (something painful or difficult) ⟨I can't *handle* much more of this foul weather⟩ — see BEAR 2
6 to be in charge of ⟨I'll be *handling* the team's workouts while the leader is on vacation⟩ — see BOSS 1

handless *adj* lacking or showing a lack of nimbleness in using one's hands ⟨she's far too *handless* to be good at needlework⟩ — see CLUMSY 1

handling *n* the act or activity of looking after and making decisions about something ⟨the *handling* of proper order in the courtroom is the job of the sergeant at arms⟩ — see CONDUCT 1

handmade *adj* created by a hand process rather than by a machine ⟨received a *handmade* sweater at the baby shower⟩
synonyms handcrafted, handwrought
related words homemade, man-made, manual; bespoke (*also* bespoken), crafted, custom-built, custom-made
near antonyms automatic, machined, mass-produced

handmaiden *also* **handmaid** *n* a female domestic servant ⟨the princess was intensely shy, and allowed only her *handmaiden* to enter her chambers⟩ — see MAID 1

hand out *vb* to give out (something) to appropriate individuals ⟨no system yet in place for *handing out* room assignments⟩ — see ADMINISTER 1

handover *n* the usually forced yielding of one's person or possessions to the control of another ⟨though the *handover* of my wallet was painful, it was better than getting shot by some trigger-happy punk⟩ — see SURRENDER

hand over *vb* **1** to give (something) over to the control or possession of another usually under duress ⟨the police officer ordered the suspect to *hand over* his weapons⟩ — see SURRENDER 1
2 to put (something) into the possession of someone for use or consumption ⟨in response to a desperate plea, we *handed over* all our extra blankets and pillows to the homeless shelter⟩ — see FURNISH 2
3 to put (something) into the possession or safekeeping of another ⟨*handed over* their valuables to the desk clerk, who put them in the hotel safe⟩ — see GIVE 2
4 to shift possession of (something) from one person to another ⟨*hand over* that screwdriver, will you please?⟩ — see PASS 1

handpick *vb* to decide to accept (someone or something) from a group of possibilities ⟨*handpicked* what she considered to be the cutest kitten from the litter⟩ — see CHOOSE 1

handpicked *adj* singled out from a number or group as more to one's liking ⟨the senator's *handpicked* campaign staff⟩ — see SELECT 1

hand running *adv, dialect* in succession without others coming in between ⟨worked on repairing the fencing for five days *hand running*⟩ — see CONSECUTIVELY

hands–down *adj* involving minimal difficulty or effort ⟨after all that worrying, the game for the championship turned out to be a *hands-down* win⟩ — see EASY 1

hands down *adv* **1** without any question ⟨she is *hands down* the most gifted musician in the class⟩ — see INDEED 1
2 without difficulty ⟨she'll win the dancing competition *hands down*⟩ — see EASILY 1

handsel *n* something given to someone without expectation of a return ⟨gave little *handsels* to their houseguests on New Year's Day⟩ — see GIFT 1

handsome *adj* **1** having or showing elegance ⟨the glass-topped table was a *handsome* addition to the room⟩ — see ELEGANT 1
2 of a size greater than average of its kind ⟨earns a *handsome* salary as senior vice president of the firm⟩ — see LARGE 1
3 very pleasing to look at ⟨a *handsome* man with finely chiseled features⟩ — see BEAUTIFUL 1
4 sufficiently large in size, amount, or number to merit attention ⟨real estate developers realized a *handsome* profit on that deal⟩ — see CONSIDERABLE 1

handsomely *adv* in a generous manner ⟨rewarded *handsomely* the kids who had found his lost dog⟩ — see WELL 2

handsomeness *n* **1** dignified or restrained beauty of form, appearance, or style ⟨a modern-style addition that detracts from the *handsomeness* of that neoclassic building⟩ — see ELEGANCE
2 the qualities in a person or thing that as a whole give pleasure to the senses ⟨she never had noticed his *handsomeness* until he got a more becoming haircut⟩ — see BEAUTY 1

hand–to–mouth *adj* less plentiful than what is normal, necessary, or desirable ⟨survived on a *hand-to-mouth* income that came from any odd job that he could find⟩ — see MEAGER

handworker *n* a person whose occupation requires skill with the hands ⟨it's hard to find a *handworker* to tailor clothes these days⟩ — see ARTISAN

handwringer *n* a person who is inclined to worry ⟨opponents of the nuclear power plant were dismissed as a bunch of *handwringers* who were standing in the way of progress⟩ — see NERVOUS NELLIE

handwriting *n* **1** the form or style of a particular person's writing ⟨she immediately recognized the *hand-*

writing on the envelope as that of her old college roommate⟩
synonyms hand, penmanship, script
related words cacography, hen scratch, hen track, scratch, scrawl, scribble; backhand, copperplate, cursive, print, running hand; autograph, John Hancock, John Henry, signature
2 writing done by hand ⟨the columnist laments the decline of fine *handwriting*, as so few people write letters by hand anymore⟩
synonyms calligraphy, longhand, manuscript, penmanship, script
related words lettering; phonography, shorthand, steno, stenography
antonyms print, type, typewriting

handwrought *adj* created by a hand process rather than by a machine ⟨ordered *handwrought* andirons for the fireplace in their restored 18th-century saltbox⟩ — see HANDMADE

handy *adj* **1** situated within easy reach ⟨keeps a box of tissue *handy* whenever she watches *Romeo and Juliet* on her home theater⟩ — see CONVENIENT
2 skillful with the hands ⟨*handy* with a needle and thread⟩ — see DEXTEROUS 1

handyman *n* a person who does general repairs or maintenance work ⟨hired a *handyman* to paint the porch, clean the gutters, and replace the broken window⟩
synonyms handyperson
related words jack-of-all-trades; doctor, mender, renovator, repairer; mechanic, repairman, serviceman, troubleshooter; tinkerer; do-it-yourselfer

handyperson *n* a person who does general repairs or maintenance work ⟨she's a real *handyperson* who can fix anything around the house⟩ — see HANDYMAN

hang *n* **1** a downward slope ⟨anyone foolish enough to ski that *hang* would end up with a broken neck⟩ — see DECLINE 3
2 the extent to which something hangs or dips below a straight line ⟨there's too much *hang* in the bunting on the parade float—nothing should be touching the ground⟩ — see SAG

hang *vb* **1** to place on an elevated point without support from below ⟨*hang* your coats on the coat rack in the hall⟩
synonyms dangle, sling, suspend, swing
related words hook, mount, pin, tack; drape, festoon, garland, string; extend (out), jut, project, stick out; overhang, protrude; cascade, depend, fall; balance, poise
2 to be determined by, based on, or subject (to) ⟨our plan to go to the amusement park has all been worked out; now it just *hangs* on the weather⟩ — see DEPEND 1
3 to be limp from lack of water or vigor ⟨as they neared the end of the long, hard march all but the most hardy were *hanging*, and some could barely put one foot in front of the other⟩ — see DROOP 1
4 to rest or move along the surface of a liquid or in the air ⟨*hanging* just above the horizon was a little pink cloud⟩ — see FLOAT 1
5 to find a basis ⟨that's very slim evidence upon which to *hang* a theory⟩ — see BASE

hang (around *or* out) *vb* **1** to come or be together as friends ⟨she still *hangs around* with her college roommate⟩ — see ASSOCIATE 1
2 to spend time doing nothing ⟨for my vacation I plan to rent a beach house and just *hang out*⟩ — see IDLE

hang (at) *vb* to go to or spend time in often ⟨most summer afternoons, we'd *hang at* the municipal pool for a few hours⟩ — see FREQUENT

hang (over) *vb* to remain poised to inflict harm, danger, or distress on ⟨as long as the possibility of having to move again was *hanging over* them, the family couldn't really settle in⟩ — see THREATEN

hang about *vb, British* **1** to spend time doing nothing ⟨a London slum where lots of unemployed young men could be seen *hanging about*⟩ — see IDLE
2 to spend time in aimless activity ⟨we'll be *hanging about* at the pub if you need us⟩ — see FIDDLE (AROUND)

hang around *vb* to continue to be in a place for a significant amount of time ⟨if you *hang around* until my husband gets home, you can meet him⟩ — see [1]STAY 1

hang back *vb* to show uncertainty about the right course of action ⟨even though the young mother wanted the job, she still *hung back* because she wasn't sure if she should spend time away from her family⟩ — see HESITATE

hangdog *adj* feeling unhappiness ⟨"Why do you look so *hangdog* today?" she asked⟩ — see SAD 1

hanger–on *n* a person who is supported by or seeks support from another without making an adequate return ⟨almost overnight, the singer was a star, and almost overnight, he was surrounded by *hangers-on* who wanted something⟩ — see LEECH

hanging *adj* **1** bending downward or forward ⟨*hanging* branches blocked our way for a good part of the trail⟩ — see NODDING
2 extending freely from a support from above ⟨light from a *hanging* chandelier filled the great hall⟩ — see DEPENDENT 1

hanging *n* a downward slope ⟨with a steep *hanging* like that, the roofers can't be too careful⟩ — see DECLINE 3

hangout *n* a place for spending time or for socializing ⟨a favorite *hangout* of the golden-agers is the local community center⟩
synonyms haunt, purlieu, rendezvous, resort, stamping ground, stomping ground
related words camp, canteen, club, clubhouse, country club, key club, service club, union; harbor, harborage, haven, nest, refuge, retreat, sanctuary

hang–up *n* a source of persistent emotional distress ⟨low self-esteem is only one of his many *hang-ups*⟩ — see DEMON 2

hanker (for *or* after) *vb* to have an earnest wish to own or enjoy ⟨*hankering for* some company in his lonely mountain cabin⟩ ⟨*hanker after* a life of leisure⟩ — see DESIRE 1

hankering *n* a strong wish for something ⟨I've had a *hankering* for pizza with anchovies all afternoon⟩ — see DESIRE 1

hankie *or* **hanky** *n* a small, often square piece of material that is used for personal hygiene purposes ⟨held a *hankie* up to his nose and blew vigorously⟩
synonyms handkerchief, kerchief
related words napkin, serviette [*chiefly British*], tissue, towel; bandanna (*or* bandana)

hanky–panky *n* the use of clever underhanded actions to achieve an end ⟨had to resort to a certain amount of *hanky-panky* to sneak away from the house without his dog seeing him⟩ — see TRICKERY

hant *n, dialect* the soul of a dead person thought of especially as appearing to living people ⟨those old ladies are so superstitious that they see *hants* everywhere⟩ — see GHOST 1

[1]**hap** *n* **1** something that happens ⟨we must make the best of both the good and the bad *haps* of life⟩ — see EVENT 1
2 the uncertain course of events ⟨by *hap* and circumstance, he ended up as a cartoonist in New York⟩ — see CHANCE 1

[2]**hap** *n, dialect* a decorative cloth used as a top covering for a bed ⟨the *hap* was a patchwork quilt that the old woman had made herself⟩ — see COUNTERPANE

hap *vb* to take place ⟨what wondrous events hath *happed* this Christmas Day?⟩ — see HAPPEN

haphazard *adj* lacking a definite plan, purpose, or pattern ⟨considering the *haphazard* way you measured the ingredients, it's a wonder the cookies came out this good⟩ — see RANDOM

haphazard *adv* without definite aim, direction, rule, or method ⟨shoes were tossed *haphazard* into the closet⟩ — see HIT OR MISS

haphazardly *adv* without definite aim, direction, rule, or method ⟨you should not begin writing *haphazardly*; first, make an outline⟩ — see HIT OR MISS

hapless *adj* having, prone to, or marked by bad luck ⟨the *hapless* motorist had barely paid his bill and driven away from the body shop when a truck sideswiped his car⟩ — see UNLUCKY 1

happen *vb* to take place ⟨did anything exciting *happen* over the summer?⟩
synonyms be, befall, betide, chance, come, come about, come down, come off, cook, do, go down [*slang*], go on, hap, occur, pass, transpire
related words break, develop, rise, shape (up); arise, come up, crop (up), materialize, spring (up); intervene; fall out, follow, result, turn out; go off, proceed
phrases come to pass

happen (on *or* upon) *vb* to come upon unexpectedly or by chance ⟨*happened on* the filming of a movie⟩
synonyms chance (upon), encounter, find, hit (upon), light (on *or* upon), meet, pitch (upon), stumble (on *or* onto), tumble (upon)
related words luck (out, on, onto, *or* into); confront, face; discover, strike, turn up
phrases bump into, come across, run across, run against, run into, run upon

happen (upon) *vb* to come upon face-to-face or as if face-to-face ⟨*happened upon* the hotel manager in the lobby and promptly complained about the room⟩ — see MEET 1

happening *adj* **1** being in the latest or current fashion ⟨those are some *happening* duds, man⟩ — see STYLISH
2 marked by much life, movement, or activity ⟨the downtown theater district is a *happening* place this autumn⟩ — see ALIVE 2
3 enjoying widespread favor or approval ⟨that might be a *happening* outfit right now, but not on a woman who'll never see 40 again⟩ — see POPULAR 1

happening *n* **1** an exciting or noteworthy event that one experiences firsthand ⟨the President's visit to the school was a real *happening* for teachers and students alike⟩ — see ADVENTURE 1
2 something that happens ⟨gave a detailed account of all the *happenings* of the weekend⟩ — see EVENT 1

happily *adv* **1** in a cheerful or happy manner ⟨*happily* accepted the invitation to dinner⟩ — see GAILY 1
2 in a manner suitable for the occasion or purpose ⟨one of those rare occasions on which business and pleasure *happily* mixed⟩ — see PROPERLY

happiness *n* **1** a feeling or state of well-being and contentment ⟨her *happiness* was complete when she got her very own house⟩
synonyms beatitude, blessedness, bliss, blissfulness, felicity, gladness, joy, warm fuzzies
related words elatedness, elation, exhilaration, exultation, high, intoxication; ecstasy, euphoria, glory, heaven, nirvana, paradise, rapture, rapturousness, ravishment, seventh heaven, transport; delectation, delight, enjoyment, pleasure; cheer, cheerfulness, comfort, exuberance, gaiety (*also* gayety), gladsomeness, glee, gleefulness, jocundity, jollity, joyfulness, joyousness, jubilance, jubilation, lightheartedness, merriness, mirth; content, contentedness, gratification, satisfaction, triumph
near antonyms agony, anguish, desolation, joylessness, sorrow, sufferance, woe, woefulness; blues, cheerlessness, dejection, depression, desolateness, despondency, disheartenment, dispiritedness, doldrums, downheartedness, gloom, gloominess, melancholy, mournfulness, plaintiveness; Gehenna, hell, purgatory
antonyms calamity, ill-being, misery, sadness, unhappiness, wretchedness
2 the feeling experienced when one's wishes are met ⟨finally found true *happiness* as a doctor in a poor rural area⟩ — see PLEASURE 1
3 the quality or state of being especially suitable or fitting ⟨the striking *happiness* of the phrase "fatal attraction" as the title for an erotic thriller⟩ — see APPROPRIATENESS

happy *adj* **1** coming or happening by good luck especially unexpectedly ⟨a *happy* discovery, finding the letter that would prove her innocence⟩ — see FORTUNATE 1
2 experiencing pleasure, satisfaction, or delight ⟨made bread for the first time and was *happy* with the tasty result⟩ — see GLAD 1
3 feeling that one's needs or desires have been met ⟨has been much *happier* ever since she moved⟩ — see CONTENT
4 having good luck ⟨the *happy* person who is both appreciated and rewarded for all his hard work⟩ — see LUCKY 1
5 meeting the requirements of a purpose or situation ⟨the wine was a *happy* complement to such a fine meal⟩ — see FIT 1
6 having extreme or relentless concern ⟨poll-*happy* pundits just care about which political candidate is winning, and never about the issues⟩ — see HUNG UP 1

happy–go–lucky *adj* **1** having a relaxed, casual manner ⟨he is completely *happy-go-lucky* on fishing trips—if he catches something, fine; if he doesn't, that's fine, too⟩ — see EASYGOING 1
2 having or showing freedom from worries or trouble ⟨went on her *happy-go-lucky* way, totally unaware that she was strewing litter behind her⟩ — see CAREFREE

harangue *n* **1** a long angry speech or scolding ⟨launched into a long *harangue* about poor customer service without realizing that I wasn't even an employee!⟩ — see TIRADE
2 a usually formal discourse delivered to an audience ⟨the dictator's lengthy *harangue* before a captive audience⟩ — see SPEECH 1

harangue *vb* **1** to give a formal often extended talk on a subject ⟨the eminent professor *harangued* for three hours on his favorite subject, the clash of East and West⟩ — see TALK 1
2 to talk as if giving an important and formal speech ⟨a talk-show guest using the interviewer's questions as an opportunity to *harangue* on a variety of pet peeves⟩ — see ORATE 1

harass *vb* to use up all the physical energy of ⟨had been visibly *harassed* by the demands of the presidency⟩ — see EXHAUST 1

harasser *n* a person who causes repeated emotional pain, distress, or annoyance to another ⟨the firm takes the issue of sexual harassment very seriously, and *harassers* are harshly disciplined⟩ — see TORMENTOR

harassment *n* the act of making unwelcome intrusions upon another ⟨he owes her a lot of money, so he shouldn't be surprised at her constant *harassment* for a repayment⟩ — see ANNOYANCE 1

harbinger *n* one that announces or indicates the later arrival of another ⟨her father's successful job interview was seen as a *harbinger* of better times to come⟩ — see FORERUNNER 1

harbinger *vb* to give a slight indication of beforehand

⟨the hope that the housing slump does not *harbinger* a general economic recession⟩ — see FORESHADOW

harbor *n* **1** a part of a body of water protected and deep enough to be a place of safety for ships ⟨the tanker stayed in Boston *harbor* three days to undergo repairs⟩
synonyms anchorage, harborage, haven, port
related words basin, dock, marina, moorage, mooring; arm, bay, bight, cove, creek [*chiefly British*], embayment, estuary, firth, fjord (*also* fiord), gulf, inlet, lagoon, loch [*Scottish*], lough [*chiefly Irish*], narrow, roads, roadstead; canal, channel, sound, strait; containerport, home port, seaport
2 something (as a building) that offers cover from the weather or protection from danger ⟨seeking a *harbor* from the drenching rain, we unfortunately chose a bank where a robbery was taking place⟩ — see SHELTER

harbor *vb* **1** to keep in one's mind or heart ⟨he had long *harbored* a grudge against his old employer, who had high-handedly fired him without cause⟩
synonyms bear, cherish, entertain, have, hold, nurse
related words cultivate, foster, nurture, support, sustain; carry, keep, maintain, preserve, remember, retain, treasure; cleave (to), cling (to), hug, stick (to); brood (about *or* over), fixate (on *or* upon), obsess (about *or* over)
phrases hang on to, hold on to
near antonyms disregard, drop, forget, ignore, neglect, overlook; abjure, decline, deny, disdain, refuse, reject, repudiate, scorn; abandon, desert, discard, forsake, give up, part (with), quit, renounce, throw out; erase, expunge
2 to provide with living quarters or shelter ⟨the woods in our suburb *harbor* deer, foxes, raccoons, and skunks⟩ — see HOUSE 1
3 to be or provide a shelter for ⟨the little cabin is *harbored* from the wind by a thick growth of pines⟩ — see SHELTER 1

harborage *n* **1** a part of a body of water protected and deep enough to be a place of safety for ships ⟨the city boasts one of the best deepwater *harborages* on the Atlantic coast⟩ — see HARBOR 1
2 something (as a building) that offers cover from the weather or protection from danger ⟨the only *harborage* from the storm was a lone pine tree, which looked like it could get hit by lightning any minute⟩ — see SHELTER

hard *adj* **1** having or showing a lack of sympathy or tender feelings ⟨a *hard* man, who never had a kind word for anyone⟩
synonyms affectless, callous, case-hardened, cold-blooded, compassionless, desensitized, hard-boiled, hard-hearted, heartless, indurate, inhuman, inhumane, insensate, insensitive, ironhearted, merciless, obdurate, pachydermatous, pitiless, remorseless, ruthless, slash-and-burn, soulless, stony (*also* stoney), stonyhearted, take-no-prisoners, thick-skinned, uncharitable, unfeeling, unmerciful, unsparing, unsympathetic
related words boorish, heedless, inconsiderate, thoughtless, uncaring, unfriendly, unloving, unthinking; grim, hard-bitten, harsh, heavy-handed, ironfisted, ironhanded, jackbooted, knock-down, drag-out (*or* knock-down-and-drag-out), oppressive, rough, rough-and-tumble, severe, sledgehammer, stern, tough, ungentle; abusive, acrimonious, disagreeable, hateful, ill-natured, ill-tempered, malevolent, malicious, mean, rancorous, spiteful, surly, virulent; barbarous, bestial, brutal, brutish, cruel, evil-minded, savage, vicious; austere, cold, frosty
near antonyms benevolent, benignant, gentle, kind; clement, indulgent, lenient, mild; cordial, friendly, good-natured, good-tempered, gracious; tolerant, understanding; affectionate, fond, loving
antonyms charitable, compassionate, humane, kindhearted, kindly, merciful, sensitive, softhearted, sympathetic, tender, tenderhearted, warm, warmhearted
2 requiring considerable physical or mental effort ⟨clearing land is *hard* work⟩ ⟨a *hard* exam to pass⟩
synonyms arduous, Augean, backbreaking, challenging, demanding, difficult, effortful, exacting, formidable, grueling (*or* gruelling), heavy, hellacious, herculean, killer, laborious, moiling, murderous, pick-and-shovel, rigorous, rough, rugged, severe, stiff, strenuous, sweaty, tall, testing, toilsome, tough, uphill
related words abstract, abstruse, complex, complicated, elusive, hairy, insoluble, intricate, involved, knotty, opaque, problematic (*also* problematical), recondite, serious, spiny, stubborn, thorny, ticklish, tricky; bruising, burdensome, exhausting, labored, onerous, oppressive, stressful, taxing, tight, trying; annoying, bothersome, distressing, irksome, troublesome, vexatious; grievous, grim, strict, stringent; brutal, cruel, inhuman, painful
near antonyms achievable, clear, doable, elementary, manageable, uncomplicated; comforting, gentle, painless, relaxed, smooth, soothing; accessible, friendly, idiotproof, user-friendly
antonyms cheap, easy, effortless, facile, light, mindless, simple, soft, undemanding
3 able to withstand hardship, strain, or exposure ⟨they were forced to import sheep of a *harder* stock, one that could thrive in the harsh climate⟩ — see HARDY 1
4 based on sound reasoning or information ⟨do you have any *hard* evidence that this was once the site of a Native American village?⟩ — see GOOD 1
5 difficult to endure ⟨the *hard* life of a migrant farm worker⟩ — see HARSH 1
6 extreme in degree, power, or effect ⟨a carpet that withstood years of *hard* wear⟩ — see INTENSE 1
7 given to exacting standards of discipline and self-restraint ⟨a *hard* disciplinarian who is quick to punish the tiniest violation of the rules⟩ — see SEVERE 1
8 having a consistency that does not easily yield to pressure ⟨*hard* candies⟩ ⟨fell on the *hard* floor and bruised her arm⟩ — see FIRM 2
9 having been established and usually not subject to change ⟨there isn't always a *hard* line between right and wrong⟩ — see FIXED 1
10 having or showing deep-seated resentment ⟨maintained *hard* feelings toward those who had cheated him⟩ — see BITTER 1
11 sticking to an opinion, purpose, or course of action in spite of reason, arguments, or persuasion ⟨a woman with a *hard* will who never budged from her chosen path⟩ — see OBSTINATE
12 restricted to or based on fact ⟨that newscast is strictly devoted to *hard* news, as the producers prefer to leave the gossip to others⟩ — see FACTUAL 1

hard *adv* **1** with great effort or determination ⟨we took a much-needed break after working *hard* all week⟩ ⟨a *hard*-won victory⟩
synonyms amain, arduously, assiduously, determinedly, diligently, doggedly, hardly, industriously, intensely, intensively, intently, laboriously, mightily, purposefully, resolutely, sedulously, slavishly, strenuously
related words actively, animatedly, briskly, busily, dynamically, energetically, feverishly, spiritedly, vehemently, vigorously, zealously; continuously, ploddingly, steadfastly, steadily, unabatedly, unrelentingly, unremittingly; ardently, attentively, conscientiously, earnestly, exhaustively, meticulously, painstakingly, seriously, thoroughly; indefatigably, tirelessly, unflaggingly, untiringly, wearilessly; obstinately, stubbornly, willfully

near antonyms casually, desultorily, halfheartedly, indolently, lackadaisically, languidly, lazily, listlessly, shiftlessly, sluggishly, spiritlessly, tiredly, wearily
2 with feelings of bitterness or grief ⟨took the news of their grandfather's death *hard*⟩
synonyms agonizingly, bitterly, dolefully, dolorously, grievously, hardly, inconsolably, lugubriously, mournfully, painfully, plaintively, regretfully, resentfully, ruefully, sadly, sorely, sorrowfully, unhappily, wailfully, woefully, wretchedly
related words abjectly, cheerlessly, crestfallenly, dejectedly, despairingly, despondently, disconsolately, dispiritedly, downheartedly, low-spiritedly; blackly, darkly, dismally, distressfully, distressingly, dourly, drearily, forlornly, gloomily, glumly, joylessly, mirthlessly, miserably, morosely, pessimistically, somberly, sullenly; acutely, harshly, keenly, piercingly, poignantly, severely, sharply; cruelly, hurtfully, ill, rancorously
near antonyms cheerfully, cheerily, delightedly, gaily (*also* gayly), gleefully, good-naturedly, lightheartedly, merrily, mirthfully, rejoicingly, sunnily; blithely, blithesomely, calmly, casually, dispassionately, easily, impassively, indifferently, lightly, nonchalantly, stoically, unconcernedly; favorably, well
antonyms blissfully, gladly, happily, joyfully, joyously
3 in a vigorous and forceful manner ⟨hit the ball *hard*, causing it to soar out of bounds⟩ ⟨the wind blew *hard* all day⟩
synonyms dynamically, energetically, explosively, firmly, forcefully, forcibly, mightily, muscularly, powerfully, roundly, stiffly, stoutly, strenuously, strongly, sturdily, vigorously
related words fiercely, hammer and tongs, robustly, roughshod, sharply, vehemently, violently; actively, animatedly, briskly, crisply, eagerly, gamely, heartily, lustily, snappily, spiritedly, spunkily, vivaciously; decidedly, determinedly, directly, emphatically, fast, fixedly, intensively, intently, purposefully, resolutely, rigidly, smartly, solidly, soundly, squarely, steadfastly, steadily, sturdily, surely; aggressively, assertively, manfully, potently
phrases like gangbusters, to beat the band, with a vengeance, with might and main
near antonyms delicately, faintly, frailly, shakily; bloodlessly, halfheartedly, languidly, lazily, listlessly, spiritlessly; impotently, ineffectively, ineffectually, lamely, nervelessly, spinelessly, uncertainly
antonyms feebly, gently, softly, weakly
4 at, within, or to a short distance or time ⟨the groom stood *hard* by, ready to help, as the lady mounted the skittish horse⟩ — see NEAR 1
5 in a manner so as to cause loss or suffering ⟨the dog had been treated *hard* by his previous owner⟩ — see HARDLY 1

hard–and–fast *adj* **1** having been established and usually not subject to change ⟨*hard-and-fast* rules that governed the corporate environment in those days included strictures regarding office dress that were rigidly enforced⟩ — see FIXED 1
2 not capable of changing or being changed ⟨*hard-and-fast* beliefs that are the rock-solid foundation of their religion⟩ — see INFLEXIBLE 1

hard–bitten *adj* able to withstand hardship, strain, or exposure ⟨a *hard-bitten* Apache chief who could endure the scorching heat of the Arizona desert⟩ — see HARDY 1

hard–boiled *adj* **1** having or showing a lack of sympathy or tender feelings ⟨a *hard-boiled* Puritan schoolmaster who was as unyielding as New England granite⟩ — see HARD 1
2 having or showing a practical cleverness or judgment ⟨made the *hard-boiled* business decision to downsize the company, thereby costing thousands of longtime employees their jobs⟩ — see SHREWD 1

hard–core *adj* firmly established over time ⟨the *hard-core* habits that generate our mountains of trash every-day will be extremely difficult to change⟩ — see INVETERATE 1

hard–driving *adj* having a strong desire for personal advancement ⟨she's the most *hard-driving* malpractice lawyer I've ever seen⟩ — see AMBITIOUS 1

harden *vb* **1** to become physically firm or solid ⟨the glue begins to *harden* as soon as it is exposed to air⟩
synonyms concrete, congeal, firm (up), freeze, indurate, set, solidify
related words cake, callus, encrust (*also* incrust); clot, coagulate, gel, gelate, gelatinize, jell, jelly, stiffen, thicken; calcify, crystallize (*also* crystalize), ossify, petrify, rigidify; anneal, case-harden, temper
near antonyms deliquesce, dissolve, flux, fuse, melt, smelt, thaw, unfreeze
antonyms liquefy (*also* liquify), soften
2 to make able to withstand physical hardship, strain, or exposure ⟨pioneer women who had been *hardened* by years of living on the plains⟩
synonyms fortify, indurate, inure, season, steel, strengthen, toughen
related words acclimate, acclimatize, adapt, adjust; anneal, temper; invigorate, vitalize; immunize; bolster, boost, brace, buttress, enforce, forearm, prop (up), reinforce (*also* reenforce), support; break in, limber (up), train; accustom, condition, habituate, naturalize
near antonyms emasculate, enervate, enfeeble, exhaust, sap, weaken; cripple, debilitate, hamstring, incapacitate; sensitize
antonyms soften
3 to increase the ability of (as a muscle) to exert physical force ⟨arm muscles that were *hardened* by all the years of casting and hauling his fishing nets⟩ — see STRENGTHEN 1
4 to make more harsh, uncompromising, or severe ⟨the government *hardened* restrictions on travel to and from the war-torn nation⟩ — see HARSHEN

hardened *adj* **1** able to withstand hardship, strain, or exposure ⟨*hardened* from years of deprivation and grief, the man regarded the house fire as just another misfortune in a life filled with them⟩ — see HARDY 1
2 sticking to an opinion, purpose, or course of action in spite of reason, arguments, or persuasion ⟨*hardened* cynics regarded those TV shows as being anything but reality-based⟩ — see OBSTINATE

hard–eyed *adj* lacking in friendliness or warmth of feeling ⟨stared back at the prisoner with a *hard-eyed* glint⟩ — see COLD 2

hardhanded *adj* difficult to endure ⟨the *hardhanded* rule of a tyrannical regime⟩ — see HARSH 1

hardhead *n* a stupid person ⟨a *hardhead* who has to learn every life lesson the hard way⟩ — see IDIOT

hardheaded *adj* **1** having or showing a practical cleverness or judgment ⟨a *hardheaded* politician who never hesitated to set aside principle in favor of expediency⟩ — see SHREWD 1
2 sticking to an opinion, purpose, or course of action in spite of reason, arguments, or persuasion ⟨Granny remained *hardheaded* about keeping her house and not moving into a nursing home⟩ — see OBSTINATE
3 willing to see things as they really are and deal with them sensibly ⟨a *hardheaded* minister who understands the difficulties teenagers face today⟩ — see REALISTIC 1

hardheadedness *n* **1** a steadfast adherence to an opinion, purpose, or course of action in spite of reason, arguments, or persuasion ⟨her unrelenting *hardheadedness* didn't win many friends, but it helped her to get her way most of the time⟩ — see OBSTINACY

2 exceptional discernment and judgment especially in practical matters ⟨the *hardheadedness* of a bean counter⟩ — see ACUMEN

hard–hearted *adj* having or showing a lack of sympathy or tender feelings ⟨a *hard-hearted* brush-off to a homeless man asking for money⟩ — see HARD 1

hardihood *n* **1** active strength of body or mind ⟨the 80-year-old grandmother attributes her *hardihood* to having eaten a cup of yogurt every day for the past 50 years⟩ — see VIGOR 1

2 strength of mind to carry on in spite of danger ⟨the explorers were driven by an almost reckless *hardihood* in the face of the unknown⟩ — see COURAGE

hard–line *adj* not allowing for any exceptions or loosening of standards ⟨a *hard-line* approach to the sentencing of repeat offenders⟩ — see RIGID 1

hard–luck *adj* having, prone to, or marked by bad luck ⟨a *hard-luck* ball club that never could get the breaks it needed⟩ — see UNLUCKY 1

hardly *adv* **1** in a manner so as to cause loss or suffering ⟨the new judge vowed to deal *hardly* with repeat offenders⟩

synonyms brutally, hard, harshly, ill, oppressively, roughly, severely, sternly, stiffly

related words callously, cold-bloodedly, heartedly, heartlessly, inhumanely, inhumanly, insensately, insensitively, mercilessly, obdurately, pitilessly, ruthlessly, tyrannically, uncharitably, unfeelingly, unmercifully, unsparingly; abusively, brutishly, savagely, viciously; aggressively, assertively, decidedly, determinedly, firmly, grimly, gruffly, resolutely, strongly, toughly

near antonyms benevolently, benignantly, considerately, cordially, graciously, kindly, lovingly, tenderly; charitably, compassionately, humanely, mercifully, softheartedly, sympathetically, tolerantly, understandingly

antonyms clemently, gently, leniently, lightly, mildly, softly

2 certainly not ⟨I would *hardly* think someone with her attitude could make a good manager⟩

synonyms ill, no, none, no way, scarcely

related words near, never, nothing, nowhere, nowise

phrases by no means, nothing doing, on no account

near antonyms awful, awfully, enormously, exceedingly (*also* exceeding), extremely, greatly, highly, hugely, immensely, mightily, mighty, most, quite, terribly, very; assuredly, clearly, hands down, perfectly, plainly, really, truly, unequivocally, unquestionably, utterly; doubtless, more or less, mostly, rather, slightly, somewhat

antonyms absolutely, certainly, completely, definitely, positively, surely

3 by a very small margin ⟨we were *hardly* able to make it back to camp before darkness set in⟩ — see JUST 2

4 with feelings of bitterness or grief ⟨his broker did not think that he would take his financial losses so *hardly*⟩ — see HARD 2

5 with great effort or determination ⟨the state championship was a *hardly* fought contest between two evenly matched teams⟩ — see HARD 1

hardness *n* **1** something that is a cause for suffering or special effort especially in the attainment of a goal ⟨the test questions were rated for *hardness*, a rating of five indicating the most difficult⟩ — see DIFFICULTY 1

2 the quality or state of being demanding or unyielding (as in discipline or criticism) ⟨the aunt's *hardness* gradually crumbled under the influence of the little orphan's endearing ways⟩ — see SEVERITY

hard–nosed *adj* sticking to an opinion, purpose, or course of action in spite of reason, arguments, or persuasion ⟨the team's *hard-nosed* coach doesn't make exceptions for anybody⟩ — see OBSTINATE

hard–pressed *adj* faced with difficulty or uncertainty about what to say, think, or do ⟨they will be *hard-pressed* to come up with any facts that actually support their argument⟩ — see HARD PUT

hard put *adj* faced with difficulty or uncertainty about what to say, think, or do ⟨she was *hard put* to explain her department's excessive expenditures⟩

synonyms baffled, confounded, hard-pressed, nonplussed (*also* nonplused), perplexed

related words bewildered, confused, disconcerted, fazed; embarrassed, flustered, put out

phrases at a loss, put to it

near antonyms undaunted, unfazed; composed, untroubled

hardscrabble *adj* producing inferior or only a small amount of vegetation ⟨it was hard to eke out even a bare existence on the *hardscrabble* lands⟩ — see BARREN 1

hardship *n* something that is a cause for suffering or special effort especially in the attainment of a goal ⟨working two jobs was a *hardship* he was willing to endure to get out of debt⟩ — see DIFFICULTY 1

hard up *adj* lacking money or material possessions ⟨despite being undeniably *hard up*, they had too much pride to accept charity⟩ — see POOR 1

hardware *n* items needed for the performance of a task or activity ⟨gathered together the *hardware* needed to set up a first aid station at the finish line for the marathon⟩ — see EQUIPMENT

hardwired *adj* being a part of the innermost nature of a person or thing ⟨a cat with a *hardwired* compulsion to knock expensive knickknacks off of shelves⟩ — see INHERENT

hardy *adj* **1** able to withstand hardship, strain, or exposure ⟨chrysanthemums are *hardy* enough to survive a light frost⟩ ⟨the settlers of the Old West were a *hardy* lot⟩

synonyms cast-iron, hard, hard-bitten, hardened, inured, rugged, stout, strong, sturdy, tough, toughened, vigorous

related words flinty, leathery, resilient, stalwart; durable, enduring, everlasting, immortal, imperishable, lasting, permanent, stable, staunch (*also* stanch), staying, tenacious, unyielding; flourishing, prospering, thriving; able-bodied, brawny, muscular; fit, fortified, hale, healthy, husky, lusty, red-blooded, robust, sound, strapping, virile; annealed, seasoned, tempered

near antonyms emasculated, enervated, enfeebled, exhausted, run-down, sapped, wasted, weakened, worn, worn out; crippled, debilitated, diseased, incapacitated, infirm, unsound; fragile, frail, puny; resistless, sensitive, susceptible, unresistant, vulnerable, yielding; mortal, perishable, temporary, transient

antonyms delicate, nonhardy, soft, tender, weak

2 inclined or willing to take risks ⟨*hardy* souls who pioneered new paths into outer space⟩ — see BOLD 1

hare *vb* to proceed or move quickly ⟨she's always *haring* off to attend to some emergency⟩ — see HURRY 2

harebrained *adj* **1** lacking in seriousness or maturity ⟨the movie follows the *harebrained* antics of a pair of stoners who seem incapable of growing up⟩ — see GIDDY 1

2 showing or marked by a lack of good sense or judgment ⟨a *harebrained* idea to go for a hike in an area where grizzly bear attacks had recently been reported⟩ — see FOOLISH 1

hark *vb* to pay attention especially through the act of hearing ⟨upon hearing the offending ringing, the teacher sarcastically cried, "*Hark*! Could that possibly be a cell phone?"⟩ — see LISTEN

hark back (to) *vb* to bring back to mind ⟨the new stadium, designed for nostalgic appeal, *harks back to* the intimate ballparks of yore⟩ — see REMEMBER

harken *vb* to pay attention especially through the act of hearing ⟨young people would do well to read this wise and witty book and *harken* to its message⟩ — see LISTEN

harken back (to) *vb* to bring back to mind ⟨let's *harken back to* what we learned last week⟩ — see REMEMBER

harlequin *n* a comically dressed performer (as at a circus) who entertains with playful tricks and ridiculous behavior ⟨among the court entertainers waiting to enter the grand hall were masked *harlequins* in brightly colored pantaloons⟩ — see CLOWN 1

harlot *n* a woman who engages in sexual activities for money ⟨the touristy port town little resembled the haven for thieves, cutthroats, and *harlots* it had once been⟩ — see PROSTITUTE

harlotry *n* the practice of engaging in sexual activities for money ⟨a city that in biblical times was infamous for licentiousness and *harlotry*⟩ — see PROSTITUTION

harm *n* something that causes loss or pain ⟨you were lucky to survive the fire without *harm*⟩ ⟨no *harm* in trying⟩ — see INJURY 1

harm *vb* **1** to cause bodily damage to ⟨though she wasn't *harmed* by the flying glass, she slipped and fell on a piece and cut her hand⟩ — see INJURE 1
2 to reduce the soundness, effectiveness, or perfection of ⟨the company's reputation has been *harmed* by allegations of crooked accounting⟩ — see DAMAGE 1

harmful *adj* causing or capable of causing harm ⟨DDT has been proven to be extremely *harmful* to the environment⟩
synonyms adverse, bad, baleful, baneful, damaging, dangerous, deleterious, detrimental, evil, hurtful, ill, injurious, mischievous, nocuous, noxious, pernicious, prejudicial, wicked
related words hostile, inimical, unfriendly; contagious, deadly, infectious, infective, pestiferous, pestilent, pestilential, poisonous, venomous; insidious, menacing, ominous, sinister, threatening; hazardous, imperiling (*or* imperilling), jeopardizing, parlous, perilous, risky, unsafe, unsound; nasty, noisome, unhealthful, unhealthy, unwholesome; destructive, fatal, killer, lethal, malignant, ruinous
near antonyms advantageous, beneficial, useful; favorable, good, propitious; curative, healthful, healthy, helpful, palliative, remedial, salubrious, salutary, wholesome; secure, sound; benignant; noncorrosive, nondestructive, nonfatal, noninfectious, nonlethal, nonpoisonous, nonpolluting, nontoxic, nonvenomous
antonyms anodyne, benign, harmless, hurtless, innocent, innocuous, inoffensive, safe

harmless *adj* not causing or being capable of causing injury or hurt ⟨a perfectly *harmless* little spider⟩
synonyms anodyne, benign, hurtless, innocent, innocuous, inoffensive, safe, white
related words healthful, healthy, salubrious, wholesome; benignant; sound, trustworthy; gentle, gracious, mild; nonthreatening, painless, unobjectionable; noncorrosive, nondestructive, nonfatal, noninfectious, nonlethal, nonpoisonous, nonpolluting, nontoxic, nonvenomous
near antonyms poisonous, venomous; menacing, ominous, sinister, threatening; hazardous, imperiling (*or* imperilling), jeopardizing, parlous, perilous, risky, unsafe, unsound; nasty, noisome, unhealthful, unhealthy, unwholesome; offensive, painful, scathing, wounding; deadly, fatal, lethal, ruinous; destructive, insidious, malignant, noxious, pestilent, polluted, tainted
antonyms adverse, bad, baleful, baneful, damaging, dangerous, deleterious, detrimental, evil, harmful, hurtful, ill, injurious, mischievous, nocuous, noxious, pernicious, prejudicial, wicked

harmonic *adj* having the parts agreeably related ⟨the desire to live the kind of *harmonic* life in which work and family are perfectly balanced⟩ — see HARMONIOUS 2

harmonious *adj* **1** having a pleasing mixture of notes ⟨the naturally *harmonious* sounds of a forest glen in springtime⟩
synonyms canorous, euphonic, euphonious, harmonizing, melodious, musical, symphonic, symphonious, tuneful
related words blending, chiming, flowing, mellifluent, mellifluous; dulcet, mellow, melodic, sweet; echoing, resonant, sonorous; quavering, trilling, warbling; agreeable, appealing, pleasant; cadenced, lilting, lyric, lyrical, rhythmic (*or* rhythmical), songful, songlike; chordal, harmonic, homophonic, orchestral, polyphonic (*or* polyphonous), tonal
near antonyms blaring, clanging, clashing, clattering, grating, harsh, jangling, jarring, metallic, raspy, raucous, scratching, screeching, shrill, squeaky, strident; disagreeable, unpleasant, unpleasing; atonal, off-key
antonyms discordant, disharmonious, dissonant, inharmonious, tuneless, unmelodious, unmusical
2 having the parts agreeably related ⟨a *harmonious* arrangement of archways and doorways in the palace courtyard⟩
synonyms balanced, congruous, consonant, eurythmic (*or* eurhythmic), harmonic
related words even, proportioned, regular, symmetrical (*or* symmetric); aesthetic (*also* esthetic *or* aesthetical *or* esthetical), artistic, becoming, elegant, graceful, tasteful; agreeable, felicitous, pleasant, pleasing, satisfying; coherent, cohesive, compatible, coordinated, correspondent, matched, matching; Apollinian, Apollonian
near antonyms asymmetrical (*or* asymmetric), disordered, irregular, skewed, unequal, uneven, unsymmetrical; distasteful, graceless, inartistic, inelegant, tasteless, unaesthetic, unbecoming, ungraceful, unlovely; disagreeable, displeasing, dissatisfying, infelicitous, unfortunate, unpleasant, unsightly; clashing, conflicting, disunited, incompatible, uncoordinated
antonyms disharmonic, disharmonious, incongruous, inharmonic, inharmonious, unbalanced
3 having or marked by agreement in feeling or action ⟨an unusually *harmonious* meeting among the leaders resulted in a quick peace agreement⟩
synonyms agreeable, amicable, compatible, congenial, frictionless, kindred, unanimous, united
related words pacific, peaceable, peaceful; collaborating, cooperative, symbiotic, synergetic, synergic; noncompetitive, nonconflicting, uncompetitive; sympathetic, tolerant, understanding; affable, amiable, cordial, friendly, genial, neighborly
near antonyms antagonistic, antipathetic, clashing, conflicting, hostile, inimical, unfriendly; belligerent, contentious, quarrelsome; contradicting, contradictory, contrary, opposing, opposite; competing, competitive, rivaling (*or* rivalling)
antonyms disagreeable, discordant, disharmonious, disunited, incompatible, inharmonious, uncongenial
4 not having or showing any apparent conflict ⟨no form of social discrimination can ever be *harmonious* with the basic principles and ideals of our nation⟩ — see CONSISTENT

harmonize *vb* **1** to form a pleasing relationship ⟨the color of the walls *harmonized* nicely with the blue tones in the carpet⟩
synonyms agree, assort, blend, chime, chime in, conform, consort, coordinate, groove

related words balance, correlate, correspond, dovetail, hang together, match; meet, parallel; bond, coalesce, cohere, conjoin, fuse, merge, square, tally
near antonyms contradict, contrast, counter, differ, diverge, jar; cancel (out), counteract, negate, offset
antonyms clash, collide, conflict
2 to bring to a state free of conflicts, inconsistencies, or differences ⟨an attempt to *harmonize* the New Testament version of events with the accounts of the ancient Romans⟩
synonyms accommodate, attune, conciliate, conform, coordinate, key, reconcile
related words adapt, tune; blend, combine, connect, correlate, dovetail, fit, fuse, integrate, join, match, merge, orchestrate, pair, square, suit, synchronize, synthesize, unify, unite; align (*also* aline), arrange, array, balance, equalize, even, order, proportion, regularize, standardize
near antonyms confuse, disarray, disorder, disorganize, disrupt, disturb, skew, upset; alienate, estrange
antonyms disharmonize
3 to be in agreement on every point ⟨interrogated in separate rooms, the two burglary suspects gave stories that didn't *harmonize* at all⟩ — see CHECK 1

harmonizing *adj* having a pleasing mixture of notes ⟨a *harmonizing* chorus of early-morning chirps arose from the bird-laden trees⟩ — see HARMONIOUS 1

harmony *n* **1** a balanced, pleasing, or suitable arrangement of parts ⟨her face had an angelic *harmony* that fascinated the leading painters of her day⟩
synonyms balance, coherence, concinnity, consonance, consonancy, orchestration, proportion, symmetry, symphony, unity
related words coordination, correlation, correspondence, equalization, equilibrium, evenness, order, orderliness, regularity, uniformity
near antonyms confusion, disorganization, dissonance, disturbance, tension; disconnectedness, disjointedness, incompatibility; irregularity, unevenness
antonyms asymmetry, discordance, disproportion, disunity, imbalance, incoherence, violence
2 peaceful coexistence ⟨the apparent inability of the party's right and left wings to resolve their conflicts and live in *harmony* at least during the convention⟩
synonyms chime, comity, compatibility, concord, peace
related words amity, companionship, compatibleness, congeniality, fellowship, fraternization, friendship; collaboration, reciprocity, symbiosis; agreement, consensus, unanimity; cohesion, cohesiveness, unity; affinity, connection, empathy, kinship, oneness, rapport, solidarity, sympathy, understanding; peacefulness, sereneness, serenity, sweetness and light, tranquillity (*or* tranquility)
near antonyms antagonism, antipathy, enmity, hatred, hostility, unfriendliness; alienation, breach, divorce, estrangement, rupture, schism, scission, severance; dissent, dissidence; anarchy, disorder, disturbance, strife, turmoil
antonyms conflict, discord, dissension (*also* dissention), variance
3 a state of consistency ⟨for once, the kids' idea of a vacation was in perfect *harmony* with their parents' notion of total relaxation⟩ — see CONFORMITY 1

harm's way *n* the state of not being protected from injury, harm, or evil ⟨got everyone out of *harm's way* just minutes before the house was ripped apart by the tornado⟩ — see DANGER 1

harness *vb* to put into action or service ⟨huge dams *harness* the power of water to produce electricity⟩ — see USE 1

harp (on) *vb* to speak or write about insistently and usually tiresomely ⟨there were so many good things about the stage production that it seems churlish to *harp on* a couple of minor missteps⟩ — see BELABOR 1

harpoon *vb* to penetrate or hold (something) with a pointed object ⟨she deftly *harpooned* a shrimp with her skewer and held it over the fire⟩ — see IMPALE

harpy *n* **1** a bad-tempered scolding woman ⟨in fairy tales stepmothers are often portrayed as *harpies* who make the lives of their stepchildren miserable⟩ — see SHREW
2 a person who habitually preys upon others ⟨having just started to make it really big in the music business, he found himself surrounded by a flock of *harpies* greedy for a piece of the action⟩ — see PREDATOR

harridan *n* a bad-tempered scolding woman ⟨if you were married to that *harridan*, you, too, would take to drink⟩ — see SHREW

harrow *vb* to cause persistent suffering to ⟨the villagers were gaunt and sickly, *harrowed* by years of disease and starvation⟩ — see AFFLICT

harrowing *adj* **1** hard to accept or bear especially emotionally ⟨a *harrowing* portrayal of the ravages of war⟩ — see BITTER 2
2 intensely or unbearably painful ⟨the *harrowing* amputations without any anesthetic that soldiers and sailors once were forced to endure⟩ — see EXCRUCIATING 1

harrying *n* the act of making unwelcome intrusions upon another ⟨the relentless *harrying* of the sensitive teen by his classmates eventually drove him to suicide⟩ — see ANNOYANCE 1

harsh *adj* **1** difficult to endure ⟨*harsh* conditions in the refugee camp⟩
synonyms bitter, brutal, burdensome, cruel, excruciating, grievous, grim, hard, hardhanded, heavy, inhuman, murderous, onerous, oppressive, rough, rugged, searing, severe, stiff, tough, trying
related words austere, bleak, comfortless, discomforting, forbidding, inhospitable, spartan, uncomfortable; biting, inclement, intemperate, wild; rigorous, strict, stringent; agonizing, heartbreaking, heartrending, painful, wretched; crushing, grinding, overwhelming, wearing; insufferable, insupportable, intolerable, unbearable, unendurable; harrowing, tortuous; bad, disagreeable, hostile, unfriendly, unpleasant
near antonyms comfortable, cozy, luxurious, snug; agreeable, friendly, genial, hospitable, pleasant; peaceful, relaxing, reposeful, restful; bearable, endurable, painless, tolerable; balmy, calm, clement, gentle, mild, moderate, temperate
antonyms easy, light, soft
2 disagreeable to one's aesthetic or artistic sense ⟨the *harsh* lighting in the cafeteria makes the food look slightly off-color⟩
synonyms grating, grotesque, jarring, unaesthetic
related words acid, flashy, garish, gaudy, loud, tawdry; tacky, tasteless, vulgar; inartistic, unartistic; artless, clumsy, crude, graceless, inelegant, rude; uncouth, uncultured, unrefined; disgusting, gross, obscene, repugnant, repulsive, ugly; disagreeable, jolting, unpleasant, unpleasing; blaring, clashing, discordant, disharmonious, dissonant, inharmonious, jangling, off-key, ragged, raspy, raucous, unmelodious, unmusical; bizarre, kinky, odd, outlandish, shocking
near antonyms artful, artistic; attractive, beautiful, becoming, comely; agreeable, appealing, felicitous, good, harmonious, harmonizing, pleasing, seemly; calming, comforting, soothing; softened, subdued; cultured, elegant, graceful, gracious, polished, refined, tasteful
antonyms aesthetic (*also* esthetic *or* aesthetical *or* esthetical)
3 causing discomfort ⟨the *harsh* northern climate⟩ — see UNCOMFORTABLE 1

4 given to exacting standards of discipline and self-restraint ⟨a *harsh* judge when it comes to drug users and especially drug dealers⟩ — see SEVERE 1
5 hard to accept or bear especially emotionally ⟨the *harsh* reality of failure⟩ ⟨*harsh* words of criticism from her music teacher⟩ — see BITTER 2
6 not giving pleasure to the mind or senses ⟨winced at the *harsh* sound that the beginner violinist was making⟩ — see UNPLEASANT

harshen *vb* to make more harsh, uncompromising, or severe ⟨recent changes to the drunk driving laws *harshen* penalties for repeat offenders⟩
synonyms harden, stiffen, strengthen, toughen
near antonyms lessen, moderate, soften
antonyms ameliorate, ease

harshly *adv* in a manner so as to cause loss or suffering ⟨treated the prisoners *harshly*, and many died⟩ — see HARDLY 1

harshness *n* **1** a harsh or sharp quality ⟨there was a *harshness* about her voice that made her an unlikely but surprisingly evocative singer of torch songs⟩ — see EDGE 1
2 the quality or state of being demanding or unyielding (as in discipline or criticism) ⟨was surprised at the *harshness* of the choirmaster's criticism, since he was usually pretty easygoing⟩ — see SEVERITY

harum–scarum *adj* having or showing a lack of concern for the consequences of one's actions ⟨a *harum-scarum* dash through the crowded terminal to make the flight⟩ — see RECKLESS 1

harum–scarum *adv* in a confused and reckless manner ⟨tossed everything *harum-scarum* from the closet in a desperate attempt to find her shoes⟩ — see HELTER-SKELTER 1

harvest *n* the quantity of an animal or vegetable product gathered at the end of a season ⟨we can thank the bountiful *harvest* of 1621 for our traditional feast of turkey and all the trimmings every November⟩ — see CROP 1

harvest *vb* to catch or collect (a crop or natural resource) for human use ⟨*harvest* salmon from nearby rivers⟩ ⟨every year we *harvest* corn from our own garden⟩
synonyms gather, pick, reap
related words clam, fish, seal, shrimp, whale; accumulate, forage, garner; glean; cut, hay, mow; bag, capture, hunt, net, snare, trap; crop, grow, raise
near antonyms plant, seed, sow

has–been *n* one that has passed the peak of effectiveness or popularity ⟨now a *has-been*, the actor's been reduced to appearing on a third-rate reality show⟩
synonyms dinosaur, relic
related words dodo, fogy (*also* fogey), fossil, old-timer; fuddy-duddy, mossback, stick-in-the-mud, stodge [*British*], troglodyte; throwback
near antonyms comer, rising star, up-and-comer

hash *n* an unorganized collection or mixture of various things ⟨the docudrama was a *hash* of facts, half-truths, speculation, and pure fiction⟩ — see MISCELLANY 1

hash *vb* **1** to cut into small pieces ⟨he *hashed* some roast beef, put it in a pie shell, and topped it with a layer of mashed potatoes⟩ — see CHOP
2 to undo the proper order or arrangement of ⟨the bookkeeper had so *hashed* the figures it took weeks to straighten out the accounts⟩ — see DISORDER

hash (over *or* out) *vb* to talk about (an issue) usually from various points of view and for the purpose of arriving at a decision or opinion ⟨for months the town councilmen *hashed over* the proposal to allow a big-box store in their rural community⟩ — see DISCUSS

hassle *n* **1** a brief clash between enemies or rivals ⟨the best way to avoid *hassles* with those aggressive panhandlers is to ignore them⟩ — see ENCOUNTER
2 a physical dispute between opposing individuals or groups ⟨the moment the police arrived, the *hassle* broke up, and no one was seriously injured⟩ — see FIGHT 1
3 an often noisy or angry expression of differing opinions ⟨had a huge *hassle* with an airline representative before she got her ticket refunded⟩ — see ARGUMENT 1
4 something that is a source of irritation ⟨it's a *hassle* to find a parking space downtown⟩ — see ANNOYANCE 3

hassle *vb* **1** to attack repeatedly with mean put-downs or insults ⟨a small group of jeering protesters *hassled* the politically active singer at every appearance she made⟩ — see TEASE 2
2 to express different opinions about something often angrily ⟨constantly *hassled* with the chef over the need to cook pork thoroughly⟩ — see ARGUE 2

haste *n* **1** a high rate of movement or performance ⟨made *haste* to get there on time⟩ — see SPEED 1
2 excited and often showy or disorderly speed ⟨*haste* makes waste⟩ ⟨in her *haste*, she forgot her keys⟩ — see HURRY 1

hasten *vb* **1** to cause to move or proceed fast or faster ⟨*hasten* the activation of yeast with heat⟩ — see HURRY 1
2 to proceed or move quickly ⟨the contractors *hastened* to complete the project before the deadline⟩ — see HURRY 2

hastily *adv* **1** with excessive or careless speed ⟨the *hastily* put together report contained a lot of errors⟩
synonyms cursorily, headlong, hotfoot, hurriedly, pell-mell, precipitately, precipitously, rashly
related words headfirst, headily, hotheadedly, impatiently, impetuously, impulsively, recklessly, thoughtlessly; automatically, glancingly, haphazardly; impromptu, spontaneously; abruptly, suddenly; offhand, offhandedly
phrases on the spur of the moment
near antonyms calculatingly, circumspectly, designedly; falteringly, haltingly, hesitantly, hesitatingly, tentatively; leisurely, slowly
antonyms deliberately, studiedly
2 with great speed ⟨the congresswoman *hastily* made her way towards the waiting elevator⟩ — see FAST 1

hastiness *n* excited and often showy or disorderly speed ⟨several council members objected to the *hastiness* with which the proposal was brought to a vote⟩ — see HURRY 1

hasty *adj* **1** acting or done with excessive or careless speed ⟨Anna later regretted her *hasty* decision to sell her car⟩
synonyms cursory, drive-by, flying, gadarene, headlong, helter-skelter, hurried, overhasty, pell-mell, precipitate, precipitous, rash, rushed
related words breakneck, breathtaking; headstrong, heady, hotheaded, impatient, impetuous, impulsive, madcap, reckless, unadvised; quick, rapid, speedy, swift; horseback, impromptu, makeshift, offhand, offhanded, off-the-cuff, rush, slapdash, snap, spontaneous, spur-of-the-moment; abrupt, sudden
near antonyms calculated, calculating, measured; circumspect, foresighted, forethoughtful; drawn-out, extended, long-term, prolonged; faltering, hesitant, hesitating, tentative; dallying, dawdling, laggard, leisurely, poky (*or* pokey), shilly-shallying, slow
antonyms deliberate, unhurried, unrushed
2 moving, proceeding, or acting with great speed ⟨we all wish our sick friend a *hasty* recovery⟩ — see FAST 1

hat *n* a covering for the head usually having a shaped crown ⟨in those days, no properly dressed person left home without a *hat*⟩

synonyms cap, chapeau, headdress, headgear, headpiece, lid [*slang*]
related words baseball cap, beret, billycock [*British*], biretta, boater, bonnet, bowler, calotte, capuche, casque, castor, cloche, cocked hat, cowboy hat, cowl, derby, fedora, fez, garrison cap, hard hat, helm, helmet, high hat, homburg, hood, kepi (*also* képi), kufi, leghorn, miter (*or* mitre), nightcap, opera hat, overseas cap, panama, picture hat, pillbox, plug hat, porkpie hat, service cap, shako, silk hat, skimmer, skullcap, sombrero, sou'wester, Stetson, stocking cap, stovepipe, sunbonnet, tam, tam-o'-shanter, ten-gallon hat, top hat, topper, toque, tricorne (*or* tricorn), turban, zucchetto; warbonnet

hatch *n* a barrier by which an entry is closed and opened ⟨watertight *hatches* provided access through the ship's bulkheads⟩ — see DOOR 1

hatch *vb* to cover and warm eggs as the young inside develop ⟨the mallards and geese have begun *hatching* in their nests down by the pond⟩ — see SET 1

hate *n* **1** a very strong dislike ⟨*hate* can sometimes be replaced with tolerance when people meet face to face⟩
synonyms abhorrence, abomination, detestation, execration, hatred, loathing
related words cattiness, despite, despitefulness, hatefulness, invidiousness, malevolence, malice, maliciousness, malignancy, malignity, meanness, spite, spitefulness; aversion, disgust, distaste, horror, odium, repugnance, repulsion, revulsion; animosity, antagonism, antipathy, bitterness, contempt, disdain, enmity, grudge, hostility, jealousy, pique, resentment, scorn; bile, jaundice, rancor, spleen, venom, virulence, vitriol
near antonyms appetite, inclination, liking; admiration, adoration, veneration, worship; acceptance, tolerance; passion, relish, taste
antonyms affection, devotion, fondness, love
2 something or someone that is hated ⟨the Alaska pipeline is a pet *hate* of environmentalists⟩
synonyms abhorrence, abomination, anathema, antipathy, aversion, bête noire, detestation, execration
related words dread, hang-up, horror, phobia; bogey (*also* bogie *or* bogy), bugaboo, bugbear; adversary, enemy; annoyance, grievance, hassle, nuisance, peeve
near antonyms beloved, darling, dear, honey, sweetheart; delight, enjoyment, felicity, joy, pleasure; favorite, like, preference; treasure
antonyms love

hate *vb* to dislike strongly ⟨she *hates* her job, she hates her friends, and she hates her life!⟩
synonyms abhor, abominate, despise, detest, execrate, loathe
related words deplore, deprecate, disapprove (of), discountenance, disdain, disfavor, scorn
phrases have it in for
near antonyms desire, fancy, favor, like, prefer; enjoy, relish; admire, adore, approve (of), esteem, hallow, idolize, revere, venerate, worship; cherish, prize, treasure
antonyms love

hateful *adj* having or showing a desire to cause someone pain or suffering for the sheer enjoyment of it ⟨the girl's classmates were bullying her online, sending her *hateful* e-mails and text messages⟩
synonyms bad [*slang*], bitchy, catty, cruel, despiteful, malevolent, malicious, malign, malignant, mean, nasty, spiteful, vicious, virulent
related words devious, scoundrelly, scurvy, snakelike; acrimonious, bitter, envious, jaundiced, jealous, rancorous, resentful, vindictive, vitriolic; contemptuous, deprecating, derogatory, disdainful, disparaging, mean-spirited, obnoxious, opprobrious, scornful, snide, snotty, unkind, unkindly, unloving; baleful, baneful, evil; harsh, hostile, inimical; acrid, caustic, poisonous, scathing, venomous
near antonyms compassionate, good, good-hearted, kind, kindhearted, kindly, sympathetic, warm, warm-hearted; affable, agreeable, amiable, cordial, friendly, genial, gracious, nice, pleasant; affectionate, amorous, sweet, tender, tenderhearted; humane; altruistic, high-minded, humanitarian, magnanimous, noble, philanthropic (*also* philanthropical)
antonyms benevolent, benign, benignant, loving, unmalicious

hatefully *adv* in a mean or spiteful manner ⟨many voters were turned off by the way the candidate *hatefully* dredged up his opponent's marital troubles⟩ — see NASTILY

hatefulness *n* the desire to cause pain for the satisfaction of doing harm ⟨her political commentary seems to be nothing more than an exercise in *hatefulness* and vicious invective⟩ — see MALICE

hat in hand *adv* in a manner showing no signs of pride or self-assertion ⟨he was forced to apologize *hat in hand* for the offensive comment⟩ — see LOWLY

hatred *n* a very strong dislike ⟨a lifelong *hatred* of war that inspired him to join a peace movement⟩ — see HATE 1

haughtiness *n* an exaggerated sense of one's importance that shows itself in the making of excessive or unjustified claims ⟨it was surprising to see such *haughtiness* in someone who had come from such humble origins⟩ — see ARROGANCE

haughty *adj* **1** having a feeling of superiority that shows itself in an overbearing attitude ⟨the *haughty* waiter smirked when I remarked that it was odd that a French restaurant didn't even have french fries on the menu⟩ — see ARROGANT
2 having or displaying feelings of scorn for what is regarded as beneath oneself ⟨the student reporter received a *haughty* letter in reply to his request for an interview with the governor⟩ — see PROUD 1

haul *n* **1** the total amount collected or obtained especially at one time ⟨our latest trip to collect shells at the beach resulted in quite a *haul*⟩
synonyms bounty, catch, take, yield
related words bag; earnings, gain, gross, income, net, payoff, proceeds, profit, receipts, return, revenue, winnings; booty, loot, plunder, spoils, swag; appropriation, collection
near antonyms deduction, loss, subtraction
2 a mass or quantity of something taken up and carried, conveyed, or transported ⟨a truck carrying a large *haul* of lumber⟩ — see LOAD 1
3 the act or an instance of applying force on something so that it moves in the direction of the force ⟨the sharp *haul* strained the rope but didn't break it⟩ — see PULL 1

haul *vb* **1** to cause to follow by applying steady force on ⟨a pair of strong oxen *hauled* the plow⟩ — see PULL 1
2 to support and take from one place to another ⟨a vast army of trucks *haul* produce across America every day⟩ — see CARRY 1

haunches *n pl* the part of the body upon which someone sits ⟨squatted down on her *haunches* to get a better shot of the ducks with her camera⟩ — see BUTTOCKS

haunt *n* **1** a place for spending time or for socializing ⟨one of their favorite after-school *haunts* is Joe's Pizza⟩ — see HANGOUT
2 *chiefly dialect* the soul of a dead person thought of especially as appearing to living people ⟨we heard the local tales of a *haunt* in the choir loft and of a specter in the graveyard⟩ — see GHOST 1

haunt *vb* to go to or spend time in often ⟨much of her time is spent *haunting* antique shops in search of unique knobs for the curio cabinets she builds⟩ — see FREQUENT

haunter *n* someone who regularly spends time in a particular place ⟨she's been a *haunter* of bookstores since her college days⟩ — see DENIZEN 1

haunting *adj* fearfully and mysteriously strange or fantastic ⟨the *haunting* tones of the Highland bagpipes⟩ — see EERIE

hauteur *n* an exaggerated sense of one's importance that shows itself in the making of excessive or unjustified claims ⟨she looked at him with the *hauteur* of someone who is accustomed to being instantly obeyed⟩ — see ARROGANCE

have *n* a wealthy person ⟨a society that discriminates between the *haves* and the have-nots⟩ — see CAPITALIST

have *vb* **1** to keep, control, or experience as one's own ⟨my uncle *has* a sizable collection of black powder rifles⟩
synonyms command, enjoy, hold, own, possess, retain
related words keep, reserve, withhold; bear, carry; boast, show off, sport
phrases rejoice in
near antonyms abandon, cede, disclaim, disown, hand over, relinquish, renounce, surrender, yield; discard, dump; decline, reject, repudiate, spurn; need, require
antonyms lack, want
2 to agree to receive whether willingly or reluctantly ⟨we decided that I would *have* the job of calling the volunteers on the phone⟩ ⟨she refused to *have* him as a husband⟩ — see TAKE 2
3 to bring forth from the womb ⟨her grandmother *had* 11 children⟩ — see BEAR 1
4 to cause to believe what is untrue ⟨he'd been *had* —the painting was a fake, and he never saw the "art dealer" or his money again⟩ — see DECEIVE
5 to come to a knowledge of (something) by living through it ⟨*had* a great time at the party⟩ ⟨*had* three operations on her leg⟩ — see EXPERIENCE
6 to give permission for or to approve of ⟨I will not *have* any more nonsense about a party in celebration of my retirement⟩ — see ALLOW 1
7 to influence someone with a bribe ⟨an upstanding judge who could not be *had* at any price⟩ — see BRIBE
8 to keep in one's mind or heart ⟨I have never *had* an unkind thought for him⟩ ⟨do you *have* an opinion?⟩ — see HARBOR 1

have (to) *vb* to be under necessity or obligation to ⟨I *have to* take out the trash before we can leave⟩ ⟨*has to* take medicine for her heart⟩ — see NEED 2

haven *n* **1** a part of a body of water protected and deep enough to be a place of safety for ships ⟨this picturesque cove is one of the most popular *havens* on all of the cape for weekend yachtsmen⟩ — see HARBOR 1
2 something (as a building) that offers cover from the weather or protection from danger ⟨the cross-country skiers hoped desperately to find a cave, as a *haven* from the blizzard⟩ — see SHELTER

have on *vb, chiefly British* to cause to believe what is untrue ⟨you're *having* me *on*, aren't you, mate?⟩ — see DECEIVE

havoc *n* **1** a state in which everything is out of order ⟨computer network problems created *havoc* throughout the office⟩ — see CHAOS
2 the state or fact of being rendered nonexistent, physically unsound, or useless ⟨the powerful hurricane wreaked *havoc* all along the coast⟩ — see DESTRUCTION 1

hawk *n* one who urges or attempts to cause a war ⟨the *hawks* were claiming that without war there could be no peace⟩ — see WARMONGER

hawk *vb* to sell from place to place usually in small quantities ⟨a determined bootstrapper who went from *hawking* newspapers on the street corner to running a media empire⟩ — see PEDDLE

hawker *n* one who sells things outdoors ⟨street corner *hawkers* selling everything from fake designer purses to original works of art⟩ — see PEDDLER

hawkeyed *adj* having unusually keen vision ⟨the *hawkeyed* driver spotted the state trooper lying in wait for unwary speeders⟩ — see SHARP-EYED

hawkshaw *n* a person not on the police force who investigates criminal or illicit activity or searches for missing persons ⟨the firm hired a *hawkshaw* to find out who was fencing stock from their warehouse⟩ — see DETECTIVE

hay *n* **1** a very small sum of money ⟨their credit card debt isn't *hay*—it'll take years to pay it off⟩ — see MITE 1
2 *slang* a place set aside for sleeping ⟨dragging myself out of the *hay* on such a cold, dreary morning seemed like an act of sheer masochism⟩ — see BED 1

haymaker *n* a hard strike with a part of the body or an instrument ⟨dealt his opponent a *haymaker* that sent him reeling across the boxing ring⟩ — see [1]BLOW

hayseed *n* an awkward or simple person especially from a small town or the country ⟨though educated and sophisticated, the country singer always put on the facade of an amiable *hayseed* when in public⟩ — see HICK

haywire *adj* having or showing a very abnormal or sick state of mind ⟨she gradually went *haywire* after the tragic death of her husband⟩ — see INSANE 1

hazard *n* **1** something that may cause injury or harm ⟨the tumbledown old barn was considered a fire *hazard*⟩ — see DANGER 2
2 the uncertain course of events ⟨it was only by *hazard* and good fortune that we found our way back to the trail⟩ — see CHANCE 1

hazard *vb* **1** to place in danger ⟨just so the tourists could see the sea lions up close, the captain needlessly *hazarded* his ship⟩ — see ENDANGER
2 to take a chance on ⟨was unwilling to *hazard* landing the plane on the small island, which didn't even have an airfield⟩ — see RISK 1

hazardous *adj* involving potential loss or injury ⟨a *hazardous* journey across the arctic ice⟩ — see DANGEROUS 1

haze *n* **1** an atmospheric condition in which suspended particles in the air rob it of its transparency ⟨Jim could barely make out the tall buildings through the *haze*⟩
synonyms brume, fog, gauze, mist, murk, reek, smog, soup
related words bank, cloud, fume, miasma, smoke, smother, steam
2 a state of mental confusion ⟨people wandered around in a *haze* in the days following the earthquake⟩
synonyms daze, dazedness, fog, muddle, spin, swoon
related words reverie, stupor, trance; befuddlement, bewilderment, perplexity, puzzlement; delirium, malaise, paralysis; cloudiness, fogginess
near antonyms alertness, levelheadedness

[1]**haze** *vb* to attack repeatedly with mean put-downs or insults ⟨the roughnecks on the oil rig would *haze* the young man for his refined manners and educated speech⟩ — see TEASE 2

[2]**haze** *vb* to make dark, dim, or indistinct ⟨unfortunately, smog was *hazing* the view of the distant city skyline⟩ — see CLOUD 1

hazed *adj* covered over by clouds ⟨*hazed* skies made the flat landscape look even duller⟩ — see OVERCAST

hazy *adj* **1** filled with or dimmed by fine particles (as of dust or water) in suspension ⟨*hazy* skies made it dangerous to fly⟩ ⟨the *hazy* sunshine so common in August⟩
synonyms beclouded, befogged, brumous, clouded,

cloudy, foggy, gauzy, misty, murky, smoggy, soupy
related words overcast, rainy, stormy, thick; dirty, miry, mucky, muddy, slimy, slushy, turbid; miasmal, miasmatic, miasmic; smoky (*also* smokey), smudgy, sooty; filmy, milky, opaque
near antonyms bright, clean; clement, fair, sunny, sunshiny; translucent, transparent
antonyms clear, cloudless, limpid, pellucid, unclouded
2 covered over by clouds ⟨when taking landscape photographs, compensate for dull, *hazy* skies by emphasizing colorful features on the ground⟩ — see OVERCAST
3 not seen or understood clearly ⟨the meaning of "you should" here is *hazy*—does it mean "you are strongly urged" or "you are commanded"?⟩ — see FAINT 1

head *adj* highest in rank or authority ⟨as *head* editor at the TV station for 17 years, he has hired and fired innumerable staff members⟩
synonyms chief, commanding, first, foremost, high, lead, leading, preeminent, premier, presiding, primary, prime, principal, supereminent, supreme, top
related words high-level, senior; controlling, directing, managing, officiating, overseeing, regnant, reigning, ruling, supervisory; main, major, paramount, predominant, predominate, sovereign (*also* sovran); ascendant (*also* ascendent), dominant, grand, superior, topmost, upmost, upper, uppermost
phrases in charge
near antonyms ancillary, inferior, last, less, lesser, lower, lowly, second, secondary, subordinate, subsidiary; assistant, assisting, coadjutor, deputy, junior, under

head *n* **1** the upper or front part of the body that contains the brain, the major sense organs, and the mouth ⟨I hit my *head* as I went through the low doorway⟩
synonyms bean, block [*slang*], dome, mazard (*or* mazzard) [*chiefly dialect*], nob, noddle, noggin, noodle, nut [*slang*], pate, poll
related words cranium, crown, scalp, skull; occiput
2 the place of leadership or command ⟨every year a different parent is placed at the *head* of the troop's cookie drive⟩
synonyms chair, driver's seat, headship, helm, rein(s)
related words chieftainship, commandership, directorship; forefront, lead, vanguard; captainship, chairmanship, deanship, dictatorship, generalship, governorship, kingship, mastership, mastery, premiership, presidency, presidentship, superintendency; dominance, dominion, jurisdiction, sovereignty (*also* sovranty), sway, upper hand; eminence, height, pedestal, pinnacle, seat, throne, top
near antonyms ranks
3 a light mass of fine bubbles formed in or on a liquid ⟨the *head* on the ice cream soda rose a good two inches above the rim of the glass⟩ — see FOAM
4 a member of the human race ⟨the tour guide counted *heads*, and everyone was present⟩ — see HUMAN
5 a time or state of affairs requiring prompt or decisive action ⟨the security issue came to a *head* when an employee was robbed in broad daylight in the company parking lot⟩ — see EMERGENCY
6 the beginning part of a stream ⟨Lake Itasca in Minnesota is the *head* of the Mississippi River⟩ — see HEADWATER
7 the highest part or point ⟨stood at the *head* of the stairs and looked down⟩ — see HEIGHT 1
8 the normal or healthy condition of the mental abilities ⟨you're out of your *head* if you think you can swim across that river⟩ — see MIND 2
9 the part of a person that feels, thinks, perceives, wills, and especially reasons ⟨challenged us to put our *heads* together and find a solution to the skyrocketing costs of the company's health insurance plans⟩ — see MIND 1
10 the person (as an employer or supervisor) who tells people and especially workers what to do ⟨as *head* of the planning committee, he had the responsibility of appointing someone to look into the parking situation⟩ — see BOSS
11 a bank of earth constructed to control water ⟨built a *head* to create a millpond⟩ — see DAM
12 a room furnished with a fixture for flushing body waste ⟨give me a chance to visit the *head*, and I'll be all set to go⟩ — see TOILET
13 a person who regularly uses drugs especially illegally ⟨a shop near campus where all the *heads* used to get their paraphernalia⟩ — see DOPER
14 a person with a strong and habitual liking for something ⟨she's a total tech *head* who adores home electronics and computers⟩ — see FAN
15 a word or series of words often in larger letters placed at the beginning of a passage or at the top of a page in order to introduce or categorize ⟨rechecked to make sure that all the *heads* were in boldface⟩ — see HEADING
16 a special and usually inborn ability ⟨I have no *head* for numbers⟩ — see TALENT

head *vb* **1** to go on a specified course or in a certain direction ⟨the migrant workers were *heading* for California for the grape harvest⟩
synonyms bear, make
related words aim, bend, direct, point, turn; beeline, light out, put, put out, set off, set out, strike, take off; face, orient, steer; about-face, back, come about, come round, cut, incline, put about, reverse, swerve, tack, turn back, veer, wheel, yaw
2 to be at the front of ⟨*heading* the procession at the dog show was a miniature poodle, followed by dogs seemingly of every breed⟩ — see LEAD 3
3 to be in charge of ⟨who *headed* the CIA when Ronald Reagan was president?⟩ — see BOSS 1
4 to be positioned along a certain course or in a certain direction ⟨the road to riches *headed* north, thought many, as off they went to Alaska to try their luck at panning gold⟩ — see RUN 3
5 to point or turn (something) toward a target or goal ⟨after a long day at the beach, we *headed* the car toward home⟩ — see AIM
6 to serve as leader of ⟨Robert La Salle *headed* the expedition that claimed Louisiana for the French king⟩ — see LEAD 2
7 to cut off the head of ⟨got a job at the slaughterhouse *heading* cattle⟩ — see DECAPITATE

headache *n* **1** a dull, unpleasant, or difficult piece of work ⟨filling out all the required forms was a real *headache*⟩ — see CHORE 2
2 something that is a source of irritation ⟨one of the *headaches* of being a band teacher is never knowing if the school's music program will be cut⟩ — see ANNOYANCE 3

head and shoulders *adv* by a considerable margin ⟨a performance that was *head and shoulders* above all the others in the talent competition⟩
synonyms far and away
related words decidedly, definitely, really, undoubtedly, unquestionably; considerably, extensively, significantly, substantially, well
phrases by all odds, by a long shot, by far, by half
near antonyms barely, hardly, just, marginally, scarcely, slightly; minimally, minutely

head case *n* **1** a person judged to be legally or medically insane ⟨while serving in the military hospital's psychiatric unit, he got to observe a wide variety of *head cases*⟩ — see LUNATIC 1
2 a person of odd or whimsical habits ⟨an area of scientific research that's a good niche for social misfits and

hard-core *head cases*⟩ — see ECCENTRIC

headdress *n* a covering for the head usually having a shaped crown ⟨most of the acrobats riding the horses and elephants wore some sort of fancy *headdress*⟩ — see HAT

header *n* a word or series of words often in larger letters placed at the beginning of a passage or at the top of a page in order to introduce or categorize ⟨why does each column have a *header* except the last one?⟩ — see HEADING

headgear *n* a covering for the head usually having a shaped crown ⟨in some states a helmet is required *headgear* for motorcycle riders⟩ — see HAT

heading *n* a word or series of words often in larger letters placed at the beginning of a passage or at the top of a page in order to introduce or categorize ⟨the recipe for turkey gumbo is under the *heading* "stews" rather than under "soups"⟩
synonyms caption, head, header, headline, rubric, title
related words banner, streamer; catch word, guide word, running head; greeting, salutation; superscript, superscription; subhead, subheading, subtitle

headland *n* **1** an area of high ground jutting out into a body of water beyond the line of the coast ⟨the lighthouse, situated on a narrow, rocky *headland*, commands an expansive view of the coast⟩
synonyms ness, point, promontory
related words cape, foreland, peninsula, spit; breakwater, jetty, levee
2 an area of land that juts out into a body of water ⟨navigation is notoriously difficult at the southernmost tip of South America, where ships must round the *headland* of Cape Horn⟩ — see [2]CAPE

headline *n* a word or series of words often in larger letters placed at the beginning of a passage or at the top of a page in order to introduce or categorize ⟨I usually just glance at the *headlines* in the morning paper before dashing off to work⟩ — see HEADING

headliner *n* the person who has the most important role in a play, movie, or TV show ⟨a *headliner* on variety shows in the early days of TV⟩ — see STAR 2

headlong *adj* acting or done with excessive or careless speed ⟨terrified forest creatures in a *headlong* retreat from the rapidly spreading fire⟩ — see HASTY 1

headlong *adv* **1** with excessive or careless speed ⟨plunged *headlong* into the crowd in pursuit of the purse snatcher⟩ — see HASTILY 1
2 without delay ⟨had barely finished the last project when we went *headlong* into the next one⟩ — see IMMEDIATELY

headman *n* the person (as an employer or supervisor) who tells people and especially workers what to do ⟨as *headman* at the newspaper 20 years ago, he hired the then-promising young reporter who won this year's Pulitzer Prize for investigative reporting⟩ — see BOSS

headmost *adj* coming before all others in time or order ⟨the *headmost* horse shied at the sight of a snake⟩ — see FIRST 1

head off *vb* to keep from happening by taking action in advance ⟨if we act quickly, we may still be able to *head off* disaster⟩ — see PREVENT

head-on *adv* in direct confrontation or competition ⟨the underdog team met its more talented opponent *head-on* and won the hockey game through sheer grit⟩ — see HEAD-TO-HEAD

headpiece *n* **1** a covering for the head usually having a shaped crown ⟨the bride will be wearing a flowing veil fastened to a pearl-covered *headpiece*⟩ — see HAT
2 the ability to learn and understand or to deal with problems ⟨she has looks and personality but not much in the way of a *headpiece*⟩ — see INTELLIGENCE 1

headquarters *n pl* **1** a place from which authority is exercised ⟨the *headquarters* of the newly established United States government was in New York City, the nation's first capital⟩ — see SEAT 1
2 the place from which a commander runs operations ⟨the scout went straight to the large tent in the center of the camp, correctly assuming that it served as the division's *headquarters*⟩ — see COMMAND 3

head-scratcher *n* something hard to understand or explain ⟨why he chose to sink all of his money into a failing business is a real *head-scratcher*⟩ — see MYSTERY

head-scratching *n* a state of mental uncertainty ⟨poorly worded instructions that must have resulted in a lot of *head-scratching*⟩ — see CONFUSION 1

headship *n* **1** the duty or function of watching or guarding for the sake of proper direction or control ⟨while he was in the hospital, the CEO had his most trusted lieutenant assume temporary *headship* of the firm⟩ — see SUPERVISION 1
2 the place of leadership or command ⟨the person at the *headship* of the firm will face daunting challenges, given the current state of the economy⟩ — see HEAD 2

headstone *n* a shaped stone laid over or erected near a grave and usually bearing an inscription to identify and preserve the memory of the deceased ⟨many of the *headstones* were for children who had died during the influenza epidemic⟩ — see TOMBSTONE

headstream *n* the beginning part of a stream ⟨the *headstreams* of the Ganges River arise in the Himalayas⟩ — see HEADWATER

headstrong *adj* **1** given to resisting control or discipline by others ⟨a *headstrong* child who likes to test the limits of his parents' patience⟩ — see UNCONTROLLABLE
2 sticking to an opinion, purpose, or course of action in spite of reason, arguments, or persuasion ⟨the tenants of the building remain *headstrong* in their determination not to be evicted by the developer⟩ — see OBSTINATE

heads-up *n* the act or an instance of telling beforehand of danger or risk ⟨thanks for the *heads-up* about the upcoming visit from the corporate big shots⟩ — see WARNING 1

head-to-head *adv* in direct confrontation or competition ⟨it's fitting that the two best teams during the regular season will go *head-to-head* for the championship⟩
synonyms eyeball-to-eyeball, face-to-face, head-on, mano a mano, one-on-one, toe-to-toe

headwater *n, usually* **headwaters** *pl* the beginning part of a stream ⟨the first exploration of the Missouri River from its mouth to its *headwaters* was made by Meriwether Lewis and William Clark in the early 1800s⟩
synonyms head, headstream, source
related words fountain, fountainhead, geyser, headspring, hot spring, spring, wellspring; branch, feeder, tributary

headway *n* forward movement in time or place ⟨the ant was making little *headway* carrying a crumb that was about five times his size⟩ — see ADVANCE 1

heady *adj* **1** experiencing or marked by overwhelming usually pleasurable emotion ⟨still *heady* from his election win, he announced his first cabinet appointments⟩ — see ECSTATIC
2 having or showing a practical cleverness or judgment ⟨one of the *headiest* politicians around, he knows how to read the public mood at any given moment⟩ — see SHREWD 1
3 having an abundance of some characteristic quality (as flavor) ⟨a rich meal full of *heady* sauces and strong spices⟩ — see FULL-BODIED

heal *vb* **1** to restore to a healthy condition ⟨a low-fat vegetarian diet, moderate exercise, and stress manage-

ment help *heal* a diseased heart⟩ ⟨*heal* the sick⟩
synonyms cure, fix, mend, rehab, rehabilitate, set up
related words attend (to), care (for), doctor, medicate, minister (to), nurse, physic, treat; fortify, rejuvenate, renew, resuscitate, revitalize, revive; alleviate, relieve, remedy, repair
near antonyms cripple, damage, disable, harm, hurt, impair, injure, lacerate, lame, maim, mangle, mutilate, wound; afflict, ail, debilitate, enervate, enfeeble, lay up, sap, sicken, waste, weaken
2 to become healthy and strong again after illness or weakness ⟨most of the soldiers could go home while they were still *healing* from their wounds⟩ — see CONVALESCE
3 to bring about recovery from ⟨time *heals* all wounds, even those of the heart⟩ — see CURE 1

healing *adj* tending to cure disease or restore health ⟨the native peoples of South America recognized the *healing* powers of the dried bark of the cinchona tree, formerly used as a specific in malaria⟩ — see MEDICINAL 1

healing *n* the process or period of gradually regaining one's health and strength ⟨the long period of *healing* following the operation⟩ — see CONVALESCENCE

health *n* **1** the condition of being sound in body ⟨Sam gradually regained his *health* after a long bout with cholera⟩
synonyms fitness, healthiness, heartiness, robustness, sap, soundness, verdure, wellness, wholeness, wholesomeness
related words fettle, shape; cleanliness, hygiene; hardiness, lustiness, robustiousness, ruggedness, stamina, strength, toughness, vigor, vigorousness, vitality; bloom, flush, flushness; activeness, agility, liveliness, spryness; weal, welfare, well-being
near antonyms debility, decrepitude, feebleness, frailness, infirmity, lameness, sickliness, weakness; ailment, condition, disease, disorder, malady, trouble
antonyms illness, sickness, unhealthiness, unsoundness
2 a state of being or fitness ⟨a country in good economic *health* now that the recession is past⟩ — see CONDITION 1

health club *n* a building or room used for sports activities and exercising ⟨plays racquetball at the nearby *health club*⟩ — see GYM

healthful *adj* beneficial to the health of body or mind ⟨one of the most *healthful* forms of exercise is a brisk walk⟩
synonyms good, healthy, medicinal, restorative, salubrious, salutary, salutiferous, sanative, tonic, wholesome
related words alleviative, corrective, curative, recuperative, refreshing, rehabilitative, rejuvenating, rejuvenescent, remedial; advantageous, useful; antiseptic, aseptic, clean, hygienic, sanitary; nourishing, nutritional, nutritious; nonpoisonous, nontoxic
near antonyms damaging, deleterious, harmful, injurious, pernicious; infectious, poisonous, sickening, toxic; insanitary, unhygienic, unsanitary
antonyms insalubrious, noxious, unhealthful, unhealthy, unwholesome

healthiness *n* the condition of being sound in body ⟨healthy teeth are an indication of a horse's overall *healthiness*⟩ — see HEALTH 1

health spa *n* a building or room used for sports activities and exercising ⟨a *health spa* offering aerobics classes for all levels of fitness⟩ — see GYM

healthy *adj* **1** enjoying health and vigor ⟨always a hard worker, Grandma has remained *healthy* into her 80s⟩
synonyms able-bodied, bouncing, fit, hale, hearty, robust, sound, well, well-conditioned, whole, wholesome
related words hard, hardy, iron, lusty, rugged, stalwart, strong, sturdy, tough; ambulatory, nondisabled, uncrippled; active, agile, chipper, lively, sprightful, sprightly, spry, vigorous, vital; blooming, clean-cut, flourishing, flush, prospering, thriving; all right, good, right
phrases in fine fettle, in shape, in the pink
near antonyms decrepit, enfeebled, feeble, infirm, rundown, sickened, sickly, weak, weakened, weakly, worn-out; challenged, crippled, debilitated, differently abled, disabled, halt, incapacitated, lame; delicate, fragile, frail; emaciated, gaunt, haggard, malnourished, undernourished; afflicted, troubled; bad, poorly
antonyms ailing, diseased, ill, sick, unfit, unhealthy, unsound, unwell
2 beneficial to the health of body or mind ⟨the air in here isn't *healthy*⟩ ⟨ads that promote *healthy* eating habits⟩ — see HEALTHFUL
3 sufficiently large in size, amount, or number to merit attention ⟨a *healthy* turnout of volunteers to plant trees on Arbor Day⟩ — see CONSIDERABLE 1
4 marked by vigorous growth and well-being especially economically ⟨coming out of a prolonged recession, the restaurant business seemed to be *healthy* again⟩ — see PROSPEROUS 1

heap *n* **1** a considerable amount ⟨she always has a *heap* of good ideas⟩ ⟨you're in a *heap* of trouble for missing curfew!⟩ — see LOT 2
2 a quantity of things thrown or stacked on one another ⟨found her shoe under a *heap* of clothes on the floor⟩ — see [1]PILE 1

heap *vb* **1** to give readily and in large quantities ⟨the critics *heaped* scorn on the wannabe blockbuster and its implausible plot⟩ — see RAIN 2
2 to lay or throw on top of one another ⟨*heaped* the stones in a corner of the yard⟩ — see PILE 1
3 to put into (something) as much as can be held or contained ⟨*heaped* her plate with spaghetti⟩ — see FILL 1

hear *vb* **1** to come to an awareness of ⟨I *heard* your sister is home from the hospital⟩ — see DISCOVER 1
2 to pay attention especially through the act of hearing ⟨at least *hear* what I have to say before you start disagreeing⟩ — see LISTEN

hearing *n* range of hearing ⟨let's make sure she's out of *hearing* before I tell you what I got her for her birthday⟩ — see EARSHOT

hearken *vb* to pay attention especially through the act of hearing ⟨*hearken*! I hear the distant beat of the hooves of many horses⟩ — see LISTEN

hearken back (to) *vb* to bring back to mind ⟨an elderly man who liked to *hearken back to* "the good old days"⟩ — see REMEMBER

hearsay *n* information or opinion that is widely disseminated without any authority or confirmation of accuracy ⟨supposedly, he's planning to quit, but that's only *hearsay*⟩ — see RUMOR

hearse *vb* to place (a dead body) in the earth, a tomb, or the sea ⟨the cemetery *hearses* an average of eight bodies a week⟩ — see BURY 1

heart *n* **1** the capacity for feeling for another's unhappiness or misfortune ⟨those who refuse to contribute to the fund for the famine victims must have no *heart*⟩
synonyms bigheartedness, charity, commiseration, compassion, feeling, good-heartedness, humanity, kindheartedness, kindliness, kindness, largeheartedness, mercy, pity, ruth, softheartedness, sympathy, warmheartedness
related words feelings, responsiveness, sensibility, sensitivity; affection, love, regard; affinity, empathy, rapport; altruism, benevolence, benignancy, benignity, generosity, goodwill, humaneness, humanism, humanitarianism, philanthropy
near antonyms callousness, coldness, disinterest, indif-

ference, unconcern; cruelty, harshness; animosity, antipathy, dislike, hatred, hostility
antonyms coldheartedness, hard-heartedness, inhumanity, inhumanness, mercilessness, pitilessness
2 a thing or place that is of greatest importance to an activity or interest ⟨the *heart* of the village economy was the outdoor market⟩ — see CENTER 1
3 strength of mind to carry on in spite of danger ⟨never lost *heart* while she was lost in the woods⟩ — see COURAGE
4 the central part or aspect of something under consideration ⟨at the *heart* of the problem is the school's outmoded computer system⟩ ⟨avoided any small talk and got right to the *heart* of the matter⟩ — see CRUX
5 the seat of one's deepest thoughts and emotions ⟨deep down in her *heart*, she knew he was telling the truth⟩ — see CORE 1

heartache *n* deep sadness especially for the loss of someone or something loved ⟨the *heartache* she felt when she saw the innocent victims of the war⟩ — see SORROW

heartbeat *n* a very small space of time ⟨I'd accept a job offer from that company in a *heartbeat*⟩ — see INSTANT

heartbreak *n* deep sadness especially for the loss of someone or something loved ⟨I understand the *heartbreak* you must feel over your grandmother's death⟩ — see SORROW

heartbreaking *adj* **1** causing unhappiness ⟨a *heartbreaking* story of a family torn asunder by war⟩ — see SAD 2
2 of a kind to cause great distress ⟨the *heartbreaking* state of Main Street now that most of the businesses have closed⟩ — see REGRETTABLE
3 deserving of one's pity ⟨a *heartbreaking* attempt to escape that ends in disaster⟩ — see PATHETIC 1

heartbroken *adj* **1** feeling unhappiness ⟨not as *heartbroken* over missing out on the trip to New York as I thought she would be⟩ — see SAD 1
2 expressing or suggesting mourning ⟨was utterly *heartbroken* when his pet dog died⟩ — see MOURNFUL 1

hearten *vb* to fill with courage or strength of purpose ⟨thinking we were hopelessly lost, we were *heartened* by the sight of a familiar farmhouse⟩ — see ENCOURAGE 1

heartening *adj* **1** having qualities which inspire hope ⟨a *heartening* visit to the hospital, where the patient was alert and sitting up⟩ — see HOPEFUL 1
2 making one feel good inside ⟨hearing how his students still appreciated him after all those years was *heartening* to the music teacher⟩ — see HEARTWARMING
3 pointing toward a happy outcome ⟨the accomplishments of the first day were a *heartening* start to our renovation of the house⟩ — see FAVORABLE 2

heartfelt *adj* genuine in feeling ⟨a number of the retiring teacher's former students have expressed their *heartfelt* appreciation for the invaluable lessons they learned in his classroom⟩ — see SINCERE 1

hearth *n* the place where one lives ⟨all were welcome, friends and strangers alike, to their humble *hearth*⟩ — see HOME 1

hearthstone *n* the place where one lives ⟨after years abroad, the eldest son returned to the family *hearthstone*, the old house in Philadelphia⟩ — see HOME 1

heartily *adv* **1** in a cheerful or happy manner ⟨the parishioners laughed *heartily* at the pastor's good-natured quips⟩ — see GAILY 1
2 to a full extent or degree ⟨I am *heartily* tired of this spring-cleaning⟩ — see FULLY 1

heartiness *n* the condition of being sound in body ⟨Granddad's *heartiness* on the hike put everyone else to shame—he wouldn't even hear of stopping to rest⟩ — see HEALTH 1

heartless *adj* **1** having or showing a lack of sympathy or tender feelings ⟨a *heartless* boss who would fire people for missing work, even if they were sick as a dog⟩ — see HARD 1
2 having or showing the desire to inflict severe pain and suffering on others ⟨his *heartless* whipping of runaway slaves virtually to the point of death shocked even other slave owners⟩ — see CRUEL 1

heartlessness *n* disposition to willfully inflict pain and suffering on others ⟨the gung ho *heartlessness* with which the secret police tortured prisoners was beyond belief⟩ — see CRUELTY

heartrending *adj* **1** causing unhappiness ⟨couldn't bear to see the *heartrending* photos of victims of the famine⟩ — see SAD 2
2 hard to accept or bear especially emotionally ⟨a *heartrending* choice between saving his daughter or his son⟩ — see BITTER 2
3 of a kind to cause great distress ⟨*heartrending* memories of all the terrible crimes he'd committed and was sorry for now⟩ — see REGRETTABLE
4 deserving of one's pity ⟨the *heartrending* sight of a starving child holding out his hands for food⟩ — see PATHETIC 1

heartsease *n* freedom from disquieting or oppressive thoughts or emotions ⟨winning such a prestigious award did not bring the artist the *heartsease* and contentment she thought it would⟩ — see PEACE 2

heartsick *adj* feeling unhappiness ⟨felt *heartsick* over having to give up the family farm⟩ — see SAD 1

heartsickness *n* a state or spell of low spirits ⟨could not begin to describe the *heartsickness* he felt when he sold the family farm⟩ — see SADNESS

heartsore *adj* feeling unhappiness ⟨a grandmother feeling *heartsore* and despondent when all her relatives left en masse after the holidays⟩ — see SAD 1

heart–stopping *adj* causing great emotional or mental stimulation ⟨the movie's climax is a *heart-stopping* chase through the streets of San Francisco⟩ — see EXCITING 1

heartstrings *n pl* **1** general emotional condition ⟨always said she didn't care much for cats, but now the little kitten was tugging at her *heartstrings*⟩ — see FEELING 2
2 the seat of one's deepest thoughts and emotions ⟨a story that will touch the very *heartstrings* of its readers⟩ — see CORE 1

heartwarming *adj* making one feel good inside ⟨Sarah was deeply touched by the *heartwarming* welcome she received from her relatives in Israel⟩
synonyms cheering, comforting, encouraging, fulfilling, gladdening, gratifying, heartening, rewarding, satisfying
related words affecting, inspiring, inspiriting, moving, poignant, stirring, touching; edifying, elevating, uplifting; sympathetic, tender; kind, kindly, loving, warm; animating, enlivening, exciting, exhilarating, invigorating, rousing, stimulating, thrilling; pleasing, pleasurable, welcoming
near antonyms cheerless, disappointing, disgruntling, displeasing, dissatisfying, heartbreaking, heartrending, saddening; discomforting, disconcerting, dismaying, distressing, disturbing, upsetting; cold, unfeeling, unfriendly, unkind, unloving, unpleasant
antonyms demoralizing, depressing, discouraging, disheartening, dispiriting

hearty *adj* **1** characterized by unqualified enthusiasm ⟨his decision to marry at long last has the whole family's *hearty* approval⟩
synonyms wholehearted, whole-souled

related words single-minded; ardent, avid, eager, enthusiastic, excited, exuberant, fervent, gung ho, impassioned, keen, mettlesome, passionate, raring, vehement, warm, zealous; animated, energetic, lively, spirited, vigorous; absolute, bona fide, earnest, genuine, heartfelt, sincere, unaffected, undisguised, unequivocal, unfeigned, unrestrained
near antonyms apathetic, disinterested, dispassionate, indifferent, uninterested; lackadaisical, listless, perfunctory, spiritless, uneager, unenthusiastic, unexcited; equivocal, hesitant, qualified, tentative, uncertain; delayed, dilatory, doubtful, hedging, hesitating; forced, reluctant, resistant, reticent, unwilling
antonyms grudging, halfhearted, lukewarm, tepid
2 enjoying health and vigor ⟨you're looking really *hearty* after that month in the clear mountain air!⟩ — see HEALTHY 1
3 having or showing kindly feeling and sincere interest ⟨the mayor gave the assembled volunteers his *hearty* thanks for their restoration of the bandstand on the town square⟩ — see FRIENDLY 1
4 not showing weakness or uncertainty ⟨gave the reins a *hearty* tug but the horse wouldn't budge⟩ — see FIRM 1

hearty *n* one who operates or navigates a seagoing vessel ⟨gather round me *hearties*, and I'll tell you a sea tale that'll shiver your timbers for sure⟩ — see SAILOR

heat *n* **1** depth of feeling ⟨informed the doctor, with considerable *heat*, that she had been kept waiting for three hours⟩ — see ARDOR 1
2 *slang* a portable weapon from which a shot is discharged by gunpowder ⟨a private detective packing *heat*⟩ — see GUN 1
3 *slang* a body of officers of the law ⟨he thought he was so slick, but the *heat* was onto him in no time⟩ — see POLICE 2

heat *vb* to cause to have or give off heat to a moderate degree ⟨*heat* water for tea⟩ ⟨*heat* the oven to 350 degrees before you put the cake in⟩ — see WARM 1

heated *adj* **1** being in a state of increased activity or agitation ⟨a *heated* discussion about who should pay for the pizza⟩ — see FEVERISH 1
2 having or giving off heat to a moderate degree ⟨early settlers put *heated* bricks under the blankets to keep warm⟩ — see WARM 1

heath *n* **1** a broad area of level or rolling treeless country ⟨not much grows on the *heath* besides heather⟩ — see PLAIN 1
2 land that is uninhabited or not fit for crops ⟨drove through a vast, empty *heath* that seemingly had no end⟩ — see WASTELAND

heathen *adj* not civilized ⟨old missionaries who mistakenly thought that they were going off to China to tame the *heathen* hordes⟩ — see SAVAGE 1

heathen *n* **1** a person who does not worship the God of the Bible ⟨a missionary sent to distant lands to convert the *heathens*⟩
synonyms gentile, idolater (*or* idolator), pagan
related words atheist, giaour, infidel, misbeliever, miscreant, nonbeliever, unbeliever; non-Christian, non-Jew, non-Muslim; neo-pagan, polytheist
near antonyms Christian, Jew, Muslim
2 an uncivilized person ⟨European colonizers, who considered the New World peoples to be *heathens*, forced them to conform to European ways⟩
synonyms barbarian, savage
related words Neanderthal, primitive; noble savage

heathenish *adj* not civilized ⟨believing that going to church in bare feet was *heathenish*, the missionaries made the natives wear shoes⟩ — see SAVAGE 1

heave *vb* **1** to lift with effort ⟨I *heaved* my duffel bag into the bus's overhead compartment⟩
synonyms boost, heft, hoist, jack (up), upheave
related words elevate, hike, pick up, raise, rear, up, uplift, upraise, uprear
near antonyms depress, drop, lower; sink, submerge, submerse
2 to discharge the contents of the stomach through the mouth ⟨*heaved* as soon as he stepped off the roller coaster⟩ — see VOMIT
3 to move from a lower to a higher place or position ⟨*heaved* the bucket from the bottom of the well⟩ — see RAISE 1
4 to send through the air especially with a quick forward motion of the arm ⟨*heaved* the brick over the fence⟩ — see THROW 1
5 to breathe hard, quickly, or with difficulty ⟨by the time he reached the top step of the tower, he was *heaving*⟩ — see GASP

heaven *n* **1** a dwelling place of perfect happiness for the soul after death ⟨prayed that the souls of the deceased would go to *heaven*⟩
synonyms above, bliss, elysian fields, Elysium, empyrean, kingdom come, New Jerusalem, paradise, sky, Zion (*also* Sion)
related words Beulah, glory, happy hunting ground, nirvana, promised land, Valhalla; afterlife, afterworld, hereafter, otherworld
phrases on high
near antonyms inferno; limbo, purgatory; hades, netherworld, underworld; abyss, pit
antonyms Gehenna, hell, Pandemonium, perdition
2 an often imaginary place or state of utter perfection and happiness ⟨compared to my old job, this new one is *heaven*⟩ — see PARADISE 1
3 a state of overwhelming usually pleasurable emotion ⟨she was in *heaven* the day she learned she was one of the finalists for the science scholarship⟩ — see ECSTASY
4 *usually* **heavens** *pl* the expanse of air surrounding the earth ⟨the starry *heavens*⟩ ⟨the space shuttle gradually disappeared into the *heavens*⟩ — see SKY 1

heavenly *adj* **1** of the very best kind ⟨had a *heavenly* time at the dance⟩ — see EXCELLENT
2 of, relating to, or being God ⟨do not concern yourself with material possessions, but with things *heavenly*, the prophet admonished⟩ — see HOLY 3
3 of, relating to, or suggesting heaven ⟨*heavenly* hosts singing "Alleluia!"⟩ — see CELESTIAL
4 giving pleasure or contentment to the mind or senses ⟨the *heavenly* aroma of chocolate fills the shop⟩ — see PLEASANT 1

heaven–sent *adj* coming or happening by good luck especially unexpectedly ⟨a *heaven-sent* offer to be the all-expenses-paid chaperone to some students on a trip to Paris⟩ — see FORTUNATE 1

heavily *adv* to a great degree ⟨*heavily* spiced sausage⟩ ⟨the family was *heavily* in debt⟩ — see VERY 1

heaviness *n* **1** the amount that something weighs ⟨the numbers on the back of each sample indicate the *heaviness* of the carpeting material⟩ — see WEIGHT 1
2 the state or quality of being heavy ⟨the backpack was filled with water bottles that gave it an extra *heaviness*⟩ — see WEIGHTINESS 1

heavy *adj* **1** having great weight ⟨this trunk full of books is much too *heavy* for one person to lift⟩
synonyms hefty, massive, ponderous, weighty
related words burdensome, leaden, lumpish; bulky, elephantine, massy, outsize (*also* outsized), voluminous; overweight, top-heavy; solid, substantial; ultraheavy
near antonyms airy, ethereal, feathery, fluffy, gossamer, gossamery; flimsy, insubstantial, slight; lightweight, undersized (*also* undersize), underweight; ultralight, ultralightweight
antonyms light, weightless

2 causing weariness, restlessness, or lack of interest ⟨the study of history doesn't have to be all about dull *heavy* reading and the memorization of dates⟩ — see BORING
3 containing much seasoning, fat, or sugar ⟨avoid *heavy* desserts like cheesecake and pecan pie⟩ — see RICH 2
4 covered over by clouds ⟨*heavy* skies threatening rain⟩ — see OVERCAST
5 difficult to endure ⟨ignoring common sense, she drank the parasite-infested pond water and paid a *heavy* penalty for it⟩ — see HARSH 1
6 extreme in degree, power, or effect ⟨*heavy* rains⟩ ⟨the *heavy* fighting has just begun, so there are no casualties to report⟩ — see INTENSE 1
7 having a matter of importance as its topic ⟨got into a *heavy* discussion about death and the afterlife⟩ — see SERIOUS 2
8 requiring considerable physical or mental effort ⟨until we find our groove, it's going to be *heavy* sledding on this project⟩ — see HARD 2
9 having great power or influence ⟨she's not among the handful of *heavy* critics who can make or break a Broadway show⟩ — see IMPORTANT 2
10 containing unborn young within the body ⟨the heifer was *heavy* with young and soon would be birthing⟩ — see PREGNANT 1

heavy *n* **1** a mean, evil, or unprincipled person ⟨she hates having to play the *heavy* all the time, but her husband refuses to be the disciplinarian in the family⟩ — see VILLAIN
2 one of high position or importance within a group ⟨in the field of secondary education, she definitely ranks as one of the *heavies*⟩ — see BIG SHOT

heavy–duty *adj* **1** extreme in degree, power, or effect ⟨some *heavy-duty* lobbying on the part of the president to get the bill passed⟩ — see INTENSE 1
2 having great power or influence ⟨a group of *heavy-duty* politicians and other notables attended the gala⟩ — see IMPORTANT 2

heavy–handed *adj* **1** given to exacting standards of discipline and self-restraint ⟨the gym teacher is *heavy-handed* with the boys and much more lenient with the girls⟩ — see SEVERE 1
2 lacking or showing a lack of nimbleness in using one's hands ⟨felt *heavy-handed* and awkward when she held the newborn infant⟩ — see CLUMSY 1

heavyhearted *adj* feeling unhappiness ⟨she was *heavyhearted* at losing the election, in which she had invested everything⟩ — see SAD 1

heavy hitter *n* one of high position or importance within a group ⟨many of the *heavy hitters* in the wine industry were boozing and schmoozing at the expo⟩ — see BIG SHOT

heavyset *adj* being compact and broad in build and often short in stature ⟨has the *heavyset* build of a weight lifter⟩ — see STOCKY

heavyweight *n* one of high position or importance within a group ⟨a *heavyweight* in the U.S. Senate, he has a lot of clout in judicial confirmations⟩ — see BIG SHOT

hebetude *n* physical or mental inertness ⟨faced with a class forever enveloped in a miasma of apathy and intellectual *hebetude*, the professor had little hope of kindling an interest in medieval European history⟩ — see LETHARGY

heck *n* a state in which everything is out of order ⟨it looks like *heck* in that boy's bedroom⟩ — see CHAOS

heckle *vb* to attack repeatedly with mean put-downs or insults ⟨a controversial player who was constantly *heckled* by the fans⟩ — see TEASE 2

heckler *n* a person who causes repeated emotional pain, distress, or annoyance to another ⟨avoided the *hecklers* who hung out on the street corner making threatening remarks to passersby⟩ — see TORMENTOR

hectic *adj* being in a state of increased activity or agitation ⟨exhausted from a *hectic* day at the office⟩ — see FEVERISH 1

hectically *adv* in a confused and reckless manner ⟨a moth kept banging *hectically* against the screen, seeking the light on the other side⟩ — see HELTER-SKELTER 1

hector *n* a person who teases, threatens, or hurts smaller or weaker persons ⟨a small-town *hector* with no job and lots of time on his hands⟩ — see BULLY 1

hector *vb* to make timid or fearful by or as if by threats ⟨the children used to constantly *hector* the poor dog, and now he growls at everybody⟩ — see INTIMIDATE

hedge *n* a physical object that blocks the way ⟨the messenger was confronted with a *hedge* of spears held aloft by the castle guards⟩ — see BARRIER

hedge *vb* **1** to avoid giving a definite answer or position ⟨she kept *hedging* whenever he asked her to go on a date with him⟩ — see EQUIVOCATE
2 to close or shut in by or as if by barriers ⟨the prison was *hedged* by a high stone wall⟩ — see ENCLOSE 1

hedonism *n* excessive pursuit of fleshly pleasures ⟨their spring break trip to Mexico became an exercise in heedless *hedonism*⟩ — see SENSUALITY

hedonist *n* a person whose life is devoted to luxury and sensual pleasures ⟨every year the Mexican resort is taken over by collegiate *hedonists* on spring break⟩ — see VOLUPTUARY

hedonistic *adj* given to or marked by excessive gratification of one's desires ⟨a *hedonistic* rock star whose life is one nonstop party⟩ ⟨a city known for its wild, *hedonistic* nightlife⟩
synonyms decadent, indulgent, luxurious, overindulgent, self-indulgent, sybaritic
related words carnal, fleshly, sensual, sensuous, voluptuous; masturbatory, onanistic, self-absorbed, self-obsessed; gluttonous, greedy, rapacious, voracious; extravagant, incontinent, intemperate, reckless, splurging, uncontrolled, wanton
near antonyms abstemious, abstinent, continent, sober, temperate; ascetic (*also* ascetical), austere, spartan; disciplined, self-controlled, self-disciplined, self-governed
antonyms self-abnegating, self-denying

heebie–jeebies *n pl* a sense of panic or extreme nervousness ⟨got a bad case of the *heebie-jeebies* before the audition⟩ — see JITTERS

heed *n* **1** a state of being aware ⟨took *heed* of the student's learning disability so as to arrive at reasonable expectations for him⟩ — see ATTENTION 2
2 strict attentiveness to what one is doing ⟨pay *heed* to what you're doing with that knife while you're talking⟩ — see CARE 1

heed *vb* **1** to take notice of and be guided by ⟨if we had *heeded* the ranger's advice, we might not have gotten lost⟩
synonyms follow, listen (to), mind, note, observe, regard, watch
related words consider, contemplate, mull, ponder, weigh; comply (with), conform (to), keep, obey, respect; attend (to), hark (to), hear, hearken (to); mark, notice, see
near antonyms brush (aside *or* off), discount, dismiss, gloss (over), gloze (over), neglect, pass over, pooh-pooh (*also* pooh), scorn, shrug off; defy, flout; slight, snub
antonyms disregard, ignore, tune out
2 to pay attention especially through the act of hearing ⟨that boy never *heeds* when I caution him about running with his shoelaces untied⟩ — see LISTEN

heedful *adj* having or showing a close attentiveness to avoiding danger or trouble ⟨*heedful* of snakes, we watched our footing while walking through the tall grass to the lake's edge⟩ — see CAREFUL 1

heedfulness *n* **1** a close attentiveness to avoiding danger ⟨despite their habitual *heedfulness*, even good drivers can get into accidents⟩ — see CAUTION 1
2 strict attentiveness to what one is doing ⟨always exercises extreme *heedfulness* when she handles her best china⟩ — see CARE 1

heedless *adj* not paying or showing close attention especially for the purpose of avoiding trouble ⟨*heedless* drivers who back out of parking spaces without looking⟩ — see CARELESS 1

heedlessness *n* failure to take the care that a cautious person usually takes ⟨the dog's lack of protection against rabies was purely due to his owner's *heedlessness*⟩ — see NEGLIGENCE 1

hee–haw *n* an explosive sound that is a sign of amusement ⟨the humor may have been corny and obvious, but the audience responded with hearty *hee-haws*⟩ — see LAUGH 1

hee–haw *vb* to show mirth with an explosive vocal sound ⟨those hayseeds will *hee-haw* at even the dumbest jokes⟩ — see LAUGH 1

heel *n* a person whose behavior is offensive to others ⟨felt like a *heel* when she found out that she'd blamed the wrong person⟩ — see JERK 1

heel *vb* to set or cause to be at an angle ⟨the strong gust *heeled* the sailboat almost to the point of capsizing, but we managed to right it⟩ — see LEAN 1

heft *n* **1** the amount that something weighs ⟨some synthetic fabrics are nice and warm, but I prefer wool because it has more *heft*⟩ — see WEIGHT 1
2 the power to direct the thinking or behavior of others usually indirectly ⟨as a former senator, he still had some *heft* in political circles⟩ — see INFLUENCE 1
3 *archaic* the main or greater part of something as distinguished from its subordinate parts ⟨the *heft* of the wainwright's business had been the building of hay wagons⟩ — see BODY 1

heft *vb* **1** to lift with effort ⟨*hefted* his growing son onto his shoulders⟩ — see HEAVE 1
2 to move from a lower to a higher place or position ⟨*heft* your baggy gym shorts a little higher—you're showing us more than we care to see⟩ — see RAISE 1

heftiness *n* **1** the quality or state of being large in size ⟨a restaurant known for the *heftiness* of its portions⟩ — see LARGENESS
2 the state or quality of being heavy ⟨clerks no longer have to deal with the *heftiness* of paper files now that everything is filed on computers⟩ — see WEIGHTINESS 1

hefty *adj* **1** having great weight ⟨that's a pretty *hefty* book bag for a tiny person like you⟩ — see HEAVY 1
2 of a size greater than average of its kind ⟨received a *hefty* donation from the local business association for holiday lights along Main Street⟩ — see LARGE 1
3 strongly and heavily built ⟨*hefty* since childhood, he became a champion wrestler⟩ — see [1]HUSKY 1

hegemony *n* controlling power or influence over others ⟨European intellectuals have long debated the consequences of the *hegemony* of American popular culture around the world⟩ — see SUPREMACY 1

height *n* **1** the highest part or point ⟨many regard the painting of the Sistine Chapel as the *height* of Michelangelo's career⟩
synonyms acme, apex, apogee, capstone, climax, crescendo, crest, crown, culmination, head, high noon, high tide, high-water mark, meridian, ne plus ultra, noon, noontime, peak, pinnacle, sum, summit, tip-top, top, zenith
related words bloom, blossom, flood tide, flower, glory, heyday, prime; cap, ceiling, roof; extreme, extremity, tip, vertex; high, highlight, highspot
near antonyms abyss, base, foot; minimum
antonyms bottom, nadir, rock bottom
2 the most extreme or advanced point ⟨the student's defiant use of a cell phone during class was regarded by the professor as the *height* of insolence⟩
synonyms depth, extremity, limit
related words consummation, epitome, quintessence, ultimate
3 the distance of something or someone from bottom to top ⟨the average *height* of the players on the volleyball team is well over six feet⟩
synonyms altitude, elevation, inches, stature
related words rise; highness, loftiness, tallness
4 an area of high ground ⟨Gulliver, standing on a *height* near the shore, saw an island suspended above the sea⟩
synonyms altitude(s), elevation, eminence, highland, hill, hump, mound, prominence, rise, upland
related words alp, mount, mountain, peak; butte, mesa, plateau, table, tableland; bluff, cliff, crag, precipice, steep, tor; ridge, sierra; dome, sugarloaf; foothill, hillock, hummock, knob, knoll; downs
near antonyms dale, dell, depression, dingle, glen, hollow, vale, valley; basin, bottom, bottomland, fen, flat, floodplain, plain, tidewater
antonyms lowland
5 the most intense or characteristic phase of something ⟨at the very *height* of the storm, someone knocked on the door⟩ — see THICK

heighten *vb* **1** to make markedly greater in measure or degree ⟨several controversial measures have *heightened* parental awareness of the impact of school policy decisions⟩ — see INTENSIFY
2 to move from a lower to a higher place or position ⟨*heightened* the hem on her skirt just a couple of inches⟩ — see RAISE 1

heightened *adj* being at a higher level than average ⟨there were *heightened* levels of lead in the drinking water⟩ — see HIGH 2

heinie *n, slang* the part of the body upon which someone sits ⟨a skirt so tight that her *heinie* was clearly outlined⟩ — see BUTTOCKS

heinousness *n* the state or quality of being utterly evil ⟨the *heinousness* of the Holocaust was only fully realized after the war⟩ — see ENORMITY 1

heir *n* a person who has the right to inherit property ⟨upon his death, Mr. Parkworth's property was divided evenly among his *heirs*, four sons and three daughters⟩
synonyms heir at law, inheritor, legatee
related words claimant; heir apparent, representative, succeeder, successor; coheir, coheiress, heiress; assignee, beneficiary, devisee, grantee; descendant (*also* descendent), scion

heir at law *n* a person who has the right to inherit property ⟨all of the *heirs at law* must be located before settlement of the estate is completed⟩ — see HEIR

heist *n* an instance of theft ⟨it was the largest jewelry *heist* in the city's history⟩ — see THEFT 2

heist *vb* to take (something) without right and with an intent to keep ⟨a professional burglar was able to *heist* a box of jewelry from the safe in the closet⟩ — see STEAL 1

helical *adj* turning around an axis like the thread of a screw ⟨Sirius, the brightest star in the heavens, travels a *helical* path through space⟩ — see SPIRAL

helicopter *n* a vehicle for traveling through the air that obtains its lift from rotors which spin horizontally ⟨took a *helicopter* tour to get a better sense of the grandeur of the Grand Canyon⟩
synonyms chopper, copter, eggbeater, helo, whirlybird
related words rotary-wing aircraft, rotorcraft; autogiro (*or* autogyro), convertiplane (*or* convertaplane), gyroplane, tilt-rotor; slick [*slang*]

hell *n* **1** the place of punishment for the wicked after

death ⟨condemned to *hell* for their sins⟩
synonyms Gehenna, Pandemonium, perdition, Tophet
related words blazes, inferno; purgatory; hades, netherworld, shades, Tartarus, underworld; Sheol; abyss, pit; fire and brimstone, hellfire
near antonyms glory, happy hunting ground, nirvana, promised land, Valhalla
antonyms bliss, elysian fields, Elysium, empyrean, heaven, kingdom come, New Jerusalem, paradise, sky, Zion (*also* Sion)
2 a situation or state that causes great suffering and unhappiness ⟨picking cotton under the hot summer sun was *hell*⟩
synonyms agony, Gehenna, horror, misery, murder, nightmare, torment, torture
related words affliction, calvary, cross, curse, ordeal, trial, tribulation; calamity, misfortune, tragedy; gall, thorn; bummer, downer, drag
near antonyms delight, diversion, entertainment, fun, joy, pleasure, recreation; lark, picnic, riot
antonyms heaven, paradise
3 a state in which everything is out of order ⟨all *hell* broke loose when the jury's verdict was announced⟩ — see CHAOS

hellacious *adj* **1** extreme in degree, power, or effect ⟨the *hellacious* heat was more than we could bear⟩ — see INTENSE 1
2 requiring considerable physical or mental effort ⟨the pioneers survived a particularly *hellacious* river crossing with their covered wagon barely in one piece⟩ — see HARD 2

hell–bent (on *or* upon) *adj* fully committed to achieving a goal ⟨she's *hell-bent on* a career in show business and heaven help anyone who gets in her way⟩ — see DETERMINED 1

hellcat *n* a mean or ugly old woman ⟨one of the two spinster sisters is said to be a *hellcat*, and the other is as sweet as can be⟩ — see CRONE

hell–for–leather *adj* having or showing a lack of concern for the consequences of one's actions ⟨having been behind for most of the race, the stock car driver made a *hell-for-leather* dash to the finish⟩ — see RECKLESS 1

hell–for–leather *adv* with great speed ⟨we ran *hell-for-leather* out of that spooky house⟩ — see FAST 1

hellhole *n* a dirty or messy place ⟨his first apartment was a *hellhole* in an unsafe neighborhood⟩ — see PIGPEN

hellion *n* an appealingly mischievous person ⟨the little *hellions* were tearing through the house squirting their water pistols⟩ — see SCAMP 1

hello *n* an expression of goodwill upon meeting ⟨we said our *hellos* and got right down to business⟩
synonyms greeting, salutation, salute, welcome
related words ave, hail; amenities, civilities, pleasantries; regards, respects, wishes
antonyms adieu, bon voyage, congé (*also* congee), farewell, Godspeed, good-bye (*or* good-by)

hell–raising *adj* being rough or noisy in a high-spirited way ⟨would often reminisce with his buddies about their *hell-raising* adventures as teenagers⟩ — see BOISTEROUS

helm *n* the place of leadership or command ⟨with a blind person at the *helm*, the city has made a lot of improvements for the physically challenged⟩ — see HEAD 2

helm *vb* to operate or control the course of ⟨a treacherous route for any weekend sailor just learning to *helm* his vessel⟩ — see NAVIGATE 1

helmsman *n* the person (as an employer or supervisor) who tells people and especially workers what to do ⟨had a complaint and demanded to talk to the *helmsman* of this vast construction project, not some underling⟩ — see BOSS

helo *n* a vehicle for traveling through the air that obtains its lift from rotors which spin horizontally ⟨the rescue *helo* swept in and landed on the roof of the skyscraper⟩ — see HELICOPTER

help *n* **1** an act or instance of helping ⟨I could use your *help* getting this tire back on the car⟩
synonyms abetment, aid, assist, assistance, backing, boost, hand, helping hand, leg up, lift, support
related words advancement, encouragement, facilitation, forwarding, furtherance, furthering, nurturance; benefaction, patronage, promotion, sponsorship; advice, care, counsel, guidance, mentoring; attendance, attention, hand-holding, service; beneficence, charity, favor, kindness, philanthropy; assuagement, palliation, relief, succor
near antonyms constraint, frustration, inhibition, interference, obstruction, repression, restraint; deterrence, discouragement
antonyms hindrance
2 a thing that helps ⟨the computer is a great *help* for writing reports⟩
synonyms advantage, aid, asset, benefit, boon
related words hand, lift, pick-me-up; support, sustenance; blessing, godsend, windfall; recourse, refuge, resort, resource
near antonyms constraint, inhibitor, liability, obstacle, obstruction, restraint, stranglehold
antonyms disadvantage, drawback, encumbrance, hindrance, impediment, minus
3 a body of persons at work or available for work ⟨it's so hard to get good *help* these days⟩ — see FORCE 1

help *vb* **1** to provide (someone) with what is useful or necessary to achieve an end ⟨offered to *help* her widowed father when he moved into an apartment⟩
synonyms abet, aid, assist, back, backstop, prop (up), support
related words advance, ease, facilitate, forward, foster, further, launch; champion, endorse (*also* indorse), patronize, promote, sponsor; attend, care (for), comfort, minister (to), succor; sustain; bolster, boost, buttress, reinforce (*also* reenforce); advise, counsel, guide, mentor, nurture; bail out, deliver, rescue, save; embolden, encourage, hearten; benefit, favor, oblige, profit, serve
phrases bear a hand, to stand one in good stead
near antonyms balk, bar, block, constrain, hamper, handicap, hold back, impede, inhibit, obstruct, restrain, strangle; baffle, foil, frustrate, inconvenience, interfere, oppose, sabotage, thwart; desert, disappoint, fail, let down; discourage, dishearten; repress, retard, stifle, straiten, stunt; damage, harm, hurt, injure
antonyms hinder
2 to make more bearable or less severe ⟨the new ointment didn't *help* Josh's sunburn one bit⟩
synonyms allay, alleviate, assuage, ease, mitigate, mollify, palliate, relieve, soothe
related words abate, lighten, moderate, soften, temper; cure, heal, remedy; amend, correct, emend, fix, mend, rectify, reform, repair; ameliorate, better, enhance, enrich, improve, meliorate, perfect, refine
near antonyms harm, hurt, impair, injure; heighten, intensify, sharpen
antonyms aggravate, exacerbate
3 to keep from happening by taking action in advance ⟨they couldn't *help* the way things turned out⟩ — see PREVENT
4 to provide with something useful or desirable ⟨being independently wealthy certainly *helped* him during his years as a struggling young artist⟩ — see BENEFIT
5 to make better ⟨some minor revisions would *help* this essay immensely⟩ — see IMPROVE

helper *n* a person who helps a more skilled person ⟨over the summer Chris worked as a carpenter's *helper*⟩
synonyms adjunct, adjutant, aid, aide, apprentice, assistant, coadjutor, deputy, helpmate, helpmeet, lieutenant, mate, sidekick
related words attendant, handmaiden (*also* handmaid), maid, maidservant, scullion, servant; auxiliary, legman, subordinate, underling; employee (*also* employe), hand, help, hireling, laborer, swamper, worker; gal Friday, girl Friday; man Friday, right hand; aide-de-camp

helpful *adj* **1** providing service or assistance ⟨a Web site that I've always found to be *helpful* for finding information on common medical problems⟩
synonyms conducive, facilitative, useful
related words advantageous, beneficial, efficacious, favorable, productive, profitable, salutary; accommodating, obliging
near antonyms ineffective, ineffectual; adverse, disadvantageous, inconvenient, profitless, unfavorable
antonyms unhelpful, useless
2 promoting or contributing to personal or social well-being ⟨it would be *helpful* to have more than one thesaurus in the classroom⟩ — see BENEFICIAL

helping hand *n* an act or instance of helping ⟨a skilled mechanic who generously provides a *helping hand* when his neighbors are plagued by car troubles⟩ — see HELP 1

helpless *adj* **1** lacking protection from danger or resistance against attack ⟨after the storm we found a *helpless* baby bird that had fallen out of its nest⟩
synonyms defenseless, exposed, susceptible, undefended, unguarded, unprotected, unresistant, vulnerable
related words indefensible, untenable; uncovered, unsafe; overcome, preyed (on *or* upon); disarmed, passive, resistless, unarmed; feeble, frail, weak; abandoned, high and dry, marooned
phrases in the lurch
near antonyms defensible; covered, fortified, safe, screened, secure, sheltered; armed, armored; immune, impenetrable, impregnable, invincible, strong, unassailable, unbeatable, unconquerable; almighty, omnipotent
antonyms guarded, invulnerable, protected, resistant, shielded
2 unable to act or achieve one's purpose ⟨we watched, feeling *helpless*, as the vase slipped from her hand and crashed to the floor⟩ — see POWERLESS

helpmate *n* **1** a person who helps a more skilled person ⟨after several years as a photographer's *helpmate*, the young man decided to pursue his own ambitions in commercial photography⟩ — see HELPER
2 the female partner in a marriage ⟨the man and his *helpmate* of 50 years decided that it was high time they took a trip around the world together⟩ — see WIFE

helpmeet *n* **1** a person who helps a more skilled person ⟨exasperated, the army surgeon requested a *helpmeet* who wouldn't faint at the sight of blood⟩ — see HELPER
2 the female partner in a marriage ⟨chose for his *helpmeet* a woman who could share his passion for rock climbing⟩ — see WIFE

helter-skelter *adj* **1** acting or done with excessive or careless speed ⟨a bill that was pushed through committee in a last-minute *helter-skelter* burst of legislative activity⟩ — see HASTY 1
2 lacking a definite plan, purpose, or pattern ⟨the offspring of unreconstructed flower children, they've been educated in a somewhat *helter-skelter* fashion⟩ — see RANDOM

helter-skelter *adv* **1** in a confused and reckless manner ⟨the sheep ran *helter-skelter* inside their pen when the coyote appeared in their midst⟩
synonyms amok (*or* amuck), berserk, berserkly, frantically, frenetically, frenziedly, harum-scarum, hectically, madly, pell-mell, wild, wildly
related words agitatedly, confusedly, crazily, desperately, feverishly, haywire, skittishly, uncontrollably; heedlessly, hotheadedly, recklessly, wantonly; chaotically, riotously, tumultuously, turbulently; aimlessly, haphazard, haphazardly, hit-or-miss, topsy-turvy
near antonyms calmly, collectedly, composedly, coolly (*also* cooly), imperturbably, peacefully, placidly, self-composedly, self-possessedly, serenely, unconcernedly; meekly, mildly, passively, tamely; methodically, orderly, systematically
2 without definite aim, direction, rule, or method ⟨goods arranged *helter-skelter* on the shelves of the variety store⟩ — see HIT OR MISS

helter-skelter *n* a state of noisy, confused activity ⟨in the *helter-skelter* at the refugee camp the child got separated from his parents⟩ — see COMMOTION

helve *n* a part by which an implement is held ⟨the head of the ax was crudely lashed to a wooden *helve*⟩ — see HANDLE 1

hem *n* the line or relatively narrow space that marks the outer limit of something ⟨the *hem* of the blouse was gold⟩ — see BORDER 1

hem (in) *vb* to close or shut in by or as if by barriers ⟨a village *hemmed in* on all sides by mountains⟩ — see ENCLOSE 1

hence *adv* **1** for this or that reason ⟨an endangered orchid species, *hence* illegal to pick⟩ — see THEREFORE
2 from this or that place ⟨the exorcist commanded, "Get thee *hence*, Satan!"⟩ — see AWAY

henceforth *adv* from this point on ⟨*henceforth*, there will be no more prolonged coffee breaks⟩
synonyms henceforward, hereafter
related words afterward (*or* afterwards), later, subsequently; hereupon, thereupon

henceforward *adv* from this point on ⟨you have sworn to tell the truth in this court, and *henceforward* you are bound by your oath⟩ — see HENCEFORTH

henpeck *vb* to subject (someone) to constant scoldings and sharp reminders ⟨neighbors say she *henpecked* him into giving up golf and selling his clubs⟩ — see NAG 1

hep *adj* keenly aware of and responsive to the latest developments especially in fashion and entertainment ⟨*hep* devotees of jazz were willing to brave any venue to hear him play⟩ — see AU COURANT 1

hepped up *adj* showing urgent desire or interest ⟨all *hepped up* about buying a new motorcycle⟩ — see EAGER

herald *n* **1** a person who actively supports or favors a cause ⟨an outspoken *herald* of prison reform⟩ — see EXPONENT 1
2 one that announces or indicates the later arrival of another ⟨the American robin—the *herald* of spring in the North⟩ — see FORERUNNER 1

herald *vb* **1** to give a slight indication of beforehand ⟨the reshuffle of the company's management *heralded* the sweeping changes to come⟩ — see FORESHADOW
2 to make known openly or publicly ⟨*herald* the great tidings to all the world⟩ — see ANNOUNCE

herbage *n* green leaves or plants ⟨added some ferns and other *herbage* to the sidewalk planters⟩ — see GREENERY

herculean *adj* **1** requiring considerable physical or mental effort ⟨the *herculean* task of grading 60 student essays over one weekend⟩ — see HARD 2
2 unusually large ⟨a *herculean* banquet table that took eight men to lift it⟩ — see HUGE

herd *n* **1** a group of domestic animals assembled or herded together ⟨the great *herds* of cattle that cowboys once drove across the plains⟩
synonyms drove, flock

related words colony, covey, gaggle, pack, plump [*chiefly dialect*], pod, school, swarm
2 the body of the community as contrasted with the elite ‹aspire to achieve something, to distinguish yourself from the *herd*› — see MASS 1
3 a great number of persons or things massed together ‹gearing up for the *herd* of holiday shoppers at the mall on the day after Thanksgiving› — see CROWD 1
herd *vb* to urge, push, or force onward ‹the guards briskly *herded* us through the museum in order to prevent overcrowding› — see DRIVE 1
herder *n* a tender of livestock ‹the nomadic reindeer *herders* of Siberia live in reindeer-skin tents›
synonyms herdsman
related words buckaroo (*also* buckeroo), cowboy, cowgirl, cowhand, cowherd, cowman, cowpoke, cowpuncher, gaucho, ranchero, vaquero; sheepherder, shepherd, shepherdess; goatherd; swineherd; wrangler; drover
herdsman *n* a tender of livestock ‹a lone *herdsman* stood with his sheep and his dog on the hillside› — see HERDER
hereafter *adv* from this point on ‹he is giving up all his worldly goods and *hereafter* will devote his life to the poor› — see HENCEFORTH
hereafter *n* **1** time that is to come ‹apologized, for being late to the meeting and assured his boss that there would be no such recurrences in the *hereafter*› — see FUTURE 1
2 unending existence after death ‹hoped to be reunited with his deceased wife in the *hereafter*› — see ETERNITY 2
here and now *n* the time currently existing or in progress ‹while we can plan for the future, we must first deal with the *here and now*› — see [1]PRESENT
here and there *adv* **1** in one place and another ‹an overgrown lawn with yellow patches of dandelions scattered *here and there*›
synonyms about, around, passim
related words all over, everyplace, everywhere, far and wide, high and low, right and left, throughout, ubiquitously
near antonyms nowhere
2 on some occasions ‹she spoke so softly that I only caught a word *here and there*› — see SOMETIMES
hereditary *adj* genetically passed or capable of being passed from parent to offspring ‹eye and hair color are *hereditary*›
synonyms genetic (*also* genetical), heritable, inborn, inheritable, inherited
related words congenital, inbred, inherent, innate, native, natural
near antonyms acquired
antonyms nonhereditary
heresiarch *n* a person who believes, teaches, or advocates something opposed to accepted beliefs ‹his about-face on welfare reform has led him to be seen as a *heresiarch* among his party's faithful› — see HERETIC 1
heresy *n* departure from a generally accepted theory, opinion, or practice ‹the *heresy* of asserting that Shakespeare was not a great writer›
synonyms dissent, dissidence, heterodoxy, nonconformity
related words error, fallacy, falsehood, misbelief, misconception, myth; apostasy, defection, infidelity, schism, scission, sectarianism, separatism; deviance, deviation, iconoclasm, unconventionality; disagreement, discord, dissension (*also* dissention)
near antonyms agreement, conformation, conventionality
antonyms conformity, orthodoxy
heretic *n* **1** a person who believes, teaches, or advocates something opposed to accepted beliefs ‹Galileo was condemned as a *heretic* for supporting Copernicus's thesis that the earth revolves around the sun and not vice versa›
synonyms dissenter, dissentient, dissident, heresiarch, nonconformist
related words apostate, defector, renegade; schismatic, sectarian, separationist, separatist; disbeliever, infidel, misbeliever, unbeliever; bohemian, individualist
near antonyms believer
antonyms conformer, conformist
2 a person who does not conform to generally accepted standards or customs ‹he's the ultimate *heretic*: a Yankees fan living deep in the heart of the Red Sox Nation› — see NONCONFORMIST 1
heretical *also* **heretic** *adj* deviating from commonly accepted beliefs or practices ‹the belief that women should be allowed to have careers outside the home was once considered *heretical*›
synonyms dissentient, dissenting, dissident, heterodox, iconoclastic, maverick, nonconformist, nonorthodox, out-there, unconventional, unorthodox
related words free-spirited, freethinking, nontraditional; apostate, defecting, renegade; schismatic (*also* schismatical), sectarian, separatist
antonyms conforming, conformist, conventional, orthodox
heretofore *adv* up to this or that time ‹having been *heretofore* unwilling to fly, he was forced to make an exception for his brother's out-of-state wedding› — see HITHERTO
heritable *adj* genetically passed or capable of being passed from parent to offspring ‹*heritable* characteristics like skin and eye and hair color› — see HEREDITARY
heritage *n* **1** an inherited or established way of thinking, feeling, or doing ‹hospitality is a cherished Southern *heritage*› — see TRADITION 1
2 something that is or may be inherited ‹this farm is my *heritage* from my father, as it was for him from his father› — see INHERITANCE
herky–jerky *adj* marked by a series of sharp quick motions ‹filmed in a *herky-jerky* style that will give many moviegoers a headache› — see JERKY 1
hermetic *also* **hermetical** *adj* difficult for one of ordinary knowledge or intelligence to understand ‹wrote *hermetic* poetry whose sole intended readership was himself› — see PROFOUND 1
hermit *n* a person who lives away from others ‹St. Jerome is said to have spent two years as a *hermit* in the desert, searching for inner peace› — see RECLUSE
hermitage *n* **1** a place where a person goes to hide or to avoid others ‹the artist's desert *hermitage* was a small adobe house at the end of a long dusty road› — see HIDEOUT
2 a residence for men under religious vows ‹monks in that *hermitage* take a vow of silence› — see MONASTERY
hero *n* **1** a person who is the object of extreme or uncritical devotion ‹fans of the sports *hero* didn't care what the facts were—in their minds, he was innocent of all criminal charges› — see IDOL
2 a large sandwich on a long split roll ‹shared a foot-long meatball *hero* with his friend› — see SUBMARINE
heroic *also* **heroical** *adj* **1** feeling or displaying no fear by temperament ‹a memorial honoring the *heroic* nurses who served in the war› — see BRAVE 1
2 large and impressive in size, grandeur, extent, or conception ‹an opera production of *heroic* proportions› — see GRAND 1
3 unusually large ‹a *heroic* statue of Alexander the Great astride his horse› — see HUGE

heroically *adv* **1** in a fearless manner ⟨struggled *heroically* to raise three children on her meager salary⟩ — see BRAVELY 1
2 in a manner befitting a person of the highest character and ideals ⟨doctors and nurses worked *heroically* through the night to keep the patient alive⟩ — see GREATLY 1

heroism *n* strength of mind to carry on in spite of danger ⟨the inspiring *heroism* of the firefighters who risked their lives to save the people trapped in the burning building⟩ — see COURAGE

hero–worship *vb* **1** to love or admire too much ⟨people who *hero-worship* celebrities are setting themselves up for disappointment⟩ — see IDOLIZE
2 to praise too much ⟨a golfing pro who is *hero-worshipped* by hordes of weekend duffers⟩ — see FLATTER 1

hero worship *n* excessive admiration of or devotion to a person ⟨once the object of uncritical *hero worship*, the aging quarterback now faces the derision of his team's fickle fans⟩ — see WORSHIP

hesitance *n* **1** a lack of willingness or desire to do or accept something ⟨sales figures for the month were up, as consumers began to overcome their *hesitance* about purchasing big-ticket items⟩ — see RELUCTANCE
2 a state or an instance of temporary inaction because of uncertainty about the right course of action ⟨she mistook my *hesitance* to mean I didn't like her poem, but I was trying to come up with appropriate words of praise⟩ — see HESITATION

hesitancy *n* **1** a lack of willingness or desire to do or accept something ⟨his appointment to the superintendency was confirmed by the school board without the least *hesitancy*⟩ — see RELUCTANCE
2 a state or an instance of temporary inaction because of uncertainty about the right course of action ⟨his *hesitancy* in pulling over into the next lane while he had a chance resulted in him missing his exit⟩ — see HESITATION

hesitant *adj* slow to begin or proceed with a course of action because of doubts or uncertainty ⟨he was *hesitant* about committing himself to the oversight of the project, which he knew would be long and difficult⟩
synonyms cagey (*also* cagy), disinclined, dubious, indisposed, loath (*also* loth *or* loathe), reluctant, reticent
related words uneager, unenthusiastic; averse, unwilling; ambivalent, conflicted, doubtful, faltering, halting, indecisive, infirm, irresolute, questioning, skeptical, uncertain, undecided, unsure, vacillating, wobbly (*also* wabbly); fainthearted, shy, timid
near antonyms eager, enthusiastic, glad, happy, keen; ready, willing; certain, decided, determined, resolute, sure, unquestioning
antonyms disposed, inclined

hesitate *vb* to show uncertainty about the right course of action ⟨I didn't *hesitate* to tell them that what they were doing was wrong and that I wanted no part of it⟩
synonyms balance, dither, falter, halt, hang back, scruple, shilly-shally, stagger, teeter, vacillate, waver, wobble (*also* wabble)
related words haw, hem; dally, dawdle, delay, linger, pause, procrastinate, wait; back down, chicken (out); consider, debate, deliberate, ponder, weigh; oscillate, sway; equivocate, hedge, pussyfoot, waffle
near antonyms decide; budge, stir; advance, continue
antonyms dive (in), plunge (in)

hesitation *n* a state or an instance of temporary inaction because of uncertainty about the right course of action ⟨one moment's *hesitation* on my part, and the elusive butterfly was lost to me forever⟩
synonyms faltering, fence-sitting, hesitance, hesitancy, indecision, irresolution, pause, shilly-shally, shilly-shallying, vacillation, wavering, wobbling (*also* wabbling)
related words delay, hawing, procrastination, waiting; arrière-pensée, misgiving, second thought; consideration, debate, deliberation, doubt, incertitude, indecisiveness, indetermination, uncertainness, uncertainty; avoidance, equivocation; aversion, disinclination, indisposition, reluctance, unwillingness; faintheartedness, shyness, timidity, timidness
near antonyms certainty, certitude, confidence, decisiveness, determination, firmness, resoluteness, resolution, sureness; alacrity, eagerness, readiness

heterodox *adj* **1** deviating from commonly accepted beliefs or practices ⟨a Christian clergyman with a very *heterodox* opinion on the divinity of Jesus⟩ — see HERETICAL
2 not rigidly following established form, custom, or rules ⟨her *heterodox* approach to teaching science initially met with some resistance from her peers⟩ — see INFORMAL 1

heterodoxy *n* departure from a generally accepted theory, opinion, or practice ⟨Copernicus's theory that the earth revolved around the sun was arrant *heterodoxy* at a time when the earth was thought to be the center of the universe⟩ — see HERESY

heterogeneity *n* the quality or state of being composed of many different elements or types ⟨the cultural *heterogeneity* of its residents is a point of pride for the city⟩ — see VARIETY 1

heterogeneous *adj* consisting of many things of different sorts ⟨the seating in the hall was a *heterogeneous* collection of old school desk chairs, wood and metal folding chairs, and even a few plush theater seats⟩ — see MISCELLANEOUS

heterogeneousness *n* the quality or state of being composed of many different elements or types ⟨the ever increasing *heterogeneousness* of the nation's population will bring about a whole new set of challenges⟩ — see VARIETY 1

het up *adj* feeling or showing uncomfortable feelings of uncertainty ⟨it won't do you any good to get all *het up* before the tryouts and lose sleep⟩ — see NERVOUS 1

hew *vb* **1** to bring down by cutting ⟨laboriously *hewed* trees to build their rude log cabins⟩ — see FELL 2
2 to hold to something firmly as if by adhesion ⟨decided to *hew* to the original plan rather than change everything⟩ — see STICK 1

hew (to) *vb* to give steadfast support to ⟨no longer was able to *hew to* the party line and so he switched political parties⟩ — see ADHERE (TO) 1

hex *n* **1** a woman believed to have often harmful supernatural powers ⟨people who used to believe that misfortune was caused by evil *hexes* and mischievous sprites⟩ — see WITCH 1
2 something that brings bad luck ⟨there seemed to be a *hex* on him, for all of his business ventures came to naught despite his hard work⟩ — see JINX
3 a spoken word or set of words believed to have magic power ⟨the wizard had put a *hex* on the evil gnome that turned him to stone⟩ — see SPELL 1

hex *vb* to cast a spell on ⟨I think our plans have been *hexed* from the start—everything is going wrong⟩ — see BEWITCH 1

hey *interj* how delightful ⟨*hey*, I won the lottery!⟩ — see HOORAY

heyday *n* a state or time of great activity, thriving, or achievement ⟨in its *heyday*, the circus was a major form of entertainment for small-town America⟩ — see BLOOM 1

hiatus *n* **1** an open space in a barrier (as a wall or hedge) ⟨steam was rising from an *hiatus* in the ground⟩ — see GAP 1

2 an incomplete or deficient area ⟨a *hiatus* in the law which prevented the district attorney from prosecuting the offenders⟩ — see GAP 3
3 a break in continuity ⟨a three-year *hiatus* before the fifth book in the series appeared⟩ — see GAP 2

hiccup *also* **hiccough** *n* a break in continuity ⟨the business has grown steadily for 14 years, with only a few minor *hiccups*⟩ — see GAP 2

hick *n* an awkward or simple person especially from a small town or the country ⟨city dwellers who looked down on their cousins from northern Maine as *hicks*⟩
synonyms bumpkin, chawbacon, churl, clodhopper, cornball, countryman, hayseed, hillbilly, provincial, rube, rustic, yokel
related words boor, clod, clown, gawk, lout, oaf; greenhorn, tenderfoot; peasant, peon; backwoodsman, mountaineer
near antonyms slicker, smoothy (*or* smoothie); metropolitan, suburbanite, urbanite
antonyms cosmopolitan, cosmopolite, sophisticate

[1]**hickey** *n* a small article the actual name of which one either does not know or cannot remember ⟨I lost the *hickey* that locks and unlocks the car's doors by remote control⟩ — see DOODAD 1

[2]**hickey** *n* a small, inflamed swelling of the skin ⟨the last thing she needed on her wedding day was a *hickey* for her radiant face⟩ — see POCK

hidden *adj* screened or sequestered from view ⟨a *hidden* beach that very few know how to get to⟩ — see SECLUDED

hide *n* **1** the outer covering of an animal removed for its commercial value ⟨seal *hides* are used by Eskimos to make footwear, boats, shelters, bags, and clothing⟩
synonyms fur, leather, pelt, skin
related words badger, beaver, chamois, chinchilla, ermine, fisher, fox, marten, mink, muskrat, otter, Persian lamb, rabbit, raccoon (*also* racoon), sable, seal; bearskin, buckskin, calfskin, coonskin, cowhide, deerskin, doeskin, goatskin, horsehide, karakul, kidskin, kolinsky, lambskin, pigskin, rawhide, sealskin, sharkskin, sheep, sheepskin, snakeskin; fleece, mouton; alligator, crocodile; cordovan, morocco, patent leather, suede
2 the hairless natural covering of an animal prepared for use ⟨boots made of shiny alligator *hide*⟩ — see LEATHER 1

[1]**hide** *vb* **1** to put into a hiding place ⟨the thief had *hidden* the stolen jewelry under the floorboards⟩
synonyms bury, cache, conceal, ensconce, secrete
related words hoard, squirrel (away), stash; entomb, inter
near antonyms bare, expose, reveal, show, uncover, unmask, unveil, unwrap; flaunt, parade, show off; disinter, unearth
antonyms display, exhibit
2 to keep secret or shut off from view ⟨he tried to *hide* his criminal past⟩ ⟨she *hid* the cat's litter box behind a screen⟩
synonyms belie, blanket, blot out, cloak, conceal, cover, curtain, disguise, enshroud, mask, obscure, occult, paper over, screen, shroud, suppress, veil
related words bury, camouflage, cover (up), smother; gild, gloss (over), varnish, whitewash; becloud, bedim, befog, block, cloud, darken, eclipse, obstruct, occlude, overcast, overshadow, shade
near antonyms bring out, present; clarify, illuminate; advertise, air, broadcast, get out, proclaim, publicize, publish, spread
antonyms bare, disclose, display, divulge, expose, reveal, show, uncloak, uncover, unmask, unveil
3 to remain out of sight ⟨he *hid* in the closet while his roommate lied to the probation officer⟩
synonyms hole up, lie, lurk, repose, skulk
related words slink, sneak; avoid, elude, evade
phrases lie low, sit tight
near antonyms come out, materialize, show up, turn up
antonyms appear

[2]**hide** *vb* **1** to strike repeatedly ⟨the grizzled quartermaster threatened to *hide* any soldier caught stealing provisions⟩ — see BEAT 1
2 to strike repeatedly with something long and thin or flexible ⟨threatened to *hide* the boys with his cane if he ever found them on his property again⟩ — see WHIP 1

hideaway *n* a place where a person goes to hide or to avoid others ⟨the novelist has a little *hideaway* in the country where he goes whenever he wants to do some serious writing⟩ — see HIDEOUT

hidebound *adj* tending to favor established ideas, conditions, or institutions ⟨the *hidebound* innkeeper refused to see the need for a Web site, insisting that the inn had done without one for over 150 years⟩ — see CONSERVATIVE 1

hideosity *n* something unpleasant to look at ⟨residents of the historic district have protested that a fast-food joint would be a *hideosity* and totally out of character with the rest of the neighborhood⟩ — see EYESORE

hideous *adj* **1** causing intense displeasure, disgust, or resentment ⟨the *hideous* way in which she treated her maid after she discovered her ring was missing⟩ — see OFFENSIVE 1
2 extremely disturbing or repellent ⟨a *hideous* crime that could not be fully described in the newspapers⟩ — see HORRIBLE 1
3 unpleasant to look at ⟨wearing a *hideous* Halloween mask that made the kids all jump with fright⟩ — see UGLY 1

hideousness *n* **1** the quality of inspiring intense dread or dismay ⟨the indescribable *hideousness* of the squalor in which the villagers are forced to live⟩ — see HORROR 1
2 the state or quality of being utterly evil ⟨the *hideousness* of the defendant's alleged crimes should not prevent him from getting a fair trial⟩ — see ENORMITY 1

hideout *n* a place where a person goes to hide or to avoid others ⟨police found the stolen jewels under the floorboards in the thief's *hideout*, a cabin deep in the woods⟩
synonyms concealment, covert, den, hermitage, hideaway, hidey-hole (*or* hidy-hole), lair, nest
related words blind, cover, nook, recess; hangout, harbor, harborage, haunt, haven, redoubt, refuge, retreat, shelter

hidey-hole *or* **hidy-hole** *n* a place where a person goes to hide or to avoid others ⟨commandos captured the deposed dictator in a carefully camouflaged cellar that he had been using as a *hidey-hole*⟩ — see HIDEOUT

hiding *n* the placing of something out of sight ⟨fearing that the enemy would soon be upon them, the museum director oversaw the *hiding* of the most valuable works of art⟩ — see CONCEALMENT 1

hie *vb* to proceed or move quickly ⟨we had best *hie* home before the snow gets worse⟩ — see HURRY 2

hierarchy *n* a scheme of rank or order ⟨honesty sits at the top of my *hierarchy* of values⟩ — see SCALE 1

hierophant *n* a person who actively supports or favors a cause ⟨as an early *hierophant* of birth control, Margaret Sanger had to face down often vehement opposition⟩ — see EXPONENT 1

higgledy-piggledy *adj* lacking in order, neatness, and often cleanliness ⟨the quilt was a *higgledy-piggledy* patchwork of odd-shaped fabric scraps, each of which held a fond memory for the family⟩ — see MESSY

high *adj* **1** extending to a great distance upward ⟨as the

highest mountain in the world, Mount Everest is mountaineering's holy grail⟩
synonyms altitudinous, lofty, tall, towering
related words dominant, dominating, eminent, prominent; elevated, lifted, raised, uplifted, upswept; high-rise, statuesque
near antonyms flat, stubby, stumpy
antonyms low, low-lying, short, squat
2 being at a higher level than average ⟨gasoline prices are *high* right now⟩ ⟨a *high* fever⟩ ⟨people with *high* incomes⟩
synonyms elevated, escalated, heightened, increased, jacked (up), raised, up
related words extreme, full, maximized, maximum, peaked, sky-high, utmost; inflated, over, overfilled, overflowing, overfull, overlarge, overloaded, oversize (*or* oversized)
near antonyms decreased, depressed, dropped, knock-down [*chiefly British*], receded, under
antonyms down, low
3 located at a greater height than average or usual ⟨an eagle's nest *high* on the cliff⟩ ⟨an old house with *high* ceilings⟩
synonyms airy, elevated, nosebleed
related words ascendant (*also* ascendent), ascending, soaring; overhead, overlooking, raised, upheld, uplifted, upraised; topmost, upmost, upper, uppermost, upward
near antonyms depressed, descendant (*also* descendent), descending, down, dropped, fallen, grounded, lowered, sunken; lowermost, nethermost, undermost; abreast, even, level
antonyms low, low-lying
4 being far along in development ⟨a cabal of self-proclaimed Luddites who argued that the evils of *high* technology far outweighed its virtues⟩ — see ADVANCED 1
5 being under the influence of alcohol ⟨not only has he never been *high*, he has never even tasted alcohol⟩ — see DRUNK
6 commanding a large price ⟨the concert tickets weren't cheap—you don't even want to know how *high* they were⟩ — see COSTLY
7 having, characterized by, or arising from a dignified and generous nature ⟨she had the *highest* intentions, but her "help" turned out to be a disaster⟩ — see NOBLE 2
8 highest in rank or authority ⟨*high* government officials⟩ ⟨lord *high* executioner⟩ — see HEAD
9 being under the influence of a recreational drug ⟨he's clean now, but when he was younger he used to get *high* every day⟩ — see STONED 1

high *adv* in a luxurious manner ⟨after he had won the lottery Philip lived pretty *high*—until all the money was gone⟩
synonyms expensively, extravagantly, fatly, grandly, large, lavishly, luxuriously, opulently, palatially, plushly, richly, sumptuously
related words imposingly, impressively, magnificently, splendidly; grandiosely, ostentatiously, pompously, pretentiously; affluently, comfortably, fine, wealthily; immoderately, indulgently, intemperately, prodigally, wantonly, wastefully
near antonyms unpretentiously; cheaply, economically, frugally, inexpensively, meagerly, poorly, skimpily, sparely, sparingly, thriftily; conservatively, moderately, prudently, reasonably, restrainedly, sensibly, temperately
antonyms austerely, humbly, modestly, plainly, simply

high *n* **1** a state of overwhelming usually pleasurable emotion ⟨it took days for the *high* of the World Series win to wear off⟩ — see ECSTASY
2 the expanse of air surrounding the earth ⟨V formations of honking geese on *high* mean winter will soon be here⟩ — see SKY 1

high and dry *adj* unable to act or achieve one's purpose ⟨the inadequate supplies of vaccine left many people *high and dry* when the flu season arrived⟩ — see POWERLESS

high and low *adv* in every place or in all places ⟨I've been looking *high and low* for my glasses⟩ — see EVERYWHERE

high–and–mighty *adj* having a feeling of superiority that shows itself in an overbearing attitude ⟨a boss so *high-and-mighty* that no one could reason with him about anything⟩ — see ARROGANT

highball *vb* to proceed or move quickly ⟨trying to make up for lost time, the train just *highballed* through the station without stopping⟩ — see HURRY 2

highborn *adj* of high birth, rank, or station ⟨skeptics have argued that these dramatic masterpieces must have been written by someone more *highborn* than one William Shakespeare of Stratford-upon-Avon⟩ — see NOBLE 1

highbred *adj* of high birth, rank, or station ⟨as the *highbred* descendant of one of the state's oldest families, he bristled at being ordered about by an uncouth upstart⟩ — see NOBLE 1

highbrow *adj* much given to learning and thinking ⟨finally, a TV series that appeals to a *highbrow* audience⟩ — see INTELLECTUAL 1

highbrow *n* a person with strong intellectual interests ⟨guests at her elegant dinner parties are a mix of the city's *highbrows* and captains of industry⟩ — see INTELLECTUAL

highbrowed *adj* much given to learning and thinking ⟨*highbrowed* readers were not bothered by the novel's lack of a conventional plot⟩ — see INTELLECTUAL 1

high–class *adj* of the very best kind ⟨had some surprisingly *high-class* food at the church supper⟩ — see EXCELLENT

high–end *adj* **1** appealing to affluent consumers ⟨a *high-end* haberdashery that serves its clients by appointment only⟩ — see UPSCALE
2 commanding a large price ⟨*high-end* digital cameras intended for professionals and serious amateurs⟩ — see COSTLY

higher *adj* being far along in development ⟨an institute of *higher* learning⟩ ⟨*higher* primates, such as the apes⟩ — see ADVANCED 1

highest *adj* **1** being at a point or level higher than all others ⟨the *highest* grade⟩ ⟨the *highest* flag on the pole⟩ — see TOP 1
2 coming before all others in importance ⟨turned to the *highest* authority for answers⟩ ⟨the *highest* official in the land⟩ — see FOREMOST 1

highfalutin *also* **hifalutin** *adj* **1** full of fine words and fancy expressions ⟨his *highfalutin* paean to the working class failed to win over a crowd that wanted to hear down-to-earth proposals for economic relief⟩ — see FLOWERY 1
2 having a feeling of superiority that shows itself in an overbearing attitude ⟨her *highfalutin* relatives from New York made the snide remark that her little house "has that lived-in look"⟩ — see ARROGANT
3 having or displaying feelings of scorn for what is regarded as beneath oneself ⟨refused to be intimidated by the *highfalutin* manner of the sales staff in the fashionable boutique⟩ — see PROUD 1
4 self-consciously trying to present an appearance of grandeur or importance ⟨"fine Southern cuisine" sounds a bit *highfalutin* for a barbecue shack⟩ — see PRETENTIOUS 1

highflier *or* **highflyer** *n* an ambitious person who eagerly goes after what is desired ⟨one of New York's largest law firms, it attracts *highfliers* looking for a big-time legal career⟩ — see GO-GETTER

high–flown *adj* **1** full of fine words and fancy expressions ⟨gave a *high-flown* reply instead of a simple "yes" or "no" answer⟩ — see FLOWERY 1
2 very dignified in form, tone, or style ⟨*high-flown* speeches about the nobleness of their cause⟩ — see ELEVATED 2

high ground *n* the more favorable condition or position in a competition ⟨one would have thought that having the superior product would have given the company the *high ground* in the video format war⟩ — see ADVANTAGE 1

high–handed *adj* **1** having a feeling of superiority that shows itself in an overbearing attitude ⟨the manager displayed a *high-handed* demeanor that increasingly demoralized the members of his staff⟩ — see ARROGANT
2 having or showing a tendency to force one's will on others without any regard to fairness or necessity ⟨that country club tends to be rather *high-handed* about whom they let in and whom they shut out⟩ — see ARBITRARY 1

high–hat *adj* **1** being or characteristic of a person who has an offensive air of superiority and tends to ignore or disdain anyone regarded as inferior ⟨at the wedding reception the bride's *high-hat* relatives did their considerable best to ignore us⟩ — see SNOBBISH
2 having a feeling of superiority that shows itself in an overbearing attitude ⟨several *high-hat* society types arrived after we did, but they got seated first⟩ — see ARROGANT

high–hat *vb* **1** to show contempt for ⟨one presidential candidate presents himself as an outsider who has long been *high-hatted* by the Beltway elite⟩ — see SCORN 1
2 to deliberately ignore or treat rudely ⟨was *high-hatted* by an old college friend who's now a power player on Wall Street⟩ — see SNUB 1

high horse *n* an exaggerated sense of one's importance that shows itself in the making of excessive or unjustified claims ⟨I won't deal with you until you get off your *high horse* and stop patronizing me⟩ — see ARROGANCE

high jinks *also* **hijinks** *n pl* wildly playful or mischievous behavior ⟨despite the team's dismal record, the players have won over many fans with their exuberant *high jinks*⟩ — see HORSEPLAY

highland *n* an area of high ground ⟨there are permanent glaciers in the cool, humid *highlands* of the Pacific Northwest⟩ — see HEIGHT 4

highlight *vb* to indicate the importance of by centering attention on ⟨according to the TV schedule, this week's "Astronomy Today" *highlights* the accomplishments of Maria Mitchell⟩ — see EMPHASIZE 1

highly *adv* **1** to a great degree ⟨though she didn't win, she was *highly* satisfied with her personal results for the marathon⟩ — see VERY 1
2 to a large extent or degree ⟨that is *highly* different from your first idea for a family vacation⟩ — see GREATLY 2

high–minded *adj* **1** having, characterized by, or arising from a dignified and generous nature ⟨*high-minded* efforts to improve the lives of people who are less fortunate⟩ — see NOBLE 2
2 self-consciously trying to present an appearance of grandeur or importance ⟨she was too *high-minded* to admit publicly to watching trashy movies, but privately she loved them⟩ — see PRETENTIOUS 1

high–mindedly *adv* in a manner befitting a person of the highest character and ideals ⟨*high-mindedly* gave his colleagues all the credit for the successful completion of the project⟩ — see GREATLY 1

high–muck–a–muck *or* **high–muckety–muck** *n* one of high position or importance within a group ⟨failed to pass muster with the country club's *high-muck-a-mucks*⟩ — see BIG SHOT

high noon *n* **1** a state or time of great activity, thriving, or achievement ⟨the *high noon* of the whaling industry occurred in the first half of the 19th century⟩ — see BLOOM 1
2 the highest part or point ⟨the exhibition showcased works painted at the *high noon* of French Impressionism⟩ — see HEIGHT 1
3 the middle of the day ⟨the dedication ceremony began at *high noon* with a 21-gun salute⟩ — see NOON 1

high–pitched *adj* having a high musical pitch or range ⟨the *high-pitched* sound of a siren⟩ — see SHRILL

high–pressure *adj* having or showing a bold forcefulness in the pursuit of a goal ⟨a *high-pressure* salesman who wouldn't take "no" for an answer⟩ ⟨"for a limited time only" and other standbys of *high-pressure* advertising⟩ — see AGGRESSIVE 1

high priest *n* **1** a person who actively supports or favors a cause ⟨the *high priest* of tax relief for the state's property owners⟩ — see EXPONENT 1
2 one who brings an art or science to full realization ⟨as the *high priest* of nouvelle cuisine, he was enormously influential in the food world⟩ — see EXPONENT 2

high road *n* a passage cleared for public vehicular travel ⟨hair-raising tales of outlaws who ambushed coaches traveling the *high roads*⟩ — see WAY 1

high roller *n* someone who spends money freely or foolishly ⟨in the carefree environment of a vacation, even a person of modest means has the urge to play the *high roller*⟩ — see PRODIGAL

high–rolling *adj* given to spending money freely or foolishly ⟨an overpriced nightclub that caters mainly to *high-rolling* tourists⟩ — see PRODIGAL

high–sounding *adj* full of fine words and fancy expressions ⟨*high-sounding* speeches full of promises that the candidates would never keep⟩ — see FLOWERY 1

high–spirited *adj* **1** joyously unrestrained ⟨a *high-spirited* crowd loudly cheering the basketball team on⟩ — see EXUBERANT
2 marked by a lively display of strong feeling ⟨the band struck up a *high-spirited* march as the President's motorcade approached⟩ — see SPIRITED 1

high–spiritedly *adv* in a quick and spirited manner ⟨the teens *high-spiritedly* donned clown costumes in preparation for the party they were giving at the Children's Hospital⟩ — see GAILY 2

high–strung *adj* easily excited by nature ⟨a dog that tends to be *high-strung* is not the best pet for young children⟩ — see EXCITABLE

hightail (it) *vb* to hasten away from something dangerous or frightening ⟨when a fight broke out, we *hightailed it* out of the bar⟩ — see RUN 2

high–ticket *adj* commanding a large price ⟨a specialty store selling *high-ticket* goods to a well-heeled clientele⟩ — see COSTLY

high–water mark *n* the highest part or point ⟨he hit the *high-water mark* of his acting career when he played Tiny Tim in a school play⟩ — see HEIGHT 1

highway *n* a passage cleared for public vehicular travel ⟨the four-lane *highway* narrows to two lanes once you leave the city⟩ — see WAY 1

highway robbery *n* the exaction of a grossly excessive charge for goods or services ⟨what some rock superstars charge for concert tickets is simply *highway robbery*⟩ — see EXTORTION

hijack *also* **highjack** *vb* to take control of (a vehicle) by force ⟨some loser tried to *hijack* the plane with a toy gun⟩ — see COMMANDEER 1

hijacking *also* **highjacking** *n* the unlawful or forcible carrying away of a person or animal ⟨a country in which *hijackings* of foreign executives has become commonplace⟩ — see ABDUCTION

hike *vb* **1** to travel by foot for exercise or pleasure ⟨she *hiked* along the trail around the pond⟩
synonyms amble, perambulate, ramble, saunter, stroll, tramp, tromp
related words roam, rove, wander; peregrinate, traipse, traverse, trek, walk; march, promenade; power walk
2 to move from a lower to a higher place or position ⟨with a determined look, he *hiked* his trousers up and buckled down to work⟩ — see RAISE 1

hiker *n* a person who travels by foot for exercise or pleasure ⟨the *hikers* set out before dawn in order to have the trail to themselves⟩
synonyms ambler, perambulator, rambler, tramper, walker
related words pedestrian; roamer, rover, trekker, wanderer, wayfarer; alpinist, backpacker, climber, mountaineer

hilarious *adj* causing or intended to cause laughter ⟨*hilarious* cartoons that the whole family can enjoy⟩ ⟨the clown's *hilarious* antics⟩ — see FUNNY 1

hilariousness *n* the amusing quality or element in something ⟨the *hilariousness* of the situation only struck us later, and we had a good laugh⟩ — see HUMOR 1

hilarity *n* a mood characterized by high spirits and amusement and often accompanied by laughter ⟨*hilarity* is the last thing you expect to find at a funeral, but we were there to celebrate his life rather than to dwell on his death⟩ — see MIRTH

hill *n* **1** a quantity of things thrown or stacked on one another ⟨the ants made little *hills* of dirt⟩ — see [1]PILE 1
2 an area of high ground ⟨a town nestled in a valley surrounded by green *hills*⟩ — see HEIGHT 4
3 an upward slope ⟨I got stuck behind a truck going up a *hill* in a no-passing zone⟩ — see ASCENT 2

hill *vb* to form into a pile or ridge of earth ⟨*hilled* peat moss around the rosebushes to protect them from the freeze⟩ — see MOUND 1

hillbilly *n* an awkward or simple person especially from a small town or the country ⟨in the skit, he was a shy *hillbilly* in love with a city girl⟩ — see HICK

Himalayan *adj* unusually large ⟨as military blunders go, the disastrous Pickett's Charge was of *Himalayan* proportions⟩ — see HUGE

hind *adj* being at or in the part of something opposite the front part ⟨the frog's long *hind* legs⟩ ⟨the hawk's reddish *hind* feathers⟩ — see BACK

hinder *adj* being at or in the part of something opposite the front part ⟨the animal's case of mange was especially bad in its *hinder* parts⟩ — see BACK

hinder *vb* to create difficulty for the work or activity of ⟨was not *hindered* by a lack of money because she could use what food she had on hand⟩ — see HAMPER

hindmost *adj* **1** being at or in the part of something opposite the front part ⟨the dance teacher had to keep reminding us to kick our *hindmost* foot when we reversed direction⟩ — see BACK
2 following all others of the same kind in order or time ⟨the *hindmost* wagon in the caravan had the roughest ride because of the deep ruts and dust created by the others⟩ — see LAST 1

hindrance *n* something that makes movement or progress difficult ⟨made a survey of all the *hindrances* to wheelchair access, such as curbs and stairs⟩ — see ENCUMBRANCE

hinge *vb* to be determined by, based on, or subject (to) ⟨the outcome of the game *hinged* on a single play⟩ — see DEPEND 1

hinky *adj, slang* **1** not feeling sure about the truth, wisdom, or trustworthiness of someone or something ⟨the cop was feeling *hinky* about the whole situation and was starting to think that it was a setup⟩ — see DOUBTFUL 1
2 feeling or showing uncomfortable feelings of uncertainty ⟨after noticing that the driver seemed *hinky*, the border guard demanded that he submit to an inspection of his vehicle⟩ — see NERVOUS 1

hint *n* **1** a slight or indirect pointing to something (as a solution or explanation) ⟨can't you give me some *hint* as to where you're taking me?⟩
synonyms clue, cue, indication, inkling, intimation, lead, suggestion
related words breath, flicker, glimmer, glimpse, mention, scent, whiff, wind; hunch, idea, inspiration, notion; allusion, implication, inference, innuendo, insinuation; denotation, evidence, guidepost, key, mark, overtone, pointer, sign, signal, telltale, token; assistance, nod, prompt, tip, tip-off, wink; feeling, foreboding, intuition, premonition, presentiment, suspicion; augury, foreshadower, foretaste, harbinger, omen, portent, prefigurement, presage, symptom
near antonyms answer, solution
2 an almost imperceptible sign of something ⟨there was the slightest *hint* of scorn in her voice⟩
synonyms breath, flicker, glimmer, suggestion, tang, touch, trace, whiff
related words inkling, intimation, scent, wind; evidence, indication, mark, sign
near antonyms permeation, pervasion, saturation
3 a piece of advice or useful information especially from an expert ⟨some helpful *hints* for cleaning carpet stains⟩ — see [1]TIP 1
4 a very small amount ⟨I detect just a *hint* of mint in the sauce⟩ — see PARTICLE 1

hint *vb* to convey an idea indirectly ⟨kept *hinting* that she wouldn't mind an invitation to spend the weekend at their beach house⟩
synonyms allude, imply, indicate, infer, insinuate, intimate, suggest
related words advert, mention, point, refer, signal, signalize, signify; smack (of), smell (of)
near antonyms announce, declare, proclaim; elucidate, explain, spell out; delineate, describe

hinterland *n* a rural region that forms the edge of the settled or developed part of a country ⟨the colonies hugged the coastline, while the *hinterland* remained largely unexplored⟩ — see FRONTIER 2

hip *adj* **1** being in the latest or current fashion ⟨*hip* sunglasses whose fancy prices will make you squint in disbelief⟩ — see STYLISH
2 having inside information ⟨he wasn't *hip* to what was going on behind the scenes and was taken totally unawares by the company shake-up⟩ — see WISE 2
3 keenly aware of and responsive to the latest developments especially in fashion and entertainment ⟨*hip* fashionistas wouldn't be caught dead in that outfit⟩ — see AU COURANT 1

hip *n* the quality or state of being fashionable ⟨kids dyeing their hair in pursuit of *hip*⟩ — see COOL 2

hip *vb* to give information to ⟨if you want to get *hipped* on what goes on behind the scenes at a television network, you should read this book⟩ — see ENLIGHTEN 1

hipness *n* the quality or state of being fashionable ⟨such *hipness* does not come cheap, and his clothes budget is out of sight⟩ — see COOL 2

hipsterism *n* the quality or state of being fashionable ⟨college *hipsterism* that year meant ragged flannel shirts and faded jeans⟩ — see COOL 2

hire *n* **1** the state of being provided with a paying job ⟨he spent most of his career in the *hire* of high-paying defense contractors⟩
synonyms employ, employment, engagement
related words appointment, assignment, conscription,

enlistment, recruitment; incumbency, tenure; occupation, place, position, post, situation, work
near antonyms boot, discharge, dismissal, firing, removal, sack, severance; demotion, suspension; furlough, layoff, leave, liberty, retirement
antonyms joblessness, nonemployment, unemployment
2 the money paid regularly to a person for labor or services ⟨used to mow lawns for *hire*⟩ — see WAGE

hire *vb* **1** to take or get the temporary use of (something) for a set sum ⟨the Youngs *hired* a limousine for their daughter's wedding⟩
synonyms charter, engage, lease, rent
related words sublease, sublet; check out; arrange (for), bespeak, book, contract (for), order, reserve, sign up (for)
2 to provide with a paying job ⟨the farm *hires* teenagers to pick blueberries in the summer⟩ — see EMPLOY 1

hireling *n* one who works for another for wages or a salary ⟨demanded to speak to the store's owner and not one of his *hirelings*⟩ — see EMPLOYEE

hirsute *adj* covered with or as if with hair ⟨wore a *hirsute* mask as part of his werewolf costume⟩ — see HAIRY 1

hiss *n* **1** a sound similar to the speech sound \s\ stretched out ⟨the *hiss* of air escaping from a balloon⟩
synonyms fizz, sizzle, swish, whish, whiz (*or* whizz)
related words swoosh, wheeze, whistle, whoosh, zip; sibilance, sibilant
2 a vocal sound made to express scorn or disapproval ⟨there was a chorus of boos and *hisses* from the fans when the umpire called the runner out⟩ — see CATCALL

hiss *vb* to make a sound like that of stretching out the speech sound \s\ ⟨the frightened kitten *hissed* at us when we tried to pick it up⟩
synonyms fizz, fizzle, sizzle, swish, whish, whiz (*or* whizz)
related words swoosh, wheeze, whistle, whoosh, zip; bubble, effervesce; buzz, drone, hum

hissy *n, chiefly Southern & southern Midland* an outburst or display of excited anger ⟨she throws a royal *hissy* whenever her food is late⟩ — see TANTRUM

hissy fit *n* an outburst or display of excited anger ⟨the demanding diva had a major *hissy fit* when she had to wait for her trailer to be ready⟩ — see TANTRUM

historian *n* a student or writer of history ⟨*historians* are still trying to sort out fact from fiction in the story of Kateri Tekakwitha, the Lily of the Mohawks⟩
synonyms annalist, chronicler
related words autobiographer, biographer; archivist, chronologist, genealogist, hagiographer

historic *adj* having great meaning or lasting effect ⟨a *historic* peace agreement between the two nations⟩ — see IMPORTANT 1

historical *adj* restricted to or based on fact ⟨a *historical* novel that tells the story of Hannibal's crossing of the Alps through the eyes of a young boy⟩ — see FACTUAL 1

history *n* **1** an account of important events in the order in which they happened ⟨a *history* of the American civil rights movement during the 1960s⟩
synonyms annals, chronicle, record
related words blog, commentary, diary, journal, memoir, reminiscence(s); autobiography, biography, life; epic, legend, narrative, saga, story, tale; archives, documentation, log, register, report; chronology, genealogy
2 a relating of events usually in the order in which they happened ⟨we heard the whole *history* of her illness in excruciating detail⟩ — see ACCOUNT 1
3 the events or experience of former times ⟨*history* has many lessons to teach us, if only we would listen⟩ — see PAST

histrionic *adj* **1** given to or marked by attention-getting behavior suggestive of stage acting ⟨a penchant for dish throwing, door slamming, and other *histrionic* displays of temper⟩ — see THEATRICAL 1
2 having the general quality or effect of a stage performance ⟨we never tired of his *histrionic* reenactment of how he found money under the floorboards of a house he was renovating⟩ — see DRAMATIC 1

hit *n* **1** a person or thing that is successful ⟨the new babysitter turned out to be a *hit* with the kids⟩
synonyms blockbuster, megahit, smash, success, supernova, winner
related words blue chip, blue chipper, corker, crackerjack (*also* crackajack), dandy, jim-dandy, pip, prizewinner; gem, jewel, treasure; marvel, natural, phenomenon, sensation, wonder; coup, triumph, victory
near antonyms disappointment, fizzle, lemon, loser
antonyms bomb, bummer, bust, catastrophe, clinker, debacle (*also* débâcle), dud, failure, fiasco, flop, misfire, turkey, washout
2 a hard strike with a part of the body or an instrument ⟨the quarterback can't take too many more *hits* like that and escape permanent injury⟩ — see [1]BLOW

hit *vb* **1** to deliver a blow to (someone or something) usually in a strong vigorous manner ⟨a good carpenter *hits* a nail just two or three times to drive it in⟩
synonyms bang, bash, bat, belt, biff, bludgeon, bob, bonk, bop, box, bust, clap, clip, clobber, clock, clout, crack, hammer, knock, nail, paste, pound, punch, rap, slam, slap, slog, slug, smack, smite, sock, strike, swat, swipe, tag, thump, thwack, wallop, whack, whale, zap
related words batter, beat, buffet, bung, chop, cuff, drub, lace, lambaste (*or* lambast), lick, mangle, maul, pelt, pepper, pommel, pummel, rough; scuff; bunt, flick, stroke, tap; bump, butt, jab, jostle, kick, knee, poke, prod, push, shove, stamp; bowl (down *or* over), cream, deck, dump [*slang*], fell, floor, knock down, level; rabbit-punch, sucker punch; cane, club, cudgel, flail, flog, lash, sap, slash, sledge, sledgehammer, spear, stab, switch, thrash, whip; bean, brain, conk, skull
phrases hang one on
2 to come into usually forceful contact with something ⟨when she fell on the ice, she *hit* hard and badly bruised her elbow⟩
synonyms bang, bash, bump, collide, crash, impact, impinge, knock, ram, slam, smash, strike, swipe, thud
related words bounce, carom, clunk, glance, rebound, ricochet, skim, skip; contact, land, touch; brush, graze, kiss, nudge, scrape, shave, sweep; bulldoze, jostle, muscle, press, push
near antonyms miss, skirt
3 to obtain (as a goal) through effort ⟨the rock band *hit* "the big time" with their third album⟩ — see ACHIEVE 1

hit (on *or* upon) *vb* to come upon after searching, study, or effort ⟨the doctor finally *hit on* what was wrong with the pain-wracked woman⟩ — see FIND 1

hit (up) *vb* to make a request of ⟨she's always *hitting* me *up* for money⟩ — see ASK 2

hit (upon) *vb* to come upon unexpectedly or by chance ⟨the popular belief that Sir Isaac Newton *hit upon* his understanding of gravity at the sight of an apple falling from a tree⟩ — see HAPPEN (ON *OR* UPON)

hitch *n* **1** a danger or difficulty that is hidden or not easily recognized ⟨there are always a few *hitches* when you launch a system as complex as this one⟩ — see PITFALL 1
2 a fixed period of time during which a person holds a job or position ⟨signed on for a three-year *hitch* in the army⟩ — see TERM 1

hitch *vb* **1** to move or cause to move with a sharp quick motion ⟨kept *hitching* up his pants because they were too big in the waist⟩ — see JERK 1

2 to put or bring together so as to form a new and longer whole ⟨she escaped out the window by using a makeshift rope of bedsheets and clothing she'd *hitched* together⟩ — see CONNECT 1
3 to put securely in place or in a desired position ⟨*hitched* the trailer to the back of the car⟩ — see FASTEN 2
4 to travel by securing free rides ⟨her brother *hitched* across the country after he graduated from college⟩ — see HITCHHIKE

hitcher *n* one who hitchhikes ⟨never stops for *hitchers* on interstates, where hitchhiking is illegal⟩ — see HITCHHIKER

hitchhike *vb* to travel by securing free rides ⟨another one of those novels in which the hero undertakes a journey of self-discovery by *hitchhiking* around the country⟩
synonyms hitch, thumb
related words bum; stow away; carjack, hijack (*also* highjack)

hitchhiker *n* one who hitchhikes ⟨police have issued warnings about a serial killer who is believed to be preying upon *hitchhikers*⟩
synonyms hitcher
related words stowaway; carjacker, hijacker

hither *adj* being the less far of two ⟨we began to explore the *hither* bank while our companions crossed the creek to explore the yonder bank⟩ — see NEAR 1

hitherto *adv* up to this or that time ⟨at the talent show Kyle revealed his *hitherto* unknown gift for doing impressions⟩
synonyms heretofore, theretofore, yet
related words before, formerly, previously
phrases so far, thus far
near antonyms afterward (*or* afterwards), later, subsequently; hereupon, thereupon
antonyms henceforth, henceforward, hereafter, thenceforth, thenceforward (*also* thenceforwards), thereafter

hit–or–miss *adj* lacking a definite plan, purpose, or pattern ⟨your *hit-or-miss* schedule for taking your medication is going to land you in the hospital again⟩ — see RANDOM

hit or miss *adv* without definite aim, direction, rule, or method ⟨I was learning Spanish *hit or miss*, mostly just by hearing my friends speak it⟩
synonyms aimlessly, anyhow, anyway, anywise, desultorily, erratically, haphazard, haphazardly, helter-skelter, irregularly, randomly, willy-nilly
related words arbitrarily, capriciously, carelessly, casually, indiscriminately, informally, offhand, offhandedly, promiscuously, whimsically; accidentally, fortuitously, inadvertently, unconsciously, unintentionally, unwittingly; disconnectedly, disjointedly, fitfully, intermittently, spottily, unpredictably; higgledy-piggledy, topsy-turvy
phrases at random
near antonyms carefully, formally, gingerly, meticulously, orderly, punctiliously; deliberately, intentionally, purposefully, purposely
antonyms methodically, systematically

hoagie *also* **hoagy** *n* a large sandwich on a long split roll ⟨had a steak-and-cheese *hoagie* for the first time in Philadelphia⟩ — see SUBMARINE

hoar *adj* dating or surviving from the distant past ⟨the *hoar* and crumbling stones of ruined temples⟩ — see ANCIENT 1

hoar *n* a covering of tiny ice crystals on a cold surface ⟨the *hoar*-covered meadow gleamed in the early-morning sun⟩ — see FROST 1

hoard *n* **1** a supply stored up and often hidden away ⟨keeps a *hoard* of empty yogurt containers in his basement workshop for storing whatnots⟩
synonyms cache, stash, stockpile, store
related words coffers, deposit, funds, nest egg, savings, sinking fund, treasure; inventory, pool, reserve, reservoir, stock; provisions, resources; accumulation, assemblage, collection, gathering, harvest; repertory
2 a collection of things kept available for future use or need ⟨she couldn't find one pencil with an eraser in her entire *hoard* of pencil stubs⟩ — see STORE 1

hoard *vb* to put (something of future use or value) in a safe or secret place ⟨he's been *hoarding* empty yogurt containers all winter, with the intention of using them to start seedlings in the spring⟩
synonyms cache, lay away, lay by, lay in, lay up, put by, salt away, squirrel (away), stash, stockpile, store, stow, treasure
related words accumulate, acquire, amass, assemble, collect, concentrate, garner, gather, pick up, round up, scrape (together); heap, pile, stack; conserve, husband, preserve; bank, coffer, deposit, hold, keep, reserve, retain, save, set by, stock, withhold; bury, conceal, ensconce, secrete
phrases set aside
near antonyms cast, discard, ditch, dump, fling (off *or* away), jettison, throw away, throw out, unload; consume, squander, use up, waste; hand out, hand over, relinquish, surrender; blow, dissipate, fritter (away), lavish, misspend, run through, spend; deplete, exhaust, expend, impoverish; dispel, disperse, dissipate, scatter

hoarfrost *n* a covering of tiny ice crystals on a cold surface ⟨the *hoarfrost* formed a delicate swirly pattern on the window⟩ — see FROST 1

hoariness *n* the state of being something old ⟨the *hoariness* of that joke is such that Noah probably used it to entertain his fellow passengers on the ark⟩ — see ANCIENTNESS 2

hoarse *adj* harsh and dry in sound ⟨the dying man spoke in a *hoarse* whisper⟩
synonyms coarse, croaking, croaky, grating, gravel, gravelly, gruff, husky, rasping, raspy, rusty, scratchy, throaty
related words growling, growly, guttural; abrasive, cacophonous, discordant, grinding, jarring, rough, scraping, scratching; cawing, raucous, screeching, squawking, strident; choked, cracked, strained, strangled; dissonant, inharmonious, unmelodious, unmusical
near antonyms gentle, gliding, golden, liquid, mellifluent, mellifluous, mellow, soothing, sweet, tender; satiny, silken, smooth, soft, velvety; euphonious, lyric, lyrical, melodic, melodious, musical

hoary *adj* dating or surviving from the distant past ⟨*hoary* oak trees with dripping moss and gnarled limbs shaded us from the sun⟩ — see ANCIENT 1

hoax *n* an imitation that is passed off as genuine ⟨the skeleton of the purported ancient hominid turned out to be a *hoax*⟩ — see FAKE 1

hoax *vb* to cause to believe what is untrue ⟨a skilled forger who *hoaxed* the art world into believing that the paintings were long-lost Vermeers⟩ — see DECEIVE

hoaxer *n* **1** a dishonest person who uses clever means to cheat others out of something of value ⟨if it sounds too good to be true, you're probably dealing with a *hoaxer* in a boiler room somewhere⟩ — see TRICKSTER 1
2 one who makes false claims of identity or expertise ⟨his college roommate turned out be a complete *hoaxer* and not the son of a wealthy shipping tycoon he said he was⟩ — see IMPOSTOR

hob *n* playful, reckless behavior that is not intended to cause serious harm ⟨our indoor Frisbee game—my dog's and mine—played *hob* with a couple of lamps and a vase⟩ — see MISCHIEF 1

hobble *vb* **1** to create difficulty for the work or activity

of ⟨we were *hobbled* by the snowstorm from getting out to do some Christmas shopping⟩ — see HAMPER
2 to walk while favoring one leg ⟨I *hobbled* home with a twisted ankle⟩ — see LIMP 1

hobby *n* an activity outside of one's regular occupation that is engaged in primarily for pleasure ⟨his ranch is just a weekend *hobby*—he makes his real money as an investment banker⟩ — see AVOCATION

hobbyhorse *n* an activity outside of one's regular occupation that is engaged in primarily for pleasure ⟨oil painting became the *hobbyhorse* of her long years of retirement⟩ — see AVOCATION

hobbyist *n* a person who regularly or occasionally engages in an activity as a pastime rather than as a profession ⟨a book on crafting fine wood furniture that is intended for the home *hobbyist*⟩ — see AMATEUR 1

hobgoblin *n* **1** an imaginary being usually having a small human form and magical powers ⟨in Shakespeare's *Midsummer Night's Dream*, Puck is a *hobgoblin* who plays pranks such as spoiling milk and tripping old ladies⟩ — see FAIRY
2 something or someone that causes fear or dread especially without reason ⟨the fear of success and the pressures that come with it can be more of a *hobgoblin* than the possibility of failure⟩ — see BOGEY 1

hobnob *vb* **1** to come or be together as friends ⟨those two have been *hobnobbing* together since freshman year⟩ — see ASSOCIATE 1
2 to take part in social activities ⟨spent some time *hobnobbing* with the rich and famous while in Los Angeles⟩ — see SOCIALIZE

hobnobber *n* a person frequently seen in the company of another ⟨the actor's agent is a *hobnobber* with a lot of big movie producers⟩ — see ASSOCIATE 1

hobo *n* a homeless wanderer who may beg or steal for a living ⟨kind folks who always gave *hoboes* who came to the farm a meal and then sent them on their way⟩ — see TRAMP 1

hock *n* a place of confinement for persons held in lawful custody ⟨some lowlife who had been in and out of *hock* most of his adult life⟩ — see JAIL

hock *vb* to leave as a guarantee of repayment of a loan ⟨the prince had to *hock* the family jewels to pay his gambling debts⟩ — see PAWN

hocus-pocus *n* the art or skill of performing tricks or illusions for entertainment ⟨with some well-crafted *hocus-pocus*, the illusionist made the dove disappear from his hands⟩ — see MAGIC 2

hodgepodge *n* an unorganized collection or mixture of various things ⟨the exhibit was a *hodgepodge* of mediocre art, bad art, and really bad art⟩ — see MISCELLANY 1

hog *n* one who eats greedily or too much ⟨if I had known that my guests were going to be such *hogs*, I would have prepared twice as much food⟩ — see GLUTTON

hoggish *adj* having a huge appetite ⟨was feeling *hoggish* after the hike and ate the whole bag of cookies⟩ — see VORACIOUS 1

hog heaven *n* a situation or state of carefree comfort ⟨a drink was in my hand, my butt was in a hot tub, and I was in *hog heaven*⟩ — see BEER AND SKITTLES

hogshead *n* an enclosed wooden vessel for holding beverages ⟨the ship's hold carried 164 *hogsheads* of molasses⟩ — see CASK

hog-tie *vb* to create difficulty for the work or activity of ⟨their principals' inflexible demands virtually *hog-tied* the diplomats' efforts to negotiate a peace treaty⟩ — see HAMPER

hog-tied *adj* unable to act or achieve one's purpose ⟨prosecutors were *hog-tied* as the convicted felon was freed on a technicality⟩ — see POWERLESS

hogwash *n* language, behavior, or ideas that are absurd and contrary to good sense ⟨the librarian told us a lot of *hogwash* about how you can go to jail for having overdue books⟩ — see NONSENSE 1

ho-hum *adj* causing weariness, restlessness, or lack of interest ⟨the characterizations are good, but the plot is just *ho-hum*⟩ — see BORING

hoick *vb* to move or cause to move with a sharp quick motion ⟨*hoicked* up his pants and hastily waded into the water⟩ — see JERK 1

hoi polloi *n pl* the body of the community as contrasted with the elite ⟨"I pay no attention to the opinions of the *hoi polloi*," the writer sniffed⟩ — see MASS 1

hoist *vb* **1** to lift with effort ⟨dockworkers *hoisted* all 164 barrels of molasses out of the ship's hold when it arrived in port⟩ — see HEAVE 1
2 to move from a lower to a higher place or position ⟨*hoisted* the flag on the flagpole⟩ — see RAISE 1
3 to swallow in liquid form ⟨I have time to *hoist* a couple beers before heading home⟩ — see DRINK 1

hokey *adj* tiresomely obvious and unsophisticated ⟨their father's sense of humor was *hokey* beyond belief and most people's endurance⟩ — see CORNY 2

hokeypokey *n* language, behavior, or ideas that are absurd and contrary to good sense ⟨every year the legislature has to go through the same *hokeypokey* before it balances the state budget⟩ — see NONSENSE 1

hokum *n* language, behavior, or ideas that are absurd and contrary to good sense ⟨a movie about the disaster that's pure Hollywood *hokum*⟩ — see NONSENSE 1

hold *n* **1** the act or manner of holding ⟨make sure you have a firm *hold* on the chain saw before you turn it on⟩
synonyms clasp, clench, grapple, grasp, grip, handgrip, handhold
related words anchorage, leverage, purchase; grab, seizure; foothold, footing, toehold; clinch, embrace, hug
near antonyms release, relinquishment
2 a structure or place from which one can resist attack ⟨the ruins of an ancient Roman *hold*⟩ — see FORT
3 the right or means to command or control others ⟨the government has no *hold* over where we live and work⟩ — see POWER 1
4 the state or fact of being able to exchange information regarding one's current situation ⟨I worry that I won't be able to get *hold* of you in an emergency⟩ — see TOUCH 1
5 a place of confinement for persons held in lawful custody ⟨upon hearing the guilty verdict, the accused realized that he would lie in that godforsaken *hold* for the remainder of his life⟩ — see JAIL
6 the knowledge gained from the process of coming to know or understand something ⟨I need to get *hold* of the situation before planning a course of action⟩ — see COMPREHENSION
7 the state of being held in lawful custody ⟨a suspected terrorist who was abducted at an airport and put in *hold* at an undisclosed location⟩ — see DETENTION 1

hold *vb* **1** to have or keep in one's hands ⟨this casserole dish is too hot to *hold*, so grab a potholder⟩
synonyms clench, cling (to), clutch, grip
related words bear, carry; bag, capture, catch, collar, corral, grab, grapple, hook, land, latch (on *or* onto), nab, nail, seize, snap (up), snare, snatch, take, trap; feel, finger, handle, paw; clasp, embrace, grasp, hug; cradle
phrases hang on to, hold on to
near antonyms drop, give, hand, unclasp, unhand; cede, deliver, give up, hand out, hand over, release, relinquish, render, turn over, yield
2 to continue to have in one's possession or power ⟨she, and she alone, *held* the keys to the mysterious chest⟩ — see KEEP 2
3 to have as an opinion ⟨"We *hold* these truths to be

self-evident, that all men are created equal"⟩ — see BELIEVE 2
4 to have within ⟨the mysterious chest *held* an ancient book on magic spells and potions⟩ — see CONTAIN 1
5 to keep in one's mind or heart ⟨still *held* her close to his heart, though they had long parted⟩ — see HARBOR 1
6 to keep, control, or experience as one's own ⟨the same family has *held* this piece of land for over 300 years⟩ — see HAVE 1
7 to make or have room for ⟨the couple needed to rent a hall that would *hold* 300 people⟩ — see ACCOMMODATE 1
8 to reach for and take hold of by embracing with the fingers or arms ⟨please *hold* my arm on these slippery stairs⟩ — see TAKE 1
9 to think of in a particular way ⟨*held* to be the best blueberry pies in the state⟩ — see CONSIDER 1
10 to keep from exceeding a desirable degree or level (as of expression) ⟨we managed to *hold* our laughter until we got outside⟩ ⟨*hold* your temper until you hear the whole story⟩ — see CONTROL 1
11 to point or turn (something) toward a target or goal ⟨*held* a gun on the store clerk and ordered him to empty the till⟩ — see AIM 1

holdall *n, chiefly British* a bag carried by hand and designed to hold a traveler's clothing and personal articles ⟨there was a forgotten *holdall* in the bus station loo⟩ — see TRAVELING BAG

holdback *n* **1** an instance or period of being prevented from going about one's business ⟨there'll be a *holdback* on production until the new machinery is fully installed⟩ — see DELAY
2 something that makes movement or progress difficult ⟨the only *holdback* to starting the new job is my contractual commitment to my current position⟩ — see ENCUMBRANCE

hold back *vb* **1** to create difficulty for the work or activity of ⟨the only thing *holding* Joe *back* from joining the swim team is lack of transportation⟩ — see HAMPER
2 to refrain from openly showing or uttering ⟨*held back* her tears until she was alone⟩ — see SUPPRESS 2

hold down *vb* to set bounds or an upper limit for ⟨efforts to *hold down* taxes keep running up against the legislature's ingrained unwillingness to cut spending⟩ — see LIMIT 1

holder *n* **1** one who has a legal or rightful claim to ownership ⟨the *holders* of the land gave us permission to camp on it⟩ — see PROPRIETOR
2 something into which a liquid or smaller objects can be put for storage or transportation ⟨her hat made a good *holder* for the shells she collected on the beach⟩ — see CONTAINER

holding *n* **1** a decision made by a court or tribunal regarding a case it has heard ⟨the *holding* of "not guilty" took everyone by surprise⟩ — see SENTENCE
2 *usually* **holdings** *pl* transportable items that one owns ⟨the museum's *holdings* of ancient manuscripts are among the rarest in the world⟩ — see POSSESSION 2

holding pattern *n* **1** a state of temporary inactivity ⟨repair work on the bridge was in a *holding pattern* for the duration of the winter⟩ — see ABEYANCE
2 an instance or period of being prevented from going about one's business ⟨the couple has been trapped in this *holding pattern* for six months, as adoption officials create more red tape⟩ — see DELAY

hold off (on) *vb* to assign to a later time ⟨we *held off on* accepting the invitation in the hopes that something better would come along⟩ — see POSTPONE

hold on *vb* **1** to remain indefinitely in existence or in the same state ⟨the ancient beliefs still *held on* in remote mountain villages⟩ — see CONTINUE 1
2 to remain in place in readiness or expectation of something ⟨*hold on* a minute—it's not your turn⟩ — see WAIT

hold out *vb* to continue to operate or to meet one's needs ⟨we hoped our supply of firewood would *hold out* until power was restored⟩ ⟨luckily, the old outboard motor *held out* till we made it to shore⟩
synonyms hold up, keep up, last, prevail, survive
related words bear up, carry on, cope, endure, fare, get along, get by, get on, go, hang in, make out, manage, persevere; abide, continue, draw out, hang on, hold on, linger, persist, remain, run on, stretch
near antonyms break, break down, collapse, conk (out), crash, cut out, die, expire, stall, stop; run down, wane
antonyms fail, fizzle, give out, go out, peter (out), run out

hold over *vb* to assign to a later time ⟨the golf tournament had to be *held over* until the line of thunderstorms had passed through⟩ — see POSTPONE

holdup *n* an instance or period of being prevented from going about one's business ⟨a *holdup* in construction due to the weather⟩ — see DELAY

hold up *vb* **1** to assign to a later time ⟨*held up* mail delivery until we had a permanent address⟩ — see POSTPONE
2 to bring (something) to a standstill ⟨traffic was *held up* for miles by the accident⟩ — see ^{1}HALT 1
3 to create difficulty for the work or activity of ⟨if lack of transportation is the only thing *holding* you *up*, I can give you a ride⟩ — see HAMPER
4 to continue to operate or to meet one's needs ⟨the air conditioner *held up* this year, but it's not going to make it through another summer⟩ — see HOLD OUT
5 to remain indefinitely in existence or in the same state ⟨the storm's hurricane-force winds did not *hold up* once it hit the coast⟩ — see CONTINUE 1
6 to withstand scrutiny and gain acceptance or approval ⟨an argument that won't *hold up* in court⟩ — see WASH 2

hole *n* **1** a place in a surface allowing passage into or through a thing ⟨line up the pegs on section A with the *holes* in section B and press the two together⟩
synonyms aperture, opening, orifice, perforation
related words loophole; breach, break, chink, cleft, crack, cranny, crevice, cut, fissure, gash, notch, rent, rift, rupture, slash, slit, split, tear; slot, space; exit, mouth, outlet, pore, vent; entrance, inlet, intake; pinhole, pinprick, punch, puncture; airhole, armhole, buttonhole, keyhole, knothole, peephole, pothole, wormhole
near antonyms fill, filler, filling, patch, plug, seal, stopper; barrier, blockage, obstacle, obstruction
2 a sunken area forming a separate space ⟨dig a *hole* big enough to plant the tree⟩
synonyms cavity, concavity, dent, depression, dint, hollow, indentation, indenture, pit, recess
related words burrow, cave, cavern, ditch, excavation, furrow, groove, gutter, trench, trough; basin, bowl, valley; alcove, cleft, niche, nook, opening, recess, socket; alveolus, dimple, gouge, impression, imprint, notch, pocket; borehole, chuckhole, crater, posthole, pothole, sinkhole, wallow, water hole, well; abyss, chasm, gulf, vacuity, vacuum, void
near antonyms hill, mound, rise; bump, bunch, hump, lump, pimple, swell, swelling, tumor
antonyms bulge, camber, convexity, jut, projection, protrusion, protuberance
3 a difficult, puzzling, or embarrassing situation from which there is no easy escape ⟨Bill dug himself into a *hole* by promising to be in two places at the same time⟩ — see PREDICAMENT

4 a dirty or messy place ⟨when people see my room, they often ask, "How can you live in this *hole*?"⟩ — see PIGPEN
5 an open space in a barrier (as a wall or hedge) ⟨found a *hole* in the chain-link fence big enough to squeeze through⟩ — see GAP 1
6 the shelter or resting place of a wild animal ⟨watched the snake slither into its *hole*⟩ — see DEN 1
7 an incomplete or deficient area ⟨there's a huge *hole* in your logic⟩ — see GAP 3

hole *vb* to make a hole or series of holes in ⟨*holed* the target with a round of shots⟩ — see PERFORATE

hole–and–corner *adj* undertaken or done so as to escape being observed or known by others ⟨a *hole-and-corner* antiterrorist operation whose very existence has been steadfastly denied by the government⟩ — see SECRET 1

hole up *vb* to remain out of sight ⟨we'll *hole up* in the cellar and wait out the hurricane⟩ — see ¹HIDE 3

holiday *n, chiefly British* a period during which the usual routine of school or work is suspended ⟨the member of parliament met his wife while on *holiday* in the south of France⟩ — see VACATION

holiday *vb* to take or spend a vacation ⟨saw kangaroos while *holidaying* in Australia⟩ — see VACATION

holiness *n* the quality or state of being spiritually pure or virtuous ⟨known throughout the world for his *holiness*, the prophet was visited daily by hundreds of pilgrims⟩
synonyms blessedness, devoutness, godliness, piety, piousness, sainthood, saintliness, saintship, sanctity
related words asceticism, devotion, morality, prayerfulness, religiousness, spirituality; priestliness; goodness, rectitude, righteousness, uprightness, virtue, virtuousness; consecration, sacredness
near antonyms blasphemousness, irreverence, sacrilegiousness; depravedness, depravity, evilness, heinousness, monstrosity, sinfulness, vileness, wickedness; hypocrisy, sanctimoniousness, sanctimony
antonyms godlessness, impiety, ungodliness, unholiness

holler *n* **1** a loud vocal expression of strong emotion ⟨heard a *holler* from somewhere in the woods and ran toward it⟩ — see SHOUT
2 an expression of dissatisfaction, pain, or resentment ⟨there didn't seem to be a thermostat setting that wouldn't bring a *holler* from somebody⟩ — see COMPLAINT 1

holler *vb* **1** to express dissatisfaction, pain, or resentment usually tiresomely ⟨another city council meeting with residents *hollering* about the unsatisfactory collection of garbage⟩ — see COMPLAIN
2 to speak so as to be heard at a distance ⟨there's no need to *holler*; I'm in the next room⟩ — see CALL 1

hollo *or* **halloo** *also* **hallo** *vb* to speak so as to be heard at a distance ⟨far into the night searchers could be heard *holloing* for the lost child⟩ — see CALL 1

hollow *adj* curved inward ⟨there's a noticeably *hollow* spot in the mattress where he has been sleeping⟩
synonyms concave, dented, depressed, dished, indented, recessed, sunken
related words alveolar, cavernous, crescentic, cuplike, cupped, cuppy, recurved; dimpled, pockmarked; compressed, condensed, contracted, diminished, reduced
near antonyms ballooning, bloated, blown up, bulbous, distended, enlarged, expanded, extended, inflated, jutting, projecting, puffed, puffy, risen, swollen; domed, global, globular, round, rounded, spherical
antonyms bulging, cambered, convex, protruding, protrusive, protuberant

hollow *n* **1** a sunken area forming a separate space ⟨made a little *hollow* in her mound of mashed potatoes and filled it with gravy⟩ — see HOLE 2
2 an area of lowland between hills or mountains ⟨a quaint village nestled in a *hollow* among green hills⟩ — see VALLEY

holocaust *n* **1** a destructive burning ⟨the *holocaust* caused by the ignited chemicals completely destroyed the factory and several surrounding homes⟩ — see FIRE 1
2 the killing of a large number of people ⟨as many as 2,000,000 people may have perished in the *holocaust* perpetrated by Cambodia's Khmer Rouge⟩ — see MASSACRE

hols *n pl, British* a period during which the usual routine of school or work is suspended ⟨my friends from university are all going abroad for the summer *hols*⟩ — see VACATION

holy *adj* **1** showing a devotion to God and to a life of virtue ⟨the *holy* monk spent many hours on his knees in prayer⟩
synonyms devout, godly, pious, religious, sainted, saintly
related words ascetic (*also* ascetical), prayerful, reverent, reverential, spiritual, worshipful; pietistic, religiose; beatified, blessed (*also* blest), canonized, venerable; angelic (*or* angelical), cherubic; chaste, moral, pure, righteous, upright, virtuous
near antonyms blasphemous, desecrating, irreverent, profanatory, profane, sacrilegious; nonreligious, secular, unspiritual, worldly; backsliding, unfaithful; black, evil, immoral, iniquitous, miscreant, sinful, sinning, unrighteous, wicked
antonyms antireligious, faithless, godless, impious, irreligious, ungodly, unholy
2 set apart or worthy of veneration by association with God ⟨the Torah contains the *holy* writings of Judaism⟩
synonyms blessed (*also* blest), consecrate, consecrated, hallowed, sacral, sacred, sacrosanct, sanctified
related words adored, enshrined, glorified, revered, venerated, worshipped (*also* worshiped); ceremonial, liturgical, priestly, religious, ritual, sacramental, spiritual; biblical, scriptural
near antonyms nonreligious, unspiritual; earthly, mundane, profane, secular, temporal, worldly
antonyms deconsecrated, desacralized, unconsecrated, unhallowed
3 of, relating to, or being God ⟨the *Holy* Trinity⟩
synonyms blessed (*also* blest), divine, godlike, godly, heavenly, sacred, supernatural
related words eternal, everlasting, immortal; all-powerful, almighty, omnipotent, omniscient, supreme
near antonyms human, mortal, natural
4 not to be violated, criticized, or tampered with ⟨the hour every Saturday she listens to her radio program is *holy* and you'd better not make her miss it⟩ — see SACRED 1

Holy Writ *n* a book made up of the writings accepted by Christians as coming from God ⟨quotes extensively from *Holy Writ* in his sermons⟩ — see BIBLE

homage *n* **1** a formal expression of praise ⟨the poem is a moving *homage* to all who have served in our nation's armed services⟩ — see ENCOMIUM
2 public acknowledgment or admiration for an achievement ⟨the unique *homage* that we grant to Olympic athletes⟩ — see GLORY 1

hombre *n* an adult male human being ⟨two tough-looking *hombres* sauntered into the bar and ordered . . . lemonade⟩ — see MAN 1

home *n* **1** the place where one lives ⟨as we entered his 34-room mansion, our host playfully exclaimed, "Welcome to my humble *home*!"⟩
synonyms abode, diggings, domicile, dwelling, fireside, habitation, hearth, hearthstone, house, lodging, pad,

place, quarters, residence, roof
related words accommodations, housing, nest, residency, shelter; bungalow, cabin, casita, chalet, cottage; duplex, ranch, ranch house, saltbox, semi [*chiefly British*], split level, townhome, town house, tract house, triplex; apartment, apartment house, condominium, flat, tenement, tenement house, walk-up; penthouse, salon, suite; barracks, billet, boardinghouse, dorm, dormitory, lodging house, lodgment (*or* lodgement), room(s), rooming house; castle, château, countryseat, estate, hall, manor, manor house, mansion, palace, villa; farmhouse, grange, hacienda, homestead; double-wide, houseboat, house trailer, mobile home, motor home, recreational vehicle, trailer; hermitage, manse, parsonage, rectory, vicarage; hooch (*or* hootch) [*slang*], hovel, hut, hutch, shack, shanty
2 the place where a plant or animal is usually or naturally found ⟨the American south, the *home* of the armadillo⟩
synonyms habitat, niche, range, territory
related words element, environment, environs, haunt, locality, milieu, neighborhood, setting, surroundings
3 the land of one's birth, residence, or citizenship ⟨people who have a common *home*, traditions, language, and food tend to form their own communities in their adopted countries⟩ — see COUNTRY 1
4 those who live as a family in one house ⟨a man who believes that a person's *home* is the most important thing in life⟩ — see HOUSEHOLD
5 a place of origin ⟨Springfield, Massachusetts, is the *home* of basketball, for it was there that the first hoops were hung in 1891⟩ — see BIRTHPLACE

homeboy *n* a violent, brutal person who is often a member of an organized gang ⟨the papers described the two youths accused of the robbery as *homeboys* whose street activities had been known to the police for some time⟩ — see HOODLUM

homeland *n* the land of one's birth, residence, or citizenship ⟨travels every year to Italy, her *homeland* for the first two decades of her life⟩ — see COUNTRY 1

homely *adj* unpleasant to look at ⟨a vast family fortune can make even the *homeliest* of women seem like good marriage material⟩ — see UGLY 1

Homeric *adj* large and impressive in size, grandeur, extent, or conception ⟨the climactic scene of the movie is a pitched battle of *Homeric* proportions⟩ — see GRAND 1

homespun *adj* having or showing an unpretentious informality ⟨dispenses his *homespun* philosophy of life in a weekly newspaper column⟩ — see CRACKER-BARREL

homesteader *n* a person who settles in a new region ⟨in the 1800s *homesteaders* in search of cheap land and a new life headed to the West in droves⟩ — see FRONTIERSMAN

home stretch *n* the last part of a process or action ⟨this project has been a lot of work, but we're finally in the *home stretch*⟩ — see FINALE

homey *or* **homie** *n* a violent, brutal person who is often a member of an organized gang ⟨the fatal shooting of a fellow *homey* was just the wake-up call he needed to get out of the drug trade⟩ — see HOODLUM

homicidal *adj* eager for or marked by the shedding of blood, extreme violence, or killing ⟨court-appointed psychiatrists have described the accused as a *homicidal* maniac who should be put away for life⟩ — see BLOODTHIRSTY

homicide *n* **1** the intentional and unlawful taking of another person's life ⟨the missing man was thought to be the victim of a *homicide*, but his body was never found⟩
synonyms blood, foul play, murder, rubout, slaying
related words chance-medley, killing, manslaughter; bloodshed, butchery, carnage, decimation, destruction, massacre, slaughter; assassination, execution, hit; euthanasia, mercy killing; filicide, fratricide, matricide, parricide, patricide, regicide, uxoricide
2 a person who kills another person ⟨throughout the ages society has stigmatized the *homicide*⟩ — see ASSASSIN

homiletic *or* **homiletical** *adj* marked by or given to preaching moral values ⟨tends to speak in *homiletic* aphorisms, which can be a little tiresome⟩ — see SERMONIC

homily *n* **1** a public speech usually by a member of the clergy for the purpose of giving moral guidance or uplift ⟨last Sunday's *homily* was about being kind to your neighbors⟩ — see SERMON
2 an idea or expression that has been used by many people ⟨a TV movie filled with the usual hokey *homilies* about people triumphing over life's adversities⟩ — see COMMONPLACE

homogenize *vb* **1** to make agree with a single established standard or model ⟨plans to *homogenize* the science curriculum in public high schools throughout the state⟩ — see STANDARDIZE
2 to turn into a single mass or entity that is more or less the same throughout ⟨chain stores and fast-food restaurants have *homogenized* the nation's highways and byways to the point where every place looks like every other place⟩ — see BLEND 1

homologate *vb* to give official acceptance of as satisfactory ⟨to be effectual, a judge must *homologate* the plea bargain between the district attorney and the defense⟩ — see APPROVE

Homo sapiens *n* the human race ⟨how far into outer reaches of the universe will *Homo sapiens* someday be able to go?⟩ — see MANKIND

hon *n* a person with whom one is in love ⟨I'm so glad you're home, *hon*⟩ — see SWEETHEART 1

honcho *n* **1** one of high position or importance within a group ⟨the office was all abuzz because some *honchos* from corporate headquarters were coming for a visit⟩ — see BIG SHOT
2 the person (as an employer or supervisor) who tells people and especially workers what to do ⟨he's definitely the head *honcho* in that company⟩ — see BOSS

hone *vb* **1** to make sharp or sharper ⟨*honed* the knife's blade to razor-like sharpness⟩ ⟨*honed* his crossword-puzzle skills by reading the dictionary as though it were a thrilling novel⟩ — see SHARPEN
2 to make smooth by friction ⟨*honed* the edge of the axe until it was amazingly sharp⟩ — see GRIND 1

honed *adj* having an edge thin enough to cut or pierce something ⟨using a finely *honed* butcher knife will make cutting meat easier⟩ — see SHARP 1

honest *adj* **1** being in the habit of telling the truth ⟨at least the weatherman is *honest* and doesn't pretend to be able to predict the unpredictable⟩ — see TRUTHFUL
2 conforming to a high standard of morality or virtue ⟨*honest* and industrious farm folk⟩ — see GOOD 2
3 following the accepted rules of moral conduct ⟨that rare, *honest* customer who doesn't hesitate to tell the cashier she's given him too much change⟩ — see HONORABLE 1
4 free from any intent to deceive or impress others ⟨the sort of person who helps others from an *honest* desire to do good, and not because she might need a favor from them someday⟩ — see GUILELESS
5 free in expressing one's true feelings and opinions ⟨appreciate your *honest* friends, who tell you what you need to hear and not what you want to hear⟩ — see FRANK
6 guided by or in accordance with one's sense of right and wrong ⟨made an *honest* attempt to return the

money she had found in the cafeteria⟩ — see CONSCIENTIOUS 1

7 being exactly as appears or as claimed ⟨a restaurant serving *honest* down-home Southern cooking⟩ — see AUTHENTIC 1

honest broker *n* one who works with opposing sides in order to bring about an agreement ⟨after all the bad blood on both sides, we need to find someone who hasn't been influenced and can act as an *honest broker*⟩ — see MEDIATOR

honestly *adv* to tell the truth ⟨*honestly*, I haven't the slightest idea what you're talking about⟩ — see ACTUALLY 1

honesty *n* **1** devotion to telling the truth ⟨George Washington has gone down in history for his *honesty*⟩
synonyms integrity, probity, truthfulness, veracity, verity
related words honor, honorableness, incorruptibility, rectitude, righteousness, right-mindedness, scrupulosity, scrupulousness, uprightness; artlessness, candidness, candor, forthrightness, frankness, good faith, guilelessness, ingenuousness, plainspokenness, sincerity, straightforwardness; dependability, reliability, reliableness, trustability, trustiness, trustworthiness; accuracy, objectivity; authenticity, correctness, genuineness, truth; credibility
near antonyms artifice, cozenage, crookedness, deception, dissembling, dissimulation, double-dealing, dupery, duplicity, fakery, falseness, falsity, fraudulentness, hypocrisy, insincerity, two-facedness; beguilement, craftiness, cunning, cunningness, furtiveness, guile, indirection, insidiousness, oiliness, perfidy, slickness, slipperiness, slyness, smoothness, treacherousness, trickery, underhandedness, unscrupulousness, wiliness; equivocation, prevarication; exaggeration, inaccuracy
antonyms deceit, deceitfulness, dishonesty, lying, mendaciousness, mendacity, untruthfulness

2 conduct that conforms to an accepted standard of right and wrong ⟨he's known for his *honesty* in business dealings⟩ — see MORALITY 1

3 faithfulness to high moral standards ⟨she knew she could count on her students' *honesty*, even if she left the classroom for a few moments during the test⟩ — see HONOR 1

4 the free expression of one's true feelings and opinions ⟨I am speaking with all *honesty* when I say that your apple pie is the best I've ever tasted⟩ — see CANDOR 1

honey *n* **1** a lovely woman ⟨she's a *honey*, all right⟩ — see BEAUTY 2

2 something very good of its kind ⟨this morning one of my employees had a real *honey* of an excuse for being late for work⟩ — see JIM-DANDY

3 a person with whom one is in love ⟨he usually gives his *honey* a dozen red roses on Valentine's Day⟩ — see SWEETHEART 1

honey *vb* to praise too much ⟨she knew that the hairstylist was *honeying* her for a reason—the expectation of a generous tip⟩ — see FLATTER 1

honker *n, slang* the part of the face bearing the nostrils and nasal cavity ⟨with a *honker* like that, you must need a hankie the size of a bedsheet⟩ — see NOSE 1

honor *n* **1** faithfulness to high moral standards ⟨the mayor, a man of *honor*, never broke a promise to the voters⟩
synonyms honesty, integrity, probity, rectitude, righteousness, uprightness
related words blamelessness, character, conscientiousness, decency, fairness, high-mindedness, incorruptibility, irreproachability, irreproachableness, justice, morality, nobility, reputability, respectability, right-mindedness, scrupulousness, virtue, virtuousness
near antonyms corruptibility, corruption, corruptness, debasement, debauchery, decadence, degeneracy, degradation, depravity, disgrace, disgracefulness, disreputableness, dissipatedness, dissipation, dissoluteness, looseness, perversion, pervertedness, profligacy, shamelessness, venality; blameworthiness, criminality, crookedness, dishonesty, immorality, unrighteousness, unscrupulousness; knavery, rascality, roguishness; meanness, reprehensibleness, rottenness, sinfulness, vileness, villainy, wickedness, wretchedness
antonyms baseness, dishonor, lowness

2 an asset that brings praise or renown ⟨a dedicated, caring teacher who is an *honor* to the teaching profession⟩ — see GLORY 2

3 public acknowledgment or admiration for an achievement ⟨the *honor* we give to our soldiers on Veterans Day⟩ — see GLORY 1

4 something given in recognition of achievement ⟨has received several *honors* from the Boy Scouts for his many years of service⟩ — see AWARD 1

5 something granted as a special favor ⟨it will be an *honor* for me to show your aunt around the city⟩ — see PRIVILEGE

honor *vb* to show appreciation, respect, or affection for (someone) with a public celebration ⟨the newlyweds were *honored* with a dinner given by the bride's grandmother⟩
synonyms fete (*or* fête), recognize
related words acknowledge, cite, commend, compliment, credit, thank; extol (*also* extoll), glorify, laud, praise, tout; acclaim, applaud, cheer, hail, laureate, salute; celebrate, commemorate, memorialize, observe; congratulate, felicitate
near antonyms discredit, disgrace, dishonor, humble, humiliate, shame; bad-mouth, defame, libel, malign, slander; boo, hiss, hoot, jeer; censure, condemn, damn, denounce, reprobate; mock, put down, ridicule, slight

honorable *adj* **1** following the accepted rules of moral conduct ⟨the only *honorable* thing to do is to admit that you were wrong and apologize⟩
synonyms decent, ethical, honest, just, noble, principled, respectable, righteous, stand-up, upright, upstanding
related words blameless, guiltless, irreproachable, unassailable, unimpeachable; chivalrous, classy, high-minded, menschy, right-minded; conscientious, fair, good, incorruptible, moral, reputable, respected, scrupulous, uncorrupted, virtuous; decorous, nice, polite, proper, seemly
near antonyms bad, blackguardly, corrupt, criminal, crooked, evil, immoral, iniquitous, knavish, mean, nefarious, rascally, reprehensible, roguish, rotten, scoundrelly, sinful; unfair, unscrupulous, vile, villainous, wicked, wretched; blamable, blameworthy, censurable, culpable; debased, debauched, decadent, degenerate, degraded, demoralized, depraved, disgraceful, disreputable, dissipated, dissolute, libertine, loose, perverse, perverted, profligate, reprobate, shameful, venal
antonyms base, dishonest, dishonorable, ignoble, low, unethical, unjust, unprincipled, unrighteous, unworthy

2 conforming to a high standard of morality or virtue ⟨it was *honorable* of you to give all the credit to your friend⟩ — see GOOD 2

3 guided by or in accordance with one's sense of right and wrong ⟨I believe that if I genuinely cannot decide fairly, I should do the *honorable* thing and decline to serve on the panel⟩ — see CONSCIENTIOUS 1

honorably *adv* in a manner befitting a person of the highest character and ideals ⟨their sons died *honorably*, fighting a war to preserve freedom for future generations⟩ — see GREATLY 1

honorary *adj* serving to preserve the memory of a person, thing, or an event ⟨an *honorary* plaque marking the site of the first public school in America⟩ — see COMMEMORATIVE

[1]hooch *n, slang* a distilled beverage that can make a person drunk ⟨during Prohibition, everybody drank homemade *hooch*⟩ — see ALCOHOL

[2]hooch *or* **hootch** *n, slang* a small, simply constructed, and often temporary dwelling ⟨the soldiers quickly threw up the *hooches* where they would be living for the next few weeks⟩ — see SHACK

hoochie *n, slang* a boldly flirtatious or sexually promiscuous woman ⟨took up with some *hoochie* he had met at a biker bar⟩ — see FLOOZY

[1]hood *n* a violent, brutal person who is often a member of an organized gang ⟨when a gang of *hoods* started hanging out in front of the store, customers went elsewhere⟩ — see HOODLUM

[2]hood *n* something that covers or conceals like a piece of cloth ⟨counterfeiters conducting their affairs under a *hood* of secrecy⟩ — see CLOAK 1

hoodlum *n* a violent, brutal person who is often a member of an organized gang ⟨a couple of *hoodlums* held up the convenience store⟩
synonyms bully, gangbanger, gangsta, gangster, goon, gorilla, homeboy, homey (*or* homie), hood, hooligan, mobster, mug, plug-ugly, punk, roughneck, rowdy, ruffian, thug, tough, toughie (*also* toughy), yob [*British*], yobbo [*British*]
related words cutthroat, scoundrel, villain; assassin, bandit, bravo, brigand, criminal, crook, desperado, felon, gunman, highwayman, lawbreaker, mafioso, malefactor, offender, outlaw, perp, perpetrator, pirate; pickpocket, racketeer, robber, swindler, thief, vandal; juvenile delinquent, tearaway [*British*]

hoodoo *n* **1** language, behavior, or ideas that are absurd and contrary to good sense ⟨some economists have characterized the proposal as economic *hoodoo* that should be hooted down⟩ — see NONSENSE 1
2 something that brings bad luck ⟨some *hoodoo* must be at work—I lost both sets of house keys⟩ — see JINX

hoodwink *vb* to cause to believe what is untrue ⟨Tom Sawyer famously *hoodwinked* the other boys into thinking there was nothing more enjoyable than whitewashing a fence⟩ — see DECEIVE

hooey *n* language, behavior, or ideas that are absurd and contrary to good sense ⟨stories about the inn being haunted are just a lot of *hooey*⟩ — see NONSENSE 1

hoof (it) *vb* **1** to go on foot ⟨I *hoofed it* to the library to save bus fare⟩ — see WALK 1
2 to perform a series of usually rhythmic bodily movements to music ⟨he *hoofs it* from seven to eight every Thursday night with other avid square dancers⟩ — see DANCE 1

hoo–ha *also* **hoo–hah** *n* a state of noisy, confused activity ⟨the media *hoo-ha* that inevitably occurs when a politician makes a gaffe, no matter how inconsequential⟩ — see COMMOTION

hook *n* a hard strike with a part of the body or an instrument ⟨delivered a hard right *hook* that struck his opponent in the eye⟩ — see [1]BLOW

hook *vb* **1** to cause to turn away from a straight line ⟨the pitcher *hooked* the ball, and the batter missed⟩ — see BEND 1
2 to put or bring together so as to form a new and longer whole ⟨*hooked* up three short chains together to make a longer necklace⟩ — see CONNECT 1
3 to take (something) without right and with an intent to keep ⟨the monkey *hooked* four bananas from the basket and scampered away to enjoy them⟩ — see STEAL 1
4 to take physical control or possession of (something) suddenly or forcibly ⟨at the clearance sale I *hooked* one of the few remaining digital cameras⟩ — see CATCH 1
5 to turn away from a straight line or course ⟨hang the bird feeder on a branch that *hooks* upward⟩ — see CURVE 1

hooker *n* a woman who engages in sexual activities for money ⟨the undercover cop's beat was a seedy stretch of town popular with the *hookers* and junkies⟩ — see PROSTITUTE

hookup *n* the state of having shared interests or efforts (as in social or business matters) ⟨the drama club's *hookup* with a local acting company provided several aspiring young actors with experience doing summer theater⟩ — see ASSOCIATION 1

hook up *vb* to come or be together as friends ⟨how that odd couple ever *hooked up* we'll never know⟩ — see ASSOCIATE 1

hooligan *n* a violent, brutal person who is often a member of an organized gang ⟨shouldn't you *hooligans* be in school instead of threatening old ladies?⟩ — see HOODLUM

hoop *n* a circular strip ⟨made Christmas garlands from *hoops* of red and green construction paper⟩ — see [1]RING 2

hoopla *n* a state of noisy, confused activity ⟨for all of the *hoopla*, very little news emerged from the governor's press conference⟩ — see COMMOTION

hooray *also* **hurrah** *or* **hurray** *interj* how delightful ⟨"*Hooray*!" he cried when he heard that his team had won⟩
synonyms glory (*or* glory be), ha (*or* hah), hallelujah, hey, hot dog, huzzah, wahoo [*chiefly West*], whee, whoopee, yahoo, yippee
related words wow, zowie; ooh; gee, gee whiz, gosh
near antonyms alack, alas, aw, boo

hoosegow *n* a place of confinement for persons held in lawful custody ⟨she ended up in the *hoosegow* for disorderly conduct⟩ — see JAIL

hoot *n* **1** a loud vocal expression of strong emotion ⟨the courtroom erupted in *hoots* of laughter upon hearing the witness's sarcastic retort⟩ — see SHOUT
2 a vocal sound made to express scorn or disapproval ⟨he ignored the *hoots* and jeers coming from the back of the crowd and kept on speaking⟩ — see CATCALL
3 the smallest amount or part imaginable ⟨I don't give a *hoot* whether you want to go or not—you're going⟩ — see JOT
4 someone or something that is very funny ⟨that stand-up comic is a *hoot* all right, if endless bathroom jokes propel you into paroxysms of laughter⟩ — see SCREAM

hop *n* **1** a social gathering for dancing ⟨back in those days taking someone to the school *hop* was a big deal⟩ — see DANCE
2 an act of leaping into the air ⟨she made it across the rocky creek in two *hops*⟩ — see JUMP 1

hop *vb* **1** to move with a light springing step ⟨a rabbit *hopped* across the frozen grass⟩ — see SKIP 1
2 to propel oneself upward or forward into the air ⟨the bus stopped, a lone passenger *hopped* on, and the driver continued on his way⟩ — see JUMP 1

hope (for) *vb* to believe in the future occurrence of (something) ⟨he was *hoping for* an A in English⟩ — see EXPECT

hopeful *adj* **1** having qualities which inspire hope ⟨economists are offering a *hopeful* forecast for a healthy economy in the coming year⟩
synonyms auspicious, bright, encouraging, fair, golden, heartening, likely, optimistic, promising, propitious, roseate, rose-colored, rosy, upbeat
related words cheering, comforting, reassuring, soothing; assured, confident, decisive, doubtless, positive, sure, unhesitating; beamish, bullish, eupeptic; favorable, good

near antonyms cheerless, comfortless; doubtful, dubious, uncertain; bearish, grim, negative, unfavorable; funereal, glum, gray (*also* grey), miserable, wretched
antonyms bleak, dark, depressing, desperate, discouraging, disheartening, dismal, downbeat, dreary, gloomy, hopeless, inauspicious, pessimistic, unencouraging, unlikely, unpromising, unpropitious
2 pointing toward a happy outcome ⟨in a *hopeful* response to the ad, several people called to say they'd seen our lost cat⟩ — see FAVORABLE 2

hopeful *n* one who seeks an office, honor, position, or award ⟨the three mayoral *hopefuls* are going to debate on local TV⟩ — see CANDIDATE

hopeless *adj* **1** not capable of being cured or reformed ⟨a *hopeless* optimist who looked for the good in everyone and everything⟩ ⟨a *hopeless* criminal who spent most of his adult life in jail⟩
synonyms incorrigible, incurable, irrecoverable, irredeemable, irreformable, irremediable, irretrievable, unrecoverable, unredeemable
related words irreparable, irreversible, uncorrectable; unencouraging, unpromising; impenitent, unreformed, unregenerate, unrepentant
near antonyms reversible; encouraging, promising; penitent, regretful, remorseful, repentant, rueful, sorry; correctable, fixable, rectifiable, repairable, reparable, salvable, salvageable
antonyms curable, reclaimable, recoverable, redeemable, reformable, remediable, retrievable, savable (*or* saveable)
2 emphasizing or expecting the worst ⟨the poor old woman was feeling *hopeless* about ever finding her lost cat⟩ — see PESSIMISTIC 1
3 incapable of being solved or accomplished ⟨keeping this desk organized is *hopeless*⟩ — see IMPOSSIBLE
4 feeling or showing no hope ⟨the *hopeless* look on the faces of the people in the refugee camp⟩ — see DESPONDENT 1

hopelessness *n* utter loss of hope ⟨the utter *hopelessness* of the people in the refugee camp⟩ — see DESPAIR 1

hophead *n, slang* a person who regularly uses drugs especially illegally ⟨in the early 20th century *hopheads* were people one expected to find only in the netherworld of jazz⟩ — see DOPER

hopped–up *adj* **1** being under the influence of a recreational drug ⟨killed in an attempted robbery by some *hopped-up* hoodlum⟩ — see STONED 1
2 showing urgent desire or interest ⟨the parents get almost as *hopped-up* about Christmas as the kids⟩ — see EAGER

hopping *adj* **1** feeling or showing anger ⟨when he saw what I'd done to his car, the other driver was *hopping*⟩ — see ANGRY
2 marked by much life, movement, or activity ⟨by the time we arrived at the club, the place was *hopping*⟩ — see ALIVE 2
3 involved in often constant activity ⟨caring for six kids always keeps her *hopping*⟩ — see BUSY 1

hop, skip, and jump *n* a very small distance or degree ⟨it looked like only a *hop, skip, and jump* on the map, but the drive took six hours⟩ — see HAIR 1

horde *n* a great number of persons or creatures massed together ⟨a *horde* of mosquitoes⟩ ⟨*hordes* of shoppers crowding the stores the week before Christmas⟩ — see CROWD 1

horizonless *adj* being or seeming to be without limits ⟨a *horizonless* array of opportunities for a young, ambitious person at the new company⟩ — see INFINITE

horn *n* something shaped like a hollow cone and used as a container ⟨musketeers carrying their gunpowder in powder *horns*⟩ — see CORNET

horniness *n* **1** intense sexual desire ⟨another movie comedy that celebrates the unbridled *horniness* of the teenage boy⟩ — see LUST 1
2 sexual appetite ⟨a sexagenarian with the *horniness* of a man half his age⟩ — see DESIRE 2

horn–mad *adj* feeling or showing anger ⟨the residents were *horn-mad* when they found out their housing project had been built on a waste dump site⟩ — see ANGRY

hornswoggle *vb* to cause to believe what is untrue ⟨I think we've been *hornswoggled* by that carnival barker⟩ — see DECEIVE

horny *adj* having a strong sexual desire ⟨in her view, "teenage boys are perpetually *horny*"⟩ — see LUSTFUL

horrendous *adj* **1** causing fear ⟨a *horrendous* explosion shook the building⟩ — see FEARFUL 1
2 causing intense displeasure, disgust, or resentment ⟨a *horrendous* breach of good manners that should not escape censure⟩ — see OFFENSIVE 1
3 extremely disturbing or repellent ⟨emergency room personnel must not flinch even from the most *horrendous* injuries⟩ — see HORRIBLE 1

horrible *adj* **1** extremely disturbing or repellent ⟨a *horrible* car accident that left eyewitnesses in a state of shock⟩
synonyms appalling, atrocious, awful, dreadful, frightful, ghastly, grisly, gruesome (*also* grewsome), hideous, horrendous, horrid, horrific, horrifying, lurid, macabre, monstrous, nightmare, nightmarish, shocking, terrible, terrific
related words alarming, bloodcurdling, dire, direful, fearful, fearsome, forbidding, formidable, frightening, gut-wrenching, hair-raising, heart-stopping, intimidating, redoubtable, scary, terrifying; abhorrent, deplorable, disagreeable, disgusting, distasteful, loathsome, nauseating, noisome, obnoxious, obscene, offensive, repugnant, repulsive, revolting, sickening; abominable, evil, foul, heinous, noxious, odious, unspeakable, vile; grotesque, ugly, unsightly
near antonyms agreeable, appealing, attractive, delectable, delicious, delightful, enjoyable, enticing, inviting, pleasant, pleasing, pleasurable, satisfying, welcome; cheering, comforting, soothing
2 causing fear ⟨a *horrible* scream that made shivers go up and down our spines⟩ — see FEARFUL 1
3 causing intense displeasure, disgust, or resentment ⟨I can never forgive her for the *horrible* way she treated her stepdaughter⟩ — see OFFENSIVE 1
4 extremely unsatisfactory ⟨I'm never going back to that restaurant; the service was *horrible*⟩ — see WRETCHED 1

horrid *adj* **1** causing intense displeasure, disgust, or resentment ⟨accused him of stealing and said mean and *horrid* things about him⟩ — see OFFENSIVE 1
2 extremely disturbing or repellent ⟨died a *horrid* death in the fire⟩ — see HORRIBLE 1

horridness *n* the quality of inspiring intense dread or dismay ⟨imagine the *horridness* of not being able to escape from the path of lava spewing from a volcano⟩ — see HORROR 1

horrific *adj* extremely disturbing or repellent ⟨*horrific* images of torture that shocked the conscience of the world⟩ — see HORRIBLE 1

horrified *adj* filled with fear or dread ⟨he sat rigid in his seat, *horrified* that the plane would crash⟩ — see AFRAID

horrify *vb* to strike with fear ⟨the news that a convicted sex offender lived in her neighborhood *horrified* her⟩ — see FRIGHTEN

horrifying *adj* **1** causing fear ⟨received *horrifying* death threats from the townspeople because he had accused

the popular football coach of sexual misconduct⟩ — see FEARFUL 1
2 extremely disturbing or repellent ⟨the *horrifying* sight of children suffering from malnutrition⟩ — see HORRIBLE 1

horror *n* **1** the quality of inspiring intense dread or dismay ⟨it's difficult to even begin to comprehend the *horror* of the Holocaust⟩
synonyms atrociousness, atrocity, awfulness, dreadfulness, frightfulness, ghastliness, grisliness, gruesomeness, hideousness, horridness, monstrosity, repulsiveness
related words badness, baseness, depravedness, depravity, diabolicalness, evil, evilness, foulness, heinousness, immorality, iniquitousness, iniquity, invidiousness, sinfulness, ungodliness, viciousness, vileness, wickedness; accursedness, cursedness, deplorableness, despicableness, detestableness, execrableness, hatefulness, loathsomeness, reprehensibleness; creepiness, eeriness, fearfulness, fearsomeness, ghostliness, ghoulishness, scariness; agony, anguish, hellishness, misery, torment, torture
near antonyms agreeableness, delightfulness, pleasantness, pleasurableness; allurement, appeal, attraction, attractiveness, desirability, desirableness
2 a situation or state that causes great suffering and unhappiness ⟨had never experienced the *horrors* of war⟩ — see HELL 2
3 something unpleasant to look at ⟨are you really going to hang that *horror* on the wall?⟩ — see EYESORE
4 the emotion experienced in the presence or threat of danger ⟨imagine my *horror* at finding myself face to face with a lion on the loose⟩ — see FEAR 1
5 a dislike so strong as to cause stomach upset or queasiness ⟨cat lover or no, she regards cleaning the litter box with *horror*⟩ — see DISGUST

horror–struck *adj* filled with fear or dread ⟨*horror-struck*, the villagers watched helplessly as the tsunami hit the shore⟩ — see AFRAID

horse *n* a large hoofed domestic animal that is used for carrying or drawing loads and for riding ⟨the mounted police stable their *horses* in the city park⟩
synonyms equine, nag, steed
related words equid; colt, filly, foal, gelding, mare, stallion; bronco, mustang, pony; charger, courser, cow pony, cutting horse, galloper, hack, hackney, mount, packhorse, prancer, quarter horse, racehorse, saddle horse, trotter, warhorse, workhorse; bay, black, buckskin, chestnut, dun, palomino, pinto, roan, skewbald, sorrel; cob, dobbin, jade, plug, skate

horse around *vb* to engage in attention-getting playful or boisterous behavior ⟨the boys were *horsing around* on the boat when one of them fell overboard⟩ — see CUT UP

horsefeathers *n pl, slang* language, behavior, or ideas that are absurd and contrary to good sense ⟨*horsefeathers*! don't believe everything you read in the papers⟩ — see NONSENSE 1

horselaugh *n* an explosive sound that is a sign of amusement ⟨even in a crowded auditorium you wouldn't have trouble picking out his earsplitting *horselaugh*⟩ — see LAUGH 1

horseless carriage *n* a self-propelled passenger vehicle on four wheels ⟨with the coming of the *horseless carriage*, distances between places were greatly reduced and the national landscape was transformed⟩ — see CAR

horseplay *n* wildly playful or mischievous behavior ⟨when he saw us spraying each other with the hose instead of washing the car, Dad yelled, "Cut out the *horseplay*!"⟩
synonyms buffoonery, clownery, clowning, foolery, high jinks (*also* hijinks), horsing around, monkey business, monkeying, monkeyshine(s), roughhouse, roughhousing, shenanigan(s), skylarking, slapstick, tomfoolery
related words childishness, clownishness, foolishness, funning, jesting, joking, nonsense, silliness, waggery; boisterousness, rambunctiousness, rowdiness, rowdyism, rumbustiousness [*chiefly British*]; devilry (*or* deviltry), impishness, knavery, mischief, mischievousness, prankishness, rascality, roguery, roguishness, trickery; cavorting, frivolity, frolicking, gamboling (*or* gambolling), merrymaking, playfulness, revelry, roistering, romping, sporting, sportiveness

horsepower *n* the ability to exert effort for the accomplishment of a task ⟨that architectural firm probably doesn't have the creative *horsepower* to produce a truly innovative design⟩ — see POWER 2

horse sense *n* the ability to make intelligent decisions especially in everyday matters ⟨pure *horse sense* should tell you not to stand so close to the space heater⟩ — see COMMON SENSE

horse–trade *vb* to talk over or dispute the terms of a purchase ⟨I *horse-traded* with the painter: I did his tax returns, and he did my kitchen⟩ — see BARGAIN 1

horsewhip *vb* to strike repeatedly with something long and thin or flexible ⟨the cruel guards promptly *horsewhipped* the prisoners if they collapsed under the heavy loads they were forced to carry⟩ — see WHIP 1

horsing around *n* wildly playful or mischievous behavior ⟨at the beach there was a lot more *horsing around* on the sand than actual swimming in the water⟩ — see HORSEPLAY

hose *n* a close-fitting covering for the foot and leg ⟨a reenactor dressed like Benjamin Franklin in waistcoat, breeches, and *hose*⟩ — see STOCKING

hose *vb, slang* to rob by the use of trickery or threats ⟨when the guy failed to return with our money, we sooned realized that we had been *hosed*⟩ — see FLEECE

hospice *n* a place that provides rooms and usually a public dining room for overnight guests ⟨the monks run a *hospice* for travelers in their mountain retreat⟩ — see HOTEL

hospitable *adj* showing a natural kindness and courtesy especially in social situations ⟨the family is unfailingly *hospitable* whenever guests show up unexpectedly at their summer cottage⟩ — see GRACIOUS 1

host *n* **1** a great number of persons or creatures massed together ⟨a *host* of people of all faiths gathered in St. Peter's Square to see the Pope⟩ — see CROWD 1
2 a large body of men and women organized for land warfare ⟨the small band of defenders was no match for the enemy's mighty *host* of thousands⟩ — see ARMY 1
3 a person who conducts a program of entertainment by making introductions and providing continuity ⟨our favorite morning TV show has a new *host*⟩ — see ANNOUNCER

hostel *n* a place that provides rooms and usually a public dining room for overnight guests ⟨in the old days, a traveler could spend the night at one of the *hostels* placed along the coach route⟩ — see HOTEL

hostelry *n* a place that provides rooms and usually a public dining room for overnight guests ⟨the grande dame of the city's *hostelries*, it has played host to presidents, kings, and Hollywood royalty⟩ — see HOTEL

hostile *adj* **1** marked by opposition or ill will ⟨our landlord has a *hostile* attitude toward foreigners and refuses to rent to them⟩
synonyms adversarial, adversary, antagonistic, antipathetic, inhospitable, inimical, jaundiced, mortal, negative, unfriendly, unsympathetic
related words adverse, argumentative, bellicose, belligerent, clashing, combative, conflicting, contentious,

contrary, disputatious, militant, opposed, pugnacious, quarrelsome, resisting, scrappy, truculent; antisocial, cold, cool, disagreeable, disapproving, distant, frigid, icy; biased, prejudiced; discourteous, ill-bred, ill-mannered, impertinent, impolite, inconsiderate, rude, surly, uncivil, unfavorable, unkind, unmannerly, unpleasant, unsociable; acrimonious, bitter, despiteful, hateful, malevolent, malicious, malign, malignant, opprobrious, rancorous, spiteful, unloving, vindictive, virulent
near antonyms affable, amiable, amicable, civil, companionable, comradely, convivial, cordial, genial, good-natured, good-tempered, gracious, gregarious, neighborly, pleasant, sociable, social, warm; affectionate, devoted, kind, kindly, loving, nice, sweet; accepting, agreeable, approving, benign, empathetic, favorable, understanding, warmhearted, welcoming
antonyms friendly, hospitable, nonantagonistic, nonhostile, sympathetic
2 opposed to one's interests ⟨the company's president vows to fight the *hostile* takeover by the giant corporation⟩ — see ADVERSE 1

hostile *n* one that is hostile toward another ⟨reports of *hostiles* in the area kept the settlers on edge⟩ — see ENEMY

hostility *n* **1** a deep-seated ill will ⟨a lingering *hostility* between the two neighbors ever since since they had that property-line dispute⟩ — see ENMITY
2 hostilities *pl* a state of armed violent struggle between states, nations, or groups ⟨both sides agreed to cease all *hostilities* for Hanukkah and Christmas⟩ — see WAR 1

hot *adj* **1** having a notably high temperature ⟨the casserole, just out of the oven, was too *hot* to eat⟩
synonyms ardent, boiling, broiling, burning, fervent, fervid, fiery, piping hot, red, red-hot, roasting, scalding, scorching, searing, sultry, superheated, sweltering, torrid, ultrahot, white-hot
related words blazing, glowing, igneous, molten, seething, sizzling; heated, overheated, reheated, warmed; snug, toasty, warm, warmish; feverish, flushed, inflamed (*also* enflamed); canicular, muggy, steamy, summerlike, summery, tropical
near antonyms chill, chilly, coldish, cool, coolish, nippy, snappy; blizzardly, frosty, snowy, subfreezing, subzero, wintry (*also* wintery); chilled, cooled, refrigerated, unheated; benumbed, numb, shivering
antonyms algid, arctic, bitter, bone-chilling, cold, freezing, frigid, frozen, glacial, ice-cold, iced, icy
2 being or involving the latest methods, concepts, information, or styles ⟨this spring it's the cool shades of lipstick that are *hot*⟩ — see MODERN
3 enjoying widespread favor or approval ⟨was surprised to learn that American jazz has long been *hot* in Russia⟩ — see POPULAR 1
4 marked by bursts of destructive force or intense activity ⟨your *hot* temper is going to get you in trouble⟩ ⟨a *hot* battle for first place in the American League⟩ — see VIOLENT 1
5 showing urgent desire or interest ⟨we were *hot* to get the baseball game started and wished it would stop raining⟩ — see EAGER
6 sexually attractive ⟨my sisters only watched the game because they think the outfielder is *hot*⟩ — see SEXY 1
7 feeling or showing anger ⟨you don't have to get all *hot* about it⟩ — see ANGRY
8 moving, proceeding, or acting with great speed ⟨bought a *hot* new car that should tear up the roadways⟩ — see FAST 1
9 of the very best kind ⟨since you're guilty as hell, you'd better get a *hot* lawyer⟩ — see EXCELLENT
10 having a strong sexual desire ⟨he admitted that the nude photos made him *hot*⟩ — see LUSTFUL

hot *adv* with great speed ⟨workers were working *hot* and heavy to repair the breach in the levee⟩ — see FAST 1

hot (up) *vb, chiefly Southern, southern Midland, & British* to cause to have or give off heat to a moderate degree ⟨with a silky Southern drawl, the waitress asked, "Want me to *hot up* that pie?"⟩ — see WARM 1

hot air *n* **1** boastful speech or writing ⟨his taking credit for the rescue was mostly *hot air*, since the boat was actually saved by the Coast Guard⟩ — see BOMBAST 1
2 language that is impressive-sounding but not meaningful or sincere ⟨her campaign promise to "fight for the people" showed a taste for stale *hot air*⟩ — see RHETORIC 1

hotbed *n* a place or environment that favors the development of something ⟨prerevolutionary Boston was viewed as a *hotbed* of treason by the British⟩ — see BREEDING GROUND

hot-blooded *adj* having or expressing great depth of feeling ⟨after watching the successful defense of Fort McHenry, Francis Scott Key quickly wrote the *hot-blooded* poem that later became known as "The Star-Spangled Banner"⟩ — see FERVENT 1

hot-button *adj* relating to or causing the expression of opposing opinions ⟨the new plan raises a number of *hot-button* issues that are sure to get voters riled up⟩ — see CONTROVERSIAL 1

hotcake *n* a flat cake made from thin batter and cooked on both sides (as on a griddle) ⟨*hotcakes* and maple syrup will be served at the church breakfast⟩ — see PANCAKE

hotchpotch *n* an unorganized collection or mixture of various things ⟨Sunday supper was a *hotchpotch* of leftovers⟩ — see MISCELLANY 1

hotdog *vb* to engage in attention-getting playful or boisterous behavior ⟨a skier who couldn't resist the urge to *hotdog* on the slopes whenever he wanted to impress a girl⟩ — see CUT UP

hot dog *interj* how delightful ⟨"*Hot dog*!" the child cried, "We're going to the circus!"⟩ — see HOORAY

hotel *n* a place that provides rooms and usually a public dining room for overnight guests ⟨for their 50th anniversary they stayed at one of the finest *hotels* in San Francisco⟩
synonyms auberge, caravansary (*or* caravanserai), hospice, hostel, hostelry, inn, lodge, public house, tavern
related words B and B, bed-and-breakfast, guesthouse; apartment hotel; accommodations, lodgings, rest; court, motel, motor court, motor inn, motor lodge, resort, spa, tourist court, youth hostel; camp, campground; bunkhouse, dorm, dormitory; boardinghouse, lodging house, rooming house; doss-house [*chiefly British*], fleabag, flophouse

hotfoot *adv* with excessive or careless speed ⟨lowered his plane *hotfoot* onto a pasture when the engine started to sputter⟩ — see HASTILY 1

hotfoot (it) *vb* to proceed or move quickly ⟨you'd better *hotfoot it* to the bus stop if you're going to catch the bus⟩ — see HURRY 2

hothouse *n* **1** a glass-enclosed building for growing plants ⟨grows tomatoes in his *hothouse* all winter long⟩ — see CONSERVATORY
2 a place or environment that favors the development of something ⟨an urban enclave of bohemians that acquired a reputation for being a *hothouse* of creativity⟩ — see BREEDING GROUND

hotness *n* the state of enjoying widespread approval ⟨the phenomenal *hotness* of the movie's stars is the driving force behind all of the advance publicity⟩ — see POPULARITY

hots *n pl* sexual appetite ⟨he has the *hots* for any woman who doesn't have the good sense to reject him⟩ — see DESIRE 2

hotshot *n* a person with a high level of knowledge or skill in a field ⟨while still in his 20s, he was known on Wall Street as an investment *hotshot*⟩ — see EXPERT

hot stuff *n* something very good of its kind ⟨wow, that dress is *hot stuff*—I've never seen anything like it!⟩ — see JIM-DANDY

hot ticket *n* a practice or interest that is very popular for a short time ⟨the *hot ticket* this season is the retro look⟩ — see FAD

hottie *n* a physically attractive person ⟨if you're not a *hottie*, you haven't a prayer of getting on that reality show⟩ — see DOLL 2

hottish *adj* having or giving off heat to a moderate degree ⟨the island's temperature is mild in winter and *hottish* in summer, but never extreme⟩ — see WARM 1

hot war *n* a state of armed violent struggle between states, nations, or groups ⟨fortunately, the cool relationship between the two nations never escalated into a *hot war*⟩ — see WAR 1

hound *n* **1** a domestic mammal that is related to the wolves and foxes ⟨in the yard an old *hound* greeted us with a single bark⟩ — see DOG 1
2 a person with a strong and habitual liking for something ⟨a camera *hound* even before the baby arrived, he's now become obsessive⟩ — see FAN
3 a mean, evil, or unprincipled person ⟨a no-good *hound* who got his girlfriend pregnant and then took off⟩ — see VILLAIN
4 a person whose behavior is offensive to others ⟨nobody could stand that low-down *hound* and his penchant for mean-spirited pranks⟩ — see JERK 1

hound *vb* **1** to go after or on the track of ⟨after she was publicly dumped by her boyfriend, the actress was *hounded* by reporters night and day⟩ — see FOLLOW 2
2 to subject (someone) to constant scoldings and sharp reminders ⟨kept *hounding* his mother to let him drive her car until she gave in⟩ — see NAG 1

hounding *n* the act of going after or in the tracks of another ⟨the rock star eventually couldn't take the constant *hounding* by reporters and fans⟩ — see PURSUIT 1

hourly *adv* many times ⟨that couple argues *hourly*, about everything⟩ — see OFTEN

house *n* **1** a commercial or industrial activity or organization ⟨a publishing *house* that specializes in school textbooks⟩ — see ENTERPRISE 1
2 a group of persons who come from the same ancestor ⟨the present British royal family belongs to the *House* of Windsor⟩ — see FAMILY 1
3 the place where one lives ⟨come over to my *house* for supper so I can show off my new stove⟩ — see HOME 1
4 those who live as a family in one house ⟨the whole *house* is in a state of excited anticipation for the holidays⟩ — see HOUSEHOLD
5 the shelter or resting place of a wild animal ⟨prairie dogs make their *house* underground⟩ — see DEN 1

house *vb* **1** to provide with living quarters or shelter ⟨some of the freshmen were temporarily *housed* in local motels while the new dorm was being finished⟩
synonyms accommodate, bestow, billet, bivouac, board, bunk, camp, chamber, domicile, encamp, harbor, lodge, put up, quarter, roof, room, shelter, take in
related words ensconce, home, roost, secure, shed, stable, tent; barrack; bed (down)
near antonyms eject, evict
2 to close or shut in by or as if by barriers ⟨*housed* the stereo speakers in attractive walnut cabinets that match the furniture⟩ — see ENCLOSE 1

house cat *n* a small domestic animal known for catching mice ⟨the *house cat* at the Cheshire Cat Bookstore has the dual responsibility of being mascot and mouser⟩ — see CAT 1

house girl *n* a female domestic servant ⟨visited the old plantation where her grandmother had long ago toiled as a *house girl*⟩ — see MAID 1

household *adj* **1** of or relating to a household or family ⟨he spent the weekend at home, helping with *household* chores⟩ — see DOMESTIC 1
2 often observed or encountered ⟨"ozone" is now a *household* word, thanks to global warming⟩ — see COMMON 1

household *n* those who live as a family in one house ⟨a *household* that consists of a single mom, her two kids, and her widowed mother⟩
synonyms extended family, home, house, ménage
related words blood, folks, kin, kindred, kinfolk (*or* kinfolks), kinsfolk, kith; brood; nuclear family; clan, community

housekeeper *n* a female domestic servant ⟨the bachelor doctor could easily afford to hire a *housekeeper* to cook and clean⟩ — see MAID 1

housemaid *n* a female domestic servant ⟨scrubbing the floors invariably fell to the lowliest *housemaid*⟩ — see MAID 1

housing *n* something that encloses another thing especially to protect it ⟨a camera with a waterproof *housing* for taking pictures of coral reefs and other underwater features⟩ — see [1]CASE 1

hovel *n* a small, simply constructed, and often temporary dwelling ⟨refugees living in crowded *hovels*⟩ — see SHACK

hover *vb* to rest or move along the surface of a liquid or in the air ⟨claimed that the UFO *hovered* a moment, then spun off into space at incredible speed⟩ — see FLOAT 1

hover (over) *vb* to remain poised to inflict harm, danger, or distress on ⟨after the first big layoff, the possibility of losing their jobs *hovered over* all of the factory's workers⟩ — see THREATEN

how *adv* in what manner or way ⟨if you show me precisely *how* this is confusing, I would be happy to explain⟩ — see WHERE 2

how *n* the means or procedure for doing something ⟨the environmental activist eagerly launched into an explanation of the *hows* and whys of developing renewable energy sources⟩ — see METHOD

howbeit *adv* in spite of that ⟨I've never written a poem before; *howbeit*, I feel my first attempt is quite good⟩ — see HOWEVER

howbeit *conj* in spite of the fact that ⟨our visit to Niagara Falls was very pleasant, *howbeit* slightly shorter than we had planned⟩ — see ALTHOUGH

however *adv* in spite of that ⟨I'm all out of eggs; *however*, I can still make us a nice breakfast⟩
synonyms even so, howbeit, nevertheless, nonetheless, notwithstanding, still, still and all, though, withal, yet
related words after all, anyhow, regardless; per contra
phrases all the same (*or* just the same), at the same time

howl *n* **1** a crying out in grief ⟨the agonized *howl* of the grief-stricken parents rose toward heaven⟩ — see LAMENT 1
2 a loud vocal expression of strong emotion ⟨heard *howls* of laughter from the children watching the clown's silly antics⟩ — see SHOUT
3 a violent shouting ⟨the crowd raised a *howl* when the notorious murderer appeared at the courthouse door⟩ — see CLAMOR 1

howl *vb* **1** to make a long loud mournful sound ⟨several coyotes began *howling* close by as the sun went down⟩ ⟨the wind *howled* on the open plain⟩
synonyms bay, keen, ululate, wail, yowl
related words bawl, caterwaul, scream, screech, shriek, shrill, squall, squeal, yawp (*or* yaup), yell, yelp
2 to cry out loudly and emotionally ⟨the boy *howled* in

pain when his baby sister bit him⟩ — see SCREAM 1

hoydenish *adj* having qualities or traits that are traditionally considered inappropriate for a girl or woman ⟨a *hoydenish* woman, who smoked cigars and wore heavy work boots to town⟩ — see UNFEMININE

hub *n* a thing or place that is of greatest importance to an activity or interest ⟨Broadway is the *hub* of theater life in New York⟩ — see CENTER 1

hubble–bubble *n* a state of noisy, confused activity ⟨amidst the *hubble-bubble* of Christmas morning we forgot to walk the dog⟩ — see COMMOTION

hubbub *n* **1** a state of noisy, confused activity ⟨imagine all the *hubbub* at the zoo when the lion escaped⟩ — see COMMOTION

2 a violent shouting ⟨the people who had been in line for tickets made a huge *hubbub* when they were told that the concert was all sold out⟩ — see CLAMOR 1

hubby *n* the male partner in a marriage ⟨my *hubby's* been gone on a business trip all week, and I really miss him⟩ — see HUSBAND

huckster *n* one who sells things outdoors ⟨*hucksters* outside the auditorium selling everything from key chains to life-size cutouts of the rock star⟩ — see PEDDLER

huddle *n* **1** a coming together of a number of persons for a specified purpose ⟨after an all-night *huddle*, the state legislature finally approved a budget for the coming year⟩ — see MEETING 1

2 a number of things considered as a unit ⟨saw a *huddle* of tents that turned out to be a Boy Scout encampment⟩ — see GROUP 1

3 a usually small number of persons considered as a unit ⟨in the lobby during intermission *huddles* of theatergoers were excitedly discussing the play⟩ — see GROUP 2

huddle *vb* **1** to gather into a closely packed group ⟨the puppies *huddled* together to keep warm⟩ — see [2]PRESS 3

2 to lie low with the limbs close to the body ⟨*huddled* under her bed when she heard an intruder⟩ — see CROUCH

hue *n* a property that becomes apparent when light falls on an object and by which things that are identical in form can be distinguished ⟨suggested she wear brighter *hues* to complement her skin tone⟩ — see COLOR 1

hue and cry *n* a violent shouting ⟨the *hue and cry* in the classroom when someone let loose a snake⟩ — see CLAMOR 1

huff *n* **1** a state of nervous or irritated concern ⟨was in a *huff* because everyone was running late and the hot breakfast she had prepared was getting cold⟩ — see FRET

2 an outburst or display of excited anger ⟨gets all in a *huff* every time anyone makes the slightest criticism⟩ — see TANTRUM

3 the feeling of being offended or resentful after a slight or indignity ⟨left the restaurant in a *huff* after waiting 15 minutes to be seated⟩ — see PIQUE

huff *vb* to talk loudly and wildly ⟨demanding to speak to the branch manager, she *huffed* about the rudeness of the bank teller⟩ — see RANT

huffiness *n* **1** an exaggerated sense of one's importance that shows itself in the making of excessive or unjustified claims ⟨her *huffiness* seemed silly, considering what a stupid question she'd just asked⟩ — see ARROGANCE

2 readiness to show annoyance or impatience ⟨there's no point in telling her what you think unless you want to put up with her *huffiness*⟩ — see PETULANCE

huffish *adj* having a feeling of superiority that shows itself in an overbearing attitude ⟨*huffish* wealthy people who expected to receive top priority in the ship's dining room⟩ — see ARROGANT

huffy *adj* **1** easily offended ⟨the comedy is about a *huffy* actress who loudly protests every perceived insult, no matter how slight⟩ — see TOUCHY 1

2 having a feeling of superiority that shows itself in an overbearing attitude ⟨he's been acting very *huffy* ever since he was named head of the department⟩ — see ARROGANT

hug *vb* **1** to express to (someone) admiration for his or her success or good fortune ⟨she *hugged* herself for having made a killing on the investment⟩ — see CONGRATULATE

2 to put one's arms around and press tightly ⟨Grandma *hugged* the grandchildren good-bye⟩ — see EMBRACE 1

huge *adj* unusually large ⟨the old stadium was replaced by a *huge* new one that seats 100,000 spectators⟩

synonyms astronomical (*also* astronomic), Brobdingnagian, bumper, colossal, cosmic (*also* cosmical), cyclopean, elephantine, enormous, galactic, gargantuan, giant, gigantesque, gigantic, grand, herculean, heroic (*also* heroical), Himalayan, humongous (*also* humungous), immense, jumbo, king-size (*or* king-sized), leviathan, mammoth, massive, mega, mighty, monster, monstrous, monumental, mountainous, oceanic, pharaonic, planetary, prodigious, super, super-duper, supersize, supersized, titanic, tremendous, vast, vasty, walloping, whacking, whopping

related words big, bulky, considerable, extensive, good, goodly, great, gross, handsome, hefty, hulking, largish, major, outsize (*also* outsized), overgrown, oversize (*or* oversized), sizable (*or* sizeable), substantial, tidy, voluminous; august, formidable, grandiose, imposing, lofty, majestic; cavernous, monolithic, overwhelming, staggering, stupendous, towering; boundless, immeasurable, infinite

near antonyms little, mini, petite, pint-size (*or* pint-sized), puny, small, smallish, undersized (*also* undersize); dinky, dwarfish, half-pint

antonyms bantam, bitty, diminutive, infinitesimal, Lilliputian, little bitty, micro, microminiature, microscopic (*also* microscopical), midget, miniature, minuscule, minute, pocket, pygmy, teensy, teensy-weensy, teeny, teeny-weeny, tiny, wee

hugely *adv* **1** to a great degree ⟨*hugely* mistaken about the character of the people he had rented the house to⟩ — see VERY 1

2 to a large extent or degree ⟨this donation has added *hugely* to the library's collection of music manuscripts⟩ — see GREATLY 2

hugeness *n* the quality or state of being very large ⟨you can only appreciate the *hugeness* of the dome when you see how tiny the people standing under it look⟩ — see IMMENSITY

hugger–mugger *adj* **1** lacking in order, neatness, and often cleanliness ⟨a *hugger-mugger* presentation of the facts of the case that left everyone confused⟩ — see MESSY

2 undertaken or done so as to escape being observed or known by others ⟨a tale of *hugger-mugger* doings and international espionage⟩ — see SECRET 1

hulk *n* a big clumsy often slow-witted person ⟨the big-boned girl felt like a *hulk* standing in line next to the slender, delicate ballerinas⟩ — see OAF 1

hulking *adj* **1** of a size greater than average of its kind ⟨a heavy, *hulking* stone blocked the way⟩ — see LARGE 1

2 strongly and heavily built ⟨I need a strong *hulking* young man to carry out the television set⟩ — see [1]HUSKY 1

hull *n* something that encloses another thing especially to protect it ⟨the coffin was placed in a cement *hull*⟩ — see [1]CASE 1

hull *vb* to remove the natural covering of ⟨*hull* the pinto beans before adding them⟩ — see PEEL

hullabaloo *n* **1** a state of noisy, confused activity ⟨there was a lot of needless *hullabaloo* as the new millennium approached⟩ — see COMMOTION

2 a violent shouting ⟨there was such a *hullabaloo* in the room that he couldn't hear himself think⟩ — see CLAMOR 1

hum *n* a monotonous sound like that of an insect in motion ⟨we heard the *hum* of an outboard motor and a few minutes later the small craft came into sight⟩

synonyms burr, buzz, chirr, churr, drone, purr, thrum, whir (*also* whirr), whiz (*or* whizz), zoom

related words babble, coo, gasp, gurgle, hiss, moan, murmur, rustle, sigh, suspiration, susurration, susurrus, whisper; whish, zing, zip

near antonyms bawl, howl, roar, scream, screech, shriek, squall, squeal, yelp, yell

hum *vb* **1** to be copiously supplied ⟨one restaurant was *humming* with diners, while a neighboring eatery was practically empty⟩ — see ABOUND

2 to fly, turn, or move rapidly with a fluttering or vibratory sound ⟨a helicopter *hummed* overhead⟩ — see WHIR

human *adj* relating to or characteristic of human beings ⟨it's *human* nature to care about what people think of us⟩

synonyms earthborn, mortal, natural

related words anthropoid, creatural, hominid, humanlike, humanoid

near antonyms angelic (*or* angelical), divine, godlike, preternatural, superhuman, supernatural, supernormal; immortal, omnipotent, omniscient; animal, beastly, bestial, brute, infrahuman; inhuman, robotic, subhuman

antonyms nonhuman

human *n* a member of the human race ⟨*humans* are the only mammals not endowed with a natural defense against the elements, such as fur or a thick hide⟩

synonyms baby, being, bird, bod [*British*], body, character, cookie (*or* cooky), creature, customer, devil, duck, egg, face, fish, guy, head, human being, individual, life, man, mortal, party, person, personage, scout, slob, sort, soul, specimen, stiff, thing, wight

related words hominid, homo, humanoid; brother, fellow, fellowman, neighbor; celebrity, personality, self, somebody

phrases son of man

near antonyms animal, beast, beastie, brute, critter

human being *n* a member of the human race ⟨we're all *human beings*, regardless of our differences⟩ — see HUMAN

humane *adj* **1** having or marked by sympathy and consideration for others ⟨*humane* guards who treated the prisoners decently⟩ ⟨the Geneva conventions spelled out standards for the *humane* treatment of prisoners of war⟩

synonyms beneficent, benevolent, benignant, compassionate, good-hearted, kind, kindhearted, kindly, softhearted, sympathetic, tender, tenderhearted, warmhearted

related words attentive, considerate, solicitous, thoughtful; affable, amicable, benign, companionable, comradely, cordial, friendly, genial, gentle, good, good-natured, good-tempered, gracious, mild, neighborly, nice, pleasant, sweet, warm; clement, forbearing, forgiving, lenient, merciful, soft; patient, pitying, tolerant, understanding; altruistic, brotherly, charitable, freehanded, generous, greathearted, humanitarian, liberal, magnanimous, munificent, noble, openhearted, philanthropic (*also* philanthropical), selfless, unselfish, unsparing; anticruelty, cruelty-free

near antonyms ironhearted, merciless, pitiless, ruthless, stonyhearted; inconsiderate, insensitive, thoughtless, uncaring, unthinking; grim, hard-boiled, harsh, heavy-handed, severe, stern, tough, unsentimental; hateful, malevolent, malicious, malign, malignant, mean, nasty, spiteful, virulent; antihumanitarian, uncharitable

antonyms atrocious, barbaric, barbarous, bestial, brutal, brute, brutish, callous, cold-blooded, cruel, fiendish, hard-hearted, heartless, inhuman, inhumane, insensate, sadistic, savage, truculent, uncompassionate, unfeeling, unkind, unkindly, unsympathetic, vicious, wanton

2 having or showing the capacity for sharing the feelings of another ⟨the movie's *humane* depiction of people who are physically and mentally challenged⟩ — see SYMPATHETIC 1

humaneness *n* sympathetic concern for the well-being of others ⟨with more *humaneness* than good sense, I decided to take in yet another stray cat⟩ — see BENIGNANCY

humanitarian *adj* having or showing a concern for the welfare of others ⟨*humanitarian* efforts to aid the earthquake victims⟩ — see CHARITABLE 1

humanity *n* **1** human beings in general ⟨all *humanity* can learn from this tragedy⟩ — see PEOPLE 1

2 the capacity for feeling for another's unhappiness or misfortune ⟨a country known for the *humanity* of its liberal immigration policy⟩ — see HEART 1

3 the human race ⟨in Greek mythology, the gods display many of the weaknesses of *humanity*, such as jealousy, foolishness, and greed⟩ — see MANKIND

humankind *n* **1** human beings in general ⟨all *humankind* shares the desire for peace⟩ — see PEOPLE 1

2 the human race ⟨perhaps someday *humankind* will find the key that unlocks the mystery of the universe⟩ — see MANKIND

humble *adj* **1** not having or showing any feelings of superiority, self-assertiveness, or showiness ⟨a medical scientist who remained remarkably *humble* even after winning the Nobel Prize⟩ ⟨even though she'd been proven wrong, her attitude was still far from *humble*⟩

synonyms demure, down-to-earth, lowly, meek, modest, unassuming, unpretentious

related words acquiescent, compliant, deferential, resigned, submissive, unaggressive, unassertive, yielding; cowering, cringing, shrinking; ingenuous, naive (*or* naïve), plain, simple, unaffected; bashful, diffident, introverted, mousy (*or* mousey), overmodest, passive, quiet, reserved, retiring, sheepish, shy, subdued, timid, unobtrusive; aw-shucks, self-deprecating, self-deprecatory, self-effacing

near antonyms aggressive, assertive, audacious, bold, brash, brassy, cheeky, forward, impertinent, impudent, saucy; cocksure, cocky, confident, hubristic, overconfident, self-confident; egocentric, egoistic (*also* egoistical), narcissistic, prideful, self-affected, self-centered, self-complacent, self-conceited, self-congratulatory, self-contented, self-engrossed, self-important, self-obsessed, self-pleased, self-satisfied, smug, stuck-up, swelled-headed; boastful, bombastic, braggy, swaggering, vain, vainglorious; condescending, disdainful, dominant, dominating, domineering, magisterial, overbearing, patronizing, pontificating; flamboyant, ostentatious, showy; extroverted (*also* extraverted), immodest, outgoing, uninhibited, unreserved

antonyms arrogant, bumptious, chesty, conceited, egotistic (*or* egotistical), fastuous, haughty, highfalutin (*also* hifalutin), high-and-mighty, high-handed, high-hat, hoity-toity, huffish, huffy, imperious, lordly, overweening, peremptory, pompous, presuming, presumptuous, pretentious, self-asserting, self-assertive, super-

cilious, superior, toplofty (*also* toploftical), uppish, uppity
2 belonging to the class of people of low social or economic rank ⟨a *humble* peasant girl who claimed she was chosen by God to restore the French king to his throne⟩ — see IGNOBLE 1
3 showing, expressing, or offered in a spirit of humility or unseemly submissiveness ⟨please accept my *humble* thanks for this unexpected favor⟩ — see ABJECT

humble *vb* to reduce to a lower standing in one's own eyes or in others' eyes ⟨Philip was utterly *humbled* by a crushing defeat in the first round of the state chess tournament⟩
synonyms abase, chasten, cheapen, debase, degrade, demean, discredit, disgrace, dishonor, foul, humiliate, lower, shame, sink, smirch, take down
related words abash, confound, confuse, discomfit, disconcert, discountenance, embarrass, faze, fluster, mortify, nonplus, rattle; belittle, castigate, criticize, cry down, decry, depreciate, detract, diminish, discount, disparage, minimize, put down, ridicule, write off; badmouth, defame, defile, libel, malign, slander; affront, insult; censure, condemn, damn, denounce, execrate, reprehend, reprobate
near antonyms acclaim, applaud, boast, celebrate, cheer, cite, commend, compliment, congratulate, decorate, eulogize, extol (*also* extoll), fete (*or* fête), hail, honor, laud, praise, salute, tout; acknowledge, recognize; highlight, play up, spotlight; dignify, ennoble, enshrine, ensky, enthrone, glorify, magnify; advance, boost, lift, promote, raise, upgrade, uplift; idealize, romanticize
antonyms aggrandize, canonize, deify, elevate, exalt

humbleness *n* the absence of any feelings of being better than others ⟨in a display of true *humbleness* he gave much of the credit for his discovery to others⟩ — see HUMILITY

humbly *adv* in a manner showing no signs of pride or self-assertion ⟨*humbly* accepted the criticism⟩ — see LOWLY

humbug *n* **1** an imitation that is passed off as genuine ⟨tests showed that the "old" map of America was a cleverly made *humbug*⟩ — see FAKE 1
2 language, behavior, or ideas that are absurd and contrary to good sense ⟨those UFO stories are a lot of *humbug*⟩ — see NONSENSE 1
3 one who makes false claims of identity or expertise ⟨one *humbug* after another claimed to be the miraculously surviving daughter of the Russian czar⟩ — see IMPOSTOR

humbug *vb* to cause to believe what is untrue ⟨*humbugged* into believing that the bones were the skeleton of a prehistoric human being⟩ — see DECEIVE

humbuggery *n* language, behavior, or ideas that are absurd and contrary to good sense ⟨a lot of *humbuggery* about a mean old witch that lives in the woods⟩ — see NONSENSE 1

humdinger *n* something very good of its kind ⟨the concert concluded with a *humdinger* of a fireworks display⟩ — see JIM-DANDY

humdrum *adj* causing weariness, restlessness, or lack of interest ⟨she leads a *humdrum* life that will never be made into a major motion picture⟩ ⟨a *humdrum* meal⟩ — see BORING

humdrum *n* a tedious lack of variety ⟨loathed the *humdrum* of daily life in a small town⟩ — see MONOTONY

humid *adj* containing or characterized by an uncomfortable amount of moisture ⟨the air was so *humid* that our beach towels hanging on the line never really got dry⟩
synonyms damp, muggy, sticky, sultry
related words steamy, summerlike, summery, sweltering, torrid; semitropical (*also* semitropic), subhumid, subtropical (*also* subtropic), tropic, tropical; close, heavy, oppressive, smothering, stifling, stuffy, suffocating; clammy, dank, moist; awash, bathed, doused (*also* dowsed), drenched, dripping, saturated, soaked, soaking, sodden, soggy, sopping, soppy, soused, washed, watered, waterlogged, watery, wet
near antonyms bracing, cool, crisp, fresh, invigorating, refreshing; arid, baked, burned (*or* burnt), dehydrated, desert, droughty, dusty, parched, scorched, seared, semiarid, sere (*also* sear), sunbaked, thirsty, waterless
antonyms dry

humidity *n* the amount of water suspended in the air in tiny droplets ⟨the oppressive *humidity* made the hot day seem even hotter⟩ — see MOISTURE

humiliate *vb* to reduce to a lower standing in one's own eyes or in others' eyes ⟨no student feels *humiliated* for not having the "right" clothes because everyone is wearing a school uniform⟩ — see HUMBLE

humility *n* the absence of any feelings of being better than others ⟨displaying genuine *humility*, the peace activist accepted the Nobel Prize on behalf of all who have worked to end the violence⟩
synonyms demureness, down-to-earthness, humbleness, lowliness, meekness, modesty
related words acquiescence, compliance, deference, passivity, resignedness, submission, submissiveness; ingenuousness, naïveté (*also* naivete *or* naiveté); directness, plainness, simpleness; bashfulness, diffidence, mousiness, quietness, reserve, reservedness, retiringness, sheepishness, shyness, timidity, timidness
near antonyms aggressiveness, assertiveness; attitude, audaciousness, boldness, brashness, brassiness, cheek, cheekiness, cockiness, cocksureness, forwardness, overconfidence, swagger, swash, temerity; impertinence, impudence, insolence, nerve, sauciness; boastfulness, chest-thumping, self-applause, self-assumption, self-centeredness, self-complacency, self-conceit, self-glorification, self-importance, self-opinion, self-partiality, self-satisfaction, vaingloriousness, vanity; condescension, disdain, scorn; flamboyance, ostentation, ostentatiousness, showiness
antonyms arrogance, assumption, bumptiousness, conceit, egoism, egotism, haughtiness, hauteur, huffiness, imperiousness, loftiness, lordliness, peremptoriness, pomposity, pompousness, presumptuousness, pretense (*or* pretence), pretension, pretentiousness, pride, pridefulness, superciliousness, superiority, toploftiness

hummer *n* **1** an ambitious person who eagerly goes after what is desired ⟨he's a real *hummer* when it comes to getting new clients for his advertising agency⟩ — see GO-GETTER
2 something very good of its kind ⟨this is the author's first mystery novel, and it's a *hummer*⟩ — see JIM-DANDY

humming *adj* marked by much life, movement, or activity ⟨the new science center is usually *humming* with school groups on Thursdays⟩ — see ALIVE 2

humongous *also* **humungous** *adj* unusually large ⟨I'm sleepy because I ate a *humongous* lunch⟩ — see HUGE

humor *n* **1** the amusing quality or element in something ⟨we failed to see any *humor* in his racially charged jokes⟩
synonyms comedy, comic, comicality, drollery, drollness, funniness, hilariousness, humorousness, richness, uproariousness
related words amusement, enjoyment, fun, pleasure; absurdity, irony, laughableness, ludicrousness, ridiculousness; whimsicality, wittiness, wryness; burlesque, caricature, farce, jest, lampoon, parody, satire, slapstick, spoof, takeoff; jocularity, jokiness, playfulness, waggishness

near antonyms agony, anguish, dolor, grief, heartache, heartbreak, misery, sorrow, torment, torture, tribulation, woe; gravity, seriousness, soberness, solemnity, solemnness, somberness
antonyms pathos
2 humorous entertainment ⟨a screenwriter best known for lowbrow *humor*⟩ — see COMEDY 1
3 a state of mind dominated by a particular emotion ⟨the prospect of going out to dinner put her in a good *humor* all day⟩ — see MOOD 1
4 a sudden impulsive and apparently unmotivated idea or action ⟨she was seized by a sudden *humor* to contact an old college friend that she hadn't seen in ages⟩ — see WHIM

humor *vb* to give in to (a desire) ⟨*humored* her grandfather by listening to his war stories for the hundredth time⟩ — see INDULGE 1

humorist *n* a person (as a writer) noted for or specializing in humor ⟨Mark Twain is perhaps America's most beloved *humorist*⟩
synonyms card, comedian, comic, droll, farceur, funnyman, gagger, gagman, gagster, jester, joker, jokester, wag, wit
related words comedienne, entertainer; banterer, cutup, kidder, knockabout, practical joker, prankster, quipper, quipster, teaser, wisecracker; buffoon, clown, fool, harlequin, zany; caricaturist, lampooner, parodist, satirist

humoristic *adj* causing or intended to cause laughter ⟨a somewhat *humoristic* scene in an otherwise dark and brooding drama⟩ — see FUNNY 1

humorless *adj* not joking or playful in mood or manner ⟨*humorless* people who can't see the lighter side of life⟩ — see SERIOUS 1

humorous *adj* **1** causing or intended to cause laughter ⟨the *humorous* moments in an otherwise somber affair⟩ ⟨"most *humorous* costume" went to the girl dressed as Little Bo Peep⟩ — see FUNNY 1
2 given to or marked by mature intelligent humor ⟨the movie's a *humorous* look at love and marriage⟩ — see WITTY

humorousness *n* the amusing quality or element in something ⟨the *humorousness* of falling on a banana peel is usually lost on the person who falls⟩ — see HUMOR 1

hump *n* **1** *British* a state of resentful silence or irritability ⟨failing her A-levels has certainly given her the *hump*⟩ — see POUT
2 an elevation of land higher than a hill ⟨a cloud-capped *hump* straddles the border separating the two countries⟩ — see MOUNTAIN 1
3 an area of high ground ⟨the grassy *hump* at the center of the park is a popular sledding spot during the winter⟩ — see HEIGHT 4

hump *vb* **1** to devote serious and sustained effort ⟨the farmers had to really *hump* to get the harvest in before the rains⟩ — see LABOR
2 to proceed or move quickly ⟨the boat was really *humping* before the motor started to sputter all of a sudden⟩ — see HURRY 2

hunch *vb* to lie low with the limbs close to the body ⟨he *hunched* next to a bush to avoid being seen⟩ — see CROUCH

hundred *n* a considerable amount ⟨it seems like we've answered this question *hundreds* of times⟩ — see LOT 2

hung *adj* bending downward or forward ⟨stood penitently before the judge with a *hung* head while he received his sentence⟩ — see NODDING

hunger *n* **1** a need or desire for food ⟨no degree of *hunger* would induce me to eat octopus⟩
synonyms appetite, belly, emptiness, famishment, munchies, stomach
related words rapaciousness, rapacity, ravenousness, voraciousness, voracity; malnutrition, starvation, undernourishment; craving, sweet tooth; famine, fast, hunger strike; gluttony, gourmandism, greed, hoggishness
near antonyms fill, fullness, glut, repleteness, repletion, satiation, satiety, satisfaction, surfeit
antonyms inappetence
2 a strong wish for something ⟨a lonely girl with a desperate *hunger* for love⟩ — see DESIRE 1
3 urgent desire or interest ⟨reads everything he can find on airplanes with a seemingly insatiable *hunger*⟩ — see EAGERNESS

hunger (for) *vb* to have an earnest wish to own or enjoy ⟨voters *hungering for* honest and upright leadership⟩ — see DESIRE 1

hungry *adj* **1** feeling a desire or need for food ⟨John was still *hungry* after eating only a muffin for breakfast⟩
synonyms empty, famished, peckish [*chiefly British*], starved, starving
related words rapacious, ravenous, voracious, wolfish; malnourished, underfed, undernourished; gluttonous, gormandizing, greedy, hoggish, insatiable, piggish, piggy
near antonyms engorged, glutted, gorged, overfed, overfull, overstuffed, replete, stuffed, surfeited
antonyms full, sated, satiate, satiated, satisfied
2 showing urgent desire or interest ⟨*hungry* for the latest news⟩ — see EAGER

hung up *adj* **1** having extreme or relentless concern ⟨parents of a toddler who are already *hung up* about her getting into a good college⟩
synonyms happy, obsessed, queer
related words absorbed, anxious, concerned, distracted, engaged, engrossed, full, involved, knee-deep, occupied, preoccupied, prepossessed, worried; ardent, crazy, dotty, fervent, fervid, feverish, foolish, impassioned, nuts, passionate, silly
near antonyms apathetic, casual, cool, detached, disinterested, dispassionate, incurious, indifferent, insouciant, nonchalant, unconcerned, uncurious, unenthusiastic, uninterested, uninvolved
2 feeling or showing uncomfortable feelings of uncertainty ⟨so *hung up* about having his tax returns audited that he can't sleep⟩ — see NERVOUS 1

hunk *n* **1** a physically attractive man ⟨her new boyfriend is quite the *hunk*⟩
synonyms beefcake, pretty boy, stud, superstud
related words babe [*slang*], dish, doll, dreamboat [*slang*], eye candy, eyeful, fox, knockout, stunner; lady-killer, sheik, womanizer
near antonyms dog, grotesquerie (*also* grotesquery), monster, nerd
2 a small uneven mass ⟨what looked like a *hunk* of potato in her stew turned out to be a pebble⟩ — see LUMP 1

hunker (down) *vb* to lie low with the limbs close to the body ⟨had to *hunker down* so no one would see him behind the gate⟩ — see CROUCH

hunkers *n pl* the part of the body upon which someone sits ⟨the tree had a stout branch, and I found the boy perched there on his *hunkers*⟩ — see BUTTOCKS

hunks *n pl* a mean grasping person who is usually stingy with money ⟨a horrible old *hunks* who refused to lend money to his destitute brother⟩ — see MISER

hunky–dory *adj* being to one's liking ⟨if she just agrees to cooperate, everything will be *hunky-dory*⟩ — see SATISFACTORY 1

hunt *n* an act or process of looking carefully or thoroughly for someone or something ⟨soon the whole family was involved in the *hunt* for Mom's car keys⟩ — see SEARCH

hunt *vb* **1** to seek out (game) for food or sport ⟨Native Americans of the plains *hunted* buffalo for food, clothing, and shelter⟩
synonyms chase, stalk
related words capture, drag, net, snare, trap; dog, ferret, hawk, hound; course, pursue, run, run down, spoor, track, trail; gun (for), harpoon, kill, shoot; poach; cull
2 to go in search of ⟨I spent all afternoon *hunting* a job for the summer⟩ — see SEEK 1
3 to go into or range over for purposes of discovery ⟨a bag lady *hunts* the neighborhood for returnable bottles⟩ — see EXPLORE 2

hunt (down *or* up) *vb* to come upon after searching, study, or effort ⟨managed to *hunt down* his ancestors, who arrived back to the 16th century⟩ — see FIND 1

hunt (through) *vb* to look through (as a place) carefully or thoroughly in an effort to find or discover something ⟨she *hunted through* old birth and marriage records to trace the family tree⟩ — see SEARCH 1

hunter *n* a person who hunts game ⟨*hunters* must have a license to shoot deer⟩
synonyms huntsman, nimrod
related words huntress, sportsman, sportswoman; archer, gunner; birder, falconer, fowler, hawker; hunter-gatherer, trapper; poacher
antonyms nonhunter

huntsman *n* a person who hunts game ⟨the *huntsman* presented the king with two pheasants for the royal table⟩ — see HUNTER

hurdle *n* something that makes movement or progress difficult ⟨the many *hurdles* he had to overcome on the road to success⟩ — see ENCUMBRANCE

hurl *vb* **1** to discharge the contents of the stomach through the mouth ⟨that meal was so gross I thought I was going to *hurl*⟩ — see VOMIT
2 to proceed or move quickly ⟨a fighter jet *hurled* through the sky⟩ — see HURRY 2
3 to send through the air especially with a quick forward motion of the arm ⟨*hurled* snowballs at each other⟩ — see THROW 1

hurly *n* a state of noisy, confused activity ⟨the high-spirited *hurly* that engulfs the college campus as students begin arriving en masse for the start of the academic year⟩ — see COMMOTION

hurly–burly *n* a state of noisy, confused activity ⟨lost sight of his children in all the *hurly-burly* of the fair⟩ — see COMMOTION

hurricane *n* a state of noisy, confused activity ⟨economic news that unleashed a *hurricane* on the trading floor⟩ — see COMMOTION

hurried *adj* acting or done with excessive or careless speed ⟨*hurried* shoppers who grab the wrong items⟩ ⟨ate a *hurried* meal⟩ — see HASTY 1

hurriedly *adv* with excessive or careless speed ⟨*hurriedly* dashed off a note to let them know she'd been called away for an emergency⟩ — see HASTILY 1

hurry *n* **1** excited and often showy or disorderly speed ⟨after all her *hurry* to get her report done on time, Elizabeth learned that it wasn't due till the following week⟩
synonyms haste, hastiness, hustle, precipitation, precipitousness, rush
related words bustle, flurry, flutter, scurry, scuttle, stir, whirl; beeline, dash, scramble, stampede; hotheadedness, impetuosity, impetuousness, impulsiveness, impulsivity, rashness; expedition, expeditiousness, fastness, fleetness, quickness, rapidity, rapidness, speed, speediness, swiftness, velocity; celerity, dispatch, promptitude, promptness
near antonyms dilatoriness, lateness, pokiness, procrastination, slowness; languor, leisureliness, lethargy, sluggishness, torpor; dormancy, inaction, inactivity, inertia, inertness, quiescence
antonyms deliberateness, deliberation
2 a high rate of movement or performance ⟨a person who does everything in a *hurry*⟩ — see SPEED 1
3 a state of noisy, confused activity ⟨in all the *hurry* of the modern world, people tend to forget what's really important⟩ — see COMMOTION

hurry *vb* **1** to cause to move or proceed fast or faster ⟨the new nurses were *hurried* through the orientation program because they were so desperately needed on the ward⟩
synonyms accelerate, bundle, fast-track, hasten, quicken, rush, speed (up), whisk
related words drive, goad, prod, propel, push, race, spur, stir, urge; aid, dispatch, ease, encourage, expedite, facilitate
near antonyms delay, encumber, fetter, hamper, hinder, hobble, hold back, hold up, impede, interfere (with), manacle, rein (in), restrain, shackle, tie up, trammel; arrest, check, stall, stay, still, stop
antonyms brake, decelerate, retard, slow (down)
2 to proceed or move quickly ⟨if we *hurry*, we'll make the four o'clock train⟩
synonyms barrel, belt, blast, blaze, blow, bolt, bomb [*slang*], bowl, breeze, bundle, bustle, buzz, cannonball, careen, career, chase, course, crack (on), dash, drive, fly, hare, hasten, hie, highball, hotfoot (it), hump, hurl, hurtle, hustle, jet, jump, motor, nip, pelt, race, ram, rip, rocket, run, rush, rustle, scoot, scurry, scuttle, shoot, speed, step, tear, travel, trot, whirl, whisk, zip, zoom
related words beetle, dart, flit, scamper, scud, scuffle; stampede, streak, whiz (*or* whizz); gallop, jog, sprint; accelerate, quicken, step out; catch up, fast-forward, outpace, outrun, outstrip, overtake; arrow, beeline
phrases beat it, get a move on, make tracks, shake a leg, step on it
near antonyms dally, dawdle, dillydally, drag, hang (around *or* out), lag, linger, loiter, poke, tarry; amble, lumber, plod, saunter, shuffle, stroll; decelerate, slow (down *or* up)
antonyms crawl, creep, poke

hurry–scurry *or* **hurry–skurry** *n* a state of noisy, confused activity ⟨for all the *hurry-scurry* you would have thought that the guests were the British royal family and not my in-laws⟩ — see COMMOTION

hurt *n* **1** a state of great suffering of body or mind ⟨in her *hurt* she said a lot of things to her boyfriend that she didn't really mean⟩ — see DISTRESS 1
2 something that causes loss or pain ⟨a totally baseless accusation that caused lasting *hurt* to his reputation⟩ — see INJURY 1

hurt *vb* **1** to feel or cause physical pain ⟨my head *hurts*⟩ ⟨a bad sprain that really *hurts*⟩ ⟨I *hurt* all over⟩
synonyms ache, pain, smart
related words bite, bleed, burn, chafe, cramp, fester, itch, nag, pinch, pound, rack, sting, swell, throb, tingle, twinge; agonize, anguish, suffer; afflict, harrow, torment, torture
2 to reduce the soundness, effectiveness, or perfection of ⟨don't worry that you'll *hurt* the new lawn by walking across it⟩ — see DAMAGE 1
3 to cause bodily damage to ⟨the common belief that reading in poor light *hurts* your eyes⟩ — see INJURE 1
4 to feel deep sadness or mental pain ⟨I know you must be *hurting* from the cruel words they said⟩ — see GRIEVE

hurtful *adj* **1** causing or capable of causing harm ⟨the most *hurtful* thing you can do to this silk dress is put it in the dryer⟩ — see HARMFUL
2 hard to accept or bear especially emotionally ⟨her ex-

husband said *hurtful* things that she could never forgive⟩ — see BITTER 2

hurting *adj* causing or feeling bodily pain ⟨a badly *hurting* finger kept her from writing neatly⟩ — see PAINFUL 1

hurtle *vb* **1** to proceed or move quickly ⟨the probe *hurtled* through space to its destination: Jupiter⟩ — see HURRY 2

2 to send through the air especially with a quick forward motion of the arm ⟨*hurtled* his spear at the tiger as it lunged toward him⟩ — see THROW 1

hurtless *adj* not causing or being capable of causing injury or hurt ⟨unlike some parodies, which are mean-spirited, this one was marked by *hurtless* humor and affectionate exaggeration⟩ — see HARMLESS

husband *n* the male partner in a marriage ⟨she and her *husband* just celebrated their 50th wedding anniversary⟩

synonyms hubby, man, mister, old man

related words better half, companion, consort, mate, partner, significant other, spouse; Mr. Right; soul mate; bridegroom, groom; benedict; widower; househusband

husband *vb* to avoid the wasteful or destructive use of ⟨*husband* our natural resources so that our children and grandchildren may benefit from them⟩ — see CONSERVE 1

husbandry *n* **1** careful management of material resources ⟨in accordance with his practice of good *husbandry*, he never buys anything on credit⟩ — see ECONOMY

2 the science or occupation of cultivating the soil, producing crops, and raising livestock ⟨a family of winemakers whose tradition of vineyard *husbandry* goes back several generations⟩ — see AGRICULTURE

hush *n* **1** a state of freedom from storm or disturbance ⟨the storm passed, and a *hush* fell over the sea⟩ — see CALM 1

2 the near or complete absence of sound ⟨a *hush* fell over the auditorium as the lights went down⟩ — see SILENCE 2

hush *vb* **1** to become still and orderly ⟨the whole room *hushed* when the queen made her entrance⟩ — see QUIET 1

2 to stop talking ⟨the talkative lady next to me on the train never *hushed* once during the whole four-hour trip⟩ — see SHUT UP 1

3 to stop the noise or speech of ⟨he tried to *hush* the baby by making a lot of silly faces⟩ — see SILENCE 1

hush (up) *vb* to keep from being publicly known ⟨the well-connected family was able to *hush up* the scandal so it never reached the papers⟩ — see SUPPRESS 1

hushed *adj* **1** free from disturbing noise or uproar ⟨entered the *hushed* interior of the Gothic church⟩ — see QUIET 1

2 free from storms or physical disturbance ⟨the *hushed* lake was smooth as glass the morning after the storm⟩ — see CALM 1

3 mostly or entirely without sound ⟨a *hushed* sickroom⟩ — see SILENT 3

4 not known or meant to be known by the general populace ⟨*hushed* negotiations between the two countries⟩ — see PRIVATE 1

hush–hush *adj* **1** not known or meant to be known by the general populace ⟨the reporter suspected there was a *hush-hush* reason why the company agreed to the deal⟩ — see PRIVATE 1

2 undertaken or done so as to escape being observed or known by others ⟨top-echelon diplomats met in a *hush-hush* conference in a last-ditch effort to head off an international crisis⟩ — see SECRET 1

husk *n* something that encloses another thing especially to protect it ⟨corn *husks*⟩ ⟨a high stone wall is the *husk* that protects the actor from prying curiosity seekers⟩ — see [1]CASE 1

husk *vb* to remove the natural covering of ⟨the tedious task of *husking* coconuts⟩ — see PEEL

[1]**husky** *adj* **1** strongly and heavily built ⟨a *husky* weight lifter⟩

synonyms beefy, brawny, burly, hefty, hulking, mesomorphic

related words able-bodied, athletic, herculean, mighty, muscle-bound, muscular, powerful, robust, rugged, sinewy, stalwart, stout, strapping, strong, sturdy; chunky, compact, heavy, heavyset, solid, squat, squatty, stocky, thickset; chubby, dumpy, lumpish, podgy [*chiefly British*], portly, pudgy, roly-poly, tubby

near antonyms lean, light, lightweight, slender, slight, slim, svelte, sylphlike, thin, willowy; bony (*also* boney), gangling, gangly, gaunt, gawky, lanky, reedy, scraggy, scrawny, skinny, spare, stringy, twiggy, waspish, weedy; spidery, wiry; debilitated, delicate, effete, emaciated, enervated, enfeebled, feeble, fragile, frail, infirm, puny, unathletic, weak, weakly, wimpy

2 of a size greater than average of its kind ⟨the neighbors bought a fairly *husky* lawn mower for their small yard⟩ — see LARGE 1

[2]**husky** *adj* harsh and dry in sound ⟨a voice that was *husky* from years of smoking⟩ — see HOARSE

hussy *n* a boldly flirtatious or sexually promiscuous woman ⟨the antiquated view that any unmarried woman who lived on her own was a *hussy*⟩ — see FLOOZY

hustle *n* **1** a scheme in which the victim is cheated out of his money after first gaining his trust ⟨finally got wise to his *hustle* and threatened to call the police⟩ — see CONFIDENCE GAME

2 excited and often showy or disorderly speed ⟨the *hustle* and bustle of the holiday season⟩ — see HURRY 1

3 readiness to engage in daring or difficult activity ⟨with his characteristic *hustle*, he had everything lined up in two days⟩ — see ENTERPRISE 2

4 an instance of the use of dishonest methods to acquire something of value ⟨a clever *hustle* that tricked people into revealing their bank account information⟩ — see FRAUD 1

hustle *vb* **1** to devote serious and sustained effort ⟨everyone really *hustled* to get the magazine out on schedule⟩ — see LABOR

2 to proceed or move quickly ⟨we'd better *hustle*, or we'll miss the train⟩ — see HURRY 2

3 to rob by the use of trickery or threats ⟨a customer *hustled* the cashier by getting her all confused while she was making change⟩ — see FLEECE

hustler *n* **1** a woman who engages in sexual activities for money ⟨a truck stop that featured cheap lodgings and even cheaper *hustlers*⟩ — see PROSTITUTE

2 an ambitious person who eagerly goes after what is desired ⟨the ad for the sales job claims that for someone who's a real *hustler*, the sky's the limit⟩ — see GO-GETTER

hut *n* a small, simply constructed, and often temporary dwelling ⟨smoke rose from a fisherman's *hut* on the shore of the lake⟩ — see SHACK

hutch *n* **1** a small, simply constructed, and often temporary dwelling ⟨the destitute family lives in a tiny *hutch* made of tin and cardboard⟩ — see SHACK

2 a storage case typically having doors and shelves ⟨keeps her best china in a *hutch* in the dining room⟩ — see CABINET

3 an enclosure with an open framework for keeping animals ⟨the owner took the rabbit out of the *hutch* so the children could pet it⟩ — see CAGE

hutment *n* **1** a place where a group of people live for a short time in tents or cabins ⟨the arriving national

guardsmen were forced to live in a *hutment* until permanent barracks could be constructed⟩ — see CAMP 1
2 a small, simply constructed, and often temporary dwelling ⟨a group of shabby *hutments* that had been erected to shelter the refugees⟩ — see SHACK

huzzah *or* **huzza** *interj* how delightful ⟨the beleaguered soldiers cried, "*Huzzah*!" as badly needed reinforcements appeared⟩ — see HOORAY

hybrid *adj* being offspring produced by parents of different races, breeds, species, or genera ⟨a *hybrid* rose called "American Beauty" was actually first developed in France⟩ — see MIXED 1

hybrid *n* an offspring of parents with different genes especially when of different races, breeds, species, or genera ⟨a tangelo is a *hybrid* of the tangerine and the grapefruit⟩
synonyms cross, crossbred, crossbreed, intercross, mongrel
related words mule; outcross; half-bred; mulatto
near antonyms full-blood, pureblood, purebred, thoroughbred

hygienic *adj* free from filth, infection, or dangers to health ⟨food packaging done under rigidly *hygienic* conditions⟩ — see SANITARY

hymn *n* **1** a religious song ⟨our Sunday church services always open with a *hymn*⟩
synonyms anthem, canticle, carol, chorale, psalm, spiritual
related words dirge, lament, requiem, threnody; Gloria Patri, hallelujah, paean; mass, oratorio; processional, recessional
2 a formal expression of praise ⟨the documentary on the Shakers is essentially a *hymn* to the simple life⟩ — see ENCOMIUM

hymn *vb* to proclaim the glory of ⟨during the honeymoon following the inauguration, newspaper articles seemed to *hymn* the president's every move⟩ — see PRAISE 1

hymnal *n* a book of hymns ⟨*hymnals* are distributed among the congregation before the church service so everyone can join in the singing⟩
synonyms hymnary, hymnbook, psalmody
related words breviary, missal, Psalter; songbook, songster; antiphonal, antiphonary

hymnary *n* a book of hymns ⟨everyone turn to page 22 in the *hymnary*, please⟩ — see HYMNAL

hymnbook *n* a book of hymns ⟨a worshipper who knew the words of all the church songs and didn't need a *hymnbook*⟩ — see HYMNAL

hype *adj, slang* of the very best kind ⟨a couple of the tracks on the album feature some really *hype* vocals⟩ — see EXCELLENT

¹hype *n, slang* **1** a person who regularly uses drugs especially illegally ⟨a derelict building that's now a shooting gallery for heroin *hypes*⟩ — see DOPER
2 a slender hollow instrument by which material is put into or taken from the body through the skin ⟨scattered inside the abandoned building were *hypes* and other signs of drug use⟩ — see NEEDLE 1

²hype *n* information released to the media that is designed to gain public attention or support for a person, business, or cause ⟨the prelaunch *hype* for the new cell phone translated into phenomenal sales numbers on release day⟩ — see PUBLICITY

¹hype *vb* to make greater in size, amount, or number ⟨the TV writers tried to *hype* interest in the fading soap opera with flashy new plotlines⟩ — see INCREASE 1

²hype *vb* to provide publicity for ⟨the auto company has been *hyping* its forthcoming line of hybrids for almost a year now⟩ — see PUBLICIZE 1

hyper *adj* easily excited by nature ⟨she's so *hyper* that she's the last person you'd want to turn to in an emergency⟩ — see EXCITABLE

hyperactive *adj* **1** being in a state of increased activity or agitation ⟨the skyrocketing price of oil resulted in a wildly fluctuating, *hyperactive* stock market⟩ — see FEVERISH 1
2 easily excited by nature ⟨*hyperactive* children who are in dire need of a guardian with a firm hand⟩ — see EXCITABLE

hyperbole *n* the representation of something in terms that go beyond the facts ⟨"enough food to feed a whole army" is a common example of *hyperbole*⟩ — see EXAGGERATION

hyperbolize *vb* to add to the interest of by including made-up details ⟨even if she did *hyperbolize* her account of an encounter with a bear, it still must have been pretty scary⟩ — see EMBROIDER

hyperbolized *adj* extended beyond normal or realistic bounds ⟨the *hyperbolized* sentiments that are so commonly found in popular love songs⟩ — see BLOATED 1

hypercritic *n* a person given to harsh judgments and to finding faults ⟨of course the *hypercritics* were quick to jump on the film for every time it deviated even slightly from the novel on which it was based⟩ — see CRITIC 1

hypercritical *adj* given to making or expressing unfavorable judgments about things ⟨if you go by what that *hypercritical* reviewer says, you are going to end up seeing very few movies⟩ — see CRITICAL 1

hyperexcitable *adj* easily excited by nature ⟨those *hyperexcitable* contestants on TV game shows who celebrate winning by jumping up and down uncontrollably⟩ — see EXCITABLE

hyperintelligent *adj* having or showing quickness of mind ⟨from an early age he showed signs of being a *hyperintelligent* child⟩ — see INTELLIGENT 1

hyperkinetic *adj* easily excited by nature ⟨an elderly couple who are unable to control their *hyperkinetic* grandson⟩ — see EXCITABLE

hypersexual *adj* having a strong sexual desire ⟨typically users of crystal meth report that the powerful stimulant leaves them feeling *hypersexual* as well as euphoric⟩ — see LUSTFUL

hyperventilate *vb* to breathe hard, quickly, or with difficulty ⟨he was so nervous he began *hyperventilating*, and the extra oxygen made him dizzy⟩ — see GASP

hypnosis *n* the art or act of inducing in a person a sleeplike state during which he or she readily follows suggestions ⟨with *hypnosis* there's some question as to just how involuntary the actions of the hypnotized person really are⟩
synonyms hypnotism, mesmerism
related words autohypnosis, automatism, autosuggestion, self-hypnosis, self-suggestion; bewitchment, enchantment, spellbinding

hypnotic *adj* tending to cause sleep ⟨her eyes soon grew heavy from the *hypnotic* rhythm of the train's wheels⟩
synonyms drowsy, narcotic, opiate, sleepy, slumberous (*or* slumbrous), somniferous, somnolent, soporific
related words depressant, relaxant, sedative, tranquilizing (*also* tranquillizing); calming, comforting, lulling, pacifying, quieting, relaxing, restful, settling, soothing; analgesic, anesthetic, anesthetizing, benumbing, deadening, dulling, numbing; hypnotizing, mesmerizing, stupefying
near antonyms arousing, awakening, energizing, invigorating, rousing, stimulating, wakening, waking; bracing, refreshing, restorative, reviving, stimulative, stimulatory
antonyms stimulant

hypnotism *n* the art or act of inducing in a person a sleeplike state during which he or she readily follows suggestions ⟨some people have undergone *hypnotism* in order to induce them to give up their smoking habit⟩ — see HYPNOSIS

hypnotize *vb* to hold the attention of as if by a spell ⟨the crowd was *hypnotized* by the powerful, eloquent speaker⟩ — see ENTHRALL 1

hypocrisy *n* the pretending of having virtues, principles, or beliefs that one in fact does not have ⟨the *hypocrisy* of people who claim to care about the environment but ride around in gas-guzzlers⟩

synonyms cant, dissembling, dissimulation, insincerity, piousness

related words deceit, deceitfulness, deception, deceptiveness, dishonesty, double-dealing, falsity, perfidy, two-facedness; affectation, affectedness, pretense (*or* pretence), pretension, pretentiousness, sanctimoniousness, self-righteousness, self-satisfaction; duplicity, fakery, falseness, fraudulentness, shamming; artificiality, glibness, oiliness, smoothness, unctuousness

near antonyms candor, directness, forthrightness, frankness, honesty, openheartedness, openness, probity, straightforwardness, truthfulness; artlessness, guilelessness, naturalness, unaffectedness

antonyms genuineness, sincereness, sincerity

hypocritical *adj* not being or expressing what one appears to be or express ⟨it's *hypocritical* to say mean things behind someone's back, and then to act nice when you want something from her⟩ — see INSINCERE

hypodermic *n* a slender hollow instrument by which material is put into or taken from the body through the skin ⟨he hardly felt it when the nurse stuck the *hypodermic* in his arm⟩ — see NEEDLE 1

hypodermic needle *n* a slender hollow instrument by which material is put into or taken from the body through the skin ⟨doesn't mind getting shots as long as he doesn't catch sight of the *hypodermic needle*⟩ — see NEEDLE 1

hypodermic syringe *n* a slender hollow instrument by which material is put into or taken from the body through the skin ⟨the nurse filled a different *hypodermic syringe* for each injection⟩ — see NEEDLE 1

hypothecate *vb* to take as true or as a fact without actual proof ⟨even before a single vote had been cast, media pundits were *hypothecating* that the former senator would be the party's nominee⟩ — see ASSUME 2

hypothesis *n* an idea that is the starting point for making a case or conducting an investigation ⟨working on the *hypothesis* that teenagers function better in the late morning, some high schools are starting classes later⟩ — see THEORY

hypothesize *vb* to take as true or as a fact without actual proof ⟨if we *hypothesize* that current population trends continue for the next 50 years⟩ — see ASSUME 2

hypothetical *adj* existing only as an assumption or speculation ⟨we talked about what we would do in various *hypothetical* emergencies⟩ — see THEORETICAL 1

hypothetical *n* something taken as being true or factual and used as a starting point for a course of action or reasoning ⟨believes that predictions of the extinction of certain species as the result of global warming are based upon too many *hypotheticals*⟩ — see ASSUMPTION 1

hysteria *n* a state of wildly excited activity or emotion ⟨the *hysteria* of the mother when she realized that she had lost her four-year-old son in the crowd⟩ — see FRENZY

hysterical *also* **hysteric** *adj* **1** causing or intended to cause laughter ⟨some of the things little kids come out with are *hysterical*⟩ — see FUNNY 1

2 feeling overwhelming fear or worry ⟨the police officer assured the mother that there was no need to get *hysterical*, for most missing children are found safe and sound⟩ — see FRANTIC 1

3 filled with fear or dread ⟨upon hearing the announcement that a shark had been sighted, *hysterical* beachgoers raced out of the water⟩ — see AFRAID

I

ice *vb* **1** to make sure, certain, or safe ⟨with that win, the team has pretty much *iced* a spot in the play-offs⟩ — see ENSURE

2 *slang* to put to death deliberately ⟨that gang leader wouldn't hesitate to *ice* anyone who tries to invade his turf⟩ — see MURDER 1

iceberg *n* a cold aloof person ⟨a brilliant doctor, no doubt, but both patients and staff complain that he is an *iceberg*⟩ — see COLD FISH

ice–cold *adj* having a low or subnormal temperature ⟨*ice-cold* hands from hours spent shoveling snow⟩ — see COLD 1

icicle *n* a cold aloof person ⟨his wife is such an *icicle* you're lucky to get so much as a greeting from her⟩ — see COLD FISH

icky *adj* not giving pleasure to the mind or senses ⟨the novel has an *icky* sentimentality that makes my skin crawl⟩ — see UNPLEASANT

icon *also* **ikon** *n* **1** a person who is the object of extreme or uncritical devotion ⟨Marilyn Monroe, Elvis Presley, the Beatles, and other *icons* of pop culture⟩ — see IDOL

2 a written or printed mark that is meant to convey information to the reader ⟨the player's remote control is very user-friendly as it doesn't use any *icons* that you haven't seen a million times before⟩ — see CHARACTER 1

3 a visible representation of something abstract (as a quality) ⟨cites Marlene Dietrich as an *icon* of old-time Hollywood glamour⟩ — see EMBODIMENT

4 a person who is widely known and usually much talked about ⟨a sports bar filled with photos of *icons* from football, basketball, and baseball⟩ — see CELEBRITY 1

5 a two dimensional design intended to look like a person or thing ⟨any *icon* of the Deity is regarded as blasphemous by adherents of that religion⟩ — see PICTURE 1

iconoclast *n* a person who does not conform to generally accepted standards or customs ⟨notorious as an *iconoclast*, that music critic isn't afraid to go after sacred cows⟩ — see NONCONFORMIST 1

iconoclastic *adj* deviating from commonly accepted beliefs or practices ⟨the book offers *iconoclastic* and irreverant portraits of some of history's most sacred cows⟩ — see HERETICAL

icy *adj* **1** having a low or subnormal temperature ⟨an *icy* drink that was especially refreshing on that hot afternoon⟩ — see COLD 1

2 lacking in friendliness or warmth of feeling ⟨she wondered why the salesclerk at the boutique had given her an *icy* glare⟩ — see COLD 2

ID *vb* to find out or establish the identity of ⟨studies that show that eyewitnesses are surprisingly unreliable when called upon to *ID* the perpetrators of crimes⟩ — see IDENTIFY 1

idea *n* **1** something imagined or pictured in the mind ⟨my *idea* of the perfect vacation spot is an uncrowded, unspoiled beach⟩

synonyms abstraction, cogitation, concept, conception, image, impression, intellection, mind's eye, notion, picture, thought

related words apprehension, premonition, presentiment; preconception, prejudice, prepossession; chimera, delusion, hallucination, illusion, phantasm (*also* fantasm); caprice, conceit, fancy, freak, kink, vagary, whim; cognition, observation, perception, reflection; assumption, belief, conclusion, conviction; conjecture, guess, hunch, hypothesis, speculation, supposition, surmise, theory; brainchild, brainstorm, brain wave, inspiration

near antonyms actuality, fact, reality

2 someone of such unequaled perfection as to deserve imitation ⟨Helen Keller remains my *idea* of a person with indomitable spirit⟩ — see IDEAL 1

3 something that one hopes or intends to accomplish ⟨the *idea* is to get the information without seeming to be nosy⟩ — see GOAL

ideal *adj* **1** dealing with or expressing a quality or idea ⟨honesty is an *ideal* entity that has more admirers than practitioners⟩ — see ABSTRACT 1

2 not real and existing only in the imagination ⟨depicts an *ideal* society in which conflict and privation are unknown⟩ — see IMAGINARY

3 being entirely without fault or flaw ⟨for years she's been searching for a man who would make an *ideal* husband, and she's still looking⟩ — see PERFECT 1

ideal *n* **1** someone of such unequaled perfection as to deserve imitation ⟨she's our *ideal* of the concerned, caring physician⟩

synonyms beau ideal, classic, eidolon, exemplar, idea, model, nonesuch, nonpareil, paragon, patron saint

related words role model; embodiment, epitome, incarnation, manifestation, personification, phantom, pink; archetype, example, mirror, paradigm, pattern; guideline, principle, rule; gauge (*also* gage), standard, touchstone; essence, quintessence; acme, apex, apotheosis, culmination, peak, pinnacle, summit, zenith

2 the most perfect type or example ⟨the Taj Mahal in India is generally regarded as the *ideal* of Mogul architectural beauty⟩ — see QUINTESSENCE 1

3 something that one hopes or intends to accomplish ⟨his *ideal* is to make enough money so that he can retire at 50⟩ — see GOAL

idealist *adj* having or marked by a tendency to be guided more by ideals than by reality ⟨an *idealist* attempt to make a go of a mom-and-pop hardware store on Main Street⟩ — see IDEALISTIC

idealist *n* one whose conduct is guided more by the image of perfection than by the real world ⟨an *idealist* sees the best in everyone, regardless of how they behave⟩

synonyms Don Quixote, dreamer, fantast, idealizer, ideologue (*also* idealogue), romantic, romanticist, utopian, visionary

related words emotionalist, sentimentalist; daydreamer, fantasizer, woolgatherer; Micawber, optimist, Pollyanna; do-gooder, reformer; perfectionist; doctrinaire, theorist, thinker

near antonyms cynic, defeatist, pessimist; empiric, empiricist

antonyms hardnose, pragmatist, realist

idealistic *adj* having or marked by a tendency to be guided more by ideals than by reality ⟨*idealistic* pacifists who thought that tyranny could be toppled by rational argument and mutual understanding⟩

synonyms idealist, quixotic, quixotical, romantic, starry, starry-eyed, utopian, visionary

related words impractical, unrealistic; crusading, messianic, zealous; dewy-eyed, moonstruck, moony, sentimental, tender-minded; hopeful, optimistic, Pollyan-

naish (*also* Pollyannish), rosy, upbeat; doctrinaire, ideological (*also* ideologic)
near antonyms hardheaded, hard-nosed, tough-minded, unsentimental; practical, pragmatic (*also* pragmatical), realistic
antonyms clear-eyed, clear-sighted

idealize *vb* to represent or think of as better than reality would warrant ‹he had a tendency to *idealize* his heroes and believe they could do no wrong›
synonyms glamorize (*also* glamourize), glamour (up), glorify, romanticize
related words heroicize, heroize; euphemize, poeticize, soften, sweeten; adulate, canonize, deify, idolize; aggrandize, dignify, ennoble, enshrine, enthrone, magnify
near antonyms belittle, decry, denigrate, deprecate, disparage, minimize, put down
antonyms deglamorize

idealizer *n* one whose conduct is guided more by the image of perfection than by the real world ‹an *idealizer*, she thinks that any convicted criminal is capable of being redeemed by the love of a good woman› — see IDEALIST

ideally *adv* without any flaws or errors ‹an *ideally* executed routine on the parallel bars that earned him perfect scores from the judges› — see PERFECTLY 1

ideate *vb* to form a mental picture of ‹the psychotic would repeatedly *ideate* the act of committing murder, and eventually he came to believe his own delusions› — see IMAGINE 1

ideation *n* the ability to form mental images of things that either are not physically present or have never been conceived or created by others ‹caregivers are trained to watch for signs of depression and suicidal *ideation*—some patients are likely to put their fantasies to action› — see IMAGINATION 1

ideational *adj* dealing with or expressing a quality or idea ‹ideograms are *ideational*—they are meant to suggest some general idea and not a particular word or phrase› — see ABSTRACT 1

idée fixe *n* something about which one is constantly thinking or concerned ‹had this bizarre *idée fixe* that people were spying on her with electromagnetic waves› — see FIXATION

identical *adj* **1** being one and not another ‹both families wanted the *identical* puppy and weren't accepting the argument that its littermates were just as good› — see SAME 2
2 resembling another in every respect ‹*identical* dresses whose only difference is a designer label that fetches a high price› — see SAME 1

identicalness *n* the state of being exactly alike ‹the *identicalness* of your answers to your friend's suggests that someone copied› — see IDENTITY 1

identify *vb* **1** to find out or establish the identity of ‹sufficient forensic evidence to allow investigators to *identify* the perpetrator›
synonyms distinguish, finger, ID, pinpoint, single (out)
related words diagnose; determine, find; locate, pick out, place, recognize, spot; check, examine, inspect, investigate, notice, observe, scrutinize; betray, disclose, discover, reveal
phrases put one's finger on
near antonyms camouflage, conceal, disguise, hide; counterfeit, feign, sham, simulate
2 to think of (something) in combination ‹for some reason, he always *identified* the color red with flowers› — see ASSOCIATE 2

identifying *adj* serving to identify as belonging to an individual or group ‹the marching band's striking black-and-silver uniforms serve as its *identifying* mark for thousands of parade spectators› — see CHARACTERISTIC 1

identity *n* **1** the state of being exactly alike ‹although the covers of the two paperback editions of the novel are different, there's a complete *identity* in the texts›
synonyms identicalness, sameness
related words oneness, selfsameness; homogeneity, homogeneousness, homology; equality, equivalence; accordance, agreement, conformity, congruity, correspondence, likeness, resemblance, similarity
near antonyms alteration, change, modification, variation; distinction, distinctiveness, distinctness, exoticness, individuality, separateness, separation, uniqueness, unusualness; deviance, divergence; variance; incompatibility, incongruence, incongruity, incongruousness; contrast
antonyms difference, disagreement, discrepancy, disparateness, disparity, dissimilarity, unlikeness
2 the set of qualities that make a person different from other people ‹children begin to form their own *identity* by the age of two› — see INDIVIDUALITY 1

ideologue *also* **idealogue** *n* **1** one who is intensely or excessively devoted to a cause ‹as long as there are *ideologues* controlling both sides of the aisle, legislative compromise is out of the question› — see ZEALOT
2 one whose conduct is guided more by the image of perfection than by the real world ‹the revolutionaries proved to be impractical *ideologues* who had no idea how to run a country› — see IDEALIST

ideology *also* **idealogy** *n* the basic beliefs or guiding principles of a person or group ‹members of that sect follow an *ideology* of nonviolence and freely given cooperation› — see CREED 1

idiocy *n* a foolish act or idea ‹trying to get that many people to agree on anything was pure *idiocy*› — see FOLLY 1

idiom *n* a sequence of words having a specific meaning ‹the English *idiom* "how are you doing?" is our version of a greeting that in some other languages can be translated as "how are you going?"› — see PHRASE

idiomatic *adj* of, relating to, or belonging to a single person ‹the new teacher's *idiomatic* approach to dealing with special-needs students is already showing signs of success› — see INDIVIDUAL 1

idiosyncrasy *n* an odd or peculiar habit ‹his only *idiosyncrasy* is his inveterate wearing of sneakers, even with business suits›
synonyms crotchet, curiosity, eccentricity, erraticism, individualism, kink, mannerism, oddity, peculiarity, quiddity, quip, quirk, singularity, tic, trick, twist
related words affectation, airs; attribute, characteristic, mark, property, trait; custom, habit, pattern, practice (*also* practise), way, wont; addiction; abnormality, neuroticism, perversion, weirdness; disposition, genius, leaning, partiality; bent, inclination, penchant, predilection, predisposition, proclivity, propensity, tendency, turn; attitude, character, humor, identity, individuality, nature, personality, temperament
near antonyms conformity, sameness

idiot *n* a stupid person ‹only an *idiot* would invest in a company just because a casual acquaintance recommended it›
synonyms airhead, birdbrain, blockhead, bonehead, bubblehead, chowderhead, chucklehead, clodpoll (*or* clodpole), clot [*British*], cluck, clunk, cretin, cuddy (*or* cuddie) [*British dialect*], deadhead, dim bulb [*slang*], dimwit, dip, dodo, dolt, donkey, doofus [*slang*], dope, dork [*slang*], dullard, dumbbell, dumbhead, dum-dum, dummkopf, dummy, dunce, dunderhead, fathead, gander, golem, goof, goon, half-wit, hammerhead, hardhead, ignoramus, imbecile, jackass, know-nothing, knucklehead, lamebrain, loggerhead [*chiefly dialect*], loon, lump, lunkhead, meathead, mome [*archaic*], moron, mug [*chiefly British*], mutt, natural, nimrod [*slang*],

nincompoop, ninny, ninnyhammer, nit [*chiefly British*], nitwit, noddy, noodle, numskull (*or* numbskull), oaf, pinhead, prat [*British*], ratbag [*chiefly Australian*], saphead, schlub (*also* shlub) [*slang*], schnook [*slang*], simpleton, stock, stupe, stupid, thickhead, turkey, woodenhead, yahoo, yo-yo
related words booby, buffoon, fool, goose, loony, lunatic, madman, nut, zany; loser; gawk; featherbrain, scatterbrain; beast, boor, cad, churl, clown, creep, cur, heel, jerk, skunk, snake, stinker, villain; bimbette [*slang*], bimbo [*slang*], himbo
phrases dumb cluck
near antonyms egghead, intellect, intellectual, sage, thinker, whiz, wizard; polymath, Renaissance man; sharpie (*or* sharpy)
antonyms brain, genius

idiot box *n* an electronic device with a screen and speakers that reproduces images and sound ⟨she huffily declared that she wouldn't have an *idiot box* in her home⟩ — see TELEVISION

idle *adj* **1** not being in a state of use, activity, or employment ⟨the car was *idle* for two weeks while they went on vacation⟩ — see INACTIVE 2
2 not easily aroused to action or work ⟨an *idle* employee who always seems to be either on break or at lunch⟩ — see LAZY 1

idle *vb* to spend time doing nothing ⟨she likes to *idle* during the summer, maintaining that there's a lot to be said for sloth⟩
synonyms bum, chill, dally, dawdle, dillydally, drone, footle, goof (off), hack (around), hang (around *or* out), hang about [*British*], kick around, kick back, laze, lazy, loaf, loll, lounge, veg out
related words fiddle (around), fool, mess, monkey, muck, piddle, play, potter (around), putter (around), trifle; doze, estivate (*also* aestivate), hibernate; lag, linger, loiter, poke, relax, rest, tarry; amble, mosey, saunter, stroll, swan; furlough, goldbrick, malinger, truant
phrases kill time, twiddle one's thumbs
near antonyms drudge, grind, grub, hump, hustle, labor, moil, peg, plod, plow, plug, slave, sweat, toil, travail, work; apply, buckle (down); exert, put out

idleness *n* **1** an inclination not to do work or engage in activities ⟨the brothers' innate *idleness* meant that neither did much, either inside or outside their ramshackle cabin⟩ — see LAZINESS
2 lack of action or activity ⟨a day spent in *idleness* is nice, but a month of doing nothing is boring!⟩ — see INACTION
3 lack of use ⟨the *idleness* of the sewing machine was apparent by its thick layer of dust⟩ — see DISUSE

idler *n* a lazy person ⟨an *idler* by nature, he expected to be waited on by his new wife⟩ — see LAZYBONES

idol *n* a person who is the object of extreme or uncritical devotion ⟨a movie *idol* whose reprehensible offscreen behavior caused him to experience a spectacular fall from grace⟩
synonyms god, hero, icon (*also* ikon)
related words beau ideal, classic, exemplar, ideal, model, nonpareil, paragon

idolater *or* **idolator** *n* a person who does not worship the God of the Bible ⟨by and large the American colonists were not particularly tolerant of those who were regarded as *idolaters*⟩ — see HEATHEN 1

idolatry *n* excessive admiration of or devotion to a person ⟨her *idolatry* of her favorite rock star is one step removed from stalking⟩ — see WORSHIP

idolization *n* excessive admiration of or devotion to a person ⟨the mass *idolization* of sports figures often results in the public's refusal to believe that they could ever do wrong⟩ — see WORSHIP

idolize *vb* to love or admire too much ⟨she blindly *idolized* her older sister, refusing to acknowledge her considerable faults⟩
synonyms adore, adulate, canonize, deify, dote (on), hero-worship, worship
related words appreciate, cherish, esteem, prize, treasure, value; fancy, favor, like, prefer; regard; hallow, respect, revere, venerate; approve, endorse (*also* indorse), support
near antonyms abhor, abominate, despise, detest, disdain, dislike, hate, loathe; belittle, deprecate, disparage, misprize, put down

idolizing *adj* reflecting great admiration or devotion ⟨gave his fiancée an *idolizing* glance⟩ — see WORSHIPFUL

idyll *also* **idyl** *n* a time or instance of carefree fun ⟨her year as a vineyard worker in the south of France was not the *idyll* that she had expected it to be⟩ — see FLING 1

if *n* **1** something taken as being true or factual and used as a starting point for a course of action or reasoning ⟨your conclusion may turn out to be accurate, but you're postulating a lot of *ifs*⟩ — see ASSUMPTION 1
2 something upon which the carrying out of an agreement or offer depends ⟨there are a number of *ifs* in the proposal⟩ — see CONDITION 2

ignitable *also* **ignitible** *adj* capable of catching or being set on fire ⟨gasoline fumes are quite *ignitable*⟩ — see COMBUSTIBLE

ignite *vb* to set (something) on fire ⟨tried using newspapers as kindling to *ignite* the logs in the fireplace⟩ — see BURN 2

ignited *adj* being on fire ⟨the *ignited* fireworks caused explosions that leveled the building⟩ — see ABLAZE 1

ignoble *adj* **1** belonging to the class of people of low social or economic rank ⟨an *ignoble* child who would one day grow up to be a prince among playwrights⟩
synonyms baseborn, common, humble, inferior, low, lowborn, lower-class, low-life, lowly, lumpen, mean, plebeian, prole, proletarian, unwashed, vulgar
related words bourgeois, middle-class; plain, poor, simple, working-class; déclassé, down-market, downscale
near antonyms eminent, illustrious, notable, prominent
antonyms aristocratic, blue-blooded, genteel, gentle, grand, great, high, highborn, highbred, lofty, noble, patrician, upper-class, upper-crust, wellborn
2 not following or in accordance with standards of honor and decency ⟨such an *ignoble* act is completely unworthy of a military officer⟩
synonyms base, contemptible, currish, despicable, detestable, dirty, dishonorable, execrable, ignominious, low, low-down, low-minded, mean, nasty, paltry, snide, sordid, vile, wretched
related words bad, black, evil, foul, immoral, iniquitous, miscreant, wicked, wrong; cruel, vicious; blamable, blameworthy, censurable, reprehensible; corrupt, debased, debauched, degenerate, depraved, dissolute, perverted; atrocious, villainous; unethical, unprincipled, unscrupulous; discreditable, disgraceful, disreputable, shameful, unworthy
near antonyms ethical, honest, just, principled, righteous, right-minded, scrupulous; commendable, excellent, exemplary, good, moral, right; decent, proper, reputable, respectable, seemly; blameless, guiltless; incorruptible, irreproachable; uncorrupted, unerring
antonyms high, high-minded, honorable, lofty, noble, straight, upright, venerable, virtuous

ignominious *adj* **1** not respectable ⟨some of his friends considered the job of janitor to be an *ignominious* fate for the laid-off executive⟩ — see DISREPUTABLE
2 not following or in accordance with standards of

honor and decency ⟨the prison guards degraded themselves with their inhumane, *ignominious* treatment of the prisoners⟩ — see IGNOBLE 2

ignominy *n* the state of having lost the esteem of others ⟨he spent the remainder of his life in *ignominy* after being involved in a bribery scandal⟩ — see DISGRACE 1

ignoramus *n* a stupid person ⟨only an *ignoramus* would be foiled by the building's security system⟩ — see IDIOT

ignorance *n* **1** the state of being unaware or uninformed ⟨*ignorance* of the law is no excuse⟩
synonyms benightedness, cluelessness, incognizance, innocence, nescience, obliviousness, unawareness, unfamiliarity
related words callowness, greenness, inexperience, naïveté (*also* naivete *or* naiveté), rawness, simpleness, unsophistication
near antonyms experience, know-how; sophistication
antonyms acquaintance, awareness, cognizance, familiarity
2 the state of being unlearned ⟨with such vast sums spent on education, the level of *ignorance* among graduating seniors is a national disgrace⟩
synonyms illiteracy
related words functional illiteracy, innumeracy; brainlessness, dumbness, idiocy, imbecility, stupidity; philistinism; foolishness, mindlessness, senselessness, witlessness
near antonyms education, instruction, training; enlightenment, knowledge; erudition, scholarship
antonyms learning, literacy

ignorant *adj* **1** lacking in education or the knowledge gained from books ⟨they may be poor, *ignorant* farmers, but they are not stupid⟩
synonyms analphabetic, benighted, dark, illiterate, nonliterate, rude, simple, uneducated, uninstructed, unlearned, unlettered, unread, unschooled, untaught, untutored
related words functionally illiterate, innumerate, semiliterate, unknowledgeable; artless, lowbrow, philistine, uncultivated, uncultured; callow, green, inexperienced, innocent, naive (*or* naïve); unsophisticated; raw, unskilled, untrained; brainless, dumb, idiotic (*also* idiotical), imbecile (*or* imbecilic), moronic, stupid, witless; foolish, senseless, silly
near antonyms brilliant, intelligent, smart; experienced, expert, trained; erudite, learned, polyhistoric, polymath (*or* polymathic), scholarly; cultivated, cultured, highbrow, intellectual; sophisticated; acquainted, aware, familiar
antonyms educated, knowledgeable, lettered, literate, schooled, well-informed, well-read
2 not informed about or aware of something ⟨he was *ignorant* of their wedding plans⟩
synonyms clueless, incognizant, innocent, insensible, nescient, oblivious, unacquainted, unaware, unconscious, uninformed, unknowing, unmindful, unwitting
related words uneducated, unschooled, untaught; absent, absentminded, abstracted, heedless, inattentive, inconscient
phrases in the dark
near antonyms au courant, hip, plugged-in, up-to-date; educated, knowledgeable, schooled, taught; heedful, observant; sensitive, sentient
antonyms acquainted, aware, cognizant, conscious, conversant, grounded, informed, knowing, mindful, witting

ignore *vb* **1** to fail to give proper attention to ⟨*ignoring* your health now will haunt you further down the road⟩ — see NEGLECT 1
2 to dismiss as of little importance ⟨although the movie is a cinematic tour de force, one can't *ignore* the fact that it seriously distorts history⟩ — see EXCUSE 1

ilk *n* a number of persons or things that are grouped together because they have something in common ⟨we're looking for chestnuts and other items of that *ilk* for our autumn decorations⟩ — see SORT 1

ill *adj* **1** affected with nausea ⟨she grew *ill* from the constant rocking motion of the boat⟩ — see NAUSEOUS 1
2 causing or capable of causing harm ⟨one of the *ill* effects of winter weather is the rapid spread of germs as people spend more time together indoors⟩ — see HARMFUL
3 temporarily suffering from a disorder of the body ⟨since I'm *ill*, I guess that I'll just have to miss that dental appointment⟩ — see SICK 1
4 falling short of a standard ⟨such *ill* behavior will not be tolerated⟩ — see BAD 1
5 being or showing a sign of evil or calamity to come ⟨the abrupt breakdown of negotiations appears to be an *ill* omen for this ongoing hostage situation⟩ — see OMINOUS

ill *adv* **1** in a manner so as to cause loss or suffering ⟨in those days society treated debtors very *ill*, even going so far as to put them in prison⟩ — see HARDLY 1
2 certainly not ⟨you can *ill* afford to miss another day of work⟩ — see HARDLY 2

ill *n* **1** an abnormal state that disrupts a plant's or animal's normal bodily functioning ⟨chicken pox and the other *ills* that were once a fixture of childhood⟩ — see DISEASE
2 that which is morally unacceptable ⟨idealistic people who try to cure all of our society's *ills*⟩ — see EVIL
3 bad luck or an example of this ⟨the travelers merrily set off on their journey, scarcely imagining the *ills* that would befall them⟩ — see MISFORTUNE

ill–advised *adj* showing poor judgment especially in personal relationships or social situations ⟨an *ill-advised* criticism of the boss at a company function⟩ — see INDISCREET

ill at ease *adj* feeling or showing uncomfortable feelings of uncertainty ⟨I'm usually *ill at ease* when addressing a large crowd of people⟩ — see NERVOUS 1

ill–boding *adj* being or showing a sign of evil or calamity to come ⟨in an *ill-boding* turn of events, the government began rounding up political dissidents⟩ — see OMINOUS

ill–bred *adj* **1** lacking in refinement or good taste ⟨the *ill-bred* habit of chewing with the mouth open⟩ — see COARSE 2
2 showing a lack of manners or consideration for others ⟨only an *ill-bred*, conceited person would demand that everyone cater to their whims⟩ — see IMPOLITE

illegal *adj* **1** contrary to or forbidden by law ⟨it is *illegal* to import those birds into this country⟩
synonyms criminal, felonious, illegitimate, illicit, lawless, unlawful, wrongful
related words bad, evil, immoral, shameful, sinful, unethical, wicked, wrong; blamable, blameworthy, censurable, reprehensible; banned, barred, contraband, criminalized, disallowed, discouraged, forbidden, interdicted, outlawed, prohibited, proscribed; adulterine, bootleg, unauthorized, unlicensed, unsanctioned; under-the-counter, under-the-table; corrupt, unprincipled, unscrupulous, villainous
near antonyms ethical, good, just, principled, right, righteous, virtuous; allowed, permitted; authorized, licensed; approved, endorsed (*also* indorsed), sanctioned; abetted, encouraged, promoted, suggested, supported; correct, decent, decorous, proper, seemly
antonyms lawful, legal, legitimate
2 not being in accordance with the rules or standards of what is fair in sport ⟨an *illegal* pass⟩ — see FOUL 2

illegalize *vb* to make or declare contrary to the law ⟨a

bill that would *illegalize* the private use of fireworks⟩
synonyms criminalize, outlaw
related words ban, bar, enjoin, forbid, interdict, prohibit, proscribe
near antonyms allow, let, permit, suffer; approve, endorse (*also* indorse), sanction
antonyms decriminalize, legalize

illegible *adj* incapable of being read or deciphered ⟨*illegible* signatures on the petition will be disregarded⟩
synonyms indecipherable, undecipherable, unreadable
related words faint, indistinct, obscure, unclear
antonyms clean, decipherable, fair, legible, readable

illegitimacy *n* the state or fact of being born out of wedlock ⟨she had learned of her *illegitimacy* while rummaging through old family records in the attic⟩
synonyms bar sinister, bastardy, spuriousness
antonyms legitimacy

illegitimate *adj* **1** born to a father and mother who are not married ⟨despite being *illegitimate*, Alexander Hamilton rose to greatness⟩
synonyms baseborn, bastard, misbegotten, natural, spurious, supposititious, unfathered
related words fatherless, motherless; nameless; adopted, orphaned
antonyms legitimate
2 contrary to or forbidden by law ⟨an *illegitimate* use of campaign contributions for personal expenses⟩ — see ILLEGAL 1
3 not using or following good reasoning ⟨made several *illegitimate* inferences⟩ — see ILLOGICAL

ill–fated *adj* having, prone to, or marked by bad luck ⟨the *ill-fated* trip ended in disaster for all⟩ — see UNLUCKY 1

ill–favored *adj* unpleasant to look at ⟨an *ill-favored* and yapping little dog that reminded people a lot of its owner⟩ — see UGLY 1

ill–humored *adj* having or showing a habitually bad temper ⟨an *ill-humored* person should probably not take a job that requires dealing with the public⟩ — see ILL-TEMPERED

illiberal *adj* **1** not broad or open in views or opinions ⟨an *illiberal* society that viewed any artistic depiction of the nude as inherently indecent⟩ — see NARROW 2
2 unwilling to grant other people social rights or to accept other viewpoints ⟨some of the more *illiberal* residents were opposed to having a hospice for AIDS patients in the neighborhood⟩ — see INTOLERANT 2
3 *archaic* lacking in refinement or good taste ⟨people who had been scorned as *illiberal* because they were poor⟩ — see COARSE 2

illiberalism *n* stubborn or intolerant adherence to one's opinions or prejudices ⟨a woman who fails to see that her unexamined faith in political liberalism actually makes her guilty of *illiberalism*⟩ — see BIGOTRY

illiberality *n* stubborn or intolerant adherence to one's opinions or prejudices ⟨liked the peace and quiet of small-town life but chafed at its social and religious *illiberality*⟩ — see BIGOTRY

illiberalness *n* stubborn or intolerant adherence to one's opinions or prejudices ⟨the *illiberalness* of her religious beliefs made any theological discussion rather pointless⟩ — see BIGOTRY

illicit *adj* contrary to or forbidden by law ⟨had a long history of using *illicit* drugs⟩ — see ILLEGAL 1

illimitable *adj* being or seeming to be without limits ⟨the *illimitable* expanse of the universe⟩ — see INFINITE

illiteracy *n* the state of being unlearned ⟨far too many children are doomed to a lifetime of *illiteracy* in that country⟩ — see IGNORANCE 2

illiterate *adj* **1** violating approved patterns of speaking and writing ⟨most of the messages left on the Web site's bulletin board are *illiterate*⟩
synonyms ungrammatical
related words unidiomatic; nonstandard, substandard
near antonyms idiomatic
antonyms grammatical
2 lacking in education or the knowledge gained from books ⟨offered menus with pictures, presumably for the many *illiterate* people who must eat there⟩ — see IGNORANT 1

ill–mannered *adj* showing a lack of manners or consideration for others ⟨an *ill-mannered* child who refuses to say "please" or "thank you"⟩ — see IMPOLITE

ill–natured *adj* having or showing a habitually bad temper ⟨an *ill-natured* and unpleasant old horse that sometimes bites⟩ — see ILL-TEMPERED

illness *n* **1** an abnormal state that disrupts a plant's or animal's normal bodily functioning ⟨suffered from a mysterious *illness* that left her weak and tired all the time⟩ — see DISEASE
2 the condition of not being in good health ⟨prone to *illness* as a child, he was sent to a western ranch with the expectation that it would toughen him up⟩ — see SICKNESS 1

illogical *adj* not using or following good reasoning ⟨the *illogical* claim that playing basketball makes people taller because one sees so many tall players⟩ ⟨*illogical* people are likely to believe every sensational claim made on TV⟩
synonyms fallacious, illegitimate, inconsequent, inconsequential, invalid, irrational, nonrational, unreasonable, unreasoning, unsound, weak
related words eristic (*also* eristical), misleading, sophistic (*or* sophistical), specious; half-baked, ill-advised, misguided, unconsidered, unreasoned; inconsistent; absurd, asinine, foolish, meaningless, nonsensical, preposterous, reasonless, senseless, silly; Kafkaesque, odd, peculiar, strange, surreal, unusual, weird; insane, mad, nutty, wacky (*also* whacky); disordered, disorganized, rambling, random; unconvincing; inexplicable, unaccountable, unexplainable
near antonyms commonsense, sane, sensible, sober, wise; enlightened, informed, just, justified, reasoned; ordered, organized; clear, cogent, compelling, convincing, credible, persuasive, plausible, satisfying, solid; certain, sure, true; confirmed, corroborated, demonstrated, established, substantiated, validated
antonyms logical, rational, reasonable, sound, valid, well-founded, well-grounded

ill–starred *adj* having, prone to, or marked by bad luck ⟨an *ill-starred* attempt to circumnavigate the earth in a balloon⟩ — see UNLUCKY 1

ill–tempered *adj* having or showing a habitually bad temper ⟨an *ill-tempered* cat will scratch with little provocation⟩
synonyms acid, bearish, bilious, bloody-minded [*chiefly British*], cantankerous, disagreeable, dyspeptic, ill-humored, ill-natured, ornery, splenetic, surly
related words choleric, crabby, cranky, crotchety, fussy, grouchy, grumpy, querulous; irascible, irritable, peevish, peppery, petulant, quick-tempered, short-tempered, snappish, snippy, testy, touchy; argumentative, contentious, contrary, cussed; angry, exasperated, indignant, irate, mad, upset, uptight; depressed, dour, glum, morose, sullen; anal, old-maidish, schoolmarmish
near antonyms agreeable, amicable, congenial, friendly, pleasant; benign, gentle, kind, nice, sweet; bubbly, cheerful, cheery, effervescent, exuberant, high-spirited, joyful, lighthearted, lively, vivacious; content, glad, happy; calm, placid, serene; long-suffering, patient, tolerant

antonyms amiable, good-humored, good-natured, good-tempered

ill–treat *vb* to inflict physical or emotional harm upon ⟨anyone who *ill-treats* their pets should not be allowed to have any⟩ — see ABUSE 1

illume *vb* **1** to provide (someone) with moral or spiritual understanding ⟨a favorite line of an Eastern Church hymn reads, "through fast-closed doors Thou camest Thy Disciples to *illume*"⟩ — see ENLIGHTEN 2

2 to supply with light ⟨during the vigil service the church's Gothic interior was *illumed* by the light of hundreds of tapers⟩ — see ILLUMINATE 1

illuminant *n* something that provides illumination ⟨at the time, a spermaceti candle was the brightest indoor *illuminant* available⟩ — see LIGHT 2

illuminate *vb* **1** to supply with light ⟨a floor lamp *illuminates* a living room rather nicely⟩

synonyms bathe, beacon, emblaze, illume, illumine, irradiate, light, lighten

related words brighten; beam, beat (down), radiate, shine; enhalo, halo; floodlight; highlight, spotlight; blaze, burn, fire, flame, glare, glow, ignite, incinerate, kindle; bedazzle, blind, daze, dazzle; gleam, glisten, glitter

near antonyms dim, dull, obscure; cover, shroud, veil; douse (*also* dowse), extinguish, put out, quench, snuff (out)

antonyms blacken, darken, obfuscate

2 to make plain or understandable ⟨the museum's exhibit on the refraction of light really *illuminated* the subject for us⟩ — see EXPLAIN 1

3 to supplement with pictorial matter for the purpose of explanation or decoration ⟨no one knows for sure the identity of the artist who *illuminated* that medieval manuscript so beautifully⟩ — see ILLUSTRATE 2

4 to indicate the importance of by centering attention on ⟨that city's total unpreparedness for the powerful hurricane *illuminated* the need for all cities to have plans in place before disaster strikes⟩ — see EMPHASIZE 1

5 to provide (someone) with moral or spiritual understanding ⟨how man is *illuminated* by a higher spirit⟩ — see ENLIGHTEN 2

illuminated *adj* filled with much light ⟨an intensely *illuminated* room is usually needed for producing live television shows⟩ — see BRIGHT 2

illuminati *n pl* individuals carefully selected as being the best of a class ⟨a book launching party to which only New York's cultural *illuminati* were invited⟩ — see ELITE 1

illuminating *adj* providing useful information or knowledge ⟨the DVD is an *illuminating* tutorial on the proper calibration of a high-definition television⟩ — see INFORMATIVE

illumination *n* **1** a statement that makes something clear ⟨the candidate's so-called *illuminations* of his views on a number of controversial issues left many voters in the dark⟩ — see EXPLANATION 1

2 the quality or state of having or giving off light ⟨in that clime the *illumination* of the full moon is such as you can practically read by it⟩ — see BRILLIANCE 1

3 the steady giving off of the form of radiation that makes vision possible ⟨a steady *illumination* from the flashlight was all I had while changing the tire⟩ — see LIGHT 1

illuminative *adj* serving to explain ⟨*illuminative* descriptions of the sights to be seen from the observatory gave us a much better idea of what we were looking at⟩ — see EXPLANATORY

illumine *vb* **1** to supply with light ⟨small table lamps *illumine* the inn's dining room in a most romantic way⟩ — see ILLUMINATE 1

2 to provide (someone) with moral or spiritual understanding ⟨readers of great literature are both entertained and *illumined*⟩ — see ENLIGHTEN 2

illumined *adj* filled with much light ⟨*illumined* display windows in the street's many shops add much to the holiday glow⟩ — see BRIGHT 2

ill–use *vb* to inflict physical or emotional harm upon ⟨the alcoholic had *ill-used* his long-suffering wife for years⟩ — see ABUSE 1

illusion *n* **1** a conception or image created by the imagination and having no objective reality ⟨the magician specializes in creating *illusions*, so that people believe they have seen something when they really haven't⟩ — see FANTASY 1

2 a false idea or belief ⟨the idea that we as a nation can ever enjoy perfect security is an *illusion*⟩ — see FALLACY 1

illusionist *n* one who practices tricks and illusions for entertainment ⟨tried to figure out how the *illusionist* made his assistant disappear from the stage⟩ — see MAGICIAN 2

illustrate *vb* **1** to show or make clear by using examples ⟨she *illustrated* her point with a story about her experiences as a field anthropologist⟩

synonyms demonstrate, exemplify, instance

related words adduce, cite, mention, quote; name, specify; analyze, break down; clarify, clear (up), explain, explicate, expound; edify, elucidate, enlighten; illuminate; construe, interpret; simplify, spell out; detail, enumerate, list

near antonyms becloud, blur, cloud, darken, fog, muddy, obscure; confuse, perplex, puzzle

2 to supplement with pictorial matter for the purpose of explanation or decoration ⟨lavishly *illustrated* the monograph on Caravaggio with color plates⟩

synonyms illuminate, pictorialize

related words image, picture, visualize

3 to make plain or understandable ⟨the recent devastating fire *illustrates* the need for improved safety codes⟩ — see EXPLAIN 1

illustration *n* **1** something that visually explains or decorates a text ⟨this book on birds has gorgeous *illustrations*⟩

synonyms diagram, figure, graphic, plate, visual

related words art, artwork; drawing, illumination, image, pictogram, pictograph, picture; caption, key, legend; inset; depiction, pictorialization, portrait, portrayal, representation; clarification, elucidation, explanation, explication, exposition

2 a statement that makes something clear ⟨forced to give several *illustrations* until she was understood⟩ — see EXPLANATION 1

3 a two-dimensional design intended to look like a person or thing ⟨the doctor sketched an *illustration* to explain the procedure to the patient⟩ — see PICTURE 1

4 one of a group or collection that shows what the whole is like ⟨chose one essay as an *illustration* of the high quality of the collection⟩ — see EXAMPLE

illustrative *adj* serving to explain ⟨an *illustrative* analogy in which the relationship between God and humanity is likened to that between a shepherd and his flock⟩ — see EXPLANATORY

illustrious *adj* standing above others in rank, importance, or achievement ⟨an *illustrious* physicist who is a sure bet for a Nobel Prize⟩ — see EMINENT

image *vb* **1** to present a picture of ⟨in the painting Sacagawea is *imaged* as an intrepid woman pointing the way for Lewis and Clark⟩ — see PICTURE 1

2 to give a representation or account of in words ⟨the brochure *images* a vacation at the resort in language that makes you want to make a reservation this instant⟩ — see DESCRIBE 1

3 to reproduce or show (an exact likeness) as a mirror would ⟨the burnished chrome fixtures *imaged* the jewelry store's glittery merchandise⟩ — see REFLECT 1
4 to form a mental picture of ⟨anyone who still *images* the cape's coastline as a scene of unspoiled beauty is in for a rude awakening⟩ — see IMAGINE 1

image *n* **1** something or someone that strongly resembles another ⟨the girl is growing up to be the perfect *image* of her mother⟩
synonyms alter ego, carbon, carbon copy, clone, counterpart, doppelgänger (*or* doppelganger), double, duplicate, duplication, facsimile, fetch, likeness, look-alike, match, mirror image, picture, replica, ringer, spit, spitting image, twin
related words Chinese copy; effigy, portrait, portrayal; companion, fellow, mate; equal, equivalent; analogue (*or* analog), parallel
near antonyms antithesis, converse, opposite, reverse
2 a two-dimensional design intended to look like a person or thing ⟨a cave with prehistoric *images* of wild animals⟩ — see PICTURE 1
3 something imagined or pictured in the mind ⟨a sentimental visit to her childhood home to see if it still matched her mental *image* of the place⟩ — see IDEA 1
4 a visible representation of something abstract (as a quality) ⟨a general who became for many the very *image* of the stoic warrior⟩ — see EMBODIMENT

imaginal *adj* **1** consisting of or relating to pictures ⟨after a desensitizing series of *imaginal* exposures to the feared object, the phobic person is then exposed to the actual object⟩ — see PICTORIAL 1
2 not real and existing only in the imagination ⟨the equator is merely an *imaginal* line⟩ — see IMAGINARY

imaginary *adj* not real and existing only in the imagination ⟨told by the psychologist that it was perfectly normal for their child to have an *imaginary* friend⟩
synonyms chimerical (*also* chimeric), fabulous, fanciful, fantasied, fantastic (*also* fantastical), fictional, fictitious, ideal, imaginal, imagined, invented, made-up, make-believe, mythical (*or* mythic), notional, phantasmal, phantasmic, phantom, pretend, unreal, visonary
related words fabled, legendary, romantic; abstract, hypothetical, theoretical (*also* theoretic); unbelievable, unconvincing, unlikely; conceived, envisaged, envisioned, pictured, visualized; daydreamlike, deceptive, delusional, delusive, hallucinatory, illusory, phantasmagoric (*or* phantasmagorical); concocted, fabricated, feigned, fictive; inexistent, nonexistent
near antonyms authentic, genuine, true; factual, verifiable, verified; believable, convincing, realistic; corporeal, material, physical, solid, substantial; palpable, tangible
antonyms actual, existent, existing, real

imagination *n* **1** the ability to form mental images of things that either are not physically present or have never been conceived or created by others ⟨a cartoonist needs a fertile *imagination* in order to create interesting cartoons on demand⟩
synonyms contrivance, creativity, fancy, fantasy (*also* phantasy), ideation, imaginativeness, invention, inventiveness, originality
related words brainstorm, brainstorming, inspiration; fecundity, fertility; ingenuity, resourcefulness; versatility; chimera, daydream, delusion, dream, figment, hallucination, illusion, mind's eye, mirage, phantasm (*also* fantasm), pipe dream; envisaging, visualization
near antonyms literality, literalness
2 the skill and imagination to create new things ⟨she lacks the *imagination* to be anything but an imitator of other directors' cinematic styles⟩ — see CREATIVITY 1

imaginative *adj* **1** having the skill and imagination to create new things ⟨an *imaginative* child who is always writing short stories about her pet cat⟩ — see CREATIVE 1
2 showing a noteworthy use of the imagination and creativity especially in inventing ⟨found an *imaginative* gadget that can grind the beans and heat the water to brew coffee⟩ — see CLEVER 1

imaginativeness *n* **1** the ability to form mental images of things that either are not physically present or have never been conceived or created by others ⟨what sets apart geniuses like Thomas Edison and Ben Franklin from the average person is their keen intellect and restless *imaginativeness*⟩ — see IMAGINATION 1
2 the skill and imagination to create new things ⟨it took exceptional *imaginativeness* and tireless dedication to invent the airplane⟩ — see CREATIVITY 1

imagine *vb* **1** to form a mental picture of ⟨she was determined to have the wedding that she had always *imagined*⟩
synonyms conceit [*chiefly dialect*], conceive, conjure (up), dream, envisage, envision, fancy, fantasize, fantasy, feature, ideate, image, picture, see, vision, visualize
related words daydream, stargaze; hallucinate; re-create, reflect, relive, reminisce; contemplate, meditate, muse, ponder, ruminate; concoct, fabricate, invent, make up, manufacture, plan, project; foresee, prefigure
2 to have as an opinion ⟨I *imagine* that's true, but you still have to prove it⟩ — see BELIEVE 2
3 to form an opinion from little or no evidence ⟨I *imagine* things will change rapidly once we begin⟩ — see GUESS 1

imagined *adj* not real and existing only in the imagination ⟨got needlessly upset about *imagined* dangers⟩ — see IMAGINARY

imbecile *n* a stupid person ⟨only an *imbecile* would leave their car unlocked, with the keys in the ignition, and then be surprised when the vehicle was stolen⟩ — see IDIOT

imbecility *n* **1** a foolish act or idea ⟨was arrested for the sheer *imbecility* of speeding down a dark road with no headlights on⟩ — see FOLLY 1
2 lack of good sense or judgment ⟨we were stunned by the *imbecility* of the ideas presented by this once-respected biologist⟩ — see FOOLISHNESS 1

imbibe *vb* **1** to swallow in liquid form ⟨an array of colorful and tasty drinks for party guests to *imbibe*⟩ — see DRINK 1
2 to take in (something liquid) through small openings ⟨plants can *imbibe* water through their roots⟩ — see ABSORB 1

imbrication *n* a partial covering of one thing by an adjoining member ⟨a scalloped pattern formed by the *imbrication* of the rounded roof tiles⟩ — see OVERLAP 1

imbroglio *n* an often noisy or angry expression of differing opinions ⟨a celebrated *imbroglio* involving some big names in the New York literary scene⟩ — see ARGUMENT 1

imbue *vb* to cause (as a person) to become filled or saturated with a certain quality or principle ⟨her training at the school for the deaf *imbued* her with a sense of purpose that she had never known before⟩ — see INFUSE

imitable *adj* constituting, serving as, or worthy of being a pattern to be imitated ⟨most readers of classic English literature could recognize Jane Austen's *imitable* style instantly⟩ — see MODEL

imitate *vb* **1** to use (someone or something) as the model for one's speech, mannerisms, or behavior ⟨teenage musicians who *imitate* whichever rock stars are hot⟩
synonyms ape, copy, copycat, emulate, mime, mimic
related words ditto, echo, reecho, repeat; burlesque, caricature, lampoon, mock, parody, travesty; imperson-

ate, perform, play; pantomime
2 to copy or exaggerate (someone or something) in order to make fun of ⟨*imitating* someone's stutter and laughing at them is a cruel thing to do⟩ — see MIMIC 1
3 to make an exact likeness of ⟨a second-rate artist who was notorious for *imitating* the works of other painters⟩ — see COPY 1

imitation *n* something that is made to look exactly like something else ⟨challenged me to tell the real roses from the silk *imitations*⟩ — see COPY

imitation *adj* being such in appearance only and made with or manufactured from usually cheaper materials ⟨the stage production uses only *imitation* diamonds, as real gems would be prohibitively expensive⟩
synonyms artificial, bogus, dummy, ersatz, factitious, fake, false, faux, imitative, man-made, mimic, mock, pretend, sham, simulated, substitute, synthetic
related words cultured, manufactured, process; unauthentic; adulterated, designer, doctored, engineered, fudged, juggled, manipulated, tampered (with); concocted, fabricated; counterfeit, deceptive, forged, fraudulent, misleading, phony (*also* phoney); affected, brummagem, feigned, pinchbeck, pseudo, spurious
near antonyms authentic, bona fide, legitimate, true; premium, quality, valuable; pure, unadulterated
antonyms genuine, natural, real

imitative *adj* **1** using or marked by the use of something else as a basis or model ⟨your writing style tends to be *imitative* of whichever author you've recently read⟩
synonyms apish, canned, emulative, epigonic (*or* epigonous), formulaic, mimetic, mimic, slavish, unoriginal
related words copied, cribbed, plagiarized; artificial, bogus, factitious, fake, false, imitation, man-made, mock, sham, simulated, substitute, synthetic; duplicated, photocopied, reduplicated, reproduced, transcribed; backup; counterfeit, deceptive, forged, fraudulent, misleading; cut-and-dried (*also* cut-and-dry), perfunctory, routine, uninspired
near antonyms authentic, bona fide, legitimate, true; genuine, natural, real; classic, ideal, model
antonyms archetypal (*also* archetypical), original
2 being such in appearance only and made with or manufactured from usually cheaper materials ⟨an *imitative* extract never has the flavor of the real thing⟩ — see IMITATION

imitator *n* **1** a person who adopts the appearance or behavior of another especially in an obvious way ⟨an Elvis *imitator* in a sequinned jumpsuit⟩ — see COPYCAT
2 a person who imitates another's voice and mannerisms for comic effect ⟨that comedian is a hilarious *imitator* of a surprising array of current celebrities⟩ — see MIMIC

immaculacy *n* the quality or state of being morally pure ⟨no one could have a heart of such *immaculacy*—she was too good to be true⟩ — see CHASTITY 1

immaculate *adj* **1** free from any trace of the coarse or indecent ⟨an *immaculate* soul⟩ — see CHASTE 1
2 free from dirt or stain ⟨somehow managed to keep the white carpet *immaculate*⟩ — see CLEAN 1
3 being entirely without fault or flaw ⟨a fussy groundskeeper who always manages to restore the football field to an *immaculate* expanse of healthy, well-manicured turf⟩ — see PERFECT 1

immaculately *adv* without any flaws or errors ⟨from a technical point of view, the songs are *immaculately* produced and engineered, but somehow they fail to emotionally engage the listener⟩ — see PERFECTLY 1

immanent *adj* being a part of the innermost nature of a person or thing ⟨a question as to whether altruism is *immanent* in all individuals or is instead acquired from without⟩ — see INHERENT

immaterial *adj* **1** not composed of matter ⟨it is only possible to study *immaterial* forces like gravity by observing their effects on the physical world⟩
synonyms bodiless, ethereal, formless, incorporeal, insubstantial, nonmaterial, nonphysical, spiritual, unbodied, unsubstantial
related words metaphysical, psychic (*also* psychical), supernatural; impalpable, insensible, intangible, invisible; airy, diaphanous, gaseous, gossamery, tenuous, thin, vaporous, wispish
near antonyms animal, carnal, fleshly; detectable, discernible (*also* discernable), noticeable, observable, palpable, sensible, tangible, visible; bulky, heavy, massive, solid
antonyms bodily, corporeal, material, physical, substantial
2 not having anything to do with the matter at hand ⟨while undoubtedly upsetting, that story is *immaterial* to the question of why you are late⟩ — see IRRELEVANT

immateriality *n* the quality or state of being unimportant ⟨the cost of such a lavish affair may be a matter of some *immateriality* to the wedding planner, but not to the person who has to foot the bill⟩ — see INSIGNIFICANCE

immature *adj* **1** being in the early stage of life, growth, or development ⟨*immature* frogs are called "tadpoles"⟩ — see YOUNG
2 having or showing the annoying qualities (as silliness) associated with children ⟨an *immature* teenager who still threw tantrums⟩ — see CHILDISH
3 lacking in adult experience or maturity ⟨many high school students are still too *immature* to foresee the consequences of their actions⟩ — see CALLOW

immeasurable *adj* being or seeming to be without limits ⟨the *immeasurable* expanse of the ocean⟩ — see INFINITE

immediacy *n* the state or condition of being near ⟨the *immediacy* of Christmas is just beginning to dawn on many last-minute shoppers⟩ — see PROXIMITY

immediate *adj* **1** done or occurring without any noticeable lapse in time ⟨felt *immediate* relief after taking the painkiller⟩ — see INSTANTANEOUS
2 done or working without something else coming in between ⟨she is my *immediate* superior, so I report to her⟩ — see DIRECT 1
3 done, carried out, or given without delay ⟨*immediate* treatment saved the victim of the massive heart attack⟩ — see PROMPT 1
4 not being distant in time, space, or significance ⟨for the victims of the terrorist attack, the incident is as *immediate* as yesterday's news⟩ — see CLOSE 2
5 existing or in progress right now ⟨we need to solve the *immediate* problems before working on the more long-term ones⟩ — see PRESENT 1

immediately *adv* without delay ⟨if we don't leave *immediately*, we'll be late for the concert⟩
synonyms bang, directly, forthwith, headlong, incontinently, instantaneously, instanter, instantly, now, PDQ, plumb, presently, promptly, pronto, right, right away, right now, right off, straightaway, straight off, straightway
related words away, freely; anon, momentarily, shortly, soon; apace, briskly, fast, fleetly, full-tilt, posthaste, quick, quickly, rapidly, readily, snappily, speedily, swift, swiftly; abruptly, presto, suddenly, unexpectedly; hastily, impetuously, impulsively, rashly, recklessly; exactly, opportunely, punctually, seasonably
phrases at once, in no time, off the bat, on a dime, on the double, on the spot
near antonyms slowly; late, tardily

immediately *conj, chiefly British* just at the moment

that ⟨give us a ring *immediately* you get back⟩ — see WHEN 2

immemorial *adj* dating or surviving from the distant past ⟨the *immemorial* Alps, where once Hannibal's army marched⟩ — see ANCIENT 1

immense *adj* **1** unusually large ⟨the elephant was simply *immense*, even as elephants go⟩ — see HUGE
2 of the very best kind ⟨we had simply an *immense* time at the luxury resort⟩ — see EXCELLENT

immensely *adv* to a great degree ⟨an *immensely* successful debut album⟩ — see VERY 1

immenseness *n* the quality or state of being very large ⟨the overwhelming *immenseness* of the stadium made me feel like an ant⟩ — see IMMENSITY

immensity *n* the quality or state of being very large ⟨the *immensity* of the mountain was awe-inspiring, especially up close⟩
synonyms enormity, enormousness, giantism, gigantism, hugeness, immenseness, magnitude, massiveness, prodigiousness, vastitude, vastness
related words bigness, extensiveness, greatness, largeness, sizableness, voluminousness, weightiness; awesomeness, grandness, stupendousness, tremendousness; boundlessness, limitlessness; ampleness, capaciousness, commodiousness, spaciousness; excessiveness, extravagance, extremeness, gaudiness, grandiosity, immoderacy
near antonyms littleness, puniness, smallness; triviality
antonyms diminutiveness, minuteness, tininess

immensurable *adj* being or seeming to be without limits ⟨a man who displayed *immensurable* courage even in the face of overwhelming adversity⟩ — see INFINITE

immerse *vb* **1** to hold the attention of ⟨that documentary on human reproduction never fails to *immerse* an audience⟩ — see ENGAGE 1
2 to sink or push (something) briefly into or as if into a liquid ⟨tried to *immerse* the balloon in the water⟩ — see DIP 1

immersed *adj* having the mind fixed on something ⟨the child was so *immersed* in a book that she didn't hear her mother calling⟩ — see ATTENTIVE 1

immersing *adj* holding the attention or provoking interest ⟨an *immersing* documentary on the array of animal species threatened with extinction⟩ — see INTERESTING

immersion *n* a focusing of the mind on something ⟨a program of complete *immersion* in the language is the only way you're going to learn it⟩ — see ATTENTION 1

immigrant *n* one that leaves one place to settle in another ⟨America was founded by *immigrants* and they have been its lifeblood ever since⟩ — see EMIGRANT

imminence *n* something that may cause injury or harm ⟨since the end of the Cold War, nuclear annihilation has seemed to be a less likely *imminence*⟩ — see DANGER 2

imminent *adj* **1** giving signs of immediate occurrence ⟨a storm is *imminent*, so you should seek shelter now⟩
synonyms impending, looming, pending, threatening
related words approaching, coming, forthcoming, future, near, nearing, oncoming, upcoming; brewing, gathering; likely, possible, probable; inevitable, unavoidable; apocalyptic (*also* apocalyptical), lowering, menacing, ominous, portentous; anticipated, awaited, expected, foreseen, predicted
phrases around the corner
near antonyms distant, far-off, remote; eventual, ultimate; bygone, former, past; late, recent
2 being soon to appear or take place ⟨an *imminent* development that should radically transform how we treat the disease⟩ — see FORTHCOMING 1

immingle *vb* to turn into a single mass or entity that is more or less the same throughout ⟨the *immingled* cries and groans of the dying soldiers were forever etched in his memory⟩ — see BLEND 1

immix *vb* to turn into a single mass or entity that is more or less the same throughout ⟨deep in her lair, the old crone *immixed* the secret ingredients into a magic potion⟩ — see BLEND 1

immobile *adj* **1** fixed in a place or position ⟨the patient must remain *immobile* while he is in the MRI unit⟩ — see STATIONARY 1
2 incapable of moving or being moved ⟨a huge, *immobile* tree of an endangered species that the creators of the theme park decided to make part of the design⟩ — see IMMOVABLE 1

immobilize *vb* to render powerless, ineffective, or unable to move ⟨town councils felt *immobilized* by the powers newly granted to the state legislation⟩ — see PARALYZE 1

immoderacy *n* a propensity for extremes in one's actions, beliefs, or habits ⟨the same *immoderacy* that caused him to become a drug addict later impelled him to embrace religious fanaticism⟩ — see EXCESS 2

immoderate *adj* going beyond a normal or acceptable limit in degree or amount ⟨the young widow remarried with what was regarded as *immoderate* haste by most observers⟩ — see EXCESSIVE

immoderation *n* a propensity for extremes in one's actions, beliefs, or habits ⟨*immoderation* seemed to inhabit every facet of the actress's over-the-top life⟩ — see EXCESS 2

immodest *adj* showing a lack of proper social reserve or modesty ⟨an *immodest* proposal for altering the town's traditional character by an uppity newcomer at his first town meeting⟩ — see PRESUMPTUOUS 1

immolate *vb* to give up as an offering to a god ⟨a ceremony in which they *immolated* their cherished possessions so that the gods would send rain⟩ — see SACRIFICE

immolation *n* something offered to a god ⟨the blood-drenched *immolations* that the ancient Aztecs annually offered by the thousands⟩ — see SACRIFICE

immoral *adj* **1** not conforming to a high moral standard; morally unacceptable ⟨blatantly *immoral* behavior by members of the clergy that should not be tolerated by the community⟩ — see BAD 2
2 not guided by or showing a concern for what is right ⟨stealing another's words, even over the Internet, remains an *immoral* act⟩ — see UNPRINCIPLED

immoralist *n* a person who commits moral wrongs ⟨among history's imperial *immoralists*, few can compare with the Roman emperor Caligula⟩ — see EVILDOER 1

immorality *n* **1** immoral conduct or practices harmful or offensive to society ⟨religious denominations that regard drinking, smoking, and even dancing as examples of *immorality*⟩ — see VICE 1
2 that which is morally unacceptable ⟨a sermon about modern society's casual acceptance of or indifference to *immorality*⟩ — see EVIL

immortal *adj* **1** lasting forever ⟨the age-old quest for *immortal* fame⟩ — see EVERLASTING 1
2 having an existence or validity that does not change or diminish ⟨vowed that his hatred of that family was *immortal* and that someday he'd get his revenge⟩ — see ABIDING

immortality *n* unending existence after death ⟨central to most religions is a belief in the *immortality* of the soul⟩ — see ETERNITY 2

immortalize *vb* to give eternal or lasting existence to ⟨*immortalized* the words "Call me Ishmael" as the novel's opening line⟩ — see PERPETUATE

immotile *adj* incapable of moving or being moved ⟨a free-form sculpture that manages to suggest movement while remaining an *immotile* object⟩ — see IMMOVABLE 1

immovable *adj* **1** incapable of moving or being moved ⟨that boulder is *immovable*, even with a bulldozer⟩
synonyms immobile, immotile, irremovable, nonmotile, nonmoving, unbudging, unmovable
related words motionless, moveless, static, stationary, still; fast, fixed, rooted, steadfast, stuck, wedged
near antonyms portable, removable (*also* removeable), transferable (*also* transferrable), transportable
antonyms mobile, motile, movable (*or* moveable), moving
2 sticking to an opinion, purpose, or course of action in spite of reason, arguments, or persuasion ⟨despite tears and pleading, the police officer was *immovable* on the matter of a hefty fine for speeding⟩ — see OBSTINATE

immunity *n* freedom from punishment, harm, or loss ⟨the suspect refused to name his partners unless he was granted *immunity*⟩ — see IMPUNITY

immure *vb* **1** to close or shut in by or as if by barriers ⟨scientists at the research station in Alaska are *immured* by the frozen wastelands that surround them⟩ — see ENCLOSE 1
2 to put in or as if in prison ⟨*immured* by a controlling, possessive mother, the young woman had no outside social life⟩ — see IMPRISON

immurement *n* **1** the act of confining or the state of being confined ⟨the *immurement* of Japanese-Americans continued for the duration of the war⟩ — see INTERNMENT
2 the state of being held in lawful custody ⟨condemned the long-term *immurement* of prisoners who have yet to be convicted of anything⟩ — see DETENTION 1

immutability *n* the state of continuing without change ⟨the *immutability* of the laws of physics is a myth, since refinements of those laws continue to be made⟩ — see CONSTANCY 1

immutable *adj* not capable of changing or being changed ⟨one of the *immutable* laws of television is that low ratings inevitably lead to cancellation⟩ — see INFLEXIBLE 1

immutableness *n* the state of continuing without change ⟨according to some behavioral scientists, a person's personality is set in early childhood and from then on nothing can challenge its essential *immutableness*⟩ — see CONSTANCY 1

imp *n* **1** an appealingly mischievous person ⟨scooped up the little *imp* and took him to bed⟩ — see SCAMP 1
2 an evil spirit ⟨a story about a crumbling mansion infested with a brood of *imps*⟩ — see DEMON 1

impact *vb* **1** to act upon (a person or a person's feelings) so as to cause a response ⟨the tragic loss of his father *impacted* the boy for the rest of his life⟩ — see [1]AFFECT 1
2 to come into usually forceful contact with something ⟨the damage sustained when a car going 40 miles an hour *impacts* with a brick wall⟩ — see HIT 2
3 to set solidly in or as if in surrounding matter ⟨the bullet was found *impacted* in the police officer's protective vest⟩ — see ENTRENCH

impact *n* **1** a forceful coming together of two things ⟨the glass shattered immediately upon *impact* with the floor⟩
synonyms bump, collision, concussion, crash, impingement, jar, jolt, jounce, kick, shock, slam, smash, strike, wallop
related words blow, buffet, hit, knock, punch, rap, slap, thump; bashing, battering, bludgeoning, clobbering, hammering, lambasting, licking, pounding, pummeling (*also* pummelling), thrashing; contact, encounter, meeting, touch
2 the power to bring about a result on another ⟨the execution had such a powerful *impact* on her that she became a crusader for the abolition of capital punishment⟩ — see EFFECT 2
3 the quality of an utterance that provokes interest and produces an effect ⟨the story has real dramatic *impact*⟩ — see [1]PUNCH 1

impactful *adj* having the power to affect the feelings or sympathies ⟨an *impactful* story of love and redemption⟩ — see MOVING

impair *vb* to reduce the soundness, effectiveness, or perfection of ⟨already *impaired* by a crack, the windshield shattered upon impact with the baseball⟩ — see DAMAGE 1

impaired *adj* **1** being under the influence of alcohol ⟨driving while *impaired* is against the law⟩ — see DRUNK
2 deprived of the power to perform one or more natural bodily activities ⟨special devices for sight-*impaired* visitors⟩ — see DISABLED

impale *vb* to penetrate or hold (something) with a pointed object ⟨*impale* a marshmallow or two on that stick and let's start toasting⟩
synonyms gore, harpoon, jab, lance, peck, pick, pierce, pink, puncture, run through, skewer, spear, spike, spit, stab, stick, transfix, transpierce
related words spindle; perforate, riddle; bayonet, dirk, gimlet, pike, poniard, prong, quill; pinprick, poke, prick, punch, thrust; cut, knife, slice

impalpable *adj* **1** not capable of being perceived by the sense of touch ⟨the rich colors used in the wall coverings and furniture give the room an *impalpable* warmth⟩ — see INTANGIBLE
2 not perceptible by a sense or by the mind ⟨any difference between the two sound systems is *impalpable* to all but the most discerning audiophiles⟩ — see IMPERCEPTIBLE

impart *vb* to cause (something) to pass from one to another ⟨*imparted* the latest information on the approaching snowstorm⟩ — see COMMUNICATE 1

impartial *adj* marked by justice, honesty, and freedom from bias ⟨an *impartial* evaluation of the job applicant's qualifications that does not consider age, gender, or race⟩ — see FAIR 2

impartiality *n* lack of favoritism toward one side or another ⟨the defense lawyers challenged the *impartiality* of the presiding judge⟩ — see DETACHMENT 1

impassable *also* **impassible** *adj* impossible to get through or into ⟨the road was *impassable* until snowplows cleared it⟩ — see IMPENETRABLE 1

impasse *n* **1** a point in a struggle where neither side is capable of winning or willing to give in ⟨in their bitter custody battle, the divorcing couple are at a total *impasse*⟩
synonyms deadlock, gridlock, halt, logjam, Mexican standoff, stalemate, standoff, standstill
related words dead end; bind, bottleneck, corner, dilemma, fix, hole, jam, morass, pickle, pinch, plight, predicament, quagmire, quandary, spot; difficulty; problem
2 a difficult, puzzling, or embarrassing situation from which there is no easy escape ⟨the impossible *impasse* faced by those who opposed the war but did not want to seem disloyal to the troops⟩ — see PREDICAMENT

impassible *adj* not feeling or showing emotion ⟨years of living behind bars had rendered him *impassible*⟩ — see IMPASSIVE 1

impassion *vb* to rouse to strong feeling or action ⟨the obvious intent of the documentary was to *impassion* viewers to do something about global warming⟩ — see PROVOKE 1

impassioned *adj* having or expressing great depth of

feeling ⟨an *impassioned* plea for justice⟩ — see FERVENT 1

impassive *adj* **1** not feeling or showing emotion ⟨she remained *impassive* as the officers informed her of her son's death⟩

synonyms affectless, apathetic, cold-blooded, emotionless, impassible, numb, passionless, phlegmatic, stoic (*or* stoical), stolid, undemonstrative, unemotional

related words cold, cool, dispassionate, unmoved; calm, collected, composed; imperturbable, unflappable; reserved, reticent, taciturn; bland, blank, deadpan, dry, empty, expressionless, inexpressive, stone-faced, straight-faced, vacant, wooden; enigmatic (*also* enigmatical), impenetrable, inscrutable; aloof, bloodless, detached, indifferent, insensible, unconcerned, unsentimental; impersonal, objective, unresponsive; hard-hearted, pitiless, unfeeling; inconsiderate, thoughtless

near antonyms blazing, burning, fiery, flaming, glowing, red-hot; ardent, enthusiastic, gung ho, warm-blooded, zealous; gushing, maudlin, mawkish, mushy, sentimental; dramatic, histrionic, melodramatic, overemotional, overheated, perfervid; compassionate, responsive, sympathetic; reactive, sensitive

antonyms demonstrative, emotional, fervent, fervid, hot-blooded, impassioned, passional, passionate, vehement

2 not expressing any emotion ⟨an *impassive* expression on the prisoner's face as his sentence was read⟩ — see BLANK 1

impassiveness *n* a lack of emotion or emotional expressiveness ⟨the child's inexplicable *impassiveness*, after all he'd been through, was a source of concern for his relatives⟩ — see APATHY 1

impassivity *n* a lack of emotion or emotional expressiveness ⟨the killer's apparent *impassivity* as he dispatched his victims⟩ — see APATHY 1

impatience *n* urgent desire or interest ⟨the child's *impatience* for Christmas morning is engaging⟩ — see EAGERNESS

impatient *adj* **1** showing urgent desire or interest ⟨she was *impatient* to give her presentation before the landmark commission⟩ — see EAGER

2 unable or unwilling to endure ⟨those airline passengers who are so *impatient* of delays, even for the most obvious of reasons⟩ — see INTOLERANT 1

impeach *vb* **1** to make a claim of wrongdoing against ⟨the company's president has been *impeached* by the Securities and Exchange Commission⟩ — see ACCUSE

2 to demand proof of the truth or rightness of ⟨questionable methodology that should cause us to *impeach* the findings of this survey on obesity⟩ — see CHALLENGE 1

impeccability *n* the quality or state of being free from guilt or blame ⟨the *impeccability* of the nun's moral character and untiring selflessness qualified her for sainthood⟩ — see INNOCENCE 1

impeccable *adj* **1** being entirely without fault or flaw ⟨the etiquette expert was celebrated for her absolutely *impeccable* manners⟩ — see PERFECT 1

2 free from guilt or blame ⟨the head of the investigation must be a person of *impeccable* probity and honesty⟩ — see INNOCENT 2

3 free from sin ⟨the belief that there can be no such thing as an *impeccable* soul⟩ — see INNOCENT 1

impeccably *adv* without any flaws or errors ⟨he speaks French *impeccably*⟩ — see PERFECTLY 1

impecuniosity *n* the state of lacking sufficient money or material possessions ⟨such was the level of my *impecuniosity* that I could not afford to eat at the cheapest greasy spoon⟩ — see POVERTY 1

impecunious *adj* lacking money or material possessions ⟨they were so *impecunious* that they couldn't afford to give one another even token Christmas gifts⟩ — see POOR 1

impecuniousness *n* the state of lacking sufficient money or material possessions ⟨her claims of *impecuniousness* rang false when we noticed the luxuries she had bought for herself⟩ — see POVERTY 1

impede *vb* to create difficulty for the work or activity of ⟨the construction work *impeded* the smooth running of the office for several months⟩ — see HAMPER

impediment *n* something that makes movement or progress difficult ⟨tough going for the burros on the canyon trail, even without the added *impediment* of heavy loads⟩ — see ENCUMBRANCE

impel *vb* **1** to set or keep in motion ⟨gasoline *impels* a car's engine⟩ — see MOVE 2

2 to cause (a person) to give in to pressure ⟨I felt *impelled* to tell the truth, however painful it might be⟩ — see FORCE 1

impend *vb* to be about to happen ⟨for confirmed pessimists some disaster always seems to be *impending*⟩ — see LOOM

impend (over) *vb* to remain poised to inflict harm, danger, or distress on ⟨fears of an economic recession *impended over* the stock market⟩ — see THREATEN

impending *adj* **1** being soon to appear or take place ⟨an *impending* celebration of the 100th anniversary of the college's founding⟩ — see FORTHCOMING 1

2 giving signs of immediate occurrence ⟨an aura of *impending* doom hung over the city⟩ — see IMMINENT 1

impenetrability *n* the quality or state of being impossible to know, understand, or explain ⟨the *impenetrability* of her prose is apparently the basis of her appeal to literary snobs⟩ — see INSCRUTABILITY 1

impenetrable *adj* **1** impossible to get through or into ⟨the ancient temple was surrounded by vast stretches of *impenetrable* jungle⟩

synonyms impassable (*also* impassible), impermeable, impervious, impregnable

related words close, compact, dense, thick, tight; compressed, condensed; sturdy, substantial, tough; firm, frozen, hard, solid, stiff; inflexible, rigid, unbending, unyielding

near antonyms soft, squishy; bendable, elastic, flexible, giving, malleable, pliable, yielding; absorbent, porous

antonyms negotiable, passable, penetrable, permeable

2 being beyond one's powers to know, understand, or explain ⟨the mysteries of that religion are completely *impenetrable* to outsiders⟩ — see MYSTERIOUS 1

3 impossible to understand ⟨the textbook's language is completely *impenetrable*, at least to me⟩ — see INCOMPREHENSIBLE

4 not allowing penetration (as by gas, liquid, or light) ⟨the container of toxic waste has an *impenetrable* seal to prevent leaks⟩ — see TIGHT 1

impenitent *adj* not sorry for having done wrong ⟨an *impenitent* criminal who said he'd do it all over again, given the chance⟩ — see REMORSELESS 1

imperative *adj* **1** forcing one's compliance or participation by or as if by law ⟨reporting signs of physical abuse is now an *imperative* duty for hospital and school personnel⟩ — see MANDATORY

2 impossible to do without ⟨proper equipment is *imperative* for the success of this chemical experiment⟩ — see ESSENTIAL 1

3 needing immediate attention ⟨an *imperative* need for medical supplies in the earthquake-ravaged country⟩ — see ACUTE 2

imperative *n* **1** a statement of what to do that must be obeyed by those concerned ⟨a secretary of defense who was fond of issuing harshly worded *imperatives*⟩ — see COMMAND 1

2 something one must do because of prior agreement ⟨although he had little taste for the social *imperatives* that come with being governor, he put on a brave face⟩ — see OBLIGATION 1

imperceptible *adj* not perceptible by a sense or by the mind ⟨a slight difference in hue between the two glasses that's *imperceptible* unless they're placed side by side⟩
synonyms impalpable, inappreciable, indistinguishable, insensible
related words inaudible, intangible, invisible; inconspicuous, indistinct, unnoticeable, unseeable, unseen; faint, insignificant, liminal, slender, slight, subtle, trivial; buried, concealed, covert, disguised, hidden, obscure, shrouded, unapparent, vague
near antonyms audible, observable, recognizable, tangible, visible; clear, conspicuous, evident, eye-catching, manifest, noticeable, obvious, plain, prominent, striking; apparent, distinct, significant, straightforward
antonyms appreciable, discernible (*also* discernable), palpable, perceptible, ponderable, sensible

imperceptive *adj* not having or showing a deep understanding of something ⟨*imperceptive* critics who failed to see that it was much more than another mindless action movie⟩
synonyms impercipient, insentient, unperceptive, unwise
related words undiscriminating; dense, dull, obtuse, sluggish, thickheaded; brainless, dumb, feebleminded, foolish, idiotic (*also* idiotical), imbecile (*or* imbecilic), moronic, silly, simple, slow, stupid, thoughtless, unintelligent, witless
near antonyms discriminating; acute, perspicacious; brainy, bright, brilliant, clever, intelligent, keen, nimble, quick, quick-witted, smart; cerebral, erudite, learned, literate, scholarly; astute, sharp, shrewd; contemplative, reflective, thoughtful
antonyms discerning, insightful, perceptive, percipient, sagacious, sage, sapient

impercipient *adj* not having or showing a deep understanding of something ⟨*impercipient* interpretations of the novel failed to note its dark humor⟩ — see IMPERCEPTIVE

imperfect *adj* having a fault ⟨an *imperfect* representation of the circumstances surrounding Paul Revere's famous ride⟩ — see FAULTY

imperfection *n* something that spoils the appearance or completeness of a thing ⟨the shirt was marked down because of a minor *imperfection*⟩ — see BLEMISH

imperial *adj* large and impressive in size, grandeur, extent, or conception ⟨envisioned an *imperial* city that would rival the capitals of Europe for beauty and magnificence⟩ — see GRAND 1

imperil *vb* to place in danger ⟨a single mistake could *imperil* the lives of everyone involved in the military operation⟩ — see ENDANGER

imperilment *n* the state of not being protected from injury, harm, or evil ⟨the city has reduced the number of its firefighters, to the *imperilment* of every homeowner⟩ — see DANGER 1

imperious *adj* **1** fond of ordering people around ⟨an *imperious* little boy who liked to tell the other scouts what to do⟩ — see BOSSY
2 having a feeling of superiority that shows itself in an overbearing attitude ⟨an *imperious* movie star who thinks she's some sort of goddess⟩ — see ARROGANT
3 having or showing a tendency to force one's will on others without any regard to fairness or necessity ⟨an office administrator with an *imperious* manner that really grates on people⟩ — see ARBITRARY 1
4 needing immediate attention ⟨as war casualties mounted, the need for trained nurses became *imperious*⟩ — see ACUTE 2

imperiousness *n* an exaggerated sense of one's importance that shows itself in the making of excessive or unjustified claims ⟨the *imperiousness* of that fashion designer irritates everyone around her⟩ — see ARROGANCE

imperishable *adj* **1** impossible to destroy ⟨energy is *imperishable*⟩ — see INDESTRUCTIBLE
2 having an existence or validity that does not change or diminish ⟨the belief that through military glory one could achieve *imperishable* fame⟩ — see ABIDING

imperium *n* controlling power or influence over others ⟨a nation whose economic *imperium* waned after the war⟩ — see SUPREMACY 1

impermanence *n* the state or quality of lasting only for a short time ⟨the ancient Roman ruins are a telling reminder of the *impermanence* of even the grandest man-made constructions⟩
synonyms ephemerality, evanescence, fleetingness, fugitiveness, impermanency, momentariness, temporariness, transience, transiency, transitoriness
related words brevity, shortness
near antonyms continuance, continuation; longevity
antonyms endurance, permanence, permanency

impermanency *n* the state or quality of lasting only for a short time ⟨builders of elaborate sand castles seem not at all bothered by the *impermanency* of their creations⟩ — see IMPERMANENCE

impermanent *adj* **1** intended to last, continue, or serve for a limited time ⟨built an *impermanent* structure to serve for the archaeologists' living quarters during the dig⟩ — see TEMPORARY 1
2 lasting only for a short time ⟨a summer romance that was an *impermanent* fancy, quickly forgotten⟩ — see MOMENTARY

impermeable *adj* **1** impossible to get through or into ⟨the wall of security people surrounding the rock band was *impermeable*⟩ — see IMPENETRABLE 1
2 not allowing penetration (as by gas, liquid, or light) ⟨an *impermeable* seal on the ancient tomb had preserved the artifacts exceptionally well⟩ — see TIGHT 1

impermissible *adj* that may not be permitted ⟨trial juries must be able to discern the difference between a permissible inference and *impermissible* speculation⟩
synonyms banned, barred, forbidden, interdicted, outlawed, prohibited, proscribed, taboo (*also* tabu), verboten
related words intolerable, unacceptable, unbearable, unendurable; illegal, illegitimate, illicit, improper, inappropriate, unauthorized, unlawful, unlicensed; ineffable, unmentionable; unseemly, unsuitable; objectionable; disallowed, disapproved, discouraged; refused, rejected, revoked, unsanctioned, vetoed; repressed, suppressed; precluded, prevented, stopped; excluded, ruled out, shut out; blocked, hindered, impeded, obstructed
near antonyms acceptable, bearable, endurable, tolerable; accepted, accredited, allowed, appropriate, approved, authorized, certified, endorsed (*also* indorsed), lawful, legal, legitimate, licensed, OK (*or* okay), permitted, warranted; accorded, granted, sanctioned, vouchsafed; brooked, condoned, countenanced; encouraged, promoted, supported; commanded, mandatory, ordered, required; proper, seemly, suitable, tolerated, unobjectionable
antonyms allowable, permissible, permissive, sufferable

impersonate *vb* **1** to pretend to be (what one is not) in appearance or behavior ⟨a school intruder was caught trying to *impersonate* a teacher⟩
synonyms act, masquerade (as), personate, play, pose (as)
related words ape, copy, imitate, mime, mimic, mock, monkey, parody, travesty; perform, portray

2 to present a portrayal or performance of ⟨interpreters at the living history museum *impersonate* figures who are known to have actually lived in the colonial town⟩ — see ACT 1

impersonator *n* **1** a person who imitates another's voice and mannerisms for comic effect ⟨a versatile *impersonator*, he conjures up a glittering array of female stars and divas in the course of his act⟩ — see MIMIC

2 one who acts professionally (as in a play, movie, or television show) ⟨a gifted *impersonator* who can convincingly portray both heroes and heels⟩ — see ACTOR 1

impertinence *n* **1** disrespectful or argumentative talk given in response to a command or request ⟨a disciplinarian of the old school, he refused to tolerate any *impertinence* from his children⟩ — see BACK TALK

2 rude behavior ⟨the *impertinence* of deliberately ignoring waiting customers while they finished their conversation⟩ — see DISCOURTESY

3 the quality or state of not having anything to do with the matter at hand ⟨the *impertinence* of that issue renders any discussion of it a waste of our time⟩ — see IRRELEVANCE

impertinency *n* rude behavior ⟨the shameless *impertinency* of the teenagers at the beach⟩ — see DISCOURTESY

impertinent *adj* **1** displaying or marked by rude boldness ⟨the *impertinent* child had a smart answer for everything⟩ — see NERVY 1

2 showing a lack of manners or consideration for others ⟨*impertinent* salesmen who telephone people during the dinner hour⟩ — see IMPOLITE

3 not having anything to do with the matter at hand ⟨your résumé needlessly lists skills that are *impertinent* to the job for which you are applying⟩ — see IRRELEVANT

imperturbability *n* evenness of emotions or temper ⟨his *imperturbability* in a crisis is legendary among hospital staffers⟩ — see EQUANIMITY

imperturbable *adj* not easily panicked or upset ⟨the chef was absolutely *imperturbable*—even when the kitchen caught on fire⟩ — see UNFLAPPABLE

impervious *adj* **1** not allowing penetration (as by gas, liquid, or light) ⟨the material for this coat is supposed to be *impervious* to rain⟩ — see TIGHT 1

2 impossible to get through or into ⟨the rain forest is *impervious* to all but the most dedicated explorers⟩ — see IMPENETRABLE 1

impetrate *vb* to make a request to (someone) in an earnest or urgent manner ⟨since deists do not believe in a Creator who interferes in human affairs, they generally regard as fruitless any effort to *impetrate* Him for divine favors⟩ — see BEG

impetus *n* something that arouses action or activity ⟨the reward money should be sufficient *impetus* for someone to come forward with information about the robbery⟩ — see IMPULSE 1

impiety *n* an act of great disrespect shown to God or to sacred ideas, people, or things ⟨the unspeakable *impiety* of spitting in a church⟩ — see BLASPHEMY

impinge *vb* to come into usually forceful contact with something ⟨hail was noisily *impinging* upon the car's exterior⟩ — see HIT 2

impingement *n* a forceful coming together of two things ⟨the *impingement* of the hailstones on the metal roof was making quite a racket⟩ — see IMPACT 1

impious *adj* not showing proper reverence for the holy or sacred ⟨an *impious* act that horrified their pious mother⟩ — see IRREVERENT

impish *adj* tending to or exhibiting reckless playfulness ⟨the gang of *impish* children ran into the street, utterly oblivious to the traffic⟩ — see MISCHIEVOUS 1

impishness *n* **1** a natural disposition for playful behavior ⟨her irrepressible *impishness* means that no one is ever safe from her practical jokes⟩ — see PLAYFULNESS

2 playful, reckless behavior that is not intended to cause serious harm ⟨the boys' *impishness* was easy to forgive, since it caused no real harm⟩ — see MISCHIEF 1

implacable *adj* **1** sticking to an opinion, purpose, or course of action in spite of reason, arguments, or persuasion ⟨an *implacable* judge who knew in his bones that the cover-up extended to the highest levels of government⟩ — see OBSTINATE

2 showing no signs of slackening or yielding in one's purpose ⟨an *implacable* dedication to the proposition that everyone is entitled to a quality education⟩ — see UNYIELDING 1

implant *vb* **1** to set permanently in the consciousness or mind-set ⟨a music teacher who strove to *implant* within his students a love of the classics⟩

synonyms breed, enroot, inculcate, infix, inseminate, instill, plant, sow

related words drive, hammer, pound; embed (*also* imbed), entrench (*also* intrench), fix, lodge, root; imbue, infuse, ingrain (*also* engrain), inoculate, invest, steep, suffuse

2 to set solidly in or as if in surrounding matter ⟨the gemstone was poorly *implanted* in the setting, so it was constantly popping out⟩ — see ENTRENCH

implausible *adj* too extraordinary or improbable to believe ⟨the terrorist attacks generated a whole passel of *implausible* conspiracy theories that dishonor the memory of those who perished⟩ — see INCREDIBLE

implement *vb* to carry out effectively ⟨*implemented* the evacuation plan without a hitch⟩ — see ENFORCE

implement *n* an article intended for use in work ⟨gardening *implements* such as hoes, spades, and pruners⟩

synonyms device, instrument, tool, utensil

related words apparatus, appliance, mechanism; contraption, contrivance, gadget, gizmo (*also* gismo), jigger; accessory (*also* accessary), accoutrement (*or* accouterment), adjunct, appendage, attachment

implementation *n* the doing of an action ⟨the *implementation* of the idea turned out to be harder than its conception⟩ — see COMMISSION 2

implicate *vb, archaic* to cause to twine about one another ⟨the *implicated* vines did form a most restful garden bower⟩ — see INTERTWINE 1

implicit *adj* **1** understood although not put into words ⟨the *implicit* agreement among members of the outing club is that everyone pays his or her own way on all trips⟩

synonyms implied, tacit, unexpressed, unspoken, unvoiced, wordless

related words inferred, presumed; construed, interpreted; unannounced, undeclared, unsaid, untold; hinted, insinuated, intimated, suggested

near antonyms apparent, blatant, evident, manifest, obvious, plain, straightforward; unambiguous, unequivocal, unmistakable

antonyms explicit, express, expressed, spoken, stated, voiced

2 having or showing a mind free from doubt ⟨members of the expedition must have *implicit* trust in their leaders⟩ — see CERTAIN 2

3 existing only as a possibility and not in fact ⟨there's a risk *implicit* in any overseas operation undertaken by the military⟩ — see POTENTIAL

implied *adj* understood although not put into words ⟨an *implied* agreement is not legally enforceable⟩ — see IMPLICIT 1

implode *vb* to fall down or in as a result of physical pressure ⟨a controlled demolition during which the entire building *imploded* in a matter of seconds⟩ — see COLLAPSE 1

implore *vb* to make a request to (someone) in an earnest or urgent manner ⟨the victims of the hurricane *implored* the governor to put the full resources of the state into the relief effort⟩ — see BEG

imploring *adj* asking humbly ⟨the *imploring* boy tearfully asked the veterinarian to do what he could to save the life of his dog⟩ — see SUPPLIANT

imply *vb* to convey an idea indirectly ⟨they may have *implied* that they'd help, but they didn't actually say so⟩ — see HINT

impolite *adj* showing a lack of manners or consideration for others ⟨the librarian was shocked that anyone could be so *impolite* as to continue talking despite repeated warnings to be quiet⟩
synonyms discourteous, disrespectful, ill-bred, ill-mannered, impertinent, inconsiderate, rude, thoughtless, uncalled-for, uncivil, ungracious, unhandsome, unmannered, unmannerly
related words arch, audacious, bold, bold-faced, brash, brassy, brazen, cheeky, fresh, impudent, insolent, lippy, sassy, saucy, shameless; boorish, caddish, churlish, clownish, loutish, uncouth, vulgar; abrupt, blunt, brusque (*also* brusk), crusty, curt, gruff, sharp, snippety, snippy; antisocial, crabbed, cross, disagreeable, grumpy, sullen, surly; improper, incorrect, indecent, indecorous, unseemly; arrogant, bumptious, conceited, haughty, high-handed, imperious, peremptory, pompous, presumptuous, pretentious, supercilious, superior
near antonyms humble, meek, modest, unassertive; deferential, dutiful, respectful, submissive, yielding; acceptable, appropriate, becoming, befitting, correct, decent, decorous, fit, fitting, good, meet, proper, respectable, right, seemly, suitable; affable, cordial, friendly, genial, hospitable, sociable; felicitous, graceful; chivalrous, courtly, gallant; ceremonious; elegant, refined
antonyms civil, considerate, courteous, genteel, gracious, mannerly, polite, thoughtful, well-bred

impoliteness *n* rude behavior ⟨such flagrant *impoliteness* must never be tolerated⟩ — see DISCOURTESY

import *n* **1** the quality or state of being important ⟨I can't overemphasize the *import* of this examination on your future academic career⟩ — see IMPORTANCE
2 the idea that is conveyed or intended to be conveyed to the mind by language, symbol, or action ⟨didn't understand all the technical jargon, but got the general *import* of the speech⟩ — see MEANING 1

import *vb* **1** to be of importance ⟨it *imports* little whether you like Grandma's gift; you should have graciously thanked her⟩ — see MATTER
2 to communicate or convey (as an idea) to the mind ⟨the word "freedom" can *import* different things to different people⟩ — see MEAN 1

importance *n* the quality or state of being important ⟨a final exam has great *importance*⟩
synonyms account, consequence, import, magnitude, moment, momentousness, significance, weight, weightiness
related words celebrity, distinction, eminence, fame, note, noteworthiness, notoriety, preeminence, prominence, renown; store, substance, substantiveness, value, worth, worthiness; gravity, seriousness; authority, control, dominion, mastery, potency, power, sway; mark, name, report, reputation, repute; centrality, essentiality, essentialness; cachet, position, prestige, rank, standing, stature, status; glory, greatness, honor, illustriousness
near antonyms paltriness, pettiness, valuelessness, worthlessness; discredit, disgrace, dishonor, disrepute, ignominy, infamy, odium, opprobrium, shame; anonymity; obscurity
antonyms insignificance, littleness, puniness, slightness, smallness, triviality

important *adj* **1** having great meaning or lasting effect ⟨the discovery of penicillin was a very *important* event in the history of medicine⟩
synonyms big, consequential, earthshaking, earthshattering, eventful, historic, major, material, meaningful, momentous, monumental, much, significant, substantial, tectonic, weighty
related words decisive, fatal, fateful, strategic; earnest, grave, heavy, serious, sincere; distinctive, exceptional, impressive, outstanding, prominent, remarkable; valuable, worthwhile, worthy; distinguished, eminent, great, illustrious, noble, notable, noteworthy, outstanding, preeminent, prestigious; famous, notorious, renowned; all-important, central, critical, crucial, essential, key, pivotal, seminal, vital
near antonyms paltry, petty, worthless; anonymous, nameless, obscure, uncelebrated, unknown
antonyms inconsequential, inconsiderable, insignificant, little, minor, negligible, slight, small, trifling, trivial, unimportant
2 having great power or influence ⟨Rachel Carson was an *important* figure in the environmental movement⟩
synonyms heavy, heavy-duty, influential, mighty, potent, powerful, puissant, significant, strong
related words high-level, senior, top; able, capable, competent, effective, efficient; authoritarian, autocratic (*also* autocratical), despotic, dictatorial, magisterial, tyrannical (*also* tyrannic); celebrated, distinguished, dominant, eminent, famed, famous, great, illustrious, noble, notable, noteworthy, notorious, outstanding, preeminent, prestigious, prominent, renowned; dynamic, energetic, forceful, high-powered, robust, vigorous
near antonyms feeble, flimsy, frail, infirm; anonymous, nameless, obscure, uncelebrated, unknown; incapable, incompetent, ineffective, inept, inexpert, unfit, unqualified, unskilled, unskillful
antonyms helpless, impotent, insignificant, little, powerless, unimportant, weak
3 having a feeling of superiority that shows itself in an overbearing attitude ⟨an *important* businessman who always expects special treatment wherever he goes⟩ — see ARROGANT
4 having too high an opinion of oneself ⟨oh, you're so *important*—you think the world revolves around you⟩ — see CONCEITED

importunate *adj* needing immediate attention ⟨the demands of the chairmanship were becoming too *importunate* for me to continue without an assistant⟩ — see ACUTE 2

importune *vb* to make a request to (someone) in an earnest or urgent manner ⟨she was always *importuning* people for favors, even when she had no right to ask⟩ — see BEG

importunity *n* **1** something that someone insists upon having ⟨overwhelmed by the often conflicting *importunities* of pressure groups⟩ — see DEMAND 1
2 the act of making unwelcome intrusions upon another ⟨resented the *importunity* of those door-to-door Bible-thumpers⟩ — see ANNOYANCE 1

impose *vb* to establish or apply as a charge or penalty ⟨that state now *imposes* a fine for text messaging while driving⟩
synonyms assess, charge, exact, fine, lay, levy, put
related words dock, excise, mulct, penalize, tax; extort, shake down, wrest, wring; bleed, fleece, gouge, milk, skin, squeeze; coerce, compel, force; inflict, wreak; set; reapply, reimpose, relay

near antonyms abate, diminish, lessen; forgive, release; condone, disregard, excuse, gloss (over), gloze (over), ignore, pardon
antonyms remit

impose (on *or* upon) *vb* to take unfair advantage of ⟨thanks for offering your own bed, but I wouldn't dream of *imposing on* you and will be perfectly happy on the couch⟩ — see EXPLOIT 1

imposing *adj* **1** having or showing a formal and serious or reserved manner ⟨the president of the bank is exactly the sort of *imposing* figure that one might expect⟩ — see DIGNIFIED
2 large and impressive in size, grandeur, extent, or conception ⟨the corporation's *imposing* headquarters were designed by one of the nation's cutting-edge architects⟩ — see GRAND 1

imposition *n* a charge usually of money collected by the government from people or businesses for public use ⟨an *imposition* of 10% on imported goods⟩ — see TAX

impossible *adj* incapable of being solved or accomplished ⟨the seemingly *impossible* problem of world hunger⟩ ⟨fitting everything in my backpack seemed an *impossible* task⟩
synonyms hopeless, insoluble, insolvable, insuperable, unattainable, undoable, unrealizable, unsolvable
related words impracticable, impractical, infeasible, unusable, unworkable; debatable, disputable, doubtable, doubtful, dubious, far-fetched, fishy, improbable, problematic (*also* problematical), questionable, shady, shaky, suspect, suspicious, unfeasible, unlikely; implausible, inconceivable, incredible, unbelievable, unimaginable, unthinkable; futile, useless; absurd, fantastic (*also* fantastical), outlandish, preposterous, ridiculous
near antonyms applicable, functional, practicable, practical, reasonable, serviceable, usable (*also* useable), useful, working; likely, probable; acceptable, believable, conceivable, credible, plausible
antonyms achievable, attainable, doable, feasible, possible, realizable, resolvable, soluble, workable

impost *n* a charge usually of money collected by the government from people or businesses for public use ⟨consumers steadfastly resisted any *impost* on merchandise purchased over the Internet⟩ — see TAX

impostor *or* **imposter** *n* one who makes false claims of identity or expertise ⟨the man who claimed to be a prince turned out to be an *impostor*⟩
synonyms charlatan, fake, faker, fakir, fraud, hoaxer, humbug, mountebank, phony (*also* phoney), pretender, quack, quacksalver, ringer, sham
related words copycat, imitator, impersonator, mimic; actor, bluffer, counterfeiter, deceiver, dissembler, duper, feigner, misleader, operator, trickster; poseur; cozener, defrauder, dodger, fraudster [*chiefly British*], scammer, scamster, sharper, sharpie (*or* sharpy), skinner, swindler
near antonyms ace, adept, authority, crackerjack (*also* crackajack), expert, maestro, master, past master, professional, virtuoso, whiz, wizard

impotence *n* the lack of sufficient ability, power, or means ⟨the congressional committee's essential *impotence* in affecting the management of the war was frustrating to its members⟩ — see INABILITY

impotent *adj* **1** not able to produce fruit or offspring ⟨most mules are *impotent*⟩ — see STERILE 1
2 unable to act or achieve one's purpose ⟨an *impotent* ruler who was just a figurehead⟩ — see POWERLESS

impoundment *n* the act of confining or the state of being confined ⟨after his *impoundment* in the garage all weekend, the family dog was ready to frolic⟩ — see INTERNMENT

impoverished *adj* **1** lacking money or material possessions ⟨the widespread hope that the lottery's record-setting jackpot is won by an *impoverished* family⟩ — see POOR 1
2 producing inferior or only a small amount of vegetation ⟨an *impoverished* field that over the years had been overgrazed⟩ — see BARREN 1

impoverishment *n* the state of lacking sufficient money or material possessions ⟨the gradual loss of manufacturing jobs plunged the area into a level of *impoverishment* it had never known⟩ — see POVERTY 1

impracticable *adj* not capable of being put to use or account ⟨an *impracticable* plan for dealing with the recent intrusion of bears in the suburban neighborhood⟩ — see IMPRACTICAL

impractical *adj* not capable of being put to use or account ⟨the flimsy little toy shovel was cute, but completely *impractical* for digging up tree stumps⟩
synonyms impracticable, inoperable, nonpractical, unserviceable, unusable, unworkable, useless
related words unsuitable; inaccessible, unattainable, unavailable, unobtainable, unreachable; dead, dormant, fallow, free, idle, inactive, inert, inoperative, latent; arrested, interrupted, suspended; unrealistic
near antonyms accessible, acquirable, available, obtainable, procurable, reachable; all-around (*also* all-round), handy; active, alive, busy, employed, functioning, operating, operative, running, working
antonyms applicable, feasible, functional, operable, operational, practicable, practical, serviceable, ultrapractical, usable (*also* useable), useful, utilizable, workable

imprecate *vb* to ask a divine power to send harm or evil upon ⟨with her dying breath the witch *imprecated* the villagers for their relentless persecution of her⟩ — see CURSE 1

imprecation *n* a prayer that harm will come to someone ⟨the defiant prisoner continued to hurl *imprecations* and insults at the guards⟩ — see CURSE 1

imprecise *adj* not precisely correct ⟨3.14 is an *imprecise* approximation of the value of pi⟩ — see INEXACT 1

impregnable *adj* **1** incapable of being defeated, overcome, or subdued ⟨an *impregnable* fortress that had foiled one invader after another over the centuries⟩ — see INVINCIBLE
2 impossible to get through or into ⟨the castle's supposedly *impregnable* walls⟩ — see IMPENETRABLE 1

impregnate *vb* to wet thoroughly with liquid ⟨*impregnated* the cloth with furniture polish⟩ — see SOAK 1

impresa *n* a device, design, or figure used as an identifying mark ⟨the family's selection of the lily as its *impresa* dates from the 16th century⟩ — see EMBLEM

impress *n* a perceptible trace left by pressure ⟨the stamp left a smudgy *impress* on the paper⟩ — see PRINT 1

impress *vb* **1** to act upon (a person or a person's feelings) so as to cause a response ⟨*impressed* him with the intensity of their musical performance⟩ — see [1]AFFECT 1
2 to produce a vivid impression of ⟨*impressed* the importance of safe driving habits by displaying photos of horrific crashes⟩ — see ENGRAVE 2
3 to cause (a person) to give in to pressure ⟨after weeks of nagging, they *impressed* her into going to the masquerade party⟩ — see FORCE 1

impression *n* **1** a perceptible trace left by pressure ⟨a shoe *impression* in the dirt that could lead police to the culprit⟩ — see PRINT 1
2 something imagined or pictured in the mind ⟨had a vague *impression* that the guide would be female⟩ — see IDEA 1

impressionist *n* a person who imitates another's voice and mannerisms for comic effect ⟨a celebrated *impres-*

sionist who can do enough rapid-fire imitations to populate an entire stage with characters⟩ — see MIMIC

impressive *adj* having the power to affect the feelings or sympathies ⟨an *impressive* play about a loving family attempting to lift themselves out of poverty⟩ — see MOVING

imprimatur *n* an acceptance of something as satisfactory ⟨could not begin the project without the boss's *imprimatur*⟩ — see APPROVAL 1

imprint *n* **1** a mark or series of marks left on a surface by something that has passed along it ⟨found an *imprint* on the road where something apparently had been dragged⟩ — see TRACK 1

2 a perceptible trace left by pressure ⟨an *imprint* of a dinosaur's foot embedded in the limestone⟩ — see PRINT 1

imprint *vb* to produce a vivid impression of ⟨that early lesson on the value of honesty permanently *imprinted* itself on my mind⟩ — see ENGRAVE 2

imprison *vb* to put in or as if in prison ⟨in this society, we try to *imprison* criminals so that they can't do any more harm⟩

synonyms commit, confine, immure, incarcerate, intern, jail, jug, lock (up)

related words constrain, limit, restrain, restrict, shut; bar, gate; apprehend, arrest, bust [*slang*], capture, catch, detain, nab, pick up, pinch, seize; impress, shanghai; hold, impound, keep; bind, enchain, fetter, handcuff, manacle, shackle, trammel

near antonyms emancipate, enfranchise, manumit, unbind, uncage, unchain, unfetter

antonyms discharge, free, liberate, release

imprisoned *adj* taken and held prisoner ⟨took up the cause of *imprisoned* political dissidents⟩ — see CAPTIVE

imprisonment *n* **1** the act of confining or the state of being confined ⟨the offense is punishable by a fine or *imprisonment*⟩ — see INTERNMENT

2 the state of being held in lawful custody ⟨the long years of *imprisonment* had taken their toll on his mind and spirit as well as his body⟩ — see DETENTION 1

improbable *adj* not likely to be true or to occur ⟨it seems *improbable* that the two writers never met since they traveled in the same social circles⟩

synonyms doubtful, dubious, far-fetched, flimsy, questionable, unapt, unlikely

related words implausible, impossible, inconceivable, incredible, unbelievable, unimaginable, unthinkable; absurd, bizarre, crazy, fantastic (*also* fantastical), foolish, insane, nonsensical, odd, outlandish, preposterous, ridiculous, unreal, wild; outside, remote, slight

near antonyms believable, conceivable, credible, earthly, imaginable, plausible; possible, potential; liable

antonyms likely, probable

impromptu *adj* made or done without previous thought or preparation ⟨our dinner guest thanked us with an *impromptu* song⟩ — see EXTEMPORANEOUS

impromptu *n* something that is performed, made, or done without preparation ⟨although five different lines had been written, the best choice turned out to be an *impromptu* from the tired actor himself⟩ — see IMPROVISATION

improper *adj* not appropriate for a particular occasion or situation ⟨an *improper* use of slang in a formal piece of writing⟩ — see INAPPROPRIATE

improperly *adv* in a mistaken or inappropriate way ⟨the manufacturer's warranty is no longer valid if the appliance is used *improperly*⟩ — see WRONGLY

improperness *n* the quality or state of being unsuitable or unfitting ⟨the *improperness* of such behavior at a religious ceremony should have been achingly obvious⟩ — see INAPPROPRIATENESS 1

impropriety *n* **1** the quality or state of not being socially proper ⟨the *impropriety* of the song that the campers sang for the visitors was embarrassing⟩

synonyms inappropriateness, incorrectness, indecency, indecorousness, indecorum, indelicateness, unbecomingness, unseemliness, untowardness

related words coarseness, crudeness, vulgarity; immodesty, naughtiness; imprudence, indiscreetness, indiscretion; churlishness, discourteousness, disrespect, impertinence, impoliteness, impudence, incivility, inconsiderateness, inconsideration, insolence, rudeness, ungraciousness

near antonyms discretion, prudence; etiquette, form, manners, proprieties; considerateness, consideration, genteelness, gentility, graciousness, thoughtfulness

antonyms appropriateness, correctness, decency, decorousness, decorum, fitness, properness, propriety, rightness, seemliness, suitability, suitableness

2 a socially improper or unsuitable act or remark ⟨such *improprieties* as asking people how much money they make⟩

synonyms familiarity, faux pas, gaff, gaffe, indiscretion, solecism

related words blunder, error, flub, fumble, goof, lapse, miscue, misstep, mistake, oversight, slip, slipup, stumble; discourtesy, incivility, offense (*or* offence); boner, howler; foul-up, muff; misapprehension, miscalculation, misconception, misjudgment, misstatement, misunderstanding

near antonyms form, manners, mores, proprieties

antonyms amenity, attention, civility, courtesy, formality, gesture, pleasantry

3 the quality or state of being unsuitable or unfitting ⟨I see no *impropriety* in referring to certain anatomical parts by their standard names⟩ — see INAPPROPRIATENESS 1

improv *n* something that is performed, made, or done without preparation ⟨the performance features a two-minute *improv* as well as scripted segments⟩ — see IMPROVISATION

improve *vb* to make better ⟨a little salt would *improve* this bland food⟩

synonyms ameliorate, amend, better, enhance, enrich, help, meliorate, perfect, refine, upgrade

related words correct, emend, rectify, reform, remediate, remedy; edit, fine-tune, redraft, refurbish, rehab, rehabilitate, revamp, revise, rework; beef (up), boost, fortify, intensify, reinforce (*also* reenforce), strengthen; fine, hone, polish; retouch, touch up

near antonyms damage, endamage, harm, hurt, impair, injure, spoil, tarnish, vitiate; blemish, blight, deface, disfigure, flaw, mar; diminish, lessen, lower, reduce

antonyms worsen

improved *adj* being far along in development ⟨an *improved* version of the software is now available⟩ — see ADVANCED 1

improvement *n* an instance of notable progress in the development of knowledge, technology, or skill ⟨there's been a great *improvement* in your handwriting—I can actually read it!⟩ — see ADVANCE 2

improvident *adj* not thinking about and providing for the future ⟨the *improvident* view that the wearing away of the ozone layer need not concern us⟩

synonyms myopic, shortsighted

related words careless, heedless, imprudent, incautious, injudicious, mindless, unguarded, unsafe, unwary, unwise; extravagant, prodigal, profligate, spendthrift, thriftless, unthrifty; indulgent, lavish, reckless, wasteful

near antonyms careful, judicious, prudent, sensible, wise; economic, economical, economizing, frugal,

scrimping, sparing, thrifty; conserving, preserving, saving
antonyms farsighted, forehanded, foreseeing, foresighted, forethoughtful, provident
improvisation *n* something that is performed, made, or done without preparation ⟨that comedy skit was a totally unrehearsed *improvisation*⟩
synonyms ad-lib, extemporization, impromptu, improv
related words concoction, contrivance, creation, innovation, invention, wrinkle
near antonyms bit, drill, routine
improvisational *adj* made or done without previous thought or preparation ⟨an *improvisational* comedy sketch that showcased his lightning-fast wit⟩ — see EXTEMPORANEOUS
improvise *vb* to perform, make, or do without preparation ⟨since the award was a complete surprise, I *improvised* an acceptance speech⟩
synonyms ad-lib, clap (together *or* up), extemporize, fake
related words concoct, contrive, cook (up), devise, fabricate, hatch, invent, make up, manufacture, think (up); cobble (together *or* up), dash (off)
near antonyms arrange, lay, prepare, ready; consider, contemplate, ponder, study; exercise, practice (*also* practise), rehearse
improvised *adj* made or done without previous thought or preparation ⟨stumbled through an *improvised* reply to an unexpected question at the press conference⟩ — see EXTEMPORANEOUS
imprudent *adj* showing poor judgment especially in personal relationships or social situations ⟨a very sweet girl, but so *imprudent* that no one trusts her with a secret⟩ — see INDISCREET
impudence *n* **1** disrespectful or argumentative talk given in response to a command or request ⟨my mother would not tolerate *impudence* from any of us⟩ — see BACK TALK
2 rude behavior ⟨their *impudence* irritated everyone at the wedding reception⟩ — see DISCOURTESY
impudent *adj* displaying or marked by rude boldness ⟨the guest's *impudent* inquiries about the cost of just about everything we had in the house⟩ — see NERVY 1
impuissant *adj* unable to act or achieve one's purpose ⟨claims that such restrictions on military interventions on foreign soil would render the nation an *impuissant* giant on the world stage⟩ — see POWERLESS
impulse *n* **1** something that arouses action or activity ⟨the new auto factory was just the *impulse* that the local economy needed⟩
synonyms boost, encouragement, goad, impetus, incentive, incitation, incitement, instigation, momentum, motivation, provocation, spur, stimulant, stimulus, yeast
related words inducement, invitation; antecedent, cause, consideration, grounds, motive, occasion, reason; catalyst, catalyzer, fuel, spark
phrases shot in the arm
antonyms counterincentive, disincentive
2 a habitual attraction to some activity or thing ⟨the universal, fundamental *impulse* of self-preservation⟩ — see INCLINATION 1
impulsive *adj* **1** caused by or suggestive of an irresistible urge ⟨an *impulsive* purchase of a very expensive jacket⟩ — see COMPULSIVE
2 prone to sudden illogical changes of mind, ideas, or actions ⟨an *impulsive* woman who never seems to have the same opinion about anything for longer than 10 minutes⟩ — see WHIMSICAL
impulsiveness *n* an inclination to sudden illogical changes of mind, ideas, or actions ⟨his irrepressible *impulsiveness* sometimes got him into trouble⟩ — see WHIMSICALITY
impunity *n* freedom from punishment, harm, or loss ⟨she mistakenly believed that she could insult people with *impunity*⟩
synonyms exemption, immunity
related words aegis (*also* egis), armor, cover, defense, guard, protection, safeguard, safety, security, shield; buffer, bumper, screen; absolution, absolving, dispensation, forgiveness
near antonyms exposure, liability, openness, susceptibility, susceptibleness, vulnerability
impure *adj* **1** containing foreign or lower-grade substances ⟨be careful, because *impure* motor oil can damage your car's engine⟩
synonyms adulterate, adulterated, alloyed, contaminated, dilute, diluted, polluted, tainted, thinned, weakened
related words unclarified, unfiltered, unrefined; befouled, begrimed, bemired, besmirched, corrupted, debased, defiled, dirtied, fouled, maculate (*or* maculated), soiled, spoiled, sullied; blended, commingled, incorporated, intermingled, intermixed, merged, mingled, mixed; coalesced, combined, compounded; cheapened, doctored
near antonyms clarified, filtered, purified, refined, ultrarefined; neat, plain, straight; concentrated, strong; uncombined; pasteurized; sterile, sterilized; clean, immaculate, spotless, stainless, unsoiled, unsullied
antonyms fine, pure, ultrapure, unadulterated, unalloyed, uncontaminated, uncut, undiluted, unmixed, unpolluted, untainted
2 depicting or referring to sexual matters in a way that is unacceptable in polite society ⟨Victorian notions of what qualified as *impure* art now strike us as laughable⟩ — see OBSCENE 1
impureness *n* the quality or state of being obscene ⟨the alleged *impureness* of a novel that was banned in the United States until 1959⟩ — see OBSCENITY 1
impurity *n* **1** something that is or that makes impure ⟨*impurities* in the water made it cloudy⟩
synonyms adulterant, contaminant, contamination, defilement, pollutant
related words blot, blotch, spot, stain, taint; dirt, filth, grime, muck, scum, sludge, smut, soil; blemish, defect, disfigurement, fault, flaw; abnormality, imperfection, irregularity
near antonyms clarifier, filter, purifier, refiner; cleanliness, immaculateness, purity
2 the quality or state of being obscene ⟨the *impurity* of her thoughts was troubling, given her strict upbringing⟩ — see OBSCENITY 1
imputation *n* a slyly or subtly derogatory remark ⟨I resent the *imputation* that I'm nice to Grandmother because she has money⟩ — see INNUENDO
impute *vb* to explain (something) as being the result of something else ⟨people often *impute* his silence to unfriendliness and not to the shyness it really represents⟩ — see CREDIT 1
in *adj* **1** being in the latest or current fashion ⟨the *in* hairstyle this spring⟩ — see STYLISH
2 enjoying widespread favor or approval ⟨the *in* thing to do is not always the right thing to do⟩ — see POPULAR 1
3 keenly aware of and responsive to the latest developments especially in fashion and entertainment ⟨*in* gearheads had already decided that the format was a loser⟩ — see AU COURANT 1
4 being within the confines of a specified place ⟨the doctor isn't *in* right now⟩ — see PRESENT 2
in *adv* at, within, or to a short distance or time ⟨the fielders closed *in*⟩ — see NEAR 1

in *n* the power to direct the thinking or behavior of others usually indirectly ⟨her years of experience with the federal regulatory agency gives her a tremendous *in* as a lobbyist for the nuclear power industry⟩ — see INFLUENCE 1

in *prep* using the means or agency of ⟨drawn on the wall *in* crayon⟩ — see BY 2

inability *n* the lack of sufficient ability, power, or means ⟨the apparent *inability* of young children to sit still⟩
synonyms impotence, inadequacy, incapability, incapacity, incompetence, incompetency, ineptitude, insufficiency, powerlessness
related words disqualification, inaptitude; ineffectiveness, ineffectuality, ineffectualness, inefficaciousness, inefficacy, inefficiency
near antonyms aptitude, bent, endowment, flair, genius, gift, knack, talent; effectiveness, effectualness, efficaciousness, efficiency; fitness, suitability, suitableness; potency, power, puissance, sinew, strength
antonyms ability, adequacy, capability, capacity, competence, competency, potency

inaccessible *adj* hard or impossible to get to or get at ⟨the tumor is centered in an *inaccessible* part of the brain⟩
synonyms inapproachable, inconvenient, unapproachable, unattainable, unavailable, unobtainable, unreachable, untouchable
related words away, distant, far, faraway, far-off, remote, removed; apart, hidden, isolated, out-of-the-way, secluded
near antonyms close, immediate, near, nearby, neighboring, next-door, nigh
antonyms accessible, acquirable, approachable, attainable, convenient, getatable, handy, obtainable, procurable, reachable

inaccuracy *n* an unintentional departure from truth or accuracy ⟨an unfortunate *inaccuracy* in the report⟩ — see ERROR 1

inaccurate *adj* **1** not being in agreement with what is true ⟨he claimed that the TV ratings were *inaccurate* because they didn't take into account all those viewers in health clubs⟩ — see FALSE 1
2 not precisely correct ⟨the estimate is *inaccurate*, but will do for our purposes⟩ — see INEXACT 1

inaccurately *adv* in a mistaken or inappropriate way ⟨*inaccurately* reported that she was absent that day⟩ — see WRONGLY

inaction *n* lack of action or activity ⟨as a result of the park department's *inaction*, the city's pools are not ready to open for the summer⟩
synonyms dormancy, idleness, inactivity, inertness, nonaction, quiescence
related words indolence, inertia, languor, lassitude, laziness, lethargy, listlessness, shiftlessness, sleepiness, sloth, sluggishness; dallying, loafing, lolling, lounging
near antonyms animateness, briskness, exuberance, jazziness, liveliness, peppiness, robustness, sprightliness, vibrancy, vivacity; assiduity, assiduousness, business, diligence, employment, industriousness, industry, occupation
antonyms action, activeness, activity

inactive *adj* **1** slow to move or act ⟨it's easiest to catch snakes early in the morning, while they're still cold and *inactive*⟩
synonyms dull, inert, lethargic, quiescent, sleepy, sluggish, torpid
related words ambitionless, apathetic, indolent, languorous, lazy, lazyish, listless, shiftless, slack, slothful, sluggard, sluggardly; dormant, inanimate, motionless, resting, sedentary, static, still; dead; dopey (*also* dopy), drugged; asleep, drowsy, somnambulant; catatonic, comatose
near antonyms busy, engaged, occupied, working; animated, bouncing, dynamic, energetic, kinetic, lively, peppy, perky, spirited, sprightly, springy, vigorous, vital, vivacious, zippy; assiduous, diligent, hardworking, industrious, sedulous
antonyms active
2 not being in a state of use, activity, or employment ⟨an *inactive* oil well⟩
synonyms dead, dormant, fallow, free, idle, inert, inoperative, latent, off, unused, vacant
related words abeyant, arrested, interrupted, suspended; unoccupied; asleep, comatose, lifeless, moribund, quiescent, sleepy; inoperable, unusable, unworkable, useless; dull, slow
phrases at rest, on the shelf, out of commission
near antonyms functional, operable, operational, workable; assiduous, industrious, sedulous; energetic, vigorous; feasible, practical, usable (*also* useable), useful, viable
antonyms active, alive, busy, employed, functioning, going, living, on, operating, operative, running, working

inactivity *n* **1** lack of action or activity ⟨the *inactivity* outside the school led me to think that it must have been vacation week⟩ — see INACTION
2 lack of use ⟨after weeks of *inactivity*, the car wouldn't start⟩ — see DISUSE

inadequacy *n* **1** a falling short of an essential or desirable amount or number ⟨the *inadequacy* of our servings was soon apparent, as hungry guests started clamoring for seconds⟩ — see DEFICIENCY
2 the lack of sufficient ability, power, or means ⟨tried to blame others in order to hide the *inadequacy* of his leadership⟩ — see INABILITY

inadequate *adj* not coming up to an expected measure or meeting a particular need ⟨an *inadequate* amount of food on hand for so many unexpected guests⟩ — see SHORT 3

inadequately *adv* in an unsatisfactory way ⟨she did the job quickly, but *inadequately*⟩ — see BADLY 1

inadequateness *n* a falling short of an essential or desirable amount or number ⟨the *inadequateness* of our emergency food supplies should have been obvious⟩ — see DEFICIENCY

inadvertent *adj* happening by chance ⟨an *inadvertent* encounter with a rattlesnake in the brush⟩ — see ACCIDENTAL 1

inadvisable *adj* showing poor judgment especially in personal relationships or social situations ⟨it's *inadvisable* to have public arguments in the hallways⟩ — see INDISCREET

inalterable *adj* not capable of changing or being changed ⟨the *inalterable* record of history, which we ignore at our peril⟩ — see INFLEXIBLE 1

inamorata *n* a female romantic companion ⟨a number of women have been suggested as the *inamorata* who inspired such passionate love poetry⟩ — see GIRLFRIEND

inane *adj* having no meaning ⟨*inane* and useless phrases, such as "have a nice day"⟩ — see MEANINGLESS

inanimate *adj* lacking animate awareness or sensation ⟨"pathetic fallacy" is the literary term for the ascription of human feelings or motives to *inanimate* natural elements⟩ — see INSENSATE 1

inanity *n* **1** a foolish act or idea ⟨quickly realized that her suggestion was an *inanity* and withdrew it⟩ — see FOLLY 1
2 lack of good sense or judgment ⟨the jaw-dropping

inanity of the singer's comments on the awards show⟩ — see FOOLISHNESS 1

inappeasable *adj* incapable of being satisfied ⟨at the time the public seemed to have an *inappeasable* appetite for reality TV shows⟩ — see INSATIABLE

inapplicability *n* the quality or state of not having anything to do with the matter at hand ⟨the sheer *inapplicability* of the comment made everyone else at the meeting stare in bewilderment⟩ — see IRRELEVANCE

inapplicable *adj* not having anything to do with the matter at hand ⟨the judge refused to allow mention of the defendant's conviction for shoplifting, ruling that it was *inapplicable* to the case at hand⟩ — see IRRELEVANT

inapposite *adj* **1** not appropriate for a particular occasion or situation ⟨that comparison is completely *inapposite*; there are no parallels between the two books at all⟩ — see INAPPROPRIATE

2 not having anything to do with the matter at hand ⟨a speech laden with *inapposite* anecdotes and unfunny jokes⟩ — see IRRELEVANT

inappositeness *n* the quality or state of being unsuitable or unfitting ⟨the *inappositeness* of the description quickly became clear⟩ — see INAPPROPRIATENESS 1

inappreciable *adj* not perceptible by a sense or by the mind ⟨an *inappreciable* change in the temperature⟩ — see IMPERCEPTIBLE

inapproachable *adj* hard or impossible to get to or get at ⟨conventional wisdom had long held that the mountain's summit was *inapproachable* from the northen slope⟩ — see INACCESSIBLE

inappropriate *adj* not appropriate for a particular occasion or situation ⟨a bathing suit is *inappropriate* dress for strolling the streets of this seaside village⟩

synonyms amiss, graceless, improper, inapposite, inapt, incongruous, incorrect, indecorous, inept, infelicitous, malapropos, perverse, unapt, unbecoming, unfit, unhappy, unseemly, unsuitable, untoward, wrong

related words inopportune, unfortunate, unseasonable, untimely; extraneous, immaterial, inapplicable, irrelative, irrelevant; misbecoming, mismatched; incompatible, inconsistent, uncongenial; bad, naughty, sinful; blamable, blameworthy, censurable; banned, barred, disallowed; forbidden, interdicted, outlawed, prohibited, proscribed; awkward, gauche, ungraceful; unacceptable, unsatisfactory

phrases out of place, out of the way

near antonyms fortunate, opportune, seasonable, timely; applicable, apposite, apropos, apt, germane, material, pat, pointed, relative, relevant; compatible, congenial, harmonious; allowed, authorized, permitted; approved, endorsed (*also* indorsed), kosher, licensed, sanctioned; abetted, encouraged, promoted, supported; acceptable, adequate, all right, decent, fine, OK (*or* okay), passable, respectable, satisfactory, tolerable; commendable, creditable, exemplary; blameless, irreproachable; balanced, companionate, congruous, consonant, harmonious

antonyms appropriate, becoming, befitting, correct, decorous, felicitous, fit, fitting, genteel, happy, meet, proper, right, seemly, suitable

inappropriately *adv* in a mistaken or inappropriate way ⟨she *inappropriately* referred to my chaperone as my father, and not as my stepfather⟩ — see WRONGLY

inappropriateness *n* **1** the quality or state of being unsuitable or unfitting ⟨I cannot even begin to describe the *inappropriateness* of such language for the dinner table⟩

synonyms improperness, impropriety, inappositeness, inaptness, incorrectness, infelicity, unfitness, wrongness

related words extraneousness, inadequacy, inadequateness, inadmissibility, inapplicability, irrelevance, meaninglessness, pointlessness, senselessness; inauspiciousness, inexpedience, inexpediency, intolerability, undesirability, undesirableness, unsatisfactoriness, uselessness; unbecomingness; unseasonability

near antonyms admissibility, applicability, bearing, connection, materiality, pertinence, pointedness, relevance, relevancy

antonyms appositeness, appropriateness, aptness, correctness, felicitousness, felicity, fitness, fittingness, properness, propriety, rightness, seemliness, suitability, suitableness

2 the quality or state of not being socially proper ⟨the *inappropriateness* of belching in a restaurant should have been apparent even to you⟩ — see IMPROPRIETY 1

inapt *adj* **1** not appropriate for a particular occasion or situation ⟨an *inapt* but well-meaning attempt to inject some humor into the proceedings⟩ — see INAPPROPRIATE

2 lacking qualities (as knowledge, skill, or ability) required to do a job ⟨a recruit who was utterly *inapt* for most soldierly duties, so he spent most of his time playing in the army band⟩ — see INCOMPETENT

inaptly *adv* in a mistaken or inappropriate way ⟨the development was *inaptly* named Apple Orchard Condominiums, presumably in honor of what was destroyed in order to build them⟩ — see WRONGLY

inaptness *n* the quality or state of being unsuitable or unfitting ⟨the *inaptness* of the ski outfit made her stand out among the somberly dressed mourners⟩ — see INAPPROPRIATENESS 1

inarguable *adj* not capable of being challenged or proved wrong ⟨the colonists presented their case for political independence with what they regarded as *inarguable* logic⟩ — see IRREFUTABLE

inarguably *adv* without any question ⟨was *inarguably* the most important factor in our victory over the other team⟩ — see INDEED 1

inarticulate *adj* unable to speak ⟨the sudden rumblings of an earthquake rendered people *inarticulate* with fear⟩ — see MUTE 1

inasmuch as *conj* **1** to the degree that ⟨the economic forecast for the coming decade looks promising, *inasmuch as* we can predict that far in advance⟩

synonyms insofar as, insomuch as, insomuch that, so far as

2 for the reason that ⟨you should not use that source, *inasmuch as* it is badly out-of-date⟩ — see SINCE

inaugural *adj* coming before all others in time or order ⟨the *inaugural* event in the city's week long festival honoring the sailing ships⟩ — see FIRST 1

inaugural *n* the process or an instance of being formally placed in an office or organization ⟨attended the *inaugurals* of the city's last three mayors⟩ — see INSTALLATION 1

inaugurate *vb* **1** to be responsible for the creation and early operation or use of ⟨*inaugurated* the college's athletic program for women⟩ — see FOUND

2 to put into an office or welcome into an organization with special ceremonies ⟨the president *inaugurated* the newest member of the club with a welcoming speech⟩ — see INSTALL 1

inauguration *n* the process or an instance of being formally placed in an office or organization ⟨the pomp and circumstance of a presidential *inauguration*⟩ — see INSTALLATION 1

inaugurator *n* a person who establishes a whole new field of endeavor ⟨the famed *inaugurator* of the assembly line in the production of automobiles⟩ — see FATHER 2

inauspicious *adj* being or showing a sign of evil or calamity to come ⟨this many problems so early in the project is a most *inauspicious* sign⟩ — see OMINOUS

inauthentic *adj* being such in appearance only and made or manufactured with the intention of committing fraud ⟨an *inauthentic* warbonnet that was probably made in an overseas factory a few months ago⟩ — see COUNTERFEIT 1

inborn *adj* **1** being a part of the innermost nature of a person or thing ⟨an *inborn* talent for dancing⟩ — see INHERENT
2 genetically passed or capable of being passed from parent to offspring ⟨certain instincts are *inborn* in mice⟩ — see HEREDITARY

inbred *adj* being a part of the innermost nature of a person or thing ⟨an *inbred* desire to do good in the world⟩ — see INHERENT

in camera *adv* in a manner intended to prevent knowledge or awareness by others ⟨the board of trustees met *in camera* to decide the fate of the embattled university president⟩ — see PRIVATELY

incandescence *n* the steady giving off of the form of radiation that makes vision possible ⟨candles made from whale oil were once highly prized because they burned with an *incandescence* superior to that of other candles⟩ — see LIGHT 1

incandescent *adj* **1** giving off or reflecting much light ⟨sitting in darkness, except for the *incandescent* coals of our campfire⟩ — see BRIGHT 1
2 having or expressing great depth of feeling ⟨a speaker *incandescent* with righteous anger over the treatment of the refugees⟩ — see FERVENT 1

incandescently *adv* in a manner marked by the shining or reflecting of much light ⟨with lights burning as *incandescently* as the midday sun, soundstages on early color films often reached 100 degrees⟩ — see BRIGHTLY 1

incantation *n* a spoken word or set of words believed to have magic power ⟨hovering over the sick child, the witch doctor muttered mysterious *incantations*⟩ — see SPELL 1

incapability *n* the lack of sufficient ability, power, or means ⟨the apparent *incapability* of the president's staff to deal with the crisis⟩ — see INABILITY

incapable *adj* lacking qualities (as knowledge, skill, or ability) required to do a job ⟨hired a supremely *incapable* assistant who only made a mess of things⟩ — see INCOMPETENT

incapacitate *vb* **1** to render powerless, ineffective, or unable to move ⟨the malfunctioning of a single component can *incapacitate* the engine⟩ — see PARALYZE 1
2 to cause severe or permanent injury to ⟨the stroke left her completely *incapacitated*⟩ — see MAIM

incapacitated *adj* deprived of the power to perform one or more natural bodily activities ⟨was temporarily *incapacitated* by the car accident⟩ — see DISABLED

incapacity *n* the lack of sufficient ability, power, or means ⟨her entrenched *incapacity* for decision-making doesn't make her a very good boss⟩ — see INABILITY

incarcerate *vb* to put in or as if in prison ⟨the state *incarcerated* over 1900 people last year⟩ — see IMPRISON

incarcerated *adj* taken and held prisoner ⟨*incarcerated* residents of that state are still allowed to vote in elections⟩ — see CAPTIVE

incarceration *n* **1** the act of confining or the state of being confined ⟨he was bored and frustrated by his *incarceration* in the quarantine⟩ — see INTERNMENT
2 the state of being held in lawful custody ⟨sentenced to six months of *incarceration* for dealing in narcotics⟩— see DETENTION 1

incarnate *vb* to represent in visible form ⟨the general view that Hitler *incarnated* extreme egotism and indeed evil itself⟩ — see EMBODY 2

incarnation *n* a visible representation of something abstract (as a quality) ⟨she is the very *incarnation* of grace and tactfulness⟩ — see EMBODIMENT

incaution *n* failure to take the care that a cautious person usually takes ⟨as a result of an agent's colossal *incaution*, a laptop filled with top-secret intelligence was missing⟩ — see NEGLIGENCE 1

incautious *adj* not paying or showing close attention especially for the purpose of avoiding trouble ⟨an *incautious* comment got her in political hot water⟩ — see CARELESS 1

incautiousness *n* failure to take the care that a cautious person usually takes ⟨a mere moment of *incautiousness* can cause an accident⟩ — see NEGLIGENCE 1

incendiary *n* **1** a person who deliberately and unlawfully sets fire to a building or other property ⟨firefighters caught the *incendiary*, who was watching the effects of his handiwork⟩ — see ARSONIST
2 a person who stirs up public feelings especially of discontent ⟨blamed the protests on outside *incendiaries* who were intent on overthrowing the government⟩ — see AGITATOR

incendiary *adj* tending to excite political disorder or insurrection ⟨recklessly made *incendiary* remarks during a period of heightened racial tensions⟩ — see INFLAMMATORY

incense *n* **1** a sweet or pleasant smell ⟨the heavenly *incense* of spring flowers⟩ — see FRAGRANCE
2 excessive praise ⟨count on the office manager to spread the *incense* whenever there's a visiting VIP from the head office⟩ — see FLATTERY

[1]**incense** *vb* to make angry ⟨the insult so *incensed* him that he had to be restrained from hitting the guy⟩ — see ANGER

[2]**incense** *vb* to fill or infuse with a pleasant odor or odor-releasing substance ⟨the gift shop was heavily *incensed* with a cloying mixture of herbal essences⟩ — see SCENT 1

incensed *adj* feeling or showing anger ⟨*incensed* residents demanded that the police apprehend the punks who vandalized the cemetery⟩— see ANGRY

incentive *n* something that arouses action or activity ⟨the handsome reward for the missing dog was an *incentive* for me to start looking⟩ — see IMPULSE 1

inception *n* the point at which something begins ⟨this seemed like a good program at its *inception*, but it isn't working out as planned⟩ — see BEGINNING

inceptive *adj* beginning to come into existence ⟨only just recently gained an *inceptive* understanding of the overwhelming vastness of the universe⟩ — see NASCENT

incertitude *n* a feeling or attitude that one does not know the truth, truthfulness, or trustworthiness of someone or something ⟨a growing *incertitude* about the honesty of the housekeeper they had just hired⟩— see DOUBT

incessant *adj* going on and on without any interruptions ⟨the *incessant* noise from an outside repair crew was a real distraction during the test⟩ — see CONTINUOUS

incessantly *adv* on every relevant occasion ⟨she *incessantly* made the same suggestion for a Roman theme whenever anyone mentioned holding a party⟩ — see ALWAYS 1

inch *n* **1** a very small distance or degree ⟨give them an *inch*, and they'll take a mile⟩ — see HAIR 1
2 an individual part of a process, series, or ranking ⟨*inch* by *inch*, we're making progress toward our fundraising goal⟩ — see DEGREE 1
3 inches *pl* the distance of something or someone from bottom to top ⟨made the most of her *inches* by standing on her tiptoes to reach the top shelf⟩ — see HEIGHT 3

inch *vb* **1** to advance gradually beyond the usual or desirable limits ⟨every year the water *inches* further up the embankments, threatening to permanently engulf the island city⟩ — see ENCROACH

2 to move slowly ⟨the car *inched* carefully across the snow-covered causeway⟩ — see CRAWL 2

inchmeal *adv* by small steps or amounts ⟨the troops moved through the village *inchmeal*, recapturing it virtually house by house⟩ — see GRADUALLY

inchoate *adj* beginning to come into existence ⟨*inchoate* feelings of affection for a man whom she had, up till now, thought of as only a friend⟩ — see NASCENT

incident *n* **1** something that happens ⟨the odd little *incident* was reported in the local paper⟩ — see EVENT 1

2 something that is found along with something else ⟨a teen discovering that taxes are the inevitable and evil *incident* of a paying job⟩ — see ACCOMPANIMENT

incidental *adj* **1** happening by chance ⟨an *incidental* meeting of two ships in the middle of the Atlantic⟩ — see ACCIDENTAL 1

2 lacking importance ⟨we still have to work out a few *incidental* details, but the proposal is largely complete⟩ — see UNIMPORTANT

incidentally *adv* by way of interjection or digression ⟨*incidentally*, have you seen the new building they're putting up?⟩ — see APROPOS

incipience *n* the point at which something begins ⟨since its *incipience*, the show has been on the cutting edge of comedy⟩ — see BEGINNING

incipiency *n* the point at which something begins ⟨from its *incipiency* the city's monthlong festival of the performing arts has been a great success⟩ — see BEGINNING

incipient *adj* beginning to come into existence ⟨I have an *incipient* dislike and distrust of that guy, and I only met him this morning⟩ — see NASCENT

incise *vb* **1** to cut (as letters or designs) on a hard surface ⟨*incised* a pattern into the copper plate⟩ — see ENGRAVE 1

2 to penetrate with a sharp edge (as a knife) ⟨*incised* the tree with a sharp ax to get the sap flowing⟩ — see CUT 1

incision *n* a long deep cut ⟨the surgeon made a thin *incision* with the scalpel⟩ — see GASH

incitation *n* **1** something that arouses a strong response from another ⟨the rabble-rousing speech was seen by many as an *incitation* to ethnic violence⟩ — see PROVOCATION 1

2 something that arouses action or activity ⟨a mild heart attack was all the *incitation* he needed to adopt an exercise regimen and a healthy diet⟩ — see IMPULSE 1

incite *vb* **1** to bring (something volatile or intense) into being ⟨the rock band's failure to show up *incited* a riot, as the crowd had waited for hours⟩

synonyms abet, brew, ferment, foment, instigate, pick, provoke, raise, stir (up), whip (up)

related words advance, cultivate, encourage, forward, foster, further, nourish, nurture, promote, sow, stimulate; detonate, set, set off, trigger; excite, galvanize, inflame (*also* enflame), inspire, motivate, rouse; activate, energize, enliven, fire, invigorate, jazz (up), liven (up), pep (up), quicken, stimulate, vitalize

phrases set in motion

near antonyms bridle, check, constrain, curb, discourage, hold, inhibit, regulate, rein (in), restrain, tame; allay, calm, quiet, settle, soothe, still, subdue, tranquilize (*also* tranquillize)

2 to rouse to strong feeling or action ⟨the demagogue's fiery rant *incited* the crowd to riot⟩ — see PROVOKE 1

incitement *n* **1** something that arouses a strong response from another ⟨the insulting remark was all the *incitement* that was needed for a fight to break out⟩ — see PROVOCATION 1

2 something that arouses action or activity ⟨the approaching deadline was certainly an *incitement* to get going on the assignment⟩ — see IMPULSE 1

inciter *n* a person who stirs up public feelings especially of discontent ⟨the governor warned that *inciters* of mob violence would be dealt with harshly⟩ — see AGITATOR

inciting *adj* serving or likely to arouse a strong reaction ⟨a deliberately *inciting* comment questioning someone's manhood started the brawl⟩ — see PROVOCATIVE

incivility *n* rude behavior ⟨I won't tolerate *incivility*, and that includes text messaging while I'm speaking⟩ — see DISCOURTESY

inclement *adj* marked by wet and windy conditions ⟨the weather report warned that the holiday weekend would be spoiled by *inclement* weather⟩ — see FOUL 1

inclination *n* **1** a habitual attraction to some activity or thing ⟨her natural *inclination* to help people in need⟩

synonyms affection, affinity, aptitude, bent, bias, bone, devices, disposition, genius, habitude, impulse, leaning, partiality, penchant, predilection, predisposition, proclivity, propensity, tendency, turn

related words favor, one-sidedness, partisanship, prejudice; endowment, faculty, flair, genius, gift, knack, talent; addiction, appetite, fancy, fondness, like, liking, preference, taste; forte, speciality, specialty; convention, custom, habit, pattern, practice (*also* practise), routine, trick, way, wont; eccentricity, idiosyncrasy, kink, oddity, peculiarity, quirk, singularity

near antonyms allergy, averseness, aversion, disfavor, disinclination, dislike, disliking, disrelish, distaste; detachment, impartiality, neutrality, objectivity; apathy, disinterestedness, indifference, insouciance, nonchalance, unconcern

2 the act of positioning or an instance of being positioned at an angle ⟨the photographer adjusted the *inclination* of the sitter's head⟩ — see TILT

3 the degree to which something rises up from a position level with the horizon ⟨the *inclination* of the hill is gentle, so walking up it isn't too bad⟩ — see SLANT

incline *n* the degree to which something rises up from a position level with the horizon ⟨the steep *incline* of the hill meant that it was impossible to ride a bicycle up it⟩ — see SLANT

incline *vb* **1** to set or cause to be at an angle ⟨carefully *inclined* the ladder against the house⟩ — see LEAN 1

2 to show a liking or proneness (for something) ⟨a good restaurant for diners who *incline* to spicy food⟩ — see LEAN 2

inclined *adj* **1** having a desire or inclination (as for a specified course of action) ⟨we couldn't have convinced her if she weren't already so *inclined*⟩ — see WILLING 1

2 having a liking or affection ⟨a nightclub strictly for those *inclined* towards loud music⟩ — see FOND 1

3 having a tendency to be or act in a certain way ⟨a kindly couple who are *inclined* to be helpful to strangers⟩ — see PRONE 1

4 running in a slanting direction ⟨the highway ramps and other *inclined* roadways were treacherous during the ice storm⟩ — see DIAGONAL

inclining *adj* bending downward or forward ⟨the *inclining* branches of the evergreens seemed almost ready to break under the weight of the heavy snow⟩ — see NODDING

include *vb* **1** to have as part of a whole ⟨the college application *included* some thought-provoking essay questions⟩

synonyms carry, comprehend, contain, embrace, encompass, entail, involve, number, subsume, take in

related words comprise, consist (of); bracket; have, hold, own, possess; admit, receive; compose, constitute, form, make; assimilate, embody, incorporate, integrate

near antonyms ban, bar, debar, preclude, prevent, pro-

hibit; deny, refuse, reject; eliminate, except, rule out; lose, mislay, misplace
antonyms exclude, leave (out), miss out [*British*], omit
2 to close or shut in by or as if by barriers ⟨that inextinguishable spark of liberty that is *included* within every human being⟩ — see ENCLOSE 1

inclusive *adj* covering everything or all important points ⟨a butterfly expert with an *inclusive* knowledge of his subject⟩ — see ENCYCLOPEDIC

inclusively *adv* with everyone or everything taken into account at the same time ⟨for the complete body makeover, a week at the spa costs, *inclusively*, $10,000⟩ — see ALL AROUND

incognito *adj* not named or identified by a name ⟨an *incognito* source in the CIA was the source of the information⟩ — see NAMELESS 1

incognizance *n* the state of being unaware or uninformed ⟨your complete *incognizance* of the inflammatory effect of such language is amazing⟩ — see IGNORANCE 1

incognizant *adj* not informed about or aware of something ⟨a bunch of loud partygoers who seemed utterly *incognizant* of the disturbance they were creating⟩ — see IGNORANT 2

incoherent *adj* **1** not clearly or logically connected ⟨the thriller's *incoherent* plot left movie audiences wondering who did what⟩
synonyms choppy, disconnected, disjointed, unconnected
related words baffling, bewildering, confounding, confused, confusing, disordered, disorderly, disorganized, muddled, perplexing, puzzling, unorganized; disconcerting, frustrating; fallacious, illogical, inconsistent, invalid, irrational, unsound; absurd, asinine, bizarre, curious, eccentric, foolish, odd, outlandish, outré, peculiar, screwy, strange, unreasonable, unusual, weird; meaningless, nonsensical, nutty, preposterous, ridiculous, senseless, silly; unconvincing; inexplicable, unaccountable, unexplainable
near antonyms ordered, orderly, organized, systematic, systematized; logical, rational, reasonable, sensible, solid, sound, valid; cogent, compelling, convincing, persuasive, plausible, satisfying; clear, clear-cut, lucid, perspicuous, transparent, unambiguous, unequivocal, unmistakable
antonyms coherent, connected
2 consisting of particles that do not stick together ⟨a driveway covered with *incoherent* gravel⟩ — see LOOSE 2

incombustible *adj* incapable of being burned ⟨we keep our important papers in an *incombustible* safe in the basement⟩
synonyms fireproof, noncombustible, nonflammable, noninflammable
related words nonexplosive
near antonyms ablaze, afire, aflame, blazing, burning, combusting, fiery, flaming, ignited, inflamed (*also* enflamed), kindled, lit (*or* lighted); consumable; explosive, incendiary, volcanic
antonyms burnable, combustible, flammable, ignitable (*also* ignitible), inflammable

income *n* **1** an increase usually measured in money that comes from labor, business, or property ⟨her summer job gave her some extra *income*⟩
synonyms earnings, gain(s), incoming(s), proceeds, profit, return, revenue, yield
related words killing, windfall; salary, take-home pay, tips, wages; bankroll, capital, coffers, exchequer, finances, funds, money, pocket, pocketbook, resources, wherewithal
near antonyms charge, cost, disbursement, expenditures, expenses, outgo, outlay
2 a flowing or coming in ⟨the *income* of matériel is still hampered by inadequate logistical support⟩ — see INFLUX

incomer *n, chiefly British* one that leaves one place to settle in another ⟨a steady stream of *incomers* to Australia from all parts of the Commonwealth⟩ — see EMIGRANT

incoming *n* **1** the act of coming upon a scene ⟨the endless succession of *incomings* had us wondering how we would ever find room for everyone⟩ — see ARRIVAL
2 *usually* **incomings** *pl* an increase usually measured in money that comes from labor, business, or property ⟨the company's *incomings* from its brick-and-mortar stores, online sales, and Web site advertising⟩ — see INCOME 1

incommode *vb* to cause discomfort to or trouble for ⟨the innkeeper tried to hide how much the request *incommoded* them⟩ — see INCONVENIENCE

incommoding *adj* causing difficulty, discomfort, or annoyance ⟨such *incommoding* features of air travel as flight delays and time-consuming security screenings⟩ — see INCONVENIENT 1

incommodity *n* a feature of someone or something that creates difficulty for achieving success ⟨cited reduced privacy as one of the *incommodities* of apartment living⟩ — see DISADVANTAGE 1

incommunicable *adj* beyond the power to describe ⟨the vastness of the universe is *incommunicable*⟩ — see INDESCRIBABLE

incommutable *adj* not capable of changing or being changed ⟨a traditionalist and staunch opponent of relativism, she argues that there is indeed a timeless and *incommutable* moral code by which all must abide⟩ — see INFLEXIBLE 1

incomparable *adj* having no equal or rival for excellence or desirability ⟨the *incomparable* jewel known as the Hope Diamond⟩ — see ONLY 1

incompatible *adj* not being in agreement or harmony ⟨the committee's *incompatible* goals—develop new projects and cut costs—meant that they got very little accomplished⟩ — see INCONSISTENT 1

incompetence *n* the lack of sufficient ability, power, or means ⟨the astounding *incompetence* of the new assistant⟩ — see INABILITY

incompetency *n* the lack of sufficient ability, power, or means ⟨the *incompetency* of the secretary was revealed only after she had left the company, and her successor discovered years of filing left undone⟩ — see INABILITY

incompetent *adj* lacking qualities (as knowledge, skill, or ability) required to do a job ⟨an *incompetent* carpenter had built the deck, and the railings were loose already⟩
synonyms inapt, incapable, inept, inexpert, unable, unfit, unfitted, unqualified, unskilled, unskillful
related words ineffective, ineffectual, inefficient; amateurish, callow, dilettantish, green, inexperienced, raw, unprofessional; unequipped, unprepared, untrained; useless, worthless; disqualified, ineligible; wanting
near antonyms prepared, ready, trained; overqualified; accomplished, ace, adept, consummate, crack, experienced, practiced (*also* practised), seasoned, veteran, virtuoso; all-around (*also* all-round), protean, versatile
antonyms able, capable, competent, expert, fit, qualified, skilled, skillful, ultracompetent

incomplete *adj* lacking some necessary part ⟨an *incomplete* puzzle that has several pieces missing⟩
synonyms deficient, fragmental, fragmentary, half, halfway, partial
related words broken, damaged, flawed, impaired, imperfect, injured, marred, spoiled; sketchy, unassembled, uncompleted, unfinished

near antonyms flawless, unbroken, undamaged, unimpaired, uninjured, unmarred; completed, finished
antonyms complete, entire, full, intact, integral, perfect, whole

incompletely *adv* in some measure or degree ⟨a physiological process that is *incompletely* understood at the present time⟩ — see PARTLY

incompliant *adj* given to resisting authority or another's control ⟨a perpetually *incompliant* employee who seemed to think that the rules did not apply to him⟩ — see DISOBEDIENT

incomprehensible *adj* impossible to understand ⟨rocket science is *incomprehensible* to most people⟩
synonyms impenetrable, unfathomable, ungraspable, unintelligible
related words abstruse, enigmatic (*also* enigmatical), esoteric, indecipherable, inscrutable, recondite, unsearchable; cryptic, darkling, deep, mysterious, mystic, oblique, obscure, occult, uncanny; unanswerable, unknowable; baffling, bewildering, confounding, confusing, mystifying, perplexing, puzzling; inconceivable, unimaginable, unthinkable
near antonyms basic, elemental, elementary, essential, fundamental, rudimentary, underlying; easy, simple; coherent, connected, ordered, orderly, organized, systematic, systematized; clear, cogent, compelling, convincing, lucid, pellucid, perspicuous, plain, straightforward
antonyms fathomable, intelligible, understandable

incomprehension *n* a failure to understand correctly ⟨the anthropologist's apparent *incomprehension* of the ceremonial rites she describes in her book surprised reviewers⟩ — see MISUNDERSTANDING 1

inconceivable *adj* too extraordinary or improbable to believe ⟨the formerly *inconceivable* idea that humans could land on the moon⟩ — see INCREDIBLE

incongruity *n* someone or something with qualities or features that seem to conflict with one another ⟨she's an *incongruity*: an impeccably groomed woman who keeps a messy house⟩ — see CONTRADICTION 1

incongruous *adj* **1** not appropriate for a particular occasion or situation ⟨there's an *incongruous* modernism to the actor's performance in this period piece⟩ — see INAPPROPRIATE
2 not being in agreement or harmony ⟨*incongruous* theories about the origins of matter⟩ — see INCONSISTENT 1

inconsequence *n* the quality or state of being unimportant ⟨up to that point his life had been one largely marked by *inconsequence*⟩ — see INSIGNIFICANCE

inconsequent *adj* not using or following good reasoning ⟨presents an *inconsequent* argument for a major reversal in the nation's policy on narcotics⟩ — see ILLOGICAL

inconsequential *adj* **1** lacking importance ⟨that's an *inconsequential* problem compared to the other issues⟩ — see UNIMPORTANT
2 so small or unimportant as to warrant little or no attention ⟨an *inconsequential* error that does nothing to lessen the value of the report⟩ — see NEGLIGIBLE
3 not using or following good reasoning ⟨an *inconsequential* line of argument that did little to further the prosecution's case⟩ — see ILLOGICAL

inconsequentiality *n* the quality or state of being unimportant ⟨the *inconsequentiality* of a question before the council seemed to have no bearing upon the amount of time wasted discussing it⟩ — see INSIGNIFICANCE

inconsiderable *adj* **1** lacking importance ⟨the duties of the club's vice president are *inconsiderable* by any standard⟩ — see UNIMPORTANT
2 so small or unimportant as to warrant little or no attention ⟨an *inconsiderable* number of complaints about the car seat⟩ — see NEGLIGIBLE 1

inconsiderableness *n* the quality or state of being unimportant ⟨the *inconsiderableness* of his duties in the make-work job was downright embarrassing⟩ — see INSIGNIFICANCE

inconsiderate *adj* showing a lack of manners or consideration for others ⟨she was *inconsiderate* by nature, never bothering to hold the door for the next person⟩ — see IMPOLITE

inconsiderateness *n* rude behavior ⟨for sheer *inconsiderateness*, that lout has everyone else beat⟩ — see DISCOURTESY

inconsideration *n* rude behavior ⟨fortunately, the *inconsideration* and self-centeredness of toddlers is eventually outgrown⟩ — see DISCOURTESY

inconsistent *adj* **1** not being in agreement or harmony ⟨*inconsistent* theories make it difficult to settle on one explanation⟩
synonyms clashing, conflicting, disagreeing, discordant, discrepant, incompatible, incongruous, inconsonant, inharmonious, mutually exclusive, repugnant
related words irreconcilable; antagonistic, antipodal, antipodean, antithetical, contradictory, contrary, diametric (*or* diametrical), opposing, opposite
phrases at odds, at variance
near antonyms akin, like, similar
antonyms accordant, agreeing, compatible, concordant, conformable (to), congruent, congruous, consistent, consonant, correspondent (with *or* to), harmonious, nonconflicting
2 likely to change frequently, suddenly, or unexpectedly ⟨an *inconsistent* breeze was our only relief from the heat⟩ — see FICKLE 1

inconsolable *adj* feeling unhappiness ⟨he was *inconsolable* after the death of his wife⟩ — see SAD 1

inconsolably *adv* with feelings of bitterness or grief ⟨she cried *inconsolably* for weeks after her dog died⟩ — see HARD 2

inconsonant *adj* not being in agreement or harmony ⟨that is *inconsonant* with established judicial tradition⟩ — see INCONSISTENT 1

inconspicuous *adj* not readily seen or noticed ⟨left an *inconspicuous* scratch on the wall⟩ — see UNOBTRUSIVE

inconstancy *n* **1** lack of faithfulness especially to one's husband or wife ⟨a wife who was long inured to the chronic *inconstancy* of her husband⟩ — see INFIDELITY 1
2 the frequent and usually sudden passing from one condition to another ⟨the *inconstancy* of public opinion is such that today's hero may be tomorrow's punching bag⟩ — see FLUX 1

inconstant *adj* **1** likely to change frequently, suddenly, or unexpectedly ⟨our windjammer sailed wherever the *inconstant* winds took us⟩ — see FICKLE 1
2 not true in one's allegiance to someone or something ⟨an *inconstant* but always entertaining friend⟩ — see FAITHLESS

incontestable *adj* not capable of being challenged or proved wrong ⟨the *incontestable* statement that every contest has a winner and a loser⟩ — see IRREFUTABLE

incontestably *adv* without any question ⟨you are *incontestably* correct that tomorrow is another day⟩ — see INDEED 1

incontinently *adv* without delay ⟨upon reading the rave review, I *incontinently* called the restaurant for a reservation⟩ — see IMMEDIATELY

incontrollable *adj* given to resisting control or discipline by others ⟨police have vowed to crack down on the speeding, racing, and other driving misdeeds being committed by the town's *incontrollable* teenagers⟩ — see UNCONTROLLABLE

incontrovertible *adj* not capable of being challenged or proved wrong ⟨*incontrovertible* facts that left the jury with no choice but to convict⟩ — see IRREFUTABLE

incontrovertibly *adv* without any question ⟨an *incontrovertibly* accurate measurement of the height of the mountain⟩ — see INDEED 1

inconvenience *n* something that is a source of irritation ⟨the *inconvenience* of having to walk everywhere until the car is fixed⟩ — see ANNOYANCE 3

inconvenience *vb* to cause discomfort to or trouble for ⟨he *inconvenienced* his sister by moving into her tiny apartment⟩
synonyms discommode, disoblige, disturb, incommode, put out, trouble
related words burden, encumber, saddle, weigh; fetter, hamper, hamstring, handicap, hinder, hobble, hold back, hold up, impede, inhibit, interfere (with), manacle, obstruct, shackle, tie up, trammel; aggravate, anger, annoy, bother, bug, chafe, exasperate, gall, get, irk, nettle, peeve, pique, rile, vex; grate, inflame (*also* enflame), provoke; agitate, perturb, upset
near antonyms abet, aid, assist, help; ease, facilitate, smooth; appease, conciliate, disarm, mollify, pacify, placate; delight, gladden, gratify, please, satisfy; comfort, console, content
antonyms accommodate, favor, oblige

inconvenient *adj* **1** causing difficulty, discomfort, or annoyance ⟨the unexpected visitors showed up at an *inconvenient* time⟩
synonyms awkward, discommoding, disobliging, incommoding
related words bothersome, burdensome, onerous, troublesome; annoying, disturbing, exasperating, frustrating, galling, irksome, irritating, maddening, nagging, nettlesome, riling, vexatious, vexing
near antonyms acceptable, bearable, endurable, sufferable, tolerable; advantageous, desirable, good, helpful
antonyms convenient, ultraconvenient
2 hard or impossible to get to or get at ⟨for some reason, the homeowners placed the dishes in an *inconvenient* cabinet⟩ — see INACCESSIBLE

inconvincible *adj* sticking to an opinion, purpose, or course of action in spite of reason, arguments, or persuasion ⟨she's *inconvincible* on the issue as she is on everything else, so don't even bother⟩ — see OBSTINATE

incorporate *vb* **1** to make a part of a body or system ⟨astronomers had to *incorporate* the existence of Pluto into their scheme of the solar system after the dwarf planet was discovered⟩ — see EMBODY 1
2 to turn into a single mass or entity that is more or less the same throughout ⟨*incorporated* all the ingredients for the cheesecake mixture⟩ — see BLEND 1
3 to represent in visible form ⟨the one-of-a-kind house *incorporates* the architect's fundamental belief that a structure should be fully integrated into its setting⟩ — see EMBODY 2

incorporation *n* a visible representation of something abstract (as a quality) ⟨the workers stood nervously before the company boss, for he was to them the *incorporation* of all that controlled their fate⟩ — see EMBODIMENT

incorporeal *adj* not composed of matter ⟨ghosts are supposed to be *incorporeal*⟩ — see IMMATERIAL 1

incorrect *adj* **1** having an opinion that does not agree with truth or the facts ⟨you're *incorrect* about the date of the final exam—it's next Tuesday, not Wednesday⟩
synonyms mistaken, wrong
related words confused, misguided, misinformed, misled; erroneous, false, inaccurate, inexact, untrue; deceived, deluded, duped, tricked
phrases all wet, full of it
near antonyms informed; accurate, exact, precise, true
antonyms correct, right
2 not appropriate for a particular occasion or situation ⟨chose the *incorrect* military uniform for the treaty ceremony⟩ — see INAPPROPRIATE
3 not being in agreement with what is true ⟨an *incorrect* but not intentionally deceitful statement⟩ — see FALSE 1

incorrectly *adv* in a mistaken or inappropriate way ⟨you *incorrectly* identified the part of speech of one of the words in the sentence⟩ — see WRONGLY

incorrectness *n* **1** the quality or state of being unsuitable or unfitting ⟨the alleged *incorrectness* of the hat she wore to her daughter's wedding mattered only to gossips⟩ — see INAPPROPRIATENESS 1
2 the quality or state of not being socially proper ⟨the utter *incorrectness* of the use of such language in a church can scarcely be expressed⟩ — see IMPROPRIETY 1

incorrigible *adj* not capable of being cured or reformed ⟨an *incorrigible* criminal who should spend the rest of his life behind bars⟩ — see HOPELESS 1

increase *n* **1** something added (as by growth) ⟨shortly after he turned 12, he had a sudden height *increase*⟩
synonyms accretion, accrual, addendum, addition, augmentation, boost, expansion, gain, increment, more, plus, proliferation, raise, rise, step-up, supplement, uptick
related words accumulation, assemblage, collection, gathering; complement; accession, appendix, continuation, extension, uptrend, upturn; jump, run-up, spike
near antonyms deduction, subtraction
antonyms abatement, decline, decrease, decrement, depletion, diminishment, diminution, drop-off, fall, falloff, lessening, loss, lowering, reduction, shrinkage, step-down
2 the act or process of becoming greater in number ⟨the *increase* in the number of students enrolled at the school was very gradual⟩ — see MULTIPLICATION

increase *vb* **1** to make greater in size, amount, or number ⟨we have to *increase* the number of season-ticket holders if the local sports franchise is to survive⟩
synonyms accelerate, add (to), aggrandize, amplify, augment, boost, build up, compound, enlarge, escalate, expand, extend, hype, multiply, pump up, raise, swell, stoke, supersize, up
related words boom, jump, skyrocket, spike; bump (up), ratchet (up) *also* rachet (up); blow up, dilate, distend, inflate; draw out, elongate, flesh (out), lengthen, prolong, protract, stretch; develop, enhance, heighten, intensify, magnify; complement, supplement; beef (up), reinforce (*also* reenforce), strengthen; maximize; accumulate, amass, collect; follow up, parlay
near antonyms abbreviate, abridge, curtail, shorten; compress, condense, constrict, contract; cut back, retrench
antonyms abate, decrease, de-escalate, diminish, downsize, dwindle, lessen, lower, minify, reduce, subtract (from)
2 to become greater in extent, volume, amount, or number ⟨the number of Internet users *increased* exponentially during the 1990s⟩
synonyms accelerate, accumulate, appreciate, balloon, boom, build up, burgeon (*also* bourgeon), climb, enlarge, escalate, expand, gain, mount, multiply, mushroom, proliferate, rise, roll up, snowball, spread, swell, wax
related words jump, rocket, skyrocket, surge; heighten, intensify, redouble; blow up, bulk, distend, inflate, puff (up); crescendo, crest, peak

antonyms contract, decrease, diminish, dwindle, lessen, recede, wane

increased *adj* being at a higher level than average ⟨an *increased* concentration of sugar in the bloodstream⟩ — see HIGH 2

incredible *adj* too extraordinary or improbable to believe ⟨tried to explain her weeklong disappearance with an *incredible* tale of abduction by a total stranger⟩
synonyms fantastic (*also* fantastical), implausible, inconceivable, incredulous, unbelievable, uncompelling, unconceivable, unconvincing, unimaginable, unthinkable
related words debatable, disputable, dodgy [*chiefly British*], doubtable, doubtful, dubious, dubitable, farfetched, fishy, flimsy, questionable, shaky, suspect, suspicious, unlikely, unreasonable; hopeless, impossible; absurd, comical, farcical, laughable, ludicrous, outlandish, preposterous, ridiculous, risible, silly; indefensible, insupportable, untenable
phrases full of it
near antonyms likely, possible, probable; reasonable; certain, incontestable, indisputable, indubitable, questionless, sure, undeniable, undoubted, unquestionable
antonyms believable, cogitable, conceivable, convincing, credible, creditable, imaginable, plausible, supposable, thinkable

incredibly *adv* to a great degree ⟨the entrance exam to the elite prep school was *incredibly* difficult⟩ — see VERY 1

incredulity *n* refusal to accept something as true ⟨the teacher's *incredulity* about the claims in the essay proved to be well-founded⟩ — see DISBELIEF

incredulous *adj* **1** inclined to doubt or question claims ⟨*incredulous* by nature, I'm of course very suspicious of anyone who claims to be able to communicate with the dead⟩ — see SKEPTICAL 1
2 too extraordinary or improbable to believe ⟨an *incredulous* account of alien abduction that the tabloids had a field day with⟩ — see INCREDIBLE

increment *n* something added (as by growth) ⟨added another big *increment* to the sales total this quarter⟩ — see INCREASE 1

incremental *adj* **1** proceeding or changing by steps or degrees ⟨the *incremental* evolution of the collection from a specialized gallery into a comprehensive art museum⟩ — see GRADUAL
2 produced by a series of additions of identical or similar things ⟨the *incremental* total for my collection of baseball cards⟩ — see CUMULATIVE

incriminate *vb* to make a claim of wrongdoing against ⟨in exchange for a reduced sentence, the thief agreed to *incriminate* his accomplice⟩ — see ACCUSE

incubate *vb* **1** to cover and warm eggs as the young inside develop ⟨the hen *incubated* her eggs for two weeks⟩ — see SET 1
2 to help the growth or development of ⟨hopefully, these youthful visits to the museum will *incubate* an enduring love of art⟩ — see FOSTER 1

inculcate *vb* **1** to cause (as a person) to become filled or saturated with a certain quality or principle ⟨dedicated teachers *inculcating* young minds with a love of learning⟩ — see INFUSE
2 to set permanently in the consciousness or mind-set ⟨a malcontent who *inculcated* in his offspring an abiding distrust of all civil authority⟩ — see IMPLANT 1

inculpable *adj* free from guilt or blame ⟨you may not have started the ugly rumor, but you helped to spread it, so you're hardly *inculpable*⟩ — see INNOCENT 2

incult *adj* lacking in refinement or good taste ⟨our *incult* ancestors, who dwelt in rude huts⟩ — see COARSE 2

incumbency *n* something one must do because of prior agreement ⟨few *incumbencies* of her office are as distasteful to the college president as fund-raising, of which there seems to be no end⟩ — see OBLIGATION 1

incumbent *adj* forcing one's compliance or participation by or as if by law ⟨it is *incumbent* upon you to attend every staff meeting⟩ — see MANDATORY

incurable *adj* not capable of being cured or reformed ⟨an *incurable* flirt at school dances⟩ — see HOPELESS 1

incuriosity *n* lack of interest or concern ⟨a teacher who is trying to overcome her students' entrenched *incuriosity* about world events⟩ — see INDIFFERENCE

incurious *adj* having or showing a lack of interest or concern ⟨a quick *incurious* glance at the pile of junk mail⟩ — see INDIFFERENT 1

incuriousness *n* lack of interest or concern ⟨her husband's utter *incuriousness* about her work was especially galling to her⟩ — see INDIFFERENCE

incursion *n* a sudden attack on and entrance into hostile territory ⟨there were *incursions* from the border every summer⟩ — see RAID 1

indebted *adj* being under obligation for a favor or gift ⟨thereafter forever felt *indebted* to the producer for giving her her lucky break⟩ — see BEHOLDEN

indebtedness *n* something (as money) which is owed ⟨his total *indebtedness* exceeded a year's income⟩ — see DEBT 1

indecency *n* **1** the quality or state of being obscene ⟨parents complained about the *indecency* of the song's lyrics⟩ — see OBSCENITY 1
2 the quality or state of not being socially proper ⟨that a remark of such indisputable *indecency* was uttered at a meeting of the school board made everyone gasp⟩ — see IMPROPRIETY 1

indecent *adj* depicting or referring to sexual matters in a way that is unacceptable in polite society ⟨paintings of nude figures are artistic, not *indecent*⟩ — see OBSCENE 1

indecipherable *adj* incapable of being read or deciphered ⟨after so many years the paper label in the drawer of the antique desk is *indecipherable*⟩ — see ILLEGIBLE

indecision *n* a state or an instance of temporary inaction about the right course of action ⟨her *indecision* about where to go for dinner, while everyone was getting hungrier by the minute, was frustrating⟩ — see HESITATION

indecorous *adj* not appropriate for a particular occasion or situation ⟨an *indecorous* joke for a solemn moment in the marriage ceremony⟩ — see INAPPROPRIATE

indecorousness *n* the quality or state of not being socially proper ⟨for sheer *indecorousness* it would be hard to beat the telling of bawdy jokes at a child's birthday party⟩ — see IMPROPRIETY 1

indecorum *n* the quality or state of not being socially proper ⟨the thoughtless *indecorum* of wearing a floor-length white dress as a guest at a wedding⟩ — see IMPROPRIETY 1

indeed *interj* how surprising, doubtful, or unbelievable ⟨*indeed*, you really did shave all your hair off!⟩ — see NO

indeed *adv* **1** without any question ⟨I know that you can *indeed* do better than that⟩
synonyms all right, alright, assuredly, certainly, clearly, definitely, doubtless, easily, forsooth, hands down, inarguably, incontestably, incontrovertibly, indisputably, plainly, really, so, sure, surely, truly, unarguably, undeniably, undoubtedly, unquestionably
related words conceivably, likely, perhaps, possibly, probably; obviously, unmistakably
phrases by all means, by all odds, damn well, for certain, for sure
2 not merely this but also ⟨that is not merely a reason, but is *indeed* the entire point⟩ — see EVEN 1

3 to tell the truth ⟨that woman can be difficult—*indeed*, she can be insufferable⟩ — see ACTUALLY 1

indefatigable *adj* showing no signs of weariness even after long hard effort ⟨an *indefatigable* laborer who can work from sunrise to sunset⟩ — see TIRELESS

indefectible *adj* being entirely without fault or flaw ⟨the *indefectible* logic of the polemist's arguments⟩ — see PERFECT 1

indefensible *adj* too bad to be excused or justified ⟨the city's lack of preparedness for a major natural disaster was utterly *indefensible*⟩ — see INEXCUSABLE

indefinable *adj* beyond the power to describe ⟨some *indefinable* quality makes that movie star very appealing⟩ — see INDESCRIBABLE

indefinite *adj* **1** being or seeming to be without limits ⟨the *indefinite* vastness of the frozen tundra⟩ — see INFINITE

2 not expressed in precise terms ⟨an *indefinite* longing for something new and exciting in her life⟩ — see VAGUE 1

3 not seen or understood clearly ⟨through the dense fog we could just barely discern the *indefinite* form of another boat⟩ — see FAINT 1

indelible *adj* not easily forgotten ⟨winning the state basketball championship was our team's most *indelible* experience⟩ — see UNFORGETTABLE

indelibly *adv* for all time ⟨the advertiser hopes that the slogan will be *indelibly* imprinted on consumers' memories⟩ — see EVER 1

indelicacy *n* the quality or state of lacking refinement or good taste ⟨the *indelicacy* of their dinner conversation made the other guests wince in embarrassment⟩ — see VULGARITY 1

indelicate *adj* showing poor judgment especially in personal relationships or social situations ⟨the company considered his *indelicate* handling of such a personal matter to be unprofessional⟩ — see INDISCREET

indelicateness *n* **1** the quality or state of lacking refinement or good taste ⟨the well-known *indelicateness* of the comedian's humor made him a poor choice for master of ceremonies⟩ — see VULGARITY 1

2 the quality or state of not being socially proper ⟨the *indelicateness* of the topic makes it a poor choice for dinner conversation⟩ — see IMPROPRIETY 1

indemnification *n* payment to another for a loss or injury ⟨that insurance company is known to be slow when processing claims for *indemnification*⟩ — see COMPENSATION 1

indemnify *vb* to provide (someone) with a just payment for loss or injury ⟨the company generously *indemnifies* workers who are injured on the job⟩ — see COMPENSATE 1

indemnity *n* payment to another for a loss or injury ⟨the widow now lives on a pension and an *indemnity* from her late husband's company⟩ — see COMPENSATION 1

indent *n* a V-shaped cut usually on an edge or a surface ⟨with the heel of his boot he made a sizable *indent* in the dirt as a temporary marker⟩ — see NOTCH 1

indentation *n* **1** a sunken area forming a separate space ⟨the previous occupant's furniture had left some fairly noticeable *indentations* in the carpet⟩ — see HOLE 2

2 a V-shaped cut usually on an edge or a surface ⟨deep *indentations* along the edge of the leaf⟩ — see NOTCH 1

indented *adj* curved inward ⟨that *indented* area of the mountainside is prone to avalanches⟩ — see HOLLOW

indenture *n* **1** a sunken area forming a separate space ⟨the dropped hammer left an *indenture* in the floor⟩ — see HOLE 2

2 a V-shaped cut usually on an edge or a surface ⟨made a small *indenture* to mark the spot where the plank was to be sawed⟩ — see NOTCH 1

independence *n* **1** the ability to care for one's self ⟨children are supposed to achieve some measure of *independence* by the time they are 18—so it's time for that 30-year-old to move out!⟩ — see SELF-SUFFICIENCY

2 the state of being free from the control or power of another ⟨college freshmen often revel in their newfound *independence*⟩ — see FREEDOM 1

independency *n* the state of being free from the control or power of another ⟨adolescence is typically an awkward time for young people, as they are making the difficult transition from the dependency of childhood to the *independency* of adulthood⟩ — see FREEDOM 1

independent *adj* **1** able to take care of oneself or itself without outside help ⟨an *independent* young man who moved out of his parents' house while still a college student⟩ — see SELF-SUFFICIENT

2 not being under the rule or control of another ⟨finally they are an *independent* people, after centuries of domination by their more powerful neighbors⟩ — see FREE 1

independently *adv* without aid or support ⟨*independently* came to the same conclusion⟩ — see ALONE 1

in–depth *adj* covering everything or all important points ⟨an *in-depth* report on the issue of violence in popular entertainment⟩ — see ENCYCLOPEDIC

indescribable *adj* beyond the power to describe ⟨the *indescribable* immensity of Mount Everest⟩
synonyms incommunicable, indefinable, ineffable, inenarrable, inexpressible, nameless, uncommunicable, unspeakable, unutterable
related words unsayable; inconceivable, incredible, unbelievable, unimaginable, unthinkable; inexplicable, unexplainable; characterless, featureless, nondescript
near antonyms conceivable, imaginable, thinkable
antonyms communicable, definable, expressible, speakable

indestructible *adj* impossible to destroy ⟨diamonds are widely considered to be *indestructible* because they are one of the hardest known substances⟩
synonyms imperishable, inextinguishable
related words incorruptible; deathless, immortal, perpetual, undying; indelible, indissoluble, ineffaceable, ineradicable, inexpungible; durable, enduring, everlasting, lasting, permanent, unbreakable; strong, sturdy, tough
near antonyms mortal; impermanent, transient, transitory; breakable, delicate, flimsy, fragile, frail
antonyms destructible, extinguishable, perishable

index *n* an arrow-shaped piece on a dial or scale for registering information ⟨the *index* on the thermometer dropped below zero⟩ — see POINTER 1

index *vb* to put (someone or something) on a list ⟨*indexed* all the books in the library by category⟩ — see [1]LIST 2

Indian sign *n, chiefly British* something that brings bad luck ⟨the *Indian sign* has apparently been put on that rugby team, which has lost 10 straight games⟩ — see JINX

indicate *vb* **1** to serve as a sign or symptom of ⟨his attitude seems to *indicate* that he has little interest in the project⟩
synonyms bespeak, betoken, denote, mean, point (to), signify, tell (of)
related words bode, foreshow, foretell, presage

2 to convey an idea indirectly ⟨her expression *indicated* that she was uncomfortably cold, but she was too polite to say so⟩ — see HINT

indication *n* a slight or indirect pointing to something (as a solution or explanation) ⟨there are *indications* that a medical breakthrough in the treatment of the disease is imminent⟩ — see HINT 1

indicative *adj* indicating something ⟨a wide-eyed look that is *indicative* of his constant curiosity⟩
synonyms denotative, denoting, reflective, significant, signifying, telltale
related words alluding, allusive, referring; characteristic, symptomatic; demonstrative, exhibiting, expressive; symbolic (*also* symbolical); connoting, hinting, implying, insinuating, suggestive

indicator *n* an arrow-shaped piece on a dial or scale for registering information ⟨you should refill when the *indicator* on the gas gauge shows that there's only a quarter of a tank left⟩ — see POINTER 1

indict *vb* to make a claim of wrongdoing against ⟨the grand jury could *indict* the mayor for fraud and embezzlement⟩ — see ACCUSE

indictment *n* a formal claim of criminal wrongdoing against a person ⟨that prosecutor gets an *indictment* for 90% of his cases⟩ — see CHARGE 1

indifference *n* lack of interest or concern ⟨an alarming *indifference* toward the well-being of his own children⟩
synonyms apathy, casualness, complacence, disinterestedness, disregard, incuriosity, incuriousness, insouciance, nonchalance, torpor, unconcern
related words halfheartedness, lukewarmness, tepidity, tepidness; carelessness, heedlessness, recklessness, unawareness; lethargy, listlessness; aloofness, coldness, cool, detachment, dispassion; callosity, callousness, hard-heartedness, hardness, insensitivity; bloodlessness, impassiveness, impassivity, phlegm, stoicism, stolidity
near antonyms attention, attentiveness, awareness, conscientiousness, curiosity, heedfulness, keenness; sensitivity, warmheartedness; bias, partiality, prejudice; ardor, desire, fervency, passion, vehemence, warmth, zeal
antonyms concern, interest, regard

indifferent *adj* **1** having or showing a lack of interest or concern ⟨*indifferent* about the result of the football game⟩
synonyms apathetic, casual, complacent, disinterested, incurious, insensible, insouciant, nonchalant, perfunctory, pococurante, unconcerned, uncurious, uninterested
related words halfhearted, lukewarm, tepid; aloof, cold, numb, remote, unemotional; callous, hardhearted, insensitive, unfeeling; calm, cool, detached, dispassionate; careless, heedless, mindless; impassive, impervious, phlegmatic, stoic (*or* stoical), stolid; lethargic, listless; unimpressed
near antonyms attentive, aware, conscientious, heedful, mindful; caring, sensitive, warmhearted; ardent, fervent, keen, passionate, warm, zealous
antonyms concerned, interested
2 of average to below average quality ⟨an *indifferent* but drinkable cup of coffee⟩ — see MEDIOCRE 1
3 marked by justice, honesty, and freedom from bias ⟨they believed their art teacher could offer an *indifferent* judgment on their works' merits⟩ — see FAIR 2

indigence *n* the state of lacking sufficient money or material possessions ⟨there are various state and federal programs to help relieve *indigence*⟩ — see POVERTY 1

indigene *also* **indigen** *n* a member of the first race to inhabit a region ⟨the *indigenes* had not merely adapted to the harsh climate, but had in fact prospered in it⟩ — see ABORIGINE

indigenous *adj* **1** belonging to a particular place by birth or origin ⟨the culture of the *indigenous* people of that country⟩ — see NATIVE 1
2 being a part of the innermost nature of a person or thing ⟨the drive to create that is *indigenous* to humanity⟩ — see INHERENT

indigent *adj* lacking money or material possessions ⟨*indigent* people who require some outside assistance⟩ — see POOR 1

indignant *adj* feeling or showing anger ⟨the poker player became *indignant* at the accusation of cheating⟩ — see ANGRY

indignation *n* an intense emotional state of displeasure with someone or something ⟨her *indignation* at the offensive television show led her to start a grassroots campaign for its cancellation⟩ — see ANGER

indignity *n* an act or expression showing scorn and usually intended to hurt another's feelings ⟨minor *indignities* such as intentionally mispronouncing a person's name⟩ — see INSULT

indirect *adj* not straightforward or direct ⟨the cab driver took a very *indirect* route to the hotel⟩ ⟨a long-winded, *indirect* answer to a very simple question⟩
synonyms circuitous, circular, roundabout
related words crooked, curvy, serpentine, sinuous, tortuous, twisting, winding; meandering, rambling, wandering; circumlocutory, long-winded, prolix, verbose; deceitful, deceptive, devious, dishonest, duplicitous, insidious, misleading, sneaky, underhand, underhanded; calculating, crafty, cunning, subtle, tricky
near antonyms candid, forthright, frank, honest, open, plain, unconcealed, undisguised
antonyms direct, straight, straightforward

indiscreet *adj* showing poor judgment especially in personal relationships or social situations ⟨telling a friend's secrets is *indiscreet*, and unkind as well⟩
synonyms brash, graceless, ill-advised, imprudent, inadvisable, indelicate, injudicious, tactless, undiplomatic, unwise
related words dumb, idiotic (*also* idiotical), moronic, stupid; careless, heedless, inconsiderate, mindless, thoughtless; ill-mannered, improper, inappropriate, indecorous, unbecoming, uncivil, unseemly; foolish, harebrained, nonsensical, preposterous, senseless, silly
near antonyms intelligent, logical, rational, sensible, smart, sound; appropriate, becoming, civil, decorous, proper, seemly; sage, sane, sapient
antonyms advisable, discreet, judicious, prudent, tactful, wise

indiscretion *n* a socially improper or unsuitable act or remark ⟨a single *indiscretion* can get someone kicked out of that exclusive club⟩ — see IMPROPRIETY 2

indiscriminate *adj* consisting of many things of different sorts ⟨donated an *indiscriminate* jumble of toys, books, and old clothes to the rummage sale⟩ — see MISCELLANEOUS

indispensable *adj* impossible to do without ⟨fully aware that he was an *indispensable* assistant, he decided that it was high time that he be paid what he was worth⟩ — see ESSENTIAL 1

indisposed *adj* **1** slow to begin or proceed with a course of action because of doubts or uncertainty ⟨one person in our reading group is very *indisposed* to choosing a racy book⟩ — see HESITANT
2 temporarily suffering from a disorder of the body ⟨stays home from work whenever he feels the least *indisposed*⟩ — see SICK 1

indisposition *n* the condition of not being in good health ⟨a brief *indisposition* made her miss the party⟩ — see SICKNESS 1

indisputable *adj* not capable of being challenged or proved wrong ⟨an *indisputable* fact that is not subject to interpretation according to one's political beliefs⟩ — see IRREFUTABLE

indisputably *adv* without any question ⟨you are *indisputably* correct in your calculations⟩ — see INDEED 1

indistinct *adj* not seen or understood clearly ⟨managed to discern a blurry, *indistinct* shadow through the downpour⟩ — see FAINT 1

indistinctive *adj* lacking in distinctive features or qualities ⟨a line of *indistinctive* sportswear that does not justify its premium price point⟩ — see NONDESCRIPT

indistinguishable *adj* **1** not perceptible by a sense or by the mind ⟨*indistinguishable* differences that can be measured only electronically⟩ — see IMPERCEPTIBLE
2 not seen or understood clearly ⟨*indistinguishable* shapes in the fog⟩ — see FAINT 1
3 resembling another in every respect ⟨a synthetic fabric that supposedly is *indistinguishable* from real silk⟩ — see SAME 1

individual *n* **1** a member of the human race ⟨every *individual* has value⟩ — see HUMAN
2 one that has a real and independent existence ⟨our general concept of what constitutes a chair is based on our experience with many *individuals* that were called chairs⟩ — see ENTITY

individual *adj* **1** of, relating to, or belonging to a single person ⟨everyone has his or her own *individual* opinion about the subject, but you will have to work together⟩
synonyms idiomatic, individualized, particular, patented, peculiar, personal, personalized, private, privy, separate, singular, subjective, unique
related words characteristic, distinctive, intimate; identifying, idiosyncratic; especial, express, special, specific; independent, nonconformist, self-directed, self-sufficient; custom, customized, specialized
near antonyms broad, prevailing, prevalent, widespread; common, normal, regular, typical
antonyms general, generic, popular, public, shared, universal
2 not the same or shared ⟨guest rooms at the inn have *individual* bathrooms⟩ — see SEPARATE 1
3 serving to identify as belonging to an individual or group ⟨he's got a highly *individual* laugh that I would know anywhere⟩ — see CHARACTERISTIC 1

individualism *n* **1** an odd or peculiar habit ⟨the novelist gives each character an assortment of *individualisms* that sets them apart⟩ — see IDIOSYNCRASY
2 the set of qualities that make a person different from other people ⟨his *individualism* and epic vision set him well apart from other architects of his generation⟩ — see INDIVIDUALITY 1

individualist *n* a person who does not conform to generally accepted standards or customs ⟨an *individualist* who steadfastly refuses to do what everyone else is doing⟩ — see NONCONFORMIST 1

individuality *n* **1** the set of qualities that make a person different from other people ⟨her *individuality* showed through in everything she did⟩
synonyms character, identity, individualism, personality, selfhood, self-identity
related words distinctiveness, idiosyncrasy, oneness, peculiarity, separateness, singleness, singularity, uniqueness; disposition, humor, nature, temper, temperament; independence
near antonyms conformity, conventionality
2 one that has a real and independent existence ⟨according to immanentism, God is not so much an *individuality* as an abstract mind or spirit that pervades the world⟩ — see ENTITY

individualized *adj* of, relating to, or belonging to a single person ⟨an *individualized* plan of study for the gifted student in the class⟩ — see INDIVIDUAL 1

indoctrinate *vb* to cause to acquire knowledge or skill in some field ⟨*indoctrinated* children in proper safety procedures⟩ — see TEACH

indolence *n* an inclination not to do work or engage in activities ⟨a general feeling of *indolence* usually overtakes them during summer vacation⟩ — see LAZINESS

indolent *adj* not easily aroused to action or work ⟨an *indolent* boy who had to be forced to help out with the chores⟩ — see LAZY 1

indomitable *adj* incapable of being defeated, overcome, or subdued ⟨an *indomitable* spirit was needed to endure the rigors of pioneer life⟩ — see INVINCIBLE

indubitable *adj* not capable of being challenged or proved wrong ⟨the *indubitable* fact that there are no more woolly mammoths or saber-toothed tigers around⟩ — see IRREFUTABLE

induce *vb* **1** to be the cause of (a situation, action, or state of mind) ⟨the medication *induced* labor⟩ — see EFFECT
2 to cause (someone) to agree with a belief or course of action by using arguments or earnest requests ⟨finally *induced* the eyewitness to the gangland slaying to cooperate with the police⟩ — see PERSUADE

inducement *n* the act of reasoning or pleading with someone to accept a belief or course of action ⟨gave up smoking only after a prolonged *inducement* by all the other family members⟩ — see PERSUASION 1

inducing *n* the act of reasoning or pleading with someone to accept a belief or course of action ⟨after the intense *inducing* of his friends, he went on a diet and joined a health club⟩ — see PERSUASION 1

induct *vb* to put into an office or welcome into an organization with special ceremonies ⟨*inducted* the pitcher into the Baseball Hall of Fame⟩ — see INSTALL 1

inductee *n* a person forced or required to enroll in military service ⟨a new crop of *inductees* produced by the draft⟩ — see CONSCRIPT

induction *n* **1** the process or an instance of being formally placed in an office or organization ⟨the formal *induction* will be tomorrow, but the college president has already started work⟩ — see INSTALLATION 1
2 an opinion arrived at through a process of reasoning ⟨the urbanologist's controversial *induction* that a thriving bohemian community is vital to a city's economic health⟩ — see CONCLUSION 1

indulge *vb* **1** to give in to (a desire) ⟨the grandparents *indulged* the child's wishes to an extent that they never did with their own children⟩
synonyms cater (to), gratify, humor
related words bask, luxuriate, revel, wallow; coddle, mollycoddle, pamper, spoil; delight, please, pleasure; sate, satiate, satisfy
near antonyms bridle, check, constrain, curb, inhibit, restrain, stifle
2 to give (oneself) over to something especially unrestrainedly ⟨conventioneers who were obviously eager to *indulge* themselves in all of the vices that Las Vegas might offer⟩ — see ABANDON 1
3 to treat with great or excessive care ⟨you *indulge* those grandkids in ways you never did with your own kids⟩ — see BABY

indulgence *n* **1** an act of kind assistance ⟨as an only child, she was used to getting every kind of *indulgence* from her doting parents⟩ — see FAVOR 1
2 something adding to pleasure or comfort but not absolutely necessary ⟨bubble baths were her one *indulgence*⟩ — see LUXURY 1

indulgent *adj* **1** tolerant and kind in the judgment of and expectations for others ⟨she was perhaps a bit too *indulgent* with her children, who always seemed to get away with everything⟩
synonyms charitable, clement, easy, soft
related words accommodating, acquiescent, amenable, obliging; easygoing, laid-back, undemanding
near antonyms demanding; uncharitable, unforgiving; inflexible, intolerant, unbending, uncompromising, unyielding
antonyms hard, harsh, severe, stern, strict

2 given to or marked by excessive gratification of one's desires ⟨inherited riches helped fuel her *indulgent* lifestyle⟩ — see HEDONISTIC
3 willing to do a favor ⟨an *indulgent* clerk who let me try on practically every size-seven shoe the store had⟩ — see ACCOMMODATING

indurate *adj* having or showing a lack of sympathy or tender feelings ⟨an *indurate* heart that admits no love or mercy⟩ — see HARD 1

indurate *vb* **1** to become physically firm or solid ⟨clay that had been *indurated* by long exposure to the summer sun⟩ — see HARDEN 1
2 to make able to withstand physical hardship, strain, or exposure ⟨such a brutal upbringing could only callous his soul and *indurate* his heart to the suffering of others⟩ — see HARDEN 2

industrious *adj* involved in often constant activity ⟨an *industrious* worker who never seems to sleep⟩ — see BUSY 1

industriously *adv* **1** with great effort or determination ⟨worked *industriously* to complete the project ahead of schedule⟩ — see HARD 1
2 in a manner involving great or constant activity ⟨she's been *industriously* putting together the plans for the charity ball⟩ — see BUSILY

industriousness *n* attentive and persistent effort ⟨she did twice as much work as anyone else through sheer *industriousness*⟩ — see DILIGENCE

industry *n* attentive and persistent effort ⟨he isn't the smartest kid in class, but he gets the best grades by determined *industry*⟩ — see DILIGENCE

inebriant *n* a distilled beverage that can make a person drunk ⟨stocking up on her in-laws' favorite *inebriants* for the holidays⟩ — see ALCOHOL

inebriate *adj* being under the influence of alcohol ⟨those *inebriate* sports fans who yell and scream throughout the game⟩ — see DRUNK

inebriate *n* a person who makes a habit of getting drunk ⟨having performed in countless bars and clubs, the stand-up comedian was used to being heckled by *inebriates* in the back of the house⟩ — see DRUNK 1

inebriated *adj* being under the influence of alcohol ⟨after a night spent partying, the fraternity brothers were all severely *inebriated*⟩ — see DRUNK

inebriation *n* the condition of being drunk ⟨students who seem to think uninhibited *inebriation* is an essential part of the college experience⟩ — see INTOXICATION 1

inebriety *n* the condition of being drunk ⟨there were times during her bouts of *inebriety* when she actually thought that her boyfriend's jokes were funny⟩ — see INTOXICATION 1

ineffable *adj* beyond the power to describe ⟨an *ineffable* beauty descends upon the canyon as the sun begins to set⟩ — see INDESCRIBABLE

ineffective *adj* **1** not producing the desired result ⟨an *ineffective* effort to reduce unemployment that only spurred inflation⟩
synonyms counterproductive, feckless, hamstrung, ineffectual, inefficacious, inefficient, inexpedient
related words abortive, bootless, fruitless, futile, nonproductive, pointless, profitless, unavailing, unproductive, unprofitable, unsuccessful, useless, worthless
near antonyms availing, beneficial, helpful, productive, profitable, successful, useful, worthwhile
antonyms effective, effectual, efficacious, efficient, expedient, operant, ultraefficient
2 producing no results ⟨an *ineffective* medication that will be denied FDA approval⟩ — see FUTILE 1

ineffectual *adj* **1** not producing the desired result ⟨an *ineffectual* effort to find the trail again did at least lead them to another stunning view of the canyon⟩ — see INEFFECTIVE 1
2 producing no results ⟨another *ineffectual* plan to lose weight without dieting or exercising⟩ — see FUTILE 1

inefficacious *adj* **1** not producing the desired result ⟨his efforts to restore the neglected houseplant back to health were belated and sadly *inefficacious*⟩ — see INEFFECTIVE 1
2 producing no results ⟨an *inefficacious* medication for a rare form of tuberculosis⟩ — see FUTILE 1

inefficient *adj* not producing the desired result ⟨*inefficient* measures to solve the problem of teenage smoking⟩ — see INEFFECTIVE 1

inelegant *adj* **1** lacking social grace and assurance ⟨*inelegant* teens still learning how to act at formal events⟩ — see AWKWARD 1
2 marked by an obvious lack of style or good taste ⟨*inelegant* furniture that looked like it belonged in a budget motel⟩ — see [1]TACKY 1

ineluctability *n* the quality or state of being impossible to avoid or evade ⟨the continuing debate over the *ineluctability* of global warming⟩ — see INEVITABILITY

ineluctable *adj* impossible to avoid or evade ⟨the *ineluctable* approach of winter had many worried about the cost of heating their homes⟩ — see INEVITABLE

ineluctably *adv* because of necessity ⟨writing poetry is an *ineluctably* solitary activity⟩ — see NEEDS

ineludible *adj* impossible to avoid or evade ⟨police officers have an *ineludible* responsibility to protect the public, and never more so than in times of natural disaster⟩ — see INEVITABLE

inenarrable *adj* beyond the power to describe ⟨the filmmaker's decision to depict the essentially *inenarrable* phenomenon called love by means of a series of lush metaphors⟩ — see INDESCRIBABLE

inept *adj* **1** lacking qualities (as knowledge, skill, or ability) required to do a job ⟨a well-meaning but *inept* secretary who can't seem to keep the boss's appointments straight⟩ — see INCOMPETENT
2 not appropriate for a particular occasion or situation ⟨an *inept* comparison between nursing-home residents and day-care children that many found offensive⟩ — see INAPPROPRIATE
3 showing or marked by a lack of skill and tact (as in dealing with a situation) ⟨an *inept* effort to become friends with their future son-in-law⟩ — see AWKWARD 2
4 showing or marked by a lack of good sense or judgment ⟨she offers one *inept* suggestion after another for saving the parish church⟩ — see FOOLISH 1

ineptitude *n* the lack of sufficient ability, power, or means ⟨the nurse's *ineptitude* made it clear that she would be happier in a different line of work⟩ — see INABILITY

inequity *n* **1** the state of being unfair or unjust ⟨the *inequity* of the punishment led many people to believe that the defendant was being punished for his political beliefs⟩ — see INJUSTICE 1
2 unfair or inadequate treatment of someone or something or an instance of this ⟨the unavoidable *inequities* of any system for distributing benefits⟩ — see DISSERVICE

inert *adj* **1** not being in a state of use, activity, or employment ⟨the *inert*, abandoned factories that are scattered all over that dying city⟩ — see INACTIVE 2
2 slow to move or act ⟨a sleepy, *inert* reptile that is no threat to people when left alone⟩ — see INACTIVE 1

inertia *n* an inclination not to do work or engage in activities ⟨the *inertia* that grips so many of the club's members is the reason why nothing ever gets done⟩ — see LAZINESS

inertness *n* lack of action or activity ⟨the noticeable *inertness* of the campus on weekends, when most of the students go home⟩ — see INACTION

inescapable *adj* impossible to avoid or evade ⟨some people believe that your fate is determined at birth and thus *inescapable*⟩ — see INEVITABLE

inescapably *adv* because of necessity ⟨*inescapably*, we must take some drastic measures to avoid a catastrophe⟩ — see NEEDS

inessential *adj* not needed by the circumstances or to accomplish an end ⟨he writes very spare prose, with nary an *inessential* word to be found⟩ — see UNNECESSARY

inestimable *adj* having a value beyond any ability to appraise or adequately appreciate ⟨Einstein's *inestimable* contributions to science⟩ — see PRICELESS 1

inevitability *n* the quality or state of being impossible to avoid or evade ⟨a hockey team that has refused to accept the *inevitability* of defeat⟩

synonyms certainty, ineluctability, inevitableness

related words likelihood, probability; inexorability, inexorableness, relentlessness

near antonyms preventability; improbability, unlikelihood, unlikeliness; doubtfulness, dubiousness

antonyms uncertainty

inevitable *adj* impossible to avoid or evade ⟨getting wet is *inevitable* if you are going to try to give your dog a bath⟩

synonyms certain, ineluctable, ineludible, inescapable, necessary, sure, unavoidable, unescapable

related words decided, definite, settled; likely, possible, probable; destined, fated, foreordained, predestined, predetermined, preordained; inexorable, relentless, unremitting, unstoppable

phrases in the bag, in the cards (*also* on the cards)

near antonyms preventable (*also* preventible); doubtful, dubious, questionable, shaky, unclear; undecided, unsettled; undependable, unreliable; improbable, unlikely

antonyms avoidable, evadable, uncertain, unsure

inevitableness *n* the quality or state of being impossible to avoid or evade ⟨given the age of her car, she has resigned herself to the *inevitableness* of its demise in the not-too-distant future⟩ — see INEVITABILITY

inevitably *adv* because of necessity ⟨we must *inevitably* make some sacrifices if we are going to save money⟩ — see NEEDS

inexact *adj* **1** not precisely correct ⟨a thousand is an *inexact* figure for the number of islands in the St. Lawrence River⟩

synonyms approximate, approximative, ballpark, imprecise, inaccurate, loose, squishy

related words erroneous, false, incorrect, off, wrong; general, indefinable, indefinite, indeterminate, indistinct, mushy, undefined, undetermined, unsettled, vague; faulty, flawed, mistaken; specious; distorted, fallacious, misleading; doubtful, dubious, questionable, uncertain; inconclusive, indecisive; debatable, disputable; invalidated, unconfirmed, unsubstantiated, unsupported

near antonyms certain, incontestable, indubitable, positive, sure, undeniable, unquestionable; correct, errorless, factual, right, sound, true, valid; clear-cut, decisive, definable, defined, definite; incontrovertible, indisputable, irrefutable; absolute, unqualified; confirmed, corroborated, determined, established, substantiated, supported, validated

antonyms accurate, dead, dead-on, exact, precise, ultraprecise, veracious

2 not being in agreement with what is true ⟨an *inexact* and misleading statement regarding the number of combat casualties⟩ — see FALSE 1

inexcusable *adj* too bad to be excused or justified ⟨spitting at a teacher is *inexcusable* behavior and will be severely punished⟩

synonyms indefensible, inexpiable, insupportable, unforgivable, unjustifiable, unpardonable, unwarrantable

related words insufferable, intolerable, unbearable, unendurable; abominable, atrocious, heinous, monstrous, outrageous, scandalous, shocking; egregious, flagrant, glaring, gross, rank; unacceptable, untenable; black, evil, iniquitous, vicious, wicked; base, contemptible, deplorable, despicable, dirty, execrable, ignoble, reprobate, vile, wretched; cruel, nasty; blamable, blameworthy, censurable, reprehensible; banned, barred, condemned, disallowed, forbidden, interdicted, outlawed, prohibited, proscribed

near antonyms acceptable, tolerable; authorized, legal, permissible; allowed, permitted, tolerated; approved, endorsed (*also* indorsed), sanctioned; abetted, encouraged, promoted, supported; ethical, good, moral, virtuous

antonyms defensible, excusable, forgivable, justifiable, pardonable, venial

inexhaustible *adj* showing no signs of weariness even after long hard effort ⟨seemingly *inexhaustible* horses that pulled heavy wagons across the wide prairies⟩ — see TIRELESS

inexpedient *adj* not producing the desired result ⟨a nutritionally dubious, *inexpedient* method for losing weight⟩ — see INEFFECTIVE 1

inexpensive *adj* costing little ⟨*inexpensive* but pretty jewelry that can be worn every day⟩ — see CHEAP 1

inexperienced *adj* **1** lacking in adult experience or maturity ⟨*inexperienced* teenagers who, naturally, thought they knew everything⟩ — see CALLOW

2 lacking or showing a lack of expert skill ⟨an *inexperienced* carpenter had obviously built the rough-hewn cabin⟩ — see AMATEURISH

inexpert *adj* **1** lacking or showing a lack of expert skill ⟨an *inexpert* attempt at putting on an outdoor concert⟩ — see AMATEURISH

2 lacking qualities (as knowledge, skill, or ability) required to do a job ⟨the *inexpert* mechanic only made the problem worse—and charged me a fortune for doing it⟩ — see INCOMPETENT

3 showing or marked by a lack of skill and tact (as in dealing with a situation) ⟨well-meaning but *inexpert* expressions of sympathy from friends after the funeral⟩ — see AWKWARD 2

inexpert *n* a person who lacks experience and competence in an art or science ⟨the shoddy tiling in the bathroom was a sure sign that it was the work of an *inexpert*⟩ — see AMATEUR 2

inexpertness *n* a lack of the level of skill associated with an expert or professional ⟨the *inexpertness* of the plasterwork is painfully obvious to all who visit that historic house⟩ — see AMATEURISHNESS

inexpiable *adj* too bad to be excused or justified ⟨apparently, the gubernatorial candidate is guilty of the *inexpiable* sin of speaking out too openly and honestly about the state's financial woes⟩ — see INEXCUSABLE

inexplainable *adj* impossible to explain ⟨a computer prone to *inexplainable* crashes⟩ — see INEXPLICABLE

inexplicable *adj* impossible to explain ⟨an *inexplicable* desire for ice cream at two in the morning⟩

synonyms inexplainable, unaccountable, unexplainable

related words indefinable, indescribable, inexpressible, unsayable; cryptic, enigmatic (*also* enigmatical), impenetrable, incomprehensible, inscrutable, mysterious, unfathomable, unknowable; irrational, unreasonable, unsound; foolish, illogical, mindless, senseless; absurd, odd, peculiar, strange, unusual, weird

near antonyms logical, rational, reasonable, tenable,

understandable; sane, sensible, wise; compelling, convincing, persuasive, plausible, satisfying; confirmed, corroborated, determined, established, explained, substantiated, validated
antonyms accountable, explainable, explicable

inexplicit *adj* not expressed in precise terms ⟨for questions like "What do you think of my new haircut?" sometimes an *inexplicit* response is safest⟩ — see VAGUE 1

inexpressible *adj* beyond the power to describe ⟨overcome by an *inexpressible* awe at the sight of the thunderous waterfall⟩ — see INDESCRIBABLE

inexpressive *adj* not expressing any emotion ⟨kept a resolutely *inexpressive* face throughout the poker game⟩ — see BLANK 1

inexpugnable *adj* having been established and usually not subject to change ⟨an *inexpugnable* belief in the essential goodness of people⟩ — see FIXED 1

inextinguishable *adj* **1** impossible to destroy ⟨freedom remains an *inextinguishable* dream for people around the world⟩ — see INDESTRUCTIBLE
2 incapable of being satisfied ⟨possesses an *inextinguishable* optimism that the voters find very appealing⟩ — see INSATIABLE

infallible *adj* **1** not being or likely to be wrong ⟨a teacher with an *infallible* memory for names⟩
synonyms unerring, unfailing
related words errorless, faultless, flawless, impeccable; certain, foolproof, inerrant, perfect, sure; dependable, reliable
near antonyms defective, faulty, flawed, imperfect; undependable, unreliable
antonyms fallible
2 not likely to fail ⟨an *infallible* cure for hiccups⟩
synonyms can't-miss, certain, fail-safe, sure, surefire, unfailing
related words dependable, reliable; deadly, unerring
near antonyms doubtful, questionable, uncertain
antonyms fallible

infamous *adj* not respectable ⟨the *infamous* criminal who remains known only by the moniker of "Jack the Ripper"⟩ — see DISREPUTABLE

infamy *n* the state of having lost the esteem of others ⟨despite her eventual pardons, she could never completely free herself of the *infamy* of being named a war criminal⟩ — see DISGRACE 1

infant *n* a recently born person ⟨*infants* should be kept warm at all times⟩ — see BABY 1

infantile *adj* having or showing the annoying qualities (as silliness) associated with children ⟨the *infantile* humor that teenage boys are justly famous for⟩ — see CHILDISH

infatuated (with) *adj* filled with an intense or excessive love for ⟨hopelessly *infatuated with* the rock band's lead singer⟩ — see ENAMORED (OF)

infatuation *n* a strong but often short-lived liking for another person ⟨had a brief *infatuation* with the captain of the ski team⟩ — see CRUSH 1

infectious *adj* exciting a similar feeling or reaction in others ⟨an *infectious* giggle that got the whole class laughing⟩ — see CONTAGIOUS 2

infelicitous *adj* not appropriate for a particular occasion or situation ⟨an *infelicitous* comment on the weight of the guest of honor at the banquet⟩ — see INAPPROPRIATE

infelicity *n* the quality or state of being unsuitable or unfitting ⟨the *infelicity* of holiday decorations at a funeral home⟩ — see INAPPROPRIATENESS 1

infer *vb* **1** to form an opinion or reach a conclusion through reasoning and information ⟨he *inferred* that she had left because her coat was gone⟩
synonyms conclude, decide, deduce, derive, extrapolate, gather, judge, make out, reason, understand
related words assume, suppose; conjecture, guess, speculate, surmise; construe, interpret, read; contemplate, philosophize, rationalize, think; ascertain, dope (out), find out
phrases draw a conclusion
2 to convey an idea indirectly ⟨the results *infer* that there might be a problem with one piece of the equipment⟩ — see HINT

inferable *also* **inferrible** *adj* being or provable by reasoning in which the conclusion follows necessarily from given information ⟨the *inferable* but unstated conclusion of the report on juvenile delinquency⟩ — see DEDUCTIVE

inference *n* an opinion arrived at through a process of reasoning ⟨that seems like a reasonable *inference*, but in this case it happens to be incorrect⟩ — see CONCLUSION 1

inferential *adj* being or provable by reasoning in which the conclusion follows necessarily from given information ⟨there is only *inferential* evidence that the ancient site was used for celebrations of the summer solstice⟩ — see DEDUCTIVE

inferior *n* one who is of lower rank and typically under the authority of another ⟨she is nice to her *inferiors* as well as to her superiors⟩ — see UNDERLING

inferior *adj* **1** situated lower down ⟨creatures that inhabit the dark, *inferior* depths of the ocean⟩
synonyms lower, nether
related words lowest, nethermost; underlying
near antonyms highest, uppermost; overhanging, overhead
antonyms higher, superior, upper
2 of little or less value or merit ⟨a girl who has always felt *inferior* to her older sister⟩
synonyms mean, minor, secondary, second-class, second-rate
related words junior, lesser, lower, low-level, petty, smaller, subordinate, under; average, common, fair, middling, ordinary; amiss, bad, defective, unsatisfactory, wrong; deficient, inadequate, insufficient, unacceptable; littler, slighter, smaller; jerkwater, low-rent, one-horse, small-time, two-bit
near antonyms major, more, primary, senior; choice, exceptional, first-class, first-rate, high-grade, premium, prime, select, selected; acceptable, adequate, sufficient
antonyms greater, higher, superior
3 belonging to the class of people of low social or economic rank ⟨at one time, the upper crust liked to believe that *inferior* people were fit only to be servants⟩ — see IGNOBLE 1
4 falling short of a standard ⟨an *inferior* science textbook that was out-of-date the day that it was published⟩ — see BAD 1
5 having not so great importance or rank as another ⟨an *inferior* officer cannot strike a superior under any circumstances⟩ — see LESSER
6 of low quality ⟨*inferior* chocolate candy that no serious chocolate lover would think of eating⟩ — see CHEAP 2

infernal *adj* deserving of one's condemnation or displeasure ⟨I detest that *infernal* machine⟩ — see DAMNABLE

inferno *n* a destructive burning ⟨the intense heat of the raging *inferno* repeatedly drove back the firefighters⟩ — see FIRE 1

infertile *adj* **1** not able to produce fruit or offspring ⟨an *infertile* cow is of limited use to a farmer⟩ — see STERILE 1
2 producing inferior or only a small amount of vegetation ⟨only parched, *infertile* fields remained after months of drought⟩ — see BARREN 1

infest *vb* to spread or swarm over in a troublesome manner ⟨in desperation, we called in an exterminator because the house was *infested* with ants⟩

synonyms overrun

related words beset, overspread, overwhelm; abound, crawl, teem; annoy, pester, plague; contaminate, infect

infidelity *n* **1** lack of faithfulness especially to one's husband or wife ⟨*infidelity* can lead to divorce⟩

synonyms disloyalty, faithlessness, falseness, falsity, inconstancy, perfidiousness, perfidy, unfaithfulness

related words adultery; betrayal, double-cross, double-dealing, duplicity, sellout, treachery, treason; deceit, deception, lying

near antonyms staunchness, steadfastness; dependability, reliability; honesty, trustworthiness

antonyms allegiance, constancy, devotedness, devotion, faith, faithfulness, fealty, fidelity, loyalty

2 the act or fact of violating the trust or confidence of another ⟨the one thing that the political boss will not forgive is *infidelity*⟩ — see BETRAYAL

3 a sexual encounter or relationship between a married person and someone other than their spouse ⟨had known about his wife's *infidelities* for years⟩ — see ADULTERY

infighting *n* a lack of agreement or harmony ⟨continued *infighting* has just completely robbed that political action committee of its effectiveness⟩ — see DISCORD

infiltrate *vb* to introduce in a gradual, secret, or clever way ⟨over time, undercover agents *infiltrated* the crime ring and eventually busted their gambling racket⟩ — see INSINUATE

infinite *adj* being or seeming to be without limits ⟨the *infinite* expanse of outer space⟩

synonyms bottomless, boundless, endless, fathomless, horizonless, illimitable, immeasurable, immensurable, indefinite, limitless, measureless, unbounded, unfathomable, unlimited

related words abysmal; countless, incalculable, incomputable, inestimable, innumerable, unmeasured; exhaustless, inexhaustible; extensive, far-flung, immense, vast

near antonyms fathomable, measurable; depthless, shallow, superficial

antonyms bounded, circumscribed, confined, definite, finite, limited, restricted

infinitesimal *adj* very small in size ⟨a soft drink with only an *infinitesimal* amount of caffeine⟩ — see TINY

infinity *n* endless time ⟨it seemed as though that meeting might extend into *infinity*⟩ — see ETERNITY 1

infirm *adj* lacking bodily strength ⟨the elderly and *infirm* have to be especially careful during the winter months⟩ — see WEAK 1

infirmity *n* **1** an abnormal state that disrupts a plant's or animal's normal bodily functioning ⟨an 18th-century quack who specialized in those mysterious *infirmities* that are known only to the idle rich⟩ — see DISEASE

2 the quality or state of lacking physical strength or vigor ⟨a period of *infirmity* left the athlete completely out of shape⟩ — see WEAKNESS 1

infix *vb* **1** to produce a vivid impression of ⟨a puzzling detail that had been *infixed* in the detective's mind for over a decade⟩ — see ENGRAVE 2

2 to set permanently in the consciousness or mind-set ⟨a football coach celebrated for *infixing* in his players an all-consuming will to win⟩ — see IMPLANT 1

inflame *also* **enflame** *vb* **1** to make angry ⟨the newspaper editorial *inflamed* her enough to inspire her to dash off a letter to the editor⟩ — see ANGER

2 to set (something) on fire ⟨a carelessly tossed cigarette *inflamed* the papers in the trash can⟩ — see BURN 2

inflamed *also* **enflamed** *adj* **1** being on fire ⟨the *inflamed* hillsides in one of the largest wildfires in the state's history⟩ — see ABLAZE 1

2 feeling or showing anger ⟨he gets red-faced when he's *inflamed* enough⟩ — see ANGRY

inflammable *adj* capable of catching or being set on fire ⟨some pajamas are made of *inflammable* material, so be careful⟩ — see COMBUSTIBLE

inflammatory *adj* tending to excite political disorder or insurrection ⟨the restless crowd was stirred up by the *inflammatory* rhetoric⟩

synonyms incendiary, seditious

related words agitational, instigative, provocative; mutinous, rebellious, revolutionary

near antonyms conciliatory, pacific; diplomatic; calming, soothing

inflated *adj* extended beyond normal or realistic bounds ⟨he's been walking around with an *inflated* ego every since he got the promotion⟩ — see BLOATED 1

inflation *n* the quality or state of appearing or trying to appear more important or more valuable than is the case ⟨the personal essay accompanying his college application was devoid of the *inflation* and self-aggrandizement that all too often is found in such writings⟩ — see PRETENSE 1

inflection *n* something that curves or is curved ⟨the *inflection* of the river is even more obvious when viewed from the summit of the nearby mountain⟩ — see BEND 1

inflexibility *n* the quality or state of being demanding or unyielding (as in discipline or criticism) ⟨the principal's *inflexibility* in matters of discipline is the stuff of school legend⟩ — see SEVERITY

inflexible *adj* **1** not capable of changing or being changed ⟨the *inflexible* law of gravity⟩

synonyms fixed, hard-and-fast, immutable, inalterable, incommutable, invariable, unalterable, unchangeable

related words changeless, constant, determinate, established, set, settled, stable, steadfast, steady, unaltered, unchanging, unvarying; immovable, unmovable

near antonyms adaptable, adjustable; fickle, fluctuating, inconstant, uncertain, unsettled, unstable, varying; plastic, pliable, pliant, supple, willowy

antonyms alterable, changeable, elastic, flexible, mutable, variable

2 incapable of or highly resistant to bending ⟨shoes made of *inflexible* plastic hurt my feet⟩ — see STIFF 1

3 not allowing for any exceptions or loosening of standards ⟨*inflexible* entry rules for the contest ban anyone who works for the company as well as any of their relatives⟩ — see RIGID 1

4 sticking to an opinion, purpose, or course of action in spite of reason, arguments, or persuasion ⟨her *inflexible* father was unmoved by tears and pleading, and he grounded her anyway⟩ — see OBSTINATE

inflow *n* a flowing or coming in ⟨the *inflow* of new students every September means that there will always be new blood for student organizations⟩ — see INFLUX

influence *vb* to act upon (a person or a person's feelings) so as to cause a response ⟨the news reports of the devastating flood *influenced* a great many people to make contributions for food and supplies⟩ — see [1]AFFECT 1

influence *n* **1** the power to direct the thinking or behavior of others usually indirectly ⟨a mayor who doesn't hesitate to use her *influence* to get business leaders behind civic improvements⟩

synonyms authority, clout, credit, heft, in, juice [*slang*], leverage, pull, sway, weight

related words counterinfluence; command, dominance, dominion, mastery, predominance, reign, scepter, sovereignty (*also* sovranty), supremacy; conse-

quence, eminence, importance, moment; impact, impress, impression, imprint, mark
near antonyms helplessness, impotence, impotency, powerlessness, weakness
2 the power to bring about a result on another ⟨the basic premise of astrology is that the position of the stars has an *influence* on human affairs⟩ — see EFFECT 2

influent *n* a stream that flows into a larger body of water ⟨along with its *influents*, the Missouri and Ohio rivers, the Mississippi River drains all or part of 31 U.S. states and two Canadian provinces⟩ — see TRIBUTARY

influential *adj* **1** having power over the minds or behavior of others ⟨in light of the effect that they have had, religious leaders such as Jesus and Muḥammad must be regarded as among the most *influential* people ever⟩
synonyms authoritative, forceful, weighty
related words cogent, controlling, dominating, masterful; dominant, predominant, regnant, sovereign (*also* sovran), supreme; eminent, important, momentous
near antonyms helpless, impotent, powerless, weak; incapable, unable
2 having great power or influence ⟨a particularly *influential* politician got the team a new ballpark⟩ — see IMPORTANT 2

influx *n* a flowing or coming in ⟨a sudden *influx* of people into the exurbs⟩
synonyms affluence, flux, income, inflow, inpouring, inrush
related words deluge, flood, flow, inundation, overflow, spate, torrent; rush, stampede; river, stream, tide
near antonyms emigration, exodus, flight
antonyms outflow, outpouring

info *n* a report of recent events or facts not previously known ⟨wondered about the fate of newspapers, seeing as so many people now go on the Internet for *info*⟩ — see NEWS

inform *vb* **1** to give information (as to the authorities) about another's improper or unlawful activities ⟨the police only caught the mastermind of the burglary because his disgruntled partner *informed*⟩ — see SQUEAL 1
2 to give information to ⟨chose teaching as a career because it affords the opportunity to *inform* a whole generation of young minds⟩ — see ENLIGHTEN 1

informal *adj* **1** not rigidly following established form, custom, or rules ⟨an *informal* meeting allowed everyone to get acquainted⟩
synonyms heterodox, irregular, unceremonious, unconventional, unorthodox
related words unauthorized, unofficial; casual, easygoing, familiar, free and easy, lax, loose, offhand, relaxed, ultracasual
near antonyms correct, decorous, proper; constrained, inhibited, restrained, rigid, stiff, stuffy, uptight
antonyms ceremonial, ceremonious, conventional, formal, orthodox, regular, routine
2 not designed to be worn only on special occasions ⟨chose an *informal* flowery dress⟩ — see CASUAL 1
3 used in or suitable for speech and not formal writing ⟨the use of *informal* language in a scholarly article is really inappropriate⟩ — see COLLOQUIAL 1

informant *n* a person who provides information about another's wrongdoing ⟨the FBI is working closely with *informants* to find out about the subversive group⟩ — see INFORMER

information *n* **1** a collection of factual knowledge about something ⟨the network correspondent spent the entire day gathering *information* for her report on the brewing scandal⟩
synonyms data, facts
related words findings, intelligence
2 a report of recent events or facts not previously known ⟨what's the latest *information* about the wildfires out in the West?⟩ — see NEWS

informational *adj* providing useful information or knowledge ⟨an *informational* presentation from the company's health care provider⟩ — see INFORMATIVE

informative *adj* providing useful information or knowledge ⟨some Web sites for family vacation resorts are very *informative* and some are practically useless⟩
synonyms educational, educative, enlightening, illuminating, informational, informatory, instructional, instructive
related words comprehensive, copious, detailed, full; communicatory, edifying, elucidative, explanatory; chatty, gossipy, newsy; availing, beneficial, constructive, helpful, profitable; practical, serviceable, usable (*also* useable), useful, worthwhile
near antonyms impractical, unhelpful, unusable, useless
antonyms unenlightening, unilluminating, uninformative, uninstructive

informatory *adj* providing useful information or knowledge ⟨an *informatory* brochure is available for first-time visitors to the historic site⟩ — see INFORMATIVE

informed *adj* **1** based on sound reasoning or information ⟨the expert's *informed* opinion persuaded many fence-sitters to get a flu shot⟩ — see GOOD 1
2 having information especially as a result of study or experience ⟨people who are *informed* about nutrition have some serious misgivings about this new diet⟩ — see FAMILIAR 2

informer *n* a person who provides information about another's wrongdoing ⟨the *informer* who told the police about that conspiracy has angered a lot of dangerous people⟩
synonyms betrayer, canary [*slang*], deep throat, fink, informant, nark [*British*], rat, rat fink, snitch, snitcher, squealer, stoolie, stool pigeon, talebearer, tattler, tattletale, telltale, whistle-blower
related words collaborator; blabber, blabbermouth, gossip, gossiper, leaker; snoop, snooper, spy; notifier

infraction *n* a failure to uphold the requirements of law, duty, or obligation ⟨speeding is only a minor *infraction*, but vehicular homicide is a serious felony⟩ — see BREACH 1

infrastructure *n* the arrangement of parts that gives something its basic form ⟨a bold plan to deal a crippling blow to the *infrastructure* of international terrorism⟩ — see FRAME 1

infrequent *adj* not often occurring or repeated ⟨a shut-in who made *infrequent* trips to the store⟩
synonyms isolated, occasional, odd, rare, sporadic
related words scarce, scattered, uncommon, unique, unusual; choppy, discontinuous, erratic, fitful, intermittent, irregular, spasmodic, spotty, unsteady
phrases few and far between
near antonyms daily, regular; common, ordinary, routine
antonyms frequent

infrequently *adv* not often ⟨their grandparents were disappointed that they visited so *infrequently*⟩ — see SELDOM

infringe (on *or* upon) *vb* to fail to keep ⟨a law that was struck down by the court for *infringing upon* the Fifth Amendment to the U.S. Constitution⟩ — see VIOLATE 1

infringement *n* a failure to uphold the requirements of law, duty, or obligation ⟨any government action limiting freedom of speech is an *infringement* of the U.S. Constitution⟩ — see BREACH 1

infuriate *vb* to make angry ⟨the quarterback's stupid mistake *infuriated* the coach⟩ — see ANGER

infuriate *adj* feeling or showing anger ⟨Casanova made

a hasty retreat from the woman's bedroom, with the *infuriate* husband in hot pursuit⟩ — see ANGRY

infuriated *adj* feeling or showing anger ⟨an *infuriated* correspondent who keeps sending increasingly vicious letters⟩ — see ANGRY

infuse *vb* to cause (as a person) to become filled or saturated with a certain quality or principle ⟨parents who *infuse* their children with strong moral values⟩
synonyms endue (*or* indue), imbue, inculcate, ingrain (*also* engrain), inoculate, invest, steep, suffuse
related words animate, charge, enliven, invigorate, leaven; implant, instill, plant; impregnate, permeate, pervade, saturate; deluge, drown, fill, flood, inundate, overwhelm, submerge
near antonyms deprive, divest, strip; clear, empty; eliminate, remove, take away

ingathering *n* a body of people come together in one place ⟨before an *ingathering* of local members of the clergy the mayor addressed some of the problems facing the city⟩ — see GATHERING

ingenious *adj* **1** having the skill and imagination to create new things ⟨an *ingenious* but rather eccentric inventor⟩ — see CREATIVE 1
2 showing a noteworthy use of the imagination and creativity especially in inventing ⟨a chair that can't tip over is quite *ingenious*⟩ — see CLEVER 1

ingeniousness *n* the skill and imagination to create new things ⟨hired a new designer whose vision demonstrates a real *ingeniousness*⟩ — see CREATIVITY 1

ingenuity *n* the skill and imagination to create new things ⟨the mystery writer's exceptional *ingenuity* enabled her to devise plots that always had readers guessing to the very end⟩ — see CREATIVITY 1

ingenuous *adj* **1** free from any intent to deceive or impress others ⟨photographs that capture the *ingenuous* smiles of young children at play⟩ — see GUILELESS
2 lacking in worldly wisdom or informed judgment ⟨the story of an *ingenuous* newcomer to the big city who outwits the slickers at their own game⟩ — see NAIVE 1

ingenuously *adv* without any attempt to impress by deception or exaggeration ⟨like some other supermodels, she *ingenuously* claims that she doesn't consider herself beautiful⟩ — see NATURALLY 3

ingenuousness *n* the quality or state of being simple and sincere ⟨his aw-shucks *ingenuousness* endeared him to his sophisticated new friends⟩ — see NAÏVETÉ 1

ingest *vb* **1** to take in as food ⟨claims that the average person *ingests* considerably more calories than is necessary or desirable⟩ — see EAT 1
2 to take into the stomach through the mouth and throat ⟨*ingested* the foul-tasting medicine with only the greatest difficulty⟩ — see SWALLOW 1

ingrain *also* **engrain** *vb* **1** to cause (as a person) to become filled or saturated with a certain quality or principle ⟨the journalism professor has long *ingrained* his students with a deep respect for their chosen profession⟩ — see INFUSE
2 to produce a vivid impression of ⟨the third-world privation he had witnessed forever *ingrained* itself upon the young doctor's memory⟩ — see ENGRAVE 2
3 to set solidly in or as if in surrounding matter ⟨tried to *ingrain* traditional values in their children⟩ — see ENTRENCH

ingrain *adj* being a part of the innermost nature of a person or thing ⟨an *ingrain* skepticism that saves him from falling for every hoax that comes along⟩ — see INHERENT

ingrained *also* **engrained** *adj* being a part of the innermost nature of a person or thing ⟨her deeply *ingrained* distrust of all authority⟩ — see INHERENT

ingratiating *adj* likely or intended to win one's affection ⟨one of the orphans had a most *ingratiating* smile⟩
synonyms disarming, endearing, insinuating, winning, winsome
related words adorable, charming, likable (*or* likeable), lovable (*also* loveable); affecting, poignant, touching; adulatory, deferential, effusive, flattering, fulsome, groveling (*or* grovelling), kowtowing, obsequious, servile, sycophantic; drooling, oleaginous, slavering, slobbering; saccharine, soapy, sugary, unctuous
near antonyms alienating, disaffecting, displeasing; repugnant, repulsive; arrogant, disdainful, haughty, insolent, proud, scornful
antonyms unendearing, uningratiating

ingratitude *n* failure or refusal to acknowledge receipt of something good from another ⟨their daughter's *ingratitude* for all that they have done for her is truly appalling⟩
synonyms thanklessness, ungratefulness
related words inappreciativeness, unappreciation
antonyms appreciation, appreciativeness, gratefulness, gratitude, thankfulness, thanks

ingredient *n* one of the parts that make up a whole ⟨one of the *ingredients* in the salad dressing is sugar⟩ — see ELEMENT 1

ingress *n* the means or right of entering or participating in ⟨with limited *ingress* and egress to the freeway, the stadium is the frequent scene of bottlenecks⟩ — see ENTRANCE 1

ingurgitate *vb* to swallow or eat greedily ⟨with no time for fine dining, we just *ingurgitated* our food and went on our way⟩ — see GOBBLE

inhabitable *adj* suitable for living in ⟨the search for an *inhabitable* planet⟩ — see LIVABLE

inhabitant *n* one who lives permanently in a place ⟨the *inhabitants* of the town don't like the tourists⟩
synonyms denizen, dweller, habitant, inhabiter, occupant, resident, resider, tenant
related words cohabitant, coresident; aborigine, native; citizen, national, subject; colonist, émigré (*also* emigré), migrant, newcomer, settler; burgher, local, localite, townee [*chiefly British*], townie (*or* towny), townsman, villager
near antonyms alien, foreigner, nonresident; guest, tourist, visitor; defector, emigrant, escaper, evacuee, exile, expatriate, refugee
antonyms transient

inhabiter *n* one who lives permanently in a place ⟨he was the sole *inhabiter* of a 60-room mansion⟩ — see INHABITANT

inhale *vb* to swallow or eat greedily ⟨*inhaled* the doughnuts so quickly that you would have missed it if you blinked⟩ — see GOBBLE

inharmonious *adj* **1** not being in agreement or harmony ⟨the inn bans young children because the owners believe that they are *inharmonious* with the quiet atmosphere other guests desire⟩ — see INCONSISTENT 1
2 marked by or producing a harsh combination of sounds ⟨a deliberately *inharmonious* piece of music in the modern idiom⟩ — see DISSONANT

inharmony *n* a lack of agreement or harmony ⟨a striking *inharmony* between the evangelist's professed spiritual concerns and his materialistic pleasures⟩ — see DISCORD

inherent *adj* being a part of the innermost nature of a person or thing ⟨an *inherent* concept of justice⟩
synonyms built-in, constitutional, constitutive, essential, hardwired, immanent, inborn, inbred, indigenous, ingrain, ingrained (*also* engrained), innate, integral, intrinsic, native, natural
related words basic, deep-rooted, elemental, fundamental; congenital, hereditary, inherited, inmost, inner, interior; internal; characteristic, distinctive, peculiar; habitual, inveterate; normal, regular, typical

phrases in one's blood
near antonyms alien, foreign; accidental, coincidental, incidental; acquired, adscititious; superficial, surface; exterior, external
antonyms adventitious, extraneous, extrinsic

inherently *adv* by natural character or ability ⟨the judge's observation that women are not *inherently* better at parenting than men⟩ — see NATURALLY 1

inheritable *adj* genetically passed or capable of being passed from parent to offspring ⟨eye color is an *inheritable* trait⟩ — see HEREDITARY

inheritance *n* something that is or may be inherited ⟨a keen sense of humor was her *inheritance* from her mother⟩
synonyms bequest, birthright, heritage, legacy, patrimony
related words heirloom; bestowal, gift, offering, present

inherited *adj* genetically passed or capable of being passed from parent to offspring ⟨hair color is *inherited*⟩ — see HEREDITARY

inheritor *n* a person who has the right to inherit property ⟨someday that little boy will become the *inheritor* of one of the largest private fortunes in the country⟩ — see HEIR

inhibit *vb* **1** to create difficulty for the work or activity of ⟨the cold *inhibited* her from getting much work done that morning⟩ — see HAMPER
2 to keep from exceeding a desirable degree or level (as of expression) ⟨laws designed to *inhibit* the powers of the intelligence organizations⟩ — see CONTROL 1
3 to steer (a person) from an activity or course of action ⟨a fundamental sense of propriety should have *inhibited* you from making a drunken spectacle of yourself⟩ — see DISCOURAGE 2

inhibition *n* **1** the checking of one's true feelings and impulses when dealing with others ⟨an innate *inhibition* made it difficult for him to tell his girlfriend what he was really feeling⟩ — see CONSTRAINT 1
2 something that makes movement or progress difficult ⟨without the *inhibition* of their jackets, the boys were able to wrestle more vigorously⟩ — see ENCUMBRANCE

inhospitable *adj* marked by opposition or ill will ⟨the proposal received an unexpectedly *inhospitable* response from the city council⟩ — see HOSTILE 1

inhuman *adj* **1** difficult to endure ⟨kept the prisoners in criminally *inhuman* conditions⟩ — see HARSH 1
2 having or showing a lack of sympathy or tender feelings ⟨an *inhuman* indifference to the sufferings of other human beings⟩ — see HARD 1
3 having or showing the desire to inflict severe pain and suffering on others ⟨a classic sociological study showing just how *inhuman* an individual can become when given absolute power over another⟩ — see CRUEL 1

inhumane *adj* **1** having or showing a lack of sympathy or tender feelings ⟨*inhumane* wardens who regularly ignored the crying children in their care⟩ — see HARD 1
2 having or showing the desire to inflict severe pain and suffering on others ⟨an *inhumane* dictator who tortured and murdered thousands of his own people⟩ — see CRUEL 1

inhumanity *n* disposition to willfully inflict pain and suffering on others ⟨man's *inhumanity* to man has been a recurring theme in human history⟩ — see CRUELTY

inhumanness *n* disposition to willfully inflict pain and suffering on others ⟨the unspeakable *inhumanness* of the pseudoscientific experiments performed on inmates of the concentration camps⟩ — see CRUELTY

inhumation *n* the act or ceremony of putting a dead body in its final resting place ⟨there is evidence that this ancient culture practiced cremation as well as *inhumation*⟩ — see BURIAL 1

inhume *vb* to place (a dead body) in the earth, a tomb, or the sea ⟨there were so many dead that it was impossible to *inhume* them all promptly⟩ — see BURY 1

inimical *adj* **1** marked by opposition or ill will ⟨received an *inimical* response rather than the anticipated support⟩ — see HOSTILE 1
2 opposed to one's interests ⟨laws designed to enhance national security that some regard as *inimical* to cherished freedoms⟩ — see ADVERSE 1

inimitable *adj* having no equal or rival for excellence or desirability ⟨an *inimitable* performer of violin solos⟩ — see ONLY 1

iniquitous *adj* not conforming to a high moral standard; morally unacceptable ⟨zero tolerance at the academy for cheating and other *iniquitous* practices⟩ — see BAD 2

iniquitousness *adj* immoral conduct or practices harmful or offensive to society ⟨a movie about an unhinged taxi driver who is disgusted by the *iniquitousness* of the city's tenderloin and goes on a murderous rampage⟩ — see VICE 1

iniquity *n* **1** immoral conduct or practices harmful or offensive to society ⟨the use of illegal narcotics is not only a destroyer of personal health but also an *iniquity* that undermines our society⟩ — see VICE 1
2 that which is morally unacceptable ⟨a nation still struggling with the aftereffects of the *iniquity* of slavery⟩ — see EVIL

initial *adj* coming before all others in time or order ⟨you've resolved my *initial* complaint, but now I have a new question⟩ — see FIRST 1

initially *adv* in the beginning ⟨we *initially* intended to rebuild our hurricane-damaged home from the ground up⟩ — see ORIGINALLY

initiate *vb* **1** to be responsible for the creation and early operation or use of ⟨no one knows who *initiated* written language⟩ — see FOUND
2 to impart knowledge of a new thing or situation to ⟨*initiated* the new recruits in the unspoken laws of military conduct⟩ — see ACQUAINT 1
3 to put into an office or welcome into an organization with special ceremonies ⟨*initiated* her as Surgeon General before an army of reporters and photographers⟩ — see INSTALL 1

initiation *n* the process or an instance of being formally placed in an office or organization ⟨the *initiation* of the newest members of the local chamber of commerce⟩ — see INSTALLATION 1

initiative *n* readiness to engage in daring or difficult activity ⟨the sentry showed remarkable *initiative* and uncommon bravery in foiling the terrorist attack⟩ — see ENTERPRISE 2

initiator *n* a person who establishes a whole new field of endeavor ⟨as the *initiator* of printing from movable type, Gutenberg revolutionized people's access to written language⟩ — see FATHER 2

inject *vb* to put among or between others ⟨*injected* one more comment into the body of the text⟩ — see INSERT

injudicious *adj* showing poor judgment especially in personal relationships or social situations ⟨lost a job because of an *injudicious* comment regarding the boss's toupee⟩ — see INDISCREET

injunction *n* a statement of what to do that must be obeyed by those concerned ⟨in the cult there were *injunctions* for and against everything, as nothing was a matter of personal choice⟩ — see COMMAND 1

injure *vb* **1** to cause bodily damage to ⟨*injured* himself while skiing⟩
synonyms damage, harm, hurt, wound
related words batter, bloody, blow out, bruise, contuse, cut, gash, gore, lacerate, scald, scar, scathe, strain, tear; crease, graze, nick; cripple, hamstring, lame,

maim, mangle, mutilate; abuse, aggrieve, afflict, maltreat, torment, torture; lay up; blemish, impair, mar, scrape, spoil
near antonyms cure, fix, heal, mend, remedy
2 to reduce the soundness, effectiveness, or perfection of ⟨the agent's treachery has *injured* our national security for years to come⟩ — see DAMAGE 1

injurious *adj* causing or capable of causing harm ⟨inaccurate news reports are *injurious* to the public's faith in the media⟩ — see HARMFUL

injury *n* **1** something that causes loss or pain ⟨the harsh words were the worst *injury* that his father could inflict⟩
synonyms affliction, damage, detriment, harm, hurt
related words disservice, injustice, outrage, wrong; affront, dart, indignity, insult, offense (*or* offence); beating, crippling, mayhem, mutilation; defacement, disability, disablement, disfigurement, impairment; lesion; rupture, strain; abrasion, chafe, scrape, scratch; booboo, bruise, contusion, swelling, wound; bump, concussion; cut, gash, laceration; burn, scald, scar, scathe, sear
near antonyms healing, recovery; cure, fix, remedy
2 unfair or inadequate treatment of someone or something or an instance of this ⟨the state did the rancher an *injury* when it destroyed his herd of cattle without adequate proof that it was diseased⟩ — see DISSERVICE

injustice *n* **1** the state of being unfair or unjust ⟨the *injustice* of the coach's accusation that I'd been lazy frustrated and angered me⟩
synonyms inequity, unfairness, unjustness
related words dirtiness, foulness
antonyms equity, fairness, justice
2 unfair or inadequate treatment of someone or something or an instance of this ⟨a group that has long suffered *injustice* at the hands of our judicial system⟩ — see DISSERVICE

ink *vb* to write one's name on (as a document) ⟨the basketball star just *inked* a two-year contract with the most celebrated franchise in the NBA⟩ — see SIGN

inkling *n* a slight or indirect pointing to something (as a solution or explanation) ⟨did not give the slightest *inkling* that he was planning to quit⟩ — see HINT 1

inlet *n* a part of a body of water that extends beyond the general shoreline ⟨went fishing in the quiet *inlets* of the coast⟩ — see GULF 1

in–migrant *n* one that leaves one place to settle in another ⟨the recent flood of *in-migrants* has completely altered the state's cultural and political landscape⟩ — see EMIGRANT

inn *n* a place that provides rooms and usually a public dining room for overnight guests ⟨we decided to stay at an *inn* rather than keep driving all night⟩ — see HOTEL

innards *n pl* **1** the internal organs of the body ⟨unpleasant memories of having to examine the *innards* of a frog for science class⟩ — see GUT 1
2 an interior or internal part ⟨consumers are warned against poking around in the *innards* of the air conditioner⟩ — see INSIDE 1

innate *adj* being a part of the innermost nature of a person or thing ⟨an *innate* athletic ability that allowed him to excel at just about any sport he tried his hand at⟩ — see INHERENT

innately *adv* by natural character or ability ⟨Anne Frank's memorable belief that most people are *innately* good⟩ — see NATURALLY 1

inner *adj* **1** situated farther in ⟨an *inner* area of the national park that is some distance from the nearest road⟩
synonyms inside, interior, internal, inward
related words inmost, innermost; central, mid, middle, midmost
near antonyms outermost, outmost; surface
antonyms exterior, external, outer, outside, outward
2 of or relating to the mind ⟨kept his *inner* life private⟩ — see MENTAL 1

inner space *n* the seat of one's deepest thoughts and emotions ⟨an intensely private individual, he treats his *inner space* as sacred ground that is off-limits to other people⟩ — see CORE 1

innkeeper *n* the owner or manager of an inn ⟨the *innkeeper* was a very genial, accommodating host⟩
synonyms boniface, landlord, taverner
related words padrone, patron; hosteler (*or* hosteller), hotelier, hotelman

innocence *n* **1** the quality or state of being free from guilt or blame ⟨the accused embezzler eventually proved her *innocence* and was released⟩
synonyms blamelessness, faultlessness, guiltlessness, impeccability, innocency, irreproachability, irreproachableness
related words decency, goodness, honesty, incorruptibility, integrity, law-abidingness, righteousness, uprightness, virtuousness; morality, virtue; chastity, purity, sinlessness; harmlessness, inoffensiveness
near antonyms blame, fault, responsibility; corruption, criminality, depravity, evil, immorality, reprehensibleness, sinfulness, wickedness; harmfulness, offensiveness
antonyms blameworthiness, culpability, guilt, guiltiness
2 the quality or state of being simple and sincere ⟨the *innocence* of the child's question touched everyone present⟩ — see NAÏVETÉ 1
3 the state of being unaware or uninformed ⟨in my *innocence* I just assumed that quoted rate was for a week's stay and not for a single night at the health spa⟩ — see IGNORANCE 1
4 the quality or state of being morally pure ⟨in Melville's novel, the sailor Billy Budd serves as a symbol of absolute *innocence*⟩ — see CHASTITY 1

innocency *n* the quality or state of being free from guilt or blame ⟨let me be the first to declare my own *innocency* in the matter: I neither spread nor believed the malicious gossip⟩ — see INNOCENCE 1

innocent *n* an innocent or gentle person ⟨an *innocent* who is often puzzled by and prey to the evils of the world⟩ — see LAMB

innocent *adj* **1** free from sin ⟨an *innocent* baby⟩
synonyms impeccable, pure, sinless, white
related words chaste, moral, virgin, virtuous; immaculate, spotless, unblemished, unstained, unsullied; decent, ethical, good, honest, honorable, righteous, upright, virtuous; blameless, guiltless
near antonyms lascivious, lecherous, lewd, libidinous, lickerish, lustful, oversexed, unchaste; evil, immoral, iniquitous, reprobate, unrighteous, virtueless, wicked; corrupt, debased, debauched, degenerate, depraved, dissolute, erring, fallen, lost, perverted; condemned, damned
antonyms impure, peccant, sinful, sinning
2 free from guilt or blame ⟨the robbery suspect was eventually found to be *innocent*⟩
synonyms blameless, cleanhanded, clear, faultless, guiltless, impeccable, inculpable, irreproachable, lilywhite
related words absolved, acquitted, cleared, exonerated, vindicated; ethical, law-abiding, moral, righteous, upright, virtuous
phrases in the clear
near antonyms blamable, blameworthy, censurable, culpable, impeachable, indictable, punishable; accused, impeached, indicted; condemned, convicted; hangdog, shamed, shamefaced
antonyms guilty
3 free from any intent to deceive or impress others ⟨an

innocent offer to sing before the gathering⟩ — see GUILELESS
4 lacking in worldly wisdom or informed judgment ⟨an *innocent* young woman who felt a little out of place among her more sophisticated roommates⟩ — see NAIVE 1
5 not causing or being capable of causing injury or hurt ⟨good-natured teasing that is just *innocent* fun⟩ — see HARMLESS
6 not informed about or aware of something ⟨a woman who seems entirely *innocent* of good manners and common courtesy⟩ — see IGNORANT 2

innocently *adv* **1** without any attempt to impress by deception or exaggeration ⟨"You look nice," she commented *innocently*⟩ — see NATURALLY 3
2 with purity of thought and deed ⟨very young children approach the world so *innocently*⟩ — see PURELY 1

innocuous *adj* not causing or being capable of causing injury or hurt ⟨those *innocuous* lies we must tell every day if society is to remain civil⟩ — see HARMLESS

innominate *adj* not named or identified by a name ⟨those *innominate* artisans and artists who built and decorated the great medieval cathedrals of Europe⟩ — see NAMELESS 1

innovate *vb* to be responsible for the creation and early operation or use of ⟨*innovated* a new system for filing books that dramatically improved efficiency in libraries⟩ — see FOUND

innovation *n* something (as a device) created for the first time through the use of the imagination ⟨the computer is one *innovation* that revolutionized the business world⟩ — see INVENTION 1

innovational *adj* having the skill and imagination to create new things ⟨in the high-tech sector, a company is either *innovational*—or it's history⟩ — see CREATIVE 1

innovative *adj* **1** having the skill and imagination to create new things ⟨an award for the most *innovative* designer of consumer electronics⟩ — see CREATIVE 1
2 showing a noteworthy use of the imagination and creativity especially in inventing ⟨*innovative* automotive technology⟩ — see CLEVER 1

innovativeness *n* the skill and imagination to create new things ⟨a surprising new product from a company that has never been a wellspring of *innovativeness*⟩ — see CREATIVITY 1

innovator *n* one who creates or introduces something new ⟨thank goodness for the *innovator* who thought up the remote control⟩ — see INVENTOR

innovatory *adj* having the skill and imagination to create new things ⟨the composer Charles Ives is remembered for his *innovatory* use of dissonance and polytonal harmonies⟩ — see CREATIVE 1

innuendo *n* a slyly or subtly derogatory remark ⟨repeatedly made *innuendos* regarding his opponent's business dealings but feigned innocence when called upon to substantiate them⟩
synonyms imputation, insinuation
related words aspersion, libel, slander, smear; affront, dig, epithet, indignity, insult, slight, slur; hint, inkling, intimation, suggestion

innumerable *adj* too many to be counted ⟨our reasons to give thanks are as *innumerable* as the stars⟩ — see COUNTLESS

innumerous *adj* too many to be counted ⟨had offered to help with the cleaning on *innumerous* occasions⟩ — see COUNTLESS

inoculate *vb* to cause (as a person) to become filled or saturated with a certain quality or principle ⟨*inoculated* them with the idea that the individual can always make a difference in this world⟩ — see INFUSE

inoffensive *adj* not causing or being capable of causing injury or hurt ⟨an *inoffensive* little joke at the opening of his speech⟩ — see HARMLESS

inoperable *adj* **1** not being in working order ⟨we have several *inoperable* cars on the property⟩
synonyms down, inoperative, kaput (*also* kaputt), malfunctioning, nonfunctional, nonfunctioning, nonoperating
related words broken; off; deactivated, deadlocked, ineffective, ineffectual, nonproductive, unproductive, unusable, unworkable, useless
phrases on the blink, on the fritz, out of commission
near antonyms effective, effectual, employable, performing, producing, productive, serving, usable (*also* useable), useful, viable, workable
antonyms functional, functioning, operable, operant, operating, operational, operative, running, working
2 not capable of being put to use or account ⟨a delightfully creative but *inoperable* plan for building a theme park in the area⟩ — see IMPRACTICAL

inoperative *adj* **1** not being in a state of use, activity, or employment ⟨be careful when putting your hands in even an *inoperative* garbage disposal⟩ — see INACTIVE 2
2 not being in working order ⟨looking for an expert to fix the *inoperative* grandfather clock⟩ — see INOPERABLE 1
3 having no legal or binding force ⟨the decision of the state's supreme court has rendered the law *inoperative*⟩ — see NULL 1

inopportune *adj* occurring before the usual or expected time ⟨their *inopportune* arrival before the house was cleaned⟩ — see EARLY 2

inopportunely *adv* before the usual or expected time ⟨dropped in *inopportunely*, before dinner was ready⟩ — see EARLY

inordinate *adj* going beyond a normal or acceptable limit in degree or amount ⟨an *inordinate* number of complaints about the slow pace of snow removal around the city⟩ — see EXCESSIVE

inordinately *adv* beyond a normal or acceptable limit ⟨taking an *inordinately* long time to finish the house⟩ — see TOO 1

inpouring *n* a flowing or coming in ⟨that small nation has been overwhelmed by an *inpouring* of refugees from its war-torn neighbor⟩ — see INFLUX

input *n* **1** matter that is fed into something ⟨at that point I was being subjected to so much sensory *input* that I had to close my eyes⟩
synonyms intake
related words accretion, accrual, addendum, addition, augmentation, gain, increment, supplement
antonyms output, outturn, production, throughput
2 an opinion suggesting a wise or proper course of action ⟨he solicited *input* from several trusted sources before making the investment⟩ — see ADVICE 1

inquest *n* a systematic search for the truth or facts about something ⟨the police conducted an *inquest* into the case⟩ — see INQUIRY 1

inquire (into) *vb* to search through or into ⟨the principal *inquired into* the possibility of holding graduation at a larger hall⟩ — see EXPLORE 1

inquire (of) *vb* to put a question or questions to ⟨casually *inquired of* the neighbors the identity of the house's previous owner⟩ — see ASK 1

inquiry *n* **1** a systematic search for the truth or facts about something ⟨an *inquiry* into the origins of the universe⟩
synonyms delving, disquisition, examen, examination, exploration, inquest, inquisition, investigation, probation, probe, probing, research, study
related words quest; audit, check; checkup, diagnosis, inspection; hearing, interrogation, trial; feeler, query, question; poll, questionary, questionnaire, survey; challenge, cross-examination, going-over, grilling, quiz; re-

hearing, reinvestigation; self-examination, self-exploration, self-questioning, self-reflection, self-scrutiny, soul-searching
2 an act or instance of asking for information ⟨one student made a hesitant *inquiry* about the assignment⟩ — see QUESTION 2

inquisition *n* a systematic search for the truth or facts about something ⟨there's no need to conduct an *inquisition* about so trivial a matter⟩ — see INQUIRY 1

inquisitive *adj* interested in what is not one's own business ⟨an *inquisitive* woman who tends to everybody's business but her own⟩ — see CURIOUS 1

inquisitiveness *n* an eager desire to find out about things that are often none of one's business ⟨his irksome *inquisitiveness* made people reluctant to socialize with him⟩ — see CURIOSITY 1

inroad *n* a sudden attack on and entrance into hostile territory ⟨the army is finally making *inroads* into enemy territory⟩ — see RAID 1

inrush *n* a flowing or coming in ⟨a sudden *inrush* of air blew my hair back⟩ — see INFLUX

insalubrious *adj* bad for the well-being of the body ⟨after inhaling the *insalubrious* city smog for a month, I was happy to once again breathe in the fresh air of the country⟩ — see UNHEALTHY 1

ins and outs *n pl* the characteristic peculiarities and technicalities of something ⟨still learning the *ins and outs* of the brokerage business⟩
synonyms mechanics, ropes, workings
related words details, incidentals, minutiae, particulars; oddities, quirks; brass tacks, nuts and bolts

insane *adj* **1** having or showing a very abnormal or sick state of mind ⟨only an *insane* person would intentionally jump off a skyscraper⟩
synonyms balmy, barmy [*chiefly British*], bats, batty, bedlam, bonkers, brainsick, bughouse [*slang*], certifiable, crackbrained, cracked, crackers, crackpot, cranky [*dialect*], crazed, crazy, cuckoo, daffy, daft, demented, deranged, fruity [*slang*], gaga, haywire, kooky (*also* kookie), loco [*slang*], loony (*also* looney), loony tunes (*or* looney tunes), lunatic, mad, maniacal (*also* maniac), mental, meshuga (*or* meshugge *also* meshugah *or* meshuggah), moonstruck, non compos mentis, nuts, nutty, psycho, psychotic, scatty [*chiefly British*], screwy, unbalanced, unhinged, unsound, wacko (*also* whacko), wacky (*also* whacky), wud [*chiefly Scottish*]
related words dotty, fey, loopy, off, potty [*chiefly British*], teched (*or* tetched), touched; aberrant, delirious, delusional, delusionary, disordered, disturbed, neurotic, obsessive-compulsive, paranoiac (*also* paranoic), paranoid (*also* paranoidal), schizoid, schizophrenic, sociopathic; eccentric, odd, oddball, pixilated (*also* pixillated), queer, strange; foolish, senseless, witless; irrational, unreasonable; amok (*or* amuck), ape, ballistic, bananas, berserk, nuclear; depressed; distracted, distraught, frantic, frenzied, haywire, hysterical (*also* hysteric), raving, wigged-out; fixated, monomaniac, monomaniacal, obsessed
phrases around the bend, off one's gourd, off one's head, off one's rocker, out of one's head (*or* mind), out to lunch [*slang*]
near antonyms clear, lucid, rational, reasonable; judicious, sensible, wise; healthy, normal, well-adjusted; unneurotic
antonyms balanced, compos mentis, sane, sound, uncrazy
2 conceived or made without regard for reason or reality ⟨a completely *insane* plan to build an opera house in the middle of nowhere⟩ — see FANTASTIC 1
3 showing or marked by a lack of good sense or judgment ⟨an *insane* plan to blow all of their savings on lottery tickets⟩ — see FOOLISH 1
4 going beyond a normal or acceptable limit in degree or amount ⟨wanted an *insane* amount of money to paint our house⟩ — see EXCESSIVE

insanity *n* **1** a serious mental disorder that prevents one from living a safe and normal life ⟨his incurable *insanity* requires that he spend the rest of his life in a mental hospital⟩
synonyms aberration, dementia, derangement, lunacy, madness, mania, rage [*archaic*]
related words neurosis, psychosis; instability, irrationality, unreasonableness; delirium, frenzy, hysteria; hallucinosis, hypomania, paranoia, schizophrenia; senile dementia; delusion, hallucination; monomania, obsession, phobia; abnormality, dementedness, unsoundness
near antonyms lucidity, rationality, rationalness, reasonability, reasonableness; normality, soundness
antonyms mind, saneness, sanity
2 a foolish act or idea ⟨everyone laughed at the latest *insanity* from the town eccentric⟩ — see FOLLY 1
3 lack of good sense or judgment ⟨had the *insanity* to think that taking over a government building in protest of our foreign policy was a good idea⟩ — see FOOLISHNESS 1

insatiable *adj* incapable of being satisfied ⟨an *insatiable* need for the approval of others⟩
synonyms inappeasable, inextinguishable, insatiate, quenchless, unappeasable, unquenchable, unslakable
related words unappeased, unsatisfied; avid, rapacious, ravenous, voracious; demanding, exigent, importunate, insistent, urgent; clamorous, crying, pressing, yearning
near antonyms satiate, satiated, satisfied; controlled, curbed, restrained
antonyms appeasable, extinguishable, satiable, satisfiable

insatiate *adj* incapable of being satisfied ⟨an *insatiate* avarice that impels him to work incessantly for a fortune that he will never have time to enjoy⟩ — see INSATIABLE

inscribe *vb* **1** to cut (as letters or designs) on a hard surface ⟨paid a jeweler to *inscribe* their names and wedding date on their wedding rings⟩ — see ENGRAVE 1
2 to add (a person) to a list or roll as a participant or member ⟨*inscribed* the couple in the society of sustaining donors to the museum⟩ — see ENROLL 1
3 to put (someone or something) on a list ⟨*inscribed* his name on the list of those to be executed⟩ — see [1]LIST 2

inscrutability *n* **1** the quality or state of being impossible to know, understand, or explain ⟨the *inscrutability* of divine intentions is something that people of faith usually just accept⟩
synonyms impenetrability, inscrutableness, mysteriousness, numinousness, obscurity, uncanniness
related words deepness, profundity; darkness, murkiness, obscurity, shadowiness, vagueness; ambiguity, equivocality, equivocalness; incomprehensibility, unintelligibility, unintelligibleness; inexplicability, inexplicableness; unanswerability; unknowability; abstruseness, abstrusity, esotericism, hermetism, reconditeness
near antonyms intelligibility, understandability; clarity, obviousness, plainness, self-evidence, straightforwardness, transparency
2 the quality or state of having a veiled or uncertain meaning ⟨the *inscrutability* of the notations in the ledger—who, for example, was the recipient of "gift to X"?⟩ — see OBSCURITY 1

inscrutable *adj* **1** being beyond one's powers to know, understand, or explain ⟨the many *inscrutable* beliefs of that ancient religion⟩ — see MYSTERIOUS 1
2 having an often intentionally veiled or uncertain meaning ⟨ancient oracles typically uttered *inscrutable*

prophecies that could be interpreted almost any way one chose⟩ — see OBSCURE 1

inscrutableness *n* **1** the quality or state of being impossible to know, understand, or explain ⟨it's the sheer *inscrutableness* of the lady's smile that has tantalized art lovers for centuries⟩ — see INSCRUTABILITY 1
2 the quality or state of having a veiled or uncertain meaning ⟨the *inscrutableness* of the inscriptions left by the doomed colonists of Roanoke Island has inspired many theories concerning their fate⟩ — see OBSCURITY 1

insculp *vb, archaic* to cut (as letters or designs) on a hard surface ⟨laid to rest under a stone *insculpt* with the figure of an angel⟩ — see ENGRAVE 1

insect *n* a person of no importance or influence ⟨the magazine's editor in chief was notorious for treating staffers as *insects*, often not even bothering to learn their names⟩ — see NOBODY

insecure *adj* **1** not tightly fastened, tied, or stretched ⟨*insecure* twine allowed the bundle of newspapers to break open as soon as it was tossed to the ground⟩ — see LOOSE 1
2 feeling or showing uncomfortable feelings of uncertainty ⟨I always feel *insecure* in those high-end highfalutin restaurants⟩ — see NERVOUS 1

insecurity *n* the quality or state of not being firmly fixed in position ⟨the *insecurity* of the bookcase made it dangerous for a household with small children who like to climb⟩ — see INSTABILITY

inseminate *vb* to set permanently in the consciousness or mind-set ⟨the notion that their monarch ruled by divine right had been *inseminated* in the people for countless generations⟩ — see IMPLANT 1

insensate *adj* **1** lacking animate awareness or sensation ⟨the belief that God is immanent in all things, even *insensate* objects⟩
synonyms inanimate, insensible, insentient, senseless, unfeeling
related words exanimate, lifeless; comatose, unconscious
near antonyms aware, cognizant, conscious; animated, lively, vibrant
antonyms animate, feeling, sensate, sensible, sensitive, sentient
2 having or showing a lack of sympathy or tender feelings ⟨an *insensate* boss who refuses to allow time off for funerals⟩ — see HARD 1

insensibility *n* **1** a lack of emotion or emotional expressiveness ⟨the husband's general *insensibility* is creating great tension in the marriage⟩ — see APATHY 1
2 a temporary state of unconsciousness ⟨knocked into *insensibility* by the blow to the head⟩ — see FAINT

insensible *adj* **1** having lost consciousness ⟨if a choking person is *insensible*, you should lay them down on their back before performing the Heimlich maneuver⟩ — see UNCONSCIOUS 1
2 not perceptible by a sense or by the mind ⟨the fragile glass flowers can be damaged by even the most *insensible* tremors⟩ — see IMPERCEPTIBLE
3 having or showing a lack of interest or concern ⟨city hall remains *insensible* to our complaints about the downtown parking situation⟩ — see INDIFFERENT 1
4 lacking animate awareness or sensation ⟨even the canyon's *insensible* rocks seemed to mock the stranded climber's utter helplessness⟩ — see INSENSATE 1
5 lacking in refinement or good taste ⟨married an *insensible* brute upon whom the niceties of life were completely lost⟩ — see COARSE 2
6 not informed about or aware of something ⟨a scientist who usually is so engrossed in his work that he is quite *insensible* of the passage of time⟩ — see IGNORANT 2

insensitive *adj* **1** having or showing a lack of sympathy or tender feelings ⟨an *insensitive* remark about his deceased wife that was incredibly rude⟩ — see HARD 1
2 lacking in sensation or feeling ⟨fingers rendered *insensitive* by the cold⟩ — see NUMB 1

insentient *adj* **1** lacking animate awareness or sensation ⟨refused to believe that the universe as we know it evolved from the random interactions of *insentient* particles of matter⟩ — see INSENSATE 1
2 not having or showing a deep understanding of something ⟨an *insentient* therapist who failed to see what the teenager's real problem was⟩ — see IMPERCEPTIVE

inseparability *n* the state of being in a very personal or private relationship ⟨never seen apart, the two women had an *inseparability* that was legendary among their friends⟩ — see FAMILIARITY 1

inseparable *adj* closely acquainted ⟨they've been *inseparable* friends since they met at summer camp years ago⟩ — see FAMILIAR 1

insert *vb* to put among or between others ⟨surreptitiously *inserted* the book in its proper place on the shelf⟩
synonyms edge in, fit (in *or* into), inject, insinuate, intercalate, interject, interpolate, interpose, intersperse, introduce, sandwich (in *or* between), work in
related words cut in, inlay, inset, install; interfile, interline, lard, weave; cram, shove, thrust, wedge; add, append, attach
near antonyms eject, eliminate, exclude, expel, extract, withdraw; deduct, detach, subtract; reject

inshore *adj* of, relating to, or situated in the waters near the shore ⟨an oil spill that was devastating to *inshore* fisheries in the area⟩
synonyms alongshore, coastal, littoral, nearshore, offshore, shoreside
related words beachside, seaside, waterside
near antonyms blue-water, deepwater, oceanic

inside *adj* **1** not known or meant to be known by the general populace ⟨made a stock trade based on *inside* information⟩ — see PRIVATE 1
2 situated farther in ⟨chose the *inside* lane to run around the track⟩ — see INNER 1

inside *n* **1** an interior or internal part ⟨the *inside* of the clock features an amazingly complex mechanism⟩
synonyms innards, interior, within
related words belly, bowels, guts; stuffing; recesses; center, core, heart
near antonyms border, boundary, brim, brink, edge, end, extremity, fringe, limit, lip, margin, perimeter, periphery, rim; surface
antonyms exterior, outside
2 *usually* **insides** *pl* the internal organs of the body ⟨medical students eager to see what people's *insides* look like⟩ — see GUT 1
3 the seat of one's deepest thoughts and emotions ⟨not one to share her fears and worries, she keeps it all on the *inside*⟩ — see CORE 1
4 information not generally available to the public ⟨a person with the *inside* on what really happened at the board meeting⟩ — see DOPE 1

inside out *adv* with attention to all aspects or details ⟨after 20 years of employment there, he has come to know the company *inside out*⟩ — see THOROUGHLY 1

inside track *n* the more favorable condition or position in a competition ⟨the applicant with actual experience in pharmaceutical sales will definitely have the *inside track* for the job⟩ — see ADVANTAGE 1

insight *n* the ability to understand inner qualities or relationships ⟨a therapist with real *insight* into people's personalities⟩ — see WISDOM 1

insightful *adj* having or showing deep understanding and intelligent application of knowledge ⟨a critical study featuring an *insightful* analysis of the novelist's recurring themes⟩ — see WISE 1

insignificance *n* the quality or state of being unimportant ⟨a tabloid newspaper devoted to people and events of astonishing *insignificance*⟩
synonyms immateriality, inconsequence, inconsequentiality, inconsiderableness, insignificancy, littleness, negligibility, nullity, pettiness, slightness, smallness, triviality
related words emptiness, valuelessness, worthlessness
near antonyms substance, value, worth
antonyms bigness, consequence, import, importance, magnitude, moment, significance, weight, weightiness

insignificancy *n* **1** a person of no importance or influence ⟨forced to face the fact that he would always be an *insignificancy* in such a large law firm, he decided to strike out on his own⟩ — see NOBODY
2 the quality or state of being unimportant ⟨we shouldn't even be talking about a matter of such patent *insignificancy*⟩ — see INSIGNIFICANCE

insignificant *adj* **1** lacking importance ⟨an *insignificant* detail that we can safely ignore⟩ — see UNIMPORTANT
2 so small or unimportant as to warrant little or no attention ⟨the *insignificant* wear on the doll's face does nothing to diminish its considerable value as an antique⟩ — see NEGLIGIBLE 1

insincere *adj* not being or expressing what one appears to be or express ⟨the *insincere* compliments of a spiteful gossip⟩
synonyms artificial, backhanded, counterfeit, double, double-dealing, double-faced, fake, feigned, hypocritical, Janus-faced, jive [*slang*], left-handed, lip, mealy, mealymouthed, Pecksniffian, phony (*also* phoney), phony-baloney (*or* phoney-baloney), pretended, two-faced, unctuous
related words affected, assumed, claptrap, contrived, forced, mechanical, put-on, simulated, strained, unnatural; empty, hollow, meaningless; deceitful, devious, dishonest, false, untruthful; facile, glib, superficial; bogus, sham; campy, facetious, jocular, tongue-in-cheek; canting, pharisaical, pious, sanctimonious, self-righteous, simon-pure
near antonyms direct, forthright, frank, heart-to-heart, open, plain, straightforward
antonyms artless, candid, genuine, heartfelt, honest, sincere, undesigning, unfeigned

insincerity *n* the pretending of having virtues, principles, or beliefs that one in fact does not have ⟨the *insincerity* of the family's professed concern for the environment is pretty much exposed by the gas-guzzler parked in the driveway⟩ — see HYPOCRISY

insinuate *vb* **1** to introduce in a gradual, secret, or clever way ⟨years were needed for the agent to *insinuate* himself into the terrorist organization⟩
synonyms infiltrate, slip, sneak, wind, work in, worm, wriggle
related words creep, edge, wiggle; insert, interpolate, interpose, introduce
2 to convey an idea indirectly ⟨are you *insinuating* that I won by cheating?⟩ — see HINT
3 to put among or between others ⟨quietly *insinuated* herself among the concertgoers raptly listening to the piano solo⟩ — see INSERT

insinuating *adj* likely or intended to win one's affection ⟨the fortune hunter's *insinuating* attentions were having their intended effect on the naive heiress⟩ — see INGRATIATING

insinuation *n* a slyly or subtly derogatory remark ⟨the *insinuation* that there were considerations other than love for the actor having such a high-profile wedding⟩ — see INNUENDO

insipid *adj* **1** lacking in taste or flavor ⟨an apple pie with a mushy, *insipid* filling that strongly resembled soggy cardboard⟩
synonyms dead, flat, flavorless, savorless, tasteless, unsavory
related words bland, dilute, thin, watery, weak; plain, unflavored
near antonyms disgusting, distasteful, loathsome, sickening, unappetizing, unpalatable; cloying, mawkish; appetizing, delectable, delicious, palatable, toothsome; keen, piquant, seasoned, spicy; flavored; heavy, rich
antonyms flavorful, flavorsome, sapid, savory (*also* savoury), tasteful, tasty
2 lacking in qualities that make for spirit and character ⟨an *insipid* and somewhat boring movie about teenagers in love⟩ — see WISHY-WASHY 1

insist *vb* to state as a fact usually forcefully ⟨she continued to *insist* that she was right, even in the face of overwhelming evidence to the contrary⟩ — see CLAIM 1

insist (on) *vb* to ask for (something) earnestly or with authority ⟨the director *insisted on* absolute quiet on the set⟩ — see DEMAND 1

insistence *n* a solemn and often public declaration of the truth or existence of something ⟨a continued *insistence* that there was a massive cover-up by the government⟩ — see PROTESTATION

insistent *adj* continuing despite difficulties, opposition, or discouragement ⟨Margaret Sanger is remembered as an *insistent* crusader for birth control⟩ — see PERSISTENT

insobriety *n* **1** a propensity for extremes in one's actions, beliefs, or habits ⟨a short, unhappy life characterized chiefly by *insobriety*⟩ — see EXCESS 2
2 habitual or excessive drinking of intoxicants ⟨her once-promising singing career was undermined by *insobriety* and emotional instability⟩ — see INTEMPERANCE 1

insofar as *conj* to the degree that ⟨*insofar as* I know, there are no other complications for obtaining the building permit⟩ — see INASMUCH AS 1

insolence *n* **1** disrespectful or argumentative talk given in response to a command or request ⟨amazed that parents would tolerate such *insolence* from their teenaged children⟩ — see BACK TALK
2 rude behavior ⟨her frequent displays of *insolence* have lowered her standing among movie fans⟩ — see DISCOURTESY

insolent *adj* displaying or marked by rude boldness ⟨an appallingly *insolent* reply to a reasonable request⟩ — see NERVY 1

insoluble *adj* incapable of being solved or accomplished ⟨the seemingly *insoluble* mystery concerning the identity of the people who built these ancient structures⟩ — see IMPOSSIBLE

insolvable *adj* incapable of being solved or accomplished ⟨faced with the perennially *insolvable* dilemma of having to choose between career and family⟩ — see IMPOSSIBLE

insolvency *n* the inability to pay one's debts ⟨unless the economy improves, many resorts in the area face *insolvency*⟩
synonyms bankruptcy, failure, ruin
related words Chapter 11
antonyms solvency

insomnia *n* the inability to obtain adequate sleep ⟨has suffered from *insomnia* virtually his entire life⟩
synonyms sleeplessness, wakefulness
related words alertness, restlessness
near antonyms drowsiness, sleepiness; narcolepsy

insomniac *adj* not sleeping or able to sleep ⟨an *insomniac* veteran tormented by his memories of the war⟩ — see WAKEFUL

insomuch as *conj* to the degree that ⟨*insomuch as* one can ever know about these things, their marriage seems solid as a rock⟩ — see INASMUCH AS 1

insomuch that *conj* to the degree that ⟨*insomuch that* it is humanely possible, I try not to lie about anything⟩ — see INASMUCH AS 1

insouciance *n* lack of interest or concern ⟨wandered into the meeting with complete *insouciance* to the fact that she was late⟩ — see INDIFFERENCE

insouciant *adj* **1** having or showing freedom from worries or trouble ⟨the *insouciant* gaiety of the idle rich⟩ — see CAREFREE

2 having or showing a lack of interest or concern ⟨an *insouciant* attitude about punctuality that is really discourteous to her coworkers⟩ — see INDIFFERENT 1

inspect *vb* to look over closely (as for judging quality or condition) ⟨*inspected* the collie before the dog show⟩

synonyms audit, check (out), con, examine, overlook, oversee, review, scan, scrutinize, survey, view

related words notice, observe, watch; comb, peruse, pore (over); analyze, dissect, parse; delve (into), explore, investigate, plumb, probe, research, study; categorize, classify; pick over; reinspect, rereview, resurvey

phrases go over

near antonyms skim; glance (at *or* over); miss, overlook

inspection *n* a close look at or over someone or something in order to judge condition ⟨a prison cell *inspection* should include looking under the bed, to say the least⟩

synonyms audit, check, checkup, examination, going-over, look-see, review, scan, scrutiny, survey, view

related words analysis, assay, close-up, deconstruction, dissection; exploration, investigation, probe, research, study; inquisition, interrogation; once-over, perusal; recheck, reinspection, resurvey; observation, surveillance, watch; checkout, test-drive, trial run

inspire *vb* **1** to fill with courage or strength of purpose ⟨the rousing campaign speech *inspired* everyone to get out the vote⟩ — see ENCOURAGE 1

2 to draw out (something hidden, latent, or reserved) ⟨what *inspired* that comment?⟩ — see EDUCE

3 to provide (someone) with moral or spiritual understanding ⟨great works of visual art can *inspire* us in ways that the written word often cannot⟩ — see ENLIGHTEN 2

inspiring *adj* causing great emotional or mental stimulation ⟨an *inspiring* idea for a national program in which young people would commit themselves to a year of community service⟩ — see EXCITING 1

inspirit *vb* to fill with courage or strength of purpose ⟨the sight of the royal family doughtily enduring the bombing raids greatly *inspirited* the rest of the population⟩ — see ENCOURAGE 1

instability *n* the quality or state of not being firmly fixed in position ⟨the *instability* of the bridge became tragically apparent when it suddenly collapsed⟩

synonyms insecurity, precariousness, shakiness, unstableness, unsteadiness

related words insubstantiality, unsoundness; changeability, inconstancy, mutability; laxness, looseness, slackness

near antonyms firmness, soundness, substantiality

antonyms fastness, fixedness, security, stability, steadiness

install *vb* **1** to put into an office or welcome into an organization with special ceremonies ⟨*installed* her as the new principal of the high school⟩

synonyms baptize, inaugurate, induct, initiate, instate, invest, seat

related words swear in; consecrate, enshrine; accept, admit, receive, take in; enlist, enroll (*also* enrol)

near antonyms can, discharge, fire, terminate; muster out

2 to establish or place comfortably or snugly ⟨*installed* herself in an easy chair by the fireplace and remained there for the rest of the afternoon⟩ — see ENSCONCE 1

installation *n* **1** the process or an instance of being formally placed in an office or organization ⟨the *installation* of a new president takes place once every four years⟩

synonyms baptism, inaugural, inauguration, induction, initiation, installment (*also* instalment), investiture, investment

related words enlistment, enrollment (*also* enrolment); promotion

near antonyms discharge, removal

2 a structure that is designed and built for a particular purpose ⟨a massive *installation* that supplies the electrical power needs for the entire state⟩ — see FACILITY

installment *also* **instalment** *n* the process or an instance of being formally placed in an office or organization ⟨attended the *installment* of the new university president⟩ — see INSTALLATION 1

instance *n* one of a group or collection that shows what the whole is like ⟨this is just one *instance* of his repeated failure to do what he promised⟩ — see EXAMPLE

instance *vb* **1** to give as an example ⟨*instanced* one particular incident as an illustration of their penchant for practical jokes⟩ — see QUOTE 1

2 to make reference to or speak about briefly but specifically ⟨*instanced* the latest astronomical research in her presentation on measuring star magnitude⟩ — see MENTION 1

3 to show or make clear by using examples ⟨*instanced* the hero's moral courage with several examples from the novel⟩ — see ILLUSTRATE 1

instant *adj* **1** done or occurring without any noticeable lapse in time ⟨an *instant* response to the cry for help⟩ — see INSTANTANEOUS

2 needing immediate attention ⟨an *instant* need for food supplies in the famine-stricken country⟩ — see ACUTE 2

3 existing or in progress right now ⟨we should be more concerned with *instant* dangers than with those in the far-off future⟩ — see PRESENT 1

instant *n* a very small space of time ⟨it all happened in an *instant*⟩

synonyms beat, eyeblink, flash, heartbeat, jiff, jiffy, minute, moment, nanosecond, New York minute, second, shake, split second, trice, twinkle, twinkling, wink

related words microsecond; snatch, spurt

near antonyms aeon (*or* eon), age, eternity, forever; infinity, lifetime

instantaneous *adj* done or occurring without any noticeable lapse in time ⟨the thunder following the flash of lightning was nearly *instantaneous*⟩

synonyms immediate, instant, split-second, straightaway

related words summary; fast, hit-and-run, prompt, quick, rapid, speedy, swift

near antonyms dilatory, tardy; slow, sluggish; prolonged, protracted; deferred, delayed

instantaneously *adv* without delay ⟨I had just slammed the car door shut when I *instantaneously* remembered that I had left the keys inside⟩ — see IMMEDIATELY

instanter *adv* without delay ⟨as soon as I had called out that answer, I *instanter* knew that it was wrong⟩ — see IMMEDIATELY

instantiate *vb* to represent in visible form ⟨his imposing mansion is intended to *instantiate* for visitors his staggering success as an entrepreneur⟩ — see EMBODY 2

instantiation *n* a visible representation of something

abstract (as a quality) ⟨a generation that regarded Susan Sontag as the *instantiation* of the modern urban intellectual⟩ — see EMBODIMENT

instantly *adv* without delay ⟨showed leadership by reacting *instantly* to the crisis⟩ — see IMMEDIATELY

instantly *conj* just at the moment that ⟨we realized there would be problems *instantly* we saw the final report⟩ — see WHEN 2

instate *vb* to put into an office or welcome into an organization with special ceremonies ⟨the new secretary of the treasury was *instated* on Monday⟩ — see INSTALL 1

instead *adv* as a substitute ⟨I was offered a ride, but I chose to walk *instead*⟩
synonyms first, rather
related words alternately, alternatively
phrases in lieu

instigate *vb* **1** to bring (something volatile or intense) into being ⟨the medical breakthrough *instigated* a whole new field of therapy⟩ — see INCITE 1
2 to rouse to strong feeling or action ⟨the charge that the scene in the movie had *instigated* teenagers to commit similar acts of vandalism⟩ — see PROVOKE 1

instigating *adj* serving or likely to arouse a strong reaction ⟨an artist who deliberately creates *instigating* works of art that are sure to arouse controversy⟩ — see PROVOCATIVE

instigation *n* **1** something that arouses a strong response from another ⟨without *instigation* of any kind, the man suddenly threw a punch⟩ — see PROVOCATION 1
2 something that arouses action or activity ⟨the promise of windfall profits was all the *instigation* they needed to invest in the scheme⟩ — see IMPULSE 1

instigative *adj* serving or likely to arouse a strong reaction ⟨she is no stranger to controversy, having penned several *instigative* and inflammatory books attacking liberals⟩ — see PROVOCATIVE

instigator *n* a person who stirs up public feelings especially of discontent ⟨an *instigator* who always managed to be innocently standing by once the fighting began⟩ — see AGITATOR

instill *vb* to set permanently in the consciousness or mind-set ⟨a charismatic leader who *instilled* in his followers a passionate commitment to the cause⟩ — see IMPLANT 1

instinctive *adj* done instantly and without conscious thought or decision ⟨the *instinctive* reaction of a mother is to protect her children⟩ — see AUTOMATIC 1

instinctual *adj* done instantly and without conscious thought or decision ⟨the birds' *instinctual* response is to fly away when startled⟩ — see AUTOMATIC 1

institute *n* **1** a group of persons formally joined together for some common interest ⟨founded an *institute* to combat the cruel treatment of animals⟩ — see ASSOCIATION 2
2 a public organization with a particular purpose or function ⟨a scientific *institute* researching a cure for cancer⟩ — see INSTITUTION 1

institute *vb* to be responsible for the creation and early operation or use of ⟨Elizabeth Cady Stanton is generally credited with *instituting* the women's-rights movement in 1848⟩ — see FOUND

instituter *or* **institutor** *n* a person who establishes a whole new field of endeavor ⟨Eli Whitney is known as the *instituter* of the American system of manufacture on account of his pioneering concept of the mass production of interchangeable parts⟩ — see FATHER 2

institution *n* **1** a public organization with a particular purpose or function ⟨a charitable *institution* devoted to raising funds to feed the hungry⟩
synonyms establishment, foundation, institute
related words body, collective, group; corporation, enterprise; charity, philanthropy; think tank
2 a person who has long been associated with a place or activity ⟨an actor who has been a Broadway *institution* for decades⟩
synonyms fixture
related words first lady, grand old man; icon (*also* ikon), symbol; dean, elder statesman
3 a group of persons formally joined together for some common interest ⟨an *institution* devoted to studying social problems and proposing solutions for them⟩ — see ASSOCIATION 2
4 a place where insane people are cared for ⟨their father was committed to an *institution* after his mental health began to rapidly deteriorate⟩ — see MADHOUSE 1

instruct *vb* **1** to cause to acquire knowledge or skill in some field ⟨spent his military career *instructing* young pilots⟩ — see TEACH
2 to give information to ⟨*instructed* everyone in the use of the new telephone system⟩ — see ENLIGHTEN 1
3 to issue orders to (someone) by right of authority ⟨the proctors *instructed* everyone to put their pencils down and hand in their tests⟩ — see COMMAND 1

instruction *n* **1** a statement of what to do that must be obeyed by those concerned ⟨needed an administrative assistant who was good at following *instructions*⟩ — see COMMAND 1
2 the act or process of imparting knowledge or skills to another ⟨the view that the *instruction* of our nation's youth should be our highest priority⟩ — see EDUCATION 1

instructional *adj* providing useful information or knowledge ⟨an *instructional* DVD on home repair for do-it-yourselfers⟩ — see INFORMATIVE

instructive *adj* providing useful information or knowledge ⟨an *instructive* demonstration of the proper way to pack a suitcase so your clothes don't arrive in a mess⟩ — see INFORMATIVE

instructor *n* a person whose occupation is to give formal instruction in a school ⟨had spent most of his adulthood as an *instructor* in the local school system⟩ — see TEACHER

instrument *n* **1** a written or printed paper giving information about or proof of something ⟨a valid will is a legal *instrument*⟩ — see CERTIFICATE
2 an article intended for use in work ⟨always choose the right *instrument* for any woodworking job⟩ — see IMPLEMENT
3 something used to achieve an end ⟨he sees scouting as an *instrument* for building character in young people⟩ — see AGENT 1
4 one that is or can be used to further the purposes of another ⟨the claim that the scientists are mere *instruments* of the tobacco companies, who pay them to produce findings that are highly suspect⟩ — see [1]PAWN

instrumentalist *n* a person who plays a musical instrument ⟨he excels as a conductor, a composer, and as an *instrumentalist*⟩ — see MUSICIAN 1

instrumentality *n* something used to achieve an end ⟨computer literacy is only an *instrumentality* for acquiring an education, and not an end in itself⟩ — see AGENT 1

insubordinate *adj* given to resisting authority or another's control ⟨the junior officer was court-martialed for being *insubordinate*⟩ — see DISOBEDIENT

insubordination *n* refusal to obey ⟨was fired for chronic *insubordination*⟩ — see DISOBEDIENCE

insubstantial *adj* **1** being of a material lacking in sturdiness or substance ⟨an *insubstantial* carton that could not possibly stand up during long-distance shipping⟩ — see FLIMSY 1

2 not composed of matter ⟨energy is *insubstantial*⟩ — see IMMATERIAL 1

insufferable *adj* more than can be put up with ⟨an *insufferable* bore whose only topic of conversation is himself⟩ — see UNBEARABLE

insufficiency *n* **1** a falling short of an essential or desirable amount or number ⟨dealt with the school's *insufficiency* of art supplies by buying materials out of her own pocket⟩ — see DEFICIENCY

2 the lack of sufficient ability, power, or means ⟨her alleged *insufficiency* for the job⟩ — see INABILITY

insufficient *adj* not coming up to an expected measure or meeting a particular need ⟨there's been an *insufficient* number of volunteers for the job, so I'll have to select someone⟩ — see SHORT 3

insular *adj* not broad or open in views or opinions ⟨an *insular* community that is not receptive of new ideas, especially from outsiders⟩ — see NARROW 2

insulate *vb* to set or keep apart from others ⟨tried to *insulate* their children from the often disturbing news in the mass media⟩ — see ISOLATE

insulation *n* the state of being alone or kept apart from others ⟨she had grown up in such rural *insulation* that she'd never met anyone of a different race⟩ — see ISOLATION

insult *n* an act or expression showing scorn and usually intended to hurt another's feelings ⟨panelists on that political talk show simply exchange *insults*, not ideas⟩
synonyms affront, barb, brickbat, cut, dart, dig, dis (*also* diss) [*slang*], epithet, gird, indignity, name, offense (*or* offence), outrage, personality, poke, put-down, sarcasm, slap, slight, slur
related words catcall, gibe (*or* jibe), jeer, mock, quip, sneer, taunt; abuse, invective, vituperation; disapproval, opprobrium; disgrace, dishonor, shame; attack, criticism, knock, slam, swipe; torment, torture
near antonyms accolade, commendation, compliment; acclaim, applause, praise; adulation, flattery

insult *vb* to cause hurt feelings or deep resentment in ⟨*insulted* their hosts by casually remarking about the outdated look of their home⟩
synonyms affront, dis (*also* diss) [*slang*], disrespect, offend, outrage, slap, slight, wound
related words cut, snub; displease, distress, disturb, hurt, miff, pain, trouble, upset; jeer, mock, ridicule, sneer (at), taunt; defame, disparage, libel, malign, revile, slander, slur, smear; oppress, persecute, torment, torture
near antonyms acclaim, applaud, approve, hail; commend, compliment, eulogize, praise; adulate, flatter, sweet-talk; exalt, glorify, honor; delight, gratify, please, satisfy

insuperable *adj* **1** incapable of being defeated, overcome, or subdued ⟨the building project ran into *insuperable* financial difficulties and had to be scrapped⟩ — see INVINCIBLE

2 incapable of being solved or accomplished ⟨*insuperable* problems have arisen which make it very unlikely that we will ever finish this project⟩ — see IMPOSSIBLE

insupportable *adj* **1** more than can be put up with ⟨the *insupportable* arrogance of that jerk is more than anyone should have to bear⟩ — see UNBEARABLE

2 too bad to be excused or justified ⟨the organization's racist views have been denounced as morally *insupportable*⟩ — see INEXCUSABLE

insure *vb* to make sure, certain, or safe ⟨took steps to *insure* the timely completion of the project⟩ — see ENSURE

insurgence *n* open fighting against authority (as one's own government) ⟨the *insurgence* eventually succeeded in undermining the corrupt dictatorship⟩ — see REBELLION 1

insurgency *n* open fighting against authority (as one's own government) ⟨there always seems to be *insurgency* of some type in that troubled country⟩ — see REBELLION 1

insurgent *adj* taking part in a rebellion ⟨any *insurgent* soldiers will be dealt with harshly⟩ — see REBELLIOUS 1

insurgent *n* a person who rises up against authority ⟨the government subjected the *insurgents* to the most inhuman torture imaginable⟩ — see REBEL

insurmountable *adj* incapable of being defeated, overcome, or subdued ⟨the familiar story of the underdog who ultimately triumphs despite *insurmountable* odds⟩ — see INVINCIBLE

insurrection *n* open fighting against authority (as one's own government) ⟨the famous *insurrection* of the slaves in ancient Rome under Spartacus⟩ — see REBELLION 1

insurrectionary *adj* taking part in a rebellion ⟨a small *insurrectionary* force that was soundly defeated by the loyalists⟩ — see REBELLIOUS 1

insurrectionary *n* a person who rises up against authority ⟨only a small band of *insurrectionaries* who were willing to stand up to the dictator⟩ — see REBEL

insurrectionist *n* a person who rises up against authority ⟨a would-be *insurrectionist* with a plan to bomb the capitol⟩ — see REBEL

intact *adj* not lacking any part or member that properly belongs to it ⟨it's rare to find such an old chess set that is *intact*⟩ — see COMPLETE 1

intake *n* matter that is fed into something ⟨the *intake* on that paper shredder is limited to five sheets at a time⟩ — see INPUT 1

intangible *adj* not capable of being perceived by the sense of touch ⟨electrical energy is completely *intangible*⟩
synonyms impalpable
related words bodiless, immaterial, incorporeal, insubstantial, unsubstantial; ethereal, spiritual, unreal
near antonyms corporeal, physical; embodied, material, real, solid, substantial
antonyms palpable, tactile, tangible, touchable

integer *n* **1** a character used to represent a mathematical value ⟨three is a positive *integer*⟩ — see NUMBER 1

2 one that has a real and independent existence ⟨an event that is seen as the point at which the gay rights movement became an *integer* and not just a smattering of protests⟩ — see ENTITY

integral *adj* **1** being a part of the innermost nature of a person or thing ⟨a car dealer respected for his *integral* honesty and straightforwardness with customers⟩ — see INHERENT

2 impossible to do without ⟨she's an *integral* member of the team of archaeologists at that dig⟩ — see ESSENTIAL 1

3 not lacking any part or member that properly belongs to it ⟨a prep school that adheres to the belief that athletics are essential to an *integral* life⟩ — see COMPLETE 1

integrate *vb* **1** to make a part of a body or system ⟨*integrate* the new developments into our understanding of cancer⟩ — see EMBODY 1

2 to turn into a single mass or entity that is more or less the same throughout ⟨*integrate* the powders thoroughly before adding them to the liquid⟩ — see BLEND 1

integrity *n* **1** conduct that conforms to an accepted standard of right and wrong ⟨demonstrated that he was a man of *integrity* by taking full responsibility for his actions⟩ — see MORALITY 1

2 devotion to telling the truth ⟨her *integrity* is such that she tells the truth even when people least want to hear it⟩ — see HONESTY 1

3 faithfulness to high moral standards ⟨a politician of great honesty and *integrity*⟩ — see HONOR 1

intellect *n* **1** a very smart person ⟨one of the finest *intel-*

lects of our time⟩ — see GENIUS 1
2 the ability to learn and understand or to deal with problems ⟨a child of great *intellect* as well as artistic talent⟩ — see INTELLIGENCE 1

intellection *n* **1** something imagined or pictured in the mind ⟨notebooks filled with his *intellections* on an amazing array of topics⟩ — see IDEA 1
2 the thought processes that have been established as leading to valid solutions to problems ⟨ever since Descartes famously declared, "I think, therefore I am," people have tended to regard acts of conscious *intellection* as proof of their own existence⟩ — see LOGIC

intellectual *adj* **1** much given to learning and thinking ⟨as the daughter of college professors, she's used to being around *intellectual* people⟩
synonyms blue, cerebral, eggheaded, geeky, highbrow, highbrowed, intellectualist, intellectualistic, longhaired (*or* longhair), nerdish, nerdy
related words cultivated, cultured; middlebrow; erudite, learned, literate, polyhistoric, polymath (*or* polymathic), scholarly, well-read; academic (*also* academical), bookish, professorial; didactic, high-toned, hyperintellectual, pedantic; high-hat, snobbish, snobby, snooty; educated, schooled; brainy, bright, brilliant, clever, intelligent, quick-witted, smart
near antonyms uncultivated, uncultured; ignorant, illiterate, uneducated, unlettered, unread; dumb, foolish, idiotic (*also* idiotical), moronic, slow, stupid, unintelligent; benighted, unenlightened
antonyms anti-intellectual, lowbrow, nonintellectual, philistine
2 of or relating to the mind ⟨*intellectual* pursuits such as reading and studying⟩ — see MENTAL 1
3 of or relating to schooling or learning especially at an advanced level ⟨research that shows that people from very *intellectual* backgrounds are happiest with spouses having comparable educations⟩ — see ACADEMIC 1

intellectual *n* a person with strong intellectual interests ⟨discovered that in politics a reputation for being an *intellectual* was regarded as a liability⟩
synonyms double-dome, egghead, geek, highbrow, intellectualist, longhair, nerd
related words blue, bluestocking; Brahmin, mandarin, sage; intellectualizer, pseud [*British*]; brain, genius, intellect, thinker, whiz, wizard
near antonyms blockhead, dolt, dope, dumbbell, dummy, dunce, fathead, half-wit, imbecile, moron, nitwit, pinhead, simpleton
antonyms anti-intellectual, lowbrow, philistine

intellectualist *adj* much given to learning and thinking ⟨a small cadre of *intellectualist* reformers who had no idea of the concerns of the common folk⟩ — see INTELLECTUAL 1

intellectualist *n* a person with strong intellectual interests ⟨being an *intellectualist*, he has little in common with the status-seeking philistines who live next door⟩ — see INTELLECTUAL

intellectualistic *adj* much given to learning and thinking ⟨while living in Paris she fell in with a coterie of self-consciously arty, *intellectualistic* bohemians⟩ — see INTELLECTUAL 1

intellectuality *n* the ability to learn and understand or to deal with problems ⟨one doesn't need the *intellectuality* of a rocket scientist to understand the problem⟩ — see INTELLIGENCE 1

intelligence *n* **1** the ability to learn and understand or to deal with problems ⟨high scores on this test supposedly demonstrate great *intelligence*⟩
synonyms brain(s), brainpower, gray matter, headpiece, intellect, intellectuality, mentality, reason, sense, smarts
related words eggheadedness, highbrowism, intellectualism; braininess, brilliance; acumen, alertness, apprehension, astuteness, discernment, discriminability, insight, judgment (*or* judgement), perception, percipience, perspicacity; common sense, horse sense, mother wit; aptitude, talent; sagacity, sapience, wisdom, wit; head, mind, skull
near antonyms denseness, density, doltishness, dopiness, dullness (*also* dulness), dumbness, fatuity, feeblemindedness, foolishness, half-wittedness, idiocy, imbecility, senselessness, simpleness, slowness, stupidity
2 a report of recent events or facts not previously known ⟨usually received the latest *intelligence* about how the war was going⟩ — see NEWS
3 exceptional discernment and judgment especially in practical matters ⟨as head of the customer service department, he has handled complaints and disputes with unfailing *intelligence* and good humor⟩ — see ACUMEN

intelligencer *n* **1** a person employed by a newspaper, magazine, or radio or television station to gather, write, or report news ⟨the student journalist asked questions as probing as those of a seasoned *intelligencer*⟩ — see REPORTER
2 a person who tries secretly to obtain information for one country in the territory of another usually unfriendly country ⟨as the nation's top *intelligencer*, the director of the CIA should have been more skeptical of the information he was being fed⟩ — see SPY

intelligent *adj* **1** having or showing quickness of mind ⟨proud parents typically insist that their child is *intelligent* way beyond his or her years⟩ ⟨his *intelligent* response to the emergency averted a disaster⟩
synonyms alert, brainy, bright, brilliant, clever, exceptional, fast, hyperintelligent, keen, nimble, quick, quick-witted, sharp, sharp-witted, smart, supersmart, ultrasmart
related words apt, ingenious, resourceful; acute, astute, discerning, heady, insightful, knowing, perceptive, percipient, perspicacious, sagacious, sapient, savvy, wise; cerebral, erudite, genial, highbrow, knowledgeable, learned, literate, scholarly, well-read; educated, informed, schooled, skilled, trained; creative, inventive, judicious, prudent, sage, sane; sapient, sensible, sound, wise; crafty, cunning, foxy, shrewd, wily; logical, rational, reasonable
near antonyms feebleminded, simpleminded; boobish, foolish, half-baked, idiotic (*also* idiotical), imbecile (*or* imbecilic), moronic, silly; ignorant, illiterate, lowbrow, nonintellectual, unacademic, uneducated, uninformed, unintellectual, untaught, unthinking; absurd, asinine, balmy, cockeyed, crackpot, crazy, cuckoo, daffy, daft, dippy, dotty, featherheaded, fool, half-baked, harebrained, insane, kooky (*also* kookie), loony (*also* looney), lunatic, mad, nonsensical, nutty, preposterous, sappy, screwball, tomfool, unwise, wacky (*also* whacky), zany
antonyms airheaded, birdbrained, boneheaded, braindead, brainless, bubbleheaded, chuckleheaded, dense, dim, dim-witted, doltish, dopey (*also* dopy), dorky [*slang*], dull, dumb, dunderheaded, empty-headed, fatuous, gormless [*chiefly British*], half-witted, knuckleheaded, lamebrain (*or* lamebrained), lunkheaded, mindless, obtuse, opaque, pinheaded, senseless, simple, slow, slow-witted, soft, softheaded, stupid, thick, thickheaded, thick-witted, unbrilliant, unintelligent, unsmart, vacuous, weak-minded, witless
2 having the ability to reason ⟨there is some debate over whether dolphins are *intelligent* animals⟩ — see RATIONAL 1
3 having or showing good judgment and restraint especially in conduct or speech ⟨the only *intelligent* response to such a tasteless joke is to quickly change the subject⟩ — see DISCREET 1

intelligentsia *n* intellectuals considered as a social class ⟨a presidential candidate who was the darling of the *intelligentsia*—and very few others⟩
synonyms clerisy, literati
related words avant-garde, culturati; chosen, illuminati; best, choice, cream, elect, elite, fat, flower, pick, prime, upper crust
near antonyms booboisie

intelligible *adj* capable of being understood ⟨speculation on the odds that a communication from a far-off planet would be *intelligible*⟩
synonyms accessible, apprehensible, coherent, comprehendible, comprehensible, fathomable, graspable, legible, scrutable, understandable
related words decipherable; plain, simple, straightforward; articulate, fluent, well-spoken
near antonyms inarticulate; cryptic, esoteric, mysterious, obscure
antonyms incoherent, incomprehensible, inscrutable, insensible

intemperance *n* **1** habitual or excessive drinking of intoxicants ⟨in his harangue on the perils of drink, the prohibitionist claimed that *intemperance* has always been the number one destroyer of marriages⟩
synonyms alcoholism, drunkenness, insobriety, intemperateness
related words inebriety, intoxication; bibulousness, dipsomania; debauchery, dissoluteness
near antonyms abstention, abstinence, teetotalism
antonyms sobriety, temperance
2 a propensity for extremes in one's actions, beliefs, or habits ⟨there's a wearisome *intemperance* in his verbal attacks against any and all who dare to disagree with him⟩ — see EXCESS 2

intemperate *adj* **1** showing no signs of being under control ⟨*intemperate* anger that is so extreme that the man should be in therapy⟩ — see RAMPANT 1
2 given to excessive use of alcoholic beverages ⟨a serious course in wine appreciation that does not welcome *intemperate* drinkers and party animals⟩ — see CRAPULOUS

intemperateness *n* **1** a propensity for extremes in one's actions, beliefs, or habits ⟨a talk show that seems to select political pundits mostly for their exhibitionistic *intemperateness*⟩ — see EXCESS 2
2 habitual or excessive drinking of intoxicants ⟨as far as the townspeople are concerned, the students at the local college seem to be far more noteworthy for their *intemperateness* than for their intellectualism⟩ — see INTEMPERANCE 1

intend *vb* **1** to have in mind as a purpose or goal ⟨an aspiring entrepreneur who *intends* to revolutionize the biotech industry⟩
synonyms aim, allow [*chiefly Southern & Midland*], aspire, calculate, contemplate, design, go [*chiefly Southern & Midland*], look, mean, meditate, plan, propose, purport, purpose
related words dream, hope, wish; consider, debate, mull (over), ponder; attempt, endeavor, strive, struggle, try; plot, scheme; accomplish, achieve, effect, execute, perform
phrases figure on
2 to communicate or convey (as an idea) to the mind ⟨lawyers for both sides argued for days about what was *intended* by a particular phrase in the law⟩ — see MEAN 1

intendance *n* the act or activity of looking after and making decisions about something ⟨his scrupulous *intendance* of the university's finances⟩ — see CONDUCT 1

intended *n* the person to whom one is engaged to be married ⟨after a bit of bickering, she and her *intended* have finally picked out a wedding site⟩ — see BETROTHED

intended *adj* made, given, or done with full awareness of what one is doing ⟨you may feign innocence, but I know that that last remark was an *intended* dig⟩ — see INTENTIONAL

intense *adj* **1** extreme in degree, power, or effect ⟨the *intense* cold of the polar regions⟩
synonyms acute, almighty, blistering, deep, dreadful, excruciating, explosive, exquisite, fearful, fearsome, ferocious, fierce, frightful, furious, ghastly, hard, heavy, heavy-duty, hellacious, intensive, keen, profound, terrible, vehement, vicious, violent
related words accentuated, aggravated, concentrated, deepened; emphasized, enhanced, heightened, intensified, magnified; stressed; exhaustive, thorough; harsh, rigorous, severe
near antonyms feeble, weak; shallow, superficial; moderated, qualified; alleviated, eased, lightened, toned (down); abated, decreased, diminished, lessened, reduced, subdued
antonyms light, moderate, soft
2 having or expressing great depth of feeling ⟨an *intense* actor who favors edgy film roles⟩ — see FERVENT 1

intensely *adv* **1** with great effort or determination ⟨struggled *intensely* to master the language of her adopted country⟩ — see HARD 1
2 to a great degree ⟨the senate race was *intensely* close⟩ — see VERY 1

intenseness *n* **1** depth of feeling ⟨she presents her religious convictions with an *intenseness* that makes some people uncomfortable⟩ — see ARDOR 1
2 the quality or state of being forceful (as in expression) ⟨every challenge that he undertakes is tackled with an *intenseness* that would exhaust most people⟩ — see VEHEMENCE 1

intensify *vb* to make markedly greater in measure or degree ⟨*intensified* her efforts to preserve the town's historic buildings and landmarks⟩
synonyms accentuate, amp (up), amplify, beef (up), boost, consolidate, deepen, enhance, heighten, magnify, redouble, step up, strengthen
related words broaden, enlarge, expand, extend, lengthen; accelerate, hasten, quicken; emphasize, point (up), sharpen, stress; augment, enforce, reinforce (*also* reenforce), restrengthen, supplement; maximize; enliven, jazz (up); aggravate, exacerbate
near antonyms decrease, diminish, lessen, let up (on), reduce, subdue, tone (down), weaken; dwindle, recede, subside, taper (off), wane; alleviate, ease, lighten
antonyms abate, moderate

intensity *n* **1** depth of feeling ⟨spoke with great *intensity* and eloquence on the need to combat racism⟩ — see ARDOR 1
2 the quality or state of being forceful (as in expression) ⟨the *intensity* of the actor's performance had theatergoers on the edge of their seats⟩ — see VEHEMENCE 1

intensive *adj* extreme in degree, power, or effect ⟨an *intensive* effort to prevent an adult bookstore from opening in town⟩ — see INTENSE 1

intensively *adv* with great effort or determination ⟨labored *intensively* in order to get the film ready for its premiere⟩ — see HARD 1

intent *adj* **1** fully committed to achieving a goal ⟨*intent* on finishing her sculpture in time for the group show⟩ — see DETERMINED 1
2 having the mind fixed on something ⟨he was so *intent* on his work that he didn't hear the dog bark⟩ — see ATTENTIVE 1

intent *n* **1** something that one hopes or intends to accomplish ⟨I'm sorry that I hurt your feelings; that wasn't my *intent*⟩ — see GOAL

2 the idea that is conveyed or intended to be conveyed to the mind by language, symbol, or action ⟨the wording was a little unclear, but I think I grasped the *intent*⟩ — see MEANING 1

intention *n* **1** something that one hopes or intends to accomplish ⟨her *intention* is to climb the highest peak in each of the 50 states⟩ — see GOAL
2 the idea that is conveyed or intended to be conveyed to the mind by language, symbol, or action ⟨she was uncertain of the *intention* of his frantic gesturing⟩ — see MEANING 1

intentional *adj* made, given, or done with full awareness of what one is doing ⟨I'm fairly sure that your "accidental" cutting down of my rosebush was really *intentional*⟩
synonyms conscious, deliberate, intended, knowing, purposeful, purposive, set, voluntary, willed, willful (*or* wilful), witting
related words designed, planned; conscious; advised, calculated, considered, measured, reasoned, studied, thoughtful, weighed; premeditated, premeditative, prepense; discretionary, elective, optional, volunteer
near antonyms inadvertent, unwitting; accidental, chance, haphazard, hit-or-miss, incidental, random; aimless, desultory, purposeless; abrupt, impetuous, sudden; coerced, forced, involuntary; compulsory, mandatory, necessary, nonelective, obligatory, ordered, required; casual; extemporaneous, impromptu, impulsive, instinctive, spontaneous, unforced, unpremeditated
antonyms nondeliberate, nonpurposive, unintentional

intentionally *adv* with full awareness of what one is doing ⟨the witness *intentionally* gave misleading answers to the questions⟩
synonyms advisedly, consciously, deliberately, designedly, knowingly, purposefully, purposely, purposively, willfully, wittingly
related words calculatedly, studiedly; voluntarily, willingly; premeditatedly
phrases on purpose
near antonyms accidentally, incidentally; haphazardly, randomly; involuntarily, unwillingly; impulsively, instinctively, spontaneously
antonyms inadvertently, unconsciously, unintentionally, unknowingly, unwittingly

intently *adv* with great effort or determination ⟨*intently* studied his notes just before the exam⟩ — see HARD 1

intentness *n* a mental state free of jesting or trifling ⟨studied the dance steps with obvious *intentness*⟩ — see EARNESTNESS

inter *vb* to place (a dead body) in the earth, a tomb, or the sea ⟨the soldier was *interred* with great honors at Arlington National Cemetery⟩ — see BURY 1

interaction *n* doings between individuals or groups ⟨she guessed from the friendly *interaction* that they were close to the other parents in the organization⟩ — see RELATION 1

intercalate *vb* to put among or between others ⟨between the recipes for hearty peasant dishes, the author *intercalates* fond reminiscences of her year in the French countryside⟩ — see INSERT

intercede *vb* to act as a go-between for opposing sides ⟨asked an old friend of the family to *intercede* in the bitter dispute over the inheritance⟩ — see INTERVENE

interceder *n* one who works with opposing sides in order to bring about an agreement ⟨respected around the world, the secretary-general of the United Nations was asked to be the *interceder* in several international disputes⟩ — see MEDIATOR

intercept *vb* to stop, seize, or interrupt while in progress or on course ⟨the cat was about to hightail it out the front door when I *intercepted* her⟩
synonyms block, interdict, pick off
related words capture, catch, collar, corral, grab, seize, snare, snatch, trap

intercessor *n* one who works with opposing sides in order to bring about an agreement ⟨eventually, they hired an *intercessor*, because they were getting nowhere on their own⟩ — see MEDIATOR

interchangeable *adj* capable of being substituted in place of one another ⟨the concept of *interchangeable* parts revolutionized the mass production of manufactured goods⟩
synonyms commutable, exchangeable, fungible, substitutable, switchable
related words replaceable
antonyms noninterchangeable

intercommunicate *vb* to engage in an exchange of information or ideas ⟨the two agencies will need to *intercommunicate* better if the nation is ever to become truly secure from international terrorism⟩ — see COMMUNICATE 2

interconnect *vb* to put or bring together so as to form a new and longer whole ⟨we *interconnected* all of our audio and video components to get the full home theater experience⟩ — see CONNECT 1

intercourse *n* **1** doings between individuals or groups ⟨the niceties of social *intercourse* are lost on that nerd⟩ — see RELATION 1
2 sexual union involving penetration of the vagina by the penis ⟨*intercourse* is one of ways by which the disease is commonly spread⟩ — see SEXUAL INTERCOURSE

intercross *n* an offspring of parents with different genes especially when of different races, breeds, species, or genera ⟨that pink rose is an *intercross* of red and white roses⟩ — see HYBRID

interdict *n* an order that something not be done or used ⟨the church's controversial *interdict* against the use of birth control devices⟩ — see PROHIBITION 2

interdict *vb* **1** to order not to do or use or to be done or used ⟨the state legislature moved to *interdict* the use of radar-detection devices by motorists⟩ — see FORBID
2 to stop, seize, or interrupt while in progress or on course ⟨federal agents are able to *interdict* only a small percentage of the narcotic shipments into the country⟩ — see INTERCEPT

interdicted *adj* that may not be permitted ⟨an *interdicted* hold in wrestling⟩ — see IMPERMISSIBLE

interdicting *n* the act of ordering that something not be done or used ⟨the *interdicting* against bullying at school, along with stiff penalties, was long overdue⟩ — see PROHIBITION 1

interdiction *n* **1** an order that something not be done or used ⟨a written *interdiction* against the wearing of clothing incorporating gang colors⟩ — see PROHIBITION 2
2 the act of ordering that something not be done or used ⟨the recent *interdiction* against open fires on the beach has riled summer revelers⟩ — see PROHIBITION 1

interest *vb* to hold the attention of ⟨the book didn't *interest* me, so I ended up watching the parade of people on the sidewalk⟩ — see ENGAGE 1

interest *n* **1** a legal right to participation in the advantages, profits, and responsibility of something ⟨all of the workers at the food cooperative have an *interest* in it⟩
synonyms claim, share, stake
related words co-ownership, ownership, part, partnership, possession, title
2 the state of doing well especially in relation to one's happiness or success ⟨make no mistake: she's determined to act in her own *interest* in this business deal⟩ — see WELFARE
3 a commercial or industrial activity or organization ⟨a

multinational corporation with *interests* on every continent⟩ — see ENTERPRISE 1

4 a group of people with a common identifying interest that they seek to protect and promote ⟨the contention that the nation's financial *interests* have too much power⟩ — see INTEREST GROUP

interest group *n* a group of people with a common identifying interest that they seek to protect and promote ⟨agricultural *interest groups* are adamantly opposed to the bill⟩

synonyms interest, pressure group, special interest

related words vested interest; political action committee

interesting *adj* holding the attention or provoking interest ⟨an *interesting* lecture on conflicts in the Middle East since the demise of the Ottoman Empire⟩

synonyms absorbing, arresting, consuming, engaging, engrossing, enthralling, fascinating, gripping, immersing, intriguing, involving, riveting

related words breathtaking, electric, electrifying, exciting, exhilarating, galvanizing, inspiring, rousing, stimulating, stirring, thrilling; provocative, tantalizing; emphatic, showy, splashy, striking; alluring, attractive, bewitching, captivating, charming, enchanting, spellbinding; hypnotizing, mesmerizing; curious, odd, unusual, weird; amazing, astonishing, astounding, eventful, eye-opening, fabulous, marvelous (*or* marvellous), surprising, wonderful, wondrous; amusing, entertaining

near antonyms operose, tiresome, tiring, wearisome, wearying; sterile, unexciting; dreary, humdrum, pedantic, pedestrian; demoralizing, discouraging, disheartening, dispiriting

antonyms boring, drab, dry, dull, heavy, monotonous, tedious, uninteresting

interfere *vb* to interest oneself in what is not one's concern ⟨a strong resentment of outsiders who attempted to *interfere* with their traditional ways of doing things⟩

synonyms butt in, interlope, intermeddle, intrude, meddle, mess, muck (about *or* around), nose, obtrude, poke, pry, snoop

related words intercede, interpose, intervene; barge (in), chisel (in), encroach, infringe, invade, trespass; fiddle, fool, monkey, play, tamper

near antonyms avoid, eschew, shun; disregard, ignore, neglect, overlook

interfere (with) *vb* to create difficulty for the work or activity of ⟨claims that the countless federal regulations *interfere with* his business and are of no benefit to anyone⟩ — see HAMPER

interference *n* something that makes movement or progress difficult ⟨without the *interference* of the rain, we could have made good time on that road trip⟩ — see ENCUMBRANCE

interferer *n* a person who meddles in the affairs of others ⟨an incurable *interferer*, she couldn't mind her own business to save her life⟩ — see BUSYBODY

interfering *adj* thrusting oneself where one is not welcome or invited ⟨an *interfering* woman by nature, she was precisely the kind of mother-in-law that every new bride dreads⟩ — see INTRUSIVE

interfuse *vb* **1** to come together to form a single unit ⟨comedy and social commentary *interfuse* seamlessly in this hilariously satirical movie⟩ — see UNITE 1

2 to turn into a single mass or entity that is more or less the same throughout ⟨an attractive cologne that *interfuses* herbal and woodsy scents⟩ — see BLEND 1

interim *adj* **1** intended to last, continue, or serve for a limited time ⟨putting up some students in local motels is obviously just an *interim* solution to the college's housing shortage⟩ — see TEMPORARY 1

2 serving in a position for the time being ⟨will serve as *interim* head of the police department until the investigation is completed⟩ — see ACTING

interim *n* a break in continuity ⟨there was a brief *interim* in the proceedings while everyone got organized⟩ — see GAP 2

interior *n* an interior or internal part ⟨the *interior* of the computer was clogged with dust⟩ — see INSIDE 1

interior *adj* **1** of or relating to the mind ⟨the novel's characters have plenty of adventures, but their *interior* lives are never explored⟩ — see MENTAL 1

2 situated farther in ⟨was given a windowless *interior* office⟩ — see INNER 1

interject *vb* to put among or between others ⟨she occasionally *interjected* comments into the conversation⟩ — see INSERT

interjection *n* a sudden short emotional utterance ⟨a chorus of angry *interjections* greeted the announcement that our flight would be delayed⟩ — see EXCLAMATION

interlace *vb* **1** to cause to twine about one another ⟨*interlaced* strands of her hair for a new look⟩ — see INTERTWINE 1

2 to scatter or set here and there among other things ⟨*interlaced* jokes between the serious passages in the speech⟩ — see THREAD 1

3 to twist together into a usually confused mass ⟨I've *interlaced* the cables on my audio-video system so confusingly that I've no idea what connects what⟩ — see ENTANGLE 1

interlink *vb* to put or bring together so as to form a new and longer whole ⟨she was idly *interlinking* paper clips into a chain as she listened⟩ — see CONNECT 1

interlope *vb* to interest oneself in what is not one's concern ⟨regarded the new couple as a pair of *interloping* parvenus who were sure to upset the town's social hierarchy⟩ — see INTERFERE

interloper *n* a person who meddles in the affairs of others ⟨summer residents were regarded as *interlopers* who had no deep commitment to the town's welfare⟩ — see BUSYBODY

interlude *n* a break in continuity ⟨there was a brief *interlude* in the performance while the stagehands shifted scenery⟩ — see GAP 2

intermeddle *vb* to interest oneself in what is not one's concern ⟨she can no more refrain from *intermeddling* than she can from breathing⟩ — see INTERFERE

intermeddler *n* a person who meddles in the affairs of others ⟨local voters regarded the out-of-state campaign workers as impertinent *intermeddlers*⟩ — see BUSYBODY

intermediary *adj* occupying a position equally distant from the ends or extremes ⟨the bridal couple were regally ensconced in *intermediary* seats at the head table⟩ — see MIDDLE 1

intermediary *n* one who works with opposing sides in order to bring about an agreement ⟨in the past he's served as an *intermediary* in several hostage situations⟩ — see MEDIATOR

intermediate *adj* **1** being about midway between extremes of amount or size ⟨with a compact being too small and a van too large, we settled on an *intermediate*-sized sedan⟩ — see MIDDLE 2

2 occupying a position equally distant from the ends or extremes ⟨although the party activists tend to back candidates with somewhat extreme views, ordinary voters generally prefer the *intermediate* aspirant⟩ — see MIDDLE 1

intermediate *n* one who works with opposing sides in order to bring about an agreement ⟨she often used her father as an *intermediate* in arguments with her mother⟩ — see MEDIATOR

intermediate *vb* to act as a go-between for opposing sides ⟨if the secretary-general chooses to *intermediate* in this dispute, he'll need all of his diplomatic skills just to get both sides in the same room⟩ — see INTERVENE

interment *n* the act or ceremony of putting a dead body in its final resting place ⟨a respectful but nonreligious *interment* in a private cemetery⟩ — see BURIAL 1

intermingle *vb* to turn into a single mass or entity that is more or less the same throughout ⟨thoroughly *intermingle* the different kinds of candy so that each bag will get a good assortment⟩ — see BLEND 1

intermission *n* a break in continuity ⟨an awkward *intermission* between speeches⟩ — see GAP 2

intermittent *adj* **1** occurring or appearing at intervals ⟨*intermittent* showers had me opening and closing my umbrella all day long⟩
synonyms continual, on-and-off, periodic, periodical, recurrent, recurring
related words alternate, alternating, cyclic (*or* cyclical), rhythmic (*or* rhythmical), seasonal, serial; aperiodic, erratic, fitful, irregular, occasional, spasmodic, sporadic, spotty, unsteady
near antonyms eternal, everlasting, interminable, perpetual
antonyms constant, continuous, incessant, unceasing
2 lacking in steadiness or regularity of occurrence ⟨the breadwinner's *intermittent* employment put the family in a difficult position financially⟩ — see FITFUL

intermix *vb* to turn into a single mass or entity that is more or less the same throughout ⟨*intermixed* the ingredients just until there were no more lumps in the batter⟩ — see BLEND 1

intermixture *n* a distinct entity formed by the combining of two or more different things ⟨the building is an intriguing *intermixture* of classical and modern elements⟩ — see BLEND

intern *vb* to put in or as if in prison ⟨some Polish citizens were *interned* in Russian camps during World War II⟩ — see IMPRISON

internal *adj* **1** situated farther in ⟨somehow grave robbers hadn't managed to locate and enter the *internal* chambers of the Egyptian tomb⟩ — see INNER 1
2 of or relating to the mind ⟨the never-ending *internal* monologue of the novel's main character⟩ — see MENTAL 1

international *adj* relating to or involving two or more nations ⟨an *international* trade agreement⟩
synonyms foreign, multinational, transnational
related words intercontinental, transcontinental
near antonyms domestic, internal, national

interned *adj* taken and held prisoner ⟨the soldiers daringly rescued their *interned* comrades without the loss of a single life⟩ — see CAPTIVE

internee *n* one that has been taken and held in confinement ⟨all *internees* were released upon the cessation of hostilities⟩ — see CAPTIVE

internment *n* the act of confining or the state of being confined ⟨the *internment* of Americans of Japanese descent during World War II is one of the more shameful chapters in United States history⟩
synonyms captivity, confinement, immurement, impoundment, imprisonment, incarceration, prison
related words bondage, enslavement, servitude; restraint, restriction; arrest, capture, entrapment; custody, detainer, detainment, detention, house arrest
near antonyms emancipation, liberation, manumission, redemption, release; freedom, independence, liberty

internship *n* a period of undergoing practical instruction in one's job or career ⟨seeking a summer *internship* at a local television station⟩ — see APPRENTICESHIP

interpenetrate *vb* to spread throughout ⟨with tie-dyeing, the dye does not *interpenetrate* the entire fabric⟩ — see PERMEATE

interpolate *vb* to put among or between others ⟨*interpolated* a new paragraph into the online encyclopedia article⟩ — see INSERT

interpose *vb* **1** to act as a go-between for opposing sides ⟨an elder statesman who has *interposed* a number of times in international conflicts⟩ — see INTERVENE
2 to cause a disruption in a conversation or discussion ⟨I hate to *interpose*, but could you tell me what you meant by that last remark?⟩ — see INTERRUPT
3 to put among or between others ⟨a solid line of police in riot gear *interposed* itself between the trade ministers and the crowd of protesters⟩ — see INSERT

interposer *n* one who works with opposing sides in order to bring about an agreement ⟨I hope that we can resolve this dispute by ourselves, without the help of some outside *interposer*⟩ — see MEDIATOR

interpret *vb* **1** to make plain or understandable ⟨a biblical passage that scholars haven't been able to *interpret* to everyone's satisfaction⟩ — see EXPLAIN 1
2 to present a portrayal or performance of ⟨*interpreted* the role of Fletcher Christian in a challengingly new way⟩ — see ACT 1

interpretation *n* **1** a statement that makes something clear ⟨that's one possible *interpretation* of that cryptic remark⟩ — see EXPLANATION 1
2 a presentation of an artistic work (as a piece of music) from a particular point of view ⟨a sensitive *interpretation* of a piece that is a touchstone for violinists⟩ — see ACCOUNT 2
3 a distinct treatment of something (as a story or a play) ⟨a very Freudian *interpretation* of *The Nutcracker*⟩ — see RIFF

interpretative *adj* serving to explain ⟨fundamentalists who believe that the Bible means exactly what it says and thus requires no *interpretative* commentary⟩ — see EXPLANATORY

interpreter *n* one who brings an art or science to full realization ⟨Monet is generally regarded as the foremost *interpreter* of pure impressionism⟩ — see EXPONENT 2

interpretive *adj* serving to explain ⟨an edition of Shakespeare's plays with many *interpretive* footnotes that students should find very helpful⟩ — see EXPLANATORY

interregnum *n* a break in continuity ⟨the democratic regime proved to be a short-lived *interregnum* between dictatorships⟩ — see GAP 2

interring *n* the act or ceremony of putting a dead body in its final resting place ⟨fittingly, the *interring* took place on a gloomy, rainy day⟩ — see BURIAL 1

interrogate *vb* **1** to put a question or questions to ⟨*interrogated* him about where he'd gone the night before⟩ — see ASK 1
2 to put a series of questions to ⟨police *interrogated* the murder suspect for hours on end⟩ — see EXAMINE 1

interrogative *n* an interrogative expression often used to test knowledge ⟨though she phrased it as an *interrogative*, it was clear that the utterance was more of a command⟩ — see QUESTION 1

interrupt *vb* to cause a disruption in a conversation or discussion ⟨it's rude to *interrupt* when someone is making an important point⟩
synonyms break in, chime in, chip in [*chiefly British*], cut in, interpose, intrude
related words barge (in), bother, horn in; add, contribute, put in

interruption *n* **1** a break in continuity ⟨an *interruption* in cable service during the lightning storm⟩ — see GAP 2
2 a momentary halt in an activity ⟨a brief *interruption* in the discussion while we all got coffee⟩ — see PAUSE 1

intersect *vb* to divide by passing through or across ⟨an elevated highway now *intersects* that old urban neighborhood⟩

synonyms bisect, cross, cut
related words crisscross, decussate
intersection *n* a place where roads meet ⟨take a left turn at the next *intersection*⟩ — see CROSSROAD 1
intersperse *vb* **1** to scatter or set here and there among other things ⟨for variety, *intersperse* some photos among the other decorations on the wall⟩ — see THREAD 1
2 to put among or between others ⟨*intersperses* some fascinating factoids about wine between his profiles of the nation's leading wineries⟩ — see INSERT
interstice *n* **1** a break in continuity ⟨there's an occasional *interstice* in the tedium, but most of the novel is boring⟩ — see GAP 2
2 an open space in a barrier (as a wall or hedge) ⟨pesky weeds growing in the *interstices* between the flagstones⟩ — see GAP 1
intertwine *vb* **1** to cause to twine about one another ⟨*intertwined* two different colors of yarn⟩
synonyms enlace, entwine, implicate [*archaic*], interlace, intertwist, interweave, inweave, lace, ply, twist, weave, wreathe, writhe
related words braid, plait, plat, pleach; blend, fuse, join, link, mix
near antonyms disentangle, uncoil, untangle, untwine, unwind
2 to twist together into a usually confused mass ⟨*intertwining* yarn is usually a bad idea, because you'll never get it all sorted out again⟩ — see ENTANGLE
intertwist *vb* **1** to cause to twine about one another ⟨*intertwisted* the cables in his roommate's entertainment system just out of spite⟩ — see INTERTWINE 1
2 to twist together into a usually confused mass ⟨the tree's *intertwisted* roots seemed to extend forever⟩ — see ENTANGLE 1
interval *n* **1** a break in continuity ⟨there were *intervals* of thousands of years between the major ice ages⟩ — see GAP 2
2 an open space in a barrier (as a wall or hedge) ⟨unable to find my way out of the maze, I cheated and squeezed through a convenient *interval* in the hedge⟩ — see GAP 1
intervene *vb* to act as a go-between for opposing sides ⟨*intervened* in the argument before any real harm was done⟩
synonyms intercede, intermediate, interpose, mediate
related words butt in, interfere, intrude, meddle, obtrude, pry, snoop; arbitrate, moderate, negotiate, referee; barge (in), bother; break (in), chime in, cut in; infringe, invade, trespass
near antonyms stand by; avoid, eschew, shun; disregard, ignore, overlook
interview *vb* to go around and approach (people) with a request for opinions or information ⟨a reporter at the scene *interviewing* witnesses to the explosion⟩ — see CANVASS 1
interviewer *n* a person who goes around and approaches people with a request for opinions or information ⟨had no time for an *interviewer* who wanted to ask me about my phone service⟩ — see CANVASSER
interweave *vb* **1** to cause to twine about one another ⟨*interweaved* garlands of red and gold beads and wrapped them around the Christmas tree⟩ — see INTERTWINE 1
2 to scatter or set here and there among other things ⟨the author artfully *interweaves* excerpts from soldiers' letters into his history of the Vietnam War⟩ — see THREAD 1
3 to twist together into a usually confused mass ⟨in our play the kitten and I managed to *interweave* the skeins of yarn into a hopeless tangle⟩ — see ENTANGLE 1
intestinal fortitude *n* **1** strength of mind to carry on in spite of danger ⟨the one person who had the *intestinal fortitude* to stand up and denounce the injustice of it all⟩ — see COURAGE
2 the strength of mind that enables a person to endure pain or hardship ⟨you'll need considerable *intestinal fortitude* to put up with that corporate diva, but the work experience will be worth it⟩ — see FORTITUDE
intimacy *n* the state of being in a very personal or private relationship ⟨there can be both rewards and regrets from *intimacy* with another person⟩ — see FAMILIARITY 1
intimate *adj* **1** closely acquainted ⟨*intimate* friends who can practically finish each other's sentences⟩ — see FAMILIAR 1
2 not known or meant to be known by the general populace ⟨they broke up after she shared *intimate* information with all 500 of her closest friends⟩ — see PRIVATE 1
intimate *n* a person who has a strong liking for and trust in another ⟨usually quite aloof in public, he's actually quite relaxed with his *intimates*⟩ — see FRIEND 1
intimate *vb* to convey an idea indirectly ⟨trying to *intimate* that there was more going on than anyone knew⟩ — see HINT
intimately *adv* in a manner intended to prevent knowledge or awareness by others ⟨*intimately* shared information that is only now being divulged in the memoirs of his sole confidant⟩ — see PRIVATELY
intimation *n* a slight or indirect pointing to something (as a solution or explanation) ⟨the newscaster could not resist giving a slight *intimation* that the voting was going contrary to predictions⟩ — see HINT 1
intimidate *vb* to make timid or fearful by or as if by threats ⟨refusing to be *intimidated* by the manager's harsh stare, I demanded my money back⟩
synonyms blackjack, bogart, browbeat, bulldoze, bully, bullyrag, cow, hector, mau-mau, strong-arm
related words bluster, trash-talk; affright, alarm (*also* alarum), frighten, horrify, scare, shock, spook, startle, terrify; menace, terrorize, threaten; badger, harass, hound; bludgeon, coerce, compel, constrain, dragoon, force, make, oblige, press, pressure, push around; demoralize, psych (out), unman, unnerve; discompose, disconcert, disquiet, distress, disturb, perturb, upset
phrases pick on
near antonyms cheer, comfort, console, reassure, solace, soothe; embolden, encourage, hearten, steel; convince, persuade
intimidating *adj* **1** causing fear ⟨the *intimidating* prospect of the college entrance exams⟩ — see FEARFUL 1
2 harsh and threatening in manner or appearance ⟨an *intimidating* bodyguard keeping the fans away from the rock star⟩ — see GRIM 1
intimidator *n* a person who teases, threatens, or hurts smaller or weaker persons ⟨the loan shark hired an *intimidator* to make sure that he got all that was owed him⟩ — see BULLY 1
intolerable *adj* **1** more than can be put up with ⟨this stifling heat is *intolerable*⟩ — see UNBEARABLE
2 going beyond a normal or acceptable limit in degree or amount ⟨the *intolerable* haste with which the press passed judgment on the accused⟩ — see EXCESSIVE
intolerably *adj* beyond a normal or acceptable limit ⟨a lot of actresses are divas, but that one is *intolerably* vain and arrogant⟩ — see TOO 1
intolerance *n* stubborn or intolerant adherence to one's opinions or prejudices ⟨a memoir of a time when racial *intolerance* was socially acceptable⟩ — see BIGOTRY
intolerant *adj* **1** unable or unwilling to endure ⟨*intolerant* of fools, she is not an easy person to work for⟩
synonyms impatient
related words uncompromising, unforgiving, unyield-

ing; complaining, fussing, griping, grumbling, kvetching, protesting, squawking, whining
near antonyms accepting, forgiving, long-suffering, resigned, uncomplaining, willing; indulgent
antonyms abiding, enduring, forbearing, patient, tolerant
2 unwilling to grant other people social rights or to accept other viewpoints ⟨*intolerant* people who callously deny others the very rights that they take for granted⟩
synonyms bigoted, illiberal, narrow, narrow-minded, prejudiced, small-minded
related words conservative, hidebound, old-fashioned, reactionary; blindfolded, blinkered, insular, parochial, provincial; biased, one-sided, partial, partisan
near antonyms extreme, progressive, radical; impartial, objective, unbiased
antonyms broad-minded, liberal, open-minded, tolerant, unprejudiced

intolerantness *n* stubborn or intolerant adherence to one's opinions or prejudices ⟨there's an element of *intolerantness* in his religious writings that many readers find unsettling⟩ — see BIGOTRY

intonate *vb* to utter in musical or drawn out tones ⟨the priest then proceeded to *intonate* the prayer's familiar opening words⟩ — see CHANT 1

intone *vb* to utter in musical or drawn out tones ⟨"The day is begun," the narrator *intoned*⟩ — see CHANT 1

intoxicant *n* a distilled beverage that can make a person drunk ⟨a religious denomination that strictly forbids the use of all *intoxicants*⟩ — see ALCOHOL

intoxicate *vb* **1** to cause a pleasurable stimulation of the feelings ⟨the stunning spectacle of this Las Vegas show is sure to *intoxicate* spectators⟩ — see THRILL
2 to fill with great joy ⟨she was *intoxicated* by the news that she'd gotten the job of her dreams⟩ — see ELATE

intoxicated *adj* **1** being under the influence of alcohol ⟨state police warned that there would be zero tolerance for *intoxicated* drivers over the long holiday weekend⟩ — see DRUNK
2 experiencing or marked by overwhelming usually pleasurable emotion ⟨the *intoxicated* moment when she found out that she'd won the award⟩ — see ECSTATIC

intoxicating *adj* causing great emotional or mental stimulation ⟨naive, young men who had once regarded the thought of going off to war as an *intoxicating* notion⟩ — see EXCITING 1

intoxication *n* **1** the condition of being drunk ⟨there's a firm distinction between the moderate consumption of alcoholic beverages and overindulgence to the point of *intoxication*⟩
synonyms drunkenness, inebriation, inebriety
related words tipsiness; insobriety, intemperance; alcoholism; bender, binge, brannigan, jag, souse, spree, toot
2 a state of overwhelming usually pleasurable emotion ⟨the *intoxication* felt by two people who have just fallen in love⟩ — see ECSTASY

intractability *n* refusal to obey ⟨the dog's frustrating *intractability* forced the family to try obedience training by a professional⟩ — see DISOBEDIENCE

intractable *adj* **1** given to resisting authority or another's control ⟨an *intractable* child who deliberately does the opposite of whatever he is told⟩ — see DISOBEDIENT
2 given to resisting control or discipline by others ⟨cats are by nature fairly *intractable* animals⟩ — see UNCONTROLLABLE

intransigence *n* a steadfast adherence to an opinion, purpose, or course of action in spite of reason, arguments, or persuasion ⟨her *intransigence* on the issue was simply frustrating⟩ — see OBSTINACY

intransigent *adj* sticking to an opinion, purpose, or course of action in spite of reason, arguments, or persuasion ⟨he has remained *intransigent*, refusing all suggestions for improvement of the process⟩ — see OBSTINATE

intrepid *adj* feeling or displaying no fear by temperament ⟨an *intrepid* explorer who probed parts of the rain forest never previously attempted⟩ — see BRAVE 1

intrepidity *n* strength of mind to carry on in spite of danger ⟨he managed to get back to camp, despite the grizzly bears, through sheer *intrepidity*⟩ — see COURAGE

intrepidly *adv* in a fearless manner ⟨spies sneaked *intrepidly* into the enemy's camp⟩ — see BRAVELY 1

intrepidness *n* strength of mind to carry on in spite of danger ⟨a globe-trotting journalist of remarkable *intrepidness* who never flinches from any challenge life has to offer⟩ — see COURAGE

intricacy *n* **1** something that makes a situation more complicated or difficult ⟨just now learning the *intricacies* of owning one's own business⟩ — see COMPLICATION 1
2 the state or quality of having many interrelated parts or aspects ⟨the *intricacy* of the puzzle requires close concentration⟩ — see COMPLEXITY 1

intricate *adj* **1** having many parts or aspects that are usually interrelated ⟨an *intricate* machine that requires some training to use it properly⟩ — see COMPLEX 1
2 made or done with great care or with much detail ⟨an *intricate* hairstyle that requires far too much maintenance to suit my taste⟩ — see ELABORATE 1

intricateness *n* the state or quality of having many interrelated parts or aspects ⟨the awesome *intricateness* of the human eye⟩ — see COMPLEXITY 1

intrigue *n* a secret plan for accomplishing evil or unlawful ends ⟨the *intrigue* was quickly discovered, and the would-be assassins were arrested⟩ — see PLOT 1

intrigue *vb* **1** to engage in a secret plan to accomplish evil or unlawful ends ⟨evidence that the leading manufacturers had *intrigued* to keep prices artificially high⟩ — see PLOT
2 to hold the attention of ⟨the mystery story *intrigued* me so that I read it in one sitting⟩ — see ENGAGE 1

intriguing *adj* holding the attention or provoking interest ⟨an *intriguing* concept that should engender much debate among climatologists⟩ — see INTERESTING

intrinsic *adj* being a part of the innermost nature of a person or thing ⟨the question of whether people have an *intrinsic* sense of right and wrong⟩ — see INHERENT

intrinsically *adv* by natural character or ability ⟨he's worked hard to be good at baseball, as he's not *intrinsically* athletic⟩ — see NATURALLY 1

intro *n* a short section (as of a book) that leads to or explains the main part ⟨in her *intro* the author offers rather precise definitions of some of the key words that she will be using throughout her book⟩ — see INTRODUCTION

introduce *vb* **1** to make (one person) known (to another) socially ⟨a friend *introduced* him to the woman who later became his wife⟩
synonyms acquaint, present
related words address, greet, hail, meet; reacquaint, reintroduce
2 to present or bring forward for discussion ⟨after about 20 minutes the moderator *introduced* a new topic for the debate⟩
synonyms bring up, broach, moot, place, raise
related words allude (to), cite, mention, name, refer (to); offer, propose, suggest; air, express, speak (of), talk (about), vent, ventilate; interject, interrupt; debate, discuss, thrash (out *or* over)
near antonyms censor, hush (up), quiet, silence, suppress
3 to be responsible for the creation and early operation

or use of ⟨Luther Burbank *introduced* the idea of plant breeding, developing over 800 new varieties of fruits, vegetables, grains, and grasses⟩ — see FOUND

4 to impart knowledge of a new thing or situation to ⟨*introduced* everyone to the company's new phone system⟩ — see ACQUAINT 1

5 to put among or between others ⟨*introduce* a new variable to the equation⟩ — see INSERT

introducer *n* one who creates or introduces something new ⟨the *introducer* of the ballpoint pen was a man by the name of John Loud⟩ — see INVENTOR

introduction *n* a short section (as of a book) that leads to or explains the main part ⟨a leading biologist wrote the *introduction* to that new textbook⟩

synonyms exordium, foreword, intro, preamble, preface, prelude, proem, prologue (*also* prolog), prolusion

related words beginning, commencement, initiation, opening, origin, origination, outset, start

near antonyms envoi (*or* envoy), postscript; aftermath; cessation, close, closing, conclusion, end, finale, finish, stop, termination

antonyms epilogue (*also* epilog)

introductory *adj* **1** coming before the main part or item usually to introduce or prepare for what follows ⟨an *introductory* paragraph to the chapter on evolution⟩ — see PRELIMINARY

2 of or relating to the simplest facts or theories of a subject ⟨an *introductory* course in computer programming⟩ — see ELEMENTARY

introspection *n* examination of one's own thoughts and feelings ⟨not a man given to *introspection*, he grew impatient with his wife's constant need to discuss their relationship⟩

synonyms self-contemplation, self-examination, self-observation, self-questioning, self-reflection, self-scrutiny, self-searching, soul-searching

related words self-analysis, self-awareness, self-consciousness, self-recognition; introversion, self-absorption, self-centeredness, self-concern, self-involvement; self-actualization, self-discovery, self-exploration, self-fulfillment, self-realization; self-knowledge, self-revelation; self-concept, self-image, self-perception; contemplation, meditation, reflection, rumination

introvert *n* a shy or reserved person ⟨although interested in the public welfare, he was too much of an *introvert* to consider personally running for political office⟩

synonyms shrinking violet, wallflower

related words mouse; cold fish, iceberg, icicle

antonyms extrovert (*also* extravert)

introverted *adj* not comfortable around people ⟨a quiet, *introverted* child who likes to sit at home and read books⟩ — see SHY 2

intrude *vb* **1** to cause a disruption in a conversation or discussion ⟨forgive me for *intruding*, but I think I know where that restaurant is⟩ — see INTERRUPT

2 to interest oneself in what is not one's concern ⟨the story of a would-be matchmaker who *intrudes* into the lives of her friends⟩ — see INTERFERE

intrude (upon) *vb* to thrust oneself upon (another) without invitation ⟨a man with an opinion on everything, he doesn't hesitate to *intrude upon* whoever happens to be standing by⟩ — see BOTHER 1

intruder *n* a person who meddles in the affairs of others ⟨an inveterate *intruder*, he needs to get a life⟩ — see BUSYBODY

intruding *adj* thrusting oneself where one is not welcome or invited ⟨a relentlessly *intruding* child who likes to interrupt adult conversations simply to get attention⟩ — see INTRUSIVE

intrusive *adj* thrusting oneself where one is not welcome or invited ⟨she's that proverbially *intrusive* neighbor who never knocks before coming in⟩

synonyms busy, interfering, intruding, meddlesome, meddling, nosy (*or* nosey), obtrusive, officious, presuming, presumptuous, protrusive, prying, pushing, pushy, snoopy

related words bold, brazen, bumptious, impertinent, impudent, insolent, rude; invading, trespassing; curious, inquisitive; annoying, harassing, pestiferous; overbearing, superserviceable

near antonyms hands-off; uninvolved; quiet, reclusive, reserved, reticent, retiring, silent, taciturn, withdrawn; inhibited, restrained, subdued

antonyms unobtrusive

intuit *vb* to have a clear idea of ⟨an imaginative genius like Shakespeare could *intuit* the thoughts, feelings, and motives of a vast array of characters⟩ — see COMPREHEND 1

inundate *vb* to cover with a flood ⟨water from the overflowing bathtub *inundated* the bathroom floor⟩ — see FLOOD

inundation *n* a great flow of water or of something that overwhelms ⟨the family's shed was washed away in the last *inundation*⟩ — see FLOOD

inure *vb* to make able to withstand physical hardship, strain, or exposure ⟨the hardship of army training *inured* her to the rigors of desert warfare⟩ — see HARDEN 2

inured *adj* able to withstand hardship, strain, or exposure ⟨the weather-beaten, *inured* faces of farmers⟩ — see HARDY 1

invade *vb* to enter for conquest or plunder ⟨a superpower that had a tendency to *invade* and take over smaller and weaker countries⟩

synonyms foray (into), overrun, raid

related words despoil, loot, maraud, pillage, plunder, ransack, ravage, sack, strip; conquer, crush, dominate, overcome, overpower, overwhelm, subdue, subject, subjugate, vanquish; assail, assault, attack, beset, charge, rush, storm, strike; battle, clash (with), combat, fight, war (with); encroach, harass, infringe, trespass; beleaguer, besiege, blockade, invest; garrison, occupy

near antonyms defend, guard, protect, safeguard, shield, ward; defy, oppose, repel, resist, withstand; capitulate (to), cede (to), submit (to), succumb (to), surrender (to), yield (to)

invader *n* one that starts armed conflict against another especially without reasonable cause ⟨vigilant defenders at the border were quick to repel the *invaders*⟩ — see AGGRESSOR

[1]**invalid** *adj* chronically or repeatedly suffering from poor health ⟨an old and now *invalid* woman who rarely gets out anymore⟩ — see SICKLY 1

[2]**invalid** *adj* **1** having no legal or binding force ⟨the treaty is *invalid* once one side violates it⟩ — see NULL 1

2 not being in agreement with what is true ⟨that's an *invalid* assumption on your part⟩ — see FALSE 1

3 not using or following good reasoning ⟨an argument which has one untrue premise is *invalid*⟩ — see ILLOGICAL

4 having no basis in reason or fact ⟨an *invalid* claim that can be easily disproved by the facts⟩ — see GROUNDLESS

invalidate *vb* to put an end to by formal action ⟨those nations eventually *invalidated* their trade agreement⟩ — see ABOLISH 1

invalidation *n* the doing away with something by formal action ⟨sought speedy *invalidation* of the contract, which had been signed without parental consent⟩ — see ABOLITION

invaluable *adj* having a value beyond any ability to appraise or adequately appreciate ⟨the list of likely donors proved to be *invaluable* to our fund-raising efforts⟩ — see PRICELESS 1

invariability *n* the state of continuing without change ⟨the *invariability* of the weather around here gets boring sometimes⟩ — see CONSTANCY 1

invariable *adj* not capable of changing or being changed ⟨an *invariable* interest rate⟩ — see INFLEXIBLE 1

invariably *adv* on every relevant occasion ⟨their slacker son *invariably* gives the same response to the questions about his career plans⟩ — see ALWAYS 1

invariant *adj* not varying ⟨an *invariant* value⟩ — see UNIFORM

invasion *n* a sudden attack on and entrance into hostile territory ⟨the *invasion* of the Soviet Union by Germany during World War II⟩ — see RAID 1

invective *n* harsh insulting language ⟨hurled curses and *invective* at the driver who heedlessly cut them off in traffic⟩ — see ABUSE 1

invective *adj* marked by harsh insulting language ⟨an overbearing, bullying boss who is fond of sending *invective* e-mails to long-suffering assistants⟩ — see ABUSIVE

inveigh *vb* to express dissatisfaction, pain, or resentment usually tiresomely ⟨always *inveighing* against the high property taxes that they were forced to pay⟩ — see COMPLAIN

invent *vb* to create or think of by clever use of the imagination ⟨they *invented* an explanation for the broken vase that would satisfy their grandmother⟩
synonyms concoct, construct, contrive, cook (up), devise, drum up, excogitate, fabricate, make up, manufacture, think (up), trump up, vamp (up)
related words coin, design, hatch, produce; daydream, dream, fantasize; conceive, envisage, envision, imagine, picture, vision, visualize; ad-lib, extemporize, improvise
phrases come up with
near antonyms clone, copy, copycat, duplicate, imitate, mimic, reduplicate, replicate, reproduce

invented *adj* not real and existing only in the imagination ⟨a daydreamer who lives mostly in her *invented* magic kingdom⟩ — see IMAGINARY

invention *n* **1** something (as a device) created for the first time through the use of the imagination ⟨his clever *invention* made people's lives easier⟩
synonyms brainchild, coinage, concoction, contrivance, creation, innovation, wrinkle
related words contraption, device, gadget, gizmo (*also* gismo), novelty; design, product, work; dream, fantasy (*also* phantasy), picture, vision; conception, imagining, origination
near antonyms carbon copy, clone, copy, dupe, duplicate, duplication, facsimile, imitation, reduplication, replica, replication, reproduction
2 something that is the product of the imagination ⟨unsurprisingly, the story about being kidnapped by aliens was pure *invention*⟩ — see FICTION
3 the ability to form mental images of things that either are not physically present or have never been conceived or created by others ⟨a writer with great *invention*, she is able to create on the page worlds that don't exist but certainly seem like they could⟩ — see IMAGINATION 1
4 the skill and imagination to create new things ⟨a person of seemingly endless *invention*, Thomas Edison held a world-record 1,093 patents⟩ — see CREATIVITY 1

inventive *adj* **1** showing a noteworthy use of the imagination and creativity especially in inventing ⟨*inventive* electronic games⟩ ⟨*inventive* ways to use leftovers⟩ — see CLEVER 1
2 having the skill and imagination to create new things ⟨an *inventive* youth, he devised an automatic feeding system for his dog⟩ — see CREATIVE 1

inventiveness *n* **1** the ability to form mental images of things that either are not physically present or have never been conceived or created by others ⟨the artist's fertile *inventiveness* allows her to put on canvas landscapes that have never been trod by mortal feet⟩ — see IMAGINATION 1
2 the skill and imagination to create new things ⟨the contention that, in order to prosper, cities must attract young, well-educated people of great *inventiveness* in both the arts and high technology⟩ — see CREATIVITY 1

inventor *n* one who creates or introduces something new ⟨the *inventor* of the electric light bulb⟩
synonyms contriver, designer, developer, deviser, formulator, innovator, introducer, originator
related words author, begetter, creator, establisher, father, founder, generator, inaugurator, initiator, instituter (*or* institutor), sire; groundbreaker, pioneer, planner, researcher, researchist; builder, maker, producer; dreamer; codeveloper, coinventer, coproducer, coresearcher
near antonyms aper, copier, copycat, duplicator, imitator, mimic

inventory *vb* to make a list of ⟨would you *inventory* the supplies in the back room?⟩ — see [1]LIST 1

inventory *n* **1** the number of individuals or amount of something available at any given time ⟨the dealership has an unusually large *inventory* of pre-owned vehicles⟩ — see SUPPLY
2 a short statement of the main points ⟨offers an informative *inventory* of everything that is known about the virus at this time⟩ — see SUMMARY

invert *vb* to change the position of (an object) so that the opposite side or end is showing ⟨if you *invert* the coin, there's a picture of a buffalo on the back⟩ — see REVERSE 2

invertebrate *adj* lacking strength of will or character ⟨an *invertebrate* Congress that blithely went along with the President's ill-conceived plan⟩ — see WEAK 2

invest *vb* **1** to cause (as a person) to become filled or saturated with a certain quality or principle ⟨*invested* the film with his own enthusiasm for the wonders of flight⟩ — see INFUSE
2 to furnish freely or naturally with some power, quality, or attribute ⟨a woman *invested* with the strong desire to make the world a better place⟩ — see ENDOW 1
3 to give official or legal power to ⟨*invested* him with power of attorney⟩ — see AUTHORIZE 1
4 to outfit with clothes and especially fine or special clothes ⟨a fashion designer who has *invested* a number of the winners of the best actress award⟩ — see CLOTHE 1
5 to put into an office or welcome into an organization with special ceremonies ⟨the beloved actor was finally *invested* as a knight by the queen⟩ — see INSTALL 1
6 to surround (as a fortified place) with armed forces for the purpose of capturing or preventing commerce and communication ⟨the city was mercilessly *invested* for an entire year, but never fell⟩ — see BESIEGE 1
7 to surround or cover closely ⟨nightfall *invested* the land⟩ — see ENFOLD 1

investigate *vb* to search through or into ⟨experts *investigating* new ways of dealing with the problem⟩ — see EXPLORE 1

investigation *n* a systematic search for the truth or facts about something ⟨officials launched an extensive *investigation* of the plane crash⟩ — see INQUIRY 1

investigator *n* **1** one who observes or studies by close examination and systematic inquiry ⟨*investigators* who discovered new evidence that the universe was much older than had been previously estimated⟩
synonyms experimenter, researcher
related words monitor, observer; empiric, empiricist, fact finder; field-worker; examiner, inspector
2 a person not on the police force who investigates criminal or illicit activity or searches for missing per-

sons ⟨the *investigator* in charge of the case was touted as an expert at tracing stolen art⟩ — see DETECTIVE

investiture *n* the process or an instance of being formally placed in an office or organization ⟨the *investiture* of a new member of parliament⟩ — see INSTALLATION 1

investment *n* **1** the cutting off of an area by military means to stop the flow of people or supplies ⟨the *investment* of Cuba was one of the decisive moments in the Cuban Missile Crisis⟩ — see BLOCKADE
2 the process or an instance of being formally placed in an office or organization ⟨the *investment* of a new diocesan bishop is typically a grand and solemn occasion⟩ — see INSTALLATION 1

inveterate *adj* **1** firmly established over time ⟨he has an *inveterate* tendency to tell some very tall tales⟩
synonyms bred-in-the-bone, confirmed, deep, deep-rooted, deep-seated, entrenched (*also* intrenched), hard-core, rooted, settled
related words firm, fixed, frozen, hard, hard-and-fast, immutable, irradicable, set, unalterable, unchangeable; embedded (*also* imbedded), implanted, inculcated, instilled; inborn, inbred, ingrained (*also* engrained), inherent, innate, integral, intrinsic, natural; accustomed, chronic, customary, habitual, regular, typical, usual; abiding, enduring, lifelong, persistent, persisting
near antonyms brief, ephemeral, fleeting, impermanent, interim, momentary, provisional, short-lived, short-term, temporary, transient
2 being such by habit and not likely to change ⟨the man is an *inveterate* liar who only rarely tells the truth⟩ — see HABITUAL 1

invidious *adj* having or showing mean resentment of another's possessions or advantages ⟨inevitably, his remarkable success attracted the *invidious* attention of the other sales representatives⟩ — see ENVIOUS

invidiousness *n* a painful awareness of another's possessions or advantages and a desire to have them too ⟨she pretended to be happy for her friend's good fortune, but there was an unmistakable *invidiousness* about her supposedly heartfelt congratulations⟩ — see ENVY

invigorate *vb* to give life, vigor, or spirit to ⟨the fresh air and sunshine *invigorated* the children after a long winter indoors⟩ — see ANIMATE

invigorated *adj* made or become fresh in spirits or vigor ⟨an *invigorated* worker returning from a relaxing vacation⟩ — see NEW 4

invigorating *adj* having a renewing effect on the state of the body or mind ⟨an *invigorating* breeze made our afternoon sail all the more enjoyable⟩ — see TONIC 1

invincible *adj* incapable of being defeated, overcome, or subdued ⟨an *invincible* wrestler who has never lost a match⟩
synonyms bulletproof, impregnable, indomitable, insuperable, insurmountable, invulnerable, unbeatable, unconquerable, unstoppable
related words inviolable, unassailable, unbreachable, untouchable; armored, defended, guarded, protected, safe, safeguarded, secure, shielded; unbeaten, unbowed, unconquered, undefeated, unsubdued
near antonyms exposed, imperiled (*or* imperilled), insecure, liable, open, susceptible, unguarded, unprotected, unsafe; defenseless, helpless, powerless, weak
antonyms superable, surmountable, vincible, vulnerable

inviolable *adj* not to be violated, criticized, or tampered with ⟨a person with *inviolable* moral standards⟩ ⟨an *inviolable* trust between lawyer and client⟩ — see SACRED 1

invisible *adj* not readily seen or noticed ⟨the stitches are *invisible*, so the mended skirt looks as good as new⟩ — see UNOBTRUSIVE

invite *vb* **1** to request the presence or participation of ⟨she's *invited* only select friends to visit her new house⟩
synonyms ask, bid
related words solicit; beckon, call, summon
2 to act so as to make (something) more likely ⟨you're just *inviting* ridicule by making such outrageous claims⟩ — see COURT 1

invocation *n* a spoken word or set of words believed to have magic power ⟨a Siberian shaman muttering mysterious *invocations* to ward off evil⟩ — see SPELL 1

invoice *n* a record of goods sold or services performed together with the costs due ⟨the *invoice* stated that we owed $1500⟩ — see [1]BILL 1

invoke *vb* to be the cause of (a situation, action, or state of mind) ⟨we should be prepared for the possibility that any solution may *invoke* another set of problems⟩ — see EFFECT

involuntary *adj* **1** not made or done willingly or by choice ⟨my long stays on the sidelines during our football games were strictly *involuntary*⟩
synonyms coerced, forced, unintended, unintentional, unwilling, will-less
related words accidental, unplanned, unpremeditated; automatic, impulsive, instinctive, spontaneous, unprompted; inadvertent, unconscious, unknowing, unwitting
near antonyms advised, conscious, considered, knowing, planned, premeditated, premeditative, prepense, purposeful; volitional; self-imposed, self-inflicted
antonyms deliberate, freewill, intentional, uncoerced, unforced, voluntary, willful (*or* wilful), willing
2 done instantly and without conscious thought or decision ⟨breathing is *involuntary*⟩ — see AUTOMATIC 1
3 forcing one's compliance or participation by or as if by law ⟨the abolition of *involuntary* servitude by civilized society⟩ — see MANDATORY

involute *adj* **1** having many parts or aspects that are usually interrelated ⟨the novel's deliberately *involute* plot is intended as a brainteaser for readers⟩ — see COMPLEX 1
2 turning around an axis like the thread of a screw ⟨the chambered nautilus is readily identified by its *involute* seashell⟩ — see SPIRAL

involution *n* the state or quality of having many interrelated parts or aspects ⟨the *involution* of the thriller's plot made it hard to follow⟩ — see COMPLEXITY 1

involve *vb* **1** to be the business or affair of ⟨this isn't something that *involves* you, so don't worry about it⟩ — see CONCERN 2
2 to have as part of a whole ⟨a tragic play usually *involves* a number of plot devices, including the hero's fatal flaw⟩ — see INCLUDE 1
3 to hold the attention of ⟨her blissful daydream so completely *involved* her that she never heard the knock on the door⟩ — see ENGAGE 1
4 to surround or cover closely ⟨a mind that was deeply *involved* in doubt about his wife's fidelity⟩ — see ENFOLD 1

involved *adj* **1** having many parts or aspects that are usually interrelated ⟨a remarkably *involved* story for a writer so young⟩ — see COMPLEX 1
2 made or done with great care or with much detail ⟨very *involved* descriptions of every last detail of the lavish wedding⟩ — see ELABORATE 1

involving *adj* holding the attention or provoking interest ⟨an *involving* book that you won't be able to put down⟩ — see INTERESTING

invulnerable *adj* incapable of being defeated, overcome, or subdued ⟨typically teenagers suppose themselves to be *invulnerable*, so they take needless risks⟩ — see INVINCIBLE

inward *adj* **1** situated farther in ⟨moved towards the *inward* room for more privacy⟩ — see INNER 1
2 closely acquainted ⟨he's more *inward* with the president than most members of the cabinet⟩ — see FAMILIAR 1

inwards *n pl* the internal organs of the body ⟨the hunter cleaned the deer by slicing open the belly and removing the *inwards*⟩ — see GUT 1

inweave *vb* to cause to twine about one another ⟨*inweave* the strips of dough to make a decorative border⟩ — see INTERTWINE 1

in–your–face *adj* having or showing a bold forcefulness in the pursuit of a goal ⟨an *in-your-face* attitude that sometimes puts people off⟩ — see AGGRESSIVE 1

iota *n* the smallest amount or part imaginable ⟨there's not an *iota* of doubt regarding the defendant's guilt⟩ — see JOT

ipso facto *adv* because of necessity ⟨if we refuse to tolerate bigotry, do we become, *ipso facto*, as intolerant as those whom we condemn?⟩ — see NEEDS

IQ *n* a highly developed skill in or knowledge of something ⟨he has a movie *IQ* that is off the charts⟩ — see COMMAND 2

irascibility *n* readiness to show annoyance or impatience ⟨his natural *irascibility* tends to make people leave him alone⟩ — see PETULANCE

irascible *adj* easily irritated or annoyed ⟨forced to endure a memorably *irascible* boss on her first job after college⟩ — see IRRITABLE

irascibleness *n* readiness to show annoyance or impatience ⟨she typically responds to stupid requests with the *irascibleness* of a black mamba⟩ — see PETULANCE

irate *adj* feeling or showing anger ⟨the big increase in cable rates prompted a flood of *irate* calls and letters⟩ — see ANGRY

irateness *n* an intense emotional state of displeasure with someone or something ⟨his *irateness* was such that we feared he might have a heart attack or stroke⟩ — see ANGER

ire *n* an intense emotional state of displeasure with someone or something ⟨the patronizing comment from the snooty waiter roused her *ire*⟩ — see ANGER

ire *vb* to make angry ⟨nothing *ires* him more than having to wait for his dinner⟩ — see ANGER 1

ireful *adj* feeling or showing anger ⟨*ireful* expressions on the faces of the protesters of the tax increase⟩ — see ANGRY

iridescent *adj* having a rainbowlike play of colors ⟨an *iridescent* soap bubble⟩
synonyms nacreous, opalescent, pearlescent
related words chatoyant; colorful, motley, multicolored, polychromatic, polychrome, varicolored, variegated

irk *vb* to disturb the peace of mind of (someone) especially by repeated disagreeable acts ⟨she *irked* her friend by chewing her gum loudly during the movie⟩ — see IRRITATE 1

irk *n* something that is a source of irritation ⟨one of the prof's major *irks* is a cell phone that rings during a lecture⟩ — see ANNOYANCE 3

irked *adj* subjected to and reacting with irritation ⟨*irked* drivers were honking and shouting at the cows in the road⟩ — see ANNOYED

irksome *adj* causing annoyance ⟨the *irksome* habit of leaving all the kitchen cabinet doors open⟩ — see ANNOYING

iron *adj* not showing weakness or uncertainty ⟨he had an *iron* determination to succeed in on Wall Street⟩ — see FIRM 1

ironhearted *adj* having or showing a lack of sympathy or tender feelings ⟨the touching reunion scene caused even the most *ironhearted* audience members to cry⟩ — see HARD 1

irons *n pl* something that physically prevents free movement ⟨guards forced the prisoners to sleep while still shackled in *irons*⟩ — see BOND 1

irradiate *vb* **1** to supply with light ⟨the light from a galaxy of flashing signs *irradiates* the heart and soul of Las Vegas⟩ — see ILLUMINATE 1
2 to throw or give off ⟨*irradiating* an aura of supreme confidence on the playing field⟩ — see EMIT 1

irrational *adj* not using or following good reasoning ⟨it's *irrational* to think that you can continue to consume an excess of calories and not gain weight⟩ — see ILLOGICAL

irrecoverable *adj* **1** not capable of being cured or reformed ⟨unfortunately, he was destined to live out his days as an *irrecoverable* alcoholic⟩ — see HOPELESS 1
2 not capable of being repaired, regained, or undone ⟨one computer file proved to be *irrecoverable* after the crash⟩ — see IRREPARABLE

irredeemable *adj* **1** not capable of being cured or reformed ⟨resigned to the fact that his in-laws are *irredeemable* practical jokers⟩ — see HOPELESS 1
2 not capable of being repaired, regained, or undone ⟨the *irredeemable* loss of innocence that the war brought about⟩ — see IRREPARABLE

irreformable *adj* not capable of being cured or reformed ⟨an *irreformable* liar who long ago lost all interest in telling the truth⟩ — see HOPELESS 1

irrefragable *adj* not capable of being challenged or proved wrong ⟨the prosecutor painstakingly built an *irrefragable* case⟩ — see IRREFUTABLE

irrefutable *adj* not capable of being challenged or proved wrong ⟨the *irrefutable* reply of "Because I like it!"⟩
synonyms accomplished, certain, inarguable, incontestable, incontrovertible, indisputable, indubitable, irrefragable, positive, sure, unanswerable, unarguable, unchallengeable, undeniable, unquestionable
related words unambiguous, unequivocal; absolute, clear, conclusive, decisive, definite, hands-down; uncontested, uncontradicted, undisputed, unquestioned
near antonyms controversial, debated, disputed; doubtful, dubious, iffy, inconclusive, indecisive, uncertain; ambiguous, equivocal; academic (*also* academical), hypothetical, speculative, theoretical (*also* theoretic)
antonyms answerable, arguable, contradictable, controvertible, debatable, disputable, doubtable, moot, negotiable, problematic (*also* problematical), questionable, refutable

irregular *adj* **1** departing from some accepted standard of what is normal ⟨it was a bank customer's slightly *irregular* behavior that made people suspicious⟩ — see DEVIANT
2 lacking in steadiness or regularity of occurrence ⟨*irregular* mail delivery to the island⟩ — see FITFUL
3 not having a level or smooth surface ⟨although the moon looks smooth from here, it actually has a very bumpy and *irregular* surface⟩ — see UNEVEN 1
4 not rigidly following established form, custom, or rules ⟨the request is *irregular*, but I'll allow it⟩ — see INFORMAL 1
5 not staying constant ⟨*irregular* gusts of wind⟩ — see UNEVEN 2

irregularly *adv* without definite aim, direction, rule, or method ⟨attended class only *irregularly*⟩ — see HIT OR MISS

irrelative *adj* not having anything to do with the matter at hand ⟨these *irrelative* points only to serve to dilute what is otherwise a strong case⟩ — see IRRELEVANT

irrelevance *n* the quality or state of not having anything to do with the matter at hand ⟨the *irrelevance* of the comment brought conversation to a standstill⟩
synonyms extraneousness, impertinence, inapplicability
related words improperness, inappositeness, inappropriateness, inaptness, unfitness, unsuitability; immateriality, inconsequentiality, insignificance; emptiness, inaneness, inanity, meaninglessness, pointlessness, uselessness
near antonyms appropriateness, aptness, fitness, suitability, suitableness; importance, significance; usefulness
antonyms applicability, bearing, connection, materiality, pertinence, relevance, relevancy

irrelevant *adj* not having anything to do with the matter at hand ⟨*irrelevant* questions that merely disrupted the classroom lesson⟩
synonyms extraneous, immaterial, impertinent, inapplicable, inapposite, irrelative
related words incidental, peripheral, tangent, tangential; dead, moot; inconsequential, insignificant, unimportant; empty, inane, meaningless, pointless, senseless, useless; inappropriate, inapt, unsuitable
phrases beside the point, neither here nor there
near antonyms important, meaningful, significant; sensible, useful; appropriate, apt, fit, suitable
antonyms applicable, apposite, apropos, germane, material, pertinent, pointed, relative, relevant

irreligious *adj* lacking religious emotions, principles, or practices ⟨raised in an *irreligious* family where the subject of God was never even discussed⟩
synonyms godless, nonreligious, religionless
related words churchless, unchurched; heathen, pagan, paganish, ungodly, unholy; blasphemous, impious, irreverent, profanatory, sacrilegious; agnostic, atheistic (*or* atheistical); unconsecrated, unhallowed; profane, secular, temporal, worldly
near antonyms devout, God-fearing, godly, holy, pious, prayerful, reverent, sainted, saintly, worshipful, worshipping (*also* worshiping); sanctimonious; blessed (*also* blest), consecrated, hallowed, sacred, sacrosanct, sanctified; devotional, spiritual
antonyms religious

irremediable *adj* **1** not capable of being cured or reformed ⟨the firm belief that no juvenile delinquent is *irremediable*⟩ — see HOPELESS 1
2 not capable of being repaired, regained, or undone ⟨it turned out that the flood damage was not *irremediable*⟩ — see IRREPARABLE

irremovable *adj* incapable of moving or being moved ⟨the driveway had to be built to curve around an *irremovable* tree⟩ — see IMMOVABLE 1

irreparable *adj* not capable of being repaired, regained, or undone ⟨*irreparable* damage to the car⟩
synonyms irrecoverable, irredeemable, irremediable, irretrievable, irreversible, unrecoverable, unredeemable
related words irreplaceable, irrevocable; unredeemed
near antonyms corrected, fixed, recovered, remedied, repaired
antonyms correctable, corrigible, fixable, redeemable, remediable, repairable, reparable, retrievable, undoable

irreproachability *n* the quality or state of being free from guilt or blame ⟨commended the children on the *irreproachability* of their table manners⟩ — see INNOCENCE 1

irreproachable *adj* **1** free from guilt or blame ⟨the captain of the force is a police officer of absolutely *irreproachable* character⟩ — see INNOCENT 2
2 being entirely without fault ⟨an *irreproachable* solution to the problem that should satisfy everyone⟩ — see PERFECT 1

irreproachableness *n* the quality or state of being free from guilt or blame ⟨the *irreproachableness* of the sergeant's conduct was in marked contrast to that of his fellow officers in the corruption-ridden precinct⟩ — see INNOCENCE 1

irresolution *n* a state or an instance of temporary inaction because of uncertainty about the right course of action ⟨after a moment of anguished *irresolution*, I raised my rifle and fired at the charging animal⟩ — see HESITATION

irresponsible *adj* having or showing a lack of concern for the consequences of one's actions ⟨it was *irresponsible* to go off and leave your baby unattended in an automobile⟩ — see RECKLESS 1

irretrievable *adj* **1** not capable of being cured or reformed ⟨an *irretrievable* drug addict who had wasted a once-promising life⟩ — see HOPELESS 1
2 not capable of being repaired, regained, or undone ⟨this is just an *irretrievable* mess, so let's start all over again⟩ — see IRREPARABLE

irreverence *n* an act of great disrespect shown to God or to sacred ideas, people, or things ⟨certain sects of Islam consider a woman showing her face in public to be a gross *irreverence*⟩ — see BLASPHEMY

irreverent *adj* not showing proper reverence for the holy or sacred ⟨*irreverent* behavior during church services⟩
synonyms blasphemous, impious, profane, sacrilegious
related words agnostic, atheistic (*or* atheistical); godless, heretical (*also* heretic), irreligious, miscreant, nonreligious, religionless, secular; ungodly, unholy; unconsecrated, unhallowed; heathen, pagan, paganish
near antonyms devout, God-fearing, godly, holy, prayerful, religious, sainted, saintly, worshipful, worshipping (*also* worshiping); consecrated, hallowed, sacred, sacrosanct, sanctified
antonyms pious, reverent

irreversible *adj* not capable of being repaired, regained, or undone ⟨fortunately, the misprint wasn't an *irreversible* error since it was discovered early⟩ — see IRREPARABLE

irrigate *vb* to pour liquid over or through in order to cleanse ⟨if you get the chemical in your eye, *irrigate* the eye thoroughly with water⟩ — see FLUSH 1

irritability *n* readiness to show annoyance or impatience ⟨the librarian's well-known *irritability* makes students hesitant to ask questions⟩ — see PETULANCE

irritable *adj* easily irritated or annoyed ⟨that *irritable* old man always yells at people to stay off of his lawn⟩
synonyms choleric, crabby, cranky, cross, crotchety, fiery, grouchy, grumpy, irascible, peevish, perverse, pettish, petulant, prickly, quick-tempered, raspy, ratty, short-tempered, snappish, snappy, snarky, snippety, snippy, stuffy, testy, waspish
related words bearish, bilious, cantankerous, cross-grained, curmudgeonly, disagreeable, dyspeptic, ill-humored, ill-natured, ill-tempered, off-color (*or* off-colored), ornery, querulous, snarly, surly; argumentative, bellicose, belligerent, combative, contentious, disputatious, fractious, fretful, pugnacious, quarrelsome, scrappy, truculent; huffy, pouty, sensitive, short, sulky, sullen, tetchy, thin-skinned, touchy; hot-blooded, passionate
phrases out of humor, out of sorts
near antonyms affable, companionable, cordial, extroverted (*also* extraverted), friendly, genial, gregarious, outgoing, sociable; agreeable, amiable, good-natured, good-tempered, sweet, well-disposed; carefree, easygoing, happy-go-lucky, relaxed; forbearing, long-suffer-

ing, obliging, patient, stoic (*or* stoical), tolerant, uncomplaining, understanding

irritableness *n* readiness to show annoyance or impatience ⟨the old man's chronic *irritableness* makes him the terror of the nursing home⟩ — see PETULANCE

irritant *n* something that is a source of irritation ⟨the whining child was a constant *irritant* to his long-suffering parents⟩ — see ANNOYANCE 3

irritate *vb* **1** to disturb the peace of mind of (someone) especially by repeated disagreeable acts ⟨constant chatter *irritated* the student, who was trying to concentrate on a hard assignment⟩

synonyms aggravate, annoy, bother, bug, burn (up), chafe, eat, exasperate, frost, gall, get, grate, gripe, hack (off), irk, itch, nark [*British*], nettle, peeve, persecute, pique, put out, rasp, rile, ruffle, spite, vex

related words hassle, heckle; nag; inflame (*also* enflame), provoke, rouse; badger, bait, bullyrag (*also* ballyrag), devil, hagride, harass, harry, pester, plague, tease; anger, antagonize, enrage, incense, infuriate, madden, rankle, roil; agitate, discomfort, discompose, disquiet, distress, exercise, freak (out), fret, perturb, undo, unhinge, unsettle, upset, worry; affront, insult, miff, offend, outrage

phrases get one's goat, get on one's nerves, get to, rub the wrong way, set one's teeth on edge, stick in one's craw, wear on

near antonyms appease, conciliate, mollify, oblige, pacify, placate, propitiate; delight, gladden, gratify, please, satisfy; assure, cheer, comfort, console, content, quiet, reassure, solace, soothe

2 to make sore by continued rubbing ⟨new shoes usually *irritate* my feet⟩ — see CHAFE 1

irritated *adj* subjected to and reacting with irritation ⟨*irritated* viewers were bombarding the station with complaints about the game's delayed start⟩ — see ANNOYED

irritating *adj* **1** causing annoyance ⟨his particularly *irritating* habit of leaving his dirty clothes on the floor⟩ — see ANNOYING

2 causing an unpleasant tingling sensation ⟨this soap leaves a residue that might be a little *irritating* if you have sensitive skin⟩ — see SCRATCHY 2

irritation *n* the feeling of impatience or anger caused by another's repeated disagreeable acts ⟨Dad's general *irritation* at the incessant complaining coming from the back seat of the car⟩ — see ANNOYANCE 2

irruption *n* a sudden attack on and entrance into hostile territory ⟨the *irruptions* of the Goths into Italy in the fifth century⟩ — see RAID 1

island *n* a fairly small area of land completely surrounded by water ⟨the *island* of Hawaii is the largest in the Hawaiian archipelago⟩

synonyms isle, islet

related words atoll, barrier reef, cay, coral reef, key

near antonyms continent, main, mainland

isle *n* a fairly small area of land completely surrounded by water ⟨the Australian seas are rife with uninhabited *isles*⟩ — see ISLAND

islet *n* a fairly small area of land completely surrounded by water ⟨landed the boat on a tiny *islet* that we had all to ourselves⟩ — see ISLAND

isolate *n* a person who lives away from others ⟨interpersonal relationships are very stressful for him, so he lives as a virtual *isolate* on the Upper West Side of Manhattan⟩ — see RECLUSE

isolate *vb* to set or keep apart from others ⟨outlying villages that had been *isolated* by the massive earthquake⟩

synonyms cut off, insulate, seclude, segregate, separate, sequester

related words quarantine; confine, immure, incarcerate, intern, jail, lock (up), restrain, restrict; abstract, detach, disengage, remove; detain, hold, keep

near antonyms assimilate, associate, connect, join, link, unite; discharge, free, liberate, loose, release

antonyms desegregate, integrate, reintegrate

isolated *adj* **1** screened or sequestered from view ⟨the hikers unexpectedly came upon an *isolated* mountain cabin⟩ — see SECLUDED

2 not often occurring or repeated ⟨fortunately for this neighborhood, the burglary was just an *isolated* incident⟩ — see INFREQUENT

isolation *n* the state of being alone or kept apart from others ⟨forced *isolation* always made the sociable child lonely⟩

synonyms aloneness, insulation, privacy, secludedness, seclusion, segregation, separateness, sequestration, solitariness, solitude

related words loneliness, lonesomeness; vacuum; confinement, incarceration, internment, quarantine; retirement, withdrawal; ghettoization

near antonyms camaraderie, companionship, company, comradeship, fellowship, society

issuable *adj* open to question or dispute ⟨an *issuable* claim that the food additive causes cancer⟩ — see DEBATABLE 1

issuance *n* the act or process of giving out something to each member of a group ⟨the *issuance* of an instruction sheet to each member of the class⟩ — see DISTRIBUTION 1

issue *n* **1** a condition or occurrence traceable to a cause ⟨one of the *issues* of the Civil War was a resolution to the question of states' rights⟩ — see EFFECT 1

2 a place or means of going out ⟨since the lake is the *issue* of the polluted river, it is becoming polluted as well⟩ — see EXIT 1

3 the descendants of a person, animal, or plant ⟨someone who dies without *issue* might have their estate turned over to the state⟩ — see OFFSPRING

issue *vb* **1** to produce and release for distribution in printed form ⟨plans to *issue* a monthly newsletter⟩ — see PUBLISH 1

2 to throw or give off ⟨a volcano *issuing* vast clouds of hot ash⟩ — see EMIT 1

Italian sandwich *n* a large sandwich on a long split roll ⟨that restaurant makes a great *Italian sandwich*⟩ — see SUBMARINE

italicize *vb* to make more apparent ⟨high-definition television *italicizes* every line and wrinkle in an actor's face⟩ — see EMPHASIZE 2

itch *n* **1** sexual appetite ⟨he has had an *itch* for that woman since the day she started working in the office⟩ — see DESIRE 2

2 a strong wish for something ⟨has an *itch* to travel to far-off and exciting places⟩ — see DESIRE 1

3 intense sexual desire ⟨sailors on shore leave looking to satisfy the *itch* with the first available woman⟩ — see LUST 1

itch *vb* to disturb the peace of mind of (someone) especially by repeated disagreeable acts ⟨don't let her snide put-downs *itch* you—just ignore her⟩ — see IRRITATE 1

itch (for) *vb* to have an earnest wish to own or enjoy ⟨a bully who's just *itching for* a fight⟩ — see DESIRE 1

itchy *adj* **1** causing an unpleasant tingling sensation ⟨the child in the pew ahead of us kept tugging at his *itchy* church clothes⟩ — see SCRATCHY 2

2 having a strong sexual desire ⟨a red-light district that was a favorite haunt of *itchy* sailors on shore leave⟩ — see LUSTFUL

item *n* **1** a separate part in a list, account, or series ⟨she got all the *items* on her grocery list except cereal⟩

synonyms detail, particular, point

related words article, belonging, object, stuff, thing; characteristic, component, constituent, element, factor,

feature, member; ingredient; division, particle, partition, piece, portion, section, segment
near antonyms aggregate, composite, compound, conglomerate; entirety, sum, summation, total, totality, whole
2 a report of recent events or facts not previously known ⟨our next *item* is about the blizzard blanketing the East Coast⟩ — see NEWS

itemize *vb* **1** to make a list of ⟨*itemized* the expenses for the business trip⟩ — see [1]LIST 1
2 to specify one after another ⟨*itemized* the potential problems if a wind farm is built there⟩ — see ENUMERATE 1

iterate *vb* to say or state again ⟨no matter how many times I *iterate* that this so-called prank is a bad idea, no one listens⟩ — see REPEAT 1

iteration *n* the act of saying or doing over again ⟨your constant *iteration* of the same piddling complaints is wearing thin⟩ — see REPEAT

itinerant *adj* traveling from place to place ⟨an *itinerant* musician can see a lot of the world⟩
synonyms ambulant, ambulatory, errant, fugitive, gallivanting (*also* galavanting), nomad, nomadic, perambulatory, peregrine, peripatetic, ranging, roaming, roving, vagabond, vagrant, wandering, wayfaring
related words drifting, footloose, meandering, rambling; sauntering, strolling, traipsing, walking; migrant, migratory
phrases on the move
near antonyms immobile, nonmoving, settled, standing, static, stationary; motionless, still

itty–bitty *or* **itsy–bitsy** *adj* very small in size ⟨maddening swarms of *itty-bitty* insects flew around our faces⟩ — see TINY

ivory–tower *adj* very learned or educated but inexperienced in practical matters ⟨a large public university that needs as its president not some *ivory-tower* intellectual but a skilled administrator⟩ — see ACADEMIC 2

ivory–towered *adj* very learned or educated but inexperienced in practical matters ⟨an *ivory-towered* elite that always favors the candidate who is idealistic but unelectable⟩ — see ACADEMIC 2

ivory–towerish *adj* very learned or educated but inexperienced in practical matters ⟨the governor dismissed his critics at the state university as a gaggle of *ivory-towerish* goo-goos⟩ — see ACADEMIC 2

J

jab *n* a quick thrust ⟨gave the jellyfish on the beach a cautious *jab* with my stick⟩ — see [1]POKE 1

jab *vb* to penetrate or hold (something) with a pointed object ⟨*jabbed* a pickle and tossed it on the plate⟩ — see IMPALE

jabber *n* unintelligible or meaningless talk ⟨to me the baby's speech was simply *jabber*, but his mother claimed to know exactly what he was saying⟩ — see GIBBERISH 1

jabber *vb* **1** to engage in casual or rambling conversation ⟨please do not *jabber* during the rabbi's sermon⟩ — see CHAT 1
2 to speak rapidly, inarticulately, and usually unintelligibly ⟨monkeys *jabbering* at each other in their cages⟩ — see BABBLE 1

jabberer *n* a person who talks constantly ⟨the sort of office *jabberer* who has an opinion on everything⟩ — see CHATTERBOX

jabberwocky *n* unintelligible or meaningless talk ⟨when he gets angry, he talks in a sort of agitated *jabberwocky* that is really quite comical⟩ — see GIBBERISH 1

jack *n* **1** *slang* something (as pieces of stamped metal or printed paper) customarily and legally used as a medium of exchange, a measure of value, or a means of payment ⟨I'd buy that watch, but I don't have the *jack* right now⟩ — see MONEY 1
2 a piece of cloth with a special design that is used as an emblem or for signaling ⟨a Portuguese ship flying the national *jack*⟩ — see FLAG 1
3 an adult male human being ⟨hey, *jack*, can you spare some change?⟩ — see MAN 1
4 one who operates or navigates a seagoing vessel ⟨the streets of the old seaport were once full of *jacks*, harlots, and other dockside denizens⟩ — see SAILOR
5 the total of the bets at stake at one time ⟨tension was mounting as the *jack* was getting bigger by the minute⟩ — see POT 1
6 a person whose job is to cut down trees ⟨we'll need to hire more *jacks* to get this forest cleared before winter⟩ — see LUMBERJACK

jack (up) *vb* **1** to lift with effort ⟨*jack up* the car so we can change that tire⟩ — see HEAVE 1
2 to move from a lower to a higher place or position ⟨local restaurants *jacked up* their prices for the summer tourist season⟩ — see RAISE 1

jackass *n* **1** a person who lacks good sense or judgment ⟨only a *jackass* would dive into a lake without first checking to see how deep the water is⟩ — see FOOL 1
2 a stupid person ⟨you don't have to act like a *jackass* just to get a girl to notice you⟩ — see IDIOT
3 a sturdy and patient domestic mammal that is used especially to carry things ⟨with our *jackasses* loaded with supplies, we slowly made our way down to the floor of the canyon⟩ — see DONKEY 1

jacked (up) *adj* being at a higher level than average ⟨the convenience store had the item I needed but at a ridiculously *jacked up* price⟩ — see HIGH 2

jacket *n* **1** something that encloses another thing especially to protect it ⟨slip the art book into its *jacket* so it won't get dirty⟩ — see [1]CASE 1
2 the hairy covering of a mammal especially when fine, soft, and thick ⟨llamas are prized for their soft, lush *jackets*⟩ — see FUR 1

jackleg *adj* **1** being such only for recreation ⟨a toolshed that can be built by any *jackleg* carpenter who's capable of hitting a nail without smashing his thumb⟩ — see AVOCATIONAL
2 lacking or showing a lack of expert skill ⟨he did such a *jackleg* installation of that door frame that now the

door won't shut⟩ — see AMATEURISH
3 having or showing lowered moral character or standards ⟨a *jackleg* lawyer whose clients consist mainly of drug dealers and child molesters⟩ — see CORRUPT

jackleg *n* a person who lacks experience and competence in an art or science ⟨you can't rely on a bunch of *jacklegs* to run your dairy farm⟩ — see AMATEUR 2

jackpot *n* **1** *chiefly West* a difficult, puzzling, or embarrassing situation from which there is no easy escape ⟨a wily dude who managed to get himself out of one *jackpot* after another⟩ — see PREDICAMENT
2 the total of the bets at stake at one time ⟨once the *jackpot* hit $100 million, everybody and his cousin was buying lottery tickets⟩ — see POT 1

jack–tar *n* one who operates or navigates a seagoing vessel ⟨a *jack-tar* swabbing the deck under the critical eye of the first mate⟩ — see SAILOR

jade *vb* to make weary and restless by being dull or monotonous ⟨a steady diet of nothing but lobster would *jade* the palate of even the most ardent lobster lover⟩ — see [2]BORE

jaded *adj* **1** depleted in strength, energy, or freshness ⟨after that long bar exam, I'm too *jaded* for anything but a nap⟩ — see WEARY 1
2 having one's patience, interest, or pleasure exhausted ⟨even *jaded* sci-fi fans are finding this new space adventure fresh and exciting⟩ — see WEARY 2

jading *adj* causing weariness, restlessness, or lack of interest ⟨the *jading* task of sorting and counting change⟩ — see BORING

jagged *adj* **1** having an uneven edge or outline ⟨it's going to be hard to repair the *jagged* tear in the tablecloth so that it doesn't show⟩ — see RAGGED 1
2 not having a level or smooth surface ⟨rode our mountain bikes down the trail's *jagged* terrain, which made for a bumpy ride⟩ — see UNEVEN 1

jail *n* a place of confinement for persons held in lawful custody ⟨sentenced to three years in *jail* for his crime⟩
synonyms bastille, big house [*slang*], bridewell, brig, calaboose, can, clink [*slang*], cooler, coop, guardroom, hock, hold, hoosegow, jailhouse, joint [*slang*], jug, lockup, nick [*British slang*], pen, penitentiary, pokey [*slang*], prison, quod [*British slang*], slam, slammer, stir [*slang*], stockade, tolbooth [*Scottish*]
related words bull pen, cage, cell, hole, tank; block, ward; glasshouse [*British*], guardhouse, hulk(s); concentration camp, gulag, labor camp, prison camp, stalag, work camp; dungeon, keep, oubliette; reformatory, reform school, training school
near antonyms outside

jail *vb* to put in or as if in prison ⟨threatened to *jail* the punks if they so much as jaywalked⟩ — see IMPRISON

jailbird *n* a person convicted as a criminal and serving a prison sentence ⟨had spent most of his sorry life as a *jailbird* in hoosegows across the South⟩ — see CONVICT

jailed *adj* taken and held prisoner ⟨the *jailed* protestors were noisily demanding to see their lawyers⟩ — see CAPTIVE

jailhouse *n* a place of confinement for persons held in lawful custody ⟨received a tip from an informant inside the county *jailhouse*⟩ — see JAIL

jake *adj, slang* being to one's liking ⟨once they hook up the game system, everything will be *jake* around here⟩ — see SATISFACTORY 1

jalopy *n* a dilapidated old automobile ⟨his parents gave him an old *jalopy* for school⟩ — see BEATER 1

jam *n* **1** a crowded mass (as of cars) that impedes or blocks movement ⟨thousands of cars trying to leave the stadium's parking lot at the same time are sure to create a *jam*⟩
synonyms backup, bottleneck, jam-up, logjam, snarl, tailback [*British*], tie-up
related words tangle; gridlock, lock; congestion, traffic; crawl, delay, slowdown, stoppage
2 a difficult, puzzling, or embarrassing situation from which there is no easy escape ⟨the heavy rain puts us in a real *jam*: all of the preparations are for a garden wedding⟩ — see PREDICAMENT

jam *vb* **1** to fit (people or things) into a tight space ⟨*jammed* his clothes into the already bulging hamper⟩ — see CROWD 1
2 to prevent passage through by filling with something ⟨firefighters found the nightclub's doorways *jammed* with trapped patrons⟩ — see CLOG 1
3 to put into (something) as much as can be held or contained ⟨the inn will *jam* a guest's picnic basket with an array of tempting foods⟩ — see FILL 1
4 to force one's way ⟨several more people *jammed* into the bus even though there was hardly room to stand⟩ — see [2]PRESS 4

jambalaya *n* an unorganized collection or mixture of various things ⟨its *jambalaya* of widely diverse nationalities and races gives the urban neighborhood a rich vitality⟩ — see MISCELLANY 1

jamboree *n* a bout of prolonged or excessive drinking ⟨he was a bit remorseful when he returned to the farm after his *jamboree* in town⟩ — see CAROUSE

jammed *adj* **1** containing or seeming to contain the greatest quantity or number possible ⟨tour buses, *jammed* with eager sightseers, invariably stop at that spot⟩ — see FULL 1
2 firmly positioned in place and difficult to dislodge ⟨this *jammed* door just won't budge⟩ — see TIGHT 2

jam–pack *vb* to put into (something) as much as can be held or contained ⟨we *jam-packed* the box with goodies for our sick friend⟩ — see FILL 1

jam–packed *adj* **1** containing or seeming to contain the greatest quantity or number possible ⟨a film *jam-packed* with spectacular action sequences⟩ — see FULL 1
2 having little space between items or parts ⟨the *jam-packed* placement of the chicken pieces in the frying pan prevented them from browning properly⟩ — see CLOSE 1

jam–up *n* a crowded mass (as of cars) that impedes or blocks movement ⟨knowing that there was a big traffic *jam-up* ahead, we took the detour that the locals always use⟩ — see JAM 1

jangle *n* friendly, informal conversation or an instance of this ⟨the hall was abuzz with the usual preconvention *jangle*⟩ — see CHAT 1

janitor *n* **1** a person who takes care of a property sometimes for an absent owner ⟨got a job as the night *janitor* at the elementary school⟩ — see CUSTODIAN 1
2 a person who tends a door ⟨according to popular Christian tradition, St. Peter acts as *janitor* at heaven's pearly gates⟩ — see DOORKEEPER

Janus–faced *adj* not being or expressing what one appears to be or express ⟨there was a *Janus-faced* quality to the interview: for all of the smiling and nodding, the interviewer's body language expressed deep boredom⟩ — see INSINCERE

jape *n* something said or done to cause laughter ⟨by the standards of today's no-holds-barred satire, Will Rogers' homespun *japes* about politicians seem awfully gentle⟩ — see JOKE 1

jape *vb* to make jokes ⟨the characters in Oscar Wilde's plays *jape* with a readiness and sophistication that is rarely, if ever, encountered in real life⟩ — see JOKE 1

jar *n* **1** a forceful coming together of two things ⟨this padded case should protect your laptop from the *jars* normally experienced while traveling⟩ — see IMPACT 1
2 something that makes a strong impression because it is so unexpected ⟨the flow of her day was interrupted

with the *jar* of an unexpected crisis⟩ — see SURPRISE 1
3 a harsh grating sound ⟨the *jar* of a stuck car door⟩ — see RASP

jar *vb* **1** to express different opinions about something often angrily ⟨those two coworkers have such incompatible personalities that it's no wonder they constantly *jar*⟩ — see ARGUE 2
2 to be out of harmony or agreement usually noticeably ⟨the bright orange of the walls *jars* with the light pastels of the furnishings⟩ — see CLASH

jargon *n* the special terms or expressions of a particular group or field ⟨I don't understand a lot of computer *jargon*⟩ — see TERMINOLOGY

jargon *vb* to make a short sharp sound like a small bird ⟨the birds who began *jargoning* to greet the dawn⟩ — see CHIRP

jarring *adj* **1** causing a strong emotional reaction because of unexpectedness ⟨the *jarring* news that major financial institutions were on the verge of collapse⟩ — see SURPRISING 1
2 disagreeable to one's aesthetic or artistic sense ⟨the final chord of that song is too *jarring* for me⟩ — see HARSH 2

jaundice *n* a deep-seated ill will ⟨the *jaundice* in the eyes of the two feuding neighbors was enough to kill crabgrass⟩ — see ENMITY

jaundiced *adj* **1** having or showing mean resentment of another's possessions or advantages ⟨took a *jaundiced* view of his opponent's triumphs on the tennis court⟩ — see ENVIOUS
2 marked by opposition or ill will ⟨environmentalists tend to cast a *jaundiced* eye on those oversized, gas-guzzling vehicles⟩ — see HOSTILE 1

jaunt *n* a short trip for pleasure ⟨took a leisurely *jaunt* up to the mountains for the day⟩ — see EXCURSION 1

jaunty *adj* having much high-spirited energy and movement ⟨oozing charm, the *jaunty* dance instructor literally swept the women off their feet⟩ — see LIVELY 1

javelin *n* a weapon with a long straight handle and sharp head or blade ⟨from atop his horse the warrior hurled a *javelin* that pierced the chest of his hapless foe⟩ — see SPEAR

jaw *n* friendly, informal conversation or an instance of this ⟨now that he's retired, he's got all afternoon for a *jaw* with his friends at the senior center⟩ — see CHAT 1

jaw *vb* **1** to criticize (someone) severely or angrily especially for personal failings ⟨you don't have to *jaw* me to death just because I bite my nails⟩ — see SCOLD
2 to engage in casual or rambling conversation ⟨just a group of girls sitting around the locker room and *jawing* about the usual stuff⟩ — see CHAT 1

jaw–dropper *n* something that makes a strong impression because it is so unexpected ⟨the underdog's victory was a *jaw-dropper* in boxing circles⟩ — see SURPRISE 1

jaw–dropping *adj* causing a strong emotional reaction because of unexpectedness ⟨the *jaw-dropping* prices for high-end modern art at the auction houses this season⟩ — see SURPRISING 1

jay *n* **1** a man extremely interested in his clothing and personal appearance ⟨a snooty little *jay* who refused to wear anything but designer labels⟩ — see DANDY 1
2 a person who talks constantly ⟨the stranger's incessant chatter was annoying, and she was the kind of *jay* that I didn't have in mind when I entered the park⟩ — see CHATTERBOX

jazz *n* language, behavior, or ideas that are absurd and contrary to good sense ⟨don't give me that *jazz* about how you didn't know that it was illegal⟩ — see NONSENSE 1

jazz (up) *vb* to give life, vigor, or spirit to ⟨your assignment is to *jazz up* the design of that Web page⟩ — see ANIMATE

jazziness *n* the quality or state of having abundant or intense activity ⟨the surprising *jazziness* of the city's art scene⟩ — see VITALITY 1

jazzy *adj* **1** attractively eye-catching in style ⟨that's a *jazzy* bathing suit, with all those spangles⟩
synonyms flashy, pizzazzy (*or* pizazzy), snazzy, splashy
related words cool, fresh (*slang*), hip, neat; à la mode (*also* a la mode), chic, chichi; dapper, dashing, natty, sharp, smart, snappy, spruce; faddish, fashionable, happening, in, modish, stylish, swish, trendy; custom, designer; showy, striking; flamboyant, garish, gaudy, glittery, glitzy, jaunty, loud, ostentatious, raffish, rakish, swank (*or* swanky), wild
near antonyms modest, plain, quiet, simple, unadorned; conservative, muted, restrained, subdued, toned-down, understated, unpretentious; styleless, unfashionable, unstylish; démodé, old-fashioned, outmoded, out-of-date, passé
2 having much high-spirited energy and movement ⟨a *jazzy* little dance routine that the aerobics instructor created⟩ — see LIVELY 1

jealous *adj* **1** intolerant of rivalry or unfaithfulness ⟨a boyfriend who became *jealous* whenever she paid attention to anyone but him⟩
synonyms possessive
related words controlling, demanding, domineering, grasping; covetous, envious, invidious, jaundiced; distrustful, mistrustful, suspicious; overprotective, protective
near antonyms undemanding; permissive, tolerant, tolerating, trustful, trusting, understanding
2 having or showing mean resentment of another's possessions or advantages ⟨was *jealous* of his friend's great popularity with the girls⟩ — see ENVIOUS

jealousy *n* a painful awareness of another's possessions or advantages and a desire to have them too ⟨her *jealousy* over her sister's singing career drove the two of them apart⟩ — see ENVY

jeer *n* a vocal sound made to express scorn or disapproval ⟨ignored the *jeers* of the other team's fans and just focused on making her free throw shot⟩ — see CATCALL

jeer *vb* to make (someone or something) the object of unkind laughter ⟨the unforgiving crowd *jeered* the magician when the final trick went awry⟩ — see RIDICULE

jefe *n* the person (as an employer or supervisor) who tells people and especially workers what to do ⟨the *jefe* of a drug cartel operating out of Central America⟩ — see BOSS

Jehovah *n* the being worshipped as the creator and ruler of the universe ⟨in the Lord *Jehovah* is everlasting strength⟩ — see DEITY 2

jejune *adj* **1** causing weariness, restlessness, or lack of interest ⟨another moralizing tale filled with *jejune* platitudes⟩ — see BORING
2 having or showing the annoying qualities (as silliness) associated with children ⟨an essay filled with *jejune*, simplistic opinions about international politics⟩ — see CHILDISH

jell *vb* **1** to take on a definite form ⟨our ideas for the marketing campaign are just beginning to *jell*⟩ — see FORM 1
2 to turn from a liquid into a substance resembling jelly ⟨the sauce will *jell* once it cools down⟩ — see COAGULATE

jelly *vb* to turn from a liquid into a substance resembling jelly ⟨this fruit juice is taking longer to *jelly* than I expected⟩ — see COAGULATE

jellyfish *n* a person without strength of character ⟨a *jellyfish* who was afraid to tell her boss that her latest brainstorm was just plain bad⟩ — see WEAKLING 2

jeopard *vb* to place in danger ⟨a scandal that could seriously *jeopard* his political career⟩ — see ENDANGER

jeopardize *vb* to place in danger ⟨don't do anything that will *jeopardize* your place on the advisory board⟩ — see ENDANGER

jeopardizing *adj* involving potential loss or injury ⟨that stupid prank could turn out to be a *jeopardizing* event in your academic career⟩ — see DANGEROUS 1

jeopardy *n* the state of not being protected from injury, harm, or evil ⟨the city's firefighters routinely put their lives in *jeopardy* by executing daring rescues⟩ — see DANGER 1

jeremiad *n* a long angry speech or scolding ⟨a *jeremiad* against the political apathy shown by so many young people⟩ — see TIRADE

jerk *n* **1** a person whose behavior is offensive to others ⟨his constant rudeness and insensitivity made everyone think he was a real *jerk*⟩
synonyms bastard, beast, bleeder [*British*], blighter [*chiefly British*], boor, bounder, bugger, buzzard, cad, chuff, churl, clown, creep, cretin, crud [*slang*], crumb [*slang*], cur, dirtbag [*slang*], dog, fink, heel, hound, joker, louse, lout, pill, rat, rat fink, reptile, rotter, schmuck [*slang*], scum, scumbag [*slang*], scuzzball [*slang*], skunk, sleaze, sleazebag [*slang*], sleazeball [*slang*], slime, slimeball [*slang*], slob, snake, so-and-so, sod [*chiefly British*], stinkard, stinker, swine, toad, varmint, vermin
related words barbarian, brute, caveman, Neanderthal, savage; loudmouth, vulgarian; lowlife, miscreant, rascal, rogue, roughneck, scab, scamp, scoundrel, villain, wretch; booby, doofus [*slang*], fool, jackass, nincompoop, ninny, nit [*chiefly British*], nitwit, nut, schmo (*or* schmoe) [*slang*]; airhead, birdbrain, blockhead, dink [*slang*], dolt, dope, dork [*slang*], goon, half-wit, idiot, imbecile, moron, turkey; brat, insolent, nuisance, pest, snip; snob, snoot, snot; dweeb [*slang*], nerd
phrases son of a gun
near antonyms hero, heroine, idol, role model; gentleman, lady; angel, saint
2 the act or an instance of applying force on something so that it moves in the direction of the force ⟨guided the rowboat with a *jerk* of the rope⟩ — see PULL 1

jerk *vb* **1** to move or cause to move with a sharp quick motion ⟨I *jerked* to one side to avoid getting hit⟩ ⟨*jerked* the leash to get the dog's attention⟩
synonyms buck, hitch, hoick, jolt, twitch, yank
related words bump, jounce, lurch, pitch, stagger; jig, jiggle, jog, joggle, shake; drag, lug, pull, tug; pluck, tweak; grab, rip, snap (up), snatch, tear, wrench, wrest, wring
2 to make jerky or restless movements ⟨you've got to quit *jerking*, or the barber will nick you by accident⟩ — see FIDGET
3 to make a series of small irregular or violent movements ⟨the car *jerked* with every shift of the gear⟩ — see SHAKE 1

jerky *adj* **1** marked by a series of sharp quick motions ⟨made *jerky* progress walking with the new crutches⟩
synonyms bumpy, choppy, herky-jerky, jouncy, rough
related words erratic, fitful, irregular, spasmodic, spastic, unsteady; jagged, ragged, uneven
near antonyms calm, placid, smooth, steady, still
2 showing or marked by a lack of good sense or judgment ⟨he's acting *jerky* just to get people's attention⟩ — see FOOLISH 1

jerry–built *adj* hastily or roughly constructed ⟨my *jerry-built* wine racks may not look pretty, but they get the job done⟩ — see RUDE 1

jerry–rigged *adj* hastily or roughly constructed ⟨a *jerry-rigged* switch to keep the machine in operation until it can be repaired⟩ — see RUDE 1

jest *n* **1** an attitude or manner not to be taken seriously ⟨you should know that our teasing was done entirely in *jest*⟩ — see FUN 2
2 something said or done to cause laughter ⟨laughed politely at his feeble *jest* about his pet mosquito⟩ — see JOKE 1
3 a playful or mischievous act intended as a joke ⟨putting a mouse in her desk drawer was intended to be a harmless *jest*⟩ — see PRANK
4 a person or thing that is made fun of ⟨his outlandish costumes made him the *jest* of the town⟩ — see LAUGHINGSTOCK

jest *vb* to make jokes ⟨when I asked my sister for a loan, she laughingly replied, "Surely you *jest*!"⟩ — see JOKE 1

jester *n* **1** a person (as a writer) noted for or specializing in humor ⟨a gentle *jester*, the cartoonist more often tries to evoke a broad smile than a hearty guffaw⟩ — see HUMORIST
2 a person formerly kept in a royal or noble household to amuse with jests and pranks ⟨the king called for some much-needed entertainment from his *jester*⟩ — see FOOL 2

jesting *adj* marked by or expressive of mild or good-natured teasing ⟨made *jesting* comments about my need for serious fashion advice⟩ — see QUIZZICAL

jesting *n* good-natured teasing or exchanging of clever remarks ⟨lots of laughter and elbow-nudging *jesting* at family reunions⟩ — see BANTER

jet *n* a usually forceful stream of fluid discharged from a narrow opening ⟨bought a new showerhead that emits a superpowerful *jet* of water⟩
synonyms spout, spurt, squirt
related words flush, gush, spew; spit, spray, spritz; geyser, spouter; blast, burst

jet *vb* **1** to flow out in great quantities or with force ⟨water *jetting* out of opened fire hydrants at a dangerously high rate⟩ — see GUSH 1
2 to violently throw out or off (something from within) ⟨the volcano has been *jetting* out fiery lava in life-threatening amounts⟩ — see ERUPT 1
3 to proceed or move quickly ⟨the presidential candidates *jetted* through the state for a week before racing off to the next primary⟩ — see HURRY 2

jettison *n* the getting rid of whatever is unwanted or useless ⟨with his ship rapidly sinking, the captain ordered a last-ditch *jettison* of much of its cargo⟩ — see DISPOSAL 1

jettison *vb* to get rid of as useless or unwanted ⟨just *jettison* that plan, because we know it won't work⟩ — see DISCARD

jetty *n* a structure used by boats and ships for taking on or landing cargo and passengers ⟨didn't see any passengers waiting for the ferry, so the captain sailed past the *jetty*⟩ — see DOCK

jewel *n* **1** a usually valuable stone cut and polished for ornament ⟨a necklace set with priceless *jewels*⟩ — see GEM 1
2 an asset that brings praise or renown ⟨an illuminated medieval manuscript that is the *jewel* of the library's collection of rare books⟩ — see GLORY 2
3 someone or something unusually desirable ⟨a star athlete who would be a *jewel* for any team⟩ — see PRIZE 1

Jezebel *n* a boldly flirtatious or sexually promiscuous woman ⟨as far as the family matriarch was concerned, her son's fiancée was a gold digger and a *Jezebel*⟩ — see FLOOZY

jibe *vb* to be in agreement on every point ⟨that doesn't *jibe* with what I know about his character⟩ — see CHECK 1

jiff *n* a very small space of time ⟨give me a *jiff* while I go to get my coat⟩ — see INSTANT

jiffy *n* a very small space of time ⟨I'll be there in a *jiffy*⟩ — see INSTANT

jig *n* a clever often underhanded means to achieve an end ⟨okay, buster, the *jig* is up⟩ — see TRICK 1

jig *vb* to make jerky or restless movements ⟨the mother could tell that her little boy had to use the bathroom because he was *jigging*⟩ — see FIDGET

jigger *n* an interesting and often novel device with a practical use ⟨a kitchen store filled with neat little *jiggers* that you didn't know you needed⟩ — see GADGET

jiggery–pokery *n* the use of clever underhanded actions to achieve an end ⟨the judge ordered the corporation to hand over all records, with no *jiggery-pokery* about unexpected problems and missing information⟩ — see TRICKERY

jiggle *vb* **1** to make a series of small irregular or violent movements ⟨the gelatin salad continued to *jiggle* after she set it on the table⟩ — see SHAKE 1
2 to make jerky or restless movements ⟨the applicant's knees constantly *jiggled*, betraying her nervousness⟩ — see FIDGET

jiggling *n* a series of slight movements by a body back and forth or from side to side ⟨the nerve-rattling *jiggling* we got when we drove over the railroad tracks⟩ — see VIBRATION 1

jilt *vb* to end a usually intimate relationship with ⟨still trying to get over being *jilted* by his longtime girlfriend⟩ — see DITCH 1

jim–dandy *n* something very good of its kind ⟨the brand new car was a *jim-dandy*⟩
synonyms beaut, beauty, bee's knees, cat's meow, corker, crackerjack (*also* crackajack), daisy, dandy, dilly, doozy (*or* doozie *also* doozer), dream, honey, hot stuff, humdinger, hummer, knockout, lollapalooza, lulu [*slang*], nifty, peach, pip, pippin, ripper, ripsnorter, snorter, sockdolager (*or* sockdologer), standout, sweetheart
related words marvel, phenomenon, prodigy, sensation, wonder; catch, crown jewel, diamond, gem, imperial, jewel, pearl, plum, treasure
phrases something else
near antonyms bust, disappointment, dud, failure, flop, lemon, letdown, loser, stinker, turkey

jim–dandy *adj* of the very best kind ⟨a *jim-dandy* guitarist who would be an asset to any garage band⟩ — see EXCELLENT

jimjams *n pl* a sense of panic or extreme nervousness ⟨heights don't give me the *jimjams*, but flying does⟩ — see JITTERS

jimmy *vb* to raise, move, or pull apart with or as if with a lever ⟨let's try to *jimmy* the door lock with my credit card⟩ — see [1]PRY 1

jingle *n* **1** a series of short high ringing sounds ⟨the *jingle* of change in my pocket⟩ — see TINKLE
2 a short musical composition for the human voice often with instrumental accompaniment ⟨loved that *jingle* in the commercial for the fast-food place⟩ — see SONG 1

jingle *vb* to make a repeated sharp light ringing sound ⟨the bell on the kitten's collar *jingled* as she walked⟩
synonyms chink, clink, tingle, tinkle
related words clang, clangor, clank, clash, crash; clack, clatter, rattle; chime, ding, ding-dong, gong, jangle, ping, plink, ring

jingo *n* **1** one who shows excessive favoritism towards his or her country ⟨a *jingo* who thought other countries should automatically follow his country's policies⟩ — see NATIONALIST
2 one who urges or attempts to cause a war ⟨the often bitter rhetoric between the *jingoes* and the committed pacifists⟩ — see WARMONGER

jingoism *n* excessive favoritism towards one's own country ⟨his loudmouthed *jingoism* will not win us any foreign allies⟩ — see CHAUVINISM

jingoist *adj* having or showing excessive favoritism towards one's own country ⟨a *jingoist* speech that just stopped short of calling for a declaration of war⟩ — see NATIONALIST 1

jingoist *n* one who urges or attempts to cause a war ⟨*jingoists* applauding the appointment of a hard-line foreign minister⟩ — see WARMONGER

jingoistic *adj* having or showing excessive favoritism towards one's own country ⟨dismissed the political action committee as a bunch of *jingoistic* extremists who never met a war they wouldn't support⟩ — see NATIONALIST 1

jink *vb* to move suddenly aside or to and fro ⟨*jinking* here and there with remarkable agility, the thieving urchin frustrated all attempts to catch him⟩ — see DODGE 1

jinx *n* something that brings bad luck ⟨believed the broken mirror was a *jinx*⟩
synonyms hex, hoodoo, Indian sign [*chiefly British*], whammy
related words Jonah; curse, evil eye, pox, spell, voodoo; augury, omen, portent
near antonyms amulet, charm, fetish (*also* fetich), talisman

jinxed *adj* having, prone to, or marked by bad luck ⟨this fishing rod must be *jinxed*, seeing as how I never catch anything⟩ — see UNLUCKY 1

jitteriness *n* a state of nervousness marked by sudden jerky movements ⟨sensing the team's *jitteriness* before the big game, the coach gave a pregame speech that was more reassuring than inspirational⟩ — see JUMPINESS

jitters *n pl* a sense of panic or extreme nervousness ⟨always got the *jitters* right before a test⟩
synonyms butterflies, dither, heebie-jeebies, jimjams, nerves, screaming meemies, shakes, shivers, whim-whams, willies
related words cold sweat, creeps, fidgets, goose bumps; agitation, anxiety, fear, hysteria, uneasiness; frazzle, nervous breakdown; edginess, jumpiness, skittishness
near antonyms aplomb, calm, composure, equanimity, imperturbability, self-possession, tranquillity (*or* tranquility)

jittery *adj* **1** easily excited by nature ⟨a *jittery* person who shouldn't even consider a career as an air traffic controller⟩ — see EXCITABLE
2 feeling or showing uncomfortable feelings of uncertainty ⟨feeling a little *jittery* before the flight⟩ — see NERVOUS 1

jive *adj, slang* not being or expressing what one appears to be or express ⟨don't give me that *jive* talk about me being your new best friend⟩ — see INSINCERE

jive *n* the special terms or expressions of a particular group or field ⟨a novel that captures dead-on the *jive* of young Hollywood hipsters⟩ — see TERMINOLOGY

jive *vb* **1** to make fun of in a good-natured way ⟨don't be upset—we're just *jiving* you⟩ — see TEASE 1
2 to make jokes ⟨our team was laughing and *jiving* after our surprise win⟩ — see JOKE 1

job *n* **1** an assignment at which one regularly works for pay ⟨a high-paying *job* as a banker⟩
synonyms appointment, berth, billet, capacity, connection, function, place, position, post, situation
related words business, employ, employment, occupation, profession; work; office, spot; calling, pursuit, trade, vocation; line, racket; engagement, gig; livelihood, living; career, lifework, practice (*also* practise); duty, mission, posting, service, task
near antonyms avocation; joblessness, unemployment
2 a piece of work that needs to be done regularly ⟨taking the trash out is one of my *jobs*⟩ — see CHORE 1

3 a specific task with which a person or group is charged ⟨your *job* on this committee is to review the curriculum and suggest changes⟩ — see MISSION
4 the action for which a person or thing is specially fitted or used or for which a thing exists ⟨a coffeemaker's *job* is to make coffee, and this overpriced machine doesn't do it very well⟩ — see ROLE
5 a dull, unpleasant, or difficult piece of work ⟨boy, doing all that filing was a real *job*⟩ — see CHORE 2

jobholder *n* one who works for another for wages or a salary ⟨more *jobholders* than the state agency has ever had in the past⟩ — see EMPLOYEE

jobless *adj* having no job ⟨having been *jobless* for six months, he was starting to get seriously discouraged⟩ — see UNEMPLOYED

jocose *adj* indicative of or marked by high spirits or good humor ⟨the comedian's *jocose* introductions kept the awards ceremony from becoming a stodgy affair⟩ — see MERRY

jocosely *adv* in a cheerful or happy manner ⟨a group of friends sitting around and commenting *jocosely* on the other wedding guests⟩ — see GAILY 1

jocular *adj* **1** given to or marked by mature intelligent humor ⟨made the *jocular* observation that the best way to make a small fortune in the wine business is to start off with a large fortune⟩ — see WITTY
2 indicative of or marked by high spirits or good humor ⟨the children at the library were charmed by the *jocular* storyteller⟩ — see MERRY

jocund *adj* indicative of or marked by high spirits or good humor ⟨old friends engaged in *jocund* teasing⟩ — see MERRY

jocundity *n* a mood characterized by high spirits and amusement and often accompanied by laughter ⟨the kind of forced *jocundity* that one finds so often at corporate events⟩ — see MIRTH

joe *n* an adult male human being ⟨your average *joe* isn't a particularly big fan of the opera⟩ — see MAN 1

Joe Blow *n* an average or ordinary man ⟨the typical *Joe Blow* can't afford to stay at the new five-star hotel⟩
synonyms everyman, Joe Six-Pack, John Doe, little guy, little man, lug, slob
related words commoner, pleb, plebeian, prole, proletarian; everywoman, plain Jane; laborer, peon, worker
phrases man in the street
near antonyms big cheese, big shot, big wheel, big wig, fat cat, mover and shaker, VIP

Joe Six–Pack *n* an average or ordinary man ⟨the political ads airing during the football game were an obvious attempt to gain the votes of the *Joe Six-Packs* in the audience⟩ — see JOE BLOW

jog *vb* **1** to go at a pace faster than a walk ⟨had to *jog* to catch up to them⟩ — see RUN 1
2 to make short up-and-down movements ⟨her purse was *jogging* against her hip as she walked⟩ — see NOD

joggle *vb* to make a series of small irregular or violent movements ⟨the old bus *joggled* as it barreled down the dirt road⟩ — see SHAKE 1

john *n* a room furnished with a fixture for flushing body waste ⟨man, that guy seems to spend hours in the *john*⟩ — see TOILET

John Barleycorn *n* a distilled beverage that can make a person drunk ⟨she blamed *John Barleycorn* for the breakdown of their marriage⟩ — see ALCOHOL

John Doe *n* an average or ordinary man ⟨to *John Doe* the most important issues in any election are usually those that affect his wallet⟩ — see JOE BLOW

John Hancock *n* a person's name written in their own handwriting often given to indicate awareness or consent ⟨let me just scribble my *John Hancock* on the bottom of the form⟩ — see SIGNATURE

join *n* a place where two or more things are united ⟨a small crack in the chalice at the *join* of the stem and the bowl⟩ — see JOINT 1

join *vb* **1** to be adjacent to ⟨the condo complex *joins* the golf course⟩ — see ADJOIN 1
2 to become a member of ⟨we're always looking for new people to *join* our book club⟩ — see ENTER 2
3 to come together to form a single unit ⟨one oxygen atom and two hydrogen atoms *join* to make one water molecule⟩ — see UNITE 1
4 to participate or assist in a joint effort to accomplish an end ⟨nations *joining* to bring aid to the earthquake-devastated region⟩ — see COOPERATE 1
5 to put or bring together so as to form a new and longer whole ⟨the plan is to *join* the various bike paths so that cyclists can travel from one end of the cape to the other⟩ — see CONNECT 1

joining *adj* having a border in common ⟨out of regard for your coworkers in the *joining* cubicles, please wear headphones when listening to electronic devices⟩ — see ADJACENT

joining *n* a place where two or more things are united ⟨the *joining* of the original house and the later addition is barely noticeable⟩ — see JOINT 1

joint *adj* used or done by a number of people as a group ⟨a *joint* effort by residents of the neighborhood to help reduce crime⟩ — see COLLECTIVE

joint *n* **1** a place where two or more things are united ⟨the leak was found at a *joint* in the pipe⟩
synonyms connection, coupling, join, joining, jointure, junction, juncture
related words link, nexus, tie; interconnection, intersection; abutment, articulation, attachment; seam, suture; concourse, confluence, meeting; union
near antonyms cleft, crack, crevice, fissure, gap, rift, separation
2 a building, room, or suite of rooms occupied by a service business ⟨let's go to the local burger *joint*⟩ — see PLACE 2
3 *slang* a place of confinement for persons held in lawful custody ⟨violate your probation and you'll be back in the *joint* in short order, loser⟩ — see JAIL

jointly *adv* in or by combined action or effort ⟨we always purchase our mother's birthday present *jointly*⟩ — see TOGETHER 2

jointure *n* a place where two or more things are united ⟨every *jointure* in the roof of the harbor tunnel shows signs of leakage⟩ — see JOINT 1

joke *n* **1** something said or done to cause laughter ⟨he was known for his hilarious *jokes*⟩
synonyms boff (*or* boffo), boffola, crack, drollery, funny, gag, giggle [*chiefly British*], jape, jest, josh, laugh, nifty, one-liner, pleasantry, quip, rib, sally, waggery, wisecrack, witticism, yuk (*or* yuck *also* yak *or* yock) [*slang*]
related words funning, joking, wisecracking; knee-slapper, panic [*slang*], riot, scream, thigh-slapper; antic, buffoonery, caper, leg-pull, monkeyshine(s), practical joke, prank, trick; burlesque, caricature, lampoon, mock, mockery, parody, put-on, riff; banter, kidding, persiflage, raillery, repartee; drollness, facetiousness, funniness, hilariousness, humorousness; comedy, humor, wit, wordplay
2 a poor, insincere, or insulting imitation of something ⟨her rendition of the national anthem is a *joke*⟩ — see MOCKERY 1
3 a person or thing that is made fun of ⟨having lost his looks and his voice years ago, these days he's just a show business *joke* and fodder for late-night comedy⟩ — see LAUGHINGSTOCK

joke *vb* **1** to make jokes ⟨he was known for his ability to *joke* about his lack of anything resembling a social life⟩
synonyms banter, chaff, fool, fun, gag, jape, jest, jive,

jolly, josh, kid, quip, wisecrack, yuk (*or* yuck) [*slang*]
related words gibe (*or* jibe), haze, jeer, mock, rag, rally, razz, rib, ridicule, tease; caricature, lampoon, parody, satirize; amuse, divert, entertain
phrases crack wise
2 to make fun of in a good-natured way ⟨oh, don't get offended, I was just *joking* you⟩ — see TEASE 1

joker *n* **1** a person (as a writer) noted for or specializing in humor ⟨he's the *joker* of the family, always making us laugh⟩ — see HUMORIST
2 a person whose behavior is offensive to others ⟨just ignore that *joker* and his rude comments⟩ — see JERK 1
3 an adult male human being ⟨sat at the bar next to some poor *joker* who had just lost his job⟩ — see MAN 1
4 a danger or difficulty that is hidden or not easily recognized ⟨read the contract carefully before signing to make sure there aren't any *jokers*⟩ — see PITFALL 1

jokester *n* a person (as a writer) noted for or specializing in humor ⟨hired the hot new Hollywood *jokester* to write the sitcom script⟩ — see HUMORIST

joking *adj* marked by or expressive of mild or good-natured teasing ⟨grinned and gave him a *joking* nudge with my elbow⟩ — see QUIZZICAL

jollies *n pl* a pleasurably intense stimulation of the feelings ⟨a provocateur who gets his *jollies* from stirring up political controversy⟩ — see THRILL

jollification *n* joyful or festive activity ⟨each year the mountain men of the Old West would gather for a week of carousing, tall tale-telling, and general *jollification*⟩ — see MERRYMAKING

jollity *n* joyful or festive activity ⟨I love all of the warm-hearted *jollity* of the holiday season⟩ — see MERRYMAKING

jolly *adj* **1** indicative of or marked by high spirits or good humor ⟨an especially *jolly* crowd of well-wishers at their wedding reception⟩ — see MERRY
2 giving pleasure or contentment to the mind or senses ⟨we always have a *jolly* time at their seaside cottage⟩ — see PLEASANT 1

jolly *adv* to a great degree ⟨I *jolly* well agree that you did the right thing⟩ ⟨has become a *jolly* careful driver since his recent accident⟩ — see VERY 1

jolly *vb* to make jokes ⟨spent their nights around the campfire good-naturedly *jollying* and telling scary stories⟩ — see JOKE 1

jolt *n* **1** a forceful coming together of two things ⟨pack the glass vase so that it won't fall victim to any hard *jolts* in transit⟩ — see IMPACT 1
2 something that makes a strong impression because it is so unexpected ⟨the news of the CEO's sudden retirement was a *jolt* to us all⟩ — see SURPRISE 1

jolt *vb* **1** to make a series of small irregular or violent movements ⟨the roller coaster car jerked and *jolted* as it coursed along the old wooden tracks⟩ — see SHAKE 1
2 to move or cause to move with a sharp quick motion ⟨she *jolted* the door open with her elbow⟩ — see JERK 1
3 to cause an unpleasant surprise for ⟨the sneak terrorist attack *jolted* the country out of its indolence and indifference⟩ — see SHOCK 1

jolting *adj* causing a strong emotional reaction because of unexpectedness ⟨the *jolting* news about our friend's premature death⟩ — see SURPRISING 1

jones *n, slang* **1** a physiological need for certain drugs ⟨that dude had a *jones* for heroin like you wouldn't believe⟩ — see ADDICTION
2 a strong wish for something ⟨I have a real *jones* for a milk shake⟩ — see DESIRE 1

jones (for) *vb, slang* to have an earnest wish to own or enjoy ⟨I'm really *jonesing for* a cup of coffee right now⟩ — see DESIRE 1

josh *n* something said or done to cause laughter ⟨a close-knit family constantly exchanging lighthearted *joshes* at the dinner table⟩ — see JOKE 1

josh *vb* **1** to make fun of in a good-natured way ⟨don't get all hot and bothered! I'm just *joshing* you⟩ — see TEASE 1
2 to make jokes ⟨a very outgoing man who *joshes* with everyone he meets⟩ — see JOKE 1

joshing *adj* marked by or expressive of mild or good-natured teasing ⟨a *joshing* response to my earnest question⟩ — see QUIZZICAL

joshing *n* good-natured teasing or exchanging of clever remarks ⟨for all his *joshing*, he can be very serious when he needs to be⟩ — see BANTER

jostle *vb* to force one's way ⟨everyone glared at the man who *jostled* to the front of the line⟩ — see [2]PRESS 4

jot *n* the smallest amount or part imaginable ⟨it's obvious that he doesn't have a *jot* of interest in history⟩
synonyms beans, bubkes (*also* bupkes *or* bupkus), continental, damn, darn (*also* durn), diddly [*slang*], diddly-squat [*slang*], doodley-squat (*or* doodly-squat), fig, ghost, hoot, iota, lick, modicum, rap, squat [*slang*], syllable, tittle, whit, whoop
related words ace, bit, crumb, dab, driblet, glimmer, hint, little, mite, nip, ounce, particle, peanuts, pin, ray, scrap, scruple, semblance, shade, shadow, shred, skosh, smidgen (*also* smidgeon *or* smidgin *or* smidge), snap, speck, spot, sprinkling, strain, streak, suspicion, touch, trace

jot (down) *vb* to make a written note of ⟨I'll *jot down* the message⟩ — see RECORD 1

jotting *n* a usually brief written reminder ⟨the judges reviewed their *jottings* one last time before selecting the pinot noir as the best wine of the tasting overall⟩ — see NOTE 1

jounce *n* a forceful coming together of two things ⟨we felt a definite *jounce* every time the car hit a pothole⟩ — see IMPACT 1

jounce *vb* **1** to make a series of small irregular or violent movements ⟨a rickety cart *jouncing* as it was being pulled over the cobblestoned streets⟩ — see SHAKE 1
2 to make short up-and-down movements ⟨her head *jounced* as the horse began to gallop⟩ — see NOD

jouncy *adj* marked by a series of sharp quick motions ⟨I'm afraid the car will give a rather *jouncy* ride until I can get the shocks repaired⟩ — see JERKY 1

journal *n* **1** a publication that appears at regular intervals ⟨a monthly scientific *journal*⟩
synonyms book, bulletin, diurnal, gazette, mag, magazine, newspaper, organ, paper, periodical, rag, review, serial, zine
related words annual, bimonthly, biweekly, daily, monthly, quarterly, semimonthly, semiweekly, triweekly, weekly, yearbook; digest, little magazine; fanzine; pictorial, slick; broadside, edition, extra, sheet, supplement, tab, tabloid; newsletter, newsmagazine, newsweekly
2 a record of personal experiences, reflections, or ideas kept regularly for private use ⟨the writer faithfully records his dreams in a *journal*, believing that they are a vital key to self-understanding⟩
synonyms daybook, diary
related words itinerary; blog, Weblog; log, logbook

journalist *n* a person employed by a newspaper, magazine, or radio or television station to gather, write, or report news ⟨a *journalist* who has won awards for two of his feature stories⟩ — see REPORTER

journey *n* a going from one place to another usually of some distance ⟨they were hungry and tired after their long *journey*⟩
synonyms expedition, passage, peregrination, travel(s), trek, trip
related words commutation, commute, errand, excursion, flight, hop, jaunt, junket, outing, sally, sortie, tour;

cruise, sail, voyage; drive, ride, spin; grand tour, odyssey, pilgrimage, progress, quest, safari; hike, slog, tramp, walk, walkabout

journey *vb* to take a trip especially of some distance ⟨an intense yearning to *journey* to distant lands⟩ — see TRAVEL 1

jovial *adj* indicative of or marked by high spirits or good humor ⟨the trip to the amusement park put everyone in a *jovial* mood⟩ — see MERRY

joviality *n* a mood characterized by high spirits and amusement and often accompanied by laughter ⟨the company's holiday parties often had an air of forced *joviality*⟩ — see MIRTH

jovially *adv* in a cheerful or happy manner ⟨*jovially* waved good morning to us⟩ — see GAILY 1

joy *n* **1** a feeling or state of well-being and contentment ⟨the inexpressible *joy* that the couple are feeling upon the birth of their first child⟩ — see HAPPINESS 1
2 a source of great satisfaction ⟨my car is my pride and *joy*⟩ — see DELIGHT 1

joy *vb* to feel or express joy or triumph ⟨the whole town is *joying* in the fact that its oldest church has been restored to its Victorian splendor⟩ — see EXULT

joyful *adj* experiencing pleasure, satisfaction, or delight ⟨the news of the child's safe return made us all *joyful*⟩ — see GLAD 1

joyless *adj* feeling unhappiness ⟨was utterly *joyless* after his bitter divorce⟩ — see SAD 1

joylessness *n* a state or spell of low spirits ⟨the inescapable *joylessness* that marred Yuletide celebrations during the war years⟩ — see SADNESS

joyous *adj* experiencing pleasure, satisfaction, or delight ⟨a *joyous* crowd eagerly awaiting the countdown to midnight on New Year's Eve⟩ — see GLAD 1

jubilant *adj* having or expressing feelings of joy or triumph ⟨the nominee's *jubilant* acceptance speech before the cheering crowd⟩ — see EXULTANT

jubilate *vb* to feel or express joy or triumph ⟨a medical researcher too committed to his work to pause and *jubilate* even upon hearing that he had won the Nobel Prize⟩ — see EXULT

jubilee *n* a time or program of special events and entertainment in honor of something ⟨the town is planning a year-long *jubilee* in celebration of its founding 200 years ago⟩ — see FESTIVAL

Judas *n* one who betrays a trust or an allegiance ⟨she heatedly called her best friend a *Judas* after she found out her secrets had been spread all over town⟩ — see TRAITOR

judder *vb, chiefly British* to make a series of small irregular or violent movements ⟨the engine began to *judder* alarmingly just a few miles outside of Brighton⟩ — see SHAKE 1

judge *n* **1** a person who impartially decides or resolves a dispute or controversy ⟨their father always played the role of *judge* when there was a disagreement between the siblings⟩
synonyms adjudicator, arbiter, arbitrator, referee, umpire
related words jurist, justice, magistrate; intermediary, intermediate, mediator, mediatrix, moderator, negotiator; conciliator, go-between, peacemaker, reconciler, troubleshooter; decider
2 a public official having authority to decide questions of law ⟨the *judge* gave the defendant a suspended sentence⟩
synonyms adjudicator, beak [*chiefly British*], bench, court, jurist, justice, magistrate
related words chief justice, circuit judge, justice of the peace, squire; auditor, master; jurisconsult, jurisprudent

judge *vb* **1** to give an opinion about (something at issue or in dispute) ⟨the committee will *judge* the case solely on the evidence⟩
synonyms adjudge, adjudicate, arbitrate, decide, determine, referee, rule (on), settle, umpire
related words consider, deem, deliberate, hear, ponder, weigh; size up; mediate, moderate, negotiate; prosecute, try; find (for *or* against); conclude, resolve; redetermine, rejudge
near antonyms equivocate, hedge, pussyfoot, skirt
2 to decide the size, amount, number, or distance of (something) without actual measurement ⟨considering the amount of dough we have, I *judge* we'll get about six dozen cookies out of it⟩ — see ESTIMATE 2
3 to form an opinion or reach a conclusion through reasoning and information ⟨I *judge* that the girl has had a troubled relationship with her mother⟩ — see INFER 1
4 to have as an opinion ⟨I *judge* that he knew what kind of woman she was when he married her⟩ — see BELIEVE 2

judgmatic *or* **judgmatical** *adj* having or showing good judgment and restraint especially in conduct or speech ⟨not the most *judgmatic* way to tell a woman that she could stand to lose a few pounds⟩ — see DISCREET 1

judgment *or* **judgement** *n* **1** a decision made by a court or tribunal regarding a case it has heard ⟨the court will give its *judgment* in this case tomorrow morning⟩ — see SENTENCE
2 a position arrived at after consideration ⟨built her fortune by making intelligent *judgments* about the performance of stocks⟩ — see DECISION 1
3 an idea that is believed to be true or valid without positive knowledge ⟨your *judgment* of the situation isn't a very good one⟩ — see OPINION 1
4 an opinion on the nature, character, or quality of something ⟨critical *judgment* on that new comedy has been overwhelmingly negative⟩ — see ESTIMATION 1

judgmental *adj* given to making or expressing unfavorable judgments about things ⟨culinary purists who tend to be *judgmental* about home cooks who take shortcuts⟩ — see CRITICAL 1

judicious *adj* **1** having or showing good judgment and restraint especially in conduct or speech ⟨a good teacher who knows how to give *judicious* criticism as well as praise⟩ — see DISCREET 1
2 suitable for bringing about a desired result under the circumstances ⟨I'll ask for the raise at a time I deem most *judicious*⟩ — see EXPEDIENT

judiciousness *n* suitability for bringing about a desired result under the circumstances ⟨the *judiciousness* of using such harsh language in a letter of complaint is questionable at best⟩ — see EXPEDIENCY

jug *n* **1** a place of confinement for persons held in lawful custody ⟨some no-good fellow who had spent most of his life in and out of the county *jug*⟩ — see JAIL
2 a handled container for holding and pouring liquids that usually has a lip or a spout ⟨put a *jug* of milk on the table⟩ — see PITCHER

jug *vb* to put in or as if in prison ⟨the luckless crooks got *jugged* before they knew what hit them⟩ — see IMPRISON

juggernaut *n* a series of activities undertaken to achieve a goal ⟨there was no escaping the *juggernaut* of hype for the studio's biggest summer blockbuster⟩ — see CAMPAIGN

juggle *n* a clever often underhanded means to achieve an end ⟨a temporary suspension of the gas tax was just a crowd-pleasing *juggle* that was not a long-term solution to the energy problem⟩ — see TRICK 1

juggle *vb* to cause to believe what is untrue ⟨everyone thinks that they are too smart to be *juggled* by con artists⟩ — see DECEIVE

jugglery *n* the use of clever underhanded actions to

achieve an end ⟨you wouldn't believe the *jugglery* I have to resort to in order to get the cat in the carrier for a trip to the vet's⟩ — see TRICKERY

jugular *n* a vulnerable point ⟨a sadistic training instructor who would seek out a recruit's *jugular* and then go for it⟩ — see ACHILLES' HEEL

juice *n* **1** active strength of body or mind ⟨the aging quarterback proved he still had the *juice* to play the whole game⟩ — see VIGOR 1

2 *slang* the power to direct the thinking or behavior of others usually indirectly ⟨those activists don't have the political *juice* to sway the vote of a single legislator⟩ — see INFLUENCE 1

3 *slang* a distilled beverage that can make a person drunk ⟨I had heard my friend was hitting the *juice* again, and I was concerned⟩ — see ALCOHOL

juiced *adj* **1** showing urgent desire or interest ⟨I've been *juiced* for this Caribbean cruise for almost a year⟩ — see EAGER

2 *slang* being under the influence of alcohol ⟨he has to get *juiced* first, but you'll find he's quite a dancer⟩ — see DRUNK

juicehead *n, slang* a person who makes a habit of getting drunk ⟨that old *juicehead* actually cleaned up his act after his wife dumped him⟩ — see DRUNK 1

juicer *n, slang* a person who makes a habit of getting drunk ⟨a perpetually hung-over *juicer* living a dead-end life⟩ — see DRUNK 1

juice up *vb* to give life, vigor, or spirit to ⟨some parlor games that will *juice up* an otherwise dull evening at home⟩ — see ANIMATE

juiciness *n* the quality or state of being full of juice ⟨the delicious *juiciness* of ripe pears⟩ — see SUCCULENCE

juicy *adj* **1** full of juice ⟨she bit into the *juicy* orange⟩
synonyms fleshy, pulpy, succulent
related words sappy, watery
near antonyms dehydrated, desiccated, dry, sere (*also* sear), shriveled (*or* shrivelled), withered
antonyms juiceless, sapless

2 yielding a profit ⟨the former president landed a *juicy* book deal⟩ — see PROFITABLE 1

juke *vb* to elude (an opponent in a sports contest) by making a deceptive or agile movement ⟨*juked* defenders with a series of spin moves and picked up 15 yards on the running play⟩
synonyms deke, fake, fake out
related words dodge, evade, sidestep, slip; pump-fake, stutter-step; maneuver (around)

jumble *n* **1** a state in which everything is out of order ⟨the house is always in a *jumble* before and after vacation trips⟩ — see CHAOS

2 an unorganized collection or mixture of various things ⟨a *jumble* of rubber bands, batteries, and pencil stubs all stuffed into that drawer⟩ — see MISCELLANY 1

jumble *vb* to undo the proper order or arrangement of ⟨the contest editor has *jumbled* the letters of some common words⟩ — see DISORDER

jumbled *adj* lacking in order, neatness, and often cleanliness ⟨a *jumbled* closet in which she could never find anything⟩ — see MESSY

jumbo *adj* unusually large ⟨a *jumbo* jet⟩ — see HUGE

jumbo *n* something that is unusually large and powerful ⟨the winner in the contest for biggest pumpkin was a *jumbo* that weighed in at over a thousand pounds⟩ — see GIANT

jump *n* **1** an act of leaping into the air ⟨took a small *jump* forward to avoid stepping in the puddle⟩
synonyms bound, hop, leap, spring, vault
related words bounce, lope, skip; caper, capriole, gambado, gambol; attack, pounce; dive, pitch, plunge

2 the more favorable condition or position in a competition ⟨get a *jump* on the competition by starting early⟩ — see ADVANTAGE 1

jump *vb* **1** to propel oneself upward or forward into the air ⟨*jumped* across the ditch⟩
synonyms bound, hop, leap, spring, vault
related words bounce, hurdle, leapfrog, lope, skip; buck; caper, capriole, cavort, frolic, gambol, romp; attack, pounce; shoot, skyrocket

2 to move suddenly and sharply (as in surprise) ⟨the sudden appearance of a mouse scurrying across the floor made me *jump*⟩ — see START 1

3 to proceed or move quickly ⟨when I tell you to do something, I expect you to *jump*⟩ — see HURRY 2

jump (on) *vb* **1** to take sudden, violent action against ⟨the robbers waited until he had passed by them and then *jumped on* him without warning⟩ — see ATTACK 1

2 to criticize harshly and usually publicly ⟨no need to *jump on* him just because he locked the keys in the car⟩ — see ATTACK 2

jumpiness *n* a state of nervousness marked by sudden jerky movements ⟨the police detective interpreted the suspect's *jumpiness* as a sign of guilt⟩
synonyms edginess, fidgetiness, fidgets, flightiness, jitteriness, restiveness, skittishness
related words agita, agitation, anxiety, anxiousness, apprehension, apprehensiveness, disquiet, feverishness, franticness, freneticism, hand-wringing, perturbation, restlessness, trepidation, unease, uneasiness, upset, worry; nerves, tenseness, tension; butterflies, dither, heebie-jeebies, jimjams, jitters, shakes, shivers, willies
near antonyms confidence, self-assurance, self-confidence, sureness; control, self-control; aplomb, calm, calmness, collectedness, composure, coolness, ease, easiness, equanimity, equilibrium, imperturbability, poise, repose, self-possession, tranquillity (*or* tranquility), tranquilness

jump–start *vb* to give life, vigor, or spirit to ⟨an intentionally provocative comment that was supposed to *jump-start* the discussion⟩ — see ANIMATE

jumpy *adj* **1** easily excited by nature ⟨a *jumpy* little terrier⟩ — see EXCITABLE

2 feeling or showing uncomfortable feelings of uncertainty ⟨flight attendants had to calm *jumpy* passengers after the plane hit unexpected turbulence⟩ — see NERVOUS 1

junction *n* **1** a place where two or more things are united ⟨situated at the *junction* of several major railways, the city has long been a transportation hub⟩ — see JOINT 1

2 the act or an instance of joining two or more things into one ⟨the *junction* of the coalition's two military forces has not been without problems⟩ — see UNION 1

3 a place where roads meet ⟨the town finally installed a traffic light at that busy *junction*⟩ — see CROSSROAD 1

juncture *n* **1** a particular and often important moment in time ⟨at the present *juncture*, I think the country is looking for a strong president⟩ — see POINT 1

2 a place where two or more things are united ⟨the water is leaking at the *juncture* of those two pipes⟩ — see JOINT 1

3 a time or state of affairs requiring prompt or decisive action ⟨we have now arrived at a *juncture* where something must be done to avert war⟩ — see EMERGENCY

jungle *n* an unorganized collection or mixture of various things ⟨clearing out the *jungle* of boxes cluttering up the garage is her project for the weekend⟩ — see MISCELLANY 1

junior *adj* having not so great importance or rank as another ⟨*junior* advisers to the governor⟩ — see LESSER

junior *n* one who is of lower rank and typically under the authority of another ⟨she's his *junior* in the company⟩ — see UNDERLING

junk *n* **1** that which is of low quality or worth ⟨couldn't believe that such *junk* was chosen to be read for the book club⟩ ⟨my car is *junk*—it spends more time in the shop than on the road⟩
synonyms cheese, crapola [*slang*], dreck (*also* drek), muck, rubbish, sleaze, slop, slush, trash, tripe
related words camp, kitsch; claptrap, humbug, nonsense; bomb, clinker, clunker, dud, lemon, stinker, turkey; mess, muddle, shambles
2 discarded or useless material ⟨*junk* on the side of the road waiting for the trash collection⟩ — see GARBAGE 1

junk *vb* to get rid of as useless or unwanted ⟨we'll have to *junk* this old car⟩ — see DISCARD

junker *n* a dilapidated old automobile ⟨they finally traded in their old *junker* for a nice new car⟩ — see BEATER 1

junket *n* a short trip for pleasure ⟨took a *junket* to the city for some sightseeing and shopping⟩ — see EXCURSION 1

junket *vb* to entertain with a fancy meal ⟨a lobbyist who regularly *junkets* politicians who are friendly toward the oil industry⟩ — see FEAST 1

junkie *also* **junky** *n* **1** a person who regularly uses drugs especially illegally ⟨heroin *junkies* wasting their lives⟩ — see DOPER
2 a person with a strong and habitual liking for something ⟨a television cartoon *junkie*⟩ — see FAN

junking *n* the getting rid of whatever is unwanted or useless ⟨that old chair needs *junking*⟩ — see DISPOSAL 1

junky *adj* **1** having no usefulness ⟨that broken watch you're wearing is *junky*⟩ — see WORTHLESS
2 of low quality ⟨a *junky* coat that is sure to fall apart after one winter⟩ — see CHEAP 2

jurisdiction *n* lawful control over the affairs of a political unit (as a nation) ⟨the United States has no *jurisdiction* over Cuba⟩ — see RULE 2

jurist *n* a public official having authority to decide questions of law ⟨earned a reputation as one of the most learned *jurists* in the federal courts⟩ — see JUDGE 2

jury–rig *vb* to make or assemble roughly or hastily ⟨we *jury-rigged* shelves out of cartons and crates until we could afford real furniture⟩ — see COBBLE (TOGETHER *OR* UP)

jury–rigged *adj* hastily or roughly constructed ⟨a *jury-rigged* system for supplying the town's water while the main pumping station is being repaired⟩ — see RUDE 1

just *adj* **1** being what is called for by accepted standards of right and wrong ⟨a *just* punishment should fit the crime⟩
synonyms competent, condign, deserved, due, fair, justified, merited, right, rightful, warranted
related words applicable, appropriate, apt, fit, fitting, meet, proper, requisite, suitable; lawful, legal, legitimate; accurate, correct, true; rhadamanthine, strict, stringent, uncompromising; equitable, impartial, square
near antonyms incoherent, incorrect, irrelative, irrelevant; improper, inapplicable, inapposite, inappropriate, inapt, indefensible, unjustifiable, unreasonable, unsuitable; biased, inequitable, partial, unequal; arbitrary, despotic; illegitimate, unlawful
antonyms undeserved, undue, unfair, unjust, unjustified, unmerited, unwarranted
2 based on sound reasoning or information ⟨there are *just* reasons for the state's ban of the private use of fireworks⟩ — see GOOD 1
3 conforming to a high standard of morality or virtue ⟨they are a *just* people who are guided by a firm belief in God and a love of traditional values⟩ — see GOOD 2
4 following the accepted rules of moral conduct ⟨the sort of *just* conduct that we expect of every soldier⟩ — see HONORABLE 1
5 guided by or in accordance with one's sense of right and wrong ⟨stopping to help a stranded motorist is simply the *just* thing to do⟩ — see CONSCIENTIOUS 1
6 marked by justice, honesty, and freedom from bias ⟨a *just* appraisal of the political situation over there⟩ — see FAIR 2

just *adv* **1** in the same manner ⟨you can do it *just* the way they do⟩
synonyms exactly, precisely
related words even, expressly, faultlessly, perfectly; identically, uniformly; alike, likewise, similarly
phrases to a T
near antonyms slightly, somewhat, vaguely; differently, variably
2 by a very small margin ⟨I was *just* over the minimum age requirement for the senior citizen discount⟩
synonyms barely, hardly, marginally, narrowly, scarcely, slightly
related words minimally, minutely, scantly; almost, approximately, closely, more or less, nearly, partly, plus or minus, roughly, somewhat
phrases by the skin of one's teeth
near antonyms definitely, easily, plainly, positively, quite, unquestionably; abundantly, completely, copiously, fully, generously, greatly
antonyms considerably, significantly, substantially, vastly, well
3 nothing more than ⟨I was *just* kidding⟩
synonyms but, merely, only, purely, simply
4 as stated or indicated without the slightest difference ⟨the length of the curtain is *just* right⟩ — see EXACTLY 1
5 for nothing other than ⟨got this present *just* for you⟩ — see SOLELY 1
6 not long ago ⟨I *just* bought this dress⟩ — see NEWLY

justice *n* **1** the practice of giving to others what is their due or an instance of this ⟨the victim's family felt that *justice* had been done in the case⟩
synonyms equity, fair shake, right
related words equitability, equitableness, evenhandedness, fair-mindedness, fairness, impartiality; goodness, righteousness, virtue; honor, integrity, uprightness
near antonyms bias, one-sidedness, partiality, prejudice; unfairness, unjustness, wrongfulness; corruption, impropiety; crime, offense (*or* offence), wrongdoing; disservice, harm
antonyms inequity, injustice, raw deal, wrong
2 a public official having authority to decide questions of law ⟨a *justice* of the U.S. Supreme Court⟩ — see JUDGE 2
3 lack of favoritism toward one side or another ⟨with scrupulous *justice*, the marriage counselor noted that both parties had much to atone for⟩ — see DETACHMENT 1

justifiable *adj* capable of being defended with good reasoning against verbal attack ⟨had *justifiable* reasons for leaving early⟩ — see TENABLE 2

justification *n* an explanation that frees one from fault or blame ⟨offered a weak *justification* for why he was so late⟩ — see EXCUSE

justified *adj* **1** based on sound reasoning or information ⟨in a well-*justified* ruling the court voted unanimously to overturn the law⟩ — see GOOD 1
2 being what is called for by accepted standards of right and wrong ⟨the use of force to capture the armed fugitive was fully *justified*⟩ — see JUST 1

justify *vb* **1** to be an acceptable reason for ⟨you seem to think that losing a basketball game *justifies* a temper tantrum⟩
synonyms excuse
related words account (for), alibi, explain, explain away, rationalize; brush (aside *or* off), condone, disregard, forgive, gloss (over), gloze (over), ignore, pardon,

pass over, remit, shrug off, wink (at)
2 to continue to declare to be true or proper despite opposition or objections ⟨failed to *justify* the need for a war at this time⟩ — see MAINTAIN 2

jut *n* a part that sticks out from the general mass of something ⟨Cape Fear is one of the more colorfully named *juts* along the North Carolina coast⟩ — see BULGE 1

jut *vb* to extend outward beyond a usual point ⟨the sandbar *juts* out into the ocean⟩ — see BULGE 1

juvenile *adj* **1** being in the early stage of life, growth, or development ⟨a *juvenile* alligator just hatched from its egg⟩ — see YOUNG
2 having or showing the annoying qualities (as silliness) associated with children ⟨throwing a tantrum is rather *juvenile* behavior for a person of your age⟩ — see CHILDISH
3 lacking in adult experience or maturity ⟨a spoiled, *juvenile* golfer who does not know how to win gracefully⟩ — see CALLOW

juvenile *n* a young person who is between infancy and adulthood ⟨a medical study that followed *juveniles* through adolescence and into adulthood⟩ — see CHILD 1

juxtaposed *adj* having a border in common ⟨the *juxtaposed* photographs of the country's richest and poorest areas are a telling commentary on inequality⟩ — see ADJACENT

K

kahuna *n* one of high position or importance within a group ⟨a big *kahuna* at a Hollywood talent agency, he's got the fancy car to prove it⟩ — see BIG SHOT

kale *n, slang* something (as pieces of stamped metal or printed paper) customarily and legally used as a medium of exchange, a measure of value, or a means of payment ⟨trying to scrape up the *kale* to buy more dope⟩ — see MONEY 1

kaleidoscopic *adj* marked by a variety of usually vivid colors ⟨a trendy bar that offers a *kaleidoscopic* array of new-wave martinis that go way beyond the colorless original⟩ — see COLORFUL

kamikaze *adj* having or showing a lack of concern for the consequences of one's actions ⟨a bike messenger who regularly cuts across busy city streets with a *kamikaze* boldness⟩ — see RECKLESS 1

kaput *also* **kaputt** *adj* **1** facing certain defeat, disaster, or death ⟨once the Germans were forced to retreat from Stalingrad, the Nazi cause was *kaput*⟩ — see DONE FOR
2 having passed its time of use or usefulness ⟨hard-line Soviet-style Communism became *kaput* in Russia⟩ — see OBSOLETE
3 not being in working order ⟨the heating system went *kaput* on the coldest day of the year⟩ — see INOPERABLE 1

karma *n* a special quality or impression associated with something ⟨as the site of a string of failed businesses, the building definitely had bad *karma*⟩ — see AURA 1

katzenjammer *n* loud, confused, and usually inharmonious sound ⟨traffic was all tied up, the kids were fighting, and in the midst of all this *katzenjammer*, the phone rang⟩ — see NOISE 1

keel *n* a large craft for travel by water ⟨for a few days at least, the Titanic was the largest and grandest *keel* afloat⟩ — see SHIP

keel (over) *vb* to lose consciousness ⟨I swear I'll *keel over* if you make me dissect a frog⟩ — see FAINT

keelhaul *vb* to criticize (someone) severely or angrily especially for personal failings ⟨there's no need to *keelhaul* him—it was an honest mistake, and a small one at that⟩ — see SCOLD

keen *adj* **1** able to sense slight impressions or differences ⟨pilots with especially *keen* eyesight⟩ — see [2]ACUTE
2 causing intense discomfort to one's skin ⟨the *keen* wind gave me chapped lips⟩ — see CUTTING 1
3 having an edge thin enough to cut or pierce something ⟨lanced the boil with a *keen* scalpel⟩ — see SHARP 1
4 having or showing quickness of mind ⟨readers who were *keen* enough to realize that the writer was being satirical⟩ — see INTELLIGENT 1
5 of the very best kind ⟨that new digital camera sure is *keen*⟩ — see EXCELLENT
6 showing urgent desire or interest ⟨a *keen* hunger for fame and fortune in the fashion industry⟩ — see EAGER
7 extreme in degree, power, or effect ⟨movies gave him *keen* enjoyment like nothing else⟩ — see INTENSE 1

keen *n* a crying out in grief ⟨the loud *keens* of the widows were heard throughout the war-ravaged city⟩ — see LAMENT 1

keen *vb* **1** to express dissatisfaction, pain, or resentment usually tiresomely ⟨victims of the disaster have been *keening* for weeks about the slowness of governmental aid⟩ — see COMPLAIN
2 to make a long loud mournful sound ⟨mourners *keening* for the victims of the bombing⟩ — see HOWL 1

keenness *n* **1** a harsh or sharp quality ⟨the *keenness* of the knife should tell you that it was sharpened recently⟩ ⟨a writer famous for the *keenness* of her wit⟩ — see EDGE 1
2 urgent desire or interest ⟨was looking forward to his birthday party with the *keenness* of a youngster⟩ — see EAGERNESS
3 exceptional discernment and judgment especially in practical matters ⟨had the financial *keenness* to know that the stock was overvalued⟩ — see ACUMEN
4 the state or quality of being able to sense slight impressions or differences ⟨there's an enhanced *keenness* of hearing that young mothers seem to develop⟩ — see ACUITY

keep *n* the act or activity of keeping something in an existing and usually satisfactory condition ⟨the *keep* of the stable is mainly left to the two equine-loving daughters⟩ — see MAINTENANCE

keep *vb* **1** to mark with an appropriate practice, rite, or

ceremony ⟨*keep* the Sabbath by not working⟩
synonyms celebrate, commemorate, observe
related words bless, consecrate, sanctify, solemnize; fete (*or* fête), honor, laud, praise; memorialize, remember
near antonyms blow off, disregard, forget, ignore, neglect, overlook
antonyms break, transgress, violate
2 to continue to have in one's possession or power ⟨the money is yours to *keep*⟩ ⟨*keep* my secret and don't tell it to anyone⟩
synonyms hold, reserve, retain, withhold
related words conserve, guard, preserve, protect, save; boast, enjoy, have, own, possess; command, control, detain, direct, manage, rule; bear, harbor; cherish, cling (to), hug, treasure
phrases hang on to, hold on to
near antonyms abandon, cede, drop; contribute, donate, give, hand out; discard, dump; decline, reject, repudiate, spurn; lose
antonyms give up, hand over, release, relinquish, surrender, yield
3 to do what is required by the terms of ⟨make sure you *keep* your promise to help out at the homeless shelter⟩ — see FULFILL 1
4 to place somewhere for safekeeping or ready availability ⟨I *keep* extra toothbrushes for unexpected overnight guests⟩ — see STORE 1
5 to pay the living expenses of ⟨looking for a sugar daddy to *keep* her in a style to which she'd dearly love to become accustomed⟩ — see SUPPORT 2
6 to look after and make decisions about ⟨enlisted a relative to *keep* the store while she was away⟩ — see CONDUCT 1
7 to keep from exceeding a desirable degree or level (as of expression) ⟨at least try to *keep* your temper during the holiday meal⟩ — see CONTROL 1
8 to drive danger or attack away from ⟨may God bless and *keep* you⟩ — see DEFEND 1

keep (from) *vb* to resist the temptation of ⟨try to *keep from* eating all the chocolate in one day!⟩ — see FORBEAR

keep (to) *vb* to give steadfast support to ⟨always *keeps to* his political positions, even when they are unpopular⟩ — see ADHERE (TO) 1

keeper *n* **1** a person or group that watches over someone or something ⟨how should I know where she is? I'm not her *keeper*⟩ — see GUARD 1
2 a person who takes care of a property sometimes for an absent owner ⟨during the winter the *keeper* of the family's beach house is a local resident who looks after the place⟩ — see CUSTODIAN 1

keeping *n* **1** responsibility for the safety and well-being of someone or something ⟨put the house keys into a neighbor's secure *keeping* while they were on vacation⟩ — see CUSTODY
2 the fact or state of having (something) at one's disposal ⟨my aunt has all of our family's old photographs in her *keeping*⟩ — see POSSESSION 1
3 the following of a custom, rule, or law ⟨the *keeping* of religious laws and traditions⟩ — see OBSERVANCE 1
4 a state of being or fitness ⟨the estate hasn't been in good *keeping* since the owner suffered financial reverses⟩ — see CONDITION 1

keepsake *n* something that serves to keep alive the memory of a person or event ⟨saved the tassel from her mortarboard as a *keepsake* of her high school graduation⟩ — see MEMORIAL

keep up *vb* **1** to continue to operate or to meet one's needs ⟨let's hope that old air conditioner *keeps up* through this heat wave⟩ — see HOLD OUT
2 to keep in good condition ⟨*kept* the house *up* while the owners were gone⟩ — see MAINTAIN 1
3 to remain indefinitely in existence or in the same state ⟨let's hope this beautiful weather *keeps up* for the rest of our vacation⟩ — see CONTINUE 1

keg *n* an enclosed wooden vessel for holding beverages ⟨a *keg* of beer⟩ — see CASK

keister *also* **keester** *n, slang* the part of the body upon which someone sits ⟨he fell right on his *keister* in front of the whole crowd⟩ — see BUTTOCKS

kempt *adj* being clean and in good order ⟨a distinguished-looking gentleman with a *kempt* beard and an old-world manner⟩ — see NEAT 1

kenspeckle *adj, chiefly Scottish* likely to attract attention ⟨the kind of *kenspeckle* performance art that is much in evidence at Edinburgh's Fringe Festival⟩ — see NOTICEABLE

kerchief *n* **1** a scarf worn on the head ⟨tied the *kerchief* around her head to keep her hair out of her face⟩ — see BANDANNA
2 a small, often square piece of material that is used for personal hygiene purposes ⟨dabbed the sweat on his brow with a *kerchief*⟩ — see HANKIE

kerf *n* a V-shaped cut usually on an edge or a surface ⟨with a handsaw I made a *kerf* in the board to mark where I needed to cut⟩ — see NOTCH 1

kerfuffle *n, chiefly British* a state of noisy, confused activity ⟨predictably, the royal scandal caused quite a *kerfuffle* on Fleet Street⟩ — see COMMOTION

kernel *n* the central part or aspect of something under consideration ⟨the *kernel* of your argument seems to be the inevitability of the division of that nation along ethnic lines⟩ — see CRUX

key *adj* **1** coming before all others in importance ⟨maintains that Sir Isaac Newton remains the *key* figure in physical science⟩ — see FOREMOST 1
2 of the greatest possible importance ⟨first—and this is *key*—I wasn't even there that evening⟩ — see CRUCIAL

key *n* **1** an explanatory list of the symbols on a map or chart ⟨in order to know what those dotted lines represent, you'll need to look at the *key*⟩ — see LEGEND 1
2 something that allows someone to achieve a desired goal ⟨a good education is the *key* to success⟩ — see PASSPORT 1
3 the means or right of entering or participating in ⟨he had found the *key* to her heart⟩ — see ENTRANCE 1

key *vb* to bring to a state free of conflicts, inconsistencies, or differences ⟨her response was perfectly *keyed* to the situation⟩ — see HARMONIZE 2

keynote *n* the central part or aspect of something under consideration ⟨the need for a greater sense of self-reliance is the *keynote* of his self-help message⟩ — see CRUX

keystone *n* an immaterial thing upon which something else rests ⟨a committed socialist who argues that greed is the *keystone* of capitalism⟩ — see BASE 1

ki *n* a spiritual force that is held to emanate from or give animation to living beings ⟨martial artists learn to use *ki* to fend off would-be attackers⟩ — see ENERGY 1

kibitz *also* **kibbitz** *vb* to engage in casual or rambling conversation ⟨a martial arts student who seemed more interested in *kibitzing* than in karate⟩ — see CHAT 1

kibitzer *also* **kibbitzer** *n* a person who meddles in the affairs of others ⟨a nosy *kibitzer* who always knows who is dating whom⟩ — see BUSYBODY

kick *n* **1** a pleasurably intense stimulation of the feelings ⟨I get a *kick* out of downhill skiing⟩ — see THRILL
2 a source of great satisfaction ⟨it was a *kick* for the parents to see their once-shy son star in a Broadway play⟩ — see DELIGHT 1
3 a feeling or declaration of disapproval or dissent ⟨nowadays there seem to be few words in the dictionary

that do not raise a *kick* from one person or another⟩ — see OBJECTION

4 a forceful coming together of two things ⟨I felt a *kick* in my hands as the jackhammer came roaring to life⟩ — see IMPACT 1

kick *vb* **1** to express dissatisfaction, pain, or resentment usually tiresomely ⟨he's been *kicking* all week about not getting the promotion⟩ — see COMPLAIN

2 to present an opposing opinion or argument ⟨fiscal conservatives have already started to *kick* about the proposed program, claiming it will increase the state's deficit substantially⟩ — see OBJECT

kick around *vb* **1** to give serious and careful thought to ⟨the board spent the afternoon *kicking around* the feasibility of opening an overseas office⟩ — see PONDER

2 to spend time in aimless activity ⟨I really can't do much but *kick around* at work until I get the rest of the submissions⟩ — see FIDDLE (AROUND)

3 to spend time doing nothing ⟨spent the afternoon *kicking around*, while his wife bought out the mall⟩ — see IDLE

4 to move about from place to place aimlessly ⟨after spending a year in Europe *kicking around*, the backpacker was ready to return home⟩ — see WANDER 1

5 to inflict physical or emotional harm upon ⟨children who were raised by an alcoholic father who regularly *kicked* them *around*⟩ — see ABUSE 1

kick back *vb* **1** to refrain from labor or exertion ⟨I plan to spend the day *kicking back* and watching television⟩ — see REST 1

2 to spend time doing nothing ⟨a good resort for people who want to *kick back* and watch others exercise strenuously⟩ — see IDLE

kick in *vb* **1** to make a donation as part of a group effort ⟨if everyone in the department *kicks in*, we can give him an especially nice present for his retirement⟩ — see CONTRIBUTE 1

2 *slang* to stop living ⟨the ornery cuss finally *kicked in* at the ripe old age of 90⟩ — see DIE 1

kickoff *n* the point at which something begins ⟨a political cycle in which an election marks not only the end of one campaign but also the *kickoff* for the next one⟩ — see BEGINNING

kick off *vb* **1** to take the first step in (a process or course of action) ⟨I'll *kick off* the discussion on ethics with this question⟩ — see BEGIN 1

2 *slang* to stop living ⟨surprisingly, the recluse was worth a cool million when he *kicked off*⟩ — see DIE 1

kick out *vb* to drive or force out ⟨*kicked out* of the game for using bad language⟩ — see EJECT 1

kickshaw *n* **1** a small object displayed for its attractiveness or interest ⟨a display case in the antiques shop filled with costume jewelry and various *kickshaws* from the 1920s⟩ — see KNICKKNACK

2 something that is pleasing to eat because it is rare or a luxury ⟨the company's holiday party always features an array of artfully confected *kickshaws*⟩ — see DELICACY 1

kickup *n* an often noisy or angry expression of differing opinions ⟨after their last *kickup*, they didn't speak to each other for a week⟩ — see ARGUMENT 1

kicky *adj* causing great emotional or mental stimulation ⟨needing one last *kicky* experience in my life, I decided to try bungee jumping⟩ — see EXCITING 1

kid *n* a young person who is between infancy and adulthood ⟨the fire was accidentally started by a couple of *kids* fooling around⟩ — see CHILD 1

kid *vb* **1** to make fun of in a good-natured way ⟨everybody's *kidding* me about my new haircut⟩ — see TEASE 1

2 to make jokes ⟨he always *kids* around about his "wild and crazy" life as an accountant⟩ — see JOKE 1

kiddie *also* **kiddy** *n* a young person who is between infancy and adulthood ⟨there are plenty of attractions at the state fair that will amuse the *kiddies*⟩ — see CHILD 1

kidding *adj* marked by or expressive of mild or good-natured teasing ⟨made *kidding* remarks about her lack of skills in the kitchen⟩ — see QUIZZICAL

kiddish *adj* having or showing the annoying qualities (as silliness) associated with children ⟨such *kiddish* behavior is not appropriate in church⟩ — see CHILDISH

kiddo *n* a young person who is between infancy and adulthood ⟨let's go out to a restaurant where there won't be any screaming *kiddos* running around⟩ — see CHILD 1

kidnap *vb* to carry away (as a person) forcibly or unlawfully ⟨the child of the wealthy industrialist was *kidnapped* and held for ransom⟩

synonyms abduct

related words capture, crimp, impress, seize, shanghai, waylay; abscond (with), snatch, spirit; hijack (*also* highjack); catch, cop [*slang*], steal, take

phrases make away with, make off with, run off with

near antonyms deliver, ransom, redeem, rescue; restore, return

kidnapping *also* **kidnaping** *n* the unlawful or forcible carrying away of a person or animal ⟨an alert system for the prompt reporting of juvenile *kidnappings*⟩ — see ABDUCTION

kidney *n* a number of persons or things that are grouped together because they have something in common ⟨her new boyfriend is of a different *kidney* than what she usually dates⟩ — see SORT 1

kid stuff *n* something easily done or dealt with ⟨sorting the books was *kid stuff*, since all I had to do was go by their size⟩ — see CINCH 1

kilderkin *n* an enclosed wooden vessel for holding beverages ⟨the *kilderkins* that line one wall of the brewpub are just for decoration—there's no beer in them⟩ — see CASK

kill *vb* **1** to deprive of life ⟨during the war more soldiers were *killed* by disease than anything else⟩

synonyms carry off, claim, croak [*slang*], destroy, dispatch, do in, fell, slay, take

related words bump off, butcher, cut down, finish, get, ice [*slang*], knock off, murder, neutralize, off [*slang*], put away, rub out, scrag, snuff, take out, waste, whack [*slang*]; annihilate, blot out, decimate, kill off, massacre, mow, slaughter, smite; assassinate, execute, martyr, terminate; euthanize (*also* euthanatize), put down; suicide

phrases do away with, do for [*chiefly British*], make away with

near antonyms raise, restore, resurrect, resuscitate, revive; nurture

antonyms animate

2 to reject by or as if by a vote ⟨the Senate *killed* the bill by a single vote⟩ — see NEGATIVE 1

3 to show (something written) to be no longer valid by drawing a cross over or a line through it ⟨I think that paragraph is irrelevant, so *kill* it⟩ — see X (OUT)

4 to use up all the physical energy of ⟨the long hike up the mountain just about *killed* us⟩ — see EXHAUST 1

5 to attract or delight as if by magic ⟨with his dark good looks he would positively *kill* the ladies⟩ — see CHARM 1

6 to cause to stop functioning ⟨*kill* the engine before it overheats⟩ — see DEACTIVATE

killer *adj* **1** likely to cause or capable of causing death ⟨*killer* viruses that claimed millions of lives⟩ — see DEADLY 1

2 requiring considerable physical or mental effort ⟨a *killer* exercise program guaranteed to whip you into shape⟩ — see HARD 2

killer *n* **1** a dull, unpleasant, or difficult piece of work

⟨weeding out that overgrown garden is going to be a *killer*⟩ — see CHORE 2
2 a person who kills another person ⟨gunned down by hired *killers*⟩ — see ASSASSIN

killing *adj* **1** causing or intended to cause laughter ⟨he's usually quiet, but occasionally unleashes some *killing* remark that cracks everyone up⟩ — see FUNNY 1
2 requiring much time, effort, or careful attention ⟨a *killing* schedule that requires the touring company to play in a different city every night⟩ — see DEMANDING 1

killjoy *n* a person who spoils the pleasure of others ⟨his perpetually negative attitude made him a real *killjoy* when others were trying to have fun⟩
synonyms drag, grinch, party pooper, spoilsport, wet blanket
related words fuddy-duddy, goody-goody, Goody Two-shoes, old maid, stick-in-the-mud; defeatist, Jeremiah, knocker, pessimist; complainer, crab, cynic, grouch, grump, sorehead, sourpuss, whiner; bore, downer, drip
near antonyms cutup, jester, live wire; carouser, celebrant, celebrator, merrymaker, rejoicer, reveler (*or* reveller), roisterer; libertine, playboy, playgirl, rake

kilter *n* a state of being or fitness ⟨since I dropped my food processor, it's been all out of *kilter*⟩ — see CONDITION 1

kin *n* **1** a group of persons who come from the same ancestor ⟨invited all of his kith and *kin* to his graduation party⟩ — see FAMILY 1
2 a person connected with another by blood or marriage ⟨since she did not appear to be *kin* to either side, we've no idea what she was doing at the wedding⟩ — see RELATIVE

kind *adj* **1** given to or made with heedful anticipation of the needs and happiness of others ⟨providing the grieving widow with a homemade meal was a *kind* deed⟩ — see THOUGHTFUL 1
2 having or marked by sympathy and consideration for others ⟨a *kind* person who regularly volunteers at the homeless shelter⟩ — see HUMANE 1

kind *n* **1** a number of persons or things that are grouped together because they have something in common ⟨I like that *kind* of candy⟩ — see SORT 1
2 one of the units into which a whole is divided on the basis of a common characteristic ⟨we looked at just about every *kind* of flooring before deciding which to use in the kitchen⟩ — see CLASS 2

kindhearted *adj* having or marked by sympathy and consideration for others ⟨a *kindhearted* young man who shoveled his elderly neighbor's driveway after the blizzard⟩ — see HUMANE 1

kindheartedness *n* **1** sympathetic concern for the well-being of others ⟨through the *kindheartedness* of a local veterinarian, the stray cat's broken leg was mended without charge⟩ — see BENIGNANCY
2 the capacity for feeling for another's unhappiness or misfortune ⟨her natural *kindheartedness* is one reason why she's thinking about becoming a medical missionary⟩ — see HEART 1

kindle *vb* to set (something) on fire ⟨worried that lightning will *kindle* the forest in the drought-striken nature preserve⟩ — see BURN 2

kindled *adj* being on fire ⟨*kindled* straw was responsible for the blaze that destroyed the barn⟩ — see ABLAZE 1

kindler *n* a person who stirs up public feelings especially of discontent ⟨a *kindler* of riots and public protests, the anarchist Emma Goldman was eventually deported to Russia⟩ — see AGITATOR

kindliness *n* **1** kindly concern, interest, or support ⟨was touched by the *kindliness* of his neighbors, who voluntarily took care of his dog while he was in the hospital⟩ — see GOODWILL 1
2 the capacity for feeling for another's unhappiness or misfortune ⟨as a result of her *kindliness*, several poor families have the makings for a Thanksgiving feast⟩ — see HEART 1
3 sympathetic concern for the well-being of others ⟨an elderly couple of modest means but infinite *kindliness*⟩ — see BENIGNANCY

kindly *adj* **1** having or marked by sympathy and consideration for others ⟨brought homemade chicken soup out of *kindly* concern for my health⟩ — see HUMANE 1
2 promoting or contributing to personal or social well-being ⟨a vegetarian diet can be very *kindly* to a person hoping to lose a few pounds⟩ — see BENEFICIAL

kindly *adv* **1** with good reason or courtesy ⟨would you *kindly* hand me the scissors?⟩ — see WELL 4
2 *chiefly Southern* to some degree or extent ⟨their visit was *kindly* a surprise⟩ — see FAIRLY 1

kindness *n* **1** an act of kind assistance ⟨what a *kindness* to allow us to use your car for the funeral⟩ — see FAVOR 1
2 the capacity for feeling for another's unhappiness or misfortune ⟨out of the *kindness* of your heart, would you at least consider adopting this stray cat?⟩ — see HEART 1
3 sympathetic concern for the well-being of others ⟨with touching *kindness*, the couple offered the stranded tourists a place to stay for the night⟩ — see BENIGNANCY

kind of *adv* to some degree or extent ⟨those sheets are *kind of* new, so use something else to cover the floor while painting⟩ — see FAIRLY 1

kindred *adj* **1** having a close connection like that between family members ⟨archaeology and the *kindred* science of anthropology⟩ — see RELATED
2 having or marked by agreement in feeling or action ⟨finally found people who were *kindred* spirits when she joined the hiking club⟩ — see HARMONIOUS 3

kindred *n* a group of persons who come from the same ancestor ⟨the kingdom's royal *kindred* actually numbers in the thousands⟩ — see FAMILY 1

kinetic *adj* **1** having much high-spirited energy and movement ⟨the novel's plot is *kinetic* and fast-paced, and its effect on the reader is much like that of a surfeit of caffeine⟩ — see LIVELY 1
2 marked by much life, movement, or activity ⟨the loft district is the locus of the city's *kinetic* arts scene⟩ — see ALIVE 2

kinfolk *or* **kinfolks** *n pl* a group of persons who come from the same ancestor ⟨let's invite all our *kinfolk* for the holidays⟩ — see FAMILY 1

king *n* **1** a person of rank, power, or influence in a particular field ⟨the undisputed *king* of automobile sales for the entire metropolitan area⟩ — see MAGNATE
2 *cap* the being worshipped as the creator and ruler of the universe ⟨all bowed their heads in worship to the *King*⟩ — see DEITY 2

kingdom *n* a region of activity, knowledge, or influence ⟨a studio head who was once the undisputed ruler of the *kingdom* of Hollywood⟩ — see FIELD 2

kingdom come *n* a dwelling place of perfect happiness for the soul after death ⟨be careful with that thing, or you'll send us all to *kingdom come*⟩ — see HEAVEN 1

kingfish *n* one of high position or importance within a group ⟨as a *kingfish* in the state's political circles, he was accustomed to being courted by presidential hopefuls⟩ — see BIG SHOT

kingliness *n* a dignified bearing or appearance befitting someone of royal status ⟨from an early age he had that special something, an aura of *kingliness* that foretold his future rise to the country's presidency⟩ — see MAJESTY 1

kingly *adj* fit for or worthy of a royal ruler ⟨a *kingly* gift of 50 million dollars to his old alma mater⟩ — see MONARCHICAL

kingpin *n* **1** one of high position or importance within a group ⟨a police sting that nabbed several *kingpins* of the city's drug trade⟩ — see BIG SHOT
2 the person (as an employer or supervisor) who tells people and especially workers what to do ⟨finally nailed the mob *kingpin* who had been controlling all the gambling rackets in the city⟩ — see BOSS

king–size *or* **king–sized** *adj* **1** unusually large ⟨built a *king-size* mansion with the money he had made in the stock market⟩ — see HUGE
2 of great extent from end to end ⟨the *king-size* snake known as the anaconda⟩ — see LONG 1

king's ransom *n* a very large amount of money ⟨that enormous diamond ring must have cost a *king's ransom*⟩ — see FORTUNE 2

kink *n* **1** a painful sudden tightening of a muscle ⟨got a *kink* in my neck from lying in that awkward position for too long⟩ — see [1]CRAMP
2 an odd or peculiar habit ⟨the boss's fondness for nicknames is one of those *kinks* that staffers just have to put up with⟩ — see IDIOSYNCRASY
3 a sudden impulsive and apparently unmotivated idea or action ⟨whenever he got a *kink* in his head, he'd drop whatever he was doing to pursue this latest obsession⟩ — see WHIM

kinky *adj* different from the ordinary in a way that causes curiosity or suspicion ⟨while passing through the airport, don't wear any *kinky* clothing that is likely to pique the interest of security⟩ — see ODD 2

kinsfolk *n pl* a group of persons who come from the same ancestor ⟨my *kinsfolk* all live in the East⟩ — see FAMILY 1

kinship *n* the fact or state of having something in common ⟨she and I have a special *kinship* since we both grew up in England⟩ — see CONNECTION 1

kinsman *n* a person connected with another by blood or marriage ⟨to protect the family honor, he sought to revenge the murder of his *kinsman*⟩ — see RELATIVE

kiosk *n* a freestanding airy structure in a scenic setting (as a park) typically offering commanding views ⟨the *kiosk* in the waterfront park is a favorite meeting place for city residents⟩ — see BELVEDERE

kip *n* **1** a place set aside for sleeping ⟨he was in *kip* when I knocked on the door⟩ — see BED 1
2 *chiefly British* a short sleep ⟨after an afternoon *kip*, we were ready to sample all the nightlife that London had to offer⟩ — see [1]NAP

kip *vb, British* to sleep lightly or briefly ⟨after a rigorous walk over the Devon moors, I needed to *kip* down a bit on the daybed⟩ — see NAP 1

kirk *n, chiefly Scottish* a building for public worship and especially Christian worship ⟨left Edinburgh early in the morning for St. John's *Kirk* in Perth⟩ — see CHURCH 1

kismet *n* a state or end that seemingly has been decided beforehand ⟨he always said that it was *kismet* that they met at a showing of their favorite movie⟩ — see FATE 1

kiss *vb* **1** to touch one another with the lips as a sign of love ⟨it's traditional for couples to *kiss* under the mistletoe at Christmastime⟩
synonyms smooch
related words buss, French-kiss, lip, osculate, smack; canoodle, make out, neck, pet, spoon; caress, embrace, fondle, hug, love; bill, cuddle, nestle, snuggle
2 to pass lightly across or touch gently especially in passing ⟨a gentle breeze *kissing* the water's surface⟩ — see [2]BRUSH

kisser *n, slang* **1** the front part of the head ⟨angrily threw the unwanted valentine back in the would-be suitor's *kisser*⟩ — see FACE 1
2 the opening through which food passes into the body of an animal ⟨how'd you like a punch right in the *kisser*?⟩ — see MOUTH 1

kiss off *vb* **1** to end a usually intimate relationship with ⟨*kisses off* every girlfriend with the line, "It's not you . . . it's me"⟩ — see DITCH 1
2 to express scornfully one's low opinion of ⟨a chef who airily *kisses off* the cuisine of his rivals as homey comfort food⟩ — see DECRY 1

kit *n, chiefly British* items needed for the performance of a task or activity ⟨soldiers were dispatched to get their *kit*⟩ — see EQUIPMENT

kit (up *or* **out)** *vb, chiefly British* to provide (someone) with what is needed for a task or activity ⟨go see the quartermaster to be *kitted out* in your new uniforms⟩ — see FURNISH 1

kit bag *n* a soft-sided case designed for carrying belongings especially on the back ⟨a soldier's *kit bag*⟩ — see PACK 1

kitchen–sink *adj* consisting of many things of different sorts ⟨many of the bartender's recipes are for *kitchen-sink* cocktails that sound like they would be a waste of good liquor⟩ — see MISCELLANEOUS

kite *n* a person who habitually preys upon others ⟨characterized the neighborhood store owners as *kites* who ruthlessly gouged their inner-city customers⟩ — see PREDATOR

kittenish *adj* affecting shyness or modesty in order to attract masculine interest ⟨the days when young ladies at a dance were supposed to be *kittenish* around young men⟩ — see COY 1

kittenishness *n* the attitude or behavior of one who insincerely courts the amorous attentions of others ⟨her cuddly *kittenishness* can get old really fast⟩ — see COQUETRY

[1]**kitty** *n* a small domestic animal known for catching mice ⟨delighted to adopt a stray *kitty* from the pound⟩ — see CAT 1

[2]**kitty** *n* a sum of money set aside for a particular purpose ⟨why don't you get us all sodas and just take the money from the party *kitty*?⟩ — see FUND 1

kitty–corner *also* **catty–corner** *or* **catercorner** *or* **kitty–cornered** *or* **catty–cornered** *or* **catercornered** *adv* in a line or direction running from corner to corner ⟨walked *kitty-corner* across the quadrangle to the registration booth⟩ — see CROSSWISE

klatch *also* **klatsch** *n* a group of people sharing a common interest and relating together socially ⟨his *klatch* of friends hasn't changed all that much since college⟩ — see GANG 2

kloof *n, South African* a narrow opening between hillsides or mountains that can be used for passage ⟨halfway up its side, the couple sat in the cool shadows of the cliff overlooking the length of the *kloof*⟩ — see CANYON

klutz *n* a clumsy, awkward person ⟨how can she be such a *klutz* after studying ballet for so many years?⟩
synonyms butterfingers, dub, looby, lubber, lummox, spaz [*slang*]
related words clodhopper, gawk, gawky, lout, lump, oaf, tawpie [*chiefly Scottish*], tyke (*also* tike) [*chiefly British*]; bungler, duffer, fumbler, stumblebum, stumbler

klutzy *adj* having or showing an inability to move in a graceful manner ⟨a *klutzy* kid who was always bumping into things⟩ — see CLUMSY 2

knack *n* **1** a clever often underhanded means to achieve an end ⟨she's tried every *knack* in Cupid's book to get her guy to marry her⟩ — see TRICK 1

2 a special and usually inborn ability ⟨a jazz musician with an incredible *knack* for improvisation⟩ — see TALENT

knackered *adj, British* depleted in strength, energy, or freshness ⟨I'm absolutely *knackered*, so no pub-crawling for me tonight⟩ — see WEARY 1

knapsack *n* a soft-sided case designed for carrying belongings especially on the back ⟨grabbed my *knapsack* from the hook and ran to catch my ride⟩ — see PACK 1

knave *n* a mean, evil, or unprincipled person ⟨he plays the role of the duplicitous *knave* who tries to foil the play's hero⟩ — see VILLAIN

knavery *n* **1** a playful or mischievous act intended as a joke ⟨the sort of frat-boy *knaveries* that become the stuff of campus legend⟩ — see PRANK

2 playful, reckless behavior that is not intended to cause serious harm ⟨suspects some *knavery* going on in the political campaign⟩ — see MISCHIEF 1

knavish *adj* tending to or exhibiting reckless playfulness ⟨a *knavish* bunch of urchins racing pell-mell through the marketplace⟩ — see MISCHIEVOUS 1

knee–jerk *adj* done instantly and without conscious thought or decision ⟨a colleague known for her *knee-jerk* rejection of any proposal that she didn't originate⟩ — see AUTOMATIC 1

knee–slapper *n* someone or something that is very funny ⟨the movie is a real *knee-slapper* if you are a fan of lowbrow humor⟩ — see SCREAM

knell *vb* to make the clear sound heard when metal vibrates ⟨the church bells *knelled* to mark the death of the nation's beloved leader⟩ — see [2]RING

knickknack *also* **nicknack** *n* a small object displayed for its attractiveness or interest ⟨a variety of pretty porcelain *knickknacks* adorned the mantel⟩

synonyms bauble, bibelot, curio, curiosity, doodad, gaud, gewgaw (*also* geegaw), gimcrack, kickshaw, novelty, ornamental, tchotchke, trinket

related words bijouterie, bric-a-brac, gimcrackery, trinketry, trumpery, virtu (*or* vertu); bagatelle, trifle; figurine, objet d'art (*also* objet), ornament; keepsake, memento, souvenir; conversation piece; collectible (*or* collectable), collector's item

knife *n* an instrument with a metal length that has a sharp edge for cutting ⟨be careful in using the *knife* to split open the cardboard box⟩

synonyms blade, cutter, shank [*slang*], shiv [*slang*]

related words cleaver, hack; bayonet, bodkin, bolo, bowie knife, cutlass, dagger, dirk, jackknife, machete, pocketknife, poniard, sheath knife, stiletto, stylet, switchblade, switch knife, yataghan; rapier, saber (*or* sabre), steel, sword; scalpel

knob *n* a small uneven mass ⟨toss a *knob* of butter into the frying pan⟩ — see LUMP 1

knock *n* **1** a hard strike with a part of the body or an instrument ⟨gave the door a good *knock*⟩ — see [1]BLOW

2 bad luck or an example of this ⟨getting his college degree was a six year adventure not without its share of *knocks* along the way⟩ — see MISFORTUNE

3 a change in status for the worse usually temporarily ⟨the geneticist's reputation took a *knock* when several of his peers were unable to confirm his research findings⟩ — see REVERSE 1

knock *vb* **1** to come into usually forceful contact with something ⟨my knee *knocked* against the table leg when I tried to get up quickly⟩ — see HIT 2

2 to deliver a blow to (someone or something) usually in a strong vigorous manner ⟨threatened to *knock* him upside the head if he didn't do as he was told⟩ — see HIT 1

3 to express one's unfavorable opinion of the worth or quality of ⟨hey, don't *knock* it until you've tried it⟩ — see CRITICIZE

knock (about) *vb* to move about from place to place aimlessly ⟨we *knocked about* from town to town, looking for work⟩ — see WANDER 1

knockabout *adj* being rough or noisy in a high-spirited way ⟨a *knockabout* game of football in the mud⟩ — see BOISTEROUS

knockabout *n* a person who roams about without a fixed route or destination ⟨the book is one writer's journey of self-discovery as a restless *knockabout*⟩ — see NOMAD

knock back *vb* to swallow in liquid form ⟨desperately thirsty, she *knocked back* an entire glass of water without pausing⟩ — see DRINK 1

knock down *vb* **1** to receive as return for effort ⟨she's *knocking down* a good salary, but she has to work very hard⟩ — see EARN 1

2 to take apart ⟨right after the holidays the stores start to *knock down* the window displays⟩ — see DISASSEMBLE 1

3 to strike (someone) so forcefully as to cause a fall ⟨the overexcited dog *knocked* the toddler *down*⟩ — see FELL 1

4 to make smaller in amount, volume, or extent ⟨they'll have to *knock down* the price of those televisions if they expect to sell any⟩ — see DECREASE 1

knock–down, drag–out *or* **knock–down–and–drag–out** *adj* marked by bursts of destructive force or intense activity ⟨the football game was a *knock-down, drag-out* battle between bitter rivals⟩ — see VIOLENT 1

knocker *n* a person given to harsh judgments and to finding faults ⟨the secretary of defense needs supporters, not *knockers*, to get through this crisis⟩ — see CRITIC 1

knock off *vb* **1** to bring (as an action or operation) to an immediate end ⟨*knock* it *off*!⟩ — see STOP 1

2 to stop doing (something) permanently ⟨decided it was time to *knock off* telling fantastic fibs about her family background⟩ — see QUIT 2

3 to take away (an amount or number) from a total ⟨a proposal to *knock* 10 cents *off* the gasoline tax⟩ — see SUBTRACT

4 to remove valuables from (a place) unlawfully ⟨Bonnie and Clyde coped with the Great Depression by *knocking off* banks⟩ — see ROB

5 to put to death deliberately ⟨various assassins have tried to *knock off* the dictator over the years⟩ — see MURDER 1

knockout *adj* very pleasing to look at ⟨a *knockout* sports car that's the talk of the neighborhood⟩ — see BEAUTIFUL 1

knockout *n* **1** a lovely woman ⟨the cosmetics company wants a model who's a real *knockout*⟩ — see BEAUTY 2

2 a temporary state of unconsciousness ⟨a splash of cold water brought the boxer out of his *knockout*⟩ — see FAINT

3 something very good of its kind ⟨the band's new album is a *knockout*⟩ — see JIM-DANDY

4 a physically attractive person ⟨only a few of the show's cast members are real *knockouts*⟩ — see DOLL 2

knock out *vb* to use up all the physical energy of ⟨the entire staff *knocked* itself *out* getting the project finished on time⟩ — see EXHAUST 1

knock over *vb* **1** to remove valuables from (a place) unlawfully ⟨he *knocked over* six convenience stores before getting caught⟩ — see ROB

2 to strike (someone) so forcefully as to cause a fall ⟨*knocked* me *over* trying to get out the door⟩ — see FELL 1

knock up *vb, British* to cause to stop sleeping ⟨I asked the clerk at the hotel to *knock* me *up* at 7:00 a.m.⟩ — see WAKE 1

knot *n* **1** a number of things considered as a unit ⟨from the summit we could see *knots* of houses up and down the river valley⟩ — see GROUP 1

2 a small rounded mass of swollen tissue ⟨felt a small *knot* on the back of his head⟩ — see BUMP 1

3 a uniting or binding force or influence ⟨their business partnership is strengthened by the *knot* of personal friendship⟩ — see BOND 2

4 a usually small number of persons considered as a unit ⟨*knots* of people were quietly chatting around the meeting hall⟩ — see GROUP 2

5 something that requires thought and skill for resolution ⟨mercy killing is generally seen as a matter fraught with legal and medical *knots*⟩ — see PROBLEM 1

knot *vb* to twist together into a usually confused mass ⟨the extension cords were hopelessly *knotted* together⟩ — see ENTANGLE 1

knottiness *n* the state or quality of having many interrelated parts or aspects ⟨the staggering *knottiness* of the legal procedure that we had to go through⟩ — see COMPLEXITY 1

knotty *adj* **1** having many parts or aspects that are usually interrelated ⟨the *knotty* problems that arise when every nation is part of the global marketplace⟩ — see COMPLEX 1

2 requiring exceptional skill or caution in performance or handling ⟨the candidates cautiously gave their views on an array of *knotty* issues⟩ — see TRICKY 1

know *vb* **1** to have a practical understanding of ⟨a career diplomat who *knows* several languages⟩

synonyms comprehend, grasp, understand

related words appreciate, apprehend, cognize, fathom, follow, ken [*chiefly Scottish*], perceive, savvy; have, possess; catch on (to), pick up

near antonyms misapprehend, misconceive, misinterpret, misknow, misperceive, misunderstand

2 to come to a knowledge of (something) by living through it ⟨a gripping news story about orphans who have come to *know* full well the horrors of war⟩ — see EXPERIENCE

3 to have a clear idea of ⟨I think I *know* what you're trying to say⟩ — see COMPREHEND 1

know–how *n* knowledge gained by actually doing or living through something ⟨you'll gain some practical *know-how* in this auto mechanics class⟩ — see EXPERIENCE 1

knowing *adj* **1** having inside information ⟨exchanged a *knowing* look with her business partner during the sales presentation⟩ — see WISE 2

2 having or showing a practical cleverness or judgment ⟨*knowing* movie producers do not invest their own money in their risky ventures⟩ — see SHREWD 1

3 made, given, or done with full awareness of what one is doing ⟨after giving *knowing* offense to people of Italian ancestry, he gave the lame excuse that it had all been a joke⟩ — see INTENTIONAL

4 decided on as a result of careful thought ⟨with *knowing* malice, she mentioned the fact that the baby's birth had been "premature"⟩ — see DELIBERATE 1

knowingly *adv* with full awareness of what one is doing ⟨cannot convict unless the defendant *knowingly* committed perjury⟩ — see INTENTIONALLY

knowingness *n* exceptional discernment and judgment especially in practical matters ⟨all the *knowingness* that comes from 20 years in the police department was evident in his appraisal of the situation⟩ — see ACUMEN

knowledge *n* **1** a body of facts learned by study or experience ⟨the forest ranger shared some of his vast *knowledge* of the woods with us⟩

synonyms lore, science, wisdom

related words dope, information, intelligence, know, lowdown, news, skinny [*slang*]; data, evidence, facts; acquaintance, awareness, familiarity, literacy; erudition, learning, scholarship; expertise, know-how

near antonyms ignorance, inexperience, innocence, nescience, unfamiliarity

2 the understanding and information gained from being educated ⟨tests evaluate how much *knowledge* you have gained in a particular subject⟩ — see EDUCATION 2

3 a state of being aware ⟨my *knowledge* that I was watching a true story made the film more compelling⟩ — see ATTENTION 2

knowledgeable *adj* **1** having information especially as a result of study or experience ⟨I'm fairly *knowledgeable* about wine⟩ — see FAMILIAR 2

2 having or displaying advanced knowledge or education ⟨*knowledgeable* historians regard that story as pure fiction⟩ ⟨a *knowledgeable* report on the latest advances in cancer research⟩ — see EDUCATED 1

know–nothing *n* a stupid person ⟨often disparaged her coworkers as a bunch of *know-nothings*⟩ — see IDIOT

knucklehead *n* a stupid person ⟨I'd like to get my hands on the *knucklehead* who designed that paper-towel dispenser⟩ — see IDIOT

knuckleheaded *adj* not having or showing an ability to absorb ideas readily ⟨the editorial lampooned the *knuckleheaded* legislation, which was yet another attempt by the government to protect people from themselves⟩ — see STUPID 1

knuckle under *vb* **1** to cease resistance (as to another's arguments, demands, or control) ⟨encouraged her to stand firm and not *knuckle under* to political pressure⟩ — see YIELD 3

2 to yield to the control or power of enemy forces ⟨the remote outpost was overrun and forced to *knuckle under*⟩ — see FALL 2

kobold *n* an imaginary being usually having a small human form and magical powers ⟨the metal cobalt gets its name from the medieval Germanic belief that its appearance in silver ore was the handiwork of mischievous, thieving *kobolds*⟩ — see FAIRY

kook *n* a person of odd or whimsical habits ⟨if you insist on painting your house bright orange, everyone will assume you are a *kook*⟩ — see ECCENTRIC

kooky *also* **kookie** *adj* **1** different from the ordinary in a way that causes curiosity or suspicion ⟨I'm not sure that someone with such *kooky* ideas on biology should be teaching the subject to high schoolers⟩ — see ODD 2

2 having or showing a very abnormal or sick state of mind ⟨if you think that drugs aren't bad for you, you haven't met that guy's *kooky* friends⟩ — see INSANE 1

3 showing or marked by a lack of good sense or judgment ⟨a *kooky* bicyclist who stubbornly refuses to wear a helmet⟩ ⟨that was a *kooky* thing to do⟩ — see FOOLISH 1

kowtow *vb* to use flattery or the doing of favors in order to win approval especially from a superior ⟨you can try *kowtowing* to the boss, but he'll see right through you⟩ — see FAWN

kudo *n* **1** something given in recognition of achievement ⟨an honorary degree from her alma mater that is simply the latest *kudo* for an outstanding career in journalism⟩ — see AWARD 1

2 an admiring personal remark ⟨a *kudo* is in order for the way the young people acquitted themselves at their first formal dance⟩ — see COMPLIMENT 1

kudos *n* public acknowledgment or admiration for an achievement ⟨the attorney did pro bono work because it was the right thing to do, and not for any future *kudos* that it might bring⟩ — see GLORY 1

kvell *vb* to feel or express joy or triumph ⟨proud grandparents who *kvell* over every thing that their precious little darlings do⟩ — see EXULT

kvetch *n* **1** a person who makes frequent complaints

usually about little things ⟨according to the *kvetch* on the bus tour, there was little about Europe that was satisfactory⟩ — see CRYBABY
2 an expression of dissatisfaction, pain, or resentment ⟨vainly hoped that his mother would spare him another *kvetch* about still being single⟩ — see COMPLAINT 1
kvetch *vb* to express dissatisfaction, pain, or resentment usually tiresomely ⟨a chronically resentful person who seems to look for things to *kvetch* about⟩ — see COMPLAIN
kvetcher *n* a person who makes frequent complaints usually about little things ⟨if that *kvetcher* is to be believed, the nursing home has yet to serve a decent meal⟩ — see CRYBABY

L

label *n* a slip (as of paper or cloth) that is attached to something to identify or describe it ⟨on its frame the painting had a *label* with its title and the name of the artist⟩
synonyms marker, tag, ticket
related words caption, legend; brand, emblem, hallmark, logo, mark, symbol, trademark; badge, decal, plaque, seal, stamp, sticker
label *vb* **1** to attach an identifying slip to ⟨he *labeled* all of the poisonous materials with the familiar skull and crossbones⟩
synonyms mark, tag, ticket
related words caption, earmark, hallmark, stamp; call, designate, identify, name, tab; entitle, style, term, title; brand, stigmatize
2 to give a name to ⟨in the past, teachers had a tendency to *label* the students "slow learners" when in fact they had treatable learning disabilities⟩ — see NAME 1
labor *n* **1** a dull, unpleasant, or difficult piece of work ⟨one of the *labors* of Hercules in classical mythology was to clean out the stables of King Augeas⟩ — see CHORE 2
2 the active use of energy in producing a result ⟨a superhuman amount of *labor* must have gone into designing and building the pyramids of Egypt⟩ — see EFFORT
3 very hard or unpleasant work ⟨a political dissident forced to do six months of hard *labor* in the salt mines as punishment⟩ — see [1]TOIL
4 the act or process of giving birth to children ⟨the mother's *labor* lasted for six hours⟩ — see CHILDBIRTH
5 something produced by physical or intellectual effort ⟨a small, personal film that was clearly a *labor* of love for the director and actors⟩ — see PRODUCT 1
labor *vb* to devote serious and sustained effort ⟨he *labored* most of the day over the difficult legal brief⟩
synonyms bang away, beaver (away), dig (away), drudge, endeavor, fag, grub, hump, hustle, moil, peg (away), plod, plow, plug, slave, slog, strain, strive, struggle, sweat, toil, travail, tug, work
related words apply (oneself), buckle (down), dig in, hammer (away), knuckle down, pitch in; attack, drive; essay, try; exercise, exert, overexert, overwork; eke out, grind (out), put out, scrabble, scratch; trudge, wade
phrases sweat blood
near antonyms break, ease (up), let up, slacken; bum, chill, dally, dillydally, footle, goldbrick, goof (off), hack (around), hang (around *or* out), idle, laze, loaf, lounge, shirk, slack (off), veg out; bask, loll, relax, repose, rest, unwind; dabble, doodle, fool around, fribble, goof (around), hang, hang about [*British*], mess around, monkey (around), play, potter (around), putter (around), trifle
laborer *n* a person who does very hard or dull work ⟨having no real skills, the men could only find work as *laborers* unloading cargo ships⟩ — see SLAVE 2
labor force *n* a body of persons at work or available for work ⟨the corporation has a *labor force* of nearly 100,000 people⟩ — see FORCE 1
laborious *adj* **1** involved in often constant activity ⟨the volunteers have been commendably *laborious* in their cleanup of the beach⟩ — see BUSY 1
2 requiring considerable physical or mental effort ⟨the *laborious* task of cleaning up the oil spill⟩ — see HARD 2
3 requiring much time, effort, or careful attention ⟨that report is the product of months of *laborious* research⟩ — see DEMANDING 1
laboriously *adv* **1** in a manner involving great or constant activity ⟨working *laboriously* late into the night in order to meet the deadline⟩ — see BUSILY
2 with great effort or determination ⟨the farmer *laboriously* pruned all season long to produce the finest crop of grapes possible⟩ — see HARD 1
laborsaving *adj* designed to replace or decrease human labor and especially physical labor ⟨a new *laborsaving* device let us clean the house in half the time⟩
synonyms automated, automatic, robotic, self-acting, self-operating, self-regulating
related words mechanical, motorized, nonmanual; computerized; aiding, helping; easing, relieving; time-saving; semiautomatic
antonyms nonautomated, nonautomatic
labyrinth *n* a confusing and complicated arrangement of passages ⟨we eventually realized that we were lost in the *labyrinth* of hallways in the museum⟩ — see MAZE 1
labyrinthian *adj* having many parts or aspects that are usually interrelated ⟨a Web site with an exceptionally *labyrinthian* procedure for ordering merchandise⟩ — see COMPLEX 1
labyrinthine *adj* having many parts or aspects that are usually interrelated ⟨the *labyrinthine* politics of Central Europe left us totally befuddled⟩ — see COMPLEX 1
lace *n* **1** a length of braided, flexible material that is used for tying or connecting things ⟨I had to replace the *lace* of my shoe because it kept breaking whenever I pulled the knot too tight⟩ — see CORD 1
2 a length of something formed of three or more strands woven together ⟨there will be gold *lace* decorating both sleeves of the new uniform⟩ — see BRAID
lace *vb* **1** to cause to twine about one another ⟨the gardener *laced* the shoots of ivy around the trellis to direct their growth⟩ — see INTERTWINE 1

2 to scatter or set here and there among other things ⟨the decorator *laced* small mirrors among the knickknacks for added effect⟩ — see THREAD 1
3 to strike repeatedly ⟨energetically *laced* the seaman's back with the cat-o'-nine-tails⟩ — see BEAT 1
4 to make more pleasant to the taste by adding something intensely flavored ⟨a savory dish *laced* with saffron and ginger⟩ — see SEASON 1
5 to alter (something) for the worse with the addition of foreign or lower-grade substances ⟨the unsuspecting woman's drink had been *laced* with a roofie⟩ — see ADULTERATE

laceration *n* a long deep cut ⟨the fall from the motocross bike left him with several *lacerations* from the sharp rocks⟩ — see GASH

lachrymose *adj* given to expressing strong emotion (as sorrow) by readily shedding tears ⟨the more *lachrymose* mourners at the funeral required a steady supply of tissues⟩ — see TEARFUL 1

lacing *n* **1** a length of braided, flexible material that is used for tying or connecting things ⟨stopped briefly to tighten the *lacing* on his shoe⟩ — see CORD 1
2 a length of something formed of three or more strands woven together ⟨the *lacing* on the uniform gives it a smart look⟩ — see BRAID

lack *n* **1** the fact or state of being absent ⟨the *lack* of news about the fate of the soldiers was frustrating⟩
synonyms absence, dearth, want
related words deficiency, deficit, failure, famine, inadequacy, inadequateness, insufficiency, meagerness, paucity, poverty, scantiness, scantness, scarceness, scarcity, shortage, skimpiness, undersupply; deprivation, loss, necessity, need, needfulness, omission; privation; blankness, emptiness, vacuity, vacuum, void
near antonyms abundance, amplitude, bounty, plenitude, plenteousness, plentifulness, plentitude, plenty, wealth; adequacy, sufficiency; excess, overabundance, oversupply, superabundance, surfeit, surplus; deluge, flood; bushel, deal, gobs, heap, loads, lot, mass, mountain, much, oodles, peck, pile, pot, quantity, raft, reams, scads, stack, volume, wad; fund, pool, stock, supply; cache, hoard, stash, stockpile
antonyms presence
2 a falling short of an essential or desirable amount or number ⟨the *lack* of eligible candidates for the jury kept the trial from getting started⟩ — see DEFICIENCY
3 a state of being without something necessary, desirable, or useful ⟨the *lack* of fresh water at the campsite definitely would be a problem⟩ — see NEED 1

lackadaisical *adj* lacking bodily energy or motivation ⟨feeling particularly *lackadaisical* in the summer heat, they lazily tossed a ball back and forth⟩ — see LISTLESS

lackey *n* a person hired to perform household or personal services ⟨the housekeeper sent the *lackey* to fetch some more coffee⟩ — see SERVANT

lacking *adj* **1** not coming up to an expected measure or meeting a particular need ⟨we felt the afternoon television offerings were somewhat *lacking* in entertainment value⟩ — see SHORT 3
2 not present or in evidence ⟨for the moment anyway, wood for the fireplace is *lacking*⟩ — see ABSENT 2

laconic *adj* **1** marked by the use of few words to convey much information or meaning ⟨the sportscaster's color commentary tends to be *laconic* but very much to the point⟩ — see CONCISE
2 tending not to speak frequently (as by habit or inclination) ⟨*laconic* by nature, he found the monastery's vow of silence was very much to his liking⟩ — see SILENT 2

laconically *adv* in a few words ⟨the witness answered the prosecutor's questions rather *laconically* and had to be coaxed into giving more details⟩ — see SHORTLY 1

lacuna *n* **1** a falling short of an essential or desirable amount or number ⟨attributes many of the nation's problems to a *lacuna* of leadership at the top⟩ — see DEFICIENCY
2 an incomplete or deficient area ⟨a *lacuna* in its collection of Impressionists that the museum is trying to fill⟩ — see GAP 3

lad *n* **1** a male person who has not yet reached adulthood ⟨fond of telling tall tales of the days when he was just a *lad*⟩ — see BOY 1
2 an adult male human being ⟨pass me another beer—will you, *lad*?⟩ — see MAN 1

ladder *n* a scheme of rank or order ⟨their team placed third on the tournament *ladder*⟩ — see [3]SCALE 1

laddie *n* a male person who has not yet reached adulthood ⟨not all the *laddies* in Scotland wear kilts, you know!⟩ — see BOY 1

lade *vb* **1** to lift out with something that holds liquid ⟨the cook *laded* the stew into small bowls⟩ — see DIP 2
2 to place a weight or burden on ⟨the trucks were heavily *laden* with produce for the market⟩ — see LOAD 1

laden *vb* to place a weight or burden on ⟨*laden* a ship with emergency medical supplies⟩ — see LOAD 1

la–di–da *also* **la–de–da** *or* **lah–de–dah** *or* **lah–dee–dah** *or* **lah–di–dah** *adj* self-consciously trying to present an appearance of grandeur or importance ⟨there's no need to be *la-di-da* with your friends—we all know that classy accent is a put-on⟩ — see PRETENTIOUS 1

lading *n* a mass or quantity of something taken up and carried, conveyed, or transported ⟨a bill of *lading* is a document issued by a carrier that lists goods being shipped and specifies the terms of their transport⟩ — see LOAD 1

ladle *n* a utensil with a bowl and a handle that is used especially in cooking and serving food ⟨the chef hunted for a *ladle* to add the chicken broth to the pot⟩ — see SPOON

ladle *vb* to lift out with something that holds liquid ⟨the server *ladled* out the soup from a large tureen⟩ — see DIP 2

lady *n* **1** an adult female human being ⟨"*ladies* and gentlemen, please observe closely," said the magician⟩ — see WOMAN 1
2 the female partner in a marriage ⟨in public the husband was frequently seen holding hands with his *lady*⟩ — see WIFE
3 a woman of high birth or social position ⟨the *ladies* of the royal court were all dressed extravagantly⟩ — see GENTLEWOMAN
4 a female romantic companion ⟨warned his fellow biker to stop messing with his *lady*⟩ — see GIRLFRIEND

ladylove *n* a female romantic companion ⟨ever the gallant, he bought an enormous bouquet of flowers for his *ladylove*⟩ — see GIRLFRIEND

lag *adj* following all others of the same kind in order or time ⟨we're now in the *lag* end of the project⟩ — see LAST 1

lag *vb* **1** to lose bodily strength or vigor ⟨during the fourth quarter the whole team seemed to *lag*⟩ — see WEAKEN 2
2 to move or act slowly ⟨the tired puppy was *lagging* behind the rest of the pack⟩ — see DELAY 1

laggard *adj* moving or proceeding at less than the normal, desirable, or required speed ⟨I hate being stuck behind *laggard* motorists on the freeway⟩ — see SLOW 1

laggard *n* someone who moves slowly or more slowly than others ⟨tried to spur on the *laggards* at the back of the line during the hike⟩ — see SLOWPOKE

laggardly *adv* at a pace that is less than usual, desirable, or expected ⟨some students *laggardly* wandered in to class, obviously dreading the upcoming quiz⟩ — see SLOW

lagger *n* someone who moves slowly or more slowly than others ⟨after 10 hours, there weren't any spectators left to cheer on the *laggers* as they finished the marathon⟩ — see SLOWPOKE

lagging *adj* moving or proceeding at less than the normal, desirable, or required speed ⟨the *lagging* pace of work on the project was worrisome⟩ — see SLOW

lagniappe *n* **1** something given in addition to what is ordinarily expected or owed ⟨the meal was served with a *lagniappe* of freshly made cornbread⟩ — see BONUS
2 something given to someone without expectation of a return ⟨the hotel threw in some free shampoo as a *lagniappe*⟩ — see GIFT 1

laid–back *adj* having a relaxed, casual manner ⟨a *laid-back* fisherman, he didn't really care if he caught anything, being content to relax and enjoy the sunshine⟩ — see EASYGOING 1

lair *n* **1** a place where a person goes to hide or to avoid others ⟨the detectives tracked the thieves to their *lair* and made immediate arrests⟩ — see HIDEOUT
2 the shelter or resting place of a wild animal ⟨we found an abandoned fox's *lair* in the woods behind the barn⟩ — see DEN 1
3 *British dialect* a place set aside for sleeping ⟨a homeless man whose usual *lair* was a bench in Hyde Park⟩ — see BED 1

lam *n* the act or an instance of getting free from danger or confinement ⟨the prisoners were recaptured after only three days on the *lam*⟩ — see ESCAPE

lam *vb* to get free from a dangerous or confining situation ⟨let's *lam* out of this hellhole while there's still time⟩ — see ESCAPE 1

lamb *n* an innocent or gentle person ⟨the new guys at football camp were *lambs* who hardly knew what awaited them⟩
synonyms angel, dove, innocent, sheep
related words babe, colt, cub, fledgling, greenhorn, ingenue (*or* ingénue), naïf (*or* naif), newbie, tenderfoot, virgin; cherub, saint; mollycoddle, sissy, softy (*or* softie), weakling, wimp; dupe, pigeon, sap, sucker
near antonyms bully, roughneck, rowdy, tough; beast, boor, cad, churl, clown, creep, cretin, cur, heel, jerk, joker, louse, lout, slob; shark, skunk, snake, stinker; devil, knave, miscreant, no-good, rapscallion, rascal, reprobate, rogue, scalawag (*or* scallywag), scamp, scoundrel, varlet, villain
antonyms wolf

lambaste *or* **lambast** *vb* **1** to criticize (someone) severely or angrily especially for personal failings ⟨the director *lambasted* them mercilessly for forgetting their lines during the final dress rehearsal⟩ — see SCOLD
2 to criticize harshly and usually publicly ⟨movie critics across the country *lambasted* the thriller for its orgy of violence⟩ — see ATTACK 2
3 to strike repeatedly ⟨stern schoolmasters who *lambasted* the boys for the smallest violation of the rules⟩ — see BEAT 1

lambency *n* the quality or state of having or giving off light ⟨the *lambency* of the sunlit stained-glass window was breathtaking⟩ — see BRILLIANCE 1

lambent *adj* giving off or reflecting much light ⟨the *lambent* flames from our campfire cast a comforting glow⟩ — see BRIGHT 1

lambently *adv* in a manner marked by the shining or reflecting of much light ⟨a single candle burned *lambently* in the window of the secluded cottage⟩ — see BRIGHTLY 1

lame *adj* **1** arousing or deserving of one's loathing and disgust ⟨just some *lame* stereotyping of ethnic minorities⟩ — see CONTEMPTIBLE 1
2 falling short of a standard ⟨the amenities at this hotel are *lame*; there's not even a television in the room⟩ — see BAD 1

lame *vb* to cause severe or permanent injury to ⟨we were afraid that the horse would be *lamed* by its horrible fall⟩ — see MAIM

lamebrain *n* a stupid person ⟨who's the *lamebrain* who put an empty coffee carafe back on a hot burner?⟩ — see IDIOT

lamebrain *or* **lamebrained** *adj* not having or showing an ability to absorb ideas readily ⟨he offended a number of people with that insensitive, *lamebrain* comment⟩ — see STUPID 1

lamella *n* a small thin piece of material that resembles an animal scale ⟨the gemstone's distinctive iridescence is caused by light passing from one *lamella* of crystal to another⟩ — see ²SCALE

lament *n* **1** a crying out in grief ⟨the national *lament* that was heard when President Kennedy was assassinated⟩
synonyms groan, howl, keen, lamentation, moan, plaint, wail
related words cry, sob, tears; agonizing, grieving, mourning, sorrowing, suffering, weeping; hand-wringing, regret; complaint, cri de coeur, outcry, protest; anguish, dolor, grief, heartache, heartbreak, sorrow, woe
near antonyms cheering, laughing, smiling
antonyms exultation, rejoicing
2 a composition expressing one's grief over a loss ⟨a poem that is her *lament* for her late grandmother⟩
synonyms dirge, elegy, requiem, threnody
related words taps; elegiac (*also* elegiacal), monody
near antonyms encomium, eulogy, paean, panegyric
3 an expression of dissatisfaction, pain, or resentment ⟨the career woman's *lament* that there aren't any good men left⟩ — see COMPLAINT 1

lament *vb* **1** to feel or express sorrow for ⟨she *lamented* the loss of her beloved pet to a degree that went way beyond words⟩
synonyms bemoan, bewail, deplore, grieve (for), mourn, wail (for)
related words elegize; cry (for), keen, moan, weep; regret, rue; bawl, blubber, sob; agonize, bleed, hurt, sorrow, suffer
near antonyms beam, cheer, grin, laugh, smile
antonyms delight, exult (in), glory (in), joy, rejoice (in)
2 to feel sorry or dissatisfied about ⟨the youth *lamented* not having spent more time with his late grandfather⟩ — see REGRET

lamentable *adj* **1** expressing or suggesting mourning ⟨the *lamentable* cries of the women for their slain sons were heard throughout the village⟩ — see MOURNFUL 1
2 of a kind to cause great distress ⟨it's a *lamentable* situation, but I don't see how it can be fixed⟩ — see REGRETTABLE

lamentation *n* a crying out in grief ⟨there was a great *lamentation* on Wall Street when the government's latest unemployment figures were published⟩ — see LAMENT 1

lamina *n* a small thin piece of material that resembles an animal scale ⟨the *laminae* of stratified rock were deposited separately, building upwards as time passed⟩ — see ²SCALE

lamp *n* something that provides illumination ⟨I didn't realize it had gotten so dark in the room until my wife came in and turned on the *lamp*, momentarily blinding me⟩ — see LIGHT 2

lampoon *n* a creative work that uses sharp humor to point up the foolishness of a person, institution, or human nature in general ⟨this classic musical is a *lampoon* of the movie business at the time when sound was introduced⟩ — see SATIRE

lanai *n* a covered structure adjoining an entrance to a building ⟨a low-slung Hawaiian beach house with an open-sided *lanai* to catch the tropical breezes⟩ — see PORCH

lance *n* a weapon with a long straight handle and sharp head or blade ⟨the *lance* struck squarely on the knight's shield, knocking him from his horse⟩ — see SPEAR

lance *vb* to penetrate or hold (something) with a pointed object ⟨doctors used to *lance* infected sores, so that they could drain clean⟩ — see IMPALE

land *n* **1** a body of people composed of one or more nationalities usually with its own territory and government ⟨the whole *land* rose up in outrage over the tyrant's unconscionable cruelties⟩ — see NATION 1
2 a broad geographical area ⟨the *land* to the west was said to have incredibly rich soil and plentiful water⟩ — see REGION 2
3 the solid part of our planet's surface as distinguished from the sea and air ⟨it's always good to be back on dry *land* after a long boat ride⟩ — see EARTH 2

land *vb* **1** to stop at or near a place along the shore ⟨the Pilgrims *landed* at Plymouth after exploring Cape Cod Bay⟩
synonyms anchor, dock
related words berth, moor, tie up; beach, ground; harbor; arrive, reach, show up, turn up; debark, disembark
phrases make port
near antonyms embark, launch, sail
2 to get to a destination ⟨we *landed* at the hotel just before midnight⟩ — see COME 2
3 to go ashore from a ship ⟨the passengers on the cruise *landed* at St. George in Bermuda⟩ — see DISEMBARK 1
4 to come to rest after descending from the air ⟨our plane is *landing* in 15 minutes, so we need to put all of our things away⟩ — see ALIGHT 1
5 to receive as return for effort ⟨because of his work on the boss's pet project, he *landed* a promotion as well as a raise⟩ — see EARN 1
6 to take physical control or possession of (something) suddenly or forcibly ⟨after struggling for half an hour, the fisherman finally *landed* a 10-pound bass⟩ — see CATCH 1

landfill *n* a place where discarded materials (as trash) are dumped ⟨we took all of our old, broken furniture to the *landfill*⟩ — see DUMP 1

landing *n* a structure used by boats and ships for taking on or landing cargo and passengers ⟨our families waved good-bye to us from the *landing* as we left on our honeymoon cruise⟩ — see DOCK

landlord *n* **1** the owner of land or housing that is rented to another ⟨agreed to pay the *landlord* the rent on the first Monday of each month⟩
synonyms lessor, letter, renter
related words landlady; laird, landholder, landowner; proprietor; slumlord
antonyms lessee, lodger, roomer, tenant
2 the owner or manager of an inn ⟨a weekend workshop that is intended to disabuse would-be *landlords* of a bed-and breakfast that the job is one long vacation⟩ — see INNKEEPER

landmark *n* a point in a chain of events at which an important change (as in one's fortunes) occurs ⟨typically, people feel that turning 21 is a *landmark* in one's life⟩ — see TURNING POINT

landmass *n* one of the great divisions of land on the globe or the main part of such a division ⟨the islands of Ireland and Great Britain were once part of the Eurasian *landmass*⟩ — see MAINLAND

land mine *n* a danger or difficulty that is hidden or not easily recognized ⟨parents of teenagers never know when they might set off an emotional *land mine*⟩ — see PITFALL 1

landscape *n* the physical features of a region as a whole ⟨radar images that map the lunar *landscape*⟩ — see GEOGRAPHY

landsman *n* a person living in or originally from the same country as another ⟨during the time he was an American in Paris he felt a special kinship with his fellow *landsmen*⟩ — see COMPATRIOT 1

language *n* **1** the stock of words, pronunciation, and grammar used by a people as their basic means of communication ⟨Great Britain, the United States, Australia, and other countries where English is the dominant *language*⟩
synonyms lingo, mother tongue, speech, tongue, vocabulary
related words acrolect; argot, cant, colloquial, dialect, idiolect, idiom, jargon, parlance, patois, patter, pidgin, slang, slanguage, vernacular; colloquialism, localism, provincialism, regionalism, shibboleth, vernacularism; terminology; coinage, modernism, neologism
2 the special terms or expressions of a particular group or field ⟨"love" means "nothing" in the *language* of tennis⟩ — see TERMINOLOGY
3 the way in which something is put into words ⟨we're finding the *language* of the legal documents to be tough going⟩ — see WORDING 1

languid *adj* **1** lacking bodily energy or motivation ⟨a few *languid* dancers swayed about on the dance floor without much enthusiasm⟩ — see LISTLESS
2 lacking bodily strength ⟨the tired athlete's *languid* movements on the tennis court⟩ — see WEAK 1
3 moving or proceeding at less than the normal, desirable, or required speed ⟨the film's *languid* pace will not be to the taste of many moviegoers⟩ — see SLOW 1

languidness *n* the quality or state of lacking physical strength or vigor ⟨the *languidness* of her sigh suggested that death would not be long in the coming⟩ — see WEAKNESS 1

languish *vb* to lose bodily strength or vigor ⟨older people, especially, were *languishing* during the prolonged heat wave⟩ — see WEAKEN 2

languishing *adj* lacking bodily energy or motivation ⟨his lingering sickness left him *languishing* and uninterested in his usual activities⟩ — see LISTLESS

languor *n* **1** physical or mental inertness ⟨the beach was packed with sunbathers wallowing in the *languor* brought on by a scorching summer day⟩ — see LETHARGY
2 the quality or state of lacking physical strength or vigor ⟨the tropical heat sapped our strength, leaving us in a state of unaccustomed *languor*⟩ — see WEAKNESS 1

languorous *adj* lacking bodily energy or motivation ⟨the drummer's *languorous* playing caused the rest of the band to keep missing the beat⟩ — see LISTLESS

lank *adj* not stiff in structure ⟨right after a shower, her *lank* hair hung down to her shoulders⟩ — see LIMP 1

lanky *adj* being tall, thin and usually loose-jointed ⟨the *lanky* basketball star was great at slam-dunking⟩
synonyms gangling, gangly, rangy, spindling, spindly
related words angular, bony (*also* boney), gaunt, lank, rawboned, scraggy, scrawny, skinny; lean, slender, slim, spare, thin; racy, reedy, spidery, stringy, twiggy, waspish, weedy, willowy, wiry; spindle-legged, spindle-shanked
near antonyms beefy, bulky, chubby, chunky, heavyset, pudgy, squat, stocky, stout, stubby, stumpy, sturdy, thick-bodied, thickset, weighty; muscle-bound; corpulent, fat, fleshy, full, gross, obese, overweight, plump, portly, roly-poly, rotund, round, tubby

lap *n* a portion of a trip ⟨we were on the last *lap* of the journey, eagerly heading for home⟩ — see LEG 2

[1]**lap** *vb* **1** to flow along or against ⟨the waves gently *lapped* the sandy shore⟩ — see WASH 1

2 to flow in a broken irregular stream ⟨the creek *lapped* along through the ravine before collecting in the pond⟩ — see GURGLE

3 to move with a splashing motion ⟨a stiff breeze that was causing the lake waters to *lap* against the hull with some force⟩ — see SLOSH 1

²lap *vb* **1** to lie over parts of one another ⟨the armadillo's plates *lap* tightly so as to form a protective shield⟩ — see OVERLAP

2 to surround or cover closely ⟨this recording of the symphony is sure to *lap* listeners in stereophonic bliss⟩ — see ENFOLD 1

lap (up) *vb* to receive or accept gladly or readily ⟨a show-off who *laps up* attention the way a kitten does milk⟩ — see WELCOME

lapping *n* a partial covering of one thing by an adjoining member ⟨the *lapping* of the roofing shingles should be several inches in order to avoid leaks⟩ — see OVERLAP

lapse *n* **1** a change in status for the worse usually temporarily ⟨the scandal caused the president to suffer a dramatic *lapse* in popularity⟩ — see REVERSE 1

2 an unintentional departure from truth or accuracy ⟨his slip of the tongue about the mayor's name was an unfortunate *lapse*⟩ — see ERROR 1

3 the stopping of a process or activity ⟨wasn't bothered by the *lapse* of her membership at the health club⟩ — see END 1

lapse *vb* to come to an end ⟨the contract will *lapse* at the end of the year unless we renew⟩ — see CEASE 1

larcenist *n* one who steals ⟨when the serial *larcenist* Willie Sutton was asked why he continued to rob banks, he supposedly replied, "because that's where the money is"⟩ — see THIEF

larceny *n* the unlawful taking and carrying away of property without the consent of its owner ⟨the security guard waited until the shoplifter had actually left the store with the item, so as to have proof of *larceny*⟩ — see THEFT 1

lardy *adj* having an excess of body fat ⟨he's become quite *lardy* since he began neglecting his exercise regimen⟩ — see FAT 1

large *adj* **1** of a size greater than average of its kind ⟨he was hungry, so he ordered the *large* pizza⟩
synonyms big, biggish, boxcar, bulky, considerable, goodly, grand, great, handsome, hefty, hulking, husky, largish, outsize (*also* outsized), oversize (*or* oversized), sizable (*or* sizeable), substantial, tidy, voluminous
related words astronomical (*also* astronomic), Brobdingnagian, bumper, Bunyanesque, cavernous, colossal, cosmic (*also* cosmical), cyclopean, elephantine, enormous, galactic, gargantuan, gigantic, gross, hellacious, herculean, heroic (*also* heroical), Himalayan, huge, humongous (*also* humungous), immense, jumbo, king-size (*or* king-sized), leviathan, major, mammoth, massive, monolithic, monstrous, monumental, mountainous, pharaonic, prodigious, staggering, stupendous, super, super-duper, supersized, titanic, tremendous, vast, vasty, walloping, whacking, whopping; excessive, exorbitant, extravagant, extreme, immoderate, inordinate; abundant, ample, appreciable, copious, plentiful; fat, thick; capacious, commodious, roomy, spacious
near antonyms diminutive, half-pint, infinitesimal, Lilliputian, little-bitty, microminiature, microscopic (*also* microscopical), mini, miniature, minuscule, minute, pint-size (*or* pint-sized), pocket-size (*also* pocket-sized), pygmy, teensy, teensy-weensy, teeny, teeny-weeny, tiny, wee; petite, slender, slight, slim, thin
antonyms bantam, dinky, dwarf, dwarfish, little, puny, shrimpy, small, smallish, undersized (*also* undersize)

2 enjoying widespread favor or approval ⟨a color that will be very *large* this spring if the fashion designers have their way⟩ — see POPULAR 1

large *adv* in a luxurious manner ⟨college students living *large* on generous allowances from indulgent parents⟩ — see HIGH

largeheartedness *n* the capacity for feeling for another's unhappiness or misfortune ⟨the famed *largeheartedness* of a city that has welcomed refugees with open arms on more than one occasion⟩ — see HEART 1

largely *adv* **1** for the most part ⟨the earth's surface is *largely* composed of water⟩ — see CHIEFLY

2 to a large extent or degree ⟨with this land purchase, the corporation *largely* increases its holdings in the area⟩ — see GREATLY 2

largeness *n* the quality or state of being large in size ⟨I was impressed by the *largeness* of the portions at the new restaurant⟩
synonyms bigness, bulkiness, grandness, greatness, heftiness, substantiality, voluminousness
related words enormity, enormousness, extensiveness, grossness, healthiness, hugeness, immenseness, immensity, magnitude, massiveness, mightiness, mountainousness, prodigiousness, stupendousness, vastness; excessiveness, extravagance, extremeness, immoderacy; abundance, ampleness, bountifulness, copiousness, generosity, handsomeness, liberality, muchness; adequacy, sufficiency; weightiness
near antonyms diminutiveness, minuteness, tininess; slightness; meagerness, poorness, scantiness, scarceness, scarcity, skimpiness, slenderness, slimness, spareness, sparseness, sparsity, stinginess; deficiency, inadequacy, inadequateness
antonyms fineness, littleness, puniness, smallness

largess *also* **largesse** *n* **1** something given to someone without expectation of a return ⟨the alumna's huge bequest was an unexpected *largess*⟩ — see GIFT 1

2 the quality or state of being generous ⟨the philanthropist was known for his *largess* to all of the city's cultural institutions⟩ — see LIBERALITY

largish *adj* **1** of a size greater than average of its kind ⟨she was hungry, so she took a somewhat *largish* portion of food from the buffet⟩ — see LARGE 1

2 sufficiently large in size, amount, or number to merit attention ⟨a *largish* amount of media attention was paid to something that was a nonstory⟩ — see CONSIDERABLE 1

lariat *n* a rope or long leather thong with a noose used especially for catching livestock ⟨the cowboy could throw a *lariat* around a running steer's head from 20 yards away⟩ — see LASSO

lark *n* a time or instance of carefree fun ⟨the kids will have a grand *lark* at the carnival⟩ — see FLING 1

lark *vb* to play and run about happily ⟨we would rather *lark* about in the summer than get part-time jobs⟩ — see FROLIC 1

larkiness *n* a natural disposition for playful behavior ⟨within the confines of the private club, these hotshot lawyers display a *larkiness* that would do a frat boy proud⟩ — see PLAYFULNESS

larky *adj* given to good-natured joking or teasing ⟨a *larky* group of youths enjoying a night out on the town⟩ — see PLAYFUL

larrup *n, dialect* a hard strike with a part of the body or an instrument ⟨he gave the ball a good *larrup* with his club, and it easily cleared the ditch⟩ — see ¹BLOW

larva *n* a young wingless often wormlike form (as a grub or caterpillar) that hatches from the egg of many insects ⟨the *larva* looked ugly, but it was destined to hatch into a beautiful butterfly⟩
synonyms naiad, nymph
related words pupa

lascivious *adj* **1** depicting or referring to sexual matters in a way that is unacceptable in polite society ⟨was

fired for making *lascivious* remarks to a coworker⟩ — see OBSCENE 1
2 having a strong sexual desire ⟨all of the debutantes were warned about the *lascivious* playboy⟩ — see LUSTFUL

lasciviousness *n* the quality or state of being obscene ⟨the minister preached a sermon against the *lasciviousness* that pervades so much of popular culture⟩ — see OBSCENITY 1

lash *n* **1** a hard strike with a part of the body or an instrument ⟨suddenly felt the *lash* of her drunken husband's hand on her cheek⟩ — see [1]BLOW
2 a long thin or flexible tool for striking ⟨the rider repeatedly struck the horse with the *lash* to force it to go faster⟩ — see WHIP

lash *vb* **1** to strike repeatedly with something long and thin or flexible ⟨the cat's tail nervously *lashed* the table leg⟩ — see WHIP 1
2 to strike repeatedly ⟨all night long sheets of rain *lashed* the windows⟩ — see BEAT 1

lashings *also* **lashins** *n pl, chiefly British* a considerable amount ⟨we've prepared *lashings* of wassail for the holiday party⟩ — see LOT 2

lass *n* a female person who has not yet reached adulthood ⟨she's only a gawky *lass* now, but she'll be a beautiful woman some day⟩ — see GIRL 2

lassie *n* a female person who has not yet reached adulthood ⟨a pretty young *lassie* of 16 years⟩ — see GIRL 2

lassitude *n* **1** a complete depletion of energy or strength ⟨our *lassitude* was such that we couldn't even be bothered to get more soda from the fridge⟩ — see FATIGUE 1
2 physical or mental inertness ⟨as his cancer progresses, his days are increasingly marked by *lassitude* and isolation from the outside world⟩ — see LETHARGY

lasso *n* a rope or long leather thong with a noose used especially for catching livestock ⟨the cowpuncher skillfully tossed the *lasso* around the calf's neck⟩
synonyms lariat, reata, riata

last *adj* **1** following all others of the same kind in order or time ⟨*last* one in the pool is a rotten egg⟩
synonyms bottommost, closing, concluding, final, hindmost, lag, latest, latter, rearmost, terminal, terminating, ultimate
related words consequent, ensuing, eventual, following, succeeding; conclusive, crowning, decisive, definitive; farthermost, farthest, furthermost, furthest, remotest; lowermost, lowest, nethermost; endmost, extreme, outermost, outmost, utmost; penultimate
near antonyms eminent, premier, superior
antonyms beginning, earliest, first, foremost, headmost, inaugural, initial, leadoff, maiden, opening, original, pioneer, primary, starting
2 serving to put an end to all debate or questioning ⟨a book on the Kennedy assassination that supposedly is the *last* statement on what happened that fateful day⟩ — see CONCLUSIVE 1
3 of the greatest or highest degree or quantity ⟨our *last* praise should be reserved for those original thinkers who expand the frontiers of science⟩ — see ULTIMATE 1

last *vb* **1** to continue to operate or to meet one's needs ⟨we were lucky that the batteries *lasted* until we could get to the store to buy more⟩ — see HOLD OUT
2 to remain indefinitely in existence or in the same state ⟨this heavy drought has *lasted* all summer⟩ — see CONTINUE 1

lasting *adj* having an existence or validity that does not change or diminish ⟨one of the few books published last year that is likely to have *lasting* significance⟩ — see ABIDING

last name *n* a name shared by members of a family ⟨please write your first name, middle initial, and *last name* at the top of the form⟩ — see SURNAME 1

last word *n* a practice or interest that is very popular for a short time ⟨a swimsuit that is the *last word* in sportswear this season⟩ — see FAD

late *adj* **1** not arriving, occurring, or settled at the due, usual, or proper time ⟨I ran as fast as I could, but was still *late* for class⟩
synonyms behind, behindhand, belated, delinquent, latish, overdue, tardy
related words delayed, detained, postponed; dallying, dawdling, dilatory, dillydallying, dragging, laggard, lagging, poky (*or* pokey), slow, sluggish, unhurried
near antonyms opportune, seasonable, timely; prompt, punctual
antonyms early, inopportune, precocious, premature, unseasonable, untimely
2 having been such at some previous time ⟨the *late* musical director said he would never have allowed such behavior while he was in charge⟩ — see FORMER 1
3 no longer living ⟨our *late* granduncle remembered us in his will⟩ — see DEAD 1
4 being far along in development ⟨*late* impressionism gave rise to pointillism⟩ — see ADVANCED 1

late *adv* **1** after the due, usual, or proper time ⟨she has a habit of arriving *late* for everything⟩
synonyms belatedly, delinquently, tardily
related words afterward (*or* afterwards), anon, eventually, later, latterly, subsequently, thereafter; dilatorily, laggardly, pokily, slow, slowly, sluggishly
near antonyms immediately, promptly, punctually; pronto, quickly, rapidly, snappily, speedily, swiftly
antonyms beforehand, early, inopportunely, precociously, prematurely, unseasonably
2 not long ago ⟨the actress, *late* of New York but now of Los Angeles, is being eagerly sought for film roles⟩ — see NEWLY

lately *adv* not long ago ⟨have you been listening to the radio much *lately*?⟩ — see NEWLY

latency *n* a state of temporary inactivity ⟨the flower bulbs went from *latency* to full bloom in a matter of days⟩ — see ABEYANCE

lateness *n* the quality or state of being late ⟨we were unable to get into the movie due to our *lateness* in arriving⟩
synonyms belatedness, delinquency, tardiness
related words dilatoriness, sluggishness
near antonyms promptitude, promptness, punctuality
antonyms earliness, prematureness, prematurity

latent *adj* not being in a state of use, activity, or employment ⟨he has a *latent* talent for acting that he hasn't had a chance to express yet⟩ — see INACTIVE 2

later *adj* being, occurring, or carried out at a time after something else ⟨the details of the plan will be filled in at a *later* date⟩ — see SUBSEQUENT

later *adv* following in time or place ⟨we're going to go to the mall *later* on⟩ — see AFTER

lateral *adj* of, relating to, or located on one side ⟨from the *lateral* view you can see how thick the wall really is⟩ — see SIDE

latest *adj* following all others of the same kind in order or time ⟨the *latest* news reveals many details we didn't know before⟩ — see LAST 1

latest *n* a practice or interest that is very popular for a short time ⟨that skirt is the absolute *latest*!⟩ — see FAD

lather *n* **1** a light mass of fine bubbles formed in or on a liquid ⟨she worked the shampoo into a *lather* before rubbing it into her pet dog's coat⟩ — see FOAM
2 a state of nervous or irritated concern ⟨he worked himself into a *lather* waiting for the results of the AIDS test⟩ — see FRET

lather *vb* to strike repeatedly ⟨the flinty rancher did not hesitate to *lather* a recalcitrant horse⟩ — see BEAT 1

lathery *adj* covered with, consisting of, or resembling foam ⟨the *lathery* crests of the waves washed up and down the sandy beach⟩ — see FOAMY

latish *adj* not arriving, occurring, or settled at the due, usual, or proper time ⟨the bus was often a little *latish*, but never more than by a few minutes⟩ — see LATE 1

latitude *n* **1** an allowable margin of freedom or variation ⟨the regulations regarding the pasteurization of dairy products don't allow for much *latitude*⟩ — see SLACK 1

2 the right to act or move freely ⟨the new laws gave the police more *latitude* in dealing with suspected criminals⟩ — see FREEDOM 2

latrine *n* a room furnished with a fixture for flushing body waste ⟨where's the nearest *latrine*, soldier?⟩ — see TOILET

latter *adj* following all others of the same kind in order or time ⟨the multiplex was showing a comedy and a horror film, and we decided that the *latter* would be more fun to watch⟩ — see LAST 1

latterly *adv* following in time or place ⟨he had been a teacher, a librarian, and some years *latterly*, a novelist⟩ — see AFTER

laud *n* public acknowledgment or admiration for an achievement ⟨an actor who in his lifetime received all the *laud* and honor that the theater world could bestow⟩ — see GLORY 1

laud *vb* **1** to declare enthusiastic approval of ⟨the critics have *lauded* the best-selling author's newest novel⟩ — see ACCLAIM

2 to proclaim the glory of ⟨the nation's people were expected to *laud* the dictator at every opportunity⟩ — see PRAISE 1

laudable *adj* deserving of high regard or great approval ⟨you showed *laudable* restraint in dealing with that ridiculously demanding customer⟩ — see ADMIRABLE

laugh *n* **1** an explosive sound that is a sign of amusement ⟨the child's frown turned into a *laugh* when he saw the clown⟩

synonyms belly laugh, boff (*or* boffo), boffola, cachinnation, cackle, chortle, chuckle, giggle, guffaw, hee-haw, horselaugh, laughter, snicker, snigger, titter, twitter

related words crow, whoop; grin, simper, smile, smirk

near antonyms cry, groan, moan, sob, wail; face, frown, grimace, lower (*also* lour), mouth, pout, scowl

2 someone or something that is very funny ⟨that new sitcom is a *laugh*⟩ — see SCREAM

3 something said or done to cause laughter ⟨the film comedy had a good *laugh* in just about every scene⟩ — see JOKE 1

laugh *vb* **1** to show mirth with an explosive vocal sound ⟨everyone *laughed* when the clown dramatically slipped and fell⟩

synonyms break up, cackle, chortle, chuckle, crack up, giggle, hee-haw, roar, scream, snicker, titter, twitter

related words grin, smile

phrases split one's sides

near antonyms bawl, blubber, cry, sob, weep; howl, scream, squall, wail, yowl; bleat, pule, whimper, whine; sniffle, snivel; groan, moan, sigh

2 to express scornful amusement by means of facial contortions ⟨you're going to try out for the football team? Don't make me *laugh*!⟩ — see SNEER

laugh (at) *vb* to make (someone or something) the object of unkind laughter ⟨most viewers seem to tune in just to *laugh at* the self-deluded souls who think that they can actually sing⟩ — see RIDICULE

laughable *adj* **1** causing or intended to cause laughter ⟨the *laughable*, boisterous antics of the circus clowns⟩ — see FUNNY 1

2 so foolish or pointless as to be worthy of scornful laughter ⟨it was simply *laughable* to see this middle-aged, hopelessly square candidate trying to appear young and hip⟩ — see RIDICULOUS 1

laughing *adj* indicative of or marked by high spirits or good humor ⟨the satisfying comedy put us in a *laughing* mood for the rest of the evening⟩ — see MERRY

laughingstock *n* a person or thing that is made fun of ⟨his nerdy clothes made him the *laughingstock* of the schoolyard⟩

synonyms butt, derision, jest, joke, mark, mock, mockery, sport, target

related words chump, dupe, fall guy, fool, gull, monkey, pigeon, sap, sucker, victim

near antonyms darling, favorite, pet

laughter *n* an explosive sound that is a sign of amusement ⟨the nervous producers were reassured by the sounds of *laughter* coming from the theater⟩ — see LAUGH 1

launch *n* **1** a rising from a surface at the start of a flight (as of a rocket) ⟨the reporters held their collective breath as they silently watched the space shuttle's *launch*⟩ — see LIFTOFF

2 the point at which something begins ⟨we are at the *launch* of a new age of space exploration⟩ — see BEGINNING

launch *vb* **1** to be responsible for the creation and early operation or use of ⟨after retiring, he *launched* a small company devoted to making medical devices⟩ — see FOUND

2 to take the first step in (a process or course of action) ⟨she *launched* a career in journalism after quitting acting school⟩ — see BEGIN 1

3 to send through the air especially with a quick forward motion of the arm ⟨infantrymen *launching* grenades at the nest of machine gunners⟩ — see THROW 1

launder *vb* to remove objectionable parts from ⟨had to *launder* the quarterback's off-the-cuff's remarks before they could be quoted in the newspaper⟩ — see CENSOR

laurels *n pl* public acknowledgment or admiration for an achievement ⟨the medics received many *laurels* for their heroic actions during the disaster⟩ — see GLORY 1

lavaliere *also* **lavalliere** *n* an ornament worn on a chain around the neck or wrist ⟨gave his girlfriend a golden *lavaliere* engraved with his name⟩ — see PENDANT 1

lavatory *n* a room furnished with a fixture for flushing body waste ⟨the school's filthy, broken-down *lavatories* were a disgrace⟩ — see TOILET

lave *vb* to flow along or against ⟨the cold water from the stream gently *laved* her burned fingers⟩ — see WASH 1

lavish *adj* **1** going beyond a normal or acceptable limit in degree or amount ⟨this *lavish* consumption of our natural resources simply cannot continue⟩ — see EXCESSIVE

2 pouring forth in great amounts ⟨the *lavish* praise that the novel was receiving had some wondering if it could ever live up to readers' expectations⟩ — see PROFUSE

3 showing obvious signs of wealth and comfort ⟨the *lavish* apartment even boasted a marble bathroom with gold-plated fixtures⟩ — see LUXURIOUS 1

lavish *vb* **1** to give readily and in large quantities ⟨doting parents *lavishing* lots of attention on their children⟩ — see RAIN 2

2 to use up carelessly ⟨a great actor who *lavished* his talent in lousy movies⟩ — see WASTE 1

lavishly *adv* **1** in a generous manner ⟨complained that the university spends *lavishly* on the football program but underfunds other sports⟩ — see WELL 2

2 in a luxurious manner ⟨Hollywood celebrities are known for living *lavishly*⟩ — see HIGH

lavishness *n* the quality or fact of being free or wasteful in the expenditure of money ⟨the lottery winner's friends were struck by the *lavishness* of his new lifestyle⟩ — see EXTRAVAGANCE 1

law *n* **1** a rule of conduct or action laid down by a governing authority and especially a legislature ⟨a record number of *laws* were passed in that legislative session⟩
synonyms act, bill, constitution, enactment, ordinance, statute
related words command, commandment, decree, dictate, directive, edict, fiat, ruling; bylaw, ground rule, regulation, rule; amendment, legislation; common law, martial law; blue law; prohibition, proscription, restriction; canon, capitulary, encyclical
near antonyms higher law
2 a collection or system of rules of conduct ⟨it's important to obey the *law* at all times, or else you might end up in jail⟩ — see CODE
3 the department of government that keeps order, fights crime, and enforces statutes ⟨a petty thief who had somehow managed to avoid the *law* for most of his life⟩ — see POLICE 1

law–abiding *adj* readily giving in to the command or authority of another ⟨the *law-abiding* citizens of the neighborhood did everything they could to help reduce street crime⟩ — see OBEDIENT

lawbreaker *n* a person who has committed a crime ⟨legislation that mandates lengthy prison sentences for chronic *lawbreakers*⟩ — see CRIMINAL

lawbreaking *adj* not restrained by or under the control of legal authority ⟨some sociologists specialize in studying the *lawbreaking* elements of society⟩ — see LAWLESS 1

lawbreaking *n* **1** a breaking of a moral or legal code ⟨even something as simple as littering is considered an example of *lawbreaking*⟩ — see OFFENSE 1
2 activities that are in violation of the laws of the state ⟨an outbreak of *lawbreaking* plagued the city in the months following the end of the war⟩ — see CRIME 1

lawful *adj* permitted by law ⟨hunting is a *lawful* activity only if you have the proper license⟩ — see LEGAL 1

lawfulness *n* the quality or state of being legal ⟨the lawyers had to work for weeks to determine the *lawfulness* of the proposed contract⟩ — see LEGALITY

lawgiver *n* a member of an organized body of persons having the authority to make laws ⟨political activists strenuously lobbied the state's *lawgivers* to expand the scope of the civil rights legislation⟩ — see LEGISLATOR

lawless *adj* **1** not restrained by or under the control of legal authority ⟨the *lawless* rioters were destroying everything in sight⟩
synonyms anarchic (*also* anarchical), disorderly, lawbreaking, unruly
related words defiant, insubordinate, mutinous, rebellious, refractory, riotous; undisciplined; criminal, felonious, illegal, illegitimate, illicit, unlawful, wrongful; disobedient, froward, intractable, recalcitrant
near antonyms lawful, legal, legalized, legitimate; amenable, compliant, docile, obedient, submissive, tractable
antonyms law-abiding, orderly
2 contrary to or forbidden by law ⟨the level of *lawless* activity in the territory had reached the point where the authorities felt compelled to act⟩ — see ILLEGAL 1

lawlessness *n* **1** a state in which there is widespread wrongdoing and disregard for rules and authority ⟨the western frontier was notorious for its *lawlessness*⟩ — see ANARCHY
2 activities that are in violation of the laws of the state ⟨*lawlessness* in the city had reached an unconscionable and intolerable level⟩ — see CRIME 1

lawmaker *n* a member of an organized body of persons having the authority to make laws ⟨the state's *lawmakers* worked long into the night drafting a bill that would be acceptable to everyone⟩ — see LEGISLATOR

lawman *n* a member of a force charged with law enforcement at the local level ⟨as the rural county's chief *lawman*, the sheriff has to patrol a vast area with only minimal manpower⟩ — see OFFICER 1

lawsuit *n* a court case for enforcing a right or claim ⟨the homeowner filed a *lawsuit* against the moving company that was refusing to be held responsible for damaging her furniture⟩
synonyms action, proceeding, suit
related words litigation; case, cause, complaint; counterclaim, countersuit, cross action, cross-claim

lawyer *n* a person whose profession is to conduct lawsuits for clients or to advise about legal rights and obligations ⟨their *lawyers* told them that they couldn't use the park for the concert without permission from the city⟩
synonyms advocate, attorney, attorney-at-law, counsel, counselor (*or* counsellor), counselor-at-law, legal eagle
related words cocounsel; district attorney, prosecuting attorney, prosecutor, solicitor; criminal lawyer, mouthpiece [*slang*], public defender, trial lawyer; solicitor; jurist; lawgiver, lawmaker, legislator, solon; ambulance chaser, pettifogger, Philadelphia lawyer, shyster

lax *adj* **1** failing to give proper care and attention ⟨*lax* parents who let their kids stay out as late as they want⟩ — see NEGLIGENT
2 not bound by rigid standards ⟨the guidelines for the essay contest were fairly *lax*, permitting a wide variety of topics⟩ — see EASYGOING 2
3 not tightly fastened, tied, or stretched ⟨the sheet on the foresail was *lax*, and so the sail was flapping wildly in the stiff wind⟩ — see LOOSE 1

laxness *n* failure to take the care that a cautious person usually takes ⟨the mountain climber's uncharacteristic *laxness* almost caused an accident⟩ — see NEGLIGENCE 1

[1]lay *n* **1** a rhythmic series of musical tones arranged to give a pleasing effect ⟨the minstrel strummed a cheerful *lay* on his lute⟩ — see MELODY
2 a short musical composition for the human voice often with instrumental accompaniment ⟨she sang a short *lay* in dedication to her husband⟩ — see SONG 1

[2]lay *n* the activity by which one regularly makes a living ⟨my main *lay* is as a general contractor, but I do side work as a carpenter⟩ — see OCCUPATION 1

lay *vb* **1** to arrange something in a certain spot or position ⟨just *lay* the book over there on the table for now⟩ — see PLACE 1
2 to cause to come to rest at the bottom (as of a liquid) ⟨the rain was just hard enough to *lay* the dust in the air⟩ — see SETTLE 1
3 to establish or apply as a charge or penalty ⟨state officials tried to *lay* a tax on merchandise sold over the Internet⟩ — see IMPOSE
4 to make ready in advance ⟨she's *laying* plans for the charity auction months ahead of time⟩ — see PREPARE 1
5 to put a layer of on a surface ⟨the mason *laid* mortar over the first row of bricks before starting the second⟩ — see SPREAD 2
6 to risk (something) on the outcome of an uncertain event ⟨I'll *lay* five dollars that you can't do it⟩ — see BET
7 to explain (something) as being the result of something else ⟨an electrical fire that was *laid* to faulty wiring⟩ — see CREDIT 1
8 to place (a dead body) in the earth, a tomb, or the sea ⟨*lay* the corpse to rest⟩ — see BURY 1

layabout *n* a lazy person ⟨she regretted ever asking that *layabout* to be her roommate, as he created the mess of two people and refused to help with anything⟩ — see LAZYBONES

lay away *vb* to put (something of future use or value) in a safe or secret place ⟨the weather forecast warned of a severe storm, so we *laid away* a generous supply of bottled water and canned food just in case⟩ — see HOARD

lay by *vb* **1** to get rid of as useless or unwanted ⟨a politician who had *laid by* his principles years ago⟩ — see DISCARD

2 to put (something of future use or value) in a safe or secret place ⟨ever since the last hurricane caught them unprepared, they have *laid by* emergency supplies⟩ — see HOARD

lay down *vb* **1** to put into effect through legislative or authoritative action ⟨the city council promises to *lay down* new ordinances that will force dog walkers to clean up after their animals⟩ — see ENACT

2 to state clearly and strongly ⟨at the risk of their popularity, the parents *laid down* the rules for the party and wouldn't accept any arguments⟩ — see ASSERT 1

3 to give the rules about (something) clearly and exactly ⟨the supervisor *laid down* the procedure for a complaint of sexual harassment⟩ — see PRESCRIBE

4 to give (something) over to the control or possession of another usually under duress ⟨commanded the surrounded troops to *lay down* their weapons⟩ — see SURRENDER 1

lay figure *n* one that is or can be used to further the purposes of another ⟨the novel's characters are not fully fleshed humans, but are simply *lay figures* strutted out to serve as mouthpieces for conflicting points of view⟩ — see [1]PAWN

lay in *vb* to put (something of future use or value) in a safe or secret place ⟨be sure to *lay in* enough food for the long Alaska winter⟩ — see HOARD

layman *n* a person who regularly or occasionally engages in an activity as a pastime rather than as a profession ⟨the discussion about investing was geared more to the *layman* than to the professional investor⟩ — see AMATEUR 1

layoff *n* **1** the termination of the employment of an employee or a work force often temporarily ⟨even senior employees lost their jobs in the massive *layoff*⟩

synonyms ax (*or* axe), discharge, dismissal, furlough, redundancy [*chiefly British*]

related words pink slip; bird [*chiefly British*], boot, bum's rush, downsizing, firing, heave-ho, sack; closing, shutdown; shakeout, shake-up

near antonyms callback, recall, reemployment, rehire, rehiring

2 a period of often involuntary inactivity or idleness ⟨after such a long *layoff* the boxer badly needed to get back into shape⟩ — see DOWNTIME

lay off *vb* to bring (as an action or operation) to an immediate end ⟨you need to *lay off* eating those jelly doughnuts, or you'll end up looking like one⟩ — see STOP 1

lay off (of) *vb* to stop doing (something) permanently ⟨we warned him to *lay off of* the cigarette smoking⟩ — see QUIT 2

lay on *vb* **1** to put a layer of on a surface ⟨she *lays* the butter *on* so thickly that you hardly taste the bagel⟩ — see SPREAD 2

2 *chiefly British* to provide with a paying job ⟨*lay on* more staff for the busy tourist season in the Lake District⟩ — see EMPLOY 1

layout *n* **1** the way in which something is sized, arranged, or organized ⟨the decorator changed the *layout* of the living room three times before declaring it finished⟩ — see FORMAT 1

2 the way in which the elements of something (as a work of art) are arranged ⟨the *layout* of his portraits typically consists of a finely drawn subject against a roughly sketched background⟩ — see COMPOSITION 3

lay out *vb* **1** to hand over or use up in payment ⟨he *laid out* big bucks for a new lawnmower that runs by itself⟩ — see SPEND 1

2 to work out the details of (something) in advance ⟨the transatlantic balloonists *laid out* a backup plan in case of an emergency⟩ — see PLAN 1

3 to put into a particular arrangement ⟨plants in the botanical gardens are *laid out* according to biogeographic region⟩ — see ORDER 1

4 to present so as to invite notice or attention ⟨for the historic celebration, the museum *laid out* its full collection of native artifacts⟩ — see SHOW 1

layover *n* a brief halt in a journey ⟨our flight from New York to San Francisco made a *layover* in Chicago⟩ — see STOP 1

lay over *vb* to assign to a later time ⟨we'll have to *lay over* a discussion of the issue until the next meeting⟩ — see POSTPONE

lay up *vb* to put (something of future use or value) in a safe or secret place ⟨an eating disorder that would impel her to *lay up* candy bars in her closet for all-night food binges⟩ — see HOARD

laze *vb* to spend time doing nothing ⟨the kind of sultry August day that makes you want to do nothing but *laze*⟩ — see IDLE

laziness *n* an inclination not to do work or engage in activities ⟨although she often talks about ambitious household projects, nothing even gets started because of her chronic *laziness*⟩

synonyms idleness, indolence, inertia, shiftlessness, sloth

related words apathy, languor, lassitude, lethargy, listlessness, sluggishness, supineness; dallying, goldbricking, loafing, lolling, lounging

near antonyms ambition, enterprise, go, hustle, initiative; assiduity, assiduousness, diligence, perseverance; animation, briskness, energy, exuberance, jazziness, liveliness, lustiness, pep, peppiness, robustness, sprightliness, vibrancy, vigor, vim, vitality, vivacity

antonyms drive, industriousness, industry

lazy *adj* **1** not easily aroused to action or work ⟨the *lazy* dog just wanted to lie on the couch all day and sleep⟩

synonyms idle, indolent, shiftless, slothful

related words apathetic, drowsy, dull, inert, languorous, lazyish, lethargic, listless, quiescent, sleepy, sluggish, supine, torpid

near antonyms ambitious, diligent, enterprising, zealous; active, animated, bouncing, brisk, dynamic, energetic, exuberant, frisky, jaunty, jazzy, lively, peppy, perky, pert, snappy, spirited, sprightly, springy, vigorous, vivacious, zippy

antonyms industrious

2 failing to give proper care and attention ⟨that cookbook author can be *lazy* about giving cooking times and temperatures⟩ — see NEGLIGENT

lazy *vb* to spend time doing nothing ⟨a good afternoon to spend *lazying* on the back porch⟩ — see IDLE

lazybones *n pl* a lazy person ⟨he's a *lazybones* who is never willing to do any work⟩

synonyms couch potato, deadbeat, do-nothing, drone, idler, layabout, loafer, lotus-eater, slouch, slug, sluga-bed, sluggard

related words bum, good-for-nothing, ne'er-do-well; crawler, creeper, dawdler, laggard, putterer, slowpoke, snail, stick-in-the-mud, straggler; clock-watcher, goldbrick, malingerer, shirker, slacker; dallier, lingerer, loiterer, loller, lounger, saunterer; delayer, procrastinator; dropout, quitter

near antonyms achiever, comer, highflier (*or* highflyer); live wire, powerhouse

antonyms doer, go-ahead, go-getter, hummer, hustler, rustler, self-starter

lea *or* **ley** *n* **1** a broad area of level or rolling treeless country ⟨across the *lea* rolls a lonely wagon⟩ — see PLAIN 1

2 open land over which livestock may roam and feed ⟨the cattle were free to range over the *lea*⟩ — see RANGE 1

lead *adj* highest in rank or authority ⟨the *lead* diplomat is responsible for making policy for the entire embassy⟩ — see HEAD

lead *n* **1** the person who has the most important role in a play, movie, or TV show ⟨the actor's career has really taken off since he became the *lead* in that prime-time drama⟩ — see STAR 2

2 the space or amount of space between two points, lines, surfaces, or objects ⟨the runner maintained a *lead* of several meters all the way around the track⟩ — see DISTANCE 1

3 a piece of advice or useful information especially from an expert ⟨my sister got a *lead* on the job opening from her neighbor, who is the human resources director for the company⟩ — see [1]TIP 1

4 a slight or indirect pointing to something (as a solution or explanation) ⟨the police are now working on several *leads* generated by the evidence gathered at the crime scene⟩ — see HINT 1

lead *vb* **1** to point out the way for (someone) especially from a position in front ⟨an enthusiastic docent *led* our group through the art museum⟩

synonyms conduct, direct, guide, marshal (*also* marshall), pilot, route, show, steer, usher

related words precede; accompany, attend, chaperone (*or* chaperon), convoy, escort, see; control, manage

near antonyms dog, hound, shadow, tail, tailgate

antonyms follow, trail

2 to serve as leader of ⟨a senior programmer is *leading* the team that is developing the new accounting software⟩

synonyms boss, captain, command, head, spearhead

related words control, dominate; direct, govern, handle, manage, oversee, regulate, run, superintend, supervise

near antonyms bow (to), comply (with), defer (to), follow, obey, serve, submit (to), yield (to)

3 to be at the front of ⟨the local high school's marching band *led* the parade⟩

synonyms head

related words precede; announce, herald; accompany, attend, escort, usher

near antonyms conclude, end, finish, stop, terminate; tail, tailgate; dog, follow, trail

4 to be positioned along a certain course or in a certain direction ⟨this old road *leads* to an abandoned quarry⟩ — see RUN 3

5 to give advice and instruction to (someone) regarding the course or process to be followed ⟨the salesclerk *led* us through the maze of options now available to television buyers⟩ — see GUIDE 1

leaden *adj* **1** causing weariness, restlessness, or lack of interest ⟨a *leaden* performance of a classic American play that nearly put us to sleep⟩ — see BORING

2 of the color gray ⟨the *leaden* sky made everything seem dark and depressing⟩ — see GRAY 1

leader *n* **1** a long hollow cylinder for carrying a substance (as a liquid or gas) ⟨the *leader* funnels water off of the roof and down into the cistern⟩ — see PIPE 1

2 the person (as an employer or supervisor) who tells people and especially workers what to do ⟨the team *leader* is good at making sure that everyone keeps busy at their assigned tasks⟩ — see BOSS

3 one that takes the lead or sets an example ⟨an architectural firm that is widely regarded as a *leader* in innovative residential design⟩ — see BELLWETHER

leading *adj* **1** coming before all others in importance ⟨they are the *leading* suppliers of processed meat in the country⟩ — see FOREMOST 1

2 highest in rank or authority ⟨served as the *leading* counsel on the defendant's legal team⟩ — see HEAD

leading edge *n* the leading or most important part of a movement ⟨an activist who is on the *leading edge* of the fight for equal marriage rights⟩ — see FOREFRONT

leadoff *adj* coming before all others in time or order ⟨the *leadoff* batter⟩ — see FIRST 1

lead off *vb* to take the first step in (a process or course of action) ⟨plans to *lead off* the news conference with a prepared statement⟩ — see BEGIN 1

lead on *vb* to lead away from a usual or proper course by offering some pleasure or advantage ⟨a con man whose dupes are usually *led on* by their own greed and eagerness to turn an easy buck⟩ — see LURE

leaf *vb* to turn over pages in an idle or cursory manner ⟨we must have spent hours *leafing* through wallpaper books before we found something we both liked⟩ — see SKIM 1

leafage *n* green leaves or plants ⟨the springtime *leafage* enveloping the park makes it seem much more private⟩ — see GREENERY

leaflet *n* a short printed publication with no cover or with a paper cover ⟨the company hires college students to work the phones and distribute *leaflets* for its clients⟩ — see PAMPHLET

leafy *adj* covered with a thick, healthy natural growth ⟨the backyard's *leafy* bushes look nice, but have a tendency to attract deer⟩ — see LUSH 1

league *n* **1** a group of persons formally joined together for some common interest ⟨a *league* of concerned parishioners who are seeking a greater voice in church affairs⟩ — see ASSOCIATION 2

2 an association of persons, parties, or states for mutual assistance and protection ⟨created to avert future wars, the *League* of Nations was a forerunner of the United Nations⟩ — see CONFEDERACY

3 one of the units into which a whole is divided on the basis of a common characteristic ⟨that falls into a different *league* of fiction—the popular novel⟩ — see CLASS 2

league *vb* **1** to form or enter into an association that furthers the interests of its members ⟨the whole block *leagued* together to keep a liquor store from opening in their neighborhood⟩ — see ALLY

2 to participate or assist in a joint effort to accomplish an end ⟨some unlikely political bedfellows *leagued* together to get the bill passed⟩ — see COOPERATE 1

leaguer *n* the cutting off of an area by military means to stop the flow of people or supplies ⟨Germany's abandonment of the *leaguer* of Stalingrad is seen as a major turning point of World War II⟩ — see BLOCKADE

leaguer *vb, archaic* to surround (as a fortified place) with armed forces for the purpose of capturing or preventing commerce and communication ⟨an impregnable fortress that not even the mightiest army on earth would venture to *leaguer*⟩ — see BESIEGE 1

leak (out) *vb* to become known ⟨the candidate's campaign didn't want his choice of a running mate to *leak out* before an official announcement was made⟩ — see GET OUT 1

leakproof *adj* unable to be penetrated by water because of construction or treated material ⟨the campers stayed dry in their *leakproof* tents⟩ — see WATERPROOF

lean *adj* having a noticeably small amount of body fat ⟨all of the marathoners are extremely *lean*⟩ — see THIN 1

lean *n* the degree to which something rises up from a

position level with the horizon ⟨the wall has enough of a *lean* that we can't set a bookcase against it⟩ — see SLANT

lean *vb* **1** to set or cause to be at an angle ⟨just *lean* the ladder against the tree and climb up it⟩
synonyms angle, cant, cock, heel, incline, list, pitch, slant, slope, tilt, tip
related words bank; bend, deviate, swerve, veer; decline, descend, recline, retreat
near antonyms even, flatten, level, straighten
2 to show a liking or proneness (for something) ⟨the family's diet *leans* toward greasy food⟩
synonyms incline, run, tend, trend
related words go, gravitate; indicate, point, suggest
near antonyms avoid, shun, shy (from *or* away from)
3 to place reliance or trust ⟨you can always *lean* on me if you need help⟩ — see DEPEND 2

lean (toward *or* towards) *vb* to show partiality toward ⟨I'm *leaning toward* sausage on our pizza tonight—we got pepperoni the last three times⟩ — see PREFER 1

leaning *adj* running in a slanting direction ⟨the *leaning* tower of Pisa is a popular tourist attraction in Italy⟩ — see DIAGONAL

leaning *n* **1** a prevailing or general movement or inclination ⟨the news media are often accused of having liberal *leanings*⟩ — see TREND 1
2 a habitual attraction to some activity or thing ⟨despite what his athletic *leanings* might suggest, he was actually a very lazy kid⟩ — see INCLINATION 1

leap *n* an act of leaping into the air ⟨the horse cleared the hurdle with a tremendous *leap*⟩ — see JUMP 1

leap *vb* to propel oneself upward or forward into the air ⟨the outfielder *leaped* into the air to catch the ball before it went over the fence⟩ — see JUMP 1

leaping *adj* passing from one topic to another ⟨we had trouble following the lecturer's *leaping* look at archaeological discoveries around the world⟩ — see DISCURSIVE

learn *vb* **1** to acquire complete knowledge, understanding, or skill in ⟨after months of trying, he finally *learned* the dance steps⟩
synonyms get, master, pick up
related words apprehend, comprehend, grasp, know, understand; absorb, assimilate, digest, drink (in), imbibe; ascertain, descry, detect, determine, dig up, discern, discover, examine, find out, hear, hit (on *or* upon), run down, scare up, search (for), see, track (down), tumble (to), unearth; major (in), study; memorize
phrases get the hang of
near antonyms forget; misunderstand; miss, overlook; disregard, ignore, neglect
antonyms unlearn
2 to come to an awareness of ⟨the directors have since *learned* that they should examine the company's financial reports a little more closely⟩ — see DISCOVER 1
3 to come upon after searching, study, or effort ⟨the police were astonished when they *learned* the identity of the students who had vandalized the school⟩ — see FIND 1
4 to commit to memory ⟨he *learned* the words to the song while performing karaoke⟩ — see MEMORIZE

learned *adj* **1** having or displaying advanced knowledge or education ⟨the *learned* professor can speak knowledgeably on a wide array of subjects⟩ — see EDUCATED 1
2 suggestive of the vocabulary used in books ⟨a teaching assistant who tries to impress us with all of his *learned* words⟩ — see BOOKISH

learnedness *n* the understanding and information gained from being educated ⟨the university's head librarian exuded an aura of *learnedness*⟩ — see EDUCATION 2

learning *n* the understanding and information gained from being educated ⟨the *learning* that you get from books is just as important as the experience you get from life⟩ — see EDUCATION 2

lease *vb* **1** to give the possession and use of (something) in return for periodic payment ⟨the landlord was willing to *lease* the apartment for less than we had expected⟩ — see RENT 1
2 to take or get the temporary use of (something) for a set sum ⟨I couldn't afford to buy a car outright, so I decided to *lease* one instead⟩ — see HIRE 1

leastways *adv, dialect* whatever else is done or is the case ⟨the minister is fixing to get married, *leastways* that's what everyone at the diner was saying⟩ — see ALWAYS 2

leastwise *adv* whatever else is done or is the case ⟨*leastwise* you have a job, and that's more than some folks can say⟩ — see ALWAYS 2

leather *n* **1** the hairless natural covering of an animal prepared for use ⟨the company claims to use only the finest *leathers* for its shoes and handbags⟩
synonyms hide, skin
related words coat, fleece, fur, pelt; alligator, antelope, buckskin, cabretta, calfskin, capeskin, chamois, cordovan, cowhide, crocodile, deerskin, doeskin, goatskin, horsehide, kid, kidskin, lambskin, morocco, ostrich, pigskin, seal, sharkskin, sheepskin, snakeskin; nubuck, patent leather, suede
2 the outer covering of an animal removed for its commercial value ⟨this jacket was made from real *leather*⟩ — see HIDE 1

leather *vb* to strike repeatedly with something long and thin or flexible ⟨an expert rider will find almost no reason to *leather* a horse⟩ — see WHIP 1

leathery *adj* not easily chewed ⟨the *leathery* meat served in the cafeteria drove many of us to start bringing our own lunches⟩ — see TOUGH 1

leave *n* **1** a period during which the usual routine of school or work is suspended ⟨the soldier was on *leave* for three days before having to report back to base⟩ — see VACATION
2 the approval by someone in authority for the doing of something ⟨the editor gave the reporters *leave* to follow up on their initial investigation of the senator's fund-raising practices⟩ — see PERMISSION
3 the act of leaving a place ⟨the party was clearly dying down, and it was time to take our *leave*⟩ — see DEPARTURE 1

leave *vb* **1** to cause to remain behind ⟨you can *leave* your lunch in the refrigerator while we're outside⟩ ⟨starry-eyed lovers who promise never to *leave* one another⟩
synonyms abandon, desert, forsake, maroon, quit, strand
related words discard, ditch, dump, fling, jettison, junk, scrap, shed, shuck (off), throw away, throw out; deliver, give up, hand over, relinquish, surrender, yield; escape, retreat (from), take off (from), vacate, withdraw (from); abjure, cut off, disown, reject, renounce, repudiate, separate (from); sacrifice; distance; disregard, forget, ignore, neglect
phrases walk away from, walk out on
near antonyms harbor, have, hold, keep, own, possess, reserve, retain, withhold; redeem, rescue, save
antonyms reclaim
2 to give by means of a will ⟨I'm going to *leave* all of my possessions to my children⟩
synonyms bequeath, will
related words deed; hand down, hand on, pass (down); devise
3 to give up (a job or office) ⟨he *left* his job in the city and moved out into the country⟩ — see QUIT 1

4 to put (something) into the possession or safekeeping of another ⟨why don't you *leave* your watch with me while you swim?⟩ — see GIVE 2
5 to end a usually intimate relationship with ⟨is there ever a good way to *leave* a lover?⟩ — see DITCH 1
6 to give permission to ⟨aw, *leave* him come⟩ — see ALLOW 2

leave off *vb* **1** to bring (as an action or operation) to an immediate end ⟨we usually *leave off* working as soon as the bell rings⟩ — see STOP 1
2 to come to an end ⟨the snow should *leave off* around midnight⟩ — see CEASE 1

leave–taking *n* **1** the act of leaving a place ⟨the *leave-taking* of the guest of honor was scheduled for 11 o'clock⟩ — see DEPARTURE 1
2 the act or process of two or more persons going off in different directions ⟨the sweethearts' *leave-taking* was filled with tearful pauses and promises to meet again⟩ — see PARTING 1

leavings *n pl* a remaining group or portion ⟨the *leavings* of the banquet were packed up and delivered to a shelter for the homeless⟩ — see REMAINDER 1

lech *n* sexual appetite ⟨a story about a detective with a nose for crime and a *lech* for redheads⟩ — see DESIRE 2

lecher *n* a man given to seducing women ⟨a friendly warning to the new assistant about the office *lecher*⟩ — see DON JUAN

lecherous *adj* having a strong sexual desire ⟨most of the male patrons at the bar appeared to be *lecherous* conventioneers looking for some action⟩ — see LUSTFUL

lecture *vb* **1** to criticize (someone) severely or angrily especially for personal failings ⟨the frustrated manager *lectured* the waitstaff about its poor level of service⟩ — see SCOLD
2 to give a formal often extended talk on a subject ⟨a physician who has *lectured* before countless women's groups on the importance of self-examination in the early detection of breast cancer⟩ — see TALK 1

lecturer *n* a person who makes usually formal public speeches ⟨this evening's *lecturer* has an uncanny ability to make highly abstruse material understandable to lay audiences⟩ — see ORATOR

leech *n* a person who is supported by or seeks support from another without making an adequate return ⟨whenever the gang went out for pizza, the *leech* in the group always had an excuse for not paying his fair share⟩
synonyms bloodsucker, freeloader, free rider, hanger-on, moocher, parasite, sponge, sponger
related words dependent; deadbeat, idler; flunky (*also* flunkey *or* flunkie), henchman, lackey, satellite, stooge, sycophant, toady, yes-man; cheapskate, miser, niggard, piker, scrooge, skinflint, tightwad
near antonyms benefactor, philanthropist, supporter

leer (at) *vb* to look at in a flirtatious or desiring way ⟨the boys would always *leer at* the girls in the swimming pool⟩ — see OGLE

leeward *adj* being in the direction that the wind is blowing ⟨we moved to the *leeward* side of the ship so that we wouldn't have the wind in our faces⟩ — see DOWNWIND

leeway *n* an allowable margin of freedom or variation ⟨you will be given some *leeway* in choosing how to carry out the project⟩ — see SLACK 1

left *n* a political belief stressing progress, the essential goodness of humankind, and individual freedom ⟨a rising politician who is being hailed as the new voice of the *left*⟩ — see LIBERALISM

left–handed *adj* **1** lacking or showing a lack of nimbleness in using one's hands ⟨I'd rather have no help at all than have his *left-handed* "assistance"⟩ — see CLUMSY 1
2 not being or expressing what one appears to be or express ⟨failed to realize that he had received a *left-handed* compliment⟩ — see INSINCERE

leftism *n* a political belief stressing progress, the essential goodness of humankind, and individual freedom ⟨the candidate's opponents are working overtime to paint him as a champion of extreme *leftism*⟩ — see LIBERALISM

leftover *n* **1** an unused or unwanted piece or item typically of small size or value ⟨that doormat is just a *leftover* from when the new carpet was installed⟩ — see [1]SCRAP 1
2 leftovers *pl* a remaining group or portion ⟨take as many of these calendars as you want, and put the *leftovers* back on the shelf⟩ — see REMAINDER 1

left wing *n* a political belief stressing progress, the essential goodness of humankind, and individual freedom ⟨the *left wing* has lost considerable influence in the party, which is now aggressively courting political moderates⟩ — see LIBERALISM

leg *n* **1** a lower limb of an animal ⟨he broke his *leg* when he accidentally stepped in that gopher hole⟩
synonyms pin
related words member; foreleg, forelimb; calf, drumstick, ham, shank, shin, thigh
2 a portion of a trip ⟨on the first *leg* of the cruise they went south to the Caribbean⟩
synonyms lap, stage
related words layover, stopover

leg (it) *vb* to go on foot ⟨the car was in the shop so we had to *leg it* to work for a couple of days⟩ — see WALK 1

legacy *n* something that is or may be inherited ⟨the old locket was part of the *legacy* from my great-great-grandmother⟩ — see INHERITANCE

legal *adj* **1** permitted by law ⟨the congressman's fund-raising efforts, though arguably unethical, were determined to be *legal*⟩
synonyms lawful, legit [*slang*], legitimate, licit
related words allowable, authorized, noncriminal, permissible; justifiable, warrantable; constitutional; de jure, regulation, statutory; good, innocent, just, proper, right
near antonyms bad, corrupt, evil, immoral, iniquitous, reprobate, sinful, wicked, wrong; banned, criminal, forbidden, guilty, impermissible, outlawed, prohibited, unauthorized, unjust; under-the-counter, under-the-table; nonconstitutional, unconstitutional
antonyms illegal, illegitimate, illicit, lawless, unlawful, wrongful
2 following or according to the rules ⟨the referee declared it a *legal* play⟩ — see FAIR 3

legal eagle *n* a person whose profession is to conduct lawsuits for clients or to advise about legal rights and obligations ⟨the actor hired a dream team of high-priced *legal eagles* to help him beat the murder rap⟩ — see LAWYER

legality *n* the quality or state of being legal ⟨the senator questioned the *legality* of the proposed espionage operation⟩
synonyms lawfulness, legitimacy
related words rightfulness, rightness; permissibility, permissibleness
near antonyms badness, immorality, iniquitousness, iniquity, sinfulness, unjustness, wickedness, wrongness; criminality, unconstitutionality
antonyms illegality, illegitimacy, unlawfulness, wrongfulness

legally *adv* according to the rules or the law ⟨that's not a move that can be made *legally* in chess⟩ — see FAIRLY 2

legal tender *n* something (as pieces of stamped metal or printed paper) customarily and legally used as a medium of exchange, a measure of value, or a means of payment ⟨coins and bills are considered *legal tender*, but postage stamps are not⟩ — see MONEY 1

legate *n* a person sent on a mission to represent another ⟨the *legate* was charged with a list of objectives to accomplish on behalf of his country⟩ — see AMBASSADOR

legatee *n* a person who has the right to inherit property ⟨the couple had no children, so they declared their nephew their only *legatee*⟩ — see HEIR

legend *n* **1** an explanatory list of the symbols on a map or chart ⟨the *legend* indicated that a large circle represented a major city, while a small circle stood for a small town⟩
synonyms key
related words scale; caption; guide, table
2 an explanation or description accompanying a pictorial illustration ⟨the *legend* in the science textbook indicated that the accompanying picture had been enlarged by 1000%⟩ — see CAPTION 1
3 a traditional but unfounded story that gives the reason for a current custom, belief, or fact of nature ⟨some ancient civilizations had *legends* about spirits that inhabited trees and rocks⟩ — see MYTH 1
4 the body of customs, beliefs, stories, and sayings associated with a people, thing, or place ⟨that story of how the world came to be has long been part of Native American *legend*⟩ — see FOLKLORE

legendary *adj* based on, described in, or being a myth ⟨the unicorn is a *legendary* creature⟩ — see MYTHICAL 1

legendry *n* the body of customs, beliefs, stories, and sayings associated with a people, thing, or place ⟨although the historic King Arthur lived in the sixth century, most of the *legendry* regarding him and the Knights of the Round Table is set in the far more romantic age of medieval chivalry⟩ — see FOLKLORE

legerdemain *n* **1** the art or skill of performing tricks or illusions for entertainment ⟨the illusionist's show is an entertaining blend of *legerdemain* and over-the-top showmanship⟩ — see MAGIC 2
2 the use of clever underhanded actions to achieve an end ⟨the reduction of the deficit is due in part to financial *legerdemain* that masks the true costs of running the government⟩ — see TRICKERY

legible *adj* capable of being understood ⟨an anxious mood that was clearly *legible* upon her face⟩ — see INTELLIGIBLE

legion *adj* being of a large but indefinite number ⟨the obstacles that the programmers had to overcome have been *legion*⟩ — see MANY

legion *n* **1** a large body of men and women organized for land warfare ⟨joined the French Foreign *Legion*⟩ — see ARMY 1
2 a great number of persons or creatures massed together ⟨*legions* of fans crowded the stadium for the rock concert⟩ — see CROWD 1

legionary *n* a person engaged in military service ⟨the daring exploits of the French *legionaries* have long been the stuff of literary and cinematic legend⟩ — see SOLDIER

legionnaire *n* a person engaged in military service ⟨the *legionnaires* are well respected for their fighting prowess⟩ — see SOLDIER

legislate *vb* to put into effect through legislative or authoritative action ⟨wants the Congress to *legislate* new laws banning the use of these types of weapons⟩ — see ENACT

legislator *n* a member of an organized body of persons having the authority to make laws ⟨the *legislators* met in an all-night session to hammer out the details of the bill⟩
synonyms lawgiver, lawmaker, solon
related words assemblyman, assemblywoman; congressman, congresswoman; senator

legit *adj, slang* permitted by law ⟨the barbershop, which appears to be a *legit* operation, is actually a front for a local mobster⟩ — see LEGAL 1

legitimacy *n* the quality or state of being legal ⟨the *legitimacy* of the military dictatorship was not recognized by most other nations⟩ — see LEGALITY

legitimate *adj* permitted by law ⟨the mistrust created among investors by the financial scandal has hurt even companies engaged in wholly *legitimate* business practices⟩ — see LEGAL 1

leg up *n* an act or instance of helping ⟨a key endorsement that would give the struggling candidate a real *leg up* right now⟩ — see HELP 1

lei *n* an ornamental chain or string (as of beads) worn around the neck ⟨we were presented with flowery *leis* as soon as we stepped off the plane in Hawaii⟩ — see NECKLACE

leisure *n* freedom from activity or labor ⟨upon retiring, the elderly couple looked forward to a life of well-deserved *leisure*⟩ — see ^{1}REST 1

leisurely *adj* moving or proceeding at less than the normal, desirable, or required speed ⟨after buying our stuff, we just wandered around the mall at a *leisurely* pace⟩ — see SLOW 1

leisurely *adv* at a pace that is less than usual, desirable, or expected ⟨the old hound dog *leisurely* sauntered over to his water bowl to take a drink⟩ — see SLOW

lemon *n* something that has failed ⟨the used car he bought turned out to be a *lemon*, and he soon had trouble starting the thing⟩ — see FAILURE 3

lend *vb* to give to another for temporary use with the understanding that it or a like thing will be returned ⟨I can *lend* you my copy of the textbook until the weekend⟩ ⟨can you *lend* me five dollars?⟩
synonyms advance, loan
related words furnish, give, grant; lease, let [*chiefly British*], rent
near antonyms receive, take
antonyms borrow

length *n* **1** a wide space or area ⟨vowed that he would journey the *lengths* of the earth to find her⟩ — see EXPANSE
2 the space or amount of space between two points, lines, surfaces, or objects ⟨the *length* of a professional tennis court is 78 feet from baseline to baseline⟩ — see DISTANCE 1

lengthen *vb* to make longer ⟨I had to *lengthen* the handle of the paint roller in order to reach the top of the wall⟩ — see EXTEND 1

lengthening *n* the act of making longer ⟨a *lengthening* of the school year is favored by many of the parents in the school district⟩ — see EXTENSION 1

lengthy *adj* **1** of great extent from end to end ⟨she used a *lengthy* piece of rope to tie her dog to a tree⟩ — see LONG 1
2 lasting for a considerable time ⟨the store manager gives new associates a *lengthy* sermon on the evils of shoplifting⟩ — see LONG 2

lenience *n* kind, gentle, or compassionate treatment especially towards someone who is undeserving of it ⟨a judge's reputation for *lenience* towards first-time criminals⟩ — see MERCY 1

leniency *n* kind, gentle, or compassionate treatment especially towards someone who is undeserving of it ⟨the defense requested *leniency* in light of their client's lack of a prior criminal record⟩ — see MERCY 1

lenity *n* kind, gentle, or compassionate treatment especially towards someone who is undeserving of it ⟨a social critic who argues that judicial *lenity* is chiefly to blame for the increased criminality that plagues us⟩ — see MERCY 1

lensman *n* one who takes photographs ⟨an expert *lensman* whose work has appeared in dozens of magazines⟩ — see PHOTOGRAPHER

leper *n* one who is cast out or rejected by society ⟨a convicted child molester who is treated as a *leper* wherever he goes⟩ — see OUTCAST

leprechaun *n* an imaginary being usually having a small human form and magical powers ⟨the story that if you follow a rainbow to its end, you'll find a *leprechaun's* pot of gold⟩ — see FAIRY

leprechaunish *adj* tending to or exhibiting reckless playfulness ⟨he broke into a *leprechaunish* grin at the mere thought of his devilish plan for revenge⟩ — see MISCHIEVOUS 1

less *adj* having not so great importance or rank as another ⟨the restaurant's chowder has been declared the state's best by no *less* a person than the governor himself⟩ — see LESSER

lessee *n* one who rents a room or apartment in another's house ⟨the *lessee* has the right to expect the lessor to make all necessary repairs in a timely manner⟩ — see TENANT 1

lessen *vb* **1** to make smaller in amount, volume, or extent ⟨we *lessened* our efforts as it became clear they weren't having an effect⟩ — see DECREASE 1

2 to grow less in scope or intensity especially gradually ⟨the pain should begin to *lessen* within minutes of taking the medication⟩ — see DECREASE 2

3 to lower in character, dignity, or quality ⟨blatant hypocrisy that *lessened* him in the eyes of the voters⟩ — see DEBASE 1

lesser *adj* having not so great importance or rank as another ⟨it was the *lesser* evil of the two choices⟩

synonyms inferior, junior, less, lower, minor, smaller, subordinate

related words little, mean, small; minute, petty; jerkwater, one-horse, second-class, second-rate, two-bit; associate, auxiliary, secondary, subsidiary

near antonyms choice, exceptional, first-class, first-rate

antonyms greater, higher, major, more, primary, prime, senior, superior, superordinate

lesson *n* something assigned to be read or studied ⟨your *lesson* for tonight will be the chapter on chemical reactions⟩

synonyms assignment, reading

related words homework, schoolwork; lecture; drill, exercise, practice (*also* practise); étude, study

lesson *vb* to cause to acquire knowledge or skill in some field ⟨would tirelessly *lesson* the children in proper manners⟩ — see TEACH

lessor *n* the owner of land or housing that is rented to another ⟨*lessors* are free to charge as much as they want for a house⟩ — see LANDLORD 1

let *n* something that makes movement or progress difficult ⟨a private resort that allows vacationers to experience without *let* the joys of nudism⟩ — see ENCUMBRANCE

let *vb* **1** to give permission to ⟨my parents would not *let* me drive until I had a job and could pay for my own gas⟩ — see ALLOW

2 *chiefly British* to give the possession and use of (something) in return for periodic payment ⟨the pensioner has begun *letting* rooms in her East End home to earn some extra money⟩ — see RENT 1

3 to make able or possible ⟨the low gravity on the moon *lets* you make enormous leaps and jumps⟩ — see ENABLE 1

4 to fail to prevent (some behavior on someone's part) especially from neglect or indifference ⟨they *let* their kids get away with murder⟩ — see ALLOW 3

let alone *conj* to say nothing of ⟨I don't have enough money for a new car, *let alone* a luxury sedan⟩

synonyms much less, never mind, still less

phrases not to mention

letch *n* **1** a strong wish for something ⟨a sudden *letch* for chocolate⟩ — see DESIRE 1

2 sexual appetite ⟨she's developed quite a *letch* for that movie star—and he's young enough to be her son⟩ — see DESIRE 2

letdown *n* **1** the emotion felt when one's expectations are not met ⟨the museum exhibit was just so-so, and we returned home with a vague sense of *letdown*⟩ — see DISAPPOINTMENT 1

2 something that disappoints ⟨the eagerly anticipated new movie starring our favorite actor turned out to be a big *letdown*⟩ — see DISAPPOINTMENT 2

let down *vb* to fall short in satisfying the expectation or hope of ⟨with my poor performance I really felt that I had *let* my teammates *down*⟩ — see DISAPPOINT

lethal *adj* likely to cause or capable of causing death ⟨we were lucky that the snake's venom wasn't *lethal*, and our friend turned out to be all right⟩ — see DEADLY 1

lethargic *adj* slow to move or act ⟨a big meal always makes me feel *lethargic* and sleepy⟩ — see INACTIVE 1

lethargy *n* physical or mental inertness ⟨the doctor suspected that the patient's depression and *lethargy* were a result of seasonal affective disorder⟩

synonyms hebetude, languor, lassitude, listlessness, stupor, torpor

related words boredom, indifference; malaise; laziness; fatigue, sleepiness; narcosis; idleness, inaction

near antonyms eagerness, enthusiasm, keenness, spiritedness; ambition, enterprise

antonyms vigor, vim, vitality, vivacity

let on *vb* to take on a false or deceptive appearance ⟨she's not half as innocent as she likes to *let on*⟩ — see PRETEND 1

let on (about) *vb* to make known (as information previously kept secret) ⟨we agreed not to *let on about* our marriage plans to anyone⟩ — see REVEAL 1

[1]**letter** *n* a message on paper from one person or group to another ⟨he faithfully wrote her a *letter* every week they were apart⟩

synonyms dispatch, epistle, memo, memorandum, missive, note

related words billet-doux, open letter; airmail, card, electronic mail, e-mail, junk mail, mail, postal card, postcard; communication, report; encyclical

[2]**letter** *n* the owner of land or housing that is rented to another ⟨it is the *letter* of the apartment—not the lessee—who is responsible for basic repair and upkeep⟩ — see LANDLORD 1

letter carrier *n* a person who delivers mail ⟨we like to leave a little gift in the mailbox around Christmas for our *letter carrier*⟩ — see POSTMAN

lettered *adj* having or displaying advanced knowledge or education ⟨the *lettered* crowd is well acquainted with the author, but the average person probably hasn't heard of him⟩ — see EDUCATED 1

letter-perfect *adj* being entirely without fault or flaw ⟨the actress's recitation was *letter-perfect*⟩ — see PERFECT 1

letup *n* a usually gradual decrease in the pace or level of activity of something ⟨the downpour continued for hours without *letup*⟩ — see SLOWDOWN

let up *vb* **1** to come to an end ⟨the rain *let up* just as we reached the house⟩ — see CEASE 1

2 to grow less in scope or intensity especially gradually ⟨the windmill slowed down as the wind *let up*⟩ — see DECREASE 2

levee *n* **1** a bank of earth constructed to control water

⟨the raging floodwaters were too much for the *levee* to handle⟩ — see DAM

2 a structure used by boats and ships for taking on or landing cargo and passengers ⟨we tied the boat up at the *levee* and started unloading the fish we had caught⟩ — see DOCK

level *adj* **1** having a surface without bends, breaks, or irregularities ⟨looked for a *level* place to land the plane⟩
synonyms even, flat, flush, plane, smooth
related words exact, uniform; aligned (*also* alined), regular, true; horizontal, tabular; plumb, straight, vertical
near antonyms inexact, irregular, unaligned, warped; undulating, undulatory, wavy; pitted, pockmarked, pocky
antonyms bumpy, coarse, lumpy, rough, uneven, unsmoothed

2 free from emotional or mental agitation ⟨in a much more *level* mood now that the worst is over⟩ — see CALM 2

level *n* the placement of someone or something in relation to others in a vertical arrangement ⟨a young karate student ready to rise to the next *level* in his chosen art of self-defense⟩ — see RANK 1

level *vb* **1** to make equal in amount, degree, or status ⟨we'll give both teams the same equipment so as to *level* the playing field⟩ — see EQUALIZE

2 to make free from breaks, curves, or bumps ⟨the construction workers *leveled* the ground before laying a foundation for the new house⟩ — see EVEN 1

3 to point or turn (something) toward a target or goal ⟨the marksman *leveled* his gun at the target and fired⟩ — see AIM 1

4 to strike (someone) so forcefully as to cause a fall ⟨the boxer *leveled* his badly outclassed opponent with a single blow⟩ — see FELL 1

5 to destroy (as a building) completely by knocking down or breaking to pieces ⟨an architectural gem that was *leveled* to build a parking lot⟩ — see DEMOLISH 1

leveler *or* **leveller** *n* one who advocates or practices social equality ⟨a nation of *levelers*, Norway has a tax structure designed to reduce the gap between the richest and the poorest⟩ — see DEMOCRAT

levelheaded *adj* based on sound reasoning or information ⟨I've always appreciated my father's *levelheaded* advice⟩ — see GOOD 1

levelheadedness *n* the ability to make intelligent decisions especially in everyday matters ⟨the judge had developed a reputation for no-nonsense *levelheadedness* in deciding cases⟩ — see COMMON SENSE

lever *vb* to raise, move, or pull apart with or as if with a lever ⟨the workers used crowbars to *lever* the heavy stone block into its new position⟩ — see [1]PRY 1

leverage *n* the power to direct the thinking or behavior of others usually indirectly ⟨lacking much of the *leverage* it once had, the union is now being forced to make some humiliating concessions⟩ — see INFLUENCE 1

leverage *vb* to take unfair advantage of ⟨a reality show contestant who's trying to *leverage* her 15 minutes of fame⟩ — see EXPLOIT 1

leviathan *adj* unusually large ⟨the Titanic was a *leviathan* ship by the standards of the time⟩ — see HUGE

leviathan *n* something that is unusually large and powerful ⟨a *leviathan* of the seas, that cruise ship is said to be the largest passenger vessel afloat⟩ — see GIANT

levity *n* a lack of seriousness often at an improper time ⟨the teachers disapprove of any displays of *levity* during school assemblies⟩ — see FRIVOLITY 1

levy *n* a charge usually of money collected by the government from people or businesses for public use ⟨the legislators approved a new *levy* on imported cattle to help protect American ranchers⟩ — see TAX

levy *vb* **1** to pick especially for required military service ⟨unprepared for war, the government was forced to *levy* men on a scale that was unprecedented in its history⟩ — see DRAFT 1

2 to establish or apply as a charge or penalty ⟨the baseball commissioner is *levying* a fine of $10,000 against every player involved in the fracas⟩ — see IMPOSE

lewd *adj* **1** depicting or referring to sexual matters in a way that is unacceptable in polite society ⟨bystanders were shocked by the *lewd* behavior of the couple in the park⟩ — see OBSCENE 1

2 having a strong sexual desire ⟨with his unwelcome advances, the *lewd* executive had alienated all of the women in the office⟩ — see LUSTFUL

3 hinting at or intended to call to mind matters regarded as indecent ⟨a nearby diner kept telling *lewd* jokes until we told him to shut up⟩ — see SUGGESTIVE 1

lewdness *n* the quality or state of being obscene ⟨the *lewdness* of the material on that Web site makes it inappropriate for children⟩ — see OBSCENITY 1

lexical *adj* of or relating to words or language ⟨a dictionary provides *lexical* information—it tells you what the word "cat" means, not all there is to know about cats⟩ — see VERBAL 1

lexicon *n* a reference book giving information about the meanings, pronunciations, uses, and origins of words listed in alphabetical order ⟨an avid word enthusiast who is compiling a *lexicon* of archaic and unusual words⟩ — see DICTIONARY

liability *n* **1** a feature of someone or something that creates difficulty for achieving success ⟨a retired football player whose chief asset—his prodigious girth—has now become a *liability*⟩ — see DISADVANTAGE 1

2 the state of being held as the cause of something that needs to be set right ⟨the *liability* for the accident is held by the person who was driving too fast⟩ — see RESPONSIBILITY 1

3 the state of being left without shelter or protection against something harmful ⟨failure to properly clean the wound could increase your *liability* to infection⟩ — see EXPOSURE 1

4 the quality or state of being likely to occur ⟨what's the *liability* that he'll file a formal complaint if he's refused admission?⟩ — see PROBABILITY 1

5 *usually* **liabilities** *pl* something (as money) which is owed ⟨your *liabilities* total about $200,000⟩ — see DEBT 1

liable *adj* **1** being in a situation where one is likely to meet with harm ⟨because of his frail constitution, he's *liable* to diseases⟩
synonyms endangered, exposed, open, sensitive, subject (to), susceptible, vulnerable
related words likely, prone; uncovered, undefended, unguarded, unprotected, unscreened, unsecured
phrases at risk, in deep water, in jeopardy
near antonyms covered, guarded, protected, safeguarded, screened, secured, sheltered, shielded, warded
antonyms insusceptible, invulnerable, unexposed, unsusceptible

2 being the one who must meet an obligation or suffer the consequences for failing to do so ⟨the owner of a pet is *liable* for any damage that that pet might do⟩ — see RESPONSIBLE 1

liaison *n* **1** the fact or state of having something in common ⟨a variety of political factions are attracted to that presidential contender, but there doesn't appear to be much of a *liaison* between them and the candidate⟩ — see CONNECTION 1

2 the state of having shared interests or efforts (as in social or business matters) ⟨the strong *liaison* between the parents and teachers is based on the fact that both have the students' best interests at heart⟩ — see ASSOCIATION 1

liar *n* a person who tells lies ⟨she knew he was a *liar* when he started claiming that he was an astronaut⟩
synonyms fabricator, fabulist, fibber, prevaricator, storyteller
related words exaggerator, mythomaniac; calumniator, defamer, libeler, libelist, slanderer; perjurer; distorter, falsifier; equivocator, palterer; gossip, gossiper, talebearer; charlatan, cheat, cheater, counterfeiter, cozener, deceiver, defrauder, dissembler, dissimulator, double-dealer, fraud, hustler, knave, mountebank, operator, pretender
near antonyms square shooter

libation *n* a liquid suitable for drinking ⟨a variety of *libations* will be available at the wedding reception⟩ — see DRINK 1

libel *n* the making of false statements that damage another's reputation ⟨the governor's office issued a statement accusing the state's largest newspaper of *libel*⟩ — see SLANDER

libel *vb* to make untrue and harmful statements about ⟨the court decided that the newspaper's reportage of the former mayor, while irresponsible, did not constitute an effort to *libel* him⟩ — see SLANDER

libeling *or* **libelling** *n* the making of false statements that damage another's reputation ⟨the underhanded politician resorted to *libeling* when it became clear that that was the only way he was going to win the election⟩ — see SLANDER

libelous *or* **libellous** *adj* causing or intended to cause unjust injury to a person's good name ⟨*libelous* statements about a celebrity for which the tabloid was sued⟩
synonyms calumnious, defamatory, scandalous, slanderous
related words erroneous, false, inaccurate, incorrect, inexact, invalid, off, unsound, untrue, wrong; denigrative, denigratory, depreciative, depreciatory, derogatory, detractive, disparaging, uncomplimentary, unfavorable, unflattering; invidious, objectionable; maligning, traducing, vilifying; hateful, malevolent, malicious, spiteful
near antonyms appreciative, complimentary, favorable; adulatory, commendatory, eulogistic, hagiographic (*also* hagiographical), laudatory; accurate, correct, errorless, factual, right, sound, true, valid

liberal *adj* **1** not bound by traditional ways or beliefs ⟨parents who take a very *liberal* attitude toward letting their children stay out late⟩
synonyms broad-minded, nonconventional, nonorthodox, nontraditional, open-minded, progressive, radical, unconventional, unorthodox
related words advanced, contemporary, modern; forbearing, indulgent, large-minded, lenient, permissive, tolerant; extreme; impartial, objective, unbiased
near antonyms hard, rigid, strict; doctrinal, dogmatic (*also* dogmatical); bigoted, blinkered, intolerant, narrow-minded; reactionary, unreconstructed
antonyms conservative, conventional, hidebound, nonprogressive, old-fashioned, orthodox, stodgy, traditional
2 being more than enough without being excessive ⟨he always puts *liberal* amounts of grated cheese on his pizza⟩ — see PLENTIFUL
3 giving or sharing in abundance and without hesitation ⟨a doctor who has been very *liberal* in dispensing low-cost care to patients who could not otherwise afford it⟩ — see GENEROUS 1

liberalism *n* a political belief stressing progress, the essential goodness of humankind, and individual freedom ⟨*liberalism* had always claimed to stand for the greatest social good⟩
synonyms left, leftism, left wing
related words neoliberalism; radicalism, socialism
near antonyms neoconservatism
antonyms conservatism, illiberalism, immobilism, right

liberality *n* the quality or state of being generous ⟨already known for his *liberality*, the billionaire continued to give away record amounts of money⟩
synonyms bigheartedness, bountifulness, bounty, generosity, generousness, largesse (*also* largess), munificence, openhandedness, openheartedness, philanthropy, unselfishness
related words beneficence, charity, kindliness, selflessness; kindness; gift, gratuity, lagniappe; tribute; extravagance, improvidence, lavishness, prodigality, wastefulness; spendthrift; dissipating, squandering
near antonyms conserving, economizing, economy, frugality, husbandry, providence, scrimping, skimping, thrift; conservation, saving; husbanding, managing; scraping; cutting back
antonyms cheapness, closeness, meanness, miserliness, parsimony, penuriousness, pinching, selfishness, stinginess, tightness, ungenerosity

liberally *adv* in a generous manner ⟨she spread frosting *liberally* over the cake until it oozed over the edges⟩ — see WELL 2

liberate *vb* **1** to set free (as from slavery or confinement) ⟨the animal rightists snuck into the laboratory in the middle of the night to *liberate* all of the monkeys⟩ — see FREE 1
2 to set free from entanglement or difficulty ⟨we were *liberated* from our financial woes when we hit the grand prize in the lottery⟩ — see EXTRICATE

liberation *n* the act of setting free from slavery ⟨the *liberation* of the slaves was one of the key results of the Civil War⟩
synonyms emancipation, enfranchisement, freeing, manumission
related words deliverance, redemption, salvation; autonomy, freedom, independence, independency, liberty, self-government, sovereignty (*also* sovranty)
near antonyms bondage, serfdom, servitude, thralldom (*or* thraldom), yoke; captivity, enchainment, imprisonment, incarceration, internment; conquest, subjugation
antonyms enslavement

libertinage *n* **1** a sinking to a state of low moral standards and behavior ⟨his frat-boy *libertinage* was abruptly halted when his fed-up father cut him off financially⟩ — see CORRUPTION 2
2 immoral conduct or practices harmful or offensive to society ⟨a young prince more interested in *libertinage* than leadership⟩ — see VICE 1

libertine *adj* having or showing lowered moral character or standards ⟨his *libertine* sister had got caught up in the urban drug scene and had died of an overdose⟩ — see CORRUPT

libertine *n* a person who has sunk below the normal moral standard ⟨the legend of Don Juan depicts him as a playboy and *libertine*⟩ — see DEGENERATE

libertinism *n* **1** a sinking to a state of low moral standards and behavior ⟨a group of urban bohemians who were better known for their *libertinism* than for their intellectualism⟩ — see CORRUPTION 2
2 immoral conduct or practices harmful or offensive to society ⟨even by the standards of ancient Rome, Caligula's reign was marked by a *libertinism* that went beyond the pale⟩ — see VICE 1

liberty *n* **1** the power, right, or opportunity to choose ⟨he doesn't want to go to the sales conference, but he doesn't have that *liberty*⟩ — see CHOICE 1
2 the state of being free from the control or power of

another ⟨the hope that the country's first-ever elections will usher in a new era of *liberty* and respect for the rule of law⟩ — see FREEDOM 1

libidinous *adj* having a strong sexual desire ⟨a novel about a *libidinous* lawyer who becomes an abject slave to his sexual addiction⟩ — see LUSTFUL

libidinousness *n* sexual appetite ⟨an expression of raging *libidinousness* that would have been worthy of a whole company of soldiers⟩ — see DESIRE 2

library *n* **1** a place where books, periodicals, and records are kept for use but not for sale ⟨I went to the *library* to do some research for my report⟩
synonyms archive
related words rental library (*or* lending library); bibliotheca; stacks
2 an organized group of objects acquired and maintained for study, exhibition, or personal pleasure ⟨a confirmed cineast with an impressive *library* of classic movies on DVD⟩ — see COLLECTION 1

license *also* **licence** *vb* to give official or legal power to ⟨a state statute *licenses* county sheriffs to choose their own deputies⟩ — see AUTHORIZE 1

license *or* **licence** *n* **1** the approval by someone in authority for the doing of something ⟨the company is seeking *license* to operate several more power plants in the state⟩ — see PERMISSION
2 the granting of power to perform various acts or duties ⟨a restaurant owner has to get a *license* to serve food and drink⟩ — see COMMISSION 1
3 the right to act or move freely ⟨military commanders on the ground must be granted considerable *license*, as wars cannot be micromanaged by people back in Washington⟩ — see FREEDOM 2

licentious *adj* having a strong sexual desire ⟨a moralist who decried what she regarded as the *licentious* and corrupt culture of the entertainment industry⟩ — see LUSTFUL

licentiousness *n* immoral conduct or practices harmful or offensive to society ⟨our minister often condemns the *licentiousness* he sees cavalierly portrayed in today's mass media⟩ — see VICE 1

licit *adj* permitted by law ⟨law enforcement agencies are demanding stricter regulation of the sale of *licit* medications that can later be used in the home manufacture of illicit drugs⟩ — see LEGAL 1

lick *n* **1** a hard strike with a part of the body or an instrument ⟨gave the ball a solid *lick* with the bat⟩ — see [1]BLOW
2 a very small amount ⟨the soup needs just a *lick* more of salt⟩ — see PARTICLE 1
3 the smallest amount or part imaginable ⟨you haven't done a *lick* of work all day⟩ — see JOT

lick *vb* **1** to strike repeatedly ⟨your father will *lick* you good if he hears you using swear words⟩ — see BEAT 1
2 to achieve a victory over ⟨he's determined to do everything he can to *lick* the cancer⟩ — see BEAT 2

lickety-split *adv* with great speed ⟨the scared dog ran *lickety-split* for home⟩ — see FAST 1

licking *n* failure to win a contest ⟨our team took a *licking* last night, but we'll get them next time⟩ — see DEFEAT 1

lickspittle *n* a person who flatters another in order to get ahead ⟨a partisan news program whose host is more of a *lickspittle* for the White House than a serious journalist⟩ — see SYCOPHANT

lid *n* **1** a piece placed over an open container to hold in, protect, or conceal its contents ⟨I had to get a screwdriver to pry the *lid* off of the paint can⟩ — see COVER 1
2 *slang* a covering for the head usually having a shaped crown ⟨as he left the field, the pitcher tipped his *lid* to the cheering crowd⟩ — see HAT

lie *n* a statement known by its maker to be untrue and made in order to deceive ⟨he wanted to deny the accusation, but he couldn't tell a *lie*⟩
synonyms fable, fabrication, fairy tale, falsehood, falsity, fib, mendacity, prevarication, story, tale, taradiddle (*or* tarradiddle), untruth, whopper
related words distortion, exaggeration, half-truth; ambiguity, equivocation, obliquity; defamation, libel, slander; perjury; bluff, fiction, pose, pretense (*or* pretence); humbug, jive, nonsense; canard, fallacy, misconception, myth; falsification, misinformation, misreport, misrepresentation, misstatement; deceit, deceitfulness, dishonesty, duplicity, fraudulence
near antonyms fact, truism, verity; honesty, truthfulness, veracity; authentication, confirmation, substantiation, validation, verification
antonyms truth

[1]lie *vb* to make a statement one knows to be untrue ⟨would I *lie* to you about that?⟩
synonyms fabricate, fib, prevaricate
related words forswear (*also* foreswear), perjure; equivocate, fudge, palter; beguile, cozen, deceive, delude, dupe, fool, gull, hoax, hoodwink, kid, snow, take in, trick; defame, libel, slander, traduce; falsify, misreport, misrepresent, misstate; distort, garble; dissemble, dissimulate; misguide, misinform, mislead
near antonyms assert, swear, testify; authenticate, confirm, substantiate, validate, verify

[2]lie *vb* **1** to be positioned along a certain course or in a certain direction ⟨the train tracks *lie* just over that hill⟩ — see RUN 3
2 to occupy a place or location ⟨I left the book *lying* on the counter⟩ — see STAND 1
3 to remain out of sight ⟨paparazzi were *lying* in wait outside the restaurant, a well-known celebrity hangout⟩ — see [1]HIDE 3

lie detector *n* an instrument for detecting physical signs of the tension that goes with lying ⟨hooked the suspect up to a *lie detector* before interrogating him about the robbery⟩
synonyms polygraph

liege man *n* one who follows the opinions or teachings of another ⟨a highly influential anthropologist whose *liege men* can now be found be a score of major universities⟩ — see FOLLOWER 1

lieutenant *n* a person who helps a more skilled person ⟨the drug lord has a pair of brutal *lieutenants* who do most of his dirty work for him⟩ — see HELPER

life *n* **1** a history of a person's life ⟨a renowned historian who has written *lives* of several early presidents⟩ — see BIOGRAPHY
2 a member of the human race ⟨an appalling number of *lives* were lost in the war⟩ — see HUMAN
3 active strength of body or mind ⟨even though he's 86 years old, he still shows a lot of *life*⟩ — see VIGOR 1
4 the period during which something exists, lasts, or is in progress ⟨the Egyptian civilization had an extremely long *life*⟩ — see DURATION 1
5 the way people live at a particular time and place ⟨frontier *life* must have been rugged, exciting, challenging, and more than a little dangerous⟩ — see CIVILIZATION 1

lifeless *adj* no longer living ⟨the kayaker's *lifeless* body was found just downstream of the rapids where he had capsized⟩ — see DEAD 1

lifelessness *n* the state of being dead ⟨the sight of her husband's corpse, in all of its embalmed *lifelessness*, was heartbreaking⟩ — see DEATH 2

lifelike *adj* closely resembling the object imitated ⟨the eyes of the *lifelike* portrait seem to follow visitors around the room⟩ — see NATURAL 2

life span *n* the period during which something exists, lasts, or is in progress ⟨I saw no need to pay more for a better-built computer that would just grow obsolete before the end of its *life span*⟩ — see DURATION 1

lifestyle *n* the way people live at a particular time and place ⟨retirees enjoying a more casual, stress-free *lifestyle*⟩ — see CIVILIZATION 1

lifetime *n* the period during which something exists, lasts, or is in progress ⟨the *lifetime* of the camera's batteries was so short we couldn't get through a day trip without having to replace them⟩ — see DURATION 1

lift *n* **1** an act or instance of helping ⟨the company's senior vice president gave his son a much-needed *lift* up the corporate ladder⟩ — see HELP 1

2 a means of getting to a destination in a vehicle driven by another ⟨I'll need a *lift* to work while my car is in the shop⟩ — see RIDE

lift *vb* **1** to move from a lower to a higher place or position ⟨I needed help *lifting* the heavy globe back up to the top shelf⟩ — see RAISE 1

2 to move or extend upward ⟨once the sun started to cut through the morning fog, the colorful hot-air balloons began to *lift* off from the field⟩ — see ASCEND

3 to take (something) without right and with an intent to keep ⟨she turned her back for just a moment, and somebody *lifted* her purse⟩ — see STEAL 1

lifted *adj* being positioned above a surface ⟨with *lifted* heels and bent knees, the runners tensely waited for the gun to go off⟩ — see ELEVATED 1

liftoff *n* a rising from a surface at the start of a flight (as of a rocket) ⟨everyone was quiet in the control room as they waited for *lift-off*⟩

synonyms blastoff, launch, takeoff

related words ascent

near antonyms crash; splashdown

antonyms landing

ligature *n* **1** something that physically prevents free movement ⟨the surgeon tied a *ligature* around the tube to keep it in place⟩ — see BOND 1

2 a uniting or binding force or influence ⟨a common language is often the *ligature* that unites the people of a nation⟩ — see BOND 2

light *n* **1** the steady giving off of the form of radiation that makes vision possible ⟨he read poetry to her by the *light* of the moon⟩

synonyms blaze, flare, fluorescence, glare, gleam, glow, illumination, incandescence, luminescence, radiance, shine

related words flash, glimmer, glint, glitter, scintillation, shimmer, sparkle, twinkle; daylight, moonlight, sunlight, sunshine; afterglow, aureole (*or* aureola), aurora, beam, halo, ray, shaft, streak, stream, sunbeam; glisten, gloss, luster (*or* lustre), polish, reflection, sheen

near antonyms blackness, dark, darkness, dimness, dusk, duskiness, gloom, night, shadow

2 something that provides illumination ⟨turn off the *light* when you go to bed⟩

synonyms beacon, illuminant, lamp

related words arc lamp (*also* arc light), candelabra, candelabrum, candle, chandelier, dark lantern, electric, flare, flash, flashbulb, flashcube, flashlight, floodlight, fluorescent lamp, gaslight, gasolier, girandole, headlight, incandescent lamp, klieg light (*or* kleig light), lantern, light bulb, lighthouse, lighting, sconce, spotlight, streetlight, sun lamp

3 a person who is widely known and usually much talked about ⟨a leading *light* in the acting profession⟩ — see CELEBRITY 1

4 the first appearance of light in the morning or the time of its appearance ⟨with the coming of *light* we could see all the damage that the storm had caused⟩ — see DAWN 1

[1]light *adj* **1** having little weight ⟨the suitcase was as *light* as a feather after all the clothes were removed⟩

synonyms featherlight, feathery, lightweight, underweight, weightless

related words bantam, diminutive, little, minute, puny, small, smallish, tiny, undersized (*also* undersize), wee; flimsy, fragile, insubstantial; petite, slender, slight, slim, thin

near antonyms big, considerable, extensive, goodly, great, handsome, huge, hulking, jumbo, king-size (*or* king-sized), large, largish, massive, overscale (*or* overscaled), oversize (*or* oversized), sizable (*or* sizeable), substantial, super, voluminous, whacking; bulky, cumbersome, unwieldy

antonyms heavy, hefty, leaden, overweight, ponderous, weighty

2 involving minimal difficulty or effort ⟨a little *light* work was all it took to straighten up the room⟩ — see EASY 1

3 less plentiful than what is normal, necessary, or desirable ⟨traffic on the highway seems to be very *light* today⟩ — see MEAGER

4 moving easily ⟨the dancer was exceptionally *light* on her feet⟩ — see GRACEFUL 1

5 not harsh or stern especially in nature or effect ⟨*light* punishment to fit a minor offense⟩ — see GENTLE 1

6 resembling air in lightness ⟨the waves had an especially *light* foam at their crests because of the strong breeze⟩ — see AIRY 1

[2]light *adj* **1** filled with much light ⟨the *light*, airy room is exceptionally cheerful⟩ — see BRIGHT 2

2 lacking intensity of color ⟨we painted the walls a *light* blue⟩ — see PALE 1

3 of light complexion ⟨her *light* skin tends to freckle easily in the sun⟩ — see FAIR 4

[1]light *vb* **1** to set (something) on fire ⟨we *lit* the kindling before adding the heavier logs⟩ — see BURN 2

2 to supply with light ⟨the lights from the TV cameras will *light* this room as though it were high noon⟩ — see ILLUMINATE 1

[2]light *vb* **1** to come to rest after descending from the air ⟨the bird *lit* on the branch and began to sing⟩ — see ALIGHT 1

2 to come down from something (as a vehicle) ⟨he hurriedly *lighted* from the bus and started walking up the street⟩ — see ALIGHT 2

light (on *or* upon) *vb* to come upon unexpectedly or by chance ⟨the novelist *lit upon* the plot for his latest thriller while visiting a remote lighthouse in Maine⟩ — see HAPPEN (ON *OR* UPON)

[1]lighten *vb* to become glad or hopeful ⟨the patient *lightened* when he heard the disease responds well to treatment⟩ — see CHEER (UP) 1

[2]lighten *vb* to supply with light ⟨the room was gradually *lightened* by the rising sun⟩ — see ILLUMINATE 1

light-footed *also* **light-foot** *adj* moving easily ⟨the *light-footed* cat crept silently through the house⟩ — see GRACEFUL 1

light-headed *adj* **1** having a feeling of being whirled about and in danger of falling down ⟨I always get *light-headed* after riding roller coasters, even when I'm standing still again⟩ — see DIZZY 1

2 lacking in seriousness or maturity ⟨we couldn't concentrate on our work because we were feeling so *light-headed*⟩ — see GIDDY 1

light-headedness *n* a lack of seriousness often at an improper time ⟨teenagers, with all of their usual *light-headedness*, are not the best audience for this serious play⟩ — see FRIVOLITY 1

lighthearted *adj* having or showing freedom from worries or trouble ⟨his *lighthearted* attitude in the face of danger was the source of some concern⟩ — see CAREFREE

lightheartedness *n* carefree freedom from constraint

⟨he approaches his medical duties with a *lightheartedness* that some patients find disturbing⟩ — see ABANDON

lighting out *n* the act of leaving a place ⟨your *lighting out* of church before the end of services did not go unnoticed⟩ — see DEPARTURE 1

lightless *adj* being without light or without much light ⟨wondered what might be lurking in the *lightless* corners of the basement⟩ — see DARK 1

lightly *adv* without difficulty ⟨you're not going to get off *lightly* if they catch you!⟩ — see EASILY 1

light–minded *adj* lacking in seriousness or maturity ⟨the movie was a *light-minded* take on the biblical story of Noah and the Flood⟩ — see GIDDY 1

light–mindedness *n* a lack of seriousness often at an improper time ⟨she displays a *light-mindedness* that might be excusable in a teenager but not in someone hoping to make it in the business world⟩ — see FRIVOLITY

[1]lightness *n* **1** the state or quality of having little weight ⟨the first thing I noticed about the little bird was its *lightness*; I could hardly tell I was holding it in my hand⟩
synonyms slightness, weightlessness
related words airiness, delicacy, ethereality, etherealness; flimsiness, fluffiness, insubstantiality
near antonyms solidity, solidness, substantiality
antonyms heaviness, heftiness, massiveness, ponderousness, weightiness
2 a lack of seriousness often at an improper time ⟨the inappropriate *lightness* of the anchorman's tone while he was reading the story of the freak accident in which people had died⟩ — see FRIVOLITY 1

[2]lightness *n* the quality or state of having or giving off light ⟨the photographer was concerned that the *lightness* of the background would cast the main subject into shadow⟩ — see BRILLIANCE 1

lightning *adj* moving, proceeding, or acting with great speed ⟨he made a *lightning* dash for the goal⟩ — see FAST 1

[1]lightsome *adj* filled with much light ⟨a lovely and *lightsome* room with huge windows⟩ — see BRIGHT 2

[2]lightsome *adj* **1** having or showing a good mood or disposition ⟨lighthearted lovers skipping along the beach with a *lightsome* gait⟩ — see CHEERFUL 1
2 having or showing freedom from worries or troubles ⟨set off on his grand tour of Europe with a *lightsome* heart⟩— see CAREFREE
3 moving easily ⟨still *lightsome* despite her advancing years, the cat continued to ignore orders not to leap onto the kitchen table⟩ — see GRACEFUL 1

lightweight *adj* having little weight ⟨it's going to be hot, so wear mostly *lightweight* clothing⟩ — see [1]LIGHT 1

lightweight *n* a person of no importance or influence ⟨among astronomers she's considered a *lightweight*⟩ — see NOBODY

light–year *n* a huge physical or conceptual distance ⟨my sister and I are close in age, but personality-wise, there are *light-years* between us⟩ — see GALAXY

[1]like *n* **1** a number of persons or things that are grouped together because they have something in common ⟨you can never trust his *like*, because they'll always let you down⟩ — see SORT 1
2 one that is equal to another in status, achievement, or value ⟨we'd never seen its *like* in any other shop in town⟩ — see EQUAL

[2]like *n* positive regard for something ⟨she thought her new boyfriend was unusually interested in her *likes* and dislikes⟩ — see LIKING

like *adj* having qualities in common ⟨you're not talking about *like* things when you compare football and golf⟩ — see ALIKE

like *adv* **1** to some degree or extent ⟨the cat would curl up, tightly *like*, and just go to sleep⟩ — see FAIRLY 1
2 close to but not exactly ⟨the distance is more *like* 500 miles⟩ — see APPROXIMATELY

like *conj* the way it would be or one would do if ⟨it looks *like* it's going to rain at any moment⟩ — see AS IF

like *vb* **1** to wish to have ⟨I'd *like* another slice of pizza, but I've already eaten more than I should have⟩
synonyms care (for), want
related words adore, delight (in), dig, enjoy, fancy, groove (on), love, relish, revel (in), welcome; covet, crave, desire, die (for), hanker (for *or* after), wish (for), yearn (for)
phrases feel like
2 to show partiality toward ⟨I *like* romantic comedies more than action movies⟩ — see PREFER 1
3 to take pleasure in ⟨an adventuresome young woman who *likes* skydiving⟩ — see ENJOY 1
4 to see fit ⟨feel free to order whatever you *like* from the menu⟩ — see CHOOSE 2

likelihood *n* the quality or state of being likely to occur ⟨the weatherman on TV said that the *likelihood* of rain today was fairly high⟩ — see PROBABILITY 1

likely *adj* **1** having a high chance of occurring ⟨if you don't graduate from high school, your *likely* fate is a low-paying job⟩
synonyms probable
related words conceivable, earthly, imaginable, possible, potential, supposable; apt, bound, certain, doubtless, imminent, inescapable, inevitable, liable, necessary, sure, unavoidable
near antonyms impossible, inconceivable, unimaginable
antonyms doubtful, dubious, improbable, questionable, unlikely
2 having qualities which inspire hope ⟨this looks like a *likely* spot for good trout fishing⟩ — see HOPEFUL 1
3 worthy of being accepted as true or reasonable ⟨we didn't find her excuse a very *likely* story⟩ — see BELIEVABLE
4 very pleasing to look at ⟨a *likely* gal such as yourself should have no trouble getting a date⟩ — see BEAUTIFUL 1

likely *adv* by reasonable assumption ⟨the picnic will *likely* be cancelled if the storm continues⟩ — see PROBABLY

liken *vb* **1** to describe as similar ⟨he generally *likened* a root canal to some horrible form of torture⟩ — see COMPARE 1
2 to regard or represent as equal or comparable ⟨I think that we can *liken* the two pianists, at least in terms of natural talent⟩ — see EQUATE 1

likeness *n* **1** a two-dimensional design intended to look like a person or thing ⟨the wealthy businessman hired a leading artist to paint his *likeness*⟩ — see PICTURE 1
2 something or someone that strongly resembles another ⟨why, you're the very *likeness* of your mother!⟩ — see IMAGE 1
3 the quality or state of having many qualities in common ⟨the forgery was difficult to detect due to the pinpoint *likeness* it bore to the original⟩ — see SIMILARITY 1

likewise *adv* **1** in addition to what has been said ⟨the owner of the restaurant is *likewise* the owner of the deli next door⟩ — see MORE 1
2 in like manner ⟨I mind my own business, and you should do *likewise*⟩ — see ALSO 1

liking *n* positive regard for something ⟨I have a *liking* for dark chocolate⟩
synonyms appetite, fancy, favor, fondness, like, love, love affair, partiality, preference, relish, shine, taste, use
related words craving, desire, hankering, longing,

thirst, yen; enthusiasm, gusto, interest, passion; bias, prejudice; bent, inclination, leaning, propensity, tendency; tooth; palate; weakness
near antonyms apathy, disinclination; indifference, unconcern
antonyms aversion, disfavor, disgust, dislike, distaste, hatred, loathing, mislike

Lilliputian *adj* **1** not broad or open in views or opinions ⟨to the *Lilliputian* minds of that small town any depiction of the nude, regardless of its artistry, was pornographic⟩ — see NARROW 2
2 of a size that is less than average ⟨a model train carrying *Lilliputian* figures through a miniature landscape⟩ — see SMALL 1

lily–livered *adj* having or showing a shameful lack of courage ⟨the pacifist was mistakenly accused of being a *lily-livered* coward⟩ — see COWARDLY

lily–white *adj* free from guilt or blame ⟨the state's lieutenant governor was the only member of the administration who could claim to have remained *lily-white* during the scandal⟩ — see INNOCENT 2

limb *n* a major outgrowth from the main stem of a woody plant ⟨we hung the swing from the highest *limb* of the tree that we could reach⟩ — see BRANCH 1

limber *adj* able to bend easily without breaking ⟨he shaped the basket out of *limber* branches that could bend easily around a frame⟩ — see WILLOWY

limelight *n* the center of public attention ⟨an actress who discovered that the *limelight* was not such a glowing experience when her privacy was invaded⟩ — see CENTER STAGE

limit *n* **1** a real or imaginary point beyond which a person or thing cannot go ⟨there was no *limit* to the number of challenges they faced⟩
synonyms bound, boundary, cap, ceiling, confines, end, extent, limitation, line, termination
related words extremity, fag end, terminus; border, brim, edge, margin, rim, verge; outside; bar, barrier, fence, hedge, restraint, stop, wall
2 the most extreme or advanced point ⟨those bratty kids have pushed my patience to the *limit*⟩ — see HEIGHT 2

limit *vb* **1** to set bounds or an upper limit for ⟨*limit* the note to a few words⟩
synonyms cap, circumscribe, confine, hold down, restrict
related words bar, block, hamper, hinder, impede, obstruct; constrict, contract, lessen, narrow, pinch, squeeze, tighten; quell, repress, suppress; number; modify, qualify
near antonyms broaden, expand, widen; overextend, overreach
antonyms exceed
2 to mark the limits of ⟨adjectives *limit* the meanings of nouns⟩
synonyms bound, circumscribe, define, delimit, demarcate, demark, mark (off), terminate
related words control, determine, govern; delineate, describe

limitation *n* **1** a real or imaginary point beyond which a person or thing cannot go ⟨the bridge has a weight *limitation* that bars heavy trucks from crossing it⟩ — see LIMIT 1
2 something that limits one's freedom of action or choice ⟨the state has some fairly strict *limitations* on the sale and use of alcoholic beverages⟩ — see RESTRICTION 1
3 the act or practice of keeping something (as an activity) within certain boundaries ⟨the *limitation* on the number of vehicles allowed on the island does not sit well with year-round residents⟩ — see RESTRICTION 2

limited *adj* **1** having distinct or certain limits ⟨to avoid overcrowding, the number of tickets to the outdoor concerts is *limited*⟩
synonyms bounded, circumscribed, defined, definite, determinate, finite, measured, narrow, restricted
related words modified, qualified; detailed, exact, precise, specific; confined, constricted, moderate, modest; minute, puny, small, tiny; determined, fixed, settled
near antonyms bottomless, countless, incalculable, inestimable, inexhaustible, innumerable, unfathomable; unqualified, unreserved; general, indeterminate, nebulous, vague; enlarged, escalated, expanded; copious, plenitudinous, plentiful; big, bulky, bumper, considerable, extensive, goodly, great, handsome, hefty, hulking, jumbo, king-size (*or* king-sized), large, largish, overscale (*or* overscaled), oversize (*or* oversized), respectable, sizable (*or* sizeable), substantial, super, vast, voluminous, whacking; epic, grandiose, major; ample, broad, comprehensive, cosmopolitan, expansive, global, inclusive, sweeping, universal, whole
antonyms boundless, dimensionless, endless, illimitable, immeasurable, indefinite, infinite, limitless, measureless, unbounded, undefined, unlimited, unmeasured
2 having a limit ⟨competition for *limited* resources among growing populations is often a source of international conflict⟩ — see FINITE 1

limitless *adj* being or seeming to be without limits ⟨the *limitless* nature of the universe is awe-inspiring⟩ — see INFINITE

limn *vb* to give a representation or account of in words ⟨he *limned* the scene in the courtroom so perfectly I could practically see it⟩ — see DESCRIBE 1

limp *adj* **1** not stiff in structure ⟨his broken arm was *limp* as he held it against his side⟩
synonyms droopy, flaccid, floppy, lank, yielding
related words flabby, mushy, semisoft, soft, squashy, squishy; delicate, flimsy, insubstantial; elastic, flexible, lax, loose, pliant, relaxed, resilient, springy, stretchy, supple
near antonyms firm, hard, indurated, solid, sound, strong; brittle, crisp; compact, dense, substantial
antonyms inflexible, resilient, rigid, stiff, sturdy, tense
2 depleted in strength, energy, or freshness ⟨the *limp* runners just dropped to the ground after crossing the finish line⟩ — see WEARY 1
3 lacking bodily energy or motivation ⟨the team's *limp* performance has many calling for the head coach's resignation⟩ — see LISTLESS

limp *vb* **1** to walk while favoring one leg ⟨she *limped* all day after stubbing her toe on the lawn sprinkler⟩
synonyms halt, hobble
related words hitch; blunder, falter, flounder, lurch, shamble, shuffle, stagger, stumble, teeter, totter, waver, wobble (*also* wabble); dodder
near antonyms breeze, glide, sail
antonyms stride
2 to proceed or act clumsily or ineffectually ⟨the damaged boat *limped* back into port⟩ — see FLOUNDER 1
3 to move slowly ⟨we'll have to stop *limping* if we are ever going to make our destination in time⟩ — see CRAWL 2

limpid *adj* **1** easily seen through ⟨her eyes are the blue of a *limpid* stream of water⟩ — see CLEAR 1
2 free from emotional or mental agitation ⟨the *limpid* conscience of a man who is at peace with himself as he awaits death⟩ — see CALM 2

limpidity *n* the state or quality of being easily seen through ⟨Crystal Lake was obviously named for the *limpidity* of its water⟩ — see CLARITY 1

limpidness *n* the state or quality of being easily seen through ⟨the *limpidness* of the water allows visitors to actually see fish swimming along the bottom⟩ — see CLARITY 1

limp–wristed *adj* lacking strength of will or character ⟨maintained that the nation's foreign policy should not be in the hands of *limp-wristed* bleeding hearts with no military experience⟩ — see WEAK 2

line *n* **1** a series of persons or things arranged one behind another ⟨the *line* for tickets stretched around the block⟩
synonyms column, cue, file, queue, range, string, train
related words echelon, rank, row, tier; chain, progression, sequence, succession; array
2 a way of acting or proceeding ⟨since the election, the president has taken a very conservative *line*⟩ — see COURSE 1
3 the activity by which one regularly makes a living ⟨my *line* of business is "pre-owned" vehicles, and have I got a deal for you!⟩ — see OCCUPATION 1
4 a region of activity, knowledge, or influence ⟨advanced mathematics is a little outside of my *line*, but I'll see what I can do to help⟩ — see FIELD 2
5 a real or imaginary point beyond which a person or thing cannot go ⟨you really crossed the *line* with that outrageous display of bad behavior⟩ — see LIMIT 1
6 a long hollow cylinder for carrying a substance (as a liquid or gas) ⟨the workers rushed to fix the leak in the gas *line*⟩ — see PIPE 1
7 a length of braided, flexible material that is used for tying or connecting things ⟨he made sure to bring extra fishing *line* in case a fish broke free⟩ — see CORD 1
8 a group of vehicles traveling together or under one management ⟨she owns a *line* of limousines⟩ — see FLEET
9 the direction along which something or someone moves ⟨the airplane took a southerly *line* toward the capital⟩ — see PATH 1
10 a group of persons who come from the same ancestor ⟨a 10th of all island residents are members of the *line* of this early settler⟩ — see FAMILY 1
11 the line of ancestors from whom a person is descended ⟨he comes from a noble *line* that goes back several centuries⟩ — see ANCESTRY

lineage *n* **1** the line of ancestors from whom a person is descended ⟨his Italian *lineage* was very important to him⟩ — see ANCESTRY
2 a group of persons who come from the same ancestor ⟨it is now generally accepted that the *lineage* of Thomas Jefferson includes black as well as white members⟩ — see FAMILY 1

linear *adj* free from irregularities or digressions in course ⟨the bullets from early firearms were notorious for not following a strictly *linear* path through the air⟩ — see STRAIGHT 1

linger *vb* to move or act slowly ⟨since they were charging by the hour, the house painters *lingered* in finishing up their work⟩ — see DELAY 1

lingerer *n* someone who moves slowly or more slowly than others ⟨he's known as a *lingerer*, always the last to arrive and the last to leave⟩ — see SLOWPOKE

lingo *n* **1** the stock of words, pronunciation, and grammar used by a people as their basic means of communication ⟨medical missionaries struggling to learn the *lingo* of the African tribe that they were treating⟩ — see LANGUAGE 1
2 the special terms or expressions of a particular group or field ⟨the shorthand medical *lingo* that the hospital staffers use with one another⟩ — see TERMINOLOGY

linguistic *also* **linguistical** *adj* of or relating to words or language ⟨the age at which children begin to acquire *linguistic* skills⟩ — see VERBAL 1

link *n* **1** a rod-shaped portion of seasoned ground meat in a casing ⟨I like to put maple syrup on my breakfast *links*⟩ — see SAUSAGE
2 a uniting or binding force or influence ⟨those old love letters were her only remaining *link* with her late grandparents⟩ — see BOND 2

link *vb* **1** to put or bring together so as to form a new and longer whole ⟨she *linked* the flowers together to form a long chain⟩ — see CONNECT 1
2 to think of (something) in combination ⟨since childhood I have always *linked* trips to the beach with the discomforts of sunburn and sand in my clothes⟩ — see ASSOCIATE 2

link (up) *vb* to come together to form a single unit ⟨carbon atoms *link up* to form a diamond crystal⟩ — see UNITE 1

linkage *n* the fact or state of having something in common ⟨the accountants noticed a *linkage* between the two supposedly independent companies⟩ — see CONNECTION 1

linking *n* the act or an instance of joining two or more things into one ⟨the *linking* of state roads and highways into one interstate highway system⟩ — see UNION 1

linkup *n* the state of having shared interests or efforts (as in social or business matters) ⟨the *linkup* of the two art museums has proved beneficial to both institutions⟩ — see ASSOCIATION 1

linn *n, chiefly Scottish* a narrow opening between hillsides or mountains that can be used for passage ⟨climb to the cairn above the loch, and from there you'll get a broad view of the *linn*⟩ — see CANYON

lint *n* a soft airy substance or covering ⟨it's important to clean the *lint* out of the dryer every time you use it⟩ — see [1]FUZZ

lion *n* a person of rank, power, or influence in a particular field ⟨the book festival brought together two *lions* of contemporary poetry for a joint reading⟩ — see MAGNATE

lionhearted *adj* feeling or displaying no fear by temperament ⟨traditionally young Masai men are consigned to a period of isolation in the bush in order to turn them into strong, *lionhearted* warriors⟩ — see BRAVE 1

lion's share *n* the largest part or quantity of something ⟨the lead actress deservedly got the *lion's share* of credit for the show's success⟩ ⟨the *lion's share* of ballots went the incumbent's way⟩ — see MAJORITY 1

lip *adj* not being or expressing what one appears to be or express ⟨part of the ritual of the awards ceremony is the nominee's *lip* praise for the performances of his or her competitors⟩ — see INSINCERE

lip *vb* to flow along or against ⟨the waves, reflecting the red glow of the sunset, gently *lipped* the prow⟩ — see WASH 1

liquefy *also* **liquify** *vb* to go from a solid to a liquid state ⟨the steel *liquefied* in the intense heat of the forge⟩
synonyms deliquesce, flux, fuse, melt, run, thaw
related words found, gutter, smelt, try; dissolve, render; soften, thin
near antonyms clot, coagulate, congeal, gel, jell, jelly, thicken
antonyms harden, set, solidify

liquid *adj* **1** capable of moving like a liquid ⟨always have in the kitchen a dispenser of *liquid* soap available for hand washing⟩ — see FLUID 1
2 easily seen through ⟨the *liquid* air of the remote mountains⟩ — see CLEAR 1

liquidate *vb* **1** to destroy all traces of ⟨a decisive act that *liquidated* all doubts and fears about his governing abilities⟩ — see ANNIHILATE 1
2 to put to death deliberately ⟨his first act as absolute ruler was to *liquidate* his opponents⟩ — see MURDER 1
3 to give what is owed for ⟨used our lottery winnings to *liquidate* our debts⟩ — see PAY 2

liquor *n* a distilled beverage that can make a person drunk ⟨you can't order *liquor* in a bar until you're 21 years old⟩ — see ALCOHOL

liquor (up) *vb* to partake excessively of alcoholic beverages ⟨the men *liquored up* at the roadhouse and then thought it would be a good idea to go hunting⟩ — see DRINK 2

lissome *also* **lissom** *adj* **1** moving easily ⟨the *lissome* actress's dance training is apparent in the way she moves on stage⟩ — see GRACEFUL 1

2 able to bend easily without breaking ⟨rattan is such a *lissome* material that it can be used for all manner of furniture and baskets⟩ — see WILLOWY

[1]list *n* a record of a series of items (as names or titles) usually arranged according to some system ⟨we put eggs, sour cream, tomatoes, roast beef, and cheddar cheese on the shopping *list*⟩

synonyms canon, catalog (*or* catalogue), checklist, listing, menu, register, registry, roll, roll call, roster, schedule, table

related words agenda, bibliography, catalogue raisonné, compendium, compilation, directory, docket, enumeration, glossary, index, inventory, manifest, payroll; calendar, chronology, timetable

[2]list *n* the act of positioning or an instance of being positioned at an angle ⟨the extreme *list* of the racing yacht made it hard for the untried crew to keep their balance⟩ — see TILT

[3]list *n* a long narrow piece of material ⟨shave a thin *list* from the side of the board⟩ — see STRIP 1

[1]list *vb* **1** to make a list of ⟨the coach *listed* the people on the team⟩

synonyms enumerate, inventory, itemize, numerate

related words count, mark, number; check (off), tick (off)

2 to put (someone or something) on a list ⟨her number isn't *listed* in the phone book⟩

synonyms catalog (*or* catalogue), enroll (*also* enrol), enter, index, inscribe, put down, record, register, schedule, slate

related words book, card, file, note; classify, compile, tabulate, tally; reschedule

near antonyms delete

3 to add (a person) to a list or roll as a participant or member ⟨our grandfather is *listed* among the war dead honored by the memorial⟩ — see ENROLL 1

4 to specify one after another ⟨do I need to *list* all of the reasons why your idea won't work?⟩ — see ENUMERATE 1

[2]list *vb* to set or cause to be at an angle ⟨the sudden shift of the load in the hull *listed* the ship badly⟩ — see LEAN 1

listen *vb* to pay attention especially through the act of hearing ⟨would you *listen* to what I have to say?⟩

synonyms attend, hark, harken, hear, hearken, heed, mind

phrases prick up one's ears

near antonyms discount, disregard

antonyms ignore, tune out

listen (to) *vb* to take notice of and be guided by ⟨you'd better *listen to* my advice!⟩ — see HEED 1

listen in (on) *vb* to listen to (another in private conversation) ⟨it's not polite to *listen in on* other people's private conversations⟩ — see EAVESDROP (ON)

listing *adj* **1** inclined or twisted to one side ⟨the *listing* battleship limped back to port for repairs⟩ — see AWRY

2 running in a slanting direction ⟨the *listing* lines of a poem scrawled on a chalkboard⟩ — see DIAGONAL

listing *n* a record of a series of items (as names or titles) usually arranged according to some system ⟨an alphabetical *listing* of all of the students currently enrolled in the school⟩ — see [1]LIST

listless *adj* lacking bodily energy or motivation ⟨when I had the flu, I felt *listless* and worn-out⟩

synonyms enervated, lackadaisical, languid, languishing, languorous, limp, spiritless

related words indolent, lazy, slothful; dull, lethargic, logy (*also* loggy), sleepy, sluggish, torpid; exhausted, knackered [*British*], tired, weary; feeble, frail, weak; apathetic, impassive, indifferent, phlegmatic, stolid; careless, heedless, thoughtless, unwary; inactive, inert

near antonyms active, dynamic, industrious, kinetic; avid, eager, enthusiastic, keen, lively, pumped, vivacious; cheerful, chipper, perky, up; agog, alert, awake, dapper, open-eyed, sleepless, vigilant, watchful, wide-awake

antonyms ambitious, animated, energetic, enterprising, motivated

listlessness *n* **1** physical or mental inertness ⟨following a couple of big mistakes early in the game, the team sank into an uncharacteristic *listlessness* and was never able to recover the lead⟩ — see LETHARGY

2 the state of being bored ⟨we searched desperately for something to jar us out of our *listlessness*⟩ — see BOREDOM

3 the quality or state of lacking physical strength or vigor ⟨general *listlessness* is often a side effect of chemotherapy⟩ — see WEAKNESS 1

[1]lit *or* **lighted** *adj* **1** filled with much light ⟨the coat room was just *lit* well enough for us to identify our jackets⟩ — see BRIGHT 2

2 being on fire ⟨some *lighted* torches lined the path to the shrine⟩ — see ABLAZE 1

[2]lit *adj* being under the influence of alcohol ⟨his wife was definitely *lit* after her night out with the girls from the office⟩ — see DRUNK

literacy *n* the understanding and information gained from being educated ⟨he impressed everyone with his general *literacy* as well as his natural intelligence⟩ — see EDUCATION 2

literal *adj* restricted to or based on fact ⟨a *literal* account of the explorer's adventures is actually a lot less interesting than his own exaggerated stories⟩ — see FACTUAL 1

literalism *n* realistic depiction in art and literature ⟨if audiences ever got the *literalism* they claim they want in movies, they'd be fast asleep by the second reel⟩ — see VERISIMILITUDE

literary *adj* suggestive of the vocabulary used in books ⟨the novel's dialogue is a little too *literary* in flavor to be entirely convincing⟩ — see BOOKISH

literate *adj* having or displaying advanced knowledge or education ⟨the columnist's witty and *literate* comments on current events make her a popular guest on political talk shows⟩ — see EDUCATED 1

literati *n pl* intellectuals considered as a social class ⟨Boston's 19th-century *literati* often referred to their city as "the Athens of America"⟩ — see INTELLIGENTSIA

lithe *adj* **1** able to bend easily without breaking ⟨the *lithe* blade of a fencing foil⟩ — see WILLOWY

2 moving easily ⟨*lithe* dancers glided across the stage⟩ — see GRACEFUL 1

3 having a noticeably small amount of body fat ⟨she has the *lithe*, sinewy body of a distance runner⟩ — see THIN 1

lithesome *adj* **1** able to bend easily without breaking ⟨stretching exercises designed to make the athlete's limbs more *lithesome*⟩ — see WILLOWY

2 moving easily ⟨the *lithesome* panther moved effortlessly and noiselessly through the rain forest⟩ — see GRACEFUL 1

litter *n* **1** an unorganized collection or mixture of vari-

ous things ⟨a *litter* of magazines covered the bedroom floor⟩ — see MISCELLANY 1
2 discarded or useless material ⟨if you get caught throwing your *litter* on the sidewalk, you'll get slapped with a fine⟩ — see GARBAGE 1

litterateur *or* **littérateur** *n* a person who creates a written work ⟨Washington Irving is generally credited as the first American *litterateur* to gain a reputation in Britain and on the Continent⟩ — see AUTHOR 1

littered *adj* lacking in order, neatness, and often cleanliness ⟨is there any wonder that you can never find anything in your *littered* desk?⟩ — see MESSY

little *adj* **1** having relatively little height ⟨there was a *little* hedge separating the two lawns⟩ — see SHORT 1
2 lacking importance ⟨there were just a few *little* details left to take care of⟩ — see UNIMPORTANT
3 not broad or open in views or opinions ⟨*little*-minded people who dislike the fact that human society is always progressing⟩ — see NARROW 2
4 not lasting for a considerable time ⟨let's take a *little* pause to relax⟩ — see SHORT 2
5 of a size that is less than average ⟨the petting zoo has a *little* horse in addition to all of the goats and sheep⟩ — see SMALL 1

little *adv* **1** in a very small quantity or degree ⟨we had *little* more than we needed to survive in the wilderness⟩
synonyms negligibly, nominally, slightly
related words meagerly, scantily; barely, hardly, just, marginally, minimally, scarcely
phrases a bit, a trifle
near antonyms completely, entirely, purely, thoroughly, totally, utterly; eminently, exceptionally; appreciably, discernibly, noticeably, palpably; abundantly, plentifully; generously, handsomely, liberally; astronomically, grandly, hugely, monstrously, monumentally
antonyms awful, awfully, beastly, considerably, deadly, especially, exceedingly (*also* exceeding), extensively, extra, extremely, far, frightfully, full, greatly, heavily, highly, jolly, mightily, mighty, mortally, most, much, particularly, rattling, real, right, significantly, so, something, substantially, super, terribly, too, very, whacking
2 not often ⟨he's been studying very *little* for the bar exam⟩ — see SELDOM

little *n* a very small amount ⟨there's just a *little* of the pie left⟩ — see PARTICLE 1

little bitty *adj* very small in size ⟨all that was left when I finally got to the dessert table was one *little bitty* piece of pie⟩ — see TINY

little by little *adv* by small steps or amounts ⟨*little by little*, we pieced together the jigsaw puzzle⟩ — see GRADUALLY

little guy *n* an average or ordinary man ⟨for a politician who likes to portray himself as a friend of the *little guy*, he sure is fond of rubbing elbows with the fat cats⟩ — see JOE BLOW

little man *n* an average or ordinary man ⟨claims that the wind farm would benefit only its developers and that the *little man* would get nothing out of it⟩ — see JOE BLOW

littleness *n* **1** the quality or state of being little in size ⟨the *littleness* of the painting hardly gives any indication of its price—which is a fortune⟩ — see SMALLNESS 1
2 the quality or state of being unimportant ⟨you can hardly imagine the appalling *littleness* of the stuff that she obsesses over⟩ — see INSIGNIFICANCE

littlest *adj* being the least in amount, number, or size possible ⟨the *littlest* kitten in the litter was also the cutest⟩ — see MINIMAL

little woman *n* the female partner in a marriage ⟨I'll check with the *little woman* about whether we can go⟩ — see WIFE

littoral *adj* of, relating to, or situated in the waters near the shore ⟨*littoral* warfare includes amphibious landings⟩ — see INSHORE

lit up *adj* being under the influence of alcohol ⟨he finally wandered in at 3:00 a.m., obviously *lit up*⟩ — see DRUNK

livable *also* **liveable** *adj* suitable for living in ⟨after we added some furniture and painted the walls, the apartment was *livable*⟩
synonyms habitable, inhabitable
related words comfortable, cozy, homelike, homey (*also* homy), intimate, snug; deluxe, lavish, luxuriant, luxurious, plush, sumptuous; opulent, palatial, rich; acceptable, bearable, endurable, sufferable, supportable, sustainable, tolerable
near antonyms uncomfortable; humble, spartan; economical, frugal, spare, thrifty; insupportable, intolerable, unacceptable, unbearable, unendurable
antonyms uninhabitable, unlivable

live *adj* **1** being in effective operation ⟨didn't realize that the microphone was *live* and proceeded to make some rather indiscreet comments⟩ — see ACTIVE 1
2 having or showing life ⟨there is a tank of *live* lobsters sitting at the front of the restaurant⟩ — see ALIVE 1

live *vb* **1** to have a home ⟨he *lives* next door to the hospital⟩
synonyms abide, dwell, reside
related words lodge, settle, stay; frequent, hang (at), haunt, visit; cohabit, inhabit, occupy; people, populate; lease, rent, sublet, tenant
2 to have life ⟨Socrates was a philosopher who *lived* in ancient Greece⟩ — see BE 1

livelily *adv* in a quick and spirited manner ⟨the boat skipped *livelily* across the lake⟩ — see GAILY 2

liveliness *n* the quality or state of having abundant or intense activity ⟨we were surprised by the *liveliness* of the crowd at the nightclub despite the early hour⟩ — see VITALITY 1

lively *adv* in a quick and spirited manner ⟨now then, step *lively* there⟩ — see GAILY 2

lively *adj* **1** having much high-spirited energy and movement ⟨the *lively* puppy was racing around the dining room floor chasing after people's shoelaces⟩
synonyms active, airy, animate, animated, bouncing, brisk, energetic, frisky, gay, jaunty, jazzy, kinetic, mettlesome, peppy, perky, pert, pizzazzy (*or* pizazzy), racy, snappy, spanking, sparky, spirited, sprightly, springy, vital, vivacious, zippy
related words dapper, dashing, spiffy; agog, alert, awake, open-eyed, up, wide-awake; agile, nimble, spry; bright, buoyant, cheerful, chipper, chirpy, chirrupy, effervescent, sparkly, upbeat; eager, enthusiastic, keen; frolicsome, impish, pixieish, playful; boisterous, bubbly, ebullient, exuberant, high-spirited; high-strung, nervous, skittish
phrases on the go
near antonyms indolent, lazy, unambitious; inert, lethargic, sleepy, sluggish, tired, torpid, weary; apathetic, impassive, phlegmatic, stolid; boring, dull, irksome, tedious
antonyms dead, inactive, inanimate, lackadaisical, languid, languishing, languorous, leaden, lifeless, limp, listless, spiritless, vapid
2 marked by much life, movement, or activity ⟨the party was a *lively* affair that lasted into the small hours of the morning⟩ — see ALIVE 2

liven (up) *vb* to give life, vigor, or spirit to ⟨the bandleader tried to *liven up* the party by playing more energetic music so people would dance⟩ — see ANIMATE

livery *n* the distinctive clothing worn by members of a particular group ⟨the limousine chauffeur was easily distinguished from the cab drivers by his *livery*⟩ — see UNIFORM

live wire *n* **1** a very energetic person ⟨the babysitter will have her hands full with those two little *live wires*⟩ — see PISTOL
2 an ambitious person who eagerly goes after what is desired ⟨that new reporter on the police beat is a real *live wire*⟩ — see GO-GETTER

livid *adj* **1** feeling or showing anger ⟨the boss was *livid* when yet another deadline was missed⟩ — see ANGRY
2 lacking a healthy skin color ⟨her face was *livid* with fear⟩ — see PALE 2

lividity *n* an intense emotional state of displeasure with someone or something ⟨the level of the boss's *lividity* was something I'd never seen outside of cartoons—I almost expected steam to rise out of his head⟩ — see ANGER

lividness *n* an intense emotional state of displeasure with someone or something ⟨their employer's titanic *lividness* over the situation had them all wondering if they'd all get fired⟩ — see ANGER

living *adj* **1** being in effective operation ⟨a *living* tradition of the holiday season⟩ ⟨a *living* culture that has survived a number of foreign invasions⟩ — see ACTIVE 1
2 having being at the present time ⟨there are fewer than a dozen *living* former presidents⟩ — see EXTANT 1
3 having or showing life ⟨is your hamster still *living*?⟩ — see ALIVE 1
4 closely resembling the object imitated ⟨an outdoor museum that is a *living* re-creation of a typical New England village circa 1840⟩ — see NATURAL 2

llano *n* a broad area of level or rolling treeless country ⟨for generations the family has raised cattle on the *llanos* of the American Southwest⟩ — see PLAIN 1

load *n* **1** a mass or quantity of something taken up and carried, conveyed, or transported ⟨hoisted a *load* of grain on the truck going to Florida⟩
synonyms burden, cargo, draft, freight, haul, lading, loading, payload, weight
related words consignment; boatload, carload, shipload, trainload, truckload, wagonload; ballast, deadweight; overload, surcharge; bale, bundle, pack, package, packet, parcel, shipment; manifest; body, bulk, mass
2 loads *pl* a considerable amount ⟨there's no rush, since we've got *loads* of time left⟩ — see LOT 2

load *vb* **1** to place a weight or burden on ⟨students complaining that their teachers were *loading* them with work⟩
synonyms burden, encumber, freight, lade, laden, lumber, saddle, weight
related words clog, clutter, fill, pack; heap, mound, pile, stack; press, weigh; strain, tax; overburden, overload, overtax, surcharge; hamper, handicap; afflict, oppress
near antonyms alleviate, ease, lighten, relieve
antonyms disburden, discharge, disencumber, unburden, unlade, unload
2 to put into (something) as much as can be held or contained ⟨she *loaded* her plate at the buffet with as much food as she could carry and with more than any sane person should eat⟩ — see FILL 1

loaded *adj* **1** containing or seeming to contain the greatest quantity or number possible ⟨the department stores were *loaded* with goods for the holiday shopping season⟩ — see FULL 1
2 having goods, property, or money in abundance ⟨the guy in the fancy foreign sports car obviously was *loaded*⟩ — see RICH 1
3 *slang* being under the influence of alcohol ⟨the departing party guest was *loaded*, so we held his car keys until he had sobered up⟩ — see DRUNK
4 *slang* being under the influence of a recreational drug ⟨wasted his life getting *loaded* and watching TV all day⟩ — see STONED 1

loading *n* a mass or quantity of something taken up and carried, conveyed, or transported ⟨the accident was caused by an 18-wheeler with a *loading* in excess of the legal limit⟩ — see LOAD 1

loaf *vb* to spend time doing nothing ⟨the kind of sultry August afternoon that makes you just want to *loaf*⟩ — see IDLE

loafer *n* a lazy person ⟨an incorrigible *loafer* who never accomplished anything⟩ — see LAZYBONES

loamy *adj* consisting or suggestive of earth ⟨that *loamy* section of the backyard is perfect for growing a garden⟩ — see EARTHY 1

loan *vb* to give to another for temporary use with the understanding that it or a like thing will be returned ⟨can you *loan* me your lawn mower this weekend?⟩ — see LEND

loath *also* **loth** *or* **lothe** *adj* slow to begin or proceed with a course of action because of doubts or uncertainty ⟨I was *loath* to accept his claim of having climbed Mount Everest⟩ — see HESITANT

loathe *vb* to dislike strongly ⟨I simply *loathe* tapioca pudding⟩ — see HATE

loathing *n* **1** a dislike so strong as to cause stomach upset or queasiness ⟨the sight of his mortal enemy getting that undeserved promotion filled him with *loathing*⟩ — see DISGUST
2 a very strong dislike ⟨I have an uncompromising *loathing* for anyone who would deliberately harm an animal⟩ — see HATE 1

loathsome *adj* causing intense displeasure, disgust, or resentment ⟨we traced the foul smell to a pile of *loathsome* garbage by the back wall⟩ — see OFFENSIVE 1

lob *vb* to send through the air especially with a quick forward motion of the arm ⟨he lightly *lobbed* the errant ball over the fence to the waiting schoolboy⟩ — see THROW 1

lobby *n* **1** a centrally located room in a building that serves as a gathering or waiting area or as a passageway into the interior ⟨our tour group met downstairs in the *lobby* of the hotel before going out to dinner⟩ — see FOYER 1
2 the entrance room of a building ⟨the ticket booth is located in the theater's outer *lobby*⟩ — see HALL 1

lobotomize *vb* to deprive of emotional or intellectual vitality ⟨fear of saying anything controversial has so *lobotomized* this book on geopolitics that it fails to say anything at all⟩ — see DEHYDRATE 1

local *n* **1** a local unit of an organization ⟨the truck drivers are members of *Local* 349 of the Teamsters' Union⟩ — see CHAPTER 1
2 a usually longtime resident of a locality ⟨few *locals* seem to patronize the city's touristy restaurants, leaving them to diners who prefer atmosphere over food⟩ — see NATIVE 1

locale *n* **1** the area or space occupied by or intended for something ⟨we found an ideal *locale* for our annual picnic⟩ — see PLACE 1
2 the place and time in which the action for a portion of a dramatic work (as a movie) is set ⟨the movie's *locale* is ambiguous, though the architecture and dress are suggestive of 19th-century Europe⟩ — see SCENE 1

localite *n* a usually longtime resident of a locality ⟨visitors to the Florida Keys soon learn that "conch" is a term for a *localite* as well as a mollusk⟩ — see NATIVE 1

locality *n* the area or space occupied by or intended for something ⟨a *locality* filled with exotic plants⟩ — see PLACE 1

locate *vb* to come upon after searching, study, or effort ⟨we were finally able to *locate* the missing cat, who had been sleeping in the closet the whole time⟩ — see FIND 1

location *n* the area or space occupied by or intended for something ⟨we chose the historic church on Main Street as the *location* for the ceremony⟩ — see PLACE 1

loch *n, Scottish* a part of a body of water that extends beyond the general shoreline ⟨in his biography of Samuel Johnson, James Boswell tells of being conducted by a Scottish boatman "across one of the *lochs*, as they call them, or arms of the sea"⟩ — see GULF 1

lock *n* one that is certain to succeed ⟨the governor is regarded as a *lock* for his party's presidential nomination⟩ — see SURE THING

lock (up) *vb* to put in or as if in prison ⟨if they catch you, they're going to *lock* you *up* and throw away the key!⟩ — see IMPRISON

locker *n* **1** a covered rectangular container for storing or transporting things ⟨the enlisted man usually stored his uniform in his *locker* at the foot of his bed⟩ — see CHEST

2 a storage case typically having doors and shelves ⟨a down-at-the heels health club where most of the *lockers* look to be unusable⟩ — see CABINET

locker–room *adj* depicting or referring to sexual matters in a way that is unacceptable in polite society ⟨keep your *locker-room* talk for your fraternity brothers⟩ — see OBSCENE 1

lockstep *n* an established and often automatic or monotonous series of actions followed when engaging in some activity ⟨followed the *lockstep* that had been in his family for generations: prep school, Ivy League university, job on Wall Street⟩ — see ROUTINE 1

lockup *n* a place of confinement for persons held in lawful custody ⟨the firm conviction that juvenile offenders should never be held in adult *lockups*⟩ — see JAIL

loco *adj, slang* having or showing a very abnormal or sick state of mind ⟨that dog's plumb *loco*, just running around in circles all day long⟩ — see INSANE 1

loco *vb* to cause to go insane or as if insane ⟨years of living alone had clearly *locoed* the old rancher⟩ — see CRACK

locomote *vb* to change one's position ⟨most babies begin to *locomote*—by crawling—when they are seven to ten months old⟩ — see MOVE 3

locum tenens *n* a person or thing that takes the place of another ⟨I'm just a *locum tenens*, so any major decisions should be deferred until your regular doctor returns from vacation⟩ — see SUBSTITUTE

locus *n* **1** a thing or place that is of greatest importance to an activity or interest ⟨an area of the Southwest that has been the *locus* of a number of New Agey movements⟩ — see CENTER 1

2 the area or space occupied by or intended for something ⟨the *locus* of brightness occurs where the rays of sunlight converge in front of the lens⟩ — see PLACE 1

locution *n* a distinctive way of putting ideas into words ⟨in the poet's somewhat affected *locution*, word order is often reversed and so we have "the sea serene"⟩ — see STYLE 1

lodestar *also* **loadstar** *n* a guiding or motivating purpose or principle ⟨a society seemingly with unbridled greed as its only *lodestar*⟩ — see COMPASS 1

lodestone *also* **loadstone** *n* something that attracts interest ⟨the young woman's wealth unfortunately made her a *lodestone* for fortune hunters⟩ — see MAGNET

lodge *n* **1** a place that provides rooms and usually a public dining room for overnight guests ⟨when we go on our country vacation, we always stay at this little *lodge* in the middle of nowhere⟩ — see HOTEL

2 an often small house for recreational or seasonal use ⟨every summer we rent a small fishing *lodge* by the lake⟩ — see COTTAGE

3 the meeting place of an organization ⟨the Masons meet at the *lodge* every Thursday evening⟩ — see CLUB 2

4 the shelter or resting place of a wild animal ⟨the family of beavers built a *lodge* near the narrow point of the river⟩ — see DEN 1

lodge *vb* **1** to provide with living quarters or shelter ⟨the landlord can legally *lodge* up to 20 people in his apartment building at one time⟩ — see HOUSE 1

2 to establish or place comfortably or snugly ⟨our pet guinea pig *lodged* himself in the far corner of his cage and simply refused to come out⟩ — see ENSCONCE 1

3 to set solidly in or as if in surrounding matter ⟨the gunman had managed to *lodge* a bullet in my back, just inches from my spine⟩ — see ENTRENCH

lodged *adj* firmly positioned in place and difficult to dislodge ⟨the rusty, old bolts were so well *lodged* that a power wrench was needed to extract them⟩ — see TIGHT 2

lodger *n* one who rents a room or apartment in another's house ⟨the mysterious *lodger* slept all day and only went out at night⟩ — see TENANT 1

lodging *n* **1** the place where one lives ⟨food and *lodging* are two of the largest expenses of living in the city⟩ — see HOME 1

2 lodgings *pl* a room or set of rooms in a private house or a block used as a separate dwelling place ⟨I've rented *lodgings* in the old boardinghouse downtown⟩ — see APARTMENT 1

3 a place to sleep and related amenities for the temporary use of a tourist or traveler ⟨*lodging* was whatever budget motel we could find for each leg of our trip⟩ — see ACCOMMODATION 1

lodgment *or* **lodgement** *n* **1** a mass or quantity that has piled up or that has been gathered over a period of time ⟨the *lodgment* of a week's worth of newspapers in the doorway was a telltale sign that the family was away⟩ — see ACCUMULATION 1

2 a place to sleep and related amenities for the temporary use of a tourist or traveler ⟨dismayed at the shabby *lodgments* that were the only option of cross-country travelers at the time⟩ — see ACCOMMODATION 1

loft *n* a room or unfinished space directly beneath the roof of a building ⟨the cottage has two bedrooms on the ground floor and a second-floor *loft* that could be converted into a third one⟩ — see ATTIC

loft *vb* to send through the air especially with a quick forward motion of the arm ⟨he *lofted* the ball down the center of the field toward a receiver⟩ — see THROW 1

loftiest *adj* being at a point or level higher than all others ⟨from the *loftiest* part of the mountain ridge you could see all the way to the next state⟩ — see TOP 1

loftiness *n* an exaggerated sense of one's importance that shows itself in the making of excessive or unjustified claims ⟨we were offended by the new club member's air of *loftiness*⟩ — see ARROGANCE

lofty *adj* **1** extending to a great distance upward ⟨the ever-increasing *lofty* heights of the world's skyscrapers⟩ — see HIGH 1

2 having a feeling of superiority that shows itself in an overbearing attitude ⟨she acts all *lofty* and superior just because she went to an Ivy League college⟩ — see ARROGANT

3 having or displaying feelings of scorn for what is regarded as beneath oneself ⟨his *lofty* attitude toward menial chores really rankles the other camp counselors⟩ — see PROUD 1

4 having, characterized by, or arising from a dignified and generous nature ⟨remained true to the cause's *lofty*

ideals, regardless of the changing winds of popular opinion⟩ — see NOBLE 2
5 very dignified in form, tone, or style ⟨the *lofty* nature of the coronation ceremony⟩ — see ELEVATED 2

log *vb* **1** to make a written note of ⟨the station captain *logged* the arrest and then left for home⟩ — see RECORD 1
2 to obtain (as a goal) through effort ⟨an actor who has *logged* a record number of Academy Award nominations in the course of her career⟩ — see ACHIEVE 1

logged *adj* containing, covered with, or thoroughly penetrated by water ⟨usually the driftwood is so *logged* with water that it needs an extended drying period before it can be used by the artist⟩ — see WET 1

logger *n* a person whose job is to cut down trees ⟨the *loggers* were obliged to plant as many trees as they cut down⟩ — see LUMBERJACK

loggerhead *n, chiefly dialect* a stupid person ⟨that *loggerhead* couldn't find the business end of a cow even if his life depended on it⟩ — see IDIOT

logic *n* the thought processes that have been established as leading to valid solutions to problems ⟨I tried to use *logic* to figure out the solution to the puzzle⟩
synonyms intellection, ratiocination, reason, reasoning, sense
related words cogency, coherence, logicality, logicalness, rationality, rationalness; convincingness, persuasiveness; syllogism, synthesis; analysis, dissection; deduction, induction; argumentation, disputation
near antonyms illogic, incoherence; absurdity, brainlessness, insanity, irrationality, nonsensicalness, preposterousness, senselessness

logical *adj* **1** according to the rules of logic ⟨the lawyer won the case with a *logical* argument about the motives of the suspect⟩
synonyms analytic (*or* analytical), coherent, consequent, good, rational, reasonable, sensible, sound, valid, well-founded, well-grounded
related words a posteriori, a priori, syllogistic; cognitive, empirical (*also* empiric); defendable, defensible, justifiable, maintainable, supportable, sustainable, tenable
near antonyms casuistic (*or* casuistical), eristic (*also* eristical), fallacious, misleading, sophistic (*or* sophistical), specious; unarticulated; unscientific; absurd, cockeyed, crazy, daffy, fatuous, half-baked, half-witted, harebrained, insane, loony (*also* looney), mad, nonsensical, nutty, preposterous, simpleminded, stupid, weak-minded, witless; senseless, thoughtless; uncompelling, unconvincing
antonyms illegitimate, illogical, incoherent, inconsequent, inconsequential, invalid, irrational, unreasonable, unsound, weak
2 based on sound reasoning or information ⟨that's the *logical* choice under the circumstances⟩ — see GOOD 1

logjam *n* **1** a crowded mass (as of cars) that impedes or blocks movement ⟨the presence of an ambulance on the side of the highway created a *logjam* of rubberneckers who just had to have a look⟩ — see JAM 1
2 a point in a struggle where neither side is capable of winning or willing to give in ⟨efforts to break the *logjam* in the talks between union and management⟩ — see IMPASSE 1

logo *n* a device, design, or figure used as an identifying mark ⟨the company's *logo* is instantly recognizable all over the world⟩ — see EMBLEM

logorrhea *n* the use of too many words to express an idea ⟨the article suffers from the *logorrhea* that infects so much academic writing⟩ — see VERBIAGE 1

logorrheic *adj* using or containing more words than necessary to express an idea ⟨his blog entries generally begin as focused and succinct arguments but too often devolve into *logorrheic* screeds⟩ — see WORDY 1

logy *also* **loggy** *adj* depleted in strength, energy, or freshness ⟨the next morning I was feeling *logy*, having stayed up half the night⟩ — see WEARY 1

loiter *vb* to move or act slowly ⟨don't *loiter* in this neighborhood after dark⟩ — see DELAY 1

loiterer *n* someone who moves slowly or more slowly than others ⟨she yelled at the *loiterers* at the end of the line to hurry up⟩ — see SLOWPOKE

loll *vb* **1** to be limp from lack of water or vigor ⟨the heads of the flowers *lolled* on their stems in the blistering heat⟩ — see DROOP 1
2 to refrain from labor or exertion ⟨farmhands *lolling* about in the shade and taking a break from the midday sun⟩ — see REST 1
3 to spend time doing nothing ⟨some members of the decorating committee were hard at work, and others were just *lolling* about⟩ — see IDLE

lollapalooza *n* something very good of its kind ⟨a huge birthday bash that promises to be a *lollapalooza* of a party⟩ — see JIM-DANDY

lollop *vb* to move with a light springing step ⟨the dog raced off and then *lolloped* back with a large stick in its mouth⟩ — see SKIP 1

lolly *n, British* something (as pieces of stamped metal or printed paper) customarily and legally used as a medium of exchange, a measure of value, or a means of payment ⟨I had to cough up the *lolly* when I lost the bet⟩ — see MONEY 1

lollygag *also* **lallygag** *vb* to move or act slowly ⟨accused the government of *lollygagging* while survivors of the earthquake continued to live in the most wretched conditions⟩ — see DELAY 1

lone *adj* **1** being the one or ones of a class with no other members ⟨the *lone* ripe apple in the entire bag⟩ — see ONLY 2
2 not being in the company of others ⟨just one *lone* cow in the middle of the field⟩ — see ALONE 1

lonely *adj* **1** not being in the company of others ⟨a single *lonely* cactus in the desert⟩ — see ALONE 1
2 sad from lack of companionship or separation from others ⟨I was *lonely* when I first got to Los Angeles, but I soon made friends⟩ — see LONESOME 1
3 causing or marked by an atmosphere lacking in cheer ⟨the *lonely* streets of a honky-tonk beach town in the off-season⟩ — see GLOOMY 1

loner *n* a person who does not conform to generally accepted standards or customs ⟨that guy in tech support is a *loner*, and never wants to hang out with the rest of us⟩ — see NONCONFORMIST 1

lone ranger *n* a person who does not conform to generally accepted standards or customs ⟨something of a *lone ranger* among anthropologists, she does her research without either a lending hand or an eye toward trendy topics⟩ — see NONCONFORMIST 1

lonesome *adj* **1** sad from lack of companionship or separation from others ⟨a *lonesome* kitten left at the pound by its hard-hearted owners⟩
synonyms desolate, forlorn, lonely, lorn
related words friendless; abandoned, deserted, forgotten, forsaken, neglected, rejected; alone, lone, solitary, solo, unaccompanied; only, sole
near antonyms accompanied, attended, escorted
2 not being in the company of others ⟨a *lonesome* cypress tree on a rocky, windswept point⟩ — see ALONE 1
3 causing or marked by an atmosphere lacking in cheer ⟨the playground seems especially *lonesome* now that there are no young children in the neighborhood⟩ — see GLOOMY 1

lone wolf *n* a person who does not conform to generally accepted standards or customs ⟨a *lone wolf* in the art world, he has his own style and paints only to please himself⟩ — see NONCONFORMIST 1

long *adj* **1** of great extent from end to end ⟨giraffes have *long* necks to help them reach leaves on tall trees⟩
synonyms elongate (*or* elongated), extended, king-size (*or* king-sized), lengthy
related words extensive, far-reaching, longish, outstretched; oblong, rectangular; big, biggish, considerable, hefty, hulking, jumbo, large, largish, overscale (*or* overscaled), oversize (*or* oversized), sizable (*or* sizeable), substantial, super
near antonyms abbreviated, abridged, curtailed, diminished, shortened; bitty, diminutive, little, miniature, minute, puny, small, smallish, teeny, tiny, undersized (*also* undersize), wee
antonyms brief, curt, short, shortish
2 lasting for a considerable time ⟨if it's boring, even a movie with a running time of 90 minutes can seem *long*⟩
synonyms extended, far, great, lengthy, long-drawn-out (*or* long-drawn), long-lived, long-term
related words aeonian (*or* aeonic), endless, everlasting, interminable, persistent; longish, overlong, prolonged, protracted; permanent; all-day, all-night; multiday, multiyear
near antonyms abrupt, sudden; abbreviated, condensed, curtailed, shortened; ephemeral, fleeting, momentary, transient, transitory; impermanent; short-range
antonyms brief, little, mini, short, shortish, short-lived, short-term

long *n* a long or seemingly long period of time ⟨they should be here before *long*⟩ — see AGE 2

long (for) *vb* to have an earnest wish to own or enjoy ⟨I *long for* the day when cancer is but a distant and unpleasant memory⟩ — see DESIRE 1

long–drawn–out *or* **long–drawn** *adj* lasting for a considerable time ⟨a *long-drawn-out* acceptance speech by an overemotional actor⟩ — see LONG 2

long green *n, slang* something (as pieces of stamped metal or printed paper) customarily and legally used as a medium of exchange, a measure of value, or a means of payment ⟨where did he get the *long green* to afford wheels like that?⟩ — see MONEY 1

longhair *n* a person with strong intellectual interests ⟨long-standing tension between the townies and the *longhairs* at the elite college⟩ — see INTELLECTUAL

long–haired *or* **longhair** *adj* much given to learning and thinking ⟨one of those *long-haired* idealists who founded short-lived utopias in rural America⟩ — see INTELLECTUAL 1

longhand *n* writing done by hand ⟨my computer was down for most of the afternoon, so I wrote out my report in *longhand*⟩ — see HANDWRITING 2

long haul *n* a long distance ⟨growing up in suburban New England, I used to think the 10 miles between our house and the mall was a *long haul*⟩ — see MILE

longing *n* a strong wish for something ⟨by four o'clock in the afternoon, I usually experience a strong *longing* for chocolate⟩ — see DESIRE 1

long–lived *adj* **1** being of advanced years and especially past middle age ⟨that sequoia tree is especially *long-lived*, having reached an age generally estimated to be at least 3,000 years⟩ — see ELDERLY
2 lasting for a considerable time ⟨much to the relief of his parents, the youth's interest in the piano proved to be *long-lived*⟩ — see LONG 2

longshoreman *n* one who loads and unloads ships at a port ⟨the *longshoremen* moved all of the fish into cold storage for shipment to the market⟩ — see DOCKWORKER

long–suffering *adj* accepting pains or hardships calmly or without complaint ⟨the *long-suffering* parents calmly waited until the tantrum had passed⟩ — see PATIENT 1

long–suffering *n* the capacity to endure what is difficult or disagreeable without complaining ⟨you will need infinite *long-suffering* to put up with that arrogant jerk⟩ — see PATIENCE

long suit *n* something for which a person shows a special talent ⟨one-on-one politicking is her *long suit*⟩ — see FORTE

long–term *adj* lasting for a considerable time ⟨before approving a new drug, the government insists on some *long-term* research to determine any possible side effects⟩ — see LONG 2

long–winded *adj* using or containing more words than necessary to express an idea ⟨his *long-winded* explanation could have been boiled down to two sentences⟩ — see WORDY 1

long–windedness *n* the use of too many words to express an idea ⟨that professor's *long-windedness* has long been legendary on campus⟩ — see VERBIAGE 1

loo *n, chiefly British* a room furnished with a fixture for flushing body waste ⟨he inquired as to whether there was a *loo* anywhere in the building⟩ — see TOILET

looby *n* a clumsy, awkward person ⟨although he was a *looby* physically, he was a towering figure in mathematics⟩ — see KLUTZ

look *n* **1** facial appearance regarded as an indication of mood or feeling ⟨you should have seen the *look* on your face when we yelled "Surprise!"⟩
synonyms cast, countenance, expression, face, visage
related words frown, grimace, lower (*also* lour), mouth, pout, scowl; grin, smile; air, appearance, aspect, bearing, demeanor, manner, mien, presence
2 an instance of looking especially briefly ⟨she gave the junk mail a quick *look* before throwing it in the wastebasket⟩
synonyms cast, eye, gander, glance, glimpse, peek, peep, regard, sight, view
related words gape, gaze, glare, leer, ogle, stare; sideglance; squinny, squint; coup d'oeil
3 the outward form of someone or something especially as indicative of a quality ⟨the bride's father has the *look* of a prosperous businessman⟩ — see APPEARANCE 1
4 looks *pl* the qualities in a person or thing that as a whole give pleasure to the senses ⟨a supermodel's career tends to be entirely based on her exceptional good *looks*⟩ — see BEAUTY 1

look *vb* **1** to give the impression of being ⟨it *looks* like it might rain⟩ — see SEEM
2 to make known (as an idea, emotion, or opinion) ⟨the music teacher *looked* her displeasure with a fierce frown⟩ — see EXPRESS 1
3 to have in mind as a purpose or goal ⟨they were *looking* to make a fast buck⟩ — see INTEND 1

look (at) *vb* to make note of (something) through the use of one's eyes ⟨I found her at the mall *looking at* the new outfits on the mannequins⟩ — see SEE 1

look (into) *vb* to search through or into ⟨the owner is being forced to *look into* new options for promoting his declining business⟩ — see EXPLORE 1

look (on *or* upon) *vb* to think of in a particular way ⟨you could call the comment mean-spirited, but I do not *look on* it that way at all⟩ — see CONSIDER 1

look (toward) *vb* to stand or sit with the face or front toward ⟨the bay window *looks toward* the park⟩ — see FACE 1

look–alike *n* something or someone that strongly resembles another ⟨at first glance these two mattresses may be *look-alikes*, but a comparison of their innards tells a different story⟩ — see IMAGE 1

look down (on *or* upon) *vb* to show contempt for ⟨I

am tired of the way they *look down on* us like we aren't good enough for them⟩ — see SCORN 1

looker *n* a physically attractive person ⟨a college campus that has its fair share of *lookers*⟩ — see DOLL 2

looking glass *n* a smooth or polished surface that forms images by reflection ⟨always remember that the image is reversed in the *looking glass*⟩ — see MIRROR

lookout *n* **1** a high place or structure from which a wide view is possible ⟨we went up to the *lookout* on the top of the hill to watch the fireworks⟩
synonyms observatory, outlook, overlook
related words aerie, crow's nest, tower, watchtower; promontory
2 all that can be seen from a certain point ⟨we were struck by the amazing beauty of the *lookout* from the top of the tower⟩ — see VIEW 1
3 a person or group that watches over someone or something ⟨make sure to post a *lookout* so that no one can sneak up on us⟩ — see GUARD 1
4 an act or period of watching for signs of activity, danger, or opportunity ⟨one of the robbers kept a *lookout* for the police⟩ — see VIGIL

look out (for) *vb* **1** to be cautious of or on guard against ⟨if you go in those woods, *look out for* snakes!⟩ — see BEWARE (OF)
2 to have an interest or concern for ⟨she *looks out for* number one, and everyone else can go hang⟩ — see CARE

look–see *n* a close look at or over someone or something in order to judge condition ⟨gave the painting a preliminary *look-see* to determine whether it could possibly be a genuine old master⟩ — see INSPECTION

look up *vb* **1** to go in search of ⟨be sure to *look* me *up* if you're ever in town⟩ — see SEEK 1
2 to become glad or hopeful ⟨by the next morning, the skies had begun to clear and we were *looking up*⟩ — see CHEER (UP) 1

loom *vb* to be about to happen ⟨he could tell that trouble was *looming* when the bullies swaggered into the park⟩
synonyms brew, impend
related words advance, approach, close in, draw on, gather, near; hang, hover, lower (*also* lour), menace, overhang, threaten
near antonyms abate, decline, de-escalate, die down, diminish, disappear, dwindle, ebb, fade, fall, lessen, let up, lower, moderate, recede, relent, remit, shrink, subside, taper, taper off, vanish, wane; fall back, pass, recede, retreat, withdraw

looming *adj* giving signs of immediate occurrence ⟨some economists see a *looming* collapse of the stock market⟩ — see IMMINENT 1

loon *n* **1** a person judged to be legally or medically insane ⟨giggled like a *loon* at his own jokes⟩ — see LUNATIC 1
2 a stupid person ⟨the *loons* at the grocery store had put the potato chips at the bottom of the bag⟩ — see IDIOT

loony *n* a person judged to be legally or medically insane ⟨his insistence that aliens from outer space were monitoring his thoughts forced doctors to conclude that he was in fact a *loony*⟩ — see LUNATIC 1

loony *also* **looney** *adj* **1** showing or marked by a lack of good sense or judgment ⟨that's got to be the *looniest* idea I've ever heard⟩ — see FOOLISH 1
2 having or showing a very abnormal or sick state of mind ⟨unfortunately, that homeless man talking to himself on the street is indeed *loony*⟩ — see INSANE 1

loony tunes *or* **looney tunes** *adj* having or showing a very abnormal or sick state of mind ⟨anyone living alone in that remote cabin would be sure to go *loony tunes*⟩ — see INSANE 1

loop *n* a circular strip ⟨cut the paper into narrow strips, and then paste those into *loops*⟩ — see [1]RING 2

looped *adj* being under the influence of alcohol ⟨I must've been *looped* when I agreed to work as a tiger exerciser at the zoo⟩ — see DRUNK

loose *adj* **1** not tightly fastened, tied, or stretched ⟨secure your neckerchief with a *loose* knot⟩
synonyms insecure, lax, loosened, relaxed, slack, slackened, unsecured
related words detached, free, unattached, unbound, undone, unfastened, untied; baggy, blousy, saggy
near antonyms constrained, restrained; attached, bound, fastened, tied; fast, firm, jammed, snug, stuck, wedged
antonyms taut, tense, tight
2 consisting of particles that do not stick together ⟨the car wheels slipped on the *loose* gravel in the driveway⟩
synonyms incoherent, unconsolidated
related words nonadhesive, nonviscous; disconnected, disjointed, separate, unconnected; coarse, granular, rough
near antonyms connected, solid; compacted, compressed; adhesive, gelatinous, gluey, glutinous, gooey, gummy, sticky, viscid, viscous
antonyms coherent, compact, dense, packed
3 not bound by rigid standards ⟨the generally *loose* discipline practiced by many weekend dads⟩ — see EASYGOING 2
4 not bound, confined, or detained by force ⟨there was a brief panic when the lion got *loose* from its cage at the zoo⟩ — see FREE 3
5 not precisely correct ⟨a *loose* guess about the size of the crowd at the outdoor concert⟩ — see INEXACT 1
6 having or showing lowered moral character or standards ⟨the *loose* life that he led in the years before his death by a drug overdose⟩ — see CORRUPT

loose *vb* **1** to cause (a projectile) to be driven forward with force ⟨the archers *loosed* a great volley of arrows at the foot soldiers charging towards them⟩ — see SHOOT 1
2 to find emotional release for ⟨do not *loose* your pent-up frustrations on the next person who happens by⟩ — see TAKE OUT 1
3 to set free (as from slavery or confinement) ⟨animal-rights activists *loosed* the monkeys from their laboratory cages⟩ — see FREE 1
4 to set free (from a state of being held in check) ⟨the storm *loosed* its full fury when it hit the coastline at high tide⟩ — see RELEASE 1

loosen *vb* **1** to make less taut ⟨the lead climber *loosened* the climbing rope so that the other climber could have more room to maneuver⟩ — see SLACKEN 1
2 to set free (as from slavery or confinement) ⟨the secret police have ways of *loosening* your tongue⟩ — see FREE 1
3 to set free (from a state of being held in check) ⟨the well-known fact that alcohol tends to *loosen* a person's inhibitions⟩ — see RELEASE 1

loosen (up) *vb* to free from obstruction or difficulty ⟨asked the school administrators to *loosen up* the rules on what can be printed on T-shirts⟩ — see EASE 1

loosened *adj* not tightly fastened, tied, or stretched ⟨the *loosened* nuts finally dropped off of the screws⟩ — see LOOSE 1

loosen up *vb* to get rid of nervous tension or anxiety ⟨a high-pressure job that makes it hard for him to *loosen up* even on weekends⟩ — see RELAX 1

loot *n* **1** valuables stolen or taken by force ⟨the burglar was caught when he foolishly stopped to examine the *loot* from the robbery⟩
synonyms booty, pillage, plunder, spoil, swag
related words prize; catch, haul, take, treasure; pilferage; windfall

2 something (as pieces of stamped metal or printed paper) customarily and legally used as a medium of exchange, a measure of value, or a means of payment ⟨a top-ranked golfer earning plenty of *loot*⟩ — see MONEY 1

loot *vb* to search through with the intent of committing robbery ⟨the bandits *looted* the archaeological dig before riding off into the night⟩ — see RANSACK 1

lop (off) *vb* to make (something) shorter or smaller with the use of a cutting instrument ⟨the hair stylist started by *lopping off* several inches from her long tresses, before beginning to shape what was left⟩ — see CLIP 1

lope *vb* to move with a light springing step ⟨the jogger happily *loped* along, just enjoying the fresh morning air⟩ — see SKIP 1

lopsided *adj* inclined or twisted to one side ⟨the portrait in the foyer was *lopsided*, so I straightened it while I was waiting⟩ — see AWRY

loquacious *adj* fond of talking or conversation ⟨sometimes the *loquacious* talk show host barely lets her guests get a word in⟩ — see TALKATIVE

lord *n* **1** a person of rank, power, or influence in a particular field ⟨as *lords* of the local real estate scene, they own nearly all of the city's prime pieces of property⟩ — see MAGNATE

2 *cap* the being worshipped as the creator and ruler of the universe ⟨at this point all that we can do is put our fate in the hands of the *Lord*⟩ — see DEITY 2

3 a man of high birth or social position ⟨*lords* and ladies arriving at the palace⟩ — see GENTLEMAN 1

lord (it over) *vb* to assume or treat with an air of superiority ⟨waiters at that fancy restaurant like to *lord it over* the customers, acting like they're doing them a favor just being there⟩ — see CONDESCEND 2

lordliness *n* an exaggerated sense of one's importance that shows itself in the making of excessive or unjustified claims ⟨the *lordliness* of his manner really got on his colleagues' nerves, as he had no real authority over them⟩ — see ARROGANCE

lordly *adj* **1** having a feeling of superiority that shows itself in an overbearing attitude ⟨one dinner guest was a little *lordly* about her status as a vegetarian, even asking the other diners how they could bear to eat dead animals⟩ — see ARROGANT

2 having or displaying feelings of scorn for what is regarded as beneath oneself ⟨his *lordly* attitude toward people who enjoy popular music⟩ — see PROUD 1

3 having, characterized by, or arising from a dignified and generous nature ⟨born to great wealth, he has always displayed a *lordly* generosity toward the less fortunate⟩ — see NOBLE 2

lore *n* **1** a body of facts learned by study or experience ⟨the home gardener had acquired her herbal *lore* from many years of trial and error⟩ — see KNOWLEDGE 1

2 the body of customs, beliefs, stories, and sayings associated with a people, thing, or place ⟨set out to study the rich *lore* of the Cajun people of Louisiana before it all vanished⟩ — see FOLKLORE

lorn *adj* sad from lack of companionship or separation from others ⟨*lorn* beyond all description, the widow struggled to cope with her crushing grief⟩ — see LONESOME 1

lose *vb* **1** to be unable to find or have at hand ⟨I always *lose* my keys⟩

synonyms mislay, misplace

related words forget, miss, overlook, pass over

near antonyms enjoy, have, hold, keep, occupy, own, possess, retain; descry, detect, find, locate, run down, scare up, scout (up), track (down)

2 to fail to win, gain, or obtain ⟨if the team *loses* this game, they're out of the play-offs⟩

synonyms drop

related words forfeit

near antonyms conquer, prevail (over), triumph (over)

antonyms nail (down), win

3 to undergo defeat ⟨she really hates to *lose* at anything, and inevitably throws tantrums when it happens⟩

synonyms bow out, fall

related words falter; tank, throw; forfeit; bomb, collapse, crack (up), fail, flop, flunk, fold, founder, miss, strike out, wash out

phrases take the count

near antonyms flourish, prosper, succeed, thrive

antonyms conquer, prevail, triumph, win

4 to get rid of as useless or unwanted ⟨we told the recent grad to *lose* the flashy shirts and dress conservatively for the job interview⟩ — see DISCARD

5 to use up carelessly ⟨we *lost* a good hour while he tried to find his keys⟩ — see WASTE 1

loser *n* something that has failed ⟨the first movie in the series was good, but all the sequels have been *losers*⟩ — see FAILURE 3

loss *n* **1** the act or an instance of not having or being able to find ⟨he was upset over the *loss* of his wedding ring⟩

synonyms mislaying, misplacement

related words deprivation, dispossession, privation; forfeit, forfeiture, penalty; sacrifice; bereavement; absence, lack, need, want

near antonyms control, hands, having, keeping, possession

antonyms acquisition, gain

2 a person or thing harmed, lost, or destroyed ⟨the platoon was able to accomplish its reconnaissance mission without any *losses*⟩ — see CASUALTY 1

3 failure to win a contest ⟨we're discouraged by our *loss* on Friday, but we're training hard for next week's game nevertheless⟩ — see DEFEAT 1

4 the amount by which something is lessened ⟨was determined to stay on the diet until he showed a *loss* of 10 pounds⟩ — see DECREASE

5 the state of being robbed of something normally enjoyed ⟨her *loss* of sleep meant that she would have trouble concentrating at work the next day⟩ — see PRIVATION

6 the state or fact of being rendered nonexistent, physically unsound, or useless ⟨the *loss* of the oil tanker was more significant than the *loss* of its cargo⟩ — see DESTRUCTION 1

lost *adj* no longer possessed ⟨we searched all over the house for the *lost* keys⟩

synonyms gone, mislaid, misplaced, missing

related words absent, castaway; irrecoverable, irretrievable; forgotten, unknown

near antonyms cherished, loved, prized, protected, treasured, valued

antonyms owned, possessed, retained

lot *n* **1** a small piece of land that is developed or available for development ⟨the softball team often plays in the vacant *lot* down at the end of the street⟩

synonyms parcel, plat, plot, property, tract

related words patch; frontage; lease; development; real estate

2 a considerable amount ⟨you'll need to do a *lot* of studying for the test⟩ ⟨you sure bought a *lot* of clothing⟩

synonyms abundance, barrel, basketful, boatload, bucket, bunch, bundle, bushel, carload, chunk, deal, dozen, fistful, gobs, good deal, heap, hundred, lashings (*also* lashins) [*chiefly British*], loads, mass, mess, mountain, much, multiplicity, myriad, oodles, pack, passel, peck, pile, plateful, plenitude, plentitude, plenty, pot, potful, profusion, quantity, raft, reams, scads, sheaf, shipload, sight, slew, spate, stack, store, ton, truckload, volume, wad, wealth, yard

related words epidemic, plague, rash; bonanza, embarrassment, excess, overabundance, overage, overkill, overmuch, oversupply, plethora, redundancy, superabundance, superfluity, surfeit, surplus; deluge, flood, overflow; army, bevy, cram, crowd, crush, drove, flock, herd, horde, host, legion, mob, multitude, press, score, sea, swarm, throng; gazillion, jillion, kazillion, million, thousands, trillion, zillion

phrases all kinds (of), quite a bit

near antonyms atom, crumb, dot, fleck, flyspeck, fragment, grain, granule, iota, jot, modicum, molecule, mote, nubbin, particle, ray, scintilla, scrap, shred, tittle, whit; smatter, smattering; dash, drop, morsel, shot; piece, portion, section; absence, dearth, famine, lack, paucity, poverty, scarceness, scarcity, shortage, undersupply, want; deficiency, deficit, inadequacy, insufficiency, meagerness, scantiness, scantness, skimpiness

antonyms ace, bit, dab, dram, driblet, glimmer, handful, hint, lick, little, mite, mouthful, nip, ounce, peanuts, pinch, pittance, scruple, shade, shadow, smidgen (*also* smidgeon *or* smidgin *or* smidge), speck, spot, sprinkle, sprinkling, strain, streak, suspicion, tad, taste, touch, trace

3 a small area of usually open land ⟨there were still plenty of Christmas trees available for sale in the *lot*⟩ — see FIELD 1

4 a number of things considered as a unit ⟨the auctioneer next introduced a *lot* containing several pieces of fine china⟩ — see GROUP 1

5 a state or end that seemingly has been decided beforehand ⟨will it always be my *lot* to be picked last in gym class?⟩ — see FATE 1

6 a group of people sharing a common interest and relating together socially ⟨you should stop hanging out with that *lot*, or you'll end up in trouble⟩ — see GANG 2

7 a usually small number of persons considered as a unit ⟨the school is indeed fortunate in its science teachers, because there's not a bad one in the *lot*⟩ — see GROUP 2

lot *vb* to give as a share or portion ⟨everyone is *lotted* opportunities in life, and it's their responsibility to take them⟩ — see ALLOT

lothario *n* a man given to seducing women ⟨a novel about the loveless existence of an aging *lothario*⟩ — see DON JUAN

lotus–eater *n* a lazy person ⟨a tropical resort that perfect for live wires and *lotus-eaters* alike⟩ — see LAZYBONES

lotusland *n* an often imaginary place or state of utter perfection and happiness ⟨the tropical resort's advertising depicts it as a *lotusland* of luxury and indolence⟩ — see PARADISE 1

louche *adj* not respectable ⟨before gentrification, it was the sort of *louche* neighborhood where people went looking for illegal drugs⟩ — see DISREPUTABLE

loud *adj* **1** marked by a high volume of sound ⟨*loud* music that could be heard all over the neighborhood⟩

synonyms blaring, blasting, booming, clamorous, clangorous, deafening, earsplitting, piercing, plangent, resounding, ringing, roaring, slam-bang, sonorous, stentorian, thundering, thunderous

related words brazen, dinning, discordant, noisy, obstreperous, raucous, rip-roaring, vociferous; grating, harsh, overloud, sharp, shrill, squealing, strident

near antonyms dead, quiet, silent, still, stilly, ultraquiet; calm, dreamy, peaceful, restful, serene, soothing, tranquil; hushed, muffled, muted, softened, toned (down)

antonyms gentle, low, soft

2 excessively showy ⟨his *loud* Hawaiian shirt made his face look especially pale⟩ — see GAUDY

lounge *n* a long upholstered piece of furniture designed for several sitters ⟨the tired youth stretched out on the *lounge* and breathed a huge sigh of relief⟩ — see COUCH

lounge *vb* **1** to refrain from labor or exertion ⟨police found the burglar *lounging* in the shade behind the building⟩ — see REST 1

2 to spend time doing nothing ⟨after putting in tons of overtime at the office, all we wanted to do on vacation was *lounge* around⟩ — see IDLE

lounge lizard *n* **1** a man extremely interested in his clothing and personal appearance ⟨a slick *lounge lizard* in a silk suit⟩ — see DANDY 1

2 a man given to seducing women ⟨a balding, paunchy *lounge lizard* whose days and nights of conquest were behind him⟩ — see DON JUAN

louse *n* a person whose behavior is offensive to others ⟨I can't believe you're willing to spend time with that lying *louse*⟩ — see JERK 1

louse up *vb* **1** to make a mistake ⟨everything is riding on this project, so we can't afford to *louse up*⟩ — see ERR 1

2 to make or do (something) in a clumsy or unskillful way ⟨I *loused up* the wallpapering job in the bedroom—the seams show too much⟩ — see BOTCH

lousily *adv* in an unsatisfactory way ⟨the new tennis racket did nothing for my game; I performed as *lousily* as ever⟩ — see BADLY 1

lousy *adj* **1** arousing or deserving of one's loathing and disgust ⟨why, you *lousy* cheater!⟩ — see CONTEMPTIBLE 1

2 falling short of a standard ⟨I actually play a pretty *lousy* game of tennis⟩ — see BAD 1

3 extremely unsatisfactory ⟨a *lousy* meal that we shouldn't have had to pay for⟩ — see WRETCHED 1

4 of low quality ⟨a tacky store selling *lousy* souvenirs that were made in some foreign sweatshop⟩ — see CHEAP 2

5 possessing or covered with great numbers or amounts of something specified ⟨a Manhattan neighborhood that is *lousy* with wannabe actors⟩ — see RIFE

lout *n* **1** a big clumsy often slow-witted person ⟨watch where you're going, you big *lout*!⟩ — see OAF 1

2 a person whose behavior is offensive to others ⟨Howard's rude behavior at the country club earned him a reputation as a *lout*⟩ — see JERK 1

loutish *adj* having or showing crudely insensitive or impolite manners ⟨the *loutish* bully didn't have a whole lot of friends⟩ — see CLOWNISH

lovable *also* **loveable** *adj* having qualities that tend to make one loved ⟨she was a *lovable* child, always helpful and kind⟩

synonyms adorable, darling, dear, disarming, endearing, lovesome, precious, sweet, winning, winsome

related words embraceable, kissable; beloved, cherished, favored, favorite, loved, treasured; attractive, beautiful, desirable, lovely; alluring, appealing, captivating, charming, enchanting, engaging, entrancing, fascinating, fetching; admirable, likable (*or* likeable), reputable, respectable; affable, agreeable, cheerful, cordial, friendly, genial, good-natured, good-tempered, gracious, kind, nice, pleasant; delightful, pleasing, well-disposed

near antonyms unloved; contemptible, disagreeable, disgusting, distasteful, heinous, horrible, lousy, nasty, offensive, unlikable, unpleasant, wretched; frightful, grotesque, hideous, ill-favored, monstrous, ogreish, repellent (*also* repellant), repugnant, repulsive; ugly, unattractive, unsightly, vile; appalling, awful, dreadful, foul, horrendous, horrid, nauseating, noisome, obnoxious, obscene, revolting, scandalous, shocking, sickening

antonyms abhorrent, abominable, detestable, hateful, loathsome, odious, unlovable

love *n* **1** a feeling of strong or constant regard for and dedication to someone ⟨her *love* for her children was truly selfless⟩
synonyms affection, attachment, devotedness, devotion, fondness, passion
related words appetite, fancy, favor, like, liking, partiality, preference, relish, taste; craving, crush, desire, infatuation, longing, lust, yearning; ardor, eagerness, enthusiasm, fervor, zeal; appreciation, esteem, estimation, regard, respect; adoration, adulation, deification, idolatry, idolization, worship; allegiance, faithfulness, fealty, fidelity, loyalty, steadfastness
near antonyms allergy, animosity, antagonism, antipathy, aversion, disfavor, dislike, enmity, hostility; abhorrence, disgust, repugnance, repulsion, revulsion; misanthropy
antonyms abomination, hate, hatred, loathing, rancor
2 a person with whom one is in love ⟨she is the *love* of my life⟩ — see SWEETHEART 1
3 positive regard for something ⟨a *love* of chocolate, which I will pay anything to indulge⟩ — see LIKING
4 a brief romantic relationship ⟨he refused to discuss past *loves*⟩ — see AFFAIR 1

love *vb* **1** to hold dear ⟨patriots who *loved* their country well enough to die for it⟩
synonyms appreciate, cherish, prize, treasure, value
related words delight (in), dig, enjoy, fancy, groove (on), like, relish, revel (in); admire, apprize, esteem, regard, respect, revere, reverence, venerate; enshrine, memorialize; adore, caress, dote (on), idolize, worship
phrases set store by (*or* set store on)
near antonyms undervalue; abhor, abominate, despise, detest, execrate, hate, loathe; disdain, high-hat, scorn, scout, slight, sniff (at), snub; bad-mouth, belittle, cry down, decry, deprecate, depreciate, disparage, kiss off, minimize, put down, write off; abandon, forget, neglect
antonyms disvalue
2 to feel passion, devotion, or tenderness for ⟨a husband who *loves* his wife more than anything⟩
synonyms adore, cherish, worship
related words adulate, canonize, deify, idealize, idolize; revere, reverence, venerate; delight (in), dote (on)
phrases carry a torch for (*or* carry the torch for), fall for, lose one's heart (to)
near antonyms antagonize, displease; disapprove (of), disfavor, dislike; disgust, nauseate, repel, repulse, revolt, sicken, turn off
antonyms abhor, abominate, despise, detest, execrate, hate, loathe
3 to take pleasure in ⟨I *love* playing Frisbee in the summer rain⟩ — see ENJOY 1
4 to touch or handle in a tender or loving manner ⟨the baby responded to my caresses and kisses by *loving* me right back⟩ — see FONDLE

love affair *n* **1** a brief romantic relationship ⟨the tabloids feel obliged to keep us informed of the *love affairs* of celebrities, whether we care to know or not⟩ — see AFFAIR 1
2 positive regard for something ⟨a group of young men united by their *love affair* with the muscle car⟩ — see LIKING

love child *n* an illegitimate child ⟨a woman who claimed to be the *love child* of two of Hollywood's most beloved stars during its golden age⟩ — see BASTARD 1

loved *adj* granted special treatment or attention ⟨her grandparents' constant doting made her feel especially *loved*⟩ — see DARLING 1

loveliness *n* the qualities in a person or thing that as a whole give pleasure to the senses ⟨our daughter was a vision of *loveliness* in her prom dress⟩ — see BEAUTY 1

lovely *adj* **1** of the very best kind ⟨thanked their hosts for the *lovely* time they had at the party⟩ — see EXCELLENT
2 very pleasing to look at ⟨a *lovely* painting of young girls in their summer dresses⟩ — see BEAUTIFUL 1

lovemaking *n* **1** sexual union involving penetration of the vagina by the penis ⟨does not allow her young daughter to watch any films in which *lovemaking* is shown, however discreetly⟩ — see SEXUAL INTERCOURSE
2 the series of social engagements shared by a couple looking to get married ⟨a series of Rococo paintings in which the *lovemaking* of French aristocrats is depicted with erotic playfulness⟩ — see COURTSHIP

lover *n* a person with a strong and habitual liking for something ⟨an enthusiastic *lover* of all kinds of team sports⟩ — see FAN

lovesome *adj* **1** having qualities that tend to make one loved ⟨a *lovesome* child that any couple would eagerly adopt⟩ — see LOVABLE
2 very pleasing to look at ⟨the kind of young and *lovesome* woman that any man would want for a wife⟩ — see BEAUTIFUL 1

lovey–dovey *adj* appealing to the emotions in an obvious and tiresome way ⟨*lovey-dovey* songs that were supposedly inspired by his feelings for his beloved wife⟩ — see CORNY 1

lovey–doveyness *n* the state or quality of having an excess of tender feelings (as of love, nostalgia, or compassion) ⟨the *lovey-doveyness* of the wedding vows, personally written by the couple, had me rolling my eyes⟩ — see SENTIMENTALITY

loving *adj* **1** feeling or showing love ⟨they were a *loving* family, supporting each other when times were bad⟩
synonyms adoring, affectionate, devoted, fond, tender, tenderhearted
related words caring, compassionate, considerate, cordial, doting, forgiving, friendly, humane, kind, understanding, warmhearted; ardent, fervent, impassioned, passionate, warm; amatory, amorous, erotic (*also* erotical); enamored, infatuated, lovesick; lovey-dovey, mushy, romantic, sappy, sentimental; brotherly, fatherly, motherly, sisterly
near antonyms aloof, antisocial, cold-eyed, cool, detached, distant, dry, frosty, hard-hearted, indifferent, offish, pitiless, remote, reserved, standoffish, unbending, uncaring, unfeeling; disaffected, unconcerned, uninvolved; cold, frigid, unfriendly; callous, cold-blooded, hard-boiled, heartless, pitiless, ruthless, soulless, unromantic, unsentimental
antonyms unloving
2 taking, showing, or involving great care and effort ⟨the homemade costume clearly showed the *loving* work that had gone into it⟩ — see PAINSTAKING

lovingness *n* attention accompanied by protectiveness and responsibility ⟨with a fierce *lovingness* she has maintained her family's cherished heirlooms for future generations⟩ — see CARE 2

low *adj* **1** being near the equator ⟨we took a cruise to the *low* northern latitudes⟩
synonyms equatorial, tropical
related words semitropical (*also* semitropic), subtropical (*also* subtropic)
near antonyms temperate
antonyms polar
2 belonging to or characteristic of an early level of skill or development ⟨once considered the latest thing, electric typewriters now look like *low* technology indeed⟩ — see PRIMITIVE 1
3 belonging to the class of people of low social or economic rank ⟨people, both high and *low*, have been wor-

shipping in this cathedral for centuries⟩ — see IGNOBLE 1
4 feeling unhappiness ⟨I was feeling *low*, and wanted to do something exciting to cheer myself up⟩ — see SAD 1
5 having a low musical pitch or range ⟨the tuba's *low* notes made the floor vibrate⟩ — see DEEP 2
6 having relatively little height ⟨the *low* hedge surrounding the garden wasn't meant to keep anything out, just to look pretty⟩ — see SHORT 1
7 lacking bodily strength ⟨the weeklong bout of chicken pox laid her *low*⟩ — see WEAK 1
8 lacking in refinement or good taste ⟨jokes about toilets are generally considered *low* humor⟩ — see COARSE 2
9 not following or in accordance with standards of honor and decency ⟨*low* tactics of that sort will not be tolerated on this hockey team⟩ — see IGNOBLE 2
10 not loud in pitch or volume ⟨murmured her answer in a *low* voice⟩ — see SOFT 1
11 costing little ⟨gas is *low* right now, but prices will inevitably rise this summer, when people start driving more⟩ — see CHEAP 1
12 of, relating to, or located at the bottom ⟨currently enjoys a *low* standing in the polls⟩ — see BOTTOM
13 not coming up to an expected measure or meeting a particular need ⟨levels for school volunteers remain *low*, at least compared to what was expected⟩ — see SHORT 3
14 no longer living ⟨thousands of the elderly were laid *low* by the deadly strain of flu⟩ — see DEAD 1

lowborn *adj* belonging to the class of people of low social or economic rank ⟨his patrician parents were very slow to accept his *lowborn* wife⟩ — see IGNOBLE 1

lowbred *adj* lacking in refinement or good taste ⟨having been brought up in a genteel family, she began to resent her fiancé's *lowbred* ways⟩ — see COARSE 2

lowbrow *adj* lacking in refinement or good taste ⟨at office gatherings his *lowbrow* humor often embarrassed his coworkers⟩ — see COARSE 2

lowbrow *n* a person who is chiefly interested in material comfort and is hostile or indifferent to art and culture ⟨the town's *lowbrows* think that the school's music program is a complete waste of taxpayers' money⟩ — see PHILISTINE

lowdown *n* information not generally available to the public ⟨have you heard the *lowdown* on the new chairman of the department?⟩ — see DOPE 1

low–down *adj* not following or in accordance with standards of honor and decency ⟨of all the *low-down* tricks that have ever been played in the history of that game⟩ — see IGNOBLE 2

low–end *adj* costing little ⟨a *low-end* stereo system that's good enough for casual listening⟩ — see CHEAP 1

lower *adj* **1** having not so great importance or rank as another ⟨a *lower* position in the company⟩ — see LESSER
2 situated lower down ⟨this book goes on the *lower* shelf⟩ — see INFERIOR 1

[1]lower *vb* **1** to cause to fall intentionally or unintentionally ⟨workmen slowly *lowered* the heavy statue into place⟩ — see DROP 1
2 to go to a lower level especially abruptly ⟨prices of the new type of televisions *lowered* considerably as competition and sales increased⟩ — see DROP 2
3 to make smaller in amount, volume, or extent ⟨decided to *lower* his career ambitions to something more achievable⟩ — see DECREASE 1
4 to grow less in scope or intensity especially gradually ⟨the noise of the jet engine *lowered* as the plane disappeared in the distance⟩ — see DECREASE 2
5 to reduce to a lower standing in one's own eyes or in others' eyes ⟨how could you *lower* yourself by passing off someone else's work as your own?⟩ — see HUMBLE
6 to diminish the price or value of ⟨over time, inflation *lowers* incomes and savings in terms of actual buying power⟩ — see DEPRECIATE 1

[2]lower *also* **lour** *vb* **1** to take on a gloomy or forbidding look ⟨the sky *lowered* overhead, threatening a fierce thunderstorm⟩ — see DARKEN 1
2 to look with anger or disapproval ⟨the motorist *lowered* at the jerk who had cut in front of her⟩ — see FROWN

lower *also* **lour** *n* a twisting of the facial features in disgust or disapproval ⟨he turned to see the scornful *lower* on her face⟩ — see GRIMACE

lower–class *adj* belonging to the class of people of low social or economic rank ⟨they were finally earning enough to get out of the *lower-class* tax bracket⟩ — see IGNOBLE 1

lowered *adj* directed down ⟨she wouldn't look at me, preferring instead to just sit there with *lowered* eyes⟩ — see DOWNCAST 1

lowering *also* **louring** *adj* **1** covered over by clouds ⟨the *lowering* sky made us think twice about going to the park⟩ — see OVERCAST
2 harsh and threatening in manner or appearance ⟨we chose our next words carefully, mindful of the *lowering* expression on his face⟩ — see GRIM 1

lowermost *adj* of, relating to, or located at the bottom ⟨even when her singing career was at its *lowermost* point, she still got gigs at small clubs⟩ — see BOTTOM

lowest *adj* being the least in amount, number, or size possible ⟨I play my radio at the *lowest* volume, but the neighbors still complain about the noise⟩ — see MINIMAL

low–grade *adj* of low quality ⟨plumbing fixtures that were made out of *low-grade* materials⟩ — see CHEAP 2

low–key *also* **low–keyed** *adj* not excessively showy ⟨hoping to make a good impression, he deliberately chose a *low-key* tie with a subtle pattern⟩ — see QUIET 2

low–life *adj* belonging to the class of people of low social or economic rank ⟨photographs of the *low-life* residents of postwar Paris⟩ — see IGNOBLE 1

lowliness *n* the absence of any feelings of being better than others ⟨that saint is often held up as a role model for her piety and unaffected *lowliness*⟩ — see HUMILITY

lowly *adj* **1** belonging to the class of people of low social or economic rank ⟨a tycoon who struggled all his life to overcome his *lowly* origins⟩ — see IGNOBLE 1
2 not having or showing any feelings of superiority, self-assertiveness, or showiness ⟨the nuns at the convent regard themselves as *lowly* servants of the Lord⟩ — see HUMBLE 1

lowly *adv* in a manner showing no signs of pride or self-assertion ⟨*lowly* bowing before his king, he accepted his knighthood⟩
synonyms abjectly, deferentially, hat in hand, humbly, meanly, meekly, modestly, sheepishly, submissively
related words obsequiously, servilely, subserviently; fearfully, mousily, timidly; bashfully, diffidently, self-deprecatingly, shyly, timorously; civilly, courteously, politely, respectfully, suppliantly
phrases cap in hand
near antonyms fearlessly; discourteously, disdainfully, disrespectfully, impertinently, rashly, recklessly, saucily; bitchily, impolitely, impudently, rudely, uncivilly, ungraciously
antonyms arrogantly, audaciously, boldly, brashly, brazenly, contemptuously, haughtily, huffily, imperiously, loftily, pompously, presumptuously, pretentiously, pridefully, proudly, scornfully, self-importantly, superciliously, swaggeringly, uppishly

low–lying *adj* having relatively little height ⟨the *low-ly-*

ing hills blocked our view of the sea only a little bit⟩ — see SHORT 1

low–minded *adj* not following or in accordance with standards of honor and decency ⟨even by the standards of our times, that was *low-minded,* gutter politics⟩ — see IGNOBLE 2

lown *adj, dialect* free from storms or physical disturbance ⟨a *lown* and pleasant valley⟩ — see CALM 1

lowness *n* **1** the quality or state of lacking refinement or good taste ⟨the shameless *lowness* of the comedian's humor is something movie fans either love or hate⟩ — see VULGARITY 1
2 the quality or state of lacking physical strength or vigor ⟨her lingering illness reduced her to a state of *lowness* she had never known before⟩ — see WEAKNESS 1

low–pressure *adj* having a relaxed, casual manner ⟨a *low-pressure* boss who lets employees do their work without looking over their shoulders⟩ — see EASYGOING 1

low–rent *adj* of low quality ⟨a store full of *low-rent* items⟩ — see CHEAP 2

low–slung *adj* having relatively little height ⟨only *low-slung* hotels have been built around the lake, so development isn't as intrusive as at other resorts⟩ — see SHORT 1

low–spirited *adj* feeling unhappiness ⟨the captain tried to cheer up her *low-spirited* teammates after their big loss⟩ — see SAD 1

loyal *adj* firm in one's allegiance to someone or something ⟨we remain *loyal* to the ideals for which this organization stands⟩ — see FAITHFUL 1

loyalist *n* a person who loves his or her country and supports its interests and policies ⟨die-hard *loyalists* engaging in espionage against the revolutionaries⟩ — see PATRIOT

loyalty *n* adherence to something to which one is bound by a pledge or duty ⟨there was no denying that dog's *loyalty* to his master⟩ — see FIDELITY

lozenge *n* a small mass containing medicine to be taken orally ⟨take one of these *lozenges* for your cold⟩ — see PILL 1

lubber *n* **1** a big clumsy often slow-witted person ⟨although he's something of a *lubber,* everyone agrees that he has a kind heart⟩ — see OAF 1
2 a clumsy, awkward person ⟨the two *lubbers* who came to deliver my furniture⟩ — see KLUTZ

lubricate *vb* to coat (something) with a slippery substance in order to reduce friction ⟨it's not a good idea to use olive oil to *lubricate* the gears in an appliance⟩
synonyms grease, oil, slick, wax
related words bathe, douse (*also* dowse), drench, soak, souse, wash, water, wet
near antonyms coarsen, rough, roughen; dehydrate, dry, parch, sear

lubricated *adj* having or being a surface so smooth as to greatly reduce traction ⟨the *lubricated* parts of the machine were whirring smoothly⟩ — see SLICK 1

lubricious *or* **lubricous** *adj* having a strong sexual desire ⟨back in the days when *lubricious* employers could, with impunity, take advantage of naive factory girls⟩ — see LUSTFUL

lucency *n* the state or quality of being easily seen through ⟨the *lucency* of the membrane⟩ — see CLARITY 1

lucent *adj* **1** easily seen through ⟨the pristine waters of *lucent* mountain streams⟩ — see CLEAR 1
2 giving off or reflecting much light ⟨the moon was a *lucent* orb in the cloudless autumn sky⟩ — see BRIGHT 1

lucid *adj* **1** giving off or reflecting much light ⟨those *lucid* bands that spread across the arctic sky and are known as the northern lights⟩ — see BRIGHT 1
2 having full use of one's mind and control over one's actions ⟨decided to make out her will while she was still *lucid*⟩ — see SANE
3 not subject to misinterpretation or more than one interpretation ⟨tried to make his instructions as *lucid* as possible so that everyone would understand what to do⟩ — see CLEAR 2

lucidity *n* clearness of expression ⟨the *lucidity* of the recipe should ensure a minimum of confusion⟩ — see SIMPLICITY 2

lucidness *n* clearness of expression ⟨she was impressed by the *lucidness* of her surgeon's explanation of the operation⟩ — see SIMPLICITY 2

Lucifer *n* the supreme personification of evil often represented as the ruler of hell ⟨*Lucifer* is depicted as a powerful but proud angel who leads a revolt against heaven⟩ — see DEVIL 1

Luciferian *adj* of, relating to, or worthy of an evil spirit ⟨the movie's villain wore a *Luciferian* expression of supreme confidence⟩ — see FIENDISH 1

luck *n* **1** success that is partly the result of chance ⟨some people have all the *luck*⟩
synonyms fortunateness, fortune, luckiness
related words blessing, boon, fluke, godsend, hit, serendipity, strike, windfall; break, chance, opportunity; coup, stroke
near antonyms knock, misadventure, mishap; adversity, curse, debacle (*also* débâcle), sorrow, tragedy, trouble; calamity, cataclysm, catastrophe, disaster; defeat, failure, fizzle, nonachievement, nonsuccess; accident, casualty; disappointment, lapse, letdown, reversal, reverse, setback, slipup; circumstance, destiny, doom, fate, lot, portion; hex, jinx
antonyms mischance, misfortune, unluckiness
2 the uncertain course of events ⟨let's plan our vacation rather than leave everything to *luck*⟩ — see CHANCE 1

luckiness *n* success that is partly the result of chance ⟨the supposed *luckiness* of a rabbit's foot—it didn't do much for the rabbit⟩ — see LUCK 1

luckless *adj* having, prone to, or marked by bad luck ⟨a bar where *luckless* gamblers go to drown their sorrows⟩ — see UNLUCKY 1

lucky *adj* **1** having good luck ⟨the *lucky* gambler waltzed out of the casino with $10,000⟩
synonyms fortunate, happy
related words blessed (*also* blest), favored, gifted, privileged; fair, golden, promising; hot
near antonyms cursed (*also* curst), disadvantaged
antonyms hapless, ill-fated, ill-starred, luckless, snakebit (*or* snakebitten), star-crossed, unfortunate, unhappy, unlucky
2 coming or happening by good luck especially unexpectedly ⟨finding this $20 bill on the way to the candy store was a *lucky* break⟩ — see FORTUNATE 1

lucrative *adj* yielding a profit ⟨the hired gun's mission was to turn the failing store into a *lucrative* operation⟩ — see PROFITABLE 1

lucre *n* **1** something (as pieces of stamped metal or printed paper) customarily and legally used as a medium of exchange, a measure of value, or a means of payment ⟨foreign coins are not acceptable *lucre* in most vending machines in this country⟩ — see MONEY 1
2 the amount of money left when expenses are subtracted from the total amount received ⟨it's usually *lucre* and not lust that motivates someone to set up a pornographic Web site⟩ — see PROFIT 1

luculent *adj* not subject to misinterpretation or more than one interpretation ⟨the district attorney's brilliant, *luculent* summation sealed the case for the prosecution⟩ — see CLEAR 2

Lucullan *also* **Lucullian** *adj* showing obvious signs of wealth and comfort ⟨a *Lucullan* lifestyle that included the requisite mansion and yacht⟩ — see LUXURIOUS 1

ludicrous *adj* **1** causing or intended to cause laughter ⟨the *ludicrous* sight of their teacher in a Halloween costume⟩ — see FUNNY 1
2 so foolish or pointless as to be worthy of scornful laughter ⟨a *ludicrous* and easily detected attempt to forge his father's signature on a note to school⟩ — see RIDICULOUS 1

lug *n* **1** a big clumsy often slow-witted person ⟨get off of my feet, you big *lug*!⟩ — see OAF 1
2 an average or ordinary man ⟨the billionaire industrialist was totally clueless about the concerns of the blue-collar *lugs* that worked for him⟩ — see JOE BLOW

lug *vb* **1** to cause to follow by applying steady force on ⟨*lugged* the lawn mower out into the backyard⟩ — see PULL 1
2 to support and take from one place to another ⟨I don't understand why he's always *lugging* all of his books around when his locker is right over there⟩ — see CARRY 1

lugubrious *adj* **1** causing or marked by an atmosphere lacking in cheer ⟨the diner's dim lighting makes eating there a particularly *lugubrious* experience⟩ — see GLOOMY 1
2 expressing or suggesting mourning ⟨in Victorian times, people who could affect particularly *lugubrious* expressions were hired to march in funeral processions as professional mourners⟩ — see MOURNFUL 1

lugubriously *adv* with feelings of bitterness or grief ⟨18th-century gravestones typically have inscriptions in which the brevity of life and the certainty of death are *lugubriously* noted⟩ — see HARD 2

lukewarm *adj* **1** having or giving off heat to a moderate degree ⟨I left the bowl of soup sitting on the counter too long, and now it's *lukewarm*⟩ — see WARM 1
2 showing little or no interest or enthusiasm ⟨the dentist's lecture on the merits of flossing got only a *lukewarm* response⟩ — see TEPID 1

lukewarmness *n* the quality or state of being moderate in temperature ⟨the *lukewarmness* of the soda pop did nothing for its taste⟩ — see WARMTH 1

lull *n* a momentary halt in an activity ⟨we took the opportunity of a *lull* in the conversation to announce that we were engaged to be married⟩ — see PAUSE 1

lull *vb* to free from distress or disturbance ⟨the absence of attacks for such an extended period had *lulled* the nation into a false sense of security⟩ — see CALM 1

lullaby *vb* to free from distress or disturbance ⟨reclining peacefully on the deck, *lullabied* by the gentle motion of the ship⟩ — see CALM 1

lulling *adj* tending to calm the emotions and relieve stress ⟨the *lulling* sound of a gently flowing stream⟩ — see SOOTHING 1

lulu *n, slang* something very good of its kind ⟨joked that the streaker gave a *lulu* of a performance⟩ — see JIM-DANDY

lumber *n* tree logs as prepared for human use ⟨a huge amount of *lumber* will be needed to build the house⟩ — see WOOD 1

lumber *vb* **1** to move heavily or clumsily ⟨the elephant *lumbered* through the jungle⟩
synonyms barge, clomp, clump, flog [*British*], flounder, galumph, lump, plod, pound, scuff, scuffle, shamble, shuffle, slog, slough, stamp, stomp, stumble, stump, tramp, tromp, trudge
related words drag, flop, haul; blunder, careen, dodder, lurch, reel, stagger, sway, teeter, totter, waddle, weave, wobble (*also* wabble)
near antonyms drift, float, hang, hover, poise, waft
antonyms breeze, coast, glide, slide, waltz, whisk
2 to proceed or act clumsily or ineffectually ⟨the novel's plot *lumbers* to its predictable conclusion after 500 long pages⟩ — see FLOUNDER 1
3 to make a low heavy rolling sound ⟨the horse-drawn wagon *lumbered* along the trail⟩ — see RUMBLE
4 to place a weight or burden on ⟨preparations that will *lumber* the expedition with unnecessary equipment and supplies⟩ — see LOAD 1

lumberjack *n* a person whose job is to cut down trees ⟨the sawmill gets most of its business from the *lumberjacks* up north⟩
synonyms jack, logger, lumberman
related words lumberer; sawyer; forester

lumberman *n* a person whose job is to cut down trees ⟨a *lumberman* who supervises the rest of the team during logging season⟩ — see LUMBERJACK

luminance *n* **1** brightness created by light reflected from a surface ⟨the emerald had a pure, icy green *luminance*⟩ — see SHINE 1
2 the quality or state of having or giving off light ⟨the landscapes of the French painter Claude Lorraine have a unique *luminance* that no other artist has quite captured⟩ — see BRILLIANCE 1

luminary *n* **1** a ball-shaped gaseous celestial body that shines by its own light ⟨awed by the vast number of *luminaries* in the night sky⟩ — see STAR 1
2 a person who is widely known and usually much talked about ⟨*luminaries* from the worlds of sports, entertainment, and politics were at the gala⟩ — see CELEBRITY 1

luminescence *n* the steady giving off of the form of radiation that makes vision possible ⟨we could see inside the cave even without a flashlight because of the *luminescence* coming from some of the fungus on the walls⟩ — see LIGHT 1

luminosity *n* the quality or state of having or giving off light ⟨the *luminosity* of the fireflies made for an enchanting nighttime show⟩ — see BRILLIANCE 1

luminous *adj* **1** giving off or reflecting much light ⟨the *luminous* moon bathed the snow-covered fields with a pearly glow⟩ — see BRIGHT 1
2 standing above others in rank, importance, or achievement ⟨some of the most *luminous* writers in the nation's history have graced that magazine's pages⟩ — see EMINENT
3 not subject to misinterpretation or more than one interpretation ⟨an author with a simple, *luminous* prose style that is free of affectation and pretention⟩ — see CLEAR 2

luminously *adv* in a manner marked by the shining or reflecting of much light ⟨in the soft candlelight her eyes sparkled *luminously* at him⟩ — see BRIGHTLY 1

luminousness *n* the quality or state of having or giving off light ⟨there's a special *luminousness* to the air over the island that painters and photographers have long sought to capture⟩ — see BRILLIANCE 1

lummox *n* a clumsy, awkward person ⟨that player is a *lummox* in the outfield, with three errors just this week⟩ — see KLUTZ

lump *n* **1** a small uneven mass ⟨she dumped a *lump* of clay on the table and started to sculpt⟩
synonyms blob, chunk, clod, clot, clump, dollop, glob, gob, gobbet, hunk, knob, nub, nubble, nugget, wad
related words bead, drop, globule; block, body, bulk; particle, piece, portion; bit, chip, crumb, granule, morsel, nubbin, patch, scrap
2 a small rounded mass of swollen tissue ⟨I got a good-sized *lump* on my head from that fall⟩ — see BUMP 1
3 an abnormal mass of tissue ⟨advised by her doctor to examine her breasts regularly for unusual *lumps*⟩ — see GROWTH 1
4 failure to win a contest ⟨you can't win all the time, so learn to take your *lumps* in stride⟩ — see DEFEAT 1
5 a stupid person ⟨gazed disgustedly at the *lump* her daughter had married⟩ — see IDIOT

6 a big clumsy often slow-witted person ⟨standing next to those ballet dancers, with their delicate features and lithe bodies, I felt like a *lump*⟩ — see OAF 1

lump *vb* **1** to bring together in one body or place ⟨when we *lumped* all of our pocket change together, we found that we had just enough a buy a carton of ice cream⟩ — see GATHER 1

2 to move heavily or clumsily ⟨while I was on crutches, I was *lumping* about the house like an elephant⟩ — see LUMBER 1

lumpen *adj* belonging to the class of people of low social or economic rank ⟨a kind of music that has traditionally appealed to the *lumpen* segment of the musical audience⟩ — see IGNOBLE 1

lumpy *adj* **1** having small pieces or lumps spread throughout ⟨the *lumpy* mashed potatoes were cold as well⟩ — see CHUNKY 1

2 not having a level or smooth surface ⟨before painting, we had to sand the *lumpy* surface to make it smooth⟩ — see UNEVEN 1

lunacy *n* **1** a foolish act or idea ⟨you want to sneak into the building after the alarm is set—what *lunacy*!⟩ — see FOLLY 1

2 a serious mental disorder that prevents one from living a safe and normal life ⟨the judge ruled that the certified *lunacy* of the accused made him incompetent to stand trial⟩ — see INSANITY 1

3 lack of good sense or judgment ⟨our friend's good-natured *lunacy* makes him of no use in an emergency but very entertaining companion nevertheless⟩ — see FOOLISHNESS 1

lunatic *adj* **1** having or showing a very abnormal or sick state of mind ⟨he had a *lunatic* obsession with personal hygiene that was genuinely disturbing⟩ — see INSANE 1

2 showing or marked by a lack of good sense or judgment ⟨such *lunatic* clowning during church services is completely inappropriate⟩ — see FOOLISH 1

lunatic *n* **1** a person judged to be legally or medically insane ⟨the *lunatic* was committed to an institution after running naked through the department store⟩

synonyms bug, crackbrain, crazy, fool, fruitcake, head case, loon, loony, maniac, nut, nutcase, nutter [*British slang*], psycho, psychopath, sickie, sicko, wacko (*also* whacko)

related words madman, madwoman; abnormal, deviant; manic-depressive, monomaniac, mythomaniac, neurotic, obsessive, obsessive-compulsive, paranoid, psychoneurotic, psychotic, schizo, schizoid, schizophrene, schizophrenic, sociopath; character, codger, crack, crackpot, crank, eccentric, fantastic (*also* fantastical), flake, kook, oddball, oddity, original, quiz, screwball, tyke (*also* tike) [*chiefly British*], weirdo, zany; case, patient

2 a person who lacks good sense or judgment ⟨we all knew she was a *lunatic*, but we never expected her to try to jump off of the roof of the school with a hang glider⟩ — see FOOL 1

lunch time *n* the middle of the day ⟨every Wednesday at *lunch time* the museum offers a free lecture or musical performance⟩ — see NOON 1

lunge *n* a quick thrust ⟨anticipated the *lunge* and jumped aside to avoid being stabbed⟩ — see [1]POKE 1

lunkhead *n* a stupid person ⟨don't let that *lunkhead* anywhere near your work tools⟩ — see IDIOT

lunkheaded *adj* **1** not having or showing an ability to absorb ideas readily ⟨a *lunkheaded* but good-hearted man⟩ — see STUPID 1

2 showing or marked by a lack of good sense or judgment ⟨the actor plays a cheerfully *lunkheaded* character in the new comedy⟩ — see FOOLISH 1

lurch *vb* **1** to make a series of unsteady side-to-side motions ⟨the room *lurched* with every jolt of the earthquake⟩ — see ROCK 1

2 to move forward while swaying from side to side ⟨dressed in his zombie costume, the boy *lurched* down the street in his quest for Halloween candy⟩ — see STAGGER 1

lure *n* **1** something that persuades one to perform an action for pleasure or gain ⟨the promise of easy money is always the *lure* for some people to take up a life of crime⟩

synonyms allurement, bait, come-on, enticement, siren song, temptation, turn-on

related words appeal, call; attraction, boost, encouragement, goad, impetus, impulse, incentive, inducement, motivation, persuasion, seducement, seduction, spur, stimulus; decoy, snare, trap; entrapment, mousetrap

near antonyms alarm (*also* alarum), alert, caution, forewarning, notice, warning

2 something used to attract animals to a hook or into a trap ⟨the fish simply didn't seem to like the *lure* I was using, so I didn't catch a thing⟩ — see BAIT 1

3 the act or pressure of giving in to a desire especially when ill-advised ⟨the *lure* of the video game was distracting me from my studies⟩ — see TEMPTATION 1

lure *vb* to lead away from a usual or proper course by offering some pleasure or advantage ⟨the hunter *lured* the lion into the open with the antelope carcass⟩

synonyms allure, bait, beguile, betray, decoy, entice, lead on, seduce, solicit, tempt

related words draw in, inveigle, persuade, rope (in), snow; catch, enmesh (*also* immesh), ensnare, entrap, mesh, snare, tangle, trap; bewitch, captivate, charm, enchant, fascinate, magnetize, wile

near antonyms alert, caution, forewarn, ward (off), warn; drive (away *or* off), repulse, turn away

lurid *adj* **1** extremely disturbing or repellent ⟨we quickly drove past the *lurid* scene of the crash⟩ — see HORRIBLE 1

2 lacking a healthy skin color ⟨the doctor was alarmed by the patient's *lurid* complexion⟩ — see PALE 2

3 arousing a strong and usually superficial interest or emotional reaction ⟨the *lurid* news reports about the romance between the two Hollywood stars⟩ — see SENSATIONAL 1

luring *adj* having an often mysterious or magical power to attract ⟨the *luring* sight of sparkling gemstones in a jewelry-store window⟩ — see FASCINATING 1

lurk *vb* **1** to move about in a sly or secret manner ⟨we caught a glimpse of someone *lurking* around the corner⟩ — see SNEAK 1

2 to remain out of sight ⟨watch out for snakes *lurking* in the tall grass⟩ — see [1]HIDE 3

lurker *n* someone who acts in a sly and secret manner ⟨suddenly, the mysterious *lurker* leapt out into the light!⟩ — see SNEAK

luscious *adj* **1** very pleasing to the sense of taste ⟨a *luscious* strawberry bursting with juice⟩ — see DELICIOUS 1

2 pleasing to the physical senses ⟨*luscious* silk fabric that slid across her hands⟩ — see SENSUAL

3 giving pleasure or contentment to the mind or senses ⟨the *luscious* thought that while she was basking on the beach, her coworkers were slaving away at the office⟩ — see PLEASANT 1

4 sexually attractive ⟨a *luscious* bod like that has spent a lot of time in the gym or under the knife of a good plastic surgeon⟩ — see SEXY 1

lusciousness *n* the quality of being delicious ⟨it was hard to resist the decadent *lusciousness* of the three-layer chocolate cake⟩ — see DELICIOUSNESS

lush *adj* **1** covered with a thick healthy natural growth

⟨they loved to go for picnics in the *lush* woodlands⟩
synonyms green, grown, leafy, luxuriant, overgrown, verdant
related words fat, fecund, fertile, fruitful, productive, prolific, rich; dense, tangled
near antonyms bleak, depleted, impoverished, infertile, poor, stark, unproductive; arid, dead, desert, dry, parched, sere (*also* sear), waterless
antonyms barren, leafless
2 growing thickly and vigorously ⟨*lush* dandelions had turned the meadow into a sea of yellow⟩ — see RANK 1
3 very pleasing to the sense of taste ⟨*lush* desserts that are well worth the boatload of calories⟩ — see DELICIOUS 1
4 marked by vigorous growth and well-being especially economically ⟨those were *lush* times for the gambling industry, which kept building ever grander casinos⟩ — see PROSPEROUS 1
5 pleasing to the physical senses ⟨I could listen to the baritone's *lush* voice for hours⟩ — see SENSUAL
6 producing abundantly ⟨his *lush* fields were the envy of neighboring farmers⟩ — see FERTILE

lush *n* **1** a person who makes a habit of getting drunk ⟨she accused him of being a *lush* and a spendthrift⟩ — see DRUNK 1
2 *slang* a distilled beverage that can make a person drunk ⟨you guys can drink if you want, but I'm laying off the *lush*⟩ — see ALCOHOL

lush (up) *vb, slang* to partake excessively of alcoholic beverages ⟨frat boys *lushing up* on beer during freshman rush⟩ — see DRINK 2

lust *n* **1** intense sexual desire ⟨he was overcome with *lust* when he saw the images⟩
synonyms ardor, concupiscence, eros, eroticism, horniness, itch, lustfulness, passion
related words erotomania, nymphomania, satyriasis; lasciviousness, lewdness, libidinousness, licentiousness, lickerishness, randiness, salaciousness, wantonness
near antonyms frigidity
2 a strong wish for something ⟨the belief that most politicians have a *lust* for power⟩ — see DESIRE 1
3 urgent desire or interest ⟨vacation tours for people with a *lust* for adventure⟩ — see EAGERNESS
4 sexual appetite ⟨a no-strings-attached relationship in which both parties were there merely for the satisfaction of their *lust*⟩ — see DESIRE 2

lust (for *or* after) *vb* to have an earnest wish to own or enjoy ⟨I'm *lusting after* that new SUV⟩ — see DESIRE 1

luster *or* **lustre** *n* **1** brightness created by light reflected from a surface ⟨the Hope diamond is famous for its brilliant *luster*⟩ — see SHINE 1
2 the quality or state of having or giving off light ⟨on a clear night at sea the stars seem to take on a magical *luster*⟩ — see BRILLIANCE 1

luster *or* **lustre** *vb* to shoot forth bursts of light ⟨her pearl necklace *lustered* softly in the candlelight of the restaurant⟩ — see FLASH 1

lusterless *adj* lacking a surface luster or gloss ⟨a small tombstone of *lusterless* granite marks his modest grave⟩ — see MATTE

lustful *adj* having a strong sexual desire ⟨a chronically *lustful* college jock who was always chasing after girls⟩
synonyms concupiscent, goatish, horny, hot, hypersexual, itchy, lascivious, lecherous, lewd, libidinous, licentious, lubricious (*or* lubricous), oversexed, passionate, randy, salacious, satyric, wanton
related words aroused, excited; easy, fast, loose, promiscuous; dissipated, dissolute, libertine; corrupt, debased, debauched, decadent, degenerate, degraded, demoralized, depraved, dissipated, dissolute, immoral, indecent
near antonyms celibate, chaste, decent, immaculate, modest, moral, pure, virtuous; monastic, monkish; maidenly, virginal; innocent, lily-white; priggish, prim, prudish, puritanical, straitlaced (*or* straightlaced), Victorian
antonyms frigid, undersexed

lustfulness *n* **1** intense sexual desire ⟨a sermon on *lustfulness* and the weakness of the flesh⟩ — see LUST 1
2 sexual appetite ⟨the legendary *lustfulness* of sailors who have been at sea for far too long⟩ — see DESIRE 2

lustihood *n* sexual appetite ⟨behind that demure facade lurked an unexpected *lustihood*⟩ — see DESIRE 2

lustiness *n* the quality or state of having abundant or intense activity ⟨campaign volunteers working for their candidate with a *lustiness* that is inspiring⟩ — see VITALITY 1

lustrous *adj* **1** giving off or reflecting much light ⟨the *lustrous* finish on the satin bedspread adds to the feeling of luxury⟩ — see BRIGHT 1
2 having a shiny surface or finish ⟨*lustrous* silver jewelry adorned her neck⟩ — see GLOSSY

lustrously *adv* in a manner marked by the shining or reflecting of much light ⟨he tenderly caressed her *lustrously* soft hair⟩ — see BRIGHTLY 1

lustrousness *n* the quality or state of having or giving off light ⟨the lovely *lustrousness* of her hair just made you want to stroke it⟩ — see BRILLIANCE 1

lusty *adj* **1** having active strength of body or mind ⟨the *lusty* young rowers on the college crew team⟩ — see VIGOROUS 1
2 not showing weakness or uncertainty ⟨a *lusty* spirit of adventure⟩ — see FIRM 1
3 having an abundance of some characteristic quality (as flavor) ⟨such a *lusty* dish calls for an equally rich wine⟩ — see FULL-BODIED

luxe *adj* showing obvious signs of wealth and comfort ⟨we stayed only in *luxe* accommodations on the trip through the Loire Valley⟩ — see LUXURIOUS 1

luxuriant *adj* **1** covered with a thick, healthy natural growth ⟨an older man who still has a *luxuriant* head of hair⟩ — see LUSH 1
2 growing thickly and vigorously ⟨a *luxuriant* coat of fur⟩ — see RANK 1
3 producing abundantly ⟨*luxuriant* soil that yields endless fields of grain⟩ — see FERTILE
4 showing obvious signs of wealth and comfort ⟨the fashion model always wore the most *luxuriant* outfits⟩ — see LUXURIOUS 1

luxurious *adj* **1** showing obvious signs of wealth and comfort ⟨the *luxurious* apartment was filled with the latest electronic gadgets and fine works of art⟩
synonyms Babylonian, deluxe, lavish, Lucullan (*also* Lucullian), luxe, luxuriant, luxury, opulent, palace, palatial, plush, plushy, silken, sumptuous
related words costly, dear, expensive, precious, premium, rich; extravagant, grandiose, ostentatious, pretentious, showy; august, awesome, awful, baronial, beautiful, gorgeous, grand, heroic (*also* heroical), imposing, impressive, kingly, magnificent, majestic, monumental, noble, proud, regal, royal, splendid, stately; comfortable, cozy, homelike, homey (*also* homy), snug
near antonyms economical, frugal, meager (*or* meagre), spare, stingy, thrifty
antonyms ascetic (*also* ascetical), austere, humble, no-frills, spartan
2 given to or marked by excessive gratification of one's desires ⟨squandered his fortune in the relentless satisfaction of his *luxurious* tastes⟩ — see HEDONISTIC

luxuriously *adv* in a luxurious manner ⟨we welcomed the opportunity to live *luxuriously* while on the ocean liner⟩ — see HIGH

luxury *adj* showing obvious signs of wealth and comfort ⟨a *luxury* ski lodge for those whose idea of roughing it includes private whirlpool baths⟩ — see LUXURIOUS 1

luxury *n* **1** something adding to pleasure or comfort but not absolutely necessary ⟨a private yacht is a *luxury*⟩
synonyms amenity, comfort, extra, frill, indulgence, superfluity
related words extravagance, nonessential; dainty, delicacy, nicety, treat; accessory (*also* accessary), accoutrement (*or* accouterment), bells and whistles, option
antonyms basic, essential, fundamental, must, necessity, requirement
2 something that adds to one's ease of living ⟨having one's own bathroom is one of life's greatest *luxuries*⟩ — see COMFORT 2

lying *adj* telling or containing lies ⟨that *lying* son of a gun told me that the used car had never been in an accident⟩ — see DISHONEST 1

lynx–eyed *adj* having unusually keen vision ⟨the *lynx-eyed* copy editor never seemed to miss an error in the reporters' work⟩ — see SHARP-EYED

lyric *adj* **1** having a pleasantly flowing quality suggestive of music ⟨they performed a slow, *lyric* dance for the audience⟩
synonyms euphonious, lyrical, mellifluent, mellifluous, mellow, melodic, melodious, musical
related words dulcet, golden, sweet
near antonyms disconnected, staccato; discordant, dissonant, grating, harsh, inharmonious, jarring, strident, unmelodious, unmusical
antonyms unlyrical
2 having qualities suggestive of poetry ⟨the film's *lyric* photography really enhanced its romantic mood⟩ — see POETIC

lyric *n* **1** a composition using rhythm and often rhyme to create a lyrical effect ⟨would you care to read your short *lyric* aloud?⟩ — see POEM
2 a short musical composition for the human voice often with instrumental accompaniment ⟨the guitarist sang a gentle *lyric* while playing⟩ — see SONG 1

lyrical *adj* **1** having a pleasantly flowing quality suggestive of music ⟨the *lyrical* cadences of voice-over narration give the film a very poignant quality⟩ — see LYRIC 1
2 having qualities suggestive of poetry ⟨the photographer achieves a very *lyrical* effect with her intentionally blurred images of flowers growing in the wild⟩ — see POETIC

M

ma *n* a female human parent ⟨I told my *ma* that on Mother's Day we'd be dining at the town's toniest restaurant⟩ — see MOTHER

mac *or* **mack** *n, British* a coat made of water-resistant material ⟨I'm glad the little nipper remembered his *mac* today, because it's supposed to rain⟩ — see RAINCOAT

macabre *adj* extremely disturbing or repellent ⟨a *macabre* movie about animated corpses⟩ — see HORRIBLE 1

macaroni *n* a man extremely interested in his clothing and personal appearance ⟨the glitter rock of the 1970s seemed more about mascaraed *macaronis* than about music⟩ — see DANDY 1

macédoine *n* an unorganized collection or mixture of various things ⟨a quirky secondhand bookstore with a *macédoine* of out-of-print titles⟩ — see MISCELLANY 1

macerate *vb* to wet thoroughly with liquid ⟨garnished with cherries that had been *macerated* in liqueur⟩ — see SOAK 1

Machiavellian *adj* not guided by or showing a concern for what is right ⟨yet another tale of a power-mad dictator with a *Machiavellian* plan to take over the world⟩ — see UNPRINCIPLED

machinate *vb* **1** to engage in a secret plan to accomplish evil or unlawful ends ⟨a trio of courtiers who were discovered to be *machinating* against the queen⟩ — see PLOT
2 to plan out usually with subtle skill or care ⟨the hackers *machinated* a way to steal credit numbers from the company's Web site⟩ — see ENGINEER

machination *n* a secret plan for accomplishing evil or unlawful ends ⟨incredibly complicated *machinations* to assassinate the president that inevitably failed⟩ — see PLOT 1

machine *n* **1** a device that changes energy into mechanical motion ⟨a *machine* that washes dishes for you⟩ — see ENGINE
2 a self-propelled passenger vehicle on four wheels ⟨that Corvette is a *machine* that any guy would love to own⟩ — see CAR

machinery *n* something used to achieve an end ⟨sincerely believes that the *machinery* of government can be used to better people's lives⟩ — see AGENT 1

machismo *n* the set of qualities considered appropriate for or characteristic of men ⟨a culture that prizes *machismo* and has rigid gender roles⟩ — see VIRILITY

macho *n* the set of qualities considered appropriate for or characteristic of men ⟨their annual guys-only hunting trip is a celebration of *macho*⟩ — see VIRILITY

mackintosh *also* **macintosh** *n, chiefly British* a coat made of water-resistant material ⟨be sure to wear a *mackintosh* while hiking over the misty mountains of England's Lake District⟩ — see RAINCOAT

macrocosm *n* the whole body of things observed or assumed ⟨almost the entirety of the vast *macrocosm* remains beyond our reach⟩ — see UNIVERSE

mad *adj* **1** feeling or showing anger ⟨the constant harassment from telemarketers finally made her good and *mad*⟩ — see ANGRY
2 having or showing a very abnormal or sick state of mind ⟨the man who thinks he's been turned into a bug is clearly *mad*⟩ — see INSANE 1
3 marked by great and often stressful excitement or activity ⟨a *mad* rush to finish the shopping before Christmas⟩ — see FURIOUS 1
4 showing or marked by a lack of good sense or judgment ⟨her *mad* decision to quit a good job and run off to the big city with a man she barely knew⟩ — see FOOLISH 1

mad *n* an intense emotional state of displeasure with someone or something ⟨watch out, the boss has got a bit of a *mad* on just now⟩ — see ANGER

mad *vb* to make angry ⟨her endless excuses for not doing the work *madded* her overburdened coworkers⟩ — see ANGER 1

mad (about) *adj* filled with an intense or excessive love for ⟨he's virtually inseparable from his new girlfriend and seems to be just *mad about* her⟩ — see ENAMORED (OF)

madam *n* the female partner in a marriage ⟨the *madam* and I are planning to go out for a nice dinner on our anniversary⟩ — see WIFE

madcap *adj* foolishly adventurous or bold ⟨a *madcap* scheme to go over Niagara Falls in a barrel⟩ — see FOOLHARDY 1

madcap *n* a person who seeks out very dangerous or foolhardy adventures with no apparent fear ⟨an incorrigible *madcap* who loves drag racing and white-water rafting⟩ — see DAREDEVIL

madden *vb* **1** to cause to go insane or as if insane ⟨the endless swarms of mosquitoes all but *maddened* the explorers⟩ — see CRAZE
2 to make angry ⟨her perpetual tardiness *maddened* her friends to no end⟩ — see ANGER

maddening *adj* causing annoyance ⟨after a few days, she found the monotonous work to be absolutely *maddening*⟩ — see ANNOYING

made-to-order *adj* made or fitted to the needs or preferences of a specific customer ⟨the manufacturer offers its online customers *made-to-order* computer systems⟩ — see CUSTOM-MADE

made-up *adj* not real and existing only in the imagination ⟨the bogeyman was one of those *made-up* monsters whose sole purpose was to threaten children⟩ — see IMAGINARY

madhouse *n* **1** a place where insane people are cared for ⟨it was hard to believe that this place with the bright cheery walls was really a *madhouse*⟩
synonyms asylum, bedlam, institution
related words hospital; halfway house, home; hospice, sanatorium, sanitarium, sanitorium
2 a place of uproar or confusion ⟨our house is always a *madhouse* on school mornings, with five kids and two dogs running around⟩
synonyms babel, bedlam, circus, scrum [*British*], three-ring circus
related words bustle, commotion, pandemonium, racket, ruckus, tumult, turmoil; brouhaha, clamor, clatter, din, hubbub, noise; chaos, confusion, disarrangement, disarray, disorder, havoc, hell, mess, muss, shambles
near antonyms arcadia, heaven, paradise, utopia; order, orderliness, organization; calm, lull, peace, respite; hush, quiet, silence, stillness

madly *adv* **1** in a confused and reckless manner ⟨dashed *madly* around the house during last-minute preparations for the party⟩ — see HELTER-SKELTER 1
2 in an enthusiastic manner ⟨the young singer has been so *madly* praised by the critics you'd think she had invented singing itself⟩ — see SKY-HIGH

madman *n* a person who seeks out very dangerous or foolhardy adventures with no apparent fear ⟨as far as I'm concerned, anyone who likes skydiving is a *madman*⟩ — see DAREDEVIL

madness *n* **1** a serious mental disorder that prevents one from living a safe and normal life ⟨nowadays certain forms of *madness* are quite treatable⟩ — see INSANITY 1

2 lack of good sense or judgment ⟨to do something so reckless would be sheer *madness*⟩ — see FOOLISHNESS 1

3 an intense emotional state of displeasure with someone or something ⟨her incessant insults goaded him to such *madness* that he would storm around breaking dishes and slamming doors⟩ — see ANGER

madras *n* a scarf worn on the head ⟨an Indian woman wearing a *madras* in bright yellow⟩ — see BANDANNA

Maecenas *n* one that helps another with gifts or money ⟨the opera company no longer has an array of moneyed *Maecenases* to which it can turn for financial support⟩ — see BENEFACTOR

maelstrom *n* water moving rapidly in a circle with a hollow in the center ⟨our rubber raft got caught in a *maelstrom* in a particularly rough stretch of white water⟩ — see WHIRLPOOL

maestro *n* a person with a high level of knowledge or skill in a field ⟨a *maestro* of the violin⟩ — see EXPERT

Mafia *n* a group involved in secret or criminal activities ⟨the local *Mafia* largely finances itself through extortion rackets and drug trafficking⟩ — see [1]RING 1

mag *n* a publication that appears at regular intervals ⟨flip through this month's fashion *mags* to find out what's in style⟩ — see JOURNAL 1

magazine *n* **1** a building for storing goods ⟨the village kept a *magazine* where people left common supplies⟩ — see STOREHOUSE

2 a place where military arms are stored ⟨the *magazine* is heavily guarded to prevent theft⟩ — see ARMORY

3 a publication that appears at regular intervals ⟨a weekly sports *magazine*⟩ — see JOURNAL 1

mage *n* a person skilled in using supernatural forces ⟨an ancient tale of a *mage* who made lush gardens grow in the desert⟩ — see MAGICIAN 1

maggot *n* a sudden impulsive and apparently unmotivated idea or action ⟨the last *maggot* he got in his head resulted in a disastrous extramarital affair⟩ — see WHIM

Magian *n* a person skilled in using supernatural forces ⟨in Shakespeare's *The Tempest*, Prospero is a benevolent *Magian* who rules over an enchanted tropical island⟩ — see MAGICIAN 1

magic *adj* **1** being or appearing to be under a magic spell ⟨a *magic* castle in which even the furniture comes to life⟩ — see ENCHANTED

2 having seemingly supernatural qualities or powers ⟨truth seekers of all sorts seem to be attracted to this *magic* spot in the desert⟩ — see MYSTIC 1

magic *n* **1** the power to control natural forces through supernatural means ⟨he claimed that he could summon a storm through *magic*⟩

synonyms bewitchery, bewitchment, conjuring, devilry (*or* deviltry), diablerie, enchantment, ensorcellment, mojo, necromancy, sorcery, thaumaturgy, voodooism, witchcraft, witchery, wizardry

related words abracadabra, amulet, charm, fetish (*also* fetich), mascot, periapt, phylactery, talisman; conjuration, glamour (*also* glamor), incantation, spell; curse, hex, jinx; augury, crystal gazing, divination, divining, forecasting, foreknowing, foreseeing, foretelling, fortune-telling, predicting, presaging, prognosticating, prophesying, soothsaying, sortilege; hexerei, hoodoo, occultism, spiritualism; augur, omen; exorcism; alchemy

near antonyms science

2 the art or skill of performing tricks or illusions for entertainment ⟨hired an entertainer to perform *magic* for their child's 10th birthday party⟩

synonyms conjuring, hocus-pocus, legerdemain, prestidigitation

related words deception, deceptiveness, trickery

phrases sleight of hand

3 the power of irresistible attraction ⟨a leader so charismatic that his appeal was like *magic*⟩ — see CHARM 2

magical *adj* **1** being or appearing to be under a magic spell ⟨the gym was decorated to resemble a *magical* wonderland for the party⟩ — see ENCHANTED

2 being so extraordinary or abnormal as to suggest powers which violate the laws of nature ⟨modern aviation must seem *magical* to someone who doesn't understand basic aeronautics⟩ — see SUPERNATURAL 2

3 having seemingly supernatural qualities or powers ⟨the child prodigy's musical talent is so spectacular that it seems *magical*⟩ — see MYSTIC 1

magician *n* **1** a person skilled in using supernatural forces ⟨the *magician* was able to summon the birds of the air and the beasts of the field with a simple spell⟩

synonyms charmer, conjurer (*or* conjuror), enchanter, mage, Magian, magus, necromancer, sorcerer, voodoo, voodooist, witch, wizard

related words enchantress, hag, hex, sorceress; warlock; occultist; thaumaturge, thaumaturgist, theurgist, wonder-worker; medicine man, shaman, shamanist, witch doctor; crystal gazer, diviner, foreseer, fortune-teller, prognosticator, prophesier, prophet, seer, soothsayer; medium; exorciser, exorcist

2 one who practices tricks and illusions for entertainment ⟨the famous *magician's* signature trick was pulling a rabbit out of a hat⟩

synonyms conjurer (*or* conjuror), illusionist, prestidigitator, trickster

related words charmer, enchanter, enchantress

magisterial *adj* being the most accurate and apparently thorough ⟨a *magisterial* biography of Thomas Jefferson that has never been superseded⟩ — see DEFINITIVE 1

magistrate *n* a public official having authority to decide questions of law ⟨chose to take their case before the local *magistrate*⟩ — see JUDGE 1

magnanimous *adj* having, characterized by, or arising from a dignified and generous nature ⟨a *magnanimous* donation to the town's animal shelter⟩ — see NOBLE 2

magnanimously *adv* in a manner befitting a person of the highest character and ideals ⟨*magnanimously* decided to forgive her former classmates, who had treated her so badly⟩ — see GREATLY 1

magnate *n* a person of rank, power, or influence in a particular field ⟨a studio *magnate* who had the biggest stars in Hollywood at his beck and call⟩

synonyms baron, captain, czar (*also* tsar *or* tzar), king, lion, lord, mogul, monarch, Napoleon, prince, tycoon

related words big boy, big cheese, bigfoot, biggie, big gun, big shot, big wheel, bigwig, fat cat, figure, heavy, heavyweight, honcho, kahuna, main man, mover and shaker, nabob, nawab, notable, personage, pooh-bah (*also* poo-bah), supremo [*chiefly British*], VIP; celebrity, personality, star, superstar; deity, demigod, god

near antonyms half-pint, lightweight, small-timer; inferior, subordinate, underling; nobody, nothing, zero

magnet *n* something that attracts interest ⟨the giant theme park is a *magnet* for tourists to the area⟩

synonyms attraction, draw, lodestone (*also* loadstone)

related words capital, center, cynosure, epicenter, mecca, pole, polestar; allure, allurement, bait, enticement, fascination, lure, temptation, turn-on; appeal, call; incentive, inducement, persuasion, spur, stimulus; curiosity, sight(s), spectacle

magnetic *adj* having an often mysterious or magical power to attract ⟨a cult leader who attracted followers with his *magnetic* gaze⟩ — see FASCINATING 1

magnetism *n* the power of irresistible attraction ⟨she managed to win the election by sheer *magnetism*⟩ — see CHARM 2

magnetize *vb* to attract or delight as if by magic ⟨the store's gorgeous window displays never fail to *magnetize* shoppers and sightseers⟩ — see CHARM 1

magnific *adj* **1** full of fine words and fancy expressions ⟨his letter to me was written in such a *magnific* style that I half wondered if he had penned it with a quill⟩ — see FLOWERY 1

2 large and impressive in size, grandeur, extent, or conception ⟨the pyramids at Giza remain among the most *magnific* edifices the world has ever seen⟩ — see GRAND 1

magnification *n* the representation of something in terms that go beyond the facts ⟨most movies don't deal in reality but in a *magnification* of reality where everything is more intense⟩ — see EXAGGERATION

magnificence *n* impressiveness of beauty on a large scale ⟨the *magnificence* of the great castle hallway is beyond description⟩

synonyms augustness, brilliance, gloriousness, glory, gorgeousness, grandeur, grandness, majesty, nobility, nobleness, resplendence, resplendency, splendidness, splendiferousness, splendor, stateliness, stupendousness, sublimeness, superbness

related words awesomeness, formidability, marvelousness, wonderfulness, wondrousness; dignity, elegance, grace; lavishness, luxuriance, luxuriousness, luxury, opulence, princeliness, richness, sumptuousness; grandiosity, ostentation, pretentiousness; elaborateness, flashiness, gaudiness, ornateness, poshness, ritziness, showiness, swankiness; extraordinariness, remarkableness

magnificent *adj* large and impressive in size, grandeur, extent, or conception ⟨a *magnificent* mansion that still takes away the breath of visitors⟩ — see GRAND 1

magnify *vb* **1** to add to the interest of by including made-up details ⟨there's no need to *magnify* the events of your trip in order to make it seem impressive⟩ — see EMBROIDER

2 to assign a high status or value to ⟨his newfound fame as an actor has finally *magnified* him in the eyes of his perennially doubting family⟩ — see EXALT 1

3 to make markedly greater in measure or degree ⟨the movie's sound effects *magnify* every crash and boom in the action scenes⟩ — see INTENSIFY

4 to proclaim the glory of ⟨imposing cathedrals that were built to *magnify* the Lord and to inspire awe in worshippers⟩ — see PRAISE 1

magniloquence *n* boastful speech or writing ⟨he's prone to fits of maudlin *magniloquence* when he's drunk⟩ — see BOMBAST 1

magnitude *n* **1** the quality or state of being important ⟨the *magnitude* of the issue can scarcely be overstated⟩ — see IMPORTANCE

2 the quality or state of being very large ⟨the mountain's sheer *magnitude* usually leaves tourists speechless⟩ — see IMMENSITY

3 the total amount of measurable space or surface occupied by something ⟨the *magnitude* of the planned skyscraper is totally disproportionate with that of the other buildings on the block⟩ — see [1]SIZE

magnum opus *n* something (as a work of art) that is a great achievement and often its creator's greatest achievement ⟨this symphony is usually considered Beethoven's *magnum opus*⟩ — see MASTERPIECE

magpie *adj* consisting of many things of different sorts ⟨a pack rat whose cramped apartment is filled with a *magpie* collection of books, old newspapers, and tchotchkes⟩ — see MISCELLANEOUS

magpie *n* a person who talks constantly ⟨media *magpies* will no doubt seize upon the president's latest gaffe and blow it all out of proportion⟩ — see CHATTERBOX

magus *n* a person skilled in using supernatural forces ⟨attributed the storms to a clash of wills between the two most powerful *magi* in the land⟩ — see MAGICIAN 1

maid *n* **1** a female domestic servant ⟨hired a *maid* to do the housework after the baby was born⟩

synonyms biddy, char [*British*], charwoman, handmaiden (*also* handmaid), house girl, housekeeper, housemaid, maidservant, skivvy [*British*], wench

related words attendant, chambermaid; abigail, lady-in-waiting, maid-in-waiting; au pair, nursemaid; domestic, menial; amah, ayah

2 a young unmarried woman ⟨a dance where the fair *maids* and handsome bucks of the village hoped to meet one another⟩ — see GIRL 1

maiden *adj* **1** coming before all others in time or order ⟨the Titanic sank on its *maiden* voyage⟩ — see FIRST 1

2 never having had sexual relations ⟨only *maiden* girls were allowed to serve as priestesses in that temple in ancient Roman times⟩ — see VIRGIN 1

maiden *n* a young unmarried woman ⟨a story about a beautiful *maiden* and her mysterious father⟩ — see GIRL 1

maidservant *n* a female domestic servant ⟨a large estate that once had many *maidservants*⟩ — see MAID 1

mail *n* communications or parcels sent or carried through the postal system ⟨began receiving lots of *mail* after he became known as a frequent donor to charities⟩

synonyms correspondence, matter, parcel post, post [*chiefly British*], snail mail

related words airmail, airpost, certified mail, registered mail, rural delivery, rural free delivery, special delivery, special handling; direct mail, junk mail, mailer; card, dispatch, epistle, letter, message, missive, note, postal card, postcard, printed matter; bundle, package, shipment

mail *vb* to send through the postal system ⟨if you don't *mail* that letter soon, it's going to arrive late⟩

synonyms post

related words airmail, frank; address, consign; direct, dispatch, forward, remit, route, ship, transmit, transport; register

near antonyms get, receive

mail carrier *n* a person who delivers mail ⟨we always give our faithful *mail carrier* a special card for Christmas⟩ — see POSTMAN

mailman *n* a person who delivers mail ⟨the *mailman* usually leaves packages outside the mailbox⟩ — see POSTMAN

maim *vb* to cause severe or permanent injury to ⟨on-the-job accidents *maim* far too many workers every year⟩

synonyms cripple, disable, incapacitate, lame, mutilate

related words dismember, hamstring, hobble, paralyze; batter, bruise, bung up, mangle, maul, rough (up); gore, lacerate, wing, wound; disfigure, scar; kneecap; break, damage, harm, hurt, impair, injure; bash, beat, belt, bludgeon, buffet, drub, hammer, lace, lambaste (*or* lambast), lick, paste, pelt, pommel, pound, pummel, thump; bang, box, hit, punch, slap, smack, smash, sock, spank, swat, swipe, thrash, thwack, whack; flog, lash, wallop, whip; kill, murder; torment, torture

near antonyms cure, heal, rehabilitate, remedy; doctor, fix, mend, patch; rejuvenate, renew, repair, restore

main *adj* coming before all others in importance ⟨this is the *main* point of the study—everything else is secondary⟩ — see FOREMOST 1

main *n* **1** muscular strength ⟨all their might and *main* could not budge the stalled car⟩ — see MUSCLE 1

2 one of the great divisions of land on the globe or the main part of such a division ⟨islanders periodically traveled back to the *main* for supplies⟩ — see MAINLAND

3 the main or greater part of something as distinguished from its subordinate parts ⟨the *main* of the tree is still healthy⟩ — see BODY 1

mainland *n* one of the great divisions of land on the globe or the main part of such a division ⟨the boat back to the *mainland* leaves once every two days⟩
synonyms continent, landmass, main
related words subcontinent, supercontinent
near antonyms island, isle, islet; atoll, barrier reef, cay, coral reef, key; cape, headland, peninsula, promontory

mainly *adv* for the most part ⟨you *mainly* need to focus on improving your golf swing⟩ — see CHIEFLY

mainstay *n* something or someone to which one looks for support ⟨Mom has been our *mainstay* in this crisis⟩ — see DEPENDENCE 2

maintain *vb* **1** to keep in good condition ⟨he repairs and *maintains* antique cars as a hobby⟩
synonyms conserve, keep up, preserve, save
related words service; support, sustain; care (for), husband, manage; defend, guard, protect, safeguard, screen, shield; cure, fix, heal, remedy; mend, patch, rebuild, reconstruct, rehabilitate, rejuvenate, restore
near antonyms disregard, ignore, neglect; break, damage, destroy, harm, hurt, impair, injure, ruin, wreck

2 to continue to declare to be true or proper despite opposition or objections ⟨part of debating is learning to *maintain* your position in the face of harsh challenges⟩
synonyms defend, justify, support, uphold
related words advocate, champion, espouse; confirm, vindicate, warrant; affirm, assert, aver, avouch, avow, claim, contend, insist, plead, proclaim, profess, protest, state; argue, debate, discuss; emphasize, stress, underline, underscore
phrases stand up for, stick up for
near antonyms abandon, abjure, forsake, recant, retract, take back, withdraw; reverse, switch; controvert, disprove, rebut, refute

3 to pay the living expenses of ⟨we simply cannot afford to *maintain* a horse⟩ — see SUPPORT 2

4 to state (something) as a reason in support of or against something under consideration ⟨she continued to *maintain* that a sewing machine would end up paying for itself since she could make her own clothes⟩ — see ARGUE 1

5 to state as a fact usually forcefully ⟨he *maintains* that there is indeed hard evidence for extraterrestrial visitors⟩ — see CLAIM 1

maintainable *adj* capable of being defended with good reasoning against verbal attack ⟨it is important to choose a *maintainable* position for your thesis⟩ — see TENABLE 2

maintenance *n* the act or activity of keeping something in an existing and usually satisfactory condition ⟨I was hired to perform basic *maintenance* until the property could be sold⟩
synonyms care and feeding, conservation, conserving, keep, preservation, preserving, sustentation, upkeep
related words conservancy; support, sustaining; care, custody, guardianship; defense, guarding, protection, safeguarding, safekeeping
near antonyms dereliction, disregard, ignoring, inattention, neglect, negligence; damage, demolition, destruction, harm, hurt, injury, ruin, ruination

majestic *adj* **1** having or showing elegance ⟨a *majestic* pillar of society who continues to entertain in grand style⟩ — see ELEGANT 1

2 large and impressive in size, grandeur, extent, or conception ⟨a *majestic* Egyptian pyramid that has enthralled travelers for aeons⟩ — see GRAND 1

3 very dignified in form, tone, or style ⟨the *majestic* language and beautiful cadences of the King James Version of the Bible⟩ — see ELEVATED 2

majesty *n* **1** a dignified bearing or appearance befitting someone of royal status ⟨even as a child, the princess possessed a certain *majesty* that would later serve her well⟩
synonyms augustness, kingliness, royalty, stateliness
related words high-mindedness, magnanimity, nobility, nobleness; haughtiness, lordliness, pomposity, pompousness; dignity, poise; gloriousness, grandeur, grandness, greatness, impressiveness, magnificence, resplendence, resplendency, splendidness, splendor; class, elegance, grace

2 dignified or restrained beauty of form, appearance, or style ⟨the bishop carries himself with an impressive *majesty*⟩ — see ELEGANCE

3 impressiveness of beauty on a large scale ⟨the *majesty* of the Roman Colosseum is breathtaking⟩ — see MAGNIFICENCE

major *adj* **1** sufficiently large in size, amount, or number to merit attention ⟨with several blockbuster hits under her belt, the actress now commands some *major* cash for appearing in a movie⟩ — see CONSIDERABLE 1

2 having great meaning or lasting effect ⟨a *major* change in how science is taught in our high schools⟩ — see IMPORTANT 1

majority *adj* held by or applicable to a majority of the people ⟨the *majority* opinion among the tour group members was that they should cancel the rest of the trip⟩ — see GENERAL 3

majority *n* **1** the largest part or quantity of something ⟨a vast *majority* of the town's residents support the proposed tax reduction⟩
synonyms bulk, generality, lion's share, mass, preponderance
related words plurality; maximum, most; abundance, heap, loads, lot, much, oodles, plenty, profusion, reams, scads, wealth
near antonyms couple, few, handful, smattering, sprinkling; least, minimum
antonyms minority

2 the state of being fully grown or developed ⟨she will inherit a fortune upon her *majority*⟩ — see MATURITY 1

major league *n* the highest level of a field of endeavor ⟨when you've landed a tenure-track position at that university, you're playing in the *major leagues*⟩ — see BIG TIME

major leaguer *n* one of high position or importance within a group ⟨it was never a *major leaguer* among book publishers⟩ — see BIG SHOT

majorly *adv* to a great degree ⟨we're *majorly* frustrated about the situation back at home⟩ — see VERY 1

make *vb* **1** to bring into being by combining, shaping, or transforming materials ⟨will you help me *make* the dough for the cookies?⟩
synonyms fabricate, fashion, form, frame, manufacture, produce
related words assemble, build, construct, erect, make up, put up, raise, rear, set up, structure, throw up; craft, handcraft; hew; forge, mold, shape; cobble (together *or* up), knock out, patch (together), throw up; prefabricate; create, invent, mint, originate; establish, father, institute, organize; concoct, contrive, cook (up), design, devise, imagine, think (up); conceive, envisage, picture, visualize; refashion, remake, remanufacture
phrases put together

near antonyms disassemble, dismantle, take apart; break up, dismember; abolish, annihilate, demolish, destroy, devastate, eradicate, exterminate, extinguish, flatten, pulverize, raze, ruin, shatter, smash, wreck; blow up, explode

2 to obtain (as a goal) through effort ⟨we finally *made* it!⟩ — see ACHIEVE 1

3 to be the cause of (a situation, action, or state of mind) ⟨the cats *made* quite a disturbance when they knocked the Christmas tree over⟩ — see EFFECT

4 to carry through (as a process) to completion ⟨one person from each department will be asked to *make* a short presentation at the meeting⟩ — see PERFORM 1

5 to cause (a person) to give in to pressure ⟨*made* him do all the work while everyone else just lounged around⟩ — see FORCE 1

6 to decide the size, amount, number, or distance of (something) without actual measurement ⟨I *make* that to be about six feet long⟩ — see ESTIMATE 2

7 to form by putting together parts or materials ⟨*make* a model airplane⟩ — see BUILD

8 to give the impression of being ⟨the family *made* merry despite their financial worries⟩ — see SEEM

9 to go on a specified course or in a certain direction ⟨the baby *made* straight for the toy lying on the rug⟩ — see HEAD 1

10 to put into effect through legislative or authoritative action ⟨the legislature failed to *make* any new laws last session⟩ — see ENACT

11 to receive as return for effort ⟨I *make* considerably more money now than I did when I first started working here⟩ — see EARN 1

12 to have a clear idea of ⟨what do you *make* of the latest information?⟩ — see COMPREHEND 1

13 *chiefly dialect* to position (something) so as to prevent passage through an opening ⟨*make* the gate when ye leave⟩ — see CLOSE 1

make–believe *adj* not real and existing only in the imagination ⟨zoomed around the house in a *make-believe* car⟩ — see IMAGINARY

make out *vb* **1** to meet one's day-to-day needs ⟨we're not rich, but we're *making out* all right⟩ — see GET ALONG 1

2 to have a clear idea of ⟨I can't quite *make out* what she is trying to say⟩ — see COMPREHEND 1

3 to take on a false or deceptive appearance ⟨he tried to *make out* that he didn't mind losing his job, but friends suspected he was desperately worried⟩ — see PRETEND 1

4 to form an opinion or reach a conclusion through reasoning and information ⟨as best as I can *make out*, the police were informed of the incident but didn't think it was worth investigating⟩ — see INFER 1

make over *vb* **1** to change in form, appearance, or use ⟨the old factory was completely *made over* and is now an upscale shopping center⟩ — see CONVERT 2

2 to give over the legal possession or ownership of ⟨*made* the deed *over* to his daughter⟩ — see TRANSFER 1

3 to make different in some way ⟨just got up one day and decided to *make over* her hairstyle and her appearance in general⟩ — see CHANGE 1

Maker *n* the being worshipped as the creator and ruler of the universe ⟨let us give thanks to our *Maker* for this meal⟩ — see DEITY 2

makeshift *adj* taking the place of one that came before ⟨turned a towel into a *makeshift* skirt⟩ — see NEW 1

makeshift *n* a temporary replacement ⟨when his belt broke, he was forced to use string as a *makeshift*⟩

synonyms expedient, stopgap

related words quick fix; recourse, refuge, resort; alternate, backup, standby, stand-in, substitute, understudy

makeup *n* **1** preparations intended to beautify the face ⟨she never left the house without applying her *makeup* and arranging her jewelry⟩

synonyms cosmetics, maquillage, paint, war paint

related words greasepaint; camo, camouflage; cold cream, cream, eye shadow, kohl, lipstick, lotion, mascara, oil, powder, rouge, vanishing cream

2 the way in which the elements of something (as a work of art) are arranged ⟨the *makeup* of the memorial is strikingly simple: a single massive globe signifying world unity⟩ — see COMPOSITION 3

make up *vb* **1** to be all the substance of ⟨the book is *made up* of 20 chapters⟩ — see CONSTITUTE 1

2 to create or think of by clever use of the imagination ⟨she keeps *making up* excuses as to why she hasn't yet finished the project⟩ — see INVENT

3 to form by putting together parts or materials ⟨we'll have to *make up* the bookcase, which came in a box marked "some assembly required"⟩ — see BUILD

make up (for) *vb* to balance with an equal force so as to make ineffective ⟨the lavish present almost *made up for* her forgetting his birthday⟩ — see OFFSET

making *n, often pl* **makings** the basic elements from which something can be developed ⟨she has all the *makings* of an excellent leader, but she needs some experience first⟩

synonyms material, raw material, stuff, substance, timber

related words possibility, potential, potentiality; matter, metal

maladminister *vb* to manage badly ⟨because the organization *maladministered* the relief effort, thousands of refugees went hungry needlessly⟩ — see MISMANAGE

maladroit *adj* **1** lacking or showing a lack of nimbleness in using one's hands ⟨some *maladroit* steering on her part caused the bicycle to go crashing into the bushes⟩ — see CLUMSY 1

2 showing or marked by a lack of skill and tact (as in dealing with a situation) ⟨the socially *maladroit* young man often has a difficult time meeting new people⟩ — see AWKWARD 2

malady *n* an abnormal state that disrupts a plant's or animal's normal bodily functioning ⟨in the olden days people were always suffering from some unknown *malady*⟩ — see DISEASE

malapropos *adj* not appropriate for a particular occasion or situation ⟨a newscaster's *malapropos* attempt at humor upon the death of a beloved figure⟩ — see INAPPROPRIATE

malarkey *also* **malarky** *n* language, behavior, or ideas that are absurd and contrary to good sense ⟨the old lady declared that everything politicians say is pure *malarkey*⟩ — see NONSENSE 1

malcontent *adj* having a feeling that one has been wronged or thwarted in one's ambitions ⟨she seems like a very *malcontent* person, always acting as if the entire world were out to get her⟩ — see DISCONTENTED

male *adj* of, relating to, or marked by qualities traditionally associated with men ⟨the radio program offers both *male* and female perspectives on many common relationship issues⟩ — see MASCULINE

male *n* an adult male human being ⟨research shows that more *males* than females are responding positively to the new ad campaign⟩ — see MAN 1

maledict *vb* to ask a divine power to send harm or evil upon ⟨a fiery televangelist who was notorious for *maledicting* liberals and their ilk on a weekly basis⟩ — see CURSE 1

malediction *n* a prayer that harm will come to someone ⟨the two old women began casting aspersions and heaping *maledictions* upon one another⟩ — see CURSE 1

malefaction *n* a breaking of a moral or legal code ⟨the town treasurer has been linked to the kickback scheme and other financial *malefactions*⟩ — see OFFENSE 1

malefactor *n* **1** a person who commits moral wrongs ⟨she regards anyone who would cause the breakup of a family as a *malefactor* of the worst sort⟩ — see EVILDOER 1
2 a person who has committed a crime ⟨the victim was able to give a clear description of the *malefactor* to the police⟩ — see CRIMINAL

malevolence *n* the desire to cause pain for the satisfaction of doing harm ⟨only mindless *malevolence* would explain this cruel vandalism⟩ — see MALICE

malevolent *adj* having or showing a desire to cause someone pain or suffering for the sheer enjoyment of it ⟨the novel grossly oversimplified the conflict as a struggle between relentlessly *malevolent* villains on one side and faultless saints on the other⟩ — see HATEFUL

malevolently *adv* in a mean or spiteful manner ⟨"I'll get you yet!" she hissed *malevolently*⟩ — see NASTILY

malfeasance *n* improper or illegal behavior ⟨a campaign to impeach the governor for *malfeasance* in office⟩ — see MISCONDUCT 1

malformed *adj* badly or imperfectly formed ⟨a clay sculpture of an eagle that was so *malformed* that it looked more like a feathered football⟩
synonyms deformed, distorted, misshapen, monstrous, shapeless
related words defaced, disfigured; aberrant, abnormal, freakish, mutant; asymmetrical (*or* asymmetric), crooked, disproportionate, irregular, lopsided, nonsymmetrical, overbalanced, unbalanced, unequal; horrible, horrific, terrible; ugly, unattractive
near antonyms shapely; flawless, perfect
antonyms undeformed

malfunctioning *adj* not being in working order ⟨a *malfunctioning* computer cost us days of work⟩ — see INOPERABLE 1

malice *n* the desire to cause pain for the satisfaction of doing harm ⟨there was no reason other than pure *malice* to spread such disgusting lies all over campus⟩
synonyms cattiness, despite, hatefulness, malevolence, maliciousness, malignance, malignancy, malignity, meanness, nastiness, spite, spitefulness, spleen, venom, viciousness
related words abusiveness, cruelty; abhorrence, abomination, execration, hate, hatred, loathing; animosity, antagonism, antipathy, bitterness, enmity, grudge, hostility, ill will, jaundice, mean-spiritedness, rancor, resentment; despicableness, invidiousness; vengefulness, vindictiveness; aversion, disgust, distaste, horror, repugnance, repulsion, revulsion; bitchery, bitchiness, contempt, disdain; jealousy, pique, resentment, scorn; bile, rancor, virulence, vitriol
near antonyms devotion, love, passion; amiability, amicability, amity, civility, cordiality, friendliness, hospitality; adoration, ardor, infatuation, veneration, worship; affection, charity, kindliness, kindness; comity, empathy, friendship, goodwill, sympathy, understanding

malicious *adj* having or showing a desire to cause someone pain or suffering for the sheer enjoyment of it ⟨the neighborhood chatterbox has again been spreading *malicious* gossip⟩ — see HATEFUL

maliciously *adv* in a mean or spiteful manner ⟨*maliciously* tried to ruin her reputation⟩ — see NASTILY

maliciousness *n* the desire to cause pain for the satisfaction of doing harm ⟨the young thugs acted with a *maliciousness* that the once-quiet neighborhood was not accustomed to⟩ — see MALICE

malign *adj* having or showing a desire to cause someone pain or suffering for the sheer enjoyment of it ⟨both parties to the divorce showed a *malign* desire to make each other's future life utterly miserable⟩ — see HATEFUL

malign *vb* to make untrue and harmful statements about ⟨a candidate who believes that it is possible to win an election without *maligning* anyone⟩ — see SLANDER

malignance *n* the desire to cause pain for the satisfaction of doing harm ⟨in meting out the harsh sentence, the judge cited the exceptional *malignance* and ruthlessness with which the rape was committed⟩ — see MALICE

malignancy *n* the desire to cause pain for the satisfaction of doing harm ⟨her irrepressible *malignancy* was such that she even attacked her friends behind their backs⟩ — see MALICE

malignant *adj* having or showing a desire to cause someone pain or suffering for the sheer enjoyment of it ⟨a *malignant* wish to lash out at everyone who was smarter, richer, or better-looking than he was⟩ — see HATEFUL

malignantly *adv* in a mean or spiteful manner ⟨she's *malignantly* conspiring to ruin her best friend's marriage⟩ — see NASTILY

maligning *n* the making of false statements that damage another's reputation ⟨public *maligning* of a person can actually be grounds for a lawsuit⟩ — see SLANDER

malignity *n* the desire to cause pain for the satisfaction of doing harm ⟨one of the characters in the novel is a slave driver of such *malignity* that he came to be one of the most famous villains in all of literature⟩ — see MALICE

malison *n* a prayer that harm will come to someone ⟨muttered terrible *malisons* against her child's murderers⟩ — see CURSE 1

mall *n* a public place for strolling ⟨the pedestrian traffic through the grassy *mall* is heaviest during the summer lunch hours⟩ ⟨the tree-lined *mall* in the city's historic district remains the favored site for strutting about in one's Easter finery⟩ — see PROMENADE

malleability *n* the quality or state of being easily molded ⟨the *malleability* and conductivity of gold makes it well-suited for use in electronic circuitry⟩ — see PLASTICITY

malleable *adj* **1** capable of being easily molded or modeled ⟨*malleable* cookie dough⟩ — see PLASTIC 1
2 capable of being readily changed ⟨the cult leader took advantage of the *malleable*, compliant personalities of his followers⟩ — see FLEXIBLE 1

malodorous *adj* having an unpleasant smell ⟨the cellar will need to be cleared of several *malodorous*, maggot-infested piles of garbage⟩
synonyms fetid, foul, frowsty [*chiefly British*], frowsy (*or* frowzy), funky, fusty, musty, noisome, rank, reeking, reeky, ripe, smelly, stenchy, stinking, stinky, strong
related words putrid, rancid, skunky, stale; bad, disgusting, offensive, repulsive, revolting, vile; decayed, decaying, decomposed, decomposing, rotted, rotten, rotting, spoiled, spoiling; dirty, filthy, nasty, noxious; odiferous, odoriferous, odorous
near antonyms flowery, fruity, spicy, woodsy
antonyms ambrosial, aromatic, fragrant, perfumed, redolent, savory (*also* savoury), scented, sweet

maltreat *vb* **1** to inflict physical or emotional harm upon ⟨emotionally *maltreated* and neglected for years by her husband, she had long ago resigned herself to a loveless marriage⟩ — see ABUSE 1
2 to abuse physically ⟨if you *maltreat* the puppy, we will take it away immediately⟩ — see MANHANDLE 1

mama *also* **mamma** *or* **momma** *n* a female human parent ⟨I'm not your *mama*—you'll have to clean up after yourself⟩ — see MOTHER

mammoth *adj* unusually large ⟨a *mammoth* book with color plates of birds native to North America⟩ — see HUGE

mammoth *n* something that is unusually large and powerful ⟨even as sport-utility vehicles go, that one is a *mammoth*⟩ — see GIANT

mammy *n* a female human parent ⟨the toddler clung to her *mammy* and eyed the strangers fearfully⟩ — see MOTHER

man *n* **1** an adult male human being ⟨several *men* will be needed to dig up the old tree stump in the backyard⟩
synonyms bastard, bloke [*chiefly British*], buck, cat, chap [*chiefly British*], chappie [*British*], dude, fella, fellow, galoot [*slang*], gent, gentleman, guy, hombre, jack, joe, joker, lad, male
related words master, mister, sir; buddy, buster
2 a male romantic companion ⟨I'm going to see my *man* again tonight⟩ — see BOYFRIEND
3 a member of the human race ⟨every *man* has a responsibility to safeguard the planet⟩ — see HUMAN
4 the human race ⟨*man* is always coming up with new advances in science and technology⟩ — see MANKIND
5 the male partner in a marriage ⟨I now pronounce you *man* and wife⟩ — see HUSBAND
6 a body of officers of the law ⟨the crowd of onlookers quickly scattered when the *man* arrived on the scene⟩ — see POLICE 2

manacle *n* **1** *usually* **manacles** *pl* something that physically prevents free movement ⟨*manacles* prevented the bear from roaming beyond a very small area⟩ — see BOND 1
2 something that makes movement or progress difficult ⟨the warring groups need to shake off the *manacle* of their troubled past and learn to live with one another in peace⟩ — see ENCUMBRANCE

manacle *vb* **1** to confine or restrain with or as if with chains ⟨*manacled* the prisoner to the wall⟩ — see BIND 1
2 to create difficulty for the work or activity of ⟨in this situation, the police are *manacled* by unnecessary regulations⟩ — see HAMPER

manage *vb* **1** to deal with (something) usually skillfully or efficiently ⟨as usual, she *managed* the crisis with a minimum of fuss⟩ — see HANDLE 1
2 to look after and make decisions about ⟨*managed* a household and a business simultaneously⟩ — see CONDUCT 1
3 to meet one's day-to-day needs ⟨it'll be hard for a few weeks, but we'll *manage*⟩ — see GET ALONG 1

management *n* the act or activity of looking after and making decisions about something ⟨fiscal *management* of the city's sports facility can be challenging⟩ — see CONDUCT 1

manager *n* a person who manages or directs something ⟨we wanted an exemption from the policy regarding refunds, but the store *manager* refused⟩ — see EXECUTIVE

managerial *adj* suited for or relating to the directing of things ⟨her *managerial* style is very direct and detail-oriented⟩ — see EXECUTIVE

man–at–arms *n* a person engaged in military service ⟨the condottieri who served as *men-at-arms* for the Italian city-states often sold their allegiance to the highest bidder⟩ — see SOLDIER

mandarin *n* a worker in a government agency ⟨the officious *mandarins* in the motor vehicles department refused to let me renew my license without all of the required forms⟩ — see BUREAUCRAT

mandate *n* the granting of power to perform various acts or duties ⟨the committee has been given a *mandate* to reform the process for admitting applicants to the university⟩ — see COMMISSION 1

mandate *vb* to request the doing of by virtue of one's authority ⟨the president of the sports league has *mandated* drug testing for all active members⟩ — see COMMAND 2

mandatory *adj* forcing one's compliance or participation by or as if by law ⟨the tests are *mandatory* for all students wishing to graduate⟩
synonyms compulsory, forced, imperative, incumbent, involuntary, necessary, nonelective, obligatory, peremptory, required
related words all-important, essential, indispensable, needed, requisite; insistent, persistent, pressing, urgent; demanded, enforced; coercive
near antonyms chosen, discretionary; dispensable, unnecessary, unneeded, unwanted; inconsequential, insignificant, nonessential, unimportant
antonyms elective, optional, voluntary

maneuver *vb* **1** to deal with (something) usually skillfully or efficiently ⟨*maneuvered* the conversation so as to avoid the touchy subject of her divorce⟩ — see HANDLE 1
2 to plan out usually with subtle skill or care ⟨successfully *maneuvered* a way to get him to ask her to the dance⟩ — see ENGINEER

manful *adj* feeling or displaying no fear by temperament ⟨he made the *manful* decision to stick by his friends when everyone else had abandoned them⟩ — see BRAVE 1

manfully *adv* in a fearless manner ⟨*manfully* accepted the responsibility of raising his deceased sister's children⟩ — see BRAVELY 1

mangle *vb* to make or do (something) in a clumsy or unskillful way ⟨you've *mangled* this so badly that we'll have to do it over⟩ — see BOTCH

mangy *adj* showing signs of advanced wear and tear and neglect ⟨a *mangy* old car that was covered in rust⟩ — see SHABBY 1

manhandle *vb* **1** to abuse physically ⟨charges that the police *manhandled* peaceful protesters⟩
synonyms maltreat, maul, mishandle, rough (up)
related words abuse, ill-treat, ill-use, mistreat, misuse; roughhouse, wrestle; bash, batter, beat, buffet, drub, lambaste (*or* lambast), lick, pommel, pound, pummel, slap, thrash; harm, hurt, injure, wound; oppress, persecute, wrong; ambush, assail, attack; clobber, fight, gang up (on), hit, jump, knock; torment, torture
near antonyms caress, fondle, pet; coddle, mollycoddle, pamper; care (for), foster, nurture
2 to inflict physical or emotional harm upon ⟨if you see anyone *manhandling* a child, you should call the authorities⟩ — see ABUSE 1

manhood *n* the set of qualities considered appropriate for or characteristic of men ⟨a society that highly values *manhood* and courage⟩ — see VIRILITY

mania *n* **1** a serious mental disorder that prevents one from living a safe and normal life ⟨that form of *mania* often manifests itself in excessive and often incoherent talkativeness⟩ — see INSANITY 1
2 something about which one is constantly thinking or concerned ⟨his wife was baffled and amused by his *mania* for old comic books⟩ — see FIXATION

maniac *n* **1** a person judged to be legally or medically insane ⟨they should permanently put away the *maniac* who is responsible for these kidnappings⟩ — see LUNATIC 1
2 a person with a strong and habitual liking for something ⟨I'm a *maniac* for anything flavored with peppermint⟩ — see FAN

maniacal *also* **maniac** *adj* having or showing a very abnormal or sick state of mind ⟨the movie's villain was a just a clichéd axe-wielding nutcase with a *maniacal* laugh⟩ — see INSANE 1

manifest *adj* not subject to misinterpretation or more than one interpretation ⟨despite the his *manifest* lack of leadership skills, the shift supervisor managed to keep his position⟩ — see CLEAR 2

manifest *vb* **1** to make known (something abstract) through outward signs ⟨a frustration that is often *manifested* by a minor facial tic⟩ — see SHOW 2
2 to represent in visible form ⟨graduates of the military academies *manifest*, we hope, the best that this country has to offer⟩ — see EMBODY 2

manifestation *n* a visible representation of something abstract (as a quality) ⟨a portrait of a mother and child that is regarded as the very *manifestation* of maternal love⟩ — see EMBODIMENT

manifold *adj* being of many and various kinds ⟨the *manifold* attractions of that state make it an ideal destination for a family vacation⟩
synonyms divers, multifarious, myriad
related words multiform, multiple, multiplex, multitudinous; heterogeneous, heterogenous, miscellaneous, mixed, sundry, various; different, diverse, unlike, varied
near antonyms homogeneous, homogenous, monolithic, unmixed, unvaried; alike, identical, same; distinct, distinctive, individual, separate; alone, lone, only, sole, solitary; singular, unique

manifoldness *n* the quality or state of being composed of many different elements or types ⟨the mind-boggling *manifoldness* of Leonardo da Vinci's genius⟩ — see VARIETY 1

manikin *also* **mannikin** *n* **1** a three-dimensional representation of the human body used especially for displaying clothes ⟨the store has *manikins* so lifelike that they have startled me on more than one occasion⟩ — see MANNEQUIN 1
2 a person who poses with or wears merchandise (as clothes) often for pictorial advertising ⟨the undulating movements of the *manikins* as they strutted down the catwalk⟩ — see MODEL 2

manipulate *vb* **1** to control or take advantage of by artful, unfair, or insidious means ⟨the con man would slyly *manipulate* the emotions of his marks in order to win their sympathy and trust⟩
synonyms exploit, play (upon)
related words engineer, finagle, jockey, maneuver; beguile, bluff, cozen, deceive, delude, dupe, fool, gull, hoax, hoodwink, kid, shanghai, snow, take in, trick; intrigue, machinate, plot, scheme; arrange, contrive, devise, finesse, mastermind; cheat, chisel, con, defraud, fleece, gyp, hustle, swindle
2 to deal with (something) usually skillfully or efficiently ⟨a scientist effortlessly *manipulating* a slew of statistics while testifying before Congress⟩ — see HANDLE 1
3 to plan out usually with subtle skill or care ⟨*manipulated* the schedule of presidential primaries so that the choice of the party elders would win the nomination⟩ — see ENGINEER

mankind *n* the human race ⟨all of *mankind* stands to gain if world peace is ever achieved⟩
synonyms Homo sapiens, humanity, humankind, man
related words being, body, creature, fellowman, human, individual, mortal, party, person

manlike *adj* **1** of, relating to, or marked by qualities traditionally associated with men ⟨some people still consider nursing to be a less *manlike* occupation⟩ — see MASCULINE
2 having qualities or traits that are traditionally considered inappropriate for a girl or woman ⟨polls have shown that strong-willed, assertive women running for public office are regarded by some voters as too *manlike*⟩ — see UNFEMININE

manliness *n* the set of qualities considered appropriate for or characteristic of men ⟨studio executives wondered if the actor possessed the *manliness* expected in an action hero⟩ — see VIRILITY

manly *adj* of, relating to, or marked by qualities traditionally associated with men ⟨a *manly* deep voice⟩ — see MASCULINE

man–made *adj* **1** being such in appearance only and made with or manufactured from usually cheaper materials ⟨*man-made* diamonds that were really just glass⟩ — see IMITATION
2 produced by humans rather than natural processes ⟨the houses in the new development are built around a *man-made* lake⟩ — see SYNTHETIC 1

manna *n* **1** a source of great satisfaction ⟨the announcement that there would be a sequel was *manna* to the many fans of the original movie⟩ — see DELIGHT 1
2 something that provides happiness or does good for a person or thing ⟨the company's Christmas bonus was especially welcome *manna* this year⟩ — see BLESSING 2

mannequin *n* **1** a three-dimensional representation of the human body used especially for displaying clothes ⟨the *mannequin* over there looks so real⟩
synonyms dummy, figure, form, manikin (*also* mannikin)
related words doll
2 a person who poses with or wears merchandise (as clothes) often for pictorial advertising ⟨several *mannequins* posing for this year's catalogue look especially emaciated⟩ — see MODEL 2

manner *n* **1 manners** *pl* personal conduct or behavior as evaluated by an accepted standard of appropriateness for a social or professional setting ⟨the young man's impeccable *manners* are an unmistakable sign of a good upbringing⟩
synonyms etiquette, form, mores, proprieties
related words amenities, civilities, pleasantries; bearing, demeanor, deportment, mien; courtesy, decorum, mannerliness, politeness; formalities, protocol, rules; air, attitude, carriage, poise, polish, pose, posture, presence; custom, habit, pattern, practice (*also* practise), trick, way, wont; convention, fashion, mode, style
2 a distinctive way of putting ideas into words ⟨the former doctor writes his novels very much in the *manner* of someone who is used to observing the smallest details⟩ — see STYLE 1
3 a number of persons or things that are grouped together because they have something in common ⟨fish and all *manner* of sea life on view at the aquarium⟩ — see SORT 1
4 the means or procedure for doing something ⟨you happened to reach the correct answer, but the *manner* by which you solved the problem was all wrong⟩ — see METHOD

mannerism *n* an odd or peculiar habit ⟨quirky *mannerisms* such as toying with her hair and tapping her toes⟩ — see IDIOSYNCRASY

mannerliness *n* speech or behavior that is a sign of good breeding ⟨the elderly gentleman comported himself with old-world, old-school *mannerliness*⟩ — see POLITENESS 1

mannerly *adj* showing consideration, courtesy, and good manners ⟨a *mannerly* child is welcome everywhere⟩ — see POLITE 1

mannish *adj* **1** of, relating to, or marked by qualities traditionally associated with men ⟨a woman with a somewhat *mannish* gait⟩ — see MASCULINE
2 having qualities or traits that are traditionally considered inappropriate for a girl or woman ⟨for her first outing as a spelunker she wore the same *mannish* jeans as the guys⟩ — see UNFEMININE

mano a mano *adv* in direct confrontation or competition ⟨the two brothers decided to go *mano a mano* in one final match to determine who was the better tennis player⟩ — see HEAD-TO-HEAD

manor *n* a large impressive residence ⟨the old family *manor* has 117 rooms⟩ — see MANSION

manor house *n* a large impressive residence ⟨entertained everyone at their *manor house* after the wedding ceremony⟩ — see MANSION

manpower *n* a body of persons at work or available for work ⟨we're a little short on *manpower* today, so we'll need you to do some extra tasks⟩ — see FORCE 1

manse *n* a large impressive residence ⟨the ivy-covered *manse* is one of the town's oldest and most prominent landmarks⟩ — see MANSION

mansion *n* a large impressive residence ⟨if I ever win the lottery, I'm going to buy a *mansion* in the hills⟩
synonyms castle, château, estate, hacienda, hall, manor, manor house, manse, palace, villa
related words showplace; abode, domicile, dwelling, habitation, hearth, home, house, lodging(s), pad, place; housing, nest, quarter(s), residency, roof; great house; country house, countryseat; aerie, penthouse; salon, suite, town house

man–size *or* **man–sized** *adj* of, relating to, or marked by qualities traditionally associated with men ⟨worked up a *man-size* appetite playing soccer⟩ — see MASCULINE

manslayer *n* a person who kills another person ⟨Cain has the distinction of being the Bible's first and most infamous *manslayer*⟩ — see ASSASSIN

manta *n* any of several extremely large rays ⟨a *manta* glided along the sea bottom⟩ — see DEVILFISH

manta ray *n* any of several extremely large rays ⟨the *manta ray* blended in beautifully with the sandy ocean floor⟩ — see DEVILFISH

manteau *n* a sleeveless garment worn so as to hang over the shoulders, arms, and back ⟨Muslim women in loose black *manteaus*⟩ — see [1]CAPE

mantilla *n* a scarf worn on the head ⟨a beautiful Spanish lady with a lace *mantilla*⟩ — see BANDANNA

mantle *n* **1** a sleeveless garment worn so as to hang over the shoulders, arms, and back ⟨a long black velvet *mantle*⟩ — see [1]CAPE
2 something that covers or conceals like a piece of cloth ⟨the *mantle* of secrecy that surrounds the operations of the organization's hierarchy⟩ — see CLOAK 1

mantle *vb* to surround or cover closely ⟨early-morning fog *mantled* the fields along the river⟩ — see ENFOLD 1

manual *n* a book used for instruction in a subject ⟨an owner's *manual* comes with the camera⟩ — see TEXTBOOK

manufactory *n* a building or set of buildings for the manufacturing of goods ⟨recent years have seen a tremendous growth in *manufactories* all along the river⟩ — see FACTORY

manufacture *vb* **1** to bring into being by combining, shaping, or transforming materials ⟨the company *manufactures* appliances and electronics⟩ — see MAKE 1
2 to create or think of by clever use of the imagination ⟨he *manufactured* some story about how his car broke down and he was unable to call home and let anyone know that he would be late⟩ — see INVENT

manumission *n* the act of setting free from slavery ⟨the official *manumission* of the slaves came after the Civil War⟩ — see LIBERATION

manumit *vb* to set free (as from slavery or confinement) ⟨though he was an outspoken defender of liberty, this son of Virginia did not *manumit* his own slaves until he was on his deathbed⟩ — see FREE 1

manuscript *n* writing done by hand ⟨beautiful, careful *manuscript* on the school's diplomas⟩ — see HANDWRITING 2

many *adj* being of a large but indefinite number ⟨a journey of *many* miles begins with a single step⟩
synonyms beaucoup [*slang*], legion, multifold, multiple, multiplex, multitudinous, numerous
related words countless, innumerable, numberless, uncountable, unnumbered, untold; several, some; miscellaneous, mixed, sundry, various; divers, manifold, multifarious, myriad
phrases all kinds of, quite a few
near antonyms countable, limited
antonyms few

map *n* an illustration of certain features of a geographical area ⟨a wall *map* of the United States⟩
synonyms chart
related words ground plan, plan, plat, plot; relief map

map (out) *vb* to work out the details of (something) in advance ⟨*mapped out* a plan for the fledgling company to become profitable within two years⟩ — see PLAN 1

maquillage *n* preparations intended to beautify the face ⟨the aging actress's thick *maquillage* made her look like a parody of her younger self⟩ — see MAKEUP 1

mar *n* something that spoils the appearance or completeness of a thing ⟨the Johnsons complained to the movers about broken dishes and *mars* on the furniture⟩ — see BLEMISH

mar *vb* **1** to affect slightly with something morally bad or undesirable ⟨*mar* a politician's reputation with scurrilous rumors⟩ — see TAINT 1
2 to reduce the soundness, effectiveness, or perfection of ⟨the once glossy surface is now *marred* by numerous small pits and abrasions⟩ — see DAMAGE 1

marathon *adj* lasting for a considerable time ⟨a *marathon* study session the night before the exam⟩ — see LONG 2

maraud *vb* to search through with the intent of committing robbery ⟨just for kicks, bored teenagers *marauded* neighborhood houses while their owners were away⟩ — see RANSACK 1

marble *vb* to mark with small spots especially unevenly ⟨*marble* the paper with several different dyes to get a striking effect⟩ — see SPOT 1

marbled *adj* having blotches of two or more colors ⟨a *marbled* chocolate and vanilla cake⟩ — see PIED

marbles *n pl* the normal or healthy condition of the mental abilities ⟨everyone thought she'd lost her *marbles* when she made such an illogical suggestion⟩ — see MIND 2

[1]march *n* a region along the dividing line between two countries ⟨when it was first built, this castle protected what was then the country's northern *march*⟩ — see FRONTIER 1

[2]march *n* forward movement in time or place ⟨the *march* of time⟩ — see ADVANCE 1

march *vb* **1** to move along with a steady regular step especially in a group ⟨the band had to practice for hours to be able to *march* in perfect step⟩
synonyms file, pace, parade, stride
related words goose-step; perambulate, step, traipse, tread; hike, tramp; lumber, plod, stamp, stomp, stride, trudge
near antonyms amble, meander, ramble, stroll, wander
2 to move forward along a course ⟨bleary-eyed commuters *marching* off to the train station for the morning commute⟩ — see GO 1

march (with) *vb* to be adjacent to ⟨on the west, Maine *marches* entirely *with* the state of New Hampshire⟩ — see ADJOIN 1

mare's nest *n* a state in which everything is out of order ⟨the lack of planning had resulted in the city's evacuation being a *mare's nest* of epic proportions⟩ — see CHAOS

margin *n* the line or relatively narrow space that marks the outer limit of something ⟨the *margins* of the paper should only be an inch wide⟩ — see BORDER 1

margin *vb* to serve as a border for ⟨the riverbed is *margined* by a flat beach of smooth rocks⟩ — see BORDER

marginal *adj* located at or near a border ⟨*marginal* locations in the open-air market are a bit cheaper⟩ — see BORDERLINE

marginally *adv* by a very small margin ⟨the team lost another game, but at least they performed *marginally* better this time out⟩ — see JUST 2

marine *adj* **1** of or relating to the sea ⟨he loves collecting little *marine* creatures while at the beach⟩
synonyms maritime, oceanic, pelagic
related words abyssal, deep-sea, deepwater, saltwater; benthic; admiralty, nautical, naval; undersea, underwater; hydrographic, oceanographic (*also* oceanographical)
2 of or relating to navigation of the sea ⟨a collection of *marine* instruments, including a sextant⟩
synonyms maritime, nautical, navigational
related words admiralty, naval; oceangoing, seafaring, seagoing; hydrographic, oceanographic (*also* oceanographical)

mariner *n* one who operates or navigates a seagoing vessel ⟨the ancient Phoenicians were outstanding *mariners* who explored and colonized much of the eastern Mediterranean⟩ — see SAILOR

marital *adj* of or relating to marriage ⟨neither of them ever forgot their *marital* vows, no matter how hard things sometimes got⟩
synonyms conjugal, connubial, married, matrimonial, nuptial, wedded
related words espoused, matched, mated; bridal, prenuptial; spousal, wifely; affianced, betrothed, committed, engaged, pledged, promised
antonyms nonmarital

maritime *adj* **1** of or relating to navigation of the sea ⟨a rare *maritime* chart from the 17th century⟩ — see MARINE 2
2 of or relating to the sea ⟨the city's extraordinary boom is almost entirely due to the increase in *maritime* commerce⟩ — see MARINE 1

mark *n* **1** a person or thing that is made fun of ⟨in the wake of the sex scandal, the governor became the favorite *mark* of late-night comedians⟩ — see LAUGHINGSTOCK
2 a person or thing that is the object of abuse, criticism, or ridicule ⟨the child's small stature and offbeat personality made her an easy *mark* for bullies⟩ — see TARGET 1
3 overall quality as seen or judged by people in general ⟨a brand of crystal that bears the *mark* of excellence⟩ — see REPUTATION
4 something set up as an example against which others of the same type are compared ⟨lately his playing hasn't been up to the *mark* expected of a concert pianist⟩ — see STANDARD 1
5 something that one hopes or intends to accomplish ⟨set *marks* for expected daily output⟩ — see GOAL
6 something that sets apart an individual from others of the same kind ⟨a sensitive expression that is the *mark* of a poet⟩ — see CHARACTERISTIC
7 something that spoils the appearance or completeness of a thing ⟨a small *mark* where the car had scraped a wall⟩ — see BLEMISH
8 the power to bring about a result on another ⟨a person of some *mark* in the field of evolutionary biology⟩ — see EFFECT 2

mark *vb* **1** to attach an identifying slip to ⟨*marked* each application with a numbered sticker⟩ — see LABEL 1
2 to be an important feature of ⟨an annual event *marked* mostly by noise and confusion⟩ — see CHARACTERIZE 2
3 to make a written note of ⟨*mark* down the names of those who are planning to attend the dinner⟩ — see RECORD 1

mark (off) *vb* to mark the limits of ⟨*marked off* the outline of the mural first⟩ — see LIMIT 2

mark down *vb* to diminish the price or value of ⟨*marked down* all seasonal goods immediately after the holidays⟩ — see DEPRECIATE 1

marked *adj* likely to attract attention ⟨walks with a *marked* limp⟩ — see NOTICEABLE

marker *n* **1** a slip (as of paper or cloth) that is attached to something to identify or describe it ⟨the *markers* on the rock and mineral specimens were old and faded⟩ — see LABEL
2 something that sets apart an individual from others of the same kind ⟨after many blind dates, he's come to realize that self-absorption is the infallible *marker* of a real loser⟩ — see CHARACTERISTIC

market *n* the state of being sought after especially for purchase ⟨a great decline in the *market* for VCRs⟩ — see DEMAND 2

market *vb* to offer for sale to the public ⟨local farmers *market* their garden-fresh produce at roadside stands all over the valley⟩
synonyms deal (in), merchandise (*also* merchandize), put up, retail, sell, vend
related words presell, wholesale; remarket, resell; hawk, peddle; barter, distribute, exchange, export, handle, trade, traffic (in); advertise, ballyhoo, boost, plug, promote, tout; bargain, chaffer, dicker, haggle, horse-trade, palter; auction; provide, supply; carry, keep, stock
antonyms buy, purchase

marketable *adj* **1** fit to be offered for sale ⟨realized that the birdhouses he enjoyed making were *marketable* and began selling them at craft fairs⟩
synonyms merchantable, salable (*or* saleable), sellable
related words commercial, profitable; costly, fancy, fine, high-grade, precious, premium, prime, valuable; dear, expensive, extravagant
near antonyms damaged, shopworn; cheap, useless, worthless; bad, inferior, low-grade, substandard, unsatisfactory
antonyms nonsalable, unmarketable, unsalable, unsellable
2 fit or likely to be sold especially on a large scale ⟨trying to turn their invention into a *marketable* product⟩ — see COMMERCIAL

marketplace *n* the buying and selling of goods especially on a large scale and between different places ⟨nations struggling to compete in the global *marketplace*⟩ — see COMMERCE 1

marksman *n* a person skilled in shooting at a target ⟨only the best *marksmen* can hit the bull's-eye at 500 feet⟩
synonyms sharpshooter, shooter, shot
related words sniper; rifleman; trapshooter; gun, gunman, gunner; markswoman

maroon *vb* to cause to remain behind ⟨pets that had been cruelly *marooned* by their owners at the end of the summer⟩ — see LEAVE 1

marriage *n* **1** a union representing a special kind of social and legal partnership between two people ⟨some religions consider *marriage* a sacrament⟩
synonyms conjugality, connubiality, match, matrimony, wedlock
related words monogamy; bigamy, polyandry, polygamy, polygyny; intermarriage, miscegenation, mixed marriage, remarriage; cohabitation, common-law marriage; civil union, domestic partnership; attachment,

commitment, relationship; betrothal, engagement, espousal, hand, pledge, promise, proposal, troth
near antonyms annulment, divorce, separation
2 a ceremony in which two people are united in matrimony ⟨just a small group of family and friends have been invited to witness the *marriage*⟩ — see WEDDING

married *adj* of or relating to marriage ⟨a sermon on the joys and responsibilities of *married* love⟩ — see MARITAL

marry *vb* **1** to perform the ceremony of marriage for ⟨they chose a priest who was a family friend to *marry* them⟩
synonyms wed
related words match, mate; conjoin, connect, unite; affiance
2 to give in marriage ⟨the couple worried about the cost of *marrying* off five daughters⟩
synonyms espouse, match, wed
related words commit, engage; affiance, betroth, pledge, promise
3 to take as a spouse ⟨he *married* his girlfriend three years ago, and they've been happy ever since⟩
synonyms espouse, wed
related words affiance, betroth, commit, engage, pledge, promise, propose; remarry
near antonyms separate (from)
antonyms divorce
4 to take a spouse ⟨she had always believed she would never *marry*, but fate proved her wrong⟩
synonyms wed
related words couple, mate; pair off, remarry
phrases tie the knot
near antonyms divorce, separate
5 to come together to form a single unit ⟨white wine and chicken *marry* especially well⟩ — see UNITE 1

marsh *n* spongy land saturated or partially covered with water ⟨the *marshes* along the coast support a remarkable profusion of plants and animals⟩ — see SWAMP 1

marshal *also* **marshall** *vb* **1** to assemble and make ready for action ⟨*marshaled* their forces for battle⟩ — see MOBILIZE
2 to point out the way for (someone) especially from a position in front ⟨*marshaling* a small group of children on a tour of the science museum⟩ — see LEAD 1
3 to put into a particular arrangement ⟨*marshal* your arguments before you stand up to speak⟩ — see ORDER 1

marshaling *or* **marshalling** *n* an act of gathering forces together to renew or attempt an effort ⟨the last-minute *marshaling* of the reserves failed to repel the onslaught⟩ — see RALLY 1

marshland *n* spongy land saturated or partially covered with water ⟨grasses, sedges, and rushes are the plant species most commonly found in *marshlands*⟩ — see SWAMP 1

martial *adj* **1** of, relating to, or suitable for war or a warrior ⟨the marching band played "The Battle Hymn of the Republic" and several other *martial* airs⟩
synonyms military, soldierly
related words aggressive, bellicose, combative, contentious, guerrilla, pugnacious, quarrelsome, scrappy, truculent, warlike; belligerent, militant, militarist, militaristic, warring; antagonistic, argumentative, fierce, gladiatorial, hot-tempered; mercenary
near antonyms civil, civilian, nonmilitary; conciliatory, nonviolent, pacific, peaceable, peaceful; affable, amiable, amicable, benevolent, complaisant, cordial, easygoing, friendly, genial, good-natured, gracious, ingratiating, obliging
antonyms unsoldierly
2 of or relating to the armed services ⟨one of the basic tenets of *martial* law⟩ — see MILITARY 1

marvel *n* something extraordinary or surprising ⟨that new electric car really is a *marvel*⟩ — see WONDER 1

marveling *or* **marvelling** *adj* filled with amazement or wonder ⟨with *marveling* stares, onlookers gathered round the remarkable invention⟩ — see OPEN-MOUTHED

marvelous *or* **marvellous** *adj* **1** causing wonder or astonishment ⟨the sheer immensity of the ancient ruin known as Stonehenge is *marvelous* to behold⟩
synonyms amazing, astonishing, astounding, awesome, awful, eye-opening, fabulous, miraculous, portentous, prodigious, staggering, stunning, stupendous, sublime, surprising, wonderful, wondrous
related words incomprehensible, inconceivable, incredible, unbelievable, unimaginable, unthinkable; extraordinary, phenomenal, rare, sensational, spectacular; singular, uncommon, unique, unusual, unwonted; conspicuous, notable, noticeable, outstanding, remarkable; impressive, smashing, striking; mind-bending, mind-blowing, mind-boggling; animating, energizing, enlightening, enlivening, exciting, galvanizing, invigorating, stimulating; alluring, attracting, attractive, beguiling, bewitching, captivating, charming, enchanting, entertaining, enthralling, fascinating, interesting
near antonyms unimpressive, uninspiring, unremarkable; boring, dull, jading, monotonous, tedious, tiring, uninspired, uninteresting, wearisome, weary, wearying; common, customary, mundane, normal, ordinary, typical, unexceptional, usual; draining, enervating, exhausting, fatiguing, wearing; debilitating, enfeebling; demoralizing, discouraging, disheartening, dispiriting
2 excitingly or mysteriously unusual ⟨old seafarers' tales of *marvelous* lands and their strange inhabitants⟩ — see EXOTIC
3 of the very best kind ⟨the novel is a *marvelous* example of a children's book which has not been dumbed down for its intended audience⟩ — see EXCELLENT

mascot *n* something worn or kept to bring good luck or keep away evil ⟨she wears a *mascot* made of ebony and silver on a chain around her neck⟩ — see CHARM 1

masculine *adj* of, relating to, or marked by qualities traditionally associated with men ⟨some people consider a deep voice to be a particularly appealing *masculine* trait⟩
synonyms male, manlike, manly, mannish, man-size (*or* man-sized), virile
related words hairy-chested, hypermasculine, macho, ultramasculine; boyish, hoydenish, tomboyish; Amazonian, butch
near antonyms metrosexual, unmacho; effeminate, girlish, sissified, sissy; feminine, womanish, womanlike, womanly; emasculated, impotent, weakened; androgynous, neuter
antonyms unmanly, unmasculine

masculinity *n* the set of qualities considered appropriate for or characteristic of men ⟨some men believe that wearing pink would undermine their *masculinity*⟩ — see VIRILITY

mash *n* a strong but often short-lived liking for another person ⟨she's usually got a *mash* on moviedom's hunk du jour⟩ — see CRUSH 1

mash *vb* **1** to apply external pressure on so as to force out the juice or contents of ⟨this press can *mash* 10 bushels of apples at a time⟩ — see [2]PRESS 2
2 to cause to become a pulpy mass ⟨*mash* the ripe banana before adding it to the mixture⟩ — see CRUSH 1

masher *n* a man given to seducing women ⟨a would-be *masher* who was more pathetic than anything else⟩ — see DON JUAN

mask *n* **1** a cover or partial cover for the face used to disguise oneself ⟨an elaborate *mask* that would be suit-

able for a fancy masquerade ball⟩
synonyms vizard
related words camouflage, costume, disguise, guise; bill, cloak, domino, hood, veil, visor (*also* vizor)
2 something that covers or conceals like a piece of cloth ⟨his unexpected friendliness is just a *mask*, for he always has an ulterior motive⟩ — see CLOAK 1

mask *vb* **1** to change the dress or looks of so as to conceal true identity ⟨the federal agents *masked* their surveillance vehicle so that it looked like an ordinary moving van⟩ — see DISGUISE 1
2 to keep secret or shut off from view ⟨*masked* his real motives for wanting to see the house that was for sale⟩ — see [1]HIDE 2

masquerade *n* a display of emotion or behavior that is insincere or intended to deceive ⟨although she was deeply bored, she maintained a *masquerade* of polite interest as her guest droned on⟩
synonyms act, airs, charade, disguise, facade (*also* façade), front, guise, playacting, pose, pretense (*or* pretence), put-on, semblance, show
related words impersonation, performance, portrayal; image, persona; appearance, color, gloss; camouflage, cloak; affectation, deceit, deception, dissembling, dissimulation, double-dealing, duplicity, fakery, fraud, guile; betrayal, double cross, faithlessness, falseness, falsity, infidelity, perfidy, treachery, treason, unfaithfulness; excuse, pretext
near antonyms bluntness, candidness, candor, directness, forthrightness, frankness, openheartedness, outspokenness, plainspokenness, sincerity, straightforwardness; artlessness, genuineness, naïveté (*also* naivete *or* naiveté)

masquerade (as) *vb* to pretend to be (what one is not) in appearance or behavior ⟨the intruder was arrested for *masquerading as* a doctor and trying to steal another woman's baby⟩ — see IMPERSONATE 1

mass *n* **1 masses** *pl* the body of the community as contrasted with the elite ⟨the *masses* demanded the elimination of tax breaks for the rich⟩
synonyms commoners, commons, crowd, herd, hoi polloi, millions, mob, multitude, people, plebeians, plebs, populace, public, rank and file
related words cattle, proletariat, rabble, rabblement, ragtag and bobtail, riffraff, rout, scum, tag, rag, and bobtail (*or* tagrag and bobtail), trash, unwashed; bourgeoisie, middle class
near antonyms gentility, gentlefolk (*also* gentlefolks), gentry, haute monde, nobility, patriciate, peerage, quality, royalty, society
antonyms A-list, aristocracy, best, choice, corps d'elite, cream, elect, elite, fat, flower, pick, pink, pride, upper crust
2 a considerable amount ⟨I have a *mass* of work to do tonight⟩ — see LOT 2
3 a distinct and separate portion of matter ⟨a *mass* of leaves in a corner of the yard⟩ — see BODY 2
4 the main or greater part of something as distinguished from its subordinate parts ⟨when taking pictures, focus your attention on the *mass* of the main subject⟩ — see BODY 1
5 the largest part or quantity of something ⟨believes that the great *mass* of voters are in the polical center and consider themselves neither conservative nor liberal⟩ — see MAJORITY 1
6 a great number of persons or creatures massed together ⟨a huge *mass* of people had gathered in the park to protest the government's latest policy⟩ — see CROWD 1

mass *vb* to gradually form into a layer, pile, or mass ⟨clouds *massing* on the western side of the mountain range⟩ — see COLLECT 2

massacre *n* the killing of a large number of people ⟨the infamous *massacre* of more than 200 Sioux at Wounded Knee, South Dakota⟩
synonyms bloodbath, butchery, carnage, death, holocaust, slaughter
related words bloodletting, bloodshed, foul play, homicide, killing, manslaughter, murder, slaying; mortality; annihilation, decimation, demolishing, destruction, devastation, eradication, extermination; genocide, pogrom; assassination, execution

massacre *vb* to kill on a large scale ⟨the country's rival ethnic groups began *massacring* one another⟩
synonyms butcher, mow (down), slaughter
related words assassinate, croak [*slang*], dispatch, do in, execute, fell, murder, slay, smite, snuff; annihilate, blot out, decimate, demolish, destroy, devastate, eradicate, exterminate, waste, wipe out

massage *vb* to praise too much ⟨a candidate who knows that you have to *massage* the voters if you want to get elected⟩ — see FLATTER 1

massive *adj* **1** having great weight ⟨a *massive* piece of furniture that was nearly impossible to move⟩ — see HEAVY 1
2 unusually large ⟨the *massive* statue took up most of the small yard⟩ — see HUGE
3 large and impressive in size, grandeur, extent, or conception ⟨the war memorial's *massive* dignity moves most visitors to reflective silence⟩ — see GRAND 1

massively *adv* to a large extent or degree ⟨I am *massively* irritated by this new development⟩ — see GREATLY 2

massiveness *n* **1** the quality or state of being very large ⟨the *massiveness* of the puppy's paws suggested that this would be a very large dog⟩ — see IMMENSITY
2 the state or quality of being heavy ⟨I need something with sufficient *massiveness* to block the wheels so this car won't roll down the ramp⟩ — see WEIGHTINESS 1

mass-market *adj* fit or likely to be sold especially on a large scale ⟨the kind of *mass-market* candy bars that connoisseurs of chocolate love to disdain⟩ — see COMMERCIAL

mass-produced *adj* made beforehand in large numbers ⟨a cheap *mass-produced* plastic toy⟩ — see READY-MADE

master *adj* **1** coming before all others in importance ⟨thought of themselves as belonging to humanity's *master* race⟩ — see FOREMOST 1
2 having or showing exceptional knowledge, experience, or skill in a field of endeavor ⟨a *master* craftsman who makes fine wood furniture of his own designs⟩ — see PROFICIENT

master *n* **1** a person with a high level of knowledge or skill in a field ⟨a *master* at chess⟩ — see EXPERT
2 one that defeats an enemy or opponent ⟨little did the tennis pro know that his new student would someday become his *master*⟩ — see VICTOR 1
3 the person (as an employer or supervisor) who tells people and especially workers what to do ⟨I'm the *master* of this operation, and you'll do what I say⟩ — see BOSS

master *vb* **1** to achieve a victory over ⟨finally *mastered* her longtime opponent at chess⟩ — see BEAT 2
2 to acquire complete knowledge, understanding, or skill in ⟨I think I've *mastered* algebra at last⟩ — see LEARN 1

masterful *adj* **1** accomplished with trained ability ⟨a *masterful* performance of a difficult piece for the violin⟩ — see SKILLFUL 1
2 fond of ordering people around ⟨a *masterful* coworker who liked to tell other people how to do their jobs⟩ — see BOSSY
3 having a feeling of superiority that shows itself in an

overbearing attitude ⟨a *masterful* businesswoman who didn't hesitate to step on a lot of people as she climbed the ladder of success⟩ — see ARROGANT
4 having or showing exceptional knowledge, experience, or skill in a field of endeavor ⟨a president who was celebrated as a *masterful* communicator of his administration's policies⟩ — see PROFICIENT

masterfully *adv* in a skillful or expert manner ⟨plays the violin *masterfully*, especially for a performer of her age⟩ — see WELL 3

masterfulness *n* **1** subtle or imaginative ability in inventing, devising, or executing something ⟨the sheer *masterfulness* of the thieves' plan could not be denied, even by the police⟩ — see SKILL 1
2 an exaggerated sense of one's importance that shows itself in the making of excessive or unjustified claims ⟨the shameless *masterfulness* that invested his every move was positively galling to his colleagues⟩ — see ARROGANCE

masterly *adj* **1** accomplished with trained ability ⟨a *masterly* performance of one of the most difficult ballets in the repertory⟩ — see SKILLFUL 1
2 having or showing exceptional knowledge, experience, or skill in a field of endeavor ⟨a *masterly* handling of a complex topic in philosophy⟩ — see PROFICIENT

masterly *adv* in a skillful or expert manner ⟨a *masterly* executed somersault⟩ — see WELL 3

mastermind *n* a person who designs and guides a plan or undertaking ⟨the real *mastermind* behind the embezzlement scheme⟩ — see ENGINEER

mastermind *vb* to plan out usually with subtle skill or care ⟨he was charged with *masterminding* a plan to redecorate the suite of offices without seriously disrupting business operations⟩ — see ENGINEER

masterpiece *n* something (as a work of art) that is a great achievement and often its creator's greatest achievement ⟨Michelangelo's frescoes in the Sistine Chapel are often considered to be his *masterpieces*⟩
synonyms chef d'oeuvre, classic, magnum opus, masterwork
related words masterstroke, pièce de résistance, showpiece, tour de force; blockbuster, megahit, smash, success, winner; gem, jewel, prize, treasure
near antonyms bomb, catastrophe, clunker, debacle (*also* débâcle), disaster, dud, failure, fiasco, fizzle, flop, loser, turkey, washout

master plan *n* a method worked out in advance for achieving some objective ⟨my neighbor assured me that the wisdom of his *master plan* for his yard would be apparent once everything was finished⟩ — see PLAN 1

mastership *n* a highly developed skill in or knowledge of something ⟨we're still working on *mastership* of the new computer system⟩ — see COMMAND 2

masterwork *n* something (as a work of art) that is a great achievement and often its creator's greatest achievement ⟨his most famous novel is regarded as a *masterwork* of Western literature⟩ — see MASTERPIECE

mastery *n* **1** a highly developed skill in or knowledge of something ⟨the exchange student returned from her year in Spain with a complete *mastery* of the language⟩ — see COMMAND 2
2 the right or means to command or control others ⟨the British monarch has only token *mastery* over the citizens of the United Kingdom⟩ — see POWER 1

masticate *vb* to crush or grind with the teeth ⟨mindlessly *masticated* peanuts while watching the baseball game on TV⟩ — see BITE (ON)

mastodon *n* something or someone that is unusually large and powerful ⟨mom-and-pop stores just can't compete with these *mastodons* of retailing⟩ — see GIANT

match *n* **1** a competitive encounter between individuals or groups carried on for amusement, exercise, or in pursuit of a prize ⟨a chess *match*⟩ — see GAME 1
2 a union representing a special kind of social and legal partnership between two people ⟨from all appearances those two have got a good *match* there⟩ — see MARRIAGE 1
3 either of a pair matched in one or more qualities ⟨I can't find the *match* to this sock⟩ — see MATE 1
4 one that is equal to another in status, achievement, or value ⟨for a wife he wants a woman who will be his *match* in every aspect of their lives⟩ — see EQUAL
5 something or someone that strongly resembles another ⟨Erin is so nearly my exact *match* you'd think she must be my twin and not just my cousin⟩ — see IMAGE 1
6 an earnest effort for superiority or victory over another ⟨the discussion soon degenerated into a pointless shouting *match*⟩ — see CONTEST 1

match *vb* **1** to be the exact counterpart of ⟨does this handbag's shade of blue *match* my navy blue pants?⟩ ⟨the rare blood type that exactly *matched* that of the transplant recipient⟩
synonyms correspond (to), equal, parallel
related words blend (with), conform (to), coordinate (with), go (with), harmonize (with); complement, supplement; counterbalance, counterpoise; echo, image, mirror, repeat; add up (to), amount (to), approach, come (to), near; measure (up), partake (of), rival, suggest
2 to give in marriage ⟨they were happy to *match* their daughter to a man from a good family⟩ — see MARRY 2
3 to produce something equal to (as in quality or value) ⟨no one has ever been able to *match* that novel for its portrayal of the horrors of war⟩ — see EQUAL 1

matching *adj* having qualities in common ⟨was fond of dressing the twins in *matching* outfits⟩ — see ALIKE

matchless *adj* having no equal or rival for excellence or desirability ⟨the *matchless* beauty and grandeur of Yosemite Valley⟩ — see ONLY 1

matchup *n* a competitive encounter between individuals or groups carried on for amusement, exercise, or in pursuit of a prize ⟨a boxing *matchup* that promises to be a sportswriter's dream⟩ — see GAME 1

mate *n* **1** either of a pair matched in one or more qualities ⟨have you seen the *mate* to this glove anywhere?⟩
synonyms companion, fellow, half, match, twin
related words coordinate; coequal, counterpart, equal, equivalent, like, parallel, peer, rival; carbon copy, double, duplicate, facsimile, identical twin, likeness, mirror image, replica, ringer; analogue (*or* analog), similarity
near antonyms antipode, antithesis, contrary, converse, opposite, reverse
2 a person frequently seen in the company of another ⟨that lout and his *mates* are known troublemakers in the neighborhood⟩ — see ASSOCIATE 1
3 *chiefly British* a person who helps a more skilled person ⟨a plumber and his *mate* showed up to fix the sink in our London hotel room⟩ — see HELPER
4 the person to whom another is married ⟨they vowed to each other that they would remain *mates* for life⟩ — see SPOUSE
5 *chiefly British* a person who has a strong liking for and trust in another ⟨spent the weekend in London with some of his *mates* from Oxford⟩ — see FRIEND 1

mate *vb* to engage in sexual intercourse ⟨cats conceive almost every time they *mate*⟩ — see COPULATE

mater *n, chiefly British* a female human parent ⟨the public school student addressed the letter to "Dear *Mater*"⟩ — see MOTHER

material *adj* **1** relating to or composed of matter ⟨there's no *material* evidence, such as a dead body, that a murder has been committed⟩

synonyms concrete, physical, substantial
related words bodily, carnal, corporal, corporeal, embodied, fleshly; apparent, appreciable, detectable, discernible (*also* discernable), noticeable, observable, palpable, perceptible, seeable, sensible, tangible, touchable, visible; objective, phenomenal; bulky, heavy, hefty, massive, ponderous, solid, weighty
near antonyms bodiless, discarnate, disembodied, formless, incorporeal, unbodied; ethereal, insubstantial, unsubstantial; impalpable, imperceptible, insensible, intangible, invisible, unnoticeable; airy, diaphanous, gossamery, tenuous, thin, vaporous, wispish; metaphysical, spiritual
antonyms immaterial, nonmaterial, nonphysical
2 having great meaning or lasting effect ⟨there's no *material* difference between the two designs for the skyscraper: one's as bad as the other⟩ — see IMPORTANT 1
3 having to do with life on earth especially as opposed to that in heaven ⟨people who worry more about *material* concerns than about spiritual ones⟩ — see EARTHLY
4 having to do with the matter at hand ⟨that information, while fascinating, is not *material* to our discussion⟩ — see PERTINENT
5 of or relating to the human body ⟨*material* needs such as food and warmth⟩ — see PHYSICAL 1

material *n* **1** the basic elements from which something can be developed ⟨she's clearly movie star *material*⟩ — see MAKING
2 *usually* **materials** *pl* items needed for the performance of a task or activity ⟨I have all the *materials* to build the mobile⟩ — see EQUIPMENT

materialist *n* a person who is chiefly interested in material comfort and is hostile or indifferent to art and culture ⟨a *materialist* who knows the price of everything and the value of nothing⟩ — see PHILISTINE

materiality *n* **1** something that actually exists ⟨preferred a single *materiality* to a slew of hypotheticals⟩ — see FACT 2
2 the fact or state of being pertinent ⟨the *materiality* of that fact is not in dispute⟩ — see PERTINENCE
3 the quality of being actual ⟨seems to question the very *materiality* of the universe⟩ — see FACT 1

materialization *n* the soul of a dead person thought of especially as appearing to living people ⟨since no one lived in the attic, the landlord suggested that the new tenant might have seen the *materialization* of a woman once murdered there⟩ — see GHOST 1

materialize *vb* **1** to come into existence ⟨the business speculator promised profits that never seemed to *materialize*⟩ — see BEGIN 2
2 to come into view ⟨the train station *materialized* through the fog⟩ — see APPEAR 1
3 to come to one's attention especially gradually or unexpectedly ⟨an unforeseen problem with this project seems to have *materialized*⟩ — see ARISE 2
4 to represent in visible form ⟨a statue of a grieving woman that seems to *materialize* the very concept of grief⟩ — see EMBODY 2

matériel *or* **materiel** *n* items needed for the performance of a task or activity ⟨the army is running short of clothing and other *matériel*⟩ — see EQUIPMENT

maternal *adj* of, relating to, or characteristic of a mother ⟨her *maternal* instincts told her that something was wrong⟩ — see MOTHERLY

maternity *n* motherly character or qualities ⟨she had such *maternity* at such a young age that all her classmates went to her for comfort⟩
synonyms motherliness
related words nurturance; fertileness, fertility, fruitfulness, productivity, richness

matey *adj, chiefly British* having or showing kindly feeling and sincere interest ⟨the pub keeper adopted a *matey* tone with me, as if he were my dearest chum⟩ — see FRIENDLY 1

math *n* the act or process of performing mathematical operations to find a value ⟨I did the *math*, and we can't afford to keeping spending like this⟩ — see CALCULATION

mathematical *adj* meeting the highest standard of accuracy ⟨produced an answer of *mathematical* precision⟩ — see PRECISE 1

mathematics *n pl* the act or process of performing mathematical operations to find a value ⟨I can't do the *mathematics* in my head, so I'll need a pen and paper⟩ — see CALCULATION

mating *n* sexual union involving penetration of the vagina by the penis ⟨if the mare doesn't get pregnant from this *mating*, you don't have to pay for the second try⟩ — see SEXUAL INTERCOURSE

matriarch *n* a dignified usually elderly woman of some rank or authority ⟨even though she was 87, the *matriarch* of the family knew everything that was going on⟩
synonyms dame, dowager, grande dame, matron
related words grandam (*or* grandame); headmistress, mistress; materfamilias; ma, mama (*also* mamma *or* momma), mammy, mom, mother

matriculate *vb* to add (a person) to a list or roll as a participant or member ⟨the college *matriculated* 1000 students for the fall semester⟩ — see ENROLL 1

matrimonial *adj* of or relating to marriage ⟨she plans to focus on *matrimonial* concerns after she's established in her career⟩ — see MARITAL

matrimony *n* a union representing a special kind of social and legal partnership between two people ⟨we intend to be joined in *matrimony* until "death do us part"⟩ — see MARRIAGE 1

matron *n* a dignified usually elderly woman of some rank or authority ⟨the *matron* firmly ordered the rowdy little boys back to their seats⟩ — see MATRIARCH

matte *also* **mat** *or* **matt** *adj* lacking a surface luster or gloss ⟨I chose a paint with a *matte* finish so the walls wouldn't be too shiny⟩
synonyms dim, dull, dulled, flat, lusterless
related words tarnished, unpolished; cloudy, dingy, dirty, drab, lackluster, mousy (*or* mousey), muddy; gray (*also* grey), leaden, pale, palish; black, dark, darkened, darkish, dimmed, dusky, gloomy, murky, obscure, obscured, pitch-black, pitch-dark, somber (*or* sombre), stygian, tenebrific, tenebrous
near antonyms buffed, burnished, glazed, lacquered, polished, rubbed, shellacked, varnished; satin, satiny; silken, silky; slick, slippery; gemmy, gleaming, glimmering, glinting, glistening, glittering, scintillating, shimmering, shining, sparkling, twinkling; beaming, bedazzling, bright, brightened, brilliant, candescent, dazzling, effulgent, fulgent, glowing, incandescent, lambent, lucent, lucid, luminous, radiant, refulgent, resplendent, shining
antonyms glossy, lustrous, shiny, sleek

matter *n* **1** a major object of interest or concern (as in a discussion or artistic composition) ⟨that is not relevant to the *matter* under discussion⟩
synonyms content, motif, motive, question, subject, theme, topic
related words subject matter; talking point; count, idea, point, purpose; consideration, issue, problem; body, bulk, burden, centerpiece, core, crux, essence, fundamental, generality, gist, grist, heart, kernel, keynote, main, marrow, mass, net, nub, nubbin, nucleus, pith, pivot, purport, quick, staple, substance, sum; basis; bottom, essential, essentiality; affair, argument, debate

near antonyms aside, digression, excursion, interjection, parenthesis, tangent
2 something to be dealt with ⟨we must take care of this *matter* before it becomes a real problem⟩
synonyms affair, business, thing
related words consideration, issue, problem; crisis, crossroad(s), crunch, emergency, exigency, flash point, head, juncture, strait, zero hour; concern, trouble, worry; care, lookout, responsibility; deadlock, halt, impasse, stalemate, standstill; corner, fix, hole, hot water, jam, pickle, pinch, predicament, scrape, spot
phrases ball of wax
3 communications or parcels sent or carried through the postal system ⟨first-class *matter*⟩ — see MAIL
4 something that requires thought and skill for resolution ⟨I've been thinking about the *matter* all night, and I believe I have a solution⟩ — see PROBLEM 1
5 an approximate amount, extent, or degree ⟨a simple meal that can be prepared in a *matter* of 20 to 30 minutes⟩ — see NEIGHBORHOOD 1

matter *vb* to be of importance ⟨she believes that doing well in school really does *matter*⟩
synonyms count, import, mean, signify, weigh
related words affect, concern, influence, sway; add up (to), amount (to)
phrases carry weight, cut ice

matter-of-fact *adj* **1** restricted to or based on fact ⟨a *matter-of-fact* recitation of the events of the last week⟩ — see FACTUAL
2 willing to see things as they really are and deal with them sensibly ⟨a *matter-of-fact* woman who didn't worry about "what ifs"⟩ — see REALISTIC 1

maturation *n* the process of becoming mature ⟨a flower's *maturation* from bud to full bloom can take weeks⟩
synonyms development, growth, maturing, ripening
related words blossoming, flourishing, flowering; mellowing, softening; evolution, evolvement, expansion, progression; coming-of-age, maturity
near antonyms decadence, decay, decaying, declension, decline, declining, degeneration, descent, deterioration; ebbing, fading, shriveling (*or* shrivelling), waning, wilting, withering; death, decease, demise, dying, end, exit, expiration, expiring, expiry, perishing; regression, retrogression, reversion

mature *adj* **1** fully grown or developed ⟨I like pears when they're still hard, before they're *mature*⟩
synonyms adult, full-blown, full-fledged, matured, ripe, ripened
related words aged, aging (*or* ageing), long-lived, old, older; golden, mellow
near antonyms blooming, blossoming, burgeoning, flourishing, flowering; undeveloped, unfinished, unfledged, unformed
antonyms adolescent, green, immature, juvenile, unripe, unripened, young, youngish, youthful
2 having reached the date at which payment is required ⟨*mature* bonds⟩ — see DUE 1
3 relating to or typical of adults; displaying proper maturity ⟨that wasn't a very *mature* response to my well-meaning criticism⟩ — see ADULT 1
4 dealing in or with explicitly sexual material ⟨a *mature* talk show that is available only on pay-cable⟩ — see ADULT 2

mature *vb* to become mature ⟨a young figure skater whose talent is still *maturing*⟩
synonyms age, develop, grow, grow up, progress, ripen
related words mellow, soften; bloom, blossom, burgeon (*also* bourgeon), flourish, flower; open, unfold; advance, evolve; get along, get on, gray (*also* grey)
near antonyms decay, decline, degenerate, deteriorate, sink, worsen; droop, dry, fade, flag, sag, shrivel, wane, waste (away), weaken, wilt, wither; regress, retrogress, revert; backslide, lapse, return

matured *adj* fully grown or developed ⟨a *matured* plant in full bloom⟩ — see MATURE 1

maturing *n* the process of becoming mature ⟨the *maturing* of young horses can take several years⟩ — see MATURATION

maturity *n* **1** the state of being fully grown or developed ⟨people are legally considered to have reached *maturity* at the age of 18 in the United States⟩
synonyms adulthood, adultness, majority
related words manhood, womanhood; bloom, flush, heyday, prime; autumn, middle age, midlife
near antonyms babyhood, infancy, toddlerhood; adolescence, childhood, youth
antonyms immaturity, minority, nonage
2 the state of being an old person ⟨special senior citizen discounts are one advantage of *maturity*⟩ — see ANCIENTNESS 1

maudlin *adj* appealing to the emotions in an obvious and tiresome way ⟨a *maudlin* movie about a lovable tramp⟩ — see CORNY 1

maul *vb* **1** to abuse physically ⟨demonstrators who claimed that they had been *mauled* by the police⟩ — see MANHANDLE 1
2 to strike repeatedly ⟨the irate store owner was *mauling* the shoplifter when the police showed up⟩ — see BEAT 1

mau-mau *vb* to make timid or fearful by or as if by threats ⟨the self-appointed guardians of political correctness have been trying to *mau-mau* the university president into rescinding everyone's freedom of speech⟩ — see INTIMIDATE

maunder *vb* **1** to move about from place to place aimlessly ⟨*maundered* all over town on his day off⟩ — see WANDER 1
2 to talk at length without sticking to a topic or getting to a point ⟨ask her a question and she'll *maunder* for half an hour⟩ — see RAMBLE 1
3 *chiefly British* to express dissatisfaction, pain, or resentment usually tiresomely ⟨a couple of mates *maundering* over their beer in a dark corner of the pub⟩ — see COMPLAIN

maunderer *n* a person who roams about without a fixed route or destination ⟨the city has many quaint alleys and backstreets to interest the urban *maunderer*⟩ — see NOMAD

maundering *adj* passing from one topic to another ⟨a long, *maundering* conversation about what was wrong with the world and how he could fix it⟩ — see DISCURSIVE

maven *also* **mavin** *n* **1** a person with a high level of knowledge or skill in a field ⟨an investment *maven*, he was doing well even when the market was doing poorly⟩ — see EXPERT
2 a person with a strong and habitual liking for something ⟨a science-fiction *maven* who could talk for hours about fictional technology⟩ — see FAN

maverick *adj* deviating from commonly accepted beliefs or practices ⟨George Sand's *maverick* views on marriage scandalized 19th-century French society⟩ — see HERETICAL

maverick *n* a person who does not conform to generally accepted standards or customs ⟨there's always one *maverick* who has to go his own way⟩ — see NONCONFORMIST 1

mawkish *adj* appealing to the emotions in an obvious and tiresome way ⟨a *mawkish* plea for donations to the charity⟩ — see CORNY 1

mawkishness *n* the state or quality of having an excess of tender feelings (as of love, nostalgia, or compassion) ⟨the grating *mawkishness* of her poetry makes me want to stamp on wildflowers⟩ — see SENTIMENTALITY

max *adj* of the greatest or highest degree or quantity ⟨the *max* number of complaints received on any given day was 15⟩ — see ULTIMATE 1

max *n* the greatest amount, number, or part ⟨at the *max* there will be 25 people at the party⟩ — see MOST

maxim *n* an often stated observation regarding something from common experience ⟨it's a common *maxim* that "a watched pot never boils," but that's not literally true⟩ — see SAYING

maximum *adj* **1** of the greatest or highest degree or quantity ⟨the *maximum* amount of time needed to complete the project⟩ — see ULTIMATE 1
2 of the highest degree ⟨he always puts out *maximum* effort⟩ — see FULL 2

maximum *n* the greatest amount, number, or part ⟨achieved the *maximum*⟩ — see MOST

maybe *adv* it is possible ⟨*maybe* we can make it to the concert, if we hurry⟩ — see PERHAPS

mayhap *adv* it is possible ⟨*mayhap* I could see you again next week? I so enjoyed our date tonight⟩ — see PERHAPS

mazard *or* **mazzard** *n, chiefly dialect* the upper or front part of the body that contains the brain, the major sense organs, and the mouth ⟨Granny threatened to whop me on the *mazard* if I didn't start minding my manners⟩ — see HEAD 1

maze *n* **1** a confusing and complicated arrangement of passages ⟨the mansion had a beautifully landscaped *maze* that was constructed of tall cypresses⟩
synonyms labyrinth, rabbit warren, warren
related words meander; jungle, quagmire; catacomb, cat's cradle, knot, snarl, tangle, web; entanglement, entrapment, snare, trap
2 *chiefly dialect* a state of mental uncertainty ⟨she's been walking around in a *maze* ever since her husband walked out on her⟩ — see CONFUSION 1

maze *vb* to throw into a state of mental uncertainty ⟨I'm completely *mazed* by the multitude of plans for health insurance⟩ — see CONFUSE 1

MC *n* a person who conducts a program of entertainment by making introductions and providing continuity ⟨when we needed an impromptu *MC* at the wedding reception, my brother volunteered⟩ — see ANNOUNCER

meager *or* **meagre** *adj* less plentiful than what is normal, necessary, or desirable ⟨ever since he started the diet, his dinners have been more *meager* than he would like⟩
synonyms exiguous, hand-to-mouth, light, niggardly, poor, scant, scanty, scarce, skimp, skimpy, slender, slim, spare, sparing, sparse, stingy
related words deficient, inadequate, insufficient, lacking, short, wanting; bare, bare-bones; least, littlest, lowest, mere, minimal, slightest; slight, small, thin; barren, infertile, sterile, unfruitful, unproductive
phrases thin on the ground
near antonyms adequate, enough, satisfactory, sufficient, tolerable; fat, fecund, fertile, fruitful, prolific, rich; lavish, luxuriant; blooming, bursting, flourishing, proliferative, swarming, teeming, thriving; excess, extra, surplus
antonyms abundant, ample, bountiful, copious, generous, liberal, plenteous, plentiful

meal *n* food eaten or prepared for eating at one time ⟨all she wants to do is sit quietly after the large Thanksgiving *meal*⟩
synonyms chow, feed, menu, mess, refection, repast, table
related words board; breakfast, buffet, collation, dinner, lunch, luncheon, refreshments, smorgasbord, snack, supper, tea; bite, gulp, morsel, serving, taste; banquet, feast, regale, spread; bake, barbecue (*also* barbeque), clambake, cookout, fry, fry-up [*British*], luau, picnic, potluck, roast

mealy *adj* **1** lacking a healthy skin color ⟨her *mealy* complexion might be OK if she were a mime, but she isn't⟩ — see PALE 2
2 not being or expressing what one appears to be or express ⟨a *mealy* apology that was really no apology at all⟩ — see INSINCERE

mealymouthed *adj* not being or expressing what one appears to be or express ⟨a *mealymouthed* compliment from a jealous competitor⟩ — see INSINCERE

[1]**mean** *adj* being about midway between extremes of amount or size ⟨for the state of Florida, what is the *mean* number of sunny days per month?⟩ — see MIDDLE 2

[2]**mean** *adj* **1** belonging to the class of people of low social or economic rank ⟨Alexander Hamilton seems to have had feelings of inferiority because of his *mean* origins⟩ — see IGNOBLE 1
2 giving or sharing as little as possible ⟨a *mean* child who hoarded all her toys⟩ — see STINGY 1
3 having or showing a desire to cause someone pain or suffering for the sheer enjoyment of it ⟨a *mean*, embittered old woman who wanted company for her misery⟩ — see HATEFUL
4 not following or in accordance with standards of honor and decency ⟨a *mean* trick to play on a trusting person⟩ — see IGNOBLE 2
5 of little or less value or merit ⟨it's no *mean* feat to memorize that long poem⟩ — see INFERIOR 2
6 of the very best kind ⟨I'm a *mean* dancer, so you could do worse than go to the prom with me⟩ — see EXCELLENT
7 showing signs of advanced wear and tear and neglect ⟨he worked hard to escape the *mean* neighborhood of his youth⟩ — see SHABBY 1
8 arousing or deserving of one's loathing and disgust ⟨that was no *mean* stunt to pull off, especially with so little advance preparation⟩ — see CONTEMPTIBLE 1

mean *n* **1** a middle point between extremes ⟨that candidate's moderate views were seen as the *mean* that voters were looking for⟩
synonyms golden mean, medium, middle, middle ground, midpoint
related words arithmetic mean, average; median, norm, par, standard
phrases middle of the road
near antonyms maximum, utmost; minimum
2 means *pl* an action planned or taken to achieve a desired result ⟨won the competition by fair and honest *means*⟩ — see MEASURE 1
3 means *pl* something used to achieve an end ⟨the ends don't justify the *means*⟩ — see AGENT 1
4 means *pl* the total of one's money and property ⟨a woman of considerable *means*⟩ — see WEALTH 1

mean *vb* **1** to communicate or convey (as an idea) to the mind ⟨the national anthem *means* various things to various people⟩
synonyms denote, express, import, intend, signify, spell
related words connote, imply, suggest; add up (to), amount (to); hint, infer, insinuate, intimate; embody, epitomize, personify, represent, symbol, symbolize; advert, allude (to), cite, instance, mention, refer (to), specify, touch (on *or* upon); designate, indicate, point (to), signal; announce, declare, proclaim; elucidate, explain
2 to be of importance ⟨your presence at my graduation would *mean* a lot to me⟩ — see MATTER
3 to have in mind as a purpose or goal ⟨I *mean* to win this race⟩ — see INTEND 1
4 to serve as a sign or symptom of ⟨these colder nights *mean* autumn has truly arrived⟩ — see INDICATE 1

meander *vb* to move about from place to place aimlessly ⟨theatergoers *meandering* around the lobby waiting for the play to start⟩ — see WANDER 1

meandering *adj* passing from one topic to another ⟨a *meandering* interview with the presidential hopeful that covered everything from his family life to his proposed foreign policy⟩ — see DISCURSIVE

meanie *also* **meany** *n* a mean, evil, or unprincipled person ⟨the class thought the substitute teacher was a big *meanie* when she assigned homework over the holidays⟩ — see VILLAIN

meaning *adj* clearly conveying a special meaning (as one's mood) ⟨gave me a *meaning* look after I said that⟩ — see EXPRESSIVE

meaning *n* **1** the idea that is conveyed or intended to be conveyed to the mind by language, symbol, or action ⟨the unmistakable *meaning* of the skier's upraised arms as he finished his spectacular run⟩
synonyms content, denotation, drift, import, intent, intention, purport, sense, significance, signification
related words connotation; clue, cue, hint, implication, indication, inkling, intimation, suggestion; message, tenor, theme; bottom, essence, essentiality, nature, soul, spirit, stuff; acceptance, acceptation, definition; burden, crux, gist; core, heart, kernel, marrow, nub, nucleus, pith, point, quick; matter, motif, motive, question, subject, topic
2 something that one hopes or intends to accomplish ⟨the people have a right to know what the president's *meaning* is in getting the nation involved in this war⟩ — see GOAL

meaningful *adj* **1** clearly conveying a special meaning (as one's mood) ⟨gave a *meaningful* sigh when I asked her how things were going⟩ — see EXPRESSIVE
2 having great meaning or lasting effect ⟨his time in office was too brief to accomplish anything *meaningful*⟩ — see IMPORTANT 1

meaningless *adj* having no meaning ⟨this argument over seating arrangements is an utterly *meaningless* bit of nonsense⟩
synonyms empty, inane, pointless, senseless
related words frivolous, inconsequential, inconsiderable, insignificant, little, minor, negligible, slight, trifling, trivial, unimportant; absurd, asinine, balmy, brainless, crackpot, crazy, cuckoo, daffy, daft, dotty, empty-headed, fatuous, foolish, half-witted, harebrained, insane, jerky, kooky (*also* kookie), loony (*also* looney), lunatic, mad, mindless, nonsensical, nutty, preposterous, sappy, silly, simpleminded, stupid, tomfool, unintelligent, unwise, wacky (*also* whacky), weak-minded, witless, zany; irrational, unreasonable; aimless, haphazard, purposeless
near antonyms eloquent, expressive, pregnant, revealing, suggestive, telling; logical, rational, reasonable, valid; consequential, eventful, important, key, major, momentous, substantial, weighty
antonyms meaningful, significant

meanly *adv* **1** in a manner showing no signs of pride or self-assertion ⟨*meanly* silent up to that point, he now felt that fair criticism was turning into gratuitous insult⟩ — see LOWLY
2 in a mean or spiteful manner ⟨in a *meanly* worded letter she told me that she never wanted to see me again⟩ — see NASTILY

meanness *n* the desire to cause pain for the satisfaction of doing harm ⟨nothing more than unprovoked *meanness* drove him to smash the child's toy⟩ — see MALICE

measly *adj* so small or unimportant as to warrant little or no attention ⟨offered her guest only one *measly* cookie⟩ — see NEGLIGIBLE 1

measure *n* **1** an action planned or taken to achieve a desired result ⟨such new security *measures* as metal detectors at all the entrances⟩
synonyms expedient, means, move, shift, step
related words act, action, deed, doing, feat, thing; course, procedure, proceeding, process; accomplishment, achievement, attainment, coup, exploit, success, triumph; activity, affair, business, dealing, enterprise, event; attempt, crack, endeavor, essay, fling, go, initiative, operation, pass, shot, stab, trial, try, undertaking, whack; effort, exertion, labor, pains, trouble, while, work; project, proposal, proposition; makeshift, resort, resource, stopgap; countermeasure, countermove, counterstep
2 a given or particular mass or aggregate of matter ⟨each day prisoners were given only a small *measure* of rice to live on⟩ — see AMOUNT
3 something set up as an example against which others of the same type are compared ⟨during the Renaissance, man came to be viewed as the *measure* of all things⟩ — see STANDARD 1
4 the recurrent pattern formed by a series of sounds having a regular rise and fall in intensity ⟨the song's soft, soothing *measures* make it a good lullaby⟩ — see RHYTHM
5 the total amount of measurable space or surface occupied by something ⟨a slipcover for the couch that was made to *measure*⟩ — see [1]SIZE

measure *vb* **1** to find out the size, extent, or amount of ⟨for this experiment, you need to carefully *measure* all the chemicals before you mix them together⟩
synonyms gauge (*also* gage), scale, span
related words weigh; calibrate, caliper; quantify, quantitate; lay off, mark (off); calculate, cipher, compute, figure, reckon, work out; appraise, assess, conjecture, estimate, evaluate, guess, guesstimate, judge, suppose, valuate, value; add up, sum, tally, total; ascertain, determine, discover, dope (out), figure out, find out
2 to keep from exceeding a desirable degree or level (as of expression) ⟨he carefully *measured* his response to the provocative question⟩ — see CONTROL 1

measured *adj* **1** decided on as a result of careful thought ⟨a *measured* response to the terrorist attack⟩ — see DELIBERATE 1
2 having distinct or certain limits ⟨the *measured* authority of the mayor in running the town's affairs⟩ — see LIMITED 1
3 marked by or occurring with a noticeable regularity in the rise and fall of sound ⟨the soldier's funeral procession moved along to the *measured* beating of a drum⟩ — see RHYTHMIC

measureless *adj* being or seeming to be without limits ⟨the bodies of the fallen sailors were consigned to the *measureless* depths of the sea⟩ — see INFINITE

measurement *n* the total amount of measurable space or surface occupied by something ⟨the *measurement* of the average house lot in that neighborhood is half an acre⟩ — see [1]SIZE

measure up (to) *vb* to come near or nearer to in character or quality ⟨he always worried about *measuring up to* his older brother⟩ — see APPROXIMATE

meat *n* **1** animal and especially mammal tissue used as food ⟨we need to go shopping; there's only enough *meat* in the freezer for one more dinner⟩
synonyms flesh
related words game, poultry, red meat, variety meat
2 substances intended to be eaten ⟨offered his guests *meat* and drink⟩ — see FOOD 1
3 the central part or aspect of something under consideration ⟨he dances all around it without ever addressing the *meat* of the issue⟩ — see CRUX

meat-and-potatoes *adj* of or relating to the simplest facts or theories of a subject ⟨a *meat-and-potatoes* knowledge of figure skating is all that a spectator really needs⟩ — see ELEMENTARY

meat and potatoes *n pl* the central part or aspect of something under consideration ⟨an article that never gets into the *meat and potatoes* of a solution to the city's rising crime rate⟩ — see CRUX

meathead *n* a stupid person ⟨he's a *meathead,* but handy to have around if there's any heavy lifting to be done⟩ — see IDIOT

mecca *n* a thing or place that is of greatest importance to an activity or interest ⟨that region of Connecticut is a *mecca* for antique hunters⟩ — see CENTER 1

mechanic *adj* done instantly and without conscious thought or decision ⟨the snapping of the handcuffs was followed by a *mechanic* reading of the suspect's rights⟩ — see AUTOMATIC 1

mechanical *adj* **1** done instantly and without conscious thought or decision ⟨the waiter's *mechanical* reply of "Everything on the menu is good"⟩ — see AUTOMATIC 1
2 lacking in natural or spontaneous quality ⟨a somewhat *mechanical* vocal performance⟩ — see ARTIFICIAL 1

mechanics *n pl* the characteristic peculiarities and technicalities of something ⟨the *mechanics* of running one's own online business⟩ — see INS AND OUTS

mechanization *n* the process of putting an apparatus, operation, or system under the control or regulation of mechanical or electronic devices ⟨a huge volume of mail that became possible only after the *mechanization* of the sorting process⟩ — see AUTOMATION

medal *n* a piece of metal given in honor of a special event, a person, or an achievement ⟨the display case held an impressive array of military *medals* from World War II⟩
synonyms medallion, order
related words decoration, honor; crown, insignia, laurel, ribbon, title; bronze, gold, silver; badge, button, chevron, clasp, cockade, color, ensign, rosette, star; distinction; award, prize, trophy; citation, commendation

medallion *n* a piece of metal given in honor of a special event, a person, or an achievement ⟨the hockey team received a gold *medallion* at the Olympics⟩ — see MEDAL

meddle *vb* to interest oneself in what is not one's concern ⟨please stop *meddling* in your sister's marriage, even though you mean well⟩ — see INTERFERE

meddler *n* a person who meddles in the affairs of others ⟨a *meddler* who stayed up all night watching the neighbors⟩ — see BUSYBODY

meddlesome *adj* thrusting oneself where one is not welcome or invited ⟨*meddlesome* neighbors kept asking the couple when they were going to have children⟩ — see INTRUSIVE

meddling *adj* thrusting oneself where one is not welcome or invited ⟨the bride's parents promised that they would never be *meddling* in-laws⟩ — see INTRUSIVE

medial *adj* occupying a position equally distant from the ends or extremes ⟨four is the *medial* number between one and seven⟩ — see MIDDLE 1

median *adj* **1** being about midway between extremes of amount or size ⟨the *median* price of a home in the area⟩ — see MIDDLE 2
2 occupying a position equally distant from the ends or extremes ⟨determine the *median* point between your two speakers, and test your stereo system from there⟩ — see MIDDLE 1

mediate *adj* occupying a position equally distant from the ends or extremes ⟨has a black-and-white view of human nature, believing that there is no *mediate* state between good and evil⟩ — see MIDDLE 1

mediate *vb* to act as a go-between for opposing sides ⟨their middle child is often asked to *mediate* between the oldest and the youngest⟩ — see INTERVENE

mediator *n* one who works with opposing sides in order to bring about an agreement ⟨if you two cannot resolve this argument on your own, we'll have to bring in a *mediator*⟩
synonyms broker, buffer, conciliator, go-between, honest broker, interceder, intercessor, intermediary, intermediate, interposer, middleman, peacemaker
related words troubleshooter; moderator; bargainer, negotiant, negotiator; appeaser, pacificator, pacifier, reconciler; agent, attorney, deputy, factor, procurator, proxy; liaison, medium; ambassador, emissary, envoy, legate, messenger; delegate, representative; busybody, interferer, meddler; arbiter, arbitrator, judge, referee, umpire; adviser (*also* advisor), counselor (*or* counsellor)

medic *n* a person specially trained in healing human medical disorders ⟨the wounded soldier called for a *medic*⟩ — see DOCTOR

medicament *n* a substance or preparation used to treat disease ⟨in the 19th century a physician's bag of *medicaments* most likely included powerful opiates⟩ — see MEDICINE

medication *n* a substance or preparation used to treat disease ⟨the doctor prescribed two different *medications* for the infection⟩ — see MEDICINE

medicinal *adj* **1** tending to cure disease or restore health ⟨even in Roman times the hot mineral springs of Bath, England, were believed to possess *medicinal* properties⟩
synonyms curative, healing, officinal, remedial, restorative, therapeutic
related words healthful, healthy, salubrious, salutary, sanative, wholesome; alleviative, corrective, tonic
near antonyms insalubrious, noisome, noxious, unhealthful, unhealthy, unwholesome; deleterious, injurious, pernicious; infectious, poisonous, toxic; adverse, bad, baleful, baneful, damaging, detrimental, harmful, hurtful, ill; insanitary, unhygienic, unsanitary
2 beneficial to the health of body or mind ⟨if gin and tonic is the *medicinal* potion that he claims, then he's done a lot of self-medication of late⟩ — see HEALTHFUL

medicinal *n* a substance or preparation used to treat disease ⟨the discovery that the plant is a potent *medicinal* once it has been refined⟩ — see MEDICINE

medicine *n* a substance or preparation used to treat disease ⟨if you don't take all the doses of your *medicine,* you might get sick again⟩
synonyms cure, drug, medicament, medication, medicinal, pharmaceutical, physic, remedy, specific
related words cure-all, nostrum, panacea; botanical, patent medicine, prescription, prescription drug; cordial, potion, tonic; miracle drug, wonder drug; cap, capsule, pill, tablet; injection, shot; embrocation, liniment, lotion, ointment, potion, poultice, salve; syrup (*also* sirup), tincture; antibiotic, antiseptic, serum; cathartic, purgative

medico *n* a person specially trained in healing human medical disorders ⟨a woman who is suspicious of all *medicos,* regardless of their credentials⟩ — see DOCTOR

medieval *also* **mediaeval** *adj* having passed its time of use or usefulness ⟨get rid of that *medieval* kerosene stove—it stinks and it's dangerous⟩ — see OBSOLETE

mediocre *adj* **1** of average to below average quality ⟨your grades are *mediocre* and barely acceptable⟩
synonyms common, fair, indifferent, medium, middling, ordinary, passable, run-of-the-mill, run-of-the-mine (*or* run-of-mine), second-class, second-rate, so-so
related words acceptable, adequate, all right, alright, decent, OK (*or* okay), reasonable, satisfactory, sufficient, sufficing, tolerable; moderate, modest; present-

able, respectable; minimal, unexceptional; fine, good, nice
near antonyms A1, capital, choice, classic, distinguished, excellent, exceptional, exquisite, fabulous, fantastic, fine, first-class, first-rate, grand, great, marvelous (*or* marvellous), matchless, maximum, nifty, number one (*also* No. 1), optimal, optimum, outstanding, par excellence, peerless, preeminent, prime, sensational, special, splendid, stellar, sterling, superb, superior, superlative, supreme, swell, terrific, tip-top, top, top-notch; unmatched, unparalleled, unsurpassed; deficient, inadequate, insufficient, lacking, unacceptable, unsatisfactory, wanting
2 of low quality ⟨*mediocre* carvings in a pseudo-African style that are sold to tourists⟩ — see CHEAP 2

meditate *vb* **1** to give serious and careful thought to ⟨I've been *meditating* a career change for months⟩ — see PONDER
2 to have in mind as a purpose or goal ⟨had *meditated* a quick return to work after having the baby, but circumstances changed⟩ — see INTEND 1

meditation *n* long or deep thinking about spiritual matters ⟨the busy executive devotes an hour a day to quiet *meditation*⟩ — see CONTEMPLATION 1

meditative *adj* given to or marked by long, quiet thinking ⟨I've been in a *meditative* mood all day⟩ — see CONTEMPLATIVE

medium *adj* **1** being about midway between extremes of amount or size ⟨taxpayers of *medium* income⟩ — see MIDDLE 2
2 occupying a position equally distant from the ends or extremes ⟨a politician who first reads the polls and then inevitably takes the *medium* stance on every issue⟩ — see MIDDLE 1
3 of average to below average quality ⟨another *medium* effort from a movie director who can do better⟩ — see MEDIOCRE 1

medium *n* **1** a middle point between extremes ⟨trying to achieve a happy *medium* as far as the demands of career and family are concerned⟩ — see MEAN 1
2 something used to achieve an end ⟨regards political activism on the local level as the best *medium* for effecting social change⟩ — see AGENT 1
3 the circumstances, conditions, or objects by which one is surrounded ⟨an artist who enjoys the cultural *medium* of the big city⟩ — see ENVIRONMENT
4 a person who claims to speak with or for the spirits of the dead ⟨the *medium* claims that she can put the grieving parents in touch with the spirit of their deceased son⟩ — see CHANNELER
5 a place or opportunity for communicating ideas and information ⟨I think a blog might be a good *medium* for sharing your reviews of local restaurants⟩ — see VENUE 1

medley *n* an unorganized collection or mixture of various things ⟨a *medley* of snack foods available on the buffet table⟩ — see MISCELLANY 1

meek *adj* not having or showing any feelings of superiority, self-assertiveness, or showiness ⟨a *meek* girl who quietly went along with whatever her circle of friends wanted⟩ — see HUMBLE 1

meekly *adv* in a manner showing no signs of pride or self-assertion ⟨the dominant personality, he is always taking advantage of his so-called best friend, who just *meekly* accepts it⟩ — see LOWLY

meekness *n* the absence of any feelings of being better than others ⟨like most other things, *meekness* is best practiced in moderation⟩ — see HUMILITY

meet *adj* meeting the requirements of a purpose or situation ⟨in this case, splitting the winnings of the contested lottery ticket seems like a *meet* solution⟩ — see FIT 1

meet *n* a competitive encounter between individuals or groups carried on for amusement, exercise, or in pursuit of a prize ⟨a swim *meet*⟩ — see GAME 1

meet *vb* **1** to come upon face-to-face or as if face-to-face ⟨we never once *met* another car on that lonely country road⟩
synonyms catch, chance (upon), encounter, happen (upon), stumble (upon)
related words accost, confront; face, greet, salute; collide (with), crash (into); crisscross, cross, pass; hit (upon), light (upon), tumble (to); reencounter, remeet
phrases bump into, cross paths (with), run across, run into, run upon
near antonyms avoid, dodge, duck, elude, escape, evade, shake, shun
2 to come together into one body or place ⟨we'll *meet* for dinner, with a discussion to follow, next week⟩ — see ASSEMBLE 1
3 to come upon unexpectedly or by chance ⟨*met* her future husband at a party⟩ — see HAPPEN (ON *OR* UPON)
4 to do what is required by the terms of ⟨a financially struggling city trying to *meet* its loans⟩ — see FULFILL 1
5 to enter into contest or conflict with ⟨the up-and-coming boxer will *meet* the reigning champ for the first time tomorrow⟩ — see ENGAGE 2
6 to produce something equal to (as in quality or value) ⟨I'll *meet* your bet, nay, I'll even raise it⟩ — see EQUAL 1
7 to put up with (something painful or difficult) ⟨trying to *meet* the challenge of going to college while working at a full-time job⟩ — see BEAR 2
8 to give what is owed for ⟨I paid a portion of the long-distance bill to keep my carrier from cutting off service until I can *meet* the remainder of the charges⟩ — see PAY 2

meeting *n* **1** a coming together of a number of persons for a specified purpose ⟨there will be another committee *meeting* next week to discuss the parish fair⟩
synonyms assembly, congress, convention, convocation, council, gathering, get-together, huddle, powwow
related words clinic, workshop; cabinet, caucus, conclave, synod; demonstration, rally; confab, conversation, dialogue (*also* dialog), discourse, discussion, palaver, talk; negotiation, parley, summit; conference, forum, round-robin, roundtable, seminar, symposium; audience, interview, session
2 a body of people come together in one place ⟨a *meeting* marked by no consensus of what needs to be done⟩ — see GATHERING 1
3 the coming together of two or more things to the same point ⟨a *meeting* of two railroad lines⟩ — see CONVERGENCE

meetly *adv* in a manner suitable for the occasion or purpose ⟨the governor *meetly* and rightly did his duty when he vetoed a bill that was clearly unconstitutional⟩ — see PROPERLY

mega *adj* unusually large ⟨I will never understand why people build those *mega* houses on tiny lots⟩ — see HUGE

megabucks *n pl* a very large amount of money ⟨a baseball player with a contract worth *megabucks*⟩ — see FORTUNE 2

megacity *n* a thickly settled, highly populated area ⟨such modern *megacities* as São Paulo and Mexico City⟩ — see CITY

megahit *n* a person or thing that is successful ⟨the band's latest album is a *megahit*⟩ — see HIT 1

megalopolis *n* a thickly settled, highly populated area ⟨what was once a series of discrete towns interspersed with countryside is now one vast *megalopolis*⟩ — see CITY

megastar *n* a person who is widely known and usually much talked about ⟨even a cast of *megastars* couldn't keep the would-be blockbuster from fizzling at the box office⟩ — see CELEBRITY 1

megrim *n* a sudden impulsive and apparently unmotivated idea or action ⟨having no sense of purpose, he was often at the mercy of the strange *megrims* that sprang into his head⟩ — see WHIM

meister *n* a person with a high level of knowledge or skill in a field ⟨asked the office's wine *meister* to recommend a good bottle for a dinner party that she was hosting⟩ — see EXPERT

melancholic *adj* feeling unhappiness ⟨she becomes quite *melancholic* when she reflects on all the lost opportunities of her life⟩ — see SAD 1

melancholy *adj* **1** causing unhappiness ⟨the *melancholy* thought of having to say good-bye to all the friends he had made over the summer⟩ — see SAD 2
2 feeling unhappiness ⟨she was a bit *melancholy* after her youngest child left for college⟩ — see SAD 1
3 given to or marked by long, quiet thinking ⟨a *melancholy* period in the artist's life that is reflected in his work⟩ — see CONTEMPLATIVE

melancholy *n* a state or spell of low spirits ⟨the bleakness of winter sometimes gives me cause for *melancholy*⟩ — see SADNESS

mélange *n* an unorganized collection or mixture of various things ⟨a *mélange* of outfits for her workouts at the gym⟩ — see MISCELLANY 1

meld *n* a distinct entity formed by the combining of two or more different things ⟨her music is a *meld* of rock and country⟩ — see BLEND

meld *vb* to turn into a single mass or entity that is more or less the same throughout ⟨a cuisine that *melds* East and West into strikingly original flavor combinations⟩ — see BLEND 1

melee *n* a rough and often noisy fight usually involving several people ⟨a verbal disagreement at the football game soon turned into a general *melee* involving scores of spectators⟩ — see BRAWL 1

meliorate *vb* to make better ⟨regulations intended to *meliorate* the working conditions of migrant farm laborers⟩ — see IMPROVE

mellifluent *adj* having a pleasantly flowing quality suggestive of music ⟨the seamless editing gives the lushly romantic film a very *mellifluent* feel⟩ — see LYRIC 1

mellifluous *adj* having a pleasantly flowing quality suggestive of music ⟨a rich, *mellifluous* voice that gets her a lot of work in radio and TV commercials⟩ — see LYRIC 1

mellow *adj* **1** having a pleasantly flowing quality suggestive of music ⟨the *mellow* tones of an old violin⟩ — see LYRIC 1
2 not harsh or stern especially in nature or effect ⟨a teacher with a *mellow* approach to classroom discipline⟩ ⟨*mellow* soaps⟩ — see GENTLE 1
3 having an easygoing and pleasing manner especially in social situations ⟨*mellow* and unflappable, the office manager greatly contributes to the work environment⟩ — see AMIABLE
4 having a relaxed, casual manner ⟨she's rather high-strung, and her boyfriend is *mellow*, so they counterbalance each other nicely⟩ — see EASYGOING 1

mellow (out) *vb* to get rid of nervous tension or anxiety ⟨I'm going to need to *mellow out* when this stressful week is finally at an end⟩ — see RELAX 1

melodic *adj* having a pleasantly flowing quality suggestive of music ⟨a sweetly *melodic* chant⟩ — see LYRIC 1

melodious *adj* **1** having a pleasantly flowing quality suggestive of music ⟨preferred the *melodious* sounds of the woodlands to anything produced in a concert hall⟩ — see LYRIC 1
2 having a pleasing mixture of notes ⟨a particularly *melodious* ringtone that was instantly recognizable⟩ — see HARMONIOUS 1

melodist *n* a person who writes musical compositions ⟨a *melodist* whose music is not likely to be very accessible to the casual listener⟩ — see COMPOSER

melodramatic *adj* **1** given to or marked by attention-getting behavior suggestive of stage acting ⟨our office drama queen yet again made the *melodramatic* declaration that he was contemplating suicide⟩ — see THEATRICAL 1
2 having the general quality or effect of a stage performance ⟨he gave his usual *melodramatic* speech that he had learned his lesson and thereafter would always remain faithful to his wife⟩ — see DRAMATIC 1

melody *n* a rhythmic series of musical tones arranged to give a pleasing effect ⟨this week, we'll learn to play a more complicated *melody* on the saxophone⟩
synonyms air, lay, song, strain, tune, warble
related words descant (*also* discant); cadence, measure, meter, rhythm; ballad, ditty, hymn, lyric, madrigal

melt *vb* **1** to cease to be visible ⟨the fog soon *melted* away with the rising of the sun⟩ — see DISAPPEAR
2 to go from a solid to a liquid state ⟨a forgotten carton of ice cream was *melting* away on the counter⟩ — see LIQUEFY

melt down *vb* to yield to mental or emotional stress ⟨apparently beset by personal problems, the actor proceeded to *melt down* before startled theatergoers⟩ — see CRACK 2

member *n* **1** one of the parts that make up a whole ⟨you're only one *member* of this group effort⟩ — see ELEMENT 1
2 one of the pieces from which something is designed to be assembled ⟨lost an indispensable *member* of the model airplane kit⟩ — see PART 1

memento *n* something that serves to keep alive the memory of a person or event ⟨kept a seashell as a *memento* of their first meeting, which happened to be at the beach⟩ — see MEMORIAL

memo *n* **1** a message on paper from one person or group to another ⟨a long series of *memos* between the two authors collaborating on the book⟩ — see [1]LETTER
2 a usually brief written reminder ⟨taped a *memo* to her computer about the upcoming meeting⟩ — see NOTE 1
3 a written communication giving information or directions ⟨*memos* were the standard means of office communication before the arrival of e-mail⟩ — see MEMORANDUM 1

memoir *n* a history of a person's life ⟨the ex-president has a lucrative contract to write his *memoirs*, in which he will supposedly set the record straight⟩ — see BIOGRAPHY

memorable *adj* **1** not easily forgotten ⟨the troupe put on the most *memorable* performance of *Hamlet* that I have ever seen⟩ — see UNFORGETTABLE
2 worth remembering or mentioning ⟨a classic Broadway musical with a raft of *memorable* songs⟩ — see NOTEWORTHY 1

memorandum *n* **1** a written communication giving information or directions ⟨I'm waiting for the *memorandum* that will explain the new vacation policy⟩
synonyms directive, memo, notice
related words announcement, bulletin, declaration, notification, posting, proclamation, pronouncement, release; dispatch, report; edict, pronunciamento, rescript; charge, command, dictate; directions, instructions, orders, word; encyclical, epistle, jotting, letter, mail, message, missive, note, post [*chiefly British*]
2 a message on paper from one person or group to another ⟨the studio executives depend on endless *memoranda* to keep track of what's going on at a movie shot on location⟩ — see [1]LETTER

3 a usually brief written reminder ⟨dispatched a *memorandum* to her secretary about the assignment⟩ — see NOTE 1

memorial *adj* serving to preserve the memory of a person, thing, or an event ⟨a *memorial* plaque on the bridge for a diver who died in the line of duty⟩ — see COMMEMORATIVE

memorial *n* something that serves to keep alive the memory of a person or event ⟨the Vietnam War *Memorial* is a starkly beautiful testimonial to the bravery of the soldiers who served in Vietnam⟩
synonyms commemorative, keepsake, memento, monument, remembrance, reminder, souvenir, token
related words memorabilia; relic, vestige; cairn, landmark, marker; testimonial, tribute; cenotaph

memorialize *vb* to be a memorial of ⟨at the entrance to the park stands a statue *memorializing* the novelist Sir Walter Scott⟩ — see COMMEMORATE 1

memorializing *adj* serving to preserve the memory of a person, thing, or an event ⟨a *memorializing* book on the sinking of the Titanic⟩ — see COMMEMORATIVE

memorial park *n* a piece of land used for burying the dead ⟨Forest Lawn in Glendale, California, is the *memorial park* that serves as the final resting place for many of Hollywood's greatest⟩ — see CEMETERY

memorize *vb* to commit to memory ⟨everyone has to *memorize* a poem for next week's class⟩
synonyms con, learn, study
related words hark back (to), mind [*chiefly dialect*], recall, recollect, relive, remember, reminisce (about), retain, think (of); accept, apprehend, comprehend, get, grasp, know, understand; absorb, digest
near antonyms disremember, forget, misremember; disregard, ignore, neglect, overlook, overpass, pass over, slight, slur (over)
antonyms unlearn

memory *n* **1** the power or process of recalling what has been previously learned or experienced ⟨a photographic *memory* makes taking tests entirely too easy⟩
synonyms mind, recollection, remembrance, reminiscence
related words hypermnesia, total recall; contemplation, meditation, musing, reflection, retrospection, thinking; awareness, cognizance, consciousness; apprehension, comprehension, grasp, grip, perception, understanding
near antonyms amnesia, repression; forgetfulness
2 a particular act or instance of recalling or the thing remembered ⟨I have only the vaguest *memory* of the family vacation we took the year I turned three⟩
synonyms anamnesis, recall, recollection, remembrance, reminiscence
related words flashback; memento, memorial, reminder, souvenir, token; association

menace *n* something that may cause injury or harm ⟨a loaded gun is a *menace* that this household doesn't need⟩ — see DANGER 2

menace *vb* **1** to place in danger ⟨*menaced* the children by leaving them in the car unattended⟩ — see ENDANGER
2 to remain poised to inflict harm, danger, or distress on ⟨stockpiles of nuclear weapons that continue to *menace* the inhabitants of this planet⟩ — see THREATEN

menacing *adj* **1** being or showing a sign of evil or calamity to come ⟨warns that the emergence of new viruses is one of the most *menacing* developments we face⟩ — see OMINOUS
2 involving potential loss or injury ⟨fears that the unemployment rate may be reaching *menacing* proportions⟩ — see DANGEROUS 1

ménage *n* those who live as a family in one house ⟨getting the whole unruly *ménage* ready for an outing takes quite a while⟩ — see HOUSEHOLD

menagerie *n* an unorganized collection or mixture of various things ⟨the living room is eclectically furnished with a *menagerie* of garage-sale finds⟩ — see MISCELLANY

mend *vb* **1** to put into good shape or working order again ⟨that shirt will be as good as new when I'm finished *mending* it⟩
synonyms doctor, fix, patch, recondition, renovate, repair, revamp
related words fix up, furbish, overhaul, rebuild, reconstruct, refurbish; aid, cure, heal, help; condition, prepare, ready; care (for), maintain, service; freshen, refresh, refreshen, regenerate, rejuvenate, renew, restore, revitalize, revive; adjust, correct, modify, rectify, redress, reform, right; ameliorate, better, enhance, enrich, improve, meliorate
near antonyms blemish, break, damage, deface, disfigure, flaw, harm, hurt, impair, injure, mar, ruin, spoil, vandalize, wreck; cripple, disable, maim, mangle, mutilate
2 to become healthy and strong again after illness or weakness ⟨she's *mending* after a particularly nasty bout of the flu⟩ — see CONVALESCE
3 to restore to a healthy condition ⟨*mended* the broken plant so that it was soon thriving again⟩ — see HEAL 1
4 to make up for (an offense) ⟨the proverb "least said, soonest *mended*" should be heeded by anyone tempted to angrily blurt out things they really don't mean⟩ — see EXPIATE
5 to change one's behavior or character for the better ⟨everyone's written her off as a liar and a thief, but I say it's never too late to *mend*⟩ — see REFORM 2
6 to bring about recovery from ⟨the old adage that only time can *mend* a broken heart⟩ — see CURE 1

mendacious *adj* telling or containing lies ⟨that tabloid routinely publishes the most moronically *mendacious* stories about celebrities⟩ — see DISHONEST 1

mendaciousness *n* the tendency to tell lies ⟨her memoirs have such an air of pervasive *mendaciousness* that she seems to have lost all sense of what truth is⟩ — see DISHONESTY 1

mendacity *n* **1** a statement known by its maker to be untrue and made in order to deceive ⟨highly fictionalized "memoirs" in which the facts were few and the *mendacities* many⟩ — see LIE
2 the tendency to tell lies ⟨you need to overcome this deplorable *mendacity*, or no one will ever believe anything you say⟩ — see DISHONESTY 1

mendicant *n* a person who lives by public begging ⟨those wretched *mendicants* on the streets of Calcutta⟩ — see BEGGAR

mending *n* the process or period of gradually regaining one's health and strength ⟨it was a long slow *mending* of his injuries from the car crash, but he's fine now⟩ — see CONVALESCENCE

menial *adj* showing, expressing, or offered in a spirit of humility or unseemly submissiveness ⟨every command was obeyed in the *menial* manner of someone who seemed grateful just to be in the presence of a celebrity⟩ — see ABJECT

menial *n* a person hired to perform household or personal services ⟨immigrants to that country faced fierce prejudice and could expect to find work only as *menials*⟩ — see SERVANT

menstruation *n* an occurrence of menstruating ⟨a first *menstruation* can be somewhat scary for girls who are unprepared⟩ — see PERIOD 1

mental *adj* **1** of or relating to the mind ⟨a funny *mental* image made him laugh out loud⟩
synonyms cerebral, inner, intellectual, interior, inter-

nal, psychological (*also* psychologic)
related words cognitive, conscious, epistemic, knowing; noetic; psychic (*also* psychical), telepathic; alert, brainy, bright, brilliant, clever, intelligent, quick-witted, rational, reasoning, sharp, sharp-witted, smart, thinking
near antonyms bodily, carnal, corporal, corporeal, fleshly, physical, somatic; unconscious; brainless, dense, doltish, dopey (*also* dopy), fatuous, half-witted, mindless, obtuse, simple, slow-witted, stupid, thick, thickheaded, unintelligent, weak-minded, witless
antonyms nonmental
2 having or showing a very abnormal or sick state of mind ⟨humane treatment of *mental* patients⟩ — see INSANE 1

mentality *n* the ability to learn and understand or to deal with problems ⟨most teenagers do not have the *mentality* to foresee the consequences of such risky behavior⟩ — see INTELLIGENCE 1

mention *n* a formal recognition of an achievement or praiseworthy deed ⟨received a special *mention* for her submission to the exhibition of local artists⟩ — see COMMENDATION 1

mention *vb* **1** to make reference to or speak about briefly but specifically ⟨you only *mentioned* in passing some of your accomplishments⟩
synonyms advert (to), cite, drop, instance, name, note, notice, quote, refer (to), specify, touch (on *or* upon)
related words allude (to), hint (at), imply, indicate, infer, intend, intimate, suggest; point (out), signal, signify; denominate, designate; indicate; bring up, broach, interject, interpolate, interpose, introduce; infiltrate, insinuate, worm; advertise, announce, broadcast, declare, proclaim, pronounce, publicize, publish, sound; clarify, clear (up), elucidate, explain, explicate, spell out
near antonyms disregard, forget, ignore, neglect, overlook, overpass, pass over, slight
2 to give as an example ⟨*mentioned* several legal precedents in support of her argument⟩ — see QUOTE 1

mentionable *adj* worth remembering or mentioning ⟨a lot of films have been relased thus far this year, but none have been *mentionable* as far as awards go⟩ — see NOTEWORTHY 1

mentor *vb* to give advice and instruction to (someone) regarding the course or process to be followed ⟨we're looking for volunteers to *mentor* students in the theater arts⟩ — see GUIDE 1

menu *n* **1** a list of foods served at or available for a meal ⟨the *menu* at the fancy restaurant listed many dishes that I had never heard of⟩
synonyms card
related words chow, chuck [*chiefly West*], cuisine, fare, grub, provender, table
phrases bill of fare
2 a record of a series of items (as names or titles) usually arranged according to some system ⟨checked the *menu* of available books⟩ — see [1]LIST
3 food eaten or prepared for eating at one time ⟨a nine-course *menu* that consisted of pocket-size portions of the chef's specialties⟩ — see MEAL

mercenariness *n* an intense selfish desire for wealth or possessions ⟨she possesses the unmistakable *mercenariness* of a confirmed gold digger⟩ — see GREED

mercenary *adj* having or marked by an eager and often selfish desire especially for material possessions ⟨they were a *mercenary* couple, who defined themselves not by what they were but by what they owned⟩ — see GREEDY 1

merchandise *n* products that are bought and sold in business ⟨we stock only the finest-quality *merchandise* in this store⟩
synonyms commodities, goods, wares
related words line; export, import; inventory, staples, stock, stuff, supply; job lot; domestics, durables (*also* durable goods), hard goods

merchandise *also* **merchandize** *vb* to offer for sale to the public ⟨the now-familiar practice of stores *merchandising* goods at dramatically lower prices on the day after Thanksgiving⟩ — see MARKET

merchandiser *n* **1** a buyer and seller of goods for profit ⟨the wholesale *merchandiser* makes a 15% profit on those toys⟩ — see MERCHANT
2 the person in a business deal who hands over an item in exchange for money ⟨a scattering of small *merchandisers* selling souvenirs around the fairgrounds⟩ — see VENDOR

merchant *n* a buyer and seller of goods for profit ⟨free trade agreements that are favored by *merchants* on both sides of the border⟩
synonyms dealer, merchandiser, trader, tradesman, trafficker
related words businessman, enterpriser, entrepreneur; buyer, marketer, purchaser; hawker, huckster, hustler, peddler (*also* pedlar); retailer, seller, shopkeeper, storekeeper, vendor (*also* vender); engrosser, monopolist; jobber, middleman, wholesaler; distributor, provider, provisioner, purveyor, supplier

merchantable *adj* fit to be offered for sale ⟨a logging operation that strips an area of all of its trees, only a small percentage of which will yield *merchantable* timber⟩ — see MARKETABLE

mercifulness *n* kind, gentle, or compassionate treatment especially towards someone who is undeserving of it ⟨preached that the *mercifulness* of the Lord is without limit⟩ — see MERCY 1

merciless *adj* having or showing a lack of sympathy or tender feelings ⟨she is a *merciless* competitor at board games of any kind⟩ — see HARD 1

mercurial *adj* likely to change frequently, suddenly, or unexpectedly ⟨the boss's mood is so *mercurial* that we never know how he's going to react to anything⟩ — see FICKLE 1

mercy *n* **1** kind, gentle, or compassionate treatment especially towards someone who is undeserving of it ⟨always show your enemies *mercy*, because it makes you a better person⟩
synonyms charity, clemency, forbearance, lenience, leniency, lenity, mercifulness, quarter
related words humanitarianism, philanthropy; empathy, pity, sympathy, understanding; commiseration, favor, grace; benevolence, care, compassion, gentleness, goodness, goodwill, humaneness, kindliness, kindness, meekness, mildness, niceness, softness, tenderness; altruism, generosity, magnanimity, nobility; affection, devotion, love, worship
near antonyms hard-heartedness, mercilessness, pitilessness, ruthlessness, uncharitableness; reprisal, requital, retaliation, retribution, revenge, vengeance; venom, vindictiveness, virulence, vitriol; atrocity, barbarity, brutality, cruelty, sadism, savageness, savagery, truculence, viciousness, violence, wantonness; castigation, chastisement, discipline, punishment, scolding; abhorrence, abomination, detestation, execration, hate, hatred, loathing; cattiness, malevolence, malice, maliciousness, malignancy, malignity, meanness, nastiness, spite, spitefulness, spleen; animosity, antagonism, antipathy, bitterness, enmity, gall, grudge, hostility, jealousy, pique, resentment; bile, jaundice, rancor; hatefulness, invidiousness; coarseness, hardness, harshness, roughness
2 an act of kind assistance ⟨did a *mercy* for the stranded motorist and was richly rewarded⟩ — see FAVOR 1
3 the capacity for feeling for another's unhappiness or misfortune ⟨a woman of such *mercy* that she's been

known to cry over dead rodents⟩ — see HEART 1

mere *adj* being this and no more ⟨the *mere* idea of your traveling alone to Europe is ridiculous⟩
synonyms bare, very
related words absolute, all-out, arrant, out-and-out, outright, pure, sheer, simple, stark, total, unadulterated, unalloyed, unmitigated, unqualified, utter; alone, lone, only, singular, sole, solitary, solo, unique

mere *n, chiefly British* a small often deep body of water ⟨one of the most scenic *meres* in England's Lake District⟩ — see [1]POOL

merely *adv* nothing more than ⟨the outside noise was *merely* a raccoon knocking over the garbage can⟩ — see JUST 3

merge *vb* to turn into a single mass or entity that is more or less the same throughout ⟨years of living side by side had failed to *merge* the various ethnic groups into one community, and the city remained more of a mosaic than a melting pot⟩ — see BLEND 1

merger *n* the act or an instance of joining two or more things into one ⟨the *merger* of the two companies will create the largest Internet service provider in the country⟩ — see UNION 1

merging *n* the act or an instance of joining two or more things into one ⟨the *merging* of the two companies resulted in a corporation with a totally different configuration⟩ — see UNION 1

meridian *n* the highest part or point ⟨a lawyer at the *meridian* of his career arguing a case before the U.S. Supreme Court⟩ — see HEIGHT 1

merit *n* **1** a quality that gives something special worth ⟨this mystery novel at least has the *merit* of an original plot⟩ — see EXCELLENCE 2
2 the relative usefulness or importance of something as judged by specific qualities ⟨that idea has some *merit*, so let's explore it⟩ — see WORTH 1

merit *vb* to be or make worthy of (as a reward or punishment) ⟨that selfless act of heroism *merited* a public ceremony to honor the young swimmer⟩ — see EARN 2

merited *adj* being what is called for by accepted standards of right and wrong ⟨the punishment, although harsh, was entirely *merited*⟩ — see JUST 1

meritorious *adj* **1** deserving of high regard or great approval ⟨worked all night with *meritorious* determination to get the project done on time⟩ — see ADMIRABLE
2 having sufficient worth or merit to receive one's honor, esteem, or reward ⟨all agreed that the most *meritorious* science project had won the competition⟩ — see WORTHY

merrily *adv* in a cheerful or happy manner ⟨our coworker *merrily* announced that it was her birthday, so we felt obligated to treat her to lunch⟩ — see GAILY 1

merriment *n* **1** a mood characterized by high spirits and amusement and often accompanied by laughter ⟨their unexpected *merriment* made him nervously inquire as to the reason for it⟩ — see MIRTH
2 joyful or festive activity ⟨the wedding reception *merriment* lasted long into the night⟩ — see MERRYMAKING

merriness *n* a mood characterized by high spirits and amusement and often accompanied by laughter ⟨I hate the forced *merriness* of so many New Year's Eve parties⟩ — see MIRTH

merry *adj* indicative of or marked by high spirits or good humor ⟨the traditional depiction of Santa Claus as a rotund man with *merry*, twinkling blue eyes⟩
synonyms blithesome, festive, gay, gleeful, jocose, jocular, jocund, jolly, jovial, laughing, mirthful, sunny
related words amused, beaming, chuckling, giggling, smiling; bright, buoyant, carefree, cheerful, cheery, chipper, lighthearted, lightsome, upbeat; animated, bouncing, frisky, jaunty, lively, peppy, perky, spirited, sprightful, sprightly, vivacious, zippy; blessed (*also* blest), blissful, delighted, ecstatic, elated, enraptured, entranced, euphoric, exhilarated, exuberant, exultant, gladsome, happy, high, joyful, joyous, jubilant, overjoyed, radiant, rapturous, ravished, thrilled, tickled; amusing, facetious, flippant, frolicsome, funny, hilarious, jesting, joking, joshing, playful, sportive, witty; cavalier, devil-may-care, easygoing, happy-go-lucky, insouciant, unconcerned; hopeful, optimistic, rosy, sanguine; antic, comic, comical, farcical, humorous, riotous, sidesplitting, uproarious
near antonyms abject, aggrieved, anguished, blue, brokenhearted, crestfallen, dejected, depressed, despondent, disconsolate, disheartened, dispirited, downcast, downhearted, forlorn, glum, heartbroken, heartsick, heavyhearted, low-spirited, melancholy, sad, saddened, sorrowful, unhappy; crying, groaning, moaning, sobbing, wailing, weeping; discontented, disgruntled, moody; doleful, dolorous, joyless, lachrymose, lugubrious, mournful, plaintive, sorry, woeful; black, bleak, cheerless, comfortless, dark, depressing, desolate, dismal, dreary, gloomy, glum, gray (*also* grey), morose, saturnine, somber (*or* sombre), sullen; miserable, woebegone, wretched; dull, lethargic, listless, sluggish, torpid

merry-go-round *n* a series of events or actions that repeat themselves regularly and in the same order ⟨weary of the daily *merry-go-round* of commuting to his job in the city⟩ — see CYCLE 1

merrymaker *n* one who engages in merrymaking especially in honor of a special occasion ⟨*merrymakers* at the country club like to celebrate New Year's Eve in an especially grand style⟩ — see CELEBRANT

merrymaking *n* joyful or festive activity ⟨Christmas Eve is always an occasion of much *merrymaking* at our home⟩
synonyms conviviality, festivity, gaiety (*also* gayety), jollification, jollity, merriment, rejoicing, reveling (*or* revelling), revelry, whoopee
related words carousal, carouse; delight, diversion, entertainment, fun, mischief, pleasure, recreation, riot; cheer, cheerfulness, cheeriness, glee, gleefulness, hilarity, joviality, merriness, mirth, mirthfulness; carnival, celebration, festival, party, revel; frolicking, gamboling (*or* gambolling), rollicking, romping; enjoyment, happiness, joy; binge, fling, frolic, gambol, lark, rollick, romp, spree; buffoonery, clownery, clownishness, flippancy, frivolity, funning, jesting, jocularity, joking, joshing, levity, lightheartedness, playfulness, zaniness
near antonyms blackness, darkness, dolefulness, dolor, gloom, gloominess, glumness, grief, heartache, heartbreak, heartsickness, miserableness, misery, mournfulness, mourning, woe, wretchedness; dejection, depression, despondence, despondency, disconsolateness, dispiritedness, doldrums, downheartedness, dumps, forlornness, joylessness, melancholy, sorrow, unhappiness

mesa *n* a broad flat area of elevated land ⟨a *mesa* in the Arizona desert⟩ — see PLATEAU

mesh *n* **1** *usually* **meshes** *pl* something that catches and holds ⟨a routine request that got hung up in the *meshes* of the state bureaucracy⟩ — see WEB 1
2 a fabric made of strands loosely twisted, knotted, or woven together at regular intervals ⟨spread a *mesh* across the doorway to keep out insects⟩ — see [1]NET 1

mesh *vb* to catch or hold as if in a net ⟨dolphins sometimes become *meshed* in fishnets⟩ — see ENTANGLE 2

meshuga *or* **meshugge** *also* **meshugah** *or* **meshuggah** *adj* having or showing a very abnormal or sick state of mind ⟨when your mother is *meshuga* like his was, a lifetime of therapy is pretty much a foregone conclusion⟩ — see INSANE 1

mesmerism *n* the art or act of inducing in a person a

sleeplike state during which he or she readily follows suggestions ⟨made a living at *mesmerism* and the selling of medical remedies of dubious value⟩ — see HYPNOSIS

mesmerize *vb* to hold the attention of as if by a spell ⟨discovered that the children were *mesmerized* by a television show⟩ — see ENTHRALL 1

mesomorphic *adj* strongly and heavily built ⟨the shot put, hammer throw, and other field events for which *mesomorhic* athletes are well-suited⟩ — see [1]HUSKY 1

mess *n* 1 a state in which everything is out of order ⟨the bachelor party had left the house in a total *mess*⟩ — see CHAOS

2 food eaten or prepared for eating at one time ⟨a *mess* of oatmeal⟩ — see MEAL

3 something unpleasant to look at ⟨the car was a *mess* after the accident⟩ — see EYESORE

4 a considerable amount ⟨an unexpected Super Bowl loss that unleashed a whole *mess* of finger-pointing and second-guessing⟩ — see LOT 2

mess *vb* to interest oneself in what is not one's concern ⟨please don't *mess* with me while I'm trying to concentrate⟩ — see INTERFERE

mess (up) *vb* 1 to make or do (something) in a clumsy or unskillful way ⟨*messed up* the drawing and had to start over⟩ — see BOTCH

2 to undo the proper order or arrangement of ⟨a nap had *messed up* her hair and she looked a sight⟩ — see DISORDER

3 to make a mistake ⟨if anyone *messes up* even once while we're recording, we have to start all over again⟩ — see ERR 1

4 to strike repeatedly ⟨"If I catch you looking at my girlfriend, I'm going to *mess* you *up*!" he threatened⟩ — see BEAT 1

mess (with) *vb* to handle thoughtlessly, ignorantly, or mischievously ⟨please don't *mess with* the buttons on the camera⟩ — see TAMPER (WITH)

message *n* a piece of conveyed information ⟨answered the phone and took a *message*⟩ — see COMMUNICATION 1

mess around *vb* 1 to spend time in aimless activity ⟨spent the vacation day just *messing around*⟩ — see FIDDLE (AROUND)

2 to show a sexual attraction for someone just for fun ⟨a guy who goes to the health club mainly to *mess around* with the women⟩ — see FLIRT 1

3 to come or be together as friends ⟨if you continue to *mess around* with such narrow-minded boobs, you'll begin to think and act like them⟩ — see ASSOCIATE 1

messed *adj* lacking in order, neatness, and often cleanliness ⟨came home to find a *messed* basement with his tools scattered about⟩ — see MESSY

messenger *n* one that carries a message or does an errand ⟨the *messenger* comes by twice a day to pick up packages⟩

synonyms courier, express [*British*], go-between, page, runner

related words forerunner, harbinger, herald; agent, ambassador, delegate, deputy, emissary, envoy, representative; bearer, carrier, deliveryman, letter carrier, mail carrier, mailman

messiness *n* a state in which everything is out of order ⟨a professional chef would not tolerate such *messiness* in the kitchen⟩ — see CHAOS

mess over *vb, slang* to inflict physical or emotional harm upon ⟨her no-good boyfriend has been *messing* her *over* for years⟩ — see ABUSE 1

messy *adj* lacking in order, neatness, and often cleanliness ⟨having a *messy* room is virtually de rigueur for a college student⟩

synonyms chaotic, cluttered, confused, disarranged, disarrayed, disheveled (*or* dishevelled), disordered, disorderly, higgledy-piggledy, hugger-mugger, jumbled, littered, messed, muddled, mussed, mussy, pell-mell, rumpled, sloppy, topsy-turvy, tousled, tumbled, unkempt, untidy, upside-down

related words bedraggled, befouled, begrimed, bemired, besmirched, blackened, cruddy, dingy, dirty, draggled, filthy, foul, grimy, grotty [*chiefly British*], grubby, grungy, mucky, nasty, smudged, soiled, spotted, squalid, stained, sullied, unclean, uncleanly; dowdy, frowsy (*or* frowzy), shaggy, slatternly, sloven, slovenly, uncombed; wrinkled; adulterated, contaminated, defiled, polluted, tainted; knotted, snarled, tangled; seedy, shabby, sleazy, sordid; neglected, neglectful, negligent

phrases at sixes and sevens, out of joint

near antonyms antiseptic, clean, cleaned, cleanly, hygienic, immaculate, sparkling, spick-and-span (*or* spic-and-span), spotless, stainless, unsoiled, unsullied; methodical (*also* methodic), regular, systematic, systematized; careful, fastidious, finicky, fussy, meticulous; combed, groomed, manicured, well-groomed; taintless, undefiled, unpolluted, untainted, wholesome

antonyms bandbox, crisp, kempt, neat, neatened, ordered, orderly, organized, shipshape, snug, tidied, tidy, trim, uncluttered, well-ordered

metamorphose *vb* to change in form, appearance, or use ⟨a science fiction story in which radiation *metamorphoses* people into giant bugs⟩ — see CONVERT 2

metamorphosis *n* a change in form, appearance, or use ⟨the *metamorphosis* of caterpillars into butterflies⟩ ⟨the *metamorphosis* of the abandoned factory into a mixed-use property⟩ — see CONVERSION 1

metaphor *n* an elaborate or fanciful way of expressing something ⟨"it's raining cats and dogs" is just a colorful *metaphor* and not a meteorological announcement⟩ — see CONCEIT 1

metaphoric *or* **metaphorical** *adj* expressing one thing in terms normally used for another ⟨an author fond of such *metaphorical* phrases as "the desert was a fiery furnace"⟩ — see FIGURATIVE

metaphysical *adj* 1 dealing with or expressing a quality or idea ⟨a work that deals with such *metaphysical* questions as the very nature of knowledge⟩ — see ABSTRACT 1

2 of, relating to, or being part of a reality beyond the observable physical universe ⟨belief in a *metaphysical* world beyond the one in which we live⟩ — see SUPERNATURAL 1

mete (out) *vb* to give out (something) to appropriate individuals ⟨determined to *mete out* an appropriate punishment for the CEO guilty of insider trading⟩ — see ADMINISTER 1

meter *n* the recurrent pattern formed by a series of sounds having a regular rise and fall in intensity ⟨the poem's heavy *meter* is meant to reinforce the atmosphere of gloom⟩ — see RHYTHM

method *n* the means or procedure for doing something ⟨the city council is stuck in the last century and needs to adopt more modern *methods* for doing things⟩

synonyms approach, fashion, form, how, manner, methodology, recipe, strategy, style, system, tack, tactics, technique, way

related words mode, modus operandi; blueprint, design, game, game plan, ground plan, intrigue, layout, line, model, plan, plot, program, route, scheme; expedient, move, shift, step; practice (*also* practise), process, routine; policy

methodical *also* **methodic** *adj* following a set method, arrangement, or pattern ⟨a *methodical* study plan that included lists of points to memorize⟩

synonyms neat, orderly, organized, regular, systematic, systematized

related words ordered, regularized, standardized, structured; accurate, clocklike, correct, exact, precise; detailed, specific

near antonyms chaotic, disordered, disorderly, shambolic [*chiefly British*], unordered

antonyms disorganized, haphazard, hit-or-miss, immethodical, irregular, nonsystematic, patternless, planless, systemless, unsystematic

methodology *n* **1** a way of acting or proceeding ⟨for solving crossword puzzles my usual *methodology* is to begin by filling in all of the answers I'm reasonably sure of⟩ — see COURSE 1

2 the means or procedure for doing something ⟨other cardiologists have questioned the *methodology* that was used to conduct the study⟩ — see METHOD

meticulosity *n* strict attentiveness to what one is doing ⟨the *meticulosity* with which she placed each piece of china, crystal, and silver on the table⟩ — see CARE 1

meticulous *adj* taking, showing, or involving great care and effort ⟨did a *meticulous* job of restoring the painting⟩ — see PAINSTAKING

meticulousness *n* strict attentiveness to what one is doing ⟨he dressed himself with uncharacteristic *meticulousness*, which made us suspect he was going on a date⟩ — see CARE 1

métier *also* **metier** *n* something for which a person shows a special talent ⟨public speaking is not my *métier*, as others can attest⟩ — see FORTE

metric *n* something set up as an example against which others of the same type are compared ⟨according to the usual *metrics* by which we judge fiction, this novel is an utter failure⟩ — see STANDARD 1

metrical *or* **metric** *adj* marked by or occurring with a noticeable regularity in the rise and fall of sound ⟨the *metrical* chugging of the machinery had a hypnotic effect⟩ — see RHYTHMIC

metropolis *n* a thickly settled, highly populated area ⟨a big, teeming *metropolis* where ambitious people from all over come to make their mark⟩ — see CITY

metropolitan *n* a person with the outlook, experience, and manners thought to be typical of big city dwellers ⟨a TV series about the lives and loves of a group of young, attractive *metropolitans*⟩ — see COSMOPOLITAN

mettlesome *adj* **1** having much high-spirited energy and movement ⟨the *mettlesome* opening dance number got the audience all jazzed up⟩ — see LIVELY 1

2 marked by a lively display of strong feeling ⟨a *mettlesome* debate on the teaching of evolution in the schools⟩ — see SPIRITED 1

mew (up) *vb* to close or shut in by or as if by barriers ⟨bored with being *mewed up* in a stuffy house all day⟩ — see ENCLOSE 1

mewl *vb* to utter feeble plaintive cries ⟨the tiny kitten *mewled* for its mother⟩ — see WHIMPER 1

Mexican standoff *n* a point in a struggle where neither side is capable of winning or willing to give in ⟨in the battle over bedtime the parents and their son are at a *Mexican standoff*⟩ — see IMPASSE 1

Mickey Mouse *adj* **1** lacking importance ⟨a woman who at town meetings insists on airing every little *Mickey Mouse* concern she has⟩ — see UNIMPORTANT

2 so small or unimportant as to warrant little or no attention ⟨as far as his schoolmarm of a boss is concerned, no rule is so *Mickey Mouse* that it can be ignored⟩ — see NEGLIGIBLE 1

microminiature *adj* very small in size ⟨a *microminiature* model of the city to be used for the movie's special effects⟩ — see TINY

microscopic *also* **microscopical** *adj* very small in size ⟨even a *microscopic* speck of dust in the eye will cause pain⟩ — see TINY

mid *adj* occupying a position equally distant from the ends or extremes ⟨her *mid* molar will have to be extracted and replaced by a bridge⟩ — see MIDDLE 1

mid *prep* in or into the middle of ⟨*mid* a tangle of weeds grew a perfect rose⟩ — see AMONG

midday *n* the middle of the day ⟨by *midday* the sun and heat were unbearable⟩ — see NOON 1

middle *adj* **1** occupying a position equally distant from the ends or extremes ⟨you must mark the exact *middle* point of each of these lines in order to solve the problem⟩

synonyms central, halfway, intermediary, intermediate, medial, median, mediate, medium, mid, midmost

related words equidistant; inmost, inner, innermost, nearest; betwixt and between, borderline, gray (*also* grey), in-between

near antonyms outer, peripheral

antonyms extreme, farthest, farthermost, furthermost, furthest, outermost, outmost, remotest, utmost

2 being about midway between extremes of amount or size ⟨a house that is *middle*-sized for that neighborhood⟩ ⟨a man of *middle* height⟩

synonyms average, intermediate, mean, median, medium, middling, midsize (*also* midsized), moderate, modest

related words reasonable; common, commonplace, conventional, normal, popular, regular, routine, standard, typical, usual; adequate, passable, tolerable

near antonyms excessive, extreme; exceptional, rare, strange, uncommon, unusual; distinctive, idiosyncratic, special, unique; individual, peculiar, private

middle *n* **1** a middle point between extremes ⟨his salary is exactly at the *middle* of the company's pay scale⟩ — see MEAN 1

2 an area or point that is an equal distance from all points along an edge or outer surface ⟨put the serving dish in the *middle* of the table⟩ — see CENTER 2

3 the middle region of the human torso ⟨clutched the football tightly against her *middle*⟩ — see MIDRIFF

4 the most intense or characteristic phase of something ⟨I'm right in the *middle* of a tax audit, so can you come back later?⟩ — see THICK

middle ground *n* a middle point between extremes ⟨both parties entered the negotiations hoping to find some *middle ground*⟩ — see MEAN 1

middleman *n* one who works with opposing sides in order to bring about an agreement ⟨the retired statesman is often asked to be a *middleman* in international disputes⟩ — see MEDIATOR

middle-of-the-road *adj* avoiding major social change or extreme political ideas ⟨a candidate with *middle-of-the-road* views on most hot-button issues⟩ — see MODERATE 2

middle-of-the-roader *n* a person who holds moderate views ⟨since the party's *middle-of-the-roaders* often lack verve, the activists inevitably nominate some extremist who can't win in the general election⟩ — see CENTRIST

middling *adj* **1** being about midway between extremes of amount or size ⟨tired of the city but not particularly interested in small-town life, he moved to a suburb of *middling* size⟩ — see MIDDLE 2

2 of average to below average quality ⟨was disappointed in the renowned historian's latest book, which is only *middling*⟩ — see MEDIOCRE 1

middlingly *adv* in a satisfactory way ⟨this vacuum handles basic jobs *middlingly*, but I'd recommend the other one for heavy-duty cleaning⟩ ⟨she's a *middlingly* successful architect, but no world-beater⟩ — see WELL 1

midget *n* a living thing much smaller than others of its kind ⟨a breed that is the *midget* of the horse world⟩ — see DWARF 1

midmost *adj* occupying a position equally distant from

the ends or extremes ⟨the *midmost* subway car is usually the most crowded one in the train, so try to avoid it⟩ — see MIDDLE 1

midpoint *n* **1** a middle point between extremes ⟨always choose a wine that is at the *midpoint* of the range of prices on the list⟩ — see MEAN 1
2 an area or point that is an equal distance from all points along an edge or outer surface ⟨that house is the precise *midpoint* of the school district⟩ — see CENTER 2

midriff *n* the middle region of the human torso ⟨*midriff*-baring tops are popular this summer⟩
synonyms middle, midsection, waist, waistline
related words trunk; abdomen, belly, gut, stomach

midsection *n* the middle region of the human torso ⟨did sit-ups to strengthen the muscles in her *midsection*⟩ — see MIDRIFF

midsize *also* **midsized** *adj* being about midway between extremes of amount or size ⟨the *midsize* company was finding it increasingly difficult to compete with the corporate giants⟩ — see MIDDLE 2

midst *n* **1** an area or point that is an equal distance from all points along an edge or outer surface ⟨stood in the *midst* of the crowd⟩ — see CENTER 2
2 the most intense or characteristic phase of something ⟨in the *midst* of illustrating a new book⟩ — see THICK

midst *prep* in or into the middle of ⟨gave a victory speech *midst* cheering supporters⟩ — see AMONG

mien *n* the outward form of someone or something especially as indicative of a quality ⟨the stern *mien* of the librarian suggested that she was not one to put up with any nonsense⟩ — see APPEARANCE 1

miff *n* the feeling of being offended or resentful after a slight or indignity ⟨"No one asked you!" she retorted, with some *miff*⟩ — see PIQUE

might *n* the ability to exert effort for the accomplishment of a task ⟨currently the President lacks the political *might* to push his programs through the Congress⟩ — see POWER 2

mightily *adv* **1** to a great degree ⟨every volunteer contributed *mightily* to the cause⟩ — see VERY 1
2 with great effort or determination ⟨struggled *mightily* to climb up the steep cliff⟩ — see HARD 1
3 in a vigorous and forceful manner ⟨it is a foregone conclusion that the President's supporters will *mightily* applaud virtually every line of his speech⟩ — see HARD 3

mighty *adj* **1** having great power or influence ⟨one of the *mighty* leaders of the U.S. financial world⟩ — see IMPORTANT 2
2 unusually large ⟨a *mighty* castle towered over everything nearby⟩ — see HUGE

mighty *adv* to a great degree ⟨he was *mighty* hungry after raking leaves all afternoon⟩ — see VERY 1

migrant *adj* having a way of life that involves moving from one region to another typically on a seasonal basis ⟨*migrant* laborers living in substandard housing⟩ — see MIGRATORY

migrant *n* one that leaves one place to settle in another ⟨the city will have to expand and upgrade its social services in order to handle the latest influx of *migrants*⟩ — see EMIGRANT

migratory *adj* having a way of life that involves moving from one region to another typically on a seasonal basis ⟨most of the apple crop is picked by *migratory* workers⟩ ⟨*migratory* birds heading south for the winter⟩
synonyms migrant, mobile
related words errant, fugitive, itinerant, nomadic, peregrine, peripatetic, ranging, roaming, roving, tramp, traveling (*or* travelling), vagabond, vagrant, wandering, wayfaring; ambulant, ambulatory, drifting, fiddle-footed, footloose, gadabout, gallivanting (*also* galavanting), meandering, rambling, sauntering, strolling, traipsing, walking
near antonyms immobile, stationary; established, fast, fixed, rooted, sedentary, set, settled
antonyms nonmigrant, nonmigrating, nonmigratory, resident

milady *n* a woman of high birth or social position ⟨the 18th-century quack Franz Anton Mesmer specialized in the curing of those mysterious ailments to which pampered *miladies* seem especially prone⟩ — see GENTLEWOMAN

mild *adj* **1** marked by temperatures that are neither too high nor too low ⟨the *mild* weather that makes springtime such a delight⟩ — see CLEMENT 1
2 not harsh or stern especially in nature or effect ⟨a quiet gentleman with a kindly soul and a *mild* disposition⟩ — see GENTLE 1

mile *n* a long distance ⟨the recluse lived in a small cabin *miles* away from his closest neighbor⟩
synonyms afar, country mile, far cry, long haul
related words infinity, light-year
antonyms hair, inch, step, stone's throw

mileage *n* the capacity for being useful for some purpose ⟨I bought this dishwasher just last year—there is still a lot of *mileage* left in it⟩ — see USE 2

milepost *n* a point in a chain of events at which an important change (as in one's fortunes) occurs ⟨a *milepost* in the development of a global economy⟩ — see TURNING POINT

milestone *n* a point in a chain of events at which an important change (as in one's fortunes) occurs ⟨the new drug was regarded as a *milestone* in the treatment of heart disease⟩ — see TURNING POINT

milieu *n* the circumstances, conditions, or objects by which one is surrounded ⟨young, innovative artists thrive in the freewheeling *milieu* that a big city offers⟩ — see ENVIRONMENT

militance *n* an inclination to fight or quarrel ⟨the level of *militance* varied significantly among the abolitionist groups⟩ — see BELLIGERENCE

militancy *n* an inclination to fight or quarrel ⟨the *militancy* of the radical organization made the authorities a little nervous⟩ — see BELLIGERENCE

militant *adj* **1** feeling or displaying eagerness to fight ⟨political radicals with a *militant* unwillingness to compromise on any issue⟩ — see BELLIGERENT
2 having or showing a bold forcefulness in the pursuit of a goal ⟨after a campaign by *militant* feminists lasting more than 70 years, American women received the right to vote in 1919⟩ — see AGGRESSIVE 1

militant *n* one who is intensely or excessively devoted to a cause ⟨*militants* within the movement insisted that there could be no compromise on the abolition of slavery⟩ — see ZEALOT

militantness *n* an inclination to fight or quarrel ⟨the *militantness* of the group's manifesto is unsettling⟩ — see BELLIGERENCE

militarist *n* one who urges or attempts to cause a war ⟨the *militarists* who dominated the Japanese government in the first half of the 20th century⟩ — see WARMONGER

military *adj* **1** of or relating to the armed services ⟨the colonel testified that revealing any more information would have required giving away *military* secrets⟩
synonyms martial, service
related words naval; GI, gladiatorial, mercenary, soldierly; militant, militarist, militaristic, warlike; enlisted, regular; paramilitary
near antonyms civil, civilian
antonyms nonmilitary
2 of, relating to, or suitable for war or a warrior ⟨after returning from the war, the college president very un-

successfully tried to impose *military* discipline on the students⟩ — see MARTIAL 1

military *n* the combined army, air force, and navy of a nation ⟨some would insist that the *military's* budget is still inadequate⟩ — see ARMED FORCES

milk *vb* to take unfair advantage of ⟨unscrupulous people trying to *milk* the welfare system for all it's worth⟩ — see EXPLOIT 1

milk–and–water *adj* **1** lacking in qualities that make for spirit and character ⟨a *milk-and-water* campaign speech that most likely did not inspire a single person⟩ — see WISHY-WASHY 1

2 lacking strength of will or character ⟨we need to elect a leader with a bold vision, not someone who's been a *milk-and-water* yes-man all his life⟩ — see WEAK 2

milk–livered *adj, archaic* having or showing a shameful lack of courage ⟨vented his spleen at those *milk-livered* men who refused to fight for king and country⟩ — see COWARDLY

mill *n* a building or set of buildings for the manufacturing of goods ⟨a steel *mill* that remains the town's principal employer⟩ — see FACTORY

mill *vb* to reduce to fine particles ⟨a demonstration of how dried kernels of corn were *milled* in colonial times⟩ — see POWDER

millions *n pl* the body of the community as contrasted with the elite ⟨intellectuals sneered that television was a medium clearly aimed at the *millions*⟩ — see MASS 1

milord *n* a man of high birth or social position ⟨a city that was a favorite stop for English *milords* on the grand tour⟩ — see GENTLEMAN 1

mime *n* **1** an actor in a story performed silently and entirely by body movements ⟨that annoying *mime* on the sidewalk is pretending to be in an invisible box again⟩

synonyms mimic, mummer, pantomime, pantomimist

related words busker [*chiefly British*], entertainer, performer, player, trouper; aper, imitator, impersonator, impressionist; clown, pantaloon

2 a movement of the body or limbs that expresses or emphasizes an idea or feeling ⟨the speech-impaired patient had to convey his wishes with *mime* or scribbled notes⟩ — see GESTURE 1

mime *vb* to use (someone or something) as the model for one's speech, mannerisms, or behavior ⟨as a joke, Eric knelt by the dinner table and began *miming* a dog begging for food⟩ — see IMITATE 1

mimetic *adj* using or marked by the use of something else as a basis or model ⟨boys have a tendency toward *mimetic* behavior, often imitating their fathers at a fairly early age⟩ — see IMITATIVE 1

mimic *adj* **1** being such in appearance only and made with or manufactured from usually cheaper materials ⟨police were concerned that the *mimic* gun, although intended only as a toy, might be confused with the real thing in certain situations⟩ — see IMITATION

2 using or marked by the use of something else as a basis or model ⟨a *mimic* battle fought by kids playing around in the schoolyard⟩ — see IMITATIVE 1

mimic *n* **1** a person who imitates another's voice and mannerisms for comic effect ⟨a gifted *mimic* who can do a terrific imitation of anyone's voice⟩

synonyms imitator, impersonator, impressionist, personator

related words burlesquer, caricaturist, lampooner, mocker, parodist, satirist; mime, mimer, mummer, pantomime, pantomimist; actor, entertainer, performer, player, trouper; ape, copycat, echo, parrot, rubber stamp

2 an actor in a story performed silently and entirely by body movements ⟨a *mimic* in black clothes and white facial makeup⟩ — see MIME 1

mimic *vb* **1** to copy or exaggerate (someone or something) in order to make fun of ⟨the comedian was famous for *mimicking* the President's distinctive lisp⟩

synonyms burlesque, caricature, do, imitate, mock, parody, send up, spoof, travesty

related words lampoon, pasquinade, satirize; deride, gibe (*or* jibe), ridicule; ape, copycat, monkey, parrot; duplicate, emulate, replicate, reproduce; act, counterfeit, dissemble, fake, feign, pretend, sham, simulate; elaborate, embellish, embroider, exaggerate, magnify, pad, play up, stretch; amplify, enhance, enlarge (on *or* upon), expand, flesh (out), overdraw, overstate, put on; mime, pantomime; impersonate, perform, personate, play

2 to use (someone or something) as the model for one's speech, mannerisms, or behavior ⟨began to learn their language by *mimicking* the sounds they made⟩ — see IMITATE 1

minatory *adj* being or showing a sign of evil or calamity to come ⟨the novel's protagonist is haunted by a *minatory* black specter⟩ — see OMINOUS

mince *vb* to cut into small pieces ⟨*minced* some garlic and added it to the stew⟩ — see CHOP

mincemeat *n* the state or fact of being rendered nonexistent, physically unsound, or useless ⟨the artillery quickly made *mincemeat* of the enemy's fortifications⟩ — see DESTRUCTION 1

mind *n* **1** the part of a person that feels, thinks, perceives, wills, and especially reasons ⟨scientists still disagree about exactly where the *mind* is located⟩

synonyms brain, cerebrum, head, psyche, thinker

related words belfry, gray matter, intellect, intelligence, loaf [*British slang*], noodle, reason, skull; acumen, alertness, astuteness, brilliance, insight, judgment (*or* judgement), mentality, perception, perspicacity, sagacity, sapience, wisdom, wit; awareness, cognizance, consciousness, self-awareness, self-consciousness

2 the normal or healthy condition of the mental abilities ⟨everyone used to tease him and tell him he was out of his *mind* when he swore he'd seen a flying saucer⟩

synonyms daylights, head, marbles, reason, saneness, sanity, wit(s)

related words rationality, reasonableness, sense; health, healthfulness, healthiness, wholesomeness; clearheadedness, lucidity, lucidness, normalcy, normality, soundness; wisdom

near antonyms delusion, hallucination; delirium, frenzy, hysteria

antonyms dementia, derangement, insanity, lunacy, madness, mania, unreason

3 an idea that is believed to be true or valid without positive knowledge ⟨please speak your *mind* freely on this matter⟩ — see OPINION 1

4 the power or process of recalling what has been previously learned or experienced ⟨call to *mind* the events of last year⟩ — see MEMORY 1

mind *vb* **1** to pay attention especially through the act of hearing ⟨you'll be in big trouble if you don't straighten up and *mind*⟩ — see LISTEN

2 *chiefly dialect* to bring back to mind ⟨I seem to *mind* such a tale from way back⟩ — see REMEMBER

3 to act according to the commands of ⟨tell the children to *mind* the babysitter⟩ — see OBEY

4 to be cautious of or on guard against ⟨*mind* the slippery steps⟩ — see BEWARE (OF)

5 to have an interest or concern for ⟨don't *mind* him; he's always complaining⟩ — see CARE

6 to take charge of especially on behalf of another ⟨the salesperson will *mind* the store while the manager goes out to lunch⟩ — see [2]TEND 1

7 to take notice of and be guided by ⟨*mind* the instructions that appear at the top of the first page of the exam⟩ — see HEED 1

mind–bending *adj* causing great emotional or mental stimulation ⟨a spy novel with a truly *mind-bending* plot⟩ — see EXCITING 1

mind–blowing *adj* causing great emotional or mental stimulation ⟨viewers will be stunned by the movie's *mind-blowing* twist ending⟩ — see EXCITING 1

mind–boggling *adj* causing great emotional or mental stimulation ⟨a big-box store with a *mind-boggling* array of home-improvement supplies for the do-it-yourselfer⟩ — see EXCITING 1

minded *adj* having a desire or inclination (as for a specified course of action) ⟨in most David vs. Goliath contests, people are generally *minded* to side with the underdog⟩ — see WILLING 1

minder *n* a person or group that watches over someone or something ⟨those self-appointed *minders* of other people's morals⟩ — see GUARD 1

mindful *adj* having specified facts or feelings actively impressed on the mind ⟨a truly considerate person, always *mindful* of the needs of others⟩ — see CONSCIOUS 1

mindfulness *n* a state of being aware ⟨his *mindfulness* of his limited education made him ill at ease around academics⟩ — see ATTENTION 2

mindless *adj* **1** not having or showing an ability to absorb ideas readily ⟨a dead-end job fit only for *mindless* drones⟩ — see STUPID 1

2 not paying or showing close attention especially for the purpose of avoiding trouble ⟨*mindless* of danger, the foolhardy skiers ignored the avalanche warnings⟩ — see CARELESS 1

mindlessness *n* the quality or state of lacking intelligence or quickness of mind ⟨despised the sheer *mindlessness* of the movie's violence⟩ — see STUPIDITY 1

mind–numbing *adj* causing weariness, restlessness, or lack of interest ⟨that movie is just a series of *mind-numbing* explosions and car chases⟩ — see BORING

mind's eye *n* something imagined or pictured in the mind ⟨there was a disturbing detail that he kept seeing in his *mind's eye* of the accident scene⟩ — see IDEA 1

mine *n* **1** an abundant source ⟨a baseball fanatic who is a *mine* of fascinating trivia about the game⟩

synonyms argosy, cornucopia, gold mine, mother lode, treasure trove, wellspring

related words armory, repository, stockpot, store, storehouse, treasure-house; cache, hoard, stash; bonanza, Golconda, gravy train, honeypot

near antonyms black hole, sinkhole

2 a usually concealed explosive device designed to go off when disturbed ⟨the soldiers were careful to disarm any *mines* they found in their path⟩ — see BOOBY TRAP 1

mine *vb* to place hidden explosive devices in or under ⟨the troops hurriedly *mined* the field before relinquishing it to the enemy⟩

synonyms booby-trap

related words blow up, bomb; ambush, snare, trap; attack

mingle *vb* **1** to turn into a single mass or entity that is more or less the same throughout ⟨the site where the river and the ocean *mingle* their waters to form a broad estuary⟩ — see BLEND 1

2 to take part in social activities ⟨*mingling* at a cocktail party⟩ — see SOCIALIZE

mingy *adj* giving or sharing as little as possible ⟨the company's *mingy* Christmas bonuses haven't exactly helped sagging employee morale⟩ — see STINGY 1

miniature *adj* very small in size ⟨a dollhouse with *miniature* furnishings⟩ — see TINY

miniature *n* an exact representation of something in greatly reduced size ⟨a diorama filled with *miniatures* of town buildings as they looked in the 19th century⟩ — see MODEL 1

minimal *adj* being the least in amount, number, or size possible ⟨the beached whales were returned to the sea with only *minimal* loss of life⟩

synonyms fewest, littlest, lowest, minimum, minutest, slightest, smallest, tiniest

related words fewer, lesser, low, minor, modest, slight, small, smaller; infinitesimal, micro, subminimal, ultramicro; irreducible

near antonyms highest

antonyms biggest, full, greatest, hugest, largest, maximum, most, top, topmost, utmost

minimize *vb* to express scornfully one's low opinion of ⟨sore losers trying to *minimize* the other team's victory⟩ — see DECRY 1

minimum *adj* being the least in amount, number, or size possible ⟨spent the *minimum* amount necessary to acquire the property⟩ — see MINIMAL

minion *n* a person or thing that is preferred over others ⟨most of the top appointments went to the new governor's personal *minions* and political cronies⟩ — see FAVORITE

minister *n* **1** a person sent on a mission to represent another ⟨the British *ministers* at the international peace conference⟩ — see AMBASSADOR

2 a person specially trained and authorized to conduct religious services in a Christian church ⟨our *minister* gives an interesting sermon every week⟩ — see CLERGYPERSON

3 a person who acts or does business for another ⟨she's merely a *minister* of the corporation⟩ — see AGENT 2

minister (to) *vb* to attend to the needs and comforts of ⟨volunteered to help *minister to* the sick at the local hospice⟩ — see NURSE 1

ministerial *adj* of, relating to, or characteristic of the clergy ⟨a priest conscientiously tending to his *ministerial* duties⟩ — see CLERICAL

ministry *n* **1** something used to achieve an end ⟨I don't care by what *ministry* it's accomplished, so long as it's done⟩ — see AGENT 1

2 the group ordained to perform clerical functions in the Christian church ⟨the ranks of the *ministry* have dwindled considerably in recent years⟩ — see CLERGY

minor *adj* **1** having not so great importance or rank as another ⟨some *minor* official with an exaggerated sense of his own importance⟩ — see LESSER

2 of little or less value or merit ⟨a *minor* poet who is little read nowadays⟩ — see INFERIOR 2

3 lacking importance ⟨only a *minor* detail, which we can easily disregard for the moment⟩ — see UNIMPORTANT

minority *n* the transitional period between childhood and adulthood ⟨a teenager during his *minority* has some of the rights of an adult, but not all⟩ — see ADOLESCENCE

minstrel *n* a person who writes poetry ⟨Edna St. Vincent Millay was unofficially the *minstrel* of Maine, as her poetry celebrates its coast and countryside⟩ — see POET

minstrelsy *n* writing that uses rhythm, vivid language, and often rhyme to provoke an emotional response ⟨the traditional forms of German *minstrelsy*⟩ — see POETRY 1

mint *adj* being in an original and unused or unspoiled state ⟨a *mint* baseball card that should be worth a lot to a collector⟩ — see FRESH 1

mint *n* a very large amount of money ⟨she made a *mint* when the real estate market was hot⟩ — see FORTUNE 2

minus *n* a feature of someone or something that creates difficulty for achieving success ⟨a plan with lots of pluses and only a few *minuses*⟩ — see DISADVANTAGE 1

minus *prep* not having ⟨the contraption was like a giant carousel *minus* the horses⟩ — see WITHOUT 1

minuscule *adj* very small in size ⟨public health officials have claimed that the chemical is harmless in such *minuscule* amounts⟩ — see TINY

minute *adj* **1** including many small descriptive features ⟨a *minute* description of the setting of the story⟩ — see DETAILED 1

2 lacking importance ⟨a person who wastes her time on the most *minute* aspects of everyday life⟩ — see UNIMPORTANT

3 so small or unimportant as to warrant little or no attention ⟨only *minute* differences between the two photographic prints⟩ — see NEGLIGIBLE 1

4 made or done with extreme care and accuracy ⟨a *minute* examination of the marine specimen⟩ — see FINE 2

5 very small in size ⟨made some *minute* adjustments to the controls⟩ — see TINY

minute *n* a very small space of time ⟨I'll be with you in just a *minute*⟩ — see INSTANT

minutely *adv* with attention to all aspects or details ⟨a *minutely* detailed analysis of the series of glitches that resulted in the blackout⟩ — see THOROUGHLY 1

minutest *adj* being the least in amount, number, or size possible ⟨a sophisticated instrument designed to pick up the *minutest* changes in temperature and humidity⟩ — see MINIMAL

minx *n* a boldly flirtatious or sexually promiscuous woman ⟨a blond actress who was usually typecast as the *minx* in melodramas⟩ — see FLOOZY

miracle *n* something extraordinary or surprising ⟨it's a *miracle* that you weren't hurt in the accident⟩ — see WONDER 1

miraculous *adj* **1** being so extraordinary or abnormal as to suggest powers which violate the laws of nature ⟨the *miraculous* nature of the revelation⟩ — see SUPERNATURAL 2

2 causing wonder or astonishment ⟨his *miraculous* escape from the burning building⟩ — see MARVELOUS 1

mire *n* **1** soft wet earth ⟨played on a football field that was thick with *mire*⟩ — see MUD

2 spongy land saturated or partially covered with water ⟨much of the land in that area is *mire* that cannot be developed⟩ — see SWAMP 1

3 a difficult, puzzling, or embarrassing situation from which there is no easy escape ⟨an abused wife who was hopelessly stuck in a *mire* of emotional dependency⟩ — see PREDICAMENT

mire *vb* **1** to make dirty ⟨the sight of the standard, which had emerged from the battle mangled and *mired*, still stirred the soldiers' hearts⟩ — see DIRTY

2 to place in conflict or difficulties ⟨the case has been *mired* in probate court for years⟩ — see EMBROIL

mirror *n* a smooth or polished surface that forms images by reflection ⟨breaking a *mirror* is supposed to bring seven years of bad luck⟩

synonyms glass, looking glass

related words cheval glass, dressing glass, hand glass, pier glass, pier mirror; reflector

mirror *vb* to reproduce or show (an exact likeness) as a mirror would ⟨the still waters of the pond *mirroring* the cloudless sky above⟩ — see REFLECT 1

mirror image *n* something or someone that strongly resembles another ⟨looking at the idealistic intern, the elderly physician could not help but see the *mirror image* of himself 40 years earlier⟩ — see IMAGE 1

mirth *n* a mood characterized by high spirits and amusement and often accompanied by laughter ⟨as charming as your mutual *mirth* is, could you refrain from nudging each other and giggling during class?⟩

synonyms cheer, cheerfulness, cheeriness, festivity, gaiety (*also* gayety), gayness, glee, gleefulness, hilarity, jocundity, joviality, merriment, merriness, mirthfulness

related words frivolity, levity; jollification, jollity, reveling (*or* revelling), revelry; brightness, buoyancy, good-humoredness, good-naturedness, humor, sunniness; gamesomeness, insouciance, lightheartedness, playfulness, sportiveness; buffoonery, clownishness, flippancy, funning, jest, jesting, jocoseness, jocosity, jocularity, joking, joshing; animation, giddiness, jauntiness, liveliness, perkiness, vivacity; joyfulness, joyousness, jubilance, rejoicing; frolicking, gamboling (*or* gambolling), rollicking, romping

near antonyms blues, dejection, depression, despondence, forlornness, sadness, sorrow, unhappiness; bile, gloom, melancholy, sourness, spleen; earnestness, graveness, gravity, grimness, seriousness, soberness, sobersidedness, solemnity, solemnness; discontent, disgruntlement, moodiness; dolefulness, dolorousness, joylessness, mournfulness, plaintiveness, woe, woefulness; blackness, darkness, gloominess, glumness; desolateness, desolation; heartbreak, miserableness, misery, mourning, wretchedness

mirthful *adj* indicative of or marked by high spirits or good humor ⟨the *mirthful* laughter of old teammates telling lame jokes and ribald stories⟩ — see MERRY

mirthfully *adv* in a cheerful or happy manner ⟨an album of bawdy songs from the Elizabethan era, all of them lustily and *mirthfully* sung⟩ — see GAILY 1

mirthfulness *n* a mood characterized by high spirits and amusement and often accompanied by laughter ⟨the *mirthfulness* of the revelers was contagious, and pretty soon everyone in the bar was laughing and singing⟩ — see MIRTH

miry *adj* full of or covered with soft wet earth ⟨*miry* fields that required a good pair of boots⟩ — see MUDDY 1

misadventure *n* bad luck or an example of this ⟨a string of financial *misadventures* eventually left him broke⟩ — see MISFORTUNE

misanthrope *n* a person who distrusts other people and believes that everything is done for selfish reasons ⟨a former *misanthrope* who now professes a newly discovered love of mankind⟩ — see CYNIC

misanthropic *adj* having or showing a deep distrust of human beings and their motives ⟨a *misanthropic* outlook on life that probably stems from a childhood filled with physical and emotional abuse⟩ — see CYNICAL

misapplication *n* incorrect or improper use ⟨this silly gossiping is a serious *misapplication* of your time⟩ — see MISUSE

misapply *vb* to put to a bad or improper use ⟨you've *misapplied* the theorem to certain problems that require a different formula⟩ ⟨kids who *misapply* their boundless energy and get into trouble⟩

synonyms abuse, misemploy, misuse, pervert, profane, prostitute

related words degrade, twist; mismanage; corrupt, debase, desecrate

near antonyms apply, employ, use, utilize; respect

misapprehend *vb* to fail to understand the true or actual meaning of ⟨unfortunately, the message that the artist was trying to convey has been *misapprehended* by many museum patrons⟩ — see MISUNDERSTAND

misapprehension *n* **1** a failure to understand correctly ⟨tried to eliminate all *misapprehensions* about the planned riverfront development⟩ — see MISUNDERSTANDING 1

2 a wrong judgment ⟨a common *misapprehension* about how our language functions⟩ — see MISTAKE 1

misappropriate *vb* to take (something) without right and with an intent to keep ⟨a financial manager *misap-*

propriating funds from her clients' accounts⟩ — see STEAL 1

misbegotten *adj* born to a father and mother who are not married ⟨a *misbegotten* child who never knew his father⟩ — see ILLEGITIMATE 1

misbehave *vb* to behave badly ⟨scolded the children for *misbehaving* and sent them to bed early⟩
synonyms act out, act up, carry on
related words misconduct; disobey, rebel; clown (around), cut up, fool around, horse around, kid (around); show off; roughhouse
phrases raise Cain (*or* raise hell), run riot
near antonyms obey; acquit, act, bear, comport, conduct, demean, deport, quit; comply, conform; check, collect, compose, constrain, contain, control, curb, handle, inhibit, move, quiet, repress, restrain

misbehaving *adj* engaging in or marked by childish misbehavior ⟨a new approach for disciplining a chronically *misbehaving* child⟩ — see NAUGHTY

misbehavior *n* improper or illegal behavior ⟨would not tolerate any *misbehavior* from her students⟩ — see MISCONDUCT 1

misbelief *n* a false idea or belief ⟨the common *misbelief* that the Great Wall of China is visible from the moon⟩ — see FALLACY 1

miscalculate *vb* to make an incorrect judgment regarding ⟨they *miscalculated* how difficult the mountainous trek would be⟩
synonyms misconceive, misdeem, misestimate, misgauge, misjudge, mismeasure, mistake
related words misapprehend, misconstrue, misinterpret, misknow, misperceive, misunderstand; overestimate, overrate, overvalue; misesteem, underestimate, underrate, undervalue; miscount, misreckon

miscalculation *n* a wrong judgment ⟨treating her opponent as an intellectual lightweight was a serious *miscalculation* on her part⟩ — see MISTAKE 1

miscarry *vb* to go wrong ⟨the scheme to save the stranded dolphins *miscarried*, and all were lost⟩
synonyms misfire
related words miss; break down, bust, conk (out), crash, die, fail, founder, stall; bomb, fizzle, flame out, flop, flunk, fold, wash out; flounder, struggle; decline, skid, slip, slump, tank, wane
phrases come a cropper, come to grief, fall flat, fall short
near antonyms prevail, succeed; flourish, prosper, thrive

miscellanea *n pl* an unorganized collection or mixture of various things ⟨searching through the *miscellanea* in the archive, she came across the draft of an unpublished and previously unknown poem by the reclusive writer⟩ — see MISCELLANY 1

miscellaneous *adj* consisting of many things of different sorts ⟨the bottom of the drawer was always a *miscellaneous* accumulation of odds and ends⟩
synonyms assorted, eclectic, heterogeneous, indiscriminate, kitchen-sink, magpie, mixed, motley, patchwork, piebald, promiscuous, raggle-taggle, ragtag, varied
related words manifold, multifarious; multiple, multiplex, myriad; disparate, divergent, diverse, sundry, various; chaotic, cluttered, confused, disarranged, disarrayed, disheveled (*or* dishevelled), disordered, farraginous, jumbled, littered, messed, messy, muddled; amalgamated, blended, combined, commingled, commixed, conglomerated, fused, incorporated, intermingled, intermixed, merged, mingled; composite, conglomerate, hybrid; unclassified, unsorted
near antonyms monolithic, uniform; alike, identical, like, same; distinct, distinctive, individual, separate
antonyms homogeneous

miscellaneousness *n* the quality or state of being composed of many different elements or types ⟨the *miscellaneousness* of the store's merchandise makes it a browser's delight⟩ — see VARIETY 1

miscellany *n* **1** an unorganized collection or mixture of various things ⟨the box from the attic contained a *miscellany* of old records, family photo albums, and long-forgotten love letters⟩
synonyms agglomerate, agglomeration, alphabet soup, assortment, botch, clutter, collage, crazy quilt, farrago, gallimaufry, grab bag, gumbo, hash, hodgepodge, hotchpotch, jambalaya, jumble, jungle, litter, macédoine, medley, mélange, menagerie, miscellanea, mishmash, mixed bag, montage, motley, muddle, olio, olla podrida, omnium-gatherum, pastiche, patchwork, patchwork quilt, potpourri, ragbag, ragout, rummage, salad, salmagundi, scramble, shuffle, smorgasbord, stew, tumble, variety, welter
related words detritus, notions, oddments, odds and ends, sundries; accumulation, aggregate, aggregation, conglomerate, conglomeration; catchall; admixture, alloy, amalgam, blend, combination, commixture, composite, compound, fusion, intermixture, mix-up; bollix, chaos, confusion, disarrangement, disarray, disorder, dog's breakfast [*chiefly British*], mess, morass, muddle, shambles; imbroglio, knot, snarl, tangle
2 a collection of writings ⟨the volume is a *miscellany* of tales and legends of the New England coast⟩ — see ANTHOLOGY

mischance *n* **1** a chance and usually sudden event bringing loss or injury ⟨the smallest *mischance* could spell disaster for our plan⟩ — see ACCIDENT 1
2 bad luck or an example of this ⟨by *mischance* she took a wrong turn and became hopelessly lost in the city⟩ — see MISFORTUNE

mischief *n* **1** playful, reckless behavior that is not intended to cause serious harm ⟨the children claimed that setting off a firecracker was harmless *mischief*, but they got a lecture anyway⟩
synonyms devilishness, devilment, devilry (*or* deviltry), diablerie, espièglerie, hob, impishness, knavery, mischievousness, rascality, roguery, roguishness, shenanigan(s), waggery, waggishness, wickedness
related words diabolicalness, misbehavior, misconduct, naughtiness, troublemaking; buffoonery, friskiness, playfulness, sportiveness; chicanery, trickery; goings-on, hanky-panky, high jinks (*also* hijinks), monkey business, monkeying, monkeyshine(s), skylarking, tomfoolery; horseplay, roughhousing; antic, caper, dido, practical joke, trick; aggravation, annoyance, exasperation, irritation
near antonyms gravitas, gravity, seriousness, solemnity, solemnness
2 a natural disposition for playful behavior ⟨your mother was full of *mischief* as a child, believe it or not⟩ — see PLAYFULNESS
3 an appealingly mischievous person ⟨he's a little *mischief* who means no harm⟩ — see SCAMP 1

mischievous *adj* **1** tending to or exhibiting reckless playfulness ⟨the children had been so *mischievous* that we had to pay the babysitter extra and then clean up the mess⟩
synonyms arch, devilish, elvish, espiègle, impish, knavish, leprechaunish, pixie (*also* pixy), pixieish, prankish, puckish, rascally, roguish, scampish, sly, tricksy, waggish, wicked
related words antic, coltish, coy, frisky, frolicsome, kittenish, playful, sportful, sportive; gay, happy, lighthearted, whimsical; energetic, lively, spirited, sprightly; artful, crafty, cunning, trickish, tricky, wily; misbehaving, naughty, troublemaking; pestering, riling, teasing

near antonyms grave, grim, sedate, sober, solemn, staid, stern

2 engaging in or marked by childish misbehavior ⟨punished for their *mischievous* tricks on the neighbors⟩ — see NAUGHTY

3 causing or capable of causing harm ⟨*mischievous* gossip that ruined a good woman's reputation⟩ — see HARMFUL

mischievousness *n* **1** a natural disposition for playful behavior ⟨as they grew older, they lost much of their youthful *mischievousness*⟩ — see PLAYFULNESS

2 playful, reckless behavior that is not intended to cause serious harm ⟨bored kids often engage in a certain amount of *mischievousness* during the long summer vacation⟩ — see MISCHIEF 1

misconceive *vb* to make an incorrect judgment regarding ⟨*misconceived* the scope of the nation's financial crisis⟩ — see MISCALCULATE

misconception *n* a false idea or belief ⟨it is a popular *misconception* that toilets flush in the opposite direction in the Southern Hemisphere⟩ — see FALLACY 1

misconduct *n* **1** improper or illegal behavior ⟨some rough play got the hockey player fined for *misconduct* on the ice⟩

synonyms malfeasance, misbehavior, misdoing, wrongdoing

related words crime, malefaction, misdeed, misdemeanor, sin, transgression, trespass, wrong; malpractice; goings-on, hanky-panky; familiarity, gaffe, impropriety, indiscretion; blunder, error, fault, flub, fumble, goof, lapse, miscue, misstep, mistake, slip, slipup, stumble

2 a sexual encounter or relationship between a married person and someone other than their spouse ⟨both parties cited *misconduct* as the reason for the divorce⟩ — see ADULTERY

misconduct *vb* to manage badly ⟨*misconducted* the polar expedition and paid for his mistakes with his life⟩ — see MISMANAGE

misconstruction *n* a failure to understand correctly ⟨his *misconstruction* of the blueprints led to some costly and time-consuming repairs⟩ — see MISUNDERSTANDING 1

misconstrue *vb* to fail to understand the true or actual meaning of ⟨claimed that the press had *misconstrued* her comments⟩ — see MISUNDERSTAND

misconstruing *n* a failure to understand correctly ⟨there are several words in English that are the result of the common *misconstruing* of singular forms as plurals⟩ — see MISUNDERSTANDING 1

miscreant *n* **1** a mean, evil, or unprincipled person ⟨halt, vile *miscreant*, and face justice!⟩ — see VILLAIN

2 a person who has committed a crime ⟨a youthful offender surrounded in prison by hard-bitten *miscreants* who had committed just about every crime imaginable⟩ — see CRIMINAL

miscue *n* an unintentional departure from truth or accuracy ⟨the slightest *miscue* could make the trapeze artist lose his grip and fall to the mat below⟩ — see ERROR 1

misdeed *n* a breaking of a moral or legal code ⟨punished for her *misdeeds* by the church elders⟩ — see OFFENSE 1

misdeem *vb* to make an incorrect judgment regarding ⟨my son is a shy, quiet boy, but you seriously *misdeem* him if you believe him to be stupid⟩ — see MISCALCULATE

misdoing *n* **1** a breaking of a moral or legal code ⟨the sordid *misdoings* of the city councilman were exposed as a result of an intense investigation by the local newspaper⟩ — see OFFENSE 1

2 improper or illegal behavior ⟨kept a watchful eye for any *misdoing* by the members of the clergy⟩ — see MISCONDUCT 1

misdoubt *n* a feeling or attitude that one does not know the truth, truthfulness, or trustworthiness of someone or something ⟨whatever *misdoubts* I had about her qualifications were erased by the interview⟩ — see DOUBT

misdoubt *vb* to have no trust or confidence in ⟨unexpectedly elevated to the throne, the new king acknowledged that many *misdoubted* his ability to lead his people⟩ — see DISTRUST

mise–en–scène *n* **1** the array of painted backgrounds and furnishings used to establish the setting in a stage production ⟨an era in which the *mise-en-scène* of Broadway musicals became ever more spectacular⟩ — see SCENERY

2 the circumstances, conditions, or objects by which one is surrounded ⟨the movie captures the *mise-en-scène* of bawdiness and ribaldry that we associate with a pirate port of call⟩ — see ENVIRONMENT

misemploy *n* to put to a bad or improper use ⟨findings in genetics that were later *misemployed* by eugenicists and racists to support the extermination of people deemed to be of "inferior" stock⟩ — see MISAPPLY

misemployment *n* incorrect or improper use ⟨the *misemployment* of genetic research to justify racist theories⟩ — see MISUSE

miser *n* a mean grasping person who is usually stingy with money ⟨the *miser* liked to sit and play with his money⟩

synonyms cheapskate, churl, hunks, niggard, penny-pincher, piker, scrooge, skinflint, tightwad

related words hoarder, pack rat, saver

near antonyms prodigal, profligate, spender, spendthrift, squanderer, waster, wastrel

miserable *adj* **1** causing or marked by an atmosphere lacking in cheer ⟨a *miserable* jail cell in which the political prisoner was left to rot⟩ — see GLOOMY 1

2 feeling unhappiness ⟨the awful news made us *miserable*⟩ — see SAD 1

3 of low quality ⟨a *miserable* meal that I wouldn't feed to a dog⟩ — see CHEAP 2

4 showing signs of advanced wear and tear and neglect ⟨a *miserable* little apartment⟩ — see SHABBY 1

5 deserving of one's pity ⟨*miserable* refugees from the war-torn country⟩ — see PATHETIC 1

6 deserving pitying scorn (as for inadequacy) ⟨that ugly mutt is one *miserable* excuse for a dog⟩ — see PITIFUL 1

miserableness *n* a state or spell of low spirits ⟨the magnitude of the parents' *miserableness* could scarcely be imagined by those who had never lost a child⟩ — see SADNESS

miserere *n* an expression of dissatisfaction, pain, or resentment ⟨an essay that is essentially a long *miserere* about the decline of good manners in our society⟩ — see COMPLAINT 1

miserliness *n* the quality or practice of being overly sparing with money ⟨some kids like to grouse about the *miserliness* of their parents as far as allowances are concerned⟩ ⟨the company's misguided *miserliness* is the reason we're still using these inefficient, outdated computers⟩ — see PARSIMONY 1

miserly *adj* giving or sharing as little as possible ⟨my brother, who is notoriously *miserly*, surprised us when he offered to pick up the tab⟩ — see STINGY 1

misery *n* **1** a situation or state that causes great suffering and unhappiness ⟨the flood brought *misery* to the many hundreds whom it had made homeless⟩ — see HELL 2

2 a state of great suffering of body or mind ⟨a medication that promises to provide greater relief to those living in chronic *misery* because of arthritis⟩ — see DISTRESS 1

misestimate *vb* to make an incorrect judgment regarding ⟨sorely *misestimated* the character of the young man they hired to look after their vacation home⟩ — see MISCALCULATE

misfire *vb* to go wrong ⟨their scheme to rob the bank *misfired* disastrously and landed them all in jail⟩ — see MISCARRY

misfortune *n* bad luck or an example of this ⟨through sheer *misfortune* our car got a flat tire and we were late for the ceremony⟩ ⟨our *misfortunes* of the last year included the loss of a beloved pet⟩
synonyms adversity, ill, knock, misadventure, mischance, mishap, tragedy
related words calamity, cataclysm, catastrophe, disaster; affliction, hardship, trial, tribulation, woe; distress, misery, suffering, unhappiness; defeat, failure, fizzle, nonsuccess; curse, evil, sorrow, trouble; accident, casualty; blow, body blow, disappointment, letdown, setback; circumstance, destiny, doom, fate, lot, portion
near antonyms break, chance, fluke, godsend, hit, opportunity, strike, stroke, windfall; accomplishment, achievement, success
antonyms fortune, luck, serendipity

misgauge *vb* to make an incorrect judgment regarding ⟨the candidate fatally *misgauged* voters' concerns, and his negative ads only served to alienate many would-be supporters⟩ — see MISCALCULATE

misgiving *n* **1** a feeling or attitude that one does not know the truth, truthfulness, or trustworthiness of someone or something ⟨I had *misgivings* about the alleged victim's story, but I was afraid to speak up⟩ — see DOUBT
2 an uneasy feeling about the rightness of what one is doing or going to do ⟨he was filled with *misgivings* about committing himself to such a huge loan⟩ — see QUALM
3 suspicion or fear of future harm or misfortune ⟨overcome by a sudden *misgiving* upon seeing the creepy old mansion⟩ — see APPREHENSION 1

misgovern *vb* to manage badly ⟨the ruling party was soundly defeated at the polls for having disastrously *misgoverned* the country⟩ — see MISMANAGE

misguide *vb* to cause to believe what is untrue ⟨we were *misguided* by the flashy advertisements for what turned out to be pretty lousy pizza⟩ — see DECEIVE

mishandle *vb* **1** to inflict physical or emotional harm upon ⟨having been shuffled from foster home to foster home, the orphaned girl felt she had been *mishandled* by an uncaring society⟩ — see ABUSE 1
2 to abuse physically ⟨adopted a sadly *mishandled* puppy from the pound⟩ — see MANHANDLE 1
3 to manage badly ⟨we took over as soon as we realized that the fill-in had been *mishandling* the situation⟩ — see MISMANAGE

mishap *n* **1** a chance and usually sudden event bringing loss or injury ⟨the usual *mishaps* of a family vacation⟩ — see ACCIDENT 1
2 bad luck or an example of this ⟨*mishap* followed wherever he went⟩ — see MISFORTUNE

mishmash *n* an unorganized collection or mixture of various things ⟨the painting was just a *mishmash* of colors and abstract shapes as far as we could tell⟩ — see MISCELLANY 1

misimpression *n* a failure to understand correctly ⟨she was under the *misimpression* that the class was for beginners, but it was actually for advanced students⟩ — see MISUNDERSTANDING 1

misinform *vb* to cause to believe what is untrue ⟨had been *misinformed* about the purpose of the meeting and walked in on what was a surprise birthday party⟩ — see DECEIVE

misinterpret *vb* **1** to change so much as to create a wrong impression or alter the meaning of ⟨his note on this passage in the novel seriously *misinterprets* the author's meaning⟩ — see GARBLE 1
2 to fail to understand the true or actual meaning of ⟨we *misinterpreted* the directions and ended up on the wrong side of town⟩ — see MISUNDERSTAND

misinterpretation *n* a failure to understand correctly ⟨his *misinterpretation* of the ambiguously worded instructions was hardly his fault⟩ — see MISUNDERSTANDING 1

misjudge *vb* to make an incorrect judgment regarding ⟨the gymnast *misjudged* her landing and sprained her ankle⟩ — see MISCALCULATE

misjudging *n* a wrong judgment ⟨a series of small *misjudgings* along the way eventually amounted to a colossal mistake⟩ — see MISTAKE 1

misjudgment *n* a wrong judgment ⟨one serious *misjudgment* at this point could cost the candidate the election⟩ — see MISTAKE 1

misknow *vb* to fail to understand the true or actual meaning of ⟨so often, for all of our presumption, we *misknow* the hearts of others⟩ — see MISUNDERSTAND

misknowledge *n* a failure to understand correctly ⟨the traveler's *misknowledge* of local customs led him to make some embarrassing faux pas⟩ — see MISUNDERSTANDING 1

mislaid *adj* no longer possessed ⟨a traveler looking for his *mislaid* passport⟩ — see LOST

mislay *vb* to be unable to find or have at hand ⟨I'm always *mislaying* my bus pass⟩ — see LOSE 1

mislaying *n* the act or an instance of not having or being able to find ⟨your *mislaying* of the car keys caused us to be late for work once again⟩ — see LOSS 1

mislead *vb* to cause to believe what is untrue ⟨the coral snake's attractive colors can *mislead* you into thinking that it is harmless⟩ — see DECEIVE

misleading *adj* tending or having power to deceive ⟨the *misleading* text of the advertisement would like you to believe that you're getting something for nothing⟩ — see DECEPTIVE 1

mislike *n* a strong feeling of not liking or approving ⟨a well-known *mislike* of stuffy, formal affairs⟩ — see DISLIKE 1

mislike *vb* **1** to feel dislike for ⟨as Shakespeare's Othello famously pleaded, *"Mislike* me not for my complexion"⟩ — see DISLIKE 1
2 to hold an unfavorable opinion of ⟨he's such a polite, friendly, and kind young man, it's hard to see how any prospective father-in-law could *mislike* him⟩ — see DISAPPROVE (OF)

mismanage *vb* to manage badly ⟨the business was *mismanaged* so seriously that it eventually had to declare bankruptcy⟩
synonyms maladminister, misconduct, misgovern, mishandle, misrule
related words abuse, ill-treat, ill-use, maltreat, mistreat, misuse; damage, harm, hurt, violate; botch, bungle
near antonyms govern, handle, husband, manage, rule; care (for), nurture; aid, help, protect, rescue

mismeasure *vb* to make an incorrect judgment regarding ⟨the television network seriously *mismeasured* public reaction to the unceremonious dismissal of the popular anchorwoman⟩ — see MISCALCULATE

misorder *n* a state in which everything is out of order ⟨the chronic *misorder* that plagued her candidancy from the very start⟩ — see CHAOS

misperceive *vb* to fail to understand the true or actual meaning of ⟨humor-challenged members of the audience *misperceived* the speaker's harmless joke as an insult to their organization⟩ — see MISUNDERSTAND

misplace *vb* to be unable to find or have at hand ⟨I seem to have *misplaced* my keys⟩ — see LOSE 1

misplaced *adj* no longer possessed ⟨we eventually found the *misplaced* tickets in his coat pocket⟩ — see LOST

misplacement *n* the act or an instance of not having or being able to find ⟨they worried that his *misplacement* of the invitation would keep them from getting in, but fortunately their names were on the list⟩ — see LOSS 1

misprision *n* **1** open dislike for someone or something considered unworthy of one's concern or respect ⟨his intense *misprision* for comic books and other "trash literature" is well known⟩ — see CONTEMPT
2 the nonperformance of an assigned or expected action ⟨an elected official charged with *misprision* and bribery⟩ — see FAILURE 1

misread *vb* to fail to understand the true or actual meaning of ⟨I *misread* her body language and thought she was becoming confrontational⟩ — see MISUNDERSTAND

misreading *n* a failure to understand correctly ⟨your *misreading* of the definition of the word is what got you into trouble⟩ — see MISUNDERSTANDING 1

misrelate *vb* to change so much as to create a wrong impression or alter the meaning of ⟨that Hollywood anecdote has been *misrelated* so many times that at this point no one knows what was actually said⟩ — see GARBLE 1

misrepresent *vb* **1** to change so much as to create a wrong impression or alter the meaning of ⟨this summary seriously *misrepresents* the general tone and substance of the speech⟩ — see GARBLE 1
2 to give a misleading impression of ⟨deliberately *misrepresented* the facts of the case⟩ — see BELIE 1

misrule *n* a state in which there is widespread wrongdoing and disregard for rules and authority ⟨the country's long period of *misrule* had made it a hotbed for terrorist organizations⟩ — see ANARCHY

misrule *vb* to manage badly ⟨accused of *misruling* his island nation to the point of economic collapse⟩ — see MISMANAGE

[1]**miss** *n* **1** a female person who has not yet reached adulthood ⟨a special perfume for the little *miss*⟩ — see GIRL 2
2 a young unmarried woman ⟨you should ask that young *miss* if she would like to dance⟩ — see GIRL 1

[2]**miss** *n* something that has failed ⟨a television season with far fewer hits than *misses*⟩ — see FAILURE 3

miss *vb* **1** to fail to attend ⟨had to *miss* work for a week because of the flu⟩ — see CUT 2
2 to fail to understand the true or actual meaning of ⟨I think you're *missing* the point⟩ — see MISUNDERSTAND
3 to be unsuccessful ⟨everyone knows that most of the new television series will *miss* and be gone before anyone notices⟩ — see FAIL 2

misshape *vb* to twist (something) out of a natural or normal shape or condition ⟨the crippling disease had grotesquely *misshaped* his formerly lithe body⟩ — see CONTORT

misshapen *adj* badly or imperfectly formed ⟨the returning camper proudly presented his mother with a *misshapen* clay bowl that he had made in crafts class⟩ — see MALFORMED

misshaping *n* the twisting of something out of a natural or normal shape or condition ⟨the rear bumper suffered some pretty noticeable *misshaping* from the accident⟩ — see CONTORTION

missing *adj* **1** no longer possessed ⟨the *missing* socks turned up in the dog's special hiding place⟩ — see LOST
2 not present or in evidence ⟨any sense of how real people talk and act is *missing* from this novel⟩ — see ABSENT 2
3 not at a certain place ⟨our church organist is *missing* this morning, so we'll have to sing without her accompaniment⟩ — see ABSENT 1

mission *n* a specific task with which a person or group is charged ⟨your *mission* is to clean up the house before company arrives⟩
synonyms assignment, brief, business, charge, detail, job, operation, post
related words burden, chore, duty, need, obligation, office, requirement, responsibility; errand, labor, work; commitment, pledge, promise; appointment, commission, designation, nomination; compulsion, constraint, restraint

missive *n* a message on paper from one person or group to another ⟨the two old friends like to fire off *missives* filled with good-natured teasing and mock insults⟩ — see [1]LETTER

misspend *vb* to use up carelessly ⟨warned that a childhood spent playing video games was a *misspent* youth indeed⟩ — see WASTE 1

misstate *vb* to change so much as to create a wrong impression or alter the meaning of ⟨a person who can be counted on to *misstate* even the simplest telephone message⟩ — see GARBLE 1

misstep *n* **1** a wrong judgment ⟨another *misstep* like that, and the company could go belly-up⟩ — see MISTAKE 1
2 an unintentional departure from truth or accuracy ⟨a *misstep* that could lead to disaster⟩ — see ERROR 1

missus *or* **missis** *n* the female partner in a marriage ⟨usually the *missus* has the final say-so on buying a house, and the mister has the last word on the purchase of a car⟩ — see WIFE

missy *n* a female person who has not yet reached adulthood ⟨and how old is the little *missy*?⟩ — see GIRL 2

mist *n* **1** a light or fine rain ⟨a *mist* was falling on the streets as we drove home⟩ — see DRIZZLE
2 an atmospheric condition in which suspended particles in the air rob it of its transparency ⟨a heavy *mist* obscured our view of the city from the observatory⟩ — see HAZE 1

mist *vb* to make dark, dim, or indistinct ⟨the damp air *misted* the window pane⟩ — see CLOUD 1

mistake *n* **1** a wrong judgment ⟨I made a *mistake* when I assumed that you were looking for a serious relationship⟩
synonyms misapprehension, miscalculation, misjudging, misjudgment, misstep, slip, slipup
related words blunder, boner, boob [*British*], clinker, errancy, error, fault, flub, fumble, gaffe, goof, inaccuracy, lapse, miscue, stumble, trip; foul-up, muff; misstatement; misconception, misconstruction, misconstruing, misimpression, misinterpretation, misprision, misunderstanding
2 an unintentional departure from truth or accuracy ⟨made a *mistake* on the exam that almost cost her a passing grade⟩ — see ERROR 1

mistake *vb* **1** to fail to understand the true or actual meaning of ⟨the auctioneer *mistook* my nod for a bid, and I ended up buying a painting I don't even like⟩ — see MISUNDERSTAND
2 to make an incorrect judgment regarding ⟨you seriously *mistake* me if you think I scare so easily⟩ — see MISCALCULATE
3 to fail to differentiate (a thing) from something similar or related ⟨she *mistook* physical attraction for love⟩ — see CONFUSE 3

mistaken *adj* having an opinion that does not agree with truth or the facts ⟨meat loaf is on the cafeteria's menu today, if I'm not *mistaken*⟩ — see INCORRECT 1

mistakenly *adv* in a mistaken or inappropriate way ⟨we *mistakenly* thought that this was our conference room⟩ — see WRONGLY

mister *n* the male partner in a marriage ⟨I'll check with the *mister* and see if we're free that weekend⟩ — see HUSBAND

mistreat *vb* to inflict physical or emotional harm upon ⟨the foster parent who had been *mistreating* his charges was sent to jail⟩ — see ABUSE 1

mistress *n* a female other than his wife with whom a married man has a continuing sexual relationship ⟨he lavished gifts upon his *mistress* but completely ignored his wife⟩
synonyms concubine, doxy (*also* doxie), other woman, woman
related words lover, paramour; courtesan, demimondaine, demirep, odalisque; harlot, prostitute, strumpet, whore; girlfriend

mistrust *n* a feeling or attitude that one does not know the truth, truthfulness, or trustworthiness of someone or something ⟨had an unfortunate *mistrust* of doctors, so her medical condition was allowed to worsen⟩ — see DOUBT

mistrust *vb* to have no trust or confidence in ⟨a recluse who *mistrusts* her neighbors and stays in her house all day⟩ — see DISTRUST

mistrustful *adj* **1** inclined to doubt or question claims ⟨we were *mistrustful* of the so-called "miracle cure" for obesity⟩ — see SKEPTICAL 1
2 not feeling sure about the truth, wisdom, or trustworthiness of someone or something ⟨inhabitants of that remote community tend to be *mistrustful* of outsiders⟩ — see DOUBTFUL 1

mistrustfully *adv* with distrust ⟨our cat tends to view strangers *mistrustfully*⟩ — see ASKANCE

mistrustfulness *n* a feeling or attitude that one does not know the truth, truthfulness, or trustworthiness of someone or something ⟨eyed the strange invention with his usual *mistrustfulness*⟩ — see DOUBT

misty *adj* **1** filled with or dimmed by fine particles (as of dust or water) in suspension ⟨enjoyed the *misty* view of the thunderous falls from the deck of the sightseeing boat⟩ — see HAZY 1
2 not seen or understood clearly ⟨I've a *misty* understanding of the issue but not so much that I could vote intelligently⟩ — see FAINT 1

misunderstand *vb* to fail to understand the true or actual meaning of ⟨you *misunderstood* that poem because you took everything so literally⟩
synonyms misapprehend, misconstrue, misinterpret, misknow, misperceive, misread, miss, mistake
related words misconceive, misdeem, misjudge; mishear
antonyms appreciate, apprehend, catch, comprehend, conceive, fathom, get, grasp, grok, know, make out, penetrate, perceive, savvy, see, seize, take in, understand

misunderstanding *n* **1** a failure to understand correctly ⟨people once thought that there were canals on Mars because of a common *misunderstanding* of a report by an Italian astronomer⟩
synonyms incomprehension, misapprehension, misconstruction, misconstruing, misimpression, misinterpretation, misknowledge, misreading
related words astigmatism, misconception, misperception, misprision, mistake
near antonyms appreciation, apprehension, comprehension, conception, grasp, grokking, knowledge, perception, prehension, understanding; awareness, consciousness, realization
2 an often noisy or angry expression of differing opinions ⟨tried to resolve their *misunderstandings* peacefully⟩ — see ARGUMENT 1

misusage *n* incorrect or improper use ⟨the teacher was appalled by the new student's *misusage* of some basic scientific terms⟩ — see MISUSE

misuse *n* incorrect or improper use ⟨the warranty for this dryer is null and void if you subject the product to deliberate *misuse*⟩
synonyms abuse, misapplication, misemployment, misusage, misutilization, perversion
related words mishandling, mismanagement, mismanaging; ill-treatment, ill-usage, maltreatment, mistreatment; damage, destruction, ruin, spoiling, wrecking; corruption, debasement, desecration, profanation, prostitution
near antonyms application, employment, use, utilization

misuse *vb* **1** to put to a bad or improper use ⟨an actor who *misused* his considerable talent by appearing in too many lousy movies⟩ — see MISAPPLY
2 to inflict physical or emotional harm upon ⟨sadly *misused* by the people he had trusted⟩ — see ABUSE 1

misutilization *n* incorrect or improper use ⟨the report documents how the *misutilization* of the drug can have serious side effects⟩ — see MISUSE

mite *n* **1** a very small sum of money ⟨I have only a *mite* left to buy lunch for the rest of the week⟩
synonyms chicken feed [*slang*], chump change, dime, hay, peanuts, pin money, pittance, shoestring, song, two cents
related words petty cash, pocket money, spending money
near antonyms bankroll, capital, funds, means, wherewithal; opulence, pelf, riches, treasure, wealth; heap, pile, pot; bonanza, mine, treasure trove, treasury
antonyms big buck(s), boodle, bundle, fortune, king's ransom, megabuck(s), mint, wad
2 a living thing much smaller than others of its kind ⟨the kitten was just a *mite*, hardly the size of my palm⟩ — see DWARF 1
3 a very small amount ⟨that speech didn't make a *mite* of sense⟩ — see PARTICLE 1

mitigate *vb* to make more bearable or less severe ⟨this medicine should *mitigate* the pain until the strained muscle heals itself⟩ — see HELP 2

mix *n* a distinct entity formed by the combining of two or more different things ⟨guacamole is usually a *mix* of avocado, tomato, onion, and spices⟩ — see BLEND

mix *vb* **1** to turn into a single mass or entity that is more or less the same throughout ⟨those ingredients should not be *mixed* until the last stage of the recipe⟩ — see BLEND 1
2 to take part in social activities ⟨happily *mixing* with the other guests at the party⟩ — see SOCIALIZE

mix (up) *vb* **1** to fail to differentiate (a thing) from something similar or related ⟨you've *mixed* piety *up* with pietism⟩ — see CONFUSE 3
2 to undo the proper order or arrangement of ⟨in my rush I had *mixed up* the files and had to sort them out later⟩ — see DISORDER

mixed *adj* **1** being offspring produced by parents of different races, breeds, species, or genera ⟨our *mixed* dog has a greyhound's body but the features of a collie⟩
synonyms cold-blooded (*or* coldblood), cross, crossbred, hybrid, mongrel
related words grade, half-bred; dihybrid, trihybrid; crossed, hybridized, interbred, outcrossed
near antonyms pedigreed (*or* pedigree); inbred, linebred, straightbred
antonyms blooded, full-blood, full-blooded, purebred, thoroughbred
2 consisting of many things of different sorts ⟨the con-

tinuing education program offers a very *mixed* selection of courses⟩ — see MISCELLANEOUS

mixed bag *n* an unorganized collection or mixture of various things ⟨a *mixed bag* of professional astronomers and amateur enthusiasts attended the conference⟩ — see MISCELLANY 1

mixed–up *adj* suffering from mental confusion ⟨I was all *mixed-up*, and I was still on page two of the instructions⟩ — see DIZZY 2

mixture *n* a distinct entity formed by the combining of two or more different things ⟨add eggs to the *mixture* of dry ingredients⟩ — see BLEND

mix–up *n* an instance of confusion ⟨there was a *mix-up* at the airport and our luggage was accidentally sent to Ohio⟩ — see FOUL-UP

mizzle *n* a light or fine rain ⟨as I wandered around the city, the late afternoon *mizzle* seemed the perfect accompaniment to my melancholy mood⟩ — see DRIZZLE

moan *n* **1** a long low sound indicating pain or grief ⟨she uttered an agonized *moan* and clutched her stomach⟩
synonyms groan, wail
related words blubbering, crying, sniveling, sobbing, weeping, whimpering, whining, yammering; keen, lament, lamentation, plaint; bawl, cry, howl, shriek, squall, whimper, whine, yelp, yowl
near antonyms cackle, chortle, chuckle, giggle, guffaw, laugh, snicker, snigger, titter, twitter
2 a crying out in grief ⟨a great *moan* arose from the crowd when the awful news was announced⟩ — see LAMENT 1
3 an expression of dissatisfaction, pain, or resentment ⟨not the sort of person who would accept without a *moan* chronic emotional abuse from a domestic partner⟩ — see COMPLAINT 1

moan *vb* **1** to utter a moan ⟨he *moaned* and cried for days after his dog, his only companion, died⟩
synonyms groan, wail
related words blubber, cry, sob, weep; sniff, snivel, whimper, whine; bemoan, bewail, deplore, keen, lament, rue; agonize, anguish, bleed, grieve, hurt, mourn, sorrow, suffer; bawl, howl, shriek, squall, yammer, yelp, yowl
near antonyms cackle, chortle, chuckle, crack up, giggle, guffaw, laugh, snicker, titter, twitter
2 to express dissatisfaction, pain, or resentment usually tiresomely ⟨their son *moaned* whenever anyone asked him to do some work⟩ — see COMPLAIN

mob *n* **1** a great number of persons or creatures massed together ⟨a *mob* of pigeons soon flocked around us after they spied the bread crumbs⟩ — see CROWD 1
2 a group involved in secret or criminal activities ⟨the club owner was accused of having connections with a *mob* of racketeers⟩ — see [1]RING 1
3 the body of the community as contrasted with the elite ⟨political speeches designed to appeal to the *mob*⟩ — see MASS 1

mob *vb* to move upon or fill (something) in great numbers ⟨the snack bar was *mobbed* as soon as the meeting was over⟩ — see CROWD 2

mobile *adj* **1** capable of being moved especially with ease ⟨a *mobile* electric generator⟩ — see MOVABLE
2 having a way of life that involves moving from one region to another typically on a seasonal basis ⟨*mobile* workers who work the New England resorts in the summer and the ones in Florida during the winter⟩ — see MIGRATORY

mobilization *n* an act of gathering forces together to renew or attempt an effort ⟨called for the prompt *mobilization* of all national resources to combat the deadly epidemic⟩ — see RALLY 1

mobilize *vb* to assemble and make ready for action ⟨we are prepared to *mobilize* the troops on very short notice⟩
synonyms marshal (*also* marshall), muster, rally
related words arrange, group, line up, order, organize; call (up), convene, summon; activate; collect, round up
near antonyms disarrange, disorder, disorganize, disrupt, disturb; deactivate, dismiss; break up, disband, dissolve, split (up)
antonyms demob [*chiefly British*], demobilize

mobster *n* a violent, brutal person who is often a member of an organized gang ⟨the *mobster* threatened to break his legs if he didn't pay up⟩ — see HOODLUM

mock *adj* **1** being such in appearance only and made with or manufactured from usually cheaper materials ⟨*mock* turtle soup⟩ — see IMITATION
2 lacking in natural or spontaneous quality ⟨since I had inadvertently learned what I was getting, I opened the present with *mock* surprise⟩ — see ARTIFICIAL 1

mock *n* **1** a person or thing that is made fun of ⟨they made a *mock* of the new recruit in front of the whole unit⟩ — see LAUGHINGSTOCK
2 something that is made to look exactly like something else ⟨obviously, the "priceless" Grecian urn that is destroyed in the movie was a *mock*⟩ — see COPY

mock *vb* **1** to copy or exaggerate (someone or something) in order to make fun of ⟨*mocked* the bully's swaggering walk behind his back⟩ — see MIMIC 1
2 to make (someone or something) the object of unkind laughter ⟨the fashion gurus loved to *mock* the first lady for her unsophisticated clothes⟩ — see RIDICULE
3 to go against the commands, prohibitions, or rules of ⟨a person willing to *mock* the religious prohibition against working on the Sabbath⟩ — see DISOBEY

mocker *n* a person who causes repeated emotional pain, distress, or annoyance to another ⟨someday, she swore, she'd get back at the *mockers* who were making her life miserable⟩ — see TORMENTOR

mockery *n* **1** a poor, insincere, or insulting imitation of something ⟨the resort's Old West show for tourists is a *mockery* of Native American culture⟩
synonyms caricature, cartoon, farce, joke, parody, sham, travesty
related words burlesque, comedy; lampoon, takeoff; counterfeit, fake, feigning, forgery, hoax, humbug, knockoff, phony (*also* phoney), pretense (*or* pretence), sham, simulation
near antonyms homage, tribute
2 a person or thing that is made fun of ⟨you won't make a *mockery* of me!⟩ — see LAUGHINGSTOCK
3 the making of unkind jokes as a way of showing one's scorn for someone or something ⟨insulted by their *mockery* of his Southern mannerisms⟩ — see RIDICULE

mod *adj* **1** being or involving the latest methods, concepts, information, or styles ⟨the young artist's converted loft is decorated in a self-consciously *mod* style⟩ — see MODERN
2 keenly aware of and responsive to the latest developments especially in fashion and entertainment ⟨a chichi boutique for *mod* dressers with deep pockets⟩ — see AU COURANT 1

mod con *n, chiefly British* something that adds to one's ease of living ⟨bedrooms at the English country inn are filled with 18th-century charm, while the bathrooms have all the *mod cons* that 21st-century tourists demand⟩ — see COMFORT 2

[1]**mode** *n* **1** a distinctive way of putting ideas into words ⟨uses a colloquial *mode* of expression for his informal essays⟩ — see STYLE 1
2 a state of mind dominated by a particular emotion ⟨when I'm in my cooking *mode*, I just have to go into the kitchen and make something⟩ — see MOOD 1

[2]**mode** *n* a practice or interest that is very popular for a

short time ⟨slim, tanned bodies are definitely the *mode* at this beach resort⟩ — see FAD

model *adj* constituting, serving as, or worthy of being a pattern to be imitated ⟨why can't you be like your sister, who is such a well-behaved *model* child?⟩
synonyms archetypal (*also* archetypical), classic, definitive, exemplary, imitable, paradigmatic, quintessential, textbook
related words ideal, nonpareil, special, unique; absolute, flawless, impeccable, perfect; A-OK, A1, bang-up, banner, capital, choice, crackerjack, dandy, excellent, fabulous, fantastic, fine, first-class, first-rate, grand, great, groovy, jim-dandy, keen, marvelous (*or* marvellous), nifty, par excellence, prime, primo [*slang*], sensational, splendid, stellar, sterling, superb, superior, superlative, swell, terrific, tip-top, top, top-notch, unsurpassed, wizard [*chiefly British*], wonderful; exceptional, fancy, high-grade
near antonyms bad, low-grade, poor, substandard, unsatisfactory; atrocious, execrable, vile, wretched; deficient, disappointing, failed, inadequate, inferior; average, normal, ordinary, representative, typical; mediocre, second-class, second-rate

model *n* **1** an exact representation of something in greatly reduced size ⟨the dollhouse was a tiny, perfect *model* of the family's actual house⟩
synonyms miniature
related words carbon, carbon copy, clone, copy, dummy, dupe, duplicate, duplication, facsimile, imitation, mock, reduplication, replica, replication, reproduction; dwarf, midget, mini, pocket edition, pygmy (*also* pigmy)
near antonyms archetype, original, prototype; blowup, enlargement
2 a person who poses with or wears merchandise (as clothes) often for pictorial advertising ⟨the most famous *models* can earn thousands of dollars an hour⟩
synonyms manikin (*also* mannikin), mannequin
related words figure, form; doll, dummy; spokesmodel, supermodel
3 someone of such unequaled perfection as to deserve imitation ⟨she's the very *model* of the dedicated teacher⟩ — see IDEAL 1

moderate *adj* **1** avoiding extremes in behavior or expression ⟨he was only a *moderate* drinker, generally stopping after a couple of glasses of wine⟩
synonyms temperate
related words controlled, curbed, disciplined, inhibited, restrained, self-controlled, self-denying, self-disciplined; calculated, deliberate, measured; levelheaded, rational, reasonable, sensible; average, mediocre, medium, modest, run-of-the-mill, run-of-the-mine (*or* run-of-mine), so-so; normal, ordinary, regular, routine, typical, usual
near antonyms excessive, extreme, inordinate, radical; irrational, unreasonable, unreasoning; extremist, fanatic (*or* fanatical), rabid; unbridled, unchecked, uncontrolled, unrestrained
antonyms immoderate, intemperate
2 avoiding major social change or extreme political ideas ⟨the principal's *moderate* position on cell phones is that students can use them at school but only for emergencies⟩
synonyms central, centrist, middle-of-the-road
related words conventional, nonrevolutionary, orthodox, traditional; levelheaded, rational, reasonable, sensible; neutral
near antonyms excessive; conservative, reactionary, rightist; leftist, liberal, progressive; fanatic (*or* fanatical), rabid, subversive, violent; agitating, exciting, fomenting, incendiary, inciting, inflammatory, instigating, provocative, provoking; rabble-rousing; dissenting
antonyms extremist, radical, revolutionary, revolutionist, ultra
3 being about midway between extremes of amount or size ⟨a *moderate* snowfall was forecast for the region⟩ — see MIDDLE 2
4 marked by temperatures that are neither too high nor too low ⟨a city that is celebrated for its *moderate* climate⟩ — see CLEMENT 1

moderate *n* a person who holds moderate views ⟨to the community's detriment, *moderates* were often shouted down at town meetings by the local hotheads⟩ — see CENTRIST

moderate *vb* to grow less in scope or intensity especially gradually ⟨the wind began to *moderate* as the night wore on⟩ — see DECREASE 2

moderately *adv* to some degree or extent ⟨it was raining *moderately* hard outside⟩ — see FAIRLY 1

moderateness *n* an avoidance of extremes in one's actions, beliefs, or habits ⟨the *moderateness* of their enthusiasm for my proposed outing suggested that they would rather do something else⟩ — see TEMPERANCE 1

moderation *n* an avoidance of extremes in one's actions, beliefs, or habits ⟨the kind of person who does everything in *moderation*⟩ — see TEMPERANCE 1

moderator *n* a person in charge of a meeting ⟨the *moderator* should make sure that everyone gets a chance to speak⟩ — see CHAIR 1

modern *adj* being or involving the latest methods, concepts, information, or styles ⟨this hairstyle is absolutely the most *modern* fashion out there⟩
synonyms contemporary, current, designer, hot, mod, modernistic, new, new age, newfangled, new-fashioned, present-day, red-hot, space-age, state-of-the-art, ultramodern, up-to-date, up-to-the-minute
related words fashionable, happening, in, modish, nouvelle, now, stylish; last, latest; modernized, updated; futuristic, high-tech (*also* hi-tech); latter-day, recent
near antonyms anachronistic; aged, age-old, ancient, antediluvian, hoary, old, venerable; bygone, former, late, olden, past; antique, historic, historical; retro, retrograde; kaput (*also* kaputt), obsolete, outmoded, outworn, unmodernized; old-world; discarded, disused, moth-eaten; forgotten, remote; ageless, dateless, timeless
antonyms antiquated, archaic, dated, fusty, musty, old-fangled, old-fashioned, old-time, out-of-date, passé

modern *n* a person with very modern ideas ⟨the leaders of the American suffragists were originally regarded by many people as uppity *moderns* who should have stayed in their place⟩
synonyms modernist, ultramodernist
related words neophiliac; leftist, lefty, liberal, progressive; extremist, radical, reformer, reformist, revolutionary, revolutionist; bohemian
near antonyms conservative, rightist, right-winger, standpatter, Tory; old hand, old-timer, veteran; conformist, traditionalist; archconservative, Bourbon, diehard, neocon, neoconservative, paleoconservative; Colonel Blimp, square, stuffed shirt
antonyms antediluvian, dodo, fogy (*also* fogey), fossil, fuddy-duddy, reactionary, stick-in-the-mud

modernist *n* a person with very modern ideas ⟨a time when Paris was the center of the universe for *modernists* in the art world⟩ — see MODERN

modernistic *adj* being or involving the latest methods, concepts, information, or styles ⟨a trendy hotel with *modernistic* room lamps that required some figuring just to turn on⟩ — see MODERN

modernize *vb* to adapt to modern needs, taste, or usage ⟨a proposal to *modernize* the old school and bring it into the 21st century⟩
synonyms contemporize, streamline, update

related words recast, redesign, redevelop, redo, reengineer, refashion, remake, remodel, revamp, revise, rework

modest *adj* **1** being about midway between extremes of amount or size ⟨he was awarded a *modest* pension when he retired⟩ — see MIDDLE 2
2 free from any trace of the coarse or indecent ⟨tended to wear more *modest* swimsuits than the thong-clad guests at the resort⟩ — see CHASTE 1
3 not comfortable around people ⟨a *modest* winner who said a quick thank-you and promptly left the stage⟩ — see SHY 2
4 not having or showing any feelings of superiority, self-assertiveness, or showiness ⟨appealingly *modest* about her success in the fashion industry⟩ — see HUMBLE 1

modestly *adv* **1** in a manner showing no signs of pride or self-assertion ⟨spoke *modestly* about his accomplishments as an entrepreneur⟩ — see LOWLY
2 with purity of thought and deed ⟨dressed *modestly* to go to church⟩ — see PURELY 1

modesty *n* **1** the absence of any feelings of being better than others ⟨his natural *modesty* makes him reluctant to run for public office⟩ — see HUMILITY
2 the quality or state of being morally pure ⟨in this day and age, that's very becoming *modesty* in a teenager⟩ — see CHASTITY 1

modicum *n* the smallest amount or part imaginable ⟨only a *modicum* of skill is necessary to put the kit together⟩ — see JOT

modifiable *adj* capable of being readily changed ⟨architects designed the arena to be easily *modifiable* for staging a variety of events⟩ — see FLEXIBLE 1

modification *n* the act, process, or result of making different ⟨the rough draft needed only a few *modifications* before it was ready to hand in⟩ — see CHANGE 1

modify *vb* **1** to limit the meaning of (as a noun) ⟨adjectives are words that *modify* nouns, while adverbs can *modify* adjectives and verbs⟩ — see QUALIFY 1
2 to make different in some way ⟨he *modified* the appliance so that it would run more quietly⟩ — see CHANGE 1

modish *adj* **1** being in the latest or current fashion ⟨the strikingly *modish* gowns that actresses wear to award shows⟩ — see STYLISH
2 enjoying widespread favor or approval ⟨a *modish* chef who is currently the darling of the restaurant reviewers⟩ — see POPULAR 1

modishness *n* **1** the quality or state of being fashionable ⟨when it comes to clothes, she prefers modesty to *modishness*⟩ — see COOL 2
2 the state of enjoying widespread approval ⟨the *modishness* of that hairstyle is now so transparent that the really hip people have moved on to something else⟩ — see POPULARITY

moggy *also* **moggie** *n, British* a small domestic animal known for catching mice ⟨an unattached schoolteacher who lives in a London flat with a *moggy* as her only companion⟩ — see CAT 1

mogul *n* a person of rank, power, or influence in a particular field ⟨movie *moguls* promising to turn young actresses into stars⟩ — see MAGNATE

moiety *n* one of two equal or nearly equal parts ⟨the lot was split into two equal *moieties*⟩ — see HALF 1

moil *n* **1** a state of noisy, confused activity ⟨went for a retreat at the monastery for a temporary respite from the *moil* of the modern world⟩ — see COMMOTION
2 very hard or unpleasant work ⟨fed up with the *moil* and moneygrubbing of Wall Street, he decided to open a bed-and-breakfast in Vermont⟩ — see [1]TOIL

moil *vb* **1** to devote serious and sustained effort ⟨miners *moiling* all day in the sunless recesses of the earth⟩ — see LABOR
2 to be in a state of violent rolling motion ⟨the angry mob *moiled* around the courthouse⟩ — see SEETHE 1

moiling *adj* requiring considerable physical or mental effort ⟨the kind of *moiling* work that was done by unskilled laborers before the age of mechanization⟩ — see HARD 2

moist *adj* slightly or moderately wet ⟨luckily, my new suede shoes are only a bit *moist* after I accidentally wore them in the rain⟩
synonyms damp, dampish, dank, wettish
related words semimoist; dewy, misty; clammy; humid, muggy, sticky; sultry, summery, sweltering, torrid, tropical; awash, bathed, doused (*also* dowsed), drenched, dripping, saturate, saturated, soaked, soaking, sodden, soggy, sopping, soppy, soused, steeped, washed, watered, waterlogged, water-soaked
near antonyms arid, dry, waterless; baked, bone-dry, burned (*or* burnt), dehydrated, desert, droughty, dusty, parched, scorched, seared, sere (*also* sear), sunbaked; hyperarid, ultradry; waterproof, water-repellent, water-resistant, watertight

moisten *vb* to make or become slightly or moderately wet ⟨*moisten* the cloth before cleaning with it⟩
synonyms bedew, damp, dampen
related words bathe, lave; douse (*also* dowse), drench, impregnate, saturate, soak, souse, steep, wash, water, wet; humidify; dip, dunk, immerge, immerse; flush, irrigate, rinse, sluice; refresh, rehydrate, remoisten
near antonyms dehumidify, dehydrate, desiccate, parch, scorch, sear
antonyms dry

moistness *n* the amount of water suspended in the air in tiny droplets ⟨the *moistness* of the limestone caves creates an ideal environment for the ripening of Roquefort cheese⟩ — see MOISTURE

moisture *n* the amount of water suspended in the air in tiny droplets ⟨dew is really just *moisture* from the air that condenses and collects when the temperature drops at night⟩
synonyms damp, dampness, humidity, moistness
related words mugginess, stickiness, stuffiness; sultriness; clamminess, dankness, soddenness, sogginess, wetness
near antonyms aridity, dehumidification, dehydration, dryness

mojo *n* **1** something worn or kept to bring good luck or keep away evil ⟨a *mojo* is a type of voodoo charm⟩ — see CHARM 1
2 the power to control natural forces through supernatural means ⟨he joked that he had worked his *mojo* to assure a sunny day for the picnic⟩ — see MAGIC 1

moke *n, British slang* a sturdy and patient domestic mammal that is used especially to carry things ⟨scolded his assistant for having no more intelligence than a *moke*⟩ — see DONKEY 1

mold *n* the loose surface material in which plants naturally grow ⟨*mold* so rich that just about anything will grow in it⟩ — see DIRT 1

mold *vb* to go through decomposition ⟨plants *molding* in the abandoned garden⟩ — see DECAY 1

moldable *adj* capable of being easily molded or modeled ⟨as the clay dries out, it becomes less and less *moldable*⟩ — see PLASTIC 1

molder *vb* to go through decomposition ⟨leaves *moldering* in the compost pile⟩ — see DECAY 1

mole *n* a person who tries secretly to obtain information for one country in the territory of another usually unfriendly country ⟨for years we have had a *mole* in the enemy's national intelligence agency⟩ — see SPY

molecule *n* a very small piece ⟨not a *molecule* of sense in that girl⟩ — see BIT 1

mollify *vb* **1** to lessen the anger or agitation of ⟨an apology would probably *mollify* your friend⟩ — see PACIFY 1

2 to make more bearable or less severe ⟨a friendly gesture that did a lot to *mollify* their suspicions about the new neighbor⟩ — see HELP 2

mollifying *adj* tending to lessen or avoid conflict or hostility ⟨a future son-in-law using *mollifying* flattery to overcome a bad first impression⟩ — see PACIFIC 1

mollycoddle *vb* to treat with great or excessive care ⟨refused to *mollycoddle* her malingering son and sent him off to school⟩ — see BABY

molt *vb* to cast (a natural bodily covering or appendage) aside ⟨a crab *molts* its shell as it grows larger⟩ — see SHED 1

mom *n* a female human parent ⟨be sure to tell your *mom* and dad that you'll be home late for supper⟩ — see MOTHER

mome *n, archaic* a stupid person ⟨he's a *mome*, but a harmless fellow for all of that⟩ — see IDIOT

moment *n* **1** a particular point at which an event takes place ⟨at that *moment* he suddenly turned around and headed toward me⟩ — see OCCASION 1

2 the quality or state of being important ⟨an event of great *moment*⟩ — see IMPORTANCE

3 a very small space of time ⟨I'll be there in just a *moment*⟩ — see INSTANT

4 the time currently existing or in progress ⟨I'm not doing anything at the *moment*⟩ — see [1]PRESENT

momentarily *adv* at or within a short time ⟨we'll be finished *momentarily*⟩ — see SHORTLY 2

momentariness *n* the state or quality of lasting only for a short time ⟨the *momentariness* of the pain from the needle prick hardly compares to the lasting good feelings that a blood donor experiences⟩ — see IMPERMANENCE

momentary *adj* lasting only for a short time ⟨the pain of the flu shot was only *momentary*⟩

synonyms brief, deciduous, ephemeral, evanescent, flash, fleeting, fugacious, fugitive, impermanent, passing, short-lived, temporary, transient, transitory

related words little, short, shortish; acting, interim, provisional, short-term

near antonyms lifelong; continuing, durable, persistent; imperishable, indefectible, indestructible

antonyms ceaseless, dateless, deathless, endless, enduring, eternal, everlasting, immortal, lasting, long-lived, permanent, perpetual, timeless, undying, unending

momentous *adj* having great meaning or lasting effect ⟨a *momentous* occasion that will go down in the history books⟩ — see IMPORTANT 1

momentousness *n* the quality or state of being important ⟨no one could fail to realize the *momentousness* of the occasion⟩ — see IMPORTANCE

momentum *n* something that arouses action or activity ⟨the former president's endorsement was all the *momentum* the campaign needed⟩ — see IMPULSE 1

mommy *n* a female human parent ⟨the little boy cried for his *mommy*⟩ — see MOTHER

monarch *n* **1** one who rules over a people with a sole, supreme, and usually hereditary authority ⟨the ruling *monarch* of Britain at that time was Queen Elizabeth I⟩

synonyms autocrat, potentate, ruler, sovereign (*also* sovran)

related words coruler; Caesar, czar (*also* tsar *or* tzar), emir (*or* amir *also* ameer), emperor, empress, kaiser, khan, khedive, king, lord, mikado, mogul, prince, queen, satrap, shah, sultan, suzerain; authoritarian, Big Brother, despot, dictator, führer (*or* fuehrer), monocrat, overlord, paramount, tyrant

2 a person of rank, power, or influence in a particular field ⟨the glitzy gala was attended by most of the reigning *monarchs* of the recording industry⟩ — see MAGNATE

monarchal *or* **monarchial** *adj* fit for or worthy of a royal ruler ⟨a singing superstar with a *monarchal* haughtiness that drives her assistants crazy⟩ — see MONARCHICAL

monarchical *also* **monarchic** *adj* fit for or worthy of a royal ruler ⟨guests who stay in the hotel's most expensive suite live in *monarchical* splendor⟩

synonyms kingly, monarchal (*or* monarchial), princely, queenly, regal, royal

related words aristocratic, baronial, imperial, lordly, noble, patrician; grandiose, heroic (*also* heroical), imposing, magnificent, majestic, monumental, splendid, stately

monastery *n* a residence for men under religious vows ⟨Gregory Mendel worked out his concepts of genetics by doing breeding experiments using pea plants in the *monastery's* garden⟩

synonyms abbey, cloister, friary, hermitage, priory

related words house; convent, nunnery; lamasery

monetary *adj* of or relating to money, banking, or investments ⟨an economist who is critical of this administration's *monetary* policies⟩ — see FINANCIAL

money *n* **1** something (as pieces of stamped metal or printed paper) customarily and legally used as a medium of exchange, a measure of value, or a means of payment ⟨are you sure you have enough *money* to buy all that?⟩

synonyms bread [*slang*], bucks, cabbage [*slang*], cash, change, chips, coin, currency, dough, gold, green, jack [*slang*], kale [*slang*], legal tender, lolly [*British*], long green [*slang*], loot, lucre, moola (*or* moolah) [*slang*], needful, pelf, scratch [*slang*], shekels (*also* sheqels *or* shekelim *or* shekalim *or* sheqalim), tender, wampum

related words coinage, specie; dead presidents [*slang*], folding money, paper money, scrip; banknote, cashier's check, check, draft, money order, note, promissory note; bill, dollar, greenback; bankroll, capital, finances, funds, roll [*slang*], wad, wallet; chump change, dibs [*slang*], dime, mite, peanuts, pittance, shoestring; big bucks, bomb [*British*], boodle, bundle, earth, fortune, king's ransom, megabucks, mint, packet [*chiefly British*], pile, pot; abundance, means, opulence, riches, treasure, wealth; resources, wherewithal; mad money, petty cash, pin money, pocket money, spending money

2 a wealthy person ⟨she had always planned to marry *money*⟩ — see CAPITALIST

moneybags *n pl* a wealthy person ⟨the old *moneybags* was used to being deferred to by his fellow townspeople⟩ — see CAPITALIST

moneyed *also* **monied** *adj* having goods, property, or money in abundance ⟨luxury goods that are purchased mainly by *moneyed* tourists from abroad⟩— see RICH 1

moneygrubbing *adj* having or marked by an eager and often selfish desire especially for material possessions ⟨works two jobs to satisfy his *moneygrubbing* wife⟩ — see GREEDY 1

moneymaking *adj* yielding a profit ⟨a celebrity chef with a *moneymaking* line of cookware⟩ — see PROFITABLE 1

money–spinning *adj, chiefly British* yielding a profit ⟨turning his stately ancestral home into a tourist attraction proved to be a *money-spinning* venture for the earl⟩ — see PROFITABLE 1

mongrel *adj* being offspring produced by parents of different races, breeds, species, or genera ⟨a *mongrel* dog⟩ — see MIXED 1

mongrel *n* an offspring of parents with different genes especially when of different races, breeds, species, or genera ⟨*mongrels* often suffer fewer health problems than purebreds⟩ — see HYBRID

moniker *also* **monicker** *n* **1** a descriptive or familiar name given instead of or in addition to the one belonging to an individual ⟨seeing as no respectable rodeo performer could possibly be known as Leslie, a suitably masculine *moniker* was created for him⟩ — see NICKNAME
2 a word or combination of words by which a person or thing is regularly known ⟨"Cornelius Jedidiah Beauregard" is his rather unwieldy *moniker*⟩ — see NAME 1

monitor *vb* to pay continued close attention to (something) for a particular purpose ⟨police regularly *monitor* that road to record traffic density and to catch speeders⟩
synonyms cover, watch
related words surveil; eye; behold, espy, look, note, notice, observe, regard, see, sight, spy, view, witness; gape, gawk, gaze, glare, goggle, peer, rubberneck, stare; glance, glimpse, peek, peep
phrases keep an eye on

monitory *adj* serving as or offering a warning ⟨historically natural disasters have often been interpreted by some as punitive or *monitory* measures against sin-ridden humanity⟩ — see CAUTIONARY

monkey *n* **1** a physiological need for certain drugs ⟨I've got this *monkey* on my back, and going to detox is the only way to get it off⟩ — see ADDICTION
2 an appealingly mischievous person ⟨come back here, you little *monkey*!⟩ — see SCAMP 1

monkey (around) *vb* **1** to engage in attention-getting playful or boisterous behavior ⟨stop *monkeying around* in the house or you'll break something⟩ — see CUT UP
2 to spend time in aimless activity ⟨would rather just *monkey around* instead of doing work⟩ — see FIDDLE (AROUND)

monkey (with) *vb* to handle thoughtlessly, ignorantly, or mischievously ⟨don't *monkey with* that broken lawnmower⟩ — see TAMPER (WITH)

monkey business *n* wildly playful or mischievous behavior ⟨the new nanny will not tolerate such *monkey business* from her charges⟩ — see HORSEPLAY

monkeying *n* wildly playful or mischievous behavior ⟨all that *monkeying* was sure to end in someone or something getting hurt⟩ — see HORSEPLAY

monkeyshine *n* **1** *usually* **monkeyshines** *pl* wildly playful or mischievous behavior ⟨hockey players who are known for their *monkeyshines* on and off the ice⟩ — see HORSEPLAY
2 *usually* **monkeyshines** *pl* a playful or mischievous act intended as a joke ⟨on the alert for paleontological *monkeyshines* ever since the unmasking of Piltdown man⟩ — see PRANK

monochromatic *adj* **1** having or consisting of a single color ⟨although marble and bronze sculptures are *monochromatic*, they can be amazingly lifelike⟩
synonyms monochrome, monochromic, self, self-colored, solid
related words achromatic, neutral
near antonyms dappled (*also* dapple), marbled, shaded; mottled, parti-color (*or* parti-colored), piebald, pied, pinto, skewbald; banded, barred, brindled (*or* brindle), streaked, striated; checkered, dotted, patterned, plaid, striped; flecked, specked, speckled, spotted; bichrome, bicolored (*or* bicolor), dichromatic, trichromatic, tricolor (*or* tricolored), two-tone
antonyms chromatic, colorful, kaleidoscopic, motley, multicolored, polychromatic, polychrome, rainbow, varicolored, varied, variegated
2 causing weariness, restlessness, or lack of interest ⟨a *monochromatic* portrayal of a hero seemingly without flaws or even distinctive traits⟩ — see BORING

monochrome *adj* having or consisting of a single color ⟨an artist who produces *monochrome* pencil drawings⟩ — see MONOCHROMATIC 1

monochromic *adj* having or consisting of a single color ⟨dull, *monochromic* decor⟩ — see MONOCHROMATIC 1

monocratic *adj* exercising power or authority without interference by others ⟨as the newspaper's *monocratic* publisher, he simply did not tolerate any dissent from his policies and decrees⟩ — see ABSOLUTE 1

monopolize *vb* to have complete control over ⟨it is illegal in the United States to *monopolize* an entire industry⟩ ⟨you shouldn't *monopolize* the exercise equipment while others are waiting to use it⟩
synonyms sew up
related words bogart, corner, hog; absorb, consume, engross; have, hold, own, possess; command, control, direct, govern, manage, reign (over), rule

monosyllabic *adj* marked by the use of few words to convey much information or meaning ⟨the sullen teenager would give only a *monosyllabic* response to even the friendliest question⟩ — see CONCISE

monotone *n* a tedious lack of variety ⟨there's a *monotone* to the landscape in that part of the state: uniformly flat land in all directions, for as far as the eye can see⟩ — see MONOTONY

monotonous *adj* causing weariness, restlessness, or lack of interest ⟨the lecturer's *monotonous* delivery threatened to put us to sleep⟩ — see BORING

monotonousness *n* a tedious lack of variety ⟨detested the mind-numbing *monotonousness* of the task but knew that it had to be done⟩ — see MONOTONY

monotony *n* a tedious lack of variety ⟨the *monotony* of the cafeteria's selections was as bad as the quality⟩
synonyms humdrum, monotone, monotonousness, sameness
related words uniformity; blahs, boredom, drabness, dullness (*also* dulness), ennui, restlessness, tediousness, tedium, tiresomeness, weariness, wearisomeness
near antonyms diversity, multiplicity, variety; variability, variation; absorption, engagement, engrossment, enthrallment, fascination, grip, interest, intrigue, involvement; animation, enlivenment, excitement, invigoration, stimulation

monster *adj* unusually large ⟨a *monster* truck competition⟩ — see HUGE

monster *n* **1** a strange or horrible and often frightening creature ⟨both children insisted that their parents check under the bed for *monsters* every night⟩
synonyms grotesque, grotesquerie (*also* grotesquery), monstrosity, ogre
related words ogress; Frankenstein; bête noire, bogey (*also* bogie *or* bogy), bugaboo, bugbear; banshee, bogeyman (*also* bogyman), demon (*or* daemon), devil, fiend, fright, imp, incubus; horror, terror; abomination, anathema; abnormality, freak; mutant, mutation
2 a person, thing, or event that is far from normal ⟨the gardener destroyed all of the *monsters* that mutated from his tomato plants⟩ — see FREAK 1
3 a mean, evil, or unprincipled person ⟨the guards at the concentration camps were *monsters* who enjoyed seeing their victims suffer⟩ — see VILLAIN 1
4 something large of its kind ⟨a *monster* of a sandwich that could easily feed two hearty eaters⟩ — see GIANT

monstrosity *n* **1** a person, thing, or event that is far from normal ⟨any *monstrosities* born to the farm animals were sent to the agricultural college for study⟩ — see FREAK 1
2 a strange or horrible and often frightening creature ⟨filled the haunted house with all sorts of spooks and mechanical *monstrosities*⟩ — see MONSTER 1
3 something unpleasant to look at ⟨we were glad when the city tore down that *monstrosity* that used to stand across from the park⟩ — see EYESORE

4 the quality of inspiring intense dread or dismay ⟨the *monstrosity* of the famine can scarcely be conveyed to those who have not witnessed it in person⟩ — see HORROR 1

5 the state or quality of being utterly evil ⟨the *monstrosity* of the terrorists' actions shocked the entire civilized world⟩ — see ENORMITY 1

monstrous *adj* **1** badly or imperfectly formed ⟨a *monstrous* melon that was clearly not fit to eat⟩ — see MALFORMED

2 extremely disturbing or repellent ⟨the *monstrous* measures taken by the dictator against anyone who opposed his regime⟩ — see HORRIBLE 1

3 unusually large ⟨a *monstrous* tomato as big as a basketball⟩ — see HUGE

4 unpleasant to look at ⟨some *monstrous* high-rises have begun to spoil that lovely residential neighborhood⟩ — see UGLY 1

monstrous *adv, chiefly dialect* to a great degree ⟨a *monstrous* pretty gal, she was⟩ — see VERY 1

monstrously *adv* **1** beyond a normal or acceptable limit ⟨our team wasn't merely bad—we were *monstrously* inept⟩ — see TOO 1

2 to a large extent or degree ⟨a *monstrously* expensive movie that nearly bankrupted the studio⟩ — see GREATLY 2

montage *n* an unorganized collection or mixture of various things ⟨my memories of the childhood trip are a *montage* of the sights, smells, and sounds of India⟩ — see MISCELLANY 1

Montezuma's revenge *n* abnormally frequent intestinal evacuations with more or less fluid stools ⟨the one person in the tour group who didn't drink the water was spared *Montezuma's revenge*⟩ — see DIARRHEA

monthlies *n pl* an occurrence of menstruating ⟨she couldn't go swimming because of her *monthlies*⟩ — see PERIOD 1

months *n pl* a long or seemingly long period of time ⟨that meeting lasted for *months*⟩ — see AGE 2

monument *n* **1** a shaped stone laid over or erected near a grave and usually bearing an inscription to identify and preserve the memory of the deceased ⟨the Quakers disapproved of *monuments*, regarding them as idolatrous, so thousands of Nantucketers spend their eternal rest in complete anonymity⟩ — see TOMBSTONE

2 something that serves to keep alive the memory of a person or event ⟨a moving *monument* to the great war and a tribute to the untold millions who died in it⟩ — see MEMORIAL

monumental *adj* **1** large and impressive in size, grandeur, extent, or conception ⟨a *monumental* misunderstanding that had far-reaching consequences⟩ — see GRAND 1

2 unusually large ⟨serves a *monumental* sundae that usually requires three people to finish it⟩ — see HUGE

3 having great meaning or lasting effect ⟨the moon landing was seen as a *monumental* event in human history⟩ — see IMPORTANT 1

monumentalize *vb* to be a memorial of ⟨adding to the appeal of the Taj Mahal is the fact that it *monumentalizes* one man's undying love for his wife⟩ — see COMMEMORATE 1

monumentally *adv* to a large extent or degree ⟨your parents will be *monumentally* disappointed if you don't go to college⟩ — see GREATLY 2

mooch *vb* **1** to live by relying on someone else's generosity or hospitality without sharing in the cost or responsibility ⟨he's always *mooching* off of his friends, even though he can easily pay his own way⟩ — see FREELOAD

2 to move about in a sly or secret manner ⟨I suspect she's *mooching* around in the background and keeping an eye on us⟩ — see SNEAK 1

3 to move about from place to place aimlessly ⟨kids on vacation *mooching* about the house and looking for something to do⟩ — see WANDER 1

moocher *n* a person who is supported by or seeks support from another without making an adequate return ⟨unfortunately, too many people at the community potluck were *moochers* who didn't bring any food of their own⟩ — see LEECH

mood *n* **1** a state of mind dominated by a particular emotion ⟨losing my favorite sweater left me in a bad *mood* for the rest of the day⟩

synonyms cheer, feather, humor, mode, spirit, temper

related words angle, attitude, mind-set, outlook, perspective, slant, standpoint, viewpoint; emotion, feeling, heart, passion, sentiment; strain; belief, conviction, judgment (*or* judgement), mind, opinion; expression, tone, vein; character, disposition, identity, individuality, makeup, mettle, personality, selfhood, self-identity, temper, temperament; responsiveness, sensibility, sensitiveness, sensitivity

phrases frame of mind

2 a special quality or impression associated with something ⟨there's a haunting *mood* of melancholy about the ruined old castle⟩ — see AURA 1

3 *archaic* an intense emotional state of displeasure with someone or something ⟨in his *mood*, the king spared no one his venomous tongue⟩ — see ANGER

moody *adj* frequently influenced by moods and especially bad moods ⟨teenagers are often both *moody* and changeable⟩

synonyms temperamental

related words capricious, changeable, changeful, fickle, fluctuating, fluid, freakish, impulsive, inconstant, mercurial, mutable, uncertain, unsettled, unstable, unsteady, variable, volatile, whimsical; pouty, sulky; choleric, crabby, cranky, cross, crotchety, grouchy, grumpy, irascible, irritable, peevish, petulant, quick-tempered, short-tempered, snappish, snippety, snippy, testy, waspish

near antonyms equable, even; immutable, inflexible, invariable, unalterable, unchangeable; changeless, constant, settled, stable, steady, unchanging

moola *or* **moolah** *n, slang* something (as pieces of stamped metal or printed paper) customarily and legally used as a medium of exchange, a measure of value, or a means of payment ⟨we dropped some serious *moola* on that home theater system⟩ — see MONEY 1

moon *n* a long or seemingly long period of time ⟨we've been planning this big event for many *moons*⟩ — see AGE 2

mooncalf *n* a person who lacks good sense or judgment ⟨he was a helpless *mooncalf* when it came to making decisions about even the most trivial things⟩ — see FOOL 1

moonshine *n* **1** illegally produced liquor ⟨during Prohibition, *moonshine* and "bathtub gin" were made secretly⟩

synonyms bootleg, mountain dew, white lightning

related words bathtub gin, red-eye, rotgut; alcohol, ardent spirits, booze, drink, firewater, grog, hooch [*slang*], John Barleycorn, juice [*slang*], potable, rum, spirits, strong drink, tipple

2 a distilled beverage that can make a person drunk ⟨serving all sorts of *moonshine* at the bar⟩ — see ALCOHOL

3 language, behavior, or ideas that are absurd and contrary to good sense ⟨a book about the so-called good old days that's sentimental *moonshine*⟩ — see NONSENSE 1

moonstruck *adj* having or showing a very abnormal or sick state of mind ⟨police asked psychiatrists to put together a portrait of the *moonstruck* marksman who was responsible for the shootings⟩ — see INSANE 1

moor *n* **1** a broad area of level or rolling treeless country ⟨as she wanders the windswept *moor*, the novel's heroine vows that she will never marry the vicar⟩ — see PLAIN 1

2 spongy land saturated or partially covered with water ⟨a mysterious figure who was said to have haunted the *moors* of southwest England⟩ — see SWAMP 1

moor *vb* to put securely in place or in a desired position ⟨*moored* the boat to the dock⟩ — see FASTEN 2

moot *adj* open to question or dispute ⟨it's a *moot* question what might have happened if the American colonies had not broken away from Great Britain⟩ — see DEBATABLE 1

moot *vb* **1** to present or bring forward for discussion ⟨conservatives had shouted down the proposal when it was first *mooted*⟩ — see INTRODUCE 2

2 to talk about (an issue) usually from various points of view and for the purpose of arriving at a decision or opinion ⟨the issue of whether a person's nature or upbringing is more important continues to be *mooted* by experts and laymen alike⟩ — see DISCUSS

mope *vb* **1** to move or act slowly ⟨we were in a rush, and the Sunday driver in front of us was just *moping* along⟩ — see DELAY 1

2 to silently go about in a bad mood ⟨she's been *moping* all weekend because her boyfriend hasn't called even once⟩ — see SULK

mopes *n pl* a state or spell of low spirits ⟨he's got the *mopes* because his girlfriend is mad at him⟩ — see SADNESS

mopey *adj* given to or displaying a resentful silence and often irritability ⟨I don't know what's made him all *mopey*, but he's getting hard to live with⟩ — see SULKY

moppet *n* a young person who is between infancy and adulthood ⟨a host of adorable *moppets* were hired for the ad campaign⟩ — see CHILD 1

mop–up *n* the last part of a process or action ⟨the general announced that the remaining fighting would be only a *mop-up* to a war that was all but over⟩ — see FINALE

moral *adj* **1** conforming to a high standard of morality or virtue ⟨the kind of *moral* behavior that is expected of everyone in the parish's youth organization⟩ — see GOOD 2

2 guided by or in accordance with one's sense of right and wrong ⟨a *moral* decision to refrain from sexual relations until after marriage⟩ — see CONSCIENTIOUS 1

moralism *n* a tendency to care a great deal about seemly behavior and morals especially in sexual matters ⟨the *moralism* that the candidate displays on the campaign trail is in stark contrast to his rumored sexual indiscretions off the stump⟩ — see PRUDERY

moralist *n* a person who is greatly concerned with seemly behavior and morality especially regarding sexual matters ⟨a smattering of *moralists* around the country tried to get the songs banned from the radio⟩ — see PRUDE

moralistic *adj* marked by or given to preaching moral values ⟨parental opinion was divided on the school's *moralistic* curriculum⟩ — see SERMONIC

morality *n* **1** conduct that conforms to an accepted standard of right and wrong ⟨given his reputation for unswerving *morality*, scandal of any kind would wreck his political career⟩
synonyms character, decency, goodness, honesty, integrity, probity, rectitude, righteousness, rightness, uprightness, virtue, virtuousness
related words high-mindedness, honor, incorruptibility, irreproachability, irreproachableness, right-mindedness, scrupulosity, scrupulousness; appropriateness, correctness, decorousness, decorum, etiquette, fitness, propriety, seemliness; ethics, morals
near antonyms impropriety, indecency, indecorum, indiscretion; debauchery, degeneracy, degradation, depravity, perversion, pervertedness, sinfulness; crookedness, dishonesty, underhandedness, unscrupulousness; lowness, meanness, viciousness, vileness; corruption
antonyms badness, evil, evildoing, immorality, iniquity, sin, villainy, wickedness

2 the code of good conduct for an individual or group ⟨the *morality* that members of the Mafia are expected to adhere to—or suffer the consequences⟩ — see ETHICS

moralizing *adj* marked by or given to preaching moral values ⟨I found the novel's *moralizing* tone a bit much for beach reading⟩ — see SERMONIC

morally *adv* with purity of thought and deed ⟨a politician who is in the habit of acting legally without behaving *morally*⟩ — see PURELY 1

morals *n pl* the code of good conduct for an individual or group ⟨at issue were the doctor's professional ethics, not her private *morals*⟩ — see ETHICS

morass *n* **1** something that catches and holds ⟨advised against becoming involved in that country's civil war, warning that escape from that *morass* might prove nigh impossible⟩ — see WEB 1

2 spongy land saturated or partially covered with water ⟨the distracted driver had driven his car off the road and into a *morass*⟩ — see SWAMP 1

moratorium *n* a state of temporary inactivity ⟨the director of the blood bank called for a *moratorium* in donations until the surplus could be used up⟩ — see ABEYANCE

morbid *adj* causing or marked by an atmosphere lacking in cheer ⟨a pessimist who is given to *morbid* introspection and thoughts of death⟩ — see GLOOMY 1

mordancy *n* biting sharpness of feeling or expression ⟨the surprising *mordancy* with which the two physicians contested each other's claim to having discovered an effective vaccine for polio⟩ — see ACRIMONY 1

mordant *adj* marked by the use of wit that is intended to cause hurt feelings ⟨a *mordant* review of the movie that compared it to having one's teeth pulled for two hours⟩ — see SARCASTIC

more *adj* resulting in an increase in amount or number ⟨bought *more* apples in order to make a bigger pie⟩ — see ADDITIONAL

more *adv* **1** in addition to what has been said ⟨the sci-fi movie was totally unbelievable and, what's *more*, it was boring⟩
synonyms additionally, again, also, besides, either, further, furthermore, likewise, moreover, then, too, withal, yet
phrases as well, for good measure, in addition to, into the bargain (*also* in the bargain), on top of, to boot, what's more

2 to a greater or higher extent ⟨the boxers for this bout are *more* evenly matched than the last two were⟩
synonyms better

more *n* something added (as by growth) ⟨add a little *more* to the mixture⟩ — see INCREASE 1

more or less *adv* **1** very close to but not completely ⟨the lot is 16 acres *more or less*⟩ — see ALMOST

2 to some degree or extent ⟨most couples in the survey said that they were *more or less* happy in their marriage⟩ — see FAIRLY 1

3 close to but not exactly ⟨the box weighs 60 pounds *more or less*⟩ — see APPROXIMATELY

moreover *adv* in addition to what has been said ⟨swimming alone is against the rules and, *moreover*, it's dangerous⟩ — see MORE 1

mores *n pl* personal conduct or behavior as evaluated by an accepted standard of appropriateness for a social or professional setting ⟨the *mores* of academic life as opposed to those of the business world⟩ — see MANNER 1

moribund *adj* **1** nearly dead ⟨with its run-down look and empty aisles, the grocery store appeared *moribund*⟩
synonyms dying
related words expiring, fading, passing away, sinking; decadent, declining, deteriorating; dead, deceased, defunct, demised, departed, fallen, gone, lifeless, passed away; terminal
phrases at death's door
near antonyms alive, animate, live, living, quick; being, breathing, existing, subsisting, surviving; booming, flourishing, prospering, roaring, thriving; animated, bouncing, energetic, frisky, jazzy, lively, peppy, perky, spirited, sprightful, sprightly, springy, vital, vivacious, zippy
2 having passed its time of use or usefulness ⟨youngsters snickering at the *moribund* slang their parents were using⟩ — see OBSOLETE

morn *n* **1** the first appearance of light in the morning or the time of its appearance ⟨my herald of the *morn* is my cat, sticking his paw in my face to wake me up⟩ — see DAWN 1
2 the time from sunrise until noon ⟨so, how are you this lovely *morn*?⟩ — see MORNING 1

morning *n* **1** the time from sunrise until noon ⟨after working in the fields all *morning*, we were ready for a hearty lunch⟩
synonyms forenoon, morn
related words aurora, dawn, dawning, daybreak, daylight; cockcrow, sunrise, sunup; day, daytime, light
near antonyms dark, darkness, night, nighttime, twilight; dusk, evening, nightfall, sundown, sunset; afternoon
2 the first appearance of light in the morning or the time of its appearance ⟨*morning* has broken⟩ — see DAWN 1
3 the point at which something begins ⟨the period when people in ancient Mesopotamia began living in cities is usually regarded as the *morning* of civilization⟩ — see BEGINNING

moron *n* a stupid person ⟨some *moron* forgot to lock the doors before going home⟩ — see IDIOT

morose *adj* causing or marked by an atmosphere lacking in cheer ⟨those *morose* job seekers who have grown accustomed to rejection⟩ — see GLOOMY 1

morsel *n* **1** a small piece or quantity of food ⟨the chef's cuisine is so good that diners will want to savor every *morsel*⟩
synonyms bite, mouthful, nibble, nugget, taste, tidbit (*also* titbit)
related words collop, medallion, noisette; nosh, snack; appetizer, canapé, hors d'oeuvre; bit, chew, crumb, dab, dribble, driblet, fleck, hint, mote, nubbin, particle, pinch, scrap, scruple, shred, smidgen (*also* smidgeon *or* smidgin *or* smidge), snip, snippet, speck, spot, sprinkling, suspicion, tittle, touch, trace; dash, drop; lap, lick; gulp, swallow, swig
2 a very small piece ⟨searching for any *morsel* of useful information⟩ — see BIT 1
3 a person of no importance or influence ⟨a *morsel* like her wouldn't last a week in the rough-and-tumble world of Wall Street⟩ — see NOBODY

mortal *adj* **1** likely to cause or capable of causing death ⟨a *mortal* wound⟩ — see DEADLY 1
2 of, relating to, or suggestive of death ⟨a wounded soldier writhing in *mortal* agony⟩ — see DEATHLY 1
3 relating to or characteristic of human beings ⟨just an ordinary guy with all the usual *mortal* limitations⟩ — see HUMAN
4 marked by opposition or ill will ⟨have always had a *mortal* aversion to narcissistic people⟩ — see HOSTILE 1

mortal *n* a member of the human race ⟨just an ordinary *mortal* living an ordinary life⟩ — see HUMAN

mortally *adv* to a great degree ⟨I'm *mortally* certain that I've seen that guy before⟩ — see VERY 1

mortgage *vb* to obligate by prior agreement ⟨I've *mortgaged* all my free time this week to the hospice and won't be able to come to the party⟩ — see PLEDGE 1

mortician *n* a person who manages funerals and prepares the dead for burial or cremation ⟨the *mortician* will take care of all of the arrangements for the funeral⟩ — see FUNERAL DIRECTOR

mortification *n* the emotional state of being made self-consciously uncomfortable ⟨the *mortification* of being dumped the night before the prom⟩ — see EMBARRASSMENT 1

mortify *vb* to throw into a state of self-conscious distress ⟨was *mortified* by her children's atrocious manners⟩ — see EMBARRASS 1

mortuary *adj* of, relating to, or suggestive of death ⟨the huge department store's *mortuary* atmosphere in its sad, last weeks of operation⟩ — see DEATHLY 1

mossback *n* a person with old-fashioned ideas ⟨those *mossbacks* at the intelligence agency didn't get the memo that the world had changed⟩ — see FOGY

mossbacked *adj* tending to favor established ideas, conditions, or institutions ⟨the restaurant's *mossbacked* owner refuses to bow to contemporary casualness and relax his dress code⟩ — see CONSERVATIVE 1

mossy *adj* having passed its time of use or usefulness ⟨*mossy* rules of etiquette that date from the Victorian era⟩ — see OBSOLETE

[1]**most** *adv* to a great degree ⟨a *most* careful driver, especially in bad weather⟩ — see VERY 1

[2]**most** *adv* very close to but not completely ⟨the cost of *most* everything is higher nowadays⟩ — see ALMOST

most *adj* of the greatest or highest degree or quantity ⟨the player with the *most* ability on the tennis team⟩ — see ULTIMATE 1

most *n* the greatest amount, number, or part ⟨this room will accommodate 50 people at the *most*⟩
synonyms max, maximum, outside
related words best, ultimate, utmost; extreme
antonyms least, minimum

mostly *adv* for the most part ⟨the weather this month has been *mostly* mild⟩ — see CHIEFLY

mote *n* a very small piece ⟨there's not a *mote* of dirt in that woman's house⟩ — see BIT 1

moth–eaten *adj* **1** having passed its time of use or usefulness ⟨*moth-eaten* scientific theories that no one's believed in ages⟩ — see OBSOLETE
2 showing signs of advanced wear and tear and neglect ⟨a man who's been wearing the same *moth-eaten* clothes for decades⟩ — see SHABBY 1
3 used or heard so often as to be dull ⟨an uncle who tells the same *moth-eaten* stories every Thanksgiving⟩ — see STALE 1

mother *adj* of, relating to, or characteristic of a mother ⟨she often offered to babysit for friends, hoping to satisfy her *mother* urges until she had children of her own⟩ — see MOTHERLY

mother *n* a female human parent ⟨he dreaded telling his *mother* that her favorite figurine had gotten broken⟩
synonyms ma, mama (*also* mamma *or* momma), mammy, mater [*chiefly British*], mom, mommy, old lady
related words materfamilias, matriarch, matron; stepmother; supermom, superwoman

mother *vb* **1** to bring forth from the womb ⟨I hope to

mother at least one child⟩ — see BEAR 1
2 to attend to the needs and comforts of ⟨*mothered* the patients with chicken soup⟩ — see NURSE 1

mother country *n* **1** a place of origin ⟨Greece can boast to being the *mother country* of democracy⟩ — see BIRTHPLACE
2 the land of one's birth, residence, or citizenship ⟨even after decades of living in their adopted nation, they maintained a strong attachment to the *mother country*⟩ — see COUNTRY 1

motherland *n* **1** a place of origin ⟨for many oenophiles, France remains the *motherland* of fine wines⟩ — see BIRTHPLACE
2 the land of one's birth, residence, or citizenship ⟨all his life he longed to return to his *motherland*⟩ — see COUNTRY 1

motherliness *n* motherly character or qualities ⟨he cherished his foster parent for her *motherliness*⟩ — see MATERNITY

mother lode *n* an abundant source ⟨the university has long been a *mother lode* of athletic talent, with many alumni joining the rarefied ranks of the professionals⟩ — see MINE 1

motherly *adj* of, relating to, or characteristic of a mother ⟨she showed a sweet *motherly* tenderness toward the tiny kitten she was taking care of⟩
synonyms maternal, mother
related words parental; female, feminine, womanish, womanlike, womanly; matriarchal, matronly; caring, giving, nurturing

mother-naked *adj* lacking or shed of clothing ⟨shocked to find that many of the participants at the spring break bacchanal were *mother-naked*⟩ — see NAKED 1

mother tongue *n* the stock of words, pronunciation, and grammar used by a people as their basic means of communication ⟨although the anthropologist could speak the local language fairly well, she was always glad to find someone who shared her *mother tongue*⟩ — see LANGUAGE 1

motif *n* **1** a major object of interest or concern (as in a discussion or artistic composition) ⟨the *motif* of mute figures standing in lonely isolation is a recurrent one in the artist's works⟩ — see MATTER 1
2 a unit of decoration that is repeated all over something (as a fabric) ⟨the fabric for the upholstery features a scallop shell *motif*⟩ — see PATTERN 1

motion *n* the act or an instance of changing position ⟨we were instructed not to make any sudden *motions* or we might scare away the deer⟩ — see MOVEMENT 1

motion *vb* to direct or notify by a movement or gesture ⟨the referee *motioned* the team captains to confer with him on the sideline⟩
synonyms beckon, flag, gesture, signal, wave
related words nod; gesticulate, mime, pantomime, sign; signalize; acquaint, advise, inform, relate, tell; flourish, shrug

motionlessly *adv* without motion ⟨could sit *motionlessly* for hours⟩ — see STILL 1

motion picture *n* **1** a story told by means of a series of continuously projected pictures and a sound track ⟨a popular novel that was made into a major *motion picture*⟩ — see MOVIE 1
2 motion pictures *pl* the art or business of making a movie ⟨to the industrialist, producing *motion pictures* seemed a lot more glamorous than manufacturing synthetics⟩ — see MOVIE 2

motivation *n* something that arouses action or activity ⟨fear of failing should be plenty of *motivation* to study for the test⟩ — see IMPULSE 1

motive *n* **1** a major object of interest or concern (as in a discussion or artistic composition) ⟨the principal *motive* of the piece was introduced in the flute section⟩ — see MATTER 1
2 a unit of decoration that is repeated all over something (as a fabric) ⟨decorated with a paisley *motive*⟩ — see PATTERN 1
3 something (as a belief) that serves as the basis for another thing ⟨the detective felt that the first suspect didn't have any *motive* for committing the crime⟩ — see REASON 2

motley *adj* **1** consisting of many things of different sorts ⟨a ship with a *motley* crew of old salts, young adventurers, and shifty characters of all ages⟩ — see MISCELLANEOUS
2 marked by a variety of usually vivid colors ⟨a tropical bird with *motley* plumage⟩ — see COLORFUL

motley *n* **1** a person formerly kept in a royal or noble household to amuse with jests and pranks ⟨the *motleys* with their colorful outfits⟩ — see FOOL 2
2 an unorganized collection or mixture of various things ⟨a *motley* of old junk stored in the attic⟩ — see MISCELLANY 1

motor *n* **1** a device that changes energy into mechanical motion ⟨the device was equipped with a small electrical *motor* to make the gears spin⟩ — see ENGINE
2 a self-propelled passenger vehicle on four wheels ⟨went shopping for a new automobile at Valley *Motors*⟩ — see CAR

motor *vb* **1** to proceed or move quickly ⟨effortlessly *motored* past the other runners for a first-place finish⟩ — see HURRY 2
2 to travel by a motorized vehicle ⟨*motoring* along the highway at the speed limit⟩ — see DRIVE 2

motorboat *n* a boat equipped with a motor ⟨*motorboats* are banned on the lake because they are a hazard to swimmers⟩
synonyms powerboat, speedboat, stinkpot [*slang*]
related words cabin cruiser, cruiser, hydrofoil, motor sailer, runabout, sedan, sportfisherman

motorcade *n* a group of vehicles traveling together or under one management ⟨the next part of the parade was a *motorcade* of fire engines⟩ — see FLEET

motorcar *n* a self-propelled passenger vehicle on four wheels ⟨a convention for those who love antique *motorcars*⟩ — see CAR

motor home *n* a motor vehicle that is specially equipped for living while traveling ⟨they lived out of their *motor home* until they found a suitable house⟩ — see CAMPER

motorist *n* a person who travels by automobile ⟨environmental organizations suggest that *motorists* get together and carpool to avoid adding to pollution levels⟩
synonyms automobilist, driver, wheelman
related words operator; codriver; chauffeur; carpooler
antonyms nondriver

motormouth *n* a person who talks constantly ⟨I had to listen to the *motormouth's* cell phone conversations for the entire commute⟩ — see CHATTERBOX

motormouthed *adj* fond of talking or conversation ⟨that *motormouthed* moron can go on endlessly about absolutely nothing⟩ — see TALKATIVE

motor vehicle *n* a self-propelled passenger vehicle on four wheels ⟨got a license to drive a *motor vehicle* the minute she turned 16⟩ — see CAR

mottle *n* a small area that is different (as in color) from the main part ⟨canvases covered with streaks and *mottles*⟩ — see SPOT 1

mottle *vb* to mark with small spots especially unevenly ⟨old papers that were *mottled* by mold⟩ — see SPOT 1

mottled *adj* **1** having blotches of two or more colors ⟨a *mottled* complexion⟩ — see PIED
2 marked with spots ⟨*mottled* leather upholstery that isn't supposed to look perfect⟩ — see SPOTTED 1

moue *n* a twisting of the facial features in disgust or disapproval ⟨a *moue* of distaste at the display of bad manners⟩ — see GRIMACE

mound *n* **1** a pile or ridge of granular matter (as sand or snow) ⟨*mounds* of snow after the plow had passed⟩ — see [2]BANK

2 a quantity of things thrown or stacked on one another ⟨an ever-growing *mound* of dirty laundry on the floor⟩ — see [1]PILE 1

3 an area of high ground ⟨a pitcher's *mound*⟩ — see HEIGHT 4

mound *vb* **1** to form into a pile or ridge of earth ⟨*mound* the mulch around the plants⟩

synonyms bank, hill

related words heap, pile, pyramid, stack; embank; bunch, bundle, clump, lump, mass, wad; accumulate, amass, assemble, collect, conglomerate, gather, group

2 to lay or throw on top of one another ⟨*mounding* slices of cheese on top of her sandwich meat⟩ — see PILE 1

[1]**mount** *n* an elevation of land higher than a hill ⟨*Mount* Everest⟩ — see MOUNTAIN 1

[2]**mount** *n* a structure that holds up or serves as a foundation for something else ⟨hammered together a *mount* for the cameras⟩ — see SUPPORT 1

mount *vb* **1** to become greater in extent, volume, amount, or number ⟨medical expenses began to *mount*⟩ — see INCREASE 2

2 to bring before the public in performance or exhibition ⟨the huge amount of money needed to *mount* an opera⟩ — see PRESENT 1

3 to move or extend upward ⟨the cable car continues to *mount* to ever higher terrain until the moment when the entire valley comes into view⟩ — see ASCEND

mountain *n* **1** an elevation of land higher than a hill ⟨my cousin likes to climb *mountains* just because she can⟩

synonyms alp, hump, mount, peak

related words cordillera, mountain range, range, sierra; inselberg, knob, seamount; aiguille, horn, mountaintop, pinnacle, summit

near antonyms basin, bowl, depression, hollow, vale, valley

2 a considerable amount ⟨receives a *mountain* of mail every year for the holidays⟩ — see LOT 2

3 a quantity of things thrown or stacked on one another ⟨he piled a *mountain* of mashed potatoes on his plate⟩ — see [1]PILE 1

mountain dew *n* illegally produced liquor ⟨one sip of the hillbilly's potent *mountain dew* left inexperienced drinkers gasping⟩ — see MOONSHINE 1

mountain lion *n* a large tawny cat of the wild ⟨the problems created by *mountain lions* coming into contact with humans in suburban developments⟩ — see COUGAR

mountainous *adj* unusually large ⟨the seemingly *mountainous* obstacles he had to overcome while growing up⟩ — see HUGE

mountebank *n* one who makes false claims of identity or expertise ⟨claimed that many doctors were frauds and *mountebanks*⟩ — see IMPOSTOR

mounting *n* a structure that holds up or serves as a foundation for something else ⟨built a new *mounting* for the engine⟩ — see SUPPORT 1

mourn *vb* **1** to feel deep sadness or mental pain ⟨we *mourned* for weeks after our beloved pet's death⟩ — see GRIEVE

2 to feel or express sorrow for ⟨an editorial that *mourns* the loss of the town's last movie theater⟩ — see LAMENT 1

mournful *adj* **1** expressing or suggesting mourning ⟨she had such a *mournful* expression that someone teasingly asked if her dog had died⟩

synonyms aching, agonized, anguished, bemoaning, bewailing, bitter, deploring, doleful, dolesome, dolorous, funeral, grieving, heartbroken, lamentable, lugubrious, plaintive, plangent, regretful, rueful, sorrowful, sorry, wailing, weeping, woeful

related words dirgelike, elegiac (*also* elegiacal), melancholy; dejected, depressed, despondent, disconsolate, dispirited, downcast, downhearted, heartsick, heartsore, inconsolable, tearful; brokenhearted, careworn, crestfallen, downcast, downhearted, forlorn, gloomy, glum, low-spirited, miserable, sad, triste, unhappy, woebegone; bawling, crying, groaning, howling, keening, moaning, yammering; bleeding, suffering; black, bleak, cheerless, comfortless, dark, darkening, desolate, dismal, dreary, funereal, gloomy, glum, gray (*also* grey), joyless, low, miserable, moody, morbid, morose, pathetic, pessimistic, piteous, saturnine, somber (*or* sombre), sullen, wretched

near antonyms delighted, exulting, glorying, happy, joyful, rejoicing, triumphant; bright, cheerful, cheering, cheery; laughing, smiling; blissful, blithe, blithesome, buoyant, jocund, jolly, joyous, lighthearted, merry, mirthful; encouraging, hopeful, optimistic; ecstatic, elated, euphoric, exhilarated, giddy, heady, rapturous, rhapsodic (*also* rhapsodical)

2 feeling unhappiness ⟨the *mournful* survivors of the disaster were faced with the grim task of burying the dead⟩ — see SAD 1

3 causing unhappiness ⟨the *mournful* death of a beloved entertainer⟩ — see SAD 2

mournfully *adv* with feelings of bitterness or grief ⟨cried out *mournfully* for the son who would never return home from the war⟩ — see HARD 2

mournfulness *n* a state or spell of low spirits ⟨the memorial to the war's dead has an aura of *mournfulness* that cannot be conveyed in words⟩ — see SADNESS

mouse *vb* to move about in a sly or secret manner ⟨a cat *mousing* along in the shadows of the garden⟩ — see SNEAK 1

mousy *or* **mousey** *adj* easily frightened ⟨a *mousy* little girl who hid behind her mother the entire time we were there⟩ — see SHY 1

mouth *n* **1** the opening through which food passes into the body of an animal ⟨the baby chicks opened their *mouths* very wide and chirped piteously when their mother came back with worms⟩

synonyms chops, gob [*chiefly British*], kisser [*slang*], mug, piehole [*slang*], trap [*slang*], yap [*slang*]

related words countenance, face, puss [*slang*], visage; muzzle; jaws, mandible, maxilla; gullet, maw

2 a twisting of the facial features in disgust or disapproval ⟨the boy usually makes a *mouth* when he gets an injection⟩ — see GRIMACE

3 disrespectful or argumentative talk given in response to a command or request ⟨I won't tolerate you giving your mother *mouth* about everything⟩ — see BACK TALK

4 a person who speaks for another or for a group ⟨the press secretary is the official *mouth* of the administration⟩ — see SPOKESPERSON

mouth *vb* **1** to distort one's face ⟨when her mother told her to mind, the little girl *mouthed* insolently and rolled her eyes⟩ — see MUG 1

2 to speak softly and unclearly ⟨the prompter *mouthed* the forgotten words under his breath⟩ — see MUMBLE

mouth (off) *vb* to talk as if giving an important and formal speech ⟨some crank *mouthing off* in the center of town to anyone who would listen⟩ — see ORATE 1

mouthful *n* a small piece or quantity of food ⟨took a

small *mouthful* of the soup to see if she liked it⟩ — see MORSEL 1

mouthpiece *n* a person who speaks for another or for a group ⟨a statement read by the official *mouthpiece* of the company⟩ — see SPOKESPERSON

mouthwatering *adj* very pleasing to the sense of taste ⟨an eye-catching display of *mouthwatering* cakes and pastries⟩ — see DELICIOUS 1

mouthy *adj* fond of talking or conversation ⟨those *mouthy* motorists who can't seem to stay off their cell phones⟩ — see TALKATIVE

movable *or* **moveable** *adj* capable of being moved especially with ease ⟨any furniture that is not *movable* will be covered with protective cloths by the painters⟩
synonyms mobile, portable
related words adjustable, flexible, modular; removable (*also* removeable), transferable (*also* transferrable), transportable; motile, moving; unbalanced, unstable, unsteady; manageable
near antonyms immotile, nonmotile, nonmoving; motionless, moveless, standing, static, stationary, still, stuck, wedged; fast, fixed, rooted, steadfast
antonyms immobile, immovable, irremovable, nonmobile, unmovable

movables *or* **moveables** *n pl* **1** the movable articles (such as tables and chairs) in a room ⟨when painting a room, you should first cover or remove all of the *movables*⟩ — see FURNITURE
2 transportable items that one owns ⟨packed our *movables* into the van and headed off to our new home⟩ — see POSSESSION 2

move *n* **1** an action planned or taken to achieve a desired result ⟨retiring early was a smart *move*⟩ — see MEASURE 1
2 the act or an instance of changing position ⟨don't make a *move*⟩ — see MOVEMENT 1

move *vb* **1** to change the place or position of ⟨I need you to *move* all your books off that chair before company gets here⟩
synonyms budge, dislocate, displace, disturb, relocate, remove, reposition, shift, transfer, transpose
related words bear, carry, cart, convey, drive, haul, lug, tote, transmit, transplant, transport; replace, supersede, supplant; alter, make over, modify, redo, refashion, remake, remodel, revamp, revise, rework, vary
near antonyms anchor, fix, freeze, moor, secure, set, stabilize; embed (*also* imbed), entrench (*also* intrench), implant, ingrain (*also* engrain), lodge, root
2 to set or keep in motion ⟨the hands of the wall clock are *moved* by battery⟩
synonyms actuate, drive, impel, propel, work
related words activate, motivate, provoke; abet, ferment, foment, incite, raise, stir (up), whip (up); set off, trigger, trip; arouse, excite, fire (up), galvanize, inflame (*also* enflame), inspire, instigate, rouse, stimulate
near antonyms bridle, check, constrain, contain, control, curb, inhibit, regulate, rein (in), restrain
3 to change one's position ⟨don't *move* while I'm trying to draw your portrait⟩
synonyms budge, locomote, shift, stir
related words fiddle, fidget, jiggle, squiggle, squirm, toss, twitch, wiggle, wriggle, writhe; rouse
near antonyms hang around, remain, stay, stick around, tarry; stabilize
antonyms freeze, still
4 to act upon (a person or a person's feelings) so as to cause a response ⟨we were deeply *moved* by the program of patriotic music⟩ — see [1]AFFECT 1
5 to rouse to strong feeling or action ⟨the heartfelt appeal *moved* the people to reach into their pockets and donate generously⟩ — see PROVOKE 1
6 to cause (someone) to agree with a belief or course of action by using arguments or earnest requests ⟨the report *moved* me to change my mind about the issue⟩ — see PERSUADE
7 to cause to function ⟨this one button *moves* the whole machine⟩ — see ACTIVATE
8 to leave a place often for another ⟨the police officer told the loiterers to *move* along⟩ — see GO 2

movement *n* **1** the act or an instance of changing position ⟨a sudden *movement* in the far corner of the room made her turn in that direction⟩
synonyms motion, move, shift, shifting, stir, stirring
related words dislocation, migration, relocation; locomotion, mobility, motility, motivity; fiddling, fidgeting, squirm, squirming, twitching, wriggling, writhing; flailing, flapping, waving
near antonyms immobility; inertia, inertness, stillness; cessation, discontinuance, ending, expiration, finish, halt, lapse, pause, shutdown, shutoff, stop, stoppage, surcease, termination
antonyms motionlessness
2 a series of activities undertaken to achieve a goal ⟨a *movement* for political reform in the city⟩ — see CAMPAIGN

movie *n* **1** a story told by means of a series of continuously projected pictures and a sound track ⟨there was much excitement when it was announced that the popular children's book would be turned into a *movie*⟩
synonyms film, flick, flicker, motion picture, moving picture, picture
related words animated cartoon, cartoon, docudrama, documentary, feature, featurette, short, short subject; silent, talkie; B movie, B picture, cofeature
2 movies *pl* the art or business of making a movie ⟨many a small-town girl has gone to Hollywood, dreaming of making it big in the *movies*⟩
synonyms big screen, cinema, film, filmdom, filmland, filmmaking, moviemaking, pictures, screen, silver screen
related words Bollywood, Hollywood; showbiz, show business

moviemaking *n* the art or business of making a movie ⟨a director with 25 years of experience at *moviemaking*⟩ — see MOVIE 2

moving *adj* having the power to affect the feelings or sympathies ⟨he gave a truly *moving* graduation speech that had some graduates in tears⟩
synonyms affecting, emotional, impactful, impressive, poignant, stirring, touching
related words eloquent, expressive, meaningful, significant; demonstrative, excitable, feeling, passionate, responsive, sensitive; exciting, inspirational, provoking, rousing, stimulating; dramatic, histrionic, melodramatic, theatrical (*also* theatric); cathartic
near antonyms cold, cool, detached, dispassionate, emotionless; deadpan
antonyms unaffecting, unemotional, unimpressive

moving picture *n* a story told by means of a series of continuously projected pictures and a sound track ⟨in the 20th century *moving pictures* became an important form of artistic expression⟩ — see MOVIE 1

mow *n* a twisting of the facial features in disgust or disapproval ⟨her *mow* suggested that she wasn't looking forward to a long evening of political speeches⟩ — see GRIMACE

mow *vb* **1** to shorten the standing leafy plant cover of ⟨you really should *mow* the lawn before it gets much higher⟩
synonyms cut
related words clip, crop, curtail, cut back, dock, hack, lop, manicure, nip, pare, prune, trim; bob, shave, shear, snip

2 to bring down by cutting ⟨an afternoon spent *mowing* hay⟩ — see FELL 2

mow (down) *vb* **1** to kill on a large scale ⟨machine guns *mowed down* the advancing troops without mercy⟩ — see MASSACRE

2 to strike (someone) so forcefully as to cause a fall ⟨the crowd rushing in for the sale *mowed down* the poor clerks standing at the front entrance⟩ — see FELL 1

moxie *n* **1** knowledge gained by actually doing or living through something ⟨it was old-fashioned military *moxie* that got medical supplies to the disaster site in record time⟩ — see EXPERIENCE 1

2 strength of mind to carry on in spite of danger ⟨a fearless journalist who denounced McCarthyism when few had the *moxie* to do so⟩ — see COURAGE

3 active strength of body or mind ⟨say, you're full of *moxie* this morning!⟩ — see VIGOR 1

Mrs. *n* the female partner in a marriage ⟨"How nice to see you! How's the *Mrs.*?" inquired the charming older gentleman⟩ — see WIFE

Mrs. Grundy *n* a person who is greatly concerned with seemly behavior and morality especially regarding sexual matters ⟨the librarian pointed out that many of the books that contain material that was once offensive to the *Mrs. Grundys* of the world are now revered as literary classics⟩ — see PRUDE

much *adj* having great meaning or lasting effect ⟨actually, nothing *much* changed⟩ — see IMPORTANT 1

much *adv* **1** to a great degree ⟨*much* gratified by the favorable response to her novel⟩ — see VERY 1

2 to a large extent or degree ⟨the new decorations made me *much* happier⟩ — see GREATLY 2

3 very close to but not completely ⟨today the old neighborhood looks *much* as it did years ago⟩ — see ALMOST

4 many times ⟨I don't do that *much* anymore⟩ — see OFTEN

5 close to but not exactly ⟨he behaves *much* the same as I did at that age⟩ — see APPROXIMATELY

much *n* a considerable amount ⟨*much* of what people think they know about words is inaccurate or downright false⟩ — see LOT 2

much as *conj* in spite of the fact that ⟨*much as* I'd like to blame you, I know I can't⟩ — see ALTHOUGH

much less *conj* to say nothing of ⟨after spraining his ankle, the gymnast hadn't been expected to appear in today's event, *much less* win it⟩ — see LET ALONE

muck *n* **1** foul matter that mars the purity or cleanliness of something ⟨spattered with *muck* from the pigpen⟩ — see FILTH 1

2 soft wet earth ⟨her shoes were covered with *muck* by the end of the soccer game⟩ — see MUD

3 that which is of low quality or worth ⟨what's this *muck* that you've been watching on TV, anyway?⟩ — see JUNK 1

4 language, behavior, or ideas that are absurd and contrary to good sense ⟨there's some solid substance in this book, but the reader has to trudge through a lot of *muck* to get to it⟩ — see NONSENSE 1

muck *vb* to make dirty ⟨you can't work in the garden and not expect to *muck* your clothes⟩ — see DIRTY

muck (about *or* around) *vb* to interest oneself in what is not one's concern ⟨regretted the day she thought that it would be a good idea to *muck about* in the neighbors' marital problems⟩ — see INTERFERE

muckety–muck *also* **muck–a–muck** *or* **mucky–muck** *n* one of high position or importance within a group ⟨the obituary mentioned that he was a *muckety-muck* in several service clubs⟩ — see BIG SHOT

muck up *vb* to make or do (something) in a clumsy or unskillful way ⟨I swear, she *mucks up* everything she tries⟩ — see BOTCH

mucky *adj* **1** full of or covered with soft wet earth ⟨the ground was very *mucky* after a night of pouring rain⟩ — see MUDDY 1

2 not clean ⟨only too happy to remove those old *mucky* clothes⟩ — see DIRTY 1

mud *n* soft wet earth ⟨we cannot play softball today because the field turned to *mud* after last night's heavy rain⟩

synonyms guck (*or* gook), mire, muck, ooze, slime, slop, sludge, slush

related words gumbo, silt; clay, dirt, gravel, humus, loam, sand, soil

muddle *n* **1** a state in which everything is out of order ⟨things at the newly built school were all in a *muddle* on opening day⟩ — see CHAOS

2 a state of mental confusion ⟨I was in such a *muddle* after the accident that I didn't know where I was⟩ — see HAZE 2

3 a state of mental uncertainty ⟨the new, supposedly improved forms simply put taxpayers in a bigger *muddle*⟩ — see CONFUSION 1

4 an unorganized collection or mixture of various things ⟨a *muddle* of old magazines piled on the shelves⟩ — see MISCELLANY 1

muddle *vb* **1** to throw into a state of mental uncertainty ⟨a car shopper thoroughly *muddled* by too much well-meaning advice⟩ — see CONFUSE 1

2 to undo the proper order or arrangement of ⟨some mischievous brat had *muddled* the household accounts⟩ — see DISORDER

muddled *adj* lacking in order, neatness, and often cleanliness ⟨a *muddled* arrangement of trophies in the display case⟩ — see MESSY

muddleheaded *adj* suffering from mental confusion ⟨a *muddleheaded* waiter gave us another party's bill⟩ — see DIZZY 2

muddy *adj* **1** full of or covered with soft wet earth ⟨please do not walk in the house with *muddy* boots on, as you will get the carpet dirty⟩

synonyms miry, mucky, oozy, slimy, sludgy, slushy

related words clayey, loamy, roily, silty; bedraggled; befouled, begrimed, cruddy, dirty, filthy, foul, grimy, grotty [*chiefly British*], grubby, grungy, gunky, impure, smutty, soiled, squalid, stained, sullied, unclean, uncleanly

near antonyms antiseptic, clean, cleanly, immaculate, pristine, sparkling, spick-and-span (*or* spic-and-span), spotless, squeaky-clean, unsoiled, unstained, unsullied

2 having visible particles in liquid suspension ⟨whether *muddy* or not, water taken from lakes and streams should be boiled by campers⟩ — see CLOUDY 1

3 not clean ⟨we were all *muddy* after playing outside⟩ — see DIRTY 1

muddy *vb* **1** to throw into a state of mental uncertainty ⟨my mind had been thoroughly *muddied* by the long hours of exacting work⟩ — see CONFUSE 1

2 to make (something) unclear to the understanding ⟨that argument is irrelevant and will just *muddy* the issue we're trying to resolve⟩ — see CONFUSE 2

3 to make dirty ⟨forgot to take off our shoes and accidentally *muddied* the kitchen floor⟩ — see DIRTY

mudslinger *n* one who makes harsh, personal attacks against opponents ⟨a local hot-button issue that has turned some normally mild-mannered neighbors into letter-writing *mudslingers*⟩ — see ATTACK DOG

mudslinging *n* the use of personal attacks or insults in order to undermine an opponent ⟨the ceaseless *mudslinging* merely convinced voters that neither candidate was worth voting for⟩ — see NAME-CALLING

muff *vb* to make or do (something) in a clumsy or unskillful way ⟨*muffed* the repair job and had to do it again⟩ — see BOTCH

muffle *vb* **1** to deaden the sound of ⟨the walls *muffled*

their conversation so that only a low murmur was heard⟩
synonyms mute, stifle
related words insulate, soundproof; pad; dampen, mellow, soften, subdue, tone (down); baffle; smother
near antonyms amplify, boost, deepen, enhance, heighten, increase, magnify, step up, strengthen
antonyms unmuffle
2 to surround or cover closely ⟨the airport had been *muffled* in fog all morning long⟩ — see ENFOLD 1

mug *n* **1** a round vessel equipped with a handle and designed for drinking ⟨a coffee *mug*⟩ — see CUP
2 a violent, brutal person who is often a member of an organized gang ⟨just a bunch of *mugs* with no respect for anyone, not even themselves⟩ — see HOODLUM
3 the front part of the head ⟨she joked about not having to see his ugly *mug* anymore⟩ — see FACE 1
4 the opening through which food passes into the body of an animal ⟨keep your *mug* shut and listen up⟩ — see MOUTH 1
5 a twisting of the facial features in disgust or disapproval ⟨an involuntary *mug* at the revolting sight⟩ — see GRIMACE
6 *chiefly British* one who is easily deceived or cheated ⟨the cardsharp was always on the lookout for a new *mug*⟩ — see [1]DUPE
7 *chiefly British* a stupid person ⟨those *mugs* couldn't blow up a balloon, let alone the Houses of Parliament⟩ — see IDIOT

mug *vb* **1** to distort one's face ⟨every time their picture was snapped, both children *mugged* by sticking out their tongues or scrunching up their faces⟩
synonyms grimace, mouth
related words pout; contort, deform, twist, warp; frown, glare, gloom, glower, lower (*also* lour), scowl; gape, gaze, ogle, stare; growl, snarl, sneer; simper, smirk
phrases make a face (*or* make faces), pull a face
near antonyms beam, grin, smile
2 to take a photograph of ⟨*mugging* captured criminals for the police records⟩ — see PHOTOGRAPH

muggy *adj* containing or characterized by an uncomfortable amount of moisture ⟨the air was so *muggy* we felt we just had to go for a swim⟩ — see HUMID

mulct *n* a sum of money to be paid as a punishment ⟨the loan shark usually imposed a *mulct* of an additional 20% on overdue payments⟩ — see FINE

mulct *vb* to rob by the use of trickery or threats ⟨trying to *mulct* the insurance company for an accident that never happened⟩ — see FLEECE

muliebrity *n* the set of qualities considered appropriate for or characteristic of women ⟨with her lovely outfit and graceful manners, she was the epitome of matronly *muliebrity*⟩ — see FEMININITY

mulish *adj* sticking to an opinion, purpose, or course of action in spite of reason, arguments, or persuasion ⟨a *mulish* determination to have his own way⟩ — see OBSTINATE

mulishness *n* a steadfast adherence to an opinion, purpose, or course of action ⟨cursed their *mulishness* for failing to own up to what seemed like an obvious mistake to him⟩ — see OBSTINACY

mull *vb* to reduce to fine particles ⟨the dentist was in the habit of *mulling* the mercury amalgam in the palm of his hand⟩ — see POWDER

mull (over) *vb* to give serious and careful thought to ⟨*mull over* the idea for a while and then let me know⟩ — see PONDER

multicolored *adj* marked by a variety of usually vivid colors ⟨displays of *multicolored* pottery from her native Mexico⟩ — see COLORFUL

multifarious *adj* being of many and various kinds ⟨the *multifarious* interests and activities in which Benjamin Franklin immersed himself⟩ — see MANIFOLD

multifariousness *n* the quality or state of being composed of many different elements or types ⟨the remarkable *multifariousness* of the conglomerate's commercial activities⟩ — see VARIETY 1

multifold *adj* being of a large but indefinite number ⟨the advantages of the new accounting system are *multifold*⟩ — see MANY

multihued *adj* marked by a variety of usually vivid colors ⟨used *multihued* dinnerware and stemware to give the table settings a casual, festive look⟩ — see COLORFUL

multinational *adj* relating to or involving two or more nations ⟨*multinational* efforts to negotiate a lasting peace in the region⟩ — see INTERNATIONAL

multiple *adj* **1** used or done by a number of people as a group ⟨*multiple* ownership of a vacation condo⟩ — see COLLECTIVE
2 being of a large but indefinite number ⟨the *multiple* achievements of her long career in public education⟩ — see MANY

multiplex *adj* being of a large but indefinite number ⟨would sometimes experience *multiplex* moods in the course of a single day⟩ — see MANY

multiplication *n* the act or process of becoming greater in number ⟨there's been a steady *multiplication* in our attic of old video equipment since the revolution in consumer electronics⟩
synonyms accumulating, accumulation, addition, increase, mushrooming, proliferation
related words doubling, quadrupling, tripling; creep, growth, rise, spread; enlargement, escalation, expansion; amplification, distension (*or* distention), inflation; accretion, accrual, augmentation, cumulation; extension, lengthening; boost, gain, hike, increment, rise
near antonyms abatement, compressing, compression, condensation, condensing, constricting, constriction, contracting, contraction, diminishing, diminishment, diminution, drop, drop-off, fall, falloff, lessening, lowering, reduction, shrinkage, shrinking; retrenching, retrenchment, shortening
antonyms decrease

multiplicity *n* **1** a considerable amount ⟨a *multiplicity* of suggestions for turning the company around⟩ — see LOT 2
2 the quality or state of being composed of many different elements or types ⟨Shakespeare's works seem to encompass the full *multiplicity* of human experience⟩ — see VARIETY 1

multiply *vb* **1** to bring forth offspring ⟨rabbits *multiply* with proverbial rapidity⟩ — see PROCREATE
2 to make greater in size, amount, or number ⟨the booming economy *multiplied* the wealth of investors⟩ — see INCREASE 1
3 to become greater in extent, volume, amount, or number ⟨with each attempt the problems *multiplied*⟩ — see INCREASE 2

multitude *n* **1** a great number of persons or creatures massed together ⟨awed by the *multitude* of stars in the night sky⟩ — see CROWD 1
2 the body of the community as contrasted with the elite ⟨the nation's idle rich frolicked while the *multitude* starved⟩ — see MASS 1

multitudinous *adj* being of a large but indefinite number ⟨the *multitudinous* questions that seem to be an inevitable part of opening day at school⟩ — see MANY

mum *adj* deliberately refraining from speech ⟨kept *mum* about the surprise bridal shower⟩ — see SILENT 1

mumble *n* speech that is not clear enough to be understood ⟨please answer the question without your usual *mumble* and try to use complete sentences⟩

synonyms grunt, grunting, murmur, murmuring, mutter, muttering
related words rumor, undertone, whisper; babble, babbling, blab, blabbing, chatter, chattering, drivel, driveling (*or* drivelling), gabble, gabbling, jabber, jabbering, maundering, prattle, prattling, rambling

mumble *vb* to speak softly and unclearly ⟨I can't understand you if you *mumble*⟩
synonyms chunter [*British*], grunt, mouth, murmur, mutter
related words babble, blab, chatter, drivel, gabble, gibber, jabber, maunder, prattle, ramble; breathe, gasp, pant, whisper; buzz
near antonyms articulate, enunciate
antonyms speak out, speak up

mumbo jumbo *n* unintelligible or meaningless talk ⟨the soothsayer's predictions were nothing but *mumbo jumbo*⟩ — see GIBBERISH 1

mummer *n* **1** an actor in a story performed silently and entirely by body movements ⟨a street festival featuring *mummers* in a pantomime⟩ — see MIME 1
2 one who acts professionally (as in a play, movie, or television show) ⟨those moonstruck *mummers* on TV soap operas who have more hair than talent⟩ — see ACTOR 1

munchies *n pl* a need or desire for food ⟨I often get the *munchies* while watching TV late at night⟩ — see HUNGER 1

mundane *adj* **1** having to do with the practical details of regular life ⟨they didn't want to be bothered with *mundane* concerns like doing the dishes while on vacation⟩
synonyms everyday, nitty-gritty, prosaic, terrestrial, workaday
related words earthly, temporal, worldly; average, common, commonplace, customary, familiar, garden, generic, normal, ordinary, plain, popular, routine, run-of-the-mill, run-of-the-mine (*or* run-of-mine), standard, typical, unexceptional, unremarkable, usual; frequent, habitual, regular; expected, predictable
near antonyms high-minded, lofty, noble, sublime; aberrant, abnormal, atypical; exceptional, extraordinary, freak, peculiar, phenomenal, rare, singular, special, uncommon, uncustomary, unique, unusual, unwonted; bizarre, curious, far-out, funny, odd, outlandish, out-of-the-way, outré, quaint, quirky, remarkable, screwy, strange, weird, wild
2 having to do with life on earth especially as opposed to that in heaven ⟨a period for reflection and penitence, when spiritual concerns should take precedence over those that are *mundane*⟩ — see EARTHLY

municipality *n* a thickly settled, highly populated area ⟨a *municipality* with an excellent police department⟩ — see CITY

munificence *n* the quality or state of being generous ⟨a number of poor communities now have school computers as a result of that billionaire's *munificence*⟩ — see LIBERALITY

munificent *adj* giving or sharing in abundance and without hesitation ⟨a *munificent* host who has presided over many charitable events at his mansion⟩ — see GENEROUS 1

munificently *adv* in a generous manner ⟨has shared her wealth *munificently* on countless occasions⟩ — see WELL 2

murder *n* **1** a situation or state that causes great suffering and unhappiness ⟨this weather is *murder* on my sinuses⟩ — see HELL 2
2 the intentional and unlawful taking of another person's life ⟨arrested for attempting to commit *murder*⟩ — see HOMICIDE 1

murder *vb* **1** to put to death deliberately ⟨those people made me so mad I felt like I wanted to *murder* them⟩
synonyms assassinate, bump off, croak [*slang*], dispatch, do in, execute, get, ice [*slang*], knock off, liquidate, neutralize, off [*slang*], put away, rub out, slay, snuff, take out, terminate, whack [*slang*]
related words blow away, shoot, shoot down; blot out, carry off, claim, cut down, destroy, fell, kill, smite, zap; butcher, massacre, mow (down), slaughter; annihilate, eliminate, eradicate, exterminate, wipe out
phrases do away with
near antonyms animate, raise, restore, resurrect, resuscitate, revive
2 to make or do (something) in a clumsy or unskillful way ⟨we listened in horror as she *murdered* our favorite song on stage⟩ — see BOTCH

murderer *n* a person who kills another person ⟨the *murderer* was sentenced to life in prison without the possibility of parole⟩ — see ASSASSIN

murdering *adj* eager for or marked by the shedding of blood, extreme violence, or killing ⟨a vow to bring down the *murdering* fiend who had destroyed his family⟩ — see BLOODTHIRSTY

murderous *adj* **1** difficult to endure ⟨the *murderous* heat of the desert⟩ — see HARSH 1
2 requiring considerable physical or mental effort ⟨those exams were *murderous*⟩ — see HARD 2
3 likely to cause or capable of causing death ⟨braved *murderous* machine-gun fire to capture the hill from the enemy⟩ — see DEADLY 1
4 eager for or marked by the shedding of blood, extreme violence, or killing ⟨Viking warriors became legendary for the *murderous* fury they displayed in battle⟩ — see BLOODTHIRSTY

murk *n* **1** a time or place of little or no light ⟨a robber lying unseen in the *murk*⟩ — see DARK 1
2 an atmospheric condition in which suspended particles in the air rob it of its transparency ⟨stuck outside in the *murk* and the rain⟩ — see HAZE 1

murkiness *n* the quality or state of having a veiled or uncertain meaning ⟨we had trouble understanding the passage because of its *murkiness*⟩ — see OBSCURITY 1

murky *adj* **1** being without light or without much light ⟨I didn't like walking around the *murky* campground without a flashlight⟩ — see DARK 1
2 causing or marked by an atmosphere lacking in cheer ⟨the *murky* shadows of the cemetery⟩ — see GLOOMY 1
3 filled with or dimmed by fine particles (as of dust or water) in suspension ⟨skies made *murky* from the smoke of forest fires that were many miles to the west⟩ — see HAZY 1
4 having an often intentionally veiled or uncertain meaning ⟨a *murky* reply to a question about his intentions⟩ — see OBSCURE 1
5 not seen or understood clearly ⟨a gubernatorial candidate with a *murky* position on the hot-button issue of capital punishment⟩ — see FAINT 1

murmur *n* **1** an expression of dissatisfaction, pain, or resentment ⟨finished the tedious job without a *murmur*⟩ — see COMPLAINT 1
2 speech that is not clear enough to be understood ⟨could just barely hear the *murmurs* of the audience⟩ — see MUMBLE

murmur *vb* **1** to express dissatisfaction, pain, or resentment usually tiresomely ⟨no prisoner dared *murmur* out loud⟩ — see COMPLAIN
2 to speak softly and unclearly ⟨a college professor who tends to *murmur*⟩ — see MUMBLE

murmurer *n* an irritable and complaining person ⟨the *murmurers* among the patients usually got fed last⟩ — see GROUCH 1

murmuring *n* speech that is not clear enough to be understood ⟨his surprising announcement brought *mur-*

murings from the crowd⟩ — see MUMBLE

muscle *n* **1** muscular strength ⟨I'm going to need someone with real *muscle* to help me move all this furniture⟩
synonyms beef, brawn, main, thew
related words force, might, potency, power, puissance, sinew; energy, vigor
near antonyms impotence, impotency, weakness; debilitation, debility, enfeeblement, faintness, feebleness, frailness, frailty, infirmity
2 the ability to exert effort for the accomplishment of a task ⟨at the time the military lacked the *muscle* to fight two wars at once⟩ — see POWER 2

muscle *vb* **1** to cause (a person) to give in to pressure ⟨he was *muscled* out of command by his opponents at military headquarters⟩ — see FORCE 1
2 to force one's way ⟨*muscling* straight through the packed crowd of people waiting to board the ship⟩ — see [2]PRESS 4

muscular *adj* **1** marked by a well-developed musculature ⟨Olympic runners tend to have very *muscular* legs⟩
synonyms brawny, sinewy
related words wiry; powerful, strong; beefy, burly, hefty, hulking, husky; able-bodied, athletic, herculean, mighty, robust, rugged, stalwart, stout, strapping, sturdy; muscle-bound; sculpted
near antonyms nonathletic; debilitated, delicate, effete, enervated, enfeebled, feeble, fragile, frail, weak, weakened, weakly, wimpy; light, lightweight, slight; lean, slender, slim, svelte, sylphlike, thin, willowy; emaciated, gaunt, lank, rawboned, scraggy, spare
antonyms scrawny, skinny
2 having muscles capable of exerting great physical force ⟨a *muscular* superhero who can easily lift a ton or more⟩ — see STRONG 1
3 marked by or uttered with forcefulness ⟨a presidential speech that promises to be a *muscular* enunciation of the nation's foreign policy⟩ — see EMPHATIC 1
4 having an abundance of some characteristic quality (as flavor) ⟨a *muscular* red wine that goes especially well with beef⟩ — see FULL-BODIED

muscularly *adv* in a vigorous and forceful manner ⟨the driving rhythms and dramatic crescendos of the *muscularly* played final movement brought concertgoers to their feet⟩ — see HARD 3

muse *n* a person who writes poetry ⟨where is the *muse* who will sing of this man's great and noble deeds?⟩ — see POET

museum *n* a building or part of a building in which objects of interest are displayed ⟨a trip to the *Museum* of Natural History⟩
synonyms gallery, salon
related words archives, assemblage, collection, library; display, exhibition; studio

museum piece *n* something belonging to or surviving from an earlier period ⟨that old wooden ironing board she uses is a *museum piece*⟩ — see ANTIQUE

mush *n* **1** something (as a work of literature or music) that is too sentimental ⟨an opera that is pure *mush*⟩ — see CORN
2 the state or quality of having an excess of tender feelings (as of love, nostalgia, or compassion) ⟨couldn't stand all the *mush* in the movie's romantic scenes⟩ — see SENTIMENTALITY

mushiness *n* the state or quality of having an excess of tender feelings (as of love, nostalgia, or compassion) ⟨prefers mindless action movies to the "*mushiness*" of romantic comedies⟩ — see SENTIMENTALITY

mushroom *vb* to become greater in extent, volume, amount, or number ⟨the suburb's population has *mushroomed* tremendously in the last decade⟩ — see INCREASE 2

mushrooming *n* the act or process of becoming greater in number ⟨this *mushrooming* of options for phone, cable, and Internet service has left me hopelessly confused⟩ — see MULTIPLICATION

mushy *adj* **1** appealing to the emotions in an obvious and tiresome way ⟨a *mushy* love story⟩ — see CORNY 1
2 giving easily to the touch ⟨*mushy* fruit that was obviously overripe⟩ — see SOFT 3

musical *adj* **1** having a pleasantly flowing quality suggestive of music ⟨the *musical* sounds of the babbling brook⟩ — see LYRIC 1
2 having a pleasing mixture of notes ⟨the song of the skylark has been celebrated for being especially *musical*⟩ — see HARMONIOUS 1

musicale *n* an entertainment featuring singing or the playing of musical instruments ⟨gathered every month in someone's home for an informal *musicale*⟩ — see CONCERT

musician *n* **1** a person who plays a musical instrument ⟨the violinist was a famous and exquisitely talented *musician*⟩
synonyms instrumentalist, player
related words minstrel; artist, performer; maestro, virtuoso; accompanist, recitalist, soloist, symphonist; accordionist, bassoonist, clarinetist (*or* clarinettist), cornetist (*or* cornettist), drummer, fiddler, flautist, flutist, guitarist, harpist, hornist, keyboardist, oboist, organ-grinder, organist, percussionist, pianist, picker, piper, reedman, saxophonist, trombonist, trumpeter, violinist, violist
2 a person who writes musical compositions ⟨that *musician* is known for having written music that is very difficult to perform⟩ — see COMPOSER

musing *adj* given to or marked by long, quiet thinking ⟨he was clearly in a *musing* mood, and did not feel like talking just then⟩ — see CONTEMPLATIVE

muskeg *n* spongy land saturated or partially covered with water ⟨local farmers can make extra money by digging peat out of the nearby *muskeg*⟩ — see SWAMP 1

musketeer *n* a person who has a strong liking for and trust in another ⟨the two little *musketeers* were never seen apart⟩ — see FRIEND 1

muss *n* a state in which everything is out of order ⟨careful planning had eliminated most of the *muss* that usually accompanies a move to a new house⟩ — see CHAOS

muss *vb* to undo the proper order or arrangement of ⟨the wind *mussed* up my hair⟩ — see DISORDER

mussed *adj* lacking in order, neatness, and often cleanliness ⟨the charmingly *mussed* look of a rock star in full rebel regalia⟩ — see MESSY

mussy *adj* lacking in order, neatness, and often cleanliness ⟨a *mussy* pile of papers and books⟩ — see MESSY

must *n* something necessary, indispensable, or unavoidable ⟨exercise is a *must* if you want to stay healthy⟩ — see ESSENTIAL 1

must *vb* to be under necessity or obligation to ⟨we *must* be quiet during the performance⟩ — see NEED 2

muster *n* **1** a body of people come together in one place ⟨a *muster* of concerned citizens⟩ — see GATHERING 1
2 a number of things considered as a unit ⟨considering the *muster* of suggestions that were submitted for "word of the year"⟩ — see GROUP 1

muster *vb* **1** to assemble and make ready for action ⟨a command to *muster* the troops⟩ — see MOBILIZE
2 to bring together in assembly by or as if by command ⟨all the supporters that I could *muster* for the fund-raising campaign⟩ — see CONVOKE
3 to be made up of ⟨the corps of regular wine drinkers *musters* only about 10% of the population⟩ — see COMPRISE 1

muster out *vb* to let go from office, service, or employment ⟨*mustered out* of the army at the end of the war⟩ — see DISMISS 1

must–have *adj* impossible to do without ⟨aprons are *must-have* accessories for the cooking class⟩ — see ESSENTIAL 1

must–have *n* something necessary, indispensable, or unavoidable ⟨hiking boots are a *must-have* for this trip⟩ — see ESSENTIAL 1

musty *adj* **1** having an unpleasant smell ⟨*musty* old gym socks⟩ — see MALODOROUS
2 used or heard so often as to be dull ⟨the *musty* prose of writers who use the same expressions over and over⟩ — see STALE 1

mutable *adj* likely to change frequently, suddenly, or unexpectedly ⟨a politician with very *mutable* positions on all the issues⟩ — see FICKLE 1

mutate *vb* to pass from one form, state, or level to another ⟨colored lights that slowly *mutate* from green to blue and so on across the color spectrum⟩ — see CHANGE 2

mute *adj* **1** unable to speak ⟨the child is both deaf and *mute* because her hearing was lost at birth⟩
synonyms inarticulate, speechless, voiceless
related words tongue-tied; incoherent, incomprehensible; closemouthed, laconic, reserved, reticent, taciturn, tight-lipped, uncommunicative; mum, nonspeaking, quiet, silent, wordless
near antonyms blabby, chatty, communicative, expansive, gabby, garrulous, loquacious, talkative, talky, vocal; expatiating, speaking out, speaking up; articulating, speaking, talking; articulate, eloquent, fluent, voluble
2 deliberately refraining from speech ⟨remained *mute* no matter how much we pleaded for an answer⟩ — see SILENT 1

mute *n* a device on a musical instrument that deadens or softens its tone ⟨I was practicing my trumpet at three in the morning when the *mute* fell out, and I managed to wake everyone up⟩
synonyms damper
related words muffler, quieter, softener, soft pedal

mute *vb* **1** to stop the noise or speech of ⟨*muted* the television while she was on the phone⟩ — see SILENCE 1
2 to deaden the sound of ⟨closing the windows *muted* the traffic noise so we could get to sleep⟩ — see MUFFLE 1

muted *adj* **1** mostly or entirely without sound ⟨the *muted* cry of a frightened witness to a murder⟩ — see SILENT 3
2 not excessively showy ⟨painted with *muted* colors⟩ — see QUIET 2
3 deliberately refraining from speech ⟨she was unexpectedly *muted* in the presence of her literary idol⟩ — see SILENT 1

muteness *n* incapacity for or restraint from speaking ⟨we were baffled by his uncharacteristic *muteness*⟩ — see SILENCE 1

mutilate *vb* to cause severe or permanent injury to ⟨was lucky not to be *mutilated* in the car crash⟩ — see MAIM

mutineer *n* a person who rises up against authority ⟨the *mutineers* were captured after they turned to piracy on the open seas⟩ — see REBEL

mutinous *adj* taking part in a rebellion ⟨vowed that he would someday see the *mutinous* crew hang⟩ — see REBELLIOUS 1

mutiny *n* open fighting against authority (as one's own government) ⟨a *mutiny* led by the ship's cook⟩ — see REBELLION 1

mutiny *vb* to rise up against established authority ⟨the party's conservative faction *mutinied* just before the election⟩ — see REBEL

mutt *n* a stupid person ⟨it's an expensive camera, and I'd rather not turn it over to some *mutt*⟩ — see IDIOT

mutter *n* speech that is not clear enough to be understood ⟨the distracting *mutter* of some member of the audience⟩ — see MUMBLE

mutter *vb* **1** to express dissatisfaction, pain, or resentment usually tiresomely ⟨a *muttering* group of workers⟩ — see COMPLAIN
2 to speak softly and unclearly ⟨*muttering* to himself under his breath⟩ — see MUMBLE

mutterer *n* an irritable and complaining person ⟨the usual *mutterers* about the food in the cafeteria⟩ — see GROUCH 1

muttering *n* speech that is not clear enough to be understood ⟨barely heard *mutterings* of discontent⟩ — see MUMBLE

mutual *adj* used or done by a number of people as a group ⟨every film is a *mutual* effort by the director, writer, actors, and a host of others⟩ — see COLLECTIVE

mutually exclusive *adj* not being in agreement or harmony ⟨the two plans are *mutually exclusive*; implementing one will automatically rule out the other⟩ — see INCONSISTENT 1

muzzy *adj* **1** not expressed in precise terms ⟨in an attempt to be all things to all people, the candidate offered to the voters an intentionally *muzzy* campaign message⟩ — see VAGUE 1
2 suffering from mental confusion ⟨with my mind still *muzzy* from the medication, I had no idea what the nurse was saying⟩ — see DIZZY 2

myopic *adj* **1** able to see near things more clearly than distant ones ⟨he became so *myopic* that he finally broke down and got contact lenses⟩ — see NEARSIGHTED
2 not thinking about and providing for the future ⟨the *myopic* city designers who did not plan for growth⟩ — see IMPROVIDENT

myriad *adj* **1** being of many and various kinds ⟨the *myriad* problems that today's cities face⟩ — see MANIFOLD
2 too many to be counted ⟨the *myriad* influences that shape a person's character⟩ — see COUNTLESS

myriad *n* a considerable amount ⟨the car can be outfitted with a *myriad* of options⟩ — see LOT 2

mysterious *adj* **1** being beyond one's powers to know, understand, or explain ⟨the huge stone statues on Easter Island are ancient, *mysterious*, and haunting⟩
synonyms arcane, cryptic, deep, enigmatic (*also* enigmatical), impenetrable, inscrutable, mystic, occult, uncanny
related words dark, darkling, fuzzy, murky, obscure, shadowy, vague; ambiguous, equivocal; imponderable, incomprehensible, unfathomable, unintelligible, unsearchable; inexplicable, unaccountable, unexplainable; unanswerable, unknowable; metaphysical, mystical, numinous, supernatural; abstruse, esoteric, recondite; baffling, befuddling, bewildering, confounding, confusing, disorienting, mystifying, perplexing, puzzling
near antonyms fathomable, intelligible, understandable; apparent, clear, evident, manifest, obvious, open-and-shut, palpable, patent, perspicuous, plain, straightforward, transparent, unambiguous, unequivocal, unmistakable
2 having an often intentionally veiled or uncertain meaning ⟨the stranger's *mysterious* prediction⟩ — see OBSCURE 1

mysteriousness *n* **1** the quality or state of being impossible to know, understand, or explain ⟨the *mysteriousness* of the nocturnal noises evaporated with the arrival of daybreak⟩ — see INSCRUTABILITY 1
2 the quality or state of having a veiled or uncertain meaning ⟨the unexpected *mysteriousness* of the phone message had them a little concerned⟩ — see OBSCURITY 1

mystery *n* something hard to understand or explain

⟨why my sister married that guy is still a *mystery* to my parents⟩
synonyms closed book, conundrum, enigma, head-scratcher, mystification, puzzle, puzzlement, riddle, secret
related words brainteaser, case, challenge, knot, matter, perplexity, poser, problem, stumper, trouble

mystic *adj* **1** having seemingly supernatural qualities or powers ⟨the notion that a cat has nine lives is based upon the belief that nine is a *mystic* number⟩
synonyms magic, magical, numinous, occult, weird
related words bewitched, enchanted, spellbound; bewitching, charming, conjuring, enchanting, wiling; amazing, astonishing, astounding, awesome, extraordinary, fabulous, marvelous (*or* marvellous), miraculous, portentous, stunning, stupendous, sublime, wondrous; divining, forecasting, foreknowing, foreseeing, foretelling, fortune-telling, predicting, presaging, prognosticating, prophesying, soothsaying; metaphysical, preternatural, unearthly; paranormal, supernormal
near antonyms commonplace, everyday, normal, ordinary, prosaic, routine, run-of-the-mill, unexceptional, unremarkable, usual, workaday
2 being beyond one's powers to know, understand, or explain ⟨the belief that there are *mystic* forces at work here⟩ — see MYSTERIOUS 1
3 having an often intentionally veiled or uncertain meaning ⟨*mystic* prophesies that are never understood until it is too late⟩ — see OBSCURE 1

mystification *n* **1** a state of mental uncertainty ⟨the new information did little to ease our *mystification*⟩ — see CONFUSION 1
2 something hard to understand or explain ⟨an event that is one of the great *mystifications* in all of maritime history⟩ — see MYSTERY

mystify *vb* to throw into a state of mental uncertainty ⟨we were *mystified* by the sudden changes in the tax code⟩ — see CONFUSE 1

myth *n* **1** a traditional but unfounded story that gives the reason for a current custom, belief, or fact of nature ⟨according to an ancient Greek *myth*, humans acquired fire from Prometheus, a Titan who had stolen it from heaven⟩
synonyms fable, legend, mythos
related words allegory, parable; fabrication, fantasy (*also* phantasy), fiction, figment, invention; narrative, saga, story, tale, yarn
2 the body of customs, beliefs, stories, and sayings associated with a people, thing, or place ⟨over the years Davy Crockett evolved from an actual person to one of the great figures of American *myth*⟩ — see FOLKLORE
3 a false idea or belief ⟨the idea that alligators can live in the sewers of New York is just a *myth*⟩ — see FALLACY 1

mythical *or* **mythic** *adj* **1** based on, described in, or being a myth ⟨for years the Spanish conquistadors searched for the *mythical* El Dorado, a place of unimaginable riches⟩
synonyms fabled, fabulous, legendary
related words famed, romanticized, storied; chimerical (*also* chimeric), fabricated, fantastic (*also* fantastical), fictional, fictitious; fanciful, imaginary, imagined, invented, made-up, make-believe, pretend, unreal; allegorical, mythological (*also* mythologic); semilegendary
near antonyms actual, existent, real, real-world; historical; factual, true; attested, authenticated, confirmed, established, proven, substantiated, validated, verified; authentic, bona fide, genuine, real-life
2 not real and existing only in the imagination ⟨the *mythical* unicorn⟩ — see IMAGINARY

mythology *n* the body of customs, beliefs, stories, and sayings associated with a people, thing, or place ⟨Ares is the god of war in Greek *mythology*⟩ — see FOLKLORE

mythos *n* **1** a traditional but unfounded story that gives the reason for a current custom, belief, or fact of nature ⟨according to one creation *mythos*, humans sprang from the forehead of a god⟩ — see MYTH 1
2 the body of customs, beliefs, stories, and sayings associated with a people, thing, or place ⟨the Superman *mythos* has long since become ingrained in popular American culture⟩ — see FOLKLORE

my word *interj* how surprising, doubtful, or unbelievable ⟨*my word*, how that child has grown!⟩ — see NO

N

nab *vb* **1** to take or keep under one's control by authority of law ⟨the officer *nabbed* the purse snatcher before he could escape⟩ — see ARREST 1
2 to take physical control or possession of (something) suddenly or forcibly ⟨a pickpocket *nabbed* my wallet⟩ — see CATCH 1

nabe *n* an area (as of a city) set apart for some purpose or having some special feature ⟨although it has undergone several transformations over the years, Times Square remains one of New York's most fabled *nabes*⟩ — see DISTRICT

nabob *n* one of high position or importance within a group ⟨dressed conservatively so as to make a good impression with the *nabobs* on the co-op's board⟩ — see BIG SHOT

nacreous *adj* having a rainbowlike play of colors ⟨the *nacreous* lining of the shell of a mollusk⟩ — see IRIDESCENT

nadir *n* **1** the lowest point or level ⟨the discussion really reached its *nadir* when people resorted to name-calling⟩
synonyms bedrock, bottom, depth, rock bottom, zero
related words abyss, armpit, pit
near antonyms bloom, flood tide, flower, glory, heyday; crescendo, high; cap, ceiling, crest, roof
antonyms acme, apex, climax, crown, culmination, head, height, high-water mark, meridian, peak, pinnacle, summit, tip-top, top, zenith
2 the lowest part, place, or point ⟨got into the stock market when it was at its *nadir* and then watched prices soar⟩ — see BOTTOM 3

nag *n* a large hoofed domestic animal that is used for carrying or drawing loads and for riding ⟨a poor farmer who could only afford one old *nag*⟩ — see HORSE

nag *vb* **1** to subject (someone) to constant scoldings and sharp reminders ⟨she kept *nagging* him to fix the furnace before the weather got any colder⟩
synonyms dog, henpeck, hound, needle, peck (at)
related words carp (at), fuss (about *or* over), nitpick; annoy, badger, bait, bother, bug, chivy (*or* chivvy), harass, harry, hassle, irk, pester, plague, ride, vex, yap (at); egg, goad, incite, prod, prompt, spur, urge; exhort, insist, press, pressure, push; blandish, cajole, coax, wheedle; beg, importune, plead
phrases pick at
near antonyms compliment; commend, laud, praise, recommend, tout; acclaim, applaud, build up, eulogize, extol (*also* extoll)
2 to express dissatisfaction, pain, or resentment usually tiresomely ⟨if all you can do is *nag*, then you are of no use to this organization at all⟩ — see COMPLAIN

nagging *adj* causing worry or anxiety ⟨I have this *nagging* feeling that something will still go wrong⟩ — see TROUBLESOME

naiad *n* **1** a mythical goddess represented as a young girl and said to live outdoors ⟨in Greek mythology, *naiads* supposedly drowned the young men with whom they became enamored⟩ — see NYMPH 1
2 a young wingless often wormlike form (as a grub or caterpillar) that hatches from the egg of many insects ⟨students in science class learning how to distinguish a dragonfly *naiad* from an earthworm⟩ — see LARVA

naïf *or* **naif** *adj* lacking in worldly wisdom or informed judgment ⟨the senator, newly elected and still *naïf*, will learn soon enough how Washington really works⟩ — see NAIVE 1

nail *vb* **1** to deliver a blow to (someone or something) usually in a strong vigorous manner ⟨the boxer *nailed* his opponent with a devastating left hook⟩ — see HIT 1
2 to make final, definite, or beyond dispute ⟨this latest infidelity *nails* it—I'm filing for divorce⟩ — see CLINCH
3 to reveal the true nature of ⟨an investigative report that *nailed* the teenage novelist as someone who had plagiarized the works of others⟩ — see EXPOSE 1
4 to take or keep under one's control by authority of law ⟨the very first time I tried to steal anything, I got *nailed*⟩ — see ARREST 1
5 to take physical control or possession of (something) suddenly or forcibly ⟨the running back saw the pass coming in and *nailed* it⟩ — see CATCH 1

nail–biter *n* something (as a close contest) that induces much suspense as to its outcome ⟨a presidential election that was one of the great *nail-biters* of all time⟩
synonyms cliff-hanger, hair-raiser, suspenser, thriller
related words photo finish, squeaker
near antonyms yawner; blowout

nail–biting *adj* marked by or causing agitation or uncomfortable feelings ⟨for a couple of *nail-biting* moments we thought that we had actually won the mega lottery⟩ — see NERVOUS 2

naive *or* **naïve** *adj* **1** lacking in worldly wisdom or informed judgment ⟨a first-time buyer who was so *naive* that he believed the salesman's spiel and paid good money for the rusty and broken-down car⟩
synonyms aw-shucks, dewy, dewy-eyed, green, ingenuous, innocent, naïf (*or* naif), primitive, simple, simpleminded, uncritical, unknowing, unsophisticated, unsuspecting, unsuspicious, unwary, unworldly, wide-eyed
related words callow, childish, immature, inexperienced, raw; childlike, idealistic, impractical, unrealistic; believing, credulous, gullible (*also* gullable), susceptible, trustful, trusting, unguarded; beguiled, duped, gulled, tricked; careless, heedless, thoughtless
near antonyms critical, cynical, doubting, incredulous, skeptical, suspecting, suspicious, unconvinced; careful, cautious, guarded, leery (*also* leary), wary, watchful; down-to-earth, hardheaded, pragmatic (*also* pragmatical), realistic, sober; street-smart, streetwise
antonyms cosmopolitan, experienced, knowing, sophisticated, worldly, worldly-wise
2 free from any intent to deceive or impress others ⟨the young girl gave honest and *naive* answers to the social worker's probing questions⟩ — see GUILELESS
3 readily taken advantage of ⟨we get piles of junk mail because you are *naive* enough to keep entering these dumb contests⟩ — see EASY 2

naively *or* **naïvely** *adv* without any attempt to impress by deception or exaggeration ⟨she *naively* admitted to the job interviewer that she actually had little work experience⟩ — see NATURALLY 3

naiveness *n* **1** readiness to believe the claims of others without sufficient evidence ⟨I can't believe the *naiveness* of people who don't realize there's always some catch to so-called free offers⟩ — see CREDULITY
2 the quality or state of being simple and sincere ⟨the innate *naiveness* of young children is one of their most endearing qualities⟩ — see NAÏVETÉ 1

naïveté *also* **naivete** *or* **naiveté** *n* **1** the quality or state of being simple and sincere ⟨her *naïveté* led her to leave her new car unlocked while she shopped at the mall⟩
synonyms artlessness, greenness, guilelessness, ingenu-

ousness, innocence, naiveness, naivety (*also* naïvety) [*chiefly British*], naturalness, simplemindedness, simpleness, simplicity, unsophistication, unworldliness, viridity
related words candor, frankness, genuineness, honesty, openness, sincerity, straightforwardness, unaffectedness, unpretentiousness; callowness, childishness, coltishness, inexperience, rawness; insularity, parochialism, provincialism; carelessness, heedlessness, thoughtlessness; ignorance, obliviousness, unawareness; credulity, credulousness, gullibility, impressionability; idealism, impracticality, optimism
near antonyms affectedness, artificiality, pretentiousness; deviousness, dishonesty, insincerity; disbelief, doubtfulness, incredulity, suspiciousness; carefulness, caution, street smarts, wariness; pessimism, skepticism; maturity
antonyms artfulness, cynicism, knowingness, sophistication, worldliness
2 readiness to believe the claims of others without sufficient evidence ⟨though he was streetwise, the investigative reporter regularly assumed an air of *naïveté* when he was interviewing confidence men, charlatans, counterfeiters, and other assorted swindlers of the general public⟩ — see CREDULITY

naivety *also* **naïvety** *n, chiefly British* the quality or state of being simple and sincere ⟨the contention that the royal family took advantage of the young Diana's *naivety*⟩ — see NAÏVETÉ 1

naked *adj* **1** lacking or shed of clothing ⟨had recurrent nightmares about being *naked* in public⟩
synonyms au naturel, bare, bottomless, disrobed, mother-naked, nude, raw, starkers [*chiefly British*], stripped, unclad, unclothed, undressed
related words seminude, topless; denuded, peeled; unveiled
phrases in the altogether (*or* the buff *or* the nude *or* one's birthday suit *or* the raw), stark naked
near antonyms covered, veiled; arrayed, caparisoned, decked (out), rigged (out), tricked (out); vested; decent
antonyms appareled (*or* apparelled), attired, clad, clothed, dressed, garbed, invested, robed, suited
2 lacking a usual or natural covering ⟨the winter trees now look so *naked* without their colorful fall foliage⟩
synonyms bald, bare, denuded, exposed, open, peeled, stripped, uncovered
related words displayed, revealed; hairless, shaven; disrobed, unclad, unclothed, undressed; furless, skinned; divested; unprotected
near antonyms mantled; overgrown, overrun, overspread; bearded, hairy
antonyms covered
3 free from all additions or embellishment ⟨a *naked* room waiting for an interior decorator's inspired touch⟩ — see PLAIN 1

nakedness *n* the state of having no clothes on one's body ⟨the sadistic guards took full advantage of the prisoner's *nakedness* to torment and humiliate him⟩ — see NUDITY

namby–pamby *adj* **1** lacking in qualities that make for spirit and character ⟨she's such a *namby-pamby* nothing that it's no wonder she's never asked out⟩ — see WISHY-WASHY 1
2 lacking strength of will or character ⟨mocked *namby-pamby* intellectuals who endlessly debate the pros and cons of everything and invariably end up accomplishing nothing⟩ — see WEAK 2

namby–pamby *n* a person without strength of character ⟨those *namby-pambies* at city hall are never going to get serious about our crime problem⟩ — see WEAKLING 2

name *adj* having a good reputation especially in a field of knowledge ⟨the university's physics department boasts a number of *name* physicists⟩ — see RESPECTABLE 1

name *n* **1** a word or combination of words by which a person or thing is regularly known ⟨introduced himself and then asked what my *name* was⟩
synonyms appellation, appellative, cognomen, compellation, denomination, denotation, designation, handle, moniker (*also* monicker), nomenclature, title
related words baptismal name, Christian name, first name, forename, given name; family name, maiden name, middle name, surname; matronymic, patronymic; byname, diminutive, epithet, hypocorism, nickname, sobriquet (*also* soubriquet); banner, rubric, tag; alias, cryptonym, nom de guerre, nom de plume, pen name, pseudonym; binomial, monomial; trivial name, vernacular; misnomer; brand name, label, trademark, trade name
2 an act or expression showing scorn and usually intended to hurt another's feelings ⟨quit calling her *names*⟩ — see INSULT
3 outward and often deceptive indication ⟨a celebrity who is the head of the charitable organization in *name* only⟩ — see APPEARANCE 2
4 overall quality as seen or judged by people in general ⟨has a good *name* among fellow marine biologists⟩ — see REPUTATION
5 a person who is widely known and usually much talked about ⟨managed to get several *names* to appear at the restaurant's opening⟩ — see CELEBRITY 1

name *vb* **1** to give a name to ⟨decided to *name* her new puppy "Bubbles"⟩
synonyms baptize, call, christen, clepe [*archaic*], denominate, designate, dub, entitle, label, nominate, style, term, title
related words brand, stigmatize, tag; denote, specify; miscall, misname, mistitle; code-name, nickname; rechristen, relabel, rename; surname
2 to make reference to or speak about briefly but specifically ⟨I don't want to *name* anyone in particular, but someone in this room fiddled with my car's radio⟩ — see MENTION 1
3 to pick (someone) by one's authority for a specific position or duty ⟨was *named* the provost of the university⟩ — see APPOINT 2
4 to decide to accept (someone or something) from a group of possibilities ⟨you don't like my offer? Just *name* your price⟩ — see CHOOSE 1
5 to decide upon (the time or date for an event) usually from a position of authority ⟨you *name* the date and I'll make sure I'm there⟩ — see APPOINT 1
6 to come to a judgment about after discussion or consideration ⟨they finally *named* a date for the wedding⟩ — see DECIDE 1

nameable *also* **namable** *adj* worth remembering or mentioning ⟨not one *nameable* accomplishment in all of her years in the senate⟩ — see NOTEWORTHY 1

name–calling *n* the use of personal attacks or insults in order to undermine an opponent ⟨the campaign quickly degenerated into *name-calling* rather than an intelligent discussion of the issues⟩
synonyms character assassination, mudslinging
related words defamation, libel, maligning, slander, smearing, vilification; belittlement, detraction, disparagement; abuse, invective, vituperation; censure, denunciation, revilement; aspersion, innuendo

nameless *adj* **1** not named or identified by a name ⟨the victim of the crime will remain *nameless* to protect his privacy⟩ ⟨those *nameless* editors who write the synopses for TV shows in the newspaper⟩
synonyms anonymous, faceless, incognito, innomi-

nate, unbaptized, unchristened, unidentified, unnamed, untitled
related words undetermined, unspecified; obscure, uncelebrated, unheard-of, unheralded, unknown, unsung; unexceptional, unremarkable
near antonyms denominated, designated, specified; labeled (*or* labelled), tabbed, titled; celebrated, famed, famous, known, notable, noted, noteworthy, remarkable, renowned, well-known; exceptional
antonyms baptized, christened, dubbed, named, termed
2 beyond the power to describe ⟨was seized with a *nameless*, vague fear that made her seek the companionship of another person⟩ — see INDESCRIBABLE
3 not widely known ⟨a *nameless* poet who has just been rediscovered by devotees of love poems⟩ — see OBSCURE 2

namelessness *n* the quality or state of being mostly or completely unknown ⟨the *namelessness* of the builders of the Mayan pyramids is no way diminishes the greatness of their achievement⟩ — see OBSCURITY 2

namely *adv* that is to say ⟨there's always one person stuck with cleaning up the mess, *namely* me⟩
synonyms scilicet, to wit, videlicet
related words especially, expressly, particularly, specially, specifically

namer *n* someone with the right or responsibility for making a selection ⟨we can't start the ceremony until the *namer* of the scholarship winners shows up⟩ — see SELECTOR

nanny *also* **nannie** *n* a girl or woman employed to care for a young child or children ⟨wrote a memoir recounting her days as a *nanny* for the rich and often indiscreet⟩ — see NURSE

nanosecond *n* a very small space of time ⟨a *nanosecond* was about all that it took her to accept his marriage proposal⟩ — see INSTANT

[1]nap *n* a short sleep ⟨so tired that she needed to take a refreshing *nap* before soccer practice⟩
synonyms catnap, doze, drowse, forty winks, kip [*chiefly British*], siesta, snooze, wink
related words repose, rest; slumber; bed

[2]nap *n* a soft airy substance or covering ⟨high-quality suede has a good, even *nap*⟩ — see [1]FUZZ

nap *vb* **1** to sleep lightly or briefly ⟨decided to let the kids *nap* for a few more minutes before waking them⟩
synonyms catnap, doze, drowse, kip [*British*], slumber, snooze
related words relax, repose, rest; couch, lay, lie, roost; lull
near antonyms arise, arouse, awake, awaken, get up, rise, rouse, uprise, wake (up), waken
2 to be in a state of sleep ⟨I'm just going to *nap* the entire afternoon⟩ — see SLEEP 1

Napoleon *n* a person of rank, power, or influence in a particular field ⟨started out as a small-time banker but ultimately became a *Napoleon* of finance⟩ — see MAGNATE

napping *adj* being in a state of suspended consciousness ⟨the *napping* children looked so peaceful⟩ — see ASLEEP 1

napping *n* a natural periodic loss of consciousness during which the body restores itself ⟨some people think that *napping* in the afternoon will keep you from sleeping well at night⟩ — see SLEEP 1

narcissism *n* excessive interest in oneself ⟨in his *narcissism*, he just assumed that everyone else wanted to hear the tiny details of his day⟩ — see EGOISM

narcissist *n* a person who is overly concerned with his or her own desires, needs, or interests ⟨with the rise of TV reality shows, attention-craving *narcissists* had a public forum for their self-infatuation⟩ — see EGOIST

narcissistic *adj* overly concerned with one's own desires, needs, or interests ⟨trying to raise the social consciousness of the normally *narcissistic* Hollywood community⟩ — see EGOCENTRIC

narcotic *adj* **1** tending to calm the emotions and relieve stress ⟨some therapists believe that certain scents can have a *narcotic* effect on people⟩ — see SOOTHING 1
2 tending to cause sleep ⟨the lecturer droned on in a *narcotic* monotone that eventually had the entire class struggling to stay awake⟩ — see HYPNOTIC

narcotic *n* something that soothes, calms, or induces passivity or a sense of security ⟨an irradicable sense of self-righteousness seems to be the *narcotic* that inures these religious fanatics from any realization of the harm they have done⟩ — see OPIATE

nark *n, British* a person who provides information about another's wrongdoing ⟨he began to suspect that there was a *nark* in his organization who was tipping off Scotland Yard⟩ — see INFORMER

nark *vb, British* to disturb the peace of mind of (someone) especially by repeated disagreeable acts ⟨during the war some of the British were *narked* by their American allies, who were perceived as arrogant⟩ — see IRRITATE 1

narked *adj, British* subjected to and reacting with irritation ⟨the greengrocer was *narked* at having to make do with what was left over⟩ — see ANNOYED

narrate *vb* to give an oral or written account of in some detail ⟨got a CD of the best-selling children's story that happened to be *narrated* by the author herself⟩ — see TELL 1

narration *n* a relating of events usually in the order in which they happened ⟨a *narration* that vastly overstates her minor role in this international affair⟩ — see ACCOUNT 1

narrative *n* **1** a relating of events usually in the order in which they happened ⟨wrote a witty, chatty *narrative* of all the happenings at the party⟩ — see ACCOUNT 1
2 a work with imaginary characters and events that is shorter and usually less complex than a novel ⟨in such *narratives* as "The Murders in the Rue Morgue" and "The Purloined Letter," Edgar Allan Poe essentially created the modern detective story⟩ — see STORY 1

narrow *adj* **1** being of less than usual width ⟨found a *narrow* opening in the fence that he was able to squeeze through⟩
synonyms fine, hairline, needlelike, paper-thin, skinny, slender, slim, slim-jim, thin, ultrathin
related words attenuate, attenuated, elongate (*or* elongated), linear; bottleneck, close, compressed, condensed, constricted, contracted, squeezed, tight, tightened; lanky, rangy, reedy, shoestring, spindly, stalky, stringy, twiggy, willowy, wispy; lank, spare
near antonyms chunky, squat, stocky, stumpy, thick, thickset; bulky, massive, voluminous; thickish, widish
antonyms broad, fat, wide
2 not broad or open in views or opinions ⟨a *narrow* person who thought that anyone who even owned a television had been morally corrupted by society⟩
synonyms illiberal, insular, Lilliputian, little, narrow-minded, parochial, petty, picayune, provincial, sectarian, small, small-minded
related words inflexible, ironbound, obdurate, obstinate, rigid, set, stubborn, unyielding, wrongheaded; bigoted, intolerant; biased, discriminating, discriminatory, jaundiced, one-sided, partial, partisan, prejudiced; brass bound, hidebound, old-fashioned, reactionary, stodgy, straitlaced (*or* straightlaced), stuffy; dogmatic (*also* dogmatical), opinionated, opinionative; limited; hick, unsophisticated
near antonyms impartial, nonpartisan, objective, unbiased, unprejudiced; freethinking

antonyms broad-minded, catholic, cosmopolitan, liberal, open, open-minded, receptive, tolerant

3 having distinct or certain limits ⟨a play about human suffering, but in a *narrower* sense, also about the modern struggles of the working-class poor⟩ — see LIMITED 1

4 showing little difference in the standing of the competitors ⟨a *narrow* gubernatorial contest, the outcome of which may depend upon a handful of votes⟩ — see CLOSE 3

5 unwilling to grant other people social rights or to accept other viewpoints ⟨a *narrow* man who wouldn't work for a woman simply because he refused to believe women had the proper temperament for management⟩ — see INTOLERANT 2

narrow (down) *vb* to reduce in size or volume by or as if by pressing parts or members together ⟨plans to *narrow down* the scope of the investigation into the government scandal⟩ — see COMPRESS 1

narrowly *adv* by a very small margin ⟨they *narrowly* escaped with their lives⟩ — see JUST 2

narrow–minded *adj* **1** unwilling to grant other people social rights or to accept other viewpoints ⟨integration of the public schools was once vigorously opposed by *narrow-minded* people who feared social change⟩ — see INTOLERANT 2

2 not broad or open in views or opinions ⟨*narrow-minded* people who instinctively feared and opposed any and all immigrants⟩ — see NARROW 2

narrow–mindedness *n* stubborn or intolerant adherence to one's opinions or prejudices ⟨the *narrow-mindedness* of the islanders prevents them from seeing that not all changes are for the worse⟩ — see BIGOTRY

narrows *n pl* a narrow body of water between two land masses ⟨we had to cautiously navigate our dinghy through the *narrows* before reaching the open water of the bay⟩ — see CHANNEL 2

nascence *n* the point at which something begins ⟨the poem's publication is often regarded as the *nascence* of the Beat movement⟩ — see BEGINNING

nascency *n* the point at which something begins ⟨witnessed firsthand the *nascency* of the American space program⟩ — see BEGINNING

nascent *adj* beginning to come into existence ⟨one of the leading figures in the *nascent* civil-rights movement⟩

synonyms aborning, budding, inceptive, inchoate, incipient

related words first, formative, inaugural, inchoative, initial, original; elementary, embryonic, fundamental, rudimentary; formless, incoherent; introductory, preliminary, preparatory; crude, primitive, rude

near antonyms advanced, developed, evolved, high, higher, improved, refined

antonyms adult, full-blown, full-fledged, mature, ripe, ripened

nastily *adv* in a mean or spiteful manner ⟨he *nastily* stuck his foot out and tripped the front runner, simply because he couldn't stand to see her win⟩

synonyms bitchily, cattily, despitefully, hatefully, malevolently, maliciously, malignantly, meanly, spitefully, viciously, villainously, virulently, wickedly

related words contemptuously, deprecatingly, disdainfully, scornfully; acrimoniously, antagonistically, caustically, envyingly, hostilely, invidiously, obnoxiously, rancorously, venomously, vindictively, vituperatively; bitterly, enviously, jealously, resentfully; balefully, caddishly, callously, cruelly, evil-mindedly, felly, hardheartedly, heartlessly, inhumanely, kindlessly, mercilessly, pitilessly, ruthlessly, soullessly, unfeelingly; disagreeably, ill, ungraciously, unkindly; ill-naturedly, inconsiderately, insensitively, thoughtlessly; diabolically, fiendishly; misanthropically

near antonyms affably, agreeably, amiably, cordially, genially, good-humoredly, good-naturedly, graciously, nicely, pleasantly; altruistically, humanely; considerately, feelingly, lovingly, mercifully, sensitively, softheartedly, solicitously, soulfully, thoughtfully; compassionately, sympathetically; angelically, divinely, gently, sweetly, tenderly

antonyms benevolently, benignantly, good-heartedly, kindheartedly, kindly

nastiness *n* **1** the desire to cause pain for the satisfaction of doing harm ⟨there was a natural *nastiness* about him that was evident from the time he was a small child⟩ — see MALICE

2 the quality or state of being obscene ⟨the *nastiness* of the graffiti required that the school remove it immediately⟩ — see OBSCENITY 1

3 the state or quality of being dirty ⟨the piles of rotting food in the kitchen were only one element in the apartment's general impression of appalling *nastiness*⟩ — see DIRTINESS 1

nasty *adj* **1** arousing or deserving of one's loathing and disgust ⟨fortunately, the story's *nasty* characters are balanced by some truly good people⟩ — see CONTEMPTIBLE 1

2 causing intense displeasure, disgust, or resentment ⟨a *nasty* video game that was so violent that I could hardly watch the opening scenes⟩ — see OFFENSIVE 1

3 causing or feeling bodily pain ⟨a *nasty* cut on my lip⟩ — see PAINFUL 1

4 depicting or referring to sexual matters in a way that is unacceptable in polite society ⟨*nasty* magazines that are not sold to minors⟩ — see OBSCENE 1

5 having or showing a desire to cause someone pain or suffering for the sheer enjoyment of it ⟨made *nasty* comments about how ugly she was⟩ — see HATEFUL

6 marked by wet and windy conditions ⟨bring your raincoat, as the weather's supposed to be *nasty*⟩ — see FOUL 1

7 not clean ⟨it's incredibly *nasty* inside that garbage bin, so stay away from there⟩ — see DIRTY 1

8 not giving pleasure to the mind or senses ⟨the smell of those old leftovers is downright *nasty*⟩ — see UNPLEASANT

9 causing worry or anxiety ⟨she had the *nasty* sense that she'd made a mistake somewhere⟩ — see TROUBLESOME

10 not being in accordance with the rules or standards of what is fair in sport ⟨a *nasty* hit got the hockey player suspended⟩ — see FOUL 2

11 not following or in accordance with standards of honor and decency ⟨that was a *nasty* trick to play on people who were so trusting⟩ — see IGNOBLE 2

12 requiring exceptional skill or caution in performance or handling ⟨given the high-ranking people involved, it will be a *nasty* job to hammer out a compromise⟩ — see TRICKY 1

natch *adv, slang* according to the usual course of things ⟨the next day the office lothario was claiming, "The chicks at the party couldn't resist a looker like myself, *natch*"⟩ — see NATURALLY 2

nates *n pl* the part of the body upon which someone sits ⟨the cleavage of his *nates* was obvious in those low-slung pants⟩ — see BUTTOCKS

nation *n* **1** a body of people composed of one or more nationalities usually with its own territory and government ⟨the American people became one *nation* when they adopted the Constitution in 1789⟩

synonyms commonwealth, country, land, sovereignty (*also* sovranty), state

related words city-state, microstate, ministate, nation-state; domain, dominion, empire, kingdom, realm, republic; duchy, dukedom, emirate, principality, seigniory (*or* seignory), sultanate; democracy, dictatorship, monarchy, monocracy, oligarchy, sovereign (*also* sovran), theocracy; client state, colony, condominium, dependency, mandate, province, settlement, soil, trust territory; fatherland, homeland, motherland; great power, power, sea power, superpower, world power; welfare state

2 a people having a common language, culture, and body of traditions ⟨an international organization dedicated to upholding the basic human rights of people from all *nations*⟩ — see NATIONALITY

national *adj* of or relating to a nation ⟨played the home team's *national* anthem before the start of the soccer game⟩
synonyms civil, public
related words civic, federal, municipal; government, governmental; domestic, internal, intestine; democratic, republican; nationwide
near antonyms global, international; alien, external, foreign
antonyms nonnational

national *n* a person who owes allegiance to a government and is protected by it ⟨recommended that foreign *nationals* living in the region evacuate immediately⟩ — see CITIZEN 1

nationalism *n* **1** excessive favoritism towards one's own country ⟨Nazism's almost epic *nationalism* appealed to downtrodden Germans still suffering the humiliation of being defeated in World War I⟩ — see CHAUVINISM
2 love and support for one's country ⟨American *nationalism* is often most visible during Fourth of July celebrations⟩ — see PATRIOTISM

nationalist *adj* **1** having or showing excessive favoritism towards one's own country ⟨a *nationalist* rant against the immigrants supposedly flooding the country⟩
synonyms chauvinist, chauvinistic, jingoist, jingoistic, nationalistic, superpatriotic
related words spread-eagle; loyal, patriotic; antiforeign, anti-immigrant, nativist, nativistic, xenophobic
near antonyms internationalist
2 having or showing love and support for one's country ⟨*nationalist* fervor is often at its highest when a country is at war⟩ — see PATRIOTIC

nationalist *n* one who shows excessive favoritism towards his or her country ⟨a staunch *nationalist* who favored any policy that would give the country more power in the international arena⟩
synonyms chauvinist, flag-waver, jingo, superpatriot
related words loyalist, patriot; hawk, warmonger; nativist
near antonyms internationalist; neutralist

nationalistic *adj* **1** having or showing love and support for one's country ⟨a *nationalistic* display of the country's flag at all civic events⟩ — see PATRIOTIC
2 having or showing excessive favoritism towards one's own country ⟨a *nationalistic* economic policy that raises up enormous barriers against the importation of goods from other countries⟩ — see NATIONALIST 1

nationality *n* a people having a common language, culture, and body of traditions ⟨New York City may have more *nationalities* than any other metropolis in the world⟩
synonyms ethnicity, nation, race
related words minority; clan, family, folk, house, kindred, tribe

native *adj* **1** belonging to a particular place by birth or origin ⟨though she now lived in the Northeast, she was a *native* Midwesterner⟩
synonyms aboriginal, autochthonous, born, domestic, endemic, indigenous
related words local, regional; original
near antonyms imported, introduced, transplanted; alien, exotic, foreign, strange; expatriate, immigrant
antonyms nonindigenous, nonnative
2 being such as found in nature and not altered by processing or refining ⟨diamonds in their *native* state are not the bright, flashy gems that one might imagine⟩ — see CRUDE 1
3 being a part of the innermost nature of a person or thing ⟨a *native* energy and ambition that would allow him to rise above his humble beginnings⟩ — see INHERENT

native *n* **1** a usually longtime resident of a locality ⟨the *natives* seem to resent the summer tourists even though they depend upon them for their livelihood⟩
synonyms local, localite, townie (*or* towny), year-rounder
related words denizen, dweller, habitant, inhabitant, occupant, resident, resider
near antonyms excursionist, sightseer, traveler (*or* traveller); holidayer, vacationer, vacationist
2 a member of the first race to inhabit a region ⟨to the missionaries, the religious beliefs of the *natives* were nothing more than superstitions that called for complete obliteration⟩ — see ABORIGINE

nativity *n* the act or instance of being born ⟨my father and grandparents were proud observers of my *nativity*⟩ — see BIRTH 1

natter *n, chiefly British* friendly, informal conversation or an instance of this ⟨a section of the park in which nannies like to gather for a relaxed *natter*⟩ — see CHAT 1

natter *vb* to engage in casual or rambling conversation ⟨could sit for hours *nattering* about nothing⟩ — see CHAT 1

nattily *adv* in a strikingly neat and trim manner ⟨he's very *nattily* dressed in a new tailored suit⟩ — see SMARTLY

natty *adj* being strikingly neat and trim in style or appearance ⟨a *natty* woman, she's usually impeccably dressed in tailored clothing from Europe⟩ — see SMART 1

natural *adj* **1** being such from birth or by nature ⟨from his first visits to the wading pool, we could tell that our little boy loved water and was a *natural* swimmer⟩
synonyms born, congenital
related words chronic, confirmed, habitual, incorrigible, ingrained (*also* engrained), inveterate, proper, regular, unreconstructed, unregenerate; constitutional, consummate; elemental, elementary, essential; connate, hereditary, inborn, inherent, innate, intimate, intrinsic, native; instinctual, intuitive
near antonyms cultivated, developed, trained; alien, foreign, unnatural
antonyms nonnatural
2 closely resembling the object imitated ⟨the diorama featuring stuffed birds and plastic plants actually looked very *natural*⟩
synonyms lifelike, living, naturalistic (*also* naturalist), near, photo-realistic, realistic, three-dimensional
related words alike, like, matching, similar, verisimilar; akin, analogous, approximate, comparable, resembling; accurate, close, faithful, true; compelling, convincing; expressive, graphic (*also* graphical), gritty, vivid
near antonyms dissimilar, off, unalike, unlike; incomparable, unmatched; contrasted, contrasting, different, disparate; fake, mock, phony (*also* phoney), sham
antonyms nonnatural, nonrealistic, unnatural, unrealistic

3 being such by blood and not by adoption or marriage ⟨an adult adoptee who has decided to search for his *natural* parents⟩
synonyms biological (*also* biologic), birth, consanguineous
related words legitimate
near antonyms illegitimate
antonyms adopted, adoptive, nonbiological
4 being a part of the innermost nature of a person or thing ⟨her *natural* talent for music first became apparent when, unbidden, she started banging on a toy piano⟩ — see INHERENT
5 being such as found in nature and not altered by processing or refining ⟨*natural* salts are not edible until they are washed and processed⟩ — see CRUDE 1
6 existing without human habitation or cultivation ⟨photographs of animals in their *natural* habitat⟩ — see WILD 2
7 free from any intent to deceive or impress others ⟨she was completely *natural* in expressing her feelings for him, unafraid of how they would be received⟩ — see GUILELESS
8 relating to or characteristic of human beings ⟨it's only *natural* to make mistakes—it's part of being human⟩ — see HUMAN
9 born to a father and mother who are not married ⟨had fathered an unknown number of *natural* children⟩ — see ILLEGITIMATE 1
10 having, characterized by, or arising from a dignified and generous nature ⟨his late grandfather was as kind and *natural* a man as one could ever hope to meet⟩ — see NOBLE 2
11 not civilized ⟨a *natural* man, unacquainted with the blessings and burdens of society⟩ — see SAVAGE 1

natural *n* a stupid person ⟨European explorers had a tendency to view the nonwhite peoples they encountered as uncivilized *naturals*⟩ — see IDIOT

naturalism *n* realistic depiction in art and literature ⟨a major exponent of *naturalism*, Theodore Dreiser depicted life's harsh realities unflinchingly and without moral judgment⟩ — see VERISIMILITUDE

naturalistic *also* **naturalist** *adj* closely resembling the object imitated ⟨the movie's volcanic eruption is so *naturalistic* that it's easy to forget that it all came out of a computer⟩ — see NATURAL 2

naturally *adv* **1** by natural character or ability ⟨tour guides who are *naturally* outgoing and can easily approach and converse with strangers⟩
synonyms congenitally, constitutionally, inherently, innately, intrinsically
related words basically, elementally, essentially, fundamentally; instinctively, intuitively; intimately
near antonyms artificially, unnaturally
2 according to the usual course of things ⟨we *naturally* like to be as comfortable as possible⟩
synonyms commonly, generally, natch [*slang*], normally, ordinarily, typically, usually
related words customarily, habitually, regularly, routinely; familiarly; conventionally, traditionally
phrases as a rule, needless to say, of course, on the whole
near antonyms funnily, oddly, peculiarly, queerly, strangely, weirdly; anomalously, irregularly; radically
antonyms abnormally, atypically, extraordinarily, uncommonly, untypically, unusually
3 without any attempt to impress by deception or exaggeration ⟨a boy trying to act *naturally* around the girl he has a crush on⟩
synonyms artlessly, guilelessly, ingenuously, innocently, naively (*or* naïvely), sincerely, unaffectedly, unfeignedly, unpretentiously
related words genuinely, honestly, simply, truly; freely, openheartedly, openly; candidly, frankly, matter-of-factly; casually, coolly (*also* cooly), nonchalantly; informally, relaxedly, unceremoniously
near antonyms artfully, cannily, deceitfully, deceptively, deviously, dishonestly, falsely; archly, calculatingly, craftily, cunningly, furtively, insidiously, sharply, shiftily, slickly, slyly (*also* slily), underhand, underhanded, underhandedly; flatteringly, sycophantically, unctuously
antonyms affectedly, artificially, hypocritically, insincerely, pretentiously, unnaturally

naturalness *n* **1** carefree freedom from constraint ⟨the children danced with a *naturalness* born of the sheer enjoyment of music and movement⟩ — see ABANDON
2 the quality or state of being simple and sincere ⟨has always admired the very *naturalness* of the Amish lifestyle⟩ — see NAÏVETÉ 1

nature *n* **1** the set of qualities that makes a person, a group of people, or a thing different from others ⟨it was the violent *nature* of his stories that got them banned from school libraries⟩ ⟨her *nature* was such that lying was never an option for her⟩ ⟨the stoic *nature* of these people enables them to endure one calamity after another⟩
synonyms character, clay, colors, complexion, constitution, genius, personality, self, tone
related words distinctiveness, distinctness, individuality, singularity, uniqueness; attribute, characteristic, earmark, essentiality, feature, flavor, hallmark, mark, point, property, savor (*also* savour), stamp, trait; disposition, grain, sort, temper, temperament; composition, makeup; essence, essentiality, interior, interiority, soul, spirit; metal, stuff, substance; habit, way
2 that part of the physical world that is removed from human habitation ⟨needed to get out of the office and back to *nature* in order to clear his head⟩
synonyms open, open air, outdoors, out-of-doors, wild, wilderness
related words backwoods, bush, country, frontier, hinterland, sticks, up-country; outside, without; badland, barren, desert, waste, wasteland
3 a number of persons or things that are grouped together because they have something in common ⟨group together anything round: buttons, lids, coins, and other things of that *nature*⟩ — see SORT 1
4 one's characteristic attitude or mood ⟨a boy of a quiet and shy *nature*⟩ — see DISPOSITION 1
5 the quality or qualities that make a thing what it is ⟨some artists maintain that color, light, and shadow are the very *nature* of painting⟩ — see ESSENCE 1
6 the whole body of things observed or assumed ⟨the belief that all of *nature* is controlled by an unseen Supreme Being⟩ — see UNIVERSE

naught *also* **nought** *n* the numerical symbol 0 or the absence of number or quantity represented by it ⟨my locker number is *naught*-seven-two⟩ — see ZERO 1

naughty *adj* engaging in or marked by childish misbehavior ⟨told her to act her age and stop throwing temper tantrums like a *naughty* little girl⟩
synonyms bad, contrary, errant, froward, misbehaving, mischievous
related words defiant, disrespectful, ill-mannered, ill-natured, impolite, improper, impudent, indecorous, insolent, rude, uncouth, unmannerly; disobedient, headstrong, intractable, obstreperous, recalcitrant, refractory, transgressing, unruly, untoward, willful (*or* wilful); balky, restive, uncontrollable, ungovernable, wayward, wild; arch, elfish, impish, knavish, monkeying, monkeyish, ornery, pixieish, prankish, rascally, roguish, waggish; dissolute, perverse, wrongheaded; disorderly, rowdy, ruffianly; corrupt, evil, wicked; insurgent, mutinous, rebellious; disobliging, inconsiderate, selfish,

thoughtless, unkind, unkindly; babyish, childish, immature, infantile, jejune, juvenile, kiddish, puerile
near antonyms acquiescent, compliant, complying, dutiful, obedient, submissive; clean, correct, decent, decorous, moral, proper, respectable; considerate, courteous, kindly, mannerly, polite, thoughtful; angelic (*or* angelical), cherubic, divine, heavenly; amenable, docile, governable, tractable; amiable, complaisant, good-natured, obliging, pleasant; discreet, modest; adult, grown-up, mature
antonyms behaved, behaving, nice, orderly

nausea *n* **1** a disturbed condition of the stomach in which one feels like vomiting ⟨symptoms include fever accompanied by a loss of appetite and *nausea*⟩
synonyms nauseousness, qualmishness, queasiness, queerness, sickness, squeamishness
related words qualm; airsickness, altitude sickness, car sickness, morning sickness, motion sickness, mountain sickness, seasickness
2 a dislike so strong as to cause stomach upset or queasiness ⟨such graphic scenes of senseless violence fill me with *nausea*⟩ — see DISGUST

nauseate *vb* to cause to feel disgust ⟨such hateful graffiti would *nauseate* anyone with an ounce of human decency⟩ — see DISGUST

nauseated *adj* **1** affected with nausea ⟨being aboard ship during that storm would make anyone but the most experienced sailor *nauseated*⟩ — see NAUSEOUS 1
2 filled with disgust ⟨*nauseated* critics panned the movie comedy for its celebration of unspeakably gross behavior⟩ — see SICK 2

nauseating *adj* causing intense displeasure, disgust, or resentment ⟨her relentlessly vicious gossiping is absolutely *nauseating*⟩ — see OFFENSIVE 1

nauseous *adj* **1** affected with nausea ⟨after eating the last four pieces of the two-week-old pizza, he was feeling a little *nauseous*⟩
synonyms ill, nauseated, qualmish, queasy (*also* queazy), queer, queerish, sick, sickish, squeamish
related words green, peaked, peaky, sickly; unsettled, upset, woozy
near antonyms settled; healthy, well
2 causing intense displeasure, disgust, or resentment ⟨it turned out that a dead mouse between the walls was causing the *nauseous* stench⟩ — see OFFENSIVE 1

nauseousness *n* a disturbed condition of the stomach in which one feels like vomiting ⟨the nervousness I experienced before getting on the roller coaster paled in comparison to the *nauseousness* I suffered soon afterwards⟩ — see NAUSEA 1

nautical *adj* of or relating to navigation of the sea ⟨collected sextants and other antique *nautical* equipment⟩ — see MARINE 2

navel *n* a thing or place that is of greatest importance to an activity or interest ⟨a city that likes to regard itself as the nation's *navel* of art and culture⟩ — see CENTER 1

navel–gazing *n* excessive interest in oneself ⟨a singer-songwriter whose compositions are too often exercises in self-important *navel-gazing*⟩ — see EGOISM

navigable *adj* capable of being traveled on ⟨this map shows which rivers are *navigable* and which aren't⟩ — see PASSABLE 1

navigate *vb* **1** to operate or control the course of ⟨the hours of training that are required before a student pilot is allowed to *navigate* an airplane solo⟩
synonyms conn (*also* con), helm, pilot, steer
related words commandeer, hijack (*also* highjack)
2 to travel on water in a vessel ⟨the months that were once required to *navigate* around South America in the days before the Panama Canal⟩ — see SAIL 1
3 to make one's way through, across, or over ⟨it will take some effort to *navigate* that stretch of hills, but we can do it⟩ — see TRAVERSE

navigational *adj* of or relating to navigation of the sea ⟨the folly of trying to sail with outdated *navigational* maps⟩ — see MARINE 2

navigator *n* one who operates or navigates a seagoing vessel ⟨our crew comprised a captain, a *navigator*, and a few deckhands⟩ — see SAILOR

nawab *n* one of high position or importance within a group ⟨a meeting with the *nawabs* on the university's board of trustees⟩ — see BIG SHOT

nay *adv* not merely this but also ⟨I was angry—*nay*, furious—at the way they were treating that poor dog⟩ — see EVEN 1

nay *n* **1** a vote or decision against something ⟨when the votes were tallied, it was 241 yeas and 54 *nays*⟩ — see NO 1
2 an unwillingness to grant something asked for ⟨gave a resounding *nay* to the request for a mixed-company camping trip⟩ — see DENIAL 1

naysayer *n* a person who distrusts other people and believes that everything is done for selfish reasons ⟨those *naysayers* who attack the integrity of the entire judicial system⟩ — see CYNIC

nazi *n* a mean, evil, or unprincipled person ⟨the guy behind the food counter is a *nazi* with an apron: you either follow his rules, or you don't get served⟩ — see VILLAIN

Neanderthal *n* **1** a big clumsy often slow-witted person ⟨they looked like a tribe of *Neanderthals* compared to the bridegroom's patrician-looking family⟩ — see OAF 1
2 a man with crude manners and habits and outmoded attitudes ⟨made the mistake of dining with some *Neanderthal* who repeatedly mistook his shirtsleeve for a napkin⟩ — see CAVEMAN

Neanderthal *or* **Neandertal** *adj* not civilized ⟨her boyfriend's *Neanderthal* tastes and manners were often embarrassing⟩ — see SAVAGE 1

near *adj* **1** being the less far of two ⟨grab the comforter from the *near* side of the bed and fold it in half⟩
synonyms closer, hither, nigher, this
related words fore, forward, front, inside
near antonyms distant, remote, remoter; back, outside
antonyms far, farther, further, opposite, other, that
2 being such only when compared to something else ⟨the incessant busyness of the family next-door makes us look like we live in *near* retirement⟩ — see COMPARATIVE
3 closely resembling the object imitated ⟨the dress is made from a *near* silk that would fool anyone but an expert⟩ — see NATURAL 2
4 not being distant in time, space, or significance ⟨the famous prediction that in the *near* future everyone will be famous for 15 minutes⟩ — see CLOSE 2
5 closely acquainted ⟨only her *nearest* friends know she's pregnant⟩ — see FAMILIAR 1

near *adv* **1** at, within, or to a short distance or time ⟨as the campers grew cold, so they gravitated *nearer* to the campfire⟩ ⟨as summer draws *near*, we usually start planning our annual vacation⟩
synonyms around, by, close, hard, in, nearby, nigh
related words hereabouts (*or* hereabout), hereaway (*or* hereaways) [*dialect*], thereabouts (*also* thereabout); along, alongside; accessibly, conveniently, handily
phrases at close quarters, at hand, on one's doorstep, within call
2 to a close degree ⟨copy the artist's drawing into your own sketchbook as *near* as you can⟩
synonyms closely, nearly
near antonyms distantly, remotely
3 very close to but not completely ⟨it's *near* six o'clock,

so we should start preparing dinner⟩ — see ALMOST
4 close to but not exactly ⟨it takes somewhere *near* an hour to get there⟩ — see APPROXIMATELY

near *prep* close to ⟨please don't cough *near* me⟩ — see AROUND 1

near *vb* **1** to come near or nearer ⟨as the procession *nears*, you'll be able to take a better picture of the graduates⟩ — see APPROACH 1
2 to move closer to ⟨as we *near* the church, you'll be able to see the bas-relief sculptures better⟩ — see COME 1

nearby *adj* not being distant in time, space, or significance ⟨grabbed the *nearby* quilt and gently laid it over the sleeping child⟩ — see CLOSE 2

nearby *adv* at, within, or to a short distance or time ⟨I'll be *nearby* if you need anything⟩ — see NEAR 1

nearing *adj* being soon to appear or take place ⟨teachers preparing for the fast-*nearing* school year⟩ — see FORTHCOMING 1

nearly *adv* **1** to a close degree ⟨copy that design as *nearly* as you can⟩ — see NEAR 2
2 very close to but not completely ⟨I *nearly* fell down the stairs⟩ — see ALMOST

near miss *n* a barely successful escape from something undesirable ⟨a *near miss* with death prompted him to give up skydiving⟩ — see CLOSE CALL

nearness *n* **1** the state of being in a very personal or private relationship ⟨my cousin and I have lost that *nearness* we had when we were kids⟩ — see FAMILIARITY 1
2 the state or condition of being near ⟨our *nearness* to the theme park has made us beloved by relatives from all over the country⟩ — see PROXIMITY

nearshore *adj* of, relating to, or situated in the waters near the shore ⟨red tide had a particularly devastating effect on *nearshore* shellfisheries⟩ — see INSHORE

nearsighted *adj* able to see near things more clearly than distant ones ⟨I am a little *nearsighted* and need to wear glasses to drive⟩
synonyms myopic, shortsighted
related words astigmatic; purblind
near antonyms presbyopic
antonyms farsighted, hypermetropic, hyperopic

neat *adj* **1** being clean and in good order ⟨keep the kitchen *neat* so the cook doesn't have to work around piles of dirty dishes⟩
synonyms antiseptic, bandbox, crisp, groomed, kempt, orderly, picked up, prim, shipshape, smug, snug, tidied, tidy, trig, trim, uncluttered, well-groomed
related words dapper, natty, saucy, smart, spiffy, spruce; immaculate, spick-and-span (*or* spic-and-span), spotless; rakish, sleek, streamlined, taut; organized, straight, systematic
near antonyms scruffy, seedy, shabby, slipshod, sloppy; dirty, filthy, foul, nasty, sordid, squalid; dowdy, frowsy (*or* frowzy), rumpled, tousled, tumbled; disorganized, unsystematic
antonyms disheveled (*or* dishevelled), disordered, disorderly, messy, mussed, mussy, sloven, slovenly, unkempt, untidy
2 free from added matter ⟨I like my soda *neat*, so skip the ice cubes⟩ — see PURE 1
3 of the very best kind ⟨that new skateboard park is *neat*⟩ — see EXCELLENT
4 following a set method, arrangement, or pattern ⟨regime change is rarely a *neat* process, particularly in a country where a coup d'état is more likely to occur than an election⟩ — see METHODICAL

neaten *vb* to make neat ⟨*neatened* the living room in anticipation of company⟩
synonyms pick up, redd (up *or* out) [*chiefly dialect*], spruce (up), straighten (up *or* out), tidy (up), trim
related words arrange, array, classify, codify, dispose, draw up, marshal (*also* marshall), order, organize, range, systematize
near antonyms disarrange, disarray, discompose, dishevel, disorder, disorganize, disrupt, disturb, jumble, mess (up), mix (up), muddle, muss, rumple, scramble, shuffle, tousle, tumble, upset

neath *prep, dialect* in a lower position than ⟨*neath* his calm surface there was seething anger⟩ — see BELOW 1

neb *n* **1** the jaws of a bird together with their hornlike covering ⟨the cardinal has a black face and a noticeable bright red *neb*⟩ — see BEAK 1
2 the part of the face bearing the nostrils and nasal cavity ⟨with her round glasses perched on her small *neb*, the librarian certainly presents an owlish appearance⟩ — see NOSE 1

nebulosity *n* the quality or state of having a veiled or uncertain meaning ⟨the stupefying *nebulosity* of his philosophical musings⟩ — see OBSCURITY 1

nebulous *adj* **1** having an often intentionally veiled or uncertain meaning ⟨made *nebulous* references to some major changes the future may hold⟩ — see OBSCURE 1
2 not seen or understood clearly ⟨could just make out the *nebulous* outline of a fishing shack in the dense fog⟩ — see FAINT 1

nebulousness *n* the quality or state of having a veiled or uncertain meaning ⟨the *nebulousness* of the imagery in his poetry seems to be part of its attraction to some readers⟩ — see OBSCURITY 1

necessarily *adv* because of necessity ⟨the argument that the existence of the universe *necessarily* implies the existence of an all-powerful being responsible for creating it⟩ — see NEEDS

necessary *adj* **1** forcing one's compliance or participation by or as if by law ⟨an emissions test is *necessary* before you can renew the registration for your car⟩ — see MANDATORY
2 impossible to avoid or evade ⟨taxes will always be a *necessary* evil⟩ — see INEVITABLE
3 impossible to do without ⟨food and water are *necessary* for survival⟩ — see ESSENTIAL 1

necessary *n* something necessary, indispensable, or unavoidable ⟨a modest income that provided the family with only the *necessaries* of life⟩ — see ESSENTIAL 1

necessitate *vb* to have as a requirement ⟨getting new shoes would *necessitate* another trip to the mall⟩ — see NEED 1

necessitous *adj* **1** impossible to do without ⟨all the dreaded, *necessitous* decisions that one must make when arranging the funeral of a loved one⟩ — see ESSENTIAL 1
2 lacking money or material possessions ⟨amidst the holiday feasting, merrymaking and spending, it was easy to overlook the *necessitous* members of the community⟩ — see POOR 1
3 needing immediate attention ⟨firmly of the belief that no matter is so *necessitous* that it cannot be put off until tomorrow⟩ — see ACUTE 2

necessity *n* **1** something necessary, indispensable, or unavoidable ⟨on any road trip, accurate maps are a *necessity*⟩ — see ESSENTIAL 1
2 the state of lacking sufficient money or material possessions ⟨two years of unemployment had reduced the family to abject *necessity*⟩ — see POVERTY 1

neck *n* **1** a broad geographical area ⟨we're going to be in your *neck* of the woods in July, so maybe we can get together then⟩ — see REGION 2
2 a narrow body of water between two land masses ⟨only a narrow *neck* of the South China Sea separates Taiwan from mainland China⟩ — see CHANNEL 2
3 a very small distance or degree ⟨for most of the race he trailed the leader by only a *neck*⟩ — see HAIR 1

neck and neck *adj* showing little difference in the standing of the competitors ⟨a *neck and neck* finish in which only a fraction of a second separated the winner from the runner-up⟩ — see CLOSE 3

necklace *n* an ornamental chain or string (as of beads) worn around the neck ⟨found a lovely *necklace* to match the bracelet and ring her mother had given her⟩
synonyms choker, collar, dog collar, lei
related words torque (*or* torc); beads, carcanet [*archaic*], rivière; rope, strand; bangle, lavaliere (*also* lavalliere), locket, pendant (*also* pendent)

necrology *n* a notice of a person's death usually with a short biographical account ⟨the club's founder recently died, and this month's newsletter includes a lengthy *necrology*⟩ — see OBITUARY

necromancer *n* a person skilled in using supernatural forces ⟨in ancient times any kind of natural disaster was apt to be regarded as the work of some evil-minded *necromancer*⟩ — see MAGICIAN 1

necromancy *n* the power to control natural forces through supernatural means ⟨in the conjuring of the souls of the dead, *necromancy* seemed to offer human beings a means of exerting some control over an uncertain world⟩ — see MAGIC 1

necropolis *n* a piece of land used for burying the dead ⟨an ancient *necropolis* that has given archaeologists valuable insights into how people once lived and died⟩ — see CEMETERY

necropsy *n* examination of a dead body especially to find out the cause of death ⟨a *necropsy* failed to definitively establish a cause of death⟩ — see AUTOPSY

need *n* **1** a state of being without something necessary, desirable, or useful ⟨when it came time to wrap the presents, he found he was in *need* of adhesive tape⟩
synonyms absence, lack, needfulness, want
related words deficiency, deficit, inadequacy, insufficiency; dearth, meagerness, paucity, poverty, scantiness, scarceness, scarcity, shortage, skimpiness; defect, minus; deprivation, famishment, privation; demand, essential, necessity, requirement, requisite
near antonyms adequacy, enough, sufficiency; fund, pool, stock, supply; excess, fill, overabundance, oversupply, plenty, surfeit, surplus; hoard, stockpile
2 something necessary, indispensable, or unavoidable ⟨got a job that barely provided for his basic *needs*⟩ — see ESSENTIAL 1
3 something one must do because of prior agreement ⟨no *need* to apologize⟩ — see OBLIGATION 1
4 the state of lacking sufficient money or material possessions ⟨donating money to help those in *need*⟩ — see POVERTY 1

need *vb* **1** to have as a requirement ⟨a national crisis that *needs* a strong leader to solve it⟩
synonyms bear, challenge, claim, demand, necessitate, require, take, want, warrant
related words entail, involve; ask, beg, claim, clamor (for), cry (for); hurt (for), lack; command, enjoin, exact, insist, press, quest, stipulate
phrases call for
near antonyms own, possess
antonyms have, hold
2 to be under necessity or obligation to ⟨you *need* not stand when she enters the room⟩
synonyms have (to), must, ought (to), shall, should
related words will

needed *adj* impossible to do without ⟨pack only what will be *needed*⟩ — see ESSENTIAL 1

needful *adj* **1** impossible to do without ⟨purchase *needful* provisions⟩ — see ESSENTIAL 1
2 lacking money or material possessions ⟨let's first help the *needful* families in our own community⟩ — see POOR 1

needful *n* **1** something (as pieces of stamped metal or printed paper) customarily and legally used as a medium of exchange, a measure of value, or a means of payment ⟨fortunately, the family had the *needful* to stock up the larder before the long hard winter⟩ — see MONEY 1
2 something necessary, indispensable, or unavoidable ⟨packed a warm jacket and other *needfuls* for an autumn weekend in the country⟩ — see ESSENTIAL 1

needfulness *n* a state of being without something necessary, desirable, or useful ⟨I can scarcely describe my *needfulness* for a hot shower after a hard-fought game of racquetball⟩ — see NEED 1

neediness *n* the state of lacking sufficient money or material possessions ⟨a family's general level of *neediness* is the determining factor in the allocation of charitable donations⟩ — see POVERTY 1

needle *n* **1** a slender hollow instrument by which material is put into or taken from the body through the skin ⟨the nurse inserted the *needle* into his vein and collected some blood for testing⟩
synonyms hype [*slang*], hypodermic, hypodermic needle, hypodermic syringe, syringe
2 an arrow-shaped piece on a dial or scale for registering information ⟨simply by reading the compass *needle* you should be able to figure out in which direction we're heading⟩ — see POINTER 1

needle *vb* **1** to attack repeatedly with mean put-downs or insults ⟨we *needled* him mercilessly for thinking that he had any chance of being the prom date for the school's most popular girl⟩ — see TEASE 2
2 to subject (someone) to constant scoldings and sharp reminders ⟨quit *needling* me! I'll take out the trash in a minute!⟩ — see NAG 1

needlelike *adj* being of less than usual width ⟨I need a *needlelike* piece of wire to finish making this wreath⟩ — see NARROW 1

needler *n* a person who causes repeated emotional pain, distress, or annoyance to another ⟨those merciless *needlers* who had the child in tears almost every day at school⟩ — see TORMENTOR

needless *adj* not needed by the circumstances or to accomplish an end ⟨*needless* expenditures that pushed the construction project way over budget⟩ — see UNNECESSARY

needlework *n* decorative stitching done on cloth with the use of a needle ⟨a visit to the art museum to see an exhibition of 18th-century *needlework*⟩
synonyms embroidery
related words crewel, cross-stitch, needlepoint; fagoting (*or* faggoting), hemstitch, smocking; fancywork

needs *adv* because of necessity ⟨the dangers of global warming must *needs* be recognized—and recognized soon—by the industrialized nations of the world⟩
synonyms ineluctably, inescapably, inevitably, ipso facto, necessarily, perforce, unavoidably
related words involuntarily
antonyms unnecessarily

needy *adj* lacking money or material possessions ⟨those generous souls who regularly give money and donate clothes to help the *needy*⟩ — see POOR 1

ne'er *adv* at no time ⟨fare thee well, for *ne'er* shall I return⟩ — see NEVER 1

ne'er–do–well *adj* having no ambition, success, or value to society ⟨the *ne'er-do-well* denizens of a seedy bar near the docks⟩ — see NO-ACCOUNT 1

ne'er–do–well *n* an idle worthless person ⟨the local *ne'er-do-wells* seem to hang out on the street corners at all hours of the day and night⟩
synonyms bum, derelict, do-nothing, good-for-nothing, no-account, no-good, no-goodnik, slacker, vagrant
related words hobo, sundowner [*Australian*], tramp,

vagabond; drifter, roamer, transient; beggar, panhandler; dodger, goldbrick, shirker; gamine, ragamuffin, urchin, waif; drone, idler, lazybones, loafer, slouch, slug, sluggard; down-and-out (*or* down-and-outer), indigent, pauper
near antonyms success, winner

nefarious *adj* not conforming to a high moral standard; morally unacceptable ⟨the chaste heroines and *nefarious* villains of old-time melodramas⟩ — see BAD 2

negate *vb* **1** to declare not to be true ⟨this evidence *negates* his claim that he was not at the scene of the crime⟩ — see DENY 1
2 to put an end to by formal action ⟨Prohibition was established by the 18th amendment to the U.S. Constitution, only to be *negated* by the 21st amendment 13 years later⟩ — see ABOLISH 1
3 to think not to be true or real ⟨you simply can't *negate* your feelings for someone, even if they don't feel the same way about you⟩ — see DISBELIEVE

negation *n* **1** a refusal to confirm the truth of a statement ⟨issued specific *negations* of all of the charges against her⟩ — see DENIAL 2
2 the doing away with something by formal action ⟨a ruling by the Supreme Court that many regarded as a *negation* of the basic right of privacy⟩ — see ABOLITION

negative *adj* **1** marked by opposition or ill will ⟨classes that hopefully will change the *negative* attitude that some students have toward the recent immigrants⟩ — see HOSTILE 1
2 opposed to one's interests ⟨the almost universally *negative* reaction to the book⟩ — see ADVERSE 1

negative *n* **1** a vote or decision against something ⟨in the absence of an unambiguous *negative* from the commander, we decided to continue on the mission⟩ — see NO 1
2 something that is as different as possible from something else ⟨the desire to control another person is actually the *negative* of real love⟩ — see OPPOSITE
3 a feature of someone or something that creates difficulty for achieving success ⟨the main *negative* of this job is that I have to get up at 4:30 a.m.⟩ — see DISADVANTAGE 1

negative *vb* **1** to reject by or as if by a vote ⟨although the rebuttal was very eloquent, the jury *negatived* it in favor of the prosecution's argument⟩ ⟨we promptly *negatived* the idea of having pizza again for dinner, noting that we had already had it for three nights that week⟩
synonyms blackball, down, kill, nix, shoot down, veto
related words decline, disallow, disapprove, dismiss, refuse; blacklist
near antonyms admit, allow, approve, assent (to), pass, sanction; elect, support
antonyms confirm, ratify
2 to declare not to be true ⟨the governor's press secretary promptly *negatived* the rumor that he was not intending to run for reelection⟩ — see DENY 1
3 to show unwillingness to accept, do, engage in, or agree to ⟨even though I had originally *negatived* the invitation, Mom thought I should go anyway⟩ — see DECLINE 1
4 to balance with an equal force so as to make ineffective ⟨no amount of flattery is likely to *negative* that overheard insult⟩ — see OFFSET
5 to be unwilling to grant ⟨ultimately, we *negatived* the request for a personal loan⟩ — see DENY 2

negativistic *adj* inclined to doubt or question claims ⟨if we were to listen to those *negativistic* bean counters, we would never have a marketing campaign of any kind⟩ — see SKEPTICAL 1

neglect *n* **1** the state of being unattended to or not cared for ⟨for years the barn sat in *neglect* until one day it finally fell down⟩
synonyms desolation, dilapidation, disrepair, seediness
related words inattention, negligence; abandonment, desertion; decay, decrepitude, dereliction, deterioration, disintegration, dumpiness, ruin, ruination
near antonyms conservation, preservation, upkeep
antonyms keeping, repair
2 the nonperformance of an assigned or expected action ⟨your ongoing *neglect* of your health is going to land you in the hospital someday⟩ — see FAILURE 1

neglect *vb* **1** to fail to give proper attention to ⟨as usual the news media *neglected* the real issues of the campaign and focused on personalities⟩
synonyms bypass, disregard, forget, ignore, overlook, overpass, pass over, slight, slur (over)
related words fail; miss, omit; brush (aside *or* off), reject, shrug off, slough (off) *also* sluff (off); disdain, pooh-pooh (*also* pooh), scorn; scant, skimp
near antonyms appreciate, cherish, prize, treasure, value; cultivate, foster, nurse, nurture; pamper; remember; listen (to), watch; follow, mark, note, notice, observe, remark
antonyms attend (to), heed, mind, regard, tend (to)
2 to leave undone or unattended to especially through carelessness ⟨I've *neglected* my garden, and now it's overgrown with weeds⟩
synonyms forget, shirk
related words slack (off)
near antonyms carry out, do, execute, perform; accomplish, achieve; keep up, maintain
antonyms attend (to), remember
3 to miss the opportunity or obligation ⟨conveniently, the job applicant *neglected* to mention his criminal record⟩
synonyms fail, forget, omit
related words disregard, ignore, overlook, overpass, pass over, pretermit, slight; slide, slip; default; skip
phrases miss out on
near antonyms heed, mind, remember; keep, observe; carry out, do, execute, perform, practice (*also* practise); discharge, fulfill (*or* fulfil), meet, satisfy; comply (with)

neglected *adj* showing signs of advanced wear and tear and neglect ⟨a *neglected* teddy bear, missing one eye and both ears, shoved into the closet⟩ — see SHABBY 1

neglectful *adj* failing to give proper care and attention ⟨he's certainly not a *neglectful* father as he takes very good care of his children⟩ — see NEGLIGENT

neglectfulness *n* failure to take the care that a cautious person usually takes ⟨as a result of the mother's chronic *neglectfulness* of their welfare, the children were placed in foster care⟩ — see NEGLIGENCE 1

neglecting *adj* failing to give proper care and attention ⟨our chronically *neglecting* custodian has let trash accumulate around the warehouse⟩ — see NEGLIGENT

negligence *n* **1** failure to take the care that a cautious person usually takes ⟨exhibiting his usual *negligence*, he failed to set the emergency brake, and the car rolled down the steep hill and crashed into the telephone pole⟩
synonyms carelessness, dereliction, heedlessness, incaution, incautiousness, laxness, neglectfulness, remissness, slackness
related words foolhardiness, rashness, recklessness, wildness; neglect, omission; delinquency, irresponsibility, irresponsibleness, malfeasance, malpractice, misconduct; misdirection, mishandling, mismanagement; forgetfulness, inadvertence, inadvertency, inattention, inattentiveness, obliviousness, shortsightedness, unwariness
near antonyms alertness, attention, attentiveness, awareness; circumspection, observance, vigilance,

watchfulness; responsibility, responsibleness
antonyms care, carefulness, caution, cautiousness, heedfulness
2 the nonperformance of an assigned or expected action ⟨the factory's owners are being charged with criminal *negligence* for the fire that killed a dozen workers⟩ — see FAILURE 1

negligent *adj* failing to give proper care and attention ⟨the youngster has been woefully *negligent* in taking care of the vacationing neighbor's dog, repeatedly forgetting to feed the poor animal⟩
synonyms careless, derelict, disregardful, lax, lazy, neglectful, neglecting, remiss, slack
related words heedless, incautious, irresponsible, reckless, wild; unguarded, unwary; forgetful; disregardful, disregarding, inattentive, oblivious, thoughtless, unheeding, unmindful, unthinking; apathetic, disinterested, indifferent, unconcerned, uninterested; delinquent; loose
near antonyms meticulous, painstaking, punctilious; cautious, chary, circumspect, gingerly, guarded; alert, heedful, heeding, mindful, observant, regardful, regarding, vigilant, wary, watchful; foresighted, forethoughtful, provident, responsible; thinking, thoughtful; concerned, interested
antonyms attentive, careful, conscientious, nonnegligent

negligibility *n* the quality or state of being unimportant ⟨the *negligibility* of so much that is churned out by weekly television⟩ — see INSIGNIFICANCE

negligible *adj* **1** so small or unimportant as to warrant little or no attention ⟨the two cents in change was such a *negligible* sum that she left the store without bothering to take it⟩
synonyms chicken, de minimis, footling, inconsequential, inconsiderable, insignificant, measly, Mickey Mouse, minute, niggling, no-account, nominal, paltry, peanut, petty, picayune, piddling, piddly, piffling, pimping, slight, trifling, trivial
related words inferior, mean; imperceptible, inappreciable; little, puny, tiny; hairsplitting, nitpicking, pettifogging, quibbling; one-horse, small-fry, two-bit
near antonyms serious, substantial, weighty; eventful, momentous, pivotal; conspicuous, noteworthy, outstanding, prominent, remarkable, striking; appreciable, discernible (*also* discernable), measurable
antonyms big, consequential, considerable, important, material, significant
2 lacking importance ⟨the results from that small study of coffee drinkers are *negligible* and can be ignored⟩ — see UNIMPORTANT
3 small in degree ⟨there's a *negligible* chance I may make it to the picnic, but don't count on it⟩ — see REMOTE 1

negligibly *adv* in a very small quantity or degree ⟨this box is *negligibly* bigger than the other one, but it's such a slight difference I don't think it matters⟩ — see LITTLE 1

negotiable *adj* **1** capable of being traveled on ⟨some of the national park's roads are not *negotiable* in winter⟩ — see PASSABLE 1
2 open to question or dispute ⟨the final judgment is not *negotiable*⟩ — see DEBATABLE 1

negotiate *vb* **1** to bring about through discussion and compromise ⟨wanted to *negotiate* a higher salary before she accepted the job offer⟩
synonyms arrange, bargain, concert, conclude
related words settle (on *or* upon); chaffer, deal, dicker, haggle, horse-trade, palter; agree; contract, covenant; argue, debate, discuss, hammer out, hash (over), reason, talk, talk over, work out; renegotiate
2 to deal with (something) usually skillfully or efficiently ⟨she's good at *negotiating* personality conflicts between coworkers⟩ — see HANDLE 1
3 to plan out usually with subtle skill or care ⟨the prisoners *negotiated* their escape by using Morse code to tap messages to each other through the walls⟩ — see ENGINEER
4 to talk over or dispute the terms of a purchase ⟨told them I'd take $8,000 for the car and wasn't in the mood to *negotiate*⟩ — see BARGAIN 1
5 to carry through (as a process) to completion ⟨scores of experiments later, the chemists managed to *negotiate* the development of a more durable polymer⟩ — see PERFORM 1

negotiation *n* the act or practice of each side giving up something in order to reach an agreement ⟨it will take some *negotiation*, but I think we can get each side to agree to a cease-fire⟩ — see CONCESSION 1

neigh *vb* to make the cry typical of a horse ⟨the horses *neighed* when the rider came into the barn⟩
synonyms nicker, whicker, whinny

neighbor *vb* to be adjacent to ⟨the baseball field *neighbors* a parking lot⟩ — see ADJOIN 1

neighborhood *n* **1** an approximate amount, extent, or degree ⟨a movie that's said to have cost in the *neighborhood* of 100 million dollars⟩
synonyms matter, tune, vicinity
related words ballpark; nearness, proximity
2 an area (as of a city) set apart for some purpose or having some special feature ⟨are you familiar with the city's Latino *neighborhood*?⟩ — see DISTRICT
3 the people living in a particular area ⟨invited practically the whole *neighborhood* over for a big party⟩ — see COMMUNITY 1
4 an adjoining region or space ⟨we were somewhere in the *neighborhood* of the Capitol because we could see the dome⟩ — see ENVIRONS 2

neighboring *adj* **1** having a border in common ⟨he and his future wife grew up on *neighboring* farms⟩ — see ADJACENT
2 not being distant in time, space, or significance ⟨the statehouse and its *neighboring* buildings⟩ — see CLOSE 2

neighborliness *n* kindly concern, interest, or support ⟨showing uncommon *neighborliness*, one of my new coworkers took me out to lunch on my first day⟩ — see GOODWILL 1

neighborly *adj* having or showing kindly feeling and sincere interest ⟨they were *neighborly* folks, always ready to lend a helping hand whenever necessary⟩ — see FRIENDLY 1

nemesis *n* **1** one who inflicts punishment in return for an injury or offense ⟨Batman is the Joker's main *nemesis* and always foils his wicked plots⟩
synonyms avenger, castigator, chastiser, punisher, scourge, vigilante
related words revenger; redresser, righter; requiter
near antonyms ransomer, redeemer, vindicator
2 suffering, loss, or hardship imposed in response to a crime or offense ⟨social ostracism was once society's *nemesis* for those who defied its sexual mores⟩ — see PUNISHMENT
3 a source of harm or misfortune ⟨irrationality is the *nemesis* of democracy, for good government depends upon the wisdom of the electorate⟩ — see BANE 1

neolithic *adj* having passed its time of use or usefulness ⟨my old manual typewriter now seems positively *neolithic*⟩ — see OBSOLETE

neonate *n* a recently born person ⟨the hospital has added a new wing especially for *neonates*⟩ — see BABY 1

neophyte *n* **1** a person who has recently been persuaded to join a religious sect ⟨*neophytes* are assigned

an experienced church member to guide them through their first year⟩ — see CONVERT 1
2 a person who is just starting out in a field of activity ⟨a *neophyte* in snowboarding⟩ — see BEGINNER

neoplasm *n* an abnormal mass of tissue ⟨removed a *neoplasm* from the patient's abdomen⟩ — see GROWTH 1

ne plus ultra *n* the highest part or point ⟨this new sports car is being billed as the *ne plus ultra* of automotive achievement⟩ — see HEIGHT 1

Neptune *n* the whole body of salt water that covers nearly three-fourths of the earth ⟨sailors shipwrecked by the wild waves of *Neptune*⟩ — see OCEAN 1

nerd *n* **1** a person slavishly devoted to intellectual or academic pursuits ⟨was such a *nerd* in college that she spent Saturday nights at the library⟩
synonyms bookworm, dink [*slang*], dork [*slang*], geek, grind, swot [*British*], weenie, wonk
related words double-dome, egghead, highbrow, intellectual; brain, genius; academic, bookman, scholar; gearhead, techie
near antonyms goldbrick, goof-off, slacker, underachiever; lowbrow
2 a person with strong intellectual interests ⟨an unlikely romance between a *nerd* and a campus beauty queen⟩ — see INTELLECTUAL

nerdish *adj* much given to learning and thinking ⟨*nerdish* students will find several university organizations where they will fit in⟩ — see INTELLECTUAL 1

nerdy *adj* much given to learning and thinking ⟨a fringe party of *nerdy* political activists who have no chance of getting elected⟩ — see INTELLECTUAL 1

nerts *n pl, slang* language, behavior, or ideas that are absurd and contrary to good sense ⟨*nerts*! that's all I have to say about that idea⟩ — see NONSENSE 1

nerve *n* **1** shameless boldness ⟨you've got a lot of *nerve* showing up here⟩ — see EFFRONTERY
2 strength of mind to carry on in spite of danger ⟨that daring rescue took some *nerve*⟩ — see COURAGE
3 nerves *pl* a sense of panic or extreme nervousness ⟨a veteran performer who still gets a case of the *nerves* before performances⟩ — see JITTERS

nerve *vb* to prepare (oneself) mentally or emotionally ⟨needs to *nerve* himself for the big game tomorrow⟩ — see FORTIFY 1

nerve center *n* a thing or place that is of greatest importance to an activity or interest ⟨Wall Street's undisputed status as the *nerve center* for the world of high finance⟩ — see CENTER 1

nerved *adj* inclined or willing to take risks ⟨a *nerved* and fearless driver of race cars⟩ — see BOLD 1

nerveless *adj* **1** lacking strength of will or character ⟨he's a *nerveless* pushover who'll be eaten alive by his own staff⟩ — see WEAK 2
2 not easily panicked or upset ⟨to be a paramedic, you need to be calm, clearheaded, and *nerveless* in emergencies⟩ — see UNFLAPPABLE

nerve-racking *or* **nerve-wracking** *adj* marked by or causing agitation or uncomfortable feelings ⟨the *nerve-racking* wait to learn the identities of the passengers who were killed in the plane crash⟩ — see NERVOUS 2

nerviness *n* shameless boldness ⟨didn't appreciate her *nerviness* in asking my boyfriend on a date⟩ — see EFFRONTERY

nervosity *n* an uneasy state of mind usually over the possibility of an anticipated misfortune or trouble ⟨a palpable feeling of *nervosity* in every corner of the city after the terrorist attack⟩ — see ANXIETY 1

nervous *adj* **1** feeling or showing uncomfortable feelings of uncertainty ⟨he was *nervous* about how he would do at the varsity basketball tryouts⟩
synonyms aflutter, antsy, anxious, atwitter, dithery, edgy, goosey, het up, hinky [*slang*], hung up, ill at ease, insecure, jittery, jumpy, nervy, perturbed, queasy (*also* queazy), tense, troubled, uneasy, unquiet, upset, uptight, worried
related words aggrieved, bothered, concerned, disquieted, distraught, distressed, disturbed, freaked, freaked-out, shook-up; apprehensive, foreboding, hesitant, misgiving; fretful, fretting, stewing, vexed; qualmish, qualmy; flustered, twittered, undone, unnerved, unstrung; obsessed, preoccupied, restless; fidgety, flighty, fluttery, high-strung, hypertense, skittish, spooky
phrases keyed up, on edge, on pins and needles, on tenterhooks
near antonyms confident, self-assured, self-confident, sure; controlled, self-controlled
antonyms calm, collected, cool, easy, happy-go-lucky, nerveless, relaxed
2 marked by or causing agitation or uncomfortable feelings ⟨a *nervous* silence filled the room as the teacher handed out the graded exams⟩
synonyms agitating, anxious, creepy, disquieting, distressful, distressing, disturbing, fraught, hairy, nail-biting, nerve-racking (*or* nerve-wracking), restless, tense, uneasy, unnerving, unsettling, worrisome
related words bothersome, troublesome; foreboding, misgiving; discouraging, disheartening, strained; restive, restless, unrestful; awkward, embarrassing
near antonyms restful; pacific
antonyms calming, comfortable, easy, peaceful, quiet, quieting, tranquil
3 easily excited by nature ⟨a *nervous* sort of person, she's completely thrown by anything unexpected⟩ — see EXCITABLE

nervous breakdown *n* a mental or nervous collapse ⟨you're going to have a *nervous breakdown* if you keep up that pace⟩ — see BREAKDOWN 1

nervous Nellie *or* **nervous Nelly** *n* a person who is inclined to worry ⟨many new parents are *nervous Nellies* when it comes to the health of their babies⟩
synonyms handwringer, worrier, worrywart
related words defeatist, fatalist, pessimist
phrases nervous wreck
near antonyms optimist, Pollyanna

nervousness *n* an uneasy state of mind usually over the possibility of an anticipated misfortune or trouble ⟨your *nervousness* over your son's safety is only natural⟩ — see ANXIETY 1

nervy *adj* **1** displaying or marked by rude boldness ⟨the *nervy* waiter held up the small tip and called out to the departing customers, "Hope it doesn't break the bank!"⟩
synonyms arch, audacious, bold, bold-faced, brash, brassbound, brassy, brazen, brazen-faced, cheeky, cocksure, cocky, fresh, impertinent, impudent, insolent, sassy, saucy, wise
related words assertive, forward, obtrusive; audacious, defiant, disrespectful; shameless, unabashed, unblushing; bluff, blunt, curt; cute, facetious, flip, flippant, pert, smart, smart-aleck, smart-alecky; lippy, mouthy
near antonyms demure, humble, modest; courteous, genteel, mannerly, polite, proper; deferential, respectful; abashed, ashamed, blushing, embarrassed, shamefaced; gentle, mild; inconspicuous, unobtrusive
antonyms meek, mousy (*or* mousey), retiring, shy, timid
2 inclined or willing to take risks ⟨*nervy* rock climbers wanting to make gravity-defying ascents⟩ — see BOLD 1
3 feeling or showing uncomfortable feelings of uncertainty ⟨I'm a little *nervy* about my first job interview⟩ — see NERVOUS 1

nescience *n* the state of being unaware or uninformed ⟨the appalling *nescience* of today's high schoolers concerning international affairs⟩ — see IGNORANCE 1

nescient *adj* not informed about or aware of something ⟨narrow-minded, provincial people who are blissfully *nescient* of the world beyond their little suburb⟩ — see IGNORANT 2

ness *n* **1** an area of high ground jutting out into a body of water beyond the line of the coast ⟨from atop the *ness*, there was a beautiful view of the coastline as it stretched for miles into the distance⟩ — see HEADLAND 1

2 an area of land that juts out into a body of water ⟨the little skiff rounded the tip of the *ness*⟩ — see [2]CAPE

nest *n* **1** a place or environment that favors the development of something ⟨suspected that the elite private universities were a *nest* of antigovernment sentiments⟩ — see BREEDING GROUND

2 a place where a person goes to hide or to avoid others ⟨headed back to her cozy *nest* in the mountains for a little rest and relaxation⟩ — see HIDEOUT

nest egg *n* a sum of money set aside for a particular purpose ⟨paid for the computer out of his *nest egg*⟩ — see FUND 1

nestle *vb* **1** to lie close ⟨*nestled* in next to the other kittens in the box⟩ — see NUZZLE

2 to sit or recline comfortably or cozily ⟨*nestling* with her children on the couch⟩ — see SNUGGLE 1

3 to establish or place comfortably or snugly ⟨we had scarcely *nestled* the children in their beds when there was a knock at the door⟩ — see ENSCONCE 1

nestor *n* the senior member of a group ⟨as the grizzled *nestor* of American film critics, he greatly influences what other reviewers write⟩ — see DEAN

[1]**net** *n* **1** a fabric made of strands loosely twisted, knotted, or woven together at regular intervals ⟨the basketball didn't go into the basket—it just hit the *net*⟩
synonyms mesh, netting, network
related words web, webbing; grille (*also* grill), lattice, screen, screening, wirework; bobbinet, Brussels lace, filigree, fishnet, lace, marquisette, tulle

2 a device or scheme for capturing another by surprise ⟨drug runners caught in an elaborate *net* set by the police⟩ — see TRAP 1

3 something that catches and holds ⟨caught in a *net* of palace intrigues⟩ — see WEB 1

[2]**net** *n* **1** the amount of money left when expenses are subtracted from the total amount received ⟨his *net* for the year was about 60% of his total income⟩ — see PROFIT 1

2 the central part or aspect of something under consideration ⟨the *net* of the report on race relations is that things are better but not good enough⟩ — see CRUX

[1]**net** *vb* **1** to catch or hold as if in a net ⟨the kite was stubbornly *netted* in the branches of the willow tree⟩ — see ENTANGLE 2

2 to take physical control or possession of (something) suddenly or forcibly ⟨a police sting that *netted* drug dealers from all parts of the city⟩ — see CATCH 1

[2]**net** *vb* to receive after charges and deductions have been made ⟨the entrepreneur *netted* millions on that deal⟩
synonyms clear
related words earn, gain, garner, get, make, realize; cash in (on), rake (in); clean up
near antonyms gross

nether *adj* situated lower down ⟨skied the *nether* slope of the mountain⟩ — see INFERIOR 1

nethermost *adj* of, relating to, or located at the bottom ⟨some strange creature from the *nethermost* region of the ocean⟩ — see BOTTOM

netherworld *n* a social sphere that exists outside of the mainstream ⟨the shadowy *netherworld* of all-night raves⟩
synonyms demimonde, demiworld, half-world, underbelly, underworld
related words abyss, depths

netizen *n* an active participant in the online community of the Internet ⟨the dismaying rudeness that so many *netizens* exhibit while online⟩
synonyms cybercitizen, cybernaut, cybersurfer
related words browser, surfer

netting *n* a fabric made of strands loosely twisted, knotted, or woven together at regular intervals ⟨wore a veil of *netting*⟩ — see [1]NET 1

nettle *vb* to disturb the peace of mind of (someone) especially by repeated disagreeable acts ⟨don't *nettle* your brother while he's trying to do his homework⟩ — see IRRITATE 1

nettlesome *adj* causing annoyance ⟨a few *nettlesome* details that still required attention⟩ — see ANNOYING

nettling *adj* causing annoyance ⟨your constant sniffling is extremely *nettling*⟩ — see ANNOYING

network *n* **1** a fabric made of strands loosely twisted, knotted, or woven together at regular intervals ⟨didn't like to embroider *network* as it tore so easily⟩ — see [1]NET 1

2 something made up of many interdependent or related parts ⟨a telephone *network*⟩ — see SYSTEM 1

3 a group of people sharing a common interest and relating together socially ⟨being gradually introduced to the *network* of African-American business leaders in the city⟩ — see GANG 2

neuter *vb* to remove the sex organs of ⟨agreed to let the children have the dog on the condition that they have her *neutered*⟩
synonyms alter, desex, fix
related words castrate, emasculate, geld; spay; sterilize

neutral *adj* **1** not favoring or joined to either side in a quarrel, contest, or war ⟨Sweden remained *neutral* during World War II, refusing to join either side in the conflict⟩
synonyms nonpartisan
related words nonaligned; hands-off, noninterventionist; autonomous, independent, sovereign (*also* sovran), unaffiliated; nonbelligerent; individualistic; disinterested, evenhanded, fair, impartial, indifferent, unbiased, uninfluenced, unprejudiced; bipartisan
phrases on the fence
near antonyms biased, partial, partisan, prejudiced, unfair; affiliated, associated, federated; belligerent
antonyms allied, confederate

2 lacking in distinctive features or qualities ⟨the hero is the novel's only fully fleshed person, all the others being rather *neutral* characters who are just there to advance the plot⟩ — see NONDESCRIPT

neutralism *n* lack of favoritism toward one side or another ⟨his *neutralism* in the matter is questionable, since he owns thousands of shares in the company⟩ — see DETACHMENT 1

neutrality *n* lack of favoritism toward one side or another ⟨his unimpeachable *neutrality* makes him the ideal person to judge which of us is right⟩ — see DETACHMENT 1

neutralize *vb* **1** to balance with an equal force so as to make ineffective ⟨a pro-government rally that is intended to *neutralize* the antiwar demonstrations⟩ — see OFFSET

2 to put to death deliberately ⟨orders to find the renegade colonel and to *neutralize* him⟩ — see MURDER 1

neutralizer *n* a force or influence that makes an opposing force ineffective or less effective ⟨a police crackdown that's intended as a *neutralizer* on the rising violence⟩ — see COUNTERBALANCE

never *adv* **1** at no time ⟨I have *never* been out of the country⟩

synonyms ne'er
related words nevermore; not; infrequently, little, rarely, seldom
near antonyms eternally, everlastingly, evermore, invariably; frequently, often, recurrently, repeatedly
antonyms always, constantly, continuously, endlessly, ever, forever, perpetually
2 not in any degree, way, or under any condition ⟨though she turned down his offer of marriage twice, he was *never* convinced that she did not love him⟩
synonyms no, none, nothing, noway (*or* noways), nowise
related words nowhere near
phrases by no means, in no wise, nothing doing, on no account
near antonyms completely, extremely, full, fully, par excellence, right, very; altogether, exactly; somehow, someway (*also* someways); out
antonyms anyhow, anyway, anywise, at all, ever, half, however

never mind *conj* to say nothing of ⟨I have a hard enough time getting out of bed before sunrise, *never mind* getting to work so early⟩ — see LET ALONE

never–never land *n* an often imaginary place or state of utter perfection and happiness ⟨a depiction of Merry Old England that debunks the popular notion that it was ever some sort of *never-never land*⟩ — see PARADISE 1

nevertheless *adv* in spite of that ⟨I really don't want to; *nevertheless*, I will do it because you asked me to⟩ — see HOWEVER

new *adj* **1** taking the place of one that came before ⟨after my bike was stolen, my scooter became my *new* mode of transportation⟩
synonyms makeshift, substitute, substitutive
related words alternate, alternative, pinch; different, other, separate; extra, spare; improvised, jury; another, second; utility; successive; equivalent
near antonyms first, former; equal, identical, same; lasting, permanent
antonyms original
2 not known or experienced before ⟨Spanish was a *new* course of study for her⟩ ⟨the Americas were *new* lands for the European explorers⟩
synonyms fresh, novel, original, strange, unaccustomed, unfamiliar, unheard-of, unknown, unprecedented
related words innovative, unique; nontraditional, unconventional, untried, unused, unworn; pathbreaking, pioneering, trailblazing
near antonyms conventional, established, traditional, tried, tried-and-true; derivative, imitative
antonyms familiar, hackneyed, old, time-honored, tired, warmed-over
3 recently made and never used before ⟨that unique scent that is the telltale sign of a *new* car⟩
synonyms brand-new, spick-and-span (*or* spic-and-span), unused
related words clean, fresh, mint, pristine, unspoiled; untouched; newfangled, new-fashioned; natural, raw, unprocessed, untreated, unworked, virgin
near antonyms dirty, soiled, spoiled, stale; aged, beat-up, old, shabby, shopworn, well-handled, worn
antonyms hand-me-down, second hand, used
4 made or become fresh in spirits or vigor ⟨a little rest made him a *new* man after the exhausting basketball game⟩
synonyms energized, freshened, invigorated, newborn, reanimated, reborn, recreated, reenergized, refreshed, regenerated, reinvigorated, renewed, resuscitated, revived
related words animated, enlivened, exhilarated, jazzed (up); resurrected; rested, untired, unwearied
near antonyms tired, weary; dampened, deadened; emasculated, unmanned; demoralized, disheartened, dispirited
antonyms drained, enervate, enervated, exhausted, knackered [*British*], weakened
5 being or involving the latest methods, concepts, information, or styles ⟨*new* techniques in plastic surgery⟩ — see MODERN

new *adv* not long ago ⟨*new*-mown grass⟩ — see NEWLY

new age *adj* being or involving the latest methods, concepts, information, or styles ⟨a kitchen crammed full of *new age* appliances⟩ — see MODERN

newbie *n* a person who is just starting out in a field of activity ⟨a *newbie* to the Internet, he was still trying to cope with the visual clutter of cyberspace⟩ — see BEGINNER

newborn *adj* made or become fresh in spirits or vigor ⟨felt like a *newborn* activist after that pep rally⟩ — see NEW 4

newborn *n* a recently born person ⟨intentionally bought clothes that were too big for her *newborn* but which undoubtedly would fit him in a few months⟩ — see BABY 1

newcomer *n* a person who is just starting out in a field of activity ⟨he's a *newcomer* to ice hockey⟩ — see BEGINNER

newfangled *adj* being or involving the latest methods, concepts, information, or styles ⟨got one of those *newfangled* espresso makers⟩ — see MODERN

new–fashioned *adj* being or involving the latest methods, concepts, information, or styles ⟨husbands staying at home to raise their children is a fairly *new-fashioned* idea⟩ — see MODERN

New Jerusalem *n* **1** a dwelling place of perfect happiness for the soul after death ⟨prayed that the those recently departed will spend eternal life in *New Jerusalem*⟩ — see HEAVEN 1
2 an often imaginary place or state of utter perfection and happiness ⟨an idealistic senator who thought that he could singlehandedly turn Washington into the *New Jerusalem*⟩ — see PARADISE 1

newly *adv* not long ago ⟨a *newly* married couple still getting to know one another⟩
synonyms freshly, just, late, lately, new, now, only, recently
related words latterly
phrases of late
near antonyms ago, before, earlier, early, erstwhile, formerly, previously; heretofore, hitherto
antonyms anciently

newness *n* the quality or appeal of being new ⟨all that the skyscraper has going for it is its *newness*, for it's an ugly, poorly designed building⟩ — see NOVELTY 1

news *n pl* a report of recent events or facts not previously known ⟨dropped by to give me the latest *news* about her daughter⟩
synonyms advice(s), 411 [*slang*], gen [*chiefly British*], info, information, intelligence, item, story, tidings, uncos [*chiefly Scottish*], word
related words announcement, bulletin, communication, correspondence, dispatch, message, reportage; dope, lowdown, scoop, tidbit (*also* titbit), tip; gossip, rumor, tale, tattle; feedback; disinformation, propaganda

newscaster *n* one who reads and introduces news reports on a news program ⟨*newscasters* were scrambling to put together an updated report after the unexpected turn of events⟩ — see ANCHORPERSON

newshound *n* a person employed by a newspaper, magazine, or radio or television station to gather, write, or report news ⟨a *newshound* of the old school, he was highly skeptical of the claim that the firings weren't politically motivated⟩ — see REPORTER

newsman *n* a person employed by a newspaper, magazine, or radio or television station to gather, write, or report news ⟨any *newsman* will tell you that if you talk to enough people, you'll eventually get a money quote⟩ — see REPORTER

newsmonger *n* a person who habitually reveals personal or sensational facts about others ⟨the neighborhood *newsmonger* came over to tell us that the Clarksons were putting in a pool⟩ — see GOSSIP 1

newspaper *n* a publication that appears at regular intervals ⟨liked to read the *newspaper* every morning⟩ — see JOURNAL 1

newsperson *n* a person employed by a newspaper, magazine, or radio or television station to gather, write, or report news ⟨the host of that morning show prefers to think of himself as a *newsperson* and not as an entertainer⟩ — see REPORTER

newsreader *n, chiefly British* one who reads and introduces news reports on a news program ⟨the legendary BBC *newsreader* now has her own current affairs program⟩ — see ANCHORPERSON

newsy *adj* having the style and content of everyday conversation ⟨a *newsy* TV program covering the local scene⟩ — see CHATTY 1

New York minute *n* a very small space of time ⟨in a *New York minute* she had signed the contract and was off on her first assignment⟩ — see INSTANT

next *adj* being the one that comes immediately after another ⟨my house is the *next* one⟩ ⟨turn at the *next* street, not this one⟩ ⟨she was *next* in line for concert tickets⟩
synonyms coming, ensuing, following, succeeding
related words consecutive, sequential, successive; posterior, subsequent; immediate; second
phrases on deck
near antonyms anterior, former; past; last
antonyms antecedent, foregoing, precedent, preceding, previous, prior

next–door *adj* not being distant in time, space, or significance ⟨a *next-door* neighbor who is always helpful and friendly⟩ — see CLOSE 2

next to *adv* very close to but not completely ⟨bought it for *next to* nothing⟩ — see ALMOST

next to *prep* **1** close to ⟨enjoys living *next to* the ocean⟩ — see AROUND 1
2 subsequent to in time or order ⟨*next to* the war, the flagging economy was the biggest campaign issue⟩ — see AFTER

nexus *n* **1** a series of things linked together ⟨the oft-repeated claim that any person on the planet can be connected to any other person through a *nexus* of six relationships⟩ — see CHAIN 1
2 a thing or place that is of greatest importance to an activity or interest ⟨as the *nexus* for three great religions, Jerusalem has had a troubled as well as illustrious history⟩ — see CENTER 1

Niagara *n* a great flow of water or of something that overwhelms ⟨that uncensored remark brought a *Niagara* of angry calls to the television station⟩ — see FLOOD

nib *n* **1** the jaws of a bird together with their hornlike covering ⟨a finch cracking seeds in its *nib*⟩ — see BEAK 1
2 the last and usually sharp or tapering part of something long and narrow ⟨make sure the *nib* has been sharpened before you try to cut anything⟩ — see POINT 2

nibble *n* a small piece or quantity of food ⟨I don't want a whole dessert, so can I just have a *nibble* of yours?⟩ — see MORSEL 1

nibble *vb* **1** to eat reluctantly and in small bites ⟨having no real appetite at all, I just *nibbled* during the party⟩
synonyms peck, pick
related words graze, nosh, snack; taste
near antonyms gorge, gormandize, overeat, pig out, swill
2 to crush or grind with the teeth ⟨*nibbling* crackers⟩ — see BITE (ON)
3 to consume or wear away gradually ⟨discovered that inflation had steadily *nibbled* their savings⟩ — see EAT 2

nibs *n pl* one of high position or importance within a group ⟨a staff appointment that must be approved by his *nibs*, the magazine's editor in chief⟩ — see BIG SHOT

nice *adj* **1** following the established traditions of refined society and good taste ⟨had *nice* manners⟩ — see PROPER 1
2 giving pleasure or contentment to the mind or senses ⟨a cool glass of lemonade sure would be *nice*⟩ — see PLEASANT 1
3 hard to please ⟨she's far too *nice* about her clothes for me to even consider giving her clothing for her birthday⟩ — see FINICKY
4 having an easygoing and pleasing manner especially in social situations ⟨such a *nice* person to have as a party guest⟩ — see AMIABLE
5 made or done with extreme care and accuracy ⟨the noticeably *nice* folding of the dinner napkins told us that we were in the home of a domestic diva⟩ — see FINE 2
6 conforming to a high standard of morality or virtue ⟨in those days *nice* people would not have been caught dead in a gambling casino⟩ — see GOOD 2
7 marked by or showing careful attention to set forms and details ⟨a gentleman's club with a *nice* code of honor that no one can breach and still remain a member⟩ — see CEREMONIOUS 1

nicely *adv* **1** in a pleasing way ⟨he's a *nicely* helpful child⟩ — see WELL 5
2 in a satisfactory way ⟨I'm doing *nicely*, and thanks for asking⟩ — see WELL 1
3 with good reason or courtesy ⟨excuse yourself *nicely* and you should be fine⟩ — see WELL 4

nice–nelly *adj* given to or marked by very conservative standards regarding personal behavior or morals ⟨the novel's wildly off base portrayal of 18th-century aristocrats as *nice-nelly* exemplars of decorum⟩ — see STRAITLACED

nice nelly *n* a person who is greatly concerned with seemly behavior and morality especially regarding sexual matters ⟨some *nice nelly* bowdlerized this collection of wartime ditties that were lustily sung by the men around the campfire⟩ — see PRUDE

nice–nellyism *n* a tendency to care a great deal about seemly behavior and morals especially in sexual matters ⟨a misguided *nice-nellyism* prompted the city-owned art museum to cancel its scheduled exhibit on the nude in photography⟩ — see PRUDERY

niceness *n* the state or quality of having a pleasant or agreeable manner in socializing with others ⟨his unfailing *niceness* makes him a great student to have in class⟩ — see AMIABILITY 1

nicety *n* **1** a single piece of information ⟨knows all the *niceties* of diplomatic protocol⟩ — see FACT 3
2 something that adds to one's ease of living ⟨a woman too fond of the *niceties* of urban living to even consider becoming a farmer's wife⟩ — see COMFORT 2
3 the quality or state of being very accurate ⟨there's a *nicety* of detail in his meticulously painted landscapes⟩ — see PRECISION

niche *n* **1** a hollowed-out space in a wall ⟨statues of various saints occupy the *niches* lining the abbey's many corridors⟩
synonyms alcove, nook, recess

related words corner, cranny, cubbyhole; cubicle; dent, embrasure, indent, indentation, indenture; ambry, housing, shrine

2 a situation or activity for which a person or thing is best suited ⟨after several false starts, she finally found her *niche* in the restaurant business⟩

synonyms groove, place, slot

related words appointment, berth, billet, capacity, function, job, position, post; rank, standing, station, status; forte, long suit, métier (*also* metier), speciality, specialty, strong suit, thing

3 the place where a plant or animal is usually or naturally found ⟨the platypus's *niche* is the waters of eastern Australia and Tasmania⟩ — see HOME 2

nick *n* **1** a V-shaped cut usually on an edge or a surface ⟨I made a *nick* in the frame when I accidentally dropped it⟩ — see NOTCH 1

2 *British slang* a place of confinement for persons held in lawful custody ⟨the blokes at the pub traded stories of nights spent in the *nick* after having lifted too many pints⟩ — see JAIL

3 *British* a state of being or fitness ⟨the princess is in excellent *nick* these days⟩ — see CONDITION 1

nick *vb, British slang* **1** to take (something) without right and with an intent to keep ⟨that lorry was a piece of rubbish, I don't know why anyone would want to *nick* it⟩ — see STEAL 1

2 to take or keep under one's control by authority of law ⟨a petty thief who was always getting *nicked* for picking the pockets of tourists outside Buckingham Palace⟩ — see ARREST 1

nicker *vb* to make the cry typical of a horse ⟨horses *nickering* in the barn⟩ — see NEIGH

nickname *n* a descriptive or familiar name given instead of or in addition to the one belonging to an individual ⟨his wavy hair earned him the *nickname* "Curly" early in life⟩

synonyms alias, byname, cognomen, epithet, handle, moniker (*also* monicker), sobriquet (*also* soubriquet), surname

related words appellation, denomination, denotation, designation, label, tag, title; anonym, nom de guerre, nom de plume, pen name, pseudonym

nidus *n* a place or environment that favors the development of something ⟨a type of contact lens that proved to be a *nidus* of infection⟩ — see BREEDING GROUND

nifty *adj* of the very best kind ⟨that popcorn popper is *nifty*⟩ — see EXCELLENT

nifty *n* **1** something said or done to cause laughter ⟨though ostensibly a drama, the play is filled with zingy little *nifties* that lighten the mood⟩ — see JOKE 1

2 something very good of its kind ⟨that joke was a *nifty*⟩ — see JIM-DANDY

niggard *adj* giving or sharing as little as possible ⟨in Shakespeare's sonnet, the narrator begs his love to give him more praise "than *niggard* truth would willingly impart"⟩ — see STINGY 1

niggard *n* a mean grasping person who is usually stingy with money ⟨such a *niggard* that he refused to hand out candy at Halloween, saying it would cost too much money⟩ — see MISER

niggardliness *n* the quality or practice of being overly sparing with money ⟨remembered for her legendary *niggardliness,* financier Hetty Green lived the life of a pauper but died with a net worth of over $100 million⟩ — see PARSIMONY 1

niggardly *adj* **1** giving or sharing as little as possible ⟨she's a *niggardly* woman, so don't expect a handout from her⟩ — see STINGY 1

2 less plentiful than what is normal, necessary, or desirable ⟨*niggardly* portions of meat for dinner⟩ — see MEAGER

niggle *vb* to make often peevish criticisms or objections about matters that are minor, unimportant, or irrelevant ⟨you know it drives me crazy when you *niggle* like that⟩ — see QUIBBLE 1

niggler *n* a person given to harsh judgments and to finding faults ⟨you can't pay attention to every *niggler*, simply because you can't please every one⟩ — see CRITIC 1

niggling *adj* so small or unimportant as to warrant little or no attention ⟨only *niggling* differences between the original Broadway musical and the film version that followed⟩ — see NEGLIGIBLE 1

nigh *adj* not being distant in time, space, or significance ⟨the end is *nigh*⟩ — see CLOSE 2

nigh *adv* **1** at, within, or to a short distance or time ⟨have worked for them for *nigh* on 10 years⟩ — see NEAR 1

2 very close to but not completely ⟨he has *nigh* completed his degree⟩ — see ALMOST

nigh *prep* close to ⟨a field *nigh* the church⟩ — see AROUND 1

nigh *vb* **1** to come near or nearer ⟨as the hour of his death was *nighing*⟩ — see APPROACH 1

2 to move closer to ⟨as the old man was *nighing* his hour of death⟩ — see COME 1

nigher *adj* being the less far of two ⟨the town has only two motels, and the one *nigher* to the train station is actually the better one⟩ — see NEAR 1

night *adj* of, relating to, or occurring in the night ⟨took a *night* flight out to the coast⟩ — see NOCTURNAL

night *n* **1** the time from sunset to sunrise when there is no visible sunlight ⟨loved to sit outside at *night* and watch the stars⟩

synonyms dark, darkness, nighttime

related words dusk, evening, gloaming, nightfall, twilight; midnight

near antonyms dawn, daybreak, sunrise, sunup; forenoon, morning; high noon, midday, noon, noonday, noontide, noontime; afternoon

antonyms day, daytime

2 a time or place of little or no light ⟨snuck out of town under the cover of *night*⟩ — see DARK 1

3 the time from when the sun begins to set to the onset of total darkness ⟨we waited until *night* to begin lighting the candles in the windows⟩ — see DUSK 1

night and day *adv* on every relevant occasion ⟨*night and day* she reminded him that if it weren't for her, he'd be a nobody⟩ — see ALWAYS 1

nightclub *n* a bar or restaurant offering special nighttime entertainment (as music, dancing, or comedy acts) ⟨decided to go dancing at a local *nightclub* after the long dinner and movie⟩

synonyms bistro, boîte, cabaret, café (*also* cafe), club, nightspot, nitery (*also* niterie), roadhouse, supper club

related words a-go-go, disco, discotheque (*or* discothèque); barroom, pub [*chiefly British*], public house [*chiefly British*], saloon, tavern; clip joint [*slang*], dive, honky-tonk, key club, speakeasy; canteen, watering hole, watering place

nightdress *n* a loose pullover garment worn in bed ⟨bought a long *nightdress* for the cold winter months ahead⟩ — see NIGHTGOWN

nightfall *n* the time from when the sun begins to set to the onset of total darkness ⟨since you aren't taking a flashlight, make sure you're back at camp by *nightfall*⟩ — see DUSK 1

nightgown *n* a loose pullover garment worn in bed ⟨decided to buy a flannel *nightgown* instead of pajamas⟩

synonyms gown, nightdress, nightshirt

related words nightclothes; pajamas, pj's; nightcap; lingerie, negligee (*also* negligé), nightie (*or* nighty)

nighthawk *n* a person who is active late at night ⟨an all-night diner that is patronized by *nighthawks* from every segment of society⟩ — see NIGHT OWL

nightly *adj* of, relating to, or occurring in the night ⟨the elderly couple's *nightly* walk around the neighborhood⟩ — see NOCTURNAL

nightmare *adj* extremely disturbing or repellent ⟨survivors of a nuclear holocaust would surely face a *nightmare* existence⟩ — see HORRIBLE 1

nightmare *n* a situation or state that causes great suffering and unhappiness ⟨that 20-page exam was a *nightmare*⟩ — see HELL 2

nightmarish *adj* extremely disturbing or repellent ⟨a photographic exhibit of *nightmarish* images from the wars of the 20th century⟩ — see HORRIBLE 1

night owl *n* a person who is active late at night ⟨a *night owl* whose spouse is more of an early bird⟩
synonyms nighthawk
related words nightclubber, pub crawler; night rider, nightwalker; noctambulist, sleepwalker
near antonyms early bird

nightshirt *n* a loose pullover garment worn in bed ⟨preferred *nightshirts* over pajama sets⟩ — see NIGHTGOWN

nightspot *n* a bar or restaurant offering special nighttime entertainment (as music, dancing, or comedy acts) ⟨one of the city's few *nightspots* featuring a dance floor and a live band⟩ — see NIGHTCLUB

nightstick *n* a heavy rigid stick used as a weapon or for punishment ⟨police officers fitted out with *nightsticks* and handcuffs⟩ — see CLUB 1

nighttime *adj* of, relating to, or occurring in the night ⟨warnings about protecting household pets from *nighttime* predators in the outer reaches of suburbia⟩ — see NOCTURNAL

nighttime *n* the time from sunset to sunrise when there is no visible sunlight ⟨before electricity, gas lamps were used for illumination during the *nighttime*⟩ — see NIGHT 1

nil *n* the numerical symbol 0 or the absence of number or quantity represented by it ⟨the difference in the audio performance of those two CD players is *nil*⟩ — see ZERO 1

nimble *adj* **1** having or showing quickness of mind ⟨possessing a *nimble* wit, he always has a cutting comeback for any intended insult thrown his way⟩ — see INTELLIGENT 1
2 moving easily ⟨her *nimble* fingers make knitting look so easy⟩ — see GRACEFUL 1

nimbleness *n* ease and grace in physical activity ⟨that dance routine requires a certain amount of *nimbleness* and flexibility⟩ — see DEXTERITY 2

nimbus *n* **1** a special quality or impression associated with something ⟨fans are inevitably disappointed when the *nimbus* of glamour about their favorite celebrity turns out to be an illusion⟩ — see AURA 1
2 an artistic rendering of radiant light around the head or body of a sacred personage ⟨the *nimbi* for the sculpted figures around the exterior of the church are simple disks about the saints' heads⟩ — see AUREOLE

nimiety *n* a propensity for extremes in one's actions, beliefs, or habits ⟨the artist's ingrained *nimiety* results in cloying pictures of cute kids holding even cuter animals⟩ — see EXCESS 2

nimrod *n* **1** a person who hunts game ⟨a mighty *nimrod* with the heads of big game mounted on his walls⟩ — see HUNTER
2 *slang* a stupid person ⟨there are lots of *nimrods* out in the woods, so always wear bright red during hunting season⟩ — see IDIOT

nincompoop *n* **1** a person who lacks good sense or judgment ⟨quit acting like a *nincompoop*, because I know you are smarter than that⟩ — see FOOL 1
2 a stupid person ⟨who wants a *nincompoop* as a business partner?⟩ — see IDIOT

ninny *n* **1** a person who lacks good sense or judgment ⟨only a *ninny* would try to cross a swollen, raging river⟩ — see FOOL 1
2 a stupid person ⟨was such a *ninny* that he kept forgetting my name, even though I was wearing a name tag⟩ — see IDIOT

ninnyhammer *n* **1** a person who lacks good sense or judgment ⟨what kind of *ninnyhammer* would believe that?⟩ — see FOOL 1
2 a stupid person ⟨don't just stand there like a *ninnyhammer* —give me some help⟩ — see IDIOT

[1]**nip** *n* **1** the quality or state of being stimulating to the mind or senses ⟨the barbecue sauce has a *nip* to it that balances out the sweetness⟩ — see PIQUANCY
2 a very small amount ⟨I'll have just a *nip* of your sandwich⟩ — see PARTICLE 1
3 an uncomfortable degree of coolness ⟨there's a *nip* in the air today⟩ — see CHILL

[2]**nip** *n* the portion of a serving of a beverage that is swallowed at one time ⟨give me just a *nip* of milk to help me swallow this pill⟩ — see DRINK 2

nip *vb* **1** to make (something) shorter or smaller with the use of a cutting instrument ⟨I'm just going to *nip* these hedges, and then I'll be done with the work outside⟩ — see CLIP 1
2 to squeeze tightly between two surfaces, edges, or points ⟨the puppy *nipped* her hand while playing⟩ — see PINCH 1
3 to take (something) without right and with an intent to keep ⟨that guy *nipped* my wallet from the restaurant table when I turned away⟩ — see STEAL 1
4 to proceed or move quickly ⟨I'll just *nip* off to the corner store for some milk⟩ — see HURRY 2

nip and tuck *adj* showing little difference in the standing of the competitors ⟨the race was *nip and tuck* to the very end, with the judges needing to look at photos of the finish three times⟩ — see CLOSE 3

nipper *n* a male person who has not yet reached adulthood ⟨the little *nipper* can't quite reach the cabinet⟩ — see BOY 1

nippiness *n* an uncomfortable degree of coolness ⟨a new *nippiness* in the mornings hinted at the coming of winter⟩ — see CHILL

nipping *adj* **1** having a low or subnormal temperature ⟨a group of campers waking up to the *nipping* air of a Rocky Mountain morning⟩ — see COLD 1
2 uncomfortably cool ⟨better wear a windbreaker if you're going sailing in this *nipping* wind⟩ — see CHILLY 1

nippy *adj* **1** having a low or subnormal temperature ⟨bring a jacket, as it's a little *nippy* outside⟩ — see COLD 1
2 having a powerfully stimulating odor or flavor ⟨blue cheese is a little too *nippy* for my taste⟩ — see SHARP 2
3 moving, proceeding, or acting with great speed ⟨racing around the neighborhood on a *nippy* scooter⟩ — see FAST 1
4 uncomfortably cool ⟨a *nippy* wind that chilled parade watchers to the bone⟩ — see CHILLY 1

nirvana *n* **1** a state of being disregardful or unconscious of one's surroundings, concerns, or obligations ⟨the spa experience was a week of pure *nirvana*⟩ — see OBLIVION
2 an often imaginary place or state of utter perfection and happiness ⟨the popular fantasy that life as a beachcomber in the South Pacific would be never-ending *nirvana*⟩ — see PARADISE 1

nit *n, chiefly British* **1** a person who lacks good sense or judgment ⟨stop being such a great *nit* and listen to what I have to say⟩ — see FOOL 1
2 a stupid person ⟨some *nit* at the bar was claiming all politicians are crooked⟩ — see IDIOT

nitery *also* **niterie** *n* a bar or restaurant offering special nighttime entertainment (as music, dancing, or comedy acts) ⟨*niteries* in this college town attract a predictably youngish crowd⟩ — see NIGHTCLUB

nitpick *vb* to make often peevish criticisms or objections about matters that are minor, unimportant, or irrelevant ⟨her husband *nitpicks* about everything: from how she puts the plates away to how she files the bills⟩ — see QUIBBLE 1

nitpicker *n* a person given to harsh judgments and to finding faults ⟨a tiresome *nitpicker* who seems to think that I can't do anything right⟩ — see CRITIC 1

nitty–gritty *adj* having to do with the practical details of regular life ⟨a look at the *nitty-gritty* aspects of putting out a newspaper⟩ — see MUNDANE 1

nitty–gritty *n* the specific practical details of something ⟨the governor tends to leave the *nitty-gritty* of running the state government to others⟩
synonyms brass tacks, nuts and bolts, ropes
related words incidentals, ins and outs, minutiae, particulars, specifics, technicalities; oddities, peculiarities, quirks; ramifications
near antonyms big picture

nitwit *n* **1** a person who lacks good sense or judgment ⟨don't be a *nitwit*—wear a seat belt!⟩ — see FOOL 1
2 a stupid person ⟨an absolute *nitwit* as far as geography is concerned⟩ — see IDIOT
3 a silly flighty person ⟨a *nitwit* who never should have been given a position of responsibility in the company⟩ — see FLIBBERTIGIBBET

nix *vb* **1** to be unwilling to grant ⟨our supervisor *nixed* my request to work from home, if only on a trial basis⟩ — see DENY 2
2 to reject by or as if by a vote ⟨movie audiences have effectively *nixed* the idea of the reviving the old-fashioned western by emphatically ignoring this latest effort⟩ — see NEGATIVE 1
3 to show unwillingness to accept, do, engage in, or agree to ⟨the committee *nixed* the additional expenditures⟩ — see DECLINE 1

no *adv* **1** not in any degree, way, or under any condition ⟨this cake is *no* better than the last one we made⟩ — see NEVER 2
2 certainly not ⟨in *no* uncertain terms we were told to leave⟩ — see HARDLY 2

no *interj* how surprising, doubtful, or unbelievable ⟨*no*—you can't possibly mean that I failed that test! I studied for days!⟩
synonyms ah, aha, come on, fie, indeed, my word, pshaw, well, what, why
related words gee, gee whiz, ha, hello, hey, lo, oh; fiddlesticks, phooey, pooh; there; oops (*or* whoops *also* woops), ugh; egad, gad, gadzooks [*archaic*], the deuce, the devil, the dickens, zounds

no *n* **1** a vote or decision against something ⟨though I wanted spaghetti for dinner, the consensus was a decisive *no*⟩
synonyms nay, negative, non placet
related words con; blackball, veto; denial, negation, refusal
near antonyms pro; acceptance, approval, grace
antonyms positive, yea, yes
2 an unwillingness to grant something asked for ⟨gave him a polite *no* when he asked her to dance⟩ — see DENIAL 1

no–account *adj* **1** having no ambition, success, or value to society ⟨only heard from his *no-account* relatives when they wanted a handout⟩
synonyms good-for-nothing, ne'er-do-well, no-good
related words idle, indolent, lazy, shiftless, slothful, unambitious; useless, worthless
near antonyms ambitious, diligent, enterprising, industrious
2 so small or unimportant as to warrant little or no attention ⟨some miscellaneous *no-account* expenses that we simply paid for with our own pocket money⟩ — see NEGLIGIBLE 1

no–account *n* an idle worthless person ⟨claims that every last one of his in-laws is a nerveless *no-account*⟩ — see NE'ER-DO-WELL

Noachian *adj* having passed its time of use or usefulness ⟨*Noachian* farm equipment that probably belongs in a museum somewhere⟩ — see OBSOLETE

[1]**nob** *n* the upper or front part of the body that contains the brain, the major sense organs, and the mouth ⟨the detective had an odd habit of scratching the side of his *nob* whenever he asked a question⟩ — see HEAD 1

[2]**nob** *n, chiefly British* one of high position or importance within a group ⟨all of the London's political *nobs* were there for the dedication of the memorial⟩ — see BIG SHOT

nobble *vb, British slang* **1** to rob by the use of trickery or threats ⟨an old scam that's been used for years to *nobble* unsuspecting London tourists⟩ — see FLEECE
2 to take physical control or possession of (something) suddenly or forcibly ⟨a London bobby *nobbled* the pickpocket just as he was about to make off with the tourist's watch⟩ — see CATCH 1

nobility *n* **1** impressiveness of beauty on a large scale ⟨was struck by the *nobility* of such an old, distinguished castle⟩ — see MAGNIFICENCE
2 the highest class in a society ⟨wealthy plantation owners constituted the *nobility* of colonial Virginia⟩ — see ARISTOCRACY 1

noble *adj* **1** of high birth, rank, or station ⟨despite his *noble* background, the prince is known for his unpretentious way with common people⟩
synonyms aristocratic, blue-blooded, genteel, gentle, grand, great, highborn, highbred, patrician, silk-stocking, upper-class, upper-crust, wellborn
related words high, lofty, superior; elevated, ennobled, exalted; gentlemanly, kingly, knightly, ladylike, lordly, princely, queenly, regal, royal; high-level, senior
near antonyms inferior, knavish; bastard, illegitimate; ordinary, plain; abased, degraded; junior, subordinate
antonyms baseborn, common, humble, ignoble, low, lower-class, lowly, mean, nonaristocratic, plebeian, ungenteel
2 having, characterized by, or arising from a dignified and generous nature ⟨the factory owner had a kind, *noble* disposition that showed in his unstinting generosity toward the poor⟩ ⟨our country was founded on the *noble* ideas that are put forth in the Founding Fathers' writings⟩
synonyms big, chivalrous, elevated, gallant, great, greathearted, high, high-minded, lofty, lordly, magnanimous, natural, sublime
related words ennobled, exalted, glorified; heroic (*also* heroical), honorable, valiant, venerable, worthy; knightly, princely, regal; inspiring, moving, numinous, uplifting; august, magnificent, majestic
near antonyms sordid, squalid, vile, wretched; abominable, contemptible, despicable, detestable, hateful, offensive, repulsive, ugly, vicious; dastardly, dirty, lousy, sorry; little, mean, narrow, small-minded; degrading, discreditable, humiliating, ignominious; coarse, crude, vulgar
antonyms base, debased, degenerate, degraded, ignoble, low
3 following the accepted rules of moral conduct ⟨his *noble* behavior even as he was being unjustly attacked by his political opponents⟩ — see HONORABLE 1
4 large and impressive in size, grandeur, extent, or con-

ception ⟨Peter the Great's plan to build for Russia a capital city as *noble* as any in Europe⟩ — see GRAND 1
5 of the very best kind ⟨a *noble* racehorse⟩ — see EXCELLENT
6 standing above others in rank, importance, or achievement ⟨a *noble* professor known internationally for his medical research⟩ — see EMINENT

noble *n* a man or woman of high birth or social position ⟨an elite school for children of *nobles*⟩ — see GENTLEPERSON

nobleman *n* a man of high birth or social position ⟨his impeccable manners immediately marked him as a *nobleman*⟩ — see GENTLEMAN 1

nobleness *n* impressiveness of beauty on a large scale ⟨these snapshots just don't convey the breathtaking *nobleness* of St. Peter's basilica in Rome⟩ — see MAGNIFICENCE

noblewoman *n* a woman of high birth or social position ⟨traditionally, *noblewomen*—whether they are titled or not—have served as great patronesses of the arts⟩ — see GENTLEWOMAN

nobly *adv* in a manner befitting a person of the highest character and ideals ⟨civil rights activists *nobly* striving for justice and equality⟩ — see GREATLY 1

nobody *n* a person of no importance or influence ⟨tired of feeling like a *nobody*, she decided to launch her own business⟩
synonyms cipher, dwarf, half-pint, insect, insignificancy, lightweight, morsel, nonentity, nothing, nullity, number, pip-squeak, pygmy (*also* pigmy), shrimp, snippersnapper, twerp, whippersnapper, zero, zilch
related words no-name, noncelebrity; least; inferior, mediocrity, obscurity; figurehead, puppet; nonperson
near antonyms chief, head, lead, leader; celebrity, luminary, notable, personality, planet, star, superstar; authority, superior; great power, party, power
antonyms big shot, big wheel, bigwig, eminence, figure, kahuna, kingpin, magnate, nabob, personage, somebody, VIP

nobody *pron* no person ⟨there is *nobody* home⟩ ⟨*nobody* wants to clean up that mess⟩
synonyms none, no one
near antonyms anybody, anyone; somebody, someone
antonyms everybody, everyone

nocturnal *adj* of, relating to, or occurring in the night ⟨he bought a new telescope so he could pursue his favorite *nocturnal* hobby of astronomy⟩
synonyms night, nightly, nighttime
related words late; midnight, overnight
near antonyms noon
antonyms daily, diurnal

nocuous *adj* causing or capable of causing harm ⟨hand washing is one of the easiest ways to help prevent the spread of *nocuous* germs⟩ — see HARMFUL

nod *vb* to make short up-and-down movements ⟨though she couldn't see the rain, she knew it had started because she could see the flowers *nod* as raindrops hit them⟩
synonyms bob, bobble, jog, jounce, pump, seesaw, wag
related words jerk, jiggle, shake, wiggle, wobble (*also* wabble); oscillate, rock, sway, swing, undulate; drop, duck

nodding *adj* bending downward or forward ⟨some students, with *nodding* heads, were helplessly falling asleep during the boring lecture⟩
synonyms bowed, bowing, declined, declining, descendant (*also* descendent), descending, drooping, droopy, hanging, hung, inclining, pendulous, sagging, stooping, weeping
related words floppy, limp; dangling, falling, pendent (*or* pendant), suspended; dipping, sinking, slumping
near antonyms erect, inflexible, rigid, stiff; elevated, raised, upraised
antonyms unbending, upright

noddle *n* the upper or front part of the body that contains the brain, the major sense organs, and the mouth ⟨tapped his *noddle* to indicate he was thinking⟩ — see HEAD 1

noddy *n* a stupid person ⟨which one of you *noddies* put an empty milk carton back in the fridge?⟩ — see IDIOT

node *n* a small rounded mass of swollen tissue ⟨the doctor examined the *node* on my knee before deciding it was the result of arthritis⟩ — see BUMP 1

nodule *n* a small rounded mass of swollen tissue ⟨a *nodule* on the leaf indicated that a worm had laid eggs there⟩ — see BUMP 1

Noel *n* the season celebrating Christmas ⟨for *Noel* the town puts on a festival of indoor and outdoor events, including strolling carolers in Victorian dress⟩ — see YULETIDE

no–frills *adj* providing only the essentials and nothing fancy or luxurious ⟨a low-cost, *no-frills* vacation during which we camped out and cooked our own meals⟩
synonyms austere, spartan, stark
related words plain, simple, unadorned, undecorated, unelaborate, unfancy
near antonyms adorned, decorated, elaborate, fancy
antonyms deluxe, Lucullan (*also* Lucullian), luxe, luxurious, plush

noggin *n* the upper or front part of the body that contains the brain, the major sense organs, and the mouth ⟨watch the lintel above the door, unless you want to bang your *noggin*⟩ — see HEAD 1

no–good *adj* **1** having no ambition, success, or value to society ⟨tired of supporting their spendthrift, *no-good* daughter, who has yet to find a job commensurate with her alleged abilities⟩ — see NO-ACCOUNT 1
2 having no usefulness ⟨that *no-good* chair should be thrown away⟩ — see WORTHLESS

no–good *n* **1** a mean, evil, or unprincipled person ⟨neighbors remembered the killer as having been an utter *no-good* since childhood⟩ — see VILLAIN
2 an idle worthless person ⟨we'll have to pay more than minimum wage for the job if we expect to get people other than *no-goods*⟩ — see NE'ER-DO-WELL

no–goodnik *n* an idle worthless person ⟨an otherwise intelligent woman who has a singular gift for picking boyfriends who invariably turn out to be *no-goodniks*⟩ — see NE'ER-DO-WELL

noise *n* **1** loud, confused, and usually inharmonious sound ⟨the incessant *noise* of traffic on Fifth Avenue made normal conversation impossible⟩
synonyms babel, blare, bluster, bowwow, brawl, bruit [*archaic*], cacophony, chatter, clamor, clangor, decibel(s), din, discordance, katzenjammer, racket, rattle, roar
related words discord, dissonance; commotion, furor, hubbub, hullabaloo, hurly-burly, rumpus, tumult, uproar; clatter, jangle; bang, blast, boom, clap, crack, crash
near antonyms calm, hush, lull; quietude, serenity, tranquillity (*or* tranquility)
antonyms quiet, silence, silentness, still, stillness
2 a violent shouting ⟨keep the *noise* down, you kids!⟩ — see CLAMOR 1
3 information or opinion that is widely disseminated without any authority or confirmation of accuracy ⟨there's been a lot of *noise* that the stock is ready to skyrocket, but I'll believe it when I see it⟩ — see RUMOR

noise (about *or* abroad) *vb* to make (as a piece of information) the subject of common talk without any authority or confirmation of accuracy ⟨for weeks afterwards, staffers *noised about* the department head's sudden, unexplained departure⟩ — see RUMOR

noiseless *adj* mostly or entirely without sound ⟨tried to remain *noiseless* as he crept up the stairs⟩ — see SILENT 3

noisome *adj* **1** bad for the well-being of the body ⟨it's no fun having asthma and living in an area with *noisome* smog⟩ — see UNHEALTHY 1
2 causing intense displeasure, disgust, or resentment ⟨a *noisome* remark about my weight that stuck with me for days⟩ — see OFFENSIVE 1
3 having an unpleasant smell ⟨the *noisome* air of the area of the city that was downwind of the dog food factory⟩ — see MALODOROUS

noisy *adj* **1** making loud, confused, and usually unharmonious sounds ⟨the *noisy* crowd marched up the street, shouting ever louder as they approached the palace⟩
synonyms clangorous, dinning, discordant, rackety
related words cacophonous, dissonant; resounding, sonorous; clamorous, uproarious; blatant, obstreperous, strident, vociferous; blaring, booming, brassy, brazen, clanging, earsplitting, jangly
near antonyms calm, hushed
antonyms noiseless, quiet, silent, soundless, still
2 full of or characterized by the presence of noise ⟨the crowded auditorium was *noisy*, packed with excited theatergoers eager for the show to start⟩ ⟨the manufacturing plant was a decidedly *noisy* place, so we wore ear protection while we toured it⟩
synonyms clamorous, clangorous, clattering, clattery, rackety, resounding, uproarious
related words resonant, sonorous; buzzing, humming, murmuring; blustery, boisterous, raucous, rip-roaring, roaring, roistering, romping, rowdy; tumultuous, woolly (*also* wooly); obstreperous, vociferous
near antonyms calm, peaceful, serene, tranquil
antonyms hushed, noiseless, quiet, silent, soundless, stilled, stilly
3 excessively showy ⟨the wallpaper was far too *noisy* for what was supposed to be a restful bedroom⟩ — see GAUDY
4 likely to attract attention ⟨the movie had been preceded by months of *noisy* hype, only to die a quick death at the box office⟩ — see NOTICEABLE

nomad *adj* traveling from place to place ⟨*nomad* caravans of Bedouins⟩ — see ITINERANT

nomad *n* a person who roams about without a fixed route or destination ⟨after college she became quite the *nomad*, backpacking through Europe with no particular destination⟩
synonyms drifter, gadabout, gypsy, knockabout, maunderer, rambler, roamer, rover, stroller, vagabond, wanderer, wayfarer
related words laggard, straggler; lingerer, loiterer, sojourner; bum, hobo, tramp; passenger, sightseer, traveler (*or* traveller); migrant, transient, vagrant; ambler, saunterer
phrases bird of passage
near antonyms homebody; denizen, dweller, habitant, inhabitant, resident, settler

nomadic *adj* traveling from place to place ⟨raised in a *nomadic* family, she attended half a dozen different high schools⟩ — see ITINERANT

no–man's–land *n* land that is uninhabited or not fit for crops ⟨the city's decayed industrial quarter is a *no-man's-land* of abandoned factories and weedy vacant lots⟩ — see WASTELAND

nom de guerre *n* a fictitious or assumed name ⟨an acerbic and provocative blogger known to most only by her online *nom de guerre*⟩ — see PSEUDONYM

nomenclature *n* a word or combination of words by which a person or thing is regularly known ⟨the *nomenclature*, "tuxedo," derives from the fact that the jacket first became popular in the resort area of Tuxedo Park, New York⟩ — see NAME 1

nominal *adj* **1** being something in name or form only ⟨he was the *nominal* head of state—everyone knew the country was actually run by one of his advisers⟩
synonyms formal, paper, titular
related words so-called; phantom, virtual; apparent, assumed, evident, ostensible, presumed, seeming, supposed
near antonyms actual, real, true
2 so small or unimportant as to warrant little or no attention ⟨when you pay $400 for an airline ticket, a ticketing fee of five dollars seems *nominal*⟩ — see NEGLIGIBLE 1

nominally *adv* in a very small quantity or degree ⟨although the more expensive TV set is *nominally* better than the other, it's not worth the big difference in price⟩ — see LITTLE 1

nominate *vb* **1** to give a name to ⟨this first drawing, which we'll *nominate* as Plan A, shows how the house would look with the smaller annex⟩ — see NAME 1
2 to pick (someone) by one's authority for a specific position or duty ⟨the U.S. Constitution directs the president to *nominate* ambassadors⟩ — see APPOINT 2

nominee *n* one who has been chosen by some authority for a specific position or duty ⟨as the club's vice presidential *nominee*, she was expected to support the president's position⟩ — see APPOINTEE

nonabrasive *adj* not harsh or stern especially in nature or effect ⟨*nonabrasive* polishes⟩ ⟨the congregation much preferred the *nonabrasive* manner of the soft-spoken curate⟩ — see GENTLE 1

nonacceptance *n* an unwillingness to grant something asked for ⟨the university's *nonacceptance* of my application for admission was accompanied by considerable regret, if you believe the rejection letter⟩ — see DENIAL 1

nonachievement *n* a falling short of one's goals ⟨a youthful drug addict who's headed for a lifetime of *nonachievement*⟩ — see FAILURE 2

nonaction *n* lack of action or activity ⟨your *nonaction* on this matter will result in an arrest warrant⟩ — see INACTION

nonage *n* **1** the state or time of being a child ⟨the short stories of the novelist's *nonage* have only recently been discovered by scholars⟩ — see CHILDHOOD
2 the transitional period between childhood and adulthood ⟨the indiscretions of his long-ago *nonage* have come back to haunt him now that he's a serious presidential contender⟩ — see ADOLESCENCE

nonambiguous *adj* not subject to misinterpretation or more than one interpretation ⟨I need a *nonambiguous* "yes" or "no"⟩ — see CLEAR 2

no–name *adj* not widely known ⟨a low-budget movie with a cast of *no-name* actors⟩ — see OBSCURE 2

nonbelief *n* refusal to accept something as true ⟨my *nonbelief* in UFO's should not be construed as an unshakable belief in their nonexistence—I'm just waiting for proof⟩ — see DISBELIEF

nonbinding *adj* having no legal or binding force ⟨a verbal agreement is considered *nonbinding* in this state⟩ — see NULL 1

nonchalance *n* lack of interest or concern ⟨with their usual *nonchalance* they arrived at the wedding ceremony half an hour late⟩ — see INDIFFERENCE

nonchalant *adj* having or showing a lack of interest or concern ⟨you shouldn't be so *nonchalant* about something that is so important to your parents⟩ — see INDIFFERENT 1

noncombustible *adj* incapable of being burned ⟨fire-fighting gear is made of *noncombustible* material⟩ — see INCOMBUSTIBLE

noncommittal *adj* lacking in distinctive features or qualities ⟨the novelist has repeatedly used bland, *noncommittal* words that lack emotional resonance⟩ — see NONDESCRIPT

non compos mentis *adj* having or showing a very abnormal or sick state of mind ⟨will seek to prove that the elderly tycoon was *non compos mentis* when he dictated that will⟩ — see INSANE 1

nonconcur *vb* to have a different opinion ⟨the one *nonconcurring* judge in the case issued his own opinion⟩ — see DISAGREE

nonconcurrence *n* variance of opinion on a matter ⟨a statement explaining the basis of the justice's *nonconcurrence* with the majority opinion⟩ — see DISAGREEMENT 1

nonconflicting *adj* not having or showing any apparent conflict ⟨there are several *nonconflicting* reports on the effectiveness of the new drug⟩ — see CONSISTENT

nonconformer *n* a person who does not conform to generally accepted standards or customs ⟨a community in which men and women were expected to conform to traditional gender roles, and *nonconformers* were socially ostracized⟩ — see NONCONFORMIST 1

nonconformist *adj* deviating from commonly accepted beliefs or practices ⟨a cattle-ranching family that took some time in getting used to their daughter's *nonconformist* adoption of vegetarianism⟩ — see HERETICAL

nonconformist *n* **1** a person who does not conform to generally accepted standards or customs ⟨always the *nonconformist*, she insisted on wearing red on St. Patrick's Day and not green like everyone else⟩

synonyms bohemian, boho, counterculturist, deviant, enfant terrible, free spirit, heretic, iconoclast, individualist, loner, lone ranger, lone wolf, maverick, nonconformer

related words freethinker; character, codger, crackbrain, crackpot, crank, eccentric, freak, kook, nut, oddball, screwball, weirdo; eight ball, misfit, outsider; aberrant, anomaly

near antonyms adherent, follower, supporter; sheep

antonyms conformer, conformist

2 a person who believes, teaches, or advocates something opposed to accepted beliefs ⟨a *nonconformist* who was excommunicated from her church for her teachings⟩ — see HERETIC 1

nonconformity *n* departure from a generally accepted theory, opinion, or practice ⟨an artistic movement that doesn't tolerate *nonconformity*⟩ — see HERESY

noncontroversial *adj* unlikely to provoke controversy or offense ⟨a *noncontroversial* proposal for increasing security at nuclear power plants⟩ — see SAFE 3

nonconventional *adj* not bound by traditional ways or beliefs ⟨his *nonconventional* cures were the subject of some controversy⟩ — see LIBERAL 1

nondescript *adj* lacking in distinctive features or qualities ⟨travelers settling for *nondescript* motel rooms that could be located anywhere⟩

synonyms beige, characterless, faceless, featureless, indistinctive, neutral, noncommital, vanilla

related words boring, drab, dreary, dry, dull, flat, humdrum, leaden, monotonous, pedestrian, stodgy, stuffy, tame, tedious, tiresome, tiring, uninteresting, wearisome, weary, wearying

near antonyms arresting, bold, catchy, dramatic, emphatic, eye-catching, flamboyant, showy, splashy, striking

nondrinker *n* a person who abstains from alcoholic beverages ⟨a variety of nonalcoholic drinks for the *nondrinkers* at the party⟩

synonyms abstainer, teetotaler (*or* teetotaller), teetotalist

related words dry, prohibitionist

near antonyms alcoholic, barfly, boozehound, boozer, drunk, drunkard, inebriate, sot, souse, tippler; wet

antonyms bibber, drinker

none *adv* **1** certainly not ⟨your help comes *none* too soon⟩ — see HARDLY 2

2 not in any degree, way, or under any condition ⟨I'll switch his mug with mine, and he'll be *none* the wiser⟩ — see NEVER 2

none *pron* no person ⟨*none* will come to the party⟩ — see NOBODY

nonelective *adj* forcing one's compliance or participation by or as if by law ⟨language arts, math, and science are *nonelective* subjects taken by all students at the school⟩ — see MANDATORY

nonentity *n* **1** a conception or image created by the imagination and having no objective reality ⟨the arctic circle is a *nonentity*—you won't see it on the way to the north pole⟩ — see FANTASY 1

2 a person of no importance or influence ⟨was so quiet he was almost a *nonentity* at the meeting⟩ — see NOBODY

nonessential *adj* not needed by the circumstances or to accomplish an end ⟨money's tight, so we'll have to skip *nonessential* purchases⟩ — see UNNECESSARY

nonesuch *n* someone of such unequaled perfection as to deserve imitation ⟨in medieval legend Sir Galahad is the *nonesuch* of the noble knight with a pure and unselfish heart⟩ — see IDEAL 1

nonetheless *adv* in spite of that ⟨sometimes you can be a real jerk, but I like you *nonetheless*⟩ — see HOWEVER

nonexistent *adj* not present or in evidence ⟨our perennially *nonexistent* computer tech is, once again, not here today⟩ — see ABSENT 2

nonexpert *n* a person who regularly or occasionally engages in an activity as a pastime rather than as a profession ⟨as a *nonexpert*, I enjoy her readable articles on physics and astronomy⟩ — see AMATEUR 1

nonextant *adj* no longer existing ⟨we know that Renaissance artwork only through copies made by other artists, the original painting being *nonextant*⟩ — see EXTINCT

nonfeasance *n* the nonperformance of an assigned or expected action ⟨you can sue for *nonfeasance* if the company doesn't fulfill the contract⟩ — see FAILURE 1

nonfictional *adj* restricted to or based on fact ⟨a *nonfictional* account of a disastrous ascent of Mount Everest⟩ — see FACTUAL 1

nonfigurative *adj* using elements of form (as color, line, or texture) with little or no attempt at creating a realistic picture ⟨the gallery owner is resigned to the fact that *nonfigurative* works generally do not appeal to tourists⟩ — see ABSTRACT 2

nonflammable *adj* incapable of being burned ⟨children's pajamas made of *nonflammable* fabric⟩ — see INCOMBUSTIBLE

nonformal *adj* used in or suitable for speech and not formal writing ⟨use of the *nonformal* "Dad" would be a little jarring in a prayer to our Heavenly Father⟩ — see COLLOQUIAL 1

nonfunctional *adj* not being in working order ⟨that gas pump is *nonfunctional*, which is the reason for the plastic bag over the nozzle⟩ — see INOPERABLE 1

nonfunctioning *adj* not being in working order ⟨the Ferris wheel is *nonfunctioning* at the moment⟩ — see INOPERABLE 1

nonidentical *adj* being not of the same kind ⟨the *nonidentical* bullet fragments were presented as evidence that more than one gun was involved⟩ — see DIFFERENT 1

noninflammable *adj* incapable of being burned ⟨*noninflammable* materials used for construction of the interior of the nightclub⟩ — see INCOMBUSTIBLE

nonliterary *adj* used in or suitable for speech and not formal writing ⟨slang words are usually considered *nonliterary*⟩ — see COLLOQUIAL 1

nonliterate *adj* lacking in education or the knowledge gained from books ⟨an organization helping *nonliterate* adults improve their reading skills⟩ — see IGNORANT 1

nonmaterial *adj* not composed of matter ⟨Newton's laws explain the effects of *nonmaterial* forces on bodies⟩ — see IMMATERIAL 1

nonmotile *adj* incapable of moving or being moved ⟨an examination of the slides of *nonmotile* cells⟩ — see IMMOVABLE 1

nonmoving *adj* **1** fixed in a place or position ⟨the casino is actually in a *nonmoving* vessel permanently docked on the city's waterfront⟩ — see STATIONARY 1
2 incapable of moving or being moved ⟨all of the machine's *nonmoving* parts⟩ — see IMMOVABLE 1

nonnative *adj* being, relating to, or characteristic of a country other than one's own ⟨*nonnative* customs that made the recent immigrants stand out in their new country⟩ — see FOREIGN 1

nonnative *n* a person who is not native to or known to a community ⟨the problems encountered by a *nonnative* after moving into a close-knit community⟩ — see STRANGER

nonnatural *adj* produced by humans rather than natural processes ⟨pure vanilla extract that was made without any *nonnatural* ingredients⟩ — see SYNTHETIC 1

nonobjective *adj* using elements of form (as color, line, or texture) with little or no attempt at creating a realistic picture ⟨the real subject of his *nonobjective* paintings is color—and the intense emotional response it can provoke in the viewer⟩ — see ABSTRACT 2

nonobjectivity *n* an attitude that always favors one way of feeling or acting especially without considering any other possibilities ⟨the judge's *nonobjectivity* in the case was apparent from the first day of the trial⟩ — see BIAS 1

no–nonsense *adj* not joking or playful in mood or manner ⟨a *no-nonsense* gymnastics coach⟩ — see SERIOUS 1

nonoperating *adj* not being in working order ⟨fixed all *nonoperating* parts⟩ — see INOPERABLE 1

nonorthodox *adj* **1** deviating from commonly accepted beliefs or practices ⟨one of the few colonies to tolerate *nonorthodox* religious beliefs⟩ — see HERETICAL
2 not bound by traditional ways or beliefs ⟨a *nonorthodox* approach to teaching music⟩ — see LIBERAL 1

nonpareil *adj* having no equal or rival for excellence or desirability ⟨the *nonpareil* beauty of Helen of Troy⟩ — see ONLY 1

nonpareil *n* someone of such unequaled perfection as to deserve imitation ⟨among the knights of the Round Table, Galahad stood alone as the *nonpareil* of nobility and selflessness⟩ — see IDEAL 1

nonpartisan *adj* **1** marked by justice, honesty, and freedom from bias ⟨made a *nonpartisan* decision that satisfied all concerned⟩ — see FAIR 2
2 not favoring or joined to either side in a quarrel, contest, or war ⟨*nonpartisan* observers who were there to ensure a fair election⟩ — see NEUTRAL 1

nonpartisanship *n* lack of favoritism toward one side or another ⟨the *nonpartisanship* of the congressional committee members is suspect, as they are all allies of the president⟩ — see DETACHMENT 1

nonphysical *adj* not composed of matter ⟨ghosts are generally thought to be *nonphysical* in nature⟩ — see IMMATERIAL 1

non placet *n* a vote or decision against something ⟨the motion to award the controversial scholar an honorary degree from the university passed by an overwhelming margin, with only two recorded *non placets*⟩ — see NO 1

nonplus *vb* to throw into a state of self-conscious distress ⟨I was *nonplussed* by his openly expressed admiration of me⟩ — see EMBARRASS 1

nonplussed *also* **nonplused** *adj* faced with difficulty or uncertainty about what to say, think, or do ⟨the self-possessed actress seemed uncharacteristically *nonplussed* after the director's harsh appraisal of her performance⟩ — see HARD PUT

nonpractical *adj* not capable of being put to use or account ⟨an inventor who seemed to be able to create only *nonpractical* gadgets⟩ — see IMPRACTICAL

nonproblem *n* something of little importance ⟨the state legislature has wasted its time on *nonproblems* and has ignored the serious challenges that we face⟩ — see TRIFLE

nonprofessional *adj* **1** being such only for recreation ⟨racing stunts that *nonprofessional* drivers should not attempt to duplicate⟩ — see AVOCATIONAL
2 lacking or showing a lack of expert skill ⟨didn't like the *nonprofessional* photos the modeling agency did for her⟩ — see AMATEURISH

nonprofessional *n* a person who regularly or occasionally engages in an activity as a pastime rather than as a profession ⟨one need not be a legal professional to join the bar association; it is open to professionals and *nonprofessionals* alike⟩ — see AMATEUR 1

nonpublic *adj* not known or meant to be known by the general populace ⟨school records are regarded as *nonpublic* information⟩ — see PRIVATE 1

nonrational *adj* not using or following good reasoning ⟨was so upset that he was completely *nonrational* for a moment⟩ — see ILLOGICAL

nonrealistic *adj* using elements of form (as color, line, or texture) with little or no attempt at creating a realistic picture ⟨a *nonrealistic* rendering of the chaos and destruction wreaked by war⟩ — see ABSTRACT 2

nonreligious *adj* **1** lacking religious emotions, principles, or practices ⟨grew up in a *nonreligious* family⟩ — see IRRELIGIOUS
2 not involving religion or religious matters ⟨a display of *nonreligious* holiday decorations on municipally owned property⟩ — see PROFANE 1

nonrepresentational *adj* using elements of form (as color, line, or texture) with little or no attempt at creating a realistic picture ⟨*nonrepresentational* photographs that are really about the play of light on rapidly moving objects⟩ — see ABSTRACT 2

nonresistant *adj* receiving or enduring without offering resistance ⟨the *nonresistant* arrest of most of the demonstrators⟩ — see PASSIVE

nonsense *n* **1** language, behavior, or ideas that are absurd and contrary to good sense ⟨told the little brat to stop his mischievous *nonsense* and start behaving properly⟩ ⟨the discussion about building a time machine was complete *nonsense*⟩ ⟨a hundred years ago, the idea that man could walk on the moon was regarded as impractical *nonsense*⟩
synonyms applesauce [*slang*], balderdash, baloney (*also* boloney), beans, bilge, blah (*also* blah-blah), blarney, blather, blatherskite, blither, bosh, bull [*slang*], bunk, bunkum (*or* buncombe), claptrap, codswallop [*British*], crapola [*slang*], crock, drivel, drool, fiddle, fiddle-faddle, fiddlesticks, flannel [*British*], flapdoodle, folderol (*also* falderal), folly, foolishness, fudge, garbage, guff, hogwash, hokeypokey, hokum, hoodoo,

hooey, horsefeathers [*slang*], humbug, humbuggery, jazz, malarkey (*also* malarky), moonshine, muck, nerts [*slang*], nuts, piffle, poppycock, punk, rot, rubbish, senselessness, silliness, slush, stupidity, taradiddle (*or* tarradiddle), tommyrot, tosh, trash, trumpery, twaddle
related words absurdity, asininity, fatuity, foolery, idiocy, imbecility, inaneness, inanity, insanity, kookiness, lunacy; absurdness, craziness, madness, senselessness, witlessness; hoity-toity, monkey business, monkeyshine(s), shenanigan(s), tomfoolery; gas, hot air, rigmarole (*also* rigamarole); double-talk, greek, hocus-pocus
near antonyms levelheadedness, rationality, reasonability, reasonableness, sensibleness; common sense, horse sense, sense; discernment, judgment (*or* judgement), wisdom
2 unintelligible or meaningless talk ⟨when you talk with your mouth full of food, everything just comes out as *nonsense*⟩ — see GIBBERISH 1

nonsensical *adj* **1** conceived or made without regard for reason or reality ⟨the idea that we could counteract global warming by opening all of the world's refrigerators at once is *nonsensical* at best⟩ — see FANTASTIC 1
2 showing or marked by a lack of good sense or judgment ⟨your plan to lose weight through total starvation is completely *nonsensical*⟩ — see FOOLISH 1

nonsensicalness *n* lack of good sense or judgment ⟨the *nonsensicalness* of your attempt to swim across the icy river is beyond words⟩ — see FOOLISHNESS 1

nonspecific *adj* relating to the main elements and not to specific details ⟨his criticism of the picture is fairly *nonspecific*, but he clearly doesn't like it⟩ — see GENERAL 2

nonstop *adj* going on and on without any interruptions ⟨*nonstop* negotiations in an eleventh-hour attempt to avert a strike⟩ — see CONTINUOUS

nonsuccess *n* a falling short of one's goals ⟨refused to let the *nonsuccess* of her bid for a seat in the state senate discourage her from a career in poltics⟩ — see FAILURE 2

nontraditional *adj* not bound by traditional ways or beliefs ⟨a *nontraditional* couple who are planning a very unconventional wedding⟩ — see LIBERAL 1

nonvalid *adj* **1** having no basis in reason or fact ⟨a *nonvalid* theory that most scientists rejected long ago⟩ — see GROUNDLESS
2 having no legal or binding force ⟨failure to inform the suspect of his rights rendered his confession *nonvalid*⟩ — see NULL 1

nonviolent *adj* not involving violence or force ⟨*nonviolent* protests⟩ — see PEACEFUL 2

noodle *n* **1** a stupid person ⟨a sweet girl, but a *noodle* whom you wouldn't want to depend on in an emergency⟩ — see IDIOT
2 the upper or front part of the body that contains the brain, the major sense organs, and the mouth ⟨since he's a seven-footer, it shouldn't be too difficult to spot his *noodle* in this crowd⟩ — see HEAD 1

nook *n* a hollowed-out space in a wall ⟨books filled every *nook* in the house⟩ — see NICHE 1

noon *n* **1** the middle of the day ⟨we eat a big lunch around *noon* then have dinner in the evening⟩
synonyms high noon, lunch time, midday, noonday, noontide, noontime
related words forenoon, morning; afternoon, evening
2 the highest part or point ⟨she died too young and never even reached the *noon* of her life⟩ — see HEIGHT 1

noonday *n* the middle of the day ⟨in the tropics the *noonday* heat can be overwhelming⟩ — see NOON 1

no one *pron* no person ⟨*no one* is home⟩ — see NOBODY

noontide *n* the middle of the day ⟨we like to work off lunch with a *noontide* ramble⟩ — see NOON 1

noontime *n* **1** the highest part or point ⟨far removed from the *noontime* of their popularity, when they had performed at sold-out arenas, the band now played at small clubs⟩ — see HEIGHT 1
2 the middle of the day ⟨listening to the radio at *noontime* for news updates⟩ — see NOON 1

noose *n* something that catches and holds ⟨a confirmed bachelor, he vows never to get caught in the *noose* of matrimony⟩ — see WEB 1

norm *n* **1** what is typical of a group, class, or series ⟨sales figures that are within the *norm* of a store of that size⟩ — see AVERAGE
2 norms *pl* the code of good conduct for an individual or group ⟨societal *norms* dictate that murder is wrong⟩ — see ETHICS

normal *adj* **1** being of the type that is encountered in the normal course of events ⟨that fateful day had begun just like any *normal* workday⟩ — see ORDINARY 1
2 having full use of one's mind and control over one's actions ⟨if you run around screaming like that, no one will think you are *normal*⟩ — see SANE
3 having or showing the qualities associated with the members of a particular group or kind ⟨she has *normal* reading abilities for a child her age⟩ — see TYPICAL 1

normal *n* what is typical of a group, class, or series ⟨a temperature chart showing the *normals* and extremes for various regions⟩ — see AVERAGE

normalcy *n* the state or fact of being the way things usually are ⟨a combat-weary soldier longing for the *normalcy* of peacetime life⟩ — see NORMALITY

normality *n* the state or fact of being the way things usually are ⟨the county slowly has returned to *normality* after a week of flash flooding⟩
synonyms normalcy, status quo
related words groove, routine, rut; currency, prevalence; conventionality; harmony, orderliness, peace
near antonyms irregularity, uncommonness, unusualness; disorderliness, disruptiveness; disruption, disturbance; anomalousness, deviance; exceptionalness, extraordinariness, noteworthiness, remarkableness; unconventionality
antonyms abnormality

normalize *vb* to make agree with a single established standard or model ⟨English spelling wasn't *normalized* until printed books became common⟩ — see STANDARDIZE

normally *adv* according to the usual course of things ⟨*normally* I go to my health club after work, but today I'm giving myself a break⟩ — see NATURALLY 2

nose *n* **1** the part of the face bearing the nostrils and nasal cavity ⟨with that *nose*, the baby sure looks like his father⟩
synonyms beak, conk [*chiefly British slang*], honker [*slang*], neb, nozzle [*slang*], proboscis, schnoz (*or* schnozz) [*slang*], schnozzle [*slang*], smeller, snoot, snout
related words pug, pugnose
2 the last and usually sharp or tapering part of something long and narrow ⟨bent the wire around the *nose* of the pliers⟩ — see POINT 2

nose *vb* **1** to become aware of by means of the sense organs in the nose ⟨could *nose* the garbage from across the street⟩ — see SMELL 1
2 to interest oneself in what is not one's concern ⟨a neighbor who likes to *nose* around and discover everyone's secrets⟩ — see INTERFERE
3 to move slowly ⟨the line to get tickets is just *nosing*, so we are going to be here for a while⟩ — see CRAWL 2

nosebleed *adj* located at a greater height than average or usual ⟨we were sitting way up in the *nosebleed* seats⟩ — see HIGH 3

nosedive *n* the act or process of going to a lower level or altitude ⟨the pilot struggled to pull his plane out of a *nosedive*⟩ — see DESCENT 1

nose–dive *vb* to go to a lower level especially abruptly ⟨prices on just about everything *nose-dived* right after the holidays⟩ — see DROP 2

nosegay *n* a bunch of flowers ⟨a stately procession of bridesmaids holding small *nosegays*⟩ — see BOUQUET 1

nose out *vb* to come upon after searching, study, or effort ⟨independent investigators eventually *nosed out* proof of White House wrongdoing⟩ — see FIND 1

nosey parker *n, chiefly British* a person who meddles in the affairs of others ⟨the *nosey parker* next door is insane with frustration because I won't take her advice about how to nurse my baby⟩ — see BUSYBODY

nosiness *n* an eager desire to find out about things that are often none of one's business ⟨your annoying *nosiness* isn't going to win you any friends⟩ — see CURIOSITY 1

nostrum *n* something that cures all ills or problems ⟨a quack *nostrum* for cancer of all types⟩ — see CURE-ALL

nosy *or* **nosey** *adj* **1** interested in what is not one's own business ⟨*nosy* in-laws asking about our finances⟩ — see CURIOUS 1

2 thrusting oneself where one is not welcome or invited ⟨a *nosy* coworker sat down right next to us as we were having an unmistakably private conversation⟩ — see INTRUSIVE

notability *n* a person who is widely known and usually much talked about ⟨an opening night that was attended by some of Broadway's biggest *notabilities*⟩ — see CELEBRITY 1

notable *adj* **1** standing above others in rank, importance, or achievement ⟨a panel made up of *notable* authorities on the virus⟩ — see EMINENT

2 worth remembering or mentioning ⟨predicts trends in the stock market with *notable* accuracy⟩ — see NOTEWORTHY 1

notable *n* a person who is widely known and usually much talked about ⟨directors, actors, and other *notables* at the annual gathering for the Academy Awards⟩ — see CELEBRITY 1

notably *adv* in regard to something mentioned explicitly or in detail ⟨some contributors to the museum, *notably* those in the past few years, have been very helpful⟩ — see SPECIFICALLY 1

notation *n* a usually brief written reminder ⟨he had scribbled his *notation* so quickly I couldn't read it⟩ — see NOTE 1

notch *n* **1** a V-shaped cut usually on an edge or a surface ⟨lifted up the fence rail and positioned it in the *notch* cut into the post⟩

synonyms chip, hack, indent, indentation, indenture, kerf, nick

related words joggle, nock, punch, snip; groove, score, undercut; slit, slot

2 a narrow opening between hillsides or mountains that can be used for passage ⟨try to get through the *notch* before the storm blows in⟩ — see CANYON

3 an individual part of a process, series, or ranking ⟨sales for the album increased, and it moved up another *notch* on the music charts⟩ — see DEGREE 1

notch (up) *vb* to obtain (as a goal) through effort ⟨a stunning performance that *notched up* a second Academy Award for the actor⟩ — see ACHIEVE 1

note *n* **1** a usually brief written reminder ⟨I'll make a *note* to myself so I don't forget to pick up some milk on the way home⟩

synonyms jotting, memo, memorandum, notation

related words bordereau, memoir, memorial, minutes, protocol, report; line; document, writing

2 a message on paper from one person or group to another ⟨write a friendly *note* to the neighbors asking them to keep the noise down⟩ — see [1]LETTER

3 a natural vocal sound made by an animal ⟨can you distinguish between the *notes* of the whippoorwill and the mockingbird?⟩ — see CALL 1

4 a piece of printed paper used as money in the United States ⟨will you be paying in coins or *notes*?⟩ — see [1]BILL 2

5 a special quality or impression associated with something ⟨spoke with a *note* of irritation in her voice⟩ — see AURA 1

6 overall quality as seen or judged by people in general ⟨a writer of *note* among readers of modern poetry⟩ — see REPUTATION

7 a briefly expressed opinion ⟨let me read a few *notes* I jotted down while you were auditioning⟩ — see REMARK

8 a state of being aware ⟨during my long convalescence I had taken *note* of which friends had helped me and which ones had found other things to do⟩ — see ATTENTION 2

9 something that sets apart an individual from others of the same kind ⟨an intense, full-bodied red wine with all of the spicy *notes* for which that grape variety is famous⟩ — see CHARACTERISTIC

note *vb* **1** to make a statement of one's opinion ⟨I'd like to *note* that I don't care for that tone of voice⟩ — see REMARK 1

2 to make a written note of ⟨a waitress hurriedly *noting* our orders⟩ — see RECORD 1

3 to make note of (something) through the use of one's eyes ⟨*note* the artist's rendering of the trees, how their leaves seem to dance in the wind⟩ — see SEE 1

4 to make reference to or speak about briefly but specifically ⟨the lecturer *noted* several sources where listeners could go for further information⟩ — see MENTION 1

5 to take notice of and be guided by ⟨please *note* that the office will be closed tomorrow⟩ — see HEED 1

noted *adj* widely known ⟨a serious play that needs a *noted* Broadway actor for the lead if it is to attract audiences⟩ — see FAMOUS 1

noteless *adj* not widely known ⟨his father was a *noteless* artist who never got the big break that he deserved⟩ — see OBSCURE 2

notepad *n* a number of sheets of writing paper glued together at one edge ⟨used a different *notepad* for each class's notes⟩ — see PAD 1

noteworthiness *n* the fact or state of being above others in rank or importance ⟨her long-standing *noteworthiness* as a neurosurgeon gets her many referrals from doctors around the country⟩ — see EMINENCE 1

noteworthy *adj* **1** worth remembering or mentioning ⟨former neighbors claimed that there was nothing *noteworthy* about the serial killer who had once quietly lived among them⟩

synonyms citable, memorable, mentionable, nameable (*also* namable), notable, observable, remarkable

related words quotable, repeatable; indelible, unforgettable; newsworthy

near antonyms average, ordinary, prosaic, routine, run-of-the-mill, standard, unexceptional

antonyms forgettable, unmemorable, unremarkable

2 standing above others in rank, importance, or achievement ⟨winner of the Nobel Prize for his *noteworthy* contributions to the field of genetics⟩ — see EMINENT

nothing *adv* not in any degree, way, or under any condition ⟨*nothing* daunted by the poor reception his first novel received, he proceeded to write another one⟩ — see NEVER 2

nothing *n* **1** a person of no importance or influence ⟨his friends couldn't understand why he'd want to marry a

girl who was an obvious *nothing*⟩ — see NOBODY
2 something of little importance ⟨you're always worrying about *nothing*⟩ — see TRIFLE
3 the numerical symbol 0 or the absence of number or quantity represented by it ⟨two minus two equals *nothing*⟩ — see ZERO 1

nothingness *n* the state of being dead ⟨the inevitable *nothingness* that awaits all of us⟩ — see DEATH 2

notice *n* **1** a published statement informing the public of a matter of general interest ⟨a public safety *notice* regarding the need for a smoke detector in the home⟩ — see ANNOUNCEMENT
2 a state of being aware ⟨this malicious e-mail will be brought to the *notice* of the department head⟩ — see ATTENTION 2
3 a written communication giving information or directions ⟨received a *notice* of promotion from the head of the company⟩ — see MEMORANDUM 1
4 an essay evaluating or analyzing something ⟨avidly reads the latest theater *notices* in the paper⟩ — see CRITICISM
5 the act or an instance of telling beforehand of danger or risk ⟨in the event of a terrorist threat, the building will be evacuated with little *notice* beforehand⟩ — see WARNING 1

notice *vb* **1** to make note of (something) through the use of one's eyes ⟨did you *notice* what she was wearing?⟩ — see SEE 1
2 to make reference to or speak about briefly but specifically ⟨briefly *noticed* in his lecture the author's first published work⟩ — see MENTION 1

noticeable *adj* likely to attract attention ⟨the stain on the new carpet was quite *noticeable*, and nothing we did made it any lighter⟩
synonyms arresting, bodacious, bold, brilliant, catchy, commanding, conspicuous, dramatic, emphatic, eye-catching, flamboyant, grabby, kenspeckle [*chiefly Scottish*], marked, noisy, prominent, pronounced, remarkable, showy, splashy, striking
related words detectable, discernible (*also* discernable), observable, perceptible, recognizable, visible; outstanding, salient; distinguished, eminent, impressive, notable, noteworthy; highlighted, spotlighted; flagrant, glaring, howling, screaming; flashy, garish, gaudy, glitzy, jazzy, loud, meretricious, swank (*or* swanky), tawdry; highfalutin (*also* hifalutin), ostentatious, pretentious; extravagant, fancy, florid, glittery, spectacular; opulent, ornate, overdone, overwrought; absorbing, engrossing, enthralling, fascinating, interesting, riveting
near antonyms subtle; concealed, hidden, shrouded; dim, faint, obscure; insignificant, undistinguished, unimportant; modest, unaffected, unassuming, unpretentious; conservative, plain, quiet, simple, understated; muted, restrained, subdued, subtle, toned-down, unflashy
antonyms inconspicuous, unemphatic, unflamboyant, unnoticeable, unobtrusive, unremarkable, unshowy

notification *n* a published statement informing the public of a matter of general interest ⟨a *notification* posted by the health board that its inspectors had cited the restaurant for several violations⟩ — see ANNOUNCEMENT

notion *n* **1 notions** *pl* small useful items ⟨the fabric store had a wide variety of thread, pins, buttons, and other *notions*⟩
synonyms etceteras, novelties, odds and ends, sundries
related words baubles, bric-a-brac, gewgaws (*also* geegaws), knickknacks (*also* nicknacks), trinkets; gadgets, gimmicks, jiggers; hodgepodge, miscellany, variety
2 a sudden impulsive and apparently unmotivated idea or action ⟨I have a *notion* to go in-line skating this afternoon⟩ — see WHIM
3 an idea that is believed to be true or valid without positive knowledge ⟨has this naive *notion* that most people are basically honest⟩ — see OPINION 1
4 something imagined or pictured in the mind ⟨that modernistic building does not match my *notion* of what a country cottage should look like⟩ — see IDEA 1
5 an idea or statement about all of the members of a group or all the instances of a situation ⟨the popular *notion* that college athletes are airheads⟩ — see GENERALIZATION

notional *adj* **1** dealing with or expressing a quality or idea ⟨she has a *notional* understanding of romantic love but no actual experience of being in love⟩ — see ABSTRACT 1
2 not real and existing only in the imagination ⟨your computer's "visits" to various parts of cyberspace are entirely *notional*—you stay put and the Web pages come to you⟩ — see IMAGINARY

notoriety *n* **1** a person who is widely known and usually much talked about ⟨a television show featuring a rogues' gallery of *notorieties* from 20 years of overhyped scandals⟩ — see CELEBRITY 1
2 the fact or state of being known to the public ⟨a lawyer of *notoriety* for the huge awards he's won in medical malpractice cases⟩ — see FAME 1

notorious *adj* **1** not respectable ⟨a *notorious* mastermind of terrorist activities⟩ — see DISREPUTABLE
2 widely known ⟨a book signing for a *notorious* author of tell-all celebrity biographies⟩ — see FAMOUS 1

notwithstanding *adv* in spite of that ⟨you're rather late getting here, but you're welcome to join us for dinner *notwithstanding*⟩ — see HOWEVER

notwithstanding *conj* in spite of the fact that ⟨the man suspected of being the serial killer is little known to his neighbors, *notwithstanding* he has lived in the apartment complex for years⟩ — see ALTHOUGH

notwithstanding *prep* without being prevented by ⟨we went to see the show, my objections *notwithstanding*⟩ — see DESPITE

nourish *vb* **1** to help the growth or development of ⟨wanted to *nourish* her students' love of art⟩ — see FOSTER 1
2 to supply with nourishment ⟨we've always been *nourished* by such good food when staying at their house⟩ — see SUSTAIN 1
3 to bring to maturity through care and education ⟨he willingly *nourished* a child that was not his own⟩ — see BRING UP 1

nourishing *adj* providing the substances necessary for health and bodily growth ⟨milk should be part of a *nourishing* breakfast⟩ — see NUTRITIOUS

nourishment *n* something that maintains or stimulates the intellect ⟨a series of fantasy novels that provide wonderful *nourishment* for a child's imagination⟩ — see SUSTENANCE

nous *n, chiefly British* the ability to make intelligent decisions especially in everyday matters ⟨an Oxford don who was long on erudition but a little short on everyday *nous*⟩ — see COMMON SENSE

nouveau riche *n* one who has recently acquired wealth and social position ⟨a *nouveau riche* who is reportedly using his money to buy his way into Palm Beach society⟩
synonyms arriviste, parvenu, upstart
related words arrivé, comer; adventurer, snob, social climber; fat cat, moneybags, nabob

novel *adj* not known or experienced before ⟨that's a *novel* idea for a TV series⟩ — see NEW 2

novelette *n* a work with imaginary characters and events that is shorter and usually less complex than a novel ⟨bought a collection of his novels and *novelettes*⟩ — see STORY 1

novelettish *adj* appealing to the emotions in an obvious and tiresome way ⟨readers will encounter surprisingly *novelettish* dialogue for a work that is supposed to be a literary novel⟩ — see CORNY 1

novella *n* a work with imaginary characters and events that is shorter and usually less complex than a novel ⟨pressed for time, many English teachers have their students read the one *novella* among the novelist's works⟩ — see STORY 1

novelty *n* **1** the quality or appeal of being new ⟨the *novelty* of having a cat wore off after the first time I had to change the litter box⟩
synonyms freshness, newness, originality
related words hipness, trendiness; bizarreness, strangeness, unfamiliarity, unusualness; progressiveness; currentness, recentness, up-to-dateness; departure, divergence, innovation, offshoot, shoot
near antonyms banality, commonness, familiarity; outdatedness, staleness
2 novelties *pl* small useful items ⟨travel kits filled with small bars of soap, a folding toothbrush, and other *novelties*⟩ — see NOTION 1
3 a small object displayed for its attractiveness or interest ⟨a shop selling souvenirs, T-shirts, and assorted *novelties* for tourists passing through⟩ — see KNICKKNACK

novice *n* a person who is just starting out in a field of activity ⟨a *novice* chess player⟩ — see BEGINNER

novitiate *n* a person who is just starting out in a field of activity ⟨a *novitiate* in the rarefied world of international diplomacy, the recently appointed ambassador is treading cautiously⟩ — see BEGINNER

now *adj* keenly aware of and responsive to the latest developments especially in fashion and entertainment ⟨questioned the moral values of the *now* generation⟩ — see AU COURANT 1

now *adv* **1** at the present time ⟨that company doesn't make those toys *now* because they are unsafe⟩
synonyms anymore, currently, nowadays, presently, right now, today
related words here
phrases at present, for the time being
near antonyms away, far, farthest, remotest; heretofore, hitherto, since; ago, previously
antonyms before, formerly, long, once, then
2 not long ago ⟨I was just *now* wondering what to do about those old clothes⟩ — see NEWLY
3 on some occasions ⟨goes *now* here, *now* there—all seemingly without plan or purpose⟩ — see SOMETIMES
4 without delay ⟨come here right *now*⟩ — see IMMEDIATELY

now *conj* for the reason that ⟨I'll repeat my question *now* that you are paying attention⟩ — see SINCE

now *n* the time currently existing or in progress ⟨I know I said you could go, but that was then and this is *now*⟩ — see [1]PRESENT

nowadays *adv* at the present time ⟨*nowadays* wives are just as likely to work outside the home as their husbands are⟩ — see NOW 1

now and then *adv* on some occasions ⟨we do go to the library *now and then*, but not as often as we should⟩ — see SOMETIMES

noway *adv* **1** *or* **noways** not in any degree, way, or under any condition ⟨that will *noway* hurt your chances of getting on the team⟩ — see NEVER 2
2 *usually* **no way** certainly not ⟨*no way* will I go with you to the dance⟩ — see HARDLY 2

nowhere *n* **1** the open rural area outside of big towns and cities ⟨from the looks of things, we're stranded in *nowhere* and most likely its proverbial middle⟩ — see COUNTRY 2
2 the quality or state of being mostly or completely unknown ⟨in a few short years he rose out of *nowhere* to prominence in the dot-com world⟩ — see OBSCURITY 2

nowheresville *n* the quality or state of being mostly or completely unknown ⟨after years of languishing in *nowheresville*, she started to make it really big in the art world⟩ — see OBSCURITY 2

nowise *adv* not in any degree, way, or under any condition ⟨her romance novels are *nowise* different from those of scores of other writers⟩ — see NEVER 2

noxious *adj* **1** bad for the well-being of the body ⟨mixing bleach and ammonia can cause *noxious* fumes that can seriously harm you⟩ — see UNHEALTHY 1
2 causing or capable of causing harm ⟨*noxious* smog that for years has been encrusting the historic cathedral with soot⟩ — see HARMFUL
3 causing intense displeasure, disgust, or resentment ⟨a *noxious* new breed of horror movie in which graphic depictions of torture are presented as entertainment⟩ — see OFFENSIVE 1

nozzle *n, slang* the part of the face bearing the nostrils and nasal cavity ⟨in this classic film noir, a private eye gets his *nozzle* sliced when he starts poking it into places where it's not welcome⟩ — see NOSE 1

nth *adj* of the greatest or highest degree or quantity ⟨exaggerates to the *nth* degree about everything she ever did⟩ — see ULTIMATE 1

nuanced *adj* **1** made or done with extreme care and accuracy ⟨a *nuanced*, shaded representation of a hot-button issue that is too often depicted in black and white⟩ — see FINE 2
2 satisfying or pleasing because of fineness or mildness ⟨a sauce with a *nuanced* lemon flavor that doesn't overwhelm the taste of the fish⟩ — see DELICATE 1

nub *n* **1** a small uneven mass ⟨throw a *nub* of butter into the frying pan⟩ — see LUMP 1
2 the central part or aspect of something under consideration ⟨the *nub* of the argument is that the intelligence agencies failed the country⟩ — see CRUX

nubbin *n* **1** a very small piece ⟨had only a *nubbin* of crayon left⟩ — see BIT 1
2 the central part or aspect of something under consideration ⟨this *nubbin* of the intelligence report is the prediction that the country's government will soon fall⟩ — see CRUX

nubble *n* a small uneven mass ⟨dropped a *nubble* of clay on the floor of the pottery⟩ — see LUMP 1

nubbly *adj* having small pieces or lumps spread throughout ⟨the walls were painted with a *nubbly* paint that was supposed to give them an interesting texture⟩ — see CHUNKY 1

nubby *adj* having small pieces or lumps spread throughout ⟨a *nubby* yarn that produces bumpy fabrics when woven⟩ — see CHUNKY 1

nucleus *n* **1** a thing or place that is of greatest importance to an activity or interest ⟨a college campus that was a *nucleus* of opposition to the war⟩ — see CENTER 1
2 the central part or aspect of something under consideration ⟨the *nucleus* of the movement's methodology has always been passive resistance⟩ — see CRUX

nude *adj* lacking or shed of clothing ⟨Picasso's paintings of *nude* art models⟩ — see NAKED 1

nude *n* the state of having no clothes on one's body ⟨the artist painted some models in the *nude*⟩ — see NUDITY

nudge *vb* **1** to pass lightly across or touch gently especially in passing ⟨accidentally *nudged* me as they squeezed past⟩ — see [2]BRUSH
2 to try to persuade (someone) through earnest appeals to follow a course of action ⟨the car salesman *nudged* me into taking a test-drive, even though I had said that I was just looking⟩ — see URGE

nudity *n* the state of having no clothes on one's body ⟨a film actress for whom *nudity* is not a problem⟩
synonyms altogether, bareness, birthday suit, bottom-

lessness, buff, nakedness, nude, raw
related words toplessness; naturism, nudism

nudnik *also* **nudnick** *n* **1** one who is obnoxiously annoying ⟨dreads family gatherings, as that *nudnik* of a brother-in-law is always sure to be there⟩ — see NUISANCE 1
2 someone or something boring ⟨nobody wants to hang around with that *nudnik*—all he wants to do is talk shop⟩ — see DRAG 1

nugatory *adj* **1** having no legal or binding force ⟨the congressional resolution has symbolic value only, as it relates to a matter governed by the states and is thus *nugatory*⟩ — see NULL 1
2 lacking importance ⟨the book is entertaining, but its contributions to Shakespearean scholarship are *nugatory*⟩ — see UNIMPORTANT

nugget *n* **1** a small piece or quantity of food ⟨*nuggets* of beef in the chow mein⟩ ⟨fried chicken *nuggets*⟩ — see MORSEL 1
2 a small uneven mass ⟨a *nugget* of gold⟩ — see LUMP 1
3 a very small piece ⟨a seemingly inconsequential *nugget* of information that proved to be the key to cracking the case⟩ — see BIT 1

nuisance *n* **1** one who is obnoxiously annoying ⟨the new neighbor is threatening to become a *nuisance*, dropping in on us several times a day⟩
synonyms annoyance, annoyer, bother, gadfly, gnawer, nudnik (*also* nudnick), pain, persecutor, pest, tease, teaser
related words headache; harrier, heckler, interrupter (*also* interruptor); hassle, plague; harasser, molester, tormentor (*also* tormenter), torturer
phrases pain in the neck
near antonyms charmer, smoothy (*or* smoothie); comforter, solacer, soother
2 something that is a source of irritation ⟨folding up this map correctly is such a *nuisance*⟩ — see ANNOYANCE 3

nuke *vb* to bring to a complete end the physical soundness, existence, or usefulness of ⟨a pretty sizable piece of real estate would be *nuked* if an asteroid struck⟩ — see DESTROY 1

null *adj* **1** having no legal or binding force ⟨the contract was *null* because one party forgot to sign it⟩
synonyms bad, inoperative, invalid, nonbinding, nonvalid, nugatory, null and void, void
related words illegal; useless, worthless; ineffective, ineffectual
near antonyms legal; working
antonyms binding, good, valid
2 having no usefulness ⟨that information is as *null* as no information at all⟩ — see WORTHLESS

null *vb* to put an end to by formal action ⟨asked the state court to *null* the election results because of widespread voting irregularities⟩ — see ABOLISH 1

null and void *adj* having no legal or binding force ⟨public disclosure of the terms of the out-of-court settlement renders it *null and void*⟩ — see NULL 1

nullification *n* the doing away with something by formal action ⟨an act aimed at curbing sedition that was perhaps the most serious attempt at *nullification* of freedom of the press in the nation's history⟩ — see ABOLITION

nullify *vb* to put an end to by formal action ⟨the constitutional amendment that *nullified* Prohibition⟩ — see ABOLISH 1

nullity *n* **1** a person of no importance or influence ⟨that tiny country's ambassador from the U.S. is usually some *nullity* who happens to be a friend or supporter of the current president⟩ — see NOBODY
2 the quality or state of being unimportant ⟨one of the basic themes of the theater of the absurd is the essential *nullity* of human existence⟩ — see INSIGNIFICANCE

numb *adj* **1** lacking in sensation or feeling ⟨I've been sitting in the same position for too long and now my feet are *numb*⟩
synonyms asleep, benumbed, dead, insensitive, numbed, torpid, unfeeling
related words chilled, nipped; anesthetized, cocainized, deadened, drugged, stupefied; blunted, dulled, obtunded; insensible, senseless, unconscious; inanimate, insensate
near antonyms awake
antonyms feeling, sensible, sensitive
2 not expressing any emotion ⟨apparently in shock, he answered the police officer's questions with a *numb* expression on his face⟩ — see BLANK 1
3 not feeling or showing emotion ⟨years of physical and emotional abuse had rendered the woman *numb* and withdrawn⟩ — see IMPASSIVE 1

numb *vb* to reduce or weaken in strength or feeling ⟨wait for the medication to *numb* your mouth⟩ — see DULL 1

numbed *adj* lacking in sensation or feeling ⟨*numbed* fingers that needed warming by the fire⟩ — see NUMB 1

number *n* **1** a character used to represent a mathematical value ⟨asked him to write out the equation in *numbers*, not letters⟩
synonyms digit, figure, integer, numeral, numeric, whole number
related words decimal, fraction; cipher; symbol
2 a literary, musical, or artistic production ⟨a doomsday novel that turns out to be one of those it-was-all-a-dream *numbers*⟩ — see COMPOSITION 1
3 a performance regularly presented by an individual or group ⟨a modern dance *number*⟩ — see ACT 1
4 a person of no importance or influence ⟨doesn't want to go to some mammoth state university where she would be just a *number*⟩ — see NOBODY
5 an act of notable skill, strength, or cleverness ⟨a stunning gymnastics *number* that really impressed the judges⟩ — see FEAT 1
6 numbers *pl* the act or process of performing mathematical operations to find a value ⟨if you believe the president's *numbers*, we can afford these new programs and still have tax cuts⟩ — see CALCULATION

number *vb* **1** to find the sum of (a collection of things) by noting each one as it is being added ⟨*number* those apples and tell me how many you have⟩ — see COUNT 1
2 to have a total of ⟨the full-time staff *numbers* 30 people⟩ — see AMOUNT (TO) 1
3 to have as part of a whole ⟨is *numbered* among the great minds of our times⟩ — see INCLUDE 1

number crunching *n* the act or process of performing mathematical operations to find a value ⟨he did a little *number crunching* and made an offer on the house⟩ — see CALCULATION

numberless *adj* too many to be counted ⟨the *numberless* stars in the universe⟩ — see COUNTLESS

number one *also* **No. 1** *adj* **1** coming before all others in importance ⟨considers international terrorism to be the *number one* threat to national security⟩ — see FOREMOST 1
2 of the very best kind ⟨the company's chocolate is rated as *number one* by serious chocoholics⟩ — see EXCELLENT

numbing *adj* **1** causing weariness, restlessness, or lack of interest ⟨an utterly *numbing* class in statistics⟩ — see BORING
2 having a low or subnormal temperature ⟨the *numbing* air of that wintry morning⟩ — see COLD 1

numbness *n* a lack of emotion or emotional expressiveness ⟨the prisoner exhibited the *numbness* of someone who had spent more years behind bars than he could remember⟩ — see APATHY 1

numeral *n* a character used to represent a mathematical value ⟨write the answer in Roman *numerals*⟩ — see NUMBER 1
numerate *vb* **1** to make a list of ⟨*numerate* the dish's ingredients for me⟩ — see ¹LIST 1
2 to specify one after another ⟨I don't have the time to *numerate* all the reasons, so I'll offer just a few⟩ — see ENUMERATE 1
numeric *n* a character used to represent a mathematical value ⟨in addition to the standard alphabetical letters and *numerics*, the keyboard features rows of special characters⟩ — see NUMBER 1
numero uno *adj* **1** coming before all others in importance ⟨she's the *numero uno* tabloid celebrity at the moment⟩ — see FOREMOST 1
2 of the very best kind ⟨if you've got the bucks, the company's hand-tooled leather boots are *numero uno*⟩ — see EXCELLENT
numerous *adj* being of a large but indefinite number ⟨received *numerous* complaints about that product⟩ — see MANY
numinous *adj* having seemingly supernatural qualities or powers ⟨some have sensed a *numinous* energy in the landscape around Sedona, Arizona⟩ — see MYSTIC 1
numinousness *n* the quality or state of being impossible to know, understand, or explain ⟨the undeniable *numinousness* of so many of the articles of faith embraced by that sect⟩ — see INSCRUTABILITY 1
numskull *or* **numbskull** *n* a stupid person ⟨don't be such a *numskull*—we can't afford a new car!⟩ — see IDIOT
nuncupative *adj* made or carried on through speaking rather than in writing ⟨the soldier left a *nuncupative* will that was witnessed by two of his comrades⟩ — see VERBAL 2
nuptial *adj* of or relating to marriage ⟨newlyweds still in a state of *nuptial* bliss⟩ — see MARITAL
nuptial *n, usually* **nuptials** *pl* a ceremony in which two people are united in matrimony ⟨their *nuptials* will take place at the university chapel⟩ — see WEDDING
nurse *n* a girl or woman employed to care for a young child or children ⟨sent his little son back to his *nurse* so that he could return to his study to work⟩
synonyms babysitter, dry nurse, nanny (*also* nannie), nursemaid, nurser, sitter
related words amah, ayah; au pair, bonne; mammy; duenna, fraulein, governess, mademoiselle
nurse *vb* **1** to attend to the needs and comforts of ⟨willingly lent a hand to *nurse* his grandmother in her final years, helping her get from one room to the other and making sure she was warm⟩
synonyms administer (to), care (for), minister (to), mother
related words cure, heal, remedy; doctor, treat; aid, conserve, preserve, provide (for), support; baby, coddle, mollycoddle, pamper, spoil; cater (to), humor; indulge
phrases do for [*chiefly British*], look after, look out for, look to, see to, take care of, wait on (*also* wait upon)
near antonyms brush (aside *or* off), forget, ignore, neglect, overlook, slight
2 to give milk to from the breast ⟨a new mother's decision to *nurse* her baby⟩
synonyms breast-feed, suckle, wet-nurse
related words bottle-feed
near antonyms wean
3 to keep in one's mind or heart ⟨he continues to *nurse* a tender affection for his first girlfriend⟩ — see HARBOR 1
4 to treat with great or excessive care ⟨*nursed* his sprained ankle for the rest of the week⟩ — see BABY
5 to bring to maturity through care and education ⟨as foster parents they accepted and *nursed* 16 needy children over the years⟩ — see BRING UP 1
6 to help the growth or development of ⟨her teachers did much to *nurse* her literary talent⟩ — see FOSTER 1
7 to use or give out in stingy amounts ⟨he carefully *nursed* his energy during the marathon so that he would have something left for the final stretch⟩ — see SPARE 1
nursemaid *n* a girl or woman employed to care for a young child or children ⟨sent the children to their *nursemaid*⟩ — see NURSE
nurser *n* a girl or woman employed to care for a young child or children ⟨volunteered at the hospital as a *nurser* to hold premature babies⟩ — see NURSE
nursery *n* **1** a place or environment that favors the development of something ⟨ancient Greece is often cited as the *nursery* of democracy⟩ — see BREEDING GROUND
2 a school for children who are generally less than five years old ⟨are asking parents not to bring their children to the *nursery* if they have the flu virus⟩ — see NURSERY SCHOOL
nursery school *n* a school for children who are generally less than five years old ⟨parents trying to find the right *nursery school* for their children⟩
synonyms crèche, day nursery, nursery, pre-K, prekindergarten, preschool
nurture *vb* **1** to help the growth or development of ⟨wanted to find the art school that would best *nurture* his artistic talent⟩ — see FOSTER 1
2 to provide (someone) with moral or spiritual understanding ⟨she feels that her lifelong practice of reading the Bible daily has *nurtured* her in ways she cannot describe⟩ — see ENLIGHTEN 2
3 to supply with nourishment ⟨*nurtured* her children through the long winters with home-cooked soup⟩ — see SUSTAIN 1
nut *n* **1** a person of odd or whimsical habits ⟨a show devoted to those lovable *nuts* who collect the weirdest things just for fun⟩ — see ECCENTRIC
2 a person who lacks good sense or judgment ⟨anyone who runs into traffic like that sure is a *nut*⟩ — see FOOL 1
3 a person with a strong and habitual liking for something ⟨a baseball *nut* who waited 86 years for the Boston Red Sox to win the World Series⟩ — see FAN
4 a person judged to be legally or medically insane ⟨the man walking down the street talking to himself looked like a *nut* until we realized he was talking into his cell phone⟩ — see LUNATIC 1
5 something that requires thought and skill for resolution ⟨the question of how to increase functionality without decreasing efficiency may prove to be a tough *nut* to crack⟩ — see PROBLEM 1
6 *slang* the upper or front part of the body that contains the brain, the major sense organs, and the mouth ⟨he didn't appreciate his friend's jibe about watching his big *nut* when getting into the car⟩ — see HEAD 1
7 **nuts** *pl* language, behavior, or ideas that are absurd and contrary to good sense ⟨responding to your opponent's every argument with "*Nuts*!" is not exactly finely reasoned refutation⟩ — see NONSENSE 1
nutcase *n* **1** a person judged to be legally or medically insane ⟨some *nutcase* was arrested for sending the threatening letters to the White House⟩ — see LUNATIC 1
2 a person of odd or whimsical habits ⟨around the condo complex she's known as the *nutcase* who consistently ignores the rules⟩ — see ECCENTRIC
3 a person who lacks good sense or judgment ⟨only a *nutcase* would try to accelerate a campfire by dousing it with gasoline⟩ — see FOOL 1
nutrient *adj* providing the substances necessary for

health and bodily growth ⟨a breakfast drink enriched with *nutrient* proteins and vitamins⟩ — see NUTRITIOUS

nutritional *adj* providing the substances necessary for health and bodily growth ⟨the doctor recommended *nutritional* supplements⟩ — see NUTRITIOUS

nutritious *adj* providing the substances necessary for health and bodily growth ⟨opted for a *nutritious* snack and bought an apple instead of a candy bar⟩
synonyms nourishing, nutrient, nutritional, nutritive
related words enriched, fortified; dietary, dietetic; beneficial, healthful, healthy, restorative, salubrious, salutary, wholesome
near antonyms fattening; insalubrious, unhealthful, unhealthy, unwholesome
antonyms nonnutritious, nonnutritive

nutritive *adj* providing the substances necessary for health and bodily growth ⟨some people contend that whole wheat bread is significantly more *nutritive* than white bread⟩ — see NUTRITIOUS

nuts *adj* **1** having or showing a very abnormal or sick state of mind ⟨the bizarre rantings in the notes left behind by the serial killer convinced the police that the guy was *nuts*⟩ — see INSANE 1
2 showing urgent desire or interest ⟨I'm *nuts* for the homecoming game⟩ — see EAGER

nuts (about) *adj* filled with an intense or excessive love for ⟨a group of old girlfriends fondly recalling teen heartthrobs that they were once *nuts about*⟩ — see ENAMORED (OF)

nuts and bolts *n pl* the specific practical details of something ⟨the *nuts and bolts* of the merger of the two companies have yet to be worked out⟩ — see NITTY-GRITTY

nutter *n, British slang* **1** a person of odd or whimsical habits ⟨rather than ostracizing them, the British seem to cherish their *nutters*⟩ — see ECCENTRIC
2 a person judged to be legally or medically insane ⟨the theory that Jack the Ripper was a *nutter* infected with venereal disease by a prostitute⟩ — see LUNATIC 1

nuttiness *n* lack of good sense or judgment ⟨her incurable *nuttiness* makes her an easy target for scam artists⟩ — see FOOLISHNESS 1

nutty *adj* **1** having or showing a very abnormal or sick state of mind ⟨the only other prisoner in the dungeon was a *nutty* soul who feasted on bugs⟩ — see INSANE 1
2 showing or marked by a lack of good sense or judgment ⟨that's a *nutty* idea that won't work at all⟩ — see FOOLISH 1

nuzzle *vb* to lie close ⟨newborn puppies *nuzzling* against their mother to stay warm⟩
synonyms cuddle, nestle, snoozle [*chiefly dialect*], snuggle
related words curl up; crouch, huddle
near antonyms blench, flinch, quail, recoil, shrink, shy, start, wince

nymph *n* **1** a mythical goddess represented as a young girl and said to live outdoors ⟨she bought the book of fairy tales for the beautiful engravings of *nymphs* and fairies featured between the stories⟩
synonyms dryad, hamadryad, naiad, oread, wood nymph
related words mermaid, Nereid, Oceanid, sea-maid (*or* sea-maiden), siren, water nymph
2 a young wingless often wormlike form (as a grub or caterpillar) that hatches from the egg of many insects ⟨mayfly *nymphs*⟩ — see LARVA
3 a female person who has not yet reached adulthood ⟨the neighborhood *nymphs* were gathered at the local pizza parlor, checking out the hot guys⟩ — see GIRL 2

O

o *n* the numerical symbol 0 or the absence of number or quantity represented by it ⟨our zip code is six-*o*-three-seven-five⟩ — see ZERO 1

oaf *n* **1** a big clumsy often slow-witted person ⟨it's not polite to call your brother a stupid *oaf*⟩
synonyms clod, clodhopper, gawk, hulk, lout, lubber, lug, lump, Neanderthal, palooka
related words chump, loser, schlemiel (*also* shlemiel), turkey; slouch; airhead, birdbrain, blockhead, blunderer, bonehead, bubblehead, chowderhead, chucklehead, clodpoll (*or* clodpole), clot [*British*], cluck, clunk, cuddy (*or* cuddie) [*British dialect*], deadhead, dim bulb [*slang*], dimwit, dip, dodo, dolt, donkey, doofus [*slang*], dope, dork [*slang*], dullard, dumbbell, dumbhead, dumdum, dummkopf, dummy, dunce, dunderhead, fathead, galoot [*slang*], gander, golem, goof, goon, half-wit, hammerhead, hardhead, idiot, ignoramus, imbecile, jackass, know-nothing, knucklehead, lamebrain, loggerhead [*chiefly dialect*], loon, lump, lunkhead, meathead, mome [*archaic*], moron, mug [*chiefly British*], mutt, natural, nimrod [*slang*], nincompoop, ninny, ninnyhammer, nit [*chiefly British*], nitwit, noddy, noodle, numskull (*or* numbskull), pinhead, prat [*British*], ratbag [*chiefly Australian*], saphead, schlub (*also* shlub) [*slang*], schnook [*slang*], simp, simpleton, stock, stupe, stupid, thickhead, turkey, woodenhead, yahoo, yo-yo; anthropoid, ape, beast, boor, brute, cad, churl, clown, creep, cretin, cur, heel, louse, skunk, snake, stinker, tyke (*also* tike) [*chiefly British*], villain; booby, fool, goose, loony (*also* looney), lunatic, madman, nut; featherbrain, scatterbrain; rascal, rogue, scamp
near antonyms brain, brainiac, egghead, genius, intellectual, sage, thinker, whiz, wizard
2 a stupid person ⟨anyone who took him for an *oaf* and tried to cheat him would be in for a nasty surprise⟩ — see IDIOT

oafish *adj* not having or showing an ability to absorb ideas readily ⟨far from being *oafish*, the professional wrestler was in fact a college graduate⟩ — see STUPID 1

oafishness *n* the quality or state of lacking intelligence or quickness of mind ⟨the *oafishness* of the investigators, who missed clues and mishandled physical evidence, is the reason why that crime was never solved⟩ — see STUPIDITY 1

oar *n* a person who drives a boat forward by means of oars ⟨"All *oars* ho!" the boatswain ordered⟩ — see OARSMAN

oar *vb* to move a boat by means of oars ⟨since the wind had completely died, they had to *oar* the sailboat back to shore⟩ — see [1]ROW

oarsman *n* a person who drives a boat forward by means of oars ⟨the only *oarsman* in a rowboat designed for two⟩
synonyms oar, rower, sculler
related words bowman, oarswoman; coxswain, crewman; puller; gob, hearty, jack, jack-tar, mariner, navigator, sailor, salt, sea dog, seafarer, seaman, shipman, swab, tar; kayaker

oath *n* a person's solemn declaration that he or she will do or not do something ⟨I need your *oath* that you won't do anything until I've had time to make a decision⟩ — see PROMISE

obbligato *n* something that is found along with something else ⟨with the babble of the brook as an *obbligato*, we enjoyed our picnic⟩ — see ACCOMPANIMENT

obduracy *n* a steadfast adherence to an opinion, purpose, or course of action in spite of reason, arguments, or persuasion ⟨the administrator was known for her unyielding *obduracy* even in the face of proof that she was wrong⟩ — see OBSTINACY

obdurate *adj* **1** having or showing a lack of sympathy or tender feelings ⟨the *obdurate* refusal of the crotchety old man to let the neighborhood kids retrieve their stray ball from his backyard⟩ — see HARD 1
2 sticking to an opinion, purpose, or course of action in spite of reason, arguments, or persuasion ⟨an *obdurate* farmer who could never be convinced to try a different method of fertilization⟩ — see OBSTINATE

obdurateness *n* a steadfast adherence to an opinion, purpose, or course of action in spite of reason, arguments, or persuasion ⟨the man clung to his views on gun control with an *obdurateness* that was peculiarly impressive⟩ — see OBSTINACY

obedience *n* **1** a bending to the authority or control of another ⟨the drill sergeant demanded complete and unquestioning *obedience* from the recruits⟩
synonyms compliance, conformity, submission, subordination
related words abidance, agreeability, amenability, teachableness, tractability, tractableness, trainability; acquiescence, capitulation, obeisance, obsequiousness, submissiveness, surrender, yielding; deference, docility, dutifulness, humility, meekness, modesty, servility, slavishness, subordinateness, subservience, subserviency; inhibition, repression, restraint, suppression; control, discipline, dutifulness, order
near antonyms noncooperation, recusancy; disrespect, impudence, insolence, rudeness; insurgence, insurgency, insurrection, mutiny, outbreak, revolt; hardheadedness, mulishness, mutinousness, obstinacy, obstinateness, perversity, pigheadedness, stubbornness; misbehavior, mischievousness, naughtiness; dissent, dissidence
antonyms balkiness, contrariness, contumacy, defiance, disobedience, frowardness, insubordination, intractability, noncompliance, obstreperousness, rebelling, rebellion, rebelliousness, recalcitrance, refractoriness, self-will, unruliness, waywardness, willfulness
2 a readiness or willingness to yield to the wishes of others ⟨the cowardly *obedience* with which the dictator's henchmen followed his every command⟩ — see COMPLIANCE 1
3 the following of a custom, rule, or law ⟨expectations of strict *obedience* to the guidelines were soon dashed⟩ — see OBSERVANCE 1

obedient *adj* readily giving in to the command or authority of another ⟨that boy is so *obedient* that he does everything the first time he is asked⟩
synonyms amenable, biddable, compliant, conformable, docile, law-abiding, submissive, tractable
related words acquiescent, agreeable, amiable, duteous, dutiful, obliging, placable; soft, surrendering, yielding; fawning, kowtowing, obeisant, obsequious, servile, slavish, subordinate, subservient; decorous, disciplined, mannerly, orderly; constrained, curbed, inhibited, repressed, restrained; controllable, disciplinable, governable, handleable, manageable, tame, teachable, tractable, trainable; gentle, meek, mild
near antonyms insurgent, mutinous; dogged, hardheaded, headstrong, mulish, obdurate, obstinate, pee-

vish, pigheaded, self-willed, stubborn, unyielding; uncontrollable, unmanageable, wild; balky, defiant, perverse, resistant; bad, disorderly, errant, misbehaving, mischievous, naughty; ill-bred, undisciplined; dissident, nonconformist; disrespectful, ill-mannered, impolite, impudent, insolent, rude
antonyms balky, contrary, contumacious, defiant, disobedient, froward, incompliant, insubordinate, intractable, noncompliant, obstreperous, rebel, rebellious, recalcitrant, refractory, restive, unamenable, ungovernable, unruly, untoward, wayward, willful (*or* wilful)

obese *adj* having an excess of body fat ⟨the basset hound was so *obese* that its stomach touched the floor⟩ — see FAT 1

obesity *n* the condition of having an excess of body fat ⟨*obesity* has been linked to a number of health risks, such as heart disease⟩ — see CORPULENCE

obey *vb* to act according to the commands of ⟨she taught her dog to *obey* her when she said "Sit!"⟩ ⟨most people *obey* the law and wear their seat belts⟩
synonyms adhere (to), comply (with), conform (to), follow, goose-step (to), mind, observe
related words defer (to), submit (to), surrender (to), yield (to); accede (to), acquiesce (to), agree (to), assent (to); attend, hear, heed, listen (to), mark, note, notice, regard, take, watch
phrases abide by, fall in with, keep to
near antonyms disoblige; challenge, dare; refuse, renounce, repudiate; direct, lead; brush off, disregard, ignore, overlook, overpass, pass over, tune out, wink (at); dismiss, pooh-pooh (*also* pooh), shrug off; breach, break, infringe, transgress, violate; deride, flout, mock, scoff (at), scorn; mutiny (against), revolt (against); buck, combat, contest, dispute, fight, oppose, resist, withstand
antonyms defy, disobey, rebel (against)

obfuscate *vb* to make (something) unclear to the understanding ⟨irrelevant matters that only serve to *obfuscate* the fundamental issue of guilt or innocence⟩ — see CONFUSE 2

obit *n* a notice of a person's death usually with a short biographical account ⟨she reads the *obits* as soon as she gets her morning paper⟩ — see OBITUARY

obituary *n* a notice of a person's death usually with a short biographical account ⟨several *obituaries* for Herman Melville portrayed him as an obscure, largely forgotten author⟩
synonyms necrology, obit
related words eulogy, memorial, testimonial, tribute; epitaph, hic jacet, inscription

object *n* **1** something material that can be perceived by the senses ⟨I kept tripping over countless little *objects* scattered about the darkened room⟩
synonyms thing
related words article, item, piece; being, entity, substance; commodity, good, ware; dingus, doohickey, thingamabob, thingamajig (*or* thingumajig), thingummy, whatchamacallit, whatnot; accessory (*also* accessary), accompaniment, bauble, curio; gaud, gewgaw (*also* geegaw), knickknack (*also* nicknack), novelty, ornamental, spangle, token, trinket
2 one that has a real and independent existence ⟨trying to determine whether communication with the dead is an *object* for study, a hoax, or a figment of the imagination⟩ — see ENTITY
3 something that one hopes or intends to accomplish ⟨the *object* of this course is to teach you algebra⟩ — see GOAL

object *vb* to present an opposing opinion or argument ⟨they *objected* to the conductor's insistence that their train tickets were not valid⟩
synonyms demur, except, expostulate, kick, protest, remonstrate
related words cavil, quibble; challenge, dare, defy, fight; conflict, debate, dispute, hassle, quarrel, squabble, wrangle; beef, bellyache, bitch, bleat, carp, caterwaul, complain, crab, croak, fuss, gripe, grizzle, grouch, grouse, growl, grumble, grump, holler, keen, maunder [*chiefly British*], moan, murmur, mutter, nag, repine, scream, squawk, squeal, wail, whimper, whine, whinge [*British*], yammer, yawp (*or* yaup), yowl; balk, gag, stick; censure, criticize, denounce; disobey, rebel, withstand; demonstrate
phrases take exception, take issue
near antonyms approve, sanction; accept; accede, acquiesce, agree, assent; adhere, comply, conform, follow, mind, obey, observe; advocate, champion, defend, maintain, support, sustain, uphold; applaud, cheer, commend

objectification *n* a visible representation of something abstract (as a quality) ⟨a statue that is often cited as an *objectification* of the ancient Greeks' notion of beauty⟩ — see EMBODIMENT

objection *n* a feeling or declaration of disapproval or dissent ⟨pardon me, but I have an *objection* to any plan that requires staying out all night⟩
synonyms challenge, complaint, demur, demurral, demurrer, difficulty, exception, expostulation, fuss, kick, protest, question, remonstrance, stink
related words compunction, doubt, misgiving, qualm, scruple; misunderstanding; cavil, niggle [*chiefly British*], quibble; argument, conflict, debate, dispute, dissent, hassle, quarrel, squabble, static; censure, criticism; defiance, disobedience, rebellion; distrust, distrustfulness, dubiety, dubitation [*archaic*], incertitude, indetermination, misdoubt, mistrust, mistrustfulness, reservation, skepticism, suspicion, uncertainty; qualmishness, unease, uneasiness; reluctance, unwillingness
near antonyms willingness; approval, sanction; acceptance, acquiescence, agreement, assent; compliance, obedience

objectionable *adj* provoking or likely to provoke protest ⟨a T-shirt with an *objectionable* image⟩
synonyms censurable, exceptionable, obnoxious, offensive, reprehensible
related words unacceptable, undesirable, unwanted, unwelcome; disagreeable, displeasing, distasteful, unpleasant; bad, execrable, lousy, miserable, terrible, unspeakable, wretched; atrocious, infamous; abhorrent, disgusting, gross, loathsome, repellent (*also* repellant), repugnant, repulsive, revolting, sickening, sickish, vile; naughty, wicked; debasing, perverted, profane; off, off-color (*or* off-colored), racy, salty, suggestive; indecent, indecorous, unbecoming; earthy, unprintable; bawdy, coarse, crude, dirty, filthy, foul, gross, lewd, nasty, obscene, smutty, vulgar; blamable, blameworthy, lascivious, pornographic, ribald, scurrilous
near antonyms acceptable, agreeable, blessed (*also* blest), congenial, darling, delectable, delicious, delightful, delightsome, dreamy, dulcet, easy, enjoyable, felicitous, good, grateful, gratifying, nice, palatable, pleasant, pleasing, pleasurable, pretty, relishable, satisfying, welcome; good; approved, endorsed (*also* indorsed), sanctioned; abetted, encouraged, promoted, supported; becoming, correct, decent, decorous, exemplary, proper, respectable, seemly; blameless, commendable, creditable; immaculate, perfect, pure, spotless; politically correct
antonyms inoffensive, unobjectionable

objective *adj* **1** based on observation or experience ⟨an *objective* assessment based solely upon the results of the experiment⟩ — see EMPIRICAL 1
2 marked by justice, honesty, and freedom from bias

⟨the judge removed herself from the case because she doubted her ability to remain *objective*, given her friendship with one of the attorneys⟩ — see FAIR 2

3 restricted to or based on fact ⟨the paper's news stories strive to be scrupulously *objective*, with opinions clearly labeled as commentary⟩ — see FACTUAL 1

objective *n* something that one hopes or intends to accomplish ⟨the summer camp's stated *objective* is to produce tournament-level tennis players⟩ — see GOAL

objectiveness *n* lack of favoritism toward one side or another ⟨in the evaluation of their children's musical talent, *objectiveness* is probably the last thing that we should expect from doting parents⟩ — see DETACHMENT 1

objectivity *n* lack of favoritism toward one side or another ⟨the teacher's *objectivity* would be seriously compromised if his own child were placed in the class⟩ — see DETACHMENT 1

objet d'art *also* **objet** *n* something strange or unusual that is an object of interest ⟨the museum's collection is strongest in *objets d'art* from the South Pacific⟩ — see CURIOSITY 2

objurgate *vb* to express public or formal disapproval of ⟨even used his last will and testament as a final opportunity to *objurgate* his prodigal son⟩ — see CENSURE 1

objurgation *n* an often public or formal expression of disapproval ⟨particularly humiliating for the general was the White House's *objurgation* of his misguided and unauthorized attempt at enunciating foreign policy⟩ — see CENSURE

obligate *vb* to cause (a person) to give in to pressure ⟨the problem is of your own making, so don't think that you can *obligate* me to help⟩ — see FORCE 1

obligated *adj* being under obligation for a favor or gift ⟨we have been their guests so many times that we feel *obligated* to return their hospitality⟩ — see BEHOLDEN

obligation *n* **1** something one must do because of prior agreement ⟨their financial *obligations* keep them from giving to charities as much as they would like⟩

synonyms burden, charge, commitment, devoir, do [*archaic*], duty, imperative, incumbency, need, office, responsibility

related words oath, pledge, promise, troth, vow, word; arrangement, prearrangement, setup; compact, contract, covenant, pact, trust; debt, payment, tribute; compulsion, constraint, restraint; must, requirement; coercion, duress, force; appointment, engagement, reservation; burden, onus

near antonyms grace, postponement, stay; discharge, ease, exemption, release, relief, waiver; loophole; alternative, choice, option, pick, preference, selection

2 something (as money) which is owed ⟨I have to pay off my current *obligations* before I can buy a new car⟩ — see DEBT 1

obligatory *adj* **1** forcing one's compliance or participation by or as if by law ⟨in this state, school attendance is *obligatory* until the age of 16⟩ — see MANDATORY

2 used or heard so often as to be dull ⟨the *obligatory* cliff-hanger endings for season finales of TV shows⟩ — see STALE 1

oblige *vb* **1** to do a service or favor for ⟨I would appreciate it greatly if you could *oblige* me by bringing a dessert to the party⟩

synonyms accommodate, favor

related words humor, indulge; coddle, mollycoddle, pamper; appease, conciliate, mollify, pacify, placate; delight, gladden, gratify, please, satisfy; abet, aid, assist, help, support; attend, care (for), comfort, minister (to), relieve, succor

near antonyms bother, discommode, disturb, incommode, inconvenience, trouble; burden, encumber, saddle, weigh; desert, disappoint, fail, let down; constrain, hamper, hamstring, hinder, hobble, hold back, impede, obstruct, restrain; frustrate, oppose, sabotage, thwart

antonyms disoblige

2 to cause (a person) to give in to pressure ⟨I know you're in a hurry, but you can't *oblige* me to drive any faster than the speed limit⟩ — see FORCE 1

obliged *adj* **1** being under obligation for a favor or gift ⟨my new neighbor gave me a Christmas present, and now I feel *obliged* to reciprocate⟩ — see BEHOLDEN

2 feeling or expressing gratitude ⟨I'd be much *obliged* if you could do me this favor⟩ — see GRATEFUL 1

obliging *adj* willing to do a favor ⟨an *obliging* concierge used her pull to get us reservations at the town's hottest restaurant⟩ — see ACCOMMODATING

obligingness *n* cheerful readiness to do something ⟨she's not exactly known for her *obligingness* when it comes time to help clean up⟩ — see ALACRITY

oblique *adj* **1** inclined or twisted to one side ⟨gave the eavesdropper an *oblique* glance out of the corner of her eye⟩ — see AWRY

2 running in a slanting direction ⟨in the painting the artist repeats the *oblique* line of the path with the *oblique* line of the outstretched arm⟩ — see DIAGONAL

obliquely *adv* in a line or direction running from corner to corner ⟨the photographer has framed the shot so that the river runs *obliquely* through it, creating a great sense of depth for the viewer⟩ — see CROSSWISE

obliqueness *n* the quality or state of having a veiled or uncertain meaning ⟨the deliberate *obliqueness* of his reply left her wondering⟩ — see OBSCURITY 1

obliquity *n* the quality or state of having a veiled or uncertain meaning ⟨her poetry is sure to satisfy those readers who readily confuse *obliquity* with profundity⟩ — see OBSCURITY 1

obliterate *vb* to destroy all traces of ⟨in a stroke, the March snowstorm *obliterated* our hopes for an early spring⟩ — see ANNIHILATE 1

obliteration *n* the state or fact of being rendered nonexistent, physically unsound, or useless ⟨the ill-advised *obliteration* of the town's historic district in order to make way for a shopping center⟩ — see DESTRUCTION 1

oblivion *n* a state of being disregardful or unconscious of one's surroundings, concerns, or obligations ⟨for two weeks each year the stressed-out couple enjoy the blissful *oblivion* that comes with a vacation at the beach⟩

synonyms forgetfulness, nirvana, obliviousness

related words ignorance, incognizance, innocence, insensibility, nescience, unawareness, unconsciousness, unfamiliarity; amnesia, blindness; absentmindedness, absorption, abstraction, inattention, inattentiveness, preoccupation

near antonyms memory, recall, recollection, remembrance; alertness, awareness, cognizance, consciousness

oblivious *adj* not informed about or aware of something ⟨the out-of-state motorist claimed to be *oblivious* of the local speed limit, even though the signs must have been hard to miss⟩ — see IGNORANT 2

obliviousness *n* **1** a state of being disregardful or unconscious of one's surroundings, concerns, or obligations ⟨her general *obliviousness* often results in her walking into walls and other hard-to-miss objects⟩ — see OBLIVION

2 the state of being unaware or uninformed ⟨*obliviousness* of a law is not an acceptable excuse for breaking it⟩ — see IGNORANCE 1

obloquy *n* **1** harsh insulting language ⟨unable to mount a rational defense of her position, she unleashed a torrent of *obloquy* on her opponent⟩ — see ABUSE 1

2 the state of having lost the esteem of others ⟨although he had beaten the murder rap, the accused murderer was condemned to live out his days in perpetual *obloquy*⟩ — see DISGRACE 1

obnoxious *adj* **1** causing intense displeasure, disgust, or resentment ⟨an *obnoxious* law that was widely flouted and engendered a whole new level of criminal activity⟩ — see OFFENSIVE 1

2 provoking or likely to provoke protest ⟨an *obnoxious* comment for which there should be an immediate apology⟩ — see OBJECTIONABLE

obscene *adj* **1** depicting or referring to sexual matters in a way that is unacceptable in polite society ⟨*obscene* gestures are totally inappropriate in the workplace⟩

synonyms bawdy, blue, coarse, crude, dirty, filthy, foul, gross, gutter, impure, indecent, lascivious, lewd, locker-room, nasty, pornographic, porny, profane, raunchy, ribald, smutty, stag, trashy, unprintable, vulgar, wanton, X-rated

related words broad, coarse-grained, gamy (*or* gamey), off, off-color (*or* off-colored), racy, risqué, salacious, salty, suggestive; barnyard, earthy, scatological; immodest, indecorous, indelicate, low, unbecoming; depraved, kinky, louche, naughty, perverse, perverted, wicked; exceptionable, objectionable, unacceptable, undesirable, unwanted, unwelcome; abhorrent, debasing, disgusting, loathsome, offensive, repellent (*also* repellant), repugnant, repulsive, revolting; distasteful, obnoxious, unpleasant; blamable, blameworthy, censurable, reprehensible; atrocious, infamous; abusive, scurrilous; hard-core, soft, soft-core

near antonyms priggish, prim, prudish, puritanical, staid, straitlaced (*or* straightlaced), Victorian; correct, decorous, genteel, nice, polite, proper, respectable, seemly; innocuous, inoffensive; acceptable, agreeable, desirable, pleasant, pleasing, welcome; appropriate, becoming, fit, meet, suitable; immaculate, perfect, pure, spotless, virginal; approved, endorsed (*also* indorsed), sanctioned

antonyms clean, decent, G-rated, nonobscene, wholesome

2 causing intense displeasure, disgust, or resentment ⟨that ugly new store is really an *obscene* bit of architecture⟩ — see OFFENSIVE 1

obscenity *n* **1** the quality or state of being obscene ⟨the issue of whether *obscenity* is a fundamental part of rap music⟩

synonyms bawdiness, blueness, coarseness, crudeness, crudity, dirt, dirtiness, filth, filthiness, foulness, grossness, impureness, impurity, indecency, lasciviousness, lewdness, nastiness, profanity, raunch, raunchiness, ribaldry, smut, smuttiness, vulgarity, wantonness

related words broadness, earthiness, gaminess, raciness, saltiness, suggestiveness; immodesty, indecorousness, indelicacy, indelicateness, lowness, unbecomingness; lechery; depravedness, depravity, kinkiness, naughtiness, perverseness, perversion, perversity, pervertedness, wickedness; exceptionability, objectionableness, unacceptability, undesirability; reprehensibility, reprehensibleness; abusiveness, scurrilousness; atrociousness, atrocity, infamy, loathsomeness, offensiveness, repellency, repugnance, repulsiveness; distastefulness, obnoxiousness, unpleasantness

near antonyms priggery, priggishness, primness, prudery, prudishness, puritanism; correctness, decency, decorousness, decorum, seemliness; appropriateness, fitness, suitability, suitableness; immaculateness, perfection, purity, spotlessness

2 a disrespectful or indecent word or expression ⟨uttered a loud *obscenity* when he dropped the hammer on his toe⟩ — see SWEARWORD

obscure *adj* **1** having an often intentionally veiled or uncertain meaning ⟨a fantasy writer who likes to put lots of *obscure* references and images in her tales of wizards and warlocks⟩

synonyms ambiguous, arcane, cryptic, dark, deep, Delphic, double-edged, elliptical (*or* elliptic), enigmatic (*also* enigmatical), equivocal, fuliginous, inscrutable, murky, mysterious, mystic, nebulous, occult, opaque

related words abstruse, esoteric, recondite; cloaked, concealed, disguised, masked, shrouded; beclouded, bedimmed, befogged, clouded, cloudy, dim, faint, foggy, fuzzy, hazy, indistinct, indistinguishable, misty, muddy, obfuscatory, obnubilated, obscurant (*or* obscurantic), shaded, shadowlike, shadowy, sphinxlike; indefinite, inexact, inexplicit, noncommittal, questionable, unclear, uncertain, undefined, undetermined, vague; impenetrable, incomprehensible, indecipherable, inexplicable; eerie (*also* eery), uncanny, weird; impalpable, inappreciable, intangible, invisible; unanswerable, unknowable; baffling, bewildering, confounding, confusing, mystifying, perplexing, puzzling, unfathomable; circuitous, indirect, roundabout; complex, complicated, difficult, obtuse

near antonyms comprehensible, fathomable, intelligible, knowable, legible, pellucid, understandable; bright, distinct, evident, self-evident, self-explanatory; certain, firm, strong, sure; defined, determined; direct, straightforward; definite, exact, explicit; appreciable, palpable, tangible, visible; blatant, patent, unmistakable

antonyms accessible, clear, nonambiguous, obvious, plain, unambiguous, unequivocal

2 not widely known ⟨he's an *obscure* artist now, but he's sure to be famous someday⟩

synonyms nameless, no-name, noteless, uncelebrated, unfamous, unknown, unrecognized, unsung

related words insignificant, minor, unimportant; undistinguished, unexceptional, unremarkable; unpopular; anonymous, faceless, unnoticeable, unrecognizable; unnewsworthy, unnoticed; forgotten, unremembered

near antonyms fabled, fabulous, legendary; infamous; distinguished, eminent, exceptional, great, illustrious, notable, outstanding, prestigious, remarkable; estimable, honorable, reputable, respectable; important, influential, leading, major, newsworthy, noteworthy, significant; favorite, popular, preferred

antonyms celebrated, famed, famous, noted, notorious, prominent, renowned, well-known

3 being without light or without much light ⟨hid in an *obscure* spot among the trees⟩ — see DARK 1

4 not seen or understood clearly ⟨a distinction so *obscure* that only the experts can really see it⟩ — see FAINT 1

obscure *vb* **1** to keep secret or shut off from view ⟨the investigative reporters *obscured* their real motives for visiting the company by pretending the story was about something else⟩ — see ^{1}HIDE 2

2 to make dark, dim, or indistinct ⟨when it isn't *obscured* by smog, the view of the city from the observatory can be spectacular⟩ — see CLOUD 1

obscured *adj* being without light or without much light ⟨an *obscured* area of the prison yard that was the perfect escape route⟩ — see DARK 1

obscurity *n* **1** the quality or state of having a veiled or uncertain meaning ⟨the 16th-century astrologer's predictions are so filled with *obscurity* that people can interpret them any way they want⟩

synonyms ambiguity, ambiguousness, darkness, equivocalness, equivocation, inscrutability, inscrutableness, murkiness, mysteriousness, nebulosity, nebulousness, obliqueness, obliquity, opacity, opaqueness

related words mystery, reconditeness; cloudiness, dimness, faintness, fogginess, fuzziness, haziness, indefiniteness, indistinctness, mistiness, shade, shadow, un-

certainty, vagueness; impenetrability, incomprehensibility, incomprehensibleness; circuitousness, circuity, indirectness; deepness, depth, profoundness; abstruseness, abstrusity, complexity, complication, difficulty, obtuseness
near antonyms comprehensibility, intelligibility, legibility; brightness, distinctness, self-evidence; certainty, surety; definiteness, exactness, explicitness, incision, incisiveness, lucidity, lucidness, perspicuity, perspicuousness; directness, forthrightness, openness, straightforwardness; palpability, tangibility, tangibleness, visibility; readability, readableness; obviousness
antonyms clarity, clearness, obviousness, plainness
2 the quality or state of being mostly or completely unknown ⟨the singer languished in relative *obscurity* for years before becoming famous⟩
synonyms anonymity, facelessness, namelessness, nowhere, nowheresville, silence
related words oblivion; inconspicuousness, invisibility, invisibleness; insignificance; unpopularity
near antonyms character, mark, name, note, rep [*slang*], report, reputation, repute; favor, popularity; importance, significance; distinction, eminence, glory, greatness, honor, illustriousness, note, preeminence, prominence; megastardom, superstardom; cachet, kudos, position, prestige, rank, standing, stature; acclaim, acknowledgment (*or* acknowledgement), praise, recognition; adoration, idolization
antonyms celebrity, fame, notoriety, renown
3 the quality or state of being impossible to know, understand, or explain ⟨her novels were favored by gullible critics who confuse *obscurity* with profundity⟩ — see INSCRUTABILITY 1

obsequy *n, usually* **obsequies** *pl* the act or ceremony of putting a dead body in its final resting place ⟨the murder victim's father was the chief mourner at the *obsequies*⟩ — see BURIAL 1

observable *adj* **1** capable of being seen ⟨scientists often work with phenomena that are not directly *observable*⟩ — see VISIBLE 1
2 worth remembering or mentioning ⟨a man who apparently was devoid of any *observable* virtue⟩ — see NOTEWORTHY 1

observance *n* **1** the following of a custom, rule, or law ⟨the *observance* of this family tradition would make your grandmother very happy⟩ ⟨*observance* of the smoking ban in public buildings⟩
synonyms abidance, adherence, compliance, conformance, conformity, keeping, obedience, observation
related words deference, honor, regard, respect, upholding; accession, acquiescence, submission, surrender; attendance, attention, heed, notice
near antonyms brush-off, disregard, ignoring; delinquency, dereliction, forgetting, neglect, overlooking; offense (*or* offence), sin, wrong; challenge, defiance, flouting, rebellion
antonyms breach, contravention, infraction, infringement, nonobservance, transgression, trespass, violation
2 an oft-repeated action or series of actions performed in accordance with tradition or a set of rules ⟨some religions require very specific *observances* on holy days⟩ — see RITE
3 a state of being aware ⟨if you've been doing any significant housecleaning, it has escaped my *observance*⟩ — see ATTENTION 2

observant *adj* **1** paying close attention usually for the purpose of anticipating approaching danger or opportunity ⟨if you were more *observant*, you would perceive that something is troubling her deeply⟩ — see ALERT 1
2 having the mind fixed on something ⟨*observant* viewers will notice that the position of hero's facial wound changes in the course of the scene⟩ — see ATTENTIVE 1

observation *n* **1** a state of being aware ⟨it has come to my *observation* that you've been missing a lot of school lately⟩ — see ATTENTION 2
2 the following of a custom, rule, or law ⟨a society in which a strict *observation* of business etiquette is expected of visiting foreigners⟩ — see OBSERVANCE 1

observational *adj* based on observation or experience ⟨her reports on the great apes were based on firsthand *observational* evidence⟩ — see EMPIRICAL 1

observatory *n* a high place or structure from which a wide view is possible ⟨the *observatory* is located on a mountaintop⟩ — see LOOKOUT 1

observe *vb* **1** to act according to the commands of ⟨you must *observe* all the rules of this school, not simply the ones that meet with your personal approval⟩ — see OBEY
2 to mark with an appropriate practice, rite, or ceremony ⟨a time when few people in New England *observed* Christmas⟩ — see KEEP 1
3 to keep one's eyes on ⟨happily spent many hours *observing* the birds at the backyard feeder⟩ — see WATCH 1
4 to make a statement of one's opinion ⟨"I think you might be mistaken," he *observed*⟩ — see REMARK 1
5 to make note of (something) through the use of one's eyes ⟨she *observed* that the weather had changed again⟩ — see SEE 1
6 to take notice of and be guided by ⟨generally *observes* the suggestions of the experts regarding baby care⟩ — see HEED 1

observer *n* someone who sees or watches something ⟨*observers* of the boxing match seemed to be divided as to who won⟩ — see SPECTATOR

obsessed *adj* having extreme or relentless concern ⟨the youngster was so *obsessed* with video games that he had little interest in playing outside⟩ — see HUNG UP 1

obsession *n* something about which one is constantly thinking or concerned ⟨her latest *obsession* is a movie star who she thinks is very handsome⟩ — see FIXATION

obsessional *adj* caused by or suggestive of an irresistible urge ⟨had an *obsessional* need to be liked by everybody⟩ — see COMPULSIVE

obsessive *adj* caused by or suggestive of an irresistible urge ⟨intrigued by the man's *obsessive* counting of everyday objects⟩ — see COMPULSIVE

obsolete *adj* having passed its time of use or usefulness ⟨I was told my old printer is *obsolete* and I can't get replacement parts⟩
synonyms antiquated, archaic, dated, démodé, demoded, fossilized, kaput (*also* kaputt), medieval (*also* mediaeval), moribund, mossy, moth-eaten, neolithic, Noachian, outdated, outmoded, out-of-date, outworn, passé, prehistoric (*also* prehistorical), rusty, Stone Age, superannuated
related words aging (*or* ageing), obsolescent; discarded, disused, inoperable, unusable, unworkable, useless; dead, defunct, expired, extinct, vanished; dormant, fallow, free, idle, inactive, inert, inoperative, latent; ancient, antediluvian, antique, dateless, fusty, musty, old; oldfangled, old-fashioned, old-time, retro, vintage; aged, age-old, hoary, venerable; atavistic, bygone, erstwhile, former, historic, historical, late, old-world, past
near antonyms contemporary, current, mod, modern, new, newfangled, new-fashioned, present-day, recent, ultramodern, up-to-date, up-to-the-minute; fresh; modernized, refurbished, remodeled, renewed; functional, operable, operational, workable; active, alive, busy, employed, functioning, operating, operative

obstacle *n* something that makes movement or progress difficult ⟨stumbling on all the *obstacles* along the path⟩ — see ENCUMBRANCE

obstinacy *n* a steadfast adherence to an opinion, purpose, or course of action in spite of reason, arguments, or persuasion ⟨the mindless *obstinacy* of those people who continue to insist that the earth is flat⟩
synonyms bullheadedness, doggedness, hardheadedness, intransigence, mulishness, obduracy, obdurateness, obstinateness, opinionatedness, pertinaciousness, pertinacity, pigheadedness, self-opinionatedness, self-will, stubbornness, willfulness
related words anal-retentiveness, perverseness, perversity, waywardness, wrongheadedness; adamancy (*also* adamance), determination, implacability, inexorability, inflexibility, inveteracy, perseverence, persistence, persistency, relentlessness, resolve, single-mindedness, steadfastness, stick-to-itiveness, tenaciousness, tenacity; firmness, hardness, rigor, rigorousness, sternness, strictness; narrow-mindedness, rigidity, rigidness; bloody-mindedness [*chiefly British*], cantankerousness, contrariness, cussedness; balkiness, contumacy, defiance, disobedience, frowardness, immovability, immovableness, insubordination, intractibility, obstreperousness, rebelliousness, recalcitrance, recalcitrancy, refractoriness, unruliness
near antonyms broad-mindedness, open-mindedness, reasonability, reasonableness, receptiveness, receptivity; acceptance, acquiescence, flexibility, pliability, pliableness, pliancy, pliantness; compliance, docility, obedience, subordinateness, subordination; submission, surrender, willingness, yielding; slavishness, subservience, subserviency

obstinate *adj* sticking to an opinion, purpose, or course of action in spite of reason, arguments, or persuasion ⟨the child was *obstinate* about wanting that specific toy, despite being offered several others⟩
synonyms adamant, adamantine, bullheaded, dogged, hard, hardened, hardheaded, hard-nosed, headstrong, immovable, implacable, inconvincible, inflexible, intransigent, mulish, obdurate, opinionated, ossified, pat, pertinacious, perverse, pigheaded, self-opinionated, self-willed, stiff-necked, stubborn, unbending, uncompromising, unrelenting, unyielding, willful (*or* wilful)
related words anal-retentive, obsessive; wayward, wrongheaded; determined, hell-bent, inexorable, persistent, relentless, resolved, set, single-minded, steadfast, stouthearted, tenacious, unflinching; firm, hard-line, hard-shell (*or* hard-shelled), iron, severe, stern, strict; hidebound, narrow-minded, rigid; bloody-minded [*chiefly British*], cantankerous; contrary, cussed; contumacious, disobedient, froward, insubordinate, intractable, recalcitrant, refractory, uncooperative, ungovernable, unmanageable, unruly; defiant, insurgent, mutinous; indomitable, invincible, unconquerable; confirmed, inveterate, unregenerate; demanding, exacting
phrases deaf to reason
near antonyms docile, obedient, placable, submissive, tractable; accepting, persuadable, receptive, responsive, willing; governable, manageable, reasonable, temperate; slavish, subservient
antonyms acquiescent, agreeable, amenable, compliant, complying, flexible, pliable, pliant, relenting, yielding

obstinateness *n* a steadfast adherence to an opinion, purpose, or course of action in spite of reason, arguments, or persuasion ⟨regardless of the issue, she holds onto her position with an *obstinateness* that would exhaust the patience of a saint⟩ — see OBSTINACY

obstreperous *adj* **1** engaging in or marked by loud and insistent cries especially of protest ⟨an *obstreperous* crowd protesting the government's immigration policy⟩ — see VOCIFEROUS
2 given to resisting authority or another's control ⟨the club's president was at his wits' end with *obstreperous* members who refused to cooperate⟩ — see DISOBEDIENT

obstreperousness *n* refusal to obey ⟨the toddler occasionally felt the need to demonstrate her independence with a foot-stamping *obstreperousness*⟩ — see DISOBEDIENCE

obstruct *vb* **1** to create difficulty for the work or activity of ⟨this would go much faster if you would stop *obstructing* me with your constant interruptions⟩ — see HAMPER
2 to prevent passage through by filling with something ⟨at the moment the city's only tunnel between downtown and the airport is *obstructed* by an overturned tanker truck⟩ — see CLOG 1

obstruction *n* something that makes movement or progress difficult ⟨an *obstruction* in the drain has the water all backed up⟩ — see ENCUMBRANCE

obtain *vb* to receive as return for effort ⟨after years of proving herself, she *obtained* recognition as a serious journalist⟩ — see EARN 1

obtainable *adj* possible to get ⟨gas was in such short supply that it was just not *obtainable* at any price⟩ — see AVAILABLE 1

obtainment *n* something added to an existing supply ⟨moving required that we sort through the mountain of *obtainments* that comes from living in the same house for 30 years⟩ — see ACCESSION 1

obtrude *vb* to interest oneself in what is not one's concern ⟨please stop *obtruding* in your brother's affairs⟩ — see INTERFERE

obtrusive *adj* thrusting oneself where one is not welcome or invited ⟨meddling in other people's romantic lives is both *obtrusive* and presumptuous⟩ — see INTRUSIVE

obtuse *adj* **1** lacking sharpness of edge or point ⟨*obtuse* scissors designed so that young users will not cut themselves⟩ — see DULL 1
2 not having or showing an ability to absorb ideas readily ⟨forgive me for being *obtuse*, but I wish you'd explain that to me again⟩ — see STUPID 1

obtuseness *n* the quality or state of lacking intelligence or quickness of mind ⟨our guest's *obtuseness* was such that he failed to take even the broadest hint that it was time to leave⟩ — see STUPIDITY 1

obverse *n* something that is as different as possible from something else ⟨the new administration had promised peace and prosperity, but what we got was the *obverse*: war and recession⟩ — see OPPOSITE

obviate *vb* to keep from happening by taking action in advance ⟨brushing regularly should *obviate* the need for frequent trips to the dentist⟩ — see PREVENT

obvious *adj* **1** not subject to misinterpretation or more than one interpretation ⟨that remark was an *obvious* joke, so lighten up⟩ — see CLEAR 2
2 very noticeable especially for being incorrect or bad ⟨*obvious* errors in the book that the editor or proofreader should have caught⟩ — see EGREGIOUS

occasion *n* **1** a particular point at which an event takes place ⟨on that *occasion*, I didn't actually meet your father⟩
synonyms moment, time
related words flash, instant, jiffy, minute, second, shake, split second, trice, twinkle, wink; bit, space, spell, stretch, while
2 a favorable combination of circumstances, time, and place ⟨the substitute violinist rose to the *occasion* and performed the piece beautifully⟩ — see OPPORTUNITY
3 someone or something responsible for a result ⟨the missing money proved to be the *occasion* of much strife between the two brothers⟩ — see CAUSE 1
4 something that happens ⟨weddings are generally

happy *occasions*⟩ — see EVENT 1

occasion *vb* to be the cause of (a situation, action, or state of mind) ⟨the announcement concerning the change in scheduling *occasioned* much confusion⟩ — see EFFECT

occasional *adj* **1** lacking in steadiness or regularity of occurrence ⟨the weekend forecast is for *occasional* showers⟩ — see FITFUL

2 not often occurring or repeated ⟨an *occasional* mechanical problem with our car, but nothing serious⟩ — see INFREQUENT

occasionally *adv* on some occasions ⟨we *occasionally* stop for ice cream on the way home⟩ — see SOMETIMES

occlude *vb* to prevent passage through by filling with something ⟨a blood clot had *occluded* a major artery in his body⟩ — see CLOG 1

occult *adj* **1** being beyond one's powers to know, understand, or explain ⟨the *occult* ways in which the human mind works⟩ — see MYSTERIOUS 1

2 having an often intentionally veiled or uncertain meaning ⟨an *occult* reference in the text that has puzzled scholars ever since⟩ — see OBSCURE 1

3 having seemingly supernatural qualities or powers ⟨Great Britain's Stonehenge is one of those *occult* places where people expect something of cosmic significance to happen⟩ — see MYSTIC 1

occult *vb* to keep secret or shut off from view ⟨*occulted* their house from prying eyes by planting large trees around it⟩ ⟨the actor's private life had long been *occulted* by a contrived public persona⟩ — see [1]HIDE 2

occupancy *n* the act or fact of residing in a place ⟨the landlord notified us of the need to cease *occupancy* in three months, when our apartment building would be sold⟩
synonyms habitation, occupation, possession, residency
related words tenancy, tenantry; ownership, proprietorship; trespass
near antonyms dispossession, ejection, ejectment; vacancy; vacating, vacation

occupant *n* one who lives permanently in a place ⟨the only *occupants* of that house are an old lady and her cat⟩ — see INHABITANT

occupation *n* **1** the activity by which one regularly makes a living ⟨my primary *occupation* is stockbroker, but I'm a drummer in a rock band on the weekends⟩
synonyms calling, employment, game, lay, line, profession, trade, vocation, work
related words call, lifework; business, enterprise, field, livelihood, living, métier (*also* metier), racket [*slang*]; assignment, engagement, gig, mission; art, craft, handcraft, handicraft; appointment, berth, billet, office, place, position, post, situation; duty, function, job, load, task, workload
near antonyms avocation, hobby, pursuit

2 the act or fact of residing in a place ⟨*occupation* of a condemned building is illegal⟩ — see OCCUPANCY

occupied *adj* involved in often constant activity ⟨the boy is constantly *occupied*, usually with sports or schoolwork⟩ — see BUSY 1

occupy *vb* to hold the attention of ⟨a puzzle will *occupy* that child for hours⟩ — see ENGAGE 1

occur *vb* to take place ⟨let me know when the lunar eclipse is scheduled to *occur*⟩ — see HAPPEN

occur (to) *vb* to enter the mind of ⟨it didn't *occur to* me to ask until much later⟩
synonyms come (to), cross, dawn (on), strike
related words recall, recollect, remember, reminisce; con, learn, memorize; appear, arrive, emerge, materialize
near antonyms forget, unlearn; disregard, ignore, neglect, overlook

occurrence *n* something that happens ⟨life is full of random *occurrences*⟩ — see EVENT 1

ocean *n* **1** the whole body of salt water that covers nearly three-fourths of the earth ⟨the *ocean* still holds mysteries that we are only beginning to unravel⟩
synonyms blue, brine, deep, Neptune, sea, seven seas
related words blue water, high seas, main, waters; basin; Davy Jones's locker, depths

2 an immeasurable depth or space ⟨with a single bound from top of the cliff, he propelled the hang glider into the *ocean* of air over the valley⟩ — see ABYSS

oceanic *adj* **1** of or relating to the sea ⟨the theory that ancient mariners took advantage of *oceanic* currents to roam the seas on primitive rafts⟩ — see MARINE 1

2 of, relating to, or occurring in the open sea ⟨during his solo crossing of the Atlantic he managed to avoid the fierce *oceanic* storms that rage in those tropical latitudes⟩ — see DEEP-SEA

3 unusually large ⟨an *oceanic* field of wheat that stretched as far as the eye could see⟩ — see HUGE

ocular *adj* of, relating to, or used in vision ⟨recommends regular eye examinations for the early detection of such *ocular* diseases as glaucoma⟩ — see VISUAL 1

odd *adj* **1** being one of a pair or set without a corresponding mate ⟨somehow, there's always at least one *odd* sock that comes out of the dryer⟩
synonyms unmatched, unpaired
related words alone, lone, only, single, singular, sole, solitary
antonyms matched, paired

2 different from the ordinary in a way that causes curiosity or suspicion ⟨*odd* behavior that prompted one of the waiting passengers to alert airport security⟩
synonyms bizarre, bizarro, cranky, crazy, curious, eccentric, erratic, far-out, funky, funny, kinky, kooky (*also* kookie), offbeat, off-kilter, off-the-wall, outlandish, out-of-the-way, outré, peculiar, quaint, queer, queerish, quirky, remarkable, rum [*chiefly British*], screwy, spaced-out, strange, wacky (*also* whacky), way-out, weird, weirdo, wild
related words aberrant, abnormal, addlepated, flaky; extraordinary, fantastic (*also* fantastical), freak, freakish, freaky, phantasmagoric (*or* phantasmagorical), phenomenal; atypical, rare, singular, uncommon, uncustomary, unique, unusual, unwonted; conspicuous, notable, noticeable, outstanding, prominent, salient, striking; atrocious, outrageous, shocking; crotchety, idiosyncratic, nonconformist, nonmainstream, out-there, unconventional, unorthodox; baffling, bewildering, confounding, mystifying, perplexing, puzzling
near antonyms average, commonplace, everyday, garden, normal, ordinary, prosaic, routine, run-of-the-mill, standard, typical, unexceptional, unremarkable, usual, workaday; conformist, conservative, conventional; expected, familiar, knee-jerk, predictable; common, customary, frequent, habitual, regular, wonted

3 being out of the ordinary ⟨the only *odd* grade for the exam was the one perfect score⟩ — see EXCEPTIONAL 1

4 noticeably different from what is generally found or experienced ⟨the *odd* occurrences in the area attracted the attention of people interested in psychic phenomena⟩ — see UNUSUAL 1

5 not often occurring or repeated ⟨with the exception of the *odd* sick day, he never takes time off from work⟩ — see INFREQUENT

oddball *n* a person of odd or whimsical habits ⟨she's known as the office *oddball*⟩ — see ECCENTRIC

oddity *n* **1** an odd or peculiar habit ⟨his one *oddity* is collecting used pencil leads⟩ — see IDIOSYNCRASY

2 something strange or unusual that is an object of interest ⟨years ago circus sideshows used to display peo-

ple with unusual physical features as *oddities*⟩ — see CURIOSITY 2
3 something that is different from what is ordinary or expected ⟨she is an *oddity* in the mostly male world of high-level corporate executives⟩ — see ANOMALY 1
4 a person of odd or whimsical habits ⟨an *oddity* with a penchant for weaving cat fur⟩ — see ECCENTRIC
oddment *n* **1** an unused or unwanted piece or item typically of small size or value ⟨the fabric store sells *oddments* left over from cutting⟩ — see [1]SCRAP 1
2 something that is different from what is ordinary or expected ⟨one of those medical *oddments* that has perplexed and intrigued generations of medical historians⟩ — see ANOMALY 1
3 something strange or unusual that is an object of interest ⟨an exhibit devoted to the incredible array of *oddments* that are collected by people the world over⟩ — see CURIOSITY 2
odds *n pl* a measure of how often an event will occur instead of another ⟨the *odds* of winning the lottery are currently 200 million to one⟩ — see PROBABILITY 2
odds and ends *n pl* **1** small useful items ⟨she's always searching among the *odds and ends* in the drawer for some tool that she needs⟩ — see NOTION 1
2 a remaining group or portion ⟨almost all of the piece of leather will be needed for upholstering the chair, so just throw away any *odds and ends*⟩ — see REMAINDER 1
odious *adj* causing intense displeasure, disgust, or resentment ⟨an *odious* and unforgivable insult⟩ — see OFFENSIVE 1
odium *n* the state of having lost the esteem of others ⟨time did nothing to diminish the *odium* in which the traitor lived out his days⟩ — see DISGRACE 1
odor *n* **1** a special quality or impression associated with something ⟨there's an *odor* of decay about the mom-and-pop amusement park, which clearly has seen better days⟩ — see AURA 1
2 the quality of a thing that makes it perceptible to the sense organs in the nose ⟨some people find the *odor* of skunk rather pleasant⟩ — see SMELL 1
3 overall quality as seen or judged by people in general ⟨her movie career has not been in good *odor* since her latest box office failure⟩ — see REPUTATION
odorize *vb* to fill or infuse with a pleasant odor or odor-releasing substance ⟨the fans are used to *odorize* the air outside the confectioner's shop in order to lure more passersby⟩ — see SCENT 1
oeuvre *n* the complete works of an author ⟨a novel that occupies a relatively minor position in the author's *oeuvre*⟩ — see CORPUS 1
of *prep* **1** earlier than ⟨it's ten minutes *of* two right now⟩ — see BEFORE 1
2 having to do with ⟨the librarian read stories *of* kings and princesses to the youngsters⟩ — see ABOUT 1
off *adj* **1** falling short of a standard ⟨the milk tasted *off*⟩ — see BAD 1
2 not being in a state of use, activity, or employment ⟨the computer is *off*, so you'll have to turn it on in order to use it⟩ — see INACTIVE 2
3 not being in agreement with what is true ⟨that claim that everyone is actually related to everyone else seems a bit *off*⟩ — see FALSE 1
4 small in degree ⟨on the *off* chance that you do get straight A's, you can skip a grade⟩ — see REMOTE 1
5 hinting at or intended to call to mind matters regarded as indecent ⟨a telltale smirk suggested that there was something *off* about his parting shot⟩ — see SUGGESTIVE 1
off *adv* from this or that place ⟨move *off* a few yards before I throw the football⟩ — see AWAY
off *vb, slang* to put to death deliberately ⟨the hit man bragged that he'd *offed* at least three people in the last year alone⟩ — see MURDER 1
offal *n* discarded or useless material ⟨a pile of *offal* from the tannery operating in the neighborhood⟩ — see GARBAGE 1
offbeat *adj* **1** different from the ordinary in a way that causes curiosity or suspicion ⟨an *offbeat* approach to the task, but it gets the job done⟩ — see ODD 2
2 noticeably different from what is generally found or experienced ⟨this writer has an enjoyably *offbeat* sense of humor⟩ — see UNUSUAL 1
off–color *or* **off–colored** *adj* hinting at or intended to call to mind matters regarded as indecent ⟨the movie was rated PG for some swearing and *off-color* jokes⟩ — see SUGGESTIVE 1
offend *vb* **1** to commit an offense ⟨since this is the first time you've *offended*, we'll let you off lightly⟩
synonyms err, fall, sin, stray, transgress, trespass, wander
related words breach, break, infringe, violate; backslide, lapse; mess up
phrases break the law, fall from grace
near antonyms forgive, justify, pardon; regret, repent, rue
2 to cause hurt feelings or deep resentment in ⟨the visitor unintentionally *offended* his hosts terribly by failing to compliment them on the elaborately prepared meal⟩ — see INSULT
3 to fail to keep ⟨keeping company without a chaperone present definitely would have *offended* the social standards of the day⟩ — see VIOLATE 1
offender *n* a person who has committed a crime ⟨juvenile *offenders* have their criminal records sealed when they turn 18⟩ — see CRIMINAL
offense *or* **offence** *n* **1** a breaking of a moral or legal code ⟨wartime *offenses* that are crimes against all of humanity⟩
synonyms breach, crime, debt, error, lawbreaking, malefaction, misdeed, misdoing, sin, transgression, trespass, violation, wrongdoing
related words bias crime, hate crime; felony, misconduct, misdemeanor, misfeasance; fault, foible, peccadillo; break, infringement; immorality, iniquitousness, iniquity, sinfulness, vice, wickedness; corruption, debauchery, depravity, licentiousness; abuse, criminality, illegality, lawlessness, unlawfulness; descent, downfall, fall
near antonyms blamelessness, faultlessness, guiltlessness, impeccability, innocence, irreproachability; goodness, morality, righteousness, virtue, virtuousness
antonyms noncrime
2 the act or action of setting upon with force or violence ⟨combat casualties grew enormously as the weapons of *offense* became far more technologically advanced than defensive armor⟩ — see ATTACK 1
3 an act or expression showing scorn and usually intended to hurt another's feelings ⟨a diplomat never deliberately gives *offense*⟩ — see INSULT
4 the feeling of being offended or resentful after a slight or indignity ⟨my mother was prone to take *offense* even at the most innocent remark⟩ — see PIQUE
offensive *adj* **1** causing intense displeasure, disgust, or resentment ⟨I find your disrespectful attitude toward religion very *offensive*⟩ ⟨the smell of rotting food is quite *offensive*⟩
synonyms abhorrent, abominable, appalling, awful, disgusting, distasteful, dreadful, evil, foul, fulsome, gross, hideous, horrendous, horrible, horrid, loathsome, nasty, nauseating, nauseous, noisome, noxious, obnoxious, obscene, odious, rancid, repellent (*also* repellant), repugnant, repulsive, revolting, scandalous, shocking, sickening, ugly

related words exceptionable, objectionable; brackish, disagreeable, dislikable (*also* dislikeable), unpleasant; contemptible, despicable, detestable, hard, hateful; unhealthy, unsavory, unwholesome; execrable, lousy, miserable; atrocious, frightful, ghastly, grim, grisly, gruesome (*also* grewsome), heinous, horrendous, horrific, horrifying, lurid, macabre, monstrous, nightmarish, shocking, sick, sickish, sickly, terrible, unspeakable, vile; off-putting, undesirable, unwanted, unwelcome; barbarous, unchristian, uncivilized, ungodly, unholy; distressing, disturbing, upsetting
near antonyms acceptable, agreeable, alluring, appealing, attractive, blessed (*also* blest), congenial, darling, delectable, delicious, delightful, delightsome, desirable, dreamy, dulcet, enjoyable, felicitous, gratifying, heavenly, inviting, likable (*or* likeable), luscious, nice, palatable, pleasant, pleasing, pleasurable, satisfying, savory (*also* savoury), sweet, welcome; unexceptionable, unobjectionable; healthful, healthy, restorative, salubrious, salutary, wholesome
antonyms innocuous, inoffensive
2 provoking or likely to provoke protest ⟨insensitive, *offensive* remarks about the plight of the homeless⟩ — see OBJECTIONABLE

offensive *n* the act or action of setting upon with force or violence ⟨the primary *offensive* by the ground forces will commence at dawn tomorrow⟩ — see ATTACK 1

offer *n* **1** an effort to do or accomplish something ⟨made the usual halfhearted *offer* to grab the check before his dinner companion could⟩ — see ATTEMPT 1
2 something which is presented for consideration ⟨a job *offer* that I couldn't refuse⟩ — see PROPOSAL

offer *vb* **1** to put before another for acceptance or consideration ⟨I *offered* my boss an alternative to the original plan, which would have required me to work overtime⟩
synonyms extend, give, proffer, tender, trot out
related words pose, propose; hold out; give in, submit; volunteer
phrases run by (*or* run past)
near antonyms accept, receive, take; accredit, approbate, approve, authorize, clear, confirm, finalize, formalize, homologate, OK (*or* okay), ratify, sanction, warrant; decline, deny, disallow, disapprove, negative, reject, turn down, veto; rebuff, rebut, refuse, spurn; retract, withdraw; disregard, ignore, neglect, overlook
2 to set before the mind for consideration ⟨*offered* the idea of a vacation at a beach resort in the Caribbean⟩ — see PROPOSE 1
3 to bring before the public in performance or exhibition ⟨a summer theater *offering* a full schedule of musicals to the vacationing public⟩ — see PRESENT 1
4 to give up as an offering to a god ⟨when fruits, flowers, or crops are *offered*, the offering is known as a bloodless sacrifice⟩ — see SACRIFICE

offering *n* something offered to a god ⟨some ancient gods were thought to demand burnt *offerings*⟩ — see SACRIFICE

offhand *adj* made or done without previous thought or preparation ⟨an *offhand* comment that later caused the politician much embarrassment⟩ — see EXTEMPORANEOUS

offhanded *adj* made or done without previous thought or preparation ⟨a quick, *offhanded* suggestion that was actually much better than any of the prepared proposals⟩ — see EXTEMPORANEOUS

office *n* **1** a large unit of a governmental, business, or educational organization ⟨the company's main *office* is in Atlanta⟩ — see DIVISION 2
2 something one must do because of prior agreement ⟨one of the chief *offices* of a friend is to be there in someone's hour of need⟩ — see OBLIGATION 1

officeholder *n* a person who holds a public office ⟨the last *officeholder* was extremely conscientious about not using public funds for his personal gain⟩ — see OFFICIAL

officer *n* **1** a member of a force charged with law enforcement at the local level ⟨if you are ever lost, find the nearest *officer* and ask for help⟩
synonyms bobby [*British*], bull [*slang*], constable [*chiefly British*], cop, copper, flatfoot [*slang*], fuzz, gendarme, lawman, policeman, police officer, shamus [*slang*]
related words patrolman, policewoman; detective, dick, gumshoe, hawkshaw, inspector, investigator, plainclothesman, sherlock, sleuth, sleuthhound; marshal (*also* marshall), sheriff, trooper; peace officer; captain, lieutenant, sergeant; constabulary, heat [*slang*], man, police, police force; operative, private detective, private eye, private investigator
near antonyms civilian
2 a person who holds a public office ⟨an *officer* of the court⟩ — see OFFICIAL

official *adj* ordered or allowed by those in authority ⟨the *official* languages for those Olympic Games were French and English⟩
synonyms authorized, sanctioned
related words lawful, legal, legit [*slang*], legitimate, licit, permissible, regulation; approved, endorsed (*also* indorsed); abetted, encouraged, promoted, suggested, supported; certified, licensed; authoritative, canonical, ex officio; semiofficial
near antonyms illegal, illegitimate, illicit, impermissible, lawless, unlawful, wrongful; unapproved, unlicensed, verboten
antonyms nonofficial, unauthorized, unofficial, unsanctioned

official *n* a person who holds a public office ⟨some of our best public *officials* do their jobs quietly and are never in the news⟩
synonyms functionary, officeholder, officer, public servant
related words bureaucrat; administrator, commissioner, director, executive, head, manager, regulator, superintendent, supervisor; chair, chairman; flunky (*also* flunkey *or* flunkie), minion, underling; co-official

officinal *adj* tending to cure disease or restore health ⟨the discovery of *officinal* plants that continues to this day⟩ — see MEDICINAL 1

officious *adj* thrusting oneself where one is not welcome or invited ⟨an *officious* little man who was always telling everyone else how to do their jobs⟩ — see INTRUSIVE

offing *n* time that is to come ⟨major changes are in the *offing* for the company⟩ — see FUTURE 1

offish *adj* having or showing a lack of friendliness or interest in others ⟨she was consistently surly and *offish* with the would-be suitors who came calling⟩ — see COOL 1

off–kilter *adj* **1** different from the ordinary in a way that causes curiosity or suspicion ⟨he's nice enough, but there's something a little *off-kilter* about him⟩ — see ODD 2
2 inclined or twisted to one side ⟨to me, the painting on the wall looks a little *off-kilter*⟩ — see AWRY

off–load *vb* to empty or rid of cargo ⟨the warehouse needs to hire more people to load and *off-load* the trucks⟩ — see UNLOAD 1

offscouring *n* **1** discarded or useless material ⟨the foundry's *offscouring* was the neighborhood's eyesore⟩ — see GARBAGE 1
2 one who is cast out or rejected by society ⟨the hills are controlled by bandits and other unsavory *offscourings*

who have taken up a life outside the law⟩ — see OUTCAST

offset *n* **1** a force or influence that makes an opposing force ineffective or less effective ⟨a better performance this time will be an *offset* to last year's dismal showing⟩ — see COUNTERBALANCE

2 the stopping of a process or activity ⟨symptoms that were striking for their abrupt onset and their equally abrupt *offset*⟩ — see END 1

offset *vb* to balance with an equal force so as to make ineffective ⟨if you get a high grade on this quiz, it will *offset* the D from your last one⟩

synonyms annul, cancel (out), compensate (for), correct, counteract, counterbalance, counterpoise, make up (for), negative, neutralize

related words invalidate, negate, neuter, nullify; atone (for); outbalance, outweigh, redeem; redress, relieve, remedy; override, overrule

offshoot *n* **1** a branch of a main stem especially of a plant ⟨we knew the rosebush had survived the harsh winter when it began producing *offshoots* and turning green again⟩

synonyms outgrowth, shoot, sprout

related words excrescence, growth; bough, branchlet, limb, twig; bud, floret; spray, sprig, spur

2 something that naturally develops or is developed from something else ⟨opened a shop selling fancy foods as an *offshoot* of their very successful restaurant⟩ — see DERIVATIVE

offshore *adj* of, relating to, or situated in the waters near the shore ⟨environmentalists adamantly opposed *offshore* drilling in the area⟩ — see INSHORE

offspring *n* the descendants of a person, animal, or plant ⟨the racehorse's *offspring* all proved to be very good racers as well⟩ ⟨the couple celebrated their 50th wedding anniversary surrounded by three generations of *offspring*⟩

synonyms fruit, get, issue, posterity, progeny, seed, spawn

related words brood, hatch, litter, young; child, scion; family, kin; lineage, stock

near antonyms ancestor, antecedent, father, forebear (*also* forbear), forebearer, forefather, grandfather, parent, primogenitor, progenitor

off-the-cuff *adj* made or done without previous thought or preparation ⟨having gotten into hot water with some unfortunate *off-the-cuff* remarks, the candidate now limits himself to his carefully prepared campaign speech⟩ — see EXTEMPORANEOUS

off-the-peg *adj, chiefly British* made beforehand in large numbers ⟨accustomed to bespoke suits, he would never condescend to wear an *off-the-peg* smoking jacket⟩ — see READY-MADE

off-the-rack *adj* made beforehand in large numbers ⟨the fashionistas were aghast that the actress would wear an *off-the-rack* dress to the Oscars⟩ — see READY-MADE

off-the-shelf *adj* made beforehand in large numbers ⟨she chose to have her computer designed to her specifications rather than buying an *off-the-shelf* machine⟩ — see READY-MADE

off-the-wall *adj* different from the ordinary in a way that causes curiosity or suspicion ⟨she does have some *off-the-wall* suggestions about home decorating⟩ — see ODD 2

oft *adv* many times ⟨as I have *oft* said, you need to look before you leap⟩ — see OFTEN

often *adv* many times ⟨I seem to stumble *often* when I try to walk in high heels⟩

synonyms again and again, constantly, continually, frequently, hourly, much, oft, oftentimes (*or* ofttimes), over and over, repeatedly

related words always, consistently, continuingly, continuously, night and day, perpetually, unceasingly, uninterruptedly; afresh, again, anew; commonly, habitually, ordinarily, regularly, routinely; intermittently, periodically, recurrently; generally, usually

phrases a lot, time after time, time and again

near antonyms now, now and then, occasionally, sometimes, sporadically; ne'er, never; once

antonyms infrequently, little, rarely, seldom

oftentimes *or* **ofttimes** *adv* many times ⟨children *oftentimes* don't realize how quickly time passes⟩ — see OFTEN

ogle *vb* to look at in a flirtatious or desiring way ⟨I do wish you two would stop *ogling* each other during class⟩

synonyms leer (at)

related words eye, gape, gawk, gaze, glare, goggle, peer, rubberneck, stare

phrases make eyes (at)

ogre *n* **1** a strange or horrible and often frightening creature ⟨a horror movie filled with *ogres* and demons of every description⟩ — see MONSTER 1

2 something or someone that causes fear or dread especially without reason ⟨the *ogre* of the standardized test keeps recurring⟩ — see BOGEY 1

oh *n* the numerical symbol 0 or the absence of number or quantity represented by it ⟨the number is one-*oh*-two-four⟩ — see ZERO 1

oil *n* a picture created with oil paint ⟨that artist is known to have created only *oils* and charcoal sketches⟩ — see PAINTING

oil *vb* to coat (something) with a slippery substance in order to reduce friction ⟨if you *oil* the machinery on a regular basis, it will operate more efficiently⟩ — see LUBRICATE

oiled *adj* **1** having or being a surface so smooth as to greatly reduce traction ⟨following the fuel spill, the resulting *oiled* stretch of roadway had to be closed to traffic⟩ — see SLICK 1

2 *slang* being under the influence of alcohol ⟨Mary will do just about anything once she's pretty well *oiled*⟩ — see DRUNK

oil painting *n* a picture created with oil paint ⟨hung a beautiful *oil painting* of the bay on the living room wall⟩ — see PAINTING

oilskin *n* a coat made of water-resistant material ⟨the *oilskins* worn by the fishing boat's crew gave them scant protection from the cold, driving rain⟩ — see RAINCOAT

oily *adj* overly or insincerely flattering ⟨an executive who surrounds herself with *oily*, sycophantic assistants⟩ — see FULSOME 1

OK *or* **okay** *adj* **1** being to one's liking ⟨that dinner was *OK*, but I liked yesterday's better⟩ — see SATISFACTORY 1

2 of a level of quality that meets one's needs or standards ⟨this latest draft of the essay is *OK* but could be better⟩ — see ADEQUATE

OK *or* **okay** *adv* **1** in a satisfactory way ⟨you did *OK* on that last test⟩ — see WELL 1

2 used to express agreement ⟨*OK*, fine, I'll go to the party⟩ — see YES

OK *or* **okay** *n* an acceptance of something as satisfactory ⟨our supervisor gave his *OK* on the project, so we can go ahead with it⟩ — see APPROVAL 1

OK *or* **okay** *vb* **1** to give official acceptance of as satisfactory ⟨a judge will have to *OK* the search warrant⟩ — see APPROVE

2 to have a favorable opinion of ⟨I'm glad that my friends *OK'd* my choice of girlfriend⟩ — see APPROVE (OF)

okeydoke *or* **okeydokey** *adv* used to express agreement ⟨*okeydoke*, we'll be there at 9:00 a.m. tomorrow⟩ — see YES

old *adj* **1** being of advanced years and especially past middle age ⟨every day the *old* fisherman set out in his small boat to brave the dangers of the sea⟩ — see ELDERLY

2 dating or surviving from the distant past ⟨an extremely *old* piece of jewelry was discovered in the Egyptian ruins⟩ — see ANCIENT 1

3 having been such at some previous time ⟨I ran into my *old* fourth-grade teacher yesterday⟩ — see FORMER 1

4 causing weariness, restlessness, or lack of interest ⟨even the most stirring speeches start to get *old* after you've heard them a few times⟩ — see BORING

older *adj* being of advanced years and especially past middle age ⟨an *older* woman was the chief librarian for the town⟩ — see ELDERLY

oldfangled *adj* pleasantly reminiscent of an earlier time ⟨those big solid-iron phones are an *oldfangled* reminder of the time when you had to rent a phone from the telephone company⟩ — see OLD-FASHIONED 1

old–fashioned *adj* **1** pleasantly reminiscent of an earlier time ⟨an elegant, *old-fashioned* bun that was held in place with pearl hairpins⟩

synonyms antique, oldfangled, old-school, old-time, old-timey, old-world, quaint, retro, retrograde, vintage

related words antiquated, moldy, obsolete, rinky-dink; historic, historical, olden, traditional; old hat, outdated, outmoded, out-of-date, outworn, passé, superannuated; dated, fusty, moth-eaten, musty, stodgy; aged, age-old, ancient, antediluvian, atavistic, fossilized, hoary, venerable; bygone, erstwhile, former, late, past; forgotten, remote; ageless, dateless; timeless; anachronistic (*also* anachronic), anachronous

near antonyms fresh, new; chic, designer, fashionable, smart, stylish; modernized, refurbished, remodeled, renewed, updated; last, latest; futuristic, high-tech (*also* hi-tech), latter-day, nontraditional; recent

antonyms contemporary, current, hot, mod, modern, modernist, modernistic, new age, newfangled, new-fashioned, present-day, red-hot, space-age, state-of-the-art, ultramodern, up-to-date

2 tending to favor established ideas, conditions, or institutions ⟨I'm so *old-fashioned* that I actually think people should use standard grammar and punctuation when composing e-mails⟩ — see CONSERVATIVE 1

old hand *n* a person with long experience in a specified area ⟨with 25 years on the job, Vinnie was the *old hand* everyone went to with their problems⟩ — see VETERAN

old lady *n* **1** a female human parent ⟨the story is that my *old lady* wanted to name me "Cecil," but the old man prevailed⟩ — see MOTHER

2 the female partner in a marriage ⟨he jokingly commented that he'd love to buy a sports car, but his *old lady* would throw a fit⟩ — see WIFE

3 a female romantic companion ⟨if he ever tried stepping out on her, his *old lady* would fill him with buckshot⟩ — see GIRLFRIEND

old–line *adj* tending to favor established ideas, conditions, or institutions ⟨an *old-line* professor who still taught as if it were 1930⟩ — see CONSERVATIVE 1

old–maidish *adj* hard to please ⟨an *old-maidish* teacher who required that every essay be written in very formal English⟩ — see FINICKY

old man *n* **1** a male human parent ⟨I'll ask my *old man* if he's up for a round of golf this weekend⟩ — see FATHER 1

2 the male partner in a marriage ⟨my *old man* and I have been together for 10 years now⟩ — see HUSBAND

3 a male romantic companion ⟨my *old man* and I have decided to move in together⟩ — see BOYFRIEND

Old Nick *n* the supreme personification of evil often represented as the ruler of hell ⟨he gave me a look that would scare *Old Nick*⟩ — see DEVIL 1

old–school *adj* **1** pleasantly reminiscent of an earlier time ⟨an *old-school* romantic comedy in which the two leads don't jump into bed at the first opportunity⟩ — see OLD-FASHIONED 1

2 tending to favor established ideas, conditions, or institutions ⟨an *old-school* gentleman who opened doors and pulled out chairs for women⟩ — see CONSERVATIVE 1

oldster *n* a person of advanced years ⟨a family film that will appeal to youngsters and *oldsters* alike⟩ — see SENIOR CITIZEN

old–time *adj* pleasantly reminiscent of an earlier time ⟨an *old-time* song that took the long-married couple back to when they were first dating⟩ — see OLD-FASHIONED 1

old–timer *n* **1** a person of advanced years ⟨a group of *old-timers* playing shuffleboard⟩ — see SENIOR CITIZEN

2 a person with long experience in a specified area ⟨*old-timers* in the fishing industry couldn't remember a time when catches were so low⟩ — see VETERAN

old–timey *adj* pleasantly reminiscent of an earlier time ⟨tourists can pose for pictures wearing *old-timey* dresses or top hats⟩ — see OLD-FASHIONED 1

old wives' tale *n* a false idea or belief ⟨the belief that going outside with wet hair will cause you to catch cold is just an *old wives' tale*⟩ — see FALLACY 1

old–world *adj* pleasantly reminiscent of an earlier time ⟨the theater has been painstakingly restored to its *old-world* elegance⟩ — see OLD-FASHIONED 1

oleaginous *adj* overly or insincerely flattering ⟨the office manager greeted the corporate bigwigs with an *oleaginous* welcome that should have embarrassed him⟩ — see FULSOME 1

olio *n* an unorganized collection or mixture of various things ⟨the performance was an old-fashioned *olio* of songs, dances, and puppetry⟩ — see MISCELLANY 1

olla podrida *n* an unorganized collection or mixture of various things ⟨the *olla podrida* of tongues that one hears on the streets of a bustling metropolis like New York City⟩ — see MISCELLANY 1

omen *n* something believed to be a sign or warning of a future event ⟨some people still believe that a black cat crossing your path is a bad *omen*⟩

synonyms augury, auspice, boding, foreboding, foreshadowing, portent, prefiguring, presage

related words forerunner, harbinger, herald, precursor; foretaste, hint, inkling, intimation, suggestion; forewarning; forecast, foretelling, prediction, prognostication, prophecy (*also* prophesy); badge, mark, note, token; divination

phrases straw in the wind

ominous *adj* being or showing a sign of evil or calamity to come ⟨that comment about downsizing from the company president sounded *ominous*⟩

synonyms baleful, dire, direful, doomy, foreboding, ill, ill-boding, inauspicious, menacing, minatory, portentous, sinister, threatening

related words black, bleak, cheerless, chill, Cimmerian, cloudy, cold, comfortless, dark, darkening, depressing, depressive, desolate, dim, disconsolate, dismal, drear, dreary, dreich [*chiefly Scottish*], elegiac (*also* elegiacal), forlorn, funereal, gloomy, glum, godforsaken, gray (*also* grey), lonely, lonesome, lugubrious, miserable, morbid, morose, murky, plutonian, saturnine, sepulchral, somber (*or* sombre), sullen, sunless, tenebrific, tenebrous, wretched; discouraging, disheartening, hopeless, unfavorable, unpromising, unpropitious; ill-fated, ill-starred, star-crossed, troubled, unfortunate, unlucky; evil, malign, malignant

near antonyms auspicious, benign, bright, encouraging, favorable, golden, heartening, hopeful, promising, propitious, prosperous
antonyms unthreatening

omission *n* something left out ⟨the disk contains a selection of deleted scenes, and a couple of the *omissions* greatly add to the intelligibility of the movie's plot⟩
synonyms deletion, elision
related words elimination; blank, skip; lapse, slip; deduction, reduction, subtraction; default, delinquency, dereliction, failure, neglect, negligence, oversight, pretermission; abbreviation, condensation
near antonyms inclusion; accretion, accrual, addendum, addition, augmentation, boost, expansion, gain, increase, increment, more, plus, raise, rise, supplement

omit *vb* to miss the opportunity or obligation ⟨you must not *omit* mentioning the sources you used in researching your paper⟩ — see NEGLECT 3

omnibus *adj* covering everything or all important points ⟨the president's state of the union speech is usually an *omnibus* look at the issues that the country is confronting⟩ — see ENCYCLOPEDIC

omnipotent *adj* having unlimited power or authority ⟨the nearly universal religious belief that God is *omnipotent* and omniscient⟩
synonyms all-powerful, almighty
related words great, sovereign (*also* sovran), supreme, towering, transcendent; authoritative, chief, majestic, master, masterful; mighty, potent, powerful, puissant, strong; divine, godlike; able, capable, competent, effective, efficient; multitalented, omnicompetent, omnificent; authoritarian, autocratic (*also* autocratical), despotic, dictatorial, magisterial, tyrannical (*also* tyrannic)
near antonyms helpless, impotent, impuissant, powerless; limited, restricted; hamstrung, handcuffed, high and dry, hog-tied, paralyzed, weak; incapable, incompetent, ineffective, ineffectual, inept, unfit, useless; feeble, frail, infirm

omnipresent *adj* present in all places and at all times ⟨seeking some much-needed relief from the *omnipresent* noise of the big city⟩
synonyms ubiquitous, universal, wall-to-wall
related words boundless, endless, fathomless, horizonless, illimitable, immeasurable, immensurable, indefinite, infinite, limitless, measureless, unbounded, unfathomable, unlimited; extensive, far-flung, widespread
near antonyms bounded, circumscribed, confined, finite, limited, measured, narrow, restricted

omnium–gatherum *n* an unorganized collection or mixture of various things ⟨the album features an *omnium-gatherum* of greatest hits from rock bands who peaked in the 1980s⟩ — see MISCELLANY 1

omphalos *n* a thing or place that is of greatest importance to an activity or interest ⟨during the Vietnam War the university's campus effectively became the area's *omphalos* for antiwar activity⟩ — see CENTER 1

on *adj* being in effective operation ⟨please don't leave the sanding machine *on* if you're not going to be near it⟩ — see ACTIVE 1

on *adv* **1** toward a point ahead in space or time ⟨we really must move *on* now if we're going to end this meeting before midnight⟩ — see ONWARD 1
2 toward or at a point lying in advance in space or time ⟨he's getting *on* in years and doesn't see or hear as well as he used to⟩ — see ALONG

on *prep* **1** having to do with ⟨books *on* sports heroes are my favorite reading matter⟩ — see ABOUT 1
2 in or into contact with ⟨don't lean *on* that ladder—you'll knock it over⟩ — see AGAINST 1

on–and–off *adj* occurring or appearing at intervals ⟨an *on-and-off* friendship over the years⟩ — see INTERMITTENT 1

once *adj* having been such at some previous time ⟨the *once* child star is now a lawyer in the entertainment industry⟩ — see FORMER 1

once *adv* at an earlier or previous time ⟨I *once* knew the quotation, but time has taken its toll on my brain cells⟩ — see FORMERLY 1

once *conj* just at the moment that ⟨you should have stopped wrestling *once* you knew someone was getting hurt, not five minutes later⟩ — see WHEN 2

oncoming *adj* being soon to appear or take place ⟨we're looking forward to your *oncoming* visit⟩ — see FORTHCOMING 1

one *adj* **1** being the one or ones of a class with no other members ⟨that's the *one* author I would stand in line for hours to get an autograph from⟩ — see ONLY 2
2 known but not named ⟨*one* person that I know said that it was the best movie he had ever seen⟩ — see CERTAIN 1

one *n* a U.S. currency bill representing 100 cents ⟨I don't have any *ones* on me just now⟩ — see DOLLAR

one–dimensional *adj* having or showing a lack of depth of understanding or character ⟨a *one-dimensional* analysis of a novel that has a lot to say about personal courage⟩ — see SUPERFICIAL 2

one–liner *n* something said or done to cause laughter ⟨the senator deftly inserted some smart *one-liners* into an otherwise sober speech⟩ — see JOKE 1

one–off *adj* **1** being the one or ones of a class with no other members ⟨an actress who commissioned a *one-off* dress from the designer for the Oscars⟩ — see ONLY 2
2 happening only once ⟨the tour is a *one-off* event to commemorate the band's 20th anniversary⟩ — see ONETIME

one–on–one *adv* in direct confrontation or competition ⟨bragged that no one could go *one-on-one* with her in a game of darts and win⟩ — see HEAD-TO-HEAD

onerous *adj* **1** difficult to endure ⟨had the *onerous* and stressful job of notifying the families of soldiers killed in action⟩ — see HARSH 1
2 requiring much time, effort, or careful attention ⟨building the scale model of the frigate was an *onerous* task⟩ — see DEMANDING 1

one–shot *adj* happening only once ⟨this offer is a *one-shot* deal; if you refuse, you won't get another chance⟩ — see ONETIME

one–sided *adj* inclined to favor one side over another ⟨my neighbor's account of how the feud got started was somewhat *one-sided*⟩ — see PARTIAL 1

one–sidedness *n* an attitude that always favors one way of feeling or acting especially without considering any other possibilities ⟨the obvious *one-sidedness* of the host means that his radio talk show isn't the open forum that he pretends it is⟩ — see BIAS 1

onetime *adj* **1** happening only once ⟨with any luck, that was a *onetime* mistake⟩
synonyms one-off, one-shot
related words nonce; inconstant, infrequent, intermittent, irregular, occasional
near antonyms common, commonplace, everyday, familiar, ordinary, routine, ubiquitous, usual; cyclic (*or* cyclical); around-the-clock, constant, continual, hourly, round-the-clock; accustomed, chronic, confirmed, customary, habitual, inveterate; expected; annual, yearly
antonyms frequent, periodic, periodical, recurrent, recurring, regular, repeated, steady
2 having been such at some previous time ⟨the *onetime* English teacher now works for a newspaper⟩ — see FORMER 1

onetime *adv* at an earlier or previous time ⟨an athlete who *onetime* competed in marathons on a regular basis⟩ — see FORMERLY 1

ongoing *adj* **1** being in progress or development ⟨we do seem to be making some headway on that *ongoing* project⟩ ⟨the ever *ongoing* quest for knowledge by men and women of science⟩
synonyms afoot, proceeding
related words functioning, happening, operating, working; afloat, alive, going; advancing, continuing, gaining
near antonyms receding, regressing, retrogressing
antonyms arrested, ended, halted, stalled, stopped
2 existing or in progress right now ⟨the *ongoing* presidential campaign⟩ — see PRESENT 1
3 having an existence or validity that does not change or diminish ⟨an *ongoing* commitment to improving their community⟩ — see ABIDING

onlooker *n* someone who sees or watches something ⟨several *onlookers* gave chase after the thief grabbed the woman's purse⟩ — see SPECTATOR

only *adj* **1** having no equal or rival for excellence or desirability ⟨the *only* way to really appreciate the beauty of the forest is to walk through it⟩
synonyms incomparable, inimitable, matchless, nonpareil, peerless, unequaled (*or* unequalled), unexampled, unmatched, unparalleled, unrivaled (*or* unrivalled), unsurpassable, unsurpassed
related words alone, singular, unique; exceptional, extraordinary, rare, uncommon, unusual; A-OK, A1, awesome, bang-up, banner, beautiful, blue-chip, boffo, bonny (*also* bonnie) [*chiefly British*], boss [*slang*], brag, brave, bully, bumper, capital, choice, classic, cool [*slang*], corking, crackerjack, cracking, dandy, divine, dope [*slang*], down [*slang*], dynamite, excellent, fab, fabulous, famous, fantabulous [*slang*], fantastic, fine, first-class, first-rate, first-string, five-star, frontline, gangbusters (*also* gangbuster), gone [*slang*], grand, great, groovy, heavenly, high-class, hot, hype [*slang*], immense, jim-dandy, keen, lovely, marvelous (*or* marvellous), mean, neat, nifty, noble, number one (*also* No. 1), numero uno, out-of-sight [*slang*], par excellence, peachy, peachy keen, phat [*slang*], prime, primo [*slang*], prize, prizewinning, quality, radical [*slang*], righteous [*slang*], sensational, splendid, stellar, sterling, superb, superior, superlative, supernal, swell, terrific, tip-top, top, top-notch, wizard [*chiefly British*], wonderful; better, preferred; exceptional, fancy, high-grade, special
phrases out of sight
near antonyms common, commonplace, everyday, familiar, frequent, garden, household, normal, ordinary, routine, ubiquitous, usual; inferior, lesser, worse, worst; bad, bastard, bush, bush-league, deficient, depressed, dissatisfactory, ill, inferior, lame, lousy, low, lower, off, paltry, poor, punk, substandard, unacceptable, unsatisfactory, wanting; low-grade, substandard; mediocre, second-class, second-rate; atrocious, awful, execrable, pathetic, rotten, terrible, vile, wretched
2 being the one or ones of a class with no other members ⟨that is the *only* possible right answer⟩ ⟨we were the *only* passengers on the tour bus⟩
synonyms alone, lone, one, one-off, singular, sole, solitary, special, sui generis, unique
related words single, solo, unaccompanied, unattended; incomparable, inimitable, matchless, peerless, unequaled (*or* unequalled), unmatched, unparalleled, unrivaled (*or* unrivalled), unsurpassable, unsurpassed; distinct, distinctive, individual, separate; nonce
near antonyms divers, manifold, multifarious, myriad; assorted, heterogenous, miscellaneous, mixed, motley, patchwork, promiscuous, varied; popular, prevailing, prevalent, rampant; perennial, recurrent, repeated

only *adv* **1** for nothing other than ⟨you're doing that *only* to annoy me⟩ — see SOLELY 1
2 not long ago ⟨we won the election *only* six days ago⟩ — see NEWLY
3 nothing more than ⟨I was *only* fooling when I said I saw a shark in the water⟩ — see JUST 3

only *conj* if it were not for the fact that ⟨that's a very nice idea, *only* it won't help⟩ — see EXCEPT

onrush *n* forward movement in time or place ⟨a sudden *onrush* of development in an area that was rural until very recently⟩ — see ADVANCE 1

onset *n* **1** the act or action of setting upon with force or violence ⟨the walls withstood the *onset* of the first battalion⟩ — see ATTACK 1
2 the point at which something begins ⟨the claim that if you take enough vitamin C at the *onset* of a cold, you'll often recover faster⟩ — see BEGINNING

onslaught *n* the act or action of setting upon with force or violence ⟨the massive *onslaught* of enemy troops caught the country by surprise⟩ — see ATTACK 1

on–target *adj* being in agreement with the truth or a fact or a standard ⟨an economic forecast for three percent growth that turned out to be entirely *on-target*⟩ — see CORRECT 1

onus *n* **1** a mark of guilt or disgrace ⟨hoping to avoid the *onus* of failure by lowering expectations ahead of time⟩ — see STAIN 1
2 responsibility for wrongdoing or failure ⟨he perpetually tries to shift the *onus* for any mistakes onto other team members⟩ — see BLAME 1

onward *also* **onwards** *adv* **1** toward a point ahead in space or time ⟨we must continue to move *onward*, or we will die in this desert⟩
synonyms ahead, forth, forward, on
near antonyms backward (*or* backwards)
2 toward or at a point lying in advance in space or time ⟨work on the project has been continuing *onward* at a steady pace⟩ — see ALONG

oodles *n pl* a considerable amount ⟨the neighbors let us know that they bought *oodles* of candy for Halloween this year⟩ — see LOT 2

oomph *n* **1** active strength of body or mind ⟨still had the *oomph* to pass other runners in the homestretch⟩ — see VIGOR 1
2 the power of irresistible attraction ⟨a supermodel with the kind of *oomph* to make you want to run out and buy the perfume⟩ — see CHARM 2

ooze *n* soft wet earth ⟨our car tires sank deep in the *ooze*⟩ — see MUD

ooze *vb* **1** to flow forth slowly through small openings ⟨maple sap *oozed* slowly from the cut in the tree and into the bucket⟩ — see EXUDE 1
2 to move slowly ⟨the line more or less *oozes* past the body lying in state, as mourners are not allowed to pause⟩ — see CRAWL 2

oozy *adj* full of or covered with soft wet earth ⟨lost a shoe in the *oozy* field⟩ — see MUDDY 1

opacity *n* the quality or state of having a veiled or uncertain meaning ⟨the *opacity* of the abstract painter's works simply baffles many gallery visitors⟩ — see OBSCURITY 1

opalescent *adj* having a rainbowlike play of colors ⟨once given away as a cheap prize at carnivals, this *opalesecent* glass is now highly prized by collectors⟩ — see IRIDESCENT

opaque *adj* **1** having an often intentionally veiled or uncertain meaning ⟨somehow listeners seem to connect with the songwriter, despite his deeply personal, often *opaque* lyrics⟩ — see OBSCURE 1
2 not seen or understood clearly ⟨an *opaque* remark that seemed to hint that there would be future retaliation⟩ — see FAINT 1
3 not having or showing an ability to absorb ideas readily ⟨people are sometimes rude to her, but fortu-

nately she's too *opaque* to realize what's happening⟩ — see STUPID 1

opaqueness *n* the quality or state of having a veiled or uncertain meaning ⟨the *opaqueness* of the narrative will not bother readers more interested in complex characters than in a gripping yarn⟩ — see OBSCURITY 1

open *adj* **1** allowing passage without obstruction ⟨thank you for clearing out the hallway so that it's *open* again⟩
synonyms clear, cleared, free, unclogged, unclosed, unobstructed, unstopped
related words enterable, navigable, passable; emptied, empty, unoccupied, vacant; exposed, revealed; gaping, wide, yawning; unbarred, unbolted, unclasped, unfastened, unlatched, unlocked, unsealed; unbuttoned, unclenched, unfolded, unfurled, unzipped
near antonyms impassable (*also* impassible); constricted, cramped, encumbered, hampered, hindered, impeded, interfered (with), trammeled (*or* trammelled); barricaded, blockaded, dammed, gated
antonyms blocked, clogged, closed, jammed, obstructed, plugged, shut, stopped, stuffed, uncleared
2 freely available for use or participation by all ⟨the lanes at the bowling alley will be *open* during the afternoon, but will be available only for league play in the evening⟩
synonyms free-for-all, public, unrestricted
related words collective, common, communal, shared; accessible, available, free; unregulated, unreserved
near antonyms limited; inaccessible, unavailable
antonyms closed, exclusive, off-limits, private, restricted
3 being in a situation where one is likely to meet with harm ⟨the country's *open* to invasion if its borders remain unguarded⟩ — see LIABLE 1
4 free in expressing one's true feelings and opinions ⟨a talkative and *open* child who tells people more than they want to know⟩ — see FRANK
5 lacking a usual or natural covering ⟨*open* wounds in his legs⟩ — see NAKED 2
6 not known by only a select few ⟨the two boxers have an *open* dislike for each other⟩ — see PUBLIC 1
7 not yet settled or decided ⟨that issue will have to remain *open* until the supervisor can decide⟩ — see PENDING 1
8 willing to consider new or different ideas ⟨she is always *open* and ready to listen to anyone's suggestions⟩ — see OPEN-MINDED 1
9 giving or sharing in abundance and without hesitation ⟨he's very *open* with his opinions, many of which are not welcome⟩ — see GENEROUS 1

open *n* that part of the physical world that is removed from human habitation ⟨a daguerreotype of a cowboy whose face is roughened from a hard life in the *open*⟩ — see NATURE 2

open *vb* **1** to change from a closed to an open position ⟨please *open* the door to let the cat out⟩
synonyms unclose
related words unbar, unbolt, unclasp, unfasten, unlatch, unlock; unbutton, unclench, unfold, unfurl, unzip; disengage, release, slip
near antonyms bar, bolt, clasp, fasten, latch, lock; button (up), zip (up)
antonyms close, shut
2 to make passage through (something) possible by removing obstructions ⟨we need to *open* this drain that's clogged with hair⟩
synonyms clear, free, unclog, unplug, unstop
related words ease, facilitate, loosen (up), smooth
near antonyms constrict, encumber, hamper, hinder, impede, interfere (with), obstruct, trammel; barricade, blockade
antonyms block, clog (up), close, dam (up), plug (up), stop
3 to arrange the parts of (something) over a wider area ⟨when we got too close, the cardinal *opened* its wings and flew to a higher branch⟩
synonyms expand, extend, fan (out), flare (out), outspread, outstretch, spread (out), stretch (out), unfold, unfurl
related words overspread
near antonyms compact, compress, condense, reduce
antonyms close, contract, fold
4 to rid the surface of (as an area) from things in the way ⟨snowplows *opened* the runway without much trouble⟩ — see CLEAR 1
5 to take the first step in (a process or course of action) ⟨we will *open* the proceedings tomorrow with a short ceremony⟩ — see BEGIN 1

open–air *adj* of, relating to, or held in the open air ⟨an *open-air* concert under the stars⟩ — see OUTDOORS

open air *n* that part of the physical world that is removed from human habitation ⟨a family of city dwellers who can't wait to go camping in the *open air*⟩ — see NATURE 2

open–and–shut *adj* not subject to misinterpretation or more than one interpretation ⟨an *open-and-shut* case of robbery⟩ — see CLEAR 2

open–eyed *adj* paying close attention usually for the purpose of anticipating approaching danger or opportunity ⟨an *open-eyed* deer cautiously grazed in the backyard⟩ — see ALERT 1

openhanded *adj* giving or sharing in abundance and without hesitation ⟨in the aftermath of the disaster, many people were exceptionally *openhanded* with their donations to charity⟩ — see GENEROUS 1

openhandedly *adv* in a generous manner ⟨the CEO *openhandedly* gave the intern advice about succeeding in the business⟩ — see WELL 2

openhandedness *n* the quality or state of being generous ⟨the governor doesn't exactly have a reputation for *openhandedness* when it comes to commuting death sentences⟩ — see LIBERALITY

openhearted *adj* free in expressing one's true feelings and opinions ⟨many therapists believe that it is better to be *openhearted* than to repress one's feelings, however hostile they may be⟩ — see FRANK

openheartedness *n* **1** the free expression of one's true feelings and opinions ⟨the *openheartedness* with which he discussed his private life often startled new acquaintances⟩ — see CANDOR 1
2 the quality or state of being generous ⟨their natural *openheartedness* made them easy prey for every trickster with a sad story⟩ — see LIBERALITY

opening *n* **1** a favorable combination of circumstances, time, and place ⟨the talk show host's usual modus operandi is to talk over his guests, thereby denying them an *opening* to articulate their positions⟩ — see OPPORTUNITY
2 a place in a surface allowing passage into or through a thing ⟨an *opening* in the roof is letting rain drip inside⟩ — see HOLE 1
3 an open space in a barrier (as a wall or hedge) ⟨the rabbit found a little *opening* in the bushes and darted through⟩ — see GAP 1

open–minded *adj* **1** willing to consider new or different ideas ⟨all I ask is that you try to be *open-minded* when we present our suggestions⟩
synonyms broad-minded, open, receptive
related words impartial, neutral, objective, unbiased, unprejudiced; easygoing, nonjudgmental, tolerant; calm, detached, dispassionate; amenable, compliant; impressionable, suggestible, susceptible; persuadable, persuasible

near antonyms biased, narrow, one-sided, partial, partisan, prejudiced; bigoted, intolerant
antonyms narrow-minded, unreceptive
2 not bound by traditional ways or beliefs ⟨younger people are often more *open-minded* on social and political issues⟩ — see LIBERAL 1

openmouthed *adj* filled with amazement or wonder ⟨the stunning view from the mountaintop left us *openmouthed* and at a loss for words⟩
synonyms amazed, astonished, astounded, awed, awestruck (*also* awestricken), dumbfounded (*also* dumfounded), flabbergasted, marveling (*or* marvelling), wondering
related words startled, surprised (*also* surprized); bemused, bewildered, puzzled; overwhelmed, staggered, stunned, stupefied
near antonyms unimpressed; disinterested, incurious, indifferent, unconcerned, uninterested; dispassionate, emotionless, impassive, unemotional; bored, jaded

openness *n* **1** the free expression of one's true feelings and opinions ⟨her *openness* was refreshing after the tiresome coyness of her friends⟩ — see CANDOR 1
2 the state of being left without shelter or protection against something harmful ⟨doctors are concerned about the population's *openness* to the new strain of the flu virus⟩ — see EXPOSURE 1

open sesame *n* something that allows someone to achieve a desired goal ⟨it turned out that a simple "please" was the *open sesame* for charming the hotel manager into giving us a room with a better view⟩ — see PASSPORT 1

operable *adj* capable of or suitable for being used for a particular purpose ⟨the historic wooden ship has been fully restored and is once again an *operable* seafaring vessel⟩ — see USABLE 1

operate *vb* **1** to control the mechanical operation of ⟨do not *operate* heavy machinery, including cars, after taking this medication⟩
synonyms handle, run, work
related words use; maneuver, manipulate, ply, wield; command, control, direct, drive, guide, pilot, steer
2 to look after and make decisions about ⟨it takes years to learn how to *operate* that kind of business so that it makes money⟩ — see CONDUCT 1
3 to produce a desired effect ⟨the medicine will take an hour or so to *operate* the first time you use it⟩ — see ACT 2
4 to put into action or service ⟨wouldn't dream of *operating* a vehicle under the influence of alcohol⟩ — see USE 1

operatic *adj* having the general quality or effect of a stage performance ⟨the fall of the scandal-ridden government seemed *operatic* in its scope and consequences⟩ — see DRAMATIC 1

operating *adj* being in effective operation ⟨the only *operating* nuclear power plant in the state⟩ — see ACTIVE 1

operation *n* **1** a specific task with which a person or group is charged ⟨a secret *operation* which, if it is discovered, the government will deny any knowledge of⟩ — see MISSION
2 a usually fixed or ordered series of actions or events leading to a result ⟨a specific mathematical *operation* is required in order to get the correct answer⟩ — see PROCESS 1
3 the act or activity of looking after and making decisions about something ⟨given the constant threat of robbery, the *operation* of a convenience store can be quite stressful⟩ — see CONDUCT 1
4 the act or practice of employing something for a particular purpose ⟨a considerable amount of training is required for the *operation* of these new high-tech weapons systems⟩ — see USE 1

operational *adj* being in effective operation ⟨a fully *operational* oil refinery⟩ — see ACTIVE 1

operative *adj* **1** being in effective operation ⟨the last *operative* bookbinder of its kind in the business⟩ — see ACTIVE 1
2 producing or capable of producing a desired result ⟨unfortunately, the *operative* amount of the medication and the lethal amount were too close for it to be used safely⟩ — see EFFECTIVE 1

operative *n* **1** a person who tries secretly to obtain information for one country in the territory of another usually unfriendly country ⟨CIA *operatives* take terrible risks to find out the secrets of foreign countries⟩ — see SPY
2 a person not on the police force who investigates criminal or illicit activity or searches for missing persons ⟨set in the 1930s, the novel is about a washed-out *operative* working for a third-rate detective agency⟩ — see DETECTIVE

opiate *adj* tending to cause sleep ⟨morphine is an *opiate* drug⟩ — see HYPNOTIC

opiate *n* something that soothes, calms, or induces passivity or a sense of security ⟨a cultural critic who argues that the Internet has now joined television as an *opiate* of the American people⟩
synonyms anesthetic, anodyne, narcotic
related words security blanket; pacifier, palliative; hypnotic, sedative, soporific, tranquilizer (*also* tranquillizer)

opine *vb* to make a statement of one's opinion ⟨the food critic *opined* that the restaurant's fare was something that one might serve a dog—if one didn't like dogs⟩ — see REMARK 1

opinion *n* **1** an idea that is believed to be true or valid without positive knowledge ⟨a number of voters expressed the *opinion* that all politicians, regardless of party affiliation, are corrupt⟩
synonyms belief, conviction, eye, feeling, judgment (*or* judgement), mind, notion, persuasion, sentiment, verdict, view
related words say; impression, perception, take; attitude; assumption, presumption, presupposition; conclusion, decision, determination; deliverance, esteem, estimate, estimation; credence, credit, faith; concept, conception, idea, thought; position, stance, stand; comment, obiter dictum, observation, reflection, remark; conjecture, guess, hunch, hypothesis, surmise, theory; advice, input, recommendation, suggestion; angle, outlook, perspective, shoes, slant, standpoint, viewpoint; counterview
near antonyms fact, truth
2 a position arrived at after consideration ⟨after reviewing the evidence, the athletic board came to the *opinion* that the team be disqualified for recruiting violations⟩ — see DECISION 1

opinionated *adj* **1** given to or marked by the forceful expression of strongly held opinions ⟨those talk shows want *opinionated* pundits, not cautious, diffident debaters⟩ — see DOGMATIC
2 sticking to an opinion, purpose, or course of action in spite of reason, arguments, or persuasion ⟨an *opinionated* professor who often clashes with students who dare to disagree with him⟩ — see OBSTINATE

opinionatedness *n* **1** a steadfast adherence to an opinion, purpose, or course of action in spite of reason, arguments, or persuasion ⟨guests on that political talk show seem to be far more prized for their uninhibited *opinionatedness* than for any trace of reasonableness⟩ — see OBSTINACY
2 stubborn or intolerant adherence to one's opinions or

prejudices ⟨in matters of religion, she seems to confuse self-righteous *opinionatedness* with godly devotion⟩ — see BIGOTRY

opinionative *adj* given to or marked by the forceful expression of strongly held opinions ⟨one particularly *opinionative* caller informed the talk show host that he was an idiot⟩ — see DOGMATIC

opinioned *adj* given to or marked by the forceful expression of strongly held opinions ⟨a theater critic who is notorious for his scathingly *opinioned* reviews⟩ — see DOGMATIC

opponent *n* **1** one that takes a position opposite another in a competition or conflict ⟨in martial arts, before the match begins, always bow to your *opponent*⟩
synonyms adversary, antagonist, foe, rival
related words equal, match; enemy; archenemy, nemesis; competitor, contestant; bane, bête noire, curse; assailant, attacker, combatant, invader
near antonyms accomplice, ally, confederate, partner; advocate, champion, exponent, proponent, supporter, sympathizer
2 one that is hostile toward another ⟨the senator has many political *opponents* who would love to ruin his career⟩ — see ENEMY

opportune *adj* especially suitable for a certain time ⟨an *opportune* rain shower gave them an excuse to leave the outdoor concert early⟩ — see TIMELY 1

opportunist *n* **1** a person who dexterously and expediently changes or adopts opinions ⟨ever the *opportunist*, she immediately set about becoming the incoming administrator's new best friend⟩ — see ACROBAT 2
2 one who does things only for his own benefit and with little regard for right and wrong ⟨an *opportunist* who makes friends and then drops them as soon as they aren't useful anymore⟩ — see SELF-SEEKER

opportunity *n* a favorable combination of circumstances, time, and place ⟨this art school could be a wonderful *opportunity* for you to finally develop your talent for painting⟩
synonyms break, chance, occasion, opening, room, shot
related words play, way; juncture, pass

oppose *vb* **1** to refuse to give in to ⟨I will continue to *oppose* any attempts to infringe upon our civil liberties⟩ — see RESIST
2 to strive to reduce or eliminate ⟨we must *oppose* ignorance and prejudice wherever and whenever they arise⟩ — see FIGHT 2

opposite *adj* being as different as possible ⟨those two are fundamentally *opposite*—she being loquacious and outgoing where he is quiet and reserved⟩
synonyms antipodal, antipodean, antithetical, contradictory, contrary, diametric (*or* diametrical), polar
related words adverse, negative, unfavorable; antagonistic, antipathetic, counter, cross, hostile; converse, inverse, obverse, reverse; alien, disparate, dissimilar, divergent, unalike, unlike
near antonyms alike, analogous, like, similar; equivalent, identical, same; synonymous
antonyms noncontradictory

opposite *n* something that is as different as possible from something else ⟨no matter what I say, you insist on the *opposite*⟩
synonyms antipode, antithesis, contrary, counter, negative, obverse, reverse
related words negation; antonym; counterpoint; converse, inverse, mirror image
near antonyms synonym; analogue (*or* analog), counterpart; carbon copy, copy, duplicate, replica

oppositeness *n* the quality or state of being as different as possible ⟨the complete *oppositeness* of the two principal meanings of the word "handicap"⟩ — see CONTRARIETY

opposition *n* **1** the inclination to resist ⟨most of the *opposition* to the proposed smoking ban is coming from bar owners worried about its impact on their businesses⟩ — see RESISTANCE 1
2 the quality or state of being as different as possible ⟨her actions stand in direct *opposition* to her words⟩ — see CONTRARIETY

oppress *vb* **1** to make sad ⟨this gloomy weather is *oppressing* all of us⟩ — see DEPRESS 1
2 to subject to incapacitating emotional or mental stress ⟨a film about a man who is haunted and *oppressed* by the secrets of his past⟩ — see OVERWHELM 1

oppressed *adj* suffering grave abuse or injustice at the hands of one in authority ⟨setting out on a quixotic quest to right wrongs and to raise up the *oppressed* peoples of the world⟩ — see DOWNTRODDEN

oppression *n* a state or spell of low spirits ⟨suffered a lingering *oppression* in the weeks after his dog died⟩ — see SADNESS

oppressive *adj* difficult to endure ⟨an *oppressive* regime that rules through terror⟩ — see HARSH 1

oppressively *adv* in a manner so as to cause loss or suffering ⟨forced to live under an *oppressively* cruel government⟩ — see HARDLY 1

oppressor *n* a person who uses power or authority in a cruel, unjust, or harmful way ⟨the dictatorship had scarcely been overthrown when the formerly oppressed suddenly abandoned their democratic ideals and became the *oppressors*⟩ — see DESPOT

opprobrious *adj* **1** marked by harsh insulting language ⟨an *opprobrious* attack on the alleged corruption in the police department⟩ — see ABUSIVE
2 not respectable ⟨contends that visiting a brothel is the sort of *opprobrious* conduct for which a public official should be censured⟩ — see DISREPUTABLE

opprobrium *n* **1** a cause of shame ⟨saw no reason why "secretary" should suddenly become a term of *opprobrium* among the politically correct⟩ — see DISGRACE 2
2 the state of having lost the esteem of others ⟨the *opprobrium* that was long attached to the convicted embezzler's name⟩ — see DISGRACE 1

oppugn *vb* **1** to demand proof of the truth or rightness of ⟨had the temerity to *oppugn* the merits of a study in a discipline that he knows nothing about⟩ — see CHALLENGE 1
2 to strive to reduce or eliminate ⟨guardians of liberty who staunchly *oppugned* tyranny, whether from the right or the left⟩ — see FIGHT 2

opt *vb* to come to a judgment about after discussion or consideration ⟨after that near catastrophe, they *opted* to reinstate the telephone service⟩ — see DECIDE 1

opt (for) *vb* to decide to accept (someone or something) from a group of possibilities ⟨I *opted for* the smaller car after I calculated how much money I would save on gas every week⟩ — see CHOOSE 1

optic *adj* of, relating to, or used in vision ⟨the *optic* nerve⟩ — see VISUAL 1

optical *adj* of, relating to, or used in vision ⟨an *optical* illusion that fools most people⟩ — see VISUAL 1

optimism *n* an inclination to believe in the most favorable outcome ⟨your perpetual *optimism* even when things look bleak⟩
synonyms bullishness, sanguinity
related words brightness, cheerfulness, perkiness, sunniness; hope, hopefulness, rosiness; idealism, meliorism
near antonyms skepticism; apprehension, caution, concern; cynicism; despair, desperation, discouragement, disheartenment, hopelessness; bleakness, cheerlessness, dreariness, gloom, gloominess; pragmatism, realism

antonyms bearishness, pessimism

optimistic *adj* having qualities which inspire hope ⟨the economic predictions for the coming year are actually quite *optimistic*⟩ — see HOPEFUL 1

option *n* **1** something that is not necessary in itself but adds to the convenience or performance of the main piece of equipment ⟨a slew of *options* that would add several thousand dollars to the base price of the car⟩ — see ACCESSORY 1

2 the power, right, or opportunity to choose ⟨you will have the *option* to select one of several quite different health insurance plans⟩ — see CHOICE 1

optional *adj* subject to one's freedom of choice ⟨at the resort all recreational activities are *optional*, and you may choose to participate in none of them⟩

synonyms discretionary, elective, voluntary

related words alternate, alternative, chosen; dispensable, unnecessary, unneeded, unwanted

near antonyms essential, indispensable, necessary, requisite

antonyms compulsory, mandatory, nonelective, nonvoluntary, obligatory, required

opulence *n* the total of one's money and property ⟨in some parts of the city nearly unimaginable *opulence* can be found side by side with nearly unthinkable poverty⟩ — see WEALTH 1

opulent *adj* **1** having goods, property, or money in abundance ⟨an *opulent* upper crust that liked to show off its possessions⟩ — see RICH 1

2 showing obvious signs of wealth and comfort ⟨an *opulent* mansion filled with priceless art and antiques⟩ — see LUXURIOUS 1

opulently *adv* in a luxurious manner ⟨an *opulently* furnished palace⟩ — see HIGH

opus *n* a literary, musical, or artistic production ⟨the composer's final *opus* was performed posthumously to great acclaim⟩ — see COMPOSITION 1

oral *adj* **1** expressed or communicated by voice ⟨a baby's crying is usually interpreted as an *oral* expression of distress⟩ — see VOCAL

2 made or carried on through speaking rather than in writing ⟨lawyers for the plaintiff will be presenting *oral* arguments before the Supreme Court next week⟩ — see VERBAL 2

orate *vb* **1** to talk as if giving an important and formal speech ⟨given the opportunity, many politicians will *orate* at considerable length on just about any subject⟩

synonyms declaim, discourse, harangue, mouth (off), perorate

related words rant, rave; bloviate, blow; lecture, preach, sermonize; advertise, announce, broadcast, declare, proclaim, pronounce; speak, speechify, talk

2 to give a formal often extended talk on a subject ⟨the respected anthropologist is expected to *orate* about her latest research findings before a packed auditorium⟩ — see TALK 1

oration *n* a usually formal discourse delivered to an audience ⟨the celebrated *orations* of Daniel Webster in unwavering support of the federal union⟩ — see SPEECH 1

orator *n* a person who makes usually formal public speeches ⟨though a brilliant wordsmith, Thomas Jefferson was by his own admission an unskilled *orator*⟩

synonyms lecturer, speaker

related words rhetorician, spellbinder; declaimer, spouter; spieler

oratorical *adj* marked by the use of impressive-sounding but mostly meaningless words and phrases ⟨a speech that was an *oratorical* endorsement of the value of education but one that refused to call for greater spending on education⟩ — see RHETORICAL 1

oratory *n* **1** the art of speaking in public eloquently and effectively ⟨a presidential hopeful with a gift for *oratory* and a highly charismatic personality⟩

synonyms elocution, public speaking

related words bombast, grandiloquence; eloquence, rhetoric; discourse, speech, talk

2 language that is impressive-sounding but not meaningful or sincere ⟨the politician's *oratory* sounded good only to people who didn't bother to think⟩ — see RHETORIC 1

orb *n* a more or less round body or mass ⟨out of the countless celestial *orbs* twirling in space, the planet Earth remains the only one we can call home, so perhaps we should take care of it⟩ — see [1]BALL 1

orbit *vb* to travel completely around ⟨the moon *orbits* the Earth⟩ — see ENCIRCLE 1

orchestra *n* a usually large group of musicians playing together ⟨the *orchestra* will be performing a selection of Beethoven pieces tomorrow night⟩ — see [2]BAND 1

orchestration *n* a balanced, pleasing, or suitable arrangement of parts ⟨the trade representatives are working towards an *orchestration* of the two countries' often competing economic interests⟩ — see HARMONY 1

ordain *vb* **1** to determine the fate of in advance ⟨he is stoic in the face of adversity, bolstered by his faith that everything in life has been *ordained* by a higher power⟩ — see DESTINE

2 to request the doing of by virtue of one's authority ⟨a new bill that would *ordain* the funding of public schools through state lottery revenues⟩ — see COMMAND 2

3 to put into effect through legislative or authoritative action ⟨the founders of the African republic *ordained* a form of government that was closely modeled on that of the United States⟩ — see ENACT

ordeal *n* a test of faith, patience, or strength ⟨the hikers were finally rescued after a three-day *ordeal* in the wilderness⟩ — see TRIAL 1

order *n* **1** the way objects in space or events in time are arranged or follow one another ⟨you always keep your books in perfect alphabetical *order*⟩ ⟨we haven't found out the *order* of the speeches yet⟩

synonyms arrangement, array, disposal, disposition, distribution, ordering, sequence, setup

related words continuity; precedence, priority; chain, procession, progression, succession; series; aligning (*also* alining), alignment (*also* alinement), lining up; design, layout, pattern, structure, system

near antonyms confusion, disorder, disorganization, disruption, upset; disconnection, disjointedness

2 a group of persons formally joined together for some common interest ⟨a religious *order*⟩ — see ASSOCIATION 2

3 a number of persons or things that are grouped together because they have something in common ⟨collects movie posters, photographs and autographs of the stars, and other memorabilia of that *order*⟩ — see SORT 1

4 a piece of metal given in honor of a special event, a person, or an achievement ⟨a book with full-color illustrations of British *orders* and decorations⟩ — see MEDAL

5 a state of being or fitness ⟨finally got the car back in working *order*⟩ — see CONDITION 1

6 a statement of what to do that must be obeyed by those concerned ⟨the commander issued an *order* that the number of guards for the prisoner be doubled⟩ — see COMMAND 1

7 one of the segments of society into which people are grouped ⟨the lower *orders* were once expected to be content living out their lives as servants to the upper classes⟩ — see CLASS 1

8 one of the units into which a whole is divided on the

basis of a common characteristic ⟨regards draftees as an entirely different *order* of soldier and less desirable than volunteers⟩ — see CLASS 2

order *vb* **1** to put into a particular arrangement ⟨I've *ordered* all of my CDs according to type of music⟩ ⟨he likes to *order* his life so that there are few surprises⟩
synonyms arrange, array, classify, codify, dispose, draw up, lay out, marshal (*also* marshall), organize, range, systematize
related words groom, make up, spruce (up), straighten (up), tidy (up); unscramble; align (*also* aline), cue, line, line up, queue; alphabetize, file, hierarchize, prioritize, sequence; emplace, place, set; display, map (out), set out
antonyms derange, disarrange, disarray, disorder, mess (up), muss (up), rumple, upset
2 to give a request or demand for ⟨the players *ordered* hamburgers for lunch⟩
synonyms ask (for), put in (for), request, requisition
related words commission, solicit; charter, hire, license (*also* licence)
phrases call for
3 to request the doing of by virtue of one's authority ⟨the teacher *ordered* that everyone sit down immediately and be quiet⟩ — see COMMAND 2
4 to issue orders to (someone) by right of authority ⟨the police officer *ordered* the crowd to back away from the suspect⟩ — see COMMAND 1

ordering *n* **1** a scheme of rank or order ⟨in the *ordering* of crimes, ripping the tags off upholstered furniture should rank fairly low⟩ — see ³SCALE 1
2 the way objects in space or events in time are arranged or follow one another ⟨the *ordering* of the children in the procession was according to height⟩ — see ORDER 1

orderly *adj* **1** being clean and in good order ⟨a small, unpretentious inn offering pleasant, *orderly* rooms⟩ — see NEAT 1
2 following a set method, arrangement, or pattern ⟨the consultant developed an *orderly* procedure that allows us to process our Internet sales much more quickly and efficiently⟩ — see METHODICAL

ordinance *n* a rule of conduct or action laid down by a governing authority and especially a legislature ⟨a local *ordinance* forbids all street parking during snowstorms⟩ — see LAW 1

ordinarily *adv* according to the usual course of things ⟨*ordinarily*, I get off work at five, but this week I'm working late to meet a project deadline⟩ — see NATURALLY 2

ordinary *adj* **1** being of the type that is encountered in the normal course of events ⟨it was a perfectly *ordinary* and undistinguished shirt⟩
synonyms average, common, commonplace, cut-and-dried (*also* cut-and-dry), everyday, garden-variety, normal, prosaic, routine, run-of-the-mill, standard, standard-issue, unexceptional, unremarkable, usual, workaday
related words regular, typical, unextraordinary; familiar, homely, plain, plain-Jane, popular, vulgar; natural; customary, wonted; insignificant, trivial, unimportant; frequent, habitual; expected, predictable
phrases par for the course
near antonyms curious, funny, peculiar, quaint, queer; aberrant, anomalous, atypical, irregular, untypical; rare, recherché, scarce; fantastic (*also* fantastical), phenomenal; bizarre, far-out, Kafkaesque, outrageous, outré, wacky (*also* whacky), way-out, weird, wild; eccentric, idiosyncratic, kooky (*also* kookie), nonconformist, oddball, offbeat, unconventional, unorthodox; freak, freakish; conspicuous, notable, novel, outstanding, prominent, salient, signal, striking, unexampled, unprecedented; singular, unique, unparalleled
antonyms abnormal, exceptional, extraordinary, odd, out-of-the-way, strange, unusual
2 of average to below average quality ⟨the pizza at that restaurant is just *ordinary*—it's nothing to write home about⟩ — see MEDIOCRE 1
3 often observed or encountered ⟨an *ordinary* hairstyle for boys of that age⟩ — see COMMON 1

ordnance *n* large firearms (as cannon or rockets) ⟨the army is waiting for the heavy *ordnance* to be brought in⟩ — see ARTILLERY

ordonnance *n* the way in which the elements of something (as a work of art) are arranged ⟨the novel's intricate *ordonnance* might not be apparent to the casual reader⟩ — see COMPOSITION 3

ordure *n* solid matter discharged from an animal's alimentary canal ⟨polite people do not discuss *ordure* in public⟩ — see DROPPING 1

oread *n* a mythical goddess represented as a young girl and said to live outdoors ⟨*oreads* supposedly prefer to live in hills and mountains⟩ — see NYMPH 1

organ *n* **1** a publication that appears at regular intervals ⟨that newspaper is intended as an *organ* for the whole university community⟩ — see JOURNAL 1
2 something used to achieve an end ⟨uses the business as an *organ* to fund a variety of political and social causes⟩ — see AGENT 1

organization *n* a group of persons formally joined together for some common interest ⟨an *organization* of people devoted to promoting world peace⟩ — see ASSOCIATION 2

organize *vb* **1** to put into a particular arrangement ⟨carefully *organized* the hotel's silverware by pattern⟩ — see ORDER 1
2 to work out the details of (something) in advance ⟨started *organizing* the anniversary party months in advance⟩ — see PLAN 1

organized *adj* following a set method, arrangement, or pattern ⟨our department is more *organized* and, therefore, more efficient in handling the tasks assigned to it⟩ — see METHODICAL

orient *vb* to impart knowledge of a new thing or situation to ⟨a training program to *orient* new employees to the requirements and dimensions of the job⟩ — see ACQUAINT 1

orientate *vb* to impart knowledge of a new thing or situation to ⟨will *orientate* all incoming freshmen to the layout of the campus⟩ — see ACQUAINT 1

orientation *n* the state or fact of facing a particular direction ⟨a building's *orientation* is an important consideration in the Chinese practice of feng shui⟩ — see EXPOSURE 2

orifice *n* a place in a surface allowing passage into or through a thing ⟨the mouth is a bodily *orifice*⟩ — see HOLE 1

origin *n* **1** a point or place at which something is invented or provided ⟨the *origins* of human language remain a matter of considerable debate⟩ — see SOURCE 1
2 the source from which something grows or develops ⟨the *origin* of the tradition of giving presents at Christmastime⟩ — see SEED 1
3 the line of ancestors from whom a person is descended ⟨they could trace their *origins* back 15 generations⟩ — see ANCESTRY

original *adj* **1** coming before all others in time or order ⟨the *original* plan had to be discarded when the situation changed drastically⟩ — see FIRST 1
2 having the skill and imagination to create new things ⟨an *original* artist who wanted his paintings to convey his emotional responses to the people, objects, and landscapes he painted⟩ — see CREATIVE 1
3 not known or experienced before ⟨separate catego-

ries for *original* and adapted screenplays⟩ — see NEW 2

original *n* **1** something from which copies are made ⟨please make copies to hand out, but keep the *original*⟩

synonyms archetype, prototype

related words source; example, mold, paradigm, pattern; beau ideal, classic, exemplar, ideal, model, nonpareil, paragon; blueprint, draft

near antonyms copy, imitation, replica, reproduction; counterfeit, fake, forgery, sham

2 a person of odd or whimsical habits ⟨the town's singing mailman is an *original*, all right⟩ — see ECCENTRIC

originality *n* **1** the quality or appeal of being new ⟨the *originality* of the war memorial sparked a heated controversy, as most people had been expecting something more traditional⟩ — see NOVELTY 1

2 the skill and imagination to create new things ⟨a poet of great *originality*, she brought a whole new range of subject matter and imagery to poetry⟩ — see CREATIVITY 1

3 the ability to form mental images of things that either are not physically present or have never been conceived or created by others ⟨a graphic novel that shows a lot of *originality* on the part of its creator⟩ — see IMAGINATION 1

originally *adv* in the beginning ⟨we *originally* planned to go out tonight, but we changed our minds⟩

synonyms firstly, initially, primarily

related words incipiently; primitively

phrases at first, to start with

near antonyms finally, lastly, ultimately

originate *vb* to come into existence ⟨the theory of relativity *originated* with Albert Einstein⟩ — see BEGIN 2

originative *adj* having the skill and imagination to create new things ⟨an *originative* genius whose mark on postmodern architecture can be seen all over the globe⟩ — see CREATIVE 1

originator *n* **1** one who creates or introduces something new ⟨Thomas Edison was the *originator* of the light bulb⟩ — see INVENTOR

2 a person who establishes a whole new field of endeavor ⟨Copernicus is sometimes hailed as the *originator* of modern astronomy, for he overturned the notion of an earth-centered universe⟩ — see FATHER 2

orison *n* an address to God or a deity ⟨a fervent *orison* asking for divine guidance in bringing about a peaceful solution to the grave international crisis⟩ — see PRAYER 1

ornament *n* something that decorates or beautifies ⟨her collection of plaster gnomes which she uses as lawn *ornaments*⟩ — see DECORATION 1

ornament *vb* to make more attractive by adding something that is beautiful or becoming ⟨delicate crystal figurines *ornament* the mantel over the fireplace⟩ — see DECORATE

ornamental *adj* serving to add beauty ⟨the trim on Victorian houses is sometimes elaborately *ornamental*⟩ — see DECORATIVE

ornamental *n* a small object displayed for its attractiveness or interest ⟨a collection of fragile *ornamentals* kept in a glass cabinet⟩ — see KNICKKNACK

ornamentation *n* something that decorates or beautifies ⟨didn't care for Victorian houses and all of their *ornamentations*⟩ — see DECORATION 1

ornate *adj* **1** elaborately and often excessively decorated ⟨an *ornate* gambling casino that is designed to look like an Italian palace⟩

synonyms bedizened, florid, fussy, gingerbread, gingerbreaded, gingerbready, overdecorated, overwrought

related words arabesque, baroque, rococo; extravagant, flamboyant, spectacular, splashy; bedaubed, flashy, garish, gaudy, glitzy, loud, ostentatious, pretentious, showy, swank (*or* swanky), tawdry; elaborate, extreme; adorned, arrayed, beautified, bedecked, decked, decorated, dressed, embellished, enriched, garnished, ornamented, trimmed; flowery, frilly, lacy; enhanced, heightened, intensified; bejeweled (*or* bejewelled), bossed, chased, emblazoned, embossed, embroidered, flounced, fringed, garlanded, gilded (*or* gilt), laced, sequined (*or* sequinned), wreathed

near antonyms bare, denuded, exposed, naked, stripped, uncovered; modest, simple, unassuming, unpretentious; conservative, muted, quiet, restrained, subdued, tasteful, toned-down, understated, unobtrusive

antonyms austere, plain, severe, stark, unadorned

2 full of fine words and fancy expressions ⟨the *ornate* prose that was standard in all diplomatic correspondence in those days⟩ — see FLOWERY 1

ornery *adj* having or showing a habitually bad temper ⟨an *ornery* old man who always yells at the neighborhood kids to keep off his lawn⟩ — see ILL-TEMPERED

orotund *adj* **1** marked by conspicuously full and rich sounds or tones ⟨the tenor's *orotund* voice was just what this soaring aria needs⟩ — see RESONANT

2 marked by the use of impressive-sounding but mostly meaningless words and phrases ⟨a master of the *orotund* prose that is favored by academic journals of literary criticism⟩ — see RHETORICAL 1

orthodox *adj* **1** following or agreeing with established form, custom, or rules ⟨schoolteachers tended to favor poets who followed a very *orthodox* style of poetry⟩ — see FORMAL 1

2 tending to favor established ideas, conditions, or institutions ⟨*orthodox* in their view of the world, the Founding Fathers subscribed to the 18th-century notion that only men with property should be allowed to vote⟩ — see CONSERVATIVE 1

oscillation *n* **1** the frequent and usually sudden passing from one condition to another ⟨fickle springtime weather in which there seemed to be an unceasing *oscillation* between unseasonable heat and unseasonable cold⟩ — see FLUX 1

2 a series of slight movements by a body back and forth or from side to side ⟨the precise *oscillations* of the quartz crystal that allows a quartz watch to keep such accurate time⟩ — see VIBRATION 1

ossified *adj* sticking to an opinion, purpose, or course of action in spite of reason, arguments, or persuasion ⟨the company's *ossified* management team failed to see the technological revolution that was sweeping their own industry⟩ — see OBSTINATE

ostensible *adj* appearing to be true on the basis of evidence that may or may not be confirmed ⟨the *ostensible* reason for the meeting turned out to be a trick to get him to the surprise party⟩ — see APPARENT 1

ostensibly *adv* to all outward appearances ⟨*ostensibly* a university student studying abroad, he was actually an espionage agent⟩ — see APPARENTLY

ostensive *adj* appearing to be true on the basis of evidence that may or may not be confirmed ⟨the *ostensive* purpose of his visit was to discuss the terms of his will⟩ — see APPARENT 1

ostensively *adv* to all outward appearances ⟨he stops by his old office periodically, *ostensively* just to say "hi"⟩ — see APPARENTLY

ostentation *n* excessive or unnecessary display ⟨the sheer *ostentation* of the rock star's mansion was overwhelming⟩

synonyms flamboyance, flash, flashiness, garishness, gaudiness, glitz, ostentatiousness, pretentiousness, showiness, swank

related words pretense (*or* pretence); éclat, extravaganza, mummery, pageant, parade, show; dazzle, fanfare, foofaraw, pageantry, pomp, razzle-dazzle, razzmatazz, spectacle; adornment, decoration, dress-

ing, embellishment, garnishment, ornamentation, trimming; extravagance, fanciness, luxuriance, luxuriousness, magnificence, opulence, richness, sumptuousness; luridness; meretriciousness, tawdriness, vulgarity
near antonyms conservativeness, moderation, modesty, restraint, simplicity, understatement; elegance, gracefulness, tastefulness; minimalism
antonyms austerity, plainness, severity

ostentatious *adj* **1** excessively showy ⟨wears an *ostentatious* diamond ring on his little finger⟩ — see GAUDY
2 self-consciously trying to present an appearance of grandeur or importance ⟨an *ostentatious* man who desperately wants to impress people with his newly acquired wealth⟩ — see PRETENTIOUS 1

ostentatiousness *n* excessive or unnecessary display ⟨the over-the-top *ostentatiousness* of the wedding banquet was in poor taste⟩ — see OSTENTATION

other *adj* **1** being not of the same kind ⟨no, I need the *other* pen, the blue one⟩ — see DIFFERENT 1
2 resulting in an increase in amount or number ⟨we'll be taking one *other* person on the trip⟩ — see ADDITIONAL
3 having been such at some previous time ⟨I was something of a celebrity in *other* days⟩ — see FORMER 1

other (than) *adv* in a different way ⟨we cannot make it to the party *other than* by canceling the previous engagement⟩ — see OTHERWISE

otherness *n* the quality or state of being different ⟨from an early age he could sense that there was an *otherness* about him—he was somehow different from the other kids⟩ — see DIFFERENCE 1

other than *prep* not including ⟨*other than* a new jacket, I bought no special clothes for the wedding⟩ — see EXCEPT

otherwise *adv* in a different way ⟨the candidate was gracious in his defeat, though he clearly wished the election had gone *otherwise*⟩
synonyms differently, else, other (than)
related words dissimilarly, diversely, variously
near antonyms similarly
antonyms likewise

other woman *n* a female other than his wife with whom a married man has a continuing sexual relationship ⟨tired of being the *other woman*, she gave him an ultimatum: divorce his wife or take a hike⟩ — see MISTRESS

otherworldly *adj* of, relating to, or being part of a reality beyond the observable physical universe ⟨a movie in which *otherworldly* beings live among us in a parallel universe⟩ — see SUPERNATURAL 1

otiose *adj* producing no results ⟨since you haven't read the book, I suppose that it would be *otiose* to inquire what you thought of it⟩ — see FUTILE 1

ought (to) *vb* to be under necessity or obligation to ⟨you *ought to* buy him a new book to replace the one you lost⟩ — see NEED 2

ounce *n* a very small amount ⟨an *ounce* of prevention is worth a pound of cure⟩ — see PARTICLE 1

oust *vb* **1** to drive or force out ⟨she was *ousted* from her job after it was proven she'd been pilfering company supplies⟩ — see EJECT 1
2 to remove from a position of prominence or power (as a throne) ⟨the people finally rose up and *ousted* the corrupt dictator⟩ — see DEPOSE 1
3 to end the occupancy or possession of ⟨the squatters were forcibly *ousted* from the abandoned building⟩ — see DISPOSSESS

out *adj* **1** fully committed to achieving a goal ⟨he's *out* to get even with the guy who beat him last time around⟩ — see DETERMINED 1
2 not at a certain place ⟨half the staff is *out* with the flu⟩ — see ABSENT 1

out *adv* **1** in or into the open air ⟨you really should get *out* more⟩ — see OUTDOORS
2 with one's normal voice speaking the words ⟨the search parties were sent in different directions and told to cry *out* if they discovered anything⟩ — see ALOUD
3 to a full extent or degree ⟨when stretched *out*, the ribbon was just long enough⟩ — see FULLY 1
4 from this or that place ⟨people staggered *out* from the burning building gasping for breath⟩ — see AWAY

out *n* the act or a means of getting or keeping away from something undesirable ⟨I really don't want to go to the party, and I've been searching for an *out*⟩ — see ESCAPE 2

out *vb* **1** to become known ⟨the truth will *out* eventually⟩ — see GET OUT 1
2 to drive or force out ⟨before moving in, we *outed* all the furry little creatures who had settled in the cabin over the winter⟩ — see EJECT 1

out–and–out *adj* **1** having no exceptions or restrictions ⟨an *out-and-out* cheater at every game she plays⟩ ⟨her story is not just an exaggeration, it's an *out-and-out* lie⟩ — see ABSOLUTE 2
2 trying all possibilities ⟨mounted an *out-and-out* effort to find the lost child⟩ — see EXHAUSTIVE 1

outback *n* a rural region that forms the edge of the settled or developed part of a country ⟨people who live in the Australian *outback* tend to be self-sufficient⟩ — see FRONTIER 2

outbrave *vb* to oppose (something hostile or dangerous) with firmness or courage ⟨completing the survival course is largely a matter of one's willingness to *outbrave* both the elements and the specter of total isolation⟩ — see FACE 2

outbreak *n* **1** a sudden and usually temporary growth of activity ⟨there was an immediate *outbreak* of paper shuffling and a pretense of work when the supervisor passed through the room⟩
synonyms burst, flare, flare-up, flash, flicker, flurry, flutter, outburst, spurt
related words recrudescence, recurrence, renewal; binge, jag, spree; boost, increase, pickup, upswing, upturn; epidemic, eruption, explosion, paroxysm; deluge, flood, rush, spate, surge, volley; commotion, furor, uproar
near antonyms calm, doldrums, slump
2 open fighting against authority (as one's own government) ⟨the government quelled the *outbreak* with ruthless efficiency⟩ — see REBELLION 1

outburst *n* **1** a sudden intense expression of strong feeling ⟨the judge directed the courtroom spectators to refrain from any *outbursts* when the verdict was read⟩
synonyms agony, blaze, burst, ebullition, eruption, explosion, fit, flare, flare-up, flash, flush, gale, gush, gust, paroxysm, spasm, storm
related words blowup, grouch, rage, tantrum; ecstasy, rapture, transport; delirium, firestorm, frenzy, furor
2 a sudden and usually temporary growth of activity ⟨there was a remarkable *outburst* of work in the office as the visiting VIPs made their tour⟩ — see OUTBREAK 1
3 the act or an instance of exploding ⟨in the *outburst* known as a supernova, the star may reach an intrinsic luminosity one billion times that of the sun⟩ — see EXPLOSION 1

outcast *n* one who is cast out or rejected by society ⟨the professor is something of an *outcast* in the halls of academe now that his former support of a dictatorial regime has become public⟩
synonyms castaway, castoff, leper, offscouring, pariah, reject
related words untouchable; outsider; deportee, exile
near antonyms insider

outclass *vb* to be greater, better, or stronger than ⟨a tennis player who *outclassed* the competition, breezing through the tournament without losing a set⟩ — see SURPASS 1

outcome *n* a condition or occurrence traceable to a cause ⟨one expected *outcome* of hard work is greater success⟩ — see EFFECT 1

outcry *n* a violent shouting ⟨I went to the window to see what the sudden *outcry* from the street below was about⟩ — see CLAMOR 1

outdated *adj* having passed its time of use or usefulness ⟨an *outdated* rotary telephone⟩ — see OBSOLETE

outdistance *vb* to be greater, better, or stronger than ⟨the new student rapidly *outdistanced* the rest of the class in math⟩ — see SURPASS 1

outdo *vb* to be greater, better, or stronger than ⟨two vaccine developers who spent years vigorously trying to *outdo* one another's research⟩ — see SURPASS 1

outdoor *also* **outdoors** *adj* of, relating to, or held in the open air ⟨an *outdoor* picnic is always at the mercy of the weather, of course⟩
synonyms alfresco, open-air, out-of-door (*or* out-of-doors), outdoorsy
related words airy; exterior, external, outer, outside, outward; outermost, outmost
near antonyms inner, inside, interior, internal, inward; inmost, innermost
antonyms indoor

outdoors *adv* in or into the open air ⟨please wait until you're *outdoors* to light up your cigarette⟩
synonyms alfresco, out, outside
related words without
near antonyms in, inside, within
antonyms indoors

outdoors *n* that part of the physical world that is removed from human habitation ⟨our family loves to hike and camp in the great *outdoors*⟩ — see NATURE 2

outdoorsy *adj* of, relating to, or held in the open air ⟨a retirement community offering tennis, golf, and other *outdoorsy* activities⟩ — see OUTDOOR

outer *adj* situated on the outside or farther out ⟨the *outer* edge of the blade of your figure skate always wears out faster than the inner because you use it more⟩
synonyms exterior, external, outside, outward
related words outermost, outlying, outmost; superficial, surface
near antonyms inmost, innermost; mid, middle, midmost
antonyms inner, inside, interior, internal, inward

outermost *adj* most distant from a center ⟨the *outermost* ring of listeners had trouble hearing the concert⟩ — see EXTREME 1

outface *vb* to oppose (something hostile or dangerous) with firmness or courage ⟨rescue workers who *outface* the daily threat of catastrophe⟩ — see FACE 2

outfit *n* **1** clothing chosen as appropriate for a specific situation ⟨the restaurant provides its waitstaff with themed *outfits*⟩ ⟨do you want to buy a new *outfit* for the Halloween party?⟩
synonyms costume, drag, dress, garb, getup, guise, togs
related words apparel, attire, clothes, duds, habiliment(s), raiment; fashion, mode, style; array, caparison, vestments
2 a commercial or industrial activity or organization ⟨they're an *outfit* specializing in travel tours for senior citizens⟩ — see ENTERPRISE 1
3 a group of people working together on a task ⟨the whole *outfit* quit early for lunch⟩ — see GANG 1
4 items needed for the performance of a task or activity ⟨for this class, you will need a professional camera *outfit* which includes at least one telephoto lens and one wide-angle lens⟩ — see EQUIPMENT
5 the distinctive clothing worn by members of a particular group ⟨the highway patrol *outfit* includes jackboots and a high-crowned hat⟩ — see UNIFORM

outfit *vb* to provide (someone) with what is needed for a task or activity ⟨*outfitted* the scuba instructors handsomely with all new gear⟩ — see FURNISH 1

outflow *n* a flowing or going out ⟨over the last year the state experienced an unprecedented brain drain as the *outflow* of highly educated professionals exceeded the inflow⟩
synonyms exodus, gush, outpour, outpouring
related words drain, flow; ebb, reflow, reflux; rush, stampede; diaspora, emigration, flight; discharge, effluence, emanation, emission
near antonyms deluge, flood, inundation, overflow, spate, torrent; river, stream, tide
antonyms flux, inflow, influx, inrush

outfox *vb* to get the better of through cleverness ⟨the prisoners *outfoxed* the guards by tunneling beneath the prison walls⟩ — see OUTWIT

out-front *adj* free in expressing one's true feelings and opinions ⟨he's always been *out-front* about his sexuality⟩ — see FRANK

outgo *n* **1** a payment made in the course of achieving a result ⟨last year the film company's *outgoes* exceeded its revenues by a wide margin⟩ — see EXPENSE
2 the act of leaving a place ⟨the *outgo* of the town's only remaining manufacturing plant was a disaster⟩ — see DEPARTURE 1

outgoing *adj* likely to seek or enjoy the company of others ⟨a salesman whose aggressively *outgoing* personality could sometimes be overbearing⟩ — see CONVIVIAL

outgrowth *n* **1** a branch of a main stem especially of a plant ⟨trimmed back some of the tree's *outgrowths* so they wouldn't interfere with the power lines⟩ — see OFFSHOOT 1
2 a condition or occurrence traceable to a cause ⟨a predictable *outgrowth* of the suburb's ever growing population will be the need for more schools⟩ — see EFFECT 1
3 something that naturally develops or is developed from something else ⟨an industry that is an *outgrowth* of the technology first developed for the U.S. space program⟩ — see DERIVATIVE

outgun *vb* to be greater, better, or stronger than ⟨a marketing firm whose innovative ad campaigns have consistently *outgunned* its rivals'⟩ — see SURPASS 1

outing *n* a short trip for pleasure ⟨an *outing* to the zoo⟩ — see EXCURSION 1

outlander *n* a person who is not native to or known to a community ⟨although we have lived in the village for years, to the natives whose families have been here for generations, we are still *outlanders*⟩ — see STRANGER

outlandish *adj* **1** different from the ordinary in a way that causes curiosity or suspicion ⟨an *outlandish* outfit made entirely out of bottle caps⟩ — see ODD 2
2 excitingly or mysteriously unusual ⟨the *outlandish* tribal rituals that astonished early explorers of that land⟩ — see EXOTIC

outlands *n pl* a rural region that forms the edge of the settled or developed part of a country ⟨missionaries to the nation's rugged *outlands*⟩ — see FRONTIER 2

outlast *vb* to last longer than ⟨I truly hope this car will *outlast* our previous one⟩ ⟨your work will probably *outlast* you⟩
synonyms outlive, outwear
related words survive; outstay; abide (beyond), endure (past), hold (past), hold out (past), last (beyond), persist (beyond); draw out, perpetuate; succeed

outlaw *vb* **1** to make or declare contrary to the law ⟨a push to *outlaw* smoking in all public buildings⟩ — see ILLEGALIZE

2 to order not to do or use or to be done or used ⟨fed up with the constant interruptions, the physician has *outlawed* all cell phone use from his office⟩ — see FORBID

outlawed *adj* that may not be permitted ⟨a refugee seeking asylum because in his home country he risks persecution as a member of an *outlawed* religious group⟩ — see IMPERMISSIBLE

outlawing *n* the act of ordering that something not be done or used ⟨the *outlawing* of open containers of beer in moving vehicles is intended to reduce drunk driving⟩ — see PROHIBITION 1

outlay *n* a payment made in the course of achieving a result ⟨the *outlays* for the couple's upcoming wedding seem to be multiplying at an incredible rate⟩ — see EXPENSE

outlay *vb* to hand over or use up in payment ⟨the nation had *outlaid* nearly 20 billion dollars on social programs at that point⟩ — see SPEND 1

outlet *n* **1** a place or means of going out ⟨this road is the only *outlet* for traffic coming from the racetrack⟩ — see EXIT 1

2 a place or opportunity for communicating ideas and information ⟨technology has provided many new *outlets* for amateur writers and artists to share their work with a global audience⟩ — see VENUE 1

outline *n* **1** a line that traces the outer limits of an object or surface ⟨place your hand on the paper and draw an *outline* around it⟩

synonyms contour, figure, silhouette

related words delineation, sketch; profile, skyline; cast, configuration, conformation, form, geometry, shape; framework, skeleton

2 a short statement of the main points ⟨a printed *outline* of the lecture has been made available for all attendees⟩ — see SUMMARY

outline *vb* **1** to draw or make apparent the outline of ⟨she carefully *outlined* the tree before she started drawing in the leaves⟩

synonyms define, delineate, silhouette, sketch, trace

related words line; bound, fringe, margin, skirt; edge, hem, rim, trim; frame; circle, compass, encircle, girdle, girth, loop, ring, round, surround; chart, diagram, draw, map (out)

2 to make into a short statement of the main points (as of a report) ⟨*outlined* the important points in the introduction⟩ — see SUMMARIZE

outlive *vb* to last longer than ⟨tortoises will *outlive* most people, as they live to be over 100 years old⟩ — see OUTLAST

outlook *n* **1** a high place or structure from which a wide view is possible ⟨the cliff-top *outlook* provides an expansive view of the sleepy village down in the valley⟩ — see LOOKOUT 1

2 a way of looking at or thinking about something ⟨tried to keep a cheerful *outlook* on life⟩ — see PERSPECTIVE 1

3 all that can be seen from a certain point ⟨the *outlook* from the tower is spectacular in all directions⟩ — see VIEW 1

out loud *adv* with one's normal voice speaking the words ⟨registered their dissatisfaction with the meal *out loud* to the waiter⟩ — see ALOUD

outmaneuver *vb* to get the better of through cleverness ⟨*outmaneuvered* his congressional opponent by co-opting his call for change in Washington⟩ — see OUTWIT

outmatch *vb* to be greater, better, or stronger than ⟨believes Secretariat would *outmatch* any other horse in racing history⟩ — see SURPASS 1

out–migrant *n* one that leaves one place to settle in another ⟨most *out-migrants* cited the state's high cost of living as their main reason for leaving⟩ — see EMIGRANT

outmoded *adj* having passed its time of use or usefulness ⟨*outmoded* computers that can be recycled⟩ — see OBSOLETE

outmost *adj* most distant from a center ⟨the *outmost* areas of the park, where few tourists venture, are still wilderness⟩ — see EXTREME 1

out–of–date *adj* having passed its time of use or usefulness ⟨the sorely *out-of-date* information that one finds all too frequently online⟩ — see OBSOLETE

out–of–door *or* **out–of–doors** *adj* of, relating to, or held in the open air ⟨an *out-of-door* performance under the stars⟩ — see OUTDOORS

out–of–doors *n* that part of the physical world that is removed from human habitation ⟨hiking in the *out-of-doors* can be a tremendous appetite builder⟩ — see NATURE 2

out–of–sight *adj, slang* of the very best kind ⟨the food at that restaurant is *out-of-sight*—but then so are the prices⟩ — see EXCELLENT

out–of–the–way *adj* **1** different from the ordinary in a way that causes curiosity or suspicion ⟨a tell-all book that focused obsessively on the *out-of-the-way* sexual activities allegedly engaged in by the film star⟩ — see ODD 2

2 noticeably different from what is generally found or experienced ⟨there was nothing *out-of-the-way* about the hitchhiker's appearance that might arouse suspicion⟩ — see UNUSUAL 1

outpour *n* a flowing or going out ⟨the roadways around the new plant are being widened to handle the expected *outpour* of vehicles at the end of the day shift⟩ — see OUTFLOW

outpouring *n* a flowing or going out ⟨an *outpouring* of affection and support for the high school athlete in need of an organ transplant⟩ — see OUTFLOW

output *n* something produced by physical or intellectual effort ⟨an author known for his prodigious literary *output*⟩ — see PRODUCT 1

outrage *n* **1** an act or expression showing scorn and usually intended to hurt another's feelings ⟨the booing during the graduation speech was an *outrage*⟩ — see INSULT

2 an intense emotional state of displeasure with someone or something ⟨the actress could barely contain her *outrage* at being passed over for an Oscar yet again⟩ — see ANGER

outrage *vb* **1** to cause hurt feelings or deep resentment in ⟨the spiteful comment *outraged* her so much that she's still holding a grudge⟩ — see INSULT

2 to make angry ⟨the vandalism in the cemetery *outraged* the entire community⟩ — see ANGER

3 to engage in sexual activity and especially intercourse with a person unwilling or unable to give consent ⟨the invading barbarians brutally *outraged* the women, killed the men, and enslaved the children⟩ — see RAPE

outraged *adj* feeling or showing anger ⟨the judge was *outraged* to discover that several jurors had disregarded her orders not to speak with members of the press⟩ — see ANGRY

outrank *vb* to be greater in importance than ⟨one hard fact *outranks* a mountain of speculation anytime⟩ — see OUTWEIGH

outré *adj* different from the ordinary in a way that causes curiosity or suspicion ⟨an actor known more for his *outré* offscreen antics than for his on-screen performances⟩ — see ODD 2

outreach *vb* to go beyond the limit of ⟨a young actress whose ambition *outreaches* her talent, unfortunately⟩ — see EXCEED 1

outrider *n* one that announces or indicates the later arrival of another ⟨sexologist Alfred Kinsey is now viewed as an *outrider* of the sexual revolution of the 1960s⟩ — see FORERUNNER 1

outright *adj* having no exceptions or restrictions ⟨that's an *outright* lie!⟩ — see ABSOLUTE 2

outrun *vb* to go beyond the limit of ⟨our expenses have been *outrunning* our revenues for some months now⟩ — see EXCEED 1

outset *n* the point at which something begins ⟨I wish you'd mentioned this problem at the *outset*⟩ — see BEGINNING

outshine *vb* to be greater, better, or stronger than ⟨the trumpeter *outshines* all of his fellow band members⟩ — see SURPASS 1

outside *adj* **1** situated on the outside or farther out ⟨slower moving vehicles should keep to the *outside* lane⟩ — see OUTER
2 small in degree ⟨though they haven't been playing at their best, they still have an *outside* chance of making it into the championship series⟩ — see REMOTE 1
3 of the greatest or highest degree or quantity ⟨the *outside* cost for repairing the item will be a thousand dollars⟩ — see ULTIMATE 1

outside *adv* in or into the open air ⟨go *outside* and smoke, if you must⟩ — see OUTDOORS

outside *n* **1** an outer part or layer ⟨painted the *outside* of the house⟩ — see EXTERIOR
2 the greatest amount, number, or part ⟨there were 300 people at the *outside* who attended the softball game⟩ — see MOST
3 the outward form of someone or something especially as indicative of a quality ⟨on the *outside*, he was the self-assured star athlete⟩ — see APPEARANCE 1

outside *prep* **1** not including ⟨*outside* that one suggestion, I haven't heard any better ideas⟩ — see EXCEPT
2 out of the reach or sphere of ⟨it is always refreshing to be assigned a project at work that is *outside* one's usual range of responsibility⟩ — see BEYOND 2

outside of *prep* **1** not including ⟨*outside of* that project you don't like, I don't think you have many choices⟩ — see EXCEPT
2 out of the reach or sphere of ⟨budget cuts will result in some teachers teaching courses *outside of* their primary areas of expertise⟩ — see BEYOND 2

outsider *n* a person who is not native to or known to a community ⟨she seems to enjoy the odd distinction of being the only *outsider* in such a small community⟩ — see STRANGER

outsize *also* **outsized** *adj* **1** unusually large ⟨an *outsize* cat who weighs 25 pounds⟩ — see HUGE
2 of a size greater than average of its kind ⟨she likes to make dramatic appearances wearing her trademark *outsize* sunglasses⟩ — see LARGE 1
3 extended beyond normal or realistic bounds ⟨I'm tired of having to deal with so many *outsize* egos at the office⟩ — see BLOATED 1

outskirts *n pl* the districts adjacent to a city ⟨some people prefer to live on the *outskirts* and work inside the city⟩ — see ENVIRONS 1

outslick *vb* to get the better of through cleverness ⟨an overly confident con man who thought that he could *outslick* anyone, even the local Mob leader⟩ — see OUTWIT

outsmart *vb* to get the better of through cleverness ⟨an inexpensive security system that would likely be *outsmarted* by anyone with a serious interest in circumventing it⟩ — see OUTWIT

outspoken *adj* free in expressing one's true feelings and opinions ⟨a newspaper columnist who has been very *outspoken* on a number of controversial issues⟩ — see FRANK

outspokenness *n* the free expression of one's true feelings and opinions ⟨some people find the celebrated *outspokenness* of that talk show host to be rather offensive⟩ — see CANDOR 1

outspread *vb* to arrange the parts of (something) over a wider area ⟨when it *outspread* its wings, a pteranodon would have had a wingspan in excess of 20 feet⟩ — see OPEN 3

outstanding *adj* **1** not yet paid ⟨there are several *outstanding* bills left, but at least we paid the rest⟩
synonyms overdue, owed, owing, payable, unpaid, unsettled
related words due, mature
near antonyms prepaid
antonyms cleared, liquidated, paid (off *or* up), repaid, settled
2 standing above others in rank, importance, or achievement ⟨the award goes to the most *outstanding* student in science⟩ — see EMINENT

outstretch *vb* **1** to arrange the parts of (something) over a wider area ⟨the dog had *outstretched* his legs and was lying across the width of the doorway⟩ — see OPEN 3
2 to make longer ⟨having *outstretched* our lunch break beyond all reason, we reluctantly headed back to work⟩ — see EXTEND 1

outstrip *vb* to be greater, better, or stronger than ⟨before he had reached his teens, the child prodigy had *outstripped* his music teacher's abilities⟩ — see SURPASS 1

out–there *adj* deviating from commonly accepted beliefs or practices ⟨the professor's *out-there* political views have made him a lightning rod for controversy on campus⟩ — see HERETICAL

outthink *vb* to get the better of through cleverness ⟨the company's growth is due in large part to its marketing division's ability to *outthink* the competition⟩ — see OUTWIT

outward *adj* situated on the outside or farther out ⟨the wall's *outward* face is painted over with a colorful mural honoring illustrious members of the community⟩ — see OUTER

outward *n* outward and often deceptive indication ⟨never was there in a man such a fine, heroic *outward* and such a cowardly interior⟩ — see APPEARANCE 2

outwear *vb* **1** to last longer than ⟨these running shoes have *outworn* any others that I have ever bought⟩ — see OUTLAST
2 to use up all the physical energy of ⟨a daily grind that would *outwear* anybody⟩ — see EXHAUST 1

outweigh *vb* to be greater in importance than ⟨in most elections the state of the economy *outweighs* all other issues⟩
synonyms outrank, overbalance, overshadow, overweigh
related words count, import, matter, mean, signify, weigh; dwarf; exceed, outstrip, surpass, transcend

outwit *vb* to get the better of through cleverness ⟨a plan to *outwit* their opponents at their own game⟩
synonyms fox, outfox, outmaneuver, outslick, outsmart, outthink, overreach
related words outguess, second-guess; baffle, balk, circumvent, foil, frustrate, thwart; cozen, deceive, dupe, fool, gull, trick; conquer, defeat, lick, overcome; bar, block, hinder, impede, obstruct

outworn *adj* having passed its time of use or usefulness ⟨*outworn* clothes with holes in them⟩ — see OBSOLETE

oval *adj* having the shape of an egg ⟨the *Oval* Office in the White House⟩
synonyms elliptical (*or* elliptic), ovate, ovoid (*also* ovoidal)

ovate *adj* having the shape of an egg ⟨the governor's bald, *ovate* head makes him an easy target for caricaturists⟩ — see OVAL

ovation *n* enthusiastic and usually public expression of approval ⟨received a standing *ovation* for the masterly performance⟩ — see APPLAUSE 1

over *adj* brought or having come to an end ⟨the play is *over* now⟩ — see COMPLETE 2

over *adv* **1** from one side to the other of an intervening space ⟨let's swim *over* to that island⟩
synonyms across, athwart, through
related words clear
2 yet another time ⟨several executives missed the presentation and would like you to do it *over* for them later this afternoon⟩ — see AGAIN 1
3 to or in a higher place ⟨I heard the noise and was startled to discover that the plane was directly *over*⟩ — see ABOVE
4 from beginning to end ⟨read it *over* until you understand it thoroughly⟩ — see THROUGH 1
5 toward or in a lower position ⟨the baby toddled two steps and then fell *over*⟩ — see DOWN 1

over *prep* **1** higher than ⟨the boy towered *over* his siblings⟩ — see ABOVE
2 in the course of ⟨the students learned a lot *over* the summer⟩ — see DURING
3 on or to the farther side of ⟨peered *over* the wall⟩ — see BEYOND 1
4 to the opposite side of ⟨hopped *over* the dropped ball⟩ — see ACROSS 1
5 in random positions within the boundaries of ⟨marbles scattered all *over* the room⟩ — see AROUND 2

overabundance *n* the state or an instance of going beyond what is usual, proper, or needed ⟨an *overabundance* of desserts at a potluck dinner⟩ — see EXCESS 1

overactive *adj* being in a state of increased activity or agitation ⟨the boy manages to panic himself by his own *overactive* imagination⟩ — see FEVERISH 1

overage *n* the state or an instance of going beyond what is usual, proper, or needed ⟨several selectmen argued that the town's cash *overage* was significant enough to warrant a reduction of the residential property tax⟩ — see EXCESS 1

overall *adj* **1** belonging or relating to the whole ⟨the *overall* view seems to be that we're doing fine economically⟩ — see GENERAL 1
2 relating to the main elements and not to specific details ⟨there's an *overall* similarity in the looks of the models for that chain of clothing stores⟩ — see GENERAL 2
3 held by or applicable to a majority of the people ⟨the *overall* mind-set among the people in our town seems to be that any increase in taxes is bad⟩ — see GENERAL 3

overall *adv* **1** with everyone or everything taken into account at the same time ⟨reduce the budget *overall* by 15 percent⟩ — see ALL AROUND
2 for the most part ⟨*overall*, this is a good speech, but it could use a little humor⟩ — see CHIEFLY

over and above *prep* in addition to ⟨we'll need another gallon of milk *over and above* what we already have⟩ — see BESIDES 1

over and over *adv* many times ⟨the little girl demanded *over and over* to be picked up so she could see the performers on stage⟩ — see OFTEN

overbalance *vb* to be greater in importance than ⟨my determination to finish the job *overbalanced* my exhaustion⟩ — see OUTWEIGH

overbear *vb* to achieve a victory over ⟨that year the football team simply *overbore* opponent after opponent with steamroller ruthlessness⟩ — see BEAT 2

overbearing *adj* **1** coming before all others in importance ⟨the *overbearing* problem in our nation's schools⟩ — see FOREMOST 1
2 fond of ordering people around ⟨the doctor's *overbearing* attitude is resented by nurses and patients alike⟩ — see BOSSY

overblown *adj* extended beyond normal or realistic bounds ⟨*overblown* predictions of financial calamity after the company had one bad quarter⟩ — see BLOATED 1

overbold *adj* foolishly adventurous or bold ⟨one *overbold* tourist almost tumbled over the rocks and into the sea⟩ — see FOOLHARDY 1

overburden *vb* to fill or load to excess ⟨it is important that you bring on the hike plenty of food and water, but don't *overburden* your pack with unnecessary gear⟩ — see OVERLOAD

overcast *adj* covered over by clouds ⟨the dark, *overcast* sky made the whole day seem depressing⟩
synonyms beclouded, clouded, cloudy, dull, hazed, hazy, heavy, lowering (*also* louring), overclouded
related words bedimmed, befogged, blackened, darkened, darksome, dim, dimmed, dulled, dusky, misty, murky, obscure, obscured, overshadowed; sunless; black, bleak, cheerless, dark, desolate, dismal, drear, dreary, funereal, gloomy, glum, gray (*also* grey), sepulchral, somber (*or* sombre), sullen
near antonyms sunlit, sunny, sunshiny; brightened, brilliant, dazzling, illuminated, illumined, lit (*or* lighted), lightened, radiant, shiny
antonyms clear, cloudless

overcast *vb* to make dark, dim, or indistinct ⟨an impenetrable fog *overcast* our view of the harbor⟩ — see CLOUD 1

overcharge *vb* **1** to charge (someone) too much for goods or services ⟨I think that store may have *overcharged* us for the shoes, which were supposed to be on sale⟩
synonyms gouge, soak, sting, surcharge
related words cheat, defraud, stick; clip, fleece, skin; mischarge
antonyms undercharge
2 to fill or load to excess ⟨*overcharged* his thesis with long, fancy words⟩ — see OVERLOAD

overcharging *n* the exaction of a grossly excessive charge for goods or services ⟨stores that were prosecuted for *overcharging* during and after the hurricane⟩ — see EXTORTION

overcloud *vb* to make dark, dim, or indistinct ⟨the eerie dusk of an approaching storm *overclouded* the plains⟩ — see CLOUD 1

overclouded *adj* covered over by clouds ⟨*overclouded* skies are a common feature in that Dutch artist's landscape paintings⟩ — see OVERCAST

overcoat *n* a warm outdoor coat ⟨put your *overcoat* on—it's freezing out there!⟩
synonyms greatcoat, surcoat, topcoat
related words chesterfield, frock coat, mackinaw, ulster; jacket, parka, surtout; oilskin, raincoat, sou'wester; wrap
near antonyms undercoat

overcome *vb* **1** to achieve a victory over ⟨the baseball team finally *overcame* their opponents in the 13th inning⟩ — see BEAT 2
2 to subject to incapacitating emotional or mental stress ⟨already under stress, she was *overcome* by news of a death in the family⟩ — see OVERWHELM 1

overconfident *adj* foolishly adventurous or bold ⟨the *overconfident* quarterback made some careless decisions that cost him the game⟩ — see FOOLHARDY 1

overcritical *adj* given to making or expressing unfavorable judgments about things ⟨an *overcritical* teacher can discourage even the most dedicated of students⟩ — see CRITICAL 1

overdecorated *adj* elaborately and often excessively decorated ⟨the room was so *overdecorated* that no one thing was shown to its best advantage⟩ — see ORNATE 1

overdo *vb* to describe or express in too strong terms

⟨the fashion designer's claim that his new line of clothing would revolutionize the way we dress was perhaps *overdoing* it just a bit⟩ — see OVERSTATE

overdraw *vb* to describe or express in too strong terms ⟨commentators have *overdrawn* the dangers of the sport in order to make it appear more exciting⟩ — see OVERSTATE

overdrawn *adj* extended beyond normal or realistic bounds ⟨*overdrawn* claims of her accomplishments that any job interviewer could see right through⟩ — see BLOATED 1

overdue *adj* **1** not arriving, or occurring, or settled at the due, usual, or proper time ⟨an *overdue* library book will be subject to daily fines⟩ — see LATE 1
2 not yet paid ⟨an *overdue* bill that's started incurring interest charges⟩ — see OUTSTANDING 1
3 going beyond a normal or acceptable limit in degree or amount ⟨spends an *overdue* percentage of her income on beauty products and services⟩ — see EXCESSIVE

overeat *vb* to eat greedily or to excess ⟨because he watches his diet for most of the year, he feels free to *overeat* during the holidays⟩ — see GORGE 2

overeater *n* one who eats greedily or too much ⟨not every fat person is actually an *overeater*⟩ — see GLUTTON

overeating *n* the excessive consumption of food ⟨the medical community's warning that the nation's most dangerous epidemic may be *overeating*⟩ — see GLUTTONY

overestimate *vb* to place too high a value on ⟨the contractors *overestimated* their ability to do the work on such short notice⟩
synonyms overrate, overvalue
related words appreciate, cherish, prize, treasure, value; admire, esteem, regard, respect; adore, idolize, revere, reverence, venerate, worship
near antonyms minimize, play down, soft-pedal; belittle, decry, depreciate, disparage; despise, disdain, scorn; abhor, abominate, detest, loathe
antonyms underestimate, underrate, undervalue

overexpose *vb* to use so much as to make less appealing ⟨seeking to capitalize on its only breakout hit, the network fatally *overexposed* the game show by scheduling it every night of the week⟩ — see HACKNEY

overextravagant *adj* going beyond a normal or acceptable limit in degree or amount ⟨no musician could live up to the *overextravagant* praise that was heaped on that promising violinist⟩ — see EXCESSIVE

overfamiliar *adj* showing a lack of proper social reserve or modesty ⟨the company cautions their managers against fraternization and being *overfamiliar* with their subordinates⟩ — see PRESUMPTUOUS 1

overfill *vb* **1** to fill or load to excess ⟨*overfilled* the wheelbarrow with bricks until finally no one could push it⟩ — see OVERLOAD
2 to flow over the brim or top of ⟨water *overfilled* the tub and poured onto the floor⟩ — see OVERFLOW 1

overflow *n* **1** a great flow of water or of something that overwhelms ⟨a great *overflow* of water from the heavy rains swept mud and silt down onto the highway⟩ — see FLOOD
2 the state or an instance of going beyond what is usual, proper, or needed ⟨an *overflow* of help actually made the job more complicated⟩ — see EXCESS 1

overflow *vb* **1** to flow over the brim or top of ⟨while the wine steward stood there gawking at the nearby celebrity, my expensive champagne was *overflowing* its glass and pouring onto our table⟩
synonyms overfill
related words boil over, run over, spill, well (up); flow, flush, gush, pour, sluice, spout, spurt, stream; deluge, drown, engulf, flood, inundate, overwhelm, submerge, submerse, swamp; wash (over); brim, cascade, slop, slosh
near antonyms recede
2 to cover with a flood ⟨the swollen river *overflowed* the surrounding land and washed several houses away⟩ — see FLOOD
3 to be copiously supplied ⟨a magazine that usually *overflows* with home-repair tips for the do-it-yourselfer⟩ — see ABOUND

overgrown *adj* covered with a thick, healthy natural growth ⟨the trail has become so *overgrown* that it is nearly impassable in spots⟩ — see LUSH 1

overhang *n* a part that sticks out from the general mass of something ⟨a recess in the face of the cliff that is hidden by the thick vines dangling from the jagged *overhang* above⟩ — see BULGE 1

overhang *vb* **1** to extend outward beyond a usual point ⟨the narrow streets of the old European city are lined with row houses often having *overhanging* second stories⟩ — see BULGE 1
2 to remain poised to inflict harm, danger, or distress on ⟨a cancer patient who refuses to put his life on hold even though the constant threat of death has been *overhanging* him for several years⟩ — see THREATEN

overhasty *adj* acting or done with excessive or careless speed ⟨an *overhasty* reading of the recipe resulted in the omission of a critical ingredient⟩ — see HASTY 1

overhaul *vb* to move fast enough to get even with ⟨in the final moments of the race, the horse in the rear sped forward at a furious pace and *overhauled* the horse that had been leading⟩ — see OVERTAKE

overhead *adv* to or in a higher place ⟨the majestic sight of eagles soaring *overhead*⟩ — see ABOVE

overhear *vb* to listen to (another in private conversation) ⟨it's not polite to try to *overhear* intimate friends sharing confidences⟩ — see EAVESDROP (ON)

overindulgent *adj* given to or marked by excessive gratification of one's desires ⟨*overindulgent* vacationers who thought the nation's strict drug laws did not apply to them⟩ — see HEDONISTIC

overinflated *adj* enlarged beyond normal from internal pressure ⟨an *overinflated* balloon will burst⟩ — see BLOATED 2

overkill *n* the state or an instance of going beyond what is usual, proper, or needed ⟨the song already borders on the maudlin—the addition of a syrupy string accompaniment would just be *overkill*⟩ — see EXCESS 1

overlap *n* a partial covering of one thing by an adjoining member ⟨the orthodontist will try to fix that *overlap* of two of your upper incisors⟩
synonyms imbrication, lapping
related words shingling; overlaying, overlying, overspreading

overlap *vb* to lie over parts of one another ⟨the brochures on the display table should *overlap* but not so much that the titles are obscured⟩
synonyms lap, overlay, overlie, overspread
related words shingle

overlay *vb* **1** to form a layer over ⟨you should apply a coat of primer first, and then *overlay* it with two coats of paint⟩ — see COVER 2
2 to lie over parts of one another ⟨cedar shingles *overlaying* one another on the roof⟩ — see OVERLAP

overlie *vb* **1** to lie over parts of one another ⟨the puzzle pieces *overlay* one another in complete disarray on the floor⟩ — see OVERLAP
2 to form a layer over ⟨there will be freezing rain tonight, so we can expect to find a thick layer of ice *overlying* the car windshield in the morning⟩ — see COVER 2

overload *vb* to fill or load to excess ⟨try not to *overload*

your backpack, or you could end up with back problems⟩
synonyms overburden, overcharge, overfill
related words stuff; burden, charge, encumber, lade, laden, load, lumber, saddle, weigh down, weight
near antonyms lighten, unburden, unload

overlook *n* a high place or structure from which a wide view is possible ⟨just down the road there's a great *overlook* where you can get a panoramic view of the valley below⟩ — see LOOKOUT 1

overlook *vb* **1** to look down on ⟨the fortress *overlooks* the city⟩
synonyms command, dominate
related words face, front
2 to fail to give proper attention to ⟨you've *overlooked* your chores again this week⟩ — see NEGLECT 1
3 to be in charge of ⟨you'll be asked to *overlook* larger projects in the future⟩ — see BOSS 1
4 to cast a spell on ⟨the superstitious grandmother actually believed that the baby had been *overlooked* by a gypsy woman⟩ — see BEWITCH 1
5 to look over closely (as for judging quality or condition) ⟨quickly *overlooked* the table of used books to see if there was anything of value⟩ — see INSPECT
6 to dismiss as of little importance ⟨definitely not the kind of spouse to *overlook* even a single instance of marital infidelity⟩ — see EXCUSE 1
7 to look after and make decisions about ⟨the engineer hired to *overlook* the construction of the canal⟩ — see CONDUCT 1

overly *adv* beyond a normal or acceptable limit ⟨there's no need to be *overly* careful about the rough draft, since we'll polish it afterwards⟩ — see TOO 1

overmaster *vb* to subject to incapacitating emotional or mental stress ⟨the student was *overmastered* by the stress of taking the college placement test and broke down crying⟩ — see OVERWHELM 1

overmastering *adj* coming before all others in importance ⟨a matter that should be given *overmastering* priority by the incoming administration⟩ — see FOREMOST 1

overmatch *vb* to achieve a victory over ⟨an indomitable spirit that no amount of adversity could *overmatch*⟩ — see BEAT 2

overmuch *adj* going beyond a normal or acceptable limit in degree or amount ⟨I think you put *overmuch* care into your personal appearance—get over yourself⟩ — see EXCESSIVE

overmuch *adv* beyond a normal or acceptable limit ⟨you worry *overmuch* about what other people think⟩ — see TOO 1

overmuch *n* the state or an instance of going beyond what is usual, proper, or needed ⟨you must not expect an *overmuch* of gratitude from a very young child⟩ — see EXCESS 1

overpass *vb* **1** to dismiss as of little importance ⟨to keep peace in the family, he was forced to *overpass* his in-laws' frequent put-downs⟩ — see EXCUSE 1
2 to go beyond the limit of ⟨a filmmaker whose technical bravura *overpasses* his ability to tell a coherent story⟩ — see EXCEED 1
3 to fail to give proper attention to ⟨army officers who had been unjustly *overpassed* for promotion⟩ — see NEGLECT 1

overplus *n* the state or an instance of going beyond what is usual, proper, or needed ⟨the store was stuck with an *overplus* of tie-ins for a movie that fizzled at the box office⟩ — see EXCESS 1

overpower *vb* **1** to bring under one's control by force of arms ⟨the invading army *overpowered* the countryside with lightning speed⟩ — see CONQUER 1
2 to subject to incapacitating emotional or mental stress ⟨*overpowered* by fear of the unknown⟩ — see OVERWHELM 1

overpowering *n* the act or process of bringing someone or something under one's control ⟨the *overpowering* of much of Europe by the Nazis during World War II⟩ — see CONQUEST

overpraise *n* excessive praise ⟨the piano instructor believes in encouraging her students but avoids any *overpraise* that might make them complacent⟩ — see FLATTERY

overpraise *vb* to praise too much ⟨proud parents are likely to *overpraise* their children for their earnest efforts at making handicrafts⟩ — see FLATTER 1

overrate *vb* to place too high a value on ⟨I think the critics seriously *overrated* that movie⟩ — see OVERESTIMATE

overreach *vb* **1** to get the better of through cleverness ⟨a real estate developer who is always trying to *overreach* his competitors, fair means or foul⟩ — see OUTWIT
2 to go beyond the limit of ⟨the mountain climbers *overreached* their abilities and paid for it dearly⟩ — see EXCEED 1

overriding *adj* coming before all others in importance ⟨the *overriding* question is how we will pay for this hurricane cleanup⟩ — see FOREMOST 1

overripe *adj* having lost forcefulness, courage, or spirit ⟨an *overripe* artist whose abstract paintings are no longer considered fresh or significant⟩ — see EFFETE 1

overrun *vb* **1** to enter for conquest or plunder ⟨waves of barbarians *overran* the Roman Empire during its long decline⟩ — see INVADE
2 to go beyond the limit of ⟨he must not *overrun* his authority as governor⟩ — see EXCEED
3 to spread or swarm over in a troublesome manner ⟨ants are *overrunning* the garden⟩ — see INFEST

oversee *vb* **1** to look after and make decisions about ⟨will *oversee* the new manufacturing division⟩ — see CONDUCT 1
2 to be in charge of ⟨looking for someone to *oversee* the project from start to finish⟩ — see BOSS 1
3 to take charge of especially on behalf of another ⟨*oversee* the household until Dad gets home⟩ — see [2]TEND 1
4 to look over closely (as for judging quality or condition) ⟨her job was to *oversee* each and every dish before it left the kitchen and was served to a customer⟩ — see INSPECT

oversexed *adj* having a strong sexual desire ⟨a raunchy movie comedy featuring the usual assortment of *oversexed* teenagers hoping to lose their virginity⟩ — see LUSTFUL

overshadow *vb* **1** to make dark, dim, or indistinct ⟨large trees *overshadow* the yard and darken the house for much of the day⟩ — see CLOUD 1
2 to be greater in importance than ⟨later you'll find that verbal skills *overshadow* any skills you have at video games⟩ — see OUTWEIGH

overshoot *vb* to go beyond the limit of ⟨don't worry if you *overshoot* the length requirement by three pages⟩ — see EXCEED 1

oversight *n* **1** the act or activity of looking after and making decisions about something ⟨*oversight* of the club's fund-raising activities⟩ — see CONDUCT 1
2 an unintentional departure from truth or accuracy ⟨claiming "three billion" instead of "three million" was just an *oversight*⟩ — see ERROR 1
3 the duty or function of watching or guarding for the sake of proper direction or control ⟨you'll have *oversight* of the troop until the scoutmaster returns⟩ — see SUPERVISION 1
4 the nonperformance of an assigned or expected ac-

tion ⟨failing to lock the car can be an expensive *oversight* if it gets stolen⟩ — see FAILURE 1

oversize *or* **oversized** *adj* **1** unusually large ⟨the woman's *oversize* hat was blocking my view of the minister⟩ — see HUGE

2 of a size greater than average of its kind ⟨a softball is an *oversize* and less densely stuffed baseball⟩ — see LARGE 1

overspread *vb* **1** to form a layer over ⟨the butter should evenly *overspread* the baking pan⟩ — see COVER 2

2 to lie over parts of one another ⟨autumn leaves *overspreading* one another on the lawn to form a colorful mosaic⟩ — see OVERLAP

overstate *vb* to describe or express in too strong terms ⟨it appears you've somewhat *overstated* your computer skills, if you can't find the "on" button!⟩

synonyms exaggerate, overdo, overdraw, put on

related words color, elaborate, embellish, embroider, magnify, pad, play up, stretch; fudge, hedge; melodramatize, overemphasize, overplay, sensationalize

near antonyms belittle, minimize, play down

antonyms understate

overstatement *n* the representation of something in terms that go beyond the facts ⟨a claim to worldwide fame is a bit of an *overstatement* on the part of that nightclub⟩ — see EXAGGERATION

overstep *vb* to go beyond the limit of ⟨the principal *overstepped* her authority in ordering everyone to remain in the unheated school⟩ — see EXCEED 1

oversupply *n* the state or an instance of going beyond what is usual, proper, or needed ⟨an *oversupply* of new homes is helping to drive down housing prices⟩ — see EXCESS 1

overtake *vb* to move fast enough to get even with ⟨she had to hurry to *overtake* her friends, who had forgotten their umbrellas⟩ ⟨the thunderstorm *overtook* them suddenly⟩

synonyms catch, catch up (with), overhaul

related words chase, pursue; gain, reach; pass, surpass

near antonyms fall short

over–the–hill *adj* being of advanced years and especially past middle age ⟨the overwhelming majority of that rock band's fans are *over-the-hill* baby boomers on a nostalgia trip⟩ — see ELDERLY

overthrow *n* failure to win a contest ⟨the surprising *overthrow* of the world's top-ranked chess player⟩ — see DEFEAT 1

overtop *vb* to be greater, better, or stronger than ⟨a manager whose arrogance was *overtopped* only by his ineptitude⟩ — see SURPASS 1

overture *n* a performance, activity, or event that precedes and sets the stage for the main event ⟨the parade down Main Street served as the *overture* for a weekend of fun and festivities⟩ — see PRELUDE 1

overturn *vb* to turn on one's side or upside down ⟨afraid that my kayak would *overturn*⟩ — see CAPSIZE

overuse *vb* to use so much as to make less appealing ⟨she had *overused* that joke to the point where it was eliciting groans and not guffaws⟩ — see HACKNEY

overvalue *vb* to place too high a value on ⟨some people *overvalue* material things⟩ — see OVERESTIMATE

overweening *adj* **1** having too high an opinion of oneself ⟨a director who has little patience for *overweening* actors who think they are above taking advice and criticism⟩ — see CONCEITED

2 going beyond a normal or acceptable limit in degree or amount ⟨*overweening* desire for wealth and fame⟩ — see EXCESSIVE

3 having a feeling of superiority that shows itself in an overbearing attitude ⟨an *overweening* administrator who simply doesn't know how to manage people⟩ — see ARROGANT

4 extended beyond normal or realistic bounds ⟨an *overweening* national pride that prompted its citizens to denigrate other countries⟩ — see BLOATED 1

overweigh *vb* to be greater in importance than ⟨proper food and sleep should *overweigh* all-night partying in your priorities⟩ — see OUTWEIGH

overweight *adj* having an excess of body fat ⟨an *overweight* person who had difficulty running even a short distance⟩ — see FAT 1

overwhelm *vb* **1** to subject to incapacitating emotional or mental stress ⟨just the thought of how much work there is to do *overwhelms* me⟩

synonyms crush, devastate, floor, grind (down), oppress, overcome, overmaster, overpower, prostrate, snow under, swamp, whelm

related words deluge, drown, sink; confute, defeat, refute; break, demoralize, distress, disturb, rock, shatter, stagger, throw, unman, unnerve, upset

2 to cover with a flood ⟨that spring the massive runoff from melting snows *overwhelmed* the valley⟩ — see FLOOD

over with *adj* brought or having come to an end ⟨we'll all be glad when this latest media obsession is *over with*⟩ — see COMPLETE 2

overwrought *adj* **1** being in a state of increased activity or agitation ⟨became *overwrought* when she heard that her child was missing⟩ — see FEVERISH 1

2 elaborately and often excessively decorated ⟨the author's prose is *overwrought* with purple passages and florid metaphors⟩ — see ORNATE 1

ovoid *adj* having the shape of an egg ⟨an *ovoid* toy that the baby couldn't tip over⟩ — see OVAL

owed *adj* not yet paid ⟨finally paid the *owed* amount⟩ — see OUTSTANDING 1

owing *adj* not yet paid ⟨there's one bill still *owing*⟩ — see OUTSTANDING 1

owing to *prep* as the result of ⟨*owing to* the extra snow days this year, we'll have to run an additional two days into June⟩ — see BECAUSE OF

own *vb* to keep, control, or experience as one's own ⟨we *own* a modest house and an equally modest car⟩ — see HAVE 1

own (up) *vb* to make an acknowledgment of something unpleasant as true or valid ⟨had a strong suspicion about which coworker stole her food from the office fridge, but the likely culprit refused to *own up*⟩ — see CONFESS 1

own (up to) *vb* to accept the truth or existence of (something) usually reluctantly ⟨*owned up to* damaging the car⟩ — see ADMIT 1

owner *n* one who has a legal or rightful claim to ownership ⟨the *owner* of the building will have to decide whether or not to sell⟩ — see PROPRIETOR

P

pa *n* a male human parent ⟨I cherish my memories of the times that I went fishing with my *pa*⟩ — see FATHER 1

pabulum *n* something that maintains or stimulates the intellect ⟨we have reached a cultural low if reality television is regarded as *pabulum* for the masses⟩ — see SUSTENANCE

pace *vb* **1** to move along with a steady regular step especially in a group ⟨six jugglers *paced* neatly alongside one another in the parade⟩ — see MARCH 1
2 to move forward along a course ⟨the couple *paced* through the motions of a marriage, but it was never more than a financial and social arrangement⟩ — see GO 1

pacemaker *n* one that takes the lead or sets an example ⟨has long been regarded as a *pacemaker* in home electronics⟩ — see BELLWETHER

pacer *n* one that takes the lead or sets an example ⟨a highly competitive industry in which any company that isn't a *pacer* quickly becomes a belly-up also-ran⟩ — see BELLWETHER

pacesetter *n* one that takes the lead or sets an example ⟨a company that has been a *pacesetter* in its field for offering health care benefits to employees⟩ — see BELLWETHER

pachydermatous *adj* having or showing a lack of sympathy or tender feelings ⟨a *pachydermatous* pop diva with little regard for punctuality or other people's schedules⟩ — see HARD 1

pacific *adj* **1** tending to lessen or avoid conflict or hostility ⟨as a *pacific* gesture, we invited our feuding neighbors to our backyard barbecue⟩
synonyms appeasing, conciliating, conciliatory, disarming, mollifying, pacifying, peacemaking, placating, placatory, propitiatory
related words endearing, ingratiating, winning, winsome; peaceable, peaceful; nonbelligerent, unaggressive, unassertive; calming, comforting, lulling, quieting, relaxing, soothing, tranquilizing (*also* tranquillizing); obliging, satisfying; affable, agreeable, amiable, amicable, benevolent, genial, gentle, good-natured, good-tempered, kind, kindly; passive, submissive, surrendering, yielding
near antonyms abrasive, aggravating, annoying, chafing, exasperating, frustrating, galling, inflammatory, irksome, irritating, maddening, nagging, nettlesome, nettling, offensive, provocative, provoking, rankling, riling, vexing; engaging, incensing, infuriating, maddening; antagonistic, antipathetic, hostile, inhospitable, inimical, unfriendly, unsympathetic; aggressive, agonistic, argumentative, assertive, bellicose, belligerent, combative, confrontational, contentious, pugnacious, quarrelsome, scrappy, truculent; martial, militant, militaristic, military, warlike
antonyms antagonizing
2 inclined to live in peace and to avoid war ⟨a *pacific* nation that has managed to remain neutral even during times of world conflict⟩ — see PEACEFUL 1

pacifist *n* a person who opposes war or warlike policies ⟨a committed *pacifist*, Gandhi succeeded in bringing about Indian independence using only nonviolence⟩ — see DOVE 1

pacifist *or* **pacifistic** *adj* inclined to live in peace and to avoid war ⟨the newspaper's editorial board has clearly staked out a *pacifist* position on the current conflict⟩ — see PEACEFUL 1

pacify *vb* **1** to lessen the anger or agitation of ⟨the only thing that would *pacify* the child and end the tantrum was a new toy⟩
synonyms appease, assuage, conciliate, disarm, gentle, mollify, placate, propitiate
related words calm, comfort, console, content, hush, quiet, soothe, tranquilize (*also* tranquillize); endear (to), ingratiate; delight, gladden, gratify, please; adulate, blarney, flatter, overpraise, soft-soap; quench, sate, satiate, satisfy; cater (to), humor, indulge; blandish, cajole, coax, sweet-talk, wheedle; baby, coddle, mollycoddle, pamper, spoil; dulcify, sweeten
near antonyms aggravate, annoy, antagonize, bother, bug, burn (up), chafe, cross, exasperate, gall, get, grate, irk, irritate, nettle, peeve, pique, put out, rankle, rile, roil, ruffle, vex; provoke, rouse; harass, harry, persecute, pester; agitate, discomfort, distress, disturb, fret, perturb, unhinge, unsettle, upset, worry; affront, insult, offend, slight
antonyms anger, enrage, incense, inflame (*also* enflame), infuriate, ire, madden, outrage
2 to bring under one's control by force of arms ⟨additional ground forces were needed to occupy those areas that had already been *pacified*⟩ — see CONQUER 1

pacifying *adj* **1** tending to calm the emotions and relieve stress ⟨a *pacifying* treat of milk and cookies⟩ — see SOOTHING 1
2 tending to lessen or avoid conflict or hostility ⟨the referee adopted a *pacifying* tone to try to calm everyone down⟩ — see PACIFIC 1

pack *n* **1** a soft-sided case designed for carrying belongings especially on the back ⟨part of basic training is becoming accustomed to taking very long hikes with an 80-pound *pack*⟩
synonyms backpack, kit bag, knapsack, packsack, rucksack
related words haversack; carryall, carry-on, grip, handbag, holdall [*chiefly British*], portmanteau, suitcase, traveling bag; fanny pack, school bag, seabag; overnight bag, overnight case, weekend bag
2 a wrapped or sealed case containing an item or set of items ⟨she tucked a small *pack* of lozenges into her bag⟩ — see PACKAGE 1
3 a considerable amount ⟨it took a *pack* of courage to stand up before that crowd and tell the truth⟩ — see LOT 2
4 a group of people sharing a common interest and relating together socially ⟨had run with a *pack* of hotrodders when he was in high school⟩ — see GANG 2

pack *vb* **1** to close up so that no empty spaces remain ⟨carefully *pack* the food containers so we'll have as much as possible for the picnic⟩ — see FILL 2
2 to put into (something) as much as can be held or contained ⟨I had *packed* the suitcase so tightly that it wouldn't close⟩ — see FILL 1
3 to support and take from one place to another ⟨remember to *pack* several changes of clothing⟩ — see CARRY 1
4 to wear or have on one's person ⟨a private detective *packing* a weapon⟩ — see CARRY 2

pack (off) *vb* to cause to go or be taken from one place to another ⟨*packed* the child *off* to a good boarding school⟩ — see SEND

pack (up *or* in) *vb* **1** to bring (as an action or operation) to an immediate end ⟨the auto company is downsizing and will be *packing up* operations at the local plant⟩ — see STOP 1
2 to stop doing (something) permanently ⟨after two years of college, he decided to *pack in* that academic stuff and join the army⟩ — see QUIT 2

pack (up *or* off) *vb* to leave a place often for another ⟨with the dinner conversation becoming more and more desultory, the time had clearly come to *pack off*⟩ — see GO 2

package *n* **1** a wrapped or sealed case containing an item or set of items ⟨got a job sorting *packages* in the mail room⟩
synonyms bundle, pack, packet, parcel
related words bag, poke [*chiefly Southern & Midland*], pouch, sack; bale; box, container, crate
2 a number of things considered as a unit ⟨ate a whole *package* of cookies at once⟩ — see GROUP 1

packed *adj* **1** containing or seeming to contain the greatest quantity or number possible ⟨the auditorium was *packed*⟩ — see FULL 1
2 having little space between items or parts ⟨a densely *packed* sequence of events⟩ — see CLOSE 1

packet *n* **1** a wrapped or sealed case containing an item or set of items ⟨a *packet* of letters that her husband wrote while he was in the army⟩ — see PACKAGE 1
2 *British* the money paid regularly to a person for labor or services ⟨of course your wage *packet* for the London job will be bigger, given the city's high cost of living⟩ — see WAGE
3 *chiefly British* a very large amount of money ⟨that town house in Mayfair cost a *packet*⟩ — see FORTUNE 2

packsack *n* a soft-sided case designed for carrying belongings especially on the back ⟨she spent weeks traveling across Europe and living out of a *packsack*⟩ — see PACK 1

pact *n* **1** a formal agreement between two or more nations or peoples ⟨a *pact* between the two small nations to defend one another in case of attack⟩ — see TREATY
2 an arrangement about action to be taken ⟨they made a *pact* to meet every week at the same time⟩ — see AGREEMENT 2

pad *n* **1** a number of sheets of writing paper glued together at one edge ⟨we'll need to buy a new *pad* for telephone messages soon⟩
synonyms notepad, tablet
related words scratch pad; album, notebook, scrapbook; booklet, pamphlet
2 a place set aside for sleeping ⟨I went back to my *pad* to get some rest⟩ — see BED 1
3 something that serves as a protective barrier ⟨a *pad* on the chair to keep it from getting scratched⟩ — see CUSHION
4 the place where one lives ⟨welcome to my *pad*⟩ — see HOME 1

[1]**pad** *vb* to add to the interest of by including made-up details ⟨the journalist was fired for *padding* certain stories to make them more interesting⟩ — see EMBROIDER

[2]**pad** *vb* to go on foot ⟨a cat *padded* silently by⟩ — see WALK 1

padding *n* **1** soft material that is used to fill the hollow parts of something ⟨the *padding* is leaking out of that pillow⟩ — see FILLING
2 the representation of something in terms that go beyond the facts ⟨that feature writer is sometimes guilty of *padding*, but he keeps it from getting out of hand⟩ — see EXAGGERATION

paddle *vb* **1** to move a boat by means of oars ⟨I like to *paddle* on the river for exercise and relaxation⟩ — see [1]ROW
2 to strike repeatedly ⟨back in those times it was acceptable for teachers to *paddle* misbehaving students⟩ — see BEAT 1

paean *n* a formal expression of praise ⟨his retirement party featured many *paeans* for his long years of service to the company⟩ — see ENCOMIUM

pagan *n* a person who does not worship the God of the Bible ⟨the Spanish conquistadores regarded the native peoples of the lands that they conquered as *pagans* who were uncivilized and inherently inferior⟩ — see HEATHEN 1

page *n* one that carries a message or does an errand ⟨dispatch a *page* to bring coffee to the senator⟩ — see MESSENGER

pageant *n* **1** a staged presentation often with music that consists of a procession of narrated or enacted scenes ⟨we always put on a Christmas *pageant* every year⟩
synonyms cavalcade
related words tableau; kaleidoscope, montage, panorama; drama, dramatization, play; demonstration, performance, presentation, production; exhibition, extravaganza, show, spectacle; parade, procession, progress
2 an elaborate, visually exciting show or event ⟨an annual summertime *pageant* depicting the town's founding and colorful early history⟩ — see EXTRAVAGANZA

pail *n* a round container that is open at the top and outfitted with a handle ⟨fetch me a *pail* full of water, please⟩
synonyms bucket
related words cauldron, kettle, pot; canteen, flagon, jar, jug, pitcher; bail, hod; tank, tub, vat; holder, receptacle, vessel

pain *n* **1** a sharp unpleasant sensation usually felt in some specific part of the body ⟨the child was crying because of a *pain* in her knee⟩
synonyms ache, pang, prick, shoot, smart, sting, stitch, throe, tingle, twinge
related words discomfort, distress, soreness, tenderness; affliction, agony, anguish, misery, sufferance, suffering, torment, torture; inflammation, sore, swelling; damage, detriment, harm, hurt, injury; backache, bellyache, charley horse, colic, complaint, earache, gripe, headache, stomachache, toothache
near antonyms comfort, ease, easiness
2 a state of great suffering of body or mind ⟨a sprained ankle caused him great *pain* for a week⟩ — see DISTRESS 1
3 pains *pl* strict attentiveness to what one is doing ⟨take *pains* to be sure that you don't damage anything while moving the furniture⟩ — see CARE 1
4 pains *pl* the active use of energy in producing a result ⟨she was at *pains* to reassure us that everything would be fine⟩ — see EFFORT
5 one who is obnoxiously annoying ⟨sometimes that child, who apparently never tires of asking questions, can be such a *pain*⟩ — see NUISANCE 1

pain *vb* to feel or cause physical pain ⟨my poor head was *paining* so from all that racket⟩ — see HURT 1

painful *adj* **1** causing or feeling bodily pain ⟨her broken arm was too *painful* for her to go on the trip⟩
synonyms aching, achy, afflictive, hurting, nasty, sore
related words agonizing, excruciating, torturous; damaging, deleterious, detrimental, harmful, hurtful, injurious, noxious, pernicious; raw, tender; bleeding, burning, chafing, cramping, festering; itching, nagging, pinching, pricking, prickling, smarting, stinging; inflamed (*also* enflamed), swollen; grievous, severe, threatening, wounding
near antonyms curative, healing, helping, remedial
antonyms indolent, painless
2 hard to accept or bear especially emotionally ⟨it's been very *painful* to accept that my father is gone forever⟩ — see BITTER 2

painfully *adv* with feelings of bitterness or grief ⟨*painfully* she recounted the years of physical abuse she had received at his hands⟩ — see HARD 2

painkiller *n* something (as a drug) that relieves pain ⟨a lot of *painkillers* have turned out to be addictive substances for patients⟩
synonyms analgesic, anesthetic, anodyne
related words sedative, tranquilizer (*also* tranquillizer); narcotic, opiate

painless *adj* involving minimal difficulty or effort ⟨getting paid to watch and review movies seems like a *painless* way to earn a living⟩ — see EASY 1

painlessly *adv* without difficulty ⟨the move to our new house was accomplished rather *painlessly*⟩ — see EASILY 1

painstaking *adj* taking, showing, or involving great care and effort ⟨she was always *painstaking* about her work⟩
synonyms careful, conscientious, fussy, loving, meticulous, scrupulous
related words assiduous, diligent, indefatigable, persevering, sedulous; exhaustive, thorough, thoroughgoing; alert, attentive, observant, vigilant, watchful; accurate, exact, precise, strict; critical, demanding, discriminating, exacting, fastidious, finicky, particular; cautious, chary, circumspect, gingerly, guarded, heedful, mindful, wary; deliberate, plodding, slow; studied, thoughtful; all-out, determined, dogged, intensive, patient, tenacious, tireless, zealous
near antonyms cursory, halfhearted; heedless, inattentive, incautious, mindless, regardless, unguarded, unsafe, unwary; lax, neglectful, negligent, slipshod, sloppy, slovenly; imprecise; inaccurate, uncritical, undemanding, undiscriminating; bold, impetuous, rash, reckless; apathetic, indifferent, lackadaisical, lazy, lazyish
antonyms careless

paint *n* preparations intended to beautify the face ⟨a woman of a certain age, as they say, who refuses to be seen in public without her *paint*⟩ — see MAKEUP 1

paint *vb* **1** to give a representation or account of in words ⟨the description *painted* a perfect image of the sun setting over the ocean⟩ — see DESCRIBE 1
2 to give color or a different color to ⟨I've decided to *paint* the bathroom walls purple⟩ — see COLOR 1

painting *n* a picture created with oil paint ⟨the *Mona Lisa* is a haunting *painting* of a woman with a most mysterious smile⟩
synonyms canvas (*also* canvass), oil, oil painting
related words fresco, mural, panorama; diptych, triptych; acrylic, aquarelle, gouache, watercolor; distemper, drawing, etching, finger painting, pastel, sketch, tempera; masterpiece; pièce de résistance, showpiece

pair *n* two things of the same or similar kind that match or are considered together ⟨a *pair* of blue socks⟩ ⟨the cheerleader and the computer nerd make quite a *pair* together⟩
synonyms brace, couple, couplet, duo, dyad, twain, twosome
related words span, yoke; partnership, team; companion, complement, doublet, fellow, half, match, mate, twin; coordinate, counterpart, equal, equivalent, like, parallel, peer, rival

pal *n* a person who has a strong liking for and trust in another ⟨I always choose my best *pal* for my softball team first⟩ — see FRIEND 1

pal (around) *vb* to come or be together as friends ⟨they began to *pal around* after discovering that they both had kids on the same soccer team⟩ — see ASSOCIATE 1

palace *adj* showing obvious signs of wealth and comfort ⟨a *palace* railroad car that was built for a 19th-century robber baron⟩ — see LUXURIOUS 1

palace *n* **1** a large impressive residence ⟨the billionaire's "summer cottage" turned out to be an over-the-top *palace*⟩ — see MANSION
2 a large, magnificent, or massive building ⟨the governor's opponents have accused him of building *palaces* to house the state government⟩ — see EDIFICE 1
3 the residence of a ruler ⟨Buckingham *Palace* flies a special flag to indicate when the monarch is in residence⟩ — see COURT 1

paladin *n* a person who actively supports or favors a cause ⟨an idealistic *paladin* seeking better treatment for the homeless⟩ — see EXPONENT 1

palatability *n* the quality of being delicious ⟨military rations that were obviously chosen for their durability and not their *palatability*⟩ — see DELICIOUSNESS

palatable *adj* **1** being to one's liking ⟨I did not find the idea of moving again very *palatable*⟩ — see SATISFACTORY 1
2 giving pleasure or contentment to the mind or senses ⟨I always associate the *palatable* aroma of roasting turkey with Thanksgiving⟩ — see PLEASANT 1
3 very pleasing to the sense of taste ⟨the vegetarian version of that classic dish turned out to be surprisingly *palatable*⟩ — see DELICIOUS 1

palatableness *n* the quality of being delicious ⟨a dish whose inventiveness greatly exceeded its *palatableness*⟩ — see DELICIOUSNESS

palatably *adv* in a pleasing way ⟨the musical play *palatably* combines sophisticated wit and tender romance⟩ — see WELL 5

palatial *adj* showing obvious signs of wealth and comfort ⟨a *palatial* penthouse apartment⟩ — see LUXURIOUS 1

palatially *adv* in a luxurious manner ⟨a premium membership in the club gives you exclusive access to a *palatially* appointed locker room and spa⟩ — see HIGH

palaver *n* **1** an exchange of views for the purpose of exploring a subject or deciding an issue ⟨seemingly endless *palaver* between the negotiating parties⟩ — see DISCUSSION 1
2 friendly, informal conversation or an instance of this ⟨we should get together and have a nice *palaver* sometime⟩ — see CHAT 1

palaver *vb* **1** to engage in casual or rambling conversation ⟨mothers *palavering* and drinking coffee while watching their children play⟩ — see CHAT 1
2 to get (someone) to do something by gentle urging, special attention, or flattery ⟨I let the salesclerk at the electronics store *palaver* me into a service contract that I didn't need⟩ — see COAX

pale *adj* **1** lacking intensity of color ⟨we chose a very *pale* pink for the walls of the room⟩
synonyms dull, dulled, faded, light, pastel, washed-out, washy
related words flat, lackluster, lusterless, matte (*also* mat *or* matt); dim, faint; dirty, muddy; achromatic, colorless, uncolored, undyed, unpainted, unstained; blanched, bleached, washed, white, whitened; gray (*also* grey), indistinct, neutral
near antonyms bright, brilliant, vibrant, vivid; chromatic, colored, dyed, painted, stained, tinged, tinted; colorful, motley, multicolored, polychromatic, polychrome, prismatic, rainbow, varicolored, variegated; flashy, garish, gaudy, loud, showy, splashy
antonyms dark, deep, gay, rich
2 lacking a healthy skin color ⟨after a week with the flu, she was deathly *pale* and noticeably thinner⟩
synonyms ashen, ashy, blanched, cadaverous, doughy, livid, lurid, mealy, paled, pallid, pasty, peaked, wan
related words sallow, sallowish, sick, sickly, waxen, waxy; white, whitened; anemic, bloodless; untanned; whey-faced, white-faced

near antonyms blushing, flushed, pink
antonyms blooming, florid, flush, full-blooded, glowing, red, rosy, rubicund, ruddy, sanguine
3 not seen or understood clearly ⟨a *pale* outline off in the distance proved to be someone out for a walk⟩ — see FAINT 1

pale *vb* to make white or whiter by removing color ⟨the sun eventually *paled* my bright blue shirt⟩ — see WHITEN

paled *adj* lacking a healthy skin color ⟨the shock of the news left him *paled* and shaking⟩ — see PALE 2

paleoconservative *adj* tending to favor established ideas, conditions, or institutions ⟨members of the religious sect are positively *paleoconservative* in their beliefs on the proper role of women⟩ — see CONSERVATIVE 1

paleoconservative *n* a person whose political beliefs are centered on tradition and keeping things the way they are ⟨*paleoconservatives* who would never sanction gambling casinos in their state⟩ — see CONSERVATIVE

palisade *n* a steep wall of rock, earth, or ice ⟨the *palisades* that line the west bank of the Hudson River for about 15 miles⟩ — see CLIFF

pall *n* **1** a boxlike container for holding a dead body ⟨bearing her husband's *pall* were her four brothers and two nephews⟩ — see COFFIN
2 an overspreading element that produces an atmosphere of gloom ⟨a persistent *pall* of distrust has overtaken this administration and will remain until the president resigns⟩ — see CLOUD
3 something that covers or conceals like a piece of cloth ⟨a *pall* of gloom overshadowed the failing theater's last production⟩ — see CLOAK 1

pall *vb* to grow less in scope or intensity especially gradually ⟨viewers' interest in the reality show eventually *palled*⟩ — see DECREASE 2

palladium *n* a measure taken to preclude loss or injury ⟨believes that a vigorously free press is one of our nation's most vital *palladia* against tyranny⟩ — see PRECAUTION

palliate *vb* **1** to make (something) seem less bad by offering excuses ⟨don't try to *palliate* your constant lying by claiming that everybody lies⟩
synonyms deodorize, excuse, explain away, extenuate, gloss (over), gloze (over), whitewash
related words sugarcoat, varnish; apologize, atone, confess; account (for), explain, justify, rationalize; minimize, play down, soft-pedal; alleviate, ease, lessen, lighten, mitigate, moderate, soften, temper; absolve, acquit, clear, exculpate, exonerate, vindicate
2 to make more bearable or less severe ⟨this medicine should *palliate* your cough at least a little⟩ — see HELP 2

pallid *adj* lacking a healthy skin color ⟨a *pallid* man who looked as though he'd never seen the sun⟩ — see PALE 2

palm *n* an instance of defeating an enemy or opponent ⟨the judges' decision was unanimous: the *palm* would go to the pianist who had played an early piece by Chopin⟩ — see VICTORY

palm *vb* to offer (something fake, useless, or inferior) as genuine, useful, or valuable ⟨another low-rent company trying to *palm* cheesy merchandise upon mail-order customers⟩ — see FOIST

palm off *vb* to offer (something fake, useless, or inferior) as genuine, useful, or valuable ⟨please stop trying to *palm off* your leftovers onto me⟩ — see FOIST

palmy *adj* **1** having attained a desired end or state of good fortune ⟨they knew her in her *palmy* days when she was living high⟩ — see SUCCESSFUL 1
2 marked by vigorous growth and well-being especially economically ⟨a *palmy* suburb with lots of new homes and shopping malls⟩ — see PROSPEROUS 1

palooka *n* a big clumsy often slow-witted person ⟨I wish he wouldn't bring over here that bunch of *palookas* he calls his friends⟩ — see OAF 1

palpable *adj* **1** able to be perceived by a sense or by the mind ⟨the tension in the negotiating room was *palpable*⟩ — see PERCEPTIBLE
2 capable of being perceived by the sense of touch ⟨a small but *palpable* lump in my neck⟩ — see TANGIBLE
3 not subject to misinterpretation or more than one interpretation ⟨a *palpable* case of lying under oath⟩ — see CLEAR 2

palpitate *vb* to expand and contract in a rhythmic manner ⟨the man's heart began to *palpitate*, and he feared another attack was coming on⟩ — see PULSATE

palpitation *n* a rhythmic expanding and contracting ⟨a *palpitation* of the blood vessels⟩ — see PULSATION

palsy *adj* having or showing kindly feeling and sincere interest ⟨the salesman changed his *palsy* attitude when he realized that I wasn't buying⟩ — see FRIENDLY 1

palsy *n* complete or partial loss of physical function (as motion or sensation) in a part of the body ⟨*palsy* can sometimes be caused by a brain injury⟩ — see PARALYSIS

palsy–walsy *adj, slang* having or showing kindly feeling and sincere interest ⟨she's gotten very *palsy-walsy* with the boss all of a sudden⟩ — see FRIENDLY 1

palter *vb* to talk over or dispute the terms of a purchase ⟨unwilling to *palter* over the price of the car⟩ — see BARGAIN 1

paltry *adj* **1** arousing or deserving of one's loathing and disgust ⟨a *paltry*, underhanded scheme to get someone fired⟩ — see CONTEMPTIBLE 1
2 falling short of a standard ⟨the hotel's shabby, outdated exercise room was its *paltry* attempt at a health spa⟩ — see BAD 1
3 not following or in accordance with standards of honor and decency ⟨just some *paltry* ruse to bilk the system⟩ — see IGNOBLE 2
4 so small or unimportant as to warrant little or no attention ⟨wanted me to sell him my old records for a *paltry* sum⟩ — see NEGLIGIBLE 1

pampa *n* a broad area of level or rolling treeless country ⟨a folktale about gauchos on the *pampas*⟩ — see PLAIN 1

pamper *vb* to treat with great or excessive care ⟨*pamper* a sick child⟩ — see BABY

pamphlet *n* a short printed publication with no cover or with a paper cover ⟨*pamphlets* about common safety precautions that we all can put into use⟩
synonyms booklet, brochure, circular, flyer (*also* flier), folder, leaflet
related words dodger, flysheet, handbill, handout, throwaway; advertisement, catalog (*or* catalogue), shopper; tract; paperback, paperbound, pocket book; guidebook, handbook, how-to, instructions, manual

pan *n, slang* the front part of the head ⟨hey, I could do without seeing your ugly *pan* for a few days⟩ — see FACE 1

pan *vb* to express one's unfavorable opinion of the worth or quality of ⟨virtually all the movie critics have *panned* this latest sequel in a tired series⟩ — see CRITICIZE

panacea *n* something that cures all ills or problems ⟨a woman who seems to believe that chicken soup is a *panacea* for nearly everything⟩ — see CURE-ALL

pancake *n* a flat cake made from thin batter and cooked on both sides (as on a griddle) ⟨every Sunday morning, we have *pancakes* and bacon for breakfast⟩
synonyms flapjack, griddle cake, hotcake, slapjack
related words oatcake, wheat cake; blin, blintze (*or* blintz), crepe (*or* crêpe); waffle

pandemonium *n* **1** a state of noisy, confused activity ⟨Christmas morning at our house is always marked by *pandemonium*⟩ — see COMMOTION
2 *cap* the place of punishment for the wicked after death ⟨a surrealist painting in which all the torments of *Pandemonium* are vividly depicted⟩ — see HELL 1

pander *n* a man who solicits clients for a woman who is willing to engage in sexual activities for money ⟨an arrest record that revealed that he had variously been a *pander*, a pickpocket, and a drug dealer⟩ — see PIMP

panegyric *n* a formal expression of praise ⟨wrote a *panegyric* on the centennial of the Nobel laureate's birth⟩ — see ENCOMIUM

panel *n* **1** a meeting featuring a group discussion ⟨there will be a discussion *panel* on Tuesday⟩ — see FORUM 1
2 a select group of persons assigned to consider or take action on some matter ⟨assembled a prestigious *panel* to investigate ways to stem the rising cost of health care⟩ — see COMMITTEE

panel discussion *n* a meeting featuring a group discussion ⟨a *panel discussion* on capital punishment⟩ — see FORUM 1

pang *n* a sharp unpleasant sensation usually felt in some specific part of the body ⟨those hunger *pangs* that strike you in the middle of the afternoon⟩ — see PAIN 1

panhandler *n* a person who lives by public begging ⟨a *panhandler* asking for money to buy food⟩ — see BEGGAR

panic *n* the emotion experienced in the presence or threat of danger ⟨the sudden sight of a grizzly bear filled the hiker with *panic*⟩ — see FEAR 1

panic *vb* to strike with fear ⟨for some reason, the herd of feeding animals at the zoo *panicked* him⟩ — see FRIGHTEN

panorama *n* all that can be seen from a certain point ⟨we admired the breathtaking *panorama* from the top of the mountain⟩ — see VIEW 1

panoramic *adj* covering everything or all important points ⟨a *panoramic* look at America's fascination with the automobile⟩ — see ENCYCLOPEDIC

pan out *vb* **1** to come to be ⟨the eagerly anticipated kayaking trip never *panned out*⟩ — see COME OUT 1
2 to turn out as planned or desired ⟨the investment scheme didn't quite *pan out*⟩ — see SUCCEED 1

pant *vb* to breathe hard, quickly, or with difficulty ⟨the dog was *panting* heavily after his breakneck run across the field⟩ — see GASP

pant (after) *vb* to have an earnest wish to own or enjoy ⟨teenage gamers *panting after* the latest video game⟩ — see DESIRE 1

pantaloons *n pl* an outer garment covering each leg separately from waist to ankle ⟨loose-fitting cotton *pantaloons* that are designed to be worn as loungewear⟩ — see PANTS

panther *n* a large tawny cat of the wild ⟨the *panther* is surprisingly difficult to spot⟩ — see COUGAR

pantomime *n* **1** a movement of the body or limbs that expresses or emphasizes an idea or feeling ⟨the game requires that you use *pantomime* to communicate an idea⟩ — see GESTURE 1
2 an actor in a story performed silently and entirely by body movements ⟨in ancient Rome *pantomimes* performed tragic love stories⟩ — see MIME 1

pantomimist *n* an actor in a story performed silently and entirely by body movements ⟨an exquisitely graceful *pantomimist*⟩ — see MIME 1

pantry *n* a built-in space for storage behind a door ⟨homemade jams and pickles are stored in a separate *pantry* off the kitchen⟩ — see CLOSET 1

pants *n pl* an outer garment covering each leg separately from waist to ankle ⟨you'll need a nice pair of *pants* for the job interview⟩
synonyms breeches, britches, pantaloons, slacks, trousers
related words baggies, bell-bottoms, blue jeans, cargo pants, cords, corduroys, denims, jeans; hose, legging (*or* leggin), sweatpants; pants suit, pantsuit; bloomers, knee breeches, knickerbockers

papa *also* **poppa** *n* a male human parent ⟨a proud *papa* of newborn twins⟩ — see FATHER 1

paper *adj* being something in name or form only ⟨there's a *paper* boycott of that company's products that nobody seems to be honoring⟩ — see NOMINAL 1

paper *n* **1** a piece of paper with information written or to be written on it ⟨handed in the correct *papers*⟩ — see FORM 2
2 a publication that appears at regular intervals ⟨we get the *paper* every morning⟩ — see JOURNAL 1
3 a short piece of writing done as a school exercise ⟨write a *paper* about your favorite author⟩ — see COMPOSITION 2
4 a short piece of writing typically expressing a point of view ⟨the *papers* written by the Founding Fathers urging adoption of the federal constitution⟩ — see ESSAY 1

paper over *vb* **1** to dismiss as of little importance ⟨the differences between the two factions are too great to be *papered over* in the name of party unity⟩ — see EXCUSE 1
2 to keep secret or shut off from view ⟨the company tried to *paper over* its red ink, issuing assurances that it was still financially sound⟩ — see [1]HIDE 2

paper–thin *adj* being of less than usual width ⟨since the wall separating our cubicles is *paper-thin*, I get way too much information about my coworker's love life⟩ — see NARROW 1

papule *n* a small, inflamed swelling of the skin ⟨the reddish, itchy *papules* that are characteristic of the rash⟩ — see POCK

par *n* **1** something set up as an example against which others of the same type are compared ⟨that last dining experience was not quite up to *par*⟩ — see STANDARD 1
2 the state or fact of being exactly the same in number, amount, status, or quality ⟨these California wines are on a *par* with the best produced in Europe⟩ — see EQUIVALENCE
3 what is typical of a group, class, or series ⟨a pulse of 70 is *par* for people of that age group⟩ — see AVERAGE

parable *n* a story intended to teach a basic truth or moral about life ⟨the *parable* in which the repentant sinner is compared to the returning prodigal son who is welcomed home⟩ — see ALLEGORY

parade *n* a body of individuals moving along in an orderly and often ceremonial way ⟨a Fourth of July *parade*⟩ — see CORTEGE 2

parade *vb* **1** to move along with a steady regular step especially in a group ⟨the marching band *paraded* past jubilant crowds⟩ — see MARCH 1
2 to present so as to invite notice or attention ⟨intends to *parade* her expensive new dress at the party⟩ — see SHOW 1

paradigmatic *adj* constituting, serving as, or worthy of being a pattern to be imitated ⟨a *paradigmatic* essay in which the writer presents his point of view clearly and engagingly⟩ — see MODEL

paradise *n* **1** an often imaginary place or state of utter perfection and happiness ⟨an idealist who trotted the globe looking for *paradise*⟩
synonyms Camelot, Cockaigne, Eden, Elysium, empyrean, fantasyland, heaven, lotusland, never-never land, New Jerusalem, nirvana, promised land, Shangri-la, utopia, Zion (*also* Sion)
related words arcadia; dreamland, dreamworld, fairyland, wonderland; blessedness, bliss, blissfulness, euphoria, gladness, joy

phrases Garden of Eden
near antonyms fool's paradise
antonyms anti-utopia, dystopia, hell
2 a dwelling place of perfect happiness for the soul after death ⟨a firm belief that good people will be rewarded in *paradise*⟩ — see HEAVEN 1
3 a state of overwhelming usually pleasurable emotion ⟨that early stage of a romance when lovers are in *paradise*⟩ — see ECSTASY

paradox *n* someone or something with qualities or features that seem to conflict with one another ⟨the *paradox* of fighting a war for peace⟩ — see CONTRADICTION 1

paragon *n* someone of such unequaled perfection as to deserve imitation ⟨in Arthurian legend, Sir Galahad is depicted as the one knight who is a *paragon* of virtue⟩ — see IDEAL 1

parallel *adj* having qualities in common ⟨*parallel* lives of two friends who first met in college⟩ — see ALIKE

parallel *n* **1** a point which two or more things share in common ⟨her professor pointed out some *parallels* between the two novels⟩ — see SIMILARITY 2
2 one that is equal to another in status, achievement, or value ⟨an advance that is without *parallel* in the history of virology⟩ — see EQUAL

parallel *vb* to be the exact counterpart of ⟨developments in the television show *paralleled* those in the lead actor's real life⟩ — see MATCH 1

parallelism *n* the quality or state of having many qualities in common ⟨the striking *parallelism* between the two crimes got police to thinking that they were committed by the same mastermind⟩ — see SIMILARITY 1

paralysis *n* complete or partial loss of physical function (as motion or sensation) in a part of the body ⟨the car accident left one athlete with *paralysis* from the waist down⟩
synonyms palsy
related words cerebral palsy, multiple sclerosis, poliomyelitis; debilitation, debility, decrepitude, enfeeblement, feebleness, frailness, frailty, weakness; infirmity, lameness; disability, impairment; diplegia, hemiplegia, paraplegia, paresis, quadriplegia, spastic paralysis
near antonyms mobility, motility, sensation

paralytic *adj* affected with paralysis ⟨at first, he would not accept that he was now *paralytic* and needed help⟩
synonyms paralyzed
related words challenged, crippled, disabled, maimed, mutilated; halt, hobbled, lame, lamed; impaired, incapacitated; hamstrung; hemiplegic, paraplegic, paretic, quadriplegic; debilitated, decrepit, enfeebled, feeble, frail, infirm, wasted, weak, weakened
near antonyms able-bodied; fit, hale, healthy, hearty, robust, sound, well, whole

paralyze *vb* **1** to render powerless, ineffective, or unable to move ⟨a blizzard *paralyzed* the city for two days⟩
synonyms cripple, disable, hamstring, immobilize, incapacitate, prostrate
related words attenuate, debilitate, enervate, enfeeble, sap, tire, undercut, undermine, weaken; hobble, lame; maim, mutilate; knock out
near antonyms energize, galvanize, invigorate, vitalize; fortify, strengthen; empower; freshen, refresh, refreshen, regenerate, rejuvenate, restore, revitalize, revive
2 to deprive of courage or confidence ⟨the school board is *paralyzed* by the threat of lawsuits for just about everything⟩ — see UNNERVE 1

paralyzed *adj* **1** affected with paralysis ⟨special ramps for *paralyzed* people in wheelchairs⟩ — see PARALYTIC
2 unable to act or achieve one's purpose ⟨a seemingly *paralyzed* mayor sat by as the city's crime rate soared⟩ — see POWERLESS

paramount *adj* **1** coming before all others in importance ⟨the *paramount* goal is to restore the colonial-era house with complete historical accuracy⟩ — see FOREMOST 1
2 of the greatest or highest degree or quantity ⟨maintaining the secrecy of the agreement is of *paramount* importance⟩ — see ULTIMATE 1

paramountcy *n* the fact or state of being above others in rank or importance ⟨a nation that has long enjoyed economic *paramountcy* in the region⟩ — see EMINENCE 1

paranormal *adj* of, relating to, or being part of a reality beyond the observable physical universe ⟨there are rumors that the old deserted mansion is the site of *paranormal* activity⟩ — see SUPERNATURAL 1

paraphernalia *n* **1** items needed for the performance of a task or activity ⟨mountain-climbing *paraphernalia*⟩ — see EQUIPMENT
2 transportable items that one owns ⟨packed up all of their *paraphernalia* for the move across the country⟩ — see POSSESSION 2

paraphrase *n* an instance of expressing something in different words ⟨your essays on human rights should have some original thought and not be simply a *paraphrase* of what's in the textbook⟩
synonyms rephrasing, restatement, restating, rewording, translating, translation
related words rehash; abstract, recap, recapitulation, reiteration, summary
near antonyms copy, transcript, transcription
antonyms quotation, quote

paraphrase *vb* to express something (as a text or statement) in different words ⟨could you *paraphrase* your diagnosis of my medical condition, using simpler language?⟩
synonyms rephrase, restate, reword, translate
related words boil down, recapitulate, reiterate, summarize, sum up
near antonyms echo, repeat; copy, reproduce, transcribe
antonyms quote

parasite *n* a person who is supported by or seeks support from another without making an adequate return ⟨a *parasite* who lived in the family's basement and refused to get a job or pay rent⟩ — see LEECH

parboil *vb* to cook in a liquid heated to the point that it gives off steam ⟨*parboil* a lobster⟩ — see BOIL 2

parcel *n* **1** a number of things considered as a unit ⟨her absurd explanation for the collision was a *parcel* of lies⟩ — see GROUP 1
2 a small area of usually open land ⟨wandered around the little *parcel* out back⟩ — see FIELD 1
3 a small piece of land that is developed or available for development ⟨subdivided the huge farm into smaller *parcels* for sale⟩ — see LOT 1
4 a usually small number of persons considered as a unit ⟨a *parcel* of kids trailing at their heels⟩ — see GROUP 2
5 a wrapped or sealed case containing an item or set of items ⟨received a mysterious *parcel* in the mail⟩ — see PACKAGE 1

parcel (out) *vb* to give out (something) to appropriate individuals ⟨*parceled out* the assignments for work on the parish fair⟩ — see ADMINISTER 1

parcel post *n* communications or parcels sent or carried through the postal system ⟨only *parcel post* bearing a return address and not exceeding size and weight limits will be accepted⟩ — see MAIL

parch *vb* to make dry ⟨the heat has really *parched* my throat⟩ — see DRY 1

pardon *n* release from the guilt or penalty of an offense ⟨the criminal is hoping for a presidential *pardon*⟩
synonyms absolution, amnesty, forgiveness, remission, remittal
related words parole; acquittal, exculpation, exoneration, vindication; condonation; exemption, immunity, impunity, indemnity; commutation, commuting, reprieve; clemency, leniency, mercy
near antonyms conviction, sentence; assessment, charge, fine, imposition, levying; castigation, chastening, chastisement, condemnation
antonyms penalty, punishment, retribution

pardon *vb* **1** to cease to have feelings of anger or bitterness toward ⟨he eventually *pardoned* his sister for interfering in his marriage⟩ — see FORGIVE 1
2 to dismiss as of little importance ⟨I'm willing to *pardon* a little sloppiness of dress in such a kind and loving person⟩ — see EXCUSE 1

pardonable *adj* worthy of forgiveness ⟨the new parents' gushing pride was *pardonable*⟩ — see VENIAL

pare *vb* to make (something) shorter or smaller with the use of a cutting instrument ⟨*pared* the stray branches on the tree⟩ — see CLIP 1

parentage *n* the line of ancestors from whom a person is descended ⟨they were pleased that their son's girlfriend was of good *parentage*⟩ — see ANCESTRY

parenthesis *n* a break in continuity ⟨regarded her husband's brief fling with a coworker as no more than a *parethesis* in an otherwise solid marriage⟩ — see GAP 2

parenthood *n* the caring for a child by its parents ⟨*parenthood* is a difficult task requiring great commitment⟩ — see PARENTING

parenting *n* the caring for a child by its parents ⟨as the big day approaches, the expectant couple are starting to get worried about their fitness for *parenting*⟩
synonyms parenthood
related words raising, rearing, upbringing; fatherhood, fathering, paternity; maternity, motherhood, mothering; caregiving, caretaking

par excellence *adj* of the very best kind ⟨sophisticated cuisine that is obviously the work of a chef *par excellence*⟩ — see EXCELLENT

pariah *n* one who is cast out or rejected by society ⟨I felt like a *pariah* when I wore the wrong outfit to the dinner party⟩ — see OUTCAST

parity *n* the state or fact of being exactly the same in number, amount, status, or quality ⟨rules requiring that there be *parity* in what schools spend on men's and women's sports⟩ — see EQUIVALENCE

park *n* the area around and belonging to a building ⟨the tycoon's country estate is surrounded by a 500-acre *park*⟩ — see GROUND 1

parley *n* **1** a meeting featuring a group discussion ⟨held a *parley* to debate the proposed change in the town's zoning laws⟩ — see FORUM 1
2 an exchange of views for the purpose of exploring a subject or deciding an issue ⟨can we meet for an informal *parley* to see if we can effect a compromise?⟩ — see DISCUSSION 1

parley *vb* to exchange viewpoints or seek advice for the purpose of finding a solution to a problem ⟨in an effort to win the goodwill of the locals, the developers *parleyed* with them before finalizing plans for the massive mall⟩ — see CONFER 2

parliament *n* the highest lawmaking body of a political unit ⟨the treaty was referred to the nation's *parliament* for ratification⟩ — see CONGRESS 1

parlor *n* a building, room, or suite of rooms occupied by a service business ⟨an ice cream *parlor* with an old-timey theme⟩ — see PLACE 2

parlous *adj* involving potential loss or injury ⟨window washing can indeed be a *parlous* occupation on a skyscraper⟩ — see DANGEROUS 1

parochial *adj* not broad or open in views or opinions ⟨the *parochial* outlook of the people in that rural backwater⟩ — see NARROW 2

parody *n* **1** a work that imitates and exaggerates another work for comic effect ⟨the musical is a *parody* of every biblical epic ever made⟩
synonyms burlesque, caricature, put-on, rib, send-up, spoof, takeoff, travesty
related words lampoon, mockery, satire; comedy, farce, humor, sketch, slapstick, squib; distortion, exaggeration; imitation, impersonation, mimicking
2 a poor, insincere, or insulting imitation of something ⟨the young man sported a feeble *parody* of a mustache in a vain attempt to make himself look older⟩ — see MOCKERY 1

parody *vb* to copy or exaggerate (someone or something) in order to make fun of ⟨*parodying* a public figure's distinctive mannerisms takes particular talent⟩ — see MIMIC 1

paroxysm *n* **1** a sudden intense expression of strong feeling ⟨a *paroxysm* of laughter greeted the pratfall⟩ — see OUTBURST 1
2 a violent disturbance (as of the political or social order) ⟨Darwin's introduction of the theory of evolution created *paroxysms* in both religion and science that are still being felt today⟩ — see CONVULSION

paroxysmal *adj* marked by bursts of destructive force or intense activity ⟨*paroxysmal* mood swings that made being around him very challenging⟩ — see VIOLENT 1

parrot *vb* to say after another ⟨the toddler *parroted* everything her father said, often to the latter's embarrassment⟩ — see REPEAT 3

parsimonious *adj* giving or sharing as little as possible ⟨a *parsimonious* woman who insists that charity begins—and ends—at home⟩ — see STINGY 1

parsimony *n* **1** the quality or practice of being overly sparing with money ⟨her *parsimony* was so extreme that she'd walk five miles to the store to save a few cents on gas⟩
synonyms cheapness, cheeseparing, closeness, miserliness, niggardliness, penny-pinching, penuriousness, pinching, stinginess, tightfistedness, tightness
related words conserving, economizing, economy, frugality, husbandry, providence, scrimping, skimping, thrift; conservation, saving; husbanding, managing
near antonyms bountifulness, bounty, generosity, largesse (*also* largess), liberality, openhandedness, openheartedness, philanthropy, unselfishness; extravagance, lavishness; dissipation, improvidence, prodigality, squandering, wastefulness
2 careful management of material resources ⟨people often think that the good times will last forever and have little interest in *parsimony*⟩ — see ECONOMY

part *adv* in some measure or degree ⟨well, you're at least *part* right about her original name⟩ — see PARTLY

part *n* **1** one of the pieces from which something is designed to be assembled ⟨the model car came in several small *parts* that had to be put together⟩
synonyms member, partition, portion, section, segment
related words component, constituent, element, factor, ingredient, moiety, parcel; cut, length; bit, fragment, particle, scrap
near antonyms whole; aggregate, composite, compound, sum, total, totality
2 something belonging to, due to, or contributed by an individual member of a group ⟨wanted no *part* of the profits⟩ — see SHARE 1
3 the action for which a person or thing is specially fit-

ted or used or for which a thing exists ⟨I'll do my *part*, so don't worry⟩ — see ROLE

4 *usually* **parts** *pl* a broad geographical area ⟨I'm not from around these *parts*⟩ — see REGION 2

part *vb* **1** to go or move in different directions from a central point ⟨after traveling together for three weeks, we *parted* at Rome⟩ — see SEPARATE 2

2 to leave a place often for another ⟨*parted* with great ceremony but with little preparation for the dangers that lay ahead⟩ — see GO 2

3 to set or force apart ⟨*parted* the prongs with pliers⟩ — see SEPARATE 1

4 to stop living ⟨before I *part*, I hope I have the opportunity to say my good-byes⟩ — see DIE 1

partake *vb* **1** to take a share or part ⟨we should all *partake* of the city's rich cultural offerings while we have the opportunity⟩

synonyms participate, share

related words endure, experience, feel, know, see, taste, undergo; encounter, meet; accept, receive

2 to take a meal ⟨"let us *partake*," our minister declared, unfolding his napkin and eyeing the feast laid out before us⟩ — see DINE 1

partake (of) *vb* to take in as food ⟨anyone planning to *partake of* the vegetarian meal needs to sign up for it beforehand⟩ — see EAT 1

partaker *n* one who takes part in something ⟨any *partaker* of forbidden activities will be severely punished by the sect's elders⟩ — see PARTICIPANT

partial *adj* **1** inclined to favor one side over another ⟨that judge is always *partial* to the defense, so be careful⟩

synonyms biased, one-sided, parti pris, partisan, prejudiced

related words hostile, inimical, jaundiced, unfriendly, unsympathetic; colored, distorted, misrepresented, shaded, warped; convinced, influenced, persuaded, predisposed, prepossessed, swayed; affected, concerned, interested

near antonyms open, open-minded, persuasible, receptive; honest, just, reasonable; bipartisan; autonomous, independent; aloof, detached, dispassionate, hardheaded, impersonal, unemotional; cold, distant, remote; apathetic, incurious, indifferent, unconcerned, uncurious, unenthusiastic, uninterested

antonyms disinterested, equal, equitable, evenhanded, fair, impartial, neutral, nonpartisan, objective, unbiased, unprejudiced

2 having a liking or affection ⟨*partial* to chocolate cake⟩ — see FOND 1

3 lacking some necessary part ⟨a *partial* answer to the problem⟩ — see INCOMPLETE

partiality *n* **1** an attitude that always favors one way of feeling or acting especially without considering any other possibilities ⟨*partiality* blinded the administrator to the benefits of the proposed system for distributing work⟩ — see BIAS 1

2 a habitual attraction to some activity or thing ⟨a person with an unfortunate *partiality* for jumping to conclusions⟩ — see INCLINATION 1

3 positive regard for something ⟨a *partiality* toward outdoor sports of all kinds⟩ — see LIKING

partially *adv* in some measure or degree ⟨the construction project is only *partially* complete⟩ — see PARTLY

participant *n* one who takes part in something ⟨he seemed to be a willing *participant* in the prank⟩

synonyms actor, partaker, participator, party, player, sharer

related words accessory (*also* accessary), aide, assistant, helper; colleague, partner

near antonyms bystander, looker-on, observer, onlooker, spectator, watcher; wallflower

antonyms nonparticipant

participate *vb* to take a share or part ⟨eager to *participate* in the city's cultural life⟩ — see PARTAKE 1

participator *n* one who takes part in something ⟨a willing *participator* in any parlor game anyone suggested⟩ — see PARTICIPANT

particle *n* **1** a very small amount ⟨there was not a *particle* of truth in what she said⟩

synonyms ace, bit, crumb, dab, dram, driblet, glimmer, hint, lick, little, mite, nip, ounce, peanuts, ray, scintilla, scruple, shade, shadow, shred, skosh, smack, smell, smidgen (*also* smidgeon *or* smidgin *or* smidge), snap, soupçon, spark, spatter, speck, splash, spot, sprinkling, strain, streak, suspicion, tad, touch, trace

related words hoot, iota, jot, minim, minimum, modicum, semblance, syllable, tittle, vestige, whit; atom, dot, fleck, flyspeck, grain, granule, molecule, morsel, mote, nubbin, patch, scrap; dash, drop, pinch; part, portion, section; bite, nibble, taste; handful, scattering, smatter, smattering; dose, shot; chip, flake, fragment, shard, shiver, sliver, smithereens, splinter; shred, tatter; clipping, paring, shaving

phrases drop in the bucket

near antonyms abundance, barrel, boatload, bucket, bundle, bushel, deal, fistful, gobs, heaps, lashings (*also* lashins) [*chiefly British*], loads, lot, mass, mess, mountain, much, oodles, passel, peck, pile, plenty, potful, profusion, quantity, raft, reams, scads, stack, wad, wealth; volume; bonanza, embarrassment, excess, overabundance, overage, overflow, overkill, overmuch, oversupply, superabundance, superfluity, surfeit, surplus; chunk, hunk, lump, slab

2 a very small piece ⟨a *particle* of cookie fell on the carpet⟩ — see BIT 1

particular *adj* **1** hard to please ⟨she's very *particular* about the cleanliness of her car⟩ — see FINICKY

2 of, relating to, or belonging to a single person ⟨that *particular* mug is Mike's⟩ — see INDIVIDUAL 1

3 tending to select carefully ⟨he's *particular* about the corn he buys⟩ — see SELECTIVE

4 including many small descriptive features ⟨a very *particular* account of the breakdown of their marriage from the husband's perspective⟩ — see DETAILED 1

particular *n* **1** a separate part in a list, account, or series ⟨requested a bill of *particulars* for the care he received in the hospital⟩ — see ITEM 1

2 a single piece of information ⟨everyone wanted to know all the *particulars* about the forthcoming merger⟩ — see FACT 3

particularity *n* **1** careful thoroughness of detail ⟨with great *particularity* she described the qualities she's looking for in a boyfriend⟩

synonyms explicitness, specificity

related words attentiveness, care, carefulness, conscientiousness, finicalness, finickiness, fussiness, meticulosity, meticulousness; alertness, cautiousness, circumspection, heedfulness, scrupulousness; discrimination, selectivity; accuracy, definitude, exactitude, exactness, fineness, preciseness, precision

near antonyms imprecision, inaccuracy, inexactness; indistinctness, vagueness

antonyms generality

2 a single piece of information ⟨I can't comment without knowing the *particularities* of the case before the court⟩ — see FACT 3

3 something that sets apart an individual from others of the same kind ⟨a novel that gets the *particularities* of life in academia exactly right⟩ — see CHARACTERISTIC

particularized *adj* including many small descriptive features ⟨the hope is that from their *particularized* descriptions of the landscape we can retrace the explorers' route⟩ — see DETAILED 1

particularly *adv* **1** in the specific case of one person or thing as distinguished from others ⟨all of you, but *particularly* anyone with a problem, should feel free to contact me at any time⟩ — see ESPECIALLY 1
2 in regard to something mentioned explicitly or in detail ⟨she complained *particularly* about the suggestion that she make a greater effort to consider other viewpoints⟩ — see SPECIFICALLY 1
3 to a great degree ⟨a *particularly* good explanation⟩ — see VERY 1

parting *adj* given, taken, or performed at parting ⟨she gave him a *parting* gift to remember her by⟩
synonyms farewell, valedictory
related words closing, concluding, final, last, ultimate; departing, leaving

parting *n* **1** the act or process of two or more persons going off in different directions ⟨although their *parting* was sad, they knew they would see each other again⟩
synonyms farewell, leave-taking, separation
related words departure, egress, exit, exiting, exodus, going, leaving, quitting, running away; decamping, decampment, flight, withdrawal; abandonment, desertion, forsaking
near antonyms reunion; arrival, greeting, salutation, welcome; gathering, joining, meeting
2 the act of leaving a place ⟨everyone waved goodbye at his *parting*⟩ — see DEPARTURE 1

parti pris *adj* inclined to favor one side over another ⟨a *parti pris* interpretation of the causes of the war⟩ — see PARTIAL 1

parti pris *n* an attitude that always favors one way of feeling or acting especially without considering any other possibilities ⟨the longer a president is dead, the better we are able to evaluate without *parti pris* his political achievements⟩ — see BIAS 1

partisan *adj* inclined to favor one side over another ⟨a shamelessly *partisan* reporter covering the primary campaign⟩ — see PARTIAL 1

partisan *also* **partizan** *n* **1** one who follows the opinions or teachings of another ⟨*partisans* of the charismatic leader refuse to tolerate any criticism of him at all⟩ — see FOLLOWER 1
2 one who is intensely or excessively devoted to a cause ⟨a *partisan* of the revolution who was even willing to give her life for it⟩ — see ZEALOT
3 one who stubbornly or intolerantly adheres to his or her own opinions and prejudices ⟨she's too much of a political *partisan* to ever concede that the other side might have a valid point⟩ — see BIGOT

partisanship *n* **1** an attitude that always favors one way of feeling or acting especially without considering any other possibilities ⟨*partisanship* can discourage any serious search for the truth⟩ — see BIAS 1
2 stubborn or intolerant adherence to one's opinions or prejudices ⟨there's a pervasive *partisanship* in the company that prevents it from acknowledging that other companies are outpacing it with innovative ideas⟩ — see BIGOTRY

partition *n* **1** one of the pieces from which something is designed to be assembled ⟨one of the *partitions* of a prefabricated house⟩ — see PART 1
2 something that divides, separates, or marks off ⟨put up a *partition* to divide the room into two⟩ — see DIVISION 1
3 the act or process of a whole separating into two or more parts or pieces ⟨the *partition* of Czechoslovakia into the Czech Republic and Slovakia⟩ — see SEPARATION 1

partly *adv* in some measure or degree ⟨you're only *partly* right⟩
synonyms half, halfway, incompletely, part, partially, partway
related words fragmentarily; enough, fairly, kindly [*chiefly Southern*], kind of, like, moderately, more or less, pretty, quite, rather, relatively, something, somewhat, sort of
phrases in part
near antonyms absolutely, dead, downright, plain; especially, exceedingly (*also* exceeding), exceptionally, extremely, greatly, highly, hugely, particularly, very
antonyms all, altogether, completely, entirely, fully, perfectly, quite, totally, utterly, wholly

partner *n* the person to whom another is married ⟨takes marriage very seriously and wants a man who will be her *partner* for life⟩ — see SPOUSE

partnership *n* the state of having shared interests or efforts (as in social or business matters) ⟨the symphony orchestra is presenting the choral piece in *partnership* with the city's leading choral society⟩ — see ASSOCIATION 1

parturition *n* the act or process of giving birth to children ⟨*parturition* can sometimes proceed more quickly than anticipated⟩ — see CHILDBIRTH

partway *adv* in some measure or degree ⟨his alibi wasn't even *partway* believable⟩ — see PARTLY

party *n* **1** a social gathering ⟨we're all invited to the big *party* to celebrate the end of the year⟩
synonyms affair, bash, binge, blast, blowout, do, event, fete (*or* fête), function, get-together, powwow, reception, shindig
related words benefit, fund-raiser; ball, dance, formal, prom; celebration, gala, occasion; bacchanal, bacchanalia, orgy, saturnalia; bake, clambake, cocktail party, hen party, house party, housewarming, icebreaker, kaffeeklatsch, kegger (*also* keg party), klatch (*also* klatsch), masquerade, meet and greet, mixer, salon, shower, social, soiree (*or* soirée), stag, supper, symposium, tea, tea party
2 a group of people acting together within a larger group ⟨a small *party* got together to protest the new chairman's decision⟩ — see FACTION
3 a group of people working together on a task ⟨a search *party*⟩ — see GANG 1
4 a member of the human race ⟨my grandfather's a determined old *party*, so don't underestimate him⟩ — see HUMAN
5 a usually small number of persons considered as a unit ⟨for *parties* of more than six people the restaurant automatically adds a 15% service charge to the bill⟩ — see GROUP 2
6 one who takes part in something ⟨a *party* to the agreement⟩ — see PARTICIPANT

partyer *also* **partier** *n* one who engages in merrymaking especially in honor of a special occasion ⟨a Mardi Gras celebration that has long attracted serious *partyers* from around the country⟩ — see CELEBRANT

partygoer *n* one who engages in merrymaking especially in honor of a special occasion ⟨chauffeured transportation was provided for those *partygoers* who had overindulged themselves at the bar⟩ — see CELEBRANT

party pooper *n* a person who spoils the pleasure of others ⟨a *party pooper* who insisted they turn the music down⟩ — see KILLJOY

parvenu *n* one who has recently acquired wealth and social position ⟨the kind of trophy house that a *parvenu* buys to prove to people, and to himself, that he has indeed arrived⟩ — see NOUVEAU RICHE

pasquinade *n* a creative work that uses sharp humor to point up the foolishness of a person, institution, or human nature in general ⟨a *pasquinade* of Washington society that features thinly disguised portraits of several political power brokers⟩ — see SATIRE

[1]**pass** *n* **1** a narrow opening between hillsides or mountains that can be used for passage ⟨a mountain *pass* that

was impassable during the winter⟩ — see CANYON
2 a passage cleared for public vehicular travel ⟨take the second *pass* on the right⟩ — see WAY 1

²pass *n* **1** a small sheet of plastic, paper, or paperboard showing that the bearer has a claim to something (as admittance) ⟨a *pass* to leave the military base for the weekend⟩ — see TICKET 1
2 an effort to do or accomplish something ⟨a final *pass* at the assignment⟩ — see ATTEMPT 1
3 the state of being actual or complete ⟨eventually, all their career goals came to *pass*⟩ — see FRUITION

pass *vb* **1** to shift possession of (something) from one person to another ⟨could you please *pass* me the phone?⟩
synonyms buck, hand, hand over, reach, transfer
related words relay; bear, carry; finger, handle, paw; cede, deliver, give, give up, release, relinquish, render, surrender, turn over, yield
2 to come to an end ⟨eventually, the storm *passed*⟩ — see CEASE 1
3 to put (something) into the possession or safekeeping of another ⟨*pass* your forms to the department head once they're filled out⟩ — see GIVE 2
4 to put into effect through legislative or authoritative action ⟨Congress cannot *pass* any law restricting free speech⟩ — see ENACT
5 to take place ⟨and the destruction of the town came to *pass*, just as the seer had predicted⟩ — see HAPPEN
6 to come to a knowledge of (something) by living through it ⟨a presidential candidate who doesn't yet know how it feels to *pass* the scrutiny of the national press⟩ — see EXPERIENCE
7 to express (a thought or emotion) in words ⟨she'll occasionally *pass* some insightful comment, but in general she doesn't have much to contribute⟩ — see SAY 1
8 to show unwillingness to accept, do, engage in, or agree to ⟨we appreciate the invitation to the party, but we'll have to *pass*⟩ ⟨I'll *pass* on the coffee⟩ — see DECLINE 1
9 to withstand scrutiny and gain acceptance or approval ⟨the finished product isn't perfect, but it will *pass*⟩ — see WASH 2

pass (for) *vb* to present a false appearance of ⟨in public they *pass for* being a loving couple, but in reality they are anything but⟩ — see FEIGN

pass (on) *vb* to stop living ⟨my grandfather *passed on* at the age of 92⟩ — see DIE 1

pass (over) *vb* to make one's way through, across, or over ⟨*passed over* two bridges⟩ — see TRAVERSE

passable *adj* **1** capable of being traveled on ⟨after the snowstorm ends, the roads might not be *passable* for the morning ride to school⟩
synonyms navigable, negotiable
related words clear, cleared, free, open, unclogged, unclosed, unobstructed, unstopped
near antonyms blocked, choked, clogged, closed, congested, dammed, jammed, obstructed, plugged (up), stopped (up), stuffed; barricaded, blockaded
antonyms impassable (*also* impassible), unnegotiable, unpassable
2 capable of being passed into or through ⟨the jungle is not *passable* without a machete⟩ — see PENETRABLE
3 of a level of quality that meets one's needs or standards ⟨that's a *passable* paper⟩ — see ADEQUATE
4 of average to below average quality ⟨the actor's Scottish accent is *passable* at best⟩ — see MEDIOCRE 1

passably *adv* in a satisfactory way ⟨looking for a husband who is rich as well as *passably* handsome⟩ — see WELL 1

passage *n* **1** an established course for traveling from one place to another ⟨the long *passage* down the Atlantic seaboard, around Cape Horn, and up the Pacific Coast to California⟩
synonyms approach, avenue, path, route, way
related words bypath, byway, lane, laneway [*British*]; artery, boulevard, bypass, drive, expressway, freeway, high road, highway, pass, passageway, pike, road, roadway, routeway [*chiefly British*], row, street, thoroughfare, turnpike; walk, walkway; trace, track, trail; airway; bikeway, cycleway [*British*]; channel, gat, watercourse, waterway; door, doorway, gate, gateway, hatch, portal
2 a going from one place to another usually of some distance ⟨an arduous *passage* across the country⟩ — see JOURNEY
3 a journey over water in a vessel ⟨the *passage* to Britain requires several days⟩ — see SAIL
4 a part taken from a longer work ⟨the news report quoted a *passage* from the novel⟩ — see EXCERPT
5 forward movement in time or place ⟨a swift *passage* from mere liking to actual love⟩ — see ADVANCE 1
6 the permanent stopping of all the vital bodily activities ⟨weary of this world, he looked forward to the next and sought *passage* with poison⟩ — see DEATH 1

passageway *n* a typically long narrow way connecting parts of a building ⟨the *passageway* to the other side of the office⟩ — see HALL 2

pass away *vb* to stop living ⟨the old woman *passed away* quietly⟩ — see DIE 1

passé *adj* having passed its time of use or usefulness ⟨that literary style is a bit *passé* nowadays⟩ — see OBSOLETE

passel *n* **1** a number of things considered as a unit ⟨reporters had a whole *passel* of questions for the new basketball coach⟩ — see GROUP 1
2 a usually small number of persons considered as a unit ⟨the young couple had a *passel* of babies in the span of a few years⟩ — see GROUP 2
3 a considerable amount ⟨a whole *passel* of unauthorized software on his computer⟩ — see LOT 2

passim *adv* in one place and another ⟨the book belonged to my father, and his trenchant comments are found *passim*—both in the margins and between the lines of text⟩ — see HERE AND THERE 1

passing *adj* lasting only for a short time ⟨his parents were willing to buy him a piano if he demonstrated that his interest in music was more than a *passing* fancy⟩ — see MOMENTARY

passing *adv* to a great degree ⟨a *passing* strange turn of events⟩ — see VERY 1

passing *n* the permanent stopping of all the vital bodily activities ⟨the precise moment of his *passing* was recorded by the machines at his bedside⟩ — see DEATH 1

passion *n* **1** a feeling of strong or constant regard for and dedication to someone ⟨married at the age of 18, they share a *passion* that has lasted for over half a century⟩ — see LOVE 1
2 a strong but often short-lived liking for another person ⟨her *passion* passed when the next hunky movie star arrived on the scene⟩ — see CRUSH 1
3 a strong wish for something ⟨a *passion* to become a doctor⟩ — see DESIRE 1
4 a subjective response to a person, thing, or situation ⟨people are sometimes slaves to their own *passions*⟩ — see FEELING 1
5 depth of feeling ⟨your *passion* for your cause is admirable, but you still can't insult people who disagree with you⟩ — see ARDOR 1
6 passions *pl* general emotional condition ⟨people who are swayed by their *passions* and not by reason⟩ — see FEELING 2
7 intense sexual desire ⟨an addiction to online pornog-

raphy that was clear proof that he had become a slave to *passion*⟩ — see LUST 1
8 sexual appetite ⟨the kind of pent-up *passion* that comes from having spent the winter in remote isolation⟩ — see DESIRE 2

passional *adj* having or expressing great depth of feeling ⟨a rather *passional* declaration of love from someone she had just started dating⟩ — see FERVENT 1

passionate *adj* **1** having a strong sexual desire ⟨a *passionate* couple plunging recklessly into an adulterous affair⟩ — see LUSTFUL
2 having or expressing great depth of feeling ⟨a *passionate* defense of the controversial play⟩ — see FERVENT 1

passionateness *n* depth of feeling ⟨delivers his sermons with a degree of *passionateness* that is positively electrifying⟩ — see ARDOR 1

passionless *adj* not feeling or showing emotion ⟨the *passionless* prose of the divorce papers gave little hint of the bitter feelings that accompanied the end of their marriage⟩ — see IMPASSIVE 1

passive *adj* receiving or enduring without offering resistance ⟨the union rank and file were surprisingly *passive* about the givebacks in the new labor contract⟩
synonyms acquiescent, nonresistant, resigned, tolerant, tolerating, unresistant, yielding
related words forbearing, impassive, long-suffering, patient, stoic (*or* stoical), uncomplaining; agreeable, amenable, compliant, complying, conformable, conformist, docile, guidable, law-abiding, obedient, pliable, pliant, subordinate, tractable, willing; obeisant, submissive, surrendering; amiable, obliging; slavish, subservient; disciplined, governable, manageable; apathetic, uncaring, unresponsive
near antonyms defiant; contrary, contumacious, disobedient, froward, incompliant, insubordinate, insurgent, intractable, mutinous, rebellious, recalcitrant, refractory, restive, uncontrollable, ungovernable, unruly, untoward; balky, perverse, wayward, wrongheaded; headstrong, willful (*or* wilful); indomitable; undisciplined, unmanageable; dissident, nonconformist
antonyms protesting, resistant, resisting, unyielding

pass off *vb* to offer (something fake, useless, or inferior) as genuine, useful, or valuable ⟨the con man tried to *pass off* a piece of blue glass as a sapphire⟩ — see FOIST

pass out *vb* to lose consciousness ⟨I *passed out* from the flu⟩ — see FAINT

pass over *vb* **1** to fail to give proper attention to ⟨you seem to have *passed over* an important e-mail notice⟩ — see NEGLECT 1
2 to dismiss as of little importance ⟨I'd be willing to *pass over* this latest episode of tardiness if there hadn't been so many before⟩ — see EXCUSE 1

passport *n* **1** something that allows someone to achieve a desired goal ⟨meeting that movie director could be your *passport* to a big acting career⟩
synonyms gateway, key, open sesame, secret, ticket
related words password; accomplishment, achievement, attainment, coup, success, triumph; approach, manner, means, method, style, system, technique, way; blueprint, design, ground plan, plan, program, scheme, strategy
2 the means or right of entering or participating in ⟨to its followers, the cult seemed like their *passport* to heaven⟩ — see ENTRANCE 1

pass up *vb* to show unwillingness to accept, do, engage in, or agree to ⟨I must *pass up* the offer to be chairman of this event⟩ — see DECLINE 1

password *n* a word or phrase that must be spoken by a person in order to pass a guard ⟨the *password* for the all-night rave will be changed next week⟩
synonyms countersign, watchword, word
related words shibboleth, sign; signal; hint, indication; parole

past *adj* having been such at some previous time ⟨a *past* editor of the newspaper⟩ — see FORMER 1

past *n* the events or experience of former times ⟨we spent a pleasant evening recalling the *past* together⟩
synonyms auld lang syne, history, yesterday, yesteryear, yore
related words bygone; flashback; annals, chronicle, record; memoir; antiquity, long ago
near antonyms by-and-by, future, futurity, hereafter, offing, tomorrow; moment, now, present, today

past *prep* **1** on or to the farther side of ⟨I drive *past* the school every day⟩ — see BEYOND 1
2 subsequent to in time or order ⟨it's ten minutes *past* six o'clock⟩ — see AFTER

paste *vb* **1** to defeat by a large margin ⟨with the economy having gone south, it was hardly surprising that the incumbent party got *pasted* in the general election⟩ — see WHIP 2
2 to deliver a blow to (someone or something) usually in a strong vigorous manner ⟨*pasted* the soccer ball halfway across the field⟩ — see HIT 1

pasteboard *n* a small sheet of plastic, paper, or paperboard showing that the bearer has a claim to something (as admittance) ⟨those *pasteboards* I got from a scalper cost me four times their face value⟩ — see TICKET 1

pastel *adj* lacking intensity of color ⟨a *pastel* blue to go with the pale pink walls⟩ — see PALE 1

pastiche *n* an unorganized collection or mixture of various things ⟨each addition to the house was done in a markedly different architectural idiom, and the result is a whimsical *pastiche*⟩ — see MISCELLANY 1

past master *n* a person with a high level of knowledge or skill in a field ⟨a movie director who was widely regarded as the *past master* of suspense⟩ — see EXPERT

pastoral *adj* **1** of, relating to, associated with, or typical of open areas with few buildings or people ⟨painted a *pastoral* scene of a flower-filled meadow⟩ — see RURAL
2 of, relating to, or characteristic of the clergy ⟨*pastoral* advice to a young couple preparing to marry⟩ — see CLERICAL

pasturage *n* open land over which livestock may roam and feed ⟨put the cows out on the back *pasturage*⟩ — see RANGE 1

pasture *n* open land over which livestock may roam and feed ⟨horses grazing in a fenced *pasture*⟩ — see RANGE 1

pasture *vb* to feed on grass or herbs ⟨*pasturing* sheep on town lands was actually a cheaper alternative to mowing⟩ — see [1]GRAZE

pasty *adj* lacking a healthy skin color ⟨she's *pasty* after a whole winter spent indoors⟩ — see PALE 2

pat *adj* sticking to an opinion, purpose, or course of action in spite of reason, arguments, or persuasion ⟨on the issue of raising taxes the governor stands *pat*⟩ — see OBSTINATE

pat *adv* without any flaws or errors ⟨after months of practicing for the competition, the cheerleaders have their moves down *pat*⟩ — see PERFECTLY 1

pat *vb* to touch or handle in a tender or loving manner ⟨affectionately *patted* the baby on the head⟩ — see FONDLE

patch *n* **1** a small area that is different (as in color) from the main part ⟨a black cat with a small *patch* of white next to her nose⟩ — see SPOT 1
2 a very small piece ⟨a *patch* of land hardly big enough for a garden⟩ — see BIT 1

patch *vb* to put into good shape or working order again ⟨*patch* the tire and it'll be as good as new⟩ — see MEND 1

patch (together) *vb* to make or assemble roughly or

hastily ⟨the stranded hikers *patched together* a shelter that afforded some protection from the wind⟩ — see COBBLE (TOGETHER *OR* UP)

patchwork *adj* consisting of many things of different sorts ⟨a *patchwork* collection of antiques from different periods⟩ — see MISCELLANEOUS

patchwork *n* an unorganized collection or mixture of various things ⟨the state's *patchwork* of outdated laws regulating commercial activity on Sundays⟩ — see MISCELLANY 1

patchwork quilt *n* an unorganized collection or mixture of various things ⟨the essay isn't so much a cogent argument as a *patchwork quilt* of the writer's random musings⟩ — see MISCELLANY 1

pate *n* the upper or front part of the body that contains the brain, the major sense organs, and the mouth ⟨plopped a cap on his bald *pate*⟩ — see HEAD 1

patent *adj* **1** not subject to misinterpretation or more than one interpretation ⟨unfortunately, the *patent* stupidity of the proposal did not deter the city council from putting it up for a vote⟩ — see CLEAR 2
2 very noticeable especially for being incorrect or bad ⟨a *patent* error that should have been caught before the book was published⟩ — see EGREGIOUS

patented *adj* of, relating to, or belonging to a single person ⟨the radio commentator went into one of his *patented* tirades after an astute caller questioned his knowledge of the facts⟩ — see INDIVIDUAL 1

pater *n, chiefly British* a male human parent ⟨*Pater* had promised to pay for military school after third form⟩ — see FATHER 1

path *n* **1** the direction along which something or someone moves ⟨try to stay out of the *path* of the golf balls while playing⟩ ⟨I tripped over a rock directly in my *path*⟩
synonyms course, line, pathway, route, routeway [*chiefly British*], steps, track, way
related words circle, circuit, loop, orbit; arc, flight path, trajectory; ascent, descent
2 a rough course or way formed by or as if by repeated footsteps ⟨a *path* worn through the library lawn by too many people walking over it⟩ — see TRAIL 1
3 an established course for traveling from one place to another ⟨the *path* along which ancient traders traveled from Europe to China was known as the Silk Road⟩ — see PASSAGE 1

pathetic *adj* **1** deserving of one's pity ⟨the plight of the homeless family was quite *pathetic*⟩
synonyms heartbreaking, heartrending, miserable, piteous, pitiable, pitiful, poor, rueful, sorry, wretched
related words deplorable, lamentable, regrettable; emotional, impressive, inspiring; affecting, moving, poignant, stirring, touching; awful, horrible, terrible; distressing, disturbing, upsetting; grievous, mournful, sad, sorrowful, woeful
near antonyms unimpressive, uninspiring
2 causing unhappiness ⟨a *pathetic* story that made her cry⟩ — see SAD 2
3 deserving pitying scorn (as for inadequacy) ⟨the crowd mercilessly booed the boxer's *pathetic* performance⟩ — see PITIFUL 1
4 so foolish or pointless as to be worthy of scornful laughter ⟨the pundit's latest book is another *pathetic* jumble of factual errors, half-baked political views, and baseless accusations⟩ — see RIDICULOUS 1

pathless *adj* not having been traveled over or through ⟨the team of scientists will use dogsleds to travel across the *pathless* Antarctic wilderness⟩
synonyms trackless, untraveled, untraversed, untrodden (*also* untrod)
related words pristine, virgin; undiscovered, unexplored
near antonyms bustling, busy, crowded; swarming, teeming, thronging
antonyms traveled (*or* travelled), trod (*or* trodden)

pathway *n* **1** a rough course or way formed by or as if by repeated footsteps ⟨we parked our car near a rambling *pathway* that led down to the pond⟩ — see TRAIL 1
2 the direction along which something or someone moves ⟨the long, winding *pathway* of the river before it meets the sea⟩ — see PATH 1

patience *n* the capacity to endure what is difficult or disagreeable without complaining ⟨the teacher's *patience* is being sorely tested this year by several parents who seem to have no interest in their children's education⟩
synonyms forbearance, long-suffering, sufferance, tolerance
related words acquiescence, resignation; passiveness, passivity; amenability, compliance, conformism, docility, obedience, subordination, tractability, willingness; discipline, self-control; submission, submissiveness
near antonyms defiance; contrariness, disobedience, insubordination, intractability, recalcitrance, resistance, willfulness
antonyms impatience

patient *adj* **1** accepting pains or hardships calmly or without complaint ⟨you were very *patient* about having to wait for me for so long⟩
synonyms forbearing, long-suffering, stoic (*or* stoical), tolerant, uncomplaining
related words lenient; acquiescent, passive, resigned, unresistant, yielding; agreeable, amenable, compliant, complying, conformist, docile, law-abiding, obedient, placable, submissive, subordinate, tractable, willing; slavish, subservient; amiable, obliging; collected, composed; constrained, contained, curbed, inhibited, repressed, restrained; disciplined, self-contained, self-controlled; apathetic, uncaring, unresponsive
near antonyms bored, tired, weary; defiant, resistant; contrary, disobedient, insubordinate, intractable, rebellious, recalcitrant, refractory, ungovernable, unmanageable, unruly
antonyms complaining, fed up, impatient, kvetching, kvetchy, protesting
2 continuing despite difficulties, opposition, or discouragement ⟨a *patient* effort to finish college despite the mounting debts⟩ — see PERSISTENT

patient *n* an individual awaiting or under medical care and treatment ⟨the nurse asked the *patient* to change into a paper gown⟩
synonyms case
related words inpatient, outpatient; rehabilitant; sufferer, victim; convalescent, nursling

patina *n* a special quality or impression associated with something ⟨although the winery is brand-new, it has been constructed and decorated to give it a *patina* of old-world quaintness⟩ — see AURA 1

patio *n* an open space wholly or partly enclosed (as by buildings or walls) ⟨there's a *patio* in the center of the apartment complex⟩ — see COURT 2

patois *n* the special terms or expressions of a particular group or field ⟨the medical *patois* that the hospital staffers used among themselves was incomprehensible to me⟩ — see TERMINOLOGY

patrician *adj* of high birth, rank, or station ⟨came from a *patrician* family⟩ — see NOBLE 1

patrician *n* a man or woman of high birth or social position ⟨the Southern *patricians* who once resided in these stately plantation homes⟩ — see GENTLEPERSON

patriciate *n* the highest class in a society ⟨the *patriciate* regarded patronage of the arts as a moral and social duty⟩ — see ARISTOCRACY 1

patrimony *n* something that is or may be inherited ⟨her *patrimony* was the family's newspaper business⟩ — see INHERITANCE

patriot *n* a person who loves his or her country and supports its interests and policies ⟨the contention that true *patriots* would be willing to do anything for their country⟩
synonyms loyalist
related words chauvinist; flag-waver, jingoist, nationalist, superpatriot; compatriot, countryman
near antonyms collaborator, quisling, spy, traitor; betrayer, deserter, recreant; renegade

patriotic *adj* having or showing love and support for one's country ⟨hanging a flag outside one's home is a *patriotic* gesture⟩
synonyms nationalist, nationalistic
related words chauvinist; jingoist, jingoistic, superpatriotic; constant, devoted, faithful, loyal, staunch (*also* stanch), steadfast, steady, true; ardent, fervent, fervid, impassioned, passionate
near antonyms traitorous, treasonous; disaffected, disloyal, faithless, false, fickle, inconstant, perfidious, recreant, treacherous, unfaithful
antonyms unpatriotic

patriotism *n* love and support for one's country ⟨her *patriotism* was so heartfelt that she quit her job to work for the war effort⟩
synonyms nationalism
related words chauvinism; jingoism; allegiance, constancy, devotion, faithfulness, fealty, loyalty, staunchness, steadfastness; fervency, fervidness, passion
near antonyms desertion, treason; disaffection, disloyalty, faithlessness, falseness, fickleness, inconstancy, perfidiousness, treachery, unfaithfulness

patron *n* **1** a person who buys a product or uses a service from a business ⟨a restaurant *patron*⟩ — see CUSTOMER 1
2 a person who takes the responsibility for some other person or thing ⟨the wealthy philanthropist is one of the city's most generous *patrons* of its symphony orchestra⟩ — see SPONSOR
3 one that helps another with gifts or money ⟨the *patron* for the museum's current blockbuster is the city's biggest banking institution⟩ — see BENEFACTOR

patronage *n* **1** the financial support and general guidance for an undertaking ⟨a symphony orchestra that had long relied upon the *patronage* of the city's moneyed old guard⟩ — see AUSPICE 1
2 transactions or economic support provided by customers ⟨he refuses to give his *patronage* to any corporation that is not socially conscious⟩ — see BUSINESS 1

patronize *vb* **1** to assume or treat with an air of superiority ⟨a director with an unpleasant habit of *patronizing* even his most gifted actors⟩ — see CONDESCEND 2
2 to promote the interests or cause of ⟨a company that loyally *patronizes* the arts⟩ — see SUPPORT 1

patron saint *n* someone of such unequaled perfection as to deserve imitation ⟨around the statehouse he's known as the *patron saint* of partisan politics⟩ — see IDEAL 1

patsy *n* one who is easily deceived or cheated ⟨an Internet newbie who's the perfect *patsy* for a cyber scam⟩ — see [1]DUPE

patter *n* **1** friendly, informal conversation or an instance of this ⟨their incessant *patter* was getting on my nerves⟩ — see CHAT 1
2 the special terms or expressions of a particular group or field ⟨the *patter* of highbrow criticism that one hears in fashionable art galleries⟩ — see TERMINOLOGY

patter *vb* to engage in casual or rambling conversation ⟨the toddler *pattered* on for what seemed like hours⟩ — see CHAT 1

pattern *n* **1** a unit of decoration that is repeated all over something (as a fabric) ⟨a coverlet with a nosegay of tiny pink roses as the *pattern*⟩
synonyms design, figure, motif, motive
related words scheme; device; adornment, caparison, decoration, embellishment, frill, garnish, ornament, trim
2 a usual manner of behaving or doing ⟨her daily *pattern* begins with coffee and a bagel every morning for breakfast⟩ — see HABIT 1
3 an established and often automatic or monotonous series of actions followed when engaging in some activity ⟨with her, everything must be done strictly according to *pattern*⟩ — see ROUTINE 1
4 the way in which the elements of something (as a work of art) are arranged ⟨many of the artist's paintings use the same *pattern* of a lone figure surrounded by a vast landscape⟩ — see COMPOSITION 3

patty *also* **pattie** *n* a small usually rounded mass of minced food that has been fried ⟨the enticing aroma of sausage *patties* sizzling in the skillet⟩ — see CAKE 1

paucity *n* a falling short of an essential or desirable amount or number ⟨a *paucity* of useful answers to the problem of traffic congestion at rush hour⟩ — see DEFICIENCY

paunch *n* an enlarged or bulging abdomen ⟨Santa is depicted as a white-bearded man with a big *paunch*⟩ — see POTBELLY

paunchy *adj* having a large protruding abdomen ⟨not surprisingly, the new Hollywood biopic casts a young, athetically trim actor in the role of the *paunchy*, balding artist⟩
synonyms beer-bellied, potbellied
related words chubby, corpulent, fat, fleshy, full, gross, obese, overweight, plump, podgy [*chiefly British*], portly, pudgy, roly-poly, rotund, round, tubby; flabby, soft
near antonyms chiseled (*or* chiselled), cut; lean, lithe, skinny, slender, slim, spare, svelte, sylphlike

pauperism *n* the state of lacking sufficient money or material possessions ⟨now discredited, the science of eugenics was once proclaimed as a means of ridding society of such undesirable traits as *pauperism* and criminality⟩ — see POVERTY 1

pauperized *adj* lacking money or material possessions ⟨out of the job and newly *pauperized*, the single father had no idea what to do next⟩ — see POOR 1

pause *n* **1** a momentary halt in an activity ⟨there was a brief *pause* for applause in her speech⟩
synonyms break, breath, breather, interruption, lull, recess
related words time-out; interim, interlude, intermission, interval, respite, rest; cessation, discontinuance, downtime, ending, expiration, finishing, hitch, lapse, stoppage, stopping, termination; abeyance, moratorium, surcease, suspension; discontinuity, gap, hiatus
near antonyms continuation, endurance, persistence, progress, progression; extension, prolongation
2 a state or an instance of temporary inaction because of uncertainty about the right course of action ⟨the question caught the professor off guard, and there was a *pause* before he responded⟩ — see HESITATION

pause *vb* to come to a temporary halt in one's activity ⟨he *paused* for a moment to regain his composure⟩
synonyms break
related words hesitate; break in, interrupt; cease, discontinue, end, finish, stop, terminate; knock off, lay off, quit; lapse, let up
phrases catch one's breath, hold one's horses
near antonyms continue, persist; advance, progress; extend, prolong, stretch

pavilion *n* a freestanding airy structure in a scenic setting (as a park) typically offering commanding views

⟨the park's *pavilions* may be rented for wedding receptions and other social gatherings⟩ — see BELVEDERE

[1]**pawn** *n* one that is or can be used to further the purposes of another ⟨though he liked to play up his influence with city hall, he was really just another *pawn* of the political bosses⟩
synonyms cat's-paw, instrument, lay figure, puppet, tool
related words chump, dupe, foil, gull, sucker, victim; minion, stooge; lap dog, yes-man

[2]**pawn** *n* something given or held to assure that the giver will keep a promise ⟨offered her license as a *pawn* that she would bring back the rental canoe⟩ — see PLEDGE 1

pawn *vb* to leave as a guarantee of repayment of a loan ⟨he *pawned* his antique watch in order to pay off his gambling debt⟩
synonyms hock, pledge
related words deposit, mortgage; bond
near antonyms buy (back), redeem, win (back)

pay *n* **1** the money paid regularly to a person for labor or services ⟨it's difficult to support two children on her *pay*⟩ — see WAGE
2 something (as money) that is given or received in return for goods or services ⟨we should demand *pay* for all the overtime we're putting in⟩ — see PAYMENT 2

pay *vb* **1** to give (someone) the sum of money owed for goods or services received ⟨we need to *pay* the cashier and then we can leave⟩
synonyms compensate, recompense, remunerate
related words refund, reimburse, repay, requite; remit; pay off, pay up, prepay
near antonyms stiff
2 to give what is owed for ⟨you ought to *pay* that bill before it's overdue⟩
synonyms ante up, balance, clear, discharge, foot, liquidate, meet, pay off, pay up, pony up, quit, recompense, settle, spring (for), stand
antonyms repudiate
3 to hand over or use up in payment ⟨rock fans were willing to *pay* enormous sums to get into the concert⟩ — see SPEND 1
4 to produce as revenue ⟨an investment *paying* six percent⟩ — see YIELD 2
5 to provide with a paying job ⟨*pay* someone to mow the lawn for the summer⟩ — see EMPLOY 1

payable *adj* not yet paid ⟨keep the bills *payable* separate from the receipts⟩ — see OUTSTANDING 1

payback *n* the act or an instance of responding to an injury with an injury ⟨we are hoping to get *payback* for the humiliating defeat we suffered at the hands of our rivals during our last matchup⟩ — see REVENGE

paycheck *n* the money paid regularly to a person for labor or services ⟨almost half of her *paycheck* goes to child care and transportation expenses⟩ — see WAGE

pay envelope *n* the money paid regularly to a person for labor or services ⟨with this recession going on, workers shouldn't be expecting fatter *pay envelopes*⟩ — see WAGE

paying *adj* yielding a profit ⟨finally found a *paying* job⟩ — see PROFITABLE 1

paying *n* the act of offering money in exchange for goods or services ⟨the actual shopping was quick, but with the long lines, *paying* for the stuff seemed to take forever⟩ — see PAYMENT 1

payload *n* a mass or quantity of something taken up and carried, conveyed, or transported ⟨the space shuttle can carry a maximum *payload* of approximately 50,000 pounds⟩ — see LOAD 1

payment *n* **1** the act of offering money in exchange for goods or services ⟨they are very prompt in the *payment* of their credit card bills⟩
synonyms compensation, disbursement, giving, paying, remitment, remittance, remuneration
related words rendering, tendering; reimbursement, repayment; paying off, paying up, prepayment; overpayment
near antonyms underpayment
antonyms nonpayment
2 something (as money) that is given or received in return for goods or services ⟨our *payment* for all the work we did barely covered our expenses⟩ ⟨we finally mailed our last car *payment* last week⟩
synonyms compensation, consideration, pay, recompense, remittance, remuneration, requital
related words salary, stipend, wage(s); disbursement, expenditure, outlay; rebate, refund; indemnity, recoupment, redress, reparation, restitution; adjustment, settlement; deposit; reimbursement, repayment; prepayment; overpayment; rent, rental
3 the money paid regularly to a person for labor or services ⟨your *payment* will be issued as a weekly check⟩ — see WAGE

payoff *n* the amount of money left when expenses are subtracted from the total amount received ⟨the *payoff* on the investment was only about $500⟩ — see PROFIT 1

pay off *vb* **1** to give what is owed for ⟨I finally *paid off* the loan⟩ — see PAY 2
2 to influence someone with a bribe ⟨she *paid off* the security guard so that she could steal whatever she liked⟩ — see BRIBE

pay up *vb* to give what is owed for ⟨for once our bills are all *paid up*⟩ — see PAY 2

PDQ *adv* without delay ⟨the boss wants the report, and he wants it *PDQ*⟩ — see IMMEDIATELY

peace *n* **1** a state without war ⟨after a long and bitter war, the troubled region finally achieved *peace*⟩
synonyms peacefulness
related words accord, amity, concord, harmony; calm, quiet, serenity, tranquillity (*or* tranquility); order, stability; pacification
near antonyms conflict, contention, discord, dissidence, strife, trouble; tumult, turmoil, unrest, upheaval; fighting, warfare; action, battle, combat
antonyms war
2 freedom from disquieting or oppressive thoughts or emotions ⟨a light, humorous novel that is good for putting my mind at *peace* right before I go to sleep⟩
synonyms calm, calmness, heartsease, peacefulness, placidity, sereneness, serenity, tranquillity (*or* tranquility)
related words content, contentment, ease; comfort, consolation, relief, solace; quiet, quietude, repose
near antonyms care, concern, perturbation; strain, stress, tenseness, tension; consternation, desperateness, desperation, discomfort, discomposure, dismay, distraction, distress, disturbance, edginess, jitters, jumpiness, nervousness; fear, fearfulness, torment, upset; doubt, dread, foreboding, incertitude, misgiving, presentiment, suspense, uncertainty
antonyms agitation, alarm (*also* alarum), anguish, anxiety, anxiousness, apprehension, apprehensiveness, uneasiness, vexation, worry
3 a state of freedom from storm or disturbance ⟨the eerie *peace* after a tornado⟩ — see CALM 1
4 peaceful coexistence ⟨can't we all just live in *peace*?⟩ — see HARMONY 2

peaceable *adj* **1** inclined to live in peace and to avoid war ⟨a *peaceable* nation that has never had any interest in conquest⟩ — see PEACEFUL 1
2 not involving violence or force ⟨trying to find a *peaceable* resolution⟩ — see PEACEFUL 2

peaceful *adj* **1** inclined to live in peace and to avoid war ⟨a *peaceful* tribe that had quietly inhabited these shores

for centuries before the arrival of the Europeans⟩
synonyms dovish, pacific, pacifist (*or* pacifistic), peaceable
related words irenic, nonaggressive, nonbelligerent, noncombative, unaggressive, unwarlike; antimilitarist, antimilitaristic, antiviolence, antiwar; calm, mild, neutral, quiet, relaxed, serene, tranquil; affable, amiable, amicable, benevolent, genial, gentle, kind, kindly; submissive, yielding
near antonyms militarist, militaristic; aggressive, bellicose, belligerent, combative, contentious, discordant, pugnacious, quarrelsome, scrappy, truculent; antagonistic, argumentative, fierce, gladiatorial, hostile, hot-tempered
antonyms bloodthirsty, hawkish, martial, warlike
2 not involving violence or force ⟨UN officials struggled to find a *peaceful* solution to the troublesome conflict⟩
synonyms nonviolent, peaceable
related words bloodless; conciliatory, irenic, pacific, peacemaking; nonbelligerent, unaggressive, unassertive; appeasing, conciliating, mollifying, pacifying, placating; calming, quieting, soothing
near antonyms armed, martial, militant, military, warlike; aggressive, assertive, bellicose, belligerent, combative, contentious, quarrelsome; antagonistic, argumentative, fierce, gladiatorial, hostile; tempestuous, volcanic
antonyms forced, violent
3 free from disturbing noise or uproar ⟨a *peaceful* house, now that the kids are all grown and departed⟩ — see QUIET 1
4 free from storms or physical disturbance ⟨a *peaceful* lake⟩ — see CALM 1
5 free from emotional or mental agitation ⟨the patient is *peaceful* and resting comfortably⟩ — see CALM 2

peacefulness *n* **1** a state of freedom from storm or disturbance ⟨the *peacefulness* of the secluded beach was refreshing⟩ — see CALM 1
2 a state without war ⟨a period of *peacefulness* that remained unbroken until World War I⟩ — see PEACE 1
3 freedom from disquieting or oppressive thoughts or emotions ⟨after coming to terms with his sexuality, he felt a *peacefulness* that he had never experienced before⟩ — see PEACE 2

peacemaker *n* one who works with opposing sides in order to bring about an agreement ⟨the former diplomat is coming out of retirement to lend his talents as a *peacemaker* to these crucial negotiations⟩ — see MEDIATOR

peacemaking *adj* tending to lessen or avoid conflict or hostility ⟨efforts at *peacemaking* overtures in the region have largely been ignored by both warring parties⟩ — see PACIFIC 1

peacenik *n* a person who opposes war or warlike policies ⟨*peaceniks* argued that all the nonmilitary options had not been exhausted⟩ — see DOVE 1

peach *n* something very good of its kind ⟨fondly remembers his old Studebaker as being a *peach* of a car⟩ — see JIM-DANDY

peachy *adj* of the very best kind ⟨a look back at those innocent days when the offerings at the local soda fountain might have been described as "simply *peachy*"⟩ — see EXCELLENT

peachy keen *adj* of the very best kind ⟨back is the days when a wienie roast was a *peachy keen* way to spend a date⟩ — see EXCELLENT

peak *n* **1** an elevation of land higher than a hill ⟨the nearest *peak* worth climbing is hundreds of miles away⟩ — see MOUNTAIN 1
2 the highest part or point ⟨a pop singer at the *peak* of her career⟩ — see HEIGHT 1
3 the projecting front part of a hat or cap ⟨accidentally stepped on the hat and crushed the *peak*⟩ — see VISOR

[1]**peaked** *adj* tapering to a thin tip ⟨the church's *peaked* spire is a prominent feature of the town's skyline⟩ — see POINTED 1

[2]**peaked** *adj* **1** lacking a healthy skin color ⟨you probably should go home, as you're looking awfully *peaked*⟩ — see PALE 2
2 temporarily suffering from a disorder of the body ⟨I'm feeling a little *peaked*, so I'm going to lie down⟩ — see SICK 1

peaky *adj* temporarily suffering from a disorder of the body ⟨her mother announced that she still looked *peaky*, and felt her forehead for a fever⟩ — see SICK 1

peal *vb* to make the clear sound heard when metal vibrates ⟨the village bells *pealed* every hour in commemoration⟩ — see [2]RING

peanut *adj* so small or unimportant as to warrant little or no attention ⟨this is a *peanut* matter, and we're fools for wasting time on it⟩ — see NEGLIGIBLE 1

peanuts *n pl* **1** a very small amount ⟨that's *peanuts* compared to what I had to deal with yesterday⟩ — see PARTICLE 1
2 a very small sum of money ⟨employees griping that they were working for *peanuts*⟩ — see MITE 1

pearl *n* someone or something unusually desirable ⟨friends who agree that his new bride is a real *pearl*⟩ — see PRIZE 1

pearlescent *adj* having a rainbowlike play of colors ⟨the sedan comes in an array of colors, with either a metallic or *pearlescent* finish⟩ — see IRIDESCENT

pebbly *adj* not having a level or smooth surface ⟨a jerky ride on a *pebbly* road⟩ ⟨the rubber handles have a *pebbly* texture that makes them easier to grip when they are wet⟩ — see UNEVEN 1

peck *n* a considerable amount ⟨now you're in a *peck* of trouble⟩ — see LOT 2

peck *vb* **1** to eat reluctantly and in small bites ⟨found out that fashion models never really eat—they just *peck* at small meals in expensive restaurants⟩ — see NIBBLE 1
2 to penetrate or hold (something) with a pointed object ⟨the bird continued to *peck* the suet cake intently⟩ — see IMPALE

peck (at) *vb* to subject (someone) to constant scoldings and sharp reminders ⟨kept *pecking at* their prodigal daughter to get off the couch and to start looking for a job⟩ — see NAG 1

pecker *n, chiefly British* strength of mind to carry on in spite of danger ⟨Churchillian speeches that encouraged Britons to keep their *pecker* up during those trying times⟩ — see COURAGE

peckish *adj, chiefly British* feeling a desire or need for food ⟨I think I'll have a snack before we go, as I'm feeling a bit *peckish*⟩ — see HUNGRY 1

Pecksniffian *adj* not being or expressing what one appears to be or express ⟨a *Pecksniffian* pandering to religious conservatives, especially in the weeks before the election⟩ — see INSINCERE

peculiar *adj* **1** being out of the ordinary ⟨a writer with a *peculiar* talent for capturing the feel of everyday conversation⟩ — see EXCEPTIONAL 1
2 different from the ordinary in a way that causes curiosity or suspicion ⟨a *peculiar* and catlike way of walking⟩ — see ODD 2
3 noticeably different from what is generally found or experienced ⟨a *peculiar* response to a polite query about his health⟩ — see UNUSUAL 1
4 of, relating to, or belonging to a single person ⟨his *peculiar* way of talking⟩ — see INDIVIDUAL 1
5 serving to identify as belonging to an individual or

group ⟨the koala is *peculiar* to Australia⟩ — see CHARACTERISTIC 1
6 of a particular or exact sort ⟨a psychopathic killer who took *peculiar* delight in torturing his victims⟩ — see EXPRESS 1

peculiarity *n* **1** an odd or peculiar habit ⟨had the *peculiarity* of constantly fussing with his hair⟩ — see IDIOSYNCRASY
2 something that sets apart an individual from others of the same kind ⟨as its name indicates, the red-winged blackbird has the distinctive *peculiarity* of a red patch on its wings⟩ — see CHARACTERISTIC

pecuniary *adj* of or relating to money, banking, or investments ⟨that makes good *pecuniary* sense⟩ ⟨the judge recused himself from the case because he had a *pecuniary* interest in the company that was being sued⟩ — see FINANCIAL

pedagogue *n* a person whose occupation is to give formal instruction in a school ⟨a *pedagogue* whose classroom lessons consisted entirely of reading directly from the textbook in a monotone⟩ — see TEACHER

peddle *vb* to sell from place to place usually in small quantities ⟨seldom saw their father, who traveled around the country *peddling* Bibles⟩
synonyms hawk
related words retail, wholesale; deal (in), distribute, high-pressure, hustle, market, merchandise (*also* merchandize), trade (in), vend

peddler *also* **pedlar** *n* one who sells things outdoors ⟨the *peddler* on the street corner selling baseball caps⟩
synonyms hawker, huckster
related words dealer, merchandiser, merchant, seller, vendor (*also* vender); costermonger [*British*]; concessionaire; black marketer (*or* black marketeer), bootlegger, fence, fencer, hustler, pusher, smuggler, trader
near antonyms buyer, purchaser; consumer, end user, user

pedestrian *adj* causing weariness, restlessness, or lack of interest ⟨a TV detective show filled with *pedestrian* plots stolen from older and better series⟩ — see BORING

pedigree *n* the line of ancestors from whom a person is descended ⟨a woman of good *pedigree*⟩ — see ANCESTRY

pedigreed *or* **pedigree** *adj* of unmixed ancestry ⟨a *pedigreed* puppy is expensive⟩ — see PUREBRED

peek *n* an instance of looking especially briefly ⟨took a *peek* at her Christmas gift hidden in the closet⟩ — see LOOK 2

peek *vb* to take a quick or hasty look ⟨*peek* out the window and see if it's raining⟩ — see GLANCE 2

peel *vb* to remove the natural covering of ⟨she *peels* apples with lightning speed⟩
synonyms bark, flay, hull, husk, shell, shuck, skin
related words bare, denude, expose, scale, strip; pare

peel (off) *vb* to rid oneself of (a garment) ⟨*peeled off* the wet clothes and tossed them over the shower rod⟩ — see REMOVE 1

peeled *adj* lacking a usual or natural covering ⟨a *peeled* banana⟩ — see NAKED 2

peel off *vb* to leave a place often for another ⟨it's rude to *peel off* like that without thanking your host⟩ — see GO 2

peep *n* an instance of looking especially briefly ⟨stole a *peep* at our neighbor's new pool⟩ — see LOOK 2

peep *vb* to make a short sharp sound like a small bird ⟨the baby *peeps* and burbles when her mother picks her up⟩ — see CHIRP

peer *n* **1** a man of high birth or social position ⟨claims to be related to an English *peer*⟩ — see GENTLEMAN 1
2 one that is equal to another in status, achievement, or value ⟨a jury of one's *peers*⟩ — see EQUAL

peer *vb* to look long and hard in wonder or surprise ⟨visitors seem mesmerized as they *peer* at the variety of marine life in the aquarium's huge tank⟩ — see GAPE

peeress *n* a woman of high birth or social position ⟨a wedding invitation eagerly sought by every peer and *peeress* in the realm⟩ — see GENTLEWOMAN

peerless *adj* having no equal or rival for excellence or desirability ⟨the show's enduring success was a testimony to the *peerless* talents of its ensemble cast⟩ — see ONLY 1

peeve *n* **1** something that is a source of irritation ⟨my main *peeve* with the animal welfare organization is the endless stream of unsolicited trinkets in my mailbox⟩ — see ANNOYANCE 3
2 the feeling of being offended or resentful after a slight or indignity ⟨he holds on to a *peeve* until the offending person apologizes⟩ — see PIQUE

peeve *vb* to disturb the peace of mind of (someone) especially by repeated disagreeable acts ⟨she is constantly *peeved* by his habit of humming show tunes while she is trying to focus on her work⟩ — see IRRITATE 1

peeved *adj* subjected to and reacting with irritation ⟨we were short a cook, and *peeved* diners were getting up and leaving before we could serve them⟩ — see ANNOYED

peeving *adj* causing annoyance ⟨a *peeving* insistence that everyone drop their work just to help him⟩ — see ANNOYING

peevish *adj* easily irritated or annoyed ⟨I would rather figure things out on my own than ask that *peevish* librarian for help⟩ — see IRRITABLE

peevishness *n* readiness to show annoyance or impatience ⟨his constant *peevishness* made everyone around him cranky as well⟩ — see PETULANCE

peewee *n* a living thing much smaller than others of its kind ⟨that particular species is the *peewee* of the salmon world⟩ — see DWARF 1

peg *n* an individual part of a process, series, or ranking ⟨took the arrogant student down a *peg*⟩ — see DEGREE 1

peg *vb* **1** to arrange or assign according to type ⟨*pegged* her as a backstabber right from the beginning⟩ — see CLASSIFY 1
2 to send through the air especially with a quick forward motion of the arm ⟨*pegged* the ball to the second baseman⟩ — see THROW 1

peg (away) *vb* to devote serious and sustained effort ⟨the writer *pegged away* at his first novel for three years before he felt that it was ready to be published⟩ — see LABOR

peg out *vb, chiefly British* to stop living ⟨when her pet pig *pegged out* she grieved for weeks⟩ — see DIE 1

pejorative *adj* intended to make a person or thing seem of little importance or value ⟨the reviewer used the *pejorative* word "versifier" to refer to the writer, whose poems had struck a responsive chord with the general public⟩ — see DEROGATORY

pelage *n* the hairy covering of a mammal especially when fine, soft, and thick ⟨color variation in the snow leopard's *pelage*⟩ — see FUR 1

pelagic *adj* **1** of or relating to the sea ⟨among *pelagic* animals the undisputed king is the blue whale, the largest creature currently roaming the face of the earth⟩ — see MARINE 1
2 of, relating to, or occurring in the open sea ⟨at one time *pelagic* whaling was the cornerstone of the island's economy⟩ — see DEEP-SEA

pelf *n* something (as pieces of stamped metal or printed paper) customarily and legally used as a medium of exchange, a measure of value, or a means of payment ⟨a politician who seems more interested in *pelf* than in policy⟩ — see MONEY 1

pellet *n* a usually round or cone-shaped little piece of lead made to be fired from a firearm ⟨the tightly packed *pellets* of a shotgun cartridge⟩ — see BULLET

pell–mell *adj* **1** acting or done with excessive or careless speed ⟨when the theater doors opened, there was a *pell-mell* rush for the best seats⟩ — see HASTY 1

2 lacking in order, neatness, and often cleanliness ⟨*pell-mell* piles of books everywhere in the professor's library⟩ — see MESSY

pell–mell *adv* **1** in a confused and reckless manner ⟨tossed stuff *pell-mell* into the dorm room⟩ — see HELTER-SKELTER 1

2 with excessive or careless speed ⟨ran *pell-mell* down the road to get help⟩ — see HASTILY 1

pellucid *adj* **1** easily seen through ⟨the *pellucid* waters that lap upon that island's beaches⟩ — see CLEAR 1

2 not subject to misinterpretation or more than one interpretation ⟨her poetry has a *pellucid* simplicity that betrays none of the sweat that went into writing it⟩ — see CLEAR 2

¹pelt *n* a hard strike with a part of the body or an instrument ⟨gave the dog a sharp *pelt* on the nose with her rolled up newspaper⟩ — see ¹BLOW

²pelt *n* the outer covering of an animal removed for its commercial value ⟨caught beavers and sold the *pelts* to fur traders⟩ — see HIDE 1

pelt *vb* **1** to proceed or move quickly ⟨*pelted* away when the cops arrived⟩ — see HURRY 2

2 to send through the air especially with a quick forward motion of the arm ⟨*pelted* snowballs at each other while waiting for the bus⟩ — see THROW 1

3 to strike repeatedly ⟨*pelted* the other kids with pebbles⟩ — see BEAT 1

¹pen *n* a place of confinement for persons held in lawful custody ⟨earned six years in a federal *pen*⟩ — see JAIL

²pen *n* an enclosure with an open framework for keeping animals ⟨a goat *pen*⟩ — see CAGE

³pen *n* a person who creates a written work ⟨Alexander Hamilton is reckoned to be the pseudonymous *pen* behind two thirds of the *Federalist Papers*⟩ — see AUTHOR 1

¹pen *vb* to close or shut in by or as if by barriers ⟨remember to *pen* up the dogs when visitors come over⟩ — see ENCLOSE 1

²pen *vb* to compose and set down on paper the words of ⟨though relatively unknown at the time of his death, the composer had *penned* some of the most memorable show tunes of his era⟩ — see WRITE 1

penal *adj* inflicting, involving, or serving as punishment ⟨Australia was once a *penal* colony⟩ — see PUNITIVE

penalize *vb* to inflict a penalty on for a fault or crime ⟨the player was *penalized* for unsportsmanlike conduct⟩ — see PUNISH

penalizing *adj* inflicting, involving, or serving as punishment ⟨forced to listen to a *penalizing* lecture on the consequences of lying⟩ — see PUNITIVE

penalty *n* **1** a sum of money to be paid as a punishment ⟨the *penalty* for speeding is $10 for every mile over the speed limit⟩ — see FINE

2 suffering, loss, or hardship imposed in response to a crime or offense ⟨in some cases, the new *penalties* for drug offenses were harsher than those for violent crimes⟩ — see PUNISHMENT

3 the negative result caused by something that creates difficulty for achieving success ⟨suffered the *penalty* of his decision to leave school without graduating⟩ — see DISADAVANTAGE 2

penchant *n* a habitual attraction to some activity or thing ⟨a *penchant* for sitting by the window and staring moodily off into space⟩ — see INCLINATION 1

pendant *also* **pendent** *n* **1** an ornament worn on a chain around the neck or wrist ⟨Navajo necklaces with *pendants* finely crafted in genuine sky-blue turquoise⟩
synonyms bangle, charm, lavaliere (*also* lavalliere)
related words locket, teardrop

2 *chiefly British* a piece of cloth with a special design that is used as an emblem or for signaling ⟨a *pendant* that once flew on Nelson's flagship⟩ — see FLAG 1

pendent *or* **pendant** *adj* extending freely from a support from above ⟨the dining area is lit by tasteful *pendent* lamps over the tables⟩ — see DEPENDENT 1

pending *adj* **1** not yet settled or decided ⟨a decision is *pending* about whether to buy computers or sports equipment with this money⟩
synonyms open, undecided, undetermined, unresolved, unsettled
related words hanging; arguable, debatable, disputable, moot, uncertain, unsure
phrases in hand
near antonyms confirmed, established; certain, sure
antonyms decided, determined, resolved, settled

2 being soon to appear or take place ⟨a *pending* review of your work so far this term⟩ — see FORTHCOMING 1

3 giving signs of immediate occurrence ⟨the sky darkened with a *pending* storm⟩ — see IMMINENT 1

pending *prep* in the course of ⟨the government must continue to function *pending* negotiations for next year's budget⟩ — see DURING

pendulous *adj* **1** bending downward or forward ⟨a cow with a *pendulous* udder⟩ — see NODDING

2 extending freely from a support from above ⟨a *pendulous* crystal chandelier dominated the ballroom⟩ — see DEPENDENT 1

penetrable *adj* capable of being passed into or through ⟨unfortunately, our netting proved to be a rather *penetrable* barrier that allowed in our cabin a steady stream of mosquitoes⟩
synonyms passable, permeable, pervious, porous
related words absorbent; breathable
near antonyms airtight, watertight; close, compact, dense, thick
antonyms impassable (*also* impassible), impenetrable, impermeable, impervious, nonporous

penetrate *vb* to go or come in or into ⟨a needle *penetrated* the heavy canvas only with great effort⟩ — see ENTER 1

penetrating *adj* causing intense discomfort to one's skin ⟨an icy, *penetrating* rain that made you feel really miserable⟩ — see CUTTING 1

peninsula *n* an area of land that juts out into a body of water ⟨the *peninsula* is constantly buffeted by storms⟩ — see ²CAPE

penitence *n* a feeling of responsibility for wrongdoing ⟨the sincerity of the player's *penitence* is questionable—he began to express remorse only after the suspension was handed down⟩ — see GUILT 1

penitent *adj* feeling sorrow for a wrong that one has done ⟨a *penitent* gossip who had come to ask for forgiveness⟩ — see CONTRITE

penitentiary *n* a place of confinement for persons held in lawful custody ⟨a sentence in the state *penitentiary* for robbery⟩ — see JAIL

penman *n* **1** a person who creates a written work ⟨the prolific *penman* of dozens of horror stories⟩ — see AUTHOR 1

2 one who writes from dictation or copies manuscripts ⟨an essay on Jacob Shallus, the *penman* who inked the United States Constitution⟩ — see SCRIBE 1

penmanship *n* **1** the form or style of a particular person's writing ⟨doctors are famous for their illegible *penmanship*⟩ — see HANDWRITING 1

2 writing done by hand ⟨the students spend far more time honing their computer skills than they do improving their *penmanship*⟩ — see HANDWRITING 2

pennant *n* a piece of cloth with a special design that is used as an emblem or for signaling ⟨the stadium was festooned with *pennants* from past championships⟩ — see FLAG 1

penniless *adj* lacking money or material possessions ⟨went from being a *penniless* girl to owner of her own restaurant⟩ — see POOR 1

pennon *n* a piece of cloth with a special design that is used as an emblem or for signaling ⟨*pennons* flew from the yachts gathered in the harbor for the festival⟩ — see FLAG 1

penny–pincher *n* a mean grasping person who is usually stingy with money ⟨we've ended up treating that *penny-pincher* to dinner three times and she's never once offered to pay⟩ — see MISER

penny–pinching *adj* giving or sharing as little as possible ⟨the new CEO's *penny-pinching* ways have helped to keep the company out of bankruptcy⟩ — see STINGY 1

penny–pinching *n* **1** careful management of material resources ⟨they'll have to practice some *penny-pinching* if they want to save for a house⟩ — see ECONOMY
2 the quality or practice of being overly sparing with money ⟨reusing your tea bags is perhaps taking *penny-pinching* too far⟩ — see PARSIMONY 1

pennyworth *n* something bought or offered for sale at a desirable price ⟨even a used lawnmower would be a *pennyworth* at that price⟩ — see BARGAIN 1

pensive *adj* given to or marked by long, quiet thinking ⟨rainy days often put her in a *pensive* mood⟩ — see CONTEMPLATIVE

penstock *n* a long hollow cylinder for carrying a substance (as a liquid or gas) ⟨a *penstock* carried water for the waterwheel⟩ — see PIPE 1

penthouse *n* a smaller structure added to a main building ⟨had a small *penthouse* built to serve as a toolshed⟩ — see ANNEX

penumbra *n* **1** partial darkness due to the obstruction of light rays ⟨the lunar eclipse began with a subtle darkening of the lunar surface as it passed within the Earth's *penumbra*⟩ — see SHADE 1
2 something that covers or conceals like a piece of cloth ⟨a *penumbra* of despair fell over the doomed city⟩ — see CLOAK 1

penurious *adj* **1** giving or sharing as little as possible ⟨the company's *penurious* management could not be convinced of the need to earmark more money for research and development⟩ — see STINGY 1
2 lacking money or material possessions ⟨the most *penurious* members of the community are forced to depend on the services of the food bank⟩ — see POOR 1

penuriousness *n* **1** the quality or practice of being overly sparing with money ⟨he daily practiced such *penuriousness* that few would have guessed that he was one of the state's wealthiest residents⟩ — see PARSIMONY 1
2 the state of lacking sufficient money or material possessions ⟨the abject *penuriousness* of so many of the city's inhabitants should be a cause for concern⟩ — see POVERTY 1

penury *n* the state of lacking sufficient money or material possessions ⟨lived in a time when single women like herself faced a lifetime of genteel *penury*⟩ — see POVERTY 1

peon *n* a person who does very hard or dull work ⟨the company had plenty of low-paying positions for people who were content to be *peons* all their lives⟩ — see SLAVE 2

people *n pl* **1** human beings in general ⟨despite the horrors she witnessed, Anne Frank never lost her faith in *people*⟩
synonyms folks, humanity, humankind, public, species, world
related words community, society; crowd, masses, mob, populace, proletariat, rabble, rabblement, riffraff
2 the body of the community as contrasted with the elite ⟨tensions mounted until the *people* rose up in rebellion⟩ — see MASS 1
3 a group of persons who come from the same ancestor ⟨introduced my new boyfriend to my *people*⟩ — see FAMILY 1

people *vb* to supply with inhabitants ⟨a science-fiction novel about a mission to *people* Mars⟩ — see SETTLE 2

pep *n* active strength of body or mind ⟨the students always display considerably more *pep* during the weeks immediately prior to the holidays⟩ — see VIGOR 1

pep (up) *vb* to give life, vigor, or spirit to ⟨the music at the party *pepped* everyone *up*⟩ — see ANIMATE

pepper *vb* **1** to cover by or as if by scattering something over or on ⟨*pepper* the costume with flecks of glitter⟩ — see SCATTER 2
2 to mark with small spots especially unevenly ⟨spilled flour *peppered* the kitchen floor⟩ — see SPOT 1

peppery *adj* marked by a lively display of strong feeling ⟨the author of several *peppery* diatribes on religious intolerance⟩ — see SPIRITED 1

peppiness *n* the quality or state of having abundant or intense activity ⟨the *peppiness* of the city's music scene in the last year has been encouraging⟩ — see VITALITY 1

peppy *adj* **1** having active strength of body or mind ⟨a *peppy* and entertaining group of young musicians⟩ — see VIGOROUS 1
2 having much high-spirited energy and movement ⟨a *peppy* dance performance⟩ — see LIVELY 1

per *adv* for each one ⟨you can have them at 50 cents *per* or three for $1.25⟩ — see APIECE

per *prep* using the means or agency of ⟨the infection is spread to the rest of the body *per* the bloodstream⟩ — see BY 2

perambulate *vb* **1** to make one's way through, across, or over ⟨we decided to lazily *perambulate* the entire length of the esplanade and enjoy the fresh air⟩ — see TRAVERSE
2 to travel by foot for exercise or pleasure ⟨long summer evenings spent *perambulating* up and down the tree-lined streets of the quaint village⟩ — see HIKE 1

perambulation *n* a relaxed journey on foot for exercise or pleasure ⟨took an invigorating *perambulation* around the lake to get some fresh air⟩ — see WALK 1

perambulator *n* **1** a person who travels by foot for exercise or pleasure ⟨counts himself among that select group of hikers who are *perambulators* of the entire Appalachian Trail⟩ — see HIKER
2 *chiefly British* a small four-wheeled vehicle designed for pushing a baby around in ⟨nannies pushing *perambulators* around London's Hyde Park⟩ — see BABY CARRIAGE

perambulatory *adj* traveling from place to place ⟨*perambulatory* groups of protesters were all over the city during the political convention⟩ — see ITINERANT

per capita *adv* for each one ⟨we expect the students to receive less funding *per capita* this year due to a marked increase in the school-age population⟩ — see APIECE

perceive *vb* **1** to have a vague awareness of ⟨I thought I *perceived* a problem, but I wasn't sure⟩ — see FEEL 1
2 to make note of (something) through the use of one's eyes ⟨*perceived* that it was going to be a nice day⟩ — see SEE 1
3 to have a clear idea of ⟨I *perceive* your point, but I still disagree⟩ — see COMPREHEND 1

percentage *n* a measure of how often an event will occur instead of another ⟨since most car thefts are never solved, there will always be greedy people ready to take advantage of this *percentage*⟩ — see PROBABILITY 2

perceptible *adj* able to be perceived by a sense or by

the mind ⟨you should note a *perceptible* temperature change when you add the second element⟩

synonyms appreciable, apprehensible, detectable, discernible (*also* discernable), distinguishable, palpable, sensible

related words audible, observable, tangible, visible; clear, conspicuous, evident, eye-catching, manifest, noticeable, obvious, plain, ponderable, prominent, striking; apparent, distinct, identifiable, significant, straightforward

near antonyms inaudible, intangible, invisible; inconspicuous, indistinct, unnoticeable, unobtrusive; faint, insignificant, slight, trivial; buried, concealed, covert, disguised, hidden, obscure, shrouded, vague

antonyms impalpable, imperceptible, inappreciable, indistinguishable, insensible, undetectable

perception *n* **1** the ability to understand inner qualities or relationships ⟨a writer of considerable *perception*, she remembers how it feels to be confused and insecure⟩ — see WISDOM 1

2 the knowledge gained from the process of coming to know or understand something ⟨a growing *perception* of the enormity of the problem⟩ — see COMPREHENSION

perceptive *adj* **1** able to sense slight impressions or differences ⟨due to their ability to rotate their ears, cats are very *perceptive* when it comes to pinpointing the source of a sound⟩ — see ACUTE 1

2 having or showing deep understanding and intelligent application of knowledge ⟨a *perceptive* therapist was able to discover what was really troubling the youth⟩ — see WISE 1

perceptiveness *n* **1** the ability to understand inner qualities or relationships ⟨the author's keen *perceptiveness* allows her some unique insights into the lives of real-life heroes⟩ — see WISDOM 1

2 the state or quality of being able to sense slight impressions or differences ⟨a drama critic who was much respected for the *perceptiveness* of his critical observations⟩ — see ACUITY

perceptivity *n* **1** the ability to understand inner qualities or relationships ⟨with great *perceptivity* the author sees that the controversy embroiling the town is really about class and cultural differences⟩ — see WISDOM 1

2 the state or quality of being able to sense slight impressions or differences ⟨the *perceptivity* of that epicure's palate is legendary in food and wine circles⟩ — see ACUITY

perch *vb* **1** to come to rest after descending from the air ⟨pigeons *perching* on the roof⟩ — see ALIGHT 1

2 to establish or place comfortably or snugly ⟨*perched* the baby in a basket⟩ — see ENSCONCE 1

perchance *adv* it is possible ⟨*perchance* he is playing the devil's advocate, and the opinions he has expressed are not actually his own⟩ — see PERHAPS

percipience *n* the knowledge gained from the process of coming to know or understand something ⟨a novelist who reveals an exceptional *percipience* of human aspirations and desires⟩ — see COMPREHENSION

percolate *vb* to flow forth slowly through small openings ⟨water *percolating* through the coffee filter⟩ — see EXUDE

percolate (into) *vb* to spread throughout ⟨the closing shot of the film is one of those iconic images that has long since *percolated into* the cultural consciousness⟩ — see PERMEATE

perdition *n* the place of punishment for the wicked after death ⟨simple stupidity is not enough to doom one to *perdition*⟩ — see HELL 1

perdure *vb* to remain indefinitely in existence or in the same state ⟨in so many ways, the influence and legacy of the Roman empire *perdures* to this very day⟩ — see CONTINUE 1

peregrinate *vb* **1** to make one's way through, across, or over ⟨Jack Kerouac's celebrated novel about penniless free spirits *peregrinating* the United States⟩ — see TRAVERSE

2 to take a trip especially of some distance ⟨a couple of backpacking college students who decided to spend the summer *peregrinating* around Ireland⟩ — see TRAVEL 1

peregrination *n* a going from one place to another usually of some distance ⟨planning a leisurely *peregrination* across Europe for our honeymoon⟩ — see JOURNEY

peregrine *adj* traveling from place to place ⟨a loyal cadre of *peregrine* workers who follow the presidential candidate from primary to primary⟩ — see ITINERANT

peremptoriness *n* an exaggerated sense of one's importance that shows itself in the making of excessive or unjustified claims ⟨the *peremptoriness* that was all too apparent in his voice irritated everyone⟩ — see ARROGANCE

peremptory *adj* **1** fond of ordering people around ⟨the governor's *peremptory* personal assistant began telling the crowd of reporters and photographers exactly where they had to stand⟩ — see BOSSY

2 forcing one's compliance or participation by or as if by law ⟨a *peremptory* summons to appear before the committee⟩ — see MANDATORY

3 having a feeling of superiority that shows itself in an overbearing attitude ⟨she had such a *peremptory* approach to running the club that people started to avoid her⟩ — see ARROGANT

4 having or showing a tendency to force one's will on others without any regard to fairness or necessity ⟨a *peremptory* insistence that the staff wait on them first⟩ — see ARBITRARY 1

perennial *adj* having an existence or validity that does not change or diminish ⟨her *perennial* pessimism was really starting to annoy her coworkers⟩ — see ABIDING

perfect *adj* **1** being entirely without fault or flaw ⟨a stunningly *perfect* performance—not the slightest mistake—won her the gold medal in women's figure skating⟩

synonyms absolute, faultless, flawless, ideal, immaculate, impeccable, indefectible, irreproachable, letter-perfect, picture-book, picture-perfect, seamless, unblemished

related words consummate, expert, masterly; classic, dandy, excellent, fabulous, fine, first-class, first-rate, grand, great, marvelous (*or* marvellous), prime, superb, superior, superlative, terrific, top, top-notch, unsurpassed; completed, finished, perfected, polished; complete, entire, intact, whole; mint, unbruised, undamaged, unimpaired, uninjured, unmarred, unspoiled; exceptional, fancy, high-grade, special; airtight, bulletproof; accurate, correct, exact, precise; inerrant, infallible, unerring, unfailing

near antonyms deficient, inadequate, incomplete, insufficient, wanting; unfinished, unpolished; fallible; blemished, blighted, broken, damaged, defaced, disfigured, impaired, injured, malformed, marred, misshapen, spoiled, vitiated; atrocious, execrable, wretched; imprecise, inaccurate, incorrect, inexact, wrong

antonyms amiss, bad, censurable, defective, faulty, flawed, imperfect, reproachable

2 having no exceptions or restrictions ⟨living in *perfect* happiness in the country⟩ — see ABSOLUTE 2

3 not lacking any part or member that properly belongs to it ⟨I have a *perfect* recollection of that conversation⟩ — see COMPLETE 1

perfect *vb* **1** to bring (something) to a state where nothing remains to be done ⟨*perfected* the arrangements for

their long-awaited European vacation⟩ — see FINISH 1
2 to make better ⟨an art teacher who seems to believe that you can always *perfect* a painting with some additional brush strokes⟩ — see IMPROVE

perfection *n* **1** exceptionally high quality ⟨Louis Comfort Tiffany produced art glass of such exquisite *perfection* that he has achieved cult status⟩ — see EXCELLENCE 1
2 the most perfect type or example ⟨Rembrandt's portraits are the *perfection* of the art of using facial expression, pose, and gesture to reveal the subject's interior life⟩ — see QUINTESSENCE 1
3 the quality or state of being very accurate ⟨audio recordings were reaching a level of *perfection* that earlier technicians had never dreamt possible⟩ — see PRECISION

perfectly *adv* **1** without any flaws or errors ⟨you did that handspring *perfectly* on your first try⟩
synonyms faultlessly, flawlessly, ideally, immaculately, impeccably, pat
related words excellently, fabulously, finely, grandly, greatly, marvelously, superbly, superiorly, superlatively, terrifically; exceptionally, fancily, specially
phrases to a nicety, to a T, to a turn, to the nines
near antonyms deficiently, inadequately, incompletely, insufficiently; fallibly; atrociously, execrably, wretchedly
antonyms amiss, badly, defectively, faultily, imperfectly
2 to a full extent or degree ⟨you know *perfectly* well what I'm talking about, so don't pretend⟩ — see FULLY 1

perfectness *n* the quality or state of being without restriction, exception, or qualification ⟨the *perfectness* of my happiness during that long-ago summer idyll can scarcely be described⟩ — see ENTIRENESS

perfervid *adj* having or expressing great depth of feeling ⟨the *perfervid* prose of a romance novel⟩ — see FERVENT 1

perfidious *adj* not true in one's allegiance to someone or something ⟨a *perfidious* campaign worker revealed the senator's strategy to his leading rival for the nomination⟩ — see FAITHLESS

perfidiousness *n* lack of faithfulness especially to one's husband or wife ⟨*perfidiousness* seems to descend to a whole other level when a husband cheats on a wife who's terminally ill⟩ — see INFIDELITY 1

perfidy *n* **1** lack of faithfulness especially to one's husband or wife ⟨he decided to forgive his wife's *perfidy*, choosing to ascribe it to a moment of uncharacteristic weakness⟩ — see INFIDELITY 1
2 the act or fact of violating the trust or confidence of another ⟨the full cost—both in compromised intelligence and in human life—of the double agent's *perfidy* is not yet known⟩ — see BETRAYAL

perforate *vb* to make a hole or series of holes in ⟨he *perforated* the sheet with his pencil and put it in his binder⟩
synonyms bore, drill, hole, pierce, punch, puncture, riddle
related words broach, tap; poke, prick, prickle; penetrate; burrow (into), excavate, gouge, groove, hollow; break, cut, gash, notch, rend, rupture, slash, slit, split
near antonyms fill, patch, plug, seal

perforation *n* **1** a mark or small hole made by a pointed instrument ⟨absentmindedly made *perforations* in his paper with his pencil⟩ — see PRICK 1
2 a place in a surface allowing passage into or through a thing ⟨poked the button through a *perforation* in the fabric⟩ — see HOLE 1

perforce *adv* because of necessity ⟨we must, *perforce*, deal with this issue immediately, as procrastination is not an option⟩ — see NEEDS

perform *vb* **1** to carry through (as a process) to completion ⟨she *performed* the task quickly and expertly⟩
synonyms accomplish, achieve, bring off, carry off, carry out, commit, compass, do, execute, follow through (with), fulfill (*or* fulfil), make, negotiate, perpetrate, prosecute, pull off, put through
related words bring about, effect, effectuate, implement; ace, nail; engage (in), practice (*also* practise); work (at); reduplicate, reenact, repeat; actualize, attain, realize; complete, end, finish, wind up
phrases go through
near antonyms fail; skimp, slight, slur
2 to have a certain purpose ⟨the kidneys *perform* as a filtering system for the blood⟩ — see FUNCTION
3 to present a portrayal or performance of ⟨has always dreamed of *performing* Hamlet on stage⟩ — see ACT 1
4 to produce a desired effect ⟨the new medication *performed* surprisingly well⟩ — see ACT 2

performance *n* **1** a presentation of an artistic work (as a piece of music) from a particular point of view ⟨a disappointing, lackluster *performance* of a classic of the musical theater⟩ — see ACCOUNT 2
2 the doing of an action ⟨the *performance* of her nightly ritual, the taking of a warm bath, calmed her⟩ — see COMMISSION 2

perfume *n* a sweet or pleasant smell ⟨the *perfume* of fresh flowers filled the room⟩ — see FRAGRANCE

perfume *vb* to fill or infuse with a pleasant odor or odor-releasing substance ⟨roses *perfumed* the wedding chapel⟩ — see SCENT 1

perfumed *adj* having a pleasant smell ⟨delicately *perfumed* stationery⟩ — see FRAGRANT

perfunctory *adj* having or showing a lack of interest or concern ⟨the violinist delivered a *perfunctory* performance that displayed none of the passion and warmth he was once known for⟩ — see INDIFFERENT 1

perhaps *adv* it is possible ⟨*perhaps* we will not have to take this exam, but I doubt it⟩
synonyms conceivably, maybe, mayhap, perchance, possibly
related words likely, probably; certainly, doubtless, sure, surely, undoubtedly; assumably, presumably, presumedly, supposably, supposedly

periapt *n* something worn or kept to bring good luck or keep away evil ⟨even rational, enlightened people have their *periapts*, which somehow make them feel a little more secure in an uncertain world⟩ — see CHARM 1

peril *n* **1** something that may cause injury or harm ⟨life is full of unexpected *perils*⟩ — see DANGER 2
2 the state of not being protected from injury, harm, or evil ⟨they were unhappy about sending their son into *peril* overseas⟩ — see DANGER 1

peril *vb* to place in danger ⟨a tribute to the men and women who, as firefighters, *peril* their lives daily⟩ — see ENDANGER

perilous *adj* involving potential loss or injury ⟨a *perilous* journey through hostile territory⟩ — see DANGEROUS 1

perimeter *n* the line or relatively narrow space that marks the outer limit of something ⟨soldiers guarding the *perimeter* of the camp⟩ — see BORDER 1

period *n* **1** an occurrence of menstruating ⟨girls having their *period* will be excused from gym class⟩
synonyms menstruation, monthlies
related words menses
2 an extent of time associated with a particular person or thing ⟨the Romantic *period* in music⟩ — see AGE 1

periodic *adj* **1** appearing or occurring repeatedly from time to time ⟨sent out *periodic* reminders about the office dress code⟩ — see REGULAR 1
2 occurring or appearing at intervals ⟨*periodic* snow

showers that might leave up to an inch⟩ — see INTERMITTENT 1

periodical *adj* **1** appearing in parts or numbers that follow regularly ⟨a *periodical* town newsletter that is supported by local advertisers⟩ — see SERIAL
2 occurring or appearing at intervals ⟨*periodical* announcements from airline personnel concerning the delay⟩ — see INTERMITTENT 1
3 appearing or occurring repeatedly from time to time ⟨*periodical* visits to the dentist will help keep your teeth healthy⟩ — see REGULAR 1

periodical *n* a publication that appears at regular intervals ⟨subscribed to three new *periodicals*⟩ — see JOURNAL 1

peripatetic *adj* traveling from place to place ⟨a *peripatetic* reporter for a cable news network⟩ — see ITINERANT

peripheral *adj* available to supply something extra when needed ⟨the IT consultant suggested that we update the drivers for all of the computer's *peripheral* devices⟩ — see AUXILIARY

periphery *n* the line or relatively narrow space that marks the outer limit of something ⟨the dogs are confined by an invisible electronic fence that runs along the *periphery* of the yard⟩ — see BORDER 1

periphrasis *n* the use of too many words to express an idea ⟨congressional hearings into the Watergate scandal were marked by an orgy of *periphrasis*, the expression "at this point in time" being a memorable example⟩ — see VERBIAGE 1

perish *vb* **1** to stop living ⟨12 people *perished* in the plane crash⟩ — see DIE 1
2 *chiefly British* to go through decomposition ⟨after being left out in the summer heat, the milk *perished* and had to be thrown out⟩ — see DECAY 1

perk *n* something given in addition to what is ordinarily expected or owed ⟨the salary's not great, but the *perks* make up for it⟩ — see BONUS

perk (up) *vb* **1** to become glad or hopeful ⟨we *perked up* once the sun came out⟩ — see CHEER (UP) 1
2 to move from a lower to a higher place or position ⟨the dog tilts her head and *perks up* her ears whenever someone speaks to her⟩ — see RAISE 1

perkily *adv* in a quick and spirited manner ⟨*perkily* took over the kitchen and whipped up a meal for her ailing aunt⟩ — see GAILY 2

perky *adj* having much high-spirited energy and movement ⟨a *perky* cheerleader⟩ — see LIVELY 1

permanent *adj* lasting forever ⟨a temporary compromise has been accepted until a more *permanent* solution can be agreed upon⟩ — see EVERLASTING 1

permanently *adv* for all time ⟨planned to stay there *permanently*⟩ — see EVER 1

permeable *adj* capable of being passed into or through ⟨a *permeable* fabric that allows your body heat to escape will be much more comfortable in the summertime⟩ — see PENETRABLE

permeate *vb* to spread throughout ⟨the smell of freshly baked bread *permeated* the house⟩
synonyms interpenetrate, percolate (into), pervade, riddle, suffuse, transfuse
related words diffuse (through), impregnate, pass (into), penetrate; fill (up); drench, imbue, infuse, saturate, soak, steep; flood, glut

permissible *adj* that may be permitted ⟨deployment overseas would be regarded as a *permissible* reason for late filing by members of the military⟩
synonyms admissible, allowable
related words acceptable, bearable, endurable, tolerable; accredited, allowed, authorized, certified, endorsed (*also* indorsed), licensed, OK (*or* okay), permitted, sanctioned, warranted; lawful, legal, licit; mandatory, ordered, required
near antonyms intolerable, unacceptable, unbearable, unendurable; objectionable; denied, disallowed, refused, rejected, vetoed; repressed, suppressed; outlawed
antonyms banned, barred, forbidden, impermissible, inadmissible, interdicted, prohibited, proscribed, verboten

permission *n* the approval by someone in authority for the doing of something ⟨she asked for *permission* to have a piece of candy⟩ ⟨the President granted *permission* for the foreign diplomats to have special quarters⟩
synonyms allowance, authorization, clearance, concurrence, consent, granting, green light, leave, license (*or* licence), sanction, sufferance, warrant
related words imprimatur, seal, signature, stamp; accreditation, certification; liberty, pass; concession, patent, permit; tolerance, toleration; acceptance, acquiescence, agreement, assent, OK (*or* okay); accord, grant
near antonyms denial, refusal, rejection, revocation; taboo (*also* tabu); injunction, veto; deterrence, discouragement, repression, suppression; ban, embargo, exclusion
antonyms interdiction, prohibition, proscription

permit *vb* **1** to give permission for or to approve of ⟨the school won't *permit* such an activity on its grounds⟩ — see ALLOW 1
2 to give permission to ⟨you are not *permitted* to swim at the town pond without a season pass⟩ — see ALLOW 2
3 to make able or possible ⟨we'll have our picnic on Thursday, weather *permitting*⟩ — see ENABLE 1
4 to fail to prevent (some behavior on someone's part) especially from neglect or indifference ⟨the college *permits* way too much drinking, in my opinion⟩ — see ALLOW 3

permit (of) *vb* to make possible especially to the exclusion of other possibilites ⟨the photo is too grainy to *permit of* anything more than a slight enlargement⟩ — see ALLOW (OF)

pernicious *adj* causing or capable of causing harm ⟨the *pernicious* effects of illegal narcotics on society⟩ — see HARMFUL

pernickety *adj, chiefly British* hard to please ⟨an Oxford don who's definitely a *pernickety* old chap⟩ — see FINICKY

perorate *vb* to talk as if giving an important and formal speech ⟨an arrogant scholar who never passes up an opportunity to posture and *perorate* on stunningly unimportant matters⟩ — see ORATE 1

peroration *n* a usually formal discourse delivered to an audience ⟨gave an eloquent *peroration* celebrating the nation's long tradition of religious tolerance and pluralism⟩ — see SPEECH 1

perpend *vb* to give serious and careful thought to ⟨spent the long weekend *perpending* what he wanted to do with his life⟩ — see PONDER

perpendicular *adj* rising straight up ⟨river rafters staring awestruck at the canyon's nearly *perpendicular* cliffs⟩ — see ERECT

perpetrate *vb* to carry through (as a process) to completion ⟨the anonymity of the Web allows pranksters to *perpetrate* their hoaxes with impunity⟩ — see PERFORM 1

perpetration *n* the doing of an action ⟨the *perpetration* of a series of pranks that resulted in an expulsion from school⟩ — see COMMISSION 2

perpetual *adj* **1** going on and on without any interruptions ⟨the *perpetual* rise and fall of the sea⟩ — see CONTINUOUS
2 having an existence or validity that does not change or diminish ⟨freedom of religion is a *perpetual* right that

is guaranteed by the nation's constitution⟩ — see ABIDING

3 lasting forever ⟨an immature jerk who seemed to be in a state of *perpetual* adolescence⟩ — see EVERLASTING 1

perpetually *adv* **1** for all time ⟨a group of jaded teenagers with their *perpetually* bored expressions⟩ — see EVER 1

2 on every relevant occasion ⟨the *perpetually* smiling host of the morning talk show⟩ — see ALWAYS 1

perpetuate *vb* to give eternal or lasting existence to ⟨we hope to *perpetuate* this holiday tradition⟩

synonyms eternalize, immortalize

related words commemorate, memorialize; celebrate, enshrine, honor; conserve, keep up, maintain, preserve, support, sustain; defend, guard, protect, safeguard

near antonyms extinguish, put out, snuff (out); annihilate, crush, decimate, demolish, destroy, devastate; eradicate, erase, expunge, extirpate, obliterate, wipe out

perpetuity *n* endless time ⟨lands that should remain in their wild state in *perpetuity*⟩ — see ETERNITY 1

perplex *vb* **1** to make complex or difficult ⟨let's not *perplex* the issue further with irrelevant concerns⟩ — see COMPLICATE 1

2 to throw into a state of mental uncertainty ⟨the question *perplexed* me⟩ — see CONFUSE 1

perplexed *adj* faced with difficulty or uncertainty about what to say, think, or do ⟨the convoluted instructions for calibrating a high-definition television will leave many consumers utterly *perplexed*⟩ — see HARD PUT

perplexity *n* a state of mental uncertainty ⟨seeing her *perplexity*, the teacher stepped in with a helpful hint⟩ — see CONFUSION 1

perquisite *n* **1** a small sum of money given for a service over and above what is due ⟨give the movers a *perquisite* if they do a good job⟩ — see [2]TIP 1

2 something given in addition to what is ordinarily expected or owed ⟨the use of a company car is one *perquisite* of the job⟩ — see BONUS

persecute *vb* **1** to cause persistent suffering to ⟨people who were *persecuted* simply for practicing their religious faith⟩ — see AFFLICT

2 to disturb the peace of mind of (someone) especially by repeated disagreeable acts ⟨she likes to *persecute* her sister with pointless, annoying questions at very inopportune times⟩ — see IRRITATE 1

persecuted *adj* suffering grave abuse or injustice at the hands of one in authority ⟨a nation that is still regarded as a refuge for *persecuted* people from around the world⟩ — see DOWNTRODDEN

persecutor *n* **1** a person who causes repeated emotional pain, distress, or annoyance to another ⟨years later his schoolyard *persecutor* would end up being one of his low-paid employees⟩ — see TORMENTOR

2 one who is obnoxiously annoying ⟨on this flight my airline-appointed *persecutor* was a chattering nitwit who could not stop talking about himself⟩ — see NUISANCE 1

persevere *vb* to continue despite difficulties, opposition, or discouragement ⟨although he was frustrated by the lack of financial resources and support, he *persevered* in his scientific research⟩

synonyms carry on, persist

related words dig in, hang on, keep up; follow through (with); knuckle down

phrases gut it out, hang in there

near antonyms give up, knock off, quit; bow, give in, submit, succumb, surrender, yield; falter, hang back, hesitate, shilly-shally, vacillate, waver, wobble (*also* wabble)

persevering *adj* continuing despite difficulties, opposition, or discouragement ⟨at the end of the long, winding trail, *persevering* hikers will be rewarded with an inviting, secluded lake⟩ — see PERSISTENT

persiflage *n* good-natured teasing or exchanging of clever remarks ⟨their tongue-in-cheek *persiflage* is sometimes mistaken for an exchange of insults by people who don't know them⟩ — see BANTER

persist *vb* **1** to continue despite difficulties, opposition, or discouragement ⟨she *persisted* in her efforts and eventually got the job she wanted⟩ — see PERSEVERE

2 to remain indefinitely in existence or in the same state ⟨my headache *persisted* for almost the entire day⟩ — see CONTINUE 1

persistence *n* uninterrupted or lasting existence ⟨the *persistence* of the fever for a week caused me great worry⟩ — see CONTINUATION

persistent *adj* continuing despite difficulties, opposition, or discouragement ⟨although his first attempts were singularly unsuccessful, he was *persistent* in his pursuit of a career in rock music⟩

synonyms dogged, insistent, patient, persevering, pertinacious, tenacious

related words assured, certain, dedicated, determined, firm, hell-bent, intent, positive, resolute, resolved, single-minded, sure; adamant, bullheaded, dogged, hardened, hardheaded, headstrong, implacable, indurate, mulish, obdurate, obstinate, opinionated, peevish, pertinacious, perverse, pigheaded, self-willed, stiff-necked, stubborn, unregenerate, unyielding, willful (*or* wilful); unfaltering, unhesitating, unwavering; resistant, wayward, wrongheaded; constant, devoted, faithful, good, loyal, staunch (*also* stanch), steadfast, steady, true; indomitable, unconquerable; hard, inflexible, relentless, stern, unbending, unflinching, unrelenting

near antonyms quitting, surrendering, yielding; faltering, hesitant, hesitating, irresolute, vacillating, wavering; disloyal, faithless, false, fickle, inconstant, perfidious, traitorous, treacherous

persnickety *adj* **1** hard to please ⟨as she got older, she got more and more *persnickety*⟩ — see FINICKY

2 requiring much time, effort, or careful attention ⟨lacked the patience to deal with such *persnickety* tasks as hanging wallpaper⟩ — see DEMANDING 1

3 being or characteristic of a person who has an offensive air of superiority and tends to ignore or disdain anyone regarded as inferior ⟨his *persnickety* attitude lost him some friends when they found out what he really thinks of "their kind"⟩ — see SNOBBISH

person *n* a member of the human race ⟨is there any *person* here who knows how to speak Spanish?⟩ — see HUMAN

personableness *n* the state or quality of having a pleasant or agreeable manner in socializing with others ⟨never exactly known for his *personableness*, our boss unexpectedly showed his warm side at the company picnic⟩ — see AMIABILITY 1

personage *n* **1** a member of the human race ⟨these sci-fi conventions attract *personages* of every description⟩ — see HUMAN

2 a person who is widely known and usually much talked about ⟨*personages* from the fields of sports and entertainment will be special guests at the political convention⟩ — see CELEBRITY 1

personal *adj* of, relating to, or belonging to a single person ⟨he kept *personal* items in a separate drawer⟩ — see INDIVIDUAL 1

personal effects *n pl* transportable items that one owns ⟨put all of your *personal effects* in the bin so that they can be x-rayed⟩ — see POSSESSION 2

personality *n* **1** a person who is widely known and usually much talked about ⟨a local television *personality*

who is beloved by area residents⟩ — see CELEBRITY 1
2 the set of qualities that make a person different from other people ⟨she's got a great *personality*⟩ — see INDIVIDUALITY 1
3 the set of qualities that makes a person, a group of people, or a thing different from others ⟨it has never been in the nation's *personality* to adhere to a rigid class system⟩ — see NATURE 1
4 an act or expression showing scorn and usually intended to hurt another's feelings ⟨every debate that was supposedly about the issues quickly degenerated into a juvenile exchange of *personalities*⟩ — see INSULT

personalize *vb* to represent in visible form ⟨in the character of the good-hearted, virtuous seaman, the author has *personalized* the concept of perfect innocence⟩ — see EMBODY 2

personalized *adj* of, relating to, or belonging to a single person ⟨a *personalized* jewelry box that had been engraved with her initials⟩ — see INDIVIDUAL 1

personally *adv* in person and usually privately ⟨the hostess told me *personally* that I was invited⟩ — see TÊTE-À-TÊTE

personal property *n* transportable items that one owns ⟨any *personal property* that is left in the lockers overnight will be impounded⟩ — see POSSESSION 2

personalty *n* transportable items that one owns ⟨and I will my *personalty* to my children⟩ — see POSSESSION 2

personate *vb* to pretend to be (what one is not) in appearance or behavior ⟨likes to *personate* the man of the world, but he's still the small-town hick that he always was⟩ — see IMPERSONATE 1

personator *n* a person who imitates another's voice and mannerisms for comic effect ⟨the science museum hired an Albert Einstein *personator* to greet guests for its special exhibit on the scientist⟩ — see MIMIC 1

personification *n* a visible representation of something abstract (as a quality) ⟨he's the *personification* of kindness⟩ — see EMBODIMENT

personifier *n* a visible representation of something abstract (as a quality) ⟨hailed the young war hero as a living *personifier* of all that is right with the generation now coming of age⟩ — see EMBODIMENT

personify *vb* to represent in visible form ⟨through her many good works she just *personifies* the spirit of charity⟩ — see EMBODY 2

personnel *n* a body of persons at work or available for work ⟨we finally have enough *personnel* to start that big project⟩ — see FORCE 1

perspective *n* **1** a way of looking at or thinking about something ⟨whether she was being rude or candid is all a matter of *perspective*⟩
synonyms angle, eye view, outlook, shoes, slant, standpoint, vantage point, viewpoint
related words interpretation, spin; belief, conviction, eye, feeling, judgment (*or* judgement), mind, mind-set, notion, opinion, perception, persuasion, sentiment, verdict, view; impression, take
phrases frame of reference, point of view
2 all that can be seen from a certain point ⟨the *perspective* from the hotel balcony was dominated by the lake and mountains⟩ — see VIEW 1

perspicuity *n* clearness of expression ⟨the *perspicuity* of this author's prose is one of the reasons why her novels are still read and those of her contemporaries are gathering dust⟩ — see SIMPLICITY 2

perspicuous *adj* not subject to misinterpretation or more than one interpretation ⟨believing that poetry need not be as *perspicuous* as prose, he writes poems that are intentionally ambiguous⟩ — see CLEAR 2

perspicuousness *n* clearness of expression ⟨the undeniable *perspicuousness* of the prosecutor's closing argument⟩ — see SIMPLICITY 2

persuade *vb* to cause (someone) to agree with a belief or course of action by using arguments or earnest request ⟨she *persuaded* us that she can indeed communicate with the dead⟩ ⟨he *persuaded* his teachers to grant an extension⟩
synonyms argue, bring, bring around, convert, convince, gain, get, induce, move, prevail (on *or* upon), satisfy, talk (into), win (over)
related words blandish, blarney, cajole, coax, entreat, exhort, fast-talk, urge, wheedle; allure, beguile, lead on, lure, seduce, snow, tempt; brainwash, overpersuade; incline, influence, move, prompt, sell, sway; attract, draw, entice, interest; chew over, converse, debate, discuss, dispute, hash (over), moot; reason (with)
near antonyms deter, discourage, dissuade, unsell

persuading *n* the act of reasoning or pleading with someone to accept a belief or course of action ⟨no amount of *persuading* could make her change her mind⟩ — see PERSUASION 1

persuasion *n* **1** the act of reasoning or pleading with someone to accept a belief or course of action ⟨the suffragists' gradual *persuasion* of the American people that voting rights had to be extended to women⟩
synonyms conversion, convincing, inducement, inducing, persuading, suasion
related words blandishment, cajolement, cajolery, coaxing, entreaty, exhortation, urging, wheedling; seduction, tempting; influencing, prompting, swaying; lobbying, pressuring; brainwashing, overpersuasion
2 a body of beliefs and practices regarding the supernatural and the worship of one or more deities ⟨debating theology with someone of a different *persuasion*⟩ — see RELIGION 1
3 an idea that is believed to be true or valid without positive knowledge ⟨he's of the *persuasion* that everything that happens in this world is part of a divine plan⟩ — see OPINION 1
4 the capacity to persuade ⟨there was an inherent *persuasion* in his sonorous voice that made listeners put aside any misgivings about his message⟩ — see COGENCY 1

persuasive *adj* having the power to persuade ⟨a *persuasive* argument for increasing funding of the city's library system⟩ — see COGENT

persuasiveness *n* the capacity to persuade ⟨the *persuasiveness* of her closing statement changed the minds of several jurors who had been leaning toward conviction⟩ — see COGENCY 1

pert *adj* **1** having much high-spirited energy and movement ⟨a *pert* girl who is a member of the cheerleading squad⟩ — see LIVELY 1
2 making light of something usually regarded as serious or sacred ⟨a *pert* retort that irritated the teacher⟩ — see FLIPPANT
3 sharp and pleasantly stimulating to the mind or senses ⟨a *pert* suggestion for a truly original marketing campaign⟩ — see PIQUANT

pertain *vb* **1** to be the property of a person or group of persons ⟨the belief that quality medical care is a right that *pertains* to everyone⟩ — see BELONG 2
2 to have a relation or connection ⟨a person who is an expert in anything *pertaining* to the history of the American theater⟩ — see APPLY 1

pertain (to) *vb* to have (something) as a subject matter ⟨where would I find books *pertaining to* birds?⟩ — see CONCERN 1

pertinacious *adj* **1** continuing despite difficulties, opposition, or discouragement ⟨a *pertinacious* little boy who was determined to catch and collect reptiles⟩ — see PERSISTENT
2 sticking to an opinion, purpose, or course of action in spite of reason, arguments, or persuasion ⟨a *pertina-*

cious salesman who would simply not take "No!" for an answer⟩ — see OBSTINATE

pertinaciousness *n* a steadfast adherence to an opinion, purpose, or course of action in spite of reason, arguments, or persuasion ⟨thanks to his *pertinaciousness*, he eventually succeeded where all others had failed⟩ — see OBSTINACY

pertinacity *n* a steadfast adherence to an opinion, purpose, or course of action in spite of reason, arguments, or persuasion ⟨without the *pertinacity* of the suffragists, voting rights for women would never have become a reality⟩ — see OBSTINACY

pertinence *n* the fact or state of being pertinent ⟨job applicants should question the *pertinence* of any questions about their personal lives⟩
synonyms applicability, bearing, connection, materiality, relevance, relevancy
related words appositeness, appropriateness, aptness, felicitousness, fitness, fittingness, rightness, seemliness, suitability, suitableness; importance, significance; usefulness
near antonyms inappositeness, inappropriateness, inaptness, infelicity, unfitness, unsuitability; insignificance; meaninglessness, pointlessness, uselessness
antonyms extraneousness, inapplicability, irrelevance, irrelevancy

pertinent *adj* having to do with the matter at hand ⟨he impressed the jury with his concise, *pertinent* answers to the attorney's questions⟩
synonyms applicable, apposite, apropos, germane, material, pointed, relative, relevant
related words appropriate, apt, fit, fitting, suitable; important, meaningful, significant; sensible, useful; admissible, allowable
phrases to the point
near antonyms frivolous, inconsequential, insignificant, little, minor, negligible, slight, trifling, trivial, unimportant; meaningless, purposeless, senseless, useless; inappropriate, inapt, unsuitable; inadmissible
antonyms extraneous, immaterial, impertinent, inapplicable, inapposite, irrelative, irrelevant, pointless

pertly *adv* in a quick and spirited manner ⟨the young girl *pertly* informed him that he was her favorite uncle⟩ — see GAILY 2

pertness *n* shameless boldness ⟨the startling *pertness* with which the waitress responded to our request to make a substitution⟩ — see EFFRONTERY

perturb *vb* to trouble the mind of; to make uneasy ⟨the caller's strange remark *perturbed* me enough to keep me awake that night⟩ — see DISTURB 1

perturbation *n* an uneasy state of mind usually over the possibility of an anticipated misfortune or trouble ⟨in her *perturbation* she kept calling her son, a freshman, to see if everything was all right at college⟩ — see ANXIETY 1

perturbed *adj* feeling or showing uncomfortable feelings of uncertainty ⟨a *perturbed* look betrayed her nervousness at her first job interview⟩ — see NERVOUS 1

perturbing *adj* causing worry or anxiety ⟨the *perturbing* news meant that we'd have to end our vacation prematurely⟩ — see TROUBLESOME

peruse *vb* to go over and mentally take in the content of ⟨*perused* the manuscript, checking for grammatical errors⟩ — see READ 1

perv *n* a person who has sunk below the normal moral standard ⟨an undercover officer visiting chat rooms in search of *pervs* preying on naive teens⟩ — see DEGENERATE

pervade *vb* to spread throughout ⟨the delicious scent of roasting turkey *pervaded* the house⟩ — see PERMEATE

perverse *adj* **1** easily irritated or annoyed ⟨how can you be so cheerful one day, and so *perverse* the next?⟩ — see IRRITABLE
2 having or showing lowered moral character or standards ⟨social conservatives who believe that Hollywood is a *perverse* world that exerts an unhealthy influence on the young⟩ — see CORRUPT
3 sticking to an opinion, purpose, or course of action in spite of reason, arguments, or persuasion ⟨a fact so self-evident that not even the most *perverse* of opponents could deny it⟩ — see OBSTINATE
4 not appropriate for a particular occasion or situation ⟨a convicted criminal seemed like a *perverse* choice for scoutmaster⟩ — see INAPPROPRIATE

perverseness *n* readiness to show annoyance or impatience ⟨the kind of *perverseness* that makes you want to snap at anyone who makes the mistake of greeting you⟩ — see PETULANCE

perversion *n* **1** a sinking to a state of low moral standards and behavior ⟨claimed that rap and rock music were responsible for the *perversion* of the nation's young people⟩ — see CORRUPTION 2
2 incorrect or improper use ⟨if there's a hidden charge for the service, then that's a *perversion* of the word "free"⟩ — see MISUSE

perversity *n* readiness to show annoyance or impatience ⟨a certain coworker's habitual *perversity* makes him unpleasant to be around⟩ — see PETULANCE

pervert *n* a person who has sunk below the normal moral standard ⟨longtime residents warned us not to go near the neighborhood *pervert*⟩ — see DEGENERATE

pervert *vb* **1** to change so much as to create a wrong impression or alter the meaning of ⟨that summary really *perverts* the other candidate's views on taxes⟩ — see GARBLE 1
2 to lower in character, dignity, or quality ⟨a movie that *perverted* the Bible story by reveling in the sinners' lewd behavior until just before the moment of divine retribution⟩ — see DEBASE 1
3 to put to a bad or improper use ⟨accused of *perverting* the Internal Revenue Service by using it to harass political opponents⟩ — see MISAPPLY

perverted *adj* having or showing lowered moral character or standards ⟨the *perverted* values of a society that had taken permissiveness to the extreme⟩ — see CORRUPT

pervertedness *n* a sinking to a state of low moral standards and behavior ⟨once hailed as a champion of the downtrodden, the cult leader is now remembered for his unspeakable *pervertedness*⟩ — see CORRUPTION 2

pervious *adj* capable of being passed into or through ⟨the new road has a *pervious* surface that will cut down on the amount of water that collects on it during heavy rains⟩ — see PENETRABLE

pesky *adj* causing annoyance ⟨the *pesky* problem of what to do with all the leftovers⟩ — see ANNOYING

pessimist *n* **1** one who emphasizes bad aspects or conditions and expects the worst ⟨she's such a *pessimist* that she's convinced she'll fail every test⟩
synonyms defeatist
related words Cassandra, Jeremiah; cynic, fatalist, nihilist; hardnose, pragmatist, realist; anti-utopian; knocker, naysayer; worrier, worrywart
near antonyms Don Quixote, dreamer, fantast, idealist, idealizer, ideologue (*also* idealogue), romantic, romanticist, utopian, visionary; sentimentalist
antonyms optimist, Pollyanna
2 a person who distrusts other people and believes that everything is done for selfish reasons ⟨a true *pessimist*, he's convinced that there will be wars as long as there are people to wage them⟩ — see CYNIC

pessimistic *adj* **1** emphasizing or expecting the worst

⟨with that *pessimistic* attitude, it's no wonder you're depressed⟩
synonyms bearish, defeatist, despairing, downbeat, hopeless
related words cynical, fatalistic, nihilist, nihilistic; desperate, discouraging, disheartening, inauspicious, unlikely, unpromising; bleak, cheerless, comfortless, depressing, desolate, dismal, dreary, funereal, gloomy, morose, saturnine, sepulchral, somber (*or* sombre), sullen; grim; contrary, hostile, negative
near antonyms auspicious, bright, encouraging, fair, golden, heartening, likely, promising, propitious; cheering, comforting, reassuring; favorable, good, positive; idealist, romantic, utopian, visionary; cheerful, cheery, chipper, sunny
antonyms hopeful, optimistic, Panglossian, Pollyanna, Pollyannaish (*also* Polyannish), rose-colored, rosy, upbeat
2 having or showing a deep distrust of human beings and their motives ⟨*pessimistic* about the prospects for a lasting peace in the area⟩ — see CYNICAL

pest *n* **1** a widespread disease resulting in a high rate of death ⟨one of the great *pests* of the 20th century was the influenza epidemic of 1918, which killed millions across the globe⟩ — see PLAGUE
2 one who is obnoxiously annoying ⟨stop being a *pest* to your sister and go find something else to do⟩ — see NUISANCE 1
3 something that is a source of irritation ⟨a never-ending construction project that continues to be a *pest* for motorists⟩ — see ANNOYANCE 3

pester *vb* to thrust oneself upon (another) without invitation ⟨one resident *pestered* the condo board about every little thing⟩ — see BOTHER 1

pestering *n* the act of making unwelcome intrusions upon another ⟨the endless *pestering* finally drove me to study at the library⟩ — see ANNOYANCE 1

pestiferous *adj* causing annoyance ⟨a *pestiferous* weed that has given gardeners no end of grief⟩ — see ANNOYING

pestilence *n* a widespread disease resulting in a high rate of death ⟨the fear that terrorists could unleash a *pestilence* that would wreak unspeakable havoc⟩ — see PLAGUE

pestilent *adj* **1** capable of being passed by physical contact from one person to another ⟨proper hand washing will help prevent the spread of most *pestilent* diseases⟩ — see CONTAGIOUS 1
2 causing annoyance ⟨*pestilent* reporters hounding him night and day⟩ — see ANNOYING
3 likely to cause or capable of causing death ⟨*pestilent* diseases such as bubonic plague and smallpox⟩ — see DEADLY 1

pestilential *adj* causing annoyance ⟨these *pestilential* little mosquitoes!⟩ — see ANNOYING

pesty *adj* causing annoyance ⟨a *pesty* toddler who never stopped asking questions⟩ — see ANNOYING

pet *adj* granted special treatment or attention ⟨spent my free time on my *pet* project⟩ — see DARLING 1

[1]pet *n* a person or thing that is preferred over others ⟨the teacher's *pet* was always getting special privileges⟩ — see FAVORITE

[2]pet *n* a state of resentful silence or irritability ⟨the teenager stalked off in a *pet* after being refused permission to go the movies⟩ — see SULK

pet *vb* to touch or handle in a tender or loving manner ⟨a cat who loves to be *petted*⟩ — see FONDLE

petition *n* an earnest request ⟨a flurry of *petitions* from eating and drinking establishments to be exempt from the new antismoking regulations⟩ — see PLEA 1

petition *vb* to make a request to (someone) in an earnest or urgent manner ⟨*petitioned* the judge to be excused from jury duty for financial hardship⟩ — see BEG

petitioner *n* one who asks earnestly for a favor or gift ⟨the lottery winner was beset by a horde of *petitioners*, all of whom thought that they were most deserving of his charity⟩ — see SUPPLICANT

petrify *vb* to deprive of emotional or intellectual vitality ⟨groupthink and peer pressure have so *petrified* the thinking of the company's top brass that they haven't produced an innovative product in years⟩ — see DEHYDRATE 1

pettiness *n* the quality or state of being unimportant ⟨the astonishing *pettiness* of most of the things that she fusses over⟩ — see INSIGNIFICANCE

pettish *adj* easily irritated or annoyed ⟨a *pettish* baby who always seemed to be crying⟩ — see IRRITABLE

pettishness *n* readiness to show annoyance or impatience ⟨his self-indulgent *pettishness* is more than his coworkers should endure⟩ — see PETULANCE

petty *adj* **1** not broad or open in views or opinions ⟨a *petty* little town that was not ethnically diverse and very happy about the situation⟩ — see NARROW 2
2 so small or unimportant as to warrant little or no attention ⟨obsessed over even *petty* problems⟩ — see NEGLIGIBLE 1

petulance *n* readiness to show annoyance or impatience ⟨I do not appreciate your *petulance* and eagerness to argue⟩
synonyms biliousness, choler, crankiness, crossness, crotchetiness, grouchiness, grumpiness, huffiness, irascibility, irascibleness, irritability, irritableness, peevishness, perverseness, perversity, pettishness, testiness, waspishness
related words cantankerousness, crustiness, curmudgeonliness, disagreeableness, dyspepsia, fretfulness, orneriness, sulkiness, surliness; aggression, aggressiveness, bellicosity, belligerence, belligerency, combativeness, contentiousness, contrariness, disputatiousness, feistiness, fight, pugnaciousness, pugnacity, quarrelsomeness, scrappiness, truculence, truculency; fussiness, querulousness, rudeness; oversensitiveness, sensitivity, supersensitivity, touchiness; animosity, antagonism, antipathy, fierceness, hostility, jaundice, rancor, unfriendliness; anger, exasperation, fury, indignation, rage, spleen, wrath; hot-bloodedness, passion
near antonyms forbearance, long-suffering, patience, tolerance, understanding; affability, agreeableness, amenity, amicability, cordiality, friendliness, geniality, sociability; amiability, amiableness, good-humoredness, good-naturedness, good-temperedness; coolness, serenity, tranquillity (*or* tranquility); easygoingness, gentleness, kindliness, mildness

petulant *adj* easily irritated or annoyed ⟨a *petulant* and fussy man who is always blaming everyone else for his problems⟩ — see IRRITABLE

pewter *adj* of the color gray ⟨a *pewter* car that's almost invisible in fog⟩ — see GRAY 1

phantasm *also* **fantasm** *n* **1** a conception or image created by the imagination and having no objective reality ⟨frightened by the *phantasms* of his own making⟩ — see FANTASY 1
2 the soul of a dead person thought of especially as appearing to living people ⟨believed that she'd seen the *phantasm* of her father on the anniversary of his death⟩ — see GHOST 1

phantasmal *adj* not real and existing only in the imagination ⟨*phantasmal* fears that have prevented her from living a normal life⟩ — see IMAGINARY

phantasmic *adj* not real and existing only in the imagination ⟨had spent a restless night during which he was visited by a series of *phantasmic* figures⟩ — see IMAGINARY

phantom *adj* not real and existing only in the imagination ⟨the company claimed that the only hazards involving its product were the *phantom* dangers created by consumer groups⟩ — see IMAGINARY

phantom *n* the soul of a dead person thought of especially as appearing to living people ⟨Halloween is supposed to be a time when *phantoms* return to walk among us⟩ — see GHOST 1

pharaoh *n* a person who uses power or authority in a cruel, unjust, or harmful way ⟨like some *pharaoh* of a third-world country, more interested in building monuments to himself than in creating a future for his people⟩ — see DESPOT

pharaonic *adj* unusually large ⟨the building of the Hoover Dam was a construction project of *pharaonic* proportions⟩ — see HUGE

pharmaceutical *n* a substance or preparation used to treat disease ⟨some *pharmaceuticals* can be quite risky unless taken correctly⟩ — see MEDICINE

pharmacist *n* a person who prepares drugs according to a doctor's prescription ⟨the *pharmacist* caught an error in the prescription's dosage⟩ — see DRUGGIST

pharmacy *n* a retail store where medicines and miscellaneous articles are sold ⟨stopped at the *pharmacy* for tissues and cold medicine⟩ — see DRUGSTORE

phase *n* **1** a certain way in which something appears or may be regarded ⟨the moral *phase* of the problem has yet to be considered⟩ — see ASPECT 1
2 an individual part of a process, series, or ranking ⟨in the final *phase* of production⟩ — see DEGREE 1

phased *adj* proceeding or changing by steps or degrees ⟨a *phased* construction of the tunnel through the heart of the city⟩ — see GRADUAL

phase down *vb* to grow less in scope or intensity especially gradually ⟨tourism along the coast *phases down* after Labor Day⟩ — see DECREASE 2

phat *adj, slang* of the very best kind ⟨fans agree that the rapper's latest CD is totally *phat*⟩ — see EXCELLENT

phenomenal *adj* **1** being out of the ordinary ⟨the *phenomenal* growth that the suburb has experienced over the last decade⟩ — see EXCEPTIONAL 1
2 being so extraordinary or abnormal as to suggest powers which violate the laws of nature ⟨the *phenomenal* ability to remember the names of thousands of people⟩ — see SUPERNATURAL 2

phenomenon *n* something extraordinary or surprising ⟨our jaws dropped when we saw this basketball *phenomenon* play for the first time⟩ — see WONDER 1

phew *interj* used to express disgust ⟨*phew*, what a stink!⟩ — see YUCK

philander *vb* to be sexually unfaithful ⟨he can't seem to stop *philandering*, even now that he's on his fifth marriage⟩ — see CHEAT 2

philanderer *n* a man given to seducing women ⟨an incorrigible *philanderer* who was often in lust and never in love⟩ — see DON JUAN

philanthropic *also* **philanthropical** *adj* having or showing a concern for the welfare of others ⟨a *philanthropic* society that has been doing good for over a century⟩ — see CHARITABLE 1

philanthropy *n* **1** a gift of money or its equivalent to a charity, humanitarian cause, or public institution ⟨among the industrialist's *philanthropies* was a college scholarship fund for deserving students from the inner city⟩ — see CONTRIBUTION
2 the giving of necessities and especially money to the needy ⟨much dedicated to *philanthropy*, the industrialist maintains a surprisingly modest lifestyle⟩ — see CHARITY 1
3 the quality or state of being generous ⟨a society dowager renowned for her *philanthropy*⟩ — see LIBERALITY

philharmonic *n* a usually large group of musicians playing together ⟨served as a conductor for the *philharmonic*⟩ — see ^{2}BAND 1

philippic *n* a long angry speech or scolding ⟨the head coach was briefly suspended after launching into a foul-mouthed *philippic* during a press conference⟩ — see TIRADE

philistine *n* a person who is chiefly interested in material comfort and is hostile or indifferent to art and culture ⟨the town's *philistines* who think that spending on the arts is a waste of taxpayers' money⟩
synonyms lowbrow, materialist
related words Babbitt; capitalist, plutocrat; bastard, boob, boor, bounder, cad, chuff, churl, clown, creep, cretin, crud [*slang*], crumb [*slang*], cur, dirtbag [*slang*], fink, heel, jerk, joker, louse, lout, rat, rat fink, rotter, scum, scumbag [*slang*]
near antonyms highbrow; middlebrow; egghead, intellectual, sage, thinker; brain, genius

philosophy *n* the basic beliefs or guiding principles of a person or group ⟨our *philosophy* is to do no harm to anyone⟩ — see CREED 1

phlegm *n* a lack of emotion or emotional expressiveness ⟨a man of remarkable *phlegm*, never showing enthusiasm nor displeasure⟩ — see APATHY 1

phlegmatic *adj* not feeling or showing emotion ⟨a strangely *phlegmatic* response to what should have been happy news⟩ — see IMPASSIVE 1

phone *vb* to make a telephone call to ⟨she *phoned* her friend to invite her over for dinner⟩ — see CALL 2

phony *also* **phoney** *adj* **1** being such in appearance only and made or manufactured with the intention of committing fraud ⟨a *phony* watch with a designer logo⟩ — see COUNTERFEIT 1
2 lacking in natural or spontaneous quality ⟨she always has this *phony* smile just before she betrays you⟩ — see ARTIFICIAL 1
3 not being or expressing what one appears to be or express ⟨her concern for our welfare is as *phony* as all get-out—she just wants to know our business⟩ — see INSINCERE

phony *also* **phoney** *n* **1** an imitation that is passed off as genuine ⟨the fancy "emerald" ring turned out to be a *phony*⟩ — see FAKE 1
2 one who makes false claims of identity or expertise ⟨the person who performed the liposuction operation was later discovered to be a *phony*⟩ — see IMPOSTOR

phony *vb* to imitate or copy especially in order to deceive ⟨the terrorists were able to move around the country using *phonied* driver's licenses⟩ — see FAKE 1

phony–baloney *or* **phoney–baloney** *adj* not being or expressing what one appears to be or express ⟨if you believe the company's *phony-baloney* press releases, it's in business solely for the benefit of mankind⟩ — see INSINCERE

phooey *interj* used to express disgust ⟨*phooey*, I can't believe we did so poorly in the rankings of the best places to live⟩ — see YUCK

photo *n* a picture created from an image recorded on a light-sensitive surface by a camera ⟨an album of wedding *photos*⟩ — see PHOTOGRAPH

photo *vb* to take a photograph of ⟨*photoed* the historic mansion for a decorating magazine⟩ — see PHOTOGRAPH

photog *n* one who takes photographs ⟨my friend's a *photog* for that supermarket tabloid⟩ — see PHOTOGRAPHER

photograph *n* a picture created from an image recorded on a light-sensitive surface by a camera ⟨the old *photograph* was faded but still clear enough to make out⟩
synonyms photo, pic, print, shot, snap, snapshot
related words blowup, close-up, enlargement, still;

telephoto; daguerreotype, ferrotype, monochrome, sepia, tintype

photograph *vb* to take a photograph of ⟨we've been *photographing* the baby virtually nonstop⟩
synonyms mug, photo, shoot, snap
related words image, picture, rephotograph, retake; film, videotape

photographer *n* one who takes photographs ⟨we'll need to choose a *photographer* for the wedding⟩
synonyms lensman, photog, shooter, shutterbug
related words cinematographer; paparazzo

photo–realistic *adj* closely resembling the object imitated ⟨*photo-realistic* portraits of birds that caused some gallerygoers to forget that they were looking at paintings⟩ — see NATURAL 2

phrase *n* a sequence of words having a specific meaning ⟨kids drawing literal representations of the *phrase* "to rain cats and dogs"⟩
synonyms expression, idiom
related words cliché (*also* cliche); locution, term; epithet, expletive, name; byword, cry, motto, shibboleth, slogan, watchword; archaism, colloquialism, euphemism, modernism, neologism, provincialism, vulgarism
phrases figure of speech

phrase *vb* to convey in appropriate or telling terms ⟨he had trouble thinking of how to *phrase* his question for the visiting dignitary⟩
synonyms articulate, clothe, couch, express, formulate, put, say, state, word
related words craft, frame; hint, imply, insinuate, intimate, suggest; paraphrase, rephrase, restate, reword, summarize, translate; communicate, disclose, speak, talk, tell, utter, verbalize, vocalize; describe, render, write up

phraseology *n* **1** a distinctive way of putting ideas into words ⟨I recognized the writer's distinctive *phraseology* even before I saw the name⟩ — see STYLE 1
2 the way in which something is put into words ⟨the unique *phraseology* of the suspect's answer stuck in my mind⟩ — see WORDING 1

phrasing *n* **1** an act, process, or means of putting something into words ⟨research has shown that the *phrasing* of the question on certain hot-button issues greatly influences the response⟩ — see EXPRESSION 1
2 the way in which something is put into words ⟨a particularly delicate and careful *phrasing* of the statement regarding the nature of the couple's relationship⟩ — see WORDING 1

phylactery *n* something worn or kept to bring good luck or keep away evil ⟨he wore a small *phylactery* on a cord around his neck⟩ — see CHARM 1

physic *n* a substance or preparation used to treat disease ⟨the museum has an exhibit on some of the strange *physics* that were once used to cure disease⟩ — see MEDICINE

physical *adj* **1** of or relating to the human body ⟨*physical* sensations such as heat and pain⟩
synonyms animal, bodily, carnal, corporal, corporeal, fleshly, material, somatic
related words anatomic (*or* anatomical), physiological (*or* physiologic); sensual, sensuous; hand-to-hand
near antonyms cerebral, inner, intellectual, mental, psychological (*also* psychologic); bodiless, immaterial, incorporeal, insubstantial, spiritual; ethereal, metaphysical, psychic (*also* psychical)
antonyms nonmaterial, nonphysical
2 relating to or composed of matter ⟨couldn't tell the difference between a *physical* object and a shadow in the dim light⟩ — see MATERIAL 1

physician *n* a person specially trained in healing human medical disorders ⟨you should always consult a *physician* if you develop a high fever⟩ — see DOCTOR

physique *n* the type of body that a person has ⟨she had a well-toned *physique*⟩
synonyms build, constitution, figure, form, frame, habit, shape
related words anatomy, structure

piazza *n, dialect* a covered structure adjoining an entrance to a building ⟨let's enjoy our mint juleps out on the *piazza*⟩ — see PORCH

pic *n* a picture created from an image recorded on a light-sensitive surface by a camera ⟨a coworker handed around some vacation *pics*⟩ — see PHOTOGRAPH

picayune *adj* **1** not broad or open in views or opinions ⟨the *picayune* ponderings of a commentator who steadfastly believes other cultures are inferior to our own⟩ — see NARROW 2
2 so small or unimportant as to warrant little or no attention ⟨irritatingly *picayune* complaints⟩ — see NEGLIGIBLE 1

picayune *n* something of little importance ⟨our lives don't amount to a *picayune* in the great scheme of things⟩ — see TRIFLE

pick *n* **1** a person or thing that is chosen ⟨that team is my *pick* to win the Super Bowl⟩ — see CHOICE 2
2 individuals carefully selected as being the best of a class ⟨the *pick* of the contestants will go on to the next competition⟩ — see ELITE 1
3 the power, right, or opportunity to choose ⟨you have first *pick* of your office mates for the softball team⟩ — see CHOICE 1
4 a hard strike with a part of the body or an instrument ⟨in the days when corporal punishment was permissible, it was not uncommon for an inattentive student to get a sharp *pick* in the head with a blackboard pointer⟩ — see [1]BLOW

pick *vb* **1** to catch or collect (a crop or natural resource) for human use ⟨*pick* peas and beans from the garden for dinner⟩ — see HARVEST
2 to decide to accept (someone or something) from a group of possibilities ⟨I *pick* you as my partner⟩ — see CHOOSE 1
3 to bring (something volatile or intense) into being ⟨he seems to be trying to *pick* a fight⟩ — see INCITE 1
4 to eat reluctantly and in small bites ⟨still suffering from the shock of his wife's death, he could do no more than *pick* halfheartedly at his food⟩ — see NIBBLE 1
5 to penetrate or hold (something) with a pointed object ⟨continued to *pick* the block of ice until she was able to extract the shrimp⟩ — see IMPALE

pick–and–shovel *adj* requiring considerable physical or mental effort ⟨she loves coming up with the "big idea" but hates the actual *pick-and-shovel* work of starting a new business⟩ — see HARD 2

picked *adj* singled out from a number or group as more to one's liking ⟨a *picked* group of people for the project⟩ — see SELECT 1

picked up *adj* being clean and in good order ⟨if your room is all *picked up*, you can go to the party⟩ — see NEAT 1

picker *n* someone with the right or responsibility for making a selection ⟨a book reviewer who is one of the *pickers* of the Pulitzer Prize for fiction⟩ — see SELECTOR

picket *n* a person or group that watches over someone or something ⟨set out a *picket* to watch the camp⟩ — see GUARD 1

picking *n* the act or process of selecting ⟨the *picking* of new recruits went on for three days⟩ — see SELECTION 1

pickle *n* a difficult, puzzling, or embarrassing situation from which there is no easy escape ⟨well, this is a bit of a *pickle* we've gotten ourselves into⟩ — see PREDICAMENT

pickled *adj* being under the influence of alcohol ⟨I must have been rather *pickled* when I agreed to your stupid scheme⟩ — see DRUNK

pick off *vb* to stop, seize, or interrupt while in progress or on course ⟨*picked off* more passes than any other player in the division⟩ — see INTERCEPT

pick up *vb* **1** to acquire complete knowledge, understanding, or skill in ⟨he has a knack for *picking up* a language in a few weeks⟩ — see LEARN 1

2 to bring together in one body or place ⟨*pick up* all of your things because we have to be off this beach before dark⟩ — see GATHER 1

3 to get possession of (something) by giving money in exchange for ⟨could you *pick up* some milk at the store?⟩ — see BUY 1

4 to gradually increase in ⟨the boat was just *picking up* speed when it was rammed by another boat⟩ — see GAIN 1

5 to move from a lower to a higher place or position ⟨*pick up* your feet while I vacuum in front of the sofa⟩ — see RAISE 1

6 to take or keep under one's control by authority of law ⟨police *picked up* the fugitive when she went out to buy food⟩ — see ARREST 1

7 to make a place neat and orderly by removing extraneous stuff ⟨I thought you said you had *picked up*, so why are these things still lying around the rec room?⟩ — see CLEAN (UP) 1

8 to begin again or return to after an interruption ⟨after the protestors were removed from the auditorium, the speaker *picked up* his lecture right where he had left off⟩ — see RESUME

9 to make neat ⟨the boy's bedroom looked like it hadn't been *picked up* in quite a while⟩ — see NEATEN

picky *adj* **1** hard to please ⟨a *picky* cat who would only eat one particular kind of food, and only if it was served in his special dish⟩ — see FINICKY

2 tending to select carefully ⟨she's *picky*, but she always finds the best quality in fresh meat and fish⟩ — see SELECTIVE

picnic *n* **1** a situation or state of carefree comfort ⟨babysitting her sister's three brats for the weekend was no *picnic*⟩ — see BEER AND SKITTLES

2 something that is easy to do ⟨this class is no *picnic*, but I've really been learning a lot⟩ — see CINCH 1

pictorial *adj* **1** consisting of or relating to pictures ⟨that photojournalist is planning to do a primarily *pictorial* report on the famine in Africa⟩
synonyms graphic (*also* graphical), imaginal, visual
related words photographic, video; drawn, painted, represented; illustrational, illustrative; hieroglyphic (*also* hieroglyphical), iconographic (*or* iconographical), ideogramic (*or* ideogrammic), ideogrammatic, ideographic, pictographic

2 producing a mental picture through clear and impressive description ⟨she writes a very *pictorial* kind of poetry, using words the way a painter applies strokes of color⟩ — see GRAPHIC 1

pictorialize *vb* to supplement with pictorial matter for the purpose of explanation or decoration ⟨N.C. Wyeth is remembered for vividly *pictorializing* a number of classic works of literature⟩ — see ILLUSTRATE 2

picture *n* **1** a two-dimensional design intended to look like a person or thing ⟨using only watercolors, she produced a strikingly lifelike *picture* of her mother⟩
synonyms icon (*also* ikon), illustration, image, likeness
related words delineation, depiction, representation, resemblance, view; portrait; daub, drawing, finger painting; etching, silhouette, sketch, watercolor; caricature, cartoon, doodle; collage, montage, photograph; hieroglyph, hieroglyphic, ideogram, ideograph; pictograph; diagram

2 a story told by means of a series of continuously projected pictures and a sound track ⟨the actor's latest *picture* is another thriller⟩ — see MOVIE 1

3 a vivid representation in words of someone or something ⟨the newspaper report gives a detailed *picture* of the current situation in that troubled country⟩ — see DESCRIPTION 1

4 position with regard to conditions and circumstances ⟨when personal opinion becomes part of the *picture*, the journalist isn't just reporting the news⟩ — see SITUATION 1

5 something or someone that strongly resembles another ⟨the young teen is the very *picture* of her mother⟩ — see IMAGE 1

6 something imagined or pictured in the mind ⟨I think I get the *picture*: you want me to leave⟩ — see IDEA 1

7 pictures *pl* the art or business of making a movie ⟨hoping for a career in *pictures*⟩ — see MOVIE 2

picture *vb* **1** to present a picture of ⟨the famous painting that *pictures* the Founding Fathers signing the Declaration of Independence⟩
synonyms depict, image, portray, represent
related words delineate, describe, document, render; outline, silhouette, sketch; illustrate, show; diagram; caricature

2 to form a mental picture of ⟨could easily *picture* the mining town from the vivid description of it in the author's memoirs⟩ see IMAGINE 1

3 to give a representation or account of in words ⟨*pictured* the sailing ship in vivid language⟩ — see DESCRIBE 1

4 to make a representation of by producing lines on a surface ⟨the next assignment is to *picture* your own face using colored pencils⟩ — see DRAW 1

picture–book *adj* being entirely without fault or flaw ⟨the players gave a *picture-book* performance that will go down in the annals of football as one of the all-time great games⟩ — see PERFECT 1

picture–perfect *adj* being entirely without fault or flaw ⟨it was a *picture-perfect* day for a picnic—the sun was shining and a light breeze stirred the air⟩ — see PERFECT 1

picturesque *adj* producing a mental picture through clear and impressive description ⟨wrote a *picturesque* tale of their journey across the country⟩ — see GRAPHIC 1

piddling *adj* so small or unimportant as to warrant little or no attention ⟨raised one final, *piddling* objection to the plan⟩ — see NEGLIGIBLE 1

piddly *adj* so small or unimportant as to warrant little or no attention ⟨there's only a *piddly* difference in price between the two paintings, so take whichever you prefer⟩ — see NEGLIGIBLE 1

piebald *adj* **1** consisting of many things of different sorts ⟨a model who owes his striking good looks to his markedly *piebald* ethnic background⟩ — see MISCELLANEOUS

2 having blotches of two or more colors ⟨a *piebald* horse that looked like it had been splashed with black and white paint⟩ — see PIED

piece *n* **1** a broken or irregular part of something that often remains incomplete ⟨a *piece* of stone fell from the crumbling wall⟩ — see FRAGMENT

2 a literary, musical, or artistic production ⟨presented a new interpretation of the *piece* by Mozart⟩ — see COMPOSITION 1

3 a portable weapon from which a shot is discharged by gunpowder ⟨carrying a *piece* under his coat⟩ — see GUN 1

4 something belonging to, due to, or contributed by an individual member of a group ⟨believes his *piece* of the profits should be higher⟩ — see SHARE 1

piece *vb* to form by putting together parts or materials ⟨you might want to *piece* together a quilt from those odd patches of cloth⟩ — see BUILD

piece by piece *adv* by small steps or amounts ⟨worked out the solution *piece by piece*⟩ — see GRADUALLY

piecemeal *adj* proceeding or changing by steps or degrees ⟨a *piecemeal* attempt to remedy the traffic congestion⟩ — see GRADUAL

piecemeal *adv* **1** by small steps or amounts ⟨remodeled their house *piecemeal* because of budgetary constraints⟩ — see GRADUALLY
2 into parts or pieces ⟨one well-aimed blow ripped the piñata *piecemeal*⟩ — see APART

pied *adj* having blotches of two or more colors ⟨although the mother's was pure black, the foal's coat was *pied*⟩
synonyms blotched, blotchy, dappled (*also* dapple), marbled, mottled, piebald, pinto, splotched, spotted
related words shaded; checkered, motley, multicolored, polychromatic, polychrome, varicolored, variegated; blotted, brindled (*or* brindle), calico, specked, speckled, streaked; colored, colorful, pigmented; dotted, peppered, sprinkled; stippled; discolored, dyed, marked, stained; flecked, streaked; bespattered, spattered
near antonyms monochromatic, monochrome, monochromic, solid

pie–eyed *adj* being under the influence of alcohol ⟨if you go out and get *pie-eyed* tonight, don't bother coming back⟩ — see DRUNK

piehole *n, slang* the opening through which food passes into the body of an animal ⟨"Shut your *piehole* or I'll shut it for you," the bully threatened⟩ — see MOUTH 1

pier *n* **1** a structure used by boats and ships for taking on or landing cargo and passengers ⟨tied the boat up at the *pier*⟩ — see DOCK
2 an upright shaft that supports an overhead structure ⟨a bridge *pier*⟩ — see PILLAR 1

pierce *vb* **1** to go or come in or into ⟨thoughts of revenge relentlessly *pierced* her mind⟩ — see ENTER 1
2 to make a hole or series of holes in ⟨*pierced* his ears with a needle⟩ — see PERFORATE
3 to penetrate or hold (something) with a pointed object ⟨the saber *pierced* his chest, releasing a spurt of blood⟩ — see IMPALE

piercing *adj* **1** causing intense discomfort to one's skin ⟨that light sweater will be no match for the *piercing* wind outside⟩ — see CUTTING 1
2 marked by a high volume of sound ⟨the frightened child emitted a *piercing* shriek that could be heard all over the house⟩ — see LOUD 1

piety *n* **1** belief and trust in and loyalty to God ⟨her *piety* is quiet but profound⟩ — see FAITH 1
2 the quality or state of being spiritually pure or virtuous ⟨among fellow clerics he is respected and admired for his *piety*⟩ — see HOLINESS
3 adherence to something to which one is bound by a pledge or duty ⟨familial *piety* keeps me from refusing to help my brother in this financial crisis⟩ — see FIDELITY

piffle *n* language, behavior, or ideas that are absurd and contrary to good sense ⟨the belief that soda is made out of acid is just *piffle*⟩ — see NONSENSE 1

piffling *adj* so small or unimportant as to warrant little or no attention ⟨from his perspective as a billionaire, what the governor got paid was a *piffling* amount⟩ — see NEGLIGIBLE 1

pig *n* one who eats greedily or too much ⟨all-you-can-eat buffets seem to encourage some people to become shameless *pigs*⟩ — see GLUTTON

pigeon *n* one who is easily deceived or cheated ⟨a confidence man in search of another *pigeon*⟩ — see [1]DUPE

piggish *adj* having a huge appetite ⟨a *piggish* dog who ate anything left within reach⟩ — see VORACIOUS 1

pigheaded *adj* sticking to an opinion, purpose, or course of action in spite of reason, arguments, or persuasion ⟨the kind of *pigheaded* person who seems to believe that facts only confuse an issue⟩ — see OBSTINATE

pigheadedness *n* a steadfast adherence to an opinion, purpose, or course of action in spite of reason, arguments, or persuasion ⟨thanks to your *pigheadedness* we missed our only chance to buy the house at a reasonable price⟩ — see OBSTINACY

pigment *n* a substance used to color other materials ⟨I'm running out of the black *pigment*⟩
synonyms color, colorant, coloring, dye, dyestuff, stain
related words tint, toner; cast, hue, shade, tinge

pigment *vb* to give color or a different color to ⟨*pigmented* varnishes⟩ — see COLOR 1

pig out *vb* to eat greedily or to excess ⟨one holiday when you're expected to *pig out* on junk food⟩ — see GORGE 2

pigpen *n* a dirty or messy place ⟨your room is a *pigpen*—so clean it up!⟩
synonyms dump, hellhole, hole, pigsty, shambles, sty
related words chaos, confusion, disarrangement, disarray, disorder, disorganization, mess, muddle, muss; havoc, hell, mare's nest, snake pit; clutter, jumble, litter, mishmash, welter

pigsty *n* a dirty or messy place ⟨the frat house was a *pigsty* the morning after the bacchanal⟩ — see PIGPEN

[1]pike *n* a passage cleared for public vehicular travel ⟨you can take the *pike* all the way to the city⟩ — see WAY 1

[2]pike *n* a weapon with a long straight handle and sharp head or blade ⟨a foot soldier armed with a *pike*⟩ — see SPEAR

[3]pike *n* the last and usually sharp or tapering part of something long and narrow ⟨the spear's metal *pike* was designed to cause a gaping wound when it was pulled out of the victim⟩ — see POINT 2

pike (out *or* off) *vb* to leave a place often for another ⟨early next morning the aloof guest just *piked out* without saying a word⟩ — see GO 2

piker *n* a mean grasping person who is usually stingy with money ⟨don't be such a *piker*—live it up a little while you're on vacation!⟩ — see MISER

pikestaff *n* a weapon with a long straight handle and sharp head or blade ⟨*pikestaffs* were in use from the Middle Ages to the 18th century⟩ — see SPEAR

pilaster *n* an upright shaft that supports an overhead structure ⟨the rectangular *pilasters* spaced along the building's facade lend an air of classical grandeur⟩ — see PILLAR 1

[1]pile *n* **1** a quantity of things thrown or stacked on one another ⟨a large *pile* of newspapers that needed to be disposed of⟩
synonyms cock, heap, hill, mound, mountain, stack
related words bank, bar, drift, embankment; bed, layer; mow, pyramid, rick; barrow, cairn, pyre; accumulation, aggregate, array, assemblage, collection, conglomeration, gathering, grouping, hoard, huddle, jumble, knot, pileup
2 a considerable amount ⟨a job that paid *piles* of money⟩ — see LOT 2
3 a very large amount of money ⟨she made a *pile* in the stock market just before it headed south⟩ — see FORTUNE 2

[2]pile *n* **1** a soft airy substance or covering ⟨the lush *pile* of the carpeting⟩ — see [1]FUZZ
2 the hairy covering of a mammal especially when fine, soft, and thick ⟨a dog with such a dense *pile* that he never minded the cold⟩ — see FUR 1

pile *vb* **1** to lay or throw on top of one another ⟨*piled* all the clothes on the chair before putting them away⟩

synonyms heap, mound, stack
related words bank; layer, pyramid; accumulate, amass, assemble, collect, concentrate, garner, gather, group, mass; bunch, clump, lump
antonyms unpile
2 to gather into a closely packed group ⟨the kids *piled* into the car⟩ — see ²PRESS 3

pile (up) *vb* to gradually form into a layer, pile, or mass ⟨snow *piling up* in the driveway at a rapid pace⟩ — see COLLECT 2

pileup *n* a mass or quantity that has piled up or that has been gathered over a period of time ⟨a *pileup* of e-mail messages that needed to be dealt with⟩ — see ACCUMULATION 1

pilfer *vb* to take (something) without right and with an intent to keep ⟨what sort of person would *pilfer* lunches from the office refrigerator?⟩ — see STEAL 1

pilgrimage *vb* to take a trip especially of some distance ⟨tourists *pilgrimaging* to all of the traditional destinations across Europe⟩ — see TRAVEL 1

pill *n* **1** a small mass containing medicine to be taken orally ⟨you'll have to take one of these *pills* every six hours for your flu⟩
synonyms cap, capsule, lozenge, tablet
related words cure, drug, medication, medicinal, pharmaceutical, physic, remedy, specific; miracle drug, wonder drug; potion, preparation; dosage, dose; drop, gelcap; bolus, pilule
2 a person whose behavior is offensive to others ⟨she can be such a *pill* when things don't go her way⟩ — see JERK 1

pillage *n* valuables stolen or taken by force ⟨the pirate ship was laden with the *pillage* of merchant ships from across the Spanish Main⟩ — see LOOT 1

pillage *vb* to search through with the intent of committing robbery ⟨soldiers *pillaging* the countryside for anything of value⟩ — see RANSACK 1

pillar *n* **1** an upright shaft that supports an overhead structure ⟨the ancient Greek temple boasted graceful marble *pillars* with richly ornamented tops⟩
synonyms column, pier, pilaster, post, stanchion
related words caryatid, pedestal; buttress, flying buttress; needle, obelisk; pile, piling
2 something or someone to which one looks for support ⟨my father has been my *pillar* throughout this crisis⟩ — see DEPENDENCE 2

pilot *adj* made or done as an experiment ⟨a new *pilot* program to train inner-city residents for jobs in the tech sector⟩ — see EXPERIMENTAL 1

pilot *n* one who flies or is qualified to fly an aircraft or spacecraft ⟨the airline is seeking experienced *pilots* to fly the new airplane⟩
synonyms airman, aviator, birdman, flier (*also* flyer)
related words ace, barnstormer, bush pilot, copilot, flyboy, test pilot; captain, skipper

pilot *vb* **1** to give advice and instruction to (someone) regarding the course or process to be followed ⟨*piloted* the figure skater through the national championships⟩ — see GUIDE 1
2 to point out the way for (someone) especially from a position in front ⟨the lead rider *piloted* the rest of the team⟩ — see LEAD 1
3 to operate or control the course of ⟨managed to *pilot* the plane to safety despite the failure of the left engine⟩ — see NAVIGATE 1

pimp *n* a man who solicits clients for a woman who is willing to engage in sexual activities for money ⟨the sting operation nabbed 15 prostitutes and two *pimps*⟩
synonyms cadet [*slang*], fancy man, pander, procurer
related words mack daddy [*slang*]; white slaver

pimp *vb* to take unfair advantage of ⟨a movie actress who *pimped* everybody she ever met as she clawed her way to the top⟩ — see EXPLOIT 1

pimping *adj* so small or unimportant as to warrant little or no attention ⟨got paid only a *pimping* amount of money as a reporter for a small newspaper⟩ — see NEGLIGIBLE 1

pimple *n* a small, inflamed swelling of the skin ⟨a painful *pimple* on his back⟩ — see POCK

pin *n* a lower limb of an animal ⟨a cat that was still a little unsteady on its *pins* after anesthesia⟩ — see LEG 1

pinch *n* **1** an instance of theft ⟨the *pinch* of my favorite sweater really bugged me!⟩ — see THEFT 2
2 the act of taking into one's control by authority of law ⟨an innocent person caught up in a city-wide *pinch* of drug dealers⟩ — see ARREST 1
3 a falling short of an essential or desirable amount or number ⟨this labor *pinch* means that there'll be long lines at the checkouts⟩ — see DEFICIENCY

pinch *vb* **1** to squeeze tightly between two surfaces, edges, or points ⟨the zipper on those jeans always *pinches* me⟩
synonyms nip
related words crimp, tweak; clasp, clutch, grasp, grip, hold, take
near antonyms drop, free, loose, loosen, release, spring
2 to take (something) without right and with an intent to keep ⟨*pinched* the earrings while the boutique owner was distracted by another customer⟩ — see STEAL 1
3 to take or keep under one's control by authority of law ⟨*pinched* the purse snatcher just two blocks from where he had robbed the old lady⟩ — see ARREST 1
4 to avoid unnecessary waste or expense ⟨if we *pinch* hard for the upcoming year, we can probably afford the vacation at that fancy resort⟩ — see ECONOMIZE

pincher *n* one who steals ⟨the *pincher* of the stolen electronics was caught by the police trying to sell them⟩ — see THIEF

pinch–hit *vb* to serve as a replacement usually for a time only ⟨assigned to *pinch-hit* as a math teacher for the remainder of the semester⟩ — see COVER 1

pinch hitter *n* a person or thing that takes the place of another ⟨the business owners brought in a *pinch hitter* until a permanent manager could be hired⟩ — see SUBSTITUTE

pinching *adj* giving or sharing as little as possible ⟨neighborhood kids who were trick-or-treating knew better than to bother to knock on that *pinching* couple's door⟩ — see STINGY 1

pinching *n* the quality or practice of being overly sparing with money ⟨this constant *pinching* is getting ridiculous—we can afford to turn on one or two lights!⟩ — see PARSIMONY 1

pinchpenny *adj* giving or sharing as little as possible ⟨her *pinchpenny* parents aren't likely to loan her the money she needs for the down payment⟩ — see STINGY 1

pine (for) *vb* to have an earnest wish to own or enjoy ⟨*pining for* a house in the mountains⟩ — see DESIRE 1

pinhead *n* a stupid person ⟨what *pinhead* put this together backwards?⟩ — see IDIOT

pinheaded *adj* not having or showing an ability to absorb ideas readily ⟨*pinheaded* leadership that got us into this mess⟩ — see STUPID 1

pinhole *n* a mark or small hole made by a pointed instrument ⟨*pinholes* in a bedsheet will look like stars if you shine a light from behind it⟩ — see PRICK 1

pining *n* a strong wish for something ⟨a sudden *pining* to have steak for dinner⟩ — see DESIRE 1

pinion *vb* to confine or restrain with or as if with chains ⟨Joan of Arc was *pinioned* to a stake and burned as a heretic⟩ — see BIND 1

pink *n* individuals carefully selected as being the best of a class ⟨the *pink* of society will be at the gala for the city's opera company⟩ — see ELITE 1

pink *vb* to penetrate or hold (something) with a pointed object ⟨accidentally *pinked* my shoulder with his fencing sword⟩ — see IMPALE

pink–slip *vb* to let go from office, service, or employment ⟨the company *pink-slipped* 300 workers in an effort to avoid bankruptcy⟩ — see DISMISS 1

pin money *n* a very small sum of money ⟨the summer intern made only *pin money* but gained valuable work experience⟩ — see MITE 1

pinnacle *n* the highest part or point ⟨a singer who has reached the *pinnacle* of success⟩ — see HEIGHT 1

pinpoint *adj* meeting the highest standard of accuracy ⟨the *pinpoint* measurement of brain tumors is critically important⟩ — see PRECISE 1

pinpoint *vb* **1** to find out or establish the identity of ⟨*pinpointed* the culprit by tracking calls from his cell phone⟩ — see IDENTIFY 1
2 to point or turn (something) toward a target or goal ⟨publishers like to be able to *pinpoint* publicity efforts where they will have the most effect⟩ — see AIM 1

pinprick *n* a mark or small hole made by a pointed instrument ⟨the nurse kindly put a decorated bandage over the *pinprick* from the injection⟩ — see PRICK 1

pinto *adj* having blotches of two or more colors ⟨somehow, the pure white mare had a *pinto* foal⟩ — see PIED

pint–size *or* **pint–sized** *adj* of a size that is less than average ⟨a *pint-size* wrestler who could defeat opponents twice his size⟩ — see SMALL 1

pinwheel *vb* to move in circles around an axis or center ⟨the kayaker had got sucked into the whirlpool, and his kayak was *pinwheeling* helplessly⟩ — see SPIN 1

pioneer *adj* coming before all others in time or order ⟨the nation's *pioneer* institution for the education of African-Americans⟩ — see FIRST 1

pioneer *n* a person who settles in a new region ⟨the hardships that the *pioneers* endured while taming the wilderness⟩ — see FRONTIERSMAN

pioneer *vb* to be responsible for the creation and early operation or use of ⟨he single-handedly *pioneered* the university's institute for medical research⟩ — see FOUND

pious *adj* **1** firm in one's allegiance to someone or something ⟨a *pious* supporter of his school's athletic teams, during winning and losing seasons alike⟩ — see FAITHFUL 1
2 showing a devotion to God and to a life of virtue ⟨a *pious* woman who decided to become a nun⟩ — see HOLY 1

piousness *n* **1** the pretending of having virtues, principles, or beliefs that one in fact does not have ⟨an outward *piousness* that was just a ploy to get him the support of religious-minded voters⟩ — see HYPOCRISY
2 the quality or state of being spiritually pure or virtuous ⟨the *piousness* with which he lived every aspect of his life was an inspiration to the other monks at the abbey⟩ — see HOLINESS

[1]**pip** *n* a small area that is different (as in color) from the main part ⟨a black horse with white *pips*⟩ — see SPOT 1

[2]**pip** *n* something very good of its kind ⟨that new sports car is a real *pip*⟩ — see JIM-DANDY

[3]**pip** *n, chiefly British* the feeling of impatience or anger caused by another's repeated disagreeable acts ⟨listening to all that chat show blather gives me the *pip*⟩ — see ANNOYANCE 2

pip *vb* to make a short sharp sound like a small bird ⟨baby birds *pipping* loudly in their nest⟩ — see CHIRP

pipe *n* **1** a long hollow cylinder for carrying a substance (as a liquid or gas) ⟨the plumber came and fixed the water *pipe* that was leaking⟩
synonyms channel, conduit, duct, leader, line, penstock, trough, tube
related words drain, drainpipe, funnel, hydrant, main, smokestack, spout, standpipe, stovepipe, tile, waste pipe, waterspout; pipage (*or* pipeage), pipeline, piping
2 an enclosed wooden vessel for holding beverages ⟨a full *pipe* of wine⟩ — see CASK

pipe *vb* **1** to cause to move to a central point or along a restricted pathway ⟨*piped* water into every house⟩ — see CHANNEL
2 to make a short sharp sound like a small bird ⟨the baby *piped* shrilly in his bed⟩ — see CHIRP

pipe down *vb* **1** to become still and orderly ⟨if you don't *pipe down*, we're turning this car around and going straight home!⟩ — see QUIET 1
2 to stop talking ⟨"*Pipe down* or I'll cancel recess!" the teacher commanded⟩ — see SHUT UP 1

pipe dream *n* a conception or image created by the imagination and having no objective reality ⟨opening our own restaurant has long been a *pipe dream*⟩ — see FANTASY 1

pipeline *n* a direct way of passing along information or supplies ⟨an equipment hauler serves as the columnist's *pipeline* for gossip about the rock band⟩ ⟨the battle was ultimately lost because the enemy had destroyed our *pipeline* for resupply⟩
synonyms channel
related words avenue, conduit, route; grapevine, outlet; fountainhead, origin, source, wellspring; supplier; connection, contact

pipe up *vb* to voice one's opinions freely with force ⟨don't worry, he'll *pipe up* if he feels he's being overlooked⟩ — see SPEAK UP

piping *adj* having a high musical pitch or range ⟨the *piping* sound of the teakettle caught my attention⟩ — see SHRILL

piping hot *adj* having a notably high temperature ⟨the appeal of *piping hot* cocoa after an afternoon of shoveling snow⟩ — see HOT 1

pippin *n* something very good of its kind ⟨gave a *pippin* of a commencement speech that earned a standing ovation⟩ — see JIM-DANDY

pip–squeak *n* a person of no importance or influence ⟨I'm not changing my job based on the advice of some *pip-squeak* who cornered me at a party⟩ — see NOBODY

piquancy *n* the quality or state of being stimulating to the mind or senses ⟨a talk show host known for the quickness and *piquancy* of his wit⟩ ⟨I appreciated the *piquancy* of the peppers in the sauce⟩
synonyms nip, pungency, spice, tang, zest, zing
related words raciness, spiciness; fieriness, hotness; acuteness, keenness, sharpness; provocativeness; excitement, invigoration, stimulant, stimulation, stimulus, thrill; bitterness, mordance, trenchancy; flavor, redolence, savor (*also* savour), savoriness, tastiness
near antonyms flatness, tastelessness; dullness (*also* dulness), insipidity, monotonousness, monotony, platitude, predictability, sameness, tediousness; blandness, thinness, weakness
antonyms insipidity

piquant *adj* sharp and pleasantly stimulating to the mind or senses ⟨a *piquant* tidbit of information about the new neighbors⟩ ⟨the *piquant* cuisine of India boasts some highly spiced dishes⟩
synonyms pert, poignant, pungent, salty, savory (*also* savoury), zesty, zingy
related words racy, spicy; fiery, gingery, hot, peppery, vinegary; acute, keen; biting, bitter, cutting, mordant, trenchant; animating, energizing, enlightening, exciting, galvanizing, invigorating, piquing, provocative, provoking; ambrosial, appetizing, delectable, delicious, luscious, palatable, scrumptious, toothsome; flavorful, savorous, tasty; absorbing, arresting, engaging, engross-

ing, enthralling, fascinating, gripping, interesting, intriguing, riveting
near antonyms flat, flavorless, savorless, tasteless; arid, banal, barren, boring, colorless, drab, dreary, dry, dull, flat, humdrum, leaden, monotonous, numbing, pedestrian, ponderous, predictable, stale, stodgy, tedious, tiring, uninteresting, wearisome, wearying; bland, dilute, thin, watery, weak
antonyms insipid, zestless

pique *n* the feeling of being offended or resentful after a slight or indignity ⟨in a fit of *pique* she posted embarrassing photos of her ex-boyfriend on the Internet⟩
synonyms dudgeon, huff, miff, offense (*or* offence), peeve, resentment, umbrage
related words aggravation, anger, annoyance, bother, botheration, discomfort, exasperation, frustration, grief, irritation, vexation; agitation, angriness, displeasure, distress, disturbance, indignation, irateness, ire, outrage, perturbation, upset; dander, temper; fit, pet, pouts, sulk(s), tantrum, tizzy; affront, barb, brickbat, dig, indignity, insult, put-down, slap, slight, slur
near antonyms satisfaction; appeasement, mollification, pacification; contentment, delight, gratification, happiness, pleasure

pique *vb* **1** to disturb the peace of mind of (someone) especially by repeated disagreeable acts ⟨her seat companion *piqued* her by repeatedly poking her in the ribs⟩ — see IRRITATE 1
2 to rouse to strong feeling or action ⟨their sarcastic comments *piqued* him to respond in kind⟩ — see PROVOKE 1
3 to think highly of (oneself) ⟨she *piques* herself on her considerable musical abilities⟩ — see PRIDE

piquing *adj* serving or likely to arouse a strong reaction ⟨*piquing* remarks that were said mainly to get a rise out of the other guests at the party⟩ — see PROVOCATIVE

piracy *n* the act or pursuit of robbing ships at sea ⟨many countries have harsh penalties for *piracy* now⟩
synonyms pirating
related words depredation, despoilment, despoliation, looting, marauding, pillaging, plunder, plundering, raiding, robbery, sacking; privateering

pirate *n* someone who engages in robbery of ships at sea ⟨Sir Francis Drake was a British *pirate* who preyed on Spanish ships with the connivance of Elizabeth I⟩
synonyms buccaneer, corsair, freebooter, rover
related words despoiler, looter, marauder, pillager, plunderer, raider, robber; privateer

pirate *vb* to take or make use of under a guise of authority but without actual right ⟨using *pirated* software that was subject to copyright⟩ — see APPROPRIATE 1

pirating *n* the act or pursuit of robbing ships at sea ⟨officially sanctioned *pirating* used to be common among warring nations⟩ — see PIRACY

pirouette *n* a rapid turning about on an axis or central point ⟨the ballerina's perfectly executed *pirouette*⟩ — see SPIN 1

pirouette *vb* to move in circles around an axis or center ⟨the ballerina *pirouetted* across the stage⟩ — see SPIN 1

pistol *n* a very energetic person ⟨a real *pistol*, she dances rings around the other performers⟩
synonyms dynamo, fireball, live wire
related words bootstrapper, go-ahead, go-getter, highflier (*or* highflyer), hummer, hustler, powerhouse, rustler, self-starter; achiever, comer, dasher; doer, enterpriser
near antonyms dawdler, idler, loafer, lounger, trifler; clock-watcher, goldbrick, shirker, slacker; couch potato, deadbeat, do-nothing, drone, layabout, lazybones, slouch, slug, slugabed, sluggard; dallier, laggard, lingerer, loiterer, slowpoke, stick-in-the-mud

pit *n* a sunken area forming a separate space ⟨removal of the tree stump left a gaping *pit* in the yard⟩ — see HOLE 2

pit–a–pat *vb* to expand and contract in a rhythmic manner ⟨her heart *pit-a-patted* with surprise⟩ — see PULSATE

pit bull *n* an aggressive and fiercely determined person ⟨a *pit bull* who won't let anyone stand in her way to the top of the corporate ladder⟩
synonyms barracuda, fire-breather, fire-eater, tiger
related words attack dog, hatchet man; aggressor, bully, shark; go-getter, hustler, live wire, self-starter; battler, fighter, scrapper; diehard, militant
near antonyms pushover, pussycat, reed, softy (*or* softie), weakling, wimp
antonyms milquetoast

pitch *n* **1** an act or instance of diving ⟨the daring *pitch* of the escaped prisoner into the swirling ocean waters at the base of the cliff⟩ — see DIVE 1
2 the degree to which something rises up from a position level with the horizon ⟨the steep *pitch* of the roof makes it too dangerous to walk on⟩ — see SLANT

pitch *vb* **1** to fix in an upright position ⟨needed help *pitching* a tent⟩ — see ERECT 1
2 to cast oneself head first into deep water ⟨when a wave hit the float, I lost my balance and *pitched* into the lake⟩ — see DIVE 1
3 to make a series of unsteady side-to-side motions ⟨the ship *pitched* in the choppy sea⟩ — see ROCK 1
4 to send through the air especially with a quick forward motion of the arm ⟨*pitched* the baseball almost 50 feet⟩ — see THROW 1
5 to get rid of as useless or unwanted ⟨we decided to *pitch* that whole system and start over again⟩ — see DISCARD
6 to provide publicity for ⟨the cutting-edge ad agency was hired to *pitch* our products to a younger generation of consumers⟩ — see PUBLICIZE 1
7 to set or cause to be at an angle ⟨the roof should be *pitched* steeply enough to prevent an excessive accumulation of snow⟩ — see LEAN 1

pitch (upon) *vb* to come upon unexpectedly or by chance ⟨at a garage sale you just might *pitch upon* a table exactly the size you need⟩ — see HAPPEN (ON *OR* UPON)

pitch–black *adj* **1** being without light or without much light ⟨finding anything in a *pitch-black* room is almost impossible⟩ — see DARK 1
2 having the color of soot or coal ⟨a *pitch-black* cat with green eyes⟩ — see BLACK 1

pitch–dark *adj* **1** being without light or without much light ⟨with its only light burned out, the closet was *pitch-dark*⟩ — see DARK 1
2 having the color of soot or coal ⟨on a whim she bleached her *pitch-dark* hair blond⟩ — see BLACK 1

pitched *adj* **1** inclined or twisted to one side ⟨*pitched* and badly weathered, the fence looked ready to fall down at any moment⟩ — see AWRY
2 running in a slanting direction ⟨a sharply *pitched* rooftop⟩ — see DIAGONAL

pitcher *n* a handled container for holding and pouring liquids that usually has a lip or a spout ⟨please bring me the *pitcher* of lemonade from the table⟩
synonyms ewer, flagon, jug
related words carafe, decanter; bucket, pail, pot; bottle, canteen, cup, fiasco, flask, jorum, mug, stein, stoup, tankard; kettle, teakettle; watering can, watering pot; beaker, cruse, vessel

pitch in *vb* to make a donation as part of a group effort ⟨everyone at the office *pitched in* to buy a gift for the soon-to-be-wed couple⟩ — see CONTRIBUTE 1

pitchy *adj* **1** being without light or without much light ⟨we stood staring into the *pitchy* dark forest, trying to determine what had made the strange cry⟩ — see DARK 1

2 having the color of soot or coal ⟨the trigger-happy soldiers couldn't see a thing in the *pitchy* darkness⟩ — see BLACK 1

piteous *adj* deserving of one's pity ⟨a *piteous* beggar huddled in the doorway of an abandoned building⟩ — see PATHETIC 1

pitfall *n* **1** a danger or difficulty that is hidden or not easily recognized ⟨buying a house can be full of *pitfalls* for the unwary⟩
synonyms booby trap, catch, catch-22, gimmick, gotcha, hitch, joker, land mine, snag
related words snare, trap, trip wire, web; hazard, peril, risk; bomb, bombshell, kicker, surprise (*also* surprize); bait, decoy, lure
2 something that may cause injury or harm ⟨one of the *pitfalls* of ignorance is that people will also assume you're stupid⟩ — see DANGER 2

pith *n* the central part or aspect of something under consideration ⟨finally got to the *pith* of the discussion⟩ — see CRUX

pithily *adv* in a few words ⟨the observation that "War is hell" is how General Sherman *pithily* summed up his experiences in combat⟩ — see SHORTLY 1

pithiness *n* the quality or state of being marked by or using only few words to convey much meaning ⟨the memorable *pithiness* of Calvin Coolidge's campaign announcement: "I do not choose to run for President in 1928"⟩ — see SUCCINCTNESS

pithy *adj* marked by the use of few words to convey much information or meaning ⟨a fairly *pithy* criticism about a notably lengthy novel⟩ — see CONCISE

pitiable *adj* **1** arousing or deserving of one's loathing and disgust ⟨the sales presentation was a *pitiable* display of ineptitude and disorganization⟩ — see CONTEMPTIBLE 1
2 deserving pitying scorn (as for inadequacy) ⟨a *pitiable* attempt at singing that generated snickers⟩ — see PITIFUL 1
3 deserving of one's pity ⟨a *pitiable*, starving old dog⟩ — see PATHETIC 1

pitiful *adj* **1** deserving pitying scorn (as for inadequacy) ⟨that piece of junk is a *pitiful* excuse for a car⟩
synonyms contemptible, despicable, miserable, pathetic, pitiable, sad, sorry, wretched
related words deplorable, discreditable, disgraceful, disreputable, ignominious, infamous, misbegotten, notorious, shameful; abhorrent, abominable, beastly, detestable, hateful, lousy, odious, stinking; bad, inferior, lame, poor; disgusting, dishonorable, shameful; meritless, unworthy, worthless; scandalous, shocking, sordid, unsavory
near antonyms admirable, commendable, creditable, laudable, meritorious, praiseworthy, redoubtable; notable, noteworthy, noticeable, outstanding, reputable, worthy; excellent; flawless, perfect; honorable, noble; honest, straight
antonyms decent, presentable, respectable
2 arousing or deserving of one's loathing and disgust ⟨a *pitiful* coward⟩ — see CONTEMPTIBLE 1
3 deserving of one's pity ⟨*pitiful* orphans who had lost everything in the war⟩ — see PATHETIC 1

pitiless *adj* having or showing a lack of sympathy or tender feelings ⟨gave the beggar in the street a *pitiless* look and kept on walking⟩ — see HARD 1

pittance *n* a very small sum of money ⟨the internship offers only a *pittance* for a salary, but it is a great opportunity to gain experience⟩ — see MITE 1

pitter–patter *vb* to expand and contract in a rhythmic manner ⟨his heart *pitter-pattered* with excitement as he waited for the right moment to propose⟩ — see PULSATE

pity *n* **1** a regrettable or blameworthy act ⟨it's a *pity* the woodchuck ate all the flowers after you put so much effort into the garden⟩ — see CRIME 2
2 the capacity for feeling for another's unhappiness or misfortune ⟨a woman of boundless *pity* who tried to care for every abandoned animal she found⟩ — see HEART 1

pity *vb* to have sympathy for ⟨I always *pity* the people who have to work in this freezing weather⟩
synonyms ache (for), bleed (for), commiserate (with), compassionate, condole (with), feel (for), sympathize (with), yearn (over)
related words care (for); grieve (for), sorrow (for); love; empathize (with), identify (with); tolerate, understand
near antonyms disregard, ignore, neglect, overlook; dislike, hate, scorn

pivot *n* the central part or aspect of something under consideration ⟨an issue that is the real *pivot* of the controversy⟩ — see CRUX

pivot *vb* to move (something) in a curved or circular path on or as if on an axis ⟨the telescope is mounted on a tripod so you can easily *pivot* it for viewing in any direction⟩ — see TURN 1

pivotal *adj* of the greatest possible importance ⟨the report was missing a *pivotal* piece of information⟩ — see CRUCIAL

pixie *also* **pixy** *adj* tending to or exhibiting reckless playfulness ⟨resorted to some *pixie* high jinks to liven up the office party⟩ — see MISCHIEVOUS 1

pixie *also* **pixy** *n* an imaginary being usually having a small human form and magical powers ⟨leave a dish of milk and some bread out for the *pixies*⟩ — see FAIRY

pixieish *adj* tending to or exhibiting reckless playfulness ⟨the actress had a *pixieish* quality that served her well in screwball comedies⟩ — see MISCHIEVOUS 1

pixilated *also* **pixillated** *adj* suffering from mental confusion ⟨a *pixilated* waitress who couldn't seem to get anything straight⟩ — see DIZZY 2

pizzazz *or* **pizazz** *n* the power of irresistible attraction ⟨he doesn't have the *pizzazz* to be a leading man in the movies⟩ — see CHARM 2

pizzazzy *or* **pizazzy** *adj* **1** attractively eye-catching in style ⟨the couple's coordinated prom outfits are witty and *pizzazzy* but still tasteful⟩ — see JAZZY 1
2 having much high-spirited energy and movement ⟨the dance company put on a well-choreographed and *pizzazzy* performance⟩ — see LIVELY 1

placard *n* a sheet bearing an announcement for posting in a public place ⟨a *placard* announcing a campaign rally at the downtown plaza⟩ — see POSTER

placard *vb* **1** to affix (as a notice) to or on a suitable place ⟨*placarded* the poster about the upcoming play to the bulletin board⟩ — see [1]POST 1
2 to make known openly or publicly ⟨*placarded* the news about the planned construction project all over the neighborhood⟩ — see ANNOUNCE

placate *vb* to lessen the anger or agitation of ⟨attempted to *placate* the screaming child by offering him a cookie⟩ — see PACIFY 1

placating *adj* tending to lessen or avoid conflict or hostility ⟨a *placating* comment that seemed to calm everyone down a bit⟩ — see PACIFIC 1

placatory *adj* tending to lessen or avoid conflict or hostility ⟨a *placatory* effort to improve relations with the townspeople, who were upset about the wild campus parties⟩ — see PACIFIC 1

place *n* **1** the area or space occupied by or intended for something ⟨the *place* chosen for the picnic⟩ ⟨there's the *place* where I left my umbrella⟩

synonyms emplacement, locale, locality, location, locus, point, position, site, spot, venue, where
related words scene; precinct, region, section, sector; here, there
2 a building, room, or suite of rooms occupied by a service business ⟨we're going to our favorite *place* to eat⟩
synonyms establishment, joint, parlor, salon
related words spot, station; facility, installation; club, house; den, dive, hole
3 an assignment at which one regularly works for pay ⟨a friend got her a *place* in a department store's clothing department⟩ — see JOB 1
4 an extent or area available for or used up by some activity or thing ⟨let's make a *place* around our campfire for the newest member of our group⟩ — see ROOM 1
5 the action for which a person or thing is specially fitted or used or for which a thing exists ⟨knew his *place* in the organization⟩ — see ROLE
6 the place where one lives ⟨they have a nice little *place* in the country⟩ — see HOME 1
7 the placement of someone or something in relation to others in a vertical arrangement ⟨came in fourth *place* in the marathon⟩ — see RANK 1
8 a situation or activity for which a person or thing is best suited ⟨with skills largely limited to those honed from endless hours of video games, he was having a hard time finding a *place* in the business world⟩ — see NICHE 2
9 an individual part of a process, series, or ranking ⟨well, in the first *place*, you shouldn't even be here⟩ — see DEGREE 1
place *vb* **1** to arrange something in a certain spot or position ⟨he carefully *placed* the flowers in a vase⟩
synonyms depose, deposit, dispose, emplace, fix, lay, position, put, set, set up, situate, stick
related words move, rearrange, reorder, shift; orient; establish, locate, plant, settle; clap, flop, plank, plop, plump, plunk (*or* plonk), plunk down, slap; ensconce, niche; assemble, collect; carry; berth, park; affix, anchor, lock, lodge, wedge; array, lay out, line up, queue, rank; set down
near antonyms relocate, remove, take; banish; dislodge, displace, replace, supersede, supplant
2 to arrange or assign according to type ⟨I'd *place* those cyclists in the advanced group for the training ride⟩ — see CLASSIFY 1
3 to decide the size, amount, number, or distance of (something) without actual measurement ⟨I'd *place* that as roughly the third largest house in the neighborhood⟩ — see ESTIMATE 2
4 to take or have a certain position within a group arranged in vertical classes ⟨*placed* second in the competition⟩ — see RANK 1
5 to pick (someone) by one's authority for a specific position or duty ⟨*placed* the recent college grad in the company's research and development division⟩ — see APPOINT 2
6 to present or bring forward for discussion ⟨once again the issue of recurrent vandalism at the high school was *placed* before the town council⟩ — see INTRODUCE 2
7 to provide with a paying job ⟨most of the trainees at the TV station are *placed* in clerical positions⟩ — see EMPLOY 1
placid *adj* **1** free from emotional or mental agitation ⟨an exceptionally *placid* mother who was rarely upset by her six children⟩ — see CALM 2
2 free from storms or physical disturbance ⟨a *placid* lake⟩ — see CALM 1
3 free from disturbing noise or uproar ⟨a vacation in the *placid* lake community⟩ — see QUIET 1
placidity *n* **1** a state of freedom from storm or disturbance ⟨the *placidity* of the area makes it a perfect vacation spot for people who just want to relax⟩ — see CALM 1
2 evenness of emotions or temper ⟨his evident lack of *placidity* makes him poorly suited for such a stressful job⟩ — see EQUANIMITY
3 freedom from disquieting or oppressive thoughts or emotions ⟨her apparent *placidity* belied an inner turmoil as she faced a life-altering decision⟩ — see PEACE 2
plague *n* a widespread disease resulting in a high rate of death ⟨the Black Death was a *plague* that killed about one third of Europe's population in the Middle Ages⟩
synonyms pest, pestilence
related words murrain; epidemic, pandemic; affection, affliction, ailment, contagion, illness, infection, infirmity, malady, sickness; blight, curse, scourge
plague *vb* to cause persistent suffering to ⟨*plagued* by a cough for all of last week⟩ — see AFFLICT
plaguey *also* **plaguy** *adj* causing annoyance ⟨I've had this *plaguey* cough for weeks now⟩ — see ANNOYING
plain *adj* **1** free from all additions or embellishment ⟨I like my hamburgers *plain*, with no ketchup or relish⟩ ⟨just give us the *plain* facts and none of your snide comments⟩
synonyms bald, bare, naked, plain-vanilla, simple, unadorned, undecorated, unembellished, unornamented, unvarnished
related words denuded, divested, stripped; au naturel, earthy, elemental, homely, natural, unsophisticated; forthright, honest, modest, unpretentious; clean; antiseptic, austere, bleak, severe, spartan, stark; minimalist; inconspicuous, muted, restrained, sober, subdued, toned (down), unobtrusive; conservative, quiet, understated
near antonyms flamboyant, flashy, garish, gaudy, glittery, glitzy, loud, ostentatious, showy, splashy, swank (*or* swanky), tawdry; bedizened, florid, lurid, ornate; exaggerated, overdecorated, overdone, overwrought; baroque, elaborate, extravagant, ornate, rococo; appareled (*or* apparelled), arrayed, bedecked, decked-out, dressed, embroidered, garnished, trimmed
antonyms adorned, decorated, embellished, fancy, ornamented
2 free from added matter ⟨I'd prefer my pasta *plain*, not flavored with tomato or spinach or anything else⟩ — see PURE 1
3 free in expressing one's true feelings and opinions ⟨their piano teacher is honest and *plain*, if not always tactful⟩ — see FRANK
4 going straight to the point clearly and firmly ⟨a *plain* report on the current situation⟩ — see STRAIGHTFORWARD 1
5 not subject to misinterpretation or more than one interpretation ⟨let me make my meaning *plain*⟩ — see CLEAR 2
plain *adv* in an honest and direct manner ⟨told her *plain* that he loved her⟩ — see STRAIGHTFORWARD
plain *n* **1** a broad area of level or rolling treeless country ⟨the first settlers in that area lived on the vast *plains* in lonely log cabins⟩
synonyms campo, champaign, down(s), grassland, heath, lea (*or* ley), llano, moor, pampa, prairie, savanna (*also* savannah), steppe, tundra, veld (*or* veldt)
related words field, meadow; floodplain; bottom, bottomland, flat, lowland; plateau, table, tableland, upland
2 a wide space or area ⟨the vast *plains* of snow-covered earth that seemed to stretch endlessly⟩ — see EXPANSE
plainly *adv* **1** in an honest and direct manner ⟨you'll have to tell your relatives very *plainly* that you don't like perfume, or they'll keep giving it to you⟩ — see STRAIGHTFORWARD
2 without any question ⟨your wife is *plainly* upset that

you didn't invite her to the game with us⟩ — see INDEED 1

plainness *n* **1** the free expression of one's true feelings and opinions ⟨his unabashed *plainness* in telling people exactly what he thought of them was often offensive⟩ — see CANDOR 1
2 the quality or state of having a form or structure of few parts or elements ⟨the *plainness* and clean lines of that coffeemaker make it a piece of modern sculpture as well as a kitchen appliance⟩ — see SIMPLICITY 1

plainspoken *adj* free in expressing one's true feelings and opinions ⟨a *plainspoken* woman who never hesitated to speak the unvarnished truth⟩ — see FRANK

plainspokenness *n* the free expression of one's true feelings and opinions ⟨a movie reviewer known for his *plainspokenness* when assessing the latest offerings from Tinseltown⟩ — see CANDOR 1

plaint *n* **1** a crying out in grief ⟨the day after the massacre the *plaints* of bereaved mothers and wives could be heard throughout the village⟩ — see LAMENT 1
2 an expression of dissatisfaction, pain, or resentment ⟨that taxes are too high is perhaps the most perennial of *plaints*⟩ — see COMPLAINT 1

plaintiff *n* the person in a legal proceeding who makes a charge of wrongdoing against another ⟨the judge ruled that the *plaintiff's* lawsuit was groundless, and he dismissed it⟩ — see COMPLAINANT

plaintive *adj* expressing or suggesting mourning ⟨the puppy's *plaintive* expression after we put the toy away was rather amusing⟩ — see MOURNFUL 1

plaintively *adv* with feelings of bitterness or grief ⟨the man sighed *plaintively* as it became clear that he was getting nowhere with the officious bureacrat⟩ — see HARD 2

plain–vanilla *adj* free from all additions or embellishment ⟨we decided to buy the *plain-vanilla* model because we don't have a lot of money to spend on extras⟩ — see PLAIN 1

plait *n* a length of something formed of three or more strands woven together ⟨she wore a *plait* down her back that reached her waist⟩ — see BRAID

plait *vb* to form into a braid ⟨*plaited* the doll's hair so it wouldn't tangle⟩ — see BRAID

plan *n* **1** a method worked out in advance for achieving some objective ⟨there is a contingency *plan* in the office for handling almost any emergency⟩
synonyms arrangement, blueprint, design, game, game plan, ground plan, master plan, program, project, road map, scheme, strategy, system
related words collusion, conspiracy, plot; contrivance, device, gambit, maneuver, ruse, stratagem, subterfuge, trick; counterplan, counterstrategy; means, tactic, technique, way; procedure, protocol; conception, idea, projet, proposal, specific(s), specification(s); aim, intent, intention, purpose; diagram, formula, layout, map, pattern, platform, policy, recipe, setup
2 something that one hopes or intends to accomplish ⟨our *plan* is to finish up by next Friday⟩ — see GOAL

plan *vb* **1** to work out the details of (something) in advance ⟨we *planned* the school dance down to the smallest detail⟩
synonyms arrange, blueprint, budget, calculate, chart, choreograph, design, frame, lay out, map (out), organize, prepare, project, scheme (out), shape, strategize (about)
related words conspire, contrive, devise, intrigue, machinate, plot, put up; concert, get up; draft, outline, sketch; aim, figure, have on, intend, mean; contemplate, meditate, premeditate
2 to have in mind as a purpose or goal ⟨I *plan* to have a party for my birthday, even if I have to throw it myself⟩ — see INTEND 1

plane *adj* having a surface without bends, breaks, or irregularities ⟨you can do these tracings on any *plane* surface⟩ — see LEVEL 1

plane *n* a vehicle for traveling through the air that has fixed wings for lift ⟨a *plane* flew overhead⟩ — see AIRPLANE

¹plane *vb* to make free from breaks, curves, or bumps ⟨*planed* the wood for the picnic table perfectly smooth so that no one would get splinters⟩ — see EVEN 1

²plane *vb* to move through the air with or as if with outstretched wings ⟨an eagle *planed* effortlessly overhead, gliding on an air current⟩ — see FLY 1

planet *n* the celestial body on which we live ⟨our collective responsibility to conserve the *planet* and its natural resources for future generations⟩ — see EARTH 1

planetary *adj* unusually large ⟨a positively *planetary* new shopping development⟩ — see HUGE

plangent *adj* **1** expressing or suggesting mourning ⟨a *plangent*, haunting song about a long-ago love⟩ — see MOURNFUL 1
2 marked by a high volume of sound ⟨*plangent* organ music filled the church⟩ — see LOUD 1
3 marked by conspicuously full and rich sounds or tones ⟨the strong, *plangent* tones of a Louis Armstrong trumpet solo⟩ — see RESONANT

plank *vb* to throw or set down clumsily or casually ⟨*planked* the carton down on the counter and left⟩ — see FLOP 1

plant *n* a building or set of buildings for the manufacturing of goods ⟨a furniture *plant* that employs hundreds of people⟩ — see FACTORY

plant *vb* **1** to put or set into the ground to grow ⟨I'll *plant* the marigold seeds in the spring⟩
synonyms drill, put in, seed, sow
related words bed; replant, transplant; broadcast, scatter; pot; overseed, reseed
near antonyms gather, harvest, reap
2 to be responsible for the creation and early operation or use of ⟨soon the sect had *planted* churches across the breadth of the colony⟩ — see FOUND
3 to set permanently in the consciousness or mind-set ⟨a profound respect for Mother Nature that had been *planted* by long experience with hurricanes⟩ — see IMPLANT 1

plantation *n* a settlement in a new country or region ⟨the struggling *plantation* almost failed during the first winter⟩ — see COLONY 1

planter *n* a person who cultivates the land and grows crops on it ⟨the *planters* are too busy around harvest time to pay the tourists much mind⟩ — see FARMER

plash *vb* **1** to flow in a broken irregular stream ⟨water *plashed* down the drain⟩ — see GURGLE
2 to move with a splashing motion ⟨a child happily *plashing* in the tub⟩ — see SLOSH 1
3 to wet or soil by striking with something liquid or mushy ⟨passing cars *plashed* us with roadside slush⟩ — see SPLASH 2

plaster *n* a medicated covering used to heal an injury ⟨put a *plaster* on the burn and don't touch it⟩ — see DRESSING 1

plastered *adj* being under the influence of alcohol ⟨I don't believe it: you're totally *plastered* at your own dinner party⟩ — see DRUNK

plastering *n* failure to win a contest ⟨our team's most recent *plastering* is just plain sad⟩ — see DEFEAT 1

plastic *adj* **1** capable of being easily molded or modeled ⟨Silly Putty is famous for being very *plastic*⟩
synonyms malleable, moldable, shapable (*or* shapeable), waxy
related words adaptable; bendable, bendy [*chiefly British*], ductile, pliable, pliant, supple, waxen, willowy; elastic, flexible, flexile, limber, resilient, workable;

bending, giving, kneadable, tractable, yielding
near antonyms inflexible, intractable, rigid, stiff
2 lacking in natural or spontaneous quality ⟨there's usually a *plastic* cordiality at these corporate events⟩ — see ARTIFICIAL 1

plasticity *n* the quality or state of being easily molded ⟨we chose that type of clay for its greater *plasticity*⟩
synonyms malleability
related words adaptability; ductility, pliability, pliableness, pliancy, pliantness, suppleness; elasticity, flexibility, limberness, resilience, workability, workableness
near antonyms inflexibility, rigidity, stiffness

[1]**plat** *n* a length of something formed of three or more strands woven together ⟨a *plat* of lace⟩ — see BRAID

[2]**plat** *n* **1** a small area of usually open land ⟨each settler was granted a *plat* to farm⟩ — see FIELD 1
2 a small piece of land that is developed or available for development ⟨plans to build a shopping center on the last undeveloped *plat* in town⟩ — see LOT 1

plat *vb* to form into a braid ⟨*plat* yarn into a cord⟩ — see BRAID

plate *n* **1** a small thin piece of material that resembles an animal scale ⟨the tiny silver *plates* on the brooch are arranged to look like fish scales⟩ — see [2]SCALE
2 something that visually explains or decorates a text ⟨the book's color *plate* illustrates the internal organs of the human body⟩ — see ILLUSTRATION 1

plateau *n* a broad flat area of elevated land ⟨Native Americans have inhabited the *plateau* for centuries⟩
synonyms altiplano, mesa, table, tableland
related words butte, dome, height, highland, upland; karoo (*or* karroo), puna

plateful *n* a considerable amount ⟨a degree in that field would give you a *plateful* of possibilities for a career⟩ — see LOT 2

platform *n* **1** a level usually raised surface ⟨you'll have to stand up there on the *platform* for your speech⟩
synonyms dais, podium, rostrum, stage, stand, tribune
related words altar, bimah (*also* bima), footpace, pulpit; riser, scaffold; balcony, gallery
2 a place or opportunity for communicating ideas and information ⟨for years the publisher has used his newspaper as a *platform* for his extreme political conservatism⟩ — see VENUE 1

platitude *n* an idea or expression that has been used by many people ⟨"blondes have more fun" is a silly *platitude*⟩ — see COMMONPLACE

platoon *n* a group of people working together on a task ⟨will need a *platoon* of assistants to mount the display at the spring flower show⟩ — see GANG 1

plaudit *n, usually* **plaudits** *pl* enthusiastic and usually public expression of approval ⟨the proud parents bragged that their daughter had received many *plaudits* for her academic achievements⟩ — see APPLAUSE 1

plausible *adj* worthy of being accepted as true or reasonable ⟨it's a *plausible* explanation for the demise of that prehistoric species⟩ — see BELIEVABLE

play *n* **1** activity engaged in to amuse oneself ⟨it's such a delight to watch the children in their *play*⟩
synonyms dalliance, frolic, frolicking, fun, fun and games, recreation, relaxation, rollicking, sport
related words gamboling (*or* gambolling), romping; amusement, diversion, entertainment; hobby, hobbyhorse, pastime; delight, enjoyment, pleasance, pleasure; friskiness, playfulness, sportiveness, wantonness; devilment, devilry (*or* deviltry), hanky-panky, hob, impishness, jinks, knavery, mischief, mischievousness, rascality, roguishness, waggery; binge, fling, kick, lark, revel, rollick, spree; hilarity, merriment, merrymaking, revelry, whoopee; buffoonery, high jinks (*also* hijinks), horseplay, tomfoolery
near antonyms drudgery, labor, work; duty, obligation, responsibility
2 a written work in which the story is told through speech and action that is intended to be acted out on stage ⟨we'll be putting on a school *play* using that stage⟩
synonyms drama, dramatization
related words interlude, playlet; comedy, comedy drama, docudrama, dramedy, melodrama, monodrama, musical, musical comedy, psychodrama, tragedy, tragicomedy; magnum opus, opus, work; adaptation
3 an attitude or manner not to be taken seriously ⟨I didn't mean to insult anyone, for it was all just *play*⟩ — see FUN 2
4 the act or practice of employing something for a particular purpose ⟨the host's sense of humor was obviously in *play* during the awards ceremony⟩ — see USE 1
5 a clever often underhanded means to achieve an end ⟨the guy at the bar made an unusually creative *play* to get her phone number⟩ — see TRICK 1

play *vb* **1** to engage in activity for amusement ⟨told her son that he needed some time to run and *play* in the yard after his hard work⟩
synonyms dally, disport, frolic, recreate, rollick, skylark, sport, toy
related words cavort, frisk, gambol, romp; dabble, trifle; amuse, divert, entertain; delight, please; dabble, fiddle (around), mess around, putter (around); bum (around), dawdle, goldbrick, hang, hang about [*British*], idle, loaf, lounge (around *or* about), relax, rest, screw around, slack (off); jest, joke, tease
near antonyms drudge, labor, plod, plug (away), slave, strain, strive, struggle, sweat, toil, work
2 to present a portrayal or performance of ⟨*played* Hamlet in the campus production of the classic⟩ — see ACT 1
3 to pretend to be (what one is not) in appearance or behavior ⟨stop *playing* the innocent, because I know that you were behind that prank⟩ — see IMPERSONATE 1
4 to spend time in aimless activity ⟨just *played* around while we waited for the bus to arrive⟩ — see FIDDLE (AROUND)
5 to deal with (something) usually skillfully or efficiently ⟨this is how we're going to *play* the situation⟩ — see HANDLE 1
6 to risk (something) on the outcome of an uncertain event ⟨figuring that she had little to lose, she *played* her last few bucks on the state lottery⟩ — see BET

play (on *or* upon) *vb* to take unfair advantage of ⟨the candidate *played on* the voters' prejudices⟩ — see EXPLOIT 1

play (upon) *vb* to control or take advantage of by artful, unfair, or insidious means ⟨*played upon* the customer's vanity to convince her to buy the expensive makeup kit⟩ — see MANIPULATE 1

play (with) *vb* to handle thoughtlessly, ignorantly, or mischievously ⟨please don't *play with* the telephone⟩ — see TAMPER (WITH)

playacting *n* a display of emotion or behavior that is insincere or intended to deceive ⟨it was clear to her friends that her reaction to the news was pure *playacting*⟩ — see MASQUERADE

play-by-play *n* a series of explanations or observations on something (as an event) ⟨on Monday mornings she usually gives her coworkers a detailed *play-by-play* on how her weekend date went⟩ — see COMMENTARY 1

play down *vb* **1** to express scornfully one's low opinion of ⟨out of sheer envy, she would always *play down* her sister's accomplishments⟩ — see DECRY 1
2 to reduce in apparent importance ⟨if you *play down* your part in the project, you won't get the credit you deserve⟩ — see SOFT-PEDAL

played out *adj* depleted in strength, energy, or freshness ⟨I'm just *played out* after the week I've had⟩ — see WEARY 1

player *n* **1** a person who plays a musical instrument ⟨a horn *player*⟩ — see MUSICIAN 1
2 one who acts professionally (as in a play, movie, or television show) ⟨a troupe of *players* used to give performances on the town green⟩ — see ACTOR 1
3 one who takes part in something ⟨a significant *player* in the negotiations⟩ — see PARTICIPANT

playful *adj* given to good-natured joking or teasing ⟨the little girl was lighthearted and *playful*⟩
synonyms antic, coltish, elfish, fay, frisky, frolicsome, larky, rollicking, sportful, sportive
related words coy, kittenish; gay, happy, lighthearted, whimsical; energetic, frolic, jocund, lively, merry, spirited, sprightly, spunky, vivacious; devilish, impish, knavish, mischievous, pixie (*also* pixy), rascally, roguish; amusing, diverting, enjoyable, entertaining, fun, pleasurable; dabbling, frivolous, goofy, silly, trifling; delightful, pleasant, pleasing; jesting, jocose, jocular, joking, prankish, teasing
near antonyms dutiful, responsible; grave, grim, serious, solemn, somber (*or* sombre), stern, stolid; no-nonsense, priggish, starchy, stuffy; decorous, formal, proper, sedate, staid; guarded, inhibited, restrained
antonyms earnest, serious-minded, sober, sobersided

playfulness *n* a natural disposition for playful behavior ⟨the *playfulness* of the kitten can be quite amusing⟩
synonyms coltishness, espièglerie, friskiness, impishness, larkiness, mischief, mischievousness, prankishness, sportfulness, sportiveness, tricksiness
related words coyness, kittenishness; archness, devilment, devilry (*or* deviltry), hob, rascality, roguishness, waggery; devilishness, diabolicalness, knavery; frivolousness; energy, liveliness, spiritedness, sprightliness, spunkiness, vivaciousness, vivacity; gaiety (*also* gayety), jocularity, jocundity, lightheartedness, mirthfulness, whimsicality
near antonyms graveness, grimness, serious-mindedness, seriousness, solemnity, solemnness, sternness; priggishness, starchiness, stuffiness; constraint, restraint, self-control
antonyms earnestness, soberness, sobersidedness

playhouse *n* a building or part of a building where movies are shown ⟨they're renovating the old *playhouse* and adding extra screens⟩ — see THEATER 1

play out *vb* to make complete use of ⟨we've finally *played out* the leftovers from that huge holiday meal⟩ — see DEPLETE 1

play up *vb* to indicate the importance of by centering attention on ⟨that TV news program *plays up* sensational stories just to get higher ratings⟩ — see EMPHASIZE 1

plea *n* **1** an earnest request ⟨the captive made an impassioned *plea* for his life to be spared⟩
synonyms adjuration, appeal, conjuration, cry, desire, entreaty, petition, pleading, prayer, solicitation, suit, suppliance, supplication
related words application, requisition; call, claim, demand, insistence
2 an explanation that frees one from fault or blame ⟨my only *plea* is that I've been overworked lately⟩ — see EXCUSE

plead *vb* to state (something) as a reason in support of or against something under consideration ⟨can I *plead* temporary insanity for having made that foolish decision?⟩ — see ARGUE 1

plead (for) *vb* to make a request for ⟨the children *pleaded for* a kitten for Christmas⟩ — see ASK (FOR) 1

plead (to) *vb* to make a request to (someone) in an earnest or urgent manner ⟨weary of charities that are always *pleading to* people of modest means to contribute even more than they already have⟩ — see BEG

pleader *n* one who asks earnestly for a favor or gift ⟨the parents finally granted the persistent *pleader* his wish: a puppy⟩ — see SUPPLICANT

pleading *adj* asking humbly ⟨a *pleading* husband seeking forgiveness once again from his long-suffering wife⟩ — see SUPPLIANT

pleading *n* an earnest request ⟨coldhearted tourists pointedly ignoring the *pleadings* of the city's many street urchins⟩ — see PLEA 1

pleasant *adj* **1** giving pleasure or contentment to the mind or senses ⟨the massage was extremely *pleasant* and relaxing⟩
synonyms agreeable, blessed (*also* blest), congenial, darling, delectable, delicious, delightful, delightsome, dreamy, dulcet, enjoyable, felicitous, good, grateful, gratifying, heavenly, jolly, luscious, nice, palatable, pleasing, pleasurable, pretty, satisfying, savory (*also* savoury), sweet, tasty, welcome
related words alluring, attractive, desirable, enviable, inviting, relishable, tempting; charming, enchanting, fascinating; calming, comforting, soothing; amusing, diverting, entertaining, recreative; affable, amiable, cheerful, cheery, comfortable, gemütlich, genial, goodly, good-natured, gracious, hospitable, kindly, personable; blissful, felicific, glad, happy, joyous; elating, exhilarating, intoxicating; ecstatic, euphoric, nirvanic, rapturous
near antonyms abominable, ghastly, god-awful, hellish, horrid, miserable, wretched; bilious, disgusting, distasteful, obnoxious, offensive, repellent (*also* repellant), repugnant, repulsive, revulsive, unsavory, vile, yucky (*also* yukky); abhorrent, detestable, hateful, odious; boring, commonplace, dull, flat, insipid, irksome, stale, tedious; displeasing, dissatisfying; depressing, disheartening, dismal, dreary, gloomy, heartbreaking, heartrending, joyless, lachrymose, sad, unhappy; deplorable, doleful, dolorous, lamentable, lugubrious, mournful, regrettable, sorrowful, tragic (*also* tragical); aggravating, annoying, exasperating, irritating, peeving, perturbing, vexing; forbidding; hostile, intimidating; angering, enraging, incensing, inflaming (*also* enflaming), infuriating, maddening, outraging, rankling, riling; distressing, disturbing, upsetting
antonyms disagreeable, pleasureless, unpalatable, unpleasant, unwelcome
2 having an easygoing and pleasing manner especially in social situations ⟨she has a reputation among the employees for being a demanding boss, but she's unexpectedly *pleasant* outside of work⟩ — see AMIABLE

pleasantly *adv* in a pleasing way ⟨we were *pleasantly* surprised by their offer to put us up for the night⟩ — see WELL 5

pleasantness *n* the state or quality of having a pleasant or agreeable manner in socializing with others ⟨his habitual *pleasantness* makes him everyone's first choice for a party guest⟩ — see AMIABILITY 1

pleasantry *n* **1** an act or utterance that is a customary show of good manners ⟨"how are you" is merely a social *pleasantry*⟩ — see CIVILITY 1
2 something said or done to cause laughter ⟨his after-dinner speeches usually include the sort of gentle *pleasantry* that raises a chuckle⟩ — see JOKE 1

please *vb* **1** to give satisfaction to ⟨fresh flowers *please* me greatly⟩
synonyms agree (with), content, delight, feast, gas [*slang*], glad [*archaic*], gladden, gratify, pleasure, rejoice, satisfy, suit, warm
related words appease, mollify, pacify, placate, soothe; assuage, quench, sate, satiate; excite, tickle, titillate; amuse, divert, entertain, treat; captivate, charm; galvanize, thrill; calm, comfort; cater (to), humor, indulge;

coddle, mollycoddle, pamper, spoil
near antonyms aggravate, annoy, bother, bug, chafe, cross, exasperate, gall, get, grate, irk, irritate, nettle, peeve, perturb, pique, put out, ruffle, vex; anger, enrage, incense, inflame (*also* enflame), infuriate, madden, outrage, rankle, rile, roil, steam up; provoke, rouse; agitate, distress, disturb, fret, upset; harass, harry, pester; affront, insult, offend
antonyms displease
2 to see fit ⟨clearly, you are going to do as you *please* no matter what I advise⟩ — see CHOOSE 2

pleased *adj* **1** experiencing pleasure, satisfaction, or delight ⟨she looked *pleased* with the gift⟩ — see GLAD 1
2 feeling that one's needs or desires have been met ⟨a sleepy, *pleased* cat⟩ — see CONTENT

pleasing *adj* giving pleasure or contentment to the mind or senses ⟨*pleasing* music in the background⟩ — see PLEASANT 1

pleasingly *adv* in a pleasing way ⟨the dining room at the inn has a *pleasingly* old-fashioned look to it⟩ — see WELL 5

pleasurable *adj* **1** giving pleasure or contentment to the mind or senses ⟨a *pleasurable* hot bath after a tiring day⟩ — see PLEASANT 1
2 providing amusement or enjoyment ⟨a number of *pleasurable* additions to the state fair this year⟩ — see FUN

pleasurably *adv* in a pleasing way ⟨we spent a *pleasurably* hectic day shopping for Christmas presents⟩ — see WELL 5

pleasure *n* **1** the feeling experienced when one's wishes are met ⟨nothing gives me more *pleasure* than a hot meal after a long day⟩
synonyms content, contentedness, contentment, delectation, delight, enjoyment, gladness, gratification, happiness, relish, satisfaction
related words afterglow; bliss, felicity, glee, gleefulness, joy, pleasance; amusement, diversion, entertainment; elatedness, elation, exhilaration, exultation, intoxication; ecstasy, euphoria, heaven, rapture; cheer, cheerfulness, exuberance, gaiety (*also* gayety), jollity, joyfulness, jubilation; joie de vivre; comfort, ease, restfulness
near antonyms misery, sadness, unhappiness, wretchedness; anguish, desolation, joylessness, sorrow, woe; dejection, depression, despondency, dispiritedness, gloom, melancholy; aggravation, annoyance, exasperation, irritation, pique, vexation; anger, fury, rage; agitation, distress, disturbance, upset; discomfort, restlessness, uneasiness
antonyms discontent, discontentedness, discontentment, displeasure, dissatisfaction, unhappiness
2 a source of great satisfaction ⟨the new car is a real *pleasure* to drive⟩ — see DELIGHT 1
3 someone or something that provides amusement or enjoyment ⟨a good-humored girl who's a *pleasure* to be around⟩ — see FUN 1

pleasure *vb* to give satisfaction to ⟨a wine that is sure to *pleasure* even the most discriminating palate⟩ — see PLEASE 1

pleat *vb* to form into a braid ⟨*pleat* ribbons⟩ — see BRAID

plebeian *adj* belonging to the class of people of low social or economic rank ⟨wondered what the people at the country club would think of his *plebeian* origins⟩ — see IGNOBLE 1

plebeians *n pl* the body of the community as contrasted with the elite ⟨the current administration evidently believes that we *plebeians* cannot withstand a dose of harsh reality⟩ — see MASS 1

plebs *n pl* the body of the community as contrasted with the elite ⟨the tabloids know that there's more money to be made from the antics of celebs than from the problems of the *plebs*⟩ — see MASS 1

pledge *n* **1** something given or held to assure that the giver will keep a promise ⟨I was required to leave my keys as a *pledge* that I would bring the car back⟩
synonyms gage, guarantee, guaranty, pawn, security
related words bail, bond; deposit, down payment, earnest, handsel; surety, warranty; assurance, oath, promise, troth, word; commitment, compact, contract, covenant; recognizance
2 a person's solemn declaration that he or she will do or not do something ⟨made a *pledge* to quit smoking⟩ — see PROMISE

pledge *vb* **1** to obligate by prior agreement ⟨I would love to go to dinner with you, but I've *pledged* myself to a play with my parents that night⟩
synonyms commit, engage, mortgage, troth
related words affiance, betroth, plight, promise, swear, vow; contract, enlist, enroll (*also* enrol), sign on, sign up; overcommit
near antonyms renege
2 to leave as a guarantee of repayment of a loan ⟨*pledged* their house against the loan⟩ — see PAWN
3 to make a solemn declaration of intent ⟨I *pledge* that I will abide by all of the rules of this organization⟩ — see PROMISE 1

plenary *adj* not lacking any part or member that properly belongs to it ⟨the delegation to the international convention was given *plenary* authority to negotiate a treaty in the nation's best interest⟩ — see COMPLETE 1

plenitude *n* **1** a considerable amount ⟨there's a *plenitude* of natural beauty in the state⟩ — see LOT 2
2 an amount or supply more than sufficient to meet one's needs ⟨a *plenitude* of food for the dinner party⟩ — see PLENTY 1

plenteous *adj* being more than enough without being excessive ⟨a *plenteous* supply of napkins for the backyard barbecue⟩ — see PLENTIFUL

plentiful *adj* being more than enough without being excessive ⟨a *plentiful* amount of strawberries that will be more than enough for a couple of pies⟩
synonyms abundant, ample, aplenty, bounteous, bountiful, comfortable, cornucopian, galore, generous, liberal, plenteous, plenty
related words extra, supernumerary, surplus; abounding, blooming, overflowing, plump, replete, rich, rife, teeming, wealthy; adequate, enough, sufficient; fat, fecund, fertile, fruitful, luxuriant, prodigal, prolific; copious, fulsome, lavish, profuse
phrases all kinds of, thick on the ground
near antonyms deficient, inadequate, insufficient, lacking, wanting; meager (*or* meagre), niggardly, stingy; skimpy; least, minimum; light, slight, small; barren, infertile, sterile, unfruitful, unproductive
antonyms bare, minimal, scant, spare

plentitude *n* **1** a considerable amount ⟨that new baby is in for a *plentitude* of love⟩ — see LOT 2
2 an amount or supply more than sufficient to meet one's needs ⟨a *plentitude* of lumber for the current housing market⟩ — see PLENTY 1

plenty *adj* being more than enough without being excessive ⟨we've picked *plenty* blueberries, so there'll be some left over after we make the pie⟩ — see PLENTIFUL

plenty *n* **1** an amount or supply more than sufficient to meet one's needs ⟨you'll have *plenty* of time to make your connecting flight⟩
synonyms abundance, cornucopia, feast, plenitude, plentitude, plethora, superabundance, wealth
related words adequacy, competence, competency, sufficiency; ampleness, amplitude, liberality; excess, overdose, overflow, overkill, oversupply, redundancy, superfluity, superfluousness, surfeit, surplus; copious-

ness, fecundity, fertility, fruitfulness, opulence, richness; lavishness, luxuriance
phrases embarrassment of riches
near antonyms paucity, poverty, scarcity; barrenness, infertility, sterility
antonyms deficiency, inadequacy, insufficiency, undersupply
2 a considerable amount ⟨*plenty* of people showed up⟩ — see LOT 2

pleonastic *adj* using or containing more words than necessary to express an idea ⟨a writer whose penchant for *pleonastic* phrasings would suggest that he is in dire need of a hard-nosed editor⟩ — see WORDY 1

plethora *n* **1** an amount or supply more than sufficient to meet one's needs ⟨a biology textbook that is helpfully illustrated with a *plethora* of excellent illustrations⟩ — see PLENTY 1
2 the state or an instance of going beyond what is usual, proper, or needed ⟨the author offers a *plethora* of detail that tends to overwhelm the reader⟩ — see EXCESS 1

plethoric *adj* going beyond a normal or acceptable limit in degree or amount ⟨the *plethoric* opulence of the mansions built by the robber barons⟩ — see EXCESSIVE

pliable *adj* **1** able to bend easily without breaking ⟨the wooden strips become more *pliable* if they are first soaked in water⟩ — see WILLOWY
2 capable of being readily changed ⟨with such iffy weather, we had to keep our vacation schedule fairly *pliable*⟩ — see FLEXIBLE 1

pliant *adj* able to bend easily without breaking ⟨a *pliant* branch bent low with the weight of ripe fruit⟩ — see WILLOWY

plod *vb* **1** to devote serious and sustained effort ⟨*plodded* night and day to get the assignment done⟩ — see LABOR
2 to proceed or act clumsily or ineffectually ⟨oxen *plodding* through deep mud⟩ — see FLOUNDER 1
3 to move slowly ⟨*plodded* reluctantly off to work⟩ — see CRAWL 2
4 to move heavily or clumsily ⟨wayfarers *plodding* across the sandy wastes⟩ — see LUMBER 1

plodder *n* someone who moves slowly or more slowly than others ⟨the guide halted the tour group so that the *plodders* who had fallen behind could catch up⟩ — see SLOWPOKE

plop *vb* to throw or set down clumsily or casually ⟨*plopped* his backpack down on a chair⟩ — see FLOP 1

plot *n* **1** a secret plan for accomplishing evil or unlawful ends ⟨the Secret Service uncovered just in time a *plot* to assassinate the President⟩
synonyms conspiracy, design, intrigue, machination, scheme
related words counterconspiracy, counterplot; frame-up; manipulation, subterfuge, trickery; artifice, contrivance, cover-up, dodge, draft, maneuver, stratagem, trick; cabal, confederacy, ring; game, gimmick, racket; ground plan, program, strategy, system; collusion, complicity, connivance, conniving, conspiration
2 a small area of usually open land ⟨grew vegetables in a little *plot*⟩ — see FIELD 1
3 a small piece of land that is developed or available for development ⟨subdivided the old farm into *plots* for tract houses⟩ — see LOT 1
4 the unfolding of events in a dramatic or literary work ⟨wrote novels in which the *plot* was always subordinate to the characterizations⟩ — see ACTION 2

plot *vb* to engage in a secret plan to accomplish evil or unlawful ends ⟨mobsters were caught *plotting* to take over the company⟩
synonyms collude, compass, connive, conspire, contrive, intrigue, machinate, put up, scheme
related words counterplot; brew, concoct, cook (up), devise, hatch; engineer, jockey, maneuver, manipulate; design, frame, lay out, map, plan, shape

plow *vb* **1** to cut into and turn over the sod of (a piece of land) using a bladed implement ⟨we'll have to get out there and *plow* and plant both fields before it rains⟩
synonyms break, furrow
related words cultivate, till; fallow; harrow, hoe, list, rake, rototill
2 to devote serious and sustained effort ⟨*plowed* determinedly through the weighty tome⟩ — see LABOR

ploy *n* **1** a clever often underhanded means to achieve an end ⟨asking me to take her shopping turned out to be a *ploy* to get me to the surprise party⟩ — see TRICK 1
2 a time or instance of carefree fun ⟨wanted one grand *ploy* through Europe before settling down and raising a family⟩ — see FLING 1

pluck *n* **1** the act or an instance of applying force on something so that it moves in the direction of the force ⟨a quick *pluck* pulled the hair right out⟩ — see PULL 1
2 the strength of mind that enables a person to endure pain or hardship ⟨it takes *pluck* to survive a crippling car accident and still go on to become successful⟩ — see FORTITUDE

pluck *vb* to rob by the use of trickery or threats ⟨the Internet opened up a whole new medium for con artists to *pluck* the gullible⟩ — see FLEECE

plug *vb* **1** to close up so that no empty spaces remain ⟨*plugged* the hole in the wall with putty⟩ — see FILL 2
2 to devote serious and sustained effort ⟨*plugged* away at solving the math problem⟩ — see LABOR
3 to provide publicity for ⟨the actress is giving lots of interviews to *plug* her latest movie⟩ — see PUBLICIZE 1
4 to strike with a missile from a gun ⟨the drug lord *plugged* the stool pigeon as a lesson for any others who were tempted to talk⟩ — see SHOOT 3

plug (up) *vb* to prevent passage through by filling with something ⟨hair *plugged up* the drain⟩ — see CLOG 1

plugger *n* a person who does very hard or dull work ⟨the quiet *pluggers* are the ones who really keep this company going⟩ — see SLAVE 2

plug–ugly *n* a violent, brutal person who is often a member of an organized gang ⟨sent over a couple of hulking *plug-uglies* to rough up the store owner⟩ — see HOODLUM

plum *n* someone or something unusually desirable ⟨that job is considered a real *plum* in the broadcasting business⟩ — see PRIZE 1

plumb *adj* **1** having no exceptions or restrictions ⟨a horror movie that's *plumb* trash and further evidence of the deterioration of popular culture⟩ — see ABSOLUTE 2
2 rising straight up ⟨the wall was not *plumb*, so everything else in the room was out of kilter⟩ — see ERECT

plumb *adv* **1** in a direct line or course ⟨I can't believe he walked *plumb* into the tree, without even seeing it!⟩ — see DIRECTLY 1
2 *chiefly dialect* to a full extent or degree ⟨I'm *plumb* tuckered out⟩ — see FULLY 1
3 without delay ⟨we had no sooner resolved that crisis than we *plumb* rushed into another one⟩ — see IMMEDIATELY

plumb *vb* to measure the depth of (as a body of water) typically with a weighted line ⟨*plumbed* the bay to make sure it was deep enough for the ship⟩ — see [2]SOUND 1

plume *n* something given in recognition of achievement ⟨the Nobel Prize for Literature is the *plume* that all authors covet⟩ — see AWARD 1

plume *vb* to think highly of (oneself) ⟨that jerk *plumes* himself on his supposed athletic skills⟩ — see PRIDE

plummet *vb* to go to a lower level especially abruptly ⟨a week in which stock prices *plummeted*⟩ — see DROP 2

plump *adj* having an excess of body fat ⟨she's been

plump all her life, and her sister has always been skinny⟩ — see FAT 1

plump *adv* in a direct line or course ⟨there was a squirrel on the sidewalk *plump* in front of us⟩ — see DIRECTLY 1

plump *n* a hard strike with a part of the body or an instrument ⟨angrily gave a *plump* of his fist against the door⟩ — see [1]BLOW

plump *vb* to throw or set down clumsily or casually ⟨*plumped* herself down on the couch and turned on the TV⟩ — see FLOP 1

plump (for) *vb* to promote the interests or cause of ⟨will *plump for* any candidate who supports stem cell research⟩ — see SUPPORT 1

plumpness *n* **1** the condition of having an excess of body fat ⟨a woman of considerable *plumpness* sat down next to me and proceeded to take up most of the bench⟩ — see CORPULENCE
2 the free expression of one's true feelings and opinions ⟨the astonishing *plumpness* that is so often found in the speech of the very young or the very old⟩ — see CANDOR 1

plunder *n* **1** valuables stolen or taken by force ⟨the thieves were promptly arrested when they tried to sell their *plunder*⟩ — see LOOT 1
2 *chiefly dialect* transportable items that one owns ⟨with all of our *plunder* in the pickup, we headed for the state that bills itself as the Last Frontier⟩ — see POSSESSION 2

plunder *vb* to search through with the intent of committing robbery ⟨the escaped convict *plundered* the house in search of valuables⟩ — see RANSACK 1

plunge *n* **1** an act or instance of diving ⟨a *plunge* off a diving board⟩ — see DIVE 1
2 the act or process of going to a lower level or altitude ⟨an overnight *plunge* in temperature sent the thermometer to below the freezing mark⟩ — see DESCENT 1

plunge *vb* **1** to cast oneself head first into deep water ⟨she took a deep breath and *plunged* from the side of the pool⟩ — see DIVE 1
2 to go to a lower level especially abruptly ⟨prices for those televisions have really *plunged* since they were first introduced⟩ — see DROP 2
3 to lead or extend downward ⟨a stairway *plunging* into darkness⟩ — see DESCEND 1

plunk *or* **plonk** *vb* to throw or set down clumsily or casually ⟨*plunked* a battered hat on his head⟩ — see FLOP 1

plunk (for) *or* **plonk (for)** *vb* to promote the interests or cause of ⟨I'm willing to *plunk for* any program that will reduce carbon emissions⟩ — see SUPPORT 1

plus *n* **1** something added (as by growth) ⟨a recalculation of the year's income that resulted in a *plus* in the company's profits⟩ — see INCREASE 1
2 the state or an instance of going beyond what is usual, proper, or needed ⟨the supply of cranberries is greatly in *plus* of the demand for them in the market⟩ — see EXCESS 1

plush *adj* **1** having an abundance of some characteristic quality (as flavor) ⟨a particularly *plush* and buttery chardonnay⟩ — see FULL-BODIED
2 showing obvious signs of wealth and comfort ⟨a *plush* estate filled with priceless art and antiques⟩ — see LUXURIOUS 1

plushly *adv* in a luxurious manner ⟨the *plushly* furnished cabin alone is worth the price we've paid for this Caribbean cruise⟩ — see HIGH

plushy *adj* showing obvious signs of wealth and comfort ⟨a *plushy* Parisian hotel where a night's stay commands a king's ransom⟩ — see LUXURIOUS 1

plus or minus *adv* close to but not exactly ⟨I have *plus or minus* five dollars in change⟩ — see APPROXIMATELY

plutocrat *n* a wealthy person ⟨the 19th-century *plutocrats* who built their enormous summer "cottages" in Newport⟩ — see CAPITALIST

plutonian *adj* causing or marked by an atmosphere lacking in cheer ⟨the rows of abandoned, boarded-up tenement houses made for a rather *plutonian* landscape⟩ — see GLOOMY 1

ply *n* an attitude that always favors one way of feeling or acting especially without considering any other possibilities ⟨since taking a *ply* to French burgundies, he's hardly even looked at anything else in the wine store⟩ — see BIAS 1

[1]**ply** *vb* to bring to bear especially forcefully or effectively ⟨she *plied* all of her charm and intelligence to convince everyone to volunteer as tutors⟩ — see EXERT

[2]**ply** *vb* to cause to twine about one another ⟨two single yarns were *plied* together to get the fabric that smooth, firm feel⟩ — see INTERTWINE 1

pneumatic *adj* having a well-proportioned feminine figure ⟨a movie star who is remembered mainly as a *pneumatic* sex symbol of the 1950s⟩ — see CURVACEOUS

poach *vb* to cook in a liquid heated to the point that it gives off steam ⟨*poaching* fish in a stock flavored with white wine⟩ — see BOIL 2

po'boy *also* **poor boy** *n* a large sandwich on a long split roll ⟨ordered a fried catfish *po'boy*⟩ — see SUBMARINE

pock *n* a small, inflamed swelling of the skin ⟨noticed strange *pocks* on his torso⟩
synonyms boil, fester, hickey, papule, pimple, pustule, whelk, zit [*slang*]
related words blackhead, blister, milium, whitehead; bump, lump, protuberance; sore, wart, weal, welt

pocket *adj* **1** of a size that is less than average ⟨a *pocket* dictionary⟩ — see SMALL 1
2 of or relating to money, banking, or investments ⟨his *pocket* involvement in the company was minimal⟩ — see FINANCIAL

pocket *n* available money ⟨the engagement ring I wanted to buy for her was beyond my *pocket*⟩ — see FUND 2

pocket *vb* **1** to refrain from openly showing or uttering ⟨*pocketed* my anger and just let the insult pass⟩ — see SUPPRESS 2
2 to take (something) without right and with an intent to keep ⟨she casually *pocketed* the note from his desk to read later⟩ — see STEAL 1
3 to put up with (something painful or difficult) ⟨meekly *pocketed* his wife's verbal abuse⟩ — see BEAR 2

pocketbook *n* a container for carrying money and small personal items ⟨she pulled some lip balm out of her *pocketbook*⟩ — see PURSE

pocket-size *also* **pocket-sized** *adj* of a size that is less than average ⟨a *pocket-size* country in the Pyrenees⟩ — see SMALL 1

pockmark *n* something that spoils the appearance or completeness of a thing ⟨the explosion left little *pockmarks* all over the face of the adjacent building⟩ — see BLEMISH

pococurante *adj* having or showing a lack of interest or concern ⟨she has put up a strangely *pococurante* front throughout this whole ordeal⟩ — see INDIFFERENT 1

pod *n* something that encloses another thing especially to protect it ⟨a fuel *pod*⟩ — see [1]CASE 1

podgy *adj, chiefly British* having an excess of body fat ⟨a *podgy* little bookseller with a shop in Notting Hill⟩ — see FAT 1

podium *n* a level usually raised surface ⟨the conductor on the *podium* tonight is one of the leading figures of classical music⟩ — see PLATFORM 1

poem *n* a composition using rhythm and often rhyme to

create a lyrical effect ⟨your assignment is to write two *poems* about springtime⟩
synonyms lyric, rune, song, verse
related words rhyme (*also* rime); ballad, lay; anacreontic, clerihew, dithyramb, eclogue, elegy, English sonnet, epic, epigram, epode, epopee, epos, georgic, idyll (*also* idyl), jingle, lament, limerick, madrigal, ode, pastoral, pastorale, psalm, rondeau, rondel (*or* rondelle), rondelet, sonnet, triolet, villanelle; haiku, senryu, tanka; blank verse, free verse, minstrelsy, poesy, poetry, versification, vers libre

poesy *n* writing that uses rhythm, vivid language, and often rhyme to provoke an emotional response ⟨in olden days young gentlemen were expected to be proficient in the art of *poesy*⟩ — see POETRY 1

poet *n* a person who writes poetry ⟨Emily Dickinson is famous as the *poet* who rarely left the house but often journeyed to the depths of the human heart⟩
synonyms bard, minstrel, muse, poetaster, rhymester (*also* rimester), versifier
related words poetess; poet laureate; scop, troubadour; epigrammatist, epigrammatizer, lyricist, rhymer, sonneteer; rhapsode, rhapsodist

poetaster *n* a person who writes poetry ⟨she's a *poetaster* whose verse never rises above what is found on greeting cards⟩ — see POET

poetic *adj* having qualities suggestive of poetry ⟨your description of the sun setting over the Grand Canyon was a particularly *poetic* piece of writing⟩
synonyms bardic, lyric, lyrical, poetical, poeticized
related words metrical (*or* metric), rhyming (*also* riming), rhythmic (*or* rhythmical); rhapsodic (*also* rhapsodical); florid, flowery, grandiloquent, highfalutin (*also* hifalutin), high-flown, ornate, purple; glamorized (*also* glamourized), idealized, romanticized; figurative, metaphoric (*or* metaphorical), symbolic (*also* symbolical)
near antonyms factual, literal, matter-of-fact; antipoetic
antonyms prosaic, prose, unlyrical, unpoetic

poetical *adj* having qualities suggestive of poetry ⟨love letters that were filled with *poetical* phrases⟩ — see POETIC

poeticized *adj* having qualities suggestive of poetry ⟨a *poeticized* depiction of Native American life before the arrival of Europeans⟩ — see POETIC

poetry *n* **1** writing that uses rhythm, vivid language, and often rhyme to provoke an emotional response ⟨not all *poetry* has to rhyme⟩
synonyms minstrelsy, poesy, song, verse
related words rhyme (*also* rime); blank verse, free verse, vers libre
antonyms prose
2 the art or power of speaking or writing in a forceful and convincing way ⟨the speeches of Dr. Martin Luther King were filled with the kind of *poetry* that touches people of all races⟩ — see ELOQUENCE

po–faced *adj, British* not joking or playful in mood or manner ⟨we rarely invite her to our parties because she's always so *po-faced*⟩ — see SERIOUS 1

poignance *n* a harsh or sharp quality ⟨there's a mean-spirited *poignance* to the novel's satiric portrait of Hollywood⟩ — see EDGE 1

poignancy *n* a harsh or sharp quality ⟨there was a *poignancy* to his wit that often left his targets smarting⟩ — see EDGE 1

poignant *adj* **1** having the power to affect the feelings or sympathies ⟨a *poignant* story of a love affair that ends in tragedy⟩ — see MOVING
2 sharp and pleasantly stimulating to the mind or senses ⟨a *poignant* truthfulness to the author's observations on marriage⟩ — see PIQUANT

point *n* **1** a particular and often important moment in time ⟨it was at that *point* that I had to stop and check on the experiment⟩
synonyms juncture
related words beat, crack, flash, heartbeat, instant, jiffy, minute, moment, nanosecond, second, shake, split second, tick, trice, twinkle, wink; bit, spell, stretch, while; brink, cusp, nick, threshold, verge; crisis, crunch time, wire
phrases moment of truth
2 the last and usually sharp or tapering part of something long and narrow ⟨be careful with the *point* on that umbrella, or you could hurt someone⟩
synonyms apex, cusp, end, nib, nose, pike, tip
related words pinpoint; prong, tine; barb, jag, prickle, snag, spike, sticker
3 an interval of time just before the onset of something ⟨was at the *point* of accepting the new job when he realized he didn't want to leave his old one⟩
synonyms brink, cusp, edge, threshold, verge
related words nick
4 a separate part in a list, account, or series ⟨went down the list *point* by *point*⟩ — see ITEM 1
5 a single piece of information ⟨two *points* that are important to remember⟩ — see FACT 3
6 a small area that is different (as in color) from the main part ⟨the little *points* of gold in the blue ceiling are supposed to represent stars⟩ — see SPOT 1
7 an area of high ground jutting out into a body of water beyond the line of the coast ⟨the racing yacht rounded the *point* far ahead of its closest rival⟩ — see HEADLAND 1
8 an area of land that juts out into a body of water ⟨*Point* Reyes, California⟩ — see [2]CAPE
9 an individual part of a process, series, or ranking ⟨at this *point* in your life, you should already be saving for retirement⟩ — see DEGREE 1
10 something that sets apart an individual from others of the same kind ⟨impeccable politeness has always been her strong *point*⟩ — see CHARACTERISTIC
11 the area or space occupied by or intended for something ⟨runners began lining up by the starting *point*⟩ — see PLACE 1
12 the quality of an utterance that provokes interest and produces an effect ⟨her jokes are often long, rambling stories that have no *point* whatsoever⟩ — see [1]PUNCH 1
13 something that one hopes or intends to accomplish ⟨what we're doing does have a *point*—doesn't it?⟩ — see GOAL
14 the central part or aspect of something under consideration ⟨that clueless reviewer seems to have missed the whole *point* of the book⟩ — see CRUX

point (to) *vb* to serve as a sign or symptom of ⟨the reduced production *points to* declining efficiency within the plant⟩ — see INDICATE 1

point (toward) *vb* to stand or sit with the face or front toward ⟨the town's monument to its lost fishermen *points toward* the sea, the source of its wealth as well as its sorrow⟩ — see FACE 1

point (up) *vb* to indicate the importance of by centering attention on ⟨*pointed up* his warning by furiously wagging his finger at them⟩ — see EMPHASIZE 1

pointed *adj* **1** tapering to a thin tip ⟨the sansevieria's long *pointed* leaves make it an easily recognized houseplant⟩
synonyms peaked, pointy, sharp, spired, tipped
related words needlelike, spiny; barbed, jagged, pronged, spiked, spikelike, spiky (*also* spikey); bladelike, knifelike
near antonyms dull, rounded
antonyms blunt
2 having to do with the matter at hand ⟨he made a num-

ber of *pointed* remarks on the crisis abroad⟩ — see PERTINENT

pointer *n* **1** an arrow-shaped piece on a dial or scale for registering information ⟨the *pointer* on my bathroom scale must be stuck—I know I lost weight⟩
synonyms hand, index, indicator, needle
related words dial, face, gauge (*also* gage)
2 a piece of advice or useful information especially from an expert ⟨the instructor gave me a few *pointers* but otherwise let me do the cooking by myself⟩ — see [1]TIP 1

pointless *adj* having no meaning ⟨a *pointless* remark that left everyone scratching their heads in confusion⟩ — see MEANINGLESS

point man *n* a person who speaks for another or for a group ⟨the *point man* for the automaker announced a recall of several models with defective parts⟩ — see SPOKESPERSON

point person *n* a person who speaks for another or for a group ⟨she's become known as the *point person* for the state department's Middle East policy⟩ — see SPOKESPERSON

pointy *adj* tapering to a thin tip ⟨wears high heels with very *pointy* toes even though they kill her feet⟩ — see POINTED 1

poise *n* **1** a condition in which opposing forces are equal to one another ⟨there must be a *poise* between the rights of the individual and the rights of society⟩ — see BALANCE 1
2 a general way of holding the body ⟨the woman's *poise* suggested that she was accustomed to having her wishes carried out promptly and without question⟩ — see POSTURE 1

poise *vb* **1** to prepare (oneself) mentally or emotionally ⟨the disgraced business executive *poised* herself for the difficult press conference⟩ — see FORTIFY 1
2 to rest or move along the surface of a liquid or in the air ⟨the falcon *poised* in the air for an instant before diving to attack its prey⟩ — see FLOAT 1

poison *adj* containing or contaminated with a substance capable of injuring or killing a living thing ⟨the witch gave Snow White a *poison* apple⟩ — see POISONOUS

poison *n* a substance that by chemical action can kill or injure a living thing ⟨the only way to get rid of rats is to leave out *poison*⟩
synonyms bane, toxic, toxin, venom
related words cancer, contagion, disease, virus; fungicide, germicide, herbicide, insecticide, microbicide, pesticide, toxicant
near antonyms antidote, antivenin, antivenom, mithridate; cure; cure-all, elixir, panacea

poison *vb* **1** to affect slightly with something morally bad or undesirable ⟨*poisoning* the minds of impressionable children with ethnic hatred⟩ — see TAINT 1
2 to make unfit for use by the addition of something harmful or undesirable ⟨exhaust fumes *poisoning* the air⟩ — see CONTAMINATE
3 to lower in character, dignity, or quality ⟨this party partisanship *poisons* the national debate we should be having about this urgent problem⟩ — see DEBASE 1
4 to cause to have often negative opinions formed without sufficient knowledge ⟨malicious rumors had *poisoned* many church members against the new pastor⟩ — see PREJUDICE

poisoned *adj* containing or contaminated with a substance capable of injuring or killing a living thing ⟨leaving *poisoned* food to try to kill the roaches⟩ — see POISONOUS

poisonous *adj* containing or contaminated with a substance capable of injuring or killing a living thing ⟨some evil person was leaving out *poisonous* meat for neighborhood dogs to eat⟩
synonyms envenomed, poison, poisoned, toxic, venomous
related words contagious, infectious, infective, pathogenic, pestilent, pestilential; baneful, deleterious, harmful, hurtful, injurious, malignant, nocuous, noxious, virulent; unhealthful, unhealthy, unwholesome; calamitous, deadly, fatal, fell, lethal, murderous
near antonyms beneficial, curative, healthful, healthy, helpful, palliative, remedial, salubrious, salutary, wholesome; benign, harmless, innocuous, inoffensive; nonfatal, nonlethal
antonyms nonpoisonous, nontoxic, nonvenomous

[1]**poke** *n* **1** a quick thrust ⟨please stop giving the cat *pokes* while it's trying to sleep⟩
synonyms dab, dig, jab, lunge
related words punch; stab, stick; push, shove; jam, jerk, jog, nudge
2 a hard strike with a part of the body or an instrument ⟨you'd better shut up if you don't want a *poke* on the nose⟩ — see [1]BLOW
3 an act or expression showing scorn and usually intended to hurt another's feelings ⟨the constantly bickering husband and wife seem unable to let five minutes pass without an exchange of gratuitous *pokes*⟩ — see INSULT

[2]**poke** *n, chiefly Southern & Midland* a container made of a flexible material (as paper or plastic) ⟨the old warning against buying a pig in a *poke*⟩ — see BAG 1

poke *vb* **1** to extend outward beyond a usual point ⟨saw his head *poking* through the window⟩ — see BULGE 1
2 to interest oneself in what is not one's concern ⟨told him to stop *poking* into other people's business⟩ — see INTERFERE
3 to move or act slowly ⟨just *poked* around all morning and didn't accomplish much⟩ — see DELAY 1
4 to move slowly ⟨they were just *poking* along home⟩ — see CRAWL 2

pokey *n, slang* a place of confinement for persons held in lawful custody ⟨joked about the time he passed out on the street and woke up in the *pokey*⟩ — see JAIL

pokily *adv* at a pace that is less than usual, desirable, or expected ⟨we wandered *pokily* around the mall while the pharmacist filled the prescription⟩ — see SLOW

poking *adj* moving or proceeding at less than the normal, desirable, or required speed ⟨the *poking* pace of the repair work has put everything way behind schedule⟩ — see SLOW 1

poky *or* **pokey** *adj* moving or proceeding at less than the normal, desirable, or required speed ⟨frustrated with the *poky* traffic during rush hour⟩ — see SLOW 1

polar *adj* **1** being as different as possible ⟨they're friends despite their *polar* positions on a number of issues⟩ — see OPPOSITE
2 having a low or subnormal temperature ⟨a *polar* air mass seemed to have settled over our area in January⟩ — see COLD 1

polarity *n* the quality or state of being as different as possible ⟨the *polarity* of the candidates' views on the issue means that the voters have a clear choice to make⟩ — see CONTRARIETY

polarize *vb* to bring (something) to a central point or under a single control ⟨we will need to *polarize* all of the fractious environmental groups into a united front if we hope to win on this issue⟩ — see CENTRALIZE

polemical *also* **polemic** *adj* **1** given to arguing ⟨during the Middle Ages even theologians could be surprisingly *polemical* in their writings⟩ — see ARGUMENTATIVE 1
2 relating to or causing the expression of opposing opinions ⟨an unnecessarily *polemical* look at the sup-

posed incompatibility between science and religion⟩ — see CONTROVERSIAL 1

polestar *n* a guiding or motivating purpose or principle ⟨under the *polestar* of progress, urban renewal programs gutted the historic districts of many cities⟩ — see COMPASS 1

police *n* **1** the department of government that keeps order, fights crime, and enforces statutes ⟨the appearance of a ransom note meant that the teenager's disappearance was now a matter for the *police*⟩
synonyms law
related words judiciary, jurisprudence, justice
2 a body of officers of the law ⟨the National Guard will serve as backup for the metropolitan *police* in the event of violent protests⟩
synonyms constabulary, finest, force, fuzz, heat [*slang*], man, police force
related words bluecoat, bobby [*British*], bull [*slang*], constable, cop, copper, gendarme, officer, peeler [*British*], policeman, police officer, policewoman, shamus [*slang*], trooper

police force *n* a body of officers of the law ⟨mobilized practically the entire *police force* to track down the escaped criminal⟩ — see POLICE 2

policeman *n* a member of a force charged with law enforcement at the local level ⟨reported the crime to the nearest *policeman*⟩ — see OFFICER 1

police officer *n* a member of a force charged with law enforcement at the local level ⟨there were *police officers* directing traffic around the scene of the accident⟩ — see OFFICER 1

policy *n* **1** a way of acting or proceeding ⟨it's always been my *policy* not to spread rumors⟩ — see COURSE 1
2 the ability to make intelligent decisions especially in everyday matters ⟨you should have exercised greater *policy* in your online relationships and not divulged so much personal information⟩ — see COMMON SENSE

polish *n* **1** a high level of taste and enlightenment as a result of extensive intellectual training and exposure to the arts ⟨acquired a great deal of *polish* during his year abroad⟩ — see CULTURE 1
2 brightness created by light reflected from a surface ⟨buffed the silver plate to a high *polish*⟩ — see SHINE 1

polish *vb* **1** to make smooth or glossy usually by repeatedly applying surface pressure ⟨you'll need to *polish* your shoes with a clean rag before the performance⟩
synonyms buff, burnish, dress, furbish, gloss, grind, rub, shine, smooth, smoothen
related words sleek, slick; coat, glaze, japan, lacquer, varnish; face, finish, veneer; brighten; file, rasp, sand, sandblast, sandpaper, scour, scrape, scrub; bob, bone, lap
near antonyms rough (up), roughen, ruffle, scuff (up)
2 to bring (something) to a state where nothing remains to be done ⟨once you *polish* the article a bit, it'll be ready to submit⟩ — see FINISH 1

polished *adj* **1** having a shiny surface or finish ⟨she could see her face reflected in the *polished* hood of the car⟩ — see GLOSSY
2 having or showing a taste for the fine arts and gracious living ⟨showing the *polished* manners of a cosmopolitan woman⟩ — see CULTIVATED

polite *adj* **1** showing consideration, courtesy, and good manners ⟨it's only *polite* to hold the door for the person behind you⟩
synonyms civil, courteous, genteel, gracious, mannerly, well-bred
related words attentive, careful, considerate, nice, solicitous, thoughtful; chivalrous, civilized, courtly, gallant, gentlemanlike, gentlemanly, ladylike; ceremonial, ceremonious, red-carpet; couth, formal, smooth, suave, unctuous, urbane; elegant, refined; deferential, dutiful, respectful, submissive, yielding; acceptable, appropriate, becoming, befitting, comme il faut, correct, decent, decorous, fit, fitting, good, meet, proper, respectable, right, seemly, suitable; affable, cordial, friendly, genial, hospitable, pleasant, sociable; felicitous, graceful; demure, humble, meek, modest, unassertive
near antonyms heedless, inconsiderate, thoughtless; audacious, bold, bold-faced, brash, brassy, disrespectful, impertinent, impudent, insolent, lippy, saucy, shameless; boorish, churlish, clodhopping, clownish, loutish, uncouth, vulgar; casual, informal, unceremonious; improper, inappropriate, incorrect, indecent, indecorous, uncalled-for, unrespectable, unseemly; arrogant, conceited, presuming, presumptuous, pretentious
antonyms discourteous, ill-bred, ill-mannered, impolite, inconsiderate, mannerless, rude, thoughtless, uncivil, ungenteel, ungracious, unmannered, unmannerly
2 following the established traditions of refined society and good taste ⟨such matters are never mentioned in *polite* conversation⟩ — see PROPER 1

politeness *n* **1** speech or behavior that is a sign of good breeding ⟨the little girl's *politeness* greatly impressed her teacher⟩
synonyms civility, courteousness, courtesy, genteelness, gentility, graciousness, mannerliness
related words attentiveness, consideration, thoughtfulness; ceremonialness, ceremoniousness, ceremony, formality; chivalrousness, chivalry, courtliness, gallantry, gentlemanliness, knighthood, knightliness; breeding, manners; suaveness, unctuousness, urbanity; elegance, refinement; deference, respect; decency, decorousness, decorum, gentilesse, polish, politesse, propriety, respectability, seemliness; affability, cordiality, friendliness, geniality, hospitality, sociability; felicitousness, gracefulness; humility, meekness, modesty, shyness
near antonyms audaciousness, audacity, boldness, brashness, brassiness, disrespect, impertinence, impudence, insolence, sauciness, shamelessness; boorishness, churlishness, clownishness, loutishness, vulgarity; casualness, informality; delinquency, improperness, impropriety, inappropriateness, incorrectness, indecency; inconsiderateness, inconsideration, thoughtlessness; arrogance, conceit, presumption, pretentiousness
antonyms discourteousness, discourtesy, impoliteness, incivility, rudeness, surliness, ungraciousness
2 an act or utterance that is a customary show of good manners ⟨inquiring after his wife was a simple *politeness*⟩ — see CIVILITY 1

politic *adj* **1** having or showing tact ⟨the actor is *politic* in discussing the aborted film project, being content to say that there were "creative differences"⟩ — see TACTFUL
2 suitable for bringing about a desired result under the circumstances ⟨it probably would not be *politic* to tell your boss that his latest idea is the worst thing you've ever heard⟩ — see EXPEDIENT

poll *n* the upper or front part of the body that contains the brain, the major sense organs, and the mouth ⟨a jaunty cap was perched on his *poll*⟩ — see HEAD 1

poll *vb* **1** to go around and approach (people) with a request for opinions or information ⟨assigned to *poll* residents on their views about a program for recycling⟩ — see CANVASS 1
2 to make (something) shorter or smaller with the use of a cutting instrument ⟨time to *poll* the sheep's wool⟩ — see CLIP 1

poller *n* a person who goes around and approaches people with a request for opinions or information ⟨data gathered by nationwide *pollers* showed the Republicans in the lead⟩ — see CANVASSER

pollster *n* a person who goes around and approaches people with a request for opinions or information ⟨he wouldn't tell the exit *pollster* whom he'd voted for⟩ — see CANVASSER

pollutant *n* something that is or that makes impure ⟨filtered the *pollutants* out of the water⟩ — see IMPURITY 1

pollute *vb* to make unfit for use by the addition of something harmful or undesirable ⟨outmoded factories *polluting* the air⟩ — see CONTAMINATE

polluted *adj* containing foreign or lower-grade substances ⟨called in to clean up the *polluted* stream⟩ — see IMPURE 1

poltergeist *n* the soul of a dead person thought of especially as appearing to living people ⟨we thought a *poltergeist* was knocking dishes off the shelves, but it turned out to just be vibrations from passing trains⟩ — see GHOST 1

poltroon *adj* having or showing a shameful lack of courage ⟨a military commander who was so *poltroon* that he surrendered without having fired so much as a single shot⟩ — see COWARDLY

poltroon *n* a person who shows a shameful lack of courage in the face of danger ⟨those *poltroons* in the state legislature who have caved in to bigotry on this important issue of basic civil rights⟩ — see COWARD

poltroonery *n* a shameful lack of courage in the face of danger ⟨decried the *poltroonery* of those politicians who caved into pressure from the special interests⟩ — see COWARDICE

polychromatic *adj* marked by a variety of usually vivid colors ⟨a *polychromatic* tropical bird⟩ — see COLORFUL

polychrome *adj* marked by a variety of usually vivid colors ⟨*polychrome* pottery featuring designs from the American Southwest⟩ — see COLORFUL

polygraph *n* an instrument for detecting physical signs of the tension that goes with lying ⟨intelligence agents were trained to fool the *polygraph*⟩ — see LIE DETECTOR

pommel *vb* to strike repeatedly ⟨the elderly woman *pommeled* the would-be thief with her handbag until he begged for mercy⟩ — see BEAT 1

pomposity *n* **1** an exaggerated sense of one's importance that shows itself in the making of excessive or unjustified claims ⟨restaurant reviews that are written with a *pomposity* that will leave a bad taste in anyone's mouth⟩ — see ARROGANCE

2 an often unjustified feeling of being pleased with oneself or with one's situation or achievements ⟨his over-the-top trophy mansion should give you some idea of his *pomposity*⟩ — see COMPLACENCE 1

pompous *adj* **1** having a feeling of superiority that shows itself in an overbearing attitude ⟨the *pompous* waiter served us in the manner of a person doing some poor soul a great favor⟩ — see ARROGANT

2 having too high an opinion of oneself ⟨a *pompous* piano teacher who thought that the music world was lucky to have her⟩ — see CONCEITED

3 self-consciously trying to present an appearance of grandeur or importance ⟨a *pompous* gambling casino decorated to look like a palace in ancient Rome⟩ — see PRETENTIOUS 1

pompousness *n* **1** an exaggerated sense of one's importance that shows itself in the making of excessive or unjustified claims ⟨offended by the *pompousness* of the minor official⟩ — see ARROGANCE

2 an often unjustified feeling of being pleased with oneself or with one's situation or achievements ⟨the *pompousness* of the self-made billionaire was evident in the gaudy mansion he built for himself⟩ — see COMPLACENCE 1

ponder *vb* to give serious and careful thought to ⟨I'm *pondering* whether or not I should join another committee⟩

synonyms chew over, cogitate, consider, contemplate, debate, deliberate, entertain, eye, kick around, meditate, mull (over), perpend, pore (over), question, revolve, ruminate, study, think (about *or* over), turn, weigh, wrestle (with)

related words muse (upon), reflect (on *or* upon), reminisce; analyze, explore, review; conclude, reason; second-guess, speculate (about); brood (about *or* over), dwell (on *or* upon), fixate (on *or* upon), fret (about *or* over), obsess (about *or* over); believe, conceive, opine; absorb, assimilate, digest, drink (in)

phrases beat one's brains out (about), chew on, cudgel one's brains (about), look at

near antonyms disregard, ignore, overlook, slight; dismiss, pooh-pooh (*also* pooh), reject

ponderous *adj* **1** causing weariness, restlessness, or lack of interest ⟨fell asleep during the *ponderous* speech⟩ — see BORING

2 having great weight ⟨those *ponderous* pachyderms more commonly known as elephants⟩ — see HEAVY 1

3 difficult to use or operate especially because of size, weight, or design ⟨lugged a *ponderous* movie camera all over China⟩ — see CUMBERSOME

ponderousness *n* the state or quality of being heavy ⟨the sheer *ponderousness* of each stone of the huge pyramid makes its construction all the more remarkable⟩ — see WEIGHTINESS 1

pontifical *adj* given to or marked by the forceful expression of strongly held opinions ⟨a theater critic known for his *pontifical* pronouncements on what is or is not worth seeing⟩ — see DOGMATIC

pony up *vb* to give what is owed for ⟨despite having good credit, the couple still had to *pony up* a large down payment for the house⟩ — see PAY 2

pooch *n* a domestic mammal that is related to the wolves and foxes ⟨walking down the street with several *pooches* on leashes⟩ — see DOG 1

pooch *vb, chiefly dialect* to extend outward beyond a usual point ⟨his lower lip *pooched* out in disappointment⟩ — see BULGE 1

pooh–bah *also* **poo–bah** *n* one of high position or importance within a group ⟨an annual clambake that attracts political *pooh-bahs* from around the state⟩ — see BIG SHOT

[1]**pool** *n* a small often deep body of water ⟨a secluded *pool* that has long been a locally favored spot for skinny-dipping⟩

synonyms billabong [*Australian*], mere [*chiefly British*], puddle, stank [*British dialect*], well

related words basin, hole, sinkhole; swimming pool; lake, pond, water hole

[2]**pool** *n* **1** a body of persons at work or available for work ⟨a large *pool* of applicants for the summer internship⟩ — see FORCE 1

2 the number of individuals or amount of something available at any given time ⟨a *pool* of ideas ready to use whenever the cartoonist needs to meet a deadline⟩ — see SUPPLY

3 a sum of money set aside for a particular purpose ⟨office workers setting up a *pool* for the collective purchase of lottery tickets⟩ — see FUND 1

4 the total of the bets at stake at one time ⟨two coworkers split last week's football *pool*⟩ — see POT 1

pooled *adj* used or done by a number of people as a group ⟨*pooled* coverage of the congressional hearings by the major broadcast networks⟩ — see COLLECTIVE

[1]**poop** *n* solid matter discharged from an animal's alimentary canal ⟨the mother cat carefully cleaned *poop* off her newborn kitten's bottom⟩ — see DROPPING 1

[2]**poop** *n, slang* information not generally available to the public ⟨the *poop* was that the ship would be headed to the war zone within a matter of weeks⟩ — see DOPE 1

pooped *adj, slang* depleted in strength, energy, or freshness ⟨“I'm really *pooped* after that hike,” she sighed⟩ — see WEARY 1

poor *adj* **1** lacking money or material possessions ⟨every year, we make up a basket of food at Thanksgiving for a *poor* family in the neighborhood⟩
synonyms beggared, beggarly, broke, destitute, dirt-poor, down-and-out, famished, hard up, impecunious, impoverished, indigent, necessitous, needful, needy, pauperized, penniless, penurious, poverty-stricken, skint [*chiefly British*], threadbare
related words deprived, disadvantaged, dispossessed, unaffluent, underprivileged; bankrupt, bankrupted, bust (*or* busted), insolvent; possessionless, ruined; depressed, distressed, hand-to-mouth, hardscrabble, pinched, poorish, reduced, straitened; cash-strapped, low, short, tapped out
phrases down on one's luck, out at elbows (*or* out at the elbows), out of pocket
near antonyms comfortable, prosperous
antonyms affluent, deep-pocketed, fat, fat-cat, flush, moneyed (*also* monied), opulent, rich, silk-stocking, wealthy, well-heeled, well-off, well-to-do
2 producing inferior or only a small amount of vegetation ⟨land that is too *poor* for farming⟩ — see BARREN 1
3 less plentiful than what is normal, necessary, or desirable ⟨a *poor* crop because of the drought this year⟩ — see MEAGER
4 falling short of a standard ⟨a pretty *poor* musician, even for a garage band⟩ — see BAD 1
5 of low quality ⟨the *poor* workmanship of the goods from that country⟩ — see CHEAP 2
6 deserving of one's pity ⟨aw, the *poor* kitten hurt its paw⟩ — see PATHETIC 1

poorly *adj* temporarily suffering from a disorder of the body ⟨she stayed home because she was feeling *poorly*⟩ — see SICK 1

poorly *adv* in an unsatisfactory way ⟨he tends to perform *poorly* on standardized tests⟩ — see BADLY 1

poor–mouth *vb* to express scornfully one's low opinion of ⟨regardless of whatever is nominated, there'll be those who will *poor-mouth* the Oscar nominees⟩ — see DECRY 1

poorness *n* the state of lacking sufficient money or material possessions ⟨each country has its own standard of *poorness*, and one nation's needy inhabitant can be another's fairly well-off citizen⟩ — see POVERTY 1

pop *adj* enjoying widespread favor or approval ⟨uninterested in the *pop* fiction that most of the other publishing houses happily churned out⟩ — see POPULAR 1

[1]**pop** *n* a loud explosive sound ⟨the soda can opened with a sharp *pop*⟩ — see CLAP 1

[2]**pop** *n* a male human parent ⟨ask your *pop* if he knows where the keys to the shed are⟩ — see FATHER 1

pop *vb* **1** to break open or into pieces usually because of internal pressure ⟨a balloon *popped* suddenly and startled us all⟩ — see EXPLODE 1
2 to break suddenly with an explosive sound ⟨the last strand *popped*, causing the chandelier to drop to the floor with a great crash⟩ — see CRACK 1
3 to cause to break open or into pieces by or as if by an explosive ⟨*popping* popcorn over a campfire⟩ — see BLAST 1
4 to strike with a missile from a gun ⟨went into the woods hoping to *pop* the rabbit that was eating our vegetables⟩ — see SHOOT 3

pop (in) *vb* to make a brief visit ⟨I just *popped in* to say hello⟩ — see CALL 3

pop off *vb* to stop living ⟨just a matter of time before the geezer *pops off*, and his gold digger of a wife gets the money⟩ — see DIE 1

poppet *n, Midland* a small figure often of a human being used especially as a child's plaything ⟨a scruffy old *poppet* that had once belonged to my great grandmother⟩ — see DOLL 1

poppycock *n* language, behavior, or ideas that are absurd and contrary to good sense ⟨starting with the cherry tree, much of what was written by Washington's early biographers was pure *poppycock*⟩ — see NONSENSE 1

populace *n* the body of the community as contrasted with the elite ⟨high officials awkwardly mingling with the general *populace*⟩ — see MASS 1

popular *adj* **1** enjoying widespread favor or approval ⟨an actor who was *popular* in the 1970s⟩
synonyms big, crowd-pleasing, du jour, faddish, faddy, fashionable, favorite, happening, hot, in, large, modish, pop, popularized, red-hot, vogue, voguish
related words semipopular; favorite, preferred, selected; desirable, liked, wanted; celebrated, famed, famous, noted, notorious, prominent, renowned, well-known; fabled, fabulous, legendary; leading, notable, outstanding, prominent, remarkable; important, significant
near antonyms washed-up; despised, detested, disliked, hated, rejected; insignificant, unimportant; indistinguished, unexceptional; anonymous, nameless, obscure, unknown; inconspicuous
antonyms out, unfashionable, unpopular
2 accepted, used, or practiced by most people ⟨the *popular* custom of exchanging greeting cards during the holiday season⟩ — see CURRENT 1
3 held by or applicable to a majority of the people ⟨*popular* opinion on that issue has changed dramatically over the years⟩ — see GENERAL 3
4 of, relating to, or favoring political democracy ⟨a truly *popular* revolution, not one that replaced one dictatorship with another⟩ — see DEMOCRATIC
5 being within the financial means of most people ⟨from their inception, DVDs were designed to be sold directly to consumers at *popular* prices⟩ — see ACCESSIBLE 1
6 costing little ⟨we also have the *popular* models, for those who prefer not to invest too much in a new TV⟩ — see CHEAP 1

popularity *n* the state of enjoying widespread approval ⟨the sudden *popularity* of low-cut blouses horrified my mother⟩
synonyms fashionability, fashionableness, favor, hotness, modishness, vogue, voguishness
related words craze, fad, mode, rage, style, trend; bandwagon, boom; fame, notoriety, prominence, renown; enthusiasm, fervor, passion
near antonyms oblivion, obscurity
antonyms disfavor, unpopularity

popularized *adj* enjoying widespread favor or approval ⟨a recently *popularized* hobby among kids⟩ — see POPULAR 1

populate *vb* to supply with inhabitants ⟨a small island *populated* only by woodland creatures⟩ — see SETTLE 2

porch *n* a covered structure adjoining an entrance to a building ⟨vacationers relaxing on the inn's spacious front *porch*⟩
synonyms gallery [*Southern & Midland*], lanai, piazza [*dialect*], stoop, veranda (*or* verandah)
related words galilee, portico; sleeping porch, solarium, sunporch, sunroom (*also* sun parlor); porte cochere

pore (over) *vb* **1** to give serious and careful thought to ⟨the committee will probably *pore over* the results of the study for a long time before making their decision⟩ — see PONDER
2 to go over and mentally take in the content of ⟨he

pored over the textbook for hours in preparation for the test⟩ — see READ 1

pornographic *adj* **1** dealing in or with explicitly sexual material ⟨opposition to a *pornographic* bookstore opening in the neighborhood⟩ — see ADULT 2
2 depicting or referring to sexual matters in a way that is unacceptable in polite society ⟨the store kept all of its *pornographic* DVDs locked up, thus ensuring that they would be accessible only to adults⟩ — see OBSCENE 1

porny *adj* **1** dealing in or with explicitly sexual material ⟨a collection of *porny* postcards of the type that American servicemen once brought back from Europe⟩ — see ADULT 2
2 depicting or referring to sexual matters in a way that is unacceptable in polite society ⟨found *porny* pinups on the walls of the serial rapist's apartment⟩ — see OBSCENE 1

porous *adj* capable of being passed into or through ⟨a cleaner that should not be used on *porous* surfaces⟩ — see PENETRABLE

port *n* a part of a body of water protected and deep enough to be a place of safety for ships ⟨the cruise ship stops at each *port* for one night only⟩ — see HARBOR 1

portable *adj* capable of being moved especially with ease ⟨a *portable* stereo system⟩ — see MOVABLE

portal *n* a barrier by which an entry is closed and opened ⟨the main *portal* to the estate is an elaborate wrought iron gate on the side facing the road⟩ — see DOOR 1

portent *n* **1** something believed to be a sign or warning of a future event ⟨a red sky in the morning can be a *portent* of a coming storm⟩ — see OMEN
2 something extraordinary or surprising ⟨a scout was sent to have a look at this teenage pitcher who was supposed to be the latest *portent* of the baseball world⟩ — see WONDER 1

portentous *adj* **1** being or showing a sign of evil or calamity to come ⟨an eerie and *portentous* stillness hung over the camp the night before the battle⟩ — see OMINOUS
2 causing wonder or astonishment ⟨in 1969 people regarded the first landing on the moon as a truly *portentous* event⟩ — see MARVELOUS 1

porter *n, chiefly British* a person who tends a door ⟨he generously tipped the *porter* for hailing a taxi⟩ — see DOORKEEPER

portion *n* **1** a state or end that seemingly has been decided beforehand ⟨he had always just assumed that lifelong bachelorhood would be his *portion*⟩ — see FATE 1
2 one of the pieces from which something is designed to be assembled ⟨equal *portions* of the students' day are devoted to study, recreation, and sleep⟩ — see PART 1
3 something belonging to, due to, or contributed by an individual member of a group ⟨each camper gets an equal *portion* of the food⟩ — see SHARE 1

portion *vb* to give out (something) to appropriate individuals ⟨*portioned* out the medical supplies equally⟩ — see ADMINISTER 1

portliness *n* the condition of having an excess of body fat ⟨the whole family was known for its *portliness*⟩ — see CORPULENCE

portly *adj* **1** having an excess of body fat ⟨a *portly* gentleman who clearly didn't get enough exercise⟩ — see FAT 1
2 having or showing a formal and serious or reserved manner ⟨walked with the *portly* grace of the grande dame that she was⟩ — see DIGNIFIED

portmanteau *n* a bag carried by hand and designed to hold a traveler's clothing and personal articles ⟨carried her possessions with her in an old *portmanteau*⟩ — see TRAVELING BAG

portrait *n* a vivid representation in words of someone or something ⟨his account created in the jurors' heads a detailed *portrait* of a lonely old man⟩ — see DESCRIPTION 1

portraiture *n* a vivid representation in words of someone or something ⟨the author's meticulous *portraiture* of a small Midwestern town at the turn of the century⟩ — see DESCRIPTION 1

portray *vb* **1** to give a representation or account of in words ⟨the author *portrays* her characters with lifelike vividness⟩ — see DESCRIBE 1
2 to point out the chief quality or qualities of an individual or group ⟨traditionally, European authors *portrayed* the natives as wise and noble⟩ — see CHARACTERIZE 1
3 to present a picture of ⟨a landscape that *portrays* the scenery near the town where the painter grew up⟩ — see PICTURE 1
4 to present a portrayal or performance of ⟨gained fame *portraying* Susan B. Anthony in a one-woman show⟩ — see ACT 1

portrayal *n* a vivid representation in words of someone or something ⟨his novel presents a moving *portrayal* of a woman searching for personal fulfillment and happiness⟩ — see DESCRIPTION 1

pose *n* a display of emotion or behavior that is insincere or intended to deceive ⟨my cheerfulness was just a *pose*, for I was feeling miserable⟩ — see MASQUERADE

[1]**pose** *vb* to set before the mind for consideration ⟨*posed* an interesting question for the visiting astronomer⟩ — see PROPOSE 1

[2]**pose** *vb* to throw into a state of mental uncertainty ⟨utterly *posed* by the barrage of questions⟩ — see CONFUSE 1

pose (as) *vb* to pretend to be (what one is not) in appearance or behavior ⟨*posing as* a soldier, the spy sneaked onto the base with surprising ease⟩ — see IMPERSONATE 1

position *n* **1** an assignment at which one regularly works for pay ⟨he holds the *position* of manager at the store⟩ — see JOB 1
2 the action for which a person or thing is specially fitted or used or for which a thing exists ⟨man's *position* in the universe⟩ — see ROLE
3 the area or space occupied by or intended for something ⟨I knew that someone had been in the room because the chair was out of its usual *position*⟩ — see PLACE 1
4 the place where someone is assigned to stand or remain ⟨the soldiers were commanded to hold their *position* on the hill at all costs⟩ — see STATION 1
5 the placement of someone or something in relation to others in a vertical arrangement ⟨holds the lead *position* in the standings⟩ — see RANK 1

position *vb* to arrange something in a certain spot or position ⟨*positioned* the chairs around the room⟩ — see PLACE 1

positive *adj* **1** expressing approval ⟨hoped for a *positive* reaction from the audience⟩ — see FAVORABLE 1
2 having or showing a mind free from doubt ⟨I'm *positive* that this is the right direction⟩ — see CERTAIN 2
3 not capable of being challenged or proved wrong ⟨seeks *positive* proof that UFO's exist⟩ — see IRREFUTABLE

positively *adv* in an approving manner ⟨for the most part audiences have responded *positively* to his avant-garde music⟩ — see ADMIRINGLY

positiveness *n* a state of mind in which one is free from doubt ⟨I can't state with any *positiveness* that I know what really happened⟩ — see CONFIDENCE 2

posse *n* a body of employees or servants who accompany and wait on a person ⟨a drug lord and his ever-present *posse* of sycophants⟩ — see CORTEGE 1

possess *vb* to keep, control, or experience as one's own ⟨she *possesses* a keen insight into people⟩ — see HAVE 1

possessed *adj* free from emotional or mental agitation ⟨remarkably poised and *possessed* in the midst of all the turmoil⟩ — see CALM 2

possession *n* **1** the fact or state of having (something) at one's disposal ⟨a student who was found to have several overdue library books in his *possession*⟩
synonyms control, enjoyment, hands, keeping
related words ownership, proprietorship; authority, command, dominion, mastery, power; repossession, retention; claiming, collaring, commandeering, confiscation, procurement
near antonyms dispossession, relinquishment, surrendering, transferal
antonyms nonpossession
2 possessions *pl* transportable items that one owns ⟨we packed up all of our *possessions* and excitedly moved into a new house⟩
synonyms belongings, chattels, duds, effects, gear, goods, holdings, movables (*or* moveables), paraphernalia, personal effects, personal property, personalty, plunder [*chiefly dialect*], stuff, things
related words treasures, valuables; appointments, fixtures, furnishings; estate, property, tangibles; collateral
near antonyms immovables, real estate
3 the act or fact of residing in a place ⟨squatters had established *possession* in the abandoned warehouse⟩ — see OCCUPANCY

possessive *adj* intolerant of rivalry or unfaithfulness ⟨he was very *possessive* of his girlfriend's attention, and it was really starting to annoy her⟩ — see JEALOUS 1

possessor *n* one who has a legal or rightful claim to ownership ⟨she was the *possessor* of several acres of land in the country⟩ — see PROPRIETOR

possibility *n* **1** something that can develop or become actual ⟨there's a *possibility* for violence in the situation⟩ — see POTENTIAL
2 something that might happen ⟨winning the championship is a real *possibility* for us⟩ — see EVENT 2

possible *adj* **1** capable of being done or carried out ⟨I think that building the entire set in two days is *possible*, albeit difficult⟩
synonyms achievable, attainable, doable, feasible, practicable, realizable, viable, workable
related words practical, reasonable, sensible; contingent, likely, probable; acceptable, believable, conceivable, creditable, plausible, thinkable; actionable, available, usable (*also* useable)
near antonyms impractical, unrealistic; doubtful, dubious, far-fetched, improbable, unlikely; implausible, inconceivable, incredible, unbelievable; futile, useless, vain; absurd, fantastic (*also* fantastical), outlandish, preposterous, ridiculous; unthinkable
antonyms hopeless, impossible, impracticable, infeasible, nonviable, unattainable, undoable, unfeasible, unrealizable, unviable, unworkable
2 existing only as a possibility and not in fact ⟨only one of several *possible* outcomes⟩ — see POTENTIAL

possibly *adv* it is possible ⟨he may *possibly* recover after such a serious mistake, but it doesn't seem likely⟩ — see PERHAPS

[1]**post** *n, chiefly British* communications or parcels sent or carried through the postal system ⟨the *post* always comes at tea time⟩ — see MAIL

[2]**post** *n* **1** a specific task with which a person or group is charged ⟨selling lemonade was my *post* at the church fair⟩ — see MISSION
2 the place where someone is assigned to stand or remain ⟨he wisely stayed at his *post* during the emergency⟩ — see STATION 1
3 an assignment at which one regularly works for pay ⟨she's held a number of teaching *posts* at local colleges⟩ — see JOB 1

[3]**post** *n* an upright shaft that supports an overhead structure ⟨hung the hammock between a tree and a *post* in the fence⟩ — see PILLAR 1

[1]**post** *vb* **1** to affix (as a notice) to or on a suitable place ⟨the student organizations generally *post* their announcements on the campus bulletin board⟩
synonyms placard
related words nail, plaster, tack (up); advertise, announce, bill, blaze, broadcast, call, declare, proclaim, promulgate, publicize, publish
near antonyms remove, take down
2 to make known openly or publicly ⟨*posted* the students' grades⟩ — see ANNOUNCE

[2]**post** *vb* to assign to a place or position ⟨the police are planning to *post* an officer outside the hospital room of the witness⟩
synonyms detail, station
related words set; appoint; place, position

[3]**post** *vb* to send through the postal system ⟨be sure to *post* the letter this afternoon⟩ — see MAIL

postdate *vb* to come after in time ⟨the inscription at the base actually *postdates* the statue itself by a number of years⟩ — see FOLLOW 1

poster *n* a sheet bearing an announcement for posting in a public place ⟨we put up a hundred *posters* announcing the concert⟩
synonyms bill, placard
related words billboard, sign, signboard; broadside, flyer (*also* flier), handbill, handout, playbill, show bill; ad, advertisement, announcement, bulletin, dispatch, release

posterior *adj* **1** being at or in the part of something opposite the front part ⟨the chapel's *posterior* location in the church serves to make it a quiet retreat⟩ — see BACK
2 being, occurring, or carried out at a time after something else ⟨artifacts dating from a *posterior* historical period⟩ — see SUBSEQUENT

posterior *n* the part of the body upon which someone sits ⟨the baseball players were always slapping one another on the *posterior*⟩ — see BUTTOCKS

posterity *n* the descendants of a person, animal, or plant ⟨an association for people who have claims for being the *posterity* of Thomas Jefferson⟩ — see OFFSPRING

posthaste *adv* with great speed ⟨ran *posthaste* for the doctor⟩ — see FAST 1

posthumous *adj* occurring after one's death ⟨the soldier was awarded a *posthumous* medal for valor⟩
synonyms postmortem
related words belated, delayed, late
antonyms antemortem

postie *n, British* a person who delivers mail ⟨the sort of small Cornish village in which the local *postie* knows everyone's business⟩ — see POSTMAN

posting *n* a published statement informing the public of a matter of general interest ⟨a *posting* in the local newspaper of the public auction of a house on which a bank had foreclosed⟩ — see ANNOUNCEMENT

postman *n* a person who delivers mail ⟨the *postman* comes at around nine every morning⟩
synonyms letter carrier, mail carrier, mailman, postie [*British*]
related words courier, messenger; postmaster, postmistress

postmortem *adj* occurring after one's death ⟨*postmortem* tests on the brain tissue of people who had been suffering from Alzheimer's disease⟩ — see POSTHUMOUS

postmortem *n* examination of a dead body especially

to find out the cause of death ⟨the *postmortem* revealed that the cause of death had been an undetected heart defect⟩ — see AUTOPSY

postmortem examination *n* examination of a dead body especially to find out the cause of death ⟨a coroner performed the *postmortem examination* with painstaking thoroughness⟩ — see AUTOPSY

postpone *vb* to assign to a later time ⟨we'll have to *postpone* a decision until we have all the information⟩
synonyms defer, delay, hold off (on), hold over, hold up, lay over, put off, put over, remit, shelve
related words suspend; hesitate, pause, stay; detain, retard, slow; extend, lengthen, prolong, protract, stretch (out); wait
near antonyms act, deal (with), decide (upon), do, work (on)

postulate *n* something taken as being true or factual and used as a starting point for a course of action or reasoning ⟨one of the *postulates* that the true agnostic rejects is the assumption that it is even possible for us to know whether God exists⟩ — see ASSUMPTION 1

postulate *vb* to take as true or as a fact without actual proof ⟨*postulates* that all people are born with certain rights that can never be taken away from them⟩ — see ASSUME 2

posture *n* **1** a general way of holding the body ⟨a good upright *posture* will prevent backaches⟩
synonyms attitude, carriage, poise, stance, station
related words attention; body language; pose, seat; bearing, behavior, conduct, demeanor, deportment; air, poise, presence; aspect, look, mien
2 position with regard to conditions and circumstances ⟨claims that the country's defense *posture* is weak⟩ — see SITUATION 1

posy *n* a bunch of flowers ⟨gathered a *posy* of wildflowers to present to his girlfriend⟩ — see BOUQUET 1

pot *n* **1** the total of the bets at stake at one time ⟨everyone got a bit nervous when the *pot* grew to more than a hundred dollars⟩
synonyms jack, jackpot, pool
related words fund, kitty; bet, stake, wager
2 a considerable amount ⟨made a *pot* of money in the real estate market⟩ — see LOT 2
3 an enlarged or bulging abdomen ⟨vowed that he would never get a *pot*, that telltale sign of middle age⟩ — see POTBELLY

potable *adj* suitable for drinking ⟨around here, the only *potable* water comes from wells⟩
synonyms drinkable
related words clean, fresh, pure, uncontaminated, unpolluted; nonpoisonous
near antonyms contaminated, dirty, foul, polluted; poison, poisonous, toxic; unhealthful, unhealthy, unwholesome
antonyms undrinkable

potable *n* **1** a distilled beverage that can make a person drunk ⟨hid the *potables* in the back hall closet⟩ — see ALCOHOL
2 a liquid suitable for drinking ⟨keeps the wet bar stocked with an array of top-shelf liquors, mixers, and other fine *potables*⟩ — see DRINK 1

potbellied *adj* having a large protruding abdomen ⟨an old, *potbellied* cat that now needs a ramp just to get on the sofa⟩ — see PAUNCHY

potbelly *n* an enlarged or bulging abdomen ⟨he began exercising to get rid of his growing *potbelly* and to improve his health⟩
synonyms bay window, beer belly, belly, corporation, gut, paunch, pot
related words breadbasket [*slang*], stomach, tummy; chubbiness, corpulence, fat, fatness, fleshiness, obesity, overweight, paunchiness, plumpness, portliness, pudginess; chunkiness, heaviness, stoutness

potence *n* the ability to exert effort for the accomplishment of a task ⟨claimed that an alliance would have a collective *potence* far greater than that of any individual nation⟩ — see POWER 2

potency *n* the ability to exert effort for the accomplishment of a task ⟨vitamins of high *potency* that should be taken only in the proper dosage⟩ — see POWER 2

potent *adj* **1** having an abundance of some characteristic quality (as flavor) ⟨a *potent* tea that is the perfect morning pick-me-up⟩ — see FULL-BODIED
2 having great power or influence ⟨a *potent* argument for expanding our program of space exploration⟩ — see IMPORTANT 2
3 producing or capable of producing a desired result ⟨*potent* medicine that can be obtained through a doctor's prescription⟩ — see EFFECTIVE 1

potentate *n* one who rules over a people with a sole, supreme, and usually hereditary authority ⟨Charles inherited the position of *potentate* of the Holy Roman Empire from his grandfather, as well that of king of Spain from his father⟩ — see MONARCH 1

potential *adj* existing only as a possibility and not in fact ⟨I can see a few *potential* problems with co-owning a beach house with another couple⟩
synonyms implicit, possible
related words conceivable, generable, imaginable, plausible, thinkable; likely, probable; conjectural, hypothetical, suppositional, theoretical (*also* theoretic); alleged, assumed, purported, reputed, supposed; achievable, attainable, doable, feasible, practicable, viable, workable
near antonyms authenticated, confirmed, demonstrated, established, proven, substantiated; authentic, bona fide, genuine, true
antonyms actual, existent, factual, real

potential *n* something that can develop or become actual ⟨a time when cloning was merely a *potential* and the stuff of science fiction⟩
synonyms capability, eventuality, possibility, potentiality, prospect
related words likelihood, probability; latency, potency
near antonyms actuality, reality; certainty

potentiality *n* something that can develop or become actual ⟨would like to see a colony on the moon as an actuality and not merely a *potentiality*⟩ — see POTENTIAL

potful *n* a considerable amount ⟨visitors to the theme park will have a *potful* of fun⟩ — see LOT 2

pother *n* **1** a state of nervous or irritated concern ⟨always in a *pother* over the state of her garden⟩ — see FRET
2 a state of noisy, confused activity ⟨the *pother* of city traffic that commuters face every day⟩ — see COMMOTION

potpourri *n* an unorganized collection or mixture of various things ⟨a *potpourri* of hit songs from the last 10 years⟩ — see MISCELLANY 1

potshot *vb* to criticize harshly and usually publicly ⟨ended the show with an extended rant in which he *potshot* an array of personages on the right⟩ — see ATTACK 2

potted *adj, slang* being under the influence of alcohol ⟨work was so awful that I'm just going to go out and get *potted* tonight⟩ — see DRUNK

potter (around) *vb* to spend time in aimless activity ⟨*pottering around* indoors on a rainy day⟩ — see FIDDLE (AROUND)

potterer *n* a person who regularly or occasionally engages in an activity as a pastime rather than as a profession ⟨a camera designed for people who don't pretend to be anything more than *potterers* at photography⟩ — see AMATEUR 1

potter's field *n* a piece of land used for burying the dead ⟨criminals and unidentified people are sometimes buried in a *potter's field*⟩ — see CEMETERY

pottery *n* articles made of baked clay ⟨we picked up some ceramic vases in a *pottery* store⟩ — see CROCKERY

potty *adj* being or characteristic of a person who has an offensive air of superiority and tends to ignore or disdain anyone regarded as inferior ⟨a ridiculous woman with pretentious airs and *potty* pronunciations for everyday words⟩ — see SNOBBISH

potty *n* a room furnished with a fixture for flushing body waste ⟨the little girl announced loudly that she needed to go to the *potty*⟩ — see TOILET

pouch *n* a container made of a flexible material (as paper or plastic) ⟨we sealed the catnip in a cloth *pouch* and tossed it to the cat⟩ — see BAG 1

pouch *vb* to extend outward beyond a usual point ⟨as he grew older, the skin on his neck *pouched*⟩ — see BULGE 1

poultice *n* a medicated covering used to heal an injury ⟨placed a *poultice* over the infected cut⟩ — see DRESSING 1

pounce (on *or* upon) *vb* to take sudden, violent action against ⟨the muggers *pounced on* the unsuspecting tourists as soon as they rounded the corner⟩ — see ATTACK 1

[1]pound *n* a hard strike with a part of the body or an instrument ⟨give the nail a final *pound* with the hammer⟩ — see [1]BLOW

[2]pound *n* an enclosure with an open framework for keeping animals ⟨stray dogs wearing tags are kept in that *pound* until their owners can be notified⟩ — see CAGE

pound *vb* **1** to move heavily or clumsily ⟨*pounding* down the road as fast as he could run⟩ — see LUMBER 1
2 to deliver a blow to (someone or something) usually in a strong vigorous manner ⟨*pounding* nails into boards all day long⟩ — see HIT 1
3 to strike repeatedly ⟨during the storm the waves furiously *pounded* the beach⟩ — see BEAT 1
4 to shape with a hammer ⟨*pounding* out a depression in the metal⟩ — see HAMMER 1
5 to reduce to fine particles ⟨the tablet may be *pounded* and mixed in with the animal's food⟩ — see POWDER

pound (down) *vb* to swallow in liquid form ⟨Friday nights were usually spent wolfing down pizza and *pounding down* beers⟩ — see DRINK 1

pour *vb* **1** to cause to flow in a stream ⟨she lifted the teakettle and *poured* some hot water from the spout⟩
synonyms stream
related words ladle, spoon; cascade, trickle; deluge, flood, inundate, overflow
2 to move in a stream ⟨water gently *pouring* down the canal toward the dam⟩ — see FLOW 1
3 to flow out in great quantities or with force ⟨tears *pouring* down his cheeks⟩ — see GUSH 1
4 to fall as water in a continuous stream of drops from the clouds ⟨it's *pouring* outside, so you'd better take an umbrella⟩ — see RAIN 1
5 to give readily and in large quantities ⟨repeatedly *poured* money into the revitalization of the downtown area⟩ — see RAIN 2

pouring *adj* marked by or abounding with rain ⟨a *pouring*, miserable day⟩ — see RAINY

pout *n* **1** a twisting of the facial features in disgust or disapproval ⟨that storekeeper's face seems to be in a permanent *pout*⟩ — see GRIMACE
2 pouts *pl* a state of resentful silence or irritability ⟨she stayed in the *pouts* all day⟩ — see SULK

pout *vb* **1** to extend outward beyond a usual point ⟨her lips *pouted* as she glared at him silently⟩ — see BULGE 1
2 to silently go about in a bad mood ⟨*pouted* and didn't say a word to anyone all morning⟩ — see SULK

pouting *adj* given to or displaying a resentful silence and often irritability ⟨stayed in a *pouting* mood until her boyfriend apologized, though he didn't have the vaguest idea what he was apologizing for⟩ — see SULKY

pouty *adj* given to or displaying a resentful silence and often irritability ⟨we could tell from the way she turned *pouty* that she'd lost the tennis match⟩ — see SULKY

poverty *n* **1** the state of lacking sufficient money or material possessions ⟨he dreamed of finding a good job and working his way out of *poverty* and debt⟩
synonyms beggary, destituteness, destitution, impecuniosity, impecuniousness, impoverishment, indigence, necessity, need, neediness, pauperism, penuriousness, penury, poorness, want
related words gutter, misery, woe, wretchedness; exigency; emergency, rainy day; austerity, deprivation, privation; bankruptcy, insolvency; belt-tightening, pinching, straitening
near antonyms luxury, prosperity
antonyms affluence, opulence, richness, wealth, wealthiness
2 a falling short of an essential or desirable amount or number ⟨a *poverty* of information about the new policies⟩ — see DEFICIENCY

poverty-stricken *adj* lacking money or material possessions ⟨*poverty-stricken* immigrants struggling to make ends meet⟩ — see POOR 1

powder *vb* to reduce to fine particles ⟨you have to *powder* the antibiotic tablet and mix it with food⟩
synonyms atomize, beat, bray, comminute, crush, disintegrate, grind, mill, mull, pound, pulverize
related words grate, kibble; crumble, crunch; break, bust, dash, fracture, fragment; shatter, smash, splinter; micronize

powder keg *n* a potentially explosive place or situation ⟨the immigration bill has become a political *powder keg* for legislators on both sides of the aisle⟩ — see TINDERBOX 1

powdery *adj* consisting of very small particles ⟨the kind of *powdery* snow that is perfect for skiing⟩ — see FINE 1

power *n* **1** the right or means to command or control others ⟨the emir has nearly complete *power* over the emirate⟩
synonyms arm, authority, clutch, command, control, death grip, dominion, grip, hold, mastery, reign, rein(s), sway
related words clout, influence, leverage, pull, voice, weight; jurisdiction; direction, management; dominance, imperium, predominance, sovereignty (*also* sovranty), supremacy; prerogative, privilege, right; eminence, importance, moment
near antonyms helplessness, weakness
antonyms impotence, impotency, powerlessness
2 the ability to exert effort for the accomplishment of a task ⟨the corporation has the *power* to accomplish almost anything⟩ ⟨you'll need to build a bit more *power* in order to be a star pitcher⟩
synonyms energy, firepower, force, horsepower, might, muscle, potence, potency, puissance, sinew, strength, vigor
related words aptitude, capability, capacity, competence, competency; adequacy, effectiveness, effectualness, usefulness
near antonyms disability, inability, inaptitude, incapability, incapableness, incapacity, incompetence, incompetency; ineffectiveness, ineffectuality, ineffectualness, inefficaciousness, inefficacy, uselessness; helplessness, paralysis
antonyms impotence, impotency, powerlessness, weakness

3 a natural ability of the mind or body ⟨dogs have a very highly developed *power* of smell⟩
synonyms faculty
related words function; capability, capacity; aptitude, endowment, flair, genius, gift, instinct, knack, talent
near antonyms inability, incapability, incapacity; inaptitude, inaptness, ineptness
4 something with a usable capacity for doing work ⟨nuclear *power*⟩ — see FUEL

powerboat *n* a boat equipped with a motor ⟨his friend had a *powerboat* and took them out waterskiing⟩ — see MOTORBOAT

powerful *adj* having great power or influence ⟨a *powerful* producer in the music business who is considered responsible for the careers of several superstars⟩ — see IMPORTANT 2

powerfully *adv* in a vigorous and forceful manner ⟨began to row *powerfully* toward the shore⟩ — see HARD 3

powerhouse *n* an ambitious person who eagerly goes after what is desired ⟨from the very start of her singing career, she had a reputation for being a very determined *powerhouse*⟩ — see GO-GETTER

powerless *adj* unable to act or achieve one's purpose ⟨I wish I could help you, but I am *powerless* in this situation⟩
synonyms hamstrung, handcuffed, helpless, high and dry, hog-tied, impotent, impuissant, paralyzed, weak
related words incapable, incompetent, ineffective, ineffectual, inept, unfit, useless; feeble, frail, infirm, passive, spineless, supine, unaggressive
near antonyms able, capable, competent, effective, efficient; authoritarian, autocratic (*also* autocratical), despotic, dictatorial, magisterial, tyrannical (*also* tyrannic); dominant, dynamic, energetic, forceful, robust, sturdy, tough, vigorous; important, major, significant; high-level, senior, top
antonyms mighty, potent, powerful, puissant, strong

powerlessness *n* the lack of sufficient ability, power, or means ⟨cursed his *powerlessness* to affect the outcome of his friend's life-threatening illness⟩ — see INABILITY

powwow *n* **1** a coming together of a number of persons for a specified purpose ⟨all the departments met for a brief *powwow* after lunch⟩ — see MEETING 1
2 a meeting featuring a group discussion ⟨the mayor's *powwow* with local business leaders to discuss downtown development⟩ — see FORUM 1
3 a social gathering ⟨our neighbors kept us up most of the night with a raucous *powwow*⟩ — see PARTY 1

powwow *vb* to exchange viewpoints or seek advice for the purpose of finding a solution to a problem ⟨civic leaders *powwowed* for hours trying to resolve the issue⟩ — see CONFER 2

practicable *adj* **1** capable of being done or carried out ⟨a solution that is not *practicable* in the time available to us⟩ — see POSSIBLE 1
2 capable of being put to use or account ⟨a *practicable* knowledge of carpentry that came in handy when he volunteered to build houses for underprivileged families⟩ — see PRACTICAL 1
3 capable of or suitable for being used for a particular purpose ⟨that flimsy little saw is not a very *practicable* tool for cutting heavy tree branches⟩ — see USABLE 1

practical *adj* **1** capable of being put to use or account ⟨a *practical* and simple solution for the town's waste disposal⟩ ⟨she has some *practical* information on sightseeing in San Francisco⟩
synonyms actionable, applicable, applicative, applied, functional, practicable, serviceable, ultrapractical, usable (*also* useable), useful, workable, working
related words down-to-earth, pragmatic (*also* pragmatical), utilitarian; banausic, mundane; accessible, available, obtainable, reachable; all-around (*also* all-round), handy; active, alive, busy, employed, functioning, operating, operative
near antonyms abstract, academic (*also* academical), armchair, theoretical (*also* theoretic); inaccessible, unattainable, unavailable, unobtainable, unreachable; unsuitable
antonyms impracticable, impractical, inapplicable, nonpractical, unusable, unworkable, useless
2 willing to see things as they really are and deal with them sensibly ⟨a *practical* caseworker who doesn't spend a lot of time philosophizing while doing social work in the inner city⟩ — see REALISTIC 1

practical joke *n* a playful or mischievous act intended as a joke ⟨friends had left the risqué message on his voice mail as a *practical joke*⟩ — see PRANK

practically *adv* very close to but not completely ⟨*practically* everyone agreed to help⟩ — see ALMOST

practice *also* **practise** *n* **1** a private performance or session in preparation for a public appearance ⟨we held one last *practice* before the big concert⟩ — see REHEARSAL
2 a usual manner of behaving or doing ⟨the store's *practice* has always been to honor all major credit cards⟩ — see HABIT 1
3 something done over and over in order to develop skill ⟨*practice* makes perfect⟩ — see EXERCISE 2

practice *also* **practise** *vb* to do over and over so as to become skilled ⟨in order to play the guitar well, you need to *practice* fingering every single day⟩
synonyms exercise, rehearse, run over
related words groove, perfect, refine; point (for), prepare (for), train (with); drill, repeat; work (at *or* on); review, study

practiced *also* **practised** *adj* **1** having or showing exceptional knowledge, experience, or skill in a field of endeavor ⟨a simple dish that any *practiced* chef should be able to produce even blindfolded⟩ — see PROFICIENT
2 accomplished with trained ability ⟨a highly *practiced* performance of a classic ballet⟩ — see SKILLFUL

practicum *n* a period of undergoing practical instruction in one's job or career ⟨she got some coaching experience through a 40-hour *practicum* with the parks department⟩ — see APPRENTICESHIP

practitioner *n* one who brings an art or science to full realization ⟨a French doctor who was once the most famous *practitioner* of natural childbirth⟩ — see EXPONENT 2

pragmatic *also* **pragmatical** *adj* willing to see things as they really are and deal with them sensibly ⟨a *pragmatic* man, not given to grand, visionary schemes⟩ — see REALISTIC 1

prairie *n* a broad area of level or rolling treeless country ⟨you can see for miles in every direction on the *prairie*⟩ — see PLAIN 1

praise *vb* **1** to proclaim the glory of ⟨hymns that *praise* God⟩
synonyms bless, carol, celebrate, emblazon, exalt, extol (*also* extoll), glorify, hymn, laud, magnify, resound
related words adore, belaud, deify, idolize, worship; acclaim, applaud, commend, compliment, hail, renown, salute; chant, cheer, eulogize, rhapsodize; cite; flatter; crack up, recommend, tout
near antonyms blame, censure, reprehend, reprobate; criticize, reprove; admonish, chide, keelhaul, rebuke, reprimand, reproach; castigate, lambaste (*or* lambast)
2 to declare enthusiastic approval of ⟨the school volunteers were *praised* for their excellent work in the reading program⟩ — see ACCLAIM

praiseworthy *adj* deserving of high regard or great approval ⟨a *praiseworthy* effort to introduce inner-city youths to the visual arts⟩ — see ADMIRABLE

pram *n, chiefly British* a small four-wheeled vehicle designed for pushing a baby around in ⟨like other trendy Notting Hill couples, they bought a fancy *pram* for the first baby⟩ — see BABY CARRIAGE

prance *vb* to walk with exaggerated arm and leg movements ⟨*pranced* across the room dressed in an outrageous costume⟩ — see STRUT 1

prank *n* a playful or mischievous act intended as a joke ⟨as a *prank*, several students managed to change all the classroom clocks to different times⟩

synonyms antic, caper, capriccio, dido, escapade, frolic, gag, jest, knavery, monkeyshine(s), practical joke, rag [*chiefly British*], roguery, shavie [*Scottish*], shine(s), trick, waggery

related words skylarking; adventure, experience, game, lark, time; high jinks (*also* hijinks), horseplay, play, roughhousing, rowdyism; shenanigan(s), tomfoolery; joking, kidding, teasing; gambit, hoax, maneuver, ploy; deed, feat, mission, performance, stunt; caprice, conceit, fancy, vagary, whim, whimsy (*also* whimsey); deceit, deception, delusion, fooling, fraud, hanky-panky, hoodwinking, ruse, sham, stratagem, subterfuge, trickery, wile

prankish *adj* tending to or exhibiting reckless playfulness ⟨told the *prankish* lad that someone would eventually get hurt if he kept it up⟩ — see MISCHIEVOUS 1

prankishness *n* a natural disposition for playful behavior ⟨her irrepressible *prankishness* sometimes got her into trouble when she was growing up⟩ — see PLAYFULNESS

prat *n, British* a stupid person ⟨I need competent people for this job, and all they send me are *prats*⟩ — see IDIOT

prate *vb* to engage in casual or rambling conversation ⟨the young executive gratingly *prated* on about his weekend hobnobbing with the rich⟩ — see CHAT 1

prattle *n* unintelligible or meaningless talk ⟨parents often claim to understand the *prattle* of their infant offspring⟩ — see GIBBERISH 1

prattle *vb* **1** to engage in casual or rambling conversation ⟨spent an hour on the phone *prattling* on about nothing in particular⟩ — see CHAT 1

2 to speak rapidly, inarticulately, and usually unintelligibly ⟨stop *prattling* and calmly tell us the news⟩ — see BABBLE 1

prattler *n* a person who talks constantly ⟨stuck next to a *prattler* in the doctor's waiting room, she found the wait interminable⟩ — see CHATTERBOX

pray *vb* to make a request to (someone) in an earnest or urgent manner ⟨I *pray* you: tell me where they went⟩ — see BEG

prayer *n* **1** an address to God or a deity ⟨he always directed a bedside *prayer* to God before going to sleep⟩

synonyms orison

related words collect, grace, invocation, litany, requiescat, thanksgiving; evensong, matins, vespers; appeal, begging, beseeching, entreaty, imploring, petition, pleading, request, soliciting, suit, supplication

2 an earnest request ⟨we hope that the governor will hear our *prayer* and do something about this pressing problem⟩ — see PLEA 1

prayerful *adj* asking humbly ⟨impressed by such *prayerful* petitioners, the governor promised that he'd see what he could do⟩ — see SUPPLIANT

preach *vb* to deliver a sermon ⟨a minister who loves to *preach*⟩

synonyms sermonize

related words evangelize; lecture, platitudinize, preachify

preacher *n* a person specially trained and authorized to conduct religious services in a Christian church ⟨the marriage will be performed by our usual *preacher*⟩ — see CLERGYPERSON

preachy *adj* marked by or given to preaching moral values ⟨the students rolled their eyes as their principal launched into another *preachy* lecture about behavior at the prom⟩ — see SERMONIC

preamble *n* **1** a performance, activity, or event that precedes and sets the stage for the main event ⟨the round of hors d'oeuvres was merely the *preamble* to an evening of lavish feasting⟩ — see PRELUDE 1

2 a short section (as of a book) that leads to or explains the main part ⟨an insightful analysis of the *preamble* to the Constitution of the United States⟩ — see INTRODUCTION

precariousness *n* the quality or state of not being firmly fixed in position ⟨she quickly moved the china teapot after noticing its *precariousness* on the shelf⟩ — see INSTABILITY

precaution *n* a measure taken to preclude loss or injury ⟨as parents of young children, they have taken the usual *precaution* of locking up their household cleansers⟩

synonyms caution, fail-safe, palladium, preventive, safeguard

related words armor, cover, guard, protection, screen, shield, wall, ward

precautionary *adj* concerned with or serving to keep something from happening ⟨prior to the game, we moved the furniture out of the way as a *precautionary* measure⟩ — see PREVENTIVE

precede *vb* to go or come before in time ⟨there are two speeches which will *precede* yours⟩

synonyms antecede, antedate, forego, predate, preexist

antonyms follow, postdate, succeed

precedence *n* the right to one's attention before other things considered less important ⟨his merchandise order takes *precedence* because we received it first⟩ — see PRIORITY

precedent *adj* going before another in time or order ⟨behavior that may be explained by a *precedent* event in her troubled life⟩ — see PREVIOUS

preceding *adj* going before another in time or order ⟨had not eaten since the *preceding* day⟩ — see PREVIOUS

preceptor *n* a person whose occupation is to give formal instruction in a school ⟨a *preceptor* at a small English boarding school⟩ — see TEACHER

precinct *n* a region of activity, knowledge, or influence ⟨a sexist attitude that was pretty common in the *precincts* of the automobile business⟩ — see FIELD 2

precious *adj* **1** commanding a large price ⟨diamonds and other *precious* stones⟩ — see COSTLY

2 granted special treatment or attention ⟨parents who refuse to hear the slightest criticism of their *precious* children⟩ — see DARLING 1

3 having qualities that tend to make one loved ⟨a *precious* friend for whom I would do anything⟩ — see LOVABLE

precipice *n* a steep wall of rock, earth, or ice ⟨scaled the steep *precipice* with the ease of an experienced climber⟩ — see CLIFF

precipitate *adj* acting or done with excessive or careless speed ⟨the army's *precipitate* withdrawal from the field of battle⟩ — see HASTY 1

precipitate *n* **1** a condition or occurrence traceable to a cause ⟨the exodus from the cities was an unexpected *precipitate* of the automobile, which effectively shrank distances⟩ — see EFFECT 1

2 matter that settles to the bottom of a body of liquid ⟨the chemist filtered out the *precipitate* from the solution⟩ — see DEPOSIT 1

precipitate *vb* to fall as water in a continuous stream of drops from the clouds ⟨the air mass was dry, as much of the moisture had *precipitated* out on the other side of the mountains⟩ — see RAIN 1

precipitately *adv* with excessive or careless speed ⟨tended to act *precipitately* when faced with an unexpected turn of events⟩ — see HASTILY 1

precipitating *adj* marked by or abounding with rain ⟨thick, *precipitating* clouds that just stayed in our region for days⟩ — see RAINY

precipitation *n* excited and often showy or disorderly speed ⟨I fear that I may have acted with some *precipitation* on this matter, so I would like to reconsider⟩ — see HURRY 1

precipitous *adj* **1** acting or done with excessive or careless speed ⟨soon regretted our *precipitous* actions in international affairs⟩ — see HASTY 1
2 having an incline approaching the perpendicular ⟨a *precipitous* ski slope that fully merits its triple diamond designation⟩ — see STEEP 1

precipitously *adv* with excessive or careless speed ⟨the sight of swimmers exiting the water *precipitously* when some joker shouted "Shark!"⟩ — see HASTILY 1

precipitousness *n* excited and often showy or disorderly speed ⟨the *precipitousness* with which he acted would soon be a cause for regret⟩ — see HURRY 1

précis *n* a short statement of the main points ⟨a *précis* of the bill that the legislature is currently considering⟩ — see SUMMARY

precise *adj* **1** meeting the highest standard of accuracy ⟨a machine which takes very *precise* measurements of brain tumors⟩
synonyms accurate, close, delicate, exact, fine, hairline, mathematical, pinpoint, refined, rigorous, spot-on
related words correct, right, strict, true; definite, definitive; nice, subtle; careful, fastidious, finical, finicky, meticulous
near antonyms approximate, round; false, incorrect, untrue, wrong; careless, loose; indefinite, unclear, vague; doubtful, dubious, questionable, unreliable, untrustworthy
antonyms coarse, imprecise, inaccurate, inexact, rough
2 being in agreement with the truth or a fact or a standard ⟨gave very *precise* answers to the members of the investigative committee⟩ — see CORRECT 1
3 being neither more nor less than a certain amount, number, or extent ⟨gave him the *precise* amount that he owed him⟩ — see EVEN 1
4 following an original exactly ⟨a *precise* translation of the original Greek⟩ — see FAITHFUL 2
5 of a particular or exact sort ⟨at that *precise* moment the lights went out⟩ — see EXPRESS 1

precisely *adv* **1** as stated or indicated without the slightest difference ⟨arrived *precisely* at noon⟩ — see EXACTLY 1
2 in the same manner ⟨I feel *precisely* the same way as you do⟩ — see JUST 1
3 without any relaxation of standards or precision ⟨measured the length of the board *precisely*⟩ — see STRICTLY

preciseness *n* the quality or state of being very accurate ⟨the final result will be determined by the *preciseness* of the measurements⟩ — see PRECISION

precision *n* the quality or state of being very accurate ⟨the company that measures TV ratings prides itself on the *precision* of its calculations⟩
synonyms accuracy, accurateness, closeness, delicacy, exactitude, exactness, fineness, nicety, perfection, preciseness, rigor, rigorousness, ultraprecision, veracity
related words correctness, fidelity, rightness, strictness, truth; definiteness, definitiveness, definitude, determinacy; nicety, subtlety; care, carefulness, fastidiousness, meticulousness, persnicketiness
near antonyms approximation, roundness; falseness, falsity, incorrectness, wrongness; carelessness, guesswork, looseness; indefiniteness, vagueness
antonyms coarseness, impreciseness, imprecision, inaccuracy, inexactitude, inexactness, roughness

preclude *vb* to keep from happening by taking action in advance ⟨issued a strict schedule for doing household chores so as to *preclude* any arguments⟩ — see PREVENT

precluding *n* the act or practice of keeping something from happening ⟨the *precluding* of any misunderstanding seemed to be her top priority⟩ — see PREVENTION

precocious *adj* occurring before the usual or expected time ⟨a *precocious* baldness makes him look older than he really is⟩ — see EARLY 2

precociously *adv* before the usual or expected time ⟨*precociously* turning gray at the age of 30, she decided to color her hair⟩ — see EARLY

preconception *n* an attitude, belief, or impression formed in advance of actual experience of something ⟨tried to go into the training sessions without any *preconceptions*⟩ — see PREPOSSESSION 1

precursor *n* **1** one that announces or indicates the later arrival of another ⟨18th-century lyric poets like Robert Burns were *precursors* of the Romantics⟩ — see FORERUNNER 1
2 something belonging to an earlier time from which something else was later developed ⟨a *precursor* of the modern eggplant⟩ — see ANCESTOR 2

precursory *adj* coming before the main part or item usually to introduce or prepare for what follows ⟨instantly recognized that chilled feeling as one of the *precursory* symptoms of a cold⟩ — see PRELIMINARY

predaceous *or* **predacious** *adj* living by killing and eating other animals ⟨the *predaceous* animals of the jungle, with the tiger at the top of the food chain⟩ — see PREDATORY

predate *vb* to go or come before in time ⟨gunpowder *predated* the invention of the gun by several centuries⟩ — see PRECEDE

predator *n* a person who habitually preys upon others ⟨measures taken to protect minors against sexual *predators*⟩
synonyms bloodsucker, buzzard, harpy, kite, shark, vampire, vulture, wolf
related words exploiter, user; leech, sponge, sponger; destroyer, devourer
antonyms prey

predatory *adj* living by killing and eating other animals ⟨hawks are *predatory* and pose a danger to rabbits and other pets⟩
synonyms predaceous (*or* predacious), rapacious, raptorial
related words carnivorous; aggressive, deadly, ferocious, fierce, savage, violent; untamed, wild
near antonyms herbivorous, vegetarian; gentle, submissive, tame

predecessor *n* something belonging to an earlier time from which something else was later developed ⟨the once-ubiquitous typewriter was the *predecessor* of today's electronic keyboard⟩ — see ANCESTOR 2

predestine *vb* to determine the fate of in advance ⟨our victory in the tournament was seemingly *predestined*⟩ — see DESTINE

predetermine *vb* to determine the fate of in advance ⟨religious sects that believe that an individual's salvation has been *predetermined* by God⟩ — see DESTINE

predicament *n* a difficult, puzzling, or embarrassing situation from which there is no easy escape ⟨if you had

told the truth in the first place, we wouldn't be in this *predicament*⟩
synonyms bind, box, catch-22, corner, dilemma, fix, hole, impasse, jackpot [*chiefly West*], jam, mire, pickle, quagmire, rabbit hole, rattrap, spot, sticky wicket, swamp
related words difficulty, node; hot water, soup; pinch, plight, quandary, scrape, trouble; deadlock, halt, logjam, stalemate, standstill; clutch, crisis, crossroad, emergency, exigency, juncture, strait
phrases kettle of fish

predicate *vb* to find a basis ⟨she has *predicated* her theory on recent findings by other astronomers⟩ — see BASE

predict *vb* to tell of or describe beforehand ⟨I can't even begin to *predict* what housing prices will be like 30 years from now⟩ — see FORETELL

predicting *n* a declaration that something will happen in the future ⟨those annual *predictings* by self-styled psychics that grace the front pages of the tabloids⟩ — see PREDICTION

prediction *n* a declaration that something will happen in the future ⟨we were all amazed when the fortune-teller's *predictions* turned out to be true⟩
synonyms auguring, augury, bodement, cast, forecast, forecasting, foretelling, predicting, presaging, prognosis, prognostic, prognosticating, prognostication, prophecy (*also* prophesy), soothsaying, vaticination
related words foreboding, harbinger, omen, portent, prevision, prospectus, sign; anticipation, foreknowledge; foresight; conjecture, guess, surmise

predictive *adj* being a sign of a later course of events ⟨unfortunately, the stock market crash of 1929 turned out to be a *predictive* event, for the next decade was consumed by the Great Depression⟩ — see PROPHETIC

predilection *n* a habitual attraction to some activity or thing ⟨a young lad with a *predilection* for telling tall tales⟩ — see INCLINATION 1

predisposition *n* a habitual attraction to some activity or thing ⟨the young woman's *predisposition* to date men who are very much like her father⟩ — see INCLINATION 1

predominance *n* controlling power or influence over others ⟨the *predominance* of the Dutch in international trade during the 17th century⟩ — see SUPREMACY 1

predominancy *n* controlling power or influence over others ⟨Asia's long rise to *predominancy* in high-tech manufacturing⟩ — see SUPREMACY 1

predominant *adj* coming before all others in importance ⟨parental involvement has been found to be the *predominant* factor in a child's success in school⟩ — see FOREMOST 1

predominantly *adv* for the most part ⟨a *predominantly* middle-class neighborhood⟩ — see CHIEFLY

preeminence *n* **1** exceptionally high quality ⟨the restaurant is known for the *preeminence* of its seafood dishes⟩ — see EXCELLENCE 1
2 controlling power or influence over others ⟨some historians contended that no nation had attained such undisputed *preeminence* since the glory days of the Roman Empire⟩ — see SUPREMACY 1
3 the fact or state of being above others in rank or importance ⟨his *preeminence* in the field of obstetrics⟩ — see EMINENCE 1

preeminent *adj* **1** coming before all others in importance ⟨the *preeminent* reason for the booming economy⟩ — see FOREMOST 1
2 highest in rank or authority ⟨the *preeminent* golfer of his generation⟩ — see HEAD
3 standing above others in rank, importance, or achievement ⟨a meeting of *preeminent* scientists from around the world⟩ — see EMINENT

preempt *vb* to take or make use of under a guise of authority but without actual right ⟨the thoughtless teenagers had *preempted* front-row seats that were reserved for the guests of honor⟩ — see APPROPRIATE 1

preemption *n* the unlawful taking or withholding of something from the rightful owner under a guise of authority ⟨longtime residents resented the *preemption* of their urban neighborhood by this influx of affluent yuppies⟩ — see APPROPRIATION 2

preexist *vb* to go or come before in time ⟨an advanced Mesoamerican civilization whose apex and collapse *preexisted* the arrival of Europeans by hundreds of years⟩ — see PRECEDE

preface *n* a short section (as of a book) that leads to or explains the main part ⟨a noted critic has written a short *preface* to her story to explain some of the historical background⟩ — see INTRODUCTION

prefatory *adj* coming before the main part or item usually to introduce or prepare for what follows ⟨in *prefatory* remarks he offered his own definition of "civilization", a word subject to a variety of interpretations⟩ — see PRELIMINARY

prefer *vb* **1** to show partiality toward ⟨I generally *prefer* chocolate ice cream over vanilla⟩
synonyms care (for), favor, lean (toward *or* towards), like
related words adore, cotton (to), delight (in), dig, enjoy, fancy, groove (on), relish, revel (in); choose, cull, handpick, name, pick, select, single (out), take; covet, crave, desire, hanker (for *or* after), want, wish (for); bias, prejudice; incline (toward), tend (to); admire, appreciate, cherish, prize, treasure, value
phrases be partial to, go in for
near antonyms disfavor, dislike, mislike; abhor, abominate, detest, hate, loathe; decline, refuse, reject, turn down; discard, jettison, throw away, throw out
2 to decide to accept (someone or something) from a group of possibilities ⟨most buyers of that vehicle have *preferred* the model with four-wheel drive⟩ — see CHOOSE 1

preferably *adv* by choice or preference ⟨I like football, but *preferably* watching from the stands rather than being down on the field⟩ — see RATHER 1

preference *n* **1** a person or thing that is preferred over others ⟨my *preference* is soul music⟩ — see FAVORITE
2 positive regard for something ⟨a *preference* for cool weather⟩ — see LIKING
3 the power, right, or opportunity to choose ⟨he was promised his *preference* when the time came to repaint his bedroom⟩ — see CHOICE 1
4 a raising or a state of being raised to a higher rank or position ⟨a long-sought *preference* to the position of naval commander⟩ — see ADVANCEMENT 1

preferment *n* a raising or a state of being raised to a higher rank or position ⟨anticipated her *preferment* to a better-paying position within the company⟩ — see ADVANCEMENT 1

preferred *adj* singled out from a number or group as more to one's liking ⟨my *preferred* means of communication is e-mail⟩ — see SELECT 1

prefigure *vb* to give a slight indication of beforehand ⟨the first crocus traditionally *prefigures* the arrival of spring⟩ — see FORESHADOW

prefiguring *n* something believed to be a sign or warning of a future event ⟨the preaching of John the Baptist is generally regarded by Christians as a *prefiguring* of the ministry of Jesus⟩ — see OMEN

pregnancy *n* the state of containing unborn young within the body ⟨an elephant's *pregnancy* can last almost a year⟩
synonyms family way, gestation, gravidity
related words conception; begetting, breeding, genera-

tion, procreation, siring, spawning
near antonyms barrenness, infertility

pregnant *adj* **1** containing unborn young within the body ⟨we only realized that our cat had been *pregnant* when she unexpectedly delivered three kittens⟩
synonyms big, caught, enceinte, expectant, expecting, gone, gravid, heavy, quick [*archaic*]
related words parturient, prenatal; childbearing, gestational; brooding; conceiving, impregnated
phrases with child, with young
near antonyms barren, infertile; aborting, miscarrying; delivered
antonyms nonpregnant
2 clearly conveying a special meaning (as one's mood) ⟨a *pregnant* silence followed the ill-advised attempt at humor⟩ — see EXPRESSIVE

prehistoric *also* **prehistorical** *adj* having passed its time of use or usefulness ⟨*prehistoric* notions about mental illness that have no place in today's world⟩ — see OBSOLETE

prejudgment *n* an attitude, belief, or impression formed in advance of actual experience of something ⟨the general public's *prejudgment* of the accused before the trial had even started⟩ — see PREPOSSESSION 1

prejudice *n* **1** an attitude that always favors one way of feeling or acting especially without considering any other possibilities ⟨her lifelong *prejudice* against doing "dirty" jobs⟩ — see BIAS 1
2 hatred of or discrimination against a person or persons based on their race ⟨fought racial *prejudice* through the use of the court system⟩ — see RACISM 2

prejudice *vb* to cause to have often negative opinions formed without sufficient knowledge ⟨all the bad stories I had heard about the incoming CEO *prejudiced* me against him even before the first meeting⟩
synonyms bias, poison, turn
related words dispose, incline, predispose; influence, prepossess; convince, persuade, suggest

prejudiced *adj* **1** inclined to favor one side over another ⟨an employer who is known to be *prejudiced* toward graduates from Ivy League schools⟩ — see PARTIAL 1
2 unwilling to grant other people social rights or to accept other viewpoints ⟨racially *prejudiced* people have existed throughout recorded history⟩ — see INTOLERANT 2

prejudicial *adj* **1** causing or capable of causing harm ⟨pretrial publicity that may be extremely *prejudicial* to a defendant's right to a fair trial⟩ — see HARMFUL
2 opposed to one's interests ⟨the defense will try to counterbalance the mass of *prejudicial* evidence presented by the prosecution⟩ — see ADVERSE 1

pre–K *n* a school for children who are generally less than five years old ⟨attends *pre-K*⟩ — see NURSERY SCHOOL

prekindergarten *n* a school for children who are generally less than five years old ⟨a single father with two children in *prekindergarten*⟩ — see NURSERY SCHOOL

prelim *adj* coming before the main part or item usually to introduce or prepare for what follows ⟨a medical assistant had done all of the *prelim* work before the physician even walked into the examining room⟩ — see PRELIMINARY

preliminarily *adv* so as to precede something in order of time ⟨the sick children were examined *preliminarily* by the nurse to determine if they had a rash⟩ — see AHEAD 1

preliminary *adj* coming before the main part or item usually to introduce or prepare for what follows ⟨we need to do some *preliminary* research in order to properly focus the experiment⟩
synonyms beginning, introductory, precursory, prefatory, prelim, prelusive, preparative, preparatory, primary
related words introducing, prefacing, preparing, readying; premonitory, warning; basic, elementary, fundamental; ahead, early, former, preceding, previous, prior
near antonyms after, behind, following, subsequent

preliminary *n* a performance, activity, or event that precedes and sets the stage for the main event ⟨a meeting to discuss seating arrangements that was merely a *preliminary* to the formal negotiating sessions⟩ — see PRELUDE 1

prelude *n* **1** a performance, activity, or event that precedes and sets the stage for the main event ⟨an eruption of sectarian violence that proved to be the *prelude* to all-out civil war⟩
synonyms curtain-raiser, overture, preamble, preliminary, prologue (*also* prolog), warm-up
related words countdown, run-up [*chiefly British*]; lead-in; kickoff, start
2 a short section (as of a book) that leads to or explains the main part ⟨the musical had a brief *prelude* to get the audience in the proper mood⟩ — see INTRODUCTION

prelusive *adj* coming before the main part or item usually to introduce or prepare for what follows ⟨after a *prelusive* dimming of the house lights intended to induce quiet, the stage curtain rose⟩ — see PRELIMINARY

premature *adj* occurring before the usual or expected time ⟨his *premature* arrival at his own surprise party almost ruined everything⟩ — see EARLY 2

prematurely *adv* before the usual or expected time ⟨a baby born three weeks *prematurely*⟩ — see EARLY

premier *adj* **1** coming before all others in time or order ⟨a space shuttle on its *premier* voyage⟩ — see FIRST 1
2 highest in rank or authority ⟨the *premier* authority on butterflies⟩ — see HEAD
3 coming before all others in importance ⟨the *premier* social occasion of the summer season⟩ — see FOREMOST 1

premise *also* **premiss** *n* **1** something taken as being true or factual and used as a starting point for a course of action or reasoning ⟨your conclusion is all wrong because you started out with a false *premise*⟩ — see ASSUMPTION 1
2 premises *pl* the area around and belonging to a building ⟨detectives painstakingly searched the *premises* for clues to the disappearance⟩ — see GROUND 1

premise *vb* to take as true or as a fact without actual proof ⟨let us *premise* certain things, such as every person's need for love, before beginning our line of reasoning⟩ — see ASSUME 2

premium *adj* commanding a large price ⟨lavish feasts at which *premium* wines flowed freely⟩ — see COSTLY

premium *n* something given in recognition of achievement ⟨encouraging Girl Scouts to sell more cookies by offering *premiums*⟩ — see AWARD 1

premonition *n* a feeling that something bad will happen ⟨she had a *premonition* that her cat would somehow get hurt that day⟩
synonyms foreboding, presage, presentiment, prognostication
related words anticipation, foreknowledge; feel, insight, intuition; augury, omen, portent, sign; impression, suspicion; agitation, alarm (*also* alarum), anxiety, anxiousness, apprehension, apprehensiveness, care, concern, disquiet, doubt, dread, fear, misgiving, nervousness, perturbation, unease, uneasiness, worry; foresight, prescience

premonitory *adj* serving as or offering a warning ⟨a moderate tremor that some seismologists have interpreted as a *premonitory* sign of the catastrophic quake that is inevitable⟩ — see CAUTIONARY

prename *n* a name that is placed before one's family name ⟨his *prename* is "Christopher," but he prefers to be called by his last name⟩ — see FORENAME

preoccupation *n* something about which one is constantly thinking or concerned ⟨the future entomologist's *preoccupation* with insects from a very early age⟩ — see FIXATION

preoccupied *adj* lost in thought and unaware of one's surroundings or actions ⟨too *preoccupied* with her worries to enjoy the meal⟩ — see ABSENTMINDED 1

preordain *vb* to determine the fate of in advance ⟨my wife and I are such soulmates, I'm convinced that our marriage was *preordained*⟩ — see DESTINE

prep *vb* to make ready in advance ⟨the cooking time is considerably shortened if you've *prepped* the chicken the night before⟩ — see PREPARE 1

preparative *adj* coming before the main part or item usually to introduce or prepare for what follows ⟨*preparative* warning that the injection was going to cause a modest amount of pain⟩ — see PRELIMINARY

preparatory *adj* coming before the main part or item usually to introduce or prepare for what follows ⟨a *preparatory* investigation to see if there is enough evidence to warrant bringing charges⟩ — see PRELIMINARY

prepare *vb* **1** to make ready in advance ⟨I think I have *prepared* myself well for this challenge⟩ ⟨we *prepared* the classroom for the important visitors by getting rid of some unsightly clutter⟩
synonyms fit, fix, groom, lay, prep, ready
related words brace, fortify, gird, steel; batten, gather, gear up, mount; educate, indoctrinate, instruct, school, train, tutor; boot (up), prime; arrange, set, spread; arm, equip, forearm, furnish, outfit, provide, supply; incline, predispose; draft, draw up, frame; warm (up)
2 to make competent (as by training, skill, or ability) for a particular office or function ⟨basic training is intended to *prepare* raw recruits for active duty in the military⟩ — see QUALIFY 2
3 to put (something) into proper and usually carefully worked out written form ⟨the CEO asked his assistant to *prepare* a statement for the press⟩ — see COMPOSE 1
4 to work out the details of (something) in advance ⟨*preparing* an escape route in case of a fire⟩ — see PLAN 1

prepared *adj* being in a state of fitness for some experience or action ⟨a marathoner completely *prepared* for the grueling race⟩ — see READY 1

preponderance *n* **1** the fact or state of being above others in rank or importance ⟨not since Rome in its glory days had a nation enjoyed such overwhelming military *preponderance*⟩ — see EMINENCE 1
2 the largest part or quantity of something ⟨a *preponderance* of the evidence points to the guilt of the defendant⟩ — see MAJORITY 1

preponderancy *n* the fact or state of being above others in rank or importance ⟨the *preponderancy* of the Democratic Party in the state's political affairs has long been accepted as a fact of life⟩ — see EMINENCE 1

prepossession *n* **1** an attitude, belief, or impression formed in advance of actual experience of something ⟨the foreign tourists' *prepossessions* about life in the U.S. had been formed by many hours of American TV shows⟩
synonyms preconception, prejudgment
related words bias, favor, partiality, prejudice; assumption, conjecture, hypothesis, imagining, predetermination, presumption, presupposition, speculation, supposition, theory, thesis; concept, conception, image, notion, picture, thought
near antonyms detachment, impartiality, neutrality, objectivity, open-mindedness, unbiasedness
2 something about which one is constantly thinking or concerned ⟨tried to cure him of his *prepossession* with money⟩ — see FIXATION

preposterous *adj* **1** conceived or made without regard for reason or reality ⟨the idea that extraterrestrials built the pyramids is *preposterous*⟩ — see FANTASTIC 1
2 showing or marked by a lack of good sense or judgment ⟨a *preposterous* suggestion to go swimming in this freezing weather⟩ — see FOOLISH 1
3 so foolish or pointless as to be worthy of scornful laughter ⟨the movie thriller had such a *preposterous* plot that we were on the edge of our seats snickering⟩ — see RIDICULOUS 1

preposterousness *n* lack of good sense or judgment ⟨laughed at the sheer *preposterousness* of the idea⟩ — see FOOLISHNESS 1

prepotency *n* the fact or state of being above others in rank or importance ⟨the magazine's *prepotency* in the world of fashion is accepted without question⟩ — see EMINENCE 1

prerogative *n* something to which one has a just claim ⟨it's your *prerogative* to refuse to attend religious services⟩ — see RIGHT 1

presage *n* **1** a feeling that something bad will happen ⟨I had a nagging *presage* that the results of my medical tests would not be good⟩ — see PREMONITION
2 something believed to be a sign or warning of a future event ⟨the sight of the first robin is always a welcome *presage* of spring⟩ — see OMEN

presage *vb* to tell of or describe beforehand ⟨people used to believe that a comet *presaged* a major event, such as the death of a king⟩ — see FORETELL

presaging *n* a declaration that something will happen in the future ⟨the far-fetched *presagings* of self-styled seers about current celebrities⟩ see PREDICTION

preschool *n* a school for children who are generally less than five years old ⟨children excited about starting *preschool*⟩ — see NURSERY SCHOOL

prescience *n* **1** the special ability to see or know about events before they actually occur ⟨most believers would probably agree that complete *prescience* is one of God's attributes⟩ — see FORESIGHT 1
2 concern or preparation for the future ⟨parents who had the *prescience* to make everything in their house childproof before the arrival of their first baby⟩ — see FORESIGHT 2

prescient *adj* having or showing awareness of and preparation for the future ⟨*prescient* environmentalists and politicians who long ago made sure that these beautiful areas would forever be spared from development⟩ — see FORESIGHTED

prescribe *vb* to give the rules about (something) clearly and exactly ⟨in chess, you can move the various pieces only in certain *prescribed* ways⟩
synonyms define, lay down, specify
related words decree, dictate, ordain; assign, direct, fix, set, settle; arrange, order; choose, select; adjure, bid, charge, command, enjoin, instruct, tell; conduct, control, govern, lead, manage; coerce, compel, constrain, force; obligate, oblige, require

prescription *n* an inherited or established way of thinking, feeling, or doing ⟨the time-honored *prescription* among hostelers that you do not mess with another person's stuff⟩ — see TRADITION 1

prescriptive *adj* based on customs usually handed down from a previous generation ⟨even in this age of e-mail the *prescriptive* response to a wedding gift is a handwritten thank-you note⟩ — see TRADITIONAL 1

presence *n* **1** a position within view ⟨men should watch their language when in the *presence* of ladies⟩
synonyms company, sight
related words closeness, contiguity, immediacy, nearness, proximity

2 the outward form of someone or something especially as indicative of a quality ⟨the orchestra's musical director has a very stately *presence*⟩ — see APPEARANCE 1

present *adj* 1 existing or in progress right now ⟨I am very busy at the *present* moment⟩
synonyms current, extant, immediate, instant, ongoing, present-day
related words contemporary, mod, modern, modernistic, new, newfangled, new-fashioned, recent, red-hot, space-age, supermodern, ultramodern, up-to-date; being, breathing, existent, existing, living
near antonyms coming, future, unborn; completed, concluded, done, ended, finished, over, terminated, through, up; ancient, antediluvian, antiquated, antique, archaic, dated, fusty, musty, noncontemporary, obsolete, old, oldfangled, old-fashioned, old-time, out-of-date, outworn, passé; ago, bygone, erstwhile, former, past
2 being within the confines of a specified place ⟨all of you are required to be *present* for every meeting⟩
synonyms attending, in
related words accompanying, observing, participating; available; abounding; latent; breathing, existent, existing, extant, live
phrases at hand, in attendance, on hand
near antonyms departed, gone, retired; nonexistent; AWOL, truant; dead, deceased, defunct, demised; lost, vanished; belated, delayed, delinquent, late, overdue, tardy
antonyms absent, away, missing, out

[1]**present** *n* the time currently existing or in progress ⟨I cannot talk to you at *present*, but perhaps in a few minutes⟩
synonyms here and now, moment, now, today
related words phase, stage, state
near antonyms history, past, yesterday, yesteryear, yore; by-and-by, future, futurity, hereafter, offing, tomorrow

[2]**present** *n* something given to someone without expectation of a return ⟨an impressive array of *presents* for the bride and groom⟩ — see GIFT 1

present *vb* 1 to bring before the public in performance or exhibition ⟨we will *present* a performance of *Our Town* tomorrow evening⟩
synonyms carry, give, mount, offer, stage
related words display, exhibit, expose, parade, show, show off, unveil; preview; act, impersonate, perform, play, portray; depict, dramatize, enact, render, represent; extend, proffer, tender
phrases come out with
2 to make (one person) known (to another) socially ⟨may I *present* my niece Sarah?⟩ — see INTRODUCE 1
3 to make a present of ⟨the company *presented* a gold watch to him on the occasion of his retirement⟩ — see GIVE 1

presentation *n* something given to someone without expectation of a return ⟨a *presentation* of much-needed money to the children's charity⟩ — see GIFT 1

present–day *adj* 1 being or involving the latest methods, concepts, information, or styles ⟨*present-day* technology has rendered yesterday's marvels obsolete⟩ — see MODERN
2 existing or in progress right now ⟨the *present-day* administration in Washington⟩ — see PRESENT 1

presentiment *n* a feeling that something bad will happen ⟨a nagging *presentiment* of danger⟩ — see PREMONITION

presently *adv* 1 at or within a short time ⟨I cannot attend to the matter this instant, but I will *presently*⟩ — see SHORTLY 2
2 at the present time ⟨we are *presently* waiting in line for our turn⟩ — see NOW 1
3 without delay ⟨the performance is starting *presently*⟩ — see IMMEDIATELY

preservation *n* 1 the act or activity of keeping something in an existing and usually satisfactory condition ⟨each curator is responsible for the *preservation* of the works of art within his or her department⟩ — see MAINTENANCE
2 the careful maintaining and protection of something valuable especially in its natural or original state ⟨the *preservation* of the tropical rainforests is a global responsibility⟩ — see CONSERVATION 1

preserve *vb* to keep in good condition ⟨vigilantly *preserving* the ancient statue for future generations to enjoy⟩ — see MAINTAIN 1

preserving *n* the act or activity of keeping something in an existing and usually satisfactory condition ⟨the *preserving* of our rights and civil liberties⟩ — see MAINTENANCE

preside (over) *vb* 1 to exercise authority or power over ⟨from 1923 to 1948 Palestine was *presided over* by Great Britain under a mandate granted by the League of Nations⟩ — see GOVERN 1
2 to look after and make decisions about ⟨he *presides over* a vast communications empire⟩ — see CONDUCT 1

presidency *n* the act or activity of looking after and making decisions about something ⟨responsibility for the *presidency* of a major television network⟩ — see CONDUCT 1

president *n* a person in charge of a meeting ⟨the *president* of the international conference on genocide⟩ — see CHAIR 1

presider *n* a person in charge of a meeting ⟨I was unaccustomed to being the *presider* of anything larger than a departmental meeting⟩ — see CHAIR 1

presiding *adj* highest in rank or authority ⟨a senator who is the *presiding* member of the armed services committee⟩ — see HEAD

press *n* 1 a built-in space for storage behind a door ⟨put the towels in the linen *press*⟩ — see CLOSET 1
2 a great number of persons or creatures massed together ⟨he pushed his way through the *press* of people outside the courthouse⟩ — see CROWD 1
3 a storage case typically having doors and shelves ⟨originally designed as a *press* for clothes, it now serves to hide the bedroom TV⟩ — see CABINET

[1]**press** *vb* to take or make use of under a guise of authority but without actual right ⟨the fleeing bank robber *pressed* a nearby taxi into service as a getaway car⟩ — see APPROPRIATE 1

[2]**press** *vb* 1 to push steadily against with some force ⟨an old doorbell that requires you to *press* the button hard⟩
synonyms bear (down on), depress, shove, weigh (on *or* upon)
related words compress, mash, punch, squash, squeeze, squish, squoosh; compel, force, pressure; lean (on *or* against), muscle; drive, propel, thrust; compact, condense, constrict, contract, crush, scrunch, wring; cram, jam, jam-pack, pack, stuff, wedge
2 to apply external pressure on so as to force out the juice or contents of ⟨my family will only drink juice from freshly *pressed* oranges⟩
synonyms crush, express, mash, squeeze
related words ream; pulp, puree (*or* purée); extract, extrude
3 to gather into a closely packed group ⟨everyone *pressed* around me to see the pictures⟩
synonyms bunch, cluster, crowd, huddle, pile
related words assemble, collect, concenter, concentrate, conglomerate, congregate, convene, converge, flock, forgather (*or* foregather), herd, swarm, throng; encircle, mob, surround; embrace, hug
near antonyms break up, disband, disperse, split (up)

4 to force one's way ⟨we continued to *press* deeper and deeper into the tangled rain forest⟩
synonyms bore, bull, bulldoze, crash, elbow, jam, jostle, muscle, push, shoulder, squeeze
related words ram, shove, thrust
5 to cause (a person) to give in to pressure ⟨a manager *pressed* by a business crisis to return from his vacation ahead of schedule⟩ — see FORCE 1
6 to try to persuade (someone) through earnest appeals to follow a course of action ⟨*pressed* us to go with them to the school board meeting⟩ — see URGE
7 to indicate the importance of by centering attention on ⟨an office e-mail that *presses* the need for greater vigilance concerning building security⟩ — see EMPHASIZE 1

press (for) *vb* to ask for (something) earnestly or with authority ⟨workers *pressing for* higher wages and better working conditions⟩ — see DEMAND 1

pressing *adj* needing immediate attention ⟨she had *pressing* business on the other side of town⟩ — see ACUTE 2

pressman *n, British* a person employed by a newspaper, magazine, or radio or television station to gather, write, or report news ⟨the only *pressman* who was invited to Downing Street for an interview with the Prime Minister⟩ — see REPORTER

pressure *n* **1** the burden on one's emotional or mental well-being created by demands on one's time ⟨a business executive who works well under *pressure*⟩ — see STRESS 1
2 the use of power to impose one's will on another ⟨*pressure* from their peers can often cause teens to do things that they normally wouldn't consider⟩ — see FORCE 2

pressure *vb* to cause (a person) to give in to pressure ⟨his father *pressured* him to go out for the swim team⟩ — see FORCE 1

pressure group *n* a group of people with a common identifying interest that they seek to protect and promote ⟨observed that if publishers gave in to every *pressure group*, nothing would ever get published⟩ — see INTEREST GROUP

prestidigitation *n* the art or skill of performing tricks or illusions for entertainment ⟨Houdini's powers of *prestidigitation* remain legendary to this very day⟩ — see MAGIC 2

prestidigitator *n* one who practices tricks and illusions for entertainment ⟨a skilled *prestidigitator* can make entire buildings seem to disappear⟩ — see MAGICIAN 2

prestigious *adj* **1** having a good reputation especially in a field of knowledge ⟨a nutritional study that has been published by a *prestigious* medical journal⟩ — see RESPECTABLE 1
2 standing above others in rank, importance, or achievement ⟨the most *prestigious* social club in town⟩ — see EMINENT

prestigiousness *n* the fact or state of being above others in rank or importance ⟨the *prestigiousness* of Le Cordon Bleu in Paris pretty much assures its graduates a meal ticket in chefdom⟩ — see EMINENCE 1

presto *adv* with great speed ⟨the hungry men dived into the food and, *presto*, it was gone⟩ — see FAST 1

presumably *adv* **1** to all outward appearances ⟨*presumably* he's going on the trip for business reasons, but we have our doubts⟩ — see APPARENTLY
2 by reasonable assumption ⟨*presumably* he'll come later⟩ — see PROBABLY

presume *vb* **1** to form an opinion from little or no evidence ⟨I *presume* you'll fly if you do go⟩ — see GUESS 1
2 to take as true or as a fact without actual proof ⟨we should *presume* that a person is innocent until proven guilty⟩ — see ASSUME 2

presumed *adj* appearing to be true on the basis of evidence that may or may not be confirmed ⟨the *presumed* culprit⟩ — see APPARENT 1

presuming *adj* **1** having a feeling of superiority that shows itself in an overbearing attitude ⟨it's rather *presuming* of you to expect to be our first choice for the award⟩ — see ARROGANT
2 showing a lack of proper social reserve or modesty ⟨I thought it *presuming* of him to think that we would invite him along⟩ — see PRESUMPTUOUS 1
3 thrusting oneself where one is not welcome or invited ⟨some *presuming* waiter thought that it was his business to tell the expectant mother that she shouldn't be having even one glass of wine⟩ — see INTRUSIVE

presumption *n* **1** shameless boldness ⟨shocked by his *presumption* in insisting that we buy his raffle tickets⟩ — see EFFRONTERY
2 something taken as being true or factual and used as a starting point for a course of action or reasoning ⟨the *presumption* of innocence⟩ — see ASSUMPTION 1

presumptive *adj* worthy of being accepted as true or reasonable ⟨in that climate of fear, an accusation alone was *presumptive* evidence of guilt⟩ — see BELIEVABLE

presumptuous *adj* **1** showing a lack of proper social reserve or modesty ⟨it's a little *presumptuous* of you to assume that I'm your new best friend just because I invited you along⟩
synonyms bold, familiar, forward, free, immodest, overfamiliar, presuming
related words arrogant, bumptious, complacent, conceited, egoistic (*also* egoistical), egomaniacal, egotistic (*or* egotistical), highfalutin (*also* hifalutin), high-and-mighty, high-hat, hoity-toity, important, overweening, pompous, prideful, proud, self-asserting, self-assertive, self-complacent, self-conceited, self-important, self-satisfied, smug, uppity, vain, vainglorious; cavalier, disdainful, haughty, lordly, pretentious, snobbish, stuck-up, supercilious, superior; audacious, bold-faced, brash, brassbound, brassy, brazen, cheeky, cocky, fresh, impertinent, impudent, insolent, overbold, pert, sassy, saucy; confident, self-assured, self-confident, sure; boastful, braggart, bragging; domineering, high-handed, imperious; self-absorbed, self-centered, self-concerned, self-engrossed, self-infatuated, self-interested, self-involved, selfish, self-obsessed, self-seeking
near antonyms demure, down-to-earth, humble, lowly, meek, unassertive, unpretentious; bashful, mousy (*or* mousey), retiring, shy, timid, timorous; diffident, self-doubting
antonyms modest, unassuming
2 having a feeling of superiority that shows itself in an overbearing attitude ⟨the *presumptuous* doctor didn't even bother to explain to me the treatment that I would be receiving⟩ — see ARROGANT
3 thrusting oneself where one is not welcome or invited ⟨the *presumptuous* salesclerk started picking out some very expensive accessories for the outfit I had just chosen⟩ — see INTRUSIVE

presumptuousness *n* **1** an exaggerated sense of one's importance that shows itself in the making of excessive or unjustified claims ⟨only a person of unparalleled *presumptuousness* would assert that she knows all there is to know about words⟩ — see ARROGANCE
2 shameless boldness ⟨he found that a certain amount of *presumptuousness* could get you in trouble, but it could also get you into places where you normally weren't allowed⟩ — see EFFRONTERY

presuppose *vb* to take as true or as a fact without actual proof ⟨the book *presupposes* its readers will already know something about the subject⟩ — see ASSUME 2

presupposition *n* something taken as being true or factual and used as a starting point for a course of action or reasoning ⟨the cynic's *presupposition* that everyone acts out of purely selfish motives⟩ — see ASSUMPTION 1

pretend *adj* **1** being such in appearance only and made with or manufactured from usually cheaper materials ⟨if you were to see the movie's *pretend* jewels in real life, you wouldn't be fooled for a minute⟩ — see IMITATION

2 not real and existing only in the imagination ⟨it's just a *pretend* gun, so please pretend that I got you and play dead⟩ — see IMAGINARY

pretend *vb* **1** to take on a false or deceptive appearance ⟨I *pretended* that I didn't care that my ex had a new man in her life⟩

synonyms dissemble, dissimulate, let on, make out

related words act, impersonate, masquerade, play, playact, pose; affect, assume, counterfeit, fake, feign, profess, put on, sham, simulate; camouflage, conceal, disguise, mask; bluff, feint

phrases make a pretense, make a show, make believe, put on an act, put up a front

2 to present a false appearance of ⟨as if I would ever *pretend* illness just to take off a day from work⟩ — see FEIGN

pretended *adj* **1** lacking in natural or spontaneous quality ⟨he shows a *pretended* affection for his girlfriend's cat⟩ — see ARTIFICIAL 1

2 not being or expressing what one appears to be or express ⟨hoped that his *pretended* interest in classical music would impress the boss⟩ — see INSINCERE

pretender *n* one who makes false claims of identity or expertise ⟨it turns out that the guy who claimed to work for a modeling agency was just a *pretender*⟩ — see IMPOSTOR

pretense *or* **pretence** *n* **1** the quality or state of appearing or trying to appear more important or more valuable than is the case ⟨she seemed to be a very down-to-earth woman who was completely free of *pretense*⟩

synonyms affectation, affectedness, grandiosity, inflation, pretension, pretentiousness

related words arrogance, bumptiousness, complacency, conceit, egotism, hauteur, imperiousness, pompousness, presumptuousness, pride, self-aggrandizement, self-assertion, self-assumption, self-conceit, self-consequence, self-glorification, self-importance, self-satisfaction, smugness, vaingloriousness, vainglory, vainness, vanity; disdain, haughtiness, lordliness, snobbery, snobbishness, superciliousness, superiority; confidence, presumption, self-assurance, self-confidence, sureness; boastfulness, braggadocio; aggressiveness, assertiveness, audaciousness, boldness, brassiness, cheekiness, cockiness, forwardness, impudence, insolence, rudeness; grandiloquence; flamboyance, flashiness, garishness, gaudiness, glitz, mummery, ostentation, ostentatiousness, show, showiness

near antonyms demureness, down-to-earthness, humbleness, humility, lowliness, meekness, modesty; bashfulness, diffidence, shyness, timidity; naturalness, sincerity

2 a display of emotion or behavior that is insincere or intended to deceive ⟨her display of bravado was just a *pretense*⟩ — see MASQUERADE

3 an entitlement to something ⟨this book on gardening makes no *pretense* at completeness⟩ — see CLAIM 1

4 an exaggerated sense of one's importance that shows itself in the making of excessive or unjustified claims ⟨the *pretense* of that woman in thinking that the other hotel guests should be inconvenienced just for her⟩ — see ARROGANCE

pretension *n* **1** an entitlement to something ⟨a *pretension* of long standing to the throne of Hungary⟩ — see CLAIM 1

2 an exaggerated sense of one's importance that shows itself in the making of excessive or unjustified claims ⟨a woman full of *pretension* and pompousness⟩ — see ARROGANCE

3 the quality or state of appearing or trying to appear more important or more valuable than is the case ⟨the *pretension* of that French restaurant is more than I can bear⟩ — see PRETENSE 1

4 something that one hopes or intends to accomplish ⟨has serious *pretensions* of becoming a writer⟩ — see GOAL

pretentious *adj* **1** self-consciously trying to present an appearance of grandeur or importance ⟨that *pretentious* couple always serves caviar at their parties, even though they themselves dislike it⟩

synonyms affected, grandiose, highfalutin (*also* hifalutin), high-minded, la-di-da (*also* la-de-da *or* lah-de-dah *or* lah-dee-dah *or* lah-di-dah), ostentatious, pompous, snippy

related words airy, grandiloquent, high-flown, high-sounding, high-toned, sententious; arrogant, bumptious, complacent, conceited, egoistic (*also* egoistical), egotistic (*or* egotistical), high-and-mighty, high-handed, high-hat, hoity-toity, imperious, important, overweening, presumptuous, prideful, proud, self-asserting, self-assertive, self-centered, self-complacent, self-conceited, self-important, self-obsessed, self-pleased, self-satisfied, smug, uppity, vain, vainglorious; self-aggrandizing, self-dramatizing, self-glorifying, self-promoting; cavalier, disdainful, haughty, lordly, snobbish, snobby, stuck-up, supercilious, superior; confident, self-assured, self-confident, sure; boastful, braggart, bragging; aggressive, assertive, audacious, bold, brassy, cheeky, cocky, forward, impudent, insolent, rude; flamboyant, flashy, flaunting, garish, gaudy, glitzy, showy, splashy

near antonyms demure, down-to-earth, homely, humble, lowly, meek, retiring, unassertive, unassuming; bashful, diffident, mousy (*or* mousey), overmodest, passive, quiet, reserved, shy, timid

antonyms modest, unpretentious

2 having a feeling of superiority that shows itself in an overbearing attitude ⟨a *pretentious* author whose books only appeal to equally *pretentious* readers⟩ — see ARROGANT

pretentiousness *n* **1** an exaggerated sense of one's importance that shows itself in the making of excessive or unjustified claims ⟨everyone took her ingrained *pretentiousness* into account when considering her statements⟩ — see ARROGANCE

2 excessive or unnecessary display ⟨the sheer *pretentiousness* of the debutante's wedding⟩ — see OSTENTATION

3 the quality or state of appearing or trying to appear more important or more valuable than is the case ⟨the utter *pretentiousness* of the movie is matched only by the incomprehensibility of its story⟩ — see PRETENSE 1

preternatural *adj* **1** being out of the ordinary ⟨an editor with a *preternatural* sense of what will interest the book-buying public⟩ — see EXCEPTIONAL 1

2 of, relating to, or being part of a reality beyond the observable physical universe ⟨an investigator of *preternatural* phenomena⟩ — see SUPERNATURAL 1

3 being so extraordinary or abnormal as to suggest powers which violate the laws of nature ⟨a *preternatural* ability to predict how the stock market will perform⟩ — see SUPERNATURAL 2

prettily *adv* in a pleasing way ⟨a white wine that balances its *prettily* fruity flavors with refreshing acidity⟩ — see WELL 5

prettiness *n* the qualities in a person or thing that as a whole give pleasure to the senses ⟨the sugary *prettiness* of the knickknacks is sure to appeal to a certain type of collector⟩ — see BEAUTY 1

pretty *adj* **1** giving pleasure or contentment to the mind or senses ⟨she was not a *pretty* sight after she fell off her horse and into the mud⟩ — see PLEASANT 1
2 meeting the requirements of a purpose or situation ⟨their misalliance is as *pretty* an example of an ill-conceived marriage as you're likely to find⟩ — see FIT 1
3 very pleasing to look at ⟨a *pretty* young girl⟩ — see BEAUTIFUL 1

pretty *adv* to some degree or extent ⟨we've had some *pretty* cold weather lately⟩ — see FAIRLY 1

pretty (up) *vb* to make more attractive by adding something that is beautiful or becoming ⟨you could *pretty up* the room rather inexpensively simply by painting it⟩ — see DECORATE

pretty boy *n* **1** a man extremely interested in his clothing and personal appearance ⟨a downtown dance club with lots of *pretty boys* in attendance⟩ — see DANDY 1
2 a physically attractive man ⟨as a musical performer, he has yet to prove that he's more than just another *pretty boy*⟩ — see HUNK 1

prevail *vb* **1** to achieve victory (as in a contest) ⟨we shall *prevail* despite the overwhelming odds⟩ — see WIN 1
2 to continue to operate or to meet one's needs ⟨a custom that still *prevails* in many areas of Africa⟩ — see HOLD OUT

prevail (on *or* **upon)** *vb* to cause (someone) to agree with a belief or course of action by using arguments or earnest requests ⟨we *prevailed on* him to sing in front of all his friends⟩ — see PERSUADE

prevail (over) *vb* to achieve a victory over ⟨*prevailed over* their traditional rivals for the first time in years⟩ — see BEAT 2

prevailing *adj* **1** accepted, used, or practiced by most people ⟨the principal disagrees with the *prevailing* attitude toward corporal punishment⟩ — see CURRENT 1
2 held by or applicable to a majority of the people ⟨the *prevailing* custom here is to leave one's doors unlocked⟩ — see GENERAL 3

prevalence *n* the fact or state of happening often ⟨the *prevalence* of rumors when hard information is withheld from the public⟩ — see FREQUENCY

prevalent *adj* accepted, used, or practiced by most people ⟨the kinds of accidents seen in places where snowmobiles are *prevalent*⟩ — see CURRENT 1

prevaricate *vb* to make a statement one knows to be untrue ⟨during the hearings the witness was willing to *prevaricate* in order to protect his friend⟩ — see [1]LIE

prevarication *n* a statement known by its maker to be untrue and made in order to deceive ⟨she knew that his account was a pure *prevarication*⟩ — see LIE

prevaricator *n* a person who tells lies ⟨she was clearly one of the more practiced *prevaricators* ever to come before the congressional committee⟩ — see LIAR

prevent *vb* to keep from happening by taking action in advance ⟨a lot of problems would have been *prevented* if we'd just prepared better⟩
synonyms avert, forestall, head off, help, obviate, preclude, stave off
related words anticipate, provide; negate, neutralize, nullify; save; baffle, balk, checkmate, deter, foil, frustrate, thwart; bar, block, hamper, hinder, impede, interfere (with), retard, stall; deflect, fend (off), stop, ward (off); avoid, circumvent, dodge, duck, elude, escape, eschew, evade, shake, shirk, shun; forbid, inhibit, prohibit; arrest, check, halt, stop; compensate (for), counteract, counterbalance, make up (for), offset
near antonyms abet, aid, assist; ease, facilitate, smooth, unclog; advance, cultivate, encourage, forward, foster, further, nurture, promote; allow, leave, let, permit

preventative *adj* concerned with or serving to keep something from happening ⟨the department in charge of taking *preventative* measures against international terrorism⟩ — see PREVENTIVE

prevention *n* the act or practice of keeping something from happening ⟨good crowd control is crucial to the *prevention* of riots⟩
synonyms averting, forestallment, precluding
related words avoidance, circumvention; negation, neutralization, nullification; baffling, balking, checkmate, crossing, debarment, determent, deterrence, foiling, frustration, thwarting; barring, enjoining, forbidding, interdicting, interdiction, outlawing, prohibiting, prohibition, proscribing, proscription
near antonyms aid, assistance, backing, support; facilitation; advancement, cultivation, encouragement, nurture, promotion

preventive *adj* concerned with or serving to keep something from happening ⟨if you start taking this *preventive* medicine now, you may not get sick after all⟩
synonyms precautionary, preventative, prophylactic
related words deterrent, deterring; negating, neutralizing, nullifying; baffling, balking, foiling, frustrating, thwarting; blocking, hampering, hindering, impeding, retardant, stalling
near antonyms abetting, aiding, assisting; easing, facilitating, smoothing; encouraging, forwarding, fostering, furthering, nurturing, promoting

preventive *n* a measure taken to preclude loss or injury ⟨if people took the simple *preventive* of frequently washing their hands, the spread of germs could be greatly reduced⟩ — see PRECAUTION

previous *adj* going before another in time or order ⟨the new instructor should consult with the *previous* teacher about the lesson plans⟩ ⟨the *previous* math problem also included a reference to store discounts⟩
synonyms antecedent, anterior, foregoing, former, precedent, preceding, prior
related words advance, early, premature; earliest, first, inaugural, initial, maiden, original, pioneer; preexisting; introductory, preliminary; erstwhile, whilom
near antonyms advanced, late; closing, concluding, final, last, latest, latter, terminal, ultimate
antonyms after, ensuing, following, later, posterior, subsequent, succeeding

previously *adv* so as to precede something in order of time ⟨he had prepared the meat stocks *previously* so as to make things easier on the day of the big dinner⟩ — see AHEAD 1

previous to *prep* earlier than ⟨his passport arrived just *previous to* his trip⟩ — see BEFORE 1

prevision *vb* to realize or know about beforehand ⟨he claimed to have *previsioned* the crash of the stock market⟩ — see FORESEE

prey *n* **1** an animal that is hunted or killed ⟨rabbits are common *prey* for owls and hawks⟩
synonyms chase, quarry
related words game; kill, victim; beast, brute, creature, critter; target
near antonyms carnivore; chaser, hunter, pursuer; killer, murderer
antonyms predator
2 a person or thing harmed, lost, or destroyed ⟨he fell *prey* to nagging—but groundless—doubts about his wife's fidelity⟩ — see CASUALTY 1
3 a person or thing that is the object of abuse, criticism, or ridicule ⟨that woman has a sharp tongue, and her favored *prey* is her long-suffering husband⟩ — see TARGET 1

prey (on *or* **upon)** *vb* to seize and eat (something) as prey ⟨a fox has been *preying on* the chickens⟩
synonyms feed (on, upon, *or* off)

related words chase, hunt, pursue, stalk; destroy, dispatch, do in, fell, kill, slay

price *n* **1** the amount of money that is demanded as payment for something ⟨I really wanted to buy that shirt, but the *price* was more money than I had⟩
synonyms ante, charge, cost, damage, fee, figure, freight, price tag
related words fair market value, market value, valuation, value; asking price, list price, sticker price; price point, rate, tariff, unit price; carrying charge, overcharge, service charge (*also* service fee), surcharge; deduction, discount, markdown, reduction, sale; deposit; down payment; account, bill, check, invoice, tab
2 the loss or penalty involved in achieving a goal ⟨I finished the project, but the *price* was losing a night's sleep⟩
synonyms cost
related words expense, toll; damages, forfeit, forfeiture, mulct, sacrifice; ante, risk
3 something offered or given in return for a service performed ⟨there was a *price* on the criminal's head⟩ — see REWARD

priceless *adj* **1** having a value beyond any ability to appraise or adequately appreciate ⟨good advice is *priceless*⟩
synonyms inestimable, invaluable
related words immeasurable, incalculable; costly, dear, expensive, high, precious, premium, pricey (*also* pricy), superexpensive, valuable
near antonyms good-for-nothing, no-good, nothing, valueless, worthless
2 commanding a large price ⟨a dealer of *priceless* antiques⟩ — see COSTLY

price tag *n* the amount of money that is demanded as payment for something ⟨a weeklong cruise on the luxury liner sounded great, but the *price tag* was enough to make me choke⟩ — see PRICE 1

pricey *also* **pricy** *adj* commanding a large price ⟨a small boutique selling *pricey* women's clothing⟩ — see COSTLY

prick *n* **1** a mark or small hole made by a pointed instrument ⟨the immunization shot left a *prick* on my arm that turned into a bruise⟩
synonyms perforation, pinhole, pinprick, punch, puncture, stab
related words gouge, groove, hollow; break, cut, gash, incision, laceration, notch, rent, rip, rupture, slash, slit, tear
2 a sharp unpleasant sensation usually felt in some specific part of the body ⟨she felt a sharp *prick* when the nurse gave her the shot⟩ — see PAIN 1

prickly *adj* **1** causing an unpleasant tingling sensation ⟨she tried to ignore the feel of the *prickly* grass against her skin⟩ — see SCRATCHY 2
2 easily irritated or annoyed ⟨she dreaded having to deal with her *prickly* boss⟩ — see IRRITABLE
3 having leaves or branches which are likely to cause a scratch ⟨waded carefully through the *prickly* bushes⟩ — see SCRATCHY 1
4 requiring exceptional skill or caution in performance or handling ⟨a *prickly* issue that will outrage at least one special interest if not handled delicately⟩ — see TRICKY 1

pride *n* **1** a reasonable or justifiable sense of one's worth or importance ⟨finishing that survival course gave me a real sense of *pride* and confidence in my abilities⟩
synonyms ego, pridefulness, self-esteem, self-regard, self-respect
related words aplomb, assurance, confidence, self-assurance, self-assuredness, self-confidence, self-pride, self-trust, self-worth; dignity, face, honor, prestige
near antonyms discredit, disesteem, disgrace, dishonor, disrepute, humiliation, ignominy, infamy, obloquy, odium, opprobrium, shame; demureness, down-to-earthness, humbleness, humility, modesty; diffidence, meekness, shyness, timidity, timidness
2 an asset that brings praise or renown ⟨an architectural and acoustical masterpiece, the concert hall is the *pride* of the whole city⟩ — see GLORY 2
3 an often unjustified feeling of being pleased with oneself or with one's situation or achievements ⟨so full of *pride* that they were ripe for a big comedown⟩ — see COMPLACENCE 1
4 individuals carefully selected as being the best of a class ⟨crackerjack test pilots who are the *pride* of the navy's air arm⟩ — see ELITE 1

pride *vb* to think highly of (oneself) ⟨he *prides* himself on the quality of his writing⟩
synonyms flatter, pique, plume
related words boast, brag, crow, gasconade, swagger, swank, swash, vapor, vaunt; congratulate, felicitate

prideful *adj* **1** having or displaying feelings of scorn for what is regarded as beneath oneself ⟨*prideful* intellectuals long considered rock music unworthy of serious study⟩ — see PROUD 1
2 having too high an opinion of oneself ⟨at the wedding the *prideful* snobs ignored their poor relations⟩ — see CONCEITED
3 having or expressing feelings of joy or triumph ⟨flashed a *prideful* smile as she received her college diploma⟩ — see EXULTANT

pridefulness *n* **1** a reasonable or justifiable sense of one's worth or importance ⟨beaming with understandable *pridefulness*, the physically challenged graduate accepted his college diploma⟩ — see PRIDE 1
2 an often unjustified feeling of being pleased with oneself or with one's situation or achievements ⟨an inordinate amount of *pridefulness* for someone who has much to be modest about⟩ — see COMPLACENCE 1

priest *n* a person specially trained and authorized to conduct religious services in a Christian church ⟨searched for a *priest* who could perform an exorcism⟩ — see CLERGYPERSON

priesthood *n* individuals carefully selected as being the best of a class ⟨a gathering of Mafia dons that was in effect a convocation of the nation's *priesthood* of organized crime⟩ — see ELITE 1

priestly *adj* of, relating to, or characteristic of the clergy ⟨majestically robed in *priestly* garments⟩ — see CLERICAL

prim *adj* **1** being clean and in good order ⟨behind the bed-and-breakfast is a *prim* little garden where guests are served afternoon tea⟩ — see NEAT 1
2 given to or marked by very conservative standards regarding personal behavior or morals ⟨a very *prim* and proper matron was in charge of the girls' dorm⟩ — see STRAITLACED

primacy *n* the fact or state of being above others in rank or importance ⟨the *primacy* of calcium for building strong bones⟩ — see EMINENCE 1

prima facie *adj* **1** appearing to be true on the basis of evidence that may or may not be confirmed ⟨a *prima facie* case of tax fraud⟩ — see APPARENT 1
2 not needing proof in order to be accepted ⟨challenged the assertion that the dearth of women on the staff constituted a *prima facie* case of sexual discrimination⟩ — see AXIOMATIC

primal *adj* **1** coming before all others in importance ⟨the *primal* theme of the essay is toleration of religious diversity⟩ — see FOREMOST 1
2 relating to or occurring near the beginning of a process, series, or time period ⟨there was a period of *primal* idealism after the founding of the republic and before the rise of partisan politics⟩ — see EARLY 1

primarily *adv* **1** in the beginning ⟨the university was *primarily* an agricultural college when it was founded over two centuries ago⟩ — see ORIGINALLY
2 for the most part ⟨ketchup is *primarily* made from tomatoes⟩ — see CHIEFLY

primary *adj* **1** coming before all others in importance ⟨the *primary* concern for many house hunters is the asking price⟩ — see FOREMOST 1
2 done or working without something else coming in between ⟨a crop failure that was the *primary* cause of the famine⟩ — see DIRECT 1
3 highest in rank or authority ⟨the movie's *primary* screenwriter⟩ — see HEAD
4 coming before the main part or item usually to introduce or prepare for what follows ⟨a few minutes of *primary* instruction in the use of our diving gear before we actually got into the water⟩ — see PRELIMINARY

prime *adj* **1** highest in rank or authority ⟨the *prime* strategist in the senator's presidential campaign⟩ — see HEAD
2 of the very best kind ⟨owns a thousand acres of *prime* farmland⟩ — see EXCELLENT

prime *n* **1** a state or time of great activity, thriving, or achievement ⟨in the *prime* of her life⟩ — see BLOOM 1
2 individuals carefully selected as being the best of a class ⟨chose the *prime* of the litter of pups⟩ — see ELITE 1

primeness *n* exceptionally high quality ⟨made no claims regarding the *primeness* of that piece of farmland⟩ — see EXCELLENCE 1

primer *n* a book used for instruction in a subject ⟨a *primer* of human anatomy⟩ — see TEXTBOOK

primeval *adj* relating to or occurring near the beginning of a process, series, or time period ⟨*primeval* forests slowly disappearing as the climate changed⟩ — see EARLY 1

primitive *adj* **1** belonging to or characteristic of an early level of skill or development ⟨*primitive* wooden tools were used before the Iron Age⟩
synonyms crude, low, rude, rudimentary
related words basic, simple, uncomplicated; homely, homespun, unsophisticated; early, embryonic, primeval, primordial; backward, underdeveloped, undeveloped; aged, ancient, antediluvian, antiquated, antique, dated, fusty, hoary, musty, obsolete, old, oldfangled, old-fashioned, old-time, out-of-date, outworn, passé, past, quaint, unmodernized
near antonyms complex, complicated, intricate, involved, sophisticated; full-blown, grown, mature, matured, perfected, ripe, ripened; civilized, cultivated, enlightened, refined; contemporary, current, latest, mod, modern, modernistic, new, newfangled, new-fashioned, novel, now, present-day, space-age, state-of-the-art, supermodern, ultramodern, up-to-date
antonyms advanced, developed, evolved, high, higher, late
2 relating to or occurring near the beginning of a process, series, or time period ⟨a *primitive* period in church history when members still lived in communes⟩ — see EARLY 1
3 lacking in worldly wisdom or informed judgment ⟨her taste in art was still *primitive*, but she knew schlock when she saw it⟩ — see NAIVE 1

primo *adj, slang* of the very best kind ⟨thanked the volunteers for a really *primo* job on the parish fund-raiser⟩ — see EXCELLENT

primogenitor *n* a person who is several generations earlier in an individual's line of descent ⟨the family held a huge reunion to mark the 200th anniversary of their *primogenitors'* arrival in America⟩ — see ANCESTOR 1

primordial *adj* relating to or occurring near the beginning of a process, series, or time period ⟨all life on Earth supposedly came from a *primordial* ooze in existence many millions of years ago⟩ — see EARLY 1

prince *n* a person of rank, power, or influence in a particular field ⟨a neighborhood in which the city's merchant *princes* built palaces that shamelessly celebrated their wealth⟩ — see MAGNATE

princely *adj* fit for or worthy of a royal ruler ⟨set a *princely* meal before their guests⟩ — see MONARCHICAL

princess *n* a usually glamorous woman who is preeminent in her field of activity ⟨as the reigning *princess* of pop music, she exerts an enormous influence over teens⟩ — see DIVA

principal *adj* **1** coming before all others in importance ⟨our *principal* reason for coming here today⟩ — see FOREMOST 1
2 highest in rank or authority ⟨the *principal* researcher in the company's chemical division⟩ — see HEAD

principal *n* the person who has the most important role in a play, movie, or TV show ⟨my cousin is one of the *principals* in a new sitcom this fall⟩ — see STAR 2

principally *adv* for the most part ⟨the tourists were *principally* concerned with the quantity of the food, and only secondarily with the quality⟩ — see CHIEFLY

principled *adj* **1** following the accepted rules of moral conduct ⟨a high-*principled* art expert who always told clients what he honestly thought their items were worth⟩ — see HONORABLE 1
2 guided by or in accordance with one's sense of right and wrong ⟨a politician widely respected for her *principled* behavior in every office she ever held⟩ — see CONSCIENTIOUS 1

principles *n pl* **1** general or basic truths on which other truths or theories can be based ⟨if you don't learn the *principles* of algebra now, you won't understand much later on⟩
synonyms ABC(s), alphabet, basics, elements, essentials, fundamentals, grammar, rudiments
related words basis, bedrock, cornerstone, foundation, groundwork, keystone, underpinning; nitty-gritty; belief, canon, doctrine, dogma, faith, philosophy; axiom, law, precept, tenet; rule, standard; theorem
near antonyms details, trivia
2 the code of good conduct for an individual or group ⟨stuck to his *principles* even in the face of extreme pressure⟩ — see ETHICS

print *n* **1** a perceptible trace left by pressure ⟨one telltale sign that I had been napping was the *print* left by the chenille bedspread on my cheek⟩
synonyms impress, impression, imprint, stamp
related words dent, hollow, indent, indentation, indenture; mark, sign
2 a picture created from an image recorded on a light-sensitive surface by a camera ⟨we now get our *prints* developed online⟩ — see PHOTOGRAPH

print *vb* to produce and release for distribution in printed form ⟨the newspaper's motto remains "All the News That's Fit to *Print*"⟩ — see PUBLISH 1

prior *adj* **1** coming before all others in importance ⟨this assignment will be *prior* to any other work you may have⟩ — see FOREMOST 1
2 going before another in time or order ⟨we've made *prior* arrangements⟩ — see PREVIOUS

priority *n* the right to one's attention before other things considered less important ⟨the committee has decided to give your request *priority*, so you'll have a meeting early tomorrow morning⟩
synonyms precedence, right-of-way
related words preference; urgency; ascendancy (*also* ascendency), preeminence, primacy, supremacy; transcendence, transcendency; order, progression, sequence, succession; front burner
near antonyms back burner

prior to *prep* earlier than ⟨make sure all revisions are approved by the author *prior to* publication⟩ — see BEFORE 1

priory *n* a residence for men under religious vows ⟨you can hear the bells from the *priory* from the other side of the village⟩ — see MONASTERY

prismatic *adj* marked by a variety of usually vivid colors ⟨with its *prismatic* plumage, the ruby-throated hummingbird is one of our garden's most prized visitors⟩ — see COLORFUL

prison *n* **1** a place of confinement for persons held in lawful custody ⟨the ongoing debate whether drug users should go to *prison*⟩ — see JAIL
2 the act of confining or the state of being confined ⟨the view that *prison* does nothing to cure the criminal—if anything, it makes him worse⟩ — see INTERNMENT

prisoner *n* one that has been taken and held in confinement ⟨the *prisoners* were fed only bread and water twice a day⟩ — see CAPTIVE

pristine *adj* **1** being in an original and unused or unspoiled state ⟨a *pristine* forest that has never been subjected to logging or development⟩ — see FRESH 1
2 free from dirt or stain ⟨one doesn't dare spill anything on his car's *pristine* upholstery⟩ — see CLEAN 1

privacy *n* the state of being alone or kept apart from others ⟨I enjoy *privacy* for a time, but eventually I miss the company of others⟩ — see ISOLATION

private *adj* **1** not known or meant to be known by the general populace ⟨that he is planning to retire is *private* information until he makes a public announcement⟩
synonyms behind-the-scenes, confidential, esoteric, hushed, hush-hush, inside, intimate, nonpublic, privy, secret
related words classified, restricted, top secret; silent, unadvertised, unannounced, undisclosed, unmentioned, unsaid, untold; clandestine, closet, collusive, conspiratorial, covert; furtive, hugger-mugger, occult, sneak, sneaking, sneaky, stealthy, surreptitious, undercover, underground, underhand, underhanded; personal; closeted, concealed, hidden; repressed, silenced, stifled, suppressed; backstage, offscreen, offstage
near antonyms well-known; advertised, aired, announced, blazed, broadcast, declared, disclosed, divulged, enunciated, heralded, proclaimed, professed, promulgated, publicized, published, reported, spotlighted; general, popular, prevailing, vulgar; current, prevalent, rife, widespread; communal, shared
antonyms common, open, public
2 undertaken or done so as to escape being observed or known by others ⟨a *private* investigation of the organization's activities⟩ — see SECRET 1
3 of, relating to, or belonging to a single person ⟨club lockers in which *private* property may be stored⟩ — see INDIVIDUAL 1

private detective *n* a person not on the police force who investigates criminal or illicit activity or searches for missing persons ⟨when the police insisted that it was an accident and not murder, she hired a *private detective*⟩ — see DETECTIVE

private eye *n* a person not on the police force who investigates criminal or illicit activity or searches for missing persons ⟨unable to get the interest of the police, they hired a *private eye* to find their missing daughter⟩ — see DETECTIVE

private investigator *n* a person not on the police force who investigates criminal or illicit activity or searches for missing persons ⟨the retired policeman decided to become a *private investigator*⟩ — see DETECTIVE

privately *adv* in a manner intended to prevent knowledge or awareness by others ⟨she confided to me *privately* that she was considering divorce⟩
synonyms backstage, confidentially, in camera, intimately, secretly
related words à deux, tête-à-tête; inwardly, sotto voce; offscreen, offstage; clandestinely, collusively, conspiratorially, covertly; furtively, secretively, sneakily, stealthily, surreptitiously, undercover, underground, underhand, underhanded, underhandedly
phrases in private
antonyms openly, publicly

privation *n* the state of being robbed of something normally enjoyed ⟨the constant *privation* of sleep was starting to affect my work⟩
synonyms deprivation, loss
related words absence, dearth, lack, need, want; dispossession; denial, forfeit, forfeiture, penalty, sacrifice; bereavement; deficiency, inadequacy, insufficiency, paucity, poverty, scarcity, shortage
near antonyms control, ownership, possession; accumulation, acquiring, gain

privilege *n* something granted as a special favor ⟨the town's oldest resident will have the *privilege* of leading the parade kicking off the Heritage Celebration⟩
synonyms appanage (*also* apanage), boon, concession, honor
related words courtesy; claim, entitlement, right; birthright; perquisite, prerogative; charter, grant, patent; exemption, immunity, waiver
near antonyms burden, duty, obligation, responsibility

privilege *vb* to give a right to ⟨only professionals who meet the education and experience requirements set by law are *privileged* to use the title "interior designer" in Oklahoma⟩ — see ENTITLE 1

privy *adj* **1** not known or meant to be known by the general populace ⟨*privy* information on the current state of the peace negotiations⟩ — see PRIVATE 1
2 undertaken or done so as to escape being observed or known by others ⟨*privy* meetings between high-level representatives from both sides for the purpose of bringing about an armistice⟩ — see SECRET 1
3 of, relating to, or belonging to a single person ⟨a *privy* seal that can be used only by the British monarch⟩ — see INDIVIDUAL 1

prize *adj* of the very best kind ⟨delighted to be guests at one of her *prize* dinner parties⟩ — see EXCELLENT

prize *n* **1** someone or something unusually desirable ⟨in the view of most of her friends, her current boyfriend is certainly no *prize*⟩
synonyms catch, gem, jewel, pearl, plum, treasure
related words blessing, find, godsend, goody (*or* goodie), valuable, windfall; booty, loot, plunder, spoil, swag; brass ring; glory, pride; gold, jackpot, prize money, treasure trove
near antonyms lemon, loser
2 something given in recognition of achievement ⟨the Pritzker Architecture *Prize* is the world's most prestigious honor in the field of architecture⟩ — see AWARD 1

[1]prize *vb* **1** to draw out by force or with effort ⟨*prizing* the stubborn nails out of the board⟩ — see EXTRACT
2 to raise, move, or pull apart with or as if with a lever ⟨trying to *prize* apart the jammed gears⟩ — see [1]PRY 1

[2]prize *vb* to hold dear ⟨veterinarians know that pets are highly *prized* by their owners⟩ — see LOVE 1

prizefighter *n* one that engages in the sport of fighting with the fists ⟨a *prizefighter* who is generally acknowledged to be one of the ring's most dangerous men⟩ — see BOXER

prizewinning *adj* of the very best kind ⟨care to try a glass of my *prizewinning* homemade wine?⟩ — see EXCELLENT

proactive *adj* having or showing awareness of and preparation for the future ⟨*proactive* decision by the city fathers to plan for the eventual withering away of the region's manufacturing base⟩ — see FORESIGHTED

probability *n* **1** the quality or state of being likely to occur ⟨the plot of the movie thriller was exciting and surprising but woefully lacking in *probability*⟩
synonyms liability, likelihood
related words credibility, plausibility, plausibleness; feasibility, feasibleness, possibility, potentiality, reasonability, reasonableness, viability
near antonyms doubtfulness, dubiousness; impracticability, impracticality; implausibility, incredibility, incredibleness
antonyms improbability, unlikelihood, unlikeliness
2 a measure of how often an event will occur instead of another ⟨the *probability* of flipping a coin and getting heads 50 times in a row is not good⟩
synonyms chance, odds, percentage
related words outlook, prospect; contingency, possibility, potential, potentiality; conditional probability

probable *adj* **1** worthy of being accepted as true or reasonable ⟨the counselor could find no *probable* reason for the girl's bizarre actions⟩ — see BELIEVABLE
2 having a high chance of occurring ⟨a *probable* outcome of the price increase will be lower consumption⟩ — see LIKELY 1

probably *adv* by reasonable assumption ⟨we would *probably* win that bet⟩
synonyms assumably, doubtless, likely, presumably
related words maybe, mayhap, perchance, perhaps, possibly; conceivably, imaginably, plausibly, practically, reasonably; potentially; assuredly, certainly, clearly, conclusively, decisively, definitely, definitively, indisputably, indubitably, positively, really, surely, truly, undeniably, undoubtedly, unquestionably; presumedly, supposably, supposedly
phrases as like as not (*or* like as not)
near antonyms implausibly, inconceivably, incredibly, unbelievably, unthinkably
antonyms improbably

probation *n* a systematic search for the truth or facts about something ⟨a candidate for the priesthood must be able to withstand an intense *probation* of his personal character⟩ — see INQUIRY 1

probative *adj* serving to give support to the truth or factualness of something ⟨no dearth of *probative* evidence for the theory of evolution⟩ — see CORROBORATIVE

probatory *adj* serving to give support to the truth or factualness of something ⟨an abundance of *probatory* data linking smoking to cancer⟩ — see CORROBORATIVE

probe *n* a systematic search for the truth or facts about something ⟨a congressional *probe* into the accusations⟩ — see INQUIRY 1

probe *vb* **1** to search through or into ⟨tabloid reporters who seem determined to *probe* every detail of the singer's private life⟩ — see EXPLORE 1
2 to go into or range over for purposes of discovery ⟨*probing* the depths of the undersea trench⟩ — see EXPLORE 2

probing *n* a systematic search for the truth or facts about something ⟨questionings and *probings* by several committees into the affair⟩ — see INQUIRY 1

probity *n* **1** conduct that conforms to an accepted standard of right and wrong ⟨a person of indisputable *probity* must head the disciplinary panel⟩ — see MORALITY 1
2 devotion to telling the truth ⟨the defense attorney questioned the *probity* of the witness⟩ — see HONESTY 1
3 faithfulness to high moral standards ⟨ideals of fairness and *probity* in journalism⟩ — see HONOR 1

problem *n* **1** something that requires thought and skill for resolution ⟨the *problem* of world hunger⟩
synonyms case, challenge, knot, matter, nut, trouble
related words issue, question; corner, fix, hole, hot water, jam, mire, pickle, predicament, quagmire, spot; crux, Gordian knot, sticky wicket, toughie (*also* toughy); catch-22, dilemma, quandary; catch, glitch, hitch, pitfall, snag; conundrum, enigma, mystery, puzzle, puzzlement, riddle; brainteaser, perplexer, poser, stumper
near antonyms magic bullet, silver bullet; cure-all, panacea
antonyms answer, solution
2 an interrogative expression often used to test knowledge ⟨there were only 10 *problems* on the exam, but they were all challenging⟩ — see QUESTION 1

problematic *also* **problematical** *adj* **1** requiring exceptional skill or caution in performance or handling ⟨the *problematic* situation of somehow having two dates for the same party⟩ — see TRICKY 1
2 giving good reason for being doubted, questioned, or challenged ⟨whether we should even bother finishing the project at this point is *problematic*⟩ — see DOUBTFUL 2

proboscis *n* the part of the face bearing the nostrils and nasal cavity ⟨if there were a direct relation between mendacity and the length of one's *proboscis*, hers would be a mile long⟩ — see NOSE 1

procedure *n* **1** a usually fixed or ordered series of actions or events leading to a result ⟨followed the *procedure* for replacing the broken part exactly as the owner's manual instructed⟩ — see PROCESS 1
2 a way of acting or proceeding ⟨followed standard *procedure* for dealing with a consumer complaint⟩ — see COURSE 1

proceed *vb* to move forward along a course ⟨you may *proceed* with your plan⟩ — see GO 1

proceed (along) *vb* to make one's way through, across, or over ⟨the hikers *proceeded along* the ridge for several hundred feet⟩ — see TRAVERSE

proceed (with) *vb* to begin again or return to after an interruption ⟨we can *proceed with* the meeting as soon as everyone has returned from lunch⟩ — see RESUME

proceeding *adj* being in progress or development ⟨currently *proceeding* projects include construction of a new school gym⟩ — see ONGOING 1

proceeding *n* **1** a court case for enforcing a right or claim ⟨a divorce *proceeding*⟩ — see LAWSUIT
2 a usually fixed or ordered series of actions or events leading to a result ⟨this is not the haphazard *proceeding* that it may seem to the casual observer⟩ — see PROCESS 1

proceeds *n pl* **1** an increase usually measured in money that comes from labor, business, or property ⟨estimated that the annual *proceeds* from an increase in the state sales tax would be enormous⟩ — see INCOME 1
2 the amount of money left when expenses are subtracted from the total amount received ⟨all *proceeds* from the special promotion will go to charity⟩ — see PROFIT 1

process *n* **1** a usually fixed or ordered series of actions or events leading to a result ⟨the *process* by which the elastic fibers spun by silkworms is turned into soft, lustrous cloth⟩
synonyms course, operation, procedure, proceeding
related words drill, routine; fashion, form, manner, method, mode, style, system, technique, way; approach, arrangement, blueprint, design, formula, game plan, ground plan, layout, plan, plot, program, project, recipe, scheme, strategy; accomplishment, achievement, attainment, enterprise, performance, undertaking, work; activity, functioning, movement
2 forward movement in time or place ⟨in the *process* of

doing this project we all learned a lot⟩ — see ADVANCE 1

3 a written notice ordering a person to appear in court ⟨the prosecutor arranged for a *process* for her appearance to be issued⟩ — see SUMMONS

procession *n* **1** a body of individuals moving along in an orderly and often ceremonial way ⟨a *procession* of mourners leaving the cemetery⟩ — see CORTEGE 2

2 forward movement in time or place ⟨watched the constant *procession* of cars headed out of the city at the start of the weekend⟩ — see ADVANCE 1

proclaim *vb* to make known openly or publicly ⟨loudly *proclaimed* her innocence, to widespread disbelief⟩ — see ANNOUNCE

proclivity *n* a habitual attraction to some activity or thing ⟨showed artistic *proclivities* at an early age⟩ — see INCLINATION 1

procreate *vb* to bring forth offspring ⟨the common perception that our Puritan forebears *procreated* more out of a sense of duty than from desire⟩

synonyms breed, multiply, propagate, reproduce

related words bear, beget, engender, gender, generate, get, have, mother, parent, produce, sire; hatch, spawn

procurable *adj* possible to get ⟨the necessary ingredients should be *procurable* at almost any grocery store⟩ — see AVAILABLE 1

procurator *n* a person who acts or does business for another ⟨he was appointed *procurator* of the church and was responsible for all of the financial arrangements⟩ — see AGENT 2

procure *vb* to receive as return for effort ⟨a reputation for integrity and incorruptibility that has *procured* for him the universal respect and admiration of his colleagues⟩ — see EARN 1

procurer *n* a man who solicits clients for a woman who is willing to engage in sexual activities for money ⟨had carved out a career as a *procurer* of high-priced call girls for wealthy, powerful men⟩ — see PIMP

prod *vb* **1** to urge or push forward with or as if with a pointed object ⟨kept *prodding* the sheep with a staff to move along faster⟩

synonyms dig, goad, spur

related words chuck, jab, jog, knock, nudge, poke; bore, drill, perforate, pierce, prick, punch, puncture, stab, stick; drive, hale, propel

2 to try to persuade (someone) through earnest appeals to follow a course of action ⟨a public outcry eventually *prodded* the politicians into action⟩ — see URGE

prodigal *adj* given to spending money freely or foolishly ⟨the *prodigal* child always spent her allowance the minute she got it⟩

synonyms extravagant, high-rolling, profligate, spendthrift, squandering, thriftless, unthrifty, wasteful

related words improvident, myopic, shortsighted; bighearted, bountiful, charitable, freehanded, freehearted, generous, lavish, liberal, munificent, openhanded, openhearted, philanthropic (*also* philanthropical), unselfish, unsparing, unstinting; careless, heedless, imprudent, incautious, injudicious, unwise; indulgent, reckless, self-indulgent, splurging, wanton

near antonyms cheap, close, closefisted, mean, miserly, niggardly, parsimonious, penurious, pinching, spare, sparing, stingy, stinting, tight, tightfisted; careful, judicious, prudent, sensible, wise; farsighted, forehanded, foreseeing, foresighted, forethoughtful, provident

antonyms conserving, economical, economizing, frugal, penny-pinching, scrimping, skimping, thrifty

prodigal *n* someone who spends money freely or foolishly ⟨the million-dollar lottery winner was such a *prodigal* that his windfall was exhausted after only a few years⟩

synonyms fritterer, high roller, profligate, spender, spendthrift, squanderer, waster, wastrel

related words dissipate

near antonyms cheapskate, miser, niggard, piker, scrooge, skinflint, tightwad; conserver, saver

antonyms economizer, penny-pincher

prodigality *n* **1** an instance of spending money or resources without care or restraint ⟨his purchase of a new yacht was only one of a series of reckless *prodigalities*⟩ — see WASTE 1

2 the quality or fact of being free or wasteful in the expenditure of money ⟨his *prodigality* eventually turned him into a pauper⟩ — see EXTRAVAGANCE 1

prodigious *adj* **1** causing wonder or astonishment ⟨stage magicians performing *prodigious* feats for rapt audiences⟩ — see MARVELOUS 1

2 unusually large ⟨a *prodigious* supply of canned food kept in the basement for emergencies⟩ — see HUGE

prodigiousness *n* the quality or state of being very large ⟨the proverbial *prodigiousness* of everything within the state of Texas⟩ — see IMMENSITY

prodigy *n* something extraordinary or surprising ⟨a new drug that is being hailed as the latest *prodigy* of the medical world⟩ — see WONDER 1

produce *n* something produced by physical or intellectual effort ⟨a book that was the *produce* of a lifetime of study on the subject⟩ — see PRODUCT 1

produce *vb* **1** to be the cause of (a situation, action, or state of mind) ⟨hopefully, the new approach to fighting substance abuse will *produce* better results⟩ — see EFFECT

2 to bring forth from the womb ⟨rabbits can potentially *produce* many offspring at once⟩ — see BEAR 1

3 to bring into being by combining, shaping, or transforming materials ⟨a factory *producing* steel⟩ — see MAKE 1

4 to present so as to invite notice or attention ⟨he *produced* his brand-new driver's license at every possible opportunity⟩ — see SHOW 1

product *n* **1** something produced by physical or intellectual effort ⟨that biography is the *product* of years of work⟩ ⟨a rebuilt car which is the *product* of several people's labor⟩

synonyms affair, fruit, handiwork, labor, output, produce, production, thing, work, yield

related words article, commodity, entry, object; goods, line, merchandise, wares; handcraft, handicraft; aftereffect, aftermath, conclusion, consequence, corollary, development, effect, issue, outcome, result, resultant, sequel, sequence, upshot; by-product, derivative, offshoot, offspring, outgrowth, residual, side effect (*also* side reaction), spin-off

2 a condition or occurrence traceable to a cause ⟨her relentless ambition is a *product* of her home environment⟩ — see EFFECT 1

production *n* something produced by physical or intellectual effort ⟨the total *production* of one week's intensive labor⟩ — see PRODUCT 1

productive *adj* **1** having a role in deciding something's final form ⟨contributed several *productive* ideas to the project⟩ — see FORMATIVE

2 producing abundantly ⟨overfishing has depleted the stock of fish in these waters, which were once so *productive*⟩ — see FERTILE

3 producing or capable of producing a desired result ⟨panicking during a crisis is not *productive* behavior⟩ — see EFFECTIVE 1

productiveness *n* the power to produce a desired result ⟨the prodigious *productiveness* of the nation's shipyards during World War II⟩ — see EFFICACY

proem *n* a short section (as of a book) that leads to or explains the main part ⟨the *proem* promises what the book does not deliver: a totally new interpretation of the French Revolution⟩ — see INTRODUCTION

profanation *n* an act of great disrespect shown to God or to sacred ideas, people, or things ⟨the First Book of the Maccabees tells of the *profanation* of the temple of Jerusalem by Antiochus IV Epiphanes in 167 B.C.⟩ — see BLASPHEMY

profane *adj* **1** not involving religion or religious matters ⟨it was hard to juggle the requirements of church and our more *profane* duties⟩
synonyms nonreligious, secular, temporal
related words atheistic, godless, irreligious, pagan, paganish, religionless; laical (*or* laic), lay, nonclerical; nondenominational, nonsectarian; earthly, mundane, terrene, terrestrial, worldly; material, physical, substantial; bodily, carnal, corporal, fleshly; blasphemous, impious, irreverent, sacrilegious; unconsecrated, unhallowed
near antonyms divine, spiritual; consecrated, hallowed, holy, sacrosanct, sanctified; churchly, devout, godly, pious, prayerful, reverent, worshipful; ethereal, insubstantial, metaphysical, unsubstantial; bodiless, immaterial, incorporeal, nonphysical
antonyms religious, sacred
2 not showing proper reverence for the holy or sacred ⟨offended by the *profane* language that her coworkers used so casually⟩ — see IRREVERENT
3 depicting or referring to sexual matters in a way that is unacceptable in polite society ⟨his idea of dinner table conversation is the telling of *profane* stories about his alleged sexual exploits⟩ — see OBSCENE 1

profane *vb* **1** to lower in character, dignity, or quality ⟨the once-lovely landscape had been *profaned* by ugly factories⟩ — see DEBASE 1
2 to put to a bad or improper use ⟨*profaned* his considerable acting talents by appearing in some wretched movies⟩ — see MISAPPLY
3 to treat (a sacred place or object) shamefully or with great disrespect ⟨invading troops *profaned* the altar by playing poker on it⟩ — see DESECRATE

profanity *n* **1** a disrespectful or indecent word or expression ⟨a rap song that is filled with *profanities*⟩ — see SWEARWORD
2 the quality or state of being obscene ⟨once notorious for its *profanity*, that 1950s best seller will strike today's readers as lamentably tame⟩ — see OBSCENITY 1

profess *vb* **1** to present a false appearance of ⟨*professed* friendship while secretly plotting revenge⟩ — see FEIGN
2 to state clearly and strongly ⟨the lonely woman *professed* her love in a series of letters to the soldier⟩ — see ASSERT 1
3 to state as a fact usually forcefully ⟨he *professed* his innocence to anyone who would listen⟩ — see CLAIM 1

professed *adj* having or showing exceptional knowledge, experience, or skill in a field of endeavor ⟨a *professed* analyst of American presidential politics⟩ — see PROFICIENT

profession *n* **1** a solemn and often public declaration of the truth or existence of something ⟨the weekly *profession* of faith by the members of the congregation⟩ — see PROTESTATION
2 the activity by which one regularly makes a living ⟨a gifted communicator, he was very good at his chosen *profession*: teaching⟩ — see OCCUPATION 1

proffer *n* something which is presented for consideration ⟨a generous *proffer* of his baronial estate for the charity gala⟩ — see PROPOSAL

proffer *vb* **1** to put before another for acceptance or consideration ⟨*proffered* his assistance in helping the two sides reach a compromise⟩ — see OFFER 1
2 to set before the mind for consideration ⟨*proffered* a novel solution for getting themselves out of debt⟩ — see PROPOSE 1

proficiency *n* **1** a highly developed skill in or knowledge of something ⟨surprised by his *proficiency* at the game after only the briefest explanation of the rules⟩ — see COMMAND 2
2 knowledge gained by actually doing or living through something ⟨acquired *proficiency* at golf through long hours of practice⟩ — see EXPERIENCE 1

proficient *adj* having or showing exceptional knowledge, experience, or skill in a field of endeavor ⟨she is quite *proficient* at computer repair⟩ ⟨a *proficient* rendition of a difficult piano piece⟩
synonyms accomplished, ace, adept, compleat, complete, consummate, crack, crackerjack, educated, experienced, expert, good, great, master, masterful, masterly, practiced (*also* practised), professed, skilled, skillful, versed, veteran, virtuoso
related words adroit, clever, deft, dexterous (*also* dextrous), handy, slick, sure-handed; gifted, talented; polished, refined; effective, effectual, efficient, workmanlike; able, capable, competent, employable, fit, fitted, habile, qualified; educated, knowledgeable, schooled, taught, trained, tutored; all-around (*also* all-round), well-rounded; long-term, old; multiskilled, multitalented
near antonyms incapable, incompetent, inept, unable, unfit, unfitted, unqualified, weak; artless, crude, rude; ineffective, ineffectual, inefficient; talentless, ungifted, untalented; ignorant, unschooled, untaught, untrained, untutored; beginning, green, inexperienced, new, raw, unseasoned, untested, untried, would-be; primitive, rough, unpolished; awkward, clumsy, ham-fisted, ham-handed, heavy-handed
antonyms amateur, amateurish, inexperienced, inexpert, jackleg, unprofessional, unseasoned, unskilled, unskillful

proficient *n* a person with a high level of knowledge or skill in a field ⟨an urgent call by the state department for *proficients* in Arabic⟩ — see EXPERT

proficiently *adv* in a skillful or expert manner ⟨an administrator who can deal with the problems quickly and *proficiently*⟩ — see WELL 3

profit *n* **1** the amount of money left when expenses are subtracted from the total amount received ⟨after we deducted the cost of sugar, lemons, and paper cups, the *profit* from a day of lemonade sales was about $20⟩
synonyms earnings, gain, lucre, net, payoff, proceeds, return
related words cleanup, killing, windfall; bottom line; gross, sales; compensation, emolument, income, pay, payment, remittal, requital, salary, wages; interest, return, revenue, yield
near antonyms charge, cost, disbursement, expenditure, expense, loss, outgo, outlay
2 an increase usually measured in money that comes from labor, business, or property ⟨found that there was a *profit* in training dogs for rich people⟩ — see INCOME 1

profit *vb* to provide with something useful or desirable ⟨an agreement that *profited* us all⟩ — see BENEFIT

profitable *adj* **1** yielding a profit ⟨selling real estate on the side turned out to be a *profitable* venture for the stay-at-home mom⟩
synonyms economic, fat, gainful, juicy, lucrative, moneymaking, money-spinning [*chiefly British*], paying, remunerative
related words advantageous, beneficial, favorable, rewarding, useful, worthwhile; bankable
near antonyms disadvantageous, unfavorable
antonyms unprofitable
2 promoting or contributing to personal or social well-

being ⟨I have always found honesty to be a *profitable* course of action⟩ — see BENEFICIAL

profitless *adj* producing no results ⟨trying to reason with her is always a *profitless* enterprise⟩ — see FUTILE 1

profligacy *n* immoral conduct or practices harmful or offensive to society ⟨a religious leader who railed against the *profligacy* of the nation's decadent aristocrats⟩ — see VICE 1

profligate *adj* given to spending money freely or foolishly ⟨*profligate* movie producers hoping to create the next blockbuster⟩ — see PRODIGAL

profligate *n* **1** someone who spends money freely or foolishly ⟨a *profligate* who could not really afford the grand style he maintained at Monticello, Jefferson died deeply in debt⟩ — see PRODIGAL

2 a person who has sunk below the normal moral standard ⟨a drunken *profligate*, he was given to wretched excess in every aspect of his life⟩ — see DEGENERATE

profound *adj* **1** difficult for one of ordinary knowledge or intelligence to understand ⟨a *profound* observation about good and evil that few listeners fully grasped⟩

synonyms abstruse, arcane, deep, esoteric, hermetic (*also* hermetical), recondite

related words erudite, learned, scholarly; academic (*also* academical), pedantic; complex, complicated, hard; darkling, enigmatic (*also* enigmatical), inscrutable, mysterious, mystic, mystical, orphic, uncanny; impenetrable, incomprehensible, unfathomable, unintelligible; ambiguous, cryptic; unanswerable, unknowable; baffling, bewildering, confounding, confusing, disorienting, mystifying, perplexing, puzzling

near antonyms easy, facile, simple, straightforward; comprehensible, fathomable, intelligible, understandable; apparent, clear, clear-cut, distinct, evident, lucid, manifest, obvious, perspicuous, plain, transparent

antonyms shallow, superficial

2 extreme in degree, power, or effect ⟨a *profound* silence fell over the audience after the last note had sounded⟩ — see INTENSE 1

3 having no exceptions or restrictions ⟨a *profound* dislike of frauds and phonies⟩ — see ABSOLUTE 2

4 extending far downward ⟨with eyes wide with disbelief, the explorers made their way through a canyon more *profound* than any they had ever imagined⟩ — see DEEP 1

profoundness *n* the quality of being great in extent (as of insight) ⟨we were struck by the *profoundness* of his observations on the ultimate meaning of life⟩ — see DEPTH 2

profundity *n* the quality of being great in extent (as of insight) ⟨a philosopher who is widely respected for the *profundity* of her thinking⟩ — see DEPTH 2

profuse *adj* pouring forth in great amounts ⟨we received *profuse* thanks for our efforts⟩ ⟨a *profuse* rush of water from the collapsing dike⟩

synonyms copious, galore, gushing, lavish, riotous

related words abounding, abundant, ample, bounteous, bountiful, liberal, plenteous, plentiful; extravagant, luxuriant; fat, fecund, fertile; free, munificent, openhanded, unsparing, unstinting; excessive, immoderate, redundant; adequate, complete, enough, sufficient

near antonyms meager (*or* meagre), niggardly, poor, scant, scanty, spare, sparse, stingy; deficient, inadequate, incomplete, insufficient, lacking, scarce, unsatisfactory, wanting; bare, mere, minimal

antonyms dribbling, trickling

profusion *n* **1** a considerable amount ⟨apples grow in *profusion* in this valley⟩ — see LOT 2

2 the quality or fact of being free or wasteful in the expenditure of money ⟨in giving gifts to his girlfriend, he was generous to the point of *profusion*⟩ — see EXTRAVAGANCE 1

progenitor *n* a person who is several generations earlier in an individual's line of descent ⟨the *progenitors* of today's Maya once ruled a mighty empire that stretched across much of Central America⟩ — see ANCESTOR 1

progeny *n* the descendants of a person, animal, or plant ⟨the rancher carefully examined the *progeny* of the new breed of cattle⟩ — see OFFSPRING

prognosis *n* a declaration that something will happen in the future ⟨the securities analyst's *prognosis* for the stock market in the new year⟩ — see PREDICTION

prognostic *n* a declaration that something will happen in the future ⟨a *prognostic* of a global pandemic that turned out to be distressingly accurate⟩ — see PREDICTION

prognosticate *vb* to tell of or describe beforehand ⟨using current trends to *prognosticate* what the workplace of the future will be like⟩ — see FORETELL

prognosticating *n* a declaration that something will happen in the future ⟨because there are always unforeseen breakthroughs in every field, in the past most *prognosticatings* have fallen short⟩ — see PREDICTION

prognostication *n* **1** a declaration that something will happen in the future ⟨the complete fulfillment of his *prognostication* surprised even him⟩ — see PREDICTION

2 a feeling that something bad will happen ⟨at the sight of the brooding mansion, her *prognostications* of ill fortune grew stronger⟩ — see PREMONITION

prognosticator *n* one who predicts future events or developments ⟨one of the best *prognosticators* in the weather business⟩ — see PROPHET 1

program *n* **1** a listing of things to be presented or considered (as at a concert or play) ⟨the *program* will tell us the scheduled order of musical numbers⟩

synonyms agenda, calendar, docket, schedule, timetable

related words card, dance card, exercises, plate; arrangement, order, ordering, organization, sequence, setup

phrases bill of fare

2 a method worked out in advance for achieving some objective ⟨we need to come up with a *program* to deal with kids skipping school⟩ — see PLAN 1

3 a way of acting or proceeding ⟨recommends a *program* of regular dental checkups⟩ — see COURSE 1

progress *n* **1** forward movement in time or place ⟨we're making slow *progress* against this stiff headwind⟩ — see ADVANCE 1

2 the act or process of going from the simple or basic to the complex or advanced ⟨the rapid *progress* of medical science in the last century⟩ — see DEVELOPMENT 1

progress *vb* **1** to become mature ⟨generally a species *progresses* from simple forms to more specialized forms⟩ — see MATURE

2 to move forward along a course ⟨our wedding plans are *progressing* nicely⟩ — see GO 1

progression *n* **1** a series of things linked together ⟨a *progression* of events that ended in utter disaster for the arctic explorers⟩ — see CHAIN 1

2 forward movement in time or place ⟨our *progression* was slow but steady⟩ — see ADVANCE 1

3 the act or process of going from the simple or basic to the complex or advanced ⟨that civilization's gradual *progression* from simple bartering to a complex economy and monetary system⟩ — see DEVELOPMENT 1

progressive *adj* **1** being far along in development ⟨*progressive* forms of animal life⟩ — see ADVANCED 1

2 not bound by traditional ways or beliefs ⟨a socially *progressive* community, it was the first to provide for the public education of girls⟩ — see LIBERAL 1

3 being or employing the latest concepts, styles, or techniques ⟨one of the founders of *progressive* dance, Isadora Duncan became an inspiration to an array of free-spirited artists⟩ — see AVANT

prohibit *vb* to order not to do or use or to be done or used ⟨the city *prohibits* swimming in the lake after dark⟩ — see FORBID

prohibited *adj* that may not be permitted ⟨there will be no toleration for smoking and other *prohibited* activities⟩ — see IMPERMISSIBLE

prohibiting *n* the act of ordering that something not be done or used ⟨not surprisingly, the *prohibiting* of the use of cell phones proved to be unpopular with patients visiting the doctor⟩ — see PROHIBITION 1

prohibition *n* **1** the act of ordering that something not be done or used ⟨the principal's *prohibition* against the use of cell phones in the school building met with unanimous approval by the teachers⟩
synonyms banning, barring, enjoining, forbidding, interdicting, interdiction, outlawing, prohibiting, proscribing, proscription
related words bidding, charging, decreeing, dictation, direction, instruction; deterrence, discouragement, dissuading; repression, suppression; coercion, compulsion, constraint, force
near antonyms allowance, permission, sufferance, toleration; approval, endorsement (*also* indorsement); authorization, clearance, license (*or* licence), sanction; encouragement, promotion, support; compliance, obedience, submission
2 an order that something not be done or used ⟨the school issued a *prohibition* against wearing clothing with obscene and provocative slogans⟩
synonyms ban, embargo, interdict, interdiction, proscription, veto
related words no-no, taboo (*also* tabu); constraint, inhibition, limitation, restraint, restriction; deterrent, discouragement; repression, suppression; prevention; denial, disallowance, negation, refusal, rejection; objection, protest; caveat, warning; no-no; commandment, decree, dictate, edict, injunction, mandate
near antonyms sufferance, tolerance, toleration; allowance, allowing, authorization, clearance, consent, granting, leave, letting, license (*or* licence), licensing (*also* licencing), permission, permitting, sanction, sanctioning; approbation, approval, blessing, endorsement (*also* indorsement), imprimatur, OK (*or* okay); enabling, encouragement, facilitation, promotion, support; compliance, obedience, submission; accession, acquiescence, agreement, assent
antonyms prescription

project *n* a method worked out in advance for achieving some objective ⟨an ambitious *project* to develop the city's waterfront⟩ — see PLAN 1

project *vb* **1** to extend outward beyond a usual point ⟨some boulders *projected* dangerously out above the trail⟩ — see BULGE 1
2 to work out the details of (something) in advance ⟨we must *project* next year's budget now⟩ — see PLAN 1

projection *n* a part that sticks out from the general mass of something ⟨filed down all the *projections* until the surface was smooth⟩ — see BULGE 1

prole *adj* belonging to the class of people of low social or economic rank ⟨the writer's *prole* origins are evident in his gritty novels about life in the inner city⟩ — see IGNOBLE 1

proletarian *adj* belonging to the class of people of low social or economic rank ⟨a self-made Internet magnate who is not at all ashamed of his *proletarian* background⟩ — see IGNOBLE 1

proletariat *n* people looked down upon as ignorant and of the lowest class ⟨the Bolsheviks believed that Russia's discontented *proletariat* made that nation ripe for revolution⟩ — see RABBLE

proliferate *vb* to become greater in extent, volume, amount, or number ⟨rumors about the incident *proliferated* on the Internet⟩ — see INCREASE 2

proliferation *n* **1** something added (as by growth) ⟨a large *proliferation* in the number of electrical appliances was placing enormous demands upon the region's power supply⟩ — see INCREASE 1
2 the act or process of becoming greater in number ⟨the *proliferation* of mistakes as both actors and crew became more and more tired⟩ — see MULTIPLICATION

prolific *adj* producing abundantly ⟨a famously *prolific* author who could produce several works of fiction and nonfiction a year⟩ — see FERTILE

prolix *adj* using or containing more words than necessary to express an idea ⟨a person known for habitually transforming brief anecdotes into *prolix* sagas that exhaust their listeners⟩ — see WORDY 1

prolixity *n* the use of too many words to express an idea ⟨*prolixity* is one of the worst offenses that a writer of any age can commit⟩ — see VERBIAGE 1

prolocutor *n* a person in charge of a meeting ⟨was chosen as *prolocutor* of the international colloquium⟩ — see CHAIR 1

prologue *also* **prolog** *n* **1** a performance, activity, or event that precedes and sets the stage for the main event ⟨unfortunately, the burglary, which he committed while still a teen, was but a *prologue* to a wasted life of crime⟩ — see PRELUDE 1
2 a short section (as of a book) that leads to or explains the main part ⟨a brief *prologue* sets the scene for the story that follows⟩ — see INTRODUCTION

prolong *vb* to make longer ⟨would like to *prolong* our vacation by any means possible⟩ — see EXTEND 1

prolongation *n* the act of making longer ⟨the indefinite *prolongation* of the cease-fire⟩ — see EXTENSION 1

prolonging *n* the act of making longer ⟨his habitual *prolonging* of any task so that it fills up an entire afternoon⟩ — see EXTENSION 1

prolusion *n* a short section (as of a book) that leads to or explains the main part ⟨in her *prolusion* she sketches the religious, cultural and political milieu in which gnosticism developed⟩ — see INTRODUCTION

prom *n* a social gathering for dancing ⟨he resolved to ask her to the school *prom* at the first opportunity⟩ — see DANCE

promenade *n* a public place for strolling ⟨a beautifully landscaped park with a wide *promenade* along the riverside⟩
synonyms boardwalk, mall, walk
related words walkway; alameda, allée; arcade, colonnade, galleria, gallery; plaza

Promethean *adj* having the skill and imagination to create new things ⟨it is only through the efforts of a *Promethean* pioneer that an art form advances⟩ — see CREATIVE 1

prominence *n* an area of high ground ⟨a rocky *prominence* that commands a stunning view of the surrounding area⟩ — see HEIGHT 4

prominent *adj* **1** likely to attract attention ⟨an attorney who occupies a *prominent* position in the town's social hierarchy⟩ — see NOTICEABLE
2 widely known ⟨*prominent* figures in the history of sports⟩ — see FAMOUS 1

promiscuous *adj* consisting of many things of different sorts ⟨since I just collect stamps that I happen to like, my collection is pretty *promiscuous*⟩ — see MISCELLANEOUS

promise *n* a person's solemn declaration that he or she will do or not do something ⟨he made a *promise* to arrive on time, come hell or high water⟩

synonyms oath, pledge, troth, vow, word
related words appointment, arrangement, commitment, engagement, obligation; agreement, compact, contract, covenant; assurance, guarantee, guaranty, undertaking; bail, bond, deposit, gage, pawn, security, token, warranty

promise *vb* **1** to make a solemn declaration of intent ⟨they *promised* to keep in touch with us after they moved away⟩
synonyms covenant, pledge, swear, vow
related words affiance, betroth, plight, troth; accede, agree, assent, consent; contract, engage, ensure, guarantee, undertake; affirm, assert, aver, avouch, avow, declare, insist, warrant
phrases give one's word
2 to show signs of a favorable or successful outcome ⟨given the cast, the new sitcom *promises* to be an excellent show⟩ — see BODE

promised *adj, chiefly dialect* pledged in marriage ⟨I cannot entertain your marriage proposal, for I am already *promised* to another⟩ — see ENGAGED 1

promised land *n* an often imaginary place or state of utter perfection and happiness ⟨finally realized that the *promised land* doesn't exist⟩ — see PARADISE 1

promising *adj* **1** having qualities which inspire hope ⟨a *promising* writer who just may write the great American novel someday⟩ — see HOPEFUL 1
2 pointing toward a happy outcome ⟨all the signs for the new business are *promising*⟩ — see FAVORABLE 2

promontory *n* **1** an area of high ground jutting out into a body of water beyond the line of the coast ⟨stood on the windswept *promontory* overlooking the bay⟩ — see HEADLAND 1
2 an area of land that juts out into a body of water ⟨Cape May is Delaware Bay's largest *promontory*⟩ — see ²CAPE

promote *vb* **1** to move higher in rank or position ⟨the navy *promoted* her to captain for her record of outstanding performance⟩
synonyms advance, elevate, raise, upgrade
related words forward, further; aggrandize, boost, heighten, improve, lift, uplift; commission, ennoble, knight; acclaim, applaud, celebrate, cite, commend, compliment, congratulate, decorate; eulogize, exalt, extol (*also* extoll), glorify, hail, honor, laud, praise, salute
phrases kick upstairs
near antonyms depose, dethrone, dismiss, expel, impeach, oust, overthrow, remove, unmake, unseat; demean, disgrace, dishonor, humble, humiliate, mortify, shame, take down; censure, condemn, damn, denounce, reprobate
antonyms abase, degrade, demote, downgrade, lower, reduce
2 to help the growth or development of ⟨a campaign *promoting* good dental hygiene⟩ — see FOSTER 1
3 to look after or assist the growth of by labor and care ⟨spends all her time now *promoting* her new business⟩ — see GROW 1
4 to provide publicity for ⟨*promoting* a new line of toys based on the popular movie⟩ — see PUBLICIZE 1

promoter *n* a person who actively supports or favors a cause ⟨a *promoter* of greater understanding and cooperation among churches⟩ — see EXPONENT 1

promotion *n* a raising or a state of being raised to a higher rank or position ⟨after 10 years at the company he was rewarded with a *promotion* to vice president⟩ — see ADVANCEMENT 1

prompt *adj* **1** done, carried out, or given without delay ⟨*prompt* treatment of snakebites is always advisable⟩
synonyms immediate, punctual, speedy, timely
related words apt, quick, ready, swift, willing; opportune, seasonable; early
near antonyms delinquent, latish, overdue; behind, behindhand, delayed, detained; dilatory, laggard, slow
antonyms belated, late, tardy
2 having or showing the ability to respond without delay or hesitation ⟨our waiter was *prompt* and courteous despite the fact that the restaurant was understaffed⟩ — see QUICK 1

prompt *vb* **1** to be the cause of (a situation, action, or state of mind) ⟨a misguided pride *prompted* the family to refuse all offers of help⟩ — see EFFECT
2 to try to persuade (someone) through earnest appeals to follow a course of action ⟨*prompted* the reluctant performer onto the stage with loud cheers and whistles⟩ — see URGE

promptitude *n* the quality or habit of arriving or being ready on time ⟨his chronic tardiness has put him in poor standing with his boss, who values hustle and *promptitude*⟩
synonyms promptness, punctuality, timeliness
related words alacrity, aptness, quickness, readiness, willingness; earliness, prematurity
near antonyms belatedness, lateness; slowness
antonyms tardiness, unpunctuality

promptly *adv* without delay ⟨shipped the package *promptly* so that it would arrive on time⟩ — see IMMEDIATELY

promptness *n* the quality or habit of arriving or being ready on time ⟨the *promptness* of the local bus line has always been reassuring⟩ — see PROMPTITUDE

promulgate *vb* to make known openly or publicly ⟨the encyclical that *promulgated* the church's position on artificial birth control⟩ — see ANNOUNCE

prone *adj* **1** having a tendency to be or act in a certain way ⟨he was *prone* to emotional outbursts under stress⟩
synonyms apt, given, inclined, tending
related words choosing, preferring; disposed, liable, likely, minded, predisposed, willing
near antonyms averse, disinclined, indisposed, loath (*also* loth *or* loathe), unwilling
2 lying with the face downwards ⟨quickly subdue the suspect and get him into a *prone* position⟩
synonyms prostrate
related words flat, recumbent; reclining, reposing; horizontal
near antonyms erect, raised, standing, upright, upstanding, vertical
antonyms supine

proneness *n* an established pattern of behavior ⟨the quarterback's *proneness* to injury has prompted team owners to offer him less lucrative terms on his new contract⟩ — see TENDENCY 1

pronounced *adj* **1** likely to attract attention ⟨a *pronounced* tendency to slurp her soup⟩ — see NOTICEABLE
2 very noticeable especially for being incorrect or bad ⟨walking with a *pronounced* limp⟩ — see EGREGIOUS

pronto *adv* **1** with great speed ⟨if they don't arrive *pronto*, we'll have to go to the movie without them⟩ — see FAST 1
2 without delay ⟨the kind of boss who wants everything *pronto*⟩ — see IMMEDIATELY

proof *n* something presented in support of the truth or accuracy of a claim ⟨she presented *proof* that she had not cheated⟩
synonyms attestation, confirmation, corroboration, documentation, evidence, substantiation, testament, testimonial, testimony, validation, voucher, witness
related words (the) goods; certificate, document, exhibit; demonstration, illustration; authentication, identification, manifestation, verification
near antonyms rebuttal, refutation; accusation, allega-

tion, charge; assumption, conjecture, guess, presumption, surmise, suspicion
antonyms disproof

prop *n* a structure that holds up or serves as a foundation for something else ⟨a *prop* kept the porch of the dilapidated house from collapsing⟩ — see SUPPORT 1

prop (up) *vb* **1** to hold up or serve as a foundation for ⟨these beams are *propping up* the entire roof⟩ — see SUPPORT 3
2 to provide (someone) with what is useful or necessary to achieve an end ⟨invariably his strong religious faith *props* him *up* in times of crisis⟩ — see HELP 1

propagate *vb* **1** to bring forth offspring ⟨the dams along the river are interfering with the salmon's ability to *propagate*⟩ — see PROCREATE
2 to cause to be known over a considerable area or by many people ⟨the various ways in which churches can *propagate* the faith⟩ — see SPREAD 1

propel *vb* **1** to apply force to (someone or something) so that it moves in front of one ⟨playfully he *propelled* his rambunctious friend into the swimming pool to cool off⟩ — see PUSH 1
2 to set or keep in motion ⟨the aircraft is *propelled* by a pair of turboprop engines⟩ — see MOVE 2

propensity *n* **1** an established pattern of behavior ⟨the criminal *propensities* of the family extended over several generations⟩ — see TENDENCY 1
2 a habitual attraction to some activity or thing ⟨a neighbor who has an unfortunate *propensity* for snooping⟩ — see INCLINATION 1

proper *adj* **1** following the established traditions of refined society and good taste ⟨the formal ball called for *proper* attire—tuxedos and full-length gowns only⟩
synonyms befitting, correct, decent, decorous, de rigueur, genteel, nice, polite, respectable, seemly
related words acceptable, adequate, satisfactory, tolerable; dress, dressy, formal; dignified, elegant, gracious; priggish, prim, stiff, stuffy; apt, material, relevant; compatible, congenial, harmonious; allowed, authorized, kosher, permitted
near antonyms intolerable, unacceptable, unsatisfactory; casual, grungy, informal; seedy, shabby, tacky; banned, barred, disallowed; forbidden, interdicted, outlawed, prohibited, proscribed; awkward, gauche, ungraceful
antonyms improper, inappropriate, incorrect, indecent, indecorous, indelicate, unbecoming, ungenteel, unseemly
2 being in agreement with the truth or a fact or a standard ⟨there is really more than one *proper* way to pronounce that word in English⟩ — see CORRECT 1
3 marked by or showing careful attention to set forms and details ⟨we had nodded and said hello to one another but had never had a *proper* introduction⟩ — see CEREMONIOUS 1
4 meeting the requirements of a purpose or situation ⟨you'll need to have a *proper* diet if you want to lose weight⟩ — see FIT 1
5 serving to identify as belonging to an individual or group ⟨malaria and other diseases that are *proper* to the tropics⟩ — see CHARACTERISTIC 1

properly *adv* in a manner suitable for the occasion or purpose ⟨the scouts were *properly* dressed for a week of camping⟩
synonyms appositely, appropriately, congruously, correctly, duly, fittingly, happily, meetly, right, rightly, suitably
related words well; acceptably, adequately, passably, satisfactorily, tolerably; decently, decorously
near antonyms unacceptably, unsatisfactorily; inopportunely, unfortunately, unseasonably; inappositely, inaptly, irrelevantly; awkwardly, ungracefully
antonyms improperly, inappropriately, incongruously, incorrectly, unseemly, unsuitably, wrongly

properness *n* the quality or state of being especially suitable or fitting ⟨questioned the *properness* of having any curfew at all for people of college age⟩ — see APPROPRIATENESS

property *n* **1** a small piece of land that is developed or available for development ⟨bought a secluded *property* in the mountains⟩ — see LOT 1
2 something that sets apart an individual from others of the same kind ⟨the ability to be magnetized is a common *property* of metals⟩ — see CHARACTERISTIC

prophecy *also* **prophesy** *n* a declaration that something will happen in the future ⟨the report on climate change included alarming *prophecies* of rising sea levels and increased storm activity⟩ — see PREDICTION

prophesier *n* one who predicts future events or developments ⟨a *prophesier* of good things for the team in the coming season⟩ — see PROPHET 1

prophesy *vb* to tell of or describe beforehand ⟨holy men were *prophesying* the coming of a new messiah⟩ — see FORETELL

prophet *n* **1** one who predicts future events or developments ⟨an economist who is regarded by many as a reliable *prophet* of future developments in the global economy⟩
synonyms augur, diviner, forecaster, foreseer, foreteller, fortune-teller, futurist, prognosticator, prophesier, seer, soothsayer, visionary
related words prophetess, sibyl, wisewoman; mystic, oracle; astrologer, crystal gazer, palmist, rhabdomancer; Cassandra, doomsayer, doomsdayer, Jeremiah
2 a person who speaks for another or for a group ⟨in the 1960s Timothy Leary gained fame as the gonzo *prophet* of the psychedelic movement⟩ — see SPOKESPERSON

prophetic *also* **prophetical** *adj* being a sign of a later course of events ⟨in retrospect, those lower-than-expected sales numbers were a *prophetic* indicator of the financial trouble the company would soon be in⟩
synonyms predictive
related words apocalyptic (*also* apocalyptical), millenarian; baleful, dire, foreboding, menacing, portentous, sinister, threatening; inauspicious, unpromising; oracular; revelatory, telling
near antonyms auspicious, promising, propitious, rosy

prophylactic *adj* concerned with or serving to keep something from happening ⟨the many *prophylactic* measures that city officials could have taken to reduce the scope of the disaster⟩ — see PREVENTIVE

propinquity *n* the state or condition of being near ⟨local housing prices, thanks to the *propinquity* of an especially picturesque beach, are out of the reach of many would-be buyers⟩ — see PROXIMITY

propitiate *vb* to lessen the anger or agitation of ⟨the temple was once the site of sacrifices—both to honor the gods in times of plenty and to *propitiate* them in times of trouble⟩ — see PACIFY 1

propitiatory *adj* tending to lessen or avoid conflict or hostility ⟨sent his girlfriend flowers as a *propitiatory* gesture for a date gone sour⟩ — see PACIFIC 1

propitious *adj* **1** having qualities which inspire hope ⟨the success of the first big movie in May was a *propitious* start for the summer season of blockbusters⟩ — see HOPEFUL 1
2 pointing toward a happy outcome ⟨a *propitious* time for starting a business⟩ — see FAVORABLE 2

proponent *n* a person who actively supports or favors a cause ⟨a vocal *proponent* of the use of electric-powered cars⟩ — see EXPONENT 1

proportion *n* **1** a balanced, pleasing, or suitable arrangement of parts ⟨the head was drawn too large, being way out of *proportion* with the body⟩ — see HARMONY 1

2 something belonging to, due to, or contributed by an individual member of a group ⟨the players argue that they aren't getting the *proportion* of the league's profits that are due to them⟩ — see SHARE 1

3 the relationship in quantity, amount, or size between two or more things ⟨the *proportion* of length to width for those screens was usually three to two⟩ — see RATIO

4 the total amount of measurable space or surface occupied by something ⟨the exact *proportions* of the room were critical⟩ — see [1]SIZE

proportional *adj* corresponding in size, amount, extent, or degree ⟨the Web site's popularity increased exponentially, resulting in a *proportional* increase in advertising revenue⟩

synonyms commensurable, commensurate, proportionate

related words balanced, symmetrical (*or* symmetric); correlative, reciprocal; contingent, dependent, relative; akin, comparable, similar

phrases in proportion

near antonyms asymmetrical (*or* asymmetric), distorted, irregular, lopsided, nonsymmetrical, twisted, unsymmetrical; unbalanced

antonyms disproportionate

proportionate *adj* corresponding in size, amount, extent, or degree ⟨expect financial returns *proportionate* to your efforts⟩ — see PROPORTIONAL

proposal *n* something which is presented for consideration ⟨the city council is accepting *proposals* for ways to use that land⟩

synonyms offer, proffer, proposition, suggestion

related words counteroffer, counterproposal, countersuggestion; feeler, overture; motion; advancement, nomination, recommendation; bid, presentation, submission, submittal, tender; arrangement, game, ground plan, layout, line, plan, plot, project, strategy, system; conception, idea, notion, theory, thought

propose *vb* **1** to set before the mind for consideration ⟨he *proposed* that we go for a walk this afternoon⟩

synonyms advance, bounce, offer, pose, proffer, propound, suggest, vote

related words move; nominate, recommend; present, submit, tender, trot out; file, lay, lodge; arrange, calculate, chart, contrive, cover, frame, map, plan, plot, shape

phrases put forth, put forward

2 to have in mind as a purpose or goal ⟨we *propose* to buy a new house within the next year⟩ — see INTEND 1

proposition *n* **1** an idea that is the starting point for making a case or conducting an investigation ⟨started the discussion with the simple *proposition* that no one ever does anything out of pure altruism⟩ — see THEORY

2 something which is presented for consideration ⟨a neighbor with a business *proposition* to tell us about⟩ — see PROPOSAL

propound *vb* to set before the mind for consideration ⟨let us *propound* the question whether mercy killing should ever be an option⟩ — see PROPOSE 1

proprietor *n* one who has a legal or rightful claim to ownership ⟨the *proprietor* of a used-car dealership⟩

synonyms holder, owner, possessor

related words co-owner, coproprietor; landlord, landowner

near antonyms squatter; lessee, renter, tenant

propriety *n* **1** socially acceptable behavior ⟨some people miss the straitlaced *propriety* that was largely abandoned in the 1960s⟩ — see DECENCY 1

2 proprieties *pl* personal conduct or behavior as evaluated by an accepted standard of appropriateness for a social or professional setting ⟨an etiquette columnist who insists that traditional *proprieties* are necessary in order to maintain a civil society⟩ — see MANNER 1

3 the quality or state of being especially suitable or fitting ⟨I'm not sure about the *propriety* of serving champagne in these glasses⟩ — see APPROPRIATENESS

props *n pl, slang* public acknowledgment or admiration for an achievement ⟨never got the *props* he deserved for being one of the pioneers of rap⟩ — see GLORY 1

prorate *vb* to give out (something) to appropriate individuals ⟨shares in the company's profits were *prorated* according to the workers' length of service⟩ — see ADMINISTER 1

prorogate *vb* to bring to a formal close for a period of time ⟨the conference was *prorogated* until the following morning⟩ — see ADJOURN

prorogue *vb* to bring to a formal close for a period of time ⟨the legislative session was *prorogued* for the summer⟩ — see ADJOURN

prosaic *adj* **1** being of the type that is encountered in the normal course of events ⟨an author with a knack for finding something of interest in the most *prosaic* details of suburban life⟩ — see ORDINARY 1

2 having to do with the practical details of regular life ⟨my job at the TV station dealt with the much more *prosaic* business of cleaning the floors⟩ — see MUNDANE 1

proscribe *vb* to order not to do or use or to be done or used ⟨regulations *proscribe* the use of electronic devices on board a plane while it is landing⟩ — see FORBID

proscribed *adj* that may not be permitted ⟨the organization lost its nonprofit status after it was determined to have engaged in several *proscribed* fund-raising activities⟩ — see IMPERMISSIBLE

proscribing *n* the act of ordering that something not be done or used ⟨the *proscribing* of the use of alcohol was to be expected⟩ — see PROHIBITION 1

proscription *n* **1** the act of ordering that something not be done or used ⟨the *proscription* against bicycles and skateboards is intended to make the plaza a more pedestrian-friendly place⟩ — see PROHIBITION 1

2 an order that something not be done or used ⟨a strongly worded *proscription* against smoking indoors⟩ — see PROHIBITION 2

prosecute *vb* to carry through (as a process) to completion ⟨the neurologists plan to *prosecute* their research for as long as funding remains available⟩ — see PERFORM 1

prosecution *n* the doing of an action ⟨oversaw the *prosecution* of the president's foreign policy⟩ — see COMMISSION 2

proselyte *n* a person who has recently been persuaded to join a religious sect ⟨an adult *proselyte* who had only recently been baptized⟩ — see CONVERT 1

proselyte *vb* to persuade to change to one's religious faith ⟨she's been trying to *proselyte* everyone in the office ever since she joined that church⟩ — see CONVERT 1

proselytize *vb* to persuade to change to one's religious faith ⟨the efforts of early missionaries to *proselytize* the Native Americans of Minnesota were largely unproductive⟩ — see CONVERT 1

prospect *n* **1** all that can be seen from a certain point ⟨gazing at the wide *prospect* spread out before me⟩ — see VIEW 1

2 one who seeks an office, honor, position, or award ⟨a good *prospect* for the position of auditor⟩ — see CANDIDATE

3 something that can develop or become actual ⟨one highly desirable *prospect* for the city is a major-league franchise⟩ — see POTENTIAL

4 the act or state of looking forward to some occurrence ⟨the *prospect* of a quiet, restful Sunday ended when our basement flooded⟩ — see EXPECTATION

prospect *vb* to go into or range over for purposes of discovery ⟨soon all manner of people had arrived in the valley to *prospect* it for gold⟩ — see EXPLORE 2

prosper *vb* **1** to grow vigorously ⟨the plants seem to be *prospering* on the new fertilizers⟩ — see THRIVE 1
2 to reach a desired level of accomplishment ⟨began to *prosper* after years of crushing setbacks⟩ — see SUCCEED 2

prospering *adj* marked by vigorous growth and well-being especially economically ⟨selling a whole range of luxury products to the *prospering* middle class⟩ — see PROSPEROUS 1

prosperous *adj* **1** marked by vigorous growth and well-being especially economically ⟨a *prosperous* business that will soon be expanding⟩
synonyms booming, boomy, flourishing, golden, halcyon, healthy, lush, palmy, prospering, roaring, successful, thriving
related words affluent, moneyed (*also* monied), opulent, rich, substantial, wealthy, well-heeled, well-off, well-to-do; comfortable
near antonyms declining, dying, failing, floundering, languishing, struggling; bankrupt, bankrupted, insolvent
antonyms depressed, unprosperous, unsuccessful
2 having attained a desired end or state of good fortune ⟨one of the most *prosperous* families in the community⟩ — see SUCCESSFUL 1
3 growing thickly and vigorously ⟨our neighbor has a real green thumb and a yard full of healthy, *prosperous* plants⟩ — see RANK 1

prostitute *n* a woman who engages in sexual activities for money ⟨the town was horrified to discover that she had once been a *prostitute*⟩
synonyms bawd, call girl, cocotte, courtesan, drab, harlot, hooker, hustler, sex worker, streetwalker, strumpet, tart, whore
related words madam, madame; white slave; bimbo [*slang*], chippie (*also* chippy), doxy (*also* doxie), floozy (*or* floozie), tramp; bitch, hussy, jade, minx; coquette, flirt, libertine, siren, tempter, temptress, vamp, wench
phrases woman of the street

prostitute *vb* **1** to lower in character, dignity, or quality ⟨a serious writer *prostituting* himself by writing pulp novels for money⟩ — see DEBASE 1
2 to put to a bad or improper use ⟨urged not to *prostitute* her musical talents by writing jingles for TV commercials⟩ — see MISAPPLY

prostitution *n* the practice of engaging in sexual activities for money ⟨*prostitution* is illegal in most states⟩
synonyms harlotry, vice, whoredom
related words demimonde; white slavery

prostrate *adj* **1** depleted in strength, energy, or freshness ⟨*prostrate* marathoners typically spend the day after the race recovering⟩ — see WEARY 1
2 lacking bodily strength ⟨*prostrate* with fear as the bombs began dropping⟩ — see WEAK 1
3 lying with the face downwards ⟨the suspects lay *prostrate* on the floor while the police searched the room⟩ — see PRONE 2

prostrate *vb* **1** to diminish the physical strength of ⟨an athlete *prostrated* for weeks by a bout of pneumonia⟩ — see WEAKEN 1
2 to render powerless, ineffective, or unable to move ⟨the huge increase in gas prices really *prostrated* the nation's economic engine⟩ — see PARALYZE 1
3 to subject to incapacitating emotional or mental stress ⟨a widow *prostrated* by crushing grief⟩ — see OVERWHELM 1
4 to strike (someone) so forcefully as to cause a fall ⟨the boxer bragged that he could *prostrate* any opponenent with a single blow⟩ — see FELL 1

prostrated *adj* lacking bodily strength ⟨patients should expect to feel very *prostrated* after the surgery⟩ — see WEAK 1

prostration *n* a complete depletion of energy or strength ⟨an outpatient suffering from fever, *prostration*, and nausea⟩ — see FATIGUE 1

protagonist *n* a person who actively supports or favors a cause ⟨Milton Friedman is usually cited as the leading American *protagonist* of monetarism⟩ — see EXPONENT 1

protean *adj* able to do many different kinds of things ⟨a *protean* actor who is equally comfortable with light comedy and serious drama⟩ — see VERSATILE

protect *vb* to drive danger or attack away from ⟨the mother bear was just trying to *protect* her cubs⟩ — see DEFEND 1

protection *n* **1** means or method of defending ⟨this small umbrella is adequate *protection* in a sudden shower⟩ — see DEFENSE 1
2 someone that protects ⟨the bodyguard was her *protection* from overzealous fans⟩ — see PROTECTOR
3 the state of not being exposed to danger ⟨the open boat offered no *protection* from the weather⟩ — see SAFETY 1

protective *adj* intended to resist or prevent attack or aggression ⟨the cat drew back its ears and sank into a *protective* posture as the dog approached it⟩ — see DEFENSIVE

protector *n* someone that protects ⟨aid workers in the war zone found it necessary sometimes to hire local gunmen as *protectors* and guides⟩
synonyms custodian, defender, guard, guardian, guardian angel, protection
related words bodyguard, champion; lookout, sentinel, sentry, warden, warder, watch, watchdog, watchman; conserver, harborer, keeper, preserver, saver

protest *n* a feeling or declaration of disapproval or dissent ⟨submitted an official *protest* about her treatment⟩ — see OBJECTION

protest *vb* **1** to state as a fact usually forcefully ⟨he *protested* that he usually was very good at baseball, and all the strikeouts were just bad luck⟩ — see CLAIM 1
2 to present an opposing opinion or argument ⟨plans to *protest* against the judge's ruling regarding admissible evidence⟩ — see OBJECT

protestation *n* a solemn and often public declaration of the truth or existence of something ⟨the governor went on television to make a passionate *protestation* of his innocence in the bribery scandal⟩
synonyms affirmation, assertion, asseveration, avouchment, avowal, claim, declaration, insistence, profession
related words allegation; announcement, proclamation, pronouncement; argument, justification, rationalization, reason; confirmation, reaffirmation, reconfirmation, vindication
near antonyms disclaimer; challenge, dispute, question; confutation, disproof, rebuttal, refutation; contradiction, denial, negation
antonyms disavowal

prototype *n* **1** one of a group or collection that shows what the whole is like ⟨a literary character who is universally regarded as the ultimate *prototype* of the spoiled, willful Southern belle⟩ — see EXAMPLE
2 something belonging to an earlier time from which something else was later developed ⟨the Greek epic that is the *prototype* of the hero myth⟩ — see ANCESTOR 2
3 something from which copies are made ⟨the manufacturer exhaustively tested the *prototype* of the vehicle before approving production⟩ — see ORIGINAL 1

protract *vb* to make longer ⟨the highway project was *protracted* by years of litigation⟩ — see EXTEND 1

protrude *vb* to extend outward beyond a usual point ⟨we spotted the kitten's tail *protruding* from beneath the dresser⟩ — see BULGE 1

protrusion *n* a part that sticks out from the general mass of something ⟨the bizarrely shaped *protrusions* of a coral reef⟩ — see BULGE 1

protrusive *adj* thrusting oneself where one is not welcome or invited ⟨his *protrusive* way of helping his co-workers usually provokes resentment, not gratitude⟩ — see INTRUSIVE

protuberance *n* a part that sticks out from the general mass of something ⟨the tree trunk had several mossy *protuberances* where branches had once grown⟩ — see BULGE 1

proud *adj* **1** having or displaying feelings of scorn for what is regarded as beneath oneself ⟨the unemployed woman was too *proud* to take a job as a maid⟩

synonyms disdainful, haughty, highfalutin (*also* hifalutin), lofty, lordly, prideful, superior

related words complacent, conceited, egoistic, egotistic (*also* egotistical), important, self-assertive, self-conceited, self-contented, self-important, self-satisfied, smug, uppity, vain, vainglorious; arrogant, pretentious, sniffy, snobbish, stuck-up, supercilious; cavalier, overbearing, overweening, peremptory, swaggering; high-sounding, pompous; condescending, patronizing; cocky, overconfident, presuming, presumptuous; bloated, boastful, bombastic, self-glorifying; audacious, bold, brash, brassy, cheeky, cocksure, forward, impertinent, impudent, saucy; confident, presuming, self-assured, self-confident, sure; bossy, domineering, high-handed, imperious; egocentric, self-centered, selfish; dominating, magisterial, masterful

near antonyms demure, homely, meek, unassuming, unpretending, unpretentious; bashful, retiring, shy, timid; diffident, self-doubting; acquiescent, compliant, deferential, ingratiating, resigned, submissive, unassertive, yielding; apologetic, cowering, cringing, shrinking; passive, quiet, reserved, subdued, unobtrusive

antonyms humble, lowly, modest

2 having too high an opinion of oneself ⟨a *proud* cheerleader who thought she should be treated like royalty⟩ — see CONCEITED

3 large and impressive in size, grandeur, extent, or conception ⟨the old neighborhood was known for its stately trees and *proud* Victorian houses⟩ — see GRAND 1

4 having or expressing feelings of joy or triumph ⟨in his acceptance letter he assured his soon-to-be boss that he was *proud* to be joining such a fine company⟩ — see EXULTANT

provable *adj* capable of being proven as true or real ⟨the police have more than enough evidence to build a *provable* case against the accused⟩ — see VERIFIABLE

prove *vb* **1** to show the existence or truth of by evidence ⟨the prosecutor used DNA evidence to *prove* the defendant's guilt⟩

synonyms demonstrate, document, establish, substantiate, validate

related words back (up), buttress, circumstantiate, corroborate; evidence, evince, record, support, uphold, witness; adduce, attest, authenticate, certify, identify; confirm, sustain, verify, vouch; clinch, nail, settle; confess, depose, testify

near antonyms challenge, dispute, object; allege, assume, conjecture, guess, presume, surmise, suspect

antonyms disprove, rebut, refute

2 to come to be ⟨the new automobile engine design *proved* impractical⟩ — see COME OUT 1

3 to gain full recognition or acceptance of ⟨*proved* herself a great actress on the Broadway stage⟩ — see ESTABLISH 1

provender *n* substances intended to be eaten ⟨a chef who prides himself on creating all of his dishes from local *provender*⟩ — see FOOD 1

proverb *n* an often stated observation regarding something from common experience ⟨her grandfather has a *proverb* for every occasion⟩ — see SAYING

provide *vb* to put (something) into the possession of someone for use or consumption ⟨this luxury hotel *provides* all the comforts of home to well-heeled vacationers⟩ — see FURNISH 2

provide (for) *vb* **1** to give consideration to (as unexpected circumstances or contingencies) ⟨the rules *provide for* emergency situations, spelling out certain exceptions⟩ — see ALLOW (FOR)

2 to pay the living expenses of ⟨sufficient income to *provide for* his ever growing family⟩ — see SUPPORT 2

providence *n* **1** careful management of material resources ⟨practicing its customary *providence*, the snowbound family was able to make the meager stores last until help arrived⟩ — see ECONOMY

2 concern or preparation for the future ⟨had the *providence* to lay in supplies before the storm hit⟩ — see FORESIGHT 2

3 *cap* the being worshipped as the creator and ruler of the universe ⟨she trusted in *Providence* to see her through the crisis⟩ — see DEITY 2

provident *adj* **1** careful in the management of money or resources ⟨it is possible to be *provident* without being miserly⟩ — see FRUGAL

2 having or showing awareness of and preparation for the future ⟨her *provident* measures kept us safe while we waited out the hurricane⟩ — see FORESIGHTED

providential *adj* coming or happening by good luck especially unexpectedly ⟨winning the lottery could not have come at a more *providential* time for the recently laid-off worker⟩ — see FORTUNATE 1

province *n* a region of activity, knowledge, or influence ⟨a legal question outside the doctor's *province*⟩ — see FIELD 2

provincial *adj* not broad or open in views or opinions ⟨some people regard a fear of new things as an unmistakable sign of a *provincial* attitude⟩ — see NARROW 2

provincial *n* an awkward or simple person especially from a small town or the country ⟨the confidence man figured that fleecing these *provincials* would be easy⟩ — see HICK

provision *n* **1** something upon which the carrying out of an agreement or offer depends ⟨loaned them the car with the *provision* that they refill the gas tank before returning it⟩ — see CONDITION 2

2 provisions *pl* substances intended to be eaten ⟨gave them ample *provisions* so they would not get hungry on the trip⟩ — see FOOD 1

provision *vb* **1** to provide (someone) with what is needed for a task or activity ⟨the climbers were sufficiently *provisioned* to withstand just about any mountaineering emergency⟩ — see FURNISH 1

2 to provide food or meals for ⟨it was the quartermaster's job to properly equip and *provision* the troops⟩ — see FEED 1

provisional *adj* **1** intended to last, continue, or serve for a limited time ⟨will form a *provisional* government until a new leader can be elected⟩ — see TEMPORARY 1

2 serving in a position for the time being ⟨he was appointed *provisional* executor of the industrialist's vast estate⟩ — see ACTING

provisionary *adj* **1** intended to last, continue, or serve for a limited time ⟨*provisionary* decrees that were issued by the junta following the coup⟩ — see TEMPORARY 1

2 serving in a position for the time being ⟨the *provision-*

ary ambassador to the United Nations⟩ — see ACTING

proviso *n* something upon which the carrying out of an agreement or offer depends ⟨released the drunken revelers with the *proviso* that they behave for the remainder of the Mardi Gras⟩ — see CONDITION 2

provisory *adj* **1** intended to last, continue, or serve for a limited time ⟨a *provisory* permit to block off the street while movie scenes were being shot⟩ — see TEMPORARY 1
2 serving in a position for the time being ⟨a *provisory* legal adviser who will be replaced by a court-appointed public defender⟩ — see ACTING

provocateur *n* a person who stirs up public feelings especially of discontent ⟨a calculating, right-wing *provocateur*, she has made a career out of controversy for its own sake⟩ — see AGITATOR

provocation *n* **1** something that arouses a strong response from another ⟨a patient man who gets angry only from the greatest of *provocations*⟩
synonyms excitement, incitation, incitement, instigation
related words encouragement, galvanization, goad, incentive, inducement, jog, prod, spur, stimulant, stimulation, stimulus; enticement, lure; induction, inspiration, motivation; aggravation, annoyance, bother, exasperation, frustration, hassle, headache, irritant, nuisance, peeve, pest
near antonyms subduing
2 something that arouses action or activity ⟨ready to retaliate at the slightest *provocation*⟩ — see IMPULSE 1

provocative *adj* serving or likely to arouse a strong reaction ⟨a *provocative* editorial that sparked a heated discussion⟩
synonyms charged, edgy, exciting, inciting, instigating, instigative, piquing, provoking, stimulating
related words explosive, fiery, incendiary, inflammatory, triggering; inducing, inspirational, inspiring, motivating, motivational, motivative; jeering, taunting, teasing; activating, energizing, galvanizing, quickening, vitalizing; angering, enraging, maddening, upsetting; aggravating, annoying, bothersome, exasperating, galling, irksome, irritating, pesky, vexatious, vexing
near antonyms subduing
antonyms noninflammatory

provoke *vb* **1** to rouse to strong feeling or action ⟨his teasing finally *provoked* her to anger⟩ ⟨bees generally will not sting unless they are *provoked*⟩
synonyms arouse, encourage, excite, fire (up), impassion, incite, instigate, move, pique, rev (up), spark, stimulate, stir
related words fan, ignite, inflame (*also* enflame), kindle, trigger; activate, animate, drive, energize, galvanize, induce, inspire, key (up), motivate, motive, pump up, quicken, set off, vitalize; abet, ferment, foment, raise, whip (up); anger, enrage, madden, upset; jeer, taunt, tease; aggravate, annoy, bother, exasperate, gall, get, irritate, vex
phrases build a fire under
near antonyms calm, soothe, subdue, tranquilize (*also* tranquillize); appease, mollify, pacify, placate
2 to bring (something volatile or intense) into being ⟨rankings that are sure to *provoke* an argument among film buffs⟩ — see INCITE 1

provoking *adj* serving or likely to arouse a strong reaction ⟨the host's *provoking* opinions are the reason why people tune in to his radio talk show in the first place⟩ — see PROVOCATIVE

prowess *n* strength of mind to carry on in spite of danger ⟨an extraordinary display of *prowess* on the battlefield⟩ — see COURAGE

proximate *adj* **1** being soon to appear or take place ⟨the *proximate* publication of his first novel⟩ — see FORTHCOMING 1
2 not being distant in time, space, or significance ⟨the husband feels that their house is a little too *proximate* to his in-laws' condo for his peace and comfort⟩ — see CLOSE 2

proximity *n* the state or condition of being near ⟨the *proximity* of the curtains to the fireplace was a cause of concern for the safety inspector⟩
synonyms adjacency, closeness, contiguity, immediacy, nearness, propinquity, vicinity
related words abutment, juxtaposition
antonyms distance, remoteness

proxy *n* a person who acts or does business for another ⟨sent a *proxy* to the meeting to cast his vote for him⟩ — see AGENT 2

prude *n* a person who is greatly concerned with seemly behavior and morality especially regarding sexual matters ⟨the racy sitcom frequently satirizes exactly the sort of *prude* who would like to see the show taken off the air⟩
synonyms bluenose, moralist, Mrs. Grundy, nice nelly, puritan, wowser [*chiefly Australian*]
related words moralizer; goody-goody, Goody Two-shoes; fuddy-duddy, old maid, prig, spoilsport, stuffed shirt
near antonyms libertarian, libertine; misbehaver
antonyms immoralist

prudence *n* **1** a close attentiveness to avoiding danger ⟨advised to use some old-fashioned *prudence* when agreeing to meet face-to-face with an online acquaintance⟩ — see CAUTION 1
2 suitability for bringing about a desired result under the circumstances ⟨*prudence* would call for a little more caution in such a delicate situation⟩ — see EXPEDIENCY
3 the ability to make intelligent decisions especially in everyday matters ⟨in the long run, *prudence* will pay off more often than taking wild risks⟩ — see COMMON SENSE

prudent *adj* **1** having or showing good judgment and restraint especially in conduct or speech ⟨her calm response was very *prudent* under the circumstances⟩ — see DISCREET 1
2 suitable for bringing about a desired result under the circumstances ⟨it wouldn't be *prudent* to ask for a raise while the company is having financial troubles⟩ — see EXPEDIENT
3 having or showing deep understanding and intelligent application of knowledge ⟨her many years of experience as a social worker have made her a *prudent* judge of character⟩ — see WISE 1

prudery *n* a tendency to care a great deal about seemly behavior and morals especially in sexual matters ⟨such *prudery* regarding artistic depictions of the nude has no place on a college campus⟩
synonyms moralism, nice-nellyism, prudishness, puritanism
related words Comstockery; old-maidishness, priggery, priggishness, primness; morality, virtue
near antonyms lechery, prurience, pruriency; libertinage, libertinism; libertarianism

prudish *adj* given to or marked by very conservative standards regarding personal behavior or morals ⟨by the *prudish* standards of the 19th century, any depiction of the nude was scandalous⟩ — see STRAITLACED

prudishness *n* a tendency to care a great deal about seemly behavior and morals especially in sexual matters ⟨the *prudishness* of the people of the Victorian era was a hindrance to the dissemination of some basic information on human health and hygiene⟩ — see PRUDERY

prune *vb* to make (something) shorter or smaller with

the use of a cutting instrument ⟨*pruned* the dead branches from the old apple tree⟩ — see CLIP 1

[1]**pry** *vb* **1** to raise, move, or pull apart with or as if with a lever ⟨it took some effort to *pry* up the trap door⟩
synonyms jimmy, lever, prize
related words elevate, hoist, lift, uplift; break, break up, detach, disengage, disjoin, divide, part, pull, separate; shift
near antonyms connect, join
2 to draw out by force or with effort ⟨a vain attempt to *pry* the cork out of a wine bottle⟩ — see EXTRACT

[2]**pry** *vb* to interest oneself in what is not one's concern ⟨don't go *prying* into other people's business⟩ — see INTERFERE

prying *adj* **1** interested in what is not one's own business ⟨as we moved into our new home, we could sense that there were *prying* eyes watching us⟩ — see CURIOUS 1
2 thrusting oneself where one is not welcome or invited ⟨*prying* neighbors who refuse to mind their own business⟩ — see INTRUSIVE

psalm *n* a religious song ⟨after the sermon we sang a brief *psalm*⟩ — see HYMN 1

psalmody *n* a book of hymns ⟨a *psalmody* containing many beloved hymns⟩ — see HYMNAL

pseudo *adj* lacking in natural or spontaneous quality ⟨the *pseudo* friendliness of a salesperson trying to sell you something⟩ — see ARTIFICIAL 1

pseudonym *n* a fictitious or assumed name ⟨the most notorious serial killer of the 19th century remains known only by the *pseudonym* of Jack the Ripper⟩
synonyms alias, nom de guerre
related words nom de plume, pen name; appellation, designation; misnomer; epithet, nickname, sobriquet (*also* soubriquet)

pshaw *interj* how surprising, doubtful, or unbelievable ⟨*pshaw*! anyone else could have done that job in half the time that it took her⟩ — see NO

psych (up) *vb* to prepare (oneself) mentally or emotionally ⟨I have to *psych* myself *up* before every swimming competition⟩ — see FORTIFY 1

psyche *n* **1** an immaterial force within a human being thought to give the body life, energy, and power ⟨disturbing, enigmatic paintings that seem to embody the *psyche* of this brilliant but troubled artist⟩ — see SOUL 1
2 the part of a person that feels, thinks, perceives, wills, and especially reasons ⟨a novel that explores the *psyche* of a depressed teen⟩ — see MIND 1

psychic *n* a person who claims to speak with or for the spirits of the dead ⟨a TV *psychic* who managed to convince at least some people that their deceased loved ones were using him to relay messages⟩ — see CHANNELER

psycho *adj* having or showing a very abnormal or sick state of mind ⟨only someone who is totally *psycho* could have committed such a heinous crime⟩ — see INSANE 1

psycho *n* a person judged to be legally or medically insane ⟨a story based on a real-life *psycho* who had serious mother-son issues⟩ — see LUNATIC 1

psychological *also* **psychologic** *adj* of or relating to the mind ⟨suffered from *psychological* disorders all of his life⟩ — see MENTAL 1

psychopath *n* a person judged to be legally or medically insane ⟨declared that he was a dangerous *psychopath* who needed to be locked up⟩ — see LUNATIC 1

psychotic *adj* having or showing a very abnormal or sick state of mind ⟨the identity of the *psychotic* murderer known as the Zodiac Killer remains an intriguing puzzle⟩ — see INSANE 1

pub *n* a place of business where alcoholic beverages are sold to be consumed on the premises ⟨coworkers enjoying the convivial atmosphere of the Irish *pub*⟩ — see BARROOM

public *adj* **1** not known by only a select few ⟨the mayor's indiscretions have been *public* knowledge for some time⟩
synonyms open
related words general, popular; nonclassified, unclassified, well-known; advertised, aired, announced, broadcast, declared, disclosed, divulged, heralded, posted, proclaimed, promulgated, publicized, published, spotlighted; current, prevalent, rife, widespread; communal, shared; reported, reputed, rumored
phrases on record
near antonyms classified; unadvertised, unannounced, undisclosed; clandestine, collusive, conspiratorial, covert; surreptitious, undercover, underhand, underhanded; intimate, personal; concealed, repressed, reserved, silenced, stifled, suppressed, withheld; recanted, retracted, revoked
antonyms confidential, private, privy, secret
2 freely available for use or participation by all ⟨a *public* swimming pool⟩ — see OPEN 2
3 of or relating to a nation ⟨a trade agreement in the *public* interest⟩ — see NATIONAL
4 held by or applicable to a majority of the people ⟨*public* sentiment was against the war⟩ — see GENERAL 3
5 used or done by a number of people as a group ⟨*public* transportation⟩ — see COLLECTIVE

public *n* **1** human beings in general ⟨a lecture open to the *public*⟩ — see PEOPLE 1
2 the body of the community as contrasted with the elite ⟨the highbrows have always disdained his horror novels, but the *public* just eats them up⟩ — see MASS 1

public house *n* **1** a place that provides rooms and usually a public dining room for overnight guests ⟨took lodging at a cheap *public house* in a seedy part of town⟩ — see HOTEL
2 *chiefly British* a place of business where alcoholic beverages are sold to be consumed on the premises ⟨visited a *public house* in London that has been welcoming customers since the time of Charles Dickens⟩ — see BARROOM

publicity *n* information released to the media that is designed to gain public attention or support for a person, business, or cause ⟨an endless flow of *publicity* for our charity event resulted in a great turnout⟩
synonyms ballyhoo, hype, puffery
related words ad, advertisement, commercial, message, plug, promotion, spot, word; banner, bill, billboard, placard, poster, sign; advertising, marketing, propaganda; pronouncement, publication, release; broadcast, bulletin, dispatch, newscast, report, story; ink [*slang*], testimonial, write-up

publicize *vb* **1** to provide publicity for ⟨the movie studios widely *publicized* their summer blockbusters⟩
synonyms ballyhoo, hype, pitch, plug, promote, talk up, tout
related words advertise, bark, merchandise (*also* merchandize), sell; push; acclaim, hail, laud, praise; endorse (*also* indorse), plump (for), plunk (for) *or* plonk (for); recommend, review; announce, broadcast, publish
phrases beat the drum (for)
2 to make known openly or publicly ⟨the city hasn't done a good job of *publicizing* the new regulations for its recycling operation⟩ — see ANNOUNCE

public servant *n* **1** a person who holds a public office ⟨the new governor vowed that he would always remember why he was called a *public servant* and not the people's master⟩ — see OFFICIAL
2 a worker in a government agency ⟨concerned that the new federal agency would just add another slew of *pub-*

lic servants to the government payroll⟩ — see BUREAUCRAT

public speaking *n* the art of speaking in public eloquently and effectively ⟨she is very experienced in *public speaking* and should do well in her campaign appearances before large crowds⟩ — see ORATORY 1

publish *vb* **1** to produce and release for distribution in printed form ⟨our local animal shelter *publishes* a newsletter⟩
synonyms get out, issue, print, put out
related words copublish; reissue, reprint, republish; serialize; contribute, edit, syndicate; manufacture, produce; distribute, market
phrases come out with
near antonyms censor, suppress
2 to make known openly or publicly ⟨will *publish* the exam scores as soon as they are available⟩ — see ANNOUNCE

puck *n* an imaginary being usually having a small human form and magical powers ⟨dreamed that her garden was the secret meeting place of *pucks* and sprites⟩ — see FAIRY

puckish *adj* tending to or exhibiting reckless playfulness ⟨he takes a *puckish* delight in teasing her about her love life, or lack thereof⟩ — see MISCHIEVOUS 1

puddle *n* a small often deep body of water ⟨splashing in the *puddles* on the way home from the bus stop⟩ — see [1]POOL

pudginess *n* the condition of having an excess of body fat ⟨started to notice a little *pudginess* around his middle⟩ — see CORPULENCE

pudgy *adj* having an excess of body fat ⟨at this point the *pudgy* toddler is still cute, but she will have health problems if she continues to be overweight⟩ — see FAT 1

puerile *adj* **1** having or showing the annoying qualities (as silliness) associated with children ⟨told the teenagers that such *puerile* behavior would not be tolerated during the ceremony⟩ — see CHILDISH
2 lacking in adult experience or maturity ⟨allowed the company to be taken over by a bunch of *puerile* whippersnappers fresh out of business school⟩ — see CALLOW
3 lacking in seriousness or maturity ⟨the kind of *puerile* jokes that teenage moviegoers apparently love⟩ — see GIDDY 1

puff *n* a slight or gentle movement of air ⟨felt a *puff* of wind on his face⟩ — see BREEZE 1

puff *vb* **1** to breathe hard, quickly, or with difficulty ⟨he came running up the stairs *puffing* and wheezing⟩ — see GASP
2 to praise too much ⟨a talk show host who can be counted on to *puff* up the celebrities who readily consent to be interviewed⟩ — see FLATTER 1

puffed *adj* enlarged beyond normal from internal pressure ⟨her eyelid was so *puffed* she couldn't see with that eye⟩ — see BLOATED 2

puffery *n* information released to the media that is designed to gain public attention or support for a person, business, or cause ⟨the newspaper's local stories are often thinly disguised *puffery* for area businesses⟩ — see PUBLICITY

pug *n* one that engages in the sport of fighting with the fists ⟨a retired *pug* with battered ears and swollen knuckles⟩ — see BOXER

pugilist *n* one that engages in the sport of fighting with the fists ⟨a *pugilist* with the trademark of the boxing ring: a nose that showed signs of having been broken on more than one occasion⟩ — see BOXER

pugnacious *adj* feeling or displaying eagerness to fight ⟨a movie reviewer who is spirited, even *pugnacious*, when defending her opinions⟩ — see BELLIGERENT

pugnacity *n* an inclination to fight or quarrel ⟨the players need to temper their *pugnacity* with a little self-restraint—their aggressive style of play too often results in penalties⟩ — see BELLIGERENCE

puissance *n* the ability to exert effort for the accomplishment of a task ⟨the president pledged to put the full *puissance* of the nation into the war effort⟩ — see POWER 2

puissant *adj* having great power or influence ⟨one of the nation's most respected and *puissant* advocates for the rights of minorities⟩ — see IMPORTANT 2

puke *vb* to discharge the contents of the stomach through the mouth ⟨the drunken reveler staggered out the door and promptly *puked* in the bushes⟩ — see VOMIT

pukka *also* **pucka** *adj* being exactly as appears or as claimed ⟨wondering whether the old-looking ivory box was *pukka*—or just something recently manufactured in China⟩ — see AUTHENTIC 1

pule *vb* to utter feeble plaintive cries ⟨a distressed baby *puling* in its crib⟩ — see WHIMPER 1

pull *n* **1** the act or an instance of applying force on something so that it moves in the direction of the force ⟨I gave the door such a *pull* that when it suddenly opened, I nearly fell backwards⟩
synonyms draw, haul, jerk, pluck, tug, wrench, yank
related words drag, tow; hitch, twitch; grab, snatch
near antonyms heave, shove, thrust
antonyms push
2 the power to direct the thinking or behavior of others usually indirectly ⟨their lawyer supposedly has a lot of *pull* with the administration in Washington⟩ — see INFLUENCE 1
3 the more favorable condition or position in a competition ⟨a political candidate with all of the *pull* that comes with a vast fortune and famous surname⟩ — see ADVANTAGE 1

pull *vb* **1** to cause to follow by applying steady force on ⟨a team of horses *pulling* a heavy wagon⟩
synonyms drag, draw, hale, haul, lug, tow, tug
related words attract; heave, jerk, yank; carry, convey, ferry, move, transport
near antonyms shove, thrust
antonyms drive, propel, push
2 to draw out by force or with effort ⟨the dentist had to struggle to *pull* the tooth⟩ — see EXTRACT
3 to injure by overuse, misuse, or pressure ⟨lift the crate carefully, or you'll *pull* a muscle⟩ — see STRAIN 1

pullback *n* an act of moving away especially from something difficult, dangerous, or disagreeable ⟨the *pullback* was necessary so that the commanders could reorganize their units and reassess the situation⟩ — see RETREAT 1

pull down *vb* **1** to bring to a complete end the physical soundness, existence, or usefulness of ⟨a powerful storm *pulled down* the old fishing shack, which had been immortalized in countless paintings⟩ — see DESTROY 1
2 to destroy (as a building) completely by knocking down or breaking to pieces ⟨an ugly billboard that was eventually *pulled down*⟩ — see DEMOLISH 1
3 to receive as return for effort ⟨he's *pulling down* six figures at that job⟩ — see EARN 1

pull in *vb* **1** to keep from exceeding a desirable degree or level (as of expression) ⟨a company that cannot manage to *pull in* costs will not be in business for very long⟩ — see CONTROL 1
2 to take or keep under one's control by authority of law ⟨he was *pulled in* after a random traffic stop turned up drugs in his car⟩ — see ARREST 1

pull off *vb* to carry through (as a process) to completion ⟨the rebel forces *pulled off* a surprisingly successful offensive against the better equipped government troops⟩ — see PERFORM 1

pullout *n* an act of moving away especially from something difficult, dangerous, or disagreeable ⟨the civil unrest has led the company to initiate a *pullout* of its operations in the region⟩ — see RETREAT 1

pull out *vb* **1** to leave a place often for another ⟨the party's been fun, but it's time to *pull out*⟩ — see GO 2
2 to move back or away (as from something difficult, dangerous, or disagreeable) ⟨the aid workers have been advised to *pull out* of those regions to which the conflict has spread⟩ — see RETREAT 1

pull round *vb, chiefly British* to become healthy and strong again after illness or weakness ⟨after a week without any relapses, it became clear that she would *pull round* eventually⟩ — see CONVALESCE

pullulate *vb* to be copiously supplied ⟨a tough city neighborhood that has a reputation for *pullulating* with prostitutes and petty criminals⟩ — see ABOUND

pull up *vb* to bring (something) to a standstill ⟨the jockey tried to *pull up* the apparently injured horse⟩ — see [1]HALT 1

pulp *vb* to cause to become a pulpy mass ⟨*pulped* three oranges to get their juice⟩ — see CRUSH 1

pulpiness *n* the quality or state of being full of juice ⟨select ripe peaches of sufficient *pulpiness* to readily yield the amount of juice required by the recipe⟩ — see SUCCULENCE

pulpy *adj* **1** full of juice ⟨good, ripe peaches will be *pulpy* and not mealy⟩ — see JUICY 1
2 giving easily to the touch ⟨the *pulpy* flesh of ripe fruit⟩ — see SOFT 3

pulsate *vb* to expand and contract in a rhythmic manner ⟨the heart muscle *pulsates* regularly to pump blood⟩
synonyms beat, palpitate, pit-a-pat, pitter-patter, pulse, throb
related words fluctuate, oscillate, vibrate; quiver, tremble

pulsation *n* a rhythmic expanding and contracting ⟨you should press against the artery in your wrist and count the *pulsations* to calculate your heart rate⟩
synonyms beat, beating, palpitation, pulse, throb
related words fluctuation, oscillation, vibration; quiver, tremble, tremor

pulse *n* a rhythmic expanding and contracting ⟨his resting *pulse* rate is much lower than that of most men his age⟩ — see PULSATION

pulse *vb* to expand and contract in a rhythmic manner ⟨blood vessels *pulsing* in time with the heartbeat⟩ — see PULSATE

pulverize *vb* **1** to bring to a complete end the physical soundness, existence, or usefulness of ⟨buildings *pulverized* by a killer tornado⟩ — see DESTROY 1
2 to reduce to fine particles ⟨*pulverize* the cement into dust for reuse⟩ — see POWDER

puma *n* a large tawny cat of the wild ⟨adult *pumas* can sometimes weigh over 200 pounds⟩ — see COUGAR

pummel *vb* to strike repeatedly ⟨*pummeled* the mugger with her fists until help arrived⟩ — see BEAT 1

pump *vb* **1** to make short up-and-down movements ⟨the thighs of the bicyclists were *pumping* furiously as they neared the finish line⟩ — see NOD
2 to put a series of questions to ⟨prying neighbors *pumped* the guileless child for information about the family's new pool⟩ — see EXAMINE 1
3 to remove (liquid) gradually or completely ⟨*pumped* water from the well⟩ — see DRAIN 1

pumped *adj* showing urgent desire or interest ⟨the whole city's so *pumped* for this championship that it's unbelievable⟩ — see EAGER

pump up *vb* **1** to cause a pleasurable stimulation of the feelings of ⟨the crowd was *pumped up* by the band's rocking performance⟩ — see THRILL
2 to make greater in size, amount, or number ⟨that pop diva is trying to *pump up* album sales with an extended publicity tour⟩ — see INCREASE 1

[1]**punch** *n* **1** the quality of an utterance that provokes interest and produces an effect ⟨the real *punch* of the speech came in its closing lines⟩
synonyms cogency, effectiveness, force, forcefulness, impact, point
related words payoff; importance, significance; appeal, attraction, charm, fascination
2 active strength of body or mind ⟨we're going to need a candidate with real *punch* if voters are ever going to get excited about this election⟩ — see VIGOR 1
3 a hard strike with a part of the body or an instrument ⟨the poor palooka wasn't able to land a single *punch* on his opponent⟩ — see [1]BLOW

[2]**punch** *n* a mark or small hole made by a pointed instrument ⟨old computers used to get information by reading the *punches* on a series of cards⟩ — see PRICK 1

punch *vb* **1** to deliver a blow to (someone or something) usually in a strong vigorous manner ⟨after the man had *punched* the bartender for eighty-sixing him, bouncers stepped in and restrained him until the police could arrive⟩ — see HIT 1
2 to make a hole or series of holes in ⟨*punch* a ticket⟩ — see PERFORATE
3 to urge, push, or force onward ⟨cowboys *punching* cattle⟩ — see DRIVE 1

punch–drunk *adj* suffering from mental confusion ⟨*punch-drunk* from having stayed up all night, she struggled through the exam⟩ — see DIZZY 2

puncheon *n* an enclosed wooden vessel for holding beverages ⟨stored the *puncheons* of rum in the cellar⟩ — see CASK

punch out *vb* to strike repeatedly ⟨you should take a course in anger management—you can't go around *punching out* people⟩ — see BEAT 1

punchy *adj* suffering from mental confusion ⟨feeling a little *punchy* after being up half the night with a crying baby⟩ — see DIZZY 2

punctilious *adj* marked by or showing careful attention to set forms and details ⟨old-money aristocrats with a *punctilious* sense of propriety⟩ — see CEREMONIOUS 1

punctual *adj* done, carried out, or given without delay ⟨the *punctual* delivery of the daily mail⟩— see PROMPT 1

punctuality *n* the quality or habit of arriving or being ready on time ⟨our boss is a real stickler for *punctuality*—he expects everyone to be at their desk by nine o'clock⟩ — see PROMPTITUDE

punctuate *vb* to indicate the importance of by centering attention on ⟨*punctuated* each and every word of his denial with a pound of his fist on the table⟩ — see EMPHASIZE 1

puncture *n* a mark or small hole made by a pointed instrument ⟨a leak caused by several small *punctures* in the rubber gasket⟩ — see PRICK 1

puncture *vb* **1** to make a hole or series of holes in ⟨a nail *punctured* the tire⟩ — see PERFORATE
2 to penetrate or hold (something) with a pointed object ⟨I could never *puncture* my own skin with a hypodermic needle⟩ — see IMPALE

pundit *n* **1** a person of deep wisdom or learning ⟨a moral question that has puzzled the *pundits* throughout the ages⟩ — see SAGE
2 a person who makes or expresses a judgment on the quality of offerings in some field of endeavor ⟨the new mini laptop has gotten a thumbs-up from industry *pundits*⟩ — see CRITIC 2

pungency *n* **1** a harsh or sharp quality ⟨the *pungency* of the vinegar gives the salad dressing the kick that it needs⟩ — see EDGE 1
2 the quality or state of being stimulating to the mind or senses ⟨theatergoers have long delighted in the *pungency* and wit of the play's dialogue⟩ — see PIQUANCY

pungent *adj* **1** having a powerfully stimulating odor or flavor ⟨a *pungent* chili that is not for those with timid taste buds⟩ — see SHARP 2
2 marked by the use of wit that is intended to cause hurt feelings ⟨a *pungent* put-down that she will not soon forget⟩ — see SARCASTIC
3 sharp and pleasantly stimulating to the mind or senses ⟨a newspaper columnist known for his *pungent* observations on everyday life⟩ — see PIQUANT

puniness *n* the quality or state of being little in size ⟨a nagging dissatisfaction with his physical *puniness* drove him to become a body builder⟩ — see SMALLNESS 1

punish *vb* to inflict a penalty on for a fault or crime ⟨the child was *punished* for breaking dishes on purpose⟩ ⟨if caught, the thief will be severely *punished*⟩
synonyms castigate, chasten, chastise, correct, discipline, penalize
related words assess, charge, dock, fine, impose, levy, mulct; convict, sentence; condemn, damn, denounce; criticize, keelhaul, rebuke, reprimand, reprove; wreak
near antonyms forfeit; get off, ransom, release; commute, reprieve; absolve, acquit, exculpate, exonerate, vindicate
antonyms excuse, pardon, spare

punisher *n* one who inflicts punishment in return for an injury or offense ⟨a father who regrets the fact that he always ends up being the household's disciplinarian and resident *punisher*⟩ — see NEMESIS 1

punishment *n* suffering, loss, or hardship imposed in response to a crime or offense ⟨he is serving five years in prison as *punishment* for aggravated assault⟩
synonyms castigation, chastisement, comeuppance, correction, desert(s), discipline, nemesis, penalty, wrath
related words reprisal, retaliation, retribution, revenge, vengeance; assessment, charge, fine, mulct; example, sentence; confinement, imprisonment, incarceration; condemnation, damnation, denouncement; censure, criticism, rebuke, reprimand, reproof
near antonyms amnesty, indemnity, pardon, parole; acquittal, exculpation, exoneration, vindication; exemption, immunity, impunity; release; commutation, reprieve; absolution, forgiveness, remission, remitment; condonation, disregard, overlooking

punitive *adj* inflicting, involving, or serving as punishment ⟨any misbehavior was immediately met with a *punitive* response⟩ ⟨the company had to pay a million dollars in *punitive* damages⟩
synonyms castigating, chastening, chastising, correcting, correctional, corrective, disciplinary, disciplining, penal, penalizing
related words retaliative, retaliatory, retributive, retributory, revengeful; vengeful, wrathful
near antonyms compensatory; acquitting, exculpating, exculpatory, exonerating, vindicating; absolving, condoning, pardoning, remitting; commuting, reprieving
antonyms nonpunitive

punk *adj* **1** falling short of a standard ⟨she plays a *punk* game of tennis, so you won't have any trouble beating her⟩ — see BAD 1
2 extremely unsatisfactory ⟨the acting in the movie ranged all the way from poor to *punk*⟩ — see WRETCHED 1
3 temporarily suffering from a disorder of the body ⟨I've been feeling *punk* today⟩ — see SICK 1

punk *n* **1** a person who is just starting out in a field of activity ⟨an impertinent *punk* who was trying to tell senior colleagues how to do their jobs⟩ — see BEGINNER
2 a violent, brutal person who is often a member of an organized gang ⟨the vigilante was hailed by some as a hero for standing up to the *punks* who had repeatedly threatened his family⟩ — see HOODLUM
3 language, behavior, or ideas that are absurd and contrary to good sense ⟨claims made by cosmetic companies about their antiaging creams that turned out to be a lot of *punk*⟩ — see NONSENSE 1

punter *n, chiefly British* **1** a person who buys a product or uses a service from a business ⟨an East End prostitute who claimed that many of her *punters* were from the upper echelons of London society⟩ — see CUSTOMER 1
2 one that bets (as on the outcome of a contest or sports event) ⟨the huge amount of money that *punters* in Britain put on football matches⟩ — see BETTOR

puny *adj* of a size that is less than average ⟨a *puny*, wrinkled apple⟩ — see SMALL 1

pupil *n* **1** one who attends a school ⟨generally there are 20 *pupils* in each class⟩ — see STUDENT
2 one who follows the opinions or teachings of another ⟨to *pupils* of the philosopher Henry David Thoreau, the shores of Walden Pond are hallowed ground⟩ — see FOLLOWER 1

puppet *n* **1** a small figure often of a human being used especially as a child's plaything ⟨gave her a *puppet* with strings for a gift⟩ — see DOLL 1
2 one that is or can be used to further the purposes of another ⟨accused the newspaper editor of being a *puppet* for the moneyed people of the town⟩ — see [1]PAWN

purchasable *adj* open to improper influence and especially bribery ⟨*purchasable* members of the state legislature whose votes could be bought, and at surprisingly cheap prices⟩ — see VENAL

purchase *vb* to get possession of (something) by giving money in exchange for ⟨I need to *purchase* a new heavy coat⟩ — see BUY 1

pure *adj* **1** free from added matter ⟨I'm allergic to any jewelry that isn't *pure* silver⟩ ⟨the solution must be kept *pure* for the experiment to work⟩
synonyms absolute, fine, neat, plain, purified, refined, straight, unadulterated, unalloyed, undiluted, unmixed
related words clarified, filtered; clean, fresh, taintless, uncontaminated, uncorrupted, undefiled, unpolluted, untainted; rendered, tried; concentrated, full-bodied, strong; uncombined
near antonyms befouled, besmirched, contaminated, corrupted, debased, defiled, fouled, polluted, soiled, spoiled, sullied, tainted; unclarified; amalgamated, blended, coalesced, combined, commingled, compounded, incorporated, intermingled, intermixed, merged, mingled; conjoined, fused, joined, linked, united; cheapened, doctored, watered-down
antonyms adulterated, alloyed, diluted, impure, mixed
2 free from any trace of the coarse or indecent ⟨the humor in the movie is as *pure* and wholesome as any parent could wish⟩ — see CHASTE 1
3 free from sin ⟨in one beatitude those who are *pure* in heart are promised the sight of God⟩ — see INNOCENT 1
4 having no exceptions or restrictions ⟨that story is *pure* nonsense⟩ — see ABSOLUTE 2

pure–blooded *or* **pure–blood** *adj* of unmixed ancestry ⟨both dogs are *pure-blooded* Chesapeake Bay retrievers⟩ — see PUREBRED

purebred *adj* of unmixed ancestry ⟨that horse is a *purebred* Arabian⟩
synonyms blooded, full-blood, full-blooded, pedigreed (*or* pedigree), pure-blooded (*or* pure-blood), thoroughbred
related words well-bred; inbred

near antonyms crossbred, crossed, half-blood (*or* half-blooded), half-bred, hybridized, interbred, outcrossed
antonyms hybrid, mixed, mongrel

purely *adv* **1** with purity of thought and deed ⟨the devout girl vowed to live her life *purely* and in the service of God⟩
synonyms chastely, innocently, modestly, morally, righteously, virtuously
related words decently, decorously, properly; priggishly, primly, prudishly
near antonyms indecently, obscenely, vulgarly; lasciviously, lewdly, lustfully
antonyms evilly, immorally, impurely, sinfully, wickedly
2 for nothing other than ⟨I fish *purely* for the fun of it—I don't care if I end up with no fish to fry⟩ — see SOLELY 1
3 nothing more than ⟨her pleasantries were *purely* for show and masked her true feelings⟩ — see JUST 3

purge *vb* to free from moral guilt or blemish especially ceremonially ⟨a day on which the faithful are expected to *purge* themselves of their sins through prayer and fasting⟩ — see PURIFY 1

purification *n* the act or fact of freeing from sin or moral guilt ⟨some people must undergo a ritual *purification* after certain activities⟩
synonyms cleansing, sanctification
related words rebirth, regeneration, restoration; grace, redemption, salvation; absolution, forgiveness, remission; acquittal, clearance, clearing, exoneration, vindication; atonement, expiation
near antonyms blasphemy, defilement, desecration, profanation, violation; corruption, debasement, perversion; contamination, pollution, sullying, tarnishing

purified *adj* free from added matter ⟨*purified* water that was now safe to drink⟩ — see PURE 1

purify *vb* **1** to free from moral guilt or blemish especially ceremonially ⟨Catholics go to confession to be *purified*⟩
synonyms cleanse, purge, sanctify
related words amend, improve, refine; heal, regenerate, restore; elevate, ennoble, uplift; absolve, acquit, clear, exonerate, vindicate
near antonyms corrupt, debase, debauch, defile, degrade, demean, deprave, pervert, stain, warp; poison, profane, prostitute; sully, tarnish
2 to remove usually visible impurities from ⟨*purify* the water by distillation⟩ — see CLARIFY 1

puritan *n* a person who is greatly concerned with seemly behavior and morality especially regarding sexual matters ⟨some of the town's *puritans* still maintain that sex education has no place in the schools⟩ — see PRUDE

puritanical *adj* given to or marked by very conservative standards regarding personal behavior or morals ⟨some of the state laws concerning sexual behavior are vestiges of a more *puritanical* time and are rarely, if ever, enforced⟩ — see STRAITLACED

puritanism *n* a tendency to care a great deal about seemly behavior and morals especially in sexual matters ⟨the Victorian era was often characterized by a hypocritical *puritanism*⟩ — see PRUDERY

purity *n* the quality or state of being morally pure ⟨struggling to live a life of *purity* while surrounded by wickedness⟩ — see CHASTITY 1

purlieu *n* **1** a place for spending time or for socializing ⟨the restaurant, the preferred *purlieu* of the theatergoing crowd, is always packed an hour or two before showtime⟩ — see HANGOUT
2 purlieus *pl* an adjoining region or space ⟨we stopped at one of the several pubs in the *purlieus* of the stadium⟩ — see ENVIRONS 2
3 purlieus *pl* the districts adjacent to a city ⟨such gated communities are common among the *purlieus* of these Midwestern cities⟩ — see ENVIRONS 1

purloin *vb* to take (something) without right and with an intent to keep ⟨the studio stepped up security, fearing that someone might attempt to *purloin* a copy of the script for the show's season finale⟩ — see STEAL 1

purloiner *n* one who steals ⟨she demanded that the pusillanimous *purloiner* of her chocolates step forward⟩ — see THIEF

purple *adj* full of fine words and fancy expressions ⟨an overwritten novel with far too many *purple* patches⟩ — see FLOWERY 1

purport *n* the idea that is conveyed or intended to be conveyed to the mind by language, symbol, or action ⟨was able to give the *purport* of the governor's speech in a few words⟩ — see MEANING 1

purport *vb* **1** to have in mind as a purpose or goal ⟨do you *purport* to spend the rest of your life on that couch, or do you think you might get a job someday?⟩ — see INTEND 1
2 to state as a fact usually forcefully ⟨he *purports* to be an expert in criminalistics⟩ — see CLAIM 1

purpose *n* **1** something that one hopes or intends to accomplish ⟨the *purpose* of the research is to discover how the virus is transmitted⟩ — see GOAL
2 the action for which a person or thing is specially fitted or used or for which a thing exists ⟨still trying to discover her *purpose* in life⟩ — see ROLE

purpose *vb* to have in mind as a purpose or goal ⟨I've been *purposing* to fix that thing for some time now⟩ — see INTEND 1

purposeful *adj* **1** fully committed to achieving a goal ⟨a soft-spoken but *purposeful* criminal investigator⟩ — see DETERMINED 1
2 made, given, or done with full awareness of what one is doing ⟨there's a difference between a *purposeful* lie and an accidental untruth⟩ — see INTENTIONAL

purposefully *adv* **1** with full awareness of what one is doing ⟨he *purposefully* chose the more difficult route to the mountain summit⟩ — see INTENTIONALLY
2 with great effort or determination ⟨strode *purposefully* into the boss's office, determined to ask for a raise⟩ — see HARD 1

purposefulness *n* firm or unwavering adherence to one's purpose ⟨approached the challenge with grim *purposefulness*⟩ — see DETERMINATION 1

purposely *adv* with full awareness of what one is doing ⟨the real estate agent *purposely* withheld information that would have discouraged us from buying the property⟩ — see INTENTIONALLY

purposive *adj* made, given, or done with full awareness of what one is doing ⟨facial tics and other unconscious movements that one would not normally call *purposive* actions⟩ — see INTENTIONAL

purposively *adv* with full awareness of what one is doing ⟨the Federal Reserve *purposively* controls the supply of money in order to keep a lid on inflation⟩ — see INTENTIONALLY

purr *n* a monotonous sound like that of an insect in motion ⟨listened to the reassuring *purr* of the car engine⟩ — see HUM

purse *n* a container for carrying money and small personal items ⟨I left my *purse* at home, so I can't buy anything after all⟩
synonyms bag, handbag, pocketbook
related words clutch, clutch bag, minaudière; billfold, wallet; compact, vanity; poke, pouch, sack; shoulder bag

pursiness *n* the condition of having an excess of body fat ⟨doctors and nutritionists have warned that a pandemic of *pursiness* poses a major threat to the health of the American public⟩ — see CORPULENCE

pursuance *n* the doing of an action ⟨until recently he has been fully engaged in *pursuance* of his duties as governor⟩ — see COMMISSION 2

pursue *vb* **1** to go after or on the track of ⟨the policeman doggedly *pursued* the pickpocket through the crowded subway station⟩ — see FOLLOW 2
2 to go in search of ⟨urged the graduates to *pursue* personal fulfillment instead of financial success⟩ — see SEEK 1

pursuing *n* the act of going after or in the tracks of another ⟨the controversy concerning the *pursuing* of criminals in speeding vehicles along busy highways⟩ — see PURSUIT 1

pursuit *n* **1** the act of going after or in the tracks of another ⟨the cat ran down the street with a pair of dogs in *pursuit*⟩
synonyms chase, chasing, dogging, following, hounding, pursuing, shadowing, tagging, tailing, tracing, tracking, trailing
related words hot pursuit; tagging along; path, track, trail; search, seeking
2 an activity outside of one's regular occupation that is engaged in primarily for pleasure ⟨a workaholic with few *pursuits* outside of the office⟩ — see AVOCATION

push *n* a series of activities undertaken to achieve a goal ⟨an unprecedented *push* to pass stronger gun control measures⟩ — see CAMPAIGN

push *vb* **1** to apply force to (someone or something) so that it moves in front of one ⟨I had to *push* my damaged bike all the way home⟩
synonyms drive, propel, shove, thrust
related words impel, move; bear (down), compress, depress, jam, pressure, squash, squeeze, weigh (upon); bulldoze, compel, force, lean (on *or* against), muscle, ram
2 to force one's way ⟨we had to *push* our way through a crowd that was mostly headed in the opposite direction⟩ — see [2]PRESS 4

push–bike *also* **push bicycle** *n, British* a two-wheeled vehicle that is propelled by the use of pedals and steered through the use of handlebars ⟨the vicar riding his sturdy *push-bike* used to be a common sight around the village⟩ — see BICYCLE

pushchair *n, chiefly British* a small four-wheeled vehicle designed for pushing a baby around in ⟨a fun festival that appeals to adults as well as tots in *pushchairs*⟩ — see BABY CARRIAGE

pushing *adj* **1** having a strong desire for personal advancement ⟨among the young associates at the law firm, he was unmistakably the most *pushing*⟩ — see AMBITIOUS 1
2 thrusting oneself where one is not welcome or invited ⟨the sort of sycophantic, *pushing* man on the make that everyone loves to hate⟩ — see INTRUSIVE

push off *vb* to leave a place often for another ⟨let's *push off* while it's still early enough to beat the evening rush⟩ — see GO 2

push on *vb* to leave a place often for another ⟨the party was getting deadly dull, so it was time was *push on*⟩ — see GO 2

pushover *n* **1** a person without strength of character ⟨*pushovers* who are afraid to discipline their little spoiled brat⟩ — see WEAKLING 2
2 one who is easily deceived or cheated ⟨scam artists mistakenly thinking that these farm families would be *pushovers*⟩ — see [1]DUPE
3 something that is easy to do ⟨though the mountain is not especially high, the climb is very arduous and is definitely not a *pushover*⟩ — see CINCH 1

pushy *adj* **1** having or showing a bold forcefulness in the pursuit of a goal ⟨he's usually very *pushy* about insinuating his own ideas into other people's projects⟩ — see AGGRESSIVE 1
2 thrusting oneself where one is not welcome or invited ⟨the *pushy* cocktail waiter kept asking me if I wanted another drink, even though I hadn't finished the first one⟩ — see INTRUSIVE

pusillanimity *n* a shameful lack of courage in the face of danger ⟨the *pusillanimity* shown by the press on this issue after the administration began applying pressure⟩ — see COWARDICE

pusillanimous *adj* having or showing a shameful lack of courage ⟨pusillanimous *politicians* who vote according to whichever way the political wind is blowing⟩ — see COWARDLY

[1]**puss** *n, slang* the front part of the head ⟨the snowball smacked him right in the *puss*⟩ — see FACE 1

[2]**puss** *n* a small domestic animal known for catching mice ⟨I don't want a purebred cat, just some playful *puss* in need of a good home⟩ — see CAT 1

pussy *n* a small domestic animal known for catching mice ⟨fed his *pussy* only the finest fish for her supper⟩ — see CAT 1

pussycat *n* a small domestic animal known for catching mice ⟨oh, look at the cute little *pussycat*, kids⟩ — see CAT 1

pussyfoot *vb* **1** to avoid giving a definite answer or position ⟨politicians who try to *pussyfoot* around hot-button issues⟩ — see EQUIVOCATE
2 to move about in a sly or secret manner ⟨*pussyfooting* through the hallways in the middle of the night⟩ — see SNEAK 1

pustule *n* a small, inflamed swelling of the skin ⟨smallpox's characteristic *pustules* typically resulted in permanent scarring for survivors of the dreaded disease⟩ — see POCK

put *vb* **1** to arrange something in a certain spot or position ⟨you can *put* this box next to the bookshelf⟩ — see PLACE 1
2 to convey in appropriate or telling terms ⟨tried to think of a good way of *putting* the news⟩ — see PHRASE
3 to decide the size, amount, number, or distance of (something) without actual measurement ⟨*put* the time of the photograph at about noon⟩ — see ESTIMATE 2
4 to establish or apply as a charge or penalty ⟨a proposal to *put* a special tax on luxuries⟩ — see IMPOSE
5 to change (something) so as to make it suitable for a new use or situation ⟨*put* the words of his patriotic poem to the tune of a well-known drinking song⟩ — see ADAPT
6 to risk (something) on the outcome of an uncertain event ⟨deciding to go for broke, he *put* $1000 on a horse that had 20 to 1 odds⟩ — see BET

putative *adj* appearing to be true on the basis of evidence that may or may not be confirmed ⟨the *putative* reason for her dismissal was poor job performance⟩ — see APPARENT 1

putatively *adv* to all outward appearances ⟨the lake's *putatively* pristine water is actually crawling with microorganisms that can wreak havoc with your gastrointestinal system⟩ — see APPARENTLY

put away *vb* **1** to place (a dead body) in the earth, a tomb, or the sea ⟨the naval authorities *put away* the body yesterday⟩ — see BURY 1
2 to put to death deliberately ⟨after a hit man had *put away* her husband, she'd be free to marry her lover⟩ — see MURDER 1
3 to take in as food ⟨can easily *put away* an entire bowl of popcorn at a single sitting⟩ — see EAT 1

put by *vb* to put (something of future use or value) in a safe or secret place ⟨have money *put by* for an emergency⟩ — see HOARD

put–down *n* **1** an act or expression showing scorn and

usually intended to hurt another's feelings ⟨new hires always have to deal with *put-downs* and practical jokes from the older employees⟩ — see INSULT
2 the act of making a person or a thing seem little or unimportant ⟨your never-ending *put-down* of my musical talents is really starting to annoy me⟩ — see DEPRECIATION

put down *vb* **1** to express scornfully one's low opinion of ⟨he has the annoying habit of *putting down* others under the guise of offering constructive criticism⟩ — see DECRY 1
2 to make a written note of ⟨we had the whole agreement *put down* on paper⟩ — see RECORD 1
3 to put (someone or something) on a list ⟨*put* her *down* as one of the chaperones for the field trip⟩ — see [1]LIST 2
4 to put a stop to (something) by the use of force ⟨a tyrant who ruthlessly *put down* uprisings⟩ — see QUELL 1
5 to explain (something) as being the result of something else ⟨a fender bender that probably can be *put down* to the young driver's inexperience⟩ — see CREDIT 1
6 to take in as food ⟨the husky youngster seemed to *put down* her own weight in food at one sitting⟩ — see EAT 1

put in *vb* to put or set into the ground to grow ⟨*put in* a crop of winter wheat⟩ — see PLANT 1

put in (for) *vb* to give a request or demand for ⟨several employees have already *put in for* vacation time during the last week of December⟩ — see ORDER 2

put off *vb* **1** to assign to a later time ⟨never *put off* until tomorrow what you can do today⟩ — see POSTPONE
2 to rid oneself of (a garment) ⟨*put off* your coat and stay awhile⟩ — see REMOVE 1
3 to cause to feel disgust ⟨she was *put off* by his blatantly sexist attitude⟩ — see DISGUST

put–on *adj* lacking in natural or spontaneous quality ⟨a *put-on* goofy voice⟩ — see ARTIFICIAL 1

put–on *n* **1** a display of emotion or behavior that is insincere or intended to deceive ⟨my bravery was all a *put-on*—I was scared out of my wits⟩ — see MASQUERADE
2 a work that imitates and exaggerates another work for comic effect ⟨for a moment, I couldn't tell if the commercial was serious or a deadpan *put-on* of ads by other insurance companies⟩ — see PARODY 1

put on *vb* **1** to place on one's person ⟨I *put on* a coat and shoes to go outside⟩
synonyms don, slip (on *or* into), throw (on)
related words apparel, array, attire, bedeck, bedizen, bundle up, caparison, clothe, doll up, dress, garb, rig, robe, suit, trick, uniform; overdress
near antonyms disrobe, strip, undress
antonyms doff, remove, take off
2 to describe or express in too strong terms ⟨some critics are *putting* it *on* when they say it's the best comedy ever made⟩ — see OVERSTATE
3 to present a false appearance of ⟨*put on* a show of anger just for fun⟩ — see FEIGN

put out *adj* subjected to and reacting with irritation ⟨he gets *put out* if anyone disturbs his dinner⟩ — see ANNOYED

put out *vb* **1** to bring to bear especially forcefully or effectively ⟨despite *putting out* her best effort, she was unable to beat her longtime tennis rival⟩ — see EXERT
2 to cause to cease burning ⟨*put out* the campfire before leaving⟩ — see EXTINGUISH 1
3 to disturb the peace of mind of (someone) especially by repeated disagreeable acts ⟨my father was *put out* by all the street noise outside our house⟩ — see IRRITATE 1
4 to cause discomfort to or trouble for ⟨if it wouldn't *put* you *out* too much, would you mind giving me a ride to the airport?⟩ — see INCONVENIENCE
5 to produce and release for distribution in printed form ⟨though most of their sales are now transacted through the Internet, the company still *puts out* a mail-order catalog⟩ — see PUBLISH 1

put over *vb* to assign to a later time ⟨as a result of a medical emergency, our dream vacation had to be *put over* to the following year⟩ — see POSTPONE

putrefaction *n* the process by which dead organic matter separates into simpler substances ⟨clearing the refrigerator of what the previous tenant had left behind was like taking a course in the advanced *putrefaction* of leftovers⟩ — see CORRUPTION 1

putrefied *adj* having undergone organic breakdown ⟨we had to throw out the *putrefied* tomatoes that had been sitting on the counter all week⟩ — see ROTTEN 1

putrefy *vb* to go through decomposition ⟨we traced the bad smell to a dead skunk *putrefying* under the house⟩ — see DECAY 1

putrescence *n* the process by which dead organic matter separates into simpler substances ⟨in the far corner of the walk-in refrigerator was a crate of cucumbers in an advanced stage of *putrescence*⟩ — see CORRUPTION 1

putrid *adj* having undergone organic breakdown ⟨the *putrid* remains of a dead raccoon on the side of the highway⟩ — see ROTTEN 1

putter (around) *vb* to spend time in aimless activity ⟨I spent all weekend at home just *puttering around*⟩ — see FIDDLE (AROUND)

putterer *n* a person who regularly or occasionally engages in an activity as a pastime rather than as a profession ⟨her husband is an inveterate *putterer*, and their garage is full of half-finished projects he has worked on over the years⟩ — see AMATEUR 1

put through *vb* to carry through (as a process) to completion ⟨the incoming university president is vowing to *put through* the sort of sweeping changes that will propel the school into the top tier academically⟩ — see PERFORM 1

put up *vb* **1** to fix in an upright position ⟨the builders *put up* the walls before starting on the roof⟩ — see ERECT 1
2 to form by putting together parts or materials ⟨plans to *put up* a pavilion in the public gardens⟩ — see BUILD
3 to offer for sale to the public ⟨*put* their possessions *up* for auction⟩ — see MARKET
4 to provide with living quarters or shelter ⟨the university *puts up* students in a variety of buildings⟩ — see HOUSE 1
5 to engage in a secret plan to accomplish evil or unlawful ends ⟨*put up* an elaborate scheme to defraud insurance companies⟩ — see PLOT
6 to place somewhere for safekeeping or ready availability ⟨I need to clear out a space in the garage to *put up* my motorcycle for the winter⟩ — see STORE 1

puzzle *n* something hard to understand or explain ⟨the final fate of the colonists at Roanoke remains a *puzzle* to this very day⟩ — see MYSTERY

puzzle *vb* to throw into a state of mental uncertainty ⟨it is the cause of the disease that *puzzles* doctors⟩ — see CONFUSE 1

puzzle (out) *vb* to find an answer for through reasoning ⟨I was able to *puzzle out* the riddle in a fairly short time⟩ — see SOLVE

puzzlement *n* **1** a state of mental uncertainty ⟨her explanation did little to relieve his *puzzlement*⟩ — see CONFUSION 1
2 something hard to understand or explain ⟨the whole situation remains a *puzzlement* to everyone who was there⟩ — see MYSTERY

pygmy *adj* of a size that is less than average ⟨a *pygmy* elephant⟩ — see SMALL 1

pygmy *also* **pigmy** *n* **1** a living thing much smaller than others of its kind ⟨hummingbirds may be the *pygmies* of the avian world, but what they lack in size they make up for in beauty⟩ — see DWARF 1
2 a person of no importance or influence ⟨regrettably, most of the candidates for the party's nomination that year were political *pygmies*⟩ — see NOBODY

pyrotechnics *n pl* a spectacular display or performance of artistic or technical skill ⟨the film's dazzling *pyrotechnics*, including dynamic editing and fluid cinematography, make it a favorite of cinephiles⟩ — see ACROBATICS

quack *n* one who makes false claims of identity or expertise ‹don't bother to see that guy, as I've heard he's a *quack* with no actual training› — see IMPOSTOR

quacksalver *n* one who makes false claims of identity or expertise ‹the medical impostors on the information superhighway are no more scrupulous than earlier *quacksalvers* who traveled along the streets of towns and villages› — see IMPOSTOR

quad *n* an open space wholly or partly enclosed (as by buildings or walls) ‹the *quad* was the college's time-honored site for protests and celebrations› — see COURT 2

quadrangle *n* an open space wholly or partly enclosed (as by buildings or walls) ‹since the weather was sunny, the convocation was held outside in the college's *quadrangle*› — see COURT 2

quadrate *adj* having four equal sides and four right angles ‹the four museum buildings surround a *quadrate* courtyard that is formally landscaped› — see SQUARE 1

quaff *n* the portion of a serving of a beverage that is swallowed at one time ‹she was so thirsty that she drank her iced tea in one long *quaff*› — see DRINK 2

quaff *vb* to swallow in liquid form ‹after digging our car out of the snowdrift, we were ready to *quaff* some hot chocolate› — see DRINK 1

quagmire *n* **1** a difficult, puzzling, or embarrassing situation from which there is no easy escape ‹the party was once again facing its quadrennial *quagmire*: the candidate sufficiently liberal to win the nomination would be too liberal for the general election› — see PREDICAMENT
2 something that catches and holds ‹a protracted custody dispute that became a judicial *quagmire*› — see WEB 1

quai *n* a structure used by boats and ships for taking on or landing cargo and passengers ‹the tour boat pulled up to the *quai* on the left bank of the Seine› — see DOCK

quail *vb* **1** to draw back in fear, pain, or disgust ‹we *quailed* when the waiter unexpectedly presented us with a hindquarter of frog's legs› — see FLINCH
2 to draw back or crouch down in fearful submission ‹brave resisters who did not *quail* before the tyrant's iron hand› — see COWER

quaint *adj* **1** different from the ordinary in a way that causes curiosity or suspicion ‹the sudden appearance of a man dressed in *quaint* clothes immediately drew the notice of passersby› — see ODD 2
2 pleasantly reminiscent of an earlier time ‹a *quaint* general store on one of the back roads of Vermont› — see OLD-FASHIONED 1

quake *n* a shaking of the earth ‹the *quake* registered 6.5 on the Richter scale, causing widespread damage› — see EARTHQUAKE 1

quake *vb* to make a series of small irregular or violent movements ‹the horror film was so scary it left us *quaking* with fear for hours afterwards› — see SHAKE 1

quaking *adj* marked by or given to small uncontrollable bodily movements ‹found the *quaking* stray dog wandering outside in the rain› — see SHAKY 1

qualification *n* **1** a skill, an ability, or knowledge that makes a person able to do a particular job ‹the fashion firm was looking for an applicant who could list superior sewing skills among his or her *qualifications*›
synonyms capability, credentials, goods, stuff
related words command, expertise, know-how, mastership, mastery, proficiency; ability, capacity, competence, competency, facility, faculty; aptitude, endowment, flair, genius, gift, knack, talent; forte, long suit, métier (*also* metier), specialism, speciality, specialty, strong suit; fitness, suitability, suitableness; makings, potentiality
2 something upon which the carrying out of an agreement or offer depends ‹will give us his permission to go to the conference with the *qualification* that we make up the time later› — see CONDITION 2

qualified *adj* having the required skills for an acceptable level of performance ‹the candidate has demonstrated that he is amply *qualified* for the position› — see COMPETENT 1

qualify *vb* **1** to limit the meaning of (as a noun) ‹*qualifying* the noun "adventure" in the title of your story with a descriptive adjective would make it more attention-grabbing›
synonyms modify
related words alter, color, distort, misrepresent, misstate, pervert, twist, warp; narrow
near antonyms broaden, expand, widen
2 to make competent (as by training, skill, or ability) for a particular office or function ‹raising five children has *qualified* her to be an advice columnist on parenting›
synonyms equip, fit, prepare, ready, season, train
related words accustom, adapt, adjust, condition, groom, habituate, shape, tailor; authorize, entitle; empower, enable; educate, indoctrinate, instruct, school, teach, tutor
3 to give a right to ‹this coupon *qualifies* the bearer for an extra 15% off the discounted price› — see ENTITLE 1
4 to give official or legal power to ‹passing the state bar exam will *qualify* you to practice law› — see AUTHORIZE 1

quality *adj* of the very best kind ‹an antiques dealer who handles nothing but *quality* pieces› — see EXCELLENT

quality *n* **1** degree of excellence ‹we expect a high *quality* of service in such a fancy restaurant›
synonyms caliber (*or* calibre), class, grade, rate
related words hallmark; mark; footing, place, position, rank, standing, stature, status; benchmark, criterion, measure, par, standard, touchstone, yardstick
2 high position within society ‹a glamorous invitation-only party for all the people of *quality* in the summer resort› — see RANK 2
3 something that sets apart an individual from others of the same kind ‹unfailing kindness is one of her many fine *qualities*› — see CHARACTERISTIC
4 the highest class in a society ‹the *quality* were inordinately proud of their bloodlines› — see ARISTOCRACY 1

qualm *n* an uneasy feeling about the rightness of what one is doing or going to do ‹she has no *qualms* about downloading pirated music files from the Internet›
synonyms compunction, misgiving, scruple
related words conscience; distrust, doubt, dubiety, incertitude, misdoubt, mistrust, reservation, skepticism, suspicion, uncertainness, uncertainty; qualmishness, unease, uneasiness; reluctance, unwillingness; demur, fuss, objection, protest, question, remonstrance; aversion, disinclination, indisposition, reluctance, unwillingness; guilt, regret, remorse, self-reproach, shame;

contrition, penitence, repentance
near antonyms aplomb, assurance, certainty, certitude, confidence, conviction, self-assurance, self-confidence, sureness

qualmish *adj* affected with nausea ⟨some passengers felt a little *qualmish* after the bumpy landing on the airstrip⟩ — see NAUSEOUS 1

qualmishness *n* **1** a disturbed condition of the stomach in which one feels like vomiting ⟨her *qualmishness* subsided after she had sipped a little ginger ale⟩ — see NAUSEA 1
2 the tendency to be or state of being squeamish ⟨I can't explain my *qualmishness* about spiders, but for some reason they really bother me⟩ — see DELICACY 3

quandary *n* a situation in which one has to choose between two or more equally unsatisfactory choices ⟨I'm in a *quandary* about whether I should try to repair my stereo or buy a new one, even though I don't have the money to do either⟩ — see DILEMMA 1

quantity *n* **1** a considerable amount ⟨I wish you *quantities* of happiness in the New Year⟩ — see LOT 2
2 a given or particular mass or aggregate of matter ⟨they prepared a huge *quantity* of mashed potatoes for the feast⟩ — see AMOUNT

quantum *n* a given or particular mass or aggregate of matter ⟨the sum of human knowledge is now so immense that even a highly educated person can hope to absorb only a tiny *quantum* of it⟩ — see AMOUNT

quarrel *n* an often noisy or angry expression of differing opinions ⟨a loud *quarrel* erupted at the next table over⟩ — see ARGUMENT 1

quarrel *vb* to express different opinions about something often angrily ⟨the coach and the referee *quarreled* about whether the ball was in bounds⟩ — see ARGUE 2

quarreler *or* **quarreller** *n* a person who takes part in a dispute ⟨known as the *quarreler* in the family, she never dropped an argument, no matter how pointless⟩ — see DISPUTANT

quarrelsome *adj* **1** feeling or displaying eagerness to fight ⟨a *quarrelsome* student who was always being sent to the principal's office for starting fights in the halls⟩ — see BELLIGERENT
2 given to arguing ⟨you're so *quarrelsome*: you can never do anything without a fuss⟩ — see ARGUMENTATIVE 1

quarrelsomeness *n* an inclination to fight or quarrel ⟨a theater critic who was more notable for his *quarrelsomeness* than for his astuteness⟩ — see BELLIGERENCE

quarry *n* an animal that is hunted or killed ⟨a hunter relentlessly tracking his *quarry*⟩ — see PREY 1

quarter *n* **1** an area (as of a city) set apart for some purpose or having some special feature ⟨lived on the edge of the central business *quarter*⟩ — see DISTRICT
2 kind, gentle, or compassionate treatment especially towards someone who is undeserving of it ⟨the coach told the team to show their opponents no *quarter* during the championship game⟩ — see MERCY 1
3 the place where someone is assigned to stand or remain ⟨call the crew to their *quarters* on deck to await further instruction⟩ — see STATION 1
4 quarters *pl* the place where one lives ⟨maintained a level of cleanliness and neatness that was unusual for a bachelor's *quarters*⟩ — see HOME 1

quarter *vb* to provide with living quarters or shelter ⟨the militia is being *quartered* just outside the city⟩ — see HOUSE 1

quarterback *vb* to be in charge of ⟨she was tapped to *quarterback* the upcoming gubernatorial campaign⟩ — see BOSS 1

[1]**quash** *vb* to put a stop to (something) by the use of force ⟨the dictator commanded the army to *quash* the uprising without mercy⟩ — see QUELL 1

[2]**quash** *vb* to put an end to by formal action ⟨attorneys asked the court to *quash* the indictment⟩ — see ABOLISH 1

quashing *n* the doing away with something by formal action ⟨the defense's latest call for the *quashing* of the indictment failed, just as the previous ones had⟩ — see ABOLITION

quaver *vb* to sing with the alternation of two musical tones ⟨know-it-alls snickered as the opera singer *quavered* on the high note⟩ — see WARBLE

quavery *adj* marked by or given to small uncontrollable bodily movements ⟨a *quavery* foal trying to stand for the first time⟩ — see SHAKY 1

quay *n* a structure used by boats and ships for taking on or landing cargo and passengers ⟨docked the ferry at the *quay* to let the passengers off⟩ — see DOCK

quean *n* a boldly flirtatious or sexually promiscuous woman ⟨in pirate tales there's always the raucous tavern and its cadre of buxom *queans*⟩ — see FLOOZY

queasiness *n* **1** a disturbed condition of the stomach in which one feels like vomiting ⟨he still battled *queasiness*, even on large cruise ships⟩ — see NAUSEA 1
2 the tendency to be or state of being squeamish ⟨a girl who has no *queasiness* about bugs at all⟩ — see DELICACY 3

queasy *also* **queazy** *adj* **1** affected with nausea ⟨the youngster felt a little *queasy* after eating too much Easter candy⟩ — see NAUSEOUS 1
2 feeling or showing uncomfortable feelings of uncertainty ⟨since I don't know much about mechanical things, I'm always *queasy* when dealing with auto mechanics⟩ — see NERVOUS 1

queen *n* **1** a usually glamorous woman who is preeminent in her field of activity ⟨during the years that she was *queen* of the figure skating world, the endorsement offers poured in⟩ — see DIVA
2 a lovely woman ⟨most men might not look at her twice, but in her lover's eyes she's a *queen*⟩ — see BEAUTY 2

queenly *adj* fit for or worthy of a royal ruler ⟨a richly appointed, *queenly* bedroom, complete with a massive four-poster bed⟩ — see MONARCHICAL

queer *adj* **1** affected with nausea ⟨eating all of that deep-fried food would make most people feel a little *queer*⟩ — see NAUSEOUS 1
2 different from the ordinary in a way that causes curiosity or suspicion ⟨one competitor had a *queer* way of running that attracted a lot of attention from the spectators⟩ — see ODD 2
3 noticeably different from what is generally found or experienced ⟨a lot of *queer* things started happening almost from the day that we moved into the house⟩ — see UNUSUAL 1
4 having extreme or relentless concern ⟨he's a little *queer* on the subject of astronomy; if you get him going, he'll talk for hours⟩ — see HUNG UP 1
5 being such in appearance only and made or manufactured with the intention of committing fraud ⟨*queer* money that was the work of a master forger⟩ — see COUNTERFEIT 1
6 giving good reason for being doubted, questioned, or challenged ⟨*queer* business practices that bear some looking into⟩ — see DOUBTFUL 2

queerish *adj* **1** affected with nausea ⟨if you don't take that antibiotic with food, you might feel a little *queerish* at first⟩ — see NAUSEOUS 1
2 different from the ordinary in a way that causes curiosity or suspicion ⟨the guy at the bar bought me a drink that left a *queerish* taste in my mouth⟩ — see ODD 2

queerness *n* a disturbed condition of the stomach in which one feels like vomiting ⟨after the roller coaster ride, I had to rest to overcome the dizziness and *queer-*

ness that I was feeling〉— see NAUSEA 1

quell *vb* **1** to put a stop to (something) by the use of force 〈the National Guard was called in to help *quell* the late-night disturbances downtown〉
synonyms clamp down (on), crack down (on), crush, put down, quash, repress, silence, slap down, snuff (out), squash, squelch, subdue, suppress
related words douse (*also* dowse), extinguish, put out, quench; smother, stifle, strangle, throttle; annihilate, decimate, demolish, desolate, destroy, devastate, nuke, rub out, ruin, smash, waste, wreck; exterminate, obliterate, wipe out; conquer, dominate, overcome, overpower, overwhelm, subdue, subjugate, vanquish
phrases sit on
near antonyms abet, aid, assist, back, help, prop up, support; foment, incite, instigate, provoke, stir, whip (up); advance, cultivate, encourage, forward, foster, further, nourish, nurture, promote
2 to stop the noise or speech of 〈the principal held up her hand to *quell* the students so they could hear the urgent announcement〉— see SILENCE 1

quench *vb* **1** to cause to cease burning 〈we thoroughly *quenched* the campfire before we headed to bed〉— see EXTINGUISH 1
2 to put a complete end to (a physical need or desire) 〈this lemonade really *quenches* my thirst〉— see SATISFY 1

quencher *n* a liquid suitable for drinking 〈marathon runners often find that plain water is the best *quencher* of all〉— see DRINK 1

quenchless *adj* incapable of being satisfied 〈the public's *quenchless* need to be entertained throughout the day〉— see INSATIABLE

querulous *adj* given to complaining a lot 〈car trips that were frequently spoiled by a couple of *querulous* passengers in the back〉— see FUSSY 1

query *n* **1** a feeling or attitude that one does not know the truth, truthfulness, or trustworthiness of someone or something 〈readers will likely have a *query* or two about some of the more remarkable episodes in the memoir〉— see DOUBT
2 an act or instance of asking for information 〈please respond to my *query* at your earliest convenience〉— see QUESTION 2

query *vb* **1** to demand proof of the truth or rightness of 〈it seems odd that someone would want two stoves, so you'd better *query* that order〉— see CHALLENGE 1
2 to put a question or questions to 〈*queried* the professor about the assignment〉— see ASK 1
3 to put a series of questions to 〈once the statement was given, the press secretary allowed reporters to *query* the President〉— see EXAMINE 1

quest *n* an act or process of looking carefully or thoroughly for someone or something 〈the Holy Grail was the object of a mystical *quest* by the knights of the Round Table〉— see SEARCH

quest *vb* **1** to ask for (something) earnestly or with authority 〈I respectfully *quest* your assistance in this matter〉— see DEMAND 1
2 to go in search of 〈many daydreamers trekked to California *questing* riches during the great gold rush of 1849〉— see SEEK 1
3 to make a request for 〈please wait until the lecturer specifically *quests* comments from the audience before chiming in〉— see ASK (FOR) 1

question *n* **1** an interrogative expression often used to test knowledge 〈because I have missed so many classes, I had a hard time answering every *question* on today's surprise quiz〉
synonyms interrogative, problem
related words brainteaser, conundrum, poser, puzzle, quiz, riddle, stickler, stumper, toughie (*also* toughy)
near antonyms answer, response, solution
2 an act or instance of asking for information 〈after reading the brief statement to the reporters, the lawyer ended the press conference by saying, "No more *questions*, please"〉 〈the dozens of *questions* researched by the reference librarians〉
synonyms call, inquiry, query, request
related words interrogatory; poll, questionnaire, survey; inquisition, interrogating, interrogation, questioning; examination, exploration, inquest, investigation, probe, probing, research, study
near antonyms answer, reply, response
3 a feeling or declaration of disapproval or dissent 〈that these measurements are accurate is beyond *question*〉— see OBJECTION
4 a major object of interest or concern (as in a discussion or artistic composition) 〈it's a *question* of personal responsibility〉— see MATTER 1

question *vb* **1** to demand proof of the truth or rightness of 〈the teenager openly *questioned* the authority of the town's police force to impose a curfew on residents under the age of 18〉— see CHALLENGE 1
2 to give serious and careful thought to 〈*question* your motives before you file the lawsuit: do you really care about the trees, or are you just trying to harass the neighbors?〉— see PONDER
3 to have no trust or confidence in 〈it was apparent that voters were *questioning* the President's ability to manage the economy〉— see DISTRUST
4 to put a question or questions to 〈the press should be allowed to *question* public officials about any matter of general interest〉— see ASK 1
5 to put a series of questions to 〈the police *questioned* the suspect before deciding that there was insufficient evidence to hold him〉— see EXAMINE 1

questionable *adj* **1** giving good reason for being doubted, questioned, or challenged 〈the runner's unexpected first-place finish is *questionable*, so a drug test has been ordered〉— see DOUBTFUL 2
2 not likely to be true or to occur 〈it's *questionable* that he will show up tonight considering all the bad weather we're having〉— see IMPROBABLE
3 open to question or dispute 〈whether it will rain today or not is *questionable*〉— see DEBATABLE 1

questioner *n* a person who is always ready to doubt or question the truth or existence of something 〈Father Henry is always happy to debate any *questioner* of the faith〉— see SKEPTIC

questioning *adj* inclined to doubt or question claims 〈a naturally *questioning* person, she demands rock-solid proof before she believes anything〉— see SKEPTICAL 1

queue *n* a series of persons or things arranged one behind another 〈join the *queue* to my left if you need to return merchandise〉— see LINE 1

quibble *vb* **1** to make often peevish criticisms or objections about matters that are minor, unimportant, or irrelevant 〈he spent the entire evening *quibbling* about the historical inaccuracies in the television series on World War II〉
synonyms carp, cavil, fuss, niggle, nitpick
related words criticize, fault; beef, bellyache, bitch, complain, crab, croak, gripe, grouse, growl, grumble, kick, kvetch, moan, squawk, squeal, wail, whimper, whine, yammer, yawp (*or* yaup), yowl; murmur, mutter
phrases split hairs
near antonyms applaud, commend, compliment, praise, recommend; approve, back, champion, endorse (*also* indorse), support
2 to express different opinions about something often angrily 〈don't *quibble* over who gets to sit in front〉— see ARGUE 2

quick *adj* **1** having or showing the ability to respond

without delay or hesitation ⟨she's a *quick* wit, always ready with a pun or joke when the moment calls for one⟩
synonyms alacritous, alert, expeditious, prompt, ready, willing
related words receptive, responsive; immediate, instant, instantaneous, summary; breakneck, breathless, brisk, fast, fleet, fleet-footed, hit-and-run, lightning, rapid, rapid-fire, rattling, snappy, speedy, swift, whirlwind; eager, keen, sharp; apt, clever, quick, quick-witted, ready-witted, sharp-witted, smart
near antonyms unresponsive; crawling, creeping, dallying, dawdling, dilatory, dillydallying, dragging, laggard, lagging, lazy, lazyish, leisurely, logy (*also* loggy), poking, poky (*or* pokey), slothful, slow, slowish, sluggish, tardy, unhurried; dormant, idle, inactive, inert
2 having or showing quickness of mind ⟨a *quick* lad, he immediately caught on to how the machinery operated⟩ — see INTELLIGENT 1
3 moving, proceeding, or acting with great speed ⟨a *quick* run through the car wash, and your vehicle will look as good as new⟩ — see FAST 1
4 having or showing life ⟨after the battle, there was a hurried accounting of the *quick* and the dead⟩ — see ALIVE 1
5 able to sense slight impressions or differences ⟨parlayed her *quick* eye for beauty into ownership of a top modeling agency⟩ — see ACUTE 1
6 *archaic* containing unborn young within the body ⟨a woman *quick* with child⟩ — see PREGNANT 1

quick *adv* with great speed ⟨watch out, as the cars pass by here pretty *quick*⟩ — see FAST 1

quick *n* the seat of one's deepest thoughts and emotions ⟨that nasty comment cut me to the *quick*⟩ — see CORE 1

quicken *vb* **1** to cause to move or proceed fast or faster ⟨she eventually *quickened* her pace so she could keep up with the others⟩ — see HURRY 1
2 to give life, vigor, or spirit to ⟨the news that we'd head to Florida for Christmas *quickened* the children, who instantly began jumping for joy⟩ — see ANIMATE

quickly *adv* with great speed ⟨*quickly* moved to block the goal⟩ — see FAST 1

quickness *n* a high rate of movement or performance ⟨his agility and overall *quickness* made him the football coach's top choice for receiver⟩ — see SPEED 1

quicksand *n* something that catches and holds ⟨mired in the *quicksand* of credit card debt⟩ — see WEB 1

quick–tempered *adj* easily irritated or annoyed ⟨a *quick-tempered* man who invariably utters threats at any kids who wander into his yard⟩ — see IRRITABLE

quick–witted *adj* having or showing quickness of mind ⟨the *quick-witted* child easily figured out the trick to making the toy work⟩ — see INTELLIGENT 1

quiddity *n* **1** an odd or peculiar habit ⟨for all of her *quiddities*, she is a very wise and generous lady⟩ — see IDIOSYNCRASY
2 the quality or qualities that make a thing what it is ⟨Rembrandt's genius was his unparalleled ability to render a person's *quiddity* in a single portrait⟩ — see ESSENCE 1

quidnunc *n* a person who habitually reveals personal or sensational facts about others ⟨with the arrival of our other friend, we at last had a quorum of *quidnuncs* and enough material to while away a long lunch hour⟩ — see GOSSIP 1

quid pro quo *n* a giving or taking of one thing of value in return for another ⟨in politics nobody does something for nothing: there's always a *quid pro quo* involved⟩ — see EXCHANGE 1

quiescence *n* **1** a state of temporary inactivity ⟨the resort community's social scene is lively during the summer but undergoes a deep *quiescence* during the long winter⟩ — see ABEYANCE
2 lack of action or activity ⟨was struck by the elk's *quiescence* as it just stood there in the clearing⟩ — see INACTION

quiescent *adj* slow to move or act ⟨a group of *quiescent* loungers recovering from the Thanksgiving feast⟩ — see INACTIVE 1

quiet *adj* **1** free from disturbing noise or uproar ⟨left the din of the rock concert and went to a *quiet* restaurant where we could hear one another talk⟩
synonyms arcadian, calm, hushed, peaceful, placid, restful, serene, still, stilly, tranquil
related words noiseless, silent, soundless; mute, speechless, wordless; dead, motionless, quiescent; muffled, muted, quieted; dull, gentle, low, soft; ultraquiet
near antonyms crazy, tempestuous, wild; blaring, blasting, booming, earsplitting, piercing, roaring, thundering, thunderous
antonyms boisterous, clamorous, clattery, deafening, loud, noisy, raucous, rip-roaring, roistering, romping, rowdy, tumultuous, unquiet, uproarious, woolly (*also* wooly)
2 not excessively showy ⟨she decided that it would be best to wear a *quiet* business suit to the job interview⟩
synonyms conservative, low-key (*also* low-keyed), muted, repressed, restrained, sober, subdued, toned-down, understated, unflashy, unpretentious
related words appropriate, becoming, fit, fitting, proper, suitable; modest, plain, simple, unadorned, undecorated; inconspicuous, unnoticeable, unobtrusive; graceful, handsome, refined, tasteful; drab, mousy (*or* mousey); practical, sensible
near antonyms meretricious; graceless, inelegant, tacky, tasteless, tawdry, trashy, vulgar; baroque, fancy, frilly, gilded (*or* gilt), ornate, rococo; overdecorated, overdone, overwrought
antonyms flamboyant, flaring, flashy, garish, gaudy, glitzy, loud, noisy, ostentatious, razzle-dazzle, splashy, swank (*or* swanky)
3 free from storms or physical disturbance ⟨a *quiet* interlude as the eye of the storm passed over us⟩ — see CALM 1
4 screened or sequestered from view ⟨a *quiet* little house set far back from the street⟩ — see SECLUDED
5 mostly or entirely without sound ⟨a diver who loves to retreat to the *quiet* world beneath the surface of the sea⟩ — see SILENT 3
6 not loud in pitch or volume ⟨*quiet* music is generally more relaxing⟩ — see SOFT 1

quiet *adv* without motion ⟨lie *quiet* and no one will guess you're hiding under the bed⟩ — see STILL 1

quiet *n* **1** a state of freedom from storm or disturbance ⟨sailors enjoying the *quiet* of a clear evening at sea⟩ — see CALM 1
2 the near or complete absence of sound ⟨new parents appreciating the blessed *quiet* that comes when their baby finally falls asleep⟩ — see SILENCE 2

quiet *vb* **1** to become still and orderly ⟨the museum docent told the rowdy youngsters to *quiet* down for the tour⟩
synonyms calm (down), chill out [*slang*], cool, hush, pipe down, settle (down)
related words dry up; relax, tranquilize (*also* tranquillize), unwind, zone out
phrases cool it
near antonyms clown (around), fool around, horse around, monkey (around), show off, skylark
antonyms act up, carry on, cut up
2 to free from distress or disturbance ⟨*quiet* a crying toddler with candy⟩ — see CALM 1
3 to stop the noise or speech of ⟨the nanny could *quiet*

unruly children with just a look⟩ — see SILENCE 1

quiet (down) *vb* to stop talking ⟨the kids *quieted down* when they realized I was about to ask them if they wanted ice cream⟩ — see SHUT UP 1

quieted *adj* mostly or entirely without sound ⟨one could hear a pin drop in the *quieted* concert hall as conductor raised his baton⟩ — see SILENT 3

quieten *vb, chiefly British* **1** to free from distress or disturbance ⟨the nanny tried to *quieten* the children with assurances that help was on its way⟩ — see CALM 1
2 to stop the noise or speech of ⟨one young chap was trying to *quieten* down the group⟩ — see SILENCE 1

quieting *adj* tending to calm the emotions and relieve stress ⟨a nice *quieting* cup of tea after a hard day at work⟩ — see SOOTHING 1

quietly *adv* without motion ⟨she stood *quietly* behind the curtains, hoping to scare her sister when she came into the room⟩ — see STILL 1

quietness *n* **1** a state of freedom from storm or disturbance ⟨preferred the relaxing *quietness* of the mall in the early morning, before the frenzy of shopping began later in the day⟩ — see CALM 1
2 the near or complete absence of sound ⟨the tense *quietness* of the crowd as it anxiously awaited the announcement of the winner⟩ — see SILENCE 2

quietude *n* **1** a state of freedom from storm or disturbance ⟨after his tantrum, the toddler lapsed into an exhausted *quietude* and fell asleep⟩ — see CALM 1
2 the near or complete absence of sound ⟨the *quietude* of the early morning was broken only by the occasional chirping of birds⟩ — see SILENCE 2

quietus *n* **1** a freeing from an obligation or responsibility ⟨was granted a *quietus* on the remainder of the debt in the old man's will⟩ — see RELEASE 1
2 the permanent stopping of all the vital bodily activities ⟨her unshakable belief in a blissful afterlife allowed her to meet her *quietus* without the slightest tinge of fear or regret⟩ — see DEATH 1

quintessence *n* **1** the most perfect type or example ⟨the Parthenon in Greece was considered the *quintessence* of the perfectly proportioned building⟩
synonyms acme, apotheosis, beau ideal, byword, classic, epitome, exemplar, ideal, perfection
related words archetype, model, prototype; paradigm, standard; nonpareil, paragon; abstract, avatar, embodier, embodiment, incarnation, incorporation, manifestation, personification; height, last word, meridian, ultimate, zenith; benchmark, criterion, touchstone, yardstick
2 the quality or qualities that make a thing what it is ⟨a selfless desire to help others is the *quintessence* of the virtue of charity⟩ — see ESSENCE 1

quintessential *adj* constituting, serving as, or worthy of being a pattern to be imitated ⟨Helen of Troy was supposedly the *quintessential* beauty of the ancient world⟩ — see MODEL

quip *n* **1** an odd or peculiar habit ⟨has his share of the *quips* that seem to come with a title of nobility⟩ — see IDIOSYNCRASY
2 something said or done to cause laughter ⟨the crowd laughed aloud at the author's clever *quip*⟩ — see JOKE 1

quip *vb* to make jokes ⟨she rolled her eyes at her brother's bragging and *quipped*, "You're a legend in your own mind, all right"⟩ — see JOKE 1

quirk *n* an odd or peculiar habit ⟨wearing red shoes every day is just one of her *quirks*⟩ — see IDIOSYNCRASY

quirky *adj* different from the ordinary in a way that causes curiosity or suspicion ⟨the waitress styles her hair in a *quirky* way that always gets her remembered by customers⟩ — see ODD 2

quisling *n* one who betrays a trust or an allegiance ⟨warned that all *quislings* would be punished without mercy⟩ — see TRAITOR

quit *adj* no longer burdened with something unpleasant or painful ⟨I am finally *quit* of that terrible task⟩ — see FREE 2

quit *vb* **1** to give up (a job or office) ⟨he decided to *quit* his job at the fast-food restaurant⟩
synonyms bag, chuck, leave, resign (from), retire (from), step aside (from), step down (from)
related words abandon, vacate; drop out (of), throw up
phrases give notice
near antonyms hire (out *or* on)
antonyms stay (at)
2 to stop doing (something) permanently ⟨her doctor told her it was high time she *quit* smoking⟩
synonyms abandon, discontinue, drop, give up, knock off, lay off (of), pack (up *or* in)
related words break off, break up, cease, close, conclude, end, expire, finish, halt, leave off, shut off; pause, taper off; throw up; round (off *or* out), terminate, wind up, wrap up
phrases hang it up, have done (with)
near antonyms go, run on; hang in, hang on, hold on, persevere, persist; follow through (with); renew, reopen, restart, resume; preserve, stay; begin, commence, start
antonyms carry on, continue, keep, keep up, maintain
3 to bring (as an action or operation) to an immediate end ⟨*quit* pestering your coworkers with pointless questions⟩ — see STOP 1
4 to cause to remain behind ⟨he *quit* the house sometime around nine this morning and hasn't been seen since⟩ — see LEAVE 1
5 to cease resistance (as to another's arguments, demands, or control) ⟨tried to persuade his daughter to remain at home, but eventually he just *quit* and let her go out on her own⟩ — see YIELD 3
6 to come to an end ⟨will this teasing ever *quit*?⟩ — see CEASE 1
7 to give what is owed for ⟨eager to *quit* all debts before starting married life⟩ — see PAY 2
8 to leave a place often for another ⟨we plan to *quit* the amusement park around seven tonight and then head to the diner for some food⟩ — see GO 2
9 to manage the actions of (oneself) in a particular way ⟨I thought the kids *quitted* themselves quite well at the concert tonight⟩ — see BEHAVE

quitclaim *n* a document containing a declaration of an intentional giving up of a right, claim, or privilege ⟨the city signed a *quitclaim* to the property, and now the company can go forward with its plans for expansion⟩ — see WAIVER

quite *adv* **1** to a full extent or degree ⟨are you *quite* sure you have permission to go?⟩ — see FULLY 1
2 to some degree or extent ⟨we camped *quite* near Mount Rushmore⟩ — see FAIRLY 1

quittance *n* **1** a freeing from an obligation or responsibility ⟨the indentured servant obtained a *quittance* from his master stating he was free to leave and was no longer required to work⟩ — see RELEASE 1
2 payment to another for a loss or injury ⟨the court awarded the plaintiff a substantial *quittance* for bodily injury and emotional distress⟩ — see COMPENSATION 1

quitting *n* the act of leaving a place ⟨we simply didn't know what to make of the couple's sudden *quitting* of the party⟩ — see DEPARTURE 1

quiver *n* an instance of shaking involuntarily with fear or cold ⟨a *quiver* ran through the audience when the monster cornered the movie's hero⟩ — see SHIVER 1

quiver *vb* to make a series of small irregular or violent movements ⟨aspen leaves *quivering* in the breeze⟩ — see SHAKE 1

quivering *adj* marked by or given to small uncontrollable bodily movements ⟨our *quivering* dog tried to hide under the bed during the thunderstorm⟩ — see SHAKY 1

quivering *n* a series of slight movements by a body back and forth or from side to side ⟨the kids were fascinated by the *quivering* of the jellyfish and kept poking it to see it wiggle⟩ — see VIBRATION 1

qui vive *n* the state of being constantly attentive and responsive to signs of opportunity, activity, or danger ⟨an army on the *qui vive* for enemy attack⟩ — see VIGILANCE

quixotic *adj* having or marked by a tendency to be guided more by ideals than by reality ⟨in this age of giant chain stores, any attempt at operating an independent bookstore must be regarded as *quixotic*⟩ — see IDEALISTIC

quixotical *adj* having or marked by a tendency to be guided more by ideals than by reality ⟨a *quixotical* attempt to bring live theater to a generation hooked on video games⟩ — see IDEALISTIC

quiz *n* **1** a person who causes repeated emotional pain, distress, or annoyance to another ⟨always eager to put everything down, my boyfriend had to be a *quiz* and make fun of the actors and costumes in our local theater troupe's latest production⟩ — see TORMENTOR
2 a set of questions or problems designed to assess knowledge, skills, or intelligence ⟨according to the magazine's marriage *quiz*, the chances that we'll have a 10th wedding anniversary are just about nil⟩ — see EXAMINATION 1
3 a person of odd or whimsical habits ⟨even by House of Lords standards, the cross-dressing earl was considered quite a *quiz*⟩ — see ECCENTRIC

quiz *vb* **1** to put a question or questions to ⟨quickly *quizzed* her about the assignment before heading off to class⟩ — see ASK 1
2 to put a series of questions to ⟨hated the way those relatives would *quiz* me about my partner and our living arrangements⟩ — see EXAMINE 1

quizzer *n* a person who causes repeated emotional pain, distress, or annoyance to another ⟨some *quizzer* in the front row was getting more laughs than the comedian on stage⟩ — see TORMENTOR

quizzical *adj* marked by or expressive of mild or good-natured teasing ⟨my puns are usually greeted with loud *quizzical* groans by my so-called friends⟩
synonyms bantering, chaffing, fooling, funning, jesting, joking, joshing, kidding, rallying, razzing, ribbing
related words bandying, quipping; baiting, deriding, derisive, derisory, hassling, heckling, jeering, mocking, needling, ridiculing, taunting; contemptuous, disdainful, sarcastic, scornful

quod *n, British slang* a place of confinement for persons held in lawful custody ⟨the robbers who made off with nearly a half million pounds will likely spend a good long time in *quod*⟩ — see JAIL

quondam *adj* having been such at some previous time ⟨a *quondam* oil baron now living comfortably in retirement⟩ — see FORMER 1

quota *n* something belonging to, due to, or contributed by an individual member of a group ⟨you need to meet your sales *quota*, or you'll be put on probation⟩ — see SHARE 1

quotation *n* a passage referred to, repeated, or offered as an example ⟨the beautiful autumn day brought to mind this *quotation* from Thoreau: "So live in each season as it passes; breathe the air, drink the drink, taste the fruit, and resign yourself to the influences of each"⟩
synonyms citation, quote
related words allusion, reference; excerpt, extract; line, part, section; snippet

quote *n* a passage referred to, repeated, or offered as an example ⟨he got a book of *quotes* from his favorite author for his birthday⟩ — see QUOTATION

quote *vb* **1** to give as an example ⟨I could *quote* to you a hundred instances in the past when you've lied to me⟩
synonyms adduce, cite, instance, mention
related words exemplify, represent; advert (to), illustrate, instance, name, refer (to), specify, touch (on *or* upon); bear out, corroborate, document, substantiate, validate; reference, source
2 to make reference to or speak about briefly but specifically ⟨*quoted* Thomas Jefferson's views on liberty in her paper on the American Revolution⟩ — see MENTION 1
3 to say after another ⟨don't *quote* this to anyone, but I think we're going to Veracruz for winter vacation⟩ — see REPEAT 3

quotidian *adj* **1** often observed or encountered ⟨not content with the *quotidian* quarrels that other couples had, they had rows that shook the entire neighborhood⟩ — see COMMON 1
2 occurring, done, produced, or appearing every day ⟨plagued by a *quotidian* coughing fit, the result of years of smoking⟩ — see DAILY

R

rabbit hole *n* a difficult, puzzling, or embarrassing situation from which there is no easy escape ⟨shoreline residents are finding themselves helplessly falling down a *rabbit hole* in their Sisyphean efforts to halt beach erosion⟩ — see PREDICAMENT

rabbit warren *n* a confusing and complicated arrangement of passages ⟨the organization's headquarters is a *rabbit warren* of small, cramped offices⟩ — see MAZE 1

rabble *n* people looked down upon as ignorant and of the lowest class ⟨the crown prince was reminded that even the *rabble* of the realm deserved his attention and compassion⟩

synonyms proletariat, rabblement, ragtag and bobtail, riffraff, rout, scum, tag, rag, and bobtail (*or* tagrag and bobtail), trash, unwashed

related words dregs; commoners, commons, herd, hoi polloi, masses, millions, mob, multitude, people, plebeians, populace, public, rank and file; bourgeoisie, middle class, working class

near antonyms elect, establishment; gentlefolk (*also* gentlefolks), nobility, peerage

antonyms A-list, aristocracy, elite, gentry, quality, society, upper class, upper crust

rabblement *n* people looked down upon as ignorant and of the lowest class ⟨haughty nobles who ignored the *rabblement* at their own peril⟩ — see RABBLE

rabble–rouser *n* a person who stirs up public feelings especially of discontent ⟨*rabble-rousers* inciting hungry people in breadlines to demand social justice⟩ — see AGITATOR

rabid *adj* **1** being very far from the center of public opinion ⟨soccer fans whose *rabid* enthusiasm makes them go berserk when their team wins⟩ — see EXTREME 2

2 feeling or showing anger ⟨he became *rabid* when the bank manager told him he would lose the family farm if he didn't pay the mortgage⟩ — see ANGRY

3 marked by bursts of destructive force or intense activity ⟨a *rabid* nationalism that leads people to attack immigrants and anyone else they perceive as being different⟩ — see VIOLENT 1

4 marked by great and often stressful excitement or activity ⟨the *rabid* witch hunts that occurred in Salem in 1692, when 150 people were accused of witchcraft and imprisoned⟩ — see FURIOUS 1

race *n* **1** a group of persons who come from the same ancestor ⟨a man, born of noble *race*, who was now living in impoverished circumstances⟩ — see FAMILY 1

2 a people having a common language, culture, and body of traditions ⟨Winston Churchill's famous hope and prediction that World War II would be remembered by future generations as the finest hour of the Britannic *race*⟩ — see NATIONALITY

race *vb* **1** to engage in a contest ⟨just how many candidates are *racing* for the senatorial seat this year?⟩ — see COMPETE

2 to proceed or move quickly ⟨was *racing* around trying to get everything done before her big trip to India⟩ — see HURRY 2

racecourse *n* an open man-made passageway for water ⟨fell into the *racecourse* for an abandoned water mill⟩ — see CHANNEL 1

raceway *n* an open man-made passageway for water ⟨the child who fell through the ice was helplessly swept along the *raceway*, still trapped under the ice, by the current⟩ — see CHANNEL 1

racial *adj* of, relating to, or reflecting the traits exhibited by a group of people with a common ancestry and culture ⟨humanitarian aid workers are often given special training to help them understand the *racial* differences between them and the people they will be serving⟩

synonyms ethnic, ethnical, tribal

related words familial; folk; kin, kindred; cultural, multiculti, multicultural, national

antonyms nonracial

racialism *n* **1** the belief that certain races of people are by birth and nature superior to others ⟨the *racialism* of some of the nation's founders seems to contradict their professed belief that "all men are created equal"⟩ — see RACISM 1

2 hatred of or discrimination against a person or persons based on their race ⟨ugly incidents of *racialism* at the school have decreased since the introduction of multiracial rap sessions⟩ — see RACISM 2

racialist *n* a person who believes that one race should control all others ⟨unfortunately, there are still *racialists* who adhere to the belief that there is one superior race⟩ — see SUPREMACIST

racism *n* **1** the belief that certain races of people are by birth and nature superior to others ⟨Hitler's declaration of his belief in a "master race" was an indication of the inherent *racism* of the Nazi movement⟩

synonyms racialism

related words apartheid, segregation, separatism; eugenics

near antonyms desegregation, integration

2 hatred of or discrimination against a person or persons based on their race ⟨the 1963 bombing of the Sixteenth Street Baptist Church in Birmingham, Alabama, was one of the most notorious incidents of *racism* that occurred during the civil rights movement of the 1960s⟩

synonyms prejudice, racialism

related words race-baiting; apartheid, jim crow, segregation, separatism; bigotry, intolerance, narrow-mindedness, narrowness

near antonyms antidiscrimination, antiracism, antisegregation; assimilationism

racist *n* a person who believes that one race should control all others ⟨after the passage of the 13th Amendment to the Constitution, *racists* still used violence and intimidation to prevent African-Americans from enjoying their new constitutional rights⟩ — see SUPREMACIST

rack *n* **1** a place set aside for sleeping ⟨the clock struck midnight, signaling that it was time to hit the *rack*⟩ — see BED 1

2 a state of great suffering of body or mind ⟨after experiencing the *rack* of a divorce, he was reluctant to commit to another relationship⟩ — see DISTRESS 1

rack *vb* **1** to cause persistent suffering to ⟨the young man was *racked* with guilt over the lie he had told to his parents⟩ — see AFFLICT

2 to injure by overuse, misuse, or pressure ⟨she *racked* her brain trying to remember where she'd put the money⟩ — see STRAIN 1

racket *n* loud, confused, and usually inharmonious sound ⟨if all the *racket* on the stairs is any indication, someone must be moving into apartment 3B⟩ — see NOISE 1

racketeer *n* a person who gets money from another by using force or threats ⟨the *racketeer* threatened to have his thugs vandalize the shop if the shopkeeper didn't pay him a monthly bribe⟩
synonyms blackmailer, extortioner, extortionist
related words blackhander, button man, gangster, hoodlum, mafioso, mobster; bully, ruffian, thug; cheat, cheater, chiseler (*or* chiseller), cozener, defrauder, dodger, double-dealer, gouger, gyp, hustler, profiteer, shark, sharper, sharpie (*or* sharpy), swindler

rackety *adj* **1** making loud, confused, and usually unharmonious sounds ⟨anyone operating that *rackety* machine had better wear earplugs⟩ — see NOISY 1
2 full of or characterized by the presence of noise ⟨the once-familiar sight of a *rackety* newspaper office with reporters pounding away at typewriters⟩ — see NOISY 2

racking *adj* intensely or unbearably painful ⟨a *racking* cough kept him awake all night⟩ — see EXCRUCIATING 1

rack up *vb* **1** to gain (as points or runs in a game) as credit towards one's total number of points ⟨having *racked up* a huge number of points in the short program, the figure skater would have to have a disastrous long program in order to miss out on a medal⟩ — see SCORE 2
2 to obtain (as a goal) through effort ⟨*racked up* their second consecutive Super Bowl victory⟩ — see ACHIEVE 1

racy *adj* **1** having much high-spirited energy and movement ⟨vivid writing and a *racy* plot that keeps readers turning the pages⟩ — see LIVELY 1
2 hinting at or intended to call to mind matters regarded as indecent ⟨a raunchy comedy with language that was a little too *racy* for an eight-year-old child⟩ — see SUGGESTIVE 1

raddled *adj* suffering from mental confusion ⟨trying to explain a mix-up in my mail order to a clearly *raddled* clerk in customer service⟩ — see DIZZY 2

radiance *n* **1** the quality or state of having or giving off light ⟨the *radiance* of the midday sun created a harsh glare for the skiers⟩ — see BRILLIANCE 1
2 the steady giving off of the form of radiation that makes vision possible ⟨had a dream in which she was steadily moving down a dark tunnel toward a *radiance* at the far end⟩ — see LIGHT 1

radiant *adj* **1** having or being an outward sign of good feelings (as of love, confidence, or happiness) ⟨she left the interview with a *radiant* smile on her face, confident she had gotten the job⟩ ⟨a *radiant* bride⟩
synonyms aglow, beaming, bright, glowing, sunny
related words brilliant, dazzling, effulgent, gleaming, luminous, refulgent, shining, starry; blithe, blithesome, bright, cheerful, cheery, chipper, gay, gladsome, lightsome, merry, mirthful, optimistic, upbeat; jocund, jovial, laughing, smiling; blooming, rosy; blissful, chuffed [*British*], delighted, gratified, happy, joyful, joyous, pleased, satisfied, thankful, tickled
near antonyms blank, flat, listless, stoic (*or* stoical), unemotional; black, dark, darkening, depressing, dismal, gloomy, glum, gray (*also* grey), melancholy, sullen; frowning, glaring, glowering, lowering (*also* louring), scowling
2 giving off or reflecting much light ⟨from the plane we could see the statehouse's *radiant* gold dome⟩ — see BRIGHT 1

radiantly *adv* in a manner marked by the shining or reflecting of much light ⟨under a *radiantly* clear sky, we raised our anchor and set off on a carefree cruise⟩ — see BRIGHTLY 1

radiate *vb* **1** to extend outwards from or as if from a central point ⟨the heat *radiating* from the fire⟩ ⟨the spokes of a bicycle wheel *radiate* from the hub towards the rim⟩
synonyms branch, fan (out), ray
related words diffuse, dispel, disperse, dissipate; fork, stem; diverge, divide, part, ramify, separate, split, uncouple, unlink, unyoke; scatter, splay, spread; arise, derive, emanate, flow, issue, proceed, spring
near antonyms approach, close in (on), near; center (on), centralize; connect, couple, join, link, unite
antonyms concentrate, converge, focus, funnel, meet
2 to emit rays of light ⟨fireflies give off their light by means of a chemical reaction that causes their abdomens to *radiate*⟩ — see SHINE 1
3 to throw or give off ⟨the sun *radiates* tiny amounts of energy in the form of microwaves⟩ — see EMIT 1

radical *adj* **1** being very far from the center of public opinion ⟨the baggy trousers that Amelia Bloomer introduced in the 1850s were considered a *radical* form of dress for women at the time⟩ — see EXTREME 2
2 not bound by traditional ways or beliefs ⟨*radical* proponents of spelling reform would have every word spelled "just the way it sounds"⟩ — see LIBERAL 1
3 *slang* of the very best kind ⟨surfing conditions at virtually all of the beaches along the coast were truly *radical*⟩ — see EXCELLENT

radical *n* a person who favors rapid and sweeping changes especially in laws and methods of government ⟨*radicals* staged large, violent protests in the hopes of toppling the government⟩
synonyms crazy, extremist, revolutionary, revolutionist
related words young Turk; leftist, lefty, red; progressive, reformer, reformist; anarch, anarchist, subversive; agitator, insurgent, insurrectionist, rebel; secessionist, separationist, separatist
near antonyms conservative, fuddy-duddy, reactionary, rightist, standpatter, Tory, traditionalist
antonyms middle-of-the-roader, moderate

raffish *adj* lacking in refinement or good taste ⟨the dowager cringed at the thought of *raffish* tourists in rough boots tromping all over her Persian rugs⟩ — see COARSE 2

raffishness *n* the quality or state of lacking refinement or good taste ⟨the *raffishness* of the crowd in the pub offended the courtly gentleman, and so he elected instead to dine at the hotel⟩ — see VULGARITY 1

raffle *n* discarded or useless material ⟨the front lawn was littered with the *raffle* that the roofers had left behind⟩ — see GARBAGE 1

raft *n* a considerable amount ⟨the babysitter had to listen to a whole *raft* of rules before she was allowed to even pick up the baby⟩ — see LOT 2

[1]rag *n* **1** a publication that appears at regular intervals ⟨the local *rag* publishes more gossip than news⟩ — see JOURNAL 1
2 rags *pl* covering for the human body ⟨the girls showed up at the prom wearing their most elegant *rags*⟩ — see CLOTHING

[2]rag *n, chiefly British* a playful or mischievous act intended as a joke ⟨a collegiate *rag* that nearly got him sent down from Oxford⟩ — see PRANK

rag *vb* to criticize (someone) severely or angrily especially for personal failings ⟨several readers called in to *rag* the editor for his paper's repeated grammatical lapses⟩ — see SCOLD

ragbag *n* an unorganized collection or mixture of various things ⟨gave away a *ragbag* of souvenirs and trinkets she had accumulated over the years⟩ — see MISCELLANY 1

rage *n* **1** a state of wildly excited activity or emotion ⟨found her at home in a *rage* of scrubbing and cleaning

in preparation for the rabbi's visit⟩ — see FRENZY
2 an intense emotional state of displeasure with someone or something ⟨boiling with *rage* at the bank teller's insult, he demanded to see the manager⟩ — see ANGER
3 a practice or interest that is very popular for a short time ⟨there was time when playing with Frisbees was all the *rage*⟩ — see FAD
4 *archaic* a serious mental disorder that prevents one from living a safe and normal life ⟨the king's last years were spent in a lonely *rage*⟩ — see INSANITY 1

rage *vb* **1** to express one's anger usually violently ⟨the bad call prompted the coach to *rage* about the refereeing, even throwing his clipboard at one referee⟩
synonyms bristle, fume, storm
related words blow up, flare (up), flip (out) [*slang*]; bluster, carry on, fulminate, rampage, rant, rave, take on; burn, foam, seethe, smolder (*or* smoulder), steam; chafe, fret, stew
phrases make a scene, run amok (*or* run amuck)
near antonyms allay, appease, pacify, soothe; check, choke (back), collect, compose, contain, curb, pocket, rein, repress, restrain, smother, stifle, strangle, subdue, suppress, swallow; moderate, temper, tone (down); ease, let up, relax; calm, cool, hush, quell, quiet, settle, still
2 to be excited or emotionally stirred up with anger ⟨still *raging* about his assistant's burnt pies, the pastry cook forgot to add the egg whites to his cake batter⟩ — see BOIL 1

ragged *adj* **1** having an uneven edge or outline ⟨the Rocky Mountains cut an angular, *ragged* profile against the sky, in contrast to the rounded silhouette of the rolling, green Adirondack Mountains⟩
synonyms broken, craggy, jagged, scraggly, scraggy
related words saw-toothed, serrate, serrated; harsh, rough, roughened, rugged; bumpy, coarse, irregular, nonuniform
near antonyms regular, uniform; flat, flush, level, plane
antonyms clean, even, smooth, soft, unbroken
2 worn or torn into or as if into rags ⟨finally convinced her to throw away her favorite pair of jeans, *ragged* from decades of yard work⟩
synonyms frayed, raggedy, ratty, seedy, shabby, tattered, threadbare, worn-out
related words dowdy, scruffy, tatterdemalion; dingy, faded; lacerate (*or* lacerated), shredded; holey, patchy; broken-down, decrepit, dilapidated, dog-eared, grungy, mangy, moth-eaten, run-down, scuzzy [*slang*], tacky
near antonyms brand-new, new, spick-and-span (*or* spic-and-span), unused
3 not having a level or smooth surface ⟨she cut herself on the *ragged* edge of the tin can's lid⟩ — see UNEVEN 1
4 wearing torn or worn out clothes ⟨*ragged* and hungry refugees emerging from the jungle where they had been in hiding for weeks⟩ — see TATTERED 1

raggedy *adj* **1** wearing torn or worn out clothes ⟨*raggedy* urchins playing in the village streets⟩ — see TATTERED 1
2 worn or torn into or as if into rags ⟨wears *raggedy* old T-shirts and jeans around the house⟩ — see RAGGED 2

raggle–taggle *adj* consisting of many things of different sorts ⟨a *raggle-taggle* assemblage of collectibles that he hopes to sell on eBay⟩ — see MISCELLANEOUS

raging *adj* intensely or unbearably painful ⟨I've had a *raging* headache⟩ — see EXCRUCIATING 1

ragout *n* an unorganized collection or mixture of various things ⟨the movie is an uncertain *ragout* of fantasy, science fiction, and old-fashioned romance⟩ — see MISCELLANY 1

ragtag *adj* **1** consisting of many things of different sorts ⟨the team was a *ragtag* bunch who had only one thing in common: a lack of skill⟩ — see MISCELLANEOUS
2 wearing torn or worn out clothes ⟨a *ragtag* and weary regiment arrived back at headquarters with the latest news from the front⟩ — see TATTERED 1

ragtag and bobtail *n* people looked down upon as ignorant and of the lowest class ⟨locals complained that rental housing would attract the *ragtag and bobtail* to their well-groomed suburb⟩ — see RABBLE

raid *n* **1** a sudden attack on and entrance into hostile territory ⟨repeated Viking *raids* wore down the defenses of the seaside village⟩
synonyms descent, foray, incursion, inroad, invasion, irruption
related words pillage, plunder; aggression, assault, coup de main, offense (*or* offence), offensive, onset, onslaught, rush, siege, storm, strike; charge, sally, sortie; ambuscade, ambush, surprise (*also* surprize), trap; air raid, blitz, blitzkrieg, bombardment; counteraggression, counterassault, counterattack, counteroffensive, counterstrike
2 the act or action of setting upon with force or violence ⟨an early morning *raid* by Federal agents took the smugglers in their hideout by surprise⟩ — see ATTACK 1

raid *vb* **1** to enter for conquest or plunder ⟨a fox has been *raiding* the chicken coop, and now we're down to eight hens⟩ — see INVADE
2 to take sudden, violent action against ⟨the enemy tribe *raided* the village just before dawn, taking everyone by surprise⟩ — see ATTACK 1

raider *n* one that starts armed conflict against another especially without reasonable cause ⟨villagers lived in constant fear of the *raiders*, who captured their women and children and sold them into slavery⟩ — see AGGRESSOR

rail *n* **1** a protective barrier consisting of a horizontal bar and its supports ⟨the stairs are icy, so hold onto the *rail*⟩ — see RAILING
2 a roadway overlaid with parallel steel rails over which trains travel ⟨an abandoned stretch of *rail* that was overgrown with brush⟩ — see RAILROAD

rail (at *or* against) *vb* to criticize (someone) severely or angrily especially for personal failings ⟨we could hear the cook in the kitchen *railing against* his assistant and wondered if we'd ever get our food⟩ — see SCOLD

railing *n* a protective barrier consisting of a horizontal bar and its supports ⟨they had to put a childproof *railing* on the balcony when the baby started walking⟩
synonyms balustrade, banister (*also* bannister), guardrail, rail
related words handrail; taffrail; fender

raillery *n* good-natured teasing or exchanging of clever remarks ⟨Luke had to put up with a lot of *raillery* from his sister the first time he asked a girl for a date⟩ — see BANTER

railroad *n* a roadway overlaid with parallel steel rails over which trains travel ⟨that *railroad* hasn't been used for passenger trains for decades⟩
synonyms rail, railway, road
related words el, elevated, elevated railroad; monorail

railway *n* a roadway overlaid with parallel steel rails over which trains travel ⟨a system of *railways* that crisscrosses the whole nation⟩ — see RAILROAD

raiment *n* covering for the human body ⟨the prince exchanged his silken *raiment* for the pauper's humble homespun⟩ — see CLOTHING

rain *n* **1** a steady falling of water from the sky in significant quantity ⟨the *rain* continued for most of the day⟩
synonyms cloudburst, deluge, downfall, downpour, rainfall, rainstorm, storm, wet
related words precipitation, shower; thundershower, thunderstorm, weather

near antonyms drizzle, mist, mizzle, scud, spit, sprinkle

2 a heavy fall of objects ⟨the Norman invaders fled when the castle's defenders threw a *rain* of stones down upon them⟩

synonyms hail, shower, storm

related words barrage, bombardment, broadside, cannonade, fusillade, salvo, volley; flood, gush, rush, spate, torrent; eruption, outbreak, outburst

rain *vb* 1 to fall as water in a continuous stream of drops from the clouds ⟨it started *raining* early this morning and hasn't let up since⟩

synonyms pour, precipitate, storm

related words shower; spit; hail, rainsquall, squall; deluge, drown, engulf, flood, inundate, swamp

phrases rain cats and dogs

near antonyms drizzle, mist, mizzle, spit, sprinkle

2 to give readily and in large quantities ⟨she *rained* praise upon her graduating students⟩ ⟨the squadron *rained* bombs on the enemy's fortifications⟩

synonyms heap, lavish, pour, shower

related words gush, stream; flood, inundate, overflow, overwhelm, swamp; bombard, hail

near antonyms hold back, keep, reserve, retain, withhold

rainbow *adj* marked by a variety of usually vivid colors ⟨the *rainbow* costumes worn by mummers at Mardi Gras⟩ — see COLORFUL

raincoat *n* a coat made of water-resistant material ⟨I grabbed my umbrella and *raincoat* before going out in the thunderstorm⟩

synonyms mac (*or* mack) [*British*], mackintosh (*also* macintosh) [*chiefly British*], oilskin, slicker, waterproof [*chiefly British*]

related words rain gear, rainwear; poncho, sou'wester, trench, trench coat

rainfall *n* a steady falling of water from the sky in significant quantity ⟨a torrential *rainfall* washed away most of the little sprouts in our vegetable garden⟩ — see RAIN 1

rainspout *n* a pipe or channel for carrying off water from a roof ⟨heavy rains had left a large puddle at the base of the *rainspout*⟩ — see GUTTER 1

rainstorm *n* a steady falling of water from the sky in significant quantity ⟨we ran into a big *rainstorm* on Highway 6, and the visibility was so poor we had to pull over⟩ — see RAIN 1

rainy *adj* marked by or abounding with rain ⟨found that the cold, *rainy* weather made his joints swell and ache⟩

synonyms pouring, precipitating, stormy, wet

related words drippy, drizzling, drizzly, misty, mizzly, spitting, sprinkling

near antonyms dry

raise *n* something added (as by growth) ⟨the school board approved a *raise* in the maximum family income for students qualifying for reduced-price lunches⟩ — see INCREASE 1

raise *vb* 1 to move from a lower to a higher place or position ⟨he asked members of the audience to *raise* their hands if they knew anyone who suffered from alcoholism⟩

synonyms boost, crane, elevate, heave, heft, heighten, hike, hoist, jack (up), lift, perk (up), pick up, take up, up, uphold, uplift, upraise

related words ascend, mount, rise; rear, upend

near antonyms descend, dip, fall, pitch, plunge, slip; bear, depress, press, push; sink, submerge

antonyms drop, lower

2 to bring to maturity through care and education ⟨since she was only two when her mother died, the girl was *raised* mainly by her aunt⟩ — see BRING UP 1

3 to bring (something volatile or intense) into being ⟨a proposal to cover the library's red brick with vinyl siding *raised* a mighty ruckus with those favoring historical preservation⟩ — see INCITE 1

4 to draw out (something hidden, latent, or reserved) ⟨the lawsuit *raised* old hatreds that had never been completely extinguished⟩ — see EDUCE

5 to fix in an upright position ⟨the mattress will fit into the moving truck only if we *raise* it on its side⟩ — see ERECT 1

6 to form by putting together parts or materials ⟨*raised* a memorial on the site of the accident in memory of those who had been killed⟩ — see BUILD

7 to look after or assist the growth of by labor and care ⟨*raises* ducks, geese, and other exotic fowl ultimately destined for the dinner table⟩ — see GROW 1

8 to make greater in size, amount, or number ⟨the multiplex *raised* the minimum age for paid admissions from four to six⟩ — see INCREASE 1

9 to move higher in rank or position ⟨he was recently *raised* to lieutenant in the fire department⟩ — see PROMOTE 1

10 to present or bring forward for discussion ⟨one member of the tour *raised* the subject of appropriate attire for visits to sacred sites in the Holy Land⟩ — see INTRODUCE 2

11 to make known (as an idea, emotion, or opinion) ⟨too afraid to *raise* an objection⟩ — see EXPRESS 1

raised *adj* 1 being at a higher level than average ⟨due to *raised* levels of mercury in the water, there is a warning against eating the local shrimp⟩ — see HIGH 2

2 being positioned above a surface ⟨directed the filming of the movie's battle scene from a *raised* platform⟩ — see ELEVATED 1

3 rising straight up ⟨the 63 Braille characters are made up of one to six *raised* dots arranged in a matrix⟩ — see ERECT

[1]rake *n* a person who has sunk below the normal moral standard ⟨a memoir that purported to be a *rake's* progress through the world of drug addiction⟩ — see DEGENERATE

[2]rake *n* the degree to which something rises up from a position level with the horizon ⟨the floor of the auditorium doesn't have much of a *rake*, so sightlines for spectators in the rear are not good⟩ — see SLANT 1

rake *vb* to look through (as a place) carefully or thoroughly in an effort to find or discover something ⟨the pathetic sight of hungry children *raking* the garbage for food⟩ — see SEARCH 1

raked *adj* running in a slanting direction ⟨the *raked* seating in the auditorium affords theatergoers an unobstructed view of the stage⟩ — see DIAGONAL

rakehell *n* a person who has sunk below the normal moral standard ⟨a resort popular with wealthy *rakehells* and the women who love their money⟩ — see DEGENERATE

rakehell *or* **rakehelly** *adj* having or showing lowered moral character or standards ⟨a *rakehell* rock band that was notorious for trashing virtually every hotel suite they ever stayed in⟩ — see CORRUPT

rakish *adj* having or showing lowered moral character or standards ⟨within a few short years their *rakish* son had squandered the family fortune on hard liquor, fast cars, and loose women⟩ — see CORRUPT

rakishness *n* a sinking to a state of low moral standards and behavior ⟨the legendary *rakishness* of the oil baron's overprivileged and underbred son⟩ — see CORRUPTION 2

[1]rally *vb* 1 to assemble and make ready for action ⟨*rallied* the Red Cross workers to deal with the devastating earthquake⟩ — see MOBILIZE

2 to become healthy and strong again after illness or weakness ⟨despite the best care that medicine could

provide, the elderly woman never really *rallied* from her fractured hip⟩ — see CONVALESCE

3 to regain a former or normal state ⟨after wavering a moment on the balance beam, she quickly *rallied* and finished with a fine dismount⟩ — see RECOVER 2

²rally *vb* to make fun of in a good-natured way ⟨his friends *rallied* him for missing an easy putt⟩ — see TEASE 1

rally *n* **1** an act of gathering forces together to renew or attempt an effort ⟨in a last-minute *rally* the Confederates at Bull Run were able to turn a near defeat into an upset victory⟩

synonyms marshaling (*also* marshalling), mobilization, rallying

related words call, call-up, summons; convening, convocation, muster, mustering

phrases call to arms

2 a mass meeting for the purpose of displaying or arousing support for a cause or person ⟨a huge *rally* for the candidate on the eve of the election⟩

synonyms demo [*British*], demonstration

related words assembly, conference, congress, convention, convocation, council, gathering; march; protest, sit-down, sit-in, strike; counterdemonstration, counterprotest, counterrally

3 the process or period of gradually regaining one's health and strength ⟨the doctors were amazed at the sick child's unexpected *rally*, which was apparently due to the new drug⟩ — see CONVALESCENCE

rallying *adj* marked by or expressive of mild or good-natured teasing ⟨he took his friends' *rallying* remarks about his girlfriend good-naturedly⟩ — see QUIZZICAL

rallying *n* an act of gathering forces together to renew or attempt an effort ⟨the *rallying* of students to support our petition for better bus service was made a lot easier by this morning's subzero temperatures⟩ — see RALLY 1

ram *vb* **1** to come into usually forceful contact with something ⟨the truck suddenly swerved and *rammed* into the side of a building⟩ — see HIT 2

2 to fit (people or things) into a tight space ⟨*rammed* as many candies into his mouth as he could fit⟩ — see CROWD 1

3 to proceed or move quickly ⟨I threw myself out of the way as a car *rammed* through the crosswalk⟩ — see HURRY 2

ramble *n* **1** a short trip for pleasure ⟨the couple's weekend *rambles* up and down the valley in search of interesting antiques⟩ — see EXCURSION 1

2 a relaxed journey on foot for exercise or pleasure ⟨our usual practice is to take a *ramble* around the neighborhood after dinner⟩ — see WALK 1

ramble *vb* **1** to talk at length without sticking to a topic or getting to a point ⟨the teenagers sat around the pizza parlor, *rambling* on about dating, homework, movies, and the local football team⟩

synonyms blather (on), go on, maunder, rattle, run on

related words deviate, digress, stray, wander; sidetrack; blab, blabber, blither, bumble, burble, chat, chatter, drivel, drool, gab, gabble, gibber, jabber, patter, prate, prattle, waffle

phrases run one's mouth

2 to move about from place to place aimlessly ⟨by tirelessly *rambling* around San Francisco for a week we probably saw more of it than many residents ever have⟩ — see WANDER 1

3 to travel by foot for exercise or pleasure ⟨we're planning to *ramble* all over the highland moors when we're in Dartmoor⟩ — see HIKE 1

rambler *n* **1** a person who roams about without a fixed route or destination ⟨a *rambler* her whole life, my aunt is likely to send me a postcard from just about any corner of the world⟩ — see NOMAD

2 a person who travels by foot for exercise or pleasure ⟨a secluded sylvan spot just waiting to be discovered by the adventurous *rambler*⟩ — see HIKER

rambling *adj* **1** passing from one topic to another ⟨I listened patiently to Mrs. Parsifal's *rambling* reminiscences, though I had no idea who "Dorothy" and "the stepson" were⟩ — see DISCURSIVE

2 using or containing more words than necessary to express an idea ⟨the new minister gives *rambling* sermons that, if they have a point, are lost on the congregation, which invariably falls asleep⟩ — see WORDY 1

rambunctious *adj* being rough or noisy in a high-spirited way ⟨that beach is often taken over by packs of *rambunctious* young people, so don't go there expecting peace and quiet⟩ — see BOISTEROUS

ramify *vb* to set or force apart ⟨the rise of cable television *ramified* the audience, creating ever smaller segments for an ever growing array of programming choices⟩ — see SEPARATE 1

rampage *n* a state of wildly excited activity or emotion ⟨some crazy guy went on a *rampage* in the public library and started grabbing books off the shelves and tossing them around⟩ — see FRENZY

rampant *adj* **1** showing no signs of being under control ⟨the mayor promised to put a stop to the *rampant* crime that plagued the city⟩

synonyms abandoned, intemperate, raw, runaway, unbounded, unbridled, unchecked, uncontrolled, unhampered, unhindered, unrestrained

related words uncontrollable, ungovernable; barbaric, hog wild, riotous, uninhibited, wild

near antonyms moderate, tempered

antonyms bridled, checked, constrained, controlled, curbed, governed, hampered, hindered, restrained, temperate

2 growing thickly and vigorously ⟨try to avoid the patch of *rampant* poison ivy near the resting spot on the trail⟩ — see RANK 1

ramrod *adj* given to exacting standards of discipline and self-restraint ⟨a *ramrod* camp director who's been known to send kids home for a minor infraction of the rules⟩ — see SEVERE 1

ranch *n* a piece of land and its buildings used to grow crops or raise livestock ⟨lives on a cattle *ranch* in Texas that's as big as the whole state of Rhode Island⟩ — see FARM

rancid *adj* causing intense displeasure, disgust, or resentment ⟨an unscrupulous food vendor who's as *rancid* as the meat that he serves⟩ — see OFFENSIVE 1

rancor *n* a deep-seated ill will ⟨controversy over use of pesticides has caused a lot of *rancor* in this agricultural community⟩ — see ENMITY

rancorous *adj* having or showing deep-seated resentment ⟨a *rancorous* autobiography in which the author heaps blame on just about everyone who had the misfortune of knowing him⟩ — see BITTER 1

random *adj* lacking a definite plan, purpose, or pattern ⟨since we were new in town, our choice of a vet for our dog was entirely *random*⟩

synonyms aimless, arbitrary, catch-as-catch-can, desultory, erratic, haphazard, helter-skelter, hit-or-miss, scattered, slapdash, stray

related words accidental, casual, chance, chancy, contingent, fluky (*also* flukey), fortuitous, inadvertent, incidental, lucky, unconsidered, unintended, unintentional, unplanned, unpremeditated; scattershot, shotgun; irregular, odd, sporadic, spot; directionless, objectless, purposeless; indiscriminate, unsystematic; undirected; disorderly, disorganized; undiscriminating, unselective

near antonyms established, fixed, regular, set, stable,

steady; constant, continuous, even; arranged, managed, orchestrated, ordered, planned; aware, conscious, deliberate, purposeful, thoughtful, willful (*or* wilful)
antonyms methodical (*also* methodic), nonrandom, orderly, organized, regular, systematic, systematized

randomly *adv* without definite aim, direction, rule, or method ⟨the winner will be *randomly* chosen from among all of the entries⟩ — see HIT OR MISS

randy *adj* having a strong sexual desire ⟨a booze-fueled off-campus party that was rife with *randy* frat boys hoping to score⟩ — see LUSTFUL

range *n* **1** open land over which livestock may roam and feed ⟨knew exactly how many head of cattle were turned out on the *range* that morning to graze⟩
synonyms lea (*or* ley), pasturage, pasture
related words ranch, station; feedlot, stockyard, yard; grassland, pampas, prairie, savanna (*also* savannah), steppe
2 an area over which activity, capacity, or influence extends ⟨didn't know she had such a wide *range* of knowledge until I talked to her⟩
synonyms ambit, amplitude, breadth, compass, confines, dimension(s), extent, reach, realm, scope, sweep, width
related words gamut, spectrum, spread; bailiwick, circle, demesne, department, discipline, domain, element, fief, fiefdom, field, province, region, specialty, sphere, terrain; frontier; horizon, panorama
3 the distance or extent between possible extremes ⟨an actor who can go through the full *range* of emotion, from joy to sorrow, in mere minutes⟩
synonyms diapason, gamut, scale, spectrum, spread, stretch
related words measure, pitch, scale; ambit, amplitude, compass, dimension(s), extent, reach, realm, scope, sweep, width
4 a relaxed journey on foot for exercise or pleasure ⟨they were stopped by security personnel while taking an innocent *range* through the palace grounds⟩ — see WALK 1
5 a series of persons or things arranged one behind another ⟨from the air, the mountain *range* stretched as far as we could see in both directions⟩ — see LINE 1
6 an appliance that prepares food for consumption by heating it ⟨the high-end appliances include a professional-quality gas *range*⟩ — see COOKER 1
7 the place where a plant or animal is usually or naturally found ⟨the American robin's winter *range* has steadily extended farther and farther north⟩ — see HOME 2

range *vb* **1** to arrange or assign according to type ⟨the campers were *ranged* in patrols, each patrol consisting of girls in a certain age group⟩ — see CLASSIFY 1
2 to move about from place to place aimlessly ⟨she let her dog off the leash and whistled for him every now and then to make sure he didn't *range* out of hearing⟩ — see WANDER 1
3 to occur within a continuous range of variation ⟨the color of Florida grapefruit can *range* anywhere from pale pink to ruby red⟩ — see RUN 4
4 to put into a particular arrangement ⟨chairs were *ranged* round the perimeter of the room⟩ — see ORDER 1

ranging *adj* traveling from place to place ⟨a *ranging* bear has been spotted at bird feeders in different parts of town⟩ — see ITINERANT

rangy *adj* **1** being tall, thin and usually loose-jointed ⟨we could use a *rangy* girl like you on our basketball team⟩ — see LANKY
2 having considerable extent ⟨a speech that took a *rangy* look at the problems facing the university⟩ — see EXTENSIVE

rank *adj* **1** growing thickly and vigorously ⟨covered with trumpet vines so *rank* you couldn't see the trellis beneath them⟩
synonyms lush, luxuriant, prosperous, rampant, weedy
related words lavish, profuse; overgrown, overrun, verdant; close, dense, tangled, thick
near antonyms dormant; blighted, stunted
antonyms sparse
2 having an unpleasant smell ⟨smokes *rank* cigars that usually send me running for fresh air⟩ — see MALODOROUS
3 very noticeable especially for being incorrect or bad ⟨the article about fairy tales was full of *rank* errors, such as a reference to "Cinderella biting into the poisoned apple"⟩ — see EGREGIOUS
4 having no exceptions or restrictions ⟨a sidewalk sale of art works by *rank* amateurs⟩ — see ABSOLUTE 2

rank *n* **1** the placement of someone or something in relation to others in a vertical arrangement ⟨attained the highest *rank* in the Freemasons⟩
synonyms degree, echelon, footing, level, place, position, ranking, reach(es), rung, situation, standing, station, status, stratum
related words condition, estate, order, walk; capacity, function; rating
2 high position within society ⟨remembered as a woman of *rank* who socialized only with other members of the elite⟩
synonyms class, dignity, fashion, quality, standing, state
related words gentility, gentleness, nobility, nobleness; grandness, highness, loftiness; distinction, dominance, precedence, preeminence, primacy, superiority; caste, station, status; preferment
near antonyms debasement, degradation; subordinateness, subordination; baseness, commonness, inferiority, lowliness, lowness
3 a series of people or things arranged side by side ⟨*rank* upon *rank* of cavalry came thundering down the hill⟩ — see [1]ROW 1
4 *usually* **ranks** *pl* one of the units into which a whole is divided on the basis of a common characteristic ⟨this book will someday join the *ranks* of the world's great novels⟩ — see CLASS 2

rank *vb* **1** to take or have a certain position within a group arranged in vertical classes ⟨my favorite pitcher *ranks* first in the league for number of consecutive outs⟩
synonyms be, grade, place, rate, stand
related words seed; count; categorize, class, classify, codify, compartmentalize, group, separate, set, sort; install, instate
2 to arrange or assign according to type ⟨most critics would *rank* him among our best actors⟩ — see CLASSIFY 1

rank and file *n* the body of the community as contrasted with the elite ⟨the chosen few might have the opportunity for a trip in the space shuttle, but it will be a while before the *rank and file* are taking space trips⟩ — see MASS 1

ranking *n* **1** a scheme of rank or order ⟨in one *ranking* of the best places to live, San Francisco surpassed all the other cities in the U.S.⟩ — see [3]SCALE 1
2 the placement of someone or something in relation to others in a vertical arrangement ⟨the President's *ranking* in the polls is at its highest level since he took office⟩ — see RANK 1

rankle *vb* **1** to be excited or emotionally stirred up with anger ⟨that kind of rude treatment from a young person makes me *rankle*⟩ — see BOIL 1
2 to make angry ⟨it *rankles* me when some schools can't

even afford paper and pencils for the students⟩ — see ANGER

rankled *adj* feeling or showing anger ⟨our supervisor was *rankled* by all the unexpected delays and problems we ran into⟩ — see ANGRY

rankling *adj* causing annoyance ⟨for some air travelers, the most *rankling* aspect of the new security measures seems to be the restrictions regarding carry-on baggage⟩ — see ANNOYING

ransack *vb* **1** to search through with the intent of committing robbery ⟨it was clear that the thieves who had *ransacked* the museum were professionals—they bypassed most of the exhibits and went straight for the vaults⟩
synonyms despoil, loot, maraud, pillage, plunder, sack
related words break in, burglarize, rip off, steal (from); comb, hunt, rake, rifle, rummage; harry, raid; ravish
2 to look through (as a place) carefully or thoroughly in an effort to find or discover something ⟨I've *ransacked* the whole house for that bracelet you lent me and it's nowhere to be found⟩ — see SEARCH 1

ransom *vb* to free from captivity or punishment by paying a price ⟨the prince emptied the treasury to *ransom* his son from the kidnappers⟩
synonyms redeem
related words bail; deliver, rescue, save; emancipate, liberate; get back, recover, regain, retrieve; release; buy; salvage

rant *n* **1** a long angry speech or scolding ⟨after complaining about the hotel's lousy service, the woman went off on another *rant* about the condition of her room⟩ — see TIRADE
2 boastful speech or writing ⟨instead of addressing the current crisis, the mayor's speech was a lot of *rant* emphasizing his accomplishments⟩ — see BOMBAST 1

rant *vb* to talk loudly and wildly ⟨when the salesclerk gave him incorrect change, he began *ranting* about the sorry state of math education today⟩
synonyms bluster, fulminate, huff, rave, spout
related words sound off, speak out, speak up; blare, blurt out, bolt; bloviate, blow, declaim, harangue, mouth (off), orate, pontificate; carry on, rage, storm, take on
near antonyms grunt, murmur, mutter, slur; breathe, whisper

rant (at) *vb* to criticize (someone) severely or angrily especially for personal failings ⟨Grandmother *ranted at* us for skipping the family holiday gathering in favor of a ski trip⟩ — see SCOLD

[1]**rap** *n* **1** a formal claim of criminal wrongdoing against a person ⟨the headlines in the paper today are all about the mayor facing an embezzlement *rap*⟩ — see CHARGE 1
2 a hard strike with a part of the body or an instrument ⟨the doctor used a little hammer to give me a *rap* on the knee to test my reflexes⟩ — see [1]BLOW
3 responsibility for wrongdoing or failure ⟨would sooner take the *rap* for the missing money than tell on his friend⟩ — see BLAME 1

[2]**rap** *n* friendly, informal conversation or an instance of this ⟨after our pickup softball game, I had a friendly *rap* with a couple of the guys in the park⟩ — see CHAT 1

[3]**rap** *n* the smallest amount or part imaginable ⟨I don't care a *rap* about losing that old jacket⟩ — see JOT

[1]**rap** *vb* **1** to deliver a blow to (someone or something) usually in a strong vigorous manner ⟨a childhood memory of the time he got his knuckles *rapped* for trying to steal candy from the corner store⟩ — see HIT 1
2 to strike or cause to strike lightly and usually rhythmically ⟨the impatient man was *rapping* his pipe on the door, hoping to wake up the sleeping attendant⟩ — see [1]TAP

[2]**rap** *vb* to engage in casual or rambling conversation ⟨the guys at the gym never seem to tire about *rapping* about basketball⟩ — see CHAT 1

[3]**rap** *vb* **1** to fill with overwhelming emotion (as wonder or delight) ⟨concertgoers were utterly *rapped* by the power of Handel's oratorio⟩ — see ENTRANCE
2 to take physical control or possession of (something) suddenly or forcibly ⟨suddenly the hawk swooped down and *rapped* the unwary rodent⟩ — see CATCH 1

rapacious *adj* **1** having a huge appetite ⟨nothing livens things up like a whole team of *rapacious* basketball players descending upon the pizza parlor⟩ — see VORACIOUS 1
2 living by killing and eating other animals ⟨*rapacious* mammals, such as coyotes, foxes, and bobcats⟩ — see PREDATORY
3 having or marked by an eager and often selfish desire especially for material possessions ⟨*rapacious* plunderers who despoiled the tombs in the ancient pyramids⟩ — see GREEDY 1

rapaciousness *n* an intense selfish desire for wealth or possessions ⟨the land developer's *rapaciousness* knew no bounds, and if what she wanted wasn't for sale, she would force the owner into selling it⟩ — see GREED

rapacity *n* an intense selfish desire for wealth or possessions ⟨the *rapacity* of the Spanish conquistadors was such that they were undeterred by the very preposterousness of the legend of El Dorado⟩ — see GREED

rape *n* **1** the act of forcing a person to engage in sexual activity and especially intercourse ⟨the brutal *rape* of a young woman⟩ ⟨a conviction for *rape*⟩
synonyms assault, ravishment, sexual assault, violation
related words acquaintance rape, date rape, statutory rape; gang rape; indecent assault, molestation; defilement, deflowering
2 the unlawful or forcible carrying away of a person or animal ⟨the legendary *rape* of the Sabine women by the ancient Romans was frequently depicted in classical art⟩ — see ABDUCTION

rape *vb* to engage in sexual activity and especially intercourse with a person unwilling or unable to give consent ⟨a woman was *raped* in that alley last night⟩
synonyms assault, force, outrage, ravish, violate
related words date rape; gang rape; molest; paw; defile, deflower

rapid *adj* moving, proceeding, or acting with great speed ⟨the *rapid* descent of the roller coaster made me feel very queasy⟩ — see FAST 1

rapid–fire *adj* moving, proceeding, or acting with great speed ⟨the witness stayed unruffled all through the prosecutor's *rapid-fire* questioning⟩ — see FAST 1

rapidity *n* a high rate of movement or performance ⟨the *rapidity* with which she can do mental math calculations is amazing⟩ — see SPEED 1

rapidly *adv* with great speed ⟨summer vacation has gone by way too *rapidly*⟩ — see FAST 1

rapidness *n* a high rate of movement or performance ⟨the *rapidness* of the response to a call for assistance is critical in saving the victim of a heart attack⟩ — see SPEED 1

rapport *n* a friendly relationship marked by ready communication and mutual understanding ⟨his good *rapport* with his students was one of the reasons why the school board named him Teacher of the Year⟩
synonyms communion, fellowship, rapprochement
related words accord, agreement, concord, harmony; oneness, solidarity, togetherness, unity; affinity, empathy, sympathy, understanding; amity, chumminess, companionship, friendliness, friendship; reciprocity, symbiosis
near antonyms alienation, disaffection, disgruntle-

ment, estrangement; coldness, cold shoulder, distance, iciness; animosity, antagonism, antipathy, bitterness, enmity, hostility, jaundice, rancor, spite

rapprochement *n* a friendly relationship marked by ready communication and mutual understanding ⟨an era of *rapprochement* between Mexico and the U.S. that was highlighted by a new trade agreement⟩ — see RAPPORT

rapscallion *n* **1** a mean, evil, or unprincipled person ⟨the city's run-down waterfront was occupied mostly by disreputable places frequented by drunkards and *rapscallions*⟩ — see VILLAIN
2 an appealingly mischievous person ⟨that little *rapscallion* kept hiding my shoes and making me go look for them⟩ — see SCAMP 1

rapt *adj* **1** experiencing or marked by overwhelming usually pleasurable emotion ⟨a rock band that still attracts *rapt* crowds of aging baby boomers⟩ — see ECSTATIC
2 having the mind fixed on something ⟨with a mixture of delight and awe, the *rapt* children stared at the chick in the incubator breaking out of its shell⟩ — see ATTENTIVE 1

raptorial *adj* living by killing and eating other animals ⟨the place of *raptorial* birds in the park's ecosystem⟩ — see PREDATORY

rapture *n* a state of overwhelming usually pleasurable emotion ⟨in *The Nutcracker* Clara gazes in *rapture* as the Christmas tree grows before her very eyes⟩ — see ECSTASY

rapture *vb* to fill with overwhelming emotion (as wonder or delight) ⟨nature lovers will be *raptured* by the documentary's breathtaking cinematography⟩ — see ENTRANCE

rapturous *adj* experiencing or marked by overwhelming usually pleasurable emotion ⟨heard the whoops of the *rapturous* fan whose quest for an autograph had met with success⟩ — see ECSTATIC

rare *adj* **1** being out of the ordinary ⟨even among the prize-winning roses, this one is a *rare* beauty⟩ — see EXCEPTIONAL 1
2 having qualities that appeal to a refined taste ⟨*rare* specialty wools, such as cashmere, prized for their fineness, lightness and exceptional warmth⟩ — see CHOICE 1
3 not often occurring or repeated ⟨the French pronunciation of the family's name is *rare*, except in Louisiana⟩ — see INFREQUENT
4 noticeably different from what is generally found or experienced ⟨"Such good manners are *rare* these days," remarked Mrs. Denby, as the young man let her go ahead of him in line⟩ — see UNUSUAL 1

raree–show *n* an elaborate, visually exciting show or event ⟨no longer the mechanisms by which nominees are actually chosen, party conventions are mostly *raree-shows* for rallying the faithful⟩ — see EXTRAVAGANZA

rarely *adv* not often ⟨summer thunderstorms occur only *rarely* along the Oregon coast⟩ — see SELDOM

raring *adj* showing urgent desire or interest ⟨we'd gotten up so early that by the time eight o'clock rolled around, we were *raring* to get started on the hike⟩ — see EAGER

rarity *n* **1** something strange or unusual that is an object of interest ⟨an American visitor in that remote Chinese village is a *rarity*⟩ — see CURIOSITY 2
2 something that is different from what is ordinary or expected ⟨a meal accompanied by wine is a *rarity* in this house⟩ — see ANOMALY 1

rascal *n* **1** a mean, evil, or unprincipled person ⟨some cold-blooded *rascal* had set the barn afire, killing all of the horses⟩ — see VILLAIN
2 an appealingly mischievous person ⟨you little *rascal*, I saw you snitching some hors d'oeuvres even though our guests haven't even arrived yet⟩ — see SCAMP 1

rascality *n* playful, reckless behavior that is not intended to cause serious harm ⟨switching the entrance and exits signs in the school parking lot may seem like harmless *rascality*, if you're not the one involved in an accident⟩ — see MISCHIEF 1

rascally *adj* tending to or exhibiting reckless playfulness ⟨those *rascally* boys had let all of the lab mice out of their cages⟩ — see MISCHIEVOUS 1

rash *adj* acting or done with excessive or careless speed ⟨that was too *rash* a move, for now I've lost my bishop and probably the whole chess game⟩ — see HASTY 1

rashly *adv* with excessive or careless speed ⟨I *rashly* agreed to babysit for the Franklin family, completely forgetting that the last time had been torture⟩ — see HASTILY 1

rasp *n* a harsh grating sound ⟨the rusted lock opened with a *rasp*⟩
synonyms creak, grind, jar, scrape, scratch
related words clang, clangor, clank, clash, jangle; scuff; croak, gargle; blast, bleat, bray, screech

rasp *vb* **1** to make smooth by friction ⟨after sawing the board in half, *rasp* the ends to remove any splinters⟩ — see GRIND 1
2 to pass roughly and noisily over or against a surface ⟨the sound of fingernails *rasping* on the blackboard makes me cringe⟩ — see SCRAPE 1
3 to disturb the peace of mind of (someone) especially by repeated disagreeable acts ⟨the two siblings seemed intent on *rasping* each other for the entire car trip⟩ — see IRRITATE 1
4 to damage or diminish by continued friction ⟨during the last ice age, glaciers *rasped* the surface, leaving the deeply scarred rock⟩ — see ABRADE 1

raspberry *n* a vocal sound made to express scorn or disapproval ⟨there were *raspberries* from the audience when the hapless actress kept forgetting her lines⟩ — see CATCALL

rasping *adj* harsh and dry in sound ⟨a patient beset by a *rasping* cough from years of smoking⟩ — see HOARSE

raspy *adj* **1** easily irritated or annoyed ⟨overwork tends to make him *raspy*⟩ — see IRRITABLE
2 harsh and dry in sound ⟨the dying man spoke in a barely audible, *raspy* voice⟩ — see HOARSE

rassle *vb* to seize and attempt to unbalance one another for the purpose of achieving physical mastery ⟨the boys would *rassle* and roughhouse for hours on end⟩ — see WRESTLE

rat *n* **1** a person who provides information about another's wrongdoing ⟨the drug mule refused to turn *rat* without a guarantee of immunity⟩ — see INFORMER
2 someone who regularly spends time in a particular place ⟨on Friday night the mall *rats* were out in full force⟩ — see DENIZEN 1
3 a person whose behavior is offensive to others ⟨no one can understand what she finds appealing in a *rat* like him⟩ — see JERK 1

rat (on) *vb* **1** to give information (as to the authorities) about another's improper or unlawful activities ⟨how much—or how little—did the fuzz have to pay you to *rat on* us?⟩ — see SQUEAL 1
2 to leave (a cause or party) often in order to take up another ⟨many party operatives *ratted on* the senator's candidacy once her poll numbers started to slip⟩ — see DEFECT (FROM)

ratbag *n, chiefly Australian* a stupid person ⟨some *ratbag* who couldn't survive a day in the outback⟩ — see IDIOT

ratchet (down) *also* **rachet (down)** *vb* to grow less in scope or intensity especially gradually ⟨news stories about the kidnapping will *ratchet down* as the weeks go by⟩ — see DECREASE 2

[1]**rate** *vb* **1** to be or make worthy of (as a reward or punishment) ⟨how does a summer intern *rate* a new computer when I've been told to make do with this clunker?⟩ — see EARN 2
2 to make an approximate or tentative judgment regarding ⟨nowadays most motorists would probably *rate* their cell phone as an "essential" piece of electronic equipment⟩ — see ESTIMATE 1
3 to take or have a certain position within a group arranged in vertical classes ⟨a restaurant that consistently *rates* high in all the standard categories⟩ — see RANK 1
4 to think of in a particular way ⟨I would *rate* her my best friend; after all, she's always been there when I needed her⟩ — see CONSIDER 1

[2]**rate** *vb* to criticize (someone) severely or angrily especially for personal failings ⟨a tyrannical father who usually spent most of dinnertime *rating* his children on their alleged multitude of failings⟩ — see SCOLD

rate *n* **1** degree of excellence ⟨not being of the first *rate*, these apples are usually sold as food for livestock⟩ — see QUALITY 1
2 the relationship in quantity, amount, or size between two or more things ⟨the exchange *rate* was 10 pesos to the dollar when we visited Mexico⟩ — see RATIO

rat fink *n* **1** a person who provides information about another's wrongdoing ⟨who's the sorry *rat fink* that went squealing to the cops?⟩ — see INFORMER
2 a person whose behavior is offensive to others ⟨regrets ever doing business with that *rat fink*, who cheated him out of gobs of money⟩ — see JERK 1

rather *adv* **1** by choice or preference ⟨I would *rather* go to the movies than stay at home⟩
synonyms fain, first, preferably, readily, soon, willingly
related words alternately, alternatively, either, instead; electively, optionally; desirably, gladly, wishfully; obligingly, voluntarily
near antonyms reluctantly; forcibly, willy-nilly
antonyms involuntarily, unwillingly
2 as a substitute ⟨don't think of the placement test as torture but *rather* as a chance to show off how much you know⟩ — see INSTEAD
3 to some degree or extent ⟨I say, don't you think that's *rather* expensive for a hamburger?⟩ — see FAIRLY 1

ratify *vb* to give official acceptance of as satisfactory ⟨Lincoln's home state of Illinois was the first to *ratify* the 13th Amendment to the U.S. Constitution, which provided for the abolition of slavery⟩ — see APPROVE

ratio *n* the relationship in quantity, amount, or size between two or more things ⟨the *ratio* of students to teachers in the school is nine to one⟩
synonyms proportion, rate
related words average; frequency; correspondence; percentage
near antonyms disproportion

ratiocination *n* the thought processes that have been established as leading to valid solutions to problems ⟨as an expert in *ratiocination*, the detective Sherlock Holmes has few rivals⟩ — see LOGIC

ration *vb* to give as a share or portion ⟨the region has had to *ration* water during times of drought⟩ — see ALLOT

rational *adj* **1** having the ability to reason ⟨human beings are *rational* creatures⟩
synonyms intelligent, reasonable, reasoning, thinking
related words analytic (*or* analytical), logical; brainy, cerebral, highbrow, highbrowed, intellectual; cognitional, cognitive, mental; levelheaded, practical, sane, sensible, sober
near antonyms brainless, dense, doltish, dopey (*also* dopy), dorky [*slang*], dull, dumb, fatuous, half-witted, mindless, obtuse, senseless, slow, stupid, thickheaded; fallacious, groundless, illogical, invalid, nonsensical
antonyms irrational, nonrational, nonthinking, unintelligent, unreasonable, unreasoning, unthinking
2 according to the rules of logic ⟨insisted there was a *rational* explanation for the strange creaking noises and that there were no such things as ghosts⟩ — see LOGICAL 1
3 based on sound reasoning or information ⟨betting all of your savings on the lottery is not a *rational* move⟩ — see GOOD 1

rationale *n* a statement given to explain a belief or act ⟨the *rationale* for starting the school day an hour later is that kids will supposedly get an extra hour of sleep⟩ — see REASON 1

rationalize *vb* to give the reason for or cause of ⟨*rationalized* his decision to buy the new car by noting that it was more fuel efficient than his old vehicle⟩ — see EXPLAIN 2

rats *interj* used to express disgust ⟨*rats*, I can't believe anyone would say such a hateful thing⟩ — see YUCK

rattle *n* loud, confused, and usually inharmonious sound ⟨I'd go nuts if I had to endure the *rattle* of that bottling plant every day⟩ — see NOISE 1

rattle *vb* **1** to make a series of short sharp noises ⟨the children tromped through the kitchen, making the plates on the shelf *rattle*⟩
synonyms clack, clatter
related words chink, chirp, clank, click, clink; clang, clash, crash; spatter, sputter; racket; clip-clop, clop, clop-clop
2 to engage in casual or rambling conversation ⟨busily *rattling* away about our vacation plans, we didn't listen to the announcements and missed our flight⟩ — see CHAT 1
3 to talk at length without sticking to a topic or getting to a point ⟨she *rattled* on and on about all her European shopping trips, but I wasn't really listening⟩ — see RAMBLE 1
4 to throw into a state of self-conscious distress ⟨don't let a little mistake *rattle* you while you're playing during the piano recital⟩ — see EMBARRASS 1

rattlebrain *n* a silly flighty person ⟨in a medical situation of this seriousness we don't need some *rattlebrain* running around in a panic⟩ — see FLIBBERTIGIBBET

rattling *adj* moving, proceeding, or acting with great speed ⟨we drove off at a *rattling* pace⟩ — see FAST 1

rattling *adv* to a great degree ⟨a *rattling* good storyteller⟩ — see VERY 1

rattrap *n* a difficult, puzzling, or embarrassing situation from which there is no easy escape ⟨although the military invasion had been a breeze, the nation soon found itself caught in a *rattrap* with no clear escape route⟩ — see PREDICAMENT

ratty *adj* **1** showing signs of advanced wear and tear and neglect ⟨some *ratty* old magazines were the only reading material in the mountaintop cabin⟩ — see SHABBY 1
2 worn or torn into or as if into rags ⟨can I use this *ratty* old T-shirt to wipe up some paint?⟩ — see RAGGED 2
3 easily irritated or annoyed ⟨I get pretty *ratty* after hours of dealing with demanding customers⟩ — see IRRITABLE
4 arousing or deserving of one's loathing and disgust ⟨that's a *ratty* way to treat an old friend who's fallen on hard times⟩ — see CONTEMPTIBLE 1

raucous *adj* being rough or noisy in a high-spirited way ⟨the partying neighbors kept up their *raucous* laughter half the night⟩ — see BOISTEROUS

raunch *n* the quality or state of being obscene ⟨the sheer *raunch* of the movie earned it a NC-17 rating⟩ — see OBSCENITY 1

raunchiness *n* the quality or state of being obscene ⟨audience members were offended by the *raunchiness* of the jokes⟩ — see OBSCENITY 1

raunchy *adj* depicting or referring to sexual matters in a way that is unacceptable in polite society ⟨inappropriately used office e-mail for an exchange of *raunchy* jokes⟩ — see OBSCENE 1

ravage *vb* to bring destruction to (something) through violent action ⟨Hurricane Andrew *ravaged* Louisiana and Florida in 1992, causing $19 billion in damage⟩
synonyms destroy, devastate, ruin, scourge
related words despoil, foray, harry, loot, maraud, pillage, plunder, sack, strip; annihilate, desolate, eradicate, expunge, extinguish, extirpate, nuke, obliterate, rub out, shatter, smash, total, vaporize, waste, wipe out, wrack, wreck; decimate, mow; demolish, raze; crush, overpower, overrun, overthrow, overwhelm
near antonyms recondition, recover, redeem, rehabilitate, restore; fix, mend, patch, repair, revamp

rave *vb* **1** to make an exaggerated display of affection or enthusiasm ⟨to break the awkward silence after my parents' argument, our guest *raved* about the canned beans and franks we'd set before him⟩ — see GUSH 2
2 to talk loudly and wildly ⟨a man stood outside city hall *raving* like a lunatic about his tax bill⟩ — see RANT

rave *n, often* **raves** *pl* enthusiastic and usually public expression of approval ⟨the books have received even more *raves* from parents than from the kids they were written for⟩ — see APPLAUSE 1

ravel (out) *vb* to separate the various strands of ⟨since the sweater is too small, you could *ravel* the yarn *out* and make something else with it⟩ — see UNRAVEL 1

raven *adj* having the color of soot or coal ⟨a black satin dress that matches her silky, *raven* hair⟩ — see BLACK 1

raven *vb* to swallow or eat greedily ⟨the rat *ravened* the poisoned bait just as we had hoped⟩ — see GOBBLE

ravenous *adj* having a huge appetite ⟨we were *ravenous* after our canoe paddling, and the chili bubbling over the campfire smelled heavenly⟩ — see VORACIOUS 1

ravine *n* a narrow opening between hillsides or mountains that can be used for passage ⟨he urged his horse down into the *ravine* where there was a thin stream of water flowing⟩ — see CANYON

ravish *vb* **1** to engage in sexual activity and especially intercourse with a person unwilling or unable to give consent ⟨tales of Caribbean pirates who abducted fair maidens and *ravished* them without mercy⟩ — see RAPE
2 to fill with overwhelming emotion (as wonder or delight) ⟨travelers have long been *ravished* with wonder and awe by the immensity of the Great Pyramid at Giza⟩ — see ENTRANCE

ravishing *adj* very pleasing to look at ⟨with her red curls falling around her shoulders, she looked *ravishing* in her green dress⟩ — see BEAUTIFUL 1

ravishment *n* the act of forcing a person to engage in sexual activity and especially intercourse ⟨the eventual *ravishment* of the heroine is one of the distinguishing features of the bodice ripper⟩ — see RAPE 1

raw *adj* **1** not cooked ⟨you should wash your hands after handling *raw* chicken⟩
synonyms uncooked
related words unheated; rare; half-baked, underdone
near antonyms well-done; overdone; baked, boiled, braised, broiled, fried, grilled, heated, roasted, sautéed (*also* sauteed); burned (*or* burnt), charred, scorched
antonyms cooked
2 being such as found in nature and not altered by processing or refining ⟨*raw* sugar is honey-colored because the crystals retain cane juices, minerals, and other impurities that haven't been refined out⟩ — see CRUDE 1
3 lacking in adult experience or maturity ⟨recruiters like to say the military turns *raw* youths into responsible men and women⟩ — see CALLOW
4 marked by wet and windy conditions ⟨the day of the funeral was one of those bleak, blustery, *raw* winter days that was as gloomy as our spirits⟩ — see FOUL 1
5 uncomfortably cool ⟨evenings in those mountains, even during the summer, tend to be a little *raw*⟩ — see CHILLY 1
6 causing intense discomfort to one's skin ⟨bundle up if you're going sailing, as there's a *raw* wind out there in the bay⟩ — see CUTTING 1
7 showing no signs of being under control ⟨a frightening display of *raw* anger⟩ — see RAMPANT 1
8 lacking or shed of clothing ⟨a private men's health club where it was common for men to swim *raw*⟩ — see NAKED 1

raw *n* the state of having no clothes on one's body ⟨a secluded swimming hole where we could swim in the *raw*⟩ — see NUDITY

raw deal *n* unfair or inadequate treatment of someone or something or an instance of this ⟨these mice are really getting a *raw deal*: after we're through using them for our science experiment, they get fed to our snake⟩ — see DISSERVICE

rawhide *vb* to strike repeatedly with something long and thin or flexible ⟨a strict disciplinarian, the rancher would *rawhide* his disobedient sons until they were black and blue⟩ — see WHIP 1

raw material *n* the basic elements from which something can be developed ⟨Canada now converts most of its *raw materials* into manufactured goods such as automobiles and auto parts⟩ — see MAKING

rawness *n* **1** an uncomfortable degree of coolness ⟨lit a fire in the hearth to combat the *rawness* of that blustery March morning⟩ — see CHILL
2 the quality or state of lacking refinement or good taste ⟨to many teens the music's *rawness* is part of its appeal⟩ — see VULGARITY 1

ray *n* **1** a narrow sharply defined line of light radiating from an object ⟨two red eyes reflected in the *ray* of light from the flashlight⟩ — see SHAFT 1
2 a very small amount ⟨the tapping sound ceased, extinguishing the last *ray* of hope that the trapped miners were still alive⟩ — see PARTICLE 1

ray *vb* **1** to emit rays of light ⟨klieg lights were *raying* against the nighttime sky at the Hollywood premiere⟩ — see SHINE 1
2 to extend outwards from or as if from a central point ⟨laugh wrinkles *rayed* out from the corners of the old man's eyes⟩ — see RADIATE 1

rayless *adj* being without light or without much light ⟨the strange creatures that lurk in the *rayless* depths of the sea⟩ — see DARK 1

raze *vb* **1** to bring to a complete end the physical soundness, existence, or usefulness of ⟨an entire city block *razed* by a terrible fire⟩ — see DESTROY 1
2 to destroy (as a building) completely by knocking down or breaking to pieces ⟨the developer *razed* the old school building and built a high-rise condominium complex⟩ — see DEMOLISH 1

razz *n* a vocal sound made to express scorn or disapproval ⟨notoriously difficult to please, opera buffs are as quick with a *razz* as with a rave⟩ — see CATCALL

razz *vb* to make fun of in a good-natured way ⟨got *razzed* all day for wearing mismatched sneakers⟩ — see TEASE 1

razzing *adj* marked by or expressive of mild or good-natured teasing ⟨his little sister made *razzing* kissing noises whenever he was on the phone with his girlfriend⟩ — see QUIZZICAL

razzle-dazzle *adj* excessively showy ⟨the *razzle-dazzle* floor show is simply further evidence that Las Vegas doesn't go in for understatement⟩ — see GAUDY

reach *n* **1** a wide space or area ⟨a wide *reach* of woods⟩ — see EXPANSE
2 an area over which activity, capacity, or influence extends ⟨she's got a good memory, but critical thinking seems to be beyond her *reach*⟩ — see RANGE 2
3 *usually* **reaches** *pl* the placement of someone or something in relation to others in a vertical arrangement ⟨there are still only a few women in the upper *reaches* of the profession⟩ — see RANK 1
reach *vb* **1** to shift possession of (something) from one person to another ⟨would you *reach* me the potatoes, please?⟩ — see PASS 1
2 to transmit information or requests to ⟨you can *reach* me by phone after 3:00 p.m. most days⟩ — see CONTACT
3 to act upon (a person or a person's feelings) so as to cause a response ⟨the movie adaptation just didn't *reach* me the way the novel did⟩ — see [1]AFFECT 1
reachable *adj* situated within easy reach ⟨placed the book at a *reachable* distance from the bed⟩ — see CONVENIENT
reacquire *vb* to get again in one's possession ⟨the hockey team is hoping to *reacquire* the Stanley Cup this year⟩ — see RECOVER 1
react *vb* to act or behave in response (as to a stimulus or influence) ⟨it was my first touchdown, and I didn't know how to *react* to the cheers of the crowd⟩
synonyms reply, respond
related words answer, return; retaliate; construe, interpret, read, take, understand; contend (with), cope (with), grapple (with), handle, manage, negotiate
near antonyms act, behave; affect, cause, draw, effect
reaction *n* action or behavior that is done in return to other action or behavior ⟨we were startled by her extreme *reaction* to being jilted by her boyfriend⟩
synonyms answer, reply, response, take
related words backlash, kickback; rebound; recoil, reflex; revulsion, rise; counterreaction, counterresponse
near antonyms action, behavior; cause, effect
reactionary *adj* tending to favor established ideas, conditions, or institutions ⟨*reactionary* guardians of proper English usage invariably regard every new coinage that comes along as a nonword⟩ — see CONSERVATIVE
reactionary *n* **1** a person whose political beliefs are centered on tradition and keeping things the way they are ⟨*reactionaries* tried to stop the passage of the legislation extending civil rights⟩ — see CONSERVATIVE 1
2 a person with old-fashioned ideas ⟨a *reactionary* in the nation's ongoing culture war, she seems to believe that watching any TV at all will rot your brain⟩ — see FOGY
reactionaryism *n* attitudes or opinions tending to favor established ideas, conditions, or institutions ⟨the region's entrenched *reactionaryism* made it one of the major battlegrounds for the civil rights movement in the 1960s⟩ — see CONSERVATISM
read *vb* **1** to go over and mentally take in the content of ⟨he always *reads* the newspaper in the morning as he eats breakfast⟩
synonyms peruse, pore (over)
related words browse, dip (into), leaf (through), scan, skim, speed-read, thumb (through), turn over; devour, gobble (up); slog (through), wade (through); reread; proofread; decipher; review, study; apprehend, comprehend, get, grasp, make, make out, perceive, see, tumble (to), understand
2 to tell of or describe beforehand ⟨the psychic claimed to be able to *read* his future⟩ — see FORETELL
readdress *vb* to consider again especially with the possibility of change or reversal ⟨the Senate will *readdress* pending gun control legislation in their next session⟩ — see RECONSIDER
reader *n* a collection of writings ⟨I picked up a book entitled "An Emerson *Reader*" because it contained one or two of his essays I hadn't read before⟩ — see ANTHOLOGY
readily *adv* **1** by choice or preference ⟨she would *readily* give up piano lessons for a season ticket at her local ski area⟩ — see RATHER 1
2 without difficulty ⟨always gives directions that are *readily* understood⟩ — see EASILY 1
reading *n* **1** a presentation of an artistic work (as a piece of music) from a particular point of view ⟨a very bizarre *reading* of one of Shakespeare's greatest tragedies by an alternative theater company⟩ — see ACCOUNT 2
2 something assigned to be read or studied ⟨make sure you do the assigned *reading* for tonight⟩ — see LESSON
ready *adj* **1** being in a state of fitness for some experience or action ⟨after studying for months, she felt *ready* for the bar exam⟩
synonyms fit, go, prepared, set
related words conditioned, primed, ripe; armed, braced, fortified, steeled; qualified, trained
near antonyms unqualified, untrained
antonyms flat-footed, half-baked, half-cocked, underprepared, unprepared, unready
2 having a desire or inclination (as for a specified course of action) ⟨I'm *ready* to help, if I can⟩ — see WILLING 1
3 having or showing the ability to respond without delay or hesitation ⟨had a *ready* response to every one of her objections regarding the feasibility of the plan⟩ — see QUICK 1
4 involving minimal difficulty or effort ⟨we're hoping you have a *ready* solution to our networking problem⟩ — see EASY 1
ready *vb* **1** to make competent (as by training, skill, or ability) for a particular office or function ⟨this advanced course should *ready* him for college⟩ — see QUALIFY 2
2 to make ready in advance ⟨we can *ready* the desserts for the party a day in advance⟩ — see PREPARE 1
3 to prepare (oneself) mentally or emotionally ⟨the basketball players sat quietly in the locker room, *readying* themselves for the final game of the season⟩ — see FORTIFY 1
ready-made *adj* made beforehand in large numbers ⟨the store carries mostly inexpensive *ready-made* clothing⟩
synonyms bought, mass-produced, off-the-peg [*chiefly British*], off-the-rack, off-the-shelf, store, store-bought
related words ready-to-wear; commercial; prefab, prefabricated; hand-me-down
near antonyms handcrafted, handmade, homemade
antonyms bespoke (*also* bespoken), custom, customized, custom-made, tailored, tailor-made
real *adj* **1** being exactly as appears or as claimed ⟨this shirt is *real* silk, not polyester⟩ — see AUTHENTIC 1
2 existing in fact and not merely as a possibility ⟨asked her parents if the Tooth Fairy was *real*⟩ — see ACTUAL
3 free from any intent to deceive or impress others ⟨*real* folk who don't put on airs⟩ — see GUILELESS
real *adv* to a great degree ⟨this fish tastes *real* good⟩ — see VERY 1
real estate *n* the largest number or amount that something can hold ⟨the enormous difference in *real estate* between a high-definition disk and one in standard definition⟩ — see CAPACITY 1
realism *n* realistic depiction in art and literature ⟨using ordinary people as models, even when depicting the greatest of saints, Caravaggio brought an unforgiving *realism* to painting that was unprecedented⟩ — see VERISIMILITUDE
realistic *adj* **1** willing to see things as they really are and deal with them sensibly ⟨high schoolers who need to be

more *realistic* in their career choices, as so few people end up as rock stars⟩
synonyms down-to-earth, earthy, hardheaded, matter-of-fact, practical, pragmatic (*also* pragmatical)
related words idealless, philistine, utilitarian; commonsensical, grounded, levelheaded, logical, no-nonsense, rational, reasonable, sane, sensible, sober, sobersided, sound; bottom-line, hard, hard-boiled, hard-edged, tough-minded, unromantic, unsentimental; cynical, disillusioned, misanthropic, pessimistic; distrustful, mistrustful, skeptical, suspicious
near antonyms fanciful, fantastic (*also* fantastical), imaginative; romantic, sentimental; cheerful, optimistic, rose-colored; trustful, trusting, unsuspicious; half-baked, illogical, insane, irrational, unreasonable; theoretical (*also* theoretic)
antonyms blue-sky, idealistic, impractical, unrealistic, utopian, visionary
2 closely resembling the object imitated ⟨those special effects look really *realistic*—I'd never guess they were all computer-generated⟩ — see NATURAL 2

reality *n* **1** something that actually exists ⟨the ambition to make his dreams a *reality*⟩ — see FACT 2
2 the fact of being or of being real ⟨no one denies the *reality* of electricity, though few people understand it fully⟩ — see EXISTENCE
3 the quality of being actual ⟨the *reality* of the situation finally dawned on her and she sat down in stunned silence⟩ — see FACT 1
4 one that has a real and independent existence ⟨you'll need to cope with a whole new set of *realities* once you've become a parent⟩ — see ENTITY

realizable *adj* capable of being done or carried out ⟨waited until their goal was *realizable* and then acted⟩ — see POSSIBLE 1

realization *n* the state of being actual or complete ⟨this research paper is the *realization* of an entire year's work⟩ — see FRUITION

realize *vb* **1** to come to an awareness of ⟨I just *realized* that I can't go out to dinner tonight because I'm supposed to babysit for our neighbor⟩ — see DISCOVER 1
2 to receive as return for effort ⟨if you deposit your paycheck in a savings account, you'll *realize* a little interest on it⟩ — see EARN 1

really *adv* **1** in actual fact ⟨I'm *really* sorry I upset you⟩ — see VERY 2
2 to tell the truth ⟨well, *really*, I'd rather go to the movies than go to dinner⟩ — see ACTUALLY 1
3 without any question ⟨that was *really* a sweet gesture on your part⟩ — see INDEED 1
4 to a great degree ⟨*really* tired after staying up all night⟩ — see VERY 1

realm *n* **1** a region of activity, knowledge, or influence ⟨medieval history is really Professor Clinton's *realm*, so I'll let her answer your question⟩ — see FIELD 2
2 an area over which activity, capacity, or influence extends ⟨a medical breakthrough that is within the *realm* of possibility⟩ — see RANGE 2

ream *vb* to rob by the use of trickery or threats ⟨*reamed* a whole new generation of suckers with a variation of the Ponzi scheme⟩ — see FLEECE

ream (out) *vb* to criticize (someone) severely or angrily especially for personal failings ⟨you are so going to get *reamed out* when the boss learns that you wrecked the company car⟩ — see SCOLD

reams *n pl* a considerable amount ⟨I have *reams* of paperwork to do before I can leave today⟩ — see LOT 2

reanalyze *vb* to consider again especially with the possibility of change or reversal ⟨you need to *reanalyze* the data, because the numbers don't tally⟩ — see RECONSIDER

reanimate *vb* to bring back to life, practice, or activity ⟨the new multiplex has begun to *reanimate* the shabby neighborhood⟩ — see REVIVE 1

reanimated *adj* made or become fresh in spirits or vigor ⟨the hikers were *reanimated* and ready to go after their brief rest along the side of the trail⟩ — see NEW 4

reanimation *n* the act or an instance of bringing something back to life, public attention, or vigorous activity ⟨a call for the *reanimation* of curfew ordinances that were discarded decades ago⟩ — see REVIVAL

reap *vb* **1** to catch or collect (a crop or natural resource) for human use ⟨my great-grandfather had to *reap* the wheat on his family farm with a hand scythe⟩ — see HARVEST
2 to receive as return for effort ⟨if you continue to work hard at musicianship, you will *reap* the rewards of being a concert pianist⟩ — see EARN 1

reappraisal *n* a usually critical look at a past event ⟨teachers are undertaking a *reappraisal* of the current grading system, as the consensus is that A's have been given out too easily of late⟩ — see REVIEW 1

rear *adj* being at or in the part of something opposite the front part ⟨go to the back of the building and look out the *rear* window and you'll see the eagle⟩ — see BACK

rear *n* **1** a behind part or surface ⟨the *rear* of the car was sleekly designed⟩
synonyms back, reverse, tail
antonyms face, forehead, forepart, front
2 the part of the body upon which someone sits ⟨fell off her skates onto her *rear*⟩ — see BUTTOCKS

rear *vb* **1** to bring to maturity through care and education ⟨watched a documentary on how wolves *rear* their young⟩ — see BRING UP 1
2 to fix in an upright position ⟨it took all the men in the village to *rear* the frame for the barn, pulling hard at the ropes until all the sides were standing⟩ — see ERECT 1
3 to form by putting together parts or materials ⟨the city has plans for *rearing* a new convention center over the next two years⟩ — see BUILD
4 to look after or assist the growth of by labor and care ⟨an amateur who *rears* rare orchids in a professional-grade greenhouse⟩ — see GROW 1

rear end *n* the part of the body upon which someone sits ⟨the mother swatted her toddler lightly on his diapered *rear end* to get his attention⟩ — see BUTTOCKS

rearmost *adj* following all others of the same kind in order or time ⟨the *rearmost* people in the cafeteria line often get the dregs that nobody wanted and for good reason⟩ — see LAST 1

rearward *adj* **1** being at or in the part of something opposite the front part ⟨got *rearward* quarters aboard the ship⟩ — see BACK
2 directed, turned, or done toward the back ⟨the tearful girl gave a *rearward* glance to her younger brother as she was being led down the street for her first day at school⟩ — see BACKWARD 1

rearward *also* **rearwards** *adv* toward the rear ⟨turned *rearward* for a moment, just for one final look at the haunting scene⟩ — see BACKWARD 1

reason *n* **1** a statement given to explain a belief or act ⟨she gave a good *reason* for her seemingly suspicious behavior⟩
synonyms account, accounting, argument, case, explanation, rationale
related words alibi, apologia, apology, defense, excuse, justification, vindication; appeal, plea; guise, pretense (*or* pretence), pretext, rationalization
2 something (as a belief) that serves as the basis for another thing ⟨a firm belief that we are here on earth to help others is the *reason* for her tireless volunteer work⟩
synonyms account, authority, grounds, motive, subject, wherefore, why

related words antecedent, cause, consideration, impetus, incentive, inspiration, instigation, occasion, stimulus

3 an explanation that frees one from fault or blame ⟨what *reason* do you have for being in such a bad mood?⟩ — see EXCUSE

4 someone or something responsible for a result ⟨what's the meteorological *reason* for tornadoes?⟩ — see CAUSE 1

5 the ability to learn and understand or to deal with problems ⟨you'll need to use all of your *reason* to get out of this tight spot⟩ — see INTELLIGENCE 1

6 the normal or healthy condition of the mental abilities ⟨was afraid that with all the stress he was under, he'd lose all *reason*⟩ — see MIND 2

7 the thought processes that have been established as leading to valid solutions to problems ⟨in a time of national crisis we need to listen to the voice of *reason*⟩ — see LOGIC

reason *vb* **1** to form an opinion or reach a conclusion through reasoning and information ⟨she *reasoned* that since all of the cakes were on sale for the same price, she might as well pick the biggest one⟩ — see INFER 1

2 to state (something) as a reason in support of or against something under consideration ⟨he tried to *reason* that no one in their right mind would buy his brother's old video games, but they were put on the online auction anyway⟩ — see ARGUE 1

reasonable *adj* **1** according to the rules of logic ⟨his answer is perfectly *reasonable*⟩ — see LOGICAL 1

2 based on sound reasoning or information ⟨those playing rules sound *reasonable* to me⟩ — see GOOD 1

3 costing little ⟨desperately trying to find *reasonable* hotel rates for the holiday weekend⟩ — see CHEAP 1

4 having the ability to reason ⟨some people once believed that women were not by nature *reasonable* beings, but generations of female scholars have proved those people wrong⟩ — see RATIONAL 1

reasonably *adv* with good reason or courtesy ⟨I expect to be treated *reasonably* by the clerks when I shop at a store⟩ — see WELL 4

reasoned *adj* **1** based on sound reasoning or information ⟨a candidate with a *reasoned* stance on this important issue⟩ — see GOOD 1

2 being or provable by reasoning in which the conclusion follows necessarily from given information ⟨given the information you have, that is the only *reasoned* solution to the problem⟩ — see DEDUCTIVE

3 decided on as a result of careful thought ⟨refusing to be swayed by the passions of the moment, the president consulted with his advisers before making a *reasoned* response to this unprovoked act of aggression⟩ — see DELIBERATE 1

reasoning *adj* having the ability to reason ⟨judged by the courts not to be a *reasoning* being who could be held accountable for his crimes⟩ — see RATIONAL 1

reasoning *n* the thought processes that have been established as leading to valid solutions to problems ⟨your *reasoning* here is faulty, for although all wives are spouses, not all spouses are wives⟩ — see LOGIC

reassurance *n* the giving of hope and strength in times of grief, distress, or suffering ⟨the governor's *reassurance* of the flood victims was seen as opportunistic⟩ — see CONSOLATION 1

reassure *vb* to ease the grief or distress of ⟨tried to *reassure* her that the dog would come back home by nightfall⟩ — see COMFORT

reata *n* a rope or long leather thong with a noose used especially for catching livestock ⟨the gauchos tied their *reatas* and rode out onto the pampas to rope calves⟩ — see LASSO

rebarbative *adj* causing annoyance ⟨there are aspects of that writer's personality that any reasonable person would regard as *rebarbative*, but we're just reading his novels—not marrying him⟩ — see ANNOYING

rebel *adj* given to resisting authority or another's control ⟨today's *rebel* chefs feel free to ignore the dictates of classic French cuisine⟩ — see DISOBEDIENT

rebel *n* a person who rises up against authority ⟨the *rebel* would not submit peacefully, even after he was captured⟩

synonyms insurgent, insurrectionary, insurrectionist, mutineer, red, revolter, revolutionary, revolutionist

related words challenger, defier, insubordinate, oppositionist, recusant, refuser, resistant, resister; anarch, anarchist; discontent, extremist, malcontent, radical

near antonyms loyalist, patriot, supporter; counterinsurgent, counterrevolutionary, counterrevolutionist

rebel *vb* to rise up against established authority ⟨the colonists *rebelled* in the wake of an onslaught of abuses⟩

synonyms mutiny, revolt

related words defy, disobey, mock; revolutionize; buck, combat, contest, fight, oppose, resist, withstand

phrases kick over the traces

near antonyms comply (with), follow, mind, obey, submit; attend, serve

rebel (against) *vb* to go against the commands, prohibitions, or rules of ⟨experts tell parents that if their once-compliant children *rebel against* them, then they should take it as a sign the kids are growing up and becoming their own persons⟩ — see DISOBEY

rebellion *n* **1** open fighting against authority (as one's own government) ⟨the *rebellion* would have failed if not for the aid sent by other countries⟩

synonyms insurgence, insurgency, insurrection, mutiny, outbreak, revolt, revolution, rising, uprising

related words coup, coup d'état (*or* coup d'etat), overthrow; misprision, sedition, treachery, treason; sabotage, subversion

near antonyms counterinsurgency, counterrevolution

2 refusal to obey ⟨the period of *rebellion* that teenagers typically go through⟩ — see DISOBEDIENCE

rebellious *adj* **1** taking part in a rebellion ⟨the *rebellious* troops fought a pitched battle with divisions still loyal to the government⟩

synonyms insurgent, insurrectionary, mutinous, revolutionary

related words seditious, traitorous, treacherous, treasonous; agitating, demagogic, rabble-rousing; defiant, disobedient, insubordinate, intractable, recalcitrant, refractory, restive, ungovernable, unruly

near antonyms constant, devoted, loyal, staunch (*also* stanch), steadfast, true, true-blue; compliant, obedient, submissive, tractable

2 given to resisting authority or another's control ⟨expected her son to grow a little more *rebellious* as he got older, but she knew he understood when to kick and when to obey⟩ — see DISOBEDIENT

rebelliousness *n* refusal to obey ⟨her habitual *rebelliousness* eventually landed her in the principal's office⟩ — see DISOBEDIENCE

rebirth *n* the act or an instance of bringing something back to life, public attention, or vigorous activity ⟨a renewed interest in long-playing records led to the *rebirth* of the turntable among audiophiles⟩ — see REVIVAL

reborn *adj* made or become fresh in spirits or vigor ⟨she felt *reborn* after the Swedish massage⟩ — see NEW 4

rebound *vb* **1** to regain a former or normal state ⟨the economy will *rebound* from this latest slump⟩ — see RECOVER 2

2 to strike and fly off at an angle ⟨the ball *rebounded* off the rim⟩ — see GLANCE 1

rebuff *n* treatment that is deliberately unfriendly ⟨took her *rebuff* in stride, and still greeted her cousin with a friendly smile the next time they met⟩ — see COLD SHOULDER

rebuke *n* an often public or formal expression of disapproval ⟨delivered a stinging *rebuke* to the Congress, calling for an end to backstabbing and arguing⟩ — see CENSURE

rebuke *vb* **1** to criticize (someone) so as to correct a fault ⟨the father was forced to *rebuke* his son for the spendthrift ways he had adopted since arriving at college⟩
synonyms admonish, chide, reprimand, reproach, reprove, tick off
related words berate, castigate, chew out, dress down, flay, harangue, jaw, keelhaul, lambaste (*or* lambast), lecture, rail (at *or* against), rate, scold, score, upbraid; abuse, assail, attack, bad-mouth, blame, blast, censure, condemn, criticize, crucify, denounce, dis (*also* diss) [*slang*], excoriate, fault, knock, lash, pan, reprehend, slam; belittle, deprecate, disparage, minimize, mock, put down; deride, ridicule, scoff, scorn
phrases burn one's ears, get after, get on
near antonyms approve, endorse (*also* indorse), OK (*or* okay), sanction; applaud, extol (*also* extoll), hail, laud, praise, salute, tout
2 to criticize (someone) severely or angrily especially for personal failings ⟨strongly *rebuked* the girl for playing with matches⟩ — see SCOLD
3 to express public or formal disapproval of ⟨in a rare move, the state's supreme court *rebuked* the governor for trying to circumvent one of its recent rulings⟩ — see CENSURE 1

rebut *vb* **1** to drive back ⟨Stalingrad's defenders were finally able to *rebut* the besiegers, but only after a horrendous loss of life⟩ — see REPEL 1
2 to prove to be false ⟨Magellan's circumnavigation of the globe effectively *rebutted* any lingering notions that the earth is flat⟩ — see DISPROVE

rebuttal *n* something (as an argument) that serves to disprove ⟨an effective *rebuttal* to her claim of having the gift of clairvoyance⟩ — see CONFUTATION

recalcitrance *n* refusal to obey ⟨punished her *recalcitrance* by taking away her driving privileges⟩ — see DISOBEDIENCE

recalcitrant *adj* **1** given to resisting authority or another's control ⟨the manager worried that the *recalcitrant* employee would try to undermine his authority⟩ — see DISOBEDIENT
2 given to resisting control or discipline by others ⟨a heart-to-heart talk with the *recalcitrant* youth revealed that he had a troubled life at home⟩ — see UNCONTROLLABLE

recall *n* **1** a particular act or instance of recalling or the thing remembered ⟨his *recall* of the events of that turbulent time is significantly different from the accounts of other eyewitnesses⟩ — see MEMORY 2
2 the act of putting an end to something planned or previously agreed to ⟨we can't get a refund on the plane tickets, so the trip is beyond *recall*⟩ — see CANCELLATION 1

recall *vb* **1** to bring back to mind ⟨I don't *recall* meeting you before⟩ — see REMEMBER
2 to put an end to (something planned or previously agreed to) ⟨I'll *recall* my purchase order if the company refuses to guarantee that it'll arrive before Christmas⟩ — see CANCEL 1

recant *vb* to solemnly or formally reject or go back on (as something formerly adhered to) ⟨the Inquisition forced Galileo to *recant* his support of the Copernican observation that the earth revolves around the sun⟩ — see ABJURE 1

recap *n* a short statement of the main points ⟨after a *recap* of this morning's meeting, we can discuss the issues that were raised⟩ — see SUMMARY

recap *vb* to make into a short statement of the main points (as of a report) ⟨please *recap* the highlights of the game for me⟩ — see SUMMARIZE

recapitulate *vb* to make into a short statement of the main points (as of a report) ⟨the professor told the students that their papers should not *recapitulate* the whole plot but should rather discuss in detail one particular incident they thought was interesting⟩ — see SUMMARIZE

recapitulation *n* a short statement of the main points ⟨will begin his presentation with a *recapitulation* of the research done on the disease up to this point⟩ — see SUMMARY

recapture *n* the act or process of getting something back ⟨the *recapture* of the territory may take longer than expected⟩ — see RECOVER 1

recapture *vb* to get again in one's possession ⟨our team managed to *recapture* the ball after the fumble⟩ — see RECOVER 1

recast *vb* to make different in some way ⟨once he *recast* the question in different terms, I understood what he was asking⟩ — see CHANGE 1

recede *vb* **1** to grow less in scope or intensity especially gradually ⟨the sound of sirens *receded* as the fire engines roared off into the distance⟩ — see DECREASE 2
2 to move back or away (as from something difficult, dangerous, or disagreeable) ⟨after the rain stops, the floodwaters should gradually *recede*⟩ — see RETREAT 1

receive *vb* to offer entrance (as to a place, school, or privilege) to ⟨a top law-school grad who was *received* by the firm with open arms⟩ — see ADMIT 2

received *adj* held by or applicable to a majority of the people ⟨traditionally the *received* opinion was that, in the event of a divorce, the mother should get custody of the children⟩ — see GENERAL 3

recently *adv* not long ago ⟨I *recently* purchased a car⟩ ⟨have you seen her *recently*?⟩ — see NEWLY

receptacle *n* something into which a liquid or smaller objects can be put for storage or transportation ⟨place all wrappers in the trash *receptacles* at the entrances of the theater⟩ — see CONTAINER

reception *n* a social gathering ⟨a wedding *reception*⟩ — see PARTY 1

receptive *adj* willing to consider new or different ideas ⟨needed a partner who was *receptive* to new ways of managing the business⟩ — see OPEN-MINDED 1

recess *n* **1** a hollowed-out space in a wall ⟨the curator placed the large vase in one of the *recesses* of the gallery wall⟩ — see NICHE 1
2 a period during which the usual routine of school or work is suspended ⟨the couple goes to Florida every January for a month-long *recess* from the rigors of winter⟩ — see VACATION
3 a momentary halt in an activity ⟨the judge called for a brief *recess* so that the witness could regain her composure⟩ — see PAUSE 1
4 a sunken area forming a separate space ⟨decided to camp in a sandy *recess* where the beach met the forest⟩ — see HOLE 2

recess *vb* to bring to a formal close for a period of time ⟨the judge *recessed* the court for lunch⟩ — see ADJOURN

recessed *adj* curved inward ⟨displayed the decorative plate on a *recessed* shelf in the wall⟩ — see HOLLOW

recession *n* **1** a period of decreased economic activity ⟨the country is just coming out of a *recession*, so expect to see fewer layoffs and more new jobs in the coming year⟩ — see DEPRESSION 1
2 an act of moving away especially from something difficult, dangerous, or disagreeable ⟨a retiring CEO mak-

ing a gradual *recession* from the daily rigors of running a major corporation⟩ — see RETREAT 1

recessive *adj* not comfortable around people ⟨a *recessive* genius who was most comfortable working alone in his chemistry lab⟩ — see SHY 2

recharge *vb* **1** to bring back to a former condition or vigor ⟨that extended vacation completely *recharged* my interest in my job⟩ — see RENEW 1

2 to bring back to life, practice, or activity ⟨the collision has *recharged* efforts to make the warning mechanisms at railroad crossings idiotproof⟩ — see REVIVE 1

recherché *adj* having qualities that appeal to a refined taste ⟨a high-end restaurant with a particularly *recherché* selection of wines⟩ — see CHOICE 1

recipe *n* the means or procedure for doing something ⟨her *recipe* for attaining financial security is to save money, invest wisely, and live well within her means⟩ — see METHOD

reciprocal *adj* related to each other in such a way that one completes the other ⟨the two nations agreed to give *reciprocal* work rights to each other's citizens, thus facilitating the daily border crossings of workers from both countries⟩ — see COMPLEMENTARY

reciprocate *vb* to make a return for ⟨*reciprocated* the favor by driving their neighbor to the airport⟩
synonyms recompense, repay, requite
related words exchange; compensate, indemnify, pay, recoup, remunerate, satisfy; give back, refund, reimburse, restitute; avenge, get back (at), retaliate, revenge
near antonyms owe

recision *n* the act of putting an end to something planned or previously agreed to ⟨the national emergency forced the immediate *recision* of all military leave⟩ — see CANCELLATION 1

recite *vb* **1** to give an oral or written account of in some detail ⟨*recited* the funny story of how he and his girlfriend met⟩ — see TELL 1

2 to give from memory ⟨after all these years, she's still able to *recite* the poems she learned as a child⟩ — see REPEAT 2

3 to specify one after another ⟨the Declaration of Independence *recites* a long list of grievances against King George III⟩ — see ENUMERATE 1

reckless *adj* **1** having or showing a lack of concern for the consequences of one's actions ⟨the *reckless* skiers were making everyone nervous by schussing down the mountainside at lightning speed⟩
synonyms daredevil, devil-may-care, foolhardy, harum-scarum, hell-for-leather, irresponsible, kamikaze
related words adventurous, audacious, bold, daring, venturesome; hasty, headlong, hotheaded, impetuous, precipitate, rash, wild; blithe, carefree, happy-go-lucky, madcap, slaphappy; nonchalant, unconcerned, unworried; careless, freewheeling, heedless, inattentive, incautious, mindless, regardless, unheeding, unmindful; feckless, inconsiderate, thoughtless, unthinking
near antonyms careful, cautious, circumspect, heedful; overcareful, overcautious, timid
antonyms responsible

2 foolishly adventurous or bold ⟨the calamitous accident was caused by a *reckless* driver who cut off the semitrailer⟩ — see FOOLHARDY 1

reckon *vb* **1** to decide the size, amount, number, or distance of (something) without actual measurement ⟨tried to *reckon* the size of the crowd at the stadium⟩ — see ESTIMATE 2

2 *chiefly dialect* to have as an opinion ⟨I *reckon* you must be new to these parts⟩ — see BELIEVE 2

3 to determine (a value) by doing the necessary mathematical operations ⟨*reckoned* the runner's pace by dividing her finishing time by the race distance⟩ — see CALCULATE 1

4 to place reliance or trust ⟨don't *reckon* on being provided with low-cost housing if you take a summer job there⟩ — see DEPEND 2

5 to think of in a particular way ⟨he was *reckoned* among the great heroes of his time⟩ — see CONSIDER 1

reckoning *n* **1** the act of placing a value on the nature, character, or quality of something ⟨that old chest isn't worth much by my *reckoning*, but an antiques dealer might think otherwise⟩ — see ESTIMATE 1

2 the act or process of performing mathematical operations to find a value ⟨you forgot about the decimal point, so your *reckoning* was way off⟩ — see CALCULATION

reclaim *vb* **1** to get again in one's possession ⟨she *reclaimed* the championship title after losing it last year⟩ — see RECOVER 1

2 to make better in behavior or character ⟨a program to *reclaim* juvenile offenders by requiring them to do community service⟩ — see REFORM 1

3 to obtain (a raw material) by separating it from a byproduct or waste product ⟨after *reclaiming* the glycerin from used vegetable oil, you can use the oil to create a fuel that burns cleaner than regular gasoline⟩ — see RECYCLE

reclamation *n* the act or process of getting something back ⟨pumped water out of the field as part of the land *reclamation* program designed to provide farmers with more farmland⟩ — see RECOVERY 1

réclame *n* **1** enthusiastic and usually public expression of approval ⟨one of those rare films that are the recipient of both critical and popular *réclame*⟩ — see APPLAUSE 1

2 public acknowledgment or admiration for an achievement ⟨the great *réclame* that the novelist enjoyed in his lifetime soon faded after his death⟩ — see GLORY 1

recluse *n* a person who lives away from others ⟨he was sick of cities and crowds, so he decided to go live by himself in the woods as a *recluse*⟩
synonyms anchorite, eremite, hermit, isolate, solitary
related words homebody, shut-in
near antonyms socialite; socializer

recognize *vb* **1** to have a clear idea of ⟨finally *recognized* that we were hopelessly lost⟩ — see COMPREHEND 1

2 to show appreciation, respect, or affection for (someone) with a public celebration ⟨an awards banquet to *recognize* local heroes⟩ — see HONOR

recognized *adj* having a good reputation especially in a field of knowledge ⟨*recognized* experts on stem cell research⟩ — see RESPECTABLE 1

recoil *vb* to draw back in fear, pain, or disgust ⟨the social worker tried not to *recoil* from the sight of the cockroach in the bathtub⟩ — see FLINCH

recollect *vb* to bring back to mind ⟨I can't *recollect* if I turned the stove off or not before leaving the house⟩ — see REMEMBER

re–collect *vb* **1** to gain emotional or mental control of ⟨she had to calm down and *re-collect* herself after being told she had won the lottery⟩ — see COLLECT 1

2 to get again in one's possession ⟨I struggled to *re-collect* the papers the wind had torn from my hands⟩ — see RECOVER 1

recollected *adj* free from emotional or mental agitation ⟨are you *recollected* enough to talk about your close call?⟩ — see CALM 2

recollection *n* **1** a particular act or instance of recalling or the thing remembered ⟨I have no *recollection* of ever saying that⟩ — see MEMORY 2

2 the power or process of recalling what has been previously learned or experienced ⟨the gradual *recollection* of that long-ago romance brought back both happy and painful feelings⟩ — see MEMORY 1

recommend *vb* **1** to put (something) into the possession or safekeeping of another ⟨serious gastronomes should *recommend* their stomachs to the restaurant's chef, giving full rein to his culinary prowess and imagination⟩ — see GIVE 2
2 to put forward (something) as one's choice for a wise or proper course of action ⟨I would *recommend* you look into that option a little more closely because I don't think it will work nearly as well as you think⟩ — see ADVISE 2

recompense *n* **1** payment to another for a loss or injury ⟨the jury awarded an additional $5,000 in *recompense* for physical pain and suffering⟩ — see COMPENSATION 1
2 something (as money) that is given or received in return for goods or services ⟨the volunteer expects nothing more than sincere thanks as *recompense* for his efforts⟩ — see PAYMENT 2

recompense *vb* **1** to give (someone) the sum of money owed for goods or services received ⟨the cash-strapped museum can *recompense* lecturers with only token honorariums⟩ — see PAY 1
2 to give what is owed for ⟨that company still needs to *recompense* the work that the contractor finished last month⟩ — see PAY 2
3 to provide (someone) with a just payment for loss or injury ⟨the government has yet to adequately *recompense* the property owners for the land taken for the new highway⟩ — see COMPENSATE 1
4 to make a return for ⟨the wealthy gentleman told the poor little girl she could *recompense* his generosity simply by enjoying her new toys⟩ — see RECIPROCATE

reconceive *vb* to consider again especially with the possibility of change or reversal ⟨will have to *reconceive* my earlier opinion about him in light of his recent behavior⟩ — see RECONSIDER

reconcile *vb* to bring to a state free of conflicts, inconsistencies, or differences ⟨historians have never been able to *reconcile* the two eyewitness accounts of the battle⟩ — see HARMONIZE 2

recondite *adj* difficult for one of ordinary knowledge or intelligence to understand ⟨geochemistry is a *recondite* subject⟩ — see PROFOUND 1

recondition *vb* to put into good shape or working order again ⟨asked my neighbor to help me *recondition* the old tractor for use on the family farm⟩ — see MEND 1

reconsider *vb* to consider again especially with the possibility of change or reversal ⟨the new intelligence forced the general to *reconsider* his plan of attack⟩
synonyms readdress, reanalyze, reconceive, redefine, reevaluate, reexamine, reexplore, rethink, review, revisit, reweigh
related words rehear; reconceptualize, reenvision, reimagine; reappraise, reassess, reinvestigate, restudy; amend, correct, emend, rectify, reform, remedy, revise
phrases change one's mind (about), go over, think better of
near antonyms assert, defend, maintain, uphold

reconsideration *n* a usually critical look at a past event ⟨the discovery of new evidence calls for a *reconsideration* of the case⟩ — see REVIEW 1

record *n* **1** a relating of events usually in the order in which they happened ⟨the town paper published a *record* of the debate, as well as a synopsis of each candidate's stance on the major questions⟩ — see ACCOUNT 1
2 an account of important events in the order in which they happened ⟨historical *records* on the rise of the Roman Empire are plentiful⟩ — see HISTORY 1

record *vb* **1** to make a written note of ⟨the reporter *recorded* the events of the evening in her notebook for later reference⟩
synonyms jot (down), log, mark, note, put down, register, report, set down, take down, write down
related words chronicle, minute, transcribe; enregister, enter, inscribe; chalk (up), notch, score
2 to put (someone or something) on a list ⟨he was *recorded* as having been a passenger on that ill-fated ship, but his body was never recovered⟩ — see [1]LIST 2

recount *vb* to give an oral or written account of in some detail ⟨a novel that *recounted* an American soldier's adventures among the samurai warriors of 19th-century Japan⟩ — see TELL 1

recoup *vb* **1** to get again in one's possession ⟨tried to *recoup* the $1,000 he had when he walked into the casino by risking his last dollar on a slot machine⟩ — see RECOVER 1
2 to provide (someone) with a just payment for loss or injury ⟨you will have to submit the proper paperwork before the insurance company will *recoup* you for the damage to your vehicle⟩ — see COMPENSATE 1
3 to become healthy and strong again after illness or weakness ⟨he's *recouping* at home after a bout of the flu⟩ — see CONVALESCE

recoupment *n* **1** payment to another for a loss or injury ⟨the jury's award included a *recoupment* for emotional distress⟩ — see COMPENSATION 1
2 the act or process of getting something back ⟨almost immediately after the new contract was signed, the company began the *recoupment* of revenue lost during the strike⟩ — see RECOVERY 1

recourse *n* something that one uses to accomplish an end especially when the usual means is not available ⟨a toddler quickly learns that a tantrum is a surefire *recourse* when a polite request for something is met with parental indifference⟩ — see RESOURCE 1

recover *vb* **1** to get again in one's possession ⟨after fishing around in the garbage for 10 minutes, I was able to *recover* my lost keys⟩
synonyms get back, reacquire, recapture, reclaim, recollect, recoup, regain, repossess, retake, retrieve
related words recruit, replenish; redeem, repurchase; rescue
near antonyms lose, mislay, misplace
2 to regain a former or normal state ⟨after a disastrous first half, the team was able to *recover* and pull off a victory⟩
synonyms bounce (back), come back, rally, rebound, snap back
related words reanimate, revitalize, revive
phrases make (*or* stage) a comeback
near antonyms decline, fail, worsen
3 to become healthy and strong again after illness or weakness ⟨I see you're *recovering* well from the accident⟩ — see CONVALESCE
4 to obtain (a raw material) by separating it from a byproduct or waste product ⟨the process of *recovering* aluminum from old cans⟩ — see RECYCLE

recovery *n* **1** the act or process of getting something back ⟨the *recovery* of the sunken boat took over a week⟩
synonyms recapture, reclamation, recoupment, repossession, retrieval
related words recruitment, replenishment; redemption, rescue
near antonyms loss, misplacement
2 the process or period of gradually regaining one's health and strength ⟨his *recovery* from the flu was remarkably quick⟩ — see CONVALESCENCE

recreant *adj* **1** having or showing a shameful lack of courage ⟨the victors had only contempt for the *recreant* enemy soldiers who surrendered without firing a shot⟩ — see COWARDLY

2 not true in one's allegiance to someone or something ⟨*recreant* campaign workers who walked out as soon as their candidate began dropping in the polls⟩ — see FAITHLESS

recreant *n* **1** a person who abandons a cause or organization usually without right ⟨traditionally armies have dealt harshly with *recreants*, with execution being a common punishment for desertion during wartime⟩ — see RENEGADE

2 a person who shows a shameful lack of courage in the face of danger ⟨the historian reserved his greatest contempt for those *recreants* who opposed the witch hunt but lacked the courage to speak out against it⟩ — see COWARD

3 one who betrays a trust or an allegiance ⟨a spy and *recreant* to his country⟩ — see TRAITOR

recreate *vb* **1** to bring back to a former condition or vigor ⟨supporters of preservation hope to *recreate* the architectural splendor that the old movie theater had when it first opened⟩ — see RENEW 1

2 to engage in activity for amusement ⟨an old summer resort where families have been *recreating* for over a century⟩ — see PLAY 1

recreated *adj* made or become fresh in spirits or vigor ⟨the club finally got some new, enthusiastic members, and the *recreated* organization actually began contributing to the community⟩ — see NEW 4

recreation *n* **1** activity engaged in to amuse oneself ⟨decided to take a bike tour of the island for *recreation* and relaxation⟩ — see PLAY 1

2 someone or something that provides amusement or enjoyment ⟨bowling is great *recreation* on a rainy afternoon⟩ — see FUN 1

3 the act or activity of providing pleasure or amusement especially for the public ⟨water parks have become a significant part of the *recreation* business⟩ — see ENTERTAINMENT 1

4 an activity outside of one's regular occupation that is engaged in primarily for pleasure ⟨as with other men of his class and income, his principal *recreations* were polo and yachting⟩ — see AVOCATION

recreational vehicle *n* a motor vehicle that is specially equipped for living while traveling ⟨sales of *recreational vehicles* typically go down when gas prices go up⟩ — see CAMPER

recruit *n* a person who is just starting out in a field of activity ⟨the skydiving instructor and other experienced jumpers tried to encourage the new *recruits* on their first jump⟩ — see BEGINNER

recruit *vb* to provide with a paying job ⟨thousands of recent immigrants were *recruited* to build the nation's rail system⟩ — see EMPLOY 1

rectifier *n* something that corrects or counteracts something undesirable ⟨a tropical vacation is a surefire *rectifier* of the midwinter blues⟩ — see CURE 1

rectify *vb* to remove errors, defects, deficiencies, or deviations from ⟨let me get the store manager, and he'll *rectify* the invoice for your order⟩ — see CORRECT 1

rectifying *adj* serving to raise or adjust something to some standard or proper condition ⟨the company is taking *rectifying* measures to address the lack of handicapped access to the building⟩ — see CORRECTIVE 1

rectitude *n* **1** conduct that conforms to an accepted standard of right and wrong ⟨encouraged the graduates to go on to live lives of unimpeachable *rectitude* and integrity⟩ — see MORALITY 1

2 faithfulness to high moral standards ⟨has a finely honed sense of *rectitude* that keeps him from cheating on exams⟩ — see HONOR 1

recuperate *vb* to become healthy and strong again after illness or weakness ⟨half the office was out today, many employees being sick or *recuperating* from the flu⟩ — see CONVALESCE

recuperation *n* the process or period of gradually regaining one's health and strength ⟨the older you get, the longer *recuperation* takes⟩ — see CONVALESCENCE

recurrent *adj* occurring or appearing at intervals ⟨had *recurrent* problems with the computer for months and finally junked it⟩ — see INTERMITTENT 1

recurring *adj* occurring or appearing at intervals ⟨death and spirituality are *recurring* themes throughout the whole of this author's work⟩ — see INTERMITTENT 1

recusant *adj* given to resisting authority or another's control ⟨several *recusant* senators refused to vote as commanded by the party leadership⟩ — see DISOBEDIENT

recycle *vb* to obtain (a raw material) by separating it from a by-product or waste product ⟨*recycling* the aluminum from soda pop cans is environmentally sound⟩
synonyms reclaim, recover
related words reuse; process, reprocess

red *adj* **1** having a healthy reddish skin tone ⟨the merry, *red*, smiling face of Santa Claus⟩ — see RUDDY

2 having a notably high temperature ⟨the streams of *red* lava were especially spectacular at night⟩ — see HOT 1

red *n* **1** a person who rises up against authority ⟨the *reds* demanded a violent overthrow of the government⟩ — see REBEL

2 *cap* an adherent or advocate of an economic system in which the means of production are owned and controlled by the state ⟨the story of John Reed, the only American *Red* buried within the Kremlin⟩ — see COMMUNIST

red alert *n* the state of being constantly attentive and responsive to signs of opportunity, activity, or danger ⟨the paparazzi were on *red alert* for sightings of the hot new Hollywood couple⟩ — see VIGILANCE

red–blooded *adj* having active strength of body or mind ⟨a *red-blooded* rugby player who always plays to win⟩ — see VIGOROUS 1

redd (up *or* out) *vb, chiefly dialect* to make neat ⟨it's time to *redd up* the garage and get rid of a lot of the junk we've accumulated⟩ — see NEATEN

redden *vb* to develop a rosy facial color (as from excitement or embarrassment) ⟨his face *reddened* when she flashed him a dazzling smile⟩ — see BLUSH

redeem *vb* **1** to do what is required by the terms of ⟨the Little League coach *redeemed* his promise to take the players out for ice cream if they improved their fielding over the season⟩ — see FULFILL 1

2 to free from captivity or punishment by paying a price ⟨the government has consistently refused to *redeem* hostages captured by terrorists⟩ — see RANSOM

3 to free from the penalties or consequences of sin ⟨the belief that sinners are *redeemed* by their faith in God⟩ — see SAVE 1

4 to make better in behavior or character ⟨the unfaithful husband made a determined effort to *redeem* himself in the eyes of his wife and children⟩ — see REFORM 1

5 to make up for (an offense) ⟨quickly *redeemed* the offending remark with a sincere and unconditional apology⟩ — see EXPIATE

redeemable *adj* capable of being corrected ⟨you made several mistakes in your report, but they're all *redeemable*⟩ — see REMEDIABLE

redeemer *n* one that saves from danger or destruction ⟨the rescued hostages profusely thanked their camouflage-clad *redeemers*⟩ — see SAVIOR

redefine *vb* to consider again especially with the possibility of change or reversal ⟨learning that he had been adopted forced him to completely *redefine* his identity⟩ — see RECONSIDER

red flag *n* something that tells of approaching danger or risk ⟨the résumé she accidentally left on the office printer was a *red flag* that she was planning to quit⟩ — see WARNING 2

red–hot *adj* **1** being or involving the latest methods, concepts, information, or styles ⟨this *red-hot* sports car uses the latest technology for its engine design⟩ — see MODERN

2 having a notably high temperature ⟨don't touch the stove—it's *red-hot*⟩ — see HOT 1

3 having or expressing great depth of feeling ⟨*red-hot* calls to action from both supporters and opponents of the war⟩ — see FERVENT 1

4 enjoying widespread favor or approval ⟨a show that is this year's *red-hot* sitcom⟩ — see POPULAR 1

red hot *n* one who is intensely or excessively devoted to a cause ⟨the inflammatory language favored by the *red hots* is simply polarizing voters and stifling all dialogue⟩ — see ZEALOT

redirect *vb* to change the course or direction of (something) ⟨upon hearing the noise, he *redirected* his gaze to the window⟩ — see TURN 2

red light *n* something that tells of approaching danger or risk ⟨the reporter took her glower as a *red light* and stopped asking questions⟩ — see WARNING 2

redo *n* the act of saying or doing over again ⟨as a way of celebrating our silver wedding anniversary, we're planning a *redo* of the trip we took on our honeymoon⟩ — see REPEAT

redo *vb* **1** to make different in some way ⟨desperately wanted to *redo* the red living room in soothing shades of green⟩ — see CHANGE 1

2 to make or do again ⟨the conductor kept asking the violinist to *redo* that passage until he was completely satisfied⟩ — see REPEAT 4

redoing *n* the act, process, or result of making different ⟨some residents objected to the *redoing* of the historic school building⟩ — see CHANGE 1

redolence *n* **1** a sweet or pleasant smell ⟨breathed in the *redolence* of the apple orchard⟩ — see FRAGRANCE

2 the quality of a thing that makes it perceptible to the sense organs in the nose ⟨the *redolence* of fir trees always reminds me of Christmas⟩ — see SMELL 1

redolent *adj* having a pleasant smell ⟨my grandmother's house always seemed to be *redolent* with the aroma of baking bread⟩ — see FRAGRANT

redouble *vb* **1** to make markedly greater in measure or degree ⟨rescuers *redoubled* their efforts to reach the people buried in the rubble after unexpectedly hearing someone call for help⟩ — see INTENSIFY

2 to make twice as great or as many ⟨if we *redouble* the recipe, we'll have enough cookies for everyone⟩ — see DOUBLE 1

redoubt *n* a structure or place from which one can resist attack ⟨a massive stone *redoubt* at the entrance of the bay guarded the city⟩ — see FORT

redoubtable *adj* **1** causing fear ⟨his next opponent, the reigning champion, would be by far the most *redoubtable* adversary the young boxer had ever faced⟩ — see FEARFUL 1

2 standing above others in rank, importance, or achievement ⟨a surprising discovery by one of the most *redoubtable* figures in Egyptian archaeology⟩ — see EMINENT

red–pencil *vb* **1** to remove errors, defects, deficiencies, or deviations from ⟨the magazine claims that every article is *red-penciled* by a team of fact checkers before it ever sees the light of print⟩ — see CORRECT 1

2 to remove objectionable parts from ⟨a television script that had been heavily *red-penciled* in abject surrender to political correctness⟩ — see CENSOR

redraft *vb* to prepare for publication by correcting, rewriting, or updating ⟨if you *redraft* that paper and include more recent data, I think we could publish it⟩ — see EDIT 1

redress *n* payment to another for a loss or injury ⟨the new skis were certainly an adequate *redress* for the lost snowboard⟩ — see COMPENSATION 1

redress *vb* to punish in kind the wrongdoer responsible for ⟨the belief that *redressing* a murder with another murder, even if carried out by the state, is not morally justified⟩ — see AVENGE

reduce *vb* **1** to bring to a lower grade or rank ⟨was *reduced* from team captain to team member as punishment for his misbehavior on the court⟩ — see DEMOTE

2 to make smaller in amount, volume, or extent ⟨you'll have to *reduce* the amount of money you spend on unnecessary purchases if you want to have any money left for retirement⟩ — see DECREASE 1

3 to diminish the price or value of ⟨a mortgage crisis that *reduced* homes to their lowest level in a decade⟩ — see DEPRECIATE 1

reduction *n* **1** something that is or may be subtracted ⟨there was a sizable *reduction* in her weekly pay when she decided to buy health insurance⟩ — see DEDUCTION 1

2 the amount by which something is lessened ⟨saw an 11% *reduction* in the number of students applying to the school⟩ — see DECREASE

3 the act or an instance of bringing to a lower grade or rank ⟨the captain was punished with a *reduction* to lieutenant⟩ — see BUMP 2

redundancy *n* **1** the use of too many words to express an idea ⟨even though the phrase "free gift" is a *redundancy*, many retailers still use it to assure customers that an item is really free⟩ — see VERBIAGE 1

2 the state or an instance of going beyond what is usual, proper, or needed ⟨there's a *redundancy* of high-priced restaurants in the area⟩ — see EXCESS 1

3 *chiefly British* the termination of the employment of an employee or a work force often temporarily ⟨several dozen employees at the London office were lost to *redundancy*⟩ — see LAYOFF 1

redundant *adj* being over what is needed ⟨this area is already chockablock with shopping malls; another one would be *redundant*⟩ — see SPARE 1

reduplicate *vb* **1** to make an exact likeness of ⟨*reduplicate* a recording of the concert for my friend⟩ — see COPY 1

2 to make or do again ⟨found out halfway through the project that I was *reduplicating* another team member's efforts, so we had to figure out who was going to do what⟩ — see REPEAT 4

reduplication *n* **1** something that is made to look exactly like something else ⟨that old-looking colonial mansion is actually a 20th-century *reduplication* of the original, which was destroyed many years ago⟩ — see COPY

2 the act of saying or doing over again ⟨ever since I was forced to do a *reduplication* of a day's work, I've been more conscientious about hitting my computer's "save" button⟩ — see REPEAT

reecho *vb* **1** to continue or be repeated in a series of reflected sound waves ⟨thunder *reechoing* through the canyon⟩ — see REVERBERATE

2 to say after another ⟨she *reechoed* an earlier speaker's points, only with a slightly different emphasis⟩ — see REPEAT 3

reed *n* a person without strength of character ⟨the congresswoman is but a *reed* who bends whichever way the political winds are blowing⟩ — see WEAKLING 2

reek *n* **1** a strong unpleasant smell ⟨a terrible *reek* com-

ing from the garbage can⟩ — see STINK 1
2 an atmospheric condition in which suspended particles in the air rob it of its transparency ⟨couldn't see through the *reek* of smog and smoke surrounding the steel plant⟩ — see HAZE 1

reek *vb* to give off an extremely unpleasant smell ⟨those old sneakers *reek* something awful⟩ — see STINK 1

reeking *adj* having an unpleasant smell ⟨I would rather not be the one to wash your *reeking* gym clothes⟩ — see MALODOROUS

reeky *adj* having an unpleasant smell ⟨a *reeky* riverbank that at low tide smells of rotting fish⟩ — see MALODOROUS

reel *n* a rapid turning about on an axis or central point ⟨she slipped and, after an out-of-control *reel*, fell on her backside⟩ — see SPIN 1

reel *vb* **1** to be in a confused state as if from being twirled around ⟨his mind *reeled* upon hearing the news that his employer had been indicted for fraud⟩ — see SPIN 2
2 to move forward while swaying from side to side ⟨got off the amusement park ride *reeling* and barely able to stand⟩ — see STAGGER 1

reeling *adj* having a feeling of being whirled about and in danger of falling down ⟨the blood donor experienced a *reeling* sensation after standing up too quickly⟩ — see DIZZY 1

reel off *vb* **1** to give from memory ⟨he's able to *reel off* the names of all the U.S. presidents, in historical order and without pausing⟩ — see REPEAT 2
2 to specify one after another ⟨her friend proceeded to *reel off* the roster of losers that she had dated over the years⟩ — see ENUMERATE 1

reenergized *adj* made or become fresh in spirits or vigor ⟨was *reenergized* after a short nap⟩ — see NEW 4

reevaluate *vb* to consider again especially with the possibility of change or reversal ⟨the senator is arguing that the government needs to *reevaluate* its budget in light of the committee's findings⟩ — see RECONSIDER

reexamination *n* a usually critical look at a past event ⟨the safety board's *reexamination* of the accident to see if it could have been prevented⟩ — see REVIEW 1

reexamine *vb* to consider again especially with the possibility of change or reversal ⟨in light of your broken leg, we should *reexamine* our decision to go on a hiking vacation this summer⟩ — see RECONSIDER

reexplore *vb* to consider again especially with the possibility of change or reversal ⟨the article *reexplores* the role of women during the American Revolution⟩ — see RECONSIDER

refashion *vb* to make different in some way ⟨*refashioned* my old pair of jeans into a cover for my scrapbook⟩ — see CHANGE 1

refashioning *n* the act, process, or result of making different ⟨the *refashioning* of the theater will make it more up-to-date and expand the seating capacity⟩ — see CHANGE 1

refection *n* food eaten or prepared for eating at one time ⟨*refections* at the monastery are as spartan as the surroundings⟩ — see MEAL

refer *vb* to have a relation or connection ⟨I don't think that rule of play *refers* to this particular situation⟩ — see APPLY 1

refer (to) *vb* **1** to make reference to or speak about briefly but specifically ⟨try not to *refer to* the recent death of her aunt⟩ — see MENTION 1
2 to use or seek out as a source of aid, relief, or advantage ⟨she studied so she wouldn't have to *refer to* the book during the exam⟩ — see RESORT (TO) 1

referee *n* a person who impartially decides or resolves a dispute or controversy ⟨served as the unofficial *referee* in disputes over the family business⟩ — see JUDGE 1

referee *vb* to give an opinion about (something at issue or in dispute) ⟨their father usually ends up *refereeing* any disputes concerning use of the big TV⟩ — see JUDGE 1

reference *n* **1** something mentioned in a text as providing related and especially supporting information ⟨the author's argument is interesting, but the lack of *references* makes me wonder if it can be proven⟩
synonyms authority, source
related words citation, excerpt, extract, quotation; caption, cross-reference, footnote, note
2 relation to or concern with something specified ⟨this reply is in *reference* to your last question⟩ — see RESPECT 1

refine *vb* to make better ⟨worked on *refining* her backhand before the big tennis match⟩ — see IMPROVE

refined *adj* **1** being far along in development ⟨a *refined* analysis of the factors that produce economic wealth in the new global economy⟩ — see ADVANCED 1
2 free from added matter ⟨*refined* gold⟩ — see PURE 1
3 having or showing a taste for the fine arts and gracious living ⟨a *refined* couple who have hosted many elegant benefits for organizations promoting the arts⟩ — see CULTIVATED
4 having or showing elegance ⟨a *refined* woman with gracious manners⟩ — see ELEGANT 1
5 made or done with extreme care and accuracy ⟨the dressmaker took a set of quite *refined* measurements before actually starting work⟩ — see FINE 2
6 satisfying or pleasing because of fineness or mildness ⟨the chef's *refined* cuisine is one that true gourmets will appreciate⟩ — see DELICATE 1
7 meeting the highest standard of accuracy ⟨this is not a *refined* calculation of the total number of calories in the dish—just a rough estimate⟩ — see PRECISE 1

refinement *n* **1** an instance of notable progress in the development of knowledge, technology, or skill ⟨the recent *refinements* in this area of medical technology⟩ — see ADVANCE 2
2 a high level of taste and enlightenment as a result of extensive intellectual training and exposure to the arts ⟨had a sense of *refinement* that her small hometown couldn't satisfy, so she moved to New York City to be closer to great museums and concert halls⟩ — see CULTURE 1
3 dignified or restrained beauty of form, appearance, or style ⟨although she can afford all the jewelry that money can buy, she dresses with the gentle *refinement* that only taste can bestow⟩ — see ELEGANCE

reflect *vb* **1** to reproduce or show (an exact likeness) as a mirror would ⟨her face was *reflected* in the waters of the still pond⟩
synonyms image, mirror
related words clone, copy, duplicate, imitate, reduplicate, repeat, replicate, reproduce
2 to make a statement of one's opinion ⟨*reflected* on the huge influence that the electronic media have on our national elections⟩ — see REMARK 1

reflection *n* **1** a briefly expressed opinion ⟨does anyone want to share their *reflections* on the passage we just read?⟩ — see REMARK
2 a cause of shame ⟨your constant lying is a serious *reflection* on your character⟩ — see DISGRACE 2
3 a careful weighing of the reasons for or against something ⟨after *reflection*, they decided to refuse the offer on the house⟩ — see CONSIDERATION 1

reflective *adj* **1** given to or marked by long, quiet thinking ⟨one of the twins was outgoing and talkative while the other was withdrawn and *reflective*⟩ — see CONTEMPLATIVE
2 indicating something ⟨this new policy is *reflective* of

the company's desire to improve customer relations⟩ — see INDICATIVE

reform *vb* **1** to make better in behavior or character ⟨volunteers at a camp that tries to *reform* troubled youths⟩
synonyms habilitate, reclaim, redeem, regenerate, rehabilitate
related words reeducate; amend, improve, refine; cleanse, purify, restore
near antonyms abase, canker, corrupt, debauch, degrade, demean, demoralize, deprave, lower, pervert, poison, profane, prostitute, subvert, warp
2 to change one's behavior or character for the better ⟨an alcoholic who's been trying to *reform* ever since he was arrested for drunk driving⟩
synonyms amend, mend, shape up, straighten (up *or* out)
related words behave, regenerate; better, improve
phrases clean up one's act
near antonyms backslide, regress
3 to remove errors, defects, deficiencies, or deviations from ⟨he had better *reform* his ways if he wants any of us to trust him⟩ — see CORRECT 1

reformative *adj* serving to raise or adjust something to some standard or proper condition ⟨took *reformative* measures to curb abuses in the state's welfare system⟩ — see CORRECTIVE 1

reformatory *adj* serving to raise or adjust something to some standard or proper condition ⟨the belief that manual labor was a *reformatory* experience for convicted felons, who would learn the value of hard work⟩ — see CORRECTIVE 1

refractoriness *n* refusal to obey ⟨I wish that teenager would grow up—she still displays the *refractoriness* of a two-year-old⟩ — see DISOBEDIENCE

refractory *adj* **1** given to resisting authority or another's control ⟨*refractory* players will be ejected from the game⟩ — see DISOBEDIENT
2 given to resisting control or discipline by others ⟨believing that rules are only for other people, he's been *refractory* virtually his entire life⟩ — see UNCONTROLLABLE

refrain *n* a part of a song or hymn that is repeated every so often ⟨I didn't know the verses of the song, so I only sang on the *refrain*⟩ — see CHORUS 2

refrain (from) *vb* to resist the temptation of ⟨couldn't *refrain from* ruffling her nephew's neatly combed hair whenever she saw him⟩ — see FORBEAR

refrainment *n* the checking of one's true feelings and impulses when dealing with others ⟨students in the class should show some generosity and *refrainment* when critiquing the work of their fellow photographers⟩ — see CONSTRAINT 1

refresh *vb* **1** to bring back to a former condition or vigor ⟨brought out some iced tea to *refresh* the spirits of the folks working out in the sun⟩ — see RENEW 1
2 to take a meal ⟨we were looking for a family-friendly restaurant where we could sit down and *refresh* before continuing⟩ — see DINE 1

refreshed *adj* made or become fresh in spirits or vigor ⟨woke the next morning *refreshed* and ready for the day⟩ — see NEW 4

refreshen *vb* to bring back to a former condition or vigor ⟨*refreshened* the wilting flowers by cutting the stems again and putting them in a vase with water⟩ — see RENEW 1

refreshing *adj* having a renewing effect on the state of the body or mind ⟨the cool wind off the ocean is *refreshing* on such a hot day⟩ — see TONIC 1

refrigerate *vb* to cause to lose heat ⟨*refrigerate* the cake after you frost it so that the frosting doesn't melt⟩ — see COOL 1

refuge *n* something (as a building) that offers cover from the weather or protection from danger ⟨hunting is strictly forbidden in the wildlife *refuge*⟩ — see SHELTER

refuge *vb* to be or provide a shelter for ⟨a nation with a long, honorable history of *refuging* political asylum seekers⟩ — see SHELTER 1

refugee *n* a person forced to emigrate for political reasons ⟨*refugees* began returning to their homeland after years of political unrest and war⟩ — see ÉMIGRÉ 1

refulgence *n* the quality or state of having or giving off light ⟨the *refulgence* of a full moon on a clear autumn night⟩ — see BRILLIANCE 1

refulgent *adj* giving off or reflecting much light ⟨*refulgent* sunlight broke through the clouds, creating huge swaths of light in the valley below us⟩ — see BRIGHT 1

refund *vb* to make a return payment to ⟨will *refund* you your money⟩ — see REPAY 1

refusal *n* an unwillingness to grant something asked for ⟨his flat *refusal* of our reasonable request was rather startling⟩ — see DENIAL 1

refuse *n* discarded or useless material ⟨*refuse* had littered the playground until our volunteer group cleaned it up⟩ — see GARBAGE 1

refuse *vb* **1** to be unwilling to grant ⟨the reclusive movie star usually *refuses* requests for interviews⟩ — see DENY 2
2 to show unwillingness to accept, do, engage in, or agree to ⟨she *refused* the award, citing the hard work of others who deserved the recognition more than she did⟩ — see DECLINE 1

refutation *n* something (as an argument) that serves to disprove ⟨these are hard scientific facts against which there can be no reasonable *refutation*⟩ — see CONFUTATION

refute *vb* **1** to declare not to be true ⟨while he was publicly *refuting* rumors of a merger, behind the scenes the CEO was working to effect that very outcome⟩ — see DENY 1
2 to prove to be false ⟨the victories of African-American athlete Jesse Owens in the 1936 Olympics effectively *refuted* the racial views of the Nazis⟩ — see DISPROVE

reg *n* a statement spelling out the proper procedure or conduct for an activity ⟨according to army *regs*, dress uniforms must be starched and boots polished at all times⟩ — see REGULATION 1

regain *vb* to get again in one's possession ⟨our team *regained* the ball with just two minutes left on the clock⟩ — see RECOVER 1

regal *adj* **1** fit for or worthy of a royal ruler ⟨the actress's *regal* bearing makes her a perfect choice to play royalty on the screen⟩ — see MONARCHICAL
2 large and impressive in size, grandeur, extent, or conception ⟨envisioned a *regal* wedding with hundreds of guests, a full choir, and a reception at the fanciest hotel in town⟩ — see GRAND 1

regale *n* a large fancy meal often accompanied by ceremony or entertainment ⟨a *regale* to honor the retiring Supreme Court justice⟩ — see FEAST 1

regale *vb* **1** to cause (someone) to pass the time agreeably occupied ⟨*regaled* his grandchildren with stories of his time in Morocco⟩ — see AMUSE
2 to entertain with a fancy meal ⟨an inn that nightly *regales* its guests with five-course meals prepared by a master chef⟩ — see FEAST 1

regalia *n* dressy clothing ⟨was impressed with the *regalia* of the women at the ball⟩ — see FINERY

regard *n* **1** a feeling of great approval and liking ⟨I have a deep *regard* for humanitarian aid workers who risk everything to help the poor⟩ — see ADMIRATION 1
2 an instance of looking especially briefly ⟨flashed the young man an imperial *regard* that clearly indicated

such behavior was out of line⟩ — see LOOK 2

3 relation to or concern with something specified ⟨with *regard* to your request for time off, go ahead and take the whole week for vacation⟩ — see RESPECT 1

4 regards *pl* best wishes ⟨give your parents my *regards*⟩ — see COMPLIMENT 2

5 a fixed intent look ⟨fixed the same magisterial *regard* on all the miscreants who appeared before her in court⟩ — see GAZE

6 *archaic* the outward form of someone or something especially as indicative of a quality ⟨Lord Warwick's noble *regard* and gallant demeanor set the innocent maid's heart aflutter⟩ — see APPEARANCE 1

regard *vb* **1** to make note of (something) through the use of one's eyes ⟨she *regarded* him with astonishment when he announced he had gotten engaged⟩ — see SEE 1

2 to take notice of and be guided by ⟨as a traveler, you should *regard* the laws and customs of whatever country you are visiting⟩ — see HEED 1

3 to think of in a particular way ⟨I wouldn't *regard* that offhand comment as a serious threat to your personal safety⟩ — see CONSIDER 1

4 to think very highly or favorably of ⟨an astronomer who is highly *regarded* by his peers⟩ — see ADMIRE

5 to give consideration to (as unexpected circumstances or contingencies) ⟨the judges *regard* the amount of effort and energy you put into the project in evaluating it⟩ — see ALLOW (FOR)

regardful *adj* marked by or showing proper regard for another's higher status ⟨his *regardful* willingness to let his elderly father carve the turkey this year⟩ — see RESPECTFUL

regarding *prep* having to do with ⟨wanted to talk to the company's vice president *regarding* a new product line⟩ — see ABOUT 1

regardless *adv* in spite of everything ⟨the weather looked bad, but they were resolved to go on with their picnic *regardless*⟩

synonyms anyhow, anyway, anyways [*chiefly dialect*], whatever

related words after all, however, nevertheless; always

phrases at all events, at any rate, in any case, in any event, no matter, whether or no (*or* whether or not)

regardless of *prep* without being prevented by ⟨*regardless of* what was previously agreed to, we now refuse to sign the contract⟩ — see DESPITE

regenerate *vb* **1** to bring back to a former condition or vigor ⟨the neighborhood was *regenerated* thanks to a government grant for restoring all the old buildings and creating studio spaces for artists⟩ — see RENEW 1

2 to bring back to life, practice, or activity ⟨dairy farming in the area was *regenerated* when new arrivals bought the old creamery⟩ — see REVIVE 1

3 to make better in behavior or character ⟨the ex-convict credits his newfound faith with *regenerating* him beyond anything that he could have imagined⟩ — see REFORM 1

regenerated *adj* made or become fresh in spirits or vigor ⟨after a cool dip in the river, the *regenerated* hikers continued on their way⟩ — see NEW 4

regeneration *n* the act or an instance of bringing something back to life, public attention, or vigorous activity ⟨the *regeneration* of knitting and crocheting is in full bloom, with Hollywood stars admitting they knit and crochet on movie sets⟩ — see REVIVAL

regime *also* **régime** *n* lawful control over the affairs of a political unit (as a nation) ⟨the *regime* of the dictator collapsed with surprising abruptness⟩ — see RULE 2

regimen *n* lawful control over the affairs of a political unit (as a nation) ⟨with the start of the new year, a new party will have *regimen* over the nation and, hopefully, bring some much-needed change⟩ — see RULE 2

region *n* **1** a part or portion having no fixed boundaries ⟨if you look in the upper left *region* of the sky, you can see the constellation Orion⟩

synonyms area, demesne, field, zone

related words corner, section; locale, locality, location, locus, place, point, position, site, space, spot

2 a broad geographical area ⟨corn is mostly grown in the central *regions* of the country⟩

synonyms belt, corridor, land, neck, part(s), tract, zone

related words district, domain, latitude(s), range, realm, terrain, territory; neighborhood, vicinity

regisseur *or* **régisseur** *n* a person who supervises the production of a stage show ⟨the ballet company's new *regisseur* plans to put a more modern spin on *The Nutcracker*⟩

synonyms director, stage director

related words auteur; impresario, producer, stage manager; directress

[1]**register** *n* an official whose job is to keep records ⟨ask the county *register* for a copy of your birth certificate⟩ — see CLERK 1

[2]**register** *n* a record of a series of items (as names or titles) usually arranged according to some system ⟨check the voter *register* to see if it has my current party affiliation⟩ — see [1]LIST

register *vb* **1** to add (a person) to a list or roll as a participant or member ⟨please *register* me for the yoga class⟩ — see ENROLL 1

2 to make a written note of ⟨the management *registered* her complaint in their log and promised to get back to her in a week⟩ — see RECORD 1

3 to put (someone or something) on a list ⟨I have to *register* my new car when I renew my driver's license⟩ — see [1]LIST 2

4 to have a clear idea of ⟨I'm not *registering* what you're saying⟩ — see COMPREHEND 1

registrar *n* an official whose job is to keep records ⟨got a copy of his transcript from the school's *registrar*⟩ — see CLERK 1

registration *n* the number of individuals registered ⟨there was a large *registration* for the popular swim classes at the community center⟩

synonyms enrollment (*also* enrolment), registry

related words class, roster; count, membership

registry *n* **1** a record of a series of items (as names or titles) usually arranged according to some system ⟨got a copy of the couple's bridal *registry* from the store's computer and scanned it for items we could afford⟩ — see [1]LIST

2 the number of individuals registered ⟨has the *registry* for the professional development seminar reached its limit yet?⟩ — see REGISTRATION

regress *vb* **1** to go back to a previous and usually lower state or level ⟨in extreme circumstances, people sometimes *regress* to the behavior they exhibited in childhood⟩

synonyms retrogress, return, revert

related words backslide, lapse, relapse; throw back; ebb; decline, degenerate, drop, fall, retrograde, worsen

near antonyms grow, mature, ripen

antonyms advance, develop, evolve, progress

2 to become worse or of less value ⟨the annual celebration has *regressed* to the point where it's nothing more than an excuse to get drunk⟩ — see DETERIORATE 1

regression *n* the act or an instance of going back to an earlier and lower level especially of intelligence or behavior ⟨the *regression* to really childish behavior that boys often undergo when put in large groups⟩

synonyms retrogression, reversion

related words backslide, lapse, relapse; atavism, re-

turn; nondevelopment; decline, degeneration
near antonyms gestation, growth, maturation, ripening
antonyms advancement, development, evolution, progression

regret *n* a feeling of responsibility for wrongdoing ⟨she was consumed with *regret* for belittling him in public and felt much better once she had apologized⟩ — see GUILT 1

regret *vb* to feel sorry or dissatisfied about ⟨we *regret* any inconvenience that we may have caused you⟩
synonyms bemoan, deplore, lament, repent, rue
related words ache (for), bewail, grieve (for), mourn, sorrow (for)
near antonyms delight (in), enjoy, relish, revel (in), savor (*also* savour)

regretful *adj* **1** expressing or suggesting mourning ⟨gave me a *regretful* look when I told him we had to move my mother to a nursing home⟩ — see MOURNFUL 1
2 feeling sorrow for a wrong that one has done ⟨was truly *regretful* that she had yelled at him⟩ — see CONTRITE

regretfully *adv* with feelings of bitterness or grief ⟨I must *regretfully* inform you that you are not among those who have been accepted for our internship program⟩ — see HARD 2

regrettable *adj* of a kind to cause great distress ⟨the explorers forged ahead despite the *regrettable* loss of some of their companions⟩
synonyms deplorable, distressful, distressing, grievous, heartbreaking, heartrending, lamentable, tragic (*also* tragical), unfortunate, unlucky, woeful
related words troublesome, vexatious; affecting, doleful, moving, piteous, poignant, ruthful, touching; awful, dire, dreadful, fearful, severe, terrible; alarming, disturbing, perturbing, traumatic, unsettling; crushing, excruciating, harrowing, horrible, horrifying, intolerable, overwhelming, shocking, sickening, unbearable; miserable, pitiful, sad, wretched; calamitous, disastrous; painful, raging, sharp
near antonyms gratifying, pleasing, rewarding, satisfying; comforting, encouraging, heartening; cheering, heartwarming, inspiring; fortunate, happy, lucky

regular *adj* **1** appearing or occurring repeatedly from time to time ⟨what with one or another of our pets having problems, we've been *regular* visitors at the animal hospital⟩
synonyms constant, frequent, habitual, periodic, periodical, repeated, steady
related words continual, intermittent, recurrent, recurring; cyclic (*or* cyclical); around-the-clock, hourly, round-the-clock, 24-7 (*or* 24/7); chronic, confirmed, inveterate; expected, usual
near antonyms episodic (*also* episodical), occasional; unexpected, unusual
antonyms inconstant, infrequent, irregular
2 following a set method, arrangement, or pattern ⟨he's followed a *regular* schedule for almost 20 years: up by 5, in bed by 10⟩ — see METHODICAL
3 following or agreeing with established form, custom, or rules ⟨thought about having a nontraditional wedding but in the end went with a *regular* ceremony instead⟩ — see FORMAL 1
4 having no exceptions or restrictions ⟨your room is a *regular* sty, and you need to clean it before you can go to the movies⟩ — see ABSOLUTE 2
5 having or showing the qualities associated with the members of a particular group or kind ⟨tantrums aren't his *regular* behavior⟩ ⟨was just a *regular* guy who preferred hanging out with friends⟩ — see TYPICAL 1

regular *n* **1** a person engaged in military service ⟨throughout the war, the *regulars* were supplemented by corps of volunteers and militiamen⟩ — see SOLDIER
2 someone who regularly spends time in a particular place ⟨the coffeehouse *regulars* were put out by the interlopers occupying their usual table⟩ — see DENIZEN 1

regularize *vb* to make agree with a single established standard or model ⟨the garment industry agreed to *regularize* women's clothing sizes so one company's size six wasn't another company's size ten⟩ — see STANDARDIZE

regulate *vb* **1** to keep from exceeding a desirable degree or level (as of expression) ⟨you would be well advised to *regulate* your enthusiasm for the venture and pause to consider the risk involved⟩ — see CONTROL 1
2 to look after and make decisions about ⟨the government agency that *regulates* the nuclear power industry in this country⟩ — see CONDUCT 1

regulation *n* **1** a statement spelling out the proper procedure or conduct for an activity ⟨it's against community *regulations* to leave your trash on the curb for more than two days⟩ — see RULE 1
2 the act or activity of looking after and making decisions about something ⟨the owner seldom visited the plant and did not take an active part in the *regulation* of the company⟩ — see CONDUCT 1
3 the duty or function of watching or guarding for the sake of proper direction or control ⟨the *regulation* of the soccer team was left entirely to the head coach and her assistants⟩ — see SUPERVISION 1

regulator *n* a mechanism for adjusting the operation of a device, machine, or system ⟨the voltage *regulator* will make sure your car's alternator gets the right amount of electricity⟩ — see CONTROL 1

rehab *n* the process or period of gradually regaining one's health and strength ⟨the accident victim had to undergo months of *rehab* before she could walk again⟩ — see CONVALESCENCE

rehab *vb* to restore to a healthy condition ⟨*rehabbing* the torture victim's battered body will be easier than restoring his emotional well-being⟩ — see HEAL 1

rehabilitate *vb* **1** to make better in behavior or character ⟨an organization that *rehabilitates* criminals so they can reenter society⟩ — see REFORM 1
2 to restore to a healthy condition ⟨underwent physical therapy to help *rehabilitate* her broken elbow⟩ — see HEAL 1

rehabilitation *n* the process or period of gradually regaining one's health and strength ⟨his *rehabilitation* from the flu was brief, and he was up and working again within a few days⟩ — see CONVALESCENCE

rehearsal *n* a private performance or session in preparation for a public appearance ⟨we made a few mistakes in *rehearsal*, but we were pretty sure that we'd be OK on opening night⟩
synonyms dry run, practice (*also* practise), trial
related words dress rehearsal; preview; run-through, walk-through; drill, exercise

rehearse *vb* **1** to do over and over so as to become skilled ⟨the orchestra *rehearsed* the symphony until they finally got it to the conductor's satisfaction⟩ — see PRACTICE
2 to give an oral or written account of in some detail ⟨wrote a letter to the management *rehearsing* in lurid detail our terrible stay at their hotel⟩ — see TELL 1
3 to say or state again ⟨*rehearsed* her story about why she was late as she walked into the meeting⟩ — see REPEAT 1
4 to specify one after another ⟨*rehearsed* the list of things he wanted for his birthday so that there would be no doubt in my mind⟩ — see ENUMERATE 1

reign *n* **1** controlling power or influence over others ⟨a start-up threatening the company's *reign* over the computer chip market⟩ — see SUPREMACY 1

2 the right or means to command or control others ⟨a democratic nation that is governed by the *reign* of law and not by the whim of its chief executive⟩ — see POWER 1

reimburse *vb* to make a return payment to ⟨make sure you keep your receipts so we can *reimburse* you for your expenses⟩ — see REPAY 1

rein *n* **1** *usually* **reins** *pl* the place of leadership or command ⟨after the president resigned, the vice president stepped in and took the *reins* of the company⟩ — see HEAD 2

2 the act or practice of keeping something (as an activity) within certain boundaries ⟨the oversight committee called on the state to keep a much tighter *rein* on the activities of its contractors⟩ — see RESTRICTION 2

3 *usually* **reins** *pl* the right or means to command or control others ⟨a peaceful transfer of the *reins* of government has always been a hallmark of our nation⟩ — see POWER 1

rein (in) *vb* to keep from exceeding a desirable degree or level (as of expression) ⟨try to *rein in* your spending, so you have some money left for saving⟩ — see CONTROL 1

reinforce *also* **reenforce** *vb* to provide evidence or information for (as a claim or idea) ⟨letters of recommendation that *reinforced* the committee's opinion of the candidate⟩ — see SUPPORT 4

reinforcement *n* a structure that holds up or serves as a foundation for something else ⟨the consulting architect suggested using additional steel *reinforcements* to counteract the bridge's design flaw⟩ — see SUPPORT 1

reinvigorated *adj* made or become fresh in spirits or vigor ⟨a *reinvigorated* political campaign that eventually made it all the way to the statehouse⟩ — see NEW 4

reiterate *vb* **1** to make or do again ⟨the pianist's valedictory concert will *reiterate* the program he played on the national tour⟩ — see REPEAT 4

2 to say or state again ⟨I want to *reiterate* that under no circumstances are you to leave the house⟩ — see REPEAT 1

reiteration *n* the act of saying or doing over again ⟨there's no need for the *reiteration* of the rules, as I know them already⟩ — see REPEAT

reiterative *adj* marked by repetition ⟨the novelist's *reiterative* style really bores some readers⟩ — see REPETITIVE

reject *n* **1** one who is cast out or rejected by society ⟨was the school *reject* as a child and has low self-esteem even today⟩ — see OUTCAST

2 something separated from a group or lot for not being as good as the others ⟨that apple has a mushy spot on it, so it's a *reject*⟩ — see CULL

reject *vb* **1** to be unwilling to grant ⟨*rejected* his request for time off⟩ — see DENY 2

2 to declare not to be true ⟨I *reject* the claim that I have ever lied about that⟩ — see DENY 1

3 to get rid of as useless or unwanted ⟨sorted through the nuts and *rejected* any that had cracked shells or were shattered⟩ — see DISCARD

4 to show unwillingness to accept, do, engage in, or agree to ⟨*rejected* his marriage proposal⟩ — see DECLINE 1

rejected *adj* left unoccupied or unused ⟨picked up the *rejected* toy to see what was wrong with it⟩ — see ABANDONED 1

rejection *n* **1** a refusal to confirm the truth of a statement ⟨made a flat *rejection* of the charges against him⟩ — see DENIAL 2

2 an unwillingness to grant something asked for ⟨the judge's swift *rejection* of the lawyer's request for a recess⟩ — see DENIAL 1

3 something separated from a group or lot for not being as good as the others ⟨that pile is for *rejections*, and this one is for applications we'll be accepting⟩ — see CULL

rejective *adj* given to making or expressing unfavorable judgments about things ⟨found that his new boss was very *rejective* of new ideas or suggestions⟩ — see CRITICAL 1

rejoice *vb* **1** to feel or express joy or triumph ⟨*rejoiced* over our unexpected victory on the soccer field⟩ — see EXULT

2 to give satisfaction to ⟨news of the enemy's surrender *rejoiced* a nation weary of war⟩ — see PLEASE 1

rejoice (in) *vb* to take pleasure in ⟨at least we can *rejoice in* the fact that the worst of the housing slump is over⟩ — see ENJOY 1

rejoicing *adj* having or expressing feelings of joy or triumph ⟨the *rejoicing* parents of the bride⟩ — see EXULTANT

rejoicing *n* joyful or festive activity ⟨there was great *rejoicing* at the launch party for the book⟩ — see MERRYMAKING

rejoin *vb* to speak or write in reaction to a question or to another reaction ⟨when I asked my daughter if she wouldn't mind picking up dinner on her way home from soccer practice, she *rejoined*, "Only if you wouldn't mind me taking out the pickup later tonight!"⟩ — see ANSWER 1

rejoinder *n* something spoken or written in reaction especially to a question ⟨he always has a smart-aleck *rejoinder* to everything⟩ — see ANSWER 1

rejuvenate *vb* **1** to bring back to a former condition or vigor ⟨the shower *rejuvenated* me after a long day of cleaning out the garage⟩ — see RENEW 1

2 to bring back to life, practice, or activity ⟨that rock star has *rejuvenated* '80s fashion for a whole new generation⟩ — see REVIVE 1

rejuvenating *adj* having a renewing effect on the state of the body or mind ⟨after a *rejuvenating* vacation, I was once again ready to slay dragons, or whatever else might spring up at the office⟩ — see TONIC 1

rejuvenation *n* the act or an instance of bringing something back to life, public attention, or vigorous activity ⟨Hollywood was seeing the *rejuvenation* of kung fu movies⟩ — see REVIVAL

rejuvenescence *n* the act or an instance of bringing something back to life, public attention, or vigorous activity ⟨the newly discovered oil deposits have led to a *rejuvenescence* of the nation's economy⟩ — see REVIVAL

rekindle *vb* to bring back to life, practice, or activity ⟨the trip to Ireland *rekindled* her interest in learning Gaelic⟩ — see REVIVE 1

relate *vb* **1** to form a close personal relationship ⟨she and I *relate* so well it's almost like we're siblings⟩ — see COMMUNE

2 to give an oral or written account of in some detail ⟨we asked our uncle to *relate* the story of his visit to communist Russia many years ago⟩ — see TELL 1

3 to have a relation or connection ⟨how does your comment *relate* to what the rest of us have been talking about for the last hour?⟩ — see APPLY 1

4 to think of (something) in combination ⟨most Americans probably *relate* tea to the United Kingdom and coffee to the U.S.⟩ — see ASSOCIATE 2

related *adj* having a close connection like that between family members ⟨the *related* fields of anthropology and archaeology⟩

synonyms affiliated, akin, allied, kindred

related words associated, connected, interconnected, interrelated, joined; alike, analogous, cognate, comparable, connate, correspondent, corresponding, ditto, like, matching, parallel, resemblant, resembling, similar, such, suchlike; identical, same; apposite, apropos, cogent, germane, material, pertinent, relevant

near antonyms diacritical (*also* diacritic), different, disparate, dissimilar, distinct, distinctive, diverse, nonidentical, other, unalike, unlike; differentiable, discriminable, distinguishable
antonyms unrelated

relation *n* **1 relations** *pl* doings between individuals or groups ⟨*relations* between the rival newspapers remained friendly despite their competition for the same stories⟩
synonyms commerce, dealings, interaction, intercourse
related words interrelationship; cross-fertilization, cross-pollination; companionship, company
antonyms nonintercourse
2 a person connected with another by blood or marriage ⟨he and I are *relations* on my mother's side⟩ — see RELATIVE
3 the fact or state of having something in common ⟨there's no *relation* between you losing your favorite baseball hat and your team losing the game⟩ — see CONNECTION 1
4 the state of having shared interests or efforts (as in social or business matters) ⟨our intramural baseball team had a *relation* with the other baseball teams in the area⟩ — see ASSOCIATION 1
5 relations *pl* sexual union involving penetration of the vagina by the penis ⟨a law that prohibits *relations* between close relatives⟩ — see SEXUAL INTERCOURSE

relationship *n* **1** the fact or state of having something in common ⟨studied the *relationship* between the phases of the moon and ocean tides⟩ — see CONNECTION 1
2 the state of having shared interests or efforts (as in social or business matters) ⟨the street's shopkeepers have a good business *relationship*⟩ — see ASSOCIATION 1

relative *adj* **1** being such only when compared to something else ⟨after being crammed into a one-bedroom apartment, they lived in *relative* comfort in a two-bedroom house⟩ — see COMPARATIVE
2 having to do with the matter at hand ⟨I don't need the whole story, just the details that are *relative* to the case⟩ — see PERTINENT

relative *n* a person connected with another by blood or marriage ⟨it's always fun to see all your *relatives* at a big family gathering⟩
synonyms cousin, kin, kinsman, relation
related words in-law; kissing cousin; kinswoman; blood, clan, family, folk, house, kindred, kinfolk (*or* kinfolks), kinsfolk, line, lineage, people, race, stock, tribe
antonyms nonrelative

relatively *adv* to some degree or extent ⟨these newly acquired in-laws felt *relatively* comfortable at our family reunion⟩ — see FAIRLY 1

relax *vb* **1** to get rid of nervous tension or anxiety ⟨she took deep breaths to *relax* before going on stage⟩
synonyms chill, chill out [*slang*], decompress, de-stress, loosen up, mellow (out), unwind, wind down
related words unbend; bask, kick back, loll, lounge, repose, rest; bum, dally, dawdle, dillydally, drone, footle, goof (off), hack (around), hang (around *or* out), idle, laze, loaf, vegetate, veg out, zone out; alleviate, comfort, ease, relieve; calm, compose, cool, quiet, settle
phrases hang loose
antonyms tense (up)
2 to make less taut ⟨*relax* the rope a bit so I can pick up the slack and tie this knot⟩ — see SLACKEN 1
3 to refrain from labor or exertion ⟨I just want to kick back and *relax* after mowing that huge lawn⟩ — see REST 1

relaxation *n* **1** activity engaged in to amuse oneself ⟨what do people in this jerkwater town do for *relaxation*?⟩ — see PLAY 1
2 freedom from activity or labor ⟨meditating in a state of total *relaxation*⟩ — see [1]REST 1

relaxed *adj* **1** enjoying physical comfort ⟨the frazzled executive was totally *relaxed* after the warm bath⟩ — see COMFORTABLE 2
2 not bound by rigid standards ⟨we're having a very *relaxed* staff meeting, and then everyone can get an early start on the long holiday weekend⟩ — see EASYGOING 2
3 not tightly fastened, tied, or stretched ⟨the fishing line was *relaxed* and looped lazily into the pond⟩ — see LOOSE 1

relaxing *adj* tending to calm the emotions and relieve stress ⟨a *relaxing* cup of chamomile tea⟩ — see SOOTHING 1

release *n* **1** a freeing from an obligation or responsibility ⟨because they had legally declared bankruptcy, they received *release* from their debt⟩
synonyms delivery, discharge, quietus, quittance
related words dispensation, exemption, immunity, waiver
2 a document containing a declaration of an intentional giving up of a right, claim, or privilege ⟨we had to sign a liability *release* before they'd let us go rock climbing on their property⟩ — see WAIVER
3 a published statement informing the public of a matter of general interest ⟨a press *release* announcing that the governor would not run for a second term⟩ — see ANNOUNCEMENT
4 reduction of or freedom from pain ⟨only sleep offered any *release* from the agony of the migraine⟩ — see EASE 1

release *vb* **1** to set free (from a state of being held in check) ⟨the losing player *released* his anger with a great yell of frustration⟩
synonyms loose, loosen, uncork, unleash, unlock, unloose, unloosen
related words discharge, emancipate, enfranchise, free, liberate, manumit, spring, unbind, uncage, unchain, unfetter, unmoor, unshackle; air, express, take out, vent
phrases let go
near antonyms handcuff, manacle, shackle, trammel; bind, confine, enchain, fetter; halter, hamper
antonyms bridle, check, constrain, contain, control, curb, govern, hold, inhibit, regulate, rein (in), restrain, smother, tame
2 to find emotional release for ⟨tried to find other ways of *releasing* tension than by chewing her fingernails⟩ — see TAKE OUT 1
3 to set free (as from slavery or confinement) ⟨*release* the prisoners immediately⟩ — see FREE 1
4 to set free from entanglement or difficulty ⟨the new governor finally managed to *release* himself from his rash campaign promise⟩ — see EXTRICATE
5 to throw or give off ⟨an air freshener that *releases* a pleasing scent into the room⟩ — see EMIT 1
6 to make known openly or publicly ⟨the panel of nutritionists *released* their findings on the safety and effectiveness of various diets⟩ — see ANNOUNCE
7 to let go from office, service, or employment ⟨they *released* the workers who couldn't handle the new technology⟩ — see DISMISS 1

relegate *vb* **1** to force to leave a country ⟨courtiers and generals who incurred the emperor's disfavor were soon *relegated* to the farther reaches of the empire⟩ — see BANISH 1
2 to arrange or assign according to type ⟨some psychologists argue that the syndrome should be *relegated* to a different class of autism⟩ — see CLASSIFY 1

relegation *n* the forced removal from a homeland ⟨the *relegation* of Japanese-Americans to internment camps during World War II⟩ — see EXILE 1

relent *vb* **1** to cease resistance (as to another's arguments, demands, or control) ⟨the supervisor finally *relented* in the face of the petition, and allowed employees to take longer lunch breaks⟩ — see YIELD 3
2 to grow less in scope or intensity especially gradually ⟨the fury of the storm *relented*, and the next day the sun finally broke through the clouds⟩ — see DECREASE 2
relentless *adj* showing no signs of slackening or yielding in one's purpose ⟨the team's offense was *relentless* in trying to score a touchdown⟩ — see UNYIELDING 1
relevance *n* the fact or state of being pertinent ⟨I appreciate that you did the dishes tonight, but that has no *relevance* to my enforcement of the punishment you got earlier this week⟩ — see PERTINENCE
relevancy *n* the fact or state of being pertinent ⟨this new information has no *relevancy* to the case⟩ — see PERTINENCE
relevant *adj* having to do with the matter at hand ⟨make sure your comments during the interview are short and *relevant*⟩ — see PERTINENT
reliability *n* worthiness as the recipient of another's trust or confidence ⟨we never had reason to question the *reliability* of the park rangers in the event of an emergency⟩
synonyms dependability, dependableness, reliableness, responsibility, solidity, solidness, sureness, trustability, trustworthiness
related words inerrancy, infallibility; credibility, creditability, creditableness
near antonyms doubtfulness, dubiousness, questionableness, shakiness, uncertainness
antonyms dodginess [*chiefly British*], unreliability
reliable *adj* worthy of one's trust ⟨I need a *reliable* car that's not going to break down constantly⟩ — see DEPENDABLE
reliableness *n* worthiness as the recipient of another's trust or confidence ⟨the proven *reliableness* of that brand of household appliances⟩ — see RELIABILITY
reliance *n* **1** something or someone to which one looks for support ⟨he's been the family's foremost *reliance* in times of trouble many times⟩ — see DEPENDENCE 2
2 the quality or state of needing something or someone ⟨a baby's *reliance* on her parents⟩ ⟨his *reliance* on his next-door neighbor for all the local gossip⟩ — see DEPENDENCE 1
relic *n* **1** a tiny often physical indication of something lost or vanished ⟨a crude stone ax and other *relics* of the Neanderthals⟩ — see VESTIGE 1
2 something belonging to or surviving from an earlier period ⟨in my grandparents' attic are many "groovy" *relics* from the 1960s⟩ — see ANTIQUE
3 one that has passed the peak of effectiveness or popularity ⟨his courtly manners marked him as a *relic* of a more refined and formal era⟩ — see HAS-BEEN
4 relics *pl* a dead body ⟨though it is believed that missionary died in New Guinea, his *relics* have never been found⟩ — see CORPSE
relief *n* **1** a feeling of ease from grief or trouble ⟨my coworkers' kind words gave me some *relief* from the grief that I was feeling upon the death of my partner⟩ — see COMFORT 1
2 a person or thing that takes the place of another ⟨I can't go home from my nursing shift until my *relief* shows up to take over⟩ — see SUBSTITUTE
3 reduction of or freedom from pain ⟨the aspirin gave him some *relief* from the headache⟩ — see EASE 1
relieve *vb* **1** to make more bearable or less severe ⟨an ice pack will *relieve* the swelling⟩ — see HELP 2
2 to set (a person or thing) free of something that encumbers ⟨the bellhop *relieved* him of his luggage and led him to the elevator⟩ — see RID
3 to take the place of ⟨at daybreak a soldier arrived to *relieve* the one who had spent the night on guard duty⟩ — see REPLACE 1
religion *n* **1** a body of beliefs and practices regarding the supernatural and the worship of one or more deities ⟨the Jewish *religion* has followers in many parts of the globe⟩
synonyms credo, creed, cult, faith, persuasion
related words church, communion, denomination, sect; doctrine, dogma, theology; deism, heathenism, monotheism, paganism, pantheism, polytheism, theism
near antonyms agnosticism, know-nothingism; atheism, godlessness, nonbelief, secularism, unbelief
2 belief and trust in and loyalty to God ⟨without his *religion*, he would not have been able to survive all the difficulties he has faced over the years⟩ — see FAITH 1
religionist *n* one who professes a religious faith ⟨makes the case that one need not be a *religionist* to have basic moral values⟩ — see BELIEVER
religionless *n* lacking religious emotions, principles, or practices ⟨some people of faith had misgivings about electing a *religionless* politician⟩ — see IRRELIGIOUS
religious *adj* **1** of, relating to, or used in the practice or worship services of a religion ⟨Johann Sebastian Bach wrote some of the most beautiful *religious* music in the world⟩
synonyms devotional, sacred, spiritual
related words blessed (*also* blest), consecrated, hallowed, holy, sacrosanct, sanctified; solemn; liturgical, ritual, sacramental; semireligious, semisacred
near antonyms earthly, mundane, terrene, terrestrial, worldly
antonyms nonreligious, profane, secular
2 showing a devotion to God and to a life of virtue ⟨a deeply *religious* woman who eventually decided to quit her job and to become a nun⟩ — see HOLY 1
3 having or expressing great depth of feeling ⟨a woman known for embracing various causes with a *religious* enthusiasm⟩ — see FERVENT 1
relinquish *vb* **1** to give (something) over to the control or possession of another usually under duress ⟨the boy reluctantly *relinquished* the illegal fireworks to the police officer⟩ — see SURRENDER 1
2 to give up (as a position of authority) formally ⟨the retiring CEO *relinquished* his position to the company's vice president with very mixed feelings⟩ — see ABDICATE
relinquishment *n* the usually forced yielding of one's person or possessions to the control of another ⟨miraculously, the *relinquishment* of the hostages was accomplished without bloodshed⟩ — see SURRENDER
relish *n* **1** positive regard for something ⟨she has great *relish* for early morning walks, which she takes nearly every day⟩ — see LIKING
2 the feeling experienced when one's wishes are met ⟨ate the bowl of ice cream with *relish*⟩ — see PLEASURE 1
relish *vb* to take pleasure in ⟨visit again real soon, for I *relish* your company⟩ — see ENJOY 1
relocate *vb* to change the place or position of ⟨those volumes have been *relocated* to the second floor of the library⟩ — see MOVE 1
reluctance *n* a lack of willingness or desire to do or accept something ⟨the mice showed an odd *reluctance* to eat the cheese we had put out for them⟩
synonyms disinclination, hesitance, hesitancy, reticence, unwillingness
related words faltering, fence-sitting, hesitation, indecision, irresolution, shilly-shallying, staggering, vacillation, wavering, wobbling (*also* wabbling); distrust, distrustfulness, doubt, incertitude, misdoubt, misgiving, mistrust, mistrustfulness, skepticism, suspicion, uncertainness, uncertainty

near antonyms assurance, assuredness, certainty, certitude, conviction, positiveness, sureness, surety
antonyms inclination, willingness

reluctant *adj* slow to begin or proceed with a course of action because of doubts or uncertainty ⟨I'm *reluctant* to let you borrow my vintage CDs since you never give back anything I lend you⟩ — see HESITANT

rely *vb* to place reliance or trust ⟨rigorously tested the rope before starting out, for the rock climbers would be *relying* on it with their very lives⟩ — see DEPEND 2

remain *vb* **1** to continue to be in a place for a significant amount of time ⟨one of the three bridges known as "the London Bridge," it was moved in the late 1960s to Lake Havasu City, Arizona, where it *remains* today⟩ — see [1]STAY 1
2 to remain indefinitely in existence or in the same state ⟨the fact *remains*: it's still impossible to be in two places at once⟩ — see CONTINUE 1

remainder *n* **1** a remaining group or portion ⟨the *remainder* of the pills were saved in case they were needed later⟩
synonyms balance, leavings, leftovers, odds and ends, remains, remnant, residue, residuum, rest
related words fragment, scrap, vestige; butt, oddment, scraping(s), stub, stump; excess, fat, overabundance, overage, overflow, overkill, overmuch, oversupply, superabundance, superfluity, surfeit, surplus
near antonyms body, bulk, main, mass, most, weight
2 an unused or unwanted piece or item typically of small size or value ⟨the *remainder* of the dough can be used to make a tartlet⟩ — see [1]SCRAP 1

remains *n pl* **1** the portion or bits of something left over or behind after it has been destroyed ⟨the *remains* of the house ripped apart by the tornado littered the block for weeks afterward⟩
synonyms ashes, debris, detritus, flotsam, residue, rubble, ruins, wreck, wreckage
related words jetsam, leavings, remnant; chaff, deadwood, dross, dust, garbage, junk, litter, refuse, riffraff, rubbish, scrap, trash, waste
2 a dead body ⟨archaeologists discovered the *remains* of an Incan woman and carefully excavated her burial site, which promised to yield important clues about her status⟩ — see CORPSE
3 a remaining group or portion ⟨gathered up the *remains* of the buffet and delivered them to a local homeless shelter⟩ — see REMAINDER 1

remake *vb* **1** to make different in some way ⟨one of those people who left the security and conformity of a small town to *remake* their lives in the big city⟩ — see CHANGE 1
2 to make or do again ⟨yesterday's soup was so good that we decided to *remake* it for today's lunch⟩ — see REPEAT 4

remaking *n* the act, process, or result of making different ⟨thought that the room looked no better for all the *remaking* and rearranging we did⟩ — see CHANGE 1

remark *n* a briefly expressed opinion ⟨the director made some short *remarks* about the new museum before officially opening the doors to visitors⟩
synonyms comment, note, observation, reflection
related words analysis, commentary, exposition; aside, obiter dictum; annotation; belief, conviction, eye, feeling, judgment (*or* judgement), mind, notion, persuasion, sentiment, verdict, view; advice, input

remark *vb* **1** to make a statement of one's opinion ⟨her date awkwardly *remarked* on the attractiveness of the background music in the restaurant⟩
synonyms allow, comment, editorialize, note, observe, opine, reflect, weigh in
related words commentate; articulate, express, say, speak, state, talk, tell, utter, verbalize, vocalize; conjecture, daresay, guess, speculate, suppose, surmise
2 to make note of (something) through the use of one's eyes ⟨I *remarked* the change in her hair color but didn't think it would be polite to say anything other than she was looking good⟩ — see SEE 1

remarkable *adj* **1** different from the ordinary in a way that causes curiosity or suspicion ⟨one participant in the race had a *remarkable* walk that was half-run, half-skip⟩ — see ODD 2
2 likely to attract attention ⟨there's a *remarkable* fixation with vanity of earthly pleasures in this author's poetry⟩ — see NOTICEABLE
3 worth remembering or mentioning ⟨just your average suburban ranch house, with nothing *remarkable* about it⟩ — see NOTEWORTHY 1

remediable *adj* capable of being corrected ⟨the problems with the local transportation system were severe but still *remediable*⟩
synonyms correctable, corrigible, fixable, redeemable, repairable, reparable
related words amendable, emendable, improvable, resolvable; reversible, undoable; reconstructible, reformable, regenerable; corrected, fixed, remedied, repaired
near antonyms irretrievable, unrecoverable; irreplaceable, irreversible, irrevocable
antonyms incorrigible, irrecoverable, irredeemable, irremediable, irreparable, unredeemable

remedial *adj* **1** serving to raise or adjust something to some standard or proper condition ⟨took a *remedial* math course over the summer so he'd be ready for algebra the following school year⟩ — see CORRECTIVE 1
2 tending to cure disease or restore health ⟨unfortunately, with a cold virus, there are few *remedial* measures besides fluids and rest⟩ — see MEDICINAL 1

remedy *n* **1** a substance or preparation used to treat disease ⟨preferred to treat colds with a homemade *remedy* made from garlic⟩ — see MEDICINE
2 something that corrects or counteracts something undesirable ⟨the mayor was desperately searching for a *remedy* to the recent surge in crime the city had been experiencing⟩ — see CURE 1

remedy *vb* **1** to bring about recovery from ⟨a little extra studying should *remedy* your poor performance in history thus far this year⟩ — see CURE 1
2 to remove errors, defects, deficiencies, or deviations from ⟨needed to wear glasses to *remedy* her bad vision⟩ — see CORRECT 1

remedying *adj* serving to raise or adjust something to some standard or proper condition ⟨I've given the engine a *remedying* tune-up that should put an end to that knocking⟩ — see CORRECTIVE 1

remember *vb* to bring back to mind ⟨I *remember* very clearly the fun we had that long-ago summer, but I can't *remember* what I had for lunch yesterday⟩
synonyms flash back (to), hark back (to), harken back (to), hearken back (to), mind [*chiefly dialect*], recall, recollect, reminisce (about), reproduce, think (of)
related words recapture, recur; educe, elicit, evoke, extract, raise, remind; relive; represent
near antonyms misremember; disregard, ignore, neglect, overlook; lose, miss; blank (out)
antonyms disremember, forget, unlearn

remembrance *n* **1** a particular act or instance of recalling or the thing remembered ⟨a happy couple with many fond *remembrances* of when they were dating in college⟩ — see MEMORY 2
2 something that serves to keep alive the memory of a person or event ⟨she gave her boyfriend on the eve of his military service one of her lockets as a *remembrance* of their abiding affection⟩ — see MEMORIAL
3 the power or process of recalling what has been previ-

ously learned or experienced ⟨*remembrance* will wane with age⟩ — see MEMORY 1

reminder *n* something that serves to keep alive the memory of a person or event ⟨the peach tree in our front yard is a living *reminder* of my late grandfather, who owned an orchard⟩ — see MEMORIAL

reminisce (about) *vb* to bring back to mind ⟨two friends *reminiscing about* those proverbial good old days⟩ — see REMEMBER

reminiscence *n* **1** a particular act or instance of recalling or the thing remembered ⟨his *reminiscences* about the war were painful to hear⟩ — see MEMORY 2
2 the power or process of recalling what has been previously learned or experienced ⟨we wondered whether she could trust her *reminiscence* of events that happened so long ago⟩ — see MEMORY 1

reminiscent *adj* provoking a memory or mental association ⟨a sparkling winter day that was oddly *reminiscent* of summer in its cheering sunniness⟩ — see SUGGESTIVE 2

remiss *adj* failing to give proper care and attention ⟨I would be *remiss* if I didn't tell you how much I appreciated the lovely gift⟩ — see NEGLIGENT

remissible *adj* worthy of forgiveness ⟨only guilty of *remissible* sins⟩ — see VENIAL

remission *n* release from the guilt or penalty of an offense ⟨the *remission* of sins⟩ — see PARDON

remissness *n* failure to take the care that a cautious person usually takes ⟨it took an incredible amount of reckless *remissness* on your part to leave the house with the front door wide open⟩ — see NEGLIGENCE 1

remit *vb* **1** to grow less in scope or intensity especially gradually ⟨waited until the rain *remitted* a little and ran to the car⟩ — see DECREASE 2
2 to dismiss as of little importance ⟨the judge refused to *remit* the young man's cavalier disregard for his pile of unpaid speeding tickets and summarily revoked his driver's license⟩ — see EXCUSE 1
3 to assign to a later time ⟨the legislature has *remitted* the matter to the next session, where it will most likely die in committee⟩ — see POSTPONE

remitment *n* the act of offering money in exchange for goods or services ⟨the charge account will be closed upon the *remitment* of the outstanding balance⟩ — see PAYMENT 1

remittable *adj* worthy of forgiveness ⟨forgetting a doctor's appointment that was made months in advance is a *remittable* offense⟩ — see VENIAL

remittal *n* release from the guilt or penalty of an offense ⟨a king who was once obliged to do public penance for the *remittal* of his sins⟩ — see PARDON

remittance *n* **1** something (as money) that is given or received in return for goods or services ⟨she always mails in her *remittance* on time so she won't ever be charged a late fee on her electric bill⟩ — see PAYMENT 2
2 the act of offering money in exchange for goods or services ⟨the *remittance* of your outstanding balance is required before you can make more purchases⟩ — see PAYMENT 1

remnant *n* **1** a remaining group or portion ⟨sailed home with just a *remnant* of the colony's original population aboard⟩ — see REMAINDER 1
2 an unused or unwanted piece or item typically of small size or value ⟨gathered together her fabric *remnants* to see if she had enough of them to sew a doll blanket for her niece⟩ — see [1]SCRAP 1

remodel *vb* to make different in some way ⟨we completely *remodeled* the house right after we moved in⟩ — see CHANGE 1

remodeling *n* the act, process, or result of making different ⟨moved out of the apartment and into a motel during the *remodeling*⟩ — see CHANGE 1

remonstrance *n* a feeling or declaration of disapproval or dissent ⟨over the vociferous *remonstrances* of my parents I decided to drop my music lessons⟩ — see OBJECTION

remonstrate (with) *vb* to present an opposing opinion or argument ⟨discouraged her from *remonstrating with* her father, whose mind was obviously made up⟩ — see OBJECT

remorse *n* a feeling of responsibility for wrongdoing ⟨he felt a deep *remorse* for having neglected his family over the years⟩ — see GUILT 1

remorseful *adj* feeling sorrow for a wrong that one has done ⟨was *remorseful* about all the trouble that he had caused in the family⟩ — see CONTRITE

remorsefulness *n* a feeling of responsibility for wrongdoing ⟨he was gnawed by an unrelenting *remorsefulness* for the pain that he had caused people⟩ — see GUILT 1

remorseless *adj* **1** not sorry for having done wrong ⟨the *remorseless* killer was sentenced to life in prison without chance of parole⟩
synonyms impenitent, shameless, unashamed, unrepentant
related words compassionless, cruel, merciless, pitiless, ruthless, unmerciful; evil, immoral, iniquitous, nefarious, reprobate, unregenerate, unrighteous, vicious, vile, villainous, wicked; callous, cold-blooded, hardhearted, heartless, inhuman, inhumane, obdurate, soulless, unfeeling
near antonyms hangdog, shamefaced; charitable, compassionate, humane, merciful, sensitive, softhearted, sympathetic, tender, tenderhearted, warm, warmhearted
antonyms apologetic, ashamed, compunctious, contrite, guilty, penitent, regretful, remorseful, repentant, rueful, shamed, sorry
2 having or showing a lack of sympathy or tender feelings ⟨a *remorseless* and implacable hit man wordlessly pursuing his victim⟩ — see HARD 1

remote *adj* **1** small in degree ⟨there's a *remote* chance that it'll rain today, so I brought an umbrella⟩
synonyms fragile, frail, negligible, off, outside, slight, slim, small
related words marginal, minimal, minor; little, tiny
near antonyms great, large; distinct, significant; considerable, goodly, healthy, largish, respectable, significant, sizable (*or* sizeable), substantial, tidy
antonyms good
2 having or showing a lack of friendliness or interest in others ⟨his grandfather had been a somewhat *remote* figure, at least until they got to spend a summer together⟩ — see COOL 1
3 screened or sequestered from view ⟨a *remote* cottage on the far side of the mountain⟩ — see SECLUDED
4 not close in time or space ⟨a permanent base on Mars is likely to happen only in the *remote* future⟩ — see DISTANT 1

remotest *adj* most distant from a center ⟨news of the emperor's death had spread even to the *remotest* corners of the empire⟩ — see EXTREME 1

removal *n* the getting rid of whatever is unwanted or useless ⟨a product for the *removal* of warts⟩ — see DISPOSAL 1

remove *n* the space or amount of space between two points, lines, surfaces, or objects ⟨their farm is just a *remove* of two miles from the town center⟩ — see DISTANCE 1

remove *vb* **1** to rid oneself of (a garment) ⟨I *removed* my coat as soon as I got inside⟩
synonyms doff, douse, peel (off), put off, shrug off, take off

related words husk, shed; kick (off); disrobe, strip, undress
near antonyms wear; apparel, array, attire, bedeck, clothe, dress, garb, rig, robe, suit
antonyms don, put on, slip (into), throw (on)
2 to take away from a place or position ⟨he carefully *removed* the old manuscript from the shelf⟩
synonyms clear, draw, take out, withdraw
related words demount, dislodge; abstract, cut, draw off, draw out, extract, pull; budge, dislocate, displace, disturb, move, shift, transfer, transpose
near antonyms mount; anchor, clamp, fix, hitch, moor, secure, set; embed (*also* imbed), entrench (*also* intrench), implant, ingrain (*also* engrain), lodge, root; set up, site, situate, stick
antonyms place, position, put
3 to change the place or position of ⟨please *remove* that chair to the other room⟩ — see MOVE 1
4 to let go from office, service, or employment ⟨voters *removed* the racist selectman from office the first chance they got⟩ — see DISMISS 1

removed *adj* not close in time or space ⟨an island far *removed* from the mainland⟩ — see DISTANT 1

remunerate *vb* **1** to give (someone) the sum of money owed for goods or services received ⟨promptly *remunerated* the repair company for fixing the dryer⟩ — see PAY 1
2 to provide (someone) with a just payment for loss or injury ⟨the negligent landlord must *remunerate* those made homeless by the fire by finding new housing for them at his own expense⟩ — see COMPENSATE 1

remuneration *n* **1** the act of offering money in exchange for goods or services ⟨customers who are tardy in their *remuneration* will be subject to extra charges⟩ — see PAYMENT 1
2 payment to another for a loss or injury ⟨the vandals were ordered to pay the property owners thousands of dollars in *remuneration*⟩ — see COMPENSATION 1
3 something (as money) that is given or received in return for goods or services ⟨we can't accept your *remuneration* for services provided until we officially bill you⟩ — see PAYMENT 2

remunerative *adj* yielding a profit ⟨made a highly *remunerative* investment that will end up paying my college tuition⟩ — see PROFITABLE 1

renaissance *n* a period of high artistic or cultural development ⟨the 19th-century literary *renaissance* that prompted people to refer to Boston as the Athens of America⟩ — see BELLE EPOQUE

rend *vb* to cause (something) to separate into jagged pieces by violently pulling at it ⟨the prophecy that the disaster would cause people to *rend* their garments in mourning⟩ — see TEAR 1

render *vb* **1** to give (something) over to the control or possession of another usually under duress ⟨a gentleman bandit who graciously asked his victims to *render* their wallets to his safe possession⟩ — see SURRENDER 1
2 to make an exact likeness of ⟨*rendered* Thomas Jefferson's signature for use on an array of gift items⟩ — see COPY 1
3 to give a representation or account of in words ⟨the witness convincingly *rendered* her version of events in just a few words⟩ — see DESCRIBE 1

rendering *n* a vivid representation in words of someone or something ⟨a poet's *rendering* of the euphoria experienced by lovers in the first blush of romance⟩ — see DESCRIPTION 1

rendezvous *n* **1** a place for spending time or for socializing ⟨the arcade was the *rendezvous* of choice for most of the teenagers in town⟩ — see HANGOUT
2 an agreement to be present at a specified time and place ⟨I have a *rendezvous* with him at lunchtime⟩ — see ENGAGEMENT 2

rendezvous *vb* to come together into one body or place ⟨we'll *rendezvous* at the entrance to the park at 6:00 p.m.⟩ — see ASSEMBLE 1

rendition *n* **1** a presentation of an artistic work (as a piece of music) from a particular point of view ⟨jazzy *renditions* of some familiar pop standards⟩ — see ACCOUNT 2
2 the usually forced yielding of one's person or possessions to the control of another ⟨the *rendition* of the prisoner to the country where the crime was committed⟩ — see SURRENDER

renegade *n* a person who abandons a cause or organization usually without right ⟨a band of *renegades* who had deserted their infantry units and were making their way to Mexico⟩
synonyms apostate, defector, deserter, recreant
related words betrayer, double-crosser, quisling, traitor, traitress (*or* traitoress), turnabout, turncoat; abandoner, come-outer, dropout, leaver; defier, insurgent, insurrectionary, insurrectionist, mutineer, rebel, red, revolter, revolutionary, revolutionist, revolutionizer; discontent, malcontent; recusant, refusenik (*also* refusnik), refuser
near antonyms adherent, disciple, follower, supporter; fanatic, militant, partisan (*also* partizan), zealot
antonyms loyalist

renege *vb* **1** to break a promise or agreement ⟨my so-called best friend promised to help me move, only to *renege* come Saturday morning⟩
synonyms back down, back off, back out, cop out, fink out
related words chicken (out), wimp out; backpedal, backtrack; abjure, abnegate, disavow, forswear (*also* foreswear), recall, recant, repudiate, retract, take back, unsay, withdraw; beg off, cry off [*chiefly British*]
phrases go back on
near antonyms adhere (to), follow through (with); comply (with), fulfill (*or* fulfil), honor, keep, satisfy
2 to solemnly or formally reject or go back on (as something formerly adhered to) ⟨refused to *renege* the principles by which she had always lived her life, even if it resulted in losing her business⟩ — see ABJURE 1

renew *vb* **1** to bring back to a former condition or vigor ⟨the trip to New York *renewed* our enthusiasm for travel⟩
synonyms freshen, recharge, recreate, refresh, refreshen, regenerate, rejuvenate, repair, restore, resuscitate, revitalize, revive, revivify
related words make over, overhaul, reclaim, recondition, reconstitute, redesign, redevelop, redo, reengineer, refurbish, rehab, rehabilitate, remake, remodel, renovate; refill, replenish, resupply; modernize, update
2 to begin again or return to after an interruption ⟨with daybreak, the rescue team will *renew* its efforts to reach the stranded mountain climbers⟩ — see RESUME
3 to bring back to life, practice, or activity ⟨the spate of recent movies based on classic comic book characters has *renewed* interest in the comics themselves⟩ — see REVIVE 1
4 to make or do again ⟨I can only *renew* my offer to help—it's up to them to accept it⟩ — see REPEAT 4

renewal *n* **1** the act of saying or doing over again ⟨a campaign season that witnessed the endless *renewal* of the same stupid charges and countercharges⟩ — see REPEAT
2 the act or an instance of bringing something back to life, public attention, or vigorous activity ⟨roller-skating experienced a major *renewal* after the introduction of in-line skates⟩ — see REVIVAL

renewed *adj* made or become fresh in spirits or vigor ⟨I was a *renewed* reader after that short nap⟩ — see NEW 4

renounce *vb* **1** to give up (as a position of authority) formally ⟨in wake of the corruption scandal, the congressman was forced to *renounce* his seat in the House⟩ — see ABDICATE

2 to solemnly or formally reject or go back on (as something formerly adhered to) ⟨after another failed romance he vowed that he was *renouncing* the world and becoming a monk⟩ — see ABJURE 1

renouncement *n* the act or practice of giving up or rejecting something once enjoyed or desired ⟨her *renouncement* of chocolate had a lot to do with the fact that it was causing her skin to break out⟩ — see RENUNCIATION

renovate *vb* to put into good shape or working order again ⟨will have to *renovate* the house extensively before we can move in⟩ — see MEND 1

renown *n* the fact or state of being known to the public ⟨a basketball icon whose *renown* is truly international⟩ — see FAME 1

renowned *adj* widely known ⟨the *renowned* painter, sculptor, architect, and engineer, Leonardo da Vinci⟩ — see FAMOUS 1

rent *n* **1** a long deep cut ⟨getting her skirt caught on a nail resulted in a four-inch *rent* that she couldn't possibly repair⟩ — see GASH

2 an open space in a barrier (as a wall or hedge) ⟨peered through the *rent* in the old garden wall for a glimpse of her mysterious new neighbor⟩ — see GAP 1

rent *vb* **1** to give the possession and use of (something) in return for periodic payment ⟨we *rented* the apartment to a college student for $500 a month⟩

synonyms lease, let [*chiefly British*]

related words charter, engage, hire; lodge; sublease, sublet; rack-rent

2 to take or get the temporary use of (something) for a set sum ⟨will need to *rent* a car while we're in Europe⟩ — see HIRE 1

renter *n* **1** one who rents a room or apartment in another's house ⟨one of the *renters* called to tell us the hot water heater was broken⟩ — see TENANT 1

2 the owner of land or housing that is rented to another ⟨left our apartment keys at the *renter's* office just before leaving in the moving truck⟩ — see LANDLORD 1

renunciation *n* the act or practice of giving up or rejecting something once enjoyed or desired ⟨his sudden *renunciation* of his smoking habit pleased his whole family⟩

synonyms abnegation, renouncement, repudiation, self-denial

related words denial, refusal; relinquishment, resignation, surrender; self-abnegation, self-renunciation

near antonyms acceptance; adoption, embrace, embracement, espousal

antonyms indulgence, self-indulgence

reopen *vb* to begin again or return to after an interruption ⟨court will *reopen* after a brief recess⟩ — see RESUME

[1]rep *n* a person who acts or does business for another ⟨the company dispatched three *reps* to the annual marketing fair⟩ — see AGENT 2

[2]rep *n, slang* overall quality as seen or judged by people in general ⟨I have a *rep* as a player to maintain, you know⟩ — see REPUTATION

repair *n* a state of being or fitness ⟨the dining table is in good *repair*, so you won't need to refinish it⟩ — see CONDITION 1

repair *vb* **1** to bring back to a former condition or vigor ⟨it will take some time to *repair* your energy after a bout with the flu⟩ — see RENEW 1

2 to put into good shape or working order again ⟨having trouble finding someone who *repairs* audio components⟩ — see MEND 1

repairable *adj* capable of being corrected ⟨the damage to her career from this scandal may not be *repairable*⟩ — see REMEDIABLE

reparable *adj* capable of being corrected ⟨whether the harm your lying has done to our friendship is *reparable* or irreparable depends a lot on you⟩ — see REMEDIABLE

reparation *n* payment to another for a loss or injury ⟨the government instituted a program of *reparations* to the descendants of Native Americans who were driven from their land⟩ — see COMPENSATION 1

repartee *n* **1** a quick witty response ⟨that *repartee* to the reporter's question drew laughs from the bystanders⟩ — see RETORT 1

2 good-natured teasing or exchanging of clever remarks ⟨I wish we weren't many miles apart, as *repartee* is harder to do with text messaging⟩ — see BANTER

repast *n* food eaten or prepared for eating at one time ⟨monks taking their evening *repast* in silence⟩ — see MEAL

repay *vb* **1** to make a return payment to ⟨I *repaid* my friend the $20 he had lent me⟩

synonyms refund, reimburse

related words give back, reciprocate, render (to); compensate, recompense, remunerate; liquidate, pay down, pay off, pay up, quit, satisfy, settle

phrases pay back

2 to make a return for ⟨how can we ever *repay* your kindness?⟩ — see RECIPROCATE

repeal *n* **1** the act of putting an end to something planned or previously agreed to ⟨the long overdue *repeal* of laws prohibiting interracial marriage⟩ — see CANCELLATION 1

2 the doing away with something by formal action ⟨the *repeal* of Prohibition during Franklin D. Roosevelt's first term⟩ — see ABOLITION

repeal *vb* **1** to put an end to (something planned or previously agreed to) ⟨the company called the furniture store to *repeal* the order for six new desks⟩ — see CANCEL 1

2 to put an end to by formal action ⟨in 1933, Congress passed the 21st Amendment which *repealed* the Prohibition Amendment of 1919, thus making the sale, distribution, and use of alcohol legal once again⟩ — see ABOLISH 1

3 to solemnly or formally reject or go back on (as something formerly adhered to) ⟨if I find that you have been lying about this, I'll instantly *repeal* every promise I made to you⟩ — see ABJURE 1

repeat *n* the act of saying or doing over again ⟨if we don't want a *repeat* of last year's disastrous celebration, we had better do some more planning⟩

synonyms duplication, iteration, redo, reduplication, reiteration, renewal, repetition, replay, replication, reprise

related words rebroadcast, rerun; recitation, rehearsal

repeat *vb* **1** to say or state again ⟨I *repeated* the address over and over until I had it memorized⟩

synonyms chime, din, iterate, rehearse, reiterate

related words paraphrase, reword; echo, reecho; mouth, parrot; abstract, encapsulate, epitomize, outline, recap, recapitulate, summarize, sum up

phrases come again

2 to give from memory ⟨*repeated* correctly all the verses she had memorized⟩

synonyms recite, reel off, say

related words con, learn, memorize, study; declaim, mouth, orate, speak

near antonyms read

3 to say after another ⟨now *repeat* the oath after me⟩

synonyms ditto, echo, parrot, quote, reecho
related words mouth; ape, copy, copycat, emulate, imitate, mime, mimic
4 to make or do again ⟨try not to *repeat* your mistakes⟩
synonyms duplicate, redo, reduplicate, reiterate, remake, renew, replicate, reprise
related words recreate, reenact, reinvent

repeated *adj* appearing or occurring repeatedly from time to time ⟨made *repeated* attempts to get in touch with her⟩ — see REGULAR 1

repeatedly *adv* many times ⟨I've told him *repeatedly* not to do that⟩ — see OFTEN

repel *vb* **1** to drive back ⟨the defenders *repelled* the attacking army after several hours of fierce fighting⟩
synonyms beat off, fend (off), rebut, repulse, stave off, turn away, turn back
related words defy, fight, hold off, oppose, resist, stand off, withstand; deflect, ward (off); rebuff, snub, spurn
near antonyms embrace, hail, welcome
2 to cause to feel disgust ⟨the idea of chocolate-covered grasshoppers *repels* me⟩ — see DISGUST
3 to refuse to give in to ⟨*repelled* the temptation to stay out late and call in sick the next day⟩ — see RESIST

repelled *adj* filled with disgust ⟨*repelled* reviewers couldn't believe how violent the movie was⟩ — see SICK 2

repellent *also* **repellant** *adj* causing intense displeasure, disgust, or resentment ⟨your snobbish behavior towards my friends is so *repellent* I can't stand to be around you anymore⟩ — see OFFENSIVE 1

repent *vb* to feel sorry or dissatisfied about ⟨after hearing what a great time you guys had at the party, I am *repenting* my decision to stay home⟩ — see REGRET

repentance *n* a feeling of responsibility for wrongdoing ⟨preached that *repentance* was the first step on the path of redemption⟩ — see GUILT 1

repentant *adj* feeling sorrow for a wrong that one has done ⟨*repentant* sinners⟩ — see CONTRITE

repercussion *n* the power to bring about a result on another ⟨your decision not to go to college will have *repercussions* you'll feel for years to come⟩ — see EFFECT 2

repertoire *n* the number of individuals or amount of something available at any given time ⟨the chef's *repertoire* of specialties seems to be limited, with several of the dishes appearing over and over again in slightly varied guises⟩ — see SUPPLY

repetition *n* the act of saying or doing over again ⟨the *repetition* of the honor society's oath at the initiation ceremonies got old really quickly⟩ — see REPEAT

repetitious *adj* marked by repetition ⟨at a real trial, *repetitious* questioning by the attorneys makes the whole affair less than thrilling⟩ — see REPETITIVE

repetitive *adj* marked by repetition ⟨the *repetitive* lyrics of so many rock songs⟩
synonyms duplicative, reiterative, repetitious
related words redundant

rephrase *vb* to express something (as a text or statement) in different words ⟨I don't understand what you're asking—could you *rephrase* your question?⟩ — see PARAPHRASE

rephrasing *n* an instance of expressing something in different words ⟨a more polite *rephrasing* of your request might get better results⟩ — see PARAPHRASE

repine *vb* to express dissatisfaction, pain, or resentment usually tiresomely ⟨there is no use *repining* over a love that's been long lost⟩ — see COMPLAIN

repine (for) *vb* to have an earnest wish to own or enjoy ⟨during the deep cold of winter, I *repine for* warm tropical beaches⟩ — see DESIRE 1

replace *vb* **1** to take the place of ⟨the old street lights were *replaced* by more energy-efficient models⟩
synonyms cut out, displace, displant, relieve, substitute, supersede, supplant
related words preempt, usurp
2 to bring, send, or put back to a former or proper place ⟨took the fragile vase down to look at it and then gently *replaced* it on the shelf⟩ — see RETURN 1

replacement *n* a person or thing that takes the place of another ⟨seeing that the starting quarterback was unable to play, the coach immediately called in his *replacement*⟩ — see SUBSTITUTE

replay *n* the act of saying or doing over again ⟨this conversation feels like a *replay* of the last time we hashed over the subject⟩ — see REPEAT

replete *adj* **1** having an excess of body fat ⟨the merchant was a richly *replete* gentleman, clearly enjoying the fruits of his success⟩ — see FAT 1
2 possessing or covered with great numbers or amounts of something specified ⟨a gym that is *replete* with the very latest in home exercise equipment⟩ — see RIFE
3 having one's appetite completely satisfied ⟨everyone settled back and relaxed, completely *replete* after the huge meal⟩ — see FULL 3

replica *n* **1** something or someone that strongly resembles another ⟨filled with the usual chain stores, the new mall is a too-familiar *replica* of hundreds of other malls⟩ — see IMAGE 1
2 something that is made to look exactly like something else ⟨assembled a small-scale *replica* of the Queen Mary ocean liner⟩ — see COPY

replicate *vb* **1** to make an exact likeness of ⟨*replicated* the famous painting in our art class⟩ — see COPY 1
2 to make or do again ⟨I can't *replicate* your results when I do the experiment myself⟩ — see REPEAT 4

replication *n* **1** something that is made to look exactly like something else ⟨bought a smaller and cheaper *replication* of the marble statue for his garden⟩ — see COPY
2 the act of saying or doing over again ⟨we'll need to do a *replication* of that experiment so we can collect more data⟩ — see REPEAT
3 something spoken or written in reaction especially to a question ⟨his carefully worded *replications* suggested that he was well aware of the punishment for perjury⟩ — see ANSWER 1

reply *n* **1** action or behavior that is done in return to other action or behavior ⟨decided the best *reply* to a wrongful discharge from employment was a lawsuit claiming discrimination⟩ — see REACTION
2 something spoken or written in reaction especially to a question ⟨I look forward to your *reply* to my request⟩ — see ANSWER 1

reply *vb* **1** to act or behave in response (as to a stimulus or influence) ⟨*replied* to the news that she had won the scholarship by jumping around the room and cheering⟩ — see REACT
2 to speak or write in reaction to a question or to another reaction ⟨please *reply* to my question at your earliest convenience⟩ — see ANSWER 1

report *n* **1** a loud explosive sound ⟨startled by the *report* of a gun⟩ — see CLAP 1
2 a relating of events usually in the order in which they happened ⟨gave a full *report* of their trip to London⟩ — see ACCOUNT 1
3 overall quality as seen or judged by people in general ⟨he's a player of good *report* in golfing circles⟩ — see REPUTATION
4 information or opinion that is widely disseminated without any authority or confirmation of accuracy ⟨the *report* is that she was caught embezzling, but no one has any evidence⟩ — see RUMOR

report *vb* **1** to give an oral or written account of in some detail ⟨will *report* the progress of the war effort before a congressional committee on Monday⟩ — see TELL 1

2 to make a written note of ⟨*reported* the lawyer's closing statement⟩ — see RECORD 1

reporter *n* a person employed by a newspaper, magazine, or radio or television station to gather, write, or report news ⟨the *reporter* was careful to ask as many questions as possible without annoying anyone⟩
synonyms correspondent, intelligencer, journalist, newshound, newsman, newsperson, pressman [*British*]
related words announcer, broadcaster, newscaster, newspaperman, newspaperwoman, newswoman; anchor, anchorman, anchorperson, anchorwoman; byliner, columnist, commentator; copyreader, editor; muckraker, photojournalist, police reporter, sportswriter, staffer, stringer

repose *n* **1** a natural periodic loss of consciousness during which the body restores itself ⟨typically the wealthy socialite spends most of the morning in *repose*, is served lunch, and then embarks on an exhaustive afternoon of shopping⟩ — see SLEEP 1
2 a state of freedom from storm or disturbance ⟨enjoyed the *repose* of a serene summer evening⟩ — see CALM 1
3 freedom from activity or labor ⟨the doctor ordered a period of *repose* for the patient recovering from pneumonia⟩ — see [1]REST 1
4 evenness of emotions or temper ⟨her *repose* in the face of the screaming demonstrators was impressive⟩ — see EQUANIMITY

[1]repose *vb* **1** to remain out of sight ⟨a little-explored region beneath which vast mineral reserves are said to *repose*⟩ — see [1]HIDE 3
2 to refrain from labor or exertion ⟨*reposed* in the Caribbean sun, enjoying her break from the world of work⟩ — see REST 1

[2]repose *vb* to put (something) into the possession or safekeeping of another ⟨the Constitution *reposes* the power to declare war to Congress, and to that body alone⟩ — see GIVE 2

reposit *vb* to place somewhere for safekeeping or ready availability ⟨the radioactive waste will be stored on-site until it can be *reposited* elsewhere⟩ — see STORE 1

reposition *vb* to change the place or position of ⟨she *repositioned* the wood before taking another swing with the ax⟩ — see MOVE 1

repository *n* a building for storing goods ⟨nurses going back and forth to the medication *repository*⟩ — see STOREHOUSE

repossess *vb* to get again in one's possession ⟨if you don't pay off the loan, the bank will come and *repossess* your car⟩ — see RECOVER 1

repossession *n* the act or process of getting something back ⟨an account of France's loss of the Louisiana Territory to Spain and its brief *repossession* of the area before selling it to the U.S. in 1803⟩ — see RECOVERY 1

reprehend *vb* **1** to declare to be morally wrong or evil ⟨that denomination *reprehends* murder in any form, contending that the taking of life is never justified⟩ — see CONDEMN 1
2 to express one's unfavorable opinion of the worth or quality of ⟨without exception, book reviewers *reprehended* the novel's tired plot⟩ — see CRITICIZE

reprehensible *adj* **1** deserving reproach or blame ⟨a *reprehensible* tyrant, who oppressed his country for decades, has finally been brought to justice⟩ — see BLAMEWORTHY
2 provoking or likely to provoke protest ⟨your behavior towards the other team was truly *reprehensible*, so you're being suspended from the next three games⟩ — see OBJECTIONABLE

represent *vb* **1** to point out the chief quality or qualities of an individual or group ⟨the writer of the magazine article *represented* the students at the academy as a bunch of spoiled brats⟩ — see CHARACTERIZE 1
2 to present a picture of ⟨a painting *representing* the ocean at sunrise⟩ — see PICTURE 1
3 to serve as a material counterpart of ⟨this orange *represents* the sun and this pea *represents* the Earth⟩ — see SYMBOLIZE 1

representational *adj* having the function or meaning of an object or figure that stands for something else ⟨a computer program with *representational* icons for different functions⟩ — see SYMBOLIC

representationalism *n* realistic depiction in art and literature ⟨the artist eventually abandoned the *representationalism* of his earlier work⟩ — see VERISIMILITUDE

representative *adj* **1** having or showing the qualities associated with the members of a particular group or kind ⟨a *representative* example of what that talented chef can do with even simple ingredients⟩ — see TYPICAL 1
2 having the function or meaning of an object or figure that stands for something else ⟨a red cross on this map is *representative* of a hospital or other medical facility⟩ — see SYMBOLIC

representative *n* **1** a person who acts or does business for another ⟨a *representative* from the car dealership called to ask how we were enjoying the new car⟩ — see AGENT 2
2 a person sent on a mission to represent another ⟨I speak on this matter as a *representative* of the people of the U.S.⟩ — see AMBASSADOR
3 one of a group or collection that shows what the whole is like ⟨this song is a fairly good *representative* of the other songs on the album⟩ — see EXAMPLE

repress *vb* **1** to put a stop to (something) by the use of force ⟨quickly *repressed* the rebellion in the provincial city and restored order⟩ — see QUELL 1
2 to refrain from openly showing or uttering ⟨you can't *repress* your feelings forever, so tell her how you feel about her⟩ — see SUPPRESS 2

repressed *adj* not excessively showy ⟨a 19th-century church in the *repressed* style favored by the strict religious sect⟩ — see QUIET 2

repression *n* the checking of one's true feelings and impulses when dealing with others ⟨psychologists talking about the *repression* of anger and how it affects one's health⟩ — see CONSTRAINT 1

reprimand *n* an often public or formal expression of disapproval ⟨while reviewing the troops, the officer delivered a curt *reprimand* to one of the soldiers⟩ — see CENSURE

reprimand *vb* **1** to criticize (someone) severely or angrily especially for personal failings ⟨*reprimanded* the summer intern for her constant tardiness⟩ — see SCOLD
2 to criticize (someone) usually gently so as to correct a fault ⟨*reprimanded* the student for using the lax grammar and punctuation of text messaging in a term paper⟩ — see REBUKE 1
3 to express public or formal disapproval of ⟨the president was forced to *reprimand* the general for publicly voicing his disagreements with the nation's foreign policy⟩ — see CENSURE 1

reprisal *n* **1** *usually* **reprisals** *pl* payment to another for a loss or injury ⟨a peace agreement that was rejected because it contained no provisions for *reprisals*⟩ — see COMPENSATION 1
2 the act or an instance of responding to an injury with an injury ⟨after defeating them last year in the finals, our team nervously awaited the expected *reprisal* by our archrivals in this year's tournament⟩ — see REVENGE

reprise *n* the act of saying or doing over again ⟨his second marriage turned out to be a *reprise* of the first one: equally disastrous, simply shorter⟩ — see REPEAT

reprise *vb* **1** to make into a short statement of the main points (as of a report) ⟨the prosecutor's closing statement effectively *reprised* the case against the defendant⟩ — see SUMMARIZE
2 to make or do again ⟨let us not *reprise* the stupid mistakes we made last time⟩ — see REPEAT 4

reproach *n* **1** a cause of shame ⟨your public display of boorish behavior is a *reproach* to this entire school⟩ — see DISGRACE 2
2 an often public or formal expression of disapproval ⟨a letter of *reproach* was added to her dossier⟩ — see CENSURE
3 the state of having lost the esteem of others ⟨nothing the traitor did in later life lessened the *reproach* in which he was universally held⟩ — see DISGRACE 1

reproach *vb* **1** to criticize (someone) severely or angrily especially for personal failings ⟨our neighbor loudly *reproached* us for tromping through his yard⟩ — see SCOLD
2 to criticize (someone) usually gently so as to correct a fault ⟨she cleared her throat as a way of *reproaching* us for having our elbows on the table⟩ — see REBUKE 1
3 to express public or formal disapproval of ⟨the governor *reproached* the legislature for failing to pass the budget on time and once again throwing the state into fiscal chaos⟩ — see CENSURE 1

reproachable *adj* deserving reproach or blame ⟨there are only a few *reproachable* lapses in a generally well-researched book⟩ — see BLAMEWORTHY

reprobate *adj* having or showing lowered moral character or standards ⟨a *reprobate* judge who could be bribed, and often with astonishing ease⟩ — see CORRUPT

reprobate *n* a mean, evil, or unprincipled person ⟨a program for rehabilitating hard-core *reprobates* and turning them into hard-working, law-abiding citizens⟩ — see VILLAIN

reprobate *vb* **1** to be unwilling to grant ⟨the board will most likely *reprobate* the request for parole⟩ — see DENY 2
2 to show unwillingness to accept, do, engage in, or agree to ⟨without hesitation she *reprobated* such an indecent idea⟩ — see DECLINE 1
3 to declare to be morally wrong or evil ⟨spent much of her talk *reprobating* the callous indifference of a materialistic society to the suffering of people in the third world⟩ — see CONDEMN 1

reproduce *vb* **1** to bring forth offspring ⟨mice *reproduce* at a much faster rate than humans do⟩ — see PROCREATE
2 to make an exact likeness of ⟨you'll have to *reproduce* that design on every tile in the bathroom⟩ — see COPY 1
3 to bring back to mind ⟨I can almost *reproduce* the information in my head, but not quite⟩ — see REMEMBER

reproduction *n* something that is made to look exactly like something else ⟨walked through a *reproduction* of the interior of the Parthenon as it must have looked when it was first built⟩ — see COPY

reproof *n* an often public or formal expression of disapproval ⟨even in church we were not free from Mother's familiar *reproof* of our ingrained tendency to fidget in our seats⟩ — see CENSURE

reprove *vb* **1** to criticize (someone) usually gently so as to correct a fault ⟨my piano teacher often *reproves* me for slouching while playing, observing that good posture helps one play better⟩ — see REBUKE 1
2 to express public or formal disapproval of ⟨the principal *reproved* the hockey team for their display of poor sportsmanship on the ice and ordered that a letter of apology be sent to the other school⟩ — see CENSURE 1
3 to hold an unfavorable opinion of ⟨the older generation has always *reproved* the younger generation's taste in music⟩ — see DISAPPROVE (OF)

reptile *n* a person whose behavior is offensive to others ⟨the actor plays a total *reptile* who's somehow still a hit with the ladies⟩ — see JERK 1

republic *n* government in which the supreme power is held by the people and used by them directly or indirectly through representation ⟨when asked by a passerby what sort of government the constitutional convention had formulated for the new nation, Benjamin Franklin memorably replied, "A *republic*, if you can keep it"⟩ — see DEMOCRACY

republican *adj* of, relating to, or favoring political democracy ⟨a small but well-organized *republican* movement working quietly to overthrow the military dictatorship⟩ — see DEMOCRATIC

repudiate *vb* **1** to declare not to be true ⟨vigorously *repudiated* the charge that she had lied on her résumé⟩ — see DENY 1
2 to refuse to acknowledge as one's own or as one's responsibility ⟨the angry mother bitterly *repudiated* her teenaged daughter, telling her that she never wanted to see or hear from her again⟩ — see DISCLAIM 1
3 to show unwillingness to accept, do, engage in, or agree to ⟨we didn't like the terms, so we *repudiated* the contract⟩ — see DECLINE 1
4 to solemnly or formally reject or go back on (as something formerly adhered to) ⟨the producers of the hit TV show threatened to take the disgruntled actor to court if he attempted to *repudiate* his contract⟩ — see ABJURE 1

repudiation *n* **1** a refusal to confirm the truth of a statement ⟨voters seemed satisfied by the candidate's public *repudiation* of the beliefs of an organization to which he had briefly belonged as a youth⟩ — see DENIAL 2
2 the act or practice of giving up or rejecting something once enjoyed or desired ⟨New Year's resolutions typically include the *repudiation* of chocolate and other indulgences and the promise to resume working out at the gym⟩ — see RENUNCIATION

repugnance *n* a dislike so strong as to cause stomach upset or queasiness ⟨could barely contain her *repugnance* of frogs and nearly threw up when she found out we'd have to dissect one in science class⟩ — see DISGUST

repugnant *adj* **1** causing intense displeasure, disgust, or resentment ⟨graffiti that featured absolutely *repugnant* racial slurs⟩ — see OFFENSIVE 1
2 not being in agreement or harmony ⟨technically speaking, it may not be a violation, but it is certainly *repugnant* to the spirit of the law⟩ — see INCONSISTENT 1

repulse *n* treatment that is deliberately unfriendly ⟨the waiter's incredibly rude *repulse* of our polite request for a better table—one that wasn't right next to the kitchen—prompted us to walk out⟩ — see COLD SHOULDER

repulse *vb* **1** to cause to feel disgust ⟨the smell of that town's paper mill totally *repulses* me⟩ — see DISGUST
2 to drive back ⟨the defense repeatedly *repulsed* all of the offense's attempts to move the ball forward, keeping them firmly planted on the 20-yard line⟩ — see REPEL 1

repulsed *adj* filled with disgust ⟨I am *repulsed* that you think it's OK to cheat on your taxes⟩ — see SICK 2

repulsion *n* a dislike so strong as to cause stomach upset or queasiness ⟨we giggled at my father, who was overcome with *repulsion* when he realized he was eating octopus⟩ — see DISGUST

repulsive *adj* causing intense displeasure, disgust, or resentment ⟨a *repulsive* display of shameless flattery that made the embarrassed actor wrinkle his nose in disgust⟩ — see OFFENSIVE 1

repulsiveness *n* the quality of inspiring intense dread or dismay ⟨horror films that seem to be trying to outdo one another in the *repulsiveness* of their monsters⟩ — see HORROR 1

reputable *adj* having a good reputation especially in a field of knowledge ⟨make sure you buy your used car from a *reputable* dealer⟩ — see RESPECTABLE 1

reputation *n* overall quality as seen or judged by people in general ⟨the college's athletic department has a good *reputation*, but the school's science facilities are a bit lacking⟩
synonyms character, fame, mark, name, note, odor, rep [*slang*], report, repute
related words credit, honor; celebrity, notoriety, renown; image, persona; admiration, regard, reverence
near antonyms discredit, disgrace, dishonor, disrepute, ignominy, infamy, obloquy, odium, opprobrium, reproach, shame

repute *n* overall quality as seen or judged by people in general ⟨that's a repair shop of good *repute*⟩ — see REPUTATION

reputed *adj* **1** appearing to be true on the basis of evidence that may or may not be confirmed ⟨this treatment is a *reputed* cure for colon cancer, but studies haven't confirmed that claim⟩ — see APPARENT 1
2 having a good reputation especially in a field of knowledge ⟨a *reputed* oceanographer whose excellent work is known internationally⟩ — see RESPECTABLE 1

request *n* **1** an act or instance of asking for information ⟨the medical columnist is unable to answer individual *requests* for specific information on various disorders⟩ — see QUESTION 2
2 the state of being sought after especially for purchase ⟨reliable babysitters are much in *request*, especially on weekends⟩ — see DEMAND 2

request *vb* **1** to give a request or demand for ⟨a notice *requesting* that I report for jury duty on Monday morning⟩ — see ORDER 2
2 to make a request for ⟨*request* extra ketchup for my fries⟩ — see ASK (FOR) 1
3 to make a request of ⟨a letter from the First Lady graciously *requesting* the chorus to perform at the White House⟩ — see ASK 2

requiem *n* a composition expressing one's grief over a loss ⟨the choir will sing Mozart's *Requiem*⟩ — see LAMENT 2

require *vb* to have as a requirement ⟨the toy *requires* four batteries, which are not included⟩ — see NEED 1

required *adj* **1** forcing one's compliance or participation by or as if by law ⟨formal instruction in driving is *required* in this state before you can get your driver's license⟩ — see MANDATORY
2 impossible to do without ⟨with these frigid winds, hats, scarves, and good mittens are *required* equipment for heading outside⟩ — see ESSENTIAL 1

requirement *n* something necessary, indispensable, or unavoidable ⟨this science course is a *requirement* for graduation⟩ — see ESSENTIAL 1

requisite *adj* impossible to do without ⟨this new CD is the *requisite* album of the year for classical music lovers⟩ — see ESSENTIAL 1

requisite *n* something necessary, indispensable, or unavoidable ⟨Art 101 is a *requisite* for Art 201⟩ — see ESSENTIAL 1

requisition *n* something that someone insists upon having ⟨a brand-new, top-notch computer was the new science teacher's first *requisition*⟩ — see DEMAND 1

requisition *vb* to give a request or demand for ⟨the invading soldiers *requisitioned* food and gasoline from the townspeople⟩ — see ORDER 2

requital *n* **1** payment to another for a loss or injury ⟨the judge ordered the landlord to pay his former tenants $100,000 each as *requital* for goods lost or damaged in the apartment fire⟩ — see COMPENSATION 1
2 something (as money) that is given or received in return for goods or services ⟨the electrician's *requital* for the used car was in the form of work on the dealer's house⟩ — see PAYMENT 2
3 the act or an instance of responding to an injury with an injury ⟨"an eye for an eye" is a form of *requital* that is still legal in some countries⟩ — see REVENGE

requite *vb* **1** to provide (someone) with a just payment for loss or injury ⟨the company *requited* the employee who had fallen on the ice while leaving work by promptly paying all his medical bills, hoping that would stave off a lawsuit⟩ — see COMPENSATE 1
2 to punish in kind the wrongdoer responsible for ⟨the future writer would later *requite* the abuse he suffered at the hands of his classmates by creating scathing portraits of them in his novels⟩ — see AVENGE
3 to make a return for ⟨I fear my love for her will never be *requited*⟩ — see RECIPROCATE

rescind *vb* **1** to put an end to (something planned or previously agreed to) ⟨the library refused to *rescind* its decision to include the controversial book in its collection⟩ — see CANCEL 1
2 to put an end to by formal action ⟨the new mayor vowed not to seek to *rescind* existing laws prohibiting smoking in the city's public places⟩ — see ABOLISH 1

rescindment *n* the doing away with something by formal action ⟨the university's controversial *rescindment* of an invitation to speak at commencement⟩ — see ABOLITION

rescission *n* the act of putting an end to something planned or previously agreed to ⟨the judge ruled that the town's *rescission* of the contract was justified due the contractor's repeated failures to meet its obligations⟩ — see CANCELLATION 1

rescript *n* an order publicly issued by an authority ⟨even though there was never an official *rescript* ordering mass genocide, that was indeed the intent and effect of the government's policy⟩ — see EDICT 1

rescue *n* the saving from danger or evil ⟨stranded people hoping for *rescue* from the rising floodwaters⟩ — see SALVATION

rescue *vb* to remove from danger or harm ⟨an all-out effort to *rescue* a beached whale⟩ — see SAVE 2

rescuer *n* one that saves from danger or destruction ⟨*rescuers* went out immediately in search of the lost child⟩ — see SAVIOR

research *n* a systematic search for the truth or facts about something ⟨I'll have to do some *research* for this project⟩ — see INQUIRY 1

research *vb* to search through or into ⟨*researched* the public record for more information about her great-grandparents⟩ — see EXPLORE 1

researcher *n* one who observes or studies by close examination and systematic inquiry ⟨medical *researchers* reported some eye-opening findings on the effectiveness of statins in the reduction of LDL in the bloodstream⟩ — see INVESTIGATOR 1

resemblance *n* **1** a point which two or more things share in common ⟨I see a family *resemblance* between you and your brother⟩ — see SIMILARITY 2
2 the quality or state of having many qualities in common ⟨the look of the director's latest film bears a strong *resemblance* to the look of his last film⟩ — see SIMILARITY 1

resemblant *adj* having qualities in common ⟨hay fever and the common cold are such *resemblant* conditions that it can be difficult to tell which one you have⟩ — see ALIKE

resembling *adj* having qualities in common ⟨*resembling* Impressionist landscapes were hung side by side so that visitors could compare how fellow artists treated the same subject matter⟩ — see ALIKE

resent *vb* to have a resentful awareness of and desire for (another's possessions or advantages) or to feel resentment toward (someone) over possessions or advantages ⟨a public prosecutor who *resents* the nice clothes, fancy car, and big house that his old law school classmate has⟩ ⟨always *resented* her baby brother, whom her parents doted on⟩ — see ENVY

resentful *adj* **1** having or showing deep-seated resentment ⟨he is still *resentful* about being passed over for a promotion⟩ — see BITTER 1
2 having or showing mean resentment of another's possessions or advantages ⟨*resentful* of her cousin's wealth⟩ — see ENVIOUS

resentfully *adv* with feelings of bitterness or grief ⟨she apologized later, but it was clear she did so *resentfully*⟩ — see HARD 2

resentment *n* **1** a lingering ill will towards a person for a real or imagined wrong ⟨if you continue to harbor *resentment* toward your father, you'll never be able to move on with your life⟩ — see GRUDGE 1
2 a painful awareness of another's possessions or advantages and a desire to have them too ⟨I don't have any *resentment* over my friend's luxurious house⟩ — see ENVY
3 the feeling of being offended or resentful after a slight or indignity ⟨my *resentment* at being spoken to like I'm stupid⟩ — see PIQUE

reservation *n* **1** a feeling or attitude that one does not know the truth, truthfulness, or trustworthiness of someone or something ⟨despite my *reservations*, we hired the young teen as a babysitter⟩ — see DOUBT
2 something upon which the carrying out of an agreement or offer depends ⟨gave us his approval without any *reservations*⟩ — see CONDITION 2

reserve *n* **1** the checking of one's true feelings and impulses when dealing with others ⟨the salesclerk showed great *reserve* in dealing with the unreasonable demands of the angry customer⟩ — see CONSTRAINT 1
2 a collection of things kept available for future use or need ⟨our fuel *reserves* are low⟩ — see STORE
3 a person or thing that takes the place of another ⟨when the first brigade fell back in retreat, the commander sent out the *reserves* to try to hold the line of battle⟩ — see SUBSTITUTE
4 an interchangeable part or piece of equipment that is kept on hand for replacement of an original ⟨don't throw that extra bike chain away, as I want to keep it as a *reserve* in case the current one breaks⟩ — see SPARE

reserve *vb* **1** to arrange to have something (as a hotel room) held for one's future use ⟨we made sure to *reserve* a kennel for our dog several months before the start of the family vacation⟩
synonyms bespeak, book
related words earmark; contract, engage, hire, retain
2 to continue to have in one's possession or power ⟨I'm *reserving* the right to work by myself if you don't do your share of the project⟩ — see KEEP 2
3 to keep or intend for a special purpose ⟨we must *reserve* this cup for ceremonial use only⟩ — see DEVOTE 1

reserved *adj* tending not to speak frequently (as by habit or inclination) ⟨a *reserved* and shy person who was wrongly thought to be stuck-up until someone finally got into a conversation with her⟩ — see SILENT 2

reservoir *n* the number of individuals or amount of something available at any given time ⟨the area boasts a large *reservoir* of college-educated people for companies to draw on⟩ — see SUPPLY

reside *vb* to have a home ⟨he's a freelance writer who *resides* in the Midwest⟩ — see LIVE 1

residence *n* the place where one lives ⟨police stopped by his *residence* to question him⟩ — see HOME 1

residency *n* the act or fact of residing in a place ⟨as much as I've enjoyed my *residency* in this state, it may be time to move on⟩ — see OCCUPANCY

resident *n* one who lives permanently in a place ⟨a *resident* of Atlanta⟩ — see INHABITANT

resider *n* one who lives permanently in a place ⟨was born in the U.S. but is now a *resider* of Dresden, Germany⟩ — see INHABITANT

residue *n* **1** the portion or bits of something left over or behind after it has been destroyed ⟨the detective noticed an ashy *residue* in the sink and deduced that a piece of paper had been burned there⟩ — see REMAINS 1
2 a remaining group or portion ⟨the *residue* of our Thanksgiving feast consisted of a denuded turkey carcass and a couple rolls⟩ — see REMAINDER 1

residuum *n* a remaining group or portion ⟨even highly decaffeinated coffee contains a tiny *residuum* of caffeine⟩ — see REMAINDER 1

resign *vb* to give up (as a position of authority) formally ⟨following the election, the incumbent cabinet members *resigned* their positions so the president could feel free to pick a new administration⟩ — see ABDICATE

resign (from) *vb* to give up (a job or office) ⟨*resigned from* the company after the news broke that he had been falsifying financial statements for years⟩ — see QUIT 1

resigned *adj* receiving or enduring without offering resistance ⟨I am *resigned* to the fact that I'll never make the list of the 400 richest Americans⟩ — see PASSIVE

resilient *adj* able to revert to original size and shape after being stretched, squeezed, or twisted ⟨after being dipped in liquid nitrogen, the rubber ball's normally *resilient* surface is as brittle as ceramic⟩ — see ELASTIC 1

resist *vb* to refuse to give in to ⟨it is important to *resist* the temptation to run away from your problems⟩
synonyms buck, defy, fight, oppose, repel, withstand
related words battle, combat, contend (with); challenge, contest, contradict, dispute; baffle, balk, foil, frustrate, thwart; check, counter, hinder, obstruct, stem
antonyms bow (to), capitulate (to), give in (to), knuckle under (to), stoop (to), submit (to), succumb (to), surrender (to), yield (to)

resistance *n* **1** the inclination to resist ⟨after some initial *resistance*, the city council warmed up to the proposed development plan⟩
synonyms defiance, opposition
related words demur, objection, protest, remonstrance; compunction, misgiving, reservation; disobedience, noncompliance, recalcitrance
near antonyms compliance, obedience; acceptance, approval
antonyms acquiescence
2 a secret organization in a conquered country fighting against enemy forces ⟨soldiers from the *resistance* were captured after a skirmish outside the foreign ministry⟩
synonyms underground
related words cabal, conspiracy

resolute *adj* fully committed to achieving a goal ⟨despite the risks involved, she was *resolute* in her decision to undergo the experimental operation⟩ — see DETERMINED 1

resolutely *adv* with great effort or determination ⟨*resolutely* championed the unpopular causes for most of his political career⟩ — see HARD 1

resoluteness *n* firm or unwavering adherence to one's purpose ⟨with a *resoluteness* that was admirable, the losing team continued to play hard until the bitter end⟩ — see DETERMINATION 1

resolution *n* **1** a position arrived at after consideration ⟨her *resolution* to become a vegetarian is based on what she recently learned about modern farming practices⟩ — see DECISION 1

2 firm or unwavering adherence to one's purpose ⟨that athlete's *resolution* to win is amazing⟩ — see DETERMINATION 1

resolvable *adj* capable of having the reason for or cause of determined ⟨I have no doubt that this mystery will turn out to be *resolvable*⟩ — see SOLVABLE

resolve *n* firm or unwavering adherence to one's purpose ⟨a naval pilot who has been unwavering in his *resolve* to become an astronaut⟩ — see DETERMINATION 1

resolve *vb* **1** to come to a judgment about after discussion or consideration ⟨I *resolved* to eat more healthily and to exercise regularly⟩ — see DECIDE 1

2 to find an answer for through reasoning ⟨*resolve* the apparent contradictions in the collected data⟩ — see SOLVE

3 to set or force apart ⟨a prism will *resolve* a beam of light into an array of colors⟩ — see SEPARATE 1

resolved *adj* fully committed to achieving a goal ⟨only the most *resolved* of explorers had any chance of finding the source of the Nile⟩ — see DETERMINED 1

resonant *adj* marked by conspicuously full and rich sounds or tones ⟨the orator's *resonant* voice filled the hall⟩

synonyms golden, orotund, plangent, resounding, reverberant, reverberating, reverberative, ringing, rotund, round, sonorous, vibrant

related words deep, full, mellifluent, mellifluous, mellow, plummy, rich; loud, powerful, stentorian, thundering, thunderous

near antonyms cavernous, hollow; faint, low, murmurous, muted, smothered, soft, weak; thin, tinny

resonate *vb* to continue or be repeated in a series of reflected sound waves ⟨the deep sounds of the bassoon *resonated* through the concert hall⟩ — see REVERBERATE

resort *n* **1** a place for spending time or for socializing ⟨the island port was once the *resort* of smugglers, pirates, and other unsavory characters⟩ — see HANGOUT

2 something that one uses to accomplish an end especially when the usual means is not available ⟨use this money only as a last *resort*⟩ — see RESOURCE 1

resort (to) *vb* **1** to use or seek out as a source of aid, relief, or advantage ⟨unable to achieve their ends politically, some of the opposition groups have begun to *resort to* violence⟩

synonyms consult, go (to), refer (to), turn (to)

related words employ, use, utilize; depend (on), rely (on)

phrases fall back on

2 to go to or spend time in often ⟨*resorted to* the library whenever he felt the need for a little peace and quiet⟩ — see FREQUENT

resound *vb* **1** to proclaim the glory of ⟨folk songs that *resound* the noble deeds of the nation's heroes of yore⟩ — see PRAISE 1

2 to continue or be repeated in a series of reflected sound waves ⟨thunder *resounded* across the plain⟩ — see REVERBERATE

resounding *adj* **1** full of or characterized by the presence of noise ⟨the *resounding* hubbub of the streets of New York City⟩ — see NOISY 2

2 marked by a high volume of sound ⟨the emcee announced the winner in a *resounding* voice that could be heard all the way to the back of the hall⟩ — see LOUD 1

3 marked by conspicuously full and rich sounds or tones ⟨a *resounding* chord⟩ — see RESONANT

4 marked by or uttered with forcefulness ⟨a *resounding* defeat for the opposition party⟩ — see EMPHATIC 1

resource *n* **1** something that one uses to accomplish an end especially when the usual means is not available ⟨we used every possible *resource* to raise the funds needed to save our town's oldest house⟩

synonyms expedient, recourse, resort

related words hope, opportunity, possibility, relief; makeshift, replacement, stopgap, substitute

2 resources *pl* available money ⟨do you have the *resources* to buy a new car or even a used car?⟩ — see FUND 2

respect *n* **1** relation to or concern with something specified ⟨with *respect* to your application⟩

synonyms reference, regard

2 a feeling of great approval and liking ⟨I have a lot of *respect* for Martin Luther King, Jr.'s steadfast courage⟩ — see ADMIRATION 1

3 respects *pl* best wishes ⟨give your mother my *respects*⟩ — see COMPLIMENT 2

respect *vb* to think very highly or favorably of ⟨an upstanding senator who is *respected* by political allies and foes alike⟩ — see ADMIRE

respectable *adj* **1** having a good reputation especially in a field of knowledge ⟨no *respectable* dietician would advise people to eat just one kind of food⟩

synonyms esteemed, estimable, name, prestigious, recognized, reputable, reputed, respected

related words honorable, venerable, worthy; creditable, good, praiseworthy; celebrated, distinguished, famed, famous, honored, illustrious, notable, prominent, redoubtable, renowned, well-known

near antonyms seedy, shadowy, shady; no-name, obscure, undistinguished, unknown

antonyms disreputable

2 following the accepted rules of moral conduct ⟨cheating is not a *respectable* thing to do under any circumstances⟩ — see HONORABLE 1

3 following the established traditions of refined society and good taste ⟨has the *respectable* manners of someone who was well brought up⟩ — see PROPER 1

4 of a level of quality that meets one's needs or standards ⟨the artwork that we commissioned from the muralist turned out to be *respectable* but was not quite what we had hoped for⟩ — see ADEQUATE

5 sufficiently large in size, amount, or number to merit attention ⟨got paid a *respectable* sum for speaking at our graduation⟩ — see CONSIDERABLE 1

respectably *adv* in a satisfactory way ⟨the stock performed *respectably*, giving us a decent return on our investment⟩ — see WELL 1

respected *adj* having a good reputation especially in a field of knowledge ⟨a *respected* oncologist whose reputation brought her patients from all over the world⟩ — see RESPECTABLE 1

respectful *adj* marked by or showing proper regard for another's higher status ⟨the children were remarkably *respectful* while in the president's office⟩

synonyms deferent, deferential, dutiful, regardful

related words reverent, reverential, venerating, worshipful; fawning, genuflecting, groveling (*or* grovelling), hagiographic (*or* hagiographical), kowtowing, obsequious, servile, subservient, sycophantic, toadying; civil, courteous, gracious, polite; kid-glove, kid-gloved

near antonyms abusive, insulting, offensive; belittling, demeaning, depreciative, depreciatory, derogatory, disparaging; contemptuous, impudent, irreverent, scornful; discourteous, insolent, rude, uncivil

antonyms disrespectful, undutiful

respecting *prep* having to do with ⟨*respecting* your earlier question, I'd like to make an additional comment⟩ — see ABOUT 1

respective *adj* not the same or shared ⟨it was late when the concert let out, so we all went our *respective* ways⟩ — see SEPARATE 1

respire *vb* to inhale and exhale air ⟨though unconscious, the patient is still *respiring*⟩ — see BREATHE 1

resplendence *n* impressiveness of beauty on a large scale ⟨the fabled *resplendence* of the Taj Mahal⟩ — see MAGNIFICENCE

resplendency *n* impressiveness of beauty on a large scale ⟨the hills of Vermont were awash in the *resplendency* of the state's celebrated autumnal foliage⟩ — see MAGNIFICENCE

respond *vb* **1** to act or behave in response (as to a stimulus or influence) ⟨doctors studying how the brain *responds* to pain⟩ — see REACT
2 to speak or write in reaction to a question or to another reaction ⟨the students energetically participated in the discussion, *responding* to the teacher's questions and comments with alacrity and enthusiasm⟩ — see ANSWER 1

response *n* **1** action or behavior that is done in return to other action or behavior ⟨my *response* to my first boxing defeat was to train even harder⟩ — see REACTION
2 something spoken or written in reaction especially to a question ⟨the real estate office's unhelpful *response* to my question about what houses in the area are renting for⟩ — see ANSWER 1

responsibility *n* **1** the state of being held as the cause of something that needs to be set right ⟨*responsibility* for the accident lies with the driver who was speeding⟩
synonyms blame, fault, liability
related words accountability, answerability
2 something one must do because of prior agreement ⟨I had the *responsibility* of closing up the shop at night⟩ — see OBLIGATION 1
3 worthiness as the recipient of another's trust or confidence ⟨the newspaper publisher should hire kids of greater *responsibility* to deliver its papers⟩ — see RELIABILITY

responsible *adj* **1** being the one who must meet an obligation or suffer the consequences for failing to do so ⟨the state laws hold pet owners *responsible* for any damage or injury done by improperly restrained animals⟩
synonyms accountable, amenable, answerable, liable
related words beholden, indebted, obligated, obliged
near antonyms exempt, immune
antonyms irresponsible, nonaccountable, unaccountable
2 worthy of one's trust ⟨our regular babysitter is very *responsible*⟩ — see DEPENDABLE

[1]**rest** *n* **1** freedom from activity or labor ⟨the coming weekend will provide some much needed *rest*⟩
synonyms decompression, ease, leisure, relaxation, repose
related words catnapping, dozing, lazing, napping, resting, sleep, slumber, slumbering, snoozing; quiet, silence, stillness; calm, peace, peacefulness, placidity, respite, restfulness, sereneness, serenity, tranquillity (*or* tranquility), tranquilness; dolce far niente, idleness
near antonyms pressure, strain, stress, tenseness, tension
antonyms exertion, labor, toil, work
2 a natural periodic loss of consciousness during which the body restores itself ⟨after a long day, I lay down on the couch for a little *rest* before dinner⟩ — see SLEEP 1

[2]**rest** *n* a remaining group or portion ⟨can you hand me the *rest* of those papers?⟩ — see REMAINDER 1

rest *vb* **1** to refrain from labor or exertion ⟨a beach resort that caters to gung ho exercisers and athletes as well as vacationers who just want to *rest*⟩
synonyms bask, kick back, loll, lounge, relax, repose
related words bum, goldbrick, hang, hang about [*British*], hang around, idle, loaf, slack (off), veg out
near antonyms drudge, grub, hump, hustle, labor, moil, peg (away), plod, plow, plug, slave, slog, strain, strive, struggle, sweat, toil, travail, work; exercise, work out
2 to be in a state of sleep ⟨the patient is currently *resting*, but as soon as he awakes, I'll tell him you called⟩ — see SLEEP 1
3 to find a basis ⟨you're *resting* your argument on a faulty premise⟩ — see BASE

restart *vb* to begin again or return to after an interruption ⟨after being shut down for three years, the power plant will *restart* operations this week⟩ — see RESUME

restate *vb* to express something (as a text or statement) in different words ⟨though I couldn't remember the exact words he used, I *restated* his message as accurately as I could⟩ — see PARAPHRASE

restatement *n* an instance of expressing something in different words ⟨the press release provides no new details—it is merely a *restatement* of information we already have⟩ — see PARAPHRASE

restating *n* an instance of expressing something in different words ⟨I think the intent of the passage comes through better in the editor's *restating*⟩ — see PARAPHRASE

restaurant *n* a public establishment where meals are served to paying customers for consumption on the premises ⟨when we get sick of cooking dinner at home, we like to go out to eat at a nice *restaurant*⟩
synonyms beanery, café (*also* cafe), caff [*British*], diner, eatery, grill
related words cafeteria, lunch counter, luncheonette, lunchroom, snack bar; greasy spoon, hash house; chophouse, steak house; pizzeria; coffeehouse, coffee shop, estaminet, teahouse, tearoom, tea shop [*chiefly British*]; bar, barroom, inn, tavern

restful *adj* free from disturbing noise or uproar ⟨I hope you had a relaxing and *restful* weekend⟩ — see QUIET 1

restfulness *n* a state of freedom from storm or disturbance ⟨enjoyed the bucolic *restfulness* of the retreat center⟩ — see CALM 1

resting *adj* being in a state of suspended consciousness ⟨the *resting* cat was curled up in my favorite chair⟩ — see ASLEEP 1

resting *n* a natural periodic loss of consciousness during which the body restores itself ⟨the hyena is ready to scavenge again after its brief *resting*⟩ — see SLEEP 1

restitution *n* payment to another for a loss or injury ⟨sought *restitution* from the other driver's insurance company for lost wages⟩ — see COMPENSATION 1

restive *adj* **1** given to resisting authority or another's control ⟨the *restive* horse threw its head and refused to move when the rider urged it forward⟩ — see DISOBEDIENT
2 lacking or denying rest ⟨spent a *restive* night worrying about the next day's exam⟩ — see RESTLESS 1

restiveness *n* **1** a disturbed or uneasy state ⟨the nighttime tornado warnings were the likely source of the *restiveness* that could be felt all over town⟩ — see UNREST
2 a state of nervousness marked by sudden jerky movements ⟨I sensed that his *restiveness* at breakfast probably had something to do with the big presentation he would be making at the sales conference⟩ — see JUMPINESS

restless *adj* **1** lacking or denying rest ⟨the worried mother spent a *restless* night, tossing and turning in bed for hours⟩
synonyms restive, uneasy, unquiet, unrestful
related words agitated, distressed, disturbed, perturbed, troubled, unsettled; aflutter, anxious, dithery, edgy, fidgety, het up, hung up, jittery, jumpy, nervous, nervy, tense, upset, uptight, worried
near antonyms calm, easy, peaceful, quiet, relaxing, tranquil

antonyms restful

2 marked by or causing agitation or uncomfortable feelings ⟨the figure skater was visibly *restless* as she waited for her scores to be posted⟩ — see NERVOUS 2

restlessness *n* **1** a disturbed or uneasy state ⟨the *restlessness* of the crowd was apparent as it waited to learn whether the football player was seriously injured⟩ — see UNREST

2 the state of being bored ⟨she began to pick at the grass near her hammock out of sheer *restlessness*⟩ — see BOREDOM

restorative *adj* **1** beneficial to the health of body or mind ⟨took a *restorative* vitamin mix to improve his immune system⟩ — see HEALTHFUL

2 having a renewing effect on the state of the body or mind ⟨I am in need of a long, *restorative* vacation⟩ — see TONIC 1

3 tending to cure disease or restore health ⟨relocation to a milder climate proved to be just the *restorative* measure that was needed for the sickly child⟩ — see MEDICINAL 1

restore *vb* **1** to bring back to a former condition or vigor ⟨*restore* an old car⟩ — see RENEW 1

2 to bring, send, or put back to a former or proper place ⟨*restored* the trophy to its proper place at the center of the shelf⟩ — see RETURN 1

restrain *vb* **1** to keep from exceeding a desirable degree or level (as of expression) ⟨the victim's family members were unable to *restrain* their emotions upon hearing the verdict⟩ — see CONTROL 1

2 to take or keep under one's control by authority of law ⟨the suspect was *restrained* and taken to an undisclosed location⟩ — see ARREST 1

restrained *adj* not excessively showy ⟨a *restrained* but elegant black purse⟩ — see QUIET 2

restraint *n* **1** the checking of one's true feelings and impulses when dealing with others ⟨it will take a great deal of *restraint* to keep from telling her how ugly that dress is⟩ — see CONSTRAINT 1

2 something that limits one's freedom of action or choice ⟨civil libertarians contend that the new laws place too many *restraints* on our constitutionally guaranteed rights⟩ — see RESTRICTION 1

3 the power to control one's actions, impulses, or emotions ⟨he shows very little *restraint* or tact when expressing his opinions about others⟩ — see WILL 1

restrict *vb* to set bounds or an upper limit for ⟨will *restrict* access to the laboratory⟩ — see LIMIT 1

restricted *adj* having distinct or certain limits ⟨the public is allowed some *restricted* access to the government-owned land⟩ — see LIMITED 1

restriction *n* **1** something that limits one's freedom of action or choice ⟨the logging company decided to relocate to another state where there would be fewer *restrictions* on its operations⟩

synonyms check, circumscription, condition, constraint, curb, fetter, limitation, restraint, stricture

related words exception, proviso, qualification, reservation, stipulation, strings; ban, prohibition, proscription

near antonyms freedom, latitude

2 the act or practice of keeping something (as an activity) within certain boundaries ⟨the *restriction* of surfing to the southern end of the beach rankled some surfers⟩

synonyms circumscription, confinement, limitation, rein, stint

related words constraint, restraint; containment, isolation, segregation

restroom *n* a room furnished with a fixture for flushing body waste ⟨I wasn't feeling well and had to make a number of trips to the *restroom*⟩ — see TOILET

result *n* **1** a condition or occurrence traceable to a cause ⟨the frequent computer crashes are an unexpected *result* of the new security software we installed⟩ — see EFFECT 1

2 something attained by mental effort and especially by computation ⟨a nonpartisan panel of experts did the math on the proposed tax cuts and spending programs and the *result* was an $800 billion federal deficit⟩ — see ANSWER 2

result (in) *vb* to be the cause of (a situation, action, or state of mind) ⟨the mix of icy conditions and rush-hour traffic *resulted in* a number of accidents on the interstate⟩ — see EFFECT

resultant *adj* coming as a result ⟨frequent trips to the ice cream parlor and the *resultant* weight gain were starting to affect my tennis game⟩

synonyms attendant, consequent, consequential, due (to)

related words accompanying, coincident, concomitant

near antonyms causal

resultant *n* a condition or occurrence traceable to a cause ⟨a person's decision to purchase a certain automobile is often the *resultant* of an array of factors, ranging from the actual performance of the vehicle to the buyer's self-image⟩ — see EFFECT 1

resume *vb* to begin again or return to after an interruption ⟨we *resumed* the game as soon as the rain had passed⟩

synonyms continue, pick up, proceed (with), renew, reopen, restart

related words resuscitate, revive; recrudesce

near antonyms complete, conclude, consummate, end, finalize, finish; belay, break, can [*slang*], cease, check, cut, desist, discontinue, drop, halt, knock off, leave off, quit, scuttle, shut off, stay, stop, terminate

résumé *or* **resume** *also* **resumé** *n* a short statement of the main points ⟨a book on the assassination that is in effect a *résumé* of all of the evidence that points to a conspiracy⟩ — see SUMMARY

resurgence *n* the act or an instance of bringing something back to life, public attention, or vigorous activity ⟨the downtown has experienced a *resurgence* since the commercial revitalization project was completed⟩ — see REVIVAL

resurrect *vb* to bring back to life, practice, or activity ⟨attempts are being made to *resurrect* the stalled arms negotiations⟩ — see REVIVE 1

resurrection *n* the act or an instance of bringing something back to life, public attention, or vigorous activity ⟨a general *resurrection* of patriotism after the war began⟩ — see REVIVAL

resuscitate *vb* **1** to bring back to a former condition or vigor ⟨she hopes to *resuscitate* the currently defunct charity organization⟩ — see RENEW 1

2 to bring back to life, practice, or activity ⟨people trying to *resuscitate* some old theories that the assassination was really an act of conspiracy⟩ — see REVIVE 1

resuscitated *adj* made or become fresh in spirits or vigor ⟨after the gloom of winter, I felt *resuscitated* by the unexpected gift of a bouquet of tulips⟩ — see NEW 4

resuscitation *n* the act or an instance of bringing something back to life, public attention, or vigorous activity ⟨the actor's appearance in a hit movie has led to the *resuscitation* of a career that had been on life support⟩ — see REVIVAL

retail *vb* to offer for sale to the public ⟨the textile manufacturer doesn't *retail* its fabrics to consumers, offering them only to wholesalers and garment makers⟩ — see MARKET

retain *vb* **1** to continue to have in one's possession or power ⟨I plan to *retain* the family heirlooms until my own children are mature enough to appreciate them, and then I will lovingly pass them on⟩ — see KEEP 2

2 to keep, control, or experience as one's own ⟨that author *retains* the right to veto any changes in his books suggested by his publisher's notoriously intrusive editor⟩ — see HAVE 1

3 to provide with a paying job ⟨her neighbor *retained* her as a nanny for the summer, thus giving her something to do until school started again⟩ — see EMPLOY 1

retainer *n* **1** a person hired to perform household or personal services ⟨knights being dressed for battle by their *retainers*⟩ — see SERVANT

2 one who works for another for wages or a salary ⟨lifelong civil service *retainers*⟩ — see EMPLOYEE

retake *vb* to get again in one's possession ⟨after some fierce fighting, government forces have *retaken* the capital⟩ — see RECOVER 1

retaliate *vb* to punish in kind the wrongdoer responsible for ⟨*retaliated* his neighbor's malicious destruction of his flower garden by cutting down the man's prize apple tree⟩ — see AVENGE

retaliation *n* the act or an instance of responding to an injury with an injury ⟨police believe that the murder was in *retaliation* for an earlier gangland execution⟩ — see REVENGE

retard *vb* to cause to move or proceed at a less rapid pace ⟨an herbicide to *retard* the growth of weeds⟩ — see SLOW 1

retardation *n* a usually gradual decrease in the pace or level of activity of something ⟨scientists discovered that they could achieve the *retardation* of light if they shined it through a variety of substances⟩ — see SLOWDOWN

retch *vb* to discharge the contents of the stomach through the mouth ⟨the smell of rotten cabbage makes me *retch*⟩ — see VOMIT

rethink *vb* to consider again especially with the possibility of change or reversal ⟨since my efforts to solve this problem aren't working, I need to *rethink* my approach⟩ — see RECONSIDER

reticence *n* a lack of willingness or desire to do or accept something ⟨the publisher's *reticence* to make content available online for free⟩ — see RELUCTANCE

reticent *adj* **1** given to keeping one's activities hidden from public observation or knowledge ⟨the panel decided to investigate the fraud charges against the company, which has always been *reticent* about its internal operations⟩ — see SECRETIVE

2 tending not to speak frequently (as by habit or inclination) ⟨her husband is by nature a *reticent* person, and she resigned herself to that fact long ago⟩ — see SILENT 2

3 slow to begin or proceed with a course of action because of doubts or uncertainty ⟨understandably, she's *reticent* about becoming involved with another evangelical religious sect⟩ — see HESITANT

retinue *n* a body of employees or servants who accompany and wait on a person ⟨a campaign bus carrying the candidate, her *retinue*, and a gaggle of reporters and bloggers⟩ — see CORTEGE 1

retire *vb* **1** to go to one's bed in order to sleep ⟨I'm exhausted, so I think I'll *retire* for the evening⟩ — see BED 1

2 to let go from office, service, or employment ⟨as a part of its restructuring, the company has begun to *retire* its older employees⟩ — see DISMISS 1

3 to move back or away (as from something difficult, dangerous, or disagreeable) ⟨the insurgents have *retired* to the outskirts of the city, but appear to be readying themselves for another offensive⟩ — see RETREAT 1

retire (from) *vb* to give up (a job or office) ⟨at the age of 72, she finally *retired from* the job she had held at the shoe factory for over 50 years⟩ — see QUIT 1

retired *adj* screened or sequestered from view ⟨hiked out to a *retired* beach and fished in the surf⟩ — see SECLUDED

retirement *n* an act of moving away especially from something difficult, dangerous, or disagreeable ⟨military historians have blamed the defeat on that battalion's *retirement* from the front lines⟩ — see RETREAT 1

retiring *adj* not comfortable around people ⟨one *retiring* young girl was sitting alone quietly in a corner during the party⟩ — see SHY 2

retort *n* **1** a quick witty response ⟨she responded to the heckler with a scathing but hilarious *retort* that instantly won over the audience⟩
synonyms comeback, repartee, riposte
related words squelch; back talk; crack, quip, sally, wisecrack, witticism, zinger; cut, insult, put-down

2 something spoken or written in reaction especially to a question ⟨the salesclerk responded to my query about the price with a brusque *retort*⟩ — see ANSWER 1

retort *vb* to speak or write in reaction to a question or to another reaction ⟨when told she couldn't have it, she *retorted*, "Fine, I didn't want it anyway!"⟩ — see ANSWER 1

retract *vb* to solemnly or formally reject or go back on (as something formerly adhered to) ⟨the newspaper was forced to *retract* the story, which turned out to be based on fabricated reporting⟩ — see ABJURE 1

retreat *n* **1** an act of moving away especially from something difficult, dangerous, or disagreeable ⟨we made a strategic *retreat* when we realized that we were outnumbered⟩
synonyms pullback, pullout, recession, retirement, withdrawal
related words rout; flinch, recoil, revulsion, shrinking; disengagement, disentanglement
antonyms advance, advancement

2 something (as a building) that offers cover from the weather or protection from danger ⟨her bedroom served as a *retreat* from the frequent arguing between her parents⟩ ⟨the abandoned cabin was a welcome *retreat* from the storm⟩ — see SHELTER

retreat *vb* **1** to move back or away (as from something difficult, dangerous, or disagreeable) ⟨we *retreated* to the safety of the cellar at the first sign of the tornado⟩
synonyms back away, drop back, fall back, pull out, recede, retire, withdraw
related words flee, fly; flinch, recoil, shrink; chicken (out); bow out; back down, backpedal, backtrack, climb down; detach, disengage, disentangle, pull away; abandon, depart, evacuate, go, leave, quit, vacate
phrases give ground, give way, lose ground
near antonyms beard, brave, brazen, breast, confront, dare, defy, face, outbrave
antonyms advance

2 to hasten away from something dangerous or frightening ⟨the untried soldiers *retreated* in humiliating disarray almost as soon as the enemy's onslaught began⟩ — see RUN 2

retribution *n* the act or an instance of responding to an injury with an injury ⟨the neighborhood is being torn apart by an endless cycle of gang violence and *retribution*⟩ — see REVENGE

retrieval *n* the act or process of getting something back ⟨a law firm that has been involved in the *retrieval* of artworks that were plundered during the war⟩ — see RECOVERY 1

retrieve *vb* to get again in one's possession ⟨needed to *retrieve* the book from my friend so I could return it to the library⟩ — see RECOVER 1

retro *adj* pleasantly reminiscent of an earlier time ⟨*retro* fashions that seek to capture the lost glamour of Hollywood in the 1930s⟩ — see OLD-FASHIONED

retrograde *adj* **1** directed, turned, or done toward the

back ⟨*retrograde* pedaling will engage the brakes on that bike⟩ — see BACKWARD 1
2 pleasantly reminiscent of an earlier time ⟨the loft's *retrograde* decor seeks to capture the look and feel of the swinging '60s⟩ — see OLD-FASHIONED

retrograde *vb* to become worse or of less value ⟨the Dark Ages, the period following the fall of the Roman Empire when Western civilization seriously *retrograded*⟩ — see DETERIORATE 1

retrogress *vb* to go back to a previous and usually lower state or level ⟨the quality of research at the university lab has begun to *retrogress* since the massive budget cuts went into effect⟩ — see REGRESS 1

retrogression *n* the act or an instance of going back to an earlier and lower level especially of intelligence or behavior ⟨social instability that has led to a *retrogression* of moral values and standards of decent behavior⟩ — see REGRESSION

retrospect *n* a usually critical look at a past event ⟨in *retrospect*, we should have saved more money for college⟩ — see REVIEW 1

retrospection *n* a usually critical look at a past event ⟨the president is confident that future *retrospections* will cast his actions in a more favorable light⟩ — see REVIEW 1

return *n* **1** something spoken or written in reaction especially to a question ⟨I was moved by my grandfather's lengthy *return* to my casual question about his experiences in the Vietnam War⟩ — see ANSWER 1
2 an increase usually measured in money that comes from labor, business, or property ⟨if we buy better equipment, we'll be able to make the product faster, thus getting a better *return* on our investment⟩ — see INCOME 1
3 the amount of money left when expenses are subtracted from the total amount received ⟨the *return* on each unit sold has increased since we streamlined the production process⟩ — see PROFIT 1

return *vb* **1** to bring, send, or put back to a former or proper place ⟨when I'm done reading a book, I always *return* it to the very shelf I got it from⟩
synonyms replace, restore
related words reconvey
near antonyms remove, take
2 to produce as revenue ⟨this technology stock is expected to *return* a healthy profit⟩ — see YIELD 2
3 to speak or write in reaction to a question or to another reaction ⟨when I asked him to sit down to dinner, he *returned* that he would come when he was good and ready⟩ — see ANSWER 1
4 to go back to a previous and usually lower state or level ⟨vowed to do anything to keep the recovering alcoholic from *returning* to his dissolute ways⟩ — see REGRESS 1

rev (up) *vb* to rouse to strong feeling or action ⟨the team was *revved up* by the coach's do-or-die locker room speech⟩ — see PROVOKE 1

revamp *vb* **1** to make different in some way ⟨the automaker is *revamping* a number of its cars in an effort to make them more appealing to younger consumers⟩ — see CHANGE 1
2 to prepare for publication by correcting, rewriting, or updating ⟨*revamped* the short story so that it would fit better with the magazine's other offerings⟩ — see EDIT 1
3 to put into good shape or working order again ⟨it will be cheaper to replace the old machinery than it would be to *revamp* it⟩ — see MEND 1

revamping *n* the act, process, or result of making different ⟨despite the extensive *revamping*, much of the factory's equipment is still obsolete⟩ — see CHANGE 1

reveal *vb* **1** to make known (as information previously kept secret) ⟨at the end of the book, the detective *reveals* the identity of the mysterious stranger⟩
synonyms bare, disclose, discover, divulge, expose, let on (about), spill, tell, unbosom, uncloak, uncover, unmask, unveil
related words confide, share; debunk, show up; unclothe, undrape; advertise, announce, blaze, bring out, broadcast, declare, placard, post, proclaim, promulgate, publicize, publish, sound; betray, blab, give away, leak; inform, squeal, talk; communicate, impart, relate; acknowledge, admit, avow, concede, confess, own; disinter, rake up, smoke out, unearth
phrases bring to light, go public (with), let the cat out of the bag (about), spill the beans (about)
near antonyms camouflage, disguise; gild, gloss (over), varnish, whitewash; becloud, bedim, befog, cloud, darken, eclipse, obscure, overcast, overshadow, shade
antonyms cloak, conceal, cover (up), enshroud, hide, mask, shroud, veil
2 to make known (something abstract) through outward signs ⟨a habitual smirk that *reveals* his contempt for other people⟩ — see SHOW 2

revealing *adj* clearly conveying a special meaning (as one's mood) ⟨the pundit's comments were particularly *revealing* and exposed some of his more distasteful prejudices⟩ — see EXPRESSIVE

revel *n* a time or instance of carefree fun ⟨in Finland, Midsummer Day ushers in a nationwide *revel* as the Finns celebrate the endless hours of sunlight with bonfires and parties⟩ — see FLING 1

revel *vb* to take part in drunken revelry ⟨*reveling* all night is not conducive to a productive next day at work⟩ — see CAROUSE

revel (in) *vb* to take pleasure in ⟨winter-weary residents *reveling in* the warm spring weather⟩ — see ENJOY 1

revelation *n* the act or an instance of making known something previously unknown or concealed ⟨the *revelation* of the movie star's secret marriage by the tabloids⟩ ⟨a new biography of the former president that contains several shocking *revelations*⟩
synonyms disclosure, divulgence, exposure
related words bombshell, kick, kicker, surprise (*also* surprize); acknowledgment (*or* acknowledgement), admission, avowal, concession, confession
near antonyms concealment, cover-up

revelatory *adj* clearly conveying a special meaning (as one's mood) ⟨ended his tall tale with a *revelatory* wink that indicated that it had all been an elaborate put-on⟩ — see EXPRESSIVE

reveler *or* **reveller** *n* one who engages in merrymaking especially in honor of a special occasion ⟨wedding *revelers* whooping it up until dawn⟩ — see CELEBRANT

reveling *or* **revelling** *n* joyful or festive activity ⟨the *reveling* was too much for her, so she went to bed early even though the party was still going strong⟩ — see MERRYMAKING

revelry *n* joyful or festive activity ⟨the lottery winner was exhausted after a long night of *revelry*⟩ — see MERRYMAKING

revenge *n* the act or an instance of responding to an injury with an injury ⟨both sides were determined to get *revenge* for perceived wrongs and showed little interest in ending the feud⟩
synonyms payback, reprisal, requital, retaliation, retribution, vengeance
related words counter, counterattack, counteroffensive; castigation, chastisement, correction; desert(s), discipline, nemesis, penalty, punishment, wrath; amends, compensation, indemnification, indemnity, quittance, recompense, recoupment, redress, remuneration, reparation(s), restitution
near antonyms clemency, grace, leniency, lenity,

mercy; forgiveness, pardon, remission

revenge *vb* to punish in kind the wrongdoer responsible for ⟨a man who took matters into his own hands and *revenged* the death of his brother⟩ — see AVENGE

revengeful *adj* likely to seek revenge ⟨the minister urged his congregation to be less *revengeful* and more forgiving in spirit⟩ — see VINDICTIVE

revenue *n* an increase usually measured in money that comes from labor, business, or property ⟨the struggling business didn't create much *revenue* during its first year of operation⟩ — see INCOME 1

reverberant *adj* marked by conspicuously full and rich sounds or tones ⟨the pastor's *reverberant* voice could be heard all over the cemetery as he read the final prayers for the deceased⟩ — see RESONANT

reverberate *vb* to continue or be repeated in a series of reflected sound waves ⟨the sound of thunder *reverberated* from one end of the mountain pass to the other⟩
synonyms echo, reecho, resonate, resound, sound
related words ring, roll
near antonyms damp, dampen, deaden, dull, quiet

reverberating *adj* marked by conspicuously full and rich sounds or tones ⟨the temple was filled with the *reverberating* sound of the gong⟩ — see RESONANT

reverberative *adj* marked by conspicuously full and rich sounds or tones ⟨the *reverberative* sounds of the pipe organ filled every corner of the majestic Gothic cathedral⟩ — see RESONANT

revere *vb* to offer honor or respect to (someone) as a divine power ⟨in some cultures people *revere* their ancestors, even leaving food offerings for them⟩ — see WORSHIP 1

revered *adj* deserving honor and respect especially by reason of age ⟨a professor who is highly *revered* at the college where she has taught for the last four decades⟩ — see VENERABLE 1

reverence *vb* to offer honor or respect to (someone) as a divine power ⟨devotees coming to *reverence* their god⟩ — see WORSHIP 1

reverend *adj* deserving honor and respect especially by reason of age ⟨our *reverend* elders should be accorded a special place of honor at the ceremonies⟩ — see VENERABLE 1

reverend *n* a person specially trained and authorized to conduct religious services in a Christian church ⟨called their *reverend* and asked if he could marry them next June⟩ — see CLERGYPERSON

reverie *also* **revery** *n* the state of being lost in thought ⟨I was lost in *reverie* and didn't realize my flight was boarding until it was almost too late⟩
synonyms daydreaming, study, trance, woolgathering
related words contemplation, meditation, musing; absentmindedness, absorption, abstraction, preoccupation; chimera, conceit, daydream, delusion, dream, fancy, fantasy (*also* phantasy), figment, hallucination, illusion, phantasm (*also* fantasm), pipe dream, unreality, vision

reversal *n* **1** a change in status for the worse usually temporarily ⟨the company's long-term strategy is sound, and they should be able to weather this latest *reversal*⟩ — see REVERSE 1
2 a changing from one policy or point of view to virtually its exact opposite ⟨parents need to be consistent in their discipline policy, as *reversals* will only undermine the whole process⟩ — see ABOUT-FACE

reverse *n* **1** a change in status for the worse usually temporarily ⟨the party has suffered some major *reverses* as a result of the corruption scandal⟩
synonyms knock, lapse, reversal, setback
related words disappointment, frustration, letdown; comedown, decline, descent, down, downfall, fall; turnabout, turnaround; recession, regression, retrogression, reversion; relapse; breakdown, collapse, crash, meltdown, ruin, undoing
near antonyms status quo
2 something that is as different as possible from something else ⟨how could you think I don't like pizza, when it's just the *reverse*: I love pizza⟩ — see OPPOSITE
3 a behind part or surface ⟨on the *reverse* of the ticket you'll find the notice that it's nontransferable⟩ — see REAR 1

reverse *vb* **1** to change (as an opinion) to the contrary ⟨the appeals court *reversed* the district court's decision⟩
synonyms switch
related words abrogate, annul, overturn, repeal, rescind, revoke, strike down; about-face, backtrack, countermand, revert
near antonyms maintain, support, uphold
2 to change the position of (an object) so that the opposite side or end is showing ⟨when one side of the cleaning cloth gets dirty, just *reverse* it⟩ ⟨you can *reverse* the jacket for a whole new look⟩
synonyms flip, invert, turn over
related words transpose; exchange, interchange, shift, switch; overturn, upset

reversion *n* the act or an instance of going back to an earlier and lower level especially of intelligence or behavior ⟨after the birth of his baby brother, the toddler temporarily underwent a kind of *reversion*, acting like a baby himself⟩ — see REGRESSION

revert *vb* to go back to a previous and usually lower state or level ⟨after the national emergency had passed, the political parties abandoned their shotgun unity and *reverted* to their partisan squabbling⟩ — see REGRESS 1

review *n* **1** a usually critical look at a past event ⟨a *review* of yesterday's football game gave us a lot of good ideas on how to improve for the next one⟩
synonyms reappraisal, reconsideration, reexamination, retrospect, retrospection
related words recap, recapitulation, rehash
near antonyms preview
2 a close look at or over someone or something in order to judge condition ⟨took the car to her mechanic for a complete mechanical *review* before she decided to sell it⟩ — see INSPECTION
3 a publication that appears at regular intervals ⟨had his poetry published in a literary *review*⟩ — see JOURNAL 1
4 an essay evaluating or analyzing something ⟨a harsh movie *review* of an expected summer blockbuster⟩ — see CRITICISM
5 the act, process, or result of making different ⟨the company decided that the 100-year-old office building could use a *review*⟩ — see CHANGE 1

review *vb* **1** to consider again especially with the possibility of change or reversal ⟨since we can't follow that plan, we'll have to *review* our options and decide on something else⟩ — see RECONSIDER
2 to look over closely (as for judging quality or condition) ⟨a consultant was brought in to *review* our security procedures⟩ — see INSPECT

reviewer *n* a person who makes or expresses a judgment on the quality of offerings in some field of endeavor ⟨many *reviewers* were unhappy with the movie's cryptic ending⟩ — see CRITIC 2

revise *n* the act, process, or result of making different ⟨that paper needs one more *revise*, and then I think it's ready to turn in⟩ — see CHANGE 1

revise *vb* **1** to make different in some way ⟨with the snow, we'll need to *revise* our travel plans⟩ — see CHANGE 1
2 to prepare for publication by correcting, rewriting, or updating ⟨*revise* the article and add more up-to-date information so we can reprint it⟩ — see EDIT 1

revision *n* the act, process, or result of making different ⟨a finicky author who makes countless *revisions* before submitting a work for publication⟩ — see CHANGE 1

revisit *vb* to consider again especially with the possibility of change or reversal ⟨this idea isn't practical now, but we probably should *revisit* it at a later time⟩ — see RECONSIDER

revitalization *n* the act or an instance of bringing something back to life, public attention, or vigorous activity ⟨the mayor was present at the ceremony marking the *revitalization* of the old industrial neighborhood as a new center for art galleries and lofts⟩ — see REVIVAL

revitalize *vb* **1** to bring back to a former condition or vigor ⟨a new cream that claims to *revitalize* sun-damaged skin⟩ — see RENEW 1
2 to bring back to life, practice, or activity ⟨the bowling alley, eager to *revitalize* interest in the sport for a younger crowd, started offering "disco bowling" every Friday night with disco music and free soda⟩ — see REVIVE 1

revival *n* the act or an instance of bringing something back to life, public attention, or vigorous activity ⟨there was a *revival* of interest in the author's classic horror stories after a film version of his best-known tale was released⟩
synonyms reanimation, rebirth, regeneration, rejuvenation, rejuvenescence, renewal, resurgence, resurrection, resuscitation, revitalization, revivification
related words renaissance, renascence; reinvention; reactivation; rally, recovery, recuperation; restoral, restoration
near antonyms death, expiration, extinction

revive *vb* **1** to bring back to life, practice, or activity ⟨an effort to *revive* the once-common custom of celebrating May 1 as a springtime festival of games and dances⟩
synonyms reanimate, recharge, regenerate, rejuvenate, rekindle, renew, resurrect, resuscitate, revitalize, revivify, rewake, rewaken
related words jump-start, kick-start; reactivate, restart; reinvent; refresh, refreshen
near antonyms extinguish, kill, quench, suppress
2 to bring back to a former condition or vigor ⟨around mid-morning, I usually need to *revive* myself with a cup of strong coffee⟩ — see RENEW 1
3 to gain consciousness again ⟨the patient eventually *revived* and was able to give us her name and address⟩ — see COME TO

revived *adj* made or become fresh in spirits or vigor ⟨the farmers felt *revived* as they headed back to the fields after a hearty lunch⟩ — see NEW 4

revivification *n* the act or an instance of bringing something back to life, public attention, or vigorous activity ⟨the runaway success of the handheld PDA led to a stunning *revivification* of the computer company's fortunes⟩ — see REVIVAL

revivify *vb* **1** to bring back to a former condition or vigor ⟨a new director hoping to *revivify* the region's oldest repertory company⟩ — see RENEW 1
2 to bring back to life, practice, or activity ⟨the new director hopes to *revivify* interest in the sports programs offered at the youth center⟩ — see REVIVE 1

reviving *adj* having a renewing effect on the state of the body or mind ⟨took a *reviving* vacation in the Caribbean⟩ — see TONIC 1

revocation *n* the act of putting an end to something planned or previously agreed to ⟨threatened the *revocation* of his son's driving privileges⟩ — see CANCELLATION 1

revoke *vb* to put an end to (something planned or previously agreed to) ⟨the judge *revoked* the jail sentence when the defendant promised to do community service instead⟩ — see CANCEL 1

revolt *n* open fighting against authority (as one's own government) ⟨soon the *revolt* had spread to every corner of the country⟩ — see REBELLION 1

revolt *vb* **1** to cause to feel disgust ⟨the jury appeared to be *revolted* by the grisly details of the murder⟩ — see DISGUST
2 to rise up against established authority ⟨the students practically *revolted* when the school cancelled the championship football game⟩ — see REBEL

revolted *adj* filled with disgust ⟨we were *revolted* when we learned about the prevalence of child labor in the Third World⟩ — see SICK 2

revolter *n* a person who rises up against authority ⟨Spartacus, who led a slave revolt in ancient Rome, has served as an inspiration for a number of other *revolters* over the centuries⟩ — see REBEL

revolting *adj* causing intense displeasure, disgust, or resentment ⟨the *revolting* sight of animals being slaughtered for no good reason⟩ — see OFFENSIVE 1

revolution *n* **1** a rapid turning about on an axis or central point ⟨revved the engine to 3000 *revolutions* per minute⟩ — see SPIN 1
2 open fighting against authority (as one's own government) ⟨the *revolution* by which the American colonies gained their independence from Great Britain necessitated going up against the world's most powerful army⟩ — see REBELLION 1

revolutionary *adj* **1** being very far from the center of public opinion ⟨a candidate with a lot of crazy, *revolutionary* ideas that no one seems to be going for⟩ — see EXTREME 2
2 taking part in a rebellion ⟨*revolutionary* forces that were soundly defeated before reaching the capital⟩ — see REBELLIOUS 1

revolutionary *n* **1** a person who favors rapid and sweeping changes especially in laws and methods of government ⟨after the collapse of the Russian monarchy, the moderate socialists briefly governed until being overthrown by the Bolshevik *revolutionaries*⟩ — see RADICAL
2 a person who rises up against authority ⟨at first the government was not worried about this small band of unarmed *revolutionaries*⟩ — see REBEL

revolutionist *adj* being very far from the center of public opinion ⟨his *revolutionist* ideas won't get him elected⟩ — see EXTREME 2

revolutionist *n* **1** a person who favors rapid and sweeping changes especially in laws and methods of government ⟨after a long series of weak leaders, the people were ready for a *revolutionist* who promised to bring sweeping change to the nation⟩ — see RADICAL
2 a person who rises up against authority ⟨historically, *revolutionists* have generally been young men willing to risk everything, even their lives, in the pursuit of their cause⟩ — see REBEL

revolve *vb* **1** to move (something) in a curved or circular path on or as if on an axis ⟨the salesclerk *revolved* the glass display case so I could see the watchbands on the reverse side⟩ — see TURN 1
2 to move in circles around an axis or center ⟨the sidereal day measures the time it takes the Earth to *revolve* completely about its axis with respect to the fixed stars⟩ — see SPIN 1
3 to give serious and careful thought to ⟨for the next several hours he kept *revolving* the cryptic message in his mind, trying to make sense of it⟩ — see PONDER

revulsion *n* a dislike so strong as to cause stomach upset or queasiness ⟨the publication of the autopsy photos prompted expressions of outrage and *revulsion*⟩ — see DISGUST

rewake *vb* to bring back to life, practice, or activity ⟨the media coverage of the dramatic escape has *rewaked* concerns about security at the prison⟩ — see REVIVE 1

rewaken *vb* to bring back to life, practice, or activity ⟨soaring gas prices have *rewakened* a demand for more fuel-efficient cars⟩ — see REVIVE 1

reward *n* something offered or given in return for a service performed ⟨there was a *reward* of $50 for the return of the missing cat⟩

synonyms bounty, price

related words bonus, lagniappe, premium; bonanza, jackpot, treasure trove; award, decoration, distinction, honor, plume, prize, trophy; gratuity, tip; desert(s), wages

reward *vb* to give something as a token of gratitude or admiration for a service or achievement ⟨the firefighters were *rewarded* by the city for their heroic actions⟩

synonyms award

related words cite, decorate, honor, remember; compensate, pay, recompense, requite; reimburse, repay; acclaim, applaud, commend, compliment, hail, praise, salute

rewarding *adj* making one feel good inside ⟨pursued a *rewarding* career providing medical care to poor children in rural areas⟩ — see HEARTWARMING

reweigh *vb* to consider again especially with the possibility of change or reversal ⟨the new study is leading doctors and nutritionists to *reweigh* the benefits of some dietary supplements⟩ — see RECONSIDER

reword *vb* to express something (as a text or statement) in different words ⟨I'll *reword* the question for you so you can better understand it⟩ — see PARAPHRASE

rewording *n* an instance of expressing something in different words ⟨I like your *rewording* of that paragraph better than the original⟩ — see PARAPHRASE

rework *vb* **1** to make different in some way ⟨the sculptor *reworked* the clay into another shape⟩ — see CHANGE 1

2 to prepare for publication by correcting, rewriting, or updating ⟨the magazine will publish your poem if you *rework* it so that it's a little shorter⟩ — see EDIT 1

reworking *n* the act, process, or result of making different ⟨the contract will need some *reworking* before it is acceptable to both parties⟩ — see CHANGE 1

rhapsodic *also* **rhapsodical** *adj* experiencing or marked by overwhelming usually pleasurable emotion ⟨the jingle used in the commercial is a humorously *rhapsodic* celebration of fast food⟩ — see ECSTATIC

rhapsodically *adv* in an enthusiastic manner ⟨*rhapsodically* described the glittering party at the billionaire's mansion⟩ — see SKY-HIGH

rhapsodize *vb* to make an exaggerated display of affection or enthusiasm ⟨*rhapsodized* about the food so as not to hurt their host's feelings⟩ — see GUSH 2

rhapsody *n* a state of overwhelming usually pleasurable emotion ⟨listening to Mozart always left him in a *rhapsody* that lingered for the remainder of the evening⟩ — see ECSTASY

rhetoric *n* **1** language that is impressive-sounding but not meaningful or sincere ⟨the mayor's promise to fight drugs was just *rhetoric*, since there was no money in the city budget for a drug program⟩

synonyms bombast, fustian, gas, grandiloquence, hot air, oratory, verbiage, wind

related words claptrap, drivel, gibberish, hogwash, humbug, jabberwocky, jazz, moonshine, nonsense; affectedness, floweriness, grandiosity, loftiness, pomposity, pretension, pretentiousness; garrulity, garrulousness, verboseness, verbosity, windiness, wordiness

2 the art or power of speaking or writing in a forceful and convincing way ⟨great leaders have often been masters of *rhetoric*, which they have used for both good and ill⟩ — see ELOQUENCE

rhetorical *also* **rhetoric** *adj* **1** marked by the use of impressive-sounding but mostly meaningless words and phrases ⟨you can skip over the *rhetorical* passages and still get the gist of the essay⟩

synonyms bombastic, flatulent, fustian, gaseous, gassy, grandiloquent, oratorical, orotund, windy

related words bloated, elevated, florid, flowery, grandiose, highfalutin (*also* hifalutin), high-flown, high-sounding, inflated, lofty, ornate, pompous, pontifical, pretentious, stilted, tumid, turgid; overdone, verbose, wordy

near antonyms eloquent, well-spoken; bald, direct, matter-of-fact, plain, plainspoken, simple, stark, straightforward, unadorned, unaffected, unpretentious

antonyms unrhetorical

2 full of fine words and fancy expressions ⟨the new governor delivered a long *rhetorical* speech about our state's bright future but laid out no specific programs for ensuring it⟩ — see FLOWERY 1

3 of or relating to words or language ⟨the next war that those two nations fight won't be *rhetorical*—it will be with bombs and bullets⟩ — see VERBAL 1

rhubarb *n* an often noisy or angry expression of differing opinions ⟨a basketball coach whose ranting *rhubarbs* with officials are the stuff of legend⟩ — see ARGUMENT 1

rhyme *also* **rime** *vb* to be in agreement on every point ⟨the new results don't *rhyme* with what we found out before⟩ — see CHECK 1

rhymester *also* **rimester** *n* a person who writes poetry ⟨reading doggerel by some *rhymester*⟩ — see POET

rhythm *n* the recurrent pattern formed by a series of sounds having a regular rise and fall in intensity ⟨the steady *rhythm* of the rain falling on the roof⟩

synonyms beat, cadence, measure, meter

related words accent, accentuation, emphasis, stress; backbeat; drum, throb; lilt, movement, sway, swing; hexameter, pentameter, tetrameter, trimeter

rhythmic *or* **rhythmical** *adj* marked by or occurring with a noticeable regularity in the rise and fall of sound ⟨lulled to sleep by the *rhythmic* sound of her mother's voice reading the Bible⟩

synonyms cadenced, cadent, measured, metrical (*or* metric)

related words even, metronomic (*also* metronomical), regular, steady, uniform; lilting, musical, swaying

antonyms arrhythmic, nonmetrical, unmeasured, unrhythmic

riata *n* a rope or long leather thong with a noose used especially for catching livestock ⟨the cowboy neatly tossed a *riata* over the head of the escaping cow⟩ — see LASSO

rib *n* **1** a work that imitates and exaggerates another work for comic effect ⟨the movie is a *rib* of the "dramatic love story" that was so popular in the 1950s⟩ — see PARODY 1

2 something said or done to cause laughter ⟨began to lose his sense of humor after being the butt of his friends' *ribs* once too often⟩ — see JOKE 1

rib *vb* to make fun of in a good-natured way ⟨*ribbed* him a bit about fumbling such an easy play⟩ — see TEASE 1

ribald *adj* **1** depicting or referring to sexual matters in a way that is unacceptable in polite society ⟨some of the movie's most *ribald*, and thus funniest, scenes were cut for showing on broadcast television⟩ — see OBSCENE 1

2 hinting at or intended to call to mind matters regarded as indecent ⟨a *ribald* tale rife with double entendres and racy innuendo⟩ — see SUGGESTIVE 1

ribaldry *n* the quality or state of being obscene ⟨there's a *ribaldry* in the works of Chaucer that generations of students of English literature have heartily enjoyed⟩ — see OBSCENITY 1

ribbing *adj* marked by or expressive of mild or good-na-

tured teasing ⟨the lightly *ribbing* tone tipped me off that this wasn't a serious reprimand⟩ — see QUIZZICAL

ribbon *n* a long narrow piece of material ⟨tied a silk *ribbon* in her hair⟩ — see STRIP 1

ribbon *vb* to cause (something) to separate into jagged pieces by violently pulling at it ⟨over the years the historic flag had become badly *ribboned* by the wind⟩ — see TEAR 1

rich *adj* **1** having goods, property, or money in abundance ⟨you would have to be quite *rich* to be able to afford a home in that neighborhood⟩

synonyms affluent, deep-pocketed, fat, fat-cat, flush, loaded, moneyed (*also* monied), opulent, silk-stocking, wealthy, well-endowed, well-fixed, well-heeled, well-off, well-to-do

related words better-off, comfortable, propertied, prosperous, substantial, successful; flourishing, prospering, thriving; advantaged, blessed (*also* blest), privileged

phrases in the chips

near antonyms unaffluent; deprived, disadvantaged, hand-to-mouth, underprivileged; bankrupt, bankrupted, beggared, broke, indebted, insolvent, pauperized, ruined, skint [*chiefly British*]; depressed, pinched, reduced, straitened; low, short

antonyms destitute, impecunious, impoverished, indigent, needy, penniless, penurious, poor, poverty-stricken

2 containing much seasoning, fat, or sugar ⟨stay away from *rich* foods before you sing tonight⟩

synonyms heavy

related words buttery, fat, fatty, greasy, oily; caloric, calorific, fattening; cloying, oversweet; filling, overfilling, satiating, sating; spicy, sugary, sweet; creamy, sauced

near antonyms natural, plain, simple; unseasoned; diet, nonfattening, slimming; nonfat

antonyms light, lite

3 having an abundance of some characteristic quality (as flavor) ⟨*rich* wines complemented the meal⟩ — see FULL-BODIED

4 producing abundantly ⟨*rich* farmland⟩ — see FERTILE

riches *n pl* the total of one's money and property ⟨industrialists who had amassed *riches* of a magnitude that few had dreamed possible⟩ — see WEALTH 1

richly *adv* in a luxurious manner ⟨a *richly* decorated penthouse that showed off the owner's art collection to its best advantage⟩ — see HIGH

richness *n* the amusing quality or element in something ⟨the *richness* of the irony—I had just contributed to the political campaign of a multimillionaire—was too much for me to ignore⟩ — see HUMOR 1

ricochet *vb* to strike and fly off at an angle ⟨the ball *ricocheted* off the fielder's glove and went over the fence for a home run⟩ — see GLANCE 1

rid *vb* to set (a person or thing) free of something that encumbers ⟨worked two jobs to *rid* himself of debt⟩

synonyms clear, disburden, disencumber, divest, free, relieve, unburden

related words discharge, emancipate, enfranchise, liberate, loose, loosen, manumit, release, spring, unbind, uncage, unchain, unfetter; bail (out), deliver, redeem, rescue; disengage, disentangle, extricate

near antonyms bog (down), fetter, hamper, restrain, shackle, subject, weigh down, weight (down)

antonyms burden, encumber, saddle

riddance *n* the getting rid of whatever is unwanted or useless ⟨the *riddance* of all the fleas from the house was a relief to everyone concerned⟩ — see DISPOSAL 1

riddle *n* something hard to understand or explain ⟨his motives for starting an argument with the coach were a complete *riddle*⟩ — see MYSTERY

riddle *vb* **1** to make a hole or series of holes in ⟨several signs along the highway were *riddled* by buckshot⟩ — see PERFORATE

2 to spread throughout ⟨the newspaper exposé revealed a gaming commission that is *riddled* with corruption⟩ — see PERMEATE

riddle (out) *vb* to find an answer for through reasoning ⟨with the discovery of the Rosetta stone, archaeologists at long last were able to *riddle out* the mystery of Egyptian hieroglyphics⟩ — see SOLVE

ride *n* a means of getting to a destination in a vehicle driven by another ⟨an organization that provides *rides* for senior citizens⟩

synonyms lift, transportation

related words drive, spin, turn; joyride; conveyance, passage, transit, transport

ride *vb* **1** to attack repeatedly with mean put-downs or insults ⟨that supervisor is always *riding* everyone for every little thing⟩ — see TEASE 2

2 to make fun of in a good-natured way ⟨his wife couldn't resist *riding* him for forgetting his own birthday⟩ — see TEASE 1

3 to rest or move along the surface of a liquid or in the air ⟨a condor *riding* high in the sky⟩ — see FLOAT 1

4 to be determined by, based on, or subject (to) ⟨our plan for the party *rides* on whether he can come⟩ — see DEPEND 1

ride (out) *vb* to come safely through ⟨just as we always have in the past, we'll *ride out* this latest crisis⟩ — see SURVIVE 1

ridge *n* the line formed when two sloping surfaces come together along their topmost edge ⟨pigeons roosting along the *ridge* of the roof⟩

synonyms crest

related words divide; backbone, ridgepole, spine; eminence, peak, prominence, promontory, rise

ridicule *n* the making of unkind jokes as a way of showing one's scorn for someone or something ⟨the early efforts by the suffragists to obtain voting rights for women were met with *ridicule*⟩

synonyms derision, mockery, sport

related words contempt, disdain, scorn; belittlement, deprecation, disparagement; catcall, insult, put-down; laughter, snickering; burlesque, caricature, mimicry, pasquinade, satire

near antonyms applause, approval, commendation, praise

ridicule *vb* to make (someone or something) the object of unkind laughter ⟨the term "big bang theory" was originally coined to *ridicule* the belief that the universe was created by a giant explosion⟩

synonyms deride, gibe (*or* jibe), jeer, laugh (at), mock, scout, shoot down, skewer

related words scoff (at), scorn, sneer (at); bad-mouth, belittle, decry, disparage, pooh-pooh (*also* pooh), put down; chaff, jive, josh, kid, quiz, rally, razz, rib, ride, tease, tweak, twit; bait, barrack [*chiefly British*], bug, catcall, harass, harry, hassle, heckle, needle, pester, rag, target, taunt, torment; ape, burlesque, caricature, imitate, lampoon, mimic, parody, parrot, pillory, satirize, take off (on), travesty

phrases cock a snook (at) *also* cock snooks (at), make fun of, make sport of, poke fun at, rag on

near antonyms applaud, approve, commend, endorse (*also* indorse), sanction

ridiculer *n* a person who causes repeated emotional pain, distress, or annoyance to another ⟨any person of great vision has his or her *ridiculers*, who inevitably fail to appreciate genius and originality⟩ — see TORMENTOR

ridiculous *adj* **1** so foolish or pointless as to be worthy

of scornful laughter ⟨a movie thriller with such a *ridiculous* plot that it gets only guffaws from audiences⟩
synonyms absurd, cockamamy (*or* cockamamie), comical, derisive, derisory, farcical, laughable, ludicrous, pathetic, preposterous, risible, silly
related words asinine, brainless, dumb, fatuous, foolish, half-baked, half-witted, harebrained, idiotic (*also* idiotical), imbecile (*or* imbecilic), inane, jerky, moronic, nonsensical, simpleminded, stupid, unwise, weak-minded, witless; balmy, cockeyed, crazy, cuckoo, daffy, daft, dotty, insane, kooky (*also* kookie), loony (*also* looney), lunatic, mad, nutty, screwball, senseless, wacky (*also* whacky); fantastic (*also* fantastical), far-fetched, inconceivable, incredible, unbelievable, unreal, unrealistic, unreasonable; illogical, irrational
phrases for the birds
near antonyms earnest, serious, solemn; believable, conceivable, credible, logical, rational, realistic, reasonable, sensible
2 causing or intended to cause laughter ⟨a movie comedian who has perfected the *ridiculous* pratfall⟩ — see FUNNY 1

rife *adj* possessing or covered with great numbers or amounts of something specified ⟨a city government that is *rife* with malfeasance and corruption⟩
synonyms abounding, abundant, awash, flush, fraught, lousy, replete, swarming, teeming, thick, thronging
related words brimming, bulging, bursting, chock-full (*or* chockful), crammed, crowded, fat, filled, full, jammed, jam-packed, loaded, packed, saturated, stuffed; clogged, congested, overcrowded, overfilled, overflowing, overfull, overladen, overloaded, overstuffed, surfeited; alive, animated, astir, bustling, busy, buzzing, humming, lively
near antonyms bare, barren, blank, devoid, empty, stark, vacant, void; depleted, drained, exhausted; deficient, incomplete, insufficient, short

riff *n* a distinct treatment of something (as a story or a play) ⟨a mock news program with humorous *riffs* on current events⟩
synonyms interpretation, take, variation
related words version; adaptation, translation

riffle *vb* to turn over pages in an idle or cursory manner ⟨Web research is convenient but doesn't offer the tactile pleasures of *riffling* through heavy old books⟩ — see SKIM 1

riffraff *n* **1** discarded or useless material ⟨the sight of piles and piles of *riffraff* at the town dump was a sobering reminder that we are indeed a society of consumers⟩ — see GARBAGE 1
2 people looked down upon as ignorant and of the lowest class ⟨local ordinances that are intended to keep the *riffraff* out of the town⟩ — see RABBLE

rifle *vb* to look through (as a place) carefully or thoroughly in an effort to find or discover something ⟨*rifled* the desk drawer in search of the insurance policy⟩ — see SEARCH 1

rift *n* **1** an irregular usually narrow break in a surface created by pressure ⟨a small *rift* opened in the earth's crust⟩ — see CRACK 1
2 an open space in a barrier (as a wall or hedge) ⟨it was possible to peek through the *rift* in the fence and see the ball game⟩ — see GAP 1

rig *n* **1** a horse-drawn wheeled vehicle for carrying passengers ⟨romantic couples enjoy being driven in the old-fashioned *rig* through the park⟩ — see CARRIAGE 1
2 covering for the human body ⟨most of the celebrants of the town's bicentennial will be in festive *rig*—so don't show up in jeans⟩ — see CLOTHING

rig *vb* to provide (someone) with what is needed for a task or activity ⟨carefully *rigged* each diver with the required equipment before starting out⟩ — see FURNISH 1

rig (out) *vb* to outfit with clothes and especially fine or special clothes ⟨everyone was *rigged out* for the country club's spring cotillion⟩ — see CLOTHE 1

rigging *n* covering for the human body ⟨even at the Ivies they dress in the standard *rigging* of the college student: T-shirt and jeans⟩ — see CLOTHING

right *adj* **1** following an original exactly ⟨a modern replica of an 18th-century British warship that is *right* in all of its details⟩ — see FAITHFUL 2
2 being exactly as appears or as claimed ⟨despite the name, New York's East River is a strait and not a *right* river⟩ — see AUTHENTIC 1
3 being in agreement with the truth or a fact or a standard ⟨the obvious answer is not always the *right* one⟩ — see CORRECT 1
4 being what is called for by accepted standards of right and wrong ⟨trying to do what is *right*⟩ — see JUST 1
5 conforming to a high standard of morality or virtue ⟨a *right* woman who did not hang around waterfront bars⟩ — see GOOD 2
6 free from irregularities or digressions in course ⟨the first city in America laid out with broad, *right* avenues⟩ — see STRAIGHT 1
7 having full use of one's mind and control over one's actions ⟨he hasn't been *right* since he suffered serious brain injury in the accident⟩ — see SANE
8 meeting the requirements of a purpose or situation ⟨the *right* tool for the job⟩ — see FIT 1

right *adv* **1** as stated or indicated without the slightest difference ⟨stay *right* where you are⟩ — see EXACTLY 1
2 in a direct line or course ⟨walk *right* over here now⟩ — see DIRECTLY 1
3 to a great degree ⟨a *right* beautiful day we're having!⟩ — see VERY 1
4 without delay ⟨we'll leave *right* after dinner⟩ — see IMMEDIATELY
5 in a manner suitable for the occasion or purpose ⟨you're not dressed *right* for an interview with a big-time law firm⟩ — see PROPERLY

right *n* **1** something to which one has a just claim ⟨everyone has the *right* to life, liberty, and the pursuit of happiness⟩
synonyms appanage (*also* apanage), birthright, prerogative
related words call, dibs, due, entitlement, perquisite, pretense (*or* pretence), pretension, privilege
2 an entitlement to something ⟨what *right* do you have to tell us what to do?⟩ — see CLAIM 1
3 the practice of giving to others what is their due ⟨activists who have fought all their lives for *right*⟩ — see JUSTICE 1

right away *adv* without delay ⟨you need to have this fixed *right away*⟩ — see IMMEDIATELY

righteous *adj* **1** conforming to a high standard of morality or virtue ⟨a *righteous* man can be trusted to act honorably regardless of the circumstances⟩ — see GOOD 2
2 following the accepted rules of moral conduct ⟨*righteous* behavior is its own reward⟩ — see HONORABLE 1
3 *slang* of the very best kind ⟨a nightspot that's a dependable venue for *righteous* jazz⟩ — see EXCELLENT

righteously *adv* with purity of thought and deed ⟨if you have acted *righteously*, you have nothing to fear⟩ — see PURELY 1

righteousness *n* **1** conduct that conforms to an accepted standard of right and wrong ⟨the laws do not always dictate *righteousness*, for what is legal is not always moral⟩ — see MORALITY 1
2 faithfulness to high moral standards ⟨a life lived with

righteousness guarantees that you will always respect yourself⟩ — see HONOR 1

rightful *adj* being what is called for by accepted standards of right and wrong ⟨in light of her admission of having lied, the only *rightful* course of action for the governor would be to resign⟩ — see JUST 1

rightist *n* a person whose political beliefs are centered on tradition and keeping things the way they are ⟨*rightists* opposed the new social programs⟩ — see CONSERVATIVE

rightly *adv* in a manner suitable for the occasion or purpose ⟨marveling at the awesome sight, we had to agree that the Grand Canyon was *rightly* named⟩ — see PROPERLY

right–minded *adj* conforming to a high standard of morality or virtue ⟨a group of *right-minded* people working for social change⟩ — see GOOD 2

rightness *n* **1** conduct that conforms to an accepted standard of right and wrong ⟨she seems to confuse *rightness* with self-righteousness⟩ — see MORALITY 1
2 the quality or state of being especially suitable or fitting ⟨the irrefutable *rightness* of the criticism didn't make it any more pleasant to hear⟩ — see APPROPRIATENESS

right now *adv* **1** at the present time ⟨*right now* we are in the middle of a major home renovation⟩ — see NOW 1
2 without delay ⟨answer my question *right now*⟩ — see IMMEDIATELY

right off *adv* without delay ⟨he had just gotten married when he was shipped *right off* to war⟩ — see IMMEDIATELY

right–of–way *n* the right to one's attention before other things considered less important ⟨the bill for emergency aid was immediately granted *right-of-way*⟩ — see PRIORITY

right–winger *n* a person whose political beliefs are centered on tradition and keeping things the way they are ⟨a staunch *right-winger* who opposes, on principle, government social programs⟩ — see CONSERVATIVE

rigid *adj* **1** not allowing for any exceptions or loosening of standards ⟨*rigid* enforcement of drug laws⟩
synonyms brassbound, cast-iron, exacting, hard-line, inflexible, rigorous, strict, stringent, uncompromising
related words close, conscientious, exact, fussy, meticulous, painstaking, punctilious, scrupulous, undeviating; adamant, adamantine, determined, dogged, firm, relentless, resolved, single-minded, steadfast, stubborn, tenacious, unbending, unflinching; immovable, implacable, unappeasable, unrelenting, unsparing, unyielding; austere, demanding, flinty, grim, hard, hardened, hard-hearted, harsh, ironbound, severe, stern, tough
near antonyms acquiescent, compliant, compromising, pliable, pliant, relenting, yielding; easy, easygoing, gentle, indulgent, kindly, lenient, merciful, mild, pampering, soft, spoiling, tolerant; neglectful, negligent, remiss, slipshod, sloppy, slovenly, unfussy
antonyms flexible, lax, loose, relaxed, slack
2 given to exacting standards of discipline and self-restraint ⟨a *rigid* man who cannot seem to relax⟩ — see SEVERE 1
3 having a consistency that does not easily yield to pressure ⟨*rigid* steel bars that should be able to hold the weight⟩ — see FIRM 2
4 incapable of or highly resistant to bending ⟨corsets, those *rigid* undergarments for women, must have been murder to wear⟩ — see STIFF 1
5 stretched with little or no give ⟨make sure that the clothesline is *rigid* so that the longer garments don't drag on the ground⟩ — see TAUT

rigidity *n* the quality or state of being demanding or unyielding (as in discipline or criticism) ⟨sometimes the *rigidity* of the headmaster's discipline was deemed excessive by even much of the faculty⟩ — see SEVERITY

rigidly *adv* without any relaxation of standards or precision ⟨the judge stuck *rigidly* to the letter of the law⟩ — see STRICTLY

rigidness *n* the quality or state of being demanding or unyielding (as in discipline or criticism) ⟨no one even asked anymore, as their father's *rigidness* regarding bedtime was legendary⟩ — see SEVERITY

rigmarole *also* **rigamarole** *n* language marked by abstractions, jargon, euphemisms, and circumlocutions ⟨the security guard gave me some kind of *rigmarole* about passes and authorizations⟩ — see GIBBERISH 2

rigor *n* **1** something that is a cause for suffering or special effort especially in the attainment of a goal ⟨hard-bitten folk who survived many *rigors* on the way to the promised land⟩ — see DIFFICULTY 1
2 the quality or state of being demanding or unyielding (as in discipline or criticism) ⟨after being coddled by his former coach, the swimmer was shocked by the *rigor* of the new training program⟩ — see SEVERITY
3 the quality or state of being very accurate ⟨said that she had heard that excuse a million times, but then she was never known for the *rigor* of her calculations⟩ — see PRECISION

rigorous *adj* **1** given to exacting standards of discipline and self-restraint ⟨a *rigorous* football coach who pushes his players to their physical and mental limits⟩ — see SEVERE 1
2 meeting the highest standard of accuracy ⟨a *rigorous* analysis of the data⟩ — see PRECISE 1
3 not allowing for any exceptions or loosening of standards ⟨a *rigorous* diet and exercise regimen⟩ — see RIGID 1
4 requiring considerable physical or mental effort ⟨studied for umpteen months for the *rigorous* exam⟩ — see HARD 2

rigorously *adv* without any relaxation of standards or precision ⟨a *rigorously* accurate accounting of the war casualties⟩ — see STRICTLY

rigorousness *n* **1** the quality or state of being demanding or unyielding (as in discipline or criticism) ⟨the *rigorousness* of the training paid off when the dance students performed brilliantly at the recital⟩ — see SEVERITY
2 the quality or state of being very accurate ⟨these days the *rigorousness* of electronic timing is necessary to measure the minute differences in the performances of Olympic athletes⟩ — see PRECISION

rile *vb* **1** to disturb the peace of mind of (someone) especially by repeated disagreeable acts ⟨one sure way to *rile* me is to keep yelling for me⟩ — see IRRITATE 1
2 to make angry ⟨her husband isn't easily *riled*, but once he is, he stays that way for days⟩ — see ANGER

riled *adj* feeling or showing anger ⟨the woman was obviously *riled*, as she kept throwing things⟩ — see ANGRY

riley *adj* **1** feeling or showing anger ⟨some visibly *riley* people were lined up in the customer service department⟩ — see ANGRY
2 having visible particles in liquid suspension ⟨take care not to stir up the bottom of the stream when you fill the dipper, or your water will be *riley*⟩ — see CLOUDY 1

riling *adj* causing annoyance ⟨a *riling* habit that drives his wife crazy⟩ — see ANNOYING

rill *n* a natural body of running water smaller than a river ⟨there are a few tiny fish in the *rill*⟩ — see CREEK 1

rim *n* the line or relatively narrow space that marks the outer limit of something ⟨the *rim* of a glass⟩ — see BORDER 1

rim *vb* to serve as a border for ⟨long lashes *rimmed* his eyes⟩ — see BORDER

rime *n* a covering of tiny ice crystals on a cold surface

⟨*rime* on the bedroom window after a bitterly cold night⟩ — see FROST 1

rime *vb* to cover with a hardened layer ⟨frost *riming* the doorknob⟩ — see ENCRUST

[1]ring *n* **1** a group involved in secret or criminal activities ⟨a *ring* of counterfeiters passing phony $20 bills⟩
synonyms cabal, conspiracy, crew, gang, Mafia, mob, syndicate
related words bunch, circle, clan, clique, coterie, coven, crowd, galère, lot, network, pack, set; junta, oligarchy
2 a circular strip ⟨a metal *ring* encircled the barrel⟩
synonyms band, circle, eye, hoop, loop, round
related words belt, cincture, collar, girdle; wreath; annulet, becket, coil, curl, furl, hank, spiral, spire, twirl, whorl
3 a group of people sharing a common interest and relating together socially ⟨a gaming *ring* that meets once a week to play⟩ — see GANG 2
4 something with a perfectly round circumference ⟨the coffee cup left a *ring* on the table⟩ — see CIRCLE 1

[2]ring *n* a communication by telephone ⟨give me a *ring* when you're ready to go⟩ — see CALL 3

[1]ring *vb* **1** to form a circle around ⟨tall cypress trees *ringing* the park⟩ — see SURROUND
2 to travel completely around ⟨the line of season ticket buyers *ringed* the block⟩ — see ENCIRCLE 1

[2]ring *vb* to make the clear sound heard when metal vibrates ⟨I didn't hear the doorbell *ring*⟩
synonyms bong, chime, knell, peal, toll
related words chink, clang, clank, clash, clink, ding, ding-dong, gong, jangle, jingle, ping, plink, plunk (*or* plonk), tang, tingle, tinkle; echo, resonate, resound, reverberate

ring (up) *vb, chiefly British* to make a telephone call to ⟨our friend *rang* us *up* to see if we wanted to go to a cricket match⟩ — see CALL 2

ringer *n* **1** one who makes false claims of identity or expertise ⟨no one was more surprised than the defendant when his lawyer turned out to be a *ringer*⟩ — see IMPOSTOR
2 something or someone that strongly resembles another ⟨he's a dead *ringer* for his grandfather⟩ — see IMAGE 1

ringing *adj* **1** marked by a high volume of sound ⟨an angry, *ringing* denial of the charges⟩ — see LOUD 1
2 marked by conspicuously full and rich sounds or tones ⟨sings in a *ringing* baritone that can be heard throughout the hall⟩ — see RESONANT
3 not subject to misinterpretation or more than one interpretation ⟨whereas other candidates hedged on that hot-button issue, he delivered a *ringing* endorsement of the pro-choice position⟩ — see CLEAR 2

ringlet *n* a length of hair that forms a loop or series of loops ⟨a little girl with perfect, golden *ringlets*⟩ — see CURL

ring up *vb* to obtain (as a goal) through effort ⟨touted the many diplomatic triumphs that the president supposedly *rang up* in his first term⟩ — see ACHIEVE 1

rinse *vb* to pour liquid over or through in order to cleanse ⟨*rinse* that shirt immediately, or the paint will set⟩ — see FLUSH 1

riot *n* someone or something that is very funny ⟨she's such a *riot* at parties⟩ — see SCREAM

riot act *n* an often public or formal expression of disapproval ⟨at a specially called meeting, he read the *riot act* to his staff for their poor handling of the crisis⟩ — see CENSURE

riotous *adj* **1** causing or intended to cause laughter ⟨his *riotous* mugging always has everyone in hysterics⟩ — see FUNNY 1
2 pouring forth in great amounts ⟨a painting by that artist is usually a *riotous* display of color⟩ — see PROFUSE

[1]rip *n* a long deep cut ⟨the hoe left *rips* in the lawn⟩ — see GASH

[2]rip *n* a person who has sunk below the normal moral standard ⟨something of a *rip* in his youth, he eventually settled down⟩ — see DEGENERATE

rip *vb* **1** to cause (something) to separate into jagged pieces by violently pulling at it ⟨the dog *ripped* the sleeve of my shirt by grabbing it with his teeth⟩ — see TEAR 1
2 to penetrate with a sharp edge (as a knife) ⟨you can see where someone *ripped* the painting with a penknife⟩ — see CUT 1
3 to proceed or move quickly ⟨the car went *ripping* down the road⟩ — see HURRY 2
4 to separate or remove by forceful pulling ⟨*rip* a sheet off the pad of paper⟩ — see TEAR 2

ripe *adj* **1** fully grown or developed ⟨a *ripe* tomato⟩ — see MATURE 1
2 having an unpleasant smell ⟨the clothes of the field hands were sweaty and *ripe* after a hard day's work⟩ — see MALODOROUS

ripen *vb* to become mature ⟨pears *ripening* on the tree⟩ — see MATURE

ripened *adj* fully grown or developed ⟨a fully *ripened* musical talent⟩ — see MATURE 1

ripening *n* the process of becoming mature ⟨the *ripening* of a pumpkin can take a whole season⟩ — see MATURATION

rip–off *n* an instance of theft ⟨a daring burglary of the art museum that resulted in one of the greatest *rip-offs* in history⟩ — see THEFT 2

rip off *vb* **1** to remove valuables from (a place) unlawfully ⟨the teens *ripped off* the store where they had been working for the summer⟩ — see ROB
2 to take (something) without right and with an intent to keep ⟨the thief *ripped off* some jewelry as soon as no one was looking⟩ — see STEAL 1
3 to rob by the use of trickery or threats ⟨an investigation revealed that a whole slew of suppliers had been *ripping off* the defense department⟩ — see FLEECE

riposte *n* a quick witty response ⟨he's known for having a brilliant *riposte* to nearly any insult⟩ — see RETORT 1

riposte *vb* to speak or write in reaction to a question or to another reaction ⟨at cocktail parties she could *riposte* with lightning speed to even the most unexpected quip⟩ — see ANSWER 1

ripped *adj, slang* **1** being under the influence of a recreational drug ⟨when I got to his house, he was already pretty *ripped*⟩ — see STONED 1
2 being under the influence of alcohol ⟨college kids who need to learn that you don't need to get *ripped* in order to have a good time⟩ — see DRUNK

ripper *n* something very good of its kind ⟨the comedian's last routine was a real *ripper*, leaving the audience in those proverbial stitches⟩ — see JIM-DANDY

ripple *vb* to flow in a broken irregular stream ⟨water *rippling* gently over the tiers of the fountain⟩ — see GURGLE

rip–roaring *adj* causing great emotional or mental stimulation ⟨a *rip-roaring* tale of the Old West⟩ — see EXCITING 1

ripsnorter *n* something very good of its kind ⟨had high hopes that the football game would be a *ripsnorter*, but it turned out to be a real snoozer⟩ — see JIM-DANDY

rise *n* **1** a raising or a state of being raised to a higher rank or position ⟨his rapid *rise* to president of the company⟩ — see ADVANCEMENT 1
2 an area of high ground ⟨if we can get to the top of that *rise*, we'll be able to see for miles⟩ — see HEIGHT 4

3 an upward slope ⟨the *rise* of the hill was relatively gentle⟩ — see ASCENT 2
4 something added (as by growth) ⟨an unexpected *rise* in prices⟩ — see INCREASE 1
5 the act or an instance of rising or climbing up ⟨unfortunately, the descent of the balloon was just as swift as its *rise*⟩ — see ASCENT 1

rise *vb* **1** to become greater in extent, volume, amount, or number ⟨the snow accumulation is *rising* at an alarming rate⟩ — see INCREASE 2
2 to leave one's bed ⟨I generally *rise* around six and leave for work by seven⟩ — see ARISE 1
3 to move or extend upward ⟨mountains majestically *rising* towards the sky⟩ — see ASCEND

risible *adj* **1** causing or intended to cause laughter ⟨a *risible* comment that made the whole class laugh⟩ — see FUNNY 1
2 so foolish or pointless as to be worthy of scornful laughter ⟨the idea that people are meant to have wings is *risible*⟩ — see RIDICULOUS 1

rising *n* **1** open fighting against authority (as one's own government) ⟨a great *rising* of the people was all it took to bring down a regime that imagined that it would endure for a thousand years⟩ — see REBELLION 1
2 the act or an instance of rising or climbing up ⟨the *rising* of the sun⟩ — see ASCENT 1

risk *n* **1** something that may cause injury or harm ⟨mountain climbing is a *risk*, but the thrill and challenge are worth it⟩ — see DANGER 2
2 the state of not being protected from injury, harm, or evil ⟨children living in poverty are considered at *risk* for a number of medical and developmental problems⟩ — see DANGER 1

risk *vb* **1** to take a chance on ⟨Colette didn't want to *risk* running out of food for her party, so she bought twice what she thought she would actually need⟩
synonyms adventure, chance, gamble (on), hazard, tempt, venture
related words beard, brave, brazen, breast, challenge, confront, dare, defy, face, outbrave; compromise, endanger, imperil, jeopardize, menace; expose, subject; bet (on), wager
phrases run the risk of
2 to place in danger ⟨we refuse to *risk* our life savings on this investment scheme⟩ — see ENDANGER

risky *adj* involving potential loss or injury ⟨a *risky* new adventure⟩ — see DANGEROUS 1

risqué *adj* hinting at or intended to call to mind matters regarded as indecent ⟨the bridal shower was filled with *risqué* banter and laughter⟩ — see SUGGESTIVE 1

rite *n* an oft-repeated action or series of actions performed in accordance with tradition or a set of rules ⟨the annual summer *rite* of loading up the car for the big family vacation⟩
synonyms ceremonial, ceremony, form, formality, observance, ritual, solemnity
related words amenities, civility, decorum, etiquette, graces, proprieties; protocol; convention, custom, habit, manners, mores, practice (*also* practise), standard, tradition, way; celebration, service

ritual *n* **1** a usual manner of behaving or doing ⟨her morning *ritual* is to enjoy a bracing cup of coffee while reading the newspaper⟩ — see HABIT 1
2 an oft-repeated action or series of actions performed in accordance with tradition or a set of rules ⟨a *ritual* that the ancient peoples of that country believed would bring rain⟩ — see RITE

ritzy *adj* being or characteristic of a person who has an offensive air of superiority and tends to ignore or disdain anyone regarded as inferior ⟨I don't appreciate your *ritzy* advice about whom I "should" associate with⟩ — see SNOBBISH

rival *n* **1** one that is equal to another in status, achievement, or value ⟨a design that is a *rival* to any produced by a professional graphic artist⟩ — see EQUAL
2 one that takes a position opposite another in a competition or conflict ⟨the boxer's toughest *rival* thus far⟩ — see OPPONENT 1
3 one who strives for the same thing as another ⟨the four cities that are the top *rivals* for the site of the next Olympic Games⟩ — see COMPETITOR

rival *vb* to engage in a contest ⟨two longtime friends who have *rivaled* for the same things at every stage of their lives⟩ — see COMPETE

rivalry *n* an earnest effort for superiority or victory over another ⟨a healthy *rivalry* in sports between the two schools⟩ — see CONTEST 1

rive *vb* **1** to cause to separate into pieces usually suddenly or forcibly ⟨road pavement that had been *riven* by the annual freeze-and-thaw cycle⟩ — see BREAK 1
2 to cause (something) to separate into jagged pieces by violently pulling at it ⟨the bitter disappointment threatened to *rive* my heart in two⟩ — see TEAR 1

rivet *vb* to fix (as one's attention) steadily toward a central objective ⟨everyone *riveted* their eyes on the trick that the magician was performing on stage⟩ — see CONCENTRATE 2

riveting *adj* holding the attention or provoking interest ⟨a *riveting* explanation of light waves that fascinated the class⟩ — see INTERESTING

rivulet *n* a natural body of running water smaller than a river ⟨small *rivulets* trickled down the side of the cliff⟩ — see CREEK 1

road *n* **1** a passage cleared for public vehicular travel ⟨I think we should take one of the less congested *roads*⟩ — see WAY 1
2 a roadway overlaid with parallel steel rails over which trains travel ⟨the railway companies are continually repairing their *roads*⟩ — see RAILROAD

roadhouse *n* a bar or restaurant offering special nighttime entertainment (as music, dancing, or comedy acts) ⟨stopped at a *roadhouse* for some drinks and a little line dancing⟩ — see NIGHTCLUB

road map *n* **1** a method worked out in advance for achieving some objective ⟨a *road map* for peace in the troubled region⟩ — see PLAN 1
2 a statement that makes something clear ⟨an article that is a good *road map* for any consumer attempting to negotiate his way through the maze of offerings in digital photography⟩ — see EXPLANATION 1

roadway *n* a passage cleared for public vehicular travel ⟨a cow wandered into the *roadway*⟩ — see WAY 1

roam *vb* to move about from place to place aimlessly ⟨he took a year off and *roamed* over Europe before going on to college⟩ — see WANDER 1

roamer *n* a person who roams about without a fixed route or destination ⟨the couple retired, sold their house, and became carefree *roamers* in an RV⟩ — see NOMAD

roaming *adj* traveling from place to place ⟨a *roaming* circus that plays small towns across the country⟩ — see ITINERANT

roar *n* **1** a violent shouting ⟨a *roar* went up from the crowd when the verdict was read⟩ — see CLAMOR 1
2 loud, confused, and usually inharmonious sound ⟨the *roar* of the machinery in the factory⟩ — see NOISE 1

roar *vb* **1** to make a long loud deep noise or cry ⟨the car's engine *roared* as it sped away⟩
synonyms bellow, boom, growl, thunder
related words grumble, roll, rumble; bang, blare, blast, peal, scream, screech, shriek, squall; bawl, call, cry, holler, hoot, shout, whoop, yell; bell, caterwaul, howl, wail, yowl
near antonyms grunt, mouth, mumble, murmur, mut-

ter, whisper; mewl, pule, squeak, whimper
2 to speak so as to be heard at a distance ⟨when we arrived at the house we could hear our friend *roaring* at someone inside, so we discreetly left⟩ — see CALL 1
3 to show mirth with an explosive vocal sound ⟨a madcap comedy that had movie audiences *roaring* all summer long⟩ — see LAUGH 1

roaring *adj* **1** marked by a high volume of sound ⟨a *roaring* party that annoyed the neighbors mightily⟩ — see LOUD 1
2 marked by vigorous growth and well-being especially economically ⟨the *roaring* mining town attracted job seekers eager to share in the boom⟩ — see PROSPEROUS 1

roaring *adv* to a great degree ⟨we had a *roaring* good time at the party⟩ — see VERY 1

roaringly *adv* to a great degree ⟨a *roaringly* successful Broadway play⟩ — see VERY 1

roast *vb* to make fun of in a good-natured way ⟨playfully *roasting* their mother for her choice of hat⟩ — see TEASE 1

roasting *adj* having a notably high temperature ⟨turn on the air conditioner—the house is *roasting* today!⟩ — see HOT 1

rob *vb* to remove valuables from (a place) unlawfully ⟨in jail for *robbing* a bank⟩
synonyms burglarize, burgle, knock off, knock over, rip off, steal (from), take off [*slang*]
related words ransack, rifle; despoil, loot, pillage, plunder, ravish, sack, spoil, strip; bleed, break in, cheat, chisel, cozen, defraud, exploit, fleece, gyp, hustle, mulct, pluck, rook, shortchange, skin, squeeze, stick, sting, swindle; hold up, mug, roll, stick up

robber *n* one who steals ⟨the *robber* wore a ski mask while holding up the bank⟩ — see THIEF

robbery *n* the unlawful taking and carrying away of property without the consent of its owner ⟨the first sign that there had been a *robbery* was the broken door lock⟩ — see THEFT 1

robe *n* something that covers or conceals like a piece of cloth ⟨with the coming of spring the hills will once again don their *robes* of green⟩ — see CLOAK 1

robe *vb* to outfit with clothes and especially fine or special clothes ⟨*robed* the queen in her ceremonial garments⟩ — see CLOTHE 1

robotic *adj* **1** designed to replace or decrease human labor and especially physical labor ⟨the dishwasher is one of the greatest *robotic* devices ever invented⟩ — see LABORSAVING
2 done instantly and without conscious thought or decision ⟨with a single *robotic* motion, she reached for a cigarette and a lighter the instant she sat down⟩ — see AUTOMATIC 1

robotization *n* the process of putting an apparatus, operation, or system under the control or regulation of mechanical or electronic devices ⟨on account of *robotization*, no human need come into direct contact with the hazardous material⟩ — see AUTOMATION

robust *adj* **1** enjoying health and vigor ⟨a *robust* and sturdy toddler⟩ — see HEALTHY 1
2 having active strength of body or mind ⟨a *robust* older man who still bicycles 10 miles a day⟩ — see VIGOROUS 1
3 having an abundance of some characteristic quality (as flavor) ⟨beef and other red meats should be accompanied by *robust* wines⟩ — see FULL-BODIED
4 not showing weakness or uncertainty ⟨a *robust* slap on the back welcoming me to the company⟩ — see FIRM 1

robustious *adj* being rough or noisy in a high-spirited way ⟨his buddies sent him off to the navy with many *robustious* and hearty toasts⟩ — see BOISTEROUS

robustness *n* **1** the condition of being sound in body ⟨she has the *robustness* of a woman half her age⟩ — see HEALTH 1
2 the quality or state of having abundant or intense activity ⟨the relentless *robustness* of the city has always inspired writers and artists⟩ — see VITALITY 1

rock *n, slang* a usually valuable stone cut and polished for ornament ⟨a trophy wife with enough *rocks* to open her own jewelry store⟩ — see GEM 1

rock *vb* **1** to make a series of unsteady side-to-side motions ⟨the boat was *rocking* so much that several passengers felt seasick⟩
synonyms careen, lurch, pitch, roll, seesaw, sway, toss, wobble (*also* wabble)
related words blunder, buck, dodder, falter, flounder, halt, hitch, hobble, jerk, jolt, reel, shake, stagger, stumble, teeter, toddle, totter, tumble, vacillate, vibrate, waddle, waver, weave; oscillate, undulate, wag, waggle
2 to swing unsteadily back and forth or from side to side ⟨the drunk *rocked* on his heels for a moment and then fell flat on his back⟩ — see TEETER 1
3 to make senseless or dizzy by a blow ⟨she *rocked* the mugger with a single punch and then ran⟩ — see STUN 1
4 to make a strong impression on (someone) with something unexpected ⟨the news of the mayor's sudden death *rocked* the city⟩ — see SURPRISE 1

rock–bottom *adj* of, relating to, or located at the bottom ⟨*rock-bottom* prices on home electronics⟩ — see BOTTOM

rock bottom *n* **1** the lowest part, place, or point ⟨when the stock market was at its *rock bottom* was the time to buy in⟩ — see BOTTOM 3
2 the lowest point or level ⟨our finances must be at *rock bottom* if we can't even afford a fast-food joint⟩ — see NADIR 1

rocket *vb* **1** to proceed or move quickly ⟨the startled cat *rocketed* out of the room⟩ — see HURRY 2
2 to rise abruptly and rapidly ⟨the child actor *rocketed* to stardom at the age of eight⟩ — see SKYROCKET

rod *n* **1** a heavy rigid stick used as a weapon or for punishment ⟨arrested for using a *rod* on his dogs in violation of the state's animal cruelty laws⟩ — see CLUB 1
2 a straight piece (as of wood or metal) that is longer than it is wide ⟨a curtain *rod*⟩ — see BAR 1

rodomontade *also* **rhodomontade** *n* boastful speech or writing ⟨for all of its jingoistic *rodomontade*, the government had no thought-out plan for the war and its aftermath⟩ — see BOMBAST 1

rogue *adj* given to or marked by cheating and deception ⟨a *rogue* administrator who took bribes to falsify paperwork⟩ — see DISHONEST 2

rogue *n* **1** a mean, evil, or unprincipled person ⟨a *rogue* who had nothing but contempt for people who made their living honestly⟩ — see VILLAIN
2 an appealingly mischievous person ⟨the little *rogue* always seems to end up being forgiven for his pranks⟩ — see SCAMP 1

roguery *n* **1** a playful or mischievous act intended as a joke ⟨those adolescent *rogueries* that seemed funny at the time—but only stupid when considered in hindsight⟩ — see PRANK
2 playful, reckless behavior that is not intended to cause serious harm ⟨the old fraternity brothers fondly recounted how their *roguery* used to rile the dean⟩ — see MISCHIEF 1

roguish *adj* tending to or exhibiting reckless playfulness ⟨a *roguish* grin was the only sign that she had something up her sleeve for the office party⟩ — see MISCHIEVOUS 1

roguishness *n* playful, reckless behavior that is not intended to cause serious harm ⟨a bit of childish *roguish-*

ness that ended up with a window being broken⟩ — see MISCHIEF 1

roil *vb* **1** to be in a state of violent rolling motion ⟨the waters of the gulf tossed and *roiled* as the hurricane surged toward the shore⟩ — see SEETHE 1
2 to make angry ⟨the clerk's brusque refusal of her request *roiled* her enough to prompt a complaint to his supervisor⟩ — see ANGER

roiled *adj* **1** feeling or showing anger ⟨he waited until he wasn't so obviously *roiled* before voicing a complaint to the manager⟩ — see ANGRY
2 having visible particles in liquid suspension ⟨the *roiled* water made more difficult the work of the divers searching the river for the missing canoeists⟩ — see CLOUDY 1

roister *vb* to take part in drunken revelry ⟨the earl's wastrel son had spent the best part of his youth *roistering* and gambling⟩ — see CAROUSE

roisterer *n* one who engages in merrymaking especially in honor of a special occasion ⟨the rowdy *roisterers* who fill the streets of New Orleans during Mardi Gras⟩ — see CELEBRANT

roisterous *adj* being rough or noisy in a high-spirited way ⟨students were told that it was possible to have a *roisterous* victory celebration without resorting to violence⟩ — see BOISTEROUS

role *also* **rôle** *n* the action for which a person or thing is specially fitted or used or for which a thing exists ⟨studying the *role* of sunlight in the body's production of vitamin D⟩
synonyms business, capacity, function, job, part, place, position, purpose, task, work
related words affair, concern, hand, involvement, participation; niche, office, post, situation; calling, occupation, pursuit, vocation; activity, assignment, charge, commission, duty, employ, mission, responsibility, service, use

[1]roll *n* a record of a series of items (as names or titles) usually arranged according to some system ⟨called the *roll* of people supposed to be in the class⟩ — see [1]LIST

[2]roll *n* a rapid turning about on an axis or central point ⟨the squirrel did a quick *roll* and vanished up a tree⟩ — see SPIN 1

roll *vb* **1** to form into a round compact mass ⟨*rolled* up the wrapper from the straw and threw it⟩ — see WAD
2 to make a low heavy rolling sound ⟨thunder *rolling* in the distance⟩ — see RUMBLE
3 to make a series of unsteady side-to-side motions ⟨the car suddenly was *rolling* as high winds swept across the bridge⟩ — see ROCK 1
4 to move (something) in a curved or circular path on or as if on an axis ⟨in order to knock your opponent off balance, you have to *roll* the log when he least expects it⟩ — see TURN 1
5 to move in a stream ⟨just lying on the beach, watching the clouds *roll* by⟩ — see FLOW 1
6 to move in circles around an axis or center ⟨*rolled* her head around her shoulders to loosen herself up⟩ — see SPIN 1
7 to move or proceed smoothly and readily ⟨once we started *rolling*, everything went perfectly⟩ — see FLOW 2

roll back *vb* to put an end to by formal action ⟨lobbyists for the industry pressured the legislators to *roll back* the new automotive safety standards⟩ — see ABOLISH 1

roll call *n* a record of a series of items (as names or titles) usually arranged according to some system ⟨the *roll call* of the fallen was read aloud at the memorial service⟩ — see [1]LIST

rollick *n* a time or instance of carefree fun ⟨enjoying a summer *rollick* before knuckling down in medical school⟩ — see FLING 1

rollick *vb* **1** to engage in activity for amusement ⟨an educator who realized that children need to *rollick* as well as to study and learn⟩ — see PLAY 1
2 to play and run about happily ⟨children *rollicking* during recess⟩ — see FROLIC 1

rollicking *adj* **1** being rough or noisy in a high-spirited way ⟨reunions with his friends from college were usually *rollicking* affairs⟩ — see BOISTEROUS
2 given to good-natured joking or teasing ⟨a *rollicking* boy who quickly charms everyone he meets⟩ — see PLAYFUL

rollicking *n* activity engaged in to amuse oneself ⟨likes to indulge in mindless *rollicking* after a day at work in order to relax⟩ — see PLAY 1

roll out *vb* to leave one's bed ⟨you'll have to *roll out* by at least 8:00 a.m. in order to get there on time⟩ — see ARISE 1

roll up *vb* to become greater in size, extent, volume, amount, or number ⟨ticket sales are expected to *roll up* as the date of the concert nears⟩ — see INCREASE 2

roly–poly *adj* having an excess of body fat ⟨a *roly-poly* baby who grew into a slender child⟩ — see FAT 1

romance *n* a brief romantic relationship ⟨an office *romance* that ended with hurt feelings on both sides⟩ — see AFFAIR 1

romantic *adj* **1** excitingly or mysteriously unusual ⟨she dreamed of meeting a tall, *romantic* stranger who would introduce her to a life of adventure⟩ — see EXOTIC
2 having or marked by a tendency to be guided more by ideals than by reality ⟨a workshop intended to disabuse would-be innkeepers of the *romantic* notion that running a bed-and-breakfast is easy⟩ — see IDEALISTIC

romantic *n* one whose conduct is guided more by the image of perfection than by the real world ⟨she's a hopeless *romantic* who believes that her one true love is somewhere waiting to be found⟩ — see IDEALIST

romanticist *n* one whose conduct is guided more by the image of perfection than by the real world ⟨those *romanticists* who seem to be perpetually surprised by mean or criminal behavior⟩ — see IDEALIST

romanticize *vb* to represent or think of as better than reality would warrant ⟨he *romanticized* what life in a small town would be like, only to be later disappointed when reality intruded⟩ — see IDEALIZE

romp *n* a time or instance of carefree fun ⟨one last *romp* before starting their new life as parents⟩ — see FLING 1

romp *vb* to play and run about happily ⟨the kids *romped* on the lawn until dinner was ready⟩ — see FROLIC 1

roof *n* **1** a raised covering over something for decoration or protection ⟨the *roof* of the pavilion leaks when it rains⟩ — see CANOPY
2 the place where one lives ⟨as long as you're living under my *roof*, you'll obey my rules⟩ — see HOME 1

roof *vb* to provide with living quarters or shelter ⟨fed and *roofed* the emergency volunteers for a week⟩ — see HOUSE 1

rook *n* a person who is just starting out in a field of activity ⟨every year the coaches have to deal with *rooks* who don't know the rules yet⟩ — see BEGINNER

rook *vb* to rob by the use of trickery or threats ⟨once you learn to recognize these swindler's tricks, no one will be able to use them to *rook* you⟩ — see FLEECE

rookie *n* a person who is just starting out in a field of activity ⟨although a star in his old sport of basketball, he was still just a *rookie* as far as baseball was concerned⟩ — see BEGINNER

room *n* **1** an extent or area available for or used up by some activity or thing ⟨I need more *room* to do a cartwheel⟩ ⟨they made *room* for him on the bench⟩
synonyms elbow room, place, space, way
related words capacity, compass, range, scope; berth, clearance, freedom, latitude, leeway, play

2 an area within a building that has been set apart from surrounding space by a wall ⟨finally had a *room* to himself when his older brother went off to college⟩
synonyms apartment, cell, chamber, closet
related words accommodation, bay, berth, booth, cabin, compartment, cubicle; alcove, niche, nook, recess; snuggery [*chiefly British*]
3 a favorable combination of circumstances, time, and place ⟨there's still *room* for improvement⟩ — see OPPORTUNITY
room *vb* to provide with living quarters or shelter ⟨we can *room* up to four visitors in our two guest bedrooms⟩ — see HOUSE 1
roomer *n* one who rents a room or apartment in another's house ⟨the new owners took in *roomers* to help pay for the house⟩ — see TENANT 1
roomy *adj* more than adequate or average in capacity ⟨a small car that's surprisingly *roomy* inside⟩ — see SPACIOUS
roost *vb* 1 to come to rest after descending from the air ⟨pigeons flying home to *roost* on the roof⟩ — see ALIGHT 1
2 to establish or place comfortably or snugly ⟨a gang of friends had *roosted* themselves around the ski lodge's massive fireplace⟩ — see ENSCONCE 1
root *n* 1 a point or place at which something is invented or provided ⟨he insists that insecurity is the *root* of all jealousy⟩ — see SOURCE 1
2 the source from which something grows or develops ⟨one would need to go back at least several hundred years to find the *root* of the entrenched hostility between the neighboring nations⟩ — see SEED 1
3 an immaterial thing upon which something else rests ⟨an implicit trust in the wisdom of the people is the *root* of democracy⟩ — see BASE 1
4 the central part or aspect of something under consideration ⟨at *root*, it's a question of the proper limits, if any, of free speech⟩ — see CRUX
root *vb* to set solidly in or as if in surrounding matter ⟨*rooted* the post securely in the dirt⟩ — see ENTRENCH
root (out) *vb* 1 to destroy all traces of ⟨a concerted effort to *root out* prejudice of any kind in the armed services⟩ — see ANNIHILATE 1
2 to draw out by force or with effort ⟨a dog *rooting out* a buried toy⟩ — see EXTRACT
3 to come upon after searching, study, or effort ⟨a journalist seeking to *root out* and expose corruption in the gaming industry⟩ — see FIND 1
rooted *adj* firmly established over time ⟨a popular, *rooted* misconception that has proved very resistant to correction⟩ — see INVETERATE 1
rope *n* 1 a length of braided, flexible material that is used for tying or connecting things ⟨used a *rope* to tie the boat to the dock⟩ — see CORD 1
2 **ropes** *pl* the characteristic peculiarities and technicalities of something ⟨needs a mentor who will show her the *ropes* of running a catering business⟩ — see INS AND OUTS
3 **ropes** *pl* the specific practical details of something ⟨still learning the *ropes* of her new job⟩ — see NITTY-GRITTY
ropy *also* **ropey** *adj* being of a consistency that resists flow ⟨because the paint was so old, it was *ropy* and couldn't be smoothly applied to the wood⟩ — see THICK 2
roseate *adj* having qualities which inspire hope ⟨one analyst who envisions a qualifiedly *roseate* future for the nation's automotive industry⟩ — see HOPEFUL 1
rose–colored *adj* having qualities which inspire hope ⟨an incurable optimist sees the world through a *rose-colored* perspective⟩ — see HOPEFUL 1
roses *n pl* something easily done or dealt with ⟨the job isn't all *roses*, but it is pretty interesting⟩ — see CINCH 1
roster *n* a record of a series of items (as names or titles) usually arranged according to some system ⟨the *roster* of subscribers to the journal⟩ — see [1]LIST
rostrum *n* a level usually raised surface ⟨stood on a *rostrum* to address the huge crowd⟩ — see PLATFORM 1
rosy *adj* 1 having a healthy reddish skin tone ⟨*rosy* and cheerful after a day outside in the snow⟩ — see RUDDY
2 having qualities which inspire hope ⟨that's a particularly *rosy* view of the economic situation, and one that may not be justified⟩ — see HOPEFUL 1
rot *n* 1 language, behavior, or ideas that are absurd and contrary to good sense ⟨I won't stand here and listen to such *rot*⟩ — see NONSENSE 1
2 the process by which dead organic matter separates into simpler substances ⟨the *rot* begins shortly after the fish are killed⟩ — see CORRUPTION 1
rot *vb* 1 to become worse or of less value ⟨the house slowly fell into disrepair and *rotted*⟩ — see DETERIORATE 1
2 to go through decomposition ⟨*rotting* vegetation on the bank of the river⟩ — see DECAY 1
rotate *vb* 1 to move (something) in a curved or circular path on or as if on an axis ⟨*rotate* the mirror 180 degrees⟩ — see TURN 1
2 to move in circles around an axis or center ⟨with mirrors on three sides, she *rotated* all around to see how the dress looked on her⟩ — see SPIN 1
rotation *n* a rapid turning about on an axis or central point ⟨the Earth completes a single *rotation* around its axis in approximately 24 hours⟩ — see SPIN 1
rote *n* an established and often automatic or monotonous series of actions followed when engaging in some activity ⟨learned the *rote* for the exercise warm-up but not the reasoning behind it⟩ — see ROUTINE 1
rotten *adj* 1 having undergone organic breakdown ⟨*rotten*, smelly meat that should have been thrown out⟩
synonyms addled, bad, corrupted, decayed, decomposed, putrefied, putrid, spoiled
related words curdled, fermented, off, rancid, rank, sour, soured, sourish, turned; contaminated, defiled, fouled, impure, polluted, tainted; corroded, crumbled, degenerated, deteriorated, disintegrated; decaying, decomposing, disintegrating, mildewy, moldering, moldy, putrefying, putrescent, rotting; gangrenous
near antonyms fresh, good, sweet; preserved, pristine, uncontaminated, undefiled, unpolluted, unspoiled, untainted, untouched
antonyms undecomposed
2 not conforming to a high moral standard; morally unacceptable ⟨played a *rotten* trick and then lied about it⟩ — see BAD 2
3 not giving pleasure to the mind or senses ⟨had a *rotten* time while on vacation⟩ — see UNPLEASANT
4 extremely unsatisfactory ⟨*rotten* housing conditions that no one should be forced to tolerate⟩ — see WRETCHED 1
5 of low quality ⟨I can't do anything with these *rotten* tools⟩ — see CHEAP 2
rotter *n* a person whose behavior is offensive to others ⟨the dirty *rotter* dumped his wife to marry his secretary⟩ — see JERK 1
rotund *adj* 1 having an excess of body fat ⟨a *rotund* little man who, predictably, was asked to play Santa every year⟩ — see FAT 1
2 marked by conspicuously full and rich sounds or tones ⟨the actor's distinct baritone and his clear and *rotund* elocution are especially effective in dramatic readings⟩ — see RESONANT
rotundity *n* the condition of having an excess of body fat ⟨finally a diet that really worked, allowing her to

leave behind a lifetime of *rotundity* and ridicule⟩ — see CORPULENCE

rough *adj* **1** covered with or as if with hair ⟨a face *rough* with a couple days' worth of beard⟩ — see HAIRY 1
2 marked by bursts of destructive force or intense activity ⟨*rough* waters that made sailing our sloop a little risky⟩ — see VIOLENT 1
3 marked by wet and windy conditions ⟨at least wear a raincoat if you're going out into that *rough* weather⟩ — see FOUL 1
4 not having a level or smooth surface ⟨a *rough* board can give you splinters⟩ — see UNEVEN 1
5 requiring considerable physical or mental effort ⟨a forensics expert who willingly takes on *rough* assignments⟩ — see HARD 2
6 difficult to endure ⟨I've had a *rough* time of it since I lost my job⟩ — see HARSH 1
7 harsh and threatening in manner or appearance ⟨the *rough* faces of hardened criminals who had spent most of their lives behind bars⟩ — see GRIM 1
8 hastily or roughly constructed ⟨made a *rough* camp as darkness fell over the forest⟩ — see RUDE 1
9 lacking in refinement or good taste ⟨he learned polite words to replace the *rough* language he had known in the slums⟩ — see COARSE 2
10 made of or resembling hair ⟨a *rough*-coated dog who was always shedding his fur⟩ — see HAIRY 2
11 marked by a series of sharp quick motions ⟨a *rough* flight that left some passengers nauseated⟩ — see JERKY 1
12 marked by turmoil or disturbance especially of natural elements ⟨after a *rough* week on the high seas, we were happy to sail through the gulf's more tranquil waters⟩ — see WILD 2

rough (up) *vb* **1** to strike repeatedly ⟨she was badly *roughed up* by a mugger in the park⟩ — see BEAT 1
2 to abuse physically ⟨the photographer claimed that he had been *roughed up* by the actor's bodyguards outside the club⟩ — see MANHANDLE 1

rough–and–ready *adj* hastily or roughly constructed ⟨a *rough-and-ready* shack that the explorers threw together as winter approached⟩ — see RUDE 1

rough–and–tumble *adj* hastily or roughly constructed ⟨the announcement of his candidacy was made from a *rough-and-tumble* stage put together just that morning⟩ — see RUDE 1

rough–and–tumble *n* a rough and often noisy fight usually involving several people ⟨a *rough-and-tumble* broke out among the fans in the stands⟩ — see BRAWL 1

roughened *adj* not having a level or smooth surface ⟨*roughened* hands from hard work⟩ — see UNEVEN 1

rough–hewn *adj* **1** hastily or roughly constructed ⟨a survivalist living in a *rough-hewn* shelter in the wilderness⟩ — see RUDE 1
2 lacking in refinement or good taste ⟨a *rough-hewn* girl who had to learn how to behave properly in polite company⟩ — see COARSE 2
3 lacking social grace and assurance ⟨*rough-hewn* military cadets feeling a little self-conscious at their first formal dance⟩ — see AWKWARD 1

roughhouse *n* wildly playful or mischievous behavior ⟨their parents simply wouldn't tolerate any *roughhouse* in the living room⟩ — see HORSEPLAY

roughhousing *n* wildly playful or mischievous behavior ⟨*roughhousing* was simply part of growing up in a family with four boys⟩ — see HORSEPLAY

roughly *adv* **1** close to but not exactly ⟨*roughly* 80% of the country's population is of that faith⟩ — see APPROXIMATELY
2 in a manner so as to cause loss or suffering ⟨if you treat the camcorder *roughly*, it will of course break⟩ — see HARDLY 1

roughneck *adj* lacking in refinement or good taste ⟨their *roughneck* antics were amusing only if you were as drunk as they were⟩ — see COARSE 2

roughneck *n* a violent, brutal person who is often a member of an organized gang ⟨a group of *roughnecks* like to hang out at the roadhouse and harass people⟩ — see HOODLUM

roughness *n* **1** a harsh or sharp quality ⟨a *roughness* to the wine that should decrease with age⟩ — see EDGE 1
2 the quality or state of lacking refinement or good taste ⟨the *roughness* of pioneer life is not glossed over in the documentary⟩ — see VULGARITY 1

round *adj* **1** having every part of the surface the same distance from the center ⟨*round* golf balls⟩ ⟨the earth is not perfectly *round*⟩
synonyms global, globular, spherical
related words annular, circular, disciform, discoid, discoidal, disklike, hooplike, ringlike; curved, looped, spiral; balled, bulbous, rotund, rounded, roundish; cylindrical (*also* cylindric), elliptical (*or* elliptic), oblong, oval, ovate, ovoid (*also* ovoidal)
antonyms nonspherical
2 having an excess of body fat ⟨a *round* little grandmother who was a natural to play Mrs. Claus⟩ — see FAT 1
3 marked by conspicuously full and rich sounds or tones ⟨an organ with a beautifully *round* sound⟩ — see RESONANT
4 being neither more nor less than a certain amount, number, or extent ⟨a *round* dozen eggs⟩ — see EVEN 1

round *adv* **1** from beginning to end ⟨people working there all year *round*⟩ — see THROUGH 1
2 on all sides or in every direction ⟨gather *round* and listen to my story⟩ — see AROUND 1
3 toward the opposite direction ⟨turned *round* to see who was calling out⟩ — see AROUND 2

round *n* **1** a circular strip ⟨a *round* of steel to reinforce the wooden beam⟩ — see [1]RING 2
2 a series of events or actions that repeat themselves regularly and in the same order ⟨a busy *round* of parties during the holiday season⟩ — see CYCLE 1
3 something with a perfectly round circumference ⟨use a cookie cutter to make the *rounds* of dough⟩ — see CIRCLE 1

round *prep* in random positions within the boundaries of ⟨talked to voters *round* the city⟩ — see AROUND 2

round *vb* **1** to form into a round compact mass ⟨carefully *rounded* the dough and placed it on a cookie tray⟩ — see WAD
2 to travel completely around ⟨a monorail for visitors that *rounds* the park⟩ — see ENCIRCLE 1
3 to turn away from a straight line or course ⟨*rounded* on the track and headed for the finish line⟩ — see CURVE 1

round (off *or* out) *vb* **1** to bring (an event) to a natural or appropriate stopping point ⟨I'll *round off* the meeting here and let everyone get an early start on the weekend⟩ — see CLOSE 3
2 to serve as a completing element to ⟨coffee and dessert *rounded out* the meal⟩ — see COMPLEMENT

roundabout *adj* not straightforward or direct ⟨took a *roundabout* route to the beach⟩ — see INDIRECT

roundel *n* something with a perfectly round circumference ⟨the windows in the colonial-era statehouse are *roundels*⟩ — see CIRCLE 1

roundly *adv* **1** in a vigorous and forceful manner ⟨*roundly* attacked the proposal to raise the state's gas tax⟩ — see HARD 3
2 with attention to all aspects or details ⟨few sitcoms were as *roundly* disliked as that one⟩ — see THOROUGHLY 1

round–robin *n* a meeting featuring a group discussion

⟨a *round-robin* to discuss the epidemic of performance-enhancing drugs plaguing professional sports⟩ — see FORUM 1

roundtable *n* a meeting featuring a group discussion ⟨an international *roundtable* of medical experts on the disease⟩ — see FORUM 1

roundup *n* a short statement of the main points ⟨I can't read 500 pages by tomorrow, so just give me the *roundup*⟩ — see SUMMARY

round up *vb* to bring together in one body or place ⟨*rounded* everyone *up* for one final training session⟩ — see GATHER 1

rouse *vb* **1** to cause to stop sleeping ⟨the honking horns *roused* her from a deep sleep⟩ — see WAKE 1
2 to cease to be asleep ⟨I finally *roused* around noon, after going to bed very late⟩ — see WAKE 2

rousing *adj* **1** causing great emotional or mental stimulation ⟨a *rousing* rendition of our national anthem⟩ — see EXCITING 1
2 marked by much life, movement, or activity ⟨during the heat wave stores were doing a *rousing* business in air conditioners⟩ — see ALIVE 2

roustabout *n* one who loads and unloads ships at a port ⟨sought work as a *roustabout* on the city's seedy waterfront⟩ — see DOCKWORKER

rouster *n* one who loads and unloads ships at a port ⟨a hard-muscled man who certainly looked like he had worked all his life as a *rouster*⟩ — see DOCKWORKER

[1]rout *n* **1** a great number of persons or creatures massed together ⟨a great *rout* of rubberneckers had gathered around the scene of the accident⟩ — see CROWD 1
2 people looked down upon as ignorant and of the lowest class ⟨at first the protests were dismissed as nothing more than the idle doings of the restless *rout*⟩ — see RABBLE

[2]rout *n* **1** failure to win a contest ⟨the championship game was a humiliating *rout* for the team that had been favored to win⟩ — see DEFEAT 1
2 the act or an instance of getting free from danger or confinement ⟨in the mad *rout* from the school shooter, it was every person for himself⟩ — see ESCAPE 1

rout *vb* **1** to defeat by a large margin ⟨as expected, the professional team had no trouble *routing* the amateurs⟩ — see WHIP 2
2 to drive or force out ⟨the nation's ground and air forces quickly *routed* the would-be invaders⟩ — see EJECT 1

rout (out) *vb* to come upon after searching, study, or effort ⟨if you give me some time, I can probably *rout out* more supplies⟩ — see FIND 1

route *n* **1** a passage cleared for public vehicular travel ⟨take *Route* 190 for six miles, then get off⟩ — see WAY 1
2 an established course for traveling from one place to another ⟨we're going to get stuck in traffic if we take the usual *route*⟩ — see PASSAGE 1
3 the direction along which something or someone moves ⟨hurricanes generally take a northerly *route* up the Atlantic seaboard⟩ — see PATH 1

route *vb* to point out the way for (someone) especially from a position in front ⟨the guide *routed* us smoothly through the jungle⟩ — see LEAD 1

routeway *n, chiefly British* the direction along which something or someone moves ⟨the courier's preferred *routeway* between the two offices takes him right past Trafalgar Square⟩ — see PATH 1

routine *adj* **1** being of the type that is encountered in the normal course of events ⟨this is just a *routine* inspection⟩ — see ORDINARY 1
2 following or agreeing with established form, custom, or rules ⟨the *routine* procedure for filing a complaint with the board⟩ — see FORMAL 1
3 often observed or encountered ⟨the movie is a *routine* thriller that has little to recommend it⟩ — see COMMON 1

routine *n* **1** an established and often automatic or monotonous series of actions followed when engaging in some activity ⟨part of my morning *routine* is drinking a cup of coffee while reading the newspaper⟩
synonyms drill, grind, groove, lockstep, pattern, rote, rut, treadmill
related words daily dozen, regimen; housekeeping; custom, fashion, habit, practice (*also* practise), trick, wont; approach, manner, method, procedure, strategy, style, tack, technique, way; design, plan, program, scheme; convention, policy, tradition
2 something done over and over in order to develop skill ⟨a weapons training *routine*⟩ — see EXERCISE 2
3 a performance regularly presented by an individual or group ⟨did a tired *routine* that's been around since the days of vaudeville⟩ — see ACT 1

rove *vb* to move about from place to place aimlessly ⟨buffalo *roving* over the vast plains⟩ — see WANDER 1

rover *n* **1** a person who roams about without a fixed route or destination ⟨ever since he developed a strong case of wanderlust in college, he's been a *rover*⟩ — see NOMAD
2 someone who engages in robbery of ships at sea ⟨a story of the days when sea *rovers* plied the Caribbean⟩ — see PIRATE

roving *adj* traveling from place to place ⟨a *roving* substitute teacher who works in a different district every day⟩ — see ITINERANT

[1]row *n* **1** a series of people or things arranged side by side ⟨stood in a *row* to have their picture taken⟩ ⟨three *rows* of eight jelly beans equals 24 jelly beans⟩
synonyms bank, rank
related words chain, column, cue, file, line, procession, queue, range, string, train; echelon, tier; array, concatenation, sequence
2 a passage cleared for public vehicular travel ⟨drive up Market *Row* and turn left⟩ — see WAY 1

[2]row *n* **1** a rough and often noisy fight usually involving several people ⟨a county fair that had a long history of bloody *rows*⟩ — see BRAWL 1
2 a state of noisy, confused activity ⟨the combination of drums and shouting contributed to the awful *row*⟩ — see COMMOTION
3 an often noisy or angry expression of differing opinions ⟨he had a *row* with his girlfriend yesterday, and now they aren't speaking⟩ — see ARGUMENT 1

[1]row *vb* to move a boat by means of oars ⟨*rowed* around the lake⟩
synonyms oar, paddle, scull
related words canoe, kayak; pole, punt; feather, pull

[2]row *vb* to express different opinions about something often angrily ⟨the couple *rows* all the time, and yet they seem happy together⟩ — see ARGUE 2

rowdy *adj* being rough or noisy in a high-spirited way ⟨a *rowdy* but good-natured group of teenagers⟩ — see BOISTEROUS

rowdy *n* a violent, brutal person who is often a member of an organized gang ⟨*rowdies* had overtaken the neighborhood and were threatening people on the street⟩ — see HOODLUM

rower *n* a person who drives a boat forward by means of oars ⟨the racing shell carries four *rowers* and a coxswain⟩ — see OARSMAN

royal *adj* **1** fit for or worthy of a royal ruler ⟨the school superintendent received a *royal* welcome⟩ — see MONARCHICAL
2 large and impressive in size, grandeur, extent, or conception ⟨had a *royal* argument over family finances⟩ — see GRAND 1
3 involving minimal difficulty or effort ⟨unfortunately,

there is no *royal* way for a person to achieve maturity⟩ — see EASY 1

royalty *n* **1** a dignified bearing or appearance befitting someone of royal status ⟨she has an air of *royalty* that belies her humble origins⟩ — see MAJESTY 1

2 individuals carefully selected as being the best of a class ⟨a political fund-raiser attended by the *royalty* of the Hollywood scene⟩ — see ELITE 1

rub *n* something that is a source of irritation ⟨even what seems to be a dream job usually turns out to have its fair share of *rubs*⟩ — see ANNOYANCE 3

rub *vb* **1** to damage or diminish by continued friction ⟨the brake pads were *rubbed* away as a result of years of use⟩ — see ABRADE 1

2 to make smooth by friction ⟨the furniture restorer *rubbed* the board perfectly smooth with sandpaper⟩ — see GRIND 1

3 to make smooth or glossy usually by repeatedly applying surface pressure ⟨the butler *rubbed* the silver tea set until it gleamed⟩ — see POLISH 1

rubbed *adj* having a shiny surface or finish ⟨the *rubbed* brass of the wall sconce showed my reflection⟩ — see GLOSSY

rubberlike *adj* able to revert to original size and shape after being stretched, squeezed, or twisted ⟨a *rubberlike* material that is used for household products⟩ — see ELASTIC 1

rubberneck *n* a person who travels for pleasure ⟨every year raucous *rubbernecks* by the busload descend upon the city for its famed Mardi Gras⟩ — see TOURIST

rubberneck *vb* to look long and hard in wonder or surprise ⟨thoughtless drivers pausing on the highway to *rubberneck* at the accident⟩ — see GAPE

rubbernecker *n* a person who travels for pleasure ⟨a shop selling the kind of tacky souvenirs that *rubberneckers* can't seem to get enough of⟩ — see TOURIST

rubber stamp *n* a person who adopts the appearance or behavior of another especially in an obvious way ⟨an author who was ultimately just another *rubber stamp* of Hemingway⟩ — see COPYCAT

rubbery *adj* able to revert to original size and shape after being stretched, squeezed, or twisted ⟨mozzarella is a *rubbery* cheese known to every pizza lover⟩ — see ELASTIC 1

rubbish *n* **1** discarded or useless material ⟨it's illegal to throw *rubbish* out of your car on the highway⟩ — see GARBAGE 1

2 that which is of low quality or worth ⟨regarded most romance novels as the lowest form of literary *rubbish*⟩ — see JUNK 1

3 language, behavior, or ideas that are absurd and contrary to good sense ⟨you're obviously no economist because what you're saying is absolute *rubbish*⟩ — see NONSENSE 1

rubbishy *adj* of low quality ⟨*rubbishy* merchandise that is mainly bought by tourists⟩ — see CHEAP 2

rubble *n* the portion or bits of something left over or behind after it has been destroyed ⟨clearing the *rubble* after the earthquake⟩ — see REMAINS 1

rube *n* an awkward or simple person especially from a small town or the country ⟨rural voters were tired of being treated as *rubes* by state officials, who showed interest in them only at election time⟩ — see HICK

rubicund *adj* having a healthy reddish skin tone ⟨the *rubicund* face of a man who clearly got a lot of fresh air and exercise⟩ — see RUDDY

rubout *n* the intentional and unlawful taking of another person's life ⟨the mafia boss ordered a *rubout* as casually as you might order a pizza⟩ — see HOMICIDE 1

rub out *vb* **1** to bring to a complete end the physical soundness, existence, or usefulness of ⟨aerial bombs *rubbed out* the oil refinery⟩ — see DESTROY 1

2 to put to death deliberately ⟨an elaborate setup to *rub out* rival mobsters⟩ — see MURDER 1

3 to destroy all traces of ⟨a promise to *rub out* the city's drug trade⟩ — see ANNIHILATE 1

rubric *n* **1** a word or series of words often in larger letters placed at the beginning of a passage or at the top of a page in order to introduce or categorize ⟨the *rubrics* at the beginning of the chapters are intended to be humorous⟩ — see HEADING

2 an inherited or established way of thinking, feeling, or doing ⟨the *rubric*, popular among jewelers anyway, that a man should spend a month's salary on his fiancée's engagement ring⟩ — see TRADITION 1

3 one of the units into which a whole is divided on the basis of a common characteristic ⟨all of these books with their conspiracy theories fall under the *rubric* of speculative fiction⟩ — see CLASS 2

rucksack *n* a soft-sided case designed for carrying belongings especially on the back ⟨hikers carrying their food and water in *rucksacks*⟩ — see PACK 1

ruckus *n* **1** a rough and often noisy fight usually involving several people ⟨the *ruckus* left one person with a sprained wrist⟩ — see BRAWL 1

2 a state of noisy, confused activity ⟨quit creating such a *ruckus*—I'm trying to sleep!⟩ — see COMMOTION

ruction *n* **1** a rough and often noisy fight usually involving several people ⟨the *ruction* ended with everyone involved getting arrested⟩— see BRAWL 1

2 a state of noisy, confused activity ⟨the *ruction* outside the door prompted me to investigate what was going on⟩ — see COMMOTION

ruddy *adj* having a healthy reddish skin tone ⟨*ruddy* complexions run in the family⟩

synonyms blooming, florid, flush, full-blooded, glowing, red, rosy, rubicund, sanguine

related words bronzed, brown, suntanned, tanned; bloomy, blowsy (*also* blowzy), blushing, flushed, pink, pinkish, warm; cherubic

near antonyms waxen, waxy; blanched, white, whitened; anemic, sick, sickly; bloodless, cadaverous; wheyfaced, white-faced

antonyms ashen, ashy, doughy, livid, lurid, mealy, pale, paled, palish, pallid, pasty, peaked, peaky, sallow, sallowish, wan

rude *adj* **1** hastily or roughly constructed ⟨a *rude* shelter built from unfinished logs by some forgotten pioneer⟩

synonyms artless, clumsy, crude, jerry-built, jerry-rigged, jury-rigged, rough, rough-and-ready, rough-and-tumble, rough-hewn, unrefined

related words defective, faulty, flawed, imperfect; imprecise, inexact; inartistic, undressed, unfinished, unpolished, unworked; amateur, amateurish, inexpert, unprofessional, unskilled, unskillful; primitive, rudimentary; unshaped, unshapen

near antonyms faultless, finished, flawless, meticulous, perfect, perfected, polished, well-done; adept, adroit, dexterous (*also* dextrous), expert, masterful, masterly, neat, practiced (*also* practised), skillful, workmanlike; artful, artistic, sophisticated; exact, precise

antonyms refined

2 belonging to or characteristic of an early level of skill or development ⟨*rude* stone tools⟩ — see PRIMITIVE 1

3 lacking in refinement or good taste ⟨a comedian who uses a lot of *rude* language in his nightclub act⟩ — see COARSE 2

4 not civilized ⟨missionaries who believed that it was their duty to convert the *rude* peoples of the world⟩ — see SAVAGE 1

5 showing a lack of manners or consideration for others ⟨it's *rude* to call someone "ugly"⟩ — see IMPOLITE

6 lacking in education or the knowledge gained from books ⟨*rude* hillbillies they might have been, but they produced music with real poignancy⟩ — see IGNORANT 1

7 being such as found in nature and not altered by processing or refining ⟨*rude* pelts that were sent to Europe to be fashioned into elegant hats and coats⟩ — see CRUDE 1

rudeness *n* **1** rude behavior ⟨such *rudeness* will not be tolerated in this office⟩ — see DISCOURTESY

2 the quality or state of lacking refinement or good taste ⟨the *rudeness* of frontier life gradually diminished with time⟩ — see VULGARITY 1

rudimental *adj* of or relating to the simplest facts or theories of a subject ⟨learned the *rudimental* concepts of math at an early age⟩ — see ELEMENTARY

rudimentary *adj* **1** belonging to or characteristic of an early level of skill or development ⟨*rudimentary* shelters built by prehistoric peoples⟩ — see PRIMITIVE 1

2 of or relating to the simplest facts or theories of a subject ⟨had only a *rudimentary* knowledge of science⟩ — see ELEMENTARY

rudiments *n pl* general or basic truths on which other truths or theories can be based ⟨learned the *rudiments* of mathematics⟩ — see PRINCIPLES 1

rue *n* a feeling of responsibility for wrongdoing ⟨a soul filled with pain and *rue*⟩ — see GUILT 1

rue *vb* to feel sorry or dissatisfied about ⟨I *rue* the day I agreed to this stupid plan⟩ — see REGRET

rueful *adj* **1** expressing or suggesting mourning ⟨the *rueful* faces of friends and family who had gathered to pay their last respects⟩ — see MOURNFUL 1

2 feeling sorrow for a wrong that one has done ⟨a *rueful* youth who had come to ask for forgiveness for online bullying⟩ — see CONTRITE

3 deserving of one's pity ⟨the *rueful*, desperate poverty of people in parts of the Third World⟩ — see PATHETIC 1

ruefully *adv* with feelings of bitterness or grief ⟨*ruefully* accepted the fact that the drunk driver would never adequately pay for his crime⟩ — see HARD 2

ruffian *n* a violent, brutal person who is often a member of an organized gang ⟨a gang of *ruffians* preying upon people who ventured into that section of town⟩ — see HOODLUM

ruffle *n* **1** a strip of fabric gathered or pleated on one edge and used as trimming ⟨likes lace curtains without *ruffles* and chintz curtains with *ruffles*⟩

synonyms flounce, frill, furbelow

related words border, edging, fringe, trim; plait, pleat, ruff; bunting, skirting

2 something that is a source of irritation ⟨a spouse's snoring is one *ruffle* that many couples must eventually come to terms with⟩ — see ANNOYANCE 3

ruffle *vb* to disturb the peace of mind of (someone) especially by repeated disagreeable acts ⟨the stream of minor complaints finally *ruffled* him into snapping, "If you don't like the way I'm doing it, do it yourself!"⟩ — see IRRITATE 1

rug *n, slang* a headpiece made of natural or synthetic hair usually worn to cover a bald area ⟨get a load of that bald guy's *rug*—who does he think he's fooling?⟩ — see HAIRPIECE

rugged *adj* **1** able to withstand hardship, strain, or exposure ⟨a *rugged* construction that survived for hundreds of years⟩ — see HARDY 1

2 difficult to endure ⟨the incredibly *rugged* conditions that the polar explorers faced⟩ — see HARSH 1

3 harsh and threatening in manner or appearance ⟨the warrior's *rugged* features frightened the child⟩ — see GRIM 1

4 having muscles capable of exerting great physical force ⟨a *rugged* athlete who's competing in weight lifting in the Olympics⟩ — see STRONG 1

5 not having a level or smooth surface ⟨*rugged* terrain that made for slow going⟩ — see UNEVEN 1

6 requiring considerable physical or mental effort ⟨even more *rugged* than most ultramarathons, this one crosses a desert⟩ — see HARD 2

7 marked by turmoil or disturbance especially of natural elements ⟨New Hampshire's Mount Washington has some of the *ruggedest* weather in all of North America⟩ — see WILD 3

8 lacking in refinement or good taste ⟨the kind of *rugged* humor that men have traditionally enjoyed at stag parties⟩ — see COARSE 2

ruin *n* **1** the state or fact of being rendered nonexistent, physically unsound, or useless ⟨a vicious bombardment that left the building in *ruins*⟩ — see DESTRUCTION 1

2 ruins *pl* the portion or bits of something left over or behind after it has been destroyed ⟨the *ruins* of an abandoned abbey⟩ — see REMAINS 1

3 the inability to pay one's debts ⟨the family faces *ruin* if the chief breadwinner doesn't find another job very soon⟩ — see INSOLVENCY

4 something that is the cause of one's ultimate failure or loss of life ⟨the politician's eventual *ruin* would be a sexual indiscretion⟩ — see DOWNFALL 1

ruin *vb* **1** to cause to lose one's fortune and become unable to pay one's debts ⟨after he was *ruined* by the Great Chicago Fire of 1871, the industrialist was forced to sell his mansion and start all over again⟩

synonyms bankrupt, break, bust

related words beggar, impoverish, pauperize; reduce, straiten; clean (out), wipe out

near antonyms enrich, richen

2 to bring destruction to (something) through violent action ⟨tornadoes *ruined* a wide swath of the county⟩ — see RAVAGE

3 to bring to a complete end the physical soundness, existence, or usefulness of ⟨a huge fire that *ruined* an entire city block⟩ — see DESTROY 1

ruination *n* **1** something that is the cause of one's ultimate failure or loss of life ⟨neglect and indifference have proved to be the *ruination* of more than one marriage⟩ — see DOWNFALL 1

2 the state or fact of being rendered nonexistent, physically unsound, or useless ⟨although this is a setback, it isn't complete *ruination* for the company⟩ — see DESTRUCTION 1

ruined *adj* facing certain defeat, disaster, or death ⟨your chances for a promotion were *ruined* the instance you started mouthing off to the boss⟩ — see DONE FOR

ruinous *adj* **1** bringing about ruin or misfortune ⟨a *ruinous* miscalculation of the financial markets left them bankrupt⟩ — see FATAL 1

2 causing or tending to cause destruction ⟨a *ruinous* windstorm destroyed the crops⟩ — see DESTRUCTIVE 1

rule *n* **1** a statement spelling out the proper procedure or conduct for an activity ⟨read the *rules* that are posted before you use the pool⟩

synonyms bylaw, ground rule, reg, regulation

related words code, constitution, decalogue, directory; act, law, ordinance, statute; behest, charge, command, commandment, decree, dictate, direction, directive, edict, fiat, instruction, order; axiom, fundamental, maxim, precept; moral, principle, value; ban, interdiction, prohibition, proscription, restriction; convention, custom, habit, manners, mores, practice (*also* practise), tradition, way; blueprint, canon, formula, guide, guideline, standard

2 lawful control over the affairs of a political unit (as a nation) ⟨the years during which Russia was under Communist *rule*⟩

synonyms administration, authority, governance, government, jurisdiction, regime (*also* régime), regimen

related words reign; dominion, power, sovereignty (*also* sovranty), supremacy, sway; command, leadership; direction, management, regulation, superintendence, supervision; autocracy, dictatorship, domination, hegemony, mastery, oppression, subjugation, tyranny

3 an inherited or established way of thinking, feeling, or doing ⟨one of the sacred *rules* of that ancient society was respect for the elderly⟩ — see TRADITION 1

rule *vb* **1** to exercise authority or power over ⟨a sea captain who *ruled* his ship sternly but justly⟩ — see GOVERN

2 to keep from exceeding a desirable degree or level (as of expression) ⟨a monarch who is known for *ruling* her emotions with an iron hand⟩ — see CONTROL 1

rule (on) *vb* to give an opinion about (something at issue or in dispute) ⟨the coach *ruled on* the question of whether an off-campus bar fight ought to disqualify someone from the team⟩ — see JUDGE 1

rule out *vb* to prevent the participation, consideration, or inclusion of ⟨another loss would *rule* them *out* of the tournament⟩ — see EXCLUDE

ruler *n* one who rules over a people with a sole, supreme, and usually hereditary authority ⟨the aging *ruler* agonized over the choice of an heir⟩ — see MONARCH 1

ruling *adj* held by or applicable to a majority of the people ⟨the *ruling* opinion on premarital sex⟩ — see GENERAL 3

ruling *n* **1** a decision made by a court or tribunal regarding a case it has heard ⟨the controversial *ruling* by the state's supreme court caused an uproar⟩ — see SENTENCE

2 an order publicly issued by an authority ⟨the FCC's *ruling* regarding the broadcasting of obscenities⟩ — see EDICT 1

rum *adj, chiefly British* different from the ordinary in a way that causes curiosity or suspicion ⟨she wears staid business suits, but prefers some quite *rum* knickers underneath⟩ — see ODD 2

rum *n* a distilled beverage that can make a person drunk ⟨a fiery sermon on the evils of demon *rum*⟩ — see ALCOHOL

rumble *vb* to make a low heavy rolling sound ⟨when thunder *rumbled* in the distant sky, we wisely began packing up our picnic⟩

synonyms growl, grumble, lumber, roll

related words boom, drum, thunder; bellow

rumbustious *adj, chiefly British* being rough or noisy in a high-spirited way ⟨while American university debates tend to be sedate affairs, their counterparts in Oxford are wholeheartedly *rumbustious*⟩ — see BOISTEROUS

ruminant *adj* given to or marked by long, quiet thinking ⟨I wandered around campus all day in a *ruminant* mood⟩ — see CONTEMPLATIVE

ruminate *vb* to give serious and careful thought to ⟨the minister hoped that the congregation would spend the remainder of the week *ruminating* the message of his sermon⟩ — see PONDER

ruminative *adj* given to or marked by long, quiet thinking ⟨a *ruminative* man, who contributed to discussions only after he had completely thought things through⟩ — see CONTEMPLATIVE

rummage *n* an unorganized collection or mixture of various things ⟨a *rummage* of textbooks, notebooks, and old school papers all over the desk⟩ — see MISCELLANY 1

rummage *vb* **1** to come upon after searching, study, or effort ⟨at the last minute she *rummaged* a costume from the attic⟩ — see FIND 1

2 to look through (as a place) carefully or thoroughly in an effort to find or discover something ⟨he *rummaged* the desk drawer trying to find the spare keys⟩ — see SEARCH 1

rummy *n* a person who makes a habit of getting drunk ⟨most mornings a dazed old *rummy* sits on the steps with a bottle in a paper bag⟩ — see DRUNK 1

rumor *n* information or opinion that is widely disseminated without any authority or confirmation of accuracy ⟨*rumor* has it that she's planning to shut down the company⟩

synonyms buzz, dish, gossip, hearsay, noise, report, scuttlebutt, talk, tattle, word

related words tale, whisper, whispering; hint, intimation, rumbling; disinformation, propaganda; urban legend (*also* urban myth); dirt, scandal

rumor *vb* to make (as a piece of information) the subject of common talk without any authority or confirmation of accuracy ⟨for years people have been *rumoring* the CEO's imminent retirement⟩

synonyms bruit (about), circulate, noise (about *or* out), whisper

related words bandy (about), blab, dish, gossip, tattle; bare, disclose, divulge, expose, let on (about), report, reveal, spill, tell; hint, imply, insinuate, intimate, suggest; blaze, broadcast, proclaim, promulgate, propagate, publicize, spread

rump *n* the part of the body upon which someone sits ⟨she plopped down on her *rump* to listen to the campfire story⟩ — see BUTTOCKS

rumple *vb* **1** to create (as by crushing) an irregular mass of creases in ⟨the guest *rumpled* the antique bedspread by lying down on it⟩ — see CRUMPLE 1

2 to develop creases or folds ⟨the linen skirt *rumpled* as soon as she started wearing it⟩ — see WRINKLE 1

3 to undo the proper order or arrangement of ⟨the aunt would invariably *rumple* the little boy's hair whenever she came to visit⟩ — see DISORDER

rumpled *adj* lacking in order, neatness, and often cleanliness ⟨a *rumpled* room that suited its teenage occupant just fine⟩ — see MESSY

rumpus *n* a state of noisy, confused activity ⟨the kids made such a *rumpus* that they woke up everyone else in the house⟩ — see COMMOTION

run *n* **1** a prevailing or general movement or inclination ⟨the company's stock has remained consistent with the overall *run* of the market⟩ — see TREND 1

2 *chiefly Midland* a natural body of running water smaller than a river ⟨a *run* full of catfish⟩ — see CREEK 1

3 the period during which something exists, lasts, or is in progress ⟨the actor has been assigned the part for the *run* of the show⟩ — see DURATION 1

4 the right to act or move freely ⟨gave the dogs the *run* of the place⟩ — see FREEDOM 2

5 runs *pl* abnormally frequent intestinal evacuations with more or less fluid stools ⟨with weekend guests in the house, it was no time to get the *runs*⟩ — see DIARRHEA

run *vb* **1** to go at a pace faster than a walk ⟨we *ran* all the way to the bus stop, but still missed the bus⟩

synonyms dash, gallop, jog, scamper, sprint, trip, trot

related words bound, canter, leap, lope, shag, skip, spring; barrel, belt, blast, blaze, blow, bolt, bomb [*slang*], bowl, breeze, bustle, buzz, cannonball, careen, course, foot (it), hare, hasten, hie, hoof (it), hotfoot (it), hump, hurl, hurry, hurtle, hustle, jet, leg (it), pelt, race, ram, rip, rocket, rush, rustle, shoot, speed, tear, whirl, whisk, zip, zoom; nip, patter, scoot, scurry, scuttle, step (along)

near antonyms amble, saunter, shamble, shuffle, stroll; crawl, creep, dally, dawdle, dillydally, drag, lag, linger, loiter, poke, tarry; lumber, plod, trudge; hobble, limp

2 to hasten away from something dangerous or fright-

ening ⟨rather than *run* from a black bear, it's better to hold your ground and make lots of noise⟩
synonyms bolt, break, bug out, flee, fly, hightail (it), retreat, run away, run off, skedaddle
related words abscond, clear out, decamp, elope, escape, get (away), get out, lam, light out, make off, mizzle [*chiefly British*], scarper [*British*], scat, scram, skip (out), skirr
phrases beat a retreat, beat it, make tracks, turn tail
near antonyms beard, brave, confront, dare, defy, face; abide, dwell, hang around, linger, remain, stay, stick around, tarry

3 to be positioned along a certain course or in a certain direction ⟨the road *runs* along the river for a while⟩
synonyms bear, extend, go, head, lead, lie
related words cross, cut, pass; course, follow, span, traverse

4 to occur within a continuous range of variation ⟨the electric bill *runs* between 30 and 50 dollars a month⟩
synonyms go, range, vary
related words alternate, fluctuate, move, shift; change, mutate; extend, reach, stretch, sweep

5 to move in a stream ⟨water *running* down the window⟩ — see FLOW 1

6 to proceed or move quickly ⟨*run* and get the nurse⟩ — see HURRY 2

7 to show a liking or proneness (for something) ⟨unfortunately, members of his family *run* to fatness⟩ — see LEAN 2

8 to urge, push, or force onward ⟨they *ran* the horses hard in order to get to the ranch quickly⟩ — see DRIVE 1

9 to control the mechanical operation of ⟨I know how to *run* that machine⟩ — see OPERATE 1

10 to eventually have as a state or quality ⟨the poor woman *ran* herself ragged trying to care for all those children⟩ — see BECOME

11 to go from a solid to a liquid state ⟨her makeup started to *run* when she got in the pool⟩ — see LIQUEFY

12 to look after and make decisions about ⟨learning to *run* the family business⟩ — see CONDUCT 1

13 to cause to function ⟨in olden days mills were *run* by flowing water⟩ — see ACTIVATE

14 to have a price of ⟨that sort of computer *runs* at least several hundred dollars⟩ — see COST

15 to come or be together as friends ⟨he's been *running* with a bad crowd lately⟩ — see ASSOCIATE 1

16 to go after or on the track of ⟨if that dog continues to *run* cars, he's going to get seriously hurt⟩ — see FOLLOW 2

run (over) *vb* to make a brief visit ⟨I could *run over* right now if that's good for you⟩ — see CALL 3

run along *vb* to leave a place often for another ⟨I'd love to stay longer, but I must be *running along*⟩ — see GO 2

runaway *adj* showing no signs of being under control ⟨a region plagued by *runaway* suburban sprawl⟩ — see RAMPANT 1

run away *vb* **1** to get free from a dangerous or confining situation ⟨*ran away* from an unhappy marriage⟩ — see ESCAPE 1

2 to hasten away from something dangerous or frightening ⟨the child *runs away* from large dogs⟩ — see RUN 2

rundlet *or* **runlet** *n* an enclosed wooden vessel for holding beverages ⟨the wine was transferred to *rundlets* for further aging in the cellar⟩ — see CASK

rundown *n* a short statement of the main points ⟨a *rundown* of the suspect's lengthy police record⟩ — see SUMMARY

run–down *adj* **1** showing signs of advanced wear and tear and neglect ⟨a *run-down* old house that really should be torn down⟩ — see SHABBY 1

2 temporarily suffering from a disorder of the body ⟨I'm afraid I'll be staying home today as I'm feeling *run-down*⟩ — see SICK 1

run down *vb* **1** to come upon after searching, study, or effort ⟨finally *ran down* the answer after hours of research⟩ — see FIND 1

2 to express scornfully one's low opinion of ⟨constantly *running down* the city's cultural life won't do anything to improve it⟩ — see DECRY 1

rune *n* a composition using rhythm and often rhyme to create a lyrical effect ⟨wrote many mournful *runes* after her lover's untimely death⟩ — see POEM

rung *n* **1** the placement of someone or something in relation to others in a vertical arrangement ⟨the greasy spoon restaurant was several *rungs* below the kind of establishment in which we usually dined⟩ — see RANK 1

2 *Scottish* a heavy rigid stick used as a weapon or for punishment ⟨the watchman usually carried a stout oak *rung*⟩ — see CLUB 1

run–in *n* a brief clash between enemies or rivals ⟨the rival gangs had a bit of a *run-in* last night⟩ — see ENCOUNTER

run in *vb* **1** to make a brief visit ⟨I just thought I'd *run in* and pick up my package⟩ — see CALL 3

2 to take or keep under one's control by authority of law ⟨if we catch you shoplifting again, we're going to *run you in*⟩ — see ARREST 1

runlet *n* a natural body of running water smaller than a river ⟨weather forecasters warned that the heavy rains might cause the area's *runlets* to overflow⟩ — see CREEK 1

runnel *n* a natural body of running water smaller than a river ⟨the fugitive made use of local *runnels* to throw the bloodhounds off his scent⟩ — see CREEK 1

runner *n* **1** a person who imports or exports goods secretly and illegally ⟨a drug *runner*⟩ — see SMUGGLER

2 one that carries a message or does an errand ⟨sent a *runner* to tell them that all was ready for the feast⟩ — see MESSENGER

running *adj* **1** being in effective operation ⟨the car has been *running* for almost an entire day⟩ — see ACTIVE 1

2 going on and on without any interruptions ⟨a *running* struggle just to make ends meet⟩ — see CONTINUOUS

running *adv* in succession without others coming in between ⟨he won the championship five times *running*⟩ — see CONSECUTIVELY

running *n* the act or activity of looking after and making decisions about something ⟨left the *running* of the corporation to his subordinates⟩ — see CONDUCT 1

running mate *n* a person frequently seen in the company of another ⟨inseparable *running mates* who first met when they were in elementary school⟩ — see ASSOCIATE 1

runny *adj* having an overly soft liquid consistency ⟨*runny* scrambled eggs⟩
synonyms soupy, watery
related words flowing, fluent, fluid, liquefied; dilute, diluted, thin, thinned, watered-down, weak, weakened; sloshy, slushy, soggy, waterlogged, wet
near antonyms ropy (*also* ropey), syrupy, viscid, viscous; creamy, heavy, thick, thickened, thickish; gelatinous, gluey, glutinous, gooey, gummy, sticky

run off *vb* **1** to drive or force out ⟨the dog often *ran off* cats and other animals that had intruded upon his owner's property⟩ — see EJECT 1

2 to get free from a dangerous or confining situation ⟨their rebellious daughter's *run off* because she was disciplined again⟩ — see ESCAPE 1

3 to hasten away from something dangerous or frightening ⟨the mouse *ran off* as soon as it saw us⟩ — see RUN 2

run–of–the–mill *adj* **1** being of the type that is encountered in the normal course of events ⟨just another *run-of-the-mill* suburb with its shopping malls and fast-food restaurants⟩ — see ORDINARY 1

2 of average to below average quality ⟨his latest offering is rather *run-of-the-mill* for this usually excellent novelist⟩ — see MEDIOCRE 1

run–of–the–mine *or* **run–of–mine** *adj* of average to below average quality ⟨so far, the job posting has attracted only *run-of-the-mine* applicants⟩ — see MEDIOCRE 1

run on *vb* **1** to engage in casual or rambling conversation ⟨we were just *running on* about how neither of us has aged a bit after all these years⟩ — see CHAT 1

2 to remain indefinitely in existence or in the same state ⟨allow the savings account to *run on* for now⟩ — see CONTINUE 1

3 to talk at length without sticking to a topic or getting to a point ⟨she's very sweet, but she does tend to *run on*⟩ — see RAMBLE 1

run over *vb* to do over and over so as to become skilled ⟨let's *run over* this dance number one more time⟩ — see PRACTICE

runt *n* a living thing much smaller than others of its kind ⟨one kitten was definitely the *runt*, weighing only six ounces at birth⟩ — see DWARF 1

run–through *n* a short statement of the main points ⟨could you give me a quick *run-through* of what the referendum question is all about?⟩ — see SUMMARY

run through *vb* **1** to penetrate or hold (something) with a pointed object ⟨before I knew what was happening, the thug had *run through* me with a knife⟩ — see IMPALE

2 to use up carelessly ⟨how did you manage to *run through* $300 in one day?⟩ — see WASTE 1

rural *adj* of, relating to, associated with, or typical of open areas with few buildings or people ⟨grew up in a *rural* community where more than half the people were farmers⟩ ⟨a painter noted for his *rural* landscapes⟩

synonyms bucolic, country, pastoral, rustic (*also* rustical)

related words backwoods, backwoodsy, countrified (*also* countryfied), provincial; agrarian, agricultural; nonurban, semirural

near antonyms citified, urbanized; metro, metropolitan, municipal; nonagricultural, nonfarm

antonyms urban

rush *n* **1** excited and often showy or disorderly speed ⟨what's the reason for all this *rush*?⟩ — see HURRY 1

2 the act or action of setting upon with force or violence ⟨the regiment recaptured the hill with a single *rush*⟩ — see ATTACK 1

3 a pleasurably intense stimulation of the feelings ⟨riding my motorcycle over these winding roads is always an adrenaline-pumping *rush*⟩ — see THRILL

rush *vb* **1** to cause to move or proceed fast or faster ⟨I wouldn't make so many mistakes if you'd stop *rushing* me⟩ — see HURRY 1

2 to flow out in great quantities or with force ⟨in the spring the stream's *rushing* waters make crossing treacherous⟩ — see GUSH 1

3 to proceed or move quickly ⟨*rushing* is a good way to slip and fall⟩ — see HURRY 2

4 to take sudden, violent action against ⟨one goat suddenly *rushed* the other and knocked it down⟩ — see ATTACK 1

rushed *adj* acting or done with excessive or careless speed ⟨a *rushed* job with a number of errors⟩ — see HASTY 1

rustic *n* an awkward or simple person especially from a small town or the country ⟨a *rustic* who was awed by the prices that city dwellers had to pay⟩ — see HICK

rustic *also* **rustical** *adj* **1** lacking social grace and assurance ⟨*rustic* yokels whose first impulse was to smirk gawkily at anyone not of their own kind⟩ — see AWKWARD 1

2 of, relating to, associated with, or typical of open areas with few buildings or people ⟨a *rustic* area that has a refreshing lack of billboards and shopping malls⟩ — see RURAL

rustle *vb* **1** to feed on grass or herbs ⟨just take the steer out to pasture and let it *rustle* for itself⟩ — see [1]GRAZE

2 to proceed or move quickly ⟨*rustled* around enthusiastically on the morning of the big trip⟩ — see HURRY 2

3 to make small sounds usually by rubbing or moving ⟨my pet peeve is candy wrappers *rustling* during a movie⟩ — see CRINKLE 1

rustler *n* an ambitious person who eagerly goes after what is desired ⟨the job requires a *rustler* who doesn't always need to be told what to do⟩ — see GO-GETTER

rusty *adj* **1** having passed its time of use or usefulness ⟨*rusty* laws still on the books because no one bothered to repeal them⟩ — see OBSOLETE

2 harsh and dry in sound ⟨in a *rusty* voice the old man ordered us off his land⟩ — see HOARSE

rut *n* an established and often automatic or monotonous series of actions followed when engaging in some activity ⟨I've fallen into a *rut*, watching television and then going to bed every night⟩ — see ROUTINE 1

ruth *n* the capacity for feeling for another's unhappiness or misfortune ⟨listening to your flippant comments about the homeless, I wonder if you have any *ruth*⟩ — see HEART 1

ruthless *adj* having or showing a lack of sympathy or tender feelings ⟨an office supervisor with a *ruthless* disregard for others' feelings⟩ — see HARD 1

RV *n* a motor vehicle that is specially equipped for living while traveling ⟨the *RV* parked in the driveway is a sure sign that their relatives from Florida have arrived⟩ — see CAMPER

S

sable *adj* having the color of soot or coal ⟨a beautiful *sable* cat⟩ — see BLACK 1

saccharine *adj* appealing to the emotions in an obvious and tiresome way ⟨the movie was funny, but it had a *saccharine* ending in which everyone lives happily ever after⟩ — see CORNY 1

saccharinity *n* the state or quality of having an excess of tender feelings (as of love, nostalgia, or compassion) ⟨the film veers into *saccharinity* as soon as the cute child star appears on screen⟩ — see SENTIMENTALITY

sacerdotal *adj* of, relating to, or characteristic of the clergy ⟨*sacerdotal* garments such as a cassock and miter⟩ — see CLERICAL

sack *n* **1** a container made of a flexible material (as paper or plastic) ⟨asked the bagger to put all the loaves of bread in the same *sack*⟩ — see BAG 1
2 a place set aside for sleeping ⟨I think I'm ready to hit the *sack*⟩ — see BED 1

[1]**sack** *vb* to let go from office, service, or employment ⟨he was *sacked* for showing up late once too often⟩ — see DISMISS 1

[2]**sack** *vb* to search through with the intent of committing robbery ⟨thieves *sacked* the house in search of the diamond necklace⟩ — see RANSACK 1

sacral *adj* set apart or worthy of veneration by association with God ⟨*sacral* laws that have been passed down for generations⟩ — see HOLY 2

sacralize *vb* to make holy through prayers or ritual ⟨*sacralizing* the cohabitation of a man and a woman by means of the marriage ceremony⟩ — see BLESS 1

sacred *adj* **1** not to be violated, criticized, or tampered with ⟨the *sacred* trust that exists between elected officials and the electorate⟩
synonyms hallowed, holy, inviolable, sacrosanct, unassailable, untouchable
related words inviolate, pure; privileged, protected, secure, shielded; exempt, immune
near antonyms blasphemous, irreverent, profane, sacrilegious
2 of, relating to, or being God ⟨a *sacred* name that must not be uttered in vain⟩ — see HOLY 3
3 of, relating to, or used in the practice or worship services of a religion ⟨a *sacred* chalice⟩ — see RELIGIOUS 1
4 set apart or worthy of veneration by association with God ⟨the *sacred* bones of a saint⟩ — see HOLY 2
5 deserving honor and respect especially by reason of age ⟨the alumni procession at graduation is one of the college's most *sacred* traditions, dating back over a hundred years⟩ — see VENERABLE 1

sacrifice *n* something offered to a god ⟨the herders selected their best lamb as a *sacrifice* in order to receive blessings from their god⟩
synonyms immolation, offering, victim
related words libation, oblation, propitiation; holocaust; contribution, donation

sacrifice *vb* to give up as an offering to a god ⟨according to the Old Testament, Abraham was willing to *sacrifice* even his son to God⟩
synonyms immolate, offer
related words consecrate, dedicate, devote; give, hand over, surrender, yield

sacrilege *n* an act of great disrespect shown to God or to sacred ideas, people, or things ⟨spitting on the temple floor would be a great *sacrilege*⟩ — see BLASPHEMY

sacrilegious *adj* not showing proper reverence for the holy or sacred ⟨a *sacrilegious*, obscene joke—and told in church at that!⟩ — see IRREVERENT

sacristy *n* a room in a church building for sacred furnishings (as vestments) ⟨our choir robes were stored in the *sacristy*⟩
synonyms vestry
related words cloakroom

sacrosanct *adj* **1** not to be violated, criticized, or tampered with ⟨the teacher's book of grades is *sacrosanct*, and someone could be expelled for changing anything in it⟩ — see SACRED 1
2 set apart or worthy of veneration by association with God ⟨believers eventually built a chapel on the *sacrosanct* spot where the miracle was thought to have taken place⟩ — see HOLY 2

sad *adj* **1** feeling unhappiness ⟨movies in which the hero dies always make us feel *sad*⟩
synonyms bad, blue, brokenhearted, cast down, crestfallen, dejected, depressed, despondent, disconsolate, doleful, down, downcast, downhearted, down in the mouth, droopy, forlorn, gloomy, glum, hangdog, heartbroken, heartsick, heartsore, heavyhearted, inconsolable, joyless, low, low-spirited, melancholic, melancholy, miserable, mournful, saddened, sorrowful, sorry, unhappy, woebegone, woeful, wretched
related words aggrieved, distressed, troubled, uneasy, unquiet, upset, worried; despairing, hopeless, sunk; disappointed, discouraged, disheartened, dispirited; suicidal; dolorous, lachrymose, lugubrious, plaintive, tearful; regretful, rueful; agonized, anguished, grieving, wailing, weeping; black, bleak, cheerless, comfortless, dark, darkening, depressing, desolate, dismal, drear, dreary, elegiac (*also* elegiacal), funereal, gray (*also* grey), morbid, morose, murky, saturnine, somber (*or* sombre), sullen
near antonyms ecstatic, elated, enraptured, entranced, euphoric, exhilarated, exuberant, exultant, overjoyed, rapturous, rhapsodic (*also* rhapsodical); blithe, blithesome, jocose, jocular, jocund, jolly, jovial, lightsome, merry, mirthful; excited, thrilled; hopeful, optimistic, rosy, sanguine; encouraged, heartened; animated, bouncing, energetic, frisky, jaunty, lively, peppy, perky, spirited, sprightful, sprightly, springy, vital, vivacious, zippy; content, gratified, pleased, satisfied; beaming, grinning, laughing, smiling; boon, carefree, careless, cavalier, devil-may-care, easygoing, happy-go-lucky, insouciant, lighthearted, unconcerned
antonyms blissful, buoyant, buoyed, cheerful, cheery, chipper, delighted, glad, gladdened, gladsome, gleeful, happy, joyful, joyous, jubilant, sunny, upbeat
2 causing unhappiness ⟨the *sad* news about our uncle's death made my father cry⟩
synonyms depressing, dismal, drear, dreary, heartbreaking, heartrending, melancholy, mournful, pathetic, saddening, sorry, tearful, teary
related words deplorable, distressful, grievous, lamentable, unfortunate, woeful; discomforting, discomposing, disquieting, distressing, disturbing, perturbing; affecting, moving, poignant, touching; discouraging, disheartening, dispiriting
near antonyms heartening, heartwarming, inspiring, stimulating, stirring, uplifting; agreeable, delightful, enjoyable, pleasant, pleasing, pleasurable, satisfying, welcome; exhilarating, thrilling
antonyms cheering, cheery, glad, happy

3 deserving pitying scorn (as for inadequacy) ⟨no one expected the supermodel to be a great actress, but her acting is *sad* beyond belief⟩ — see PITIFUL 1

sadden *vb* to make sad ⟨the arrival of winter always *saddens* me⟩ — see DEPRESS 1

saddened *adj* feeling unhappiness ⟨we were all *saddened* when our minister retired⟩ — see SAD 1

saddening *adj* causing unhappiness ⟨the *saddening* discovery that something is threatening the birds in the area⟩ — see SAD 2

saddle *vb* to place a weight or burden on ⟨to the social worker it seemed as though her supervisor had once again *saddled* her with a truly hopeless case⟩ — see LOAD 1

saddle *n* a narrow opening between hillsides or mountains that can be used for passage ⟨the next day's hike was a stiff climb out of the *saddle* where they had camped for the night⟩ — see CANYON

sadism *n* disposition to willfully inflict pain and suffering on others ⟨a troubled youth with a streak of *sadism* in him⟩ — see CRUELTY

sadistic *adj* having or showing the desire to inflict severe pain and suffering on others ⟨the troubled youth is being treated by a psychotherapist for his *sadistic* urges to hurt animals⟩ — see CRUEL 1

sadly *adv* with feelings of bitterness or grief ⟨*sadly* she told us how her dog died⟩ — see HARD 2

sadness *n* a state or spell of low spirits ⟨she was filled with *sadness* at the thought of having to leave her family⟩
synonyms blue devils, blues, dejection, depression, desolation, despond, despondence, despondency, disconsolateness, dispiritedness, doldrums, dolefulness, downheartedness, dreariness, dumps, forlornness, gloom, gloominess, glumness, heartsickness, joylessness, melancholy, miserableness, mopes, mournfulness, oppression, sorrowfulness, unhappiness
related words melancholia, self-pity; anguish, dolor, grief, mourning, somberness, sorrow, woefulness; agony, distress, pain; misery, woe, wretchedness; discouragement, disheartenment; moodiness; despair, desperation, hopelessness, self-despair; boredom, ennui, tedium; dismalness, drear, morbidness, moroseness, morosity; regret, rue
near antonyms gaiety (*also* gayety), gayness, glee, gleefulness, humor, jollity, joviality, lightheartedness, merriment, mirth, mirthfulness; cheer, cheerfulness, cheeriness, hopefulness, optimism, sunniness; content, contentedness, contentment, satisfaction; delight, gratification
antonyms bliss, blissfulness, ecstasy, elatedness, elation, euphoria, exhilaration, exuberance, exultation, felicity, gladness, gladsomeness, happiness, heaven, intoxication, joy, joyfulness, joyousness, jubilation, rapture, rapturousness

safe *adj* **1** not exposed to the threat of loss or injury ⟨the minute the rain started, we looked for a place where we would be *safe* from a drenching downpour⟩
synonyms all right, alright, secure
related words hale, healthy, intact, sound, well, whole; scatheless, unharmed, unhurt, uninjured, unscathed
phrases home free
near antonyms damaged, harmed, hurt, injured, scathed, wounded
antonyms endangered, exposed, imperiled (*or* imperilled), insecure, liable, open, subject (to), susceptible, threatened, unsafe, violable, vulnerable
2 providing safety ⟨we tried to find a *safe* place to hide our valuables while we went swimming⟩
synonyms secure, snug
related words guarding, protecting, safeguarding, sheltering, shielding; defended, guarded, protected, sheltered, shielded; impregnable, inviolable, invulnerable, unassailable, unconquerable
near antonyms menacing, minatory, parlous, perilous, threatening; undefended, unguarded, unprotected, vulnerable; precarious, treacherous, uncertain
antonyms dangerous, hazardous, insecure, risky, unsafe
3 unlikely to provoke controversy or offense ⟨when chatting with strangers, she prefers to stick to *safe* topics such as the weather⟩
synonyms noncontroversial, uncontroversial
related words politically correct; hands-down, incontestable, incontrovertible, indisputable, indubitable, undeniable, unquestionable; irrefutable; certain, definite, positive, sure; uncontested, undisputed
near antonyms arguable, contestable, controvertible, debatable, disputable, doubtable, doubtful, moot, questionable; debated, disputed
antonyms controversial, hot-button
4 having or showing a close attentiveness to avoiding danger or trouble ⟨rewarded *safe* drivers with lower insurance rates⟩ — see CAREFUL 1
5 not causing or being capable of causing injury or hurt ⟨that pain reliever is *safe* for most people to take⟩ — see HARMLESS
6 worthy of one's trust ⟨she always offers *safe* advice⟩ — see DEPENDABLE

safe *n* a specially reinforced container to keep valuables safe ⟨the hotel recommended that we keep all our valuables in its *safe* during our stay⟩
synonyms coffer, safe-deposit box, strongbox
related words lockbox; vault; locker, storeroom, treasury; box, caddy, case, casket, chest, footlocker, locker, trunk

safe–deposit box *n* a specially reinforced container to keep valuables safe ⟨kept the deed to the house in a *safe-deposit box* at the bank⟩ — see SAFE

safeguard *n* **1** means or method of defending ⟨with these *safeguards* in place, no one should be able to break into our computers⟩ — see DEFENSE 1
2 a measure taken to preclude loss or injury ⟨*safeguards* that were intended to assure our security, but not at the expense of our liberty⟩ — see PRECAUTION

safeguard *vb* to drive danger or attack away from ⟨sheepdogs *safeguard* the flock from attacks by wolves⟩ — see DEFEND 1

safekeeping *n* responsibility for the safety and well-being of someone or something ⟨while she was away on business, the single mom entrusted her daughter into her in-laws' *safekeeping*⟩ — see CUSTODY

safeness *n* the state of not being exposed to danger ⟨the *safeness* of her children was something that she worried about constantly⟩ — see SAFETY 1

safety *n* **1** the state of not being exposed to danger ⟨we were lucky to make it to *safety* just as the lions broke loose from their cage at the zoo⟩
synonyms protection, safeness, security
related words aegis (*also* egis), cover, defense, guardianship, ward; guard, safeguard, screen, shield; asylum, harbor, haven, refuge, retreat, shelter; impregnability, impregnableness, invincibility, invincibleness, inviolability, inviolableness, invulnerability, invulnerableness
near antonyms hazard, risk, threat; instability, precariousness; harm's way; exposure, liability, openness, violability, vulnerability, vulnerableness; susceptibility, susceptibleness
antonyms danger, distress, endangerment, imperilment, jeopardy, peril, trouble
2 a protective device (as on a weapon) to prevent accidental operation ⟨the gun couldn't be fired as long as the *safety* was on⟩
synonyms guard

related words fail-safe; lock; defense, protection, safeguard, shield

sag *vb* **1** to be limp from lack of water or vigor ⟨the plant's leaves were *sagging* feebly in the intense heat⟩ — see DROOP 1

2 to decline gradually from a standard level ⟨sales figures have *sagged* slightly over the past six months⟩ — see SLIP 1

3 to lose bodily strength or vigor ⟨after a whole day of working in the hot sun, he began to *sag*⟩ — see WEAKEN 2

sag *n* the extent to which something hangs or dips below a straight line ⟨if there's too much *sag* in the rod, the curtains will drag on the floor⟩

synonyms droop, hang, slack, slackness

related words floppiness, laxity, laxness, limpness, looseness

near antonyms rigidity, rigidness, tautness, tenseness, tension, tightness

sagacious *adj* having or showing deep understanding and intelligent application of knowledge ⟨a *sagacious* critique of the current social climate in our nation⟩ — see WISE 1

sagaciousness *n* the ability to understand inner qualities or relationships ⟨a woman of such down-to-earth *sagaciousness* that she ought to be writing an advice column for the newspaper⟩ — see WISDOM 1

sagacity *n* the ability to understand inner qualities or relationships ⟨a novelist of surprising *sagacity* considering his youthfulness⟩ — see WISDOM 1

sage *adj* having or showing deep understanding and intelligent application of knowledge ⟨a *sage* suggestion that she think long and hard before deciding to marry at such a young age⟩ — see WISE 1

sage *n* a person of deep wisdom or learning ⟨the young prince made a pilgrimage to the *sage*, hoping to learn the meaning of life⟩

synonyms pundit, savant, scholar

related words seer, wise man; polyhistor, polymath, Renaissance man; brain, egghead, genius, highbrow, intellect, intellectual, thinker, whiz, wizard; guru, mahatma, pandit, swami, yogi (*also* yogin); rabbi; master, mentor, teacher

near antonyms blockhead, dodo, dolt, donkey, dope, dumbbell, dummy, dunce, fathead, fool, goon, half-wit, idiot, ignoramus, imbecile, jackass, know-nothing, moron, nincompoop, ninny, nitwit, numskull (*or* numbskull), pinhead, simpleton, stock, turkey

sageness *n* the ability to understand inner qualities or relationships ⟨her father has always shown an unpretentious *sageness* about the practicalities of life⟩ see WISDOM 1

sagging *adj* bending downward or forward ⟨*sagging* branches that were weighted down with snow⟩ — see NODDING

said *adj* mentioned previously ⟨with *said* guidebook in hand, we set off to explore the city⟩ — see AFORESAID

sail *n* a journey over water in a vessel ⟨we went for a brief *sail* on the bay to relax⟩

synonyms crossing, cruise, passage, voyage

sail *vb* **1** to travel on water in a vessel ⟨I can't *sail* when there's any breeze at all because I get seasick easily⟩

synonyms boat, cruise, ferry, navigate, ship (out), voyage

related words canoe, kayak, yacht; coast

phrases make sail, take ship

2 to move or proceed smoothly and readily ⟨*sailed* through the latest assignment⟩ — see FLOW 2

3 to rest or move along the surface of a liquid or in the air ⟨a leaf *sailed* by, carried by the breeze⟩ — see FLOAT 1

sailboat *n* a boat equipped with one or more sails ⟨we were stuck in the *sailboat* for an hour until the wind came up and we could move again⟩

synonyms bark, dinghy, windjammer

related words bugeye, brigantine, caïque, caravel, catamaran, catboat, cat rig, clipper, corvette, cutter, frigate, galleon, galley, junk, keelboat, ketch, knockabout, lugger, outrigger, pinnace, piragua, sailer, schooner, shallop, sharpie (*or* sharpy), ship, sloop, square-rigger, xebec, yacht, yawl; bottom, craft, vessel

sailor *n* one who operates or navigates a seagoing vessel ⟨the *sailors* were glad to be arriving in port after their long voyage⟩

synonyms gob, hearty, jack, jack-tar, mariner, navigator, salt, sea dog, seafarer, seaman, shipman, swab, swabbie (*also* swabby) [*slang*], tar

related words coxswain, crewman, deckhand, shipmate; able-bodied seaman, able seaman, lubber; powerboater, sailboater; lime-juicer [*slang*], limey [*slang*]

sainted *adj* showing a devotion to God and to a life of virtue ⟨renowned as theologian as well as for his work as medical missionary in Africa, Dr. Albert Schweitzer was widely regarded as one of the most *sainted* individuals of his time⟩ — see HOLY 1

sainthood *n* the quality or state of being spiritually pure or virtuous ⟨while you're a perfectly nice person, you're not exactly an example of *sainthood*⟩ — see HOLINESS

saintliness *n* the quality or state of being spiritually pure or virtuous ⟨true *saintliness* requires utter selflessness and devotion to others⟩ — see HOLINESS

saintly *adj* showing a devotion to God and to a life of virtue ⟨a *saintly* man who devoted his life to caring for the dying⟩ — see HOLY 1

saintship *n* the quality or state of being spiritually pure or virtuous ⟨a man who always maintained that his mother's *saintship* was beyond question⟩ — see HOLINESS

salable *or* **saleable** *adj* **1** fit or likely to be sold especially on a large scale ⟨an item that would be too expensive to produce, and attractive to too few people, to ever be considered a *salable* commodity⟩ — see COMMERCIAL

2 fit to be offered for sale ⟨the car has to be put in better condition before it will be at all *salable*⟩ — see MARKETABLE 1

salacious *adj* having a strong sexual desire ⟨the *salacious* Greek god Pan is generally portrayed as having the legs, horns, and ears of a goat⟩ — see LUSTFUL

salaciousness *n* sexual appetite ⟨a rapist whose *salaciousness* was of a particularly sadistic stripe⟩ — see DESIRE 2

salad *n* an unorganized collection or mixture of various things ⟨the state senate must contend with a veritable *salad* of legislative measures before it can adjourn for the session⟩ — see MISCELLANY 1

salad days *n pl* a state or time of great activity, thriving, or achievement ⟨he worked for NASA in its *salad days*⟩ — see BLOOM 1

salary *n* the money paid regularly to a person for labor or services ⟨signed a contract for a new job with a *salary* of $40,000 per year⟩ — see WAGE

sale *n* the transfer of ownership of something from one person to another for a price ⟨my neighbor tried to make a *sale*, but no one was interested in buying his old car⟩

synonyms deal, trade, transaction

related words auction, silent auction; haggle, horse-trading, negotiation; bargain, buy, steal; purchase; clearance, closeout, fire sale; fair; garage sale, jumble sale [*British*], rummage sale, tag sale, yard sale

salesclerk *n* a person employed to sell goods or services especially in a store ⟨the *salesclerk* told us where to find the jewelry department⟩ — see SALESPERSON

salesman *n* a person employed to sell goods or services especially in a store ⟨a furniture *salesman* followed us around the whole time we looked for a new couch⟩ — see SALESPERSON

salesperson *n* a person employed to sell goods or services especially in a store ⟨we asked the *salesperson* to see if there were any shoes in our size in the stockroom⟩
synonyms clerk, salesclerk, salesman
related words salespeople; salesgirl, saleslady, saleswoman, shopgirl; pitchman, pitchwoman; floorwalker

saline *adj* of, relating to, or containing salt ⟨tears are *saline*⟩ — see SALTY 1

salinity *n* the quality or state of being salty ⟨distilling will eliminate the *salinity* of seawater⟩ — see SALTINESS

saliva *n* the fluid that is secreted into the mouth by certain glands ⟨our mouths filled with *saliva* when we smelled the delicious dinner⟩
synonyms drool, slaver, slobber, spit, spittle
related words foam, froth; expectoration, salivation, sputum

salivate *vb* to let saliva or some other substance flow from the mouth ⟨the dog *salivated* at the sight of the raw meat⟩ — see DROOL 1

salivate (for) *vb* to have an earnest wish to own or enjoy ⟨I've been *salivating for* a high-definition TV for some time⟩ — see DESIRE 1

sallow *adj* lacking the warm skin color indicative of or associated with good health ⟨he was still a bit *sallow* after a week spent in bed with the flu⟩ — see SICKLY 2

sally *n* **1** a short trip for pleasure ⟨a morning *sally* out to see the historic monuments around the city⟩ — see EXCURSION 1
2 something said or done to cause laughter ⟨the final *sally* made her laugh, and that ended the argument⟩ — see JOKE 1

sally (forth) *vb* to leave a place often for another ⟨he eagerly *sallied forth* from his small town to seek a new life in the bustling city⟩ — see GO 2

salmagundi *n* an unorganized collection or mixture of various things ⟨the downtown area has a *salmagundi* of one-of-a-kind shops, where you can find almost anything you might need—and many things you don't⟩ — see MISCELLANY 1

salon *n* **1** a building or part of a building in which objects of interest are displayed ⟨at its headquarters the company maintains a fashionable *salon* filled with works of modern art⟩ — see MUSEUM
2 a building, room, or suite of rooms occupied by a service business ⟨a hair *salon*⟩ — see PLACE 2

saloon *n* a place of business where alcoholic beverages are sold to be consumed on the premises ⟨cowboys drinking in the *saloon* after their work was done for the day⟩ — see BARROOM

salt *adj* of, relating to, or containing salt ⟨the oceans are *salt* water⟩ — see SALTY 1

salt *n* one who operates or navigates a seagoing vessel ⟨an old *salt* who taught me everything I know about sailing and the sea⟩ — see SAILOR

salt *vb* to scatter or set here and there among other things ⟨the old sailor *salted* his tale of the voyage with crude anecdotes and rough language⟩ — see THREAD 1

salt away *vb* to put (something of future use or value) in a safe or secret place ⟨*salted away* some jewels in a safe-deposit box for the lean times⟩ — see HOARD

saltiness *n* the quality or state of being salty ⟨the *saltiness* of the pretzels went well with the soda pop we were drinking⟩
synonyms brininess, salinity, saltness
near antonyms freshness, purity; sweetness

saltness *n* the quality or state of being salty ⟨the excessive *saltness* of the soup made it inedible⟩ — see SALTINESS

salty *adj* **1** of, relating to, or containing salt ⟨*salty* sea water is safe to swim in, but you really shouldn't swallow it⟩
synonyms brackish, briny, saline, salt
related words hard
near antonyms sweet; clear, pure; freshwater
antonyms nonsaline
2 hinting at or intended to call to mind matters regarded as indecent ⟨*salty* language that earned the movie an R rating⟩ — see SUGGESTIVE 1
3 sharp and pleasantly stimulating to the mind or senses ⟨a *salty*, insightful analysis of male-female relationships⟩ — see PIQUANT

salubrious *adj* beneficial to the health of body or mind ⟨fresh air and exercise are always *salubrious*⟩ — see HEALTHFUL

salutary *adj* **1** promoting or contributing to personal or social well-being ⟨the low interest rates should have a *salutary* effect on business⟩ — see BENEFICIAL
2 good for the health ⟨increasing scientific evidence that a glass of wine a day is quite *salutary*⟩ — see HEALTHFUL

salutation *n* **1** a formal expression of praise ⟨the speaker introduced the evening's honored guest with a lavish *salutation*⟩ — see ENCOMIUM
2 an expression of goodwill upon meeting ⟨began the discussion with a gracious *salutation* to the distinguished assembly⟩ — see HELLO

salute *n* an expression of goodwill upon meeting ⟨offered a cheery *salute* as they passed the soldiers on the street⟩ — see HELLO

salute *vb* to declare enthusiastic approval of ⟨I *salute* the idea of healthier lunch options for our students⟩ — see ACCLAIM

salutiferous *adj* beneficial to the health of body or mind ⟨the thirsty wayfarer eagerly took a drink of the spring's *salutiferous* water⟩ — see HEALTHFUL

salvation *n* the saving from danger or evil ⟨we spent the night in the cellar praying for *salvation* from the tornadoes⟩
synonyms deliverance, rescue
related words ransom, recovery, redemption; extrication; defense, guard, protection, safeguard, safeguarding, security; conservation, guardianship, preservation, safekeeping

salve *vb* to free from distress or disturbance ⟨attempting to *salve* her conscience, she anonymously sent the store a sum of cash sufficient to cover the merchandise she had shoplifted⟩ — see CALM 1

salvo *n* a rapid or overwhelming outpouring of many things at once ⟨attacked the manager with a *salvo* of complaints before she even managed to say "hello"⟩ — see BARRAGE

same *adj* **1** resembling another in every respect ⟨I bought the *same* shirt at the mall for five dollars less⟩
synonyms coequal, duplicate, equal, even, identical, indistinguishable
related words akin, alike, analogous, comparable, coordinate, correspondent, corresponding, equivalent, like, look-alike, matching, parallel, similar, such, suchlike, synonymous, tantamount
phrases much of a muchness
near antonyms differentiable, discriminable; divers, miscellaneous, sundry, varied, various
antonyms different, disparate, dissimilar, distant, distinct, distinctive, distinguishable, diverse, nonidentical, other, unalike, unlike
2 being one and not another ⟨that's the *same* guy I saw down at the beach yesterday⟩
synonyms identical, selfsame, very

near antonyms differentiable, discriminable, disparate, dissimilar, distinct, distinctive, distinguishable, diverse, unalike, unlike, varied, various
antonyms another, different, other

sameness *n* **1** a tedious lack of variety ⟨the endless *sameness* of what we keep having for dinner is starting to bore me⟩ — see MONOTONY
2 the state of being exactly alike ⟨the *sameness* of the two essays made the teacher immediately suspect plagiarism⟩ — see IDENTITY 1
3 the state or fact of being exactly the same in number, amount, status, or quality ⟨the striking *sameness* of the results for both experiments suggests that this is a real discovery⟩ — see EQUIVALENCE

sample *vb* to put (something) to a test ⟨*sampled* the soup to see if it tasted good⟩ — see TRY (OUT)

sample *n* **1** a number of things selected from a group to stand for the whole ⟨based on a *sample* of the menu items, we decided that this was the best restaurant in town⟩
synonyms cross section, sampler, sampling, selection, slice
related words case, example, exemplar, exemplification, illustration, instance, representative, specimen; archetype, classic, locus classicus, paradigm, prototype; microcosm
2 one of a group or collection that shows what the whole is like ⟨this vase is a *sample* of the high-quality glassware that the glassblowers can produce⟩ — see EXAMPLE

sampler *n* a number of things selected from a group to stand for the whole ⟨she put together a *sampler* of works in the police procedural genre⟩ — see SAMPLE 1

sampling *n* a number of things selected from a group to stand for the whole ⟨a *sampling* of shoppers said they preferred fresh orange juice over frozen⟩ — see SAMPLE 1

sanative *adj* beneficial to the health of body or mind ⟨there's nothing like the *sanative* value of a good night's sleep⟩ — see HEALTHFUL

sanctification *n* **1** the act of making something holy through religious ritual ⟨the sacred site required another *sanctification* after it had been defiled by the invaders⟩ — see CONSECRATION
2 the act or fact of freeing from sin or moral guilt ⟨the Christian belief that the suffering and death of Jesus was responsible for the *sanctification* of all humankind⟩ — see PURIFICATION

sanctified *adj* set apart or worthy of veneration by association with God ⟨a *sanctified* site where the faithful believe that a young girl had visions of the Virgin Mary⟩ — see HOLY 2

sanctify *vb* **1** to free from moral guilt or blemish especially ceremonially ⟨received the sacrament of penance, whereby they were *sanctified* and restored to divine grace⟩ — see PURIFY 1
2 to make holy through prayers or ritual ⟨*sanctify* the bread for Communion⟩ — see BLESS 1

sanction *n* the approval by someone in authority for the doing of something ⟨you cannot make a student video without your faculty advisor's *sanction* of its subject matter prior to shooting⟩ — see PERMISSION

sanction *vb* to give official acceptance of as satisfactory ⟨the administration will *sanction* almost any field trip with educational value⟩ — see APPROVE

sanctioned *adj* ordered or allowed by those in authority ⟨I cannot believe that this religious cult is a *sanctioned* student organization⟩ — see OFFICIAL

sanctity *n* the quality or state of being spiritually pure or virtuous ⟨the *sanctity* of the elderly nun shone through in her every word and gesture⟩ — see HOLINESS

sanctuary *n* **1** a place that is considered sacred (as within a religion) ⟨by law, anyone who sought refuge in a religious *sanctuary* was safe from arrest by the civil authorities⟩ — see SHRINE
2 something (as a building) that offers cover from the weather or protection from danger ⟨the marshland has been set aside as a *sanctuary* for shorebirds along that section of the coast⟩ — see SHELTER

sanctum *n* **1** a place that is considered sacred (as within a religion) ⟨the city of Jerusalem is an important *sanctum* for Christians, Jews, and Muslims alike⟩ — see SHRINE
2 something (as a building) that offers cover from the weather or protection from danger ⟨used the cabin in the woods as a *sanctum* from the commotion and interference of his family⟩ — see SHELTER

sand *vb* to make smooth by friction ⟨painstakingly *sanded* down the wooden floors of the old house⟩ — see GRIND 1

sand *n, often* **sands** *pl* the usually sandy or gravelly land bordering a body of water ⟨we went for a moonlight walk on the *sands*⟩ — see BEACH

sandbag *vb* to cause (a person) to give in to pressure ⟨always manages to *sandbag* her sister into joining her in these foolish schemes⟩ — see FORCE 1

sandwich *vb* to fit (people or things) into a tight space ⟨*sandwiched* six kids into the backseat somehow⟩ — see CROWD 1

sandwich (in *or* **between)** *vb* to put among or between others ⟨could we *sandwich in* one more speaker during the morning session of the conference?⟩ — see INSERT

sandy *adj* of a pale yellow or yellowish brown color ⟨the child with *sandy* hair really stood out among the brunettes⟩ — see BLOND

sane *adj* having full use of one's mind and control over one's actions ⟨the court ruled that the woman was indeed *sane* when she made out her will⟩
synonyms balanced, clearheaded, compos mentis, lucid, normal, right, stable
related words analytic (*or* analytical), clear, coherent, logical, rational, reasonable; even-keeled, judicious, levelheaded, sensible, wise; healthy, sound, unneurotic; well-adjusted, well-balanced
near antonyms balmy, bananas, batty, bughouse [*slang*], certifiable, crackbrained, cracked, crackpot, cranky [*dialect*], cuckoo, daffy, daft, dotty, fruity [*slang*], gaga, loco [*slang*], loony (*also* looney), loopy, meshuga (*or* meshugge *also* meshugah *or* meshuggah), moonstruck, nuts, nutty, scatty [*chiefly British*], screwy, wacko (*also* whacko), wacky (*also* whacky); aberrant, delirious, disordered; delusional, delusionary, disturbed, neurotic, obsessive-compulsive, paranoiac (*also* paranoic), paranoid (*also* paranoidal), psycho, psychotic, schizo, schizoid, schizophrenic, schizy (*or* schizzy); eccentric, odd, oddball, off, pixilated (*also* pixillated), potty [*chiefly British*], queer, strange; foolish, senseless, witless; irrational, mixed-up, unreasonable; depressed, despondent; distracted, distraught, frantic, frenzied, haywire, hysterical (*also* hysteric), raving, wigged-out; amok (*or* amuck), ape, ballistic, berserk, nuclear; fixated, monomaniac, monomaniacal, obsessed
antonyms brainsick, crazed, crazy, demented, deranged, insane, lunatic, mad, maniacal (*also* maniac), mental, unbalanced, unsound

saneness *n* the normal or healthy condition of the mental abilities ⟨a woman of remarkable *saneness*, considering the fact that she had just spent a rainy week in a cabin with four kids⟩ — see MIND 2

sangfroid *n* evenness of emotions or temper ⟨the professional gambler seemed to take both his wins and his losses with remarkable *sangfroid*⟩ — see EQUANIMITY

sanguinary *adj* eager for or marked by the shedding of blood, extreme violence, or killing ⟨a movie so *sanguinary* that I covered my eyes during at least half of it⟩ — see BLOODTHIRSTY

sanguine *adj* **1** eager for or marked by the shedding of blood, extreme violence, or killing ⟨the Civil War remains America's most *sanguine* conflict⟩ — see BLOODTHIRSTY

2 having a healthy reddish skin tone ⟨a baby with a *sanguine* complexion is more likely to leave the hospital early than a sickly-looking one⟩ — see RUDDY

3 having or showing a mind free from doubt ⟨I'm reasonably *sanguine* about the adoption of the latest proposal⟩ — see CERTAIN 2

sanguineous *adj* eager for or marked by the shedding of blood, extreme violence, or killing ⟨in the *sanguineous* culture of ancient Sparta, military glory was prized above all else⟩ — see BLOODTHIRSTY

sanguinity *n* an inclination to believe in the most favorable outcome ⟨Pollyanna had so great a tendency to look for the good in everyone and everything that her name has become a synonym for someone of irrepressible *sanguinity*⟩ — see OPTIMISM

sanitary *adj* free from filth, infection, or dangers to health ⟨the nurse made sure that everything in the room was *sanitary* so that the baby wouldn't get sick⟩

synonyms aseptic, germfree, hygienic, sterile

related words germproof; antibacterial, antibiotic, antiseptic, germicidal, microbicidal; clean, immaculate, pristine, spick-and-span (*or* spic-and-span), spotless, squeaky-clean, stainless, unsoiled, unstained, unsullied; beneficial, healthful, healthy, restorative, salubrious, salutary, salutiferous, wholesome; pure, taintless, undefiled, unpolluted, untainted; abluted, bleached, cleansed, purified, scrubbed, washed, whitened

near antonyms infectious, miasmic, pathogenetic, pathogenic, poisonous, sickening, toxic; bedraggled, besmirched, dingy, dirty, draggled, dusty, filthy, foul, grimy, grubby, grungy, mucky, muddy, nasty, smirched, soiled, sordid, stained, sullied, unclean, uncleanly, unwashed; insalubrious, noxious, unhealthful, unhealthy, unwholesome; defiled, polluted, tainted, unsterilized

antonyms germy, insanitary, unhygienic, unsanitary, unsterile

sanitary landfill *n* a place where discarded materials (as trash) are dumped ⟨even after many years in *sanitary landfills*, disposable diapers have proven to be resistant to decomposition⟩ — see DUMP 1

sanity *n* the normal or healthy condition of the mental abilities ⟨these working conditions are threatening my *sanity*!⟩ — see MIND 2

sans *prep* not having ⟨anyone *sans* shirt will not be allowed in the restaurant⟩ — see WITHOUT 1

sap *n* **1** active strength of body or mind ⟨a child full of *sap* and vivacity⟩ — see VIGOR 1

2 one who is easily deceived or cheated ⟨some poor *sap* would probably fall for that telephone scam⟩ — see [1]DUPE

3 a heavy rigid stick used as a weapon or for punishment ⟨the sadistic prison guards freely used their *saps* to enforce discipline⟩ — see CLUB 1

4 the condition of being sound in body ⟨I may no longer have the *sap* of youth, but I do have the sapience that comes only with advanced years⟩ — see HEALTH 1

sap *vb* to diminish the physical strength of ⟨weeks of hard work had *sapped* her and left her exhausted⟩ — see WEAKEN 1

saphead *n* a stupid person ⟨an important diplomatic post that is no place for a *saphead*⟩ — see IDIOT

sapience *n* the ability to understand inner qualities or relationships ⟨the kind of *sapience* that comes from a lifetime of experience as an educator⟩ — see WISDOM 1

sapient *adj* having or showing deep understanding and intelligent application of knowledge ⟨an uncle who is always good for valuable insights and some *sapient* advice⟩ — see WISE 1

sapped *adj* lacking bodily strength ⟨I was completely *sapped* after the first day of hauling logs⟩ — see WEAK 1

sappiness *n* the state or quality of having an excess of tender feelings (as of love, nostalgia, or compassion) ⟨the over-the-top *sappiness* of the verse on the Valentine's Day card⟩ — see SENTIMENTALITY

sappy *adj* **1** appealing to the emotions in an obvious and tiresome way ⟨a *sappy* letter filled with silly romantic clichés⟩ — see CORNY 1

2 showing or marked by a lack of good sense or judgment ⟨a *sappy* plan to try to get her divorced parents back together again⟩ — see FOOLISH 1

sarcasm *n* an act or expression showing scorn and usually intended to hurt another's feelings ⟨I know you're not happy, but there's no need to resort to petty *sarcasms* to make your point⟩ — see INSULT

sarcastic *adj* marked by the use of wit that is intended to cause hurt feelings ⟨her *sarcastic* comments that my singing reminded her of the time her dog was sick⟩

synonyms acerb, acerbic, acid, acidic, acidulous, acrid, barbed, biting, caustic, corrosive, cutting, mordant, pungent, sardonic, satiric (*or* satirical), scalding, scathing, sharp, smart-aleck, smart-alecky, smart-mouthed, snarky, tart

related words brisk, cross, sharp-tongued, sour, sourish, spiky (*also* spikey), tartish; incisive, keen, poignant, trenchant; cynical, dry, ironic (*also* ironical), wry; facetious, flippant, tongue-in-cheek; acrimonious, bitter, resentful, vitriolic; harsh, rough, severe, stringent; abrupt, blunt, brusque (*also* brusk), concise, crisp, curt, gruff, pithy, snippety, snippy, succinct, terse; backhanded, insincere

near antonyms amusing, droll, merry, playful, sportive, waggish; gentle, mild; bland; good-humored, good-natured; diplomatic, polite, smooth, suave, urbane; affable, cordial, genial, gracious, hospitable, sociable

sarcophagus *n* a boxlike container for holding a dead body ⟨the crypt under the abbey church contains the *sarcophagus* of the monastery's founding abbot⟩ — see COFFIN

sardonic *adj* marked by the use of wit that is intended to cause hurt feelings ⟨a *sardonic* little jab that made her visitor quiet and subdued for the rest of the night⟩ — see SARCASTIC

sash *n* a strip of flexible material (as leather) worn around the waist ⟨a dress with a flowered silk *sash*⟩ — see [2]BELT 1

sashay *n* a short trip for pleasure ⟨just a little weekend *sashay* we took to get away from it all⟩ — see EXCURSION 1

sashay *vb* to walk with exaggerated arm and leg movements ⟨the svelte young models *sashayed* down the catwalk with practiced insouciance⟩ — see STRUT 1

sass *n* disrespectful or argumentative talk given in response to a command or request ⟨an old-fashioned diner where getting *sass* from the waitstaff is part of the experience⟩ — see BACK TALK

sassy *adj* displaying or marked by rude boldness ⟨*sassy* kids shouting, "Out of our way, you old geezer!"⟩ — see NERVY 1

Satan *n* the supreme personification of evil often represented as the ruler of hell ⟨some people believe that *Satan* can successfully tempt almost anyone with lies and flattery⟩ — see DEVIL 1

satanic *adj* of, relating to, or worthy of an evil spirit

⟨the cat's eyes reflected a *satanic* red in the dark⟩ — see FIENDISH 1

sate *vb* **1** to fill with food to capacity ⟨I *sated* myself with an array of diet-busting offerings from the dessert table⟩ — see GORGE 1

2 to put a complete end to (a physical need or desire) ⟨a huge meal that should have *sated* everyone's hunger⟩ — see SATISFY 1

sated *adj* having one's appetite completely satisfied ⟨the *sated* baby fell instantly to sleep⟩ — see FULL 3

satiate *adj* having one's appetite completely satisfied ⟨a couple of *satiate* dinner guests had ensconced themselves on the living room sofa⟩ — see FULL 3

satiate *vb* to put a complete end to (a physical need or desire) ⟨a long drink of water at last *satiated* my thirst⟩ — see SATISFY 1

satiated *adj* having one's appetite completely satisfied ⟨he was too *satiated* even to consider the proffered cookie⟩ — see FULL 3

satin *adj* **1** having a shiny surface or finish ⟨*satin* paint⟩ — see GLOSSY

2 smooth or delicate in appearance or feel ⟨the *satin* petals of a rose⟩ — see SOFT 2

satiny *adj* **1** having a shiny surface or finish ⟨the *satiny* short coat of an Arabian horse⟩ — see GLOSSY

2 smooth or delicate in appearance or feel ⟨a lovely *satiny* fabric that feels so good next to the skin⟩ — see SOFT 2

satire *n* a creative work that uses sharp humor to point up the foolishness of a person, institution, or human nature in general ⟨a *satire* about the music industry in which a handsome but untalented youth is turned into a rock star⟩

synonyms lampoon, pasquinade

related words burlesque, caricature, parody, spoof, takeoff; comedy, farce, sketch, skit, slapstick, squib; derision, ridicule; cartoon, mockery, travesty

satiric *or* **satirical** *adj* marked by the use of wit that is intended to cause hurt feelings ⟨a *satiric* story about the movie business⟩ — see SARCASTIC

satisfaction *n* **1** the feeling experienced when one's wishes are met ⟨readers will close the covers of this mystery novel with complete *satisfaction*⟩ — see PLEASURE 1

2 payment to another for a loss or injury ⟨he's demanding *satisfaction* from his neighbor for running over his prize tulips⟩ — see COMPENSATION 1

3 a state of mind in which one is free from doubt ⟨he proved to my *satisfaction* that he could not have done it⟩ — see CONFIDENCE 2

satisfactorily *adv* **1** in a satisfactory way ⟨the matter has been resolved *satisfactorily*⟩ — see WELL 1

2 in or to a degree or quantity that meets one's requirements or satisfaction ⟨supplied us *satisfactorily*, if not lavishly, with meals during our stay⟩ — see ENOUGH 1

satisfactoriness *n* the quality or state of meeting one's needs adequately ⟨the overall *satisfactoriness* of the service led us to leave a reasonable tip⟩ — see SUFFICIENCY

satisfactory *adj* **1** being to one's liking ⟨we found the meal most *satisfactory*⟩

synonyms agreeable, all right, alright, copacetic (*also* copasetic *or* copesetic), ducky, fine, good, hunky-dory, jake [*slang*], OK (*or* okay), palatable

related words delectable, delicious, delightful, dreamy, felicitous, gratifying, nice, pleasant, pleasing, scrumptious, welcome; acceptable, adequate, decent, passable, tolerable

near antonyms bad, deficient, inferior, lousy, poor, punk, substandard, unacceptable, wanting, wretched; mediocre, middling, second-class, second-rate

antonyms disagreeable, unsatisfactory

2 of a level of quality that meets one's needs or standards ⟨the newlyweds' first attempt at cooking dinner was actually quite *satisfactory*⟩ — see ADEQUATE

satisfied *adj* **1** experiencing pleasure, satisfaction, or delight ⟨*satisfied* customers tend to come back over and over⟩ — see GLAD 1

2 feeling that one's needs or desires have been met ⟨a *satisfied* vacationer is one who has spent the time doing exactly what he or she wanted⟩ — see CONTENT

satisfy *vb* **1** to put a complete end to (a physical need or desire) ⟨the players *satisfied* their hunger after the game with a big pasta dinner⟩

synonyms assuage, quench, sate, satiate, slake

related words cater (to), gratify, humor, indulge; alleviate, lighten, relieve; cloy, saturate, surfeit

near antonyms arouse, excite, pique, stimulate; tantalize, tease

2 to cause (someone) to agree with a belief or course of action by using arguments or earnest requests ⟨it took me a while to *satisfy* my attorney that I had good grounds for a lawsuit⟩ — see PERSUADE

3 to do what is required by the terms of ⟨the contractor had clearly failed to *satisfy* the terms of the agreement⟩ — see FULFILL 1

4 to give satisfaction to ⟨a hot dinner and a relaxing massage never fails to *satisfy* her husband⟩ — see PLEASE 1

5 to provide (someone) with a just payment for loss or injury ⟨the owners of the restaurant were generously *satisfied* for any business lost during the filming⟩ — see COMPENSATE 1

satisfying *adj* **1** giving pleasure or contentment to the mind or senses ⟨a *satisfying* and relaxing bubble bath after a long day⟩ — see PLEASANT 1

2 having the power to persuade ⟨"I don't feel like it" is not a *satisfying* reason for skipping your chores⟩ — see COGENT

3 making one feel good inside ⟨received many *satisfying* compliments on her gardening efforts⟩ — see HEARTWARMING

satisfyingly *adv* in a pleasing way ⟨capped the story with a *satisfyingly* happy ending⟩ — see WELL 5

saturate *vb* to wet thoroughly with liquid ⟨*saturate* your hair with water before applying the dye⟩ — see SOAK 1

saturate *adj* containing, covered with, or thoroughly penetrated by water ⟨the test will only work if the sample cloth is *saturate* with solution⟩ — see WET 1

saturated *adj* containing, covered with, or thoroughly penetrated by water ⟨the carpet should be damp but not entirely *saturated*⟩ — see WET 1

saturnine *adj* causing or marked by an atmosphere lacking in cheer ⟨the men awaiting interrogation by the police shared a *saturnine* silence⟩ — see GLOOMY 1

satyr *n* a man given to seducing women ⟨the legendary conquests of a suburban *satyr*⟩ — see DON JUAN

satyric *adj* having a strong sexual desire ⟨*satyric* frat boys letting loose in the annual bacchanalia known as spring break⟩ — see LUSTFUL

sauce *n* **1** a savory fluid food used as a topping or accompaniment to a main dish ⟨the chef poured *sauce* over the meat just before he served it⟩

synonyms dressing, gravy

related words condiment, relish, seasoning; fixing(s), garnish, topping; dip, marinade

2 disrespectful or argumentative talk given in response to a command or request ⟨if you put up with any *sauce* from them, they'll only get worse⟩ — see BACK TALK

3 shameless boldness ⟨the woman was shocked by the *sauce* of the child who ran right up to her and asked for money⟩ — see EFFRONTERY

4 *slang* a distilled beverage that can make a person

drunk ⟨as soon as she returned home from the graveyard shift, she'd be hitting the *sauce*⟩ — see ALCOHOL

sauciness *n* shameless boldness ⟨it takes an incredible amount of *sauciness* to ask a total stranger what her age is⟩ — see EFFRONTERY

saucy *adj* displaying or marked by rude boldness ⟨irritated his fellow travelers with *saucy* questions and comments⟩ — see NERVY 1

saunter *n* a relaxed journey on foot for exercise or pleasure ⟨tourists on a morning *saunter* around the old section of the city⟩ — see WALK 1

saunter *vb* to travel by foot for exercise or pleasure ⟨he lazily *saunters* about the French countryside, mostly photographing birds and flowers⟩ — see HIKE 1

sausage *n* a rod-shaped portion of seasoned ground meat in a casing ⟨a couple of *sausages* and eggs make a good breakfast⟩
synonyms banger [*British*], link, wurst
related words bologna, frank, frankfurter, hot dog, kielbasa, knockwurst (*also* knackwurst), liver sausage (*also* liver pudding), liverwurst, pepperoni, salami, Vienna sausage, weenie, wiener (*also* weiner), wienerwurst; blood sausage (*also* blood pudding)

savage *n* **1** a mean, evil, or unprincipled person ⟨what kind of *savage* would hurt a baby?⟩ — see VILLAIN 1
2 an uncivilized person ⟨inhabitants of exotic lands were invariably portrayed by early travel writers as *savages*⟩ — see HEATHEN 2

savage *adj* **1** not civilized ⟨Tarzan is usually portrayed as a noble but *savage* warrior of the jungle⟩
synonyms barbarian, barbaric, barbarous, heathen, heathenish, natural, Neanderthal (*or* Neandertal), rude, uncivil, uncivilized, uncultivated, wild
related words coarse, crude, primitive, rough; uncouth, uncultured
near antonyms cultured, enlightened, humane, sophisticated; genteel, polished, polite, refined, urbane, well-bred; semicivilized
antonyms civilized
2 having or showing the desire to inflict severe pain and suffering on others ⟨a *savage* attack on a helpless person⟩ — see CRUEL 1
3 living outdoors without taming or domestication by humans ⟨*savage* beasts that seemed threatening to the tourists⟩ — see WILD 1
4 violently unfriendly or aggressive in disposition ⟨early explorers avoided those areas that were rumored to be inhabited by *savage* natives⟩ — see FIERCE 1

savage *vb* to criticize harshly and usually publicly ⟨book reviewers mercilessly *savaged* his latest novel⟩ — see ATTACK 2

savageness *n* disposition to willfully inflict pain and suffering on others ⟨the unthinkable *savageness* that must be required to torture a prisoner⟩ — see CRUELTY

savagery *n* disposition to willfully inflict pain and suffering on others ⟨a study of the *savagery* shown by soldiers in wartime⟩ — see CRUELTY

savanna *also* **savannah** *n* a broad area of level or rolling treeless country ⟨lions roaming the *savanna*⟩ — see PLAIN 1

savant *n* a person of deep wisdom or learning ⟨a *savant* in the field of medical ethics⟩ — see SAGE

save *prep* not including ⟨everyone *save* me is going to the party⟩ — see EXCEPT

save *vb* **1** to free from the penalties or consequences of sin ⟨the Christian belief that Jesus lived and died to *save* humanity⟩
synonyms deliver, redeem
related words reclaim, reform; forgive, pardon, remit, shrive; bless, hallow; consecrate, purify, sanctify
2 to remove from danger or harm ⟨the firefighters managed to *save* the family just as the burning building was collapsing⟩
synonyms bail out, bring off, deliver, rescue
related words salvage; emancipate, free, liberate, manumit, release; disentangle, extricate; recover
antonyms adventure, compromise, endanger, gamble (with), hazard, imperil, jeopardize, peril, risk, venture
3 to avoid unnecessary waste or expense ⟨we'll have to scrimp and *save* to be able to afford college⟩ — see ECONOMIZE
4 to keep in good condition ⟨lovingly *saved* the classic car and even upgraded its engine⟩ — see MAINTAIN 1
5 to keep or intend for a special purpose ⟨I'm *saving* this dress for a formal occasion⟩ — see DEVOTE 1

saver *n* one that saves from danger or destruction ⟨of all the *savers* of Jews during the Holocaust, none was more heroic than the Swedish diplomat Raoul Wallenberg⟩ — see SAVIOR

saving *conj* if it were not for the fact that ⟨I would be ready, *saving* the fact that I can't find my missing shoe⟩ — see EXCEPT

saving *prep* not including ⟨*saving* three members, the club is now fully committed to the fund-raising project⟩ — see EXCEPT

savior *or* **saviour** *n* one that saves from danger or destruction ⟨the policeman proved to be our *savior*, arriving on the scene just as we were about to be mugged⟩
synonyms deliverer, redeemer, rescuer, saver
related words custodian, defender, guard, guardian, keeper, lookout, protector, sentinel, sentry, warden, warder, watch, watcher, watchman; ransomer; salvager, salvor

savor *also* **savour** *n* **1** the property of a substance that can be identified by the sense of taste ⟨a gourmet who can identify the ingredients in any dish solely by their *savor*⟩ — see TASTE 1
2 the quality of being delicious ⟨the wonderful *savor* of Mom's apple pie⟩ — see DELICIOUSNESS

savor *also* **savour** *vb* **1** to make more pleasant to the taste by adding something intensely flavored ⟨cuisine that has been generously *savored* with southern India's rich array of spices⟩ — see SEASON 1
2 to take pleasure in ⟨as a terminal cancer patient, she's vowed to *savor* every moment of the time she has left⟩ — see ENJOY 1

savoriness *n* the quality of being delicious ⟨the *savoriness* of freshly baked bread simply cannot be overrated⟩ — see DELICIOUSNESS

savorless *adj* lacking in taste or flavor ⟨the white rice was filling, but rather *savorless*⟩ — see INSIPID 1

savory *also* **savoury** *adj* **1** having a pleasant smell ⟨cedar is one of the most *savory* of all woods⟩ — see FRAGRANT
2 very pleasing to the sense of taste ⟨a *savory* beef stew that really hit the spot⟩ — see DELICIOUS 1
3 giving pleasure or contentment to the mind or senses ⟨having to fire someone was not a task that the manager found at all *savory*⟩ — see PLEASANT 1
4 sharp and pleasantly stimulating to the mind or senses ⟨a *savory* new book on a subject that seemingly had been done to death⟩ — see PIQUANT

savvy *n* knowledge gained by actually doing or living through something ⟨she's an excellent scholar of political science, but lacks the kind of *savvy* needed to run for public office⟩ — see EXPERIENCE 1

savvy *adj* having or showing a practical cleverness or judgment ⟨a particularly *savvy* investor, he was among the first to see the potential in tech stocks⟩ — see SHREWD 1

savvy *vb* to have a clear idea of ⟨the man growled, "Don't ever date my daughter again—you *savvy*?"⟩ — see COMPREHEND 1

saw *n* an often stated observation regarding something from common experience ⟨it's an old *saw* that a red sunset presages fair skies the next day⟩ — see SAYING

sawbones *n, slang* a person specially trained in healing human medical disorders ⟨a real old-timer who remembers when you could expect a *sawbones* to make a house call⟩ — see DOCTOR

sawed–off *adj* having relatively little height ⟨he was an unpleasant, *sawed-off* man who seemed to believe that aggressiveness could make up for his perceived deficiency⟩ — see SHORT 1

saw–toothed *adj* notched or toothed along the edge ⟨a *saw-toothed* barrette⟩ — see SERRATED

say *adv* close to but not exactly ⟨a person consumes, *say*, 2000 calories a day⟩ — see APPROXIMATELY

say *n* the right to express a wish, choice, or opinion ⟨even if they decide otherwise, at least I had my *say*⟩ — see VOICE 1

say *vb* **1** to express (a thought or emotion) in words ⟨why don't you just *say* what's on your mind?⟩

synonyms articulate, bring out, enunciate, pass, speak, state, talk, tell, utter, verbalize, vocalize

related words air, discuss, give, look, share, sound, vent, ventilate, voice; blabber, bolt, blurt, get off, shoot; advertise, announce, blaze, broadcast, declare, post, proclaim, promulgate, publicize, publish; affirm, allege, assert, aver, avouch, avow; breathe, chirp, drawl, gasp, lip, mouth, murmur, purr, shout, splutter, spout, whisper; clothe, couch, formulate, formulize, phrase, put, word; comment, pipe up (with), remark; rip (out), snarl

phrases put into words

near antonyms stifle, suppress

2 to convey in appropriate or telling terms ⟨I'm not quite sure how to *say* this, but that's the worst essay I've ever read⟩ — see PHRASE

3 to give from memory ⟨*say* your prayers⟩ — see REPEAT 2

4 to take as true or as a fact without actual proof ⟨let's *say*, for the sake of argument, that this is true⟩ — see ASSUME 2

saying *n* an often stated observation regarding something from common experience ⟨there's an old *saying* that you should let sleeping dogs lie⟩

synonyms adage, aphorism, apothegm, byword, epigram, maxim, proverb, saw, sententia, word

related words bromide, cliché (*also* cliche), commonplace, platitude, wheeze; expression, felicity; axiom, motto, precept, truism, truth; formula; comment, note, reflection, remark

say–so *n* the right to express a wish, choice, or opinion ⟨some of the members complained they didn't have any *say-so* in how the organization spent its funds⟩ — see VOICE 1

scabby *adj* arousing or deserving of one's loathing and disgust ⟨that's a *scabby* trick to play on someone trying to help⟩ — see CONTEMPTIBLE 1

scads *n pl* a considerable amount ⟨*scads* of people showed up for the party⟩ — see LOT 2

scalawag *or* **scallywag** *n* a mean, evil, or unprincipled person ⟨a *scalawag* who had taken to begging on street corners while posing as a blind person⟩ — see VILLAIN

scalding *adj* **1** having a notably high temperature ⟨the *scalding* water of a geyser⟩ — see HOT 1

2 marked by the use of wit that is intended to cause hurt feelings ⟨*scalding* reviews for the overproduced horror movie⟩ — see SARCASTIC

[1]**scale** *n* a device for measuring weight ⟨I hate getting on the bathroom *scale*⟩

synonyms balance

related words gravimeter

[2]**scale** *n* a small thin piece of material that resembles an animal scale ⟨*scales* of mica were embedded in the granite⟩

synonyms lamella, lamina, plate

related words chip, flake, sliver, splint, splinter; leaf, sheet, slice

[3]**scale** *n* **1** a scheme of rank or order ⟨a student who scored very highly on a standard intelligence *scale*⟩

synonyms graduation, hierarchy, ladder, ordering, ranking

related words food chain, pecking order (*also* peck order); arrangement, array, disposal, disposition, distribution, sequence, series, setup; degree, echelon, footing, level, place, position, reaches, rung, situation, spot, standing, station, status

2 the distance or extent between possible extremes ⟨with the *scale* going from one to ten, what did you think of the movie?⟩ — see RANGE 3

scale *vb* to find out the size, extent, or amount of ⟨*scaled* the logs to get a rough idea of the amount of usable lumber they were likely to yield⟩ — see MEASURE 1

scaled *adj* composed of or covered with scales ⟨the fossilized form of a *scaled* reptile from the Triassic period⟩ — see SCALY

scaly *adj* composed of or covered with scales ⟨the snake's *scaly* skin was dry to the touch⟩

synonyms scaled, squamous

related words scalelike

near antonyms smooth

antonyms scaleless

scam *n* an instance of the use of dishonest methods to acquire something of value ⟨that's just a *scam* to bilk insurance companies for staged accidents⟩ — see FRAUD 1

scammer *n* a dishonest person who uses clever means to cheat others out of something of value ⟨Internet *scammers* who never seem to run out of swindles⟩ — see TRICKSTER 1

scamp *n* **1** an appealingly mischievous person ⟨those little *scamps* are always getting into trouble, but no one has the heart to punish them⟩

synonyms devil, hellion, imp, mischief, monkey, rapscallion, rascal, rogue, urchin

related words cutup, larker, madcap, skylarker; ragamuffin; brat, disrupter, misbehaver, nuisance; juvenile delinquent; gamin, gamine

near antonyms beast, boor, cad, churl, clown, creep, cretin, cur, heel, joker, louse, lout, skunk, snake, stinkard, stinker; knave, miscreant, reprobate, scalawag (*or* scallywag), scapegrace, scoundrel, varlet, villain

2 a mean, evil, or unprincipled person ⟨an insincere and ruthlessly ambitious *scamp* who was willing to do anything to win the reality show's grand prize⟩ — see VILLAIN

scamper *vb* to go at a pace faster than a walk ⟨the child *scampered* off to play⟩ — see RUN 1

scampish *adj* tending to or exhibiting reckless playfulness ⟨warned the *scampish* youth that those frat-boy pranks could get him into real trouble someday⟩ — see MISCHIEVOUS 1

scamster *n* a dishonest person who uses clever means to cheat others out of something of value ⟨an ever-growing swarm of *scamsters* of which the Internet user should be wary⟩ — see TRICKSTER 1

scan *n* a close look at or over someone or something in order to judge condition ⟨gave the car a good *scan* to see if it was worth buying⟩ — see INSPECTION

scan *vb* to look over closely (as for judging quality or condition) ⟨*scanned* the manuscript carefully for any overlooked errors⟩ — see INSPECT

scandal *n* a cause of shame ⟨a *scandal* that for many years haunted the family of the banker convicted of embezzlement⟩ — see DISGRACE 2

scandalous *adj* **1** causing intense displeasure, disgust, or resentment ⟨the *scandalous* news that police officers had been taking bribes⟩ — see OFFENSIVE 1

2 causing or intended to cause unjust injury to a person's good name ⟨spread a *scandalous* rumor about a coworker that almost cost him his job⟩ — see LIBELOUS

scant *adj* less plentiful than what is normal, necessary, or desirable ⟨jobs for teenagers were *scant* that summer⟩ — see MEAGER

scant *vb* to use or give out in stingy amounts ⟨don't *scant* the peanut butter on those sandwiches!⟩ — see SPARE 1

scantiness *n* a falling short of an essential or desirable amount or number ⟨the *scantiness* of grass meant that we had to feed the cows extra hay⟩ — see DEFICIENCY

scanty *adj* less plentiful than what is normal, necessary, or desirable ⟨the camera's *scanty* instructions left me somewhat confused⟩ — see MEAGER

scape *vb* to get or keep away from (as a responsibility) through cleverness or trickery ⟨the queen has vowed that none of the traitors shall *scape* the gallows, be their station ever so high⟩ — see ESCAPE 2

scapegoat *n* a person or thing taking the blame for others ⟨companies often use the economy as a *scapegoat* to avoid taking responsibility for dropping sales⟩

synonyms fall guy, goat, whipping boy

related words victim; butt, dupe, fool, laughingstock, mark, mockery, monkey; excuse

scapegrace *n* a mean, evil, or unprincipled person ⟨a whoring, drunken *scapegrace* who was blackening the family's name⟩ — see VILLAIN

[1]**scar** *n* something that spoils the appearance or completeness of a thing ⟨the *scars* left by carelessly scratching the car door with one's keys⟩ — see BLEMISH

[2]**scar** *n* a steep wall of rock, earth, or ice ⟨at the next bend in the river, a *scar* of red sandstone steeply rises to over 100 feet⟩ — see CLIFF

scarce *adj* **1** less plentiful than what is normal, necessary, or desirable ⟨food was a bit *scarce* last winter⟩ — see MEAGER

2 not coming up to an expected measure or meeting a particular need ⟨help is always *scarce* in the resort town during the busy summer season⟩ — see SHORT 3

scarcely *adv* **1** by a very small margin ⟨was *scarcely* able to walk after the near-fatal accident⟩ — see JUST 2

2 certainly not ⟨I *scarcely* think that one person being sick is an "epidemic"⟩ — see HARDLY 2

scarceness *n* a falling short of an essential or desirable amount or number ⟨the continuing *scarceness* of supplies means that we will have to ration ourselves⟩ — see DEFICIENCY

scarcity *n* a falling short of an essential or desirable amount or number ⟨the *scarcity* of good restaurants around here is surprising⟩ — see DEFICIENCY

scare *vb* to strike with fear ⟨thunderstorms have always *scared* her⟩ — see FRIGHTEN

scare *n* the emotion experienced in the presence or threat of danger ⟨fired over their heads in order to throw a *scare* into them⟩ — see FEAR 1

scared *adj* filled with fear or dread ⟨at the sight of the grizzly bear he froze, being too *scared* to even run away⟩ — see AFRAID

scare up *vb* to come upon after searching, study, or effort ⟨I can probably *scare up* my old textbooks if you need them⟩ — see FIND 1

scarf *vb* to swallow or eat greedily ⟨the college students *scarfed* the entire contents of the care package in one sitting⟩ — see GOBBLE

scarify *vb* to strike with fear ⟨that foolish woman would be *scarified* by a mouse⟩ — see FRIGHTEN

scarp *n* a steep wall of rock, earth, or ice ⟨years of violent ocean storms had heavily eroded the beach, creating a *scarp* along one end of it⟩ — see CLIFF

scarper *vb, British* to leave a place often for another ⟨I went looking for Sally at the pub, but she'd *scarpered*⟩ — see GO 2

scary *adj* **1** causing fear ⟨a *scary* movie that gave the child nightmares for weeks afterwards⟩ — see FEARFUL 1

2 easily frightened ⟨a *scary* horse who spooked and kicked at its own shadow⟩ — see SHY 1

3 filled with fear or dread ⟨I got a little *scary* when I heard the noise in the basement⟩ — see AFRAID

scat *n* solid matter discharged from an animal's alimentary canal ⟨a tracker who could identify any animal from its *scat* alone⟩ — see DROPPING 1

scathe *vb* to criticize harshly and usually publicly ⟨newspaper cartoonists *scathed* the lecherous governor with a series of cruel caricatures⟩ — see ATTACK 2

scathing *adj* marked by the use of wit that is intended to cause hurt feelings ⟨a *scathing* rebuttal of the latest theory concerning the assassination⟩ — see SARCASTIC

scatter *n* a small number ⟨played before only a *scatter* of spectators in that huge stadium⟩ — see FEW

scatter *vb* **1** to cause (members of a group) to move widely apart ⟨the noise of the backfiring car *scattered* the pigeons⟩

synonyms clear out, disband, dispel, disperse, dissipate, squander

related words break up, isolate, part, segregate, separate, split (up); diffuse, disseminate, diverge, spread

near antonyms agglutinate, conglomerate; unify, unite

antonyms assemble, cluster, collect, concentrate, congregate, gather, ingather

2 to cover by or as if by scattering something over or on ⟨the hillside was *scattered* with boulders deposited by the last ice age⟩

synonyms bestrew, dot, pepper, sow, spot, spray, sprinkle, strew

related words blanket, drizzle, dust; stud; dapple, fleck, speckle, stipple; bespatter, spatter

3 to go off in different directions and cease to exist as a body or unified whole ⟨these drunken revelers will quickly *scatter* when the police arrive⟩ — see DISPERSE 1

scatterbrain *n* a silly flighty person ⟨don't be such a *scatterbrain*—it's only a wedding, not the invasion of Normandy⟩ — see FLIBBERTIGIBBET

scatterbrained *adj* lacking in seriousness or maturity ⟨a *scatterbrained* child who couldn't seem to pay attention or stop fooling around⟩ — see GIDDY 1

scattered *adj* lacking a definite plan, purpose, or pattern ⟨a hodgepodge of *scattered* ideas that didn't add up to a clear hypothesis⟩ — see RANDOM

scattering *n* **1** an act or process in which something scatters or is scattered ⟨the *scattering* of the protesters suddenly turned violent and chaotic⟩

synonyms disbandment, dispersal, dispersion, dissipation

related words diffusion, dissemination; breakup, dissolution, disunion, separation, split

near antonyms assembly, collection, concentration, gathering

2 a small number ⟨a *scattering* of people in the mostly empty theater⟩ — see FEW

scatty *adj, chiefly British* having or showing a very abnormal or sick state of mind ⟨any number of individuals have been fingered as the *scatty* serial killer known to history as Jack the Ripper⟩ — see INSANE 1

scenario *n* the written form of a story prepared for film production ⟨submitted a *scenario* to the producers⟩ — see SCREENPLAY

scene *n* **1** the place and time in which the action for a

portion of a dramatic work (as a movie) is set ⟨the first *scene* was the kitchen of a fancy restaurant during dinner⟩
synonyms background, locale, setting
related words backdrop, scenery, set; mise-en-scène, tableau
2 an outburst or display of excited anger ⟨please don't make a *scene* while we're at the restaurant⟩ — see TANTRUM
3 position with regard to conditions and circumstances ⟨one of the leading figures in the current political *scene*⟩ — see SITUATION 1
4 the array of painted backgrounds and furnishings used to establish the setting in a stage production ⟨helped build and paint *scenes* for the school play⟩ — see SCENERY

scenery *n* the array of painted backgrounds and furnishings used to establish the setting in a stage production ⟨the musical was worth seeing just for the elaborate *scenery*⟩
synonyms decor (*or* décor), mise-en-scène, scene, set
related words backdrop, drop; background; set piece; prop, property

scent *n* **1** a sweet or pleasant smell ⟨the delightful *scent* of her perfume⟩ — see FRAGRANCE
2 the quality of a thing that makes it perceptible to the sense organs in the nose ⟨dogs are able to detect *scents* that are far below the threshold detectable by the human nose⟩ — see SMELL 1

scent *vb* **1** to fill or infuse with a pleasant odor or odor-releasing substance ⟨fancy bars of soap *scented* with lavender⟩
synonyms incense, odorize, perfume
near antonyms deodorize
antonyms stink up
2 to become aware of by means of the sense organs in the nose ⟨the dog *scented* a rabbit and suddenly took off⟩ — see SMELL 1
3 to have a vague awareness of ⟨he *scented* danger⟩ — see FEEL 1

scented *adj* having a pleasant smell ⟨a bowl of *scented* petals used to perfume a room⟩ — see FRAGRANT

schedule *n* **1** a listing of things to be presented or considered (as at a concert or play) ⟨the *schedule* of events for the conference⟩ — see PROGRAM 1
2 a record of a series of items (as names or titles) usually arranged according to some system ⟨a *schedule* of arrivals and departures⟩ — see [1]LIST

schedule *vb* to put (someone or something) on a list ⟨I've *scheduled* you for an appointment tomorrow⟩ — see [1]LIST 2

scheduled *adj* being in accordance with the prescribed, normal, or logical course of events ⟨a *scheduled* stop for the train⟩ — see DUE 2

scheme *n* **1** a clever often underhanded means to achieve an end ⟨an e-mail *scheme* to trick unwary Internet users into disclosing passwords and financial information⟩ — see TRICK 1
2 a secret plan for accomplishing evil or unlawful ends ⟨a *scheme* to kidnap the president's daughter⟩ — see PLOT 1
3 a method worked out in advance for achieving some objective ⟨a *scheme* to upgrade the city's mass transit system⟩ — see PLAN 1

scheme *vb* to engage in a secret plan to accomplish evil or unlawful ends ⟨the town inspector had *schemed* to overlook the contractor's code violations in exchange for a substantial bribe⟩ — see PLOT

scheme (out) *vb* to work out the details of (something) in advance ⟨the campaign operatives *schemed out* a plan for dealing with bombshells about the candidate's past indiscretions⟩ — see PLAN 1

scheming *adj* clever at attaining one's ends by indirect and often deceptive means ⟨the novel is about an elderly man and his *scheming* son who is impatient to inherit the family fortune⟩ — see ARTFUL 1

schism *n* **1** a lack of agreement or harmony ⟨*schism* within the charitable organization was preventing it from achieving its goals⟩ — see DISCORD
2 the act or process of a whole separating into two or more parts or pieces ⟨the *schism* of the Christian church into the Roman Catholic and Eastern Orthodox churches⟩ — see SEPARATION 1

schlock *or* **schlocky** *also* **shlock** *or* **shlocky** *adj* of low quality ⟨a tourist trap selling *schlock* souvenirs⟩ — see CHEAP 2

schlub *also* **shlub** *n, slang* a stupid person ⟨you're a complete *schlub*—you should do great around here⟩ — see IDIOT

schmaltz *also* **schmalz** *n* something (as a work of literature or music) that is too sentimental ⟨the love song was a typical example of overproduced *schmaltz*⟩ — see CORN

schmaltzy *adj* appealing to the emotions in an obvious and tiresome way ⟨a *schmaltzy* television commercial featuring a photogenic, perfect family⟩ — see CORNY 1

schmooze *n* friendly, informal conversation or an instance of this ⟨had to master the art of the *schmooze* if she wanted to get ahead in the business⟩ — see CHAT 1

schmooze *or* **shmooze** *vb* to engage in casual or rambling conversation ⟨spent every spare minute of the conference *schmoozing* with the industry's power players⟩ — see CHAT 1

schmuck *n, slang* a person whose behavior is offensive to others ⟨don't be a *schmuck* and create an embarrassing scene in public⟩ — see JERK 1

schnook *n, slang* a stupid person ⟨don't be a *schnook* and just stand there while your mother needs help⟩ — see IDIOT

schnoz *or* **schnozz** *n, slang* the part of the face bearing the nostrils and nasal cavity ⟨another smart remark like that and you'll get a bop on the *schnoz*⟩ — see NOSE 1

schnozzle *n, slang* the part of the face bearing the nostrils and nasal cavity ⟨endowed with a *schnozzle* as big as his talent, the comedian Jimmy Durante was affectionately dubbed "the Schnozzola"⟩ — see NOSE 1

scholar *n* **1** a person of deep wisdom or learning ⟨*scholars* have long debated whether there is ever such a thing as a truly selfless act⟩ — see SAGE
2 a person with a high level of knowledge or skill in a field ⟨a *scholar* who is a specialist in the history of ancient Greece⟩ — see EXPERT
3 one who attends a school ⟨a competition for promising young *scholars* from across the country⟩ — see STUDENT

scholarly *adj* **1** having or displaying advanced knowledge or education ⟨a *scholarly* analysis of the historical document⟩ — see EDUCATED 1
2 of or relating to schooling or learning especially at an advanced level ⟨a *scholarly* essay making comparisons between 18th-century French authors and their German counterparts⟩ — see ACADEMIC 1

scholarship *n* the understanding and information gained from being educated ⟨the historian's new book displays a remarkable level of *scholarship*⟩ — see EDUCATION 2

scholastic *adj* of or relating to schooling or learning especially at an advanced level ⟨a college that gives a higher priority to *scholastic* endeavors than to athletic pursuits⟩ — see ACADEMIC 1

school *vb* to cause to acquire knowledge or skill in some field ⟨*schooled* their children in proper etiquette for formal occasions⟩ — see TEACH

school *n* a place or establishment for teaching and

learning ⟨one of the first *schools* in the country to admit girls as students⟩
synonyms academe, academy, seminary
related words boarding school, prep, preparatory school, prep school; common school, elementary school, grammar school, high school, junior high school, kindergarten, middle school, primary school, public school, secondary school, senior high school, trade school, training school; charter school, magnet school, minischool; madrassa (*or* madrasa *also* madrassah *or* madrasah), Sunday school, yeshiva (*also* yeshivah)

schooling *n* the act or process of imparting knowledge or skills to another ⟨the extended *schooling* needed for a horse to be able to make those precision movements⟩ — see EDUCATION 1

schoolteacher *n* a person whose occupation is to give formal instruction in a school ⟨*schoolteachers* don't always get the summers off, for some teach during that period as well⟩ — see TEACHER

science *n* a body of facts learned by study or experience ⟨the *science* of medicine grew tremendously in the course of the 19th century⟩ — see KNOWLEDGE 1

scilicet *adv* that is to say ⟨the journal cites the spot, *scilicet* present-day Provincetown, as the location of the Pilgrims' first landfall⟩ — see NAMELY

scintilla *n* a very small amount ⟨there is not a *scintilla* of evidence for your outrageous claims⟩ — see PARTICLE 1

scintillate *vb* **1** to give off sparks ⟨we watched contentedly as our campfire *scintillated* in the darkness⟩ — see SPARK 1
2 to shoot forth bursts of light ⟨the diamond ring *scintillated* in the sunlight⟩ — see FLASH 1

scission *n* the act or process of a whole separating into two or more parts or pieces ⟨fears that the *scission* of the labor union will compromise the workers' bargaining power⟩ — see SEPARATION 1

scoff *vb* to swallow or eat greedily ⟨*scoffed* dinner before running off to the basketball game⟩ — see GOBBLE

scold *vb* to criticize (someone) severely or angrily especially for personal failings ⟨he *scolded* the kids for not cleaning up the mess they had made in the kitchen⟩
synonyms baste, bawl out, berate, call down, castigate, chastise, chew out, dress down, flay, hammer, jaw, keelhaul, lambaste (*or* lambast), lecture, rag, rail (at *or* against), rant (at), rate, ream (out), rebuke, reprimand, reproach, score, tongue-lash, upbraid
related words admonish, chide, remonstrate (with), reprove; abuse, assail, attack, bad-mouth, blame, blast, censure, condemn, criticize, crucify, denounce, dis (*also* diss) [*slang*], excoriate, fault, harangue, knock, lace (into), lash, pan, reprehend, revile, scourge, slam, vituperate; belittle, disparage, mock, put down; ridicule, scoff, scorn
phrases lay into, read the riot act (to), take to task
near antonyms approve, endorse (*also* indorse), sanction; extol (*also* extoll), laud, praise

scoop *n* **1** a utensil with a bowl and a handle that is used especially in cooking and serving food ⟨an ice cream *scoop*⟩ — see SPOON
2 information not generally available to the public ⟨come on, I know you've got the *scoop* on their breakup⟩ — see DOPE 1

scoop *vb* to lift out with something that holds liquid ⟨*scooped* broth out of the pan with a spoon⟩ — see DIP 2

scoot *vb* to proceed or move quickly ⟨now we've got to *scoot*, or we'll be late⟩ — see HURRY 2

scope *n* an area over which activity, capacity, or influence extends ⟨the company's *scope* of operations now spans two continents⟩ — see RANGE 2

scorch *vb* **1** to burn on the surface ⟨the picnickers kept *scorching* their marshmallows, deliberately sticking their skewers into the licking flames of the campfire⟩
synonyms char, sear, singe
related words fire, ignite, inflame (*also* enflame), kindle, light; bake, cremate, incinerate; scald, scathe
2 to make dry ⟨weeks of drought had badly *scorched* the soil⟩ — see DRY 1

scorching *adj* having a notably high temperature ⟨we keep indoors as much as possible during the day so as to avoid the *scorching* summer heat⟩ — see HOT 1

score *n* **1** a lingering ill will towards a person for a real or imagined wrong ⟨a whistle-blower who was more interested in settling a *score* with his employers than in exposing an injustice⟩ — see GRUDGE 1
2 something (as money) which is owed ⟨we'll pay the full *score* next week⟩ — see DEBT 1

score *vb* **1** to mark with or as if with a line or groove ⟨the glassblower *scored* the glass rod first so that it would break cleanly⟩
synonyms groove, scribe, seam
related words abrade, file, graze, mill, rasp, scarify, scratch; bevel, chamfer, flute
2 to gain (as points or runs in a game) as credit towards one's total number of points ⟨he *scored* the winning goal in the final minute of play⟩
synonyms rack up, tally
related words triumph, win; best, defeat
near antonyms lose
3 to obtain (as a goal) through effort ⟨finally *scored* a good job after years of hard work⟩ — see ACHIEVE 1
4 to criticize (someone) severely or angrily especially for personal failings ⟨*scored* her for failing to report the security breach immediately⟩ — see SCOLD

scorn *n* open dislike for someone or something considered unworthy of one's concern or respect ⟨has nothing but *scorn* for newfangled ideas of any kind⟩ — see CONTEMPT

scorn *vb* **1** to show contempt for ⟨*scorned* the religious traditions of their ancestors⟩
synonyms contemn, dis (*also* diss) [*slang*], disdain, disrespect, high-hat, look down (on *or* upon), slight, sniff (at), snoot, snub
related words scout; abhor, abominate, despise, detest, execrate, hate, loathe; belittle, deplore, deprecate, disparage; disapprove (of), discountenance, disfavor, frown (on *or* upon)
phrases look down one's nose (at), sneeze at, thumb one's nose (at), walk over
near antonyms cherish, prize, treasure, value; admire, esteem, lionize; hallow, revere, venerate, worship; accept, appreciate, approve (of), care (for), countenance, favor, OK (*or* okay), subscribe (to)
antonyms honor, respect
2 to ignore in a disrespectful manner ⟨she *scorned* the advice of her ophthalmologist and had the laser eye surgery anyway⟩
synonyms despise, disregard, flout
related words dismiss, forget, neglect, overlook, overpass, pass over, slur (over); belittle, deprecate, disparage, slight
near antonyms accept, approve; use

scornful *adj* **1** feeling or showing open dislike for someone or something regarded as undeserving of respect or concern ⟨the actress gave the paparazzi a *scornful* glare before breezing on by them⟩ — see CONTEMPTUOUS 1
2 intended to make a person or thing seem of little importance or value ⟨the tenant's complaints were met with the *scornful* observation that he expected too much for the rent he was paying⟩ — see DEROGATORY

scoundrel *n* a mean, evil, or unprincipled person ⟨some *scoundrel* stole my wallet⟩ — see VILLAIN

scour *vb* to look through (as a place) carefully or thoroughly in an effort to find or discover something ⟨the police *scoured* the city for the Typhoid Mary of this latest epidemic⟩ — see SEARCH 1

scourge *n* **1** a long thin or flexible tool for striking ⟨the museum display included a *scourge*, thumbscrews, and other notorious instruments of torture⟩ — see WHIP
2 one who inflicts punishment in return for an injury or offense ⟨the attorney general, who just happens to be a candidate for governor, is a self-proclaimed *scourge* of organized crime⟩ — see NEMESIS 1
3 a source of harm or misfortune ⟨the sheer ubiquity of food is proving to be the *scourge* of humanity, as evidenced by the obesity epidemic⟩ — see BANE 1

scourge *vb* **1** to bring destruction to (something) through violent action ⟨barbarians *scourged* the countryside, leaving village after village burned to the ground⟩ — see RAVAGE
2 to strike repeatedly with something long and thin or flexible ⟨*scourge* the tree with a whip to loosen the bark⟩ — see WHIP 1

scout *n* a member of the human race ⟨you're a good *scout*⟩ — see HUMAN

scout *vb* to make (someone or something) the object of unkind laughter ⟨the actor's attempt to rationalize his racist comments were roundly *scouted* by the media⟩ — see RIDICULE

scout (up) *vb* to come upon after searching, study, or effort ⟨I think I've *scouted up* a way for us to manage this⟩ — see FIND 1

scowl *n* a twisting of the facial features in disgust or disapproval ⟨the man across the street never seems to wear anything but a *scowl*⟩ — see GRIMACE

scowl *vb* to look with anger or disapproval ⟨*scowled* down at the misbehaving child⟩ — see FROWN

scrabble *n* a forceful effort to reach a goal or objective ⟨it'll be a long *scrabble* to pull ourselves out of poverty⟩ — see STRUGGLE 1

scrabble *vb* **1** to move (as up or over something) often with the help of the hands in holding or pulling ⟨we *scrabbled* up a sand dune to get a better view of the sea⟩ — see CLIMB 1
2 to search for something blindly or uncertainly ⟨he frantically *scrabbled* through the storage chest looking for the needed documents⟩ — see GROPE

scraggly *adj* having an uneven edge or outline ⟨a *scraggly* little tree⟩ — see RAGGED 1

scraggy *adj* **1** having an uneven edge or outline ⟨a *scraggy* beard⟩ — see RAGGED 1
2 not having a level or smooth surface ⟨climbers badly scraped their limbs on the *scraggy* cliffs⟩ — see UNEVEN 1

scramble *n* an unorganized collection or mixture of various things ⟨a *scramble* of pens and pencils in the desk drawer⟩ — see MISCELLANY 1

scramble *vb* **1** to move (as up or over something) often with the help of the hands in holding or pulling ⟨the toddler *scrambled* up the stairs⟩ — see CLIMB 1
2 to undo the proper order or arrangement of ⟨*scrambled* the letters of the word⟩ — see DISORDER

[1]**scrap** *n* **1** an unused or unwanted piece or item typically of small size or value ⟨only a *scrap* of silk was left on the sewing table after they had finished the project⟩
synonyms end, fag end, leftover, oddment, remainder, remnant, stub
related words leavings, odds and ends, pickings, refuse, remains, residual, residue, scraping(s), stump, vestige; balance, rest; chip, flake, fragment, piece, sliver, splinter; ribbon(s), shred, tatter
near antonyms whole
2 a broken or irregular part of something that often remains incomplete ⟨a *scrap* of paper fluttered to the floor⟩ — see FRAGMENT
3 a very small piece ⟨brushed away a *scrap* of lint⟩ — see BIT 1
4 discarded or useless material ⟨the rest of this stuff is just *scrap*, so sweep it up and throw it away⟩ — see GARBAGE 1

[2]**scrap** *n* **1** an often noisy or angry expression of differing opinions ⟨the state legislature's annual *scrap* over the budget⟩ — see ARGUMENT 1
2 a physical dispute between opposing individuals or groups ⟨several drunken revelers were involved in a *scrap* outside of the nightclub⟩ — see FIGHT 1

[1]**scrap** *vb* to express different opinions about something often angrily ⟨the young couple often *scrapped* about money and their very disparate spending habits⟩ — see ARGUE 2

[2]**scrap** *vb* **1** to get rid of as useless or unwanted ⟨we've decided to *scrap* the second car⟩ — see DISCARD
2 to put an end to (something planned or previously agreed to) ⟨we *scrapped* our plans to go to Paris, and set out the next day for Prague⟩ — see CANCEL 1

scrape *n* **1** a brief clash between enemies or rivals ⟨he's had his share of *scrapes* with the law in the past⟩ — see ENCOUNTER
2 a harsh grating sound ⟨the *scrape* of a shovel on concrete⟩ — see RASP
3 an area of skin roughened or worn away by harsh rubbing against another surface ⟨*scrapes* that were caused by a too-tight harness⟩ — see ABRASION

scrape *vb* **1** to pass roughly and noisily over or against a surface ⟨the rusty old gate *scrapes* against the pavement whenever anyone opens it⟩
synonyms grate, grind, rasp, scratch
related words rub; groan, whine
near antonyms glide, skate, slide
2 to damage by rubbing against a sharp or rough surface ⟨she *scraped* her knee when she fell down⟩
synonyms abrade, graze, scratch, scuff
related words bark, skin; chafe, fret, gall; claw, cut, lacerate; bruise, contuse
near antonyms polish, smooth, soften, wax
3 to press or strike against or together so as to make a scraping sound ⟨she *scraped* her fingernails across the chalkboard to get everyone's attention⟩ — see GRIND 2

scrape (up *or* together) *vb* to get with great difficulty ⟨we're barely *scraping together* a living on the farm⟩ — see EKE (OUT)

scrapper *n* a person who takes part in a dispute ⟨both movie critics are real *scrappers*, so their on-air discussions of the latest releases are often heated⟩ — see DISPUTANT

scrappiness *n* an inclination to fight or quarrel ⟨his natural *scrappiness* serves him well as an aggressive defense attorney⟩ — see BELLIGERENCE

scrapping *n* the getting rid of whatever is unwanted or useless ⟨the *scrapping* of the park's last horse-drawn carriage marks the end of an era⟩ — see DISPOSAL 1

scrappy *adj* **1** feeling or displaying eagerness to fight ⟨she was a *scrappy* girl despite—or, perhaps, because of—her small size⟩ — see BELLIGERENT
2 given to arguing ⟨a pair of *scrappy* movie critics who can never agree on anything⟩ — see ARGUMENTATIVE 1

scratch *n* **1** a harsh grating sound ⟨the *scratch* of metal on metal is not a good sound for a car to make⟩ — see RASP
2 *slang* something (as pieces of stamped metal or printed paper) customarily and legally used as a medium of exchange, a measure of value, or a means of payment ⟨she treated her buddies to a drink whenever she had the *scratch* for it⟩ — see MONEY 1

scratch *vb* **1** to damage by rubbing against a sharp or

rough surface ⟨*scratched* his arm on a branch⟩ — see SCRAPE 2
2 to pass roughly and noisily over or against a surface ⟨the branches of the willow tree *scratch* against the windowpane whenever the wind blows⟩ — see SCRAPE 1
3 to write or draw hastily or carelessly ⟨*scratched* a quick doodle in the margins⟩ — see SCRIBBLE 1

scratch (out) *vb* **1** to compose and set down on paper the words of ⟨*scratched out* a poem for his beloved wife on the home front⟩ — see WRITE 1
2 to show (something written) to be no longer valid by drawing a cross over or a line through it ⟨*scratched out* the old phone number and wrote in the new one⟩ — see X (OUT)

scratchy *adj* **1** having leaves or branches which are likely to cause a scratch ⟨*scratchy* shrubbery that's intended to keep kids and pets off the old man's property⟩
synonyms brambly, prickly, thistly, thorny
related words burred; bristly, coarse, jagged, rough
2 causing an unpleasant tingling sensation ⟨the wool pants are so *scratchy* that I can't stand to wear them⟩
synonyms irritating, itchy, prickly
related words coarse, harsh, rough
near antonyms silken, silky, soft, soothing
3 harsh and dry in sound ⟨her voice was *scratchy* from a cold⟩ — see HOARSE

scrawl *vb* to write or draw hastily or carelessly ⟨*scrawled* a quick note, stuck it in their mailbox, and hurried off⟩ — see SCRIBBLE 1

scream *n* someone or something that is very funny ⟨that new comedy is a *scream*⟩
synonyms hoot, knee-slapper, laugh, riot
related words boner, howler; crack, gag, jest, joke, pleasantry, quip, sally, waggery, wisecrack, witticism; caution, sight
near antonyms bummer, downer

scream *vb* **1** to cry out loudly and emotionally ⟨we *screamed* when the roller coaster began its 30-foot plunge⟩
synonyms howl, screech, shriek, shrill, squall, squeal, yelp, yell
related words bay, caterwaul, keen, squawk, wail, yawp (*or* yaup), yowl; bawl, call, cry, holler, shout, thunder, vociferate
near antonyms murmur, mutter, whisper
2 to show mirth with an explosive vocal sound ⟨you'll *scream* when you see the outfit that she's wearing⟩ — see LAUGH 1
3 to express dissatisfaction, pain, or resentment usually tiresomely ⟨angry residents *screamed* that their neighborhood still hadn't been plowed a week after the snowstorm⟩ — see COMPLAIN

screaming *adj* **1** arousing a strong and usually superficial interest or emotional reaction ⟨*screaming* headlines about the latest showbiz scandal⟩ — see SENSATIONAL 1
2 causing or intended to cause laughter ⟨a *screaming* picture of everyone making silly faces⟩ — see FUNNY 1

screaming meemies *n pl* a sense of panic or extreme nervousness ⟨had the *screaming meemies* on his wedding day⟩ — see JITTERS

screech *vb* to cry out loudly and emotionally ⟨the toddler *screeched* in anger when her stuffed rabbit was taken away⟩ — see SCREAM 1

screeching *adj* having a high musical pitch or range ⟨the *screeching* blast of the factory whistle hurt my ears⟩ — see SHRILL

screen *n* **1** the art or business of making a movie ⟨he was a star of both stage and *screen*⟩ — see MOVIE 2
2 means or method of defending ⟨the target will be difficult to reach as it is behind a *screen* of anti-aircraft batteries⟩ — see DEFENSE 1

screen *vb* **1** to drive danger or attack away from ⟨attack helicopters were called in to help *screen* the troops from further attacks⟩ — see DEFEND 1
2 to keep secret or shut off from view ⟨bushes *screened* the swimming pool from passersby on the street⟩ — see [1]HIDE 2
3 to pass through a filter ⟨you should *screen* the cooking oil to remove impurities⟩ — see STRAIN 2
4 to place a protective layer over ⟨*screened* his eyes with his hand to block the sun⟩ — see COVER 3

screenplay *n* the written form of a story prepared for film production ⟨each actor will be given a copy of the *screenplay* to study⟩
synonyms scenario, script
related words shooting script; story, text

screw *vb* **1** to twist (something) out of a natural or normal shape or condition ⟨*screwed* up his face at the taste of the medicine⟩ — see CONTORT
2 to rob by the use of trickery or threats ⟨managed to *screw* his siblings out of their share of the inheritance⟩ — see FLEECE

screw around *vb* to be sexually unfaithful ⟨he hired a private detective because he thought his wife was *screwing around*⟩ — see CHEAT 2

screwball *adj* showing or marked by a lack of good sense or judgment ⟨she's always off on some *screwball* plan⟩ — see FOOLISH 1

screwball *n* a person of odd or whimsical habits ⟨a *screwball* who liked to save lint and bits of string⟩ — see ECCENTRIC

screwing *n* the twisting of something out of its natural or normal shape or condition ⟨you'll regret the constant *screwing* of your face—someday it's going to freeze in that position!⟩ — see CONTORTION

screwlike *adj* turning around an axis like the thread of a screw ⟨performed a *screwlike* dive into the pool⟩ — see SPIRAL

screwup *n* **1** an unintentional departure from truth or accuracy ⟨clearly, there's been some sort of *screwup* about what time we were supposed to meet⟩ — see ERROR 1
2 someone who bungles an effort ⟨don't ask the office *screwup* to arrange the holiday party⟩ — see BUTCHER

screw up *vb* **1** to make a mistake ⟨we all *screw up* from time to time, so don't sweat it⟩ — see ERR 1
2 to make or do (something) in a clumsy or unskillful way ⟨you've totally *screwed up* the spreadsheet⟩ — see BOTCH

screwy *adj* **1** different from the ordinary in a way that causes curiosity or suspicion ⟨the counterfeit bills are poorly done and would look *screwy* to even the untrained eye⟩ — see ODD 2
2 having or showing a very abnormal or sick state of mind ⟨I was accosted on the downtown street by a woman who seemed to be a bit *screwy* in the head⟩ — see INSANE 1

scribble *vb* **1** to write or draw hastily or carelessly ⟨she *scribbled* a quick note on the pad by the door before leaving⟩
synonyms scratch, scrawl, squiggle
related words doodle; jot (down); ink, inscribe, letter, pen, pencil, print, write
2 to compose and set down on paper the words of ⟨he *scribbled* a quick note to his wife and taped it to the front door⟩ — see WRITE 1

scribe *n* **1** one who writes from dictation or copies manuscripts ⟨variations between the different manuscripts attest to the fallibility of the *scribes* who transmitted them⟩

synonyms amanuensis, calligrapher, copyist, penman, scrivener
2 an official whose job is to keep records ⟨the *scribe* keeps the minutes of the club's meetings⟩ — see CLERK 1
3 a person who creates a written work ⟨a book of dusty poems by some now-forgotten *scribe*⟩ — see AUTHOR 1

scribe *vb* to mark with or as if with a line or groove ⟨carefully *scribed* two lines into the wood⟩ — see SCORE 1

scrimmage *n* a physical dispute between opposing individuals or groups ⟨the two players got into a *scrimmage* off the court and got suspended⟩ — see FIGHT 1

scrimmage (with) *vb* to oppose (someone) in physical conflict ⟨growing up in the inner city he had often *scrimmaged with* neighborhood toughs⟩ — see FIGHT 1

scrimp *vb* to avoid unnecessary waste or expense ⟨had to *scrimp* and save for years in order to be able to afford a house⟩ — see ECONOMIZE

scrimping *adj* careful in the management of money or resources ⟨a *scrimping* homemaker⟩ — see FRUGAL

scrimping *n* careful management of material resources ⟨she had grown tired of *scrimping* and was glad to finally have a job with a decent paycheck⟩ — see ECONOMY

script *n* **1** the form or style of a particular person's writing ⟨has a neat, careful *script* with delicate loops⟩ — see HANDWRITING 1
2 the written form of a story prepared for film production ⟨sold two *scripts* to the movie studio⟩ — see SCREENPLAY
3 writing done by hand ⟨sending a thank-you note in *script*—and not just an e-mail—is the only proper way to express one's gratitude⟩ — see HANDWRITING 2

Scripture *n* a book made up of the writings accepted by Christians as coming from God ⟨one of the greatest commandments from *Scripture* is "Love thy neighbor"⟩ — see BIBLE

scrivener *n* **1** a person who creates a written work ⟨the roomful of unsung *scriveners* that it takes to churn out a weekly sitcom⟩ — see AUTHOR 1
2 one who writes from dictation or copies manuscripts ⟨the details of the contract were worked out by a lawyer, I being involved with it merely as a *scrivener*⟩ — see SCRIBE 1

scrooge *n* a mean grasping person who is usually stingy with money ⟨her father is a real *scrooge* and refuses to pay her way through college, even though he can easily afford it⟩ — see MISER

scrounge *vb* to get with great difficulty ⟨*scrounged* up the money to pay his dental bills⟩ — see EKE (OUT)

scrub *n* a living thing much smaller than others of its kind ⟨that *scrub* of a mutt turned out to be the smartest dog we ever had⟩ — see DWARF 1

scrub *vb* to put an end to (something planned or previously agreed to) ⟨the outdoor art project was *scrubbed* when the organizers found out they needed permission from city hall⟩ — see CANCEL 1

scrubby *adj* showing signs of advanced wear and tear and neglect ⟨changed into an old flannel shirt and a *scrubby* pair of jeans to clean out the garage⟩ — see SHABBY 1

scruffy *adj* showing signs of advanced wear and tear and neglect ⟨dressed in *scruffy* old clothes to clean out the garage⟩ — see SHABBY 1

scrum *n* **1** a great number of persons or creatures massed together ⟨I had to fight my way through the *scrum* of holiday shoppers at the mall⟩ — see CROWD 1
2 a physical dispute between opposing individuals or groups ⟨when the server spilled a drink on a customer, they got into a bit of a *scrum* before being separated⟩ — see FIGHT 1
3 *British* a place of uproar and confusion ⟨London's tube is quite a *scrum* during rush hour⟩ — see MADHOUSE 2

scrumptious *adj* very pleasing to the sense of taste ⟨baked a *scrumptious* chocolate cake⟩ — see DELICIOUS 1

scrunch *vb* **1** to create (as by crushing) an irregular mass of creases in ⟨*scrunched* up the shirt and tossed it in the laundry⟩ — see CRUMPLE 1
2 to lie low with the limbs close to the body ⟨the climbers *scrunched* down on the leeward side of a large boulder and waited for the storm to pass⟩ — see CROUCH
3 to press or strike against or together so as to make a scraping sound ⟨*scrunched* loose gravel with every footstep⟩ — see GRIND 2

[1]scruple *n* **1** a very small amount ⟨went about her business without even a *scruple* of suspicion⟩ — see PARTICLE 1
2 a very small piece ⟨left just a *scruple* of asparagus on the plate⟩ — see BIT 1

[2]scruple *n* an uneasy feeling about the rightness of what one is doing or going to do ⟨the survey showed that many students had few *scruples* about cheating on papers or exams⟩ — see QUALM

scruple *vb* to show uncertainty about the right course of action ⟨a tabloid journalist who has never *scrupled* to reveal the most intimate details about the lives of celebrities⟩ — see HESITATE

scrupulous *adj* **1** guided by or in accordance with one's sense of right and wrong ⟨an exemplar of morality who was *scrupulous* in all of his dealings⟩ — see CONSCIENTIOUS 1
2 taking, showing, or involving great care and effort ⟨a *scrupulous* attention to detail is evident in all of his reporting⟩ — see PAINSTAKING

scrupulousness *n* strict attentiveness to what one is doing ⟨the admirable *scrupulousness* with which they performed every step of the experiment⟩ — see CARE 1

scrutable *adj* capable of being understood ⟨she thinks that she's a sly and subtle schemer, but her machinations and motives are all too *scrutable* to those of us who know her⟩ — see INTELLIGIBLE

scrutinize *vb* to look over closely (as for judging quality or condition) ⟨the project's time constraints make it impossible for the programmers to *scrutinize* every line of code, so some bugs should be expected⟩ — see INSPECT

scrutiny *n* **1** a close look at or over someone or something in order to judge condition ⟨his performance on the football field is seemingly unaffected by the media's intense *scrutiny* of his tumultuous personal life⟩ — see INSPECTION
2 a fixed intent look ⟨began to squirm under the penetrating *scrutiny* of the judge⟩ — see GAZE

scud *n* a sudden brief rush of wind ⟨a cold *scud* sent leaves skittering down from the trees⟩ — see GUST 1

scuff *vb* **1** to damage by rubbing against a sharp or rough surface ⟨*scuffed* up her shoes by rubbing her feet under the rung of the chair⟩ — see SCRAPE 2
2 to move heavily or clumsily ⟨the miners *scuffed* past in heavy boots⟩ — see LUMBER 1

scuffle *n* a physical dispute between opposing individuals or groups ⟨several chairs were knocked over in the *scuffle*⟩ — see FIGHT 1

scuffle *vb* **1** to move heavily or clumsily ⟨she *scuffled* along in shoes that were much too large for her⟩ — see LUMBER 1
2 to seize and attempt to unbalance one another for the purpose of achieving physical mastery ⟨the burglar and the homeowner briefly *scuffled* together in the dark⟩ — see WRESTLE

scull *vb* to move a boat by means of oars ⟨a couple *sculled* past in a racing shell⟩ — see [1]ROW

sculler *n* a person who drives a boat forward by means of oars ⟨*scullers* tend to have well-developed arm muscles⟩ — see OARSMAN

sculpt *vb* to create a three-dimensional representation of (something) using solid material ⟨the colossal statue was *sculpted* from a single block of marble⟩
synonyms carve, sculpture
related words chisel, engrave, etch, grave, incise, inscribe; knap; cast, form, model, mold, shape

sculpture *vb* to create a three-dimensional representation of (something) using solid material ⟨the artist used a hammer and chisel to *sculpture* the horse out of ice⟩ — see SCULPT

scum *n* **1** people looked down upon as ignorant and of the lowest class ⟨claimed that only *scum* lived in that part of town⟩ — see RABBLE
2 a person whose behavior is offensive to others ⟨ignore the heckler—he's complete *scum*⟩ — see JERK 1

scumbag *n, slang* a person whose behavior is offensive to others ⟨don't romanticize that con artist, as she's nothing more than a *scumbag* who cheats the most vulnerable⟩ — see JERK 1

scummy *adj* arousing or deserving of one's loathing and disgust ⟨the jury was disgusted by the defense attorney's *scummy* attempt to portray the victim as deserving of what she got⟩ — see CONTEMPTIBLE 1

scunnered *adj, chiefly Scottish* subjected to and reacting with irritation ⟨my mates are fair *scunnered* with me⟩ — see ANNOYED

scurrile *or* **scurril** *adj* marked by harsh insulting language ⟨performs a *scurrile* comedy routine that is guaranteed to rile people on the right⟩ — see ABUSIVE

scurrility *n* harsh insulting language ⟨a discussion on some hot-button social issues in which any pretense to civility quickly gave way to intransigence and *scurrility*⟩ — see ABUSE 1

scurrilous *adj* marked by harsh insulting language ⟨a *scurrilous* satire on the scandal that enveloped Washington⟩ — see ABUSIVE

scurry *vb* to proceed or move quickly ⟨everyone *scurried* back to work as soon as they saw the boss's car pull into the parking lot⟩ — see HURRY 2

scurvy *adj* arousing or deserving of one's loathing and disgust ⟨after winning the lottery, she was beset by a whole *scurvy* swarm of con artists, ne'er-do-wells, and hangers-on⟩ — see CONTEMPTIBLE 1

scuttle *vb* to proceed or move quickly ⟨mice *scuttling* across the barn floor to escape the cats⟩ — see HURRY 2

scuttlebutt *n* information or opinion that is widely disseminated without any authority or confirmation of accuracy ⟨according to *scuttlebutt* in the financial markets, the company will be downsizing soon⟩ — see RUMOR

scuzzball *n, slang* a person whose behavior is offensive to others ⟨as you might expect, the owner of that sweatshop is a total *scuzzball*⟩ — see JERK 1

sea *n* the whole body of salt water that covers nearly three-fourths of the earth ⟨millions of plants and animals live in the *sea*⟩ — see OCEAN 1

sea devil *n* any of several extremely large rays ⟨a *sea devil* glided along the ocean floor⟩ — see DEVILFISH

sea dog *n* one who operates or navigates a seagoing vessel ⟨the tale of a grizzled old *sea dog* who sets out for one last voyage⟩ — see SAILOR

seafarer *n* one who operates or navigates a seagoing vessel ⟨ships and the intrepid *seafarers* who man them remain a vital part of the world economy⟩ — see SAILOR

seam *vb* to mark with or as if with a line or groove ⟨in fencing circles it is a mark of honor to have one's face *seamed* with saber cuts⟩ — see SCORE 1

seaman *n* one who operates or navigates a seagoing vessel ⟨a weathered old *seaman* who now captains a tour boat⟩ — see SAILOR

seamless *adj* being entirely without fault or flaw ⟨the conductor's *seamless* interpretation of Mozart's *Jupiter* symphony was greeted with a standing ovation⟩ — see PERFECT 1

seamster *n* a person who sews ⟨a talented *seamster* who dreams of launching his own clothing line⟩ — see SEWER

sear *vb* **1** to burn on the surface ⟨lightly *sear* the steaks, but don't cook them all the way through⟩ — see SCORCH 1
2 to make dry ⟨the clear desert air is *seared* by the summer sun⟩ — see DRY 1

search *n* an act or process of looking carefully or thoroughly for someone or something ⟨the *search* for the missing hikers lasted several days⟩
synonyms hunt, quest
related words shakedown; sweep; chase, pursuit; recon, reconnaissance, scout; canvass (*also* canvas), survey; exploration, probe; forage

search *vb* **1** to look through (as a place) carefully or thoroughly in an effort to find or discover something ⟨archaeologists have begun to *search* the southern end of the valley, where they believe the underground tombs are located⟩
synonyms comb, dig (through), dredge, hunt (through), rake, ransack, rifle, rummage, scour, sort (through), troll
related words frisk, pat down, shake down; audit, check (out), examine, inspect, investigate, review, scan, scrutinize, survey; ascertain, descry, detect, determine, discover, ferret (out), find, find out, get, hit (on *or* upon), learn, locate, run down, scare up, track (down); grub (about), poke (around); explore, probe, prospect, skirmish, snoop; browse, glance (over), look over; peruse, study
near antonyms hide; abandon, lose; ignore, neglect
2 to go into or range over for purposes of discovery ⟨the Spanish conquistadors *searched* vast areas of the Southwest in their quest for the fabled cities of gold⟩ — see EXPLORE 2

search (for *or* **out)** *vb* to go in search of ⟨every year major league scouts crisscross the country to *search for* young players with promising talent⟩ — see SEEK 1

searing *adj* **1** having a notably high temperature ⟨in our air-conditioned office, we were oblivious to the *searing* heat outside⟩ — see HOT 1
2 difficult to endure ⟨the undersecretary looked chastened as he listened to the congressman's *searing* rebuke⟩ — see HARSH 1

season *vb* **1** to make more pleasant to the taste by adding something intensely flavored ⟨the chef *seasoned* the vegetables as soon as they came out of the oven⟩
synonyms flavor, lace, savor (*also* savour), spice
related words enhance, enrich, sauce; pepper, salt; aromatize, perfume
2 to bring to a proper or desired state of fitness ⟨carefully *seasoned* the cast iron pan with vegetable oil before using it for the first time⟩ — see CONDITION 1
3 to make able to withstand physical hardship, strain, or exposure ⟨troops that had been *seasoned* by months of heavy fighting⟩ — see HARDEN 2
4 to make competent (as by training, skill, or ability) for a particular office or function ⟨her campaign manager has been *seasoned* by several hotly contested gubernatorial campaigns⟩ — see QUALIFY 2

seasonable *adj* especially suitable for a certain time ⟨*seasonable* advice is more likely to be listened to⟩ — see TIMELY 1

seasoning *n* **1** something (as a spice or herb) that adds an agreeable or interesting taste to food ⟨the stew was

too bland before they added the *seasoning*〉
synonyms flavor, flavoring, spice
related words sauce
2 something used to enhance the flavor of cooked or prepared food 〈she thinks salt is the ideal *seasoning* for all batter-fried foods〉 — see CONDIMENT

seat *n* **1** a place from which authority is exercised 〈all applications had to be submitted at the county *seat* for proper processing〉
synonyms command, headquarters
related words high command; center, home; capital
2 the part of the body upon which someone sits 〈fell down on his well-padded *seat*〉 — see BUTTOCKS
3 a thing or place that is of greatest importance to an activity or interest 〈a capital that is the *seat* of culture for the whole nation〉 — see CENTER 1

seat *vb* **1** to cause to sit down 〈the usher *seated* them in the third row〉
synonyms set down, sit
related words ensconce, settle; lay, lie, rest; place, put; recline, repose
2 to put into an office or welcome into an organization with special ceremonies 〈one of the first appointments that he made after being *seated* as president of the state senate〉 — see INSTALL 1

secern *vb* to understand or point out the difference in 〈those philistines who seemingly cannot *secern* artistic depiction of the nude from blatant pornography〉 — see DISTINGUISH 1

seclude *vb* to set or keep apart from others 〈the patients will be *secluded* until they are no longer contagious〉 — see ISOLATE

secluded *adj* screened or sequestered from view 〈we stayed in a *secluded* resort, far away from the regular tourist crowds〉
synonyms cloistered, covert, hidden, isolated, quiet, remote, retired, secret, sheltered
related words lone, lonely, lonesome, reclusive, solitary; private
near antonyms obvious, visible; exposed

secludedness *n* the state of being alone or kept apart from others 〈the inn's greatest appeal for guests was its woodland *secludedness*〉 — see ISOLATION

seclusion *n* the state of being alone or kept apart from others 〈she went into *seclusion* in order to focus entirely on writing her book〉 — see ISOLATION

[1]**second** *n* a very small space of time 〈I'll be ready in a *second*〉 — see INSTANT

[2]**second** *n* something separated from a group or lot for not being as good as the others 〈the slightly flawed linens were sold as *seconds*〉 — see CULL

secondary *adj* **1** taken or created from something original or basic 〈history textbooks are *secondary* sources for historical information and do not represent original research〉
synonyms derivative, secondhand
related words unoriginal; consequent, resultant
near antonyms fundamental, nonderivative; first, primary
antonyms basic, original
2 of little or less value or merit 〈we need to focus on getting the groceries bought and the rent paid—everything else is *secondary*〉 — see INFERIOR 2

second childhood *n* the state or period of mental decline that typically accompanies old age 〈whenever she makes a mistake, Grandmother just reminds everyone she's in her *second childhood* and children shouldn't be held accountable〉 — see DOTAGE

second–class *adj* **1** of little or less value or merit 〈a playwright who produced only *second-class* work when he turned his hand to poetry〉 — see INFERIOR 2
2 of average to below average quality 〈it's only a *second-class* restaurant and not worth the high prices〉 — see MEDIOCRE 1

secondhand *adj* taken or created from something original or basic 〈memoirs filled with *secondhand* stories about show-business celebrities〉 — see SECONDARY 1

second nature *n* a usual manner of behaving or doing 〈speaking and thinking in Japanese simply became *second nature* to her during the years she spent in Kyoto〉 — see HABIT 1

second–rate *adj* **1** of average to below average quality 〈a *second-rate* song from a songwriter who has done much better〉 — see MEDIOCRE 1
2 of little or less value or merit 〈a *second-rate* company that was never considered among the top manufacturers of televisions〉 — see INFERIOR 2
3 of low quality 〈*second-rate* goods specifically manufactured for the low end of the market〉 — see CHEAP 2

second sight *n* the power of seeing or knowing about things that are not present to the senses 〈the fairy world was believed to be visible to people blessed with *second sight*〉 — see CLAIRVOYANCE

secrecy *n* the practice or habit of keeping secrets or keeping one's affairs secret 〈this administration's steadfast adherence to *secrecy* is beginning to cost it the trust of the voters〉
synonyms closeness, secretiveness
related words confidentiality, privacy; discreetness, discretion, prudence; circumspection, wariness; reserve, reticence, silence, taciturnity; furtiveness, shiftiness, slyness, sneakiness, underhandedness; concealment, covertness, stealth, subterfuge
near antonyms candor, frankness, honesty, openness; imprudence, indiscretion

secret *adj* **1** undertaken or done so as to escape being observed or known by others 〈a *secret* operation to rescue captive soldiers behind enemy lines〉
synonyms backstairs, behind-the-scenes, clandestine, covert, furtive, hole-and-corner, hugger-mugger, hush-hush, private, privy, sneak, sneaking, sneaky, stealth, stealthy, surreptitious, undercover, underground, underhand, underhanded
related words back-channel, closed-door, off-the-books, off-the-record; classified, confidential, restricted, top secret, undisclosed; concealed, hidden, secreted, subterranean, unadvertised, unexposed
near antonyms acknowledged, avowed; aboveboard, straightforward, unconcealed, undisguised; unclassified, unrestricted; clear, evident, manifest, obvious, patent, plain
antonyms open, overt, public
2 working on missions in which one's objectives, activities, or true identity are not publicly revealed 〈*secret* agents whose wartime exploits were known only by top government officials〉
synonyms undercover
related words covert, private, secretive, subterranean
near antonyms overt
3 screened or sequestered from view 〈a *secret* cave that is screened by trees〉 — see SECLUDED
4 not known or meant to be known by the general populace 〈proprietary information that the company does its best to keep *secret*〉 — see PRIVATE 1

secret *n* **1** information shared only with another or with a select few 〈you didn't really expect him to keep a *secret* from his wife, did you?〉
synonyms confidence
related words dope, lowdown
near antonyms open secret
2 something hard to understand or explain 〈the *secrets* of the Egyptian pyramids include the construction

methods used to lift the huge blocks of stone in place⟩ — see MYSTERY
3 something that allows someone to achieve a desired goal ⟨the *secret* to advancement in this company is to appear dedicated⟩ — see PASSPORT 1

secretary *n* an official whose job is to keep records ⟨file your intent to run for office with the city *secretary*⟩ — see CLERK 1

secrete *vb* to put into a hiding place ⟨the police found the weapon *secreted* under the driver's seat of the getaway car⟩ — see [1]HIDE 1

secretion *n* the placing of something out of sight ⟨the *secretion* of their money in the backyard turned out to be a huge mistake⟩ — see CONCEALMENT 1

secretive *adj* given to keeping one's activities hidden from public observation or knowledge ⟨the intelligence agency remained *secretive* despite the media's demands for more openness in government⟩
synonyms close, closemouthed, dark, reticent, tightmouthed, uncommunicative
related words quiet, reserved, silent, taciturn, tightlipped; discreet, prudent; clandestine, covert, furtive, hugger-mugger, secret, sneak, sneaky, stealthy, surreptitious, undercover, underhand, underhanded
near antonyms candid, frank, honest, out-front, upfront; blunt, outspoken, tactless
antonyms communicative, open

secretiveness *n* the practice or habit of keeping secrets or keeping one's affairs secret ⟨his *secretiveness* about his past always made some people suspicious of what he might be hiding⟩ — see SECRECY

secretly *adv* in a manner intended to prevent knowledge or awareness by others ⟨the girl *secretly* told her best friend about the pregnancy but kept everyone else in the dark⟩ — see PRIVATELY

sect *n* a group of people acting together within a larger group ⟨one *sect* of medical researchers holds the minority view that the disease is not caused by that virus⟩ — see FACTION

sectarian *adj* not broad or open in views or opinions ⟨there are people on both the left and the right who have staked out unyielding *sectarian* positions in this debate⟩ — see NARROW 2

sectarian *n* one who stubbornly or intolerantly adheres to his or her own opinions and prejudices ⟨charged that the work of Congress has been stymied by *sectarians* who are indifferent to reason and intolerant of compromise⟩ — see BIGOT

sectarianism *n* stubborn or intolerant adherence to one's opinions or prejudices ⟨an ideological *sectarianism* that prevented the political party from ever being anything more than a fringe group⟩ — see BIGOTRY

section *n* **1** an area (as of a city) set apart for some purpose or having some special feature ⟨several abandoned warehouses in the city's industrial *section* are being converted into art galleries and artists' lofts⟩ — see DISTRICT
2 one of the pieces from which something is designed to be assembled ⟨had trouble fitting the *sections* of the bookcase together⟩ — see PART 1

secular *adj* not involving religion or religious matters ⟨that's an issue for the *secular* authorities, not the church⟩ — see PROFANE 1

secure *adj* **1** having or showing great faith in oneself or one's abilities ⟨he's so *secure* about winning the marathon that he's practically spent the prize money⟩ — see CONFIDENT 1
2 not exposed to the threat of loss or injury ⟨the fortress was thought to be *secure* against attack⟩ — see SAFE 1
3 providing safety ⟨escaped to a *secure* location⟩ — see SAFE 2
4 worthy of one's trust ⟨a fund that should provide them with a *secure* income in their retirement⟩ — see DEPENDABLE

secure *vb* **1** to drive danger or attack away from ⟨sent troops to *secure* the city⟩ — see DEFEND 1
2 to make sure, certain, or safe ⟨a retirement account that will help to *secure* our future⟩ — see ENSURE
3 to put securely in place or in a desired position ⟨candidates for admission are asked to *secure* a recent photo to their application forms⟩ — see FASTEN 2
4 to receive as return for effort ⟨finally *secured* a job after sending out dozens of applications⟩ — see EARN 1

security *n* **1** means or method of defending ⟨measures taken to beef up our national *security*⟩ — see DEFENSE 1
2 something given or held to assure that the giver will keep a promise ⟨their house will serve as *security* for the loan⟩ — see PLEDGE 1
3 the state of not being exposed to danger ⟨after the burglaries, police presence in the neighborhood was enhanced to give residents a stronger sense of *security*⟩ — see SAFETY 1

sedate *adj* **1** not joking or playful in mood or manner ⟨while not exactly cold, the doctor does maintain a *sedate* and purely professional demeanor with his patients⟩ — see SERIOUS 1
2 free from emotional or mental agitation ⟨her expression remained *sedate* as I told her the bad news⟩ — see CALM 2

sedative *adj* tending to calm the emotions and relieve stress ⟨some people find a glass of wine to be a civilized and *sedative* addition to an evening meal⟩ — see SOOTHING 1

sediment *vb* to cause to come to rest at the bottom (as of a liquid) ⟨the water flowing into the reservoir is *sedimenting* silt faster than was originally expected⟩ — see SETTLE 1

sediment *n* matter that settles to the bottom of a body of liquid ⟨the *sediment* at the bottom of the river needs to be routinely dredged so that it doesn't interfere with barge traffic⟩ — see DEPOSIT 1

seditious *adj* tending to excite political disorder or insurrection ⟨several dissidents were jailed for leading protests that the government branded as *seditious*⟩ — see INFLAMMATORY

seduce *vb* to lead away from a usual or proper course by offering some pleasure or advantage ⟨I wasn't going to buy the car, but was *seduced* by the low-interest payment plan⟩ — see LURE

seducer *n* one that tries to get a person to give in to a desire ⟨fabled as a land of endless opportunity, California continues to be a *seducer* of dreamers and doers⟩ — see TEMPTER

seduction *n* the act or pressure of giving in to a desire especially when ill-advised ⟨the swift *seduction* of the college freshman into a life of drinking and partying⟩ — see TEMPTATION 1

seductive *adj* having an often mysterious or magical power to attract ⟨people always remarked on the cult leader's *seductive* personality⟩ — see FASCINATING 1

seductiveness *n* the power of irresistible attraction ⟨she exuded a *seductiveness* that enabled her to attract a succession of six husbands⟩ — see CHARM 2

seductress *n* a woman whom men find irresistibly attractive ⟨in the movie she played Cleopatra, one of history's most famous *seductresses*⟩ — see SIREN

sedulity *n* attentive and persistent effort ⟨her *sedulity* was rewarded when the U.S. Supreme Court agreed to hear the case⟩ — see DILIGENCE

sedulous *adj* involved in often constant activity ⟨an impressively *sedulous* suitor, he was constantly sending her flowers and other tokens of his affection⟩ — see BUSY 1

sedulously *adv* with great effort or determination ⟨*sedulously* devoted herself to completing the project on time⟩ — see HARD 1

sedulousness *n* attentive and persistent effort ⟨many of the volunteers at the dig discovered that they lacked the *sedulousness* that archaeology demands⟩ — see DILIGENCE

see *vb* **1** to make note of (something) through the use of one's eyes ⟨out of the corner of my eye I *saw* the deer run into the woods⟩
synonyms behold, catch, descry, discern, distinguish, espy, eye, look (at), note, notice, observe, perceive, regard, remark, sight, spot, spy, view, witness
related words identify, make out, pick out, pick up; attend (to), consider, heed, mark, mind; study, watch; examine, inspect, scan, scrutinize, survey; glance (at), glimpse, peer (at)
phrases get a load of [*slang*], lay eyes on, set eyes on
near antonyms disregard, ignore, neglect, overpass, pass over; miss, overlook
2 to come to a knowledge of (something) by living through it ⟨a writer who *saw* World War II through the eyes of a common soldier⟩ — see EXPERIENCE
3 to come to an awareness of ⟨I bought the best seller just to *see* what all the fuss was about⟩ — see DISCOVER 1
4 to have a vague awareness of ⟨I *see* a certain sadness in his letters to his relatives back home⟩ — see FEEL 1
5 to make a social call upon ⟨you should go and *see* Father at the hospital this afternoon⟩ — see VISIT 1
6 to have a clear idea of ⟨I *see* your point⟩ — see COMPREHEND 1
7 to go along with in order to provide assistance, protection, or companionship ⟨thanks for coming, and I'll *see* you to the door⟩ — see ACCOMPANY 1
8 to form a mental picture of ⟨I can't *see* that spoiled brat as a soldier at all⟩ — see IMAGINE 1

seeable *adj* capable of being seen ⟨a *seeable* flaw in the windowpane⟩ — see VISIBLE 1

seed *n* **1** the source from which something grows or develops ⟨ancient Greece provided the *seed* for much of Western civilization's political and philosophical thought⟩
synonyms fountainhead, germ, origin, root, seedbed
related words font, fountain, spring, well, wellhead, wellspring; beginning, birth, commencement, dawn, genesis, inception, incipiency, launch, morning, onset, outset, start, threshold; creation, inauguration, origination
2 the descendants of a person, animal, or plant ⟨the famous stallion's *seed* can be found on racetracks all over the world⟩ — see OFFSPRING

seed *vb* to put or set into the ground to grow ⟨*seeded* grass in the backyard⟩ — see PLANT 1

seedbed *n* **1** a place or environment that favors the development of something ⟨a social and political environment that would later become a *seedbed* of the abolition movement⟩ — see BREEDING GROUND
2 the source from which something grows or develops ⟨that think tank has served as a *seedbed* for American conservatism since the Cold War era⟩ — see SEED 1
3 a point or place at which something is invented or provided ⟨the historic role of the Middle East as a *seedbed* for new religions⟩ — see SOURCE 1

seediness *n* the state of being unattended to or not cared for ⟨the general *seediness* of the neighborhood suggested that its residents had no pride in the place they called home⟩ — see NEGLECT 1

seedy *adj* **1** showing signs of advanced wear and tear and neglect ⟨a *seedy* but historic neighborhood that's just waiting for some new homeowners to come in and rehabilitate it⟩ — see SHABBY 1
2 worn or torn into or as if into rags ⟨chose old, *seedy* clothes to wear while painting the bathroom⟩ — see RAGGED 2

seeing *conj* for the reason that ⟨*seeing* as we're already running late, there's no reason to waste any more time⟩ — see SINCE

seek *vb* **1** to go in search of ⟨Henry Hudson was set adrift by mutinous crewmen while *seeking* the Northwest Passage to the Pacific Ocean⟩
synonyms cast about (for), cast around (for), chase (down), forage (for), hunt, look up, pursue, quest, search (for *or* out), shop (for)
related words ferret (out), root (out)
phrases look for
near antonyms hide, lose; ignore, neglect
2 to make a request for ⟨came *seeking* financial advice⟩ — see ASK (FOR) 1
3 to make an effort to do ⟨*seek* to find the best solution⟩ — see ATTEMPT

seeker *n* one who seeks an office, honor, position, or award ⟨predicted a tough year for summer job *seekers*⟩ — see CANDIDATE

seem *vb* to give the impression of being ⟨I tried to cheer them up because they *seemed* depressed⟩
synonyms act, appear, come across (as), come off (as), feel, look, make, sound
related words dissemble, pretend; recall, resemble, suggest; hint, imply, insinuate

seeming *adj* appearing to be true on the basis of evidence that may or may not be confirmed ⟨a *seeming* contradiction that disappeared upon closer analysis of the text⟩ — see APPARENT 1

seeming *n* outward and often deceptive indication ⟨her altruism is all *seeming*—she cares only about herself⟩ — see APPEARANCE 2

seemingly *adv* to all outward appearances ⟨a *seemingly* contented baby who was fast asleep in his crib⟩ — see APPARENTLY

seemliness *n* the quality or state of being especially suitable or fitting ⟨the *seemliness* of that outfit for church is debatable⟩ — see APPROPRIATENESS

seemly *adj* **1** following the established traditions of refined society and good taste ⟨it would not be *seemly* to use the memorial service as a forum for your political views⟩ — see PROPER 1
2 very pleasing to look at ⟨a young man of *seemly* appearance, robust health, and keen intelligence⟩ — see BEAUTIFUL 1

seep *vb* to flow forth slowly through small openings ⟨water *seeping* through the basement walls⟩ — see EXUDE

seer *n* one who predicts future events or developments ⟨several leading Wall Street *seers* have cautioned investors to prepare for a downturn in the economy⟩ — see PROPHET 1

seesaw *vb* **1** to make a series of unsteady side-to-side motions ⟨as their boat *seesawed* in the rough water, the rescue team tried to get the passengers off the sinking ship⟩ — see ROCK 1
2 to make short up-and-down movements ⟨the price of the stock has been *seesawing* all week⟩ — see NOD

seethe *vb* **1** to be in a state of violent rolling motion ⟨the water *seethed* with schools of feeding piranha⟩
synonyms boil, churn, moil, roil
related words reel, spin, swirl, whirl; agitate, stir
near antonyms abate, calm, subside
2 to be excited or emotionally stirred up with anger ⟨she *seethed* at the very thought of the staff's staggering incompetence⟩ — see BOIL 1

see-through *adj* **1** easily seen through ⟨consumers

pretty much expect *see-through* packaging for bacon⟩ — see CLEAR 1
2 very thin and easy to see through ⟨a designer whose *see-through* clothes scandalized the fashion world back in the 1960s⟩ — see SHEER 1

segment *n* one of the pieces from which something is designed to be assembled ⟨I think I lost one *segment* of this model kit⟩ — see PART 1

segregate *vb* to set or keep apart from others ⟨the sick cows were *segregated* from the remainder of the herd⟩ — see ISOLATE

segregation *n* the state of being alone or kept apart from others ⟨the forced *segregation* of racial minorities was once widely accepted as a fact of life⟩ — see ISOLATION

seize *vb* 1 to have a clear idea of ⟨a critic with a sharp intellect that is able to *seize* the most subtle nuances of a work of art⟩ — see COMPREHEND 1
2 to take or keep under one's control by authority of law ⟨*seized* the leaders of one of the city's major drug rings⟩ — see ARREST 1
3 to take physical control or possession of (something) suddenly or forcibly ⟨*seized* the escaping balloon just before it got out of reach⟩ — see CATCH 1
4 to take or make use of under a guise of authority but without actual right ⟨Richard III *seized* the English throne from his brother Edward in 1483⟩ — see APPROPRIATE 1

seizure *n* 1 a sudden experiencing of a physical or mental disorder ⟨an epileptic *seizure*⟩ — see ATTACK 2
2 the unlawful taking or withholding of something from the rightful owner under a guise of authority ⟨secret intrigues with the czar's ministers that culminated in the czarina's *seizure* of the throne⟩ — see APPROPRIATION 2

seldom *adv* not often ⟨we *seldom* go to the theater downtown because its prices are so high⟩
synonyms infrequently, little, rarely
related words ne'er, never; episodically, irregularly, now and then, occasionally, sometimes, sporadically
phrases once in a blue moon
near antonyms customarily, generally, habitually, ordinarily, routinely, usually; always, constantly, continually, continuously, endlessly, eternally, ever, everlastingly, evermore, forever, invariably, perennially, perpetually, unceasingly; chronically, recurrently, repeatedly
antonyms frequently, oft, often, oftentimes (*or* ofttimes)

select *vb* to decide to accept (someone or something) from a group of possibilities ⟨*selected* only two people out of 300 applicants for the summer internship⟩ — see CHOOSE 1

select *adj* 1 singled out from a number or group as more to one's liking ⟨the company claims to use only *select* beans to make its coffee⟩
synonyms cherry-picked, choice, chosen, elect, favored, favorite, first-line, handpicked, picked, preferred, selected
related words fashionable; exclusive; culled, picked over, screened, weeded (out), winnowed (out)
phrases of choice
near antonyms average, common, commonplace, ordinary, run-of-the-mill
2 having qualities that appeal to a refined taste ⟨*select* fabrics that the shop makes into expensive suits for its well-heeled clientele⟩ — see CHOICE 1

selected *adj* singled out from a number or group as more to one's liking ⟨a *selected* brand of ice cream with an exceptionally high butterfat content⟩ — see SELECT 1

selectee *n* 1 a person forced or required to enroll in military service ⟨had the dubious distinction of being the last *selectee* to serve in the Vietnam War⟩ — see CONSCRIPT
2 one who has been chosen by some authority for a specific position or duty ⟨NASA's roster of *selectees* for its astronaut training program⟩ — see APPOINTEE

selecting *n* the act or process of selecting ⟨the *selecting* of the party's nominee took three days and half a dozen votes⟩ — see SELECTION 1

selection *n* 1 the act or process of selecting ⟨his *selection* of a running mate was a long, tedious affair⟩
synonyms choice, choosing, election, picking, selecting
related words option; appointment, assignment, designation, naming, nomination; decision
2 a person or thing that is chosen ⟨our *selection* was the third entrant in the dog show⟩ — see CHOICE 2
3 the power, right, or opportunity to choose ⟨the inn's table d'hôte is excellent, but there's very limited *selection*⟩ — see CHOICE 1
4 a number of things selected from a group to stand for the whole ⟨a *selection* of the company's latest line of products for display at the trade show⟩ — see SAMPLE 1

selective *adj* tending to select carefully ⟨we were highly *selective* about the music we listened to while trying out loudspeakers⟩
synonyms choosy (*or* choosey), particular, picky
related words nice; fastidious, finical, finicking, finicky, fussy; discerning, discriminating, judicious
near antonyms indiscriminate, indiscriminating
antonyms nonselective, unselective

selector *n* someone with the right or responsibility for making a selection ⟨the librarians who are the *selectors* of the annual award for best children's book⟩
synonyms chooser, namer, picker
related words elector, voter; nominator; decider

self *adj* having or consisting of a single color ⟨a *self*-red rose of a shade that hasn't been seen before⟩ — see MONOCHROMATIC 1

self *n* the set of qualities that makes a person, a group of people, or a thing different from others ⟨some believe that it's only in times of great stress that a person's true *self* is revealed⟩ — see NATURE 1

self–abnegating *adj* given to or marked by restraint in the satisfaction of one's appetites ⟨obviously not for the *self-abnegating* vacationer, this luxury resort is for those whose budgets and appetites know no limit⟩ — see ABSTEMIOUS

self–abnegation *n* voluntary restraint in the satisfaction of one's appetites ⟨even after acquiring great wealth, he continued to practice a kind of puritanical *self-abnegation*⟩ — see ABSTINENCE 1

self–absorbed *adj* overly concerned with one's own desires, needs, or interests ⟨a *self-absorbed* man who seems utterly oblivious to the social problems of his own urban neighborhood⟩ — see EGOCENTRIC

self–absorption *n* excessive interest in oneself ⟨the novel's major characters all suffer from *self-absorption*, and they are every bit as insufferable as such people are in real life⟩ — see EGOISM

self–acting *adj* designed to replace or decrease human labor and especially physical labor ⟨*self-acting* machines that were ushered in with the industrial revolution⟩ — see LABORSAVING

self–admiration *n* an often unjustified feeling of being pleased with oneself or with one's situation or achievements ⟨his overweening *self-admiration* blinded him to constructive criticism of any kind⟩ — see COMPLACENCE 1

self–asserting *adj* 1 having a feeling of superiority that shows itself in an overbearing attitude ⟨a bunch of *self-asserting* upstarts who thought that they could buy their way into high society⟩ — see ARROGANT

2 having or showing great faith in oneself or one's abilities ‹it takes a rather *self-asserting* young man to start a business at such a tender age› — see CONFIDENT 1
3 having or showing a bold forcefulness in the pursuit of a goal ‹just the kind of cocky, *self-asserting* person that you'd expect a sports agent to be› — see AGGRESSIVE 1
self–assertive *adj* 1 having or showing a bold forcefulness in the pursuit of a goal ‹we need to hire *self-assertive* salespeople who don't require constant supervision› — see AGGRESSIVE 1
2 having a feeling of superiority that shows itself in an overbearing attitude ‹we chose a less *self-assertive* and more self-effacing applicant› — see ARROGANT
self–assumption *n* an often unjustified feeling of being pleased with oneself or with one's situation or achievements ‹the *self-assumption* of the young Internet entrepreneur was positively stunning› — see COMPLACENCE 1
self–assurance *n* great faith in oneself or one's abilities ‹her *self-assurance* led her to quit her dead-end job and start her own company› — see CONFIDENCE 1
self–assured *adj* having or showing great faith in oneself or one's abilities ‹he's a *self-assured* yachtsman who's not at all intimidated by the competition› — see CONFIDENT 1
self–assuredness *n* great faith in oneself or one's abilities ‹with the *self-assuredness* of an old pro, the young gymnast executed the difficult feat› — see CONFIDENCE 1
self–belt *n* a strip of flexible material (as leather) worn around the waist ‹the *self-belt* is covered with the same faux suede as the dress› — see [2]BELT 1
self–centered *adj* overly concerned with one's own desires, needs, or interests ‹a group of *self-centered* residents with no interest or involvement in their community› — see EGOCENTRIC
self–centeredness *n* excessive interest in oneself ‹in her extreme *self-centeredness* she hadn't even noticed that her friend was depressed› — see EGOISM
self–colored *adj* having or consisting of a single color ‹although a *self-colored* cat is most frequently black, it may also be brown, cream, lilac, blue, or red› — see MONOCHROMATIC 1
self–command *n* 1 the checking of one's true feelings and impulses when dealing with others ‹the discredited belief that young men and women lacked the *self-command* to serve alongside one another in the military› — see CONSTRAINT 1
2 the power to control one's actions, impulses, or emotions ‹an aloof man of great *self-command* but little charm› — see WILL 1
self–composed *adj* free from emotional or mental agitation ‹appeared remarkably *self-composed* for someone who had just been sentenced to life imprisonment› — see CALM 2
self–composedness *n* evenness of emotions or temper ‹with the *self-composedness* of a brain surgeon, the contestant gave his answer for the million-dollar question› — see EQUANIMITY
self–conceit *n* an often unjustified feeling of being pleased with oneself or with one's situation or achievements ‹the movie star became a victim of her own *self-conceit*, having deluded herself into believing that she was as great as her press agent said she was› — see COMPLACENCE 1
self–conceited *adj* having too high an opinion of oneself ‹a *self-conceited* medical researcher who never acknowledges her colleagues' contributions› — see CONCEITED
self–concern *n* excessive interest in oneself ‹the expectation was that her *self-concern* would diminish once she had a baby to take care of› — see EGOISM
self–concerned *adj* overly concerned with one's own desires, needs, or interests ‹doubted that her *self-concerned* coworkers wanted to hear about her marital problems› — see EGOCENTRIC
self–confession *n* an open declaration of something (as a fault or the commission of an offense) about oneself ‹by his own *self-confession*, he cravenly betrayed his wife› — see CONFESSION
self–confidence *n* great faith in oneself or one's abilities ‹for so young a pianist, he has remarkable composure and *self-confidence* on stage› — see CONFIDENCE 1
self–confident *adj* having or showing great faith in oneself or one's abilities ‹only a *self-confident* person can win the trust of the people and serve as an effective leader› — see CONFIDENT 1
self–congratulation *n* an often unjustified feeling of being pleased with oneself or with one's situation or achievements ‹the air of *self-congratulation* that pervades the songwriter's memoirs› — see COMPLACENCE 1
self–consequence *n* an exaggerated sense of one's importance that shows itself in the making of excessive or unjustified claims ‹had the *self-consequence* of someone who was born wealthy and never had to work a day in his life› — see ARROGANCE
self–containment *n* the power to control one's actions, impulses, or emotions ‹a man of extraordinary *self-containment*, he refused to lose his temper even in the most trying of circumstances› — see WILL 1
self–contemplation *n* examination of one's own thoughts and feelings ‹she doesn't seem to see the difference between a reasonable amount of *self-contemplation* and total self-absorption› — see INTROSPECTION
self–control *n* 1 the power to control one's actions, impulses, or emotions ‹toddlers have very little *self-control*› — see WILL 1
2 the checking of one's true feelings and impulses when dealing with others ‹she could be passionate and intense, but generally exercised steely *self-control* in the company of strangers› — see CONSTRAINT 1
self–denial *n* 1 the act or practice of giving up or rejecting something once enjoyed or desired ‹dieting is an endless exercise in *self-denial*› — see RENUNCIATION
2 voluntary restraint in the satisfaction of one's appetites ‹self-indulgent even when she was poor, she wasn't about to practice *self-denial* after getting rich› — see ABSTINENCE 1
self–denying *adj* given to or marked by restraint in the satisfaction of one's appetites ‹found the *self-denying* life of the monks at the monastery unexpectedly appealing› — see ABSTEMIOUS
self–dependence *n* the ability to care for one's self ‹encouraged her children to develop *self-dependence* at a relatively early age› — see SELF-SUFFICIENCY
self–dependent *adj* able to take care of oneself or itself without outside help ‹a program to help teenage parents become *self-dependent*› — see SELF-SUFFICIENT
self–destruction *n* the act of deliberately killing oneself ‹the controversy over *self-destruction* accomplished with the assistance of a physician or other person› — see SUICIDE
self–determination *n* 1 the act or power of making one's own choices or decisions ‹the United States officially recognizes 18 as the age at which someone is entitled to *self-determination*› — see FREE WILL
2 the state of being free from the control or power of another ‹rebels fighting for the territory's *self-determination*› — see FREEDOM 1
self–discipline *n* the power to control one's actions,

impulses, or emotions ⟨it takes *self-discipline* not to yell out when someone makes you angry⟩ — see WILL 1

self–educated *adj* having skills or knowledge acquired through one's own efforts without formal training ⟨a *self-educated* computer programmer who launched a successful business online⟩ — see SELF-TAUGHT

self–effacing *adj* not comfortable around people ⟨he's dating a sweet, *self-effacing* girl⟩ — see SHY 2

self–esteem *n* **1** a reasonable or justifiable sense of one's worth or importance ⟨friends and family have tried to help the shy child develop some *self-esteem*⟩ — see PRIDE 1

2 an often unjustified feeling of being pleased with oneself or with one's situation or achievements ⟨his towering *self-esteem* made praise from other people entirely unnecessary⟩ — see COMPLACENCE 1

3 great faith in oneself or one's abilities ⟨the kind of *self-esteem* that a struggling actor needs to keep going in the face of constant discouragement and rejection⟩ — see CONFIDENCE 1

self–evident *adj* not needing proof in order to be accepted ⟨the *self-evident* truth that all people have the right of self-determination⟩ — see AXIOMATIC

self–examination *n* examination of one's own thoughts and feelings ⟨many people use the dawning of a new year as an occasion for some quiet *self-examination*⟩ — see INTROSPECTION

self–glory *n* an often unjustified feeling of being pleased with oneself or with one's situation or achievements ⟨the movie star's memoirs come across as being one unending exercise in *self-glory*⟩ — see COMPLACENCE 1

self–governance *n* the state of being free from the control or power of another ⟨despite pessimistic predictions, *self-governance* has worked out well for the former colony⟩ — see FREEDOM 1

self–governed *adj* not being under the rule or control of another ⟨far beyond the reach of civil or military authorities, the settlers on the frontier were essentially *self-governed*⟩ — see FREE 1

self–governing *adj* **1** not being under the rule or control of another ⟨she left home and became entirely *self-governing* and financially independent at the age of 18⟩ — see FREE 1

2 of, relating to, or favoring political democracy ⟨a *self-governing* nation that could be a role model for other countries in the region⟩ — see DEMOCRATIC

self–government *n* **1** government in which the supreme power is held by the people and used by them directly or indirectly through representation ⟨*self-government* implies faith in the wisdom and essential goodness of the people⟩ — see DEMOCRACY

2 the power to control one's actions, impulses, or emotions ⟨steely *self-government* was all that kept her from lashing out at the rude customer⟩ — see WILL 1

3 the state of being free from the control or power of another ⟨championed *self-government* for the nation's indigenous peoples⟩ — see FREEDOM 1

selfhood *n* the set of qualities that make a person different from other people ⟨he spent a year in a monastery determining the core of his *selfhood*⟩ — see INDIVIDUALITY 1

self–identity *n* the set of qualities that make a person different from other people ⟨twins making an effort to establish their separate *self-identities*⟩ — see INDIVIDUALITY 1

self–importance *n* **1** an exaggerated sense of one's importance that shows itself in the making of excessive or unjustified claims ⟨the boxer's flamboyant *self-importance* often made for a colorful prefight press conference⟩ — see ARROGANCE

2 an often unjustified feeling of being pleased with oneself or with one's situation or achievements ⟨her overbearing *self-importance* has given her a sense of entitlement⟩ — see COMPLACENCE 1

self–important *adj* having too high an opinion of oneself ⟨a *self-important* businessman who believed his schedule mattered more than anyone else's⟩ — see CONCEITED

self–imposed *adj* done, made, or given with one's own free will ⟨if the candidates all follow *self-imposed* campaign-spending limits, government oversight is unnecessary⟩ — see VOLUNTARY 1

self–indulgent *adj* given to or marked by excessive gratification of one's desires ⟨a reality show about *self-indulgent* twentysomethings whose sole concerns seem to be getting down and getting drunk⟩ — see HEDONISTIC

self–infatuated *adj* overly concerned with one's own desires, needs, or interests ⟨a physician who specializes in cosmetic surgery mainly for *self-infatuated* socialites⟩ — see EGOCENTRIC

self–instructed *adj* having skills or knowledge acquired through one's own efforts without formal training ⟨a *self-instructed* carpenter who does quality work⟩ — see SELF-TAUGHT

self–interest *n* excessive interest in oneself ⟨her degree of *self-interest* is perhaps best reflected in her favorite topic of conversation—herself⟩ — see EGOISM

self–interested *adj* overly concerned with one's own desires, needs, or interests ⟨a staggeringly *self-interested* careerist who is eminently indifferent to anything that does not affect his personal well-being⟩ — see EGOCENTRIC

self–involved *adj* overly concerned with one's own desires, needs, or interests ⟨most of the local teenagers seem too *self-involved* to care much about the world that lies beyond their affluent suburb⟩ — see EGOCENTRIC

self–involvement *n* excessive interest in oneself ⟨in their *self-involvement*, they never noticed that one of their coworkers was on the verge of an emotional breakdown⟩ — see EGOISM

selfish *adj* overly concerned with one's own desires, needs, or interests ⟨a *selfish* desire to succeed at the expense of others⟩ — see EGOCENTRIC

selfishness *n* excessive interest in oneself ⟨the only reason for constantly ignoring everyone else's problems is *selfishness*⟩ — see EGOISM

self–love *n* an often unjustified feeling of being pleased with oneself or with one's situation or achievements ⟨nurtured a *self-love* that was far greater than any affection she ever felt for another person⟩ — see COMPLACENCE 1

self–loving *adj* overly concerned with one's own desires, needs, or interests ⟨she's too *self-loving* an individual to ever have feelings of real love for another person⟩ — see EGOCENTRIC

self–mastery *n* the power to control one's actions, impulses, or emotions ⟨she had remarkable *self-mastery* for one so young⟩ — see WILL 1

self–murder *n* the act of deliberately killing oneself ⟨how to deter terrorists who are willing to commit *self-murder* as well as the mass murder of innocent people⟩ — see SUICIDE

selfness *n* excessive interest in oneself ⟨there's a relentless *selfness* about her poetry that is wearisome to readers who do not find her endlessly fascinating⟩ — see EGOISM

self–observation *n* examination of one's own thoughts and feelings ⟨some *self-observation* might give you some insights into how others perceive you⟩ — see INTROSPECTION

self–obsessed *adj* overly concerned with one's own

desires, needs, or interests ⟨a *self-obsessed* television journalist, she has a penchant for making herself the focus of every story⟩ — see EGOCENTRIC

self–operating *adj* designed to replace or decrease human labor and especially physical labor ⟨vehicular access to the building complex is controlled by a *self-operating* gate opener⟩ — see LABORSAVING

self–opinion *n* an often unjustified feeling of being pleased with oneself or with one's situation or achievements ⟨an editor of sufficient *self-opinion* to include some of her own work in an anthology of the best American short stories⟩ — see COMPLACENCE 1

self–opinionated *adj* **1** given to or marked by the forceful expression of strongly held opinions ⟨a *self-opinionated* jerk who can't wait to tell you what he thinks about everything⟩ — see DOGMATIC

2 sticking to an opinion, purpose, or course of action in spite of reason, arguments, or persuasion ⟨he's too *self-opinionated* to even consider the possibility that he could be wrong⟩ — see OBSTINATE

3 having too high an opinion of oneself ⟨that *self-opinionated* book reviewer deludes himself in thinking that his reviews really matter⟩ — see CONCEITED

self–opinionatedness *n* a steadfast adherence to an opinion, purpose, or course of action in spite of reason, arguments, or persuasion ⟨*self-opinionatedness* is what callers to that call-in show seem to have in spades⟩ — see OBSTINACY

self–oriented *adj* overly concerned with one's own desires, needs, or interests ⟨trying to sell the virtues of carpooling and public transportation to traditionally *self-oriented* commuters⟩ — see EGOCENTRIC

self–possessed *adj* free from emotional or mental agitation ⟨a supremely *self-possessed* teacher who could handle any crisis⟩ — see CALM 2

self–possession *n* **1** evenness of emotions or temper ⟨that neurosurgeon's *self-possession* in the operating room is legendary⟩ — see EQUANIMITY

2 the power to control one's actions, impulses, or emotions ⟨the little girl's *self-possession* very occasionally gave way to crying fits⟩ — see WILL 1

self–preoccupation *n* excessive interest in oneself ⟨the smug *self-preoccupation* of a generation that had grown up experiencing nothing but affluence⟩ — see EGOISM

self–preoccupied *adj* overly concerned with one's own desires, needs, or interests ⟨one *self-preoccupied* subject in the psychological study was found to use "I" in 80% of his sentences⟩ — see EGOCENTRIC

self–protective *adj* intended to resist or prevent attack or aggression ⟨a *self-protective* gesture to ward off the blow⟩ — see DEFENSIVE

self–questioning *n* examination of one's own thoughts and feelings ⟨so consumed with *self-questioning* that he was virtually paralyzed by self-doubt⟩ — see INTROSPECTION

self–reflection *n* examination of one's own thoughts and feelings ⟨after some *self-reflection* I realized that I hadn't been honest with my partner⟩ — see INTROSPECTION

self–regard *n* **1** excessive interest in oneself ⟨her *self-regard* meant that she assumed everyone wanted to hear about every tiny detail of her life⟩ — see EGOISM

2 a reasonable or justifiable sense of one's worth or importance ⟨people with enough *self-regard* to keep their modest home in spotless condition⟩ — see PRIDE 1

self–regarding *adj* overly concerned with one's own desires, needs, or interests ⟨many residents of that community seem to be into psychoanalysis, a luxury that few but the *self-regarding* wealthy can afford⟩ — see EGOCENTRIC

self–regulating *adj* designed to replace or decrease human labor and especially physical labor ⟨a *self-regulating* thermostat runs the home's heating and cooling system⟩ — see LABORSAVING

self–reliance *n* the ability to care for one's self ⟨some people don't achieve *self-reliance* until they're over 30 years old⟩ — see SELF-SUFFICIENCY

self–reliant *adj* able to take care of oneself or itself without outside help ⟨a surprisingly calm and *self-reliant* child⟩ — see SELF-SUFFICIENT

self–reproach *n* a feeling of responsibility for wrongdoing ⟨he was filled with *self-reproach* for causing the accident⟩ — see GUILT 1

self–respect *n* a reasonable or justifiable sense of one's worth or importance ⟨getting a job and moving out of his parents' house did a lot to increase his *self-respect*⟩ — see PRIDE 1

self–restraint *n* **1** the power to control one's actions, impulses, or emotions ⟨she demonstrated an almost unnatural *self-restraint* during the fight⟩ — see WILL 1

2 the checking of one's true feelings and impulses when dealing with others ⟨we must practice *self-restraint* even with people who are deliberately rude⟩ — see CONSTRAINT 1

self–rule *n* government in which the supreme power is held by the people and used by them directly or indirectly through representation ⟨the newly created United States opted for *self-rule* rather than monarchy⟩ — see DEMOCRACY

self–ruling *adj* **1** of, relating to, or favoring political democracy ⟨having rid itself of the yoke of colonialism, the new nation chose to be a *self-ruling* state⟩ — see DEMOCRATIC

2 not being under the rule or control of another ⟨was granted special status as a *self-ruling* province⟩ — see FREE 1

selfsame *adj* being one and not another ⟨that's the *selfsame* man who once helped me⟩ — see SAME 2

self–satisfaction *n* an often unjustified feeling of being pleased with oneself or with one's situation or achievements ⟨so many of the Web site's self-portraits give the impression of clueless *self-satisfaction*⟩ — see COMPLACENCE 1

self–satisfied *adj* having too high an opinion of oneself ⟨a *self-satisfied* woman who thought that if she could balance two careers, everyone else should too⟩ — see CONCEITED

self–scrutiny *n* examination of one's own thoughts and feelings ⟨not one for *self-scrutiny*, the president was known for never looking back or second-guessing himself⟩ — see INTROSPECTION

self–searching *n* examination of one's own thoughts and feelings ⟨the author seems to use poetry as a medium for her restless *self-searching*⟩ — see INTROSPECTION

self–seeker *n* one who does things only for his own benefit and with little regard for right and wrong ⟨he's a *self-seeker* who is nice only to people who can do him favors⟩

synonyms bottom-feeder, chancer [*British*], opportunist, temporizer

related words egocentric, egoist, egotist; conniver, machinator, plotter, schemer; barracuda, shark; hanger-on, leech

near antonyms altruist

self–seeking *adj* **1** having a strong desire for personal advancement ⟨a *self-seeking* schemer who claimed others' ideas and achievements as his own⟩ — see AMBITIOUS 1

2 overly concerned with one's own desires, needs, or interests ⟨a *self-seeking* woman who could be counted on to sidetrack all conversation into a discussion of her problems⟩ — see EGOCENTRIC

self–serving *adj* overly concerned with one's own desires, needs, or interests ⟨she's just another *self-serving* politician who puts her own ambitions above the public good⟩ — see EGOCENTRIC

self–slaughter *n* the act of deliberately killing oneself ⟨members of the cult decided to hasten the end of their time in this world—and the start of their life in the next—with an orgy of *self-slaughter*⟩ — see SUICIDE

self–starter *n* an ambitious person who eagerly goes after what is desired ⟨hired a *self-starter* who instantly saw what needed to be done, and did it⟩ — see GO-GETTER

self–subsistence *n* the ability to care for one's self ⟨the goal of the program is to help these people achieve *self-subsistence* and to end their dependence on government aid⟩ — see SELF-SUFFICIENCY

self–subsistent *adj* able to take care of oneself or itself without outside help ⟨that country was agronomically *self-subsistent* before industrialization⟩ — see SELF-SUFFICIENT

self–subsisting *adj* able to take care of oneself or itself without outside help ⟨proud that their nonprofit theater was *self-subsisting* and didn't rely on government funding⟩ — see SELF-SUFFICIENT

self–sufficiency *n* the ability to care for one's self ⟨*self-sufficiency* is a goal that all teenagers should work towards⟩
synonyms independence, self-dependence, self-reliance, self-subsistence, self-support
related words autonomy, freedom, self-determination; potency, power, resilience, strength
near antonyms helplessness, impotence, impotency, inadequacy, weakness
antonyms dependence (*also* dependance), reliance

self–sufficient *adj* able to take care of oneself or itself without outside help ⟨the college student worked nights so that he would be *self-sufficient*⟩
synonyms independent, self-dependent, self-reliant, self-subsistent, self-subsisting, self-supported, self-supporting, self-sustained, self-sustaining
related words autonomous, free, self-determining; potent, powerful, resilient, strong
near antonyms helpless, inadequate, incompetent, insufficient; impotent, weak
antonyms dependent, reliant

self–support *n* the ability to care for one's self ⟨hopes to achieve full *self-support* within a year of graduating from college⟩ — see SELF-SUFFICIENCY

self–supported *adj* able to take care of oneself or itself without outside help ⟨only *self-supported* performing arts organizations will survive the huge cut in government subsidies⟩ — see SELF-SUFFICIENT

self–supporting *adj* able to take care of oneself or itself without outside help ⟨she had to take a higher-paying job in order to be *self-supporting*⟩ — see SELF-SUFFICIENT

self–sustained *adj* able to take care of oneself or itself without outside help ⟨each new colony was expected to develop a *self-sustained* economy⟩ — see SELF-SUFFICIENT

self–sustaining *adj* able to take care of oneself or itself without outside help ⟨with its own farm, the estate was largely *self-sustaining*⟩ — see SELF-SUFFICIENT

self–taught *adj* having skills or knowledge acquired through one's own efforts without formal training ⟨the cellist's success is all the more remarkable because she is *self-taught*⟩
synonyms autodidactic, self-educated, self-instructed
related words naïf (*or* naif), naive (*or* naïve), primitive; natural, unschooled, untutored; amateur
near antonyms educated, lettered, schooled, taught, trained

self–trust *n* great faith in oneself or one's abilities ⟨he had the *self-trust* to quit his secure job and start his own business⟩ — see CONFIDENCE 1

self–will *n* a steadfast adherence to an opinion, purpose, or course of action in spite of reason, arguments, or persuasion ⟨a schoolboy with a streak of *self-will* and rebellion⟩ — see OBSTINACY

self–willed *adj* sticking to an opinion, purpose, or course of action in spite of reason, arguments, or persuasion ⟨a *self-willed* toddler who refused to take her shoes off in the examining room⟩ — see OBSTINATE

sell *vb* to offer for sale to the public ⟨used to *sell* groceries in a small neighborhood market⟩ — see MARKET

sell (for) *vb* to have a price of ⟨the house is *selling for* $200,000⟩ — see COST

sell (out) *vb* to be unfaithful or disloyal to ⟨the band *sold out* its faithful followers, abandoning its edgy style for a more commercial sound⟩ — see BETRAY 1

sellable *adj* fit to be offered for sale ⟨the abandoned house is not *sellable* in its current condition⟩ — see MARKETABLE

seller *n* the person in a business deal who hands over an item in exchange for money ⟨the *seller* ceremoniously gave me the title to the car when I handed him my check⟩ — see VENDOR

sellout *n* the act or fact of violating the trust or confidence of another ⟨the *sellout* makes it much harder for me to trust you ever again⟩ — see BETRAYAL

semblance *n* **1** a display of emotion or behavior that is insincere or intended to deceive ⟨tried to project some *semblance* of confidence even though public speaking terrified her⟩ — see MASQUERADE
2 outward and often deceptive indication ⟨a used-car dealer with only a *semblance* of honesty⟩ — see APPEARANCE 2

semidarkness *n* a time or place of little or no light ⟨fumbling around in the *semidarkness*⟩ — see DARK 1

seminar *n* a meeting featuring a group discussion ⟨a *seminar* bringing together the world's leading epidemiologists⟩ — see FORUM 1

seminary *n* **1** a place or establishment for teaching and learning ⟨a *seminary* exclusively for women⟩ — see SCHOOL
2 a place or environment that favors the development of something ⟨some claimed that orphanages were *seminaries* of sin and petty crime, turning out juvenile delinquents by the score⟩ — see BREEDING GROUND

send *vb* to cause to go or be taken from one place to another ⟨they promised to *send* the package in the morning⟩
synonyms consign, dispatch, pack (off), ship, shoot, transfer, transmit, transport
related words convey, deliver, hand over, pass, render; advance, drop, launch; address, forward; export, import; bestow, contribute, donate, give, present; resend, return
near antonyms acquire, draw, earn, gain, garner, get, obtain, procure, secure
antonyms accept, receive

send (out) *vb* to throw or give off ⟨strangely, the air conditioner is *sending out* warm air⟩ — see EMIT 1

send–up *n* a work that imitates and exaggerates another work for comic effect ⟨a singer-comedian who specializes in *send-ups* of pop hits⟩ — see PARODY 1

send up *vb* to copy or exaggerate (someone or something) in order to make fun of ⟨the sitcom *sends up* the "trials and tribulations" of the rich and famous⟩ — see MIMIC 1

senescent *adj* being of advanced years and especially past middle age ⟨symptoms most often seen in *senescent* people⟩ — see ELDERLY

senility *n* the state or period of mental decline that typically accompanies old age ⟨with his increasing *senility*,

Granddad is beginning to have more and more senior moments⟩ — see DOTAGE

senior *adj* being of advanced years and especially past middle age ⟨bought special food intended for *senior* dogs⟩ — see ELDERLY

senior *n* **1** one who is older than another ⟨since the man next door is my *senior* by a number of years, I always address him as "Mr. Barton"⟩
synonyms elder
related words ancestor, forerunner, predecessor
near antonyms contemporary, peer; descendant (*also* descendent), successor
antonyms junior
2 one who is above another in rank, station, or office ⟨the young attorney benefited from the mentorship of one of his *seniors* at the firm⟩ — see SUPERIOR
3 the senior member of a group ⟨when he retires, she will be the *senior* on the faculty⟩ — see DEAN
4 a person of advanced years ⟨weekday movie matinees are often popular with *seniors*⟩ — see SENIOR CITIZEN

senior citizen *n* a person of advanced years ⟨more and more *senior citizens* are living active, rewarding lives⟩
synonyms ancient, elder, geriatric, golden-ager, oldster, old-timer, senior
related words gaffer, graybeard, patriarch, whitebeard; beldam (*or* beldame), dowager, grandam (*or* grandame); adult, grown-up; dotard
near antonyms adolescent, minor; child, cub, juvenile, kid, kiddie (*also* kiddy)
antonyms youngster, youth

sensation *n* **1** an indefinite physical response to a stimulus ⟨we felt just the smallest *sensation* of warmth when we leaned against the radiator⟩
synonyms feel, feeling, sense
related words impression, perception; hint, suggestion, touch
2 a practice or interest that is very popular for a short time ⟨the satirical video was a short-lived online *sensation*⟩ — see FAD
3 something extraordinary or surprising ⟨the first clone was considered a *sensation*⟩ — see WONDER 1

sensational *adj* **1** arousing a strong and usually superficial interest or emotional reaction ⟨the *sensational* news story caused a stir, but after a few days everyone forgot about it⟩
synonyms catchpenny, gee-whiz, lurid, screaming, sensationalist, sensationalistic
related words catchy; colorful, juicy, racy, suggestive; dramatic, histrionic, melodramatic, theatrical (*also* theatric); coarse, vulgar; gory, shocking
near antonyms innocuous, inoffensive, tame; dignified, formal, proper, restrained
antonyms nonsensational
2 of or relating to physical sensation or the senses ⟨*sensational* hallucinations⟩ — see SENSORY
3 of the very best kind ⟨this ice cream is *sensational*⟩ — see EXCELLENT

sensationalist *adj* arousing a strong and usually superficial interest or emotional reaction ⟨a *sensationalist* daytime talk show featuring an endless parade of freaks⟩ — see SENSATIONAL 1

sensationalistic *adj* arousing a strong and usually superficial interest or emotional reaction ⟨letters to the editor criticizing the newspaper's *sensationalistic* reporting⟩ — see SENSATIONAL 1

sense *n* **1** an indefinite physical response to a stimulus ⟨a strange *sense* of discomfort brought on by the room's strong colors⟩ — see SENSATION 1
2 the ability to learn and understand or to deal with problems ⟨although he has little formal education, he is a man of considerable practical *sense*⟩ — see INTELLIGENCE 1
3 the ability to make intelligent decisions especially in everyday matters ⟨you have the *sense* to handle anything that comes up⟩ — see COMMON SENSE
4 the idea that is conveyed or intended to be conveyed to the mind by language, symbol, or action ⟨got the general *sense* of the poem⟩ — see MEANING 1
5 the thought processes that have been established as leading to valid solutions to problems ⟨your argument simply shows no *sense*⟩ — see LOGIC

sense *vb* **1** to have a vague awareness of ⟨the deer seemed to *sense* danger⟩ — see FEEL 1
2 to have a clear idea of ⟨I did not *sense* the full meaning of his cryptic warning until much later⟩ — see COMPREHEND 1

senseless *adj* **1** having lost consciousness ⟨she collapsed, *senseless*, after hitting her head⟩ — see UNCONSCIOUS 1
2 having no meaning ⟨a pretty but *senseless* phrase⟩ — see MEANINGLESS
3 not having or showing an ability to absorb ideas readily ⟨he may be a little absentminded, but he's really not as *senseless* as he seems⟩ — see STUPID 1
4 showing or marked by a lack of good sense or judgment ⟨a *senseless* decision to risk his life on a practical joke⟩ — see FOOLISH 1
5 lacking animate awareness or sensation ⟨even the *senseless* sea seemed determined to swamp the storm-tossed ship⟩ — see INSENSATE 1

senselessness *n* **1** lack of good sense or judgment ⟨who had the *senselessness* to mix these dangerous chemicals together?⟩ — see FOOLISHNESS 1
2 language, behavior, or ideas that are absurd and contrary to good sense ⟨babbled some *senselessness* about being eaten by horses⟩ — see NONSENSE 1
3 the quality or state of lacking intelligence or quickness of mind ⟨the *senselessness* of his decision to drive after drinking so much⟩ — see STUPIDITY 1

sensibilities *n pl* general emotional condition ⟨the violent movie upset their *sensibilities*⟩ — see FEELING 2

sensible *adj* **1** able to be perceived by a sense or by the mind ⟨a *sensible* change in temperature⟩ — see PERCEPTIBLE
2 according to the rules of logic ⟨this is the only *sensible* conclusion⟩ — see LOGICAL 1
3 based on sound reasoning or information ⟨a *sensible* decision to delay marriage until they knew one another better⟩ — see GOOD 1
4 having specified facts or feelings actively impressed on the mind ⟨*sensible* of the shift in attitude by the general public on the issue⟩ — see CONSCIOUS 1

sensibleness *n* the ability to make intelligent decisions especially in everyday matters ⟨proud of their teenage daughter's unfailing *sensibleness* and maturity⟩ — see COMMON SENSE

sensitive *adj* **1** able to sense slight impressions or differences ⟨a scale that is *sensitive* to the smallest change in weight⟩ — see ACUTE 1
2 being in a situation where one is likely to meet with harm ⟨she's very *sensitive* to the sun and will burn if she's outside for any amount of time⟩ — see LIABLE 1
3 easily injured without careful handling ⟨the *sensitive* skin of a newborn mouse⟩ — see TENDER 1
4 of or relating to physical sensation or the senses ⟨*sensitive* data⟩ — see SENSORY
5 requiring exceptional skill or caution in performance or handling ⟨pointing out to the boss that she's wrong is always a *sensitive* task⟩ — see TRICKY 1

sensitiveness *n* the state or quality of being able to sense slight impressions or differences ⟨the extreme *sensitiveness* of the detection mechanism means that the alarm is always going accidentally⟩ — see ACUITY

sensitivity *n* the state or quality of being able to sense slight impressions or differences ⟨the *sensitivity* needed for a microphone that will be used in a recording studio⟩ — see ACUITY

sensor *n* a device that detects some physical quantity and responds usually with a transmitted signal ⟨the thief accidentally triggered the motion *sensor*, which set off the alarm⟩
synonyms detector
related words eye; electric eye, photoelectric cell; alarm (*also* alarum), trigger

sensorial *adj* of or relating to physical sensation or the senses ⟨the art installation combines light and sound effects to create a unique *sensorial* experience⟩ — see SENSORY

sensory *adj* of or relating to physical sensation or the senses ⟨trying to listen to music while watching the TV and eating dinner caused a sort of *sensory* overload⟩
synonyms sensational, sensitive, sensorial, sensuous
related words afferent, receptive; sensate, sensual
near antonyms extrasensory, intuitional

sensual *adj* pleasing to the physical senses ⟨the *sensual* feel of a velvet shirt against the skin⟩
synonyms carnal, fleshly, luscious, lush, sensuous, voluptuous
related words bodily, corporeal; agreeable, delectable, delicious, delightful, dreamy, gratifying, palatable, pleasant, pleasing, pleasurable, scrumptious; epicurean, luxurious, self-indulgent
near antonyms harsh, painful, uncomfortable; disgusting, foul, hideous, icky

sensualist *n* a person whose life is devoted to luxury and sensual pleasures ⟨a sumptuous resort that will satisfy even the most demanding *sensualists*⟩ — see VOLUPTUARY

sensuality *n* excessive pursuit of fleshly pleasures ⟨some readers objected to the novel's graphic depiction of *sensuality*⟩
synonyms carnality, debauchery, hedonism, sybaritism, voluptuousness
related words venery, wantonness; greed, rapaciousness, rapacity, ravenousness; dissipation, gluttony, immoderation, intemperance, self-indulgence
antonyms abstinence, asceticism, sobriety, temperance

sensuous *adj* **1** of or relating to physical sensation or the senses ⟨the *sensuous* pleasure of a massage⟩ — see SENSORY
2 pleasing to the physical senses ⟨a gentle, *sensuous* breeze⟩ — see SENSUAL

sentence *n* a decision made by a court or tribunal regarding a case it has heard ⟨the court-martial pronounced a *sentence* of not guilty on all counts of cowardice⟩
synonyms doom, finding, holding, judgment (*or* judgement), ruling
related words inquest, verdict; authority; decree, edict, injunction, order; arbitrament, award, declaration, deliverance, dictum, pronouncement; conclusion, decision, determination, opinion, resolution; discipline, penalty, punishment

sentence *vb* to impose a judicial punishment on ⟨the judge *sentenced* him to a fine of $50 and time served⟩
synonyms condemn, damn, doom
related words adjudge, judge; castigate, censure, chasten, chastise, correct, discipline, penalize, punish; conclude, decide, decree, determine, find, opine, resolve, rule
near antonyms pardon, reprieve

sententia *n* an often stated observation regarding something from common experience ⟨a handbook of *sententiae* and advice for those about to enter the state of matrimony⟩ — see SAYING

sententious *adj* **1** marked by or given to preaching moral values ⟨a *sententious* crank who has written countless letters to the editor about the decline in family values⟩ — see SERMONIC
2 marked by the use of few words to convey much information or meaning ⟨memoirs that are filled with *sententious* observations on love, marriage, and happiness⟩ — see CONCISE

sententiousness *n* the quality or state of being marked by or using only few words to convey much meaning ⟨the *sententiousness* of the state's motto, "Live Free or Die," has not rendered it any less controversial⟩ — see SUCCINCTNESS

sentient *adj* having specified facts or feelings actively impressed on the mind ⟨*sentient* of the danger posed by the approaching hurricane⟩ — see CONSCIOUS 1

sentiment *n* **1** a subjective response to a person, thing, or situation ⟨a *sentiment* of happiness and goodwill⟩ — see FEELING 1
2 an idea that is believed to be true or valid without positive knowledge ⟨antiwar *sentiments*⟩ — see OPINION 1

sentimental *adj* appealing to the emotions in an obvious and tiresome way ⟨a *sentimental* story about unrequited love⟩ — see CORNY 1

sentimentalism *n* the state or quality of having an excess of tender feelings (as of love, nostalgia, or compassion) ⟨the novel's *sentimentalism* bored me⟩ — see SENTIMENTALITY

sentimentality *n* the state or quality of having an excess of tender feelings (as of love, nostalgia, or compassion) ⟨the *sentimentality* of the story of star-crossed lovers only made it even more popular with moviegoers⟩
synonyms bathos, gooeyness, lovey-doveyness, mawkishness, mush, mushiness, saccharinity, sappiness, sentimentalism, sloppiness, soppiness, syrup (*also* sirup)
related words emotion; sentiment; corn, corniness, hokeyness (*or* hokiness), schmaltz (*also* schmalz)
near antonyms cynicism, hardheadedness, hardheartedness

sentinel *n* a person or group that watches over someone or something ⟨a lone *sentinel* kept watch over the fort⟩ — see GUARD 1

sentry *n* a person or group that watches over someone or something ⟨a *sentry* posted to watch for intruders⟩ — see GUARD 1

separable *adj* capable of being split into two or more parts or pieces ⟨the outdated belief that the atom is the smallest particle of matter and is not *separable*⟩
synonyms divisible
related words detachable, dissociable
near antonyms combinable, joinable
antonyms indivisible, inseparable

separate *adj* **1** not the same or shared ⟨we stayed in *separate* apartments on our vacation⟩
synonyms different, individual, respective
related words disparate, dissimilar, distinct, distinctive, distinguishable, divergent, diverse, unalike, varied, various
near antonyms identical, selfsame, very
antonyms same
2 not physically attached to another unit ⟨the housing development has 200 *separate* homes, each with its own enclosed yard⟩
synonyms detached, disconnected, discrete, free, freestanding, single, unattached, unconnected
related words independent, self-contained; individual, private
near antonyms adjoining
antonyms attached, connected, joined, linked
3 not being under the rule or control of another ⟨the former Soviet republic is now a *separate* country⟩ — see FREE 1
4 of, relating to, or belonging to a single person ⟨the

husband and wife each have *separate* interests⟩ — see INDIVIDUAL 1

separate *vb* **1** to set or force apart ⟨we tried to *separate* the gluey pages, but they were stuck tight⟩

synonyms break up, decouple, disassociate, disconnect, disjoin, disjoint, dissever, dissociate, disunite, divide, divorce, part, ramify, resolve, sever, split, sunder, uncouple, unlink, unyoke

related words break down, decompose, disassemble, disintegrate, dissolve; bifurcate, bisect, cleave, dichotomize, dissect, fractionalize, fractionate, halve, partition, quarter, segment, subdivide, trisect; fragment, fragmentate, fragmentize; break, fracture, pull, rend, rift, rip, rive, rupture, tear; cut off, insulate, isolate, seclude, segregate, sequester; detach, disengage, disentangle, unravel, untie

near antonyms assemble, associate, blend, combine, mingle, mix; connect, couple; accumulate, agglutinate, attach, bind, cement, close, fasten, fuse, knit, stick, weld

antonyms join, link, unify, unite

2 to go or move in different directions from a central point ⟨the searchers *separated* in order to cover more ground⟩

synonyms branch (out), diverge, divide, fork, part, spread

related words bestrew, break up, broadcast, clear out, disband, dispel, disperse, dissipate, distribute, scatter, sow; distance, recede, retreat

near antonyms assemble, gather, meet

antonyms converge, join

3 to arrange or assign according to type ⟨*separate* the students by reading ability⟩ — see CLASSIFY 1

4 to set or keep apart from others ⟨*separated* the injured calf from the herd⟩ — see ISOLATE

5 to understand or point out the difference in ⟨trying to *separate* science from religion on one specific point⟩ — see DISTINGUISH 1

separateness *n* the state of being alone or kept apart from others ⟨the *separateness* of the island community has given it a distinct culture⟩ — see ISOLATION

separation *n* **1** the act or process of a whole separating into two or more parts or pieces ⟨the *separation* of Norway and Sweden into two independent nations in 1905⟩

synonyms bifurcation, breakup, cleavage, dissolution, disunion, division, fractionalization, fractionation, partition, schism, scission, split, sundering

related words breach, rupture; divorce, severance; decomposition, disassembly, dismemberment, segmentation, subdivision; atomization, dichotomization, polarization; diffusion, dispersal, dispersion, scattering; administration, apportionment, distribution; isolation, seclusion, segregation, sequestration

near antonyms assemblage, association; attachment, conjunction, connection, link, linkage, linkup; aggregation, combination, consolidation, fusion

antonyms unification, union

2 the state of being kept distinct ⟨the *separation* of church and state is an important concept in the United States⟩

synonyms demarcation, discreteness, discrimination, distinction

related words differentiation; isolation, segregation

near antonyms blurring, confusion

3 a movement in different directions away from a common point ⟨a sudden *separation* of the herd of deer when they were startled⟩ — see DIVERGENCE 1

4 an open space in a barrier (as a wall or hedge) ⟨the narrow *separation* between posts in the fence⟩ — see GAP 1

5 the act or process of two or more persons going off in different directions ⟨friends who dreaded the inevitable *separation* after graduation⟩ — see PARTING 1

6 something that divides, separates, or marks off ⟨a filing cabinet with lots of adjustable *separations*⟩ — see DIVISION 1

separator *n* something that divides, separates, or marks off ⟨the toddler insisted on a dinner plate with *separators* so that different foods would never touch one another⟩ — see DIVISION 1

sepulchral *adj* causing or marked by an atmosphere lacking in cheer ⟨the decrepit mansion had a *sepulchral* tone that gave everyone a chill⟩ — see GLOOMY 1

sepulchre *or* **sepulcher** *n* a final resting place for a dead person ⟨a poem describing the forgotten *sepulcher* of a valiant knight of the Middle Ages⟩ — see GRAVE 1

sepulture *n* **1** a final resting place for a dead person ⟨opened the *sepulture* and examined the mummy⟩ — see GRAVE 1

2 the act or ceremony of putting a dead body in its final resting place ⟨the final *sepulture* of the body had to wait until the ground thawed⟩ — see BURIAL 1

sequel *n* a condition or occurrence traceable to a cause ⟨higher prices are a logical *sequel* to higher costs for manufacturers⟩ — see EFFECT 1

sequence *n* **1** a condition or occurrence traceable to a cause ⟨the attempt to help was a natural *sequence* to her charitable nature⟩ — see EFFECT 1

2 a series of things linked together ⟨a *sequence* of events that no one predicted⟩ — see CHAIN 1

3 the way objects in space or events in time are arranged or follow one another ⟨police are trying to reconstruct the *sequence* of events⟩ — see ORDER 1

sequent *adj* following one after another without others coming in between ⟨answered three *sequent* questions from one reporter before turning to the others⟩ — see CONSECUTIVE

sequential *adj* following one after another without others coming in between ⟨explained that if the two required algebra semesters weren't *sequential*, the students would likely forget the material⟩ — see CONSECUTIVE

sequentially *adv* in succession without others coming in between ⟨number the art prints in the limited edition *sequentially* so that collectors will know which one they have⟩ — see CONSECUTIVELY

sequester *vb* **1** to set or keep apart from others ⟨*sequestered* the woman until she was no longer contagious⟩ — see ISOLATE

2 to take ownership or control of (something) by right of one's authority ⟨police found and *sequestered* several illegal weapons⟩ — see CONFISCATE

sequestration *n* the state of being alone or kept apart from others ⟨what would you bring for *sequestration* on a desert island?⟩ — see ISOLATION

sequitur *n* an opinion arrived at through a process of reasoning ⟨a reasonable *sequitur* from that announcement is that you'll be leaving the company⟩ — see CONCLUSION 1

sere *also* **sear** *adj* marked by little or no precipitation or humidity ⟨a *sere* region that can't support agriculture⟩ — see DRY 1

serene *adj* **1** free from disturbing noise or uproar ⟨a *serene* vacation spot⟩ — see QUIET 1

2 free from emotional or mental agitation ⟨a *serene* woman who was everyone's source of support⟩ — see CALM 2

3 free from storms or physical disturbance ⟨a *serene* lake⟩ — see CALM 1

sereneness *n* **1** a state of freedom from storm or disturbance ⟨the inviting *sereneness* of the secluded monastery⟩ — see CALM 1

2 freedom from disquieting or oppressive thoughts or emotions ⟨with the *sereneness* of someone who has not the slightest fear of rejection, he asked her to marry him⟩ — see PEACE 2

serenity *n* **1** a state of freedom from storm or disturbance ⟨the *serenity* in the aftermath of the tornado was remarkable⟩ — see CALM 1

2 evenness of emotions or temper ⟨his *serenity* calmed those around him⟩ — see EQUANIMITY

3 freedom from disquieting or oppressive thoughts or emotions ⟨the momentary *serenity* experienced during his lunchtime rambles gets him through the rest of the workday⟩ — see PEACE 2

serial *adj* appearing in parts or numbers that follow regularly ⟨"Uncle Tom's Cabin" first appeared as a *serial* novel from 1851 to 1852⟩

synonyms episodic (*also* episodical), periodical, serialized

related words sequential; successive; periodic, recurrent, recurring, regular

serial *n* a publication that appears at regular intervals ⟨the university library has a vast collection of *serials*⟩ — see JOURNAL 1

serialized *adj* appearing in parts or numbers that follow regularly ⟨a *serialized* made-for-TV movie⟩ — see SERIAL

seriatim *adv* in succession without others coming in between ⟨objections will be dealt with *seriatim*⟩ — see CONSECUTIVELY

serious *adj* **1** not joking or playful in mood or manner ⟨I'm *serious* when I say that no one should be walking in that neighborhood at night⟩

synonyms earnest, grave, humorless, no-nonsense, po-faced [*British*], sedate, severe, sober, sobersided, solemn, staid, uncomic, unsmiling, weighty

related words harsh, stern, strict; businesslike, professional; dignified, distinguished, elevated, serious-minded; gloomy, grim

near antonyms antic, comic, comical, droll, farcical, funny, hilarious, hysterical (*also* hysteric), laughable, light, light-headed, ludicrous, ridiculous, riotous, risible, screaming, sidesplitting, uproarious; featherbrained, flighty, frivolous, goofy, harebrained, lighthearted, puerile, scatterbrained; absurd, asinine, balmy, brainless, cockeyed, crazy, cuckoo, daffy, daft, dotty, fatuous, foolish, half-witted, insane, jerky, kooky (*also* kookie), loony (*also* looney), lunatic, mad, nonsensical, nutty, preposterous, sappy, screwball, senseless, silly, unwise, wacky (*also* whacky), weak-minded, witless, zany

antonyms facetious, flip, flippant, humorous, jesting, jocular, joking, kittenish, ludic, playful

2 having a matter of importance as its topic ⟨a very *serious* film that dealt with the aftermath of the Gulf War⟩

synonyms grave, heavy, weighty

related words big, consequential, eventful, important, major, material, meaningful, momentous, portentous, significant, solid, substantial

near antonyms frivolous, insignificant, lite, little, Mickey Mouse, minor, silly, slight, small, trivial, unimportant

antonyms light, unserious

3 involving potential loss or injury ⟨a *serious* accident⟩ — see DANGEROUS 1

seriously *adv* to a great degree ⟨that's some *seriously* good pie⟩ — see VERY 1

serious–mindedness *n* a mental state free of jesting or trifling ⟨she approached the task with her usual *serious-mindedness*⟩ — see EARNESTNESS

seriousness *n* a mental state free of jesting or trifling ⟨we knew from the doctor's *seriousness* that she didn't have good news⟩ — see EARNESTNESS

sermon *n* a public speech usually by a member of the clergy for the purpose of giving moral guidance or uplift ⟨a *sermon* whose message was that we should love our neighbors as much as we love ourselves⟩

synonyms homily

related words sermonette; address, lecture, speech, talk; exhortation, preachment; lesson

sermonic *adj* marked by or given to preaching moral values ⟨the *sermonic* quality of many 19th-century novels written for young women⟩

synonyms didactic, homiletic (*or* homiletical), moralistic, moralizing, preachy, sententious

related words dogmatic (*also* dogmatical), prescriptive; admonishing, admonitory, cautionary; advisory, enlightening, instructive; holier-than-thou, self-righteous

sermonize *vb* to deliver a sermon ⟨did not believe that it was the president's place to *sermonize*, especially to other world leaders⟩ — see PREACH

serpent *n* **1** a limbless reptile with a long body ⟨an Aztec carving of a feathered *serpent* representing the god Quetzalcoatl⟩ — see SNAKE 1

2 the supreme personification of evil often represented as the ruler of hell ⟨beware the temptations of the *serpent*⟩ — see DEVIL 1

3 one who betrays a trust or an allegiance ⟨a *serpent* in their midst had betrayed the revolutionaries to the authorities⟩ — see TRAITOR

serpentine *adj* marked by a long series of irregular curves ⟨the country inn lies at the end of a rather *serpentine* road, but it's worth the trip⟩ — see CROOKED 1

serrate *adj* notched or toothed along the edge ⟨a *serrate* saw⟩ — see SERRATED

serrated *adj* notched or toothed along the edge ⟨you should use a *serrated* knife when cutting bread, so you don't squash the loaf⟩

synonyms saw-toothed, serrate

related words serried; jagged, ragged; wavy

near antonyms flat, smooth

serried *adj* having little space between items or parts ⟨a sterile subdivision with *serried* rows of cookie-cutter houses⟩ — see CLOSE 1

servant *n* a person hired to perform household or personal services ⟨the wealthy family had *servants* to clean and cook for them⟩

synonyms daily [*British*], domestic, flunky (*also* flunkey *or* flunkie), lackey, menial, retainer, slavey, steward

related words butler, footman, groom, houseboy, houseman, majordomo, man, manservant, servitor, valet; handmaiden (*also* handmaid), housekeeper, housemaid, lady-in-waiting, maid, maidservant, wench, woman; assistant, attendant, companion, factotum, follower; dogsbody [*chiefly British*], drudge, gofer (*or* gopher)

near antonyms boss, captain, chief, foreman, head, headman, helmsman, kingpin, leader, taskmaster

antonyms master, mistress

serve *vb* **1** to be a servant for ⟨he *served* his master faithfully for 20 years⟩

synonyms slave (for), work (for)

related words attend, minister (to), tend (to)

phrases dance attendance (upon), wait on (*also* wait upon)

2 to be enough ⟨they made the pasta *serve* for eight guests⟩

synonyms do, suffice

related words answer, suit; assuage, content, quench, sate, satiate, satisfy

3 to be fitting or proper ⟨those old riding boots will *serve* for now, but you'll need newer ones for the horse show⟩ — see DO 1

4 to behave toward in a stated way ⟨my parents *served* me well in preparing me for life⟩ — see TREAT 1

5 to have a certain purpose ⟨the harsh punishment *served* to teach everyone a lesson⟩ — see FUNCTION
6 to provide with something useful or desirable ⟨an excellent college that *served* her with the skills necessary to make it in today's job market⟩ — see BENEFIT

server *n* a person who serves food or drink ⟨we had barely finished ordering when the *server* brought our salads⟩
synonyms garçon, waiter, waitperson
related words waitress; barkeep (*also* barkeeper), barman [*chiefly British*], bartender; sommelier; steward, stewardess; headwaiter, maître d' (*or* maitre d'), maître d'hôtel

service *adj* of or relating to the armed services ⟨spent his time in the army as a correspondent for *service* newspapers⟩ — see MILITARY 1

service *n* 1 an act of kind assistance ⟨performed many *services* for the charitable organization⟩ — see FAVOR 1
2 the capacity for being useful for some purpose ⟨that broom is worn out beyond all *service*⟩ — see USE 2
3 the combined army, air force, and navy of a nation ⟨at the time the country had about a million men and women in the *service*⟩ — see ARMED FORCES
4 a large unit of a governmental, business, or educational organization ⟨the OSS, the nation's wartime intelligence *service*⟩ — see DIVISION 2

serviceability *n* the capacity for being useful for some purpose ⟨I have doubts about the *serviceability* of some of the junk we've accumulated⟩ — see USE 2

serviceable *adj* 1 capable of being put to use or account ⟨be sure to wear *serviceable* shoes if you're going to be walking on the rocks along the shore⟩ — see PRACTICAL 1
2 capable of or suitable for being used for a particular purpose ⟨a perfectly *serviceable*, if old, set of screwdrivers worked fine for repairing the door⟩ — see USABLE 1
3 of a level of quality that meets one's needs or standards ⟨the acting was *serviceable*, although not particularly inspired⟩ — see ADEQUATE

serviceableness *n* the capacity for being useful for some purpose ⟨the *serviceableness* of most of the junk that my grandfather had been hoarding was very doubtful⟩ — see USE 2

serviceably *adv* in a satisfactory way ⟨although this sleeping bag works *serviceably* for summer camping, it won't do for wintertime outings⟩ — see WELL 1

serviceman *n* a person engaged in military service ⟨wishing our *servicemen* overseas the best of luck⟩ — see SOLDIER

servile *adj* showing, expressing, or offered in a spirit of humility or unseemly submissiveness ⟨had always maintained a *servile* attitude around people with money⟩ — see ABJECT

servility *n* the state of being a slave ⟨the joy that emancipation must have brought to people who had known only *servility* since birth⟩ — see SLAVERY 1

servitude *n* the state of being a slave ⟨the Fugitive Slave Act had the effect of returning slaves who had made it to freedom in the North to a brutal life of *servitude* in the South⟩ — see SLAVERY 1

set *adj* 1 being in a state of fitness for some experience or action ⟨we're all *set* to go⟩ — see READY 1
2 firmly positioned in place and difficult to dislodge ⟨that rock is really *set* in the hillside⟩ — see TIGHT 2
3 fully committed to achieving a goal ⟨*set* on being the first in her family to graduate from college⟩ — see DETERMINED 1
4 having been established and usually not subject to change ⟨the library is only open during *set* hours⟩ — see FIXED 1
5 of a particular or exact sort ⟨international law has *set* rules for the treatment of prisoners of war⟩ — see EXPRESS 1
6 made, given, or done with full awareness of what one is doing ⟨it was not my *set* purpose to cause trouble for anyone⟩ — see INTENTIONAL

set *n* 1 a group of people acting together within a larger group ⟨the younger *set* is less likely to volunteer for the church's annual rummage sale⟩ — see FACTION
2 a group of people sharing a common interest and relating together socially ⟨they rarely associate with anyone outside their social *set*⟩ — see GANG 2
3 a number of things considered as a unit ⟨a *set* of tools⟩ — see GROUP 1
4 one of the units into which a whole is divided on the basis of a common characteristic ⟨the next *set* of job applicants had far more education and practical experience⟩ — see CLASS 2
5 the array of painted backgrounds and furnishings used to establish the setting in a stage production ⟨built *sets* for the play⟩ — see SCENERY

set *vb* 1 to cover and warm eggs as the young inside develop ⟨the hen *set* for days⟩
synonyms brood, hatch, incubate, sit
related words lay, spawn
2 to decide upon (the time or date for an event) usually from a position of authority ⟨*set* a date for the wedding⟩ — see APPOINT 1
3 to make an approximate or tentative judgment regarding ⟨fire losses were *set* at a million dollars⟩ — see ESTIMATE 1
4 *chiefly dialect* to rest on the buttocks or haunches ⟨come over and *set* for a spell⟩ — see SIT 1
5 to point or turn (something) toward a target or goal ⟨determined to see the West, she *set* her car towards the sun and drove off⟩ — see AIM 1
6 to come to an agreement or decision concerning the details of ⟨finally *set* some plans for the luncheon⟩ — see ARRANGE 1
7 to put securely in place or in a desired position ⟨had the jeweler *set* the diamond again⟩ — see FASTEN 2
8 to turn from a liquid into a substance resembling jelly ⟨the gelatin is just starting to *set* now⟩ — see COAGULATE
9 to arrange something in a certain spot or position ⟨*set* a book on the table⟩ — see PLACE 1
10 to become physically firm or solid ⟨the concrete must *set* completely before anyone can walk on it⟩ — see HARDEN 1

setback *n* a change in status for the worse usually temporarily ⟨the colonists persevered despite suffering *setbacks* that would have discouraged lesser souls⟩ — see REVERSE 1

set by *vb* to keep or intend for a special purpose ⟨I have *set by* the earnings from my weekend job to use as vacation money⟩ — see DEVOTE 1

set down *vb* 1 to cause to sit down ⟨*set* the toddler *down* in her seat⟩ — see SEAT 1
2 to make a written note of ⟨*set down* the names of those in attendance⟩ — see RECORD 1
3 to think of in a particular way ⟨early in the campaign, voters *set* the senator *down* as an opportunist, and the perception stuck⟩ — see CONSIDER 1

set in *vb* to come into existence ⟨a cold spell *set in* sometime last week⟩ — see BEGIN 2

setoff *n* something that decorates or beautifies ⟨the architect used stone carvings as *setoffs* for the building's marble facing⟩ — see DECORATION 1

set off *vb* to cause to function ⟨*set off* a bomb⟩ — see ACTIVATE

set on *vb* to take sudden, violent action against ⟨without warning, bandits would *set on* unwary merchants as they traveled along the Silk Road⟩ — see ATTACK 1

setout *n* the way in which something is sized, arranged, or organized ⟨the *setout* of the stations at the polling place was a little confusing⟩ — see FORMAT 1

set out *vb* to give a representation or account of in words ⟨in his inaugural address, the president *set out* his vision for the nation over the next four years⟩ — see DESCRIBE 1

settee *n* a long upholstered piece of furniture designed for several sitters ⟨the young couple snuggled on the *settee*⟩ — see COUCH

setting *n* **1** the circumstances, conditions, or objects by which one is surrounded ⟨the novice camper felt lost outside of his familiar urban *setting*⟩ — see ENVIRONMENT

2 the place and time in which the action for a portion of a dramatic work (as a movie) is set ⟨the *setting* for the novel is Victorian England⟩ — see SCENE 1

settle *vb* **1** to cause to come to rest at the bottom (as of a liquid) ⟨the light rain will *settle* the dust in the air⟩ ⟨careful handling will *settle* the lees in the bottom of the wine bottle⟩

synonyms lay, sediment

related words filter, screen, sieve, sift, strain; clarify, clear; resettle

near antonyms agitate, disturb, mix, stir

antonyms raise

2 to supply with inhabitants ⟨the region was originally *settled* by farmers⟩

synonyms colonize, people, populate

related words inhabit; move (to), relocate (to)

antonyms depopulate, unpeople

3 to give an opinion about (something at issue or in dispute) ⟨*settled* the lawsuit in favor of the defendant⟩ — see JUDGE 1

4 to come to an agreement or decision concerning the details of ⟨*settled* their wedding plans without any major disagreements⟩ — see ARRANGE 1

5 to come to rest after descending from the air ⟨birds *settling* on the branches of the maple tree⟩ — see ALIGHT 1

6 to establish or place comfortably or snugly ⟨*settled* the sleeping baby into her crib⟩ — see ENSCONCE 1

7 to free from distress or disturbance ⟨a hot meal *settled* the children down⟩ — see CALM 1

8 to gain emotional or mental control of ⟨*settled* himself only with visible effort after the angry outburst⟩ — see COLLECT 1

9 to give what is owed for ⟨*settle* a debt⟩ — see PAY 2

10 to make final, definite, or beyond dispute ⟨this information should *settle* the question of who is right⟩ — see CLINCH

11 to stop the noise or speech of ⟨*settled* the class with a firm "quiet!"⟩ — see SILENCE 1

settle (down) *vb* to become still and orderly ⟨*settle down* and get to work, please⟩ — see QUIET 1

settle (on *or* upon) *vb* to come to a judgment about after discussion or consideration ⟨the car buyer *settled on* that brand only after a lot of research⟩ — see DECIDE 1

settled *adj* **1** firmly established over time ⟨a remote village with a *settled* distrust of outsiders⟩ — see INVETERATE 1

2 having been established and usually not subject to change ⟨*settled* rules that cannot be disregarded when it is convenient to do so⟩ — see FIXED 1

settlement *n* an arrangement about action to be taken ⟨eventually reached a peace *settlement*⟩ — see AGREEMENT 2

settler *n* **1** a person who settles in a new region ⟨*settlers* learning to live in peace with the natives⟩ — see FRONTIERSMAN

2 one that leaves one place to settle in another ⟨in 1889 Jane Addams, in an effort to provide Chicago's latest wave of *settlers* with much-needed services, founded the city's first settlement house⟩ — see EMIGRANT

settlings *n pl* matter that settles to the bottom of a body of liquid ⟨a wine of that advanced age is likely to have a fair amount of *settlings*⟩ — see DEPOSIT 1

set–to *n* an often noisy or angry expression of differing opinions ⟨they had a brief *set-to* about money, but they seem to have resolved it⟩ — see ARGUMENT 1

setup *n* **1** the way in which something is sized, arranged, or organized ⟨the textbook's *setup* calls for a list of questions at the end of each chapter⟩ — see FORMAT 1

2 the way objects in space or events in time are arranged or follow one another ⟨changed the *setup* of the living room furniture several times before being satisfied⟩ — see ORDER 1

set up *vb* **1** to arrange something in a certain spot or position ⟨*set up* tables in the living room for the party⟩ — see PLACE 1

2 to be responsible for the creation and early operation or use of ⟨*set up* a scholarship fund for deserving students from the inner city⟩ — see FOUND

3 to fix in an upright position ⟨*set up* a post from which to hang the sign⟩ — see ERECT 1

4 to form by putting together parts or materials ⟨*set up* the prefabricated shed by following the instructions⟩ — see BUILD

5 to restore to a healthy condition ⟨don't worry, the doctor will *set* you *up* in no time⟩ — see HEAL 1

seven seas *n pl* the whole body of salt water that covers nearly three-fourths of the earth ⟨sailing the *seven seas* in search of adventure⟩ — see OCEAN 1

seventh heaven *n* a state of overwhelming usually pleasurable emotion ⟨she was in *seventh heaven* when she received the acceptance letter to medical school⟩ — see ECSTASY

sever *vb* to set or force apart ⟨disapproving parents who were willing to do anything to *sever* the young lovers⟩ — see SEPARATE 1

severe *adj* **1** given to exacting standards of discipline and self-restraint ⟨a *severe*, uncompromising teacher who locked the classroom door precisely when the bell rang and let no one in afterward⟩

synonyms austere, authoritarian, flinty, hard, harsh, heavy-handed, ramrod, rigid, rigorous, stern, strict, tough

related words demanding, exacting; uncharitable, unforgiving; adamant, adamantine, callous, hardened, hard-hearted, hard-line, immovable, implacable, inflexible, merciless, ossified, pitiless, relentless, rock-ribbed, stiff, unbending, uncompromising, unrelenting, unsparing, unyielding; dour, gruff; ascetic (*also* ascetical), monastic, monkish; browbeating, bullying; determined, firm, resolved, single-minded, steadfast, unflinching; dogged, intractable, obstinate, relentless

near antonyms easy, easygoing, laid-back, undemanding; charitable, kind, merciful, mild, patient, soft, softhearted; accepting, compromising, yielding; responsive, willing; acquiescent, agreeable, amenable, complaisant, compliant, flexible, pliable, pliant

antonyms clement, forbearing, gentle, indulgent, lax, lenient, tolerant

2 harsh and threatening in manner or appearance ⟨clergymen who dressed in *severe* clothing⟩ — see GRIM 1

3 not joking or playful in mood or manner ⟨the judge maintained a *severe* expression throughout the trial⟩ — see SERIOUS 1

4 difficult to endure ⟨a *severe* winter that was among the coldest on record⟩ — see HARSH 1

5 requiring considerable physical or mental effort ⟨a *severe* test of courage⟩ — see HARD 2

severely *adv* **1** in a manner so as to cause loss or suffer-

ing ⟨the building was *severely* damaged by the explosion⟩ — see HARDLY 1
2 to a great degree ⟨the rescued mountain climbers were *severely* dehydrated⟩ — see VERY 1

severity *n* the quality or state of being demanding or unyielding (as in discipline or criticism) ⟨even though no one expected the film to be a hit with the critics, the director was taken aback by the *severity* of the criticism⟩
synonyms exactingness, hardness, harshness, inflexibility, rigidity, rigidness, rigor, rigorousness, sternness, strictness, stringency
related words callousness, hard-heartedness, implacability, obduracy, obdurateness, pitilessness; dourness, gruffness; asceticism, austereness, austerity, monasticism; determination, firmness, resolve, steadfastness; obstinacy, stubbornness
near antonyms forbearance, indulgence, kindness, lenience, patience, softness, tenderness, tolerance; responsiveness, willingness; compliance, pliability, pliancy
antonyms flexibility, gentleness, laxness, mildness

sew *vb* to close up with a series of interlacing stitches ⟨luckily, I was able to *sew* the tear so skillfully that my pants looked as good as new⟩
synonyms darn, stitch, suture
related words mend, patch, repair; baste, ease, fell, finish, overcast; cross-stitch, embroider; crochet, knit, quilt
near antonyms unsew

sewer *n* a person who sews ⟨a good *sewer* who designs her own clothing⟩
synonyms seamster, stitcher
related words needlewoman, seamstress; tailor; embroiderer, needleworker; knitter, weaver

sew up *vb* to have complete control over ⟨*sewed up* the available openings so that no one else had a chance to play golf⟩ — see MONOPOLIZE

sex *n* sexual union involving penetration of the vagina by the penis ⟨the students learned about the mechanics of *sex* and reproduction in health class⟩ — see SEXUAL INTERCOURSE

sex act *n* sexual union involving penetration of the vagina by the penis ⟨the infection can be communicated through the *sex act*⟩ — see SEXUAL INTERCOURSE

sexual assault *n* the act of forcing a person to engage in sexual activity and especially intercourse ⟨convicted of *sexual assault* of a minor⟩ — see RAPE 1

sexual intercourse *n* sexual union involving penetration of the vagina by the penis ⟨many people believe that it's best to wait to experience *sexual intercourse* until you're mature enough to handle it⟩
synonyms coition, coitus, commerce, congress, copulating, copulation, coupling, intercourse, lovemaking, mating, relations, sex, sex act, sexual relations
related words fornication; safe sex; carnality, sexuality; breeding, insemination; dalliance, hanky-panky, whoopee
phrases getting it on, making love

sexual relations *n pl* sexual union involving penetration of the vagina by the penis ⟨adultery is defined as a married person engaging in *sexual relations* with someone other than their spouse⟩ — see SEXUAL INTERCOURSE

sex worker *n* a woman who engages in sexual activities for money ⟨a group that serves as an advocate for the health and welfare of *sex workers*⟩ — see PROSTITUTE

sexy *adj* **1** sexually attractive ⟨even after 30 years of marriage, he still finds his wife *sexy*⟩
synonyms bodacious, desirable, dishy, hot, luscious, toothsome
related words foxy, nubile; hunky, studly [*slang*]; alluring, seductive, sultry, vampish, vampy
2 of, relating to, exciting, or expressing sexual attraction or desire ⟨he found her new dress very *sexy* while still being tasteful⟩ — see EROTIC

shabby *adj* **1** showing signs of advanced wear and tear and neglect ⟨*shabby* wallpaper that was peeling from the walls⟩
synonyms beat-up, bombed-out, dilapidated, dog-eared, down-at-the-heels (*or* down-at-heel *also* down-at-the-heel *or* down-at-heels), dumpy, grungy, mangy, mean, miserable, moth-eaten, neglected, ratty, run-down, scrubby, scruffy, seedy, sleazy, tacky, tatterdemalion, tatty, threadbare, timeworn, tumbledown
related words abandoned, uncared-for, unkept; desolate, forlorn, godforsaken; broken-down, decrepit, tired, worn-out; bedraggled, dingy, ragged, tattered; decaying, deteriorated, deteriorating, rackety, ramshackle, rattletrap, rickety, tumbledown; broken, damaged, destroyed, harmed, hurt, impaired, injured, ruined, wrecked
phrases gone to seed
near antonyms brand-new, fresh, new; cared-for, kept-up, maintained; mended, patched, rebuilt, reconstructed; smart, spiffy, spruce
2 worn or torn into or as if into rags ⟨*shabby*, stained clothes that are barely better than rags⟩ — see RAGGED 2

shack *n* a small, simply constructed, and often temporary dwelling ⟨a farmer's *shack* out in the fields that's used for lambing and as a shelter from storms⟩
synonyms cabin, camp, hooch (*or* hootch) [*slang*], hovel, hut, hutch, hutment, shanty
related words lean-to, shed; cot, cottage, lodge; cabana; bungalow, chalet; hogan, wickiup, wigwam; tent

shackle *n* **1** something that physically prevents free movement ⟨placed *shackles* on the legs of the prisoners⟩ — see BOND 1
2 shackles *pl* something that makes movement or progress difficult ⟨the *shackles* of illiteracy can be just as confining as leg irons⟩ — see ENCUMBRANCE

shackle *vb* **1** to confine or restrain with or as if with chains ⟨unwilling to *shackle* the dogs to the wall of the house⟩ — see BIND 1
2 to create difficulty for the work or activity of ⟨*shackled* by poverty and ignorance⟩ — see HAMPER

shade *n* **1** partial darkness due to the obstruction of light rays ⟨it was hard to see in the *shade* after being in the brilliant sunlight⟩ ⟨the trees cast *shade*⟩
synonyms dusk, penumbra, shadiness, shadow, umbra
related words blackness, dimness, duskiness, gloom, gloominess, murkiness, obscurity, semidarkness, somberness; cloudiness
near antonyms brightness, brilliance, effulgence, illumination, incandescence, light, lightness, lucidity, lucidness, luminance, luminosity, luminousness, radiance, radiancy
2 a time or place of little or no light ⟨enjoying the cool *shade* of the evening⟩ — see DARK 1
3 a property that becomes apparent when light falls on an object and by which things that are identical in form can be distinguished ⟨a lovely *shade* of blue⟩ — see COLOR 1
4 a very small amount ⟨just a *shade* taller than his dance partner⟩ — see PARTICLE 1
5 the soul of a dead person thought of especially as appearing to living people ⟨spirits and *shades* haunting the night⟩ — see GHOST 1

shade *vb* to shelter (something) from light and heat ⟨the trees *shaded* us quite nicely from the noonday sun⟩
synonyms shadow
related words cloud, darken, dim, dull, overcast, over-

shadow; canopy, cover, protect, screen
near antonyms illuminate, light, lighten; expose

shaded *adj* protected from the sun's rays ⟨walking along the park's *shaded* pathway⟩ — see SHADY 1

shadiness *n* partial darkness due to the obstruction of light rays ⟨the inviting *shadiness* of a woodland grove⟩ — see SHADE 1

shadow *n* **1** partial darkness due to the obstruction of light rays ⟨the valley was in *shadow*⟩ — see SHADE 1
2 shadows *pl* a time or place of little or no light ⟨lurking in the *shadows*⟩ — see DARK 1
3 a tiny often physical indication of something lost or vanished ⟨a run-down mansion that is only a *shadow* of its former glory⟩ — see VESTIGE 1
4 a very small amount ⟨not even a *shadow* of a doubt about the defendant's guilt⟩ — see PARTICLE 1
5 the soul of a dead person thought of especially as appearing to living people ⟨rumors of a *shadow* haunting the castle⟩ — see GHOST 1
6 an overspreading element that produces an atmosphere of gloom ⟨the husband's adulterous affair had cast over their marriage a *shadow* from which there was no escape⟩ — see CLOUD

shadow *vb* **1** to go after or on the track of ⟨*shadowing* the suspect to see what he was up to⟩ — see FOLLOW 2
2 to make dark, dim, or indistinct ⟨thickening clouds *shadowed* the countryside⟩ — see CLOUD 1
3 to shelter (something) from light and heat ⟨a pathway *shadowed* by a canopy of arching branches⟩ — see SHADE

shadowed *adj* protected from the sun's rays ⟨sat in a *shadowed* corner of the garden⟩ — see SHADY 1

shadowing *n* the act of going after or in the tracks of another ⟨the submarine's relentless *shadowing* of the destroyer⟩ — see PURSUIT 1

shadowy *adj* **1** not seen or understood clearly ⟨the *shadowy* area between tough interrogation and torture⟩ — see FAINT 1
2 protected from the sun's rays ⟨a *shadowy* lane that is a mosaic of colors during the autumn foliage season⟩ — see SHADY 1

shady *adj* **1** protected from the sun's rays ⟨a lovely *shady* spot in the park that was pleasantly cool⟩
synonyms shaded, shadowed, shadowy, umbrageous
related words canopied, covered, sheltered; cloudy; dark, darkened, darkish, darkling, darksome, dim, dimmed, dusky, gloomy, inky, moonless, murky, obscure, obscured, penumbral, pitch-black, pitch-dark, somber (*or* sombre), sunless
near antonyms bedazzling, bright, brightened, brilliant, dazzling, effulgent, illuminated, illumined, incandescent, light, lit (*or* lighted), lucent, lucid, luminary, luminous; beaming, lambent, radiant, shining; lustrous
antonyms exposed, shadeless, sunny
2 given to or marked by cheating and deception ⟨a *shady* business deal⟩ — see DISHONEST 2
3 giving good reason for being doubted, questioned, or challenged ⟨cited some *shady* statistics to back up his argument⟩ — see DOUBTFUL 2
4 given to acting in secret and to concealing one's intentions ⟨*shady* characters hanging out in the park after nightfall⟩ — see SNEAKY 1
5 not respectable ⟨a courtesan who lived on the *shady* fringe of society⟩ — see DISREPUTABLE

shaft *n* **1** a narrow sharply defined line of light radiating from an object ⟨*shafts* of late-afternoon sunlight pierced the blinds and streaked the floor⟩
synonyms beam, ray
related words moonbeam, sunbeam, sunburst; laser, spotlight
2 a weapon with a long straight handle and sharp head or blade ⟨the footmen set their *shafts* so as to form a bank of steel against the enemy's charging cavalry⟩ — see SPEAR
3 unfair or inadequate treatment of someone or something or an instance of this ⟨the homeowners who were bought out are convinced they got the *shaft* in that deal⟩ — see DISSERVICE

shaggy *adj* **1** covered with or as if with hair ⟨a big, *shaggy* dog kept trying to lick my face⟩ — see HAIRY 1
2 made of or resembling hair ⟨a *shaggy* carpet that was a relic of the 1970s⟩ — see HAIRY 2

shaitan *n* an evil spirit ⟨her fate was sealed once she let the *shaitan* out of the bottle⟩ — see DEMON 1

shake *n* **1** a very small space of time ⟨I'll be there in two *shakes*⟩ — see INSTANT
2 shakes *pl* a sense of panic or extreme nervousness ⟨I get the *shakes* every time I hear her voice⟩ — see JITTERS
3 a shaking of the earth ⟨the *shake* was a modest 3.1 on the Richter scale⟩ — see EARTHQUAKE 1

shake *vb* **1** to make a series of small irregular or violent movements ⟨the bus rattled and *shook* as it barreled down a rutted road⟩
synonyms agitate, bucket, convulse, jerk, jiggle, joggle, jolt, jounce, judder [*chiefly British*], quake, quiver, shudder, vibrate, wobble (*also* wabble)
related words rock, sway, swing; chatter, quaver, shiver, thrill, tremble; twitch; dodder, waver; flicker, fluctuate, flutter, oscillate, undulate, wave; beat, palpitate, pit-a-pat, pitter-patter, pulsate, pulse, throb
2 to get or keep away from (as a responsibility) through cleverness or trickery ⟨we *shook* our pursuers by cutting through the abandoned lot⟩ — see ESCAPE 2

shake down *vb* to rob by the use of trickery or threats ⟨the rumor is that he started his career *shaking* people *down* as an enforcer for the mob⟩ — see FLEECE

shake out *vb* to come to be ⟨after hearing about all the elaborate planning, I can't wait to see how that wedding *shakes out*⟩ — see COME OUT 1

shake up *vb* to cause an unpleasant surprise for ⟨the news that we had failed the auto inspection *shook* us *up*⟩ — see SHOCK 1

shakiness *n* the quality or state of not being firmly fixed in position ⟨we added a couple more ropes to help reduce the *shakiness* of the footbridge⟩ — see INSTABILITY

shaking *adj* marked by or given to small uncontrollable bodily movements ⟨suffered a *shaking* chill during his bout with the flu⟩ — see SHAKY 1

shaking *n* **1** a series of slight movements by a body back and forth or from side to side ⟨gave the bottle of salad dressing a good *shaking*⟩ — see VIBRATION 1
2 the act or a means of getting or keeping away from something undesirable ⟨condemned the government's *shaking* of its overseas responsibilities⟩ — see ESCAPE 2

shaky *adj* **1** marked by or given to small uncontrollable bodily movements ⟨the old man's hands were so *shaky* that I was afraid he'd drop the glass⟩
synonyms aquiver, atremble, quaking, quavery, quivering, shaking, shuddering, shuddery, tottering, tottery, trembling, trembly, tremulous, wobbling (*also* wabbling), wobbly (*also* wabbly)
related words convulsive; shivering, shivery; rocky, staggery, unstable, unsteady, wavering, wavery; palpitating, pulsating, throbbing
near antonyms controlled, firm, settled, stable, steady
2 giving good reason for being doubted, questioned, or challenged ⟨results that were arrived at using some *shaky* experimental procedures⟩ — see DOUBTFUL 2

shall *vb* to be under necessity or obligation to ⟨you *shall* do as I say⟩ — see NEED 2

shallow *n, usually* **shallows** *pl* a place where a body of water (as a sea or river) is shallow ⟨we waded through the *shallows* looking for tadpoles⟩ — see SHOAL

shallow *adj* **1** lacking significant physical depth ⟨the dog quickly dug a *shallow* hole that was barely deep enough to accommodate his bone⟩
synonyms depthless, shoal
related words skin-deep, superficial, surface; fathomable, measurable; finite, limited, measured, restricted; even, flat, flush, horizontal, level, plane, smooth; two-dimensional
near antonyms abysmal, abyssal, bottomless, boundless, endless, immeasurable, inestimable, infinite, limitless, measureless, profound, unfathomable, unlimited, vast; navigable
antonyms deep
2 having or showing a lack of depth of understanding or character ⟨how *shallow* of the driver to be worrying about his car while the pedestrian was in need of medical attention⟩ — see SUPERFICIAL 2

sham *adj* **1** being such in appearance only and made with or manufactured from usually cheaper materials ⟨a sofa upholstered in *sham* leather⟩ — see IMITATION
2 being such in appearance only and made or manufactured with the intention of committing fraud ⟨street vendors selling *sham* designer handbags to gullible tourists⟩ — see COUNTERFEIT 1
3 lacking in natural or spontaneous quality ⟨the *sham* friendliness of a salesman trying to sell you something⟩ — see ARTIFICIAL 1

sham *n* **1** a poor, insincere, or insulting imitation of something ⟨condemned the rigged election as a total *sham*⟩ — see MOCKERY 1
2 an imitation that is passed off as genuine ⟨the bank robber's "gun" turned out to be a *sham*⟩ — see FAKE 1
3 one who makes false claims of identity or expertise ⟨that supposed French movie star was a *sham*⟩ — see IMPOSTOR

sham *vb* to present a false appearance of ⟨*shammed* a most unconvincing limp just to get sympathy⟩ — see FEIGN

shamble *vb* to move heavily or clumsily ⟨disconsolate and exhausted after losing the match, the wrestler *shambled* toward the locker room⟩ — see LUMBER 1

shambles *n pl* **1** a dirty or messy place ⟨this room is a *shambles*—clean it up right now!⟩ — see PIGPEN
2 a state in which everything is out of order ⟨the earthquake left the whole town in a *shambles*⟩ — see CHAOS

shame *n* **1** a feeling of responsibility for wrongdoing ⟨racked with *shame* over her actions of the previous week⟩ — see GUILT 1
2 a regrettable or blameworthy act ⟨it's a *shame* you won't be able to come to the party⟩ — see CRIME 2
3 the state of having lost the esteem of others ⟨left the room in *shame* after his angry outburst⟩ — see DISGRACE 1

shame *vb* to reduce to a lower standing in one's own eyes or in others' eyes ⟨*shamed* the family name with his conviction for embezzlement⟩ — see HUMBLE

shamed *adj* suffering from or expressive of a feeling of responsibility for wrongdoing ⟨the *shamed* look of someone who knows that he is being given credit he doesn't deserve⟩ — see GUILTY

shamefaced *adj* suffering from or expressive of a feeling of responsibility for wrongdoing ⟨the newspaper offered a *shamefaced* apology for having published photographs that were later exposed as fakes⟩ — see GUILTY

shameful *adj* not respectable ⟨*shameful* behavior by a bunch of drunken boors⟩ — see DISREPUTABLE

shameless *adj* **1** not embarrassed or ashamed ⟨she's truly *shameless* in the seemingly endless self-promotion of herself⟩ — see UNABASHED
2 not sorry for having done wrong ⟨a *shameless* exploiter of impoverished workers in overseas sweatshops⟩ — see REMORSELESS 1

shamus *n, slang* **1** a member of a force charged with law enforcement at the local level ⟨a hard-bitten L.A. *shamus* who, when he's not battling crooks, is bedding chicks⟩ — see OFFICER 1
2 a person not on the police force who investigates criminal or illicit activity or searches for missing persons ⟨he's a sleazy *shamus* who mostly finds evidence to use in divorce cases⟩ — see DETECTIVE

Shangri–la *n* an often imaginary place or state of utter perfection and happiness ⟨a dreamer who spent much of his life roaming the world in search of his personal *Shangri-la*⟩ — see PARADISE 1

shank *n, slang* an instrument with a metal length that has a sharp edge for cutting ⟨slashed at the prison guard with a *shank* he had secretly made from a scrap of metal⟩ — see KNIFE

shanty *n* a small, simply constructed, and often temporary dwelling ⟨lived just off the beach in a crude *shanty*⟩ — see SHACK

shapable *or* **shapeable** *adj* capable of being easily molded or modeled ⟨add just enough water to the flour so that it becomes a *shapable* mass⟩ — see PLASTIC 1

shape *n* **1** a state of being or fitness ⟨she was in good *shape* after having worked outdoors all summer long⟩ — see CONDITION 1
2 the outward appearance of something as distinguished from its substance ⟨that part of the state is known as the panhandle because of its *shape*⟩ — see FORM 1
3 the type of body that a person has ⟨most fashion models have the kind of *shape* that shows elegant clothes to their best advantage⟩ — see PHYSIQUE

shape *vb* **1** to change (something) so as to make it suitable for a new use or situation ⟨a dress *shaped* to the customer's particular figure⟩ — see ADAPT
2 to work out the details of (something) in advance ⟨over the winter the committee *shaped* the company's new marketing strategy⟩ — see PLAN 1

shape (up) *vb* to take on a definite form ⟨this group of summer interns is *shaping up* to be one of the best we've ever hired⟩ — see FORM 1

shapeless *adj* **1** badly or imperfectly formed ⟨a *shapeless* old hat⟩ — see MALFORMED
2 having no definite or recognizable form ⟨right now this clay is just a *shapeless* lump, but wait until I'm done sculpting it⟩ — see FORMLESS 1

shapely *adj* having a well-proportioned feminine figure ⟨a *shapely* blonde who served as eye candy in numerous Hollywood movies⟩ — see CURVACEOUS

shape up *vb* to change one's behavior or character for the better ⟨angrily told his son that if he didn't *shape up*, he'd be grounded for a month⟩ — see REFORM 2

share *vb* to take a share or part ⟨everyone in the enterprise will *share* in the profits⟩ — see PARTAKE 1

share *n* **1** something belonging to, due to, or contributed by an individual member of a group ⟨my *share* of the lottery winnings is over a million dollars⟩ ⟨her *share* of the bill comes to $13.44⟩
synonyms allotment, allowance, cut, end, part, piece, portion, proportion, quota, slice, take
related words lot, ration; commission, percentage; member, partition, section, segment
phrases piece of the action
near antonyms aggregate, composite, compound, pool, sum, total, totality; whole
2 a legal right to participation in the advantages, profits, and responsibility of something ⟨she sold her *share* in the business to her partner⟩ — see INTEREST 1

shared *adj* used or done by a number of people as a group ⟨*shared* resources⟩ — see COLLECTIVE

sharer *n* one who takes part in something ⟨all pilots are *sharers* of the same air space⟩ — see PARTICIPANT

shark *n* **1** a dishonest person who uses clever means to cheat others out of something of value ⟨a card *shark*⟩ — see TRICKSTER 1
2 a person with a high level of knowledge or skill in a field ⟨a *shark* at calculus⟩ — see EXPERT
3 a person who habitually preys upon others ⟨being a new arrival in Hollywood, she was easy prey for the *sharks* in the movie business⟩ — see PREDATOR

sharp *adv* as stated or indicated without the slightest difference ⟨be there at four o'clock *sharp*⟩ — see EXACTLY 1

sharp *adj* **1** having an edge thin enough to cut or pierce something ⟨be careful, as that knife is *sharp* enough to slice off a finger⟩
synonyms cutting, edged, edgy, ground, honed, keen, sharpened, stropped, trenchant, whetted
related words clawlike, daggerlike, knifelike; jabbing, jagged, lacerating, piercing, scratching, stabbing; pointed, pointy, spiky (*also* spikey)
near antonyms rounded, smooth; soft; even, flat, level, slick
antonyms blunt, blunted, dull, dulled, obtuse
2 having a powerfully stimulating odor or flavor ⟨that cheese is so *sharp* that its rank aroma can practically clear a room⟩
synonyms nippy, pungent, strong, tangy
related words acid, acidic; acrid, bitter, harsh; gingery, hot, peppery, piquant, spicy, tart, zesty, zingy; putrid, rancid, rank, skunky; acute, keen; animating, energizing, exciting, galvanizing, invigorating, provocative; appetizing, delectable, delicious, palatable, toothsome; flavorful, savory (*also* savoury), tasty; aromatic, redolent
near antonyms aged, mellow, ripe; gentle, soft; flat, flavorless, insipid; savorless, tasteless, zestless; dilute, thin, watery, weak
antonyms bland, mild, smooth
3 tapering to a thin tip ⟨tipped with a *sharp* arrowhead⟩ — see POINTED 1
4 being in the latest or current fashion ⟨wore a *sharp* suit to his first big job interview⟩ — see STYLISH
5 being strikingly neat and trim in style or appearance ⟨a television personality who's known as a *sharp* dresser⟩ — see SMART 1
6 causing intense discomfort to one's skin ⟨I got chapped lips from sailing all day in that *sharp* wind⟩ — see CUTTING 1
7 given to or marked by cheating and deception ⟨*sharp* business practices that are being investigated by the state's consumer protection agency⟩ — see DISHONEST 2
8 having or showing a practical cleverness or judgment ⟨a *sharp* customer who wasn't about to be taken in by that smooth-tongued salesman⟩ — see SHREWD 1
9 having or showing quickness of mind ⟨any *sharp* student would have noticed the error immediately⟩ — see INTELLIGENT 1
10 marked by the use of wit that is intended to cause hurt feelings ⟨an unnecessarily *sharp* retort to a perfectly civil question⟩ — see SARCASTIC
11 able to sense slight impressions or differences ⟨you have *sharp* eyes⟩ — see ACUTE 1
12 uncomfortably cool ⟨a spell of unusually *sharp* weather for this time of year⟩ — see CHILLY 1

sharp *n* a person with a high level of knowledge or skill in a field ⟨the computer *sharp* that the rest of the staff turns to whenever their PCs act up⟩ — see EXPERT

sharpen *vb* to make sharp or sharper ⟨you need to *sharpen* your penknife's blade frequently in order to be able to whittle properly⟩
synonyms edge, grind, hone, stone, strop, whet
related words file
near antonyms buff, burnish, gloss, polish, round, smooth
antonyms blunt, dull

sharpened *adj* having an edge thin enough to cut or pierce something ⟨the *sharpened* blade of a lawn mower⟩ — see SHARP 1

sharper *n* a dishonest person who uses clever means to cheat others out of something of value ⟨carnival *sharpers* eager to relieve the yokels of their money⟩ — see TRICKSTER 1

sharp–eyed *adj* having unusually keen vision ⟨a very *sharp-eyed* child found the last Easter egg, which was hidden in the flower arrangement⟩
synonyms clear-sighted, eagle-eyed, hawkeyed, lynx-eyed, sharp-sighted
related words sighted; alert, attentive, aware, observant, observing, vigilant, watchful
near antonyms blind, eyeless, sightless, stone-blind, visionless; astigmatic, myopic, nearsighted, shortsighted; purblind

sharpie *or* **sharpy** *n* a dishonest person who uses clever means to cheat others out of something of value ⟨those poolroom *sharpies* cleaned them out⟩ — see TRICKSTER 1

sharply *adv* in a strikingly neat and trim manner ⟨*sharply* dressed groomsmen at a formal wedding⟩ — see SMARTLY

sharpness *n* **1** a harsh or sharp quality ⟨he found that the bland crackers helped cut the *sharpness* of the cheese⟩ — see EDGE 1
2 an uncomfortable degree of coolness ⟨dress warmly; there's a bit of *sharpness* in the air today⟩ — see CHILL
3 exceptional discernment and judgment especially in practical matters ⟨possesses a political *sharpness* that most campaign managers would envy⟩ — see ACUMEN
4 the state or quality of being able to sense slight impressions or differences ⟨possesses the proverbial *sharpness* of an eagle's eye⟩ — see ACUITY

sharpshooter *n* a person skilled in shooting at a target ⟨the police stationed *sharpshooters* on rooftops all along the route of the presidential motorcade⟩ — see MARKSMAN

sharp–sighted *adj* having unusually keen vision ⟨the *sharp-sighted* hunter spotted the deer and motioned to his companions⟩ — see SHARP-EYED

sharp–witted *adj* **1** having or showing a practical cleverness or judgment ⟨her *sharp-witted* questions always cut right to the core of the issue⟩ — see SHREWD 1
2 having or showing quickness of mind ⟨a TV game show that allows *sharp-witted* contestants to show their stuff⟩ — see INTELLIGENT 1

shatter *vb* **1** to bring to a complete end the physical soundness, existence, or usefulness of ⟨tried to restore their *shattered* hopes⟩ — see DESTROY 1
2 to cause to break open or into pieces by or as if by an explosive ⟨*shattered* the sealed clay pot to find out what was inside⟩ — see BLAST 1
3 to cause to break with violence and much noise ⟨*shattered* the priceless vase in one clumsy fall⟩ — see SMASH 1

shattered *adj* forcibly separated into many pieces ⟨the glass mirror lay *shattered* on the floor⟩ — see BROKEN 1

shave *vb* **1** to make (something) shorter or smaller with the use of a cutting instrument ⟨he always *shaves* most of his hair off when the weather starts getting warmer⟩ — see CLIP 1
2 to pass lightly across or touch gently especially in passing ⟨just *shaved* the concrete post as the car turned the corner⟩ — see [2]BRUSH

shaveling *n* a male person who has not yet reached

adulthood ⟨ever since he was a *shaveling*, he's wanted to be an airline pilot, just like his dad⟩ — see BOY 1

shaver *n* a male person who has not yet reached adulthood ⟨back in the old days when my dad was just a little *shaver*⟩ — see BOY 1

shavie *n, Scottish* a playful or mischievous act intended as a joke ⟨some *shavie* he is alleged to have been involved in while a student at Saint Andrews⟩ — see PRANK

sheaf *n* a considerable amount ⟨contends that casino gambling would generate a *sheaf* of social problems for the state⟩ — see LOT 2

shear *vb* **1** to make (something) shorter or smaller with the use of a cutting instrument ⟨it took almost a week to *shear* all the wool off the flock of sheep⟩ — see CLIP 1
2 to penetrate with a sharp edge (as a knife) ⟨the shark's razor-sharp teeth *sheared* the swimmer's flesh right down to the bone⟩ — see CUT 1

sheath *n* something that encloses another thing especially to protect it ⟨he removed his knife from its *sheath* and started to whittle⟩ — see ^{1}CASE 1

sheathe *also* **sheath** *vb* to cover with something that protects ⟨sometimes shipbuilders *sheathe* a ship's bottom with copper for extra protection from barnacles and other threats⟩
synonyms clad, face
related words apparel, array, clothe, dress, garb, robe; side, skin; embosom, embower, embrace, encase, enclose (*also* inclose), encompass, enshroud, envelop, enwrap, invest, lap, mantle, shroud, surround, swathe, veil, wrap; blanket, overlay, overspread
near antonyms bare, denude, expose, strip; unswathe

shed *vb* **1** to cast (a natural bodily covering or appendage) aside ⟨a snake's skin doesn't grow as the snake does, so every so often the snake will *shed* its old skin⟩
synonyms exfoliate, molt, slip, slough (*also* sluff)
related words flake, peel, scale; chuck, discard, ditch, fling (off *or* away), jettison, junk, scrap, shuck (off), throw away, throw out, unload
2 to get rid of as useless or unwanted ⟨you need to *shed* your old notions of propriety and have some fun for a change⟩ — see DISCARD

sheen *n* brightness created by light reflected from a surface ⟨polished the metal until it had an even *sheen*⟩ — see SHINE 1

sheeny *adj* giving off or reflecting much light ⟨wore a dress of some *sheeny* material that looked spectacular under the stage lights⟩ — see BRIGHT 1

sheep *n* an innocent or gentle person ⟨he came to see that the members of the cult were *sheep* who naively went along with whatever their leader dictated⟩ — see LAMB

sheepish *adj* not comfortable around people ⟨a *sheepish* scholar who is most comfortable when surrounded by books⟩ — see SHY 2

sheepishly *adv* in a manner showing no signs of pride or self-assertion ⟨the younger boy, who idolized the older one, would *sheepishly* follow him around and be at his beck and call⟩ — see LOWLY

sheer *vb* **1** to change one's course or direction ⟨the cruise ship *sheered* to the northwest, putting it safely out of the path of the hurricane⟩ — see TURN 3
2 to depart abruptly from a straight line or course ⟨the car *sheered* to avoid hitting the dog⟩ — see SWERVE 1

sheer *adj* **1** very thin and easy to see through ⟨we had to get window shades because passersby could see right through our *sheer* curtains⟩
synonyms cobwebby, diaphanous, filmy, gauzelike, gauzy, gossamer, gossamery, see-through, transparent
related words peekaboo; clear, crystal, crystalline, limpid, liquid, lucent, pellucid; lucid, translucent; dainty, delicate, flimsy, fragile, frail, insubstantial, unsubstantial; colorless, uncolored
near antonyms opaque; cloudy, foggy, hazy, misty, murky, nebulous, smoky (*also* smokey); drab, dull, lackluster, lusterless
2 having no exceptions or restrictions ⟨survivors of the earthquake told of experiencing *sheer* terror⟩ — see ABSOLUTE 2
3 having an incline approaching the perpendicular ⟨the *sheer* slopes of the ravine⟩ — see STEEP 1

sheet *vb* to form a layer over ⟨dust *sheeted* the floors of the old, abandoned house⟩ — see COVER 2

sheet *n* a wide space or area ⟨from the bow of our ship all we could see was an impenetrable *sheet* of fog⟩ — see EXPANSE

sheila *n, Australia & New Zealand* a female person who has not yet reached adulthood ⟨two blonde *sheilas* were splashing in the water at Bondi Beach while their mother looked on⟩ — see GIRL 2

shekels *also* **sheqels** *or* **shekelim** *or* **shekalim** *or* **sheqalim** *n pl* something (as pieces of stamped metal or printed paper) customarily and legally used as a medium of exchange, a measure of value, or a means of payment ⟨if I had the *shekels*, I'd be first in line to buy one of the new vehicles⟩ — see MONEY 1

shell *n* **1** something that encloses another thing especially to protect it ⟨eating oysters straight out of their *shells*⟩ — see ^{1}CASE 1
2 the arrangement of parts that gives something its basic form ⟨workers at the shipyard have thus far erected the *shell* of the ship⟩ — see FRAME 1
3 an outer part or layer ⟨the *shell* of the building is all glass, making it conspicuous on a street with mostly limestone facades⟩ — see EXTERIOR

shell *vb* **1** to remove the natural covering of ⟨*shelling* peanuts⟩ — see PEEL
2 to use bombs or artillery against ⟨the enemy *shelled* the city for days without letup⟩ — see BOMBARD 1

shellac *vb* to defeat by a large margin ⟨the local soccer team was *shellacked* 35–0 in their final outing for the season⟩ — see WHIP 2

shellacking *n* failure to win a contest ⟨suffered a *shellacking* at the hands of a vastly superior opposition⟩ — see DEFEAT 1

shell game *n* an instance of the use of dishonest methods to acquire something of value ⟨it's amazing how intelligent people fall for that investment-fund *shell game*⟩ — see FRAUD 1

shell out *vb* to hand over or use up in payment ⟨we *shelled out* an obscene amount of money for those concert tickets⟩ — see SPEND 1

shell–shocked *adj* **1** suffering from high levels of physical and especially psychological stress ⟨even after the long furlough, the returning soldiers still felt a little *shell-shocked*⟩ — see STRESSED-OUT
2 suffering from mental confusion ⟨*shell-shocked* survivors who were in dire need of every kind of help⟩ — see DIZZY 2

shelter *n* something (as a building) that offers cover from the weather or protection from danger ⟨the sudden fierce storm forced us to run to the nearest *shelter*⟩
synonyms asylum, bolt-hole [*chiefly British*], harbor, harborage, haven, refuge, retreat, sanctuary, sanctum
related words oasis; anchorage, mooring, port; cover, screen; abode, diggings, domicile, dwelling, habitation, house, housing, lodging, lodgment (*or* lodgement), pad, place, quarters, residence, rest, roof; cloister, closet, covert, den, hermitage, hideaway, hideout, lair; castle, fastness, fort, fortress, palisade, redoubt, stronghold; lean-to, lee, shed, windbreak

shelter *vb* **1** to be or provide a shelter for ⟨the abandoned barn *shelters* a colony of stray cats⟩

synonyms harbor, refuge
related words cover, defend, protect, safeguard, screen, secure, shield, ward; domicile, house, place, quarter; shade, shadow
near antonyms expose
2 to provide with living quarters or shelter ⟨*sheltered* the troops in tents until permanent barracks could be built⟩ — see HOUSE 1

sheltered *adj* screened or sequestered from view ⟨moored the sailboat in a *sheltered* cove⟩ — see SECLUDED

shelve *vb* to assign to a later time ⟨let's *shelve* the project for now⟩ — see POSTPONE

shenanigan *n* **1** *usually* **shenanigans** *pl* playful, reckless behavior that is not intended to cause serious harm ⟨students engaging in youthful *shenanigans* on the last day of school⟩ — see MISCHIEF 1
2 *usually* **shenanigans** *pl* wildly playful or mischievous behavior ⟨an act of vandalism that went way beyond the usual *shenanigans* at summer camp⟩ — see HORSEPLAY
3 a clever often underhanded means to achieve an end ⟨the street-corner huckster of pirated DVDs had all sorts of *shenanigans* to keep the cops off of his tail⟩ — see TRICK 1

shepherd *vb* to give advice and instruction to (someone) regarding the course or process to be followed ⟨*shepherding* her through the procedure of taking out a loan⟩ — see GUIDE 1

sherlock *n* a person not on the police force who investigates criminal or illicit activity or searches for missing persons ⟨one of literature's most eccentric *sherlocks*, Nero Wolfe manages to solve mysteries without so much as leaving the confines of his own home⟩ — see DETECTIVE

sheugh *n, chiefly Scottish* a long narrow channel dug in the earth ⟨fell into a *sheugh* while rambling over the Scottish moors⟩ — see DITCH

shibboleth *n* **1** an attention-getting word or phrase used to publicize something (as a campaign or product) ⟨we knew that their claim of giving "the best deal in town" was just a *shibboleth*⟩ — see SLOGAN
2 an idea or expression that has been used by many people ⟨there's a lot of truth in the *shibboleth* that if you give some people an inch, they'll take a mile⟩ — see COMMONPLACE

shield *n* means or method of defending ⟨the slightly built boy used his sharp wit as a *shield* against the school's bullies⟩ — see DEFENSE 1

shield *vb* **1** to drive danger or attack away from ⟨celebrities who are *shielded* by a cluster of bodyguards whenever they appear in public⟩ — see DEFEND 1
2 to place a protective layer over ⟨she *shielded* her eyes from the sun with her hand⟩ — see COVER 3

shift *n* **1** an action planned or taken to achieve a desired result ⟨desperate *shifts* to stave off financial disaster⟩ — see MEASURE 1
2 the act or an instance of changing position ⟨made a small *shift* to the left to make more room on the bench⟩ — see MOVEMENT 1

shift *vb* **1** to change the place or position of ⟨he *shifted* the vase closer to the wall so that it wouldn't get knocked over⟩ — see MOVE 1
2 to change one's position ⟨she *shifted* uncomfortably in her seat throughout the interview⟩ — see MOVE 3
3 to pass from one form, state, or level to another ⟨she watched the aurora in fascination as its colors *shifted* from green to blue⟩ — see CHANGE 2
4 to give up (something) and take something else in return ⟨my brother and I *shifted* seats just before takeoff so that he could sit by the window⟩ — see CHANGE 3
5 to meet one's day-to-day needs ⟨left the others to *shift* for themselves⟩ — see GET ALONG 1

shifting *n* the act or an instance of changing position ⟨the *shifting* of the toys to the front of the display was a direct result of their sudden popularity⟩ — see MOVEMENT 1

shiftless *adj* not easily aroused to action or work ⟨*shiftless* spongers who never thought to do anything for themselves⟩ — see LAZY 1

shiftlessness *n* an inclination not to do work or engage in activities ⟨with the start of the warm weather, combating the students' *shiftlessness* was a constant ordeal⟩ — see LAZINESS

shifty *adj* **1** given to acting in secret and to concealing one's intentions ⟨*shifty* politicians making deals to channel federal funds into their districts⟩ — see SNEAKY 1
2 given to or marked by cheating and deception ⟨*shifty* practices such as turning back the odometers on used cars⟩ — see DISHONEST 2

shillelagh *also* **shillalah** *n* a heavy rigid stick used as a weapon or for punishment ⟨the bartender in the Irish pub keeps a *shillelagh* behind the bar just in case there's trouble⟩ — see CLUB 1

shilly–shally *vb* **1** to show uncertainty about the right course of action ⟨I didn't *shilly-shally* but instead raced to the hospital as soon as I heard the news⟩ — see HESITATE
2 to move or act slowly ⟨with dinner guests due in two hours, there was no time to *shilly-shally* in front of the TV set⟩ — see DELAY 1

shilly–shally *n* a state or an instance of temporary inaction because of uncertainty about the right course of action ⟨the construction project was once again delayed by the bureacratic *shilly-shally* of regulatory agencies⟩ — see HESITATION

shilly–shallying *n* a state or an instance of temporary inaction because of uncertainty about the right course of action ⟨fortunately, during the crisis there was no *shilly-shallying* on the part of the president⟩ — see HESITATION

shimmer *vb* to shoot forth bursts of light ⟨a sequined dress *shimmering* under the studio lights⟩ — see FLASH 1

shindig *n* a social gathering ⟨we're hosting a little *shindig* this weekend for some friends⟩ — see PARTY 1

shindy *n* a state of noisy, confused activity ⟨the prime minister created a brief *shindy* with his unexpected appearance⟩ — see COMMOTION

shine *n* **1** brightness created by light reflected from a surface ⟨the troop inspector insisted on nothing less than a dazzling *shine* from every pair of shoes in the line of review⟩
synonyms burnish, gloss, luminance, luster (*or* lustre), polish, sheen
related words glare, gleam, glimmer, glint, glisten, glow, shimmer; blink, flicker, sparkle, twinkle; illumination, irradiation; iridescence, luminescence; brilliance, luminosity, radiance, radiancy, refulgence; finish, glaze
near antonyms dimness, dinginess, dirtiness, drabness, dullness (*also* dulness), flatness; grayness, paleness; cloudiness, gloom, murkiness, obscureness, obscurity, somberness
2 the steady giving off of the form of radiation that makes vision possible ⟨by the *shine* of the full moon we could see the rabbit helping himself to our garden vegetables⟩ — see LIGHT 1
3 positive regard for something ⟨took quite a *shine* to the new neighbors⟩ — see LIKING
4 *usually* **shines** *pl* a playful or mischievous act intended as a joke ⟨the *shines* they pulled at summer

camp have become embellished with each retelling⟩ — see PRANK

shine *vb* **1** to emit rays of light ⟨the sun appears to *shine* particularly brightly in summer because that is when it's closest to the Earth⟩
synonyms beam, radiate, ray
related words blaze, burn, fire, flame, gleam, glimmer, glint, glisten, glister, glitter, glow, luminesce, sheen, shimmer; blink, coruscate, flare, flash, flicker, luster (*or* lustre), scintillate, spangle, sparkle, twinkle, wink, winkle; beat (down), glare; brighten, illuminate, illumine, irradiate, light, lighten; bedazzle, blind, daze, dazzle
near antonyms blacken, darken; lower (*also* lour)
2 to make smooth or glossy usually by repeatedly applying surface pressure ⟨the salesman *shined* his shoes every morning before leaving the house⟩ — see POLISH 1

shining *adj* giving off or reflecting much light ⟨the *shining* moon formed a nice backdrop for our outdoor concert⟩ — see BRIGHT 1

shiny *adj* giving off or reflecting much light ⟨we could see our reflections in the *shiny* surface of the marble walls⟩ — see BRIGHT 1

ship *n* a large craft for travel by water ⟨a cruise *ship* plying the warm waters of the Caribbean⟩
synonyms boat, keel, vessel
related words aircraft carrier, argosy, barge, coaster, collier, containership, corvette, cruiser, cutter, destroyer, ferryboat, flagship, freighter, icebreaker, ironclad, lightship, liner, man-of-war (*also* man-o'-war), merchantman, merchant ship, motor ship, packet, steamer, steamship, superliner, supertanker, tanker, trader, tramp, transport, warship, watercraft; bark (*or* barque), brig, brigantine, caravel, clipper, junk, ketch, sailboat, schooner, square-rigger, tall ship, windjammer, xebec, yacht

ship *vb* to cause to go or be taken from one place to another ⟨we *shipped* those books out yesterday⟩ — see SEND

ship (out) *vb* to travel on water in a vessel ⟨after college he decide to *ship out* on a tramp steamer and see the world⟩ — see SAIL 1

shipload *n* a considerable amount ⟨it must have taken a *shipload* of money to build that mansion⟩ — see LOT 2

shipman *n* one who operates or navigates a seagoing vessel ⟨in the middle of the vasty deep the *shipman* enjoys a splendid isolation that the landsman will never know⟩ — see SAILOR

shippable *adj* capable of being taken from one place to another by public carrier ⟨only boxes of five pounds and under are *shippable* by the postal service⟩
synonyms transferable (*also* transferrable), transmittable, transportable
related words addressable; mailable
antonyms nontransferable, receivable

shipshape *adj* being clean and in good order ⟨made everything *shipshape* for the inspection⟩ — see NEAT 1

shipwreck *n* **1** the destruction or loss of a ship ⟨the *shipwreck* of much of the Spanish Armada ended Spain's plans for invading England⟩
synonyms shipwrecking, wreck, wreckage, wrecking
related words beaching, grounding, stranding; foundering, sinking; scuttling
near antonyms recovery, salvage, salvaging
2 something that has failed ⟨finally admitted that their marriage was a *shipwreck* and that the time had come to bail out⟩ — see FAILURE 3

shipwreck *vb* to cause irreparable damage to (a ship) by running aground or sinking ⟨the yachtsman fell asleep at the wheel and *shipwrecked* his ketch on the rocks⟩
synonyms strand, wreck
related words beach; founder; scuttle
near antonyms recover, salvage

shipwrecking *n* the destruction or loss of a ship ⟨the *shipwrecking* of the Titanic by an iceberg ranks as one of the greatest disasters in the annals of the sea⟩ — see SHIPWRECK 1

shirk *vb* **1** to get or keep away from (as a responsibility) through cleverness or trickery ⟨you always try to *shirk* paying your fair share of the bill by claiming you "forgot" your wallet⟩ — see ESCAPE 2
2 to leave undone or unattended to especially through carelessness ⟨a deadbeat who has been *shirking* his duty to his family for years⟩ — see NEGLECT 2
3 to move about in a sly or secret manner ⟨given the multitude of auditoriums at the multiplex, it's not too difficult for underaged kids to *shirk* into R-rated movies⟩ — see SNEAK 1

shirker *n* one who deliberately avoids work or duty ⟨even before we weighed anchor, the captain forcefully served notice that there would be no *shirkers* on his ship⟩ — see SLACKER 1

shirty *adj, chiefly British* feeling or showing anger ⟨the visiting businessman was beginning to feel as though he had encountered every *shirty* bloke in London⟩ — see ANGRY

shiv *n, slang* an instrument with a metal length that has a sharp edge for cutting ⟨watch yourself in Cell Block 8, or you'll end up with a *shiv* in your back⟩ — see KNIFE

shiver *n* **1** an instance of shaking involuntarily with fear or cold ⟨the prisoner experienced a sudden *shiver* when confronted with the sight of the dark basement⟩
synonyms quiver, shudder, tremble
related words agitation, convulsing, jolt, quake, shake, tremor, vibration, wobble (*also* wabble); fluctuation, flutter, oscillation, wave; beat, palpitation, pulsation, pulse, throb
2 shivers *pl* a sense of panic or extreme nervousness ⟨looking down from the window ledge sent *shivers* up my spine⟩ — see JITTERS

shivering *n* a series of slight movements by a body back and forth or from side to side ⟨the *shivering* of the crystal chandeliers while there was construction work next door⟩ — see VIBRATION 1

shivery *adj* having a low or subnormal temperature ⟨those *shivery* days of January⟩ — see COLD 1

shoal *adj* lacking significant physical depth ⟨*shoal* waters of the bay meant that our ship had to be moored a considerable distance from shore⟩ — see SHALLOW 1

shoal *n* a place where a body of water (as a sea or river) is shallow ⟨the *shoals* off Nantucket Island are famous as the final resting places of many ill-fated ships⟩
synonyms ford, shallow(s)
related words bank, bar, sandbank, sandbar, towhead
near antonyms trench; abyss, deep, depth, gulf

shock *n* **1** a forceful coming together of two things ⟨the whole railway platform shook from the *shock* of the two trains colliding⟩ — see IMPACT 1
2 the state of being strongly impressed by something unexpected or unusual ⟨were in *shock* after they heard the news of the death of the president⟩ — see SURPRISE 2

shock *vb* **1** to cause an unpleasant surprise for ⟨Mom was *shocked* by the terrible news that her cousin had died in an accident⟩ ⟨I was *shocked* to find out that I was the victim of identity theft⟩
synonyms appall (*also* appal), floor, jolt, shake up
related words astonish, bowl over, dumbfound (*also* dumfound), flabbergast, freak (out), stun, stupefy; affright, alarm (*also* alarum), dismay, fright, frighten, horrify, panic, scare, scarify, spook, startle, terrify, terrorize; disgust, nauseate, repel, revolt, sicken, turn off; displease, offend, outrage, scandalize; amaze, astound,

awe; chill, daunt, demoralize, dispirit, emasculate, undo, unman, unnerve, unstring; discomfort, discompose, disconcert, disquiet, distress, disturb, perturb, shake, unsettle, upset, weird out; crush, overpower, overwhelm
phrases knock for a loop
near antonyms buffer, cushion; delight, gratify, please, rejoice, tickle; charm, entice, tempt; assure, cheer, comfort, console, solace, soothe; reassure
2 to make a strong impression on (someone) with something unexpected ⟨were *shocked* by the way the law against public intoxication was constantly being broken⟩ — see SURPRISE 1
3 to strike with fear ⟨the sudden appearance of the ghost *shocked* us to the core⟩ — see FRIGHTEN

shocked *adj* **1** affected with sudden and great wonder or surprise ⟨the escaping bridegroom bid farewell to the *shocked* wedding guests as he ran out the door⟩ — see THUNDERSTRUCK
2 filled with disgust ⟨we were *shocked* at the appalling conditions in the prison⟩ — see SICK 2
3 filled with fear or dread ⟨the hikers were so *shocked* at the sight of a bear that they didn't dare move⟩ — see AFRAID

shocking *adj* **1** causing a strong emotional reaction because of unexpectedness ⟨we all clustered around to hear the *shocking* news of our colleague's sudden death⟩ — see SURPRISING 1
2 causing fear ⟨the *shocking* appearance of a shark just a few yards off shore⟩ — see FEARFUL 1
3 causing intense displeasure, disgust, or resentment ⟨the *shocking* behavior of some rowdies at the dance⟩ — see OFFENSIVE 1
4 extremely disturbing or repellent ⟨a soldier who had witnessed the *shocking* sight of his best friend being killed⟩ — see HORRIBLE 1

shoddy *adj* **1** of low quality ⟨*shoddy* merchandise that soon fell to pieces⟩ — see CHEAP 2
2 not respectable ⟨a waterfront area filled with *shoddy* saloons, tattoo parlors, and houses of prostitution⟩ — see DISREPUTABLE

shoehorn *vb* to fit (people or things) into a tight space ⟨the organizers of the county fair *shoehorned* the craft booths between the midway and the farm exhibits⟩ — see CROWD 1

shoes *n pl* a way of looking at or thinking about something ⟨what would you do if you were in your friend's *shoes*?⟩ — see PERSPECTIVE 1

shoestring *n* a very small sum of money ⟨trying to start a business on a *shoestring*⟩ — see MITE 1

shoo–in *n* one that is certain to succeed ⟨a *shoo-in* for the position of secretary of state⟩ — see SURE THING

shoot *n* **1** a branch of a main stem especially of a plant ⟨collected the most tender *shoots* for the vegetable dish he was making⟩ — see OFFSHOOT 1
2 a sharp unpleasant sensation usually felt in some specific part of the body ⟨there'd be a *shoot* of pain from that molar whenever I bit down⟩ — see PAIN 1

shoot *vb* **1** to cause (a projectile) to be driven forward with force ⟨BB guns *shoot* small round metal pellets⟩
synonyms blast, discharge, fire, loose, squeeze off
related words launch, project; blaze (at), snipe (at); cast, catapult, fling, heave, hurl, hurtle, lob, pelt, pitch, sling, throw, toss
2 to cause a weapon to release a missile with great force ⟨soldiers train extensively to learn to *shoot* accurately and quickly⟩
synonyms blast, discharge, fire
related words blaze, pepper; plink, potshot, snipe
3 to strike with a missile from a gun ⟨hunters can *shoot* deer only during the legally specified open season⟩
synonyms drill, gun, plug, pop
related words blow away, bring down, drop, pick off, shoot down; blaze, pepper, potshot, snipe (at); blast (at), fire (at); pistol, shotgun; machine-gun, tommy-gun; croak [*slang*], destroy, dispatch, do in, fell, ice [*slang*], kill, slay; annihilate, blot out, butcher, decimate, massacre, slaughter, wipe out
4 to proceed or move quickly ⟨some show-off *shot* past all the other skiers on the slope⟩ — see HURRY 2
5 to take a photograph of ⟨*shooting* the lakeside scene while the light lasted⟩ — see PHOTOGRAPH
6 to throw or give off ⟨suddenly the old, broken-down toaster began *shooting* out sparks⟩ — see EMIT 1
7 to voice one's opinions freely with force ⟨you've been wanting to say something since this meeting started, so *shoot*⟩ — see SPEAK UP
8 to mark with small spots especially unevenly ⟨hazel eyes that were brown *shot* with green⟩ — see SPOT 1
9 to cause to go or be taken from one place to another ⟨*shot* a congratulatory e-mail to his friend as soon as he heard the good news⟩ — see SEND

shoot (up) *vb* to rise abruptly and rapidly ⟨gas prices *shot up* seemingly overnight⟩ — see SKYROCKET

shoot down *vb* **1** to make (someone or something) the object of unkind laughter ⟨nowadays the aging activist is routinely *shot down* in most quarters of the media and dismissed as an irrelevant crank⟩ — see RIDICULE
2 to reject by or as if by a vote ⟨every one of my fund-raising ideas was *shot down* by the other club members⟩ — see NEGATIVE 1
3 to prove to be false ⟨the results of several studies *shoot down* the hypothesis that coffee causes heart attacks⟩ — see DISPROVE

shooter *n* **1** a person skilled in shooting at a target ⟨there were eight *shooters* taking turns at the same target in the final competition⟩ — see MARKSMAN
2 one who takes photographs ⟨he's one of the best *shooters* of wildlife in all of professional photography⟩ — see PHOTOGRAPHER

shop *n* **1** *also* **shoppe** an establishment where goods are sold to consumers ⟨the only *shop* that has that video game in stock is halfway across the state⟩
synonyms bazaar, emporium, store
related words market, marketplace, outlet, showroom; boutique, chain store, department store, dime store, exchange, five-and-ten (*also* five-and-dime), mart, minimart, thrift shop, variety store; big box, supercenter, superstore
2 a building or set of buildings for the manufacturing of goods ⟨a machine *shop*⟩ — see FACTORY
3 the special terms or expressions of a particular group or field ⟨the patient impressed her cardiologist with her ability to talk *shop*⟩ — see TERMINOLOGY

shop (for) *vb* to go in search of ⟨engineers are still *shopping* around *for* solutions to several critical flaws in the aircraft's design⟩ — see SEEK 1

shoptalk *n* the special terms or expressions of a particular group or field ⟨eventually, he got bored with the *shoptalk* of the nuclear engineers, which he barely understood⟩ — see TERMINOLOGY

shopworn *adj* used or heard so often as to be dull ⟨the *shopworn* suggestion to job applicants to "just be yourself"⟩ — see STALE 1

shore *n* a structure that holds up or serves as a foundation for something else ⟨the carpenter placed a *shore* underneath the sagging roof of the porch⟩ — see SUPPORT 1

shore (up) *vb* **1** to hold up or serve as a foundation for ⟨a highway tunnel *shored up* by massive columns of concrete⟩ — see SUPPORT 3
2 to provide evidence or information for (as a claim or idea) ⟨used an avalanche of statistics to *shore up* his

claim that the state's economy is in fine shape⟩ — see SUPPORT 4

shoreside *adj* of, relating to, or situated in the waters near the shore ⟨*shoreside* recreation contributes mightily to the region's economy⟩ — see INSHORE

short *adj* **1** having relatively little height ⟨a lot of boys are *shorter* than the girls in middle school, but they quickly catch up by high school⟩
synonyms little, low, low-lying, low-slung, sawed-off
related words dwarf, dwarfish; compact, petite, slight; diminutive, half-pint, pint-size (*or* pint-sized), pocket, pocket-size (*also* pocket-sized), pygmy, small, smallish; bantam, bitty, dinky, mini, miniature, minimized, minute, puny, teeny, teeny-weeny, tiny, undersized (*also* undersize), wee; dumpy, flat, scrubby, squat, squatty, stubby, stumpy, stunted
near antonyms elevated, lifted, raised, uplifted, upswept; high-rise, statuesque; gangling, gangly, lanky, rangy; big, bulky, hefty, hulking, large, largish, outsize (*also* outsized), oversize (*or* oversized), sizable (*or* sizeable), voluminous
antonyms altitudinous, high, lofty, tall, towering
2 not lasting for a considerable time ⟨fortunately for those of us in the hot sun, the graduation speech was *short* and to the point⟩
synonyms brief, fast, little
related words shortish; abbreviated, abridged, curtailed, cut-back, shortened, syncopated; compact, condensed; abrupt, sudden; ephemeral, fleeting, momentary, short-lived, transient, transitory; impermanent; compendious, concise, crisp, epigrammatic, laconic, pithy, succinct, summary, terse; short-range, short-term
near antonyms endless, everlasting, interminable, persistent, unending; longish, overlong, prolonged, protracted; permanent; enlarged, expanded, supplemented; long-range, long-term
antonyms extended, far, great, lengthy, long, long-drawn-out (*or* long-drawn), long-lived
3 not coming up to an expected measure or meeting a particular need ⟨regrettably, the art supplies are *short* this year, so you'll have to share⟩
synonyms deficient, inadequate, insufficient, lacking, low, scarce, shy, wanting
related words substandard, unacceptable, unsatisfactory; hand-to-mouth, lean, light, meager (*or* meagre), niggardly, poor, scant, scanty, skimp, skimpy, slender, slim, spare, sparse, stingy; bare, mere, minimum; slight, small
near antonyms abundant, ample, bounteous, bountiful, copious, generous, liberal, plenteous, plentiful, plentitudinous; enlarged, expanded, supplemented; abounding, overflowing, teeming; satisfactory, tolerable; lavish, luxuriant, rich; big, considerable, hefty, jumbo, king-size (*or* king-sized), large, largish, oversize (*or* oversized), sizable (*or* sizeable), substantial, super
antonyms adequate, enough, sufficient
4 having a texture that readily breaks into little pieces under pressure ⟨*short* pastry⟩ — see CRISP 1
5 being or characterized by direct, brief, and potentially rude speech or manner ⟨I didn't mean to be so *short* with you by responding to your request with a snippy "I'm busy!"⟩ — see BLUNT 1

short *adv* with great suddenness ⟨the bicyclist ahead of me unexpectedly pulled up *short* and I unavoidably plowed into him⟩
synonyms abruptly, suddenly
related words surprisingly, unexpectedly; directly, immediately, incontinently, instantaneously, instantly, promptly, pronto, right, right away, right off, straightaway; fast, full-tilt, posthaste, quick, quickly, rapidly, readily, snappily, speedily, swift, swiftly; hastily, impetuously, impulsively, rashly, recklessly
phrases all of a sudden (*also* on a sudden)
near antonyms gradually, slowly; hesitantly

short *vb* to rob by the use of trickery or threats ⟨charged that the used-car dealer had been *shorting* customers for years⟩ — see FLEECE

shortage *n* a falling short of an essential or desirable amount or number ⟨there was a troubling *shortage* of supplies for the troops overseas this year⟩ — see DEFICIENCY

shortchange *vb* to rob by the use of trickery or threats ⟨was *shortchanged* out of a promotion⟩ — see FLEECE

short–circuit *vb* to create difficulty for the work or activity of ⟨for decades the maverick filmmaker was *short-circuited* by a chronic lack of funds⟩ — see HAMPER

shortcoming *n* a defect in character ⟨a wife who never tires of listing her husband's perceived *shortcomings*⟩ — see FAULT 1

shortcut *vb* to avoid having to comply with (something) especially through cleverness ⟨are you sure there's no way to *shortcut* the entrance requirements?⟩ — see CIRCUMVENT 1

shorten *vb* to make less in extent or duration ⟨we decided to *shorten* the distance we had to walk home by cutting across the neighbor's lawn⟩ ⟨if Grandma has to go shopping today, you'll need to *shorten* your visit⟩
synonyms abbreviate, abridge, curtail, cut back, dock, elide, syncopate, truncate
related words abstract, digest, encapsulate, epitomize, recapitulate, summarize, sum up; abate, compress, constrict, contract, cut, cut down, pare, prune, trim; decrease, de-escalate, deflate, diminish, downsize, dwindle, lessen, lower, moderate, modify, reduce, retrench, shrink, slash, subtract (from), taper
near antonyms enlarge, expand, supplement; add, aggrandize, amplify, augment, balloon, boost, dilate, escalate, heighten, increase, maximize, pump up, raise; blow up, distend, inflate, swell
antonyms elongate, extend, lengthen, prolong, protract

short–lived *adj* lasting only for a short time ⟨the skier's triumph turned out to be *short-lived*, as the next competitor bested her time⟩ — see MOMENTARY

shortly *adv* **1** in a few words ⟨the sudden closing of the restaurant was announced only with a *shortly* worded sign: "Out of Business"⟩
synonyms briefly, compactly, concisely, crisply, curtly, elliptically, laconically, pithily, succinctly, summarily, tersely
related words aphoristically, sententiously; exactly, precisely; abruptly, bluffly, bluntly, brusquely; monosyllabically
phrases in a nutshell, in a word, in brief, in short, in sum
near antonyms redundantly, repetitiously
antonyms diffusely, long-windedly, verbosely, wordily
2 at or within a short time ⟨the meeting will begin *shortly*, so don't go too far away to find a bathroom⟩
synonyms anon, before long, by and by, directly, momentarily, presently, soon
related words forthwith, immediately, incontinently, instantaneously, instantly, now, promptly, pronto, right away, right now, right off, straightaway, straightway

shortness *n* the condition of being short ⟨the *shortness* of the commencement speech was much appreciated by the impatient graduates⟩ — see BREVITY 1

shortsighted *adj* **1** able to see near things more clearly than distant ones ⟨because she's so *shortsighted*, she's forced to wear her glasses every waking moment⟩ — see NEARSIGHTED
2 not thinking about and providing for the future ⟨*shortsighted* investors who failed to see that the boom couldn't last⟩ — see IMPROVIDENT

short–spoken *adj* being or characterized by direct, brief, and potentially rude speech or manner ⟨don't expect much information or friendly chitchat from the *short-spoken* villagers⟩ — see BLUNT 1

short story *n* a work with imaginary characters and events that is shorter and usually less complex than a novel ⟨her very first *short story* was accepted for publication in a local journal⟩ — see STORY 1

short–tempered *adj* easily irritated or annoyed ⟨shop customers learned not to bother the *short-tempered* dog on their way out⟩ — see IRRITABLE

short–term *adj* intended to last, continue, or serve for a limited time ⟨this is only a *short-term* solution to a long-term problem⟩ — see TEMPORARY 1

shot *n* **1** a directed propelling of a missile by a firearm or artillery piece ⟨cannon operators often had to use several *shots* to figure out the range of their targets⟩
synonyms blasting, discharge, firing
related words potshot; barrage, blitz, blitzkrieg, bombardment, broadside, burst, cannonade, drumfire, fusillade, hail, salvo, shower, storm, volley
2 an effort to do or accomplish something ⟨let's take another *shot* at the puzzle⟩ — see ATTEMPT 1
3 a picture created from an image recorded on a light-sensitive surface by a camera ⟨took a *shot* of his family for the scrapbook⟩ — see PHOTOGRAPH
4 a person skilled in shooting at a target ⟨a soldier who's an excellent *shot* with a rifle⟩ — see MARKSMAN
5 the portion of a serving of a beverage that is swallowed at one time ⟨drank a *shot* of whisky⟩ — see DRINK 2
6 an opinion or judgment based on little or no evidence ⟨I have no idea what's different about you, but I'll take a *shot*: you cut your hair?⟩ — see CONJECTURE
7 a favorable combination of circumstances, time, and place ⟨we have a real *shot* at getting into the championship if we win this next match⟩ — see OPPORTUNITY

should *vb* to be under necessity or obligation to ⟨you *should* stop smoking⟩ — see NEED 2

shoulder *vb* **1** to take to or upon oneself ⟨agreed to *shoulder* the burden of caring for their elderly father⟩ — see ASSUME 1
2 to force one's way ⟨*shouldered* through the crowd at the bar and ordered a drink⟩ — see [2]PRESS 4

shout *vb* to speak so as to be heard at a distance ⟨well-wishers *shouted* to departing passengers from the dock⟩ — see CALL 1

shout *n* a loud vocal expression of strong emotion ⟨I gave a sudden *shout* of surprise when the shower abruptly turned ice-cold⟩
synonyms cry, holler, hoot, howl, whoop, yell, yowl
related words ejaculation, interjection; scream, screech, shriek, shrill, squall, squeak, squeal, yelp; bawl, bellow, clamor, outcry, roar; caterwaul, plaint, wail
near antonyms mumble, murmur, mutter; gasp, whimper, whisper

shouting distance *n* a very small distance or degree ⟨he's within *shouting distance* of being the winningest coach in college basketball history⟩ — see HAIR 1

shove *vb* **1** to apply force to (someone or something) so that it moves in front of one ⟨I had to keep *shoving* my heavy suitcase as I slowly made my way to the head of the line⟩ — see PUSH 1
2 to push steadily against with some force ⟨quit *shoving* your hand in my face⟩ — see [2]PRESS 1

shove (off) *vb* to leave a place often for another ⟨time to *shove off* for home⟩ — see GO 2

shovel *vb* to hollow out or form (something) by removing earth ⟨the troops quickly *shoveled* a trench⟩ — see DIG 1

show *n* **1** an outward and often exaggerated indication of something abstract (as a feeling) for effect ⟨the children made a *show* of disgust when confronted with asparagus⟩
synonyms demonstration, display, exhibition, flaunting
related words act, charade, facade (*also* façade), front, guise, pretense (*or* pretence), put-on, semblance, simulation; affectation, pose, sham; betrayal, disclosure
2 a display of emotion or behavior that is insincere or intended to deceive ⟨her "concern" for the less fortunate is all just a big *show*⟩ — see MASQUERADE
3 outward and often deceptive indication ⟨a false *show* of strength that fooled the enemy⟩ — see APPEARANCE 2
4 a public showing of objects of interest ⟨a boat *show* at the convention center⟩ — see EXHIBITION 1

show *vb* **1** to present so as to invite notice or attention ⟨fishing for compliments, the neighbors *showed* their new SUV to everyone on the block⟩
synonyms display, disport, exhibit, expose, flash, flaunt, lay out, parade, produce, show off, sport, strut, unveil
related words brandish, flourish, wave; advertise, air, announce, blaze, broadcast, herald, placard, post, proclaim, publicize, sound, trumpet; divulge, talk (about), tell (of); bare, discover, reveal, uncloak, uncover, unmask
near antonyms camouflage, disguise, mask; conceal, cover, curtain, enshroud, hide, obscure, occlude, occult, shroud, veil
2 to make known (something abstract) through outward signs ⟨the actor's expressive face *shows* his every thought and emotion clearly⟩
synonyms bespeak, betray, communicate, declare, demonstrate, display, evince, expose, give away, manifest, reveal
related words bare, disclose, unbosom, uncloak, uncover; advertise, air, announce, blaze, broadcast, placard, proclaim, publicize, sound, trumpet; project
near antonyms belie, misrepresent; distort, falsify, garble, twist; camouflage, disguise; gild, gloss (over), varnish, whitewash; conceal, counterfeit, cover, hide, mask, obscure, occlude, veil
3 to gain full recognition or acceptance of ⟨that *shows* we're right⟩ — see ESTABLISH 1
4 to give advice and instruction to (someone) regarding the course or process to be followed ⟨*showed* me how to play the guitar⟩ — see GUIDE 1
5 to point out the way for (someone) especially from a position in front ⟨*showed* them the way to get home⟩ — see LEAD 1
6 to come into view ⟨another car *showed* just as we were thinking we'd have the whole place to ourselves⟩ — see APPEAR 1

showboat *vb* to engage in attention-getting playful or boisterous behavior ⟨the gymnast was *showboating* for the cameras when she lost her balance and fell⟩ — see CUT UP

shower *n* **1** a heavy fall of objects ⟨a *shower* of books fell from the collapsing shelves⟩ — see RAIN 2
2 a rapid or overwhelming outpouring of many things at once ⟨a *shower* of insults and curses rained down on the criminal as he was led through the crowd⟩ — see BARRAGE

shower *vb* to give readily and in large quantities ⟨*showered* gifts on the guests of honor⟩ — see RAIN 2

showiness *n* excessive or unnecessary display ⟨we were somewhat put off by the saber-rattling *showiness* of the military parade⟩ — see OSTENTATION

show–me *adj* inclined to doubt or question claims ⟨the financial scandals may lead investors to take a more *show-me* attitude toward reported corporate earnings⟩ — see SKEPTICAL

show off *vb* **1** to engage in attention-getting playful or boisterous behavior ⟨the athletes warmed up, happily *showing off* for the crowd before the match officially started⟩ — see CUT UP
2 to present so as to invite notice or attention ⟨she just wants to *show off* her new jewelry⟩ — see SHOW 1

showstopper *n* a physically attractive person ⟨at the modeling agency everyone was a *showstopper*⟩ — see DOLL 2

show up *vb* **1** to come into view ⟨normally, one doesn't see them, but the actress's wrinkles *show up* in the close-ups⟩ — see APPEAR 1
2 to get to a destination ⟨the band *showed up* an hour late⟩ — see COME 2
3 to reveal the true nature of ⟨were *shown up* for what they really are⟩ — see EXPOSE 1

showy *adj* likely to attract attention ⟨orchid plants are known for their huge *showy* flowers⟩ — see NOTICEABLE

shred *n* a very small amount ⟨the vandals showed not a *shred* of decency⟩ — see PARTICLE 1

shred *vb* to cause (something) to separate into jagged pieces by violently pulling at it ⟨*shredded* some cooked chicken for the soup⟩ — see TEAR 1

shrew *n* a bad-tempered scolding woman ⟨Rip Van Winkle went off into the mountains to escape his wife, a *shrew* who made his life miserable⟩
synonyms battle-ax (*or* battle-axe), dragon lady, fury, harpy, harridan, termagant, virago, vixen
related words fishwife, gorgon; carper, castigator, caviler (*or* caviller), censurer, critic, faultfinder, nitpicker, railer, scold; belittler, derider, detractor; pettifogger, quibbler

shrewd *adj* **1** having or showing a practical cleverness or judgment ⟨a *shrewd* used car dealer who knew how to make the best possible deal⟩ ⟨*shrewd* investments that paid off big⟩
synonyms astute, canny, clear-eyed, clear-sighted, hard-boiled, hardheaded, heady, knowing, savvy, sharp, sharp-witted, smart
related words artful, cagey (*also* cagy), crafty, cunning, devious, dodgy [*chiefly British*], foxy, guileful, pawky [*chiefly British*], slick, sly, subtle, tricky, wily; discerning, insightful, perceptive, percipient, perspicacious, sagacious, sage, sapient, wise; experienced, veteran; discriminating, discriminative; agile, alert, brainy, bright, brilliant, clever, intelligent, keen, nimble, quick, quick-witted, sharp-eyed, sharp-sighted; apt, ingenious, resourceful; calculating, scheming
near antonyms artless, guileless, ingenuous, innocent, naive (*or* naïve); exploitable, gullible (*also* gullable); unperceptive, unwise; dense, dull, obtuse; airheaded, birdbrained, brain-dead, brainless, dim-witted, dopey (*also* dopy), dumb, empty-headed, feebleminded, gormless [*chiefly British*], half-witted, knuckleheaded, lamebrain (*or* lamebrained), lunkheaded, simple, slow, slow-witted, softheaded, stupid, thickheaded, thick-witted, unintelligent, weak-minded; foolish, idiotic (*also* idiotical), imbecile (*or* imbecilic), moronic, silly, thoughtless, witless; ignorant, uninformed
antonyms unknowing
2 causing intense discomfort to one's skin ⟨she pulled her coat tighter against the *shrewd* breeze whipping down the alley⟩ — see CUTTING 1
3 clever at attaining one's ends by indirect and often deceptive means ⟨a *shrewd* operator in the real estate game, she made every buyer think they were getting the deal of the century⟩ — see ARTFUL 1

shrewdness *n* exceptional discernment and judgment especially in practical matters ⟨a woman with the thick-skinned *shrewdness* to survive in a tough business⟩ — see ACUMEN

shriek *vb* to cry out loudly and emotionally ⟨the children *shrieked* with excitement⟩ — see SCREAM 1

shrieking *adj* having a high musical pitch or range ⟨*shrieking* horns of impatient drivers stuck in a traffic jam⟩ — see SHRILL

shrill *vb* to cry out loudly and emotionally ⟨the mud-splattered bystanders were *shrilling* with outrage at the inconsiderate motorist⟩ — see SCREAM 1

shrill *adj* having a high musical pitch or range ⟨the *shrill* sound of a policeman's whistle⟩
synonyms high-pitched, piping, screeching, shrieking, squeaking, squeaky, treble, whistling
related words peeping, thin, tinny; earsplitting, nasal, penetrating, piercing, sharp, strident; squealing, whining, whiny (*also* whiney), yapping, yelping
near antonyms gruff, hoarse, husky, rough, smoky (*also* smokey)
antonyms bass, deep, grave, low, throaty

shrimp *n* **1** a living thing much smaller than others of its kind ⟨the boy was just a *shrimp* until his teens, when he had a growth spurt⟩ — see DWARF 1
2 a person of no importance or influence ⟨you have no business telling me what to do, you little *shrimp*!⟩ — see NOBODY

shrimpy *adj* of a size that is less than average ⟨a couple of *shrimpy* bushes in the front are the house's only landscaping⟩ — see SMALL 1

shrine *n* a place that is considered sacred (as within a religion) ⟨for centuries pilgrims have traveled to the *shrine* of Saint Thomas à Becket in Canterbury, England⟩
synonyms sanctuary, sanctum
related words reliquary; martyry

shrink *vb* **1** to become smaller in size or volume through the drawing together of particles of matter ⟨the sweater will *shrink* a little when washed⟩ — see CONTRACT 2
2 to draw back in fear, pain, or disgust ⟨*shrinking* back from the approaching flames⟩ — see FLINCH
3 to grow less in scope or intensity especially gradually ⟨his crush on her is likely to *shrink* after they start their new lives on different college campuses⟩ — see DECREASE 2

shrinkage *n* the amount by which something is lessened ⟨she knew that her diet was working by the striking *shrinkage* of her waist⟩ — see DECREASE

shrinking violet *n* a shy or reserved person ⟨a reality show that wants shameless exhibitionists, not *shrinking violets*⟩ — see INTROVERT

shroud *n* something that covers or conceals like a piece of cloth ⟨the truth of the affair will always be hidden under a *shroud* of secrecy⟩ — see CLOAK 1

shroud *vb* **1** to keep secret or shut off from view ⟨*shrouded* the fact that the child had been adopted⟩ — see [1]HIDE 2
2 to make dark, dim, or indistinct ⟨the smog *shrouded* our aerial view of the city⟩ — see CLOUD 1
3 to surround or cover closely ⟨during rainy season the summit of the mountain is *shrouded* in mist⟩ — see ENFOLD 1

shrug off *vb* **1** to dismiss as of little importance ⟨an administration that was willing to *shrug off* the problem⟩ — see EXCUSE 1
2 to rid oneself of (a garment) ⟨she *shrugged off* her coat and hung it up neatly⟩ — see REMOVE 1

shtick *also* **schtick** *or* **shtik** *n* a performance regularly presented by an individual or group ⟨his *shtick* as a falling-down drunk isn't funny to people battling alcoholism⟩ — see ACT 1

shuck *n, usually* **shucks** *pl* something of little importance ⟨it doesn't matter *shucks* to her what anyone else earns⟩ — see TRIFLE

shuck *vb* to remove the natural covering of ⟨*shucking* peas⟩ — see PEEL

shuck (off) *vb* to get rid of as useless or unwanted ⟨bad habits are hard to *shuck off*⟩ — see DISCARD

shudder *n* an instance of shaking involuntarily with fear or cold ⟨a *shudder* ran through him as he stepped outside into the snow⟩ — see SHIVER 1

shudder *vb* to make a series of small irregular or violent movements ⟨huddled in the basement, we *shuddered* with fear as we heard the approaching tornado⟩ — see SHAKE 1

shuddering *adj* marked by or given to small uncontrollable bodily movements ⟨with a *shuddering* extension of his hand, the poor beggar asked for a little charity⟩ — see SHAKY 1

shuddering *n* a series of slight movements by a body back and forth or from side to side ⟨tried to control the *shuddering* of his hand⟩ — see VIBRATION 1

shuddery *adj* marked by or given to small uncontrollable bodily movements ⟨with a few *shuddery* strokes of a pen, she signed her last will and testament⟩ — see SHAKY 1

shuffle *n* **1** an unorganized collection or mixture of various things ⟨the paper got lost in the *shuffle* on his desk⟩ — see MISCELLANY 1
2 deliberate evasion in speech ⟨no matter how directly we asked the question, all we got was *shuffle* in return⟩ — see CIRCUMLOCUTION 1

shuffle *vb* **1** to move heavily or clumsily ⟨the old man *shuffled* across the floor in his slippers⟩ — see LUMBER 1
2 to undo the proper order or arrangement of ⟨*shuffle* the cards and deal five to each player⟩ — see DISORDER

shuffle (out of) *vb* to get or keep away from (as a responsibility) through cleverness or trickery ⟨I don't know how the CEO managed to *shuffle out of* being held responsible for his company's weak performance⟩ — see ESCAPE 2

shun *vb* to get or keep away from (as a responsibility) through cleverness or trickery ⟨just a ruse to *shun* the debt collectors⟩ — see ESCAPE 2

shunning *n* the act or a means of getting or keeping away from something undesirable ⟨this *shunning* of your financial responsibilities cannot continue indefinitely⟩ — see ESCAPE 2

shush *vb* to stop the noise or speech of ⟨*shushed* the crying baby⟩ — see SILENCE 1

shut *vb* **1** to position (something) so as to prevent passage through an opening ⟨please *shut* the door when you leave⟩ — see CLOSE 1
2 to stop the operations of ⟨*shut* both stores for a week⟩ — see CLOSE 2

shut (of) *adj* no longer burdened with something unpleasant or painful ⟨I cannot wait to be *shut of* this social obligation⟩ — see FREE 2

shutdown *n* the stopping of a process or activity ⟨the factory resumed operation after a brief *shutdown* for repairs⟩ — see END 1

shut–eye *n* a natural periodic loss of consciousness during which the body restores itself ⟨I can usually get some extra *shut-eye* on the weekends⟩ — see SLEEP 1

shutoff *n* the stopping of a process or activity ⟨the utility company threatened them with the *shutoff* of electricity if the bills weren't paid⟩ — see END 1

shut off *vb* **1** to bring (as an action or operation) to an immediate end ⟨threatened to *shut off* peace talks if the other side kept making unreasonable demands⟩ — see STOP 1
2 to cause to stop functioning ⟨*shut off* the computer to save electricity⟩ — see DEACTIVATE

shut out *vb* to prevent the participation, consideration, or inclusion of ⟨local residents feel that they have been *shut out* of the debate for expanding the airport⟩ — see EXCLUDE

shutterbug *n* one who takes photographs ⟨an avid *shutterbug* who takes her camera with her everywhere⟩ — see PHOTOGRAPHER

shut up *vb* **1** to stop talking ⟨you have no right to tell the rest of us to *shut up*⟩
synonyms belt up [*British*], clam up, dry up, dummy up, hush, pipe down, quiet (down)
related words calm (down), cool (down), settle (down); haw, hem
phrases hold one's tongue (*or* hold one's peace)
near antonyms pipe up, sound off, speak out, speak up, spout (off), talk up
antonyms speak, talk
2 to stop the noise or speech of ⟨nothing I said would *shut* them *up*⟩ — see SILENCE 1

shy *adj* **1** easily frightened ⟨a *shy* cat who hid under the bed every time she heard any loud noise⟩
synonyms fainthearted, fearful, fearsome, mousy (*or* mousey), scary, skittish, timid, timorous, tremulous
related words chicken, chickenhearted, chicken-livered, cowardly, craven, dastardly, gutless, lily-livered, milk-livered [*archaic*], poltroon, pusillanimous, spineless, unheroic, yellow; jittery, jumpy, spooky; anxious, apprehensive, nervous; afraid, alarmed, horrified, panicked, panicky, panic-stricken, scared, shocked, spooked, startled, terrified, terrorized, unnerved
near antonyms brave, courageous, dauntless, doughty, fearless, gallant, greathearted, heroic (*also* heroical), intrepid, lionhearted, stalwart, stout, stouthearted, undaunted, valiant, valorous; assured, confident, self-assured, self-confident; determined, firm, game, plucky, resolute, undeterred, unflinching, unswerving; mettlesome, spirited, spunky
antonyms adventuresome, adventurous, audacious, bold, daring, dashing, gutsy, hardy, venturesome, venturous
2 not comfortable around people ⟨a *shy* person who finds talking to anyone but a close friend to be an awkward and unpleasant experience⟩
synonyms backward, bashful, coy, demure, diffident, introverted, modest, recessive, retiring, self-effacing, sheepish, withdrawn
related words antisocial, lone, lone-wolf, unsociable, unsocial; awkward, embarrassed, self-conscious, unadventurous, unassertive, unenterprising; inhibited, reserved, uneasy, uptight
near antonyms boon, clubbable (*also* clubable), companionable, convivial, gregarious, sociable, social; bold, dashing, forceful; brash, forward, overbold, uninhibited, unreserved
antonyms extroverted (*also* extraverted), immodest, outgoing
3 not coming up to an expected measure or meeting a particular need ⟨the team is *shy* a couple of players because of illness⟩ — see SHORT 3
4 not respectable ⟨she was nervous about being left alone in a *shy* bar in a bad section of town⟩ — see DISREPUTABLE

sic *also* **sick** *vb* to take sudden, violent action against ⟨commanded the pit bull to "*sic* 'em"⟩ — see ATTACK 1

sick *adj* **1** temporarily suffering from a disorder of the body ⟨those coworkers who always seem to get *sick* immediately before or after long holiday weekends⟩
synonyms ailing, bad, down, ill, indisposed, peaked, peaky, poorly, punk, run-down, sickened, unhealthy, unsound, unwell
related words symptomatic; cruddy, lousy, seedy, sickish; nauseated, nauseous, qualmish, queasy (*also*

queazy), squeamish; airsick, carsick, seasick; dizzy, light-headed, shaky, woozy; achy, feverish; diseased, disordered; decrepit, feeble, fragile, frail, infirm, invalid, sickly, weak, weakly; afflicted, troubled; challenged, debilitated, disabled, halt, incapacitated, lame; hypochondriac, hypochondriacal
phrases out of sorts, under the weather
near antonyms able-bodied, conditioned, fit, well-conditioned; cured; better, convalescing, improved, mending, recovering, recuperating, rehabilitated; hardy, hearty, lusty, robust, rugged, stalwart, strong, tough; blooming, bouncing, chipper, flourishing, flush, thriving
antonyms hale, healthful, healthy, sound, well, whole, wholesome
2 filled with disgust ⟨it makes me *sick* to think of someone hurting a helpless animal⟩
synonyms disgusted, nauseated, repelled, repulsed, revolted, shocked, sickened
related words fed up, weary; angered, angry, apoplectic, cheesed off [*chiefly British*], displeased, enraged, fuming, furious, horn-mad, incensed, indignant, infuriated, irate, livid, mad, outraged, rankled, riled, roiled, shirty [*chiefly British*], sore, steaming, teed off, ticked, upset, worked up, wrought (up)
near antonyms delighted, gratified, pleased, satisfied, thankful, thrilled, tickled; beguiled, bewitched, captivated, charmed, enchanted, enthralled, entranced, fascinated, mesmerized, spellbound
3 affected with nausea ⟨the bumpy ride made her *sick* to her stomach⟩ — see NAUSEOUS 1
4 having one's patience, interest, or pleasure exhausted ⟨I'm *sick* of listening to this radio station⟩ — see WEARY 2
5 having or showing lowered moral character or standards ⟨some people insisted that only a *sick* soul could write such perverted books⟩ — see CORRUPT

sick and tired *adj* having one's patience, interest, or pleasure exhausted ⟨was *sick and tired* of wasting her time at long, pointless meetings⟩ — see WEARY 2

sicken *vb* to cause to feel disgust ⟨*sickened* by the awful sight of abused animals⟩ — see DISGUST

sicken (with) *vb* to become affected with (a disease or disorder) ⟨a number of the passengers on the cruise ship had *sickened with* food poisoning⟩ — see CONTRACT 1

sickened *adj* **1** temporarily suffering from a disorder of the body ⟨the *sickened* passengers were rushed to the emergency room for treatment⟩ — see SICK 1
2 filled with disgust ⟨many audience members, *sickened* by the movie's graphic violence, stormed out of the theater⟩ — see SICK 2

sickening *adj* causing intense displeasure, disgust, or resentment ⟨a *sickening* display of emotion⟩ — see OFFENSIVE 1

sickie *n* a person judged to be legally or medically insane ⟨the police suspect it is some *sickie* with an obsession for the actress⟩ — see LUNATIC 1

sickish *adj* affected with nausea ⟨the fumes from the freshly applied paint made her feel *sickish*⟩ — see NAUSEOUS 1

sickly *adj* **1** chronically or repeatedly suffering from poor health ⟨a *sickly* foal that seemed to catch everything that the other horses had⟩
synonyms ailing, invalid, weakly
related words bedfast, bedridden; delicate, fragile, frail; dying, fading, incurable, moribund; challenged, debilitated, incapacitated, lame; decrepit, enfeebled, feeble, infirm, weak, weakened, worn-out; ill, indisposed, peaked, poorly, run-down, sick, unhealthy, unsound, unwell
near antonyms able-bodied, fit, hale, hearty, sound, well-conditioned, whole, wholesome
antonyms healthy, well
2 bad for the well-being of the body ⟨lungs scarred by years of exposure to the *sickly* air of the coal mines⟩ — see UNHEALTHY 1

sickness *n* **1** the condition of not being in good health ⟨she was plagued by *sickness* most of her adult life⟩
synonyms illness, indisposition, unhealthiness, unsoundness
related words malaise, sickishness; affliction, ailment, condition, disease, disorder, dysfunction (*also* disfunction), malady, trouble, upset; debility, decrepitude, feebleness, frailness, infirmity, invalidism, invalidity, lameness, sickliness, weakliness, weakness; hypochondria
near antonyms comeback, convalescence, healing, mending, rally, recovery, recuperation, rehab, rehabilitation, snapback; fettle, fitness, shape; hardiness, heartiness, lustiness, robustness, ruggedness, stamina, strength, toughness, vigor, vigorousness, vitality; bloom, flush, flushness; weal, welfare, well-being
antonyms health, healthiness, soundness, wellness, wholeness, wholesomeness
2 an abnormal state that disrupts a plant or animal's normal bodily functioning ⟨a *sickness* that resulted in the death of millions of the nation's elm trees⟩ — see DISEASE 1
3 a disturbed condition of the stomach in which one feels like vomiting ⟨the *sickness* that women typically feel upon rising during the early months of a pregnancy⟩ — see NAUSEA 1

sicko *n* a person judged to be legally or medically insane ⟨some *sicko* kidnapped and murdered as many as a dozen young women⟩ — see LUNATIC 1

side *adj* of, relating to, or located on one side ⟨please bring all deliveries to the *side* door⟩
synonyms lateral
related words left, right; one-sided

side *n* **1** a place, space, or direction away from or beyond a central point or line ⟨will everyone who wants to sign up for volleyball please stand off to this *side* of the gym?⟩
synonyms flank, hand
related words outside; face, top; bottom, foot, underbelly, underbody, underpart, underside, undersurface; lee, leeward, windward; left, right
near antonyms center, inside, interior, middle, midway
2 a certain way in which something appears or may be regarded ⟨examined the problem from all *sides*⟩ — see ASPECT 1
3 a group of people acting together within a larger group ⟨our *side* won, and the club will have a holiday party after all⟩ — see FACTION

sideboard *n* a storage case typically having doors and shelves ⟨all of the silverware was kept in the *sideboard*⟩ — see CABINET

sidekick *n* a person who helps a more skilled person ⟨movie heroes invariably have a trusty *sidekick*, who often provides comic relief⟩ — see HELPER

sidesplitting *adj* causing or intended to cause laughter ⟨his *sidesplitting* jokes usually have audiences helpless with laughter⟩ — see FUNNY 1

sidestep *vb* **1** to avoid having to comply with (something) especially through cleverness ⟨the eager enlistee *sidestepped* the regulations by lying about his age⟩ — see CIRCUMVENT 1
2 to move suddenly aside or to and fro ⟨the startled spectator *sidestepped* away from the oncoming ball⟩ — see DODGE 1

sideways *adv* **1** with one side faced forward ⟨I had to walk *sideways* to get between the two towering piles of boxes⟩

synonyms broadside, crabwise, edgeways [*chiefly British*], edgewise, sidewise
related words aslant, indirectly, obliquely; laterally, sideward (*or* sidewards)
near antonyms dead, direct, right, straight
2 with distrust ⟨she glanced at us *sideways* when she heard us claim we weren't there that night⟩ — see ASKANCE

sidewise *adv* with one side faced forward ⟨standing *sidewise* in the doorway⟩ — see SIDEWAYS 1

siege *n* **1** a sudden experiencing of a physical or mental disorder ⟨a devastating *siege* of typhoid fever hit the city⟩ — see ATTACK 2
2 the cutting off of an area by military means to stop the flow of people or supplies ⟨after a *siege* of six weeks, the city of Vicksburg surrendered to General Grant and his Union forces⟩ — see BLOCKADE

siesta *n* a short sleep ⟨he typically takes a *siesta* after lunch, waiting for it to become a little cooler until resuming work⟩ — see [1]NAP

sigh *vb* to take in and let out a deep audible breath or to make a similar sound ⟨Mom always used to *sigh* loudly whenever she found a mess on the floor—which was often⟩ ⟨a breeze *sighed* through the leaves⟩
synonyms sough
related words gasp, huff, pant, puff, wheeze; breathe, respire; exhale, expire, inhale, inspire; sniff, snort, snuffle; yawn

sigh (for) *vb* to have an earnest wish to own or enjoy ⟨people have always been *sighing for* the "good old days"⟩ — see DESIRE 1

sight *n* **1** a position within view ⟨get out of my *sight*!⟩ — see PRESENCE 1
2 an instance of looking especially briefly ⟨he always fainted at the merest *sight* of blood⟩ — see LOOK 2
3 something unpleasant to look at ⟨the frat house was a *sight* the morning after the party⟩ — see EYESORE
4 the ability to see ⟨lost his *sight* in an accident when he was young⟩ — see EYESIGHT
5 a considerable amount ⟨this place sure is a good *sight* better than that last motel⟩ — see LOT 2

sight *vb* to make note of (something) through the use of one's eyes ⟨the crew felt a rush of excitement upon hearing that the lookout had *sighted* land⟩ — see SEE 1

sightless *adj* lacking the power of sight ⟨bats are often thought to be completely *sightless*, but this is not really true⟩ — see BLIND 1

sightliness *n* the qualities in a person or thing that as a whole give pleasure to the senses ⟨never known for their *sightliness*, prisons and landfills are unwelcomed in most communities⟩ — see BEAUTY 1

sightly *adj* very pleasing to look at ⟨the calligrapher's *sightly* handwriting would be desirable on the diplomas⟩ — see BEAUTIFUL 1

sightseer *n* a person who travels for pleasure ⟨we shared the bus with a group of *sightseers* from out of town⟩ — see TOURIST

sign *n* **1** a movement of the body or limbs that expresses or emphasizes an idea or feeling ⟨made a *sign* for the audience to be quiet⟩ — see GESTURE 1
2 a written or printed mark that is meant to convey information to the reader ⟨an "and" *sign*⟩ — see CHARACTER 1

sign *vb* to write one's name on (as a document) ⟨you'll have to *sign* the contract for it to be legal⟩
synonyms autograph, ink, subscribe
related words sign up; cosign, countersign, endorse (*also* indorse), register, sign on; inscribe; author, pen, pencil (in), scratch (out), scrawl, scribble; notarize

sign (up *or* on) *vb* to provide with a paying job ⟨the sports shoe company recently *signed up* the nation's top female college basketball player to plug its products⟩ — see EMPLOY 1

signal *adj* standing above others in rank, importance, or achievement ⟨the Louisiana Purchase is cited by many historians as one of the most *signal* events in American history⟩ — see EMINENT

signal *vb* to direct or notify by a movement or gesture ⟨*signaled* the oncoming traffic to stop while the wrecked car was being towed away⟩ — see MOTION

signal *n* **1** an object intended to give public notice or warning ⟨stop signs are *signals* for vehicles to come to a full stop—not suggestions for slowing down, as some drivers seem to think⟩
synonyms flag, tocsin
related words red light; knell
2 a movement of the body or limbs that expresses or emphasizes an idea or feeling ⟨quietly waiting for the *signal* to advance⟩ — see GESTURE 1

signature *n* a person's name written in their own handwriting often given to indicate awareness or consent ⟨I'll just need your *signature* on the application, and then we're all set⟩
synonyms autograph, hand, John Hancock
related words frank, mark; countersign; endorsement (*also* indorsement)

significance *n* **1** the idea that is conveyed or intended to be conveyed to the mind by language, symbol, or action ⟨the *significance* of that word is much debated by biblical scholars⟩ — see MEANING 1
2 the quality or state of being important ⟨the political *significance* of the special commission's report⟩ — see IMPORTANCE

significant *adj* **1** clearly conveying a special meaning (as one's mood) ⟨after remarking that tardiness was on the rise, our boss cast a *significant* glance my way⟩ — see EXPRESSIVE
2 indicating something ⟨the town's generous library budget is *significant* of the value its residents place on learning⟩ — see INDICATIVE
3 having great meaning or lasting effect ⟨made a *significant* change in the procedure for applying for citizenship⟩ — see IMPORTANT 1
4 having great power or influence ⟨a producer who is playing a *significant* role in the creation of the new film⟩ — see IMPORTANT 2
5 sufficiently large in size, amount, or number to merit attention ⟨paid a *significant* amount of money for the movie rights to the book⟩ — see CONSIDERABLE 1

significant other *n* the person to whom another is married ⟨she has threatened to divorce her *significant other* if he doesn't stop gambling⟩ — see SPOUSE

signification *n* the idea that is conveyed or intended to be conveyed to the mind by language, symbol, or action ⟨we should assume that the author is using the word in its ordinary *signification*⟩ — see MEANING 1

signify *vb* **1** to be of importance ⟨never mind, as the color of the room doesn't *signify* in the least⟩ — see MATTER
2 to communicate or convey (as an idea) to the mind ⟨the symbol failed to *signify* anything to me—until I realized that it was upside down⟩ — see MEAN 1
3 to serve as a sign or symptom of ⟨the opening of the new mall *signifies* the city's overdue emergence from economic depression⟩ — see INDICATE 1

signifying *adj* indicating something ⟨his tendency to use weasel words is seen as a *signifying* character trait⟩ — see INDICATIVE

sign on (for) *vb* to become a member of ⟨I *signed on for* the crew team simply as a lark⟩ — see ENTER 2

sign up (for) *vb* to become a member of ⟨they both *signed up for* a Spanish class⟩ — see ENTER 2

silence *n* **1** incapacity for or restraint from speaking

⟨the violinist expects complete *silence* from the audience during his concerts⟩
synonyms dumbness, muteness, speechlessness, stillness
related words inarticulacy, inarticulateness, voicelessness; reserve, reticence, reticency, taciturnity
near antonyms communication, speaking, talking; eloquence, fluency, volubility; chattiness, garrulousness, loquaciousness, loquacity, talkativeness, talkiness; verboseness, verbosity, windiness, wordiness
2 the near or complete absence of sound ⟨the *silence* of the garden was refreshing after the din of the party inside⟩
synonyms hush, quiet, quietness, quietude, still, stillness
related words calm, lull, peace, peacefulness, tranquillity (*or* tranquility)
near antonyms babel, blare, bluster, cacophony, chatter, clamor, clangor, din, hubbub, racket, rattle, roar, tumult, uproar
antonyms noise, sound, unquietness
3 the quality or state of being mostly or completely unknown ⟨the book eventually vanished into the *silence* that awaits best sellers whose time has past⟩ — see OBSCURITY 2

silence *vb* **1** to stop the noise or speech of ⟨the instructor quickly *silenced* anyone who tried to interrupt⟩ ⟨we need to have a repairman come and *silence* that door alarm⟩
synonyms dumb, extinguish, hush, mute, quell, quiet, quieten [*chiefly British*], settle, shush, shut up, squelch, still
near antonyms agitate, stir
2 to put a stop to (something) by the use of force ⟨brutally *silenced* all political dissent in the country⟩ — see QUELL 1

silent *adj* **1** deliberately refraining from speech ⟨the suddenly *silent* child had to be prompted to say hello⟩
synonyms dumb, mum, mute, muted, speechless, uncommunicative, wordless
related words inarticulate, tongue-tied; nonvocal, voiceless; dumbstruck; sulking, sulky, sullen
near antonyms articulate, eloquent, fluent, voluble, well-spoken; gabby, garrulous, loquacious, talkative, talky; outspoken, unreserved, vocal; facile, glib, silver-tongued, smooth-tongued
antonyms communicative, speaking, talking
2 tending not to speak frequently (as by habit or inclination) ⟨a naturally *silent* boy, he was often overshadowed by his louder siblings⟩
synonyms closemouthed, dumb, laconic, reserved, reticent, taciturn, tight-lipped, uncommunicative
related words aloof, indrawn, inhibited, introverted, reserved, restrained; sedate, self-contained, sober, staid; backward, bashful, coy, demure, diffident, modest, retiring, self-effacing, sheepish
near antonyms free-spoken, outspoken, vocal; gossipy, talebearing; diffuse, long-winded, prolix, rambling, verbose, windy, wordy; extroverted (*also* extraverted), gregarious, outgoing, sociable
antonyms blabby, chatty, communicative, conversational, gabby, garrulous, loquacious, motormouthed, mouthy, talkative, talky, unreserved
3 mostly or entirely without sound ⟨the room was so *silent* that you could have heard the proverbial pin drop⟩
synonyms hushed, muted, noiseless, quiet, quieted, soundless, still, stilly
related words calm, peaceable, peaceful, serene, tranquil
near antonyms boisterous, clamorous, clangorous, clattering, clattery, raucous, rip-roaring, roaring, roistering, tumultuous
antonyms noisy, rackety, unquiet, uproarious

silent treatment *n* treatment that is deliberately unfriendly ⟨ever since our run-in at the party she's been giving me the *silent treatment*⟩ — see COLD SHOULDER

silhouette *n* a line that traces the outer limits of an object or surface ⟨cartoonists often try to give their characters recognizable *silhouettes*⟩ — see OUTLINE 1

silhouette *vb* to draw or make apparent the outline of ⟨in the photograph the majestic mountain is strikingly *silhouetted* against the setting sun⟩ — see OUTLINE 1

silken *adj* **1** smooth or delicate in appearance or feel ⟨the *silken* texture of the synthetic fabric⟩ — see SOFT 2
2 showing obvious signs of wealth and comfort ⟨she was unaccustomed to living in such *silken* surroundings⟩ — see LUXURIOUS 1

silklike *adj* smooth or delicate in appearance or feel ⟨the lemon mousse's *silklike* texture⟩ — see SOFT 2

silk–stocking *adj* **1** having goods, property, or money in abundance ⟨the luxurious resort caters exclusively to a *silk-stocking* clientele⟩ — see RICH 1
2 of high birth, rank, or station ⟨detectives assigned to investigate crimes among the *silk-stocking* types found on the city's gold coast⟩ — see NOBLE 1

silk stocking *n* a wealthy person ⟨made her reputation as an interior designer for the *silk stockings* of Nob Hill⟩ — see CAPITALIST

silky *adj* **1** smooth or delicate in appearance or feel ⟨the plant's fibers feel *silky* to the touch⟩ — see SOFT 2
2 covered with or as if with hair ⟨the tops of the leaves are a dark glossy green, but the undersides are light and *silky*⟩ — see HAIRY 1

silliness *n* **1** lack of good sense or judgment ⟨she was both amused and irritated by the *silliness* of his comments regarding the movie they has just seen⟩ — see FOOLISHNESS 1
2 language, behavior, or ideas that are absurd and contrary to good sense ⟨stop this *silliness* at once!⟩ — see NONSENSE 1
3 a lack of seriousness often at an improper time ⟨this inability to refrain from *silliness* is a distressing sign of professional immaturity⟩ — see FRIVOLITY

silly *adj* **1** lacking in seriousness or maturity ⟨the matinee show was filled with a bunch of *silly* children making noise⟩ — see GIDDY 1
2 showing or marked by a lack of good sense or judgment ⟨those *silly* movie producers who thought that audiences would fall for that gimmick all over again⟩ — see FOOLISH 1
3 so foolish or pointless as to be worthy of scornful laughter ⟨had the *silly* notion that her latest marriage might last longer than her three previous ones⟩ — see RIDICULOUS 1
4 suffering from mental confusion ⟨stunning news that knocked me *silly*⟩ — see DIZZY 2

silver *adj* of the color gray ⟨a distinguished-looking gentleman with *silver* hair⟩ — see GRAY 1

silver *n* eating and serving utensils ⟨laid out the *silver* for the dinner guests⟩ — see TABLEWARE 1

silver screen *n* the art or business of making a movie ⟨a list of the top 100 stars of the *silver screen*⟩ — see MOVIE 2

silver–tongued *adj* able to express oneself clearly and well ⟨famed as a *silver-tongued* orator, Daniel Webster used his oratorical gifts in vigorous support of the Union⟩ — see ARTICULATE

silverware *n* eating and serving utensils ⟨we keep the *silverware* in a separate drawer⟩ — see TABLEWARE 1

silvery *adj* of the color gray ⟨a *silvery* metal of some kind⟩ — see GRAY 1

similar *adj* having qualities in common ⟨the two actresses accidentally wore *similar* outfits to the same gala⟩ — see ALIKE

similarity *n* **1** the quality or state of having many qualities in common ⟨the *similarity* between the two essays is too great to be coincidental—one author virtually copied the other⟩
synonyms alikeness, community, comparability, correspondence, likeness, parallelism, resemblance, similitude
related words semblance; affinity, analogousness; equation, equivalence, equivalency, par, parity; identicalness, identity, sameness; correlation, relationship; exchangeability, interchangeability; accordance, agreement, compatibility, conformity, congruity
near antonyms inequality; conflict, polarity; incompatibility, incongruence, incongruity, incongruousness, nonconformity; differentiability, discriminability, distinguishability; anomalousness, dichotomy; disproportion, imbalance, inequality, nonequivalence
antonyms difference, disagreement, discrepancy, disparateness, disparity, dissimilarity, dissimilitude, distinctiveness, distinctness, unlikeness
2 a point which two or more things share in common ⟨the only *similarity* between this project and the last one is that both will involve some lab work⟩
synonyms commonality, common denominator, congruity, correspondence, parallel, resemblance, similitude
related words counterpart, equal, equivalent; analogy; homology
near antonyms difference, discrepancy; deviance, divergence, incongruence, incongruity; change, modification, variation
antonyms dissimilarity

similarly *adv* in like manner ⟨all the other men were removing their ties, so I did *similarly*⟩ — see ALSO 1

similitude *n* **1** the quality or state of having many qualities in common ⟨the striking *similitude* between that modern city and the Rome of ancient times⟩ — see SIMILARITY 1
2 a point which two or more things share in common ⟨the two robberies, committed on opposite ends of the country, show some curious *similitudes*⟩ — see SIMILARITY 2

simmer *vb* to cook in a liquid heated to the point that it gives off steam ⟨I gently *simmered* the chili for an hour⟩ — see BOIL 2

simp *n* a person who lacks good sense or judgment ⟨a popular movie about a sweet *simp* from Alabama⟩ — see FOOL 1

simple *adj* **1** free from all additions or embellishment ⟨a *simple* design, and one that never goes out of fashion⟩ — see PLAIN 1
2 free from any intent to deceive or impress others ⟨growing up in *simple* innocence⟩ — see GUILELESS
3 having no exceptions or restrictions ⟨that's the *simple* truth⟩ — see ABSOLUTE 2
4 involving minimal difficulty or effort ⟨I got all of the answers right because it was such a *simple* test⟩ — see EASY 1
5 lacking in worldly wisdom or informed judgment ⟨developers mistakenly thought that the local residents were *simple* people who would sell their land for practically nothing⟩ — see NAIVE 1
6 lacking in education or the knowledge gained from books ⟨the fact that he didn't go to college doesn't mean he's *simple*⟩ — see IGNORANT 1
7 not having or showing an ability to absorb ideas readily ⟨don't be so quick to characterize people who have trouble with computers as *simple*⟩ — see STUPID 1

simpleminded *adj* **1** lacking in worldly wisdom or informed judgment ⟨a *simpleminded* view of a complex problem⟩ — see NAIVE 1
2 showing or marked by a lack of good sense or judgment ⟨scornful of their *simpleminded* belief that their parents would always be there to take care of them⟩ — see FOOLISH 1

simplemindedness *n* the quality or state of being simple and sincere ⟨the *simplemindedness* of the villagers was at times winning and at others worrisome⟩ — see NAÏVETÉ 1

simpleness *n* **1** the quality or state of being simple and sincere ⟨the *simpleness* of the villagers was so disarming that she temporarily abandoned her natural cynicism⟩ — see NAÏVETÉ 1
2 the quality or state of lacking intelligence or quickness of mind ⟨we must always remember that the often frustrating *simpleness* of the mentally challenged does not alter the fact that they deserve respect⟩ — see STUPIDITY 1
3 readiness to believe the claims of others without sufficient evidence ⟨there's a good-hearted *simpleness* about her that makes her easy prey for scams⟩ — see CREDULITY

simpleton *n* **1** a person who lacks good sense or judgment ⟨his silly antics at office parties have earned him a reputation as a *simpleton*⟩ — see FOOL 1
2 a stupid person ⟨she felt like such a *simpleton* for needing help to install her home theater⟩ — see IDIOT

simplicity *n* **1** the quality or state of having a form or structure of few parts or elements ⟨the *simplicity* of this machine should ensure ease of use by almost anyone⟩
synonyms plainness, unsophistication
related words homogeneity, homogeneousness, uniformity, unity
antonyms complexity, complexness, complicacy, complicatedness, complication, elaborateness, intricacy, intricateness, sophistication
2 clearness of expression ⟨the *simplicity* of this poem is beautiful⟩
synonyms clarity, explicitness, lucidity, lucidness, perspicuity, perspicuousness
related words incision, incisiveness; directness, forthrightness, openness, straightforwardness; readability, readableness; comprehensibility, intelligibility, legibility
near antonyms ambiguity, ambiguousness, equivocalness, equivocation, inscrutability, inscrutableness, obliqueness, obliquity, opacity, opaqueness; impenetrability, incomprehensibility, incomprehensibleness, unintelligibility, unintelligibleness; circuitousness, deviousness, indirectness, indistinctness; dimness, disjointedness, incoherence; faintness, fuzziness, muddiness, nebulousness, vagueness
antonyms obscureness, obscurity, unclarity
3 lack of good sense or judgment ⟨the stupefying *simplicity* of the generals who thought that war would be over in a month!⟩ — see FOOLISHNESS 1
4 the quality or state of being simple and sincere ⟨answered the judge's questions with childlike *simplicity*⟩ — see NAÏVETÉ 1

simplify *vb* **1** to make less complex ⟨you need to *simplify* this process somewhat or you'll never finish it today⟩
synonyms streamline
related words dumb down, oversimplify; prune, strip (down), trim; purify, refine
near antonyms elaborate
antonyms complex, complexify, complicate, perplex, sophisticate
2 to make plain or understandable ⟨the book *simplifies* for the layman some concepts of economics⟩ — see EXPLAIN 1

simply *adv* **1** for nothing other than ⟨uninterested in food, she eats *simply* to keep alive⟩ — see SOLELY 1
2 nothing more than ⟨it's *simply* smart to shop around

before buying an item⟩ — see JUST 3

simulate *vb* to present a false appearance of ⟨cosmetics that *simulate* a suntan⟩ — see FEIGN

simulated *adj* **1** being such in appearance only and made with or manufactured from usually cheaper materials ⟨a *simulated* leopard skin rug⟩ — see IMITATION

2 lacking in natural or spontaneous quality ⟨the *simulated* friendliness in public of two politicians who can't stand each other in private⟩ — see ARTIFICIAL 1

simultaneous *adj* existing or occurring at the same period of time ⟨a *simultaneous* release of the movie and its soundtrack on CD⟩ — see CONTEMPORARY 1

simultaneously *adv* at one and the same time ⟨fires broke out *simultaneously* in several parts of town⟩ — see TOGETHER 1

sin *n* **1** a breaking of a moral or legal code ⟨a child old enough to know that lying is a *sin*⟩ — see OFFENSE 1

2 that which is morally unacceptable ⟨a minister who worries that modern society has abandoned the concept of *sin*⟩ — see EVIL

3 immoral conduct or practices harmful or offensive to society ⟨a sordid section of the city that is mainly known for *sin* and degradation⟩ — see VICE 1

4 a regrettable or blameworthy act ⟨it's a *sin* to waste food when people are starving⟩ — see CRIME 2

5 a defect in character ⟨my besetting *sin* is impatience—I hate to wait for anything⟩ — see FAULT 1

sin *vb* to commit an offense ⟨bless me, Father, for I have *sinned*⟩ — see OFFEND 1

since *adv* earlier than the present time ⟨an ancient marking whose meaning is long *since* forgotten⟩ — see AGO

since *conj* for the reason that ⟨*since* you are already here, we might as well get the meeting started⟩

synonyms as, as long as, because, being (as *or* as how *or* that) [*chiefly dialect*], 'cause, considering, for, inasmuch as, now, seeing, whereas

sincere *adj* **1** genuine in feeling ⟨she offered a *sincere* apology for her angry outburst⟩

synonyms heartfelt, unfeigned

related words unaffected, unforced; artless, honest, ingenuous, translucent, transparent, true; authentic, genuine; hearty, wholehearted, whole-souled

near antonyms backhanded, double-dealing, hypocritical, left-handed, mealy, mealymouthed, two-faced, unctuous

antonyms affected, artificial, false, feigned, insincere

2 free from any intent to deceive or impress others ⟨done out of a *sincere* desire to help others⟩ — see GUILELESS

sincerely *adv* without any attempt to impress by deception or exaggeration ⟨thanked them *sincerely* for their help⟩ — see NATURALLY 3

sine qua non *n* something necessary, indispensable, or unavoidable ⟨an extensive grounding in mathematics is a *sine qua non* for a career in architecture⟩ — see ESSENTIAL 1

sinew *n* the ability to exert effort for the accomplishment of a task ⟨the justices displayed great intellectual depth and *sinew* in writing their opinion on this case⟩ — see POWER 2

sinewy *adj* **1** having muscles capable of exerting great physical force ⟨the lithe, *sinewy* body of the ballet company's leading male dancer⟩ — see STRONG 1

2 marked by a well-developed musculature ⟨the *sinewy* arms of the weight lifter⟩ — see MUSCULAR 1

sinful *adj* not conforming to a high moral standard; morally unacceptable ⟨chastised by his minister for his *sinful* behavior⟩ — see BAD 2

sinfulness *n* the state or quality of being utterly evil ⟨private diaries reveal that the torturers came to realize the unspeakable *sinfulness* of their actions and were ever afterwards haunted by nightmares⟩ — see ENORMITY 1

sing *vb* **1** to produce musical sounds with the voice ⟨it's relatively rare to find actors who can also *sing* well⟩

synonyms carol, chant, descant, vocalize

related words belt, croon, harmonize, hum, lilt, quaver, scat, sharp, slur, trill, troll, warble, yodel; serenade

2 to utter in musical or drawn out tones ⟨the cantor *sang* the prayers before the entire congregation⟩ — see CHANT 1

3 to utter one's distinctive animal sound ⟨I can hear a bird *singing* in the distance⟩ — see CRY 2

4 to give information (as to the authorities) about another's improper or unlawful activities ⟨once he saw the kind of jail time he was facing, the suspect was *singing* loud and clear to the police⟩ — see SQUEAL 1

singe *vb* to burn on the surface ⟨the marshmallows got a bit *singed* over the campfire, but we like them that way⟩ — see SCORCH 1

singer *n* one who sings ⟨a famous opera *singer* will be performing at the gala opening of the arts center⟩

synonyms caroler (*or* caroller), songster, vocalist, vocalizer, voice

related words belter; crooner, harmonizer, hummer, warbler, yodeler; serenader; cantor, chanter, chorister; chansonnier; chanteuse, songstress; bard, troubador

single *adj* **1** not married ⟨there was such a shortage of *single* men in the neighborhood that he had his pick of girlfriends⟩

synonyms unattached, unmarried, unwed

related words fancy-free, footloose; marriageable, unpaired; divorced, separated

near antonyms mated, paired; affianced, betrothed, committed, engaged, pledged, promised; remarried

antonyms attached, espoused, hitched, married, wedded (*also* wed)

2 belonging only to the one person, unit, or group named ⟨any view expressed on the newspaper's editorial pages is the *single* opinion of the writer of the column⟩ — see SOLE 1

3 not physically attached to another unit ⟨the average price of *single* homes in the area⟩ — see SEPARATE 2

4 not being in the company of others ⟨a restaurant where the *single* diner is made to feel welcome and given the same level of service as couples or groups⟩ — see ALONE 1

single (out) *vb* **1** to decide to accept (someone or something) from a group of possibilities ⟨she quickly *singled out* the most qualified candidate from the pool of the applicants⟩ — see CHOOSE 1

2 to find out or establish the identity of ⟨through careful reasoning and the process of elimination, neighbors *singled* her *out* as the writer of the anonymous letter⟩ — see IDENTIFY 1

single-handed *adv* without aid or support ⟨she was adamant that if she was expected to do the project *single-handed*, she should not have to share the credit afterward⟩ — see ALONE 1

single-handedly *adv* without aid or support ⟨the team's star slugger hit three home runs, effectively winning the game *single-handedly*⟩ — see ALONE 1

single-minded *adj* fully committed to achieving a goal ⟨every successful reform movement has been spearheaded by a *single-minded* activist who refused to accept defeat⟩ — see DETERMINED 1

singly *adv* without aid or support ⟨either *singly* or with the cooperation of other nations, we must do something about this pressing environmental issue⟩ — see ALONE 1

singular *adj* **1** being out of the ordinary ⟨the novelist's *singular* command of the language makes her a compelling voice in contemporary fiction⟩ — see EXCEPTIONAL 1

2 noticeably different from what is generally found or experienced ⟨appearing on the game show has been the most *singular* experience of my life⟩ — see UNUSUAL 1

3 of, relating to, or belonging to a single person ⟨preserving our national heritage is not a *singular* responsibility but our collective duty⟩ — see INDIVIDUAL 1

4 being the one or ones of a class with no other members ⟨this crime was a *singular* case, and using it as a reason for revising the criminal code would be ill-advised⟩ — see ONLY 2

singularity *n* an odd or peculiar habit ⟨a college professor with *singularities* of dress and speech that have long endeared him to his students⟩ — see IDIOSYNCRASY

sinister *adj* being or showing a sign of evil or calamity to come ⟨the movie relies too much on *sinister* background music to create the suspense that the plot sorely lacks⟩ — see OMINOUS

sink *vb* **1** to become worse or of less value ⟨his fortunes have steadily *sunk* since the breakup of his marriage⟩ — see DETERIORATE 1

2 to go to a lower level especially abruptly ⟨I had just bought a bundle of shares of the stock when its price *sank* like a rock⟩ — see DROP 2

3 to refrain from openly showing or uttering ⟨*sinks* his pride and makes the first step towards a reconciliation⟩ — see SUPPRESS 2

4 to cease to be visible ⟨that evening we sat on the beach, dreamily watching the sun *sink* beneath the horizon⟩ — see DISAPPEAR

5 to diminish the price or value of ⟨the slightest nick will *sink* the price of a piece of Tiffany glass⟩ — see DEPRECIATE 1

6 to reduce to a lower standing in one's own eyes or in others' eyes ⟨the revelation that he has been embezzling for years definitely *sinks* him in my opinion⟩ — see HUMBLE

7 to lead or extend downward ⟨the road *sinks* abruptly after that curve⟩ — see DESCEND 1

8 to lose bodily strength or vigor ⟨the old woman only *sunk* further after she was moved to the nursing home⟩ — see WEAKEN 2

sink *n* a place of great vice and corruption ⟨was able to rise above the inner-city *sink* that was his birthplace⟩ — see AUGEAN STABLE

sinless *adj* free from sin ⟨the belief that limbo is the place where *sinless* but unbaptized souls abide until Judgment Day⟩ — see INNOCENT 1

sinner *n* a person who commits moral wrongs ⟨even the worst *sinner* can be redeemed⟩ — see EVILDOER 1

sinuous *adj* marked by a long series of irregular curves ⟨the river flowed in a *sinuous* path through the lush valley⟩ — see CROOKED 1

sip *vb* to swallow in liquid form ⟨slowly *sipping* the hot soup⟩ — see DRINK 1

sip *n* the portion of a serving of a beverage that is swallowed at one time ⟨there are a few *sips* left in the glass⟩ — see DRINK 2

siphon *also* **syphon** *vb* **1** to remove (liquid) gradually or completely ⟨I let the stranded motorist *siphon* some of my gas so he could be on his way⟩ — see DRAIN 1

2 to cause to move to a central point or along a restricted pathway ⟨investigators discovered that the so-called charitable organization was *siphoning* funds to a terrorist group⟩ — see CHANNEL

sire *vb* to become the father of ⟨the champion racehorse went on to *sire* a long line of winners⟩ — see FATHER

sire *n* **1** a male human parent ⟨his *sire* had been a renowned Wall Street lawyer⟩ — see FATHER 1

2 a person who establishes a whole new field of endeavor ⟨the revered *sire* of the impressionist movement in art⟩ — see FATHER 2

siren *n* a woman whom men find irresistibly attractive ⟨one of history's most famous *sirens*, Cleopatra charmed both Julius Caesar and Mark Antony⟩

synonyms enchantress, femme fatale, seductress, temptress

related words beguiler, charmer, seducer, vamp; sexpot, sex symbol

siren song *n* something that persuades one to perform an action for pleasure or gain ⟨the opportunity for fame and fortune is the *siren song* that has long lured the ambitious to the big city⟩ — see LURE 1

sissified *adj* of or relating to a man who has or displays qualities considered more suitable for women ⟨what kind of *sissified* jocks play a sport like that?⟩ — see EFFEMINATE

sissy *adj* of or relating to a man who has or displays qualities more suitable for women ⟨thought it was *sissy* for a boy to like flowers⟩ — see EFFEMINATE

sissy *n* a person who shows a shameful lack of courage in the face of danger ⟨the candidate touts his wartime service as evidence that he is not a *sissy*⟩ — see COWARD

sit *vb* **1** to rest on the buttocks or haunches ⟨everybody needs to *sit* down, or no one will be able to see the movie⟩

synonyms set [*chiefly dialect*]

related words perch; lounge, slouch, sprawl, squat, straddle

near antonyms arise, get up, rise, stand

2 to cause to sit down ⟨the host had to *sit* some of the guests on the porch⟩ — see SEAT 1

3 to cover and warm eggs as the young inside develop ⟨we didn't want to disturb the hens, as they were *sitting*⟩ — see SET 1

4 to occupy a place or location ⟨the large monument that *sits* at the entrance to the battlefield⟩ — see STAND 1

site *n* the area or space occupied by or intended for something ⟨this field is the intended *site* for a new shopping mall⟩ — see PLACE 1

sitter *n* a girl or woman employed to care for a young child or children ⟨we'll be going to the movie if we can get a *sitter* for the kids⟩ — see NURSE

sitting duck *n* a person or thing that is the object of abuse, criticism, or ridicule ⟨those stupid comments just made him a *sitting duck* for comedians⟩ — see TARGET 1

situate *vb* to arrange something in a certain spot or position ⟨the new industrial complex is *situated* near the highway⟩ — see PLACE 1

situation *n* **1** position with regard to conditions and circumstances ⟨the school's *situation* is improving with additional financial help⟩

synonyms ball game, deal, footing, picture, posture, scene, status, story

related words rank, standing; place, spot, state; score, status quo

2 an assignment at which one regularly works for pay ⟨there were the usual "*situation* wanted" postings in the local newspaper⟩ — see JOB 1

3 the placement of someone or something in relation to others in a vertical arrangement ⟨in earlier times people were unable to alter their *situation* in life, so if you were born a servant, you stayed a servant⟩ — see RANK 1

sixth sense *n* the power of seeing or knowing about things that are not present to the senses ⟨a filmmaker with a *sixth sense* for knowing which stories the general public will find irresistible⟩ — see CLAIRVOYANCE

sizable *or* **sizeable** *adj* **1** of a size greater than average of its kind ⟨a *sizable* sum of money⟩ — see LARGE 1

2 sufficiently large in size, amount, or number to merit attention ⟨a *sizable* increase in attendance since the team began its winning streak⟩ — see CONSIDERABLE 1

sizably *adv* to a large extent or degree ⟨we need to *sizably* increase production if we want to finish this project on time⟩ — see GREATLY 2

[1]**size** *n* the total amount of measurable space or surface occupied by something ⟨we worried that the immense *size* of the sofa would make getting it through the doorway impossible⟩
synonyms bulk, dimension, extent, magnitude, measure, measurement, proportion
related words area; capaciousness, commodiousness, roominess, spaciousness; ampleness, amplitude, bigness, bulkiness, enormousness, grandness, greatness, grossness, heftiness, hugeness, immenseness, immensity, largeness, mass, massiveness, monstrousness, stupendousness, tremendousness, vastness, volume, voluminousness

[2]**size** *n* a substance used to stick things together ⟨coated the fabric with *size* before applying it to the wall⟩ — see GLUE

sizzle *n* a sound similar to the speech sound \s\ stretched out ⟨there was a brief *sizzle* as the moth flew into the flame⟩ — see HISS 1

sizzle *vb* **1** to make a sound like that of stretching out the speech sound \s\ ⟨from my bed I could hear the bacon *sizzling* in the frying pan⟩ — see HISS
2 to be excited or emotionally stirred up with anger ⟨she was really *sizzling* about being passed over for the promotion, and nearly quit⟩ — see BOIL 1

skank *n, slang* a person of low moral character ⟨while her clueless husband was at work, the *skank* was doing every guy in the trailer park⟩ — see SLEAZE 1

skanky *adj, slang* having loose sexual morals ⟨a pop star who cultivates an image that is more *skanky* than sexy⟩ — see SLEAZY 1

skedaddle *vb* to hasten away from something dangerous or frightening ⟨we *skedaddled* as soon as we saw the snake entering our campsite⟩ — see RUN 2

skeletal *adj* suffering extreme weight loss as a result of hunger or disease ⟨the stray kitten's *skeletal* body was pitiful to look at⟩ — see EMACIATED

skeleton *n* the arrangement of parts that gives something its basic form ⟨Native Americans covered the *skeletons* of their wigwams with bark, rush mats, or hides⟩ — see FRAME 1

skeptic *n* a person who is always ready to doubt or question the truth or existence of something ⟨the demand by *skeptics* that believers in Bigfoot produce some hard evidence of that hairy humanoid⟩
synonyms disbeliever, doubter, doubting Thomas, questioner, unbeliever
related words agnostic; cynic, misanthrope, pessimist; derider, ridiculer, scoffer
near antonyms chump, dupe, gull, pigeon, sucker

skeptical *adj* **1** inclined to doubt or question claims ⟨it's good to be *skeptical* about what you see on TV⟩
synonyms disbelieving, distrustful, doubting, incredulous, mistrustful, negativistic, questioning, show-me, suspecting, suspicious, unbelieving
related words paranoid (*also* paranoidal); critical, puzzled, quizzical; careful, cautious, guarded, gun-shy, leery (*also* leary), wary, watchful; cynical, experienced, knowing, sophisticated, worldly, worldly-wise; curious, inquiring, inquisitive, nosy (*or* nosey), snoopy; uncertain, unconvinced, undecided, undetermined, unsettled, unsure; hesitant
near antonyms green, ingenuous, innocent, naive (*or* naïve), simple, simpleminded, unknowing, unsophisticated, unworldly, wide-eyed; certain, confident, positive, sure; callow, inexperienced, raw; childlike, idealistic, impractical; beguiled, deceived, duped, gulled, tricked; careless, heedless, unsuspecting, unsuspicious, unwary
antonyms credulous, gullible (*also* gullable), trustful, trusting, uncritical, unquestioning
2 not feeling sure about the truth, wisdom, or trustworthiness of someone or something ⟨I'm a little *skeptical* of this low bid, since it's way below what the other contractors said that they would charge⟩ — see DOUBTFUL 1

skeptically *adv* with distrust ⟨the researchers' findings should be received *skeptically* until they can be replicated by other scientists⟩ — see ASKANCE

skepticism *n* a feeling or attitude that one does not know the truth, truthfulness, or trustworthiness of someone or something ⟨our alibi was met with *skepticism* at first, but we gradually convinced them of the truth⟩ — see DOUBT

sketch *n* **1** a picture using lines to represent the chief features of an object or scene ⟨made a quick *sketch* from which she would create a more detailed painting later⟩ — see DRAWING
2 a vivid representation in words of someone or something ⟨gave her boss quick *sketches* of the personalities of the clients he was about to meet⟩ — see DESCRIPTION 1

sketch *vb* **1** to draw or make apparent the outline of ⟨*sketched* the garden pavilion on a pad of paper so the homeowners would have a rough idea of how it was going to look⟩ — see OUTLINE 1
2 to give a representation or account of in words ⟨briefly *sketched* the intent of the reorganization plan⟩ — see DESCRIBE 1

skewed *adj* inclined or twisted to one side ⟨he could see that the ropes had gotten all *skewed* in the collision⟩ — see AWRY

skewer *vb* **1** to penetrate or hold (something) with a pointed object ⟨let's *skewer* our marshmallows on these sticks and start toasting⟩ — see IMPALE
2 to make (someone or something) the object of unkind laughter ⟨the satirical comic strip gleefully *skewers* many of society's sacred cows⟩ — see RIDICULE

skid *vb* to go to a lower level especially abruptly ⟨the local economy *skidded* when the last manufacturing plant moved away⟩ — see DROP 2

skill *n* **1** subtle or imaginative ability in inventing, devising, or executing something ⟨with unbelievable *skill*, the expert in origami transformed a few sheets of paper into a menagerie of exotic animals⟩
synonyms adeptness, adroitness, art, artfulness, artifice, artistry, cleverness, craft, cunning, deftness, masterfulness, skillfulness
related words dexterity, ease, finesse, handiness; experience, expertise, expertness, know-how, proficiency; creativity, ingenuity, inventiveness, knowledge, learning; aptitude, bent, flair, gift, knack, talent
near antonyms amateurishness, awkwardness, clumsiness, crudeness, klutziness, rudeness; inability, inadequacy, inadequateness, incapability, incapacity, incompetence, ineffectiveness, ineffectuality, ineffectualness, inefficacy, inefficiency
antonyms artlessness, ineptitude, ineptness, maladroitness
2 skills *pl* knowledge gained by actually doing or living through something ⟨he had acquired valuable *skills* during his life at sea⟩ — see EXPERIENCE 1

skilled *adj* having or showing exceptional knowledge, experience, or skill in a field of endeavor ⟨a delicate brain operation requiring the services of a highly *skilled* surgeon⟩ — see PROFICIENT

skillful *adj* **1** accomplished with trained ability ⟨the ice skater performed a *skillful* and graceful series of jumps⟩

synonyms adroit, artful, bravura, deft, delicate, dexterous (*also* dextrous), expert, masterful, masterly, practiced (*also* practised), virtuoso, workmanlike
related words facile, smooth; artistic, creative, fancy, ingenious, neat; adept, clever, cunning; able, adequate, capable, competent
near antonyms awkward, clumsy, crude, klutzy; ineffective, ineffectual; incompetent, inept
antonyms amateur, amateurish, artless, rude, unprofessional, unskillful
2 having or showing exceptional knowledge, experience, or skill in a field of endeavor ⟨performance testing of automobiles that should be done only by *skillful* drivers on a closed course⟩ — see PROFICIENT
skillfully *adv* in a skillful or expert manner ⟨*skillfully* guided the powerboat around the obstacles⟩ — see WELL 3
skillfulness *n* subtle or imaginative ability in inventing, devising, or executing something ⟨the *skillfulness* with which she handled that touchy situation is indeed admirable⟩ — see SKILL 1
skim *vb* **1** to turn over pages in an idle or cursory manner ⟨I'll just *skim* through a few styling magazines and see if something interesting catches my eye⟩
synonyms flip, leaf, riffle, thumb
related words browse, dip; glance (at), look over, scan
near antonyms pore (over); study
2 to move or proceed smoothly and readily ⟨a lone hang glider *skimming* along just above the treetops⟩ — see FLOW 2
3 to pass lightly across or touch gently especially in passing ⟨her hand just barely *skimmed* the wall as she ran down the hallway⟩ — see [2]BRUSH
4 to strike and fly off at an angle ⟨the rock just *skimmed* the surface of the water⟩ — see GLANCE 1
5 to take a quick or hasty look ⟨he impatiently *skimmed* through the book, looking for the specific passage he remembered seeing⟩ — see GLANCE 2
skimp *adj* less plentiful than what is normal, necessary, or desirable ⟨a dieter complaining about *skimp* meals that were served at the fat farm⟩ — see MEAGER
skimp *vb* to avoid unnecessary waste or expense ⟨we must *skimp* and save if we are going to afford a vacation this summer⟩ — see ECONOMIZE
skimp (on) *vb* to use or give out in stingy amounts ⟨I'd like a baked potato, and don't *skimp on* the sour cream⟩ — see SPARE 1
skimping *n* careful management of material resources ⟨after years of *skimping* and saving, he was finally able to afford the sports car he had always wanted⟩ — see ECONOMY
skimpy *adj* less plentiful than what is normal, necessary, or desirable ⟨the information in the user's manual for the microwave is *skimpy* and not particularly helpful⟩ — see MEAGER
skin *n* **1** an outer part or layer ⟨space-age materials used on the *skin* of the aircraft⟩ — see EXTERIOR
2 the outer covering of an animal removed for its commercial value ⟨hats made from beaver *skins* were once fashionable⟩ — see HIDE 1
3 the hairless natural covering of an animal prepared for use ⟨calf*skin* gloves⟩ — see LEATHER 1
skin *vb* **1** to remove the natural covering of ⟨I prefer not to *skin* potatoes before mashing them⟩ — see PEEL
2 to rob by the use of trickery or threats ⟨got his revenge on the dirty swindler who had *skinned* him⟩ — see FLEECE
3 to defeat by a large margin ⟨we simply got *skinned* in the interoffice softball tournament⟩ — see WHIP 2
skin-deep *adj* **1** lying on or affecting only the outer layer of something ⟨fortunately, the cut was only *skin-deep*⟩ — see SUPERFICIAL 1
2 having or showing a lack of depth of understanding or character ⟨the book provides some interesting anecdotes but only offers a *skin-deep* analysis of the events it chronicles⟩ — see SUPERFICIAL 2
skinflint *n* a mean grasping person who is usually stingy with money ⟨the team's owner is a *skinflint* whose penny-pinching ways keeps the team from acquiring any real talent⟩ — see MISER
skinner *n* a dishonest person who uses clever means to cheat others out of something of value ⟨he's proven himself to be a *skinner* of guys who are a lot smarter than you, so be wary of any deals you make with him⟩ — see TRICKSTER 1
skinny *adj* **1** being of less than usual width ⟨the tree swing was supported only by a couple of *skinny* branches⟩ — see NARROW 1
2 having a noticeably small amount of body fat ⟨her grandmother was always insisting that she was too *skinny* and never tired of trying to force more food on her⟩ — see THIN 1
skinny *n, slang* information not generally available to the public ⟨a TV show that offers all the *skinny* on Tinseltown and the stars that light it up⟩ — see DOPE 1
skint *adj, chiefly British* lacking money or material possessions ⟨an area of London where *skint* punk rockers would hang out⟩ — see POOR 1
skip *n* a person in overall command of a ship ⟨the *skip's* barking orders again⟩ — see CAPTAIN 1
skip *vb* **1** to move with a light springing step ⟨children *skipping* along the woodland path⟩
synonyms bounce, bound, hop, lollop, lope, trip
related words caper, frisk, gambol, romp; skim, skitter; jump, leap, vault
near antonyms lumber, plod, trudge
2 to fail to attend ⟨the day was so nice that we decided to *skip* class and go to the beach⟩ — see CUT 2
3 to strike and fly off at an angle ⟨the soap slipped out of my hand and went *skipping* across the bathroom floor⟩ — see GLANCE 1
skipper *n* a person in overall command of a ship ⟨we asked the *skipper* how long it would be before we reached port⟩ — see CAPTAIN 1
skirmish *n* **1** a brief clash between enemies or rivals ⟨the candidates' first debate was only a *skirmish* in a very long campaign⟩ — see ENCOUNTER
2 a physical dispute between opposing individuals or groups ⟨throughout the week of the convention, riot police engaged in *skirmishes* with the demonstrators⟩ — see FIGHT
skirmish (with) *vb* to oppose (someone) in physical conflict ⟨for years the Apache leader had been *skirmishing with* the Mexicans, who were responsible for his nickname, Geronimo⟩ — see FIGHT 1
skirr *vb* to go into or range over for purposes of discovery ⟨the film company will soon *skirr* the area looking for locations⟩ — see EXPLORE 2
skirt *n* **1** the line or relatively narrow space that marks the outer limit of something ⟨an old shack on the *skirts* of the town⟩ — see BORDER 1
2 *slang* an adult female human being ⟨a pathetic old lecher who was still chasing *skirts*⟩ — see WOMAN 1
skirt *vb* **1** to avoid by going around ⟨*skirted* the construction zone⟩ — see DETOUR 1
2 to avoid having to comply with (something) especially through cleverness ⟨the new bill would make it harder for companies to *skirt* environmental regulations⟩ — see CIRCUMVENT 1
3 to be adjacent to ⟨the commercial district *skirts* the river's edge⟩ — see ADJOIN 1
4 to serve as a border for ⟨the wooden fence that *skirts* the construction site⟩ — see BORDER
skirting *adj* having a border in common ⟨the house

hunters loved the property, but they were a bit leery of the *skirting* swamp⟩ — see ADJACENT

skirting *n* the line or relatively narrow space that marks the outer limit of something ⟨the *skirting* on the saddle was a slightly darker shade of leather⟩ — see BORDER 1

skittery *adj* easily excited by nature ⟨chickadees are *skittery* creatures, so don't expect them to linger at the bird feeder⟩ — see EXCITABLE

skittish *adj* **1** easily excited by nature ⟨the *skittish* colt leapt up when we approached⟩ — see EXCITABLE
2 easily frightened ⟨the cat is *skittish* around people she doesn't know⟩ — see SHY 1
3 likely to change frequently, suddenly, or unexpectedly ⟨a *skittish* housing market had both buyers and sellers on edge⟩ — see FICKLE 1

skittishness *n* a state of nervousness marked by sudden jerky movements ⟨because of the horse's *skittishness* and temperamental nature, only experienced riders should ride him⟩ — see JUMPINESS

skivvy *n, British* a female domestic servant ⟨the pop star's image as a working-class hero strains credulity now that he owns a large estate with an army of cooks, butlers, and *skivvies* to attend to his every want⟩ — see MAID 1

skosh *n* a very small amount ⟨add just a *skosh* more blue to the paint mixture⟩ — see PARTICLE 1

skulduggery *or* **skullduggery** *n* the use of clever underhanded actions to achieve an end ⟨the company's apparently healthy bottom line was merely an illusion, the result of years of accounting *skulduggery*⟩ — see TRICKERY

skulk *vb* **1** to move about in a sly or secret manner ⟨I thought I saw someone *skulking* about in the shadows⟩ — see SNEAK 1
2 to remain out of sight ⟨the officers caught the hapless robber *skulking* behind some trash cans⟩ — see [1]HIDE 3

skulk *n* someone who acts in a sly and secret manner ⟨around campus he was seen as a solitary *skulk* who seemed to be a little too interested in news reports of school shootings⟩ — see SNEAK

skulker *n* someone who acts in a sly and secret manner ⟨she surprised the *skulker* eavesdropping beneath her window⟩ — see SNEAK

skull *n* the case of bone that encloses the brain and supports the jaws of vertebrates ⟨paleoanthropologists recently found the *skull* of a prehistoric man in a remote area of the desert⟩
synonyms cranium
related words braincase; death's-head; head, noddle, noggin, pate, poll; crown, scalp

skunk *n* a person whose behavior is offensive to others ⟨he's nothing but a dirty, rotten *skunk*⟩ — see JERK 1

skunk *vb* **1** to defeat by a large margin ⟨we ended up *skunking* them, as our goalie was able to prevent the other team from scoring a single goal⟩ — see WHIP 2
2 to achieve a victory over ⟨our football team consistently *skunks* our traditional rivals Thanksgiving after Thanksgiving⟩ — see BEAT 2
3 to rob by the use of trickery or threats ⟨unwilling to let suppliers *skunk* him, the restaurant owner inspected every shipment before signing off on it⟩ — see FLEECE

sky *n* **1** the expanse of air surrounding the earth ⟨the *sky* usually looks deep blue on a bright clear day⟩
synonyms blue, firmament, heaven(s), high, welkin
related words midair; horizon, skyline
2 a dwelling place of perfect happiness for the soul after death ⟨a belief that warriors felled in battle will be raised to the *sky*⟩ — see HEAVEN 1

sky–high *adv* in an enthusiastic manner ⟨some reviewers had praised the movie *sky-high*, but we thought that it was just a so-so comedy⟩
synonyms enthusiastically, exuberantly, madly, rhapsodically
related words avidly, eagerly, excitedly, impatiently, keenly; fanatically, rabidly, warmly, zealously
near antonyms aloofly, disinterestedly, impassively, incuriously; hesitantly, reluctantly, unwillingly
antonyms apathetically, indifferently, lukewarmly, perfunctorily

skylark *vb* **1** to engage in attention-getting playful or boisterous behavior ⟨couldn't resist the temptation to *skylark* as commencement ceremonies came to a close⟩ — see CUT UP
2 to engage in activity for amusement ⟨he spends his time joking and *skylarking*, but his brother is serious and industrious⟩ — see PLAY 1

skylarking *n* wildly playful or mischievous behavior ⟨the players often engaged in a bit of roughhousing and *skylarking* before big games⟩ — see HORSEPLAY

skyrocket *vb* to rise abruptly and rapidly ⟨the crisis has caused oil prices to *skyrocket*⟩
synonyms rocket, shoot (up), soar, zoom
related words accumulate, appreciate, balloon, build up, burgeon (*also* bourgeon), enlarge, escalate, expand, increase, mount, multiply, mushroom, proliferate, snowball, swell, wax; crest, peak, surge; heighten, intensify
near antonyms collapse, fall; contract, decrease, diminish, drop, lessen, wane
antonyms nose-dive, plummet, plunge, slump, tumble

slack *adj* **1** failing to give proper care and attention ⟨a building contractor known mainly for his firm's *slack* workmanship and slipshod construction⟩ — see NEGLIGENT
2 not bound by rigid standards ⟨*slack* supervision on the project⟩ — see EASYGOING 2
3 not tightly fastened, tied, or stretched ⟨left the ropes *slack*⟩ — see LOOSE 1

slack *n* **1** an allowable margin of freedom or variation ⟨our boss doesn't cut us any *slack* when it comes to being back from lunch on time⟩
synonyms latitude, leeway, space, wiggle room
related words license (*or* licence), rein, swing
2 the extent to which something hangs or dips below a straight line ⟨take up the *slack* of a rope⟩ — see SAG
3 slacks *pl* an outer garment covering each leg separately from waist to ankle ⟨she prefers wearing *slacks* instead of a dress⟩ — see PANTS

slack *vb* to make less taut ⟨the skipper ordered the crew to *slack* off the sheets on the mainsail⟩ — see SLACKEN 1

slacken *vb* **1** to make less taut ⟨you'll need to *slacken* the rope a bit to get it free of that post⟩
synonyms ease, loosen, relax, slack
related words detach, free, unbind, undo, unfasten, untie
near antonyms attach, bind, fasten, tie; constrain, restrain
antonyms strain, stretch, tense, tension, tighten
2 to cause to move or proceed at a less rapid pace ⟨drivers need to *slacken* their speed as they approach the sharp curve⟩ — see SLOW

slackened *adj* not tightly fastened, tied, or stretched ⟨*slackened* lines⟩ — see LOOSE 1

slacker *n* **1** one who deliberately avoids work or duty ⟨there will be no *slackers* tolerated in this group—anyone who doesn't do their share will get booted out⟩
synonyms goldbrick, shirker
related words malingerer; dropout, quitter; drone, idler, lazybones, loafer, slouch, slug, slugabed, sluggard; dallier, lingerer, loiterer, lounger, saunterer; dawdler, laggard, putterer, slowpoke
near antonyms live wire, pistol, powerhouse; doer, go-

getter, hummer, hustler, rustler, self-starter
2 an idle worthless person ⟨views the under-30 generation as a bunch of *slackers*⟩ — see NE'ER-DO-WELL

slackness *n* **1** failure to take the care that a cautious person usually takes ⟨considering the chemical company's *slackness* when it comes to safety, it's a wonder there hasn't been a catastrophe⟩ — see NEGLIGENCE 1
2 the extent to which something hangs or dips below a straight line ⟨there's simply too much *slackness* in this clothesline⟩ — see SAG

slag *vb, chiefly British* to express one's unfavorable opinion of the worth or quality of ⟨London reviewers *slagged* off the new play for being another kitchen-sink drama⟩ — see CRITICIZE

slake *vb* to put a complete end to (a physical need or desire) ⟨a harrowing experience while mountain climbing has largely *slaked* my desire for high adventure⟩ — see SATISFY 1

slalom *vb* to move suddenly aside or to and fro ⟨*slalomed* through the crowd with the ease of an Olympic skier⟩ — see DODGE 1

slam *n* **1** a hard strike with a part of the body or an instrument ⟨gave the stubborn nail one last *slam* with the hammer⟩ — see BLOW 1
2 a loud explosive sound ⟨shut the door with a loud *slam*⟩ — see CLAP 1
3 a place of confinement for persons held in lawful custody ⟨sported a gang tattoo on his arm that had gotten him plenty of respect in the *slam*⟩ — see JAIL
4 a forceful coming together of two things ⟨the sudden *slam* of my head against the trunk of the car⟩ — see IMPACT 1

slam *vb* **1** to shove into a closed position with force and noise ⟨please don't *slam* the door every time you step out⟩
synonyms bang
related words close, shut, stop; bar, batten (down), bolt, chain, fasten, latch, lock, seal, secure
near antonyms open; unbar, unbolt, unfasten, unlatch, unlock, unseal
2 to deliver a blow to (someone or something) usually in a strong vigorous manner ⟨she *slammed* the ball deep into center field⟩ — see HIT 1
3 to come into usually forceful contact with something ⟨the car *slammed* into the wall with a fearful crunch⟩ — see HIT 2
4 to criticize harshly and usually publicly ⟨*slammed* the cast members for forgetting their lines on opening night⟩ — see ATTACK 2

slam–bang *adj* marked by a high volume of sound ⟨heard a *slam-bang* crash from the garage⟩ — see LOUD 1

slam dunk *n* one that is certain to succeed ⟨since he was trying his first case, the assistant district attorney was assigned a burglary case that was a *slam dunk*⟩ — see SURE THING

slammer *n* a place of confinement for persons held in lawful custody ⟨the Mafia capo ultimately landed in the *slammer* on a conviction of income tax evasion⟩ — see JAIL

slander *n* the making of false statements that damage another's reputation ⟨instead of resorting to *slander*, the candidates should be outlining their plans for getting us out of this mess⟩
synonyms aspersing, blackening, calumniation, calumny, character assassination, defamation, defaming, libel, libeling (*or* libelling), maligning, smearing, traducing, vilification, vilifying
related words aspersion, innuendo, muck, mud, smear; backbiting, detraction; abuse, invective, vituperation; attack, censure, criticism, denunciation, hatchet job; contempt, disdain, scorn; belittlement, denigration, disparagement; cattiness, despite, hatefulness, malevolence, malice, maliciousness, malignancy, malignity, meanness, nastiness, spite, spitefulness, spleen, venom, viciousness
near antonyms acclaim, accolade, applause, commendation, praise; esteem, honor, respect; adulation, flattery; adoration, reverence, veneration, worship

slander *vb* to make untrue and harmful statements about ⟨for some reason, that newspaper seems determined to *slander* one particular celebrity⟩
synonyms asperse, blacken, calumniate, defame, libel, malign, smear, traduce, vilify
related words belittle, denigrate, detract, disparage; discredit, disgrace, dishonor, shame; abase, debase, degrade, humble, humiliate; disdain, scorn
near antonyms exalt, glorify, honor; acclaim, applaud, commend, praise; esteem, respect; admire, regard; adore, revere, venerate, worship

slanderous *adj* causing or intended to cause unjust injury to a person's good name ⟨made *slanderous* comments about his opponent's military record⟩ — see LIBELOUS

slang *n* the special terms or expressions of a particular group or field ⟨tends to use too much hacker's *slang* when talking to coworkers about their computer problems⟩ — see TERMINOLOGY

slant *adj* running in a slanting direction ⟨as they poked through the blinds, the *slant* rays of the setting sun created interesting patterns on the room's far wall⟩ — see DIAGONAL

slant *n* **1** the degree to which something rises up from a position level with the horizon ⟨the road has just enough of a *slant* to make bicycling up it a little strenuous⟩
synonyms cant, diagonal, grade, gradient, inclination, incline, lean, pitch, rake, slope, tilt, upgrade
related words ascent, bank, climb, rise
near antonyms declension, declination, decline, declivity, descent, dip, downgrade, fall, hang, hanging, receding
2 a way of looking at or thinking about something ⟨an interesting *slant* on the problem of underage drinking⟩ — see PERSPECTIVE 1

slant *vb* **1** to change so much as to create a wrong impression or alter the meaning of ⟨reporters who *slant* the truth in order to push a political agenda⟩ — see GARBLE 1
2 to set or cause to be at an angle ⟨a ramp *slanted* at a 20 degree angle⟩ — see LEAN 1

slanted *adj* **1** inclined or twisted to one side ⟨a *slanted* fence post⟩ — see AWRY
2 running in a slanting direction ⟨*slanted* stripes⟩ — see DIAGONAL

slanting *adj* inclined or twisted to one side ⟨an old, torn flag hanging from a *slanting* flagpole⟩ — see AWRY

slantways *adv* so as to slant ⟨the temporary supports were placed *slantways* against the side of the sagging wall⟩ — see SLANTWISE

slantwise *adj* **1** inclined or twisted to one side ⟨a hodgepodge of *slantwise* postcards tacked to the wall of his cubicle⟩ — see AWRY
2 running in a slanting direction ⟨the *slantwise* cables that run between the roadway and the towers give the bridge a cathedral-like appearance⟩ — see DIAGONAL

slantwise *adv* so as to slant ⟨be careful not to lay the first boards *slantwise*, or the whole bookcase won't be straight⟩
synonyms slantways
related words down, downward (*or* downwards), up, upward (*or* upwards)

slap *n* **1** a hard strike with a part of the body or an instrument ⟨doctors used to give newborns a light *slap* to

get them to start breathing⟩ — see [1]BLOW
2 an act or expression showing scorn and usually intended to hurt another's feelings ⟨that comment is a *slap* to anyone who has ever served in the military⟩ — see INSULT

slap *vb* **1** to deliver a blow to (someone or something) usually in a strong vigorous manner ⟨she was so mad that she *slapped* him right across the face⟩ — see HIT 1
2 to cause hurt feelings or deep resentment in ⟨tired of jokes that *slap* people of faith⟩ — see INSULT

slapdash *adj* lacking a definite plan, purpose, or pattern ⟨the investigation of the charges against the mayor was *slapdash* and not very thorough⟩ — see RANDOM

slap down *vb* to put a stop to (something) by the use of force ⟨public protests against the government were always promptly *slapped down*⟩ — see QUELL 1

slaphappy *adj* **1** having or showing freedom from worries or troubles ⟨plays the role of a *slaphappy* guy with a hot dog cart who dispenses wisecracks and wit along with his wieners⟩ — see CAREFREE
2 suffering from mental confusion ⟨we were *slaphappy* with exhaustion after the nightlong train ride⟩ — see DIZZY 2

slapjack *n* a flat cake made from thin batter and cooked on both sides (as on a griddle) ⟨had a big plate of *slapjacks* with syrup for breakfast⟩ — see PANCAKE

slapstick *n* **1** humorous entertainment ⟨an actor whose roles range from *slapstick* to serious drama⟩ — see COMEDY 1
2 wildly playful or mischievous behavior ⟨a lowbrow comedy that relies heavily on *slapstick* for its laughs⟩ — see HORSEPLAY

slash *n* a long deep cut ⟨made a *slash* in the fabric with a knife⟩ — see GASH

slash *vb* **1** to penetrate with a sharp edge (as a knife) ⟨the tire appears to have been deliberately *slashed*⟩ — see CUT 1
2 to strike repeatedly with something long and thin or flexible ⟨wildly *slashing* the ground with his club and never once hitting the golf ball he was aiming at⟩ — see WHIP 1

slash–and–burn *adj* having or showing a lack of sympathy or tender feelings ⟨under his *slash-and-burn* management ethic, even longtime employees were summarily downsized for the sake of corporate competitiveness⟩ — see HARD 1

slate *adj* of the color gray ⟨the *slate* sky was a sure sign of rain⟩ — see GRAY 1

[1]slate *vb* to put (someone or something) on a list ⟨you've been *slated* for a three o'clock interview⟩ — see [1]LIST 2

[2]slate *vb* to strike repeatedly ⟨ready to *slate* anyone who disagreed⟩ — see BEAT 1

slated *adj* being in accordance with the prescribed, normal, or logical course of events ⟨*slated* to arrive at five o'clock⟩ — see DUE 2

slatternly *adj* having loose sexual morals ⟨the biography portrays the poet as a debauched scoundrel whose companions were *slatternly* women and not the chaste maids he celebrated in his lyrics⟩ — see SLEAZY 1

slaty *also* **slatey** *adj* of the color gray ⟨*slaty* stones in the riverbed⟩ — see GRAY 1

slaughter *n* the killing of a large number of people ⟨all civilized nations should protest this senseless *slaughter*⟩ — see MASSACRE

slaughter *vb* to kill on a large scale ⟨modern poultry farms *slaughter* a vast number of chickens every day⟩ — see MASSACRE

slave *n* **1** a person who is considered the property of another person ⟨many American *slaves* reached freedom in the North through the network known as the Underground Railroad⟩
synonyms bondman (*also* bondsman), chattel, thrall
related words bondwoman (*also* bondswoman), odalisque; helot, serf; bond servant, indentured servant; attendant, domestic, drudge, handmaiden (*also* handmaid), lackey, menial, servant, slavey
near antonyms freedman, freedwoman; enslaver, slave driver, slaveholder, slaver; master, taskmaster
antonyms freeman
2 a person who does very hard or dull work ⟨unappreciated office *slaves* who perform the necessary but tedious task of filing paperwork⟩
synonyms dogsbody [*chiefly British*], drone, drudge, drudger, fag, foot soldier, grub, grubber, grunt, laborer, peon, plugger, slavey, slogger, toiler, worker
related words workhorse; coolie, serf
near antonyms goldbrick, shirker; drone, idler, lazybones, loafer, slouch, slug, sluggard

slave *vb* to devote serious and sustained effort ⟨*slaving* over a hot stove⟩ — see LABOR

slave (for) *vb* to be a servant for ⟨why would you waste your time *slaving for* a boss you can't stand?⟩ — see SERVE 1

slave driver *n* a boss who assigns much work ⟨the director is a real *slave driver*, but actors still clamor for the opportunity to work with him⟩ — see TASKMASTER 1

slaver *vb* to let saliva or some other substance flow from the mouth ⟨a dog *slavering* over a bone⟩ — see DROOL 1

slaver *n* the fluid that is secreted into the mouth by certain glands ⟨*slaver* dripped from the snarling dog's jaws⟩ — see SALIVA

slavery *n* **1** the state of being a slave ⟨a child born into *slavery* was considered simply another addition to the master's wealth and property⟩
synonyms bondage, enslavement, servility, servitude, thrall, thralldom (*or* thraldom), yoke
related words peonage, serfdom; dependence (*also* dependance), subjection, subjugation; captivity, enchainment, imprisonment, incarceration
near antonyms emancipation, enfranchisement, liberation, manumission; autonomy, independence, self-government, sovereignty (*also* sovranty)
antonyms freedom, liberty
2 very hard or unpleasant work ⟨endured the *slavery* of working in the coal mines every day of his adult life⟩ — see [1]TOIL

slavey *n* **1** a person hired to perform household or personal services ⟨I'm not your *slavey*, so pick up after yourself⟩ — see SERVANT
2 a person who does very hard or dull work ⟨on the day of the feast the cook and the kitchen *slaveys* were bustling about well before dawn⟩ — see SLAVE 2

slavish *adj* **1** using or marked by the use of something else as a basis or model ⟨*slavish* imitations of the great masters will never make you a painter in your own right⟩ — see IMITATIVE 1
2 showing, expressing, or offered in a spirit of humility or unseemly submissiveness ⟨the wife's *slavish* agreement with her husband's every thought⟩ — see ABJECT

slavishly *adv* with great effort or determination ⟨detectives *slavishly* devoted themselves to the case, pursuing every lead and tracking down every suspect⟩ — see HARD 1

slay *vb* **1** to deprive of life ⟨millions have been *slain* worldwide by this dreadful disease⟩ — see KILL 1
2 to put to death deliberately ⟨vowed to *slay* without mercy whoever was responsible for murdering his family⟩ — see MURDER 1

slaying *n* the intentional and unlawful taking of another person's life ⟨a man wanted for the *slaying* of seven people during an armed robbery⟩ — see HOMICIDE 1

sleaze *n* **1** a person of low moral character ⟨some *sleaze* will try to make a buck off of this tragic murder⟩
synonyms skank [*slang*], sleazebag [*slang*], sleazeball [*slang*], slime, slimeball [*slang*]
related words slattern, slut, tramp; degenerate, libertine, perv, pervert, reprobate; creep, scumbag [*slang*], scuzzball [*slang*]; pettifogger, shyster
2 a person whose behavior is offensive to others ⟨at least her newest boyfriend isn't the kind of *sleaze* she usually dates⟩ — see JERK 1
3 that which is of low quality or worth ⟨the TV networks wouldn't be airing such *sleaze* if the public wasn't watching it⟩ — see JUNK 1

sleazebag *n, slang* **1** a person of low moral character ⟨the *sleazebags* who run the porn studios wouldn't hesitate to use their own mothers⟩ — see SLEAZE 1
2 a person whose behavior is offensive to others ⟨a Mardi Gras celebration that was spoiled by a bunch of drunken *sleazebags*⟩ — see JERK 1

sleazeball *n, slang* **1** a person of low moral character ⟨don't post your private info and revealing pics online—there are some real *sleazeballs* out there⟩ — see SLEAZE 1
2 a person whose behavior is offensive to others ⟨despite the constant rebuffs, the *sleazeball* at the bar kept hitting on all the single women⟩ — see JERK 1

sleazy *adj* **1** having loose sexual morals ⟨a *sleazy* lothario who is always on the make⟩
synonyms skanky [*slang*], slatternly, sluttish, slutty, trampy
related words whorish; indecent, lascivious, lewd, wanton; indecorous, unbecoming; corrupt, debased, debauched, degenerate, depraved, dissolute, libertine, perverted, reprobate
near antonyms priggish, prim, prudish, puritanical, straitlaced (*or* straightlaced); decent, decorous, genteel, polite, proper, seemly; celibate, chaste, modest, moral, pure, virtuous
2 of low quality ⟨a *sleazy* yellow coat that was marked down to practically nothing and not worth even that⟩ — see CHEAP 2
3 being of a material lacking in sturdiness or substance ⟨these cheap, *sleazy* curtains would do a poor job of blocking those wintertime blasts of cold air⟩ — see FLIMSY 1
4 showing signs of advanced wear and tear and neglect ⟨several letters in the *sleazy* motel's neon "vacancy" sign had burned out⟩ — see SHABBY 1

sleek *adj* having a shiny surface or finish ⟨a striking beauty with *sleek* raven hair⟩ — see GLOSSY

sleep *n* **1** a natural periodic loss of consciousness during which the body restores itself ⟨neither of them has been getting much *sleep* since the baby was born⟩
synonyms bed, catnapping, dozing, napping, repose, rest, resting, shut-eye, slumber, slumbering, snoozing, z's (*or* zs)
related words catnap, doze, drowse, forty winks, nap, siesta, snooze, wink; oversleeping; dreaming, rapid eye movement
near antonyms insomnia, sleeplessness
antonyms consciousness, wake, wakefulness
2 the state of being dead ⟨a grieving widower longing to join his beloved wife in her eternal *sleep*⟩ — see DEATH 2
3 the permanent stopping of all the vital bodily activities ⟨regretfully put their terminally ill dog to *sleep*⟩ — see DEATH 1

sleep *vb* **1** to be in a state of sleep ⟨the baby *slept* for the entire length of the car trip⟩
synonyms catnap, doze, nap, rest, slumber, snooze
related words drop off, drowse (off), nod off; oversleep, sleep in; dream, hibernate
near antonyms arise, arouse, awake, rise, wake
2 to engage in sexual intercourse ⟨if I don't read the tabloids, how will I know who is *sleeping* with whom this week?⟩ — see COPULATE

sleeper *n* one who sleeps ⟨she's a light *sleeper* and usually wakes up when I get in late⟩
synonyms dozer, slumberer
related words nodder
near antonyms insomniac; riser, waker

sleepiness *n* the quality or state of desiring or needing sleep ⟨the truck driver keeps a thermos of coffee with him to stave off *sleepiness*⟩
synonyms doziness, drowsiness, somnolence
related words fatigue, tiredness, weariness; lassitude, lethargy, sluggishness, torpidity, torpor; dozing, resting, sleeping, slumbering; oversleeping
near antonyms awareness, consciousness
antonyms insomnia, sleeplessness, wakefulness

sleeping *adj* being in a state of suspended consciousness ⟨a roomful of *sleeping* preschoolers at a daycare center⟩ — see ASLEEP 1

sleepless *adj* not sleeping or able to sleep ⟨lay *sleepless* with worry⟩ — see WAKEFUL

sleeplessness *n* the inability to obtain adequate sleep ⟨the prolonged bouts of *sleeplessness* were starting to affect his work⟩ — see INSOMNIA

sleepy *adj* **1** desiring or needing sleep ⟨the *sleepy* children were carried up to bed⟩
synonyms dozy, drowsy, slumberous (*or* slumbrous), somnolent
related words asleep, dormant, dozing, resting, sleeping, slumbering; nodding, yawning
near antonyms restive, restless, sleepless; insomniac
antonyms alert, awake, conscious, wakeful, wide-awake
2 slow to move or act ⟨a *sleepy* little town on the coast⟩ — see INACTIVE 1
3 tending to cause sleep ⟨the *sleepy* drone of his voice made staying awake a challenge⟩ — see HYPNOTIC
4 lacking in gaiety, movement, or animation ⟨a *sleepy* party that was mostly attended by the same boring people I work with⟩ — see DEAD 2

sleight *n* **1** a clever often underhanded means to achieve an end ⟨must have employed some sophisticated *sleight* to con that wary couple out of their money⟩ — see TRICK 1
2 mental skill or quickness ⟨a brilliant new theory that pays tribute to his remarkable *sleight* of mind⟩ — see DEXTERITY 1
3 ease and grace in physical activity ⟨a muscle-bound weight lifter known more for his might than his *sleight*⟩ — see DEXTERITY 2

slender *adj* **1** being of less than usual width ⟨graceful, *slender* table legs⟩ — see NARROW 1
2 having a noticeably small amount of body fat ⟨unsurprisingly, the aerobics instructor is *slender* and athletic⟩ — see THIN 1
3 less plentiful than what is normal, necessary, or desirable ⟨people of *slender* means simply can't afford those prices⟩ — see MEAGER

sleuth *n* a person not on the police force who investigates criminal or illicit activity or searches for missing persons ⟨the popular TV *sleuth* lives a much more action-packed life than do his real-world counterparts⟩ — see DETECTIVE

sleuthhound *n* a person not on the police force who investigates criminal or illicit activity or searches for missing persons ⟨the fictional *sleuthhound* Miss Marple is notable for her age as well as for her understanding of human nature, both of them being rather advanced⟩ — see DETECTIVE

slew *n* a considerable amount ⟨we still have a *slew* of work to do on this project⟩ — see LOT 2

slice *vb* **1** to cut into long slender pieces ⟨*slice* the carrot into tiny strips⟩ — see SLIVER
2 to penetrate with a sharp edge (as a knife) ⟨the shard of glass *sliced* my hand, and I started bleeding profusely⟩ — see CUT 1

slice *n* **1** a number of things selected from a group to stand for the whole ⟨the novel's multitudinous array of characters constitute a veritable *slice* of humanity⟩ — see SAMPLE 1
2 a piece that has been separated from the whole by cutting ⟨took a *slice* from the cake before passing it down the table⟩ — see CUT 1
3 something belonging to, due to, or contributed by an individual member of a group ⟨there's a pile of money to be made on this land deal, and everybody's trying to get their *slice*⟩ — see SHARE 1

slick *vb* to coat (something) with a slippery substance in order to reduce friction ⟨*slicking* the bottom of their skis with wax⟩ — see LUBRICATE

slick *adj* **1** having or being a surface so smooth as to greatly reduce traction ⟨roads are often *slick* during the first hour of a rainstorm⟩
synonyms greased, greasy, lubricated, oiled, slicked, slippery, slippy, slithery
related words brushed, buffed, burnished, glossed, ground, polished, rubbed, shined; coated, glazed, waxed; soapy, waxy; rasped, sandblasted, sanded, sandpapered, scoured, scraped, scrubbed
near antonyms coarsened, rough, roughened, scuffed, uneven
2 clever at attaining one's ends by indirect and often deceptive means ⟨a *slick* ad campaign that made smoking look cool and sexy⟩ — see ARTFUL 1
3 of the very best kind ⟨that's a *slick* new suit you have on⟩ — see EXCELLENT

slicked *adj* having or being a surface so smooth as to greatly reduce traction ⟨area roadways, *slicked* with ice, were absolutely treacherous for driving⟩ — see SLICK 1

slicker *n* **1** a coat made of water-resistant material ⟨he put on his *slicker* and boots and headed out into the rain⟩ — see RAINCOAT
2 a person with the outlook, experience, and manners thought to be typical of big city dwellers ⟨dressed in their designer duds, the out-of-state *slickers* stood out amongst the locals at the harvest supper⟩ — see COSMOPOLITAN

slickness *n* skill in achieving one's ends through indirect, subtle, or underhanded means ⟨we were both impressed and outraged by the expert *slickness* with which the swindler fooled us⟩ — see CUNNING 1

slide *vb* **1** to move about in a sly or secret manner ⟨*slid* gently into his seat without anyone else in church noticing⟩ — see SNEAK 1
2 to move or proceed smoothly and readily ⟨at this point the river *slides* along its banks with barely a ripple⟩ — see FLOW 2
3 to move slowly with the body close to the ground ⟨the convict escaped by *sliding* through the prison's ductwork⟩ — see CRAWL 1

slight *adj* **1** lacking bodily strength ⟨a small lad with a *slight* build⟩ — see WEAK 1
2 lacking importance ⟨a *slight* comedy that did nothing to further her career⟩ — see UNIMPORTANT
3 of a size that is less than average ⟨the *slight* youth packed a surprisingly solid punch⟩ — see SMALL 1
4 so small or unimportant as to warrant little or no attention ⟨apart from a *slight* fishy taste, the dish was fine⟩ — see NEGLIGIBLE 1
5 small in degree ⟨only a *slight* chance of success⟩ — see REMOTE 1

slight *n* an act or expression showing scorn and usually intended to hurt another's feelings ⟨refused to respond to their petty *slights*⟩ — see INSULT

slight *vb* **1** to cause hurt feelings or deep resentment in ⟨the dancers felt *slighted* by the harsh comments of the judges⟩ — see INSULT
2 to deliberately ignore or treat rudely ⟨as a temp worker, she often feels *slighted* by the people she has to work with⟩ — see SNUB 1
3 to show contempt for ⟨music critics who *slight* any style of music that doesn't fit their personal taste⟩ — see SCORN 1
4 to fail to give proper attention to ⟨*slighted* several major authors in her survey of 20th-century fiction⟩ — see NEGLECT 1

slightest *adj* being the least in amount, number, or size possible ⟨there's not the *slightest* chance that your plan will work⟩ — see MINIMAL

slighting *adj* intended to make a person or thing seem of little importance or value ⟨*slighting* remarks about the general lack of musical talent among the contestants⟩ — see DEROGATORY

slightly *adv* **1** by a very small margin ⟨I thought the first one was *slightly* better⟩ — see JUST 2
2 in a very small quantity or degree ⟨he was *slightly* curious about the identity of the wine, but not enough to bother asking⟩ — see LITTLE 1

slightness *n* **1** the quality or state of being little in size ⟨the old photograph shows a man whose *slightness* of build seems at variance with his reputation as a robust outdoorsman⟩ — see SMALLNESS 1
2 the state or quality of having little weight ⟨his *slightness* will serve him well if he ever decides to become a jockey⟩ — see [1]LIGHTNESS 1
3 the quality or state of being unimportant ⟨most moviegoers were not in the least bothered by the *slightness* of the plot—they were there for the special effects in any event⟩ — see INSIGNIFICANCE

slim *adj* **1** being of less than usual width ⟨a *slim* volume of poetry⟩ — see NARROW 1
2 having a noticeably small amount of body fat ⟨the pressure on ballet dancers to remain gracefully *slim*⟩ — see THIN 1
3 less plentiful than what is normal, necessary, or desirable ⟨*slim* pickings at the garage sale⟩ — see MEAGER
4 small in degree ⟨a *slim* chance is still better than none⟩ — see REMOTE 1

slime *n* **1** soft wet earth ⟨she picked her steps carefully so as not to get any *slime* on her new shoes⟩ — see MUD
2 a person whose behavior is offensive to others ⟨that guy's a real *slime*, so avoid him at all costs⟩ — see JERK 1
3 a person of low moral character ⟨he's the kind of *slime* that TV reality shows love to cast as a villain⟩ — see SLEAZE 1

slimeball *n, slang* **1** a person of low moral character ⟨a real *slimeball*, that shyster has happily defended, for a healthy fee, drug dealers and child molesters⟩ — see SLEAZE 1
2 a person whose behavior is offensive to others ⟨*slimeballs* love the anonymity of the Internet, which allows them to post incredibly vile messages without having to identify themselves⟩ — see JERK 1

slim–jim *adj* being of less than usual width ⟨an author whose published works are limited to one *slim-jim* volume of poetry⟩ — see NARROW 1

slimy *adj* full of or covered with soft wet earth ⟨please remove your *slimy* boots before coming into the house⟩ — see MUDDY 1

[1]sling *vb* to place on an elevated point without support from below ⟨*sling* a hammock between the trees⟩ — see HANG 1

[2]sling *vb* to send through the air especially with a quick forward motion of the arm ⟨*slinging* stones at the fence post⟩ — see THROW 1

slink *vb* to move about in a sly or secret manner ⟨like a thief *slinking* about in the middle of the night⟩ — see SNEAK 1

[1]**slip** *n* a long narrow piece of material ⟨baskets woven from *slips* of wicker⟩ — see STRIP 1

[2]**slip** *n* **1** an unintentional departure from truth or accuracy ⟨a careless *slip* of the tongue⟩ — see ERROR 1
2 the act of going down from an upright position suddenly and involuntarily ⟨had a nasty *slip* on the ice⟩ — see FALL 1
3 the act or an instance of getting free from danger or confinement ⟨gave her pursuers the *slip*⟩ — see ESCAPE 1
4 a wrong judgment ⟨that's not the sort of *slip* that a prudent person would have made⟩ — see MISTAKE 1

slip *vb* **1** to decline gradually from a standard level ⟨the store's quality of service began to *slip* after the new owners took over⟩
synonyms sag
related words drop, fall, slump; flag, sink, slacken, slow (down), weaken; abate, contract, decrease, deescalate, die (down), diminish, dwindle, ebb, lessen, let up, lower, moderate, recede, relent, shrink, subside, taper, taper off, wane
near antonyms rocket, shoot (up), soar; balloon, burgeon (*also* bourgeon), enlarge, escalate, expand, increase, mount, multiply, mushroom, proliferate, snowball, swell, wax; crest, peak, surge
2 to go down from an upright position suddenly and involuntarily ⟨be careful not to *slip* on the spilled oil⟩ — see FALL 1
3 to introduce in a gradual, secret, or clever way ⟨casually *slipped* it into the conversation⟩ — see INSINUATE
4 to move about in a sly or secret manner ⟨*slipped* behind the cover of the trees⟩ — see SNEAK 1
5 to move or proceed smoothly and readily ⟨jumped into the car and *slipped* behind the wheel⟩ — see FLOW 2
6 to cast (a natural bodily covering or appendage) aside ⟨periodically crabs *slip* their shells and grow new ones⟩ — see SHED 1

slip (on *or* into) *vb* to place on one's person ⟨wait here while I *slip into* something more comfortable⟩ — see PUT ON 1

slippery *adj* **1** given to acting in secret and to concealing one's intentions ⟨a bar where a lot of *slippery* characters were known to hang out⟩ — see SNEAKY 1
2 hard to find, capture, or isolate ⟨a *slippery* concept that we had trouble understanding⟩ — see ELUSIVE
3 having or being a surface so smooth as to greatly reduce traction ⟨had trouble keeping upright on the *slippery* ice⟩ — see SLICK 1

slippy *adj* having or being a surface so smooth as to greatly reduce traction ⟨bathtubs are a little too *slippy* for the elderly residents, so grab rails are standard fixtures⟩ — see SLICK 1

slipup *n* **1** an unintentional departure from truth or accuracy ⟨the marketing director made sure there were no *slipups* for the important presentation⟩ — see ERROR 1
2 a wrong judgment ⟨ran a flawless campaign—not a single *slipup*⟩ — see MISTAKE 1

slip up *vb* to make a mistake ⟨if you *slip up* in copying the data, the final result will of course be wrong⟩ — see ERR 1

slit *n* a long deep cut ⟨made a *slit* in the fabric about nine inches long⟩ — see GASH

slit *vb* to penetrate with a sharp edge (as a knife) ⟨I *slit* my finger open while cleaning up the broken glass⟩ — see CUT 1

slither *vb* to move slowly with the body close to the ground ⟨a snake *slithering* through the garden⟩ — see CRAWL 1

slithery *adj* having or being a surface so smooth as to greatly reduce traction ⟨low tide exposes a stretch of beach strewn with seaweed and *slithery* rocks⟩ — see SLICK 1

sliver *n* a small flat piece separated from a whole ⟨I got a *sliver* of wood stuck in my finger⟩ — see CHIP 1

sliver *vb* to cut into long slender pieces ⟨carefully *slivered* the rattan stems into strips for basketry⟩
synonyms slice, splinter
related words chip, chop, dice, hash, julienne, mince; saw, scissor; cleave, rive, split; gash, incise, rip, slash, slit

slob *n* **1** a dirty or sloppy person ⟨a *slob* of a professor whose office was littered with a decade's worth of notes and student papers⟩
synonyms sloven
related words slattern, slut [*chiefly British*]
antonyms neatnik, old maid
2 a person whose behavior is offensive to others ⟨he's easy enough to get along with when he's not being a loudmouthed *slob*⟩ — see JERK 1
3 a member of the human race ⟨you just know some poor *slob* is going to get blamed for this mix-up⟩ — see HUMAN
4 an average or ordinary man ⟨I don't know much about trust funds, as I'm just some poor *slob* who has to work hard for a living⟩ — see JOE BLOW

slobber *n* **1** the fluid that is secreted into the mouth by certain glands ⟨the dog got *slobber* all over our tennis ball⟩ — see SALIVA
2 unintelligible or meaningless talk ⟨I couldn't make out any of the panhandler's *slobber*, but I gave the poor soul a buck anyway⟩ — see GIBBERISH 1

slobber *vb* **1** to let saliva or some other substance flow from the mouth ⟨our dog always starts to *slobber* whenever we open a can of food⟩ — see DROOL 1
2 to make an exaggerated display of affection or enthusiasm ⟨right on cue, his entourage of sycophants began to *slobber* over every inane thing he said⟩ — see GUSH 2

slobbish *adj* lacking neatness in dress or person ⟨the memoir portrays her father as a *slobbish* lout who was a constant embarrassment to her fastidious mother⟩ — see SLOPPY 1

slobby *adj* lacking neatness in dress or person ⟨an unlikely romance between a *slobby*, bighearted galoot and an uptight career woman⟩ — see SLOPPY 1

slog *vb* **1** to deliver a blow to (someone or something) usually in a strong vigorous manner ⟨the two boxers were so exhausted they just *slogged* each other indiscriminately⟩ — see HIT 1
2 to devote serious and sustained effort ⟨*slogging* their way through a pile of paperwork⟩ — see LABOR
3 to strike repeatedly ⟨the feisty woman was still *slogging* her would-be attacker when the police arrived⟩ — see BEAT 1
4 to move heavily or clumsily ⟨Gramps never tired of telling how he had to *slog* through the snow in order to get to school⟩ — see LUMBER 1

slogan *n* an attention-getting word or phrase used to publicize something (as a campaign or product) ⟨within days, virtually everyone was familiar with the newest advertising *slogan* for that brand of soda⟩
synonyms banner, catchphrase, cry, shibboleth, tagline, watchword
related words expression, idiom; catchword, cliché (*also* cliche); maxim, motto; battle cry, war cry

slogger *n* a person who does very hard or dull work ⟨nothing but respect for the *sloggers* who work in the basement archives⟩ — see SLAVE 2

slop *n* **1** soft wet earth ⟨slipped and fell in the *slop* behind the shed⟩ — see MUD
2 slops *pl* solid matter discharged from an animal's alimentary canal ⟨cleaned the *slops* out of the cow barn⟩ — see DROPPING 1
3 that which is of low quality or worth ⟨that songwriter turns out nothing but *slop*, and record buyers eat it up⟩ — see JUNK 1
4 a thick semiliquid substance (as food) that is unattractive ⟨some *slop* that the cafeteria staff claims is edible⟩ — see GLOP

slop *vb* **1** to cause (something liquid or mushy) to move along in sheets ⟨she *slopped* water everywhere when she picked up the full pan⟩ — see SPLASH 1
2 to swallow or eat greedily ⟨watched the game while *slopping* prodigious quantities of beer⟩ — see GOBBLE

slope *n* the degree to which something rises up from a position level with the horizon ⟨the next stretch of the trail had a gentle *slope* which made it easier to climb⟩ — see SLANT

slope *vb* to set or cause to be at an angle ⟨they *sloped* our new driveway too steeply and now my car scrapes bottom whenever I back out onto the street⟩ — see LEAN 1

sloped *adj* running in a slanting direction ⟨the *sloped* arrangement of the pictures along the staircase wall should follow the line of the banister⟩ — see DIAGONAL

sloping *adj* running in a slanting direction ⟨a *sloping* ray of light that illuminates the painting's central figure is symbolic of heavenly inspiration⟩ — see DIAGONAL

sloppily *adv* in a careless or unfashionable manner ⟨when she arrived at work this morning she was *sloppily* dressed, and her hair was unkempt⟩
synonyms dowdily, slovenly
related words slatternly; chaotically, messily, untidily; shabbily, sleazily; dingily, dirtily, filthily, foully, grubbily, nastily
near antonyms neatly, orderly, tidily; fashionably, modishly; carefully, fastidiously, fussily, meticulously; cleanly, immaculately, spotlessly
antonyms nattily, sharply, smart, smartly, sprucely

sloppiness *n* the state or quality of having an excess of tender feelings (as of love, nostalgia, or compassion) ⟨the tearful *sloppiness* that you find in so many country-and-western songs⟩ — see SENTIMENTALITY

sloppy *adj* **1** lacking neatness in dress or person ⟨a *sloppy* child who always seems to have spilled something on his clothes⟩
synonyms blowsy (*also* blowzy), dowdy, frowsy (*or* frowzy), slobbish, slobby, sloven, slovenly, unkempt, untidy
related words slatternly; chaotic, cluttered, confused, disarranged, disheveled (*or* dishevelled), disordered, messed, messy, muddled, mussed, mussy, rumpled, shaggy, uncombed, wrinkled; shabby, sleazy; besmirched, blackened, dingy, dirty, filthy, foul, grimy, grubby, grungy, mucky, nasty, scroungy, scuzzy [*slang*], soiled, spotted, squalid, stained, sullied, unclean, uncleanly
near antonyms chic, fashionable, modish, stylish; combed, groomed; neat, ordered, orderly, tidy; careful, fastidious, fussy, meticulous; clean, cleaned, cleanly, immaculate, sparkling, spotless, stainless, unsoiled, unsullied
antonyms dapper, dashing, dolled up, sharp, smart, spruce
2 lacking in order, neatness, and often cleanliness ⟨dumped the papers in a *sloppy* pile on the desk⟩ — see MESSY
3 appealing to the emotions in an obvious and tiresome way ⟨a cinematic romance with a *sloppy* musical score that will have audiences reaching for their handkerchiefs⟩ — see CORNY 1

slosh *vb* **1** to move with a splashing motion ⟨the baby gurgled contentedly as the water *sloshed* gently around him in the bathtub⟩
synonyms lap, plash, splash, swash
related words babble, bubble, gurgle, ripple
2 to cause (something liquid or mushy) to move along in sheets ⟨while painting the Windsor chair, he carelessly *sloshed* paint all over the adjacent wall⟩ — see SPLASH 1

sloshed *adj, slang* being under the influence of alcohol ⟨her idiot husband makes even less sense when he's *sloshed*⟩ — see DRUNK

slot *n* a situation or activity for which a person or thing is best suited ⟨called an old friend to see if he could find a *slot* for his college-age son in the construction business that summer⟩ — see NICHE 2

sloth *n* an inclination not to do work or engage in activities ⟨a youth inclined more toward *sloth* than athletics⟩ — see LAZINESS

slothful *adj* not easily aroused to action or work ⟨his overly lax managerial style has resulted in a department that is *slothful* and unproductive⟩ — see LAZY 1

slouch *n* a lazy person ⟨is no *slouch* when it comes to cooking⟩ — see LAZYBONES

slouch *vb* to move slowly ⟨*slouched* towards the church as if going to his own funeral⟩ — see CRAWL 2

slough *also* **slew** *or* **slue** *n* spongy land saturated or partially covered with water ⟨the land for miles around the lake is strewn with ponds, *sloughs*, and mudflats⟩ — see SWAMP 1

[1]slough *vb* to move heavily or clumsily ⟨the unpleasant task of *sloughing* through the muck to retrieve the ball⟩ — see LUMBER 1

[2]slough *also* **sluff** *vb* to cast (a natural bodily covering or appendage) aside ⟨the snake is *sloughing* its old skin⟩ — see SHED 1

slough (off) *also* **sluff (off)** *vb* to get rid of as useless or unwanted ⟨finally *sloughed off* the depression that had been weighing him down for months⟩ — see DISCARD

sloven *n* a dirty or sloppy person ⟨she's a *sloven* and he's a neat freak—it's a wonder they are able to live together⟩ — see SLOB 1

sloven *adj* lacking neatness in dress or person ⟨the lawyer's *sloven* appearance led me to question his professionalism⟩ — see SLOPPY 1

slovenly *adj* lacking neatness in dress or person ⟨for the sake of their image, the band members transformed themselves from clean-cut lads to *slovenly* rockers⟩ — see SLOPPY 1

slovenly *adv* in a careless or unfashionable manner ⟨an employee who went overboard on dress-down day and was reprimanded for dressing *slovenly* on the job⟩ — see SLOPPILY

slow *adj* **1** moving or proceeding at less than the normal, desirable, or required speed ⟨because of the holiday, traffic to the beach was particularly *slow*⟩ ⟨*slow* readers⟩
synonyms crawling, creeping, dallying, dawdling, dilatory, dillydallying, dragging, laggard, lagging, languid, leisurely, poking, poky (*or* pokey), sluggish, snaillike, snail-paced, tardy, unhurried
related words deliberate, measured; inactive, inert, lethargic, loafing, lounging; lingering, loitering, tarrying; ambling, heavy-footed, inching, plodding, shuffling, slow-footed; strolling; decelerating, slowing; filibustering, procrastinating, stalling
near antonyms expeditious, prompt, ready; accelerated, hastened, quickened; hurried, rushed
antonyms barreling, bolting, breakneck, breathless, brisk, careering, dizzy, fast, fleet, flying, hasty, hurry-

ing, lightning, meteoric, quick, racing, rapid, rocketing, running, rushing, scooting, scudding, scurrying, snappy, speeding, speedy, swift, warp-speed, whirling, whirlwind, whisking, zipping
2 not having or showing an ability to absorb ideas readily ⟨the *slower* students worked together in a separate group⟩ — see STUPID 1
3 lacking in gaiety, movement, or animation ⟨a *slow* day on Wall Street⟩ — see DEAD 2
4 causing weariness, restlessness, or lack of interest ⟨the first half of the movie is *slow*, but then it gets exciting⟩ — see BORING

slow *adv* at a pace that is less than usual, desirable, or expected ⟨you need to go *slow* with this experiment, or you'll make mistakes⟩
synonyms laggardly, leisurely, pokily, slowly, sluggishly, tardily
related words carefully, cautiously, deliberately, purposefully; heavily, ploddingly
near antonyms immediately, posthaste, presto, promptly, pronto, readily, soon; impetuously, impulsively, rashly, recklessly; abruptly, suddenly
antonyms apace, briskly, fast, fleetly, full tilt, hastily, meteorically, quick, quickly, rapidly, snappily, speedily, swift, swiftly

slow *vb* to cause to move or proceed at a less rapid pace ⟨if you don't *slow* your delivery down a bit, your speech will be over too soon⟩
synonyms brake, decelerate, retard, slacken
related words halt, stop; encumber, hamper, handicap, hinder, hobble, hold back, hold up, impede, inhibit, obstruct, set back, tie up; bottleneck; arrest, check, constrain, curb, rein, restrain; baffle, foil, frustrate, sabotage, thwart
near antonyms drive, encourage, goad, propel, push, spur, stir, urge; advance, aid, dispatch, ease, expedite, facilitate, forward, further, help
antonyms accelerate, hasten, hurry, quicken, rush, speed (up), step up

slowdown *n* a usually gradual decrease in the pace or level of activity of something ⟨disease experts are encouraged by the recent *slowdown* in the spread of the virus⟩
synonyms braking, deceleration, downshift, letup, retardation
related words decline, drop, slump; ebb, remission, retreat, wane; flagging, weakening; arrest, check, halt, stoppage; collapse, crash, fall, plunge
antonyms acceleration, hastening, quickening

slowly *adv* at a pace that is less than usual, desirable, or expected ⟨walked *slowly* toward the ringing phone⟩ — see SLOW

slowness *n* the quality or state of lacking intelligence or quickness of mind ⟨her natural shyness was sometimes mistaken for *slowness* by people who did not know her well⟩ — see STUPIDITY 1

slowpoke *n* someone who moves slowly or more slowly than others ⟨quit being such a *slowpoke* this morning, or you'll be late⟩
synonyms crawler, dallier, dawdler, dragger, laggard, lagger, lingerer, loiterer, plodder, snail, straggler
related words latecomer; idler, lazybones, loafer, lounger, slouch, slug, sluggard; delayer, procrastinator
near antonyms go-getter, hustler, scrambler; hurrier, rusher, speeder
antonyms speedster

slow–witted *adj* not having or showing an ability to absorb ideas readily ⟨all but the most *slow-witted* readers will have solved the mystery long before they reach the book's final chapter⟩ — see STUPID 1

sludge *n* **1** soft wet earth ⟨after a day of heavy rain, the fairgrounds had turned into pure *sludge*⟩ — see MUD
2 something (as a work of literature or music) that is too sentimental ⟨I can't bring myself to read that *sludge*⟩ — see CORN

sludgy *adj* full of or covered with soft wet earth ⟨a *sludgy* riverbed⟩ — see MUDDY 1

[1]**slug** *n* a hard strike with a part of the body or an instrument ⟨one well aimed *slug* on the head knocked him out⟩ — see [1]BLOW

[2]**slug** *n* **1** a lazy person ⟨he's always a *slug* in the morning, which is why he prefers to sleep late⟩ — see LAZYBONES
2 the portion of a serving of a beverage that is swallowed at one time ⟨knocked back another *slug* of whiskey⟩ — see DRINK 2

slug *vb* to deliver a blow to (someone or something) usually in a strong vigorous manner ⟨she got so angry that she *slugged* the back of the chair and knocked it over⟩ — see HIT 1

slug (down) *vb* to swallow in liquid form ⟨*slugging down* endless bottles of water in the intense heat⟩ — see DRINK 1

slugabed *n* a lazy person ⟨he's always so busy that he would make anyone look like a *slugabed* by comparison⟩ — see LAZYBONES

sluggard *n* a lazy person ⟨tried to wake up the *sluggards* who were still sleeping at that late hour⟩ — see LAZYBONES

sluggish *adj* **1** moving or proceeding at less than the normal, desirable, or required speed ⟨the *sluggish* pace of the project is worrisome⟩ — see SLOW 1
2 slow to move or act ⟨reptiles are naturally *sluggish* at low temperatures⟩ — see INACTIVE 1

sluggishly *adv* at a pace that is less than usual, desirable, or expected ⟨the car responds *sluggishly* until it warms up⟩ — see SLOW

sluice *vb* to pour liquid over or through in order to cleanse ⟨he *sluiced* the gutters with lots of water in order to make sure they were clear⟩ — see FLUSH 1

slumber *n* a natural periodic loss of consciousness during which the body restores itself ⟨a toddler looking so innocent and peaceful in *slumber*⟩ — see SLEEP 1

slumber *vb* **1** to be in a state of sleep ⟨she *slumbered* for hours while the train rolled on⟩ — see SLEEP 1
2 to sleep lightly or briefly ⟨*slumbering* restlessly in the tropical heat⟩ — see NAP 1

slumberer *n* one who sleeps ⟨Rip Van Winkle is one of literature's most famous *slumberers*⟩ — see SLEEPER

slumbering *adj* being in a state of suspended consciousness ⟨made a comparison between the inattentive nation and a *slumbering* giant⟩ — see ASLEEP 1

slumbering *n* a natural periodic loss of consciousness during which the body restores itself ⟨my peaceful *slumbering* was interrupted by a ring of the doorbell⟩ — see SLEEP 1

slumberous *or* **slumbrous** *adj* **1** desiring or needing sleep ⟨parents putting their *slumberous* children to bed⟩ — see SLEEPY 1
2 tending to cause sleep ⟨the *slumberous* murmer of the wind in the trees⟩ — see HYPNOTIC

slump *n* a period of decreased economic activity ⟨the stock market is in a bit of a *slump*, but analysts expect things to pick up in the next fiscal quarter⟩ — see DEPRESSION 1

slur *n* **1** an act or expression showing scorn and usually intended to hurt another's feelings ⟨she brushed off the sexist *slurs* and proceeded to go about her business⟩ — see INSULT
2 a mark of guilt or disgrace ⟨your drunken behavior at the wedding has cast a *slur* on this family⟩ — see STAIN 1

slur (over) *vb* to fail to give proper attention to ⟨a documentary that *slurs over* certain important facts as it offers a very biased case for a conspiracy theory⟩ — see NEGLECT 1

slurp *vb* to swallow in liquid form ⟨his dinner date *slurped* her soup directly from the bowl⟩ — see DRINK 1

slush *n* **1** language, behavior, or ideas that are absurd and contrary to good sense ⟨how can you stand to read that *slush* in the tabloids?⟩ — see NONSENSE 1
2 soft wet earth ⟨he paused in front of the doorway to wipe the *slush* off of his boots⟩ — see MUD
3 something (as a work of literature or music) that is too sentimental ⟨a musical that has been reviled as pure *slush* by the New York critics⟩ — see CORN
4 that which is of low quality or worth ⟨discovered that *slush* is what publishers want, so that's exactly what she'll write⟩ — see JUNK 1

slushy *adj* **1** full of or covered with soft wet earth ⟨the *slushy* racetrack resulted in a significantly slower time for the winning horse⟩ — see MUDDY 1
2 appealing to the emotions in an obvious and tiresome way ⟨*slushy* music underscores the movie's emotional scenes⟩ — see CORNY 1

slut *n* a boldly flirtatious or sexually promiscuous woman ⟨had a reputation around town for being something of a *slut*⟩ — see FLOOZY

sluttish *adj* having loose sexual morals ⟨the stand-up comic developed her *sluttish* persona as a way to satirize sexual double standards⟩ — see SLEAZY 1

slutty *adj* having loose sexual morals ⟨you might be taken more seriously if you didn't wear that *slutty* outfit⟩ ⟨a TV reality show that appears to be nothing more than an endless celebration of a household of *slutty* alcoholics⟩ — see SLEAZY 1

sly *adj* **1** clever at attaining one's ends by indirect and often deceptive means ⟨the movie pairs a *sly*, dissembling ex-con with an upstanding, straight-arrow cop⟩ — see ARTFUL 1
2 given to acting in secret and to concealing one's intentions ⟨why, you *sly* fellow! I had no idea you were planning my birthday party⟩ — see SNEAKY 1
3 tending to or exhibiting reckless playfulness ⟨a *sly* sense of humor⟩ — see MISCHIEVOUS 1

slyboots *n pl* someone who acts in a sly and secret manner ⟨the whole family adored the impish little *slyboots*, despite his endless pranks⟩ — see SNEAK

slyness *n* skill in achieving one's ends through indirect, subtle, or underhanded means ⟨the *slyness* with which the FBI agent infiltrated the subversive organization was indeed impressive⟩ — see CUNNING 1

[1]**smack** *n* a very small amount ⟨add just a *smack* of vanilla to the whipped cream⟩ — see PARTICLE 1

[2]**smack** *n* a hard strike with a part of the body or an instrument ⟨the cook gave him a *smack* on the wrist when he tried to sneak an early taste of the sauce⟩ — see [1]BLOW

smack *vb* to deliver a blow to (someone or something) usually in a strong vigorous manner ⟨he *smacked* the punching bag one final time before heading to the showers⟩ — see HIT 1

smack–dab *adv* as stated or indicated without the slightest difference ⟨a restaurant that's *smack-dab* in the center of town⟩ — see EXACTLY 1

smacker *n, slang* a U.S. currency bill representing 100 cents ⟨one lousy *smacker* was all she left for a tip⟩ — see DOLLAR

small *adj* **1** of a size that is less than average ⟨a *small* cat who never weighed more than five pounds⟩
synonyms bantam, diminutive, dinky, dwarfish, fine, half-pint, Lilliputian, little, pint-size (*or* pint-sized), pocket, pocket-size (*also* pocket-sized), puny, pygmy, shrimpy, slight, smallish, subnormal, toylike, undersized (*also* undersize)
related words dwarf, toy; runtish, runty, scrubby, stunted; bitty, inappreciable, infinitesimal, little bitty, micro, microscopic (*also* microscopical), mini, miniature, miniaturized, minikin, minim, minuscule, minute, pinpoint, teensy, teensy-weensy, teeny, teeny-weeny, tiny, wee, weeny (*also* weensy); meager (*or* meagre), niggardly, poor, scant, scanty, scarce, skimp, skimpy, slender, slim, spare, sparse, stingy; deficient, inadequate, insufficient, lacking, wanting; bite-size (*also* bite-sized), capsule
near antonyms bulky, hefty, hulking, massive, voluminous; boxcar, Brobdingnagian, Bunyanesque, cavernous, colossal, cyclopean, elephantine, enormous, galactic, gargantuan, giant, gigantic, gross, Himalayan, herculean, heroic (*also* heroical), huge, humongous (*also* humungous), immense, jumbo, leviathan, mammoth, monolithic, monstrous, monumental, mountainous, pharaonic, prodigious, staggering, stupendous, titanic, tremendous, vast; abundant, ample, appreciable, bountiful, copious, generous, healthy, liberal, plenteous, plentiful; fat, thick; broad, wide; boundless, cosmic (*also* cosmical), immeasurable, incalculable, infinite; adequate, enough, sufficient
antonyms big, biggish, considerable, goodly, grand, great, handsome, husky, king-size (*or* king-sized), large, largish, outsize (*also* outsized), overscale (*or* overscaled), oversize (*or* oversized), sizable (*or* sizeable), substantial, tidy, whacking, whopping
2 small in degree ⟨your chances of winning the lottery are so *small* that it's best not to count on it⟩ — see REMOTE 1
3 lacking importance ⟨reluctant to bring such a *small* matter to the boss's attention⟩ — see UNIMPORTANT
4 not broad or open in views or opinions ⟨townspeople who were helpful to one another but who also could be *small* and intolerant⟩ — see NARROW 2

small arm *n* a portable weapon from which a shot is discharged by gunpowder ⟨the soldiers keep their *small arms* securely in their holsters when not on patrol⟩ — see GUN 1

small beer *n* something of little importance ⟨the money we spend on cable is *small beer* compared to the mortgage payment we have to come up with every month⟩ — see TRIFLE

small change *n* something of little importance ⟨he rightfully dismissed his woes as *small change* compared to the life-threatening problems faced by others⟩ — see TRIFLE

smaller *adj* having not so great importance or rank as another ⟨a *smaller* task but one that needs to be done nevertheless⟩ — see LESSER

smallest *adj* being the least in amount, number, or size possible ⟨severely reprimanded employees even for the *smallest* mistakes⟩ — see MINIMAL

small–fry *adj* lacking importance ⟨some *small-fry* official in the state government with a big-time ego⟩ — see UNIMPORTANT

smallish *adj* of a size that is less than average ⟨a *smallish* row of bushes lining the yard⟩ — see SMALL 1

small–minded *adj* **1** unwilling to grant other people social rights or to accept other viewpoints ⟨a *small-minded* man only concerned with his own well-being⟩ — see INTOLERANT 2
2 not broad or open in views or opinions ⟨resented the *small-minded* people who automatically opposed every new idea⟩ — see NARROW 2

small–mindedness *n* stubborn or intolerant adherence to one's opinions or prejudices ⟨the *small-mindedness* of her parents would never allow them to accept a son-in-law of a different religion⟩ — see BIGOTRY

smallness *n* **1** the quality or state of being little in size

⟨my grandmother was surprised by the *smallness* of the latest electronic devices⟩
synonyms diminutiveness, fineness, littleness, puniness, slightness
related words petiteness; minuteness, tininess; meagerness, poorness, scantiness, scantness, scarceness, scarcity, skimpiness, slenderness, slimness, spareness, sparseness, sparsity, stinginess; deficiency, inadequacy, inadequateness
near antonyms enormity, enormousness, grossness, hugeness, immenseness, immensity, magnitude, mountainousness, prodigiousness, stupendousness; extensiveness, vastness; excessiveness, extravagance, extremeness, immoderacy; abundance, ampleness, bountifulness, copiousness, generosity, healthiness, liberality; adequacy, sufficiency; heaviness, heftiness, weightiness; bulkiness, massiveness, voluminousness
antonyms bigness, grandness, greatness, largeness, magnitude
2 the quality or state of being unimportant ⟨regardless of its *smallness*, each act of kindness is ultimately rewarded⟩ — see INSIGNIFICANCE

small talk *n* friendly, informal conversation or an instance of this ⟨at the corporate get-together we made the obligatory *small talk* with some people from the home office⟩ — see CHAT 1

smart *n* **1** a sharp unpleasant sensation usually felt in some specific part of the body ⟨the toddler was whining over the *smart* from the cut⟩ — see PAIN 1
2 smarts *pl* the ability to learn and understand or to deal with problems ⟨she had the *smarts* to start college at age 16, but perhaps not the emotional maturity⟩ — see INTELLIGENCE 1

smart *vb* to feel or cause physical pain ⟨the injection only *smarted* for a moment⟩ — see HURT 1

smart *adj* **1** being strikingly neat and trim in style or appearance ⟨dressed in their *smart* new uniforms, the cadets proudly paraded around the grounds of the military school⟩
synonyms dapper, natty, sharp, snappy, spruce
related words dolled up, dressy, elegant, formal, spiffed-up; orderly, tidy; à la mode (*also* a la mode), chic, fashionable, in, modish, stylish; careful, fastidious, fussy, meticulous; combed, groomed; clean, immaculate, pristine, spotless, squeaky-clean
near antonyms messy, mussed, rumpled, uncombed, untidy, wrinkled; shabby, sleazy; dingy, dirty, filthy, foul, grimy, grubby, nasty, scroungy, scrubby, scruffy, scuzzy [*slang*], smirched, soiled, spotted, stained, sullied, unclean; dowdy, inelegant, unfashionable, unstylish
antonyms disheveled (*or* dishevelled), frowsy (*or* frowzy), sloppy, slovenly, unkempt
2 being in the latest or current fashion ⟨boutiques specializing in *smart* clothes for cosmopolitan women⟩ — see STYLISH
3 given to or marked by mature intelligent humor ⟨something one sees so rarely on TV: a *smart* sitcom⟩ — see WITTY
4 making light of something usually regarded as serious or sacred ⟨just joked and made *smart* comments during the ceremony⟩ — see FLIPPANT
5 having or showing a practical cleverness or judgment ⟨a *smart* investment that has really paid off⟩ — see SHREWD 1
6 having or showing quickness of mind ⟨a *smart* child who will do well in school⟩ — see INTELLIGENT 1
7 having a wide and refined knowledge of the world especially from personal experience ⟨a novelist who got much of the material for his works by hanging out with the *smart* set⟩ — see WORLDLY-WISE

smart-aleck *adj* **1** making light of something usually regarded as serious or sacred ⟨a talk show host who's known for his quick quips and *smart-aleck* observations on current events⟩ — see FLIPPANT
2 marked by the use of wit that is intended to cause hurt feelings ⟨a *smart-aleck* reply that was met with a slap in the face⟩ — see SARCASTIC

smart aleck *also* **smart alec** *n* a person who likes to show off in a clever but annoying way ⟨some *smart aleck* in the audience kept shouting clever insults at the nervous speaker⟩
synonyms smarty (*or* smartie), smarty-pants, wiseacre, wiseass, wise guy, wisenheimer (*also* weisenheimer)
related words know-all [*chiefly British*], know-it-all; wisecracker; hotshot, show-off

smart-alecky *adj* **1** making light of something usually regarded as serious or sacred ⟨you wouldn't be so *smart-alecky* if you were the one having the surgery⟩ — see FLIPPANT
2 marked by the use of wit that is intended to cause hurt feelings ⟨*smart-alecky* comments from a coworker about her new clothes⟩ — see SARCASTIC

smart-ass *adj* making light of something usually regarded as serious or sacred ⟨it's easy to make *smart-ass* jokes about death when you're not the one who's dying⟩ — see FLIPPANT

smart-assed *adj* making light of something usually regarded as serious or sacred ⟨*smart-assed* collegians making jokes at the expense of devout churchgoers⟩ — see FLIPPANT

smarting *adj* causing intense discomfort to one's skin ⟨we had to press on, despite the *smarting* sleet that was blowing in our faces⟩ — see CUTTING 1

smartly *adv* in a strikingly neat and trim manner ⟨the *smartly* dressed scouts marched at the head of the Memorial Day parade⟩
synonyms dashingly, nattily, sharply, snappily, sprucely
related words neatly, orderly, tidily, trimly; elegantly, fashionably, modishly, stylishly, swankily; carefully, fastidiously, fussily, meticulously; cleanly, immaculately, pristinely, spotlessly
near antonyms dowdily, inelegantly; slatternly; messily, mussily, untidily; scruffily, shabbily, sleazily; dingily, dirtily, filthily, foully, grubbily, nastily
antonyms sloppily, slovenly

smart-mouthed *adj* marked by the use of wit that is intended to cause hurt feelings ⟨your *smart-mouthed* remarks aren't at all helping the situation⟩ — see SARCASTIC

smarty *or* **smartie** *n* a person who likes to show off in a clever but annoying way ⟨think so, *smarty*? Well, you're wrong, and I can prove it!⟩ — see SMART ALECK

smarty-pants *adj* making light of something usually regarded as serious or sacred ⟨your *smarty-pants* comments aren't helping matters any⟩ — see FLIPPANT

smarty-pants *n pl* a person who likes to show off in a clever but annoying way ⟨I don't need to hear from some *smarty-pants* second-guesser that the theme for the party is all wrong⟩ — see SMART ALECK

smash *n* **1** a forceful coming together of two things ⟨the awful *smash* when his dreams got hit by reality⟩ — see IMPACT 1
2 the violent coming together of two bodies into destructive contact ⟨the sound of the *smash* made all of the bystanders immediately whip their heads around⟩ — see CRASH 1
3 a hard strike with a part of the body or an instrument ⟨she gave the tennis ball a *smash* and sent it flying over the other side of the net⟩ — see [1]BLOW
4 a loud explosive sound ⟨the bikes collided with a huge *smash*⟩ — see CLAP 1
5 a person or thing that is successful ⟨the new Broad-

way musical is a *smash*〉 — see HIT 1

smash *vb* **1** to cause to break with violence and much noise 〈the drunken guest deliberately *smashed* a glass against the brick fireplace〉
synonyms break down, crash, shatter
related words bust, fracture, fragment; annihilate, bash, decimate, demolish, desolate, destroy, devastate, nuke, pulverize, ruin, tear down, total, vaporize, waste, wrack, wreck; shiver, splinter, split; crack, crunch, crush, snap
2 to cause to break open or into pieces by or as if by an explosive 〈the firecracker *smashed* the clay pot〉 — see BLAST 1
3 to bring to a complete end the physical soundness, existence, or usefulness of 〈the invading troops *smashed* the resistance and went on to conquer the country〉 — see DESTROY 1
4 to come into usually forceful contact with something 〈we nearly *smashed* into each other on the skating rink〉 — see HIT 2

smashed *adj* **1** forcibly separated into many pieces 〈the *smashed* figurine left bits of china all over the rug〉 — see BROKEN 1
2 *slang* being under the influence of alcohol 〈on his 21st birthday, he went out and got *smashed*—before wrapping his car around a tree〉 — see DRUNK

smashup *n* the violent coming together of two bodies into destructive contact 〈three cars were involved in a *smashup* on my street last night〉 — see CRASH 1

smatter *n* a small number 〈we received only a *smatter* of complaints about the book〉 — see FEW

smattering *n* a small number 〈a *smattering* of guests at the art exhibit〉 — see FEW

smear *vb* **1** to rub an oily or sticky substance over 〈the toddler gleefully *smeared* her hair and face with maple syrup〉
synonyms anoint, bedaub, besmear, daub
related words coat, paint, plaster; grease, oil; gum, lard, pitch, tar; befoul, begrime, bemire, besmirch, blacken, dirty, foul, gaum [*dialect*], grime, mire, muck, muddy, smirch, smudge, soil, stain, sully
2 to make untrue and harmful statements about 〈he is willing to *smear* his opponent if doing so would win the election〉 — see SLANDER

smearing *n* the making of false statements that damage another's reputation 〈this *smearing* has got to stop, or the voters will conclude that there's absolutely no one worth voting for〉 — see SLANDER

smell *n* **1** the quality of a thing that makes it perceptible to the sense organs in the nose 〈the *smell* of vanilla is supposed to be very soothing〉
synonyms aroma, odor, redolence, scent, sniff
related words whiff; attar (*also* otto), bouquet, fragrance, fragrancy, perfume; ambrosia, lusciousness, savor (*also* savour), savoriness, spice, tang; acridness, fetidness, fetor, foulness, funk, gaminess, malodor, noisomeness, rancidity, rankness, reek, stench, stink; aromaticity, odoriferousness, odorousness; incense, musk
2 a very small amount 〈the pie has barely a *smell* of ginger, but lots of cinnamon〉 — see PARTICLE 1
3 a special quality or impression associated with something 〈a law firm with a mahogany-lined boardroom that has the discernible *smell* of money and power〉 — see AURA 1

smell *vb* **1** to become aware of by means of the sense organs in the nose 〈we *smelled* the aroma of freshly baked cookies as soon as we walked in the house〉
synonyms nose, scent, sniff, snuff, whiff
related words breathe, drink (in), inhale, respire; snort, snuffle; savor (*also* savour)
2 to have a vague awareness of 〈I *smell* something fishy about this situation〉 — see FEEL 1
3 to be objectionable or unsatisfactory 〈that movie *smells*—I wouldn't waste my money on it if I were you〉 — see STINK 2

smeller *n* the part of the face bearing the nostrils and nasal cavity 〈a sensitive *smeller* is just as important as a fine palate when evaluating wine〉 — see NOSE 1

smelly *adj* having an unpleasant smell 〈your *smelly* sneakers are enough to raise the dead〉 — see MALODOROUS

smidgen *also* **smidgeon** *or* **smidgin** *or* **smidge** *n* a very small amount 〈the maid cleaned the house until there wasn't even a *smidgen* of dust left〉 — see PARTICLE 1

smile *vb* **1** to express an emotion (as amusement) by curving the lips upward 〈the soldier *smiled* in pleasure when he saw the giant sign welcoming him home〉
synonyms beam, grin
related words laugh, simper; smirk, sneer
near antonyms grimace; frown, glare, gloom, glower, lower (*also* lour), scowl; pout, sulk
2 to express scornful amusement by means of facial contortions 〈*smiled* at their ridiculous antics and walked away in disgust〉 — see SNEER

smilingly *adv* in a cheerful or happy manner 〈puts up with the old woman's complaints *smilingly*〉 — see GAILY 1

smirch *n* a mark of guilt or disgrace 〈corruption charges that were a *smirch* on her reputation〉 — see STAIN 1

smirch *vb* **1** to make dirty 〈their clothes were *smirched* by dust from the trail〉 — see DIRTY
2 to reduce to a lower standing in one's own eyes or in others' eyes 〈this scandal will forever *smirch* the name of a once-great family〉 — see HUMBLE

smite *vb* to deliver a blow to (someone or something) usually in a strong vigorous manner 〈he shall *smite* his enemies with a mighty fist〉 — see HIT 1

smog *n* an atmospheric condition in which suspended particles in the air rob it of its transparency 〈the city's *smog* was once so bad that darkness often prevailed, even at noon〉 — see HAZE 1

smoggy *adj* filled with or dimmed by fine particles (as of dust or water) in suspension 〈it was hard to see through the *smoggy* afternoon sky〉 — see HAZY 1

smoke *vb, slang* to defeat by a large margin 〈man, they totally *smoked* us today!〉 — see WHIP 2

smooch *vb* to touch one another with the lips as a sign of love 〈a couple *smooching* in a dark corner〉 — see KISS 1

smooth *adj* **1** having or showing very polished and worldly manners 〈a *smooth* salesman of expensive jewelry〉 — see SUAVE
2 involving minimal difficulty or effort 〈it should be *smooth* going from this point on〉 — see EASY 1
3 having a surface without bends, breaks, or irregularities 〈a *smooth* skating rink〉 — see LEVEL 1
4 free from emotional or mental agitation 〈his *smooth* disposition and leadership qualities lend themselves well to the position〉 — see CALM 2

smooth *vb* **1** to free from obstruction or difficulty 〈a willingness to compromise will *smooth* the way to an early agreement〉 — see EASE 1
2 to make free from breaks, curves, or bumps 〈the workers *smoothed* the surface of the concrete before letting it dry〉 — see EVEN 1
3 to make smooth or glossy usually by repeatedly applying surface pressure 〈used fine sandpaper to *smooth* the face of the wood〉 — see POLISH 1

smoothen *vb* **1** to make free from breaks, curves, or bumps 〈*smoothen* the wood for the table thoroughly, or the legs will be uneven〉 — see EVEN 1
2 to make smooth or glossy usually by repeatedly applying surface pressure 〈*smoothen* the edges of the two

parts before trying to join them together⟩ — see POLISH 1

smoothly *adv* without difficulty ⟨we proceeded *smoothly* to the next stage of the project⟩ — see EASILY 1

smorgasbord *n* an unorganized collection or mixture of various things ⟨every day the director has to first deal with a *smorgasbord* of problems before he can begin filming⟩ — see MISCELLANY 1

smother *vb* **1** to be or cause to be killed by lack of breathable air ⟨children should never play inside discarded appliances because they could become trapped and *smother*⟩

synonyms choke, stifle, strangle, suffocate

related words garrote (*or* garotte), throttle; asphyxiate; drown; croak [*slang*], destroy, dispatch, do in, fell, slay

near antonyms breathe, exhale, expire, inhale, inspire; resuscitate, revive

2 to refrain from openly showing or uttering ⟨he quickly *smothered* his inappropriate laughter at the funeral ceremony⟩ — see SUPPRESS 2

3 to defeat by a large margin ⟨the soccer team *smothered* their first few opponents in the championships, but lost narrowly in the final round⟩ — see WHIP 2

smudge *vb* to make dirty ⟨she accidentally *smudged* her collar with the lipstick⟩ — see DIRTY

smudge *n* a mark of guilt or disgrace ⟨the president's spouse must not have the slightest *smudge* of scandal⟩ — see STAIN 1

smudged *adj* not clean ⟨every copy of the book that the store had was *smudged*⟩ — see DIRTY 1

smug *adj* **1** having too high an opinion of oneself ⟨a winner who was so *smug* that he lost the goodwill of the crowd⟩ — see CONCEITED

2 being clean and in good order ⟨the suburb's *smug* lawns and tree-lined streets bespeak a comfortable affluence⟩ — see NEAT 1

smuggler *n* a person who imports or exports goods secretly and illegally ⟨during Prohibition, *smugglers* of alcohol did a brisk business⟩

synonyms bootlegger, contrabandist, courier, runner

related words coyote, gunrunner, mule [*slang*]

smugness *n* an often unjustified feeling of being pleased with oneself or with one's situation or achievements ⟨the sense of *smugness* that can come with too many easy victories⟩ — see COMPLACENCE 1

smut *n* **1** foul matter that mars the purity or cleanliness of something ⟨once a year they cleaned all of the *smut* out of the chimney⟩ — see FILTH 1

2 the quality or state of being obscene ⟨the talk-show host is famous for shows filled with *smut* and scandal⟩ — see OBSCENITY 1

smuttiness *n* **1** the quality or state of being obscene ⟨we were offended by the *smuttiness* of the jokes that the comedian was telling⟩ — see OBSCENITY 1

2 the state or quality of being dirty ⟨appalled by the unspeakable *smuttiness* of the rental apartments that they were shown⟩ — see DIRTINESS 1

smutty *adj* **1** depicting or referring to sexual matters in a way that is unacceptable in polite society ⟨the movie was rated R because of some nude scenes and *smutty* dialogue⟩ — see OBSCENE 1

2 not clean ⟨a street urchin with a *smutty* face⟩ — see DIRTY 1

snag *n* a danger or difficulty that is hidden or not easily recognized ⟨we ran into a slight *snag* the night before the show⟩ — see PITFALL 1

snag *vb* to take physical control or possession of (something) suddenly or forcibly ⟨often late for work, I generally *snag* a bagel as I run out the door in the morning⟩ — see CATCH 1

snail *n* someone who moves slowly or more slowly than others ⟨go and tell the *snails* in the back to hurry up⟩ — see SLOWPOKE

snail *vb* to move slowly ⟨the highway construction work created a bottleneck that had cars *snailing* for the next five miles⟩ — see CRAWL 2

snaillike *adj* moving or proceeding at less than the normal, desirable, or required speed ⟨the application process for an overseas adoption has been moving at a *snaillike* pace⟩ — see SLOW 1

snail mail *n* communications or parcels sent or carried through the postal system ⟨even though she has an e-mail account, she still prefers to send *snail mail*⟩ — see MAIL

snail–paced *adj* moving or proceeding at less than the normal, desirable, or required speed ⟨my *snail-paced* dial-up connection is essentially worthless for video downloads⟩ — see SLOW 1

snake *vb* **1** to move about in a sly or secret manner ⟨*snaking* softly through the brush⟩ — see SNEAK 1

2 to move slowly with the body close to the ground ⟨commandos *snaking* through the grass toward the house⟩ — see CRAWL 1

snake *n* **1** a limbless reptile with a long body ⟨*snakes* are cold-blooded, so they regulate their body temperature by alternately basking in sunlight and seeking shade⟩

synonyms serpent, viper

related words adder, anaconda, asp, black racer, blacksnake, blue racer, boa, bull snake, bushmaster, chicken snake, cobra, constrictor, copperhead, coral snake, cottonmouth moccasin, diamondback rattlesnake, fer-de-lance, garter snake, gopher snake, green snake, hognose snake, horned viper, indigo snake, king cobra, king snake, krait, mamba, milk snake, moccasin, pine snake, pit viper, puff adder, python, racer, rat snake, rattlesnake, sea serpent, sea snake, sidewinder, taipan, water moccasin, water snake, worm snake

2 a person whose behavior is offensive to others ⟨why, that dirty, rotten *snake*!⟩ — see JERK 1

3 one who betrays a trust or an allegiance ⟨what a *snake* she was—having an affair with my husband while I was in the hospital!⟩ — see TRAITOR

snakebit *or* **snakebitten** *adj* having, prone to, or marked by bad luck ⟨in retrospect, our assault on the mountain's summit seems to have been *snakebit* from the get-go⟩ — see UNLUCKY 1

snake pit *n* a state in which everything is out of order ⟨finally managed to crawl out of the *snake pit* of her drug addiction⟩ — see CHAOS

snap *adj* **1** involving minimal difficulty or effort ⟨a *snap* course that even an idiot could pass⟩ — see EASY 1

2 made or done without previous thought or preparation ⟨made a *snap* decision⟩ — see EXTEMPORANEOUS

snap *n* **1** a loud explosive sound ⟨the plastic coat hook broke off with a loud *snap* when he tried to hang the heavy bag on it⟩ — see CLAP 1

2 a picture created from an image recorded on a light-sensitive surface by a camera ⟨took several *snaps* of his family for the scrapbook⟩ — see PHOTOGRAPH

3 active strength of body or mind ⟨the team is showing a lot of *snap* tonight⟩ — see VIGOR 1

4 a weather condition marked by low temperatures ⟨a prolonged cold *snap*⟩ — see COLD

5 a very small amount ⟨I don't care a *snap* about gossip⟩ — see PARTICLE 1

6 something that is easy to do ⟨this test will be a *snap*⟩ — see CINCH 1

snap *vb* **1** to speak sharply or irritably ⟨the shopkeeper finally *snapped* at one customer who couldn't seem to make up his mind⟩

synonyms bark, snarl

related words growl, grumble; roar, scream, shout, shriek, yell; fulminate, rage, rant, rave, sputter, storm,

tee off, vent, vituperate; blow up, explode, flare (up), flip (out) [*slang*]
near antonyms calm (down), simmer down
2 to break suddenly with an explosive sound ⟨the fragile twig *snapped* in her hands⟩ — see CRACK 1
3 to take a photograph of ⟨be sure to *snap* everything you see on your vacation, and then you can show us⟩ — see PHOTOGRAPH
4 to pass from one form, state, or level to another ⟨she abruptly *snapped* alert⟩ — see CHANGE 2

snap (up) *vb* to take physical control or possession of (something) suddenly or forcibly ⟨I *snapped up* the last remaining cupcake before anyone else could get their mitts on it⟩ — see CATCH 1

snapback *n* the process or period of gradually regaining one's health and strength ⟨the doctor predicted a quick *snapback* for the rugged young soldier⟩ — see CONVALESCENCE

snap back *vb* **1** to become healthy and strong again after illness or weakness ⟨teenagers will often *snap back* remarkably quickly⟩ — see CONVALESCE
2 to regain a former or normal state ⟨analysts hoped that the economy would *snap back* over the next few months⟩ — see RECOVER 2

snappily *adv* **1** with great speed ⟨she *snappily* completed the job application and handed it to the receptionist⟩ — see FAST 1
2 in a strikingly neat and trim manner ⟨the *snappily* attired male dancers wore top hats and tails⟩ — see SMARTLY
3 in a quick and spirited manner ⟨sang out the square dance calls *snappily*⟩ — see GAILY 2

snappish *adj* easily irritated or annoyed ⟨I always start feeling *snappish* whenever I get really hungry⟩ — see IRRITABLE

snappy *adj* **1** being in the latest or current fashion ⟨that *snappy* outfit really should impress your date⟩ — see STYLISH
2 easily irritated or annoyed ⟨we tried to avoid her when she was acting *snappy*, which was all too often⟩ — see IRRITABLE
3 having a low or subnormal temperature ⟨typically *snappy* weather for March⟩ — see COLD 1
4 having much high-spirited energy and movement ⟨much *snappy* repartee at the party celebrating the new art gallery's opening⟩ — see LIVELY 1
5 moving, proceeding, or acting with great speed ⟨bring us some more french fries, and make it *snappy*!⟩ — see FAST 1
6 being strikingly neat and trim in style or appearance ⟨the *snappy* outfits worn by the young, attractive staff at the hotel⟩ — see SMART 1

snapshot *n* a picture created from an image recorded on a light-sensitive surface by a camera ⟨fans excitedly took *snapshots* of the rock star as he dashed into the hotel⟩ — see PHOTOGRAPH

snare *n* **1** a device or scheme for capturing another by surprise ⟨you fell for my clever *snare*, you fool!⟩ — see TRAP 1
2 something that catches and holds ⟨someday you'll find that your lies are a *snare* from which you can't escape⟩ — see WEB 1

snare *vb* **1** to catch or hold as if in a net ⟨easily distracted by any bright object that *snared* his eye⟩ — see ENTANGLE 2
2 to take physical control or possession of (something) suddenly or forcibly ⟨campers trying to *snare* brook trout for supper⟩ — see CATCH 1

snarky *adj* **1** easily irritated or annoyed ⟨working all day with such *snarky* jerks is exhausting⟩ — see IRRITABLE
2 marked by the use of wit that is intended to cause hurt feelings ⟨with champagne as a lubricant, she unleashed an unending series of *snarky* comments for the duration of the wedding reception⟩ — see SARCASTIC

[1]**snarl** *vb* to speak sharply or irritably ⟨she *snarled* at me after I kept badgering her with questions⟩ — see SNAP 1

[2]**snarl** *vb* to twist together into a usually confused mass ⟨you'll be awfully sorry if you *snarl* your fishing line⟩ — see ENTANGLE 1

snarl *n* a crowded mass (as of cars) that impedes or blocks movement ⟨to no avail, the city promotes carpooling to help ease the traffic *snarls* that always accompany rush hour⟩ — see JAM 1

snatch *vb* to take physical control or possession of (something) suddenly or forcibly ⟨the brazen seagull *snatched* the french fry right from my hand⟩ — see CATCH 1

snatch *n, slang* the unlawful or forcible carrying away of a person or animal ⟨to the police chief, it didn't look like a *snatch*, but another case of a bride-to-be getting cold feet⟩ — see ABDUCTION

snatching *n* an instance of theft ⟨an industry in which the *snatching* of trade secrets is greatly feared⟩ — see THEFT 2

snazzy *adj* attractively eye-catching in style ⟨fond of tooling around town in a *snazzy* car⟩ — see JAZZY 1

sneak *adj* undertaken or done so as to escape being observed or known by others ⟨a *sneak* attack on the nation's capitol⟩ — see SECRET 1

sneak *n* someone who acts in a sly and secret manner ⟨"Why, you little *sneak*," the mother exclaimed, "you made my birthday present right under my nose!"⟩
synonyms lurker, skulk, skulker, slyboots, sneaker
related words skunk, snake, weasel; sharper, sharpie (*or* sharpy), slicker, swindler; snoop, snooper, spy; stalker

sneak *vb* **1** to move about in a sly or secret manner ⟨the little kids *sneak* around upstairs when they're supposed to be in bed⟩
synonyms lurk, mooch, mouse, pussyfoot, shirk, skulk, slide, slink, slip, snake, steal
related words crawl, creep, edge, inch, worm; ghost, pad, tiptoe
2 to introduce in a gradual, secret, or clever way ⟨*sneak* the topic into the conversation any way you can⟩ — see INSINUATE

sneaker *n* someone who acts in a sly and secret manner ⟨she's such a *sneaker* I wouldn't trust her any farther than I could throw her⟩ — see SNEAK

sneakiness *n* skill in achieving one's ends through indirect, subtle, or underhanded means ⟨she was impressed by the *sneakiness* with which they had planned the surprise party⟩ — see CUNNING 1

sneaking *adj* **1** given to acting in secret and to concealing one's intentions ⟨never let one of those *sneaking* salespeople into your house⟩ — see SNEAKY 1
2 undertaken or done so as to escape being observed or known by others ⟨harbored a *sneaking* admiration for his chief business rival⟩ — see SECRET 1
3 arousing or deserving of one's loathing and disgust ⟨a *sneaking* two-timer who has completely lost his wife's trust⟩ — see CONTEMPTIBLE 1

sneaky *adj* **1** given to acting in secret and to concealing one's intentions ⟨his opponent's *sneaky* campaign manager was clearly up to something⟩
synonyms furtive, shady, shifty, slippery, sly, sneaking, stealthy
related words artful, crafty, cunning, devious, foxy, guileful, slick, wily; close, closemouthed, reticent, secretive; clandestine, covert, dark; deceitful, deceiving, deceptive, devious, duplicitous, trickish, tricky, underhand, underhanded; cheating, crooked, defrauding, dishonest, dissembling, double-dealing, knavish, two-

faced; lying, mendacious, untrustworthy, untruthful; insidious, perfidious, serpentine, treacherous
near antonyms aboveboard, forthright, plainspoken, straightforward; candid, direct, foursquare, frank, open, plain; honest, trustworthy, truthful
2 undertaken or done so as to escape being observed or known by others ⟨a *sneaky* plan to replace the priceless painting with a copy⟩ — see SECRET 1

sneer *vb* to express scornful amusement by means of facial contortions ⟨in high school the in crowd would invariably *sneer* every time they passed the hapless nerds⟩
synonyms laugh, smile, snicker, snigger
related words sniff, snort; catcall, deride, gibe (*or* jibe), hoot, insult, jeer, mock, ridicule; decry, despise, disdain; scoff (at), scorn; bad-mouth, belittle, disparage, pooh-pooh (*also* pooh), put down; heckle, jive, razz, rib, ride, taunt, tease, torment

snicker *n* an explosive sound that is a sign of amusement ⟨a *snicker* of derision when we heard their offer on the house⟩ — see LAUGH 1

snicker *vb* **1** to express scornful amusement by means of facial contortions ⟨he *snickered* at the puzzled look on her face⟩ — see SNEER
2 to show mirth with an explosive vocal sound ⟨only hard-core fans of teen sex comedies will *snicker* at this lame attempt⟩ — see LAUGH 1

snide *adj* **1** not following or in accordance with standards of honor and decency ⟨a *snide* trick to get the old woman to sell her antiques for practically nothing⟩ — see IGNOBLE 2
2 being such in appearance only and made or manufactured with the intention of committing fraud ⟨some small-time crook who was selling *snide* gems to gullible tourists⟩ — see COUNTERFEIT 1

sniff *n* the quality of a thing that makes it perceptible to the sense organs in the nose ⟨we took a good *sniff* of the sauce, trying to guess its ingredients⟩ — see SMELL 1

sniff *vb* to become aware of by means of the sense organs in the nose ⟨a curious cat *sniffing* the flowers in the garden⟩ — see SMELL 1

sniff (at) *vb* to show contempt for ⟨her carpentry skills are nothing to *sniff at*⟩ — see SCORN 1

sniffy *adj* having a feeling of superiority that shows itself in an overbearing attitude ⟨she was *sniffy* about anyone who didn't live up to her standards for "good manners"⟩ — see ARROGANT

snigger *n* an explosive sound that is a sign of amusement ⟨a love scene that unintentionally drew *sniggers* from the audience⟩ — see LAUGH 1

snigger *vb* to express scornful amusement by means of facial contortions ⟨we *sniggered* as the actor kept forgetting his lines⟩ — see SNEER

snip *vb* to make (something) shorter or smaller with the use of a cutting instrument ⟨*snipped* the loose ends⟩ — see CLIP 1

snip *n* **1** a very small piece ⟨cleared out the *snips* of paper that had been clogging the machine⟩ — see BIT 1
2 *British* something bought or offered for sale at a desirable price ⟨that antique urn that we bought at London's Portobello Road Market was a real *snip*⟩ — see BARGAIN 1

snippersnapper *n* a person of no importance or influence ⟨an old hand who regards these kids right out of business school as a bunch of *snippersnappers* who don't know beans⟩ — see NOBODY

snippet *n* a very small piece ⟨read them a *snippet* of his latest poem⟩ — see BIT 1

snippety *adj* easily irritated or annoyed ⟨we complained to the manager about the *snippety*, uncooperative waitress⟩ — see IRRITABLE

snippy *adj* **1** being or characterized by direct, brief, and potentially rude speech or manner ⟨*snippy* remarks about the quality of the food at the church picnic⟩ — see BLUNT 1
2 easily irritated or annoyed ⟨feeling *snippy* after a long day of work⟩ — see IRRITABLE
3 self-consciously trying to present an appearance of grandeur or importance ⟨I get tired of his *snippy* insistence that emulating the rich and famous is the only way to appear successful⟩ — see PRETENTIOUS 1

snit *n* a state of resentful silence or irritability ⟨don't bother him; he's still in a *snit* after this morning's reprimand⟩ — see POUT

[1]snitch *vb* to give information (as to the authorities) about another's improper or unlawful activities ⟨the prison gang had its own ways of dealing with those inmates who *snitched*⟩ — see SQUEAL 1

[2]snitch *vb* to take (something) without right and with an intent to keep ⟨*snitched* some paper from the office supply room for use with her printer at home⟩ — see STEAL 1

snitch *n* a person who provides information about another's wrongdoing ⟨several men were sentenced to prison based on the now-questionable testimony of a jailhouse *snitch*⟩ — see INFORMER

snitcher *n* a person who provides information about another's wrongdoing ⟨the prison inmate swore that he'd get revenge if he ever found out who the *snitcher* was⟩ — see INFORMER

sniveler *n* a person who makes frequent complaints usually about little things ⟨the worst supermarket *snivelers* were the ones who tried to redeem coupons for items they hadn't even bought⟩ — see CRYBABY

snob *n* a person who has an offensive air of superiority and tends to ignore or disdain anyone regarded as inferior ⟨the *snobs* at the museum fund-raiser turned their little noses up at us because we weren't wearing designer outfits⟩
synonyms snoot, snot
related words elitist, name-dropper, social climber

snobbish *adj* being or characteristic of a person who has an offensive air of superiority and tends to ignore or disdain anyone regarded as inferior ⟨he gave us one *snobbish* glance and then disregarded us⟩
synonyms aristocratic, elitist, high-hat, persnickety, potty, ritzy, snobby, snooty, snotty, toffee-nosed [*chiefly British*]
related words aloof, arrogant, bumptious, haughty, high-and-mighty, highfalutin (*also* hifalutin), high-handed, hoity-toity, huffish, huffy, imperious, lordly, overweening, peremptory, pompous, presumptuous, pretentious, supercilious, superior, toplofty (*also* topliftical), uppity; biggety (*or* biggity) [*Southern & Midland*], bigheaded, egoistic (*also* egoistical), egotistic (*or* egotistical), prideful, self-conceited, self-important, self-satisfied, smug, stuck-up, swelled-headed, swell-headed
near antonyms democratic, egalitarian; egoless, humble, modest, unpretentious; antielitist, antisnob

snobby *adj* being or characteristic of a person who has an offensive air of superiority and tends to ignore or disdain anyone regarded as inferior ⟨the *snobby* waiter gave me a withering look when I ordered the cheapest wine on the list⟩ — see SNOBBISH

snooker *vb* to cause to believe what is untrue ⟨I can't believe you managed to *snooker* me with that story about being an orphan⟩ — see DECEIVE

snoop *vb* to interest oneself in what is not one's concern ⟨a private investigator *snooping* around the abandoned warehouse⟩ — see INTERFERE

snoopy *adj* **1** interested in what is not one's own business ⟨she feels that being *snoopy* is a desirable, even essential, trait in a reporter⟩ — see CURIOUS 1
2 thrusting oneself where one is not welcome or invited

⟨put a fence around the yard to keep out *snoopy* neighbors⟩ — see INTRUSIVE

snoot *n* **1** a person who has an offensive air of superiority and tends to ignore or disdain anyone regarded as inferior ⟨our neighbor is a tiresome old *snoot* who keeps talking about how the neighborhood is going downhill⟩ — see SNOB
2 the part of the face bearing the nostrils and nasal cavity ⟨an overbearing snob who walks around with her *snoot* up in the air⟩ — see NOSE 1
3 a twisting of the facial features in disgust or disapproval ⟨a *snoot* that suggested that she thought that she was better than the rest of us⟩ — see GRIMACE

snoot *vb* to show contempt for ⟨after some modest success, the singer began to *snoot* the very people who had helped her get her career off the ground⟩ — see SCORN 1

snooty *adj* being or characteristic of a person who has an offensive air of superiority and tends to ignore or disdain anyone regarded as inferior ⟨the actress plays a genteel yet faintly *snooty* older woman⟩ — see SNOBBISH

snooze *n* **1** a short sleep ⟨took a *snooze* after lunch to refresh himself⟩ — see [1]NAP
2 someone or something boring ⟨man, that novel is a *snooze*—there's not one interesting character in it⟩ — see DRAG 1

snooze *vb* **1** to be in a state of sleep ⟨*snoozed* through those long winter nights under a thick down comforter⟩ — see SLEEP 1
2 to sleep lightly or briefly ⟨she was just *snoozing* when she heard the knock at the door⟩ — see NAP 1

snoozer *n* someone or something boring ⟨the supposed farce turned out to be a numbingly slow *snoozer*⟩ — see DRAG 1

snoozing *n* a natural periodic loss of consciousness during which the body restores itself ⟨all that *snoozing* should have you well rested and ready for some hard work⟩ — see SLEEP 1

snoozle *vb, chiefly dialect* to lie close ⟨a trio of kittens were *snoozling* comfortably in the basket⟩ — see NUZZLE

snort *n* **1** a vocal sound made to express scorn or disapproval ⟨made a *snort* of derision at the lame suggestion⟩ — see CATCALL
2 the portion of a serving of a beverage that is swallowed at one time ⟨the old cowpoke asked for a *snort* of whiskey⟩ — see DRINK 2

snorter *n* something very good of its kind ⟨a real *snorter* of an action movie that lives up to all the hype⟩ — see JIM-DANDY

snot *n* a person who has an offensive air of superiority and tends to ignore or disdain anyone regarded as inferior ⟨that patronizing little *snot* at the vintage record store openly smirks when someone asks for something from the Top 40⟩ — see SNOB

snotty *adj* being or characteristic of a person who has an offensive air of superiority and tends to ignore or disdain anyone regarded as inferior ⟨a *snotty* contempt for those brash parvenus who moved into the cookie-cutter mansion next door⟩ — see SNOBBISH

snout *n* the part of the face bearing the nostrils and nasal cavity ⟨dogs and their owners must grow to resemble one another, as that man and his basset hound have remarkably similar *snouts*⟩ — see NOSE 1

snow *vb* **1** to cause to believe what is untrue ⟨easily *snowed* by her glib talk⟩ — see DECEIVE
2 to make white or whiter by removing color ⟨the years had *snowed* his hair to a silvery white, making it difficult at first to recognize her old high school crush⟩ — see WHITEN

snowball *vb* to become greater in extent, volume, amount, or number ⟨the little problems we ignored began to *snowball* into huge headaches⟩ — see INCREASE 2

snow under *vb* **1** to defeat by a large margin ⟨the challenger *snowed* the incumbent *under* in a big upset⟩ — see WHIP 2
2 to subject to incapacitating emotional or mental stress ⟨*snowed under* by the huge pile of paperwork⟩ — see OVERWHELM 1

snub *n* treatment that is deliberately unfriendly ⟨he tolerated the *snubs* from his in-laws because the holidays come but once a year, thankfully⟩ — see COLD SHOULDER

snub *vb* **1** to deliberately ignore or treat rudely ⟨the snob in town always *snubbed* anyone she thought was beneath her⟩
synonyms cold-shoulder, cut, high-hat, slight, stiff, stiff-arm
related words isolate, ostracize; brush (aside *or* off), disdain, rebuff, reject, repel, repulse, scorn, spurn; disregard, forget, neglect, overlook, overpass, pass over, shrug off
2 to show contempt for ⟨a social set that *snubs* anyone below their income bracket⟩ — see SCORN 1

snuff *vb* **1** to become aware of by means of the sense organs in the nose ⟨the dog began barking as soon as she *snuffed* the scent of squirrel⟩ — see SMELL 1
2 to put to death deliberately ⟨the proprietor of the boarding house had apparently *snuffed* almost 50 old men before she was caught⟩ — see MURDER 1

snuff (out) *vb* **1** to cause to cease burning ⟨*snuff out* the candle⟩ — see EXTINGUISH 1
2 to destroy all traces of ⟨the forest fire *snuffed out* all of the animal life in the immediate area⟩ — see ANNIHILATE 1
3 to put a stop to (something) by the use of force ⟨brutally *snuffed out* the movement for democratic rule⟩ — see QUELL 1

snug *adj* **1** being clean and in good order ⟨a *snug* military cadet in dress uniform⟩ — see NEAT 1
2 providing physical comfort ⟨a *snug* cottage that's the perfect retreat for a rustic vacation⟩ — see COMFORTABLE 1
3 enjoying physical comfort ⟨while *snug* in our warm beds, we listened to the winter storm raging outside⟩ — see COMFORTABLE 2
4 firmly positioned in place and difficult to dislodge ⟨make sure that all screws and nuts in the shelving unit are *snug*⟩ — see TIGHT 2
5 providing safety ⟨yachtsmen looking for a *snug* harbor in which to anchor for the night⟩ — see SAFE 2

snug *vb* to sit or recline comfortably or cozily ⟨the farmhand *snugged* down in the hay and proceeded to go to sleep⟩ — see SNUGGLE 1

snuggle *vb* **1** to sit or recline comfortably or cozily ⟨it's particularly nice to *snuggle* next to the fire on a snowy day⟩
synonyms curl up, nestle, snug
related words burrow; couch, crouch, huddle, hunch, hunker (down), scrunch, squat, squinch
2 to lie close ⟨*snuggle* up to a friendly cat⟩ — see NUZZLE

so *adj* being in agreement with the truth or a fact or a standard ⟨I'm afraid that some of what you've said just isn't *so*⟩ — see CORRECT 1

so *adv* **1** for this or that reason ⟨it was raining, *so* we stayed inside⟩ — see THEREFORE
2 in like manner ⟨the boss works very hard, and *so* does everyone else⟩ — see ALSO 1
3 to a great degree ⟨it's *so* cold outside⟩ — see VERY 1
4 without any question ⟨you are *so* in trouble if I catch you sneaking out of the house again⟩ — see INDEED 1

soak *n* a person who makes a habit of getting drunk ⟨felt sorry for the town *soak*, who couldn't hold a job⟩ — see DRUNK 1

soak *vb* **1** to wet thoroughly with liquid ⟨we ran for home as soon as the rain started, but our clothes still ended up *soaked*⟩
synonyms drench, drown, impregnate, macerate, saturate, sodden, sop, souse, steep
related words waterlog, water-soak; marinate, seethe; presoak; dip, immerse, inundate, submerge, swamp; bathe, douse (*also* dowse), hydrate, swill, wash, water; infiltrate, penetrate, permeate; damp, dampen, humidify, moisten
near antonyms dehydrate, desiccate, dry, parch, sear; drain, empty, void; dehumidify
antonyms wring (out)
2 to charge (someone) too much for goods or services ⟨a merchant who *soaks* the tourists every summer⟩ — see OVERCHARGE 1
3 to make wet ⟨that downpour *soaked* my hair, and now I look like a sight⟩ — see WET
4 to partake excessively of alcoholic beverages ⟨depressed about his love life, he repaired to a bar to *soak*⟩ — see DRINK 2

soak (up) *vb* to take in (something liquid) through small openings ⟨this sponge should *soak up* the spilled juice very nicely⟩ — see ABSORB 1

soaked *adj* containing, covered with, or thoroughly penetrated by water ⟨a miserable, *soaked* cat who looked like a drowned rat⟩ — see WET 1

soaker *n* a person who makes a habit of getting drunk ⟨that *soaker* couldn't pass a Breathalyzer test if his life depended on it⟩ — see DRUNK 1

soaking *adj* containing, covered with, or thoroughly penetrated by water ⟨the fisherman couldn't wait to take off his *soaking* socks⟩ — see WET 1

so–and–so *n* a person whose behavior is offensive to others ⟨I'm never talking to that nasty *so-and-so* again after what he said to me last time!⟩ — see JERK 1

soap *n* a substance used for cleaning ⟨a little *soap* and water should clean this in no time⟩ — see CLEANER

soapbox *n* a place or opportunity for communicating ideas and information ⟨some readers don't appreciate that she sometimes uses her book blog as a *soapbox* for her political views⟩ — see VENUE 1

soap opera *n* something (as a work of literature or music) that is too sentimental ⟨the movie started out well, but quickly devolved into improbable *soap opera*⟩ — see CORN

soapy *adj* overly or insincerely flattering ⟨a typically *soapy* introduction for the guest speaker at the organization's annual banquet⟩ — see FULSOME 1

soar *n* the act or an instance of rising or climbing up ⟨the *soar* of the space shuttle never fails to inspire⟩ — see ASCENT 1

soar *vb* **1** to move or extend upward ⟨the Eiffel Tower *soaring* into the skies above Paris⟩ — see ASCEND
2 to move through the air with or as if with outstretched wings ⟨bats *soaring* and swooping through the night air⟩ — see FLY 1
3 to rise abruptly and rapidly ⟨gas prices *soared* overnight because of the shortage⟩ — see SKYROCKET

sob *vb* to shed tears often while making meaningless sounds as a sign of pain or distress ⟨the child *sobbed* when she found the dead frog⟩ — see CRY 1

sober *adj* **1** not having one's mind affected by alcohol ⟨it's important to stay *sober* if you're going to be driving a car⟩
synonyms clearheaded, straight
related words abstemious, abstinent, dry, teetotal, temperate; cool, level, steady
near antonyms alcoholic, bibulous, crapulous, dipsomaniacal; maudlin, tiddly [*chiefly British*]; befuddled, besotted, dopey (*also* dopy); debauched, dissipated, dissolute
antonyms blasted [*slang*], blind, blitzed [*slang*], blotto [*slang*], bombed, boozy, canned [*slang*], cockeyed, crocked, drunk, drunken, fried, gassed, hammered [*slang*], high, inebriate, inebriated, intoxicated, juiced [*slang*], lit, lit up, loaded [*slang*], looped, oiled [*slang*], pickled, pie-eyed, plastered, potted [*slang*], ripped [*slang*], sloshed [*slang*], smashed [*slang*], sottish, soused, sozzled, squiffed (*or* squiffy), stewed, stiff, stinking [*slang*], stoned, tanked [*slang*], tight, tipsy, wasted [*slang*], wiped out [*slang*]
2 based on sound reasoning or information ⟨a *sober* assessment of the situation⟩ — see GOOD 1
3 not joking or playful in mood or manner ⟨a *sober* reply to what was only a teasing comment⟩ — see SERIOUS 1
4 not excessively showy ⟨if you don't have anything in black, at least wear a *sober* outfit to the funeral⟩ — see QUIET 2
5 given to or marked by restraint in the satisfaction of one's appetites ⟨cruise passengers of *sober* dispositions will be put off by the focus on nonstop dining⟩ — see ABSTEMIOUS

soberness *n* a mental state free of jesting or trifling ⟨the unexpected *soberness* of the class clown at the memorial service was startling⟩ — see EARNESTNESS

sobersided *adj* not joking or playful in mood or manner ⟨a surprisingly *sobersided* biography of a great comedian⟩ — see SERIOUS 1

sobriety *n* **1** a mental state free of jesting or trifling ⟨an abrupt *sobriety* fell over the group when they heard the news⟩ — see EARNESTNESS
2 voluntary restraint in the satisfaction of one's appetites ⟨although she can afford to wear anything, she practices a sartorial *sobriety* that bespeaks class and taste⟩ — see ABSTINENCE 1

sobriquet *also* **soubriquet** *n* a descriptive or familiar name given instead of or in addition to the one belonging to an individual ⟨tagged her with the *sobriquet* "peanut" because of her diminutive size⟩ — see NICKNAME

sociability *n* the quality or state of being social ⟨her *sociability* was called into question when she said she hated parties⟩
synonyms conviviality, gregariousness
related words amiability, cordiality, folksiness, friendliness, neighborliness; camaraderie, companionship, fellowship; boldness, brashness, extroversion (*or* extraversion), forwardness, immodesty
near antonyms bashfulness, coyness, diffidence, shyness, timidity, timidness; introversion, reclusion; modesty, retiringness
antonyms unsociability, unsociableness

sociable *adj* **1** likely to seek or enjoy the company of others ⟨he's an intensely *sociable* child, even prone to fits of depression when he's left alone⟩ — see CONVIVIAL
2 showing a natural kindness and courtesy especially in social situations ⟨a pleasant and *sociable* hostess who puts everyone instantly at ease⟩ — see GRACIOUS 1
3 tending to group with others of the same kind ⟨the *sociable* weaverbird breeds in large umbrella-shaped nests⟩ — see COLONIAL

social *adj* **1** likely to seek or enjoy the company of others ⟨not exactly the *social* sort, our boss generally stays in his office and keeps to himself⟩ — see CONVIVIAL
2 tending to group with others of the same kind ⟨dogs are *social* animals, preferring by nature to be part of a pack⟩ — see COLONIAL

socialist *n* an adherent or advocate of an economic system in which the means of production are owned and controlled by the state ⟨a lifelong *socialist* who never lost faith in his cause⟩ — see COMMUNIST

socialize *vb* to take part in social activities ⟨he likes to *socialize* with his coworkers after work ends⟩
synonyms associate, fraternize, go out, hobnob, mingle, mix, step out
related words carouse, party, revel; circulate
phrases rub elbows (*or* rub shoulders)
near antonyms avoid, eschew, shun; slight, snub

society *n* **1** a group of persons formally joined together for some common interest ⟨a debate *society*⟩ — see ASSOCIATION 2
2 the feeling of closeness and friendship that exists between companions ⟨an evening marked by a lovely dinner and the *society* of our closest friends⟩ — see COMPANIONSHIP
3 the way people live at a particular time and place ⟨a pre-automobile *society* in which ordinary people rarely strayed far from home⟩ — see CIVILIZATION 1

[1]**sock** *n* a close-fitting covering for the foot and leg ⟨black *socks* to go with black pants and shoes⟩ — see STOCKING

[2]**sock** *n* a hard strike with a part of the body or an instrument ⟨a wiseacre who deserves a good *sock* in the face⟩ — see [1]BLOW

sock *vb* to deliver a blow to (someone or something) usually in a strong vigorous manner ⟨kept *socking* the punching bag until he was exhausted⟩ — see HIT 1

sockdolager *or* **sockdologer** *n* something very good of its kind ⟨the professor called it one *sockdolager* of a short story, but he seemed to be the only one in the room amused by this description⟩ — see JIM-DANDY

[1]**sod** *n* the land of one's birth, residence, or citizenship ⟨a sentimental journey back to the old *sod*⟩ — see COUNTRY 1

[2]**sod** *n, chiefly British* a person whose behavior is offensive to others ⟨he's a nasty old *sod* who never has a nice thing to say about anybody⟩ — see JERK 1

sodality *n* **1** a group of persons formally joined together for some common interest ⟨a 19th-century observer of American society noted that Americans had a fondness for forming *sodalities*⟩ — see ASSOCIATION 2
2 the body of people in a profession or field of activity ⟨a tragic loss of life that was felt throughout the *sodality* of firefighters⟩ — see CORPS

sodden *adj* containing, covered with, or thoroughly penetrated by water ⟨eyes peering out between strands of *sodden* hair⟩ — see WET 1

sodden *vb* **1** to make wet ⟨soldiers' boots that were *soddened* by endless hours in muddy trenches⟩ — see WET
2 to wet thoroughly with liquid ⟨cornflakes that had been *soddened* in milk to the point of mush⟩ — see SOAK 1

sofa *n* a long upholstered piece of furniture designed for several sitters ⟨I curled up on the *sofa* with a book⟩ — see COUCH

so far as *conj* to the degree that ⟨the idea works *so far as* you've thought it out, but there may be angles you haven't considered⟩ — see INASMUCH AS 1

soft *adj* **1** not loud in pitch or volume ⟨*soft* music played in the background while we ate⟩
synonyms dull, gentle, low, quiet
related words dead, silent, still; calm, dreamy, hushed, peaceful, restful, serene, soothing, stilly, tranquil; muffled, muted, softened, toned (down)
near antonyms brazen, crashing, dinning, discordant, noisy, obstreperous, raucous, rip-roaring, vociferous; grating, harsh, shrill, squealing, strident; clarion, clear, trumpetlike
antonyms blaring, blasting, booming, clamorous, clangorous, deafening, earsplitting, loud, overloud, piercing, plangent, resounding, ringing, roaring, sonorous, stentorian, thundering, thunderous
2 smooth or delicate in appearance or feel ⟨I like this sweater the best because it is so *soft* and comfortable⟩
synonyms cottony, downy, satin, satiny, silken, silklike, silky, velvetlike, velvety
related words creamy; chiffon, delicate, fine, slick; ultrasoft
near antonyms bumpy, irregular, jagged, lumpy, pebbly; broken, jagged, ragged, roughened, rugged, scraggy; grainy, granular, gritty
antonyms coarse, harsh, rough, scratchy
3 giving easily to the touch ⟨*soft* mattresses make it very easy to fall asleep, but they have a tendency to get lumpy⟩
synonyms flabby, mushy, pulpy, spongy, squashy, squishy, squooshy
related words doughy, fleshy; droopy, flaccid, floppy, lank, limp, slack, yielding; bendable, compressible, crushable, elastic, flexible, kneadable, malleable, pliable, pliant, resilient, supple, willowy, workable; airy, light
near antonyms inelastic, inflexible, rigid, stiff, tense, unbending, unyielding; resistant, sound, strong, sturdy, tough; case-hardened, crush-proof, hardened, indurated, stiffened, tempered; compacted, compressed, condensed; adamantine, rock, rocklike; sturdy, substantial
antonyms firm, hard, solid
4 involving minimal difficulty or effort ⟨looking for a *soft* job in local government⟩ — see EASY 1
5 lacking bodily strength ⟨*soft* recruits who will get toughened up in the army⟩ — see WEAK 1
6 lacking strength of will or character ⟨a *soft* person who tends to yield to stronger personalities⟩ — see WEAK 2
7 not harsh or stern especially in nature or effect ⟨a *soft* breeze coming off the lake⟩ — see GENTLE 1
8 providing physical comfort ⟨a warm, *soft* bed to rest my weary bones⟩ — see COMFORTABLE 1
9 tolerant and kind in the judgment of and expectations for others ⟨felt that his wife had been a little too *soft* on their son, and that more discipline was in order⟩ — see INDULGENT 1
10 marked by temperatures that are neither too high nor too low ⟨it was a lovely *soft* spring evening⟩ — see CLEMENT 1
11 not having or showing an ability to absorb ideas readily ⟨sometimes I wonder if you've gone *soft* in the head⟩ — see STUPID 1

soften *vb* **1** to diminish the physical strength of ⟨three weeks of being sick in bed had noticeably *softened* her⟩ — see WEAKEN 1
2 to lessen the shock of ⟨had tried to *soften* the blow of her rejection to his marriage proposal⟩ — see CUSHION

softened *adj* lacking bodily strength ⟨the athlete, *softened* by the long period of convalescence, had to begin his training program almost from scratch⟩ — see WEAK 1

softhead *n* a silly flighty person ⟨gave his son-in-law a position in the company where the *softhead* could do little harm⟩ — see FLIBBERTIGIBBET

softheaded *adj* not having or showing an ability to absorb ideas readily ⟨serious scientists who regard UFO followers as *softheaded* and gullible⟩ — see STUPID 1

softhearted *adj* having or marked by sympathy and consideration for others ⟨a *softhearted* person who never hesitates to help anyone in trouble⟩ — see HUMANE 1

softheartedness *n* **1** the capacity for feeling for another's unhappiness or misfortune ⟨the kind of *softheartedness* that makes him an easy target for anyone with a tale of woe⟩ — see HEART 1

2 sympathetic concern for the well-being of others ⟨the widow's naive *softheartedness* makes it hard for her to say "no" to charitable appeals⟩ — see BENIGNANCY

softness *n* the quality or state of lacking strength of will or character ⟨*softness* is the one quality that the public will not tolerate in a leader⟩ — see WEAKNESS 2

soft–pedal *vb* to reduce in apparent importance ⟨she politely tries to *soft-pedal* her accomplishments when talking to less fortunate people⟩
synonyms de-emphasize, downplay, play down
related words underplay, understate; bad-mouth, belittle, cry down, decry, denigrate, deprecate, depreciate, derogate, dismiss, disparage, kiss off, minimize, poormouth, put down, run down, talk down, trash, trash-talk
near antonyms exaggerate, overdo, overdraw, overstate; elaborate, embellish, embroider, magnify, pad, stretch; fudge, hedge; melodramatize, overemphasize, overplay, sensationalize

soft–soap *vb* **1** to get (someone) to do something by gentle urging, special attention, or flattery ⟨she cunningly *soft-soaped* her parents into letting her go on the trip⟩ — see COAX
2 to praise too much ⟨shrewd voters who know when a politician is trying to *soft-soap* them⟩ — see FLATTER 1

soft soap *n* excessive praise ⟨a salesman who knows the value of *soft soap* in making a sale⟩ — see FLATTERY

soft spot *n* a vulnerable point ⟨a huge trade imbalance continued to be the *soft spot* in the nation's economy⟩ — see ACHILLES' HEEL

soft touch *n* one who is easily deceived or cheated ⟨the kindly old woman was a *soft touch* for any con man with a hard-luck story⟩ — see [1]DUPE

softy *or* **softie** *n* a person lacking in physical strength ⟨a *softy* who usually needs someone else's strong hands to open bottles and jars⟩ — see WEAKLING 1

soggy *adj* containing, covered with, or thoroughly penetrated by water ⟨spread the *soggy* papers out to dry⟩ — see WET 1

[1]**soil** *n* **1** foul matter that mars the purity or cleanliness of something ⟨got some sort of *soil* on my white pants⟩ — see FILTH 1
2 solid matter discharged from an animal's alimentary canal ⟨the horse lifted its tail and deposited its *soil* on the grass⟩ — see DROPPING 1

[2]**soil** *n* **1** the loose surface material in which plants naturally grow ⟨bought rich *soil* to plant flowers in⟩ — see DIRT 1
2 the solid part of our planet's surface as distinguished from the sea and air ⟨happy to have *soil* under my feet after that long sea voyage⟩ — see EARTH 2

soil *vb* to make dirty ⟨oil and grease *soiled* the mechanic's shirt⟩ — see DIRTY

soilage *n* the state or quality of being dirty ⟨the fee for cleaning the carpet will depend upon the extent of the *soilage*⟩ — see DIRTINESS 1

soiled *adj* not clean ⟨a *soiled* carpet in need of a good shampooing⟩ — see DIRTY 1

sojourn *n* a temporary residing as another's guest ⟨spent a relaxing *sojourn* in her friend's summer home⟩ — see VISIT 1

sojourn *vb* to reside as a temporary guest ⟨began their retirement by leisurely *sojourning* with friends and relatives scattered across the country⟩ — see VISIT 2

solace *n* **1** a feeling of ease from grief or trouble ⟨the kind words brought a little *solace* to the grieving widow⟩ — see COMFORT 1
2 the giving of hope and strength in times of grief, distress, or suffering ⟨the selfless *solace* of the sick by the workers at the hospice⟩ — see CONSOLATION 1

solace *vb* **1** to ease the grief or distress of ⟨counselors did their best to *solace* the bereaved children⟩ — see COMFORT
2 to cause (someone) to pass the time agreeably occupied ⟨I *solaced* myself with a book while I waited for the bus⟩ — see AMUSE

solacing *n* the giving of hope and strength in times of grief, distress, or suffering ⟨I will be forever grateful for my friend's *solacing* of me when my mother died⟩ — see CONSOLATION 1

solar plexus *n* the part of the body between the chest and the pelvis ⟨a punch in the *solar plexus* knocked the air out of him⟩ — see STOMACH 1

soldier *n* a person engaged in military service ⟨one of the goals of war is to keep as many *soldiers* as possible from being killed⟩
synonyms dogface, fighter, legionary, legionnaire, man-at-arms, regular, serviceman, trooper, warrior
related words servicewoman; carabineer (*or* carabinier), cavalier, cavalryman, cuirassier, dragoon; doughboy, footman, foot soldier, grunt, infantryman; commando, raider; jarhead [*slang*], marine, ranger; artilleryman, cannoneer, gunner, mortarman, musketeer, rifleman; archer, crossbowman; lancer, pikeman, spearman; Confederate, Continental, Federal, GI, guardsman, militiaman, minuteman; counterguerrilla (*also* counterguerilla), guerrilla (*or* guerilla), irregular, paramilitary, partisan (*also* partizan); combatant, noncombatant; lifer, veteran, warhorse; conscript, draftee, enrollee, recruit; reservist; champion, knight; digger [*chiefly Australian & New Zealand*], gallowglass, gendarme
antonyms civilian

soldierly *adj* of, relating to, or suitable for war or a warrior ⟨Noah Webster's brief contribution to the Revolutionary cause suggests that his *soldierly* skills were few⟩ — see MARTIAL 1

sole *adj* **1** belonging only to the one person, unit, or group named ⟨the landowner has *sole* rights to the property, so he can do whatever he wants to with it⟩
synonyms exclusive, single, unshared
related words proprietary; personal, private
near antonyms common, communal, conjoint, cooperative, joint, multiple, mutual, pooled, public, shared, united
antonyms nonexclusive
2 being the one or ones of a class with no other members ⟨the eldest son became the family's *sole* support⟩ — see ONLY 2

solecism *n* a socially improper or unsuitable act or remark ⟨the *solecism* of asking one's hosts how much something in their house cost them⟩ — see IMPROPRIETY 2

solely *adv* **1** for nothing other than ⟨I fight *solely* for my country, not for money!⟩
synonyms alone, exclusively, just, only, purely, simply
related words basically, by and large, chiefly, generally, largely, mainly, mostly, predominantly, primarily, principally, substantially
near antonyms additionally, also, besides, likewise
2 without aid or support ⟨you undertook that project *solely* on your own, and you will finish it likewise⟩ — see ALONE 1

solemn *adj* **1** having or showing a formal and serious or reserved manner ⟨the director of the funeral home has a fittingly *solemn* demeanor⟩ — see DIGNIFIED
2 not joking or playful in mood or manner ⟨*solemn* as a judge⟩ — see SERIOUS 1
3 causing or marked by an atmosphere lacking in cheer ⟨the Capitol's rotunda was draped in *solemn* decorations of a state funeral⟩ — see GLOOMY 1

solemnity *n* **1** a mental state free of jesting or trifling

⟨the coronation ceremony requires absolute *solemnity*⟩ — see EARNESTNESS
2 an oft-repeated action or series of actions performed in accordance with tradition or a set of rules ⟨the *solemnities* of the Easter vigil service⟩ — see RITE
solemnness *n* a mental state free of jesting or trifling ⟨laid the wreath at the Tomb of the Unknown Soldier with all the *solemnness* that the occasion requires⟩ — see EARNESTNESS
solicit *vb* **1** to go around and approach (people) with a request for opinions or information ⟨*solicited* several opinions about which job he should accept⟩ — see CANVASS 1
2 to make a request for ⟨always ready to *solicit* donations for a charity⟩ — see ASK (FOR) 1
3 to make a request of ⟨*solicited* him to join the team⟩ — see ASK 2
4 to make a request to (someone) in an earnest or urgent manner ⟨*solicit* the President for relief funds⟩ — see BEG
5 to lead away from a usual or proper course by offering some pleasure or advantage ⟨how many men have been *solicited* into purchasing bogus aids for "male enhancement" by shameless appeals to their vanity?⟩ — see LURE
solicitation *n* an earnest request ⟨the mail is always full of *solicitations* from worthy causes⟩ — see PLEA 1
soliciting *adj* asking humbly ⟨a *soliciting* tone is better when asking for lenient treatment you don't deserve⟩ — see SUPPLIANT
solicitor *n* **1** one that tries to get a person to give in to a desire ⟨money, that great *solicitor* that has often succeeded in persuading people to sell their very souls⟩ — see TEMPTER
2 one who asks earnestly for a favor or gift ⟨even a billionaire doesn't have the wherewithal to grant the wish of every deserving *solicitor* who comes his way⟩ — see SUPPLICANT
solicitous *adj* **1** given to or made with heedful anticipation of the needs and happiness of others ⟨a most *solicitous* husband, he had already cleaned the house and cooked dinner by the time his wife returned home from work⟩ — see THOUGHTFUL 1
2 showing urgent desire or interest ⟨a family that is *solicitous* to put this whole unfortunate affair behind them and to move on with their lives⟩ — see EAGER
solicitousness *n* attention accompanied by protectiveness and responsibility ⟨the touching *solicitousness* with which he watched over his younger brother⟩ — see CARE 2
solicitude *n* **1** an uneasy state of mind usually over the possibility of an anticipated misfortune or trouble ⟨a growing *solicitude* over the possible results of the criminal investigation⟩ — see ANXIETY 1
2 attention accompanied by protectiveness and responsibility ⟨she shows much more *solicitude* toward her aging parents than any of her siblings do⟩ — see CARE 2
solid *adj* **1** based on sound reasoning or information ⟨the only *solid* conclusion that the jury could have reached⟩ — see GOOD 1
2 having a consistency that does not easily yield to pressure ⟨the ice cream is too *solid* to scoop right now⟩ — see FIRM 2
3 having or consisting of a single color ⟨both kittens are black, but one has a *solid* coat and the other has a few white patches⟩ — see MONOCHROMATIC 1
4 not showing weakness or uncertainty ⟨some people see a *solid* handshake as a sign of strong character⟩ — see FIRM 1
5 worthy of one's trust ⟨a *solid* source of information to reporters⟩ — see DEPENDABLE
solidify *vb* **1** to become physically firm or solid ⟨water *solidifying* into ice⟩ — see HARDEN 1
2 to take on a definite form ⟨my ideas on this topic are just starting to *solidify*⟩ — see FORM 1
solidity *n* worthiness as the recipient of another's trust or confidence ⟨the *solidity* of his word is such that I don't need a written contract—or anything else⟩ — see RELIABILITY
solidness *n* worthiness as the recipient of another's trust or confidence ⟨her proven *solidness* as a friend is something that I can't even begin to describe⟩ — see RELIABILITY
solipsistic *adj* overly concerned with one's own desires, needs, or interests ⟨regards today's young people as *solipsistic* slackers who have no knowledge of or interest in the world at large⟩ — see EGOCENTRIC
solitariness *n* the state of being alone or kept apart from others ⟨it was the overwhelming *solitariness* of his existence that caused the marooned sailor to go mad⟩ — see ISOLATION
solitary *adj* **1** being the one or ones of a class with no other members ⟨a *solitary* example of truth-stretching is hardly grounds for branding the man a congenital liar⟩ — see ONLY 2
2 not being in the company of others ⟨a *solitary* sailboat was the only object on the horizon⟩ — see ALONE 1
solitary *n* a person who lives away from others ⟨weary of European civilization, the painter Paul Gauguin famously abandoned France to become a *solitary* in the South Seas⟩ — see RECLUSE
solitude *n* the state of being alone or kept apart from others ⟨sought the kind of *solitude* where his thoughts would be his only companions⟩ — see ISOLATION
solo *adj* not being in the company of others ⟨a *solo* flight in a hot-air balloon⟩ — see ALONE 1
solon *n* a member of an organized body of persons having the authority to make laws ⟨one of the most politically adept *solons* in the state legislature⟩ — see LEGISLATOR
so long as *conj* at or during the time that ⟨*so long as* you're staying with us, you may not smoke indoors⟩ — see WHEN 1
soluble *adj* capable of having the reason for or cause of determined ⟨one murder case that proved to be *soluble* after all⟩ — see SOLVABLE
solution *n* something attained by mental effort and especially by computation ⟨the *solution* to a math problem⟩ — see ANSWER 2
solvable *adj* capable of having the reason for or cause of determined ⟨I'm sure that the mystery of what happened to the missing pizza is *solvable*⟩
synonyms answerable, explainable, explicable, resolvable, soluble
related words analyzable, decipherable; feasible, workable
near antonyms difficult, inextricable, knotty; impossible, insuperable; absurd, fantastic (*also* fantastical), outlandish, preposterous, ridiculous
antonyms hopeless, inexplicable, insoluble, insolvable, unexplainable, unresolvable, unsolvable
solve *vb* to find an answer for through reasoning ⟨it took me half an hour to *solve* the logic puzzle⟩
synonyms answer, break, crack, dope (out), figure out, puzzle (out), resolve, riddle (out), unravel, unriddle, work, work out
related words conclude, decide, deduce, gather, infer, judge, reason; clear (up), iron out, straighten (out), unscramble, untangle, untie; assume, conjecture, divine, guess, presume, speculate; decipher, decode
somatic *adj* of or relating to the human body ⟨a *somatic* disorder that was once thought to be "all in the patient's head"⟩ — see PHYSICAL 1
somber *or* **sombre** *adj* **1** being without light or without

much light ⟨the prison's *somber* interrogation room has the desired effect of striking fear and despair into the prisoner⟩ — see DARK 1
2 causing or marked by an atmosphere lacking in cheer ⟨the *somber* occasion of a dear friend's funeral⟩ — see GLOOMY 1

some *adj* known but not named ⟨*some* people won't be able to come⟩ — see CERTAIN 1

some *adv* close to but not exactly ⟨*some* 300 people showed up for the giveaway⟩ — see APPROXIMATELY

somebody *n* a person who is widely known and usually much talked about ⟨a small-town girl who hopes to become a *somebody* someday⟩ — see CELEBRITY 1

someday *adv* at a later time ⟨the dream that we'll get to the other planets *someday*⟩ — see YET 1

something *adv* to some degree or extent ⟨a person of *something* less than total honesty⟩ — see FAIRLY 1

something *n* one that has a real and independent existence ⟨I heard *something* fall off the counter⟩ — see ENTITY

sometime *adj* having been such at some previous time ⟨a *sometime* athlete who's gotten awfully fat⟩ — see FORMER 1

sometime *adv* at a later time ⟨we'll get around to it *sometime*⟩ — see YET 1

sometimes *adv* on some occasions ⟨*sometimes* I like to go skiing, and *sometimes* I prefer to stay inside where it's warm⟩
synonyms here and there, now, now and then, occasionally
related words intermittently, off and on, periodically, recurrently; infrequently, little, rarely, seldom; irregularly, sporadically, variously
phrases at times, ever and anon, every now and then (*or* every now and again *or* every so often), from time to time, once in a while, on occasion
near antonyms frequently, hourly, much, oft, often, oftentimes (*or* ofttimes); commonly, ordinarily, regularly, routinely, usually; always, consistently, constantly, invariably; continually, continuingly, continuously, incessantly, perpetually, unceasingly, uninterruptedly; endlessly, ever, interminably

somewhat *adv* to some degree or extent ⟨wear a jacket as it's *somewhat* chilly today⟩ — see FAIRLY 1

somewhere *adv* very close to but not completely ⟨*somewhere* around 15,000 people live in town⟩ — see ALMOST

somniferous *adj* tending to cause sleep ⟨a *somniferous* enumeration of details that I could have done without⟩ — see HYPNOTIC

somnolence *n* the quality or state of desiring or needing sleep ⟨*somnolence* is likely to be the most typical and telling reaction to this novel⟩ — see SLEEPINESS

somnolent *adj* **1** desiring or needing sleep ⟨trying to teach *somnolent* students on a very hot day⟩ — see SLEEPY 1
2 tending to cause sleep ⟨the *somnolent* hum of insects in the grass⟩ — see HYPNOTIC

song *n* **1** a short musical composition for the human voice often with instrumental accompaniment ⟨she sang a little-known *song* for the talent show⟩
synonyms ballad, ditty, jingle, lay, lyric, vocal
related words anthem, cantata, canticle, carol, chorale, hymn, noel, psalm, spiritual; dirge, lament, requiem, threnody; hallelujah, paean; aria, art song, barcarole (*or* barcarolle), blues, chanson, chant, chantey (*or* chanty *or* shanty), chorus, croon, descant (*also* discant), folk song, glee, lullaby, madrigal, motet, part-song, pop, rocker, round, roundelay, serenade, standard; drinking song, fight song; torch song; cover, medley, remix
2 a composition using rhythm and often rhyme to create a lyrical effect ⟨the *songs* of Shakespeare⟩ — see POEM
3 a rhythmic series of musical tones arranged to give a pleasing effect ⟨whistle a *song* as accompaniment to your work⟩ — see MELODY
4 a very small sum of money ⟨developers bought the land for a *song*⟩ — see MITE 1
5 writing that uses rhythm, vivid language, and often rhyme to provoke an emotional response ⟨a hero honored in *song* and story⟩ — see POETRY 1

song and dance *n* language marked by abstractions, jargon, euphemisms, and circumlocutions ⟨instead of simply denying our request, the mayor's representative gave us a *song and dance* about legal issues and municipal liability⟩ — see GIBBERISH 2

songsmith *n* a person who writes popular musical compositions for the human voice ⟨among American *songsmiths* Irving Berlin has assumed legendary status⟩ — see SONGWRITER

songster *n* one who sings ⟨one of the most popular *songsters* during the World War II era⟩ — see SINGER

songwriter *n* a person who writes popular musical compositions for the human voice ⟨he's both a singer and a *songwriter*⟩
synonyms songsmith, tunesmith
related words cocomposer, composer, melodist, musician; symphonist; arranger, orchestrator (*also* orchestrater), scorer; librettist, lyricist, lyrist

sonny *n* a male person who has not yet reached adulthood ⟨come over here, *sonny*, and help me clean up⟩ — see BOY 1

sonorous *adj* **1** marked by a high volume of sound ⟨a *sonorous* waterfall that can be heard from a considerable distance⟩ — see LOUD 1
2 marked by conspicuously full and rich sounds or tones ⟨a baritone with a particularly *sonorous* voice⟩ — see RESONANT

soon *adv* **1** at or within a short time ⟨we'll be done *soon*⟩ — see SHORTLY 2
2 by choice or preference ⟨I'd *sooner* have a cavity filled than suffer through that opera again⟩ — see RATHER 1
3 with great speed ⟨as *soon* as possible⟩ — see FAST 1

sooner or later *adv* at a later time ⟨*sooner or later*, the police are going to track down the burglar⟩ — see YET 1

sooth *n* agreement with fact or reality ⟨I doubt not the *sooth* of what you say, but there may be other facts of which we are unaware⟩ — see TRUTH

soothe *vb* **1** to ease the grief or distress of ⟨there seemed to be no words sufficient to *soothe* the bereaved parents⟩ — see COMFORT
2 to free from distress or disturbance ⟨*soothed* the baby with a bottle⟩ — see CALM 1
3 to make more bearable or less severe ⟨hot tea with honey will *soothe* a sore throat⟩ — see HELP 2

soothing *adj* **1** tending to calm the emotions and relieve stress ⟨the *soothing* music eventually put the entire yoga class in the proper mood⟩
synonyms calming, comforting, dreamy, lulling, narcotic, pacifying, quieting, relaxing, sedative, tranquilizing (*also* tranquillizing)
related words hypnotic, opiate; analgesic, anesthetic, anodyne, deadening, depressant, numbing; antianxiety, antidepressant, antidepression, antistress
near antonyms painful, stressful, tiresome, troubling, trying, unsettling, worrisome; energizing, invigorating, stimulant, stimulating; aggravating, annoying, bothersome, disturbing, exasperating, frustrating, galling, grating, harassing, irksome, irritating, maddening, nettlesome, troublesome, vexatious, vexing
2 not harsh or stern especially in nature or effect ⟨spoke to the boy in a *soothing* voice⟩ — see GENTLE 1

soothsayer *n* one who predicts future events or developments ⟨a *soothsayer* predicted that I would meet the man of my dreams online, assuming of course that I became a subscriber to the Web site's dating service⟩ — see PROPHET 1

soothsaying *n* a declaration that something will happen in the future ⟨took the *soothsayings* published in the tabloids with a grain of salt⟩ — see PREDICTION

sop *n* something given or promised in order to improperly influence a person's conduct or decision ⟨as a *sop* to the teachers' union for supporting his reelection campaign, the mayor promised to push for the abolition of the residency requirement⟩ — see BRIBE

sop *vb* **1** to wet thoroughly with liquid ⟨*sopped* the sponge with the detergent and began scrubbing the floor vigorously⟩ — see SOAK 1
2 to make wet ⟨my book fell in the swimming pool and was thoroughly *sopped* before I could fish it out⟩ — see WET
3 to sink or push (something) briefly into or as if into a liquid ⟨hesitant to *sop* his bread in gravy, no matter how delicious, at such a formal banquet⟩ — see DIP 1

sophisticate *n* a person with the outlook, experience, and manners thought to be typical of big city dwellers ⟨*sophisticates* laughing at people they thought of as hicks⟩ — see COSMOPOLITAN

sophisticate *vb* **1** to make complex or difficult ⟨there's no need to *sophisticate* something that is beautiful in its simplicity⟩ — see COMPLICATE 1
2 to alter (something) for the worse with the addition of foreign or lower-grade substances ⟨vanilla extract that has been *sophisticated* with corn syrup⟩ — see ADULTERATE

sophisticated *adj* **1** having a wide and refined knowledge of the world especially from personal experience ⟨a surprisingly *sophisticated* and widely traveled child⟩ — see WORLDLY-WISE
2 having many parts or aspects that are usually interrelated ⟨a very *sophisticated* machine that is a marvel of modern design⟩ — see COMPLEX 1
3 having or showing very polished and worldly manners ⟨a *sophisticated* gentleman, he is a welcomed guest at dinner parties all over town⟩ — see SUAVE
4 made or done with great care or with much detail ⟨a *sophisticated* plan for totally redesigning the city's complicated traffic patterns⟩ — see ELABORATE 1

sophistication *n* the state or quality of having many interrelated parts or aspects ⟨the engine's *sophistication* requires that all repairs be done by an experienced mechanic⟩ — see COMPLEXITY 1

soporific *adj* tending to cause sleep ⟨this medication is *soporific*, so do not drive after taking it⟩ — see HYPNOTIC

soppiness *n* the state or quality of having an excess of tender feelings (as of love, nostalgia, or compassion) ⟨sees Valentine's Day as just an excuse for unbridled displays of *soppiness*⟩ — see SENTIMENTALITY

sopping *adj* containing, covered with, or thoroughly penetrated by water ⟨my hair and clothes were absolutely *sopping* after the unexpected downpour⟩ — see WET 1

soppy *adj* **1** containing, covered with, or thoroughly penetrated by water ⟨trudging over *soppy* ground at the county fair⟩ — see WET 1
2 appealing to the emotions in an obvious and tiresome way ⟨scanned the racks looking for the *soppiest* valentine the store had⟩ — see CORNY 1

sorcerer *n* a person skilled in using supernatural forces ⟨a *sorcerer* who used his power for evil ends⟩ — see MAGICIAN 1

sorceress *n* a woman believed to have often harmful supernatural powers ⟨asked the *sorceress* to cast an evil spell over the village⟩ — see WITCH 1

sorcery *n* the power to control natural forces through supernatural means ⟨in olden times people suspected of *sorcery* were often put to death⟩ — see MAGIC 1

sordid *adj* **1** not clean ⟨he managed to rise above the *sordid* streets upon which he grew up⟩ — see DIRTY 1
2 not following or in accordance with standards of honor and decency ⟨a *sordid* affair involving bribery and corruption in high places⟩ — see IGNOBLE 2

sordidness *n* the state or quality of being dirty ⟨the *sordidness* of the neighborhood betrayed a general lack of self-respect⟩ — see DIRTINESS 1

sore *adj* **1** causing or feeling bodily pain ⟨my legs are *sore* after that long walk yesterday⟩ — see PAINFUL 1
2 feeling or showing anger ⟨promise not to get *sore* if I tell you what I really think of your new hairstyle?⟩ — see ANGRY
3 having or showing deep-seated resentment ⟨he's been *sore* ever since she insulted him⟩ — see BITTER 1

sore *adv* to a great degree ⟨I was *sore* afraid we'd never make it home⟩ — see VERY 1

sorely *adv* **1** with feelings of bitterness or grief ⟨our company president, who is retiring at the end of the year, will be *sorely* missed⟩ — see HARD 2
2 to a great degree ⟨completed some *sorely* needed repairs to the boat⟩ — see VERY 1

sorghum *n* something (as a work of literature or music) that is too sentimental ⟨a once-popular children's book that today's tots would likely regard as tiresome *sorghum*⟩ — see CORN

sorriness *n* deep sadness especially for the loss of someone or something loved ⟨the *sorriness* she felt upon the untimely death of her father can scarcely be described or even imagined⟩ — see SORROW

sorrow *vb* to feel deep sadness or mental pain ⟨the soldier's widow continued to *sorrow* long after her husband's last letter had turned yellow with age⟩ — see GRIEVE

sorrow *n* deep sadness especially for the loss of someone or something loved ⟨he felt great *sorrow* at the loss of his beloved dog⟩
synonyms affliction, anguish, dolefulness, dolor, grief, heartache, heartbreak, sorriness, woe
related words agony, distress, pain, suffering, torment; blue devils, blues, dejection, depression, desolateness, desolation, despair, despondence, despondency, disconsolateness, dispiritedness, distress, doldrums, downheartedness, dreariness, dumps, forlornness, gloom, gloominess, glumness, heartsickness, joylessness, melancholy, miserableness, misery, mopes, oppression, sorrowfulness, unhappiness, woefulness, wretchedness; contrition, guilt, regret, remorse, rue, self-reproach, shame; melancholia, self-pity
near antonyms gaiety (*also* gayety), gayness, humor, jollity, joviality, lightheartedness, merriment, merrymaking, mirth, mirthfulness; hopefulness, optimism, sunniness; enjoyment; content, contentedness, contentment
antonyms blessedness, bliss, blissfulness, cheer, cheerfulness, cheeriness, delight, ecstasy, elatedness, elation, euphoria, exhilaration, exuberance, exultation, felicity, gladness, gladsomeness, glee, gleefulness, happiness, joy, joyfulness, joyousness, jubilation, pleasure, rapture, rapturousness

sorrowful *adj* **1** expressing or suggesting mourning ⟨adopted a *sorrowful* tone of voice to read the news story about the former governor's death⟩ — see MOURNFUL 1
2 feeling unhappiness ⟨the cult seemed to be a *sorrowful* assemblage of emotionally scarred people seeking love and redemption⟩ — see SAD 1

sorrowfully *adv* with feelings of bitterness or grief ⟨in a *sorrowfully* worded statement she announced that she was dropping out of the race for governor⟩ — see HARD 2

sorrowfulness *n* a state or spell of low spirits ⟨with a *sorrowfulness* that can only be described as heart-wrenching, she read the elegy⟩ — see SADNESS

sorry *adj* **1** arousing or deserving of one's loathing and disgust ⟨one more *sorry* stunt like that and you'll be fired⟩ — see CONTEMPTIBLE 1

2 causing unhappiness ⟨we have *sorry* news to report tonight⟩ — see SAD 2

3 deserving pitying scorn (as for inadequacy) ⟨the ragtag circus was a *sorry* spectacle indeed⟩ — see PITIFUL 1

4 feeling sorrow for a wrong that one has done ⟨she's genuinely *sorry* for hurting his feelings⟩ — see CONTRITE

5 feeling unhappiness ⟨was *sorry* to see the family farm being sold⟩ — see SAD 1

6 expressing or suggesting mourning ⟨those *sorry* rituals that we go through when somebody dies are not for the dead but for the living⟩ — see MOURNFUL 1

7 deserving of one's pity ⟨some *sorry* wretch had the task of putting all of those files back in order⟩ — see PATHETIC 1

sort *n* **1** a number of persons or things that are grouped together because they have something in common ⟨I prefer jackets with zippers to the *sort* that close with buttons⟩

synonyms breed, class, description, feather, genre, ilk, kidney, kind, like, manner, nature, order, species, strain, stripe, type, variety

related words model; sample, specimen; bracket, bunch, category, division, family, grade, group, grouping, lot, persuasion, rank(s), set, suite

2 a member of the human race ⟨he's a decent *sort*⟩ — see HUMAN

sort *vb* **1** to come or be together as friends ⟨you should be careful about whom you *sort* with⟩ — see ASSOCIATE 1

2 to be in agreement on every point ⟨that doesn't *sort* with what you said the last time⟩ — see CHECK 1

3 to arrange or assign according to type ⟨*sorted* the mail into bills to be paid and junk to be thrown out⟩ — see CLASSIFY 1

sort (through) *vb* to look through (as a place) carefully or thoroughly in an effort to find or discover something ⟨I *sorted through* the pile of magazines until I found the article I was looking for⟩ — see SEARCH 1

sortie *n* a short trip for pleasure ⟨an occasional *sortie* to the city to rummage through some of its numerous used-book stores⟩ — see EXCURSION 1

sort of *adv* to some degree or extent ⟨you've been acting *sort of* funny all week⟩ — see FAIRLY 1

so–so *adj* of average to below average quality ⟨a *so-so* production of a great play⟩ — see MEDIOCRE 1

so–so *adv* in a satisfactory way ⟨I think I did *so-so* on the test⟩ — see WELL 1

sot *n* a person who makes a habit of getting drunk ⟨a *sot* who was arrested after a bar fight⟩ — see DRUNK 1

sottish *adj* **1** being under the influence of alcohol ⟨you could smell the whiskey on her *sottish* aunt's breath from a block away!⟩ — see DRUNK

2 given to excessive use of alcoholic beverages ⟨a comic actor who frequently played the *sottish* curmudgeon⟩ — see CRAPULOUS

sough *vb* to take in and let out a deep audible breath or to make a similar sound ⟨all night long the patient was *soughing* in her sleep⟩ — see SIGH

soul *n* **1** an immaterial force within a human being thought to give the body life, energy, and power ⟨many religions teach that the *soul* is immortal⟩

synonyms psyche, spirit

related words life, vitality; being, essence, quintessence

near antonyms body, flesh

2 a member of the human race ⟨I promise I won't tell another *soul*⟩ — see HUMAN

3 the quality or qualities that make a thing what it is ⟨a kind act that was the very *soul* of charity⟩ — see ESSENCE 1

4 the seat of one's deepest thoughts and emotions ⟨knew in her *soul* that it was true⟩ — see CORE 1

soulless *adj* having or showing a lack of sympathy or tender feelings ⟨the public's *soulless* response to the news about the latest famine overseas⟩ — see HARD 1

soul–searching *n* examination of one's own thoughts and feelings ⟨after much *soul-searching*, they both realized that their marriage was essentially over⟩ — see INTROSPECTION

[1]**sound** *vb* **1** to continue or be repeated in a series of reflected sound waves ⟨the stranded hiker's cries for help *sounded* throughout the canyon⟩ — see REVERBERATE

2 to give the impression of being ⟨the idea at least *sounds* plausible⟩ — see SEEM

3 to make known (as an idea, emotion, or opinion) ⟨a person who certainly isn't shy about *sounding* her opinions⟩ — see EXPRESS 1

4 to make known openly or publicly ⟨the grand opening of the region's newest and largest mall has been loudly *sounded* for months⟩ — see ANNOUNCE

[2]**sound** *vb* **1** to measure the depth of (as a body of water) typically with a weighted line ⟨the pilot *sounded* the river to make sure we weren't in any danger of running aground⟩

synonyms fathom, plumb

related words gauge (*also* gage), scale, span; remeasure, replumb

2 to cast oneself head first into deep water ⟨a whale suddenly surfaced and then, just as suddenly, *sounded*⟩ — see DIVE 1

[1]**sound** *n* range of hearing ⟨wandered off, out of her parents' sight and *sound*⟩ — see EARSHOT

[2]**sound** *n* a narrow body of water between two land masses ⟨Long Island *Sound* is between Long Island, New York, and Connecticut⟩ — see CHANNEL 2

sound *adj* **1** according to the rules of logic ⟨*sound* reasoning alone should tell you that the result is invalid⟩ — see LOGICAL 1

2 enjoying health and vigor ⟨the horse is getting along in years, but still perfectly *sound*⟩ — see HEALTHY 1

3 marked by the ability to withstand stress without structural damage or distortion ⟨the shed looks flimsy, but it's actually surprisingly *sound*⟩ — see STABLE 1

soundless *adj* mostly or entirely without sound ⟨crept in on *soundless* little feet⟩ — see SILENT 3

soundly *adv* to a full extent or degree ⟨we'll keep working at it until you're *soundly* satisfied with the result⟩ — see FULLY 1

soundness *n* **1** the ability to withstand force or stress without being distorted, dislodged, or damaged ⟨the car manufacturer tested the *soundness* of the new model in various types of collisions⟩ — see STABILITY 1

2 the condition of being sound in body ⟨his athletic *soundness* is open to question since he's been away from the sport for so long⟩ — see HEALTH 1

sound off *vb* **1** to voice one's opinions freely with force ⟨she never missed a chance to *sound off* about the latest "stupid" political decisions⟩ — see SPEAK UP

2 to speak so as to be heard at a distance ⟨the guard captain commanded each sentry to *sound off*⟩ — see CALL 1

soup *n* an atmospheric condition in which suspended particles in the air rob it of its transparency ⟨in *soup* like this, amateur pilots can easily become disoriented⟩ — see HAZE 1

soupçon *n* a very small amount ⟨the book is filled with cynicism and sarcasm, along with a *soupçon* of existentialist angst⟩ — see PARTICLE 1

soupy *adj* **1** filled with or dimmed by fine particles (as of dust or water) in suspension ⟨the *soupy* skies over the island make a nighttime landing a very risky business⟩ — see HAZY 1

2 having an overly soft liquid consistency ⟨*soupy* ice cream that had been left out on the counter⟩ — see RUNNY

3 appealing to the emotions in an obvious and tiresome way ⟨once starred as the virginal ingenue in a string of *soupy* operettas⟩ — see CORNY 1

sour *vb* to cause to change from friendly or loving to unfriendly or uncaring ⟨a misunderstanding that *soured* their relationship for a long time⟩ — see ESTRANGE

sour *adj* **1** causing or characterized by the one of the four basic taste sensations that is produced chiefly by acids ⟨the *sour* candy made our mouths all wrinkly inside⟩

synonyms acid, acidic, acidulous, sourish, tart, tartish, vinegary

related words dry, soured, unsweetened; pungent, sharp, tangy, zestful, zesty, zingy; astringent, puckery hyperacid

near antonyms sweet; bland, smooth; flat, flavorless, insipid, savorless, tasteless, zestless; dilute, thin, watery, weak

2 not giving pleasure to the mind or senses ⟨you'll have to face up to the *sour* truth of the matter⟩ — see UNPLEASANT

3 falling short of a standard ⟨things started off well, but now it's all gone *sour*⟩ — see BAD 1

source *n* **1** a point or place at which something is invented or provided ⟨we were uncertain as to the *source* of the rumors⟩ ⟨a *source* of inspiration⟩

synonyms cradle, font, fountain, fountainhead, origin, root, seedbed, spring, well, wellspring

related words beginning, commencement, dawn, day one, genesis, get-go (*also* git-go), inception, incipience, incipiency, kickoff, launch, morning, nascence, nascency, onset, outset, start, threshold; baseline, first base, ground zero, square one

2 the beginning part of a stream ⟨19th-century explorers who sought the *source* of the Nile⟩ — see HEADWATER

3 something mentioned in a text as providing related and especially supporting information ⟨the professor asked the students to have at least five different *sources* for their papers⟩ — see REFERENCE 1

souring *n* the loss of friendship or affection ⟨the *souring* of the business partnership led to an ugly legal battle⟩ — see ESTRANGEMENT

sourish *adj* causing or characterized by the one of the four basic taste sensations that is produced chiefly by acids ⟨real French Chablis is going to taste *sourish* to someone who's had only the jug wine marketed under that name⟩ — see SOUR 1

sourpuss *n* an irritable and complaining person ⟨that old *sourpuss* must spend all his time making sure no one traipses across his lawn⟩ — see GROUCH 1

souse *n* a person who makes a habit of getting drunk ⟨an old *souse* who lumbered home with a full bottle of gin in him every night⟩ — see DRUNK 1

souse *vb* **1** to make wet ⟨a passing car barreled through the puddle and *soused* us good⟩ — see WET

2 to sink or push (something) briefly into or as if into a liquid ⟨repeatedly *soused* the tools in the tub to get the dirt off⟩ — see DIP 1

3 to wet thoroughly with liquid ⟨firefighters *soused* the neighboring houses so that they wouldn't catch fire as well⟩ — see SOAK 1

soused *adj* **1** being under the influence of alcohol ⟨he stumbled off to bed, completely *soused* as usual⟩ — see DRUNK

2 containing, covered with, or thoroughly penetrated by water ⟨peeled off his *soused* socks and instantly felt much more comfortable⟩ — see WET 1

souvenir *n* something that serves to keep alive the memory of a person or event ⟨kept their love letters as *souvenirs* of their courtship⟩ — see MEMORIAL

sovereign *also* **sovran** *adj* **1** coming before all others in importance ⟨the *sovereign* issue for voters is the inadequate performance of the local schools⟩ — see FOREMOST 1

2 not being under the rule or control of another ⟨a *sovereign* state whose domestic policies are its own business⟩ — see FREE 1

sovereign *also* **sovran** *n* one who rules over a people with a sole, supreme, and usually hereditary authority ⟨after the current *sovereign* dies, the monarchy may be abolished⟩ — see MONARCH 1

sovereignty *also* **sovranty** *n* **1** the state of being free from the control or power of another ⟨upon leaving home she felt that she had achieved *sovereignty* for the first time in her life⟩ — see FREEDOM 1

2 a body of people composed of one or more nationalities usually with its own territory and government ⟨as parts of the same *sovereignty*, the states should not enact laws intended to harm one another economically⟩ — see NATION 1

3 controlling power or influence over others ⟨the gradual *sovereignty* of English as the language of international communcation⟩ — see SUPREMACY 1

sow *vb* **1** to cover by or as if by scattering something over or on ⟨*sow* the fields with maize in early spring, and the crop should be ready by late summer⟩ — see SCATTER 2

2 to put or set into the ground to grow ⟨first *sow* the seeds in potting soil⟩ — see PLANT 1

3 to set permanently in the consciousness or mind-set ⟨a malicious neighbor who *sowed* within him nagging suspicions about his wife⟩ — see IMPLANT 1

sozzled *adj* being under the influence of alcohol ⟨reportedly, the legendary actor John Barrymore was *sozzled* when he gave his most memorable performances⟩ — see DRUNK

spa *n* a building or room used for sports activities and exercising ⟨a six-month membership in a health *spa* with the specific purpose of losing weight⟩ — see GYM

space *n* **1** an extent or area available for or used up by some activity or thing ⟨how much *space* will you need for the art project?⟩ — see ROOM 1

2 an indefinite but usually short period of time ⟨in the *space* of a few minutes the room had filled up⟩ — see WHILE 1

3 an incomplete or deficient area ⟨the cancellation created a huge *space* in the dentist's schedule for that day⟩ — see GAP 3

4 an allowable margin of freedom or variation ⟨the children should be given some *space* to express themselves in their schoolwork⟩ — see SLACK 1

space–age *adj* being or involving the latest methods, concepts, information, or styles ⟨*space-age* technology that totally transformed the news-gathering business⟩ — see MODERN

spaced–out *adj* **1** different from the ordinary in a way that causes curiosity or suspicion ⟨that was a seriously *spaced-out* movie about an alternate reality⟩ — see ODD 2

2 *or* **spaced** suffering from mental confusion ⟨a *spaced-out* representative from customer service who knew less than we did⟩ — see DIZZY 2

3 *or* **spaced** being under the influence of a recreational drug ⟨the mindless ramblings of a *spaced-out*, over-the-hill hippie⟩ — see STONED 1

spacey *also* **spacy** *adj* suffering from mental confusion ⟨feeling a little *spacey* in the moments following the freak accident⟩ — see DIZZY 2

spacing *n* the space or amount of space between two points, lines, surfaces, or objects ⟨the *spacing* of the houses was a little tight⟩ — see DISTANCE 1

spacious *adj* more than adequate or average in capacity ⟨almost all of the guests were able to fit into the *spacious* living room⟩
synonyms ample, capacious, commodious, roomy
related words cavernous, voluminous; broad, wide; big, biggish, bulky, considerable, generous, goodly, grand, great, handsome, hefty, hulking, large, largish, outsize (*also* outsized), overscale (*or* overscaled), oversize (*or* oversized), sizable (*or* sizeable), substantial, tidy; Brobdingnagian, Bunyanesque, colossal, elephantine, enormous, gargantuan, gigantic, herculean, heroic (*also* heroical), Himalayan, huge, humongous (*also* humungous), immense, jumbo, king-size (*or* king-sized), leviathan, mammoth, massive, monolithic, monstrous, monumental, mountainous, pharaonic, prodigious, staggering, stupendous, super, titanic, tremendous; expansive, extended, extensive, vast; boundless, limitless, unbounded
near antonyms confined, cramped, incommodious, limited, narrow, restricted; small, snug, tight, tiny

spall *n* a small flat piece separated from a whole ⟨found a variety of uses for the *spalls* left over from their stonecutting operations⟩ — see CHIP 1

span *vb* to find out the size, extent, or amount of ⟨tried to *span* the distance between the two trees by eye alone⟩ — see MEASURE 1

spangle *vb* to shoot forth bursts of light ⟨in typical Las Vegas fashion, the showgirls' sequined costumes *spangled* gloriously⟩ — see FLASH 1

spank *n* a hard strike with a part of the body or an instrument ⟨delivered a quick *spank* to the child's bottom for disobedience⟩ — see [1]BLOW

spanking *adj* having much high-spirited energy and movement ⟨a *spanking* and speedy little horse⟩ — see LIVELY 1

spanking *adv* to a great degree ⟨the bathroom tiles were *spanking* white when she finished cleaning them⟩ — see VERY 1

span–new *adj* being in an original and unused or unspoiled state ⟨I love the smell of a *span-new* book⟩ — see FRESH 1

spare *adj* **1** being over what is needed ⟨I had some *spare* time to kill, so I cleaned up my cubicle a bit⟩
synonyms excess, extra, redundant, supererogatory, superfluous, supernumerary, surplus
related words accessory, additional, supplemental, supplementary; de trop, dispensable, extraneous, gratuitous, needless, nonessential, uncalled-for, unessential, unnecessary, unneeded, unwanted; abundant, ample, bountiful, copious, plenteous, plentiful
near antonyms deficient, inadequate, insufficient, meager (*or* meagre), niggardly, poor, scant, scanty, scarce, short, shortish, skimpy, sparse
2 giving or sharing as little as possible ⟨a man who is kind and gentle but definitely *spare* of speech⟩ — see STINGY 1
3 having a noticeably small amount of body fat ⟨a tall, *spare* man⟩ — see THIN 1
4 less plentiful than what is normal, necessary, or desirable ⟨*spare* vegetation that made foraging very difficult⟩ — see MEAGER

spare *n* an interchangeable part or piece of equipment that is kept on hand for replacement of an original ⟨we promptly replaced the burnt-out lightbulb with a *spare*⟩
synonyms extra, reserve
related words backup, substitute; stock; carbon copy, clone, copy, double, dummy, dupe, duplicate, replacement, replica, replication, reproduction
near antonyms archetype, original, prototype

spare *vb* **1** to use or give out in stingy amounts ⟨I'll have a banana split—and don't *spare* the whipped cream⟩
synonyms nurse, scant, skimp (on), stint (on)
related words dole out, mete (out), portion (out), ration (out); pinch, shortchange; conserve, preserve
near antonyms heap, lavish, pour, rain, shower
2 to avoid unnecessary waste or expense ⟨she had grown up during the Great Depression, so she was no stranger to *sparing*⟩ — see ECONOMIZE

sparing *adj* **1** careful in the management of money or resources ⟨a *sparing* couple who are trying to save up enough for a house⟩ — see FRUGAL
2 giving or sharing as little as possible ⟨a government agency that has always been *sparing* of public information⟩ — see STINGY 1
3 less plentiful than what is normal, necessary, or desirable ⟨unfortunately, the explanation of the health insurance plan was somewhat *sparing* on details⟩ — see MEAGER

spark *n* a very small amount ⟨not a *spark* of interest in the actress's memoirs⟩ — see PARTICLE 1

spark *vb* **1** to give off sparks ⟨the broken radio *sparked* and smoked the instant it was plugged in⟩
synonyms scintillate, sparkle
related words flash, shine, twinkle; blaze, burn, combust, flame, flare (up), glow, light (up), radiate, scintillate
2 to cause to function ⟨interesting questions that are designed to *spark* the reader's brain⟩ — see ACTIVATE
3 to rouse to strong feeling or action ⟨President Kennedy's inspirational speeches *sparked* a generation of young idealists to enter the public arena⟩ — see PROVOKE 1

sparkily *adv* in a quick and spirited manner ⟨the dancers tripped *sparkily* across the stage⟩ — see GAILY 2

sparkle *vb* **1** to give off sparks ⟨while fireworks that *sparkle* may be entertaining to look at, they can be highly dangerous when used indoors⟩ — see SPARK 1
2 to shoot forth bursts of light ⟨the crystal *sparkled* in the sunlight⟩ — see FLASH 1

sparky *adj* having much high-spirited energy and movement ⟨that *sparky* little kid tires me out just looking at him⟩ — see LIVELY 1

sparse *adj* less plentiful than what is normal, necessary, or desirable ⟨open land is *sparse* around here⟩ — see MEAGER

spartan *adj* providing only the essentials and nothing fancy or luxurious ⟨accommodations on the windjammer are *spartan* but clean and comfortable nevertheless⟩ — see NO-FRILLS

spasm *n* **1** a painful sudden tightening of a muscle ⟨he suffers terribly from back *spasms*⟩ — see [1]CRAMP
2 a sudden intense expression of strong feeling ⟨a *spasm* of love that he had never experienced before⟩ — see OUTBURST 1

spasmodic *adj* **1** lacking in steadiness or regularity of occurrence ⟨*spasmodic* problems that we will have to deal with as they crop up⟩ — see FITFUL
2 easily excited by nature ⟨a talk show host who was famed for his edgy, *spasmodic* manner⟩ — see EXCITABLE

spastic *adj* lacking in steadiness or regularity of occurrence ⟨even after the formal surrender, *spastic* violence erupted in scattered quarters of the city⟩ — see FITFUL

spat *n* an often noisy or angry expression of differing opinions ⟨like any couple, they have their *spats*⟩ — see ARGUMENT 1

spat *vb* to express different opinions about something often angrily ⟨we tend to *spat* over money more than anything else⟩ — see ARGUE 2

spate *n* **1** a great flow of water or of something that overwhelms ⟨a *spate* of words has been published on this controversial topic⟩ — see FLOOD
2 a considerable amount ⟨an off-color remark that drew a *spate* of complaints from TV viewers⟩ — see LOT 2

spatter *vb* **1** to cause (something liquid or mushy) to move along in sheets ⟨a passing car *spattered* mud on her clothes⟩ — see SPLASH 1
2 to wet or soil by striking with something liquid or mushy ⟨the dog vigorously shook himself, *spattering* the carpet and walls with water⟩ — see SPLASH 2

spatter *n* a very small amount ⟨a *spatter* of praise for her work was mixed in with quite a lot of criticism⟩ — see PARTICLE 1

spawn *n* the descendants of a person, animal, or plant ⟨sometimes I think those little brats are the *spawn* of Satan himself⟩ — see OFFSPRING

spawn *vb* to be the cause of (a situation, action, or state of mind) ⟨these artists *spawned* a whole new movement in painting⟩ — see EFFECT

spaz *n, slang* a clumsy, awkward person ⟨I haven't played tennis in years, so don't be surprised if I am a total *spaz* on the court⟩ — see KLUTZ

speak *vb* **1** to express (a thought or emotion) in words ⟨finally *spoke* her fears⟩ — see SAY 1
2 to give a formal often extended talk on a subject ⟨the Mayanists have been invited to *speak* about their latest archaeological discoveries⟩ — see TALK 1

speak (for) *vb* to make a request for ⟨she has already *spoken for* the position, so it should go to her⟩ — see ASK (FOR) 1

speak (to *or* **with)** *vb* to communicate with by means of spoken words ⟨we *spoke to* the mall's leasing agent about opening a shop⟩ — see TALK 1

speaker *n* **1** a person in charge of a meeting ⟨the *speaker* announced that it was time for the club to move on to another matter⟩ — see CHAIR 1
2 a person who speaks for another or for a group ⟨unofficially chose a *speaker* to broach the subject with the supervisor of the department⟩ — see SPOKESPERSON
3 a person who makes usually formal public speeches ⟨the after-dinner *speaker* was a career diplomat who regaled us with humorous anecdotes from his travels abroad⟩ — see ORATOR

speak out *vb* to voice one's opinions freely with force ⟨it's a free country, so anyone can *speak out*⟩ — see SPEAK UP

speak up *vb* to voice one's opinions freely with force ⟨she's never been afraid to *speak up* at town meetings⟩
synonyms pipe up, shoot, sound off, speak out, spout (off), talk up
related words bawl, bay, bellow, call, cry, holler, roar, shout, sing (out), thunder, vociferate, yell; articulate, enounce, enunciate
phrases speak one's mind
near antonyms belt up [*British*], clam up, dummy up, hush, shut up, suppress; quiet

spear *vb* to penetrate or hold (something) with a pointed object ⟨she *speared* a pea with her fork and angrily flung it⟩ — see IMPALE

spear *n* a weapon with a long straight handle and sharp head or blade ⟨the Roman gladiator thrust his *spear* triumphantly into the lion's side⟩
synonyms javelin, lance, pike, pikestaff, shaft
related words dart, spike; gaff, halberd (*also* halbert), harpoon, leister, trident

spearhead *vb* to serve as leader of ⟨unofficially at least, Martin Luther King *spearheaded* the civil rights movement⟩ — see LEAD 2

special *adj* **1** being the one or ones of a class with no other members ⟨the President claimed that international terrorism was a *special* threat that required a *special* way of dealing with it⟩ — see ONLY 2
2 granted special treatment or attention ⟨one student who was treated as *special* by the teacher⟩ — see DARLING 1
3 of a particular or exact sort ⟨you'll need *special* permission from the fire department to do that⟩ — see EXPRESS 1

special interest *n* a group of people with a common identifying interest that they seek to protect and promote ⟨promised that as governor he would never be beholden to *special interests*⟩ — see INTEREST GROUP

speciality *n* something for which a person shows a special talent ⟨my *speciality* is linguistics⟩ — see FORTE

specialized *adj* used by or intended for experts in a particular field of knowledge ⟨highly *specialized* terms that have very specific meanings in legal documents⟩ — see TECHNICAL

specially *adv* **1** in regard to something mentioned explicitly or in detail ⟨the supplementary material was *specially* intended to address earlier accusations of cultural bias⟩ — see SPECIFICALLY 1
2 to a great degree ⟨a *specially* gifted pianist⟩ — see VERY 1

specialty *n* **1** a region of activity, knowledge, or influence ⟨a doctor with a *specialty* in internal medicine⟩ — see FIELD 2
2 something for which a person shows a special talent ⟨singing operatic works is my *specialty*⟩ — see FORTE

species *n* **1** one of the units into which a whole is divided on the basis of a common characteristic ⟨a music that is now generally regarded as a distinct *species* of rap⟩ — see CLASS 2
2 a number of persons or things that are grouped together because they have something in common ⟨in the late 1960s there emerged a new *species* of actor: edgy and not conventionally handsome⟩ — see SORT 1
3 human beings in general ⟨the future of the *species* may well depend on our willingness to limit the impact of an ever-increasing population⟩ — see PEOPLE 1

specific *adj* **1** of a particular or exact sort ⟨we need a *specific* type of pen to sign the diplomas⟩ — see EXPRESS 1
2 so clearly expressed as to leave no doubt about the meaning ⟨*specific* instructions regarding the interrogation of prisoners⟩ — see EXPLICIT

specific *n* **1** a substance or preparation used to treat disease ⟨quinine is a *specific* for malaria⟩ — see MEDICINE
2 a single piece of information ⟨although the speech was long on rhetoric and platitudinous generalities, it lacked *specifics*⟩ — see FACT 3
3 something that sets apart an individual from others of the same kind ⟨the two submissions differ only in certain *specifics*⟩ — see CHARACTERISTIC

specifically *adv* **1** in regard to something mentioned explicitly or in detail ⟨*specifically*, I object to the second point⟩
synonyms especially, notably, particularly, specially
related words concretely, expressly
phrases in particular
near antonyms altogether, basically, by and large, chiefly, largely, mainly, mostly, overall, predominantly, primarily, principally, substantially
antonyms generally
2 in the specific case of one person or thing as distinguished from others ⟨the medical study is focused on

women, and *specifically* older women⟩ — see ESPECIALLY 1

specificity *n* careful thoroughness of detail ⟨the *specificity* of your description of your medical condition was a bit more than I needed⟩ — see PARTICULARITY 1

specify *vb* **1** to give the rules about (something) clearly and exactly ⟨the document *specifies* precisely how you may use the information it contains⟩ — see PRESCRIBE
2 to make reference to or speak about briefly but specifically ⟨police reports didn't *specify* the model of car the robbers were driving⟩ — see MENTION 1

specimen *n* **1** a member of the human race ⟨he's a particularly handsome *specimen*⟩ — see HUMAN
2 one of a group or collection that shows what the whole is like ⟨chose one frog as a good *specimen* of the breed⟩ — see EXAMPLE

specious *adj* tending or having power to deceive ⟨a *specious* argument that really does not stand up under close examination⟩ — see DECEPTIVE 1

speck *n* **1** a small area that is different (as in color) from the main part ⟨a lizard with *specks* of white against a green body⟩ — see SPOT 1
2 a very small amount ⟨not a *speck* of explanation to accompany the book's pictures⟩ — see PARTICLE 1
3 a very small piece ⟨a *speck* of dust was preventing the laser from reading the disc⟩ — see BIT 1

speck *vb* to mark with small spots especially unevenly ⟨dirt that had *specked* the windows of the factory for ages⟩ — see SPOT 1

specked *adj* marked with spots ⟨a *specked* hound⟩ — see SPOTTED 1

speckle *n* a small area that is different (as in color) from the main part ⟨the cat has a *speckle* of orange right at her whiskers⟩ — see SPOT 1

speckle *vb* to mark with small spots especially unevenly ⟨*speckled* the cookies with colored sugar⟩ — see SPOT 1

speckled *adj* marked with spots ⟨a *speckled* dog⟩ — see SPOTTED 1

specs *n pl* a pair of lenses set in a frame that is held in place with ear supports and which are usually worn to correct vision ⟨I wear *specs* to read⟩ — see GLASS 1

spectacle *n* **1** an elaborate, visually exciting show or event ⟨the multimedia *spectacles* that have become established parts of the opening and closing ceremonies for the Olympic Games⟩ — see EXTRAVAGANZA
2 spectacles *pl* a pair of lenses set in a frame that is held in place with ear supports and which are usually worn to correct vision ⟨bought a pair of *spectacles* with nonprescription lenses simply to look more intelligent⟩ — see GLASS 1

spectacular *n* an elaborate, visually exciting show or event ⟨the larger-than-life *spectaculars* that make Las Vegas attractive to people with little interest in gambling⟩ — see EXTRAVAGANZA

spectator *n* someone who sees or watches something ⟨a building demolition that drew a crowd of *spectators* even at 3:00 a.m.⟩
synonyms bystander, observer, onlooker, viewer, watcher
related words eyewitness, witness; peeper, spy, voyeur

specter *or* **spectre** *n* the soul of a dead person thought of especially as appearing to living people ⟨feeling so terrified that every shadow became a *specter*⟩ — see GHOST 1

spectrum *n* the distance or extent between possible extremes ⟨the complete *spectrum* of opinions on this hotly debated subject⟩ — see RANGE 3

speculate *vb* to form an opinion from little or no evidence ⟨I *speculate* that someone has been using this cabin as a trysting place⟩ — see GUESS 1

speculation *n* a risky undertaking ⟨the couple lost all their money in real estate *speculations*⟩ — see GAMBLE

speculative *adj* existing only as an assumption or speculation ⟨a *speculative* explanation of why this ancient pottery was found hundreds of miles from where it was made⟩ — see THEORETICAL 1

speech *n* **1** a usually formal discourse delivered to an audience ⟨the guest of honor gave a short *speech* in appreciation of the award⟩
synonyms address, declamation, harangue, oration, peroration, talk
related words diatribe, rant, tirade; eulogy, panegyric, tribute; keynote address (*or* keynote speech), lecture, salutatory; homily, sermon; monologue (*also* monolog), soliloquy; pitch, presentation, spiel
2 the stock of words, pronunciation, and grammar used by a people as their basic means of communication ⟨wanting to develop a writing system for his people, Sequoya created a system of 86 symbols representing all the syllables of Cherokee *speech*⟩ — see LANGUAGE 1

speechless *adj* **1** deliberately refraining from speech ⟨he remained *speechless*, even in the face of outrageous accusations⟩ — see SILENT 1
2 unable to speak ⟨if only this poor, *speechless* animal could tell us what's wrong with it⟩ — see MUTE 1

speechlessness *n* incapacity for or restraint from speaking ⟨the *speechlessness* of our cat never seemed so frustrating as the time that it was seriously sick⟩ — see SILENCE 1

speed *n* **1** a high rate of movement or performance ⟨we dashed off the remaining paperwork with as much *speed* as possible so we could leave for the long weekend⟩
synonyms celerity, fastness, fleetness, haste, hurry, quickness, rapidity, rapidness, speediness, swiftness, velocity
related words clip, gait, pace, rate, tempo; drive, hustle; acceleration, hastiness, precipitation, precipitousness, rush; alacrity, dispatch, expedition, expeditiousness, promptitude, promptness; warp speed
near antonyms languidness, languor, leisureliness, lethargy, torpidity, torpor; reluctance; deliberateness, deliberation; dilatoriness, lateness, pokiness, procrastination
antonyms slowness, sluggishness
2 a person or thing that is preferred over others ⟨that kind of old-fashioned horror movie is just my *speed*⟩ — see FAVORITE

speed *vb* to proceed or move quickly ⟨a bullet train *speeding* across the lush countryside⟩ — see HURRY 2

speed (up) *vb* to cause to move or proceed fast or faster ⟨we have to *speed up* production if we are ever going to make the deadline⟩ — see HURRY 1

speedboat *n* a boat equipped with a motor ⟨*speedboats* leaving wakes that cause damage to docked vessels and the shoreline⟩ — see MOTORBOAT

speedily *adv* with great speed ⟨he *speedily* finished the yard work and left to play ball⟩ — see FAST 1

speediness *n* a high rate of movement or performance ⟨the *speediness* with which she types is simply amazing⟩ — see SPEED 1

speedy *adj* **1** moving, proceeding, or acting with great speed ⟨a *speedy* worker but not a very careful one, unfortunately⟩ — see FAST 1
2 done, carried out, or given without delay ⟨I was surprised by and pleased with the company's *speedy* response to my complaints⟩ — see PROMPT 1

spell *vb* **1** to cast a spell on ⟨it was as if he had *spelled* the public into believing his ridiculous claims⟩ — see BEWITCH 1
2 to communicate or convey (as an idea) to the mind ⟨that summertime combination of hot temperatures and equally hot tempers can *spell* trouble⟩ — see MEAN 1

spell *n* **1** a spoken word or set of words believed to have magic power ⟨the witch cast a *spell* that turned the prince into a toad⟩
synonyms abracadabra, bewitchment, charm, conjuration, enchantment, glamour (*also* glamor), hex, incantation, invocation, whammy
related words cantrip [*chiefly Scottish*], curse, jinx; bewitchery, conjuring, magic, mojo, necromancy, sorcery, voodoo, voodooism, witchcraft, witchery, wizardry; amulet, charm, fetish (*also* fetich), phylactery, talisman
2 a sudden experiencing of a physical or mental disorder ⟨a dizzy *spell* that caused me to fall⟩ — see ATTACK 2
3 an indefinite but usually short period of time ⟨come rest a *spell*⟩ — see WHILE 1

spellbind *vb* to hold the attention of as if by a spell ⟨the tale about pirates and their buried treasure had completely *spellbound* the children⟩ — see ENTHRALL 1

spellbound *adj* being or appearing to be under a magic spell ⟨*spellbound* audiences never tire of this annual Christmas favorite⟩ — see ENCHANTED

spell out *vb* to make plain or understandable ⟨the dating applicant *spelled out* exactly what she wanted in a man⟩ — see EXPLAIN 1

spend *vb* **1** to hand over or use up in payment ⟨I always end up *spending* too much money at the mall⟩
synonyms disburse, drop, expend, fork (over, out, *or* up), give, lay out, outlay, pay, shell out
related words lavish, rain; blow, dissipate, fritter (away), run through, squander, throw away, waste
near antonyms cache, hoard, lay up, save; acquire, earn, gain, garner, make, procure, realize, secure, win
2 to make complete use of ⟨the town has already *spent* its budget for snow removal, and it's only January⟩ — see DEPLETE 1
3 to use up carelessly ⟨*spent* all his energy on impractical schemes⟩ — see WASTE 1

spender *n* someone who spends money freely or foolishly ⟨he's a *spender* and she's a tightwad, so naturally they quarrel about money a lot⟩ — see PRODIGAL

spendthrift *adj* given to spending money freely or foolishly ⟨*spendthrift* consumers had amassed a mountain of debt on their credit cards⟩ — see PRODIGAL

spendthrift *n* someone who carelessly spends money ⟨the *spendthrift* managed to blow all of his inheritance in a single year⟩ — see PRODIGAL

spendy *adj, chiefly Northwest* commanding a large price ⟨Seattle is generally credited with transforming coffee from a workaday drink to a trendy and *spendy* beverage⟩ — see COSTLY

spent *adj* depleted in strength, energy, or freshness ⟨he plopped down in his chair, completely *spent*, and then fell asleep⟩ — see WEARY 1

spew *vb* **1** to flow out in great quantities or with force ⟨water *spewing* violently from the broken pipe⟩ — see GUSH 1
2 to violently throw out or off (something from within) ⟨a volcano *spewing* out lava⟩ — see ERUPT 1
3 to discharge the contents of the stomach through the mouth ⟨"I'm going to *spew* right here in the car if you don't pull over!" she wailed to her friend⟩ — see VOMIT

sphere *n* **1** a more or less round body or mass ⟨this *sphere* that we live on is just a tiny speck in the universe⟩ — see [1]BALL 1
2 a region of activity, knowledge, or influence ⟨higher mathematics is a little outside my *sphere*⟩ — see FIELD 2
3 a ball-shaped gaseous celestial body that shines by its own light ⟨perhaps there is indeed life on planets circling *spheres* in galaxies far, far away⟩ — see STAR 1

spherical *adj* having every part of the surface the same distance from the center ⟨the planet Earth is not, in fact, perfectly *spherical*⟩ — see ROUND 1

spice *n* **1** a sweet or pleasant smell ⟨a cologne for men that captures all of the *spice* of the sea⟩ — see FRAGRANCE
2 something (as a spice or herb) that adds an agreeable or interesting taste to food ⟨Europe in Columbus's time imported rare and valuable *spices* from the Indies⟩ — see SEASONING 1
3 the quality or state of being stimulating to the mind or senses ⟨a new hobby will add *spice* to your life⟩ — see PIQUANCY

spice *vb* to make more pleasant to the taste by adding something intensely flavored ⟨*spice* the stew with more pepper⟩ — see SEASON 1

spick–and–span *or* **spic–and–span** *adj* **1** free from dirt or stain ⟨let's make the house *spick-and-span* for our visitors⟩ — see CLEAN 1
2 recently made and never used before ⟨a *spick-and-span* waffle iron that our host was obviously using for the first time⟩ — see NEW 3

spicy *adj* hinting at or intended to call to mind matters regarded as indecent ⟨a *spicy* suggestion that earned him a slap in the face⟩ — see SUGGESTIVE 1

spigot *n* a fixture for controlling the flow of a liquid ⟨the plumber has installed a new *spigot* over the kitchen sink⟩ — see FAUCET

spike *vb* **1** to penetrate or hold (something) with a pointed object ⟨scorpions use their stinger-equipped tails to *spike* their prey⟩ — see IMPALE
2 to give life, vigor, or spirit to ⟨he *spiked* what otherwise would have been a dry economic lecture with some jokes and anecdotes⟩ — see ANIMATE

spill *n* the act of going down from an upright position suddenly and involuntarily ⟨she tripped over the toy and had a nasty *spill* on the stairs⟩ — see FALL 1

spill *vb* to make known (as information previously kept secret) ⟨the actor's butler *spilled* the secret to a tabloid for $40,000⟩ — see REVEAL 1

spilth *n* discarded or useless material ⟨factories heedlessly spewing *spilth* into our waterways⟩ — see GARBAGE 1

spin *n* **1** a rapid turning about on an axis or central point ⟨the ice skater moved into a tight *spin* at the end of her routine⟩
synonyms gyration, pirouette, reel, revolution, roll, rotation, twirl, wheel, whirl
related words circuit, circulation, ring, round; coil, curl, curve, spiral, twist, whorl; circle, orbit; eddy, swirl
2 a state of mental confusion ⟨the news left me all in a *spin*⟩ — see HAZE 2
3 a short trip for pleasure ⟨a family out for a *spin* on a beautiful Sunday afternoon⟩ — see EXCURSION 1

spin *vb* **1** to move in circles around an axis or center ⟨*spinning* on its axis, the Earth makes one complete rotation every 23 hours 56 minutes 4 seconds⟩
synonyms gyrate, pinwheel, pirouette, revolve, roll, rotate, turn, twirl, wheel, whirl
related words coil, curl, curve, round, spiral, swirl, twine, twist, wind; circle, circulate, encircle, orbit, ring; pivot, swivel
2 to be in a confused state as if from being twirled around ⟨my head *spun* as I contemplated all the possible problems this restructuring could cause⟩
synonyms reel, swim, turn, whirl
related words swirl
near antonyms calm, collect; settle, steady
3 to move (something) in a curved or circular path on or as if on an axis ⟨*spun* the child around until he was hopelessly dizzy⟩ — see TURN 1

spinal column *n* a column of bones supporting the

trunk of a vertebrate animal ⟨a diagram of the *spinal column*⟩ — see SPINE

spindling *adj* being tall, thin and usually loose-jointed ⟨a sickly, *spindling* child who spent most of his time indoors⟩ — see LANKY

spindly *adj* being tall, thin and usually loose-jointed ⟨*spindly*, underfed dogs roamed the poverty-stricken village⟩ — see LANKY

spine *n* a column of bones supporting the trunk of a vertebrate animal ⟨he hurt his *spine* in the accident, but the doctor says he'll be walking again in no time⟩
synonyms backbone, chine, spinal column, vertebral column
related words back, spinal cord, vertebra

spine–chilling *adj* causing fear ⟨the soldiers let out a *spine-chilling* yell just before charging the enemy⟩ — see FEARFUL 1

spineless *adj* **1** lacking strength of will or character ⟨a *spineless* man who let his wife make all the decisions⟩ — see WEAK 2
2 having or showing a shameful lack of courage ⟨*spineless* seamen who trembled at the first roar of the cannon⟩ — see COWARDLY

spinelessness *n* **1** the quality or state of lacking strength of will or character ⟨the *spinelessness* that the grown woman has shown in dealing with her overbearing mother⟩ — see WEAKNESS 2
2 a shameful lack of courage in the face of danger ⟨charged the midshipman with sickening *spinelessness* under fire⟩ — see COWARDICE

spin–off *n* something that naturally develops or is developed from something else ⟨a *spin-off* of the popular television series⟩ — see DERIVATIVE

spiny *adj* requiring exceptional skill or caution in performance or handling ⟨this promises to be a *spiny* problem to negotiate⟩ — see TRICKY 1

spiral *vb* to follow a circular or spiral course ⟨a narrow road *spiraling* up the mountain to the summit⟩ — see WIND 1

spiral *adj* turning around an axis like the thread of a screw ⟨a *spiral* staircase takes visitors up into the Statue of Liberty⟩
synonyms coiling, corkscrew, helical, involute, screwlike, winding
related words circular; curling, curving, swirly, twisting
near antonyms lineal, linear, right, straight

spired *adj* tapering to a thin tip ⟨the *spired* mountain peaks known as the Teton Range⟩ — see POINTED 1

spirit *n* **1** an immaterial force within a human being thought to give the body life, energy, and power ⟨the theological and philosophical belief that the *spirit* is superior to the body⟩ — see SOUL 1
2 a state of mind dominated by a particular emotion ⟨had been in a combative *spirit* all week⟩ — see MOOD 1
3 the soul of a dead person thought of especially as appearing to living people ⟨Hamlet's late father appears to him in the form of a *spirit* and with the revelation that he was in fact murdered⟩ — see GHOST 1
4 spirits *pl* a distilled beverage that can make a person drunk ⟨a hotel bar that's well stocked with *spirits*⟩ — see ALCOHOL

spirited *adj* **1** marked by a lively display of strong feeling ⟨the town meeting featured a *spirited* debate about the proposed ban on skateboarding in the plaza downtown⟩
synonyms fiery, gingery, high-spirited, mettlesome, peppery, spunky
related words aggressive, ambitious, assertive, high-pressure, in-your-face, militant, pushy; animate, animated, bouncing, bouncy, brisk, energetic, feisty, frisky, jaunty, jazzy, kinetic, peppy, perky, pert, racy, scrappy, snappy, spanking, sparky, sprightly, springy, vital, vivacious, zippy; ardent, fervent, impassioned, passionate; emphatic, obtrusive
near antonyms bloodless, boring, dull, lifeless; dead, inanimate, lackadaisical, languid, languorous, limp, listless; inert, lethargic, sleepy, sluggish, tired, torpid; low-pressure, nonassertive, unaggressive, unambitious, unassertive, unenterprising
antonyms halfhearted, leaden, spiritless
2 having much high-spirited energy and movement ⟨a team known for its *spirited* and in-your-face basketball⟩ — see LIVELY 1

spiritedly *adv* in a quick and spirited manner ⟨the two spaniels ran *spiritedly* into the surf⟩ — see GAILY 2

spiritist *n* a person who claims to speak with or for the spirits of the dead ⟨a 19th-century *spiritist* whose claims of communicating with spirits through rapping sounds were eventually debunked⟩ — see CHANNELER

spiritless *adj* lacking bodily energy or motivation ⟨he was *spiritless* and depressed for weeks after being fired⟩ — see LISTLESS

spiritual *adj* **1** not composed of matter ⟨a staunch skeptic and realist, he scoffs at the very notion of ghosts and other *spiritual* entities⟩ — see IMMATERIAL 1
2 of, relating to, or used in the practice or worship services of a religion ⟨*spiritual* songs that have been sung by generations of worshippers⟩ — see RELIGIOUS 1

spiritual *n* a religious song ⟨sang a *spiritual* at the funeral⟩ — see HYMN 1

spiritualist *n* a person who claims to speak with or for the spirits of the dead ⟨the *spiritualist* claims merely to be the agency through which the spirit—or "control"—conveys its messages to the living⟩ — see CHANNELER

spirituality *n* the group ordained to perform clerical functions in the Christian church ⟨the archbishop was opposed to the marriage, and the king needed the support of the *spirituality* if his rule was to be considered legitimate⟩ — see CLERGY

spiritualty *n* the group ordained to perform clerical functions in the Christian church ⟨a long history of conflict between that nation's *spiritualty* and its temporal leaders⟩ — see CLERGY

[1]**spit** *n* an area of land that juts out into a body of water ⟨at the northeast end of the island is a long *spit* whose terminal is crowned by a towering lighthouse⟩ — see [2]CAPE

[2]**spit** *n* **1** something or someone that strongly resembles another ⟨the *spit* and image of his father⟩ — see IMAGE 1
2 the fluid that is secreted into the mouth by certain glands ⟨so dry that he felt as if he had no *spit* left in his mouth⟩ — see SALIVA

spit *vb* to penetrate or hold (something) with a pointed object ⟨according to the propaganda put out by the war ministry, enemy soldiers were *spitting* innocent babies on bayonets⟩ — see IMPALE

spite *n* the desire to cause pain for the satisfaction of doing harm ⟨spread cruel lies out of pure *spite*⟩ — see MALICE

spite *vb* to disturb the peace of mind of (someone) especially by repeated disagreeable acts ⟨sometimes, I swear, she keeps doing that just to *spite* me⟩ — see IRRITATE 1

spiteful *adj* having or showing a desire to cause someone pain or suffering for the sheer enjoyment of it ⟨the gossip would utter the most vicious things with a *spiteful* smile⟩ — see HATEFUL

spitefully *adv* in a mean or spiteful manner ⟨*spitefully* told the orphans that they'd never amount to anything⟩ — see NASTILY

spitefulness *n* the desire to cause pain for the satisfaction of doing harm ⟨cut down their neighbors' tree out of sheer *spitefulness*⟩ — see MALICE

spitting image *n* something or someone that strongly resembles another ⟨with the help of either movie magic or makeup, the actress appeared to be the *spitting image* of the queen⟩ — see IMAGE 1

spittle *n* the fluid that is secreted into the mouth by certain glands ⟨unaware that *spittle* was leaking out of his mouth while he slept⟩ — see SALIVA

spit up *vb* to discharge the contents of the stomach through the mouth ⟨the baby finished nursing and promptly *spit up*⟩ — see VOMIT

splash *n* a very small amount ⟨at least you have a *splash* of common sense—which is more than we can say for your mother⟩ — see PARTICLE 1

splash *vb* **1** to cause (something liquid or mushy) to move along in sheets ⟨rowdy teenagers *splashing* water at each other in the community pool⟩
synonyms dash, slop, slosh, spatter, swash
related words dabble, lap, plash, wash; spray, sprinkle, spritz; squirt
2 to wet or soil by striking with something liquid or mushy ⟨the bus *splashed* us as it barrelled through the puddles⟩
synonyms bespatter, dash, plash, spatter, splatter
related words drench, drown, impregnate, saturate, soak, sop, souse, steep; bathe, douse (*also* dowse), wash, water; slop, slush, spray, sprinkle, squirt
3 to flow along or against ⟨water constantly *splashing* the wooden pilings eventually weakened them⟩ — see WASH 1
4 to flow in a broken irregular stream ⟨the spilled juice *splashed* over the counter and onto the floor⟩ — see GURGLE
5 to move with a splashing motion ⟨a baby *splashing* about in the tub⟩ — see SLOSH 1

splashy *adj* **1** likely to attract attention ⟨a *splashy* new restaurant that's currently the in place to go⟩ — see NOTICEABLE
2 attractively eye-catching in style ⟨a *splashy* ad for the new brand of blue jeans⟩ — see JAZZY 1
3 excessively showy ⟨a *splashy* outfit that was definitely out of place in church⟩ — see GAUDY

splatter *vb* to wet or soil by striking with something liquid or mushy ⟨the house painters accidentally *splattered* my car with paint⟩ — see SPLASH 2

spleen *n* **1** an intense emotional state of displeasure with someone or something ⟨vented her *spleen* and felt much better for having done so⟩ — see ANGER
2 the desire to cause pain for the satisfaction of doing harm ⟨the bill's failure to pass in the legislature was due to nothing more than partisan *spleen*⟩ — see MALICE

splendid *adj* **1** large and impressive in size, grandeur, extent, or conception ⟨a *splendid* mansion in the Georgian style⟩ — see GRAND 1
2 of the very best kind ⟨the restaurant's chef can always be relied upon to prepare a *splendid* dinner⟩ — see EXCELLENT
3 giving off or reflecting much light ⟨a *splendid* diamond that must have been worth a king's ransom⟩ — see BRIGHT 1

splendidly *adv* **1** in a pleasing way ⟨the graduation party went *splendidly*⟩ — see WELL 5
2 in a manner marked by the shining or reflecting of much light ⟨the windjammer's *splendidly* white sails billowed against a deep blue sky⟩ — see BRIGHTLY 1

splendidness *n* impressiveness of beauty on a large scale ⟨the *splendidness* of the view from Mount Holyoke's summit inspired a number of 19th-century landscape painters to make the ascent⟩ — see MAGNIFICENCE

splendiferousness *n* impressiveness of beauty on a large scale ⟨the jaw-dropping *splendiferousness* of the cathedral has attracted pilgrims since the 13th century⟩ — see MAGNIFICENCE

splendor *n* **1** impressiveness of beauty on a large scale ⟨the *splendor* of the ancient monument awed us into silence⟩ — see MAGNIFICENCE
2 the quality or state of having or giving off light ⟨the *splendor* of the huge diamond can scarcely be described⟩ — see BRILLIANCE 1
3 something extraordinary or surprising ⟨some of the many *splendors* of the reign of Tutankhamen are on display in this new travelling exhibition⟩ — see WONDER 1

splenetic *adj* having or showing a habitually bad temper ⟨the newspaper publisher's *splenetic* editorials often struck fear into local politicians⟩ — see ILL-TEMPERED

splint *n* a small flat piece separated from a whole ⟨a *splint* off the board⟩ — see CHIP 1

splinter *n* a small flat piece separated from a whole ⟨she got a *splinter* from the unfinished wall⟩ — see CHIP 1

splinter *vb* to cut into long slender pieces ⟨*splintered* the carrots into little sticks⟩ — see SLIVER

split *adj* disagreeing with each other ⟨opinions are *split* on the subject⟩ — see DIVIDED

split *n* **1** an irregular usually narrow break in a surface created by pressure ⟨an earthquake left a *split* in the ground⟩ — see CRACK 1
2 the act or process of a whole separating into two or more parts or pieces ⟨the *split* of the group into two factions marked the beginning of the end of the organization⟩ — see SEPARATION 1

split *vb* to set or force apart ⟨*split* logs for the winter's supply of wood⟩ — see SEPARATE 1

split (on) *vb, British* to give information (as to the authorities) about another's improper or unlawful activities ⟨promise you won't *split on* us, and we'll tell you what happened⟩ — see SQUEAL 1

split-second *adj* done or occurring without any noticeable lapse in time ⟨a day trader who is used to making *split-second* decisions⟩ — see INSTANTANEOUS

split second *n* a very small space of time ⟨a devastating accident can cause everything in your life to change in a *split second*⟩ — see INSTANT

splitting *adj* moving, proceeding, or acting with great speed ⟨the horse took off at a *splitting* gallop⟩ — see FAST 1

splore *n, Scottish* a state of noisy, confused activity ⟨the *splore* that annually accompanies the Edinburgh Festival⟩ — see COMMOTION

splotch *n* a small area that is different (as in color) from the main part ⟨the bleach left a small white *splotch* on my shirt⟩ — see SPOT 1

splotch *vb* to mark with small spots especially unevenly ⟨ink from a leaking pen had badly *splotched* his shirt pocket⟩ — see SPOT 1

splotched *adj* having blotches of two or more colors ⟨a *splotched* tan and white puppy⟩ — see PIED

splotchy *adj* marked with spots ⟨a country road *splotchy* with patches of snow⟩ — see SPOTTED 1

spoil *n* valuables stolen or taken by force ⟨the bandits escaped with their lives but not with the *spoils*⟩ — see LOOT 1

spoil *vb* **1** to affect slightly with something morally bad or undesirable ⟨too much coddling will *spoil* the child⟩ — see TAINT 1
2 to go through decomposition ⟨the meat has *spoiled*⟩ — see DECAY 1
3 to reduce the soundness, effectiveness, or perfection of ⟨know when to stop, for an unnecessary brushstroke can *spoil* a painted portrait⟩ — see DAMAGE 1
4 to treat with great or excessive care ⟨when they were newlyweds, the wife tended to *spoil* her husband, but she soon got over that⟩ — see BABY

spoilage *n* the process by which dead organic matter

separates into simpler substances ⟨in the days before refrigeration, *spoilage* was a constant problem⟩ — see CORRUPTION 1

spoiled *adj* having undergone organic breakdown ⟨*spoiled* milk⟩ — see ROTTEN 1

spoilsport *n* a person who spoils the pleasure of others ⟨if you don't want to play, at least don't be a *spoilsport*⟩ — see KILLJOY

spoken *adj* **1** made or carried on through speaking rather than in writing ⟨a *spoken* agreement is too easily broken⟩ — see VERBAL 2
2 expressed or communicated by voice ⟨a politician who knows the power of the *spoken* word⟩ — see VOCAL

spokesman *n* a person who speaks for another or for a group ⟨a *spokesman* for the cattle industry⟩ — see SPOKESPERSON

spokesperson *n* a person who speaks for another or for a group ⟨the *spokesperson* for the protesting students presented their demands to the administration⟩
synonyms mouth, mouthpiece, point man, point person, prophet, speaker, spokesman
related words spokesmodel, spokeswoman; front, promoter, shill; communicator, sayer, talker; agent, ambassador, delegate, emissary, envoy, representative

sponge *n* a person who is supported by or seeks support from another without making an adequate return ⟨finally told the *sponge* to move out of their house and to get a job⟩ — see LEECH

sponge *vb* **1** to take in (something liquid) through small openings ⟨the ground quickly *sponged* up the much-needed rain⟩ — see ABSORB 1
2 to live by relying on someone else's generosity or hospitality without sharing in the cost or responsibility ⟨she's been *sponging* off of her friends while she tries to land an entry-level job on Wall Street⟩ — see FREELOAD

sponger *n* a person who is supported by or seeks support from another without making an adequate return ⟨a spoiled *sponger* who, after college, moved back in with her parents and seems to be in no hurry to get a job⟩ — see LEECH

spongy *adj* **1** giving easily to the touch ⟨*spongy* moss covered the ground⟩ — see SOFT 3
2 able to soak up liquids especially readily ⟨generously pour the brandy over the cake, which is so *spongy* that it will absorb most of the liquid⟩ — see ABSORBENT

sponsor *n* a person who takes the responsibility for some other person or thing ⟨you'll need a *sponsor* to recommend you in order to get into the exclusive country club⟩
synonyms backer, guarantor, patron, surety
related words chaperone (*or* chaperon); advocate, champion, supporter; angel, benefactor, underwriter; coach, mentor, teacher; cosponsor; cosignatory, cosigner

sponsorship *n* the financial support and general guidance for an undertaking ⟨a youth softball league under the *sponsorship* of local businesses⟩ — see AUSPICE 1

spontaneity *n* carefree freedom from constraint ⟨the couple sacrificed some of the *spontaneity* in their lives when they had a baby⟩ — see ABANDON

spontaneous *adj* done instantly and without conscious thought or decision ⟨hugging a crying child is simply a *spontaneous* reaction⟩ — see AUTOMATIC 1

spontaneousness *n* carefree freedom from constraint ⟨her friends loved her for her natural *spontaneousness*⟩ — see ABANDON

spoof *n* a work that imitates and exaggerates another work for comic effect ⟨many viewers thought that the *spoof* of a television newscast was the real thing⟩ — see PARODY 1

spoof *vb* **1** to copy or exaggerate (someone or something) in order to make fun of ⟨*spoofed* overly competitive parents in a mockumentary about tryouts for a national T-ball team⟩ — see MIMIC 1
2 to cause to believe what is untrue ⟨the newspaper was *spoofed* by a supposedly plausible claim of a UFO encounter⟩ — see DECEIVE

spook *n* **1** a person who tries secretly to obtain information for one country in the territory of another usually unfriendly country ⟨Russia recalled its *spooks* after the collapse of the Soviet Union⟩ — see SPY
2 the soul of a dead person thought of especially as appearing to living people ⟨Halloween is the night when *spooks* and goblins are said to roam abroad⟩ — see GHOST 1

spook *vb* to strike with fear ⟨the sudden noise *spooked* her out of her skin⟩ — see FRIGHTEN

spooked *adj* filled with fear or dread ⟨Ichabod Crane was so *spooked* that he left Sleepy Hollow for good⟩ — see AFRAID

spookish *adj* fearfully and mysteriously strange or fantastic ⟨the *spookish* interior of a Victorian mansion that had seen better days⟩ — see EERIE

spooky *adj* **1** easily excited by nature ⟨a *spooky* horse shying at shadows⟩ — see EXCITABLE
2 fearfully and mysteriously strange or fantastic ⟨a *spooky* tale of strange hauntings and mysterious reincarnations⟩ — see EERIE

spoon *vb* to lift out with something that holds liquid ⟨lovingly *spooned* the homemade stew out of the pot⟩ — see DIP 2

spoon *n* a utensil with a bowl and a handle that is used especially in cooking and serving food ⟨an assortment of metal and wooden *spoons* should be part of every cook's culinary arsenal⟩
synonyms dipper, ladle, scoop
related words skimmer; dessertspoon, soupspoon, tablespoon, teaspoon

spoony *or* **spooney** *adj* appealing to the emotions in an obvious and tiresome way ⟨the *spoony* verses of a lovesick soldier to his girl back home⟩ — see CORNY 1

sporadic *adj* **1** lacking in steadiness or regularity of occurrence ⟨*sporadic* loud noises kept startling everyone⟩ — see FITFUL
2 not often occurring or repeated ⟨so long as the complaints remain *sporadic*, we're doing fine⟩ — see INFREQUENT

sport *n* **1** activity engaged in to amuse oneself ⟨I don't care terribly whether I actually catch any fish, as I'm just doing this for *sport*⟩ — see PLAY 1
2 an attitude or manner not to be taken seriously ⟨teasing that began in *sport* ended with some hateful words being exchanged⟩ — see FUN 2
3 the making of unkind jokes as a way of showing one's scorn for someone or something ⟨several of the kids routinely made *sport* of their classmate's speech impediment⟩ — see RIDICULE
4 a person or thing that is made fun of ⟨in a society where unmarried women had no status, a spinster was often the long-suffering *sport* of the village⟩ — see LAUGHINGSTOCK

sport *vb* **1** to engage in activity for amusement ⟨from sailing to snorkeling, each day we *sported* at a different activity offered by the beach resort⟩ — see PLAY 1
2 to play and run about happily ⟨the millionaire's grandchildren *sporting* on the estate's spacious grounds⟩ — see FROLIC 1
3 to present so as to invite notice or attention ⟨*sported* his flashy new car by driving it all over town⟩ — see SHOW 1

sportful *adj* given to good-natured joking or teasing ⟨a *sportful* brother who loved teasing his little sister⟩ — see PLAYFUL

sportfulness *n* a natural disposition for playful behavior ⟨I find my business partner's *sportfulness* charming, but I worry that it might lead clients to view him as unprofessional⟩ — see PLAYFULNESS

sporting house *n* a building in which prostitutes are available ⟨had a long career as a madam in a New Orleans *sporting house*⟩ — see BORDELLO

sportive *adj* given to good-natured joking or teasing ⟨a *sportive* pastor who began every sermon with a joke⟩ — see PLAYFUL

sportiveness *n* a natural disposition for playful behavior ⟨her high-spirited *sportiveness* can sometimes distract her and others from serious work⟩ — see PLAYFULNESS

sportsmanlike *adj* following or according to the rules ⟨admired by the fans for his *sportsmanlike* conduct on the ice⟩ — see FAIR 3

sportsmanly *adj* following or according to the rules ⟨in wrestling, biting is not *sportsmanly*, and will result in a forfeit⟩ — see FAIR 3

spot *n* **1** a small area that is different (as in color) from the main part ⟨in summer the white coat of the snow leopard is studded with brownish black *spots*⟩
synonyms blotch, dapple, dot, eyespot, fleck, mottle, patch, pip, point, speck, speckle, splotch
related words birthmark, freckle, mole; blob, blot, mark, smear, smudge, smutch, stain; spatter, splash; polka dot
2 a difficult, puzzling, or embarrassing situation from which there is no easy escape ⟨we're in a bit of a *spot* right now with our mortgage payments⟩ — see PREDICAMENT
3 a mark of guilt or disgrace ⟨scandalous conduct that will forever be a *spot* upon the family name⟩ — see STAIN 1
4 a very small amount ⟨had only a *spot* of stew for dinner, as he wasn't very hungry⟩ — see PARTICLE 1
5 the area or space occupied by or intended for something ⟨the cat grabbed my *spot* on the couch the minute I stood up⟩ — see PLACE 1

spot *vb* **1** to mark with small spots especially unevenly ⟨to give the effect of sunlight on water, the artist *spotted* the lake in his painting with flecks of gold paint⟩
synonyms blotch, dapple, dot, fleck, freckle, marble, mottle, pepper, shoot, speck, speckle, splotch, sprinkle, stipple
related words blot, dye, stain; band, bar, streak, stripe; intersperse, set, stud; bespatter, spatter
2 to make note of (something) through the use of one's eyes ⟨I *spotted* both of them as they tried to sneak out the back door⟩ — see SEE 1
3 to cover by or as if by scattering something over or on ⟨the TV networks had *spotted* reporters all over the state for the election⟩ — see SCATTER 2

spotless *adj* free from dirt or stain ⟨a *spotless* white dress⟩ — see CLEAN 1

spotlight *n* the center of public attention ⟨reality show contestants who become addicted to the *spotlight*⟩ — see CENTER STAGE

spot–on *adj* **1** being in agreement with the truth or a fact or a standard ⟨for an inside mount for window blinds, your measurements had better be *spot-on*⟩ — see CORRECT 1
2 meeting the highest standard of accuracy ⟨a *spot-on* prediction of the movie's gross on its opening weekend⟩ — see PRECISE 1

spotted *adj* **1** marked with spots ⟨the *spotted* tablecloth clashed with the stripes on the wallpaper⟩
synonyms dappled (*also* dapple), dotted, flecked, freckled, mottled, specked, speckled, splotchy, spotty, stippled, variegated
related words spangled; marbled, moiré (*or* moire), veined; chromatic, colored, colorful, motley, multicolored, multihued, polychromatic, polychrome, prismatic, rainbow, varicolored, variegated; blotched, blotchy, piebald, pinto, roan
near antonyms solid
antonyms unspotted
2 having blotches of two or more colors ⟨not surprisingly, the white cow and black bull had a *spotted* calf⟩ — see PIED

spotting *n* the act or process of sighting or learning the existence of something for the first time ⟨the *spotting* of a new bird is always a thrill for an avid bird-watcher⟩ — see DISCOVERY 1

spotty *adj* **1** lacking in steadiness or regularity of occurrence ⟨only *spotty* business failures marred the economic boom⟩ — see FITFUL
2 marked with spots ⟨Dalmatians are *spotty* dogs⟩ — see SPOTTED 1

spouse *n* the person to whom another is married ⟨employees and their *spouses* are covered by the health plan⟩
synonyms better half, consort, mate, partner, significant other
related words soul mate; domestic partner; bridegroom, groom, hubby, husband, man, mister, old man; bride, helpmate, helpmeet, lady, wife
near antonyms ex; single; bachelor; bachelorette, maid, maiden, spinster

spout *n* **1** a pipe or channel for carrying off water from a roof ⟨during the winter, runoff from the *spout* tends to freeze over and form a dangerous patch of ice on the walkway⟩ — see GUTTER 1
2 a usually forceful stream of fluid discharged from a narrow opening ⟨kids cooling off under the *spout* of water from an opened fire hydrant⟩ — see JET

spout *vb* **1** to flow out in great quantities or with force ⟨water *spouting* from the hose⟩ — see GUSH 1
2 to talk loudly and wildly ⟨a self-important loudmouth who is always *spouting* about the mess that politicians have made of everything⟩ — see RANT
3 to violently throw out or off (something from within) ⟨the drain suddenly *spouted* water and debris⟩ — see ERUPT 1

spout (off) *vb* to voice one's opinions freely with force ⟨got in trouble for *spouting off* in class in a disrespectful way⟩ — see SPEAK UP

sprat *n* a young person who is between infancy and adulthood ⟨planning to spend their vacation at a couples-only resort where they would not be bothered by snotty-nosed *sprats*⟩ — see CHILD 1

spray *vb* to cover by or as if by scattering something over or on ⟨*sprayed* the lawn with pesticides⟩ — see SCATTER 2

spread *n* **1** a decorative cloth used as a top covering for a bed ⟨bought a brightly colored *spread* for summer⟩ — see COUNTERPANE
2 a large fancy meal often accompanied by ceremony or entertainment ⟨they really know how to put out a good *spread*⟩ — see FEAST 1
3 a wide space or area ⟨a vast *spread* of land just waiting to be settled⟩ — see EXPANSE
4 the distance or extent between possible extremes ⟨the *spread* of grades was from 15 to 79 on that quiz⟩ — see RANGE 3
5 the space or amount of space between two points, lines, surfaces, or objects ⟨a *spread* of nearly 100 miles between farms⟩ — see DISTANCE 1

spread *vb* **1** to cause to be known over a considerable area or by many people ⟨*spread* the news!⟩

synonyms broadcast, circulate, disseminate, propagate
related words radiate, sprawl; diffuse, dispense, disperse, dissipate, scatter, sow; communicate, convey, impart, pass (on), transmit
near antonyms cloak, conceal, enshroud, hide, hold (in), mask, obscure, secrete, shroud, veil; contain, limit, restrict
2 to put a layer of on a surface ⟨we *spread* the fertilizer over the lawn evenly until it was fully covered⟩
synonyms apply, lay, lay on
related words anoint, bedaub, besmear, dab, daub, plaster, slather, smear; blanket, carpet, coat, cover, layer, mantle, overlay, overlie, overspread, sheet, surface
near antonyms bare, expose, peel, strip, uncover
3 to become known ⟨once news of the war's end had *spread*, spontaneous celebrations broke out everywhere⟩ — see GET OUT 1
4 to cause (something) to pass from one to another ⟨living conditions that help to *spread* chicken pox⟩ — see COMMUNICATE 1
5 to go or move in different directions from a central point ⟨the walls of the old barn *spread* under the weight of the snow on the roof⟩ — see SEPARATE 2
6 to become greater in size, extent, volume, amount, or number ⟨dissatisfaction with the new administration is *spreading* rapidly⟩ — see INCREASE 2
spread (out) *vb* to arrange the parts of (something) over a wider area ⟨let's *spread* the puzzle *out* on the floor and see what we've got⟩ — see OPEN 3
spreading *adj* exciting a similar feeling or reaction in others ⟨*spreading* enthusiasm that got our club rolling again⟩ — see CONTAGIOUS 2
spree *n* **1** a time or instance of carefree fun ⟨went on a spending *spree*⟩ — see FLING 1
2 a bout of prolonged or excessive drinking ⟨after a lifetime of self-destructive *sprees*, the poet Dylan Thomas died at last of an alcoholic overdose⟩ — see CAROUSE
sprightliness *n* the quality or state of having abundant or intense activity ⟨the *sprightliness* of the young girl made us tired just watching her⟩ — see VITALITY 1
sprightly *adj* having much high-spirited energy and movement ⟨a *sprightly* child who often claims to be too tired to move when it's time to do chores⟩ — see LIVELY 1
sprightly *adv* in a quick and spirited manner ⟨every morning the elderly couple *sprightly* sets out on a walk⟩ — see GAILY 2
spring *n* **1** an act of leaping into the air ⟨the deer gave a sudden *spring* and disappeared into the woods⟩ — see JUMP 1
2 a point or place at which something is invented or provided ⟨the *springs* of this time-honored tradition run too deep to allow for easy explanation⟩ — see SOURCE 1
spring *vb* **1** to come into existence ⟨when it comes to love and romance, hope *springs* eternally⟩ — see BEGIN 2
2 to propel oneself upward or forward into the air ⟨the cat *sprang* and pounced on the mouse⟩ — see JUMP 1
3 to set free (as from slavery or confinement) ⟨had to spend a night in jail until their lawyer could come to *spring* them⟩ — see FREE 1
spring (for) *vb* to give what is owed for ⟨offered to *spring for* dinner for the whole gang⟩ — see PAY 2
spring (up) *vb* to come to one's attention especially gradually or unexpectedly ⟨a new issue *sprang up* at yesterday's meeting of the school board⟩ — see ARISE 2
springtime *n* **1** a state or time of great activity, thriving, or achievement ⟨a *springtime* of entrepreneurship in the old Soviet bloc after the fall of the Iron Curtain⟩ — see BLOOM 1
2 the state or time of being a child ⟨a man in the winter of his life reminiscing about his *springtime* and wondering where all the years went⟩ — see CHILDHOOD
springy *adj* **1** able to revert to original size and shape after being stretched, squeezed, or twisted ⟨pillows made with *springy* foam that bounces right back⟩ — see ELASTIC 1
2 having much high-spirited energy and movement ⟨walks with a *springy* step⟩ — see LIVELY 1
sprinkle *n* **1** a light or fine rain ⟨decided it was not worth carrying an umbrella for just a *sprinkle*⟩ — see DRIZZLE
2 a small number ⟨received only a *sprinkle* of suggestions for the name of the school mascot⟩ — see FEW
sprinkle *vb* **1** to cover by or as if by scattering something over or on ⟨*sprinkle* the newly seeded lawn with water⟩ — see SCATTER 2
2 to mark with small spots especially unevenly ⟨*sprinkled* the cake with bits of coconut⟩ — see SPOT 1
sprinkling *n* **1** a small number ⟨a *sprinkling* of fans showed up at the airport⟩ — see FEW
2 a very small amount ⟨just a *sprinkling* of experience with the computer program⟩ — see PARTICLE 1
sprint *vb* to go at a pace faster than a walk ⟨he *sprinted* off to class so as to avoid being late⟩ — see RUN 1
sprite *n* **1** an imaginary being usually having a small human form and magical powers ⟨the child insisted that he'd seen a *sprite* hiding in the garden⟩ — see FAIRY
2 the soul of a dead person thought of especially as appearing to living people ⟨told hair-raising stories of *sprites* and spectral ships⟩ — see GHOST 1
sprout *n* **1** a young person who is between infancy and adulthood ⟨he earned the admiration of the neighborhood *sprouts* when he showed them how to make a slingshot⟩ — see CHILD 1
2 a branch of a main stem especially of a plant ⟨the raspberry bushes began sending out *sprouts* in early spring⟩ — see OFFSHOOT 1
spruce *adj* being strikingly neat and trim in style or appearance ⟨a slim, *spruce* man in a tailor-made business suit⟩ — see SMART 1
spruce (up) *vb* to make neat ⟨hurriedly *sprucing up* the hotel dining room before the breakfast crowd began showing up⟩ — see NEATEN
sprucely *adv* in a strikingly neat and trim manner ⟨*sprucely* dressed, I set out for my first job interview⟩ — see SMARTLY
spry *adj* moving easily ⟨an older woman who's still surprisingly *spry*⟩ — see GRACEFUL 1
spryness *n* ease and grace in physical activity ⟨has the *spryness* and flexibility of a professional athlete⟩ — see DEXTERITY 2
spume *n* a light mass of fine bubbles formed in or on a liquid ⟨*spume* floating on the ocean⟩ — see FOAM
spunk *n* the strength of mind that enables a person to endure pain or hardship ⟨had the *spunk* to overcome a severe physical disability⟩ — see FORTITUDE
spunky *adj* marked by a lively display of strong feeling ⟨a *spunky* determination to make the best of a bad situation⟩ — see SPIRITED 1
spur *n* **1** something that arouses action or activity ⟨the threat of losing its only sports franchise was the *spur* the city council needed to finally do something about the rising crime rate⟩ — see IMPULSE 1
2 a structure that holds up or serves as a foundation for something else ⟨a weak wall that might need a *spur*⟩ — see SUPPORT 1
spur *vb* to urge or push forward with or as if with a pointed object ⟨gently *spurred* the horse with his heels⟩ — see PROD 1
spurious *adj* **1** being such in appearance only and made or manufactured with the intention of committing

fraud ⟨a *spurious* Picasso painting that wouldn't have fooled an art expert for a second⟩ — see COUNTERFEIT 1

2 lacking in natural or spontaneous quality ⟨claimed that the governor's election-year enthusiasm for conservation was *spurious*, since he had cut funding for state parks⟩ — see ARTIFICIAL 1

3 born to a father and mother who are not married ⟨the *spurious* son of Charles II, the Duke of Monmouth would later mount a rebellion in a disastrous attempt to claim the throne⟩ — see ILLEGITIMATE 1

spuriousness *n* the state or fact of being born out of wedlock ⟨the *spuriousness* of her birth had always bothered her⟩ — see ILLEGITIMACY

spurn *vb* to show unwillingness to accept, do, engage in, or agree to ⟨fiercely independent, the elderly couple *spurned* all offers of financial help⟩ — see DECLINE 1

spur–of–the–moment *adj* made or done without previous thought or preparation ⟨a *spur-of-the-moment* trip to the zoo⟩ — see EXTEMPORANEOUS

spurt *n* **1** a sudden and usually temporary growth of activity ⟨a *spurt* of economic growth for the first quarter of the year⟩ — see OUTBREAK 1

2 a usually forceful stream of fluid discharged from a narrow opening ⟨a sudden *spurt* of blood rushed out from the opened wound⟩ — see JET

spurt *vb* **1** to flow out in great quantities or with force ⟨water *spurted* from the garden hose just as I was checking the nozzle⟩ — see GUSH 1

2 to throw out or off (something from within) often violently ⟨the pipe suddenly cracked and began *spurting* water⟩ — see ERUPT 1

sputter *vb* to speak rapidly, inarticulately, and usually unintelligibly ⟨she was so shocked that, for a moment, all she could do was *sputter*⟩ — see BABBLE 1

spy *vb* to make note of (something) through the use of one's eyes ⟨I *spy* a motel off in the distance, so let's spend the night there⟩ — see SEE 1

spy *n* a person who tries secretly to obtain information for one country in the territory of another usually unfriendly country ⟨the government *spy* risked his life every day in the fight against global terrorism⟩

synonyms agent, asset, emissary, intelligencer, mole, operative, spook, undercover

related words courier; counterspy, double agent, sleeper; infiltrator, informer, stool pigeon; spymaster, superspy

phrases secret agent, undercover agent

spying *n* the secret gathering of information on others ⟨traditionally, anyone caught engaging in *spying* during wartime was shot or hanged⟩ — see ESPIONAGE

squab *n* a long upholstered piece of furniture designed for several sitters ⟨at one point Robinson Crusoe tells of making a rough-hewn *squab* with the skins of animals he had killed⟩ — see COUCH

squabble *n* an often noisy or angry expression of differing opinions ⟨frightened by noise of the *squabble*, the cat hid under the couch⟩ — see ARGUMENT 1

squabble *vb* to express different opinions about something often angrily ⟨the children *squabbled* loudly over who got to play with the toy first⟩ — see ARGUE 2

squabbler *n* a person who takes part in a dispute ⟨the neighbors can be *squabblers* sometimes, but they're really no worse than most couples⟩ — see DISPUTANT

squad *n* a group of people working together on a task ⟨the cleaning *squad* usually arrives after regular business hours⟩ — see GANG 1

squalidness *n* the state or quality of being dirty ⟨the *squalidness* of the laborers' shack made my stomach turn⟩ — see DIRTINESS 1

squall *n* **1** a disturbance of the atmosphere accompanied by wind and often by precipitation (as rain or snow) ⟨a snow *squall* is expected tonight⟩ — see STORM 1

2 a state of noisy, confused activity ⟨the annual *squall* created when the store holds its biggest sale of the year⟩ — see COMMOTION

squall *vb* to cry out loudly and emotionally ⟨the baby *squalled* in pain⟩ — see SCREAM 1

squally *adj* **1** marked by wet and windy conditions ⟨be careful driving in this *squally* weather⟩ — see FOUL 1

2 marked by strong wind or more wind than usual ⟨this coastal region often experiences wet, *squally* weather⟩ — see [1]WINDY 1

squamous *adj* composed of or covered with scales ⟨a *squamous* plant bulb⟩ — see SCALY

squander *vb* **1** to use up carelessly ⟨*squandered* all her money gambling in casinos⟩ — see WASTE 1

2 to cause (members of a group) to move widely apart ⟨a single blast of the shotgun *squandered* the herd of deer⟩ — see SCATTER 1

squanderer *n* someone who spends money freely or foolishly ⟨the elderly woman refused to leave any money to the family's most notorious *squanderer*⟩ — see PRODIGAL

squandering *adj* given to spending money freely or foolishly ⟨the nightclub's ridiculous prices seem geared to *squandering* revelers with more money than sense⟩ — see PRODIGAL

square *adj* **1** having four equal sides and four right angles ⟨a *square* room⟩

synonyms foursquare, quadrate

related words blockish, blocky, boxlike, boxy, cubic, cubical, cuboid; squarish; rectangular

2 marked by justice, honesty, and freedom from bias ⟨received a *square* hearing from the disciplinary panel⟩ — see FAIR 2

square *vb* **1** to be in agreement on every point ⟨that explanation *squares* entirely with the evidence that we've seen⟩ — see CHECK 1

2 to influence someone with a bribe ⟨tried to *square* the police officer into ignoring the illegal operation⟩ — see BRIBE

squarely *adv* as stated or indicated without the slightest difference ⟨a line that is *squarely* in the middle⟩ — see EXACTLY 1

squash *vb* **1** to cause to become a pulpy mass ⟨the sort of person who couldn't even *squash* a bug⟩ — see CRUSH 1

2 to put a stop to (something) by the use of force ⟨*squashed* any effort to reform the country's power structure⟩ — see QUELL 1

squashy *adj* giving easily to the touch ⟨a bed covered in big *squashy* pillows⟩ — see SOFT 3

squat *adj* being compact and broad in build and often short in stature ⟨a short, *squat* woman⟩ — see STOCKY

squat *vb* to lie low with the limbs close to the body ⟨a detective *squatting* to examine something on the ground⟩ — see CROUCH

squat *n, slang* the smallest amount or part imaginable ⟨he doesn't do *squat* all day long and is by far the laziest worker in the company⟩ — see JOT

squatty *adj* being compact and broad in build and often short in stature ⟨a *squatty* little wrestler⟩ — see STOCKY

squawk *n* an expression of dissatisfaction, pain, or resentment ⟨if we don't receive any *squawks*, we can assume the change was acceptable⟩ — see COMPLAINT 1

squawk *vb* to express dissatisfaction, pain, or resentment usually tiresomely ⟨she *squawked* on for hours about how salespeople were always rude to her⟩ — see COMPLAIN

squawking *adj* engaging in or marked by loud and insistent cries especially of protest ⟨the PTA meeting was filled with *squawking* parents, voicing their dislike of the new vice-principal⟩ — see VOCIFEROUS

squeak *vb* to give information (as to the authorities) about another's improper or unlawful activities ⟨one of the robbers eventually *squeaked* about the others⟩ — see SQUEAL 1

squeaking *adj* having a high musical pitch or range ⟨a baby bird making little *squeaking* cries⟩ — see SHRILL

squeaky *adj* having a high musical pitch or range ⟨a child with a *squeaky* voice⟩ — see SHRILL

squeaky–clean *adj* free from dirt or stain ⟨feeling *squeaky-clean* and smelling nice after her bath⟩ — see CLEAN 1

squeal *vb* **1** to give information (as to the authorities) about another's improper or unlawful activities ⟨that stool pigeon *squealed* to the police about the whole smuggling operation⟩
synonyms fink, grass (on) [*British slang*], inform, rat (on), sing, snitch, split (on) [*British*], squeak, talk, tell (on)
related words betray, give away, turn in; backstab, cross, double-cross, sell (out), two-time; blab, tattle; tip (off)
phrases drop a dime (on)
2 to cry out loudly and emotionally ⟨the child *squealed* with frustration⟩ — see SCREAM 1
3 to express dissatisfaction, pain, or resentment usually tiresomely ⟨hoped that a DVD player in the backseat would keep the kids from *squealing* about long car rides⟩ — see COMPLAIN

squealer *n* a person who provides information about another's wrongdoing ⟨after finding out who told on them, the hoodlums proceeded to give the *squealer* the beating of his life⟩ — see INFORMER

squeamish *adj* affected with nausea ⟨the rolling of the ship made her *squeamish*⟩ — see NAUSEOUS 1

squeamishness *n* **1** a disturbed condition of the stomach in which one feels like vomiting ⟨an ever-rising *squeamishness* suddenly overwhelmed her, and she ran for the bathroom⟩ — see NAUSEA 1
2 the tendency to be or state of being squeamish ⟨his general *squeamishness* makes him a terrible choice as a lab partner for a dissection⟩ — see DELICACY 3

squeeze *vb* **1** to apply external pressure on so as to force out the juice or contents of ⟨kept *squeezing* the bottle until the ketchup squirted all over the table⟩ — see [2]PRESS 2
2 to fit (people or things) into a tight space ⟨I think we can *squeeze* a bit more into the washing machine⟩ — see CROWD 1
3 to get with great difficulty ⟨managed to *squeeze* a living by cleaning houses⟩ — see EKE (OUT)
4 to reduce in size or volume by or as if by pressing parts or members together ⟨*squeezed* the blanket until it fit into the box⟩ — see COMPRESS 1
5 to rob by the use of trickery or threats ⟨the mob *squeezes* all the local merchants by threatening violence⟩ — see FLEECE
6 to force one's way ⟨I was able to *squeeze* through the people clustered around the luggage carousel⟩ — see [2]PRESS 4

squeeze *n* **1** the act or process of reducing the size or volume of something by or as if by pressing ⟨he gave the plastic bag a *squeeze* and then folded it up for storage⟩ — see COMPRESSION
2 *slang* a person with whom one is in love ⟨she and her main *squeeze* are spending Valentine's Day at a romantic country inn⟩ — see SWEETHEART 1

squeeze off *vb* to cause (a projectile) to be driven forward with force ⟨the hunter waited for the deer to start feeding, then *squeezed off* several rounds⟩ — see SHOOT 1

squeezing *n* the act or process of reducing the size or volume of something by or as if by pressing ⟨the tight *squeezing* of his hands on hers made her face turn red⟩ — see COMPRESSION

squelch *vb* **1** to put a stop to (something) by the use of force ⟨immediately *squelched* any signs of rebellion⟩ — see QUELL 1
2 to stop the noise or speech of ⟨his irritated glare *squelched* any other potential objectors⟩ — see SILENCE

squiffed *or* **squiffy** *adj* being under the influence of alcohol ⟨the Scotsman was *squiffed* when he passed out by the roadside⟩ — see DRUNK

squiggle *vb* **1** to make jerky or restless movements ⟨a pediatrician's waiting room full of *squiggling* toddlers⟩ — see FIDGET
2 to write or draw hastily or carelessly ⟨there are some illegible notes *squiggled* in the margins of the old book⟩ — see SCRIBBLE 1

squinch *vb* **1** to lie low with the limbs close to the body ⟨*squinched* down to fit under the table⟩ — see CROUCH
2 to twist (something) out of a natural or normal shape or condition ⟨*squinched* up her eyes in disgust⟩ — see CONTORT
3 to draw back in fear, pain, or disgust ⟨didn't *squinch* a bit when the intruder pulled a knife on him⟩ — see FLINCH

squinching *n* the twisting of something out of its natural or normal shape or condition ⟨warned him that the constant *squinching* of his face would someday leave him with a permanently deformed look⟩ — see CONTORTION

squire *vb* to go along with in order to provide assistance, protection, or companionship ⟨her father *squired* her to the dance to make sure she got there all right⟩ — see ACCOMPANY 1

squirm *vb* to make jerky or restless movements ⟨the toddler *squirmed* the whole time we were in the waiting room⟩ — see FIDGET

squirmy *adj* making jerky or restless movements ⟨a *squirmy* baby⟩ — see FIDGETY

squirrel (away) *vb* to put (something of future use or value) in a safe or secret place ⟨*squirreled* the information *away* for future reference⟩ — see HOARD

squirt *vb* to flow out in great quantities or with force ⟨water *squirting* out of the faucet⟩ — see GUSH 1

squirt *n* **1** a usually forceful stream of fluid discharged from a narrow opening ⟨added a *squirt* of lemon juice to the baked haddock⟩ — see JET
2 a young person who is between infancy and adulthood ⟨I am fond of the little *squirt*, I'll admit⟩ — see CHILD 1

squishy *adj* **1** giving easily to the touch ⟨a *squishy* beanbag chair⟩ — see SOFT 3
2 not precisely correct ⟨those are awfully *squishy* estimates for the final cost of a new football stadium⟩ — see INEXACT 1

squooshy *adj* giving easily to the touch ⟨a toddler clutching a *squooshy* teddy bear⟩ — see SOFT 3

stab *n* **1** a mark or small hole made by a pointed instrument ⟨the injection left a small *stab* on her upper arm⟩ — see PRICK 1
2 an effort to do or accomplish something ⟨everybody will get a *stab* at solving the problem⟩ — see ATTEMPT 1

stab *vb* to penetrate or hold (something) with a pointed object ⟨*stabbed* the pesky leaf with the tines of the rake⟩ — see IMPALE

stability *n* **1** the ability to withstand force or stress without being distorted, dislodged, or damaged ⟨the bridge was designed with such great *stability* that it supposedly will not collapse even under the harshest weather conditions⟩
synonyms firmness, soundness, strength, sturdiness

related words dependability, durability, reliability; solidity, solidness; cohesion, toughness
near antonyms insubstantiality, unsoundness, unsubstantiality; weakness
antonyms insecurity, instability, precariousness, shakiness, unstableness, unsteadiness
2 the state of continuing without change <the *stability* of the regime is in jeopardy> — see CONSTANCY 1

stable *adj* **1** marked by the ability to withstand stress without structural damage or distortion <the observation tower is *stable* enough to withstand the strongest winds without collapsing>
synonyms bombproof, fast, firm, sound, stalwart, strong, sturdy
related words dependable, durable, reliable; infrangible, irrefragable, unbreakable; beefy, solid; cohesive, tough
near antonyms infirm, insecure, weak; shaky, tottering, tottery, unbalanced, wobbly (*also* wabbly); unsubstantial
antonyms rickety, unsound, unstable, unsteady
2 having been established and usually not subject to change <a troubled nation badly in need of a *stable* government> — see FIXED 1
3 having full use of one's mind and control over one's actions <she made some strange decisions back when she wasn't entirely *stable*> — see SANE
4 not undergoing a change in condition <a *stable* economic climate is best for business> — see CONSTANT 1

stack *n* **1** a considerable amount <earned a *stack* of money for writing the screenplay> — see LOT 2
2 a quantity of things thrown or stacked on one another <a *stack* of playing cards> — see [1]PILE 1

stack *vb* to lay or throw on top of one another <*stacked* the split logs by the house> — see PILE 1

stack (up) *vb* to gradually form into a layer, pile, or mass <those newspapers have been *stacking up* in the basement since we moved here> — see COLLECT 2

stack up (against *or* with) *vb* to come near or nearer to in character or quality <how does the new car *stack up against* your old one?> — see APPROXIMATE

stadium *n* a large usually roofless building for sporting events with tiers of seats for spectators <the football game will be held at the new *stadium*, which seats 100,000 people>
synonyms bowl, circus, coliseum, colosseum
related words ballpark, park; gym, gymnasium, spa; arena, dome, hippodrome

staff *n* **1** a body of persons at work or available for work <we're working with a short *staff* at the office today> — see FORCE 1
2 a heavy rigid stick used as a weapon or for punishment <carried a *staff* for self-defense when walking alone at night> — see CLUB 1

stag *adj* depicting or referring to sexual matters in a way that is unacceptable in polite society <a stash of *stag* flicks that were hidden in the basement> — see OBSCENE 1

stage *n* **1** a level usually raised surface <spoke to the audience from a small *stage* in front> — see PLATFORM 1
2 a portion of a trip <this is only the first *stage* of the journey> — see LEG 2
3 an individual part of a process, series, or ranking <in the last *stage* of the project> — see DEGREE 1
4 the public performance of plays <drawn to the *stage* as a career> — see DRAMA 1

stage *vb* to bring before the public in performance or exhibition <*staged* the full body of Shakespeare's plays in the course of a year> — see PRESENT 1

stage director *n* a person who supervises the production of a stage show <the *stage director* spent most of the rehearsal working with the actors to block out the scene> — see REGISSEUR

stager *n* a person with long experience in a specified area <an old *stager* who resented the young upstarts in the brokerage firm> — see VETERAN

stagger *vb* **1** to move forward while swaying from side to side <I was so tired last night that I just *staggered* upstairs to bed without eating dinner>
synonyms careen, dodder, lurch, reel, teeter, totter, waddle
related words rock, roll, seesaw, swag, sway, waver, weave, wobble (*also* wabble); barge, blunder, clomp, clump, flounder, galumph, lumber, lump, pound, scuff, scuffle, shamble, shuffle, stamp, stomp, stumble, tramp, tromp
2 to show uncertainty about the right course of action <a daunting problem that would make even the most decisive person *stagger* just a bit> — see HESITATE

staggering *adj* causing wonder or astonishment <the *staggering* scope of the new construction on campus> — see MARVELOUS 1

staggeringly *adv* to a large extent or degree <a *staggeringly* inappropriate comment to make at a funeral> — see GREATLY 2

stagy *or* **stagey** *adj* **1** given to or marked by attention-getting behavior suggestive of stage acting <a motivational speaker whose *stagy* presentations motivate some listeners to head for the nearest exit> — see THEATRICAL 1
2 having the general quality or effect of a stage performance <the president's and the prime minister's public display of mutual admiration was a little too *stagy* to be convincing> — see DRAMATIC 1

staid *adj* **1** not joking or playful in mood or manner <everyone was surprised by the racy joke from the usually *staid* professor> — see SERIOUS 1
2 having or showing a formal and serious or reserved manner <*staid* colors that would be good for business attire> — see DIGNIFIED

staidness *n* a mental state free of jesting or trifling <the *staidness* of the Quaker meeting was surprising to those accustomed to more exuberant services> — see EARNESTNESS

stain *vb* **1** to affect slightly with something morally bad or undesirable <her poor choice of companions *stained* her reputation somewhat> — see TAINT 1
2 to give color or a different color to <*stained* the table to look like cherry> — see COLOR 1
3 to make dirty <oil *stained* his work pants> — see DIRTY

stain *n* **1** a mark of guilt or disgrace <the *stain* of this cowardly act would haunt him for the rest of his career>
synonyms blot, brand, onus, slur, smirch, smudge, spot, stigma, taint
related words black eye, discredit, disesteem, disgrace, dishonor, disrepute, guilt, ignominy, infamy, obloquy, odium, opprobrium, reproach, shame; corruption, debauchery, depravity, immorality, iniquity, licentiousness, sin, unscrupulousness, vice
near antonyms award, credit, honor; chasteness, chastity, modesty, purity, stainlessness; good, right; honesty, integrity, legitimacy, probity, rectitude, scrupulousness, uprightness; goodness, righteousness, virtuousness; fame, glory, renown, repute
2 a substance used to color other materials <applied several coats of *stain* to the wood> — see PIGMENT

stained *adj* not clean <always seen wearing *stained* clothes, which he apparently hoped would mark him as an antibourgeois bohemian> — see DIRTY 1

stainless *adj* free from dirt or stain <nothing less than a

perfectly *stainless* sheet of parchment would do for a diploma⟩ — see CLEAN 1

stake *n* **1** a legal right to participation in the advantages, profits, and responsibility of something ⟨if I invest in your business, I expect a *stake* in it in return⟩ — see INTEREST 1

2 the money or thing risked on the outcome of an uncertain event ⟨lost his entire *stake* with a single roll of the dice⟩ — see BET 1

stake *vb* **1** to provide money for ⟨the actor *staked* the entire production of the film with his own money⟩ — see FINANCE 1

2 to risk (something) on the outcome of an uncertain event ⟨I'd *stake* a year's salary that she'll win the general election⟩ — see BET

stale *adj* **1** used or heard so often as to be dull ⟨viewers were bored by the *stale* story lines of the new crop of sitcoms⟩

synonyms banal, cliché (*also* cliche), clichéd, cobwebby, commonplace, hack, hackney, hackneyed, moth-eaten, musty, obligatory, shopworn, stereotyped, threadbare, timeworn, tired, trite, well-worn

related words twice-told; bromidic, platitudinal, platitudinous; canned, cardboard, conventional, cookie-cutter, derivative, imitative, ready-made, tried-and-true, unimaginative, uninspired, unoriginal; normal, ordinary, rote, routine, standard, stock, typical, usual; arid, barren, boring, colorless, drab, dreary, drudging, dry, dull, dusty, flat, heavy, ho-hum, humdrum, jading, jejune, leaden, mind-numbing, monotonous, numbing, old, pedantic, pedestrian, ponderous, prosaic, stodgy, stuffy, tame, tedious, tiresome, tiring, undramatic, uninteresting, vapid, wearisome, weary, wearying; old-fashioned, old hat

near antonyms animating, energizing, enlivening, exciting, galvanizing, invigorating, stimulating; absorbing, engaging, engrossing, gripping, interesting, intriguing, involving, riveting; atypical, extraordinary, strange, unaccustomed, uncommon, unfamiliar, unheard-of, unknown, unprecedented, unusual; pathbreaking, pioneering, trailblazing

antonyms fresh, new, novel, original, unclichéd, unhackneyed

2 causing weariness, restlessness, or lack of interest ⟨the sequel is basically a *stale* remake of the first movie⟩ — see BORING

stalemate *n* **1** a point in a struggle where neither side is capable of winning or willing to give in ⟨a new negotiator finally got both sides past the *stalemate*⟩ — see IMPASSE 1

2 a situation in which neither participant in a contest, competition, or struggle comes out ahead of the other ⟨after playing chess for 16 hours, we ended the game in a *stalemate*⟩ — see TIE 1

stalk *vb* **1** to seek out (game) for food or sport ⟨lions *stalking* gazelles on the plains⟩ — see HUNT 1

2 to walk with exaggerated arm and leg movements ⟨the irate customer *stalked* off in a huff⟩ — see STRUT 1

stall *vb* **1** to bring (something) to a standstill ⟨endless complaints *stalled* the process of selecting the winning design for the memorial⟩ — see [1]HALT 1

2 to stop functioning ⟨the engine *stalls* sometimes when it's very cold outside⟩ — see FAIL 1

stalwart *adj* **1** feeling or displaying no fear by temperament ⟨the *stalwart* soldiers in the army of Alexander the Great, who willingly followed him to the ends of the known world⟩ — see BRAVE 1

2 having muscles capable of exerting great physical force ⟨a *stalwart* yet lithe athlete⟩ — see STRONG 1

3 marked by the ability to withstand stress without structural damage or distortion ⟨the *stalwart* walls of the castle⟩ — see STABLE 1

stalwartly *adv* in a fearless manner ⟨Rachel Carson *stalwartly* championed the cause of environmentalism long before it was popular⟩ — see BRAVELY 1

stamp *n* **1** a perceptible trace left by pressure ⟨a *stamp* left in the mud by some prehistoric beast⟩ — see PRINT 1

2 something that sets apart an individual from others of the same kind ⟨virtually without exception Van Gogh's portraits bear the *stamp* of genius⟩ — see CHARACTERISTIC

stamp *vb* **1** to move heavily or clumsily ⟨*stamping* around in oversized boots⟩ — see LUMBER 1

2 to tread on heavily so as to crush or injure ⟨*stamped* the grass down in a circle⟩ — see TRAMPLE

stamp (out) *vb* to destroy all traces of ⟨working to *stamp out* racism in this country⟩ — see ANNIHILATE 1

stamping ground *n* a place for spending time or for socializing ⟨if she isn't at home, you can usually find her at the local library, her favorite *stamping ground*⟩ — see HANGOUT

stance *n* a general way of holding the body ⟨a slightly aggressive *stance*⟩ — see POSTURE 1

stanchion *n* an upright shaft that supports an overhead structure ⟨the *stanchion* of an arch⟩ — see PILLAR 1

stand *n* a level usually raised surface ⟨marchers passed by the reviewing *stand*⟩ — see PLATFORM 1

stand *vb* **1** to occupy a place or location ⟨the monument *stands* in the middle of the town plaza⟩

synonyms be, bear, lie, sit

related words command, overlook; hang around, remain, rest, stay, stick around, tarry; await, wait; post, station; dwell, reside

2 to put up with (something painful or difficult) ⟨I don't know how you can *stand* that job⟩ — see BEAR 2

3 to give what is owed for ⟨I'll *stand* lunch, and you can pay me back later⟩ — see PAY 2

4 to take or have a certain position within a group arranged in vertical classes ⟨if the city's baseball team wins today, they will *stand* first in the league⟩ — see RANK 1

standard *adj* **1** being of the type that is encountered in the normal course of events ⟨a *standard* bandage is all that that wound needs⟩ — see ORDINARY 1

2 having or showing the qualities associated with the members of a particular group or kind ⟨he's pretty much your *standard* high-school jock⟩ — see TYPICAL 1

3 accepted, used, or practiced by most people ⟨*standard* procedure⟩ — see CURRENT 1

standard *n* **1** something set up as an example against which others of the same type are compared ⟨the animation in that movie set the *standard* against which all later animated cartoons were judged⟩

synonyms bar, barometer, benchmark, criterion, gold standard, grade, mark, measure, metric, par, touchstone, yardstick

related words case, example, instance; average, norm, rule; acme, apex, meridian, peak, pinnacle, summit, zenith

near antonyms aberration, abnormality, deviation

2 a piece of cloth with a special design that is used as an emblem or for signaling ⟨a ship flying the queen's *standard*⟩ — see FLAG 1

3 what is typical of a group, class, or series ⟨somewhat shorter than the *standard* for boys that age⟩ — see AVERAGE

4 standards *pl* the code of good conduct for an individual or group ⟨a life guided by high *standards*⟩ — see ETHICS

standard–issue *adj* being of the type that is encountered in the normal course of events ⟨another *standard-issue* thriller with a man on the run desperately trying to find the baddie who framed him for murder⟩ — see ORDINARY 1

standardize *vb* to make agree with a single established standard or model ⟨the plan is to *standardize* the test for reading comprehension so that we can see how students across the state compare⟩
synonyms formalize, homogenize, normalize, regularize
related words codify, marshal (*also* marshall), methodize, order, organize, systematize, systemize; average, equalize, even; square; accredit, certify; control, govern, regulate, rule; conciliate, conform, coordinate, harmonize, integrate, reconcile, synthesize
near antonyms customize, individualize, tailor

standby *n* something or someone to which one looks for support ⟨our old *standby* in times of trouble⟩ — see DEPENDENCE 2

stand by *vb* to give steadfast support to ⟨no matter how much people object, I will *stand by* my decision⟩ — see ADHERE (TO) 1

stand–in *n* a person or thing that takes the place of another ⟨hired him at the last minute as a *stand-in* for the person who quit⟩ — see SUBSTITUTE

stand in *vb* to serve as a replacement usually for a time only ⟨she will be *standing in* for the regular teacher for a week⟩ — see COVER 1

standing *adj* **1** fixed in a place or position ⟨bought the house and all *standing* appliances and fixtures⟩ — see STATIONARY 1
2 rising straight up ⟨all *standing* timbers are in sound condition⟩ — see ERECT

standing *n* **1** high position within society ⟨a man of *standing* in his community⟩ — see RANK 2
2 the period during which something exists, lasts, or is in progress ⟨a tradition of long *standing*⟩ — see DURATION 1
3 the placement of someone or something in relation to others in a vertical arrangement ⟨my *standing* in the class at the time of graduation⟩ — see RANK 1

standoff *n* **1** a situation in which neither participant in a contest, competition, or struggle comes out ahead of the other ⟨after two hours they had played to a 5–5 *standoff*⟩ — see TIE 1
2 a point in a struggle where neither side is capable of winning or willing to give in ⟨the *standoff* continued for three days before the fugitive gave himself up to the authorities⟩ — see IMPASSE 1

standoff *adj* having or showing a lack of friendliness or interest in others ⟨the client's *standoff* attitude suggested that this was going to be a strictly business relationship⟩ — see COOL 1

standoffish *adj* having or showing a lack of friendliness or interest in others ⟨she proved to be simply shy, not *standoffish*⟩ — see COOL 1

standout *n* **1** a person who is widely known and usually much talked about ⟨several *standouts* from showbiz were at the gala⟩ — see CELEBRITY 1
2 something very good of its kind ⟨his debut novel was a *standout* in an otherwise lackluster year⟩ — see JIM-DANDY

stand out *vb* to extend outward beyond a usual point ⟨the relief figures *stand out* from the wall quite strikingly⟩ — see BULGE 1

standpat *adj* tending to favor established ideas, conditions, or institutions ⟨the *standpat* chefs were having none of this low-calorie stuff that the food police were pushing⟩ — see CONSERVATIVE 1

standpoint *n* a way of looking at or thinking about something ⟨I never thought about it from that *standpoint* before⟩ — see PERSPECTIVE 1

standstill *n* a point in a struggle where neither side is capable of winning or willing to give in ⟨battled each other to a *standstill*⟩ — see IMPASSE 1

stand–up *adj* **1** following the accepted rules of moral conduct ⟨a real *stand-up* guy, he's willing to raise the child—by himself if necessary⟩ — see HONORABLE 1
2 rising straight up ⟨a puppy with *stand-up* ears⟩ — see ERECT

stand up *vb* to withstand scrutiny and gain acceptance or approval ⟨a hypothesis that won't *stand up* to close analysis⟩ — see WASH 2

stank *n, British dialect* a small often deep body of water ⟨the Scottish innkeeper advised swimming in the nearby *stank* only if the prospect of hypothermia seemed appealing⟩ — see [1]POOL

staple *n* the main or greater part of something as distinguished from its subordinate parts ⟨reading is the very *staple* of a person's education⟩ — see BODY 1

star *adj* **1** of or relating to the stars ⟨*star* observations⟩ — see STELLAR 1
2 standing above others in rank, importance, or achievement ⟨the teacher's *star* pupil⟩ — see EMINENT
3 widely known ⟨looking for *star* actors to play the leads⟩ — see FAMOUS 1

star *n* **1** a ball-shaped gaseous celestial body that shines by its own light ⟨it's difficult to see the *stars* at night in the middle of the city because of all the streetlights⟩
synonyms luminary, sphere, sun
related words cluster, constellation, galaxy; binary star, brown dwarf, dwarf, fixed star, gasser, giant star, lodestar (*also* loadstar), neutron star, nova, pulsar, quasar, red dwarf, red giant, red star, subdwarf, supercluster, supergiant, supernova, variable, variable star, white dwarf
2 the person who has the most important role in a play, movie, or TV show ⟨when the *star* of the school play came down with the flu on opening night, her understudy got to go on⟩
synonyms headliner, lead, principal
related words leading lady, leading man; superstar; ingenue (*or* ingénue), starlet; star turn [*chiefly British*]; co-principal, costar
near antonyms extra, supernumerary
3 a person who is widely known and usually much talked about ⟨the public's endless fascination with *stars*⟩ — see CELEBRITY 1

starch *n* active strength of body or mind ⟨a middle-aged woman who has retained the *starch* of youth⟩ — see VIGOR 1

starchy *adj* marked by or showing careful attention to set forms and details ⟨a *starchy* and demanding teacher⟩ — see CEREMONIOUS 1

star–crossed *adj* having, prone to, or marked by bad luck ⟨Romeo and Juliet are among literature's most famous *star-crossed* lovers⟩ — see UNLUCKY 1

stare *vb* to look long and hard in wonder or surprise ⟨her friends *stared* in disbelief upon seeing her walking arm in arm with her ex-husband⟩ — see GAPE

stare *n* a fixed intent look ⟨caught the child's wide-eyed *stare* on film⟩ — see GAZE

stark *adj* **1** harsh and threatening in manner or appearance ⟨*stark* and forbidding mountains that the settlers knew that they would have to cross⟩ — see GRIM 1
2 having no exceptions or restrictions ⟨the school's *stark* prohibition against obscene slogans on clothing⟩ — see ABSOLUTE 2
3 lacking contents that could or should be present ⟨house buyers trying to imagine what those *stark* rooms would look like when filled with furniture⟩ — see EMPTY 1
4 producing inferior or only a small amount of vegetation ⟨a once-lush landscape rendered depressingly *stark* by strip-mining and deforestation⟩ — see BARREN 1
5 providing only the essentials and nothing fancy or

luxurious ⟨monks who have committed themselves to living in *stark* cells and working and praying in silence⟩ — see NO-FRILLS

starkers *adj, chiefly British* lacking or shed of clothing ⟨room service in one London hotel informs its employees to get used to the idea of walking in on guests who are *starkers*⟩ — see NAKED 1

starry *adj* **1** of or relating to the stars ⟨the *starry* light of the firmament on a clear night⟩ — see STELLAR 1
2 having or marked by a tendency to be guided more by ideals than by reality ⟨had the *starry* idea the Western military forces would waltz in there and put an end to rivalries that have been raging for hundreds of years⟩ — see IDEALISTIC

starry–eyed *adj* having or marked by a tendency to be guided more by ideals than by reality ⟨the *starry-eyed* notion that international sports competitions actually help foster global harmony⟩ — see IDEALISTIC

start *n* the point at which something begins ⟨knew from the *start* of the game that he would win easily⟩ — see BEGINNING

start *vb* **1** to move suddenly and sharply (as in surprise) ⟨I *started* from my chair when I heard the sudden scream⟩
synonyms bolt, jump, startle
related words jerk, jolt, twitch; blench, cringe, flinch, quail, recoil, shrink, spook, squinch, wince; bound, leap, spring; react, respond
2 to be responsible for the creation and early operation or use of ⟨*started* the impressionist movement in art⟩ — see FOUND
3 to cause to function ⟨trying to *start* the car on a frigid morning⟩ — see ACTIVATE
4 to come into existence ⟨the fight *started* when one child tripped the other⟩ — see BEGIN 2
5 to extend outward beyond a usual point ⟨frightened horses with *starting* eyes⟩ — see BULGE 1
6 to take the first step in (a process or course of action) ⟨we'll be ready to *start* the concert in a moment⟩ — see BEGIN 1

startle *vb* **1** to make a strong impression on (someone) with something unexpected ⟨the lightning *startled* the children and sent them scurrying for cover⟩ — see SURPRISE 1
2 to move suddenly and sharply (as in surprise) ⟨the cat *startled* when the door slammed shut with a bang⟩ — see START 1
3 to strike with fear ⟨loud noises always *startle* her⟩ — see FRIGHTEN

startlement *n* the state of being strongly impressed by something unexpected or unusual ⟨the look of *startlement* in her eyes when she found herself at the wedding seated next to her ex-boyfriend⟩ — see SURPRISE 2

startling *adj* causing a strong emotional reaction because of unexpectedness ⟨the *startling* news that my sister will be having a baby⟩ — see SURPRISING 1

starved *adj* feeling a desire or need for food ⟨after that long soccer practice, the children were really *starved*⟩ — see HUNGRY 1

starving *adj* feeling a desire or need for food ⟨I missed lunch, and now I'm *starving*⟩ — see HUNGRY 1

stash *n* a supply stored up and often hidden away ⟨keeps a *stash* of tissues in her desk in case anyone needs one⟩ — see HOARD 1

stash *vb* to put (something of future use or value) in a safe or secret place ⟨*stashed* the extra antifreeze in the trunk of the car⟩ — see HOARD

stashing *n* the placing of something out of sight ⟨the *stashing* of the title to the house in a strongbox that wasn't fireproof was foolish⟩ — see CONCEALMENT 1

stasis *n* a condition in which opposing forces are equal to one another ⟨for the time being, the populations of the national park's predators and prey remain in *stasis*⟩ — see BALANCE 1

state *n* **1** a body of people composed of one or more nationalities usually with its own territory and government ⟨the British monarch is the head of *state*, while the prime minister is the head of the government⟩ — see NATION 1
2 high position within society ⟨Sir Thomas More was accorded an execution befitting his *state*: a beheading and not the hanging that common criminals received⟩ — see RANK 2

state *vb* **1** to convey in appropriate or telling terms ⟨please *state* the vehicle's mechanical problem as clearly and briefly as possible⟩ — see PHRASE
2 to express (a thought or emotion) in words ⟨"I believe this theory is wrong," she *stated*⟩ — see SAY 1
3 to make known (as an idea, emotion, or opinion) ⟨everyone has a right to *state* his or her opinion, no matter how unpopular it may be⟩ — see EXPRESS 1

statehouse *n* the building in which a state legislature meets ⟨a field trip to the *statehouse* to see the legislature in session⟩ — see CAPITOL

stateliness *n* **1** a dignified bearing or appearance befitting someone of royal status ⟨the princess has a *stateliness* that will serve her well when she becomes queen⟩ — see MAJESTY 1
2 dignified or restrained beauty of form, appearance, or style ⟨the refined *stateliness* of the mansion that has served as the official home of the state's governors since the 18th century⟩ — see ELEGANCE
3 impressiveness of beauty on a large scale ⟨the *stateliness* of this mountain range is best appreciated from one of its summits⟩ — see MAGNIFICENCE

stately *adj* **1** having or showing a formal and serious or reserved manner ⟨the governor watched with *stately* aloofness as his wife charmed the party guests⟩ — see DIGNIFIED
2 having or showing elegance ⟨a *stately* dowager in an evening gown⟩ — see ELEGANT 1
3 large and impressive in size, grandeur, extent, or conception ⟨*stately* plantation homes that are now open to the public as museums⟩ — see GRAND 1
4 very dignified in form, tone, or style ⟨a *stately* composition that has served as the musical accompaniment for countless graduations and other ceremonial occasions⟩ — see ELEVATED 2

statement *n* **1** a record of goods sold or services performed together with the costs due ⟨received a *statement* from the plumber in the mail⟩ — see [1]BILL 1
2 an act, process, or means of putting something into words ⟨a careful *statement* of the legal case before the court⟩ — see EXPRESSION 1
3 something that is said ⟨her *statement* was met with considerable skepticism⟩ — see WORD 2

state–of–the–art *adj* **1** being or employing the latest concepts, styles, or techniques ⟨a medical center that prides itself on being a leader in *state-of-the-art* microsurgery⟩ — see AVANT
2 being or involving the latest methods, concepts, information, or styles ⟨he spent a boatload of money on a *state-of-the-art* home theater⟩ — see MODERN

static *adj* fixed in a place or position ⟨the *static* installation of the statue in that niche means that no one will ever see its back, which is also of interest⟩ — see STATIONARY 1

station *vb* to assign to a place or position ⟨*stationed* guards around the perimeter of the encampment⟩ — see [2]POST

station *n* **1** the place where someone is assigned to stand or remain ⟨the soldiers remained at their *station* even though a huge enemy force was approaching⟩
synonyms position, post, quarter

related words assignment, brief, business, charge, detail, job, operation
2 a regular stopping place ⟨the historic house was once a *station* on the Underground Railroad, the network that helped slaves reach freedom in the North⟩
synonyms stop, way station
related words depot, terminal; layover, stopover; outstation
3 the placement of someone or something in relation to others in a vertical arrangement ⟨in colonial America, women occupied the lowest *station* in society and were not allowed to take part in public life⟩ — see RANK 1
4 a general way of holding the body ⟨the palace guards are required to maintain a rigid *station*⟩ — see POSTURE 1

stationary *adj* 1 fixed in a place or position ⟨a *stationary* bicycle is good for exercise, but you won't enjoy the scenery very much⟩
synonyms immobile, nonmoving, standing, static
related words immotile, immovable, irremovable, nonmotile, unmovable; frozen, motionless, moveless, stagnant, still; stuck, unbudging, wedged; fast, rooted, steadfast
phrases in place
near antonyms motile; adjustable, flexible, modular; displaceable, portable, removable (*also* removeable), transferable (*also* transferrable), transportable; unbalanced, unstable, unsteady
antonyms mobile, movable (*or* moveable), moving, nonstationary
2 not undergoing a change in condition ⟨auction prices for that artist's works have been *stationary* for some time⟩ — see CONSTANT 1

statuette *n* a small statue ⟨won a gold-plated *statuette* as the prize⟩ — see FIGURINE

stature *n* the distance of something or someone from bottom to top ⟨a man of surprisingly great *stature*⟩ — see HEIGHT 3

status *n* 1 position with regard to conditions and circumstances ⟨let me know if your *status* changes and you're available to work⟩ — see SITUATION 1
2 the placement of someone or something in relation to others in a vertical arrangement ⟨resented her lowly *status* in the organization⟩ — see RANK 1

status quo *n* the state or fact of being the way things usually are ⟨civic leaders who are afraid to do anything that might change the town's *status quo*⟩ — see NORMALITY

statute *n* a rule of conduct or action laid down by a governing authority and especially a legislature ⟨a new antilittering *statute*⟩ — see LAW 1

staunch *also* **stanch** *adj* firm in one's allegiance to someone or something ⟨a *staunch* believer in the democratic system⟩ — see FAITHFUL 1

stave off *vb* 1 to drive back ⟨managed to *stave off* the invaders⟩ — see REPEL 1
2 to keep from happening by taking action in advance ⟨the quartermaster *staved off* a shortage by requisitioning more than enough supplies⟩ — see PREVENT

[1]**stay** *n* 1 a temporary residing as another's guest ⟨my mother-in-law is coming for a brief *stay* next week⟩ — see VISIT 1
2 the stopping of a process or activity ⟨we must work without *stay* if we are ever to reach our goal of equal rights for everyone⟩ — see END 1

[2]**stay** *n* a structure that holds up or serves as a foundation for something else ⟨a free press is one of the principal *stays* of a democratic society⟩ — see SUPPORT 1

[1]**stay** *vb* 1 to continue to be in a place for a significant amount of time ⟨let's *stay* inside this pavilion until it stops raining⟩
synonyms abide, dwell, hang around, remain, stick around, tarry
related words await, hang on, hold on, wait; dally, dawdle, linger, loiter; outstay, overstay
near antonyms abscond, book [*slang*], decamp, escape, evacuate, flee, fly, get out, run away, scat, scram, skip; abandon, desert, forsake, vacate
antonyms bail, bail out, bug out, buzz (off), clear off [*chiefly British*], clear out, cut out, depart, exit, get off, go, go off, leave, move, pack (up *or* off), peel off, pike (out *or* off), pull out, push off, push on, quit, shove (off), take off, vamoose, walk out
2 to bring (something) to a standstill ⟨*stay* the trial until this new evidence has been processed⟩ — see [1]HALT 1
3 to remain in place in readiness or expectation of something ⟨we'll *stay* for a while longer and see if anyone shows up⟩ — see WAIT
4 to reside as a temporary guest ⟨let's *stay* at a quaint inn rather than at some generic motel⟩ — see VISIT 2

[2]**stay** *vb* to hold up or serve as a foundation for ⟨beams being used to *stay* the bridge while it is undergoing repairs⟩ — see SUPPORT 3

stead *n* the more favorable condition or position in a competition ⟨a summer internship will stand you in good *stead* when applying to college⟩ — see ADVANTAGE 1

steadfast *adj* firm in one's allegiance to someone or something ⟨a *steadfast* supporter of women's rights⟩ — see FAITHFUL 1

steadfastness *n* adherence to something to which one is bound by a pledge or duty ⟨his refusal to be swayed on this issue is more the result of stubbornness than principled *steadfastness*⟩ — see FIDELITY

steadiness *n* the state of continuing without change ⟨the *steadiness* of the weather is something that every New Englander knows not to trust⟩ — see CONSTANCY 1

steady *adj* 1 firm in one's allegiance to someone or something ⟨even as wild accusations were circulating, she remained *steady* in her support for the candidate⟩ — see FAITHFUL 1
2 appearing or occurring repeatedly from time to time ⟨a popular author who produces a *steady* output of best sellers year after year⟩ — see REGULAR 1
3 not undergoing a change in condition ⟨a *steady* breeze from the west⟩ — see CONSTANT 1
4 not varying ⟨support for her presidential bid has been *steady*⟩ — see UNIFORM
5 worthy of one's trust ⟨a quiet but *steady* man who is one of the pillars of the community⟩ — see DEPENDABLE

steal *n* something bought or offered for sale at a desirable price ⟨at 50% off, that shirt is a real *steal*⟩ — see BARGAIN 1

steal *vb* 1 to take (something) without right and with an intent to keep ⟨the guy who tried to *steal* my car was sentenced to a year in jail⟩
synonyms appropriate, boost [*slang*], filch, heist, hook, lift, misappropriate, nick [*British slang*], nip, pilfer, pinch, pocket, purloin, rip off, snitch, swipe, thieve
related words burglarize, knock over, rob; loot, pillage, plunder, sack; carjack, hijack (*also* highjack); pick, rifle; poach, rustle, shoplift; collar, grab, grasp, nail, seize, snatch, take; mooch, sponge; abduct, kidnap, shanghai, spirit
phrases make away with, make off with, run off with, walk off with
near antonyms buy, purchase; bestow, contribute, donate, give, hand over, present
2 to move about in a sly or secret manner ⟨the teenagers were able to *steal* past a security guard and enter the fairgrounds without paying admission⟩ — see SNEAK 1

steal (from) *vb* to remove valuables from (a place) unlawfully ⟨little wonder that the store went out of business, as its employees had been *stealing from* it for years⟩ — see ROB

stealer *n* one who steals ⟨the Internet has simply provided *stealers* and scammers with a new venue for their crimes⟩ — see THIEF

stealing *n* the unlawful taking and carrying away of property without the consent of its owner ⟨in those days the *stealing* of a horse was a very serious crime⟩ — see THEFT 1

stealth *adj* undertaken or done so as to escape being observed or known by others ⟨the SWAT team carried out a *stealth* raid on the house, which was believed to be harboring a terrorist cell⟩ — see SECRET 1

stealthy *adj* **1** given to acting in secret and to concealing one's intentions ⟨cats are among the *stealthiest* of stalkers⟩ — see SNEAKY 1
2 undertaken or done so as to escape being observed or known by others ⟨constantly harassed the enemy with *stealthy* raids⟩ — see SECRET 1

steam *vb* to be excited or emotionally stirred up with anger ⟨the newspaper's blatantly biased coverage made a lot of readers *steam*⟩ — see BOIL 1

steamed up *adj* feeling or showing anger ⟨I'm really *steamed up* over his latest outrageous behavior⟩ — see ANGRY

steaming *adj* feeling or showing anger ⟨she was *steaming* after hearing that she was being slandered by someone who had once been her best friend⟩ — see ANGRY

steam up *vb* to make angry ⟨finding yet another mistaken charge on his hospital bill really *steamed* him *up*⟩ — see ANGER 1

steamy *adj* of, relating to, exciting, or expressing sexual attraction or desire ⟨a *steamy* scene that earned the movie an R rating⟩ — see EROTIC

steed *n* a large hoofed domestic animal that is used for carrying or drawing loads and for riding ⟨the knight mounted his trusty *steed*⟩ — see HORSE

steek *vb, chiefly Scottish* to position (something) so as to prevent passage through an opening ⟨Macleod threatened to *steek* the door in my face if I ever said a word against the Scots again⟩ — see CLOSE 1

steel *n* a hand weapon with a length of metal sharpened on one or both sides and usually tapered to a sharp point ⟨drew *steel* on the bandits, who immediately fled for their lives⟩ — see SWORD

steel *vb* **1** to fill with courage or strength of purpose ⟨hoped that his inspirational talk would *steel* the youths in the pursuit of their dreams⟩ — see ENCOURAGE 1
2 to make able to withstand physical hardship, strain, or exposure ⟨years of running a farm had *steeled* the hard-bitten woman⟩ — see HARDEN 2
3 to prepare (oneself) mentally or emotionally ⟨he had spent the previous night *steeling* himself for the moment when he would demand a raise⟩ — see FORTIFY 1

steely *adj* **1** harsh and threatening in manner or appearance ⟨pinned them with a *steely* gaze and demanded to know what they were doing⟩ — see GRIM 1
2 of the color gray ⟨*steely* eyes that are the color of a stormy sky⟩ — see GRAY 1

steep *adj* **1** having an incline approaching the perpendicular ⟨a very *steep* rock face that is nearly impossible to climb⟩
synonyms abrupt, bold, precipitous, sheer
related words perpendicular, plumb, straight, vertical; craggy, hillocky, hilly, mountainous, scarped; angled, canted, cocked, heeled, inclined, listed, slanted, sloped, tilted, tipped
near antonyms gentle, gradual, moderate, soft; even, flat, flush, horizontal, level, plane, smooth, unruffled, unwrinkled
antonyms easy
2 going beyond a normal or acceptable limit in degree or amount ⟨we would like to hire him, but his salary demands are just too *steep*⟩ — see EXCESSIVE

steep *vb* **1** to cause (as a person) to become filled or saturated with a certain quality or principle ⟨grew up *steeped* in the ways of his ancestors⟩ ⟨a town *steeped* in history⟩ — see INFUSE
2 to wet thoroughly with liquid ⟨chew fresh ginger that has been *steeped* in hot water to aid digestion⟩ — see SOAK 1

steer *vb* **1** to point out the way for (someone) especially from a position in front ⟨the man in the train station was able to *steer* us in the right direction⟩ — see LEAD 1
2 to operate or control the course of ⟨first needed to learn how to *steer* her personal watercraft before going out on the crowded lake⟩ — see NAVIGATE 1

stellar *adj* **1** of or relating to the stars ⟨humankind's dream of *stellar* navigation is hampered by the vast distances between the stars, even in our own galaxy⟩
synonyms astral, star, starry
related words celestial, empyrean, heavenly; intergalactic, interstellar; astronomical (*also* astronomic), astrophysical; astronautic (*or* astronautical); starlike, star-spangled
2 of the very best kind ⟨this miniature palm tree is a *stellar* example of the art of bonsai⟩ — see EXCELLENT

stench *n* a strong unpleasant smell ⟨we finally discovered the dead rat that was causing the *stench* in the basement⟩ — see STINK 1

stenchy *adj* having an unpleasant smell ⟨the soft, *stenchy* cheese is considered by turophiles to be quite delectable⟩ — see MALODOROUS

stentorian *adj* marked by a high volume of sound ⟨the professor's *stentorian* voice was enough to keep even the drowsiest student awake⟩ — see LOUD 1

step *n* **1** an action planned or taken to achieve a desired result ⟨took *steps* to ensure that there would be no more incidences of food poisoning⟩ — see MEASURE 1
2 an individual part of a process, series, or ranking ⟨the manual enumerates every *step* in the procedure for shutting down the assembly line⟩ — see DEGREE 1
3 the mark or impression made by a foot ⟨*steps* in the sand leading into the water and back out again⟩ — see FOOTPRINT
4 steps *pl* the direction along which something or someone moves ⟨their *steps* led them through a long corridor⟩ — see PATH 1
5 a very small distance or degree ⟨he lives just a *step* away from his elderly mother, so he's there if she needs him for any reason⟩ — see HAIR 1

step *vb* **1** to go on foot ⟨I *stepped* across the street for a quick lunch at the new diner⟩ — see WALK 1
2 to perform a series of usually rhythmic bodily movements to music ⟨she was in her element, happily *stepping* around the dance floor⟩ — see DANCE 1
3 to proceed or move quickly ⟨many people wanted to linger before the president's bier, but guards kept the line of mourners *stepping* forward⟩ — see HURRY 2

step (along) *vb* to leave a place often for another ⟨now that my ride's here, I'll be *stepping along*⟩ — see GO 2

step aside (from) *vb* **1** to give up (a job or office) ⟨a newscaster who knew when it was time to *step aside from* the anchor desk and let a younger person take over⟩ — see QUIT 1
2 to give up (as a position of authority) formally ⟨the prime minister was compelled to *step aside from* his office when it was demonstrated that he had violated the public trust⟩ — see ABDICATE

step–by–step *adj* proceeding or changing by steps or degrees ⟨the incessant *step-by-step* advance of the enemy's troops could no longer be resisted⟩ — see GRADUAL

step–down *n* the amount by which something is lessened ⟨took a huge *step-down* in income when she switched from a law career to one in social work⟩ — see DECREASE

step down (from) *vb* **1** to give up (a job or office) ⟨with the advent of his 90th birthday, he could no longer resist calls for him to *step down from* chairmanship of the board⟩ — see QUIT 1

2 to give up (as a position of authority) formally ⟨even in the face of a palace revolt, Queen Elizabeth I refused to *step down from* the throne⟩ — see ABDICATE

step in *vb* **1** to make a brief visit ⟨I just *stepped in* to say hi on my way to class⟩ — see CALL 3

2 to serve as a replacement usually for a time only ⟨couldn't find anyone to *step in* for me so that I could take a break from my caregiving duties⟩ — see COVER 1

step out *vb* **1** to be sexually unfaithful ⟨if she catches him *stepping out* on her, she'll divorce him without a moment's hesitation⟩ — see CHEAT 2

2 to stop living ⟨my greedy relatives are only being nice to me because they expect me to *step out* any time now⟩ — see DIE 1

3 to take part in social activities ⟨waited until a year after her husband's death before *stepping out* again⟩ — see SOCIALIZE

steppe *n* a broad area of level or rolling treeless country ⟨nomads have long grazed yaks on the *steppes* of Mongolia⟩ — see PLAIN 1

step–up *n* something added (as by growth) ⟨there's been a *step-up* in productivity since regular breaks were offered⟩ — see INCREASE 1

step up *vb* to make markedly greater in measure or degree ⟨candidates *stepping up* their campaigns as election day draws near⟩ ⟨*stepped up* the pace to catch up with the others⟩ — see INTENSIFY

stereotype *n* an idea or statement about all of the members of a group or all the instances of a situation ⟨the noble savage was a *stereotype* that appealed to 18th-century intellectuals, who viewed European civilization as decadent and corrupt⟩ — see GENERALIZATION

stereotype *vb* to use so much as to make less appealing ⟨movies have *stereotyped* the hooker with a heart of gold ad nauseam⟩ — see HACKNEY

stereotyped *adj* used or heard so often as to be dull ⟨the wacky neighbor and other *stereotyped* characters seen on TV sitcoms⟩ — see STALE 1

sterile *adj* **1** not able to produce fruit or offspring ⟨*sterile* couples sometimes choose to adopt needy children⟩ ⟨the apple tree turned out to be *sterile*, never yielding a crop of apples⟩

synonyms barren, fruitless, impotent, infertile, unfruitful

related words altered, desexed, neutered, sterilized; castrated, emasculated, gelded; spayed; unproductive

near antonyms fecund, luxuriant, productive, prolific; enriched, fertilized, rich; impregnated, pregnant; potent; bearing, producing, yielding; blooming, bursting, flourishing, swarming, teeming

antonyms fat, fertile, fruitful

2 free from filth, infection, or dangers to health ⟨the hospitals in the war-torn city often lack necessary drugs and *sterile* surgical supplies⟩ — see SANITARY

sterling *adj* of the very best kind ⟨credited the win to the pitcher's *sterling* performance on the mound⟩ — see EXCELLENT

stern *adj* **1** given to exacting standards of discipline and self-restraint ⟨the army post's *stern* commander always had the utmost respect of those who served under him⟩ — see SEVERE 1

2 harsh and threatening in manner or appearance ⟨a *stern* receptionist took our names without even looking up⟩ — see GRIM 1

sternly *adv* in a manner so as to cause loss or suffering ⟨*sternly* reprimanded the prosecuting attorney for making comments that never should have been heard by the jury⟩ — see HARDLY 1

sternness *n* the quality or state of being demanding or unyielding (as in discipline or criticism) ⟨the company's new president has a reputation for granitelike *sternness* and monkish austerity⟩ — see SEVERITY

sternward *or* **sternwards** *adv* near, toward, or in the stern of a ship or the tail of an aircraft ⟨a flight attendant hurried *sternward* to attend to the disturbance⟩ — see AFT

stevedore *n* one who loads and unloads ships at a port ⟨on the wharves, *stevedores* were unloading cargo from the far corners of the world⟩ — see DOCKWORKER

stew *n* **1** a state of nervous or irritated concern ⟨many in town are in a *stew* about the proposed plan to close at least one of the elementary schools⟩ — see FRET

2 a state of noisy, confused activity ⟨the audience went into a *stew* when the evacuation order was announced⟩ — see COMMOTION

3 an unorganized collection or mixture of various things ⟨the documentary looks at the *stew* of conspiracy theories inspired by the assassination⟩ — see MISCELLANY 1

4 a building in which prostitutes are available ⟨a red-light district full of down and dirty *stews*⟩ — see BORDELLO

stew *vb* **1** to cook in a liquid heated to the point that it gives off steam ⟨*stew* the chicken till tender, and then remove the meat from the bones⟩ — see BOIL 2

2 to experience concern or anxiety ⟨stop *stewing* over that game and just try to do better next time⟩ — see WORRY 1

steward *n* a person hired to perform household or personal services ⟨the earl couldn't imagine how he'd manage without his *steward*⟩ — see SERVANT

steward *vb* to look after and make decisions about ⟨will *steward* the city's library programs⟩ — see CONDUCT 1

stewardship *n* **1** the act or activity of looking after and making decisions about something ⟨generally the dean left the day-to-day *stewardship* of the college to the assistant dean⟩ — see CONDUCT 1

2 the duty or function of watching or guarding for the sake of proper direction or control ⟨she believes that *stewardship* of the environment is everyone's responsibility⟩ — see SUPERVISION 1

stewed *adj* being under the influence of alcohol ⟨it was clear from the caller's voice that she was fairly *stewed*⟩ — see DRUNK

stick *vb* **1** to hold to something firmly as if by adhesion ⟨those magnets are strong enough to *stick* to the refrigerator without any problems⟩

synonyms adhere, cleave, cling, hew

related words bind, cohere, fasten, fuse, glue, unite

near antonyms loosen; drop, fall

2 to arrange something in a certain spot or position ⟨you can *stick* that box in the corner until I figure out where to put everything⟩ — see PLACE 1

3 to penetrate or hold (something) with a pointed object ⟨could hardly feel the needle when the nurse *stuck* my arm with it⟩ — see IMPALE

4 to rob by the use of trickery or threats ⟨she got *stuck* by an unscrupulous seller while using the online auction site⟩ — see FLEECE

stick (to *or* with) *vb* to give steadfast support to ⟨thanks for *sticking with* me after all my other so-called friends turned their backs⟩ ⟨the governor has sworn to *stick to* his campaign promises⟩ — see ADHERE (TO) 1

stick around *vb* to continue to be in a place for a significant amount of time ⟨we *stuck around* afterwards to help clean up⟩ — see [1]STAY 1

stick–in–the–mud *n* a person with old-fashioned ideas ⟨the committee is dominated by old *stick-in-the-muds* who have little interest in bringing new ideas to the table⟩ — see FOGY

stick out *vb* **1** to extend outward beyond a usual point ⟨no feet *sticking out* in the aisles, please⟩ — see BULGE 1
2 to put up with (something painful or difficult) ⟨managed to *stick out* the whole race despite her bad knee⟩ — see BEAR 2

sticks *n pl* the open rural area outside of big towns and cities ⟨grew up in the *sticks* and is used to traveling miles just to get a loaf of bread⟩ — see COUNTRY 2

stick–to–itiveness *n* firm or unwavering adherence to one's purpose ⟨I wonder if he really has the *stick-to-itiveness* to finish law school⟩ — see DETERMINATION 1

sticky *adj* **1** tending to adhere to objects upon contact ⟨both sides of the tape are *sticky*, making it a little tricky to work with⟩
synonyms adherent, adhesive, clingy, gluey, glutinous, gummy, tacky, tenacious, viscid
related words gelatinous, gooey, ropy (*also* ropey), syrupy, viscous; pitchy, tarry
near antonyms nonviscous
antonyms nonadhesive
2 containing or characterized by an uncomfortable amount of moisture ⟨a warm *sticky* day when all we wanted to do was sit somewhere with air-conditioning⟩ — see HUMID
3 requiring exceptional skill or caution in performance or handling ⟨an especially *sticky* conversation about money matters⟩ — see TRICKY 1
4 appealing to the emotions in an obvious and tiresome way ⟨*sticky* love scenes that will bore unreconstructed cynics to death⟩ — see CORNY 1

sticky wicket *n* a difficult, puzzling, or embarrassing situation from which there is no easy escape ⟨with both sets of in-laws insisting that we spend Thanksgiving with them, we were on a *sticky wicket* indeed⟩ — see PREDICAMENT

stiff *adj* **1** incapable of or highly resistant to bending ⟨use a *stiff* piece of paper for the project⟩
synonyms inflexible, rigid, stiffened, unyielding
related words inelastic; firm, hard, solid, sound, strong; brittle, crisp; compact, dense, substantial; arthritic, rheumatic; nonelastic, nonmalleable
near antonyms elastic, resilient, springy, stretchy, workable; malleable, plastic; semiflexible; droopy, flabby, flaccid, mushy, semisoft, soft, squashy, squishy; lank, limber, limp, lissome (*also* lissom), lithe, lithesome, willowy
antonyms flexible, floppy, pliable, pliant, supple, yielding
2 difficult to endure ⟨*stiff* winds⟩ — see HARSH 1
3 going beyond a normal or acceptable limit in degree or amount ⟨don't you think that's a pretty *stiff* fine for such a minor infraction?⟩ — see EXCESSIVE
4 having a consistency that does not easily yield to pressure ⟨stir two cups of flour with the remaining ingredients to make a *stiff* dough⟩ — see FIRM 2
5 lacking social grace and assurance ⟨felt *stiff* and ill-at-ease whenever she was introduced to her father's friends⟩ — see AWKWARD 1
6 requiring considerable physical or mental effort ⟨we'll have a *stiff* climb to actually reach the summit⟩ — see HARD 2
7 marked by or showing careful attention to set forms and details ⟨the *stiff* politeness with which I was greeted suggested that they weren't truly happy to see me⟩ — see CEREMONIOUS 1
8 being under the influence of alcohol ⟨seeing that the customer was more than a little *stiff*, the bartender offered to call a cab for him⟩ — see DRUNK

stiff *n* **1** a dead body ⟨to the mortician, a *stiff* was a *stiff* and they were all pretty much alike⟩ — see CORPSE
2 a member of the human race ⟨one lucky *stiff* will get the biggest jackpot in the lottery's history⟩ — see HUMAN

stiff *vb* **1** to deliberately ignore or treat rudely ⟨the actress has a reputation for *stiffing* the press at red-carpet events⟩ — see SNUB 1
2 to rob by the use of trickery or threats ⟨customers who were too embarrassed to admit that they had been *stiffed* by an Internet company selling sexual aids⟩ — see FLEECE

stiff–arm *vb* to deliberately ignore or treat rudely ⟨in his sad and lonely old age, he *stiff-armed* even once-beloved friends⟩ — see SNUB 1

stiffen *vb* to make more harsh, uncompromising, or severe ⟨plans to further *stiffen* the already onerous requirements for admission to the elite military unit⟩ — see HARSHEN

stiffened *adj* incapable of or highly resistant to bending ⟨*stiffened* corpses⟩ ⟨an old-fashioned dress with a *stiffened* lace collar⟩ — see STIFF 1

stiffly *adv* **1** in a manner so as to cause loss or suffering ⟨*stiffly* criticized for making such indiscreet comments in public⟩ — see HARDLY 1
2 in a vigorous and forceful manner ⟨a *stiffly* fought battle⟩ — see HARD 3

stiff–necked *adj* **1** having a feeling of superiority that shows itself in an overbearing attitude ⟨he was too *stiff-necked* to admit that "underlings" might have useful ideas⟩ — see ARROGANT
2 marked by or showing careful attention to set forms and details ⟨her dinner parties are typically *stiff-necked* affairs, more to be endured than enjoyed⟩ — see CEREMONIOUS 1
3 sticking to an opinion, purpose, or course of action in spite of reason, arguments, or persuasion ⟨obviously uninterested in hearing any excuses, the *stiff-necked* officer handed me my speeding ticket with a flourish⟩ — see OBSTINATE

stifle *vb* **1** to be or cause to be killed by lack of breathable air ⟨unfortunately, the robbers were *stifled* when they got trapped in the airless bank vault⟩ — see SMOTHER 1
2 to refrain from openly showing or uttering ⟨*stifled* a yawn⟩ — see SUPPRESS 2
3 to deaden the sound of ⟨he *stifled* a cough with his hand⟩ — see MUFFLE 1

stifling *adj* lacking fresh air ⟨the lecture hall was *stifling* until we opened several windows⟩ — see STUFFY 1

stigma *n* a mark of guilt or disgrace ⟨the *stigma* of slavery remained long after it had been abolished⟩ — see STAIN 1

still *adj* **1** free from disturbing noise or uproar ⟨the town's streets are usually *still* and peopleless in the early morning hours⟩ — see QUIET 1
2 free from storms or physical disturbance ⟨the air was ominously *still* as dark clouds gathered in the distance⟩ — see CALM 1
3 mostly or entirely without sound ⟨in his paintings Paul Gauguin depicts a *still* tropical paradise inhabited by mute and motionless natives⟩ — see SILENT 3

still *n* **1** a state of freedom from storm or disturbance ⟨in the *still* of the forest he could relax and forget his worries⟩ — see CALM 1
2 the near or complete absence of sound ⟨a loud noise shattered the *still* of the night⟩ — see SILENCE 2

still *vb* **1** to bring (something) to a standstill ⟨it seemed

as though nothing could *still* the fighting⟩ — see [1]HALT 1
2 to free from distress or disturbance ⟨reading a book helps me to relax and *still* my mind before going to bed⟩ — see CALM 1
3 to stop the noise or speech of ⟨the conversation was abruptly *stilled* by a loud crash from the next room⟩ — see SILENCE 1

still *adv* **1** without motion ⟨the cat sat absolutely *still*, watching as the mouse began to make its way across the floor⟩
synonyms motionlessly, quiet, quietly
related words immovably; inactively
near antonyms movably
2 in spite of that ⟨their star player was injured in yesterday's game; *still*, it looks like he will be able to play today⟩ — see HOWEVER

still and all *adv* in spite of that ⟨she's none too enthusiastic about the project; *still and all*, she seems willing to cooperate⟩ — see HOWEVER

still less *conj* to say nothing of ⟨I never suggested that he was incompetent, *still less* that he was dishonest⟩ — see LET ALONE

stillness *n* **1** a state of freedom from storm or disturbance ⟨dozing in the warm *stillness* of a summer afternoon⟩ — see CALM 1
2 incapacity for or restraint from speaking ⟨from the couple's tense *stillness* I sensed that they had been quarreling just before I arrived⟩ — see SILENCE 1
3 the near or complete absence of sound ⟨the only thing that broke the *stillness* of the garden was the droning of a bee⟩ — see SILENCE 2

stilly *adj* **1** free from disturbing noise or uproar ⟨bats taking flight in the *stilly* summer evening⟩ — see QUIET 1
2 free from storms or physical disturbance ⟨dipping my paddle into the *stilly* water, I began canoeing across the pond⟩ — see CALM 1
3 mostly or entirely without sound ⟨the blissful peace of a star-filled, *stilly* night⟩ — see SILENT 3

stilted *adj* **1** lacking social grace and assurance ⟨the conversation was somewhat *stilted* as we didn't seem to share any interests⟩ — see AWKWARD 1
2 marked by or showing careful attention to set forms and details ⟨a *stilted* letter of apology that was written and accepted with equal measures of insincerity⟩ — see CEREMONIOUS 1

stimulant *n* **1** something that arouses action or activity ⟨the relaxed zoning regulations should serve as a *stimulant* for development in the area⟩ — see IMPULSE 1
2 a distilled beverage that can make a person drunk ⟨I always take a bottle of *stimulant* along on trips, for emergencies like plane crashes or earthquakes⟩ — see ALCOHOL

stimulate *vb* **1** to give life, vigor, or spirit to ⟨research into alternative energy sources has been *stimulated* by this funding increase⟩ — see ANIMATE
2 to rouse to strong feeling or action ⟨the government crackdown has only *stimulated* the citizenry to more acts of violence⟩ — see PROVOKE 1

stimulating *adj* **1** causing great emotional or mental stimulation ⟨enjoys the good food and *stimulating* conversation at his best friend's house⟩ — see EXCITING 1
2 having a renewing effect on the state of the body or mind ⟨a brisk, *stimulating* walk on a bright, clear wintry day⟩ — see TONIC 1
3 serving or likely to arouse a strong reaction ⟨an article containing a *stimulating* argument for raising, not lowering, the tax on gasoline⟩ — see PROVOCATIVE

stimulative *adj* having a renewing effect on the state of the body or mind ⟨the supposed *stimulative* power of herbal teas⟩ — see TONIC 1

stimulus *n* something that arouses action or activity ⟨seeing a Broadway play for the first time was the *stimulus* for her career in the theater⟩ — see IMPULSE 1

sting *vb* **1** to charge (someone) too much for goods or services ⟨a nightclub that's been *stinging* patrons for years⟩ — see OVERCHARGE 1
2 to rob by the use of trickery or threats ⟨swindlers who *sting* unwary tourists by posing as officials demanding money⟩ — see FLEECE

sting *n* **1** an instance of the use of dishonest methods to acquire something of value ⟨the pawn shop operation turned out to be a *sting* by undercover police officers to catch the ring of burglars⟩ — see FRAUD 1
2 a sharp unpleasant sensation usually felt in some specific part of the body ⟨the *sting* of cold air against my face⟩ — see PAIN 1

stinger *n* a hard strike with a part of the body or an instrument ⟨in the eighth round he delivered a *stinger* that knocked his opponent flat⟩ — see [1]BLOW

stinginess *n* the quality or practice of being overly sparing with money ⟨refusing to tip poorly paid restaurant servers is a particularly petty form of *stinginess*⟩ — see PARSIMONY 1

stinging *adj* causing intense discomfort to one's skin ⟨these cold, *stinging* winds are not just a discomfort—they can be dangerous to exposed flesh⟩ — see CUTTING 1

stingy *adj* **1** giving or sharing as little as possible ⟨until his redemption, Ebenezer Scrooge is the classic example of a very *stingy*, heartless miser⟩
synonyms cheap, chintzy, close, closefisted, mean, mingy, miserly, niggard, niggardly, parsimonious, penny-pinching, penurious, pinching, pinchpenny, spare, sparing, stinting, tight, tightfisted, uncharitable, ungenerous
related words careful, chary, conserving, economical, economizing, frugal, saving, scrimping, skimping, thrifty; acquisitive, avaricious, avid, coveting, covetous, desirous, grasping, greedy, hoggish, itchy, mercenary, rapacious, selfish, shabby, small, sordid; begrudging, envious, grudging, resentful; inhospitable
near antonyms altruistic, selfless, unselfish; extravagant, free, handsome, lavish, overgenerous, profuse; beneficent, benevolent, hospitable, humanitarian, philanthropic (*also* philanthropical); compassionate, goodhearted, greathearted, kindly, magnanimous, openhearted; thriftless, unthrifty; dissipating, frittering, prodigal, profligate, spendthrift, splurging, squandering, wasteful, wasting
antonyms bounteous, bountiful, charitable, freehanded, generous, liberal, munificent, openhanded, unsparing, unstinting
2 less plentiful than what is normal, necessary, or desirable ⟨a *stingy* serving of mashed potatoes⟩ — see MEAGER

stink *n* **1** a strong unpleasant smell ⟨the *stink* of burned plastic lingered in the kitchen for days after we accidentally melted a spatula on the stove⟩
synonyms funk, reek, stench
related words acridness, fetidness, foulness, fustiness, malodorousness, mustiness, odoriferousness, odorousness, rancidity, rankness, staleness; badness, vileness; dirt, dirtiness, filth, filthiness, nastiness; effluvium (*also* effluvia), emission; odor, redolence, scent, sniff
near antonyms floweriness, lusciousness, savoriness, spiciness, sweetness; bouquet; ambrosia
antonyms aroma, fragrance, perfume
2 a feeling or declaration of disapproval or dissent ⟨many town residents raised an unholy *stink* about the proposal to increase taxes yet again⟩ — see OBJECTION

stink *vb* **1** to give off an extremely unpleasant smell ⟨the dog *stinks* because she tangled with a skunk again⟩

synonyms reek
related words exhale, savor (*also* savour), smell; decay, decompose, rot, spoil; disgust, offend, repulse, revolt
2 to be objectionable or unsatisfactory ⟨their team really *stinks* this year⟩
synonyms bite [*slang*], smell, suck [*slang*]
antonyms rock [*slang*], rule [*slang*]

stinkard *n* a person whose behavior is offensive to others ⟨that *stinkard* asked his wife for a divorce while she was dying from cancer⟩ — see JERK 1

stinker *n* a person whose behavior is offensive to others ⟨some *stinker* nearly crashed his SUV into me because he was yakking on his cell phone⟩ — see JERK 1

stinking *adj* **1** having an unpleasant smell ⟨came home from their trip to find *stinking* garbage that had been left in the kitchen⟩ — see MALODOROUS
2 *slang* being under the influence of alcohol ⟨warned her husband not to come home *stinking*—or he'd be sleeping on the couch⟩ — see DRUNK

stinking *adv* to a great degree ⟨a huge, showy house that screams, "We're *stinking* rich!"⟩ — see VERY 1

stinkpot *n, slang* a boat equipped with a motor ⟨if I ever get filthy rich, I'm going to buy myself a *stinkpot* and take up fishing⟩ — see MOTORBOAT

stinky *adj* having an unpleasant smell ⟨a *stinky* plant that attracts certain insects and then devours them⟩ — see MALODOROUS

stint *n* **1** a fixed period of time during which a person holds a job or position ⟨signed up for a three-year *stint* in the army⟩ — see TERM 1
2 the act or practice of keeping something (as an activity) within certain boundaries ⟨his parents have always supported him without *stint*, no matter what interests he has chosen to pursue⟩ — see RESTRICTION 2

stint (on) *vb* to use or give out in stingy amounts ⟨the entrées would be worth these prices if the restaurant didn't *stint on* the side dishes so much⟩ — see SPARE 1

stinting *adj* giving or sharing as little as possible ⟨a *stinting* boss who doesn't give paid sick leave no matter how long you've worked for him⟩ — see STINGY 1

stipend *n* the money paid regularly to a person for labor or services ⟨the *stipend* you'll receive as an intern will just barely cover your housing costs⟩ — see WAGE

stipple *vb* to mark with small spots especially unevenly ⟨the sunlight falling through the lace curtain *stippled* her face⟩ — see SPOT 1

stippled *adj* marked with spots ⟨create a *stippled* effect by dabbing a contrasting color of paint over an undercoat with a rag or sponge⟩ — see SPOTTED 1

stipulate (for) *vb* to ask for (something) earnestly or with authority ⟨the contract *stipulates for* a renegotiation of the terms after two years⟩ — see DEMAND 1

stipulation *n* something upon which the carrying out of an agreement or offer depends ⟨their proposal for a baseball franchise includes several *stipulations* that are unacceptable⟩ — see CONDITION 2

[1]**stir** *n* **1** a state of noisy, confused activity ⟨the plane's first jolt caused a *stir* among the passengers, and by the third one they were in a panic⟩ — see COMMOTION
2 the act or an instance of changing position ⟨we were warned that the slightest *stir* would scare the mother bird so we hardly dared to breathe⟩ — see MOVEMENT 1

[2]**stir** *n, slang* a place of confinement for persons held in lawful custody ⟨the mule had just got out of *stir* and was being followed by the feds, who had their sights set on the kingpin of the operation⟩ — see JAIL

stir *vb* **1** to cause (as a liquid) to move about in a circle especially repeatedly ⟨the recipe says to *stir* the mixture carefully until it's properly blended⟩
synonyms agitate, churn, swirl, wash, whirl
related words beat, paddle, whip, whisk; reel, shake, wheel
2 to change one's position ⟨the cat *stirred*, then opened its eyes and slowly got to its feet⟩ — see MOVE 3
3 to rouse to strong feeling or action ⟨news coverage of the fire *stirred* many to send donations to a fund for the families who had lost their homes⟩ — see PROVOKE 1

stir (up) *vb* to bring something (volatile or intense) into being ⟨couldn't *stir up* any interest in a Saturday morning outing to the art museum⟩ — see INCITE 1

stirring *adj* **1** causing great emotional or mental stimulation ⟨the message of brotherhood in Martin Luther King's *stirring* "I Have a Dream" speech still resonates today⟩ — see EXCITING 1
2 having the power to affect the feelings or sympathies ⟨a *stirring* rendition of the national anthem⟩ — see MOVING
3 marked by much life, movement, or activity ⟨spring has arrived, and the meadow is *stirring* with life⟩ — see ALIVE 2

stirring *n* the act or an instance of changing position ⟨I thought I detected a slight *stirring* of the leaves, and yet there wasn't a breath of wind⟩ — see MOVEMENT 1

stitch *n* a sharp unpleasant sensation usually felt in some specific part of the body ⟨had to drop out of the race when the *stitch* in his side became too painful⟩ — see PAIN 1

stitch *vb* to close up with a series of interlacing stitches ⟨the doctor *stitched* the wound so adroitly that the scar was barely visible after the stitches were removed⟩ — see SEW

stitcher *n* a person who sews ⟨worked as an apparel *stitcher* for years⟩ — see SEWER

stock *adj* accepted, used, or practiced by most people ⟨the conversation became interesting once we got beyond the *stock* niceties and observations about the weather⟩ — see CURRENT 1

stock *n* **1** a group of persons who come from the same ancestor ⟨the bride comes from good *stock*⟩ — see FAMILY 1
2 a stupid person ⟨just sat there like a *stock*, staring at me blankly whenever I asked him a question⟩ — see IDIOT
3 firm belief in the integrity, ability, effectiveness, or genuineness of someone or something ⟨don't put any *stock* in her promises—she'll just tell you what she thinks you want to hear⟩ — see TRUST 1
4 the line of ancestors from whom a person is descended ⟨his family is of mixed northern European *stock*⟩ — see ANCESTRY
5 the number of individuals or amount of something available at any given time ⟨the new study adds to the general *stock* of knowledge about genetic disorders⟩ — see SUPPLY

stockade *n* a place of confinement for persons held in lawful custody ⟨prisoners of war confined in a *stockade*⟩ — see JAIL

stocking *n* a close-fitting covering for the foot and leg ⟨thick wool *stockings* designed to be worn with hiking boots⟩
synonyms hose, sock
related words hosiery; support hose; anklet, bobby socks, bootee, kneesock

stockpile *n* a supply stored up and often hidden away ⟨an emergency *stockpile* of potable water and canned goods in the cellar⟩ — see HOARD 1

stockpile *vb* to put (something of future use or value) in a safe or secret place ⟨we should be able to *stockpile* enough vaccine for the upcoming flu season⟩ — see HOARD

stocky *adj* being compact and broad in build and often short in stature ⟨the *stocky* boxer's strength and speed

more than make up for his opponent's longer reach⟩
synonyms chunky, dumpy, heavyset, squat, squatty, stout, stubby, stumpy, thickset
related words beefy, brawny, bulky, burly, husky, sturdy, thick, thickish, weighty; chubby, corpulent, fat, fleshy, full, gross, heavy, obese, overweight, plump, portly, pudgy, roly-poly, rotund, round, tubby; paunchy, potbellied; flabby, soft
near antonyms delicate, fragile, frail, puny; lean, skinny, slender, slim, spare, thin; angular, bony (*also* boney), gaunt, lank, lanky, rawboned, sinewy; scraggy, scrawny, slight; anorexic, cadaverous, emaciated, haggard, skeletal, wasted; spindly, twiggy, waspish, weedy, willowy, wiry

stodgy *adj* causing weariness, restlessness, or lack of interest ⟨the sitcom was offbeat and interesting in its first season, but has since become predictable and *stodgy*⟩ — see BORING

stoic *or* **stoical** *adj* **1** accepting pains or hardships calmly or without complaint ⟨after waiting six years for permission to immigrate to the U.S., the family is *stoic* about a six-month postponement⟩ — see PATIENT 1
2 not feeling or showing emotion ⟨at her husband's funeral she remained *stoic*, and only a few imagined the depth of her grief⟩ — see IMPASSIVE 1

stoke *vb* to make greater in size, amount, or number ⟨hopefully, offering stock options will *stoke* workers' commitment to the company⟩ — see INCREASE 1

stoked *adj, slang* showing urgent desire or interest ⟨we're pretty *stoked* about the upcoming benefit concert featuring a galaxy of rock stars⟩ — see EAGER

stolid *adj* **1** not expressing any emotion ⟨the butler responded to the duchess's constant demands with *stolid* indifference⟩ — see BLANK 1
2 not feeling or showing emotion ⟨the actor's turn as a *stolid*, impersonal bureaucrat was an interesting departure from his more impassioned roles⟩ — see IMPASSIVE 1

stomach *vb* to put up with (something painful or difficult) ⟨I could no longer *stomach* working for such a petty tyrant⟩ — see BEAR 2

stomach *n* **1** the part of the body between the chest and the pelvis ⟨please don't lean on my *stomach*—I just had a big meal⟩
synonyms abdomen, belly, breadbasket [*slang*], gut, solar plexus, tummy
related words middle, midriff, waist; paunch, potbelly; thorax
2 a need or desire for food ⟨the cake looks delicious, but I'm afraid that I have no *stomach* for sweets right now⟩ — see HUNGER 1

stomachache *n* abdominal pain especially when focused in the digestive organs ⟨all that fried food gave me a *stomachache*⟩
synonyms bellyache, collywobbles
related words colic, cramps, gripes

stomp *vb* **1** to move heavily or clumsily ⟨came *stomping* up the stairs and tossed her backpack on the bed⟩ — see LUMBER 1
2 to tread on heavily so as to crush or injure ⟨*stomping* the burning leaves in a vain attempt to put out the fire⟩ — see TRAMPLE

stomping ground *n* a place for spending time or for socializing ⟨a major part of the fun of alumni weekend is visiting the old *stomping grounds*⟩ — see HANGOUT

stone *adj* having no exceptions or restrictions ⟨the *stone* stupidity of the senator's statements embarrassed even her staffers⟩ — see ABSOLUTE 2

stone *n* a shaped stone laid over or erected near a grave and usually bearing an inscription to identify and preserve the memory of the deceased ⟨an engraved *stone* identified the grave as that of a man who had died in the Influenza Epidemic of 1918–19⟩ — see TOMBSTONE

stone *vb* to make sharp or sharper ⟨the diorama showed a villager *stoning* a scythe⟩ — see SHARPEN

Stone Age *adj* having passed its time of use or usefulness ⟨*Stone Age* attitudes about the raising of children⟩ — see OBSOLETE

stone–blind *adj* lacking the power of sight ⟨he's so oblivious to everything around him that you'd think he was *stone-blind*⟩ — see BLIND 1

stoned *adj* **1** being under the influence of a recreational drug ⟨the young actor, in his first comic role, plays a *stoned* slacker⟩
synonyms blasted [*slang*], blitzed [*slang*], bombed, high, hopped-up, loaded [*slang*], ripped [*slang*], spaced-out (*or* spaced), strung out, wasted [*slang*], wiped out [*slang*], zonked, zonked-out
related words addicted, hooked
near antonyms abstemious, abstinent, clean, temperate; clearheaded, cool, level, steady
antonyms sober, straight
2 being under the influence of alcohol ⟨his alcohol tolerance was low enough that one glass of champagne could get him *stoned*⟩ — see DRUNK

stoner *n* a person who regularly uses drugs especially illegally ⟨a comedy about aging *stoners* who are still trying to get their act together⟩ — see DOPER

stone's throw *n* a very small distance or degree ⟨the cottage is a *stone's throw* from the beach⟩ — see HAIR 1

stoneware *n* articles made of baked clay ⟨collects 19th-century English *stoneware*, especially soup tureens⟩ — see CROCKERY

stony *also* **stoney** *adj* having or showing a lack of sympathy or tender feelings ⟨the judge's *stony* demeanor didn't raise the defendant's hopes for a more lenient sentence⟩ — see HARD 1

stonyhearted *adj* having or showing a lack of sympathy or tender feelings ⟨a less *stonyhearted* person would not have been so indifferent to the dying man's pleas for forgiveness⟩ — see HARD 1

stoolie *n* a person who provides information about another's wrongdoing ⟨told the mule that if he ever turned *stoolie*, he'd end up spilling his guts in more ways than one⟩ — see INFORMER

stool pigeon *n* a person who provides information about another's wrongdoing ⟨the FBI finally got a break when one of the mob boss's top henchmen turned *stool pigeon*⟩ — see INFORMER

stoop *vb* to descend to a level that is beneath one's dignity ⟨the debate would be more enlightening if both sides didn't *stoop* to name-calling⟩ — see CONDESCEND 1

stoop *n* a covered structure adjoining an entrance to a building ⟨the *stoop* at the front entrance is just big enough to shield a resident from the elements as he fumbles for his keys⟩ — see PORCH

stooping *adj* bending downward or forward ⟨rested under the *stooping* branches of the willow tree⟩ — see NODDING

stop *n* **1** a brief halt in a journey ⟨our guide called for a *stop* at the trail hut so we could eat and rest a bit⟩
synonyms layover, stopover
related words break, pause, rest
2 a regular stopping place ⟨had lunch on a picnic table at a shady rest *stop* along the highway⟩ — see STATION 2
3 something that makes movement or progress difficult ⟨pulled out all the *stops* and presented the most spectacular show ever⟩ — see ENCUMBRANCE
4 the stopping of a process or activity ⟨put a *stop* to this nonsense⟩ — see END 1

stop *vb* **1** to bring (as an action or operation) to an immediate end ⟨the manufacturer will *stop* selling the toy

and will immediately recall all the units that have already been sold⟩
synonyms break, break off, break up, can [*slang*], cease, cut off, cut out, desist (from), discontinue, drop, end, give over, halt, knock off, lay off, leave off, pack (up *or* in), quit, shut off
related words complete, conclude, finish; close (down); deactivate; block, blockade, dam, delay, detain, hinder, hold, hold back, impede, kibosh, obstruct, stem; call, suspend; arrest, brake, check, clamp down, rein (in), squash, squelch, stamp, stanch (*or* staunch), stunt, suppress, turn back; pause, stay, suspend; abolish, abort, annul, demolish, destroy, dissolve, kill, ruin, scuttle, snuff
phrases have done with, put the kibosh on
near antonyms carry on, continue, follow through (with), keep up, run on; advance, proceed, progress; actuate, drive, impel, propel, stir
2 to bring (something) to a standstill ⟨traffic was *stopped* for over an hour by the overturned truck⟩ — see [1]HALT 1
3 to close up so that no empty spaces remain ⟨I *stopped* the mouse hole with plaster⟩ — see FILL 2
4 to come to an end ⟨the music *stopped* but we kept on dancing⟩ — see CEASE 1
5 to achieve a victory over ⟨they were eventually *stopped* by the best team in the league⟩ — see BEAT 2

stop (by *or* in) *vb* to make a brief visit ⟨*stop by* on your way to the game so we can go there together⟩ — see CALL 3

stop (up) *vb* to prevent passage through by filling with something ⟨clear the leaves out of the rain gutters so they don't *stop up* the downspouts again⟩ — see CLOG 1

stopcock *n* a fixture for controlling the flow of a liquid ⟨a mechanical engineer who designs industrial valves and *stopcocks*⟩ — see FAUCET

stopgap *n* a temporary replacement ⟨the coach we have now was only hired as a *stopgap* until someone with more experience is found⟩ — see MAKESHIFT

stopover *n* a brief halt in a journey ⟨I've been to Belgium—if you count a *stopover* in Brussels on my way to Istanbul⟩ — see STOP 1

stoppage *n* the stopping of a process or activity ⟨yet another *stoppage* in play for some unexplained reason⟩ — see END 1

storage *n* a building for storing goods ⟨in colonial times the granary was one of the community's most important *storages*⟩ — see STOREHOUSE

store *adj* made beforehand in large numbers ⟨preferred homemade bread to *store* brands⟩ — see READY-MADE

store *n* **1** a collection of things kept available for future use or need ⟨her husband has a *store* of old magazines that he has been collecting for years⟩
synonyms cache, deposit, hoard, reserve
related words budget, fund, nest egg; armory, arsenal, bank, pool, reservoir, stock, stockpile, supply; accumulation, assemblage, collection, gathering
2 a supply stored up and often hidden away ⟨keeps a *store* of quarters in the glove compartment for the parking meters⟩ — see HOARD 1
3 an establishment where goods are sold to consumers ⟨go to the grocery *store* for orange juice and eggs⟩ — see SHOP 1
4 a considerable amount ⟨we laid by a *store* of food for the party⟩ — see LOT 2

store *vb* **1** to place somewhere for safekeeping or ready availability ⟨we decided to *store* the lawn mower in the shed instead of the garage⟩
synonyms keep, put up, reposit, stow
related words cellar, garage, hangar, house, warehouse; file, pack, shelve
2 to put (something of future use or value) in a safe or secret place ⟨squirrels commonly *store* nuts in the hollows of trees and other places to prepare for the winter⟩ — see HOARD

store–bought *adj* made beforehand in large numbers ⟨he served *store-bought* biscuits and airily pretended he had baked them himself⟩ — see READY-MADE

storehouse *n* a building for storing goods ⟨the company has a large *storehouse* filled with lumber for manufacturing its line of furniture⟩
synonyms depository, depot, magazine, repository, storage, warehouse
related words cache, stockroom, storeroom; bank, bin, container, locker, safe-deposit box, strongbox; arsenal, dump; stowage

storm *vb* **1** to express one's anger usually violently ⟨the chef spent the morning *storming* at his staff about the ruined sauces⟩ — see RAGE 1
2 to fall as water in a continuous stream of drops from the clouds ⟨it *storms* so frequently up in the mountains that the peaks are rarely visible from the valley below⟩ — see RAIN 1
3 to take sudden, violent action against ⟨the pirates *stormed* the ship, easily taking the whole crew as their prisoners⟩ — see ATTACK 1
4 to be excited or emotionally stirred up with anger ⟨by the time we arrived, our hostess was *storming* because dinner was ruined⟩ — see BOIL 1

storm *n* **1** a disturbance of the atmosphere accompanied by wind and often by precipitation (as rain or snow) ⟨a winter *storm* bringing about six inches of snow⟩
synonyms squall, tempest
related words blizzard, ice storm, snowstorm; cloudburst, hailstorm, rainsquall, rainstorm, thundershower, thunderstorm, weather, windstorm; northeaster (*or* nor'easter), norther, southeaster, southwester; cyclone, hurricane, typhoon; sandstorm
2 a heavy fall of objects ⟨police had to endure a *storm* of rocks and bricks hurled by the rioters⟩ — see RAIN 2
3 a rapid or overwhelming outpouring of many things at once ⟨the army's spokesperson faced a *storm* of questions from reporters⟩ — see BARRAGE
4 a state of noisy, confused activity ⟨a few minutes of calm before the *storm*, when the store would open its doors on the busiest day of the year⟩ — see COMMOTION
5 a steady falling of water from the sky in significant quantity ⟨the *storm* caused major damage to our barn⟩ — see RAIN 1
6 a sudden intense expression of strong feeling ⟨a *storm* of indignation and demands for his resignation arose when the mayor's dishonesty was exposed⟩ — see OUTBURST 1
7 a violent disturbance (as of the political or social order) ⟨civil wars and other *storms* of unrest swept through the African continent⟩ — see CONVULSION

stormy *adj* **1** marked by bursts of destructive force or intense activity ⟨a small nation, but one with a long and *stormy* history⟩ — see VIOLENT 1
2 marked by or abounding with rain ⟨*stormy* weather was forecast for the next three days, so we cancelled our camping trip⟩ — see RAINY
3 marked by sudden or violent disturbance ⟨that couple has had a long but *stormy* relationship⟩ — see CONVULSIVE 1
4 marked by turmoil or disturbance especially of natural elements ⟨Neptune has the *stormiest* atmosphere of any planet, with winds of up to 900 miles per hour⟩ — see WILD 3
5 marked by wet and windy conditions ⟨*stormy* seas forced the schooner far off its intended course⟩ — see FOUL 1

story *n* **1** a work with imaginary characters and events that is shorter and usually less complex than a novel ⟨he's a talented writer, but his quirky *stories* will never find a wide readership⟩
synonyms narrative, novelette, novella, short story, tale, yarn
related words bedtime story; exemplum, fable, parable; anecdote, joke; fairy tale, folktale, legend, myth, romance; account, annals, chronicle, history, record, report
2 a brief account of something interesting that happened especially to one personally ⟨Grandpa is always telling *stories* about what it was like growing up on a farm⟩
synonyms anecdote, tale, yarn
related words episode, event, happening, incident, occurrence; recital, recitation
3 a report of recent events or facts not previously known ⟨a *story* in the morning paper about plans for a new library⟩ — see NEWS
4 a relating of events usually in the order in which they happened ⟨gave us the whole *story* of the accident⟩ — see ACCOUNT 1
5 a rumor or report of a personal or sensational nature ⟨*stories* going around that the old man had died with thousands of dollars hidden under his mattress⟩ — see TALE 1
6 a statement known by its maker to be untrue and made in order to deceive ⟨she tells *stories* just to get attention, so don't believe that stuff about her father being somebody important⟩ — see LIE
7 the unfolding of events in a dramatic or literary work ⟨the *story* proceeds at a pace that many readers will find a bit too leisurely⟩ — see ACTION 2
8 position with regard to conditions and circumstances ⟨management is trying to figure out what the *story* is with the accident down in the warehouse⟩ — see SITUATION 1

story line *n* the unfolding of events in a dramatic or literary work ⟨the *story line* is clumsily interrupted several times to provide some much-needed background information⟩ — see ACTION 2

storyteller *n* a person who tells lies ⟨he's something of a *storyteller*, so I wouldn't put too much stock in anything he says⟩ — see LIAR

stout *adj* **1** able to withstand hardship, strain, or exposure ⟨erected a *stout* wooden fence to keep the wild animals out⟩ — see HARDY 1
2 being compact and broad in build and often short in stature ⟨the wrestler is *stout* in build, so he is frequently underestimated by his opponents⟩ — see STOCKY
3 feeling or displaying no fear by temperament ⟨*stout* souls who boldly ventured forward, not knowing what kinds of danger they faced⟩ — see BRAVE 1
4 having muscles capable of exerting great physical force ⟨covered wagons drawn by *stout* oxen⟩ — see STRONG 1
5 not showing weakness or uncertainty ⟨a *stout* defender of women's rights in the third world⟩ — see FIRM 1

stouthearted *adj* feeling or displaying no fear by temperament ⟨*stouthearted* men and women who served in the army medical corps⟩ — see BRAVE 1

stoutheartedly *adv* in a fearless manner ⟨those early settlers who *stoutheartedly* faced the rigors of a Rocky Mountain winter⟩ — see BRAVELY 1

stoutly *adv* in a vigorous and forceful manner ⟨a settler *stoutly* defending his right to be on the land⟩ — see HARD 3

stoutness *n* strength of mind to carry on in spite of danger ⟨even in the face of insurmountable odds, the troops displayed a *stoutness* of heart that was inspiring⟩ — see COURAGE

stow *vb* **1** to place somewhere for safekeeping or ready availability ⟨*stow* the extra life jackets in the chest⟩ — see STORE 1
2 to put (something of future use or value) in a safe or secret place ⟨*stowed* candy bars, which were forbidden at the summer camp, under a board in the cabin's floor⟩ — see HOARD

straggler *n* someone who moves slowly or more slowly than others ⟨by three o'clock, only a few *stragglers* were still making their painful way to the marathon's finish⟩ — see SLOWPOKE

straight *adv* **1** in a direct line or course ⟨when we got to the airport, we went *straight* to the baggage claim area⟩ — see DIRECTLY 1
2 in an honest and direct manner ⟨we gave it to him *straight*: his performance would have to improve—or he was out⟩ — see STRAIGHTFORWARD

straight *adj* **1** free from irregularities or digressions in course ⟨in the wide, open spaces of the West some rural roads are incredibly *straight*⟩
synonyms direct, linear, right, straightaway, straightforward
related words unbent, uncurled, untwisted; undeviating, unswerving
near antonyms bowed, rounded; entwined, kinked, swirled, turned, turning, twined, twining, twisted, twisting, veering, warped; bending, coiled, coiling, corkscrew, curled, curling, curved, curving, looped, looping, spiral, spiraling (*or* spiralling), wavy, winding; meandering, weaving; devious, serpentine, sinuous; crooked, zigzag, zigzagging
2 conforming to a high standard of morality or virtue ⟨a store owner known and trusted for his *straight* dealings⟩ — see GOOD 2
3 free from added matter ⟨would you like that whiskey *straight* or with soda?⟩ — see PURE 1
4 free in expressing one's true feelings and opinions ⟨you should be *straight* with your boss and tell him that you're not happy with the current situation⟩ — see FRANK
5 going straight to the point clearly and firmly ⟨a politician who can never give a *straight* answer to questions about his positions⟩ — see STRAIGHTFORWARD 1
6 not having one's mind affected by alcohol ⟨I'll drive the car, since I seem to be the only one of us who is *straight* at the moment⟩ — see SOBER 1
7 following one after another without others coming in between ⟨I was awake for two *straight* days⟩ — see CONSECUTIVE

straightaway *adj* **1** done or occurring without any noticeable lapse in time ⟨her first novel was a *straightaway* success⟩ — see INSTANTANEOUS
2 free from irregularities or digressions in course ⟨the doomed ship was headed on a *straightaway* course in the path of the iceberg⟩ — see STRAIGHT 1

straightaway *adv* without delay ⟨he got to the hospital, and *straightaway* he was admitted and given intravenous fluids⟩ — see IMMEDIATELY

straighten *vb* to cause to follow a line that is without bends or curls ⟨*straighten* that extension cord—it should be just long enough to reach the wall outlet⟩
synonyms unbend, uncurl, unkink
related words uncoil, unroll, unwind; disentangle, untangle, untwine, untwist
near antonyms arc, bend, bow, hook, round; entwine, kink, swirl, turn, twine, twist; coil, loop, spiral, wind
antonyms bend, crook, curl, curve

straighten (up *or* **out)** *vb* **1** to change one's behavior or character for the better ⟨I hope that rehab will help her *straighten up* for good⟩ — see REFORM 2

2 to make neat ⟨a directive for everyone to *straighten up* their cubicle in preparation for a visit from some corporate VIPs⟩ — see NEATEN

straightforward *adj* **1** going straight to the point clearly and firmly ⟨a *straightforward* account of the football game with no digressions or personal comments⟩
synonyms direct, forthright, foursquare, plain, straight
related words aboveboard, candid, frank, free-spoken, honest, open, openhearted, outspoken, plainspoken, unguarded, unreserved; artless, earnest, sincere; uninhibited, unrestrained; abrupt, bluff, blunt, brusque (*also* brusk), curt, gruff, point-blank, sharp; impolite, inconsiderate, rude, tactless, undiplomatic; true, truthful, veracious
near antonyms circumlocutory, long-winded, prolix, verbose, wordy; inhibited, reserved, restrained; civil, courteous, polite, tactful; deceitful, lying, mendacious, untruthful; erroneous, fallacious, false; ambiguous, equivocal, evasive, misleading; double-dealing, hypocritical, two-faced
antonyms circuitous, indirect, roundabout
2 free from irregularities or digressions in course ⟨the missile continued on its *straightforward* path toward the enemy's command post⟩ — see STRAIGHT 1
3 free in expressing one's true feelings and opinions ⟨I want you to be *straightforward* with me and tell me if this dress looks awful⟩ — see FRANK
4 not subject to misinterpretation or more than one interpretation ⟨the distinction between the two types of offenses is pretty *straightforward*⟩ — see CLEAR 2

straightforward *also* **straightforwards** *adv* in an honest and direct manner ⟨she finally told him *straightforward* that she wasn't interested in a date⟩
synonyms directly, forthrightly, foursquare, plain, plainly, straight, straightforwardly
related words baldly, bluffly, candidly, frankly, honestly, openheartedly, openly, unguardedly, unreservedly; artlessly, earnestly, simply, sincerely; abruptly, bluntly, brusquely, curtly, gruffly, point-blank, sharply; impolitely, inconsiderately, rudely, tactlessly; truthfully, veraciously
near antonyms long-windedly, verbosely, wordily; civilly, courteously, diplomatically, politely, tactfully; deceitfully, mendaciously, untruthfully; erroneously, fallaciously, falsely, hypocritically, insincerely; ambiguously, circuitously, equivocally, evasively, indirectly

straightforwardly *adv* in an honest and direct manner ⟨*straightforwardly* yet compassionately, the doctor tells his cancer patients what their odds for survival are⟩ — see STRAIGHTFORWARD

straightforwardness *n* the free expression of one's true feelings and opinions ⟨not all of her voice students appreciate the *straightforwardness* with which she tells them that they're not going to make it as professional singers⟩ — see CANDOR 1

straight off *adv* without delay ⟨I told her *straight off* that I was not going to do that⟩ — see IMMEDIATELY

straight–out *adj* having no exceptions or restrictions ⟨the *straight-out* enmity between the two tennis players was unmistakable⟩ — see ABSOLUTE 2

straightway *adv* **1** without delay ⟨*straightway*, the decorator told us that the old couch had to go⟩ — see IMMEDIATELY
2 in a direct line or course ⟨disgusted by his coworker's offensive e-mail, he marched *straightway* to the boss's office to lodge a complaint⟩ — see DIRECTLY 1

[1]**strain** *n* **1** the line of ancestors from whom a person is descended ⟨descended from a *strain* of Irish seafarers⟩ — see ANCESTRY
2 a rhythmic series of musical tones arranged to give a pleasing effect ⟨the *strain* of an old Irish ballad rose up from the revelers downstairs⟩ — see MELODY
3 a very small amount ⟨detected a *strain* of panic in her voice when she asked if the substance was poisonous⟩ — see PARTICLE 1
4 a number of persons or things that are grouped together because they have something in common ⟨writes mystery novels of a more sophisticated *strain*⟩ — see SORT 1

[2]**strain** *n* the burden on one's emotional or mental well-being created by demands on one's time ⟨the family's constant moving is putting a real *strain* on the children⟩ — see STRESS 1

strain *vb* **1** to injure by overuse, misuse, or pressure ⟨in order to lift something heavy, squat down and lift with your legs, or you'll *strain* your back⟩
synonyms pull, rack, stretch, wrench
related words fray, tax, weaken; damage, harm, hurt, impair, wound; batter, bruise, tear; cripple, lame, mangle, mutilate
2 to pass through a filter ⟨better *strain* that coffee thoroughly to get all the grounds out⟩
synonyms filter, screen
related words leach, percolate
3 to devote serious and sustained effort ⟨the whole department is *straining* to complete the project before the deadline⟩ — see LABOR
4 to flow forth slowly through small openings ⟨put the cooked fruit in a cheesecloth bag and let the juice *strain* into a pan⟩ — see EXUDE
5 to subject (a personal quality or faculty) to often excessive stress ⟨*strained* her memory but the name just wouldn't come to her⟩ — see TRY 1
6 to draw tight ⟨the dog *strained* its leash trying to get to the cat⟩ — see TIGHTEN
7 to put one's arms around and press tightly ⟨the woman tenderly *strained* to her breast the child that she had long ago given up for dead⟩ — see EMBRACE 1

strained *adj* lacking in natural or spontaneous quality ⟨I took the complaint manager's *strained* smile to mean I wasn't a welcome sight⟩ — see ARTIFICIAL 1

strait *n* **1** a narrow body of water between two land masses ⟨as the ship headed east through the *Strait* of Gibraltar, Spain was on our left and Africa on our right⟩ — see CHANNEL 2
2 *often* **straits** *pl* a state of great suffering of body or mind ⟨in great *straits* over the loss of her mother's cherished necklace⟩ — see DISTRESS 1

straitlaced *or* **straightlaced** *adj* given to or marked by very conservative standards regarding personal behavior or morals ⟨a very *straitlaced* old lady who believed that cleavage was something that should be shown by rock crystals, not respectable women⟩
synonyms bluenosed, nice-nelly, prim, prudish, puritanical, Victorian
related words priggish, staid, stuffy; genteel, proper, refined; decent, honest, moral, right, righteous, upright, virtuous
near antonyms liberated, permissive; bad, immoral, improper, indecent, lax, lecherous, lickerish, loose, prurient, wicked; skanky [*slang*], slatternly, sleazy, sluttish, slutty, trampy; debauched, degenerate, degraded, depraved, perverted

strand *n* the usually sandy or gravelly land bordering a body of water ⟨the wishful dream of living an indolent, idyllic existence on some far-off *strand*⟩ — see BEACH

strand *vb* **1** to cause irreparable damage to (a ship) by running aground or sinking ⟨the ghostly remains of ships that had been *stranded* by the reef⟩ — see SHIPWRECK
2 to cause to remain behind ⟨he just drove off, *stranding* her in some dinky town with just a few bucks and the clothes she was wearing⟩ — see LEAVE 1

stranded *adj* resting on the shore or bottom of a body of water ⟨*stranded* whales often die because their bodies overheat on the hot sand⟩ — see AGROUND

strange *adj* **1** different from the ordinary in a way that causes curiosity or suspicion ⟨the *strange* smell we'd noticed turned out, unhappily, to be from the dinner our host was making⟩ — see ODD 2

2 excitingly or mysteriously unusual ⟨*strange* fruits from faraway lands⟩ — see EXOTIC

3 not known or experienced before ⟨using public transportation was all very *strange* to a rural girl like her⟩ — see NEW 2

4 noticeably different from what is generally found or experienced ⟨a rather *strange* story about a garden filled with poisonous plants⟩ — see UNUSUAL 1

stranger *n* a person who is not native to or known to a community ⟨the people of the island are quick to make *strangers* feel at home⟩

synonyms foreigner, nonnative, outlander, outsider

related words alien, nonresident; outcast, pariah; drifter, transient, wanderer

near antonyms buddy, chum, comrade, confidant, crony, familiar, friend, intimate, pal; acquaintance, associate, cohort, colleague, companion, fellow, hearty, hobnobber, mate, partner, peer; citizen, habitant, inhabitant, resident

antonyms native

strangle *vb* **1** to be or cause to be killed by lack of breathable air ⟨the gull got tangled in a piece of fishing line on the beach and was *strangled*⟩ — see SMOTHER 1

2 to keep (someone) from breathing by exerting pressure on the windpipe ⟨the boy complained that he was being *strangled* by his tie⟩ — see CHOKE 1

3 to refrain from openly showing or uttering ⟨*strangled* a gasp of surprise upon hearing the news⟩ — see SUPPRESS 2

stratagem *n* a clever often underhanded means to achieve an end ⟨tried various *stratagems* to get the cat into the carrier, but the feisty feline was wise to them all⟩ — see TRICK 1

strategize (about) *vb* to work out the details of (something) in advance ⟨*strategized about* how they would arrange seating if the event had to be moved inside⟩ — see PLAN 1

strategy *n* **1** a method worked out in advance for achieving some objective ⟨a statewide *strategy* to raise students' achievement test scores over the next three years⟩ — see PLAN 1

2 the means or procedure for doing something ⟨you'll need a better *strategy* than just knocking on doors if you want to sell that many magazines⟩ — see METHOD

stratum *n* **1** one of the segments of society into which people are grouped ⟨the lower *strata* of society have been hit especially hard by this economic downturn⟩ — see CLASS 1

2 the placement of someone or something in relation to others in a vertical arrangement ⟨the level of writing in that pop novel is several *strata* beneath that of serious fiction⟩ — see RANK 1

straw *adj* of a pale yellow or yellowish brown color ⟨the cheese maker told us that the best Parmesan cheeses are *straw*, not white, in color⟩ — see BLOND

stray *adj* lacking a definite plan, purpose, or pattern ⟨*stray* sightings of UFO's, none of which have been rigorously analyzed by scientists⟩ — see RANDOM

stray *vb* to commit an offense ⟨our *straying* son swears he's returned to the straight and narrow⟩ — see OFFEND 1

streak *n* **1** a line or long narrow section differing in color from the background ⟨the flower has white petals with red *streaks*⟩ — see [1]STRIPE 1

2 a very small amount ⟨there's just a *streak* of stubbornness in that child⟩ — see PARTICLE 1

streak *vb* to make stripes on ⟨light from the setting sun *streaked* the clouds in brilliant bands of pink and orange⟩ — see STRIPE

streaked *adj* having stripes ⟨hair *streaked* with gray⟩ — see STRIPED

stream *vb* **1** to cause to flow in a stream ⟨his eyes were *streaming* tears⟩ — see POUR 1

2 to move in a stream ⟨blood *streaming* out of a wound⟩ — see FLOW 1

3 to move or proceed smoothly and readily ⟨cars *streaming* along the freeway⟩ — see FLOW 2

streamer *n* a piece of cloth with a special design that is used as an emblem or for signaling ⟨*streamers* in the team's colors hung from the top of the stadium⟩ — see FLAG 1

streamlet *n* a natural body of running water smaller than a river ⟨the raging brook of last spring is a mere *streamlet* now that it's July⟩ — see CREEK 1

streamline *vb* **1** to make less complex ⟨*streamline* the work of mailing out flyers by using computer-generated labels⟩ — see SIMPLIFY 1

2 to adapt to modern needs, taste, or usage ⟨in an effort to compete against online vendors, many traditional retailers have had to *streamline* their brick-and-mortar stores⟩ — see MODERNIZE

street *n* a passage cleared for public vehicular travel ⟨going the wrong way on a one-way *street*⟩ — see WAY 1

streetwalker *n* a woman who engages in sexual activities for money ⟨the *streetwalkers* and adult movie theaters that once populated the tenderloin have been replaced by upscale shoppers and expensive restaurants and boutiques⟩ — see PROSTITUTE

strength *n* **1** the ability to exert effort for the accomplishment of a task ⟨the murdered man's wife didn't have the emotional *strength* to face reporters⟩ — see POWER 2

2 the ability to withstand force or stress without being distorted, dislodged, or damaged ⟨this cheap shelving unit doesn't have the *strength* to hold all those books⟩ — see STABILITY 1

strengthen *vb* **1** to increase the ability of (as a muscle) to exert physical force ⟨lifting weights every day will eventually *strengthen* your muscles⟩ ⟨the army makes new recruits run for miles in order to *strengthen* them⟩

synonyms beef (up), fortify, harden, toughen

related words anneal, temper; firm (up), tone (up); energize, invigorate, vitalize; restrengthen

near antonyms cripple, incapacitate, paralyze; damage, harm, hurt, impair, injure; break down, wear out; sap, undercut, undermine

antonyms debilitate, enervate, enfeeble, weaken

2 to make able to withstand physical hardship, strain, or exposure ⟨required weeks of physical therapy to *strengthen* his arm enough to pitch for the team again⟩ — see HARDEN 2

3 to make markedly greater in measure or degree ⟨encouraged the boarding school students to *strengthen* their ties with the community by doing public service⟩ — see INTENSIFY

4 to prepare (oneself) mentally or emotionally ⟨*strengthened* herself for the moment she'd have to tell her friend that she had lost the borrowed necklace⟩ — see FORTIFY 1

5 to make more harsh, uncompromising, or severe ⟨a bill was introduced to *strengthen* punishments for hate crimes⟩ — see HARSHEN

strenuous *adj* **1** marked by or uttered with forcefulness ⟨parents who voiced *strenuous* objections to the new textbooks⟩ — see EMPHATIC 1

2 requiring considerable physical or mental effort ⟨a

strenuous workout on the obstacle course⟩ — see HARD 2

strenuously *adv* **1** in a vigorous and forceful manner ⟨argued *strenuously* in favor of easing the academic requirements for participation in school sports⟩ — see HARD 3

2 with great effort or determination ⟨the IT staff worked *strenuously* to get the network back online⟩ — see HARD 1

stress *n* **1** the burden on one's emotional or mental well-being created by demands on one's time ⟨with a full-time job and her college courses, the young woman is under a lot of *stress* right now⟩

synonyms pressure, strain, tension

related words load, weight; anxiety, concern, uneasiness, worry; aggravation, anger, annoyance, exasperation, irritation, persecution, trouble

near antonyms comfort, consolation

2 a special notice or importance given to something ⟨the company's orientation program places considerable *stress* on workplace safety⟩ — see EMPHASIS 1

stress *vb* **1** to experience concern or anxiety ⟨the restaurant manager has a tendency to *stress* about every little thing that goes wrong⟩ — see WORRY 1

2 to make more apparent ⟨his bad performance only *stressed* what I'd been saying all along⟩ — see EMPHASIZE 2

3 to indicate the importance of by centering attention on ⟨the doctor *stressed* the importance of exercise⟩ — see EMPHASIZE 1

stressed *adj* suffering from high levels of physical and especially psychological stress ⟨you seem really *stressed* right now, so maybe you should try to do something more relaxing⟩ — see STRESSED-OUT

stressed–out *adj* suffering from high levels of physical and especially psychological stress ⟨the demands of this job are enough to make anyone *stressed-out*⟩

synonyms shell-shocked, stressed

related words burned-out (*or* burnt-out), exhausted, knackered [*British*], tired, worn-out; undone, unmanned, unnerved, unstrung; edgy, nervous, tense, uneasy; agitated, disturbed, perturbed, troubled, upset; aggravated, angry, annoyed, exasperated, irritated

phrases on the rack

near antonyms laid-back, relaxed, rested; carefree, devil-may-care, happy-go-lucky, lighthearted, unconcerned

stretch *adj* able to revert to original size and shape after being stretched, squeezed, or twisted ⟨*stretch* fabrics that don't wrinkle or sag⟩ — see ELASTIC 1

stretch *n* **1** a wide space or area ⟨a narrow *stretch* of beach below the cliffs⟩ — see EXPANSE

2 an indefinite but usually short period of time ⟨there was a cardinal at our bird feeder for a short *stretch* last spring⟩ — see WHILE 1

3 the distance or extent between possible extremes ⟨the stories were written over a considerable *stretch* of time⟩ — see RANGE 3

4 the space or amount of space between two points, lines, surfaces, or objects ⟨the longest *stretch* of the drive without any place to get gas⟩ — see DISTANCE 1

stretch *vb* **1** to add to the interest of by including made-up details ⟨it was *stretching* the truth to say she'd been in the movies: she was once an extra whose scene was cut in the final version⟩ — see EMBROIDER

2 to injure by overuse, misuse, or pressure ⟨I *stretched* a back muscle, and the pain is killing me⟩ — see STRAIN 1

3 to make longer ⟨the time it would take to fix the car got *stretched* from three hours to two days when the part we needed had to be ordered⟩ — see EXTEND 1

4 to subject (a personal quality or faculty) to often excessive stress ⟨your whining is *stretching* my patience to the limit⟩ — see TRY 1

5 to draw tight ⟨if the canvas isn't properly *stretched* over the frame, there will be sagging over time⟩ — see TIGHTEN

stretch (out) *vb* to arrange the parts of (something) over a wider area ⟨you can't *stretch out* your legs to the point where you're blocking the aisle⟩ — see OPEN 3

stretchable *adj* able to revert to original size and shape after being stretched, squeezed, or twisted ⟨*stretchable* gloves⟩ ⟨*stretchable* bandages⟩ — see ELASTIC 1

stretching *n* **1** the act of making longer ⟨excessive *stretching* can cause the fabric to tear or lose its elasticity⟩ — see EXTENSION 1

2 the representation of something in terms that go beyond the facts ⟨your constant *stretching* of the truth is going to get you in trouble someday⟩ — see EXAGGERATION

stretchy *adj* able to revert to original size and shape after being stretched, squeezed, or twisted ⟨a *stretchy* hair band⟩ — see ELASTIC 1

strew *vb* to cover by or as if by scattering something over or on ⟨sidewalks *strewed* with trash left by the parade watchers⟩ — see SCATTER 2

strict *adj* **1** following an original exactly ⟨not a *strict* translation, because a lot of the humor is in the wordplay⟩ — see FAITHFUL 2

2 given to exacting standards of discipline and self-restraint ⟨that piano teacher is notoriously *strict*, but students make great strides under her tutelage⟩ — see SEVERE 1

3 not allowing for any exceptions or loosening of standards ⟨on a *strict* diet⟩ ⟨*strict* adherence to the letter of the law⟩ — see RIGID 1

strictly *adv* without any relaxation of standards or precision ⟨*strictly* speaking, Columbus did not discover America—the people living there had long known about it⟩ ⟨the rules must be *strictly* obeyed⟩

synonyms exactly, precisely, rigidly, rigorously

related words carefully, conscientiously, meticulously, scrupulously

antonyms imprecisely, inexactly, loosely

strictness *n* the quality or state of being demanding or unyielding (as in discipline or criticism) ⟨his stoic temperament suited him well to the demands and *strictness* of military life⟩ — see SEVERITY

stricture *n* **1** an often public or formal expression of disapproval ⟨the church's *strictures* on the morals and mores of contemporary society⟩ — see CENSURE

2 something that limits one's freedom of action or choice ⟨the new zoning *strictures* effectively make further development along the riverfront commercially unviable⟩ — see RESTRICTION 1

stride *vb* to move along with a steady regular step especially in a group ⟨a gang of armed men *strode* into the bank and approached the teller⟩ — see MARCH 1

strife *n* **1** a lack of agreement or harmony ⟨in order to avoid family *strife*, the children spend equal time during the holidays with both of their grandmothers⟩ — see DISCORD

2 an earnest effort for superiority or victory over another ⟨bitter *strife* between the two political factions⟩ — see CONTEST 1

strike *n* **1** a work stoppage by a body of workers intended to force an employer to meet their demands ⟨the nurses will go on *strike* tomorrow unless they're finally given a pay raise⟩

synonyms walkout

related words sympathetic strike, sympathy strike; go-slow [*British*], job action, sick-out, sit-down, sit-in, slow-down; lockout

2 the act or action of setting upon with force or vio-

lence ⟨the first *strike* was directed at a munitions warehouse⟩ — see ATTACK 1
3 a feature of someone or something that creates difficulty for achieving success ⟨kids born into poverty already have a *strike* against them⟩ — see DISADVANTAGE 1
4 a forceful coming together of two things ⟨the *strike* of a hammer against a nail always has a satisfying sound when you're building something yourself⟩ — see IMPACT 1
5 an unexpected benefit or advantage resulting from the uncertain course of events ⟨she's made one *strike* after another since she began speculating in real estate⟩ — see FLUKE

strike *vb* **1** to refuse to work in order to force an employer to meet demands ⟨the union is calling for its members to *strike* until the mining company agrees to meet safety standards⟩
synonyms walk, walk out
related words sit in; lock out
2 to act upon (a person or a person's feelings) so as to cause a response ⟨we were *struck* by the willingness of total strangers to go out of their way to help us⟩ — see [1]AFFECT 1
3 to enter the mind of ⟨it *struck* her later that no one at the bank had asked for identification⟩ — see OCCUR (TO)
4 to come into usually forceful contact with something ⟨the thump of hailstones *striking* the cars in the parking lot⟩ — see HIT 2
5 to deliver a blow to (someone or something) usually in a strong vigorous manner ⟨the driver of the car behind me applied his brakes too late and *struck* my car from the rear⟩ — see HIT 1
6 to take apart ⟨the stagehands *struck* the sets the morning after the play closed⟩ — see DISASSEMBLE 1
7 to take sudden, violent action against ⟨a rattlesnake *strikes* its prey with lightning speed⟩ — see ATTACK 1
8 to cast a spell on ⟨the only way that she's going to get a man is if she *strikes* one⟩ — see BEWITCH 1

strike (into) *vb* to take the first step in (a process or course of action) ⟨before you actually *strike into* your speech, you should introduce yourself⟩ — see BEGIN 1

strike (out) *vb* to show (something written) to be no longer valid by drawing a cross over or a line through it ⟨*struck out* all references to indecent matters⟩ — see X (OUT)

strike down *vb* to put an end to by formal action ⟨a law that was later *struck down* by the U.S. Supreme Court as unconstitutional⟩ — see ABOLISH 1

strike out *vb* to be unsuccessful ⟨their joint venture in Las Vegas *struck out*, and they hurriedly dissolved the partnership⟩ — see FAIL 2

striking *adj* **1** likely to attract attention ⟨you'd be amazed what a *striking* difference new wallpaper can make in a room⟩ — see NOTICEABLE
2 very noticeable especially for being incorrect or bad ⟨several *striking* contradictions in her argument⟩ — see EGREGIOUS

string *n* **1** a length of braided, flexible material that is used for tying or connecting things ⟨a piece of *string* won't hold that gate shut if a big wind comes along⟩ — see CORD 1
2 a series of persons or things arranged one behind another ⟨a *string* of cars stretching as far as we could see⟩ — see LINE 1
3 a series of things linked together ⟨recounted the *string* of events that led to the murder⟩ — see CHAIN 1

string *vb* to put together into a series by means of or as if by means of a thread ⟨the prosecuting attorney *strung* the evidence together so that the accused man really did look guilty⟩ — see THREAD 2

string along *vb* to cause to believe what is untrue ⟨the student succeeded in *stringing* even his teachers *along* with his tales of family hardships⟩ — see DECEIVE

stringency *n* the quality or state of being demanding or unyielding (as in discipline or criticism) ⟨some people objected to the *stringency* of the new regulations regarding the alteration of building exteriors in the historic district⟩ — see SEVERITY

stringent *adj* not allowing for any exceptions or loosening of standards ⟨*stringent* rules against unauthorized persons being in the building⟩ — see RIGID 1

stringy *adj* resembling or having the texture of a mass of strings ⟨*stringy* hair that clearly needs a good washing⟩
synonyms fibrous
related words knotty, ropy (*also* ropey), thready; sinewy, wiry

strip *vb* **1** to remove clothing from ⟨the nurse told the nervous mother to *strip* her screaming baby down to his diaper for the exam⟩ — see UNDRESS 1
2 to take something away from ⟨an indiscretion that resulted in her being *stripped* of her authority⟩ — see DEPRIVE 1

strip *n* **1** a long narrow piece of material ⟨now tear the paper into *strips* and fold them up carefully⟩
synonyms list, ribbon, slip
related words slat; band, bandage, belt, binding, girth, strap, swatch, swath (*or* swathe), tape
2 a series of drawings that tell a story or part of a story ⟨a cartoonist who uses his daily *strip* to make his political points⟩ — see COMIC STRIP

[1]**stripe** *n* **1** a line or long narrow section differing in color from the background ⟨the United States flag has seven red *stripes*⟩
synonyms band, bar, streak
related words blaze, crossbar, pinstripe
2 a number of persons or things that are grouped together because they have something in common ⟨singers of every *stripe* will perform at the benefit concert⟩ — see SORT 1

[2]**stripe** *n* a hard strike with a part of the body or an instrument ⟨the prisoner was sentenced to receive 20 *stripes* with a bamboo pole⟩ — see [1]BLOW

stripe *vb* to make stripes on ⟨the children carefully *striped* the paper with red and blue paint⟩
synonyms band, bar, streak
related words blaze

striped *adj* having stripes ⟨the zebra is a black-and-white *striped* animal⟩
synonyms banded, barred, streaked
related words corded, tabby

stripling *n* a male person who has not yet reached adulthood ⟨the young boxer looked like a mere *stripling* next to his larger, more seasoned opponent⟩ — see BOY 1

stripped *adj* **1** lacking a usual or natural covering ⟨bought matching end tables of *stripped* pine⟩ — see NAKED 2
2 lacking or shed of clothing ⟨highway construction workers, *stripped* to the waist, toiled away in the sweltering heat⟩ — see NAKED 1

strive *vb* **1** to devote serious and sustained effort ⟨not only must we *strive* for peace in time of war, we must *strive* mightily to maintain that peace⟩ — see LABOR
2 to make an effort to do ⟨let us *strive* to make the most of this opportunity⟩ — see ATTEMPT

stroke *n* a hard strike with a part of the body or an instrument ⟨all it took was one hard *stroke* to knock the ball out of the tree⟩ — see [1]BLOW

stroke *vb* **1** to touch or handle in a tender or loving manner ⟨the young mother gently *stroked* the sleeping

child's brow and then leaned over and kissed him⟩ — see FONDLE
2 to praise too much ⟨a politician with a special gift for *stroking* fat-cat donors⟩ — see FLATTER 1

stroke (out) *vb* to show (something written) to be no longer valid by drawing a cross over or a line through it ⟨if you make a mistake on the form, just *stroke* it *out*⟩ — see X (OUT)

stroll *n* a relaxed journey on foot for exercise or pleasure ⟨we arrived early and took a *stroll* through the park before dinner⟩ — see WALK 1

stroll *vb* to travel by foot for exercise or pleasure ⟨people who like to *stroll* along the beach would seem to be well-represented among the clientele for dating services⟩ — see HIKE 1

stroller *n* **1** a person who roams about without a fixed route or destination ⟨back in olden days when *strollers* and vagabonds wandered the Scottish countryside⟩ — see NOMAD
2 a small four-wheeled vehicle designed for pushing a baby around in ⟨a collapsible *stroller*⟩ — see BABY CARRIAGE

strong *adj* **1** having muscles capable of exerting great physical force ⟨I need some *strong* people to help me move furniture⟩
synonyms brawny, muscular, rugged, sinewy, stalwart, stout
related words forceful, forcible, mighty, potent, powerful, puissant; able-bodied, athletic, fit, trim; beefy, burly, husky, strapping; masculine, virile; hard, inured, strengthened, sturdy, tough, toughened; energetic, energized, invigorated, lusty, red-blooded, robust, vigorous, vitalized; hale, healthy, hearty, sound
near antonyms challenged, disabled, incapacitated, paralyzed; impotent, powerless; puny, slight, small, unathletic, unfit, unhealthy
antonyms delicate, feeble, frail, weak, weakling, wimpy
2 able to withstand hardship, strain, or exposure ⟨the doctor soon declared her *strong* enough to go home from the hospital⟩ — see HARDY 1
3 having a powerfully stimulating odor or flavor ⟨the garlic in the sauce is almost too *strong*⟩ ⟨that's mighty *strong* perfume you're wearing⟩ — see SHARP 2
4 having an abundance of some characteristic quality (as flavor) ⟨*strong* coffee⟩ — see FULL-BODIED
5 having an unpleasant smell ⟨the dog's *strong* breath nearly bowled me over⟩ — see MALODOROUS
6 having great power or influence ⟨a time when the country needs a *strong* leader⟩ — see IMPORTANT 2
7 having the power to persuade ⟨made a *strong* argument for starting school an hour later each day⟩ — see COGENT
8 marked by the ability to withstand stress without structural damage or distortion ⟨buildings *strong* enough to withstand an earthquake⟩ — see STABLE 1
9 not showing weakness or uncertainty ⟨a *strong* belief in the value of hard work⟩ — see FIRM 1

strong–arm *vb* to make timid or fearful by or as if by threats ⟨developers trying to *strong-arm* homeowners into selling their houses at below-market prices⟩ — see INTIMIDATE

strongbox *n* a specially reinforced container to keep valuables safe ⟨keeps her jewelry in a *strongbox*⟩ — see SAFE

strong drink *n* a distilled beverage that can make a person drunk ⟨he's been known to partake of *strong drink* now and then⟩ — see ALCOHOL

stronghold *n* a structure or place from which one can resist attack ⟨the island was the pirates' last *stronghold* in the West Indies⟩ — see FORT

strongly *adv* in a vigorous and forceful manner ⟨in the past, the senator has always *strongly* opposed any suggested increase in taxes⟩ — see HARD 3

strongman *n* a person who uses power or authority in a cruel, unjust, or harmful way ⟨a Latin-American *strongman* who basically treated his nation's coffers as his personal bank account⟩ — see DESPOT

strong suit *n* something for which a person shows a special talent ⟨languages are definitely the diplomat's *strong suit*⟩ — see FORTE

strop *vb* to make sharp or sharper ⟨at the museum they showed us how men used to *strop* razors with leather bands before the days of disposable blades⟩ — see SHARPEN

stropped *adj* having an edge thin enough to cut or pierce something ⟨I was surprised at how sharp the *stropped* razor was⟩ — see SHARP 1

structure *n* **1** something built as a dwelling, shelter, or place for human activity ⟨the only *structure* on the island is an old Spanish fort—or what's left of it⟩ — see BUILDING
2 something put together by arranging or connecting an array of parts ⟨the Egyptian pyramids are among the most remarkable *structures* ever built⟩ — see CONSTRUCTION 1
3 the arrangement of parts that gives something its basic form ⟨the basic *structure* of all those tract houses is the same: basically, a box⟩ — see FRAME 1

struggle *n* **1** a forceful effort to reach a goal or objective ⟨a physically challenged child's determined *struggle* to make straight A's in school⟩
synonyms battle, fight, fray, scrabble, throes
related words effort, exertion, labor, pains, trouble, work; drudgery, grind, sweat, toil, travail; combat, conflict, contest, strife, tussle, war, warfare; attempt, endeavor, essay, try
2 a physical dispute between opposing individuals or groups ⟨there was a *struggle* between the armed robber and the shopkeeper, and the gun went off⟩ — see FIGHT 1
3 an earnest effort for superiority or victory over another ⟨her staunchest supporters in her *struggle* for the office⟩ — see CONTEST 1

struggle *vb* **1** to proceed or act clumsily or ineffectually ⟨each week I would *struggle* through my piano lesson, keenly aware that I wasn't getting any better⟩ — see FLOUNDER 1
2 to devote serious and sustained effort ⟨the financially strapped couple *struggled* to make ends meet⟩ — see LABOR

strumpet *n* a woman who engages in sexual activities for money ⟨the portrait painter's muse for the goddess of love was apparently a common *strumpet*⟩ — see PROSTITUTE

strung out *adj* being under the influence of a recreational drug ⟨she seems to have been *strung out* for most of the 1960s⟩ — see STONED 1

strut *vb* **1** to walk with exaggerated arm and leg movements ⟨the cat *strutted* proudly onto the porch with a bird in its mouth⟩
synonyms prance, sashay, stalk, swagger
related words flounce, mince, traipse; pussyfoot, tiptoe; sweep; parade, promenade; pad, step, tread; pace, stride; lumber, lurch, pound, shamble, shuffle, stagger
2 to present so as to invite notice or attention ⟨*strutting* his blue ribbon for all to see⟩ — see SHOW 1

stub *n* an unused or unwanted piece or item typically of small size or value ⟨an ashtray full of cigarette *stubs*⟩ ⟨ticket *stubs*⟩ — see [1]SCRAP 1

stubborn *adj* sticking to an opinion, purpose, or course of action in spite of reason, arguments, or persuasion ⟨he's just being *stubborn*, refusing even to try the new toothpaste⟩ — see OBSTINATE

stubbornness *n* a steadfast adherence to an opinion, purpose, or course of action in spite of reason, arguments, or persuasion ⟨between my brother's *stubbornness* and my own, it's amazing when we come to an agreement about anything⟩ — see OBSTINACY

stubby *adj* being compact and broad in build and often short in stature ⟨seven *stubby* little fellows carried the sleeping Snow White back to their home in a cave⟩ — see STOCKY

stuck *adj* firmly positioned in place and difficult to dislodge ⟨the car was hopelessly *stuck* in the mud⟩ — see TIGHT 2

stuck–up *adj* having too high an opinion of oneself ⟨thought that the kids at his new school were snobbish and *stuck-up*⟩ — see CONCEITED

stud *n* a physically attractive man ⟨she promised her friend that the blind date would be a real *stud*⟩ — see HUNK 1

student *n* one who attends a school ⟨a straight-A *student* at the local high school⟩
synonyms pupil, scholar
related words reader, studier; day student, preppy (*or* preppie), schoolboy, schoolchild, schoolgirl; schoolfellow, schoolmate; coed, collegian, postgraduate, undergraduate; high schooler, kindergartner (*also* kindergartener), middler, middle schooler; freshman, junior, senior, sophomore; underclassman, undergrad, upperclassman; exchange student
antonyms nonstudent

studied *adj* decided on as a result of careful thought ⟨a *studied* move by the company that was designed to put the competition out of business⟩ — see DELIBERATE 1

study *n* **1** a systematic search for the truth or facts about something ⟨conducted a *study* to determine the sleep needs of adolescents⟩ — see INQUIRY 1
2 the state of being lost in thought ⟨found her staring at the fire in a deep *study*⟩ — see REVERIE
3 a careful weighing of the reasons for or against something ⟨the idea is under *study* by the city council⟩ — see CONSIDERATION 1

study *vb* **1** to use the mind to acquire knowledge ⟨you'll have to *study* hard and learn all about the Revolutionary War in order to pass the history test⟩
synonyms bone (up)
related words cram; grind, swot [*British*]; analyze, deduce, find out; con, learn, memorize, read; research, restudy; apprehend, comprehend, grasp, know, understand; absorb, digest
phrases go over, go through
2 to commit to memory ⟨having carefully *studied* the document, he could repeat what it said exactly⟩ — see MEMORIZE
3 to give serious and careful thought to ⟨scientists who *study* the origin of the universe⟩ — see PONDER

stuff *n* **1** a skill, an ability, or knowledge that makes a person able to do a particular job ⟨a guy who has the *stuff* it takes to be head of a major corporation⟩ — see QUALIFICATION 1
2 the basic elements from which something can be developed ⟨reading, writing, and arithmetic—the *stuff* of an education⟩ — see MAKING
3 the quality or qualities that make a thing what it is ⟨the real *stuff* of nobility of character isn't riches or a title, but honor and integrity⟩ — see ESSENCE 1
4 transportable items that one owns ⟨gather up your *stuff* so that we can get going⟩ — see POSSESSION 2
5 items needed for the performance of a task or activity ⟨missed a great photo opportunity because all of my camera *stuff* was at home⟩ — see EQUIPMENT

stuff *vb* **1** to close up so that no empty spaces remain ⟨*stuffed* the box with tissue paper so the contents wouldn't rattle around⟩ — see FILL 2
2 to fill with food to capacity ⟨kids who *stuff* themselves with junk food after school and then don't have any room for supper⟩ — see GORGE 1
3 to fit (people or things) into a tight space ⟨*stuffed* all the kids into the back of the car⟩ — see CROWD 1
4 to prevent passage through by filling with something ⟨I can't smell anything, as my nose is all *stuffed*⟩ — see CLOG 1
5 to put into (something) as much as can be held or contained ⟨*stuffed* a whole suitcase with gifts for her relatives in Mexico⟩ — see FILL 1

stuffed *adj* **1** containing or seeming to contain the greatest quantity or number possible ⟨had never seen shelves so *stuffed* with books⟩ — see FULL 1
2 having one's appetite completely satisfied ⟨we were still *stuffed* from our huge breakfast and didn't want lunch⟩ — see FULL 3

stuffed shirt *n* a person with old-fashioned ideas ⟨the *stuffed shirts* in this organization don't seem to realize that without new blood our extinction is inevitable⟩ — see FOGY

stuffer *n* one who eats greedily or too much ⟨the different kinds of hot dog eaters: the *stuffer* who downs it in two bites; the nibbler; the mustard loader⟩ — see GLUTTON

stuffing *n* soft material that is used to fill the hollow parts of something ⟨never heard of using goose down as *stuffing* for comforters until she moved to a cold climate⟩ — see FILLING

stuffy *adj* **1** lacking fresh air ⟨the house was very *stuffy* after being closed up for a month⟩
synonyms breathless, close, stifling, suffocating
related words airless, unventilated; fuggy; heavy, oppressive, thick
near antonyms bracing, brisk, invigorating, refreshed, refreshing, restorative, reviving, sweet; ventilated
antonyms airy, breezy, unstuffy
2 causing weariness, restlessness, or lack of interest ⟨nothing *stuffy* about this science museum—it's all interactive and fun⟩ — see BORING
3 easily irritated or annoyed ⟨those nursing home residents with a reputation for being chronically *stuffy* were usually the last to receive attention⟩ — see IRRITABLE

stumble *n* **1** an unintentional departure from truth or accuracy ⟨was his hurtful remark a regrettable *stumble*, or was it made with artful intention?⟩ — see ERROR 1
2 the act of going down from an upright position suddenly and involuntarily ⟨has bones so brittle that a minor *stumble* could result in a serious break⟩ — see FALL 1

stumble *vb* **1** to go down from an upright position suddenly and involuntarily ⟨the bride *stumbled* on the altar steps and landed smack in the arms of the minister⟩ — see FALL 1
2 to proceed or act clumsily or ineffectually ⟨*stumbled* twice while she was reciting the "Gettysburg Address"⟩ — see FLOUNDER 1
3 to move heavily or clumsily ⟨the tipsy revelers left the path and wearily *stumbled* through the tangled undergrowth⟩ — see LUMBER 1
4 to make a mistake ⟨that network announcer rarely *stumbles* when he's on the air⟩ — see ERR 1

stumble (on *or* onto) *vb* to come upon unexpectedly or by chance ⟨*stumbled on* some old family photos when she was cleaning out a drawer⟩ — see HAPPEN (ON *OR* UPON)

stumble (upon) *vb* to come upon face-to-face or as if face-to-face ⟨*stumbled upon* an old acquaintance at the airport⟩ — see MEET 1

stumbling block *n* something that makes movement or progress difficult ⟨the only *stumbling block* to our move across the country was finding someone to adopt our cats⟩ — see ENCUMBRANCE

stump *vb* **1** to move heavily or clumsily ⟨the seemingly endless parade finally ended, and the drummers and tuba players *stumped* wearily to their buses⟩ — see LUMBER 1

2 to invite (someone) to take part in a contest or to perform a feat ⟨when my grandfather was a kid, he and his friends would *stump* one another to dive into the local swimming hole⟩ — see CHALLENGE 2

stumpy *adj* being compact and broad in build and often short in stature ⟨*stumpy* penguins become agile swimmers the moment they hit the water⟩ — see STOCKY

stun *vb* **1** to make senseless or dizzy by a blow ⟨a powerful uppercut to the jaw *stunned* the boxer and sent him crashing to the canvas⟩

synonyms daze, rock

related words deaden, knock out, paralyze; benumb, numb, stupefy; bowl over, knock down; bang, bash, belt, bludgeon, bonk, bop, clobber, clock, clout, hammer, hit, paste, pound, punch, rap, slam, slap, slug, smack, smite, sock, strike, swat, thump, thwack, wallop, whack, whale; batter, beat, buffet, bung, chop, cuff, drub, mangle, maul, pelt, pummel

phrases knock for a loop, knock silly

2 to make a strong impression on (someone) with something unexpected ⟨the news of President Kennedy's assassination *stunned* the nation⟩ — see SURPRISE 1

stunned *adj* **1** affected with sudden and great wonder or surprise ⟨realizing that they had been left out of the will, the billionaire's relatives just sat there, *stunned*⟩ — see THUNDERSTRUCK

2 suffering from mental confusion ⟨the loud blast left her momentarily *stunned*⟩ — see DIZZY 2

stunner *n* **1** a lovely woman ⟨not only is she smart, she's a real *stunner*⟩ — see BEAUTY 2

2 something that makes a strong impression because it is so unexpected ⟨as expected, the box-office champ was another superhero actioner, but the real *stunner* was the second-place finish for the low-budget comedy⟩ — see SURPRISE 1

stunning *adj* **1** causing a strong emotional reaction because of unexpectedness ⟨we suffered a *stunning* defeat at the hands of the bottom-ranked team in the division⟩ — see SURPRISING 1

2 causing wonder or astonishment ⟨the *stunning* beauty of the star-filled sky on a cloudless night⟩ — see MARVELOUS 1

3 very pleasing to look at ⟨how *stunning* the performers look in their costumes⟩ — see BEAUTIFUL 1

stunt *n* an act of notable skill, strength, or cleverness ⟨performs mental *stunts*, such as pronouncing words backwards as soon as you say them⟩ — see FEAT 1

stunt *vb* to hold back the normal growth of ⟨unfortunately, an unusually dry summer seems to have permanently *stunted* the tree⟩

synonyms dwarf, suppress

related words arrest, catch, check, halt, hold up, stall, stay, still, stop; balk, block, hold back, impede, obstruct, stem; diminish, downsize, shrink

near antonyms advance, boost, encourage, forward, foster, nourish, nurture, promote

stupe *n* a stupid person ⟨with *stupes* like that, no wonder city hall is a mess⟩ — see IDIOT

stupefaction *n* the state of being strongly impressed by something unexpected or unusual ⟨upon hearing the diagnosis of cancer, she just sat there in total *stupefaction*⟩ — see SURPRISE 2

stupefied *adj* **1** affected with sudden and great wonder or surprise ⟨gazed, *stupefied*, as humanoids with large heads emerged from the crashed UFO⟩ — see THUNDERSTRUCK

2 suffering from mental confusion ⟨when the plane began to nose-dive, the *stupefied* passengers were unsure how to act⟩ — see DIZZY 2

stupefy *vb* to make a strong impression on (someone) with something unexpected ⟨*stupefied* by the ruling that he could not compete because his missed the qualifying age by two days⟩ — see SURPRISE 1

stupefying *adj* causing a strong emotional reaction because of unexpectedness ⟨the *stupefying* figures for poverty and starvation in some parts of the third world⟩ — see SURPRISING 1

stupendous *adj* causing wonder or astonishment ⟨the *stupendous* engineering feats achieved by the ancient Romans⟩ — see MARVELOUS 1

stupendously *adv* to a large extent or degree ⟨a *stupendously* successful Broadway debut⟩ — see GREATLY 2

stupendousness *n* impressiveness of beauty on a large scale ⟨for stunning *stupendousness* the world had never seen anything the equal of the Palace of Versailles⟩ — see MAGNIFICENCE

stupid *adj* **1** not having or showing an ability to absorb ideas readily ⟨the child, who was once thought to be just *stupid*, was discovered to be suffering from dyslexia⟩ ⟨don't ask *stupid* questions⟩

synonyms airheaded, birdbrained, bonehead, boneheaded, brain-dead, brainless, bubbleheaded, chuckleheaded, dense, dim, dim-witted, doltish, dopey (*also* dopy), dorky [*slang*], dull, dumb, dunderheaded, emptyheaded, fatuous, gormless [*chiefly British*], half-witted, knuckleheaded, lamebrain (*or* lamebrained), lunkheaded, mindless, oafish, obtuse, opaque, pinheaded, senseless, simple, slow, slow-witted, soft, softheaded, thick, thickheaded, thick-witted, unintelligent, unsmart, vacuous, weak-minded, witless

related words cretinous, feebleminded, simpleminded; boobish, foolish, idiotic (*also* idiotical), imbecile (*or* imbecilic), moronic; ignorant, illiterate, lowbrow, uneducated, uninformed, unintellectual, untaught, unthinking; absurd, asinine, balmy, cockeyed, crackpot, crazy, cuckoo, daffy, daft, dippy, dotty, featherheaded, fool, half-baked, harebrained, insane, kooky (*also* kookie), loony (*also* looney), lunatic, mad, nonsensical, nutty, preposterous, sappy, screwball, silly, tomfool, unwise, wacky (*also* whacky), zany; fallacious, illogical, invalid, irrational, unreasonable

near antonyms ingenious, resourceful; acute, astute, discerning, insightful, keen, knowing, perceptive, percipient, perspicacious, sagacious, sage, sapient, savvy, wise; cerebral, erudite, highbrow, intellectual, knowledgeable, learned, literate, scholarly, thinking, well-read; educated, informed, schooled, skilled, trained; crafty, cunning, foxy, shrewd, wily; judicious, prudent, sane, sensible, sound; logical, rational, reasonable, valid

antonyms apt, brainy, bright, brilliant, clever, fast, hyperintelligent, intelligent, keen, nimble, quick, quick-witted, sharp, sharp-witted, smart, supersmart, ultrasmart

2 causing weariness, restlessness, or lack of interest ⟨I can't believe we sat through the whole *stupid* movie⟩ — see BORING

3 showing or marked by a lack of good sense or judgment ⟨not liking the captain is a *stupid* reason to quit the team⟩ — see FOOLISH 1

stupid *n* a stupid person ⟨a genius at math, but a total *stupid* when it came to his love life⟩ — see IDIOT

stupidity *n* **1** the quality or state of lacking intelligence or quickness of mind ⟨the *stupidity* of the dialogue between the two romantic leads had movie audiences giggling uncontrollably⟩

synonyms boneheadedness, brainlessness, denseness, density, dim-wittedness, doltishness, dopiness, dorkiness, dullness (*also* dulness), dumbness, fatuity, foolish-

ness, gormlessness [*chiefly British*], mindlessness, oafishness, obtuseness, senselessness, simpleness, slowness, stupidness, thickness, vacuity, weak-mindedness, witlessness
related words feeblemindedness, simplemindedness; absurdity, asininity, balminess, craziness, daftness, dippiness, dottiness, fatuousness, folly, idiocy, inaneness, inanity, insanity, lunacy, madness, nincompoopery, nonsensicalness, nuttiness, preposterousness, silliness, simplicity, wackiness, zaniness; fallacy, irrationality, unreasonableness; mental deficiency, mental retardation
near antonyms acumen, alertness, astuteness, discernment, insight, judgment (*or* judgement), perception, percipience, perspicacity; sagacity, sageness, sapience, wisdom, wit; logicality, logicalness, rationality, rationalness, reasonableness, soundness, validity
antonyms braininess, brightness, brilliance, cleverness, intelligence, keenness, quickness, quick-wittedness, sharpness, smartness
2 a foolish act or idea ⟨the succession of *stupidities* by the company's owners was bound to result in bankruptcy⟩ — see FOLLY 1
3 language, behavior, or ideas that are absurd and contrary to good sense ⟨leaving her bags unguarded inside the airport terminal was nothing but *stupidity* on her part⟩ — see NONSENSE 1

stupidness *n* the quality or state of lacking intelligence or quickness of mind ⟨I'm not sure if he leaves his front door unlocked from carelessness or just plain *stupidness*⟩ — see STUPIDITY 1

stupor *n* physical or mental inertness ⟨shocked by news of impending layoffs, the workers shuffled through their shift in a quiet *stupor*⟩ — see LETHARGY

sturdily *adv* in a vigorous and forceful manner ⟨no longer so *sturdily* maintained his innocence when his alibi proved to be a fabrication⟩ — see HARD 3

sturdiness *n* the ability to withstand force or stress without being distorted, dislodged, or damaged ⟨demonstrated the suitcase's *sturdiness* by dropping it from a third-floor window⟩ — see STABILITY 1

sturdy *adj* **1** able to withstand hardship, strain, or exposure ⟨it took a *sturdy* person to endure the life of a pioneer⟩ — see HARDY 1
2 marked by the ability to withstand stress without structural damage or distortion ⟨wear *sturdy* boots because we will be going over sharp rocks and uneven terrain⟩ — see STABLE 1
3 not showing weakness or uncertainty ⟨you'll need a *sturdy* grasp of the concepts of algebra before you can take calculus⟩ — see FIRM 1

Sturm und Drang *n* a disturbed or uneasy state ⟨in a year filled with corporate *Sturm und Drang*, the company was headed by no fewer than three different CEOs⟩ — see UNREST

sty *n* a dirty or messy place ⟨"That house is such a *sty* that I'm never setting foot in there again," she said with a shudder⟩ — see PIGPEN

stygian *adj* being without light or without much light ⟨lost in the *stygian* reaches of the deep forest⟩ — see DARK 1

style *vb* to give a name to ⟨although nowadays he's often *styled* a biologist, he's probably better thought of as a classic 19th-century naturalist⟩ — see NAME 1

style *n* **1** a distinctive way of putting ideas into words ⟨I correctly identified the quotation because I recognized Mark Twain's inimitable *style*⟩
synonyms fashion, locution, manner, mode, phraseology, tone, vein
related words address, delivery, elocution; archaism, colloquialism, regionalism; acceptation, connotation, denotation, expression, idiom
2 the means or procedure for doing something ⟨unfortunately, the club president's usual *style* is to make decisions without asking anyone's advice or approval⟩ — see METHOD
3 a practice or interest that is very popular for a short time ⟨parents who were very relieved when the *style* for having one's nose pierced faded⟩ — see FAD

styleless *adj* marked by an obvious lack of style or good taste ⟨forced to wear a *styleless* uniform for her restaurant job, she loves to dress up on weekends⟩ — see [1]TACKY 1

stylish *adj* being in the latest or current fashion ⟨a pretty, *stylish* dress⟩
synonyms à la mode (*also* a la mode), au courant, chic, cool [*slang*], exclusive, fashionable, fresh [*slang*], happening, hip, in, modish, sharp, smart, snappy, supercool, swell, swish, trendy, voguish
related words downtown, edgy, funky; dapper, dashing, dressy, kicky, natty, rakish, sassy, saucy, spiffy, spruce; chichi, classy, flossy, haute (*also* haut), nobby, posh, ritzy, soigné (*or* soignée), swank (*or* swanky); elegant, graceful, handsome, majestic, refined, sophisticated, stately, tasteful, understated; doggish, doggy, flashy, gallant; dandyish, dudish, foppish; ultrachic, ultracool, ultrahip, ultraposh, ultrasmart, ultrasophisticated
near antonyms cheesy, tacky, unattractive, unbecoming; graceless, inelegant, tasteless, trashy, unhandsome; frowsy (*or* frowzy), sloppy, slovenly, unkempt, untidy; disheveled (*or* dishevelled), messy, mussy, rumpled, wrinkled; shabby, sleazy
antonyms dowdy, out, outmoded, styleless, unchic, uncool, unfashionable, unmodish, unstylish

stylishness *n* the quality or state of being fashionable ⟨the *stylishness* of the new coat was questionable⟩ — see COOL 2

stylist *n* a person who cuts and arranges hair ⟨although she usually dresses her own hair, the bride-to-be decided to go to a professional *stylist* before the big day⟩ — see HAIRDRESSER

stymie *vb* to create difficulty for the work or activity of ⟨the raging blizzard *stymied* the rescuers' attempts to find the stranded mountain climbers⟩ — see HAMPER

suasion *n* the act of reasoning or pleading with someone to accept a belief or course of action ⟨a defense lawyer uses not only legal arguments but also moral *suasion* to appeal to a jury's sense of right and wrong⟩ — see PERSUASION 1

suasiveness *n* the capacity to persuade ⟨there's a certain *suasiveness* in her imposing looks and demeanor that gives her an advantage as a trial lawyer⟩ — see COGENCY 1

suave *adj* having or showing very polished and worldly manners ⟨the *suave* gentleman was a great favorite of the elegant ladies who attended parties at the embassy⟩
synonyms debonair, smooth, sophisticated, svelte, urbane
related words cavalier, glib, slick, unctuous; civilized, couth, cultivated, cultured, genteel, graceful, gracious, poised, polished, refined, well-bred; cosmopolitan, metro, metropolitan, smart, worldly-wise; experienced, knowing, practiced (*also* practised), schooled, seasoned; amiable, appealing, attractive; assured, calm, collected, composed, confident, cool, placid, secure, self-assured, self-confident, self-possessed, serene, tranquil, undisturbed, unperturbed
near antonyms awkward, clumsy, gauche, graceless, stiff, stilted, uncomfortable, uneasy, ungraceful, wooden; callow, green, inexperienced, puerile, raw; hick, parochial, provincial, rough-hewn, rustic (*also* rustical); inelegant, philistine, uncivilized, uncultured, unrefined; unsophisticated, unworldly; gawky, lub-

berly, stodgy, ungainly; diffident, insecure
antonyms boorish, churlish, classless, clownish, loutish, uncouth

[1]sub *n* a large sandwich on a long split roll ⟨we shared a tuna *sub* at lunch⟩ — see SUBMARINE

[2]sub *n* a person or thing that takes the place of another ⟨we had a *sub* in English today, so we didn't get our test results back⟩ — see SUBSTITUTE

sub *vb* to serve as a replacement usually for a time only ⟨the weekend anchor is *subbing* for the TV station's main anchor all this week⟩ — see COVER 1

subdue *vb* **1** to achieve a victory over ⟨*subdued* her fear of the dark by joining a club for spelunkers⟩ — see BEAT 2
2 to bring under one's control by force of arms ⟨*subdued* the rebels and sent their leaders to the gallows⟩ — see CONQUER 1
3 to put a stop to (something) by the use of force ⟨labored through the night to *subdue* the river's rising waters by building a wall of sandbags around their property⟩ — see QUELL 1

subdued *adj* not excessively showy ⟨the wedding was a *subdued* affair, with only close family and friends attending⟩ — see QUIET 2

subduer *n* one that defeats an enemy or opponent ⟨time and again Native Americans made treaties with the whites, only to see their *subduers* break those treaties⟩ — see VICTOR 1

subduing *n* the act or process of bringing someone or something under one's control ⟨the *subduing* of the nomadic tribes was accomplished, not by force of arms, but by a drought that eventually destroyed their grazing lands⟩ — see CONQUEST

subhuman *adj* having or showing the nature and appetites of a lower animal ⟨years of grinding poverty that had reduced them to a *subhuman* existence⟩ — see BESTIAL

subject *n* **1** a major object of interest or concern (as in a discussion or artistic composition) ⟨the *subject* of our discussion switched from who would be the next president to who was the greatest president in the nation's history⟩ — see MATTER 1
2 a person who owes allegiance to a government and is protected by it ⟨because of the tense situation in that country, British *subjects* were advised to return home as soon as possible⟩ — see CITIZEN 1
3 something (as a belief) that serves as the basis for another thing ⟨he has no *subject* to protest this time, but that's never stopped him before⟩ — see REASON 2

subject *vb* to bring under one's control by force of arms ⟨Attila the Hun *subjected* most of Europe to his barbaric pillage⟩ — see CONQUER 1

subject (to) *adj* **1** determined by something else ⟨your extra piano lesson on Tuesdays is *subject to* the availability of the music room⟩ — see DEPENDENT 2
2 being in a situation where one is likely to meet with harm ⟨this type of wound is highly *subject to* infection⟩ — see LIABLE 1

subjecting *n* the act or process of bringing someone or something under one's control ⟨a time when the *subjecting* of Asian and African peoples to European rule was regarded as acceptable⟩ — see CONQUEST

subjection *n* the act or process of bringing someone or something under one's control ⟨a holy man for whom the *subjection* of earthly desires is the path to spiritual perfection⟩ — see CONQUEST

subjective *adj* of, relating to, or belonging to a single person ⟨even seemingly unbiased judges are influenced by their own *subjective* assumptions and interpretations of the law⟩ — see INDIVIDUAL 1

subjoin *vb* to join (something) to a mass, quantity, or number so as to bring about an overall increase ⟨*subjoined* an epilogue that informs the reader of the current doings and whereabouts of the participants in this real-life mystery⟩ — see ADD 1

subjugate *vb* to bring under one's control by force of arms ⟨explorers who *subjugated* the natives in the name of religion⟩ — see CONQUER 1

subjugating *n* the act or process of bringing someone or something under one's control ⟨a military occupation that was seen by the people of that country as just another *subjugating* by an outside power⟩ — see CONQUEST

subjugation *n* the act or process of bringing someone or something under one's control ⟨the *subjugation* of much of Europe by Napoléon⟩ — see CONQUEST

sublime *adj* **1** causing wonder or astonishment ⟨the *sublime* beauty of the firmament⟩ — see MARVELOUS 1
2 having, characterized by, or arising from a dignified and generous nature ⟨the *sublime* virtue of having given all one's worldly goods to the poor⟩ — see NOBLE 2

sublimeness *n* impressiveness of beauty on a large scale ⟨the awe-inspiring *sublimeness* of Yosemite Valley⟩ — see MAGNIFICENCE

sublunary *adj* having to do with life on earth especially as opposed to that in heaven ⟨like all *sublunary* things, this misery will one day end⟩ — see EARTHLY

submarine *adj* living, lying, or occurring below the surface of the water ⟨the *submarine* fossils that are to be found in coral reefs⟩ — see UNDERWATER

submarine *n* a large sandwich on a long split roll ⟨always orders a roast beef *submarine* with the works⟩
synonyms Cuban sandwich, grinder, hero, hoagie (*also* hoagy), Italian sandwich, po'boy (*also* poor boy), sub, torpedo

submerge *vb* **1** to cover with a flood ⟨*submerged* by requests to babysit after she received a favorable write-up in the local newspaper⟩ — see FLOOD
2 to sink or push (something) briefly into or as if into a liquid ⟨*submerge* the tomatoes in boiling hot water for a few seconds and they will be easier to peel⟩ — see DIP 1
3 to refrain from openly showing or uttering ⟨learned to *submerge* her ego and became a better teammate for doing so⟩ — see SUPPRESS 2

submerged *adj* living, lying, or occurring below the surface of the water ⟨*submerged* local roadways made for hazardous driving⟩ — see UNDERWATER

submerse *vb* **1** to cover with a flood ⟨a week of nonstop rain that *submersed* the cornfields and delayed planting for days⟩ — see FLOOD
2 to sink or push (something) briefly into or as if into a liquid ⟨those hardy souls who daily *submerse* themselves in icy cold water for its invigorating effect⟩ — see DIP 1

submission *n* **1** a bending to the authority or control of another ⟨not given to unquestioning *submission*, he often came in conflict with his superiors⟩ — see OBEDIENCE 1
2 the usually forced yielding of one's person or possessions to the control of another ⟨the judge ordered the *submission* of all of the company's records to the prosecutors⟩ — see SURRENDER

submissive *adj* readily giving in to the command or authority of another ⟨it's not in her nature to be *submissive*⟩ — see OBEDIENT

submissively *adv* in a manner showing no signs of pride or self-assertion ⟨all of the extended family was expected to be *submissively* amenable to the matriarch's wishes⟩ — see LOWLY

submissiveness *n* a readiness or willingness to yield to the wishes of others ⟨his uncharacteristic *submissiveness* to the doctor's advice must mean he's really sick⟩ — see COMPLIANCE 1

submit *vb* **1** to cease resistance (as to another's argu-

ments, demands, or control) ⟨in the end he *submitted* and agreed to take that awful-tasting medicine⟩ — see YIELD 3
2 to give up and cease resistance (as to a liking, temptation, or habit) ⟨refusing to *submit* to sleep, she stayed by her son's hospital bed the whole night⟩ — see YIELD 1
3 to yield to the control or power of enemy forces ⟨the fort's commander received orders not to *submit* under any circumstances, as reinforcements were on the way⟩ — see FALL 2

submitting *n* the usually forced yielding of one's person or possessions to the control of another ⟨his *submitting* of his own desires to the will of God⟩ — see SURRENDER

subnormal *adj* of a size that is less than average ⟨because of the summer drought, harvests have definitely been *subnormal* this year⟩ — see SMALL 1

suboptimal *adj* falling short of a standard ⟨yes, living on junk food generally means that you have a *suboptimal* diet⟩ — see BAD 1

subordinate *adj* having not so great importance or rank as another ⟨his contention is that environment plays a *subordinate* role to heredity in determining what we become⟩ — see LESSER

subordinate *n* one who is of lower rank and typically under the authority of another ⟨*subordinates* do most of the actual creation of the famous designer's clothing designs⟩ — see UNDERLING

subordinate *vb* to bring under one's control by force of arms ⟨it is one of the lessons of history that more powerful civilizations often *subordinate* weaker ones⟩ — see CONQUER 1

subordination *n* a bending to the authority or control of another ⟨an oligarchy requires *subordination* by the masses to the will of a tiny elite⟩ — see OBEDIENCE 1

subpar *adj* falling short of a standard ⟨the service at the restaurant was *subpar*, to say the least⟩ — see BAD 1

subpoena *n* a written notice ordering a person to appear in court ⟨received a *subpoena* to appear as a witness for the prosecution⟩ — see SUMMONS

subscribe *vb* 1 to give or express one's approval (as to a proposal) ⟨promised that as president he would never *subscribe* to the use of torture as an interrogation method, regardless of the circumstances⟩ — see ACCEDE
2 to write one's name on (as a document) ⟨they dutifully *subscribed* several dozen forms at the mortgage closing⟩ — see SIGN

subscribe (to) *vb* to have a favorable opinion of ⟨I don't *subscribe to* the belief that some people are predestined to eternal happiness and others to eternal punishment⟩ — see APPROVE (OF)

subsequent *adj* being, occurring, or carried out at a time after something else ⟨I'll do the first problem as an example, but all *subsequent* efforts must be done on your own⟩
synonyms after, ensuing, later, posterior
related words behind, belated, delayed, late, slow; closing, concluding, eventual, final, last, latest, latter, terminal, ultimate; following
near antonyms advance, advanced, early, premature
antonyms antecedent, anterior, fore, foregoing, former, precedent, preceding, previous, prior

subsequently *adv* following in time or place ⟨*subsequently* found the missing glove⟩ — see AFTER

subside *vb* to grow less in scope or intensity especially gradually ⟨as the noise of the siren *subsided*, I was able to fall back to sleep⟩ — see DECREASE 2

subsidize *vb* 1 to furnish (as an institution) with a regular source of income ⟨the museum is annually *subsidized* by funds from several major corporations⟩ — see ENDOW 2
2 to provide money for ⟨housing for the elderly that was *subsidized* by the federal government⟩ — see FINANCE 1

subsidy *n* a sum of money allotted for a specific use by official or formal action ⟨government *subsidies* for farmers in case of crop failure⟩ — see APPROPRIATION 1

subsist *vb* to have life ⟨a love that was as great as any that ever did *subsist*⟩ — see BE 1

subsistence *n* 1 the fact of being or of being real ⟨believes in the *subsistence* of a soul as a separate entity from the body⟩ — see EXISTENCE
2 uninterrupted or lasting existence ⟨the *subsistence* of the patient's infection, even after the use of antibiotics, had the doctors puzzled⟩ — see CONTINUATION

substance *n* 1 the basic elements from which something can be developed ⟨many thought that the mayor's speech lacked *substance* because specific proposals for solving the city's problems were few⟩ — see MAKING
2 the quality or qualities that make a thing what it is ⟨tireless caring and nurturing that was the very *substance* of maternal love⟩ — see ESSENCE 1
3 the total of one's money and property ⟨measure the worth of a person not by his earthly *substance* but by his good deeds⟩ — see WEALTH 1
4 one that has a real and independent existence ⟨the question of whether the soul is a *substance* entirely independent of the body⟩ — see ENTITY

substance abuser *n* a person who regularly uses drugs especially illegally ⟨arranges for former *substance abusers* to give talks to school groups⟩ — see DOPER

substandard *adj* falling short of a standard ⟨a teacher who rejects *substandard* work without hesitation⟩ — see BAD 1

substantial *adj* 1 having great meaning or lasting effect ⟨*substantial* changes to the school dress code that made a lot of people unhappy⟩ — see IMPORTANT 1
2 of a size greater than average of its kind ⟨the amount he inherited was quite *substantial*, so he quit his job and set out to see the world⟩ — see LARGE 1
3 relating to or composed of matter ⟨the Land of Oz turned out to be a world of dreams, even less *substantial* than a rainbow⟩ — see MATERIAL 1
4 sufficiently large in size, amount, or number to merit attention ⟨there's been a *substantial* increase in attendance at girls' volleyball games ever since the start of their winning streak⟩ — see CONSIDERABLE 1

substantiality *n* the quality or state of being large in size ⟨their donation may not be impressive in its *substantiality*, but it did come from the heart, and that is what is really important⟩ — see LARGENESS

substantially *adv* for the most part ⟨the *Little House* books are *substantially* based on the memories of Laura Ingalls Wilder⟩ — see CHIEFLY

substantiate *vb* 1 to gain full recognition or acceptance of ⟨*substantiated* his claim to local mountaineering fame with a photo of himself on the summit of Mount McKinley⟩ — see ESTABLISH 1
2 to give evidence or testimony to the truth or factualness of ⟨Mr. MacGregor couldn't *substantiate* that it was Peter, and not some other rabbit, in the cabbage patch⟩ — see CONFIRM 1
3 to represent in visible form ⟨the artist's intense feelings are *substantiated* by his paintings' bold colors and broad brush strokes⟩ — see EMBODY 2
4 to show the existence or truth of by evidence ⟨*substantiate* the need for a tuition increase with some concrete figures⟩ — see PROVE 1
5 to provide evidence or information for (as a claim or idea) ⟨Darwin spent the rest of his life gathering evi-

dence to *substantiate* his theory of the origin of species〉 — see SUPPORT 4

substantiating *adj* serving to give support to the truth or factualness of something 〈without some *substantiating* evidence, such as a stub from a bus ticket, who's going to believe your alibi?〉 — see CORROBORATIVE

substantiation *n* something presented in support of the truth or accuracy of a claim 〈the signature of a witness provides *substantiation* that a person's will is genuine〉 — see PROOF

substantive *adj* sufficiently large in size, amount, or number to merit attention 〈they've made *substantive* changes in the nightly newscast〉 — see CONSIDERABLE 1

substitutable *adj* capable of being substituted in place of one another 〈for our purposes, the quart and the liter are close enough to be *substitutable* for one another〉 — see INTERCHANGEABLE

substitute *adj* **1** being such in appearance only and made with or manufactured from usually cheaper materials 〈*substitute* wools that supposedly have the look and feel of cashmere〉 — see IMITATION

2 taking the place of one that came before 〈had to find *substitute* transportation during the bus strike〉 — see NEW 1

substitute *vb* **1** to give up (something) and take something else in return 〈can I *substitute* coleslaw for potato salad if I order the chicken plate?〉 — see CHANGE 3

2 to serve as a replacement usually for a time only 〈*substituting* for the talk show host while she is on vacation〉 — see COVER 1

3 to take the place of 〈"John Doe," "Jane Doe," and "Baby Doe" *substituted* the real names of the parties involved to preserve their privacy〉 — see REPLACE 1

substitute *n* a person or thing that takes the place of another 〈you'll be getting a *substitute* until your regular teacher is feeling better〉 〈if you like, you can use nuts as a *substitute* for coconut in that recipe〉

synonyms backup, cover, designated hitter, fill-in, locum tenens, pinch hitter, relief, replacement, reserve, stand-in, sub

related words alternate, understudy; apology, makeshift, stopgap; agent, assignee, attorney, commissary, delegate, deputy, envoy, factor, procurator, proxy, rep, representative, surrogate; assistant, reliever, second; successor, superseder

substitutive *adj* taking the place of one that came before 〈his recent religious fanaticism is only the latest *substitutive* addiction of a person with an addictive personality〉 — see NEW 1

subsume *vb* to have as part of a whole 〈games and team sports are *subsumed* under the classification of "recreation"〉 — see INCLUDE 1

subsurface *adj* being, situated, or operating beneath the surface of the earth 〈a sandy wasteland that gave little hint of its *subsurface* wealth〉 — see BELOWGROUND

subterfuge *n* the use of clever underhanded actions to achieve an end 〈propagandists who use a kind of photographic *subterfuge*, superimposing one image on another to create a false "reality"〉 — see TRICKERY

subterranean *adj* being, situated, or operating beneath the surface of the earth 〈a *subterranean* bunker that supposedly could withstand even an atomic blast〉 — see BELOWGROUND

subtle *adj* **1** clever at attaining one's ends by indirect and often deceptive means 〈used *subtle* methods of persuasion〉 — see ARTFUL 1

2 made or done with extreme care and accuracy 〈the *subtle* strokes of the painter's brush〉 — see FINE 2

3 satisfying or pleasing because of fineness or mildness 〈a *subtle* suggestion of the Near East in the soup's flavoring〉 — see DELICATE 1

subtleness *n* skill in achieving one's ends through indirect, subtle, or underhanded means 〈the *subtleness* with which the boutique owner convinces you that you have to have that outrageously priced article of clothing〉 — see CUNNING 1

subtlety *n* skill in achieving one's ends through indirect, subtle, or underhanded means 〈we appreciated the *subtlety* with which our host indicated that it was time to leave: he volunteered to pack us a little lunch for the road〉 — see CUNNING 1

subtract *vb* to take away (an amount or number) from a total 〈if you *subtract* 10 from 23, you get 13〉 〈you can *subtract* the time you spent daydreaming from your total homework time〉

synonyms abate, deduct, knock off, take off

related words decrease, diminish, discount, downsize, dwindle, knock down, lessen, lower, reduce; abbreviate, abridge, clip, crop, curtail, cut, cut back, cut down, dock, pare, prune, retrench, shorten, slash, trim, truncate, whittle

near antonyms adjoin, annex, append; complement, supplement; enhance, heighten, intensify, magnify; aggrandize, amplify, augment, beef (up), boost, compound, enlarge, escalate, expand, increase, multiply, raise

antonyms add, tack (on)

subtraction *n* the act or an instance of taking away from a total 〈the restaurant may not have raised the price, but there's definitely been a *subtraction* in the number of fries in a side order〉

synonyms deduction

related words discount, giveback, kickback, rebate; abatement, decline, decrement, detraction, diminishment, diminution, drop, fall, loss, reduction, shrinkage; curtailment, cut, cutback

near antonyms boost, enlargement, gain, increase, increment, raise, rise; accretion, accrual, accumulation, addendum, appendix, augmentation, supplement, supplementation

antonyms accession, addition

suburbia *n* the districts adjacent to a city 〈the migration of families to *suburbia* and the resulting disintegration of inner-city neighborhoods〉 — see ENVIRONS 1

subvention *n* a sum of money allotted for a specific use by official or formal action 〈the committee receives an annual *subvention* from the foundation to run the museum〉 — see APPROPRIATION 1

subvert *vb* to lower in character, dignity, or quality 〈by insisting that she pay me for helping her, she *subverted* my noble desire to do a good deed without reward〉 — see DEBASE 1

succeed *vb* **1** to turn out as planned or desired 〈the advertising campaign that finally *succeeded* used humor to sell the product〉

synonyms click, come off, deliver, go, go over, pan out, work out

related words catch on; flourish, prosper, thrive; cook, percolate

phrases bear fruit, catch fire, deliver the goods, do the trick, go like clockwork

near antonyms languish; flounder, struggle; decline, sink, skid, slip, slump, wane; crash, crater, crumble, flame out; choke, crack up, miscarry, misfire; fall down, go under; implode, self-destruct

antonyms bomb, collapse, fail, flop, flunk, fold, founder, miss, strike out, wash out

2 to reach a desired level of accomplishment 〈if you want to *succeed* in show business, you have to feel comfortable in front of an audience〉

synonyms arrive, flourish, prosper, thrive

related words prevail, triumph, win; excel

phrases come into one's own, cut it, cut the mustard,

get ahead, get somewhere, get there, hack it, hit it big, make good, make it, make one's mark, make the grade
near antonyms flounder, struggle
antonyms fail
3 to come after in time ⟨only the results on election day will tell who will *succeed* the current president⟩ — see FOLLOW 1

succeeding *adj* **1** being the one that comes immediately after another ⟨the couple purchased some land, and in the course of the *succeeding* year built a house on it⟩ — see NEXT
2 following one after another without others coming in between ⟨that land remained in the family for five *succeeding* generations⟩ — see CONSECUTIVE

success *n* **1** a person or thing that is successful ⟨their homemade jellies have been such a *success* that they are now distributed nationwide⟩ — see HIT 1
2 a successful result brought about by hard work ⟨a long list of *successes* that the retiring president of the college can point to with pride⟩ — see ACCOMPLISHMENT 1

successful *adj* **1** having attained a desired end or state of good fortune ⟨the play had a *successful* run on Broadway⟩
synonyms flourishing, going, palmy, prosperous, thriving, triumphant
related words coming, promising; booming, growing, roaring, robust; boffo, gangbusters (*also* gangbuster), runaway, socko
phrases in clover (*also* in the clover)
near antonyms futureless, hopeless, inauspicious, no-good, unpromising; collapsing, failing, flopping, flunking, folding, washing-out; declining, slipping, slumping, waning; bankrupt, kaput (*also* kaputt), kerflooey; destroyed, ruined, wrecked
antonyms failed, unsuccessful
2 marked by vigorous growth and well-being especially economically ⟨sold their *successful* dry-cleaning business and retired to Hawaii⟩ — see PROSPEROUS 1

successional *adj* following one after another without others coming in between ⟨the *successional* stages that an area goes through following a devastating forest fire⟩ — see CONSECUTIVE

successionally *adv* in succession without others coming in between ⟨the bumptious reporter asked three questions *successionally* before anyone else could get a word in⟩ — see CONSECUTIVELY

successive *adj* following one after another without others coming in between ⟨made the honor roll for three *successive* school terms⟩ — see CONSECUTIVE

successively *adv* in succession without others coming in between ⟨as he moved up the corporate ladder, he ensconced his family in *successively* larger homes⟩ — see CONSECUTIVELY

succinct *adj* marked by the use of few words to convey much information or meaning ⟨a pocket guide that provides *succinct* explanations for rules of grammar and punctuation⟩ — see CONCISE

succinctly *adv* in a few words ⟨found it difficult to explain *succinctly* to the technician the nature of the problems she was having with her computer⟩ — see SHORTLY 1

succinctness *n* the quality or state of being marked by or using only few words to convey much meaning ⟨Caesar's observation, "I came, I saw, I conquered," is famous for its *succinctness*⟩
synonyms brevity, briefness, compactness, conciseness, concision, crispness, pithiness, sententiousness, terseness
related words abruptness, bluntness, brusqueness, curtness, shortness
near antonyms periphrasis, pleonasm, redundancy, repetitiousness, repetitiveness, tautology
antonyms diffuseness, long-windedness, prolixity, verbosity, wordiness

succulence *n* the quality or state of being full of juice ⟨the *succulence* of the apple was such that the first bite sent juice running down my chin⟩
synonyms fleshiness, juiciness, pulpiness
related words sap, sappiness
near antonyms dryness, waterlessness

succulent *adj* **1** full of juice ⟨vines weighted down with plump, *succulent* grapes⟩ — see JUICY 1
2 very pleasing to the sense of taste ⟨a buffet table set with an array of *succulent* roasts⟩ — see DELICIOUS 1

succumb *vb* **1** to cease resistance (as to another's arguments, demands, or control) ⟨he finally *succumbed* and let his wife get rid of his dilapidated easy chair⟩ — see YIELD 3
2 to give up and cease resistance (as to a liking, temptation, or habit) ⟨refused to *succumb* to her fears and defiantly walked through the dark cemetery⟩ — see YIELD 1
3 to stop living ⟨the patient lay so still and pale that everyone thought he had *succumbed*, and then he opened his eyes⟩ — see DIE 1
4 to yield to the control or power of enemy forces ⟨the doctor worked tirelessly until finally he, too, *succumbed* to the fever⟩ — see FALL 2

such *adj* having qualities in common ⟨all *such* questions should be saved until the end of the class⟩ — see ALIKE

such *adv* to a great degree ⟨she wears *such* stylish clothes⟩ — see VERY 1

suchlike *adj* having qualities in common ⟨kept asking me how long I'd lived here, and how I liked it, and *suchlike* questions⟩ — see ALIKE

suck *vb, slang* to be objectionable or unsatisfactory ⟨it's amazing that a song that *sucks* so bad can be so popular⟩ — see STINK 2

suck (up) *vb* **1** to use flattery or the doing of favors in order to win approval especially from a superior ⟨a young lieutenant constantly *sucking up* to the commanding officer⟩ — see FAWN
2 to take in (something liquid) through small openings ⟨these lilacs *sucked up* all the water I added to the vase yesterday⟩ — see ABSORB 1

sucker *n* **1** one who is easily deceived or cheated ⟨I was a *sucker* and believed them when they said the only tickets they could get were double the price⟩ — see [1]DUPE
2 a person with a strong and habitual liking for something ⟨I'm a *sucker* for cheesy horror movies⟩ — see FAN

sucker *vb* **1** to cause to believe what is untrue ⟨a notorious imposter who at one time *suckered* a lot of people into believing that she was the Grand Duchess Anastasia⟩ — see DECEIVE
2 to rob by the use of trickery or threats ⟨*suckered* millions of desperate dieters with their grossly inflated claims of successful weight loss⟩ — see FLEECE

suck in *vb* to cause to believe what is untrue ⟨she was *sucked in* by a scam that was run by a shady outfit selling time-shares⟩ — see DECEIVE

suckle *vb* to give milk to from the breast ⟨the image of a mother *suckling* her babe is a standard artistic symbol of maternal love and nurturing⟩ — see NURSE 2

suck–up *n* a person who flatters another in order to get ahead ⟨I'd like to give my boss a birthday present, but I don't want to look like a shameless *suck-up*⟩ — see SYCOPHANT

sucky *adj, slang* extremely unsatisfactory ⟨I'm tired of driving around in a *sucky* car that is always breaking down⟩ — see WRETCHED 1

sudden *adj* not expected ⟨the *sudden* snowstorm resulted in thousands of evening commuters abandoning their cars on impassable highways⟩ — see UNEXPECTED

suddenly *adv* **1** with great suddenness ⟨the bus stopped *suddenly*, and somebody's lunch landed in the aisle⟩ — see SHORT
2 without warning ⟨*suddenly*, something fell out of the sky and landed in the field a few feet away⟩ — see UNAWARES

suds *n pl* a light mass of fine bubbles formed in or on a liquid ⟨I can't seem to get any *suds* to form with this cheap dish detergent⟩ — see FOAM

sudsy *adj* covered with, consisting of, or resembling foam ⟨came out of the bathroom with her hair all *sudsy* because someone had turned off the water⟩ — see FOAMY

sue (for) *vb* to make a request for ⟨after another devastating attack, the nation *sued for* peace⟩ — see ASK (FOR) 1

suer *n* the person in a legal proceeding who makes a charge of wrongdoing against another ⟨the landlord was suing his *suers* in return, with each side alleging wrongdoing on the other's part⟩ — see COMPLAINANT

suffer *vb* **1** to come to a knowledge of (something) by living through it ⟨willingly *suffered* hardships so that their children would have a better life⟩ — see EXPERIENCE
2 to feel deep sadness or mental pain ⟨the husband *suffered* deeply at the mere suggestion that he had been unfaithful⟩ — see GRIEVE
3 to give permission for or to approve of ⟨contends that the death penalty is something that no civilized society should *suffer*⟩ — see ALLOW 1
4 to fail to prevent (some behavior on someone's part) especially from neglect or indifference ⟨I will not *suffer* you to insult me so!⟩ — see ALLOW 3

sufferable *adj* capable of being endured ⟨the only thing that makes visiting my in-laws *sufferable* is their gigantic TV⟩ — see BEARABLE

sufferance *n* **1** the approval by someone in authority for the doing of something ⟨was pointedly reminded that he was at the private beach on *sufferance* and could be kicked out at any time⟩ — see PERMISSION
2 the capacity to endure what is difficult or disagreeable without complaining ⟨spending a whole day with my airheaded sister-in-law is beyond *sufferance*⟩ — see PATIENCE

suffice *vb* to be enough ⟨I was told I have to wear shoes—will thong sandals *suffice*?⟩ — see SERVE 2

sufficiency *n* the quality or state of meeting one's needs adequately ⟨the *sufficiency* of the portions is such that you will leave the restaurant with a full stomach but without doggie bags⟩
synonyms acceptability, adequacy, satisfactoriness
related words appropriateness, correctness, fitness, goodness, properness, rightness, seemliness, suitability, suitableness, tolerability; bountifulness, copiousness; excess, overabundance, oversupply, surfeit, surplus; abundance, amplitude, opulence, plenitude, plenteousness, plentifulness, plentitude, plenty
near antonyms lack, want; crunch, dearth, deficit, famine, lack, shortage; meagerness, paucity, poorness, poverty, rareness, rarity, scantiness, scantness, scarceness, scarcity, skimpiness; necessity, need, privation
antonyms inadequacy, inadequateness, insufficiency, unsatisfactoriness

sufficiently *adv* **1** in or to a degree or quantity that meets one's requirements or satisfaction ⟨after eight tutoring sessions, I felt *sufficiently* prepared for the entrance exam⟩ — see ENOUGH 1
2 in a satisfactory way ⟨it's not great literature, but this whodunit is *sufficiently* suspenseful⟩ — see WELL 1

suffocate *vb* **1** to be or cause to be killed by lack of breathable air ⟨the law requires the owner of a discarded refrigerator to remove its door so that a child won't get trapped inside and *suffocate*⟩ — see SMOTHER 1
2 to keep (someone) from breathing by exerting pressure on the windpipe ⟨temporarily *suffocated* by the seat belt⟩ — see CHOKE 1
3 to experience complete or partial blockage of the windpipe ⟨*suffocating* in the thick, black smoke of the burning building⟩ — see CHOKE 2

suffocating *adj* lacking fresh air ⟨inside the bunker it was *suffocating*, and some of the men had already passed out⟩ — see STUFFY 1

suffrage *n* the right to formally express one's position or will in an election ⟨even as the world entered the 21st century, some nations still did not permit women's *suffrage*⟩ — see VOTE 1

suffuse *vb* **1** to cause (as a person) to become filled or saturated with a certain quality or principle ⟨she was *suffused* with an overwhelming feeling of liberation as her horse broke into a gallop⟩ — see INFUSE
2 to spread throughout ⟨a living room *suffused* with warm sunlight⟩ — see PERMEATE

sugarcoated *adj* appealing to the emotions in an obvious and tiresome way ⟨those *sugarcoated* versions of family life that old TV sitcoms portrayed⟩ — see CORNY 1

sugar daddy *n* one that helps another with gifts or money ⟨the only reason the town has any Independence Day fireworks in the first place is because the Internet tycoon has willingly become the event's de facto *sugar daddy*⟩ — see BENEFACTOR

sugary *adj* appealing to the emotions in an obvious and tiresome way ⟨writes *sugary* lyrics for singers of country music⟩ — see CORNY 1

suggest *vb* **1** to convey an idea indirectly ⟨this letter *suggests* that there's more going on than she's telling us⟩ — see HINT
2 to put (something) forward as one's choice for a wise or proper course of action ⟨I *suggested* that they talk to a therapist about their marital problems⟩ — see ADVISE 2
3 to set before the mind for consideration ⟨might I *suggest*, for an appetizer, our jumbo shrimp cocktail?⟩ — see PROPOSE 1

suggestion *n* **1** a slight or indirect pointing to something (as a solution or explanation) ⟨if you don't want to give the *suggestion* that you're evading the truth, you must look your questioner in the eye⟩ — see HINT 1
2 something which is presented for consideration ⟨no one had any better *suggestions*, so as usual we spent the afternoon at the basketball court⟩ — see PROPOSAL
3 an almost imperceptible sign of something ⟨we took care to avoid so much as even a *suggestion* of impropriety⟩ — see HINT 2

suggestive *adj* **1** hinting at or intended to call to mind matters regarded as indecent ⟨making unwelcome *suggestive* remarks to a subordinate will be regarded as sexual harassment⟩
synonyms bawdy, blue, gamy (*or* gamey), lewd, off, off-color (*or* off-colored), racy, ribald, risqué, salty, spicy
related words leering; barnyard, coarse, coarse-grained, crude, earthy, foul, gross, vulgar; dirty, filthy, gutter, indecent, lascivious, locker-room, nasty, obscene, pornographic, porny, prurient, raunchy, smutty, stag, unprintable, unpublishable, warm, X-rated; immodest, indecorous, indelicate, naughty
near antonyms clean, decent, G-rated, nonobscene; innocuous, inoffensive; priggish, prim, prudish, puritani-

cal, staid, straitlaced (*or* straightlaced), Victorian; correct, decorous, genteel, nice, polite, proper, respectable, seemly
2 provoking a memory or mental association ⟨a haunting and *suggestive* song about a long-lost love⟩
synonyms evocative, reminiscent
related words eloquent, expressive, meaningful, pregnant, revealing, significant; affecting, emotional, impressive, moving, poignant, stirring, touching; exciting, provocative, provoking, rousing, stimulating
antonyms unreminiscent
3 clearly conveying a special meaning (as one's mood) ⟨the dog's aggressive behavior is *suggestive* of some past mistreatment⟩ — see EXPRESSIVE

suicide *n* the act of deliberately killing oneself ⟨teenagers are more prone to *suicide* because they mistakenly believe their troubles are insurmountable⟩
synonyms self-destruction, self-murder, self-slaughter
related words hara-kiri (*also* hari-kiri); martyrdom; blood, foul play, homicide, murder, rubout, slaying; chance-medley, dispatch, killing, manslaughter; assassination, execution; euthanasia, mercy killing

sui generis *adj* being the one or ones of a class with no other members ⟨among history's greats Leonardo da Vinci is often considered *sui generis*—a man of such stupendous genius that the world may never see his like again⟩ — see ONLY 2

suit *n* **1** a court case for enforcing a right or claim ⟨filed a *suit* against the company that had manufactured the faulty heater, claiming they were responsible for the fire⟩ — see LAWSUIT
2 an earnest request ⟨O Lord of Heaven, hear our humble *suit*⟩ — see PLEA 1
3 the series of social engagements shared by a couple looking to get married ⟨a rather old-fashioned fellow, he first sought the consent of the girl's father for the *suit*⟩ — see COURTSHIP

suit *vb* **1** to be fitting or proper ⟨no, a second-floor room won't *suit* if there's no elevator, since one of us has a disability⟩ — see DO 1
2 to give satisfaction to ⟨the location of our hotel *suited* us just fine⟩ — see PLEASE 1
3 to outfit with clothes and especially fine or special clothes ⟨went to the party *suited* in a strange getup that he'd picked out himself⟩ — see CLOTHE 1
4 to change (something) so as to make it suitable for a new use or situation ⟨a bohemian by nature, she would have to *suit* her behavior to the corporate culture⟩ — see ADAPT

suitability *n* the quality or state of being especially suitable or fitting ⟨the *suitability* of the accommodations will ultimately depend on whether they're accessible for someone in a wheelchair⟩ — see APPROPRIATENESS

suitable *adj* **1** having the required skills for an acceptable level of performance ⟨with only one *suitable* candidate it's not difficult to decide for whom to vote⟩ — see COMPETENT 1
2 meeting the requirements of a purpose or situation ⟨I don't have anything *suitable* to wear to a bar mitzvah⟩ — see FIT 1

suitableness *n* the quality or state of being especially suitable or fitting ⟨questioned the *suitableness* of bringing a dog to a wedding⟩ — see APPROPRIATENESS

suitably *adv* **1** in a manner suitable for the occasion or purpose ⟨tried to appear *suitably* amused by his well-intentioned anecdote⟩ — see PROPERLY
2 in or to a degree or quantity that meets one's requirements or satisfaction ⟨I need someone who's *suitably* versed in computers to help me decide what to buy⟩ — see ENOUGH 1

suitcase *n* a bag carried by hand and designed to hold a traveler's clothing and personal articles ⟨it'll be much easier to carry a backpack than to lug that *suitcase* all over the place⟩ — see TRAVELING BAG

suite *n* **1** a body of employees or servants who accompany and wait on a person ⟨an athlete accompanied everywhere by a *suite* of attendants, including his personal trainer, a dietician, and a massage therapist⟩ — see CORTEGE 1
2 a number of things considered as a unit ⟨replaced the mismatched bed and chests of drawers with a handsome new bedroom *suite*⟩ — see GROUP 1
3 a room or set of rooms in a private house or a block used as a separate dwelling place ⟨whenever he visits the city, he stays in his uncle's 10th-floor *suite*⟩ — see APARTMENT 1

suitor *n* **1** a man who courts a woman usually with the goal of marrying her ⟨my sister finally married her *suitor* of six years on Sunday⟩
synonyms gallant, swain, wooer
related words beau, boyfriend, fellow, man, old man, significant other, squeeze [*slang*]; admirer, crush, steady; beloved, darling, dear, favorite, flame, honey, love, lover, spark, sweet, sweetheart, sweetie, sweetie pie, valentine; date, escort; fiancé, intended
2 one who asks earnestly for a favor or gift ⟨the inventor had several *suitors* for his patent, but he wasn't interested in dealing with a big company⟩ — see SUPPLICANT

sulk *n* a state of resentful silence or irritability ⟨a child sitting in a *sulk* over a minor disagreement⟩
synonyms grouch, hump [*British*], pet, pouts, snit, sulkiness, sullenness
related words blues, dumps, mopes; surliness; biliousness, choler, crankiness, crossness, crotchetiness, fantods, grouchiness, grumpiness, huffiness, irascibility, irascibleness, irritability, irritableness, peevishness, perverseness, perversity, pettishness, petulance, surliness, testiness, waspishness; cantankerousness, disagreeableness, dyspepsia, fretfulness, orneriness; fussiness, querulousness; oversensitiveness, sensitivity
near antonyms cheerfulness, gaiety (*also* gayety), gladsomeness, high-spiritedness, lightheartedness, perkiness; affability, agreeableness, amenity, amicability, cordiality, friendliness, geniality, graciousness, pleasantness, sociability, sociality; amiability, amiableness, good-humoredness, good-naturedness, good-temperedness

sulk *vb* to silently go about in a bad mood ⟨the toddler would *sulk* for hours whenever he didn't get his way⟩
synonyms grump, mope, pout
related words brood, dwell (on), mull (over), muse (over), ponder; frown, glower, lower (*also* lour), scowl; carry on, take on; pet

sulkiness *n* a state of resentful silence or irritability ⟨turned into a very pleasant adult when she finally outgrew her adolescent *sulkiness*⟩ — see SULK

sulky *adj* given to or displaying a resentful silence and often irritability ⟨our teenage daughter turns *sulky* if we refuse to let her borrow the car⟩
synonyms glum, mopey, pouting, pouty, sullen, surly
related words dour, gloomy, morose; choleric, crabby, cranky, cross, crotchety, grouchy, grumpy, irascible, irritable, peevish, perverse, pettish, petulant, prickly, quick-tempered, raspy, ratty, short-tempered, snappish, snappy, snarky, snippety, snippy, testy, waspish; brooding, moping; bearish, bilious, cantankerous, disagreeable, dyspeptic, ill-humored, ill-natured, ill-tempered, ornery; huffy, sensitive, temperamental, tetchy, thin-skinned, touchy
phrases down in the mouth
near antonyms sociable; cheerful, cheery, gladsome, good-humored, good-natured, good-tempered, perky, sunny; carefree, easygoing, happy-go-lucky, relaxed

sullen *adj* **1** causing or marked by an atmosphere lacking in cheer ⟨*sullen* skies that matched our mood on the day of the funeral⟩ — see GLOOMY 1
2 given to or displaying a resentful silence and often irritability ⟨*sullen* and bored at his in-laws' house, he couldn't wait for the holidays to end⟩ — see SULKY

sullenness *n* a state of resentful silence or irritability ⟨her mother-in-law managed to dispel her *sullenness* with a gals-only shopping spree⟩ — see SULK

sullied *adj* not clean ⟨lying in *sullied* bed linens that had not seen the inside of a washing machine for some time⟩ — see DIRTY 1

sully *vb* to make dirty ⟨people that *sully* our state parks with their trash⟩ ⟨a once-gleaming marble interior *sullied* by decades of exposure to cigarette smoke⟩ — see DIRTY

sultry *adj* **1** containing or characterized by an uncomfortable amount of moisture ⟨on really *sultry* days we go to the mall to hang out and cool off⟩ — see HUMID
2 having a notably high temperature ⟨the incredibly dry, *sultry* desert air⟩ — see HOT 1

sum *n* **1** a complete amount of something ⟨the *sum* of human knowledge on that subject⟩ — see WHOLE
2 a short statement of the main points ⟨the district attorney delivered a *sum* of the evidence against the accused that was simply staggering⟩ — see SUMMARY
3 the highest part or point ⟨he declared that he had reached the *sum* of joy when his newborn daughter was laid in his arms⟩ — see HEIGHT 1
4 the central part or aspect of something under consideration ⟨the *sum* of the issue is: who will pay for this?⟩ — see CRUX

sum *vb* to combine (numbers) into a single sum ⟨can *sum* figures in his head faster than I can punch them into a calculator⟩ — see ADD 2

sum (to *or* **into)** *vb* to have a total of ⟨a lifetime of charitable contributions that *sum into* the millions⟩ — see AMOUNT (TO) 1

summa *n* a short statement of the main points ⟨the director's book is basically a *summa* of his views on the nature of the theatrical experience⟩ — see SUMMARY

summarily *adv* in a few words ⟨*summarily* informed us that our help was not welcome⟩ — see SHORTLY 1

summarization *n* a short statement of the main points ⟨what you wrote goes way beyond a *summarization* of the speech⟩ — see SUMMARY

summarize *vb* to make into a short statement of the main points (as of a report) ⟨the closing minute of the newscast *summarizes* the main story of the day⟩
synonyms abstract, boil down, brief, digest, encapsulate, epitomize, outline, recap, recapitulate, reprise, sum up, synopsize, wrap up
related words abridge, condense, curtail, cut back, shorten; downsize, shrink; concentrate, consolidate; decoct, essentialize; simplify, streamline
near antonyms elongate, extend, lengthen, prolong, protract; amplify, elaborate (on *or* upon), enlarge (on *or* upon), expand, supplement

summary *adj* marked by the use of few words to convey much information or meaning ⟨obviously a one-volume encyclopedia can offer only a very *summary* account of the American Civil War⟩ — see CONCISE

summary *n* a short statement of the main points ⟨many book reports choose to begin with a *summary* of the book⟩
synonyms abstract, breviary, brief, capsule, conspectus, digest, encapsulation, epitome, inventory, outline, précis, recap, recapitulation, résumé (*or* resume *also* resumé), roundup, rundown, run-through, sum, summa, summarization, summing-up, sum-up, synopsis, wrap-up
related words abbreviation, abridgment (*or* abridgement), compend, compendium, condensation, curtailment, shortening; simplification, streamlining; rehash, reprise; conclusion, epilogue (*also* epilog)
near antonyms amplification, enlargement, expansion; addendum, supplement

summate *vb* to combine (numbers) into a single sum ⟨*summate* all of the expenses that you incurred on your last business trip⟩ — see ADD 2

summation *n* a complete amount of something ⟨the *summation* of climatic conditions that affect plant growth⟩ — see WHOLE

summerhouse *n* a freestanding airy structure in a scenic setting (as a park) typically offering commanding views ⟨the sudden shower had wedding guests scurrying to the safety of the garden's *summerhouse*⟩ — see BELVEDERE

summing–up *n* a short statement of the main points ⟨there's no time to get into all the details, so could you give me a quick *summing-up*?⟩ — see SUMMARY

summit *n* the highest part or point ⟨a new movie that some enthusiastic reviewers are already calling the *summit* of cinematic achievement⟩ — see HEIGHT 1

summon *vb* **1** to demand or request the presence or service of ⟨without explanation, the managing editor *summoned* me to his office⟩
synonyms call, hail
related words cite, subpoena; assemble, call out, call up, convene, convoke, muster; ask, bid, invite; command, order, request, requisition; beckon, demand, invoke; buzz, knell, page, ring, whistle
phrases send for
near antonyms dismiss, send (away), turn away; banish, boot (out), cast out, drum (out), eject, expel, kick out, oust, out, rout, run off, throw out, turf (out) [*chiefly British*]
2 to call into being through the use of one's inner resources or powers ⟨managed to *summon* a bright smile despite the gloomy day⟩
synonyms conjure (up), gather, get up
related words educe, elicit, evoke, raise
3 to bring together in assembly by or as if by command ⟨*summoned* a special session of parliament⟩ — see CONVOKE

summons *n* a written notice ordering a person to appear in court ⟨if you ignore a court *summons*, you will be fined⟩
synonyms process, subpoena
related words capias, warrant, writ; ticket

sumptuous *adj* showing obvious signs of wealth and comfort ⟨the cruise ship claims to offer *sumptuous* furnishings, exquisitely prepared cuisine, and stellar entertainment⟩ — see LUXURIOUS 1

sumptuously *adv* in a luxurious manner ⟨a history book *sumptuously* illustrated with maps, drawings, and photographs⟩ — see HIGH

sum total *n* a complete amount of something ⟨in this case the *sum total* of physical evidence that a crime has been committed wouldn't fill a thimble⟩ — see WHOLE

sum–up *n* a short statement of the main points ⟨a *sum-up* of the main themes of the Romantic movement⟩ — see SUMMARY

sum up *vb* to make into a short statement of the main points (as of a report) ⟨in *summing up* the evidence against the defendant, the district attorney presented fact after damning fact⟩ — see SUMMARIZE

sun *n* **1** the light given off by the star around which the planet Earth revolves ⟨be sure to wear sunscreen if you plan to spend more than a few minutes in the *sun*⟩
synonyms sunlight, sunshine
related words sunburst; daylight; glare, shine
near antonyms cloudiness; penumbra, shade, shadiness, shadow, umbra

2 a ball-shaped gaseous celestial body that shines by its own light ⟨the incomprehensible vastness of a universe filled with billions of *suns*⟩ — see STAR 1
3 the first appearance of light in the morning or the time of its appearance ⟨I'm afraid that for this long trip we shall have to leave with the *sun*⟩ — see DAWN 1
4 public acknowledgment or admiration for an achievement ⟨Olympians basking in the *sun* of athletic achievement while the public still remembers them⟩ — see GLORY 1

Sunday *adj* being such only for recreation ⟨a charity auction of works by some of the town's more socially prominent *Sunday* painters⟩ — see AVOCATIONAL

sundeck *n* a flat roofless structure attached to a building ⟨the girls spent the afternoon reading and tanning on the *sundeck*⟩
synonyms balcony, deck, terrace
related words gallery; lanai, porch, stoop, veranda (*or* verandah)

sunder *vb* to set or force apart ⟨during the cold war East and West Berlin were *sundered* by an impenetrable wall⟩ — see SEPARATE 1

sundering *n* the act or process of a whole separating into two or more parts or pieces ⟨the *sundering* of the nation by bloody civil war⟩ — see SEPARATION 1

sundown *n* the time from when the sun begins to set to the onset of total darkness ⟨we were told that the best time to see elk is at *sundown*⟩ — see DUSK 1

sundowner *n, Australian* a homeless wanderer who may beg or steal for a living ⟨*sundowners* showing up at a sheep station looking for work⟩ — see TRAMP 1

sundries *n pl* small useful items ⟨the only things she needed for her overnight stay were her carryall and a small bag for *sundries*⟩ — see NOTION 1

sunk *adj* facing certain defeat, disaster, or death ⟨all our savings went for lottery tickets, and now we're *sunk*⟩ — see DONE FOR

sunken *adj* **1** curved inward ⟨our convalescing guest's *sunken* cheeks soon filled out on a diet of my mother's cooking⟩ — see HOLLOW
2 living, lying, or occurring below the surface of the water ⟨diving for *sunken* treasure⟩ — see UNDERWATER

sunless *adj* causing or marked by an atmosphere lacking in cheer ⟨mental patients who were once condemned to spend their lives in the *sunless* confines of a state asylum⟩ — see GLOOMY 1

sunlight *n* the light given off by the star around which the planet Earth revolves ⟨let's raise the shades and let in some *sunlight*⟩ — see SUN 1

sunny *adj* **1** having or being an outward sign of good feelings (as of love, confidence, or happiness) ⟨her *sunny* laughter filled the house with joy⟩ — see RADIANT 1
2 having or showing a good mood or disposition ⟨momentarily forgot their worries at the sight of the baby's *sunny* smile⟩ — see CHEERFUL 1
3 indicative of or marked by high spirits or good humor ⟨the good-natured waitresses enhance the restaurant's *sunny* and cheery atmosphere⟩ — see MERRY
4 not stormy or cloudy ⟨we are hoping for a *sunny* weekend so we can spend time at the beach⟩ — see FAIR 1

sunrise *n* the first appearance of light in the morning or the time of its appearance ⟨a job that requires him to get up before *sunrise*⟩ — see DAWN 1

sunset *n* the time from when the sun begins to set to the onset of total darkness ⟨the glow of the western sky at *sunset*⟩ — see DUSK 1

sunshine *n* the light given off by the star around which the planet Earth revolves ⟨spent a week at the shore soaking up the *sunshine* and salt air⟩ — see SUN 1

sunshiny *adj* not stormy or cloudy ⟨we're due for a *sunshiny* weekend after all the rain we've had⟩ — see FAIR 1

sunup *n* the first appearance of light in the morning or the time of its appearance ⟨have you ever actually heard a rooster crow at *sunup*?⟩ — see DAWN 1

sup *n* the portion of a serving of a beverage that is swallowed at one time ⟨the old mariner took a *sup* of grog and began his tale⟩ — see DRINK 2

sup *vb* to swallow in liquid form ⟨*supped* the broth slowly⟩ — see DRINK 1

super *adj* unusually large ⟨drinks come in three sizes: medium, large, or *super*⟩ — see HUGE

super *adv* to a great degree ⟨my computer is *super* slow this morning⟩ — see VERY 1

superabundance *n* **1** an amount or supply more than sufficient to meet one's needs ⟨a *superabundance* of donations flowed in after the family's plight was seen on national TV⟩ — see PLENTY 1
2 the state or an instance of going beyond what is usual, proper, or needed ⟨a *superabundance* of applicants for a limited number of jobs⟩ — see EXCESS 1

superannuated *adj* having passed its time of use or usefulness ⟨a periodical that insists on using largely *superannuated* terms like "editress" and "aviatrix"⟩ — see OBSOLETE

superb *adj* of the very best kind ⟨the restaurant's baker makes a *superb* chocolate cake⟩ — see EXCELLENT

superbness *n* **1** exceptionally high quality ⟨the *superbness* of the orchestra's performance was such that the music critics were straining for superlatives⟩ — see EXCELLENCE 1
2 impressiveness of beauty on a large scale ⟨climbers rave about the *superbness* of the view from the mountain's summit⟩ — see MAGNIFICENCE

supercilious *adj* having a feeling of superiority that shows itself in an overbearing attitude ⟨the *supercilious* art dealer rolled her eyes when we asked if she had anything for under $1,000⟩ — see ARROGANT

superciliousness *n* an exaggerated sense of one's importance that shows itself in the making of excessive or unjustified claims ⟨can't bear the *superciliousness* of her cousin, who lives in New York City and thinks everybody in Tennessee is a hick⟩ — see ARROGANCE

supercool *adj* being in the latest or current fashion ⟨the teen picked out some *supercool*, superexpensive sneakers⟩ — see STYLISH

super–duper *adj* unusually large ⟨their *super-duper* ice cream sundaes are true diet busters⟩ — see HUGE

supereminent *adj* highest in rank or authority ⟨the *supereminent* authority in the field of Shakespearean scholarship⟩ — see HEAD

supererogatory *adj* being over what is needed ⟨now that the dress code has been e-mailed to everyone and posted on our intranet site, a paper memo about it seems *supererogatory*⟩ — see SPARE 1

superficial *adj* **1** lying on or affecting only the outer layer of something ⟨a *superficial* scratch that barely even broke the skin⟩
synonyms skin-deep, surface
related words depthless, shallow, shoal; two-dimensional; external
near antonyms deep, deep-seated
2 having or showing a lack of depth of understanding or character ⟨a *superficial* analysis of how the violence in video games affects young people⟩
synonyms facile, one-dimensional, shallow, skin-deep
related words cursory, hasty, oversimple, passing, sketchy; aimless, desultory, haphazard, hit-or-miss, random; limited, narrow, restricted
near antonyms discerning, penetrant, penetrating; definitive, hard; broad, complete, comprehensive, exhaustive, extensive, far-reaching, wide; general, global, in-

clusive; detailed, in-depth; critical
antonyms deep, profound

superfluity *n* **1** something adding to pleasure or comfort but not absolutely necessary ⟨spends most of her money on designer clothes and other *superfluities*⟩ — see LUXURY 1
2 the state or an instance of going beyond what is usual, proper, or needed ⟨a *superfluity* of wire coat hangers from all of those trips to the dry cleaner⟩ — see EXCESS 1

superfluous *adj* being over what is needed ⟨cleared off all the *superfluous* stuff on his desk to make room for the new computer⟩ — see SPARE 1

superheated *adj* **1** having a notably high temperature ⟨certain *superheated* liquids change to gas with almost explosive violence⟩ — see HOT 1
2 having or expressing great depth of feeling ⟨a *superheated*, rancorous argument on how the child should be raised⟩ — see FERVENT 1

superhuman *adj* being so extraordinary or abnormal as to suggest powers which violate the laws of nature ⟨in his dreams the boy can always perform *superhuman* feats⟩ — see SUPERNATURAL 2

superintend *vb* **1** to be in charge of ⟨*superintends* the construction of all scenery at the summer theater⟩ — see BOSS 1
2 to look after and make decisions about ⟨homeschooling parents who *superintend* their children's education⟩ — see CONDUCT 1
3 to take charge of especially on behalf of another ⟨whoever's *superintending* the warehouse will know what's been delivered today⟩ — see [2]TEND 1

superintendence *n* **1** the act or activity of looking after and making decisions about something ⟨under her lax *superintendence* the company eventually went bankrupt⟩ — see CONDUCT 1
2 the duty or function of watching or guarding for the sake of proper direction or control ⟨the *superintendence* of the local music festival is handled jointly by the city and the county⟩ — see SUPERVISION 1

superintendency *n* **1** the duty or function of watching or guarding for the sake of proper direction or control ⟨*superintendency* of the polling places is largely carried out by retired citizens⟩ — see SUPERVISION 1
2 the act or activity of looking after and making decisions about something ⟨currently a faculty member is needed for *superintendency* of the program⟩ — see CONDUCT 1

superintendent *n* a person who manages or directs something ⟨the office of the *superintendent* of parks issues camping permits⟩ — see EXECUTIVE

superior *adj* **1** having a feeling of superiority that shows itself in an overbearing attitude ⟨that *superior* sportscaster lets it be known that he thinks all foreign baseball teams are second-rate⟩ — see ARROGANT
2 having or displaying feelings of scorn for what is regarded as beneath oneself ⟨the *superior* attitude of the store owner's son drove the other employees crazy⟩ — see PROUD 1
3 of the very best kind ⟨a five-star restaurant known for its *superior* wine list⟩ — see EXCELLENT
4 standing above others in rank, importance, or achievement ⟨a university known for attracting *superior* scientists and mathematicians⟩ — see EMINENT

superior *n* one who is above another in rank, station, or office ⟨if a customer is rude to you, report it to your *superior* and she'll handle it⟩
synonyms better, elder, senior
related words boss, chief, head, leader, master
near antonyms assistant, deputy
antonyms inferior, subordinate, underling

superiority *n* **1** an exaggerated sense of one's importance that shows itself in the making of excessive or unjustified claims ⟨the *superiority* of some of the customers at the exclusive beauty salon is enough to curl your hair⟩ — see ARROGANCE
2 exceptionally high quality ⟨the *superiority* of tree-ripened mangoes might make you want to spend the rest of your life in a tropical climate⟩ — see EXCELLENCE 1
3 the fact or state of being above others in rank or importance ⟨the *superiority* of the nation in military might⟩ — see EMINENCE 1

superlative *adj* of the very best kind ⟨the New England town meeting is a *superlative* example of grassroots democracy⟩ — see EXCELLENT

supernal *adj* **1** of the very best kind ⟨an absolutely *supernal* performance of the concerto by a 16-year old prodigy⟩ — see EXCELLENT
2 of, relating to, or suggesting heaven ⟨a couple enjoying the *supernal* joys of parenthood for the first time⟩ — see CELESTIAL

supernatural *adj* **1** of, relating to, or being part of a reality beyond the observable physical universe ⟨believes in ghosts, guardian angels, and other *supernatural* beings⟩
synonyms metaphysical, otherworldly, paranormal, preternatural, transcendent, transcendental, unearthly
related words mystic, mystical, occult, psychic (*also* psychical), spiritistic, spiritualistic; extrasensory, supersensible, supersensory; celestial, divine, ethereal, heavenly, numinous, spiritual, unworldly
near antonyms earthly, mundane
antonyms natural
2 being so extraordinary or abnormal as to suggest powers which violate the laws of nature ⟨he seems to read books with *supernatural* speed⟩
synonyms magical, miraculous, phenomenal, preternatural, superhuman, supernormal, transcendent, transcendental, uncanny, unearthly
related words bizarre, curious, eerie (*also* eery), far-out, funny, grotesque, kinky, outlandish, out-of-the-way, outrageous, outré, peculiar, quaint, queer, queerish, quirky, remarkable, screwy, strange, wacky (*also* whacky), way-out, weird, wild; baffling, bewildering, confounding, mystifying, perplexing, puzzling, shocking; aberrant, atypical, fantastic (*also* fantastical), flaky, freak, freakish, idiosyncratic, marvelous (*or* marvellous), prodigious, rare, singular, uncommon, unique, unnatural, unusual, unwonted; unconventional, uncustomary, unorthodox; conspicuous, notable, noticeable, outstanding, prominent, salient, striking
near antonyms average, commonplace, everyday, garden, ordinary, prosaic, routine, run-of-the-mill, typical, unexceptional, unremarkable, usual, workaday; expected, familiar, predictable; common, customary, frequent, habitual, regular, wonted
3 of, relating to, or being God ⟨believed he had a *supernatural* calling to join the ministry⟩ — see HOLY 3

supernormal *adj* being so extraordinary or abnormal as to suggest powers which violate the laws of nature ⟨the little boy pretended to be a comic book hero with *supernormal* powers⟩ — see SUPERNATURAL 2

supernova *n* a person or thing that is successful ⟨tragically, a shoulder injury cut short the pitching career of one of baseball's brightest *supernovas*⟩ — see HIT 1

supernumerary *adj* being over what is needed ⟨a third, *supernumerary* witness to the signing of the will⟩ — see SPARE 1

superpatriot *n* one who shows excessive favoritism towards his or her country ⟨too much of a *superpatriot* to acknowledge the achievements of athletes from other nations⟩ — see NATIONALIST

superpatriotic *adj* having or showing excessive favoritism towards one's own country ⟨such *superpatriotic* displays of triumphalism should be discouraged at international sporting events〉 — see NATIONALIST 1

superpatriotism *n* excessive favoritism towards one's own country 〈her *superpatriotism* causes her to assume that countries desperately long to be just like her own〉 — see CHAUVINISM

supersede *vb* to take the place of 〈that edition of the dictionary that you have has been *superseded* by a more recent one〉 — see REPLACE 1

supersize *adj* unusually large 〈a *supersize* truck with an impressive towing capacity〉 — see HUGE

supersize *vb* to make greater in size, amount, or number 〈we'll have to *supersize* our contributions to our retirement fund〉 — see INCREASE 1

supersized *adj* unusually large 〈a ship too *supersized* to fit through the Panama Canal〉 — see HUGE

supersmart *adj* having or showing quickness of mind 〈a *supersmart* guy in college, he later founded a dot-com that's now worth gazillions〉 — see INTELLIGENT 1

superstar *n* a person who is widely known and usually much talked about 〈a basketball *superstar*〉 — see CELEBRITY 1

superstud *n* a physically attractive man 〈wanting to be taken seriously as an actor, he's unhappy with his image as a *superstud*〉 — see HUNK 1

supervene *vb* to come after in time 〈it was not the slow-spreading cancer that caused his death but a *supervening* heart attack〉 — see FOLLOW 1

supervenient *adj* not being a vital part of or belonging to something 〈he painted his landscapes for self-fulfillment, regarding financial rewards as *supervenient* to his reason for doing them〉 — see EXTRINSIC

supervise *vb* **1** to be in charge of 〈for each sailboat an experienced hand is assigned to *supervise* a novice seaman〉 — see BOSS 1
2 to look after and make decisions about 〈*supervises* all the affairs of the athletic club, including hiring someone to run the summer tennis camp〉 — see CONDUCT 1
3 to take charge of especially on behalf of another 〈we need someone to *supervise* the construction project while the foreman is in the hospital〉 — see ²TEND 1

supervision *n* **1** the duty or function of watching or guarding for the sake of proper direction or control 〈one of your responsibilities will be the *supervision* of all fund-raising activities for the club〉
synonyms care, charge, guidance, headship, oversight, regulation, stewardship, superintendence, superintendency, surveillance
related words monitoring, observance, observation, observing, policing; administration, control, direction, generalship, hand(s), management, running; leadership, piloting, shepherding, steering; government, reign, rule; aegis (*also* egis), auspices, guardianship, protection, trusteeship, tutelage
2 the act or activity of looking after and making decisions about something 〈one of the senior editors took over *supervision* of the project while the editor-in-chief was on maternity leave〉 — see CONDUCT 1

supervisor *n* a person who manages or directs something 〈the salesclerk said she would have to ask her *supervisor* if I could return the defective CD without a receipt〉 — see EXECUTIVE

supervisory *adj* suited for or relating to the directing of things 〈was promoted to a *supervisory* position with several assistants working under him〉 — see EXECUTIVE

supper club *n* a bar or restaurant offering special nighttime entertainment (as music, dancing, or comedy acts) 〈a posh suburban *supper club* that caters to a generally well-heeled clientele〉 — see NIGHTCLUB

supplant *vb* to take the place of 〈old traditions that were fading away and being *supplanted* by modern ways〉 — see REPLACE 1

supple *adj* **1** able to bend easily without breaking 〈a dome tent outfitted with *supple* fiberglass tent poles〉 — see WILLOWY
2 able to revert to original size and shape after being stretched, squeezed, or twisted 〈shoes made from *supple* leather〉 — see ELASTIC 1

supplement *n* **1** something added (as by growth) 〈this new rule restricting e-mail to job-related activity is only a *supplement* to the preexisting policy regarding personal use of company resources〉 — see INCREASE 1
2 something that serves to complete or make up for a deficiency in something else 〈recommends taking a vitamin C *supplement* to prevent colds〉 — see COMPLEMENT 1
3 a part added at the end of a book or periodical 〈a *supplement* containing biographical articles on women who had died since the publication of the original three-volume encyclopedia〉 — see ADDENDUM 1

supplemental *adj* **1** available to supply something extra when needed 〈the new program will provide *supplemental* health insurance to thousands of workers〉 — see AUXILIARY
2 related to each other in such a way that one completes the other 〈an astronomer who regards science and religion not as antithetical but as *supplemental* belief systems〉 — see COMPLEMENTARY

supplementary *adj* **1** available to supply something extra when needed 〈the teacher's edition of the textbook comes with a lot of *supplementary* material〉 — see AUXILIARY
2 related to each other in such a way that one completes the other 〈regards theology and philosophy as *supplementary* fields of study〉 — see COMPLEMENTARY

suppliance *n* an earnest request 〈with arms raised in humble *suppliance*, the priest asked for blessings from above〉 — see PLEA 1

suppliant *n* one who asks earnestly for a favor or gift 〈didn't like being in the position of a *suppliant*, having to ask her parents to help her pay the rent on her apartment〉 — see SUPPLICANT

suppliant *adj* asking humbly 〈the *suppliant* thief pleaded for a second chance〉
synonyms beseeching, entreating, imploring, pleading, prayerful, soliciting, supplicant, supplicating, supplicatory
related words begging, importunate, insistent, persistent

supplicant *adj* asking humbly 〈hated having to go before his boss like a *supplicant* beggar whenever he needed some time off to attend to personal matters〉 — see SUPPLIANT

supplicant *n* one who asks earnestly for a favor or gift 〈the new governor soon had to deal with a long line of *supplicants* asking for jobs and other political favors〉
synonyms petitioner, pleader, solicitor, suitor, suppliant
related words beggar, mendicant, panhandler; cadger, moocher, schnorrer; asker, requester, suer

supplicate *vb* to make a request to (someone) in an earnest or urgent manner 〈the minister reminded his flock that God is a being to be obeyed and worshipped always and not just someone to be *supplicated* in times of trouble〉 — see BEG

supplicating *adj* asking humbly 〈in a *supplicating* gesture, he got down on his knees and asked, "Will you marry me?"〉 — see SUPPLIANT

supplication *n* an earnest request 〈the Red Cross made an urgent *supplication* for donations of food and blankets for the earthquake victims〉 — see PLEA 1

supplicatory *adj* asking humbly ⟨knelt in *supplicatory* prayer⟩ — see SUPPLIANT

supply *vb* **1** to provide (someone) with what is needed for a task or activity ⟨be sure to pack your own towels in case the hostel doesn't *supply* them⟩ — see FURNISH 1

2 to put (something) into the possession of someone for use or consumption ⟨the stable will *supply* safety helmets, but we need to bring our own riding boots⟩ — see FURNISH 2

supply *n* the number of individuals or amount of something available at any given time ⟨the *supply* of parents willing to coach youth soccer seems to be shrinking⟩

synonyms budget, force, fund, inventory, pool, repertoire, reservoir, stock

related words reserve, resource; cache, hoard, stockpile; refill, renewal, replacement; kitty, nest egg, pot, purse; fountain, mine, source, spring, well, wellspring

support *n* **1** a structure that holds up or serves as a foundation for something else ⟨if you don't add a couple more *supports* to that tower of blocks, it's going to fall down⟩

synonyms brace, buttress, mount, mounting, prop, reinforcement, shore, spur, stay, underpinning

related words shoring; column, pedestal, pilaster, pillar; arch, bolster, bracket, cantilever, girder; bearing; crutch, peg, post, stake, stanchion, stand, stilt, strut, truss; base, foundation, frame

2 an act or instance of helping ⟨the team's victory owes a lot to Joe's strong *support* in left field⟩ — see HELP 1

support *vb* **1** to promote the interests or cause of ⟨though childless themselves, they *support* the local schools both by volunteering and by fiercely opposing funding cuts⟩

synonyms advocate, back, champion, endorse (*also* indorse), patronize, plump (for), plunk (for) *or* plonk (for)

related words adopt, embrace, espouse; abet, aid, assist, help, prop (up), second, side (with); backstop, bolster, boost, buttress, reinforce (*also* reenforce); advance, forward, further; plug, preach, talk up; bail out, deliver, rescue, save

phrases go in for, go to bat for, hold a brief for, stand up for, stick up for

near antonyms baffle, foil, frustrate, interfere, oppose, sabotage, thwart; desert, disappoint, fail, let down

2 to pay the living expenses of ⟨a young widow *supporting* a sick mother as well as two small children on a teacher's salary⟩

synonyms keep, maintain, provide (for)

related words finance, fund, patronize, set up, sponsor, stake, underwrite

phrases foot the bill (for), take care of

3 to hold up or serve as a foundation for ⟨pillars *supporting* the bridge⟩

synonyms bear, bolster, brace, buttress, carry, prop (up), shore (up), stay, sustain, undergird, underpin, uphold

related words steady, truss, underlie

4 to provide evidence or information for (as a claim or idea) ⟨studies that *support* the claim that red wine drinkers have a reduced risk of coronary disease and cancer⟩

synonyms back, bolster, buttress, corroborate, reinforce (*also* reenforce), shore (up), substantiate

related words confirm, establish, prove, verify; affirm, avouch, validate

near antonyms undercut, undermine, weaken

5 to continue to declare to be true or proper despite opposition or objections ⟨we *support* the students' right to speak out on local issues that affect them⟩ — see MAINTAIN 2

6 to give evidence or testimony to the truth or factualness of ⟨new evidence *supports* the original researchers' unexpected conclusions⟩ — see CONFIRM 1

7 to provide (someone) with what is useful or necessary to achieve an end ⟨sent reinforcements to *support* the troops deployed overseas⟩ — see HELP 1

8 to put up with (something painful or difficult) ⟨he simply cannot *support* the thought of having to go on living without his beloved wife at his side⟩ — see BEAR 2

supportable *adj* **1** capable of being defended with good reasoning against verbal attack ⟨are there ever circumstances where laws that restrict a person's freedom of speech are *supportable*?⟩ — see TENABLE 2

2 capable of being endured ⟨her beloved cat had been rescued from the burning house, making her other losses at least *supportable*⟩ — see BEARABLE

3 capable of being proven as true or real ⟨the news editor simply assumed the facts of the story were *supportable* and did not assign it to a fact checker⟩ — see VERIFIABLE

supporter *n* **1** a person who actively supports or favors a cause ⟨President Lyndon B. Johnson was a strong *supporter* of civil rights⟩ — see EXPONENT 1

2 someone associated with another to give assistance or moral support ⟨even the President's *supporters* acknowledge that some of the criticism is justified⟩ — see ALLY

supporting *adj* serving to give support to the truth or factualness of something ⟨scientists looking for direct *supporting* evidence of microscopic black holes, the existence of which is theoretical⟩ — see CORROBORATIVE

supportive *adj* serving to give support to the truth or factualness of something ⟨the jimmied window latch is *supportive* of the theory that there was forced entry into the house⟩ — see CORROBORATIVE

suppose *vb* **1** to decide the size, amount, number, or distance of (something) without actual measurement ⟨if we *suppose* a minimum profit of $10,000 from the charity auction, we should be able to pay for the family's medical expenses⟩ — see ESTIMATE 2

2 to form an opinion from little or no evidence ⟨what do you *suppose* he's going to do with the prize money he won?⟩ — see GUESS 1

3 to have as an opinion ⟨voters wrongly *supposed* that the new mayor would be opposed to letting hazardous waste be transported through the city⟩ — see BELIEVE 2

4 to take as true or as a fact without actual proof ⟨had always *supposed* that her father would bequeath the family farm to her⟩ — see ASSUME 2

supposed *adj* appearing to be true on the basis of evidence that may or may not be confirmed ⟨this new computer program is a *supposed* improvement over the old one⟩ — see APPARENT 1

supposedly *adv* to all outward appearances ⟨she's *supposedly* too sick to come—or so she says⟩ — see APPARENTLY

supposition *n* **1** an idea that is the starting point for making a case or conducting an investigation ⟨my *supposition* is that this grape variety, which flourishes in southern France, should do equally well here, given the similar climate⟩ — see THEORY

2 an opinion or judgment based on little or no evidence ⟨it's pure *supposition* on your part that there's something illegal going on next door⟩ — see CONJECTURE

3 something taken as being true or factual and used as a starting point for a course of action or reasoning ⟨worthless genetic research that was based on the erroneous *supposition* that acquired characteristics can be passed on to offspring⟩ — see ASSUMPTION 1

suppositional *adj* existing only as an assumption or speculation ⟨concepts regarding the origin and structure of the universe must perforce be *suppositional*⟩ — see THEORETICAL 1

supposititious *adj* born to a father and mother who are not married ⟨entered the world as the *supposititious* son of a housemaid⟩ — see ILLEGITIMATE 1

suppress *vb* **1** to keep from being publicly known ⟨the government tried to *suppress* the truth about that incident⟩
synonyms burke, cover (up), hush (up)
related words black out, censor, gag, muzzle, silence; quash, repress, smother, spike, squash, squelch, stifle, strangle, throttle
near antonyms debunk, expose, reveal, show up, uncloak, uncover, unmask; blab, disclose, divulge, spill, tell, unveil; broadcast, circulate, publish, spread; describe, narrate, recite, recount, rehearse, relate, report
2 to refrain from openly showing or uttering ⟨he managed to *suppress* a scream at the sight of the dead body⟩ ⟨*suppressed* her anger⟩
synonyms choke (back), hold back, pocket, repress, sink, smother, stifle, strangle, submerge, swallow
related words control, govern, manage; bridle, check, curb, quash, quell; bottle up, contain; muffle, squelch
near antonyms express, loose, release, take out, unleash, vent
3 to hold back the normal growth of ⟨pruning helps *suppress* buds at the ends of developed branches and encourages new growth elsewhere⟩ — see STUNT
4 to put a stop to (something) by the use of force ⟨nothing could *suppress* the rising tide of protest against the dictator's latest injustices⟩ — see QUELL 1
5 to keep secret or shut off from view ⟨the defense attorney is openly accusing the prosecutor of attempting to *suppress* vital evidence⟩ — see [1]HIDE 2

suppression *n* the checking of one's true feelings and impulses when dealing with others ⟨learned that *suppression* of her angry feelings didn't necessarily make them go away⟩ — see CONSTRAINT 1

supremacist *n* a person who believes that one race should control all others ⟨white *supremacists* were arrested for painting racial slurs on a church⟩
synonyms racialist, racist
related words segregationist; bigot, sectarian
antonyms antiracist

supremacy *n* **1** controlling power or influence over others ⟨the Roman empire had *supremacy* over the entire Mediterranean world⟩
synonyms ascendance (*also* ascendence), ascendancy (*also* ascendency), dominance, domination, dominion, hegemony, imperium, predominance, predominancy, preeminence, reign, sovereignty (*also* sovranty)
related words primacy, superiority; lordship, scepter; arm, authority, choke hold, clutch, command, control, grip, hold, mastery, sway; takeover; direction, jurisdiction, management; clout, might, pull, weight; eminence, importance, moment; prerogative, privilege, right
near antonyms helplessness, weakness; impotence, impotency, powerlessness
2 exceptionally high quality ⟨the *supremacy* of cashmere among wools accounts for its high price⟩ — see EXCELLENCE 1
3 the fact or state of being above others in rank or importance ⟨England's maritime *supremacy* in the 18th century⟩ — see EMINENCE 1

supreme *adj* **1** highest in rank or authority ⟨the *supreme* commander of the multinational force⟩ — see HEAD
2 coming before all others in importance ⟨in our house, watching baseball reigns *supreme* as the activity of choice on summer evenings⟩ — see FOREMOST 1
3 of the greatest or highest degree or quantity ⟨considers a letter of gratitude from a former student the *supreme* reward for his years of teaching⟩ — see ULTIMATE 1

Supreme Being *n* the being worshipped as the creator and ruler of the universe ⟨anthropologists have found that most cultures around the world believe in a *Supreme Being*⟩ — see DEITY 2

supremely *adv* to a great degree ⟨climbing Mount Everest is *supremely* difficult⟩ — see VERY 1

surcease *n* the stopping of a process or activity ⟨hoping the new medicine would bring *surcease* to his pain⟩ — see END 1

surcharge *vb* to charge (someone) too much for goods or services ⟨contends that with the present tax structure, the state's lower-income residents are being *surcharged* and the wealthiest residents are getting off too lightly⟩ — see OVERCHARGE 1

surcoat *n* a warm outdoor coat ⟨a knight in a fur-lined and hooded *surcoat* over a long tunic stood in the forest clearing⟩ — see OVERCOAT

sure *adj* **1** having or showing a mind free from doubt ⟨are you absolutely *sure* that she said she was coming today?⟩ — see CERTAIN 2
2 impossible to avoid or evade ⟨the joke's a *sure* dud if you don't pause in the right places⟩ — see INEVITABLE
3 not likely to fail ⟨a *sure* cure for the winter blues—a week in the Bahamas⟩ — see INFALLIBLE 2
4 worthy of one's trust ⟨a sister is a *sure* friend for life⟩ — see DEPENDABLE
5 not capable of being challenged or proved wrong ⟨no *sure* evidence that life exists on other planets⟩ — see IRREFUTABLE

sure *adv* without any question ⟨we *sure* could use your help here⟩ — see INDEED 1

sure–enough *adj* **1** being exactly as appears or as claimed ⟨a *sure-enough* ghost town that is a relic of the gold rush days⟩ — see AUTHENTIC 1
2 existing in fact and not merely as a possibility ⟨the inventor showed that he did have a *sure-enough* death ray⟩ — see ACTUAL

surefire *adj* not likely to fail ⟨pizza seems like a *surefire* choice for a food that everyone at the party will be happy with⟩ — see INFALLIBLE 2

surely *adv* without any question ⟨*surely* there's something I can do to help⟩ — see INDEED 1

sureness *n* **1** a state of mind in which one is free from doubt ⟨unfortunately, he lacked the *sureness* of his opponent in the tennis match⟩ — see CONFIDENCE 2
2 worthiness as the recipient of another's trust or confidence ⟨investors in those risky foreign enterprises were gambling on the *sureness* of their instincts⟩ — see RELIABILITY

sure thing *n* one that is certain to succeed ⟨he's a *sure thing* for the promotion: he's the most qualified candidate by far⟩
synonyms cinch, lock, shoo-in, slam dunk
related words certainty, inevitability; eventuality; foregone conclusion
phrases lead-pipe cinch
near antonyms dark horse, long shot

surety *n* **1** a formal agreement to fulfill an obligation ⟨gave his *surety* that he would pay back the loan if his sister was unable to for any reason⟩ — see GUARANTEE 1
2 a person who takes the responsibility for some other person or thing ⟨a mutual friend agreed to act as *surety* if I lent my cousin some money, since I wasn't certain that she'd be able to pay it back⟩ — see SPONSOR
3 a state of mind in which one is free from doubt ⟨I can't tell you the year in which that event happened with any great *surety*⟩ — see CONFIDENCE 2

surf *n* a light mass of fine bubbles formed in or on a liquid ⟨beachgoers romping in the swirling *surf*⟩ — see FOAM

surface *adj* lying on or affecting only the outer layer of something ⟨a *surface* stain on the wood that can easily be removed with a mild detergent⟩ — see SUPERFICIAL 1

surface *n* an outer part or layer ⟨the *surface* of just about everything in the kitchen was covered with soot after we put the grease fire out⟩ — see EXTERIOR

surface *vb* **1** to come to one's attention especially gradually or unexpectedly ⟨no information regarding the stolen car has *surfaced* since the police found it abandoned on a country road⟩ — see ARISE 2

2 to penetrate the surface (as of water) from below ⟨a submarine *surfaced* on the starboard side of the aircraft carrier⟩ — see BROACH 1

surfeit *n* the state or an instance of going beyond what is usual, proper, or needed ⟨ended up with a *surfeit* of volunteers who simply got in each other's way⟩ — see EXCESS 1

surfeit *vb* to fill with food to capacity ⟨having *surfeited* ourselves on raw oysters, we had to decline the rest of the restaurant's offerings⟩ — see GORGE 1

surfeited *adj* having one's appetite completely satisfied ⟨*surfeited* by the Thanksgiving repast, the grown-ups dozed off in front of the TV while the children raised Cain around the house⟩ — see FULL 3

surge *n* a moving ridge on the surface of water ⟨a huge *surge* nearly capsized the boat and drenched the hapless fishermen⟩ — see WAVE

surly *adj* **1** given to or displaying a resentful silence and often irritability ⟨went about his chores in a *surly* huff, totally annoyed that he was stuck at home on this beautiful Saturday⟩ — see SULKY

2 having or showing a habitually bad temper ⟨the *surly* receptionist told us we'd have to wait outside in the rain⟩ — see ILL-TEMPERED

surmise *n* an opinion or judgment based on little or no evidence ⟨my *surmise* is that the couple's "good news" is the announcement that they are going to have a baby⟩ — see CONJECTURE

surmise *vb* to form an opinion from little or no evidence ⟨we *surmised* that she had purchased the apple pie since there was a bakery box on the kitchen counter⟩ — see GUESS 1

surmount *vb* to achieve a victory over ⟨an Olympic swimmer who *surmounted* endless obstacles to achieve her goals⟩ — see BEAT 2

surname *n* **1** a name shared by members of a family ⟨judging from your *surname*, I'd guess that your family is Italian⟩

synonyms family name, last name

related words maiden name, married name; cognomen, epithet, sobriquet (*also* soubriquet)

2 a descriptive or familiar name given instead of or in addition to the one belonging to an individual ⟨"da Vinci" was Leonardo's *surname* but not his family name, Vinci being the town near Florence where the great artist was born⟩ — see NICKNAME

surpass *vb* **1** to be greater, better, or stronger than ⟨she always tried to *surpass* her older brother at anything he did⟩

synonyms beat, better, eclipse, exceed, excel, outclass, outdistance, outdo, outgun, outmatch, outshine, outstrip, overtop, top, tower (over), transcend

related words one-up, outpace, outrace, outrun, overpass; best, clobber, conquer, crush, defeat, drub, lick, master, outcompete, outperform, overcome, overmatch, prevail (over), rout, shame, skunk, subdue, surmount, thrash, trim, triumph (over), trounce, wallop, whip, win (against), worst; outbalance, outweigh, overbear, overshadow, trump

phrases go one better, run circles around (*or* run rings around)

near antonyms lose (to)

2 to go beyond the limit of ⟨the sales of the band's newest CD have *surpassed* the combined sales of its last two albums⟩ — see EXCEED 1

surpassingly *adv* to a great degree ⟨a *surpassingly* beautiful view from the summit⟩ — see VERY 1

surplus *adj* being over what is needed ⟨*surplus* stock gets shipped to the warehouse and is eventually sold at auction⟩ — see SPARE 1

surplus *n* the state or an instance of going beyond what is usual, proper, or needed ⟨we have a *surplus* of plastic knives, but we're short on forks and spoons for the picnic⟩ — see EXCESS 1

surplusage *n* the state or an instance of going beyond what is usual, proper, or needed ⟨a mall with a *surplusage* of stores all selling the same lines of clothing⟩ — see EXCESS 1

surprise *also* **surprize** *n* **1** something that makes a strong impression because it is so unexpected ⟨the anniversary party was such a complete *surprise* that the couple was speechless for a moment⟩

synonyms bombshell, jar, jaw-dropper, jolt, stunner

related words shock, thunderclap; eye-opener, revelation, shocker; amazement, marvel, wonder; fillip, kick, kicker, twist, wrinkle

phrases bolt from the blue (*also* bolt out of the blue)

2 the state of being strongly impressed by something unexpected or unusual ⟨stared in utter *surprise* at the deer in his cabin⟩

synonyms amazement, astonishment, shock, startlement, stupefaction

related words awe, wonder, wonderment; startle; bewilderment, confusion, consternation, discomfiture, dismay

3 a setup in which hidden attackers lie in wait ⟨waited under cover of darkness and took the enemy encampment by *surprise* at dawn⟩ — see AMBUSH 1

surprise *also* **surprize** *vb* **1** to make a strong impression on (someone) with something unexpected ⟨I was very *surprised* when my parents offered to pay the down payment on our house⟩

synonyms amaze, astonish, astound, bowl over, dumbfound (*also* dumfound), flabbergast, floor, rock, shock, startle, stun, stupefy, thunderstrike

related words befuddle, bewilder, blindside, blow away, confound, confuse, daze, discomfit, disconcert, dismay, jar, muddle, nonplus, perplex, shake up

phrases knock for a loop, take aback, take by surprise

2 to lie in wait for and attack by surprise ⟨FBI agents *surprised* the counterfeiters in their own base of operations⟩ — see AMBUSH

surprising *adj* **1** causing a strong emotional reaction because of unexpectedness ⟨the *surprising* news that they were going to have a baby had them rushing to buy nursery furniture⟩

synonyms amazing, astonishing, astounding, blindsiding, dumbfounding (*also* dumfounding), eye-opening, flabbergasting, jarring, jaw-dropping, jolting, shocking, startling, stunning, stupefying

related words unannounced, unanticipated, unexpected, unforeseen; awesome, awful, breathtaking, fabulous, heart-stopping, marvelous (*or* marvellous), miraculous, portentous, prodigious, staggering, stupendous, sublime, wonderful, wondrous; extraordinary, phenomenal, rare, sensational, spectacular; befuddling, bewildering, confounding, confusing, discomfiting, disconcerting, dismaying, flustering, muddling, nonplussing (*also* nonplusing), perplexing, upsetting; incomprehensible, inconceivable, incredible, unbelievable, unimaginable, unlikely, unthinkable; singular, uncom-

mon, unique, unusual, unwonted; conspicuous, notable, noticeable, outstanding, remarkable; impressive, striking
near antonyms common, customary, mundane, normal, ordinary, typical, unexceptional, unremarkable, usual
antonyms unsurprising
2 causing wonder or astonishment ⟨it's *surprising* how much knowledge of physics the architects of those immense medieval cathedrals must have had⟩ — see MARVELOUS 1

surrender *n* the usually forced yielding of one's person or possessions to the control of another ⟨the police demanded the *surrender* of all hostages as a condition for allowing the hijackers safe passage out of the country⟩
synonyms capitulating, capitulation, cession, handover, relinquishment, rendition, submission, submitting
related words acceptance, acquiescence, concession; compromise; appeasement, conciliation, reconcilement, reconciliation; capture, fall
near antonyms resistance

surrender *vb* **1** to give (something) over to the control or possession of another usually under duress ⟨the toddler *surrendered* the doll to her mother after a brief struggle⟩ ⟨the commander *surrendered* the garrison without having fired a single shot⟩
synonyms cede, cough up, deliver, give up, hand over, lay down, relinquish, render, turn in, turn over, yield
related words commit, consign, entrust (*also* intrust), transfer; forfeit, release, waive; abnegate, renounce, resign; abandon, desert, discard, forsake, part (with), shed
near antonyms keep, retain, withhold
2 to cease resistance (as to another's arguments, demands, or control) ⟨the father refused to *surrender* to his son's constant begging for a BB gun⟩ — see YIELD 3
3 to give up (as a position of authority) formally ⟨the aging queen refused to *surrender* the throne to her increasingly impatient heir⟩— see ABDICATE
4 to give up and cease resistance (as to a liking, temptation, or habit) ⟨determined to give up smoking, she so far has not *surrendered* to her incessant desire to have a cigarette⟩— see YIELD 1
5 to yield to the control or power of enemy forces ⟨General Robert E. Lee *surrendered* to General Ulysses S. Grant on April 9, 1865, thus ending the Civil War⟩ — see FALL 2
6 to give (oneself) over to something especially unrestrainedly ⟨laid-off workers who *surrender* themselves to despair will almost certainly never regain their footing⟩ — see ABANDON 1

surreptitious *adj* undertaken or done so as to escape being observed or known by others ⟨a private investigator adept at taking *surreptitious* pictures of adulterous couples⟩— see SECRET 1

surround *n* the circumstances, conditions, or objects by which one is surrounded ⟨the vast, featureless *surround* of the desert was strangely appealing to him⟩ — see ENVIRONMENT

surround *vb* to form a circle around ⟨she was *surrounded* by cheering fans within moments of scoring the winning goal⟩
synonyms circle, compass, embrace, encircle, enclose (*also* inclose), encompass, environ, gird, girdle, ring, wreathe
related words circumscribe, close in, cordon (off), fence (in), hem (in), wall; beset, besiege, entrench (*also* intrench), invest, swarm

surroundings *n pl* the circumstances, conditions, or objects by which one is surrounded ⟨we relaxed and forgot our worries for a while in the plush *surroundings* of the hotel⟩— see ENVIRONMENT

surveillance *n* **1** the duty or function of watching or guarding for the sake of proper direction or control ⟨a neutral country charged with the *surveillance* of the post-war rebuilding effort⟩ — see SUPERVISION 1
2 an act or period of watching for signs of activity, danger, or opportunity ⟨government *surveillance* of suspected terrorists⟩ — see VIGIL

survey *n* a close look at or over someone or something in order to judge condition ⟨a *survey* of the premises revealed that four of the exit doors were locked⟩ — see INSPECTION

survey *vb* **1** to go around and approach (people) with a request for opinions or information ⟨*surveyed* the medical residents and found out that 60% of them don't think they get enough sleep⟩ — see CANVASS 1
2 to look over closely (as for judging quality or condition) ⟨*surveyed* the books at the estate sale, fondly hoping to find a rare first edition⟩ — see INSPECT

survive *vb* **1** to come safely through ⟨the cat miraculously *survived* a two-story fall⟩
synonyms ride (out), weather
related words outlast, outlive, wear out; pull through; abide, continue, endure, hang on, hold on, hold out, hold up, last, lead, persist, stand, stick out, withstand; be, breathe, exist, live, subsist; flourish, prosper, thrive
phrases make it (through)
near antonyms croak [*slang*], decease, depart, die, expire, pass (on), pass away, perish, succumb; disappear, evaporate, fade, vanish; cease, end, stop
2 to continue to operate or to meet one's needs ⟨some old-world customs still *survive* in modern-day America⟩ — see HOLD OUT

susceptibility *n* the quality or state of having little resistance to some outside agent ⟨his aunt's unfortunate *susceptibility* to viruses meant she was nearly always sick⟩ ⟨a country parson who had a well-known *susceptibility* to anyone with a hard-luck story⟩
synonyms defenselessness, vulnerability, weakness
related words helplessness, powerlessness; passiveness, passivity; feebleness, frailness, frailty, infirmity; exposure, liability, openness, predisposition, proneness, sensitivity; receptiveness, receptivity; easiness, gullibility, naïveté (*also* naivete *or* naiveté); credulity, credulousness
near antonyms immunity; impenetrability, indomitability, indomitableness, invincibility
antonyms invulnerability

susceptible *adj* **1** being in a situation where one is likely to meet with harm ⟨some people are more *susceptible* to depression during the winter because of reduced exposure to sunlight⟩ — see LIABLE 1
2 lacking protection from danger or resistance against attack ⟨completely *susceptible* and totally defenseless against the imploring eyes of the puppy in the pet store⟩ — see HELPLESS 1
3 readily taken advantage of ⟨having recently lost his job, he was more *susceptible* to the illusory promises of get-rich-quick schemes⟩ — see EASY 2

suspect *adj* giving good reason for being doubted, questioned, or challenged ⟨since she was carrying no cash or credit cards, her claim to the store's detectives that she had intended to pay for the items was *suspect*⟩ — see DOUBTFUL 2

suspect *vb* **1** to form an opinion from little or no evidence ⟨we *suspected* that the runaway was a little younger than the 16 she claimed to be—more like 13⟩ — see GUESS 1
2 to have no trust or confidence in ⟨I *suspected* him from the moment he said he was an old friend of my sister's, since I probably would have heard about him⟩ — see DISTRUST

suspecting *adj* inclined to doubt or question claims ⟨*suspecting* dieters probably wouldn't fall for a weight-loss plan that claims you can eat as much as you want⟩ — see SKEPTICAL 1

suspend *vb* **1** to bring to a formal close for a period of time ⟨the judge *suspended* the hearing to give the district attorney more time to process evidence⟩ — see ADJOURN
2 to place on an elevated point without support from below ⟨*suspended* a banner proclaiming the town's "Heritage Days" from the archway⟩ — see HANG 1

suspended *adj* extending freely from a support from above ⟨a tree decorated with an array of *suspended* ornaments⟩ — see DEPENDENT 1

suspended animation *n* a state of temporary inactivity ⟨the husband's feeling that their love life was in *suspended animation* while his wife lavished all her attention on the new baby⟩ — see ABEYANCE

suspense *n* a state of temporary inactivity ⟨the lawsuit is in *suspense* until the court makes a decision concerning a related lawsuit⟩ — see ABEYANCE

suspenser *n* something (as a close contest) that induces much suspense as to its outcome ⟨Alfred Hitchcock was the acknowledged master of the cinematic *suspenser* that craftily manipulates its audience⟩ — see NAIL-BITER

suspension *n* a state of temporary inactivity ⟨trading with that nation is in *suspension* until it improves its record on human rights⟩ — see ABEYANCE

suspicion *n* **1** a feeling or attitude that one does not know the truth, truthfulness, or trustworthiness of someone or something ⟨all his promises were received with well-deserved *suspicion*⟩ — see DOUBT
2 a very small amount ⟨new parents who were alarmed by just a *suspicion* of a rash on their baby's chest⟩ — see PARTICLE 1

suspicion *vb, chiefly dialect* to form an opinion from little or no evidence ⟨no one will ever *suspicion* that I'm the one who pulled the prank⟩ — see GUESS 1

suspicious *adj* **1** giving good reason for being doubted, questioned, or challenged ⟨*suspicious* claims of being the rightful owner of the property⟩ — see DOUBTFUL 2
2 inclined to doubt or question claims ⟨*suspicious* of any menu dish having a name she can't pronounce⟩ — see SKEPTICAL 1
3 not feeling sure about the truth, wisdom, or trustworthiness of someone or something ⟨you should be very *suspicious* of those telephone calls from people telling you that you're the winner of a contest you never entered⟩ — see DOUBTFUL 1

suspiciously *adv* with distrust ⟨eyed me *suspiciously* when I snapped my book shut and hurriedly stuffed it into my bag⟩ — see ASKANCE

sustain *vb* **1** to supply with nourishment ⟨a granola bar should *sustain* you long enough to last until lunch⟩
synonyms nourish, nurture
related words sate, satiate, satisfy; nurse, suckle; cloy, fill, surfeit; fortify, replenish, strengthen; feed; board, cater, provision, victual
2 to come to a knowledge of (something) by living through it ⟨*sustained* serious injuries in the car crash⟩ — see EXPERIENCE
3 to put up with (something painful or difficult) ⟨I won't *sustain* such insolence!⟩ — see BEAR 2
4 to hold up or serve as a foundation for ⟨that old chair won't *sustain* your weight⟩ — see SUPPORT 3

sustainable *adj* **1** capable of being defended with good reasoning against verbal attack ⟨a line of argument that is probably not *sustainable* in a public forum against skilled debaters⟩ — see TENABLE 2
2 capable of being proven as true or real ⟨has no *sustainable* claim to the property without a deed or some other document⟩ — see VERIFIABLE
3 capable of being endured ⟨the general didn't think that such heavy casualties could be *sustainable* for much longer⟩ — see BEARABLE

sustenance *n* something that maintains or stimulates the intellect ⟨my only *sustenance* on the long flight was a trashy novel I'd bought in the airport⟩
synonyms aliment, food, nourishment, pabulum
related words refection
near antonyms candy, fluff, pablum, pap, trash

sustentation *n* **1** the act or activity of keeping something in an existing and usually satisfactory condition ⟨argues that a new toll is needed to pay for the long-term *sustentation* of the city's bridges⟩ — see MAINTENANCE
2 the careful maintaining and protection of something valuable especially in its natural or original state ⟨the all-important *sustentation* of Mount Vernon, Monticello, and other national treasures⟩ — see CONSERVATION 1

suture *vb* to close up with a series of interlacing stitches ⟨the doctor cleaned, *sutured*, and bandaged the wound⟩ — see SEW

svelte *adj* **1** having a noticeably small amount of body fat ⟨the *svelte* dancer seemed to float across the stage⟩ — see THIN 1
2 having or showing very polished and worldly manners ⟨the interior designer spoke in a low, *svelte* voice⟩ — see SUAVE

swab *n* one who operates or navigates a seagoing vessel ⟨old *swabs* swapping sea stories as they spend their last days in the veterans' home⟩ — see SAILOR

swabbie *also* **swabby** *n, slang* one who operates or navigates a seagoing vessel ⟨the pirate captain cried, "Ahoy, me *swabbies*, 'tis time to hoist the Jolly Roger!"⟩ — see SAILOR

swag *n* valuables stolen or taken by force ⟨robbed a bank and hid the *swag* under the floorboards⟩ — see LOOT 1

swag *vb* to be limp from lack of water or vigor ⟨the days of endless worrying had taken their toll, and the old woman's face *swagged* with exhaustion⟩ — see DROOP 1

swagger *vb* **1** to praise or express pride in one's own possessions, qualities, or accomplishments often to excess ⟨I, too, would *swagger* if I'd won first place in the bowling tournament⟩ — see BOAST 1
2 to walk with exaggerated arm and leg movements ⟨hoping to impress the women at the bar, the young man confidently *swaggered* across the room⟩ — see STRUT 1

swaggerer *n* someone who boasts ⟨despite his reputation for being a swellheaded *swaggerer*, he's actually quite insecure⟩ — see BRAGGART

swaggie *n, chiefly Australian* a homeless wanderer who may beg or steal for a living ⟨some *swaggies* were known to take occasional odd jobs at bush stations⟩ — see TRAMP 1

swagman *n, chiefly Australian* a homeless wanderer who may beg or steal for a living ⟨the *swagman* who roams through the outback is a mythic figure in Australia⟩ — see TRAMP 1

swain *n* **1** a male romantic companion ⟨a romanticized portrait of a bygone era of beauteous Southern belles and their gallant *swains*⟩ — see BOYFRIEND
2 a man who courts a woman usually with the goal of marrying her ⟨Grandma claims that she had several *swains* pursuing her, but it was only Grandpa who won her heart⟩ — see SUITOR 1

swallow *n* the portion of a serving of a beverage that is swallowed at one time ⟨drank the cool refreshing water in two *swallows* and held out her cup for more⟩ — see DRINK 2

swallow *vb* **1** to take into the stomach through the

mouth and throat ⟨try not to *swallow* the toothpaste⟩
synonyms down, get down, ingest
related words drink, guzzle, imbibe, knock back, sip; bolt, devour, gobble (up *or* down), gulp, ingurgitate; consume, eat, mouth (down), put away, sup; gorge, scarf, scoff, wolf; chew, gnaw (at *or* on), lap, lick, munch, nibble (on), peck (at), ruminate; dispatch, finish, polish off
2 to refrain from openly showing or uttering ⟨*swallowed* his pride and asked for help⟩ — see SUPPRESS 2
3 to regard as right or true ⟨my little niece *swallows* everything I tell her⟩ — see BELIEVE 1

swamp *vb* **1** to cover with a flood ⟨the boat was *swamped* by the huge wave⟩ ⟨has been *swamped* with paperwork since she returned from vacation⟩ — see FLOOD
2 to subject to incapacitating emotional or mental stress ⟨parents feeling *swamped* by work and family obligations⟩ — see OVERWHELM 1

swamp *n* **1** spongy land saturated or partially covered with water ⟨be careful in the *swamp*, because alligators sometimes lurk there⟩
synonyms bog, fen, marsh, marshland, mire, moor, morass, muskeg, slough (*also* slew *or* slue), swampland, wash, wetland
related words swale; quagmire; guck (*or* gook), muck, mud, ooze, slime, slop, sludge, slush
2 a difficult, puzzling, or embarrassing situation from which there is no easy escape ⟨with her credit cards maxed out, and the making of minimum payments a challenge, debt seemed to be an ever-deepening *swamp*⟩ — see PREDICAMENT

swampland *n* spongy land saturated or partially covered with water ⟨much of the county's *swampland* was drained for agriculture⟩ — see SWAMP 1

swank *n* excessive or unnecessary display ⟨service that is the essence of *swank*: the waiters pull out your chair for you and even place your napkin on your lap⟩ — see OSTENTATION

swank *or* **swanky** *adj* excessively showy ⟨drove up in a red sports car, the *swank* interior of which was decorated in silver and black⟩ — see GAUDY

swap *n* a giving or taking of one thing of value in return for another ⟨we made a *swap*: I'll do the dishes tonight and she'll do them for me tomorrow⟩ — see EXCHANGE 1

swap *vb* to give up (something) and take something else in return ⟨we *swapped* our other lawn mower for our neighbors' old snowblower⟩ — see CHANGE 3

swarm *n* a great number of persons or creatures massed together ⟨a *swarm* of tourists descends upon the island every summer⟩ — see CROWD 1

[1]**swarm** *vb* **1** to move upon or fill (something) in great numbers ⟨meeting little resistance, the pirates *swarmed* the decks of the merchant ship⟩ — see CROWD 2
2 to be copiously supplied ⟨at this time of year that Mexican resort *swarms* with college students on spring break⟩ — see ABOUND

[2]**swarm** *vb* to move (as up or over something) often with the help of the hands in holding or pulling ⟨one of the physical challenges had competitors *swarming* over a pile of logs⟩ — see CLIMB 1

swarming *adj* possessing or covered with great numbers or amounts of something specified ⟨the museum was *swarming* with schoolchildren on a field trip⟩ — see RIFE

swart *adj* not having a pale complexion ⟨in bodice rippers the hero is often a *swart* man of passion and mystery⟩ — see DARK 2

swarthy *adj* not having a light complexion ⟨a dark-eyed, *swarthy* young man with killer looks⟩ — see DARK 2

swash *vb* **1** to move with a splashing motion ⟨waves gently *swashing* against the shore⟩ — see SLOSH 1
2 to cause (something liquid or mushy) to move along in sheets ⟨every bump in the road *swashed* a little more of my soda on the car's upholstery⟩ — see SPLASH 1

swat *n* a hard strike with a part of the body or an instrument ⟨the impatient toddler got a *swat* on his wrist for stepping into the street by himself⟩ — see [1]BLOW

swat *vb* to deliver a blow to (someone or something) usually in a strong vigorous manner ⟨didn't sleep a wink all night because she was too busy *swatting* mosquitoes⟩ — see HIT 1

swathe *vb* **1** to surround or cover closely ⟨handed me an odd-shaped package *swathed* in bright pink tissue paper⟩ — see ENFOLD 1
2 to cover with a bandage ⟨tenderly *swathed* the soldier's wounds⟩ — see BANDAGE

sway *n* **1** the power to bring about a result on another ⟨under the *sway* of euphoria, she offered to take us all out to dinner in celebration of her new job⟩ — see EFFECT 2
2 the power to direct the thinking or behavior of others usually indirectly ⟨outdated attitudes that still hold *sway* in some communities⟩ — see INFLUENCE 1
3 the right or means to command or control others ⟨a time when Rome held *sway* over a vast empire that stretched from Britain to the Near East⟩ — see POWER 1

sway *vb* **1** to act upon (a person or a person's feelings) so as to cause a response ⟨how can you not be *swayed* by that precious kitten, meowing as if to say, "Please take me home with you?"⟩ — see [1]AFFECT 1
2 to make a series of unsteady side-to-side motions ⟨the way the ski lift was *swaying* in the wind made me nervous⟩ — see ROCK 1
3 *archaic* to exercise authority or power over ⟨an epic novel set in the days when Rome *swayed* the Western world⟩ — see GOVERN 1

swear *n* a disrespectful or indecent word or expression ⟨can't you express your frustration without using *swears*?⟩ — see SWEARWORD

swear *vb* **1** to use offensive or indecent language ⟨no one is allowed to *swear* in this house⟩
synonyms blaspheme, curse, cuss
related words anathematize, confound, damn, execrate, imprecate; fulminate, rail, rant, revile
2 to make a solemn declaration of intent ⟨*swear* to tell the truth, the whole truth, and nothing but the truth⟩ — see PROMISE 1
3 to make a solemn declaration under oath for the purpose of establishing a fact ⟨the *sworn* statement of the witness was presented as evidence⟩ — see TESTIFY

swearword *n* a disrespectful or indecent word or expression ⟨this is a list of *swearwords* that are not permitted on this radio program⟩
synonyms curse, cuss, cussword, dirty word, expletive, four-letter word, obscenity, profanity, swear, vulgarism
related words bawdry, language, scurrility; execration, imprecation, malediction; epithet, name; oath

sweat *n* **1** the active use of energy in producing a result ⟨save your *sweat*: no one will appreciate your efforts anyway⟩ — see EFFORT
2 very hard or unpleasant work ⟨it took years of *sweat* to bring the farm to the point where it is now⟩ — see [1]TOIL
3 an uneasy state of mind usually over the possibility of an anticipated misfortune or trouble ⟨my boss told me not to get in a *sweat* about the accident—she'd make sure I wasn't blamed for it⟩ — see ANXIETY 1
4 a state of nervous or irritated concern ⟨he always ends up in a *sweat* during tax season⟩ — see FRET

sweat *vb* **1** to devote serious and sustained effort ⟨spent the afternoon *sweating* over her tax returns⟩ — see LABOR

2 to experience concern or anxiety ⟨don't *sweat* over getting the application in a day late, as it probably doesn't matter⟩ — see WORRY 1

3 to work hard and long ⟨after *sweating* so hard to build the business out of nothing, we lost everything⟩ — see TOIL

4 to flow forth slowly through small openings ⟨the oil coat may *sweat* through this varnish⟩ — see EXUDE

5 *slang* to put a series of questions to ⟨the narcotics squad tried *sweating* the mule, but he was genuinely clueless about the inner workings of the drug operation⟩ — see EXAMINE 1

sweat out *vb* to put up with (something painful or difficult) ⟨I can *sweat out* one more year of this job—before I totally flip out⟩ — see BEAR 2

sweaty *adj* requiring considerable physical or mental effort ⟨exhausted after a day of *sweaty* yard work⟩ — see HARD 2

sweep *n* an area over which activity, capacity, or influence extends ⟨Mrs. Griswold has been a teacher for so long that the *sweep* of her influence extends across three generations of the townspeople⟩ — see RANGE 2

sweep *vb* **1** to move or proceed smoothly and readily ⟨the wind *swept* across the plain without respite⟩ — see FLOW 2

2 to turn away from a straight line or course ⟨from this point the mountain range *sweeps* to the northeast and extends into the next state⟩ — see CURVE 1

sweep (away) *vb* to destroy all traces of ⟨some priceless works of literature were *swept away* when the library at Alexandria burned⟩ — see ANNIHILATE 1

sweeping *adj* having considerable extent ⟨calls for *sweeping* changes in the way the nation manages security in its major ports⟩ — see EXTENSIVE

sweepingly *adv* with attention to all aspects or details ⟨in a bold move, the secretary of the treasury *sweepingly* transformed the nation's banking system⟩ — see THOROUGHLY 1

sweepstakes *also* **sweep–stake** *n pl* **1** an earnest effort for superiority or victory over another ⟨in last week's box office *sweepstakes* a quirky little comedy handily bested Hollywood's latest special effects extravaganza⟩ — see CONTEST 1

2 a competitive encounter between individuals or groups carried on for amusement, exercise, or in pursuit of a prize ⟨regards the music awards as nothing more than a popularity *sweepstakes*⟩ — see GAME 1

sweet *adj* **1** granted special treatment or attention ⟨promised his dying mother that he would always take care of his *sweet* sister⟩ — see DARLING 1

2 having a pleasant smell ⟨breathed in the *sweet* air of the azalea garden⟩ — see FRAGRANT

3 having an easygoing and pleasing manner especially in social situations ⟨a very *sweet* man directed us to the lost and found⟩ — see AMIABLE

4 having qualities that tend to make one loved ⟨a *sweet* little kitten⟩ — see LOVABLE

5 giving pleasure or contentment to the mind or senses ⟨the glowing reviews of his novel were the *sweetest* things the writer had ever read⟩ — see PLEASANT 1

sweet *n* **1** a food having a high sugar content ⟨remember to brush your teeth after eating *sweets*⟩

synonyms confection, sweetmeat

related words confectionary, confectionery, sweeties [*British*]; afters [*British*], candy, dessert, entremets, pastry

2 a person with whom one is in love ⟨my darling, my *sweet*, won't you be mine?⟩ — see SWEETHEART 1

sweeten *vb* to make more desirable ⟨we really want you to work for our company—what can we do to *sweeten* the job offer?⟩

synonyms candy, dress up, enhance

related words ameliorate, enrich, improve, meliorate; embellish, soup up, trick; cosmeticize, doll up, spruce

sweetheart *n* **1** a person with whom one is in love ⟨I married my high-school *sweetheart* as soon as we both finished college⟩

synonyms beloved, darling, dear, flame, hon, honey, love, squeeze [*slang*], sweet, sweetie, sweetie pie, truelove

related words beau, boy, boyfriend, fellow, man, swain; gal, girl, girlfriend, inamorata, ladylove, lass, mistress, tootsie; amour, lover, paramour; doll, duck(s) [*chiefly British*], pet; date, escort, steady; admirer, gallant, suitor, wooer; groom, husband; bride, wife; significant other; fiancé, intended; crush, heartthrob

2 something very good of its kind ⟨a charming waterfront cottage that's a real *sweetheart*⟩ — see JIM-DANDY

sweetie *n* a person with whom one is in love ⟨brought flowers home to his *sweetie*⟩ — see SWEETHEART 1

sweetie pie *n* a person with whom one is in love ⟨do you want to tell them how we met, *sweetie pie*, or should I?⟩ — see SWEETHEART 1

sweetly *adv* in a pleasing way ⟨a *sweetly* silly summer movie⟩ — see WELL 5

sweetmeat *n* a food having a high sugar content ⟨16th-century Naples carried on a vast export trade in silks and *sweetmeats*⟩ — see SWEET 1

sweetness *n* the state or quality of having a pleasant or agreeable manner in socializing with others ⟨one sister's *sweetness* was offset by the other's crotchetiness⟩ — see AMIABILITY 1

sweet–talk *vb* to get (someone) to do something by gentle urging, special attention, or flattery ⟨she can *sweet-talk* her besotted boyfriend into just about anything⟩ — see COAX

sweet talk *n* excessive praise ⟨enough of this *sweet talk*—just give me your honest opinion of my performance⟩ — see FLATTERY

swell *adj* **1** of the very best kind ⟨what a *swell* time we had at the country club dance⟩ — see EXCELLENT

2 being in the latest or current fashion ⟨in its heyday as a summer resort, the town was known for its swanky hotels and *swell* restaurants⟩ — see STYLISH

swell *vb* **1** to become greater in extent, volume, amount, or number ⟨the club membership has really *swelled* in recent months⟩ — see INCREASE 2

2 to make greater in size, amount, or number ⟨more layoffs will *swell* the ranks of the unemployed to unprecedented levels⟩ — see INCREASE 1

3 to extend outward beyond a usual point ⟨at that point the Congo River *swells* and forms Malebo Pool⟩ — see BULGE 1

swell *n* **1** a part that sticks out from the general mass of something ⟨the graceful *swell* of the bottle was meant to be evocative of the female figure⟩ — see BULGE 1

2 a moving ridge on the surface of water ⟨huge *swells* overwhelmed the tiny craft⟩ — see WAVE

swelled head *n* an often unjustified feeling of being pleased with oneself or with one's situation or achievements ⟨coming in first in a couple of tennis tournaments was enough to give him a *swelled head*⟩ — see COMPLACENCE 1

swellheaded *adj* having too high an opinion of oneself ⟨the child has become *swellheaded* from his parents' constant praise⟩ — see CONCEITED

swellheadedness *n* an often unjustified feeling of being pleased with oneself or with one's situation or achievements ⟨the staggering degree of *swellheadedness* that must be necessary to nominate oneself for person of the year⟩ — see COMPLACENCE 1

swelling *n* a small rounded mass of swollen tissue ⟨was worried that the *swelling* on her neck was cancerous⟩ — see BUMP 1

swelter *n* a state of nervous or irritated concern ⟨the set designer spent the entire week before opening night in a *swelter*⟩ — see FRET

sweltering *adj* having a notably high temperature ⟨the air conditioning was broken, and it was *sweltering* in the office⟩ — see HOT 1

swerve *vb* **1** to depart abruptly from a straight line or course ⟨the car *swerved* sharply to avoid the squirrel in the road⟩
synonyms break, cut, sheer, veer, yaw, zag, zig
related words skew, slew (*also* slue); arc, arch, bend, bow, crook, curve, hook, round, sweep, wheel; about-face, pivot; circle, coil, curl, loop, spiral; turn, twist, wind; weave, zigzag; deviate, stray, wander, waver
antonyms straighten
2 to turn away from a straight line or course ⟨the bike path gently *swerves* to the right⟩ — see CURVE 1
3 to cause to turn away from a straight line ⟨a dog dashed out in front of me and made me *swerve* my bike into the path of an oncoming car⟩ — see BEND 1
4 to change one's course or direction ⟨the hurricane had been following the coastline before it *swerved* and headed inland⟩ — see TURN 3

swift *adj* moving, proceeding, or acting with great speed ⟨the sleekest, *swiftest* boat ever to have sailed in the regatta⟩ — see FAST 1

swift *adv* with great speed ⟨tried to cross the *swift*-flowing river⟩ — see FAST 1

swiftly *adv* with great speed ⟨*swiftly* established himself as a star in Hollywood⟩ — see FAST 1

swiftness *n* a high rate of movement or performance ⟨with amazing *swiftness*, the airline agent got our ticket changed, and we boarded the plane just as it was about to leave⟩ — see SPEED 1

swig *n* the portion of a serving of a beverage that is swallowed at one time ⟨can I have just a *swig* of your lemonade to wash down these french fries?⟩ — see DRINK 2

swig *vb* to swallow in liquid form ⟨the only way he can stay awake at his night job is by constantly *swigging* drinks containing caffeine⟩ — see DRINK 1

swill *n* **1** the portion of a serving of a beverage that is swallowed at one time ⟨took his daily *swill* of the foul-tasting medicine⟩ — see DRINK 2
2 a thick semiliquid substance (as food) that is unattractive ⟨I don't know what's in this *swill*, but I know that I'm not eating it⟩ — see GLOP

swill *vb* **1** to eat greedily or to excess ⟨they can spend hours at the pub, drinking, chatting, and *swilling*⟩ — see GORGE 2
2 to swallow in liquid form ⟨considering the way she *swills* carbonated drinks, she ought to own stock in a soda company⟩ — see DRINK 1

swiller *n* one who eats greedily or too much ⟨after the swinish *swiller* had finally had his fill, he belched loudly⟩ — see GLUTTON

swim *vb* **1** to be in a confused state as if from being twirled around ⟨once they were in the elevator, the scent of the woman's perfume was so overpowering that it made his head *swim*⟩ — see SPIN 2
2 to rest or move along the surface of a liquid or in the air ⟨there appeared to be an oily film *swimming* on the water⟩ — see FLOAT 1

swim *n* a temporary state of unconsciousness ⟨the merest glimpse of blood sends him into a *swim*⟩ — see FAINT

swimmingly *adv* in a pleasing way ⟨the rehearsals were going *swimmingly* until half the cast came down with the flu⟩ — see WELL 5

swimmy *adj* having a feeling of being whirled about and in danger of falling down ⟨the planetarium's dazzling light show left my head *swimmy* with delight⟩ — see DIZZY 1

swindle *n* **1** a scheme in which the victim is cheated out of his money after first gaining his trust ⟨a *swindle* that involved selling a lot of land that really didn't exist⟩ — see CONFIDENCE GAME
2 an instance of the use of dishonest methods to acquire something of value ⟨identity theft has become one of the most frequent and feared *swindles* of our time⟩ — see FRAUD 1

swindle *vb* to rob by the use of trickery or threats ⟨hundreds of people were *swindled* out of their savings, and all they had to show for it were fake land deeds⟩ — see FLEECE

swindler *n* a dishonest person who uses clever means to cheat others out of something of value ⟨the *swindlers*, representing themselves as land developers, produced a glossy brochure showing beaches, palm trees, and golf links⟩ — see TRICKSTER 1

swine *n* a person whose behavior is offensive to others ⟨you really are a *swine*—you have no sense of decency at all!⟩ — see JERK 1

swing *vb* **1** to change one's course or direction ⟨thinking that we were being followed, we abruptly *swung* to the left at the next intersection⟩ — see TURN 3
2 to change the course or direction of (something) ⟨at the sound of gunfire, the cavalry officer *swung* his horse around and galloped rapidly back to the fort⟩ — see TURN 2
3 to deal with (something) usually skillfully or efficiently ⟨a man who's able to *swing* two full-time jobs⟩ — see HANDLE 1
4 to move (something) in a curved or circular path on or as if on an axis ⟨*swung* the bat and missed the ball⟩ ⟨don't let the wind *swing* that gate shut⟩ — see TURN 1
5 to place on an elevated point without support from below ⟨beach towels *swung* up to dry on the lifeguard's high chair⟩ — see HANG 1
6 to have enough money for ⟨I don't think that we can *swing* that hefty a mortgage⟩ — see AFFORD

swinish *adj* **1** having a huge appetite ⟨the more *swinish* diners attacked the all-you-can-eat buffet with gusto⟩ — see VORACIOUS 1
2 having or showing the nature and appetites of a lower animal ⟨*swinish* frat boys for whom a night on the town invariably included binge drinking and strip club hopping⟩ — see BESTIAL

swinishness *n* the manifestation of the traits or the gratification of the appetites of a lower animal ⟨a fraternity party that may well have reached a new low for alcohol-fueled *swinishness*⟩ — see BESTIALITY

swipe *n* a hard strike with a part of the body or an instrument ⟨one *swipe* of a grizzly's paw can do a person in⟩ — see [1]BLOW

swipe *vb* **1** to come into usually forceful contact with something ⟨a blindfolded partygoer *swiping* at the piñata with a stick⟩ — see HIT 2
2 to deliver a blow to (someone or something) usually in a strong vigorous manner ⟨that car just *swiped* the fender of our car⟩ — see HIT 1
3 to take (something) without right and with an intent to keep ⟨somebody *swiped* the stop sign that used to be on the corner⟩ — see STEAL 1

swiping *n* an instance of theft ⟨when the cheese *swipings* abruptly stopped, we wondered if the mouse had met his end elsewhere⟩ — see THEFT 2

swirl *vb* **1** to cause (as a liquid) to move about in a circle especially repeatedly ⟨kept *swirling* her lemonade until I thought the sound of clinking ice would drive me insane⟩ — see STIR 1

2 to move (something) in a curved or circular path on or as if on an axis ⟨*swirled* her skirts as she danced the tango⟩ — see TURN 1

swish *n* **1** a sound similar to the speech sound \s\ stretched out ⟨the steady *swish* of the windshield wipers⟩ — see HISS 1

2 a quick jerky movement from side to side or up and down ⟨the mare brushed away the flies with a sweeping *swish* of her tail⟩ — see [1]WAG

swish *vb* **1** to make a sound like that of stretching out the speech sound \s\ ⟨with their satin costumes *swishing*, the little ballerinas pirouetted onto the stage⟩ — see HISS

2 to move from side to side or up and down with quick jerky motions ⟨the horse's tail *swishes* after every jump⟩ — see WAG 1

swish *adj* being in the latest or current fashion ⟨a trendy boutique filled with *swish* accessories for the urban fashionista⟩ — see STYLISH

switch *n* **1** a long thin or flexible tool for striking ⟨struck the horse's hide with a leather *switch*, and it took off at a gallop⟩ — see WHIP

2 a quick jerky movement from side to side or up and down ⟨that telltale *switch* of the cat's tail meant there was a mouse under the piano⟩ — see [1]WAG

3 a hard strike with a part of the body or an instrument ⟨in frustration, he gave the mule a sharp *switch* on the rump, but it still wouldn't budge⟩ — see [1]BLOW

switch *vb* **1** to give up (something) and take something else in return ⟨*switched* the real grapes for fake ones⟩ ⟨*switched* the day of his flight from Thursday to Friday⟩ — see CHANGE 3

2 to move from side to side or up and down with quick jerky motions ⟨cows lazily *switching* their tails and chewing their cud⟩ — see WAG 1

3 to strike repeatedly with something long and thin or flexible ⟨a stern schoolmaster who would *switch* any boy who misbehaved⟩ — see WHIP 1

4 to change (as an opinion) to the contrary ⟨a politician who has *switched* his position on a number of issues⟩ — see REVERSE 1

5 to strike repeatedly ⟨a prank for which the youngsters were soundly *switched*⟩ — see BEAT 1

switchable *adj* capable of being substituted in place of one another ⟨baking powder and baking soda are definitely not *switchable* ingredients⟩ — see INTERCHANGEABLE

swivel *vb* to move (something) in a curved or circular path on or as if on an axis ⟨the cat *swiveled* one ear to listen to a sound outside⟩ — see TURN 1

swivet *n* a state of nervous or irritated concern ⟨she's all in a *swivet* over the wedding planning⟩ — see FRET

swollen *adj* enlarged beyond normal from internal pressure ⟨a *swollen* ankle from a sprain⟩ — see BLOATED 2

swoon *vb* to lose consciousness ⟨whenever the young woman *swooned*, she always seemed to manage falling into the arms of a good-looking man⟩ — see FAINT

swoon *n* **1** a state of mental confusion ⟨she wandered about in a *swoon* for several days after receiving the tragic news⟩ — see HAZE 2

2 a temporary state of unconsciousness ⟨fell into a *swoon* at the sight of the handsome movie star⟩ — see FAINT

3 a state of overwhelming usually pleasurable emotion ⟨her boyfriend's proposal sent her into a joyous *swoon*⟩ — see ECSTASY

swoosh *vb* to flow out in great quantities or with force ⟨water *swooshed* powerfully from the fire hose⟩ — see GUSH 1

sword *n* a hand weapon with a length of metal sharpened on one or both sides and usually tapered to a sharp point ⟨once upon a time dueling with *swords* was the gentlemanly way to settle a point of honor⟩

synonyms blade, brand, steel

related words broadsword, cutlass, rapier, saber (*or* sabre), scimitar, smallsword

swot *n, British* a person slavishly devoted to intellectual or academic pursuits ⟨every time he begged off a night at the pub—saying he had to study—his mates teased him for being a *swot*⟩ — see NERD 1

sybarite *n* a person whose life is devoted to luxury and sensual pleasures ⟨the prince was remembered as a self-indulgent *sybarite*, not as a statesman or warrior⟩ — see VOLUPTUARY

sybaritic *adj* given to or marked by excessive gratification of one's desires ⟨after putting in long hours for months on end, she was ready for a *sybaritic* sojourn at some ridiculously expensive spa⟩ — see HEDONISTIC

sybaritism *n* excessive pursuit of fleshly pleasures ⟨the billionaire's extravagant parties were marked by a degree of *sybaritism* not seen since the days of decadent Rome⟩ — see SENSUALITY

sycophant *n* a person who flatters another in order to get ahead ⟨when her career was riding high, the self-deluded actress often mistook *sycophants* for true friends⟩

synonyms apple-polisher, bootlicker, brownnoser, fawner, flunky (*also* flunkey *or* flunkie), lickspittle, suck-up, toady

related words yes-man; apparatchik, company man; hanger-on, leech, parasite, sponge, sponger; henchman, lackey, lapdog, minion, running dog, satellite, slave, stooge; admirer, cultist, devotee, enthusiast, fan, groveler, idolater (*or* idolator), worshipper (*or* worshiper), zealot; adherent, camp follower, convert, disciple, follower, me-tooer, partisan (*also* partizan), pupil, votary

syllable *n* the smallest amount or part imaginable ⟨you're not making a *syllable* of sense⟩ — see JOT

symbol *n* **1** a device, design, or figure used as an identifying mark ⟨the traditional physician's *symbol* of a staff entwined with a snake⟩ — see EMBLEM

2 a written or printed mark that is meant to convey information to the reader ⟨the *symbol* ¶ indicates where a new paragraph should begin⟩ — see CHARACTER 1

symbolic *also* **symbolical** *adj* having the function or meaning of an object or figure that stands for something else ⟨the butterfly in the poem is *symbolic* of the impermanence of youth⟩

synonyms emblematic (*also* emblematical), representational, representative

related words figural, figurative, metaphoric (*or* metaphorical), tropological; allegorical

near antonyms actual, literal

antonyms nonsymbolic

symbolize *vb* to serve as a material counterpart of ⟨the flag *symbolizes* our country⟩

synonyms emblematize, represent

related words body, embody, epitomize, incarnate, manifest, materialize, objectify, personalize, personify; exemplify, illustrate

phrases stand for

symmetry *n* a balanced, pleasing, or suitable arrangement of parts ⟨planted azalea bushes on both sides of the front steps for *symmetry*⟩ — see HARMONY 1

sympathetic *adj* **1** having or showing the capacity for sharing the feelings of another ⟨a *sympathetic* smile⟩ ⟨needed a *sympathetic* listener who would understand her marital woes⟩

synonyms commiserative, compassionate, empathetic, empathic, humane, understanding

related words feeling, perceptive, sensitive; considerate, gentle, softhearted, tender, tenderhearted, warm, warmhearted; benevolent, benignant, bighearted, chari-

table, kind, kindhearted, kindly, largehearted, magnanimous; clement, lenient, merciful, tolerant; pitying, ruthful; congenial, cordial, friendly, genial, good-natured, good-tempered, gracious, well-disposed; affectionate, loving
near antonyms inconsiderate, insensitive, thoughtless, unthinking; aloof, cool, indifferent, uncaring, uninterested; unaffectionate, unfriendly, unloving; merciless, pitiless, ruthless; bigoted, blinkered, narrow-minded, small-minded; brutal, grim, hard-bitten, hard-boiled, harsh, oppressive, rough, severe, stern, tough, ungentle, unrelenting; abusive, acrimonious, disagreeable, hateful, hostile, ill-natured, ill-tempered, malevolent, malicious, mean, rancorous, spiteful, surly, unkind, virulent
antonyms callous, cold-blooded, coldhearted, hard, hard-hearted, heartless, inhuman, inhumane, insensate, obdurate, unfeeling, unsympathetic
2 having or marked by sympathy and consideration for others ⟨a *sympathetic* store manager who let us use the telephone⟩ ⟨*sympathetic* letters from supporters after the disappointing verdict⟩ — see HUMANE 1

sympathize (with) *vb* to have sympathy for ⟨don't expect me to *sympathize with* you—each month you should have paid off your credit card in full⟩ — see PITY

sympathizer *n* someone associated with another to give assistance or moral support ⟨doesn't have many *sympathizers* since everyone knows he brought his troubles on himself⟩ — see ALLY

sympathy *n* **1** sorrow or the capacity to feel sorrow for another's suffering or misfortune ⟨since losing her own brother to lung disease, the nurse has had greater *sympathy* for families going through the same agony⟩
synonyms commiseration, compassion, feeling
related words condolence, regret; humaneness, humanity, kindheartedness, kindliness, kindness, mercy, pity, ruth, softheartedness, warmheartedness; affinity, empathy, rapport, sensitivity, understanding; altruism, benevolence, benignity, bigheartedness, charity, generosity, goodwill, humanitarianism, largeheartedness, largesse (*also* largess), magnanimity, philanthropy
near antonyms indifference, insensitivity, unconcern; cruelty, harshness, inhumanity; animosity, antipathy, dislike, hatred, hostility
antonyms callousness, coldheartedness, hardheartedness, heartlessness
2 the capacity for feeling for another's unhappiness or misfortune ⟨the least you could do is have some *sympathy* for me if I have to stay home⟩ — see HEART 1

symphonic *adj* having a pleasing mixture of notes ⟨the *symphonic* chorus of frogs in the spring⟩ — see HARMONIOUS 1

symphonious *adj* having a pleasing mixture of notes ⟨the composer is known for his *symphonious* orchestrations of instruments from diverse musical traditions⟩ — see HARMONIOUS 1

symphony *n* **1** a balanced, pleasing, or suitable arrangement of parts ⟨the satisfying *symphony* of color in Renoir's canvases⟩ — see HARMONY 1
2 a usually large group of musicians playing together ⟨a performance of a Bach concerto by the San Antonio *Symphony*⟩ — see [2]BAND 1

symphony orchestra *n* a usually large group of musicians playing together ⟨plays oboe in the local *symphony orchestra*⟩ — see [2]BAND 1

symposium *n* a meeting featuring a group discussion ⟨recently attended a daylong *symposium* on new methods of chromatography⟩ — see FORUM 1

symptomatic *adj* serving to identify as belonging to an individual or group ⟨a fever's refusal to respond to antibiotics is *symptomatic* of a viral infection⟩ — see CHARACTERISTIC 1

synchronic *adj* existing or occurring at the same period of time ⟨to musical accompaniment, the swimmers' *synchronic* movements form a kaleidoscope of artistic patterns⟩ — see CONTEMPORARY 1

synchronize *vb* to occur or exist at the same time ⟨the subtitles must *synchronize* with the movie's spoken dialogue⟩ — see COINCIDE 1

synchronous *adj* existing or occurring at the same period of time ⟨the *synchronous* arrival of a baby sister and loss of a beloved grandmother strongly affected the child⟩ — see CONTEMPORARY 1

syncopate *vb* to make less in extent or duration ⟨she tried to *syncopate* her gasp of shock⟩ — see SHORTEN

syncope *n* a temporary state of unconsciousness ⟨*syncope* has been reported in a small percentage of patients taking the drug⟩ — see FAINT

syndicate *n* **1** a group involved in secret or criminal activities ⟨a *syndicate* of counterfeiters⟩ — see [1]RING 1
2 a number of businesses or enterprises united for commercial advantage ⟨a powerful banking *syndicate* that controls loans in the small country⟩ — see CARTEL

syne *adv, chiefly Scottish* earlier than the present time ⟨a poem by Robert Louis Stevenson that begins with "From the bonny bells of heather / They brewed a drink long *syne*"⟩ — see AGO

synopsis *n* a short statement of the main points ⟨I don't need to know every little plot twist; just give me a *synopsis* of the movie⟩ — see SUMMARY

synopsize *vb* to make into a short statement of the main points (as of a report) ⟨before I agree to read the novel, could you at least *synopsize* its plot?⟩ — see SUMMARIZE

synthesis *n* a distinct entity formed by the combining of two or more different things ⟨a philosophy that is a kind of *synthesis* of several schools of Western and Eastern thought⟩ — see BLEND

synthetic *adj* **1** produced by humans rather than natural processes ⟨that organic farm doesn't use any pesticides or *synthetic* fertilizers⟩
synonyms artificial, man-made, nonnatural
related words fabricated, manufactured; cultivated, processed, refined; industrial, mechanical; ersatz, faux, imitation
near antonyms crude, raw
antonyms natural
2 being such in appearance only and made with or manufactured from usually cheaper materials ⟨*synthetic* fur collars⟩ ⟨boots of waterproof *synthetic* leather⟩ — see IMITATION

syringe *n* a slender hollow instrument by which material is put into or taken from the body through the skin ⟨the *syringe* the nurse was leveling at my arm looked to me to be at least 10 inches long⟩ — see NEEDLE 1

syrup *also* **sirup** *n* the state or quality of having an excess of tender feelings (as of love, nostalgia, or compassion) ⟨a television show for toddlers that is nothing more than pure *syrup*⟩ — see SENTIMENTALITY

syrupy *adj* being of a consistency that resists flow ⟨instead of neat squares of fudge we had *syrupy* goo⟩ — see THICK 2

system *n* **1** something made up of many interdependent or related parts ⟨the national highway *system* allows travel from one end of the country to the other⟩ ⟨the democratic *system* of checks and balances in government⟩
synonyms complex, network
related words interlacement, mesh, meshwork, net, plexus, web; aggregate, conglomerate, totality, whole; sequence, series; supersystem
2 a method worked out in advance for achieving some objective ⟨if you're going to wrap all these presents in

one afternoon, you'll need a *system*⟩ — see PLAN 1
3 the means or procedure for doing something ⟨not the best *system* perhaps, but it gets the job done⟩ — see METHOD

systematic *adj* following a set method, arrangement, or pattern ⟨the first *systematic* effort to find witnesses to the crime⟩ ⟨*systematic* elimination and reintroduction of certain foods to determine what he's allergic to⟩ — see METHODICAL

systematically *adv* with attention to all aspects or details ⟨the program's safety procedures were *systematically* analyzed for flaws⟩ — see THOROUGHLY 1

systematize *vb* to put into a particular arrangement ⟨Carl Linnaeus was the first to *systematize* the plant and animal kingdoms by creating a uniform system for naming genera and species of organisms⟩ — see ORDER 1

systematized *adj* following a set method, arrangement, or pattern ⟨a *systematized* arrangement of books⟩ — see METHODICAL

T

tab *n* **1** a record of goods sold or services performed together with the costs due ⟨I don't have any cash on me, so can you put this on my *tab*?⟩ — see [1]BILL 1
2 the amount owed at a bar or restaurant or the slip of paper stating the amount ⟨asked the server to put our dinners on separate *tabs* so we could each pay for our own meal⟩ — see CHECK 1

tabernacle *n* a building for public worship and especially Christian worship ⟨worshippers gathering at the Baptist *tabernacle* on a bright Sunday morning⟩ — see CHURCH 1

table *n* **1** a leg-mounted piece of furniture with a broad flat top designed for the serving of food ⟨we sat at the kitchen *table*, playing cards for hours on end⟩
synonyms board
related words coffee table, refectory table, tea table; bar, counter; buffet, sideboard, side table; bed table, card table
2 food eaten or prepared for eating at one time ⟨always offers a well-prepared *table* for his guests⟩ — see MEAL
3 a broad flat area of elevated land ⟨the area between the two canyons forms one broad *table*⟩ — see PLATEAU
4 a record of a series of items (as names or titles) usually arranged according to some system ⟨the periodic *table* of chemical elements⟩ — see [1]LIST
5 substances intended to be eaten ⟨the *table* that the innkeeper set out each morning made for a bountiful breakfast indeed⟩ — see FOOD 1

tableland *n* a broad flat area of elevated land ⟨to the east of the valley lies a vast, fertile *tableland*⟩ — see PLATEAU

tablet *n* **1** a number of sheets of writing paper glued together at one edge ⟨you'll need to use your writing *tablet* to record all the information that the real estate agent is likely to reel off⟩ — see PAD 1
2 a small mass containing medicine to be taken orally ⟨take two *tablets* of the medication every eight hours⟩ — see PILL 1

table talk *n* friendly, informal conversation or an instance of this ⟨he thought he weathered the *table talk* over dinner with his future in-laws rather well⟩ — see CHAT 1

tableware *n* **1** eating and serving utensils ⟨during the party we ran short of *tableware*, so I went next door and borrowed some forks and knives⟩
synonyms flatware, silver, silverware
related words place setting, setting, setup; silver plate; cutlery; chopstick, fork, knife, spoon, tablespoon, teaspoon
2 dishes used for eating or serving food or drink ⟨the couple would take out their good *tableware* only on special occasions⟩
synonyms dinnerware
related words place setting, setting, setup; china, chinaware, crockery, earthenware, porcelain, pottery, stoneware, ware; crystal, glassware; plate, saucer; cup, demitasse, glass, goblet, mug, teacup; bowl, casserole, charger, platter, tureen

taboo *also* **tabu** *adj* that may not be permitted ⟨asking a guest how much money he or she makes is strictly *taboo* because it's a rude question to ask a stranger⟩ — see IMPERMISSIBLE

tacit *adj* understood although not put into words ⟨we have a *tacit* agreement that if I wash the dishes, she dries them and puts them away⟩ — see IMPLICIT 1

taciturn *adj* tending not to speak frequently (as by habit or inclination) ⟨a *taciturn* man, he almost never initiates a conversation⟩ — see SILENT 2

tack *n* the means or procedure for doing something ⟨this clearly isn't working, so let's take a different *tack* in trying to solve the problem⟩ — see METHOD

tack (on) *vb* to join (something) to a mass, quantity, or number so as to bring about an overall increase ⟨the ticket agency *tacked on* a hefty surcharge to what was already a hefty price for the theater tickets⟩ — see ADD 1

tackle *n* items needed for the performance of a task or activity ⟨grabbed my fishing *tackle* and headed out early one morning⟩ — see EQUIPMENT

tackle *vb* to start work on energetically ⟨once I clean the kitchen, I think I'll *tackle* the bathroom⟩ — see ATTACK 3

[1]**tacky** *adj* **1** marked by an obvious lack of style or good taste ⟨it was *tacky* to wear sneakers to the wedding⟩ ⟨*tacky* plastic flowers⟩
synonyms cheesy, dowdy, inelegant, styleless, tasteless, ticky-tacky (*also* ticky-tack), trashy, unfashionable, unstylish
related words graceless, inappropriate, incorrect, unbecoming, unseemly, unsuitable, wrong; outmoded, out-of-date, passé; coarse, crude, unrefined, vulgar; cheap, common, inferior, junky, lousy, low-grade, second-rate, shoddy, sleazy, tawdry; flashy, garish, gaudy, glitzy, grotesque, kitsch, kitschy, loud, ostentatious, overdone, showy, splashy
near antonyms appropriate, becoming, correct, fitting, proper, right, seemly, suitable; conservative, genteel, handsome, neat, quiet, refined, restrained, simple, understated; contemporary, modern, up-to-date; à la mode (*also* a la mode), happening, in, modish, swank (*or* swanky)
antonyms chic, classic, classy, elegant, exquisite, fashionable, fine, posh, ritzy, smart, sophisticated, stylish, tasteful
2 showing signs of advanced wear and tear and neglect ⟨a *tacky* old couch that needed new upholstery⟩ — see SHABBY 1

[2]**tacky** *adj* tending to adhere to objects upon contact ⟨don't touch the walls while the fresh paint is still *tacky*⟩ — see STICKY 1

tact *n* the ability to deal with others in touchy situations without offending them ⟨with supreme *tact*, Isabel suggested to her neighbor that her flower garden was probably not the best place for his dog to use as a bathroom⟩
synonyms diplomacy, tactfulness
related words considerateness, consideration, courteousness, courtesy, delicacy, graciousness, sensitivity, thoughtfulness; civility, etiquette, mannerliness, manners, politeness; charm, gallantry, gentility, grace, gracefulness, poise, savoir faire, suaveness, suavity; adroitness, deftness, dexterity, finesse; deference, regard, respect
near antonyms discourteousness, discourtesy, impoliteness, inconsiderateness, inconsideration, indelicacy, thoughtlessness, ungraciousness; impoliteness, incivility; boorishness, brashness, brassiness, loutishness; awkwardness, gaucheness, gracelessness, maladroitness; disregard, disrespect, disrespectfulness, impertinence, impudence, insolence, rudeness

antonyms clumsiness, insensitivity, tactlessness

tactful *adj* having or showing tact ⟨tried to be *tactful* when asked if the dress made her friend look fat⟩
synonyms diplomatic, politic
related words considerate, courteous, delicate, graceful, gracious, thoughtful; civil, mannerly, polite; charming, gallant, genteel, suave; deferential, dutiful, regardful, respectful; affable, cordial, friendly, genial, hospitable, kind, kindhearted
near antonyms discourteous, inconsiderate, indelicate, thoughtless, ungracious; ill-bred, ill-mannered, impolite, uncalled-for, uncivil, unhandsome, unmannered, unmannerly; boorish, brash, brassy, caddish, churlish, clodhopping, clownish, loutish, uncouth; disregardful, disrespectful, impertinent, impudent, insolent, rude
antonyms gauche, impolitic, tactless, undiplomatic, untactful

tactfulness *n* the ability to deal with others in touchy situations without offending them ⟨the *tactfulness* with which the secretary of state has handled that diplomatic crisis is commendable⟩ — see TACT

tactical *adj* suitable for bringing about a desired result under the circumstances ⟨made the *tactical* move of becoming friendly with the journalism teacher, hoping that this would get him appointed editor of the school newspaper⟩ — see EXPEDIENT

tactics *n pl* the means or procedure for doing something ⟨used dishonest *tactics* to win election to the town council⟩ — see METHOD

tactless *adj* showing poor judgment especially in personal relationships or social situations ⟨made a *tactless* remark about how the woman's dress had that "homemade" look⟩ — see INDISCREET

tad *n* **1** a very small amount ⟨there's more than just a *tad* of hyperbole in the critics' praise for the promising young pianist⟩ — see PARTICLE 1
2 a male person who has not yet reached adulthood ⟨grandfather never tires of telling us about the days when he was just a *tad*⟩ — see BOY 1

taffy *n* excessive praise ⟨the magazine's profiles of showbiz celebrities tend to be pure *taffy*⟩ — see FLATTERY

tag *n* a slip (as of paper or cloth) that is attached to something to identify or describe it ⟨read the *tag* on the shirt to find out if I could wash it or if it had to be dry-cleaned⟩ — see LABEL

[1]tag *vb* **1** to attach an identifying slip to ⟨*tagged* all the dresses with sale stickers before putting them on the rack⟩ — see LABEL 1
2 to go after or on the track of ⟨wildlife experts surreptitiously *tagged* the timber wolf, carefully keeping a safe distance so the wolf wouldn't catch their scent and run⟩ — see FOLLOW 2

[2]tag *vb* **1** to deliver a blow to (someone or something) usually in a strong vigorous manner ⟨he *tagged* me with a right hook and blackened my eye⟩ — see HIT 1
2 to decide to accept (someone or something) from a group of possibilities ⟨she *tagged* her most experienced operative for the special mission⟩ — see CHOOSE 1

tagging *n* the act of going after or in the tracks of another ⟨after a weeklong *tagging* of the suspect, the detective had the all the evidence he needed that there was a smuggling operation going on⟩ — see PURSUIT 1

tagline *n* an attention-getting word or phrase used to publicize something (as a campaign or product) ⟨the *tagline* from the drug company's ad campaign backfired and quickly became fodder for late-night comedians⟩ — see SLOGAN

tag, rag, and bobtail *or* **tagrag and bobtail** *n* people looked down upon as ignorant and of the lowest class ⟨in an apparent effort to keep out the city's *tag, rag, and bobtail*, the restaurant charges royally high prices for mediocre food⟩ — see RABBLE

tag sale *n* a sale of used household and personal items ⟨on weekends the bargain-minded couple likes to drive around looking for *tag sales*⟩ — see YARD SALE

tail *n* **1** a body of employees or servants who accompany and wait on a person ⟨the *tail* that accompanies the prince wherever he goes⟩ — see CORTEGE 1
2 the part of the body upon which someone sits ⟨get your *tail* in here⟩ — see BUTTOCKS
3 a behind part or surface ⟨the *tail* of the ship⟩ — see REAR 1

tail *vb* to go after or on the track of ⟨*tailed* my brother-in-law to see where he was going at that time of the evening⟩ — see FOLLOW 2

tailback *n, British* a crowded mass (as of cars) that impedes or blocks movement ⟨stuck in a five-mile *tailback* on the southbound carriageway⟩ — see JAM 1

tail end *n* the part of the body upon which someone sits ⟨all I saw was his *tail end* vanishing around the door⟩ — see BUTTOCKS

tailing *n* the act of going after or in the tracks of another ⟨my attempt at secretly *tailing* the girls was ruined by my loud and uncontrollable hiccups⟩ — see PURSUIT 1

tailor *vb* to change (something) so as to make it suitable for a new use or situation ⟨the stand-up comic refused to *tailor* his often raunchy routine for network television⟩ — see ADAPT

tailored *adj* made or fitted to the needs or preferences of a specific customer ⟨pants bought off the rack never fit me so I have to buy *tailored* ones instead⟩ — see CUSTOM-MADE

tailor-made *adj* made or fitted to the needs or preferences of a specific customer ⟨took my measurements for the *tailor-made* bridal gown⟩ — see CUSTOM-MADE

tailspin *n* a mental or nervous collapse ⟨the simultaneous death of his wife and loss of his job caused him to go into a *tailspin*⟩ — see BREAKDOWN 1

taint *n* a mark of guilt or disgrace ⟨that rare political campaign that wasn't marred by the *taint* of false accusations⟩ — see STAIN 1

taint *vb* **1** to affect slightly with something morally bad or undesirable ⟨criticism of her sister's singing that was *tainted* by envy⟩ ⟨a tendency toward conceitedness *taints* that athlete's status as a role model⟩
synonyms blemish, darken, mar, poison, spoil, stain, tarnish, touch, vitiate
related words begrime, besmear, besmirch, blacken, blur, cloud, dirty, discolor, pollute, smear, smirch, smudge, smut, soil, sully, tar; abase, cheapen, debase, degrade, demean, discredit, disgrace, dishonor, foul, lower, shame, sink; bastardize, corrupt, debauch, demoralize, deprave, pervert, subvert; color, distort, twist
near antonyms cleanse, purify; dignify, elevate, ennoble, enshrine, glorify, hallow, magnify, uplift
2 to make unfit for use by the addition of something harmful or undesirable ⟨smog has long *tainted* the air of that city, making it difficult to breathe⟩ — see CONTAMINATE

tainted *adj* containing foreign or lower-grade substances ⟨*tainted* groundwater that is unfit to drink⟩ — see IMPURE 1

take *n* **1** action or behavior that is done in return to other action or behavior ⟨what's your *take* on the announcement that the senior vice president is taking an early retirement?⟩ — see REACTION
2 the total amount collected or obtained especially at one time ⟨who will win the poker tournament and collect the whole *take*?⟩ — see HAUL 1
3 something belonging to, due to, or contributed by an individual member of a group ⟨because there were so many winners of the jackpot, each person's *take* will be

smaller than expected⟩ — see SHARE 1
4 a distinct treatment of something (as a story or a play) ⟨despite its contemporary setting, this *take* on *King Lear* isn't particularly novel or insightful⟩ — see RIFF

take *vb* **1** to reach for and take hold of by embracing with the fingers or arms ⟨*take* my hand, or we'll get separated in this crowd⟩
synonyms clasp, grasp, grip, hold
related words clench, cling (to), clutch, hold on (to); catch, nab, seize, snatch
phrases hang on to, lay hold of
near antonyms discharge, drop, free, liberate, release; deliver, entrust (*also* intrust), give, hand, hand over, pass, relinquish, transfer, transmit, turn over, unhand
2 to agree to receive whether willingly or reluctantly ⟨will you *take* that call?⟩ ⟨*took* a cut in pay⟩
synonyms accept, have
related words accede (to), assent (to), concede (to), confirm, consent (to), OK (*or* okay), ratify, sanction, warrant; acquiesce (to), bow (to), capitulate (to), give in (to), submit (to), succumb (to), surrender (to), yield (to); abide, bear, brook, countenance, endure, shoulder, stand, stick out, stomach, support, sustain, swallow, sweat out, tolerate; adopt, embrace, welcome
near antonyms dissent (to), object (to), oppose, protest; hold off, resist, withstand; combat, contest, fight
antonyms decline, deny, disallow, disapprove, negative, refuse, reject, spurn, turn down, veto
3 to become affected with (a disease or disorder) ⟨if you don't cover your head in this weather, you'll *take* cold and be stuck inside all weekend⟩ — see CONTRACT 1
4 to decide to accept (someone or something) from a group of possibilities ⟨you can *take* the white side this time, since I got to be white for our last chess game⟩ — see CHOOSE 1
5 to get possession of (something) by giving money in exchange for ⟨I'll *take* two cheeseburgers to go, please⟩ — see BUY 1
6 to have as a requirement ⟨it will *take* a lot of courage to stand up for what is right⟩ — see NEED 1
7 to make or have room for ⟨I think we can *take* two more in this elevator⟩ — see ACCOMMODATE 1
8 to produce a desired effect ⟨it will be a few hours before this medication *takes*⟩ — see ACT 2
9 to put up with (something painful or difficult) ⟨I can't *take* anymore of your whining about your former boyfriend⟩ — see BEAR 2
10 to regard as right or true ⟨I think we can *take* his word for it⟩ — see BELIEVE 1
11 to achieve a victory over ⟨I know we can *take* that team⟩ — see BEAT 2
12 to deal with (something) usually skillfully or efficiently ⟨let's *take* each problem separately⟩ — see HANDLE 1
13 to offer entrance (as to a place, school, or privilege) to ⟨the school *takes* only a small percentage of the thousands of applicants⟩ — see ADMIT 2
14 to deprive of life ⟨I never thought heart disease would *take* such an athletic and health-conscious person⟩ — see KILL 1

take back *vb* to solemnly or formally reject or go back on (as something formerly adhered to) ⟨I *take back* what I said about her: she's not the fool I thought she was⟩ — see ABJURE 1

take down *vb* **1** to reduce to a lower standing in one's own eyes or in others' eyes ⟨there's no need to *take* us *down* by making fun of our clothes⟩ — see HUMBLE
2 to take apart ⟨electricians will *take down* all the lights for the set after the play has finished its run⟩ — see DISASSEMBLE 1
3 to make a written note of ⟨*took down* the customer's contact information⟩ — see RECORD 1

take in *vb* **1** to cause to believe what is untrue ⟨a fellow passenger on the cruise completely *took* me *in* when he claimed to be the owner of a major software company⟩ — see DECEIVE
2 to have as part of a whole ⟨this report *takes in* all the latest information on the subject⟩ — see INCLUDE 1
3 to provide with living quarters or shelter ⟨*took in* the stray dog⟩ — see HOUSE 1

take-no-prisoners *adj* having or showing a lack of sympathy or tender feelings ⟨a theater critic with a *take-no-prisoners* approach to reviewing Broadway's latest offerings⟩ — see HARD 1

takeoff *n* **1** a rising from a surface at the start of a flight (as of a rocket) ⟨make sure your tray table is safely put away during *takeoff*⟩ — see LIFTOFF
2 a work that imitates and exaggerates another work for comic effect ⟨a sitcom that's a *takeoff* of an old TV show from the 1960s⟩ — see PARODY 1

take off *vb* **1** to leave a place often for another ⟨I can only stay for a few minutes, and then I'll need to *take off* again⟩ — see GO 2
2 to rid oneself of (a garment) ⟨*take off* your coat and stay awhile⟩ — see REMOVE 1
3 to take away (an amount or number) from a total ⟨the store will *take* an additional 20% *off* if you bring in this coupon⟩ — see SUBTRACT
4 *slang* to remove valuables from (a place) unlawfully ⟨a gangbanger who decided to *take off* some fast-food joint⟩ — see ROB

take on *vb* **1** to enter into contest or conflict with ⟨will *take on* his chief opponent in the next political debate⟩ — see ENGAGE 2
2 to provide with a paying job ⟨decided to *take* her *on* as store manager⟩ — see EMPLOY 1
3 to take for one's own use (something originated by another) ⟨recently arrived immigrants who are eager to *take on* the language and culture of their adopted homeland⟩ — see ADOPT

take out *vb* **1** to find emotional release for ⟨he *took out* his frustrations by splitting a cord of firewood⟩
synonyms loose, release, unleash, vent
related words act out; air, express, state, ventilate, voice
phrases give way (to)
near antonyms control, govern, handle, manage; bridle, check, constrain, contain, curb, hold back, pull in, quell, rein (in), restrain, smother, tame; allay, lull, quiet, soothe, still; choke, inhibit, muffle, pocket, repress, stifle, strangle, swallow
antonyms bottle (up), repress, suppress
2 to go on a social engagement with ⟨she'd like to *take* the new boy *out* to the movies sometime⟩ — see DATE 1
3 to take away from a place or position ⟨the airline passenger *took* his laptop computer *out* of its carrying case⟩ — see REMOVE 2
4 to put to death deliberately ⟨the rumor is that the CIA is planning to *take* him *out* before he can seize control of the country⟩ — see MURDER 1

takeover *n* the unlawful taking or withholding of something from the rightful owner under a guise of authority ⟨the new government's high-handed *takeover* of private industries⟩ — see APPROPRIATION 2

take over *vb* **1** to serve as a replacement usually for a time only ⟨I'll *take over* for her until she gets back from her morning break⟩ — see COVER 1
2 to take to or upon oneself ⟨*took over* the responsibility of caring for the animals⟩ — see ASSUME 1
3 to take or make use of under a guise of authority but without actual right ⟨students protesting the war *took over* the college's radio station⟩ — see APPROPRIATE 1

take up *vb* **1** to move from a lower to a higher place or

position ⟨please *take up* the blanket so I can look underneath it⟩ — see RAISE 1
2 to take in (something liquid) through small openings ⟨the soil was so dry that the plant seemed to *take up* the much-needed water instantly⟩ — see ABSORB 1
3 to take for one's own use (something originated by another) ⟨one cluster of fans started chanting the team name of the champions, and the crowd quickly *took up* the cry⟩ — see ADOPT

taking *adj* very pleasing to look at ⟨had never seen such a *taking* city as Venice⟩ — see BEAUTIFUL 1

tale *n* **1** a rumor or report of a personal or sensational nature ⟨don't believe the *tales* you hear about our neighbor's kid⟩
synonyms canard, story, whisper
related words dirt, gossip, scuttlebutt, talebearing, talk, tattle; dirty laundry, dirty linen; defamation, libel, slander; hearsay; fable, fabrication, fairy tale, falsehood, falsity, fib, lie, mendacity, prevarication, untruth, whopper
2 a brief account of something interesting that happened especially to one personally ⟨asked Dad to tell once again the *tale* of how, as a kid, he broke his arm jumping out of a tree⟩ — see STORY 2
3 a statement known by its maker to be untrue and made in order to deceive ⟨told tall *tales* in an attempt to impress me with her supposedly upper-crust background⟩ — see LIE
4 a work with imaginary characters and events that is shorter and usually less complex than a novel ⟨the oft-told *tale* of Sleeping Beauty⟩ — see STORY 1
5 a total number obtained or recorded by noting each thing as it was being added ⟨when the *tale* of the dead from the disaster is announced, the city will be in shock⟩ — see COUNT 1

talebearer *n* **1** a person who habitually reveals personal or sensational facts about others ⟨statehouse *talebearers* had long spread stories about the governor's extramarital affairs⟩ — see GOSSIP 1
2 a person who provides information about another's wrongdoing ⟨the teacher told him not to be such a *talebearer*, as she was quite capable of detecting student misbehavior on her own⟩ — see INFORMER

talent *n* a special and usually inborn ability ⟨Liza's musical *talent* was already apparent by the time she was five⟩ ⟨a *talent* for coming up with really funny answers to stupid questions⟩
synonyms aptitude, bent, endowment, faculty, flair, genius, gift, head, knack
related words affinity, bias, disposition, habitude, impulse, inclination, leaning, partiality, penchant, predilection, predisposition, proclivity, propensity, tendency, turn; ear, eye, mind, nose; feel, hang, instinct, touch, way; capability, competence, facility, proficiency, skill; capacity, potential, power; forte, specialism, speciality, specialty
near antonyms disability, handicap, inability, incapacity; shortcoming, weakness

tale–teller *n* a person who habitually reveals personal or sensational facts about others ⟨the reasons for the couple's divorce aren't terribly juicy, but they will be by the time the *tale-tellers* are through⟩ — see GOSSIP 1

talisman *n* something worn or kept to bring good luck or keep away evil ⟨a pendant of white nephrite jade is often worn by Indians as a *talisman* to ward off heart disease⟩ — see CHARM 1

talk *n* **1** a usually formal discourse delivered to an audience ⟨the noted author's *talk* on the state of the modern novel⟩ — see SPEECH 1
2 an exchange of views for the purpose of exploring a subject or deciding an issue ⟨what good will all this *talk* do when we need to take action now?⟩ — see DISCUSSION 1
3 friendly, informal conversation or an instance of this ⟨sat down by the fire and had a nice little *talk* about what was new in the village⟩ — see CHAT 1
4 information or opinion that is widely disseminated without any authority or confirmation of accuracy ⟨her wild behavior is exciting some lurid *talk*⟩ — see RUMOR

talk *vb* **1** to give a formal often extended talk on a subject ⟨the fire chief often *talks* at school assemblies about fire safety⟩
synonyms declaim, descant, discourse, expatiate, harangue, lecture, orate, speak
related words recite, soliloquize; dissert, expound, pontificate, sermonize; mouth, spout; filibuster
phrases hold forth, take the floor
2 to engage in casual or rambling conversation ⟨*talked* with our neighbor as we unloaded the groceries from the car⟩ — see CHAT 1
3 to express (a thought or emotion) in words ⟨you're *talking* nonsense: take a minute and think about what you are trying to say, and then start speaking⟩ — see SAY 1
4 to give information (as to the authorities) about another's improper or unlawful activities ⟨after being threatened, the eyewitness started *talking* at length about what he had seen in the alley⟩ — see SQUEAL 1
5 to relate sometimes questionable or secret information of a personal nature ⟨you're a fine one to *talk* about your sister's marital problems when you have had plenty of your own⟩ — see GOSSIP

talk (into) *vb* to cause (someone) to agree with a belief or course of action by using arguments or earnest request ⟨the salesman *talked* us *into* buying a new vacuum⟩ — see PERSUADE 1

talk (to) *vb* to communicate with by means of spoken words ⟨I had never *talked to* a real live cowboy before⟩
synonyms chat (with), converse (with), speak (to *or* with)
related words accost, address, board, collar, greet, hail, herald; inform, notify, tell
phrases engage in conversation

talkative *adj* fond of talking or conversation ⟨a *talkative* outgoing tour guide showed our school group around the city⟩
synonyms blabby, chatty, conversational, gabby, garrulous, loquacious, motormouthed, mouthy, talky
related words communicative, expansive; demonstrative, effusive, gushing; free-spoken, outspoken, unreserved, vocal; articulate, fluent, glib, voluble, well-spoken; gossipy, talebearing, tale-telling; long-winded, prolix, rambling, verbose, windy, wordy; extroverted (*also* extraverted), gregarious, outgoing, sociable
near antonyms quiet, shy; mum, mute, silent, speechless, tongue-tied, wordless; evasive, nonvocal, secretive, self-contained; aloof, indrawn, inhibited, introverted, retiring, unsociable, withdrawn
antonyms closemouthed, laconic, reserved, reticent, taciturn, tight-lipped, uncommunicative

talk down *vb* to express scornfully one's low opinion of ⟨a company that prefers to talk up its own products rather than *talk down* those of its competitors⟩ — see DECRY 1

talk down (to) *vb* to assume or treat with an air of superiority ⟨just because I don't have extensive experience in the field is no reason to *talk down to* me as if I were a child⟩ — see CONDESCEND 2

talker *n* a person who talks constantly ⟨your brother is quite a *talker*—he wouldn't let me get a word in edgewise⟩ — see CHATTERBOX

talk over *vb* to talk about (an issue) usually from various points of view and for the purpose of arriving at a decision or opinion ⟨your father and I will have to *talk* it *over* before agreeing to let you go on the class trip⟩ — see DISCUSS

talk up *vb* **1** to provide publicity for ⟨the director and actors are making the obligatory rounds of the late-night shows to *talk up* their new movie⟩ — see PUBLICIZE 1
2 to voice one's opinions freely with force ⟨feel free to *talk up* if you have any objections⟩ — see SPEAK UP

talky *adj* fond of talking or conversation ⟨a *talky* coworker who will corner you at your desk for hours with stories about his vacation⟩ — see TALKATIVE

tall *adj* **1** extending to a great distance upward ⟨*tall* skyscrapers that cast long shadows over the park⟩ — see HIGH 1
2 requiring considerable physical or mental effort ⟨that's a pretty *tall* order⟩ — see HARD 2

tally *n* a total number obtained or recorded by noting each thing as it was being added ⟨the final *tally* for worshippers at Sunday services was 126⟩ — see COUNT 1

tally *vb* **1** to be in agreement on every point ⟨our lists for best movies of the year *tally* perfectly⟩ — see CHECK 1
2 to gain (as points or runs in a game) as credit towards one's total number of points ⟨our team *tallied* four touchdowns and gained a total of 435 yards last game⟩ — see SCORE 2

tame *adj* **1** changed from the wild state so as to become useful and obedient to humans ⟨every evening, a wild Canada goose is at the food trough with our *tame* geese⟩
synonyms domestic, domesticated, tamed
related words broken, halterbroken, housebroken, trained; docile, familiar, gentle, semidomesticated; subdued, submissive
near antonyms unbroken, untrained; wildish
antonyms feral, nondomesticated, savage, undomesticated, untamed, wild
2 causing weariness, restlessness, or lack of interest ⟨that action movie was so *tame* I fell asleep about 20 minutes into it⟩ — see BORING

tame *vb* to keep from exceeding a desirable degree or level (as of expression) ⟨try to *tame* your language when you're in front of the kids⟩ — see CONTROL 1

tamed *adj* changed from the wild state so as to become useful and obedient to humans ⟨circus trainers work with *tamed* tigers and elephants⟩ — see TAME 1

tamper (with) *vb* to handle thoughtlessly, ignorantly, or mischievously ⟨someone has *tampered with* my computer files⟩
synonyms diddle (with), fiddle (with), fool (with), mess (with), monkey (with), play (with), tinker (with), toy (with), twiddle (with)
related words abuse, alter, doctor, manhandle, manipulate, mistreat, misuse; butt in, interfere, intrude, meddle, muck (about *or* around)

tan *vb* **1** to strike repeatedly with something long and thin or flexible ⟨Grandpa told us that when he was a kid, if he misbehaved at all, his father would *tan* his backside with a belt⟩ — see WHIP 1
2 to strike repeatedly ⟨a time when children were routinely *tanned* for misbehavior⟩ — see BEAT 1

tang *n* **1** an almost imperceptible sign of something ⟨the young author's novel is surprisingly earnest, tackling its subject without the slightest *tang* of irony⟩ — see HINT 2
2 the quality or state of being stimulating to the mind or senses ⟨there's a real *tang* to her poetry—it's not all sweetness and light⟩ — see PIQUANCY

tangent *n* a departure from the subject under consideration ⟨in the middle of her description of her dog's symptoms, she went off on a *tangent* about its cute behavior⟩
synonyms aside, digression, divagation, excursion
related words excursus, parenthesis; rambling; circuitousness, circularity, circumlocution, diffuseness, prolixity, verbosity, windiness, wordiness

tangible *adj* capable of being perceived by the sense of touch ⟨a firm belief in the existence of the soul, even though it is not at all *tangible*⟩
synonyms palpable, touchable
related words tactile; corporeal, physical; actual, concrete, embodied, existent, material, real, substantial; appreciable, detectable, discernible (*also* discernable), noticeable, observable, perceptible, seeable, sensible, visible
near antonyms bodiless, formless, immaterial, incorporeal, insubstantial, nonmaterial, nonphysical, unbodied, unsubstantial; abstract, ethereal, spiritual, unreal, virtual; imperceptible, insensible
antonyms impalpable, intangible

tangle *n* a state of mental uncertainty ⟨my mind's been in a *tangle* ever since I learned some disturbing information about an online acquaintance⟩ — see CONFUSION 1

tangle *vb* **1** to catch or hold as if in a net ⟨was at last *tangled* in the web of lies that he had told to everyone⟩ — see ENTANGLE 2
2 to twist together into a usually confused mass ⟨that darn cat *tangled* the yarn I was trying to knit with⟩ — see ENTANGLE 1

tangled *adj* having many parts or aspects that are usually interrelated ⟨it helps to have a lawyer to sort out the *tangled* contracts that home buyers typically have to contend with⟩ — see COMPLEX 1

tanglement *n* something that catches and holds ⟨legal *tanglements* stemming from the museum's refusal to return the looted carvings⟩ — see WEB 1

tangy *adj* having a powerfully stimulating odor or flavor ⟨a *tangy* sauce with a strong aftertaste⟩ — see SHARP 2

tank *vb* to be unsuccessful ⟨her intended comeback movie *tanked* at the box office, and once again she was relegated to TV guest spots⟩ — see FAIL 2

tanked *adj, slang* being under the influence of alcohol ⟨we can count on those jerks getting *tanked* tonight after the game⟩ — see DRUNK

tantrum *n* an outburst or display of excited anger ⟨had a *tantrum* when he found his little sister using his model paints⟩
synonyms blowup, explosion, fireworks, fit, hissy [*chiefly Southern & southern Midland*], hissy fit, huff, scene
related words eruption, flare-up, outburst, storm, uproar; agitation, delirium, distraction, frenzy, furor, furore, fury, hysteria, rage, rampage; convulsion(s), paroxysm, seizure, spasm, upheaval; angriness, choler, indignation, irateness, ire, lividity, lividness, spleen, wrath, wrathfulness; reaction, rise; dander, temper; grouch, hump [*British*], pet, pouts, snit, sulk(s), sulkiness, sullenness

[1]**tap** *vb* to strike or cause to strike lightly and usually rhythmically ⟨*tapped* her foot in time to the music⟩ ⟨kept *tapping* the desk with his pencil⟩
synonyms beat, drum, rap
related words bang, bash, bat, bonk, bop, hammer, hit, knock, paste, pound, slam, smack, sock, strike, swat, thud, thump, thwack, wallop, whack; chink, clatter, clink, ping; pat, pit-a-pat, pitter-patter; chuck, clap, click, flick, tip

[2]**tap** *vb* to remove (liquid) gradually or completely ⟨the oil company *tapped* that first well completely dry⟩ — see DRAIN 1

tap *n* a fixture for controlling the flow of a liquid ⟨turn the *tap* to the right for cold water and to the left for hot water⟩ — see FAUCET

tape *n* a recording (as of a movie) on magnetic tape for playback on a TV ⟨the rival campaign leaked a *tape* of the senator angrily reprimanding a little boy for stepping on his foot⟩ — see VIDEO

taper *vb* to grow less in scope or intensity especially gradually ⟨you'll find the symptoms begin *tapering* gradually about 24 hours after you take the medicine⟩ — see DECREASE 2

tape recording *n* a recording (as of a movie) on magnetic tape for playback on a TV ⟨the documentary included a *tape recording* of one of the actor's earliest performances⟩ — see VIDEO

taper off *vb* to grow less in scope or intensity especially gradually ⟨at this time of the year, light begins to *taper off* a little earlier each day⟩ — see DECREASE 2

tapped out *adj* depleted in strength, energy, or freshness ⟨the prosecutor was mentally and physically *tapped out* after the long trial⟩ — see WEARY 1

taproom *n* a place of business where alcoholic beverages are sold to be consumed on the premises ⟨the local *taproom* is required by law to serve food as well⟩ — see BARROOM

tar *n* one who operates or navigates a seagoing vessel ⟨a book about the adventurous lives of *tars*, skippers, and pirates of the 18th century⟩ — see SAILOR

taradiddle *or* **tarradiddle** *n* **1** a statement known by its maker to be untrue and made in order to deceive ⟨his tales of adventure are peppered with tongue-in-cheek *taradiddles* and obvious fabrications⟩ — see LIE

2 language, behavior, or ideas that are absurd and contrary to good sense ⟨regards literary deconstruction as so much tenure-track *taradiddle*⟩ — see NONSENSE 1

tardily *adv* **1** after the due, usual, or proper time ⟨she submitted her scholarship application *tardily*, so she was not considered⟩ — see LATE 1

2 at a pace that is less than usual, desirable, or expected ⟨the money that I had lent him for the CDs came *tardily* and only after I told him that if he didn't repay me, I was taking the CDs back⟩ — see SLOW

tardiness *n* the quality or state of being late ⟨habitual *tardiness* will be recorded in your personnel file⟩ — see LATENESS

tardy *adj* **1** moving or proceeding at less than the normal, desirable, or required speed ⟨thus far progress on the project has been *tardy*⟩ — see SLOW 1

2 not arriving, occurring, or settled at the due, usual, or proper time ⟨explained that I was *tardy* because my car had broken down on the way to work⟩ — see LATE 1

target *n* **1** a person or thing that is the object of abuse, criticism, or ridicule ⟨the hapless vice president quickly became the favorite *target* of late-night comedians⟩

synonyms butt, mark, prey, sitting duck, victim

related words laughingstock, mockery, pilgarlic; lightning rod; fall guy, goat, scapegoat, whipping boy

near antonyms gossip, gossiper, talebearer, tattler, tattletale, troublemaker; defamer, libeler, libelist, traducer; baiter, heckler, needler, ribber, taunter, tease, teaser, tormentor (*also* tormenter), torturer; derider, insulter, mocker, ridiculer, scoffer, scorner; caricaturist, lampooner, parodist, satirist

2 a person or thing that is made fun of ⟨after my botched haircut, I became the *target* of lots of jokes at school⟩ — see LAUGHINGSTOCK

3 something that one hopes or intends to accomplish ⟨our *target* is to raise $100,000 for a new playground by August⟩ — see GOAL

tarnish *vb* to affect slightly with something morally bad or undesirable ⟨an arrest for shoplifting *tarnished* her reputation for many years afterwards⟩ — see TAINT 1

tarry *n* a temporary residing as another's guest ⟨a fable about the *tarry* of two Americans in a Scottish village that every century magically comes into existence for a day⟩ — see VISIT 1

tarry *vb* **1** to continue to be in a place for a significant amount of time ⟨upon seeing the sun beginning to sink in the sky, we realized we had *tarried* too long on the summit of the mountain⟩ — see [1]STAY 1

2 to move or act slowly ⟨the dean *tarried* in making his decision, still not sure if he should suspend the student or not⟩ — see DELAY 1

3 to reside as a temporary guest ⟨he *tarried* with us all summer, sleeping on the screened-in porch most nights⟩ — see VISIT 2

tart *adj* **1** causing or characterized by the one of the four basic taste sensations that is produced chiefly by acids ⟨I didn't add enough sugar to the lemonade, and now it's way too *tart*⟩ — see SOUR 1

2 marked by the use of wit that is intended to cause hurt feelings ⟨stood ready with a *tart* comeback in case the lout asked her if she wanted to dance⟩ — see SARCASTIC

tart *n* a woman who engages in sexual activities for money ⟨the sort of skimpy outfit that could cause a girl to be mistaken for a *tart*⟩ — see PROSTITUTE

tartish *adj* causing or characterized by the one of the four basic taste sensations that is produced chiefly by acids ⟨for this pie, use firm, *tartish* apples and not one of those mushy, insipid varieties⟩ — see SOUR 1

tartness *n* **1** a harsh or sharp quality ⟨there's a *tartness* to this movie critic's reviews that's a little tiresome⟩ — see EDGE 1

2 biting sharpness of feeling or expression ⟨there's a telltale *tartness* between these two teams that nobody could miss⟩ — see ACRIMONY 1

task *n* **1** a piece of work that needs to be done regularly ⟨one of my *tasks* in the morning is to make lunches for everyone in the family⟩ — see CHORE 1

2 the action for which a person or thing is specially fitted or used or for which a thing exists ⟨the forklift's *task* is to stack pallets of goods in the warehouse⟩ — see ROLE

task *vb* to give a task, duty, or responsibility to ⟨I have been *tasked* by the host with bringing the pies for Thanksgiving this year⟩ — see ENTRUST 1

taskmaster *n* **1** a boss who assigns much work ⟨pitiless *taskmaster* that he was, Ebenezer Scrooge only reluctantly let his ill-paid clerk have Christmas Day off⟩

synonyms slave driver

related words enslaver; authoritarian, disciplinarian, discipliner, martinet, stickler; despot, dictator, oppressor, tyrant; dominator, overlord; taskmistress; micromanager

2 the person (as an employer or supervisor) who tells people and especially workers what to do ⟨known as a tough but fair *taskmaster*⟩ — see BOSS

taste *n* **1** the property of a substance that can be identified by the sense of taste ⟨I can't stand the *taste* of cherry-flavored cough syrup⟩

synonyms flavor, savor (*also* savour)

related words relish, smack, tang; savoriness, tastiness; aftertaste

near antonyms tastelessness

2 a small piece or quantity of food ⟨I'll just have a *taste* of your dessert⟩ — see MORSEL 1

3 positive regard for something ⟨trying to develop a *taste* for classical music⟩ — see LIKING

taste *vb* **1** to come to a knowledge of (something) by living through it ⟨an adventurer who has *tasted* danger and lived to tell the tale⟩ — see EXPERIENCE

2 to have a vague awareness of ⟨by your language I can *taste* that something is wrong⟩ — see FEEL 1

tasteful *adj* **1** having or showing elegance ⟨a *tasteful* ar-

rangement of white flowers and dark greenery⟩ — see ELEGANT 1
2 very pleasing to the sense of taste ⟨a line of microwavable frozen entrées that are surprisingly *tasteful*⟩ — see DELICIOUS 1

tasteless *adj* **1** lacking in refinement or good taste ⟨a completely *tasteless* comment about her slight amount of facial hair⟩ — see COARSE 2
2 lacking in taste or flavor ⟨breakfast was usually plain, *tasteless* oatmeal⟩ — see INSIPID 1
3 marked by an obvious lack of style or good taste ⟨a *tasteless* suit that he wore to the party as a joke⟩ — see [1]TACKY 1

tastelessness *n* the quality or state of lacking refinement or good taste ⟨the *tastelessness* of his comments about some of the women in the office was appalling⟩ — see VULGARITY 1

tastiness *n* the quality of being delicious ⟨the *tastiness* of homemade bread⟩ — see DELICIOUSNESS

tasty *adj* **1** giving pleasure or contentment to the mind or senses ⟨the *tasty* prospect of getting his revenge after all those years⟩ — see PLEASANT 1
2 very pleasing to the sense of taste ⟨a selection of *tasty* doughnuts from the corner bakery⟩ — see DELICIOUS 1

tatter *vb* to cause (something) to separate into jagged pieces by violently pulling at it ⟨the kids will *tatter* that doll beyond repair if they don't quit yanking on it⟩ — see TEAR 1

tatterdemalion *adj* **1** showing signs of advanced wear and tear and neglect ⟨one of those *tatterdemalion* towns of the rust belt where the factories closed down decades ago⟩ — see SHABBY 1
2 wearing torn or worn out clothes ⟨an ill-equipped, *tatterdemalion* army⟩ — see TATTERED 1

tattered *adj* **1** wearing torn or worn out clothes ⟨arrived at the refugee camp *tattered* and exhausted⟩
synonyms ragged, raggedy, ragtag, tatterdemalion
related words bedraggled, scroungy, scruffy, shabby, threadbare; down-at-the-heels (*or* down-at-heel *also* down-at-the-heel *or* down-at-heels)
phrases out at elbows (*or* out at the elbows)
near antonyms decked (out), dolled up, dressed up; spiffy
2 worn or torn into or as if into rags ⟨a hobo in *tattered* old clothes and worn-out shoes⟩ — see RAGGED 2

tattle *n* information or opinion that is widely disseminated without any authority or confirmation of accuracy ⟨she claims to have picked up some juicy *tattle* about the candidate⟩ — see RUMOR

tattle *vb* to relate sometimes questionable or secret information of a personal nature ⟨those neighborhood busybodies, constantly *tattling* and whispering over their backyard fences⟩ — see GOSSIP

tattler *n* a person who provides information about another's wrongdoing ⟨as the office's resident *tattler*, she can be counted on to report any unauthorized use of the photocopiers⟩ — see INFORMER

tattletale *n* a person who provides information about another's wrongdoing ⟨don't be such a *tattletale* and tell me about every little thing your sister does⟩ — see INFORMER

tatty *adj* showing signs of advanced wear and tear and neglect ⟨the owner has let the restaurant become increasingly *tatty* over the years⟩ — see SHABBY 1

taunt *vb* to attack repeatedly with mean put-downs or insults ⟨*taunted* the newly arrived immigrants about their broken English⟩ — see TEASE 2

taunter *n* a person who causes repeated emotional pain, distress, or annoyance to another ⟨tired of always being the butt of their jokes, he decided to get back at his *taunters*⟩ — see TORMENTOR

taut *adj* stretched with little or no give ⟨a *taut* clothesline⟩
synonyms rigid, tense, tight
related words firm, inflexible, stiff, tightened, unrelaxed, unyielding
near antonyms drooping, droopy, flaccid, floppy, hanging, lank, limp, loosened, relaxed, sagging, slackened, yielding; elastic, flexible, pliant, resilient, springy, stretchy, supple
antonyms lax, loose, slack

tauten *vb* to draw tight ⟨he *tautened* the rope and then tied it off⟩ — see TIGHTEN

tavern *n* **1** a place of business where alcoholic beverages are sold to be consumed on the premises ⟨a seedy section of the city's waterfront that was rife with cheap *taverns*, tattoo parlors, and run-down flophouses⟩ — see BARROOM
2 a place that provides rooms and usually a public dining room for overnight guests ⟨a colonial-era *tavern* that has been serving weary travelers for two and a half centuries⟩ — see HOTEL

taverner *n* the owner or manager of an inn ⟨in Longfellow's *Tales of a Wayside Inn* a *taverner* tells a series of tales in verse to a group of travelers⟩ — see INNKEEPER

tawny *adj* of a pale yellow or yellowish brown color ⟨the *tawny* coat of a lion⟩ — see BLOND

tax *n* a charge usually of money collected by the government from people or businesses for public use ⟨the state sales *tax* boosted the final cost of my new computer⟩
synonyms assessment, duty, imposition, impost, levy
related words direct tax, personal tax; capitation, custom(s), excise, hidden tax, income tax, poll tax, property tax, sales tax, single tax, sin tax, tariff, toll, tribute, value-added tax, withholding tax; supertax, surcharge, surtax; death tax, estate tax, inheritance tax; flat tax, proportional tax

tax *vb* to subject (a personal quality or faculty) to often excessive stress ⟨your constant arguing is starting to *tax* my patience⟩ — see TRY 1

taxi *n* an automobile that carries passengers for a fare usually determined by the distance traveled ⟨couldn't hail a *taxi* so I had to run in the rain to make my appointment⟩ — see TAXICAB

taxicab *n* an automobile that carries passengers for a fare usually determined by the distance traveled ⟨took a *taxicab* to the airport⟩
synonyms cab, hack, taxi
related words hackney; limousine; gharry, rickshaw (*also* ricksha), water taxi; gypsy cab, jitney

taxing *adj* requiring much time, effort, or careful attention ⟨a very *taxing* workload that is taking a lot of time to finish⟩ — see DEMANDING 1

tchotchke *n* a small object displayed for its attractiveness or interest ⟨a bedroom with polka-dot curtains, flowery wallpaper, and shelves cluttered with *tchotchkes* from a lifetime of vacations⟩ — see KNICKKNACK

teach *vb* to cause to acquire knowledge or skill in some field ⟨*taught* us about the basics of organic gardening⟩
synonyms educate, indoctrinate, instruct, lesson, school, train, tutor
related words coach, mentor; drill, fit, ground, habilitate, prepare, prime, qualify; direct, guide, lead, rear; catechize, lecture, moralize, preach; implant, inculcate, instill (*also* instil); homeschool; edify, enlighten; brief, familiarize, impart (to), inform, verse; initiate, introduce, show; reeducate, reschool, reteach, retrain

teacher *n* a person whose occupation is to give formal instruction in a school ⟨a young man who ardently wants to become a *teacher* and teach first grade⟩
synonyms educationist [*chiefly British*], educator, instructor, pedagogue (*also* pedagog), preceptor, schoolteacher

related words headmaster, master, rector, schoolmaster; headmistress, instructress, mistress [*chiefly British*], schoolmarm (*or* schoolma'am), schoolmistress; coach, guide, guru, preparer, trainer; mentor, tutor, tutoress; drillmaster, inculcator; dean, docent, doctor, don, prof, professor, regius professor; academe, academic, academician, didact, pedant; governess, homeschooler; intern (*also* interne), practice teacher, reader, student teacher; catechist, lecturer, moralizer, preacher

teaching *n* the act or process of imparting knowledge or skills to another ⟨a chemist who has devoted his career to *teaching*, even though he could have made a lot more money in an industrial job⟩ — see EDUCATION 1

team *n* a group of people working together on a task ⟨asked the Boy Scouts to split into *teams* and begin pitching their tents⟩ — see GANG 1

team (up) *vb* to participate or assist in a joint effort to accomplish an end ⟨the television broadcast networks will be *teaming up* for joint coverage of the event⟩ — see COOPERATE 1

teamwork *n* the work and activity of a number of persons who individually contribute toward the efficiency of the whole ⟨it takes *teamwork* to pull off a successful fund-raiser⟩

synonyms collaboration, cooperation, coordination

related words collegiality, fellowship, partnership; community, mutualism, reciprocity, symbiosis; synergism, synergy; communion, cooperativeness, kinship, oneness, solidarity, togetherness, unity

antonyms noncooperation

tear *n* a long deep cut ⟨repaired a *tear* in the theater curtain just before the start of the show⟩ — see GASH

tear *vb* **1** to cause (something) to separate into jagged pieces by violently pulling at it ⟨angrily *tore* the letter to shreds⟩

synonyms rend, ribbon, rip, rive, shred, tatter

related words break, cleave, rupture, split; cut, gash, incise, lacerate, slash; butcher, dismember, dissect, hack, mangle

2 to separate or remove by forceful pulling ⟨*tore* the book from his hand⟩

synonyms rip, wrench, wrest, yank

related words grab, nab, seize, snap (up), snatch; lop (off), nip; amputate, cut (off), dissever, sever; extract, force, jerk, prize, pry, pull, root (out), uproot

near antonyms reattach

3 to proceed or move quickly ⟨she *tore* out of the room as soon as the phone started to ring⟩ — see HURRY 2

tear (out) *vb* to draw out by force or with effort ⟨you'll never *tear* that secret *out* of me⟩ — see EXTRACT

tear down *vb* **1** to bring to a complete end the physical soundness, existence, or usefulness of ⟨vandals *tore down* the wooden fence blocking the entrance to the beach⟩ — see DESTROY 1

2 to destroy (as a building) completely by knocking down or breaking to pieces ⟨the new owners apparently bought the house just to *tear* it *down* and build a lavish mansion in its place⟩ — see DEMOLISH 1

tearful *adj* **1** given to expressing strong emotion (as sorrow) by readily shedding tears ⟨a *tearful* woman who can be counted on to cry at every wedding, anniversary, and funeral⟩

synonyms lachrymose, teary, weepy

related words demonstrative, effusive, emotional; maudlin, mawkish, sentimental; bawling, blubbering, crying, keening, sniffling, sniveling, sobbing, wailing, weeping, whimpering; misty, misty-eyed, moist; bemoaning, bewailing; doleful, dolorous, grieving, mournful, plaintive; funereal, gloomy, lugubrious; brokenhearted, dejected, depressed, despondent, disconsolate, downcast, downhearted, heartbroken, heartsick, heavyhearted, inconsolable, miserable, sad, sorrowful, woebegone, woeful, wretched

near antonyms beaming, chuckling, giggling, grinning, laughing, smiling; blithe, blithesome, cheerful, cheery, gay, happy, jocose, jovial, lighthearted, lightsome, merry, mirthful, sunny

2 causing unhappiness ⟨the *tearful* end to what had once been a close friendship⟩ — see SAD 2

teary *adj* **1** causing unhappiness ⟨a *teary* ending to what had been up to that point a lighthearted movie⟩ — see SAD 2

2 given to expressing strong emotion (as sorrow) by readily shedding tears ⟨he's one of those *teary* drunks who sees fit to bore the other bar patrons with his sad stories⟩ — see TEARFUL 1

tease *n* **1** a person who causes repeated emotional pain, distress, or annoyance to another ⟨she can be a very cruel *tease* when she happens upon an unpopular girl who is easily hurt⟩ — see TORMENTOR

2 one who is obnoxiously annoying ⟨my youngest brother is a complete *tease*, following me around everywhere and aping my every move⟩ — see NUISANCE 1

tease *vb* **1** to make fun of in a good-natured way ⟨likes to *tease* her twin brother about his seemingly endless string of girlfriends⟩

synonyms chaff, jive, joke, josh, kid, rally, razz, rib, ride, roast

related words banter; fool, fun, string along; jest, quip, wisecrack; gag, jape, jolly, yuk (*or* yuck) [*slang*]

phrases goof on [*slang*], take the mickey out of [*British*]

2 to attack repeatedly with mean put-downs or insults ⟨grew up being *teased* because his parents were hog farmers⟩

synonyms bait, hassle, haze, heckle, needle, ride, taunt

related words deride, gibe (*or* jibe), jeer, mock, ridicule; annoy, bother, bug, burn (up), chafe, fret, frost, gall, get, gnaw (at), grate, gripe, hack (off), hagride, irk, irritate, itch, nag, nark [*British*], nettle, peeve, pester, pique, put out, rasp, rile, ruffle, spite, trouble, vex; aggravate, exasperate, goad, test, try; aggrieve, agitate, bedevil, beleaguer, discomfort, disturb, perturb; badger, dog, hound; browbeat, bully, hector; harass, harry, persecute, plague, terrorize, torment, torture

phrases make game of, pick on

teaser *n* **1** a person who causes repeated emotional pain, distress, or annoyance to another ⟨the *teasers* were never satisfied until they had caused their victim to burst into tears⟩ — see TORMENTOR

2 one who is obnoxiously annoying ⟨he was by nature a *teaser*, someone who kept testing people to see if they could calmly bear his put-downs⟩ — see NUISANCE 1

teasing *n* the act of making unwelcome intrusions upon another ⟨stop that *teasing* before you make the baby cry⟩ — see ANNOYANCE 1

technical *adj* used by or intended for experts in a particular field of knowledge ⟨although the owner's manual for the receiver was supposedly written for the average consumer, it's filled with *technical* language⟩

synonyms specialized

related words esoteric, especial, exclusive, limited, narrow, peculiar, restricted, special, specific, unique; authoritative, expert, professional, specialist (*or* specialistic); technicalized

near antonyms common, generalized, generic, nonexclusive, nonspecific, ordinary, overall, universal; inexpert, lay, nonprofessional, unprofessional; self-evident, self-explanatory, straightforward

antonyms general, nontechnical, untechnical

technique *n* the means or procedure for doing something ⟨showed me a different knitting *technique*⟩ — see METHOD

tectonic *adj* having great meaning or lasting effect ⟨a *tectonic* shift in societal trends occurred in the 1960s⟩ — see IMPORTANT 1

tedious *adj* causing weariness, restlessness, or lack of interest ⟨a long and *tedious* staff meeting⟩ — see BORING

tedium *n* the state of being bored ⟨the *tedium* of spending a hot afternoon trapped inside the house⟩ — see BOREDOM

teed off *adj* **1** feeling or showing anger ⟨the boss is really *teed off* about the loss of one of our most important clients, so don't go near him⟩ — see ANGRY
2 subjected to and reacting with irritation ⟨she gets really *teed off* if you touch anything on her desk⟩ — see ANNOYED

teem *vb* to be copiously supplied ⟨the area *teems* with entrepreneurs hoping to hit upon the next big thing⟩ — see ABOUND

teeming *adj* possessing or covered with great numbers or amounts of something specified ⟨oceans *teeming* with life⟩ — see RIFE

teensy *adj* very small in size ⟨for years we lived in a *teensy* apartment that was the size of the proverbial broom closet⟩ — see TINY

teensy–weensy *adj* very small in size ⟨she wore a *teensy-weensy* bikini that was appropriately likened to dental floss⟩ — see TINY

teeny *adj* very small in size ⟨had to look closely to see the *teeny* splinter in her foot⟩ — see TINY

teeny–weeny *adj* very small in size ⟨kept losing the *teeny-weeny* coffee mugs for the kitchen in her dollhouse⟩ — see TINY

teeter *vb* **1** to swing unsteadily back and forth or from side to side ⟨he drunkenly *teetered* at the edge of the pool⟩
synonyms falter, rock, totter, waver, wobble (*also* wabble)
related words flounder, lurch, stumble, toddle; quake, quaver, quiver, shake, shudder, tremble, vibrate; careen, reel, stagger, weave
2 to move forward while swaying from side to side ⟨the toddler *teetered* down the stairs on her mother's high heels⟩ — see STAGGER 1
3 to show uncertainty about the right course of action ⟨was *teetering* on the brink of making a decision about college⟩ — see HESITATE

teetotaler *or* **teetotaller** *n* a person who abstains from alcoholic beverages ⟨in a quandary about what to serve for the wedding toast since his future in-laws are *teetotalers*⟩ — see NONDRINKER

teetotalist *n* a person who abstains from alcoholic beverages ⟨not exactly looking forward to spending the holidays, including New Year's, with relatives who are strict *teetotalists*⟩ — see NONDRINKER

telegraphic *adj* marked by the use of few words to convey much information or meaning ⟨when dealing with her staff, she communicated mostly in *telegraphic* sentences and meaningful looks⟩ — see CONCISE

telephone *vb* to make a telephone call to ⟨I'll try to *telephone* the office and make an appointment today⟩ — see CALL 2

telescope *vb* to reduce in size or volume by or as if by pressing parts or members together ⟨for dramatic purposes, the film *telescopes* the years over which the events occurred into a few short months⟩ — see COMPRESS 1

telescoping *n* the act or process of reducing the size or volume of something by or as if by pressing ⟨the *telescoping* of the season for movie awards into a couple of months⟩ — see COMPRESSION

television *n* an electronic device with a screen and speakers that reproduces images and sound ⟨people who turn on the *television* the minute they walk in the door⟩
synonyms boob tube, box, idiot box, telly [*chiefly British*], tube, TV
related words LCD, plasma; home theater, home video

tell *vb* **1** to give an oral or written account of in some detail ⟨they *told* the story of how they had met⟩
synonyms chart, chronicle, describe, narrate, recite, recount, rehearse, relate, report
related words deliver, give, reel off, state, utter, voice; detail, enumerate, itemize, particularize; bare, disclose, divulge, expose, let on (about), reveal; delineate, depict, express, render, sketch
phrases set forth
2 to express (a thought or emotion) in words ⟨just *tell* us what is in your heart⟩ — see SAY 1
3 to find the sum of (a collection of things) by noting each one as it is being added ⟨who can *tell* the number of grains of sand in the world?⟩ — see COUNT 1
4 to give information to ⟨*tell* me, when did you begin playing the violin?⟩ — see ENLIGHTEN 1
5 to issue orders to (someone) by right of authority ⟨*told* us to sit still and wait⟩ — see COMMAND 1
6 to make known (as information previously kept secret) ⟨I won't *tell* your secret to anyone⟩ — see REVEAL 1

tell (of) *vb* to serve as a sign or symptom of ⟨his shoddy performance in the debate *tells of* too little preparation⟩ — see INDICATE 1

tell (on) *vb* **1** to act upon (a person or a person's feelings) so as to cause a response ⟨the pressure of final exams is beginning to *tell on* the students in the dorm⟩ — see [1]AFFECT 1
2 to give information (as to the authorities) about another's improper or unlawful activities ⟨in that neighborhood, you wouldn't even think about *telling on* the drug dealers⟩ — see SQUEAL 1

telling *adj* having the power to persuade ⟨presented us with *telling* evidence that convinced us he was right⟩ — see COGENT

telltale *adj* indicating something ⟨I know you've been eating chocolate because of the *telltale* smudges on your face⟩ — see INDICATIVE

telltale *n* **1** a person who habitually reveals personal or sensational facts about others ⟨the media's professional *telltales* have basically decided that today's celebrities have no right to privacy⟩ — see GOSSIP 1
2 a person who provides information about another's wrongdoing ⟨the department *telltale* told the boss that his coworkers were taking extra long breaks⟩ — see INFORMER

telly *n, chiefly British* an electronic device with a screen and speakers that reproduces images and sound ⟨has had the same *telly* since the Thatcher administration⟩ — see TELEVISION

temblor *n* a shaking of the earth ⟨a *temblor* knocked down many of the buildings in the village⟩ — see EARTHQUAKE 1

temerarious *adj* foolishly adventurous or bold ⟨*temerarious* people rush in without forethought⟩ — see FOOLHARDY 1

temerity *n* shameless boldness ⟨she had the *temerity* to ask my boyfriend if she could go out with him should he and I ever break up⟩ — see EFFRONTERY

temper *n* **1** a special quality or impression associated with something ⟨there's a *temper* of tranquillity about the retreat that visitors find very inviting⟩ — see AURA 1
2 a state of mind dominated by a particular emotion ⟨was in quite a bad *temper* after spilling his juice all over his new shirt⟩ — see MOOD 1
3 one's characteristic attitude or mood ⟨she has an even

temper and a calm manner that sets everyone all at ease⟩ — see DISPOSITION 1

temperament *n* one's characteristic attitude or mood ⟨looking for a dog with a sweet *temperament*⟩ — see DISPOSITION 1

temperamental *adj* **1** frequently influenced by moods and especially bad moods ⟨one of those *temperamental* actresses who can make life difficult for everyone around her⟩ — see MOODY

2 likely to change frequently, suddenly, or unexpectedly ⟨stock prices have been pretty *temperamental* lately, often fluctuating wildly⟩ — see FICKLE 1

temperance *n* **1** an avoidance of extremes in one's actions, beliefs, or habits ⟨my father attributes his ripe old age to *temperance* in all things, especially eating and drinking⟩

synonyms moderateness, moderation, temperateness

related words constraint, control, discipline, restraint, self-control, self-discipline; middle-of-the-roadism; asceticism, austerity, frugality, mortification, sacrifice, self-command, self-containment, self-denial, self-mastery; abnegation, abstention, avoidance, eschewal, forbearance; rationality, rationalness, reasonability, reasonableness, sensibility, sensibleness; abstinence, soberness, sobriety, teetotalism

near antonyms excess, superfluity; extremeness, extremity; unconstraint, unrestraint; extremism, radicalness; irrationality, unreasonableness; insobriety

antonyms excessiveness, immoderacy, immoderateness, immoderation, intemperance, intemperateness

2 voluntary restraint in the satisfaction of one's appetites ⟨practices a blue-blooded *temperance* that his parvenu neighbors will never understand⟩ — see ABSTINENCE 1

temperate *adj* **1** avoiding extremes in behavior or expression ⟨rather *temperate* in his appraisal of the movie, calling it good but not great⟩ — see MODERATE 1

2 marked by temperatures that are neither too high nor too low ⟨escaped a cold Midwestern winter by vacationing in a more *temperate* climate down south⟩ — see CLEMENT 1

3 given to or marked by restraint in the satisfaction of one's appetites ⟨a soft-spoken, serious-minded person of *temperate* habits⟩ — see ABSTEMIOUS

temperateness *n* an avoidance of extremes in one's actions, beliefs, or habits ⟨there was a steadfast *temperateness* about every aspect of his life⟩ — see TEMPERANCE 1

tempest *n* **1** a disturbance of the atmosphere accompanied by wind and often by precipitation (as rain or snow) ⟨the sudden summertime *tempest* drove us off the golf course and into the clubhouse⟩ — see STORM 1

2 a violent disturbance (as of the political or social order) ⟨the town council handled the *tempest* over cuts to the school budget as well as could be expected⟩ — see CONVULSION

tempestuous *adj* **1** marked by bursts of destructive force or intense activity ⟨order was restored to the court after the judge put a stop to the defendant's *tempestuous* outburst⟩ — see VIOLENT 1

2 marked by sudden or violent disturbance ⟨in terms of social change, the 1960s are generally considered the most *tempestuous* decade in recent American history⟩ — see CONVULSIVE 1

3 marked by turmoil or disturbance especially of natural elements ⟨we spent a *tempestuous* night stranded on the summit of the mountain⟩ — see WILD 3

4 marked by wet and windy conditions ⟨stay indoors this weekend as the weather promises to be *tempestuous*⟩ — see FOUL 1

temple *n* a building for public worship and especially Christian worship ⟨the largest *temple* in the Gothic style in the country⟩ — see CHURCH 1

temporal *adj* **1** having to do with life on earth especially as opposed to that in heaven ⟨do not worry about *temporal* concerns, but instead focus on spiritual matters⟩ — see EARTHLY

2 not involving religion or religious matters ⟨administrators on campus are in place to deal with students' *temporal* needs, and spiritual advisors are available to help students with their nontemporal needs⟩ — see PROFANE 1

temporariness *n* the state or quality of lasting only for a short time ⟨the *temporariness* of the job is probably the reason why so few people are applying for it⟩ — see IMPERMANENCE

temporary *adj* **1** intended to last, continue, or serve for a limited time ⟨summer workers looking for *temporary* accommodations in private homes⟩

synonyms ad interim, impermanent, interim, provisional, provisionary, provisory, short-term

related words acting; alternate, proxy, substitute; expedient, improvised, makeshift; intermediary, intermediate, transitional; ephemeral, fleeting, fugitive, short-lived, transitory; conditional, contingent, limited, qualified, short-range, tentative; replaceable, terminable, terminate

near antonyms final, fixed, set, settled; unconditional, unlimited, unqualified; extended, lasting, long-range, standing; dateless, deathless, endless, enduring, eternal, everlasting, immortal, perpetual, timeless, undying, unending

antonyms long-term, permanent

2 lasting only for a short time ⟨a *temporary* lapse of memory⟩ — see MOMENTARY

3 serving in a position for the time being ⟨the *temporary* head of the sales division⟩ — see ACTING

temporizer *n* **1** a person who dexterously and expediently changes or adopts opinions ⟨the kind of *temporizer* who determines his position on a political issue by taking a look at the polls⟩ — see ACROBAT 2

2 one who does things only for his own benefit and with little regard for right and wrong ⟨a lifelong *temporizer*, he was for the war as long as it was popular and against it the minute the tide of public opinion went the other way⟩ — see SELF-SEEKER

tempt *vb* **1** to lead away from a usual or proper course by offering some pleasure or advantage ⟨that chocolate dessert sure *tempts* me, but I should stick with my diet⟩ — see LURE

2 to take a chance on ⟨refusing to lay in enough food for the long winter *tempts* the dangers of starvation⟩ — see RISK 1

temptation *n* **1** the pressure to give in to a desire for easy or immediate pleasure ⟨he felt the *temptation* to go sailing, but did his chores instead⟩

synonyms allurement, enticement, lure, seduction

related words siren song; allure, appeal, attraction, attractiveness, charm, enchantment, glamour (*also* glamor); beckoning, invitation; bait, inducement, influence, persuasion, power, sway

2 something that persuades one to perform an action for pleasure or gain ⟨money, power, and other overwhelming *temptations* can seduce a person to a life of crime⟩ — see LURE 1

tempter *n* one that tries to get a person to give in to a desire ⟨there is no greater *tempter* to put off studying than my dog when he wants to play⟩

synonyms baiter, seducer, solicitor

related words beguiler, enchantress, siren, temptress; tantalizer; briber, inducer, inveigler, persuader; corrupter (*also* corruptor), debaser, debaucher, degrader, depraver, perverter, undoer

temptress *n* a woman whom men find irresistibly attractive ⟨Greta Garbo, one of the most famous *temptresses* ever to appear on screen, died in 1990⟩ — see SIREN

ten *n* a physically attractive person ⟨promised me that she would fix me up with a *ten*⟩ — see DOLL 2

tenable *adj* **1** capable of being defended against physical attack ⟨the soldiers' encampment on the open plain was not *tenable*, so they retreated to higher ground⟩
synonyms defendable, defensible
related words defended, guarded, protected, safeguarded, secure, secured, shielded; bulletproof, impregnable, indomitable, invincible, inviolable, invulnerable, unassailable, unbeatable, unconquerable, untouchable
near antonyms vincible, vulnerable; assailable, exposed, imperiled (*or* imperilled), insecure, liable, open, susceptible, undefended, unguarded, unprotected, unsecured; defenseless, helpless, powerless, weak
antonyms indefensible, untenable
2 capable of being defended with good reasoning against verbal attack ⟨the *tenable* theory that a giant meteor strike set off a chain of events resulting in the demise of the dinosaurs⟩
synonyms defendable, defensible, justifiable, maintainable, supportable, sustainable
related words rational, reasonable, sensible, well-grounded; acceptable, admissible, allowable, exceptionable, legitimate, passable, unobjectionable, viable, warrantable; confirmable, provable, verifiable; explainable, explicable
near antonyms absurd, illogical, irrational, ridiculous, unsound; extreme, outrageous, unreasonable; groundless, objectionable, unacceptable, unfounded; inexplicable, unexplainable
antonyms indefensible, insupportable, unjustifiable, unsustainable, untenable

tenacious *adj* **1** continuing despite difficulties, opposition, or discouragement ⟨a *tenacious* trainer, she adheres to her grueling swimming schedule no matter what⟩ — see PERSISTENT
2 tending to adhere to objects upon contact ⟨you'll have a devil of a time getting those *tenacious* burrs off of your wool sweater⟩ — see STICKY 1

tenant *n* **1** one who rents a room or apartment in another's house ⟨the laundry in the basement is for *tenants* only⟩
synonyms boarder, lessee, lodger, renter, roomer
related words cotenant, subtenant; flatmate [*chiefly British*], roommate (*also* roomie); guest, visitor; occupant, occupier, resident, resider
near antonyms laird [*chiefly Scottish*], landholder, landowner, proprietor; landlady; slumlord; host, innkeeper, proprietor
antonyms landlord, lessor, letter
2 one who lives permanently in a place ⟨the abandoned warehouse's only *tenants* are a band of squatters⟩ — see INHABITANT

[1]**tend** *vb* to show a liking or proneness (for something) ⟨her wardrobe *tends* toward dark colors and heavy fabrics⟩ — see LEAN 2

[2]**tend** *vb* **1** to take charge of especially on behalf of another ⟨*tend* the store while I run an errand⟩
synonyms attend, care (for), mind, oversee, superintend, supervise, watch
related words administrate, conduct, control, direct, govern, guide, manage, operate, preside (over), regulate, run, steward; guard, patrol, protect, safeguard, shield; baby, babysit, chaperone (*or* chaperon), mother, shepherd
phrases look after, see after, see to, take care of
near antonyms abandon, disregard, forget, ignore, neglect, pass over
2 to look after or assist the growth of by labor and care ⟨lately I haven't been doing a good job of *tending* my garden⟩ — see GROW 1
3 to work by plowing, sowing, and raising crops on ⟨plots that during the war were *tended* by city dwellers as vegetable gardens⟩ — see FARM
4 to look after and make decisions about ⟨the dying patriarch wondered who would *tend* the family business after he was gone⟩ — see CONDUCT 1

tendency *n* **1** an established pattern of behavior ⟨a *tendency* to drop things⟩ ⟨a *tendency* to make snap judgments⟩
synonyms aptness, proneness, propensity, way
related words affinity, aptitude, bent, disposition, inclination, leaning, mind-set, partiality, penchant, predilection, predisposition, proclivity, turn; custom, habit, pattern, practice (*also* practise), routine, wont; eccentricity, idiosyncrasy, oddity, peculiarity, quirk, singularity, trick
near antonyms averseness, disinclination, dislike, indisposition
2 a prevailing or general movement or inclination ⟨we'll be seeing a *tendency* for skirt lengths to get shorter this coming season⟩ — see TREND 1
3 a habitual attraction to some activity or thing ⟨a youth with a natural *tendency* toward arts and crafts instead of sports⟩ — see INCLINATION 1

tendentiousness *n* an attitude that always favors one way of feeling or acting especially without considering any other possibilities ⟨the palpable and unrelenting *tendentiousness* that pervades her every political pronouncement⟩ — see BIAS 1

tender *adj* **1** easily injured without careful handling ⟨a *tender* wound⟩ ⟨*tender* plants that cannot take the cold⟩ ⟨*tender* pride that got bruised when his girlfriend dumped him⟩
synonyms delicate, fragile, frail, sensitive
related words breakable, brittle, crushable, eggshell, frangible, friable; feeble, flimsy, puny, slight, soft, tenuous, weak; nonhardy, perishable, resistless, susceptible, unresistant, vulnerable, yielding
near antonyms durable, firm, flinty, hard, hardy, resistant, robust, rugged, solid, sound, stiff, stout, strong, sturdy, substantial; infrangible, nonbreakable, unbreakable; hardened, inured, strengthened, tempered, toughened
antonyms tough
2 feeling or showing love ⟨a *tender* embrace between father and daughter⟩ — see LOVING 1
3 having or marked by sympathy and consideration for others ⟨an especially *tender* teacher who loves having kids with special educational needs in her class⟩ — see HUMANE 1
4 lacking bodily strength ⟨a very *tender* child who always seems to be sick⟩ — see WEAK 1
5 not harsh or stern especially in nature or effect ⟨his *tender* comments on how to improve her writing style were gratefully received⟩ — see GENTLE 1

tender *n* something (as pieces of stamped metal or printed paper) customarily and legally used as a medium of exchange, a measure of value, or a means of payment ⟨money from that board game is not legal *tender* and can't be exchanged for goods or services⟩ — see MONEY 1

tender *vb* to put before another for acceptance or consideration ⟨the coach *tendered* his resignation and started a new career as a physical therapist⟩ — see OFFER 1

tenderfoot *n* a person who is just starting out in a field of activity ⟨skateboarders who are *tenderfeet* will inevitably fall as they learn their first moves⟩ — see BEGINNER

tenderhearted *adj* **1** feeling or showing love ⟨a *tender-*

hearted new mother⟩ — see LOVING 1
2 having or marked by sympathy and consideration for others ⟨a *tenderhearted* offer of help for the victims of the earthquake⟩ — see HUMANE 1

tenderheartedness *n* sympathetic concern for the well-being of others ⟨a hard-nosed businessman, better known for his tough-mindedness than for his *tenderheartedness*⟩ — see BENIGNANCY

tenderness *n* sympathetic concern for the well-being of others ⟨a self-made business powerhouse, she didn't make her fortune by womanly displays of *tenderness*⟩ — see BENIGNANCY

tending *adj* having a tendency to be or act in a certain way ⟨men *tending* toward daily exercise will significantly reduce their risk of cardiac arrest⟩ — see PRONE 1

tenebrific *adj* **1** being without light or without much light ⟨a man unexpectedly emerged from the *tenebrific* shadows of the cave⟩ — see DARK 1
2 causing or marked by an atmosphere lacking in cheer ⟨soldiers who had lived for months in the *tenebrific* trenches that stretched along the western front⟩ — see GLOOMY 1

tenebrous *adj* **1** being without light or without much light ⟨a *tenebrous* night with no moon⟩ — see DARK 1
2 causing or marked by an atmosphere lacking in cheer ⟨in the midst of those *tenebrous* days Thomas Paine penned the immortal words "These are the times that try men's souls"⟩ — see GLOOMY 1

tenement *n* a room or set of rooms in a private house or a block used as a separate dwelling place ⟨an exhibit of pictures showing the *tenements* of the New York City neighborhood of Hell's Kitchen during the 1920s⟩ — see APARTMENT 1

tense *adj* **1** feeling or showing uncomfortable feelings of uncertainty ⟨was *tense* about the upcoming bar exam⟩ — see NERVOUS 1
2 marked by or causing agitation or uncomfortable feelings ⟨a *tense* relationship existed between the two teachers⟩ — see NERVOUS 2
3 stretched with little or no give ⟨a *tense* rope⟩ — see TAUT

tense *vb* to draw tight ⟨he *tensed* his muscles and attempted to lift the heavy appliance onto the truck⟩ — see TIGHTEN

tension *n* the burden on one's emotional or mental well-being created by demands on one's time ⟨under a lot of *tension* right now about her decision not to go to college⟩ — see STRESS 1

tent *n* a raised covering over something for decoration or protection ⟨a huge *tent* was erected for the outdoor wedding reception⟩ — see CANOPY

tentative *adj* determined by something else ⟨our plans are only *tentative* at this point and will depend on whether you can come⟩ — see DEPENDENT 2

tenty *also* **tentie** *adj, Scottish* paying close attention usually for the purpose of anticipating approaching danger or opportunity ⟨I warn ye now, ye best be *tenty*⟩ — see ALERT 1

tenure *n* a fixed period of time during which a person holds a job or position ⟨during his *tenure* as president the college experienced steady growth⟩ — see TERM 1

tepid *adj* **1** showing little or no interest or enthusiasm ⟨the proposed table tennis club met with only a *tepid* response⟩
synonyms halfhearted, lukewarm, uneager, unenthusiastic
related words apathetic, disinterested, dispassionate, emotionless, impassive, indifferent, neutral, uncaring, uninterested; lackadaisical, languid, listless, perfunctory, undemonstrative, unemotional, unresponsive; unfeeling, unsympathetic; chill, chilly, cold, cool, frigid, frosty, glacial, icy, unfriendly, wintry (*also* wintery)
near antonyms agog, ardent, avid, exuberant, fervid, feverish, fiery, gung ho, hot-blooded, impassioned, intense, raring, red-hot, vehement; engaged, engrossed, interested; ready, willing; cordial, friendly, genial, warmhearted
antonyms eager, enthusiastic, hearty, keen, passionate, warm, wholehearted
2 having or giving off heat to a moderate degree ⟨make sure the water for the footbath is just *tepid* or you'll burn yourself⟩ — see WARM 1

tepidity *n* the quality or state of being moderate in temperature ⟨bathers enjoying the soothing *tepidity* of the waters at the health spa⟩ — see WARMTH 1

tepidness *n* the quality or state of being moderate in temperature ⟨the *tepidness* of the soup suggested it had been sitting on the counter for a while⟩ — see WARMTH 1

tergiversate *vb* to avoid giving a definite answer or position ⟨shamelessly *tergiversating*, the witness replied, "Well, it depends upon what your definition of 'truth' is"⟩ — see EQUIVOCATE

tergiversation *n* deliberate evasion in speech ⟨like most politicians, he has the gift for *tergiversation*⟩ — see CIRCUMLOCUTION 1

term *n* **1** a fixed period of time during which a person holds a job or position ⟨elected for a two-year *term* as mayor⟩
synonyms hitch, stint, tenure, tour
related words shift, watch; go, turn; duration, standing, time; cycle, span, spell, stretch; life, life span, lifetime, run
2 a pronounceable series of letters having a distinct meaning especially in a particular field ⟨what's the *term* for the odd feeling that you've experienced an event before?⟩ — see WORD 1

term *vb* to give a name to ⟨the armed forces began a rescue mission *termed* Operation In and Out⟩ — see NAME 1

termagant *n* a bad-tempered scolding woman ⟨living with that *termagant* was almost as bad as living with a rabid dog⟩ — see SHREW

terminal *adj* **1** following all others of the same kind in order or time ⟨took me to the *terminal* point of that bus route⟩ — see LAST 1
2 likely to cause or capable of causing death ⟨a form of cancer that is usually *terminal*⟩ — see DEADLY 1

terminate *vb* **1** to bring (an event) to a natural or appropriate stopping point ⟨we need to *terminate* the discussion for this evening, but we'll resume tomorrow morning⟩ — see CLOSE 3
2 to come to an end ⟨this class will *terminate* with the arrival of Memorial Day⟩ — see CEASE 1
3 to mark the limits of ⟨*terminated* the area set aside for the runners to change their clothes with a series of folding screens⟩ — see LIMIT 2
4 to put to death deliberately ⟨the operative's covert mission was to *terminate* the leader of the opposition⟩ — see MURDER 1
5 to let go from office, service, or employment ⟨he was *terminated* for constantly coming in to work late⟩ — see DISMISS 1

terminated *adj* brought or having come to an end ⟨peace talks have now been *terminated*⟩ — see COMPLETE 2

terminating *adj* following all others of the same kind in order or time ⟨the *terminating* speech of the political convention turned out to be the most inspiring⟩ — see LAST 1

termination *n* **1** a real or imaginary point beyond which a person or thing cannot go ⟨I've reached the *termination* of my patience with you bratty kids⟩ — see LIMIT 1

2 the act of ceasing to exist ⟨feels that the voluntary *termination* of one's life should be left entirely up to the patient⟩ — see DEATH 3
3 the stopping of a process or activity ⟨at the *termination* of the movie, please throw away any empty food containers in the appropriate bins⟩ — see END 1

terminology *n* the special terms or expressions of a particular group or field ⟨the *terminology* favored by sportscasters⟩ ⟨medical *terminology* that can be hard for the patient to understand⟩
synonyms argot, cant, dialect, jargon, jive, language, lingo, patois, patter, shop, shoptalk, slang, vocabulary
related words colloquial, colloquialism, idiom, localism, parlance, pidgin, provincialism, regionalism, speech, vernacular, vernacularism; slanguage; bureaucratese, computerese, cyberspeak, educationese, governmentese, journalese, technobabble

terrace *n* a flat roofless structure attached to a building ⟨from their *terraces* residents of the high-rise have panoramic views of the city⟩ — see SUNDECK

terra firma *n* the solid part of our planet's surface as distinguished from the sea and air ⟨after that nightmarish storm, the sailors were grateful to reach *terra firma*⟩ — see EARTH 2

terrain *n* **1** a region of activity, knowledge, or influence ⟨we're moving into unfamiliar *terrain* if we bring pre-Columbian art into our discussion⟩ — see FIELD 2
2 the physical features of a region as a whole ⟨an analysis of the *terrain* revealed that an invasion force of paratroopers would have their work cut out for them⟩ — see GEOGRAPHY
3 the circumstances, conditions, or objects by which one is surrounded ⟨a new senator getting lost in the foggy *terrain* of double-dealing and deception⟩ — see ENVIRONMENT

terrene *adj* having to do with life on earth especially as opposed to that in heaven ⟨in the expenditure of his psychic energies, he strives to strike a balance between the celestial and the *terrene*⟩ — see EARTHLY

terrestrial *adj* **1** having to do with life on earth especially as opposed to that in heaven ⟨scientists haven't even found all the *terrestrial* life on our planet⟩ — see EARTHLY
2 having to do with the practical details of regular life ⟨let's focus on *terrestrial* issues—such as how to pay the bills⟩ — see MUNDANE 1

terrible *adj* **1** causing fear ⟨a *terrible* nightmare that woke me up⟩ — see FEARFUL 1
2 extreme in degree, power, or effect ⟨I have a *terrible* headache⟩ — see INTENSE 1
3 extremely disturbing or repellent ⟨that is a *terrible* movie to let your six-year-old watch⟩ — see HORRIBLE 1
4 extremely unsatisfactory ⟨this nonfat ice cream is *terrible*⟩ — see WRETCHED 1
5 of low quality ⟨manufactures *terrible* clothes that often tear after a single wash⟩ — see CHEAP 2

terribly *adv* to a great degree ⟨I'm *terribly* sorry to bother you⟩ — see VERY 1

terrific *adj* **1** of the very best kind ⟨you've done a *terrific* job on this report⟩ — see EXCELLENT
2 extremely disturbing or repellent ⟨a *terrific* murder that sickened even hard-bitten police officers⟩ — see HORRIBLE 1

terrified *adj* filled with fear or dread ⟨*terrified* dogs hiding under the couch⟩ — see AFRAID

terrify *vb* to strike with fear ⟨the prospect of speaking in front of a huge crowd of people absolutely *terrifies* me⟩ — see FRIGHTEN

terrifying *adj* causing fear ⟨heard a *terrifying* noise coming from the next room⟩ — see FEARFUL 1

territory *n* the place where a plant or animal is usually or naturally found ⟨that plant's *territory* extends from Georgia all the way north to Maine⟩ — see HOME 2

terror *n* **1** a source of persistent emotional distress ⟨after the death of her father, fear of developing cancer became one of the *terrors* of her life⟩ — see DEMON 2
2 the emotion experienced in the presence or threat of danger ⟨the reports of a serial killer on the loose struck *terror* into our hearts⟩ — see FEAR 1

terrorize *vb* to strike with fear ⟨thunderstorms *terrorize* our cats, who all scamper downstairs when lightning flashes⟩ — see FRIGHTEN

terrorized *adj* filled with fear or dread ⟨the *terrorized* victims didn't know where to run during the bombing raid⟩ — see AFRAID

terse *adj* marked by the use of few words to convey much information or meaning ⟨could tell from his *terse* replies to my questions that he was in no mood to talk⟩ — see CONCISE

tersely *adv* in a few words ⟨she stated her dissatisfaction rather *tersely* with a simple "I don't approve"⟩ — see SHORTLY 1

terseness *n* the quality or state of being marked by or using only few words to convey much meaning ⟨the *terseness* of my replies simply meant that I was too busy to talk at that time⟩ — see SUCCINCTNESS

test *n* **1** a procedure or operation carried out to resolve an uncertainty ⟨will need to run some *tests* on the blood sample to rule out blood poisoning⟩ — see EXPERIMENT
2 a set of questions or problems designed to assess knowledge, skills, or intelligence ⟨applicants for the cashier's position must first take a simple math *test*⟩ — see EXAMINATION 1

test *vb* **1** to put (something) to a test ⟨please *test* this sample for the presence of lead⟩ — see TRY (OUT)
2 to subject (a personal quality or faculty) to often excessive stress ⟨all of these unnecessary questions are *testing* my patience⟩ — see TRY 1

testament *n* **1** something presented in support of the truth or accuracy of a claim ⟨the "before" and "after" pictures are a *testament* to the effectiveness of the weight loss program⟩ — see PROOF
2 the basic beliefs or guiding principles of a person or group ⟨Jefferson's collected writings constitute his political *testament*⟩ — see CREED 1

testify *vb* to make a solemn declaration under oath for the purpose of establishing a fact ⟨several witnesses *testified* that they had seen the accused in the vicinity of the crime scene⟩
synonyms attest, depose, swear, witness
related words verify; vouch; promise, vow
phrases bear witness

testify (to) *vb* to declare (something) to be true or genuine ⟨that auction house will always *testify to* a painting's authenticity⟩ — see CERTIFY 1

testimonial *n* something presented in support of the truth or accuracy of a claim ⟨her performance in this tournament has been a *testimonial* to the dedication and talent she brings to the tennis court⟩ — see PROOF

testimony *n* something presented in support of the truth or accuracy of a claim ⟨the plaintiff's case rests largely on the *testimony* of several scientists with no known expertise in that field⟩ — see PROOF

testiness *n* readiness to show annoyance or impatience ⟨attributed his unusual *testiness* this morning to being hungry⟩ — see PETULANCE

testing *adj* requiring considerable physical or mental effort ⟨beginning rock climbers should choose a less *testing* route to the summit⟩ — see HARD 2

testy *adj* easily irritated or annoyed ⟨that coworker would be easier to get along with if she weren't so *testy* all the time⟩ — see IRRITABLE

tetchy *adj* easily offended ⟨a morose and *tetchy* resident of a nursing home⟩ — see TOUCHY 1

tête–à–tête *adv* in person and usually privately ⟨met *tête-à-tête* with the student's parents to discuss his disciplinary problems in class⟩

synonyms face-to-face, personally

related words familiarly, intimately; confidentially, secretly; directly, immediately

phrases in private, in secret

near antonyms distantly, indirectly; openly, publicly

tête–à–tête *n* friendly, informal conversation or an instance of this ⟨had a quick *tête-à-tête* with my neighbor before heading off to work⟩ — see CHAT 1

text *n* a book used for instruction in a subject ⟨the school's science curriculum suffers from a serious lack of up-to-date *texts*⟩ — see TEXTBOOK

textbook *adj* constituting, serving as, or worthy of being a pattern to be imitated ⟨a *textbook* example of a film that captures the feel of the novel on which it is based⟩ — see MODEL

textbook *n* a book used for instruction in a subject ⟨one shelf in my bookcase is crammed full of my old college *textbooks*⟩

synonyms handbook, manual, primer, text

related words schoolbook; grammar, reader, speller; tract, treatise; dictionary, lexicon, vocabulary, wordbook; casebook, encyclopedia, reference; bible, guide, guidebook

textile *n* a woven or knitted material (as of cotton or nylon) ⟨brought back a whole suitcase of beautiful *textiles* from India⟩ — see CLOTH 1

thankful *adj* **1** experiencing pleasure, satisfaction, or delight ⟨we were *thankful* that someone else was footing the bill for the lavish wedding banquet⟩ — see GLAD 1

2 feeling or expressing gratitude ⟨I am *thankful* for all your help⟩ — see GRATEFUL 1

thankfulness *n* acknowledgment of having received something good from another ⟨expressed her *thankfulness* for helping her move by taking us all out for dinner⟩ — see THANKS

thankless *adj* **1** not showing gratitude ⟨a *thankless* boss who seems oblivious to the extra effort his subordinates have made⟩

synonyms unappreciative, ungrateful

related words rude, thoughtless, ungracious

near antonyms beholden, indebted; gratified, pleased; courteous, gracious, thoughtful

antonyms appreciative, grateful, obliged, thankful

2 not likely to be appreciated by those who benefit ⟨the *thankless* job of cleaning up after a party⟩

synonyms unappreciated, ungrateful

related words uncredited, underappreciated, underrated, undervalued, unnoticed, unrecognized, unrewarded, unsung, unvalued

near antonyms credited, esteemed, honored, prized, recognized, regarded, rewarded, valued; creditable, meritorious, praiseworthy

antonyms appreciated

thanklessness *n* failure or refusal to acknowledge receipt of something good from another ⟨the mayor has become used to the unthinking *thanklessness* of the people he's trying to serve⟩ — see INGRATITUDE

thanks *n pl* acknowledgment of having received something good from another ⟨to express our *thanks*, we'd like to present you with this plaque⟩

synonyms appreciation, appreciativeness, gratefulness, gratitude, thankfulness

related words thanksgiving; gratification, indebtedness, satisfaction; acknowledgment (*or* acknowledgement), recognition, tribute

antonyms ingratitude, thanklessness, unappreciation, ungratefulness

that *adv* to a great degree ⟨the hotel isn't *that* far from the beach⟩ — see VERY 1

thaumaturgy *n* the power to control natural forces through supernatural means ⟨a macabre tale about a woman who uses *thaumaturgy* to bring her dead lover back to life⟩ — see MAGIC 1

thaw *vb* to go from a solid to a liquid state ⟨will have to let the apple juice concentrate *thaw* before you can mix it with water⟩ — see LIQUEFY

thawed *adj* freed from a frozen state by exposure to warmth ⟨recommends cooking *thawed* fish within 24 hours⟩

synonyms defrosted, unfrozen

related words liquefied, melted, molten; deiced; heated, warmed

near antonyms chilled, iced, refrigerated; quick-frozen, refrozen, supercooled; congealed, glaciated, semisolid; frostbitten, frosty, icy

antonyms frozen

theater *or* **theatre** *n* **1** a building or part of a building where movies are shown ⟨there's still one *theater* in town that shows independent films⟩

synonyms cinema, playhouse

related words nickelodeon; megaplex, multiplex, plex (*or* 'plex); art house, art theater, cinematheque; fleapit [*British*], grind house; drive-in

2 the public performance of plays ⟨have been fascinated by the *theater* ever since I was a child⟩ — see DRAMA 1

3 a large room or building for enclosed public gatherings ⟨the lecturer waited until the *theater* was full before beginning⟩ — see HALL 3

theatrical *also* **theatric** *adj* **1** given to or marked by attention-getting behavior suggestive of stage acting ⟨after stepping out of their hired limousine, the prom couple made a *theatrical* entrance in their evening clothes⟩

synonyms dramatic, hammy, histrionic, melodramatic, stagy (*or* stagey)

related words actorish, actorly, actressy; overacted, overdone, sensational, staged; conspicuous, elaborate, flamboyant, grandiose, ostentatious, showy; affected, artificial, exaggerated, mannered, pretentious, self-conscious, studied, unnatural

near antonyms nondramatic, nontheatrical, unaffected, underplayed, unpretentious; muted, restrained, subdued, toned (down); conservative, discreet, inconspicuous; modest, plain, quiet, simple

antonyms undramatic

2 having the general quality or effect of a stage performance ⟨in a very *theatrical* voice the actress announced to the gathering that she did not sign autographs⟩ — see DRAMATIC 1

theatricals *n pl* the public performance of plays ⟨has been involved in amateur *theatricals* for most of his adult life⟩ — see DRAMA 1

theatrics *n pl* the public performance of plays ⟨before her first film role, her acting experience had been limited to amateur *theatrics*⟩ — see DRAMA 1

theft *n* **1** the unlawful taking and carrying away of property without the consent of its owner ⟨while violent crime in the city has decreased dramatically, rates of *theft* and vandalism have risen slightly⟩

synonyms larceny, robbery, stealing, thievery

related words burglary, housebreaking; embezzlement, embezzling, graft, misapplication, misappropriation, peculation; petit larceny, petty larceny; filching, pilferage, pilfering, purloining, shoplifting; abduction, carjacking, hijacking (*also* highjacking), kidnapping (*also* kidnaping), shanghaiing; despoilment, despoliation, looting, pillage, plundering, rapine, spoliation; poaching, rustling; black marketeering, smuggling; banditry, piracy

2 an instance of theft ⟨the police found the stolen car an hour after the *theft* was reported⟩
synonyms grab, heist, pinch, rip-off, snatching, swiping
related words break-in, burglary, holdup, mugging, stickup

theme *n* **1** a major object of interest or concern (as in a discussion or artistic composition) ⟨this dance piece deals with the timeless *themes* of birth and death⟩ — see MATTER 1
2 a short piece of writing done as a school exercise ⟨please write a one page *theme* on the main character of this book⟩ — see COMPOSITION 2
3 a short piece of writing typically expressing a point of view ⟨the magazine will award a scholarship to the student who writes the best *theme* on the concept of personal freedom⟩ — see ESSAY 1

then *adv* in addition to what has been said ⟨there's the cost of the car itself, and *then* there's the cost of insurance and maintenance⟩ — see MORE 1

theoretical *also* **theoretic** *adj* **1** existing only as an assumption or speculation ⟨the merits of the new testing procedures are purely *theoretical*, since no one has ever used them before⟩
synonyms academic (*also* academical), conjectural, hypothetical, speculative, suppositional
related words alleged, assumed, presumed, presupposed, proposed, supposed, unproved, unproven, untested; debatable, moot; abstract, conceptual, intellectual, metaphysical; nonclinical, nonpractical; nonempirical
near antonyms clinical, practical; concrete, defined, definite, distinct; attested, authenticated, confirmed, demonstrated, established, proven, substantiated, tested, time-tested, validated, verified; empirical (*also* empiric), nonspeculative, nontheoretical, observational
antonyms actual, factual, real
2 dealing with or expressing a quality or idea ⟨the *theoretical* musings in his new book are less engaging than the anecdote-driven arguments of his previous works⟩ — see ABSTRACT 1

theory *n* an idea that is the starting point for making a case or conducting an investigation ⟨set out to prove her *theory* that people can't really taste any difference between colas, so they buy according to the product's image⟩
synonyms hypothesis, proposition, supposition, thesis
related words assumption, concession, premise (*also* premiss), presumption, presupposition, theorem; conjecture, generalization, guess, guesswork, inference, speculation, surmise; proffer, proposal, suggestion; feeling, hunch, impression, inkling, notion, suspicion; abstraction, concept, conception, construct
near antonyms assurance, certainty, fact, knowledge

therapeutic *adj* tending to cure disease or restore health ⟨gentle exercise can be *therapeutic* for hospital patients⟩ — see MEDICINAL 1

therapeutic *n* something that corrects or counteracts something undesirable ⟨some charitable work might be the best *therapeutic* for that guy's total self-absorption⟩ — see CURE 1

therapy *n* something that corrects or counteracts something undesirable ⟨talking over my problem with you has been good *therapy*⟩ — see CURE 1

thereafter *adv* following in time or place ⟨gave his farewell speech and left the room shortly *thereafter*⟩ — see AFTER

therefore *adv* for this or that reason ⟨it's snowing hard; *therefore* I think we should stay home⟩
synonyms accordingly, consequently, ergo, hence, so, thereupon, thus, wherefore
phrases in consequence

theretofore *adv* up to this or that time ⟨*theretofore* the couple hadn't given much thought to marriage, but the unplanned pregnancy changed everything⟩ — see HITHERTO

thereupon *adv* for this or that reason ⟨she didn't get into the college of her choice and *thereupon* decided to study for a year before retaking the college entrance exams⟩ — see THEREFORE

theriac *n* something that cures all ills or problems ⟨the wizard's attempts to concoct a *theriac* for the king came to naught⟩ — see CURE-ALL

thesis *n* **1** an idea or opinion that is put forth in a discussion or debate ⟨put forth the *thesis* that the electronic media's coverage of politics trivializes the workings of our democracy⟩ — see CONTENTION 1
2 an idea that is the starting point for making a case or conducting an investigation ⟨it is not clear how the arguments you make actually support your *thesis*⟩ — see THEORY

thesp *n* one who acts professionally (as in a play, movie, or television show) ⟨a brawling actor who is in danger of becoming better known as a thug than as a *thesp*⟩ — see ACTOR 1

thespian *n* one who acts professionally (as in a play, movie, or television show) ⟨although she's "acted" in a couple of horror movies, I'd hardly call her one of our more promising *thespians*⟩ — see ACTOR 1

thew *n* muscular strength ⟨a prizefighter of unparalleled *thew* in the boxing world⟩ — see MUSCLE 1

thick *adj* **1** having or being of relatively great depth or extent from one surface to its opposite ⟨a *thick* board was laid across the pit⟩
synonyms chunky, fat
related words blockish, blocky, bulky, dense, hefty, thickish; broad, deep, wide
near antonyms narrow, shallow
antonyms skinny, slender, slim, thin
2 being of a consistency that resists flow ⟨*thick* maple syrup for pancakes⟩
synonyms ropy (*also* ropey), syrupy, viscid, viscous
related words creamy, heavy, slushy, thickened, thickish, turbid, undiluted; semifluid, semiliquid; gluey, glutinous, sticky; gelatinous, gooey, gummy, jellylike; concentrated, condensed
near antonyms flowing, fluid; dilute, diluted, liquid, watered-down, weak
antonyms runny, soupy, thin, watery
3 closely acquainted ⟨those two have been *thick* since grade school⟩ — see FAMILIAR 1
4 having a greater than usual measure across ⟨cross your name off the list with a really *thick* line so I can see it⟩ — see WIDE 1
5 having little space between items or parts ⟨a hedge *thick* with gorse bushes⟩ — see CLOSE 1
6 not having or showing an ability to absorb ideas readily ⟨couldn't believe that his guests were so *thick* that they were missing his hints that it was time to leave⟩ — see STUPID 1
7 possessing or covered with great numbers or amounts of something specified ⟨a meadow *thick* with wildflowers⟩ — see RIFE

thick *n* the most intense or characteristic phase of something ⟨in the *thick* of winter many Northerners are dreaming of tropical islands⟩
synonyms deep, depth, height, middle, midst
related words center, heart

thicket *n* a thick patch of shrubbery, small trees, or underbrush ⟨flushed a pheasant from a *thicket* of willows⟩
synonyms boscage (*also* boskage), bosk (*or* bosque), bosquet, brake, brushwood, chaparral, coppice, copse, covert
related words canebrake; brush, bush, scrub, scrub-

land; bramble, jungle, tangle; grove, hedge, stand, woodlot; forest, greenwood, wildwood, wood, woodland

thickhead *n* a stupid person ⟨a real *thickhead* when confronted with anything mechanical⟩ — see IDIOT

thickheaded *adj* not having or showing an ability to absorb ideas readily ⟨don't suppose that he's *thickheaded* just because he doesn't understand English very well⟩ — see STUPID 1

thickness *n* **1** the degree to which a fluid can resist flowing ⟨beat the eggs and sugar until the mixture has the *thickness* of heavy cream⟩ — see CONSISTENCY

2 the quality or state of lacking intelligence or quickness of mind ⟨he's an incredibly bright engineer, but he displays all the *thickness* of a turkey when it comes to personal relationships⟩ — see STUPIDITY 1

thickset *adj* being compact and broad in build and often short in stature ⟨a short, *thickset* bulldog⟩ — see STOCKY

thick–skinned *adj* having or showing a lack of sympathy or tender feelings ⟨was so *thick-skinned* that she was clueless about the fact that the joke had hurt her friend's feelings⟩ — see HARD 1

thick–witted *adj* not having or showing an ability to absorb ideas readily ⟨one of the most time-honored clichés of teen comedies: the *thick-witted* high school jock⟩ — see STUPID 1

thief *n* one who steals ⟨a *thief* has been stealing wallets and valuables from the lockers at the gym⟩

synonyms larcenist, pincher, purloiner, robber, stealer

related words burglar, cat burglar, cracksman, housebreaker, picklock, safecracker; embezzler, grafter; klepto, kleptomaniac; sneak thief; cutpurse, dip [*slang*], pickpocket, pilferer, shoplifter; abductor, carjacker, hijacker, kidnapper (*also* kidnaper), skyjacker; despoiler, looter, pillager, plunderer, ransacker, ravisher; poacher, rustler, smuggler; bandit, footpad, highwayman, pirate; mugger

thieve *vb* to take (something) without right and with an intent to keep ⟨someone's been *thieving* my cookies!⟩ — see STEAL 1

thievery *n* the unlawful taking and carrying away of property without the consent of its owner ⟨a man who has a history of petty *thievery* and narcotics peddling⟩ — see THEFT 1

thimblerig *vb* to rob by the use of trickery or threats ⟨had the feeling that I had just been *thimblerigged* by the sweetest-looking old lady⟩ — see FLEECE

thin *adj* **1** having a noticeably small amount of body fat ⟨after her bout with pneumonia, she looked *thinner*⟩

synonyms bony (*also* boney), fatless, lean, lithe, skinny, slender, slim, spare, svelte

related words clean-limbed, trim; sylphlike, willowy; angular, rawboned, scraggy, scrawny, sinewy, wiry; lank, lanky, rangy, reedy, spindling, spindly, stringy, twiggy, waspish, weedy; anorectic (*also* anoretic), anorexic, cadaverous, emaciated, gaunt, haggard, pinched, skeletal, wasted, wizened; meager (*or* meagre), puny, slight

near antonyms beefy, bulky, chunky, fleshy, heavy, heavyset, stocky, stout, thick, thickset, weighty; brawny, burly, husky; dumpy, pudgy, roly-poly, squat, stubby; paunchy, potbellied; flabby, soft; buxom, zaftig (*also* zoftig); fleshed-out, full, hippy, round

antonyms chubby, corpulent, fat, gross, obese, overweight, plump, portly, rotund, tubby

2 being of less than usual width ⟨the *thin* threads of a cobweb⟩ — see NARROW 1

3 not containing very much of some important element ⟨the evidence for that oddball theory is pretty *thin*⟩ — see WEAK 3

thin *vb* to alter (something) for the worse with the addition of foreign or lower-grade substances ⟨*thinned* the cream with milk but didn't tell anyone⟩ — see ADULTERATE

thing *n* **1** a member of the human race ⟨you poor *thing*, you must be exhausted⟩ — see HUMAN

2 one that has a real and independent existence ⟨the *thing* to which the subject of the sentence refers⟩ — see ENTITY

3 something done by someone ⟨one of the *things* you can do is to help me clean up⟩ — see ACTION 1

4 something material that can be perceived by the senses ⟨can you hand me that *thing* over there?⟩ — see OBJECT 1

5 something produced by physical or intellectual effort ⟨just the latest *thing* from her fertile imagination⟩ — see PRODUCT 1

6 something that happens ⟨the burglary was just one of those *things* that can happen anywhere⟩ — see EVENT 1

7 something that one hopes or intends to accomplish ⟨the important *thing* is that we get the project back on schedule⟩ — see GOAL

8 something to be dealt with ⟨I have lots of *things* to do this afternoon⟩ — see MATTER 2

9 things *pl* transportable items that one owns ⟨gather your *things* and get out⟩ — see POSSESSION 2

10 something for which a person shows a special talent ⟨math just isn't my *thing*⟩ — see FORTE

thingamabob *n* a small article the actual name of which one either does not know or cannot remember ⟨a drawer for all the *thingamabobs* that have fallen or broken off various items around the house⟩ — see DOODAD 1

thingamajig *or* **thingumajig** *n* a small article the actual name of which one either does not know or cannot remember ⟨reattach that *thingamajig* and the machine should work⟩ — see DOODAD 1

thingness *n* the fact of being or of being real ⟨conceptual artists have taken the *thingness* out of art, asserting that the artistic vision is embodied in the concept and not in any particular object⟩ — see EXISTENCE

thingummy *n* a small article the actual name of which one either does not know or cannot remember ⟨an antiques store filled with *thingummies* from the horse-and-buggy days⟩ — see DOODAD 1

think *vb* to have as an opinion ⟨I *think* we should wait for someone to come help us out⟩ — see BELIEVE 2

think (about *or* **over)** *vb* to give serious and careful thought to ⟨I'll have to *think over* everything you've said before deciding what to do⟩ — see PONDER

think (of) *vb* to bring back to mind ⟨that postcard from Florida makes me *think of* all the fun we used to have there as kids⟩ — see REMEMBER

think (up) *vb* to create or think of by clever use of the imagination ⟨the marketing department is trying to *think up* better ways to pitch our product to younger consumers⟩ — see INVENT

thinker *n* **1** a very smart person ⟨she's a very nice person, but she's no great *thinker*⟩ — see GENIUS 1

2 the part of a person that feels, thinks, perceives, wills, and especially reasons ⟨loves crossword puzzles, bridge, and other pastimes that makes her use the old *thinker*⟩ — see MIND 1

thinking *adj* having the ability to reason ⟨it's surprising to find *thinking* people who believe such nonsense⟩ — see RATIONAL 1

thinned *adj* **1** containing foreign or lower-grade substances ⟨genuine maple syrup *thinned* with corn syrup⟩ — see IMPURE 1

2 not containing very much of some important element ⟨the *thinned* iced tea that the restaurant serves is barely distinguishable from water⟩ — see WEAK 3

thin–skinned *adj* easily offended ⟨she only laughed at

the teasing, but a more *thin-skinned* person would have gotten angry⟩ — see TOUCHY 1

thirst *n* **1** a strong wish for something ⟨his *thirst* for knowledge is evident in his book-filled house⟩ — see DESIRE 1
2 urgent desire or interest ⟨an unquenchable *thirst* for travel that has led her to the far corners of the globe⟩ — see EAGERNESS

thirst (for) *vb* to have an earnest wish to own or enjoy ⟨his wife has always *thirsted for* a more affluent lifestyle than their salaries would allow⟩ — see DESIRE 1

thirstiness *n* a strong wish for something ⟨the only way to satisfy that *thirstiness* for a new job is to start looking⟩ — see DESIRE 1

thirsty *adj* **1** marked by little or no precipitation or humidity ⟨struggling to survive in that hot and *thirsty* climate⟩ — see DRY 1
2 showing urgent desire or interest ⟨young athletes *thirsty* for a chance to prove themselves⟩ — see EAGER
3 able to soak up liquids especially readily ⟨guest bathrooms are furnished with luxuriously thick, *thirsty* towels⟩ — see ABSORBENT

this *adj* being the less far of two ⟨some of the best restaurants are on *this* side of town⟩ — see NEAR 1

thistly *adj* having leaves or branches which are likely to cause a scratch ⟨caught her sleeve on a *thistly* bush⟩ — see SCRATCHY 1

thorn *n* something that is a source of irritation ⟨your constant questions are a *thorn* in my side⟩ — see ANNOYANCE 3

thorny *adj* **1** having leaves or branches which are likely to cause a scratch ⟨stay out of the *thorny* brambles unless you want a ton of scratches⟩ — see SCRATCHY 1
2 requiring exceptional skill or caution in performance or handling ⟨the candidate tried to avoid discussing his views on the *thorny* issue of abortion⟩ — see TRICKY 1

thorough *adj* **1** having no exceptions or restrictions ⟨had *thorough* access to the files for her research⟩ — see ABSOLUTE 2
2 including many small descriptive features ⟨*thorough* analysis of the current crisis in Asia⟩ — see DETAILED 1
3 trying all possibilities ⟨a *thorough* search of the building that turned up no evidence of a bomb⟩ — see EXHAUSTIVE 1
4 covering everything or all important points ⟨a very *thorough* textbook on respiratory disorders⟩ — see ENCYCLOPEDIC

thoroughbred *adj* of unmixed ancestry ⟨a *thoroughbred* dog⟩ — see PUREBRED

thoroughfare *n* a passage cleared for public vehicular travel ⟨one of the city's main *thoroughfares*⟩ — see WAY 1

thoroughgoing *adj* **1** having no exceptions or restrictions ⟨civil rights advocates are hoping for a *thoroughgoing* rejection of the proposed bill⟩ — see ABSOLUTE 2
2 trying all possibilities ⟨a *thoroughgoing* attempt to solve the puzzle and still no luck⟩ — see EXHAUSTIVE 1

thoroughly *adv* **1** with attention to all aspects or details ⟨they searched the grounds *thoroughly* for any sign of the intruder⟩
synonyms completely, comprehensively, detailedly, exhaustively, fully, inside out, minutely, roundly, sweepingly, systematically, through and through, totally
related words meticulously, microscopically; all-out, full blast, intensively; broadly, encyclopedically, extensively, generally, globally, widely; conclusively, consummately, definitely, perfectly
phrases at length, from stem to stern, from the ground up, in detail
near antonyms aimlessly, desultorily, haphazardly, hit-or-miss, randomly; cursorily, imperfectly, inadequately, narrowly, shallowly, sketchily, summarily, superficially; indeterminately, nebulously, vaguely
2 to a full extent or degree ⟨I am *thoroughly* satisfied with her explanation of the events of that evening⟩ — see FULLY 1

though *adv* in spite of that ⟨I know we didn't win, but I was happy with how we played, *though*⟩ — see HOWEVER

though *conj* in spite of the fact that ⟨*though* it has no well-known actors in it, the movie has become the sleeper hit of the summer⟩ — see ALTHOUGH

thought *n* **1** a careful weighing of the reasons for or against something ⟨I'll give your request some *thought* and then let you know what my decision is⟩ — see CONSIDERATION 1
2 something imagined or pictured in the mind ⟨I just had a *thought*: what if we both pitched in and bought him one big present instead of two smaller presents for his birthday?⟩ — see IDEA 1

thoughtful *adj* **1** given to or made with heedful anticipation of the needs and happiness of others ⟨a *thoughtful* offer to watch the neighbors' children on moving day⟩ ⟨a *thoughtful* manager who understands that people's families should be more important than their jobs⟩
synonyms attentive, considerate, kind, solicitous
related words brotherly, good, good-hearted, helpful, hospitable, kindhearted, kindly, neighborly, nice; caring, compassionate, sympathetic, tender; chivalrous, courteous, courtly, gallant, gracious, polite; diplomatic, tactful; deferential, dutiful, obliging, regardful, respectful; altruistic, beneficent, benevolent, benignant, humane, selfless, unselfish; charitable, generous, magnanimous
near antonyms inattentive, uncaring, unheeding; inhospitable, unkind, unkindly; ill-bred, ill-mannered, impolite, rude, uncivil, unmannerly; unhelpful; malevolent, malicious, mean, spiteful
antonyms heedless, inconsiderate, thoughtless, unthinking
2 decided on as a result of careful thought ⟨a *thoughtful* argument for military action⟩ — see DELIBERATE 1
3 given to or marked by long, quiet thinking ⟨was a quiet and *thoughtful* child who rarely spoke but when he did, he almost always had something worthwhile to say⟩ — see CONTEMPLATIVE

thoughtfully *adv* with good reason or courtesy ⟨a restaurant that *thoughtfully* provides the diners with a basket of bread while they await their meals⟩ — see WELL 4

thoughtless *adj* showing a lack of manners or consideration for others ⟨always making *thoughtless* comments that hurt other people's feelings⟩ — see IMPOLITE

thought–out *adj* decided on as a result of careful thought ⟨following an obviously well *thought-out* plan, the terrorists simultaneously exploded eight bombs around the city⟩ — see DELIBERATE 1

thrall *n* **1** a person who is considered the property of another person ⟨I'm not your *thrall*, so you'll have to pick up after yourself⟩ — see SLAVE 1
2 the state of being a slave ⟨a people who still bear the scars of having been in *thrall* for so many years⟩ — see SLAVERY 1

thralldom *or* **thraldom** *n* the state of being a slave ⟨having known only *thralldom*, the newly emancipated had little idea how to live as freedmen⟩ — see SLAVERY 1

thrash *vb* **1** to defeat by a large margin ⟨the incumbent has been *thrashing* his opponents for so long that there's never any real contest for the Senate seat⟩ — see WHIP 2
2 to strike repeatedly with something long and thin or

flexible ⟨*thrashed* the poor horse with a riding crop⟩ — see WHIP 1

3 to strike repeatedly ⟨the tree branches *thrashed* the sides of the house as the storm continued to rage⟩ — see BEAT 1

4 to make jerky or restless movements ⟨in obvious pain, the wounded soldier *thrashed* about his cot⟩ — see FIDGET

thrash (out) *vb* to produce or bring about especially by long or repeated effort ⟨after hours of brainstorming, the writers finally *thrashed out* an extended story arc for the sitcom⟩ — see HAMMER OUT

thread *n* **1** a thin, flexible structure that resembles a hair ⟨the unwary bug was snared in the sticky *threads* of the spider's web⟩ — see HAIR 2

2 threads *pl* covering for the human body ⟨a number of people at the prom complimented me on my "nice *threads*"⟩ — see CLOTHING

thread *vb* **1** to scatter or set here and there among other things ⟨this history book *threads* excerpts from the diaries of pioneer women into its account of the settlement of the West⟩

synonyms interlace, intersperse, interweave, lace, salt, weave, wreathe

related words insert, intermingle, mingle, mix; alternate, juxtapose; amalgamate, assimilate, blend, combine, commingle, embody, fuse, incorporate, integrate, merge

2 to put together into a series by means of or as if by means of a thread ⟨the reporter *threaded* his newspaper articles about the basketball team into a book that was essentially a chronicle of their championship season⟩

synonyms concatenate, string

related words chain, connect, join, link, unite; interlace, intersperse, intertwine, interweave, lace, weave, wreathe

threadbare *adj* **1** showing signs of advanced wear and tear and neglect ⟨bought a *threadbare* couch at a garage sale⟩ — see SHABBY 1

2 used or heard so often as to be dull ⟨a novel filled with nothing but *threadbare* clichés⟩ — see STALE 1

3 worn or torn into or as if into rags ⟨I loved that *threadbare* shirt, but after 10 years of wear, it was time to throw it away⟩ — see RAGGED 2

4 lacking money or material possessions ⟨never knew that she had so many *threadbare* relatives until she won the lottery⟩ — see POOR 1

threat *n* something that may cause injury or harm ⟨terrorism is a *threat* to the safety of people everywhere⟩ — see DANGER 2

threaten *vb* to remain poised to inflict harm, danger, or distress on ⟨the powerful hurricane continues to *threaten* the southern coastline⟩

synonyms hang (over), hover (over), impend (over), menace, overhang

related words endanger, hazard, imperil, jeopardize, peril

threatening *adj* **1** giving signs of immediate occurrence ⟨economists warning of a *threatening* recession⟩ — see IMMINENT 1

2 being or showing a sign of evil or calamity to come ⟨a *threatening* silence followed the loud thump in the adjoining motel room⟩ — see OMINOUS

3 involving potential loss or injury ⟨*threatening* rocks lined that narrow stretch of the river through which we would be rafting⟩ — see DANGEROUS 1

three–dimensional *adj* closely resembling the object imitated ⟨an actress who has been acclaimed for her *three-dimensional* portrayal of the celebrated monarch⟩ — see NATURAL 2

threefold *adj* having three units or parts ⟨a *threefold* approach to solving the problem⟩ — see TRIPLE

three–ring circus *n* a place of uproar and confusion ⟨the house has been a *three-ring circus* ever since the kids got back from summer camp⟩ — see MADHOUSE 2

threesome *n* a group of three ⟨the *threesome* has been playing music together since all three were in high school⟩ ⟨you don't see many *threesomes* at honeymoon resorts, but one bride had brought along her mother⟩

synonyms triad, trifecta, trinity, trio, triple, triplet, triumvirate

related words trilogy, triptych; triple crown; triplicate; triplex

threnody *n* a composition expressing one's grief over a loss ⟨the composer's cello concerto was composed as a moving *threnody* for his late wife⟩ — see LAMENT 2

thresh *vb* **1** to make jerky or restless movements ⟨the poor dog *threshed* against his chain⟩ — see FIDGET

2 to strike repeatedly ⟨he *threshed* the whimpering dog with his cane⟩ — see BEAT 1

threshold *n* **1** an interval of time just before the onset of something ⟨on the *threshold* of a new age of green technology⟩ — see POINT 3

2 the point at which something begins ⟨at the *threshold* of the new year, it's time to look back and make resolutions for the future⟩ — see BEGINNING

thrift *n* careful management of material resources ⟨through hard work and *thrift* our father was able to raise the money to put all four of us through college⟩ — see ECONOMY

thriftless *adj* given to spending money freely or foolishly ⟨a *thriftless* girl who didn't keep track of her finances and overspent constantly⟩ — see PRODIGAL

thrifty *adj* careful in the management of money or resources ⟨if you are *thrifty*, you can find ways to decorate your room stylishly yet inexpensively⟩ — see FRUGAL

thrill *n* a pleasurably intense stimulation of the feelings ⟨everyone gets a real *thrill* out of the Independence Day fireworks⟩

synonyms bang, boot, charge, exhilaration, frisson, jollies, kick, rush, titillation, wallop

related words arousal, buzz, electrification, high, intoxication; jolt, shock, surprise (*also* surprize); delectation, delight, enjoyment, joy, lift, pleasure; amusement, diversion, entertainment, fun, treat

thrill *vb* to cause a pleasurable stimulation of the feelings of ⟨I was *thrilled* to hear that you got the promotion that you'd been so desperately wanting⟩

synonyms charge, electrify, excite, exhilarate, galvanize, intoxicate, pump up, titillate, turn on

related words arouse, incite, inspire, provoke, stimulate; bewitch, captivate, charm, delight, enchant, enthrall (*or* enthral), hypnotize, mesmerize, rivet, spellbind; interest, intrigue, tantalize

near antonyms bore, jade, pall, tire, weary; deject, demoralize, discourage, dishearten, dispirit

thriller *n* something (as a close contest) that induces much suspense as to its outcome ⟨those televison awards are hardly *thrillers* since the same people win year after year⟩ — see NAIL-BITER

thrilling *adj* causing great emotional or mental stimulation ⟨a *thrilling* adventure movie⟩ — see EXCITING 1

thrive *vb* **1** to grow vigorously ⟨these plants *thrive* with relatively little sunlight⟩

synonyms burgeon (*also* bourgeon), flourish, prosper

related words luxuriate, overgrow, proliferate, shoot up; germinate, root, sprout; bloom, flower, fruit, produce, propagate, regenerate, seed

2 to reach a desired level of accomplishment ⟨going to a school for gifted students will help him *thrive* as a musical prodigy⟩ — see SUCCEED 2

thriving *adj* **1** having attained a desired end or state of

good fortune ⟨our new landscaping business is *thriving*⟩ — see SUCCESSFUL 1
2 marked by much life, movement, or activity ⟨the once *thriving* downtown has fallen into steep decline since the new mall was built⟩ — see ALIVE 2
3 marked by vigorous growth and well-being especially economically ⟨a *thriving* manufacturing community that is experiencing a tremendous growth in new jobs⟩ — see PROSPEROUS 1

throaty *adj* **1** harsh and dry in sound ⟨had a bad cold and a *throaty* cough to go with it⟩ — see HOARSE
2 having a low musical pitch or range ⟨a *throaty* alto⟩ — see DEEP 2

throb *n* a rhythmic expanding and contracting ⟨I seemed to feel anew the pain of her death with each *throb* of my heart⟩ — see PULSATION

throb *vb* to expand and contract in a rhythmic manner ⟨the car's stereo speakers *throbbing* with the song's bass line⟩ — see PULSATE

throe *n* **1** a sharp unpleasant sensation usually felt in some specific part of the body ⟨collapsed in the *throes* of agony⟩ — see PAIN 1
2 throes *pl* a forceful effort to reach a goal or objective ⟨that third-world country is caught up in the *throes* of a democratic revolution⟩ — see STRUGGLE 1

throng *n* a great number of persons or creatures massed together ⟨grabbed a megaphone and addressed the vast *throng*⟩ — see CROWD 1

throng *vb* to move upon or fill (something) in great numbers ⟨fans *thronged* the field to celebrate the win⟩ — see CROWD 2

thronging *adj* possessing or covered with great numbers or amounts of something specified ⟨the theme park is *thronging* with tourists during the summer⟩ — see RIFE

throttle *vb* to keep (someone) from breathing by exerting pressure on the windpipe ⟨I was so angry at what he was saying that I could have *throttled* him!⟩ — see CHOKE 1

through *adj* brought or having come to an end ⟨a standing ovation for the cast when the play was *through*⟩ — see COMPLETE 2

through *adv* **1** from beginning to end ⟨read the letter *through* twice⟩ ⟨never once missed class the whole year *through*⟩
synonyms around, over, round, throughout
2 from one side to the other of an intervening space ⟨the bullet struck the door and went right *through*⟩ — see OVER 1

through *prep* **1** in or into the middle of ⟨lost control of the car and drove *through* the crowd⟩ — see AMONG
2 in random positions within the boundaries of ⟨the numerous small towns scattered *through* these hills⟩ — see AROUND 2
3 in the course of ⟨thoughtless people talking *through* the whole movie⟩ — see DURING
4 to the opposite side of ⟨walked *through* the room⟩ — see ACROSS 1
5 along the way of ⟨the quickest way out of the building is *through* that hall there⟩ — see BY 1
6 as the result of ⟨won the tournament *through* practice and hard work⟩ — see BECAUSE OF
7 using the means or agency of ⟨apparently got his money *through* theft and deception⟩ — see BY 2

through and through *adv* **1** to a full extent or degree ⟨I know him *through and through*, and he would never do such a cowardly thing⟩ — see FULLY 1
2 with attention to all aspects or details ⟨those UFO claims were examined *through and through* and were found to be completely bogus⟩ — see THOROUGHLY 1

throughout *adv* **1** from beginning to end ⟨while some fans deserted the singer during her troubled years, others remained loyal *throughout*⟩ — see THROUGH 1
2 in every place or in all places ⟨a cake studded *throughout* with raisins⟩ — see EVERYWHERE

throughout *prep* **1** in random positions within the boundaries of ⟨saw red-tailed hawks *throughout* the game preserve⟩ — see AROUND 2
2 in the course of ⟨the actress revealed that she has struggled with depression *throughout* her adult life⟩ — see DURING

throw *n* a risky undertaking ⟨a desperate *throw*, that could jump-start his presidential campaign or end it right there⟩ — see GAMBLE

throw *vb* **1** to send through the air especially with a quick forward motion of the arm ⟨*threw* a life preserver to the drowning man⟩
synonyms cast, catapult, chuck, dash, fire, fling, heave, hurl, hurtle, launch, lob, loft, peg, pelt, pitch, sling, toss
related words bowl, dart, flip, gun, hook, pass, roll, shoot; buck, eject, impel, precipitate, project, propel, rifle, thrust
phrases let fly
2 to cause to fall intentionally or unintentionally ⟨the attacker *threw* his victim to the ground⟩ — see DROP 1

throw (on) *vb* to place on one's person ⟨*threw on* a sweater and headed outside⟩ — see PUT ON 1

throw away *vb* **1** to get rid of as useless or unwanted ⟨I should *throw away* that torn shirt⟩ — see DISCARD
2 to use up carelessly ⟨if you buy a high-end computer, you'll just be *throwing away* money on a bunch of features you'll never use⟩ — see WASTE 1

throw down *vb* to cause to fall intentionally or unintentionally ⟨*throw down* the gun, and put your hands up⟩ — see DROP 1

throw–in *n* something given in addition to what is ordinarily expected or owed ⟨anyone who buys a book today will get a bookmark as a *throw-in*⟩ — see BONUS

throwing away *n* the getting rid of whatever is unwanted or useless ⟨the *throwing away* of her old stuffed animals marked the beginning of her mental preparation for an independent life as a college student⟩ — see DISPOSAL 1

throw off *vb* to draw the attention or mind to something else ⟨the sudden noise just *threw* me *off* completely, and I missed my shot⟩ — see DISTRACT 1

throw out *vb* **1** to drive or force out ⟨the player was *thrown out* of the game after assaulting the ref⟩ — see EJECT 1
2 to get rid of as useless or unwanted ⟨would you mind if I *threw out* that leftover pizza that's been in the fridge for two weeks?⟩ — see DISCARD
3 to throw or give off ⟨the charcoal grill is *throwing out* big billows of black smoke⟩ — see EMIT 1
4 to show unwillingness to accept, do, engage in, or agree to ⟨he'll *throw out* any acting offers that don't meet his standards⟩ — see DECLINE 1

throw over *vb* to show unwillingness to accept, do, engage in, or agree to ⟨if the U.S. Senate *throws over* the treaty, the President's prestige will be in shambles⟩ — see DECLINE 1

throw up *vb* **1** to discharge the contents of the stomach through the mouth ⟨she must have eaten something that didn't agree with her because she *threw up* right after dinner⟩ — see VOMIT
2 to make or assemble roughly or hastily ⟨when the townspeople realized that the President's motorcade would be coming through on its way to the conference, they *threw up* a hasty "Welcome" sign⟩ — see COBBLE (TOGETHER *OR* UP)

thrum *n* a monotonous sound like that of an insect in motion ⟨the steady *thrum* of the turbines in the power plant⟩ — see HUM

thrust *vb* **1** to apply force to (someone or something) so that it moves in front of one ⟨the cat *thrust* her paw under the couch, trying to reach her toy mouse⟩ — see PUSH 1
2 to move or extend upward ⟨the butte *thrusts* up 300 feet from the floor of the valley⟩ — see ASCEND

thruway *n* a passage cleared for public vehicular travel ⟨we took back roads on the way out, and the *thruway* on the way back⟩ — see WAY 1

thud *n* a hard strike with a part of the body or an instrument ⟨the *thud* of his head against the cabinet door brought tears to his eyes⟩ — see [1]BLOW

thud *vb* to come into usually forceful contact with something ⟨the snowball *thudded* against the side of my car⟩ — see HIT 2

thug *n* a violent, brutal person who is often a member of an organized gang ⟨the Mob boss regularly sent his *thugs* after people who were slow to pay their debts⟩ — see HOODLUM

thumb *vb* **1** to travel by securing free rides ⟨thought I'd *thumb* into town instead of paying for a cab⟩ — see HITCHHIKE
2 to turn over pages in an idle or cursory manner ⟨I *thumbed* through the book during the flight but was too distracted to really read it⟩ — see SKIM 1

thumbnail *adj* marked by the use of few words to convey much information or meaning ⟨a *thumbnail* outline of the plot of the novel⟩ — see CONCISE

thump *n* a hard strike with a part of the body or an instrument ⟨gave her boyfriend a *thump* against the side of his head whenever he said something obnoxious⟩ — see [1]BLOW

thump *vb* **1** to deliver a blow to (someone or something) usually in a strong vigorous manner ⟨*thumped* the desk with his hand as he delivered his speech⟩ — see HIT 1
2 to strike repeatedly ⟨playfully knocked his younger brother down and began to *thump* him with a foam bat⟩ — see BEAT 1

thumping *adv* to a great degree ⟨wrote several *thumping* big books on World War II⟩ — see VERY 1

thunder *vb* **1** to make a long loud deep noise or cry ⟨as we got closer, the waterfall *thundered* louder and louder⟩ — see ROAR 1
2 to speak so as to be heard at a distance ⟨a hotheaded man who was always *thundering* about the crooks and idiots running the government⟩ — see CALL 1

thunderclap *n* a loud explosive sound ⟨awakened by the *thunderclap* of a large branch falling on the roof⟩ — see CLAP 1

thundering *adj* marked by a high volume of sound ⟨the preacher delivered a *thundering* speech on the decline of morality in modern society⟩ — see LOUD 1

thunderous *adj* marked by a high volume of sound ⟨the last *thunderous* chord of the symphony rang throughout the hall⟩ — see LOUD 1

thunderstrike *vb* to make a strong impression on (someone) with something unexpected ⟨everyone was *thunderstruck* when she quit her job without warning⟩ — see SURPRISE 1

thunderstruck *adj* affected with sudden and great wonder or surprise ⟨the teen was *thunderstruck* when his parents told him he had been adopted⟩
synonyms amazed, astonished, astounded, awestruck (*also* awestricken), bowled over, dumbfounded (*also* dumfounded), dumbstruck, flabbergasted, shocked, stunned, stupefied
related words blindsided, startled, surprised (*also* surprized); aghast, appalled, dismayed, horrified; bewildered, confused, dazed, overwhelmed; agape, awed, awesome, openmouthed, wide-eyed, widemouthed
near antonyms blasé (*also* blase), casual, nonchalant, unruffled

thus *adv* for this or that reason ⟨we didn't have room for all seven of us in my car and *thus* took two cars to go to the movies⟩ — see THEREFORE

thwack *n* **1** a hard strike with a part of the body or an instrument ⟨he gave the ball a hard *thwack* with the bat and sent it deep into the outfield⟩ — see [1]BLOW
2 a loud explosive sound ⟨even from the top of the bleachers we could hear the loud *thwack* of the ball being hit⟩ — see CLAP 1

thwack *vb* to deliver a blow to (someone or something) usually in a strong vigorous manner ⟨*thwacked* the growling dog on the nose with a rolled-up newspaper⟩ — see HIT 1

thwart *vb* to prevent from achieving a goal ⟨a coalition of grassroots organizations *thwarted* the company's efforts to get approval for a new power plant⟩ — see FRUSTRATE 1

tic *n* an odd or peculiar habit ⟨constantly playing with her hair is one of her more annoying *tics*⟩ — see IDIOSYNCRASY

tick (off) *vb* to specify one after another ⟨*ticked off* everything she would need to buy while her daughter wrote the items down on a list⟩ — see ENUMERATE 1

ticked *adj* feeling or showing anger ⟨the boss is really *ticked* about this latest snafu, so now might not be a good time to ask for a raise⟩ — see ANGRY

ticket *n* **1** a small sheet of plastic, paper, or paperboard showing that the bearer has a claim to something (as admittance) ⟨only people with *tickets* will be allowed past the front gates⟩
synonyms check, coupon, pass, pasteboard
related words certificate, note, token, voucher
2 a slip (as of paper or cloth) that is attached to something to identify or describe it ⟨the price on the *ticket* is $20 more than the advertised price⟩ — see LABEL
3 the means or right of entering or participating in ⟨people to whom a green card represents a *ticket* to a better life⟩ — see ENTRANCE 1
4 something that allows someone to achieve a desired goal ⟨that entry-level job could be her *ticket* to a career in big-time advertising⟩ — see PASSPORT 1

ticket *vb* to attach an identifying slip to ⟨the attendant quickly *ticketed* my coat and handed the claim stub back to me⟩ — see LABEL 1

tickled *adj* experiencing pleasure, satisfaction, or delight ⟨I'm *tickled* that you like the present so much⟩ — see GLAD 1

ticklish *adj* **1** easily offended ⟨he's *ticklish* about his looks, so it's wisest to avoid the subject altogether⟩ — see TOUCHY 1
2 requiring exceptional skill or caution in performance or handling ⟨trying to tell him that his zipper is down without embarrassing him will be a *ticklish* task⟩ — see TRICKY 1

tick off *vb* **1** to criticize (someone) so as to correct a fault ⟨she royally *ticked* the babysitter *off* for letting the child play outside unsupervised⟩ — see REBUKE 1
2 to make angry ⟨it really *ticks* me *off* when someone says something like that⟩ — see ANGER 1

ticky–tacky *also* **ticky–tack** *adj* marked by an obvious lack of style or good taste ⟨her house is full of *ticky-tacky* figurines⟩ — see [1]TACKY 1

tidbit *also* **titbit** *n* **1** something that is pleasing to eat because it is rare or a luxury ⟨gave her an expensive box of chocolate *tidbits*⟩ — see DELICACY 1
2 a small piece or quantity of food ⟨I'll just have a *tidbit* of the dessert, nothing too big⟩ — see MORSEL 1

tiddly *adj, chiefly British* being under the influence of alcohol ⟨after sampling the single malts at several Scottish distilleries, by day's end we were definitely a little *tiddly*⟩ — see DRUNK

tide *n* a prevailing or general movement or inclination

⟨the *tide* of the battle turned suddenly, and the would-be invaders were forced to retreat⟩ — see TREND 1

tidied *adj* being clean and in good order ⟨that rare teenager who keeps a nicely-*tidied* room⟩ — see NEAT 1

tidings *n pl* a report of recent events or facts not previously known ⟨any *tidings* from the front, soldier?⟩ — see NEWS

tidy *adj* **1** being clean and in good order ⟨could easily find everything on her *tidy* desk⟩ — see NEAT 1

2 of a size greater than average of its kind ⟨paid a *tidy* sum for a painting that may not even be a genuine Titian⟩ — see LARGE 1

3 sufficiently large in size, amount, or number to merit attention ⟨signed a three-year contract for a *tidy* amount⟩ — see CONSIDERABLE 1

tidy (up) *vb* **1** to make a place neat and orderly by removing extraneous stuff ⟨just give me a minute to *tidy up* before you bring company over⟩ — see CLEAN (UP) 1

2 to make neat ⟨we'll work more efficiently if we *tidy up* our work area after completing the first phase of our experiment⟩ — see NEATEN

tie *n* **1** a situation in which neither participant in a contest, competition, or struggle comes out ahead of the other ⟨the competition for first place in the dessert division ended in a *tie* between the chocolate pecan pie and the walnut fudge tart⟩

synonyms dead heat, draw, stalemate, standoff

related words deadlock, impasse; seesaw; photo finish; horse race, toss-up

2 a uniting or binding force or influence ⟨their marriage will serve to form a very strong *tie* between our families⟩ — see BOND 2

tie *vb* **1** to gather into a tight mass by means of a line or cord ⟨*tied* the newspapers into a bundle⟩

synonyms band, bind, truss

related words cinch, cord, rope, strap, thread, wire; gird, girt; lash, leash, tether; interlace, intertwine, interweave; lace; entangle, knot, snarl, tangle, twist; coil, wind

near antonyms undo, unfasten, unlace, unlash, unloose, unloosen, unstrap, unstring, unthread; unleash, untether; disentangle, unravel, unsnarl, untangle, untwine, untwist; uncoil, unspool, unwind

antonyms unbind, untie

2 to produce something equal to (as in quality or value) ⟨at the class reunion we learned that he had won the Nobel Prize in medicine—how could the rest of us *tie* that?⟩ — see EQUAL 1

tied–up *adj* involved in often constant activity ⟨we'll be *tied-up* with work for the next several days⟩ — see BUSY 1

tier *n* one of the units into which a whole is divided on the basis of a common characteristic ⟨the bottom *tier* of entrants⟩ — see CLASS 2

tie–up *n* **1** a crowded mass (as of cars) that impedes or blocks movement ⟨a *tie-up* at the junction of Main and Central has slowed traffic to a crawl⟩ — see JAM 1

2 the state of having shared interests or efforts (as in social or business matters) ⟨in a *tie-up* with the film studio, the toy company is producing a whole line of figures featuring characters from the animated movie⟩ — see ASSOCIATION 1

tie up *vb* to create difficulty for the work or activity of ⟨an accident is *tying up* traffic at 5th and Broadway⟩ — see HAMPER

tiff *n* an often noisy or angry expression of differing opinions ⟨got into a little *tiff* about what color sheets to buy for their bed⟩ — see ARGUMENT 1

tiff *vb* to express different opinions about something often angrily ⟨like any couple, they occasionally *tiff*, but it's never anything serious⟩ — see ARGUE 2

tiger *n* an aggressive and fiercely determined person ⟨even the best defense can't keep that *tiger* from scoring⟩ — see PIT BULL

tight *adj* **1** not allowing penetration (as by gas, liquid, or light) ⟨the lid forms a *tight* seal with the canister that will keep the spices fresh⟩

synonyms impenetrable, impermeable, impervious

related words close, compact, dense, snug, thick; airtight, hermetic (*also* hermetical), leakproof, watertight; lightproof, soundproof, waterproof

near antonyms absorbent, leaky, porous, unsealed

antonyms penetrable, permeable, pervious

2 firmly positioned in place and difficult to dislodge ⟨a *tight* screw that won't come loose⟩ ⟨a jar with a *tight* lid⟩

synonyms fast, firm, frozen, jammed, lodged, set, snug, stuck, wedged

related words bonded, cemented, glued; anchored, clamped; embedded (*also* imbedded), entrenched (*also* intrenched), impacted, implanted; attached, bound, fastened, secured; immovable, unyielding

near antonyms detached, dislodged, freed, loosened, unattached, unbound, undone, unfastened, unsecured; movable (*or* moveable), yielding

antonyms insecure, loose

3 giving or sharing as little as possible ⟨is fairly *tight* with his money⟩ — see STINGY 1

4 having little space between items or parts ⟨the traffic on the freeway was so *tight* we couldn't get over to the exit we wanted⟩ — see CLOSE 1

5 showing little difference in the standing of the competitors ⟨a *tight* race for governor⟩ — see CLOSE 3

6 stretched with little or no give ⟨the rope was pulled *tight*⟩ — see TAUT

7 closely acquainted ⟨supposedly he and the rock star have been totally *tight* since they went to high school together⟩ — see FAMILIAR 1

8 being under the influence of alcohol ⟨having spent several hours getting nice and *tight*, the campus Romeo was having performance problems⟩ — see DRUNK

tighten *vb* to draw tight ⟨*tighten* the straps on the backpack so that the load doesn't shift while hiking⟩

synonyms strain, stretch, tauten, tense

related words elongate, extend, lengthen; cinch, constrict

near antonyms ease, relax

antonyms loosen, slack, slacken

tightfisted *adj* giving or sharing as little as possible ⟨the company is pretty *tightfisted* when it comes to bonuses⟩ — see STINGY 1

tightfistedness *n* the quality or practice of being overly sparing with money ⟨longing for the occasional luxury, they bitterly complained about their father's *tightfistedness*⟩ — see PARSIMONY 1

tight–lipped *adj* tending not to speak frequently (as by habit or inclination) ⟨the cabinet official is usually *tight-lipped* about her private life⟩ — see SILENT 2

tight–mouthed *adj* given to keeping one's activities hidden from public observation or knowledge ⟨the studio has been *tight-mouthed* about how the show's cliffhanger season finale will be resolved⟩ — see SECRETIVE

tightness *n* the quality or practice of being overly sparing with money ⟨a man of legendary *tightness*, he has plenty of money in his savings account⟩ — see PARSIMONY 1

tightwad *n* a mean grasping person who is usually stingy with money ⟨you're always such a *tightwad* when charity comes calling⟩ — see MISER

till *vb* to work by plowing, sowing, and raising crops on ⟨farmers *tilling* the soil from sunup to sunset⟩ — see FARM

tiller *n* a person who cultivates the land and grows crops on it ⟨in his paintings farmers are invariably depicted as brawny yet noble *tillers* of the land⟩ — see FARMER

tilt *n* the act of positioning or an instance of being positioned at an angle ⟨indicated her approval with a slight *tilt* of her head⟩
synonyms angling, bend, cock, inclination, list, tip
related words turn, twist, veer; bow, dip, nod

tilt *vb* to set or cause to be at an angle ⟨the robin *tilts* its head as it hunts for worms in the grass⟩ — see LEAN 1

tilted *adj* **1** inclined or twisted to one side ⟨stared at me with a *tilted* head and a quizzical look⟩ — see AWRY
2 running in a slanting direction ⟨the floors of the old house were *tilted* slightly⟩ — see DIAGONAL

tilting *adj* running in a slanting direction ⟨a rickety, *tilting* staircase that did not look safe⟩ — see DIAGONAL

timber *n* **1** a dense growth of trees and shrubs covering a large area ⟨upon our approach the deer disappeared back into the *timber* from whence it had come⟩ — see FOREST
2 tree logs as prepared for human use ⟨needed a new load of *timber* to finish building the house⟩ — see WOOD 1
3 the basic elements from which something can be developed ⟨a novel with the *timber* to become a best seller, if marketed correctly⟩ — see MAKING

timberland *n* a dense growth of trees and shrubs covering a large area ⟨the wildfire burned through a large swath of *timberland*⟩ — see FOREST

time *n* **1** a particular point at which an event takes place ⟨remember that one *time* you tried to wash the dog in the sink⟩ — see OCCASION 1
2 an exciting or noteworthy event that one experiences firsthand ⟨enjoys telling us about the *times* he had while he was in the army⟩ — see ADVENTURE 1
3 an extent of time associated with a particular person or thing ⟨back in my parents' *time*, families usually had only one car⟩ — see AGE 1
4 the period during which something exists, lasts, or is in progress ⟨how much *time* will the project take?⟩ — see DURATION 1

time bomb *n* a potentially explosive place or situation ⟨the region's political instability has turned it into a ticking *time bomb*⟩ — see TINDERBOX 1

timekeeper *n* a device to measure time ⟨the museum includes some ancient water clocks and sundials in its collection of historical *timekeepers*⟩ — see TIMEPIECE

timeless *adj* having an existence or validity that does not change or diminish ⟨views the church's message and mission as *timeless* and not subject to the whim of the people⟩ — see ABIDING

timeliness *n* the quality or habit of arriving or being ready on time ⟨your *timeliness* will make a good impression on the person interviewing you for the job⟩ — see PROMPTITUDE

timely *adj* **1** especially suitable for a certain time ⟨a *timely* invitation to lunch that came just as I was starting to feel hungry⟩
synonyms opportune, seasonable, well-timed
related words appropriate, apt, fit, fitting, meet, pat, proper, suitable; pertinent, relative, relevant; fortunate, lucky, propitious; anticipated, expected; prompt, punctual
near antonyms improper, inappropriate, irrelative, irrelevant, unfit, unseemly, unsuitable; unfortunate, unlucky; behind, behindhand, belated, delayed, delinquent, late, latish, overdue, postponed, slow, tardy; anticipatory, early, precocious, premature; abrupt, sudden, unanticipated, unexpected
antonyms inopportune, unseasonable, untimely
2 done, carried out, or given without delay ⟨when I order a pizza, I expect it to be delivered in a *timely* manner⟩ — see PROMPT 1

time-out *n* a period of often involuntary inactivity or idleness ⟨we need to take a *time-out* from our relationship to think things over⟩ — see DOWNTIME

timepiece *n* a device to measure time ⟨the only *timepiece* she used at the cabin was a garden sundial⟩
synonyms chronometer, clock, timekeeper, timer
related words alarm clock, atomic clock, cuckoo clock, grandfather clock, time clock; clepsydra, hourglass, sandglass, sundial, water clock; chronograph, stopwatch, watch

timer *n* a device to measure time ⟨set the kitchen *timer* to 30 minutes⟩ — see TIMEPIECE

timeserver *n* a person who dexterously and expediently changes or adopts opinions ⟨a classic *timeserver*, she switched her position on the war the instant it began losing public support⟩ — see ACROBAT 2

timetable *n* a listing of things to be presented or considered (as at a concert or play) ⟨checked the *timetable* of events to see if I'd be able to get something to eat beforehand⟩ — see PROGRAM 1

timeworn *adj* **1** showing signs of advanced wear and tear and neglect ⟨the wooden steps to the *timeworn* cottage had rotted and several shutters were missing⟩ — see SHABBY 1
2 used or heard so often as to be dull ⟨I'm sick of the *timeworn* "How you've grown!" every time she sees me⟩ — see STALE 1

timid *adj* easily frightened ⟨a *timid* rabbit hopped cautiously out of the hedge⟩ — see SHY 1

timidity *n* lack of willingness to assert oneself and take risks ⟨none of the scouts showed the least *timidity* about rappeling down the cliff⟩
synonyms faintheartedness, timidness, timorousness
related words bashfulness, constraint, embarrassment, inhibition, restraint, shyness, skittishness; hesitation, indecision, indecisiveness, irresoluteness, irresolution; alarm (*also* alarum), anxiety, apprehension, concern, discomposure, dismay, fear, panic, upset, worry; cowardice, cowardliness, cravenness, spinelessness
near antonyms assurance, confidence, self-assertiveness, self-assurance, self-confidence; composure, coolness, insouciance, nonchalance, unconcern; backbone, decisiveness, determination, fiber, firmness, fortitude, gameness, grit, gumption, mettle, resoluteness, resolution, spunk; bravery, courage, courageousness, daring, dauntlessness, doughtiness, fearlessness, gutsiness, intrepidity, intrepidness, valor; brazenness, cheek, effrontery, gall, temerity
antonyms audaciousness, audacity, boldness, cojones [*slang*], guts, nerve

timidness *n* lack of willingness to assert oneself and take risks ⟨such *timidness* is surprising in a man as physically imposing as he is⟩ — see TIMIDITY

timorous *adj* easily frightened ⟨sensational news stories that seem designed to needlessly alarm an already *timorous* public⟩ — see SHY 1

timorousness *n* lack of willingness to assert oneself and take risks ⟨the *timorousness* with which so many politicians approach hot-button issues⟩ — see TIMIDITY

tin *n* a metal container in the shape of a cylinder ⟨row upon row of *tins* containing food for an emergency that never happened⟩ — see CAN 1

tincture *n* a property that becomes apparent when light falls on an object and by which things that are identical in form can be distinguished ⟨a ragged shirt that seemed to be stained with the *tincture* of blood⟩ — see COLOR 1

tincture *vb* to give color or a different color to ⟨clouds *tinctured* by the rays of the setting sun⟩ — see COLOR 1

tinderbox *n* **1** a potentially explosive place or situation

⟨the city has been a *tinderbox* ever since racial profiling became an issue⟩
synonyms flash point, powder keg, time bomb, volcano
related words hot button, third rail
2 a time or state of affairs requiring prompt or decisive action ⟨while the country's prime minister was meeting with the U.S president, a political *tinderbox* was igniting at home⟩ — see EMERGENCY

tinge *n* a property that becomes apparent when light falls on an object and by which things that are identical in form can be distinguished ⟨there's a bluish *tinge* to your lips—you must be freezing!⟩ — see COLOR 1

tinge *vb* to give color or a different color to ⟨just slightly *tinge* the frosting with yellow food coloring to give it a lemony look⟩ — see COLOR 1

tingle *n* a sharp unpleasant sensation usually felt in some specific part of the body ⟨can't stand those funny *tingles* I get when my foot falls asleep⟩ — see PAIN 1

tingle *vb* to make a repeated sharp light ringing sound ⟨awoke to the steady pitter-patter of raindrops *tingling* on the rooftop⟩ — see JINGLE

tiniest *adj* being the least in amount, number, or size possible ⟨at one time atoms were thought to be the *tiniest* particles of matter⟩ — see MINIMAL

tinker (with) *vb* to handle thoughtlessly, ignorantly, or mischievously ⟨the camera hasn't worked properly ever since our son *tinkered with* it⟩ — see TAMPER (WITH)

tinkerer *n* a person who regularly or occasionally engages in an activity as a pastime rather than as a profession ⟨he's been tinkering with cars since he was a kid, and now he's a *tinkerer* who knows nearly as much as a mechanic⟩ — see AMATEUR 1

tinkle *n* a series of short high ringing sounds ⟨the soothing *tinkle* of the wind chime on the back porch⟩
synonyms chime(s), jingle, tintinnabulation
related words clatter, jangle, rattle; chink, clang, clank, clink, ding-dong, ping, ring; chirr, ripple, trill, warble

tinkle *vb* to make a repeated sharp light ringing sound ⟨the bell around the cat's neck *tinkled* as he ran across the yard⟩ — see JINGLE

tinsel *n* something attractive but lacking in substance ⟨a book that examines popular fame and finds it to be very disposable *tinsel*⟩ — see COTTON CANDY

tint *n* a property that becomes apparent when light falls on an object and by which things that are identical in form can be distinguished ⟨her eyes have a greenish *tint*⟩ — see COLOR 1

tint *vb* to give color or a different color to ⟨if you *tint* that blue paint with this yellow paint, you should get a nice shade of green⟩ — see COLOR 1

tintinnabulation *n* a series of short high ringing sounds ⟨the merry *tintinnabulation* of church bells⟩ — see TINKLE

tintless *adj, archaic* lacking an addition of color ⟨the *tintless* light of the midwinter sun⟩ — see COLORLESS 1

tiny *adj* very small in size ⟨the forest ranger showed us how every square foot of forest is alive with *tiny* creatures⟩
synonyms atomic, bitsy, bitty, infinitesimal, itty-bitty (*or* itsy-bitsy), little bitty, microminiature, microscopic (*also* microscopical), miniature, minuscule, minute, teensy, teensy-weensy, teeny, teeny-weeny, wee, weeny (*also* weensy)
related words baby, diminutive, dwarf, elfin, half-pint, Lilliputian, little, micro, mini, minikin, model, petite, pocket, pocket-size (*also* pocket-sized), pygmy, small, smallish; dinky, dwarfish, insignificant, pint-size (*or* pint-sized), puny, scrubby, undersized (*also* undersize)
near antonyms big, bulky, bumper, considerable, extensive, good, goodly, grand, great, gross, handsome, hefty, hulking, jumbo, king-size (*or* king-sized), large, largish, major, outsize (*also* outsized), overgrown, overscale (*or* overscaled), oversize (*or* oversized), sizable (*or* sizeable), substantial, super, whacking, whopping; formidable, grandiose, imposing, lofty, majestic, monolithic, staggering, stupendous, towering; boundless, cavernous, immeasurable, infinite, vast, vasty, voluminous
antonyms astronomical (*also* astronomic), colossal, cosmic (*also* cosmical), elephantine, enormous, giant, gigantic, herculean, heroic (*also* heroical), huge, immense, mammoth, massive, monster, monstrous, monumental, mountainous, planetary, prodigious, titanic, tremendous

[1]**tip** *n* **1** a piece of advice or useful information especially from an expert ⟨got some *tips* from a horticulturist on how to get my violets to bloom⟩
synonyms hint, lead, pointer
related words advice, advisement, assistance, counsel, guidance, recommendation, suggestion; caution, cautioning, sign, signal, telltale, tip-off, warning; brief, direction, feedback, instruction, observation; prompt, reminder, urging; answer, clue, solution
2 information not generally available to the public ⟨investigators are trying to determine whether the investor illegally received a *tip* that the company's stock was about to plunge⟩ — see DOPE 1

[2]**tip** *n* **1** a small sum of money given for a service over and above what is due ⟨gave our waiter an extra large *tip* for such fantastic service⟩
synonyms gratuity, perquisite
related words donation, gift, lagniappe, largesse (*also* largess), present; bonus, favor, reward; contribution, offering
2 something given in addition to what is ordinarily expected or owed ⟨a customer who always gives his paper carrier a very generous *tip* at Christmastime⟩ — see BONUS

[3]**tip** *n* **1** the act of positioning or an instance of being positioned at an angle ⟨she didn't say anything but just acknowledged our presence with a *tip* of her head⟩ — see TILT
2 *chiefly British* a place where discarded materials (as trash) are dumped ⟨you simply cannot dispose of leftover petrol at the *tip*⟩ — see DUMP 1

[4]**tip** *n* the last and usually sharp or tapering part of something long and narrow ⟨the *tip* of a knitting needle⟩ — see POINT 2

tip *vb* to set or cause to be at an angle ⟨be careful because if you *tip* your cup any more, you'll spill your tea⟩ — see LEAN 1

tip–off *n* something that tells of approaching danger or risk ⟨the retreat of the island's wildlife to higher ground was a *tip-off* that a tsunami was about to strike⟩ — see WARNING 2

tipped *adj* tapering to a thin tip ⟨a round-*tipped* needle⟩ — see POINTED 1

tipping *adj* inclined or twisted to one side ⟨a boat *tipping* under the weight of a lopsided load⟩ — see AWRY

tipple *n* a distilled beverage that can make a person drunk ⟨they had a nanny who was rather too fond of *tipple*⟩ — see ALCOHOL

tipple *vb* to partake excessively of alcoholic beverages ⟨I do *tipple* now and then⟩ — see DRINK 2

tippler *n* a person who makes a habit of getting drunk ⟨her husband was a closet *tippler* who had hidden small stashes of liquor all over the house⟩ — see DRUNK 1

tipsy *adj* being under the influence of alcohol ⟨our uncle had too much to drink and was a little *tipsy*⟩ — see DRUNK

tip–top *adj* of the very best kind ⟨the doctor told me I was in *tip-top* shape⟩ — see EXCELLENT

tip–top *n* the highest part or point ⟨this trail will take you to the fire tower at the *tip-top* of that hill⟩ — see HEIGHT 1

tirade *n* a long angry speech or scolding ⟨after the inspection by the health department, we had to listen to the manager's *tirade* about keeping the restaurant's kitchen cleaner⟩

synonyms diatribe, harangue, jeremiad, philippic, rant

related words assault, attack, broadside, invective, lambasting, lashing, tongue-lashing, vituperation; berating, chewing out, rebuke, reprimand, reproach, reproof; abuse, castigation, censure, condemnation, criticism, denunciation; belittlement, deprecation, depreciation, disparagement, dissing; excoriation, execration, revilement; admonishment, admonition, lecture, sermon

near antonyms encomium, eulogy, panegyric, rhapsody, tribute; acclaim, acclamation, accolade, citation, homage, honor, praise; approval, blessing, commendation, endorsement (*also* indorsement), sanction; ovation, plaudit, rave

tire *vb* **1** to diminish the physical strength of ⟨I don't want our walk to *tire* you too much⟩ — see WEAKEN 1

2 to make weary and restless by being dull or monotonous ⟨this long dry lecture will *tire* the audience if you don't insert some jokes into it⟩ — see [2]BORE

3 to use up all the physical energy of ⟨this pentathlon will *tire* all but the hardiest athletes⟩ — see EXHAUST 1

tired *adj* **1** depleted in strength, energy, or freshness ⟨I'm usually *tired* after a long day of working in the yard⟩ — see WEARY 1

2 having one's patience, interest, or pleasure exhausted ⟨I'm sick and *tired* of your antics⟩ — see WEARY 2

3 used or heard so often as to be dull ⟨such *tired* phrases won't hold your reader's interest⟩ — see STALE 1

tiredness *n* a complete depletion of energy or strength ⟨your *tiredness* will go away after a good rest⟩ — see FATIGUE 1

tireless *adj* showing no signs of weariness even after long hard effort ⟨a *tireless* advocate for human rights⟩

synonyms indefatigable, inexhaustible, unflagging, untiring, weariless

related words assiduous, conscientious, diligent, meticulous, painstaking, sedulous; determined, dogged, patient, persevering, persistent, pertinacious, plodding, relentless, steadfast, steady, stubborn, tenacious, unabating, unfailing, unfaltering, unflinching, unrelenting, unremitting, unwavering; active, busy, dynamic, energetic, feverish, spirited, vigorous; hard, industrious, intense, laborious, slavish, strenuous

near antonyms indolent, lackadaisical, laggard, lazy, listless, shiftless, slothful, sluggish; apathetic, casual, desultory, languid, spiritless; beat, broken, burned-out (*or* burnt-out), done in, drained, enervated, jaded, overtaxed, overworked, played out, sapped, spent, tuckered (out), wearied, worn-out

tiresome *adj* causing weariness, restlessness, or lack of interest ⟨what a *tiresome* church service that turned out to be⟩ — see BORING

tiring *adj* causing weariness, restlessness, or lack of interest ⟨the seminar was *tiring* and not particularly helpful or informative⟩ — see BORING

titan *n* something that is unusually large and powerful ⟨this newest ocean liner is a true *titan* of the sea⟩ — see GIANT

titanic *adj* unusually large ⟨the *titanic* new skyscraper dwarfs every other building around it⟩ — see HUGE

titillate *vb* to cause a pleasurable stimulation of the feelings ⟨tabloids *titillate* their readers with racy details about the private lives of media-created celebrities⟩ — see THRILL

titillation *n* a pleasurably intense stimulation of the feelings ⟨a cultural critic who argues that people have become too dependent upon the instant gratification and *titillation* that television and the Internet provide⟩ — see THRILL

title *n* **1** a word or combination of words by which a person or thing is regularly known ⟨about the only thing the book and the movie have in common are their *titles*⟩ — see NAME 1

2 a word or series of words often in larger letters placed at the beginning of a passage or at the top of a page in order to introduce or categorize ⟨a humorous illustration appears above the *title* of every chapter in the book⟩ — see HEADING

3 the position occupied by the one who comes in first in a competition ⟨won the singles *title* three years in a row⟩ — see CROWN 2

title *vb* to give a name to ⟨what do you plan on *titling* your latest album?⟩ — see NAME 1

titleholder *n* the person who comes in first in a competition ⟨became the youngest *titleholder* in the sport's history⟩ — see CHAMPION 1

titlist *n* the person who comes in first in a competition ⟨the boxing *titlist* with the most knockouts to his credit⟩ — see CHAMPION 1

titter *n* an explosive sound that is a sign of amusement ⟨a *titter* swept through the crowd at his verbal slip⟩ — see LAUGH 1

titter *vb* to show mirth with an explosive vocal sound ⟨even as students in the sex ed class continued to *titter*, the lecturer plowed ahead⟩ — see LAUGH 1

tittle *n* **1** a very small piece ⟨we have examined every last *tittle* of evidence available and can find nothing to support his claims⟩ — see BIT 1

2 the smallest amount or part imaginable ⟨there's not a *tittle* of sense in that book⟩ — see JOT

titular *adj* being something in name or form only ⟨he's the *titular* head of the department, though it's the assistant managers who largely run things around here⟩ — see NOMINAL 1

tizzy *n* a state of nervous or irritated concern ⟨all in a *tizzy* because she can't find her car keys⟩ — see FRET

to *prep* earlier than ⟨right now it's 25 minutes *to* 10:00⟩ — see BEFORE 1

toad *n* a person whose behavior is offensive to others ⟨that miserable *toad* is lucky to have even a single friend⟩ — see JERK 1

toady *n* a person who flatters another in order to get ahead ⟨no one liked the office *toady*, who spent most of her time complimenting the boss on what a great job he was doing⟩ — see SYCOPHANT

toady *vb* to use flattery or the doing of favors in order to win approval especially from a superior ⟨a satirical novel about an amoral go-getter who *toadies* his way to the top of the corporate ladder⟩ — see FAWN

toast *vb* to cause to have or give off heat to a moderate degree ⟨come over and *toast* your toes by the fire⟩ — see WARM 1

toasty *adj* having or giving off heat to a moderate degree ⟨I'm nice and *toasty* in front of the fire⟩ — see WARM 1

tocsin *n* **1** an object intended to give public notice or warning ⟨the *tocsin* rang out, warning us of the approaching tornado⟩ — see SIGNAL 1

2 something that tells of approaching danger or risk ⟨noted that a sudden drop in a student's grades may be a *tocsin* of a serious personal problem⟩ — see WARNING 2

today *adv* at the present time ⟨even *today*, arranged marriages remain a common practice in some parts of the world⟩ — see NOW 1

today *n* the time currently existing or in progress ⟨live for *today* and let tomorrow worry about itself⟩ — see [1]PRESENT

to–do *n* a state of noisy, confused activity ⟨there was such a *to-do* when the mice got loose from the science room that I thought the principal was going to close the school⟩ — see COMMOTION

toe–to–toe *adv* in direct confrontation or competition ⟨mom-and-pop grocery stores are usually wildly outmatched when they go *toe-to-toe* with large chain stores⟩ — see HEAD-TO-HEAD

toff *n, chiefly British* a man extremely interested in his clothing and personal appearance ⟨the *toffs* were everywhere to be seen on opening day at Ascot⟩ — see DANDY 1

toffee–nosed *adj, chiefly British* being or characteristic of a person who has an offensive air of superiority and tends to ignore or disdain anyone regarded as inferior ⟨having come from the middle class, he suffered at the hands of the *toffee-nosed* twits at Eton⟩ — see SNOBBISH

tog (up *or* out) *vb* to outfit with clothes and especially fine or special clothes ⟨*togged out* in obviously brand-new hiking garb, she was quite a sight⟩ — see CLOTHE 1

together *adj* free from emotional or mental agitation ⟨she's one of the most *together* people I know⟩ — see CALM 2

together *adv* **1** at one and the same time ⟨the two packages, although sent on different days, arrived *together*⟩
synonyms coincidentally, coincidently, concurrently, contemporaneously, simultaneously
related words close, immediately, narrowly, near
phrases at once, in unison
near antonyms apart, independently, individually, singly; consecutively, successively
antonyms separately
2 in or by combined action or effort ⟨working *together*, we can get this project done on time⟩
synonyms concertedly, conjointly, hand in glove (*or* hand and glove), jointly
related words collectively, mutually, reciprocally, unanimously, unitedly; cooperatively, symbiotically
phrases in concert
antonyms apart, independently, individually, separately, severally, single-handed, single-handedly, singly, solely, unaided, unassisted, unilaterally
3 with everyone or everything taken into account at the same time ⟨*together*, the properties are worth more than five million⟩ — see ALL AROUND
4 in succession without others coming in between ⟨for three days *together* the stubborn child refused to eat⟩ — see CONSECUTIVELY

toggery *n* covering for the human body ⟨inmates wearing regulation prison *toggery*⟩ — see CLOTHING

togs *n pl* **1** clothing chosen as appropriate for a specific situation ⟨put on your party *togs* and come over to our place for an all-night dance party⟩ — see OUTFIT 1
2 covering for the human body ⟨hey, those are some snazzy *togs* you're wearing⟩ — see CLOTHING

[1]**toil** *n* very hard or unpleasant work ⟨after years of *toil* in a sweatshop, Kim was finally able to start her own dressmaking business⟩
synonyms donkeywork, drudge, drudgery, fatigue, grind, labor, moil, slavery, sweat, travail
related words spadework; effort, exertion, pains, struggle, trouble; chore, duty, job, obligation, responsibility; routine, tedium, treadmill
near antonyms decompression, ease, leisure, relaxation, repose, rest; amusement, dalliance, diversion, entertainment, recreation, sport; dormancy, idleness, inactivity, inertia, inertness; dallying, goldbricking, loafing, lolling, lounging
antonyms fun, play

[2]**toil** *n, usually* **toils** *pl* something that catches and holds ⟨a married woman hopelessly caught in the *toils* of an extramarital affair⟩ — see WEB 1

toil *vb* to devote serious and sustained effort ⟨*toiled* for many years on the mammoth outdoor sculpture⟩ — see LABOR

toiler *n* a person who does very hard or dull work ⟨on Labor Day we should give a thought to those *toilers* who work long hours at low-paying jobs⟩ — see SLAVE 2

toilet *n* a room furnished with a fixture for flushing body waste ⟨we were directed to the *toilets* in the church basement⟩
synonyms bath, bathroom, bog [*British*], can, cloakroom [*British*], comfort station, convenience [*chiefly British*], head, john, latrine, lavatory, loo [*chiefly British*], potty, restroom, washroom, water closet
related words commode, pan [*British*], pot; garderobe, jakes, outhouse, privy; half bath, powder room; ladies [*chiefly British*], ladies' room, men's room

toilet *vb* to outfit with clothes and especially fine or special clothes ⟨the princess required at least a dozen maids to *toilet* her for formal occasions⟩ — see CLOTHE 1

toilsome *adj* **1** requiring considerable physical or mental effort ⟨faced with the *toilsome* task of cleaning out her deceased father's homestead⟩ — see HARD 2
2 requiring much time, effort, or careful attention ⟨this is the most *toilsome* part of the construction, so we'll go slowly to make sure we're doing it right⟩ — see DEMANDING 1

token *n* something that serves to keep alive the memory of a person or event ⟨please accept this parting gift as a *token* of our lasting affection⟩ — see MEMORIAL

tolbooth *n, Scottish* a place of confinement for persons held in lawful custody ⟨Deacon Brodie, thought to be the inspiration for Robert Louis Stevenson's *Strange Case of Dr. Jekyll and Mr. Hyde*, was publicly hung at the site of the old *tolbooth* of Edinburgh⟩ — see JAIL

tolerable *adj* **1** capable of being endured ⟨stubbing your toe is at least a more *tolerable* pain than breaking your foot⟩ — see BEARABLE
2 of a level of quality that meets one's needs or standards ⟨the accommodations are *tolerable* though not exactly luxurious⟩ — see ADEQUATE

tolerably *adv* in a satisfactory way ⟨I'm doing *tolerably*, thanks for asking⟩ — see WELL 1

tolerance *n* the capacity to endure what is difficult or disagreeable without complaining ⟨showed great *tolerance* in dealing with the child's tantrums⟩ — see PATIENCE

tolerant *adj* **1** accepting pains or hardships calmly or without complaint ⟨this job requires a *tolerant* person who is used to dealing with complaints and angry customers⟩ — see PATIENT 1
2 receiving or enduring without offering resistance ⟨a *tolerant* acceptance of the terrible way that his wife has always treated him⟩ — see PASSIVE

tolerate *vb* **1** to fail to prevent (some behavior on someone's part) especially from neglect or indifference ⟨my boss simply doesn't *tolerate* tardiness⟩ — see ALLOW 3
2 to put up with (something painful or difficult) ⟨suffering a terrible headache, the poor woman couldn't *tolerate* all the noise the neighbors were making⟩ — see BEAR 2

tolerating *adj* receiving or enduring without offering resistance ⟨old pictures of a graciously *tolerating* father letting his young children climb all over him⟩ — see PASSIVE

toll *vb* to make the clear sound heard when metal vibrates ⟨let the church bells joyously *toll* on this most happy occasion⟩ — see [2]RING

tomb *n* a final resting place for a dead person ⟨explored the historic graveyard and saw *tombs* that dated back two centuries⟩ — see GRAVE 1

tomb *vb* to place (a dead body) in the earth, a tomb, or the sea ⟨Forest Lawn is where many of Tinseltown's immortals are *tombed* for all eternity⟩ — see BURY 1

tomboyish *adj* having qualities or traits that are traditionally considered inappropriate for a girl or woman ⟨her father thought that ice hockey was a little too *tomboyish* for her, but her mother and older brother encouraged her to take it up⟩ — see UNFEMININE

tombstone *n* a shaped stone laid over or erected near a grave and usually bearing an inscription to identify and preserve the memory of the deceased ⟨the historic cemetery's many *tombstones* marking the graves of children are telling reminders of the harshness of pioneer life⟩
synonyms gravestone, headstone, monument, stone
related words cross, marker, plaque, table, tablet; monolith, obelisk, pillar; memorial, shrine; burial, sepulchre (*or* sepulcher), sepulture, tomb

tome *n* a set of printed sheets of paper bound together between covers and forming a work of fiction or nonfiction ⟨picked up a thick *tome* on the Roman Empire at a used book store⟩ — see BOOK 1

tomfool *adj* showing or marked by a lack of good sense or judgment ⟨what kind of *tomfool* idea is this?⟩ — see FOOLISH 1

tomfoolery *n* wildly playful or mischievous behavior ⟨the open bar may have had something to do with the *tomfoolery* at the wedding reception⟩ — see HORSEPLAY

tommyrot *n* language, behavior, or ideas that are absurd and contrary to good sense ⟨no genuinely intelligent and educated person would believe such *tommyrot*⟩ — see NONSENSE 1

tomorrow *n* time that is to come ⟨today's college graduates are the leaders of *tomorrow*⟩ — see FUTURE 1

Tom Thumb *n* a living thing much smaller than others of its kind ⟨a tiny *Tom Thumb* of a hamster⟩ — see DWARF 1

[1]ton *n* a considerable amount ⟨I received a *ton* of advice on the problem—all of it unsolicited⟩ — see LOT 2

[2]ton *n* a practice or interest that is very popular for a short time ⟨granite countertops became all the *ton* in kitchen decor⟩ — see FAD

tone *n* **1** a distinctive way of putting ideas into words ⟨the angry *tone* of his letter makes it clear he doesn't want to speak to me ever again⟩ — see STYLE 1
2 a property that becomes apparent when light falls on an object and by which things that are identical in form can be distinguished ⟨fall fashions in deep jewel *tones*⟩ — see COLOR 1
3 the set of qualities that makes a person, a group of people, or a thing different from others ⟨all that showbiz glitz is out of keeping with the *tone* of the college⟩ — see NATURE 1

toned–down *adj* not excessively showy ⟨after such a heated argument, it was a relief to hear someone use *toned-down* language to state their position⟩ — see QUIET 2

tongue *n* the stock of words, pronunciation, and grammar used by a people as their basic means of communication ⟨he spoke in a *tongue* that I didn't understand⟩ — see LANGUAGE 1

tongue–lash *vb* to criticize (someone) severely or angrily especially for personal failings ⟨the drill sergeant *tongue-lashed* the recruits with a colorful litany of foul-mouthed invectives⟩ — see SCOLD

tonic *adj* **1** having a renewing effect on the state of the body or mind ⟨breathe in clear *tonic* mountain air⟩ ⟨never underestimate the *tonic* power of humor on a sick person⟩
synonyms bracing, cordial, invigorating, refreshing, rejuvenating, restorative, reviving, stimulating, stimulative, vital, vitalizing
related words life-giving; conditioning, strengthening; animating, exhilarating, exhilarative, quickening, sharp; corrective, curative, curing, medicinal, rectifying, recuperative, reformative, reformatory, rehabilitative, remedial, remedying, reparative, therapeutic; beneficial, healthful, healthy, helpful, salubrious, salutary, wholesome
near antonyms deadening, debilitating, draining, enervating, enfeebling, exhausting, numbing, sapping, weakening, wearying; deleterious, injurious, pernicious; insalubrious, noxious, unhealthful, unhealthy, unwholesome
2 beneficial to the health of body or mind ⟨the *tonic* air of the mountains is just what you need after being cooped up in the city for so long⟩ — see HEALTHFUL

too *adv* **1** beyond a normal or acceptable limit ⟨ticket prices for the rock concert are simply *too* high⟩
synonyms devilishly, excessively, exorbitantly, inordinately, intolerably, monstrously, overly, overmuch, unacceptably, unduly
related words extravagantly, immoderately, intemperately; extortionately, inexcusably, obscenely, unbearably, unconscionably, unreasonably; improperly, inappropriately; abnormally, extraordinarily, freakishly, singularly, uncommonly, uncustomarily, unusually; astronomically, considerably, deadly, eminently, especially, exceedingly (*also* exceeding), exceptionally, extensively, extra, extremely, greatly, highly, hugely, incredibly, mightily, remarkably, significantly, substantially, super, terribly, very, whacking
phrases to a fault, to death, with a vengeance
near antonyms acceptably, moderately, modestly, reasonably, temperately; barely, hardly, just, marginally, meagerly, minimally, scantily, scarcely, slightly
antonyms deficiently, inadequately, insufficiently
2 in addition to what has been said ⟨I want to buy this sweater—and that sweater *too*!⟩ — see MORE 1
3 to a great degree ⟨the audience didn't seem *too* interested in what the speaker had to say⟩ — see VERY 1

tool *n* **1** an article intended for use in work ⟨needed a special *tool* to open the case of the CD player⟩ — see IMPLEMENT
2 one that is or can be used to further the purposes of another ⟨a ruthless leader using his trusting followers as *tools* in his quest for power⟩ — see [1]PAWN
3 one who is easily deceived or cheated ⟨you're just a pathetic *tool* of the advertising industry if you believe everything you see in TV commercials⟩ — see [1]DUPE

tool *vb* to travel by a motorized vehicle ⟨I spent some time *tooling* around town today⟩ — see DRIVE 2

toom *adj, chiefly Scottish* lacking contents that could or should be present ⟨the little shop in Edinburgh now stood *toom*⟩ — see EMPTY 1

toot *n* a bout of prolonged or excessive drinking ⟨about every six months he disappears for a week and goes on a *toot*⟩ — see CAROUSE

tooth and nail *adv* with all power or resources being used ⟨I'll fight *tooth and nail* to win the finals⟩ — see FULL BLAST

toothsome *adj* **1** very pleasing to the sense of taste ⟨a *toothsome* chocolate dessert⟩ — see DELICIOUS 1
2 sexually attractive ⟨the movie star and his supermodel girlfriend are considered the most *toothsome* couple in Hollywood⟩ — see SEXY 1

toothsomeness *n* the quality of being delicious ⟨people once delighted in feasting on peacock, a bird not known for its *toothsomeness*⟩ — see DELICIOUSNESS

toothy *adj* very pleasing to the sense of taste ⟨a selection of gourmet cookies and other *toothy* delights⟩ — see DELICIOUS 1

top *adj* **1** being at a point or level higher than all others ⟨an office in the *top* story of the building⟩ ⟨the *top* student in our graduating class⟩
synonyms highest, loftiest, topmost, upmost, uppermost
related words higher, loftier, upper; consummate, maximal, maximized, maximum, peaked, supreme, utmost, uttermost; chief, dominant, first, foremost, head, leading, predominant, preeminent, premier, principal; dominant, dominating, eminent, prominent, towering; elevated, escalated, heightened, jacked (up), lifted, raised, uplifted, upraised
near antonyms below, lower, nether, under, underneath; low, lowered, low-lying, sunken
antonyms bottommost, lowermost, lowest, nethermost, rock-bottom, undermost
2 of the greatest or highest degree or quantity ⟨your safety is our *top* priority⟩ — see ULTIMATE 1
3 of the highest degree ⟨going at *top* speed⟩ — see FULL 2
4 of the very best kind ⟨he's one of the tennis club's *top* players⟩ — see EXCELLENT
5 highest in rank or authority ⟨nearly all of the *top* officials in the state's department of corrections resigned after the scandal⟩ — see HEAD

top *n* **1** a piece placed over an open container to hold in, protect, or conceal its contents ⟨make sure the *top* is on the juice blender before you turn it on⟩ — see COVER 1
2 the highest part or point ⟨a hawk's nest at the very *top* of the tree⟩ — see HEIGHT 1

top *vb* to be greater, better, or stronger than ⟨the next contender's javelin throw *topped* the reigning champion's and set a new world record⟩ — see SURPASS 1

top billing *n* the center of public attention ⟨despite being of epic proportions, the African famine rarely received *top billing* in the American press⟩ — see CENTER STAGE

topcoat *n* a warm outdoor coat ⟨threw on a wool *topcoat* and headed out into the snow⟩ — see OVERCOAT

toper *n* a person who makes a habit of getting drunk ⟨most evenings her husband could be found at the local tavern with all of the town's other *topers*⟩ — see DRUNK 1

topflight *adj* of the very best kind ⟨he insists on buying a *topflight* computer system, money being no object⟩ — see EXCELLENT

Tophet *n* the place of punishment for the wicked after death ⟨a vision in which the souls of the damned plunged into *Tophet* like rocks falling down a mountainside⟩ — see HELL 1

topic *n* a major object of interest or concern (as in a discussion or artistic composition) ⟨the *topic* of his poem is the bitter conflict in Northern Ireland⟩ — see MATTER 1

toploftiness *n* an exaggerated sense of one's importance that shows itself in the making of excessive or unjustified claims ⟨a drama critic who delivers his judgments with the *toploftiness* of an infallible deity⟩ — see ARROGANCE

toplofty *also* **toploftical** *adj* having a feeling of superiority that shows itself in an overbearing attitude ⟨those *toplofty* history professors who sneeringly use the term "popularizer" to describe any historian whose works are read with pleasure⟩ — see ARROGANT

topmost *adj* **1** being at a point or level higher than all others ⟨his kite got tangled in the *topmost* branches of the tree⟩ — see TOP 1
2 of the highest degree ⟨our *topmost* goal is to help students learn foreign languages in an easy and natural way⟩ — see FULL 2

top–notch *adj* of the very best kind ⟨a *top-notch* violinist who had no trouble getting a position with the symphony⟩ — see EXCELLENT

top–of–the–line *adj* of the very best kind ⟨gourmet chefs who insist on *top-of-the-line* cookware and are willing to pay for it⟩ — see EXCELLENT

topography *n* the physical features of a region as a whole ⟨a map of the *topography* of the coastline shows a significant loss of wetlands⟩ — see GEOGRAPHY

topper *n* something (as a fact or argument) that is decisive or overwhelming ⟨there are lots of good reasons we can't go to the concert, but the fact that the tickets are all sold out is the *topper*⟩ — see CLINCHER

topping *adj, chiefly British* of the very best kind ⟨I know a *topping* new pub in Southwark where we won't run into any toffs⟩ — see EXCELLENT

topple *vb* to go down from an upright position suddenly and involuntarily ⟨the tower of blocks *toppled* even though I bumped into it ever so slightly⟩ — see FALL 1

top–shelf *adj* of the very best kind ⟨hoping to impress the new neighbors, she brought a *top-shelf* wine as a housewarming gift⟩ — see EXCELLENT

topsy–turvy *adj* lacking in order, neatness, and often cleanliness ⟨the office is still *topsy-turvy* even though we moved in months ago⟩ — see MESSY

torch *n* a person who deliberately and unlawfully sets fire to a building or other property ⟨in an insurance scam, the slumlord hired a *torch* to burn the tenement down⟩ — see ARSONIST

torch *vb* to set (something) on fire ⟨police suspect that the owner *torched* the house for the insurance money⟩ — see BURN 2

torment *n* **1** a situation or state that causes great suffering and unhappiness ⟨the released soldiers gave interviews trying to explain to civilians the *torment* that prisoners of war experience⟩ — see HELL 2
2 a state of great suffering of body or mind ⟨was in *torment* for weeks after he broke up with his girlfriend⟩ — see DISTRESS 1
3 a source of persistent emotional distress ⟨insomnia that was caused by a host of nighttime *torments*⟩ — see DEMON 2

torment *vb* to cause persistent suffering to ⟨he was *tormented* by nightmares about the accident⟩ — see AFFLICT

tormenting *adj* **1** hard to accept or bear especially emotionally ⟨it was a *tormenting* moment as they helplessly watched the other team score in the final seconds of the game⟩ — see BITTER 2
2 intensely or unbearably painful ⟨a *tormenting* injury⟩ — see EXCRUCIATING 1

tormentor *also* **tormenter** *n* a person who causes repeated emotional pain, distress, or annoyance to another ⟨shocked by the news that his chief *tormentor* from elementary school had committed suicide at the age of 30⟩
synonyms baiter, harasser, heckler, mocker, needler, persecutor, quiz, quizzer, ridiculer, taunter, tease, teaser, torturer
related words belittler, derider, detractor, giber (*or* jiber), insulter, jeerer, scoffer, scorner; trash-talker; smart aleck (*also* smart alec), smarty (*or* smartie), smarty-pants, wiseacre, wiseguy; kidder, lampooner, satirist; accuser, blamer, troublemaker; assailant, attacker, molester, victimizer; bother, disturber, pest
near antonyms defender, deliverer, guard, protector, rescuer, savior (*or* saviour); comforter, consoler, solace, soother, succorer; bodyguard, champion

torpedo *n* a large sandwich on a long split roll ⟨that deli's *torpedoes* are big enough to serve two people⟩ — see SUBMARINE

torpid *adj* **1** slow to move or act ⟨a *torpid* sloth that refused to budge off its tree branch⟩ — see INACTIVE 1

2 lacking in sensation or feeling ⟨my tongue and throat remained *torpid* for a time following the endoscopy⟩ — see NUMB 1

torpor *n* **1** lack of interest or concern ⟨after a lifetime of setbacks, defeats, and failures, he could only greet the latest bad news with a resigned fatalism and dull *torpor*⟩ — see INDIFFERENCE

2 physical or mental inertness ⟨following a gut-busting Thanksgiving dinner, we spent the rest of the day lounging about in a contented *torpor*⟩ — see LETHARGY

torrent *n* a great flow of water or of something that overwhelms ⟨the dam broke, unleashing a *torrent* down the dry riverbed⟩ — see FLOOD

torrid *adj* **1** having a notably high temperature ⟨the dry, *torrid* summers in southern Arizona⟩ — see HOT 1

2 having or expressing great depth of feeling ⟨a *torrid* love affair⟩ — see FERVENT 1

tortuous *adj* marked by a long series of irregular curves ⟨a *tortuous* mountain road marked by numerous hairpin turns⟩ — see CROOKED 1

torture *n* **1** a situation or state that causes great suffering and unhappiness ⟨it's *torture* for me to see you so unhappy⟩ — see HELL 2

2 a state of great suffering of body or mind ⟨spent an afternoon in *torture* waiting to hear whether her brother had made it home safely⟩ — see DISTRESS 1

torture *vb* **1** to cause persistent suffering to ⟨the neighbor's dog constantly *tortures* our cat, barking at him and chasing him down the street⟩ — see AFFLICT

2 to twist (something) out of a natural or normal shape or condition ⟨*tortured* her naturally straight hair into curls⟩ — see CONTORT

torturer *n* a person who causes repeated emotional pain, distress, or annoyance to another ⟨a sadistic *torturer* of men he regarded as weak, the drillmaster really had it in for one recruit⟩ — see TORMENTOR

torturing *adj* intensely or unbearably painful ⟨watched the final *torturing* moments of the game as the lead constantly shifted between the two teams⟩ — see EXCRUCIATING 1

torturing *n* the twisting of something out of a natural or normal shape or condition ⟨fans of the natural look frown on the *torturing* of garden trees and shrubs into fantastic shapes⟩ — see CONTORTION

torturous *adj* **1** hard to accept or bear especially emotionally ⟨relatives had to make the *torturous* decision to disconnect the patient's life-support system⟩ — see BITTER 2

2 intensely or unbearably painful ⟨the post-infection treatment for rabies was as notoriously *torturous* as the disease itself⟩ — see EXCRUCIATING 1

Tory *n* a person whose political beliefs are centered on tradition and keeping things the way they are ⟨a small-town *Tory* who saw that society was changing, much to his regret⟩ — see CONSERVATIVE

tosh *n* language, behavior, or ideas that are absurd and contrary to good sense ⟨people who believe such *tosh* have the analytical skills of a toddler⟩ — see NONSENSE 1

toss *vb* **1** to make a series of unsteady side-to-side motions ⟨the boat *tossed* to and fro in the heavy seas⟩ — see ROCK 1

2 to make jerky or restless movements ⟨*tossed* and turned in bed all night, unable to sleep in the heat⟩ — see FIDGET

3 to send through the air especially with a quick forward motion of the arm ⟨*toss* that football over here⟩ — see THROW 1

4 to get rid of as useless or unwanted ⟨we need to go through the basement and *toss* whatever we don't use⟩ — see DISCARD

toss (down *or* **off)** *vb* to swallow in liquid form ⟨*tossed off* the last of the medicine⟩ — see DRINK 1

tosspot *n* a person who makes a habit of getting drunk ⟨a bar filled with the same old *tosspots* night after night⟩ — see DRUNK 1

tot (up) *vb* to combine (numbers) into a single sum ⟨*tot up* the prices of the individual pieces and see if buying the whole set makes more sense⟩ — see ADD 2

total *adj* **1** having no exceptions or restrictions ⟨had *total* power over the people of that country⟩ — see ABSOLUTE 2

2 not lacking any part or member that properly belongs to it ⟨gave us a *total* rundown of the events⟩ — see COMPLETE 1

3 trying all possibilities ⟨this was *total* war as far as the military was concerned, and no weapons system was off-limits⟩ — see EXHAUSTIVE 1

total *n* a complete amount of something ⟨that's the *total* for our wheat harvest this year⟩ — see WHOLE

total *vb* **1** to have a total of ⟨two and two *total* four⟩ — see AMOUNT (TO) 1

2 to combine (numbers) into a single sum ⟨*total* all the receipts and tell me how much I owe you⟩ — see ADD 2

3 to bring to a complete end the physical soundness, existence, or usefulness of ⟨a powerful hurricane *totaled* the house some years ago⟩ — see DESTROY 1

totalism *n* a system of government in which the ruler has unlimited power ⟨warned that forfeiture of civil liberties for the sake of security would only result in the terror of *totalism*⟩ — see DESPOTISM

totalitarianism *n* a system of government in which the ruler has unlimited power ⟨in times of crisis, when a nation's people are frightened, there are often calls for *totalitarianism*⟩ — see DESPOTISM

totality *n* a complete amount of something ⟨the *totality* of the stars in the universe can only be loosely guessed at⟩ — see WHOLE

totalize *vb* to combine (numbers) into a single sum ⟨when we *totalized* our restaurant receipts for a month, the result was a little startling⟩ — see ADD 2

totally *adv* **1** to a full extent or degree ⟨I am *totally* upset you can't make it to the celebration⟩ — see FULLY 1

2 with attention to all aspects or details ⟨he made *totally* sure the door was locked when he left the house⟩ — see THOROUGHLY 1

tote *vb* to support and take from one place to another ⟨*toted* his dog from the muddy backyard to the bathtub for a thorough washing⟩ — see CARRY 1

tote (up) *vb* to combine (numbers) into a single sum ⟨he *toted up* each person's costs to see what we had spent as a group⟩ — see ADD 2

totem *n* a device, design, or figure used as an identifying mark ⟨the bald eagle, that universally recognized *totem* of our country⟩ — see EMBLEM

totter *vb* **1** to move forward while swaying from side to side ⟨*tottered* around the house as she practiced walking in high heels⟩ — see STAGGER 1

2 to swing unsteadily back and forth or from side to side ⟨the figurine *tottered* precariously for a moment before falling off the shelf⟩ — see TEETER 1

tottering *adj* marked by or given to small uncontrollable bodily movements ⟨after the accident, she was only able to take a few *tottering* steps at a time⟩ — see SHAKY 1

tottery *adj* marked by or given to small uncontrollable bodily movements ⟨with a *tottery* gait the frail, elderly woman slowly climbed the steps of the church⟩ — see SHAKY 1

touch *n* **1** the state or fact of being able to exchange information regarding one's current situation ⟨everyone promised to keep in *touch* over the summer⟩
synonyms communication, contact, hold

related words commerce, communion, intercommunication, intercourse
2 a very small amount ⟨added just a *touch* of parsley to the dish⟩ — see PARTICLE 1
3 something that sets apart an individual from others of the same kind ⟨each designer has his or her own personal *touches*⟩ — see CHARACTERISTIC
4 an almost imperceptible sign of something ⟨a *touch* of irritation tinged his voice as the candidate fielded yet another question about his personal finances⟩ — see HINT 2

touch *vb* **1** to come into bodily contact with (something) so as to perceive a slight pressure on the skin ⟨be careful not to *touch* this pan—it's still hot⟩
synonyms feel
related words caress, embrace, finger, fondle, hug, kiss, lip, nose, nudge, nuzzle, paw, rub, stroke; palp, palpate; brush, graze, shave, skim; clasp, clench, cling (to), clutch, grasp, grip, handle, hold, palm; chuck, clap, dab, flick, pat, tag, tap, tip; hit, knock, pound, rap, whack
2 to act upon (a person or a person's feelings) so as to cause a response ⟨your speech on the true meaning of patriotism *touched* me deeply⟩ — see [1]AFFECT 1
3 to affect slightly with something morally bad or undesirable ⟨unfortunately, his insufferable arrogance tends to *touch* even the good deeds that he does⟩ — see TAINT 1
4 to be adjacent to ⟨our property *touches* theirs right where that big elm tree is⟩ — see ADJOIN 1
5 to be the business or affair of ⟨I don't think this decision *touches* you, so butt out⟩ — see CONCERN 2

touch (on) *vb* to come very close to being ⟨that behavior *touches on* insanity⟩ — see BORDER (ON) 1

touch (on *or* upon) *vb* to make reference to or speak about briefly but specifically ⟨I do want to briefly *touch upon* the medieval view of the world before talking about Gothic architecture⟩ — see MENTION 1

touchable *adj* capable of being perceived by the sense of touch ⟨not very comfortable with abstractions, I usually relate better to *touchable* things⟩ — see TANGIBLE

touch down *vb* to come to rest after descending from the air ⟨the plane will *touch down* in about 30 minutes⟩ — see ALIGHT 1

touching *adj* **1** having a border in common ⟨*touching* lots in the housing development will eventually be separated by hedges for privacy⟩ — see ADJACENT
2 having the power to affect the feelings or sympathies ⟨a *touching* movie about two lost animals who try to find their way home⟩ — see MOVING

touching *prep* having to do with ⟨there has been an objection *touching* the last of the proposed new bylaws⟩ — see ABOUT 1

touch off *vb* to cause to function ⟨his obscene comment *touched off* a heated debate about the need for censorship on live broadcasts⟩ — see ACTIVATE

touchstone *n* something set up as an example against which others of the same type are compared ⟨his book has long been a *touchstone* for travel writing that aspires to be literature⟩ — see STANDARD 1

touchy *adj* **1** easily offended ⟨watch what you say around him, as he's very *touchy* about every little thing⟩
synonyms huffy, tetchy, thin-skinned, ticklish
related words hypersensitive, oversensitive, sensitive, supersensitive, tender; choleric, crabby, cranky, cross, cross-grained, crotchety, grouchy, grumpy, irascible, irritable, peevish, perverse, pettish, petulant, prickly, quick-tempered, raspy, ratty, short-tempered, snappish, snappy, snarky, snippety, snippy, stroppy [*British*], stuffy, testy, waspish; bearish, bilious, cantankerous, curmudgeonly, disagreeable, dyspeptic, ill-humored, ill-natured, ill-tempered, ornery, querulous, surly
near antonyms agreeable, amiable, good-natured, good-tempered, well-disposed; carefree, easygoing, happy-go-lucky, relaxed, unconcerned; forbearing, long-suffering, obliging, understanding
antonyms thick-skinned
2 requiring exceptional skill or caution in performance or handling ⟨money is a *touchy* subject for many people and shouldn't be discussed casually⟩ — see TRICKY 1
3 capable of catching or being set on fire ⟨the experiment involves the use of some *touchy* chemicals, so caution is required⟩ — see COMBUSTIBLE

touchy–feely *adj* showing feeling freely ⟨she is too *touchy-feely* and he is too stiff-upper-lip for their relationship to ever work out⟩ — see DEMONSTRATIVE 1

tough *adj* **1** not easily chewed ⟨her steak was so *tough* that she suggested the waiter use it as a hockey puck⟩
synonyms chewy, leathery
related words fibrous, gristly, sinewy, stringy; brittle, crunchy, hard; cardboardy
near antonyms mushy, soft
antonyms tender
2 able to withstand hardship, strain, or exposure ⟨this is a *tough* plant that easily withstands harsh winters⟩ — see HARDY 1
3 difficult to endure ⟨*tough* weather conditions on the top of the mountain all year long⟩ — see HARSH 1
4 requiring considerable physical or mental effort ⟨even if you study for it, it's still a *tough* exam⟩ — see HARD 2
5 requiring exceptional skill or caution in performance or handling ⟨handled a *tough* situation with the aplomb and tact of a true diplomat⟩ — see TRICKY 1
6 given to exacting standards of discipline and self-restraint ⟨a *tough* supervisor who docked the pay of anyone who punched in late, no matter what the reason⟩ — see SEVERE 1

tough *n* a violent, brutal person who is often a member of an organized gang ⟨didn't want her son hanging out with the neighborhood *toughs*⟩ — see HOODLUM

toughen *vb* **1** to increase the ability of (as a muscle) to exert physical force ⟨weight lifting will help *toughen* those flabby muscles of yours⟩ — see STRENGTHEN 1
2 to make able to withstand physical hardship, strain, or exposure ⟨hiking every morning through snow and ice *toughened* him considerably⟩ — see HARDEN 2
3 to make more harsh, uncompromising, or severe ⟨attempts to *toughen* conditions under which waivers from military service would be permitted⟩ — see HARSHEN

toughened *adj* able to withstand hardship, strain, or exposure ⟨a group of *toughened* mountain bikers barreling up the hill⟩ — see HARDY 1

toughie *also* **toughy** *n* a violent, brutal person who is often a member of an organized gang ⟨after numerous suspensions, the school *toughies* were finally expelled for gang activities on campus⟩ — see HOODLUM

toupee *n* a headpiece made of natural or synthetic hair usually worn to cover a bald area ⟨the weatherman calmly adjusted his *toupee* after the wind nearly blew it off⟩ — see HAIRPIECE

tour *n* a fixed period of time during which a person holds a job or position ⟨asked the soldiers to consider signing up for a second *tour* of duty⟩ — see TERM 1

tour *vb* to take a trip especially of some distance ⟨thought it would be lots of fun to *tour* all over Europe this summer⟩ — see TRAVEL 1

tour de force *n* an act of notable skill, strength, or cleverness ⟨her performance as a woman impaired by a stroke was a theatrical *tour de force*⟩ — see FEAT 1

tourist *n* a person who travels for pleasure ⟨*tourists* from all over like to take pictures of the alligators in the bayou⟩
synonyms excursionist, rubberneck, rubbernecker,

sightseer, traveler (*or* traveller), tripper [*chiefly British*]
related words holidayer, holidaymaker [*chiefly British*], vacationer, vacationist; guest, hosteler (*or* hosteller), visitor; transient; journeyer, pilgrim, wayfarer; snowbird, sunseeker

tournament *n* a competitive encounter between individuals or groups carried on for amusement, exercise, or in pursuit of a prize ⟨a golf *tournament* in which professionals compete against amateurs⟩ — see GAME 1

tourney *n* a competitive encounter between individuals or groups carried on for amusement, exercise, or in pursuit of a prize ⟨progressed to the final round of the tennis *tourney*⟩ — see GAME 1

tousle *vb* to undo the proper order or arrangement of ⟨his grandfather would always *tousle* the boy's neatly combed hair⟩ — see DISORDER

tousled *adj* lacking in order, neatness, and often cleanliness ⟨a *tousled* pile of yarn and material scraps at the bottom of her craft box⟩ — see MESSY

tout *vb* **1** to praise or publicize lavishly and often excessively ⟨a new cleaning agent *touted* as the only product a homeowner needs for all his or her cleaning chores⟩
synonyms ballyhoo, blow up, crack up, cry up, glorify, trumpet, tub-thump
related words acclaim, applaud, extol (*also* extoll), laud, magnify; commend, compliment, eulogize; advance, advertise, announce, blare, blaze, blazon, boost, herald, offer, plug, promote, publicize; assert, aver, claim, declare, lay down, make out, proclaim, pronounce
2 to declare enthusiastic approval of ⟨statements from several former patients *touting* the doctor's alleged cancer cure⟩ — see ACCLAIM
3 to provide publicity for ⟨an avalanche of ads *touting* the new movie⟩ — see PUBLICIZE 1

tow *vb* to cause to follow by applying steady force on ⟨*towed* the car into the shop for repair⟩ — see PULL 1

toward *or* **towards** *prep* having to do with ⟨didn't know what his attitude *toward* women in the military was⟩ — see ABOUT 1

tower *n* a large, magnificent, or massive building ⟨a hill from which one can gaze upon the *towers* of that great and historic city⟩ — see EDIFICE 1

tower (over) *vb* to be greater, better, or stronger than ⟨that actor's performance *towered over* all others in the film⟩ — see SURPASS 1

towering *adj* **1** extending to a great distance upward ⟨the *towering* mountain peaks of the Rockies⟩ — see HIGH 1
2 going beyond a normal or acceptable limit in degree or amount ⟨doting parents who tend to give their children *towering* praise for very minor accomplishments⟩ — see EXCESSIVE
3 very dignified in form, tone, or style ⟨an article that in *towering* language decries the evils of modern society⟩ — see ELEVATED 2

to wit *adv* that is to say ⟨if we keep spending money like it's water, we're sure to end up in the same place as it often does, *to wit*, down the drain⟩ — see NAMELY

town *n* a thickly settled, highly populated area ⟨after driving for miles with nothing but corn and wheat fields to look at, we were relieved to roll into a small *town* and have a bite to eat at the local diner⟩ — see CITY

townie *or* **towny** *n* **1** a usually longtime resident of a locality ⟨the *townies* are dismayed that all the venerable manses around the village green are being bought as vacation homes by rich interlopers⟩ — see NATIVE 1
2 a person who lives in a town on a permanent basis ⟨the university board met with an association representing the *townies* to figure out a solution to the problems created by off-campus parties⟩ — see BURGHER

townlet *n* a small residential settlement ⟨we passed through several sleepy *townlets* on the long drive to the ski lodge⟩ — see VILLAGE

townsman *n* a person who lives in a town on a permanent basis ⟨thousands of *townsmen* turned out to vote on the school budget⟩ — see BURGHER

toxic *adj* containing or contaminated with a substance capable of injuring or killing a living thing ⟨certain plants are *toxic* if eaten⟩ — see POISONOUS

toxic *n* a substance that by chemical action can kill or injure a living thing ⟨tested for *toxics* in the water supply⟩ — see POISON

toxin *n* a substance that by chemical action can kill or injure a living thing ⟨read a pamphlet on the *toxin* responsible for botulism, a food poisoning that can cause paralysis and even death in some cases⟩ — see POISON

toy *vb* **1** to engage in activity for amusement ⟨the cat *toyed* with the mouse it had caught, batting it about⟩ — see PLAY 1
2 to show a sexual attraction for someone just for fun ⟨likes to *toy* with men whom she has no intention of actually dating⟩ — see FLIRT 1

toy (with) *vb* to handle thoughtlessly, ignorantly, or mischievously ⟨that microscope is a delicate instrument, not something to be *toyed with*⟩ — see TAMPER (WITH)

toylike *adj* of a size that is less than average ⟨the emergency kit comes with a *toylike* wrench, which supposedly is better than nothing⟩ — see SMALL 1

trace *n* **1** a mark or series of marks left on a surface by something that has passed along it ⟨the wolf came and went without leaving a *trace* on the hard, dry ground⟩ — see TRACK 1
2 a passage cleared for public vehicular travel ⟨an old *trace* that dates back to the days of the covered wagon⟩ — see WAY 1
3 a rough course or way formed by or as if by repeated footsteps ⟨stay on the *trace*, or you'll get lost in these thick woods⟩ — see TRAIL 1
4 a tiny often physical indication of something lost or vanished ⟨a ship that appears to have vanished without a *trace* on the high seas⟩ — see VESTIGE 1
5 a very small amount ⟨doctors detected only a *trace* of bacteria in the blood sample but put the patient on antibiotics just in case⟩ — see PARTICLE 1
6 an almost imperceptible sign of something ⟨there didn't seem to be so much as a *trace* of the truth to anything he said⟩ — see HINT 2
7 the mark or impression made by a foot ⟨followed the *traces* of the deer into the deep woods⟩ — see FOOTPRINT

trace *vb* **1** to draw or make apparent the outline of ⟨*trace* your hand onto this piece of paper⟩ — see OUTLINE 1
2 to go after or on the track of ⟨police *traced* the burglar back to his apartment, where they discovered a ton of stolen loot⟩ — see FOLLOW 2

tracing *n* the act of going after or in the tracks of another ⟨the *tracing* of this mountain lion is going to be difficult if the rain washes away all of the tracks⟩ — see PURSUIT 1

track *n* **1** a mark or series of marks left on a surface by something that has passed along it ⟨a muddy *track* across the kitchen floor⟩
synonyms imprint, trace, trail
related words footmark, footprint, footstep, hoofprint, path, print, pug, rut, step, tread; artifact, evidence, leavings, relic, remain(s), remainder, reminder, remnant, residual, residue, sign, spoor, telltale, token, vestige; clue, cue, hint, indication, inkling, intimation, lead, suggestion; scent, shadow, whiff
2 a rough course or way formed by or as if by repeated footsteps ⟨there was still a faint *track* through the un-

derbrush that indicated where the path used to be⟩ — see TRAIL 1

3 the direction along which something or someone moves ⟨I followed the *track* of the thief's eyes as he watched the woman put the money into her purse and walk away⟩ — see PATH 1

track *vb* **1** to go after or on the track of ⟨predators stealthily *tracking* their prey⟩ — see FOLLOW 2

2 to make one's way through, across, or over ⟨once upon a time, millions of buffalo *tracked* the wide open plains⟩ — see TRAVERSE

track (down) *vb* to come upon after searching, study, or effort ⟨I'll try to *track down* his last known address⟩ — see FIND 1

tracking *n* the act of going after or in the tracks of another ⟨took a class in the *tracking* of game that the hunters' association offers⟩ — see PURSUIT 1

trackless *adj* not having been traveled over or through ⟨the *trackless* desert is no place for unequipped, unprepared travelers⟩ — see PATHLESS

tract *n* **1** a broad geographical area ⟨a vast and fertile *tract* of farmland⟩ — see REGION 2

2 a small area of usually open land ⟨the town had planned on turning that *tract* of meadow into a park⟩ — see FIELD 1

3 a small piece of land that is developed or available for development ⟨had a number of small *tracts* for sale, but we couldn't afford to buy land and then build a house⟩ — see LOT 1

tractable *adj* readily giving in to the command or authority of another ⟨put the dog in obedience classes, with the hopes of making her a little more *tractable*⟩ — see OBEDIENT

trade *n* **1** a giving or taking of one thing of value in return for another ⟨when the other team unexpectedly offered to hand over its top pitcher for our star shortstop, our coach agreed to the *trade*⟩ — see EXCHANGE 1

2 an occupation requiring skillful use of the hands ⟨a youth eager to learn the *trade* of cabinetmaking⟩ — see CRAFT 1

3 the activity by which one regularly makes a living ⟨writing is my *trade*⟩ — see OCCUPATION 1

4 the buying and selling of goods especially on a large scale and between different places ⟨a bill regulating *trade* with that country⟩ — see COMMERCE 1

5 the transfer of ownership of something from one person to another for a price ⟨the *trade* of all of her holdings in the company just before the stock plunged in value immediately aroused suspicions⟩ — see SALE

trade *vb* **1** to carry on the business of buying and selling goods or other property ⟨the U.S. agreed to *trade* with China⟩

synonyms deal, traffic

related words bargain, barter, horse-trade, negotiate, transact; auction, exchange, merchandise (*also* merchandize), rebuy, resell, swap; buy, pick up, purchase, take; distribute, fair-trade, market, peddle, retail, sell, supply, vend, wholesale; black-market, bootleg, fence, smuggle; corner, engross, monopolize, undersell; day-trade, invest, speculate

near antonyms black [*chiefly British*], blackball, boycott

2 to give up (something) and take something else in return ⟨I'll *trade* my chocolate chip cookie for your bag of chips⟩ — see CHANGE 3

trademark *n* **1** a device (as a word) identifying the maker of a piece of merchandise and legally reserved for the exclusive use of that person or company ⟨"Kleenex" is a *trademark* for a cleansing tissue⟩

synonyms brand

related words brand name, trade name; collective mark, emblem, hallmark, imprint, label, logo, mark, service mark, stamp; copyright, patent

2 a device, design, or figure used as an identifying mark ⟨the golden arches are a *trademark* of McDonald's⟩ — see EMBLEM

trade–off *n* a giving or taking of one thing of value in return for another ⟨a *trade-off* in which a company got a celebrity spokesperson and a fading star got some much-needed cash⟩ — see EXCHANGE 1

trader *n* a buyer and seller of goods for profit ⟨a coffee *trader*⟩ — see MERCHANT

tradesman *n* **1** a buyer and seller of goods for profit ⟨an antique dealer who's known as a good *tradesman*, buying his items cheaply and selling them for a hefty profit⟩ — see MERCHANT

2 a person whose occupation requires skill with the hands ⟨carpenters joining the *tradesmen's* union⟩ — see ARTISAN

tradition *n* **1** an inherited or established way of thinking, feeling, or doing ⟨the town *tradition* of having the oldest resident ride at the head of the parade⟩

synonyms convention, custom, heritage, prescription, rubric, rule

related words ethic, form, mode, mores, norm, principles, standards, values; birthright, inheritance, legacy; folklore, lore, superstition; culture, lifestyle

2 the body of customs, beliefs, stories, and sayings associated with a people, thing, or place ⟨according to *tradition*, this field was the site of a skirmish between the first settlers and the Native Americans living in the area⟩ — see FOLKLORE

traditional *adj* **1** based on customs usually handed down from a previous generation ⟨a *traditional* Passover meal at his grandparents' house⟩

synonyms classical, conventional, customary, prescriptive

related words authentic, established, fixed, historical; common, habitual, orthodox, usual; ancestral, historic, old-time, old-world; aged, age-old, ancient, antediluvian, hoary, old, venerable; ageless, dateless, immemorial, timeless

near antonyms contemporary, current, modern, modernized, new, new-age, present-day, updated, up-to-date; futuristic, high-tech (*also* hi-tech), hot, latest, mod, modernistic, newfangled, new-fashioned, red-hot, space-age, state-of-the-art, supermodern, ultramodern; nonconformist, nonorthodox, original, progressive, revolutionary, unorthodox, unprecedented, unusual

antonyms nontraditional, unconventional, uncustomary, untraditional

2 tending to favor established ideas, conditions, or institutions ⟨a family that is very *traditional* when it comes to institutions like marriage⟩ — see CONSERVATIVE 1

traditionalism *n* attitudes or opinions tending to favor established ideas, conditions, or institutions ⟨a staunch supporter of grammatical *traditionalism*, my English teacher didn't care what the experts in linguistics said⟩ — see CONSERVATISM

traditionalist *n* a person whose political beliefs are centered on tradition and keeping things the way they are ⟨a *traditionalist* who doesn't believe in expanding government⟩ — see CONSERVATIVE

traditionalistic *adj* tending to favor established ideas, conditions, or institutions ⟨*traditionalistic* bartenders tend to cringe at the sweet concoctions that nowadays pass for cocktails⟩ — see CONSERVATIVE 1

traduce *vb* **1** to fail to keep ⟨a law that *traduces* one of our most cherished rights: the right to privacy⟩ — see VIOLATE 1

2 to make untrue and harmful statements about ⟨my opponent in this campaign may villainously *traduce* me, but I will not stoop to his level⟩ — see SLANDER

traducing *n* the making of false statements that damage another's reputation ⟨this endless *traducing* of candidates has got to stop, or the public will lose all faith in the electoral process⟩ — see SLANDER

traffic *n* the buying and selling of goods especially on a large scale and between different places ⟨the United Nations released a report on countries that still condone the *traffic* of women and children⟩ — see COMMERCE 1

traffic *vb* to carry on the business of buying and selling goods or other property ⟨arrested him for *trafficking* in drugs⟩ — see TRADE 1

trafficker *n* a buyer and seller of goods for profit ⟨a *trafficker* who sold pirated DVDs from the back of his car⟩ — see MERCHANT

tragedy *n* **1** a sudden violent event that brings about great loss or destruction ⟨the earthquake was only the latest in a series of *tragedies* for the city⟩ — see DISASTER 1

2 bad luck or an example of this ⟨it's the *tragedy* of many great artists not to be recognized for their genius until after they're dead⟩ — see MISFORTUNE

tragic *also* **tragical** *adj* of a kind to cause great distress ⟨in a *tragic* turn of events the area's sole remaining steel mill suddenly closed⟩ — see REGRETTABLE

trail *n* **1** a rough course or way formed by or as if by repeated footsteps ⟨took a *trail* through the woods to get to the main road⟩

synonyms footpath, path, pathway, trace, track

related words bridle path; towpath; alley, alleyway, bypath, byroad, bystreet, byway, passageway, walkway; cutoff, shortcut; lane, pass, passage, road, roadway, route, row, run, runway, street, thoroughfare

2 a mark or series of marks left on a surface by something that has passed along it ⟨the slugs left a slimy *trail* on the sidewalk⟩ — see TRACK 1

trail *vb* to go after or on the track of ⟨we *trailed* our friend into the woods, inadvertently spoiling his plans for a solitary hike⟩ — see FOLLOW 2

trailer *n* a motor vehicle that is specially equipped for living while traveling ⟨the band packed their equipment back into their *trailer* and headed off to their next gig⟩ — see CAMPER

trailing *n* the act of going after or in the tracks of another ⟨did you think I didn't know about your constant *trailing* of me?⟩ — see PURSUIT 1

train *n* **1** a body of employees or servants who accompany and wait on a person ⟨a movie star who never goes anywhere without a *train* of personal assistants to cater to his every whim and need⟩ — see CORTEGE 1

2 a group of vehicles traveling together or under one management ⟨a *train* of supply trucks making its way to the army encampment⟩ — see FLEET

3 a series of persons or things arranged one behind another ⟨already a long *train* of ticket buyers waiting outside the stadium⟩ — see LINE 1

4 a series of things linked together ⟨you've broken my *train* of thought—now what were we talking about?⟩ — see CHAIN 1

train *vb* **1** to bring to a proper or desired state of fitness ⟨has been *training* track-and-field athletes at the school for years⟩ — see CONDITION 1

2 to cause to acquire knowledge or skill in some field ⟨will *train* the students in good study habits⟩ — see TEACH

3 to fix (as one's attention) steadily toward a central objective ⟨*train* all your thoughts on imagining how you'd score the winning goal in the game⟩ — see CONCENTRATE 2

4 to point or turn (something) toward a target or goal ⟨*trained* his eyes on the distant bull's-eye⟩ — see AIM 1

5 to make competent (as by training, skill, or ability) for a particular office or function ⟨he's so experienced that they usually use him to *train* new recruits⟩ — see QUALIFY 2

trainer *n* a person who trains performers or athletes ⟨hired a personal *trainer* to help her get in shape⟩ — see COACH

training *n* **1** something done over and over in order to develop skill ⟨a boxer who's been doing a lot of *training* with his footwork⟩ — see EXERCISE 2

2 the act or process of imparting knowledge or skills to another ⟨entered a convent for religious *training*⟩ — see EDUCATION 1

3 a period of undergoing practical instruction in one's job or career ⟨on-the-job *training*⟩ ⟨teacher *training*⟩ — see APPRENTICESHIP

traipse *vb* **1** to go on foot ⟨*traipsed* down the hall to get her printout from the computer room⟩ — see WALK 1

2 to move about from place to place aimlessly ⟨a group of friends *traipsing* around the country the summer after graduation⟩ — see WANDER 1

trait *n* something that sets apart an individual from others of the same kind ⟨honesty is one of her defining *traits*⟩ — see CHARACTERISTIC

traitor *n* one who betrays a trust or an allegiance ⟨accused by her family of being a *traitor* when she sold their traditionally animal-friendly business to a competitor known to use animals for testing its products⟩

synonyms apostate, backstabber, betrayer, double-crosser, double-dealer, Judas, quisling, recreant, serpent, snake, turncoat

related words accommodationist, collaborationist, collaborator, sellout, subversive, subverter; coconspirator, conspirator, intriguer, plotter, schemer; defector, deserter, renegade; blabbermouth, gossip, gossiper, gossipmonger, informant, informer, rat, rumormonger, snitch, snitcher, squealer, stool pigeon, talebearer, talker, tattler, tattletale, telltale

traitorous *adj* not true in one's allegiance to someone or something ⟨when our coach took a job at a rival college, a few *traitorous* players went right along with him⟩ — see FAITHLESS

trammel *n* something that makes movement or progress difficult ⟨students and parents who want to throw off the *trammels* of outdated school policies⟩ — see ENCUMBRANCE

trammel *vb* **1** to confine or restrain with or as if with chains ⟨years after his death, she was still *trammeled* by inconsolable grief for her deceased husband⟩ — see BIND 1

2 to create difficulty for the work or activity of ⟨the new paperwork requirements will only *trammel* us and lower our productivity⟩ — see HAMPER

tramp *n* **1** a homeless wanderer who may beg or steal for a living ⟨the police encouraged the *tramps* who were sleeping in the park to spend the bitterly cold night in the homeless shelter⟩

synonyms bindle stiff, bum, bummer, hobo, sundowner [*Australian*], swaggie [*chiefly Australian*], swagman [*chiefly Australian*], vagabond, vagrant

related words drifter, roamer, transient; beggar, derelict, mendicant, panhandler, stiff; dodger, malingerer, shirker, slacker; gamine, ragamuffin, urchin, waif

2 a boldly flirtatious or sexually promiscuous woman ⟨no daughter of hers was going to go to the dance dressed like a *tramp*⟩ — see FLOOZY

tramp *vb* **1** to move heavily or clumsily ⟨*tramped* wearily up the stairs after a long day at work⟩ — see LUMBER 1

2 to tread on heavily so as to crush or injure ⟨didn't mean to *tramp* your toes as I was running past you⟩ — see TRAMPLE

3 to travel by foot for exercise or pleasure ⟨we would have happily *tramped* through the forest for the rest of the day if it hadn't started to rain⟩ — see HIKE 1

tramper *n* a person who travels by foot for exercise or pleasure ⟨though inaccessible to most vehicles, the boggy backcountry is popular with intrepid *trampers*⟩ — see HIKER

trample *vb* to tread on heavily so as to crush or injure ⟨Isabel looked out her window and beheld the neighbor's Labrador retriever *trampling* her begonias⟩
synonyms champ, stamp, stomp, tramp, tromp
related words override, run down, run over, step (on); mash, pulp, smash, squash, squelch; boot, hoof, kick

trampy *adj* having loose sexual morals ⟨an author who mostly wrote hard-boiled fiction about macho men and *trampy* women⟩ — see SLEAZY 1

trance *n* the state of being lost in thought ⟨lulled by the sound of the train, she stared out the window in a *trance*, oblivious to the fact that the conductor was taking tickets⟩ — see REVERIE

tranquil *adj* **1** free from disturbing noise or uproar ⟨the house was once again *tranquil* after the kids moved outside to play⟩ — see QUIET 1
2 free from emotional or mental agitation ⟨though she should have been upset, she felt oddly *tranquil* upon learning that she would not be receiving the scholarship⟩ — see CALM 2
3 free from storms or physical disturbance ⟨drifting dreamily through *tranquil* seas⟩ — see CALM 1

tranquilize *also* **tranquillize** *vb* to free from distress or disturbance ⟨at long last the crying baby was *tranquilized* by the steady rocking of her cradle⟩ — see CALM 1

tranquilizing *also* **tranquillizing** *adj* tending to calm the emotions and relieve stress ⟨a woman who put a lot of faith in the *tranquilizing* effects of a cup of tea⟩ — see SOOTHING 1

tranquillity *or* **tranquility** *n* **1** a state of freedom from storm or disturbance ⟨enjoyed the *tranquillity* of the snow-covered field at dusk⟩ — see CALM 1
2 evenness of emotions or temper ⟨a psychotherapist valued for her *tranquillity* and ability to listen⟩ — see EQUANIMITY
3 freedom from disquieting or oppressive thoughts or emotions ⟨a mountain climber who finds inner *tranquillity* as he looks out from the edge of some lofty precipice⟩ — see PEACE 2

tranquilness *n* evenness of emotions or temper ⟨he maintained his gentle *tranquilness* despite the provocations⟩ — see EQUANIMITY

transaction *n* the transfer of ownership of something from one person to another for a price ⟨if you want to return any merchandise, make sure you keep the receipt for the initial sales *transaction*⟩ — see SALE

transcend *vb* **1** to be greater, better, or stronger than ⟨a man whose practical knowledge of botany *transcends* that of his more educated colleagues⟩ — see SURPASS 1
2 to go beyond the limit of ⟨a person who believes that any true understanding of God *transcends* human intelligence⟩ — see EXCEED 1

transcendence *n* the fact or state of being above others in rank or importance ⟨makes a case for the *transcendence* of Louis Armstrong's contributions to the field of jazz⟩ — see EMINENCE 1

transcendent *adj* **1** of, relating to, or being part of a reality beyond the observable physical universe ⟨a firm belief in angels, demons, and other *transcendent* beings⟩ — see SUPERNATURAL 1
2 being so extraordinary or abnormal as to suggest powers which violate the laws of nature ⟨the star player's *transcendent* performance helped the team to a surprise victory⟩ — see SUPERNATURAL 2

transcendental *adj* **1** of, relating to, or being part of a reality beyond the observable physical universe ⟨the concept of the soul as a *transcendental* entity that exists entirely apart from the body⟩ — see SUPERNATURAL 1
2 being so extraordinary or abnormal as to suggest powers which violate the laws of nature ⟨in his speeches he manifests a *transcendental* ability to inspire people from all points on the political spectrum⟩ — see SUPERNATURAL 2

transfer *vb* **1** to give over the legal possession or ownership of ⟨Claire's grandfather agreed to *transfer* certain stocks to her when she turned 18⟩
synonyms alien, alienate, assign, cede, convey, deed, make over
related words bequeath, hand down, leave, pass (down), will; bestow, commend, commit, confer, contribute, deliver, donate, grant, hand over, move, pass, present, release, relinquish, surrender, transmit, turn in, turn over, vest, yield; consign, entrust (*also* intrust), trust; lease, lend, let [*chiefly British*], loan, rent
phrases dispose of
near antonyms expropriate
2 to cause (something) to pass from one to another ⟨they used Morse Code to *transfer* the message from one ship to another⟩ — see COMMUNICATE 1
3 to cause to go or be taken from one place to another ⟨will have to *transfer* you from our San Francisco office to our New York headquarters⟩ — see SEND
4 to change the place or position of ⟨*transferred* the car keys from my pocket to my purse⟩ — see MOVE 1
5 to put (something) into the possession or safekeeping of another ⟨before she left the country, she *transferred* all her record books and important papers to her mother⟩ — see GIVE 2
6 to shift possession of (something) from one person to another ⟨*transferred* the ball to the running back⟩ — see PASS 1

transferable *also* **transferrable** *adj* capable of being taken from one place to another by public carrier ⟨supplemental charges for oversized *transferable* goods like pianos⟩ — see SHIPPABLE

transfiguration *n* a change in form, appearance, or use ⟨after his *transfiguration* into a Buddhist monk, all his family and friends were amazed by his newly found patience and tranquillity⟩ — see CONVERSION 1

transfigure *vb* to change in form, appearance, or use ⟨married life has seemingly *transfigured* his formerly aimless existence⟩ — see CONVERT 2

transfix *vb* to penetrate or hold (something) with a pointed object ⟨*transfixed* the inanimate butterfly specimens to the collection board⟩ — see IMPALE

transform *vb* to change in form, appearance, or use ⟨by clicking a few buttons, this toy car can be *transformed* into a robot⟩ — see CONVERT 2

transformation *n* a change in form, appearance, or use ⟨a raven-haired starlet who underwent an attention-getting *transformation* and showed up at the awards ceremony as a blonde⟩ — see CONVERSION 1

transfuse *vb* **1** to cause (something) to pass from one to another ⟨a teacher who is able to *transfuse* his enthusiasm and passion for history to his students⟩ — see COMMUNICATE 1
2 to spread throughout ⟨light *transfused* the room as the sun rose⟩ — see PERMEATE

transgress *vb* **1** to commit an offense ⟨I didn't realize I was *transgressing* when I told your sister she looked like she had lost weight⟩ — see OFFEND 1
2 to fail to keep ⟨don't even think about *transgressing* the drug laws of that Asian country, for punishments are severe and there's nothing that our government can do to intervene⟩ — see VIOLATE 1

transgression *n* **1** a breaking of a moral or legal code ⟨acts that are *transgressions* against the laws of civilized societies everywhere⟩ — see OFFENSE 1
2 a failure to uphold the requirements of law, duty, or

obligation ⟨a dying woman asking for divine forgiveness for a lifetime of *transgressions*⟩ — see BREACH 1

transience *n* the state or quality of lasting only for a short time ⟨wary of the *transience* of popular enthusiasms, the writers of the U.S. Constitution made changing the document a long and difficult process⟩ — see IMPERMANENCE

transiency *n* the state or quality of lasting only for a short time ⟨because of the *transiency* of their residency, college students often display little interest in the welfare of the towns where they go to school⟩ — see IMPERMANENCE

transient *adj* lasting only for a short time ⟨had *transient* thoughts of suicide but never acted upon them⟩ — see MOMENTARY

transit *vb* to make one's way through, across, or over ⟨once you *transit* that stretch of dense woods, the hiking should be much easier⟩ — see TRAVERSE

transitoriness *n* the state or quality of lasting only for a short time ⟨given the *transitoriness* of most teen romances, the parents probably have little to worry about⟩ — see IMPERMANENCE

transitory *adj* lasting only for a short time ⟨a *transitory* panic struck me when I realized that we had left the baby in the car⟩ — see MOMENTARY

translate *vb* to express something (as a text or statement) in different words ⟨would you mind *translating* this German article for me?⟩ — see PARAPHRASE

translate (into) *vb* to be the cause of (a situation, action, or state of mind) ⟨it remains to be seen whether the policy changes will *translate into* true progress⟩ — see EFFECT

translating *n* an instance of expressing something in different words ⟨his insightful *translating* of that passage really captured the tone of the original⟩ — see PARAPHRASE

translation *n* an instance of expressing something in different words ⟨had to read Dante's *Divine Comedy* in *translation* since I don't know Italian⟩ — see PARAPHRASE

translucence *n* the state or quality of being easily seen through ⟨the exceptional *translucence* of the sapphire adds to its value⟩ — see CLARITY 1

translucency *n* the state or quality of being easily seen through ⟨the *translucency* of a wine can only be appreciated if it is served in uncolored glasses, preferably of fine crystal⟩ — see CLARITY 1

transmissible *adj* capable of being passed by physical contact from one person to another ⟨don't worry, the genetic disorder isn't *transmissible* from one generation to the next⟩ — see CONTAGIOUS 1

transmit *vb* **1** to cause (something) to pass from one to another ⟨sneezing and coughing can *transmit* disease⟩ — see COMMUNICATE 1
2 to cause to go or be taken from one place to another ⟨I'll *transmit* this information over the airwaves⟩ — see SEND
3 to put (something) into the possession or safekeeping of another ⟨*transmitted* the deed of his house to his lawyer⟩ — see GIVE 2

transmittable *adj* **1** capable of being passed by physical contact from one person to another ⟨that disease is only *transmittable* through direct contact with an infected person, not through contact with something the infected person has touched⟩ — see CONTAGIOUS 1
2 capable of being taken from one place to another by public carrier ⟨I doubt that animals are legally *transmittable* through the mail⟩ — see SHIPPABLE

transmute *vb* to change in form, appearance, or use ⟨in his elegy on his deceased wife, the poet has *transmuted* inconsolable grief into high art⟩ — see CONVERT 2

transnational *adj* relating to or involving two or more nations ⟨global warming is a *transnational* problem that requires a *transnational* solution⟩ — see INTERNATIONAL

transparency *n* the state or quality of being easily seen through ⟨because of the *transparency* of the Caribbean waters, we could see sharks and tropical fish swimming 20 or 30 feet below the surface⟩ — see CLARITY 1

transparent *adj* **1** easily seen through ⟨bottles of blue *transparent* glass⟩ — see CLEAR 1
2 not subject to misinterpretation or more than one interpretation ⟨his meaning in leaving the conversation is *transparent*: he doesn't want to talk about his combat experiences⟩ — see CLEAR 2
3 very thin and easy to see through ⟨told her she had to wear a slip under that nearly *transparent* skirt⟩ — see SHEER 1

transpierce *vb* to penetrate or hold (something) with a pointed object ⟨got a thrill out of *transpiercing* butterflies with hat pins⟩ — see IMPALE

transpire *vb* to take place ⟨please tell me what *transpired* on the night of October 1⟩ — see HAPPEN

transport *n* **1** a state of overwhelming usually pleasurable emotion ⟨was in *transports* of joy after winning the championship⟩ — see ECSTASY
2 something used to carry goods or passengers ⟨rising gas prices will impel more people to use public *transport*⟩ — see CONVEYANCE

transport *vb* **1** to cause to go or be taken from one place to another ⟨I'll have to *transport* the car to our new home overseas by public carrier⟩ — see SEND
2 to fill with great joy ⟨was absolutely *transported* when she heard that her brother was getting married⟩ — see ELATE
3 to fill with overwhelming emotion (as wonder or delight) ⟨was *transported* with wonder when she saw the Matterhorn for the first time⟩ — see ENTRANCE
4 to force to leave a country ⟨the offending journalist was *transported* out of the country and ordered to never return⟩ — see BANISH 1
5 to support and take from one place to another ⟨will you *transport* this heavy casserole dish to the dining room for me?⟩ — see CARRY 1

transportable *adj* capable of being taken from one place to another by public carrier ⟨you'll need to see if that food is *transportable* overseas before you send boxes of it to your relatives in the military⟩ — see SHIPPABLE

transportation *n* **1** a means of getting to a destination in a vehicle driven by another ⟨I'm without *transportation* tonight, so I can't meet you at the movies⟩ — see RIDE
2 something used to carry goods or passengers ⟨right now my bike is my only *transportation*⟩ — see CONVEYANCE

transpose *vb* **1** to change in form, appearance, or use ⟨contends that popular culture has *transposed* Christmas from a religious feast into a celebration of consumerism⟩ — see CONVERT 2
2 to change the place or position of ⟨after the ex-governor's scandals belatedly came to light, his portrait was *transposed* to a quiet corner of the statehouse⟩ — see MOVE 1

transubstantiate *vb* to change in form, appearance, or use ⟨the novelist *transubstantiated* the joys and sorrows of his early years into a charming fable about childhood⟩ — see CONVERT 2

transude *vb* to flow forth slowly through small openings ⟨sweat was *transuding* from the pores of his face despite his best efforts to look cool and collected during the interview⟩ — see EXUDE

transversely *adv* in a line or direction running from corner to corner ⟨the coat of arms had a line of white horses running *transversely* from one corner to another on a blue background⟩ — see CROSSWISE

trap *n* **1** a device or scheme for capturing another by surprise ⟨undercover agents devised a *trap* to catch the counterfeiters⟩ ⟨a bear *trap*⟩
synonyms ambush, net, snare, web
related words enmeshment, entanglement, entrapment, envelopment; booby trap, catch, hazard, land mine, pitfall, snag; artifice, cheat, cheating, deception, double-dealing, duplicity, ploy, ruse, subterfuge, trick
2 a setup in which hidden attackers lie in wait ⟨an overland route to the Far East that was once notorious for the many robbers who laid *traps* for unsuspecting wayfarers⟩ — see AMBUSH 1
3 something that catches and holds ⟨the promotion is really just a *trap* to keep her from taking a new job elsewhere⟩ — see WEB 1
4 *slang* the opening through which food passes into the body of an animal ⟨shut your *trap* before someone belts you one!⟩ — see MOUTH 1

trap *vb* **1** to catch or hold as if in a net ⟨an ambitious young man who was now *trapped* in a series of shady business deals⟩ — see ENTANGLE 2
2 to take physical control or possession of (something) suddenly or forcibly ⟨finally *trapped* the annoying fly in the palm of his hand⟩ — see CATCH 1

trash *n* **1** discarded or useless material ⟨the neighbor's dog was rooting around in our *trash* this morning⟩ — see GARBAGE 1
2 language, behavior, or ideas that are absurd and contrary to good sense ⟨don't talk *trash* to me!⟩ — see NONSENSE 1
3 people looked down upon as ignorant and of the lowest class ⟨snooty people who thought that we were *trash* because we were in the cleaning business⟩ — see RABBLE
4 that which is of low quality or worth ⟨the souvenirs in the gift shop are nothing but *trash*⟩ — see JUNK 1

trash *vb* **1** to criticize harshly and usually publicly ⟨a stand-up comedian who humorously *trashes* the motley crew of people who bug her⟩ — see ATTACK 2
2 to deliberately cause the damage or destruction of another's property ⟨someone had broken into the gym and *trashed* the decorations for the dance⟩ — see VANDALIZE
3 to express scornfully one's low opinion of ⟨a club member who *trashes* every idea that isn't hers⟩ — see DECRY 1
4 to take sudden, violent action against ⟨gangs of young punks would *trash* the encampment of homeless men just for sport⟩ — see ATTACK 1

trashing *n* deliberate damaging or destroying of another's property ⟨the *trashing* of his apartment was the work of his ex-girlfriend, who apparently did not take the breakup very well⟩ — see VANDALISM

trash–talk *vb* to express scornfully one's low opinion of ⟨began to *trash-talk* the opposing players the minute they got on the field⟩ — see DECRY 1

trashy *adj* **1** marked by an obvious lack of style or good taste ⟨I know that sequined shirt cost a lot of money, but I still think it looks kind of *trashy*⟩ — see [1]TACKY 1
2 of low quality ⟨*trashy* furniture that fell apart after a few weeks⟩ — see CHEAP 2
3 depicting or referring to sexual matters in a way that is unacceptable in polite society ⟨a *trashy* skin magazine with no pretense to subtlety⟩ — see OBSCENE 1

travail *n* **1** a state of great suffering of body or mind ⟨no greater *travail* than that of parents who have suffered the death of a child⟩ — see DISTRESS 1
2 very hard or unpleasant work ⟨these villagers now have decent housing, so our *travail* has not been in vain⟩ — see [1]TOIL
3 the act or process of giving birth to children ⟨a midwife assisted her throughout her long *travail*⟩ — see CHILDBIRTH

travail *vb* to devote serious and sustained effort ⟨Labor Day is the day on which we recognize those men and women who daily *travail* with little appreciation or compensation⟩ — see LABOR

travel *n, often* **travels** *pl* a going from one place to another usually of some distance ⟨in all his *travels* he never met pleasanter people than he had in that village⟩ — see JOURNEY

travel *vb* **1** to take a trip especially of some distance ⟨the couple loves to *travel* and has been to 34 countries⟩
synonyms journey, peregrinate, pilgrimage, tour, trek, trip, voyage
related words gallivant (*also* galavant), hop, jaunt, knock (about), perambulate, ramble, roam, rove, traipse, wander; migrate, road-trip; bus, cab, coach, cruise, drive, fly, gig, jet, motor, navigate, ride, roll, sail, trundle; barnstorm
2 to make one's way through, across, or over ⟨will *travel* the river for a while and then continue on land⟩ — see TRAVERSE
3 to proceed or move quickly ⟨that racehorse can definitely *travel*⟩ — see HURRY 2
4 to come or be together as friends ⟨he *traveled* with a fast crowd when he was in college⟩ — see ASSOCIATE 1

traveler *or* **traveller** *n* a person who travels for pleasure ⟨a company that offers guidebooks and maps for *travelers*⟩ — see TOURIST

traveling bag *n* a bag carried by hand and designed to hold a traveler's clothing and personal articles ⟨*traveling bags* made of lightweight but tough fabrics⟩
synonyms carryall, carry-on, grip, handbag, holdall [*chiefly British*], portmanteau, suitcase, wallet
related words overnight bag (*also* overnight case), weekend bag (*also* weekend case), weekender; cosmetic case, traveling case; carpetbag, duffel bag, kit, kit bag; backpack, haversack, knapsack, packsack, rucksack; attaché, attaché case, briefcase, valise; baggage, bags, luggage

traverse *vb* to make one's way through, across, or over ⟨the spider *traversed* the wall from end to end⟩
synonyms course, cover, cross, cut (across), follow, go, navigate, pass (over), perambulate, peregrinate, proceed (along), track, transit, travel
related words hike, traipse, tramp, tread, walk; ride, run; crisscross

travesty *n* **1** a poor, insincere, or insulting imitation of something ⟨rigged from the start, his trial was a *travesty* of justice⟩ — see MOCKERY 1
2 a work that imitates and exaggerates another work for comic effect ⟨the big-screen version of the classic sitcom is actually a good-natured *travesty* of the TV series⟩ — see PARODY 1

travesty *vb* to copy or exaggerate (someone or something) in order to make fun of ⟨this comedy sketch mindlessly *travesties* the hard work of relief workers around the world⟩ — see MIMIC 1

treacherous *adj* not true in one's allegiance to someone or something ⟨a *treacherous* "friend," she's been known to turn against people in the blink of an eye⟩ — see FAITHLESS

treachery *n* the act or fact of violating the trust or confidence of another ⟨was furious that she revealed his secret and never forgave her for the *treachery*⟩ — see BETRAYAL

tread *vb* to go on foot ⟨to protect the fragile environment of the beach dunes, we must *tread* cautiously and lightly⟩ — see WALK 1

treadmill *n* an established and often automatic or monotonous series of actions followed when engaging in some activity ⟨the *treadmill* of the morning commute to work⟩ — see ROUTINE 1

treason *n* the act or fact of violating the trust or confidence of another ⟨reading a friend's diary without permission would have to be regarded as the ultimate act of personal *treason*⟩ — see BETRAYAL

treasure *n* **1** an asset that brings praise or renown ⟨ancient archaeological *treasures* that today would never be allowed out of the country of origin⟩ — see GLORY 2
2 someone or something unusually desirable ⟨in thanking them for their contributions, the mayor referred to the volunteers at the homeless shelter as the city's greatest *treasures*⟩ — see PRIZE 1

treasure *vb* **1** to hold dear ⟨I'll always *treasure* the time my friend and I spent together this past summer⟩ — see LOVE 1
2 to put (something of future use or value) in a safe or secret place ⟨a trove of fine wines that he had lovingly *treasured* over the years⟩ — see HOARD

treasure trove *n* an abundant source ⟨the ancient city, having been almost perfectly preserved under volcanic ash for nearly 2,000 years, is proving to be a *treasure trove* of archaeological information⟩ — see MINE 1

treat *n* **1** a source of great satisfaction ⟨spending a long weekend at a ski resort is a real *treat*⟩ — see DELIGHT 1
2 something that is pleasing to eat because it is rare or a luxury ⟨for us sushi is a real *treat* since no restaurant around here makes it⟩ — see DELICACY 1

treat *vb* **1** to behave toward in a stated way ⟨she tries to *treat* all of her students fairly and equally, regardless of her personal feelings toward them⟩
synonyms act (toward), be (to), deal (with), handle, serve, use
related words consider, esteem, rate, reckon, regard, view; engage (with), react (to), respond (to)
phrases do by
2 to deal with (something) usually skillfully or efficiently ⟨school officials *treated* the vandalism of the students' artwork as a very serious matter⟩ — see HANDLE 1
3 to exchange viewpoints or seek advice for the purpose of finding a solution to a problem ⟨I will *treat* with my lawyer and let you know what we decide⟩ — see CONFER 2
4 to give medical treatment to ⟨a nurse *treating* a patient⟩ — see DOCTOR 1

treat (of) *vb* to have (something) as a subject matter ⟨his paper *treats of* the ethical dilemmas that doctors face every day in the emergency rooms of urban hospitals⟩ — see CONCERN 1

treaty *n* a formal agreement between two or more nations or peoples ⟨in accordance with a *treaty* between the United States and the tribes of the Pacific Northwest, commercial fishing of certain kinds of salmon is limited to Native Americans⟩
synonyms accord, alliance, compact, convention, covenant, pact
related words entente, entente cordiale; bargain, bond, charter, concord, contract, deal, settlement, understanding; projet

treble *adj* **1** having a high musical pitch or range ⟨the *treble* shrieks of children at play⟩ — see SHRILL
2 having three units or parts ⟨a *treble* painting, with each panel telling a different part of the Nativity story⟩ — see TRIPLE

trek *n* a going from one place to another usually of some distance ⟨started on our *trek* up the mountain before the sun rose⟩ — see JOURNEY

trek *vb* to take a trip especially of some distance ⟨adventurers *trekking* across the desert in search of a fabled city of gold⟩ — see TRAVEL 1

tremble *n* an instance of shaking involuntarily with fear or cold ⟨with a *tremble*, she ventured out into the snow⟩ — see SHIVER 1

trembling *adj* marked by or given to small uncontrollable bodily movements ⟨*trembling* from the cold⟩ — see SHAKY 1

trembling *n* a series of slight movements by a body back and forth or from side to side ⟨at the first sign of the room's *trembling*, I ducked for cover, for I was certain that it was the start of the big quake⟩ — see VIBRATION 1

trembly *adj* marked by or given to small uncontrollable bodily movements ⟨the inexperienced lecturer tried to control her *trembly* hands as she walked onstage⟩ — see SHAKY 1

tremendous *adj* unusually large ⟨that's a *tremendous* amount of work for one person⟩ — see HUGE

tremendously *adv* to a large extent or degree ⟨I'm *tremendously* upset I didn't get into that university⟩ — see GREATLY 2

tremor *n* a shaking of the earth ⟨smaller *tremors* continued for days after the major earthquake⟩ — see EARTHQUAKE 1

tremulous *adj* **1** easily frightened ⟨a *tremulous* girl somehow mustered up the courage to ask a question of the governor⟩ — see SHY 1
2 marked by or given to small uncontrollable bodily movements ⟨the frail woman extended a *tremulous* hand in welcome⟩ — see SHAKY 1

trench *n* a long narrow channel dug in the earth ⟨dug a *trench* and filled it with water in an attempt to keep the forest fire off her property⟩ — see DITCH

trench (on) *vb* to come very close to being ⟨that response *trenches on* outright rudeness⟩ — see BORDER (ON) 1

trenchant *adj* having an edge thin enough to cut or pierce something ⟨even the most *trenchant* sword could not sever the bonds of loyalty between them⟩ — see SHARP 1

trend *n* **1** a prevailing or general movement or inclination ⟨according to the survey, there's a growing *trend* for companies to run their own day-care centers for the benefit of employees⟩
synonyms current, direction, drift, leaning, run, tendency, tide, wind
related words curve, downside, shift, swing, turn, turnabout, upside; custom, habit, propensity, tenor, way; countercurrent, countertrend; undercurrent, undertow
2 a practice or interest that is very popular for a short time ⟨still had a coat from the last *trend* for fake fur, when the material lined everything from boots to coats to bracelets⟩ — see FAD

trend *vb* **1** to show a liking or proneness (for something) ⟨during the winter our school system *trends* toward canceling school at the drop of a hat—or at least a snowflake⟩ — see LEAN 2
2 to turn away from a straight line or course ⟨the river *trends* east, then west again, forming an oxbow⟩ — see CURVE 1

trendiness *n* the quality or state of being fashionable ⟨*trendiness* is something that I don't think about when choosing clothes⟩ — see COOL 2

trendsetter *n* one that takes the lead or sets an example ⟨a closely watched *trendsetter* in women's fashions⟩ — see BELLWETHER

trendy *adj* **1** being in the latest or current fashion ⟨if what's in the stores is any indication, shorter skirts are *trendy* again this year⟩ — see STYLISH
2 keenly aware of and responsive to the latest developments especially in fashion and entertainment ⟨*trendy* foodies always looking for the hottest chefs and the coolest restaurants⟩ — see AU COURANT 1

trepidation *n* the emotion experienced in the presence

or threat of danger ⟨shaking with *trepidation*, I stepped into the old abandoned house⟩ — see FEAR 1

trespass *n* **1** a breaking of a moral or legal code ⟨forgive us our *trespasses* as we forgive those who trespass against us⟩ — see OFFENSE 1
2 a failure to uphold the requirements of law, duty, or obligation ⟨plagiarism is a serious *trespass* of academic integrity⟩ — see BREACH 1

trespass *vb* to commit an offense ⟨I consider him to be *trespassing* against all of us when he *trespasses* against any one of us⟩ — see OFFEND 1

triad *n* a group of three ⟨a *triad* of candlesticks on the mantle⟩ — see THREESOME

triadic *adj* having three units or parts ⟨the application to this music school is *triadic* in structure: there's the written application, then the audition, and finally an interview with the admissions board⟩ — see TRIPLE

trial *adj* made or done as an experiment ⟨a *trial* medical procedure that should be considered only after all other options have been exhausted⟩ — see EXPERIMENTAL 1

trial *n* **1** a test of faith, patience, or strength ⟨living with her insufferable relatives was a real *trial*⟩
synonyms cross, crucible, fire, gauntlet (*also* gantlet), ordeal
related words baptism, initiation; adversity, affliction, asperity, misadventure, mischance, misfortune, mishap, privation, tragedy, tribulation, trouble, vicissitude, woe; acid test, litmus test; challenge, complication, difficulty, grief, grievance, hardship, rigor; annoyance, discomfort, inconvenience, nuisance
phrases baptism of fire
2 a private performance or session in preparation for a public appearance ⟨ran another *trial* of the aerial performance before opening night⟩ — see REHEARSAL
3 a procedure or operation carried out to resolve an uncertainty ⟨*trials* by medical researchers haven't determined whether the medication is safe or not⟩ — see EXPERIMENT
4 an effort to do or accomplish something ⟨will rest and make another *trial* at climbing the mountain⟩ — see ATTEMPT 1
5 something that is a source of irritation ⟨trying to have a coherent phone conversation with his senile father was always a *trial*⟩ — see ANNOYANCE 3

tribal *adj* of, relating to, or reflecting the traits exhibited by a group of people with a common ancestry and culture ⟨a *tribal* solidarity that transcends all other loyalties or bonds⟩ — see RACIAL

tribe *n* a group of persons who come from the same ancestor ⟨the wedding joined the two *tribes* together⟩ — see FAMILY 1

tribulation *n* a state of great suffering of body or mind ⟨a documentary chronicling the lasting *tribulation* of Holocaust survivors⟩ — see DISTRESS 1

tribunal *n* an assembly of persons for the administration of justice ⟨was tried before a military *tribunal* and found not guilty of the charges⟩ — see COURT 3

tribune *n* a level usually raised surface ⟨addressed the vast crowd from the *tribune*⟩ — see PLATFORM 1

tributary *n* a stream that flows into a larger body of water ⟨the Amazon and its more than 1,000 known *tributaries* form the world's largest drainage basin⟩
synonyms affluent, bayou, branch, confluent, feeder, influent
related words backwater; brook, brooklet, creek, rill, rivulet, run [*chiefly Midland*], streamlet; fountainhead, head, headstream, headwater, source
antonyms distributary, effluent

tribute *n* a formal expression of praise ⟨*tributes* were received from all over the world at the opera singer's farewell concert⟩ — see ENCOMIUM

trice *n* a very small space of time ⟨it's just a scrape on the knee—we'll have you fixed up in a *trice*⟩ — see INSTANT

trick *n* **1** a clever often underhanded means to achieve an end ⟨her husband used every *trick* in the book to get out of appearing in his parish's fashion show⟩
synonyms artifice, device, dodge, fetch, flimflam, gambit, gimmick, jig, juggle, knack, play, ploy, scheme, shenanigan, sleight, stratagem, wile
related words bluff, end run, feint; cheating, chicanery, cozenage, craft, crookery, cunning, deception, dupery, duplicity, fakery, jugglery, legerdemain, skulduggery (*or* skullduggery), subterfuge, swindling, trickery; fraud, gaff, hoax, sham, swindle; blind, front, smoke screen
phrases sleight of hand
2 a playful or mischievous act intended as a joke ⟨thought that gluing the silver dollar to the floor and watching him struggle to pick it up would be a good *trick*⟩ — see PRANK
3 a usual manner of behaving or doing ⟨that deadbeat is up to his usual *tricks*: once again he's claiming the check is in the mail⟩ — see HABIT 1
4 an act of notable skill, strength, or cleverness ⟨it'd be quite a *trick* to hit that target from here⟩ — see FEAT 1
5 an odd or peculiar habit ⟨a dog with the *trick* of eating cabbage⟩ — see IDIOSYNCRASY

trick *vb* to cause to believe what is untrue ⟨you *tricked* me into thinking my ex wasn't coming to the party tonight⟩ — see DECEIVE

tricker *n* a dishonest person who uses clever means to cheat others out of something of value ⟨they're equal-opportunity con artists: *trickers* of plutocrats and pensioners alike⟩ — see TRICKSTER 1

trickery *n* the use of clever underhanded actions to achieve an end ⟨Delia resorted to *trickery*—even loading up the fishing equipment—to induce her dog into the car for his vet appointment⟩
synonyms artifice, chicane, chicanery, gamesmanship, hanky-panky, jiggery-pokery, jugglery, legerdemain, skulduggery (*or* skullduggery), subterfuge, wile
related words artfulness, caginess (*also* cageyness), craftiness, cunning, deviousness, foxiness, oiliness, shadiness, sharpness, shiftiness, shrewdness, slickness, slipperiness, slyness, sneakiness, treachery, underhandedness, wiliness; crookedness, crookery, cunning, deceit, deceitfulness, deception, deceptiveness, dishonesty, dissimulation, double-dealing, dupery, duplicity, guile, guilefulness, hypocrisy, insincerity; fakery, humbuggery, imposture, quackery; dirty pool, dirty tricks; design, plotting, scheming, secrecy, stealth
near antonyms artlessness, forthrightness, guilelessness, ingenuousness, sincerity; candidness, candor, directness, openness, plainness, plainspokenness

trickle *vb* **1** to fall or let fall in or as if in drops ⟨*trickled* a little honey into her tea⟩ — see DRIP
2 to flow in a broken irregular stream ⟨the brook *trickled* along the glade⟩ — see GURGLE

tricksiness *n* a natural disposition for playful behavior ⟨the novelist has a known weakness for literary *tricksiness*, so the reader should be skeptical of the narrator's trustworthiness⟩ — see PLAYFULNESS

trickster *n* **1** a dishonest person who uses clever means to cheat others out of something of value ⟨a heartless *trickster* swindled the elderly woman out of her life savings⟩
synonyms bilk, bilker, cheat, cheater, chiseler (*or* chiseller), confidence man, cozener, defrauder, dodger, fakir, finagler, fraudster [*chiefly British*], hoaxer, scammer, scamster, shark, sharper, sharpie (*or* sharpy), skinner, swindler, tricker
related words double-crosser, double-dealer; bluffer, charlatan, fake, faker, humbug, impostor (*or* imposter),

mountebank, phony (*also* phoney), pretender, quack, quacksalver, ringer, sham; adventurer, fox, gamesman, knave, prankster, rascal, rogue; fast-talker, slick, slicker, slickster, slyboots, smoothy (*or* smoothie), wheeler-dealer; plotter, schemer, sneak, sneaker; blackleg, cardsharp (*or* cardsharper)
2 one who practices tricks and illusions for entertainment ⟨a very adept *trickster* who used mirrors to make huge items—even buildings—seem to disappear⟩ — see MAGICIAN 2

tricksy *adj* **1** requiring exceptional skill or caution in performance or handling ⟨it's a bit *tricksy* to have a candid conversation with the company president without appearing to be either presumptuous or obsequious⟩ — see TRICKY 1
2 tending to or exhibiting reckless playfulness ⟨a *tricksy* provocateur who will make the most outrageous statements just to get a reaction⟩ — see MISCHIEVOUS 1

tricky *adj* **1** requiring exceptional skill or caution in performance or handling ⟨a *tricky* musical passage for the woodwind section⟩
synonyms catchy, delicate, difficult, dodgy [*chiefly British*], hairy, knotty, nasty, prickly, problematic (*also* problematical), sensitive, spiny, sticky, thorny, ticklish, touchy, tough, tricksy
related words abstract, abstruse, complex, complicated, hard, intricate, involved, recondite, serious; problem, scabrous, stubborn, troublesome, troublous, vexatious, vexing, worrisome; burdensome, demanding, discommoding, exacting, exhausting, importunate, inconvenient, onerous, oppressive, painful, stressful
near antonyms easy, effortless, manageable, painless, simple, straightforward, uncomplicated, undemanding, unproblematic
2 clever at attaining one's ends by indirect and often deceptive means ⟨he's a *tricky* one, so be careful when dealing with him⟩ — see ARTFUL 1

tried *adj* worthy of one's trust ⟨a *tried* method for catching sport fish⟩ — see DEPENDABLE

tried–and–true *adj* worthy of one's trust ⟨a *tried-and-true* friend who has always been there for me⟩ — see DEPENDABLE

trifecta *n* a group of three ⟨that summertime *trifecta* for meteorologically induced misery: hazy, hot, and humid⟩ — see THREESOME

trifle *n* something of little importance ⟨let us not speak of *trifles* when our nation may be going to war⟩
synonyms bagatelle, child's play, frippery, nonproblem, nothing, picayune, shuck(s), small beer, small change, triviality
related words naught (*also* nought), nothingness, smoke, zero; peanuts, pittance, song, straw, two bits; bunk, claptrap, drivel, folly, fribble, fudge, hogwash, humbug, humbuggery, nonsense, piffle, rot, trash, trivia; bit, crumb, dab, dram, lick, mite, ounce, particle, pinhead, scintilla, shred, smidgen (*also* smidgeon *or* smidgin *or* smidge), soupçon, speck, spot, tad, touch, trace

trifle *vb* **1** to show a sexual attraction for someone just for fun ⟨do not *trifle* with me unless you mean to ask me to marry you⟩ — see FLIRT 1
2 to spend time in aimless activity ⟨spent a lazy afternoon *trifling* on the front porch⟩ — see FIDDLE (AROUND)

trifle (away) *vb* to use up carelessly ⟨*trifled away* his hard-earned professional respect with a single act of plagiarism⟩ — see WASTE 1

trifler *n* a person who lacks experience and competence in an art or science ⟨he was never taken seriously as a comic book artist, with most illustrators regarding him as a mere *trifler*⟩ — see AMATEUR 2

trifling *adj* **1** lacking importance ⟨deciding what you want to do for a living is no *trifling* matter⟩ — see UNIMPORTANT
2 so small or unimportant as to warrant little or no attention ⟨*trifling* differences between the theatrical and DVD versions of the movie⟩ — see NEGLIGIBLE 1

trig *adj* being clean and in good order ⟨to the office she wears *trig* two-piece suits that are fashionable but still businesslike⟩ — see NEAT 1

trigger *vb* to cause to function ⟨mold *triggers* my allergies⟩ — see ACTIVATE

trill *vb* to sing with the alternation of two musical tones ⟨a bluebird *trilled* outside our window⟩ — see WARBLE

trim *adj* being clean and in good order ⟨kept his journal entries *trim*, never crossing out words or scribbling, but printing exactly and nicely⟩ — see NEAT 1

trim *n* **1** a state of being or fitness ⟨the doctor declared her to be in good *trim* for the race⟩ — see CONDITION 1
2 something that decorates or beautifies ⟨added a little *trim* to her cocktail dress to make it a little fancier⟩ — see DECORATION 1

trim *vb* **1** to achieve a victory over ⟨a speed skater who consistently *trimmed* all his competition⟩ — see BEAT 2
2 to defeat by a large margin ⟨they *trimmed* our team by 40 points⟩ — see WHIP 2
3 to make (something) shorter or smaller with the use of a cutting instrument ⟨*trimmed* her bangs⟩ — see CLIP 1
4 to make more attractive by adding something that is beautiful or becoming ⟨*trim* a tree for Christmas⟩ — see DECORATE
5 to make neat ⟨*trimmed* the shrubbery in order to enhance the house's curb appeal⟩ — see NEATEN

trimmer *n* **1** a person who dexterously and expediently changes or adopts opinions ⟨gradually fading in the primaries, the former front-runner watched helplessly as the *trimmers* rushed to embrace the party's newest rising star⟩ — see ACROBAT 2
2 one that defeats an enemy or opponent ⟨last year's winner of the tournament unexpectedly got trimmed in the first round, and the *trimmer* was a young player that no one had ever heard of⟩ — see VICTOR 1

trimming *n* failure to win a contest ⟨our football team suffered a pretty severe *trimming*⟩ — see DEFEAT 1

trinity *n* a group of three ⟨read novels and poetry produced by that sisterly *trinity* of English literature: Charlotte, Anne, and Emily Brontë⟩ — see THREESOME

trinket *n* a small object displayed for its attractiveness or interest ⟨the top of his desk was littered with *trinkets* that were collected as souvenirs from various vacations⟩ — see KNICKKNACK

trio *n* a group of three ⟨the band was just a *trio* of musicians on piano, drums, and saxophone⟩ — see THREESOME

trip *n* **1** a going from one place to another usually of some distance ⟨I'd like to book a *trip* to Greece with your travel agency⟩ — see JOURNEY
2 an unintentional departure from truth or accuracy ⟨even a small *trip* in the bomb-making calculations could lead to disaster⟩ — see ERROR 1

trip *vb* **1** to go at a pace faster than a walk ⟨went *tripping* up the steps of city hall in their eagerness to get married⟩ — see RUN 1
2 to go down from an upright position suddenly and involuntarily ⟨*tripped* over a chair and landed on her face⟩ — see FALL 1
3 to move with a light springing step ⟨dancers *tripping* lightly across the stage⟩ — see SKIP 1
4 to take a trip especially of some distance ⟨while he was growing up, the family *tripped* to New England every summer⟩ — see TRAVEL 1
5 to make a mistake ⟨the press has had it in for the new

governor, and they are just waiting for her to *trip*⟩ — see ERR 1

tripartite *adj* having three units or parts ⟨negotiated a *tripartite* agreement with its trading partner, with the first and second parts coming into effect immediately and the last part five years later⟩ — see TRIPLE

tripe *n* that which is of low quality or worth ⟨it's shocking that an esteemed newspaper like this one would publish such *tripe*⟩ — see JUNK 1

triple *adj* having three units or parts ⟨a *triple* scoop of chocolate ice cream⟩
synonyms threefold, treble, triadic, tripartite, triplex
related words triplicate

triple *n* a group of three ⟨that *triple* of terrors for the wintertime driver: snow, ice, and sleet⟩ — see THREESOME

triplet *n* a group of three ⟨the theater piece is actually a *triplet* of comedy sketches, all of them having romantic love as their theme⟩ — see THREESOME

triplex *adj* having three units or parts ⟨a *triplex* house that features a separate apartment on each floor⟩ — see TRIPLE

tripper *n, chiefly British* a person who travels for pleasure ⟨day *trippers* who come to spend a few hours on the island⟩ — see TOURIST

trippingly *adv* in a quick and spirited manner ⟨loves words that roll *trippingly* off the tongue⟩ — see GAILY 2

trite *adj* used or heard so often as to be dull ⟨by the time the receiving line had ended, the bride and groom's thanks sounded *trite* and tired⟩ — see STALE 1

triumph *n* **1** a successful result brought about by hard work ⟨getting into Harvard is quite a *triumph*⟩ — see ACCOMPLISHMENT 1
2 an instance of defeating an enemy or opponent ⟨our stunning *triumph* on the field won us the title of regional champs⟩ — see VICTORY

triumph *vb* **1** to achieve victory (as in a contest) ⟨despite an accident early on, the runner persevered and ultimately *triumphed*⟩ — see WIN 1
2 to feel or express joy or triumph ⟨in that part of the world it's customary for people to *triumph* by firing guns into the air⟩ — see EXULT

triumph (over) *vb* to achieve a victory over ⟨with teamwork, we can *triumph over* anything⟩ — see BEAT 2

triumphant *adj* **1** having attained a desired end or state of good fortune ⟨the *triumphant* bidder on the house⟩ — see SUCCESSFUL 1
2 having or expressing feelings of joy or triumph ⟨he was positively *triumphant* when the school troublemaker finally got expelled⟩ — see EXULTANT

triumvirate *n* a group of three ⟨among the city's cultural institutions, the art museum, the symphony orchestra, and the opera company reign as the supreme *triumvirate*⟩ — see THREESOME

trivial *adj* **1** lacking importance ⟨why spend so much time on *trivial* decisions, like whether the soda should be regular or diet?⟩ — see UNIMPORTANT
2 so small or unimportant as to warrant little or no attention ⟨figured that restaurant customers wouldn't notice such a *trivial* surcharge on their bill⟩ — see NEGLIGIBLE 1

triviality *n* **1** something of little importance ⟨overlooked such *trivialities* as haphazardly folded napkins when rating the quality of restaurants⟩ — see TRIFLE
2 the quality or state of being unimportant ⟨the only thing the complaints have in common is their undeniable *triviality*⟩ — see INSIGNIFICANCE

troglodyte *n* a man with crude manners and habits and outmoded attitudes ⟨the *troglodytes* who believed that women had no place in the military, except perhaps as nurses⟩ — see CAVEMAN

troll *n* an imaginary being usually having a small human form and magical powers ⟨"The Three Billy Goats Gruff," is the story of three goats trying to cross a bridge guarded by a nasty *troll* living beneath it⟩ — see FAIRY

troll *vb* to look through (as a place) carefully or thoroughly in an effort to find or discover something ⟨the owner of the bed-and-breakfast often *trolls* antique stores for furniture and knickknacks⟩ — see SEARCH 1

trollop *n* a boldly flirtatious or sexually promiscuous woman ⟨in some countries a woman traveling alone was traditionally regarded as a *trollop*⟩ — see FLOOZY

tromp *vb* **1** to move heavily or clumsily ⟨sleepily *tromped* into the kitchen to answer the ringing phone, tripping over an array of clothes and books along the way⟩ — see LUMBER 1
2 to tread on heavily so as to crush or injure ⟨the kids *tromped* my flowers to smithereens⟩ — see TRAMPLE
3 to defeat by a large margin ⟨sure, I lost the election, but I didn't get *tromped*, so I'll see you again in four years⟩ — see WHIP 2
4 to travel by foot for exercise or pleasure ⟨the scouts *tromped* through the dell, mostly just following the course of the creek⟩ — see HIKE 1
5 to strike repeatedly ⟨*tromped* the bully, giving him a taste of his own medicine⟩ — see BEAT 1

troop *n* **1** an organized group of stage performers ⟨a celebrated acting *troop* will be coming to town next month to perform one of Shakespeare's plays⟩ — see COMPANY 1
2 troops *pl* the combined army, air force, and navy of a nation ⟨the *troops* overseas are grateful for the support of so many at home⟩ — see ARMED FORCES

trooper *n* a person engaged in military service ⟨a moving Memorial Day service honoring our fallen *troopers*⟩ — see SOLDIER

trope *n* an idea or expression that has been used by many people ⟨a screenplay that reads like a catalog of mystery-thriller *tropes*⟩ — see COMMONPLACE

trophy *n* an asset that brings praise or renown ⟨the mogul's latest *trophies* include an oversized mansion and a 20-years-younger wife⟩ — see GLORY 2

tropical *adj* **1** being near the equator ⟨wanted to escape winter and visit some *tropical* location where freezing to death would not be a possibility⟩ — see LOW 1
2 expressing one thing in terms normally used for another ⟨an author given to high-flown *tropical* phrasings and convoluted symbology⟩ — see FIGURATIVE

tropological *adj* expressing one thing in terms normally used for another ⟨a *tropological* construct that no reader of the Bible should take literally⟩ — see FIGURATIVE

trot *n* **1** a mean or ugly old woman ⟨a gossipy old *trot* who never had a good word to say about anyone⟩ — see CRONE
2 trots *pl* abnormally frequent intestinal evacuations with more or less fluid stools ⟨pick a caterer who is very conscientious about the preparation and refrigeration of food if you'd rather not give your guests the *trots* as a parting gift⟩ — see DIARRHEA

trot *vb* **1** to go at a pace faster than a walk ⟨had to *trot* to keep up with the tour guide's quick pace⟩ — see RUN 1
2 to proceed or move quickly ⟨now *trot* along and get washed up for supper⟩ — see HURRY 2

troth *n* **1** a person's solemn declaration that he or she will do or not do something ⟨by my *troth*, I will not trespass on your precious property⟩ — see PROMISE
2 the act or state of being engaged to be married ⟨solemnly announced their *troth* before the church's congregation⟩ — see ENGAGEMENT 1
3 adherence to something to which one is bound by a pledge or duty ⟨the knight pledged his eternal *troth* to the defense of the kingdom⟩ — see FIDELITY

troth *vb* to obligate by prior agreement ⟨I *troth* myself eternally to your service⟩ — see PLEDGE 1

trot out *vb* to put before another for acceptance or consideration ⟨after no one bought the first explanation, they *trotted out* another⟩ — see OFFER 1

trouble *n* **1** an abnormal state that disrupts a plant's or animal's normal bodily functioning ⟨hoping that the doctor will be able to accurately diagnose my *trouble*⟩ — see DISEASE
2 something that may cause injury or harm ⟨that wild dog is *trouble*, so stay away⟩ — see DANGER 2
3 something that requires thought and skill for resolution ⟨the police officers first broke up the fight and then asked what the *trouble* was⟩ — see PROBLEM 1
4 the active use of energy in producing a result ⟨please, don't go to all that *trouble* just for me⟩ — see EFFORT
5 the state of not being protected from injury, harm, or evil ⟨if you think your brother might be in *trouble*, then let's go check up on him⟩ — see DANGER 1

trouble *vb* **1** to experience concern or anxiety ⟨don't *trouble* about me—I'll be fine⟩ — see WORRY 1
2 to cause discomfort to or trouble for ⟨I hate to *trouble* you, but would you mind moving for a minute so I can sweep under your chair?⟩ — see INCONVENIENCE

troubled *adj* feeling or showing uncomfortable feelings of uncertainty ⟨the *troubled* looks on their faces showed that they were still waiting for news about the accident⟩ — see NERVOUS 1

troublesome *adj* causing worry or anxiety ⟨the *troublesome* news that there will be more cuts in the school budget⟩
synonyms discomforting, discomposing, disquieting, distressing, disturbing, nagging, nasty, perturbing, troubling, troublous, unsettling, upsetting, worrisome
related words daunting, demoralizing, discomfiting, disconcerting, discouraging, disheartening, dismaying, dispiriting; chilling, frightening, scary; harassing, persecutive, persecutory; alarming, dire, direful, dread, dreadful, fearful, fearsome, forbidding, formidable, frightening, frightful, ghastly, hair-raising, horrendous, horrible, horrifying, intimidating, scary, shocking, terrible, terrifying
near antonyms calming, quieting, settling, soothing; comforting, consoling, dreamy, inviting, lulling, narcotic, pacifying, relaxing, sedative, tranquilizing (*also* tranquillizing)
antonyms reassuring

troubling *adj* causing worry or anxiety ⟨the most *troubling* sign of all is that he's stopped returning my phone calls⟩ — see TROUBLESOME

troublous *adj* causing worry or anxiety ⟨a *troublous* teen whose antisocial antics had us all on edge⟩ — see TROUBLESOME

trough *n* **1** a long hollow cylinder for carrying a substance (as a liquid or gas) ⟨all of the wiring for the converted residential loft is concealed in a vertical *trough*⟩ — see PIPE 1
2 a long narrow channel dug in the earth ⟨I slid and fell into the *trough* by the side of the road, scraping my leg⟩ — see DITCH
3 a pipe or channel for carrying off water from a roof ⟨the *troughs* on the eaves of the house were clogged with leaves⟩ — see GUTTER 1

trounce *vb* to defeat by a large margin ⟨our candidate *trounced* her opponent in the election, winning with 76% of the vote⟩ — see WHIP 2

trouncing *n* failure to win a contest ⟨took a serious *trouncing* during the last three minutes of the game⟩ — see DEFEAT 1

troupe *n* an organized group of stage performers ⟨I desperately want to join our regional theater's acting *troupe* and perhaps get a lead role⟩ — see COMPANY 1

trouper *n* one who acts professionally (as in a play, movie, or television show) ⟨had been a well-known Broadway *trouper* before making his screen debut⟩ — see ACTOR 1

trousers *n pl* an outer garment covering each leg separately from waist to ankle ⟨picked up his *trousers* from the dry cleaners⟩ — see PANTS

truce *n* a temporary stopping of fighting ⟨both sides agreed to a 24-hour *truce* beginning at midnight on Christmas Eve⟩
synonyms armistice, cease-fire
related words accord, reconcilement, reconciliation; détente (*or* detente); peace, peacetime
near antonyms conflict, hostilities, hot war, war

truck *n* **1** a giving or taking of one thing of value in return for another ⟨for centuries African slaves were sold in the West Indies in *truck* for molasses, which was then shipped to New England to be made into rum⟩ — see EXCHANGE 1
2 discarded or useless material ⟨filled a dozen large garbage bags with all the *truck* we collected when we cleaned the place out⟩ — see GARBAGE 1

truckle *vb* to use flattery or the doing of favors in order to win approval especially from a superior ⟨the kind of guy who *truckles* to anyone who has even a suspicion of money⟩ — see FAWN

truckload *n* a considerable amount ⟨the guy who marries her is in for a *truckload* of misery⟩ — see LOT 2

truculence *n* **1** an inclination to fight or quarrel ⟨a congenital *truculence* that resulted in his spending most of his adolescence in juvenile detention homes⟩ — see BELLIGERENCE
2 disposition to willfully inflict pain and suffering on others ⟨beneath his suave, polished exterior lay the *truculence* of a common street thug⟩ — see CRUELTY

truculent *adj* **1** feeling or displaying eagerness to fight ⟨die-hard fans who became *truculent* and violent after their team's loss⟩ — see BELLIGERENT
2 marked by harsh insulting language ⟨a theater critic who was notorious for his titanically *truculent* reviews⟩ — see ABUSIVE
3 having or showing the desire to inflict severe pain and suffering on others ⟨*truculent* warlords who spared not even the children⟩ — see CRUEL 1

trudge *vb* **1** to move heavily or clumsily ⟨flooded residents who were forced to *trudge* through waist-deep water⟩ — see LUMBER 1
2 to proceed or act clumsily or ineffectually ⟨no expert on taxes, I spent the whole weekend *trudging* through Form 1040⟩ — see FLOUNDER 1

true *adj* **1** being exactly as appears or as claimed ⟨his claim that he's the heir to the throne of Greece can't be *true*⟩ — see AUTHENTIC 1
2 being in agreement with the truth or a fact or a standard ⟨if that is *true*, then we can't get in without a key⟩ — see CORRECT 1
3 existing in fact and not merely as a possibility ⟨the *true* scope of this environmental problem is far greater than anyone imagined⟩ — see ACTUAL
4 firm in one's allegiance to someone or something ⟨he will be *true* to his word⟩ — see FAITHFUL 1
5 following an original exactly ⟨it's not a *true* reproduction of the painting because the original is much larger⟩ — see FAITHFUL 2
6 free from any intent to deceive or impress others ⟨may our love for one another always be *true*⟩ — see GUILELESS
7 restricted to or based on fact ⟨that news story is completely *true*, for the station released a list of its sources to back it up⟩ — see FACTUAL 1
8 worthy of one's trust ⟨a *true* friend when you need one⟩ — see DEPENDABLE

9 having or showing the qualities associated with the members of a particular group or kind ⟨paleontologists are still debating whether the fossil is that of a *true* dinosaur or a precursor⟩ — see TYPICAL 1
10 conforming to a high standard of morality or virtue ⟨a person of great integrity, he was the *truest* person I've ever met⟩ — see GOOD 2

true believer *n* **1** one who is intensely or excessively devoted to a cause ⟨it's impossible to argue with those *true believers,* as they think any counterevidence is proof of an evil conspiracy⟩ — see ZEALOT
2 a person who actively supports or favors a cause ⟨*true believers* who fought the good fight even when it was out of fashion⟩ — see EXPONENT 1

true–blue *adj* firm in one's allegiance to someone or something ⟨a *true-blue* patriot even during the revolution's darkest hours⟩ — see FAITHFUL 1

truelove *n* a person with whom one is in love ⟨has been married to his *truelove* for 50 years⟩ — see SWEETHEART 1

trueness *n* agreement with fact or reality ⟨the *trueness* or falseness of that statement can be easily determined⟩ — see TRUTH

truism *n* an idea or expression that has been used by many people ⟨ended his letter with the overused *truism,* "You can't win them all!"⟩ — see COMMONPLACE

truly *adv* **1** not merely this but also ⟨he is a kind, *truly* generous man⟩ — see EVEN 1
2 to tell the truth ⟨*truly,* I had no idea you were throwing me a party⟩ — see ACTUALLY 1
3 without any question ⟨I very much appreciate your gift—*truly,* I can't thank you enough!⟩ — see INDEED 1
4 in actual fact ⟨this is *truly* the nicest thing anyone has done for me⟩ — see VERY 2

trumpery *adj* of low quality ⟨*trumpery* knickknacks from some souvenir shop⟩ — see CHEAP 2

trumpery *n* language, behavior, or ideas that are absurd and contrary to good sense ⟨claims for weight-loss products that are based much more on Madison-Avenue *trumpery* than on bariatric science⟩ — see NONSENSE 1

trumpet *vb* **1** to make known openly or publicly ⟨the losing party lost no time in *trumpeting* allegations of election fraud⟩ — see ANNOUNCE
2 to praise or publicize lavishly and often excessively ⟨critics *trumpeted* the band's latest album as the best of the decade⟩ — see TOUT 1

trump up *vb* to create or think of by clever use of the imagination ⟨a wife who was always *trumping up* little projects for her husband to do around the house⟩ — see INVENT

truncate *vb* to make less in extent or duration ⟨a *truncated* version of the 11 o'clock newscast followed the awards show, which ran over its time slot—as it always does⟩ — see SHORTEN

truncheon *n* a heavy rigid stick used as a weapon or for punishment ⟨police officers were forced to use their *truncheons* on the rioters⟩ — see CLUB 1

trunk *n* a covered rectangular container for storing or transporting things ⟨threw the rest of her books and tapes in the *trunk* and closed the lid⟩ — see CHEST

truss *vb* to gather into a tight mass by means of a line or cord ⟨after stuffing the turkey, the chef quickly *trussed* it so the forcemeat wouldn't fall out during roasting⟩ — see TIE 1

trust *n* **1** firm belief in the integrity, ability, effectiveness, or genuineness of someone or something ⟨a relationship of mutual *trust* between lawyer and client⟩
synonyms confidence, credence, faith, stock
related words acceptance, assurance, assuredness, certainty, certitude, conviction, positiveness, sureness, surety; credit, dependence (*also* dependance), hope, reliance
near antonyms disbelief, incredulity, unbelief; distrustfulness, doubt, dubiety, dubiousness, incertitude, misdoubt, misgiving, mistrustfulness, nonconfidence, skepticism, suspicion, uncertainness, uncertainty; disenchantment, disillusion, disillusionment
antonyms distrust, mistrust
2 a number of businesses or enterprises united for commercial advantage ⟨government lawyers argued against allowing the telephone companies to merge, asserting that such a merger would result in a *trust* that would stifle competition⟩ — see CARTEL
3 responsibility for the safety and well-being of someone or something ⟨left her cat in the *trust* of her neighbors while she was on vacation⟩ — see CUSTODY
4 the right to take possession of goods before paying for them ⟨as his inner-city customers are chronically short on money, the neighborhood grocer frequently has to sell on *trust*⟩ — see CREDIT 1

trust *vb* **1** to give a task, duty, or responsibility to ⟨*trusted* the eldest child with walking the dog every morning⟩ — see ENTRUST 1
2 to put (something) into the possession or safekeeping of another ⟨I wouldn't *trust* my wallet with a complete stranger if I were you⟩ — see GIVE 2
3 to regard as right or true ⟨don't *trust* everything you read in the newspaper⟩ — see BELIEVE 1

trustability *n* worthiness as the recipient of another's trust or confidence ⟨the ethical journalist should not publish if there is any uncertainty regarding the *trustability* of his anonymous source⟩ — see RELIABILITY

trustable *adj* worthy of one's trust ⟨a Web site that is a *trustable* source of biographical information⟩ — see DEPENDABLE

trustful *adj* having or showing trust in another ⟨a *trustful* child quietly sleeping, sure in the knowledge that his parents would be there when he woke⟩ — see TRUSTING 1

trusting *adj* **1** having or showing trust in another ⟨Delia couldn't look into her dog's *trusting* eyes as she drove him to the vet⟩
synonyms confiding, trustful
related words artless, childlike, credulous, guileless, gullible (*also* gullable), innocent, naive (*or* naïve), simple, unsophisticated; dependent, hopeful, reliant; accepting, believing, certain, confident, convinced, overconfident, secure, sure, unquestioning, unsuspecting, unsuspicious, unwary
near antonyms disbelieving, incredulous, unbelieving, unconvinced, undecided, unpersuaded; dubious, hesitant, leery (*also* leary), oversuspicious, skeptical, suspicious, uncertain, unsure, wary
antonyms distrustful, doubtful, doubting, mistrustful, trustless, untrusting
2 readily taken advantage of ⟨a corrupt stockbroker who preyed upon *trusting* customers⟩ — see EASY 2

trustless *adj* not feeling sure about the truth, wisdom, or trustworthiness of someone or something ⟨with time the missionary doctor won the trust of even the most *trustless* villagers⟩ — see DOUBTFUL 1

trustworthiness *n* worthiness as the recipient of another's trust or confidence ⟨you have to prove your *trustworthiness* before I will tell you my secrets⟩ — see RELIABILITY

trustworthy *adj* worthy of one's trust ⟨a *trustworthy* bodyguard who would never blab to the tabloids⟩ — see DEPENDABLE

trusty *adj* worthy of one's trust ⟨movie cowboys always get on their *trusty* horses and ride off into the sunset⟩ — see DEPENDABLE

truth *n* agreement with fact or reality ⟨there is no *truth* to the rumor that the couple is getting a divorce⟩

synonyms facticity, factuality, sooth, trueness, verity

related words accuracy, accurateness, actuality, authenticity, correctness; credibility, honesty, trustability, trustiness, trustworthiness, truthfulness, veracity; dependability, reliability

near antonyms erroneousness, fallaciousness, fallacy; falsehood, fiction, half-truth, lie; impreciseness, imprecision, inaccuracy, incorrectness, inexactitude, inexactness; deceit, dishonesty, equivocation, lying, mendaciousness, mendacity, prevarication, untruthfulness

antonyms falseness, falsity, untruth

truthful *adj* being in the habit of telling the truth ⟨a *truthful* youngster who wouldn't just make up a story like that⟩

synonyms honest, veracious

related words candid, direct, forthcoming, forthright, foursquare, frank, freehearted, free-spoken, open, openhearted, out-front, outspoken, plain, plainspoken; believable, credible, true, veritable; artless, earnest, genuine, guileless, unaffected, unpretending, unpretentious; conscientious, moral, principled, scrupulous; aboveboard, dependable, reliable, trustable, trustworthy, trusty

near antonyms fallacious, false, untrue; unbelievable, undependable, unreliable, unscrupulous, untrustworthy; bluffing, dissembling, dissimulating, duplicitous, equivocating, hypocritical, insincere, posing, pretending; artful, deceitful, deceptive, devious, evasive, slick, slippery, sly, sneaky, treacherous, tricky, underhanded, wily

antonyms dishonest, fibbing, lying, mendacious, prevaricating, untruthful

truthfully *adv* to tell the truth ⟨*truthfully*, I'd rather go to the amusement park than to the museum, but I'll go along with the rest of the group⟩ — see ACTUALLY 1

truthfulness *n* devotion to telling the truth ⟨given the fact that used-car dealers are not renowned for their *truthfulness*, I had an independent mechanic check out the vehicle⟩ — see HONESTY 1

try *n* an effort to do or accomplish something ⟨was granted another *try* at the field goal⟩ — see ATTEMPT 1

try *vb* **1** to subject (a personal quality or faculty) to often excessive stress ⟨you're *trying* my patience⟩

synonyms strain, stretch, tax, test

related words demand, exact, importune, press, pressure, push; aggravate, agitate, annoy, bother, exasperate, gall, get (to), gnaw (at), grate, harass, harry, hassle, irk, irritate, nettle, pain, peeve, pester, rile, spite, vex

2 to make an effort to do ⟨*try* to unlock the door⟩ ⟨will *try* to call later tonight⟩ — see ATTEMPT

try (out) *vb* to put (something) to a test ⟨want to *try out* my new skateboard?⟩ ⟨*tried out* his skill at archery⟩

synonyms sample, test

related words check (out), examine, experiment (with), explore, feel (out), investigate, research, study; resample, retest

trying *adj* difficult to endure ⟨a harrowing account of the *trying* conditions experienced by the hostages prior to their release⟩ — see HARSH 1

tryst *n* an agreement to be present at a specified time and place ⟨both lovers had to hurry to keep their noontime *tryst* in the park⟩ — see ENGAGEMENT 2

tsk–tsk *vb* to hold an unfavorable opinion of ⟨some guests *tsk-tsked* the fact that the bride was visibly pregnant for the wedding⟩ — see DISAPPROVE (OF)

tubby *adj* having an excess of body fat ⟨in America, Santa Claus is portrayed as a jolly but *tubby* older gentleman⟩ — see FAT 1

tube *n* **1** a long hollow cylinder for carrying a substance (as a liquid or gas) ⟨watched the liquid move through the *tube* between the flasks and recorded the movement in his chemistry notebook⟩ — see PIPE 1

2 an electronic device with a screen and speakers that reproduces images and sound ⟨we plan to relax and spend some time in front of the *tube* tonight⟩ — see TELEVISION

tub–thump *vb* to praise or publicize lavishly and often excessively ⟨the studio is going all out to *tub-thump* its latest summer blockbuster⟩ — see TOUT 1

tub–thumper *n* a person who actively supports or favors a cause ⟨advances in civil rights that came about only because of the relentless clamor of the *tub-thumpers*⟩ — see EXPONENT 1

tuck (away *or* **in)** *vb* to take in as food ⟨after *tucking away* that huge meal, I was feeling a little sleepy⟩ — see EAT 1

tucker *n, chiefly Australian* substances intended to be eaten ⟨you can get some downright peculiar *tucker* deep in the outback⟩ — see FOOD 1

tucker (out) *vb* to use up all the physical energy of ⟨we're hoping that the mountain bike ride will *tucker* the kids *out* so they'll sleep well tonight⟩ — see EXHAUST 1

tuckered (out) *adj* depleted in strength, energy, or freshness ⟨*tuckered out* after a long day of playing tennis⟩ — see WEARY 1

tug *n* the act or an instance of applying force on something so that it moves in the direction of the force ⟨gave the man in front a *tug* on his shirtsleeve as a sign that he was supposed to step aside⟩ — see PULL 1

tug *vb* **1** to cause to follow by applying steady force on ⟨*tugged* on the door until it opened⟩ — see PULL 1

2 to devote serious and sustained effort ⟨she's *tugged* all her life to get to where she is now in the business world⟩ — see LABOR

tug–of–war *n* an earnest effort for superiority or victory over another ⟨the effort to get their teenage son to keep his room clean is a constant *tug-of-war*⟩ — see CONTEST 1

tuition *n* the act or process of imparting knowledge or skills to another ⟨they hired a private tutor to handle the *tuition* of their children in French⟩ — see EDUCATION 1

tumble *n* **1** an unorganized collection or mixture of various things ⟨cleaned a crazy *tumble* of buttons, hair bands, loose change, and old candy wrappers out from the couch cushions⟩ — see MISCELLANY 1

2 the act of going down from an upright position suddenly and involuntarily ⟨took a little *tumble* on the ice⟩ — see FALL 1

3 a state in which everything is out of order ⟨her office is a *tumble* of books and papers, but somehow she can find everything⟩ — see CHAOS

tumble *vb* **1** to go down from an upright position suddenly and involuntarily ⟨the infant stood for a moment and then *tumbled* on the carpet⟩ — see FALL 1

2 to go to a lower level especially abruptly ⟨prices for those stocks have really *tumbled*⟩ — see DROP 2

3 to undo the proper order or arrangement of ⟨*tumbled* all the clothes in her closet as she furiously searched for her favorite pair of jeans⟩ — see DISORDER

4 to fall down or in as a result of physical pressure ⟨all we need is one strong wind, and that old barn is going to *tumble*⟩ — see COLLAPSE 1

tumble (to) *vb* to have a clear idea of ⟨I finally *tumbled to* the fact that I had been duped into getting involved in a phony investment scheme⟩ — see COMPREHEND 1

tumble (upon) *vb* to come upon unexpectedly or by chance ⟨while we were out on a drive in the country, we *tumbled upon* a farm stand selling the best peaches I've ever tasted⟩ — see HAPPEN (ON *OR* UPON)

tumbled *adj* lacking in order, neatness, and often cleanliness ⟨a *tumbled* entryway filled with the usual jumble of sports equipment, backpacks, papers, and shoes⟩ — see MESSY

tumbledown *adj* showing signs of advanced wear and tear and neglect ⟨lived alone on a *tumbledown* farm that had seen better days⟩ — see SHABBY 1

tumescent *adj* enlarged beyond normal from internal pressure ⟨our pregnant kitty's *tumescent* middle⟩ — see BLOATED 2

tumid *adj* enlarged beyond normal from internal pressure ⟨he'd just been in a fight, and was nursing his *tumid* lip⟩ — see BLOATED 2

tummy *n* the part of the body between the chest and the pelvis ⟨tickled the toddler's *tummy*⟩ — see STOMACH 1

tumor *n* an abnormal mass of tissue ⟨the scan showed a small *tumor* in her abdomen⟩ — see GROWTH 1

tumult *n* **1** a state of noisy, confused activity ⟨in the *tumult* of the evacuation from the coast, we accidentally left on the television, which was of course tuned to the local newscast breathlessly reporting on the hurricane we were fleeing⟩ — see COMMOTION
2 a violent disturbance (as of the political or social order) ⟨the political *tumult* that swept the American colonies in the late 1700s⟩ — see CONVULSION
3 a violent shouting ⟨went to the window to see what the great *tumult* was and discovered a crowd of demonstrators marching down the street⟩ — see CLAMOR 1

tumultuous *adj* **1** marked by sudden or violent disturbance ⟨one of the most *tumultuous* periods in the history of the region⟩ — see CONVULSIVE 1
2 marked by turmoil or disturbance especially of natural elements ⟨watched the *tumultuous* weather from the dry safety of our house⟩ — see WILD 3
3 marked by bursts of destructive force or intense activity ⟨after a *tumultuous* day of trading, the stock market was down 500 points⟩ — see VIOLENT 1

tun *n* an enclosed wooden vessel for holding beverages ⟨in olden days an English ship's capacity was measured by the number of *tuns* of wine it could hold⟩ — see CASK

tundra *n* a broad area of level or rolling treeless country ⟨a report on the arctic *tundra* of Alaska and the polar bears that inhabit that vast, frozen plain⟩ — see PLAIN 1

tune *n* **1** a rhythmic series of musical tones arranged to give a pleasing effect ⟨hummed a little *tune* while I sorted the laundry⟩ — see MELODY
2 a state of consistency ⟨your negative assessment of the restaurant seems to be in *tune* with the opinions of the critics⟩ — see CONFORMITY 1
3 an approximate amount, extent, or degree ⟨retail rents on the fashionable street can run to the *tune* of $100,000 a year⟩ — see NEIGHBORHOOD 1

tuneful *adj* having a pleasing mixture of notes ⟨some especially *tuneful* songs have been written for this new animated film⟩ — see HARMONIOUS 1

tunesmith *n* a person who writes popular musical compositions for the human voice ⟨a British *tunesmith* whose songs were equally popular in America⟩ — see SONGWRITER

turbid *adj* having visible particles in liquid suspension ⟨the pond water became *turbid* from our swimming and splashing⟩ — see CLOUDY 1

turbulent *adj* **1** marked by bursts of destructive force or intense activity ⟨the *turbulent* struggle for civil rights that shook up American society in the 1960s⟩ — see VIOLENT 1
2 marked by turmoil or disturbance especially of natural elements ⟨the *turbulent* rapids of the river were certainly daunting to those of us who were new to river rafting⟩ — see WILD 3
3 marked by wet and windy conditions ⟨expect *turbulent* weather as the cold front brings rain and sleet⟩ — see FOUL 1
4 marked by sudden or violent disturbance ⟨these are *turbulent*, dangerous times in a region known for being a powder keg⟩ — see CONVULSIVE 1

turf (out) *vb, chiefly British* to drive or force out ⟨the pub keeper doesn't hesitate to *turf out* anyone who gets too drunk⟩ — see EJECT 1

turgid *adj* enlarged beyond normal from internal pressure ⟨*turgid* leeches having had their fill of blood⟩ — see BLOATED 2

turista *n* abnormally frequent intestinal evacuations with more or less fluid stools ⟨the entire family came down with the dreaded *turista* three days into their long-awaited vacation⟩ — see DIARRHEA

turkey *n* **1** a person who lacks good sense or judgment ⟨only a *turkey* would think it's a good idea to go for a jog when the weather drops below zero⟩ — see FOOL 1
2 a stupid person ⟨you *turkey*, that wasn't my boyfriend—it was my brother!⟩ — see IDIOT
3 something that has failed ⟨his business venture ended up being a *turkey*, and he lost quite a bit of money on it⟩ — see FAILURE 3

turmoil *n* **1** a disturbed or uneasy state ⟨was in *turmoil* most of the night, trying to convince himself he had made the right decision⟩ — see UNREST
2 a state of noisy, confused activity ⟨avoided the *turmoil* of the mall during the holiday season⟩ — see COMMOTION

turn *n* **1** a relaxed journey on foot for exercise or pleasure ⟨would you care to take a *turn* around the garden?⟩ — see WALK 1
2 an act of kind assistance ⟨one good *turn* deserves another⟩ — see FAVOR 1
3 a habitual attraction to some activity or thing ⟨an adventurous *turn* of mind that led him toward more physical activities like biking and skateboarding⟩ — see INCLINATION 1
4 something that curves or is curved ⟨right after this *turn* in the road you'll find the antiques shop on the right⟩ — see BEND 1
5 a sudden experiencing of a physical or mental disorder ⟨a sudden *turn* of dizziness that may have been brought on by a change in her medication⟩ — see ATTACK 2
6 a performance regularly presented by an individual or group ⟨between the show's two major musical acts, there was a short *turn* by a juggling troupe⟩ — see ACT 1

turn *vb* **1** to move (something) in a curved or circular path on or as if on an axis ⟨*turned* the doorknob as quietly as possible⟩
synonyms pivot, revolve, roll, rotate, spin, swing, swirl, swivel, twirl, twist, wheel, whirl
related words screw, unscrew; twiddle; coil, crank, reel, wind; circulate
2 to change the course or direction of (something) ⟨the dog *turned* the stampeding flock of sheep around⟩ ⟨he *turned* his cart uphill⟩
synonyms deflect, divert, redirect, swing, veer, wheel, whip
related words avert, deviate, move, rechannel, shift, shunt, sidetrack, swerve, switch, transfer; swivel, twist, whirl, zigzag; bend, curve, sway; reverse, turn back
3 to change one's course or direction ⟨we *turned* left at the light⟩ ⟨the storm unexpectedly *turned* south and missed our area⟩
synonyms detour, deviate, diverge, sheer, swerve, swing, turn off, veer, wheel
related words tack, zigzag; double (back), turn back
4 to eventually have as a state or quality ⟨will *turn* 12 in six months⟩ — see BECOME
5 to move in circles around an axis or center ⟨the wheels *turned*, but the car was hopelessly stuck and wasn't moving⟩ — see SPIN 1

6 to give serious and careful thought to ⟨*turned* the question every which way but could find no answer⟩ — see PONDER

7 to be determined by, based on, or subject (to) ⟨what we do next *turns* on your answer to the following question⟩ — see DEPEND 1

8 to be in a confused state as if from being twirled around ⟨all the new information made his head *turn*⟩ — see SPIN 2

9 to cause to have often negative opinions formed without sufficient knowledge ⟨he did his best to *turn* his new friends against his ex-wife⟩ — see PREJUDICE

turn (on) *vb* to take sudden, violent action against ⟨it is dangerous to keep tigers as house pets, as they often *turn on* their masters without warning⟩ — see ATTACK 1

turn (to) *vb* to use or seek out as a source of aid, relief, or advantage ⟨no need to *turn to* violence when we can talk things out peacefully⟩ — see RESORT (TO) 1

turnabout *n* a changing from one policy or point of view to virtually its exact opposite ⟨employees regarded the latest *turnabout* as a sure sign that management hadn't a clue as to what it was doing⟩ — see ABOUT-FACE

turnaround *n* a changing from one policy or point of view to virtually its exact opposite ⟨we were at a loss to explain this *turnaround* in our daughter's attitude toward her studies⟩ — see ABOUT-FACE

turn away *vb* to drive back ⟨using tree branches, the campers were able to *turn away* the charging fox, which was apparently rabid⟩ — see REPEL 1

turn back *vb* to drive back ⟨a cavalry charge that was *turned back* by withering fire⟩ — see REPEL 1

turncoat *n* one who betrays a trust or an allegiance ⟨the plot of the story revolved around the gangster's relentless determination to learn the identity of the *turncoat*⟩ — see TRAITOR

turndown *n* an unwillingness to grant something asked for ⟨the request to use the restroom was just a formality—I really didn't expect a *turndown*⟩ — see DENIAL 1

turn down *vb* to show unwillingness to accept, do, engage in, or agree to ⟨I'm afraid that I will have to *turn down* your invitation⟩ — see DECLINE 1

turned–on *adj* keenly aware of and responsive to the latest developments especially in fashion and entertainment ⟨a film genre that today's *turned-on* moviegoers seem little interested in⟩ — see AU COURANT 1

turner *n* one who performs feats of physical strength, balance, and agility on special apparatus ⟨in the days before physical fitness became part of the mainstream, *turners* in athletic clubs were often regarded as social oddities⟩ — see ACROBAT 1

turn in *vb* **1** to give (something) over to the control or possession of another usually under duress ⟨*turned in* the banned assault rifle to the police⟩ — see SURRENDER 1

2 to go to one's bed in order to sleep ⟨it's almost midnight, so it's time to *turn in*⟩ — see BED 1

turning point *n* a point in a chain of events at which an important change (as in one's fortunes) occurs ⟨the *turning point* came when Victor finally admitted he was a werewolf⟩

synonyms climacteric, climax, corner, landmark, milepost, milestone, watershed

related words break, capper, clincher, crusher, highlight, topper; conversion, metamorphosis, transfiguration, transformation, turnabout, turnaround; boiling point, breaking point, clutch, conjuncture, crisis, crossroad(s), crunch, crunch time, Dunkirk, emergency, exigency, extremity, flash point, head, juncture, zero hour

turn off *vb* **1** to cause to feel disgust ⟨that memorably bad meal *turned* me *off* about restaurant food for a while⟩ — see DISGUST

2 to change one's course or direction ⟨*turn off* at the third exit and follow the ramp to your left⟩ — see TURN 3

3 to let go from office, service, or employment ⟨eventually, the supervisor *turned off* the insubordinate employee⟩ — see DISMISS 1

4 to cause to stop functioning ⟨please *turn off* the fan when you're done⟩ — see DEACTIVATE

turn–on *n* something that persuades one to perform an action for pleasure or gain ⟨knew the offer of free pizza would be a major *turn-on* to the pair of teenagers she had just asked to help her move⟩ — see LURE 1

turn on *vb* **1** to cause a pleasurable stimulation of the feelings ⟨unsurprisingly, the fanboys were *turned on* by the movie's amazing special effects and slam-bang plot⟩ — see THRILL

2 to cause to function ⟨would you *turn on* the TV?⟩ — see ACTIVATE

turn out *vb* **1** to leave one's bed ⟨we *turn out* early on workdays⟩ — see ARISE 1

2 to remove the dirt from ⟨it's our practice to *turn out* the room after guests stay over⟩ — see CLEAN 1

3 to drive or force out ⟨angrily *turned* their adult son *out* of their home for using drugs⟩ — see EJECT 1

4 to come to be ⟨everything will *turn out* fine in the end⟩ — see COME OUT 1

turn over *vb* **1** to give (something) over to the control or possession of another usually under duress ⟨reluctantly *turned* the ship *over* to the first mate while he went below to try to stop the leak⟩ — see SURRENDER 1

2 to put (something) into the possession or safekeeping of another ⟨*turned* the evidence *over* to the police⟩ — see GIVE 2

3 to turn on one's side or upside down ⟨don't try to tell me the bucket *turned over* all by itself⟩ — see CAPSIZE

4 to change the position of (an object) so that the opposite side or end is showing ⟨would you mind *turning* the picture *over* so I can see if the backing needs to be replaced⟩ — see REVERSE 2

turnpike *n* a passage cleared for public vehicular travel ⟨the *turnpike* was jammed with people heading south for the long weekend⟩ — see WAY 1

turn up *vb* **1** to come into view ⟨my missing car keys *turned up* just in time⟩ — see APPEAR 1

2 to get to a destination ⟨when do you think our guests will *turn up*?⟩ — see COME 2

3 to come upon after searching, study, or effort ⟨it took days to *turn up* the original documents⟩ — see FIND 1

turpitude *n* a sinking to a state of low moral standards and behavior ⟨pictorial advertisements for chic clothing and fragrances in which drug addiction and other forms of moral *turpitude* are depicted as alternative fashion statements⟩ — see CORRUPTION 2

tush *n, slang* the part of the body upon which someone sits ⟨exercises that are guaranteed to give you a great *tush*⟩ — see BUTTOCKS

tussle *n* a physical dispute between opposing individuals or groups ⟨a small *tussle* on the basketball court was quickly broken up⟩ — see FIGHT 1

tussle *vb* to seize and attempt to unbalance one another for the purpose of achieving physical mastery ⟨puppies *tussling* with one another, rolling over and over on the carpet⟩ — see WRESTLE

tut (over *or* about) *vb* to hold an unfavorable opinion of ⟨Aunt Marge *tuts over* almost everything the younger generation does⟩ — see DISAPPROVE (OF)

tutelage *n* the act or process of imparting knowledge or skills to another ⟨a governess overseeing the *tutelage* of the family's children⟩ — see EDUCATION 1

tutor *vb* **1** to cause to acquire knowledge or skill in some

field ⟨*tutored* me in Spanish⟩ — see TEACH
2 to give advice and instruction to (someone) regarding the course or process to be followed ⟨bought a video series designed to *tutor* a person in the fine art of decorating cakes⟩ — see GUIDE 1

tutoring *n* the act or process of imparting knowledge or skills to another ⟨found his calling in the *tutoring* of children with special educational needs⟩ — see EDUCATION 1

tut–tut (over *or* about) *vb* to hold an unfavorable opinion of ⟨ever since the invention of talkies, someone or other has been *tut-tutting about* the bad language heard in movies⟩ — see DISAPPROVE (OF)

TV *n* an electronic device with a screen and speakers that reproduces images and sound ⟨turn off the *TV* and go outside for a change⟩ — see TELEVISION

twaddle *n* language, behavior, or ideas that are absurd and contrary to good sense ⟨the novel's elaborate theory detailing a supposed 2,000-year-old conspiracy is mostly tiresome *twaddle*⟩ — see NONSENSE 1

twain *n* two things of the same or similar kind that match or are considered together ⟨I like rap and my parents like country music, and never the *twain* shall meet in our house⟩ — see PAIR

tweet *vb* to make a short sharp sound like a small bird ⟨the computer *tweeted* again, signaling another error⟩ — see CHIRP

twerp *n* a person of no importance or influence ⟨in high school he was just a little *twerp*, and now he's a big Internet entrepreneur⟩ — see NOBODY

twice *adv* to two times the amount or degree ⟨having been turned down before, he is *twice* shy about making any more marriage proposals⟩ — see DOUBLY

twiddle (with) *vb* to handle thoughtlessly, ignorantly, or mischievously ⟨don't allow the kids to *twiddle with* the air conditioner⟩ — see TAMPER (WITH)

twig *vb* to have a clear idea of ⟨it took me a while to *twig* the true nature of the relationship between the two women⟩ — see COMPREHEND 1

twilight *n* 1 a time or place of little or no light ⟨stumbled around the *twilight* of the shuttered room, unable to see where she was going⟩ — see DARK 1
2 the time from when the sun begins to set to the onset of total darkness ⟨watched as *twilight* descended and the woods fell silent⟩ — see DUSK 1

twin *adj* consisting of two members or parts that are usually joined ⟨a *twin*-cylinder engine⟩ — see DOUBLE 1

twin *n* 1 either of a pair matched in one or more qualities ⟨I've found one sock but can't find its *twin*⟩ — see MATE 1
2 something or someone that strongly resembles another ⟨some of these people who think that they're a given movie star's *twin* are kidding themselves⟩ — see IMAGE 1

twine *vb* to follow a circular or spiral course ⟨the snake silently *twined* around the tree trunk⟩ — see WIND 1

twinge *n* a sharp unpleasant sensation usually felt in some specific part of the body ⟨felt a *twinge* in her knee on that cold, rainy morning⟩ — see PAIN 1

twinkle *n* a very small space of time ⟨in just a *twinkle*, the shooting star was gone⟩ — see INSTANT

twinkle *vb* 1 to shine with light at regular intervals ⟨holiday decorations *twinkled* in the shop windows⟩ — see BLINK 1
2 to shoot forth bursts of light ⟨stars *twinkling* on a crisp September night⟩ — see FLASH 1

twinkling *n* a very small space of time ⟨in a *twinkling*, the rabbit had disappeared⟩ — see INSTANT

twirl *n* a rapid turning about on an axis or central point ⟨the *twirl* of the dancer's skirt mesmerized me⟩ — see SPIN 1

twirl *vb* 1 to move (something) in a curved or circular path on or as if on an axis ⟨absentmindedly *twirled* a lock of her hair around her finger⟩ — see TURN 1
2 to move in circles around an axis or center ⟨an ice-skater *twirling* in place⟩ — see SPIN 1

twist *n* 1 a forceful rotating or pulling motion for the purpose of dislodging something ⟨with a forceful *twist* she loosened the bolt⟩ — see WRENCH 1
2 an odd or peculiar habit ⟨my roommate has his little *twists*, and I have mine, so things should balance out⟩ — see IDIOSYNCRASY

twist *vb* 1 to change so much as to create a wrong impression or alter the meaning of ⟨my enemies will *twist* my words, but you'll only hear the truth out of me⟩ — see GARBLE 1
2 to follow a circular or spiral course ⟨the path gently *twisted* down the hill⟩ — see WIND 1
3 to move (something) in a curved or circular path on or as if on an axis ⟨*twisted* my wrist around to stretch it⟩ — see TURN 1
4 to move by or as if by a forceful rotation ⟨kept *twisting* the cap until it came free⟩ — see WRENCH 1
5 to make jerky or restless movements ⟨the dental patient *twisted* nervously in the chair⟩ — see FIDGET
6 to cause to twine about one another ⟨has the habit of idly *twisting* the strands of her hair while daydreaming⟩ — see INTERTWINE 1

twisted *adj* marked by a long series of irregular curves ⟨a *twisted* walking stick made from a blackthorn sapling⟩ — see CROOKED 1

twisting *adj* marked by a long series of irregular curves ⟨a *twisting* mountain road that requires extra careful driving⟩ — see CROOKED 1

twisting *n* a forceful rotating or pulling motion for the purpose of dislodging something ⟨it took some *twisting*, but I finally got the top off the jar⟩ — see WRENCH 1

twitch *vb* 1 to make jerky or restless movements ⟨the dog *twitched* in her sleep⟩ — see FIDGET
2 to move or cause to move with a sharp quick motion ⟨the rabbit *twitched* its nose⟩ — see JERK 1

twitching *n* a series of slight movements by a body back and forth or from side to side ⟨the *twitching* of my cat's ears was a signal that I should stop petting her before she got any angrier⟩ — see VIBRATION 1

twitchy *adj* making jerky or restless movements ⟨examining the *twitchy* little poodle was a challenge for the vet⟩ — see FIDGETY

twitter *n* 1 a state of nervous or irritated concern ⟨our grandmother gets all in a *twitter* if she doesn't get her weekly phone call right on time⟩ — see FRET
2 an explosive sound that is a sign of amusement ⟨the sort of lame double entendres that invariably provoke *twitters* among the immature⟩ — see LAUGH 1

twitter *vb* 1 to engage in casual or rambling conversation ⟨a local diner where the town gossips like to *twitter*⟩ — see CHAT 1
2 to make a short sharp sound like a small bird ⟨his two-way radio *twittered* as he answered it⟩ — see CHIRP
3 to show mirth with an explosive vocal sound ⟨has this grating habit of *twittering* helplessly whenever she's nervous⟩ — see LAUGH 1

two cents *n pl* a very small sum of money ⟨a passionate environmentalist who would work for *two cents* if her job did something to reduce global warming⟩ — see MITE 1

two–faced *adj* not being or expressing what one appears to be or express ⟨a *two-faced* friend who was just using me to advance her career⟩ — see INSINCERE

twofold *adj* 1 being twice as great or as many ⟨my reasons for buying the condo are *twofold*: first, it will serve as my vacation home, and second, it should turn out to be a good investment⟩ — see DOUBLE 2

2 consisting of two members or parts that are usually joined ⟨the mission of the campaign is *twofold*: to reduce underage drinking and to reduce alcohol-related traffic accidents⟩ — see DOUBLE 1

twofold *adv* to two times the amount or degree ⟨with the start of the recession, home foreclosures began increasing *twofold*⟩ — see DOUBLY

twosome *n* two things of the same or similar kind that match or are considered together ⟨those sisters are a constant *twosome*, going everywhere together⟩ — see PAIR

two–time *vb* to be unfaithful or disloyal to ⟨an entrepreneur who's supposedly *two-timed* every business partner she's ever had⟩ — see BETRAY 1

two–timing *adj* relating to or being a sexual encounter or relationship between a married person and someone other than their spouse ⟨her husband's compulsive *two-timing* behavior is the reason she left⟩ — see ADULTEROUS

two–timing *n* **1** a sexual encounter or relationship between a married person and someone other than their spouse ⟨he found out about the *two-timing* when he found a love letter stuffed in the dresser⟩ — see ADULTERY

2 the act or fact of violating the trust or confidence of another ⟨this repudiation of her campaign pledges is an unconscionable *two-timing* of the electorate⟩ — see BETRAYAL

two–wheeler *n* a two-wheeled vehicle that is propelled by the use of pedals and steered through the use of handlebars ⟨a committed environmentalist, he doggedly rides his *two-wheeler* to work⟩ — see BICYCLE

tycoon *n* a person of rank, power, or influence in a particular field ⟨an oil *tycoon* who's widely considered the most powerful man in the county⟩ — see MAGNATE

tyke *also* **tike** *n* a domestic mammal that is related to the wolves and foxes ⟨adopted a lovable *tyke* from the local animal shelter⟩ — see DOG 1

type *n* **1** a number of persons or things that are grouped together because they have something in common ⟨what *type* of people do you generally hang out with?⟩ — see SORT 1

2 one of the units into which a whole is divided on the basis of a common characteristic ⟨a music store that has a good selection of all *types* of music, not just pop, rock, and rap⟩ — see CLASS 2

type *vb* to arrange or assign according to type ⟨*type* the birds by geographical range⟩ — see CLASSIFY 1

typical *adj* **1** having or showing the qualities associated with the members of a particular group or kind ⟨*typical* behavior for a two-year-old⟩

synonyms archetypal (*also* archetypical), average, characteristic, normal, regular, representative, standard, true

related words common, commonplace, conventional, customary, everyday, ordinary, usual, wonted, workaday; classic, textbook, vintage; expected, familiar, habitual, predictable, routine, unexceptional, unremarkable; predominant, preponderant

near antonyms uncommon, unconventional, uncustomary, unusual, unwonted; distinctive, especial, exceptional, extraordinary, infrequent, noteworthy, rare, remarkable, singular, special, unexpected, unfamiliar, unique, unpredictable; eccentric, idiosyncratic, nonconformist, peculiar, unknown, unorthodox; curious, erratic, funky, funny, odd, oddball, offbeat, outlandish, quirky, screwy, strange, wacky (*also* whacky), way-out; bizarre, fantastic (*also* fantastical), far-out, freak, freakish, kooky (*also* kookie), out-of-the-way, outrageous, outré, rare, singular, unnatural, weird, wild

antonyms aberrant, abnormal, anomalous, atypical, deviant, irregular, nonrepresentative, nontypical, untypical

2 serving to identify as belonging to an individual or group ⟨when I asked what he had learned in school that day, he gave me the *typical* answer of teenagers: "I don't know"⟩ — see CHARACTERISTIC 1

typically *adv* according to the usual course of things ⟨prairie dogs *typically* live in open spaces⟩ — see NATURALLY 2

tyrannical *also* **tyrannic** *adj* **1** exercising power or authority without interference by others ⟨a *tyrannical* ruler whose terrible reign was marked by unceasing violence⟩ — see ABSOLUTE 1

2 fond of ordering people around ⟨even when he was still a toddler, he tended to be a *tyrannical* playmate⟩ — see BOSSY

tyrannized *adj* suffering grave abuse or injustice at the hands of one in authority ⟨when the *tyrannized* masses could take no more, a violent and bloody revolution became inevitable⟩ — see DOWNTRODDEN

tyrannizer *n* a person who uses power or authority in a cruel, unjust, or harmful way ⟨a petty *tyrannizer*, the alcoholic father made his family suffer the cost of his many personal failures⟩ — see DESPOT

tyrannous *adj* **1** exercising power or authority without interference by others ⟨studied the *tyrannous* rule of Stalin, communist dictator of the Soviet Union⟩ — see ABSOLUTE 1

2 fond of ordering people around ⟨my older sister is a *tyrannous* bore who isn't happy unless she's in charge⟩ — see BOSSY

tyranny *n* a system of government in which the ruler has unlimited power ⟨a popular uprising replaced that nation's *tyranny* with freedom and democracy⟩ — see DESPOTISM

tyrant *n* a person who uses power or authority in a cruel, unjust, or harmful way ⟨the people universally feared the *tyrant*, who was notorious for his frequent use of torture⟩ — see DESPOT

tyro *n* a person who is just starting out in a field of activity ⟨he's a good musician, but at 14, he's still a *tyro* and has a lot to learn⟩ — see BEGINNER

U

ubiquitous *adj* **1** often observed or encountered ⟨by that time cell phones had become *ubiquitous*, and people had long ceased to be impressed by the sight of one⟩ — see COMMON 1
2 present in all places and at all times ⟨was weary of the *ubiquitous* noise of the big city and longed for the quiet of the country⟩ — see OMNIPRESENT

ugh *interj* used to express disgust ⟨*ugh*, this oven desperately needs to be cleaned⟩ — see YUCK

ugly *adj* **1** unpleasant to look at ⟨her first attempt at painting was pretty *ugly*—a portrait of her sister that was not at all flattering⟩
synonyms grotesque, hideous, homely, ill-favored, monstrous, unappealing, unattractive, unbeautiful, uncomely, unhandsome, unlovely, unpleasing, unpretty, unsightly, vile
related words abhorrent, abominable, appalling, awful, disgusting, distasteful, dreadful, gross, horrible, horrid, loathsome, nauseating, nauseous, noisome, repellent (*also* repellant), repugnant, repulsive, revolting, sickening; frumpish, frumpy, plain, unaesthetic, unbecoming, unshapely
near antonyms shapely; imposing, impressive, prepossessing
antonyms aesthetic (*also* esthetic *or* aesthetical *or* esthetical), attractive, beauteous, beautiful, bonny (*also* bonnie) [*chiefly British*], comely, cute, drop-dead, fair, fetching, good-looking, goodly, gorgeous, handsome, knockout, lovely, pretty, ravishing, seemly, sightly, stunning, taking, well-favored
2 causing intense displeasure, disgust, or resentment ⟨an *ugly* suggestion for controlling the overpopulation of deer in the area⟩ — see OFFENSIVE 1

ukase *n* an order publicly issued by an authority ⟨she brazenly ignored the company's *ukase* about entering by the back door⟩ — see EDICT 1

ultimate *adj* **1** of the greatest or highest degree or quantity ⟨the *ultimate* speed yet attained by a land-based vehicle⟩
synonyms consummate, last, max, maximum, most, nth, outside, paramount, supreme, top, utmost, uttermost
related words unequaled (*or* unequalled), unmatched, unparalleled, unrivaled (*or* unrivalled), unsurpassed; biggest, hugest, largest; topmost, upmost, uppermost
near antonyms littlest, minutest, smallest, tiniest; lowest; fewest
antonyms least, minimal, minimum, slightest
2 following all others of the same kind in order or time ⟨the *ultimate* speaker at today's meeting⟩ — see LAST 1
3 most distant from a center ⟨the *ultimate* edges of the universe⟩ — see EXTREME 1

ultimately *adv* at a later time ⟨we'll *ultimately* renovate this section of the house, but for now it will stay as it is⟩ — see YET 1

ultimatum *n* something that someone insists upon having ⟨issued the *ultimatum* that the project be finished by the following week, or it would be terminated⟩ — see DEMAND 1

ultra *adj* being very far from the center of public opinion ⟨espouses a kind of *ultra* conservatism that even some members of his own party cannot support⟩ — see EXTREME 2

ultraconservatism *n* attitudes or opinions tending to favor established ideas, conditions, or institutions ⟨a radio talk show host who has become for many listeners the national voice of *ultraconservatism*⟩ — see CONSERVATISM

ultraconservative *adj* tending to favor established ideas, conditions, or institutions ⟨under the leadership of its *ultraconservative* musical director, the symphony orchestra almost never played modern pieces⟩ — see CONSERVATIVE 1

ultraexpensive *adj* commanding a large price ⟨*ultraexpensive* medical equipment that only the largest hospitals can afford⟩ — see COSTLY

ultrahot *adj* having a notably high temperature ⟨*ultrahot* by any standard, a bolt of lightning can attain a temperature of 50,000 degrees Fahrenheit⟩ — see HOT 1

ultramodern *adj* being or involving the latest methods, concepts, information, or styles ⟨an *ultramodern* design for the company's new line of automobiles⟩ — see MODERN

ultramodernist *n* a person with very modern ideas ⟨an *ultramodernist* in interior decoration, she freely uses materials that are recognizably man-made to achieve a look that enthusiastically embraces the 21st century⟩ — see MODERN

ultrapractical *adj* capable of being put to use or account ⟨modular furniture was once touted as the *ultrapractical* solution to any and all interior layout problems⟩ — see PRACTICAL 1

ultraprecision *n* the quality or state of being very accurate ⟨an instrument that can measure changes in the size of tumors with an *ultraprecision* that is astonishing⟩ — see PRECISION

ultrasmart *adj* having or showing quickness of mind ⟨those *ultrasmart* investors who got out of the stock market before it collapsed⟩ — see INTELLIGENT 1

ultrathin *adj* being of less than usual width ⟨a new generation of flat-panel TVs that were *ultrathin*⟩ — see THIN 1

ululate *vb* to make a long loud mournful sound ⟨Arab women *ululating* with grief⟩ — see HOWL 1

umbra *n* **1** a time or place of little or no light ⟨strange noises were coming from the wooded *umbra* beyond our campfire⟩ — see DARK 1
2 partial darkness due to the obstruction of light rays ⟨during a solar eclipse observers located within the *umbra* experience a complete blocking of the sun by the moon⟩ — see SHADE 1

umbrage *n* the feeling of being offended or resentful after a slight or indignity ⟨took *umbrage* at the slightest suggestion of disrespect⟩ — see PIQUE

umbrageous *adj* protected from the sun's rays ⟨the estate's grounds include a delightfully *umbrageous* grove⟩ — see SHADY 1

umpire *n* a person who impartially decides or resolves a dispute or controversy ⟨usually acts as *umpire* in the all-too-frequent squabbles between the two other roommates⟩ — see JUDGE 1

umpire *vb* to give an opinion about (something at issue or in dispute) ⟨in our family disputes regarding the use of our home entertainment system are *umpired* by Dad⟩ — see JUDGE 1

unabashed *adj* not embarrassed or ashamed ⟨*unabashed* by their booing and hissing, he continued with his musical performance⟩
synonyms shameless, unashamed, unblushing, unembarrassed

related words prideful, proud; bold, brassy, brazen, cheeky, impudent, insolent, saucy; unapologetic, undaunted, undeterred, undismayed; unblinking, unflinching; impenitent, remorseless, unrepentant
near antonyms confounded, confused, discomfited, disconcerted, discountenanced, fazed, flustered, mortified, nonplussed (*also* nonplused), rattled; apologetic, contrite, penitent, remorseful, repentant, sorry
antonyms abashed, ashamed, embarrassed, hangdog, shamed, shamefaced, sheepish

unable *adj* lacking qualities (as knowledge, skill, or ability) required to do a job ⟨a celebrated author of serious plays, he turned out to be a particularly *unable* writer of comedies⟩ — see INCOMPETENT

unacceptable *adj* falling short of a standard ⟨this work is entirely *unacceptable*⟩ — see BAD 1

unacceptably *adv* **1** beyond a normal or acceptable limit ⟨the ski lodge was *unacceptably* cold⟩ — see TOO 1
2 in an unsatisfactory way ⟨she does her chores quickly but usually *unacceptably*⟩ — see BADLY 1

unacclimated *adj* not having acquired a habit or tolerance ⟨*unacclimated* to the intense heat of the tropics⟩ — see UNUSED 1

unaccompanied *adj* not being in the company of others ⟨an *unaccompanied* child on the airplane flight⟩ — see ALONE 1

unaccountable *adj* impossible to explain ⟨the decorator's client has an *unaccountable* dislike for that color⟩ — see INEXPLICABLE

unaccustomed *adj* **1** not having acquired a habit or tolerance ⟨pampered youngsters who were *unaccustomed* to such hard work⟩ — see UNUSED 1
2 not known or experienced before ⟨the *unaccustomed* friendliness of my relatives after I won the lottery⟩ — see NEW 2
3 noticeably different from what is generally found or experienced ⟨*unaccustomed* styles of cooking that the tourists had to be persuaded to try⟩ — see UNUSUAL 1

unacquainted *adj* not informed about or aware of something ⟨*unacquainted* with the latest developments in the field of astronomy⟩ — see IGNORANT 2

unadapted *adj* not having acquired a habit or tolerance ⟨the animals that were *unadapted* to extreme cold quickly died out during the Ice Age⟩ — see UNUSED 1

unadjusted *adj* not having acquired a habit or tolerance ⟨still *unadjusted* to the lifestyle of an air force cadet⟩ — see UNUSED 1

unadorned *adj* free from all additions or embellishment ⟨the completely *unadorned* clothing favored by members of that religious sect⟩ — see PLAIN 1

unadulterated *adj* **1** free from added matter ⟨an *unadulterated* solution is required for the experiment⟩ — see PURE 1
2 having no exceptions or restrictions ⟨the *unadulterated* nonsense that you sometimes hear from political pundits on TV⟩ — see ABSOLUTE 2

unaesthetic *adj* disagreeable to one's aesthetic or artistic sense ⟨believes that even industrial buildings need not have *unaesthetic* designs⟩ — see HARSH 2

unaffected *adj* free from any intent to deceive or impress others ⟨a relaxed and *unaffected* style of public speaking⟩ — see GUILELESS

unaffectedly *adv* without any attempt to impress by deception or exaggeration ⟨writes *unaffectedly* simple love poems⟩ — see NATURALLY 3

unaided *adv* without aid or support ⟨took pictures of the first time that the baby was able to walk *unaided*⟩ — see ALONE 1

unalike *adj* being not of the same kind ⟨our opinions of the movie couldn't have been more *unalike*⟩ — see DIFFERENT 1

unalloyed *adj* **1** free from added matter ⟨*unalloyed* chemicals⟩ — see PURE 1
2 having no exceptions or restrictions ⟨the *unalloyed* happiness that marriage has brought them⟩ — see ABSOLUTE 2

unalterable *adj* not capable of changing or being changed ⟨the rules of the game are *unalterable*, regardless of who is playing⟩ — see INFLEXIBLE 1

unambiguous *adj* **1** not subject to misinterpretation or more than one interpretation ⟨looked at his neighbor's new car with *unambiguous* envy⟩ — see CLEAR 2
2 so clearly expressed as to leave no doubt about the meaning ⟨an *unambiguous* declaration of his love for her⟩ — see EXPLICIT

unambivalent *adj* not subject to misinterpretation or more than one interpretation ⟨that comment is an *unambivalent* insult⟩ — see CLEAR 2

unanimity *n* the state of being of one opinion about something ⟨in a rare moment of *unanimity* the club members decided to throw a party for themselves⟩ — see AGREEMENT 1

unanimous *adj* having or marked by agreement in feeling or action ⟨a *unanimous* vote to upgrade the school's computer facilities⟩ — see HARMONIOUS 3

unanswerable *adj* not capable of being challenged or proved wrong ⟨the *unanswerable* assertion that she didn't know much about art but she knew what she liked⟩ — see IRREFUTABLE

unanticipated *adj* not expected ⟨ran into some *unanticipated* difficulties with the computer program⟩ — see UNEXPECTED

unanticipatedly *adv* without warning ⟨the *unanticipatedly* high fuel prices had many people wondering how they were going to keep warm that winter⟩ — see UNAWARES

unappealing *adj* unpleasant to look at ⟨an *unappealing* mess of dirt and trash in the corner of the room⟩ — see UGLY 1

unappeasable *adj* **1** incapable of being satisfied ⟨it turned out that the public's appetite for sadistic horror movies was not *unappeasable* after all⟩ — see INSATIABLE
2 showing no signs of slackening or yielding in one's purpose ⟨warned that the nation was dealing with an *unappeasable* enemy⟩ — see UNYIELDING 1

unappetizing *adj* disagreeable or disgusting to the sense of taste ⟨the array of *unappetizing* foods that we encountered at that cheap roadside restaurant⟩ — see DISTASTEFUL 1

unappreciated *adj* not likely to be appreciated by those who benefit ⟨a number of *unappreciated* little favors that we had done for the neighbors⟩ — see THANKLESS 2

unappreciative *adj* not showing gratitude ⟨vowed that his *unappreciative* niece would never receive another birthday present from him⟩ — see THANKLESS 1

unapproachable *adj* hard or impossible to get to or get at ⟨a nearly *unapproachable* fortress in the mountains⟩ — see INACCESSIBLE

unapt *adj* **1** not appropriate for a particular occasion or situation ⟨has a knack for saying the most *unapt* things at the worst possible moments⟩ — see INAPPROPRIATE
2 not likely to be true or to occur ⟨at this point an admission of guilt from him would be most *unapt*⟩ — see IMPROBABLE

unarguable *adj* not capable of being challenged or proved wrong ⟨I will not challenge your *unarguable* expertise in the field of lepidopterology⟩ — see IRREFUTABLE

unarguably *adv* without any question ⟨he is *unarguably* a better tennis player than his wife⟩ — see INDEED 1

unashamed *adj* **1** not embarrassed or ashamed ⟨*unashamed* of her religious beliefs and values⟩ — see UNABASHED
2 not sorry for having done wrong ⟨even after being convicted of housing violations, the slumlord remained as *unashamed* as ever⟩ — see REMORSELESS 1

unasked *adj* not searched or asked for ⟨received a lot of *unasked* advice on the project⟩ — see UNSOUGHT

unassailable *adj* not to be violated, criticized, or tampered with ⟨one of the *unassailable* beliefs of that political party⟩ — see SACRED 1

unassisted *adv* without aid or support ⟨managed to do the group project *unassisted* after his partners got sick⟩ — see ALONE 1

unassuming *adj* not having or showing any feelings of superiority, self-assertiveness, or showiness ⟨a talented but surprisingly *unassuming* musician⟩ — see HUMBLE 1

unattached *adj* **1** not married ⟨everyone was surprised when the *unattached* woman finally fell in love⟩ — see SINGLE 1
2 not physically attached to another unit ⟨preferred an *unattached* house to a townhome⟩ — see SEPARATE 2

unattainable *adj* **1** hard or impossible to get to or get at ⟨an eagle's nest in an *unattainable* location⟩ — see INACCESSIBLE
2 incapable of being solved or accomplished ⟨unfortunately, world peace is probably an *unattainable* ideal⟩ — see IMPOSSIBLE

unattractive *adj* unpleasant to look at ⟨an *unattractive*, awkward baby bird⟩ — see UGLY 1

unauthentic *adj* being such in appearance only and made or manufactured with the intention of committing fraud ⟨trying to sell *unauthentic* autographs of American presidents⟩ — see COUNTERFEIT 1

unavailable *adj* hard or impossible to get to or get at ⟨the commander is *unavailable* right now⟩ — see INACCESSIBLE

unavailing *adj* producing no results ⟨an *unavailing* effort to avert a war⟩ — see FUTILE 1

unavoidable *adj* impossible to avoid or evade ⟨unfortunately, kitchen duty will be *unavoidable* tonight⟩ — see INEVITABLE

unavoidably *adv* because of necessity ⟨we'll be *unavoidably* late this evening⟩ — see NEEDS

unaware *adj* not informed about or aware of something ⟨she was *unaware* of the change in travel plans⟩ — see IGNORANT 2

unaware *adv* without warning ⟨the predawn attack took the airmen completely *unaware*⟩ — see UNAWARES

unawareness *n* the state of being unaware or uninformed ⟨the college-educated couple's smug *unawareness* of current events was both surprising and sad⟩ — see IGNORANCE 1

unawares *adv* without warning ⟨the thunderstorm caught us *unawares*, and we scrambled to get off the ridge as lightning started to flash⟩
synonyms aback, suddenly, unanticipatedly, unaware, unexpectedly
related words abruptly, short; amazingly, astoundingly, surprisingly
phrases all of a sudden, off base
near antonyms laggardly, leisurely, pokily, slowly, sluggishly, tardily; obviously

unbalance *vb* to cause to go insane or as if insane ⟨the shock of the loss of his wife and children completely *unbalanced* him⟩ — see CRAZE

unbalanced *adj* **1** having or showing a very abnormal or sick state of mind ⟨horrific crimes that obviously were committed by a very *unbalanced* person⟩ — see INSANE 1
2 not being in or able to maintain a state of balance ⟨in such an *unbalanced* political situation, the probability of war increases⟩ — see UNSTABLE 1

unbaptized *adj* not named or identified by a name ⟨thus far the novel I've been working on remains *unbaptized*⟩ — see NAMELESS 1

unbearable *adj* more than can be put up with ⟨this heat is *unbearable*—when are we going to get air-conditioning?⟩
synonyms insufferable, insupportable, intolerable, unendurable, unsupportable
related words unacceptable; crushing, overwhelming; comfortless, hard, harsh, painful, uncomfortable; appalling, dreadful, excruciating, gruesome (*also* grewsome), harrowing, horrendous, horrible, horrid, horrifying, nightmarish, shocking, terrible, tormenting, torturous, vile, wretched; acute, extreme, intense, piercing; disgusting, distasteful, loathsome, nauseating, obnoxious, offensive, repugnant, repulsive, revolting, sickening; heinous, noxious, odious, unspeakable
near antonyms livable (*also* liveable); acceptable; adequate, admissible, allowable, reasonable, satisfactory
antonyms endurable, sufferable, supportable, sustainable, tolerable

unbeatable *adj* incapable of being defeated, overcome, or subdued ⟨a seemingly *unbeatable* baseball team⟩ — see INVINCIBLE

unbeautiful *adj* unpleasant to look at ⟨a makeshift shelter that was *unbeautiful* perhaps, but it kept us out of the rain⟩ — see UGLY 1

unbecoming *adj* not appropriate for a particular occasion or situation ⟨boorish behavior that is *unbecoming* to an officer⟩ — see INAPPROPRIATE

unbecomingness *n* the quality or state of not being socially proper ⟨the *unbecomingness* of such behavior at a White House dinner should be painfully obvious⟩ — see IMPROPRIETY 1

unbeknownst *also* **unbeknown** *adj* happening or existing without one's knowledge ⟨*unbeknownst* to me, my mother was planning a party⟩ — see UNKNOWN 1

unbelief *n* refusal to accept something as true ⟨a natural-born skeptic, she typically greets the latest conspiracy theory with head-shaking *unbelief*⟩ — see DISBELIEF

unbelievable *adj* too extraordinary or improbable to believe ⟨a completely *unbelievable* story about why there was lipstick on his collar⟩ — see INCREDIBLE

unbeliever *n* a person who is always ready to doubt or question the truth or existence of something ⟨a hardheaded *unbeliever* who demanded to see concrete evidence of any alleged UFO activity⟩ — see SKEPTIC

unbelieving *adj* inclined to doubt or question claims ⟨*unbelieving* scientists who demand that all phenomena be subjected to rigorous scientific scrutiny⟩ — see SKEPTICAL

unbend *vb* to cause to follow a line that is without bends or curls ⟨the new highway will largely *unbend* that twisting path that the old road used to follow⟩ — see STRAIGHTEN

unbending *adj* **1** having or showing a lack of friendliness or interest in others ⟨the commanding officer's *unbending* reserve when dealing with subordinates⟩ — see COOL 1
2 sticking to an opinion, purpose, or course of action in spite of reason, arguments, or persuasion ⟨the school's new headmaster is reputed to be an *unbending* disciplinarian⟩ — see OBSTINATE

unbiased *adj* marked by justice, honesty, and freedom from bias ⟨offered an *unbiased* judgment of the dancer's performance⟩ — see FAIR 2

unbidden *also* **unbid** *adj* not searched or asked for ⟨she arrived, *unbidden*, to help out at the Red Cross center⟩ — see UNSOUGHT

unbind *vb* **1** to disengage the knotted parts of ⟨*unbind* a rope⟩ — see UNTIE
2 to set free (as from slavery or confinement) ⟨a newly elected democratic government whose first act was to *unbind* the nation's vast horde of political prisoners⟩ — see FREE 1

unblemished *adj* being entirely without fault or flaw ⟨a modeling agency looking for people with *unblemished* complexions⟩ — see PERFECT 1

unblock *vb* to rid the surface of (as an area) from things in the way ⟨*unblock* the road so that the convoy can proceed⟩ — see CLEAR 1

unblushing *adj* not embarrassed or ashamed ⟨an *unblushing* patriotism that is manifested in the family's public display of the flag⟩ — see UNABASHED

unbodied *adj* not composed of matter ⟨ghosts are often depicted as *unbodied*, yet somehow visible, beings⟩ — see IMMATERIAL 1

unbookish *adj* used in or suitable for speech and not formal writing ⟨a refreshingly *unbookish* talk on how dictionaries get made⟩ — see COLLOQUIAL 1

unborn *adj* of a time after the present ⟨a home entertainment system that can be adapted for products as yet *unborn*⟩ — see FUTURE

unbosom *vb* to make known (as information previously kept secret) ⟨*unbosomed* his fear of dying only to his closest friends⟩ — see REVEAL 1

unbound *adj* not bound, confined, or detained by force ⟨a dog left *unbound* in the yard⟩ — see FREE 3

unbounded *adj* **1** being or seeming to be without limits ⟨the *unbounded* enthusiasm shown by the new club members⟩ — see INFINITE
2 showing no signs of being under control ⟨*unbounded* terror that was caused by the simultaneous detonation of seven car bombs around the city⟩ — see RAMPANT 1

unbraid *vb* to separate the various strands of ⟨*unbraided* the line⟩ — see UNRAVEL 1

unbridled *adj* showing no signs of being under control ⟨a case that was solved only because of one detective's *unbridled* determination to bring the killer to justice⟩ — see RAMPANT 1

unbroken *adj* **1** going on and on without any interruptions ⟨just mile after mile of *unbroken* woodland⟩ — see CONTINUOUS
2 living outdoors without taming or domestication by humans ⟨a young, *unbroken* horse⟩ — see WILD 1

unbudging *adj* incapable of moving or being moved ⟨the massive old bed was simply *unbudging*, despite our best efforts⟩ — see IMMOVABLE 1

unbuild *vb* to destroy (as a building) completely by knocking down or breaking to pieces ⟨beavers were busily building dams, and local landowners were just as diligently *unbuilding* them⟩ — see DEMOLISH 1

unburden *vb* **1** to empty or rid of cargo ⟨the crew was frantically *unburdening* the ship in an attempt to save it⟩ — see UNLOAD 1
2 to set (a person or thing) free of something that encumbers ⟨a generous friend *unburdened* her of that particular financial worry⟩ — see RID

unburdened *adj* no longer burdened with something unpleasant or painful ⟨now *unburdened* of his painful secret, he felt free for the first time in years⟩ — see FREE 2

uncage *vb* to set free (as from slavery or confinement) ⟨*uncaged* the bird and let it fly away⟩ — see FREE 1

uncalled-for *adj* **1** not needed by the circumstances or to accomplish an end ⟨*uncalled-for* restrictions on freedom of the press during the national emergency⟩ — see UNNECESSARY
2 showing a lack of manners or consideration for others ⟨hurtful remarks about a person's looks that are simply *uncalled-for*⟩ — see IMPOLITE

uncanniness *n* the quality or state of being impossible to know, understand, or explain ⟨a sly smile only added to the *uncanniness* of her cryptic response to my innocent question⟩ — see INSCRUTABILITY 1

uncanny *adj* **1** being beyond one's powers to know, understand, or explain ⟨a number of *uncanny* parallels in the lives of the twins who had been separated at birth⟩ — see MYSTERIOUS 1
2 being so extraordinary or abnormal as to suggest powers which violate the laws of nature ⟨an *uncanny* gift for knowing when someone, no matter how distant, needed help⟩ — see SUPERNATURAL 2
3 fearfully and mysteriously strange or fantastic ⟨*uncanny* and unexpected shadows along the mountainsides⟩ — see EERIE

uncataloged *adj* not appearing on a list ⟨hundreds of *uncataloged* runners ran in the marathon⟩ — see UNLISTED

unceasing *adj* going on and on without any interruptions ⟨this *unceasing* rain will turn me into a mushroom!⟩ — see CONTINUOUS

uncelebrated *adj* not widely known ⟨a gifted but *uncelebrated* poet⟩ — see OBSCURE 2

unceremonious *adj* **1** being or characterized by direct, brief, and potentially rude speech or manner ⟨my polite request was met with an *unceremonious* refusal⟩ — see BLUNT 1
2 not rigidly following established form, custom, or rules ⟨her *unceremonious* approach to her hosting duties puts party guests immediately at ease⟩ — see INFORMAL 1

uncertain *adj* **1** likely to change frequently, suddenly, or unexpectedly ⟨the stifling heat would occasionally be relieved by an *uncertain* breeze⟩ — see FICKLE 1
2 not feeling sure about the truth, wisdom, or trustworthiness of someone or something ⟨never *uncertain* of her political beliefs or judgment, she was a decisive and fearless leader⟩ — see DOUBTFUL 1

uncertainty *n* a feeling or attitude that one does not know the truth, truthfulness, or trustworthiness of someone or something ⟨*uncertainty* about her job prospects has her worried⟩ — see DOUBT

unchain *vb* to set free (as from slavery or confinement) ⟨activists for animal rights who would like to *unchain* zoo animals and return them to the wild⟩ — see FREE 1

unchallengeable *adj* not capable of being challenged or proved wrong ⟨the contention that there are certain *unchallengeable* rules governing proper grammar⟩ — see IRREFUTABLE

unchangeable *adj* not capable of changing or being changed ⟨I'm afraid that my opinion on this matter is *unchangeable*⟩ — see INFLEXIBLE 1

unchangeableness *n* the state of continuing without change ⟨the endless days of sunshine were certainly pleasant, but the *unchangeableness* of the weather got to be boring after a while⟩ — see CONSTANCY 1

unchanging *adj* **1** not undergoing a change in condition ⟨took comfort in *unchanging* family traditions⟩ — see CONSTANT 1
2 not varying ⟨wore an *unchanging* expression of boredom throughout the entire lecture⟩ — see UNIFORM

uncharitable *adj* **1** giving or sharing as little as possible ⟨an *uncharitable* couple who wouldn't even donate food to needy families at Thanksgiving⟩ — see STINGY 1
2 having or showing a lack of sympathy or tender feelings ⟨an *uncharitable* attitude towards people who give in to alcohol or other temptations⟩ — see HARD 1

unchecked *adj* showing no signs of being under control ⟨*unchecked* corruption in the state's prison system⟩ — see RAMPANT 1

unchristened *adj* not named or identified by a name ⟨some *unchristened* dog that we just adopted from the local pound⟩ — see NAMELESS 1

uncivil *adj* **1** not civilized ⟨the *uncivil* and wild land that the pioneers tamed and settled⟩ — see SAVAGE 1
2 showing a lack of manners or consideration for others ⟨such *uncivil* behavior will not be tolerated⟩ — see IMPOLITE

uncivilized *adj* not civilized ⟨unfairly branded as *uncivilized* by European explorers, they had created a culture that was actually quite advanced⟩ — see SAVAGE 1

unclad *adj* lacking or shed of clothing ⟨drawings and sculptures of the *unclad* human figure⟩ — see NAKED 1

unclean *adj* **1** having or showing lowered moral character or standards ⟨there's something *unclean* about this whole business⟩ — see CORRUPT
2 not clean ⟨a lackadaisical waiter who tried to set our table with smudged glasses and *unclean* silverware⟩ — see DIRTY 1

uncleanliness *n* the state or quality of being dirty ⟨the *uncleanliness* of the restaurant's windows wasn't very appetizing either⟩ — see DIRTINESS 1

uncleanly *adj* not clean ⟨the *uncleanly* uniforms of the restaurant's staff⟩ — see DIRTY 1

uncleanness *n* the state or quality of being dirty ⟨the general *uncleanness* of the doctor's office turned my stomach⟩ — see DIRTINESS 1

unclear *adj* **1** not expressed in precise terms ⟨their suggestion for correcting the problem is a bit *unclear*⟩ — see VAGUE 1
2 not seen or understood clearly ⟨obtained at best an *unclear* glimpse of the rarely seen bird from across the road⟩ — see FAINT 1

uncloak *vb* **1** to make known (as information previously kept secret) ⟨*uncloaked* the latest plan for improvements to the state capitol⟩ — see REVEAL 1
2 to reveal the true nature of ⟨investigative reporters *uncloaked* the real estate tycoon, revealing him to be nothing more than a slumlord⟩ — see EXPOSE 1

unclog *vb* **1** to make passage through (something) possible by removing obstructions ⟨*unclog* a bathroom drain with a cleaner⟩ — see OPEN 2
2 to free from obstruction or difficulty ⟨*unclog* the way for more people to take advantage of the government program⟩ — see EASE 1

unclogged *adj* allowing passage without obstruction ⟨an *unclogged* pipe works much more efficiently⟩ — see OPEN 1

unclose *vb* to change from a closed to an open position ⟨one nurse closed the window in my room, and a minute later another nurse *unclosed* it⟩ — see OPEN 1

unclosed *adj* allowing passage without obstruction ⟨escaped through the one remaining *unclosed* passageway⟩ — see OPEN 1

unclothe *vb* to remove clothing from ⟨partially *unclothed* the patient for treatment⟩ — see UNDRESS 1

unclothed *adj* lacking or shed of clothing ⟨an artist's drawings of clothed and *unclothed* figures⟩ — see NAKED 1

unclouded *adj* not stormy or cloudy ⟨campers awaking to the sight of a completely *unclouded* blue sky⟩ — see FAIR 1

unclubbable *adj* having or showing a lack of friendliness or interest in others ⟨for such a decidedly *unclubbable* man, politics was an odd career choice⟩ — see COOL 1

uncluttered *adj* being clean and in good order ⟨I work better with an *uncluttered* desk⟩ — see NEAT 1

unco *adv* to a great degree ⟨has written an *unco* fine novel about the war⟩ — see VERY 1

uncoerced *adj* done, made, or given with one's own free will ⟨the therapist noted that *uncoerced* behavioral changes can sometimes strengthen relationships⟩ — see VOLUNTARY 1

uncolored *adj* lacking an addition of color ⟨the walls will be left *uncolored*, so you can choose your own color scheme⟩ — see COLORLESS 1

uncomely *adj* unpleasant to look at ⟨behind his somewhat *uncomely* face lay a sweet and charming personality⟩ — see UGLY 1

uncomfortable *adj* **1** causing discomfort ⟨unfortunately, dressing up for the dance meant wearing an *uncomfortable* shirt⟩
synonyms comfortless, discomforting, harsh
related words aching, hurting, miserable, nasty, painful, sore; agonizing, excruciating, torturous; distressing, disturbing, upsetting; awkward, cumbersome, inconvenient, ungainly; uneasy; chafing, cramping, itching, pinching, pricking, prickling, smarting, stinging
near antonyms easy, soothing; cozy, cushy, snug, soft; easeful, relaxing, reposeful, restful
antonyms comfortable, comfy
2 causing embarrassment ⟨the *uncomfortable* situation of running into an ex-friend at a social gathering⟩ — see AWKWARD 3
3 lacking social grace and assurance ⟨a person who is *uncomfortable* at parties with lots of strangers⟩ — see AWKWARD 1

uncomic *adj* not joking or playful in mood or manner ⟨the movie takes a very *uncomic* approach to underage drinking, finding nothing funny about drunken teens⟩ — see SERIOUS 1

uncommon *adj* **1** being out of the ordinary ⟨a landscape of *uncommon* beauty⟩ — see EXCEPTIONAL 1
2 noticeably different from what is generally found or experienced ⟨backyard swimming pools are not an *uncommon* sight in that neighborhood⟩ — see UNUSUAL 1

uncommonly *adv* to a great degree ⟨he's *uncommonly* well-read for a boy his age⟩ — see VERY 1

uncommunicable *adj* beyond the power to describe ⟨the book attempts to communicate the *uncommunicable* horrors of war⟩ — see INDESCRIBABLE

uncommunicative *adj* **1** deliberately refraining from speech ⟨the child was *uncommunicative* and unhelpful to school investigators⟩ — see SILENT 1
2 given to keeping one's activities hidden from public observation or knowledge ⟨intelligence agencies must be *uncommunicative* about their operations if they are to be at all effective⟩ — see SECRETIVE
3 tending not to speak frequently (as by habit or inclination) ⟨resigned to the fact that her husband was always going to be an *uncommunicative* partner⟩ — see SILENT 2

uncompelling *adj* too extraordinary or improbable to believe ⟨a diet supplement that makes some rather *uncompelling* health claims⟩ — see INCREDIBLE

uncomplaining *adj* accepting pains or hardships calmly or without complaint ⟨an *uncomplaining* hardworking single mother of five⟩ — see PATIENT 1

uncomplimentary *adj* intended to make a person or thing seem of little importance or value ⟨an *uncomplimentary* description of the town in which the writer grew up⟩ — see DEROGATORY

uncompromising *adj* **1** not allowing for any exceptions or loosening of standards ⟨an *uncompromising* adherence to the rules that would do a schoolmarm proud⟩ — see RIGID 1
2 sticking to an opinion, purpose, or course of action in spite of reason, arguments, or persuasion ⟨the professor is generally an *uncompromising* stickler for deadlines, but he will make exceptions for genuine need⟩ — see OBSTINATE

unconceivable *adj* too extraordinary or improbable to believe ⟨it's *unconceivable* that a once-promising actor could end up this way⟩ — see INCREDIBLE

unconcern *n* lack of interest or concern ⟨wore an expression of general *unconcern* throughout the trial⟩ — see INDIFFERENCE

unconcerned *adj* **1** having or showing freedom from worries or troubles ⟨playful and *unconcerned* despite his medical emergency⟩ — see CAREFREE

2 having or showing a lack of interest or concern ⟨a featherbrain completely *unconcerned* about the important issues of the day⟩ — see INDIFFERENT 1

unconditional *adj* having no exceptions or restrictions ⟨demanded an *unconditional* surrender⟩ — see ABSOLUTE 2

unconfined *adj* not bound, confined, or detained by force ⟨residents of the camp for drug rehabilitation are completely *unconfined*—no one is there unless they want to be⟩ — see FREE 3

uncongenial *adj* not giving pleasure to the mind or senses ⟨a dank and *uncongenial* castle that makes one question just how merry old England really was⟩ — see UNPLEASANT

unconnected *adj* **1** not clearly or logically connected ⟨a delirious inmate whose *unconnected* ramblings frustrated the staff⟩ — see INCOHERENT 1

2 not physically attached to another unit ⟨the *unconnected* houses in the private development have common areas and share certain facilities⟩ — see SEPARATE 2

unconquerable *adj* incapable of being defeated, overcome, or subdued ⟨an *unconquerable* spirit that got the family through some hard times⟩ — see INVINCIBLE

unconscionable *adj* **1** going beyond a normal or acceptable limit in degree or amount ⟨an *unconscionable* number of errors for an important government report⟩ — see EXCESSIVE

2 not guided by or showing a concern for what is right ⟨a politician with an *unconscionable* disregard for the truth⟩ — see UNPRINCIPLED

unconscious *adj* **1** having lost consciousness ⟨the guard was knocked *unconscious* by a blow to the head⟩
synonyms cold, insensible, senseless
related words semiconscious; anesthetized; collapsed
near antonyms alert, awake, aware, up; resuscitated, revived
antonyms conscious

2 not informed about or aware of something ⟨*unconscious* of the somber expression she wore⟩ — see IGNORANT 2

unconsidered *adj* made or done without previous thought or preparation ⟨regretted some *unconsidered* comments that she made during a live TV interview⟩ — see EXTEMPORANEOUS

unconsolidated *adj* consisting of particles that do not stick together ⟨*unconsolidated* soil⟩ — see LOOSE 2

unconstraint *n* carefree freedom from constraint ⟨the actor plays the role of the comic drunkard with the kind of crowd-pleasing *unconstraint* that has made him a stage legend⟩ — see ABANDON

uncontrollable *adj* given to resisting control or discipline by others ⟨the *uncontrollable* child kept throwing tantrums in public and creating scenes⟩
synonyms froward, headstrong, incontrollable, intractable, recalcitrant, refractory, ungovernable, unmanageable, unruly, untoward, wayward, willful (*or* wilful)
related words bullheaded, contrary, difficult, hardheaded, incorrigible, intransigent, mulish, obdurate, obstinate, opinionated, perverse, pigheaded, self-willed, stiff, stiff-necked, stubborn; undisciplined, unpunished; uncontrolled, wild; boisterous, irrepressible, rambunctious, rowdy; disobedient, indocile, insubordinate, rebellious; misbehaving, naughty
phrases out of hand
near antonyms docile, obedient, well-behaved; compliant, placable, pliable, submissive, yielding; accepting, persuadable, receptive, responsive, willing; reasonable, temperate, trainable
antonyms controllable, governable, manageable, tractable

uncontrolled *adj* showing no signs of being under control ⟨a tirade filled with *uncontrolled* anger about what the government was doing⟩ — see RAMPANT 1

uncontroversial *adj* unlikely to provoke controversy or offense ⟨*uncontroversial* legislation, such as designating the cranberry the official state fruit⟩ — see SAFE 3

unconventional *adj* **1** deviating from commonly accepted beliefs or practices ⟨the Shakers acquired their name because of their *unconventional* practice of dancing with shaking movements during worship⟩ — see HERETICAL

2 not bound by traditional ways or beliefs ⟨had *unconventional* opinions on the raising of children⟩ — see LIBERAL 1

3 not rigidly following established form, custom, or rules ⟨young, creative people who lead *unconventional* but fulfilling lifestyles⟩ — see INFORMAL 1

unconvinced *adj* not feeling sure about the truth, wisdom, or trustworthiness of someone or something ⟨*unconvinced* that the prosecution had proven guilt beyond a reasonable doubt⟩ — see DOUBTFUL 1

unconvincing *adj* too extraordinary or improbable to believe ⟨the excuse for her tardiness was too *unconvincing* to be accepted⟩ — see INCREDIBLE

uncooked *adj* not cooked ⟨crunching on *uncooked* carrots⟩ — see RAW 1

uncoordinated *adj* having or showing an inability to move in a graceful manner ⟨my swimming instructor had never seen anyone so *uncoordinated*—in or out of the water⟩ — see CLUMSY 2

uncordial *adj* lacking in friendliness or warmth of feeling ⟨extended a correct but decidedly *uncordial* welcome to the other nation's diplomats at the peace negotiations⟩ — see COLD 2

uncork *vb* to set free (from a state of being held in check) ⟨*uncorked* her emotions once she was alone in her room⟩ — see RELEASE 1

uncos *n pl, chiefly Scottish* a report of recent events or facts not previously known ⟨*uncos* of recent sightings of the Loch Ness Monster always seem to increase with the start of the tourist season⟩ — see NEWS

uncountable *adj* too many to be counted ⟨an *uncountable* number of mosquitoes in the yard⟩ — see COUNTLESS

uncounted *adj* too many to be counted ⟨gazed in wonder at the *uncounted* stars of the sky⟩ — see COUNTLESS

uncouple *vb* to set or force apart ⟨*uncoupled* the two railroad cars⟩ — see SEPARATE 1

uncouth *adj* **1** having or showing crudely insensitive or impolite manners ⟨will not tolerate any *uncouth* behavior, such as eating with one's mouth open⟩ — see CLOWNISH

2 lacking in refinement or good taste ⟨the movie's *uncouth* humor seemed to be purposely offensive⟩ — see COARSE 2

uncover *vb* **1** to make known (as information previously kept secret) ⟨*uncovered* the location of the secret documents⟩ — see REVEAL 1

2 to reveal the true nature of ⟨a magazine article that purports to *uncover* the inner operations of what many regard as a religious cult⟩ — see EXPOSE 1

uncovered *adj* lacking a usual or natural covering ⟨the famed snows of Mount Kilimanjaro are receding, leaving behind much *uncovered* ground⟩ — see NAKED 2

uncritical *adj* lacking in worldly wisdom or informed

judgment ⟨had an *uncritical* trust in the nation's leaders⟩ — see NAIVE 1

uncrown *vb* to remove from a position of prominence or power (as a throne) ⟨Edward VIII effectively *uncrowned* himself when he insisted upon marrying an American divorcée⟩ — see DEPOSE 1

unctuous *adj* **1** not being or expressing what one appears to be or express ⟨an *unctuous* effort to appear religious to the voters⟩ — see INSINCERE
2 overly or insincerely flattering ⟨an *unctuous* appraisal of the musical talent shown by the boss's daughter⟩ — see FULSOME 1

uncultivated *adj* **1** existing without human habitation or cultivation ⟨miles of *uncultivated* land that had never been touched by a plow or an ax⟩ — see WILD 2
2 lacking in refinement or good taste ⟨an *uncultivated* and ignorant philistine who cared only about money⟩ — see COARSE 2
3 not civilized ⟨an *uncultivated* age when people lived just to meet their day-to-day needs⟩ — see SAVAGE 1

uncultured *adj* lacking in refinement or good taste ⟨an unlettered and *uncultured* society that still had the manners of the frontier⟩ — see COARSE 2

uncurious *adj* having or showing a lack of interest or concern ⟨how can you be so *uncurious* about the world around you?⟩ — see INDIFFERENT 1

uncurl *vb* to cause to follow a line that is without bends or curls ⟨*uncurled* the ribbon and flattened it out⟩ — see STRAIGHTEN

uncustomary *adj* **1** being out of the ordinary ⟨has *uncustomary* grace and poise for a girl of her age⟩ — see EXCEPTIONAL 1
2 noticeably different from what is generally found or experienced ⟨anger that was very *uncustomary* for such an even-tempered man⟩ — see UNUSUAL 1

undauntable *adj* feeling or displaying no fear by temperament ⟨the *undauntable* adventurers who crossed the trackless wilderness in search of El Dorado⟩ — see BRAVE 1

undaunted *adj* feeling or displaying no fear by temperament ⟨*undaunted* despite their repeated failures at starting a business⟩ — see BRAVE 1

undeceive *vb* to free from mistaken beliefs or foolish hopes ⟨promptly *undeceived* the young woman about the sincerity of the man's intentions⟩ — see DISILLUSION

undecided *adj* **1** not yet settled or decided ⟨a number of *undecided* matters still before the committee⟩ — see PENDING 1
2 not feeling sure about the truth, wisdom, or trustworthiness of someone or something ⟨voters still seem to be *undecided* about that candidate's fitness for the office of president⟩ — see DOUBTFUL 1

undecipherable *adj* incapable of being read or deciphered ⟨*undecipherable* stone inscriptions that have inspired a wide assortment of theories⟩ — see ILLEGIBLE

undecorated *adj* free from all additions or embellishment ⟨left the room simple and *undecorated* so that she'd be able to concentrate when she studied there⟩ — see PLAIN 1

undefended *adj* lacking protection from danger or resistance against attack ⟨the cowardly soldiers fled, leaving the palace *undefended*⟩ — see HELPLESS 1

undefined *adj* not seen or understood clearly ⟨plagued by *undefined* worries that kept her awake at night⟩ — see FAINT 1

undemonstrative *adj* not feeling or showing emotion ⟨an *undemonstrative* person by nature, he nevertheless loved his wife very much⟩ — see IMPASSIVE 1

undeniable *adj* not capable of being challenged or proved wrong ⟨*undeniable* evidence of guilt⟩ — see IRREFUTABLE

undeniably *adv* without any question ⟨*undeniably* handsome, he's never been conceited about his looks⟩ — see INDEED 1

under *adv* in or to a lower place ⟨crouch down *under* where they won't see you⟩ — see BELOW 1

under *prep* in a lower position than ⟨the cat is hiding *under* the bed⟩ — see BELOW 1

underbelly *n* **1** a social sphere that exists outside of the mainstream ⟨unable to get work in mainstream films, the actor ended up in Hollywood's *underbelly*—the porn industry⟩ — see NETHERWORLD
2 the side or part facing downward from something ⟨the *underbelly* of the old submarine is in bad shape⟩ — see BOTTOM 1
3 a vulnerable point ⟨the vast, thinly guarded southern border was obviously the *underbelly* of the nation's line of defense⟩ — see ACHILLES' HEEL

underbody *n* the side or part facing downward from something ⟨the *underbody* of the car was starting to rust⟩ — see BOTTOM 1

underclothes *n pl* clothing intended to be worn underneath other clothing ⟨keeps her *underclothes* in a separate drawer⟩ — see UNDERWEAR

underclothing *n* clothing intended to be worn underneath other clothing ⟨he changes his *underclothing* every day⟩ — see UNDERWEAR

undercover *adj* **1** undertaken or done so as to escape being observed or known by others ⟨an *undercover* operation to infiltrate the terrorist organization⟩ — see SECRET 1
2 working on missions in which one's objectives, activities, or true identity are not publicly revealed ⟨for months she's been an *undercover* agent pretending to be a drug dealer⟩ — see SECRET 2

undercover *n* a person who tries secretly to obtain information for one country in the territory of another usually unfriendly country ⟨within the city was a well-organized fifth column, and these *undercovers* would make themselves known as soon as the invading forces breached the city limits⟩ — see SPY

underestimate *vb* to place too low a value on ⟨we had *underestimated* her ability to raise the start-up money for her own design firm⟩
synonyms underrate, undervalue
related words de-emphasize, minimize, play down, soft-pedal; belittle, decry, depreciate, disparage; despise, disdain, scorn
phrases sell short
near antonyms appreciate, cherish, prize, treasure, value; admire, esteem, regard, respect; adore, idolize, revere, reverence, venerate, worship
antonyms overestimate, overrate, overvalue

undergarments *n pl* clothing intended to be worn underneath other clothing ⟨pack plenty of warm *undergarments* for the ski vacation⟩ — see UNDERWEAR

undergird *vb* to hold up or serve as a foundation for ⟨the theory of evolution *undergirds* virtually all of modern biology⟩ — see SUPPORT 3

undergo *vb* to come to a knowledge of (something) by living through it ⟨some people *undergo* a complete transformation while away at college⟩ — see EXPERIENCE

underground *adj* **1** undertaken or done so as to escape being observed or known by others ⟨an *underground* operation to smuggle ancient artifacts out of the country⟩ — see SECRET 1
2 being, situated, or operating beneath the surface of the earth ⟨an *underground* shopping mall that is part of the city's subway system⟩ — see BELOWGROUND

underground *n* a secret organization in a conquered country fighting against enemy forces ⟨joined the *underground* while still a teenager⟩ — see RESISTANCE 2

underhand *adj* **1** given to or marked by cheating and deception ⟨willing to stoop to *underhand* methods in order to win⟩ — see DISHONEST 2
2 undertaken or done so as to escape being observed or known by others ⟨the congressman's *underhand* attempt to slip several pork barrel items into the bill⟩ — see SECRET 1

underhanded *adj* **1** given to or marked by cheating and deception ⟨the commercial is a part of an *underhanded* PR campaign to whitewash the company's environmental record⟩ — see DISHONEST 2
2 undertaken or done so as to escape being observed or known by others ⟨an *underhanded* attempt at infiltrating the other party's headquarters⟩ — see SECRET 1

underline *vb* to indicate the importance of by giving prominent display ⟨a report that *underlines* the contributions of fathers to successful, happy families⟩ — see EMPHASIZE 3

underling *n* one who is of lower rank and typically under the authority of another ⟨the real estate tycoon has a whole army of *underlings* to attend to the details⟩
synonyms inferior, junior, subordinate
related words attendant, follower, retainer; domestic, menial, steward; flunky (*also* flunkey *or* flunkie), henchman, lackey, minion; adjutant, aid, aide, assistant, coadjutor, deputy, second, second fiddle; helpmate, helpmeet, mate, sidekick
near antonyms boss, captain, chief, foreman, head, headman, helmsman, kingpin, leader, master, taskmaster
antonyms senior, superior

underlying *adj* of or relating to the simplest facts or theories of a subject ⟨the *underlying* differences between democracy and dictatorship⟩ — see ELEMENTARY

undermining *n* a gradual weakening, loss, or destruction ⟨the view that the constant mudslinging and negative campaigning contributes to the *undermining* of the public's faith in politics and government⟩ — see CORROSION

undermost *adj* of, relating to, or located at the bottom ⟨the *undermost* layer of the mattress filling should provide firm back support⟩ — see BOTTOM

underneath *adv* in or to a lower place ⟨the ball rolled under the porch, so you'll have to crawl *underneath* to get it⟩ — see BELOW 1

underpart *n* the side or part facing downward from something ⟨the bird's *underparts* were white⟩ — see BOTTOM 1

underpin *vb* to hold up or serve as a foundation for ⟨the central beliefs that *underpin* a free society⟩ — see SUPPORT 3

underpinning *n* **1** an immaterial thing upon which something else rests ⟨the *underpinnings* of the theory have recently been called into question⟩ — see BASE 1
2 a structure that holds up or serves as a foundation for something else ⟨the *underpinnings* of the bridge were seriously damaged in the collision⟩ — see SUPPORT 1

underprivileged *adj* kept from having the necessities of life or a healthful environment ⟨*underprivileged* children often don't do as well on standardized tests as more privileged students⟩ — see DEPRIVED

underrate *vb* to place too low a value on ⟨it's perhaps the most *underrated* film of the last decade⟩ — see UNDERESTIMATE

underscore *vb* to indicate the importance of by giving prominent display ⟨a history of the Old West that *underscores* the role that pioneer women had in bringing order and stability to the wild frontier⟩ — see EMPHASIZE 2

underscoring *n* a special notice or importance given to something ⟨the *underscoring* we've given the play's local setting will hopefully increase ticket sales⟩ — see EMPHASIS 1

underside *n* the side or part facing downward from something ⟨the *underside* of the cat's coat is pure white⟩ — see BOTTOM 1

undersized *also* **undersize** *adj* of a size that is less than average ⟨though a football all-star in high school, he was just a mediocre, *undersized* player at the college level⟩ — see SMALL 1

understand *vb* **1** to form an opinion or reach a conclusion through reasoning and information ⟨as I *understand* it, this is the best plan that we have⟩ — see INFER 1
2 to have a practical understanding of ⟨I think I *understand* how an engine works now⟩ — see KNOW 1
3 to have a clear idea of ⟨after a few weeks in Russia I began to *understand* the language a little bit⟩ — see COMPREHEND 1

understandable *adj* capable of being understood ⟨with *understandable* pain and anger, the victim's family lashed out at the convicted murderer⟩ — see INTELLIGIBLE

understanding *adj* having or showing the capacity for sharing the feelings of another ⟨a kind and *understanding* teacher who often helps troubled students⟩ — see SYMPATHETIC 1

understanding *n* **1** an arrangement about action to be taken ⟨the landlord came to an *understanding* with the tenants about his obligations for maintaining the property⟩ — see AGREEMENT 2
2 the knowledge gained from the process of coming to know or understand something ⟨a social observer with a deep *understanding* of the problems that the nation's cities face in the 21st century⟩ — see COMPREHENSION

understated *adj* not excessively showy ⟨the actor's *understated* interpretation of the lead role is surprisingly compelling⟩ — see QUIET 2

undersupply *n* a falling short of an essential or desirable amount or number ⟨an *undersupply* of nutritious foods at the party⟩ — see DEFICIENCY

undersurface *n* the side or part facing downward from something ⟨painted the *undersurface* of the plane blue⟩ — see BOTTOM 1

undertake *vb* to take to or upon oneself ⟨*undertook* the responsibility of raising the orphaned children as their own⟩ — see ASSUME 1

undertaker *n* a person who manages funerals and prepares the dead for burial or cremation ⟨the *undertaker* wore black clothes and a solemn expression⟩ — see FUNERAL DIRECTOR

undervalue *vb* to place too low a value on ⟨you shouldn't *undervalue* your talent—you are a very gifted singer⟩ — see UNDERESTIMATE

underwater *adj* living, lying, or occurring below the surface of the water ⟨*underwater* plants don't require as much light to grow as surface plants⟩ ⟨a vessel designed for *underwater* exploration⟩
synonyms aquatic, submarine, submerged, sunken
related words oceanic; undersea; abysmal, abyssal, deep, deep-sea, deepwater

under way *adv* in progress ⟨construction of the new shopping mall is *under way*⟩
synonyms afoot, under weigh
near antonyms deferred, delayed, postponed; suspended

underwear *n* clothing intended to be worn underneath other clothing ⟨*underwear* has got to be the most boring thing that one could ever receive as a birthday present!⟩
synonyms underclothes, underclothing, undergarments, undies, unmentionables
related words lingerie; panties, scanties; slip, underskirt; boxers, boxer shorts, briefs, drawers, long johns,

pants, shorts, underdrawers, underpants, undershirt, undershorts, union suit; nightdress, nightgown, nightshirt, pajamas, pj's
near antonyms outerwear

under weigh *adv* in progress ⟨registration for the summer session is *under weigh*⟩ — see UNDER WAY

underweight *adj* having little weight ⟨the long illness left him frail and *underweight*⟩ — see [1]LIGHT 1

underworld *n* a social sphere that exists outside of the mainstream ⟨a magazine article taking an insightful look at the *underworld* inhabited by street people⟩ — see NETHERWORLD

underwrite *vb* to provide money for ⟨a university willing to *underwrite* an archaeological expedition⟩ — see FINANCE 1

undetermined *adj* **1** not seen or understood clearly ⟨an *undetermined* form seen only from a distance⟩ — see FAINT 1
2 not yet settled or decided ⟨the fate of the prisoners is still *undetermined*⟩ — see PENDING 1

undeviating *adj* not varying ⟨an *undeviating* dedication to duty⟩ — see UNIFORM

undies *n pl* clothing intended to be worn underneath other clothing ⟨likes to wear silk *undies*⟩ — see UNDERWEAR

undiluted *adj* free from added matter ⟨*undiluted* cranberry juice would be too strong for anyone to drink⟩ — see PURE 1

undiplomatic *adj* showing poor judgment especially in personal relationships or social situations ⟨the reporter's *undiplomatic* references to the state's overweight governor⟩ — see INDISCREET

undisturbed *adj* free from emotional or mental agitation ⟨didn't tell him the sad news until after the test, so he would remain *undisturbed*⟩ — see CALM 2

undivided *adj* not divided or scattered among several areas of interest or concern ⟨a teacher who insists on the *undivided* attention of her students⟩ — see WHOLE 1

undo *vb* **1** to deprive of courage or confidence ⟨the sudden shriek *undid* the campers⟩ — see UNNERVE 1
2 to disengage the knotted parts of ⟨*undo* a tangled shoelace⟩ — see UNTIE
3 to trouble the mind of; to make uneasy ⟨the mere mention of the home invasion still had the power to *undo* her⟩ — see DISTURB 1

undoable *adj* incapable of being solved or accomplished ⟨a combat mission of that type is not only *undoable*, it's foolish⟩ — see IMPOSSIBLE

undoing *n* something that is the cause of one's ultimate failure or loss of life ⟨an intractable drug habit proved to be her sad *undoing*⟩ — see DOWNFALL 1

undomesticated *adj* living outdoors without taming or domestication by humans ⟨domesticated rats are more tolerable companions than are their *undomesticated* cousins⟩ — see WILD 1

undoubtedly *adv* without any question ⟨we will *undoubtedly* have to do some editing of our home video⟩ — see INDEED 1

undress *vb* **1** to remove clothing from ⟨I quickly *undressed* myself and pulled on a set of dry clothes⟩
synonyms disrobe, strip, unclothe
related words bare, denude, divest, expose, uncover, undrape, unveil; bark, flay, peel, skin
near antonyms apparel, array, attire, caparison, clothe, costume, cover, deck, dress, feather, garb, garment, invest, rig (out), vest; cloak, mantle; drape, swaddle, swathe; accoutre (*or* accouter), equip, furnish, outfit
antonyms dress, gown, robe
2 to reveal the true nature of ⟨a self-styled financial investor who was eventually *undressed* as a con artist running a pyramid scheme⟩ — see EXPOSE 1

undressed *adj* **1** being such as found in nature and not altered by processing or refining ⟨*undressed* animal hides⟩ — see CRUDE 1
2 lacking or shed of clothing ⟨an *undressed* patient waiting to be examined by the doctor⟩ — see NAKED 1

undue *adj* going beyond a normal or acceptable limit in degree or amount ⟨try to avoid *undue* delay responding to e-mails⟩ — see EXCESSIVE

unduly *adv* beyond a normal or acceptable limit ⟨*unduly* upset by the slight delay of our departure⟩ — see TOO 1

undyed *adj* lacking an addition of color ⟨pieces of *undyed* leather⟩ — see COLORLESS 1

undying *adj* **1** having an existence or validity that does not change or diminish ⟨his *undying* devotion to his terminally ill wife is truly inspiring⟩ — see ABIDING
2 lasting forever ⟨a duet in which the singers swear *undying* love for one another⟩ — see EVERLASTING 1

uneager *adj* showing little or no interest or enthusiasm ⟨received the usual *uneager* response when she asked for volunteers to help clean up⟩ — see TEPID 1

unearth *vb* to remove from place of burial ⟨*unearthed* a hoard of treasures from the Egyptian tomb⟩— see EXHUME

unearthing *n* the act or process of sighting or learning the existence of something for the first time ⟨the *unearthing* of a prehistoric man who had been preserved in an Alpine glacier proved to be a great boon to science⟩ — see DISCOVERY 1

unearthly *adj* **1** being so extraordinary or abnormal as to suggest powers which violate the laws of nature ⟨an *unearthly* knack for picking winning lottery numbers⟩ — see SUPERNATURAL 2
2 fearfully and mysteriously strange or fantastic ⟨an *unearthly* wail came from out of the darkness⟩ — see EERIE
3 of, relating to, or being part of a reality beyond the observable physical universe ⟨*unearthly* messages that she believed were coming from her deceased father⟩ — see SUPERNATURAL 1

unease *n* an uneasy state of mind usually over the possibility of an anticipated misfortune or trouble ⟨although we'd been assured that everything would be fine, we couldn't shake our feeling of *unease*⟩ — see ANXIETY 1

uneasiness *n* **1** a disturbed or uneasy state ⟨a general *uneasiness* has descended over the city in the wake of the murders⟩ — see UNREST
2 an uneasy state of mind usually over the possibility of an anticipated misfortune or trouble ⟨his *uneasiness* lasted until his son's plane had returned safely to the ground⟩ — see ANXIETY 1

uneasy *adj* **1** feeling or showing uncomfortable feelings of uncertainty ⟨I'm a bit *uneasy* about taking a baby on such a long trip⟩ — see NERVOUS 1
2 lacking or denying rest ⟨spent an *uneasy* night sleeping in his car⟩ — see RESTLESS 1
3 lacking social grace and assurance ⟨a shy lad, he's always a bit *uneasy* at parties⟩ — see AWKWARD 1
4 marked by or causing agitation or uncomfortable feelings ⟨an *uneasy* calm descended over the city as inhabitants waited for the attack that was sure to come⟩ — see NERVOUS 2

uneducated *adj* lacking in education or the knowledge gained from books ⟨a literary reference that could not be grasped by an *uneducated* person⟩ — see IGNORANT 1

unembarrassed *adj* not embarrassed or ashamed ⟨he seemed thoroughly *unembarrassed* by his sycophantic behavior at the company party⟩ — see UNABASHED

unembellished *adj* free from all additions or embellishment ⟨an *unembellished* vase is best because it won't take attention away from the flowers⟩ — see PLAIN 1

unemotional *adj* not feeling or showing emotion ⟨a surprisingly *unemotional* expression for someone who was just informed that his wife was missing⟩ — see IMPASSIVE 1

unemployed *adj* having no job ⟨the plant closings left a significant portion of the town's population *unemployed*⟩
synonyms jobless
related words subemployed, underemployed
phrases out of work
near antonyms self-employed
antonyms employed, working

unending *adj* lasting forever ⟨the writer's latest memoir is a seemingly *unending* exercise in narcissistic rambling⟩ — see EVERLASTING 1

unendurable *adj* more than can be put up with ⟨people used to travel along this stretch of the highway by night so as to avoid the *unendurable* heat of the day⟩ — see UNBEARABLE

unenjoyable *adj* not giving pleasure to the mind or senses ⟨an *unenjoyable* evening spent plowing through a backlog of office paperwork⟩ — see UNPLEASANT

unenthusiastic *adj* showing little or no interest or enthusiasm ⟨my suggestion that we go to see the new action flick was greeted with an *unenthusiastic* shrug⟩ — see TEPID 1

unequal *adj* not staying constant ⟨*unequal* pulsations of the heart that might be a sign of trouble⟩ — see UNEVEN 2

unequaled *or* **unequalled** *adj* having no equal or rival for excellence or desirability ⟨a horse of *unequaled* beauty⟩ — see ONLY 1

unequivocal *adj* **1** not subject to misinterpretation or more than one interpretation ⟨few of the candidates have yet staked out *unequivocal* positions on the hot-button issues⟩ — see CLEAR 2
2 so clearly expressed as to leave no doubt about the meaning ⟨the directions on the vial state in clear and *unequivocal* language that the drug should not be taken by pregnant women⟩ — see EXPLICIT

unerring *adj* not being or likely to be wrong ⟨an *unerring* taste in interior decoration⟩ — see INFALLIBLE 1

unescapable *adj* impossible to avoid or evade ⟨you will make some mistakes—that is just one of the *unescapable* realities of this job⟩ — see INEVITABLE

unessential *adj* not needed by the circumstances or to accomplish an end ⟨don't pack any *unessential* items until we're sure we have room for everything we'll actually need⟩ — see UNNECESSARY

unethical *adj* **1** not conforming to a high moral standard; morally unacceptable ⟨*unethical* treatment of prisoners of war that was a clear violation of international law⟩ — see BAD 2
2 not guided by or showing a concern for what is right ⟨an *unethical* attorney, he had no qualms about getting off clients who he knew were guilty⟩ — see UNPRINCIPLED

uneven *adj* **1** not having a level or smooth surface ⟨the driveway is *uneven* and collects water in several large puddles whenever it rains⟩
synonyms broken, bumpy, coarse, irregular, jagged, lumpy, pebbly, ragged, rough, roughened, rugged, scraggy
related words lopsided, unbalanced; inexact, unaligned; rutted, rutty, undulating, undulatory, wavy; pitted, pocked; knobbly, knobby, knurled, knurly, nubbly, nubby; burred, harsh, sandpapery, scraggly, scratchy; nonuniform
near antonyms exact, uniform; aligned (*also* alined), regular, true; horizontal, tabular; plumb, straight, vertical; flush
antonyms even, flat, level, plane, smooth
2 not staying constant ⟨the level of attendance at the ballpark has been very *uneven* this season⟩
synonyms changing, erratic, fluctuating, irregular, unequal, unstable, unsteady, varying
related words capricious, changeable, changeful, choppy, fickle, fluid, inconsistent, inconstant, mercurial, mutable, uncertain, unsettled, variable, volatile
near antonyms regular
antonyms changeless, constant, stable, steady, unchanging, unvarying
3 inclined or twisted to one side ⟨a goofy guy with an *uneven* grin⟩ — see AWRY

unexampled *adj* having no equal or rival for excellence or desirability ⟨her performance in the Olympics was an *unexampled* display of athletic prowess⟩ — see ONLY 1

unexceptional *adj* being of the type that is encountered in the normal course of events ⟨the physicist, now regarded as one of the brightest minds in science, was an *unexceptional* student as a child⟩ — see ORDINARY 1

unexpected *adj* not expected ⟨the failure of the backup generator was *unexpected* and a contingency for which we weren't prepared⟩
synonyms abrupt, sudden, unanticipated, unforeseen, unlooked-for
related words unintended, unplanned; improbable, unlikely; startling, surprising
near antonyms predicted, prophesied; unsurprising
antonyms anticipated, expected, foreseen

unexpectedly *adv* without warning ⟨the snow started *unexpectedly*⟩ — see UNAWARES

unexplainable *adj* impossible to explain ⟨a series of *unexplainable* weather events⟩ — see INEXPLICABLE

unexpressed *adj* understood although not put into words ⟨they shared an *unexpressed* but nevertheless deep affection⟩ — see IMPLICIT 1

unfailing *adj* **1** not being or likely to be wrong ⟨an *unfailing* judge of personal character⟩ — see INFALLIBLE 1
2 not likely to fail ⟨the writer's *unfailing* sense of humor is again evident in his newest book⟩ — see INFALLIBLE 2

unfailingly *adv* on every relevant occasion ⟨she has been *unfailingly* optimistic throughout this ordeal⟩ — see ALWAYS 1

unfair *adj* not being in accordance with the rules or standards of what is fair in sport ⟨a team that is notorious throughout the league for its record of *unfair* play⟩ — see FOUL 2

unfairness *n* **1** the state of being unfair or unjust ⟨the transparent *unfairness* of the referee's decision made her furious⟩ — see INJUSTICE 1
2 unfair or inadequate treatment of someone or something or an instance of this ⟨it would be no *unfairness* to the article's second author to characterize his contributions as minimal⟩ — see DISSERVICE

unfaithful *adj* not true in one's allegiance to someone or something ⟨colonists who later proved to be *unfaithful* to the cause of independence⟩ — see FAITHLESS

unfaithfulness *n* **1** lack of faithfulness especially to one's husband or wife ⟨he eventually forgave his wife's *unfaithfulness*⟩ — see INFIDELITY 1
2 the act or fact of violating the trust or confidence of another ⟨the jaw-dropping *unfaithfulness* of the person she had considered her best friend was deeply hurtful⟩ — see BETRAYAL
3 a sexual encounter or relationship between a married person and someone other than their spouse ⟨there were charges of *unfaithfulness* on both sides⟩ — see ADULTERY

unfamiliar *adj* not known or experienced before ⟨ordered an *unfamiliar* wine and was surprised to find that it was much drier than what they were used to⟩ — see NEW 2

unfamiliarity *n* the state of being unaware or uninformed ⟨some intense studying rapidly remedied my *unfamiliarity* with the subject⟩ — see IGNORANCE 1

unfamous *adj* not widely known ⟨the influenza epidemic of 1918 was eminently egalitarian: it struck down the famous and the *unfamous* with equal fervor⟩ — see OBSCURE 2

unfashionable *adj* marked by an obvious lack of style or good taste ⟨an old and *unfashionable* jacket that someone had donated to charity⟩ — see ¹TACKY 1

unfasten *vb* to disengage the knotted parts of ⟨gently *unfastened* the strings of the baby's hood⟩ — see UNTIE

unfathered *adj* born to a father and mother who are not married ⟨grew up in the straitened circumstances that are typical for *unfathered* children⟩ — see ILLEGITIMATE 1

unfathomable *adj* **1** being or seeming to be without limits ⟨the *unfathomable* reaches of space⟩ — see INFINITE

2 impossible to understand ⟨for some *unfathomable* reason the family decided to venture out into the blizzard⟩ — see INCOMPREHENSIBLE

unfavorable *adj* opposed to one's interests ⟨the company chose to accept the *unfavorable* settlement rather than spend more money on legal fees⟩ — see ADVERSE 1

unfeeling *adj* **1** having or showing a lack of sympathy or tender feelings ⟨gave the homeless people on the street only an *unfeeling* glance⟩ — see HARD 1

2 lacking in sensation or feeling ⟨her heart was as cold and hard as the *unfeeling* marble statue in her garden⟩ — see NUMB 1

3 lacking animate awareness or sensation ⟨worked as an embalmer, usually with an *unfeeling* corpse as his only companion⟩ — see INSENSATE 1

unfeigned *adj* genuine in feeling ⟨the young soprano retains an *unfeigned* humility that is surprising, given the critical acclaim she has received⟩ — see SINCERE 1

unfeignedly *adv* without any attempt to impress by deception or exaggeration ⟨parents who are *unfeignedly* enthusiastic about the man their daughter has chosen to marry⟩ — see NATURALLY 3

unfeminine *adj* having qualities or traits that are traditionally considered inappropriate for a girl or woman ⟨in bygone days pants were considered *unfeminine*, and even women bicycling were expected to wear skirts⟩

synonyms hoydenish, manlike, mannish, tomboyish, unladylike, unwomanly

related words gentlemanly, male, manly, masculine

near antonyms effeminate, girlish, sissified, sissy, unmanly, unmasculine, womanish, womanlike; distaff, petticoat

antonyms female, feminine, ladylike, womanly

unfertile *adj* producing inferior or only a small amount of vegetation ⟨struggling to make a living with the region's *unfertile* fields⟩ — see BARREN 1

unfetter *vb* to set free (as from slavery or confinement) ⟨authorities eventually *unfettered* the menagerie of wild animals that had been kept illegally as pets⟩ — see FREE 1

unfit *adj* **1** lacking qualities (as knowledge, skill, or ability) required to do a job ⟨just because I don't have actual work experience doesn't mean I'm *unfit* for the job⟩ — see INCOMPETENT

2 not appropriate for a particular occasion or situation ⟨those flimsy shoes are *unfit* for the hike we're about to take⟩ — see INAPPROPRIATE

unfitness *n* **1** the quality or state of being unsuitable or unfitting ⟨her *unfitness* for a managerial position is apparent in the abusive way she treats her subordinates⟩ — see INAPPROPRIATENESS 1

2 the quality or state of not being socially proper ⟨the manifest *unfitness* of such a coarse gesture at an elegant party⟩ — see IMPROPRIETY 1

unfitted *adj* lacking qualities (as knowledge, skill, or ability) required to do a job ⟨a restless free spirit, he was temperamentally *unfitted* for a desk job⟩ — see INCOMPETENT

unflagging *adj* showing no signs of weariness even after long hard effort ⟨being rewarded for the *unflagging* zeal with which she led the fund-raising campaign⟩ — see TIRELESS

unflappable *adj* not easily panicked or upset ⟨the *unflappable* teacher never even blinked when the wall map came crashing down⟩

synonyms imperturbable, nerveless, unshakable

related words calm, collected, composed, cool, coolheaded, icy, nonchalant, placid, self-collected, self-composed, self-possessed, serene, steely, tranquil, undisturbed, unperturbed, unruffled, unshaken, untroubled, unworried

near antonyms panicky; aflutter, anxious, dithery, edgy, het up, hung up, jittery, jumpy, nervous, nervy, perturbed, shaky, tense, troubled, uneasy, upset, uptight, worried

antonyms perturbable, shakable (*or* shakeable)

unflashy *adj* not excessively showy ⟨a family man who drives a serviceable, decidedly *unflashy* car⟩ — see QUIET 2

unfledged *adj* lacking in adult experience or maturity ⟨the kind of mistake in judgment that an *unfledged* youth could be expected to make⟩ — see CALLOW

unflinching *adj* showing no signs of slackening or yielding in one's purpose ⟨he was *unflinching* in his determination to see that justice was done⟩ — see UNYIELDING 1

unfold *vb* **1** to arrange the parts of (something) over a wider area ⟨carefully *unfold* that antique map so that it doesn't tear⟩ — see OPEN 3

2 to gradually become clearer or more detailed ⟨as the situation *unfolded*, it became clear that more help would be needed⟩ — see DEVELOP 1

3 to produce flowers ⟨the rosebud *unfolded* literally overnight⟩ — see BLOOM

4 to come into view ⟨the majestic landscape *unfolded* before us⟩ — see APPEAR 1

unforced *adj* done, made, or given with one's own free will ⟨the participation of the people on the project must be *unforced*, or it really isn't a volunteer effort⟩ — see VOLUNTARY 1

unforeseen *adj* not expected ⟨there are almost always *unforeseen* consequences for any major endeavor⟩ — see UNEXPECTED

unforgettable *adj* not easily forgotten ⟨an *unforgettable* evening of dining and dancing⟩

synonyms indelible, memorable

related words notable, noteworthy, remarkable

near antonyms unremarkable

antonyms forgettable

unforgivable *adj* too bad to be excused or justified ⟨an *unforgivable* crime that society must seek just punishment for⟩ — see INEXCUSABLE

unformed *adj* **1** having no definite or recognizable form ⟨what was once an *unformed* lump of clay is now an attractive, useful bowl⟩ — see FORMLESS 1

2 lacking in adult experience or maturity ⟨under his care and tutelage, young men, *unformed* in mind and body, became battle-worthy soldiers⟩ — see CALLOW

unfortunate *adj* **1** bringing about ruin or misfortune ⟨an *unfortunate* chain of events destroyed the business⟩ — see FATAL 1

2 having, prone to, or marked by bad luck ⟨up to that point in her life she had been *unfortunate* in love⟩ — see UNLUCKY 1

3 of a kind to cause great distress ⟨an *unfortunate* choice of words that would later prove to be embarrassing for the talk show host⟩ — see REGRETTABLE

unfounded *adj* having no basis in reason or fact ⟨the accusation proved to be *unfounded*⟩ — see GROUNDLESS

unfriendly *adj* 1 lacking in friendliness or warmth of feeling ⟨the *unfriendly* looks quickly warmed when we were recognized as long-unseen relatives⟩ — see COLD 2

2 marked by opposition or ill will ⟨an *unfriendly* nation⟩ — see HOSTILE 1

3 opposed to one's interests ⟨the claim that the state's numerous regulations create a climate *unfriendly* to small businesses⟩ — see ADVERSE 1

unfrozen *adj* freed from a frozen state by exposure to warmth ⟨there should be a couple of *unfrozen* chicken breasts in the refrigerator⟩ — see THAWED

unfruitful *adj* not able to produce fruit or offspring ⟨disappointed to discover that the mare was *unfruitful*⟩ — see STERILE 1

unfurl *vb* to arrange the parts of (something) over a wider area ⟨after the protestors had *unfurled* their banner, it stretched from one side of the visitors' gallery to the other⟩ — see OPEN 3

ungainly *adj* 1 difficult to use or operate especially because of size, weight, or design ⟨getting the *ungainly* couch up the stairs was a real chore⟩ — see CUMBERSOME

2 having or showing an inability to move in a graceful manner ⟨the tree cutter was crushing any unlucky petunias that lay in the path of his *ungainly* tread⟩ — see CLUMSY 2

ungenerous *adj* giving or sharing as little as possible ⟨it is *ungenerous* for someone of his ample means not to provide more for the care of his aging parents⟩ — see STINGY 1

ungentle *adj* harsh and threatening in manner or appearance ⟨a demanding and *ungentle* land that was not for the fainthearted⟩ — see GRIM 1

ungovernable *adj* 1 given to resisting authority or another's control ⟨a handful of *ungovernable* students are disrupting the learning environment for everyone else⟩ — see DISOBEDIENT

2 given to resisting control or discipline by others ⟨resigned to the fact that my cat is basically is an *ungovernable* beast with a will of his own⟩ — see UNCONTROLLABLE

ungraceful *adj* lacking social grace and assurance ⟨an *ungraceful* but well-meaning hostess⟩ — see AWKWARD 1

ungracious *adj* showing a lack of manners or consideration for others ⟨we were taken aback by our aunt's *ungracious* reply to the invitation we had sent her⟩ — see IMPOLITE

ungraciousness *n* rude behavior ⟨the former champion's unbecoming *ungraciousness* in defeat: he refused to shake the new champion's hand⟩ — see DISCOURTESY

ungrammatical *adj* violating approved patterns of speaking and writing ⟨the résumé and its *ungrammatical* cover letter were summarily thrown in the trash⟩ — see ILLITERATE 1

ungraspable *adj* impossible to understand ⟨advanced scientific theories of *ungraspable* complexity for the layperson⟩ — see INCOMPREHENSIBLE

ungrateful *adj* 1 not likely to be appreciated by those who benefit ⟨the park's custodial staff has the *ungrateful* job of cleaning up after the Independence Day party is over⟩ — see THANKLESS 2

2 not showing gratitude ⟨although the food was being provided for free, the *ungrateful* recipients could not refrain from complaining that it was not to their liking⟩ — see THANKLESS 1

ungratefulness *n* failure or refusal to acknowledge receipt of something good from another ⟨we'll keep your *ungratefulness* in mind the next time you ask for our assistance⟩ — see INGRATITUDE

unguarded *adj* 1 free in expressing one's true feelings and opinions ⟨the swimming coach quickly regretted his *unguarded* comments about the young swimmer's limitations⟩ — see FRANK

2 lacking protection from danger or resistance against attack ⟨an *unguarded* gate that would later prove to be the fatal weakness in the city's defenses⟩ — see HELPLESS 1

3 not paying or showing close attention especially for the purpose of avoiding trouble ⟨in an *unguarded* moment I let my mind wander and smashed my car into a tree⟩ — see CARELESS 1

unguardedness *n* the free expression of one's true feelings and opinions ⟨chastised by the other royals for her *unguardedness* when talking to the press⟩ — see CANDOR 1

unhampered *adj* showing no signs of being under control ⟨the freeway system needs to be expanded to meet the demands of the city's *unhampered* growth⟩ — see RAMPANT 1

unhandsome *adj* 1 unpleasant to look at ⟨a character actor with a distinctively craggy, *unhandsome* face⟩ — see UGLY 1

2 showing a lack of manners or consideration for others ⟨in an interview the free-spoken actor made some *unhandsome* remarks about his costars⟩ — see IMPOLITE

unhandy *adj* 1 difficult to use or operate especially because of size, weight, or design ⟨the new SUV is particularly *unhandy* and difficult to maneuver in parking lots and narrow streets⟩ — see CUMBERSOME

2 lacking or showing a lack of nimbleness in using one's hands ⟨an *unhandy* person should be kept away from knives and other sharp objects⟩ — see CLUMSY 1

unhappily *adv* with feelings of bitterness or grief ⟨an *unhappily* married couple being counseled by a professional⟩ — see HARD 2

unhappiness *n* a state or spell of low spirits ⟨with time the young woman got over the *unhappiness* caused by the breakup⟩ — see SADNESS

unhappy *adj* 1 feeling unhappiness ⟨he's been *unhappy* ever since his family's move, which took him away from all his friends⟩ — see SAD 1

2 having, prone to, or marked by bad luck ⟨she's trying to forget that whole *unhappy* attempt to start a business⟩ — see UNLUCKY 1

3 not appropriate for a particular occasion or situation ⟨a guest unintentionally made *unhappy* reference to what is a painful situation for the family⟩ — see INAPPROPRIATE

unhealthful *adj* bad for the well-being of the body ⟨the *unhealthful* level of smog in the city⟩ — see UNHEALTHY 1

unhealthiness *n* the condition of not being in good health ⟨remedied his general *unhealthiness* with a long-overdue change to a healthy diet and exercise⟩ — see SICKNESS 1

unhealthy *adj* 1 bad for the well-being of the body ⟨we knew that the junk food at the carnival was *unhealthy*, but it tasted so good!⟩

synonyms insalubrious, noisome, noxious, sickly, unhealthful, unwholesome

related words germy, insanitary, unhygienic, unsanitary; nonnutritious; poisonous, toxic; fatal, lethal, mortal

near antonyms hygienic, sanitary; nutritious
antonyms healthful, healthy
2 involving potential loss or injury ⟨criticism of the military dictatorship has proved to be *unhealthy* for several of that nation's journalists⟩ — see DANGEROUS 1
3 temporarily suffering from a disorder of the body ⟨she's been *unhealthy* for almost a week now⟩ — see SICK 1

unheard–of *adj* not known or experienced before ⟨houses selling at *unheard-of* prices⟩ — see NEW 2

unheroic *adj* having or showing a shameful lack of courage ⟨the new biography casts the romanticized outlaw in a much more vicious and *unheroic* light⟩ — see COWARDLY

unhindered *adj* showing no signs of being under control ⟨in the absence of appropriate oversight, the *unhindered* deforestation of the region continues⟩ — see RAMPANT 1

unhinge *vb* **1** to cause to go insane or as if insane ⟨the endless harassment by the guards completely *unhinged* the prisoners of war⟩ — see CRAZE
2 to trouble the mind of; to make uneasy ⟨I was momentarily *unhinged* by the unexpected question⟩ — see DISTURB 1

unhinged *adj* having or showing a very abnormal or sick state of mind ⟨destined to become one of the nation's most notorious serial killers, he apparently became *unhinged* as a result of being abandoned as a young teen⟩ — see INSANE 1

unhurried *adj* moving or proceeding at less than the normal, desirable, or required speed ⟨we cycled at an *unhurried* pace and saved our strength for the hills up ahead⟩ — see SLOW 1

unidentified *adj* **1** known but not named ⟨an *unidentified* worker reported the security breach⟩ — see CERTAIN 1
2 not named or identified by a name ⟨some *unidentified* person helped them and then left quietly⟩ — see NAMELESS 1

unification *n* the act or an instance of joining two or more things into one ⟨the political *unification* of several Central European states into a German empire dominated by Prussia⟩ — see UNION 1

uniform *adj* not varying ⟨with flat-screen TVs, picture sharpness is *uniform* over the entire screen, even in the corners⟩
synonyms even, invariant, steady, unchanging, undeviating, unvarying, unwavering
related words fixed, immutable, invariable, set, unalterable, unchangeable
antonyms changing, deviating, nonuniform, unsteady, varying

uniform *n* the distinctive clothing worn by members of a particular group ⟨the band *uniform* was brown with red and white stripes⟩
synonyms livery, outfit
related words fatigues, full dress, regimentals; costume, finery, regalia

unify *vb* **1** to bring (something) to a central point or under a single control ⟨will *unify* the several departments into a single operation⟩ — see CENTRALIZE
2 to come together to form a single unit ⟨the two labor unions *unified* in order to strengthen their bargaining position with the manufacturers⟩ — see UNITE 1

unimaginable *adj* too extraordinary or improbable to believe ⟨a nearly *unimaginable* string of coincidences⟩ — see INCREDIBLE

unimportant *adj* lacking importance ⟨we figured that the details were *unimportant* as long as we got the basic design correct⟩
synonyms fiddling, foolish, frivolous, incidental, inconsequential, inconsiderable, insignificant, little, Mickey Mouse, minor, minute, negligible, nugatory, slight, small, small-fry, trifling, trivial
related words jerkwater, one-horse; nickel-and-dime, paltry, petty, small-time, worthless; anonymous, nameless, obscure, uncelebrated, unknown
phrases neither here nor there
near antonyms decisive, fatal, fateful; chief, dominant, overbearing, overmastering, overriding, principal; distinctive, exceptional, impressive, outstanding, prominent, remarkable; valuable, worthwhile, worthy; distinguished, eminent, great, illustrious, preeminent, prestigious; famous, notorious, renowned; all-important, basic, essential, fundamental, key
antonyms big, consequential, eventful, important, major, material, meaningful, momentous, significant, substantial, unfrivolous, weighty

uninflammable *adj* incapable of being burned ⟨an *uninflammable* stage curtain⟩ — see INCOMBUSTIBLE

uninformed *adj* not informed about or aware of something ⟨the mayor is clearly *uninformed* when it comes to the state of the city's schools⟩ — see IGNORANT 2

uninhibited *adj* showing feeling freely ⟨an *uninhibited* child who laughed and cried with equal abandon⟩ — see DEMONSTRATIVE 1

uninhibitedness *n* carefree freedom from constraint ⟨reserved by nature, she simply lacks the kind of *uninhibitedness* that producers of reality shows are looking for⟩ — see ABANDON

uninstructed *adj* lacking in education or the knowledge gained from books ⟨gathered the village's children, who were *uninstructed* for the most part, and formed a school⟩ — see IGNORANT 1

unintelligent *adj* not having or showing an ability to absorb ideas readily ⟨you're not *unintelligent*, so you must just be stubbornly resisting all attempts to teach you something⟩ — see STUPID 1

unintelligible *adj* impossible to understand ⟨uttered only a string of *unintelligible* murmurs⟩ — see INCOMPREHENSIBLE

unintended *adj* **1** happening by chance ⟨backyard digging that resulted in *unintended* damage to buried phone wires⟩ — see ACCIDENTAL 1
2 not made or done willingly or by choice ⟨a response that yielded an *unintended* insight into her personal character⟩ — see INVOLUNTARY 1

unintentional *adj* **1** happening by chance ⟨an *unintentional* encounter with an old classmate at the mall⟩ — see ACCIDENTAL 1
2 not made or done willingly or by choice ⟨an *unintentional* insult that nevertheless was very hurtful⟩ — see INVOLUNTARY 1

uninterested *adj* having or showing a lack of interest or concern ⟨the teacher decided to make a career change after having to teach yet another class of *uninterested* teens⟩ — see INDIFFERENT 1

uninteresting *adj* causing weariness, restlessness, or lack of interest ⟨the tour guide's spiel was *uninteresting* and not particularly informative⟩ — see BORING

uninterrupted *adj* going on and on without any interruptions ⟨a movie comedy that is 90 minutes of *uninterrupted* hilarity⟩ — see CONTINUOUS

uninvited *adj* not searched for or asked for ⟨I always ignore *uninvited* advice⟩ — see UNSOUGHT

union *n* **1** the act or an instance of joining two or more things into one ⟨the *union* of East Germany and West Germany that became possible after the fall of communism⟩
synonyms combination, combining, connecting, connection, consolidation, coupling, junction, linking, merger, merging, unification
related words agglomeration, amalgamation, blend, coalescence, commingling, compounding, fusion, inter-

mingling, intermixture, mingling, mix, mixture, synthesis; reunification, reunion
near antonyms detachment, divorcement, separation, severance
antonyms breakup, disconnection, dissolution, disunion, division, parting, partition, schism, scission, split
2 an association of persons, parties, or states for mutual assistance and protection ⟨in 1949 the U.S. and Canada joined their European allies in a transatlantic *union* to defend Western Europe from aggression by the Soviet Union⟩ — see CONFEDERACY
3 the state of having shared interests or efforts (as in social or business matters) ⟨the movie studio is producing the blockbuster in *union* with another studio because of the tremendous cost involved⟩ — see ASSOCIATION 1

unique *adj* **1** of, relating to, or belonging to a single person ⟨a comedian who brings a *unique* and twisted perspective to contemporary social issues⟩ — see INDIVIDUAL 1
2 being out of the ordinary ⟨the restaurant, specializing in fusion cuisine, provides a truly *unique* dining experience for those who can afford it⟩ — see EXCEPTIONAL 1
3 being the one or ones of a class with no other members ⟨the Mapparium, a huge glass globe that visitors can walk through, is *unique*—there's not another one like it anywhere⟩ — see ONLY 2
4 noticeably different from what is generally found or experienced ⟨a *unique* ability to add large sums in his head⟩ — see UNUSUAL 1

unisex *adj* suitable to or for either sex ⟨the new *unisex* fragrances that appeal to today's metrosexuals⟩ ⟨*unisex* restrooms⟩ — see GENDERLESS

unisexual *adj* suitable to or for either sex ⟨bought *unisexual* toys for the couple's new baby⟩ — see GENDERLESS

unison *n* the state of being of one opinion about something ⟨the members of the committee are in *unison* on this point⟩ — see AGREEMENT 1

unite *vb* **1** to come together to form a single unit ⟨using the microscope, we watched the water droplets *unite* into a single pool⟩
synonyms associate, coalesce, combine, conjoin, conjugate, connect, couple, fuse, interfuse, join, link (up), marry, unify
related words mate, yoke; ally, confederate, league; chain, compound, hitch, hook, splice; assemble, cluster, congregate, constellate, convene, gather, meet; recombine, reconnect, rejoin, reunify, reunite
near antonyms detach, disaffiliate, disconnect, disjoin, disjoint, dissociate, disunite, divide, divorce, fractionate, isolate, resolve, uncouple, unyoke; disband, disperse, scatter
antonyms break up, dissever, part, section, separate, sever, split, sunder, unlink
2 to bring (something) to a central point or under a single control ⟨*united* several teams under the reorganization plan⟩ — see CENTRALIZE
3 to form or enter into an association that furthers the interests of its members ⟨parents *united* to reform the school's curriculum⟩ — see ALLY
4 to participate or assist in a joint effort to accomplish an end ⟨only if private investors and public officials *unite* for the common good, will this city experience an economic revival⟩ — see COOPERATE 1

united *adj* **1** having or marked by agreement in feeling or action ⟨the party must present a *united* front if it hopes to win the election⟩ — see HARMONIOUS 3
2 used or done by a number of people as a group ⟨when a campaign to raise funds is this successful, it's only because of the *united* effort of all concerned⟩ — see COLLECTIVE

unity *n* a balanced, pleasing, or suitable arrangement of parts ⟨there's an aesthetic *unity* to the sculpture garden that makes it an ideal spot for quiet relaxing⟩ — see HARMONY 1

universal *adj* **1** able to do many different kinds of things ⟨a *universal* wrench⟩ — see VERSATILE
2 belonging or relating to the whole ⟨mankind's *universal* need for affection⟩ — see GENERAL 1
3 covering everything or all important points ⟨the genius of Leonardo da Vinci was *universal*: he was an artist, an architect, an engineer, and a scientist, among other things⟩ — see ENCYCLOPEDIC
4 present in all places and at all times ⟨after the home team won the national championship, throughout the city a sense of pride was as *universal* as the air⟩ — see OMNIPRESENT

universe *n* the whole body of things observed or assumed ⟨the theory that the *universe* is constantly expanding⟩
synonyms cosmos, creation, macrocosm, nature, world
related words existence, reality
near antonyms nothingness, void

univocal *adj* so clearly expressed as to leave no doubt about the meaning ⟨those who believe that the language of the Bible is *univocal*: it is never metaphorical but intended to be taken literally⟩ — see EXPLICIT

unjustifiable *adj* too bad to be excused or justified ⟨an *unjustifiable* attack that must be avenged⟩ — see INEXCUSABLE

unjustness *n* **1** the state of being unfair or unjust ⟨the sheer *unjustness* of the accusation infuriated her beyond words⟩ — see INJUSTICE 1
2 unfair or inadequate treatment of someone or something or an instance of this ⟨life seemed to treat him with an *unjustness* that was immensely frustrating⟩ — see DISSERVICE

unkempt *adj* **1** lacking in order, neatness, and often cleanliness ⟨an *unkempt* and cluttered room⟩ — see MESSY
2 lacking neatness in dress or person ⟨the stereotype of the *unkempt* but brilliant scientist⟩ — see SLOPPY 1

unkink *vb* to cause to follow a line that is without bends or curls ⟨you should *unkink* the garden hose before you turn on the water⟩ — see STRAIGHTEN

unknowing *adj* **1** lacking in worldly wisdom or informed judgment ⟨those *unknowing* people who think that the world is a kindly place are in for a rude awakening⟩ — see NAIVE 1
2 not informed about or aware of something ⟨the poor woman has been the *unknowing* target of some pretty vicious gossip⟩ — see IGNORANT 2

unknown *adj* **1** happening or existing without one's knowledge ⟨*unknown* to me was the fact that while I was out, my family was hurriedly preparing a surprise birthday party⟩
synonyms unbeknownst (*also* unbeknown)
related words unperceived, unrecognized, unsuspected; unaware, unconscious, unmindful; unknowing, unsuspecting, unwitting; ignorant, unacquainted, unfamiliar
2 not known or experienced before ⟨becoming a father brought *unknown* joy to his life⟩ — see NEW 2
3 not widely known ⟨looking for a relatively *unknown* singer to record the song⟩ — see OBSCURE 2

unlade *vb* to empty or rid of cargo ⟨permission will not be given to *unlade* the ship until it can be thoroughly inspected⟩ — see UNLOAD 1

unladylike *adj* having qualities or traits that are traditionally considered inappropriate for a girl or woman ⟨the female boxers were pummeling one another in decidedly *unladylike* fashion⟩ — see UNFEMININE

unlash *vb* to disengage the knotted parts of ⟨*unlashed* the ropes which secured the crate in the bed of the truck⟩ — see UNTIE

unlawful *adj* **1** contrary to or forbidden by law ⟨it is *unlawful* to set off fireworks within the city limits⟩ — see ILLEGAL 1

2 not conforming to a high moral standard; morally unacceptable ⟨a sympathetic look at the *unlawful* love between a married physician and an adoring colleague⟩ — see BAD 2

unlay *vb* to separate the various strands of ⟨our tour guide at the maritime museum showed us how sailors used to *unlay* rope⟩ — see UNRAVEL 1

unlearn *vb* to be unable to recall or think of ⟨let's hope that over the summer I don't *unlearn* everything I learned over the course of this past year⟩ — see FORGET 1

unlearned *adj* lacking in education or the knowledge gained from books ⟨although the people of the farming community were largely an *unlearned* lot, they wanted an advanced education for their children⟩ — see IGNORANT 1

unleash *vb* **1** to set free (from a state of being held in check) ⟨*unleashed* all of his unspoken love for her in a long letter that he hoped he would have the courage to mail⟩ — see RELEASE 1

2 to find emotional release for ⟨lifting weights is a way for me to *unleash* all the frustrations of the workday⟩ — see TAKE OUT 1

unlettered *adj* lacking in education or the knowledge gained from books ⟨*unlettered* moviegoers could scarcely imagine how little resemblance the film bore to the novel on which it was supposedly based⟩ — see IGNORANT 1

unlike *adj* being not of the same kind ⟨you're trying to compare very *unlike* things—like those proverbial apples and oranges⟩ — see DIFFERENT 1

unlikely *adj* not likely to be true or to occur ⟨in the *unlikely* event that the file is deleted or corrupted, you will want to have backup copies available⟩ — see IMPROBABLE

unlikeness *n* the quality or state of being different ⟨because of the general *unlikeness* of their features, most new acquaintances are surprised to learn that they are brothers⟩ — see DIFFERENCE 1

unlimited *adj* **1** being or seeming to be without limits ⟨no ruler should ever be given *unlimited* power⟩ — see INFINITE

2 not limited or specialized in application or purpose ⟨an insurance policy that offers *unlimited* coverage in case of loss⟩ — see GENERAL 4

unlink *vb* to set or force apart ⟨*unlinked* the railroad cars⟩ — see SEPARATE 1

unlisted *adj* not appearing on a list ⟨she kept her phone number *unlisted* so as to reduce the number of unwanted calls⟩

synonyms uncataloged, unrecorded, unregistered

related words unwritten; unidentified, unspecified; undisclosed, unknown, unrevealed

antonyms cataloged (*or* catalogued), listed, recorded, registered

unlit *adj* being without light or without much light ⟨she stumbled over something in the *unlit* hallway⟩ — see DARK 1

unliterary *adj* used in or suitable for speech and not formal writing ⟨poems written in a natural, *unliterary* voice⟩ — see COLLOQUIAL 1

unload *vb* **1** to empty or rid of cargo ⟨the dockworkers *unloaded* the ship⟩

synonyms disburden, discharge, disencumber, offload, unburden, unlade, unpack

related words free, lighten, relieve; clear, empty, evacuate, vacate, void

near antonyms charge, cram, fill, heap, jam, jam-pack, stuff

antonyms load, pack

2 to get rid of as useless or unwanted ⟨I can't seem to *unload* this old car—even the charities won't take it!⟩ — see DISCARD

unlock *vb* to set free (from a state of being held in check) ⟨that last insult *unlocked* her tongue, and she finally said what she really thought⟩ — see RELEASE 1

unlooked–for *adj* not expected ⟨the interesting stuff found in the attic was an *unlooked-for* bonus for the new homeowners⟩ — see UNEXPECTED

unloose *vb* to set free (from a state of being held in check) ⟨the familiar scent *unloosed* a flood of pleasant memories from her childhood⟩ — see RELEASE 1

unloosen *vb* to set free (from a state of being held in check) ⟨a relaxing bath *unloosened* all the mental and physical tension that had been building throughout the day⟩ — see RELEASE 1

unlovely *adj* **1** not giving pleasure to the mind or senses ⟨Sunday night is often spoiled by the *unlovely* thought of having to go back to school or work the next morning⟩ — see UNPLEASANT

2 unpleasant to look at ⟨an *unlovely* but efficient little machine⟩ — see UGLY 1

unlucky *adj* **1** having, prone to, or marked by bad luck ⟨the *unlucky* campers had rain all week⟩ ⟨I'm so *unlucky* I don't bother to play the lottery⟩ ⟨an *unlucky* throw of the dice⟩

synonyms hapless, hard-luck, ill-fated, ill-starred, jinxed, luckless, snakebit (*or* snakebitten), star-crossed, unfortunate, unhappy

related words adverse, ill, inauspicious, unfavorable, unpromising, untoward; calamitous, catastrophic, disastrous; accursed (*or* accurst), damned, doomed, tragic (*also* tragical)

near antonyms blessed (*also* blest), favored, gifted, privileged; auspicious, fair, favorable, golden, promising, propitious

antonyms fortunate, happy, lucky

2 of a kind to cause great distress ⟨the settlers made the *unlucky* decision to cross the dangerous mountain pass in the middle of winter⟩ — see REGRETTABLE

unmake *vb* to remove from a position of prominence or power (as a throne) ⟨a movie studio chief who likes to boast that he can *unmake* any star in Hollywood if he wishes⟩ — see DEPOSE 1

unman *vb* **1** to deprive of courage or confidence ⟨the near crash of the airliner was a completely *unmanning* experience for the passengers⟩ — see UNNERVE 1

2 to lessen the courage or confidence of ⟨players who wouldn't let themselves be *unmanned* by the loss of a single game⟩ — see DISCOURAGE 1

unmanageable *adj* given to resisting control or discipline by others ⟨an *unmanageable* dog who had to be returned to the pound⟩ — see UNCONTROLLABLE

unmanly *adj* of or relating to a man who has or displays qualities considered more suitable for women ⟨there is nothing *unmanly* about letting your emotions show⟩ — see EFFEMINATE

unmannered *adj* showing a lack of manners or consideration for others ⟨we will never again invite such *unmannered* guests⟩ — see IMPOLITE

unmannerly *adj* showing a lack of manners or consideration for others ⟨in an *unmannerly* disregard for anyone else's comfort, she turned up the heat without saying a word⟩ — see IMPOLITE

unmarried *adj* not married ⟨a girl who swore she'd remain *unmarried* for her whole life⟩ — see SINGLE 1

unmask *vb* **1** to make known (as information previously kept secret) ⟨the killer's identity won't be *un-*

masked until the season's final episode⟩ — see REVEAL 1

2 to reveal the true nature of ⟨*unmasked* the motives of the people advocating the sale of the publicly owned land⟩ — see EXPOSE 1

unmatched *adj* **1** being one of a pair or set without a corresponding mate ⟨a drawer full of *unmatched* socks⟩ — see ODD 1

2 having no equal or rival for excellence or desirability ⟨the house cat is a mouse-hunting machine of *unmatched* efficiency⟩ — see ONLY 1

unmediated *adj* done or working without something else coming in between ⟨photoshopped images have made people aware that a digital photograph is not necessarily an *unmediated* depiction of reality⟩ — see DIRECT 1

unmelodious *adj* marked by or producing a harsh combination of sounds ⟨I awoke to the *unmelodious* clatter of jackhammers at the construction site next door⟩ — see DISSONANT

unmentionables *n pl* clothing intended to be worn underneath other clothing ⟨he was standing there in the cold, clad only in his *unmentionables*⟩ — see UNDERWEAR

unmerciful *adj* **1** going beyond a normal or acceptable limit in degree or amount ⟨she went into an *unmerciful* level of detail about her latest health problems⟩ — see EXCESSIVE

2 having or showing a lack of sympathy or tender feelings ⟨the critics were *unmerciful* in their assessments of the young actress's performance⟩ — see HARD 1

unmindful *adj* not informed about or aware of something ⟨*unmindful* of the consequences of such a rash decision⟩ — see IGNORANT 2

unmistakable *adj* not subject to misinterpretation or more than one interpretation ⟨a glint in his eye that was an *unmistakable* expression of greed⟩ — see CLEAR 2

unmitigated *adj* having no exceptions or restrictions ⟨it looks like another one of your get-rich-quick schemes has ended in *unmitigated* failure⟩ — see ABSOLUTE 2

unmixed *adj* free from added matter ⟨chocolate has a great taste, but I prefer my milk *unmixed*⟩ — see PURE 1

unmovable *adj* incapable of moving or being moved ⟨the tree was *unmovable*, so we designed the garden pond around it⟩ — see IMMOVABLE 1

unmusical *adj* marked by or producing a harsh combination of sounds ⟨a very *unmusical* chorus of squawks from the angry ravens⟩ — see DISSONANT

unnamed *adj* **1** known but not named ⟨used some *unnamed* procedure for testing the accuracy of the device⟩ — see CERTAIN 1

2 not named or identified by a name ⟨the newspaper article quoted several *unnamed* sources⟩ — see NAMELESS 1

unnatural *adj* **1** departing from some accepted standard of what is normal ⟨the documentary evinces an *unnatural* obsession with the gruesome details of the disaster⟩ — see DEVIANT

2 lacking in natural or spontaneous quality ⟨just before the debate, the candidates flashed *unnatural* smiles for the cameras⟩ — see ARTIFICIAL 1

unnecessary *adj* not needed by the circumstances or to accomplish an end ⟨that large suitcase is *unnecessary*—we are only going to be away for a couple of days⟩

synonyms dispensable, gratuitous, inessential, needless, nonessential, uncalled-for, unessential, unwarranted

related words discretionary, elective, optional; extra, extraneous, irrelative, irrelevant, redundant, superfluous

near antonyms all-important, crucial, important, vital; imperative, pressing, urgent

antonyms essential, indispensable, necessary, needed, needful, required

unnerve *vb* **1** to deprive of courage or confidence ⟨the riding accident so *unnerved* me that for a while I was afraid to get back on a horse⟩

synonyms demoralize, emasculate, paralyze, undo, unman, unstring

related words debilitate, enervate, enfeeble, neuter, weaken; prostrate, sap, soften, tire, waste; frighten, intimidate, psych (out), scare, terrify, terrorize; daunt, discourage, dishearten, dismay, dispirit; craze, derange, madden, unbalance, unhinge; discompose, disquiet, disturb, faze, perturb, unsettle, upset, weird out

near antonyms fortify, strengthen; embolden, encourage, hearten

antonyms nerve

2 to lessen the courage or confidence of ⟨a figure skater can't afford to be *unnerved* by an occasional slipup⟩ — see DISCOURAGE 1

unnerving *adj* marked by or causing agitation or uncomfortable feelings ⟨the *unnerving* news of yet another murder⟩ — see NERVOUS 2

unnoticeable *adj* not readily seen or noticed ⟨a nearly *unnoticeable* change in the color⟩ — see UNOBTRUSIVE

unnumbered *adj* too many to be counted ⟨the *unnumbered* stars wheeled overhead⟩ — see COUNTLESS

unobstructed *adj* allowing passage without obstruction ⟨only one road remained *unobstructed* after the storm⟩ — see OPEN 1

unobtainable *adj* hard or impossible to get to or get at ⟨that information is *unobtainable* as long as my computer is down⟩ — see INACCESSIBLE

unobtrusive *adj* not readily seen or noticed ⟨the notice that an 18% tip would be automatically added was so *unobtrusive* we almost didn't see it at the bottom of the menu⟩

synonyms discreet, inconspicuous, invisible, unnoticeable

related words unnoticed, unremarked, unseen; impalpable, imperceptible, inappreciable, indistinguishable, insensible; faint, indistinct, obscure; concealed, hidden

near antonyms arresting, eye-catching, showy, striking; flashy, loud, noisy; apparent, clear, discernible (*also* discernable), distinct, evident, manifest, obvious, patent, plain, prominent, unmistakable; blatant, flagrant, glaring, gross, screaming

antonyms conspicuous, noticeable, visible

unoriginal *adj* using or marked by the use of something else as a basis or model ⟨critics faulted the novel for having a painfully *unoriginal* plot⟩ — see IMITATIVE 1

unornamented *adj* free from all additions or embellishment ⟨the *unornamented* interior of an old New England church⟩ — see PLAIN 1

unorthodox *adj* **1** deviating from commonly accepted beliefs or practices ⟨a time when people with *unorthodox* religious views were banished from the colony⟩ — see HERETICAL

2 not bound by traditional ways or beliefs ⟨raised by an aunt, whose *unorthodox* parenting practices made for a strange but fun childhood⟩ — see LIBERAL 1

3 not rigidly following established form, custom, or rules ⟨an *unorthodox* but effective procedure for opening a wine bottle without a corkscrew⟩ — see INFORMAL 1

unpack *vb* to empty or rid of cargo ⟨*unpacked* the car the minute they got back from vacation⟩ — see UNLOAD 1

unpaid *adj* not yet paid ⟨my goal is to have no *unpaid* balances on my credit cards⟩ — see OUTSTANDING 1

unpainted *adj* lacking an addition of color ⟨the wooden shingles on the island's houses are usually left *unpainted*, and over time the salt air turns them a soft gray⟩ — see COLORLESS 1

unpaired *adj* being one of a pair or set without a corresponding mate ⟨found an *unpaired* shoe in the back of the closet⟩ — see ODD 1

unpalatable *adj* **1** disagreeable or disgusting to the sense of taste ⟨pasta and honey is an *unpalatable* combination⟩ — see DISTASTEFUL 1
2 not giving pleasure to the mind or senses ⟨hesitated before sharing some of the more *unpalatable* details of his captivity⟩ — see UNPLEASANT

unparalleled *adj* having no equal or rival for excellence or desirability ⟨an antique vase of *unparalleled* beauty⟩ — see ONLY 1

unpardonable *adj* too bad to be excused or justified ⟨regards cruelty to animals as an *unpardonable* sin⟩ — see INEXCUSABLE

unperceptive *adj* not having or showing a deep understanding of something ⟨*unperceptive* readers failed to see that the "news story" was an elaborate put-on⟩ — see IMPERCEPTIVE

unperturbed *adj* free from emotional or mental agitation ⟨remained *unperturbed* despite the latest problems in the construction of their new house⟩ — see CALM 2

unplanned *adj* **1** happening by chance ⟨an *unplanned* change in our itinerary—we got lost!⟩ — see ACCIDENTAL 1
2 made or done without previous thought or preparation ⟨stumbled through a completely *unplanned* acceptance speech⟩ — see EXTEMPORANEOUS

unpleasant *adj* not giving pleasure to the mind or senses ⟨the burnt pot roast had a very *unpleasant* odor⟩
synonyms bad, bitter, disagreeable, displeasing, distasteful, harsh, icky, nasty, rotten, sour, uncongenial, unlovely, unpalatable, unpleasing, unsavory, unwelcome, wicked, yucky (*also* yukky)
related words abhorrent, abominable, appalling, awful, beastly, bilious, disgusting, dreadful, foul, ghastly, gnarly [*slang*], god-awful, gross, hateful, hellish, hideous, horrendous, horrible, horrid, invidious, loathsome, nauseating, nauseous, noisome, obnoxious, obscene, odious, offensive, repellent (*also* repellant), repugnant, repulsive, revolting, revulsive, scandalous, seamy, shocking, sick, sickening, ugly, unholy, vile, villainous; aggravating, annoying, galling, irritating, vexing; crappy [*slang*], cruddy, crummy (*also* crumby), lousy, miserable, sucky [*slang*], wretched
near antonyms delectable, delicious, delightful, dreamy, felicitous; amiable, charming, cheery, friendly, jolly, kindly, sweet
antonyms agreeable, congenial, good, grateful, gratifying, nice, palatable, pleasant, pleasing, pleasurable, satisfying, welcome

unpleasing *adj* **1** not giving pleasure to the mind or senses ⟨an *unpleasing* combination of flavors in the dish⟩ — see UNPLEASANT
2 unpleasant to look at ⟨an *unpleasing* combination of fuchsia and orange⟩ — see UGLY 1

unplug *vb* to make passage through (something) possible by removing obstructions ⟨the chimney should work just fine once it is *unplugged* and cleaned out⟩ — see OPEN 2

unpolished *adj* lacking in refinement or good taste ⟨an *unpolished* but well-meaning young man⟩ — see COARSE 2

unprecedented *adj* not known or experienced before ⟨this is an *unprecedented* request for the reference desk⟩ — see NEW 2

unpredictable *adj* likely to change frequently, suddenly, or unexpectedly ⟨*unpredictable* spring weather that makes it really hard to know what to wear⟩ — see FICKLE 1

unprejudiced *adj* marked by justice, honesty, and freedom from bias ⟨an *unprejudiced* judicial opinion⟩ — see FAIR 2

unpremeditated *adj* **1** happening by chance ⟨an *unpremeditated* encounter with an old boyfriend⟩ — see ACCIDENTAL 1
2 made or done without previous thought or preparation ⟨an *unpremeditated* verbal attack that was prompted by an unexpected question at the press conference⟩ — see EXTEMPORANEOUS

unprepared *adj* made or done without previous thought or preparation ⟨an obviously *unprepared* acceptance speech by the surprise winner⟩ — see EXTEMPORANEOUS

unpretending *adj* free from any intent to deceive or impress others ⟨an *unpretending* manner that makes her quite a winning performer⟩ — see GUILELESS

unpretentious *adj* **1** free from any intent to deceive or impress others ⟨a simple and *unpretentious* account about growing up in the rural South⟩ — see GUILELESS
2 not excessively showy ⟨lives in a rather *unpretentious* house for someone so wealthy⟩ — see QUIET 2
3 not having or showing any feelings of superiority, self-assertiveness, or showiness ⟨the *unpretentious* disposition of an award-winning scientist who has nothing to prove to anyone⟩ — see HUMBLE 1

unpretentiously *adv* without any attempt to impress by deception or exaggeration ⟨that rare restaurant reviewer who writes engagingly but *unpretentiously* about food⟩ — see NATURALLY 3

unpretty *adj* unpleasant to look at ⟨an *unpretty* accumulation of trash right next to the entrance to the restaurant⟩ — see UGLY 1

unprincipled *adj* not guided by or showing a concern for what is right ⟨an *unprincipled* businessman who made a lot of money—and didn't care how he did it⟩
synonyms cutthroat, immoral, Machiavellian, unconscionable, unethical, unscrupulous
related words merciless, pitiless, remorseless, ruthless; crooked, deceitful, dishonest, jackleg, knavish; corrupt, debased, debauched, decadent, degenerate, degraded, demoralized, depraved, dissipated, libertine, licentious, profligate; cheapjack, dog-eat-dog, opportunistic; calculating, scheming, sharp
near antonyms conscientious, good, honorable, just, noble, righteous, virtuous
antonyms ethical, moral, principled, scrupulous

unprintable *adj* depicting or referring to sexual matters in a way that is unacceptable in polite society ⟨uttered an *unprintable* oath when he saw stocks take their worst slide ever⟩ — see OBSCENE 1

unprocessed *adj* being such as found in nature and not altered by processing or refining ⟨*unprocessed* foods that still have much of their original flavor⟩ — see CRUDE 1

unproductive *adj* **1** producing inferior or only a small amount of vegetation ⟨crop rotation had prevented the farmland from becoming *unproductive*⟩ — see BARREN 1
2 producing no results ⟨her attempts to write a novel have been *unproductive*⟩ — see FUTILE 1

unprofessional *adj* lacking or showing a lack of expert skill ⟨an *unprofessional* carelessness about the accuracy of the news story⟩ — see AMATEURISH

unprofitable *adj* producing no results ⟨an *unprofitable* effort to find the information⟩ — see FUTILE 1

unprogressive *adj* tending to favor established ideas, conditions, or institutions ⟨a candidate with *unprogres-*

sive ideas about public education⟩ — see CONSERVATIVE 1

unprotected *adj* lacking protection from danger or resistance against attack ⟨I was uncomfortable about leaving my house *unprotected*, so I bought a dog⟩ — see HELPLESS 1

unqualified *adj* **1** having no exceptions or restrictions ⟨the new play is an *unqualified* success⟩ — see ABSOLUTE 2

2 lacking qualities (as knowledge, skill, or ability) required to do a job ⟨if we hire an *unqualified* candidate, we'll just be wasting our time⟩ — see INCOMPETENT

3 not limited or specialized in application or purpose ⟨an *unqualified* denial of the charges⟩ — see GENERAL 4

unquenchable *adj* incapable of being satisfied ⟨from a very early age she displayed an *unquenchable* curiosity about the natural world⟩ — see INSATIABLE

unquestionable *adj* not capable of being challenged or proved wrong ⟨a person of *unquestionable* integrity⟩ — see IRREFUTABLE

unquestionably *adv* without any question ⟨given his experience, he is *unquestionably* the right person for this job⟩ — see INDEED 1

unquiet *adj* **1** feeling or showing uncomfortable feelings of uncertainty ⟨plagued with an *unquiet* mind the whole time her son was stationed overseas⟩ — see NERVOUS 1

2 lacking or denying rest ⟨an *unquiet* curiosity that impelled him to study the world about him relentlessly⟩ — see RESTLESS 1

unquietness *n* a disturbed or uneasy state ⟨on the night before his wedding, the groom paced the floor with an *unquietness* befitting a man awaiting his own execution⟩ — see UNREST

unravel *vb* **1** to separate the various strands of ⟨it took us forever to *unravel* the jumbled mass of Christmas tree lights⟩

synonyms disentangle, ravel (out), unbraid, unlay, unsnarl, untangle, untwine, untwist, unweave

related words fray, fret; smooth, straighten (out); uncoil, undo, unknot, unlace, unroll, unstring, unthread, untie, unwind

near antonyms braid, knot, lace, plait, ply, splice, tie, wind

antonyms entangle, snarl, tangle

2 to find an answer for through reasoning ⟨*unraveled* the mystery⟩ — see SOLVE

unreachable *adj* hard or impossible to get to or get at ⟨bothered by an *unreachable* itch on her back⟩ — see INACCESSIBLE

unread *adj* lacking in education or the knowledge gained from books ⟨an officer who seemed to be completely *unread* in military theory⟩ — see IGNORANT 1

unreadable *adj* incapable of being read or deciphered ⟨those *unreadable* scribbles that one encounters so frequently with medical prescriptions⟩ — see ILLEGIBLE

unreal *adj* **1** conceived or made without regard for reason or reality ⟨an *unreal* claim that is distant from the slightest hint of truth⟩ — see FANTASTIC 1

2 not real and existing only in the imagination ⟨the *unreal* world of TV sitcoms⟩ — see IMAGINARY

unreality *n* a conception or image created by the imagination and having no objective reality ⟨a sci-fi author who seems to have preferred the *unrealities* of his own fiction to the realities of the world about him⟩ — see FANTASY 1

unrealizable *adj* incapable of being solved or accomplished ⟨an *unrealizable* dream for a severely impoverished nation⟩ — see IMPOSSIBLE

unreasonable *adj* **1** having no basis in reason or fact ⟨an *unreasonable* assumption⟩ — see GROUNDLESS

2 not using or following good reasoning ⟨an *unreasonable* respect for a man who did not deserve it⟩ — see ILLOGICAL

unreasoning *adj* not using or following good reasoning ⟨an *unreasoning* argument based on some false assumptions⟩ — see ILLOGICAL

unrecognized *adj* not widely known ⟨a still mostly *unrecognized* but nevertheless significant pioneer in the field of science fiction⟩ — see OBSCURE 2

unrecorded *adj* not appearing on a list ⟨an *unrecorded* contribution to the scholarship fund⟩ — see UNLISTED

unrecoverable *adj* **1** not capable of being cured or reformed ⟨believed that there was no such thing as an *unrecoverable* criminal⟩ — see HOPELESS 1

2 not capable of being repaired, regained, or undone ⟨the flood caused *unrecoverable* damage to our home⟩ — see IRREPARABLE

unredeemable *adj* **1** not capable of being cured or reformed ⟨*unredeemable* sinners⟩ — see HOPELESS 1

2 not capable of being repaired, regained, or undone ⟨assured the senior citizens that there was no such thing as an *unredeemable* error when operating a computer⟩ — see IRREPARABLE

unrefined *adj* **1** being such as found in nature and not altered by processing or refining ⟨*unrefined* sugar⟩ — see CRUDE 1

2 hastily or roughly constructed ⟨an *unrefined* mountaineer's hut⟩ — see RUDE 1

3 lacking in refinement or good taste ⟨guilty of such *unrefined* behavior as eating with their mouths open⟩ — see COARSE 2

unregistered *adj* not appearing on a list ⟨an *unregistered* car⟩ — see UNLISTED

unrehearsed *adj* made or done without previous thought or preparation ⟨an *unrehearsed* speech of thanks⟩ — see EXTEMPORANEOUS

unrelenting *adj* **1** sticking to an opinion, purpose, or course of action in spite of reason, arguments, or persuasion ⟨that professor tends to be *unrelenting* about deadlines⟩ — see OBSTINATE

2 showing no signs of slackening or yielding in one's purpose ⟨*unrelenting* in the pursuit of equality for all races⟩ — see UNYIELDING 1

unremarkable *adj* being of the type that is encountered in the normal course of events ⟨a quiet and *unremarkable* child⟩ — see ORDINARY 1

unremitting *adj* going on and on without any interruptions ⟨*unremitting* rain that lasted for six days⟩ — see CONTINUOUS

unrepentant *adj* not sorry for having done wrong ⟨she was *unrepentant* about selling her ex-boyfriend's prized guitar⟩ — see REMORSELESS 1

unreserve *n* the free expression of one's true feelings and opinions ⟨with an *unreserve* perhaps never before witnessed in the halls of Congress, the general gave his unvarnished assessment of the war effort⟩ — see CANDOR 1

unreserved *adj* **1** free in expressing one's true feelings and opinions ⟨the politician was criticized for being too *unreserved* in his pronouncements on touchy subjects⟩ — see FRANK

2 showing feeling freely ⟨people in that part of the world tend to be *unreserved* mourners, and funerals are marked by loud wailing⟩ — see DEMONSTRATIVE 1

unreservedness *n* the free expression of one's true feelings and opinions ⟨the withering *unreservedness* of his critique of my musical talent caught me off guard⟩ — see CANDOR 1

unresistant *adj* **1** lacking protection from danger or resistance against attack ⟨a weakened immune system that rendered him *unresistant* to pneumonia⟩ — see HELPLESS 1

2 receiving or enduring without offering resistance ⟨the kitten was surprisingly *unresistant* when the vet examined her⟩ — see PASSIVE

unresolved *adj* not yet settled or decided ⟨we have to deal with several *unresolved* issues⟩ — see PENDING 1

unrespectable *adj* not respectable ⟨in the minds of her straitlaced parents, acting was still an *unrespectable* profession⟩ — see DISREPUTABLE

unrest *n* a disturbed or uneasy state ⟨*unrest* gripped the city as the people nervously awaited the expected bombardment⟩ ⟨his stomach *unrest* was just a sign of stage fright⟩

synonyms disquiet, ferment, fermentation, restiveness, restlessness, Sturm und Drang, turmoil, uneasiness, unquietness

related words fidgets; agitation, commotion, confusion, excitement, hubbub, moil, stir, storm, trouble, tumult, tumultuousness, turbulence, upheaval, uproar, unsettlement; disruption, perturbation; agitation, anxiety, disquietude, inquietude, queasiness, tension, unease; anarchy, chaos, disorder, welter

near antonyms order, orderliness

antonyms calm, ease, peace, peacefulness, quiet, tranquillity (*or* tranquility)

unrestful *adj* lacking or denying rest ⟨spent an *unrestful* night worrying about her children⟩ — see RESTLESS 1

unrestrained *adj* **1** not bound by rigid standards ⟨he homeschooled his children because he believed that they would do best in an *unrestrained* learning environment⟩ — see EASYGOING 2

2 not bound, confined, or detained by force ⟨*unrestrained* dogs⟩ — see FREE 3

3 showing feeling freely ⟨very reserved when she's around strangers, but quite *unrestrained* in the company of friends⟩ — see DEMONSTRATIVE 1

4 showing no signs of being under control ⟨*unrestrained* laughter that had been fueled by a liberal dose of alcohol⟩ — see RAMPANT 1

unrestraint *n* carefree freedom from constraint ⟨the cheerful *unrestraint* of children⟩ — see ABANDON

unrestricted *adj* **1** freely available for use or participation by all ⟨it's an *unrestricted* marathon—anyone can run in it⟩ — see OPEN 2

2 not bound by rigid standards ⟨the author of the book has an *unrestricted* view of what qualifies as "art"⟩ — see EASYGOING 2

3 not limited or specialized in application or purpose ⟨an *unrestricted* license to operate a motor vehicle⟩ — see GENERAL 4

unriddle *vb* **1** to find an answer for through reasoning ⟨I managed to *unriddle* the novel's central mystery before the main character did⟩ — see SOLVE

2 to make plain or understandable ⟨the all-encompassing genius of Leonardo da Vinci is something that no biographer could ever hope to *unriddle*⟩ — see EXPLAIN 1

unrighteous *adj* not conforming to a high moral standard; morally unacceptable ⟨an *unrighteous* act that cannot go unpunished by the congregation⟩ — see BAD 2

unripe *adj* lacking in adult experience or maturity ⟨*unripe* and unprepared recruits who were sent into battle as cannon fodder⟩ — see CALLOW

unripened *adj* lacking in adult experience or maturity ⟨the *unripened* thoughts of a young writer with limited life experiences⟩ — see CALLOW

unrivaled *or* **unrivalled** *adj* having no equal or rival for excellence or desirability ⟨a violinist who is hailed for his *unrivaled* musicianship⟩ — see ONLY 1

unruffled *adj* free from emotional or mental agitation ⟨remained *unruffled* by the news that stocks were in a free fall⟩ — see CALM 2

unruliness *n* refusal to obey ⟨frustrated by the boys' *unruliness*, the lifeguard asked them to leave the pool⟩ — see DISOBEDIENCE

unruly *adj* **1** given to resisting authority or another's control ⟨*unruly* pupils were given detention as a matter of course⟩ — see DISOBEDIENT

2 given to resisting control or discipline by others ⟨a camp that was known as a place where *unruly* youths were given their last chance to shape up⟩ — see UNCONTROLLABLE

3 not restrained by or under the control of legal authority ⟨*unruly* mobs roamed the streets of the capital after the government leaders had fled⟩ — see LAWLESS 1

unsafe *adj* **1** involving potential loss or injury ⟨workers are forbidden from engaging in *unsafe* activities on company time⟩ — see DANGEROUS 1

2 not paying or showing close attention especially for the purpose of avoiding trouble ⟨people who have a record of being *unsafe* drivers usually have to pay higher insurance premiums⟩ — see CARELESS 1

unsatisfactorily *adv* in an unsatisfactory way ⟨*unsatisfactorily* prepared entrées should be immediately returned to the kitchen and replaced with something more acceptable⟩ — see BADLY 1

unsatisfactory *adj* falling short of a standard ⟨an *unsatisfactory* first attempt at building a birdhouse⟩ — see BAD 1

unsavory *adj* **1** disagreeable or disgusting to the sense of taste ⟨an *unsavory* blend of spices that simply overwhelmed the fish's delicate flavor⟩ — see DISTASTEFUL 1

2 not conforming to a high moral standard; morally unacceptable ⟨*unsavory* doings that ruined the couple's good name in the community⟩ — see BAD 2

3 not giving pleasure to the mind or senses ⟨hated the whole *unsavory* business of firing people⟩ — see UNPLEASANT

4 lacking in taste or flavor ⟨the *unsavory* food dished up at the rest area's restaurant should be consumed only by the truly desperate⟩ — see INSIPID 1

unsay *vb* to solemnly or formally reject or go back on (as something formerly adhered to) ⟨the witness tried to *unsay* the very testimony that he had given a few days earlier⟩ — see ABJURE 1

unschooled *adj* lacking in education or the knowledge gained from books ⟨an *unschooled* but nevertheless intelligent woman who desperately wanted to learn how to read⟩ — see IGNORANT 1

unscrupulous *adj* not guided by or showing a concern for what is right ⟨an *unscrupulous* businessman manipulated them into selling their land for practically nothing⟩ — see UNPRINCIPLED

unseasonable *adj* occurring before the usual or expected time ⟨an *unseasonable* snowstorm in early November⟩ — see EARLY 2

unseasonably *adv* before the usual or expected time ⟨it's been *unseasonably* hot this spring⟩ — see EARLY

unseat *vb* to remove from a position of prominence or power (as a throne) ⟨a governor who was *unseated* by the first successful recall in the state's history⟩ — see DEPOSE 1

unsecured *adj* not tightly fastened, tied, or stretched ⟨an *unsecured* luggage rack on top of the car that was a hazard to other vehicles on the road⟩ — see LOOSE 1

unseemliness *n* the quality or state of not being socially proper ⟨I should not have to explain the *unseemliness* of wearing a red miniskirt to a funeral⟩ — see IMPROPRIETY 1

unseemly *adj* not appropriate for a particular occasion or situation ⟨an *unseemly* interest in their host's income and expenses⟩ — see INAPPROPRIATE

unselfish *adj* giving or sharing in abundance and without hesitation ⟨an *unselfish* man who spends much of his time helping his community⟩ — see GENEROUS 1

unselfishness *n* the quality or state of being generous ⟨her natural *unselfishness* sometimes attracts those who would take advantage⟩ — see LIBERALITY

unserviceable *adj* not capable of being put to use or account ⟨the dairy farm comes with a lot of equipment, but most of it is antiquated or *unserviceable*⟩ — see IMPRACTICAL

unsettle *vb* to trouble the mind of; to make uneasy ⟨the news that the local grocery store had sold contaminated produce *unsettled* many shoppers⟩ — see DISTURB 1

unsettled *adj* **1** likely to change frequently, suddenly, or unexpectedly ⟨we've been having a lot of *unsettled* weather lately⟩ — see FICKLE 1

2 not yet paid ⟨I keep *unsettled* bills next to the checkbook⟩ — see OUTSTANDING 1

3 not yet settled or decided ⟨we can't move on as long as this important question remains *unsettled*⟩ — see PENDING 1

4 not feeling sure about the truth, wisdom, or trustworthiness of someone or something ⟨I'm still *unsettled* about whether I should take that job⟩ — see DOUBTFUL 1

unsettling *adj* **1** causing worry or anxiety ⟨*unsettling* new developments in the effort to bring peace and stability to that region⟩ — see TROUBLESOME

2 marked by or causing agitation or uncomfortable feelings ⟨had the *unsettling* task of picking out a coffin and making the other funeral arrangements for his father⟩ — see NERVOUS 2

unshakable *adj* not easily panicked or upset ⟨we need the kind of leader who will be *unshakable* in a national crisis⟩ — see UNFLAPPABLE

unshaken *adj* free from emotional or mental agitation ⟨the hostage remained *unshaken* throughout the ordeal⟩ — see CALM 2

unshaped *adj* having no definite or recognizable form ⟨an *unshaped* mass of clay that was just in need of some inspiration from the modeler⟩ — see FORMLESS 1

unshared *adj* belonging only to the one person, unit, or group named ⟨with her older sister off to college, she was thrilled to have an *unshared* bedroom for the first time in her life⟩ — see SOLE 1

unshorn *adj* covered with or as if with hair ⟨the sight of their *unshorn* heads is something that these male recruits will not see during their basic training⟩ — see HAIRY 1

unsightly *adj* unpleasant to look at ⟨strip-mining leaves an *unsightly* gash in the landscape⟩ — see UGLY 1

unskilled *adj* **1** lacking or showing a lack of expert skill ⟨an *unskilled* handling of the facial features in the portrait explains why it is attributed to "school of Velázquez" and not to the master himself⟩ — see AMATEURISH

2 lacking qualities (as knowledge, skill, or ability) required to do a job ⟨hired *unskilled* workers because they would work for lower wages⟩ — see INCOMPETENT

unskillful *adj* **1** lacking qualities (as knowledge, skill, or ability) required to do a job ⟨an *unskillful* editor can be worse than none at all⟩ — see INCOMPETENT

2 lacking or showing a lack of expert skill ⟨some painfully *unskillful* playing by the band's guitarist⟩ — see AMATEURISH

unslakable *adj* incapable of being satisfied ⟨an *unslakable* yearning to explore the far-off corners of the globe⟩ — see INSATIABLE

unsmart *adj* not having or showing an ability to absorb ideas readily ⟨she's not a complete idiot, just kind of *unsmart*⟩ — see STUPID 1

unsmiling *adj* not joking or playful in mood or manner ⟨delivered the reprimand with a harsh and *unsmiling* face⟩ — see SERIOUS 1

unsnarl *vb* to separate the various strands of ⟨*unsnarled* the fishing lines⟩ — see UNRAVEL 1

unsociable *adj* having or showing a lack of friendliness or interest in others ⟨an *unsociable* but not an overtly rude child⟩ — see COOL 1

unsoiled *adj* free from dirt or stain ⟨never managed to make it through a day at the packing plant with *unsoiled* shoes⟩ — see CLEAN 1

unsolicited *adj* not searched or asked for ⟨tired of the *unsolicited* advice from friends and family regarding her love life⟩ — see UNSOUGHT

unsolvable *adj* incapable of being solved or accomplished ⟨an apparently *unsolvable* problem⟩ — see IMPOSSIBLE

unsophisticated *adj* lacking in worldly wisdom or informed judgment ⟨mistakenly believed that the tribe was *unsophisticated* and would sell their land for a fraction of its worth⟩ — see NAIVE 1

unsophistication *n* **1** the quality or state of being simple and sincere ⟨the *unsophistication* of the plea touched his heart⟩ — see NAÏVETÉ 1

2 the quality or state of having a form or structure of few parts or elements ⟨the *unsophistication* of the coffeemaker's design is part of its appeal⟩ — see SIMPLICITY 1

unsought *adj* not searched or asked for ⟨the meddling neighbor insisted on giving us *unsought* advice⟩

synonyms unasked, unbidden (*also* unbid), uninvited, unsolicited

related words undesired, unwanted, unwelcome; objectionable, offensive, unacceptable, undesirable; uncalled-for, unnecessary

near antonyms necessary, needed, required; desired, wanted, welcome

antonyms requested, solicited

unsound *adj* **1** having or showing a very abnormal or sick state of mind ⟨disgruntled relatives tried to prove that the woman was of *unsound* mind when she made her will⟩ — see INSANE

2 not being in agreement with what is true ⟨an *unsound* and pernicious stereotype⟩ — see FALSE 1

3 not using or following good reasoning ⟨it is clearly *unsound* to argue that just because a scientific explanation for that phenomenon does not currently exist, no such explanation is possible⟩ — see ILLOGICAL

4 temporarily suffering from a disorder of the body ⟨an *unsound* horse that will have to be disqualified from the race⟩ — see SICK 1

unsoundness *n* the condition of not being in good health ⟨the overall *unsoundness* of her health in her last years greatly limited what she could do⟩ — see SICKNESS 1

unsparing *adj* **1** giving or sharing in abundance and without hesitation ⟨neighbors were *unsparing* in their charity when a local family was rendered homeless by a fire⟩ — see GENEROUS 1

2 having or showing a lack of sympathy or tender feelings ⟨*unsparing* in his criticism of the welfare state⟩ — see HARD 1

unspeakable *adj* beyond the power to describe ⟨continually encountered *unspeakable* beauty in their travels through the Alps⟩ — see INDESCRIBABLE

unspecialized *adj* not limited or specialized in application or purpose ⟨preferred to have one *unspecialized* tool rather than buy 16 specialized ones⟩ — see GENERAL 4

unspecified *adj* known but not named ⟨some *unspecified* person is expected to replace him temporarily as director of operations until a permanent director can be found⟩ — see CERTAIN 1

unspoken *adj* understood although not put into words ⟨an *unspoken* promise to remain faithful to one another⟩ — see IMPLICIT 1

unsportsmanlike *adj* not being in accordance with the rules or standards of what is fair in sport ⟨was suspended for *unsportsmanlike* conduct⟩ — see FOUL 2

unstable *adj* **1** not being in or able to maintain a state of balance ⟨the minute we put the books down on the *unstable* desk, the whole stack went crashing to the floor⟩
synonyms unbalanced, unsteady
related words rocky, shaky, tippy, tipsy, wavery, wobbly (*also* wabbly), wonky [*British*]; infirm, insecure, precarious, unsound; doddering, doddery, jiggling, jiggly, rickety, staggery, teetering, tottering, tottery; askew, awry, cockeyed, lopsided, off-kilter, uneven
near antonyms even, level, straight; sound, sturdy, substantial
antonyms balanced, equilibrated, stabilized, stable, steady
2 likely to change frequently, suddenly, or unexpectedly ⟨financial investors don't like an *unstable* economy⟩ — see FICKLE 1
3 not staying constant ⟨*unstable* temperatures are not ideal storage conditions for wine⟩ — see UNEVEN 2

unstableness *n* the quality or state of not being firmly fixed in position ⟨if the tunnel had been properly inspected, the *unstableness* of the overhead concrete panels would have been discovered in time⟩ — see INSTABILITY

unstained *adj* **1** free from dirt or stain ⟨you should be wearing a tie, preferably an *unstained* one⟩ — see CLEAN 1
2 lacking an addition of color ⟨bought an *unstained* picnic table that they planned to finish themselves⟩ — see COLORLESS 1

unsteadiness *n* the quality or state of not being firmly fixed in position ⟨blamed the poor quality of the video on the tripod's *unsteadiness*⟩ — see INSTABILITY

unsteady *adj* **1** lacking in steadiness or regularity of occurrence ⟨a year of *unsteady* economic growth⟩ — see FITFUL
2 likely to change frequently, suddenly, or unexpectedly ⟨in the days of sailing ships, mariners were constantly at the mercy of *unsteady* winds⟩ — see FICKLE 1
3 not being in or able to maintain a state of balance ⟨cautiously climbed up the *unsteady* ladder⟩ — see UNSTABLE 1
4 not staying constant ⟨*unsteady* business conditions that rattled investors⟩ — see UNEVEN 2

unstinting *adj* giving or sharing in abundance and without hesitation ⟨a group of school volunteers who are *unstinting* with their time⟩ — see GENEROUS 1

unstintingly *adv* in a generous manner ⟨parishoners gave *unstintingly* to the overseas disaster relief fund⟩ — see WELL 2

unstop *vb* to make passage through (something) possible by removing obstructions ⟨the plumber *unstopped* the drain⟩ — see OPEN 2

unstoppable *adj* incapable of being defeated, overcome, or subdued ⟨at this point she's so far ahead in the polls that she's *unstoppable*⟩ — see INVINCIBLE

unstopped *adj* allowing passage without obstruction ⟨an *unstopped* hole was the cause of the leakage⟩ — see OPEN 1

unstring *vb* **1** to cause to go insane or as if insane ⟨the kind of fierce combat that can *unstring* even hardened soldiers⟩ — see CRAZE
2 to deprive of courage or confidence ⟨a little *unstrung* by the fact that he was on his first job interview⟩ — see UNNERVE 1

unstructured *adj* having no definite or recognizable form ⟨writes *unstructured* compositions that some people might not even regard as poems⟩ — see FORMLESS 1

unstudied *adj* made or done without previous thought or preparation ⟨has an *unstudied* effervescence that is rare in show business⟩ — see EXTEMPORANEOUS

unstylish *adj* marked by an obvious lack of style or good taste ⟨chose a bizarrely *unstylish* hairstyle for the Halloween party⟩ — see [1]TACKY 1

unsubstantial *adj* **1** not composed of matter ⟨as thin and *unsubstantial* as the wind⟩ — see IMMATERIAL 1
2 being of a material lacking in sturdiness or substance ⟨*unsubstantial* wisps of lace⟩ — see FLIMSY 1
3 lacking bodily strength ⟨an *unsubstantial* child who was unfit to play sports of any kind⟩ — see WEAK 1

unsubstantiated *adj* having no basis in reason or fact ⟨an *unsubstantiated* claim that was thrown out of court⟩ — see GROUNDLESS

unsuccessful *adj* producing no results ⟨an *unsuccessful* attempt to fix the faucet ourselves⟩ — see FUTILE 1

unsuitable *adj* not appropriate for a particular occasion or situation ⟨all the movies playing now are violent or otherwise *unsuitable* for a child's birthday party⟩ — see INAPPROPRIATE

unsuitably *adv* in a mistaken or inappropriate way ⟨dressed *unsuitably* for the unexpectedly cold weather⟩ — see WRONGLY

unsullied *adj* free from dirt or stain ⟨only *unsullied* vestments are ever appropriate for church services⟩ — see CLEAN 1

unsung *adj* not widely known ⟨an *unsung* hero of the Holocaust⟩ — see OBSCURE 2

unsupportable *adj* more than can be put up with ⟨these high taxes are just *unsupportable*⟩ — see UNBEARABLE

unsupported *adj* having no basis in reason or fact ⟨an *unsupported* claim that the structure was built by Vikings⟩ — see GROUNDLESS

unsure *adj* not feeling sure about the truth, wisdom, or trustworthiness of someone or something ⟨*unsure* of her ability to handle the pressure of competing in the Olympic Games⟩ — see DOUBTFUL 1

unsurpassable *adj* having no equal or rival for excellence or desirability ⟨the *unsurpassable* splendor of the palace⟩ — see ONLY 1

unsurpassed *adj* **1** having no equal or rival for excellence or desirability ⟨an artist who is *unsurpassed* at painting portraits that reveal the subject's inner life⟩ — see ONLY 1
2 of the very best kind ⟨a French restaurant known for its *unsurpassed* cuisine⟩ — see EXCELLENT

unsuspecting *adj* lacking in worldly wisdom or informed judgment ⟨sidewalk vendors selling bogus gems to *unsuspecting* tourists⟩ — see NAIVE 1

unsuspicious *adj* lacking in worldly wisdom or informed judgment ⟨a happy-go-lucky, *unsuspicious* fellow who was easy prey for confidence men⟩ — see NAIVE 1

unsympathetic *adj* **1** having or showing a lack of sympathy or tender feelings ⟨gave them an *unsympathetic* look and pointed out that they'd brought the problem on themselves⟩ — see HARD 1
2 lacking in friendliness or warmth of feeling ⟨an aloof and *unsympathetic* man who does not engage in small talk⟩ — see COLD 2
3 marked by opposition or ill will ⟨a bohemian artist who found the *unsympathetic* environment of the small town too much to bear⟩ — see HOSTILE 1
4 opposed to one's interests ⟨an *unsympathetic* reaction to her proposal to ban trans fats from the company cafeteria⟩ — see ADVERSE 1

untamed *adj* **1** existing without human habitation or cultivation ⟨a dangerous and *untamed* land⟩ — see WILD 2

2 living outdoors without taming or domestication by humans ⟨tried to capture the *untamed* horse⟩ — see WILD 1

untangle *vb* **1** to separate the various strands of ⟨gently *untangled* the baby's hair⟩ — see UNRAVEL 1

2 to set free from entanglement or difficulty ⟨I was finally able to *untangle* myself from my credit problems⟩ — see EXTRICATE

untaught *adj* lacking in education or the knowledge gained from books ⟨an *untaught* artist whose primitive paintings are now prized by collectors⟩ — see IGNORANT 1

unthinkable *adj* too extraordinary or improbable to believe ⟨to most people it seemed *unthinkable* that such a gentle man could be guilty of such awful crimes⟩ — see INCREDIBLE

unthrifty *adj* given to spending money freely or foolishly ⟨the *unthrifty* couple ended up having to declare bankruptcy⟩ — see PRODIGAL

unthrone *vb* to remove from a position of prominence or power (as a throne) ⟨the board of directors *unthroned* the CEO when it became clear that he was not going to reverse the company's sagging fortunes anytime soon⟩ — see DEPOSE 1

untidy *adj* **1** lacking in order, neatness, and often cleanliness ⟨I can never find anything in this *untidy* office⟩ — see MESSY

2 lacking neatness in dress or person ⟨neighbors gossiped about the woman's rumpled and *untidy* children⟩ — see SLOPPY 1

untie *vb* to disengage the knotted parts of ⟨she always makes sure to *untie* her shoelaces before removing her shoes⟩

synonyms unbind, undo, unfasten, unlash

related words unbraid, unlace; disentangle, ravel, unravel, unsnarl, untangle, unwind; loose, loosen

near antonyms braid, interlace, interweave, lace, wind; entangle, snarl, tangle

antonyms bind, fasten, knot, lash, tie

untimely *adj* occurring before the usual or expected time ⟨the *untimely* arrival of our guests caught us by surprise⟩ — see EARLY 2

untiring *adj* showing no signs of weariness even after long hard effort ⟨the camel's reputation as an *untiring* beast of burden⟩ ⟨the detective's *untiring* investigation of the crime finally led to several arrests⟩ — see TIRELESS

untitled *adj* not named or identified by a name ⟨the band is working on a new album which is still *untitled*⟩ — see NAMELESS 1

untold *adj* too many to be counted ⟨*untold* generations have lived and died in this ancient land⟩ — see COUNTLESS

untouchable *adj* **1** hard or impossible to get to or get at ⟨*untouchable* oil lying deep within the earth⟩ — see INACCESSIBLE

2 not to be violated, criticized, or tampered with ⟨an *untouchable* target for criticism as far as the local newspaper was concerned⟩ — see SACRED 1

untoward *adj* **1** given to resisting authority or another's control ⟨tried to reason with the *untoward* child⟩ — see DISOBEDIENT

2 given to resisting control or discipline by others ⟨a program for *untoward* teenagers that is designed to give them the kind of discipline that their parents were unable or unwilling to administer⟩ — see UNCONTROLLABLE

3 opposed to one's interests ⟨achieved great success as an artist despite growing up in a very *untoward* milieu⟩ — see ADVERSE 1

4 not appropriate for a particular occasion or situation ⟨unfortunately, one of the symptoms of dementia can be a tendency to make *untoward* and often shocking remarks⟩ — see INAPPROPRIATE

untowardness *n* the quality or state of not being socially proper ⟨the *untowardness* of the politically biased speech raised some eyebrows at the charity fund-raiser⟩ — see IMPROPRIETY 1

untraveled *adj* not having been traveled over or through ⟨to some it seemed plausible that in the relatively *untraveled* vastnesses of the Pacific Northwest a creature such as Sasquatch could lurk⟩ — see PATHLESS

untraversed *adj* not having been traveled over or through ⟨the documentary captures the mountainous wilderness in all of its untamed and *untraversed* glory⟩ — see PATHLESS

untreated *adj* being such as found in nature and not altered by processing or refining ⟨*untreated* wool⟩ — see CRUDE 1

untrodden *also* **untrod** *adj* not having been traveled over or through ⟨the fields in the valley are newly carpeted in an expanse of *untrodden* snow⟩ — see PATHLESS

untroubled *adj* **1** free from emotional or mental agitation ⟨she remains *untroubled* despite the chaos around her⟩ — see CALM 2

2 free from storms or physical disturbance ⟨quietly canoeing on the *untroubled* waters of the lake⟩ — see CALM 1

untrue *adj* **1** not being in agreement with what is true ⟨"the sky is purple" is an *untrue* statement⟩ — see FALSE 1

2 not true in one's allegiance to someone or something ⟨*untrue* to his country in its time of need⟩ — see FAITHLESS

untruth *n* **1** a false idea or belief ⟨their argument rests on a fundamental *untruth* which has long been discredited⟩ — see FALLACY 1

2 a statement known by its maker to be untrue and made in order to deceive ⟨the Web site is rife with *untruths* and misleading information⟩ — see LIE

3 the quality or state of being false ⟨there is an element of *untruth* in all forms of art: works of art provide only a semblance of reality⟩ — see FALLACY 2

untruthful *adj* **1** not being in agreement with what is true ⟨an unintentionally *untruthful* statement that the candidate later corrected⟩ — see FALSE 1

2 telling or containing lies ⟨the political action committee was slammed for spreading *untruthful* smears about the candidate and his wife⟩ — see DISHONEST 1

untruthfulness *n* the tendency to tell lies ⟨consistent *untruthfulness* on your part will result in consistent distrustfulness on other people's part⟩ — see DISHONESTY 1

untutored *adj* lacking in education or the knowledge gained from books ⟨to the *untutored* observer these works of art must seem strange indeed⟩ — see IGNORANT 1

untwine *vb* to separate the various strands of ⟨*untwined* his shoelaces⟩ — see UNRAVEL 1

untwist *vb* to separate the various strands of ⟨*untwisted* the ball of thread⟩ — see UNRAVEL 1

untypical *adj* departing from some accepted standard of what is normal ⟨the plant displays some *untypical* characteristics⟩ — see DEVIANT

unusable *adj* not capable of being put to use or account ⟨a completely *unusable* gadget that's just taking up space in the drawer⟩ — see IMPRACTICAL

unused *adj* **1** not having acquired a habit or tolerance ⟨the runner's performance suffered because he was *unused* to running at such high elevations⟩

synonyms unacclimated, unaccustomed, unadapted, unadjusted
related words unseasoned
near antonyms unaffected, uninfluenced
antonyms acclimated, accustomed, adapted, adjusted, habituated, used
2 recently made and never used before ⟨preferred to start with *unused* pencils⟩ — see NEW 3
3 not being in a state of use, activity, or employment ⟨is there an *unused* cubicle that the temp could work out of?⟩ — see INACTIVE 2

unusual *adj* **1** noticeably different from what is generally found or experienced ⟨we found some *unusual* shells by the high-tide mark while combing the beach⟩
synonyms curious, extraordinary, funny, odd, offbeat, out-of-the-way, peculiar, queer, rare, singular, strange, unaccustomed, uncommon, uncustomary, unique, weird
related words bizarre, eccentric, far-out, kooky (*also* kookie), oddball, outlandish, outré, way-out; aberrant, abnormal, atypical, exceptional, irregular; newsworthy, notable, noteworthy, noticeable, particular, remarkable, special
near antonyms unexceptional; expected, predictable; familiar, normal, regular, typical
antonyms common, ordinary, plain, usual
2 being out of the ordinary ⟨the famously arrogant actor accepted his award with *unusual* grace and humility⟩ — see EXCEPTIONAL 1

unutterable *adj* beyond the power to describe ⟨*unutterable* joy that a baby can bring to a household⟩ ⟨the *unutterable* suffering brought on by the war⟩ — see INDESCRIBABLE

unvarnished *adj* free from all additions or embellishment ⟨I'm telling the *unvarnished* truth⟩ — see PLAIN 1

unvarying *adj* **1** not undergoing a change in condition ⟨an *unvarying* dedication to the welfare of her community⟩ — see CONSTANT 1
2 not varying ⟨*unvarying* temperatures and humidity are best for the preservation of ancient artifacts⟩ — see UNIFORM

unveil *vb* **1** to make known (as information previously kept secret) ⟨*unveiled* the techniques that the self-styled clairvoyant used to trick her clients⟩ — see REVEAL 1
2 to present so as to invite notice or attention ⟨*unveiled* the new sculpture before a gathering of dignitaries⟩ — see SHOW 1

unvocal *adj* marked by or producing a harsh combination of sounds ⟨the nursery full of crying toddlers made a most *unvocal* din⟩ — see DISSONANT

unvoiced *adj* understood although not put into words ⟨an *unvoiced* promise to be waiting for him when he returned from the war⟩ — see IMPLICIT 1

unwarrantable *adj* too bad to be excused or justified ⟨the *unwarrantable* arrogance of that man⟩ — see INEXCUSABLE

unwarranted *adj* **1** not needed by the circumstances or to accomplish an end ⟨the committee concluded that any further revisions to the regulations were currently *unwarranted*⟩ — see UNNECESSARY
2 having no basis in reason or fact ⟨don't leap to *unwarranted* conclusions⟩ — see GROUNDLESS

unwary *adj* **1** lacking in worldly wisdom or informed judgment ⟨e-mail scams that take advantage of *unwary* computer users⟩ — see NAIVE 1
2 not paying or showing close attention especially for the purpose of avoiding trouble ⟨a dangerous stretch of desert that has claimed many *unwary* travelers⟩ — see CARELESS 1
3 readily taken advantage of ⟨*unwary* consumers who unquestioningly swallow the dubious claims of TV pitchmen⟩ — see EASY 2

unwashed *adj* belonging to the class of people of low social or economic rank ⟨a TV producer who knew what the *unwashed* masses wanted—and unhestitatingly gave it to them⟩ — see IGNOBLE 1

unwashed *n* people looked down upon as ignorant and of the lowest class ⟨Aunt Edna was fond of snootily reminding us that we need not take our manners from the great *unwashed*⟩ — see RABBLE

unwavering *adj* not varying ⟨an *unwavering* commitment to social justice⟩ — see UNIFORM

unweave *vb* to separate the various strands of ⟨if you want the scarf to be perfect, you're going to have to *unweave* the last three inches and fix the mistake⟩ — see UNRAVEL 1

unwed *adj* not married ⟨called for new social programs to aid *unwed* teenage mothers⟩ — see SINGLE 1

unwelcome *adj* not giving pleasure to the mind or senses ⟨the *unwelcome* news ruined what had been a fine day⟩ — see UNPLEASANT

unwell *adj* temporarily suffering from a disorder of the body ⟨she missed work because she was *unwell*⟩ — see SICK 1

unwholesome *adj* **1** bad for the well-being of the body ⟨health inspectors shut down several food stands that were using tainted and *unwholesome* meat⟩ — see UNHEALTHY 1
2 having or showing lowered moral character or standards ⟨despite having been raised in such *unwholesome* environments as a brothel and a traveling circus, singer Edith Piaf rose to international stardom⟩ — see CORRUPT

unwieldy *adj* difficult to use or operate especially because of size, weight, or design ⟨an *unwieldy* machine that requires two people to operate it⟩ — see CUMBERSOME

unwilling *adj* not made or done willingly or by choice ⟨*unwilling* contributions from city employees who felt pressured to do so⟩ — see INVOLUNTARY 1

unwillingness *n* a lack of willingness or desire to do or accept something ⟨your *unwillingness* to help with the cooking means that you won't be sharing in the eating⟩ — see RELUCTANCE

unwind *vb* to get rid of nervous tension or anxiety ⟨soft music and a good book help me *unwind*⟩ — see RELAX 1

unwisdom *n* lack of good sense or judgment ⟨you find both wisdom and *unwisdom* in his writings, and it's your job to discover which is which⟩ — see FOOLISHNESS 1

unwise *adj* **1** showing or marked by a lack of good sense or judgment ⟨made the *unwise* decision to invest in a brand-new company⟩ — see FOOLISH 1
2 showing poor judgment especially in personal relationships or social situations ⟨an *unwise* urge to confide in total strangers⟩ — see INDISCREET
3 not having or showing a deep understanding of something ⟨a stunningly *unwise* observer of the political scene⟩ — see IMPERCEPTIVE

unwitting *adj* **1** happening by chance ⟨an *unwitting* mistake made in copying the material⟩ — see ACCIDENTAL 1
2 not informed about or aware of something ⟨an *unwitting* accomplice to the crime⟩ — see IGNORANT 2

unwomanly *adj* having qualities or traits that are traditionally considered inappropriate for a girl or woman ⟨aggression and assertiveness were once considered *unwomanly*⟩ — see UNFEMININE

unwonted *adj* being out of the ordinary ⟨honored for the *unwonted* courage he showed in battle⟩ — see EXCEPTIONAL 1

unworkable *adj* not capable of being put to use or account ⟨the company decided that the proposed reorganization of its operations was *unworkable* due to high costs⟩ — see IMPRACTICAL

unworldliness *n* the quality or state of being simple and sincere ⟨there's a sweet *unworldliness* about her that makes men want to be her protector⟩ — see NAÏVETÉ 1

unworldly *adj* lacking in worldly wisdom or informed judgment ⟨the guy's *unworldly* enough to think that any stranger who would approach him on a city street is simply trying to help him⟩ — see NAIVE 1

unworried *adj* free from emotional or mental agitation ⟨remained *unworried* despite the panic all around her⟩ — see CALM 2

unwritten *adj* made or carried on through speaking rather than in writing ⟨an *unwritten* contract may not be enforceable⟩ — see VERBAL 2

unyielding *adj* **1** showing no signs of slackening or yielding in one's purpose ⟨the pioneers faced the challenge of settling the frontier with *unyielding* courage⟩
synonyms determined, dogged, grim, implacable, relentless, unappeasable, unflinching, unrelenting
related words persevering, persistent, tenacious; hard, hardheaded, headstrong, intractable, mulish, obdurate, opinionated, peevish, pertinacious, perverse, pigheaded, self-willed, stubborn, uncooperative, willful (*or* wilful); merciless, ruthless, unforgiving
near antonyms slackening, softening, yielding; impotent, invertebrate, slack, spineless, weak; complaisant, obliging, pliable, pliant
2 having a consistency that does not easily yield to pressure ⟨knead the dough until it feels reasonably *unyielding*⟩ — see FIRM 2
3 incapable of or highly resistant to bending ⟨an *unyielding* steel bar⟩ — see STIFF 1
4 sticking to an opinion, purpose, or course of action in spite of reason, arguments, or persuasion ⟨despite studies showing that limits on development would hurt the local economy, the town council remained *unyielding* in their support for these limits⟩ — see OBSTINATE

unyoke *vb* to set or force apart ⟨*unyoke* these two boats and tie them to the dock separately⟩ — see SEPARATE 1

unyoung *adj* being of advanced years and especially past middle age ⟨the park has walking trails that are suitable for both the young and the *unyoung*⟩ — see ELDERLY

up *adj* **1** being at a higher level than average ⟨the level of the lake is *up* this spring⟩ — see HIGH 2
2 brought or having come to an end ⟨okay, time is *up*⟩ — see COMPLETE 2
3 having information especially as a result of study or experience ⟨she's always *up* on the latest developments in fashion⟩ — see FAMILIAR 2

up *vb* **1** to make greater in size, amount, or number ⟨climbing fuel prices have forced the delivery company to *up* its prices⟩ — see INCREASE 1
2 to move from a lower to a higher place or position ⟨*upped* the catboat's sail⟩ — see RAISE 1
3 to move or extend upward ⟨the road constantly *ups* and downs as it makes its way over the hills⟩ — see ASCEND

upbeat *adj* **1** having or showing a good mood or disposition ⟨an *upbeat* attitude about life⟩ — see CHEERFUL 1
2 having qualities which inspire hope ⟨several *upbeat* signs that the economy is improving⟩ — see HOPEFUL 1

upbraid *vb* to criticize (someone) severely or angrily especially for personal failings ⟨his wife *upbraided* him for his irresponsible handling of the family finances⟩ — see SCOLD

upchuck *vb* to discharge the contents of the stomach through the mouth ⟨a speaker so nervous that he had *upchucked* backstage⟩ — see VOMIT

upcoming *adj* being soon to appear or take place ⟨an *upcoming* election⟩ — see FORTHCOMING 1

up–country *n* a rural region that forms the edge of the settled or developed part of a country ⟨built a cabin in the *up-country*⟩ — see FRONTIER 2

update *vb* to adapt to modern needs, taste, or usage ⟨the movie is basically a retelling of the tried-and-true Cinderella story, *updated* for today's hipper audiences⟩ — see MODERNIZE

upend *vb* **1** to achieve a victory over ⟨the team won the division play-offs, but was *upended* in the final championship game⟩ — see BEAT 2
2 to fix in an upright position ⟨we had to *upend* the sofa in order to fit it into the elevator⟩ — see ERECT 1

up–front *adj* free in expressing one's true feelings and opinions ⟨some hurt feelings could have been spared if he'd been more *up-front* about whom he was inviting to the party⟩ — see FRANK

upgrade *n* **1** an upward slope ⟨had to walk our bicycle on the *upgrades* on our ride through the hills⟩ — see ASCENT 2
2 a raising or a state of being raised to a higher rank or position ⟨received an *upgrade* to lieutenant⟩ — see ADVANCEMENT 1
3 the degree to which something rises up from a position level with the horizon ⟨there's a steep *upgrade* to some of the hills on that route⟩ — see SLANT

upgrade *vb* **1** to move higher in rank or position ⟨*upgraded* them to first class⟩ — see PROMOTE 1
2 to make better ⟨that restaurant had better *upgrade* its service—and fast—if it wants to stay in business⟩ — see IMPROVE

upgrading *n* a raising or a state of being raised to a higher rank or position ⟨she was surprised by the unannounced *upgrading* to the position of supervisor⟩ — see ADVANCEMENT 1

upheaval *n* a violent disturbance (as of the political or social order) ⟨the government can no longer control the social *upheaval* brought about by the collapse of the country's economy⟩ — see CONVULSION

upheave *vb* to lift with effort ⟨exactly how the builders of the pyramids at Giza *upheaved* such massive blocks of stone remains a mystery⟩ — see HEAVE 1

uphill *adj* requiring considerable physical or mental effort ⟨an *uphill* battle to eradicate poverty in an area of the state that has never known anything else⟩ — see HARD 2

uphill *n* an upward slope ⟨no matter where you go bicycle touring, the *uphills* always seem to outnumber the downhills⟩ — see ASCENT 2

uphold *vb* **1** to continue to declare to be true or proper despite opposition or objections ⟨determined to *uphold* her views in the face of all challenges⟩ — see MAINTAIN 2
2 to hold up or serve as a foundation for ⟨an entablature *upheld* by a series of gracefully slender columns⟩ — see SUPPORT 3
3 to move from a lower to a higher place or position ⟨worshippers *upheld* their joined hands and sang the praises of the Lord⟩ — see RAISE 1

upkeep *n* the act or activity of keeping something in an existing and usually satisfactory condition ⟨the *upkeep* of the old place was costing a fortune⟩ — see MAINTENANCE

upland *n* an area of high ground ⟨the animals huddled on the *upland* as the floodwater rose⟩ — see HEIGHT 4

uplift *vb* to move from a lower to a higher place or position ⟨a mountain range that was *uplifted* millions of years ago by the collision of continental plates⟩ — see RAISE 1

uplifted *adj* being positioned above a surface ⟨an *uplifted* area of ground⟩ — see ELEVATED 1

upmarket *adj* appealing to affluent consumers ⟨an *up-*

market restaurant that is quite pricey but also quite good⟩ — see UPSCALE

upmost *adj* being at a point or level higher than all others ⟨the *upmost* floor of the building⟩ — see TOP 1

upon *prep* in or into contact with ⟨leaned *upon* the desk⟩ — see AGAINST 1

upper–class *adj* of high birth, rank, or station ⟨*upper-class* boys who had an entrenched sense of entitlement⟩ — see NOBLE 1

upper class *n* the highest class in a society ⟨a school founded to educate the children of the *upper class*⟩ — see ARISTOCRACY 1

upper–crust *adj* of high birth, rank, or station ⟨an interior designer who has intimate knowledge of the tastes of her *upper-crust* clientele⟩ — see NOBLE 1

upper crust *n* **1** individuals carefully selected as being the best of a class ⟨the conference was a gathering of the *upper crust* of the computer programming industry⟩ — see ELITE 1
2 the highest class in a society ⟨a specialty clothing store for the *upper crust*⟩ — see ARISTOCRACY 1

upper hand *n* the more favorable condition or position in a competition ⟨finally gained the *upper hand* in the argument⟩ — see ADVANTAGE 1

uppermost *adj* being at a point or level higher than all others ⟨the *uppermost* floor of the house gets very hot in the summer⟩ — see TOP 1

uppish *adj* having a feeling of superiority that shows itself in an overbearing attitude ⟨the new employee's *uppish* airs aren't winning him many friends among his colleagues⟩ — see ARROGANT

uppity *adj* having a feeling of superiority that shows itself in an overbearing attitude ⟨*uppity* social climbers who were the biggest snobs in town⟩ — see ARROGANT

upraise *vb* **1** to move from a lower to a higher place or position ⟨the runner's arms were *upraised* in a sign of victory as he crossed the finish line⟩ — see RAISE 1
2 to fix in an upright position ⟨archaeologists are still not sure how the mysterious statues on Easter Island were *upraised*⟩ — see ERECT 1

upraised *adj* being positioned above a surface ⟨these *upraised* earthworks are believed to have been built by Native Americans hundreds of years ago and used for enclosure, burial, religious rites, or defense⟩ — see ELEVATED 1

uprear *vb* to move or extend upward ⟨trees *uprearing* towards the sky⟩ — see ASCEND

upright *adj* **1** conforming to a high standard of morality or virtue ⟨an honest and *upright* people⟩ — see GOOD 2
2 following the accepted rules of moral conduct ⟨informing the clerk that he had just given me back too much in change was the only *upright* thing to do⟩ — see HONORABLE 1
3 rising straight up ⟨only one pillar of the ruined temple remained *upright*⟩ — see ERECT

uprightness *n* **1** conduct that conforms to an accepted standard of right and wrong ⟨the *uprightness* of our cause is not what is being called into question here⟩ — see MORALITY 1
2 faithfulness to high moral standards ⟨the members of this special investigative committee must be personages of unquestionable *uprightness*⟩ — see HONOR 1

uprise *n* an upward slope ⟨the sharp *uprise* leading up to the fortress would make an assault extremely difficult⟩ — see ASCENT 2

uprise *vb* **1** to leave one's bed ⟨*uprise*! we have lots of work to do today!⟩ — see ARISE 1
2 to move or extend upward ⟨as we went from the coast into the state's interior, the land gradually began *uprising* and eventually we were on mountainous terrain⟩ — see ASCEND

uprising *n* open fighting against authority (as one's own government) ⟨the *uprising* was quickly and brutally suppressed⟩ — see REBELLION 1

uproar *n* **1** a state of noisy, confused activity ⟨the house is always in a jubilant *uproar* during the holidays⟩ — see COMMOTION
2 a state of wildly excited activity or emotion ⟨the ref's controversial call sent the crowd into an *uproar*⟩ — see FRENZY
3 a violent disturbance (as of the political or social order) ⟨the *uproar* following the corrupt election nearly toppled the government⟩ — see CONVULSION
4 a violent shouting ⟨an *uproar* arose from the crowd when it was announced that the concert was cancelled and refunds might not be available⟩ — see CLAMOR 1

uproarious *adj* **1** causing or intended to cause laughter ⟨the movie follows the comic duo through a series of outrageous and *uproarious* escapades⟩ — see FUNNY 1
2 full of or characterized by the presence of noise ⟨visited the site where the action movie was being filmed only to find a chaotic, *uproarious* set⟩ — see NOISY 2

uproariousness *n* the amusing quality or element in something ⟨the supposed *uproariousness* of the situation was lost on the people who fell for the scam⟩ — see HUMOR 1

uproot *vb* to draw out by force or with effort ⟨*uprooted* the old bridge's pilings upon the completion of its replacement⟩ — see EXTRACT

upscale *adj* appealing to affluent consumers ⟨a new *upscale* shopping center is under construction on the west end of town⟩
synonyms exclusive, high-end, upmarket
related words elegant, fashionable, posh; extravagant, ostentatious, showy; deluxe, lavish, luxuriant, luxurious, opulent, plush, sumptuous; costly, expensive
near antonyms cheap, inexpensive
antonyms dime-store, discount, down-market, downscale, low-end

upset *adj* feeling or showing uncomfortable feelings of uncertainty ⟨she was *upset* by the unexplained change in plans⟩ — see NERVOUS 1

upset *n* an act or instance of the order of things being disturbed ⟨the move to a new town is just the latest in a series of *upsets* for my family over the last year⟩
synonyms derangement, dislocation, disruption, disturbance
related words convulsion, revolution, unsettledness, unsettlement, upheaval

upset *vb* **1** to trouble the mind of; to make uneasy ⟨the smallest things can *upset* us if we're already stressed⟩ — see DISTURB 1
2 to turn on one's side or upside down ⟨the narrow boat *upsets* easily and should be handled with care⟩ — see CAPSIZE
3 to undo the proper order or arrangement of ⟨the change in the bus schedule *upset* our daily routine⟩ — see DISORDER

upsetting *adj* causing worry or anxiety ⟨the constant arguing is *upsetting* to a sensitive person like your grandmother⟩ — see TROUBLESOME

upshot *n* a condition or occurrence traceable to a cause ⟨the *upshot* of the court's ruling is that a number of communities will now have to change their gun laws⟩ — see EFFECT 1

upside–down *adj* lacking in order, neatness, and often cleanliness ⟨the frantic search left the room *upside-down*⟩ — see MESSY

upstanding *adj* **1** following the accepted rules of moral conduct ⟨a fine, *upstanding* woman who deserves to be nominated to the state's highest court⟩ — see HONORABLE 1
2 rising straight up ⟨not a single wall remained *upstanding* after the tornado had passed⟩ — see ERECT

upstart *n* one who has recently acquired wealth and social position ⟨having made their money in oil decades ago, they consider these billionaire dot-commers mere *upstarts*⟩ — see NOUVEAU RICHE

upthrust *vb* to move or extend upward ⟨an *upthrusting* seamount⟩ — see ASCEND

uptick *n* something added (as by growth) ⟨an *uptick* in sales over the last fiscal year⟩ — see INCREASE 1

uptight *adj* feeling or showing uncomfortable feelings of uncertainty ⟨he has a tendency to fret and get *uptight* whenever his usual routine is disrupted⟩ — see NERVOUS 1

up–to–date *adj* **1** being or involving the latest methods, concepts, information, or styles ⟨demanded the most *up-to-date* computer system available⟩ — see MODERN
2 having information especially as a result of study or experience ⟨I'm afraid that I'm not *up-to-date* on that issue⟩ — see FAMILIAR 2

up–to–the–minute *adj* being or involving the latest methods, concepts, information, or styles ⟨the company insists on having *up-to-the-minute* firewall and antivirus software⟩ — see MODERN

upturn *vb* to move or extend upward ⟨at this point the road *upturns* steeply, the trees become scarcer, and the valley unfolds before you⟩ — see ASCEND

urbane *adj* having or showing very polished and worldly manners ⟨a gentlemanly and *urbane* host of elegant dinner parties⟩ — see SUAVE

urbanize *vb* to accustom to the ways of the city ⟨every September the city of Boston *urbanizes* a new crop of college students from small towns across the country⟩ — see CITIFY

urchin *n* an appealingly mischievous person ⟨we could never resist the little *urchin's* pleas for candy⟩ — see SCAMP 1

urge *n* a strong wish for something ⟨I'm trying to resist the *urge* to eat another piece of cake⟩ — see DESIRE 1

urge *vb* to try to persuade (someone) through earnest appeals to follow a course of action ⟨the public service announcement *urges* pet owners to spay or neuter their pets⟩
synonyms egg (on), encourage, exhort, goad, nudge, press, prod, prompt
related words drive, propel, spur, stimulate; hurry, hustle, push, rush; adjure, beseech, implore, importune; blandish, cajole, coax, soft-soap, wheedle; high-pressure, nag, needle, pressure; foment, incite, instigate, provoke, stir (up)
near antonyms deter, discourage, dissuade; brake, check, constrain, curb, hold back, inhibit, restrain

urgent *adj* needing immediate attention ⟨I will need to put off everything but the most *urgent* issues⟩ — see ACUTE 2

usable *also* **useable** *adj* **1** capable of or suitable for being used for a particular purpose ⟨although the spade is *usable* as a snow shovel, it doesn't do a very good job⟩
synonyms available, employable, exploitable, fit, functional, operable, practicable, serviceable, useful
related words applicable, relevant; doable, feasible, viable, workable; reusable
antonyms impracticable, inoperable, nonfunctional, unavailable, unemployable, unusable
2 capable of being put to use or account ⟨there's not a scrap of *usable* information in that article on finding the right pet for one's family⟩ — see PRACTICAL 1

usage *n* the act or practice of employing something for a particular purpose ⟨the machine's warranty does not cover malfunctions that result from improper *usage*⟩ — see USE 1

use *n* **1** the act or practice of employing something for a particular purpose ⟨the *use* of boom boxes is strictly prohibited in the park⟩
synonyms application, employment, exercise, operation, play, usage
related words exertion; reuse
near antonyms disuse, nonuse
2 the capacity for being useful for some purpose ⟨the broken grill isn't going to be of much *use* in cooking the hamburgers⟩
synonyms account, avail, mileage, service, serviceability, serviceableness, usefulness, utility
related words advantage, benefit, gain; aid, assistance, help; applicability, appropriateness, fitness, relevance; profit, value, worth
near antonyms inapplicability, inappropriateness
antonyms uselessness, worthlessness
3 positive regard for something ⟨I have no *use* for slackers⟩ — see LIKING

use *vb* **1** to put into action or service ⟨I will need to *use* the large hammer for this project⟩
synonyms apply, employ, exercise, exploit, harness, operate, utilize
related words handle, manipulate, wield; direct, run, work; cannibalize, recycle, reuse
phrases bring to bear, draw on (*or* upon), make use of
near antonyms ignore, neglect; misapply, misuse
2 to behave toward in a stated way ⟨the factory workers were underpaid and poorly *used* by their employers⟩ — see TREAT 1
3 to take unfair advantage of ⟨I was paying for everything on our little outing, and I was starting to feel like I was being *used*⟩ — see EXPLOIT 1

used *adj* being in the habit or custom ⟨my grandmother has spent her whole life on the farm and is *used* to working hard⟩ — see ACCUSTOMED

useful *adj* **1** capable of being put to use or account ⟨*useful* suggestions for limiting the amount of food we eat⟩ — see PRACTICAL 1
2 capable of or suitable for being used for a particular purpose ⟨I've found this tool really *useful* for making sure all my pictures are hung straight⟩ — see USABLE 1
3 providing service or assistance ⟨hopefully, the consultant's financial advice will prove *useful* in planning for our retirement⟩ — see HELPFUL 1

usefulness *n* the capacity for being useful for some purpose ⟨the well-known *usefulness* of thick phone books as seat boosters for short diners⟩ — see USE 2

useless *adj* **1** not capable of being put to use or account ⟨a garage full of *useless* junk⟩ — see IMPRACTICAL
2 producing no results ⟨a *useless* attempt to reach an agreement⟩ — see FUTILE 1

user *n* a person who regularly uses drugs especially illegally ⟨a person who started out as a *user* and is now a drug dealer as well⟩ — see DOPER

use up *vb* to make complete use of ⟨we *used up* the last of the flour when we made the waffles⟩ — see DEPLETE 1

usher *vb* to point out the way for (someone) especially from a position in front ⟨*ushered* the job applicant into the room and then left⟩ — see LEAD 1

usual *adj* **1** accepted, used, or practiced by most people ⟨that's not the *usual* method, but it works⟩ — see CURRENT 1
2 being of the type that is encountered in the normal course of events ⟨the characters in this novel are drawn with greater depth than is *usual* for a work of science fiction⟩ — see ORDINARY 1
3 often observed or encountered ⟨the *usual* reaction to the sight of the falls is one of absolute awe⟩ — see COMMON 1

usually *adv* according to the usual course of things ⟨we *usually* go out to eat on Fridays⟩ — see NATURALLY 2

usurp *vb* to take or make use of under a guise of authority but without actual right ⟨the mayor *usurped* the school board's authority when he fired the principal⟩ — see APPROPRIATE 1

usurpation *n* the unlawful taking or withholding of something from the rightful owner under a guise of authority ⟨the government's *usurpation* of the tribe's hunting grounds left them without a source of food⟩ — see APPROPRIATION 2

utensil *n* an article intended for use in work ⟨participants in the class must supply their own writing *utensils*⟩ — see IMPLEMENT

utility *n* the capacity for being useful for some purpose ⟨the store specializes in gee-whiz gadgetry of dubious *utility*⟩ — see USE 2

utilize *vb* to put into action or service ⟨we must *utilize* all the tools at our disposal⟩ — see USE 1

utmost *adj* **1** most distant from a center ⟨supreme power that extended to the *utmost* points of the empire⟩ — see EXTREME 1

2 of the greatest or highest degree or quantity ⟨inhabitants of the war-ravaged region are experiencing the *utmost* misery imaginable⟩ — see ULTIMATE 1

3 of the highest degree ⟨an intelligence operation that must be conducted with the *utmost* secrecy⟩ — see FULL 2

utopia *n* an often imaginary place or state of utter perfection and happiness ⟨dreamed of one day retiring to a tropical *utopia*⟩ — see PARADISE 1

utopian *adj* having or marked by a tendency to be guided more by ideals than by reality ⟨a plan to revitalize the city's decaying downtown that proved to be overly ambitious and *utopian*⟩ — see IDEALISTIC

utopian *n* one whose conduct is guided more by the image of perfection than by the real world ⟨in the 19th century *utopians* founded a number of short-lived socialist communities⟩ — see IDEALIST

utter *adj* **1** having no exceptions or restrictions ⟨our attempt to reform the school system was an *utter* failure⟩ — see ABSOLUTE 2

2 of the highest degree ⟨spoke with *utter* certainty⟩ — see FULL 2

utter *vb* **1** to send forth using the vocal chords ⟨she tried not to *utter* a sound as the doctor gave her a flu shot⟩

synonyms emit

related words deliver; blurt (out), ejaculate, exclaim; gasp, groan, heave, hoot, moan, pant, quaver, snarl, sob, sputter, squawk, squeak, squeal, stammer, stutter, whimper, yowl; lip, mouth, whisper

2 to express (a thought or emotion) in words ⟨never *uttered* a single comment at the meeting⟩ — see SAY 1

utterance *n* **1** an act, process, or means of putting something into words ⟨many writers have used poetry as a means to give *utterance* to their deepest thoughts⟩ — see EXPRESSION 1

2 something that is said ⟨celebrities whose every *utterance* is treated as though it were newsworthy⟩ — see WORD 2

uttered *adj* expressed or communicated by voice ⟨her first *uttered* cry for help since the start of the ordeal⟩ — see VOCAL

utterly *adv* **1** to a full extent or degree ⟨we are in fact *utterly* out of food⟩ — see FULLY 1

2 to a large extent or degree ⟨was *utterly* overwhelmed by the demands on her time⟩ — see GREATLY 2

uttermost *adj* of the greatest or highest degree or quantity ⟨I have the *uttermost* faith in your abilities⟩ — see ULTIMATE 1

U-turn *n* a changing from one policy or point of view to virtually its exact opposite ⟨did an abrupt *U-turn* when she learned that her would-be suitor was a dot-commer worth millions⟩ — see ABOUT-FACE

V

vacancy *n* **1** empty space ⟨the vast *vacancy* that exists between our solar system and the nearest star having its own orbiting planets⟩
synonyms black hole, blank, blankness, emptiness, vacuity, void
related words nothingness; inane, vacuum; air, open, waste; bareness, barrenness, bleakness, desolateness, hollowness; cavity, gap, hole, hollow
near antonyms fullness (*also* fulness), repleteness
2 the quality or state of being empty ⟨the *vacancy* of the cavernous gymnasium was eerily apparent to me as I shot baskets alone⟩
synonyms bareness, emptiness, vacantness, vacuity
related words hollowness; blankness, vacuum, void; nothingness; barrenness, bleakness, desolateness; availability, clearness, openness; depletion, dryness, exhaustion
near antonyms completeness; abundance, fatness, repleteness
antonyms fullness (*also* fulness)

vacant *adj* **1** lacking contents that could or should be present ⟨a *vacant* room that could be converted into a classroom⟩ — see EMPTY 1
2 not being in a state of use, activity, or employment ⟨looking for *vacant* land on which to build a house⟩ — see INACTIVE 2
3 not expressing any emotion ⟨the prisoner's *vacant* and distracted expression⟩ — see BLANK 1
4 left unoccupied or unused ⟨police discovered that vagrants had been sleeping in the *vacant* warehouse⟩ — see ABANDONED 1

vacantness *n* the quality or state of being empty ⟨there's a melancholy air of *vacantness* that seems to hang over a beach town during the long lull of winter⟩ — see VACANCY 2

vacate *vb* **1** to put an end to by formal action ⟨the contract was *vacated* by the court on the grounds that the signer was underage⟩ — see ABOLISH 1
2 to remove the contents of ⟨*vacated* the house⟩ — see EMPTY

vacated *adj* left unoccupied or unused ⟨*vacated* cottages that are easy targets for burglars during the winter⟩ — see ABANDONED 1

vacation *n* a period during which the usual routine of school or work is suspended ⟨area schools are on *vacation* that week in February so local ski resorts do a booming business⟩
synonyms break, holiday [*chiefly British*], hols [*British*], leave, recess
related words sabbatical; furlough, liberty; breather, relaxation, respite, rest; interim, intermission, interval; feast, holy day, legal holiday; idling, loafing, lounging, slacking

vacation *vb* to take or spend a vacation ⟨hoping to *vacation* in Spain this summer⟩
synonyms holiday
related words escape, get (away), get off; break, recess; ease (up), let up; relax, repose, rest; bum, goldbrick, idle, laze, loaf, lounge, slack (off)
near antonyms drudge, endeavor, grub, hump, hustle, labor, moil, peg (away), plod, plow, plug, slave, slog, strain, strive, struggle, sweat, toil, travail, work

vacillate *vb* to show uncertainty about the right course of action ⟨*vacillated* for so long that someone else stepped in and made the decision⟩ — see HESITATE

vacillation *n* a state or an instance of temporary inaction because of uncertainty about the right course of action ⟨the president was soundly criticized for his *vacillation* before responding to the crisis⟩ — see HESITATION

vacuity *n* **1** empty space ⟨the seemingly endless *vacuity* between settlements in the desert⟩ — see VACANCY 1
2 the quality or state of being empty ⟨the *vacuity* of the house after everyone had moved out was both striking and depressing⟩ — see VACANCY 2
3 the quality or state of lacking intelligence or quickness of mind ⟨the monumental *vacuity* of the starlet's comments on the important issues of the day⟩ — see STUPIDITY 1

vacuous *adj* **1** lacking contents that could or should be present ⟨a great *vacuous* space that should have been filled with an audience⟩ — see EMPTY 1
2 not having or showing an ability to absorb ideas readily ⟨a movie that was enthusiastically derided for its *vacuous* dialogue⟩ — see STUPID 1

vagabond *adj* traveling from place to place ⟨a *vagabond* group of entertainers that performed in rough-and-tumble mining towns⟩ — see ITINERANT

vagabond *n* **1** a homeless wanderer who may beg or steal for a living ⟨be wary of the *vagabonds* in that corner of the city⟩ — see TRAMP 1
2 a person who roams about without a fixed route or destination ⟨after they retired, the couple bought an RV and became footloose *vagabonds*⟩ — see NOMAD

vagary *n* a sudden impulsive and apparently unmotivated idea or action ⟨the *vagaries* of a rather eccentric, elderly lady⟩ — see WHIM

vagrancy *n* a sudden impulsive and apparently unmotivated idea or action ⟨a frequent victim to the *vagrancies* of the heart, she had a succession of passionate but short-lived romances⟩ — see WHIM

vagrant *adj* traveling from place to place ⟨bands of *vagrant* children in the streets of the impoverished city⟩ — see ITINERANT

vagrant *n* **1** a homeless wanderer who may beg or steal for a living ⟨*vagrants* sleeping in cardboard boxes on the sidewalk⟩ — see TRAMP 1
2 an idle worthless person ⟨the *vagrants* who are a familiar sight at the city's bus terminal⟩ — see NE'ER-DO-WELL

vague *adj* **1** not expressed in precise terms ⟨gave as *vague* a reply as he could, hoping not to give away the surprise⟩
synonyms fuzzy, indefinite, inexplicit, muzzy, unclear
related words ambiguous, cryptic, dark, enigmatic (*also* enigmatical), equivocal, murky, nebulous, obscure, unintelligible; bleary, blurry, dim, faint, foggy, gauzy, hazy, misty, woozy; indeterminate, indistinct, indistinguishable, uncertain, undefinable, undefined, undetermined; inexplicable, inscrutable, mysterious; baffling, bewildering, confounding, confusing, mystifying, obfuscatory, perplexing, puzzling, unfathomable
near antonyms candid, direct, forthright, foursquare, frank, honest, open, openhearted, outspoken, plainspoken, straight, straightforward, unguarded; obvious, plain, unambiguous, understandable, unequivocal; comprehensible, fathomable, intelligible; defined, distinct, well-defined; blatant, patent, unmistakable
antonyms clear, definite, explicit, specific
2 not seen or understood clearly ⟨I have only a *vague*

idea of what you're talking about⟩ — see FAINT 1

vain *adj* **1** having too high an opinion of oneself ⟨a man so *vain* that he spent hours admiring himself in the mirror⟩ — see CONCEITED
2 producing no results ⟨all their efforts to escape proved *vain*⟩ — see FUTILE 1
3 having no usefulness ⟨having tired of the *vain* pleasures of life in the fast lane, he returned to the small town he had grown up in⟩ — see WORTHLESS

vainglorious *adj* having too high an opinion of oneself ⟨a *vainglorious* woman who always insists on being the center of attention⟩ — see CONCEITED

vaingloriousness *n* an often unjustified feeling of being pleased with oneself or with one's situation or achievements ⟨a tiresome *vaingloriousness* that manifested itself in the old general's incessant boasting about his battlefield victories⟩ — see COMPLACENCE 1

vainglory *n* an often unjustified feeling of being pleased with oneself or with one's situation or achievements ⟨the *vainglory* that nations have historically shown after they have achieved military supremacy⟩ — see COMPLACENCE 1

vainness *n* an often unjustified feeling of being pleased with oneself or with one's situation or achievements ⟨the vexing *vainness* that seemed to fill every page of his memoirs⟩ — see COMPLACENCE 1

vale *n* an area of lowland between hills or mountains ⟨settled in a lush *vale* in the shadow of the mountains⟩ — see VALLEY

valedictory *adj* given, taken, or performed at parting ⟨a *valedictory* address given by the college president upon his retirement⟩ — see PARTING

valiant *adj* feeling or displaying no fear by temperament ⟨*valiant* soldiers marching off to war⟩ — see BRAVE 1

valiantly *adv* in a fearless manner ⟨*valiantly* they plowed forward through the dense jungle⟩ — see BRAVELY 1

valid *adj* **1** according to the rules of logic ⟨your argument isn't *valid* because you're taking what should be the conclusion and using it as a premise⟩ — see LOGICAL 1
2 based on sound reasoning or information ⟨only further investigation will show whether your theory is *valid*⟩ — see GOOD 1

validate *vb* **1** to give evidence or testimony to the truth or factualness of ⟨a witness independently *validated* the policeman's version of events⟩ — see CONFIRM 1
2 to show the existence or truth of by evidence ⟨the booming economy in and of itself *validated* the soundness of the government's economic policies⟩ — see PROVE 1

validation *n* something presented in support of the truth or accuracy of a claim ⟨I'm afraid we cannot act on your claim without *validation*⟩ — see PROOF

valley *n* an area of lowland between hills or mountains ⟨the *valley* will be the first to flood if the river rises⟩
synonyms dale, dene [*British*], hollow, vale
related words canyon (*also* cañon), combe (*also* coombe *or* coomb) [*British*], dell, depression, dingle, glen, gorge, gulch, gully (*also* gulley), kloof [*South African*], ravine, rift valley; basin, bowl
near antonyms alp, mount, mountain, peak; height, mountaintop, pinnacle, summit; plateau, tableland

valor *n* strength of mind to carry on in spite of danger ⟨the absence of indecision even in the face of death is the true mark of *valor*⟩ — see COURAGE

valorous *adj* feeling or displaying no fear by temperament ⟨*valorous* deeds that will be long remembered⟩ — see BRAVE 1

valorously *adv* in a fearless manner ⟨they fought *valorously* for a cause that most people were too timid to support⟩ — see BRAVELY 1

valuable *adj* commanding a large price ⟨an extremely *valuable* diamond necklace⟩ — see COSTLY

valuate *vb* to make an approximate or tentative judgment regarding ⟨the house is *valuated* at six million dollars, pending an official assessment⟩ — see ESTIMATE 1

valuation *n* **1** the act of placing a value on the nature, character, or quality of something ⟨my *valuation* of your musical talent has nothing to do with our friendship⟩ — see ESTIMATE 1
2 the amount of money for which something will find a buyer ⟨the final auction bid was still less than the minimum *valuation* that we had specified as acceptable, so the painting was withdrawn⟩ — see VALUE 1
3 the relative usefulness or importance of something as judged by specific qualities ⟨the low *valuation* that society places on knowledge for the sake of knowledge⟩ — see WORTH 1

value *n* **1** the amount of money for which something will find a buyer ⟨the real *value* of that house is close to a million dollars⟩
synonyms valuation, worth
related words charge, cost, fee, figure, price, rate; appraisal, assessment, estimate, estimation, evaluation; face value, list price, unit price
2 a quality that gives something special worth ⟨defending the democratic system's intrinsic *values*⟩ — see EXCELLENCE 2
3 the relative usefulness or importance of something as judged by specific qualities ⟨the *value* of a good education cannot be overstated⟩ — see WORTH 1

value *vb* **1** to hold dear ⟨a nation that *values* individualism and self-reliance⟩ — see LOVE 1
2 to make an approximate or tentative judgment regarding ⟨*values* his stocks at $150,000 or thereabouts⟩ — see ESTIMATE 1

value judgment *n* an opinion on the nature, character, or quality of something ⟨lexicographers do not make *value judgments* about words when deciding whether they should be entered in the dictionary⟩ — see ESTIMATION 1

valueless *adj* having no usefulness ⟨a fish that was once regarded as *valueless* and routinely thrown away by fishermen⟩ — see WORTHLESS

valve *n* a fixture for controlling the flow of a liquid ⟨a hot water *valve*⟩ — see FAUCET

vamoose *vb* to leave a place often for another ⟨it's getting late, so we had better *vamoose*⟩ — see GO 2

vamp (up) *vb* to create or think of by clever use of the imagination ⟨political spin doctors who can *vamp up* a justification for just about anything⟩ — see INVENT

vampire *n* a person who habitually preys upon others ⟨regarded debt collectors as *vampires* who made a living from the misery of others⟩ — see PREDATOR

van *n* **1** the innovators of new concepts, styles, and techniques especially in the arts ⟨an artist who was in the *van* of abstract expressionism⟩ — see AVANT-GARDE
2 the leading or most important part of a movement ⟨a company that is considered by some to be in the *van* of the latest technology for renewable energy⟩ — see FOREFRONT

vandal *n* a person who damages or destroys property on purpose ⟨a group of *vandals* broke into the school and painted graffiti on the walls⟩
synonyms defacer
related words graffitist, tagger; demolisher, desecrater (*or* desecrator), despoiler, destroyer, ravager, ruiner, saboteur, waster, wrecker; depredator, looter, marauder, pillager, plunderer, ransacker, sacker, spoiler, spoliator

near antonyms conserver, preserver, protector, saver; conservator, preservationist

vandalism *n* deliberate damaging or destroying of another's property ⟨anyone guilty of *vandalism* to university property will be expelled⟩
synonyms defacement, defacing, trashing, vandalization
related words demolishing, demolishment, desecrating, desecration, destruction, ravage, ravaging, ruin, ruination, wrecking; sabotage; depredation, despoiling, despoilment, looting, marauding, pillage, pillaging, plunder, plundering, predation, ransacking, sacking, spoliation
near antonyms conservation, preservation, protection, salvage, saving

vandalization *n* deliberate damaging or destroying of another's property ⟨colorizing that classic black-and-white film would be an unforgivable act of cinematic *vandalization*⟩ — see VANDALISM

vandalize *vb* to deliberately cause the damage or destruction of another's property ⟨he decided to *vandalize* the store because the owner had kicked him out⟩
synonyms deface, trash
related words desecrate, violate; graffiti, tag; bang up, break, damage, harm, hurt, impair, mar, shatter, spoil; annihilate, demolish, destroy, devastate, ravage, raven, raze, ruin, scourge, smash, tear down, total, waste, wipe out, wrack, wreck; sabotage; depredate, despoil, loot, maraud, pillage, plunder, ransack, sack, spoliate
near antonyms conserve, preserve, protect, save; salvage; build, rebuild

vanguard *n* **1** the innovators of new concepts, styles, and techniques especially in the arts ⟨a style of jazz that the *vanguard* quickly recognized as new and exciting⟩ — see AVANT-GARDE
2 the leading or most important part of a movement ⟨talk radio is often regarded as being in the *vanguard* of the conservative movement⟩ — see FOREFRONT

vanilla *adj* lacking in distinctive features or qualities ⟨a plain *vanilla* version of a song that's been recorded more times than necessary⟩ — see NONDESCRIPT

vanish *vb* to cease to be visible ⟨the house *vanished* into the fog as we drove away⟩ — see DISAPPEAR

vanished *adj* no longer existing ⟨the *vanished* tradition of the maypole as the center for May Day festivities⟩ — see EXTINCT

vanity *n* an often unjustified feeling of being pleased with oneself or with one's situation or achievements ⟨an all-consuming *vanity* that made him hunger for constant praise from others⟩ — see COMPLACENCE 1

vanquish *vb* to bring under one's control by force of arms ⟨*vanquished* nation after nation in his relentless conquest of Europe⟩ — see CONQUER 1

vanquisher *n* one that defeats an enemy or opponent ⟨a parade for the triumphal return of the empire's most celebrated *vanquisher*⟩ — see VICTOR 1

vanquishing *n* the act or process of bringing someone or something under one's control ⟨a movie about the *vanquishing* of Egypt by Rome⟩ — see CONQUEST

vantage *n* the more favorable condition or position in a competition ⟨the *vantage* had all been ours for the first half of the contest⟩ — see ADVANTAGE 1

vantage point *n* a way of looking at or thinking about something ⟨who started the argument apparently depends on your *vantage point*⟩ — see PERSPECTIVE 1

vapor *vb* to praise or express pride in one's own possessions, qualities, or accomplishments often to excess ⟨a faded Southern belle tiresomely *vaporing* about all the handsome beaux she had in her long-ago youth⟩ — see BOAST 1

vaporize *vb* to bring to a complete end the physical soundness, existence, or usefulness of ⟨a lightning strike *vaporized* the tree⟩ — see DESTROY 1

variable *adj* **1** capable of being readily changed ⟨a *variable* expense that we could reduce if we needed to⟩ — see FLEXIBLE 1
2 likely to change frequently, suddenly, or unexpectedly ⟨highly *variable* income from his job as a real estate agent⟩ — see FICKLE 1

variance *n* a lack of agreement or harmony ⟨persistent *variance* within the rock band eventually caused it to break up⟩ — see DISCORD

variation *n* **1** a distinct treatment of something (as a story or a play) ⟨the movie begins with a somewhat irreverent *variation* on the Nativity story⟩ — see RIFF
2 the act, process, or result of making different ⟨the latest in a long line of *variations* in her hair color⟩ — see CHANGE 1

varicolored *adj* marked by a variety of usually vivid colors ⟨a brilliantly *varicolored* tapestry⟩ — see COLORFUL

varicose *also* **varicosed** *adj* enlarged beyond normal from internal pressure ⟨*varicose* blood vessels⟩ — see BLOATED 2

varied *adj* **1** consisting of many things of different sorts ⟨the museum's highly *varied* collection of works of art⟩ — see MISCELLANEOUS
2 marked by a variety of usually vivid colors ⟨an annual springtime event during which birders get to observe these migratory birds in their *varied* breeding plumage⟩ — see COLORFUL

variegated *adj* **1** marked by a variety of usually vivid colors ⟨the *variegated* costumes of the dancers in the nightclub⟩ — see COLORFUL
2 marked with spots ⟨a variety of *variegated* tulip that is highly prized by gardeners⟩ — see SPOTTED 1

variety *n* **1** the quality or state of being composed of many different elements or types ⟨the sheer *variety* of the city's ethnic restaurants was dazzling⟩
synonyms assortment, diverseness, diversity, heterogeneity, heterogeneousness, manifoldness, miscellaneousness, multifariousness, multiplicity, variousness
related words disparateness, disparity, dissimilarity, distinction, distinctiveness, distinctness, otherness, unlikeness
near antonyms homogeneity, homogeneousness, likeness, sameness, similarity; fewness, paucity
2 an unorganized collection or mixture of various things ⟨every kitchen has a drawer crammed with a *variety* of things for which there just doesn't seem to be any other place⟩ — see MISCELLANY 1
3 a number of persons or things that are grouped together because they have something in common ⟨I prefer movies of the horror *variety*⟩ — see SORT 1

various *adj* marked by a variety of usually vivid colors ⟨for their *various* and bizarrely shaped plumage, males of the bird of paradise species have few rivals⟩ — see COLORFUL

variousness *n* the quality or state of being composed of many different elements or types ⟨the outfits that he wears are always interesting for their *variousness* and unpredictability⟩ — see VARIETY 1

varlet *n* a mean, evil, or unprincipled person ⟨challenged the dastardly *varlet* to a duel⟩ — see VILLAIN

varmint *n* a person whose behavior is offensive to others ⟨a seedy saloon that attracts the most low-down, dirty *varmints* in town⟩ — see JERK 1

vary *vb* **1** to be unlike; to not be the same ⟨opinions by experts on the subject *vary*⟩ — see DIFFER 1
2 to make different in some way ⟨*varied* the method occasionally for the sake of experimentation⟩ — see CHANGE 1
3 to occur within a continuous range of variation ⟨the appliance store is offering discounts that *vary* from 10

to 40 percent, depending upon the brand⟩ — see RUN 4
4 to pass from one form, state, or level to another ⟨terrain that constantly *varied* as we traveled from the coast to the interior⟩ — see CHANGE 2

varying *adj* not staying constant ⟨a *varying* commitment to the cause that meant that one could never be sure if the volunteers would show up⟩ — see UNEVEN 2

vast *adj* unusually large ⟨a *vast* expanse of land just waiting to be settled⟩ — see HUGE

vastitude *n* the quality or state of being very large ⟨the *vastitude* of the ocean, especially when contemplated from the deck of a small boat⟩ — see IMMENSITY

vastly *adv* **1** to a great degree ⟨the team has *vastly* improved in the course of the season⟩ — see VERY 1
2 to a large extent or degree ⟨*vastly* underestimated the cost of advertising the new product⟩ — see GREATLY 2

vastness *n* the quality or state of being very large ⟨awed by the *vastness* of the prairie⟩ — see IMMENSITY

vasty *adj* unusually large ⟨the days when intrepid explorers sailed the *vasty* deep in small vessels⟩ — see HUGE

vaticinate *vb* to tell of or describe beforehand ⟨if he could really *vaticinate* the course of the stock market, he'd be rich enough to own Manhattan⟩ — see FORETELL

vaticination *n* a declaration that something will happen in the future ⟨the myopic prewar *vaticinations* that the conflict would be brief and relatively painless⟩ — see PREDICTION

[1]vault *n* an underground burial chamber ⟨archaeologists were thrilled to discover an ancient *vault* that hadn't been looted by grave robbers⟩ — see CRYPT

[2]vault *n* an act of leaping into the air ⟨a *vault* over the car's hood by the frightened deer⟩ — see JUMP 1

vault *vb* to propel oneself upward or forward into the air ⟨*vaulted* over the obstacle with ease⟩ — see JUMP 1

vaunt *vb* to praise or express pride in one's own possessions, qualities, or accomplishments often to excess ⟨even the noblest of fellows have been known to *vaunt* a bit⟩ — see BOAST 1

vaunter *n* someone who boasts ⟨like so many *vaunters* of the nation's military might, he never personally felt the need to serve in the armed forces⟩ — see BRAGGART

veer *vb* **1** to change one's course or direction ⟨at this point the river *veers* to the southwest before finally emptying into the Atlantic Ocean⟩ — see TURN 3
2 to change the course or direction of (something) ⟨*veered* the ship abruptly to the right to avoid a collision⟩ — see TURN 2
3 to depart abruptly from a straight line or course ⟨without warning the car *veered* to the left and into an oncoming truck⟩ — see SWERVE 1

vegetation *n* green leaves or plants ⟨the local *vegetation* is flourishing as a result of the recent rains⟩ — see GREENERY

veg out *vb* to spend time doing nothing ⟨after an exhausting week at work, I just want to spend the weekend *vegging out*⟩ — see IDLE

vehemence *n* **1** the quality or state of being forceful (as in expression) ⟨the *vehemence* in her voice when she insisted that she never gossiped surprised me⟩
synonyms aggressiveness, assertiveness, emphasis, fierceness, forcefulness, intenseness, intensity, vigorousness, violence
related words potency, power, strength; eloquence; ardency, ardor, fervency, fervidness, fervor, insistence, passion, warmth; stridency, vociferousness; absoluteness, clearness, directness, incision, incisiveness, plainness, straightforwardness, vividness
near antonyms ambiguity, equivocation; delicacy, lightness, subtlety
antonyms feebleness, mildness, weakness
2 depth of feeling ⟨every cause that she pursues is pursued with great *vehemence*⟩ — see ARDOR 1

vehement *adj* **1** marked by or uttered with forcefulness ⟨*vehement* complaints about the restaurant's poor service⟩ — see EMPHATIC 1
2 extreme in degree, power, or effect ⟨despite the *vehement* opposition of the club's treasurer, the motion was passed⟩ — see INTENSE 1
3 having or expressing great depth of feeling ⟨a *vehement* defender of the rights of minorities⟩ — see FERVENT 1

vehicle *n* **1** something used to achieve an end ⟨used organized protests as a *vehicle* for change⟩ — see AGENT 1
2 something used to carry goods or passengers ⟨bought a larger *vehicle* after they had a third baby⟩ — see CONVEYANCE

veil *n* something that covers or conceals like a piece of cloth ⟨under the *veil* of descending darkness the thieves began their operation⟩ — see CLOAK 1

veil *vb* **1** to keep secret or shut off from view ⟨a thicket of bushes *veils* the private beach from the road⟩ — see [1]HIDE 2
2 to surround or cover closely ⟨morning fog *veiled* the fields⟩ — see ENFOLD 1

vein *n* a distinctive way of putting ideas into words ⟨the author goes on in that sarcastic *vein* for pages⟩ — see STYLE 1

veld *or* **veldt** *n* a broad area of level or rolling treeless country ⟨lions prowling the African *veld*⟩ — see PLAIN 1

velocipede *n, archaic* a two-wheeled vehicle that is propelled by the use of pedals and steered through the use of handlebars ⟨a museum with an interesting collection of 19th-century *velocipedes*⟩ — see BICYCLE

velocity *n* a high rate of movement or performance ⟨the *velocity* of light is about 186,000 miles per second⟩ — see SPEED 1

velvetlike *adj* smooth or delicate in appearance or feel ⟨the growing antlers of a young deer are covered with a *velvetlike* skin⟩ — see SOFT 2

velvety *adj* smooth or delicate in appearance or feel ⟨a dog's *velvety* ears⟩ — see SOFT 2

venal *adj* open to improper influence and especially bribery ⟨that judge is known for being *venal* and easily bought⟩
synonyms bribable, corruptible, dirty, purchasable
related words temptable; hack, mercenary; crooked, cutthroat, dishonest, Machiavellian, unethical, unmoral, unprincipled, unscrupulous; corrupt, corrupted, debased, debauched, defiled, degenerate, degraded, demoralized, depraved, dissipated, dissolute, perverse, perverted, reprobate, sleazy, vitiated, warped; bad, evil, immoral, iniquitous, nefarious, sinful, vicious, wicked
near antonyms ethical, honest, principled, scrupulous; good, moral, righteous, upright, virtuous
antonyms incorruptible

vend *vb* to offer for sale to the public ⟨*vends* snack foods and novelties at fairs⟩ — see MARKET

vendor *also* **vender** *n* the person in a business deal who hands over an item in exchange for money ⟨we're thinking of making a deal with that other software *vendor*⟩
synonyms broker, dealer, merchandiser, seller
related words merchant, trader, tradesman; auctioneer, concessionaire; black marketer (*or* black marketeer), bootlegger, fence, fencer, hustler, scalper, smuggler, trafficker; discounter, distributor, e-tailer, exporter, jobber, reseller, retailer, wholesaler; chapman [*British*], hawker, huckster, peddler (*also* pedlar); salesclerk, salesman, salesperson, saleswoman, shopgirl; bargainer, haggler, horse trader, palterer
near antonyms consumer, end user, user

antonyms buyer, purchaser

veneer *n* **1** a deceptively attractive external appearance ⟨the *veneer* of civility that the neighbors had maintained over the years disappeared with the filing of the first lawsuit⟩ — see GLOSS 1

2 an outer part or layer ⟨the top and sides of the desk are overlaid with cherry *veneers*, while the interior wood is white pine⟩ — see EXTERIOR

venerable *adj* **1** deserving honor and respect especially by reason of age ⟨the *venerable* old man was a cherished source of advice and wisdom for the villagers⟩

synonyms hallowed, revered, reverend, sacred, venerated

related words honorable, reputable, respectable; considered, esteemed, honored, respected, reverenced; admirable, distinguished, estimable, redoubtable, worthy; good, moral, noble, righteous

near antonyms bad, discreditable, disgraceful, dishonorable, disreputable, ignominious, infamous, loose, notorious, shameful; immoral, seamy, shadowy, shady, sordid, unsavory, vile, wicked; base, contemptible, despicable, detestable, dirty, low, mean, wretched

2 dating or surviving from the distant past ⟨a *venerable* tradition that colleges have been maintaining for centuries⟩ — see ANCIENT 1

venerate *vb* to offer honor or respect to (someone) as a divine power ⟨a proper setting in which to *venerate* God⟩ — see WORSHIP 1

venerated *adj* deserving honor and respect especially by reason of age ⟨a beloved and *venerated* professor who has been a fixture on campus for decades⟩ — see VENERABLE 1

venge *vb, archaic* to punish in kind the wrongdoer responsible for ⟨a romance novel featuring a hotheaded hero who is ever ready to *venge* every affront to the family's honor⟩ — see AVENGE

vengeance *n* the act or an instance of responding to an injury with an injury ⟨sought *vengeance* after his sister was murdered⟩ — see REVENGE

vengeful *adj* likely to seek revenge ⟨a *vengeful* person never lets go of a grudge⟩ — see VINDICTIVE

venial *adj* worthy of forgiveness ⟨taking the restaurant's menu as a souvenir seems like a *venial* offense⟩

synonyms condonable, excusable, forgivable, pardonable, remissible, remittable

related words justifiable, redeemable; allowable, permissible; insignificant, minor, petty, trifling, trivial, unimportant; harmless, ignorable, tolerable

near antonyms abominable, criminal, damning, evil, heinous; sinful, vile, wicked

antonyms indefensible, inexcusable, mortal, unforgivable, unjustifiable, unpardonable

venom *n* **1** a substance that by chemical action can kill or injure a living thing ⟨an antidote to snake *venom*⟩ — see POISON

2 the desire to cause pain for the satisfaction of doing harm ⟨a neighborhood gossip of such *venom* that she was feared by all and genuinely liked by no one⟩ — see MALICE

venomous *adj* containing or contaminated with a substance capable of injuring or killing a living thing ⟨a *venomous* arrow⟩ — see POISONOUS

vent *vb* **1** to find emotional release for ⟨*vented* her anger and then quickly calmed down⟩ — see TAKE OUT 1

2 to make known (as an idea, emotion, or opinion) ⟨*vented* his opinions freely and loudly at town meetings⟩ — see EXPRESS 1

3 to throw or give off ⟨a clothes dryer *venting* steam⟩ — see EMIT 1

ventilate *vb* to make known (as an idea, emotion, or opinion) ⟨a person who tends to *ventilate* opinions without first thinking them through⟩ — see EXPRESS 1

ventilated *adj* open to the free circulation of air ⟨if the barn isn't kept *ventilated*, the hay can ignite⟩ — see AIRY 2

venture *n* a risky undertaking ⟨their latest business *venture* failed big-time⟩ — see GAMBLE

venture *vb* **1** to place in danger ⟨don't *venture* more money than you can afford to lose⟩ — see ENDANGER

2 to take a chance on ⟨*ventured* to speak plainly at the meeting⟩ — see RISK 1

venturesome *adj* **1** inclined or willing to take risks ⟨a *venturesome* child tried to climb the huge tree⟩ — see BOLD 1

2 involving potential loss or injury ⟨the first solo pilot to undertake the *venturesome* crossing of the Atlantic Ocean by air⟩ — see DANGEROUS 1

venturous *adj* inclined or willing to take risks ⟨at the time, any woman *venturous* enough to want to be an astronaut faced ridicule⟩ — see BOLD 1

venue *n* **1** a place or opportunity for communicating ideas and information ⟨a cable show might the perfect *venue* for your opinions about local politics⟩

synonyms forum, medium, outlet, platform, soapbox

related words channel, conduit, pipeline; showcase, stage

2 the area or space occupied by or intended for something ⟨the historic library is a perfect *venue* for the series of poetry readings⟩ — see PLACE 1

veracious *adj* **1** being in the habit of telling the truth ⟨he has a reputation for being *veracious*, so people generally take his word for things⟩ — see TRUTHFUL

2 following an original exactly ⟨most readers have accepted the book as a *veracious* account of Samuel Johnson's table talk⟩ — see FAITHFUL 2

3 being in agreement with the truth or a fact or a standard ⟨a novel that presents a fairly *veracious* and unvarnished picture of the lives of affluent suburbanites⟩ — see CORRECT 1

veracity *n* **1** devotion to telling the truth ⟨her innate *veracity* is beyond question⟩ — see HONESTY 1

2 the quality or state of being very accurate ⟨I challenge the *veracity* of many of the quotations in his memoirs, for he recreates conversations that occurred decades ago⟩ — see PRECISION

veranda *or* **verandah** *n* a covered structure adjoining an entrance to a building ⟨whiling away the afternoon from the inn's wide *veranda*⟩ — see PORCH

verbal *adj* **1** of or relating to words or language ⟨the child didn't yet have the *verbal* skills needed to tell the doctor about the pain he was experiencing⟩

synonyms lexical, linguistic (*also* linguistical), rhetorical (*also* rhetoric), vocabular, wordy

related words communicative, conversational

antonyms nonlexical, nonlinguistic, nonverbal

2 made or carried on through speaking rather than in writing ⟨a *verbal* agreement carries less force than a written contract⟩

synonyms nuncupative, oral, spoken, unwritten, viva voce, word-of-mouth

related words consensual, implicit, informal; articulated, verbalized; given, pronounced, said, sounded, stated, told, voiced

near antonyms explicit, formal

antonyms paper, written

verbalism *n* **1** an act, process, or means of putting something into words ⟨the meticulous *verbalism* of the senator's prepared statement suggests that she knew that it would spark controversy⟩ — see EXPRESSION 1

2 the use of too many words to express an idea ⟨prose that is lean, uncluttered, and utterly devoid of any trace of *verbalism*⟩ — see VERBIAGE 1

verbalize *vb* to express (a thought or emotion) in words

⟨couldn't quite *verbalize* the cause of his mental distress⟩ — see SAY 1

verbatim *adv* in the same words ⟨you can't just copy the encyclopedia article *verbatim* for your report—that's plagiarism⟩
synonyms ad verbum, directly, exactly, word for word
related words accurately, precisely; identically; literally
near antonyms basically, essentially, virtually; carelessly, freely, imprecisely, inaccurately, loosely
antonyms inexactly

verbiage *n* **1** the use of too many words to express an idea ⟨teachers loathe the *verbiage* that students resort to in order to pad a paper⟩
synonyms circumlocution, diffuseness, diffusion, garrulity, garrulousness, logorrhea, long-windedness, periphrasis, prolixity, redundancy, verbalism, verboseness, verbosity, windiness, wordage, wordiness
related words circuitousness, circularity, digressiveness; pleonasm, tautology; reiteration, repetition, repetitiousness, repetitiveness; embellishment, embroidering, exaggeration, hyperbole, overstatement
near antonyms brevity, briefness, compactness, conciseness, concision, crispness, pithiness, succinctness, terseness
2 language that is impressive-sounding but not meaningful or sincere ⟨the pretentious *verbiage* that one finds in the reviews of self-important art critics⟩ — see RHETORIC 1
3 the way in which something is put into words ⟨as per the standard *verbiage* of military reports, the assault was launched at "0700 hours"⟩ — see WORDING 1

verbose *adj* using or containing more words than necessary to express an idea ⟨had to wade through a *verbose* letter of complaint⟩ — see WORDY 1

verboseness *n* the use of too many words to express an idea ⟨the *verboseness* of the essay is obviously the result of being forced to meet a minimum-page requirement⟩ — see VERBIAGE 1

verbosity *n* the use of too many words to express an idea ⟨your ideas are good, but your penchant for *verbosity* is unfortunate⟩ — see VERBIAGE 1

verboten *adj* that may not be permitted ⟨a college campus on which any form of hate speech was strictly *verboten*⟩ — see IMPERMISSIBLE

verdant *adj* covered with a thick, healthy natural growth ⟨a beautiful, *verdant* field⟩ — see LUSH 1

verdict *n* **1** a position arrived at after consideration ⟨the marketing consultant's *verdict* was that we were doing just fine⟩ — see DECISION 1
2 an idea that is believed to be true or valid without positive knowledge ⟨was anxious to hear her best friend's *verdict* on her new boyfriend⟩ — see OPINION 1

verdure *n* **1** green leaves or plants ⟨a good time to tour the wine country is when it is clothed with the *verdure* of midsummer⟩ — see GREENERY
2 the condition of being sound in body ⟨a portrait of a fresh-faced teenage girl in all of her youthful *verdure* and irrepressible joie de vivre⟩ — see HEALTH 1

verge *n* **1** an interval of time just before the onset of something ⟨the suspect was on the *verge* of confessing when the officers realized that he hadn't been read his rights⟩ — see POINT 3
2 the line or relatively narrow space that marks the outer limit of something ⟨the southern *verge* of the national park⟩ — see BORDER 1

verge (on) *vb* **1** to be adjacent to ⟨our land *verges on* a wildlife refuge⟩ — see ADJOIN 1
2 to come very close to being ⟨a comment that *verged on* an insult⟩ — see BORDER (ON) 1

verging *adj* having a border in common ⟨the two brothers bought *verging* properties⟩ — see ADJACENT

verifiable *adj* capable of being proven as true or real ⟨we're not sure whether that's a *verifiable* hypothesis⟩ ⟨you need a *verifiable* letter from your doctor to file a claim for short-term disability⟩
synonyms checkable, confirmable, demonstrable, empirical (*also* empiric), provable, supportable, sustainable
related words certifiable, documentable, well-founded; defensible, excusable, justifiable, vindicable, warrantable; alleged, assumed, conjectured, guessed, presumed, surmised, suspected
near antonyms debatable, disprovable, disputable, refutable
antonyms indemonstrable, insupportable, unprovable, unsupportable, unsustainable, unverifiable

verify *vb* to give evidence or testimony to the truth or factualness of ⟨the dispatcher was able to *verify* the caller's location⟩ — see CONFIRM 1

verifying *adj* serving to give support to the truth or factualness of something ⟨failed to produce any *verifying* evidence⟩ — see CORROBORATIVE

verily *adv* **1** to tell the truth ⟨*verily*, I don't remember a single thing about that course⟩ — see ACTUALLY 1
2 not merely this but also ⟨I shall pay back your loan and *verily* do so with considerable interest⟩ — see EVEN 1

verisimilitude *n* realistic depiction in art and literature ⟨the novel's degree of *verisimilitude* is compromised by 18th-century characters who speak in very 21st-century English⟩
synonyms literalism, naturalism, realism, representationalism, verismo
related words photo-realism; authenticity, grittiness

verismo *n* realistic depiction in art and literature ⟨the author of this crime novel uses profuse profanity in the name of *verismo*, but its effectiveness palls after a couple of chapters⟩ — see VERISIMILITUDE

veritably *adv* in actual fact ⟨the view from the summit of the mountain is *veritably* breathtaking⟩ — see VERY 2

verity *n* **1** agreement with fact or reality ⟨the local tourist bureau is less concerned with the *verity* of the legend than the fact that it attracts visitors to the area⟩ — see TRUTH
2 devotion to telling the truth ⟨no one is questioning your *verity*—just your memory of events that happened long ago⟩ — see HONESTY 1

vermin *n* a person whose behavior is offensive to others ⟨the *vermin* who looted abandoned houses after the hurricane⟩ — see JERK 1

vernacular *adj* used in or suitable for speech and not formal writing ⟨writes essays in a very easy-to-read, *vernacular* style⟩ — see COLLOQUIAL 1

versatile *adj* able to do many different kinds of things ⟨a *versatile* baseball player can play any position⟩ ⟨this tool is *versatile* enough to serve as a wrench or pliers⟩
synonyms adaptable, all-around (*also* all-round), protean, universal
related words general-purpose, mixed-use, multipurpose; well-rounded; able, ace, adept, experienced, expert, masterful, proficient, skilled, skillful; adjustable, alterable, changeable, elastic, flexible, fluid, malleable, modifiable, plastic, pliable, pliant, supple, variable
near antonyms limited; amateur, inexperienced

verse *n* **1** a composition using rhythm and often rhyme to create a lyrical effect ⟨composed a short *verse* for his mother's birthday⟩ — see POEM
2 writing that uses rhythm, vivid language, and often rhyme to provoke an emotional response ⟨skilled at *verse*⟩ — see POETRY 1

verse *vb* to give information to ⟨while in prison, he

versed himself in the rights of the incarcerated⟩ — see ENLIGHTEN 1

versed *adj* **1** having information especially as a result of study or experience ⟨*versed* in the latest developments in aeronautics⟩ — see FAMILIAR 2

2 having or showing exceptional knowledge, experience, or skill in a field of endeavor ⟨well *versed* in the techniques of laser surgery⟩ — see PROFICIENT

versifier *n* a person who writes poetry ⟨I may not be a great poet, but I'm as good as those *versifiers* hired by the greeting card companies⟩ — see POET

version *n* a presentation of an artistic work (as a piece of music) from a particular point of view ⟨a very Freudian *version* of the ballet "The Nutcracker"⟩ — see ACCOUNT 2

vertebral column *n* a column of bones supporting the trunk of a vertebrate animal ⟨carefully reconstructed the *vertebral column* of the dinosaur⟩ — see SPINE

vertical *adj* rising straight up ⟨a *vertical* cliff face⟩ — see ERECT

vertiginous *adj* having a feeling of being whirled about and in danger of falling down ⟨a 3-D effect that is likely to leave some audience members feeling *vertiginous*⟩ — see DIZZY 1

verve *adj* active strength of body or mind ⟨the actor plays the part of the superhero with tremendous *verve* and obvious enjoyment⟩ — see VIGOR 1

very *adj* **1** being one and not another ⟨we stayed in the *very* hotel my parents stayed in for their honeymoon⟩ — see SAME 2

2 being this and no more ⟨the *very* thought of having to go through that again is scary⟩ — see MERE

3 existing in fact and not merely as a possibility ⟨tourism is the *very* lifeblood of this community—the town would surely die without it⟩ — see ACTUAL

4 having no exceptions or restrictions ⟨the *very* nerve of that woman—telling me how to raise my own children⟩ — see ABSOLUTE 2

very *adv* **1** to a great degree ⟨that was a *very* brave thing to do⟩

synonyms achingly, almighty, archly, awful, awfully, badly, beastly, blisteringly, bone, colossally, corking, cracking, damn, damned, dang, deadly, desperately, eminently, enormously, especially, ever, exceedingly (*also* exceeding), extra, extremely, fabulously, fantastically, far, fiercely, filthy, frightfully, full, greatly, heavily, highly, hugely, immensely, incredibly, intensely, jolly, majorly, mightily, mighty, monstrous [*chiefly dialect*], mortally, most, much, particularly, passing, rattling, real, really, right, roaring, roaringly, seriously, severely, so, sore, sorely, spanking, specially, stinking, such, super, supremely, surpassingly, terribly, that, thumping, too, unco, uncommonly, vastly, vitally, way, whacking, wicked, wildly

related words absolutely, altogether, completely, downright, entirely, flat-out, fully, positively, purely, radically, thoroughly, totally, utterly, wholly; deeply, profoundly; exceptionally, notably, remarkably; considerably, extensively, significantly, substantially; appreciably, discernibly, markedly, noticeably, obviously, palpably, plainly, visibly; abundantly, plentifully; astronomically, grandly, monstrously, monumentally; excessively, obscenely, overmuch; amazingly, astonishingly, staggeringly

phrases a lot, as all get-out, good and

near antonyms meagerly, scantily; barely, hardly, just, marginally, minimally, scarcely

antonyms little, negligibly, nominally, slightly, somewhat

2 in actual fact ⟨the *very* same thing happened to me⟩

synonyms actually, authentically, certifiably, genuinely, really, truly, veritably

related words accurately, exactly, just, precisely, right, sharp, smack-dab, squarely; almost, nearly, practically, virtually; literally, positively, simply

phrases in actuality, in reality, in truth

near antonyms apparently, ostensibly, outwardly, plausibly, seemingly

antonyms professedly, supposedly

vessel *n* **1** a large craft for travel by water ⟨a new ocean liner that claims to be the largest commercial *vessel* afloat⟩ — see SHIP

2 a small buoyant structure for travel on water ⟨any *vessel* that is buoyant and steerable can be entered in the annual race down the river⟩ — see BOAT 1

3 a usually circular utensil for holding something (as food) ⟨uses a large copper *vessel* for beating egg whites⟩ — see DISH 1

4 something into which a liquid or smaller objects can be put for storage or transportation ⟨any watertight *vessel* can be used for mixing the paints⟩ — see CONTAINER

vest *vb* **1** to give official or legal power to ⟨"By the power *vested* in me by the state," intoned the minister, "I now pronounce that you are married"⟩ — see AUTHORIZE 1

2 to put (something) into the possession or safekeeping of another ⟨*vested* the power to access their retirement accounts with their attorney⟩ — see GIVE 2

3 to give the ownership or benefit of (something) formally or publicly ⟨the U.S. Constitution *vests* the power to declare war with Congress⟩ — see CONFER 1

vestal *adj* free from any trace of the coarse or indecent ⟨a schoolteacher who dresses with almost *vestal* modesty while on the job⟩ — see CHASTE 1

vestiary *n* covering for the human body ⟨in Gainsborough's paintings women are almost always portrayed in a varicolored *vestiary* of satin and silk⟩ — see CLOTHING

vestibule *n* the entrance room of a building ⟨please leave your wet boots in the *vestibule*⟩ — see HALL 1

vestige *n* **1** a tiny often physical indication of something lost or vanished ⟨a few strange words carved on a tree were the only *vestige* of the lost colony of Roanoke⟩

synonyms echo, ghost, relic, shadow, trace

related words memento, remembrance, reminder; artifact; afterimage, aftertaste; balance, corpse, hangover, leftover, oddment, remainder, remnant, scrap; dreg(s), leavings, remain(s), residual, residue, rest

2 the mark or impression made by a foot ⟨the fossilized *vestige* of a dinosaur that traversed that muddy landscape millions of years ago⟩ — see FOOTPRINT

vestments *n pl* covering for the human body ⟨nowadays at adult Halloween parties a lot of women like to wear *vestments* that reveal their inner vixen⟩ — see CLOTHING

vestry *n* a room in a church building for sacred furnishings (as vestments) ⟨the priest returned the chalice to the *vestry*⟩ — see SACRISTY

vesture *n* covering for the human body ⟨the man's sober *vesture* contrasted sharply with his companion's festive finery⟩ — see CLOTHING

vesture *vb* to outfit with clothes and especially fine or special clothes ⟨*vestured* like a queen for her grand birthday party⟩ — see CLOTHE 1

vet *n* a person with long experience in a specified area ⟨he's a hardened *vet* of many political campaigns⟩ — see VETERAN

veteran *adj* having or showing exceptional knowledge, experience, or skill in a field of endeavor ⟨a *veteran* teacher who mentors new teachers⟩ — see PROFICIENT

veteran *n* a person with long experience in a specified area ⟨as a *veteran* of overseas travel, she gave us solid

advice about planning our trip⟩
synonyms doyen, old hand, old-timer, stager, vet, warhorse
related words doyenne; adept, dab hand [*chiefly British*], expert, guru, hand, master, maven (*also* mavin), past master, pro, professional
near antonyms apprentice, cub; boot, novitiate; amateur, dilettante; learner, student, trainee; candidate, entrant, probationer
antonyms beginner, colt, fledgling, freshman, greenhorn, neophyte, newbie, newcomer, novice, recruit, rookie, tenderfoot, tyro

veto *n* an order that something not be done or used ⟨management's *veto* of our suggestion about allowing casual dress on Fridays⟩ — see PROHIBITION 2

veto *vb* to reject by or as if by a vote ⟨my husband quickly *vetoed* my suggestion that we adopt the stray dog⟩ — see NEGATIVE 1

vex *vb* **1** to disturb the peace of mind of (someone) especially by repeated disagreeable acts ⟨my coworkers' loud, endless conversations *vexed* me⟩ — see IRRITATE 1
2 to throw into a state of mental uncertainty ⟨a mystery novel that is sure to *vex* even the canniest readers⟩ — see CONFUSE 1

vexation *n* **1** the act of making unwelcome intrusions upon another ⟨the repeated *vexations* guaranteed that she wouldn't get any work done⟩ — see ANNOYANCE 1
2 the feeling of impatience or anger caused by another's repeated disagreeable acts ⟨he suppressed his rising *vexation* and answered as politely as he could⟩ — see ANNOYANCE 2
3 something that is a source of irritation ⟨add cell phones to the list of *vexations* that theatergoers have to contend with⟩ — see ANNOYANCE 3

vexatious *adj* causing annoyance ⟨those *vexatious* phone calls from telemarketers during the dinner hour⟩ — see ANNOYING

vexed *adj* subjected to and reacting with irritation ⟨my dog was clearly *vexed* with me for having been gone all week, and hardly greeted me when I came home⟩ — see ANNOYED

vexing *adj* causing annoyance ⟨the constantly changing schedule was somewhat *vexing*, but I coped⟩ — see ANNOYING

via *prep* **1** along the way of ⟨we're going to their house *via* the back roads⟩ — see BY 1
2 using the means or agency of ⟨contacted her *via* telephone⟩ — see BY 2

viable *adj* capable of being done or carried out ⟨more research will be required to see if this is a *viable* solution⟩ — see POSSIBLE 1

viand *n* **1** something that is pleasing to eat because it is rare or a luxury ⟨a shop selling caviar, foie gras, designer chocolates, and other pricey *viands*⟩ — see DELICACY 1
2 viands *pl* substances intended to be eaten ⟨the inn serves its choice *viands* on delicate china and its selection of vintage wines in the finest crystal available⟩ — see FOOD 1

vibe *n, usually* **vibes** *pl* a spiritual force that is held to emanate from or give animation to living beings ⟨a book by a professor of physiological science about her experiments with human energy fields and the *vibes* they emanate⟩ — see ENERGY 1

vibrance *n* the quality or state of having abundant or intense activity ⟨new legislation to help small businesses and restore the *vibrance* of the local economy⟩ — see VITALITY 1

vibrancy *n* the quality or state of having abundant or intense activity ⟨the addition of several new stores enhances the *vibrancy* of the town⟩ — see VITALITY 1

vibrant *adj* **1** marked by much life, movement, or activity ⟨was rather overwhelmed by the *vibrant* environment of the big city⟩ — see ALIVE 2
2 marked by conspicuously full and rich sounds or tones ⟨a throaty, *vibrant* singing voice⟩ — see RESONANT

vibrate *vb* to make a series of small irregular or violent movements ⟨the glasses and knickknacks on the shelves *vibrated* during the slight earthquake⟩ — see SHAKE 1

vibration *n* **1** a series of slight movements by a body back and forth or from side to side ⟨the *vibration* of the floor caused by thundering feet in the hallway⟩
synonyms jiggling, oscillation, quivering, shaking, shivering, shuddering, trembling, twitching
related words juddering [*chiefly British*], quaking, rocking; jiggle, palpitation, quiver, shake, shiver, shudder, tremble, tremor, twitch
2 *often* **vibrations** *pl* a spiritual force that is held to emanate from or give animation to living beings ⟨the Eastern holisitc philosophy that unhappy thoughts disrupt the *vibrations* from one's energy field, causing illness⟩ — see ENERGY 1
3 *usually* **vibrations** *pl* a special quality or impression associated with something ⟨although the murders happened long ago, visitors to the house claim that it still gives off unsettling *vibrations*⟩ — see AURA 1

vice *n* **1** immoral conduct or practices harmful or offensive to society ⟨that section of the city is legendary for crime and *vice*⟩
synonyms corruption, debauchery, depravity, immorality, iniquitousness, iniquity, libertinage, libertinism, licentiousness, profligacy, sin
related words bad, badness, blackness, evil, evildoing, ill, turpitude, villainy, wickedness, wrong; atrociousness, evilness, heinousness, sinfulness, unscrupulousness, viciousness, vileness, villainousness; devilry (*or* deviltry), fiendishness; corruptness, debasement, degeneracy, degeneration, depravedness, dissoluteness, dissolution; indecency, lasciviousness, lechery, lewdness, looseness, perversion, pervertedness, wantonness; abomination, anathema, taboo (*also* tabu); criminality, reprehensibleness; baseness, despicableness, dirtiness, lowness, meanness; lousiness, miserableness, wretchedness
near antonyms good, right; honesty, honor, integrity, legitimacy, probity, rectitude, scrupulosity, scrupulousness, uprightness; goodness, righteousness, virtuousness; blamelessness; chastity, innocence, perfection, pureness, purity, spotlessness; cleanness, correctness, decency, decorousness, propriety, rightness, seemliness
antonyms morality, virtue
2 a defect in character ⟨curiosity in children is not a *vice*, but something to be encouraged⟩ — see FAULT 1
3 the practice of engaging in sexual activities for money ⟨a seedy section of the city where *vice* is rampant and very much out in the open⟩ — see PROSTITUTION

vicinage *n* an adjoining region or space ⟨potential jurors were to be drawn from the *vicinage* in which the crime occurred⟩ — see ENVIRONS 2

vicinity *n* **1** an adjoining region or space ⟨there are no hotels in the *vicinity* of the hospital⟩ — see ENVIRONS 2
2 the state or condition of being near ⟨the *vicinity* of the town's only elementary school was one reason why the young couple bought the house⟩ — see PROXIMITY
3 an approximate amount, extent, or degree ⟨starting salaries in that field are in the *vicinity* of $50,000 a year⟩ — see NEIGHBORHOOD 1

vicious *adj* **1** extreme in degree, power, or effect ⟨a *vicious* winter storm ripped through the region⟩ — see INTENSE 1
2 having or showing the desire to inflict severe pain and suffering on others ⟨she made a *vicious* effort to destroy

the lives of the people who had wronged her⟩ — see CRUEL 1

3 not conforming to a high moral standard; morally unacceptable ⟨the truly *vicious* philosophy of that racist organization⟩ — see BAD 2

4 violently unfriendly or aggressive in disposition ⟨a *vicious* dog that has already bitten several people⟩ — see FIERCE 1

5 having or showing a desire to cause someone pain or suffering for the sheer enjoyment of it ⟨he spread *vicious* rumors about his ex-wife after their bitter divorce⟩ — see HATEFUL

viciously *adv* in a mean or spiteful manner ⟨the administrator *viciously* denied me the time off that I needed to attend my dear aunt's funeral⟩ — see NASTILY

viciousness *n* **1** the desire to cause pain for the satisfaction of doing harm ⟨simple *viciousness* can be the only reason for spreading such vile, unfounded rumors⟩ — see MALICE

2 disposition to willfully inflict pain and suffering on others ⟨the unspeakable *viciousness* of the medical experiments carried out at the concentration camps⟩ — see CRUELTY

victim *n* **1** a person or thing harmed, lost, or destroyed ⟨helped the *victims* of the fire⟩ — see CASUALTY 1

2 a person or thing that is the object of abuse, criticism, or ridicule ⟨the *victim* of schoolyard teasing⟩ — see TARGET 1

3 something offered to a god ⟨the Aztecs are believed to have sacrificed thousands of *victims* annually to the sun⟩ — see SACRIFICE

victimize *vb* to rob by the use of trickery or threats ⟨*victimized* by a confidence man with a slick story⟩ — see FLEECE

victor *n* **1** one that defeats an enemy or opponent ⟨the computer is usually the *victor* in a chess match against a human opponent⟩

synonyms beater, conqueror, master, subduer, trimmer, vanquisher, whipper, winner

related words champ, champion, finalist, placer; dominator, overdog, ruler, subjugator, top dog

near antonyms punching bag, pushover, quitter; failure, flop, washout; underdog

antonyms loser

2 the person who comes in first in a competition ⟨the *victor* in the science fair had constructed a functioning telescope⟩ — see CHAMPION 1

Victorian *adj* given to or marked by very conservative standards regarding personal behavior or morals ⟨a conservative Christian sect with a code of sexual morality that is often seen as quaintly *Victorian* by outsiders⟩ — see STRAITLACED

victory *n* an instance of defeating an enemy or opponent ⟨with great effort, our team managed an upset *victory* in the final moments⟩

synonyms palm, triumph, win

related words capture, conquest, mastery, subjugation, vanquishing; blowout, landslide, laugher, romp, runaway, shutout, sweep, walkaway, walkover; squeaker; success; takeover

near antonyms upset; collapse, debacle (*also* débâcle), disaster, failure, fizzle, flop, nonsuccess, washout; decline, slip, slump, wane; lurch, setback

antonyms beating, defeat, drubbing, licking, loss, overthrow, rout, shellacking, trimming, whipping

victual *vb* **1** to provide food or meals for ⟨the navy was usually equipped, clothed and *victualled* by the Crown⟩ — see FEED 1

2 to take a meal ⟨that evening the travelers *victualed* sumptuously on partridge and venison⟩ — see DINE 1

victuals *n pl* substances intended to be eaten ⟨sat down with a plate of hearty *victuals* and a mug of ale⟩ — see FOOD 1

vid *n* a recording (as of a movie) on magnetic tape for playback on a TV ⟨a *vid* of the pop star performing her latest hit single⟩ — see VIDEO

videlicet *adv* that is to say ⟨the meaning of the Constitution is determined by one—and only one—body, *videlicet*, the U.S. Supreme Court⟩ — see NAMELY

video *n* a recording (as of a movie) on magnetic tape for playback on a TV ⟨every Thanksgiving, our family watches *videos* of past holiday gatherings⟩

synonyms tape, tape recording, vid, videotape

related words DVD, laser disc; videocassette, videodisc (*or* videodisk)

videotape *n* a recording (as of a movie) on magnetic tape for playback on a TV ⟨watched a *videotape* of her daughter's first ballet recital⟩ — see VIDEO

vie *vb* to engage in a contest ⟨*vied* with his colleagues for the coveted promotion⟩ — see COMPETE

view *n* **1** all that can be seen from a certain point ⟨the *view* of the mountains from the inn's porch is spectacular⟩

synonyms command, lookout, outlook, panorama, perspective, prospect, vista

related words landscape, scene, scenery; ken, sight; visual field

2 an idea that is believed to be true or valid without positive knowledge ⟨that's one *view*, but I happen to disagree⟩ — see OPINION 1

3 an instance of looking especially briefly ⟨took a quick *view* of the Web page and decided that it didn't have what he was looking for⟩ — see LOOK 2

4 a close look at or over someone or something in order to judge condition ⟨upon closer *view* the painting was an obvious forgery⟩ — see INSPECTION

view *vb* **1** to look over closely (as for judging quality or condition) ⟨I'll have to *view* all of the evidence before making a decision⟩ — see INSPECT

2 to make note of (something) through the use of one's eyes ⟨*viewed* the latest changes and approved them⟩ — see SEE 1

3 to think of in a particular way ⟨I *view* housework as a necessary evil⟩ — see CONSIDER 1

viewer *n* someone who sees or watches something ⟨*viewers* of the police videotape are divided in their opinions as to what it actually shows⟩ — see SPECTATOR

viewpoint *n* a way of looking at or thinking about something ⟨from my *viewpoint* the rule against slogans on T-shirts infringes on my right to free speech⟩ — see PERSPECTIVE 1

vigil *n* an act or period of watching for signs of activity, danger, or opportunity ⟨kept *vigil* at their ailing son's bedside the entire time he was in the hospital⟩

synonyms lookout, surveillance, watch

related words observance, observation, supervision; inspection, scrutiny

vigilance *n* the state of being constantly attentive and responsive to signs of opportunity, activity, or danger ⟨eternal *vigilance* is the price of freedom⟩

synonyms alert, alertness, attentiveness, qui vive, red alert, watch, watchfulness

related words aliveness, awareness, consciousness, mindfulness, receptiveness, receptivity, sensitivity; care, carefulness, cautiousness, chariness, heedfulness, wariness; preparation, readiness

near antonyms absentmindedness, abstraction, daydreaming, daze, distraction; absorption, engrossment, obliviousness, preoccupation; unawareness, unconsciousness; carelessness, heedlessness, inattention, inattentiveness, inobservance; unwariness

vigilant *adj* paying close attention usually for the purpose of anticipating approaching danger or opportunity ⟨the night watchman, who was usually *vigilant*, apparently dozed off and didn't notice the vandals sneaking in⟩ — see ALERT 1

vigilante *n* one who inflicts punishment in return for an injury or offense ⟨the danger of these self-appointed *vigilantes* is that they sometimes go after innocent people⟩ — see NEMESIS 1

vignette *n* a vivid representation in words of someone or something ⟨the general's memoirs are filled with revealing *vignettes* of some of the war's most compelling personalities⟩ — see DESCRIPTION 1

vigor *n* **1** active strength of body or mind ⟨she was picked to lead the volunteer group because of her *vigor* and enthusiasm⟩
synonyms beans, bounce, brio, dash, drive, dynamism, energy, esprit, gas, get-up-and-go, ginger, go, gusto, hardihood, juice, life, moxie, oomph, pep, punch, sap, snap, starch, verve, vim, vinegar, vitality, zing, zip
related words animal spirits, animation, briskness, jauntiness, liveliness, snappiness, spirit, spiritedness, sprightliness, spunk, spunkiness, vibrance, vibrancy, vivaciousness, vivacity; ardor, élan, fervor, fire, passion, zeal; main, metal, mettle, might, muscle, potency, power, puissance, stamina, strength; brawniness, fitness, hardiness, huskiness, sturdiness, virility; health, healthiness, soundness, verdure, wellness
near antonyms indolence, laziness; debilitation, debility, delicacy, disablement, enfeeblement, faintness, feebleness, frailness, frailty, impotence, impotency, infirmity, powerlessness, puniness, slightness, softness, tenderness, weakness; enervation, exhaustion, inanition, prostration
antonyms lethargy, listlessness, sluggishness, torpidity
2 the ability to exert effort for the accomplishment of a task ⟨a drug for lowering cholesterol that acts with proven *vigor*⟩ — see POWER 2

vigorous *adj* **1** having active strength of body or mind ⟨he remains healthy and *vigorous* despite being over 80 years old⟩
synonyms dynamic, energetic, flush, gingery, lusty, peppy, red-blooded, robust, vital
related words animated, brisk, dashing, kinetic, lively, punchy, spirited, sprightly, vivacious; energized, enlivened, invigorated, vitalized; firm, fortified, mettlesome, mighty, powerful, puissant, strong; refreshed, rejuvenated, revitalized; able-bodied, athletic, beefy, brawny, burly, fit, hardy, husky, muscular, robustious, rugged, stalwart, stout, strapping, sturdy, tough, virile; hale, healthy, hearty, sound; capable, competent
near antonyms delicate, effete, enervated, faint, feeble, frail, infirm, wan, weak, weakened; impotent, powerless, prostrate, prostrated, sapped, tired; indolent, lackadaisical, languid, lazy; invertebrate, nerveless, soft, spineless, wimpy; ill, unhealthy, unsound, unwell; broken-down, debilitated, decrepit, disabled, wasted, worn-out
antonyms dull, lethargic, listless, sluggish, torpid
2 able to withstand hardship, strain, or exposure ⟨*vigorous* and sturdy little sheep bred to live in mountainous regions⟩ — see HARDY 1
3 marked by or uttered with forcefulness ⟨offered a *vigorous* dissent to the proposal⟩ — see EMPHATIC 1
4 not showing weakness or uncertainty ⟨gave the bottle of sauce a *vigorous* shaking⟩ — see FIRM 1

vigorously *adv* in a vigorous and forceful manner ⟨*vigorously* shook my hand and told me how happy he was to be there⟩ — see HARD 3

vigorousness *n* **1** the quality or state of being forceful (as in expression) ⟨the *vigorousness* of the ideas in the essay was surpassed only by the vibrancy of its language⟩ — see VEHEMENCE 1
2 the quality or state of having abundant or intense activity ⟨the record-breaking holiday sales reflect the *vigorousness* of the economy⟩ — see VITALITY 1

vile *adj* **1** not conforming to a high moral standard; morally unacceptable ⟨a *vile* plot to murder their political enemies⟩ — see BAD 2
2 not following or in accordance with standards of honor and decency ⟨a *vile* trick to play on someone⟩ — see IGNOBLE 2
3 unpleasant to look at ⟨an outfit with a truly *vile* combination of colors⟩ — see UGLY 1

vileness *n* the state or quality of being utterly evil ⟨no one can question the sheer *vileness* of this act of terrorism⟩ — see ENORMITY 1

vilification *n* the making of false statements that damage another's reputation ⟨warned that the constant *vilification* of candidates for public office was undermining the people's faith in the political system⟩ — see SLANDER

vilify *vb* to make untrue and harmful statements about ⟨claimed that she had been *vilified* by the press because of her conservative views⟩ — see SLANDER

vilifying *n* the making of false statements that damage another's reputation ⟨the nonstop *vilifying* had the effect of making some people sympathetic to the victim⟩ — see SLANDER

vilipend *vb* to express scornfully one's low opinion of ⟨one of those elitists who regularly *vilipends* popular culture⟩ — see DECRY 1

vill *n* a small residential settlement ⟨an ancient *vill* nestled midst the verdant hills⟩ — see VILLAGE

villa *n* a large impressive residence ⟨a millionaire with a luxurious *villa* in Mexico⟩ — see MANSION

village *n* a small residential settlement ⟨we stayed in a charming bed-and-breakfast in a lakeside *village*⟩
synonyms bourg, hamlet, townlet, vill, whistle-stop
related words cow town, Podunk; outpost

villager *n* a person who lives in a town on a permanent basis ⟨the *villagers* have a reputation for being polite and helpful to the tourists⟩ — see BURGHER

villain *n* a mean, evil, or unprincipled person ⟨only a heartless *villain* would kidnap a baby for ransom⟩
synonyms baddie (*or* baddy), beast, brute, caitiff, devil, evildoer, fiend, heavy, hound, knave, meanie (*also* meany), miscreant, monster, nazi, no-good, rapscallion, rascal, reprobate, rogue, savage, scalawag (*or* scallywag), scamp, scapegrace, scoundrel, varlet, wretch
related words villainess; blackguard; criminal, crook, culprit, felon, lawbreaker, malefactor, offender, perp, perpetrator, transgressor; sinner, trespasser, wrongdoer; cad, heel, serpent, snake, viper; bandit, bravo, desperado, outlaw; con, convict, jailbird; assassin, cutthroat, gangster, goon, gunman, hoodlum, hooligan, racketeer, ruffian, thug; rough, rowdy, tough; loser, lowlife, ne'er-do-well, stinker, trash
near antonyms angel, innocent, saint; hero

villainous *adj* not conforming to a high moral standard; morally unacceptable ⟨*villainous* behavior that made him one of the most notorious figures in history and gave rise to the legend of Dracula⟩ — see BAD 2

villainously *adv* in a mean or spiteful manner ⟨the robber *villainously* snatched the necklace from the old woman's throat⟩ — see NASTILY

villainy *n* that which is morally unacceptable ⟨psychologists and sociologists have tried to discover the roots of such unspeakable *villainy*⟩ — see EVIL

vim *n* active strength of body or mind ⟨some food and a little rest should give me back some of my *vim*⟩ — see VIGOR 1

vindicate *vb* **1** to free from a charge of wrongdoing

⟨vowed that the evidence would completely *vindicate* him⟩ — see EXCULPATE

2 to give evidence or testimony to the truth or factualness of ⟨recent discoveries have generally *vindicated* the physicist's theories⟩ — see CONFIRM 1

vindicating *adj* serving to give support to the truth or factualness of something ⟨*vindicating* documents have turned up only recently⟩ — see CORROBORATIVE

vindication *n* a setting free from a charge of wrongdoing ⟨recanted testimony that resulted in a long-overdue *vindication*⟩ — see ACQUITTAL

vindictive *adj* likely to seek revenge ⟨be careful not to annoy the *vindictive* old woman who lives down the street⟩

synonyms revengeful, vengeful

related words avenging, retaliatory; resentful, uncharitable, unforgiving; catty, cruel, despiteful, hateful, malevolent, malicious, malign, malignant, mean, nasty, sadistic, spiteful, venomous, vicious, viperish, virulent; narrow-minded, petty, small-minded; grim, implacable, merciless, pitiless, relentless, unrelenting; baleful, baneful, evil; harsh, hostile, inimical, wrathful

near antonyms charitable, forgiving, merciful, relenting; benevolent, benign, benignant, loving; brotherly, compassionate, good, good-hearted, kind, kindhearted, kindly, sympathetic, warm, warmhearted; altruistic, humane, humanitarian, philanthropic (*also* philanthropical); sweet, tender, tenderhearted; high-minded, magnanimous, noble

vinegar *n* active strength of body or mind ⟨glad to see his old friend was still full of *vinegar* after so many years⟩ — see VIGOR 1

vinegary *adj* causing or characterized by the one of the four basic taste sensations that is produced chiefly by acids ⟨*vinegary* potato salad⟩ — see SOUR 1

vintage *adj* pleasantly reminiscent of an earlier time ⟨the designer's bracelets and necklaces have the *vintage* look of jewelry from the 1920s⟩ — see OLD-FASHIONED 1

violate *vb* **1** to fail to keep ⟨you've *violated* the company's new rule against smoking within 30 feet of the building⟩

synonyms breach, break, contravene, fracture, infringe, offend, traduce, transgress

related words disobey, rebel; blow off, brush (off), disregard, flout, ignore, neglect, overlook, overpass, pass over, slight, tune out, wink (at); dismiss, pooh-pooh (*also* pooh), scorn, shrug off; defy, resist, withstand

near antonyms defer (to), serve, submit (to), surrender (to), yield (to); attend, hear, heed, listen (to), mark, note, notice, regard, watch

antonyms comply (with), conform (to), follow, mind, obey, observe

2 to treat (a sacred place or object) shamefully or with great disrespect ⟨the invaders *violated* the temple by using it to stable their horses⟩ — see DESECRATE

3 to engage in sexual activity and especially intercourse with a person unwilling or unable to give consent ⟨the youthful offender had been in prison barely a week when he was *violated* in the shower room⟩ — see RAPE

violation *n* **1** a breaking of a moral or legal code ⟨in colonial times blasphemy was considered a serious civil *violation* that merited harsh punishment⟩ — see OFFENSE 1

2 a failure to uphold the requirements of law, duty, or obligation ⟨a military action that must be regarded as a *violation* of the treaty⟩ — see BREACH 1

3 the act of forcing a person to engage in sexual activity and especially intercourse ⟨the time-honored brutalities of war include the *violation* of the enemy's womenfolk⟩ — see RAPE 1

violence *n* **1** the use of brute strength to cause harm to a person or property ⟨the police believe that the woman died of natural causes rather than as a result of *violence*⟩

synonyms force, foul play

related words coercion, compulsion, constraint, duress, pressure; barbarity, brutality, savagery; damage, detriment, harm, hurt, impairment, injury; crippling, maiming, mayhem, mutilation; assault, attack, bashing, battering, battery, batting, beating, belting, bludgeoning, buffeting, clubbing, cudgeling (*or* cudgelling), drubbing, flogging, hammering, lacing, licking, mauling, paddling, pelting, pommeling (*or* pommelling), pounding, pummeling (*also* pummelling), smashing, socking, thrashing, thumping, tromping, walloping, whaling, whipping; frenzy, fury, onslaught, outbreak, outrage, paroxysm, rage, rampage, revolt, riot, rupture, shock, storm, terror, threat, tumult, turbulence, upheaval, uproar; browbeating, bulldozing, bullying, hectoring, strong-arming

near antonyms pacificism, pacifism

antonyms nonviolence

2 the quality or state of being forceful (as in expression) ⟨taken aback by the *violence* of her denial of any wrongdoing⟩ — see VEHEMENCE 1

3 depth of feeling ⟨some people were taken aback by the *violence* with which the magazine's art critic attacked the exhibition⟩ — see ARDOR 1

violent *adj* **1** marked by bursts of destructive force or intense activity ⟨a *violent* fight that left several people badly hurt⟩

synonyms bang-bang, blood-and-guts, convulsive, cyclonic, explosive, ferocious, fierce, furious, hammer-and-tongs, hot, knock-down, drag-out (*or* knock-down-and-drag-out), paroxysmal, rabid, rough, stormy, tempestuous, tumultuous, turbulent, volcanic

related words barbarous, brutal, savage, vicious; antagonistic, hostile; aggressive, assertive, bellicose, belligerent, combative, contentious, gladiatorial, pugnacious, quarrelsome, truculent; combustible, volatile; agitated, frantic, frenzied, mad; cataclysmal (*or* cataclysmic), destructive, ruinous

near antonyms calm, halcyon, pacific, serene, tranquil; nonbelligerent, unaggressive

antonyms nonviolent, peaceable, peaceful

2 extreme in degree, power, or effect ⟨a *violent* thunderstorm⟩ — see INTENSE 1

3 marked by great and often stressful excitement or activity ⟨our guest's imminent arrival provoked a *violent* effort to get the place cleaned up⟩ — see FURIOUS 1

4 marked by or uttered with forcefulness ⟨prone to *violent* denunciation of anyone who disagrees with her⟩ — see EMPHATIC 1

VIP *n* a person who is widely known and usually much talked about ⟨the *VIPs* insisted on being seated in the restaurant's private dining room⟩ — see CELEBRITY 1

viper *n* a limbless reptile with a long body ⟨a *viper* sliding silently through the field⟩ — see SNAKE 1

virago *n* a bad-tempered scolding woman ⟨fairy tales that typically portray stepmothers as *viragoes*⟩ — see SHREW

virgin *adj* **1** never having had sexual relations ⟨*virgin* boys are sometimes unfairly teased⟩

synonyms maiden, virginal

related words chaste, modest, pure, vestal; innocent, untouched; abstinent, celibate, continent; unmarried, unwed

antonyms deflowered

2 being in an original and unused or unspoiled state ⟨the state's only remaining *virgin* forest⟩ — see FRESH 1

3 free from any trace of the coarse or indecent ⟨his photographs of nudes have such a *virgin* purity about them that only a prude would find them objectionable⟩ — see CHASTE 1

4 existing without human habitation or cultivation ⟨a vast expanse of *virgin* territory⟩ — see WILD 2

5 coming before all others in time or order ⟨the political analyst's *virgin* effort at a cloak-and-dagger thriller⟩ — see FIRST 1

virgin *n* a person who is just starting out in a field of activity ⟨a *virgin* in the world of comedy clubs, he's still learning to deal with hecklers⟩ — see BEGINNER

virginal *adj* **1** being in an original and unused or unspoiled state ⟨one of the state's few remaining tracts of *virginal* prairie⟩ — see FRESH 1

2 never having had sexual relations ⟨a *virginal* girl who would not permit any liberties to be taken with her body⟩ — see VIRGIN 1

3 free from any trace of the coarse or indecent ⟨the romance between the young boy and girl is portrayed with *virginal* innocence that is touching in this day and age⟩ — see CHASTE 1

viridity *n* the quality or state of being simple and sincere ⟨a heroine beset by the vacuous *viridity* that is so typical of romance novels⟩ — see NAÏVETÉ 1

virile *adj* of, relating to, or marked by qualities traditionally associated with men ⟨men were once expected to be interested only in such *virile* activities as hunting⟩ — see MASCULINE

virility *n* the set of qualities considered appropriate for or characteristic of men ⟨many cultures value *virility* as a sign of power⟩

synonyms machismo, macho, manhood, manliness, masculinity

related words maleness; boyishness, mannishness, tomboyishness

near antonyms girlishness; femaleness; girlhood, maidenhood; effeminacy, effeteness; emasculation

antonyms femininity, muliebrity, womanhood, womanliness

virtually *adv* very close to but not completely ⟨fell in love with a man who was *virtually* penniless⟩ — see ALMOST

virtue *n* **1** a quality that gives something special worth ⟨the *virtue* of wool as a clothing material is that it can provide insulation from the cold even when wet⟩ — see EXCELLENCE 2

2 conduct that conforms to an accepted standard of right and wrong ⟨a lady of honor and *virtue*⟩ — see MORALITY 1

3 strength of mind to carry on in spite of danger ⟨a military hero whose *virtue* inspired a nation⟩ — see COURAGE

virtuoso *adj* **1** accomplished with trained ability ⟨a *virtuoso* performance of a piano concerto⟩ — see SKILLFUL

2 having or showing exceptional knowledge, experience, or skill in a field of endeavor ⟨a *virtuoso* director, he is known for using every resource and technique known to film to tell a story⟩ — see PROFICIENT

virtuoso *n* a person with a high level of knowledge or skill in a field ⟨a violin *virtuoso*⟩ — see EXPERT

virtuous *adj* conforming to a high standard of morality or virtue ⟨*virtuous* behavior is its own reward⟩ — see GOOD 2

virtuously *adv* with purity of thought and deed ⟨lived simply and *virtuously*⟩ — see PURELY 1

virtuousness *n* conduct that conforms to an accepted standard of right and wrong ⟨once a cleric's *virtuousness* is seriously called into doubt, he loses his authority as a moral leader⟩ — see MORALITY 1

virulence *n* biting sharpness of feeling or expression ⟨I was surprised by the *virulence* of the criticism⟩ — see ACRIMONY 1

virulency *n* biting sharpness of feeling or expression ⟨the *virulency* of his critical judgments became the stuff of Broadway legend⟩ — see ACRIMONY 1

virulent *adj* having or showing a desire to cause someone pain or suffering for the sheer enjoyment of it ⟨the *virulent* look on her face warned me that she was about to say something unkind⟩ — see HATEFUL

virulently *adv* in a mean or spiteful manner ⟨an organization that is even more *virulently* bigoted than others of its kind⟩ — see NASTILY

visage *n* **1** facial appearance regarded as an indication of mood or feeling ⟨an old man with a noticeably happy *visage*⟩ — see LOOK 1

2 the front part of the head ⟨visitors to the mountain range had long noted that the natural rock formation bore a striking resemblance to the *visage* of a man⟩ — see FACE 1

viscera *n pl* the internal organs of the body ⟨the researchers examined the *viscera* of the infected rat⟩ — see GUT 1

viscid *adj* **1** being of a consistency that resists flow ⟨honey that turned even more *viscid* in the cold⟩ — see THICK 2

2 tending to adhere to objects upon contact ⟨*viscid* tree resin⟩ — see STICKY 1

viscidity *n* the degree to which a fluid can resist flowing ⟨a method for determining the *viscidity* of the substance⟩ — see CONSISTENCY

viscosity *n* the degree to which a fluid can resist flowing ⟨conducted an experiment to determine the *viscosity* of motor oil⟩ — see CONSISTENCY

viscous *adj* being of a consistency that resists flow ⟨*viscous* syrup that takes forever to pour from a narrow-neck bottle⟩ — see THICK 2

visible *adj* **1** capable of being seen ⟨the *visible* light spectrum runs from red to violet⟩

synonyms apparent, observable, seeable, visual

related words viewable; detectable, discernible (*also* discernable), noticeable, perceptible; clear, conspicuous, evident, eye-catching, manifest, obvious, overt, patent, perceivable, plain, prominent, striking; exposed, external, outer, outward, superficial

near antonyms disappeared, dissolved, evanesced, evaporated, melted, vanished, vaporized; imperceptible, indiscernible, indistinct, unnoticeable, unobservable; faint, inconspicuous, insignificant, slight, unobtrusive, vague; buried, concealed, covert, disguised, hidden, latent, obscure, shrouded

antonyms invisible, sightless, viewless

2 widely known ⟨although he had been kicking around Hollywood for years, he only became a highly *visible* actor after his starring role in that year's biggest movie⟩ — see FAMOUS 1

vision *n* **1** a conception or image created by the imagination and having no objective reality ⟨a *vision* of the future that no other film director had ever created⟩ — see FANTASY 1

2 the ability to see ⟨the bright light temporarily robbed me of *vision*⟩ — see EYESIGHT

3 the soul of a dead person thought of especially as appearing to living people ⟨believed he'd seen a *vision* of his mother⟩ — see GHOST 1

4 concern or preparation for the future ⟨a company president with the long-range *vision* that his firm needs to survive in the global economy⟩ — see FORESIGHT 2

vision *vb* to form a mental picture of ⟨*visioned* her idea of the perfect meal⟩ — see IMAGINE 1

visionary *adj* **1** having or marked by a tendency to be guided more by ideals than by reality ⟨a *visionary* plan for a manned flight to Mars even though there are pressing problems right here on earth⟩ — see IDEALISTIC

2 not real and existing only in the imagination ⟨one of several Christian saints who claimed to have had *visionary* experiences of hell⟩ — see IMAGINARY
3 having or showing awareness of and preparation for the future ⟨in a *visionary* move, the developer bought large tracts of the waterfront just before property values skyrocketed⟩ — see FORESIGHTED

visionary *n* **1** one who predicts future events or developments ⟨according to Greek myth, Cassandra was a *visionary* who was endowed with the gift of inerrant prophecy but fated to never be believed⟩ — see PROPHET 1
2 one whose conduct is guided more by the image of perfection than by the real world ⟨19th-century *visionaries* who founded short-lived communities in which everyone was supposed to live in perfect peace and harmony⟩ — see IDEALIST

visionless *adj* lacking the power of sight ⟨her assailant may have known about her *visionless* right eye because he approached from that direction⟩ — see BLIND 1

visit *n* **1** a temporary residing as another's guest ⟨my aunt always looks forward to her weeklong annual *visit* with her mother⟩
synonyms sojourn, stay, tarry
related words field trip, homestay, sleepover; layover, stop, stopover
2 a coming to see another briefly for social or business reasons ⟨came by for a quick *visit*⟩ — see CALL 2

visit *vb* **1** to make a social call upon ⟨the club ladies make a point of *visiting* everyone who moves into the neighborhood⟩
synonyms call (on *or* upon), drop in (on), see
related words look up, seek (out); drop by
near antonyms brush (aside *or* off), cold-shoulder, ignore, snub
2 to reside as a temporary guest ⟨an old friend who comes to *visit* for a month every summer⟩
synonyms crash [*slang*], sojourn, stay, tarry
related words come by, come over, drop by, drop in, run in, step in, stop (by); frequent, hang (around *or* out), haunt; inhabit, occupy
near antonyms abide, dwell, live, reside
3 to engage in casual or rambling conversation ⟨tries to *visit* with her best friend on the phone at least once a week⟩ — see CHAT 1
4 to go to or spend time in often ⟨*visit* Ireland for a few weeks every year⟩ — see FREQUENT
5 to make a brief visit ⟨stopped to *visit* with my father on the way out of town⟩ — see CALL 3

visitant *n* **1** a person who visits another ⟨the groundless theory that these ancient monuments were built by extraterrestrial *visitants*⟩ — see GUEST 1
2 the soul of a dead person thought of especially as appearing to living people ⟨a nocturnal *visitant* that must have been the shade of his late brother, crying out for vengeance against his murderers⟩ — see GHOST 1

visitation *n* a coming to see another briefly for social or business reasons ⟨the pastor and curate could hardly express how honored they were to receive this *visitation* from the bishop⟩ — see CALL 2

visitor *n* a person who visits another ⟨put nicer clothes on because they had *visitors* coming⟩ — see GUEST 1

visor *also* **vizor** *n* the projecting front part of a hat or cap ⟨the *visor* on your baseball cap should provide adequate shade for your eyes⟩
synonyms bill, brim, peak
related words shade

vista *n* all that can be seen from a certain point ⟨a gorgeous *vista* of the mountains from the front window⟩ — see VIEW 1

visual *adj* **1** of, relating to, or used in vision ⟨the eyes are the primary *visual* organs in humans⟩
synonyms ocular, optic, optical
related words seeing, sighted; focusing (*also* focussing)
antonyms nonvisual
2 capable of being seen ⟨that funny expression was a *visual* hint that she was getting bored⟩ — see VISIBLE 1
3 consisting of or relating to pictures ⟨*visual* evidence that could be presented in court⟩ — see PICTORIAL 1
4 producing a mental picture through clear and impressive description ⟨accounts of Civil War battles that are so grippingly *visual* that the reader recoils from the sight of so much blood⟩ — see GRAPHIC 1

visual *n* something that visually explains or decorates a text ⟨the strong *visuals* in the beginning biology book compensate somewhat for the weak text⟩ — see ILLUSTRATION 1

visualize *vb* to form a mental picture of ⟨*visualized* herself executing a perfect dive⟩ — see IMAGINE 1

vital *adj* **1** having active strength of body or mind ⟨a man who remained *vital* well into his 90s⟩ — see VIGOROUS 1
2 having much high-spirited energy and movement ⟨the child is *vital* and active again after being sick⟩ — see LIVELY 1
3 impossible to do without ⟨I forgot one *vital* ingredient, and now the biscuits taste strange⟩ — see ESSENTIAL 1
4 likely to cause or capable of causing death ⟨received a *vital* wound in the abdomen⟩ — see DEADLY 1
5 of the greatest possible importance ⟨a matter that is *vital* to our national security⟩ — see CRUCIAL
6 having a renewing effect on the state of the body or mind ⟨after the long, dreary winter, we welcomed the *vital* rays of the summer sun⟩ — see TONIC 1

vitality *n* **1** the quality or state of having abundant or intense activity ⟨a city known for the *vitality* of its music scene⟩
synonyms animation, briskness, exuberance, jazziness, liveliness, lustiness, peppiness, robustness, sprightliness, vibrance, vibrancy, vigorousness
related words buoyancy, jauntiness, springiness; brightness, cheer, cheerfulness, chirpiness, effervescence, friskiness, pizzazz (*or* pizazz), sparkle, spirit, verve, vivaciousness, vivacity; eagerness, ebullience, ebulliency, enthusiasm, keenness, spiritedness; friskiness, impishness, pertness, playfulness
near antonyms indolence, laziness; anemia, bloodlessness; languidness, languor, lethargy, limpness, listlessness, sleepiness, sluggishness, spiritlessness, torpidity, torpor, weariness; apathy, impassivity; dullness (*also* dulness), pallidness, tediousness, tedium, vapidity, vapidness
antonyms inactivity, lifelessness
2 active strength of body or mind ⟨her *vitality* seemed to spread to everyone around her⟩ — see VIGOR 1

vitalize *vb* to give life, vigor, or spirit to ⟨a hearty lunch and a long nap afterwards *vitalized* him again⟩ — see ANIMATE

vitalizing *adj* having a renewing effect on the state of the body or mind ⟨a *vitalizing* steam bath⟩ — see TONIC 1

vitally *adv* to a great degree ⟨it's *vitally* important that you deliver this message to the general⟩ — see VERY 1

vitals *n pl* the internal organs of the body ⟨remember to wear a full vest to protect your *vitals* while sparring⟩ — see GUT 1

vitiate *vb* **1** to affect slightly with something morally bad or undesirable ⟨believed that luxury *vitiates* even the most principled person⟩ — see TAINT 1
2 to reduce the soundness, effectiveness, or perfection of ⟨numerous grammatical errors *vitiate* the effectiveness of your writing⟩ — see DAMAGE 1
3 to lower in character, dignity, or quality ⟨a penchant

for coarse language *vitiates* what is otherwise a refined literary style⟩ — see DEBASE 1

vitriol *n* **1** biting sharpness of feeling or expression ⟨a film critic noted for the *vitriol* and sometimes outright cruelty of his pronouncements⟩ — see ACRIMONY 1
2 harsh insulting language ⟨the review was more than just unfavorable—it was loaded with *vitriol*⟩ — see ABUSE 1

vitriolic *adj* marked by harsh insulting language ⟨braced himself for another *vitriolic* dressing-down by his perennially displeased father⟩ — see ABUSIVE

vittles *n pl* substances intended to be eaten ⟨claimed that the chitlins were just about the tastiest *vittles* he ever ate⟩ — see FOOD 1

vituperate *vb* to criticize harshly and usually publicly ⟨every week the minister would ascend the pulpit and *vituperate* the parishioners for a litany of vices⟩ — see ATTACK 2

vituperation *n* harsh insulting language ⟨sick of the *vituperation* coming from ungrateful visitors, the put-upon webmaster took down the site's free webcam, which had afforded views of the town's picturesque harbor⟩ — see ABUSE 1

vituperative *adj* marked by harsh insulting language ⟨the type of provocative magazine article that is guaranteed to engender *vituperative* threats of subscription cancellations⟩ — see ABUSIVE

vituperatory *adj* marked by harsh insulting language ⟨the kind of *vituperatory* speeches that are designed to rouse the rank-and-file at political conventions⟩ — see ABUSIVE

vivacious *adj* **1** having much high-spirited energy and movement ⟨an outgoing, *vivacious* girl who became a successful sales rep⟩ — see LIVELY 1
2 joyously unrestrained ⟨the poem is a *vivacious* expression of his love for her⟩ — see EXUBERANT

vivaciously *adv* in a quick and spirited manner ⟨a night of drinking songs that were sung lustily and *vivaciously*⟩ — see GAILY 2

viva voce *adj* made or carried on through speaking rather than in writing ⟨the students are required to write two papers and take a *viva voce* examination⟩ — see VERBAL 2

vivid *adj* producing a mental picture through clear and impressive description ⟨*vivid* language that made the scene come alive in my mind⟩ — see GRAPHIC 1

vivify *vb* to give life, vigor, or spirit to ⟨this re-creation of a town in the Old West really *vivifies* the history that visitors learned in school⟩ — see ANIMATE

vixen *n* a bad-tempered scolding woman ⟨why anyone puts up with that *vixen's* sharp tongue is beyond me⟩ — see SHREW

vizard *n* a cover or partial cover for the face used to disguise oneself ⟨in those days it was not uncommon for street prostitutes to wear *vizards*⟩ — see MASK 1

vocabular *adj* of or relating to words or language ⟨the school banned the book for *vocabular* reasons, as some parents objected to the author's use of profanity⟩ — see VERBAL 1

vocabulary *n* **1** the special terms or expressions of a particular group or field ⟨scientific *vocabulary*⟩ — see TERMINOLOGY
2 the stock of words, pronunciation, and grammar used by a people as their basic means of communication ⟨children learn enough of the common *vocabulary* to make themselves understood by around the age of two⟩ — see LANGUAGE 1

vocal *adj* expressed or communicated by voice ⟨our cat is given to making strange *vocal* noises in the dead of night⟩
synonyms oral, spoken, uttered, voiced
related words articulated, enunciated, pronounced, sonant; breathed, chirped, drawled, gasped, intoned, mouthed, mumbled, murmured, muttered, purred, shouted, spluttered, sputtered, squeaked, whispered
near antonyms inarticulate; mute, quiet, silent; unexpressed, unsaid, unspoken, unuttered, unvoiced; surd, voiceless
antonyms nonvocal

vocal *n* a short musical composition for the human voice often with instrumental accompaniment ⟨a recording artist who arranges his own *vocals*⟩ — see SONG 1

vocalist *n* one who sings ⟨hired a *vocalist* for their jazz band⟩ — see SINGER

vocalize *vb* **1** to express (a thought or emotion) in words ⟨she's not one to *vocalize* her worries⟩ — see SAY 1
2 to produce musical sounds with the voice ⟨spent some time *vocalizing* before the concert⟩ — see SING 1

vocalizer *n* one who sings ⟨a critic who disdains many of today's pop singers as mere *vocalizers* with little artistry⟩ — see SINGER

vocation *n* **1** the activity by which one regularly makes a living ⟨finally made sculpting her *vocation* instead of just a hobby⟩ — see OCCUPATION 1
2 the body of people in a profession or field of activity ⟨she says that although she respects certain journalists, she despises the *vocation*⟩ ⟨politics has its honest and its dishonest practitioners, just like any other *vocation*⟩ — see CORPS

vociferant *adj* engaging in or marked by loud and insistent cries especially of protest ⟨a lawyer known for his *vociferant* theatrics in the courtroom⟩ — see VOCIFEROUS

vociferate *vb* to speak so as to be heard at a distance ⟨he can never seem to voice his opinions at a decent decibel level; he has to *vociferate*⟩ — see CALL 1

vociferating *adj* engaging in or marked by loud and insistent cries especially of protest ⟨*vociferating* union members angrily marched outside corporate headquarters⟩ — see VOCIFEROUS

vociferation *n* a violent shouting ⟨a sudden *vociferation* in the back of the room drew everyone's attention to the dispute⟩ — see CLAMOR 1

vociferous *adj* engaging in or marked by loud and insistent cries especially of protest ⟨*vociferous* opponents of the bill protested angrily outside the chambers of the legislature⟩
synonyms blatant, caterwauling, clamant, clamorous, obstreperous, squawking, vociferant, vociferating, yawping (*or* yauping), yowling
related words clangorous, dinning, discordant, noisy; loudmouthed, outspoken, vocal; boisterous, rackety, raucous, robustious, rowdy, uproarious; cacophonous, dissonant, earsplitting, grating, shrill, strident; blaring, blustering, booming, brassy, brazen
near antonyms noiseless, quiet, silent, soundless, still; calm, hushed, subdued

vogue *adj* enjoying widespread favor or approval ⟨always tries to use the *vogue* words of the moment so as to appear cool⟩ — see POPULAR 1

vogue *n* **1** a practice or interest that is very popular for a short time ⟨it was then the *vogue* to curl one's hair and wear dark lipstick⟩ — see FAD
2 the state of enjoying widespread approval ⟨she's the sort of person who does whatever is in *vogue*⟩ — see POPULARITY

voguish *adj* **1** being in the latest or current fashion ⟨that boutique always has the most *voguish* shoes⟩ — see STYLISH
2 enjoying widespread favor or approval ⟨an art critic with an unfortunate penchant for throwing around a lot of *voguish* words⟩ — see POPULAR 1

voguishness *n* **1** the quality or state of being fashionable ⟨the in-your-face *voguishness* of his new hairstyle certainly got our attention⟩ — see COOL 2
2 the state of enjoying widespread approval ⟨the short-lived *voguishness* of so much of what that artist produced⟩ — see POPULARITY

voice *n* **1** the right to express a wish, choice, or opinion ⟨everyone will have a *voice* in the decision of where to go for our vacationp⟩
synonyms say, say-so, vote
related words part, role (*also* rôle), share; ballot, enfranchisement, franchise, suffrage; belief, conviction, judgment (*or* judgement), opinion, sentiment, view
2 an act, process, or means of putting something into words ⟨a publisher who used his newspaper as a *voice* for his extreme conservatism⟩ — see EXPRESSION 1
3 one who sings ⟨one of the great *voices* of her generation⟩ — see SINGER

voice *vb* to make known (as an idea, emotion, or opinion) ⟨*voiced* a suggestion about where to go⟩ — see EXPRESS 1

voiced *adj* expressed or communicated by voice ⟨a loudly *voiced* expression of pain⟩ — see VOCAL

voiceless *adj* unable to speak ⟨believes that animals deserve basic rights even though they are *voiceless*⟩ — see MUTE 1

void *adj* **1** having no legal or binding force ⟨an agreement is *void* if obtained by force⟩ — see NULL 1
2 lacking contents that could or should be present ⟨a nuclear explosion that would leave the landscape as *void* and lifeless as one could imagine⟩ — see EMPTY 1
3 utterly lacking in something needed, wanted, or expected ⟨entirely *void* of common sense⟩ — see DEVOID 1
4 left unoccupied or unused ⟨the cornfields lay *void* under a blanket of snow⟩ — see ABANDONED 1

void *n* **1** an incomplete or deficient area ⟨a repressed memory that left a huge *void* in her recollection of her adolescent years⟩ — see GAP 3
2 empty space ⟨those ancient travelers who traversed those vast watery *voids* between the islands of Oceania⟩ — see VACANCY 1
3 an open space in a barrier (as a wall or hedge) ⟨the client wanted an old-fashioned stone wall and did not want the *voids* filled in with mortar⟩ — see GAP 1

void *vb* **1** to put an end to by formal action ⟨the court's decision *voided* the will⟩ — see ABOLISH 1
2 to remove the contents of ⟨the seller has promised to *void* the house of all furniture⟩ — see EMPTY

voiding *n* the doing away with something by formal action ⟨the judge's *voiding* of the decision by the jury sparked public outcry⟩ — see ABOLITION

volatile *adj* likely to change frequently, suddenly, or unexpectedly ⟨a boss of *volatile* moods is frustrating to work for⟩ — see FICKLE 1

volcanic *adj* marked by bursts of destructive force or intense activity ⟨a man with a *volcanic* temper that could go off at any moment⟩ — see VIOLENT 1

volcano *n* a potentially explosive place or situation ⟨beset by prolonged heat and lingering racial tension, the city was like a seething *volcano*⟩ — see TINDERBOX 1

volition *n* **1** the act or power of making one's own choices or decisions ⟨Tourette's syndrome is a neurological disorder marked by recurrent tics and vocalizations that are beyond the sufferer's *volition* or control⟩ — see FREE WILL
2 the power, right, or opportunity to choose ⟨left the church of her own *volition*, not because she was excommunicated⟩ — see CHOICE 1

volitional *adj* done, made, or given with one's own free will ⟨believes in destiny and doubts that most decisions are truly *volitional*⟩ — see VOLUNTARY 1

volley *n* a rapid or overwhelming outpouring of many things at once ⟨surprised by the *volley* of complaints about cable service in the area⟩ — see BARRAGE

volte–face *n* a changing from one policy or point of view to virtually its exact opposite ⟨the novelist's unexpected *volte-face* from experimentalism to traditional narrative form⟩ — see ABOUT-FACE

volume *n* **1** a considerable amount ⟨we can only make money if we sell our goods in *volume*⟩ — see LOT 2
2 a given or particular mass or aggregate of matter ⟨produces great *volumes* of work each day⟩ — see AMOUNT
3 a set of printed sheets of paper bound together between covers and forming a work of fiction or nonfiction ⟨reissued the trilogy in a single *volume*⟩ — see BOOK 1
4 the largest number or amount that something can hold ⟨state the barrel's *volume* in terms of gallons⟩ — see CAPACITY 1

voluminous *adj* of a size greater than average of its kind ⟨decorating tips to help make *voluminous* rooms feel cozy⟩ — see LARGE 1

voluminousness *n* the quality or state of being large in size ⟨the awesome *voluminousness* of the garment made it look more like a tent than a dress⟩ — see LARGENESS

voluntarily *adv* of one's own free will ⟨you took part in this *voluntarily*, so you have no cause to complain⟩
synonyms freely, willingly
related words consciously, deliberately, intentionally, knowingly, wittingly; acquiescently, consentingly; electively, optionally
phrases of one's own accord
near antonyms unconsciously, unintentionally, unknowingly, unwittingly; reluctantly
antonyms involuntarily, unwillingly

voluntary *adj* **1** done, made, or given with one's own free will ⟨a *voluntary* contribution to the school's fund-raising drive⟩
synonyms freewill, self-imposed, uncoerced, unforced, volitional, volunteer, willing
related words discretionary, elective, optional; impulsive, instinctive, spontaneous, unpremeditated; conscious, deliberate, intentional, knowing, willful (*or* wilful)
near antonyms compulsory, enforced, mandatory, necessary, nonelective, obligatory, ordered, required
antonyms coerced, compelled, forced, involuntary, nonvoluntary, unwilled, will-less
2 subject to one's freedom of choice ⟨participation in the resort's recreational activities is strictly *voluntary*⟩ — see OPTIONAL
3 made, given, or done with full awareness of what one is doing ⟨the legal distinctions between *voluntary* and involuntary manslaughter⟩ — see INTENTIONAL

volunteer *adj* done, made, or given with one's own free will ⟨*volunteer* work at the hospital⟩ — see VOLUNTARY 1

volunteer *vb* to make a present of ⟨trained tax consultants who *volunteer* their services at tax time⟩ — see GIVE 1

voluptuary *n* a person whose life is devoted to luxury and sensual pleasures ⟨a fin de siècle novel about dandies and *voluptuaries*⟩
synonyms debauchee, decadent, hedonist, sensualist, sybarite
related words Cyrenaic, Epicurean; bon vivant, epicure, glutton, gourmand; libertine, playboy, rake, roué; playgirl
near antonyms killjoy, spoilsport, wet blanket; fuddy-duddy, prude, straight arrow
antonyms ascetic

voluptuous *adj* pleasing to the physical senses ⟨the *voluptuous* richness of the music⟩ — see SENSUAL

voluptuousness *n* excessive pursuit of fleshly pleasures ⟨a painting by the 19th-century artist Ingres that vividly portrays the languorous *voluptuousness* of a sultan's seraglio⟩ — see SENSUALITY

vomit *vb* to discharge the contents of the stomach through the mouth ⟨the children with the flu *vomited* every time they tried to eat something⟩
synonyms barf, gag, heave, hurl, puke, retch, spew, spit up, throw up, upchuck
related words disgorge, regurgitate; eject, expel; nauseate
phrases lose one's lunch [*slang*], toss one's cookies

voodoo *n* a person skilled in using supernatural forces ⟨found a *voodoo* who was willing to put a hex on the man who had jilted her⟩ — see MAGICIAN 1

voodooism *n* the power to control natural forces through supernatural means ⟨*voodooism* is condemned by several religions⟩ — see MAGIC 1

voodooist *n* a person skilled in using supernatural forces ⟨a *voodooist* whose remarkable feats seemingly defy rational explanation⟩ — see MAGICIAN 1

voracious *adj* **1** having a huge appetite ⟨it seemed like the *voracious* kitten was eating her weight in food every day⟩
synonyms edacious, esurient, gluttonous, greedy, hoggish, piggish, rapacious, ravenous, swinish
related words hearty, wolfish; devouring, gobbling, gorging, gormandizing, gulping; insatiable, unquenchable, unslakable; empty, famished, hungry, peckish [*chiefly British*], starved, starving; malnourished, underfed, undernourished
near antonyms content, full, glutted, sated, satiated, satisfied, stuffed
2 showing urgent desire or interest ⟨a *voracious* reader⟩ — see EAGER

vortex *n* water moving rapidly in a circle with a hollow in the center ⟨a boat sucked down into the *vortex*⟩ — see WHIRLPOOL

votarist *n* one who follows the opinions or teachings of another ⟨*votarists* of the literary critic seemed to have penetrated the English department of every university in the country⟩ — see FOLLOWER 1

votary *n* one who follows the opinions or teachings of another ⟨a *votary* of the religious leader⟩ — see FOLLOWER 1

vote *n* **1** the right to formally express one's position or will in an election ⟨in the United States, women were granted the *vote* by the 19th Amendment in 1920⟩
synonyms ballot, enfranchisement, franchise, suffrage
related words say, say-so, voice
antonyms disenfranchisement
2 a piece of paper indicating a person's preferences in an election ⟨dropped her *vote* into the ballot box⟩ — see BALLOT 1
3 the right to express a wish, choice, or opinion ⟨he argued for a *vote* in the matter, since he was going to be affected by the final decision⟩ — see VOICE 1

vote *vb* to set before the mind for consideration ⟨I *vote* we quit working and go out for lunch⟩ — see PROPOSE 1

vouch (for) *vb* to declare (something) to be true or genuine ⟨a scientist who can *vouch for* the accuracy of the results⟩ — see CERTIFY 1

voucher *n* something presented in support of the truth or accuracy of a claim ⟨a rock band's overpriced T-shirt has become the universally recognized *voucher* for one's attendance at a sold-out concert⟩ — see PROOF

vow *n* a person's solemn declaration that he or she will do or not do something ⟨we need your *vow* that you won't damage anything while we're gone⟩ — see PROMISE

vow *vb* to make a solemn declaration of intent ⟨she *vowed* to love him forever⟩ — see PROMISE 1

voyage *n* a journey over water in a vessel ⟨the long, perilous *voyage* down the Atlantic seaboard, around Cape Horn, and up South America's Pacific coast⟩ — see SAIL

voyage *vb* **1** to take a trip especially of some distance ⟨*voyaged* to the ends of the earth in search of adventure⟩ — see TRAVEL 1
2 to travel on water in a vessel ⟨*voyaging* on a cruise ship for the first time⟩ — see SAIL 1

vulgar *adj* **1** belonging to the class of people of low social or economic rank ⟨paintings that appeal to *vulgar* tastes⟩ — see IGNOBLE 1
2 depicting or referring to sexual matters in a way that is unacceptable in polite society ⟨a warning about the movie's *vulgar* language⟩ — see OBSCENE 1
3 held by or applicable to a majority of the people ⟨the *vulgar* opinion is that the nation is in decline⟩ — see GENERAL 3
4 lacking in refinement or good taste ⟨*vulgar* behavior shown by someone who's made a lot of money and wants everyone to know it⟩ — see COARSE 2
5 used in or suitable for speech and not formal writing ⟨Latin was once the language of scholars, and English the *vulgar* language used by the common people⟩ — see COLLOQUIAL 1

vulgarism *n* a disrespectful or indecent word or expression ⟨used *vulgarisms* that embarrassed his family⟩ — see SWEARWORD

vulgarity *n* **1** the quality or state of lacking refinement or good taste ⟨our cousins' general *vulgarity* and poor manners irritate my mother⟩
synonyms coarseness, commonness, crassness, crudeness, crudity, grossness, indelicacy, indelicateness, lowness, raffishness, rawness, roughness, rudeness, tastelessness
related words boorishness, brutishness, churlishness, clownishness, loutishness, rowdiness, rusticity, uncouthness; artlessness, gracelessness, inelegance, unsophistication; insensitiveness, insensitivity, thoughtlessness; kitsch, tackiness
near antonyms courtliness, urbanity; elegance, grace, graciousness; consideration, sensitivity, thoughtfulness
antonyms cultivation, genteelness, gentility, polish, refinement, tastefulness
2 the quality or state of being obscene ⟨the pointless *vulgarity* of the joke disgusted her⟩ — see OBSCENITY 1

vulgarize *vb* to use so much as to make less appealing ⟨the composer's masterpiece has been hopelessly *vulgarized* by its use in countless TV commercials⟩ — see HACKNEY

vulnerability *n* **1** the quality or state of having little resistance to some outside agent ⟨*vulnerability* to infection⟩ — see SUSCEPTIBILITY
2 the state of being left without shelter or protection against something harmful ⟨the *vulnerability* of the car to vandalism when it's parked on the street⟩ — see EXPOSURE 1

vulnerable *adj* **1** being in a situation where one is likely to meet with harm ⟨I'm *vulnerable* to sunburn whenever I go out in the sun⟩ — see LIABLE 1
2 lacking protection from danger or resistance against attack ⟨*vulnerable* baby chicks⟩ — see HELPLESS 1

vulture *n* a person who habitually preys upon others ⟨noted that the paparazzi are *vultures* who could not exist without the connivance of the tabloid-buying public⟩ — see PREDATOR

wack *adj, slang* falling short of a standard ⟨that movie was *wack*, even by the standards of popcorn flicks⟩ — see BAD 1

wackiness *n* lack of good sense or judgment ⟨what world-class *wackiness* made you think this was a good idea?⟩ — see FOOLISHNESS 1

wacko *also* **whacko** *adj* having or showing a very abnormal or sick state of mind ⟨the governor's staff spread rumors that his opponent's wife was *wacko*, as she had once undergone shock therapy for depression⟩ — see INSANE 1

wacko *also* **whacko** *n* a person judged to be legally or medically insane ⟨some *wacko* has been sending the actress increasingly disturbing letters⟩ — see LUNATIC 1

wacky *also* **whacky** *adj* **1** different from the ordinary in a way that causes curiosity or suspicion ⟨raised by an uncle with a rather *wacky* philosophy of parenting⟩ — see ODD 2

2 having or showing a very abnormal or sick state of mind ⟨a series of bizarre letters that the killer sent to the police, detailing his *wacky*, disturbed view of the world⟩ — see INSANE 1

3 showing or marked by a lack of good sense or judgment ⟨one club member whose *wacky* ideas for fundraisers usually produced groans⟩ — see FOOLISH 1

wad *n* **1** a considerable amount ⟨a starlet who usually gets a big *wad* of publicity for her nonstop antics⟩ — see LOT 2

2 a small uneven mass ⟨a *wad* of gum stuck to the desk⟩ — see LUMP 1

3 a very large amount of money ⟨amassed—and lost—a *wad* playing the stock market⟩ — see FORTUNE 2

wad *vb* to form into a round compact mass ⟨disgusted, she *wadded* up the paper and threw it in the wastebasket⟩

synonyms agglomerate, ball, roll, round

related words bunch, clump, lump; bead, pearl, pellet, pelletize; sphere

near antonyms flatten, open, smooth, spread, unfold

antonyms unroll

wadding *n* soft material that is used to fill the hollow parts of something ⟨the last step is to fill the pillow with *wadding* and stitch it closed⟩ — see FILLING

waddle *vb* to move forward while swaying from side to side ⟨the duck *waddled* back into the water⟩ — see STAGGER 1

[1]**waddy** *n, Australian* a heavy rigid stick used as a weapon or for punishment ⟨an aborigine armed with a *waddy* was a formidable foe⟩ — see CLUB 1

[2]**waddy** *or* **waddie** *n, West* a hired hand who tends cattle or horses at a ranch or on the range ⟨the *waddies* were preparing to start branding⟩ — see COWBOY

wade (in *or* **into)** *vb* to start work on energetically ⟨*waded* deep *into* the repair project and didn't come out of it until four hours later⟩ — see ATTACK 3

waffle *vb* to avoid giving a definite answer or position ⟨she *waffled* when asked what she thought of her sister's new boyfriend⟩ — see EQUIVOCATE

waft *n* a slight or gentle movement of air ⟨*wafts* carrying the scent of spring flowers⟩ — see BREEZE 1

waft *vb* to rest or move along the surface of a liquid or in the air ⟨a feather *wafted* past us and settled on the grass⟩ — see FLOAT 1

[1]**wag** *n* a quick jerky movement from side to side or up and down ⟨the dog gave its tail a single *wag* before it flopped back down⟩

synonyms swish, switch, waggle, whisk

related words oscillation, rock, sway, swing, waver; flap, flutter, wave, whip; flick, jerk, jolt, snap, twitch; jiggle, shake, wiggle; bob, nod

[2]**wag** *n* a person (as a writer) noted for or specializing in humor ⟨some *wag* wrote a droll satire on the scandal for the newspaper⟩ — see HUMORIST

wag *vb* **1** to move from side to side or up and down with quick jerky motions ⟨the cat's tail *wagged* back and forth in annoyance⟩

synonyms swish, switch, waggle

related words oscillate, rock, sway, swing, waver; beat, flail, flap, flop, lash, whip; flick, flicker, flutter, wave; jerk, jolt; jig, jiggle, joggle, shake, twitch, wiggle; bob, jog, nod

2 to relate sometimes questionable or secret information of a personal nature ⟨tongues will *wag* as soon as word of the house's selling price gets around⟩ — see GOSSIP

3 to make short up-and-down movements ⟨the bird's head *wagged* jerkily as it looked for worms⟩ — see NOD

wage *n, often* **wages** *pl* the money paid regularly to a person for labor or services ⟨the *wage* you earn is more than enough to support us comfortably⟩

synonyms emolument, hire, packet [*British*], pay, paycheck, pay envelope, payment, salary, stipend

related words living wage, minimum wage, nominal wages, take-home pay; double time, overtime, time and a half; compensation, recompense, remittance, remuneration, requital, return; recoupment, redress, reparation, restitution; reimbursement, repayment; earnings, profit, takings, yield

wager *n* the money or thing risked on the outcome of an uncertain event ⟨lost her *wager* when the horse dropped out of the race⟩ — see BET 1

wager *vb* to risk (something) on the outcome of an uncertain event ⟨*wagered* 20 dollars that his favorite team would win⟩ — see BET

wagerer *n* one that bets (as on the outcome of a contest or sports event) ⟨as a *wagerer* of very small amounts, my uncle regards a visit to the racetrack as simply a pleasant way to spend the afternoon⟩ — see BETTOR

waggery *n* **1** playful, reckless behavior that is not intended to cause serious harm ⟨tossing lighted firecrackers around is not the kind of harmless *waggery* that it might seem⟩ — see MISCHIEF 1

2 something said or done to cause laughter ⟨Will Rogers' homespun *waggeries* struck a chord with audiences during the Great Depression⟩ — see JOKE 1

3 a playful or mischievous act intended as a joke ⟨her innocent little *waggeries* included sending slightly risqué e-mails to coworkers⟩ — see PRANK

waggish *adj* tending to or exhibiting reckless playfulness ⟨a *waggish* disposition that often got him into trouble as a child⟩ — see MISCHIEVOUS 1

waggishness *n* playful, reckless behavior that is not intended to cause serious harm ⟨he exhibits the *waggishness* of a teenage boy, which is rather sad, since he's now in his 50s⟩ — see MISCHIEF 1

waggle *n* a quick jerky movement from side to side or up and down ⟨a quick *waggle* of her head to indicate "no"⟩ — see [1]WAG

waggle *vb* to move from side to side or up and down

with quick jerky motions ⟨the rabbit *waggled* its ears and hopped away⟩ — see WAG 1

wagon *n* a wheeled usually horse-drawn vehicle used for hauling ⟨harness the horses up to the *wagon* so I can bring in the hay⟩ — see CART

wahoo *interj, chiefly West* how delightful ⟨the rodeo rider shrieked, "*Wahoo!*" as he collected his prize money⟩ — see HOORAY

wail *n* **1** a crying out in grief ⟨a prolonged *wail* arose from every corner of the city as the victims of the earthquake were unearthed from the rubble⟩ — see LAMENT 1

2 a long low sound indicating pain or grief ⟨rescuers heard a faint *wail* coming from the pile of rubble, a sure sign that one of the victims was still alive⟩ — see MOAN 1

3 an expression of dissatisfaction, pain, or resentment ⟨a transit fare increase that is sure to bring *wails* from the straphangers⟩ — see COMPLAINT 1

wail *vb* **1** to express dissatisfaction, pain, or resentment usually tiresomely ⟨the state's residents are always *wailing* about their high taxes⟩ — see COMPLAIN

2 to make a long loud mournful sound ⟨the women stood beside the coffins, *wailing* for their fallen sons and daughters⟩ — see HOWL 1

3 to utter a moan ⟨the patient lay in her bed, occasionally softly *wailing* in pain⟩ — see MOAN 1

wail (for) *vb* to feel or express sorrow for ⟨her grandfather asked her not to *wail for* him, saying that he had had a good life and was at peace⟩ — see LAMENT 1

wailfully *adv* with feelings of bitterness or grief ⟨the lost child *wailfully* kept asking for his mother⟩ — see HARD 2

wailing *adj* expressing or suggesting mourning ⟨a *wailing* quality in her voice that makes her a natural for country music⟩ — see MOURNFUL 1

wain *n* a wheeled usually horse-drawn vehicle used for hauling ⟨an antique *wain* that was once used for delivering milk⟩ — see CART

waist *n* the middle region of the human torso ⟨bent at the *waist* to catch his breath⟩ — see MIDRIFF

waistline *n* the middle region of the human torso ⟨used a belt to define her *waistline*⟩ — see MIDRIFF

wait *n* an instance or period of being prevented from going about one's business ⟨there was a long *wait* for the manager to come and help us⟩ — see DELAY

wait *vb* to remain in place in readiness or expectation of something ⟨please *wait* here, and we'll seat you shortly⟩
synonyms await, bide, hold on, stay
related words hang around, linger, remain, stick around, tarry; stand by; anticipate, expect, watch (for)
phrases bide one's time, cool one's heels, hold one's breath, sit tight

waiter *n* a person who serves food or drink ⟨*waiters* at that elegant restaurant must go through an extended training program before being allowed to serve customers⟩ — see SERVER

waitperson *n* a person who serves food or drink ⟨asked the *waitperson* what she would recommend on the menu⟩ — see SERVER

waiver *n* a document containing a declaration of an intentional giving up of a right, claim, or privilege ⟨before the hospital will treat you, you have to sign a *waiver* in which you give up your right to sue⟩
synonyms disclaimer, quitclaim, release
related words dispensation, exemption, indemnity; abdication, relinquishment, renouncement; handover, renunciation, surrender

wake *vb* **1** to cause to stop sleeping ⟨my banging around in the kitchen *woke* my wife⟩
synonyms arouse, awake, awaken, knock up [*British*], rouse, waken
related words roust, rout; raise, revive; reawaken, rewake; agitate, bestir, disturb, excite, provoke, stimulate, stir
near antonyms hypnotize, mesmerize
antonyms lull

2 to cease to be asleep ⟨I *woke* with a start when the door slammed⟩
synonyms arouse, awake, awaken, rouse, waken
related words arise, get up, rise, roll out, turn out, uprise; watch; revive; reawaken, rewake; shift, stir
near antonyms catnap, conk (off *or* out), doze, drop off, nap, nod, rest, sleep, slumber, snooze; bed (down), couch, doss (down) [*chiefly British*], flop, kip (down) [*British*], retire, sack out, turn in; lie up, sleep in; oversleep

3 to give notice to beforehand especially of danger or risk ⟨a public service announcement designed to *wake* people to the dangers of aggressive driving⟩ — see WARN

wakeful *adj* not sleeping or able to sleep ⟨the mother remained *wakeful* until her child returned home⟩
synonyms awake, insomniac, sleepless, wide-awake
related words aroused, awakened, roused, rousted, wakened; about, astir, up; aware, conscious; revived; reawakened
near antonyms dozy, drowsy, nodding, sleepy, slumberous (*or* slumbrous), somnolent; dreaming; hypnotized, mesmerized
antonyms asleep, dormant, dozing, napping, resting, sleeping, slumbering, unawakened

wakefulness *n* the inability to obtain adequate sleep ⟨a nagging *wakefulness* that seemed resistent to all of the standard home remedies⟩ — see INSOMNIA

waken *vb* **1** to cause to stop sleeping ⟨a sudden loud noise *wakened* us⟩ — see WAKE 1

2 to cease to be asleep ⟨she usually *wakens* when sunlight begins to stream through the windows⟩ — see WAKE 2

wake–up call *n* something that tells of approaching danger or risk ⟨his high blood pressure was a *wake-up call* that he needed to do something about his health⟩ — see WARNING 2

walk *n* **1** a relaxed journey on foot for exercise or pleasure ⟨we went for a long *walk* outside because it was such a nice night⟩
synonyms amble, constitutional, perambulation, ramble, range, saunter, stroll, turn, wander
related words parade, paseo, promenade; expedition, hike, march, peregrination, traipse, tramp, travel, traversal, traverse, trek, trip, walkabout; excursion, jaunt, junket, outing, sally, sashay, spin, tour; pilgrimage, progress, safari

2 a region of activity, knowledge, or influence ⟨a nondenominational church that attracts worshippers from every *walk* of life⟩ — see FIELD 2

3 a public place for strolling ⟨San Antonio's famous River *Walk* ranks among the city's foremost attractions⟩ — see PROMENADE

walk *vb* **1** to go on foot ⟨I *walked* slowly to school⟩
synonyms ambulate, foot (it), hoof (it), leg (it), pad, step, traipse, tread
related words parade, promenade; march, pace, step out, stride, troop; power walk; hike, peregrinate, trek; amble, mosey, perambulate, ramble, saunter, stroll, wander; clump, stomp, stump, tramp, trample, tromp; footslog, plod, trudge; gimp, hobble, limp; mince, prance, pussyfoot, tiptoe; bounce, sashay, stalk, strut, swagger; falter, lumber, lurch, pound, scuff, shamble, shuffle, stagger, stumble, toddle, waddle; nip, tap, trip, trot

2 to refuse to work in order to force an employer to meet demands ⟨workers threatened to *walk* unless management agreed to shoulder more of the cost of health insurance⟩ — see STRIKE 1

walker *n* a person who travels by foot for exercise or pleasure ⟨I began to lose weight after I gave up my sedentary lifestyle and became a daily *walker*⟩ — see HIKER

walking out *n* the act of leaving a place ⟨your unexplained *walking out* like that was rude⟩ — see DEPARTURE 1

walkout *n* a work stoppage by a body of workers intended to force an employer to meet their demands ⟨after four weeks of the *walkout*, management gave in⟩ — see STRIKE 1

walk out *vb* **1** to leave a place often for another ⟨we simply *walked out* after waiting half an hour for someone to come and serve us⟩ — see GO 2

2 to refuse to work in order to force an employer to meet demands ⟨the salesclerks *walked out* upon learning of the second pay cut in six months⟩ — see STRIKE 1

wall *n* **1** a physical object that blocks the way ⟨an ancient *wall* that was built to block the invading barbarians⟩ — see BARRIER

2 means or method of defending ⟨investigators faced a *wall* of silence from the members of the police department⟩ — see DEFENSE 1

wall (in) *vb* to close or shut in by or as if by barriers ⟨a lake almost entirely *walled in* by mountains⟩ — see ENCLOSE 1

wall (off) *vb* to disallow entry into (a place) by means of a physical barrier at the entry point ⟨big orange barrels *walled off* the highway exit⟩ — see CLOSE (OFF)

wallet *n* a bag carried by hand and designed to hold a traveler's clothing and personal articles ⟨with their humble belongings tucked into *wallets* of simple cloth, the pilgrims began their journey to one of Christendom's holiest shrines⟩ — see TRAVELING BAG

wallflower *n* a shy or reserved person ⟨there were too many *wallflowers* at the party, so things never really got lively⟩ — see INTROVERT

wallop *n* **1** a forceful coming together of two things ⟨felt the *wallop* of a car crashing into their front porch⟩ — see IMPACT 1

2 a hard strike with a part of the body or an instrument ⟨gave the ball a good *wallop* with the bat⟩ — see [1]BLOW

3 a pleasurably intense stimulation of the feelings ⟨she really got a *wallop* out of finding a rare first edition by her favorite author⟩ — see THRILL

wallop *vb* **1** to strike repeatedly ⟨*walloped* the branches of the pear tree with a stick in an effort to knock down some fruit⟩ — see BEAT 1

2 to defeat by a large margin ⟨*walloped* their traditional rivals 20 to nothing⟩ — see WHIP 2

3 to deliver a blow to (someone or something) usually in a strong vigorous manner ⟨arrested for *walloping* a police officer⟩ — see HIT 1

walloping *adj* unusually large ⟨he needed help to mount such a *walloping* horse⟩ — see HUGE

wall–to–wall *adj* present in all places and at all times ⟨television programming feels as if there are *wall-to-wall* sitcoms these days⟩ — see OMNIPRESENT

wampum *n* something (as pieces of stamped metal or printed paper) customarily and legally used as a medium of exchange, a measure of value, or a means of payment ⟨made some real *wampum* on that last business deal⟩ — see MONEY 1

wan *adj* lacking a healthy skin color ⟨she looks a little *wan* after all that tiring work⟩ — see PALE 2

wander *n* a relaxed journey on foot for exercise or pleasure ⟨a *wander* through the woods⟩ — see WALK 1

wander *vb* **1** to move about from place to place aimlessly ⟨we just went outside and *wandered* around until it was time to go⟩

synonyms bat, cruise, drift, float, gad (about), gallivant (*also* galavant), kick around, knock (about), maunder, meander, mooch, ramble, range, roam, rove, traipse

related words amble, saunter, stroll; dawdle, mope; gypsy, hobo, tramp, vagabond; mill (about *or* around); straggle, stray

2 to commit an offense ⟨we have all *wandered* from the path of righteousness at least once in our lives⟩ — see OFFEND 1

wanderer *n* a person who roams about without a fixed route or destination ⟨a *wanderer* who reasoned that he could never be lost, as he didn't care where he was going⟩ — see NOMAD

wandering *adj* **1** passing from one topic to another ⟨your decidedly *wandering* essay loses its punch—stick to one theme⟩ — see DISCURSIVE

2 traveling from place to place ⟨a *wandering* carnival that visited small towns all over the South⟩ — see ITINERANT

wane *vb* to grow less in scope or intensity especially gradually ⟨in the course of the evening the storm steadily *waned*⟩ — see DECREASE 2

wangle *vb* to plan out usually with subtle skill or care ⟨*wangled* a way to get free tickets to the show⟩ — see ENGINEER

wannabe *also* **wannabee** *n* a person who adopts the appearance or behavior of another especially in an obvious way ⟨an entrepreneur who seems to have made his fortune mainly by giving how-to-get-rich lectures to entrepreneurial *wannabes*⟩ — see COPYCAT

want *n* **1** the fact or state of being absent ⟨the proverb that begins, "for *want* of a nail, the shoe was lost"⟩ — see LACK 1

2 a falling short of an essential or desirable amount or number ⟨there's a notable *want* of teachers in that rural school district⟩ — see DEFICIENCY

3 a state of being without something necessary, desirable, or useful ⟨those children are in *want* of some good discipline⟩ — see NEED 1

4 the state of lacking sufficient money or material possessions ⟨grew up in extreme *want*⟩ — see POVERTY 1

5 a defect in character ⟨she's well-meaning and kind, but her besetting *want* is a complete lack of tact⟩ — see FAULT 1

want *vb* **1** to have an earnest wish to own or enjoy ⟨I *want* a new car so badly!⟩ — see DESIRE 1

2 to have as a requirement ⟨that stray cat *wants* food and a clean place to sleep⟩ — see NEED 1

3 to see fit ⟨do what you *want*⟩ — see CHOOSE 2

4 to wish to have ⟨I *want* some ice cream for dessert, please⟩ — see LIKE 1

wanting *adj* **1** falling short of a standard ⟨we tried her cooking and found it to be very *wanting*⟩ — see BAD 1

2 not coming up to an expected measure or meeting a particular need ⟨at this time of year food for many wild animals is *wanting*⟩ — see SHORT 3

3 not present or in evidence ⟨grass is almost entirely *wanting* in that arid wasteland⟩ — see ABSENT 2

wanting *prep* not having ⟨a mitten *wanting* its mate⟩ — see WITHOUT 1

wanton *adj* **1** depicting or referring to sexual matters in a way that is unacceptable in polite society ⟨that novel was once regarded as a *wanton* tale of forbidden love⟩ — see OBSCENE 1

2 having a strong sexual desire ⟨in earlier times, novelists usually portrayed *wanton* women as coming to a bad end⟩ — see LUSTFUL

3 having or showing the desire to inflict severe pain and suffering on others ⟨a *wanton* attack on unarmed civilians⟩ — see CRUEL 1

wanton *n* a person who playfully shows another amorous attention ⟨at the office party, count on her to get drunk and play the *wanton*⟩ — see FLIRT

wantonness *n* **1** disposition to willfully inflict pain and suffering on others ⟨the barbaric *wantonness* with which the guards treated the prisoners of war⟩ — see CRUELTY

2 the quality or state of being obscene ⟨novels characterized chiefly by their sheer *wantonness*⟩ — see OBSCENITY 1

war *n* **1** a state of armed violent struggle between states, nations, or groups ⟨the *war* was the result of ethnic tensions that had been building in the region for decades⟩

synonyms conflagration, conflict, hostilities, hot war

related words civil war, cold war, holy war, limited war, police action, world war; action, battle, engagement, skirmish; combat, fighting, warfare

near antonyms demilitarization, demobilization, disarmament; pacification; cease-fire, truce; calm, peacefulness, tranquillity (*or* tranquility)

antonyms peace

2 a lack of agreement or harmony ⟨the siblings always seemed to be at *war* with one another⟩ — see DISCORD

3 an earnest effort for superiority or victory over another ⟨only the latest round in the never-ending class *war*⟩ — see CONTEST 1

war (against) *vb* to oppose (someone) in physical conflict ⟨continually *warring against* their neighbors in an effort to expand their territory⟩ — see FIGHT 1

warble *n* a rhythmic series of musical tones arranged to give a pleasing effect ⟨whistled a cheerful *warble* as he strolled down the street⟩ — see MELODY

warble *vb* to sing with the alternation of two musical tones ⟨the skylark *warbled* prettily outside our window⟩

synonyms quaver, trill

related words slur; yodel; belt, carol, chant, chorus, croon, descant, harmonize, troll, vocalize; lilt, scat

ward *n* **1** means or method of defending ⟨frequent hand washing is an oft-recommended *ward* against the spread of common germs⟩ — see DEFENSE 1

2 responsibility for the safety and well-being of someone or something ⟨gained the *ward* of his cousin upon the death of her parents⟩ — see CUSTODY

ward *vb* to drive danger or attack away from ⟨vowed that he would take whatever measures were necessary to *ward* the nation's people⟩ — see DEFEND 1

warden *n* **1** a person or group that watches over someone or something ⟨in his role as *warden* of the school, a principal must provide a safe environment for the students⟩ — see GUARD 1

2 a person who takes care of a property sometimes for an absent owner ⟨served as *warden* for the country estate⟩ — see CUSTODIAN 1

warder *n* a person or group that watches over someone or something ⟨as *warder* of the velvet rope, he decides who gets into the fashionable nightclub and who doesn't⟩ — see GUARD 1

ware *adj* having specified facts or feelings actively impressed on the mind ⟨he's *ware* of the dangers that await him in the Antarctic⟩ — see CONSCIOUS 1

ware *vb* to be cautious of or on guard against ⟨a hunter yelling to his dog, "*Ware* the porcupine!"⟩ — see BEWARE (OF)

warehouse *n* a building for storing goods ⟨when the *warehouse* burned down, we lost most of our merchandise⟩ — see STOREHOUSE

wares *n pl* products that are bought and sold in business ⟨a merchant proudly displaying his *wares*⟩ — see MERCHANDISE

warfare *n* **1** a lack of agreement or harmony ⟨that troubled household seems to be almost constantly in a state of *warfare*⟩ — see DISCORD

2 an earnest effort for superiority or victory over another ⟨companies engaged in constant *warfare* for dominance in the market for home computers⟩ — see CONTEST 1

war hawk *n* one who urges or attempts to cause a war ⟨*war hawks* in the cabinet who urged the President to respond to the threat with armed force⟩ — see WARMONGER

warhorse *n* a person with long experience in a specified area ⟨a *warhorse* who's survived far nastier campaigns in his long political career⟩ — see VETERAN

wariness *n* a close attentiveness to avoiding danger ⟨only his unceasing *wariness* saved the party of skiers from an avalanche⟩ — see CAUTION 1

warlike *adj* feeling or displaying eagerness to fight ⟨a seafarer's legend that the remote island was inhabited by a *warlike* and uncivilized tribe⟩ — see BELLIGERENT

warm *adj* **1** having or giving off heat to a moderate degree ⟨the pan was still *warm*, but no longer too hot to touch⟩

synonyms heated, hottish, lukewarm, tepid, toasty, warmed, warmish

related words thawed; boiling, broiling, burning, fiery, hot, piping hot, red-hot, roasting, scalding, scorching, searing, steamy, sultry, sweltering, torrid, white-hot; overheated, roasted, superheated, sweltering; blazing, glowing, molten, sizzling; reheated, rewarmed, warmed-over

near antonyms arctic, bitter, bleak, chill, chilly, cold, freezing, frigid, frosty, gelid, glacial, ice-cold, iced, icy, nippy, polar, raw, sharp, snappy, snowy, subfreezing, subzero, ultracold, winterly, wintry (*also* wintery); frosted; benumbed, nipped, numb

antonyms chilled, coldish, cool, cooled, coolish, refrigerated, unheated

2 having or expressing great depth of feeling ⟨a *warm* hug of welcome from our grandmother⟩ — see FERVENT 1

3 having or showing kindly feeling and sincere interest ⟨a *warm* inquiry after his parents' health⟩ — see FRIENDLY 1

warm *vb* **1** to cause to have or give off heat to a moderate degree ⟨you'll need to *warm* the food in the microwave⟩

synonyms heat, hot (up) [*chiefly Southern, southern Midland, & British*], toast

related words overheat, superheat; reheat, rewarm; thaw; bake, cook, roast; burn, char, fire, parch, scald, scorch, sear

near antonyms freeze, frost, ice, supercool

antonyms chill, cool, refrigerate

2 to give satisfaction to ⟨my dance instructor's generous praise *warmed* my heart⟩ — see PLEASE 1

warm–blooded *adj* having or expressing great depth of feeling ⟨a *warm-blooded* defense of everyone's right to free speech⟩ — see FERVENT 1

warmed *adj* having or giving off heat to a moderate degree ⟨the *warmed* towels that the attendant handed us were a nice touch⟩ — see WARM 1

warm fuzzies *n pl* a feeling or state of well-being and contentment ⟨the *warm fuzzies* that one typically gets from having done a good deed⟩ — see HAPPINESS 1

warmhearted *adj* **1** having or marked by sympathy and consideration for others ⟨a *warmhearted*, understanding pastor from whom many sought guidance⟩ — see HUMANE 1

2 having or showing kindly feeling and sincere interest ⟨a *warmhearted* welcome from the staff on my first day at work⟩ — see FRIENDLY 1

warmheartedness *n* **1** sympathetic concern for the well-being of others ⟨*warmheartedness* has never been one of the CEO's strong points⟩ — see BENIGNANCY

2 the capacity for feeling for another's unhappiness or misfortune ⟨after our disastrous fire we were overwhelmed by the *warmheartedness* of the neighbors⟩ — see HEART 1

warmish *adj* having or giving off heat to a moderate degree ⟨having been on the kitchen counter for some time, the glass of juice had become rather *warmish*⟩ — see WARM 1

warmness *n* the quality or state of being moderate in temperature ⟨the cozy *warmness* of a house can be so nice after an hour spent shoveling snow⟩ — see WARMTH 1

warmonger *n* one who urges or attempts to cause a war ⟨fortunately, the *warmongers* met with overwhelming opposition⟩
synonyms hawk, jingo, jingoist, militarist, war hawk
related words agitator, firebrand, fomenter, instigator, rabble-rouser; belligerent, combatant, militant; chauvinist
near antonyms peacemaker; peacekeeper
antonyms dove, pacifist, peacenik

warmth *n* **1** the quality or state of being moderate in temperature ⟨the cozy *warmth* of the inn's parlor was a welcome relief from the wintry weather outside⟩
synonyms lukewarmness, tepidity, tepidness, warmness
related words balminess, mildness, temperateness; glow, radiance, radiancy; heat, hotness, stuffiness, sultriness, torridity, torridness
near antonyms bitterness, bleakness, cold, coldness, frigidity, frigidness, frostiness, iciness, rawness, sharpness; frost
antonyms chill, chilliness, coolness
2 depth of feeling ⟨I was surprised by the *warmth* of the greeting⟩ — see ARDOR 1

warm–up *n* a performance, activity, or event that precedes and sets the stage for the main event ⟨the couple's initial exchange of insults proved to be only a *warm-up* for their booze-fueled fight later that night⟩ — see PRELUDE 1

warn *vb* to give notice to beforehand especially of danger or risk ⟨the lifeguard *warned* the boys that if they continued playing so rough, someone was sure to get hurt⟩
synonyms advise, alert, caution, forewarn, wake
related words augur, forecast, foretell, harbinger, predict, presage, prognosticate, prophesy; apprise, inform, notify, tip (off); admonish; bode, forebode (*also* forbode), foreshadow, foretoken, portend
near antonyms imperil, risk

warning *adj* serving as or offering a warning ⟨usually gave her trademark *warning* look when the children were getting out of hand⟩ — see CAUTIONARY

warning *n* **1** the act or an instance of telling beforehand of danger or risk ⟨she delivered a strict *warning* that anyone who was caught stealing would be fired⟩
synonyms admonishment, admonition, alarm (*also* alarum), alert, caution, forewarning, heads-up, notice
related words auguring, augury, forecasting, foretelling, predicting, prediction, premonition, presaging, prognosticating, prophecy (*also* prophesy), prophesying; apprising, informing, notification, notifying, tip-off; advice, counsel, guidance, recommendation, suggestion, tip; announcement, declaration
2 something that tells of approaching danger or risk ⟨the ominously darkening sky was a *warning* that a tornado was approaching⟩
synonyms caution, red flag, red light, tip-off, tocsin, wake-up call
related words omen, portent, premonition, presage; notice, notification; buoy, indicator, knell, sign, signal; foretaste, foretoken; announcement, declaration
phrases handwriting on the wall
near antonyms all clear

warp *n* an immaterial thing upon which something else rests ⟨an unshakable belief in the essential goodness of humankind is the *warp* of his philosophy⟩ — see BASE 1

warp *vb* **1** to change so much as to create a wrong impression or alter the meaning of ⟨the faulty English translation really *warps* the meaning of the original Russian text⟩ — see GARBLE 1
2 to lower in character, dignity, or quality ⟨claims that violent movies *warp* the values of our young people⟩ — see DEBASE 1
3 to twist (something) out of a natural or normal shape or condition ⟨freezing *warped* the plastic, and now the cover won't fit⟩ — see CONTORT

war paint *n* preparations intended to beautify the face ⟨when I was young, I loved to watch Mom put on her *war paint* before a fancy evening out⟩ — see MAKEUP 1

warp and woof *n* an immaterial thing upon which something else rests ⟨regards individual freedom and democracy as the *warp and woof* of any civilized society⟩ — see BASE 1

warped *adj* having or showing lowered moral character or standards ⟨tired of his sick jokes and *warped* sense of humor⟩ — see CORRUPT

warping *n* the twisting of something out of its natural or normal shape or condition ⟨the *warping* of the door frame over the years means there's always a draft now⟩ — see CONTORTION

warrant *n* the approval by someone in authority for the doing of something ⟨some employees suspected that the supervisor had no *warrant* from the CEO for instituting the draconian work rules⟩ — see PERMISSION

warrant *vb* **1** to assume responsibility for the satisfactory quality or performance of ⟨the computer company unconditionally *warrants* all of its products for one full year⟩
synonyms guarantee, guaranty
related words attest, authenticate, avouch, certify, testify (to), vouch (for), witness; assure, bond, contract, covenant; pledge, plight, stipulate, swear, undertake, vow; adhere, assert, aver, avow, declare, insist; insure
2 to give official acceptance of as satisfactory ⟨the state constitution *warrants* these measures⟩ — see APPROVE
3 to have as a requirement ⟨the situation *warrants* your immediate attention⟩ — see NEED 1
4 to state as a fact usually forcefully ⟨we'll all be dead before that happens, I *warrant*⟩ — see CLAIM 1
5 to give official or legal power to ⟨bailiffs are *warranted* to enforce the subpoena⟩ — see AUTHORIZE 1

warranted *adj* being what is called for by accepted standards of right and wrong ⟨a *warranted* use of force by the police⟩ — see JUST 1

warranty *n* a formal agreement to fulfill an obligation ⟨a one-year *warranty* for the refrigerator⟩ — see GUARANTEE 1

warren *n* a confusing and complicated arrangement of passages ⟨got lost in the *warren* of interconnected side streets⟩ — see MAZE 1

warrior *n* a person engaged in military service ⟨a program of tough training and discipline that turns untried civilians into *warriors*⟩ — see SOLDIER

wary *adj* having or showing a close attentiveness to avoiding danger or trouble ⟨kept a *wary* eye out for signs of the enemy⟩ — see CAREFUL 1

wash *n* spongy land saturated or partially covered with water ⟨an invasive species threatening the plants native to the region's *washes*⟩ — see SWAMP 1

wash *vb* **1** to flow along or against ⟨crystal-clear waters gently *wash* the island's unspoiled beaches⟩
synonyms bathe, lap, lave, lip, splash
related words bubble, gurgle, plash, ripple, slosh

2 to withstand scrutiny and gain acceptance or approval ⟨the employee's story about missing the bus didn't *wash* with her manager⟩
synonyms fly, hold up, pass, stand up
related words get through, go down, go over, go through, play, take, work
phrases hold water, pass muster
3 to flow in a broken irregular stream ⟨soapy water *washing* down the drain⟩ — see GURGLE
4 to make wet ⟨rain *washed* the countryside for days on end⟩ — see WET
5 to pour liquid over or through in order to cleanse ⟨*washed* the baby's hair⟩ — see FLUSH 1
6 to cause (as a liquid) to move about in a circle especially repeatedly ⟨she absentmindedly *washed* her tea by tipping her cup, until the honey was at last mixed in⟩ — see STIR 1

washed *adj* containing, covered with, or thoroughly penetrated by water ⟨*washed* city streets glistened with the light of the lampposts⟩ — see WET 1

washed–out *adj* **1** lacking intensity of color ⟨*washed-out* blond hair⟩ — see PALE 1
2 depleted in strength, energy, or freshness ⟨feeling *washed-out* after the endless primary season, the party's nominee needs a vacation more than anything⟩ — see WEARY 1

washed–up *adj* having lost forcefulness, courage, or spirit ⟨he felt rather *washed-up* after this latest business failure⟩ — see EFFETE 1

washout *n* something that has failed ⟨the fashion designer's last showing was a complete *washout*⟩ — see FAILURE 3

wash out *vb* **1** to be unsuccessful ⟨most of the participants in the tough training program *washed out*⟩ — see FAIL 2
2 to make white or whiter by removing color ⟨the bright lights of the TV studio *washed out* her facial features, making her look as white as a ghost⟩ — see WHITEN
3 to use up all the physical energy of ⟨that last illness *washed* the child *out* completely⟩ — see EXHAUST 1
4 to pour liquid over or through in order to cleanse ⟨*wash out* your bathing suit in the sink⟩ — see FLUSH 1

washroom *n* a room furnished with a fixture for flushing body waste ⟨could you tell me where the *washroom* is?⟩ — see TOILET

washy *adj* **1** lacking intensity of color ⟨the supposedly rich rose she had chosen for the house unexpectedly came out a *washy* pinkish shade⟩ — see PALE 1
2 not containing very much of some important element ⟨the economy needs some strong medicine right now, and our leaders are offering only *washy* gruel⟩ — see WEAK 3

waspish *adj* easily irritated or annoyed ⟨extremely *waspish*, she uses her wit viciously when irritated⟩ — see IRRITABLE

waspishness *n* readiness to show annoyance or impatience ⟨his perpetual *waspishness* only served to make those around him cranky as well⟩ — see PETULANCE

wassail *n* a bout of prolonged or excessive drinking ⟨woke up with a terrible headache from a wild *wassail* the night before⟩ — see CAROUSE

wassail *vb* to take part in drunken revelry ⟨the knights feasted and *wassailed* for three days after the battlefield victory⟩ — see CAROUSE

wastage *n* the state or fact of being rendered nonexistent, physically unsound, or useless ⟨the slash-and-burn *wastage* of the surrounding countryside as the army made its way to the sea⟩ — see DESTRUCTION 1

waste *adj* producing inferior or only a small amount of vegetation ⟨*waste* acreage that was not fit for anything⟩ — see BARREN 1

waste *n* **1** an instance of spending money or resources without care or restraint ⟨it seems like a *waste* to spend my entire paycheck on a bigger TV⟩
synonyms extravagance, prodigality
related words indulgence, luxury, splurge; loss, wastage; dissipation, profligacy, profusion, squandering, wastefulness; overindulgence, self-indulgence; excess, immoderacy, overkill
near antonyms necessity; belt-tightening, conservation, economizing, economy, frugality, parsimony, penny-pinching, saving, scrimping, skimping, thrift; austerity, moderation, restraint, temperance, temperateness
2 discarded or useless material ⟨gathered up the *waste* when he was finished sewing⟩ — see GARBAGE 1
3 land that is uninhabited or not fit for crops ⟨an area that was a barren *waste* after the strip-mining had ended⟩ — see WASTELAND
4 solid matter discharged from an animal's alimentary canal ⟨a local ordinance requiring dog owners to properly dispose of their pet's *waste*⟩ — see DROPPING 1
5 a wide space or area ⟨a legendary mariner doomed to sail the watery *wastes* of the world until Judgment Day⟩ — see EXPANSE
6 a gradual weakening, loss, or destruction ⟨the slow *waste* of the once broad beach by the relentless tide⟩ — see CORROSION

waste *vb* **1** to use up carelessly ⟨he *wasted* his lottery winnings on booze-soaked nights with gold diggers⟩
synonyms blow, dissipate, fiddle away, fritter (away), lavish, lose, misspend, run through, spend, squander, throw away, trifle (away)
related words splurge; consume, deplete, exhaust, impoverish, overspend, shoot; indulge, overindulge; disburse, expend, lay out
phrases play ducks and drakes with (*or* make ducks and drakes of)
near antonyms economize, scrimp, skimp; preserve, protect, save; hoard, lay up
antonyms conserve
2 to bring to a complete end the physical soundness, existence, or usefulness of ⟨one country attempting to *waste* another⟩ — see DESTROY 1
3 to diminish the physical strength of ⟨endless months of inactivity *wasted* him⟩ — see WEAKEN 1

waste (away) *vb* to lose bodily strength or vigor ⟨the tuberculosis resulted in her simply *wasting away*⟩ — see WEAKEN 2

wasted *adj* **1** lacking bodily strength ⟨a *wasted* frame—a shadow of the man he once was⟩ — see WEAK 1
2 suffering extreme weight loss as a result of hunger or disease ⟨a frail and *wasted* famine victim⟩ — see EMACIATED
3 *slang* being under the influence of a recreational drug ⟨the documentary portrays the comedian as someone who was often too *wasted* to function socially⟩ — see STONED 1
4 *slang* being under the influence of alcohol ⟨unfortunately, his college years were largely spent getting *wasted*⟩ — see DRUNK

wasteful *adj* given to spending money freely or foolishly ⟨my one *wasteful* child always seemed to run out of money by midweek⟩ — see PRODIGAL

wastefulness *n* the quality or fact of being free or wasteful in the expenditure of money ⟨considering he has a family, his *wastefulness* is downright irresponsible⟩ — see EXTRAVAGANCE 1

wasteland *n* land that is uninhabited or not fit for crops ⟨with proper irrigation and fertilizer, they turned the desert *wasteland* into a fertile plain⟩
synonyms barren, desert, desolation, heath, no-man's-land, waste

related words badland; brush, bush; dust bowl; open, open air, outdoors, out-of-doors; nature, wild, wilderness

waster *n* someone who spends money freely or foolishly ⟨we want you to get a job so that you'll be a *waster* of your own money and not ours⟩ — see PRODIGAL

wastrel *n* someone who spends money freely or foolishly ⟨the black sheep of the family, he ended up being a *wastrel* and a drunkard⟩ — see PRODIGAL

watch *n* **1** a person or group that watches over someone or something ⟨the neighborhood crime *watch*⟩ — see GUARD 1

2 the state of being constantly attentive and responsive to signs of activity, opportunity, or danger ⟨kept a *watch* over the sick baby⟩ — see VIGILANCE

3 an act or period of watching for signs of activity, danger, or opportunity ⟨the little boy kept *watch* at the window for signs of Santa and his sleigh⟩ — see VIGIL

watch *vb* **1** to keep one's eyes on ⟨I turned my head to continue *watching* the bird as it flew away⟩

synonyms eye, follow, observe

related words behold, look, perceive, regard, see, view; gape, gawk, gaze, glare, goggle, look on, peer, rubberneck, stare; guard, wake, ward; bird-dog, monitor, study; spy; espy, glance, glimpse, peek, peep

phrases have one's eye on

near antonyms blink, wink

2 to take notice of and be guided by ⟨*watch* what I do when I run into that kind of problem⟩ — see HEED 1

3 to pay continued close attention to (something) for a particular purpose ⟨*watched* the situation to see if it improved⟩ — see MONITOR

4 to have an interest or concern for ⟨you should *watch* what you eat if you want a long, healthy life⟩ — see CARE

5 to take charge of especially on behalf of another ⟨hired a high school girl to *watch* their daughter until they got home from work⟩ — see TEND 1

watch (for) *vb* to believe in the future occurrence of (something) ⟨*watch for* all the latest news on this Web site⟩ — see EXPECT

watcher *n* **1** a person or group that watches over someone or something ⟨the inexperienced babysitter turned out to be a well-meaning but hopelessly incompetent *watcher* of young children⟩ — see GUARD 1

2 someone who sees or watches something ⟨a safari that affords wildlife *watchers* plenty of opportunities to see Africa's grandest creatures in their natural habitat⟩ — see SPECTATOR

watchful *adj* paying close attention usually for the purpose of anticipating approaching danger or opportunity ⟨the toddler played under the *watchful* eye of her parents⟩ — see ALERT 1

watchfulness *n* the state of being constantly attentive and responsive to signs of opportunity, activity, or danger ⟨it was only her motherly *watchfulness* that saved the boy from an accident⟩ — see VIGILANCE

watchman *n* **1** a person or group that watches over someone or something ⟨hired a *watchman* to patrol the factory at night⟩ — see GUARD 1

2 a person who takes care of a property sometimes for an absent owner ⟨a *watchman* lives next door to scare off prowlers⟩ — see CUSTODIAN 1

watch out (for) *vb* to be cautious of or on guard against ⟨*watch out for* hazards in the road⟩ — see BEWARE (OF)

watchword *n* **1** a word or phrase that must be spoken by a person in order to pass a guard ⟨the *watchword* is changed every day⟩ — see PASSWORD

2 an attention-getting word or phrase used to publicize something (as a campaign or product) ⟨their latest *watchword* turns up in every ad from that company⟩ — see SLOGAN

water *vb* to make wet ⟨*watered* the plants⟩ — see WET

water closet *n* a room furnished with a fixture for flushing body waste ⟨the first house in town to have an indoor *water closet*⟩ — see TOILET

watercourse *n* an open man-made passageway for water ⟨the Erie Canal was the first *watercourse* to connect the Hudson River with the Great Lakes⟩ — see CHANNEL 1

watercraft *n* a small buoyant structure for travel on water ⟨just about any kind of *watercraft* can be seen on the lake during the summer⟩ — see BOAT 1

water down *vb* to alter (something) for the worse with the addition of foreign or lower-grade substances ⟨*watered down* the cocktails while jacking up their prices⟩ — see ADULTERATE

watered *adj* containing, covered with, or thoroughly penetrated by water ⟨a heavily *watered* lawn⟩ — see WET 1

waterfall *n* a fall of water usually from a great height ⟨I used to like to throw sticks in the stream and watch them go over the *waterfall*⟩

synonyms cascade, cataract, fall(s)

related words flume; chute (*also* shute), rapid(s), shoot, white water

watering hole *n* a place of business where alcoholic beverages are sold to be consumed on the premises ⟨supposedly, that Broadway hangout was the favorite *watering hole* for 1940s celebrities⟩ — see BARROOM

watering place *n* a place of business where alcoholic beverages are sold to be consumed on the premises ⟨die-hard fans gathered at the local *watering place* to watch the Super Bowl⟩ — see BARROOM

waterless *adj* marked by little or no precipitation or humidity ⟨cacti prefer a nearly *waterless* environment⟩ — see DRY 1

waterlog *vb* to make wet ⟨the wood was too *waterlogged* by the downpour to be used for a fire⟩ — see WET

waterlogged *adj* containing, covered with, or thoroughly penetrated by water ⟨*waterlogged* soil that caused the roots of the potted plant to rot⟩ — see WET 1

waterproof *adj* made of or treated with material that does not allow water to penetrate ⟨luckily, my backpack is *waterproof*, so my clothes didn't get wet⟩

synonyms leakproof, waterproofed

related words rainproof; water-repellent, water-resistant; staunch (*also* stanch), watertight; nonabsorbent, nonporous; weatherproof

near antonyms absorbent, porous; leaky

waterproof *n, chiefly British* a coat made of water-resistant material ⟨remember your *waterproof* if you're walking around London in the winter⟩ — see RAINCOAT

waterproofed *adj* made of or treated with material that does not allow water to penetrate ⟨a *waterproofed* fabric that is used for outerwear⟩ — see WATERPROOF

watershed *n* a point in a chain of events at which an important change (as in one's fortunes) occurs ⟨a *watershed* moment in her life came when she inherited a reasonable sum of money and was able to start her own coffee shop⟩ — see TURNING POINT

water-soak *vb* to make wet ⟨the fire is out, but the firefighters *water-soaked* most of the house in the process⟩ — see WET

water-soaked *adj* containing, covered with, or thoroughly penetrated by water ⟨make sure that the bandages don't get *water-soaked* when you take a shower⟩ — see WET 1

waterspout *n* a pipe or channel for carrying off water from a roof ⟨the *waterspout* became clogged, and then the roof leaked⟩ — see GUTTER 1

waterway *n* an open man-made passageway for water ⟨the Erie Canal was superseded by a much larger *waterway*, the New York State Barge Canal⟩ — see CHANNEL 1

watery *adj* **1** containing, covered with, or thoroughly penetrated by water ⟨the soft, *watery* earth of the marshland⟩ — see WET 1
2 having an overly soft liquid consistency ⟨*watery* oatmeal⟩ — see RUNNY
3 not containing very much of some important element ⟨a *watery* lemonade⟩ — see WEAK 3
4 lacking in qualities that make for spirit and character ⟨political correctness has resulted in a lot of history books being written in very *watery* prose⟩ — see WISHY-WASHY 1

wave *n* a moving ridge on the surface of water ⟨the toddler was almost knocked down by the *waves* created by the speedboat⟩
synonyms billow, surge, swell
related words sea(s); surf; breaker, whitecap; comber, curl; riffle, ripple, wavelet; ground swell, roller; tidal wave, tsunami

wave *vb* to direct or notify by a movement or gesture ⟨*waved* them over to the side of the road⟩ — see MOTION

waver *vb* **1** to show uncertainty about the right course of action ⟨he's still *wavering* about whether to take the job⟩ — see HESITATE
2 to swing unsteadily back and forth or from side to side ⟨the steel tower *wavered* for a moment before falling over⟩ — see TEETER 1

wavering *n* a state or an instance of temporary inaction because of uncertainty about the right course of action ⟨after a moment's *wavering*, she accepted his proposal⟩ — see HESITATION

[1]**wax** *vb* **1** to coat (something) with a slippery substance in order to reduce friction ⟨*waxing* a surfboard⟩ — see LUBRICATE
2 *slang* to defeat by a large margin ⟨I can't believe I bet on a football team that ended up getting *waxed* 45–0⟩ — see WHIP 2

[2]**wax** *vb* **1** to become greater in extent, volume, amount, or number ⟨the commitment of the young volunteers to the cause seems to *wax* and wane⟩ — see INCREASE 2
2 to eventually have as a state or quality ⟨*waxed* poetic whenever he wrote to his girlfriend⟩ — see BECOME

waxy *adj* capable of being easily molded or modeled ⟨the children made little animals with the colorful, *waxy* modeling clay⟩ — see PLASTIC 1

way *adv* to a great degree ⟨"Oh, I'm just *way* thrilled to be here!" the pageant contestant gushed⟩ — see VERY 1

way *n* **1** a passage cleared for public vehicular travel ⟨the town honored the local sports hero by naming after him a short *way* connecting two shopping centers⟩
synonyms arterial, artery, avenue, boulevard, carriageway [*British*], drag, drive, expressway, freeway, high road, highway, pass, pike, road, roadway, route, row, street, thoroughfare, thruway, trace, turnpike
related words causeway; autobahn, autoroute, autostrada, dual carriageway [*chiefly British*], interstate, motorway [*chiefly British*], superhighway; beltway, bypass, parkway, ring road [*chiefly British*]; corniche, switchback; through street; high street [*British*], Main Street; backstreet, branch, bystreet, byway, crossroad, secondary road, shunpike, side road, side street; alley, alleyway; circle, lane, laneway [*British*], mews [*chiefly British*], place; close [*chiefly British*], cul-de-sac, dead end; corridor; track, trail
2 a usual manner of behaving or doing ⟨she's set in her *ways* and is not about to change⟩ — see HABIT 1
3 an established course for traveling from one place to another ⟨took the regular *way* to work⟩ — see PASSAGE 1
4 an established pattern of behavior ⟨that's just his *way*, so pay him no mind⟩ — see TENDENCY 1
5 an extent or area available for or used up by some activity or thing ⟨made *way* for them to pass⟩ — see ROOM 1
6 the direction along which something or someone moves ⟨go the same *way* that the school bus does⟩ — see PATH 1
7 the means or procedure for doing something ⟨figured out the best *way* to accomplish the task⟩ — see METHOD
8 the opening through which one can enter or leave a structure ⟨we came in the back *way*⟩ — see DOOR 2
9 the power, right, or opportunity to choose ⟨have it your *way*⟩ — see CHOICE 1
10 the space or amount of space between two points, lines, surfaces, or objects ⟨it's just a little *way* down the road⟩ — see DISTANCE 1

wayfarer *n* a person who roams about without a fixed route or destination ⟨one of the great *wayfarers* of American folklore, Johnny Appleseed wandered across the country, always planting apple seeds⟩ — see NOMAD

wayfaring *adj* traveling from place to place ⟨a *wayfaring* folksinger⟩ — see ITINERANT

waylay *vb* to lie in wait for and attack by surprise ⟨a lonely stretch of highway along which unsuspecting tourists are often *waylaid* by gangs⟩ — see AMBUSH

way–out *adj* different from the ordinary in a way that causes curiosity or suspicion ⟨some new and *way-out* suggestions for naming the baby⟩ — see ODD 2

way station *n* a regular stopping place ⟨a *way station* for truck drivers⟩ — see STATION 2

wayward *adj* **1** given to resisting authority or another's control ⟨had always been the most *wayward* of their three children⟩ — see DISOBEDIENT
2 given to resisting control or discipline by others ⟨an institution to which *wayward* teens were often sent⟩ — see UNCONTROLLABLE

waywardness *n* refusal to obey ⟨the unremitting *waywardness* of the child frustrated her parents at times⟩ — see DISOBEDIENCE

weak *adj* **1** lacking bodily strength ⟨the little boy was simply too *weak* to lift the box⟩
synonyms asthenic, debilitated, delicate, down-and-out, effete, enervated, enfeebled, faint, feeble, frail, infirm, languid, low, prostrate, prostrated, sapped, slight, soft, softened, tender, unsubstantial, wasted, weakened, wimpish, wimpy
related words challenged, disabled, incapacitated, invalid; paralyzed; broken-down, decrepit; impotent, powerless; breakable, flimsy, fragile; dizzy, groggy, rocky, unsteady, woozy; drained, exhausted, flagging, tired, weary, worn-out; damaged, harmed, hurt, impaired, injured, lame, unsound; resistless, susceptible, unresistant, vulnerable, yielding
near antonyms able-bodied, athletic, beefy, brawny, fit, husky, muscular, sinewy, strapping, virile; hard, hardy, lusty, red-blooded, robust, sturdy, tough; fortified, hardened, inured, strengthened, toughened; energetic, energized, invigorated, vigorous, vitalized; hale, healthy, sound; capable, competent; convalescing, recovering, recuperating
antonyms mighty, powerful, rugged, stalwart, stout, strong
2 lacking strength of will or character ⟨the opinion that overweight people are just *weak* individuals who easily give in to temptation⟩
synonyms characterless, effete, frail, invertebrate, limp-wristed, milk-and-water, namby-pamby, nerve-

less, soft, spineless, weakened, weak-kneed, weakling, wet [*British*], wimpish, wimpy, wishy-washy
related words flabby, flaccid, forceless, ineffective, ineffectual; impotent, impuissant, powerless; emasculated, unnerved; lamblike, meek, pliable, submissive; corrupt, dastardly, unprincipled, unscrupulous, villainous; cowardly, craven, fainthearted, lily-livered, nebbishy, poltroon, pusillanimous, sissy, timid; infirm, irresolute, vacillating
near antonyms ethical, good, moral, principled, right, righteous, upright, virtuous; determined, mettlesome, resolute, unrelenting; courageous, stalwart, stouthearted
antonyms backboned, firm, hard, strong, tough
3 not containing very much of some important element ⟨the coffee came out too *weak* because I didn't use enough ground beans⟩
synonyms dilute, diluted, thin, thinned, washy, watery, weakened
related words adulterated, watered-down
near antonyms enriched, fortified; concentrated, condensed, evaporated
antonyms full-bodied, rich, strong
4 not using or following good reasoning ⟨your argument is *weak*⟩ — see ILLOGICAL
5 unable to act or achieve one's purpose ⟨the vice president is a relatively *weak* official⟩ — see POWERLESS

weaken *vb* **1** to diminish the physical strength of ⟨weeks of hardship in the desert had greatly *weakened* them⟩
synonyms debilitate, devitalize, enervate, enfeeble, etiolate, prostrate, sap, soften, tire, waste
related words cripple, disable, hamstring, incapacitate; deplete, depress, exhaust, impoverish, unman, wash out; damage, harm, hurt, impair, injure, invalid, lay up; break down, grind (down), wear down, wear out; paralyze
near antonyms energize, invigorate, recruit, rejuvenate, vitalize; harden, season, toughen
antonyms beef (up), fortify, strengthen
2 to lose bodily strength or vigor ⟨the bodybuilder *weakened* once she eased off on her workouts⟩
synonyms decay, droop, emaciate, fade, fail, flag, go, lag, languish, sag, sink, waste (away), wilt, wither
related words break down, wear out; yield; degenerate, deteriorate, rot, run down
near antonyms convalesce, rally, rebound, recover, recuperate; gain
3 to alter (something) for the worse with the addition of foreign or lower-grade substances ⟨*weakened* the juice with too much water⟩ — see ADULTERATE

weakened *adj* **1** containing foreign or lower-grade substances ⟨the pharmacist, motivated by pure greed, would pass off the *weakened* drugs to unsuspecting customers, some of whom had life-threatening illnesses⟩ — see IMPURE 1
2 lacking bodily strength ⟨left *weakened* by a prolonged illness⟩ — see WEAK 1
3 lacking strength of will or character ⟨the nation's people, *weakened* by years of tyranny, tended to automatically obey anyone with an authoritative manner⟩ — see WEAK 2
4 not containing very much of some important element ⟨some experts recommend that runners drink a *weakened* mixture of juice and water⟩ — see WEAK 3

weakening *n* a gradual sinking and wasting away of mind or body ⟨the all-too-apparent *weakening* of our grandfather was hard on our mother⟩ — see DECLINE 1

weak–kneed *adj* lacking strength of will or character ⟨management is too *weak-kneed* to effectively enforce even a minimal dress code⟩ — see WEAK 2

weakling *adj* lacking strength of will or character ⟨argues that in a time of war, the country can't afford to have a *weakling* president⟩ — see WEAK 2

weakling *n* **1** a person lacking in physical strength ⟨he had been a *weakling* until high school, when he started working out to put on muscle⟩
synonyms softy (*or* softie), wimp, wuss (*also* wussy)
related words pushover; milksop, mollycoddle, sissy
antonyms powerhouse
2 a person without strength of character ⟨only a *weakling* would be willing to lie to save himself from punishment⟩
synonyms doormat, jellyfish, namby-pamby, pushover, reed, wimp
related words coward, milquetoast, mouse, nebbish, nervous Nellie (*or* nervous Nelly), pussy [*slang*], wuss (*also* wussy); sheep
near antonyms mensch
antonyms stalwart

weakly *adj* chronically or repeatedly suffering from poor health ⟨a *weakly* baby who required repeated hospitalizations⟩ — see SICKLY 1

weak–minded *adj* **1** not having or showing an ability to absorb ideas readily ⟨was written off as *weak-minded* until it was discovered that he had a learning disability⟩ — see STUPID 1
2 showing or marked by a lack of good sense or judgment ⟨a *weak-minded* decision to use all of their savings to buy lottery tickets in the hopes of hitting the jackpot⟩ — see FOOLISH 1

weak–mindedness *n* the quality or state of lacking intelligence or quickness of mind ⟨doctors mistook the boy's inability to follow instructions for *weak-mindedness*, until they realized he was deaf⟩ — see STUPIDITY 1

weakness *n* **1** the quality or state of lacking physical strength or vigor ⟨the flu left me with such overwhelming *weakness* that I could hardly stand⟩
synonyms asthenia, debilitation, debility, delicacy, enervation, enfeeblement, faintness, feebleness, fragility, frailness, frailty, infirmity, languidness, languor, listlessness, lowness, wimpiness
related words decay, decrepitude; breakdown, collapse, prostration; exhaustion, fatigue, lassitude, weariness; defenselessness, helplessness, impotence, impuissance, powerlessness; effeteness, softness, tenderness; disablement, incapacitation, invalidism; damage, harm, hurt, impairment, injury
near antonyms energy, vitality; browniness, fitness, heftiness, huskiness, lustiness, muscularity, virility; hardness, ruggedness, stoutness, sturdiness, toughness; health, healthiness, soundness, wellness
antonyms hardihood, hardiness, robustness, strength, vigor
2 the quality or state of lacking strength of will or character ⟨in a moment of *weakness* he shoplifted the comic book⟩
synonyms frailness, frailty, softness, spinelessness, wimpiness, wimpishness, wishy-washiness
related words collapse; failing, flaw, foible, peccadillo; evil, immorality, wickedness; corruption, corruptness
near antonyms discipline, self-discipline; goodness, integrity, morality, rectitude, righteousness, rightness, uprightness, virtuousness
antonyms backbone, chutzpah (*also* chutzpa *or* hutzpah *or* hutzpa), firmness, fortitude, hardihood, mettle, moxie, nerve, resoluteness, strength, toughness
3 a defect in character ⟨his one *weakness* is his cockeyed optimism about everything⟩ — see FAULT 1
4 the quality or state of having little resistance to some outside agent ⟨the devastating *weakness* of the immune system that is experienced by people with AIDS⟩ — see SUSCEPTIBILITY

weal *n* the state of doing well especially in relation to one's happiness or success ⟨the belief that somehow it is the nation's president who is responsible for the *weal* or woe of the people⟩ — see WELFARE

wealth *n* **1** the total of one's money and property ⟨her *wealth* increased to the point where she could afford several luxurious homes⟩
synonyms assets, capital, fortune, means, opulence, riches, substance, wherewithal, worth
related words belongings, chattels, effects, holdings, paraphernalia, possessions, things; bankroll, deep pockets, finances, funds, money, wallet; abundance, affluence, prosperity, success; treasure, valuables; accession, acquisition, personal property, personalty, property; nest egg, reserve, resources, savings, treasury
near antonyms debts, liabilities; indebtedness
2 a considerable amount ⟨a *wealth* of advice from all quarters on how they should spend their lottery winnings⟩ — see LOT 2
3 an amount or supply more than sufficient to meet one's needs ⟨a *wealth* of documentation to support her thesis⟩ — see PLENTY 1

wealthy *adj* having goods, property, or money in abundance ⟨a *wealthy* man who likes to collect antique cars⟩ — see RICH 1

wear *n* **1** the result of long and hard use ⟨after several years, the carpet was finally showing *wear*⟩
synonyms wear and tear
related words abrasion, corrosion, erosion; decomposition, deterioration, disintegration; fatigue
near antonyms fixing, mending, patching, rebuilding, reconditioning, reconstruction, renovation, repair, revamping
2 covering for the human body ⟨the latest in fashionable *wear*⟩ — see CLOTHING

wear *vb* **1** to use up all the physical energy of ⟨the job of running their own business *wears* them sometimes⟩ — see EXHAUST 1
2 to damage or diminish by continued friction ⟨all that walking every day *wore* the soles of my shoes very quickly⟩ — see ABRADE 1
3 *British* to put up with (something painful or difficult) ⟨her marriage is so bad—I don't know how she *wears* it⟩ — see BEAR 2

wearables *n pl* covering for the human body ⟨models showing off vintage *wearables* from the swinging '60s⟩ — see CLOTHING

wear and tear *n* the result of long and hard use ⟨my favorite jeans finally succumbed to *wear and tear* and had to be replaced⟩ — see WEAR 1

wearied *adj* **1** depleted in strength, energy, or freshness ⟨fell into bed *wearied* and desperate for sleep⟩ — see WEARY 1
2 having one's patience, interest, or pleasure exhausted ⟨*wearied* by her son's endless excuses for not having cleaned his room⟩ — see WEARY 2

weariless *adj* showing no signs of weariness even after long hard effort ⟨the *weariless* efforts to bring peace to that troubled region⟩ — see TIRELESS

weariness *n* **1** a complete depletion of energy or strength ⟨the kind of satisfying *weariness* that comes from a good day's labor⟩ — see FATIGUE 1
2 the state of being bored ⟨faces showing *weariness* and irritation at the long graduation speech⟩ — see BOREDOM

wearisome *adj* causing weariness, restlessness, or lack of interest ⟨a *wearisome* lecture on civic responsibility⟩ — see BORING

wear out *vb* to use up all the physical energy of ⟨keeping up with twin toddlers *wears* me *out*⟩ — see EXHAUST 1

weary *adj* **1** depleted in strength, energy, or freshness ⟨I am just too *weary* to do any more work tonight⟩
synonyms all in, aweary [*archaic*], beat, beaten, bleary, burned-out (*or* burnt-out), bushed, dead, done, done in, drained, exhausted, fatigued, jaded, knackered [*British*], limp, logy (*also* loggy), played out, pooped [*slang*], prostrate, spent, tapped out, tired, tuckered (out), washed-out, wearied, wiped out, worn, worn-out
related words overfatigued, overtaxed, overworked; broken-down, run-down; debilitated, enervate, enervated, enfeebled, sapped, weakened; drowsy, heavy, sleepy; lethargic, sluggish
phrases worn to a frazzle
near antonyms fresh, refreshed, rejuvenated, relaxed, rested, revitalized; active, energetic, invigorated, peppy, strengthened, strong, tireless, vitalized, weariless
antonyms unwearied
2 having one's patience, interest, or pleasure exhausted ⟨I am totally *weary* of this constant bickering⟩
synonyms bored, fed up, jaded, sick, sick and tired, tired, wearied
related words apathetic, disinterested, uninterested; glutted, sated, satiated, surfeited; dejected, demoralized, discouraged, disheartened, dispirited; beat, burned-out (*or* burnt-out), bushed, done in, drained, enervated, exhausted, fatigued, limp, played out, tuckered (out), worn-out; annoyed, exasperated, frustrated, irritated; disgusted, nauseated, repulsed; blasé (*also* blase), world-weary
near antonyms animated, energized, enlivened, excited, galvanized, invigorated, stimulated, vitalized; amused, entertained; beguiled, bewitched, captivated, charmed, enchanted, enthralled, fascinated, hypnotized, mesmerized; delighted, pleased, thrilled
antonyms absorbed, engaged, engrossed, interested, intrigued, rapt
3 causing weariness, restlessness, or lack of interest ⟨a *weary* march through a lot of boring facts and figures⟩ — see BORING

weary *vb* **1** to make weary and restless by being dull or monotonous ⟨these constant complaints are really *wearying* me⟩ — see [2]BORE
2 to use up all the physical energy of ⟨a whole day of hard physical labor had thoroughly *wearied* her⟩ — see EXHAUST 1

wearying *adj* causing weariness, restlessness, or lack of interest ⟨a *wearying* effort to sort through years of records⟩ — see BORING

weasel *vb* to avoid giving a definite answer or position ⟨the polite guest chose to *weasel* rather than admit that he didn't like the meal⟩ — see EQUIVOCATE

weasel (out of) *vb* to get or keep away from (as a responsibility) through cleverness or trickery ⟨you won't be able to *weasel out of* your share of the work by feigning illness⟩ — see ESCAPE 2

weather *vb* to come safely through ⟨we've *weathered* worse crises, and so we'll survive this one⟩ — see SURVIVE 1

weathercock *n* a person who dexterously and expediently changes or adopts opinions ⟨when the winds suddenly shifted on social values, the *weathercocks* wasted no time in proclaiming their newfound passion for conservatism⟩ — see ACROBAT 2

weave *vb* **1** to cause to twine about one another ⟨as they have for the past two centuries, crafters continue to *weave* osiers into the distinctive baskets that are the island's trademark⟩ — see INTERTWINE 1
2 to scatter or set here and there among other things ⟨a political commentator who slyly *weaves* lies into the truth⟩ — see THREAD 1
3 to move suddenly aside or to and fro ⟨a van *weaving* through traffic with reckless speed⟩ — see DODGE 1

web *n* **1** something that catches and holds ⟨he was

caught in the *web* of branches⟩ ⟨she was trapped by her own *web* of lies⟩
synonyms entanglement, mesh(es), morass, net, noose, quagmire, quicksand, snare, tanglement, toil(s), trap
related words knot, snarl, tangle; cat's cradle, labyrinth, maze; cobweb, spiderweb
2 a device or scheme for capturing another by surprise ⟨an ingenious *web* that was spun by undercover agents going after drug dealers⟩ — see TRAP 1

wed *vb* **1** to give in marriage ⟨the king wished to *wed* his favorite daughter to the bravest knight in the realm⟩ — see MARRY 2
2 to perform the ceremony of marriage for ⟨the priest usually *weds* six to eight couples a month⟩ — see MARRY 1
3 to take a spouse ⟨she swore that she would never *wed*⟩ — see MARRY 4
4 to take as a spouse ⟨a true romantic, he intends to *wed* her on Valentine's Day⟩ — see MARRY 3

wedded *adj* of or relating to marriage ⟨living in *wedded* bliss⟩ — see MARITAL

wedding *n* a ceremony in which two people are united in matrimony ⟨the couple chose to have a garden *wedding*⟩
synonyms bridal, espousal, marriage, nuptial(s)
related words match, matrimony, wedlock; union

wedge *vb* to fit (people or things) into a tight space ⟨managed to *wedge* one last book onto the bookshelf⟩ — see CROWD 1

wedged *adj* firmly positioned in place and difficult to dislodge ⟨the pebble in the heel of his shoe was pretty well *wedged*⟩ — see TIGHT 2

wedlock *n* a union representing a special kind of social and legal partnership between two people ⟨joined the happy couple in holy *wedlock*⟩ — see MARRIAGE 1

wee *adj* very small in size ⟨a *wee* baby⟩ — see TINY

weeds *n pl* covering for the human body ⟨a poor, miserable beggar clad in tattered *weeds*⟩ — see CLOTHING

weedy *adj* growing thickly and vigorously ⟨*weedy* vegetation in the abandoned lot⟩ — see RANK 1

weenie *n* a person slavishly devoted to intellectual or academic pursuits ⟨an inner-directed individual who could have cared less if others stuck the dreaded "*weenie*" label on him⟩ — see NERD 1

weeny *also* **weensy** *adj* very small in size ⟨stumbled upon a *weeny* frog in the front yard⟩ — see TINY

weep *vb* **1** to flow forth slowly through small openings ⟨water *weeping* through the basement wall⟩ — see EXUDE
2 to shed tears often while making meaningless sounds as a sign of pain or distress ⟨the child was *weeping* over the death of his dog⟩ — see CRY 1

weeping *adj* **1** bending downward or forward ⟨with its long, *weeping* fronds, this plant makes a nice ornamental⟩ — see NODDING
2 expressing or suggesting mourning ⟨a *weeping* song about a long-lost love⟩ — see MOURNFUL 1

weepy *adj* given to expressing strong emotion (as sorrow) by readily shedding tears ⟨I'm *weepy* enough that I even cry at happy endings to movies and books⟩ — see TEARFUL 1

weigh *vb* **1** to be of importance ⟨evidence that will *weigh* heavily against the defendant⟩ — see MATTER
2 to give serious and careful thought to ⟨*weighed* the options for weeks before making a decision⟩ — see PONDER

weigh (on *or* **upon)** *vb* to push steadily against with some force ⟨the bulky backpack *weighed upon* my back uncomfortably⟩ — see [2]PRESS 1

weigh down *vb* to make sad ⟨all these tragedies occurring simultaneously are *weighing* me *down*⟩ — see DEPRESS 1

weighed *adj* decided on as a result of careful thought ⟨a carefully *weighed* decision to take the company in a new direction⟩ — see DELIBERATE 1

weigh in *vb* to make a statement of one's opinion ⟨self-appointed pundits immediately *weighed in* on the latest political scandal⟩ — see REMARK 1

weight *n* **1** the amount that something weighs ⟨because of a back condition, I'm not allowed to lift anything with a *weight* of over 10 pounds⟩
synonyms avoirdupois, heaviness, heft
related words bulk, mass; poundage, tonnage; deadweight; heftiness, massiveness, ponderousness, weightiness; solidity, solidness, substantiality, substantialness
2 the quality or state of being important ⟨a matter of little *weight* that is a preoccupation solely of the news media⟩ — see IMPORTANCE
3 a mass or quantity of something taken up and carried, conveyed, or transported ⟨those books are a heavy *weight* to have to carry around all day⟩ — see LOAD 1
4 a special notice or importance given to something ⟨put extra *weight* on the matter by putting it at the top of the agenda⟩ — see EMPHASIS 1
5 the main or greater part of something as distinguished from its subordinate parts ⟨the *weight* of the evidence supports my conclusion⟩ — see BODY 1
6 the power to direct the thinking or behavior of others usually indirectly ⟨as a critic he has great *weight* in the theater world⟩ — see INFLUENCE 1
7 the condition of having an excess of body fat ⟨finally decided to do something about his *weight* and began a rigorous program of diet and exercise⟩ — see CORPULENCE

weight *vb* to place a weight or burden on ⟨*weighted* the car with a ton of furniture and then headed off for college⟩ — see LOAD 1

weightiness *n* **1** the state or quality of being heavy ⟨the *weightiness* of the bookcase made it difficult to move⟩
synonyms avoirdupois, heaviness, heftiness, massiveness, ponderousness
related words overweight; solidity, solidness, substantiality, substantialness; bulk, bulkiness, hugeness; cumbersomeness
near antonyms airiness, delicacy, ethereality, etherealness; flimsiness, fluffiness, insubstantiality, slightness
antonyms lightness, weightlessness
2 the quality or state of being important ⟨first judged the *weightiness* of a case before deciding to hear it⟩ — see IMPORTANCE

weightless *adj* having little weight ⟨the kitten seemed nearly *weightless* when I picked her up⟩ — see [1]LIGHT 1

weightlessness *n* the state or quality of having little weight ⟨the relative *weightlessness* of the suitcase surprised me⟩ — see [1]LIGHTNESS 1

weighty *adj* **1** having a matter of importance as its topic ⟨interrupted a *weighty* discussion with a silly question⟩ — see SERIOUS 2
2 having great meaning or lasting effect ⟨choosing a college is a *weighty* decision⟩ — see IMPORTANT 1
3 having great weight ⟨lifted the *weighty* sack and wondered what was in it⟩ — see HEAVY 1
4 not joking or playful in mood or manner ⟨the police office looked at me with a rather *weighty* expression⟩ — see SERIOUS 1
5 having power over the minds or behavior of others ⟨one of the *weightiest* figures in the field of pediatric medicine⟩ — see INFLUENTIAL 1

weird *adj* **1** different from the ordinary in a way that causes curiosity or suspicion ⟨always has a somewhat *weird* opinion of what's happening in the news⟩ — see ODD 2
2 fearfully and mysteriously strange or fantastic ⟨*weird*

sounds from the woods just beyond our campsite⟩ — see EERIE
3 having seemingly supernatural qualities or powers ⟨a self-styled, contemporary witch, she sells herbal mixtures that she claims are *weird* potions⟩ — see MYSTIC 1
4 noticeably different from what is generally found or experienced ⟨a *weird* little plant that we found growing in the garden⟩ — see UNUSUAL 1

weirdo *adj* different from the ordinary in a way that causes curiosity or suspicion ⟨he saw some *weirdo* lights in the sky and immediately concluded that it had to be a UFO⟩ — see ODD 2

weirdo *n* a person of odd or whimsical habits ⟨one of those *weirdos* that the rest of the town always seemed to be talking about⟩ — see ECCENTRIC

weird out *vb* to trouble the mind of; to make uneasy ⟨as a curious observer, he was *weirded out* by the fact that members of the sect seemed to have no life outside of it⟩ — see DISTURB 1

welcome *adj* giving pleasure or contentment to the mind or senses ⟨a *welcome* chance to rest after a long journey⟩ — see PLEASANT 1

welcome *n* an expression of goodwill upon meeting ⟨offered a warm *welcome* to the stranger⟩ — see HELLO

welcome *vb* to receive or accept gladly or readily ⟨the eager recruits *welcomed* every new project with which they were presented⟩
synonyms drink (in), eat (up), embrace, lap (up)
related words adopt, espouse, take up; greet, hail; enjoy, like, prefer; cherry-pick, choose, cull, decide (on), elect, handpick, name, opt (for), pick, select, single (out), take
near antonyms balk (at), decline, pass up, refuse, reject, spurn, throw over, turn down; demur (to), object (to)

welcomely *adv* in a pleasing way ⟨the commencement speaker's *welcomely* brief speech⟩ — see WELL 5

welfare *n* the state of doing well especially in relation to one's happiness or success ⟨the social worker was pleased at the improvement in the child's *welfare*⟩
synonyms good, interest, weal, well-being
related words fortune, prosperity, prosperousness, success, successfulness; fitness, health, healthiness, robustness, soundness, wellness, wholeness, wholesomeness; bliss, felicity, happiness, joy; advantage, benefit, gain, sake; content, contentedness, gratification, satisfaction
near antonyms unhealthiness, unsoundness; misery, sadness, suffering, unhappiness, wretchedness
antonyms ill-being

welkin *n* the expanse of air surrounding the earth ⟨the movie has been so overhyped that one half expects its opening to be accompanied by the proverbial ringing of the *welkin*⟩ — see SKY 1

well *adj* enjoying health and vigor ⟨my mother is quite *well*, thank you⟩ — see HEALTHY 1

well *adv* **1** in a satisfactory way ⟨our current system for dividing household chores works *well*, so let's keep it⟩
synonyms acceptably, adequately, all right, alright, creditably, decently, fine, good, middlingly, nicely, OK (*or* okay), passably, respectably, satisfactorily, serviceably, so-so, sufficiently, tolerably
related words appropriately, aptly, congruously, correctly, decorously, felicitously, fittingly, happily, meetly, rightly, seemly, suitably; gratifyingly, satisfyingly; effectively, effectually, efficiently, neatly, tidily
near antonyms unbearably; inappropriately, incorrectly, indecently, unsuitably; awfully, deplorably, disastrously, dreadfully, horrendously, horribly, horridly, miserably, terribly
antonyms bad, badly, deficiently, ill, inadequately, insufficiently, intolerably, poorly, unacceptably, unsatisfactorily
2 in a generous manner ⟨a warm and gracious host who always treats guests *well*⟩
synonyms amply, bounteously, bountifully, freehandedly, freeheartedly, generously, handsomely, lavishly, liberally, munificently, openhandedly, unstintingly
related words considerately, courteously, hospitably, kindly, nicely, reasonably, sweetly, thoughtfully; affably, amiably, cheerfully, cheerily, congenially, cordially, friendlily, genially, good-heartedly, good-naturedly, graciously; selflessly, ungrudgingly, unselfishly; altruistically, beneficently, benevolently, bigheartedly, charitably, humanely, kindheartedly, magnanimously, philanthropically
near antonyms contemptuously, disdainfully, rudely, scornfully; obnoxiously, provocatively; coldly, coolly (*also* cooly), frigidly, hostilely; angrily, belligerently; begrudgingly, grudgingly
antonyms parsimoniously, stingily, ungenerously
3 in a skillful or expert manner ⟨she plays the piano very *well*⟩
synonyms ably, adeptly, adroitly, artfully, capably, competently, consummately, deftly, expertly, masterfully, masterly, proficiently, skillfully
related words aptly, fluently; cleanly, cleverly, dexterously, neatly, nimbly; easily, facilely, handily
near antonyms inaptly; awkwardly, clumsily, crudely
antonyms amateurishly, artlessly, incapably, incompetently, inefficiently, ineptly, inexpertly, poorly, unskillfully
4 with good reason or courtesy ⟨we cannot *well* get out of going to your cousin's wedding⟩
synonyms considerately, courteously, graciously, kindly, nicely, reasonably, thoughtfully
related words pleasantly; excusably, fairly, justifiably, validly; discreetly, judiciously, prudently, sensibly, wisely; chivalrously, decorously, deferentially, gallantly, politely, respectfully, solicitously; compassionately, humanely, kindheartedly, sweetly, sympathetically
near antonyms contemptuously, disdainfully, disrespectfully, impolitely, rudely, scornfully, snootily; cruelly, heartlessly, nastily, viciously; shabbily, unfairly
antonyms discourteously, inconsiderately, thoughtlessly
5 in a pleasing way ⟨the day went *well*, despite the rough beginning⟩
synonyms agreeably, charmingly, delectably, deliciously, delightfully, dreamily, enchantingly, enjoyably, favorably, felicitously, fetchingly, gloriously, gratifyingly, great, nicely, palatably, pleasantly, pleasingly, pleasurably, prettily, satisfyingly, splendidly, sweetly, swimmingly, welcomely, winningly
related words finely, grandly, magnificently; advantageously, helpfully; blessedly, fortunately, happily, luckily; excellently, superbly; marvelously, sensationally, wonderfully; attractively, beautifully, handsomely; appealingly, appetizingly, enticingly, invitingly, temptingly
near antonyms abominably, appallingly, awfully, dreadfully, horrendously, horribly, horridly, shockingly, sickeningly, terribly, vilely; annoyingly, disgustingly, distressingly, irritatingly, vexingly
antonyms badly, disagreeably, ill, unpleasantly
6 to a full extent or degree ⟨we are *well* aware that this home renovation is going to be costly⟩ — see FULLY 1
7 without difficulty ⟨he can *well* afford to spare the time⟩ — see EASILY 1

well *interj* how surprising, doubtful, or unbelievable ⟨*well*, that is odd!⟩ — see NO

well *n* **1** a point or place at which something is invented or provided ⟨his quirkily dysfunctional family proved to be a bottomless *well* of inspiration for the novelist⟩ — see SOURCE 1

2 a small often deep body of water ⟨the spot where the spring bubbles up to the surface and forms a deep *well*⟩ — see [1]POOL

well–being *n* the state of doing well especially in relation to one's happiness or success ⟨we're only doing this for your own *well-being*⟩ — see WELFARE

well–bred *adj* showing consideration, courtesy, and good manners ⟨a *well-bred* young woman who is unfailingly polite to everyone⟩ — see POLITE 1

wellborn *adj* of high birth, rank, or station ⟨the *wellborn* men among the colonists had no experience with physical labor⟩ — see NOBLE 1

well–conditioned *adj* enjoying health and vigor ⟨frequent trips to the gym keep her *well-conditioned*⟩ — see HEALTHY 1

well–disposed *adj* having an easygoing and pleasing manner especially in social situations ⟨a bachelor who has a reputation for being *well-disposed*, especially towards the ladies⟩ — see AMIABLE

well–endowed *adj* having goods, property, or money in abundance ⟨that independent company is not so *well-endowed* that it could afford to fight a protracted lawsuit⟩ — see RICH 1

well–favored *adj* very pleasing to look at ⟨a *well-favored* young man who would make a great catch⟩ — see BEAUTIFUL 1

well–fixed *adj* having goods, property, or money in abundance ⟨she was always hitting up her *well-fixed* relatives for "loans"⟩ — see RICH 1

well–founded *adj* **1** according to the rules of logic ⟨even a *well-founded* argument can lead to an erroneous conclusion if one of the premises is incorrect⟩ — see LOGICAL 1

2 based on sound reasoning or information ⟨a *well-founded* complaint about the business's treatment of its customers⟩ — see GOOD 1

well–groomed *adj* being clean and in good order ⟨the famously *well-groomed* farms of the Amish⟩ — see NEAT 1

well–grounded *adj* according to the rules of logic ⟨counsel for the defense presented a *well-grounded* case for acquittal⟩ — see LOGICAL 1

well–heeled *adj* having goods, property, or money in abundance ⟨the resort caters to a *well-heeled* clientele that demands the best and has the money to pay for it⟩ — see RICH 1

well–informed *adj* having information especially as a result of study or experience ⟨patients considering LASIK surgery should be *well-informed* about the risks and possible complications⟩ — see FAMILIAR 2

well–known *adj* widely known ⟨an anchorwoman so *well-known* that she passes for a local celebrity⟩ — see FAMOUS 1

wellness *n* the condition of being sound in body ⟨discounted gym memberships are part of the company's employee *wellness* program⟩ — see HEALTH 1

well–nigh *adv* very close to but not completely ⟨it was *well-nigh* dark, but I could still see a little⟩ — see ALMOST

well–off *adj* having goods, property, or money in abundance ⟨a *well-off* couple adopted the baby⟩ — see RICH 1

well–read *adj* having or displaying advanced knowledge or education ⟨any *well-read* person would recognize the quotation⟩ — see EDUCATED 1

well–spoken *adj* able to express oneself clearly and well ⟨a *well-spoken* advocate for the legal rights of the underprivileged⟩ — see ARTICULATE

wellspring *n* **1** a point or place at which something is invented or provided ⟨the nation's colleges and universities were a *wellspring* for political activism and unrest⟩ — see SOURCE 1

2 an abundant source ⟨a gossip who is a *wellspring* of juicy information about the latest goings-on around town⟩ — see MINE 1

well–timed *adj* especially suitable for a certain time ⟨the release of the novel was *well-timed*: a week later the author was awarded the Nobel Prize for literature⟩ — see TIMELY 1

well–to–do *adj* having goods, property, or money in abundance ⟨a doctor who is now quite *well-to-do* as a result of his successful medical practice⟩ — see RICH 1

well–worn *adj* used or heard so often as to be dull ⟨people at the funeral offered the grieving family *well-worn* platitudes and expressions of sympathy⟩ — see STALE 1

welt *n* a hard strike with a part of the body or an instrument ⟨I'll hand ye a few *welts* with me stick and then we'll see how ye feel!⟩ — see [1]BLOW

welter *n* **1** a state of noisy, confused activity ⟨there was a *welter* of pushing and shoving as people rushed to grab the best seats for the outdoor concert⟩ — see COMMOTION

2 an unorganized collection or mixture of various things ⟨a *welter* of junk in the closet, most of which needed to be thrown out⟩ — see MISCELLANY 1

3 a state in which everything is out of order ⟨the claim that a troop withdrawal would plunge the country into a *welter* of anarchy and endless civil war⟩ — see CHAOS

wench *n* **1** a boldly flirtatious or sexually promiscuous woman ⟨a "sexy French maid" costume for the woman who wants to get in touch with her inner *wench*—at least on Halloween⟩ — see FLOOZY

2 a female domestic servant ⟨a fairytale about the transformation of a lowly kitchen *wench* into an elegant lady⟩ — see MAID 1

wet *adj* **1** containing, covered with, or thoroughly penetrated by water ⟨I left the car windows open while it rained, and the seats got all *wet*⟩

synonyms awash, bathed, bedraggled, doused (*also* dowsed), drenched, dripping, logged, saturate, saturated, soaked, soaking, sodden, soggy, sopping, soppy, soused, washed, watered, waterlogged, water-soaked, watery

related words deluged, drowned, flooded, inundated, overflowed; submerged, swamped; hydrated; dipped, dunked, splashed; aqueous; steeped; flushed, irrigated, laved, rinsed, sluiced; clammy, damp, dampish, dank, humid, moist, semimoist, wettish; boggy, miry, seepy, sloppy, squashy

near antonyms bone-dry, hyperarid, ultradry; waterproof, water-repellent, water-resistant, watertight; baked, dehydrated, freeze-dried; droughty, parched, sere (*also* sear), sunbaked, thirsty; wrung

antonyms arid, dry, unwatered, waterless

2 marked by or abounding with rain ⟨a *wet* and dreary day⟩ — see RAINY

3 being under the influence of alcohol ⟨she says a party's no fun unless she ends up *wet*⟩ — see DRUNK

4 appealing to the emotions in an obvious and tiresome way ⟨things get more than a little *wet* during the opera's big death scene⟩ — see CORNY 1

5 *British* lacking strength of will or character ⟨employees of the company despised their boss as a *wet* and ineffectual bloke⟩ — see WEAK 2

wet *n* a steady falling of water from the sky in significant quantity ⟨winced as he walked out into the *wet* without any protection⟩ — see RAIN 1

wet *vb* to make wet ⟨you need to *wet* your hair thoroughly first⟩

synonyms bathe, bedraggle, douse (*also* dowse), drench, drown, soak, sodden, sop, souse, wash, water,

waterlog, water-soak, wet down
related words asperse, bedew, damp, dampen, drizzle, humidify, hydrate, mist, moisten, moisturize, shower, sprinkle; deluge, flood, hose (down), inundate, overflow; submerge, swamp; splash; impregnate, saturate, steep; flush, irrigate, lave, rinse, slosh, sluice; dip, duck, dunk; rehydrate, rewash, rewet
near antonyms dewater, evaporate, freeze-dry; drip-dry, wring; dehumidify
antonyms dehydrate, desiccate, dry, parch, scorch, sear

wet blanket *n* a person who spoils the pleasure of others ⟨I'd love to go to the party, but with my cold, I'm afraid I'd just be a *wet blanket*⟩ — see KILLJOY

wet down *vb* to make wet ⟨it will be easier to clean up if you *wet down* the surfaces first⟩ ⟨the stylist began by *wetting down* my hair⟩ — see WET

wetland *n* spongy land saturated or partially covered with water ⟨the conservation board has not always been rigorous in protecting the *wetlands* from development⟩ — see SWAMP 1

wet–nurse *vb* **1** to give milk to from the breast ⟨*wet-nursed* the woman's baby until she was well enough to do it herself⟩ — see NURSE 2
2 to treat with great or excessive care ⟨recent college grads quickly learn that employers won't *wet-nurse* them the way that their teachers did⟩ — see BABY

wettish *adj* slightly or moderately wet ⟨the ground is still rather *wettish* after last night's downpour⟩— see MOIST

whack *n* **1** an effort to do or accomplish something ⟨took a *whack* at solving the math problem⟩ — see ATTEMPT 1
2 a hard strike with a part of the body or an instrument ⟨gave the wasp's nest a good *whack* with the bat⟩ — see [1]BLOW
3 a loud explosive sound ⟨the *whack* echoed around the field⟩ — see CLAP 1

whack *vb* **1** to deliver a blow to (someone or something) usually in a strong vigorous manner ⟨*whacked* the vending machine to get the candy bar to fall⟩ — see HIT 1
2 *slang* to put to death deliberately ⟨without a second thought the mob boss had them *whacked*⟩ — see MURDER 1

whacking *adj* unusually large ⟨harvested a *whacking* number of zucchini from the garden⟩ — see HUGE

whacking *adv* to a great degree ⟨the clown wore a *whacking* big pair of shoes⟩ — see VERY 1

whale *n* something that is unusually large and powerful ⟨a *whale* of a pickup truck⟩ — see GIANT

whale *vb* **1** to deliver a blow to (someone or something) usually in a strong vigorous manner ⟨*whaled* the ball so hard that it sailed over the fence and into the neighbor's yard⟩ — see HIT 1
2 to strike repeatedly with something long and thin or flexible ⟨*whaled* the rug with a broom to knock the dirt out of it⟩ — see WHIP 1
3 to strike repeatedly ⟨mercilessly *whaled* the pickpocket for stealing from her purse⟩ — see BEAT 1

wham *n* a hard strike with a part of the body or an instrument ⟨gave the TV a good *wham* with her fist, and suddenly the picture came back on⟩ — see [1]BLOW

whammy *n* **1** a spoken word or set of words believed to have magic power ⟨if you tell anyone about this, I swear I'll put the *whammy* on you⟩ — see SPELL 1
2 something that brings bad luck ⟨put the *whammy* on herself by publicly predicting that she would win the tennis tournament⟩ — see JINX

whang *n* the loud sound made when metal strikes metal ⟨the incessant *whang* of a wrench on the exhaust pipe as she fixed the car⟩ — see CLANG

wharf *n* a structure used by boats and ships for taking on or landing cargo and passengers ⟨tied the rowboat up at the *wharf*⟩ — see DOCK

what *interj* how surprising, doubtful, or unbelievable ⟨*what*! I can't believe we won!⟩ — see NO

what all *pron* any of various other things that might also be mentioned ⟨the book was about family, social differences, and I don't know *what all* else⟩ — see WHATNOT

whatchamacallit *n* a small article the actual name of which one either does not know or cannot remember ⟨I need one of those *whatchamacallits* to connect the two patch cords⟩ — see DOODAD 1

whatever *adv* in spite of everything ⟨*whatever* the reviews say, I still think it was a great play⟩ — see REGARDLESS

whatever *pron* any of various other things that might also be mentioned ⟨looking for a job as writer or editor—or *whatever*—with a TV network newscast⟩ — see WHATNOT

whatnot *n* a small article the actual name of which one either does not know or cannot remember ⟨the store sells an array of *whatnots* for the do-it-yourself plumber⟩ — see DOODAD 1

whatnot *pron* any of various other things that might also be mentioned ⟨the drawer is full of spare pens, paper clips, stray elastics and *whatnot*⟩
synonyms what all, whatever
related words anything; whichever
phrases what have you

whatsit *also* **whatsis** *or* **what–is–it** *n* a small article the actual name of which one either does not know or cannot remember ⟨there's always one random *whatsit* left over every time I put a bookcase together⟩ — see DOODAD 1

whee *interj* how delightful ⟨*whee*! that was a fun ride⟩ — see HOORAY

wheedle *vb* to get (someone) to do something by gentle urging, special attention, or flattery ⟨*wheedled* him into doing their work for them⟩ — see COAX

wheel *n* **1** a rapid turning about on an axis or central point ⟨the *wheel* of the tape reel⟩ — see SPIN 1
2 one of high position or importance within a group ⟨she's a major *wheel* in that state's Democratic Party⟩ — see BIG SHOT
3 a series of events or actions that repeat themselves regularly and in the same order ⟨the *wheel* of time turns: the children are now the parents, and their children have taken their place at the school desks⟩ — see CYCLE 1
4 wheels *pl slang* a self-propelled passenger vehicle on four wheels ⟨now that I've got *wheels*, I can go to the outlet mall⟩ — see CAR

wheel *vb* **1** to change the course or direction of (something) ⟨*wheeled* the bike around sharply to see what had fallen off⟩ — see TURN 2
2 to move (something) in a curved or circular path on or as if on an axis ⟨*wheeled* the bicycle's tires around to see if they were balanced⟩ — see TURN 1
3 to move in circles around an axis or center ⟨she *wheeled* around and around until finally she got dizzy and fell down⟩ — see SPIN 1
4 to turn away from a straight line or course ⟨the highway *wheels* to the west as it forms an arc that bypasses the city⟩ — see CURVE 1
5 to change one's course or direction ⟨upon hearing the construction workers' suggestive remarks, she *wheeled* around to glare at them⟩ — see TURN 3

wheelman *n* a person who travels by automobile ⟨we'll need someone to be our *wheelman* for the heist⟩ — see MOTORIST

wheeze *vb* to breathe hard, quickly, or with difficulty ⟨he was *wheezing* rapidly after a hard run⟩ — see GASP

whelk *n* a small, inflamed swelling of the skin ⟨unsightly *whelks* covered the beggar's face⟩ — see POCK

whelm *vb* to subject to incapacitating emotional or mental stress ⟨the news so *whelmed* them that they were stunned into silence⟩ — see OVERWHELM 1

whelp *n* a young person who is between infancy and adulthood ⟨playtime's over, it's time to gather up the *whelps* and head home⟩ — see CHILD 1

when *conj* **1** at or during the time that ⟨she complained that no one was paying attention to her *when* she gave her speech⟩
synonyms as, so long as, while, whilst [*chiefly British*]
near antonyms after
2 just at the moment that ⟨you should say hello *when* you answer the phone⟩
synonyms as soon as, immediately [*chiefly British*], instantly, once
near antonyms after, directly [*chiefly British*], since
3 in spite of the fact that ⟨she quit writing *when* she could have been a fine author⟩ — see ALTHOUGH

where *adv* **1** at, in, or to what place ⟨*where* will you be tonight?⟩
synonyms whereabouts (*also* whereabout), whither
related words wherever
near antonyms whence
2 in what manner or way ⟨I cannot see *where* the explanation is mistaken⟩
synonyms how, wherein
related words thus, thusly; accordingly, consequently, ergo, hence, so, thereupon, wherefore

where *n* the area or space occupied by or intended for something ⟨we've decided on the when, but we still haven't resolved the *where* for the party⟩ — see PLACE 1

whereabouts *also* **whereabout** *adv* at, in, or to what place ⟨*whereabouts* do you expect to be on your journey tonight?⟩ — see WHERE 1

whereas *conj* **1** for the reason that ⟨*whereas* you chose to participate in this stupid prank, you will be held responsible as well⟩ — see SINCE
2 in spite of the fact that ⟨*whereas* there are many good reasons to switch to Plan B, we must stick with Plan A as long as it is feasible⟩ — see ALTHOUGH

wherefore *adv* for this or that reason ⟨it was getting late, and *wherefore* we decided to move on⟩ — see THEREFORE

wherefore *n* something (as a belief) that serves as the basis for another thing ⟨demanded to know the whys and *wherefores* for the decision⟩ — see REASON 2

wherein *adv* in what manner or way ⟨*wherein* this document can be demonstrated to be out of compliance with current standards, that section will be considered null and void⟩ — see WHERE 2

wherewithal *n* **1** available money ⟨had the *wherewithal* to pay cash for the car⟩ — see FUND 2
2 the total of one's money and property ⟨people with the *wherewithal* to be able to afford such a lavish lifestyle⟩ — see WEALTH 1

whet *vb* to make sharp or sharper ⟨*whetted* the knife with the grindstone⟩ — see SHARPEN

whetted *adj* having an edge thin enough to cut or pierce something ⟨I'll need a well-*whetted* axe to split the wood⟩ — see SHARP 1

whicker *vb* to make the cry typical of a horse ⟨*whickering* as they waited at the starting gate, the horses seemed to sense the excitement of the crowd⟩ — see NEIGH

whiff *n* an almost imperceptible sign of something ⟨even a *whiff* of appreciation for everything I've done for her would have been nice⟩ — see HINT 2

whiff *vb* to become aware of by means of the sense organs in the nose ⟨*whiffed* the pot of chili on the stove and announced that he was staying for dinner⟩ — see SMELL 1

while *conj* **1** at or during the time that ⟨pay attention *while* I'm explaining how the new phone system works⟩ — see WHEN 1
2 in spite of the fact that ⟨*while* this term paper is very well done, it's still late⟩ — see ALTHOUGH

while *n* **1** an indefinite but usually short period of time ⟨we stayed at the fair for a *while* longer⟩
synonyms bit, space, spell, stretch
related words lapse; season, span; day, epoch, era; beat, eyeblink, flash, heartbeat, instant, jiff, jiffy, minute, moment, nanosecond, New York minute, second, shake, split second, spurt, trice, twinkle, twinkling, wink; aeon (*or* eon), age, eternity, infinity, perpetuity; interim, interlude, intermission, interval
2 the active use of energy in producing a result ⟨it's not worth my *while* to fix it, so we'll get a new one⟩ — see EFFORT

whilom *adj* having been such at some previous time ⟨pointedly ignored the *whilom* friends who had turned on her⟩ — see FORMER 1

whilst *conj, chiefly British* **1** at or during the time that ⟨I like to get my knitting done *whilst* watching the telly⟩ — see WHEN 1
2 in spite of the fact that ⟨*whilst* a good worker, he's not a very good manager⟩ — see ALTHOUGH

whim *n* a sudden impulsive and apparently unmotivated idea or action ⟨on a *whim*, we stopped at the roadside stand to get ice cream⟩
synonyms bee, caprice, crank, fancy, freak, humor, kink, maggot, megrim, notion, vagary, vagrancy, whimsy (*also* whimsey)
related words capriciousness, fancifulness, fantasy (*also* phantasy), freakishness, impetuosity, whimsicality; conceit; concept, conception, image, impression, mind's eye, picture, thought; brainstorm, inspiration
phrases bee in one's bonnet

whimper *n* an expression of dissatisfaction, pain, or resentment ⟨patiently posed for dozens of photographs without so much as a *whimper*⟩ — see COMPLAINT 1

whimper *vb* **1** to utter feeble plaintive cries ⟨the dog *whimpered* to be let in⟩
synonyms bleat, mewl, pule
related words fuss, sniffle, snivel, snuffle, whine; bawl, blub [*chiefly British*], blubber, cry, sob, weep; peep, squeak; yelp; mumble, murmur, mutter; groan, moan, sigh
near antonyms scream, screech, shriek, squeal; howl, squall, wail, yowl; call, caterwaul, squawk; bellow, roar
2 to express dissatisfaction, pain, or resentment usually tiresomely ⟨a good-hearted person, but given to *whimpering* about trifles⟩ — see COMPLAIN

whimsical *adj* prone to sudden illogical changes of mind, ideas, or actions ⟨it's hard to make plans with such a *whimsical* best friend⟩
synonyms capricious, freakish, impulsive
related words impetuous, mercurial, moody, temperamental, volatile; crankish, eccentric, flaky, quirky; arbitrary, erratic, fickle, inconstant, irregular, shaky, willful (*or* wilful); impractical, quixotic, quixotical, romantic, unrealistic, utopian, visionary
near antonyms equable; down-to-earth, earthy, hardboiled, hardheaded, levelheaded, matter-of-fact, practical, pragmatic (*also* pragmatical), reasonable, sensible, tough-minded; commonsensical, grounded, logical, nononsense, rational, sane, sober, sobersided, sound; fast, fixed, hard-and-fast, immutable, inflexible, invariable, unalterable, unbending, unchangeable uncompromising, unrelenting, unyielding; changeless, constant, established, set, settled, stable, steadfast, steady, unchanging, unvarying

whimsicality *n* an inclination to sudden illogical changes of mind, ideas, or actions ⟨her *whimsicality*

made her an unpredictable companion⟩
synonyms caprice, capriciousness, freakishness, impulsiveness, whimsicalness
related words mercurialness, moodiness, unpredictability, willfulness; eccentricity, flakiness; arbitrariness, fickleness, inconstancy, irregularity, volatileness, volatility; changeability, flexibility, mutability, variability, variableness
near antonyms levelheadedness, practicality, reasonability, reasonableness; fastness, firmness, fixedness, immovability, immovableness, immutability, inflexibility, invariability; changelessness, constancy, stability, steadfastness, steadiness

whimsicalness *n* an inclination to sudden illogical changes of mind, ideas, or actions ⟨at times she displays a certain *whimsicalness* that is charming⟩ — see WHIMSICALITY

whimsy *also* **whimsey** *n* a sudden impulsive and apparently unmotivated idea or action ⟨the pop singer's latest *whimsy* is that she has acting talent⟩ — see WHIM

whim–whams *n pl* a sense of panic or extreme nervousness ⟨just the sight of a roller coaster gives him the *whim-whams*⟩ — see JITTERS

whine *n* an expression of dissatisfaction, pain, or resentment ⟨the perennial *whine* that movies aren't as good as they used to be⟩ — see COMPLAINT 1

whine *vb* to express dissatisfaction, pain, or resentment usually tiresomely ⟨for the whole of our vacation, the kids *whined* on and on about the weather⟩ — see COMPLAIN

whiner *n* **1** a person who makes frequent complaints usually about little things ⟨don't be a *whiner*—the hike's not that difficult⟩ — see CRYBABY
2 an irritable and complaining person ⟨among the hospital staff the patient in 504 had acquired a reputation for being a *whiner*⟩ — see GROUCH 1

whinge *n, British* an expression of dissatisfaction, pain, or resentment ⟨that bloke always has some *whinge* about how women don't understand him⟩ — see COMPLAINT 1

whinge *vb, British* to express dissatisfaction, pain, or resentment usually tiresomely ⟨dutifully cares for his elderly mum, despite her tendency to *whinge* about everything⟩ — see COMPLAIN

whinny *vb* to make the cry typical of a horse ⟨the father *whinnied* and reared as his young daughter pretended to ride him⟩ — see NEIGH

whip *n* a long thin or flexible tool for striking ⟨please do not use your belt as a *whip*⟩
synonyms flogger, lash, scourge, switch
related words birch, blacksnake, bullwhip, cat-o'-nine-tails, cowhide, crop, hickory, knout, quirt, rattan, rawhide, strap; bastinado (*or* bastinade), bat, baton, billy, billy club, bludgeon, cane, club, cudgel, flail, nightstick, staff

whip *vb* **1** to strike repeatedly with something long and thin or flexible ⟨*whipped* the animal when it did not move fast enough to please him⟩
synonyms birch, cowhide, flagellate, flail, flog, hide, horsewhip, lash, leather, rawhide, scourge, slash, switch, tan, thrash, whale
related words knout, quirt, strap; cut; flick, touch up; blackjack, cane, club, cudgel, fustigate; pistol-whip; bang, bop, box, bust, clap, clip, clobber, clout, crack, cuff, hit, knock, lam, paste, punch, slap, slug, smack, smite, sock, spank, swat, swipe, thwack, wallop, whack; bash, baste, bat, batter, beat, belabor, belt, bludgeon, buffet, bung, drub, fib [*British*], hammer, lace, lambaste (*or* lambast), lather, lick, mangle, maul, paddle, pelt, pommel, pound, pummel, rough, slate, slog, thresh, thump, tromp, whop (*or* whap), whup, work over
2 to defeat by a large margin ⟨we *whipped* them 13-0 in the last game⟩
synonyms annihilate, blow away, bomb, bury, clobber, cream, drub, dust, flatten, paste, rout, shellac, skin, skunk, smoke [*slang*], smother, snow under, thrash, trim, tromp, trounce, wallop, wax [*slang*], whomp, whop (*or* whap), whup
related words sweep, upset; beat, best, conquer, dispatch, hurdle, lick, master, overbear, overcome, overmatch, prevail (over), subdue, surmount, take, throw, triumph (over), win (against), worst; crush, knock off, knock over, overpower, overthrow, overwhelm, subjugate, upend, vanquish; ace (out), better, eclipse, exceed, outdistance, outdo, outfight, outshine, outstrip, overtop, surpass, top, transcend; edge (out), nose out, pip [*British*]; cap, excel, flourish, score, succeed; break, destroy, do in, finish, sink, slaughter
phrases beat the pants off, eat alive, run circles around (*or* run rings around), wipe the floor with (*or* wipe the ground with)
3 to change the course or direction of (something) ⟨any more complaints and I'm *whipping* this car around and heading back home⟩ — see TURN 2
4 to move or cause to move with a striking motion ⟨her hair *whipped* in the wind⟩ — see FLAP
5 to strike repeatedly ⟨threatened to *whip* them if they didn't behave⟩ — see BEAT 1

whip (up) *vb* to bring (something volatile or intense) into being ⟨*whipped up* protests against the proposed amendment to the state's constitution⟩ — see INCITE 1

whip hand *n* the more favorable condition or position in a competition ⟨unquestionably the company has the *whip hand* in negotiations with the labor union⟩ — see ADVANTAGE 1

whipper *n* one that defeats an enemy or opponent ⟨as the *whippers* of teams from much larger schools, our players have much to be proud of⟩ — see VICTOR 1

whippersnapper *n* a person of no importance or influence ⟨some young *whippersnapper* piped up with a pointless comment⟩ — see NOBODY

whipping *n* failure to win a contest ⟨suffered a *whipping* that took them out of competition⟩ — see DEFEAT 1

whipping boy *n* a person or thing taking the blame for others ⟨used the government's economic policies as the *whipping boy* for every bad decision the company made⟩ — see SCAPEGOAT

whippy *adj* able to revert to original size and shape after being stretched, squeezed, or twisted ⟨the *whippy* branches of a weeping willow⟩ — see ELASTIC 1

whir *also* **whirr** *n* a monotonous sound like that of an insect in motion ⟨a *whir* coming from the refrigerator⟩ — see HUM

whir *also* **whirr** *vb* to fly, turn, or move rapidly with a fluttering or vibratory sound ⟨the hummingbird *whirred* as it hovered over a flower⟩ ⟨our tires *whirred* as we traveled over the rough road⟩
synonyms bumble, burr, buzz, drone, hum, whish, whiz (*or* whizz), zip, zoom
related words chirr, churr; thrum; fizz, hiss, murmur, purr, rustle, sigh, sizzle, swish, whisper; coo, curr; wheeze, whistle, whoosh

whirl *n* **1** a rapid turning about on an axis or central point ⟨the *whirl* of the mechanical ride made him dizzy⟩ — see SPIN 1
2 a state of mental uncertainty ⟨so many changes at once had her all in a *whirl*⟩ — see CONFUSION 1
3 a state of noisy, confused activity ⟨lost an earring in the *whirl* of the party⟩ — see COMMOTION
4 an effort to do or accomplish something ⟨I'm pretty good at fixing things, so how about if I give it a *whirl*?⟩ — see ATTEMPT 1

whirl *vb* **1** to cause (as a liquid) to move about in a circle especially repeatedly ⟨*whirled* the chocolate syrup into the milk with a spoon⟩ — see STIR 1
2 to move (something) in a curved or circular path on or as if on an axis ⟨the figure skater *whirled* his partner with effortless grace⟩ — see TURN 1
3 to move in circles around an axis or center ⟨the gambler held his breath as the roulette wheel *whirled*⟩ — see SPIN 1
4 to proceed or move quickly ⟨cars *whirling* by on the highway⟩ — see HURRY 2
5 to be in a confused state as if from being twirled around ⟨my mind *whirled* from all of the excitement⟩ — see SPIN 2
whirling *adj* having a feeling of being whirled about and in danger of falling down ⟨still *whirling* from the amusement park ride, I needed to sit down⟩ — see DIZZY 1
whirlpool *n* water moving rapidly in a circle with a hollow in the center ⟨in *The Odyssey*, Ulysses is trapped between the six-headed monster Scylla and Charybdis, a deadly *whirlpool* that threatens to suck in his ship⟩
synonyms gulf, maelstrom, vortex
related words tourbillion (*or* tourbillon); eddy, swirl, whirl
whirlwind *adj* moving, proceeding, or acting with great speed ⟨after a *whirlwind* romance of only a few weeks, the couple decided to get married⟩ — see FAST 1
whirlybird *n* a vehicle for traveling through the air that obtains its lift from rotors which spin horizontally ⟨from the sky a police *whirlybird* was able to track the fleeing carjacker⟩ — see HELICOPTER
whish *n* a sound similar to the speech sound \s\ stretched out ⟨the *whish* of tires on wet pavement⟩ — see HISS 1
whish *vb* **1** to fly, turn, or move rapidly with a fluttering or vibratory sound ⟨seemingly out of nowhere, a baseball *whished* past my head⟩ — see WHIR
2 to make a sound like that of stretching out the speech sound \s\ ⟨the match *whished* as it burst into flame⟩ — see HISS
whisk *n* a quick jerky movement from side to side or up and down ⟨with a *whisk* of the broom, the dirt was gone⟩ — see [1]WAG
whisk *vb* **1** to cause to move or proceed fast or faster ⟨the museum guide kept *whisking* us along, telling us there was much more we had to see⟩ — see HURRY 1
2 to move or proceed smoothly and readily ⟨now that the highway has been widened, traffic just *whisks* along⟩ — see FLOW 2
3 to proceed or move quickly ⟨*whisked* through the crowd and delivered the urgent message⟩ — see HURRY 2
whisper *n* a rumor or report of a personal or sensational nature ⟨there were *whispers* that the starlet was secretly married⟩ — see TALE 1
whisper *vb* to make (as a piece of information) the subject of common talk without any authority or confirmation of accuracy ⟨assistants *whispered* that the two singers were having a secret relationship⟩ — see RUMOR
whistle–blower *n* a person who provides information about another's wrongdoing ⟨there are laws to protect *whistle-blowers* who reveal corporate malfeasance⟩ — see INFORMER
whistle–stop *n* a small residential settlement ⟨for that all-important primary election, candidates are willing to go to every *whistle-stop* in the state⟩ — see VILLAGE
whistling *adj* having a high musical pitch or range ⟨the *whistling* sound of missiles as they sped toward their targets⟩ — see SHRILL
whit *n* the smallest amount or part imaginable ⟨I care not a *whit* about what other people think⟩ — see JOT
white *adj* **1** lacking an addition of color ⟨dazzlingly *white* paint on the walls of the new house⟩ — see COLORLESS 1
2 not causing or being capable of causing injury or hurt ⟨told a little *white* lie to spare her feelings⟩ — see HARMLESS
3 free from sin ⟨the tendency to see everything and everyone as morally black or *white*⟩ — see INNOCENT 1
white–haired *adj* granted special treatment or attention ⟨the company's top salesman was certainly the *white-haired* boy of the office⟩ — see DARLING 1
white heat *n* depth of feeling ⟨claims that the novel was written at *white heat* in a tremendous, unbroken burst of creativity⟩ — see ARDOR 1
white–hot *adj* having a notably high temperature ⟨the molten mass was still *white-hot* when the glassblower began to work his magic⟩ — see HOT 1
white knight *n* a person who actively supports or favors a cause ⟨a deserving cause in need of a charismatic *white knight* who will galvanize public support⟩ — see EXPONENT 1
white lightning *n* illegally produced liquor ⟨college students secretly mixing up a batch of *white lightning* in the school lab⟩ — see MOONSHINE 1
whiten *vb* to make white or whiter by removing color ⟨years of sunlight had almost completely *whitened* the flag⟩
synonyms blanch, bleach, blench, decolorize, dull, fade, pale, snow, wash out
related words brighten, lighten; dim, mat (*also* matte *or* matt); etiolate; whitewash; frost, silver
near antonyms blacken; blotch, checker, dapple, daub, discolor, fleck, marble, mottle, pattern, polychrome, shade, speck, speckle, splotch, spot, streak, striate, stripe, tarnish, variegate; color, dye, paint, pigment, stain, tincture, tinge, tint; burnish, polish, shine
antonyms darken, deepen, embrown
whitewash *vb* **1** to dismiss as of little importance ⟨refused to *whitewash* the governor's chronic disregard for the truth⟩ — see EXCUSE 1
2 to make (something) seem less bad by offering excuses ⟨don't try to *whitewash* your rudeness by claiming that you were having a bad day⟩ — see PALLIATE 1
whither *adv* at, in, or to what place ⟨*whither* are you going, my lady?⟩ — see WHERE 1
[1]**whiz** *or* **whizz** *n* **1** a sound similar to the speech sound \s\ stretched out ⟨the *whiz* of an arrow flying by at an uncomfortably close range⟩ — see HISS 1
2 a monotonous sound like that of an insect in motion ⟨the irritating *whiz* of a bee in the room⟩ — see HUM
[2]**whiz** *n* **1** a person with a high level of knowledge or skill in a field ⟨the computer *whiz* to whom we all go when we're having problems, which is fairly often⟩ — see EXPERT
2 a very smart person ⟨one of those *whizzes* who does very well in every subject⟩ — see GENIUS 1
whiz *or* **whizz** *vb* **1** to make a sound like that of stretching out the speech sound \s\ ⟨just hearing the bullets *whiz* as they fly by their heads must be terrifying for soldiers⟩ — see HISS
2 to fly, turn, or move rapidly with a fluttering or vibratory sound ⟨many vehicles were *whizzing* past us at breakneck speeds⟩ — see WHIR
whole *adj* **1** not divided or scattered among several areas of interest or concern ⟨you'll need to put your *whole* effort into this project⟩
synonyms all, concentrated, entire, exclusive, focused (*also* focussed), undivided
related words absolute, complete, full, lump, teetotal, thorough, total, unadulterated, unalloyed, unqualified, utter; comprehensive, intact, integral, perfect, unbroken

near antonyms deficient, fragmental, fragmentary, halfway, incomplete, partial
antonyms diffuse, divided, scattered
2 enjoying health and vigor ⟨*whole* and happy again after months of recuperation⟩ — see HEALTHY 1
3 not lacking any part or member that properly belongs to it ⟨the puzzle isn't quite *whole*, but close enough⟩ — see COMPLETE 1

whole *n* a complete amount of something ⟨the landlord eventually refunded the *whole* of our deposit⟩
synonyms aggregate, full, sum, summation, sum total, total, totality
related words gross; completeness, comprehensiveness, cumulativeness, entirety; bulk, lion's share, mass; enchilada, schmear
phrases grand total, the whole bit, the whole kit and caboodle, the whole nine yards, the whole shebang
near antonyms net

wholehearted *adj* characterized by unqualified enthusiasm ⟨*wholehearted* praise for the novel by the leading critics⟩ — see HEARTY 1

wholeness *n* **1** the condition of being sound in body ⟨young people who don't appreciate their *wholeness* and youthfulness while they have it⟩ — see HEALTH 1
2 the quality or state of being without restriction, exception, or qualification ⟨the *wholeness* of my faith in our new governor is not lessened by these early missteps⟩ — see ENTIRENESS

whole number *n* a character used to represent a mathematical value ⟨since percentages have been rounded off to *whole numbers*, the total will not be exactly equal to 100%⟩ — see NUMBER 1

wholesome *adj* **1** enjoying health and vigor ⟨a *wholesome* young woman in the prime of her life⟩ — see HEALTHY 1
2 beneficial to the health of body or mind ⟨trying to eat a more *wholesome* diet⟩ — see HEALTHFUL

wholesomeness *n* the condition of being sound in body ⟨after the physical exam the doctor declared that I appeared to be enjoying the *wholesomeness* of a man half my age⟩ — see HEALTH 1

whole–souled *adj* characterized by unqualified enthusiasm ⟨expressed their *whole-souled* commitment to the cause of peace⟩ — see HEARTY 1

wholly *adv* to a full extent or degree ⟨not *wholly* convinced by the evidence that the prosecutor presented⟩ — see FULLY 1

whomp *n* a loud explosive sound ⟨the dish fell off the table and hit the hardwood floor with a *whomp*⟩ — see CLAP 1

whomp *vb* to defeat by a large margin ⟨the basketball team was *whomped* in the last game of the regular season and missed out on the playoffs⟩ — see WHIP 2

whoop *n* **1** a loud vocal expression of strong emotion ⟨let out a *whoop* of joy⟩ — see SHOUT
2 the smallest amount or part imaginable ⟨he acts so rudely that I doubt he gives a *whoop* about other people's feelings⟩ — see JOT

whoopee *interj* how delightful ⟨another sitcom featuring wisecracking kids? *whoopee*⟩ — see HOORAY

whoopee *n* joyful or festive activity ⟨for New Year's Eve I'm planning to make *whoopee* at several clubs⟩ — see MERRYMAKING

whop *also* **whap** *n* a hard strike with a part of the body or an instrument ⟨the doctor gave my knee a little *whop* with his mallet to test my reflexes⟩ — see [1]BLOW

whop *or* **whap** *vb* **1** to defeat by a large margin ⟨despite high hopes, the hometown favorites got *whopped* again⟩ ⟨maybe if that television station replaced its obnoxious news anchor, it wouldn't get consistently *whopped* in the ratings⟩ — see WHIP 2
2 to strike repeatedly ⟨he called me a name and I *whopped* him good⟩ — see BEAT 1

whopper *n* **1** a statement known by its maker to be untrue and made in order to deceive ⟨told a *whopper* to get out of jury duty⟩ — see LIE
2 something that is unusually large and powerful ⟨a *whopper* of a fish that won first prize in the derby⟩ — see GIANT

whopping *adj* unusually large ⟨delivered a *whopping* 10-pound baby⟩ — see HUGE

whore *n* **1** a woman who engages in sexual activities for money ⟨a historic district of the seaport that was once notorious for the *whores* who gathered there⟩ — see PROSTITUTE
2 a boldly flirtatious or sexually promiscuous woman ⟨a society in which men commonly regard women as either Madonnas or *whores*⟩ — see FLOOZY

whoredom *n* the practice of engaging in sexual activities for money ⟨Nell Gwyn is remembered as one of the most infamous courtesans in the annals of *whoredom*⟩ — see PROSTITUTION

whorehouse *n* a building in which prostitutes are available ⟨he visited a *whorehouse* for the first time at age 19⟩ — see BORDELLO

whoreson *n* an illegitimate child ⟨a notorious 17th-century libertine who supposedly left a brood of *whoresons* across the breadth of England⟩ — see BASTARD 1

whump *n* a loud explosive sound ⟨the crate of oranges landed on the floor with a *whump*⟩ — see CLAP 1

whup *vb* **1** to defeat by a large margin ⟨in the summer box office sweepstakes, most of the Hollywood blockbusters got *whupped* by a small indie movie with no stars⟩ — see WHIP 2
2 to strike repeatedly ⟨we'll be *whupped* for this stupid prank⟩ — see BEAT 1

why *interj* how surprising, doubtful, or unbelievable ⟨*why*, what a strange thing to say!⟩ — see NO

why *n* **1** something (as a belief) that serves as the basis for another thing ⟨asked the *whys* behind the surprising decision⟩ — see REASON 2
2 something hard to understand or explain ⟨how one decides that a certain he or she is "the one" is one of the great *whys* of life⟩ — see MYSTERY

wicked *adj* **1** not conforming to a high moral standard; morally unacceptable ⟨a *wicked* urge to steal just for the sake of stealing⟩ — see BAD 2
2 tending to or exhibiting reckless playfulness ⟨a *wicked* grin on his face when he said that⟩ — see MISCHIEVOUS 1
3 not giving pleasure to the mind or senses ⟨rotting eggs create a truly *wicked* stench⟩ — see UNPLEASANT
4 causing or capable of causing harm ⟨the contention that prostitution is not a victimless crime but a *wicked* assault on family values⟩ — see HARMFUL

wicked *adv* to a great degree ⟨we were *wicked* excited when our team finally won the pennant after so many years⟩ — see VERY 1

wickedly *adv* in a mean or spiteful manner ⟨she *wickedly* whispered amusing but snide comments about the other performers in the talent show⟩ — see NASTILY

wickedness *n* **1** playful, reckless behavior that is not intended to cause serious harm ⟨a couple of live wires who got into all kinds of *wickedness* during their vacation in Las Vegas⟩ — see MISCHIEF 1
2 the state or quality of being utterly evil ⟨the movie featured a villain of unadulterated *wickedness*⟩ — see ENORMITY 1

wide *adj* **1** having a greater than usual measure across ⟨the river is so *wide* that building a bridge across it would be impractical⟩
synonyms broad, fat, thick
related words expansive, extensive, sweeping; commo-

dious, roomy, spacious; outsize (*also* outsized), oversize (*or* oversized), sizable (*or* sizeable), substantial, tidy, voluminous
near antonyms fine, hairlike, reedlike; elongate (*or* elongated), needlelike; bottleneck, close, compressed, condensed, constricted, contracted, squeezed, tight, tightened; attenuate, attenuated; small, smallish, undersized (*also* undersize)
antonyms hairline, narrow, paper-thin, skinny, slender, slim, slim-jim, thin
2 having considerable extent ⟨a *wide* and detailed knowledge of the issue⟩ — see EXTENSIVE

wide *adv* to a full extent or degree ⟨the door was *wide* open⟩ — see FULLY 1

wide–awake *adj* **1** not sleeping or able to sleep ⟨was *wide-awake* with worry for most of the night⟩ — see WAKEFUL
2 paying close attention usually for the purpose of anticipating approaching danger or opportunity ⟨investors who were *wide-awake* bought the stock as soon as it was offered⟩ — see ALERT 1

wide–eyed *adj* **1** lacking in worldly wisdom or informed judgment ⟨a *wide-eyed* and trusting child⟩ — see NAIVE 1
2 readily taken advantage of ⟨the sort of phony UFO "artifacts" that *wide-eyed* tourists fall for⟩ — see EASY 2

wide–ranging *adj* having considerable extent ⟨his *wide-ranging* business interests and real estate holdings make him one of the most powerful men in the state⟩ — see EXTENSIVE

widespread *adj* having considerable extent ⟨a *widespread* area of drought⟩ — see EXTENSIVE

widget *n* an interesting and often novel device with a practical use ⟨manufacturers of all kinds of *widgets* for the do-it-yourselfer⟩ — see GADGET

width *n* an area over which activity, capacity, or influence extends ⟨surprised by the *width* of his power and influence in the oil business⟩ — see RANGE 2

wield *vb* to bring to bear especially forcefully or effectively ⟨*wields* considerable influence in the field of women's sports⟩ — see EXERT

wife *n* the female partner in a marriage ⟨a husband and *wife* who treat each other as equals in their marriage⟩
synonyms helpmate, helpmeet, lady, little woman, madam, missus (*or* missis), Mrs., old lady, wifey, woman [*chiefly dialect*]
related words bride; better half, companion, consort, mate, partner, significant other, soul mate, spouse; dowager, matron; hausfrau, homemaker, housekeeper, housewife, stay-at-home; widow

wifey *n* the female partner in a marriage ⟨she sternly informed her husband that she did not appreciate being introduced as "the *wifey*" at gatherings⟩ — see WIFE

wig *n* a headpiece made of natural or synthetic hair usually worn to cover a bald area ⟨the cancer patient started wearing a *wig* after losing all of her hair from chemotherapy⟩ — see HAIRPIECE

wig (out) *vb, slang* to yield to mental or emotional stress ⟨with her claustrophobia, it wouldn't take a day for her to *wig out* on a submarine⟩ — see CRACK 2

wiggle *vb* to make jerky or restless movements ⟨the baby *wiggled* in her sleep⟩ — see FIDGET

wiggle room *n* an allowable margin of freedom or variation ⟨the language of the contract is vague and leaves too much *wiggle room*⟩ — see SLACK 1

wiggly *adj* making jerky or restless movements ⟨a can of *wiggly* worms⟩ — see FIDGETY

wight *n* a member of the human race ⟨what unfortunate *wight* would be out and about in such foul weather?⟩ — see HUMAN

wild *adj* **1** living outdoors without taming or domestication by humans ⟨*wild* animals can be shy or aggressive when confronted by humans⟩
synonyms feral, savage, unbroken, undomesticated, untamed, wilding
related words uncontrolled, undocile, unsubdued, untrained; bestial, brutal, brute; barbarous, uncivilized
near antonyms controlled, docile, familiar, semidomesticated, subdued, submissive; halterbroken, housebroken, trained; civilized, semicivilized, socialized
antonyms broken, busted, domestic, domesticated, gentled, tame, tamed
2 existing without human habitation or cultivation ⟨that land has been completely *wild* since the owners abandoned it⟩
synonyms natural, uncultivated, untamed, virgin
related words native; uninhabited, unpeopled, unsettled; overgrown, spontaneous, untended; waste; undeveloped; desolate, forlorn, howling
near antonyms inhabited; developed; seminatural
antonyms cultivated, tamed
3 marked by turmoil or disturbance especially of natural elements ⟨a *wild* night, full of wind and rain⟩
synonyms rough, rugged, stormy, tempestuous, tumultuous, turbulent
related words blustering, blustery, raging, violent; brutal, harsh, severe; roily, unquiet, unsettled; bleak, inclement, nasty, raw, squally
near antonyms calm, halcyon, peaceful, placid, quiet, serene, tranquil; bright, clear, clement, cloudless, fair, sunny, sunshiny, unclouded
4 conceived or made without regard for reason or reality ⟨some *wild* claim that he was abducted by aliens⟩ — see FANTASTIC 1
5 different from the ordinary in a way that causes curiosity or suspicion ⟨public speakers in the park typically spout some *wild* ideas⟩ — see ODD 2
6 marked by great and often stressful excitement or activity ⟨the holidays were especially *wild* around here this year⟩ — see FURIOUS 1
7 not civilized ⟨ancient traces of a *wild* people who lived in mountain caves⟩ — see SAVAGE 1
8 showing urgent desire or interest ⟨they're just *wild* to go on the ecotour through the Amazon rain forest⟩ — see EAGER

wild *adv* in a confused and reckless manner ⟨as soon as the doors opened, early-morning bargain hunters ran *wild* through the store⟩ — see HELTER-SKELTER 1

wild *n* that part of the physical world that is removed from human habitation ⟨some animals aren't meant to live outside of the *wild*⟩ — see NATURE 2

wilderness *n* that part of the physical world that is removed from human habitation ⟨released the wolf back into the *wilderness*⟩ — see NATURE 2

wilding *adj* living outdoors without taming or domestication by humans ⟨a herd of *wilding* mustangs⟩ — see WILD 1

wildly *adv* **1** in a confused and reckless manner ⟨upon being dismissed, the students dashed *wildly* off in all directions⟩ — see HELTER-SKELTER 1
2 to a great degree ⟨trespassers make the recluse *wildly* angry⟩ — see VERY 1

wile *n* **1** a clever often underhanded means to achieve an end ⟨had to use all of her *wiles* to convince her guests to stay for dinner⟩ — see TRICK 1
2 the use of clever underhanded actions to achieve an end ⟨it took both *wile* and cajolery to talk him into it⟩ — see TRICKERY

wile *vb* to attract or delight as if by magic ⟨her stories of the Old South could *wile* anyone⟩ — see CHARM 1

wiliness *n* **1** skill in achieving one's ends through indirect, subtle, or underhanded means ⟨admired the politi-

cian's *wiliness*, but questioned his ethics⟩ — see CUNNING 1
2 the inclination or practice of misleading others through lies or trickery ⟨her reputation for Machiavellian *wiliness* made people disinclined to trust her⟩ — see DECEIT 1

will *n* **1** the power to control one's actions, impulses, or emotions ⟨she kept her face still by sheer force of *will*⟩
synonyms continence, restraint, self-command, self-containment, self-control, self-discipline, self-government, self-mastery, self-possession, self-restraint, willpower
related words self-abnegation, self-denial, self-deprivation; moderateness, moderation, temperance, temperateness; determination, nerve; command, control, discipline, mastery; abnegation, abstention, avoidance, eschewal, forbearance; abstinence, soberness, sobriety; aplomb, assurance, composure, confidence, coolness, equanimity, poise, self-confidence; discretion
near antonyms gratification, indulgence, self-indulgence; excessiveness, immoderacy, intemperance, intemperateness, overindulgence; demerit, failing, fault, feebleness, foible, frailty, shortcoming, vice, weakness; indiscipline, unconstraint, unreserve, unreservedness, unrestraint
2 the act or power of making one's own choices or decisions ⟨you cannot force me to do anything against my own *will*⟩ — see FREE WILL

will *vb* **1** to give by means of a will ⟨*willed* their house to their adult children⟩ — see LEAVE 2
2 to see fit ⟨do as you *will*—I wash my hands of the whole affair⟩ — see CHOOSE 2

willed *adj* made, given, or done with full awareness of what one is doing ⟨a hard-nosed industrialist with a *willed* indifference to public opinion⟩ — see INTENTIONAL

willful *or* **wilful** *adj* **1** given to resisting authority or another's control ⟨a particularly *willful* horse that took weeks to break to saddle⟩ — see DISOBEDIENT
2 given to resisting control or discipline by others ⟨finally the parents sought professional counseling for the *willful* child⟩ — see UNCONTROLLABLE
3 having or showing a tendency to force one's will on others without any regard to fairness or necessity ⟨a *willful* disregard for the rights of others⟩ — see ARBITRARY 1
4 made, given, or done with full awareness of what one is doing ⟨a *willful* attempt to cheat her siblings out of their rightful inheritance⟩ — see INTENTIONAL
5 sticking to an opinion, purpose, or course of action in spite of reason, arguments, or persuasion ⟨the kind of *willful* person who can never bring himself to admit that he made a mistake⟩ — see OBSTINATE

willfully *adv* with full awareness of what one is doing ⟨*willfully* chose to risk pneumonia by jumping into a freezing lake on a dare⟩ — see INTENTIONALLY

willfulness *n* **1** a steadfast adherence to an opinion, purpose, or course of action in spite of reason, arguments, or persuasion ⟨her unceasing *willfulness* eventually wore down her critics and opponents⟩ — see OBSTINACY
2 refusal to obey ⟨*willfulness* was dealt with harshly at the orphanage⟩ — see DISOBEDIENCE

willies *n pl* a sense of panic or extreme nervousness ⟨spiders give me the *willies* for some reason⟩ — see JITTERS

willing *adj* **1** having a desire or inclination (as for a specified course of action) ⟨I'm a little confused, but perfectly *willing* to do as you ask⟩
synonyms amenable, disposed, fain, game, glad, inclined, minded, ready
related words predisposed, prone; accommodating, agreeable, compliant, cooperative, obedient, obliging, submissive; favorable, receptive; prepared, prompt, quick, responsive, swift; desirous, eager, enthused, enthusiastic, excited
near antonyms averse, loath (*also* loth *or* loathe), reluctant, reticent
antonyms disinclined, unamenable, unwilling
2 having or showing the ability to respond without delay or hesitation ⟨she's always lent a *willing* hand whenever a neighbor needed help or a friend a favor⟩ — see QUICK 1
3 done, made, or given with one's own free will ⟨a *willing* sacrifice of her limited free time for a good cause⟩ — see VOLUNTARY 1

willingly *adv* **1** by choice or preference ⟨I would not *willingly* eat liver, but sometimes I have no choice⟩ — see RATHER 1
2 of one's own free will ⟨I *willingly* made the campaign contribution; no one pressured me into doing so⟩ — see VOLUNTARILY

willingness *n* cheerful readiness to do something ⟨his unhesitating *willingness* to take on the tough assignments has earned him the status of the president's right-hand man⟩ — see ALACRITY

williwaw *n* **1** a state of noisy, confused activity ⟨the surprise verdict of the jury created a wild *williwaw* as reporters rushed to file their stories⟩ — see COMMOTION
2 a sudden brief rush of wind ⟨a *williwaw* rose up seemingly out of nowhere and wreaked havoc with our campsite⟩ — see GUST 1

will-less *adj* not made or done willingly or by choice ⟨the wife's involvement in the physical abuse of the children was not *will-less*—she could have called the police at any time⟩ — see INVOLUNTARY 1

willowy *adj* able to bend easily without breaking ⟨the rattan's stems are split into *willowy* staves that are woven together to produce exquisite baskets⟩
synonyms bendy [*chiefly British*], flexible, limber, lissome (*also* lissom), lithe, lithesome, pliable, pliant, supple
related words adaptable, ductile, elastic, fluid, kneadable, malleable, modifiable, plastic, variable, yielding; droopy, flaccid, floppy, limp; semiflexible
near antonyms inelastic, nonmalleable, unyielding; breakable, brittle, fragile
antonyms inflexible, rigid, stiff, stiffened

willpower *n* the power to control one's actions, impulses, or emotions ⟨trying to summon the *willpower* to resist eating a huge piece of cake⟩ — see WILL 1

willy-nilly *adv* without definite aim, direction, rule, or method ⟨they were in a hurry, so they just tossed everything into the room *willy-nilly*, leaving it to be all sorted out later⟩ — see HIT-OR-MISS

wilt *vb* **1** to be limp from lack of water or vigor ⟨the plants *wilted* after I forgot to water them for three whole days⟩ — see DROOP 1
2 to lose bodily strength or vigor ⟨she had *wilted* a bit after walking around the hot and humid city⟩ — see WEAKEN 2
3 to lose liveliness, force, or freshness ⟨after six solid hours of painting, his energy was starting to *wilt*⟩ — see WITHER 1

wily *adj* clever at attaining one's ends by indirect and often deceptive means ⟨a *wily* judge of character, she takes advantage of car buyers' insecurities to sell them a bigger machine than they really need⟩ — see ARTFUL 1

wimp *n* **1** a person lacking in physical strength ⟨just because you can't lift 300 pounds doesn't mean you're a *wimp*⟩ — see WEAKLING 1
2 a person without strength of character ⟨what kind of *wimp* would just give in to peer pressure?⟩ — see WEAKLING 2

wimpiness *n* **1** the quality or state of lacking physical strength or vigor ⟨in the annals of boxing, a sport where participants are not exactly known for their *wimpiness*, he is remembered as a particularly powerful slugger⟩ — see WEAKNESS 1
2 the quality or state of lacking strength of will or character ⟨her desire to do the right thing was countered by a moral *wimpiness*⟩ — see WEAKNESS 2

wimpish *adj* **1** lacking bodily strength ⟨not impressed by his *wimpish* physique⟩ — see WEAK 1
2 lacking strength of will or character ⟨it's *wimpish* to blame someone else for your mistakes⟩ — see WEAK 2

wimpishness *n* the quality or state of lacking strength of will or character ⟨the galling *wimpishness* of the legislator who votes "present" whenever there's a vote on a hot-button issue⟩ — see WEAKNESS 2

wimpy *adj* **1** lacking bodily strength ⟨a *wimpy* person is not the best choice for a job with a moving company⟩ — see WEAK 1
2 lacking strength of will or character ⟨a *wimpy* effort to change the law that was doomed to failure⟩ — see WEAK 2

win *n* an instance of defeating an enemy or opponent ⟨a team with 12 *wins* and two losses⟩ — see VICTORY

win *vb* **1** to achieve victory (as in a contest) ⟨the kind of person who always has to *win*—even if the game is just for fun⟩
synonyms conquer, prevail, triumph
related words overcome, sweep; squeak, squeeze; contend, vie; succeed; breeze, romp
phrases carry the day; kick butt
near antonyms collapse, fail, flop, fold, wash out; flounder, struggle; decline, slip, slump, wane
antonyms lose
2 to receive as return for effort ⟨*win* a gold medal in swimming⟩ — see EARN 1
3 to obtain (as a goal) through effort ⟨*won* a substantial victory in the struggle for civil rights for all⟩ — see ACHIEVE 1

win (against) *vb* to achieve a victory over ⟨a child prodigy who has already *won against* a number of more experienced chess players⟩ — see BEAT 2

win (over) *vb* to cause (someone) to agree with a belief or course of action by using arguments or earnest requests ⟨a combination of solid reasoning and outright begging *won* my parents *over*, and I became an exchange student for a year⟩ — see PERSUADE

wince *vb* to draw back in fear, pain, or disgust ⟨*winced* at the movie's graphic depiction of combat injuries⟩ — see FLINCH

[1]**wind** *n* **1** noticeable movement of air in a particular direction ⟨there's a *wind* coming from underneath the front door⟩
synonyms current, draft
related words blast, blow, flurry, gale, gust, headwind, squall, tailwind, tempest, tornado, windstorm; breath, breeze, puff, waft, zephyr
2 a prevailing or general movement or inclination ⟨the *winds* of public opinion are changing on this issue⟩ — see TREND 1
3 language that is impressive-sounding but not meaningful or sincere ⟨the speech contained nothing of substance and was just a lot of *wind*⟩ — see RHETORIC 1

[2]**wind** *n* something that curves or is curved ⟨there's one last easterly *wind* to the river before it empties into the sea⟩ — see BEND 1

wind *vb* **1** to follow a circular or spiral course ⟨flowering vines *wind* around the porch's graceful columns⟩
synonyms coil, corkscrew, curl, entwine, spiral, twine, twist
related words arc, arch, bend, crook, curve, hook, sweep, swerve, turn, veer, wheel; swirl, whirl; circle, encircle, loop; enlace, interlace, intertwine, lace; bow, bulge; meander, weave, zigzag
near antonyms straighten
2 to introduce in a gradual, secret, or clever way ⟨self-interest *winds* itself into everything that he does—even his alleged favors for other people⟩ — see INSINUATE 1

windbag *n* a person who talks constantly ⟨with a *windbag* like that, who needs a wind farm to meet our energy needs?⟩ — see CHATTERBOX

windblast *n* a sudden brief rush of wind ⟨a *windblast* from the hovering helicopter made it difficult to even stand up⟩ — see GUST 1

wind down *vb* to get rid of nervous tension or anxiety ⟨not being one for alcoholic beverages, I prefer to *wind down* with a cup of tea every night⟩ — see RELAX 1

windfall *n* something that provides happiness or does good for a person or thing ⟨hitting the lottery jackpot was an incredible *windfall* for the recently laid-off worker⟩ — see BLESSING 2

windiness *n* the use of too many words to express an idea ⟨he's a brilliant thinker, but his *windiness* tends to overwhelm his ideas⟩ — see VERBIAGE 1

winding *adj* **1** marked by a long series of irregular curves ⟨a long and *winding* path through the woods⟩ — see CROOKED 1
2 turning around an axis like the thread of a screw ⟨a *winding* staircase leads to the top of the lighthouse⟩ — see SPIRAL

windjammer *n* a boat equipped with one or more sails ⟨with no set course to follow, a *windjammer* sails wherever the wind and the captain's whim takes it⟩ — see SAILBOAT

window dressing *n* a deceptively attractive external appearance ⟨the crime-does-not-pay moralizing is just *window dressing* for nasty hard-boiled stories⟩ — see GLOSS 1

windup *n* the last part of a process or action ⟨wait until the *windup* of your sales pitch before giving up any information about the product's price point⟩ — see FINALE

wind up *vb* **1** to bring (an event) to a natural or appropriate stopping point ⟨try to *wind up* the performance, as we're almost out of time⟩ — see CLOSE 3
2 to come to an end ⟨her speeches usually *wind up* with one last joke⟩ — see CEASE 1

[1]**windy** *adj* **1** marked by strong wind or more wind than usual ⟨one particularly *windy* day should shake the last of the autumn leaves from the trees⟩
synonyms blowy, blustery, breezy, gusty, squally
related words drafty; stormy, tempestuous
near antonyms breathless, calm, motionless, still
2 marked by the use of impressive-sounding but mostly meaningless words and phrases ⟨gave his usual *windy* speech about working for the common people⟩ — see RHETORICAL 1
3 using or containing more words than necessary to express an idea ⟨a *windy* saleswoman who told us a lot more than we wanted to know about vacuum cleaners⟩ — see WORDY 1

[2]**windy** *adj* marked by a long series of irregular curves ⟨a *windy* little creek⟩ — see CROOKED 1

wing *n* a group of people acting together within a larger group ⟨the conservative *wing* of the party⟩ — see FACTION

wing *vb* to move through the air with or as if with outstretched wings ⟨watched the flocks of birds as they *winged* southward for the winter⟩ — see FLY 1

wink *n* **1** a short sleep ⟨I wasn't able to catch a *wink* during the entire flight⟩ — see [1]NAP
2 a very small space of time ⟨I turned to look away, and in a *wink* he was gone⟩ — see INSTANT

wink *vb* **1** to rapidly open and close one's eyes ⟨she

winked several times to get the dust and grit out of her eyes⟩
synonyms blink
related words bat, flutter; squint
2 to shine with light at regular intervals ⟨a lighthouse was *winking* in the distance⟩ — see BLINK 1
3 to shoot forth bursts of light ⟨fireflies *winking* in the darkness beyond our campfire⟩ — see FLASH 1
4 to secretly sympathize with or pretend ignorance of something improper or unlawful ⟨the whole sporting world seems to *wink* as untold sums are bet on the outcome of the Super Bowl⟩ — see CONNIVE 1

wink (at) *vb* to dismiss as of little importance ⟨for too long the school just *winked at* the young athletes' hooliganism, dismissing it as a case of "boys being boys"⟩ — see EXCUSE 1

wink (out) *vb* to come to an end ⟨she mused that it was as if her affection for him had just *winked out* one day⟩ — see CEASE 1

winkle *vb* to shoot forth bursts of light ⟨under a canopy of *winkling* stars, the campers bedded down for the night⟩ — see FLASH 1

winner *n* **1** a person or thing that is successful ⟨the movie was panned by the critics but has been a *winner* at the box office⟩ — see HIT 1
2 one that defeats an enemy or opponent ⟨the *winner* of any given war is usually the one who gets to write the history of that war⟩ — see VICTOR 1
3 the person who comes in first in a competition ⟨the other finalists graciously congratulated the *winner*⟩ — see CHAMPION 1

winning *adj* **1** having qualities that tend to make one loved ⟨a particularly pretty and *winning* child⟩ — see LOVABLE
2 likely or intended to win one's affection ⟨flashed a *winning* smile that soon had us at her beck and call⟩ — see INGRATIATING

winningly *adv* in a pleasing way ⟨won the debate with incisive yet *winningly* witty responses⟩ — see WELL 5

winsome *adj* **1** having or showing a good mood or disposition ⟨she was a bright, *winsome* gamine who could draw a smile out of anyone⟩ — see CHEERFUL 1
2 likely or intended to win one's affection ⟨in her new role, the actress again displays the *winsome* charm that has made her an audience favorite⟩ — see INGRATIATING
3 having qualities that tend to make one loved ⟨an actress who specialized in playing *winsome* ingenues in romantic comedies⟩ — see LOVABLE

winter *n* a period of often involuntary inactivity or idleness ⟨during the long *winter* when the party was out of power, it had plenty of time to reconsider its political priorities⟩ — see DOWNTIME

wintry *also* **wintery** *adj* **1** having a low or subnormal temperature ⟨a *wintry* and snowy day⟩ — see COLD 1
2 lacking in friendliness or warmth of feeling ⟨the doorman gave the uninvited visitors a *wintry* smile and escorted them out⟩ — see COLD 2

winze *n, Scottish* a prayer that harm will come to someone ⟨uttered a bitter *winze* upon the laird who had cast them off the land⟩ — see CURSE 1

wiped out *adj* **1** depleted in strength, energy, or freshness ⟨felt *wiped out* for several weeks after getting the flu⟩ — see WEARY 1
2 *slang* being under the influence of alcohol ⟨thought that it'd be nice to attend a fraternity party in which everyone wasn't *wiped out*⟩ — see DRUNK
3 *slang* being under the influence of a recreational drug ⟨most of the club patrons were too *wiped out* to know or care what was happening⟩ — see STONED 1

wipe out *vb* to destroy all traces of ⟨he didn't get his gambling under control until he had already *wiped out* his entire life savings⟩ — see ANNIHILATE 1

wire *n* a length of braided, flexible material that is used for tying or connecting things ⟨a telephone *wire*⟩ — see CORD 1

wirra *interj, Irish* used to express sorrow or distress ⟨*wirra, wirra,* me sweet colleen, lying in her cold grave!⟩ — see ALAS

wisdom *n* **1** the ability to understand inner qualities or relationships ⟨with age and experience comes *wisdom*—hopefully⟩ ⟨neither book learning nor simple intelligence should be confused with *wisdom*⟩
synonyms discernment, insight, perception, perceptiveness, perceptivity, sagaciousness, sagacity, sageness, sapience
related words acuity, acumen, astuteness, clear-sightedness, keenness, penetration, percipience, perspicacity, sensitivity, understanding; appreciation, apprehension, comprehension, grasp; brain(s), braininess, brightness, brilliance, canniness, cleverness, gray matter, intellect, intelligence, judgment (*or* judgement), mentality, power, reason, sense, smartness, wit; discrimination, foresight, foresightedness, judiciousness, prudence, sanity; logic, rationality
near antonyms density, dullness (*also* dulness), obtuseness; brainlessness, folly, foolishness, idiocy, imbecility, mindlessness, silliness, simplemindedness, simpleness, stupidity, witlessness; illogic, irrationality, unreasonableness, unsoundness; craziness, insanity, lunacy, madness; preposterousness, senselessness, silliness, zaniness
2 a body of facts learned by study or experience ⟨the orientation meetings will provide the company's old hands with an opportunity to pass on their *wisdom* to the new employees⟩ — see KNOWLEDGE 1
3 the ability to make intelligent decisions especially in everyday matters ⟨had overstayed her welcome and lacked the *wisdom* to know it⟩ — see COMMON SENSE
4 suitability for bringing about a desired result under the circumstances ⟨wondered about the *wisdom* of hiring such an inexperienced girl to care for the children⟩ — see EXPEDIENCY

wise *adj* **1** having or showing deep understanding and intelligent application of knowledge ⟨a respected and *wise* old judge famous for her sensible rulings⟩
synonyms discerning, insightful, perceptive, prudent, sagacious, sage, sapient
related words acute, penetrating, percipient, perspicacious; experienced; discriminating, discriminative; brainy, bright, brilliant, clever, intelligent, keen, nimble, quick, quick-witted, smart; cerebral, erudite, knowledgeable, learned, literate, scholarly; astute, clearheaded, piercing, sharp, shrewd; contemplative, reflective, thoughtful
near antonyms dense, dull, obtuse, purblind, woodenheaded; brainless, dumb, feebleminded, foolish, idiotic (*also* idiotical), imbecile (*or* imbecilic), knuckleheaded, moronic, silly, simple, slow, slow-witted, stupid, thoughtless, unintelligent, witless; undiscriminating
antonyms unperceptive, unwise
2 having inside information ⟨they fooled everyone else, but I'd heard them talking and was *wise* to their true intentions⟩
synonyms hip, knowing
related words alerted, aware, clued (in), forewarned, informed, prepared, ready, warned; observant, observing, sharp, sharp-eyed; alert, attentive, open-eyed, vigilant, watchful; plugged-in, with-it
phrases in the know
near antonyms oblivious, unaware, unconscious, uninformed, unwitting; heedless, unmindful; unprepared, unready, unwary
antonyms unknowing

3 suitable for bringing about a desired result under the circumstances ⟨selling the stock just before it plunged in value was a *wise* move on your part⟩ — see EXPEDIENT

4 making light of something usually regarded as serious or sacred ⟨you wouldn't be so *wise* if you were the one suffering from hemorrhoids⟩ — see FLIPPANT

5 displaying or marked by rude boldness ⟨she is competent, but she's always getting *wise* with the boss⟩ — see NERVY 1

wise (up) *vb* **1** to give information to ⟨*wised* him *up* to some of the more effective tricks of salesmanship⟩ — see ENLIGHTEN 1

2 to come to an awareness of ⟨she eventually *wised up* to the fact that he was taking advantage of her⟩ — see DISCOVER 1

wiseacre *n* a person who likes to show off in a clever but annoying way ⟨a loudmouthed *wiseacre* who thinks he is more amusing than he really is⟩ — see SMART ALECK

wiseass *adj* making light of something usually regarded as serious or sacred ⟨the comedian's *wiseass* monologue about terrorism was greeted with stony silence⟩ — see FLIPPANT

wiseass *n* a person who likes to show off in a clever but annoying way ⟨fine, you're right, but there was no reason to be such a *wiseass* while pointing out the error⟩ — see SMART ALECK

wisecrack *n* something said or done to cause laughter ⟨a whispered *wisecrack* doubled them over in laughter⟩ — see JOKE 1

wisecrack *vb* to make jokes ⟨*wisecracked* to hide his nervousness during the auditions⟩ — see JOKE 1

wise guy *n* a person who likes to show off in a clever but annoying way ⟨if you weren't such a *wise guy* all the time, people might be more interested in hearing what you have to say⟩ — see SMART ALECK

wisenheimer *also* **weisenheimer** *n* a person who likes to show off in a clever but annoying way ⟨it seems like every time we go to the movies, sitting behind us is some *wisenheimer* making snide cracks⟩ — see SMART ALECK

wish *vb* **1** to offer (something fake, useless, or inferior) as genuine, useful, or valuable ⟨despite my protestations, the dreaded position of club secretary was *wished* on me⟩ — see FOIST

2 to see fit ⟨you're free to sit wherever you *wish*⟩ — see CHOOSE 2

wish (for) *vb* to have an earnest wish to own or enjoy ⟨having her own home was something she had *wished for* since she was a child⟩ — see DESIRE 1

wishy-washiness *n* the quality or state of lacking strength of will or character ⟨this is no time for *wishy-washiness*: our country needs a leader who's not afraid to act decisively⟩ — see WEAKNESS 2

wishy-washy *adj* **1** lacking in qualities that make for spirit and character ⟨this story is too *wishy-washy*; you need to add some verve to it⟩

synonyms banal, flat, insipid, milk-and-water, namby-pamby, watery

related words unexciting, uninspiring, unrewarding; bland, boring, drab, dreary, dry, dull, heavy, humdrum, jading, leaden, lifeless, monotonous, pedestrian, ponderous, tedious, tiresome, tiring, uninteresting, vapid, wearisome, weary, wearying; inane; innocuous, inoffensive; mild, soft, subdued, tame, weak; common, commonplace, ordinary, stale, unexceptional

near antonyms piquant, poignant, pungent, racy, spicy; meaty, substantial; entertaining, exciting, galvanizing, inspiring, invigorating, thrilling

2 lacking strength of will or character ⟨in a time of crisis the nation can ill afford *wishy-washy* leaders⟩ — see WEAK 2

wit *n* **1** a person (as a writer) noted for or specializing in humor ⟨the pundits and political *wits* will get a lot of mileage out of the senator's latest gaffe⟩ — see HUMORIST

2 the ability to make intelligent decisions especially in everyday matters ⟨he doesn't even have the *wit* to know when to come in out of the rain⟩ — see COMMON SENSE

3 *usually* **wits** *pl* the normal or healthy condition of the mental abilities ⟨scared out of her *wits*⟩ — see MIND 2

4 exceptional discernment and judgment especially in practical matters ⟨lacked the *wit* to see that the war was unwinnable⟩ — see ACUMEN

witch *n* **1** a woman believed to have often harmful supernatural powers ⟨the 17th-century house had once belonged to a woman who was hanged as a *witch*⟩

synonyms enchantress, hag, hex, sorceress

related words charmer, conjurer (*or* conjuror), enchanter, necromancer, voodoo, voodooist; magician, sorcerer, warlock, wizard

2 a mean or ugly old woman ⟨a foul-tempered old *witch* who is constantly at odds with her neighbors⟩ — see CRONE

3 a person skilled in using supernatural forces ⟨freakish storms that were once thought to be the work of *witches*⟩ — see MAGICIAN 1

witch *vb, archaic* to attract or delight as if by magic ⟨the woman did *witch* me with her gentle smile⟩ — see CHARM 1

witchcraft *n* the power to control natural forces through supernatural means ⟨taught all of her daughters *witchcraft*⟩ — see MAGIC 1

witchery *n* **1** the power of irresistible attraction ⟨the movie star's violet eyes are frequently cited as the source of her cinematic *witchery*⟩ — see CHARM 2

2 the power to control natural forces through supernatural means ⟨a tale of horror replete with eerie hauntings and evil *witchery*⟩ — see MAGIC 1

with *prep* **1** as the result of ⟨the young man was overcome *with* grief⟩ — see BECAUSE OF

2 using the means or agency of ⟨was able to finish the project *with* her help⟩ — see BY 2

3 without being prevented by ⟨*with* all his tough talk, he is still a very gentle person⟩ — see DESPITE

withal *adv* **1** in addition to what has been said ⟨a successful businessman and *withal* a major contributor to local charities⟩ — see MORE 1

2 in spite of that ⟨a homely face that was *withal* rather compelling⟩ — see HOWEVER

withdraw *vb* **1** to move back or away (as from something difficult, dangerous, or disagreeable) ⟨the army was forced to *withdraw* from the line of battle⟩ — see RETREAT 1

2 to solemnly or formally reject or go back on (as something formerly adhered to) ⟨*withdrew* the offer of surrender upon hearing the terms⟩ — see ABJURE 1

3 to take away from a place or position ⟨*withdrew* her hand from the table⟩ — see REMOVE 2

withdrawal *n* an act of moving away especially from something difficult, dangerous, or disagreeable ⟨the army's orderly *withdrawal* from the city turned into a rout as the enemy's shock troops surged forward⟩ — see RETREAT 1

withdrawn *adj* not comfortable around people ⟨a therapist who is especially good with *withdrawn*, emotionally troubled children⟩ — see SHY 2

wither *vb* **1** to lose liveliness, force, or freshness ⟨shortly after the moon landing, interest in the space program *withered*⟩ ⟨the old man seemed to *wither* suddenly upon turning 80⟩

synonyms dry, wilt

related words mummify, shrivel, wizen; decline, fade, wane; decrease, diminish, lessen
near antonyms freshen, revive; bloom, flourish, prosper, thrive; develop, grow, increase, wax; crest, peak, surge
2 to lose bodily strength or vigor ⟨if he's left on his own, he'll just *wither* and die⟩ — see WEAKEN 2

withhold *vb* **1** to be unwilling to grant ⟨must *withhold* official approval until all the proper forms have been submitted⟩ — see DENY 2
2 to continue to have in one's possession or power ⟨*withhold* some money for your own expenses⟩ — see KEEP 2

withhold (from) *vb* to resist the temptation of ⟨please see if you can *withhold from* criticizing every little thing she says⟩ — see FORBEAR

within *n* an interior or internal part ⟨structural decay had started from *within*⟩ — see INSIDE 1

with–it *adj* keenly aware of and responsive to the latest developments especially in fashion and entertainment ⟨a brand of humor that the comedy club's *with-it* clientele very much appreciates⟩ — see AU COURANT 1

without *prep* **1** not having ⟨spent two days *without* food⟩
synonyms absent, minus, sans, wanting
2 out of the reach or sphere of ⟨a goal *without* our grasp⟩ — see BEYOND 2

withstand *vb* to refuse to give in to ⟨trying to *withstand* the temptation to use the beautiful weather as an excuse to take a mental health day⟩ — see RESIST

witless *adj* **1** not having or showing an ability to absorb ideas readily ⟨a dog so *witless* that it is barely trainable⟩ — see STUPID 1
2 showing or marked by a lack of good sense or judgment ⟨a *witless* decision to relocate to the other side of the country without even the prospect of a job⟩ — see FOOLISH 1

witlessness *n* **1** lack of good sense or judgment ⟨his astounding feats of *witlessness* are the stuff of family legend⟩ — see FOOLISHNESS 1
2 the quality or state of lacking intelligence or quickness of mind ⟨for sheer *witlessness* the movie's dialogue deserves some sort of award⟩ — see STUPIDITY 1

witness *n* something presented in support of the truth or accuracy of a claim ⟨the ruins are a compelling *witness* of the ancient civilization's cultural and aesthetic achievements⟩ — see PROOF

witness *vb* **1** to declare (something) to be true or genuine ⟨a notary public *witnessing* wills and other important documents⟩ — see CERTIFY 1
2 to make note of (something) through the use of one's eyes ⟨*witnessed* the crime⟩ — see SEE 1
3 to make a solemn declaration under oath for the purpose of establishing a fact ⟨I *witnessed* to the fact that I had seen them together that night⟩ — see TESTIFY
4 to come to a knowledge of (something) by living through it ⟨war changes anyone who has ever *witnessed* it first hand⟩ — see EXPERIENCE

witticism *n* something said or done to cause laughter ⟨a drama critic who is best remembered for his biting *witticisms*⟩ — see JOKE 1

witting *adj* **1** having specified facts or feelings actively impressed on the mind ⟨she was a *witting* partner; he had told her about the risk involved⟩ — see CONSCIOUS 1
2 made, given, or done with full awareness of what one is doing ⟨your *witting* assistance in helping the robber escape makes you an accessory after the fact⟩ — see INTENTIONAL

wittingly *adv* with full awareness of what one is doing ⟨whether he hurt her feelings *wittingly* or unwittingly isn't important; he should still apologize⟩ — see INTENTIONALLY

witty *adj* given to or marked by mature intelligent humor ⟨a *witty* and sardonic blogger who never fails to amuse his legion of readers⟩ ⟨he's well-known for his *witty* retorts⟩
synonyms clever, facetious, humorous, jocular, smart
related words cerebral, highbrow, highbrowed, intellectual; bantering, frivolous, jesting, joking, joshing, teasing; antic, comic, comical, droll, farcical, funny, hysterical, laughable, ludicrous, ridiculous, riotous, risible, rollicking, screaming, sidesplitting, uproarious; amusing, diverting, entertaining; mischievous, playful, prankish; jocose, jocund, jolly, jovial, laughing, merry, mirthful, sunny; scintillating, sparkling; flip, flippant, pert, smart-aleck, smart-alecky, waggish; whimsical
near antonyms brainless, lowbrow, stupid, witless; corny, hackney, hackneyed, lame; humorless, unamusing, uncomic, unfunny; earnest, grave, serious, serious-minded, sober, solemn, somber (*or* sombre); doleful, dolorous, lachrymose, plaintive, sorry, tearful, woeful

wiz *n* a very smart person ⟨he must be some kind of *wiz* to have graduated college at age 19⟩ — see GENIUS 1

wizard *adj, chiefly British* of the very best kind ⟨a young Brit who's a *wizard* tennis player, although not ready for Wimbledon just yet⟩ — see EXCELLENT

wizard *n* **1** a person skilled in using supernatural forces ⟨the old *wizard* who introduces the young naïf to a life of adventure is one of the most overworked tropes in fantasy literature⟩ — see MAGICIAN 1
2 a person with a high level of knowledge or skill in a field ⟨a *wizard* at fixing cars⟩ — see EXPERT
3 a very smart person ⟨a *wizard* who never studied for tests⟩ — see GENIUS 1

wizardry *n* the power to control natural forces through supernatural means ⟨a movie about *wizardry* and bizarre creatures⟩ — see MAGIC 1

wobble *also* **wabble** *vb* **1** to make a series of small irregular or violent movements ⟨the patient's hand *wobbles* so much that he can scarcely hold a glass of water⟩ — see SHAKE 1
2 to make a series of unsteady side-to-side motions ⟨the table *wobbled* whenever I leaned on it⟩ — see ROCK 1
3 to show uncertainty about the right course of action ⟨we cannot afford to have the governor *wobble* at this critical time⟩ — see HESITATE
4 to swing unsteadily back and forth or from side to side ⟨the drunk stood up, *wobbled* for a moment, and fell forward⟩ — see TEETER 1

wobbling *also* **wabbling** *adj* marked by or given to small uncontrollable bodily movements ⟨her *wobbling* gait is due to Parkinson's disease⟩ — see SHAKY 1

wobbling *also* **wabbling** *n* a state or an instance of temporary inaction because of uncertainty about the right course of action ⟨the mayor's apparent *wobbling* on the issue of increased property taxes⟩ — see HESITATION

wobbly *also* **wabbly** *adj* marked by or given to small uncontrollable bodily movements ⟨all *wobbly* from the chills associated with the flu⟩ — see SHAKY 1

woe *interj* used to express sorrow or distress ⟨ah, *woe*, with the death of the last of my siblings I am alone in this world!⟩ — see ALAS

woe *n* **1** a state of great suffering of body or mind ⟨a tale of misery and *woe*⟩ — see DISTRESS 1
2 deep sadness especially for the loss of someone or something loved ⟨the incessant *woe* that has haunted her since the death of her husband⟩ — see SORROW

woebegone *adj* feeling unhappiness ⟨the most *woebegone* people that I had ever seen in my life⟩ — see SAD 1

woeful *adj* **1** expressing or suggesting mourning ⟨the *woeful* expressions of the players after the humiliating loss⟩ — see MOURNFUL 1

2 feeling unhappiness ⟨never saw a more *woeful*-looking bunch than those campers sitting there in the drenching rain⟩ — see SAD 1

3 of a kind to cause great distress ⟨the restaurant patron made the *woeful* discovery that he had left his wallet at home⟩ — see REGRETTABLE

woefully *adv* with feelings of bitterness or grief ⟨*woefully* recounted the many injustices that the family had endured at the hands of the dictator⟩ — see HARD 2

wolf *n* **1** a man given to seducing women ⟨she threatened to geld the *wolf* if he didn't stop making passes at her⟩ — see DON JUAN

2 a person who habitually preys upon others ⟨no sooner had the lottery winner's name been made public than the *wolves* with their investment schemes showed up on her doorstep⟩ — see PREDATOR

wolf *vb* to swallow or eat greedily ⟨the way you *wolf* your food it's no wonder you have intestinal distress⟩ — see GOBBLE

woman *n* **1** an adult female human being ⟨the first *woman* to become governor of the state⟩

synonyms female, lady, skirt [*slang*]

related words dame, gentlewoman; madam, madame, senora (*or* señora); babe [*slang*], beauty, belle, chick [*slang*], damsel, doll, gal, girl, ingenue (*or* ingénue), lass, lassie, mademoiselle, maid, maiden, miss, senorita (*or* señorita)

2 a female other than his wife with whom a married man has a continuing sexual relationship ⟨eventually she found out that her husband had a *woman* in the city and that she was the real reason for all of those "late nights at the office"⟩ — see MISTRESS

3 a female romantic companion ⟨wanted to give his *woman* all the finer things in life⟩ — see GIRLFRIEND

4 *chiefly dialect* the female partner in a marriage ⟨along the American frontier it was not uncommon to encounter a mountain man traveling with his Native American *woman* in tow⟩ — see WIFE

womanhood *n* the set of qualities considered appropriate for or characteristic of women ⟨she was the ideal of traditional Southern *womanhood*⟩ — see FEMININITY

womanish *adj* **1** of or relating to a man who has or displays qualities considered more suitable for women ⟨such displays of emotion were once considered *womanish* and unseemly for a man⟩ — see EFFEMINATE

2 of, relating to, or marked by qualities traditionally associated with women ⟨she had a *womanish* gentleness, especially when dealing with children, that he loved⟩ — see FEMININE

womanishness *n* the set of qualities considered appropriate for or characteristic of women ⟨what constitutes *womanishness* varies by culture and era⟩ — see FEMININITY

womanizer *n* a man given to seducing women ⟨the candidate's reputation as a *womanizer* really cost him with female voters⟩ — see DON JUAN

womanlike *adj* of, relating to, or marked by qualities traditionally associated with women ⟨the photograph shows the silhouette of a full, *womanlike* figure framed against the backlight from an open farmhouse door⟩ — see FEMININE

womanliness *n* the set of qualities considered appropriate for or characteristic of women ⟨some cultures consider demureness and submissiveness essential elements of *womanliness*⟩ — see FEMININITY

womanly *adj* of, relating to, or marked by qualities traditionally associated with women ⟨the novelist displays a *womanly* sensitivity to the characters' feelings⟩ — see FEMININE

wonder *n* **1** something extraordinary or surprising ⟨the cunningly crafted miniature of our house is a *wonder*, perfect in every detail⟩

synonyms caution, flash, marvel, miracle, phenomenon, portent, prodigy, sensation, splendor

related words curiosity, sight, spectacle; beauty, corker, crackerjack (*also* crackajack), dandy, jim-dandy, knockout; apparition, appearance

2 the rapt attention and deep emotion caused by the sight of something extraordinary ⟨when we first saw the pyramids of Egypt, we gazed with openmouthed *wonder*⟩

synonyms admiration, amazement, astonishment, awe, wonderment

related words dread; fear; respect, reverence, veneration; curiosity, interest; shock, surprise; disbelief, incomprehension, incredulity; beguilement, bewitchment, captivation, enchantment, fascination; animation, enlightenment, enlivenment, excitement, invigoration, stimulation; absorption, engagement, engrossment, enthrallment, immersion, involvement

near antonyms apathy, disinterest, incuriosity, indifference, unconcern; boredom, doldrums, ennui, listlessness, restlessness, tedium, tiredness, weariness, weltschmerz; cheerlessness, dispiritedness, joylessness, melancholy

wonderful *adj* **1** causing wonder or astonishment ⟨the mountaintop city of Machu Picchu is unquestionably a *wonderful* sight to behold⟩ — see MARVELOUS 1

2 of the very best kind ⟨that bakery makes *wonderful* cannoli⟩ — see EXCELLENT

wondering *adj* filled with amazement or wonder ⟨with *wondering* expressions on our faces, we watched the acrobats perform their daring feats⟩ — see OPENMOUTHED

wonderment *n* the rapt attention and deep emotion caused by the sight of something extraordinary ⟨gazed in *wonderment* at the holiday decorations⟩ — see WONDER 2

wondrous *adj* causing wonder or astonishment ⟨what a *wondrous* discovery fire must have been⟩ — see MARVELOUS 1

wonk *n* a person slavishly devoted to intellectual or academic pursuits ⟨the candidate has an army of policy *wonks* ready to write for him a position paper on virtually any issue⟩ — see NERD 1

wont *adj* being in the habit or custom ⟨she paced about the room, as she is *wont* to do whenever she is agitated⟩ — see ACCUSTOMED

wont *n* a usual manner of behaving or doing ⟨he got up early, as is his *wont*⟩ — see HABIT 1

woo *vb* to act so as to make (something) more likely ⟨his attempts to *woo* approval from working-class voters has not met with much success⟩ — see COURT 1

wood *n* **1** tree logs as prepared for human use ⟨a huge load of *wood* outside the furniture maker's factory⟩

synonyms lumber, timber

related words beam, brace, pile, post, ridgepole, sill, splint, stake, stave, stick; bar, billet, block; cordwood, firewood

2 *often* **woods** *pl* a dense growth of trees and shrubs covering a large area ⟨deer and mountain lions live in those *woods*⟩ — see FOREST

wooden *adj* lacking social grace and assurance ⟨an eminent scientist who was *wooden* in front of television cameras⟩ — see AWKWARD 1

woodenhead *n* a stupid person ⟨you're not a *woodenhead*, so there's no reason why you can't learn this⟩ — see IDIOT

woodland *n* a dense growth of trees and shrubs covering a large area ⟨the house is perched atop a hill amid a stretch of dense *woodland*⟩ — see FOREST

wood nymph *n* a mythical goddess represented as a young girl and said to live outdoors ⟨*wood nymphs* were usually conceived as being both beautiful and amorous⟩ — see NYMPH 1

wooer *n* a man who courts a woman usually with the goal of marrying her ⟨of all her *wooers*, he was the only one who met with her father's approval⟩ — see SUITOR 1

wool *n* the hairy covering of a mammal especially when fine, soft, and thick ⟨the *wool* from cashmere goats is considered by many to be the finest available⟩ — see FUR 1

woolgathering *n* the state of being lost in thought ⟨my *woolgathering* was abruptly interrupted by a question from the flight attendant⟩ — see REVERIE

woolly *also* **wooly** *adj* **1** made of or resembling hair ⟨the dog's *woolly* coat will require a lot of grooming⟩ — see HAIRY 2
2 covered with or as if with hair ⟨still had a water bed and a *woolly* coverlet on top of it⟩ — see HAIRY 1

woozy *adj* having a feeling of being whirled about and in danger of falling down ⟨the blood donor started to feel a little *woozy* after rising too quickly from the cot⟩ — see DIZZY 1

word *n* **1** a pronounceable series of letters having a distinct meaning especially in a particular field ⟨my doctor used all of these medical *words* that I didn't understand⟩
synonyms expression, term
related words linguistic form, monosyllable, morpheme, speech form; polysyllable; collocation, idiom, locution, phrase; archaism, coinage, colloquialism, euphemism, loanword, modernism, neologism, vernacularism
2 something that is said ⟨people who believe that the Bible is the literal *word* of God⟩
synonyms statement, utterance
related words communication, message; announcement, declamation, declaration, manifesto, proclamation, pronouncement; verbalization, vocalization
3 a report of recent events or facts not previously known ⟨what's the latest *word* on the airplane crash?⟩ — see NEWS
4 a person's solemn declaration that he or she will do or not do something ⟨I give you my *word* that I won't try to escape⟩ — see PROMISE
5 a statement of what to do that must be obeyed by those concerned ⟨the troops waited for their commanding officer to give the *word*⟩ — see COMMAND 1
6 information or opinion that is widely disseminated without any authority or confirmation of accuracy ⟨don't tell anyone I told you about the shake-up, but that's the *word* right now⟩ — see RUMOR
7 a word or phrase that must be spoken by a person in order to pass a guard ⟨"What's the *word*?" demanded the sentry⟩ — see PASSWORD
8 an often stated observation regarding something from common experience ⟨are there truer *words* than "never look a gift horse in the mouth"?⟩ — see SAYING

word *vb* to convey in appropriate or telling terms ⟨tried to *word* the declaration exactly right⟩ — see PHRASE

wordage *n* the use of too many words to express an idea ⟨somewhere, lost within all that *wordage*, is a modestly worthwhile idea⟩ — see VERBIAGE 1

wordbook *n* a reference book giving information about the meanings, pronunciations, uses, and origins of words listed in alphabetical order ⟨a *wordbook* of nautical slang⟩ — see DICTIONARY

word for word *adv* in the same words ⟨you don't have to record the professor's comments *word for word* in your notes⟩ — see VERBATIM

wordiness *n* the use of too many words to express an idea ⟨*wordiness* will only detract from what you are trying to say⟩ — see VERBIAGE 1

wording *n* **1** the way in which something is put into words ⟨it's important to get the *wording* of this law precisely correct⟩
synonyms diction, language, phraseology, phrasing, verbiage
related words expression, formulation, locution; enunciation, phrase, speech, style, utterance, voice
2 an act, process, or means of putting something into words ⟨the *wording* of the pollster's questions seemed to reflect a built-in bias⟩ — see EXPRESSION 1

wordless *adj* **1** deliberately refraining from speech ⟨he stood *wordless* before his accusers⟩ — see SILENT 1
2 understood although not put into words ⟨a *wordless* fondness for each other⟩ — see IMPLICIT 1

word-of-mouth *adj* made or carried on through speaking rather than in writing ⟨not having the money to run ads, the restaurant relies on *word-of-mouth* publicity⟩ — see VERBAL 2

wordy *adj* **1** using or containing more words than necessary to express an idea ⟨her writing style is far too *wordy* for my tastes⟩
synonyms circuitous, circumlocutory, diffuse, garrulous, logorrheic, long-winded, pleonastic, prolix, rambling, verbose, windy
related words chatty, communicative, conversational, gabby, loquacious, talkative, talky, voluble; periphrastic; redundant, repetitious, tautological, tautologous; embellished, embroidered, exaggerated; bombastic, gaseous, gassy, grandiloquent, highfalutin (*also* hifalutin)
near antonyms brief, short; aphoristic, epigrammatic, sententious; compendious, summary; abbreviated, abridged, condensed, shortened; abrupt, blunt, brusque (*also* brusk), curt, laconic, snippy
antonyms compact, concise, crisp, pithy, succinct, terse
2 of or relating to words or language ⟨the neighborhood dispute escalated into a *wordy* war conducted through angry letters to the editor in the local paper⟩ — see VERBAL 1

work *n* **1** a literary, musical, or artistic production ⟨unfortunately, many of her *works* are now out of print⟩ — see COMPOSITION 1
2 something produced by physical or intellectual effort ⟨the new Web application is the *work* of a pair of young but highly gifted programmers⟩ — see PRODUCT 1
3 the action for which a person or thing is specially fitted or used or for which a thing exists ⟨the *work* of a movie director is to tell a story through a series of striking images⟩ — see ROLE
4 the active use of energy in producing a result ⟨put a lot of *work* into the project⟩ — see EFFORT
5 the activity by which one regularly makes a living ⟨what line of *work* are you in?⟩ — see OCCUPATION 1
6 works *pl* a building or set of buildings for the manufacturing of goods ⟨a glass *works* where high quality glassware is made⟩ — see FACTORY

work *vb* **1** to be the cause of (a situation, action, or state of mind) ⟨this new drug can really *work* wonders⟩ — see EFFECT
2 to find an answer for through reasoning ⟨finally figured out how to *work* the math problem⟩ — see SOLVE
3 to have a certain purpose ⟨the human kidneys *work* as a filtering system for the blood⟩ — see FUNCTION
4 to produce a desired effect ⟨this headache remedy takes half an hour to *work*⟩ — see ACT 2
5 to set or keep in motion ⟨this pump is *worked* by hand⟩ — see MOVE 2
6 to control the mechanical operation of ⟨show me how to *work* the machine⟩ — see OPERATE 1
7 to devote serious and sustained effort ⟨the organization has *worked* for years to raise people's awareness of

human rights issues⟩ — see LABOR
8 to take unfair advantage of ⟨a woman not afraid to *work* her sex appeal in order to get ahead⟩ — see EXPLOIT 1
work (for) *vb* to be a servant for ⟨*worked for* a rich and powerful family⟩ — see SERVE 1
workable *adj* **1** capable of being done or carried out ⟨a *workable* plan for attracting a minor league team to the city⟩ — see POSSIBLE 1
2 capable of being put to use or account ⟨a *workable* solution to the state's growing financial woes⟩ — see PRACTICAL 1
workaday *adj* **1** being of the type that is encountered in the normal course of events ⟨just a *workaday* guy living a *workaday* life⟩ — see ORDINARY 1
2 having to do with the practical details of regular life ⟨wished that she could afford servants so as not to be bothered with such *workaday* matters as cooking, cleaning, and grocery shopping⟩ — see MUNDANE 1
3 not designed to be worn only on special occasions ⟨a *workaday* outfit that I could afford to get dirty⟩ — see CASUAL 1
worker *n* **1** a person who does very hard or dull work ⟨a champion of the rights of the farm *workers* who pick the nation's fruits and vegetables⟩ — see SLAVE 2
2 one who works for another for wages or a salary ⟨a factory owner who is known for his fair and generous treatment of his *workers*⟩ — see EMPLOYEE
workforce *n* a body of persons at work or available for work ⟨the office's entire *workforce* is devoted to a single project right now⟩ — see FORCE 1
work in *vb* **1** to put among or between others ⟨I think that we can *work in* one more interview in the afternoon lineup⟩ — see INSERT
2 to introduce in a gradual, secret, or clever way ⟨managed to *work in* several references to baseball in his paper on the merits of teamwork⟩ — see INSINUATE
working *adj* **1** being in effective operation ⟨the only *working* coal mine in the area⟩ — see ACTIVE 1
2 capable of being put to use or account ⟨as a would-be independent filmmaker, you'll need a *working* knowledge of motion picture photography and editing⟩ — see PRACTICAL 1
3 involved in often constant activity ⟨a boss who is of the opinion that a *working* employee is a needed employee, as idleness is a sign of dispensability⟩ — see BUSY 1
workings *n pl* the characteristic peculiarities and technicalities of something ⟨the byzantine *workings* of the auction business for high-end art⟩ — see INS AND OUTS
workmanlike *adj* accomplished with trained ability ⟨the pitcher gave a *workmanlike* performance, allowing the other team to score only a single run⟩ — see SKILLFUL 1
workout *n* something done over and over in order to develop skill ⟨a *workout* with dumbbells for building the muscles of the hands⟩ — see EXERCISE 2
work out *vb* **1** to find an answer for through reasoning ⟨by putting our heads together, we were able to *work out* the problem⟩ — see SOLVE
2 to produce or bring about especially by long or repeated effort ⟨*worked out* a compromise between the warring factions⟩ — see HAMMER OUT
3 to turn out as planned or desired ⟨our plans for a ski vacation just didn't *work out*⟩ — see SUCCEED 1
4 to determine (a value) by doing the necessary mathematical operations ⟨after *working out* the cost of a college education, we've decided that it's never too early to start saving⟩ — see CALCULATE 1
work over *vb* to strike repeatedly ⟨those thugs really *worked* him *over*⟩ — see BEAT 1
workshop *n* a building or set of buildings for the manufacturing of goods ⟨a *workshop* for making high-end furniture⟩ — see FACTORY
work up *vb* to produce or bring about especially by long or repeated effort ⟨spent years *working up* a period novel that was historically accurate in every detail⟩ — see HAMMER OUT
world *n* **1** human beings in general ⟨the whole *world* is waiting to see how this crisis will play out⟩ — see PEOPLE 1
2 the celestial body on which we live ⟨worried about the effects of pollution on the *world*⟩ — see EARTH 1
3 the whole body of things observed or assumed ⟨theories about the origin of the *world*⟩ — see UNIVERSE
4 a huge physical or conceptual distance ⟨liberal attitudes that are a *world* away from his neighbors' backward mentality⟩ — see GALAXY
worldly *adj* **1** having a wide and refined knowledge of the world especially from personal experience ⟨she returned from her year as an exchange student a much more *worldly* person⟩ — see WORLDLY-WISE
2 having to do with life on earth especially as opposed to that in heaven ⟨preoccupied with *worldly* concerns⟩ — see EARTHLY
worldly–wise *adj* having a wide and refined knowledge of the world especially from personal experience ⟨her long career as a globe-trotting journalist has made her very *worldly-wise* and even a little jaded⟩
synonyms cosmopolitan, smart, sophisticated, worldly
related words suave, urbane; civilized, cultivated, cultured, polished, refined; experienced, knowing, practiced, schooled, seasoned; bored, cynical, jaded, skeptical; down-to-earth, pragmatic (*also* pragmatical), realistic, sober
near antonyms callow, green, inexperienced, raw; parochial, provincial, rustic (*also* rustical); philistine, uncivilized, uncultured, unrefined; childlike, simple, simpleminded; idealistic, impractical; uncritical, unknowing
antonyms guileless, ingenuous, innocent, naive (*or* naïve), unsophisticated, untutored, unworldly, wide-eyed
worm *vb* **1** to advance gradually beyond the usual or desirable limits ⟨settlements *worming* into lands reserved for the natives⟩ — see ENCROACH
2 to introduce in a gradual, secret, or clever way ⟨over a period of several years, the undercover agent was able to *worm* his way into the drug kingpin's confidence⟩ — see INSINUATE
3 to move slowly with the body close to the ground ⟨the cat silently *wormed* along the ground as it snuck up on the bird⟩ — see CRAWL 1
worn *adj* depleted in strength, energy, or freshness ⟨she was feeling very *worn* after a long day at work⟩ — see WEARY 1
worn–out *adj* **1** depleted in strength, energy, or freshness ⟨*worn-out* tourists heading back to their hotel after a hard day of sightseeing⟩ — see WEARY 1
2 worn or torn into or as if into rags ⟨used a *worn-out* T-shirt for dusting the furniture⟩ — see RAGGED 2
worried *adj* feeling or showing uncomfortable feelings of uncertainty ⟨the soldier's father had a *worried* expression as he listened to the news⟩ — see NERVOUS 1
worrier *n* a person who is inclined to worry ⟨she's a mother—being a *worrier* is part of the job description⟩ — see NERVOUS NELLIE
worrisome *adj* **1** causing worry or anxiety ⟨the patient's erratic behavior has become increasingly *worrisome*⟩ — see TROUBLESOME
2 marked by or causing agitation or uncomfortable feelings ⟨*worrisome* looks passed between the two coworkers as the personnel manager began to enumerate the company's financial woes⟩ — see NERVOUS 2
worry *n* an uneasy state of mind usually over the possi-

bility of an anticipated misfortune or trouble ⟨she can only concentrate on something when she is free of *worry*⟩ — see ANXIETY 1

worry *vb* **1** to experience concern or anxiety ⟨they *worried* for days about whether the loan would be approved⟩
synonyms bother, fear, fret, fuss, stew, stress, sweat, trouble
related words agonize; long, pine, yearn; chafe; despair
phrases give a hang (*or* care a hang), sweat blood
near antonyms accept; abide, bear, endure, stick out, stomach, sustain, take, tolerate
2 to trouble the mind of; to make uneasy ⟨those strange noises outside the house *worry* me⟩ — see DISTURB 1

worrywart *n* a person who is inclined to worry ⟨tends to dismiss people concerned about global warming as a bunch of *worrywarts*⟩ — see NERVOUS NELLIE

worsen *vb* **1** to become worse or of less value ⟨the condition of the house *worsened* with every year of neglect⟩ — see DETERIORATE 1
2 to make more severe ⟨the harsh winter only *worsened* the fuel shortage⟩ — see EXACERBATE

worship *n* excessive admiration of or devotion to a person ⟨the *worship* of professional athletes who often turn out to be all too fallible⟩
synonyms adulation, deification, hero worship, idolatry, idolization, worshipping (*also* worshiping)
related words adoration, deference, glorification, reverence, veneration; idealization, romanticization; affection, fancy, favor, fondness, like, liking, love; appreciation, esteem, regard, respect; approval
near antonyms condemnation, disapproval, disfavor, dislike, dismissal, disregard, hatred, loathing, scorn

worship *vb* **1** to offer honor or respect to (someone) as a divine power ⟨the ancient Greeks *worshipped* many different gods⟩
synonyms adore, deify, glorify, revere, reverence, venerate
related words admire, honor, love, regard, respect; apotheosize, canonize, dignify, exalt, lionize, magnify; extol (*also* extoll), laud, praise; delight, gratify, please, satisfy
near antonyms blaspheme, desecrate, profane, violate; affront, dishonor, disrespect, insult, offend, outrage, pique, ridicule, scorn, slight; displease; defame, disparage, libel, malign, slander, slur, smear
2 to feel passion, devotion, or tenderness for ⟨the single father *worships* his young daughter, and would do anything for her⟩ — see LOVE 2
3 to love or admire too much ⟨thought that some of her fellow senior citizens *worshipped* the old days too much, observing that they weren't all good⟩ — see IDOLIZE

worshipful *adj* reflecting great admiration or devotion ⟨a movie fan's *worshipful* stare upon finally meeting her idol⟩ ⟨a teacher surrounded by *worshipful* little children⟩
synonyms adoring, adulatory, deifying, idolizing, worshipping (*also* worshiping)
related words glorifying, reverent, reverential, venerating; hagiographic (*also* hagiographical); affectionate, fond, loving; appreciative, deferential, respectful; approving
near antonyms condemning, contemptuous, disapproving, hateful, loathing, scornful

worshipping *also* **worshiping** *adj* reflecting great admiration or devotion ⟨impressionable young men with a *worshipping* regard for professional athletes⟩ — see WORSHIPFUL

worshipping *also* **worshiping** *n* excessive admiration of or devotion to a person ⟨feels that there is just too much *worshipping* of rock stars⟩ — see WORSHIP

worst *vb* to achieve a victory over ⟨how humiliating for a tennis champ to be *worsted* by a player no one had ever heard of⟩ — see BEAT 2

worth *n* **1** the relative usefulness or importance of something as judged by specific qualities ⟨money alone cannot determine the true *worth* of some things⟩
synonyms account, merit, valuation, value
related words assessment, estimation, evaluation; excellence, greatness, perfection; consequence, importance, significance, weight; desirability
near antonyms emptiness, valuelessness, worthlessness; baseness, cheapness, crumminess, inferiority, lousiness, meanness, paltriness, pettiness, poorness; deficiency, inadequacy, inadequateness, insufficiency, unacceptability
2 the amount of money for which something will find a buyer ⟨one surefire way to determine the actual *worth* of a painting is to sell it at auction⟩ — see VALUE 1
3 the total of one's money and property ⟨the entrepreneur's *worth* is well over 100 million dollars⟩ — see WEALTH 1

worthless *adj* having no usefulness ⟨that expensive toy is *worthless* now that it's broken⟩
synonyms chaffy, empty, junky, no-good, null, vain, valueless
related words base, cheap, cheapjack, duff [*British*], inferior, lousy, low-grade, second-rate; bad, defective, dud, flawed, imperfect, substandard, unsatisfactory; deficient, inadequate, insufficient, unacceptable
near antonyms invaluable, precious, priceless; cherished, esteemed, prized, treasured; choice, exceptional, fancy, high-grade, special
antonyms useful, valuable, worthy

worthy *adj* having sufficient worth or merit to receive one's honor, esteem, or reward ⟨made charitable contributions to the American Red Cross and other *worthy* causes⟩ ⟨a *worthy* opponent in a tennis match⟩
synonyms deserving, good, meritorious
related words admirable, commendable, creditable, laudable, praiseworthy; invaluable, priceless; cherished, prized, treasured; choice, excellent, exceptional, fancy, high-grade, primary, prime, special
near antonyms base, cheap, inferior, second-rate, substandard; bad, defective, flawed, imperfect; deficient, inadequate, insufficient, unacceptable, unsatisfactory
antonyms no-good, undeserving, valueless, worthless

wound *vb* **1** to cause bodily damage to ⟨an arrow had *wounded* the animal, but the vet was able to save it⟩ — see INJURE 1
2 to cause hurt feelings or deep resentment in ⟨that callous comment really *wounded* me⟩ — see INSULT

wowser *n, chiefly Australian* a person who is greatly concerned with seemly behavior and morality especially regarding sexual matters ⟨*wowsers* would be well-advised to avoid Sydney's annual Gay and Lesbian Mardi Gras⟩ — see PRUDE

wrack *vb* to bring to a complete end the physical soundness, existence, or usefulness of ⟨it's amazing how a raging sea can *wrack* a seemingly sturdy beachfront home⟩ — see DESTROY 1

wraith *n* the soul of a dead person thought of especially as appearing to living people ⟨the people who once lived here believed that their world was populated by *wraiths* and witches⟩ — see GHOST 1

wrangle *n* an often noisy or angry expression of differing opinions ⟨there was a bit of a *wrangle* over how much money to give the high school for its sports programs⟩ — see ARGUMENT 1

wrangle *vb* to express different opinions about something often angrily ⟨a town meeting at which local residents *wrangled* for hours about property taxes⟩ — see ARGUE 2

wrangler *n* **1** a hired hand who tends cattle or horses at a ranch or on the range ⟨a rough-hewn *wrangler* who never says much⟩ — see COWBOY

2 a person who takes part in a dispute ⟨known as a petty, unrelenting *wrangler* who likes argument for the sake of argument⟩ — see DISPUTANT

wrap *vb* **1** to encircle or bind with or as if with a belt ⟨*wrapped* her waist with a colorful silk sash⟩ — see GIRD 1

2 to surround or cover closely ⟨a sinister darkness seemed to *wrap* the lonely cabin⟩ — see ENFOLD 1

wraps *n pl* something that covers or conceals like a piece of cloth ⟨kept the whole plan under *wraps* until they were ready to make a public announcement⟩ — see CLOAK 1

wrap–up *n* **1** a short statement of the main points ⟨a postelection *wrap-up* of the campaign's high points and many low points⟩ — see SUMMARY

2 the last part of a process or action ⟨the opening of the museum's modern art wing marks the *wrap-up* of its decade-long expansion plan⟩ — see FINALE

wrap up *vb* **1** to bring (an event) to a natural or appropriate stopping point ⟨a grand parade will *wrap up* the weeklong celebration⟩ — see CLOSE 3

2 to make into a short statement of the main points (as of a report) ⟨a reporter *wrapped up* the mayor's speech in a few sentences⟩ — see SUMMARIZE 1

wrath *n* **1** an intense emotional state of displeasure with someone or something ⟨waited until my initial *wrath* had eased before voicing my complaint⟩ — see ANGER

2 suffering, loss, or hardship imposed in response to a crime or offense ⟨the evangelist warned the gathering that unrepentant sinners would suffer the *wrath* of God⟩ — see PUNISHMENT

wrathful *adj* feeling or showing anger ⟨in a *wrathful* voice she demanded to know what had happened⟩ — see ANGRY

wrathfulness *n* an intense emotional state of displeasure with someone or something ⟨the *wrathfulness* with which he voiced his complaint was shocking⟩ — see ANGER

wreathe *vb* **1** to cause to twine about one another ⟨decided to *wreathe* the grapevines into a beribboned swag to give the room the "country look"⟩ — see INTERTWINE 1

2 to scatter or set here and there among other things ⟨*wreathed* small flowers into the design for the wallpaper⟩ — see THREAD 1

3 to form a circle around ⟨pretty ribbons *wreathed* the flower girl's braided bun⟩ — see SURROUND

wreck *n* **1** the portion or bits of something left over or behind after it has been destroyed ⟨found the *wreck* of the ship lying on the floor of the ocean⟩ — see REMAINS 1

2 the destruction or loss of a ship ⟨the *wreck* cost the insurance company millions of dollars⟩ — see SHIPWRECK 1

3 the violent coming together of two bodies into destructive contact ⟨a dangerous stretch of roadway that has been the scene of numerous car *wrecks*⟩ — see CRASH 1

wreck *vb* **1** to cause irreparable damage to (a ship) by running aground or sinking ⟨many an unwary captain has *wrecked* his ship on the shoals that surround the island⟩ — see SHIPWRECK

2 to bring to a complete end the physical soundness, existence, or usefulness of ⟨most of the furniture on the ground floor was *wrecked* by the floodwaters⟩ — see DESTROY 1

wreckage *n* **1** the state or fact of being rendered nonexistent, physically unsound, or useless ⟨the *wreckage* of those ancient statues represents a great loss to the art world⟩ — see DESTRUCTION 1

2 the portion or bits of something left over or behind after it has been destroyed ⟨the *wreckage* of the cathedral was kept as a memorial and as a reminder of war's terrible cost⟩ — see REMAINS 1

3 the destruction or loss of a ship ⟨debris floated ashore for weeks after the *wreckage*⟩ — see SHIPWRECK 1

wrecking *n* the destruction or loss of a ship ⟨the *wrecking* of the freighter was one of the worst disasters ever on the Great Lakes⟩ — see SHIPWRECK 1

wrench *n* **1** a forceful rotating or pulling motion for the purpose of dislodging something ⟨with a sharp *wrench* of the hammer I pulled the nail from the board⟩

synonyms twist, twisting, wrenching, wresting, wringing

related words draft, draw, extraction, pull, tug, yank; dislocation, displacement

2 the act or an instance of applying force on something so that it moves in the direction of the force ⟨with one final hard *wrench* I was able to pull the cork from the bottle⟩ — see PULL 1

wrench *vb* **1** to move by or as if by a forceful rotation ⟨with one last sharp yank, he *wrenched* the lid off the bottle of ketchup⟩

synonyms twist, wrest, wring

related words draw, dredge (up), extract, jerk, lug, pluck, pull, tug, tweak, yank; jimmy, lever, pry; budge, dislocate, displace, disturb, remove; shift, transfer, transpose

2 to injure by overuse, misuse, or pressure ⟨*wrenched* her shoulder by all of that heavy lifting⟩ — see STRAIN 1

3 to separate or remove by forceful pulling ⟨*wrenched* the post out of the ground⟩ — see TEAR 2

wrenching *adj* intensely or unbearably painful ⟨forced to make the emotionally *wrenching* decision to place her mother in a nursing home⟩ — see EXCRUCIATING 1

wrenching *n* a forceful rotating or pulling motion for the purpose of dislodging something ⟨after a lot of *wrenching* and tugging, the plumber managed to pull the stubborn pipe free⟩ — see WRENCH 1

wrest *vb* **1** to draw out by force or with effort ⟨the boy *wrested* the book out of his sister's hands⟩ — see EXTRACT 1

2 to get (as money) by the use of force or threats ⟨vowed that the bully had *wrested* his lunch money from him for the last time⟩ — see EXTORT

3 to get with great difficulty ⟨farmers who were used to *wresting* a living from the harsh land⟩ — see EKE (OUT)

4 to move by or as if by a forceful rotation ⟨I need a strong arm to *wrest* the lid off this pickle jar⟩ — see WRENCH 1

5 to separate or remove by forceful pulling ⟨*wrested* open the stuck door of the cabinet⟩ — see TEAR 2

wresting *n* a forceful rotating or pulling motion for the purpose of dislodging something ⟨no amount of *wresting* could loosen the rusted bolt⟩ — see WRENCH 1

wrestle *vb* to seize and attempt to unbalance one another for the purpose of achieving physical mastery ⟨the sisters *wrestled* on the floor over the last cookie⟩

synonyms grapple, rassle, scuffle, tussle

related words battle, clash (with), combat, contend, duel, fight, war (against); bash, batter, beat, buffet, hit, punch, slug, strike; box, spar; brawl, skirmish

wrestle (with) *vb* to give serious and careful thought to ⟨I've been *wrestling with* the idea of switching careers for quite some time⟩ — see PONDER

wretch *n* a mean, evil, or unprincipled person ⟨the clerk was an ungrateful *wretch* who stole money from his employer's cash register⟩ — see VILLAIN

wretched *adj* **1** extremely unsatisfactory ⟨this report is simply *wretched*—you'll have to rewrite it⟩

synonyms atrocious, awful, dismal, execrable, horri-

ble, lousy, punk, rotten, sucky [*slang*], terrible
related words bad, deficient, inferior, off, poor, substandard, wanting; contemptible, miserable, shameful; defective, faulty, flawed; low-grade, mediocre, reprehensible, second-rate; bum, useless, valueless, worthless; inadequate, insufficient, lacking; abominable, damnable, fiendish, odious, vile
near antonyms choice, excellent, exceptional, first-class, first-rate, premium, prime, superior; adequate, sufficient; acceptable, satisfactory
antonyms bitchin' [*slang*], great, marvelous (*or* marvellous), wonderful
2 arousing or deserving of one's loathing and disgust ⟨a *wretched* lie⟩ — see CONTEMPTIBLE 1
3 causing or marked by an atmosphere lacking in cheer ⟨lived alone in a *wretched* room in a run-down hotel⟩ — see GLOOMY 1
4 falling short of a standard ⟨a *wretched* attempt at writing an original song⟩ — see BAD 1
5 feeling unhappiness ⟨she was *wretched* for weeks after breaking up with her boyfriend⟩ — see SAD 1
6 not following or in accordance with standards of honor and decency ⟨his *wretched* treatment of women earned him a bad reputation⟩ — see IGNOBLE 2
7 of low quality ⟨*wretched* goods that aren't even worth half of what the store is charging for them⟩ — see CHEAP 2
8 deserving of one's pity ⟨those *wretched* souls who cannot even afford a decent roof over their heads⟩ — see PATHETIC 1
9 deserving pitying scorn (as for inadequacy) ⟨the pampered socialite complained that the only room available was in a *wretched* little motel by the highway⟩ — see PITIFUL 1

wretchedly *adv* **1** in an unsatisfactory way ⟨the whole hockey team played *wretchedly* that night⟩ — see BADLY 1
2 with feelings of bitterness or grief ⟨we're *wretchedly* disappointed in you for behaving so irresponsibly⟩ — see HARD 2

wriggle *vb* **1** to make jerky or restless movements ⟨a toddler *wriggling* in his seat all throughout the church service⟩ — see FIDGET
2 to move slowly with the body close to the ground ⟨a worm slowly *wriggled* across the sidewalk⟩ — see CRAWL 1
3 to introduce in a gradual, secret, or clever way ⟨within a month of his arrival, this social upstart had *wriggled* himself into the family's good graces⟩ — see INSINUATE 1

wriggly *adj* making jerky or restless movements ⟨after a while, the little girl got *wriggly* and had to be taken outside to the church vestibule⟩ — see FIDGETY

wring *vb* **1** to get (as money) by the use of force or threats ⟨that bill collector is willing to do anything to *wring* money out of deadbeats⟩ — see EXTORT
2 to get with great difficulty ⟨after years of trying to *wring* a decent profit out of the business, he is finally giving up⟩ — see EKE (OUT)
3 to move by or as if by a forceful rotation ⟨I'm so mad I could *wring* your neck⟩ — see WRENCH 1
4 to draw out by force or with effort ⟨willing to use torture if necessary in order to *wring* the information out of the terrorist⟩ — see EXTRACT

wringing *n* a forceful rotating or pulling motion for the purpose of dislodging something ⟨a firm *wringing* of the shoe got it off⟩ — see WRENCH 1

wrinkle *n* **1** a small fold in a soft and otherwise smooth surface ⟨the old woman's face creased into *wrinkles* as she smiled⟩ ⟨the curtains cascaded onto the floor in ripples and *wrinkles*⟩
synonyms crease, crimp, crinkle, furrow
related words corrugation, layer, loop, plait, pleat, ply, pucker, seam, tuck; crow's-foot
2 something (as a device) created for the first time through the use of the imagination ⟨the latest *wrinkle* in digital photography⟩ — see INVENTION 1

wrinkle *vb* **1** to develop creases or folds ⟨if you don't fold clothes promptly after drying, they'll *wrinkle*⟩
synonyms crease, crinkle, furrow, rumple
related words collapse, crumple, double, fold
2 to create (as by crushing) an irregular mass of creases in ⟨sitting down on the bedspread *wrinkled* it⟩ — see CRUMPLE 1

write *vb* **1** to compose and set down on paper the words of ⟨a staunch supporter of the old school, he prefers to *write* all of his letters by hand⟩
synonyms author, pen, scratch (out), scribble
related words cast, compose, craft, draft, draw up, formulate, frame, prepare; recast, redraft, revise, rewrite; letter, print, type, typewrite; record, take down, transcribe; autograph, pencil (in), register, sign; couch, express, phrase, put, word
2 to engage in an exchange of written messages ⟨promise you'll *write* while you're away⟩ — see CORRESPOND 1

write down *vb* **1** to diminish the price or value of ⟨a company forced to *write down* its assets⟩ — see DEPRECIATE 1
2 to make a written note of ⟨*write down* what you remember about that day⟩ — see RECORD 1

write off *vb* **1** to express scornfully one's low opinion of ⟨most critics have already *written off* that director as a hack incapable of turning out anything but schlock⟩ — see DECRY 1
2 to diminish the price or value of ⟨that one blunder will *write off* to nothing all the goodwill we've been building up⟩ — see DEPRECIATE 1

writer *n* a person who creates a written work ⟨a *writer* who is still trying to get published⟩ — see AUTHOR 1

writhe *vb* **1** to cause to twine about one another ⟨tends to *writhe* his fingers together when he's nervous or upset⟩ — see INTERTWINE 1
2 to make jerky or restless movements ⟨*writhing* in pain from his injuries⟩ — see FIDGET

wrong *adj* **1** falling short of a standard ⟨there is something *wrong* with this cake—it has a funny taste⟩ — see BAD 1
2 having an opinion that does not agree with truth or the facts ⟨I'm sorry, but the latest research proves you *wrong*⟩ — see INCORRECT 1
3 not appropriate for a particular occasion or situation ⟨has a knack for saying just the *wrong* thing⟩ — see INAPPROPRIATE
4 not being in agreement with what is true ⟨her answer that Thomas Jefferson was the second president of the United States is *wrong*—it was John Adams, of course⟩ — see FALSE 1
5 not conforming to a high moral standard; morally unacceptable ⟨was caught doing something *wrong*⟩ — see BAD 2

wrong *adv* off the desired or intended path or course ⟨all of our carefully laid plans have gone *wrong*⟩
synonyms afield, amiss, astray, awry
related words badly; faultily, improperly, inappropriately, incorrectly, mistakenly, wrongly; inadequately, insufficiently, unpromisingly
near antonyms perfectly; auspiciously, favorably, promisingly; correctly, properly, rightly; appropriately, fittingly, suitably
antonyms aright, right, well

wrong *n* **1** that which is morally unacceptable ⟨any reasonable person should be expected to know the differ-

ence between right and *wrong*⟩ — see EVIL
2 unfair or inadequate treatment of someone or something or an instance of this ⟨trying to right all the *wrongs* in the world⟩ — see DISSERVICE

wrongdoer *n* a person who commits moral wrongs ⟨anticorruption crusaders are going after *wrongdoers* at every level of the nation's government⟩ — see EVILDOER 1

wrongdoing *n* **1** a breaking of a moral or legal code ⟨a local newspaper exposed the contractor's elaborate attempts to cover up his *wrongdoings*⟩ — see OFFENSE 1
2 improper or illegal behavior ⟨the police officer was found to be completely innocent of any *wrongdoing*⟩ — see MISCONDUCT 1

wrongful *adj* contrary to or forbidden by law ⟨charged with *wrongful* possession of narcotics⟩ — see ILLEGAL 1

wrongly *adv* in a mistaken or inappropriate way ⟨you have *wrongly* interpreted this passage in the Bible⟩
synonyms amiss, erroneously, faultily, improperly, inaccurately, inappropriately, inaptly, incorrectly, mistakenly, unsuitably
related words misguidedly; fallibly, imperfectly; extraneously, irrelevantly, meaninglessly, pointlessly, senselessly; inadequately, insufficiently; undesirably, unsatisfactorily; foolishly, unwisely
near antonyms infallibly, perfectly; germanely, meaningfully, pertinently, relevantly, sensibly; acceptably, adequately, satisfactorily, sufficiently; prudently, sagely, wisely
antonyms appropriately, aptly, correctly, fittingly, properly, right, rightly, suitably, well

wrongness *n* the quality or state of being unsuitable or unfitting ⟨arguments about the rightness or *wrongness* of the satirical skit drowned out any discussion of the points it attempted to raise⟩ — see INAPPROPRIATENESS 1

wroth *adj* feeling or showing anger ⟨I've been waxing *wroth* all afternoon!⟩ — see ANGRY

wud *adj, chiefly Scottish* having or showing a very abnormal or sick state of mind ⟨an old miser whose obsession with money had driven him *wud*⟩ — see INSANE 1

wurst *n* a rod-shaped portion of seasoned ground meat in a casing ⟨spicy *wurst* mixed with chopped potatoes is delicious⟩ — see SAUSAGE

wuss *also* **wussy** *n* a person lacking in physical strength ⟨teased him for being a *wuss* when he failed the push-up test in gym class⟩ — see WEAKLING 1

X

x (out) *vb* to show (something written) to be no longer valid by drawing a cross over or a line through it ⟨*x out* the names of the people who have already left⟩
synonyms blue-pencil, cancel, cross (out), dele, delete, edit (out), elide, kill, scratch (out), strike (out), stroke (out)
related words blot out, efface, eradicate, erase, expunge, obliterate, root (out), rub out, wipe out; bleep, blip, clip, cut, excise, remove; bowdlerize, censor, clean (up), expurgate, launder, redact, red-pencil; abbreviate, crop, shorten; black out, repress, silence, suppress
near antonyms stet

X–rated *adj* **1** dealing in or with explicitly sexual material ⟨for his comedy-club performances the stand-up comic's routines are definitely *X-rated*⟩ — see ADULT 2
2 depicting or referring to sexual matters in a way that is unacceptable in polite society ⟨the jerk should have known better than to tell an *X-rated* joke at a company function⟩ — see OBSCENE 1

Y

yahoo *interj* how delightful ⟨you mean we were accepted for the reality show? *yahoo!*⟩ — see HOORAY

yahoo *n* a stupid person ⟨those *yahoos* who go skiing despite avalanche warnings deserve what they get⟩ — see IDIOT

Yahweh *also* **Jahveh** *or* **Yahveh** *n* the being worshipped as the creator and ruler of the universe ⟨a count of the number of times *Yahweh* is mentioned in the Old Testament⟩ — see DEITY 2

yammer *n* an expression of dissatisfaction, pain, or resentment ⟨a soccer coach having to endure the endless *yammers* from parents that their kids weren't getting enough time on the field⟩ — see COMPLAINT 1

yammer *vb* to express dissatisfaction, pain, or resentment usually tiresomely ⟨customers *yammered* on for what seemed like days about the billing mistake⟩ — see COMPLAIN

yank *n* the act or an instance of applying force on something so that it moves in the direction of the force ⟨had to give the shoe a good *yank* to get it off⟩ — see PULL 1

yank *vb* **1** to move or cause to move with a sharp quick motion ⟨she stupidly *yanked* the wheel while I was driving⟩ — see JERK 1
2 to draw out by force or with effort ⟨*yanked* out a tooth with a pair of pliers⟩ — see EXTRACT
3 to separate or remove by forceful pulling ⟨grab the other one, and let's see if we can't *yank* these two grocery carriages apart⟩ — see TEAR 2

yap *n slang* the opening through which food passes into the body of an animal ⟨a dope with a talent for opening his *yap* at exactly the wrong moment⟩ — see MOUTH 1

[1]yard *n* **1** an open space wholly or partly enclosed (as by buildings or walls) ⟨inmates are allowed an hour of exercise in the prison's inner *yard*⟩ — see COURT 2
2 the area around and belonging to a building ⟨we're looking for a house with a big *yard*⟩ — see GROUND 1

[2]yard *n* a considerable amount ⟨a composer who produced *yards* of gorgeous music over the course of a long career⟩ — see LOT 2

yard sale *n* a sale of used household and personal items ⟨there are signs up all over town advertising *yard sales*⟩
synonyms garage sale, tag sale
related words jumble sale [*British*], rummage sale

yardstick *n* something set up as an example against which others of the same type are compared ⟨this essay will be the *yardstick* by which I grade the others⟩ — see STANDARD 1

yarn *n* **1** a brief account of something interesting that happened especially to one personally ⟨Grandpa likes to tell *yarns* about when he was young⟩ — see STORY 2
2 a work with imaginary characters and events that is shorter and usually less complex than a novel ⟨a ripping *yarn* about space travel and alien monsters⟩ — see STORY 1

yaw *vb* to depart abruptly from a straight line or course ⟨the ship *yawed* hard to the right when the rogue wave hit it broadside⟩ — see SWERVE 1

yawn *n* someone or something boring ⟨as neither candidate was willing to make an unequivocal statement about anything, the debate proved to be a complete *yawn*⟩ — see DRAG 1

yawner *n* someone or something boring ⟨even die-hard opera fans are finding this production to be a real *yawner*⟩ — see DRAG 1

yawp *or* **yaup** *vb* to express dissatisfaction, pain, or resentment usually tiresomely ⟨stop *yawping* about your problems and try doing something to fix them⟩ — see COMPLAIN

yawping *or* **yauping** *adj* engaging in or marked by loud and insistent cries especially of protest ⟨the ticket agent spent hours dealing with *yawping* customers, furious that their flights had been canceled⟩ — see VOCIFEROUS

yea *adv* **1** not merely this but also ⟨we will go to the new land, and, *yea*, we will pursue our dreams!⟩ — see EVEN 1
2 used to express agreement ⟨I vote *yea* on the proposed increase in the school budget⟩ — see YES

yea *n* a vote or decision for something ⟨the measure passed with 50 *yeas* and 17 nays⟩ — see YES

yeah *adv* used to express agreement ⟨*yeah*, we'll be there⟩ — see YES

yearn (for) *vb* to have an earnest wish to own or enjoy ⟨*yearned for* a little house in the country⟩ — see DESIRE 1

yearn (over) *vb* to have sympathy for ⟨who wouldn't *yearn over* the poor little girl who just became an orphan?⟩ — see PITY

yearning *n* a strong wish for something ⟨had a sudden *yearning* for something sweet⟩ — see DESIRE 1

year–rounder *n* a usually longtime resident of a locality ⟨*year-rounders* love the off-season, when the tourists are a bittersweet memory and once again they have the island all to themselves⟩ — see NATIVE 1

yeast *n* something that arouses action or activity ⟨taxation without representation proved to be the *yeast* of rebellion⟩ — see IMPULSE 1

yeasty *adj* lacking in seriousness or maturity ⟨the *yeasty* chatter at a cocktail party on New Year's Eve⟩ — see GIDDY 1

yech *also* **yecch** *interj* used to express disgust ⟨*yech*, I hate those bugs!⟩ — see YUCK

yell *n* a loud vocal expression of strong emotion ⟨the crowd gave a *yell* of approval⟩ — see SHOUT

yell *vb* **1** to cry out loudly and emotionally ⟨*yelled* with fear when the speeding car veered onto the crowded sidewalk⟩ — see SCREAM 1
2 to speak so as to be heard at a distance ⟨I *yelled* to the kids in the backyard that it was time to go home⟩ — see CALL 1

yellow *adj* having or showing a shameful lack of courage ⟨you'll come with us into the cave, unless you're *yellow*⟩ — see COWARDLY

yelp *vb* to cry out loudly and emotionally ⟨*yelped* with surprise when everything fell off the closet shelf and onto his head⟩ — see SCREAM 1

yen *n* a strong wish for something ⟨I have a strange *yen* to take the day off from work⟩ — see DESIRE 1

yen (for) *vb* to have an earnest wish to own or enjoy ⟨what car lover doesn't *yen for* a new car at the start of every model year⟩ — see DESIRE 1

yenta *n* a person who habitually reveals personal or sensational facts about others ⟨the couple's loud quarrel had the building's *yentas* yapping for a week⟩ — see GOSSIP 1

yep *adv* used to express agreement ⟨"That's really what she said?" "*Yep*"⟩ — see YES

yes *adv* used to express agreement ⟨*yes*, I'll be ready for the test tomorrow⟩
synonyms all right, alright, aye (*also* ay), exactly, OK (*or* okay), okeydoke (*or* okeydokey), yea, yeah, yep, yo
related words absolutely, assuredly, certainly, indeed, indisputably, positively, undoubtedly, unquestionably
antonyms nay, no, no way, scarcely

yes *n* a vote or decision for something ⟨the bill passed with 50 "*yeses*" and 12 "noes."⟩
synonyms affirmative, yea
related words pro; acceptance, accession, acquiescence, agreement, approval, assent, concurrence, consent, permission, sanction
near antonyms con; blackball, veto; declination, denial, disallowance, negation, refusal, rejection, turndown
antonyms nay, negative, no, non placet

yesterday *n* the events or experience of former times ⟨my grandparents are always reminiscing about *yesterday*⟩ — see PAST

yesteryear *n* the events or experience of former times ⟨the simple games of *yesteryear* that kept children entertained for hours⟩ — see PAST

yet *adv* **1** at a later time ⟨we may *yet* figure it out⟩
synonyms eventually, finally, someday, sometime, sooner or later, ultimately
related words anon, before long, by and by, directly, imminently, momentarily, presently, shortly, soon; forthwith, immediately, promptly, pronto, right away, right now, right off, straightaway, straightway
phrases at last (*or* at long last), at length, in the end, in the fullness of time, in time
near antonyms ne'er, never, nevermore
2 in addition to what has been said ⟨offered *yet* another option for our planned tour of Europe⟩ — see MORE 1
3 in spite of that ⟨the hikers were scared, and *yet* they continued to go deeper into the cave⟩ — see HOWEVER
4 up to this or that time ⟨we have *yet* to win a single game⟩⟨she had *yet* to accomplish a single thing⟩ — see HITHERTO

yet *conj* if it were not for the fact that ⟨it feels like summer, *yet* according to the calendar we're still in early spring⟩ — see EXCEPT

yield *n* **1** an increase usually measured in money that comes from labor, business, or property ⟨the stock's *yield* has increased over the years⟩ — see INCOME 1
2 something produced by physical or intellectual effort ⟨wheat farmers were able to increase the *yield* per acre substantially⟩ — see PRODUCT 1
3 the total amount collected or obtained especially at one time ⟨the *yield* from the police department's buy-back program for firearms was staggering⟩ — see HAUL 1

yield *vb* **1** to give up and cease resistance (as to a liking, temptation, or habit) ⟨I finally *yielded* to temptation and had a bowl of ice cream⟩
synonyms bow, cave (in), give in, submit, succumb, surrender
related words cater (to), gratify, indulge, wallow; acquiesce (to), concede (to); buckle (under), knuckle under; give over (to)
near antonyms battle, breast, combat, confront, counter, defy, face, fight, meet, object, oppose, repel; thwart, withstand; reject; bridle, check, constrain, curb, inhibit, restrain, stifle
antonyms hold off, resist
2 to produce as revenue ⟨I expect that stock to *yield* at least 14% profit this year⟩
synonyms bear, give, pay, return
related words bring in, net; afford, furnish, provide, supply; pay off
3 to cease resistance (as to another's arguments, demands, or control) ⟨after initially balking at the order, the soldier *yielded* when the commanding officer threatened a formal charge of insubordination⟩
synonyms blink, bow, budge, capitulate, concede, give in, knuckle under, quit, relent, submit, succumb, surrender
related words acquiesce; defer
phrases say uncle, throw in the towel (*also* throw in the sponge)
near antonyms contend, fight, hold off; battle, breast, combat, confront, counter, defy, face, meet, object, oppose, repel; thwart, withstand
antonyms resist
4 to be the cause of (a situation, action, or state of mind) ⟨the sort of embarrassing question that seldom *yields* an honest answer⟩ — see EFFECT
5 to fall down or in as a result of physical pressure ⟨the door soon *yielded* to the battering ram⟩ — see COLLAPSE 1
6 to give (something) over to the control or possession of another usually under duress ⟨refusing to *yield* the city to enemy troops⟩ — see SURRENDER 1
7 to give (oneself) over to something especially unrestrainedly ⟨weak-willed by nature, she *yielded* herself to every dietary temptation and then whined about it afterwards⟩ — see ABANDON 1

yielding *adj* **1** receiving or enduring without offering

resistance ⟨a person too *yielding* to even stand up for his own rights⟩ — see PASSIVE
2 not stiff in structure ⟨after sitting on a hard bench for hours, I was happy to sink into the sofa's *yielding* cushions⟩ — see LIMP 1

yippee *interj* how delightful ⟨she took one look at the new car in the driveway and exclaimed, "*Yippee*!"⟩ — see HOORAY

yo *adv* used to express agreement ⟨"So, are you coming with me?" "*Yo*"⟩ — see YES

yob *n, British* a violent, brutal person who is often a member of an organized gang ⟨the complaint that English football has been taken over by the *yobs*, who make the stadiums unfit for families⟩ — see HOODLUM

yobbo *n, British* a violent, brutal person who is often a member of an organized gang ⟨some *yobbo* has been threatening shopkeepers in the East End⟩ — see HOODLUM

yoke *n* the state of being a slave ⟨a people able at last to throw off the *yoke* and to embrace freedom⟩ — see SLAVERY 1

yoke *vb* to put or bring together so as to form a new and longer whole ⟨*yoked* several ideas together to come up with a new theory⟩ — see CONNECT 1

yokel *n* an awkward or simple person especially from a small town or the country ⟨a lame comedy about the misadventures of *yokels* in the big city⟩ — see HICK

yon *adv* at or to a greater distance or more advanced point ⟨the belief that it is the destiny of the human race to explore our solar system and *yon*⟩ — see FARTHER

yonder *adv* at or to a greater distance or more advanced point ⟨look *yonder* and you'll see the skyline of the city⟩ — see FARTHER

yore *n* the events or experience of former times ⟨my favorite stories are about gallant knights and fair maidens in the days of *yore*⟩ — see PAST

young *adj* being in the early stage of life, growth, or development ⟨a *young* cat requires more food than an older one⟩ ⟨a *young* tree that will eventually reach 50 feet tall⟩
synonyms adolescent, immature, juvenile, youngish, youthful
related words ephebic, minor, preteen, subadult, teenage (*or* teenaged), underage; embryonic, emergent; callow, green, inexperienced, puerile, raw; babyish, childish, childlike, infantile, infantine, kiddish; undeveloped, unfinished, unfledged, unformed, unripe, unripened; blooming, blossoming, burgeoning, flourishing, flowering
near antonyms aged, aging (*or* ageing), ancient, elderly, geriatric, long-lived, old, older, oldish, senescent, senior; full-blown, full-fledged; golden, mellow, ripe, ripened; middle-aged; anile, decrepit, doddering, over-the-hill, senile, spavined, tottery
antonyms adult, grown-up, mature, matured

youngish *adj* being in the early stage of life, growth, or development ⟨a *youngish* but surprisingly mature audience showed up to watch the serious film⟩ — see YOUNG

youngling *n* a young person who is between infancy and adulthood ⟨she quit babysitting when she got tired of wrangling *younglings* who weren't even her own⟩ — see CHILD 1

youngster *n* a young person who is between infancy and adulthood ⟨a herd of *youngsters* following their nature guide like ducklings after a mother duck⟩ — see CHILD 1

youth *n* **1** a male person who has not yet reached adulthood ⟨a big, strapping *youth* who, even at his relatively young age, knew the meaning of hard work⟩ — see BOY 1
2 a young person who is between infancy and adulthood ⟨rounded up the neighborhood *youths* and organized them into a softball team⟩ — see CHILD 1
3 the state or time of being a child ⟨told the young people to enjoy their *youth* while they could⟩ — see CHILDHOOD

youthful *adj* being in the early stage of life, growth, or development ⟨it's still a *youthful* nation with a lot of promise and potential⟩ — see YOUNG

yowl *n* a loud vocal expression of strong emotion ⟨the cat gave a *yowl* of anger⟩ — see SHOUT

yowl *vb* **1** to express dissatisfaction, pain, or resentment usually tiresomely ⟨a bitterly cold winter that had people *yowling* about their heating bills⟩ — see COMPLAIN
2 to make a long loud mournful sound ⟨coyotes *yowling* at the moon⟩ — see HOWL 1

yowling *adj* engaging in or marked by loud and insistent cries especially of protest ⟨town meeting is always full of *yowling* residents who never seem to be happy with anything the town does⟩ — see VOCIFEROUS

yo–yo *n* **1** a person who lacks good sense or judgment ⟨some *yo-yo* cut the electricity off while I still had unsaved data⟩ — see FOOL 1
2 a stupid person ⟨those *yo-yos* who insist upon using their cell phones while speeding down the highway⟩ — see IDIOT

yuck *also* **yuk** *interj* used to express disgust ⟨*yuck*, I really hate brussels sprouts⟩
synonyms faugh, fie, phew, phooey, rats, ugh, yech (*or* yecch)
related words ah, bah, boo, humph, pish, pooh, pshaw, sheesh, tush, tut, tut-tut; alack, alas, woe
near antonyms yum-yum

yucky *also* **yukky** *adj* **1** disagreeable or disgusting to the sense of taste ⟨a child at that age where every unfamiliar and untried food is preemptively dismissed as "*yucky*"⟩ — see DISTASTEFUL 1
2 not giving pleasure to the mind or senses ⟨the weather is supposed to be *yucky*, so bring your jacket and umbrella⟩ — see UNPLEASANT

yuk *or* **yuck** *also* **yak** *or* **yock** *n, slang* something said or done to cause laughter ⟨the *yuks* on this new sitcom are so pathetic that the souped-up laugh track merely adds insult to injury⟩ — see JOKE 1

yuk *or* **yuck** *vb, slang* to make jokes ⟨pay no mind to those clowns—they are just *yukking* it up and don't mean any harm⟩ — see JOKE 1

yuletide *n* the season celebrating Christmas ⟨these days, as far as the stores are concerned, *yuletide* starts in September⟩
synonyms Christmastide, Christmastime, Noel
related words Advent; Christmas, nativity, Xmas, yule

yummy *adj* very pleasing to the sense of taste ⟨a *yummy* meal that is also nutritious⟩ — see DELICIOUS 1

Z

zag *vb* to depart abruptly from a straight line or course ⟨the crowd roared as the clown on the bicycle *zagged* while the other clowns, in hot pursuit, zigged⟩ — see SWERVE 1

zaniness *n* lack of good sense or judgment ⟨what *zaniness* possessed you to take a mental health day when you knew that the head honcho would be visiting?⟩ — see FOOLISHNESS 1

zany *adj* showing or marked by a lack of good sense or judgment ⟨a *zany* plan to drive cross-country on a motorized scooter⟩ — see FOOLISH 1

zany *n* **1** a comically dressed performer (as at a circus) who entertains with playful tricks and ridiculous behavior ⟨hired a *zany* to entertain the children at the birthday party⟩ — see CLOWN 1
2 a person of odd or whimsical habits ⟨one of the challenges of hosting a radio call-in program is preventing the *zanies* from completely taking over the discussion⟩ — see ECCENTRIC

zap *vb* to deliver a blow to (someone or something) usually in a strong vigorous manner ⟨*zapped* the annoying bug with a swatter⟩ — see HIT 1

zealot *n* one who is intensely or excessively devoted to a cause ⟨*zealots* on both sides of the issue resorted to name-calling and scare tactics⟩
synonyms crusader, fanatic, ideologue (*also* idealogue), militant, partisan (*also* partizan), red hot, true believer
related words activist; dreamer, idealist, visionary; cultist, disciple, follower, hanger-on, idolizer, votary; addict, aficionado (*also* afficionado), buff, bug, devotee, enthusiast, fan, fancier, fiend, fool, freak, habitué (*also* habitue), head, hound, junkie (*also* junky), lover, maniac, maven (*also* mavin), nut, sucker; advocate, apostle, backer, champion, evangelist, patron, promoter, stalwart, supporter; booster, rooter, well-wisher; faddist
near antonyms dabbler, dilettante
antonyms nonmilitant

zenith *n* the highest part or point ⟨at the *zenith* of her career as a dancer⟩ — see HEIGHT 1

zephyr *n* a slight or gentle movement of air ⟨a summer *zephyr* gently stirred her hair⟩ — see BREEZE 1

zero *n* **1** the numerical symbol 0 or the absence of number or quantity represented by it ⟨anything multiplied by *zero* comes out to *zero*⟩
synonyms aught, cipher, goose egg, naught (*also* nought), nil, nothing, o, oh, zilch, zip
related words blank, void
2 a person of no importance or influence ⟨those snobs on the cruise ship tried to make me feel like a complete *zero*⟩ — see NOBODY
3 the lowest point or level ⟨after several dating disasters, my confidence with the opposite sex is at *zero*⟩ — see NADIR 1

zero hour *n* a time or state of affairs requiring prompt or decisive action ⟨we're at the *zero hour*, so someone has to make a decision⟩ — see EMERGENCY

zest *n* the quality or state of being stimulating to the mind or senses ⟨dumped in more spices to add some *zest* to the marinade⟩ — see PIQUANCY

zesty *adj* sharp and pleasantly stimulating to the mind or senses ⟨bland pasta that needs a *zesty* sauce⟩ — see PIQUANT

zig *vb* to depart abruptly from a straight line or course ⟨the fox *zigged* to the right, and the hounds followed⟩ — see SWERVE 1

zigzag *vb* to move suddenly aside or to and fro ⟨the fleeing car *zigzagged* down the highway at breakneck speed⟩ — see DODGE 1

zilch *n* **1** a person of no importance or influence ⟨a passive and retiring little *zilch* of a person⟩ — see NOBODY
2 the numerical symbol 0 or the absence of number or quantity represented by it ⟨the amount of money that we have coming in right now is *zilch*⟩ — see ZERO 1

zine *n* a publication that appears at regular intervals ⟨a small cadre of students have taken to producing their own underground *zine* in order to satirize many of the university's most sacred cows⟩ — see JOURNAL 1

zing *n* **1** active strength of body or mind ⟨has the youthful, adventurous *zing* to go out and conquer mountains⟩ — see VIGOR 1
2 the quality or state of being stimulating to the mind or senses ⟨the razor-sharp repartee puts some *zing* into the movie⟩ ⟨an addition of ginger to give the marmalade a little extra *zing*⟩ — see PIQUANCY

zingy *adj* sharp and pleasantly stimulating to the mind or senses ⟨recipes for a *zingy* meal that is sure to wow your guests⟩ — see PIQUANT

Zion *also* **Sion** *n* **1** a dwelling place of perfect happiness for the soul after death ⟨found the path to *Zion* by doing penance for the wayward ways of her youth⟩ — see HEAVEN 1
2 an often imaginary place or state of utter perfection and happiness ⟨Robert Owen's New Harmony, Indiana, was but one of many attempts to establish an American *Zion*⟩ — see PARADISE 1

[1]zip *n* active strength of body or mind ⟨he has surprising *zip* for a man his age⟩ — see VIGOR 1

[2]zip *n* the numerical symbol 0 or the absence of number or quantity represented by it ⟨I've got *zip* as far as new ideas go⟩ — see ZERO 1

zip *vb* **1** to fly, turn, or move rapidly with a fluttering or vibratory sound ⟨a dragonfly *zipped* by my ear⟩ — see WHIR
2 to make an irregular series of quick, sudden movements ⟨the fly *zipped* around the room, trying to find a way to the outside⟩ — see FLIT
3 to proceed or move quickly ⟨knowing that she was already late, she went *zipping* off to meet her next client⟩ — see HURRY 2

zip (up) *vb* to give life, vigor, or spirit to ⟨the newscaster asked the writer if there was a way to *zip up* the story a little⟩ — see ANIMATE

zippy *adj* **1** having much high-spirited energy and movement ⟨a crowd of *zippy* children who'd been cooped up all day⟩ — see LIVELY 1
2 moving, proceeding, or acting with great speed ⟨she just bought a *zippy* new computer that should enable her to work more efficiently⟩ — see FAST 1

zit *n, slang* a small, inflamed swelling of the skin ⟨"Look at all these *zits*—I'm hideous!" wailed the high schooler⟩ — see POCK

zodiac *n* a series of events or actions that repeat themselves regularly and in the same order ⟨a political candidate dealing with the never-ending *zodiac* of rubber-chicken dinners and meet and greets⟩ — see CYCLE 1

zone *n* **1** a broad geographical area ⟨a tropical *zone*⟩ — see REGION 2
2 a part or portion having no fixed boundaries ⟨at that

point we were out of the danger *zone* for avalanches⟩ — see REGION 1

zonked *adj* **1** being under the influence of a recreational drug ⟨later claimed that she was *zonked* for the entire recording session⟩ — see STONED 1
2 suffering from mental confusion ⟨her only living relative is a permanently *zonked* sister who can't even care for herself⟩ — see DIZZY 2

zonked–out *adj* **1** being under the influence of a recreational drug ⟨the perpetually *zonked-out* writer Hunter S. Thompson created the genre now known as gonzo journalism⟩ — see STONED 1
2 suffering from mental confusion ⟨overmedicated, *zonked-out* residents of a nursing home⟩ — see DIZZY 2

zoo *n* a state of noisy, confused activity ⟨the post office is always a *zoo* the day that tax returns are due⟩ — see COMMOTION

zoom *n* a monotonous sound like that of an insect in motion ⟨the *zoom* of a motorboat off in the distance⟩ — see HUM

zoom *vb* **1** to fly, turn, or move rapidly with a fluttering or vibratory sound ⟨a squadron of fighter planes *zooming* over our heads prompted thoughts of a terrorist attack⟩ — see WHIR
2 to proceed or move quickly ⟨race cars *zooming* around a track at breakneck speeds⟩ — see HURRY 2
3 to rise abruptly and rapidly ⟨*zoomed* to a supervisory position after only a few short months⟩ — see SKYROCKET

z's *or* **zs** *n pl* a natural periodic loss of consciousness during which the body restores itself ⟨I'm going to try and catch a few *z's* before we go out tonight⟩ — see SLEEP 1